THE
AMERICAN
ENCYCLOPEDIC
DICTIONARY

THE AMERICAN ENCYCLOPEDIC DICTIONARY

Salem House Publishers

COMPILED IN ASSOCIATION WITH
THE OXFORD UNIVERSITY PRESS

Credits

Photographs and Illustrations
Popperfoto; Bay Books Pty Ltd; Bay Picture Library; Adelaide
Festival Centre Trust; Antarctic Division of D.S.I.R.; Australian
Army; Australian Broadcasting Commission; Australian Glass
Manufactures Company; Australian Information Service;
Australian Inland Mission; Australian Jaycees; Australian News
and Information Bureau; The Australian Opera; Australian
Tourist Commission; A. Bradley; Broken Hill Prop. Company
Ltd; Bullers Book of Birds; J. Cann; Carlton United Breweries;
Marshall Cavendish; Cement and Concrete Association of New
South Wales; M. C. Cohen and Company; Neville Coleman;
Colonial Sugar Refinery; Commonwealth Science and
Industrial Research Organization, Australia; Consulate
Republic of Cuba; Ben Cropp; B. Cummins; Dairy Industry
Authority of New South Wales; Department of Agriculture,
Australia; Department of Information and Extension Services,
PNG; Department of Main Roads, New South Wales;
Department of Mines, New South Wales; Department of
Overseas Trade, Victoria; Department of Science, Victoria;
Douglass Baglin Photography; Alan Foley; A. M. Fox; Fritz
Prenzel Photo Library; Garuda Indonesian Airways; Keith
Gillet; Globe Theatre (NZ); John Goode; Robert Goodman;
Hong Kong Government Information Service; Robert Horton;
Alan Hutchison; Japan National Tourist Organisation; Lan
Chile Airways; Lutheran Publishing House; Magic Carpet
Tours, Sydney; Malaysian Airline System; Malaysian
Government; Metropolitan Water Sewerage and Drainage
Board, Sydney; Motor Cycle Weekly; New South Wales Tourist
Bureau; New Zealand Lamb Information Bureau; New Zealand
Travel Commission; New Zealand Wildlife Service; Northern
Territory Tourist Board; Old Tote Theatre Company, Sydney;
Overseas Telecommunications Centre, Sydney; P&O Australia;
Photographic Library of Australia; Rentokil; Royal Australian
Navy; A. J. Salter; Salvation Army; Scoopix, Victoria; Brian
Shirley; Sir Colin Mackenzie Sanctuary; Snowy Mountains
Hydro-electric Authority, New South Wales; South Australian
Government Tourist Bureau; Spasm Australia Pty. Ltd.; State
Electricity Commission of Victoria; State Library of Victoria;
TAA Australia; Telecom Australia; UTA French Airlines;
Victorian Ministry of Tourism; Water Conservation and
Irrigation Committee, New South Wales; Western Australian
Department of Development and Decentralization; Eric Worrell.

First published in the U.S.A. by
Salem House Publishers Ltd. 1987
462 Boston Street, Topsfield,
Massachusetts 01983

Library of Congress Cataloging-in-
Publication Data
The American Encyclopedic Dictionary.
Includes index.
1. Encyclopedias and dictionaries
AG5.A53 1987 031 86-26187
ISBN 0-88162-231-1

How to use the Dictionary

A dictionary normally takes the uses of words and phrases as such for its subject-matter and is concerned with giving information about the things for which these words and phrases stand only so far as correct use of the words depends upon knowledge of the things. In an encyclopaedia, on the other hand, the emphasis will be much more on the nature of the things for which the words and phrases stand. That is the distinction between a dictionary and an encyclopaedia made by H. W. Fowler in the preface to the *Concise Oxford Dictionary*.

This new work attempts to combine in a form that can be easily and pleasurably used the essential features of dictionary and encyclopaedia. As well as giving the meanings of words in common or not-so-common currency, the work contains hundreds of entries on famous people and places, animals and plants. Some things are more easily explained by pictures or diagrams than by words and prolific use is made throughout this encyclopaedic dictionary of illustrations as an aid to definition and as visual amplification of the text entries. As well as colour photographs, explanatory cut-away and other diagrams, and maps, the dictionary contains reproductions of many famous paintings and specially commissioned original illustrations.

Vocabulary

The general reader for whom the book is intended may not always have another dictionary or encyclopaedia to hand and so the vocabulary has been chosen with an eye to the needs of one who may require either type of information.

The vocabulary should be more than adequate for the reader who consults the book for ordinary dictionary purposes. But it also contains terms in everyday use which would be excluded from an ordinary dictionary because of their technical and scientific character or which would be very briefly dealt with; familiar words in semi-technical use (e.g. *vertical trust, combine*, etc.); the names of famous people (e.g. statesmen, explorers, inventors, artists, and writers), historical, contemporary, or fictitious; and the names of important places and events.

Special pains have been taken to ensure that scientific and technical terms are up to date and accurate in selection and in definition, and at the same time intelligible to the user, but the present pace of development in science and technology is so swift that no reference book which deals with them in even the most general way can ever be completely up to date: between the time the book is compiled and its publication new words and senses will have come into use and existing words and senses will have acquired fresh shades of meaning or become obsolescent.

In order to keep the work within reasonable compass obsolete words and phrases have been omitted except for a few which some special interest has made it desirable to retain.

Illustrations

The illustrations have been planned to complement the text. Each of them is independent but adjacent to or near the relevant text entry, and is fully captioned. Each is intended to show the meaning of a word or indicate the character of the thing for which the word stands; to bring a diffuse subject into sharp visual focus or explain diagrammatically how a complex piece of machinery or technical process works. To avoid wasteful repetition some subjects have been grouped together, especially where the members of the group help to explain one another: the picture of a machine, for example, may not only illustrate the machine itself but exhibit the nature of its parts, and their relation to one another and to the whole.

Words are often best defined in general terms but a drawing has to be of a particular thing and therefore gives an example of the particular use of the word rather than a generalized statement. Thus the human body may be chosen to show the different bones of the skeleton, although the same terms are used for comparable bones in other vertebrates.

The subjects chosen for illustration are those of general interest, many of them being easier to define by illustration than verbally. Examples with a wide range of reference have usually been chosen; thus the illustrations of animals show at least one example from each major group.

Abbreviations

Abbreviations in current use appear in their alphabetical place in the body of the text to save a separate alphabet. But there is a separate list (see page xiii) of those abbreviations used in the dictionary itself.

Etymology

For the sake of space, derivations have been omitted with a few exceptions. These occur where the etymology is especially interesting or unexpected (e.g. *penicillin, derrick*), or when a thing has been named after its inventor or place of origin (e.g. *Fortin barometer, Borstal*). In these cases the etymology is given in square brackets at the end of the entry.

Cross-references

Where a word is given in small capitals in a definition, this indicates that reference to the word in its alphabetical place will provide further information (e.g. INSULIN in the entry for *pancreas*) or discuss the term which is given in comparison or contradistinction (e.g. NOBLE or PRECIOUS metals as opposed to *base* metals).

Pronunciation

1. **Accent** The accentuation mark ´ is placed after the vowel or vowel sound in the stressed syllable.

2. **Phonetic system** Where the pronunciation of a word or part of a word cannot be shown by the ordinary spelling and markings, a phonetic spelling is given in round brackets immediately after the black-type word. The phonetic scheme is as follows:

CONSONANTS: b; ch (ch*in*); d; dh (dh*e* = the); f; g (g*o*); h; j; k; l; m; n; ng (s*i*ng); ngg (fi*n*ger); p; r; s (s*i*p); sh (sh*i*p); t; th (th*in*); v; w; y; z; zh (v*i*zh*o*n = vision).

ṅ indicates French nasalization of preceding vowel.

The symbol χ represents the ch in B*a*ch, l*o*ch, pronounced as a guttural sound or as k.

VOWEL COMBINATIONS:

ā ē ī ō ū o͞o (mate mete mite mote mute moot)
ă ĕ ĭ ŏ ŭ o͝o (rack reck rick rock ruck rook)
ār ēr īr ūr (mare mere mire mure)
ȧr ėr ȯr (part pert port)
ah aw oi oor ow (bah bawl boil boor brow)

Vowels and combinations (as *er*) printed in italic within the brackets indicate vague sounds frequently indistinguishable from each other.

Vowels marked ⁓ may be pronounced either way, e.g. **pā̆´trĭot** (pā- or pă-).

3. **Pronunciation without respelling.** As far as possible pronunciation is shown without respelling by placing symbols over the words (e.g. **ā, ĕ, ār, ēr, o͞o,** etc.) in the black type. Unmarked vowels in the black-type words indicate vague sounds.

(a) The ordinary spelling often coincides with the phonetic system described in paragraph 2.

(b) The following additional symbols are used in the black type:

ė=ĭ (nā´kėd, rėlȳ´, cŏ´llėge, prĭ´vėt)
ir, ur=ēr (birth, burn)
ȳ y̆=ī, ĭ (implȳ´, sŭ´nny̆)
ȳr =īr (lȳre)

(c) Final *e* when unmarked is mute, i.e. not to be pronounced. Thus **āpe** is to be pronounced āp. Where final *e* is pronounced, it is marked as in **rĕ´cĭpė.** Where *e* is mute in the headword it is mute also (unless marked) in derivatives placed in the same entry, e.g. **bāre, bār´ely̆, bār´enėss.**

(d) A double consonant is pronounced as single **(sĭ´lly̆, mă´nnĭsh)** unless indicated as in **plai´nnėss** (-n-n-).

(e) The following letters and combinations have the usual values in American spelling which are shown alongside them:

Vowel Combinations

ae=ē (aegis)
ai=ā (pain)
air=ār (fair)
au=aw (maul)
ay=ā (say)
ea, ee=ē (mean, meet)
ear, eer=ēr (fear, beer)
ei=ē (ceiling)

eu, ew=ū (feud, few)
ey= ĭ(donkey)
ie=ē (thief)
ier=ēr (pier)
oa=ō (boat)
ou=ow (bound)
our=ower (flour)
oy=oi (boy)

Consonants

c is hard and=k (cob, cry, talc) *but* **c** before **e, i, y,** is soft and=s (ice, icy, city)
ck=k (back)
dg before **e, i, y,**=j (judgement)
g before **e, i, y,** is soft and=j (age, gin, orgy), except when doubled (digger, haggis, baggy)

n before **k,** hard **c, q, x**=ng (zinc, uncle, tank, banquet, minx)
ph=f (photo)
qu=kw (quit)
tch=ch (batch)
wh=w or hw (when)
x=ks (fox)

Thus in **gĕm** the pronunciation of *g* is not marked because it comes under the rule above for soft *g*, but **gĕt** is followed by (g-) to show that here exceptionally **g** before **e** is hard as in *go*.

The following combinations have the values shown:

-age=-ĭj (garbage)
-al, -el preceded by *d, n, t*=-l (Handel, mental)
-en, -ent preceded by *d, t,*=-n, -nt (madden, fatten, student)
-nch when final=-nsh or -nch (trench)
-ous=-*us* (furious)
-sion after consonants=-shon (passion, tension)
-sion after vowels=-zhon (division)
-sm=-zm (atheism, spasm)
-tion=-shon (salvation)
-tual, -tue, -ture=-chōoal, -chōo, -cher as well as -tūal, -tū, -tūr, esp. in common words

Swung Dash (~)

The 'swung dash' or 'tilde' is frequently used to save space in the body of the entry. It represents the headword (or a derivative of the headword printed in black type in the same entry) when this is repeated as a different part of speech or when it is used in combination with another word, either hyphenated or detached (but not when it has become part of a complete new word). For example, in the article **pitch**[1] *n.* we have ~ *v.t.* when the headword becomes a new part of speech, and ~ *black* and ~ -*pine* when it is in combination (but *pitchblende* as a whole word). The addition of an initial letter to the swung dash indicates a change from a small letter in the headword to a capital or vice versa (e.g. *F*~ in the article **flood** represents the Flood recorded in Genesis).

Contents

Contents

Abbreviations used
in the dictionary

A
Ab./original
abbrev./iation, -iated
abl./ative
abs./olute(ly)
acc./ording
accus./ative
act./ive
adj(s)., adjective(s)
adv(s)., adverb(s)
aeron./autics
AF, Anglo-French
Afr./ican
alg./ebra
allus./ive(ly)
Amer./ican
anal./ogy
anat./omy
Anglo-Ind./ian
anon./ymous
antiq./uities
anthrop./ology
app./arently
Arab./ic
Aram./aic
arbitr./ary
archaeol./ogy
archit./ecture
arith./metic
assim./ilated
assoc./iated
astrol./ogy
astron./omy
at. wt, atomic weight
attrib./utive(ly)
augment./ative
Austral./ian
av./oirdupois

B
b./orn
back form./ation
bibl./ical
bibliog./raphy
biochem./istry

biol./ogy
Boh./emian
bot./any
Br./itish
Braz./ilian
Bulg./arian
Burm./ese
Byz./antine

C
c./entury
Camb./ridge
c/irca
cap./ital
Celt./ic
cf., compare
Ch./urch
chem./istry
Chin./ese
chronol./ogy
cinemat./ography
cogn./ate
collect./ive(ly)
colloq./uial(ly)
com./mon
comb./ination
commerc./ial
comp., compar./ative
compl./ement
conch./ology
confus./ion
conj., conjunction, conjugation
conn./ected
constr./uction
contempt./uous(ly)
contr./action
cop./ulative
correl./ative
corresp./onding
corrupt./ion
cryst./allography
cu./bic

D
d./ied

Dan./ish
dat./ive
demonstr./ative
deriv./ative
derog./atory
dial./ect
dict./ionary
diff./erent
dim./inutive
diplom./acy
dist./inct, -inguished
distrib./utive
Du./tch
dub./ious

E
E., east(ern)
eccles./iastical
ecol./ogy
econ./omics
Egyptol./ogy
E. Ind., East Indian
  (i.e. of the East Indies)
elect./ricity
ellipt./ical
embryol./ogy
emphat./ic(ally)
eng., engin./eering
Engl., England, English
entom./ology
erron./eous(ly)
esp./ecial(ly)
ethnol./ogy
etym./ology
euphem./ism
Eur./ope(an)
exagg./eration
exc./ept
exch./ange
excl., exclamation, exclusive
expr./essing etc.

F
f./rom
facet./ious etc.

Abbreviations used
in the dictionary

fam./iliar etc.
fem./inine etc.
fig./urative etc.
Fl./emish
foll./owing (word)
footb./all
fort./ification
Fr./ench
freq./uent(ly)
frequent./ative(ly)
fut./ure (tense)

G Gael./ic
gen., general(ly), genitive
geog./raphy
geol./ogy
geom./etry
Ger./man
Gk, Greek
govt., government
gram./mar

H Heb./rew
her./aldry
Hind./ustani
hist./orical, history
hort./iculture

I i., intransitive
Icel./andic
ill./ustration
illit./erate
imit./ative
imp., imper./ative
imperf./ect
impers./onal
improp./er(ly)
incl./uding, inclusive
Ind./ian (i.e. of the Indian
    sub-continent)
ind., indicative, indirect
indecl./inable
indef./inite

inf./initive
infl./uence(d)
instr./umental (case)
int./erjection
interrog./ative(ly)
intrans./itive
Ir./ish
iron./ically
irreg./ular(ly)
It., Ital./ian

J Jap./anese
Jew/ish
joc./ular(ly)

L L, Latin
lang./uage
l.c., lower case
LG, Low German
lit./eral(ly)
Lith./uanian
LL, late Latin

M magn./etism
manuf./acture
masc./uline
math./ematics
MDu., Middle Dutch
ME, Middle English
mech./anics
med./icine
med. L, medieval Latin
metall./urgy
metaph./or(ically)
metaphys./ics
meteor./ology
Mex./ican
MG, Middle German
MHG, Middle High German
mil./itary
min./eralogy
MLG, Middle Low German
mod./ern

morphol./ogy
mus./ic
myth./ology

N N., north(ern)
n./oun
N. Amer., North America(n)
nat. hist., natural history
naut./ical
nav./al
nec./essary, -essarily
neg./ative(ly)
neut./er
nom./inative
Norm./an
north./ern
Norw./egian
ns., nouns
N.T., New Testament
num./eral

O obj./ect
obl./ique
obs./olete
obsolesc./ent
occas./ional(ly)
OE, Old English
OF, Old French
OHG, Old High German
OIr., Old Irish
OLG, Old Low German
ON, Old Norse
onomat./opoeic
ophthalm./ology
opp., (as) opposed (to), opposite
ord./inary, -inarily
orig./inal(ly)
ornith./ology
O.T., Old Testament

P p./age
paint./ing
palaeog./raphy

palaeont./ology
parenth./etic(ally)
parl./iament(ary)
part./iciple, -icipial
pass./ive(ly)
past t./ense
path./ology
pedant./ic(ally)
perf./ect (tense)
perh./aps
Pers./ian
pers./on(al)
Peruv./ian
pharm./acy, -acology
philol./ogy
philos./ophy
phon., phonet./ics
phot., photog./raphy
phr./ase
phrr., phrases
phys./ics
phys. chem., physical chemistry
physiol./ogy
pl./ural
pluperf./ect
poet./ical
Pol./ish
pol./itics etc.
pol. econ., political economy
pop./ular(ly)
Port./uguese
poss./essive
pp., pages
pr./onounced
prec., (the) preceding (word)
pred./icate, -icative
pref./ix
prep./osition(al)
pres./ent (tense)
pret./erite
print./ing
prob./able, -ably
pron., pronoun, pronounced,

pronunciation
prop./er(ly)
pros./ody
psych., psychol./ogy
psychoanal./ysis

R railw./ay
R.C./Roman Catholic
ref./erence
refl./exive(ly)
rel./ative
repr./esent
rhet./oric
Rom./an
Russ./ian

S S., south(ern)
S. Afr., South African
Sansk./rit
Sax./on
Sc./ottish
Scand./inavian
sculp./ture
sent./ence
Serb./ian
sing./ular
Slav./onic
sociol./ogy
sp./elling
Span./ish
spec./ial(ly)
specif./ic(ally)
sport./ing
Stock Exch., Stock Exchange
subj., subject, subjunctive
superl./ative
surg./ery
surv./eying
Swed./ish
syn./onym

T tech./nical (ly)
teleg./raphy

term./ination
Teut./onic
theatr./ical
theol./ogy
trans./itive
transf., in transferred sense
transl./ation
trig./onometry
Turk./ish
typ./ography

U U.K., United Kingdom
ult./imate(ly)
unexpl./ained
Univ./ersity
Univv., Universities
U.S., United States
usu./al(ly)

V v./erb
var., variant, various
varr., variants
v. aux., verb auxiliary
vbl, verbal
vbs., verbs
v.i., verb intransitive
voc./ative
v.r., verb reflexive
v.t., verb transitive
vulg./ar(ly)

W W., west(ern)
w./ith
W. Afr., West African
wd, word
wds, words
W. Ind., West Indian
(i.e. of the West Indies)

Y yr(s), year(s)

Z zool./ogy

Form of the letter **A, a** has evolved with successive cultures (see examples on right). Originally the letter may have been based on the symbol of an ox head. Left: construction of capital A in 1525 by Albrecht Durer, the great Renaissance artist. He designed the strokes within a square according to geometrical ratios.

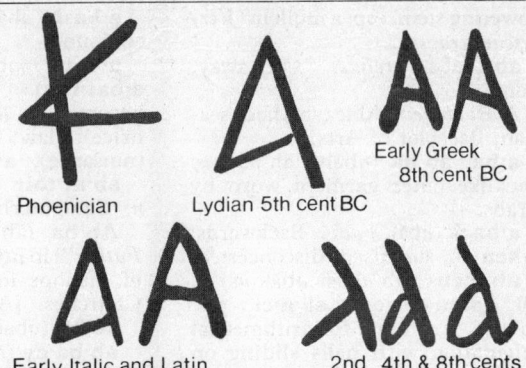

Phoenician

Lydian 5th cent BC

Early Greek 8th cent BC

Early Italic and Latin

2nd 4th & 8th cents

Many abbreviations, especially those consisting of initial letters, may be written with or without points.

A, a (ā) (pl. **A's, a's** or **As, as**). 1. First letter of modern English and ancient Roman alphabet, descended, through Greek and Latin, from first letter, **a·leph** (ah′lĕf) (א), of Hebrew and Phoenician alphabets, in English representing orig. a low–back–wide vowel sound and now a number of vowel sounds. 2. First in series, order, or class, esp. (alg. etc.) first known quantity. 3. Grade or mark indicating highest quality. 4. **A**, (mus.) sixth note of natural scale (C major); scale or key with this note for tonic. 5. **A 1** (ā′-wŭn′), applied in Lloyd's Register to ships in first-class condition in regard to both hull (designated by A) and equipment (1); hence, (also **A one**), first class, prime, perfect.

6. **A-frame**, building with main frame or shape forming inverted V; **A–O.K.** (slang), in perfect order.

A *abbrev.* Ampere(s); angstrom(s).

a (a; emphat. ā), **an** *indefinite articles.* One; some, any; (in, to, for) each.

a- *prefix.* 1. On, in, at. 2. (also **an-**) Without, not.

A.A. *abbrev.* Anti-aircraft; Alcoholics Anonymous; Associate in Arts.

A.A.A. *abbrev.* American Automobile Association; anti-aircraft artillery.

Aa·chen (ah′ken, -χen). (Fr. *Aix-la-Chapelle*) Ancient city of Germany near Belgian and Dutch borders, scene of coronation of German kings until 16th c.

Aal·borg (awl′boorg). Historic city and port of N. Denmark.

Aal·to (ahl′taw), **Alvar** (1898–1976). Finnish architect, designer, and planner; his works have influenced modern design throughout the world.

Aar (ār), **Aa·re** (ār′e). River in Switzerland flowing from the Bernese Alps NE. to the Rhine.

aard·vark (ārk′vārk) *n.* S. Afr. ant-eating quadruped (*Orycteropus afer*) with long extensile tongue. [Du., = "earth-pig"]

aard·wolf (ārd′woolf) *n.* (pl. **-wolves** pr. -woolvz). Carnivorous mammal (*Proteles cristatus*) resembling the hyena.

Aar·on (ār′on, ăr′-). Brother of Moses and traditional founder of Jewish priesthood; ~'s **rod**, (Numbers 17) plant with tall

Aardwolf

Aardvark

The Cape anteater, **aardvark,** reaches its prey first by destroying the nests with its large claws, then by grubbing with its tapering snout. It has a long thread-like tongue.

The 'earth-wolf' of southern Africa, **aardwolf** resembles the hyena but is smaller. It lives chiefly off termites, eggs and lizards. Glands release a musk smell when it is attacked.

flowering stem, esp. a mullein (*Verbascum trapsus*).

ab-, abs- *prefixes.* Off, away, from.

A.B. *abbrev.* Able (-bodied) seaman; Bachelor of Arts.

a·ba, ab·ba (abah´, ah´ba) *ns.* Sacklike outer garment worn by Arabs.

a·back (abăk´) *adv.* Backwards; **taken** ~, surprised, disconcerted.

ab·a·cus (ăb´akus; abăk´us) *n.* (pl. **ab·a·cus·es, ab·a·ci** pr. ăb´asī). 1. Frame for arithmetical calculation with balls sliding on wires, used before the adoption of the nine figures and zero, and still used in China etc. and in elementary teaching. 2. (archit.) Upper member, often a square flat slab, of capital, supporting architrave.

A·ba·dan (ahbahdahn´). Port and oil-refining center on the Persian Gulf in SW. Iran.

A·bad·don (abăd´on). Hebrew name of APOLLYON.

a·baft (abăft´) *adv.* On or toward stern of ship. ~ *prep.* Aft of, behind.

ab·a·lo·ne (ăbalō´nē) *n.* Edible mollusk of genus *Haliotis*, with ear-shaped shell lined with mother-of-pearl.

a·ban·don (abăn´don) *v.t.* Give up, surrender, forsake. ~ *n.* Careless freedom. **a·ban´don·ment** *n.* **a·ban·doned** (abăn´dond) *adj.* (esp.) Profligate.

a·base (abās´) *v.t.* (**a·based, a·bas·ing**). Humiliate, lower, make base. **a·base´ment** *n.*

a·bash (abăsh´) *v.t.* Embarrass, confound.

a·bate (abāt´) *v.* (**a·bat·ed, a·bat·ing**). Diminish, make or become less; lower; deduct (part of price); (law) quash (action), end (nuisance). **a·bate´ment** *n.*

ab·at·toir (ăb´atwār, ăbatwār´) *n.* Slaughterhouse.

Ab·ba (ăb´a). Used (in "~, *Father*") in invocations to God; title of bishops in Syriac and Coptic Churches. [Aram. = "father"]

ab·ba (abah´, ah´ba) = ABA.

ab·ba·cy (ăb´asē) *n.* (pl. **-cies**). Office, jurisdiction, or tenure of abbot or abbess.

Ab·bas (ăb´as, abahs´) (566–652). Uncle of Muhammad.

Ab·bas·id (ăb´asĭd, abăs´ĭd) *n.* Member of dynasty of caliphs ruling in Baghdad 750–1258, claiming descent from ABBAS.

ab·ba·tial (abā´shal) *adj.* Of an abbey, abbot, or abbess.

ab·bé (ăbā´, ăb´ā) *n.* 1. (esp. in France) Abbot. 2. Title of respect for a priest or any ecclesiastical figure.

ab·bess (ăb´es) *n.* Female superior of community of nuns, in those orders in which monks are governed by abbots.

Abbe·vil·li·an (ăbvĭl´ēan) *adj.* & *n.* (Culture) of the earliest paleolithic period in Europe, represented by the remains found at Abbeville, N. France (formerly called CHELLEAN).

ab·bey (ăb´ē) *n.* (pl. **-beys**). Body of monks or nuns governed by an abbot or abbess; monastic buildings; church or house once an abbey or part of it.

Ab·bey (ăb´ē) **Theatre.** Irish national theater, located since 1904 on Abbey St., Dublin.

ab·bot (ăb´ot) *n.* Superior of community of monks (now chiefly in Benedictine and Augustinian orders), usu. elected by the monks for life or period of years, and freq. holding certain episcopal rights. [Aram. *abba* father]

abbr., abbrev. *abbrevs.* Abbreviated; abbreviation.

ab·bre·vi·ate (abrē´vēāt) *v.t.* (**-at·ed, -at·ing**). Shorten, contract (esp. word, by writing part for the whole). **ab·bre·vi·a·tion** (abrēvēā´shon) *n.*

ABC (ābēsē´) *n.* (pl. **ABC's, ABCs**). Alphabet, rudiments of subject.

ab·di·cate (ăb´dĭkāt) *v.* (**-cat·ed, -cat·ing**). Renounce, relinquish (esp. crown) formally or by default. **ab·di·ca·tion** (ăbdĭkā´shon) *n.*

ab·do·men (ăb´domen, ăbdō´-) *n.* 1. (anat.) Part of body between diaphragm and floor of pelvis, containing digestive and other organs. 2. (zool.) Hind part, not bearing walking limbs, of insects, spiders, etc. **ab·dom·i·nal** (ăbdŏm´inal) *adj.*

ab·duct (ăbdŭkt´) *v.t.* Carry off person (esp. by force), kidnap; (of muscle etc.) draw limb from normal position. **ab·duc´tion, ab·duc´tor** *ns.*

a·beam (abēm´) *adv.* On a line

*Above: Earliest calculating device of the ancient world before adoption of the nine figures and zero, the **abacus** is still commonly used in the East for commercial purposes. The word is thought to derive from the Hebrew 'abāq', which described sand strewn on a surface to be written on.*

*Right: St. Mary's Abbey, York, U.K. Historically an **abbey** housed a religious community governed by an abbot or abbess. Before the Reformation, abbeys were dominant locally.*

LIVER

STOMACH

COLON

ILEUM

All the organs of the **abdomen** shown in the illustration are crucial to digestion. When food is eaten, its digestion starts in the stomach and is continued in the ileum and the colon. The liver stores products of digestion and converts them into other substances needed by the body, or to be excreted.

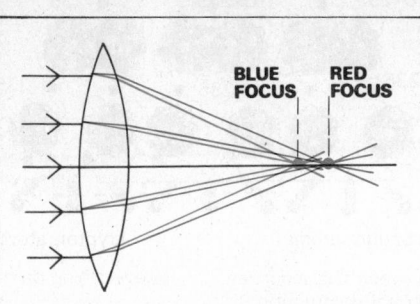

BLUE FOCUS   RED FOCUS

*Left: In chromatic **aberration**, when light passes through a convex lens the rays of various colors in the light are variously bent. Not a single focus but a sequence of foci results.*

*Below: **Aberdeen Angus,** famous breed of beef cattle notable for its quality of flesh. The Angus won world rank after its introduction to the U.S.A. in 1873.*

at right angles to ship's or aircraft's length; opposite the middle of ship's or aircraft's side.

a·be·ce·dar·i·an (ābēsēdār'ēan) *adj.* 1. Arranged alphabetically, as the 119th Psalm. 2. Elementary. ~ *n.* Pupil learning the alphabet; beginner, novice.

à Beck·et (a bĕk'ĭt), **Thomas**: see BECKET.

a·bed (abĕd') *adv.* (archaic, poet.) In bed.

A·bed·ne·go (abĕd'negō). Jewish youth who, with Shadrach and Meshach, came unharmed from a furnace into which they had been thrown by Nebuchadnezzar (Dan. 3).

A·bel (ā'bel). Second son of Adam, killed by his brother Cain (Gen. 4).

Ab·é·lard (ăb'elård; *Fr.* ăbālår'), **Pierre** (1079–1142). French philosopher; advocate of rational theological inquiry and founder of scholastic theology. (See also HÉLOÏSE.)

a·bele (abēl', ā'bel) *n.* White poplar (*Populus alba*).

Ab·er·deen (ăberdēn'). City on E. coast of N. Scotland; university, 1494; ~ (ăb'erdēn) **Angus,** (one of) a breed of polled black beef cattle; **Ab·er·do·ni·an** (ăberdō'nēan) *adj.* & *n.*

ab·er·rant (abĕr'ant) *adj.* 1. Wandering, straying from moral standard. 2. Diverging from normal type. **ab·er'rance** *n.*

ab·er·ra·tion (ăberā'shon) *n.* 1. Mental or moral slip or error; deviation from type. 2. (optics) Nonconvergence of rays to one focus. 3. (astron., also ~ **of light**) Displacement of true position of heavenly body to observer on Earth, due to Earth's motion and noninstantaneous transmission of light; **plane·tary** ~, aberration due to motion of the planet itself.

a·bet (abĕt') *v.t.* (**a·bet·ted, a·bet·ting**). Help or encourage, esp. in wrongdoing. **a·bet'ter, a·bet'tor** *ns.*

a·bey·ance (abā'ans) *n.* State of suspension, dormant condition (of rights etc.).

ab·hor (ăbhōr') *v.t.* (**-horred, -hor·ring**). Regard with disgust and hatred. **ab·hor·rent** (ăbhōr'ent, -hăr'-) *adj.* Inspiring disgust, repugnant, detestable. **ab·hor'rent·ly** *adv.* **ab·hor'rence** *n.*

a·bide (abīd') *v.* (**a·bode** pr. abōd', **a·bid·ed, a·bid·ing**). Re-

main; continue; dwell (archaic);
wait for (archaic); (with neg.)
tolerate; ~ **by**, remain faithful to.
a·bid'ing *adj.* Enduring, permanent. **a·bid'ing·ly** *adv.*

Ab·i·djan (ăbĭjahn'). Seaport on
the Gulf of Guinea; capital of the
Ivory Coast.

Ab·i·gail (ăb'igāl). 1. Wife of
Nabal and subsequently of David
(I Sam. 25). 2. In Beaumont and
Fletcher's *Scornful Lady*, the wait-
ing gentlewoman (cf. I Sam. 25)
hence (**a** ~), lady's maid.

Ab·i·lene (ăb'ilēn). City in
Kansas west of Topeka; boyhood
home of Dwight D. Eisenhower.

a·bil·i·ty (*a*bĭl'ĭtē) *n.* (pl. **-ties**)
Sufficient power, capacity (*to* do)
legal competency (to act); cleverness, talent, mental power.

A·bim·e·lech (*a*bĭm'elĕk). 1
Son of Gideon, one of the judges of
Israel (Judges 8, 9). 2. King of
Gerar, southern Palestine (Gen. 20
26).

tail cone

stabilizing tail fins

air pressure detonator

air inlet tube

airstream deflectors

pressure sensors

detonating head

conventional explosive charge

packing

neutron reflector

battery stores

cast bomb casing

lead shield container

fuses

incoming neutron

U-235 (stable)

U-236 (unstable)

barium atom   krypton atom

free neutrons

U-235   U-235   U-235

U-236   U-236   U-236

barium atoms   krypton atoms

everything vaporized   everything damage

total destruction

severe blast damage   serious fires

HIROSHIMA

Japan

0 miles   3

0 kilometres   5

Inside view of uranium bomb 'Little Boy'
(U-235), first **A-bomb** *which was*
dropped on and destroyed Hiroshima,
August 1945. Shown also: chain re-
action that fuelled it. Atomic bombs
work by nuclear fission (splitting
atoms); hydrogen bombs by fusion.
Atomic energy is now harnessed to
engineering projects and mining.

ab·in·i·ti·o (ăb ĭnĭsh´ēō). From the beginning (abbrev. *ab init.*). [L.]

a·bi·o·gen·e·sis (ābīōjĕn´ĭsĭs, ăbē-) *n.* T.H. Huxley's term for spontaneous generation (opp. BIO-GENESIS).

ab·ject (ăb´jĕkt, ăbjĕkt´) *adj.* Brought low, miserable, craven, degraded. **ab·ject´ly** *adv.*

ab·jure (ăbjoor´) *v.t.* (**-jured, -jur·ing**). Renounce on oath.
ab·ju·ra·tion (ăbjoorā´shon) *n.*

abl. *abbrev.* Ablative.

ab·la·tion (ăblā´shon) *n.* 1. Removal (esp. in surgery, of part of body). 2. (geol.) Waste of a glacier by evaporation and melting. 3. (of a rocket) Burning away of nose material on reentry into Earth's atmosphere.

ab·la·tive (ăb´latĭv) *adj.* (gram.) Of the case (in Latin and other languages) denoting direction from a place, also time and source, agent, or instrument. ~ *n.* (Word in) ablative case; ~ **absolute**, Latin construction of noun and participle (both in ablative case) expressing time, occasion, or circumstances.

ab·laut (ahb´lowt; ăb´-) *n.* (philol.) Systematic vowel permutation (not due to influence of contiguous sounds) in root of word to show changes in tense, meaning, etc., as in s*i*ng, s*a*ng, s*u*ng.

a·blaze (ablāz´) *adv.* Blazing; on fire; gleaming, brilliant.

a·ble (ā´bel) *adj.* (**a·bler, a·blest**). Having the power or ability; talented, clever; ~ **-bodied**, physically fit, robust; ~ **(-bodied) seaman**, (abbrev. A.B.) certified merchant seaman.

-able *suffix.* Close in meaning to the word *able*; by addition to nouns and verbs used to form many adjectives with sense "that can, may or must be" (*bearable, readable, washable*); "that can be made the subject of" (*objectionable*); "that is in accordance with" (*fashionable, reasonable*).

ab·lu·tion (ăbloo´shon, abloo´-) *n.* Ceremonial washing; water or wine used in this; (pl.) process of washing oneself.

ABM *abbrev.* Antiballistic missile.

ab·ne·gate (ăb´negāt) *v.t.* (**-gat·ed, -gat·ing**). Deny oneself (thing), renounce (right, belief).
ab·ne·ga·tion (ăbnega´shon) *n.*

ab·nor·mal (ăbnōr´mal) *adj.* Deviating from type, exceptional, irregular. **ab·nor´mal·ly** *adv.*
ab·nor·mal·i·ty (ăbnōrmăl´ĭtē) *n.* (pl. **-ties**).

ab·nor·mi·ty (ăbnōr´mĭtē) *n.* (pl. **-ties**). Irregularity; monstrosity.

a·board (abōrd´, abōrd´) *adv.* & *prep.* On board (ship, train, etc.).

a·bode (abōd´) *n.* 1. Dwelling place. 2. See ABIDE.

a·bol·ish (abŏl´ĭsh) *v.t.* Put an end to.

ab·o·li·tion (ăbolĭsh´on) *n.* Action or fact of abolishing; in 18th and 19th centuries esp. in U.S. history, movement against slavery, usu. A~. **ab·o·li´tion·ism** *n.* **ab·o·li·tion·ist** *n.* One advocating abolition, esp. of slavery.

ab·o·ma·sum (ăbomā´sum) *n.* (pl. **-sa** pr. -s*a*). Fourth stomach of ruminant.

Australian **Aboriginal** *hunter stands poised to spear fish in a swamp. The Aboriginals have been in Australia for at least 40,000 years. They now number about 160,000.*

A-bomb (ā´bŏm) *n.* Atom(ic) bomb.

a·bom·i·na·ble (abŏm´inabel) *adj.* Morally or physically loathsome, detestable, odious, revolting; **A ~ Snowman** = YETI. **a·bom´i·na·bly** *adv.*

a·bom·i·nate (abŏm´ināt) *v.t.* (**-nat·ed, -nat·ing**). Loathe, dislike strongly.

a·bom·i·na·tion (abŏminā´shon) *n.* Loathing; object or practice deserving of aversion or disgust.

ab·o·rig·i·nal (ăborĭj´inal) *adj.* Indigenous, existing or present at dawn of history or before arrival of colonists or invaders. ~ *n.* Aboriginal inhabitant (esp. of Australia).

ab·o·rig·i·nes (ăborĭj´inēz) *n.pl.* Aboriginal inhabitants, plants, etc. **ab·o·rig´i·ne** *n.* (colloq.) Aboriginal inhabitant.

a·bort (abōrt´) *v.* 1. (Cause to) miscarry; (biol.) become sterile, remain undeveloped. 2. Fail, cease prematurely. 3. (aeronaut.) Terminate (mission, flight) prematurely. ~ *n.* (aeronaut.) Premature termination of mission flight.

a·bor·ti·fa·cient (abōrtĭfā´shent) *adj.* & *n.* (Drug etc.) causing abortion.

a·bor·tion (abōr´shon) *n.* 1. Termination of pregnancy by expulsion of fetus, esp. before 28th week of pregnancy; (pop.) operation etc. inducing this. 2. Fetus expelled in abortion. 3. Misshapen creature; failed project or action. **a·bor´tion·ist** *n.* One who performs abortion.

a·bor·tive (abōr´tĭv) *adj.* Premature; fruitless; rudimentary. **a·bor´tive·ly** *adv.* **a·bor´tive·ness** *n.*

A·bou·kir (ahbōokēr´) **Bay** = ABUKIR BAY.

a·bou·li·a (abōo´lēa) = ABULIA.

a·bound (abownd´) *v.i.* Be plentiful; be rich (*in*), teem or be infested (*with*).

a·bout (abowt´) *adv.* On every side; near; somewhere around; here and there; astir; almost; (naut.) on or to the opposite tack (so **come, put ~**, = TACK[1] *v.* def. 2); **be ~ to** (do), be on the point of doing; **come ~**, happen; **~ face**, (mil.) turn so as to face in opposite direction. **about** *prep.* 1. On every side of; near; with. 2. Concerning. 3. Occupied with. 4. Here and there in, on, etc.

a·bout·face (abowt´fās´) *n.* Reversal of direction, opinion, policy, or behavior.

a·bove (abŭv´) *adv.* Higher up, overhead; upstream; earlier in a book etc. ~ *prep.* Over, higher than, of higher rank, etc., than; in addition to; ~ **all**, more important than everything else; of higher rank than. **a·bove´board**, without concealment; fair, open, honest.

ab·ra·ca·dab·ra (ăbrakadăb'ra) *n.* Cabalistic word formerly used as charm, orig. by Gnostics, and believed to have power of curing agues etc., esp. when written on amulet; (now) spell, mysterious formula, gibberish.

a·brade (abrād') *v.t.* (**a·brad·ed, a·brad·ing**). Scrape off, wear away, injure, by rubbing.

A·bra·ham (ā'brahăm). Hebrew patriarch, from whom all Jews trace their descent (Gen. 11); **~'s bosom**, heavenly abode of the blessed dead (Luke 16); **Plains of ~**, plateau near Quebec, scaled from St. Lawrence River by English army under WOLFE[1] (1759) and scene of subsequent battle with French under MONTCALM, which decided fate of Canada.

a·bra·sion (abrā'zhon) *n.* Rubbing or scraping off; rough or sore place on skin caused by this; (geol.) wearing away of Earth's surface by wind-borne particles of rock or sand (cf. EROSION).

a·bra·sive (abrā'sĭv, -zĭv) *adj.* Tending to produce abrasion. **~** *n.* Any substance, as emery, Carborundum, etc., used for grinding or polishing.

ab·re·ac·tion (ăbrēăk'shon) *n.* (psychiatry) Removal, by revival and expression, of the emotion associated with an event that has undergone repression in memory.

a·breast (abrĕst') *adv.* Side by side and facing the same way; **~ of**, keeping up with, not behind (times etc.).

a·bridge (abrĭj') *v.t.* (**a·bridged, a·bridg·ing**). Condense, shorten, curtail. **a·bridg'ment,** Brit. **a·bridge'ment** *ns.* Curtailment; epitome, abstract.

a·broad (abrawd') *adv.* In or to foreign lands; broadly, in different directions; out of doors; (of rumor etc.) current; **from ~**, from foreign countries.

ab·ro·gate (ăb'rogāt) *v.t.* (**-gat·ed, -gat·ing**). Repeal, cancel. **ab·ro·ga·tion** (ăbrogā'shon) *n.*

ab·rupt (abrŭpt') *adj.* Sudden, hasty; brusque; disconnected; steep; (bot.) truncated. **ab·rupt'ly** *adv.* **ab·rupt'ness** *n.*

A·bruz·zi e Mo·li·se (ahbrōōt'sē ĕ mawlē'zĕ). Region of central Italy between the Apennines and the Adriatic.

abs-: see AB-.

Ab·sa·lom (ăb'salom). Third and favorite son of DAVID[1], killed while leading rebellion against his father (2 Sam.).

ab·scess (ăb'sĕs) *n.* Local inflammation of body tissues with deep suppuration caused by bacteria that destroy the cells in the center of the area and leave a cavity filled with pus.

ab·scis·sa (ăbsĭs'a) *n.* (pl.

*'Improvisation', by Kandinsky is an example of **abstract** art, a term which covers the non-figurative painting and sculpture of this century. Abstract art rejects dominance of subject matter.*

-scis·sas, -scis·sae pr. -sĭs'ē). (geom.) Part of line between fixed point on it and ordinate to it from any other point; coordinate parallel to *x*-axis (horizontal axis) in a system of coordinates.

ab·scis·sion (ăbsĭzh'on) *n.* Cutting off; (bot.) separation.

ab·scond (ăbskŏnd') *v.i.* Go away secretly, fly from the law.

ab·sence (ăb'sens) *n.* Being away or absent; nonexistence, lack (*of*); abstracted state.

ab·sent (ăb'sent) *adj.* Not present; not existing; abstracted in mind; **~-minded**, abstracted, preoccupied; forgetful; **~-mindedly** (*adv.*), **~-mindedness** (*n.*); **absent without leave**, (mil.) absent from military duties without authorization, but without intending to desert, abbrev. AWOL or A.W.O.L. **absent** (ăbsĕnt') *v.t.* Keep (oneself) away, withdraw (oneself).

ab·sen·tee (ăbsentē') *n.* Person not present; person who absents himself or herself from duties etc.;

~ ballot, ballot cast by mail by a voter away from his or her usual voting place; **~ vote**, absentee ballots collectively. **ab·sen·tee'·ism** *n.*

ab·sinthe, ab·sinth (ăb'sĭnth) *ns.* Wormwood, the plant or its essence; strong greenish-gray liqueur flavored with wormwood and anise.

ab·so·lute (ăb'solōōt) *adj.* Complete, perfect, pure; unrestricted, independent; despotic, ruling arbitrarily; not in (the usual) grammatical relation with other words; real, not relative or comparative; unqualified; self-existent and conceivable without relation to other things; **~ alcohol**, containing at least 99% pure alcohol by weight; **~ magnitude**, magnitude of a star as it would appear at a distance of 10 parsecs; **~ music**, self-dependent instrumental music without literary or other extraneous suggestions (opp. PROGRAM music); **~ pitch**, (mus.) ability to recognize or reproduce pitch of notes; pitch of a note defined scientifically in terms of vibrations per second; **~ temperature**, temperature measured on a Centigrade (Celsius) scale, which has its zero at absolute zero; **~ zero**: see ZERO. **ab·so·lute·ly** (ăb'solōōtlē, ăbsolōōt'-) *adv.*

Completely, independently; yes, quite so.

ab·so·lu·tion (ăbsoloo͞o'shon) *n.* Formal forgiveness, esp. ecclesiastical declaration of forgiveness of sins; remission of penance.

ab·so·lut·ism (ăb'soloo͞otĭzem) *n.* (pol.) Principle of absolute government, despotism. **ab'so·lut·ist** *n.*

ab·solve (ăbzŏlv', -sŏlv') *v.t.* (**-solved, -solv·ing**). Set or pronounce free from blame etc.; acquit.

ab·sorb (ăbsôrb', -zôrb') *v.t.* Swallow up, incorporate; engross the attention of; suck in (liquid); take in (heat, light, etc.); assume (an expense). **ab·sorb'a·ble** *adj.* That can be absorbed.

ab·sorb·ent (ăbsôr'bent, -zôr'-) *adj.* Having a tendency to absorb. ~ *n.* Absorbent substance.

ab·sorp·tion (ăbsôrp'shon, -zôrp'-) *n.* Action of absorbing, fact of being absorbed.

ab·stain (ăbstān') *v.i.* Keep oneself from doing something, esp. from drinking alcohol. **ab·stain'er** *n.*

ab·ste·mi·ous (ăbstē'mēus) *adj.* Sparing or moderate in food, drink, etc. **ab·ste'mi·ous·ly** *adv.* **ab·ste'mi·ous·ness** *n.*

ab·sten·tion (ăbstĕn'shon) *n.* Refraining or holding back; not using one's vote.

ab·sti·nence (ăb'stinens) *n.* Abstaining from food, pleasure, alcohol, etc. **ab'sti·nent** *adj.* Practicing abstinence.

ab·stract (ăb'străkt) *adj.* Not concrete; theoretical, not practical; (of art etc.) concerned with pure form and pattern, free from representational qualities; ~ **expressionism**, form of abstract art in which paint is applied by spontaneous or random action of artist. **abstract** *n.* 1. **the** ~, ideal or theoretical way of regarding things. 2. Epitome, summary. 3. Abstraction, abstract term. ~ (ăbstrăkt') *v.t.* Deduct, remove; steal; disengage (attention etc.); summarize. **ab·stract'ed** *adj.* Withdrawn in thought, not attending.

ab·strac·tion (ăbstrăk'shon) *n.* Withdrawal, removal; abstract idea; absent-mindedness; abstract art.

ab·struse (ăbstroo͞os') *adj.* Hard to understand, profound. **ab·struse'ly** *adv.* **ab·struse'ness** *n.*

ab·surd (ăbserd', -zerd') *adj.* Incongruous, unreasonable, ridiculous.

A·bu Dha·bi (aboo͞o' dah'bē). City on the Persian Gulf; capital of the United Arab Emirates.

A·bu·kir (ahboo͞oker') **Bay, Aboukir Bay.** Bay at the mouth of the Nile, N. Egypt; British fleet defeated French fleet here in 1798.

a·bu·li·a (abū'lēa), **a·bou·li·a** (aboo͞o'lēa) *ns.* Loss of willpower (as mental disorder).

a·bun·dance (abŭn'dans) *n.* Plenty, more than enough; affluence; (phys.) amount present.

a·bun'dant *adj.* Plentiful, rich, in abundance. **a·bun'dant·ly** *adv.*

a·buse (abūz') *v.t.* (**a·bused, a·bus·ing**). Make bad use of, misuse; speak insultingly to or about. ~ (abūs') *n.* Misuse, perversion; unjust or corrupt practice; insulting speech. **a·bu'sive** *adj.* **a·bu'sive·ly** *adv.* **a·bu·sive·ness** *n.*

A·bu Sim·bel (aboo͞o' sĭm'bĕl). Village on the Nile S. of Aswan, Egypt; site of ancient Egyptian rock temples built by Rameses II.

a·but (abŭt') *v.* (**a·but·ted, a·but·ting**). Have common boundary with; border (*on*); end *on*, lean *against*. **a·but'ment** *n.* (archit.) Support from which arch, vault, etc. springs, and which receives the lateral thrust. **a·but'ter** *n.*

a·bysm (abĭz'em) *n.* (poet.) Abyss.

a·bys·mal (abĭz'mal) *adj.* Bottomless (esp. fig.); extremely bad. **a·bys'mal·ly** *adv.*

a·byss (abĭs') *n.* Primal chaos; bottomless chasm; deep gorge.

a·bys·sal (abĭs'al) *adj.* Of lowest depths of ocean.

Ab·ys·sin·i·a (ăbĭsĭn'ēa). Former name of Ethiopia. **Ab·ys·sin'i·an** *adj. & n.*

AC, A.C., ac *abbrevs.* Alternating current.

A/C, a/c *abbrevs.* Account; account current.

a.c. *abbrev.* (in prescriptions) Before meals.

*A large genus of trees and shrubs belonging to the pea family, the **acacia** is most commonly found in Africa and Australia. Of some 900 species, about 650 grow only in Australia.*

*Trail down the Grand Canyon, Arizona, the immense **abyss** cut by the Colorado River. The winding course of the gorge extends to 217 miles and in width it ranges from some 4 to 18 miles.*

a·ca·cia (*akā′sha*) *n.* 1. Leguminous shrub or tree of genus *A* ~ (subfamily Mimoseae), found in warmer regions of Europe and Australia, some species of which yield gum arabic, dyes, etc. 2. N. Amer. locust tree (*Robinia pseudo-acacia,* false ~), with sweet-scented pea-like flowers.

ac·a·deme (*ăk′adēm*) *n.* (properly) = ACADEMUS; (used by mistake in poet. style for) the Greek ACADEMY, hence, college, university. [Gk.; mistake perh. caused by Milton's "grove of Academe," (in *Paradise Regained*) i.e. Academus]

ac·a·dem·ic (*ăkadĕm′ĭk*) *adj.* 1. Of an academy or academician; of a university or college. 2. Of the philosophic school of Plato, skeptical. 3. Scholarly; abstract, cold, merely logical; impractical; theoretical, conventional. ~ *n.* Member of university.

ac·a·dem·i·cal (*ăkadĕm′ĭkal*) *adj.* Of a college or university. **ac·a·dem′i·cal·ly** *adv.*

a·cad·e·mi·cian (*akădemĭsh′an,* *ăkade-*) *n.* Member of art, literary, or scientific academy; teacher.

A·ca·dé·mie Fran·çaise (*ăkă-dāmē frahńsĕz′*). French honorary literary academy, founded by Richelieu (1635); membership, limited to 40, is considered the highest distinction for men of letters.

Ac·a·de·mus (*ăkadē′mus*). (Gk. legend) Hero who revealed hiding place of their sister Helen to the Dioscuri when they invaded Attica.

a·cad·e·my (*akăd′emē*) *n.* (pl. **-mies**). 1. **A** ~ , pleasure garden near Athens (said to have belonged to ACADEMUS) in which Plato taught; Plato's followers, the philosophical school founded by him. 2. A secondary or high school (esp. private). 3. Place of training in a special art. 4. Society for cultivating literature, art, etc.; **the A** ~ , (esp.) the Royal Academy of Arts, the *Académie Française,* the U.S.S.R. Academy of Science, etc.

A·ca·di·a (*akā′dēa*). Name given by French to district in what is now known as Nova Scotia, first settled by them at end of 16th c. **A·ca′-di·an** *adj.* & *n.* (Native, inhabitant) of Acadia; (descendant) of Acadians. **Acadia National Park**, scenic recreation area on Mount Desert Island off the S. coast of Maine.

ac·an·thop·ter·yg·i·an (*ăkan-thŏpterĭj′ēan*) *adj.* & *n.* (Fish) of group Acanthopterygii, usu. with hard spiny rays in dorsal and anal fins.

a·can·thus (*akăn′thus*) *n.* (pl. **-thus·es, -thi** pr. **-thī**). 1. Herbaceous plant of genus *A* ~ with large, deeply cut, hairy, shining leaves, native to southern Europe, Asia, and Africa. 2. (archit.) Conventionalized leaf of

A. mollis or *A. spinosus* (with narrower spiny-toothed leaves) used as ornament, esp. on the Corinthian and Composite capitals.

a cap·pel·la (ah kapĕl′a). (of choral music) Unaccompanied.

A·ca·pul·co (*ăkapōōl′kō; Sp.* ahkahpōōl′kaw). Port and resort city on the Pacific coast of Mexico.

ac·a·rid (*ăk′arĭd*) *n.* Arachnid of family Acaridae, a mite or tick.

acc. *abbrev.* Account; accusative.

Ac·cad (*ăk′ăd,* ah′kahd), **Ac·ca·di·an** (*akā′dēan,* akah′-): see AKKAD.

ac·cede (*ăksēd′*) *v.i.* (**-ced·ed,** **-ced·ing**). Consent, agree (*to*); (also ~ *to*) enter upon office.

ac·ce·le·ran·do (ahchĕlerahn′-dō) *adv., adj.,* & *n.* (pl. **-dos**). (mus.) (Passage performed) with gradual increase of speed. [It.]

ac·cel·er·ate (*ăksĕl′erāt*) *v.* (**-at·ed, -at·ing**). Make, become, quicker; cause to happen earlier; **accelerated particle,** (phys.) one subjected to acceleration, esp. by electrical or magnetic means.

ac·cel·er·a·tion (*ăksĕlerā′shon*) *n.* Accelerating; vehicle's power to accelerate; (phys.) rate of increase in velocity of moving body (written, e.g., 10 fps/sec. if body moves 10 feet per second faster in every second).

ac·cel·er·a·tor (*ăksĕl′erāter*) *n.*

Thing that increases anything's speed; pedal that operates throttle of internal combustion engine; substance added to mixture to reduce time taken by chemical reaction; electrical or magnetic apparatus (also *atom smasher*) giving high velocities to free electrons or other atomic particles.

ac·cent (*ăk′sĕnt*) *n.* Prominence given to syllable by stress or pitch; mark used to indicate syllabic pitch, vowel quality, etc. (see ACUTE, CIRCUMFLEX, GRAVE[2], ~); individual, local, or national mode of pronunciation; (pl.) speech; (pros.) rhythmical stress; (mus.) stress recurring at intervals; (fig.) distinctive character; emphasis *on.*

ac·cent (*ăk′sĕnt, ăksĕnt′*) *v.t.* Pronounce with accent or stress, emphasize; mark with (written) accents; intensify, make conspicuous.

ac·cen·tu·al (*ăksĕn′chōōal*) *adj.* Of accent; (esp. of verse) in which meter or rhythm results from alternation of strong and weak (not long and short) syllables. **ac·cen′-tu·al·ly** *adv.*

ac·cen·tu·ate (*ăksĕn′chōōāt*) *v.t.* (**-at·ed, -at·ing**). Accent (esp. in fig. senses). **ac·cen·tu·a·tion** (*ăksĕnchōōā′shon*) *n.*

ac·cept (*ăksĕpt′*) *v.t.* Consent to receive; answer (invitation etc.) affirmatively; receive or regard as

*1968: 'Saturn' rocket blasts off with a supreme feat of **acceleration** — the rate of change, with time, in the velocity of a moving object.*

Acadia National Park *in south-east Maine on the Atlantic coast was established in 1919. An abundance of wildlife inhabits the area and there are several museums and nature centers.*

adequate, satisfactory, or true; tolerate; agree to pay; undertake (office, responsibility). **ac·cept'- ance, ac·cep'tor** *ns.*

ac·cept·a·ble (ăksĕp'tabel) *adj.* Worth accepting; adequate; satisfactory. **ac·cept'a·bly** *adv.* **ac·cept·a·bil·i·ty** (ăksĕptabĭl'ĭtē) *n.*

ac·cept·ed (ăksĕp'tĭd) *adj.* Generally approved, recognized, or believed in.

ac·cess (ăk'sĕs) *n.* 1. Approach; addition; right or means of approach; being approached. 2. Attack or outburst.

ac·ces·si·ble (ăksĕs'ibel) *adj.* Able to be reached, entered, or obtained; open to influence (of). **ac·ces'si·bly** *adv.* **ac·ces·si·bil·i·ty** (ăksĕsibĭl'ĭtē) *n.*

ac·ces·sion (ăksĕsh'on) *n.* Acceding or attaining (esp. to throne or manhood); joining, addition; (law) addition to property by natural growth or artificial improvement.

ac·ces·so·ry (ăksĕs'erē) *adj.* Additional, subordinately contributive, adventitious. ~ *n.* (pl. **-ries**). 1. Person who aids or encourages lawbreaker before (~ **before the fact**) or after (~ **after the fact**) the commission of a criminal act. 2. Accompaniment, adjunct; (pl., commerc.) smaller articles of (esp. woman's) dress, as shoes, gloves, etc.; minor fittings for car, camera, etc.

ac·ci·dent (ăk'sĭdent) *n.* 1. Event without apparent cause, the unexpected; unintentional act, chance misfortune, mishap. 2. Property or quality not essential to our conception of a substance, attribute; mere accessory. **ac·ci·den·tal** (ăksĭdĕn'tal) *adj.* **ac·ci·den'tal·ly** *adv.* **ac·ci·dent'al** *n.* (mus.) Sharp ♯, flat ♭, or natural ♮ sign occurring not in key signature but before particular note.

ac·ci·die (ăk'sĭdē) *n.* Sloth; laziness or indifference.

ac·claim (aklām') *v.t.* Welcome or applaud loudly, hail. ~ *n.* Shout or applause or welcome.

ac·cla·ma·tion (ăklamā'shon) *n.* Loud and eager assent; (pl.) shouting in person's honor.

ac·cli·mate (aklī'mit, ăk'limāt) *v.t.* (**-mat·ed, -mat·ing**). Habituate to new climate or surroundings. **ac·cli·ma·tion** (ăklimā'shon) *n.*

ac·cli·ma·tize (aklī'matīz) *v.t.* (**-tized, -tiz·ing**) = ACCLIMATE. **ac·cli·ma·ti·za·tion** (ăklīmatīzā'- shon) *n.* Fact, process, of acclimatizing, esp. (biol.) in ref. to transference of plants or animals to a new environment.

ac·cliv·i·ty (aklĭv'ĭtē) *n.* (pl. **-ties**). Upward slope.

ac·co·lade (ăk'olād, ăkolād') *n.* 1. Ceremony of conferring knighthood, formerly an embrace, now usu. by stroke on shoulder with flat

Arch of Independence enshrining the eternal flame in **Accra**, *seaport and capital of Ghana, West Africa. Accra developed from Dutch and English forts established in the 17th century.*

of sword. 2. Expression of praise or approval.

ac·com·mo·date (akŏm'odāt) *v.t.* (**-dat·ed, -dat·ing**). 1. Adapt (*to*); harmonize; reconcile, settle differences between. 2. Equip, supply (*with*); oblige, confer favor on; find lodging for; contain comfortably. **ac·com'mo·dat·ing** *adj.* Obliging.

ac·com·mo·da·tion (akŏmodā'- shon) *n.* 1. Adaptation, adjustment; (of eye) adjustment of shape of lens to bring light rays from various distances to focus upon retina. 2. Settlement, compromise. 3. Serviceable thing, convenience. 4. Lodgings. 5. Loan.

ac·com·pa·ni·ment (akŭm'- panēment) *n.* Accompanying thing; appendage; (mus.) subsidiary part, gen. instrumental, supporting a solo instrument or voice, choir, etc.

ac·com·pa·nist (akŭm'panĭst) *n.* Performer of accompaniment.

ac·com·pa·ny (akŭm'panē) *v.t.* (**-nied, -ny·ing**). Go with, escort, attend; coexist with; (mus.) support (player, singer, chorus, etc.) by performing subsidiary part.

ac·com·plice (akŏm'plĭs) *n.* Associate, usu. subordinate, in guilt or crime.

ac·com·plish (akŏm'plĭsh) *v.t.* Perform, carry out, succeed in doing. **ac·com'plished** *adj.* Done, existing; skilled, having accomplishments. **ac·com'plish- ment** *n.* Achievement, fulfillment; social attainment.

ac·cord (akôrd') *v.* 1. Agree, be consistent (*with*). 2. Grant (indulgence, request, etc.). ~ *n.* Consent; mutual agreement; harmonious correspondence in color, tone, etc.; volition (as **of one's own** ~). **ac·cord'ance** *n.* Conformity, agreement. **ac·cord'ant** *adj.*

ac·cord·ing (akôr'dĭng) *adv.* ~ **to**, in a manner consistent with; on the authority of. **ac·cord'ing·ly** *adv.* Correspondingly; in accordance with what might be expected;

in due course; therefore.

ac·cor·di·on (akôr'dēon) *n.* Small portable musical instrument with bellows and keyboard admitting wind to metal reeds when keys are depressed; ~ **door,** ~ **file,** having a series of folds like the bellows of an accordion.

ac·cost (akawst, akŏst') *v.t.* Approach and address (esp. boldly); (of prostitute) solicit.

ac·couche·ment (ăkooshmahn') *n.* Lying-in, delivery. **ac·cou- cheur** (ăkooshēr') *n.* Male midwife. **ac·cou·cheuse** (ăkooshöz') *n.* Midwife. [Fr.]

ac·count (akownt') *n.* 1. Counting, reckoning. 2. Amount of money deposited with a bank; credit facilities allowed by shop etc. to customer; statement of money received and expended, with balance; statement of discharge of responsibilities generally, answering for conduct; final account at judgment seat of God; **balance, square** ~ **s** (*with*), settle account by payment of money due (freq. fig.); **for** ~ **of,** to be sold on behalf of; **give** (*good*) ~ **of oneself,** be successful, give favorable impression; **keep** ~ **s,** keep statement of expenditure and receipts; **on** ~ , as interim payment; **on** ~ **of,** in consideration of, because of; **on no** ~ , not for any reason, certainly not; **on one's own** ~ , for one's own purposes and at one's own risk; **on someone's** ~ , in a person's interest, for someone's sake. 3. Reckoning in one's favor, profit, advantage. 4. Estimation; **leave out of, take into,** ~ , (fail to) take into consideration. 5. Narration, report, description (*of*). 6. ~ **executive,** person in an advertising agency or other service business who is responsible for managing a client's account. **account** *v.* 1. Consider, regard as. 2. ~ **for,** give reckoning for; answer for; explain cause of, serve as explanation of.

ac·count·a·ble (akown'tabel) *adj.* 1. Bound to give account, responsible, liable. 2. Explicable. **ac·count·a·bil·i·ty** (akowntabĭl'- ĭtē) *n.*

ac·count·an·cy (akown'tansē) *n.* Profession or duties of accountant.

ac·count·ant (akown'tant) *n.* Professional keeper or inspector of accounts, esp. **certified public** ~ , one having official certificate as ~ .

ac·cou·ter (akoo'ter) *v.t.* Attire, equip. esp. for military duty (chiefly in past part. **accoutered**).

ac·cou·ter·ment (akoo'terment) *n.* (usu. *n.pl.*) Equipment, trappings.

ac·cou·tre (akoo'ter) *v.t.* (**-tred, -tring**). (esp. Brit.) = ACCOUTER. **ac·cou·tre·ment** (akoo'trement) *n.*

Ac·cra (ăk'ra, akrah'). W. Afr. seaport on Gulf of Guinea, capital

The **acetylene** torch is used in the welding and cutting of practically all industrial metals. This colorless, gaseous hydrocarbon is mixed with oxygen for use in industry.

of Ghana.

ac·cred·it (akrĕd´ĭt) *v.t.* Gain credit for; provide with credentials, as an ambassador; certify as meeting specific requirements; attribute *to*. **ac·cred'it·ed** *adj.* Officially recognized; generally accepted.

ac·crete (akrēt´) *v.i.* (**-cret·ed, -cret·ing**). Grow together or into one; form around or on (*to*), as around a nucleus. **ac·cre·tion** (akrē´shon) *n.* Growth by organic enlargement; increase by external additions; adhesion of extraneous matter; matter so added, extraneous addition.

ac·crue (akrōō´) *v.i.* (**-crued, -cru·ing**). Fall (*to* one) as a natural growth, advantage, or result (esp. of interest on invested money).

ac·cu·mu·late (akū´myulāt) *v.* (**-lat·ed, -lat·ing**). Heap up, amass; grow numerous, form increasing mass or heap. **ac·cu·mu·la·tion** (akūmyulā´shon) *n.* **ac·cu·mu·la·tive** (akū´myulātĭv, -latĭv) *adj.*

ac·cu·mu·la·tor (akū´myulāter) *n.* 1. One who collects. 2. Equipment for collecting and storing energy. 3. (Brit.) Storage battery.

ac·cu·rate (ăk´yerĭt) *adj.* Precise, exact, correct. **ac'cu·rate·ly** *adv.* **ac'cu·ra·cy** *n.* (pl. **-cies**).

ac·curs·ed (aker´sĭd, akerst´), **ac·curst** (akerst´) *adjs.* Lying under a curse; execrable, detestable.

ac·cu·sa·tion (ăkyuzā´shon) *n.* Accusing; allegation, indictment.

ac·cu·sa·tive (akū´zatĭv) *adj.* (gram.) Of the case (also *objective* case) chiefly denoting the direct object of a verb or used following certain prepositions. ~ *n.* (Word in) accusative case. **ac·cu'sa·tive·ly** *adv.*

ac·cu·sa·to·ry (akū´zatōrē, -tōrē) *adj.* Conveying or implying accusation.

ac·cuse (akūz´) *v.t.* (**-cused, -cus·ing**). Charge with fault, indict; blame, lay fault on; **the accused**, defendant in criminal case.

ac·cus·tom (akŭs´tom) *v.t.* Familiarize by habit or custom. **ac·cus'tomed** *adj.* Customary, usual; used.

ace (ās) *n.* 1. Card, die face, etc., with one pip. 2. Fighter pilot who has shot down many enemy planes; person excelling in any sport or skill; (tennis etc.) unreturnable service; point thus scored; (golf) a hole in one; the hole thus made; ~ **in the hole**, ~ **up one's sleeve**, something effective kept in reserve. **ace** *v.t.* (**aced, ac·ing**). 1. (tennis) Score an ace against (one's

opponent). 2. (golf) Reach (a hole) from the tee in a single stroke. ~ *adj.* (colloq.) Excellent, of high quality, outstanding.

a·ce·di·a (asē´dēa) = ACCIDIE.

a·ceph·a·lous (asĕf´alus) *adj.* Headless; (zool.) having no part of body specially organized as head; (bot.) with head aborted or cut off; (pros.) lacking the regular first syllable.

a·cer·bi·ty (aser´bĭtē) *n.* Astringent sourness; bitterness of speech, manner, or temper.

ac·e·tal (ăs´etăl) *n.* Colorless pleasant-smelling liquid formed by slow oxidation of alcohol; class of complex ethers, derivatives of aldehyde, of which this is the type.

ac·et·al·de·hyde (ăsĭtăl´dehīd) *n.* Aldehyde.

ac·et·an·i·lide (ăsĭtăn´ĭlĭd) *n.* White crystalline solid made by action of acetic acid on aniline and used as febrifuge and analgesic.

ac·e·tate (ăs´ĭtāt) *n.* Salt of acetic acid; synthetic material in the manufacture of which acetic acid is used; ~ **fiber**, textile fiber made from cellulose acetate.

a·ce·tic (asē´tĭk, asĕt´ĭk) *adj.* Of, producing, vinegar; ~ **acid**, colorless pungent biting organic acid (CH_3COOH) which gives vinegar its characteristic taste.

a·cet·i·fy (asĕt´ifī) *v.* (**-fied, -fy·ing**). Turn into vinegar, make or become sour. **a·cet·i·fi·ca·tion** (asĕtifīkā´shon) *n.*

aceto-, acet- *prefixes.* (chem.) Derived from, connected with, acetic acid or acetyl.

In a lead–acid **accumulator** (diagram), chemical reactions between lead plate, and lead dioxide plate, both immersed in dilute sulphuric acid, produce electrical energy.

ac·e·tone (ăs´ĭton) *n.* Colorless fragrant inflammable liquid ketone (CH_3COCH_3) widely used as an organic solvent and in making chloroform etc.

a·ce·tyl (asē´tĭl, ăs´e-) *n.* Monovalent radical (CH_3CO) of acetic acid. **a·cet·y·la·tion** (asĕtĭlā´shon) *n.* Introduction of acetyl group(s) into a compound by means of a chemical reaction. **a·cet·y·late** (asĕt´ĭlāt) *v.* (**-lat·ed, -lat·ing**).

a·cet·y·lene (asĕt´ĭlēn, -lĭn) *n.* Colorless, nearly odorless (when pure), highly inflammable gaseous hydrocarbon, usu. prepared by adding water to calcium carbide (impurities in which produce the characteristic unpleasant smell), and used for lighting, for welding, and for cutting metals, etc., hence, ∼ **torch.**

a·ce·tyl·sal·i·cyl·ic (asē´tĭlsălĭsĭl´ĭk) **acid.** Aspirin.

A·chae·a (akē´a). 1. District of ancient Greece along S. shore of Gulf of Corinth. 2. Roman province comprising all the southern part of Greece. **A·chae·an** *adj. & n.* 1. In Homer, apparently = Greek; hence, (one) of the early Greeks; of the early Greek civilization. 2. In classical times, (inhabitant) of Achaea.

A·cha·tes (akā´tēz). (Gk. & Rom. legend) Faithful friend of Aeneas.

ache (āk) *v.i.* (**ached, ach·ing**). 1. Suffer, be a source of continuous dull pain. 2. Yearn, long *for.* ∼ *n.* Continuous or prolonged dull pain.

Ach·er·on (ăk´erŏn). (Gk. myth.) One of the rivers of Hades, over which the dead were carried by Charon's ferry.

A·cheu·le·an, A·cheu·li·an (ashoo´lēan) *adjs. & ns.* (Of) the paleolithic period succeeding the Abbevillian. [*St. Acheul*, Amiens, France]

a·chieve (achēv´) *v.t.* (**a·chieved, a·chiev·ing**). Accomplish; acquire; reach (an end). **a·chieve´ment** *n.* Completion, accomplishment; thing accomplished.

A·chil·les (akĭl´ēz). (Gk. legend) Hero of the Trojan war, son of Peleus and Thetis; was killed by Paris with a poisoned arrow that pierced his heel where his mother held him in infancy when she plunged him into the Styx to make him invulnerable; hence, **Achilles' heel,** vulnerable part; ∼ **tendon,** tendon in heel by which calf muscles extend foot.

ach·ro·mat·ic (ăkromăt´ĭk) *adj.* Colorless; transmitting light without dispersing it into its constituent colors; ∼ **lens,** pair of lenses, the dispersion of one correcting the dispersion of the other. **a·chro·ma·tism** (ăkrō´matĭzem) *n.* Achromatic quality. **a·chro´ma·tize** *v.t.* (**-tized, -tiz·ing**).

ac·id (ăs´ĭd) *adj.* 1. Sour, sharp to the taste; (fig.) biting, severe. 2. Having properties of an acid. ∼ *n.* 1. Sour substance. 2. (chem.) One of a class of compounds in which hydrogen may be replaced by metals to form salts, neutralizing alkalis, usu. corroding or dissolving metals, and having sour taste. 3. (slang) The drug LSD; **ac´idhead,** user of this. 4. **acid test,** testing for gold by means of aqua fortis; (fig.) crucial test.

a·cid·ic (asĭd´ĭk) *adj.* Acid; acid forming.

a·cid·i·fy (asĭd´ĭfī) *v.* (**-fied, -fy·ing**). Change or make into acid; become or make sour.

a·cid·i·ty (asĭd´ĭtē) *n.* Acid property.

ac·i·do·sis (ăsĭdō´sĭs) *n.* (path.) Acid condition of blood and body tissues.

a·cid·u·lous (asĭj´ulus) *adj.* Somewhat acid; sharp, caustic.

-acious *suffix.* Forming adjs. with sense "inclined to" (*pugnacious*), "abounding in" (*capacious*).

-acity *suffix.* Forming nouns of quality corresponding to adjectives in **-acious.**

ac·knowl·edge (ăknŏl´ĭj) *v.t.* (**-edged, -edg·ing**). Admit the truth of, admit, own; announce receipt of; express appreciation of. **ac·knowl´edg·ment,** Brit. **ac·knowl´edge·ment** *ns.* Acknowledging; thing given or done in return for service etc.

A.C.L.U. *abbrev.* American Civil Liberties Union.

A loudspeaker being tested in the anechoic chamber of E.M.I. laboratories, Middlesex, U.K. A building's **acoustical** *quality governs audibility and clarity equally with quality of transmission.*

ac·me (ăk´mē) *n.* Highest point or pitch, culmination; (fig.) point of perfection.

ac·ne (ăk´nē) *n.* Skin eruption due to inflammation of sebaceous glands, common in adolescence, and characterized by pimples esp. on face.

ac·o·lyte (ăk´olīt) *n.* Altar attendant, esp. of priests and deacons, lighting and carrying candles etc.; assistant.

ac·o·nite (ăk´onīt) *n.* Plant of poisonous ranunculaceous genus *Aconitum,* with five blue or yellow sepals, of which one is helmet shaped, as *A. lycoctonum,* wolfsbane; dried root of this plant used in treatment of disease and as poison.

a·corn (ā´kõrn) *n.* Fruit of oak, oval nut growing in shallow woody cup; ∼ **squash,** acorn-shaped type of squash.

a·cot·y·le·don (ākŏtelē´don) *n.* (bot.) Plant with no distinct cotyledons or seed leaves, as fern, moss, etc. **a·cot·y·le´don·ous** *adj.*

a·cous·tic (akoo´stĭk) *adj.* Of the sense of hearing; of sound, of acoustics; (of building material) sound-absorbent; operated by sound waves. **a·cous´tics** *n.* 1. (usu. considered sing.) Science of sound. 2. (considered pl.) Properties of building, room, etc., in regard to audibility of sounds. **a·cous'ti·cal** *adj.* **a·cous'ti·cal·ly** *adv.*

ac·quaint (akwānt') *v.t.* Make aware or familiar, inform; **be acquainted with**, have personal knowledge of. **ac·quaint'ance** *n.* Personal knowledge; person with whom one is acquainted but not intimate. **ac·quaint'ance·ship** *n.*

ac·qui·esce (ăkwēēs') *v.t.* (**-esced, -esc·ing**). Agree, esp. tacitly; not object. **ac·qui·es'cence** *n.* **ac·qui·es'cent** *adj.*

ac·quire (akwīr') *v.t.* (**-quired, -quir·ing**). Gain, get, come to have; **acquired characteristic**, characteristic gained through influence of environment, and not inherited from parents. **ac·quire'ment** *n.* Acquiring.

ac·qui·si·tion (ăkwĭzĭsh'on) *n.* Acquiring; thing acquired, useful or pleasant addition.

ac·quis·i·tive (akwĭz'ĭtĭv) *adj.* Inclined or disposed to acquire things. **ac·quis'i·tive·ly** *adj.* **ac·quis'i·tive·ness** *n.*

ac·quit (akwĭt') *v.t.* (**-quit·ted, -quit·ting**). Pay (debt); declare not guilty, free from blame or obligation; ~ **oneself** (*well, ill,* etc.), perform one's part or duty.

ac·quit·tal (akwĭt'al) *n.* Discharge from debt; performance (of duty); deliverance from a charge by verdict etc.

A·cre (ah'ker, ā'ker). Seaport of Israel; captured by Christians in Third Crusade, 1191. **Bay of ~**, inlet of the Mediterranean in NW.

Israel.

a·cre (ā'ker) *n.* Land measure, legally 4,840 sq. yds. (4,047 sq. m); (pl.) lands, fields. **a·cre·age** (ā'kerĭj) *n.* Amount of acres, acres collectively.

ac·rid (ăk'rĭd) *adj.* Bitterly pungent, irritating; of bitter temper or manner. **ac'rid·ly** *adv.* **a·crid·i·ty** (akrĭd'ĭtē) *n.*

ac·ri·dine (ăk'rĭdēn) *n.* Colorless crystalline compound derived from coal tar, source of dyes and drugs.

ac·ri·mo·ni·ous (ăkrĭmō'nēus) *adj.* Marked by acrimony. **ac·ri·mo'ni·ous·ly** *adv.* **ac·ri·mo'ni·ous·ness** *n.*

ac·ri·mo·ny (ăk'rĭmōnē) *n.* Bitterness of temper or manner.

ac·ro·bat (ăk'rōbăt) *n.* Performer of daring and spectacular gymnastic feats. **ac·ro·bat·ic** (ăkrōbăt'ĭk) *adj.* **ac·ro·bat'i·cal·ly** *adv.* **ac·ro·bat'ics** *n.*

ac·ro·meg·a·ly (ăkrōmĕg'alē) *n.* Disease due to overactivity of pituitary gland, resulting in overgrowth of bones esp. of extremities and skull.

ac·ro·nym (ăk'ronĭm) *n.* Word formed from initial letters of words in a phrase, e.g. *NATO* (*N*orth *A*tlantic *T*reaty *O*rganization), *scuba* (*s*elf-contained *u*nderwater *b*reathing *a*pparatus).

ac·ro·pho·bi·a (ăkrofō'bēa) *n.*

General view of the Acropolis, Athens, with the Parthenon crowning the classical hill site. In Greek, acropolis means 'city at the top'.

(psych.) Pathological dread of high places.

a·crop·o·lis (akrŏp'olĭs) *n.* Citadel or upper fortified part of ancient Greek city, esp. (**A~**) that of Athens, situated on a hill about 250 ft. high and richly adorned, esp. in 5th c. B.C., with architecture and sculpture

a·cross (akraws', akrŏs') *prep. & adv.* From side to side (of), to or on the other side (of), forming a cross with, making angles with; ~ **the board**, generally.

a·cros·tic (akraw'stĭk, akrŏs'tĭk) *n.* Poem or series of written lines in which first or first and last letters or other letters of lines form word(s), the alphabet, etc.; puzzle so made.

a·cryl·ic (akrĭl'ĭk) *adj.* ~ **acid**, monobasic acid (CH_2:CH. COOH); ~ **fiber, resin**, synthetic substance prepared from acrylic acid or its derivatives. **acrylic** *n.* Acrylic fiber, resin, etc.; artist's paint with acrylic resin as a vehicle.

act (ăkt) *n.* 1. Thing done, deed; process of doing something. 2. Decree passed by legislative body, court of justice, etc.; statute. 3. Each of main divisions of dramatic work, in which definite part of whole action is completed. 4. Short performance that is part of variety show, circus, etc. 5. **Acts (of the Apostles)**, fifth book of New Testament, relating early history of Christian Church and dealing largely with the lives and work of the Apostles Peter and Paul; traditionally ascribed to St. Luke. 6. ~ **of God**, (law) sudden and

*Composing an **action painting,** a form of abstract art in which the artist works spontaneously, perhaps throwing a can of paint at the composition or impressing the rim of a tyre across it.*

with atomic number between 89 (actinium) and 103.

ac·ti·nism (ăk′tĭnĭzem) *n.* That property of radiant energy, found esp. in the shorter wavelengths of the spectrum, by which chemical changes are produced, as in photography.

ac·tin·i·um (ăktĭn′ēum) *n.* (chem.) Radioactive element, found in pitchblende; symbol Ac, at. no. 89, principal isotope at. wt. 227.

ac·ti·nom·e·ter (ăktĭnŏm′ĭter) *n.* Instrument for measuring heat radiation.

ac·ti·no·mor·phic (ăktĭnōmōr′fĭk) *adj.* (biol.) Radially symmetrical. **ac·ti·no·mor′phism** *n.*

ac·ti·no·my·cet·es (ăktĭnōmī-sē′tēz) *n.pl.* Group of minute organisms of the order Actinomycetales, commonly held to be filamentous bacteria.

ac·tion (ăk′shon) *n.* 1. Process of acting, exertion of energy or influence; **out of** ~, not functioning. 2. Thing done. 3. Series of events represented (in drama). 4. Mode of acting; mechanism of instruments etc. 5. Legal process; **take** ~, institute legal proceedings; take steps in regard to any matter. 6. Battle, engagement between opposing forces. 7. (slang) Activity, usu. of pleasurable or illicit nature. **ac′tion·a·ble** *adj.* Affording ground for action at law.

Ac·ti·um (ăk′tēum). Promontory of W. coast of Greece (opposite modern Preveza on Gulf of Amurakia), near which, in 31 B.C., the fleets of Mark Antony and Cleopatra were decisively defeated by Octavian (Augustus).

ac·ti·vate (ăk′tĭvāt) *v.t.* (**-vat·ed, -vat·ing**). Make active, esp. (phys.) radioactive; render (molecules) capable of reacting chemically; **activated charcoal,** charcoal treated to increase its adsorptive power. **ac·ti·va·tion** (ăktĭvā′shon) *n.*

ac·tive (ăk′tĭv) *adj.* 1. Working, acting, operative; consisting in or marked by action; energetic, busy, diligent; (of volcano) liable to erupt; ~ **service,** full-time service in one of the armed forces. 2. (gram.) Applied to a voice of the verb comprising all forms of intransitive verbs, and those forms of transitive verbs that attribute the verbal action to the person or thing it precedes; (loosely, of verb) in which the subject acts on or affects something else. ~ *n.* Active voice or form of verb. **ac′tive·ly** *adv.*

ac·tiv·ism (ăk′tĭvĭzem) *n.* Policy of vigorous action in politics.

*Deployment of forces at the **Battle of Actium.** Near this Greek promontory in 31 B.C., Octavian (Augustus) defeated Mark Antony and Cleopatra to become master of the Roman world.*

overwhelming natural occurrence (hurricane, earthquake, etc.) that could not reasonably have been expected or prevented. **act** *v.* 1. Represent in mimic action, perform (play); play part of (on stage or fig. in real life); perform on stage. 2. Perform actions, do things; perform special functions; (of things) work, fulfill functions; ~ **as,** serve as; ~ **on,** influence, affect; regulate one's conduct by, put into practice.

Ac·tae·on (ăktē′on). (Gk. myth.) Hunter who, because he accidentally saw Artemis bathing, was changed into a stag and killed by his own hounds.

ACTH *abbrev.* Adrenocorticotropic hormone.

act·ing (ăk′tĭng) *adj.* (esp., prefixed to title) Temporarily doing duties of; doing alone duties nominally shared with others. ~ *n.* Art or profession of performing parts in plays, films, etc.

ac·tin·ic (ăktĭn′ĭk) *adj.* Of actinism; ~ **rays,** rays possessing actinism, as the green, blue, violet, and ultraviolet rays of sunlight, which have a marked photochemical effect.

ac·ti·nide (ăk′tĭnīd) *n.* Element

Above: Preparing a patient for Caesarean operation without anesthetic, using the techniques of **acupuncture,** a medical procedure of Chinese origin. Needles of various sizes are inserted into prescribed places on the body.
Right: A patient undergoing treatment by acupuncture. In this instance, the needles have been inserted in lines parallel to the spine.

ac′tiv·ist *n.*

ac·tiv·i·ty (ăktĭv′ĭtē) *n.* (pl. **-ties**). Exertion of energy; state or quality of being active, energy, diligence, liveliness; active force or operation; specific deed or action; work or occupation.

Ac·ton (ăk′ton), (**Emerich Edward Dalberg-Acton**) **Lord John**, 1st Baron (1834–1902). English historian; leader of English Roman Catholics.

ac·tor (ăk′ter), fem. **ac·tress** (ăk′trĭs) *ns.* Dramatic performer.

ac·tu·al (ăk′chōōal) *adj.* Existing, real, present, current. **ac′tu·al·ly** *adv.* In actual fact, really, even, as a matter of fact.

ac·tu·al·i·ty (ăkchōōăl′ĭtē) *n.* (pl. **-ties**). Reality.

ac·tu·al·ize (ăk′chōōalīz) *v.t.* (**-ized, -iz·ing**). Realize in action. **ac·tu·al·i·za·tion** (ăkchōōalĭzā′shon) *n.*

ac·tu·ar·y (ăk′chōōĕrē) *n.* (pl. **-ar·ies**). Expert on insurance who calculates risks and premiums. **ac·tu·ar·i·al** (ăkchōōār′ēal) *adj.*

ac·tu·ate (ăk′chōōāt) *v.t.* (**-at·ed, -at·ing**). Serve as motive to; put into action. **ac·tu·a·tion** (ăkchōōā′shon), **ac′tu·a·tor** *ns.*

a·cu·i·ty (akū′ĭtē) *n.* (pl. **-ties**). Sharpness, acuteness.

a·cu·men (akū′men, ăk′yu-) *n.* Keen discernment, penetration.

ac·u·punc·ture (ăk′yōōpŭngk-cher) *n.* (med.) Practice of puncturing areas of skin or tissues with needles for therapeutic purposes.

a·cute (akūt´) *adj.* 1. Sharp, keen, penetrating; clever. 2. (of disease) Coming sharply to a crisis, not chronic. 3. (of sound) Sharp, shrill; having acute accent. 4. (fig.) Severe, crucial. 5. ~ **accent**, accent ´, originally indicating a high or rising pitch on the vowel so marked; ~ **angle**: see angle¹. **a·cute´ly** *adv.* **a·cute´ness** *n.*

ad (ăd) *n.* (colloq.) Advertisement.

ad- *prefix.* To, with sense of motion or direction to, reduction or change into, addition, adherence, increase, or intensification.

A.D. *abbrev.* Anno Domini, (of the Christian era). [f. L. *Anno Domini*, "in the year of our Lord"]

ad·age (ăd´ĭj) *n.* Traditional maxim.

a·da·gio (adah´jō, -zhēō) *adv., adj., n.* (pl. **-gios**). (mus.) Leisurely (passage or movement); ~ **dancing**, that involving feats of balance etc. [It.]

Ad·al·bert (ăd´albert), **St.** (c955-97). Missionary in N.

Germany and Poland, called "apostle of the Prussians," martyred in Bremen, commemorated April 23.

Ad·am¹ (ăd´am). (in Hebrew tradition) The first man (Gen. 2 and 3), who lived with Eve in the Garden of Eden, but was driven from it for eating the fruit (traditionally an apple) of "the tree of the knowledge of good and evil"; ~ **'s ale**, water; ~ **'s apple**, projection formed by the thyroid cartilage, particularly prominent in males. [Heb., = "man"]

Ad·am² (ăd´am). 1. **Robert** (1728–92). The best known of a family of Scottish architects; introduced into Britain a neoclassical style of decoration, furniture, etc., based on ancient Roman and Italian Renaissance designs. 2. **James** (1730–94), architect, his brother.

ad·a·mant¹ (ăd´amant, -mănt) *n.* Legendary stone of extreme hardness. **ad·a·man·tine** (ădamăn´tĭn, -tēn) *adj.*

ad·a·mant² (ăd´amant, -mănt) *adj.* 1. Of extreme hardness. 2.

Unshakable, inflexible. **ad´a·mant·ly** *adv.*

Ad·a·mite (ăd´amīt) *n.* Child of Adam, human being; unclothed man.

Ad·ams¹ (ăd´amz). Name of a family of American politicians, statesmen, and writers, including: 1. **John** (1735–1826) 2nd president of U.S. (1797–1801); member of committee formed to draft Declaration of Independence; 2. his wife, **Abigail Smith** (1744–1818); 3. his son, **John Quincy** (1767–1848) 6th president of U.S. (1825–9); 4. John Quincy's grandson, **Henry Brooks** (1838–1918) historian and philosopher.

Ad·ams² (ăd´amz), **Maude** (1872–1953). American actress; best known for starring role in *Peter Pan.*

Ad·ams³ (ăd´amz), **Mount.** A mountain in the Cascade Range of S. Washington.

Ad·ams⁴ (ăd´amz), **Samuel** (1722–1803). American propagandist, statesman, and leader in the American Revolution.

a·dapt (adăpt´) *v.* Suit, make suitable, fit (*to, for*); alter, modify, so as to make suitable for new surroundings, purpose, etc. **a·dapt·a·bil·i·ty** (ădăptabĭl´ĭtē) *n.* **a·dapt´a·ble** *adj.* **a·dapt´er, a·dap´tor** *ns.* (esp.) Device allowing connection of pieces of equipment not orig. designed to be connected.

ad·ap·ta·tion (ădaptā´shon) *n.* (esp. biol.) Process, characteristic of living matter, by which organism or species becomes adjusted to its environment; that which is so adapted.

A.D.C. *abbrev.* Aide-de-camp.

add (ăd) *v.* Join by way of increase or supplement; perform arithmetical process of addition; say or write further; ~ **up**, add a column of figures; find sum of; make desired total; (colloq.) seem logical or reasonable; **adding machine**, machine that performs arithmetical processes.

Ad·dams (ăd´amz), **Jane** (1860–1935). American social worker and peace advocate; founded Hull House in Chicago, 1889; shared Nobel Peace Prize, 1931.

ad·dax (ăd´ăks) *n.* Large light-colored antelope (*Addax nasomaculatus*) of N. Afr. deserts, with spiral horns.

ad·den·dum (adĕn´dum) *n.* (pl. **-da** pr. -da). Something to be added, addition, appendix.

ad·der (ăd′er) *n.* Small venomous snake, viper (*Vipera berus*); **death ~, horned ~, puff ~,** highly poisonous African and Australian species of Viperidae; **adder's-tongue** *n.* fern (*Ophioglossum vulgatum*); white- or yellow-flowered dogtooth violet.

ad·dict (ăd′ĭkt) *n.* One addicted to drugs etc.; devotee of pastime etc. **~** (adĭkt′) *v.t.* Apply habitually or compulsively (*to* a practice). **ad·dict′ed** *adj.* Devoted *to* or physiologically or psychologically dependent on drug, pastime, etc. **ad·dic′tion** *n.* **ad·dic′tive** *adj.* Causing addiction.

Ad·dis Ab·a·ba (ah′dĭs ah′babah). Capital of and largest city in Ethiopia.

Ad·di·son[1] (ăd′ĭson), **Joseph** (1672–1719). English essayist and poet; contributor to *Tatler* and joint author (with STEELE) of *Spectator*.

Ad·di·son[2] (ăd′ĭson), **Thomas** (1793–1860). English physician; first to recognize **A~'s disease**, disease connected with defective functioning of suprarenal glands and freq. characterized by bronzy pigmentation of skin.

ad·di·tion (adĭsh′on) *n.* Adding; arithmetical process of putting together two or more numbers or amounts to form a total; thing added; **in ~,** as an added thing etc. (*to*). **ad·di′tion·al** *adj.* **ad·di′tion·al·ly** *adv.*

ad·di·tive (ăd′ĭtĭv) *adj.* Of addition; to be added. **~** *n.* Substance added to mixture or alloy in order to impart specific qualities to the resulting product.

ad·dle (ăd′el) *v.* (**-dled, -dling**). Make or become addled. **~** *adj.*

Festival Theatre, Adelaide, Australia, where many international artists have performed. Adelaide, encircled by parkland, is the capital of South Australia.

ad′dlebrained, ad′dleheaded, ad′dlepated, *adjs.* Confused in mind. **ad′dled** *adj.* (of egg) Rotten; muddled, crazy.

ad·dress (adrĕs′, ăd′rĕs) *n.* 1. (obs.) Readiness, skill, adroitness. 2. Place to which letters etc. are directed; place of residence. 3. Manner, bearing, in conversation; way of addressing person. 4. Discourse delivered to audience. 5. (pl.) Courteous approach, courtship. **~** (adrĕs′) *v.t.* 1. Direct in speech or writing; speak to; send as written message (*to*); write address on outside of (letter etc.) 2. Apply *oneself,* direct one's skill or energies (*to*). 3. (golf) **~ the ball,** take aim, prepare to make a stroke.

ad·dress·ee (ădrĕsē′) *n.* Person to whom letter etc. is addressed.

ad·duce (adōos′, adūs′) *v.t.* (**-duced, -duc·ing**). Cite as proof or instance.

ad·duct (adŭkt′) *v.t.* Draw to a common center or toward median line or long axis of body. **ad·duc′tion, ad·duc′tor** *ns.*

-ade *suffix.* Forming nouns with following senses: 1. action done (*blockade, tirade*). 2. body or person concerned in action or process (*cavalcade, renegade*). 3. product of material or action (*arcade, lemonade, masquerade*).

Ad·e·laide (ăd′elād). Seaport and capital of South Australia.

A·dé·lie (adā′lē) **Land.** French territory in coastal region of Antarctica, south of Australia.

Aden, near entrance to Red Sea, was of strategic importance in 1939–45 war. Until 1967 a British colony, Aden is capital of People's Democratic Republic of Yemen.

A·den (ah′den, ā′den). Seaport in SW. Arabia near entrance to Red Sea; capital city of the People's Democratic Republic of Yemen.

A·de·nau·er (ăd′enower, ah′de-), **Konrad** (1876–1967). First chancellor, Federal Republic of Germany.

ad·e·noids (ăd′enoidz) *n.pl.* Pathological enlargement of lymphoid tissue between back of nose and throat, occurring usu. in children and often obstructing breathing. **ad·e·noi·dal** (ădenoi′dal) *adj.*

a·dept (adĕpt′) *adj.* Thoroughly proficient (*in*). **ad·ept** (ăd′ĕpt, adĕpt′) *n.* Adept person.

ad·e·quate (ăd′ekwĭt) *adj.* Proportionate to what is necessary; sufficient. **ad′e·quate·ly** *adv.* **ad·e·qua·cy** (ăd′ekwase) *n.*

ad·here (ăd-hēr′) *v.i.* (**-hered, -her·ing**). Stick fast, cleave (*to*); give support *to* (agreement, opinion, party).

ad·her·ent (ăd-hēr′ent, -hĕr′-) *adj.* Sticking; adhering. **~** *n.* Supporter (of party etc.). **ad·her′ence** *n.*

ad·he·sion (ăd-hē′zhon) *n.* Adhering; (chem.) molecular force of attraction between different kinds of molecules (opp. COHESION); (med.) abnormal union of tissue as a result of inflammation.

ad·he·sive (ăd-hē′sĭv, -zĭv) *adj.* & *n.* Adhering, sticky or gummed (substance or material); **~ tape,** tape coated on one side with a sticky

substance. **ad·he'sive·ly** *adv.*
ad·he'sive·ness *n.*

ad hoc (ăd hŏk´). Arranged for this purpose; special(ly). [L.]

ad·i·a·bat·ic (ădēabăt´ĭk, ādīa-) *adj.* (of physical change) Involving neither loss nor gain of heat.

a·dieu (adoō´, adū; *Fr.* ădyö´) *int.* & *n.* (pl. **a·dieus, a·dieux** pr. adoōz´, adūz´; *Fr.* ădyö´) Goodby. [*Fr. à Dieu* to God]

ad in·fi·ni·tum (ăd ĭnfĭnī´tum). Without limit, for ever. [L.]

ad·i·os (ădēōs´, ahdē-) *int.* Goodby. [Sp.]

ad·i·pose (ăd´ĭpōs) *adj.* Of fat, fatty; ~ **tissue**, connective tissue cells in animal body containing large globules of fat. **ad·i·pos·i·ty** (ădĭpŏs´ĭtē) *n.*

Ad·i·ron·dack (ădĭrŏn´dăk) **Mountains.** (also **Adirondacks**) Group of mountains in NE. New York.

ad·it (ăd´ĭt) *n.* Horizontal entrance to, or passage in, mine.

adj. *abbrev.* Adjutant; adjective.

ad·ja·cent (ajā´sent) *adj.* Lying near *to*, contiguous. **ad·ja·cen·cy** *n.*

ad·jec·tive (ăj´ĭktĭv) *n.* (gram.) Name of attribute added to noun to describe it more fully or definitely; modifier of noun. **ad·jec·ti·val** (ăjĭktī´val) *adj.* **ad·jec·ti·val·ly** *adv.*

ad·join (ajoin´) *v.* Be contiguous or connected (with).

ad·journ (ajẽrn´) *v.* Suspend the meeting or proceedings of (a legislature etc.); move *to* another place (esp. during such a suspension). **ad·journ'ment** *n.*

ad·judge (ajŭj´) *v.t.* (**-judged, -judg·ing**). Adjudicate upon; pronounce or award judicially.

ad·ju·di·cate (ajoō´dĭkāt) *v.* (**-cat·ed, -cat·ing**). Decide upon; pronounce; sit in judgment and pronounce sentence. **ad·ju·di·ca·tion** (ajoōdĭkā´shon), **ad·ju'di·ca·tor** *ns.*

ad·junct (ăj´ŭngkt) *n.* Subordinate or incidental thing, accompaniment; (gram.) amplification of the predicate, subject, etc.; (logic) nonessential attribute. **ad·junc·tive** (ajŭngk´tĭv) *adj.* **ad·junc'tive·ly** *adv.*

ad·jure (ajoor´) *v.t.* (**-jured, -jur·ing**). Charge under oath or penalty of curse *to* do; request earnestly. **ad·ju·ra·tion** (ăjoōrā´shon) *n.*

ad·just (ajŭst´) *v.* Arrange, put in order; harmonize; adapt (*to*); settle; (insurance) determine the amount to be paid to settle (a claim). **ad·just'a·ble** *adj.* **ad·just'ment** *n.*

ad·ju·tant (ăj´utant) *n.* 1. (mil.) Officer assisting commanding officer by communicating orders, conducting correspondence, etc.; ~ **general**, adjutant of a U.S. Army

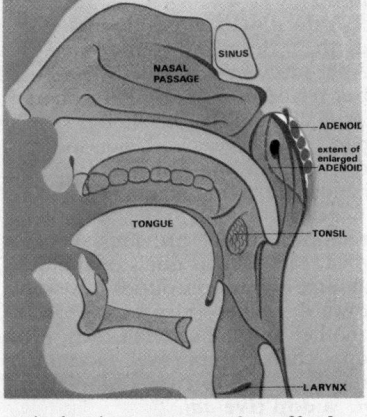

Diagram shows **adenoids,** enlargement of tissue between back of nose and throat. Large adenoids tend to obstruct breathing through the nose. Normally they decrease in size after childhood.

unit having a general staff; **A ~ General,** chief administrative officer of the U.S. Army. 2. (also ~ **stork,** ~ **bird**) Large stork of genus *Leptoptilos,* esp. Indian *L. dubius,* walking with stiff-legged gait.

Ad·ler[1] (ăd´ler), **Alfred** (1870–1937). Austrian psychiatrist; put forward theory of inferiority complex.

Ad·ler[2] (ăd´ler), **Felix** (1851–1933). German-born American educator and reformer; founder of

the Society for Ethical Culture.

ad lib (ăd lĭb´) *n.* Words, gestures, etc. ad-libbed. ~ *adv.* To any desired extent. **ad-lib** *v.* (**-libbed, -lib·bing**). Speak, act, etc. without preparation; improvise. **ad-lib** *adj.* Extemporaneous; improvised; spontaneous. **ad-lib'ber** *n.*

ad lib·i·tum (ăd lĭb´ĭtum). 1. To the extent etc. desired. 2. (mus.) That can be omitted. [L.]

Adm. *abbrev.* Admiral.

adm., admin. *abbrevs.* Administration; administrative.

Ad·me·tus (ădmē´tus). (Gk. legend) Husband of ALCESTIS.

ad·min·is·ter (ădmĭn´ĭster) *v.* 1. Manage (affairs, estate, etc.); dispense (justice, sacraments, etc.); act as administrator. 2. Formally present (oath to be sworn) *to.* 3. Furnish, give; apply (remedies). 4. Contribute *to* (one's comfort etc.).

ad·min·is·tra·tion (ădmĭnĭstrā´shon) *n.* 1. Administering; management; management of public affairs, government; (law) management of deceased person's estate. 2. Body of administrators; government. **ad·min·is·trate** (ădmĭn´ĭstrāt) *v.* (**-trat·ed, -trat·ing**). Administer. **ad·min·is·tra·tive** (ădmĭn´istrātĭv, -stra-) *adj.* Of administration; executive. **ad·min'is·tra·tor** *n.*

ad·mi·ra·ble (ăd´merabel) *adj.* Worthy of admiration; estimable, excellent. **ad'mi·ra·bly** *adv.*

ad·mi·ral (ăd´meral) *n.* Naval officer commanding fleet or subdivision of fleet; (hist.) commander in chief of navy; **A ~ of the Fleet,** highest rank of British naval officers; **Fleet ~:** see FLEET. [Arab. ´amīr commander]

Ad·mi·ral·ty (ăd´meraltē) *n.* (Brit.) Former name of government department superintending the Royal Navy.

Ad·mi·ral·ty (ăd´meraltē) **Island.** Island in the Alexander Archipelago of southeastern Alaska; **Admiralties,** group of small islands of Bismarck Archipelago, under Australian administration; **Admiralty Range,** mountain range in Victoria, Antarctica, NW. of Ross Sea.

ad·mire (admīr´) *v.t.* (**-mired, -mir·ing**). Regard with pleased surprise or approval; express admiration of. **ad·mir'er** *n.* One

The **adjutant bird** is a large stork with a stiff-legged gait. There are species in Africa, India and S.E. Asia. The largest adjutant bird, *Leptotilus dubius,* is between 6 and 7 ft. tall.

who admires. **ad·mi·ra·tion** (ăd-merā´shon) *n.*

ad·mis·si·ble (ădmĭs´ibel) *adj.* 1. That may be accepted or considered. 2. (law) That may be allowed as evidence in court. **ad·mis·si·bil·i·ty** (ădmĭsibĭl´ĭtē) *n.* **ad·mis´si·bly** *adv.*

ad·mis·sion (ădmĭsh´on) *n.* Admitting, being admitted, fee for this; acknowledgement that something is true.

ad·mit (ădmĭt´) *v.* (**-mit·ted, -mit·ting**). 1. Allow entrance or access (*to*). 2. Allow, permit; accept as valid or true; acknowledge; ~ **of**, be capable of or compatible with; leave room for. **ad·mit´tance** *n.* **ad·mit´ted·ly** *adv.*

ad·mix (ădmĭks´) *v.* Add as an ingredient, mingle *with.* **ad·mix·ture** (ădmĭks´cher) *n.*

ad·mon·ish (ădmŏn´ĭsh) *v.t.* Urge; give advice; warn; remind, inform. **ad·mon´ish·ment** *n.*

ad·mo·ni·tion (ădmonĭsh´on) *n.* Admonishing; warning, reproof. **ad·mon·i·to·ry** (ădmŏn´itōrē, -tōrē) *adj.*

ad nau·se·am (ăd naw´zēam, -ăm, -shē-, -zhē-). To a disgusting extent. [L.]

a·do (adōō´) *n.* Fuss; confused activity, bustling.

a·do·be (adō´bē) *n.* Sun-dried clay used for building etc.; house made of such clay bricks. [Span., f. *adobar* daub, plaster]

ad·o·les·cent (ădolĕs´ent) *adj. & n.* (Person) between childhood and maturity. **ad·o·les´cence** *n.*

A·do·nai (ahdōnoi´, -nī´). Hebrew title of reverence for God, pronounced as substitute for the tetragrammaton. [Heb., = "my lord(s)"]

A·do·nis (adŏn´ĭs, adō´nĭs). (Gk. myth.) Beautiful youth loved by Aphrodite; he was killed by a boar but restored to life by Persephone; Zeus decreed that he should spend part of each year with her and the rest on earth with Aphrodite; hence, handsome young man.

a·dopt (adŏpt´) *v.t.* Take into relationship not previously occupied, esp. take as one's own child, assume rights and duties of parent toward; take (idea etc.) from another and use as one's own; take up, choose; approve (accounts, report). **a·dop·tion** (adŏp´shon) *n.* **a·dop´tive** *adj.*

a·dore (adōr´, adŏr´) *v.t.* (**a·dored, a·dor·ing**). Regard with very deep respect and affection; worship as a deity; like very much; (R.C. Ch.) offer form of reverence to. **a·dor´a·ble** *adj.* **a·dor´a·bly** *adv.* **ad·o·ra·tion** (ădera´shon) *n.*

a·dor·er (adōr´er, -dŏr´-) *n.* Worshipper; ardent admirer, lover.

a·dorn (adŏrn´) *v.t.* Add beauty or luster to, esp. with ornament(s). **a·dorn´ment** *n.*

a·dre·nal (adrē´nal) *adj.* At or near kidney; of, produced by the adrenal glands; ~ **gland**, suprarenal gland, one of two yellowish-brown ductless glands lying on upper anterior surface of kidneys. ~ *n.* Adrenal gland.

a·dren·a·line (adrĕn´alĭn) *n.* Hormone secreted by adrenal glands and affecting circulation and muscular action; this obtained from these glands in animals or prepared synthetically, used in medicine as a stimulant.

a·dre·no·cor·ti·co·trop·ic (a-

A frenzied reaction to pop groups is one mark of **adolescence,** which has been described as the period when a youngster starts learning to control and properly direct sexual urges. Various hormones are responsible for the physical changes of adolescence both in males and females.

drē´nōkōrtikōtrŏp´ĭk) **hormone.** Hormone secreted by pituitary gland and stimulating adrenal cortex.

A·dri·an (ā´drēan). Name of six popes including **Adrian IV** (Nicholas Breakspear), pope 1154-1159, the only English pope.

A·dri·at·ic (ādrēăt´ĭk, ădrē-) *adj.* ~ **Sea**, arm of Mediterranean lying between Italy and Balkan peninsula. **Adriatic** *n.* Adriatic Sea.

a·drift (adrĭft´) *adj.* Drifting; at mercy of wind and tide or of circumstances.

a·droit (adroit´) *adj.* Dextrous, deft. **a·droit´ly** *adv.* **a·droit´ness** *n.*

ad·sorb (ădsōrb´, -zōrb´) *v.t.* Act as adsorbent of. **ad·sor´bent** *adj. & n.* (Substance) producing adsorption.

ad·sorp·tion (ădsōrp´shon, -zōrp´-) *n.* Process by which specific gases, vapors, or substances in solution adhere to exposed surfaces of certain, usu. solid, materials. **ad·sorp´tive** *adj.*

ad·u·late (ăj´ulāt) *v.t.* (**-lat·ed, -lat·ing**). Flatter, admire excessively. **ad·u·la·tion** (ăjulā´shon) *n.* **ad·u·la·to·ry** (ăj´ulatōrē, -tōrē) *adj.*

a·dult (adŭlt´, ăd´ŭlt) *adj.* Fully grown, mature; befitting adults; intended for or restricted to adults only. ~ *n.* Adult person, animal,

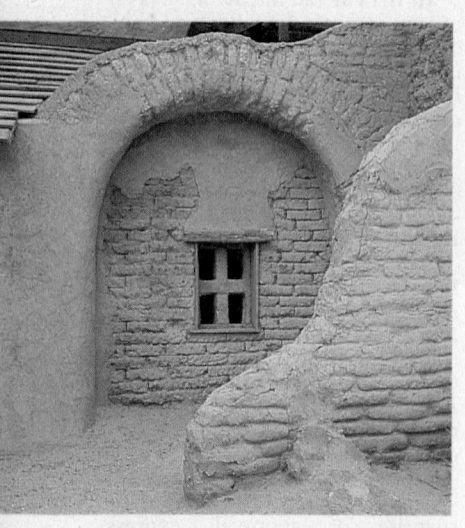

Adobe bricks have been used for centuries by the American Indians as a convenient, durable building material.

*The **Adriatic Sea** forms a part of the Mediterranean lying between Italy and the Balkan Peninsula. The average width of the Adriatic is 110 miles and it is a rich fishing ground.*

*Mangrove trees with bared **adventitious** roots: Biscayne Bay, Florida. In addition to the main root, adventitious roots are secondary roots which can grow from other parts of the plant.*

plant, etc.; ~ **education**, courses etc. provided for persons over school age.

a·dul·ter·ant (adŭl´terant) *adj.* & *n.* (Thing) employed in adulterating.

a·dul·ter·ate (adŭl´terāt) *v.t.* (**-at·ed, -at·ing**). Falsify, corrupt, debase, esp. by admixture of baser ingredients. **a·dul·ter·a·tion** (adŭlterā´shon) *n.*

a·dul·ter·er (adŭl´terer), fem. **a·dul·ter·ess** (adŭl´terĭs, -trĭs) *ns.* Person guilty of adultery.

a·dul·ter·y (adŭl´tere) *n.* (pl. **-ter·ies**). Voluntary sexual intercourse of married person with one who is not his or her spouse. **a·dul´ter·ous** *adj.* **a·dul´ter·ous·ly** *adv.*

ad·um·brate (ăd´umbrāt, ădŭm´-) *v.t.* (**-brat·ed, -brat·ing**). Represent in outline; faintly indicate; typify, foreshadow; overshadow. **ad·um·bra·tion** (ădumbrā´shon) *n.*

adv. *abbrev.* Adverb; advertisement.

ad va·lo·rem (ăd valōr´em, -lōr´-). (of taxes or duties) In proportion to (estimated) value of goods. [L.]

ad·vance (ădvăns´ -vahns´) *n.* 1. Going forward, progress; improvement, promotion. 2. Personal approach, overture; (pl.) amorous approaches. 3. Increase, as in a figure, price, etc. 4. Payment beforehand; loan. 5. **in** ~, in front, ahead; beforehand; ~ **copy**, copy of book etc., supplied before publication; ~ **guard**, guard before main body of army. **advance** *v.* (**-vanced, -vanc·ing**). Move or put forward; bring forward (claims etc.); present for consideration; accelerate (events); pay (money) before it is due; lend; help on, promote; make progress; improve, show improvement; raise (price), rise (in price). **ad·vanced´** *adj.* Far on in progress; ahead of times, others, etc. **ad·vance´ment** *n.* (esp.) Promotion, preferment; furtherance, improvement.

ad·van·tage (ădvăn´tĭj) *n.* Better position, precedence, superiority; favorable circumstance; (tennis) next point won after deuce; **mechanical** ~: see MECHANICAL; **take** ~ **of**, use (circumstance) profitably; exploit (person) unfairly. **ad·van·ta·geous** (ădvantā´jus) *adj.* **ad·van·ta´geous·ly** *adv.*

ad·vent (ăd´věnt) *n.* 1. Arrival, esp. important one. 2. Coming into being. 3. **A~**, season before Christmas, beginning on 4th Sunday before it; coming of Christ.

*Neon signs in the heart of the city. The first **advertisements** were by public criers. A 3,000-year-old written advertisement, found in ruins of*

ad·ven·ti·tious (ădventĭsh´us) *adj.* 1. Accidental, casual; not essential or intrinsic. 2. (bot.) In an unusual position, sporadic. **ad·ven·ti´tious·ly** *adv.*

ad·ven·ture (ădvĕn´cher) *n.* Unexpected or exciting experience; daring enterprise, hazardous activity. ~ *v.i.* (**-tured, -tur·ing**). 1. Venture. 2. Venture to say. **ad·ven·tur·er** (ădvĕn´cherer), fem. **ad·ven·tur·ess** (ădvĕn´cherĭs) *ns.* One who seeks adventure;

Thebes, offered a gold coin for return of a runaway slave. Advertising media include newspapers, magazines, posters, T.V., radio and illuminated signs.

speculator; one who lives by his or her wits.

ad·ven·tur·ous (ădvĕn´cherus) *adj.* Venturesome, enterprising. **ad·ven´tur·ous·ly** *adv.*

ad·verb (ăd´vĕrb) *n.* (gram.) Word that modifies a verb, adjective, or another adverb, expressing any relation of place, time, circumstance, causality, manner, or degree. **ad·ver·bi·al** (ădvĕr´bēal) *adj.* **ad·ver´bi·al·ly** *adv.*

ad·ver·sar·y (ăd´versĕre) *n.* (pl.

ad·vise (ădvīz´) v. (**-vised, -vis·ing**). Offer advice (to); recommend; notify, inform. **ad·vised'** adj. Deliberate, considered. **ad·vis·ed·ly** (ădvī´zĭdlē) adv.

ad·vis·er, ad·vi·sor (ădvī´zer) ns. Counselor, esp. person habitually consulted; **legal** ~, lawyer.

ad·vi·so·ry (ădvī´zerē) adj. Giving advice; consisting in giving advice. ~ n. (pl. **-ries**). An announcement, esp. a warning, such as a radio weather forecast.

ad·vo·ca·cy (ăd´vokasē) n. (pl. **-cies**). Function of advocate; pleading in support of.

ad·vo·cate (ăd´vokĭt, -kāt) n. Professional pleader in court of justice, counsel (technical title in Roman law courts and in countries retaining Roman law, as Scotland, France, etc.); one who pleads for another; one who speaks for cause etc. ~ (ăd´vokāt) v.t. (**-cat·ed, -cat·ing**). Plead for, support (policy etc.).

advt. abbrev. Advertisement.

ad·y·tum (ăd´ĭtum) n. (pl. **-ta** pr. -ta) Innermost part of ancient temple. [Gk. aduton not to be entered (duō enter)]

adz, adze (ădz) ns. Carpenter's tool for cutting away surface of wood, like ax with arched blade at right angles to handle.

A. E. Pseudonym of G(eorge) W(illiam) Russell (1867–1935). Irish poet and painter.

ae·dile (ē´dīl) n. (Rom. hist.) Magistrate who superintended public buildings, games, shows, etc.

A.E.F. abbrev. American Expeditionary Forces.

Ae·ge·an (ĭjē´an) adj. ~ **Sea**, arm of Mediterranean between Greece and Asia Minor; ~ **Civilization**, Bronze Age civilization of the coasts and islands of the Aegean Sea, the Minoan and Mycenaean civilizations. **Aegean** n. Aegean Sea.

Ae·gir (ā´jĭr). (Scand. myth.) Chief of the sea giants, representing the peaceful ocean.

ae·gis (ē´jĭs) n. (Gk. myth.) Shield of Zeus or Athena; **under the** ~ **of**, under the protection or sponsorship of.

Ae·gis·thus (ĭjĭs´thus). (Gk. legend) Nephew of Atreus, whom he murdered, and lover of Clytemnestra, who helped him murder her husband Agamemnon.

Æl·fric (ăl´frĭk) (c955–1020). English abbot and writer, chiefly of homilies and lives of saints.

-sar·ies). Opponent, enemy.

ad·verse (ădvers´, ăd´vers) adj. Contrary, hostile to; hurtful, injurious. **ad·verse'ly** adv.

ad·ver·si·ty (ădver´site) n. (pl. **-ties**). Condition of adverse fortune; misfortune.

ad·vert (ădvert´) v.i. Refer to.

ad·ver·tise (ăd´vertīz) v. (**-tised, -tis·ing**). Notify, warn, inform; make generally or publicly known; proclaim merits of; esp., try to encourage sales of (product) by public announcement; ~ **for**, ask for by public notice. **ad'ver·tis·er** n.

ad·ver·tise·ment (ădvertīz´-ment, -ver´tĭs-) n. Advertising; public announcement (in newspapers, by posters, etc.).

ad·vice (ădvīs´) n. Opinion given or offered as to action; information given, news.

ad·vis·a·ble (ădvī´zabel) adj. To be recommended; expedient. **ad·vis·a·bil·i·ty** (ădvīzabĭl´ĭtē) n.

Ae·ne·as (ĭnē′as). (Gk. & Rom. legend) Trojan hero; son of Anchises and Aphrodite; escaped after fall of Troy and after long wandering reached the Tiber; regarded by Romans as founder of Rome.

Ae·ne·id (ĭnē′ĭd). Epic poem by Virgil in twelve books of Latin hexameters relating story of Aeneas after fall of Troy.

Ae·o·li·an (ēō′lēan) adj. 1. Of Aeolis. 2. Of Aeolus; caused by, relating to, wind; ~ **harp**, musical instrument consisting of rectangular box on or in which are stretched strings or wires producing musical sounds as the wind passes across them; ~ **Islands**, ancient name of Lipari Islands; ~ **mode**, (mus.) ancient Greek mode; ninth of ecclesiastical modes, with A as final and E as dominant.

Ae·o·lis (ē′olĭs). Coastal district

Aerobatic displays are a common sight at most airshows today, but never fail to excite the crowds. In the early days of flight, aerobatic displays were an important way for pilots to make some extra money.

of NW. Asia Minor colonized by Greeks at very early date.

Ae·o·lus (ē′olus). (Gk. myth.) God of the winds.

ae·on, e·on (ē′on, ē′ŏn) ns. Immeasurable period; eternity.

aer·ate (ār′āt, ā′erāt) v.t. (-at·ed, -at·ing). Expose to mechanical or chemical action of air; charge, treat, or supply with air or a gas. **aer·a·tion** (ārā′shon), **aer′a·tor** ns.

aer·i·al (ār′ēal, āēr′ēal) adj. Of air, gaseous; ethereal; immaterial, imaginary; atmospheric; existing, moving, happening, in the air; conducted by aircraft. **aerial** (ār′ēal)

n. Radio or television antenna. **aer′i·al·ist** n. Performer on high wire or trapeze.

aer·ie (ār′ē, ēr′ē), **ey·rie** ns. 1. Nest of bird of prey, esp. eagle, or of other bird that nests at high elevations. 2. Human residence located high on mountain etc.

aero-, aer- prefixes. Air-; of aircraft.

aer·o·bat·ics (ārobăt′ĭks) n.pl. Spectacular feats of flying performed by airplanes. **aer·o·bat′ic** adj.

aer·obe (ār′ōb) n. Microorganism capable of living only in the presence of atmospheric oxygen; opp. ANAEROBE. **aer·o·bic** (ārō′bĭk) adj. **aerobic exercise**, sustained physical exercise that increases the body's intake of oxygen.

aer·o·drome (ār′odrōm) (Brit.) = AIRDROME.

*Radio Australia repeater station at Cox Peninsula, near Darwin. An **aerial** has identical transmitting and receiving properties and may be used simultaneously for both functions.*

aer·o·dy·nam·ics (ārōdīnăm´- ĭks) *n.* (usu. considered sing.) Branch of dynamics dealing with the effects produced in air by the motion of solid bodies through it and the effects produced on such bodies by the air through which they pass. **aer·o·dy·nam´ic, aer·o·dy·nam´i·cal** *adjs.* **aer·o·dy·nam´i·cal·ly** *adv.* **aer·o·dy·nam·i·cist** (ārōdīnăm´ĭsĭst) *n.*

aer·o·naut (âr´onawt, -nŏt) *n.* Navigator or pilot of balloon or other lighter-than-air craft. **aer·o·nau·tic** (âronaw´tĭk, -nŏt´ĭk), **aer·o·nau´ti·cal** *adjs.* Of, pertaining to, aeronautics. **aer·o·nau´tics** *n.pl.* (usu. considered sing.) Science or practice of flight.

aer·o·plane (âr´oplān) (Brit.) = AIRplane.

aer·o·sol (âr´osōl, -sawl, -sŏl) *n.* System of colloidal particles dispersed in a gas, as mist, fog, etc.; container, also called ~ **bomb,** holding substance packed under pressure with spraying device; this substance.

*Boeing 747 Jumbo Jet is powered by 4 turbo-fan engines. Front-mounted fan blows air through ducts around the jet exhausts, improving quietness and fuel economy. the Jumbo **aeroplane** can take 450 passengers.*

1 glass fiber radar cone
2 flight engineer's seat
3 flt eng electronics panel
4 upper first class lounge
5 retraction jacks
6 brake reaction link
7 undercarriage door
8 center passenger door
9 air conditioning ducts
10 galley
11 freight floor
12 freight hold door

21 spoilers
22 triple slotted flaps
23 aileron
24 HF aerial
25 fan
26 cooler
27 thrust reversers
28 thrust cone

13 rear door
14 crew wardrobe
15 toilets
16 two piece rudder
17 two piece elevator
18 auxiliary power unit (APU)
19 APU air inlets
20 main torsion box (fuel tank)

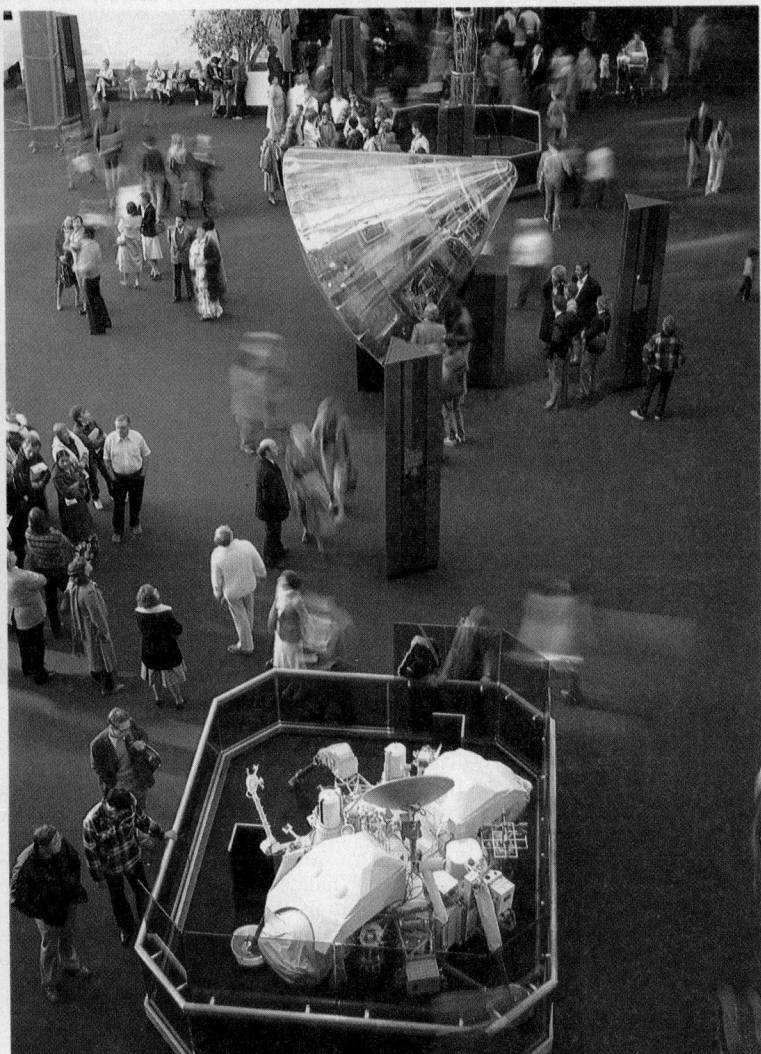

The displays in Washington's National Air and Space Museum cover many aspects of the U.S. **aerospace** program. Exhibits include space exploration equipment and moon rock samples.

approach and converse with; courteous, friendly. **af′fa·bly** *adv.* **af·fa·bil·i·ty** (ăfabĭl′ĭtē) *n.*

af′fair (afār′) *n.* Business, concern; love affair; social event; (pl.) ordinary pursuits of life; (pl.) public commercial, or professional business or transactions.

af·fect[1] (afĕkt′) *v.t.* Practice, use, assume (character); pretend to have or feel; pretend (*to* do). **af·fect′ed** *adj.* Artificially assumed or displayed; full of affectation. **af·fect′ed·ly** *adv.*

af·fect[2](afĕkt′) *v.t.* Attack (as disease); move, touch; produce (material effect on). **af·fect′ing** *adj.* Emotionally moving. **af·fect′ing·ly** *adv.*

af·fect[3] (ăf′ĕkt) *n.* (psychol.) Emotion, feeling, as antecedent of action.

af·fec·ta·tion (ăfĕktā′shon) *n.* Studied display *of*; artificiality of manner; pretense.

af·fec·tion (afĕk′shon) *n.* 1. Affecting, being affected. 2. Mental state, emotion; kindly feeling, love. 3. Bodily state due to any influence; (esp.) malady, disease. **af·fec·tion·ate** (afĕk′shonĭt) *adj.* Loving, fond; showing love or tenderness. **af·fec′tion·ate·ly** *adv.*

af·fec′tive (afĕk′tĭv) *adj.* Of the affections, emotional.

af·fer·ent (ăf′erent) *adj.* (of blood and lymph vessels, nerves, etc.) Bringing, conducting, inwards or towards.

af·fi·ance (afī′ans) *v.t.* (-anced, -anc·ing). Promise solemnly in marriage, betroth.

af·fi·da·vit (ăfĭdā′vĭt) *n.* Written statement, confirmed by oath, to be used as judicial proof. [L., = "has stated on oath"]

af·fil·i·ate (afĭl′ēāt) *v.t.* (-at·ed, -at·ing). 1. (of institution) Adopt (persons as members, societies as branches); attach *to*, connect *with* (a society). 2. (law) Fix paternity of (illegitimate child) for purpose of maintenance; father (thing) *upon*, trace *to*. **af·fil·i·ate** (afĭl′ēĭt, -āt) *n.* Person, group, business, etc. that is affiliated. **af·fil·i·a·tion** (afĭlēā′shon) *n.*

af·fin·i·ty (afĭn′ĭtē) *n.* (pl. **-ties**). Relationship, relations, by marriage or in general; structural resemblance; similarity of character suggesting relationship; liking, attraction; (chem.) tendency of substance to combine with others.

af·firm (afĕrm′) *v.* Assert strongly; make formal declaration or affirmation; state in the affirmative; ratify (judgment). **af·fir·ma·tion** (ăfermā′shon) *n.* Affirming.

---

aer·o·space (ār′ospās) *n.* Earth's atmosphere and outer space; (attrib.) of (industry concerned with) missiles, satellites, vehicles, etc. for operation in aerospace.

Aes·chy·lus (ĕs′kĭlus) (525–456 B.C.). Athenian poet regarded as founder of Greek tragic drama; of his many tragedies only seven are extant: *The Persians, Seven Against Thebes, Prometheus Bound, The Suppliant Maidens*, and the Orestes trilogy: *Agamemnon, Choephori, Eumenides.*

Aes·cu·la·pi·us (ĕskyulā′pēus). (Rom. myth.) = ASCLEPIUS.

Æ·sir (ā′sĭr). (Scand. myth.) Collective name of the gods.

Ae·sop (ē′sŏp, ē′sop) (6th c. B.C.). Semilegendary Phrygian teller of fables about animals, said to have been a slave in Samos; the fables attributed to him are prob. compiled from various sources.

*The Atlas Centaur rocket was originally designed by **aerospace** engineers as a missile but is now used as a booster for spacecraft.*

aes·thete (ĕs′thēt) *n.* Professed lover of beauty.

aes·thet·ic (ĕsthĕt′ĭk) *adj.* Of appreciation of the beautiful; having such appreciation; in accordance with principles of good taste; **A ~ Movement**, movement in late 19th-c. England advocating "art for art's sake." **aes·thet′i·cal·ly** *adv.* **aes·thet′i·cism** *n.* **aes·thet′ics** *n.* (usu. considered sing.) Philosophy of the beautiful; philosophy of art.

aes·ti·val (ĕs′tival) *adj.* Of summer.

aes·ti·vate (ĕs′tivāt) *v.i.* (-vat·ed, -vat·ing). Spend the summer, esp. (zool.) in state of torpor.

aes·ti·va·tion (ĕstivā′shon) *n.* (zool.) Aestivating; (bot.) arrangement of petals in flower bud before expansion.

Æth·el·red (ĕth′elrĕd) = ETHELRED.

AF *abbrev.* Air Force.

A.F. *abbrev.* Air Force; audio frequency.

a·far (afār′) *adv.* At, to, a distance; **from ~**, from a distance.

af·fa·ble (ăf′abel) *adj.* Easy to

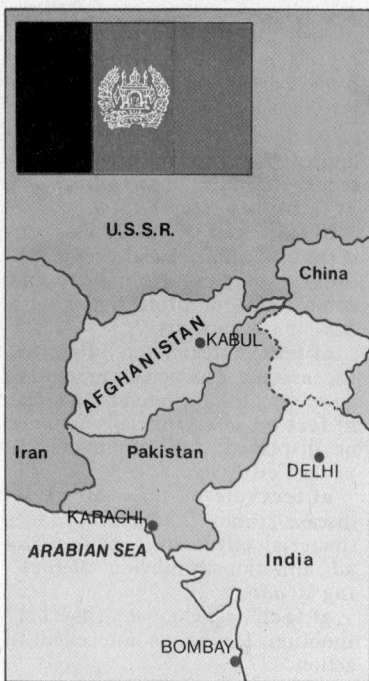

*Map and flag of **Afghanistan** and view of its rugged landscape: Salang Pass crosses Hindu Kush, at a height of 11,000 ft. Since 1979 there has been fighting between government forces backed by the U.S.S.R. and the Muslim tribesmen.*

af·firm·a·tive (afēr´matĭv) *adj.* Affirming, expressing assent; (logic) expressing agreement of the two terms of a proposition; ~ **action**, (law) process to counteract the effects of previously unfavorable allotment or refusal of jobs to persons because of their race or sex. **affirmative** *n.* Affirmative answer; the side that affirms a proposition in a debate. **af·firm´a·tive·ly** *adv.*

af·fix (afĭks´) *v.t.* Fasten, append, attach. ~ (ăf´ĭks) *n.* Appendage, addition; (gram.) prefix or suffix.

af·fla·tus (aflā´tus) *n.* Divine or creative inspiration.

af·flict (aflĭkt´) *v.t.* Distress with bodily or mental suffering. **af·flic·tion** (aflĭk´shon) *n.* Misery, distress; pain, calamity.

af·flu·ent (ăf´lo͞oent) *adj.* Flowing freely; abounding; wealthy. ~ *n.* Tributary stream. **af´flu·ence** *n.* Wealth, abundance.

af·flux (ăf´lŭks) *n.* Flow toward a point; accession.

af·ford (afôrd´, afōrd´) *v.t.* 1. (with *can*) Have the means, be rich enough, manage to spare (time etc.). 2. Supply, provide. 3. Bestow. 4. Yield supply of. 5. Be in a position *to* do.

af·for·est (afôr´ĭst; afär´-) *v.t.* Convert into a forest; plant with trees. **af·for·est·a·tion** (afôrĭstā´shon, afär-) *n.*

af·fray (afrā´) *n.* Breach of peace caused by fighting or rioting in public place.

af·front (afrŭnt´) *v.t.* Insult openly; face defiantly. **af·front´ed** *adj.* **affront** *n.* Open insult.

Af·ghan (ăf´găn, -gan) *adj.* Of Afghanistan or its people; (strictly) of a tribe of Pathans who inhabit E. Afghanistan and speak Pashto; of the Pashto language; ~ **hound**, hunting dog of ancient breed with long silky hair and tuft on head. **Afghan** *n.* 1. Afghan person or language. 2. (a~) knitted or crocheted woolen coverlet.

Af·ghan·i·stan (ăfgăn´ĭstăn). Inland republic of SW. Asia bounded on W. by Iran, on S. and E. by Pakistan and on N. by U.S.S.R.; founded in 18th c. by tribe of Pathans who broke away from Mogul Empire; later under British protection but declared a sovereign state in 1921; inhabited by various chiefly Muslim peoples, including Afghans and Tajiks, speaking several languages of which the principal are Pashto and Persian (the official language); capital, Kabul.

a·fi·cio·na·do (afĭsēeonah´dō, -fĭsho-; *Sp.* ahfēthyawnah´dhaw) *n.* (pl. **-dos**). Devotee of bullfighting (or other sport or pastime). [Sp.]

a·field (afēld´) *adv.* On, in, or to the field; away, at a distance, astray.

a·fire (afīr´) *adv.* & *pred. adj.* On fire.

a·flame (aflām´) *adv.* & *pred. adj.* In flames; in a glow of light.

AFL-CIO *abbrev.* American Federation of Labor and Congress of Industrial Organizations.

a·float (aflōt´) *adv.* & *pred. adj.* Floating, drifting; at sea, on board ship; full of water.

a·flut·ter (aflŭt´er) *adj.* In a flutter.

a·foot (afo͞ot´) *adv.* & *pred. adj.* On one's feet; astir; in the process of being done.

a·fore (afôr´, afōr´) *adv.* & *prep.* (naut.) In front (of); (archaic, dial.) before, previously. **afore´-mentioned** *adj.* Mentioned previously or earlier. **afore´said** *adj.* Spoken of or named earlier or above. **afore´thought** *adj.* Thought out or planned beforehand, premeditated.

a for·ti·o·ri (ā fôrshēōr´ē, ä fôrshēōr´ē; *Lat.* ah fôrtēōr´ē). With stronger reason, all the more. [L.]

a·foul (afowl´) *adj.* & *adv.* In a state of collision, conflict, or entanglement; **run** (or **fall**) ~ **of**, come into conflict with.

Afr. *abbrev.* Africa; African.

a·fraid (afrād´) *pred. adj.* Alarmed, frightened; sorry to say or suspect.

a·fresh (afrĕsh´) *adv.* Anew, with fresh beginning.

Af·ri·ca (ăf´rĭka). Continent between Atlantic and Indian oceans extending nearly as far southward of equator as northward; its indigenous inhabitants are darkskinned peoples varying in color from light copper in N. to black in equatorial and southern parts; it was visited by Portuguese from

*Face of an **African** tribesman, member of the pastoral Samburu tribe in northern Kenya. The political face of the African continent has changed rapidly since 1946 with former colonies gaining independence and then rejecting Europeans and their influence.*

The second largest continent (after Asia). **Africa** stretches about the same distance north and south of the Equator. Although archaeological evidence suggests East Africa was a center of early human evolution, to the outside world Africa remained the unex- plored 'Dark Continent' until the mid-19th century. 1. Giraffe in the protected terrain of Amboseli Reserve, Kenya. Wildlife reserves may save many species from extinction. 2. View from the Escom building of Johannesburg, largest city of the Republic of South Africa. 3. Victoria Falls, Zambesi River. The chasm is 355 ft. deep and water falls almost vertically with a deafening roar in a cloud of spray. 4. Looking as though sculpted by human hands: a sand dune at Tassili, near Djanet in Algeria.

15th c. onwards but remained largely unknown, except for limited colonization by the Dutch and British in the Cape region and by the French in Algeria, until mid-19th c.; in the 1880s the leading European nations competed for colonies, and the continent was divided between them, Liberia and Ethiopia alone remaining independent; after World War II most former colonies secured political independence.
Af·ri·can (ăf′rĭkan) *adj.* Of Africa or its people; ~ **violet**, a widely cultivated house plant (*Saintpaulia ionantha*) having white, pink, or violet flowers. **African** *n.* African person, esp. dark-skinned person as dist. from European or Asiatic settlers or their descendants. **Af·ri·can·ism** *n.* (esp.) African nationalism. **Af·ri-**

can·ist *adj. & n.* **Af·ri·can·ize** (ăf′rĭkanīz) *v.t.* (**-ized, -iz·ing**). Subject to rule of African blacks. **Af·ri·can·i·za·tion** (ăfrĭkanĭzā′-shon) *n.*
Af·ri·kaans (ăfrĭkahns′, -kahnz′) *n.* Language, derived from 17th-century Dutch, used in the Republic of South Africa. ~ *adj.* Of Afrikaans or its speakers.
Af·ri·kan·der (ăfrĭkăn′der) *n.* 1. (hist.) Afrikaner. 2. (One of) a breed of hump-backed, large-horned beef cattle developed in South Africa.
Af·ri·ka·ner (ăfrĭkah′ner) *n.* (Esp. Afrikaans-speaking) descendant of Dutch settlers of South Africa.
Af·ro (ăf′rō) *adj.* Of Afro-Americans, black traditions, etc. ~ *n.* Bushy hairstyle.
Afro- *prefix.* African; African

and —.
Af·ro-A·mer·i·can (ăfrōamĕr′-ĭkan) *adj. & n.* (An American, esp. a black) from Africa or descended from Africans.
aft (ăft) *adv.* In, to, or toward stern of ship or tail of aircraft.
af·ter (ăf′ter) *adv.* Behind; later. ~ *prep.* Behind; in pursuit of; following in point of time; in view of; below in importance or rank; according to; in imitation of; ~ **all**, in spite of everything that has happened, been said, done, etc. **after** *conj.* In or at a time subsequent to that when. ~ *adj.* Later, following; nearer stern of ship or tail of aircraft; **af′terbirth**, placenta and membrane enveloping fetus in womb, extruded after the child; **af′terburner**, device for increasing jet-engine thrust by burning extra fuel through use of hot ex-

haust gases; device for burning undesirable exhaust fumes, as from internal combustion engine or incinerator; **af'tercare**, attention given to person after discharge from hospital, prison, etc.; **af'tereffect**, delayed effect; effect following after an interval; **af'terglow**, glow in west after sunset; pleasant remembrance; **af'terlife**, life after death; later period of person's life; **af'termath**, (fig.) results, consequences; **af'terpains**, pains caused by uterine contraction after childbirth; **af'tertaste**, taste remaining or recurring after eating or drinking (freq. fig.); **af'terthought**, reflection after the act; later expedient or explanation.

af·ter·noon (ăfternoōn') *n.* Time between noon and evening.

af·ter·ward (ăf'terwerd), **af·ter·wards** (ăf'terwerdz) *advs.* Later, subsequently.

Ag *symbol.* Silver.

A.G. *abbrev.* Adjutant General.

a·ga (ah'ga) *n.* Commander or chief officer in Ottoman Empire; **Aga Khan**, title given to Hasan Ali Shah (1800–81) when he fled from Persia and settled in Bombay under British protection, and subsequently held by his successors; as direct descendant of Muhammad's son-in-law Ali, the Aga Khan is spiritual leader (Imam) of the Ismaili sect of Muslims. [Turk. *aghā* master, *khan* ruler, king]

a·gain (agen') *adv.* Another time, once more; further, besides; on the other hand; in return, in response; ~ **and** ~, repeatedly; **as much** ~, twice as much; **half as much** ~, one-and-a-half times as much.

a·gainst (agĕnst') *prep.* In opposition to; in contrast to; in anticipation of; into collision with; in contact with; as a protection from; in payment towards; opposite to (usu. **over** ~).

Ag·a·mem·non (ăgamĕm'nŏn, -non). (Gk. legend) King of Argos, brother of Menelaus and commander of the Greeks in the Trojan War; murdered on his return from Troy by his wife Clytemnestra and her lover Aegisthus.

a·gape¹ (agāp', agăp') *adv. & pred. adj.* Gaping.

a·ga·pe² (ahgah'pā, ah'ga-) *n.* 1. Love feast held by early Christians in connection with Lord's Supper. 2. Spiritual love (opp. EROS). [Gk., = "brotherly love"]

a·gar (ah'gār, ăg'er), **a'gar-a'gar** *ns.* Gelatinous substance obtained from various seaweeds and used as laxative, as solidifying agent in culture media for bacteria etc., and in East as food. [Malay]

Ag·as·siz (ăg'ase), **(Jean) Louis (Rodolphe)** (1807–73). Swiss-born American naturalist, educator, and writer.

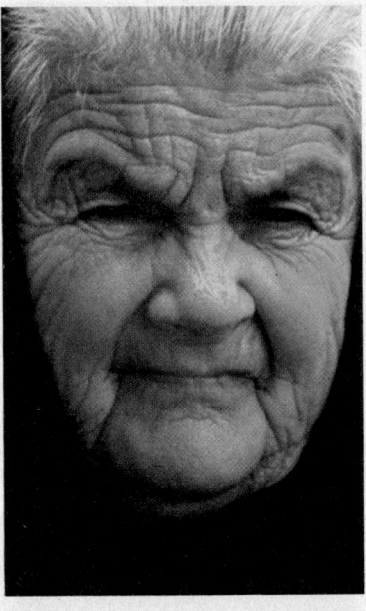

Portrait of age. Average length of the human life has much increased. The average in N.W. Europe and N. America in late 18th century was 35–40 years. By 1970 it exceeded 70 years.

a·gate (ăg'ĭt) *n.* 1. Any of various semiprecious stones, semipellucid and variegated, usu. having a banded appearance and consisting largely of silica. 2. (print.) 5½-point type.

a·ga·ve (agah've, agā'-) *n.* Tropical American plant of genus *A* ~ (family Amaryllidaceae), including century plant, of which some species are ornamental, and some yield rope and other fibers and are sources of beverages.

age (āj) *n.* 1. Length of life or of existence; a generation; (colloq., esp. in pl.) long time. 2. Particular length of life qualifying one for a purpose; ~ **of consent**, (law) age at which consent is valid; **come of** ~, (law) attain age of 18 (formerly 21) years, assume rights and

A variety of semi-precious stones, the **agate,** *found in eruptive rocks, consists largely of silica. Uses vary from jewelry and paper-knives to laboratory mortars and pestles.*

responsibilities of adult; **under** ~, not of full age; of less than age required. 3. Latter part of life (also **old** ~). 4. Great period, as **Ice A** ~; ~**-old**, having existed for a very long time. **age** *v.* (**aged, ag·ing** or **age·ing**). 1. (Cause to) grow old. 2. Become mature. **ag'ing, age'ing** *ns.* (esp.) Change of properties occurring in some metals after heat treatment or cold working. **aged** *adj.* 1. (ājd) Of the age of. 2. (ā'jĭd) Old; **the** ~, old persons. **age'less** *adj.* Never becoming old or outmoded. **age'less·ness** *n.*

a·gen·cy (ā'jensē) *n.* (pl. **-cies**). Active operation, action; instrumentality; action personified; office of agent; agent's business establishment; government bureau.

a·gen·da (ajĕn'da) *n.* List of things to be done, items of business to be considered at a meeting.

a·gent (ā'jent) *n.* One who, thing that, exerts power or produces effect; one acting for another in business, law, politics, etc.; spy; natural force acting on matter.

a·gent pro·vo·ca·teur (ăzhahn' prawvawkătör'). Person employed to detect suspected offenders by tempting them to overt action. [Fr.]

ag·glom·er·ate¹ (aglŏm'erāt) *v.* (**-at·ed, -at·ing**). Collect into a mass. **ag·glom·er·a·tion** (aglŏmerā'shon) *n.* **ag·glom·er·a·tive** (aglŏm'erātĭv, -erativ) *adj.*

ag·glom·er·ate² (aglŏm'erĭt, -rāt) *adj.* Collected into a mass. ~ *n.* Mass; (geol.) aggregate of angular fragments of rock (of any or of several kinds) that has been shattered by volcanic action and subsequently consolidated into a mass.

ag·glu·ti·nate (agloō'tināt) *v.* (**-nat·ed, -nat·ing**). 1. Unite as with glue; combine simple words to express compound ideas without important change of form or loss of meaning. 2. Turn into glue. **ag·glu·ti·na·tion** (agloōtinā'shon) *n.* **ag·glu·ti·na·tive** (agloō'tĭnātĭv) *adj.* (of languages) Characterized by the joining of simple roots to express compound ideas without material change of form or loss of meaning.

ag·gran·dize (agrăn'dīz, ăg'-ran-) *v.t.* (**-dized, -diz·ing**). Increase the power, rank, wealth, etc., of; exaggerate. **ag·gran·dize·ment** (agrăn'dĭzment) *n.*

ag·gra·vate (ăg'ravāt) *v.t.* (**-vat·ed, -vat·ing**). Increase the severity of; make more serious or worse; (colloq.) exasperate; annoy. **ag·gra·va·tion** (ăgravā'shon) *n.*

ag·gre·gate¹ (ăg'regāt) *v.* (**-gat·ed, -gat·ing**). Collect together; unite; amount to. **ag·gre·ga·tion** (ăgregā'shon) *n.*

ag·gre·gate² (ăg'regĭt, -gāt) *adj.*

How the opposing forces lined up at the **Battle of Agincourt** (Pas-de-Calais). The St. Crispin's Day battle was won in 1415 by the English under Henry V against the French in a crucial encounter of the Hundred Years War.

Collected into one body; collective total; (law) composed of associated individuals; (bot., of fruit) formed from carpels of one flower (as raspberry). ~ *n.* Total; assemblage, collection; (phys.) mass formed by union of homogeneous particles; (geol.) mass of minerals formed into one rock; (building) material mixed with lime, cement, bitumen, etc., to make concrete.

ag·gres·sion (agrĕsh'on) *n.* Unprovoked attack; (psych.) Hostile or destructive tendency or behavior. **ag·gres·sor** (agrĕs'er) *n.*

ag·gres·sive (agrĕs'ĭv) *adj.* Of attack, offensive; disposed to attack; self-assertive. **ag·gres'sive·ly** *adv.* **ag·gres'sive·ness** *n.*

ag·grieved (agrēvd') *pred. adj.* Distressed, oppressed; injured, having a grievance.

a·ghast (agăst') *adj.* Terrified; struck with amazement.

ag·ile (ăj'ĭl) *adj.* Quick-moving; nimble, active. **ag'ile·ly** *adv.* **a·gil·i·ty** (ajĭl'ĭtē) *n.*

Ag·in·court (ăj'ĭnkōrt; *Fr.* ăzhahṅkoor'). Village of NW. France, scene of victory (1415) of Henry V of England over French.

ag·i·tate (ăj'ĭtāt) *v.* (-tat·ed, -tat·ing). 1. Shake, move; disturb, excite. 2. Revolve mentally, keep up an agitation (*for*).

ag·i·ta·tion (ăjĭtā'shon) *n.* 1. Shaking. 2. Commotion, disturbance. 3. Keeping of matter constantly before public; public excitement.

ag·i·ta·to (ăjĭtah'tō) *adv.* (mus.) In an agitated manner. [It.]

ag·i·ta·tor (ăj'ĭtāter) *n.* 1. Person who creates excitement or disturbance, esp. for political ends. 2. Mechanical device for keeping liquid etc. in motion.

A·gla·ia (aglā'a). (Gk. myth.) One of the three Graces (see GRACE *n.* def. 3).

a·glit·ter (aglĭt'er) *adj.* Glittering; sparkling.

Ag·nes (ăg'nĭs), **St.** (4th c.). Patron saint of virgins, martyred in the persecution of Diocletian and commemorated Jan. 21.

Ag·new (ăg'noo, -nū), **Spiro Theodore** (1918–). Vice president of the U.S. (1969–1973) under Richard Nixon; resigned Oct. 10, 1973.

Ag·ni (ăg'nē). (Vedic myth.) God of fire.

ag·nos·tic (ăgnos'tĭk) *n.* One who holds that nothing is known, or likely to be known, of the existence of God or gods or of anything beyond material phenomena.

~ *adj.* Pertaining to agnostics or agnosticism. **ag·nos·ti·cism** (ăgnos'tĭsĭzem) *n.* [Gk. *agnostos* (*theos*) unknown (god); taken by T. H. Huxley f. Acts 17]

Ag·nus De·i (ăg'nus dē'ī, ahn'yoos dē'ē). Part of the Mass beginning with these words; figure of lamb as emblem of Christ bearing cross or banner; small disk of wax stamped with this figure and blessed by pope. [L., = "lamb of God"]

a·go (agō') *adv.* Past, gone by; since.

a·gog (agog') *adv. & pred. adj.* Eager(ly), expectant(ly).

ag·o·nize (ăg'onīz) *v.* (-nized, -niz·ing). Torture; suffer agony, writhe in anguish; make desperate efforts for effect.

ag·o·ny (ăg'onē) *n.* (pl. **-nies**). Extreme bodily or mental suffering; the last sufferings of Jesus Christ before the Crucifixion; **death ~**, **last ~**, death pangs.

ag·o·ra·pho·bi·a (ăgerafō'bēa *n.* Morbid dread of open spaces.

a·gou·ti (agoo'tē) *n.* (pl. **-tis**, **-ties**). Rodent (several species in genus *Dasyprocta*) of tropical

Taj Mahal, **Agra**, India, erected 1631-45. Thought by some to be the world's most sublime building, it was built by the Mogul emperor Shah Jahan as a mausoleum in memory of his beloved wife.

America, related to guinea pig.

agr. *abbrev.* Agricultural; agriculture.

A·gra (ah'gra). City on river Jumna in Uttar Pradesh, capital of Mogul emperors from early 16th to mid-17th c.; site of the TAJ MAHAL.

a·grar·i·an (agrār'ēan) *adj.* Of landed property or cultivated land. **a·grar'i·an·ism** *n.*

a·gree (agrē') *v.* (**a·greed**, **a·gree·ing**). Consent (*to*); be in accord, harmonize in opinion etc. (*with*); (gram.) have same number, gender, case, or person.

a·gree·a·ble (agrē'abel) *adj.* Pleasing (*to*); (colloq.) well disposed (*to, to* do); **a·gree'a·bly** *adv.*

a·gree·ment (agrē'ment) *n.* Mutual understanding, covenant; (law) contract legally binding on parties; accordance in opinion; (gram.) concord in number, gender, case, person.

A·gric·o·la (agrĭk'ola), **Gnaeus**

*Contrasts in present day **agriculture**.
Left: A cotton harvester in Louisiana
collects the cotton bolls for processing.
Above: In Cordova, Spain, a peasant
plows a furrow with two mules — in
much the same way that his ancestors
have done over the centuries.*

Julius (40–93 A.D.). Roman general; governor of Britain for several years from 78.

ag·ri·cul·ture (ăg′rĭkŭlchẹr) *n.* Cultivation of the soil. **ag·ri·cul·tur·al** (ăgrĭkŭl′cherạl) *adj.* **ag·ri·cul′tur·ist, ag·ri·cul′tur·al·ist** *ns.*

ag·ri·mo·ny (ăg′rĭmōnē) *n.* (pl. **-nies**). Perennial plant of the rose family, esp. *Agrimonia eupatoria*, which has yellow flowers and hooked clinging fruit; **hemp** ~, see HEMP.

A·grip·pa (agrĭp′a), **Marcus Vipsanius** (c63–12 B.C.). Roman general, son-in-law of the Emperor Augustus.

a·gron·o·my (agrŏn′omē) *n.* Rural economy, husbandry. **ag·ro·nom·ic** (ăgronŏm′ĭk), **ag·ro·nom′i·cal** *adjs.* **a·gron′o·mist** *n.*

a·ground (agrownd′) *adv. & pred. adj.* On the bottom of shallow water.

a·gue (ā′gū) *n.* Malarial fever; cold shivering stage of this; shivering fit.

ah (ah) *int.* Exclamation of joy, sorrow, surprise, entreaty, etc.

a·ha (ah-hah′) *int.* Exclamation of surprise, triumph, mockery.

A·hab (ā′hăb). King of Israel (1 Kings 16–22).

A·haz (ā′hăz). King of Judah (2 Kings 16).

a·head (ahĕd′) *adv. & pred. adj.* In advance *of*, in or direct line forward, onward; in or toward a more advantageous position or situation.

a·hoy (ahoi′) *int.* (naut.) Call used in hailing.

Ah·ri·man (ah′rĭman). Principle of evil in the Zoroastrian system.

A·hu·ra Maz·da (ah′hoora măz′da) = ORMAZD.

ai (ah′ē) *n.* (pl. **a·is**). Three-toed sloth (*Bradypus tridactylus*) of S. America. [f. its cry]

AID *abbrev.* Agency for International Development.

aid (ād) *v.t.* Help, assist, promote. ~ *n.* Help, assistance; helper; material source of help.

aide (ād) *n.* Aide-de-camp; assistant.

aide-de-camp (ād′dekămp′) *n.* (pl. **aides-de-camp**). Military officer acting as confidential assistant to senior officer. [Fr.]

ai·grette (ā′grĕt, āgrĕt′) *n.* Ornamental tuft of upright plumes, esp. from the long white tail feathers of egret; spray of gems or other ornaments resembling this.

ail (āl) *v.* Trouble, afflict; be ill. **ail′ment** *n.* Illness, esp. slight one.

ai·le·ron (ā′lerŏn) *n.* Hinged flap on trailing edge of aircraft wing, providing variation of lift on either side and used, for example, to execute the movement known as banking. [Fr., = "little wing, fin," dim. of *aile* wing]

ai·lu·ro·pho·bi·a (īloorofō′bēa) *n.* Morbid fear of cats. **ai·lu·ro·phobe** (īloor′ofōb) *n.* One having this fear.

aim (ām) *v.* Direct *at*; point (gun etc.); deliver blow, discharge missile *at*; form designs, try. ~ *n.* Direction of or act of directing a missile or weapon towards an object; design, purpose, object. **aim′less** *adj.* **aim′less·ly** *adv.* **aim′less·ness** *n.*

ain't (ānt) 1. Contraction of *am not*. 2. Also contraction of *is not*, *are not*, *has not*, *have not*. In all senses *ain't* is considered substandard usage in speech or writing.

Ai·nu (ī′nōō) *n.* (pl. **-nus**, collect. **-nu**). (Member of) a Caucasoid people in Japan and U.S.S.R. with hairy bodies; their language.

air (ār) *n.* 1. Invisible, odorless, and tasteless mixture of gases enveloping Earth, consisting chiefly of oxygen and nitrogen, with some carbon dioxide and traces of other gases, and breathed by all land animals; atmosphere; unconfined space; breeze; **on the** ~, broadcast(ing) by radio or television transmission. 2. Appearance; mien; affected manner. 3. (mus.) Melody, tune, aria. 4.

(attrib.) Of aircraft or flying; containing air or inflated by air. 5. ~ **bag**, safety device filling with air to protect automobile passengers in a collision; ~ **base**, center for military aircraft; **air'borne**, transported by air; in air after taking off; **air brake**, brake operated by piston driven by compressed air; also, brake consisting of flaps or other movable surfaces, normally lying parallel to airflow, turned through 90° to retard progress of aircraft or automobile; **air'brush**, fine spray for paint used in commercial art and for retouching photographs; **air cavalry**, airborne troops; **air conditioning**, process of controlling temperature and humidity of air before it enters a room, building, etc.; **air-cooled**, (*adj.*) cooled by exposure to stream of air; **air'craft**, (pl. same) any kind of flying machine, including airplanes, airships, helicopters, etc.; these collectively; **aircraft carrier**, ship designed to carry airplanes with special deck for take-off and landing; **air cushion**, cushion inflated by air; body of air serving to provide support, esp. in **air-cushion vehicle**, hovercraft; **air'-drome, air'field**, area of land where aircraft are accommodated and maintained and may take off or land; **air'foil**, any or all of the lift-producing surfaces of an aircraft, as wings, ailerons, fins, etc.;

*The ancients believed that the air sustained flight; da Vinci and later Galileo established that, on the contrary, it resisted movement of a solid object. That was the spur to the development of aerodynamics. Right: An **aircraft carrier** with support ships. Below: One of the 160-ton hovercraft that ply across the English Channel. Bottom right: Goodyear **airship** 'Europa'. Photographing sports events is one role of airships today.*

air force, branch of armed forces using aircraft in fighting; **air'-frame**, body of aircraft as distinct from engine(s); **air freight**, freight carried by aircraft; charge for this service; **air gun**, gun from which missile is discharged by compressed air; **air lane**, regular route of travel for aircraft; **air'lift**, transportation of troops, supplies, etc. by air to or from an area cut off from normal communications; (*v.t.*) transport thus; **air'line**, line of aircraft for public service; **air'liner**, large passenger airplane; **air lock**, stoppage of flow of liquid in pump or pipe by bubble of air; also, see LOCK² *n.* def. 2; **air mail**, mail carried by aircraft; **air'man**, member of crew of aircraft; enlisted man or woman in air force; **air mattress**, inflatable pad used as mattress; **air piracy**, hijacking an airplane; **air'-plane**, powered winged heavier-

than-air flying machine; **air pocket**, local condition of atmosphere, as a down current or sudden change of wind velocity, that causes aircraft to lose altitude suddenly; **air'port**, airdrome for transport of passengers and goods by air; **air power**, power of offensive and defensive action dependent upon a supply of aircraft; **air pressure**, atmospheric pressure, see ATMOSPHERE; pressure exerted by compressed air; **air pump**, pump for exhausting vessel etc. of its air; (also compressor); **air raid**, attack by aircraft; **air rifle**, air gun with rifled barrel; **air shaft**, passage for ventilating mine, tunnel, or building; **air'ship**, self-propelled lighter-than-air craft; dirigible balloon; **air'sickness**, nausea sometimes affecting airplane crew or passengers; **air'space**, space containing air; air lying over a particular territory and considered subject to its jurisdiction; **air'-speed**, speed of aircraft in relation to the air, as dist. from *groundspeed*; **air'strip**, strip of land prepared for the taking off and landing of aircraft, often for temporary use; **air terminal**, airport building equipped for reception of passengers; **air'tight**, impermeable to air; **air traffic control**, regulation of aircraft operating in air lanes; **air'waves**, medium for transmission of radio and television signals; **air'way**, ventilating passage in mine; air lane; **air'worthy**, (of aircraft) in fit condition to be flown. **air** *v.t.* Expose to open air, ventilate; express (one's grievances, opinions, etc.).

Aire·dale (ār'dāl) *n.* One of a breed of large terriers with rough reddish-brown coats. [valley of river Aire, West Yorkshire]

air·less (ār'lĭs) *adj.* Stuffy; breezeless, still. **air'less·ness** *n.*

air·y (ār'ē) *adj.* (**air·i·er, air·i·est**). Breezy; light, thin; immaterial; sprightly, graceful, delicate; superficial, flippant. **air'i·ly** *adv.*

aisle (īl) *n.* Division of church, esp. parallel to nave, choir, or transept, and divided from it by pillars; passage between rows of seats, in church, theater, etc. [L. *ala* wing]

Aix-en-Pro·vence (ĕks-ahǹ-prawvahǹs'). City in S. France, N. of Marseilles.

Aix-la-Cha·pelle (ĕks-lah-shahpĕl'). French name of AACHEN.

a·jar (ajär') *adv.* (of a door) Slightly open.

A·jax (ā'jăks). (Gk. legend) 1. Greek hero of the Trojan war, son of Telamon king of Salamis. 2.

Another Greek, son of Oileus king of Locris, who was killed after a shipwreck on his homeward journey after the fall of Troy.

AK *abbrev.* Alaska.

a.k.a. *abbrev.* Also known as.

Ak·bar (ăk'băr). **Jalaludin Muhammad** (1542–1605), Mogul emperor; enlarged the Mogul Empire in India to its greatest extent.

à Kempis, Thomas: see THOMAS À KEMPIS.

Akh·na·ton (ahknah'ton), **Ikhnaton.** Name (lit. "glory of the sun") taken by Amenhotep IV, king of Egypt of 18th dynasty (14th c. B.C.), husband of NEFERTITI, who tried to replace the worship of Ammon by that of Ra, and built a new capital at Tell el Amarna, away from Thebes where the old priesthood was established.

a·kim·bo (akĭm'bō) *adv. & adj.* (of arms) With hands on hips and elbows out.

a·kin (akĭn') *pred. adj.* Related by blood; (fig.) of similar character.

Ak·kad (ăk'ăd, ah'kahd). Northern part of ancient Babylonia; also, the city (Agade) founded by Sargon *c*2300 B.C. **Ak·ka·di·an** (akā'dēan) *adj. & n.* (Native or inhabitant) of Akkad; (of) the language of this people, the oldest known Semitic language.

Ak·ron (ăk'ron). Manufacturing and industrial city in NE. Ohio.

ak·va·vit (ahk'vahvēt) = AQUAVIT.

AL *abbrev.* Alabama.

Al *symbol.* Aluminum.

-al *suffix.* 1. Forming adjectives from L. (*general, central*), Gk. (*tropical*) etc. 2. Forming nouns (*animal, rival*), esp. of verbal action (*arrival, withdrawal*).

à la, a la (ah'lah, ăl'a). After the manner of. [Fr.]

Ala. *abbrev.* Alabama.

A.L.A. *abbrev.* American Library Association.

Al·a·bam·a (ălabăm'a). State in southeastern U.S., admitted to the Union in 1819; capital, Montgomery.

al·a·bas·ter (ăl'abăster) *n.* Translucent granular gypsum rock of white, pink, or yellowish color, used for statues etc. ~ *adj.* Of alabaster; resembling it in whiteness or smoothness.

à la carte (ăl *a* kärt', ah la). (of meal) Ordered by separate items from the bill of fare, with a stated price for each item (opp. *table d' hôte*). [Fr.]

a·lac·ri·ty (alăk'rĭtē) *n.* Briskness, cheerful readiness.

*This **alabaster** rock in Denver, Colorado, is a good example of the translucent gypsum rock that has been used for centuries to make statues, carvings and other ornaments.*

A·lad·din (aläd´in). Hero of a story in *Arabian Nights*, who acquired a lamp the rubbing of which brought a genie to do the will of the owner.

à la king (ah la kĭng´, äl a). (of food) Creamed with green pepper or pimento etc.

Al·a·mo (ăl´amō). Fort and former Franciscan mission in San Antonio, Texas; site of a massacre of Texans by Mexican troops in 1836, from which came the battle-cry "Remember the Alamo!"

à la mode (äl a mōd´, ah la). In the fashion, fashionable; (of pie etc.) served with ice cream on top; (of beef) braised with vegetables in wine and/or with a brown sauce.

Å·land (aw´land) **Islands.** Group of islands in the Gulf of Bothnia constituting a department of Finland.

a·lar (ā´ler) *adj.* Pertaining to wings; wing-shaped, winglike; axillary.

Al·a·ric (ăl´erĭk) (*c*370–410). A Visigoth, the first Germanic conqueror of Rome (410 A.D.).

a·larm (alärm´) *n.* Call to arms; warning sound giving notice of danger; warning; frightened anticipation of danger; sudden uneasiness; mechanism that sounds alarm; ~ **clock**, clock with apparatus that can be set to ring at predetermined time; **~s and excursions**, (joc.) noise and bustle. **alarm** *v.t.* Arouse to sense of danger; disturb, agitate. **a·larm´ing** *adj.* **a·larm´ing·ly** *adv.* [It. *all´ arme* to arms]

a·larm·ist (alär´mĭst) *n.* One who raises alarm on slight grounds; panic monger.

a·lar·um (alär´um, alär´-) *n.* (archaic) Alarm.

a·las (alăs´) *int.* Exclamation of grief, pity, concern.

A·las·ka (alăs´ka). State of the U.S. in the extreme NW. of N. America, with coasts on Arctic Ocean, Bering Sea, and North Pacific; discovered by Russian explorers (under Vitus Bering) in 1741, and further explored by Cook, Vancouver, and others during the last quarter of 18th c.; the territory was purchased from Russia in 1867 and admitted to the Union in 1959; capital, Juneau. Construction of new capital, at Willow, is planned. **A·las´kan** *adj.* & *n.* **Gulf of Alaska**, inlet of the Pacific Ocean between the Alaska Peninsula and the Alexander Archipelago; **Alaska Highway**, also called "Alcan Highway," highway 1,671 miles (2,689 km) long built by the U.S. and Canada between Dawson Creek, B.C., and Fairbanks, Alaska.

alb (ălb) *n.* Vestment reaching to feet, worn by celebrant at Eucharist over the cassock and by some consecrated kings.

At 20,300 ft. Mt. McKinley, in the south of **Alaska,** is the highest mountain in North America. Alaska, the largest State of U.S.A., was once known as Russian America.

Map of **Albania** with its flag. Proclaimed People's Republic in 1946, it was first a satellite of Yugoslavia, then of U.S.S.R. It is now more closely aligned with communist China.

al·ba·core (ăl´bakōr, -kōr) *n.* (pl. **-cores**, collect. **-core**). Large species of fish of E. and W. coasts of North America (*Thunnus alalunga*) allied to tuna; other fish of the same genus. [Arab. *al* the, *bakr* young camel]

Al·ba·ni·a (ălbā´nēa, awl-). Balkan state between Greece and Yugoslavia; under Turkish rule 16th c. until 1912; a republic from 1925 until 1928 when it was changed into a monarchy; again proclaimed a republic, the People's Republic of Albania, in 1946; capital, Tirana. **Al·ba´ni·an** *adj.* & *n.* (Native, inhabitant, language) of Albania.

Al·ba·ny[1] (awl´banē). Ancient poetic name, of Gaelic origin, for the N. part of Britain.

Al·ba·ny[2] (awl´banē). Capital of New York State, on the Hudson River 145 miles (233 km) N. of New York City.

al·ba·tross (ăl´batraws, -trŏs) *n.* Very long-winged oceanic bird (genus *Diomedea*), allied to petrel, found chiefly in the S. hemisphere; **wandering ~**, one of the largest sea-birds (*D. exulans*), white when adult, with dark wings and hooked beak. [f. obs. *alcatras* frigate bird, f. Span. and Port., f. Arab *al-qadus* the bucket (name for the pelican, from its supposed water-carrying habit)]

Al·bee (awl´bē), **Edward** (1928–). American playwright; author of *Who's Afraid of Virginia Woolf?* etc.

al·be·it (awlbē´ĭt) *conj.* Though.

Al·be·marle (ăl´bemärl) **Sound.** Inlet (about 50 miles long) of the Atlantic Ocean in North Carolina.

Al·bé·niz (ahlbā´nĭs; *Sp.* ahlvĕ´-nēth), **Isaac** (1860–1909). Spanish pianist and composer, famous

The long-winged oceanic **albatross** ranges the high seas for months on end. Inset: Courtship dance of the wandering albatross (Diomedea exulans). The male claps its bill, waves its neck and spreads its wings.

Calgary Stampede, **Alberta,** annual rodeo that attracts visitors from all over North America. Alberta, prairie province of Canada, is bordered on the west by the Rocky Mountains.

chiefly for works based on the rhythm of Spanish popular music.

Al·ber·ich (ăl′berĭk). (Scand. myth.) King of the elves, guardian of the treasure of the Nibelungs, stolen from him by Siegfried.

Al·bert (ăl′bert), **Prince** (1819–1861). Prince of Saxe-Coburg-Gotha; cousin and consort (1840) of Queen Victoria; **Lake ∼,** large shallow lake in Uganda, discovered in 1864, renamed *Lake Mobutu Sese Seko,* 1973.

Al·ber·ta (ălbẽr′ta). Western prairie province of Canada, bounded on the south by the U.S., and on the west by the Rocky Mountains; capital, Edmonton.

Al·ber·tus Mag·nus (ălbẽr′tus măg′nus) (1193 or 1206–1280). Swabian Dominican monk, one of the great scholastic philosophers; known as "Doctor Universalis."

Al·bi·gen·ses (ălbĭjĕn′sēz) *n.pl.* Members of a heretical sect preaching a form of Manichaean dualism in S. France, 11th–13th c. **Al·bi·gen·si·an** (ălbĭjĕn′sēan, -shan) *adj. & n.* [L. f. town of *Albi*]

Snowball, the **albino** gorilla. Albinotic animals and humans lack pigments in skin, hair, eyes. The condition is inherited. 'Albus' is Latin for white.

al·bi·no (ălbī′nō) *n.* (pl. **-nos**). Animal or human being marked by congenital absence of pigment in skin and hair, which is white, and eyes, which are pink or very pale blue and unduly sensitive to light; plant lacking normal coloring. **al·bi·not·ic** (ălbĭnŏt′ik) *adj.* **al·bi·nism** (ăl′bĭnĭzem) *n.*

Al·bi·on (ăl′bēon). Ancient poetical name for Britain.

al·bum (ăl′bum) *n.* Blank book for insertion of autographs, photographs, etc.; long-playing record or set of records.

al·bu·men (ălbū′men) *n.* White of egg.

al·bu·me·nize (ălbū′meniz) *v.t.* (**-nized, -niz·ing**). Coat (paper) with an albuminous solution.

al·bu·min (ălbū′min) *n.* Any of a class of water-soluble proteins, including the main constituent of white of egg; (bot.) substance found between skin and embryo of many seeds, usu. the edible part. **al·bu·mi·nose** (ălbū′minōs), **al·bu′mi·nous** *adjs.*

al·bu·mi·noid (ălbū′minoid) *n.* Any of a class of organic compounds forming chief parts of organs and tissues of animals and plants; protein. **al·bu·mi·noid·al** (ălbūminoi′dal) *adj.*

Al·bu·quer·que[1] (ăl′bukẽrkē), **Alfonso d'** (1453–1515). Portuguese navigator, founder of Portuguese power in India.

Al·bu·quer·que[2] (ăl′bukẽrkē). City on the Rio Grande in central New Mexico; established as a Spanish settlement in 1706.

al·bur·num (ălbẽr′num) *n.* Recently formed wood in trees, sapwood.

Al·cae·us (ălsē′us) (b. *c*620 B.C.). Greek lyric poet of Mitylene in Lesbos. **al·ca·ic** (ălkāĭk) *adj.* (esp.) Of a meter invented by Alcaeus, a stanza of four lines.

Al·can (ăl'kăn) **Highway** = ALASKA Highway.

Al·ca·traz (ăl'kătrăz). Island in San Francisco Bay, California; former site of U.S. federal prison.

Al·ces·tis (ălsĕs'tĭs). (Gk. legend) Wife of Admetus, whose life she saved by giving her own; she was brought back from Hades by Hercules.

al·che·my (ăl'kemē) n. Medieval forerunner of chemistry, primarily the attempt to transmute base metals into gold or silver. **al·chem·ic** (ălkĕm'ĭk), **al·chem'i·cal** adjs. **al·che·mist** (ăl'kemĭst) n. [Arab. al-kimia, f. al the, Gk. khēmeia transmutation of metals]

Al·ci·bi·a·des (ălsĭbī'adēz) (c450–404 B.C.). Athenian general and politician to whose irresponsibility the defeat of Athens in the Peloponnesian War was partly due.

Al·cin·o·üs (ălsĭn'ōus). (Gk. legend) King of Phaeacia and father of Nausicaa; entertained Ulysses during his journey home from Troy.

Alc·me·ne (ălkmē'nē). (Gk. myth.) Wife of Amphitryon and mother of Hercules by Zeus.

al·co·hol (ăl'kohawl, -hŏl) n. 1. Colorless volatile inflammable liquid, also called **ethyl** ~ (C_2H_5OH), formed by fermentation of sugars and contained in wine, beer, whiskey, etc., of which it is the intoxicating principle, also used in medicine and industry as a solvent for fats, oils, etc., and as a fuel. 2. Any liquor containing alcohol. 3. (chem.) Any of a class of compounds analogous to alcohol in constitution and derived from hydrocarbons by the replacement of hydrogen atoms by hydroxyl groups. [Arab. al the, koh'l powder (for staining eyelids)]

al·co·hol·ic (ălkohaw'lĭk, -hŏl'ĭk) adj. Pertaining to, containing, alcohol. ~ n. Person suffering from alcoholism.

al·co·hol·ism (ăl'kohawlĭzem, -hŏlĭz-) n. Diseased condition caused by excessive consumption of alcoholic liquors.

Al·cott (awl'kot), **Louisa May** (1832–88). American writer of popular novels; author of Little Women, Little Men, etc.

al·cove (ăl'kōv) n. Recess in room wall; recess in garden wall or hedge; summer house or secluded garden enclosure. [Arab. al-qobbah the vault]

Al·cy·o·ne (ălsī'onē). (Gk. legend) Wife of Ceyx; threw herself into the sea after finding the body of her shipwrecked husband on the shore; the gods changed both into kingfishers, and the sea is said to be calm while they are nesting; hence the expression "halcyon days."

al·de·hyde (ăl'dehīd) n. Any of

The **alder** tree with its leaf and catkins, male and female. The alder group of trees and shrubs belongs to the birch family and is found throughout the N. hemisphere and in western S. America.

a class of organic compounds containing the group CHO— in their structures, esp. acetaldehyde, CH_3CHO. [abbrev. of L. alcohol dehydrogenatum (deprived of hydrogen)]

Al·den (awl'den), **John** (1599?–1687). A signer of the Mayflower Compact and a founder of the Plymouth Colony in Massachusetts, 1620; married Priscilla Mullens.

al·der (awl'der) n. Shrub or tree (genus Alnus) of birch family, esp. A. glutinosa, growing by lakes and streams and in marshy ground.

al·der·man (awl'derman) n. (pl. **-men** pr. -men). 1. (hist.) Co-opted member of an English county or borough council, next in dignity to mayor; as an Anglo-Saxon title, a noble or person of high rank. 2. In some U.S. towns and cities, a member of municipal governing body. **al·der·man·ic** (awldermăn'-ĭk) adj.

Al·drin (awl'drin), **Edwin Eugene, Jr.** (1930–). American astronaut; second man to walk on moon (1969).

ale (āl) n. Liquor made from an infusion of malt by fermentation, flavored with hops etc., similar to but stronger and more bitter than beer; **ale'wife** n. (pl. **-wives** pr. -wīvz) Fish of N. Amer. Atlantic waters, Alosa pseudoharengus, allied to the herring.

A·lec·to (alĕk'tō). (Gk. myth.) One of the Furies (see FURY).

a·lee (alē') adv. & pred. adj. On the lee side of a ship, to leeward.

A·len·çon (alĕn'son; Fr. ălahn-sawn'). Town in NW. France, famous for the manufacture of needlepoint lace orig. copied from Venetian lace.

A·lep·po (alĕp'ō). Ancient city in Syria, twice besieged (though not taken) during the Crusades.

a·lert (alĕrt') adj. Watchful, vigilant; lively, nimble. ~ n. Warning call, alarm; warning of air raid etc., period of warning; **on the** ~, on the lookout. **a·lert'ly** adv. **a·lert'ness** n. **alert** v.t. Make alert, warn. [It. all' erta to the watchtower]

A·leu·tian (alōō'shan) **Islands** (also **Aleutians**). Group of islands in U.S. possession extending SW. from Alaska. **Aleutian Range,** volcanic mountain range extending along the Alaska Peninsula and into the Aleutian Islands; site of Katmai National Monument.

Al·ex·an·der[1] (ălĭgzăn'der) (356–323 B.C.), "the Great." King of Macedon; son of Philip II of Macedon; educated by Aristotle;

Alcatraz was a U.S. prison from 1868, originally for military purposes. Between 1934–63 it held the most dangerous federal prisoners. Since 1972 it has been a National Recreation Area.

became king 336 B.C.; was nominated by the Greek states to conduct the war against Persia, in which he was victorious; he extended his conquests to Egypt (where he founded Alexandria) and India.

Al·ex·an·der[2] (ălĭgzăn'der). Name of three emperors of Russia: **Alexander I** (1777–1825), emperor 1801–25 during the Napoleonic Wars; sponsor of the Holy Alliance; **Alexander II** (1818–81), emperor 1855–81; emancipated serfs 1861; assassinated in St. Petersburg; **Alexander III** (1845–94), emperor 1881–94.

Al·ex·an·der Nev·ski (ălĭgzăn'der nĕv'skē, nĕf'-) (1220–63). Russian Saint and national hero, called "Nevski" from the river Neva, on the banks of which he defeated the Swedes.

Al·ex·an·dri·a (ălĭgzăn'drēa). City and seaport of Egypt, founded by Alexander the Great 332 B.C.; capital of Egypt under the Ptolemies; until the Roman conquest of Egypt it was a center of Greek culture. **Al·ex·an'dri·an** *adj.* Of Alexandria; ~ **period**, period of Hellenistic literature with Alexandria as its chief center from end of the time of Alexander the Great to the Roman conquest of Greece, 300–146 B.C.

al·ex·an·drine (ălĭgzăn'drĭn, -drēn) *adj. & n.* (pros.) (Line) of six iambic feet, or 12 syllables, the French heroic verse. [so called because it was used in early poems on the subject of Alexander the Great]

al·fal·fa (ălfăl'fa) *n.* Leguminous plant (*Medicago sativa*) with trifoliate leaves and bluish-purple

Alfalfa, *also called lucerne, is a native of Europe but grown widely in the U.S.A. as a fodder crop of great economic value. Crops are pollinated by strategically placing bee colonies in the fields.*

cloverlike flowers, used for fodder.

Al·fon·so (ălfŏn'sō). Name of several kings of Spain, the last of whom, **Alfonso XIII** (1886–1941), was deposed in 1931 when Spain became a republic.

Al·fon·so I (ălfŏn'sō) (1112–85). First king of independent Portugal (1139–85).

Al·fred (ăl'frĭd) (849–899), **the Great.** King of the West Saxons 871; drove the Danes from his territories; built a navy; composed a code of laws; encouraged the revival of letters in the W. of England, himself translating Latin works into English.

al·fres·co (ălfrĕs'kō) *adv. & adj.* In the open air, out of doors.

al·gae (ăl'jē) *n.pl.* (sing. **al·ga** pr. ăl'ga). Any of the Algae, a division of primitive cryptogamic plants including green, brown, and red seaweeds, pond scums, and many microscopic water plants showing immense diversity of structure.

Al·gar·ve (ahlgär'vē). Province on the S. coast of Portugal; originally a Moorish kingdom.

al·ge·bra (ăl'jebra) *n.* Branch of mathematics dealing with relations and properties of numbers by means of letters and other general symbols. **al·ge·bra·ic** (ăljebrā'ĭk), **al·ge·bra'i·cal** *adjs.* **al·ge·bra'i-cal·ly** *adv.* **al·ge·bra·ist** (ăl'jebrā-ĭst) *n.* [Arab. *al–jebr* the reunion of fragments]

Vegetative state

A   B   C   D

Male Gamete
Female Gamete
Method of
Zygote   reproduction

Floating masses of sargasso seaweed, a form of **algae,** *gather in Sargasso Sea, North Atlantic. Diagram shows (left) method of reproduction of algae and (right) vegetative state.*

Key: A = Chlamydomonas; B = Spirogyra; C = Bladderwrack; D = Diatom. Some marine algae are used in food, 'Irish moss' seaweed, for example, in blancmange and other puddings.

Al·ge·ri·a (ăljēr´ēa). Republic in N. Africa; under French rule until 1962; capital, Algiers. **Al·ge´-ri·an** adj. & n.

Al·giers (ăljērz´). City and port on the Mediterranean; capital of Algeria.

ALGOL (ăl´gŏl) n. International algebraic language for use in programming computers. [*algo*rithmic *l*anguage]

Al·gon·qui·an (ălgŏng´kēan, -kwēan) n. (pl. **-ans**, collect. **-an**) & adj. (One) of a group of languages spoken by N. Amer. Indians from Labrador to the Carolinas and west to the Mississippi; Algonquin.

Al·gon·quin (ălgŏng´kĭn,-kwĭn) n. (pl. **-quins**, collect. **-quin**) & adj. (Member) of a group of Algonquian-speaking N. Amer. Indian tribes; Algonquian.

al·go·rism (ăl´gerĭzem) n. Arabic system of notation. [med. L. *algorismus*, f. Arab. *al-Khowa-razmi* the man of Khiva, surname of a 9th-c. Muslim mathematician]

al·go·rithm (ăl´gerĭdhem) n. 1. = ALGORISM. 2. Process or rules, usu. expressed algebraically, for (esp. machine) calculation etc. **al·go·rith·mic** (ălgerĭdh´mĭk) adj.

Al·ham·bra (ălhăm´bra). Palace of the Moorish kings at Granada, built in 13th c. [Arab. *al* the *hamra*' red: thought to refer to the color of the bricks or the name of the founder]

A·li (ah´lē, ahlē´). Cousin and son-in-law of Muhammad; regarded by some Muslims as the first caliph, his three predecessors being considered interlopers.

a·li·as (ā´lēas) n. (pl.**-as·es**). Assumed name, esp. of criminal. ~ adv. Otherwise named; called as assumed name.

A·li Ba·ba (ah´lē bah´ba, ăl´ē băb´a). Hero of a story supposed to be from the *Arabian Nights*; discovered the magic formula ("Open Sesame!") which opened the cave in which 40 robbers kept the treasures they had accumulated.

a·li·bi (ăl´ibī) n. (pl. **-bis**). Defense by an accused person that when an act allegedly took place he or she was elsewhere; (colloq.) excuse. ~ v. (colloq.) Make an excuse.

al·i·dade (ăl´ĭdād) n. Movable arm of quadrant etc. carrying the sights and indicating degrees cut off on the arc. [Arab. *al-'idada* the revolving radius (upper arm)]

al·ien (āl´yen, ā´lēen) adj. Not one's own; foreign; differing in nature (*from*); repugnant (*to*). ~ n. Person born in, citizen of, a country other than the one he or she lives in; foreigner, stranger. **al'ien·a·ble** adj. Capable of being sold. **al·ien·a·bil·i·ty** (ālyenabĭl´ĭtē, ālēena-) n.

al·ien·ate (āl´yenāt, ā´lēe-) v.t. (**-at·ed, -at·ing**). Estrange, (law) transfer ownership of; divert (*from*). **al·ien·a·tion** (ālyenā´shon, ālēe-) n. Estrangement; (law) transference of ownership; diversion to different purpose.

A·li·ghie·ri (ălĭgyar´ē): see DANTE.

a·light[1] (alīt´) v.i. (**a·light·ed, a·lit** pr. alīt´, **a·light·ing**). Dismount, descend (*from*); settle, come to earth (from the air).

a·light[2] (alīt´) pred. adj. Kindled, on fire, lighted up.

a·lign (alīn´) v. Place, lay, in a line; bring into line; form a line; ally (oneself) *with* a cause, group, side, etc. **a·lign'ment** n. Act of aligning; formation in a straight line.

a·like (alīk´) adj. Similar, like ~ adv. In like manner.

al·i·ment (ăl´iment) n. Food mental sustenance. **al·i·men·ta** (ălimĕn´tal) adj. **al·i·men'tal·l** adv.

al·i·men·ta·ry (ălimĕn´terē,-trē adj. Nourishing; performing func tions of nutrition; providing main tenance; ~ **canal**, channel i animal body through which foo passes, including whole length fror mouth through the intestines to th anus.

al·i·men·ta·tion (ălimĕntā shon) n. Nourishment; mainte nance.

al·i·mo·ny (ăl´imōnē) n. Main tenance allowance made to divorcee person by (former) spouse afte legal separation or divorce.

al·i·phat·ic (ălifăt´ĭk ad, (chem.) Fatty; belonging to th group of organic compounds i which the carbon atoms are linke in open chains as opposed to rings

al·i·quot (ăl´ĭkwŏt, -kwot) ad, & n. (math.) (Part) contained b the whole an integral number o times, thus, 6 is an aliquot part o 18.

a·lit (alĭt´) v.i. past t. and pas part. of ALIGHT.[1]

a·live (alīv´) pred. adj. Living active, brisk; fully susceptible to swarming *with*.

al·ka·li (ăl´kalī) n. (pl. **-lies -lis**). (chem.) Any of a numbe of substances having strongly basi properties and including the car bonates and hydroxides of the alka metals of ammonium and th hydroxides of some other reactiv metals; ~ **metal**, any of a group o highly reactive metallic element including lithium, sodium, and potassium. **al·ka·line** (ăl´kalīn

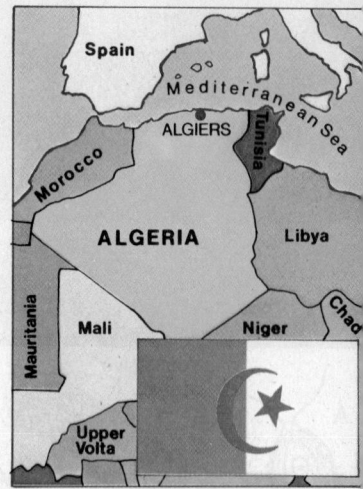

*View of Beni Izzgen, in the Algeriar Sahara, with map and flag of **Algeria** which became a republic in 1962 despite bitter opposition by French set tlers. Four retired generals led a revol against French secession in 1961: failed.*

Morphine, quinine, nicotine, cocaine and strychnine are **alkaloids**, complex compounds in plants that may affect men and animals physiologically. Alkaline plants illustrated are: Tobacco plant, pomegranate, deadly nightshade, opium poppy, henbane and hemlock. The number of alkaloids identified is nearly 1,000.

Tobacco plant

Pomegranate

Deadly nightshade

Opium poppy

Hemlock

Henbane

'Birth of Venus' by Botticelli (Uffizi, Florence), is an example of what may be termed **allegorical** painting. Botticelli (1444–1510) was one of the greatest Renaissance painters.

the greatest possible; the entire number of; ~-**American**, adj. of Americans only; typically American; chosen as best in any U.S. sport; n. all-American player; **all but**, nearly; **all clear**, signal giving information that there is no danger; esp., signal that hostile aircraft have left the neighborhood; **All Fools' Day** = APRIL Fools' Day: **All Hallows**, (archaic) All Saints' Day; **All Saints' Day**, Nov. 1, day on which there is a general celebration of all Christian saints; **All Souls' Day**, Nov. 2, day on which Roman Catholics and some Anglicans offer prayers for the souls of all the faithful deceased; **all-star**, made up of star performers; **all-time**, (colloq.) (of records) hitherto unsurpassed; of all time; **all** n. All people; the whole, every one, everything; **at ~**, in any way; in any degree; of any kind; ~ **one**, just the same. **all** adv. Wholly, quite; ~ **in**, (colloq.) quite exhuasted; ~ **in** ~, taken as a whole; of supreme importance; ~ **out**, using or involving all resources; fully extended; at top speed; **allover**, (colloq.) finished; everywhere; in characteristic behavior; **all right**, safe and sound, in good state; satisfactorily; (as sentence) I consent; all is well; **all-around**, adj. having ability and skill of all kinds, esp. in a game; **all there**, (colloq.) having all one's wits about one; **all the same**, in spite of this, notwithstanding.

Al·lah (ăl´a, ah´la). Muslim name of God. [Arab., f. al the, ilah god, cf. Heb. eloah]

Al·lah·a·bad (ălahabăd´, ahlahabahd´). Indian city at the confluence of the Jumna with the Ganges; capital of Uttar Pradesh; a place of Hindu pilgrimage.

al·lay (alā´) v.t. Put down, repress; alleviate; diminish.

al·le·ga·tion (ăligā´shon) n. Alleging; assertion (esp. one not proved).

al·lege (alĕj´) v.t. (**-leged, -leging**). Assert; affirm, advance as argument or excuse.

Al·le·ghe·ny (ălegā´nē) **Mountains** (also **Al·le·ghe´nies**). Ranges of the Appalachian system in eastern U.S. **Allegheny River**, river flowing S. through Pennsylvania; it unites with the Monongahela at Pittsburgh to form the Ohio River.

al·le·giance (alē´jans) n. Loyalty of citizen to government or

al·kane (ăl´kān) n. Any member of the paraffin series of hydrocarbons.

al·kene (ăl´kēn) n. Any member of the ethylene series of hydrocarbons; olefin.

al·kyl (ăl´kil) adj. Derived from, or related to, the paraffin series of hydrocarbons; ~ **radical**, any of the series of radicals derived from paraffin hydrocarbons by removal of a hydrogen atom, e.g. methyl (CH_3), ethyl (C_2H_5).

all (awl) adj. Entire, every, any;

-lĭn) adj. **al·ka·lin·i·ty** (ălkalĭn´ĭtē) n. [Arab. al the, qily cinders, lye]

al·ka·loid (ăl´kaloid) n. Any of a large group of nitrogenous organic substances of vegetable origin having basic or alkaline properties, many, as morphine, strychnine, cocaine, etc., being used as drugs.

sovereign; devotion to group or cause.

al·le·go·rize (ăl´egerīz) v. (**-rized, -riz·ing**). Treat as an allegory, make allegories.

al·le·go·ry (ăl´egōrē, -gŏrē) n. (pl. **-ries**). Narrative description of subject under guise of another suggestively similar; figurative story. **al·le·gor·ic** (ălegŏr´ĭk, -gār´-), **al·le·gor´i·cal** adjs. **al·le·gor´i·cal·ly** adv.

al·le·gret·to (ălegrĕt´ō, ahle-) adv., adj., & n. (pl. **-tos**). (mus.) (Passage or movement played) somewhat briskly. [It.]

al·le·gro (alĕg´rō, alā´grō) adj., adv., & n. (pl. **-gros**). (mus.) Lively, gay (passage or movement), in brisk time. [It.]

al·lele (alēl´), **a·le·lo·morph** (alē´lomōrf, alĕl´e-) ns. Gene that occupies the same relative position on homologous chromosomes.

al·le·lu·ia (ălelōō´ya) = HALLELUJAH.

Al·len (ăl´en), **Ethan** (1738–89). American Revolutionary War hero and commander of the Green Mountain Boys of Vermont.

al·ler·gen (ăl´erjĕn) n. Substance causing allergic reaction; **al·ler·gen´ic** adj.

al·ler·gist (ăl´erjĭst) n. Physician who specializes in the treatment of allergies.

al·ler·gy (ăl´erjē) n. (pl. **-gies**). Hypersensitivity of body tissues esp. to the action of some particular foreign material, as certain foods, pollens, microorganisms, etc.; (fig.) antipathy; **al·ler·gic** (alĕr´jĭk) adj. Of, possessing, allergy; susceptible to (also fig.).

al·le·vi·ate (alē´vēāt) v.t. (**-at·ed, -at·ing**). Make less burdensome or severe. **al·le·vi·a·tion** (alēvēā´shon) n. **al·le·vi·a·tive** (alē´vēātĭv, -ātĭv), **al·le·vi·a·to·ry** (alē´eātorē, -torē) adjs.

al·ley (ăl´ē) n. (pl. **-leys**). Narrow street between or behind buildings; walk, path; also **al´leyway**; ~ **cat**, homeless city cat; **bowling** ~: see BOWLING; **up one's** ~, (slang) fitting one's interests or abilities.

al·li·ance (alī´ans) n. Act, state, of allying or being allied; union by

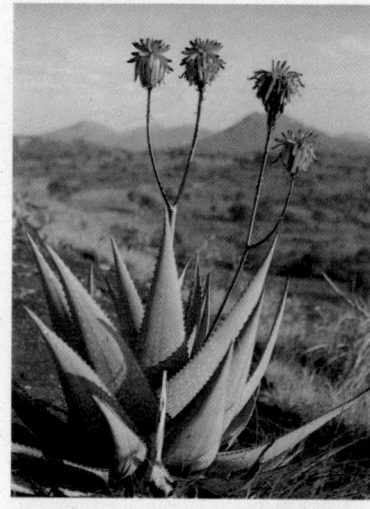

Aloe ukambaniensis. There are about 180 species of the plant. The leaves of some yield a bitter juice containing the substance called aloes, used medically as a purgative.

marriage; relationship; confederation, league (esp. between nations); **Holy A~**: see HOLY; **Triple ~**: see TRIPLE.

al·lied (alīd´, ăl´īd) adj. Combined, united (to, with), unrelated, linked by treaty.

al·li·ga·tor (ăl´igāter) n. Crocodilian (genera *Alligator* and *Cayman*) of New World and China, having certain teeth in lower jaw which fit into pits, not into notches as in crocodiles proper; ~ **pear** = AVOCADO. [Span. *el lagarto*, f. L. *lacerta* lizard]

al·lit·er·a·tion (alĭterā´shon) n. Commencement of two or more words in close connection with the same letter or sound, esp. as a device in verse. **al·lit·er·ate** (alĭt´erāt) v.i. (**-at·ed, -at·ing**). (Contain words that) begin with the same sound. **al·lit·er·a·tive** (alĭt´erātĭv, -ātĭv) adj. **al·lit·er·a·tive·ly** adv.

al·lo·cate (ăl´okāt) v.t. (**-cat·ed, -cat·ing**). Assign (to). **al·lo·ca·tion** (ălokā´shon) n. Apportionment.

al·lop·a·thy (alŏp´athē) n. Traditional medical practice that aims at curing disease by remedies having opposite effect to that

caused by the disease (opp. HOMEOPATHY). **al·lo·path·ic** (ălopăth´ĭk) adj. **al·lo·path´i·cal·ly** adv. **al·lop´a·thist** n.

al·lot (alŏt´) v.t. (**-lot·ted, -lot·ting**). Give as due share or portion; assign for special purpose.

al·lot·ment (alŏt´ment) n. Apportioning; lot in life; share allotted to one.

al·lo·trope (ăl´otrōp) n. One form of an element, differing from another or others in crystal form, or in chemical properties, or in molecular complexity, or in all three (as oxygen and ozone; yellow and red phosphorus; graphite and diamond). **al·lo·trop·ic** (ălotrŏp´ĭk) adj. **al·lot·ro·py** (alŏt´ropē) n. Existence of elements in allotropic form.

al·low (alow´) v. Admit; (colloq.) form the opinion (that); permit; admit of; give (limited periodical sum); add, deduct, in consideration of something; ~ **for**, take into consideration. **al·low´a·ble** adj.

al·low·ance (alow´ans) n. 1. Permission; tolerance. 2. Limited portion, esp. yearly income; addition to salary to cover special expenses, as **entertainment** ~, overseas ~. 3. Deduction, discount; **make ~(s) for**, allow for; forgive, excuse.

al·low·ed·ly (alow´ĭdlē) adv. Admittedly.

al·loy (ăl´oi, aloi´) n. Metal consisting of a metallic element with admixture of another metal or nonmetals, usu. having more useful properties than its constituents (e.g. brass is an alloy of copper and zinc). ~ (aloi´) v.t. 1. Form an alloy (of). 2. Debase.

all·spice (awl´spīs) n. Berry of *Pimenta officinalis*, supposed to combine flavor of cinnamon, nutmeg, and cloves.

al·lude (alōōd´) v.i. (**-lud·ed, -lud·ing**). Make indirect or passing reference to.

al·lure (aloor´) v.t. (**-lured, -lur·ing**). Tempt, entice; fasci-

*Swamps, rivers and lakes of the tropics and sub-tropics are habitat of the **alligator**. Alligator mississippiensis (U.S.A.) averages 10 ft. in length; the Chinese species averages 5 ft.*

nate, charm. ~ *n.* Personal charm.
al·lure′ment *n.*

  al·lu·sion (aloo′zhon) *n.* Indirect or passing reference.

  al·lu·sive (aloo′sĭv) *adj.* Containing an allusion, full of allusions. **al·lu′sive·ly** *adv.* **al·lu′sive·ness** *n.*

  al·lu·vi·on (aloo′vēon) *n.* Wash of sea against shore or of river against banks; flood; (esp.) alluvium; (law) formation of new land by action of water.

  al·lu·vi·um (aloo′vēum) *n.* (pl. **-vi·ums, -vi·a** pr. **-vēa**). Deposit of earth, sand, etc., left by flood esp. in river valleys and deltas. **al·lu′vi·al** *adj.* ~ **fan, cone,** deposit left by swift stream entering a valley or plain. **al·lu′vi·al·ly** *adv.*

  al·ly (alī′) *v.t.* (**-lied, -ly·ing**). Combine, unite, for special object. ~ (ăl′ī, alī′) *n.* (pl. **-lies**). Person, nation, etc., allied with another; **the Allies,** U.S., France, Britain, Russia, etc., united against Central Powers in World War I, and against Axis Powers in World War II.

  al·ma ma·ter (ăl′ma mah′ter, ahl′-, mā′ter). Title used in reference to one's university, college, or school. [L., = "fostering mother"]

  al·ma·nac (awl′manăk) *n.* Annual publication with calendar of months and days, and with astronomical and other data.

  Al·me·ri·a (ahlmĕrē′ah). Seaport in SE. Spain on the Mediterranean.

  al·might·y (awlmī′tē) *adj.* All-powerful; **the A** ~, God.

  al·mond (ah′mond, ăm′-) *n.* Kernel or stone of two varieties of *Prunus amygdalus* (**sweet, bitter** ~), allied to plum and peach; the tree; anything almond-shaped.

  al·most (awl′mōst, awlmōst′) *adv.* Very nearly.

  alms (ahmz) *n.* (sing. or pl.). Charitable relief of the poor; donation; **alms′house** (chiefly Brit.), institution founded by charity for reception of poor, usu. old, people; **alms′man,** one supported by alms.

  al·oe (ăl′ō) *n.* Liliaceous plant of genus *A* ~, with erect spikes of flowers, rosettes of fleshy leaves (often spiny), and bitter juice; (pl.) purgative drug procured from juice of aloes. **al·o·et·ic** (ălōĕt′ik) *adj.* (med.) Containing aloes.

  a·loft (alawft′, alŏft′) *adv. & adj.* High up; upward; in the air; esp. in(to) the upper parts of a ship's rigging.

  a·lo·ha (alō′a, ahlō′hah) *int. & n.* Greetings; farewell; love; friendship. [Hawaiian]

  a·lone (alōn′) *pred. adj.* Not with others, solitary. ~ *adv.* Only, exclusively.

  a·long (alawng′) *prep.* From end to end of, through any part of the length of; **along′side,** close to the side of (ship, car, etc.); **alongside of,** side by side with. **along** *adv.* In company or conjunction *with;* **all** ~, all the time; **be** ~, (colloq.) arrive.

  a·loof (alōof′) *adv. & adj.* Away, apart; reserved, indifferent.

  al·o·pe·ci·a (ălōpē′shēa, -sha) *n.* (med.) Baldness. [Gk. *alopekia* fox

An **almond** *orchard in springtime. There are two types of nut. The sweet variety is edible and used in confectionery or for its oil; the bitter almond is processed for flavoring extracts.*

mange f. *alopex* fox]

  a·loud (alowd′) *adv.* Audibly, not in a whisper; (archaic) loudly.

  alp (ălp) *n.* Mountain peak; a high mountain, esp. in the Alps.

  al·pa·ca (ălpăk′a) *n.* S. Amer. domesticated camel-like hoofed mammal, bred in Andes for its long woolly hair; its fleece; fabric of alpaca hair mixed with cotton; any of various silk, cotton or rayon fabrics more or less resembling this. [Arab *al* the, Peruvian name *paco*]

  al·pen·horn (ăl′penhorn) *n.* Long wooden horn used by Swiss herdsmen.

  al·pen·stock (ăl′penstŏk) *n.* Staff with iron point used in mountain climbing.

  al·pha (ăl′fa) *n.* First letter of Greek alphabet (A, α), corresponding to *a*, used in enumerations etc.; (astron.) chief or brightest star of constellation; ~ **and omega,** first and last letters of Greek alphabet; hence, beginning and end (Rev. I); ~ **particles, rays,** first of three types of radiation emitted by radioactive substances, consisting of positively charged particles.

  al·pha·bet (ăl′fabĕt) *n.* Set of letters (in customary order) used in a language; first rudiments; symbols representing speech sounds (**phonetic** ~); ~ **soup,** broth containing small noodles shaped like

*Gentians are among the most beautiful **alpine** flowering plants, of which there are about 1,000 species. Most summer-flowering gentians are easy to grow in a sunny position in any soil.*

*Petit France in Strasbourg, made capital of **Alsace** when the French occupied it in 1681. Alsace-Lorraine went to Germany in 1871, to France 1919, Germany 1940, France 1946.*

letters; (*joc.*) profusion of alphabetic and acronymic government agencies; **deaf-and-dumb** ~: see DEAF. **al·pha·bet·i·cal** (ălfabĕt´-ĭkal) *adj.* Of the alphabet; esp. in ~ **order. al·pha·bet´i·cal·ly** *adv.* [Gk. *alpha, beta,* first two letters of alphabet]

al·pha·bet·ize (ăl´fabetīz) *v.t.* (**-ized, -iz·ing**). Arrange in alphabetical order.

al·pha·nu·mer·ic (ălfanoōmĕr´-ĭk, -nū-) *adj.* Consisting of letters, numbers, and other symbols for computer work.

al·pine (ăl´pīn) *adj.* Of the Alps or other lofty mountains; (geol.) of a European episode of mountain formation during the Tertiary era; ~ **plant,** plant native to these regions, or (loosely) to mountain districts, or suited to similar conditions. **al·pin·ist** (ăl´pīnĭst) *n.* Alpine climber.

Alps (ălps). Mountain range extending from Ligurian Sea and Rhône valley through Switzerland to the western Hungarian plain.

al·ready (awlrĕd´ē) *adv.* Beforehand; by this time, thus early.

Al·sace (ăl´săs, ălsăs´, -sās´). French province W. of the Rhine; annexed with part of Lorraine (the annexed territory was known as Alsace-Lorraine) by Germany after the Franco-Prussian war of 1870; restored to France after the 1914–18 war.

Al·sa·tia (ălsā´sha). Old name of Alsace. **Al·sa´tian** *adj & n.* (Native, inhabitant) of Alsace; (Brit.) German shepherd dog.

al·so (awl´sō) *adv.* In addition to; ~**-ran,** horse not among first three in a race; (fig.) person etc. not distinguished in contest.

alt (ălt) *n.* (mus.) High note; **in** ~, in the octave (beginning with G) above the treble stave.

alt. *abbrev.* Altitude.

Al·tai (ăl´tī, ahl´-) **Mountains.** A major mountain system of central Asia, in the Soviet Union, Mongolia and China.

Al·ta·ic (ăltā´ĭk) *adj. & n.* (Of) a family of languages comprising Turkish, Mongol, and Tungus.

Al·ta·mi·ra (ăltamēr´a). A cave in N. Spain famous for prehistoric paintings.

al·tar (awl´ter) *n.* Flat-topped block for offerings to deity; Communion table; **lead to the** ~, marry (a woman); ~ **boy,** acolyte; ~ **cloth,** linen cloth used at Communion or Mass; silk frontal and super frontal; **al´tarpiece,** painting or sculpture above back of altar.

al·ter (awl´ter) *v.* Change in size, appearance, character, etc.; castrate or spay. **al·ter·a·tion** (awlterā´shon) *n.*

al·ter·cate (awl´terkāt) *v.i.* (**-cat·ed, -cat·ing**). Dispute hotly, wrangle. **al·ter·ca·tion** (awlterkā´shon) *n.*

al·ter e·go (awl´ter ē´gō, ĕg´ō). One's other self, intimate friend. [L.]

al·ter·nate (awl´ternĭt, ăl´-) *adj.* (of things of two kinds) Coming each after one of the other kind; placed on alternate sides (of line, stem, etc.). ~ *n.* Deputy, sub-

stitute. **al·ter·nate·ly** *adv.* **al·ter·nate** (awl´ternāt, ăl´-) *v.* (**-nat·ed, -nat·ing**). Arrange, perform, alternately; interchange (one thing) alternately *with,* by another; succeed each other by turns; consist of alternate things; **al´ternating current,** (abbrev. A.C. or a.c.) electric current reversing its direction at regular intervals. **al·ter·na·tion** (awlternā´shon, ăl-) *n.*

al·ter·na·tive (awltēr´natĭv, ăl-) *adj.* Available in place of another (thing); (of two things) mutually exclusive. ~. *n.* Permission to choose between two things; either of two possible courses; one of more than two possibilities. **al·ter´na·tive·ly** *adv.*

al·ter·na·tor (awl´ternāter, ăl´-) *n.* Generator producing alternating current.

al·tho (awldhō´) = ALTHOUGH.

alt·horn (ălt´hōrn), **alto horn** *ns.* Alto saxhorn, brass wind instrument like the French horn.

al·though (awldhō´) *conj.* Though.

al·tim·e·ter (ăltĭm´ĭter, ăl´tĭmēter) *n.* Aneroid barometer indicating altitude reached, as in aviation.

al·ti·tude (ăl´tĭtoōd, -tūd) *n.* 1. Height. 2. (geom.) Length of perpendicular from vertex to base. 3. (geog.) Height above mean sea level. 4. (astron., of heavenly body) Angular distance above horizon. 5. High place, (fig.) eminence.

al·to (ăl´tō) *n.* (pl. **-tos**). Highest adult male voice; female voice of

---

*Grandeur of the **Alps**. The village of Les Praz nestles at the foot of Aiguille Rouge and La Flegere Mountains. The mountain system extends from the Gulf of Genoa in the west to Vienna in the east.*

similar range, contralto; singer with alto voice; musical part for this. ~ *adj.* (of instrument) Tenor.

al·to·cu·mu·lus (ăltōkū′my*ulu*s) *n.* (meteor.) Type of cloud, of medium height, in form of thin patches often very close together or almost joined.

al·to·geth·er (awlt*o*gĕdh′*er*, awl′t*o*gĕdh*er*) *adv.* Totally; on the whole. ~ *n.* **in the ~**, completely naked.

al·to·stra·tus (ăltōstrā′t*u*s) *n.* (meteor.) Continuous veil of cloud, thin or thick, of medium height.

al·tru·ism (ăl′trōŏĭzem) *n.* Unselfish concern for others as a principle of action. **al·tru·is′tic** *adj.* **al·tru·is′ti·cal·ly** *adv.*

al·um (ăl′*u*m) *n.* One of series of double sulfates, esp. that of potassium and aluminum, used industrially, esp. in paper-making and leather tanning, and medically, as astringent and styptic.

a·lu·mi·na (al̄oo′mina) *n.* Aluminum oxide (Al_2O_3), which occurs as ruby, sapphire, etc., and as bauxite from which aluminum is obtained. **a·lu·mi·nate** (al̄oo′-mĭnāt) *n.* Compound of alumina with one of the stronger bases.

a·lu·min·i·um (ălyumĭn′ē*u*m) (Brit.) = ALUMINUM.

a·lu·mi·nize (al̄oo′mĭnīz) *v.t.* **(-nized, -niz·ing).** Coat with aluminum.

a·lu·mi·num (al̄oo′mĭn*u*m) *n.* (chem.) Light silvery white metallic element (symbol Al, at. no. 13, at. wt. 26.9815), not found naturally but widely distributed in the form of compounds, obtained by electrolysis and widely used esp. in alloys for construction of aircraft etc.

a·lum·na (al̆ŭm′na) *n.* (pl. **-nae** pr. -nē). Female former student of a school or college.

a·lum·nus (al̆ŭm′n*u*s) *n.* (pl. **-ni** pr. -nī). Male former student of a school or college. [L., = "foster child"]

al·ve·o·lar (ălvē′*o*ler) *adj.* Of an alveolus; (of a consonant) pronounced with tongue tip·behind upper teeth; ~ *n.* alveolar sound or consonant.

al·ve·o·late (ălvē′olĭt, -lāt) *adj.* Honeycombed, pitted with small cavities.

al·ve·o·lus (ălvē′olus) *n.* (pl. **-li** pr. lī). Small cavity, socket of a tooth; terminal air sac of lung in which exchange of gases between lung and blood takes place; cell of honeycomb; conical chamber of belemnite.

al·ways (awl′wāz, -wĭz) *adv.* At all times, on all occasions, in all circumstances; forever, constantly.

am (ăm) *v.* First pers. sing. pres. indicative of BE.

A.M. *abbrev.* Master of Arts;

Altocumulus (patchy) cloud over the Aspen Pass, Colorado. There are 1(main cloud groups, classified according to height (up to 45,000 ft.). Sighting aids weather forecasts.

Skyscrapers in Dallas, with aluminum cladding. Aluminum was developed ir 1855. Use of decorative aluminum sheeting on external walls became popular from the 1950s.

amplitude modulation.

a.m. *abbrev. Anno mundi* (L., = in the year of the world); *ant(meridiem* (L., = before noon).

Am·a·lek·ite (ăm′alĕkīt, amăl′-ekīt) *adj. & n.* (Member) of (nomadic people descended from Esau (Gen. 36), proverbial for treachery.

a·mal·gam (amăl′g*a*m) *n.* Allo(of a metal or metals, with mercury freq. plastic and used, e.g., ir dentistry; (fig.) a mixture, combination.

a·mal·ga·mate (amăl′g*a*māt) *v* **(-mat·ed, -mat·ing).** Combine unite (esp. of business firms); mix (of metals) alloy with mercury **a·mal·ga·ma·tion** (amălgamā′-sh*o*n) *n.*

a·man·u·en·sis (amănūĕn′sĭs) *n* (pl. **-ses** pr. -sēz). One wh(writes from dictation, or copies literary assistant.

am·a·ranth (ăm′arănth) *n* Imaginary unfading flower; plan(of genus *Amaranthus*, as pigweed tumbleweed, etc.; purple color **am·a·ran·thine** (ămarăn′thĭn -thīn) *adj.* (poet.) Unfading purple.

Am·a·ril·lo (ămarĭl′ō). Commercial and industrial city in NW. Texas.

am·a·ryl·lis (ămarĭl′ĭs) *n.*

Autumn–flowering bulbous plant of genus *A* ~ comprising only one species, *A. belladonna* from Cape of Good Hope, also called belladonna lily. [Gk. *Amarullis* name of a country girl in Theocritus and Virgil]

a·mass (amăs´) *v.t.* Heap together; accumulate.

am·a·teur (ăm´ater, -choor, -tūr, -cher) *n.* One who engages in an activity, esp. an art or sport, for pleasure rather than financial benefit; inexperienced, unskillful person (freq. opp. *professional*). **am·a·teur′ish** *adj.* Like an amateur; imperfect in execution, unskillful. **am·a·teur′ish·ly** *adv.* **am·a·teur′ish·ness, am′a·teur-ism** *ns.*

A·ma·ti (ahmah´tē). Name of a family of violin makers of Cremona, flourishing *c*1550–*c*1700: **Nicola** ~ (1596–1684) taught Antonio Stradivari.

am·a·tive (ăm´atĭv) *adj.* Disposed to loving. **am′a·tive·ness** *n.*

am·a·tory (ăm´atōrē, -tōrē) *adj.* Pertaining to a lover, making love, or expressions of sexual love.

a·maze (amāz´) *v.t.* (**a·mazed, a·maz·ing**). Overwhelm with wonder. **a·maz′ed·ly, a·maz′-ing·ly** *advs.* **a·maze′ment** *n.*

Am·a·zon[1] (ăm´azŏn, -zon). (Gk. myth.) One of a race of female warriors alleged by Herodotus to exist in Scythia; hence, tall, strong, or athletic woman.

Am·a·zon[2] (ăm´azŏn, -zon). Great river of S. America, flowing into the southern Atlantic on N. coast of Brazil; it was named because of a legend that a tribe of female warriors lived somewhere on its banks.

Am·a·zo·ni·an (ămazō´nēan) *adj.* Of the Amazons; of the Amazon River.

am·bas·sa·dor (ămbăs´ader) *n.* Diplomatic official of the highest rank sent by one country to another as its representative. **am·bas·sa·do·ri·al** (ămbăsadōr´ēal -dōr´-) *adj.* **am·bas·sa·dress** (ămbăs´a-drĭs) *n.* Female ambassador; ambassador's wife.

am·ber (ăm´ber) *n. & adj.* (Made of, colored like) yellow translucent fossil resin found chiefly on S. shore of Baltic and valued as ornament. **am·ber·jack** (ăm´berjăk) *n.* Any of several large food and game marine fishes of genus *Seriola*. [Fr. *ambre,* f. Arab. *anbar ambergris,* to which the name originally belonged]

am·ber·gris (ăm´bergrĭs, -grēs) *n.* Waxlike gray or blackish substance found floating in tropical seas, and in intestines of sperm whale, odoriferous and used in perfumery. [Fr. *ambre gris* gray amber]

am·bi·dex·trous (ămbĭdek´-

*Course of the mighty **Amazon**, largest river in the world. For centuries a challenge to explorers, the river drains 40 per cent of South America, including a vast belt of tropical forest.*

strus) *adj.* Able to use both hands equally well. **am·bi·dex′trous·ly** *adv.* **am·bi·dex′trous·ness** *n.*

am·bi·ent (ăm´bēent) *adj.* Surrounding. **am·bi·ence, am·bi-ance** (ăm´bēens, ahmbēahns´) *n.* Environment, surroundings; atmosphere.

am·big·u·ous (ămbĭg´ūus) *adj.* Obscure; of double meaning; of doubtful classification. **am·big′u·ous·ly** *adv.* **am·big′u·ous·ness** *n.* **am·bi·gu·i·ty** (ămbĭgū´ĭtē) *n.* (pl. **-ties**). Double meaning; expression capable of more than one meaning.

am·bi·tion (ămbĭsh´on) *n.* Ardent desire for distinction; aspiration *to* (be or do); object of such desire.

am·bi·tious (ămbĭsh´us) *adj.* Full of or showing ambition; strongly desirous. **am·bi′tious·ly** *adv.* **am·bi′tious·ness** *n.* [L. *ambitio* canvassing for votes, f. *ambire* go round]

am·biv·a·lence (ămbĭv´alens) *n.* State of having either or both of two contrary values or qualities; coexistence in one person of contradictory emotions (as love and hatred) toward the same person or thing. **am·biv′a·lent** *adj.*

am·ble (ăm´bel) *v.i.* (**-bled, -bling**). (of horse, etc.) Move by lifting two feet on one side together; walk at a leisurely pace. ~ *n.* Pace of an ambling horse; easy pace.

am·bly·o·pi·a (ămblēō´pēa) *n.* Dimness of vision without discernible change in the eye. **am·bly·op·ic** (ămblēŏp´ĭk) *adj.*

am·bro·sia (ămbrō´zha) *n.* (myth.) Food of the gods; anything delightful to taste or smell; beebread. **am·bro′sial** *adj.* [L. f. Gk. f. *ambrotos* immortal]

am·bu·lance (ăm´byulans) *n.* Vehicle for conveyance of sick or injured persons.

am·bu·lant (ăm´byulant) *adj.* (med.) Walking, not confined to bed.

am·bu·la·to·ry (ăm´byulatōrē, -tōrē) *adj.* Pertaining to, adapted for, or capable of walking, movable; not permanent. ~ *n.* (pl. **-ries**). Place for walking; arcade, cloister; esp., aisle around apse at east end of church.

am·bus·cade (ămbuskād´) *n. & v.* (**-cad·ed, -cad·ing**). Ambush.

am·bush (ăm´bŏŏsh) *v. & n.* (Make) a surprise attack from concealment; (wait in) a concealed position.

a·meer (amēr´) = EMIR.

a·mel·io·rate (amēl´yerāt) *v.* (**-rat·ed, -rat·ing**). (Cause to) become better. **a·mel·io·ra·tion** (amēlyerā´shon) *n.* **a·mel·io·ra·tive** (amēl´yerătĭv; -ātĭv) *adj.*

A·men (ah´men). Supreme god of the ancient Egyptians in the Theban religion, represented as a man with a ram's head; his worship spread to Greece, where he was identified with Zeus, and to Rome, where he was known as Jupiter Ammon.

a·men (ā´měn´, ah´-) *int.* So be it (used at end of prayer etc.). ~ **n.** Utterance of "amen"; expression of assent. [Heb. *āmēn* certainly, truly]

a·me·na·ble (amē´nabel, amĕn´a-) *adj.* Responsive, willing to listen or yield; responsible, liable, or subject (*to*). **a·me·na·ble·ness, a·me·na·bil·i·ty** (amēnabĭl´ĭtē) *ns.* **a·me·na·bly** *adv.*

a·mend (amĕnd´) *v.t.* Correct an error in (document), modify (measure before a legislature, proposal, etc.); make better, rectify.

a·mend·ment (amĕnd´ment) *n.* Improvement; addition to or correction of a document, bill, or law.

a·mends (amĕndz´) *n.* (sing. or pl.) Reparation, restitution, compensation.

A·men·ho·tep (ahmenhō´tĕp, ăm´en-). Name of four pharaohs of the 18th dynasty in Egypt; ~ **IV**: see AKHNATON.

a·men·i·ty (amĕn´ĭtē) *n.* (pl. **-ties**). Quality of being pleasant, agreeable; (characteristic of) situation, climate, disposition, etc., that is agreeable or pleasant (often pl.); (in pl.) pleasant manners or features; agreeableness.

Am·e·no·phis (ămenō´fĭs) = AMENHOTEP.

a·men·or·rhe·a (āmĕnorē´a) *n.* (physiol). Absence of menstruation.

am·ent (ăm´ent, ā´ment) *n.* Catkin. **am·en·ta·ceous** (ămentā´shus), **am·en·tif·er·ous** (ămentĭf´erus) *adjs.*

Amer. *abbrev.* America, American.

A·mer·i·ca (amĕr´ĭka). Continent of the New World or western hemisphere, consisting of great land masses, **North** ~ and **South** ~, joined by the narrow isthmus of **Central** ~; N. America comprises Canada, the U.S., and Mexico; Central and S. America are divided into a number of independent nations. N. America was prob. visited by Norse seamen *c*1000 A.D., but for the modern world the con-

tinent was discovered by Christopher Columbus, who reached the W. Indies in 1492 and the S. American mainland in 1498. (See also UNITED STATES OF AMERICA.) [named after *Amerigo* VESPUCCI]

A·mer·i·can (amĕr´ĭkan) *adj.* Of the continents of N. or S. America or their people; of the United States or its people; ~ **Beauty**, a type of rose with purplish-red flowers; ~ **cheese**, a mild cheddar; ~ **eagle** = BALD eagle; ~ **English**, English spoken in the U.S., also called **American**; ~ **Expeditionary Forces**, abbreviated A.E.F., U.S. troops in Europe in World War I; ~ **Falls**, the section of Niagara Falls within the U.S.; ~ **Federation of Labor** (A.F.L.), a federation of U.S. labor unions founded in 1886, merged with the C.I.O. in 1955; ~ **Indian**: see INDIAN; ~ **Legion**, organization of veterans of U.S. armed forces, establ. 1919; ~ **plan**, (rate for) hotel room with inclusion of meals; ~ **Revolution**, ~ **War of Independence**, war (1775–83) between Great Britain and her

The bald eagle, Haliaetus leucocephalus, commonly known as the **American Eagle,** *has been the U.S. national emblem since 1782. It is the only eagle native solely to N. America.*

colonies in N. America in which 13 colonies won independence and subsequently formed the U.S.; ~ **Samoa**, seven islands in the S. Pacific with a combined area of 76 square miles, a U.S. possession since 1951; capital, Pago Pago (see also SAMOA); ~ **Spanish**, Spanish as spoken in the Americas; ~ **Standard Version**, also called ~ **Revised Version**, a U.S. revision of the King James Bible, published in 1901. **American** *n.* 1. Citizen of the Americas. 2. Citizen of the U.S. 3. American English.

A·mer·i·ca·na (amĕrĭkăn´a, -kah´na) *n.* Books, memorabilia, etc., relating to America, esp. to U.S. history.

A·mer·i·can·ism (amĕr´ikanĭzem) *n.* 1. Devotion to U.S. and its institutions. 2. Word or idiom characteristic of American English. 3. Something peculiar to U.S.

A·mer·i·can·ize (amĕr´ikanīz) *v.* (**-ized, -iz·ing**). Naturalize as an American; make, become American in character. **A·mer·i·can·i·za·tion** (amĕrĭkanĭzā´shon) *n.*

America's Cup. Yachting trophy orig. won by schooner *America* for race around Isle of Wight (1851); later offered as challenge trophy for international matches.

Map of the continent of **America** — in cultural terms two widely different worlds. Canada and U.S.A. share a largely British heritage. Central (Caribbean) America and South America reflect Spanish and Portuguese influences and a Latin culture.

1 Manhattan, New York City, overlooking Central Park. Skyscraper hub of the city, Manhattan (31 sq. miles) is easy for the visitor to explore because of the numbered grid-plan streets.

2 View of Panama City, capital of the Panama republic. Sited near the Pacific entrance of the Panama Canal, the city has a turbulent history. In 1595 Sir Francis Drake tried to sack it.

3 Rio de Janeiro against the Sugar Loaf Mountain, a conical rock 1,296 ft. high. Early Portuguese settlers developed Rio, until 1960 Brazil's capital. The capital is now Brasilia.

a·mer·i·ci·um (ămerĭsh′ēum) n. (chem.) Metallic radioactive element; symbol Am, at. no. 95, principal isotope at. wt. 241. [f. *America* (first made at Berkeley, California)]

Am·er·ind (ăm′erĭnd) n., **Am·er·in·di·an** (ămerĭn′dēan) adj. & n. See INDIAN.

am·e·thyst (ăm′ĭthĭst) n. Purple or violet precious stone, a variety of quartz colored by manganese; purplish color. **am·e·thys·tine** (ămĭthĭs′tĭn, -tīn) adj. [Gk. *amethustos* not drunken (*methu* wine), because the stone was supposed to have the power of preventing intoxication]

Am·har·a (ahmhār′a). Former province of NW. Ethiopia, the dominant province from the 12th c.–19th c.

Am·har·ic (ămhăr′ĭk, ahmhār′-) adj. & n. (Of) the official and court language of Ethiopia, a Semitic language related to ancient Ethiopic.

a·mi·a·ble (ā′mēabel) adj. Friendly, good-natured. **a·mi·a·bil·i·ty** (āmēabĭl′ĭtē) n. **a′mi·a·bly** adv.

am·i·ca·ble (ăm′ĭkabel) adj. Friendly. **am·i·ca·bil·i·ty** (ămĭkabĭl′ĭtē) n. **am′i·ca·bly** adv.

a·mi·cus cu·ri·ae (amī′kus kūr′ēē) (pl. **a·mi·ci cu·ri·ae** pr. amī′kī). Disinterested adviser. [L., = "friend of the court"]

a·mid (amĭd′) prep. In the middle of; in the course of.

am·ide (ăm′īd, -ĭd) n. Compound formed from ammonia by replacement of one or more hydro-gen atoms by a metal or acid radical.

a·mid·ships (amĭd′shĭps) adv. In or toward the middle part of a ship or aircraft.

a·midst (amĭdst′) prep. (poet.) Amid.

a·mine (amēn′, ăm′ĭn) n. (chem.) Compound derived from ammonia by replacing one or more of the hydrogen atoms by certain aliphatic or aromatic radicals.

a·mi·no (amē′nō, ăm′inō) adj. (chem.) Pertaining to or containing the group NH_2; ~ **acid**, any organic compound containing both an amino group and a carboxyl group; some are the building blocks of proteins.

amino- prefix. Containing an amino group.

a·mir (amēr′) = EMIR.

A·mish (ah′mĭsh, ăm′ĭsh, ā′mĭsh) *adj. & n.* (Of) any of the strict Mennonite sects in the U.S. and Canada, chiefly in Pennsylvania.

a·miss (amĭs′) *adv. & pred. adj.* Out of order; wrongly; **take ~**, take offense at.

am·i·to·sis (ămĭtō′sĭs) *n.* (pl. **-ses** pr. -sēz). (biol.) Direct division of a nucleus or cell without mitosis. **am·i·tot·ic** (ămĭtŏt′ĭk) *adj.*

am·i·ty (ăm′ĭtē) *n.* Friendship, friendly relations.

Am·man (ah′mahn, ahmahn′). Capital city of Jordan.

am·me·ter (ăm′ēter) *n.* Instrument for measuring electric currents. [am-(pere) + meter]

am·mo (ăm′ō) *n.* (colloq.) Ammunition.

Am·mon[1] (ăm′on) = AMEN.

Am·mon[2] (ăm′on). Ancient country of the Ammonites, in S. Trans-Jordan. **Am·mo·nite** (ăm′onīt) *adj. & n.* (Member) of a Semitic people traditionally descended from Lot (Gen. 19), living in Ammon.

am·mo·nia (amōn′ya, amō′nēa)

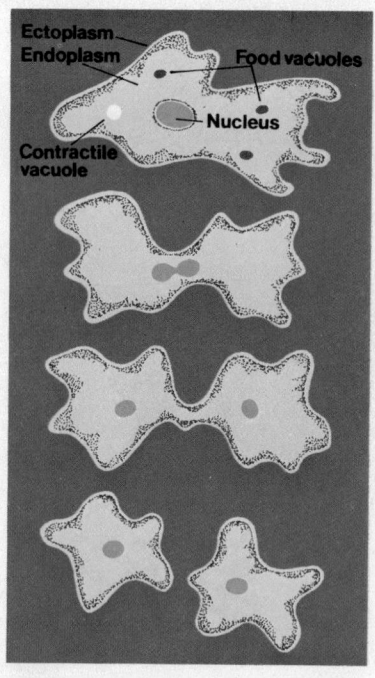

Ectoplasm
Endoplasm
Food vacuoles
Nucleus
Contractile vacuole

Amoeba is a microscopic primitive single-celled animalcule perpetually changing shape and reproducing by fission. Illustrated: An amoeba nucleus dividing into two parts.

n. Colorless gas (NH_3) with pungent smell, very soluble in water, giving alkaline solution; aqueous solution of this gas. [f. Jupiter Ammon (see AMEN), near whose temple sal ammoniac is said to have been prepared]

am·mo·ni·ac (amō′nĕăk) *adj.* Of the nature of ammonia; **sal ~**, old name for ammonium chloride (NH_4Cl), a hard white crystalline salt used in electric batteries etc. **am·mo·ni·a·cal** (ămonī′akal) *adj.* Of or resembling ammonia.

am·mo·ni·at·ed (amō′nēātĭd) *adj.* Combined with ammonia.

Am·mo·nite (ăm′onīt): see AMMON[2].

am·mo·nite (ăm′onīt) *n.* Member of an extinct group of cephalopods with chambered shell coiled in a flat spiral, freq. found fossilized in some Mesozoic rocks. [L. *cornu Ammonis* horn of AMMON[1]]

am·mo·ni·um (amō′nēum) *n.* (chem.) Radical (NH_4), whose compounds resemble those of the alkali metals; **~ chloride** = sal AMMONIAC; **~ hydroxide**, aqueous solution of ammonia, NH_4OH, used as household cleanser and in manufacturing.

am·mu·ni·tion (ămyunĭsh′on) *n.* Military stores (now only of projectiles with their necessary propellants, detonators, fuses, etc.); (fig.) facts, arguments, etc. used in attack or defense.

am·ne·sia (ămnē′zha) *n.* Loss of memory.

am·nes·ty (ăm′nĭstē) *n.* (pl. **-ties**). General pardon, usu. to a group and often before trial, for

The male crested newt, a tailed **amphibian**. European species pair on land but the female then deposits her young, 10 to 50 in number, in the water of cool streams. Below: An amphibious version of the Jeep, the ¼-ton G.P.A. Amphibian used during the 1939–45 war. The land Jeep chassis was fitted with a watertight boat hull, a rudder, operated by the steering wheel, and a propeller.

radio transceiver aerial

lever for closing vent when in water

air intake to radiator

spray shield

USA 703426·S

rudder

propeller

propeller gearbox

exhaust outlet

4-wheel-drive-lever

Above: A Roman **amphitheater**. Key: 1. Arena. 2. Emperor's or consul's box. 3. Podium. 4. Animals' entrance. 5. Animals' dens. Left: General view of the Coliseum in Rome, so named because of its size. It was erected by the emperors Vespasian and Titus on the site of Nero's Golden House. The Coliseum could seat up to 50,000 people.

offenses usu. political. ~ *v.t.* (**-tied, -ty·ing**). Give amnesty to.

am·ni·on (ăm′nē˘on, -on) *n.* (pl. **-ni·ons, -ni·a** pr. -nēa). (zool., physiol.) Membrane enclosing embryo or fetus. **am·ni·ot·ic** (ămnēot′ĭk) *adj.* Of the amnion; ~ **fluid**, fluid filling amniotic sac; ~ **sac**, cavity enclosed by amnion.

a·moe·ba (amē′ba) *n.* (pl. **-bas, -bae** pr. -bē). Single-celled protozoan, constantly changing shape, occurring in water and soil and as internal parasite. **a·moe′bic, a·moe′boid** *adjs.*

a·mok (amŭk′, amŏk) = AMUCK.

a·mong (amŭng′), **a·mongst** (amŭngst′) *preps.* In the assemblage or number of; surrounded by, within the limits of; by joint action of; between.

a·mon·til·la·do (amŏntĭlah′dō) *n.* One of the principal types of dry sherry, with nutty flavor. [Span., = "made like (the wine of) *Montilla*" (place in Cordova)]

a·mor·al (āmōr′al, ă-, -mār′-) *adj.* Nonmoral; outside the sphere of morals.

Am·o·rite (ăm′orīt) *adj.* & *n.* (Member) of an ancient Semitic people of the Middle East.

am·o·rous (ăm′erus) *adj.* Inclined to (esp. sexual) love; in love; of or pertaining to love. **am′o·rous·ly** *adv.* **am′o·rous·ness** *n.*

a·mor·phous (amōr′fus) *adj.* Formless; indeterminate; (chem., min.) not crystalline. **a·mor′phism** *n.* **a·mor′phous·ly** *adv.* **a·mor′phous·ness** *n.*

am·or·tize (ăm′ertīz, amōr′-) *v.t.* (**-tized, -tiz·ing**). Pay off (debt, mortgage) by periodic payments; gradually write off initial cost of (asset). **am·or·ti·za′tion**

(ămertīzā′shon, amōr-) *n.*

A·mos (ā′mos) (*c*760 B.C.). Hebrew minor prophet; book of Old Testament containing his prophecies.

a·mount (amownt′) *v.t.* Be equivalent *to*; add up *to*. ~ *n.* Total, quantity.

a·mour (amoor′) *n.* Love affair, esp. an illicit one.

amp (ămp) = AMPERE.

am·pe·lop·sis (ămpelŏp′sĭs) *n.* Climbing plant allied to vine, esp. Virginia creeper. [Gk., = "looking like a vine" (*ampelos* vine, *opsis* appearance)]

am·per·age (ăm′perĭj, ămpēr′-) *n.* Strength of current of electricity measured in amperes.

Am·père (ahṅpār′), **Andre-Marie** (1775–1836). French physicist and mathematician; established the relation between magnetism and electricity.

am·pere (ăm′pēr, ămpēr′) *n.* Unit of electric current; the current produced by one volt acting through resistance of one ohm (abbreviation A). [f. AMPÈRE]

am·per·sand (ăm′persănd, ămpersănd′) *n.* The sign "&" (= *and*). [f. phrase "and *per se* (= by itself) *and*"]

am·phet·a·mine (ămfět′amēn, -mĭn) *n.* Powerful synthetic drug that stimulates the heart and respiration, constricts blood vessels, and induces sleeplessness.

amphi-, amph- *prefixes.* Both, of both kinds, on both sides, around.

am·phib·i·an (ămfĭb′ēan) *adj.* & *n.* 1. (Animal) living both on land and in water; (animal) of the Amphibia, a class of vertebrates intermediate between reptiles and

fishes and including anurans and caecilians. 2. (*adj.*) Amphibious. [Gk. *amphibios* leading a double life]

am·phib·i·ous (ămfĭb′ēus) *adj.* Living both on land and in water, connected with both; (airplane, car, tank, etc.) able to operate both on land and water; (mil.) involving both land and sea forces.

am·phi·brach (ăm′fibrăk) *n.* Metrical foot of three syllables, one long between two short, or one accented between two unaccented (˘ — ˘).

am·phip·ro·style (ămfĭp′rostĭl, -fiprō′-) *adj.* & *n.* (Building) with portico at both ends.

am·phis·bae·na (ămfĭsbē′na) *n.* 1. Fabulous serpent with head at each end. 2. (zool.) Wormlike lizard of genus *A* ~. [Gk. *amphis* both ways, *baino* go]

am·phi·the·a·ter, am·phi·the·a·tre (ăm′fĭthēater) *ns.* 1. Oval, circular, or semicircular building or arena with seats rising in tiers around a central open space; natural formation resembling this; (fig.) scene of a contest. 2. Room having tiers of seats arranged above a central area for students and others to listen to lectures and observe surgery etc.

Am·phi·tri·te (ămfitrī′tē). (Gk. myth.) Sea goddess, the wife of Poseidon.

Am·phit·ry·on (ămfĭt′rēon). (Gk. myth.) Husband of Alcmene, while he was absent Zeus impersonated him and became the father of Hercules by Alcmene.

am·pho·ra (ăm′fera) *n.* (pl. **-rae** pr. -rē, **-ras**). Greek or Roman two-handled vase, esp. used to store wine, oil, etc.

Capital of the Netherlands, Amsterdam, 'Venice of the North'. Some 50 miles of canals divide the city into 70 islands linked by 500 bridges. Highstep gables characterize old houses.

am·ple (ăm′pel) *adj.* (**-pler, -plest**). Spacious, extensive; abundant; quite enough. **am′ply** *adv.*

am·pli·fy (ăm′plifī) *v.* (**-fied, -fy·ing**). Enlarge; increase strength of (electric current, signal, etc.); add details. **am·pli·fi·ca·tion** (ămplifīkā′shon) *n.* **am′pli·fi·er** *n.* (esp.) Appliance for increasing strength of electrical signals.

am·pli·tude (ăm′plitŏod, -tūd) *n.* 1. Breadth; abundance; wide range. 2. (astron.) Distance from due east or west at which celestial body rises or sets. 3. (phys.) Maximum displacement from mean position of vibrating body etc.; ~ **modulation**: see MODULATE.

am·pule, am·pul, am·poule (ăm′pūl) *ns.* (med.) Small sealed glass vessel used for storing sterilized materials prepared for injection.

am·pu·tate (ăm′pyutāt) *v.t.* (**-tat·ed, -tat·ing**). Cut off (esp. part of animal body). **am·pu·ta·tion** (ămpyutā′shon) *n.*

am·pu·tee (ămpyutē′) *n.* One who has lost limb etc. by amputation.

Am·ster·dam (ăm′sterdăm). Capital of the Netherlands.

Am·trak (ăm′trăk) *n.* A U.S. national rail-passenger system.

a·muck (amŭk′) *adv.* **run ~,** run about in murderous frenzy; get out of control. [Malay *amok*, rushing in frenzy]

a·mu·let (ăm′yulit) *n.* Thing worn as charm against evil.

A·mund·sen (ah′mundsen), **Roald** (1872–1928). Norwegian explorer; explored Northwest Passage 1903–6; reached S. Pole 1911.

A·mund·sen (ah′mundsen) **Sea.** Arm of the South Pacific Ocean, off the Antarctic coast W. of the Ross Sea.

A·mur (ahmoor′). River in NE. Asia rising in Mongolia, flowing to the Sea of Okhotsk, forming part of the Soviet-Chinese border.

a·muse (amūz′) *v.t.* (**a·mused, a·mus·ing**). Cause laughter or smiles; be or find diversion or light occupation for; entertain. **a·mus·ing** *adj.* **a·mus·ing·ly** *adv.* **a·muse′ment** *n.* Pleasant diversion; excitement of laughter or smiles; pastime; ~ **park**, park with refreshments and merry-go-rounds, roller coasters, etc.

AMVETS (ăm′vĕts) *n.* Organization of U.S. veterans of World War II and Korean War.

am·yl (ăm′il) *n.* (chem.) Radical (C_5H_{11}) occurring in the structure of various isomeric alcohols (~ **alcohols**), some of which are constituents of fusel oil; ~ **acetate**, colorless volatile liquid derived from amyl alcohol and acetic acid, with odor of pears, used in making artificial fruit essences and as solvent of cellulose acetate. [Gk. *amulon* fine meal]

am·y·la·ceous (ămilā′shus) *adj.* Of starch, starchy.

an (an; emphat. ăn) *indef. article:* see A.

an-[1]: see A- def. 2.

-an *suffix.* Forming adjectives or nouns, esp. names of places, systems, zool. classes, and founders (e.g., *Canadian, Anglican, crusta-*

A boa inhabiting swamps and rivers in South America, the non-venomous ana- conda up to 30 ft. in length, rivals the reticulated python as world's largest snake. There are 35 boa species.

an, Lutheran).

an·a-, an-[2] *prefixes.* Up, back, again, anew.

a·na (ā′na, ah′na) *n.* Collection of person's sayings; anecdotes, literary gossip, about a person.

-ana *suffix.* Appended to a name with the meaning: sayings of, anecdotes about, publications bearing on, persons or places.

An·a·bap·tist (ănabăp′tĭst) *n.* & *adj.* (Member) of a sect that arose in Germany in 1521, was heavily persecuted by both Catholics and Protestants, and suppressed (lit., = "one who baptizes over again" because the Anabaptists held that infant baptism was ineffectual, and some of them rebaptized adults); also (opprobriously) = BAPTIST. **An·a·bap′tism** *n.*

a·nab·o·lism (anăb′olĭzem) *n.* Synthesis by living things of complex molecules from simpler ones.

a·nach·ro·nism (anăk′ronĭzem) *n.* Error in computing time; event or thing that would be incongruous in the period in which it is supposed to have happened or existed. **a·nach·ro·nis′tic** *adj.*

an·a·con·da (ănakŏn′da) *n.* Tropical S. Amer. aquatic and arboreal boa (*Eunectes murinus*).

A·nac·re·on (anăk′rēon) (*c*563–78 B.C.). Greek lyric poet, of whose poems very few genuine fragments survive. **A·nac·re·on·ic** (anăkrēōn′tĭk) *adj.* & *n.* (Poem) in the manner or meter of Anacreon's lyrics; convivial and amatory.

a·nae·mi·a (anē′mēa) = ANE-MIA.

an·aer·obe (ăn′erōb, ănār′-) *n.* Microorganism that can live and reproduce in the absence of atmospheric oxygen. **an·aer·o·bic** (ănerō′bĭk, ănĕrō′-) *adj.*

an·aes·the·sia (ănĭsthē′zha) = ANESTHESIA.

an·aes·thet·ic (ănĭsthĕt′ĭk) = ANESTHETIC.

a·naes·the·tist (anĕs′thetĭst) = ANESTHETIST.

a·naes·the·tize (anĕs′thetīz) = ANESTHETIZE.

an·a·gram (ăn′agrăm) *n.* Word or phrase formed by transposing letters of another.

An·a·heim (ăn′ahīm). City in S. California, near Los Angeles; site of Disneyland.

a·nal (ā′nal) *adj.* Of or near the anus; (psych.) of or pertaining to infantile psychosexual development in which attention is centered on the anus.

an·a·lects (ăn′alĕkts), **an·a·lec·ta** (ănalĕk′ta) *ns.pl.* Literary gleanings.

an·al·ge·si·a (ănaljē′zēa, -sēa) *n.* Absence of pain; relief of pain. **an·al·ge·sic** (ănaljē′zĭk, -sĭk) *adj.* & *n.* (Drug) giving analgesia.

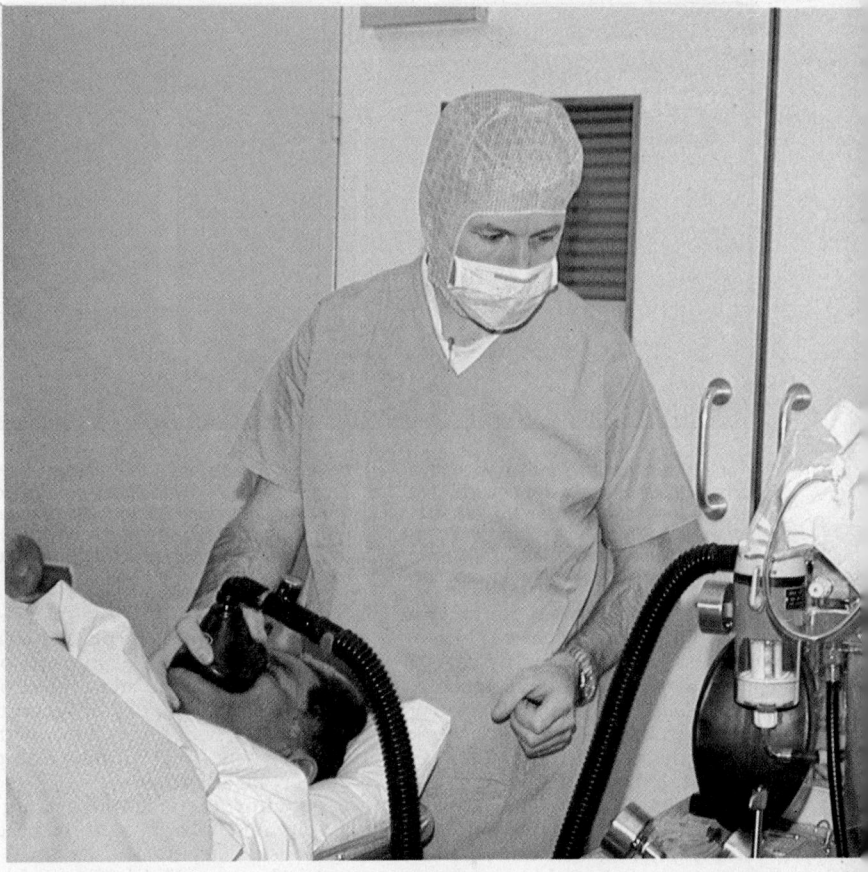

*Administering **anesthetic** before a surgical operation. Ether to desensitize pain was first demonstrated in 1846; local anesthesia in 1884, using cocaine for eye surgery.*

a·nal·o·gous (anăl′ogus) *adj.* Similar, parallel (*to*); (biol., of limb or organ) similar in function but not necessarily in structure or position (cf. HOMOLOGOUS). **a·nal·o·gous·ly** *adv.*

an·a·logue, an·a·log (ăn′alawg, -lŏg) *ns.* Analogous word or thing; ~ **computer**: see COMPUTER.

a·nal·o·gy (anăl′ojē) *n.* (pl. **-gies**). Agreement, similarity; analogue; (math.) proportion; (logic) process of reasoning from parallel cases; (gram.) process whereby words and grammatical forms are built up on the model of others.

an·a·lyse (ăn′alīz) (*Brit.*) = ANALYZE.

a·nal·y·sis (anăl′ĭsĭs) *n.* (pl. **-ses** pr. -sēz). Resolution into simple elements; PSYCHOANALYSIS; (math.) branch of mathematics using algebraic and calculus methods; (philos.) clarification of concepts and knowledge; **chemical** ~, determination of composition of substances; **qualitative** ~, identification of elements or compounds present; **quantitative** ~, determination of precise amounts of elements etc. present. **an·a·lyst**

(ăn′alĭst) *n.* One skilled in (chemical) analysis; PSYCHO-ANALYSIS. **an·a·lyt·ic** (ănalĭt′ĭk) *adj.* Pertaining to analysis; **an·a·lyt′i·cal** *adj.* Employing the method of analysis; (of language) using separate words instead of inflections; ~ **psychology**: see PSYCHOLOGY. **an·a·lyt′i·cal·ly** *adv.*

an·a·lyze (ăn′alīz) *vbs.* (**-lyzed, -lyzing**). Examine minutely the constitution of; conduct a PSYCHO-ANALYSIS; (chem.) ascertain the elements present in a compound or the constituents of a mixture, sample of food, etc.; (gram.) resolve into grammatical elements.

An·a·ni·as (ănanī′as). 1. Jewish high priest before whom Paul was brought (Acts 23). 2. Husband of Sapphira, struck dead because he "lied unto God" (Acts 5).

an·a·pest (ăn′apĕst) *n.* Metrical foot of three syllables, the first two short and the last long (◡◡–). **an·a·pes′tic** *adj.*

a·naph·o·ra (anăf′era) *n.* 1. (also **A ~**) Part of Eucharistic service in the Greek Orthodox Church; (R.C. Ch.) Canon of the Mass. 2. Repetition of words or phrases at beginning of a succession of clauses.

an·ar·chist (ăn′erkĭst) *n.* Advocate of anarchism. **an·ar·chism** *n.* System or theory that conceives of society without government.

an·ar·chy (ăn′erkē) *n.* Absence of government; disorder, political

ring
stock
Common
Anchor
Admiralty Anchor
Trotman
Grapnel
Stockless
shank
fluke
crown

A ship's **anchor** is shaped so that a horizontal pull on the cable secures it to the sea bed and an upward pull dislodges it easily. Shown (left to right): Traditional anchor with flukes (digging ends); admiralty or stowing anchor, held in place by the metal key; Trotman's anchor with flukes on pivoted arms for angled anchorage; the grapnel with arms to grasp sea-bed projections; stockless anchor as used in most large modern ships.

and social confusion. **an·ar·chic** (ănär´kĭk), **an·ar´chi·cal** adjs. Lawless. **an·ar´chi·cal·ly** adv.

an·as·tig·mat·ic (ănastĭgmăt´ĭk, anăs-) adj. Free from astigmatism (used esp. of photographic lenses in which this error is corrected).

anat. abbrev. Anatomy.

a·nath·e·ma (anăth´ema) n. Accursed thing; curse of God; curse of the Church, excommunication; imprecation. **a·nath´e·ma·tize** v. (**-tized, -tiz·ing**). Curse. [Gk. anathema thing devoted, (later) accursed thing]

An·a·to·li·a (ănatō´lēa). Asiatic part of Turkey; (in ancient usage) Asia Minor. **An·a·tol·ic** (ănatŏl´ĭk) adj. **An·a·to´li·an** adj. & n.

an·a·tom·i·cal (ănatŏm´ĭkal) adj. Belonging to anatomy; structural. **an·a·tom´i·cal·ly** adv.

a·nat·o·mist (anăt´omĭst) n. Dissecter of bodies; one skilled in anatomy. **a·nat´o·mize** v. (**-mized, -miz·ing**). Dissect; (fig.) analyze.

a·nat·o·my (anăt´omē) n. (pl. **-mies**). (Science of) bodily structure; dissection; analysis.

An·ax·ag·o·ras (ănăksăg´eras) (5th c. B.C.). Greek philosopher and scientist; he explained solar eclipses.

-ance suffix. Forming nouns of quality (e.g., arrogance) or action (e.g., assistance).

an·ces·tor (ăn´sĕster) n. Any of those from whom one's father or mother is descended, progenitor.

an·ces·tral (ănsĕs´tral) adj. Belonging to, inherited from, ancestors.

an·ces·try (ăn´sĕstrē) n. (pl. **-tries**). Ancestral lineage; ancient descent; ancestors.

an·chor (ăng´ker) n. Heavy implement consisting usu. of long shank and (curved) barbed arms, used for mooring ship to bottom of sea etc.; **at ~**, thus moored; **~ man, ~ woman**, one playing vital or central part in a team game or broadcast. **~ plate**, heavy piece of metal or timber as point of support. **anchor** v. Secure (ship) with anchor; (fig.) fix firmly; drop anchor, lie at anchor.

An·chor·age (ăng´kerĭj). Largest city in Alaska, in S. at the head of Cook Inlet.

an·chor·age (ăng´kerĭj) n. Anchoring; lying at anchor; anchoring ground.

an·cho·rite (ăng´kerīt), **an·cho·ress** (ăng´kerĭs) ns. fem. Hermit, recluse. **an·cho·rit·ic** (ăngkerĭt´ĭk) adj.

an·cho·vy (ăn´chōvē, ănchō´-) n. (pl. **-vies**). Small fish of herring family, esp. the Mediterranean Engraulis encrasicholus, used as food fish.

an·cien ré·gime (ahṅsyăṅ´ra zhēm´). System of government i France before the Revolutio (transf.) former regime. [Fr., = "old rule"]

an·cient (ān´shent) adj. Belonging to times long past; havin existed, lived, long; ~ **history**: se HISTORY. **ancient** n. **the ~ s** civilized people of antiquity **an´cient·ly** adv. **an´cient·ness** n.

an·cil·lar·y (ăn´sĭlĕrē, ănsĭl´erē adj. Subordinate; auxiliary.

-ancy suffix. Indicating state o quality but not action (e.g., infancy constancy).

and (and; emphat. ănd) con, Word connecting words, clauses and sentences.

An·da·man (ăn´daman) **Is lands.** Large group of islands i Bay of Bengal; administered (wit

View of Colombian **Andes**. The mou tain system ranges the length of wes ern S. America from Tierra del Fueg 4,000 miles north to Caribbean coas Ten peaks top 22,000 ft.

Nicobar Islands) by India; chief city, Port Blair.

an·dan·te (ahndahn´tā) *adv. & n.* (mus.) (Movement) in moderately slow time.

An·der·sen (ăn´dersen), **Hans Christian** (1805–75). Danish poet and dramatist, best known for his fairy tales.

An·der·son[1] (ăn´derson), **Carl David** (1905–). American physicist; discovered the positron in cosmic rays; shared Nobel Prize for physics, 1936.

An·der·son[2] (ăn´derson), **Marian** (1902–). American concert contralto.

An·der·son[3] (ăn´derson), **Maxwell** (1888–1959). American playwright; author of *Elizabeth the Queen, Winterset, Key Largo*, etc.

An·der·son[4] (ăn´derson), **Sherwood** (1878–1941). American novelist and short story writer; author of *Winesburg, Ohio; Dark Laughter*, etc.

An·der·son·ville (ăn´dersonvĭl). Village in SW. Georgia; site of an infamous Confederate prison for Union troops during the Civil War.

An·des (ăn´dēz). Mountain range running from N. to S. along the whole of the Pacific coast of S. America.

An·dhra Pra·desh (ahn´dra pradāsh´). State of SE. India; chief city, Hyderabad.

and·i·ron (ănd´ī´ern, -īrn) *n.* One of a pair of stands for logs in a fireplace; fire dog.

and/or (ănd´ôr´) *conj.* Indicating

that either of two things named may be applicable, or both.

An·dor·ra (ăndôr´a). Small republic in the Pyrenees, on the border between France and Spain; capital, Andorra la Vella. **An·dor´-ran** *adj. & n.*

An·dre (ahn´drā), **John** (1751–1780). British army major hanged as a spy during the Revolutionary War for conspiring with Benedict Arnold to betray West Point.

An·dre·a del Sar·to (ahndrā´a dĕl sär´tō) (1486–1531). Florentine painter.

An·drew (ăn´drōo), **St.** Apostle and patron saint of Scotland, commemorated, Nov. 30; **St. ~'s cross,** cross shaped like the letter ×.

An·dro·cles (ăn´droklēz). Runaway slave in story by Aulus Gellius (2nd c. A.D.) who extracted a thorn from the paw of a lion that later recognized and refrained from attacking him in the arena.

an·dro·gen (ăn´drojen) *n.* Any organic compound that promotes development of masculine characteristics. **an·dro·gen·ic** (ăndrojĕn´ĭk) *adj.*

an·drog·y·nous (ăndrŏj´inus) *adj.* Hermaphroditic; (bot.) with both staminate and pistillate flowers in a cluster. **an·drog´y·ny** *n.*

an·droid (ăn´droid) *n.* Robot with human form.

An·drom·a·che (ăndrŏm´akē). (Gk. legend) Wife of HECTOR, captured by the Greeks at the fall of Troy.

An·drom·e·da (ăndrŏm´ida). 1.

(Gk. legend) Daughter of Cassiopeia; was rescued by Perseus from a sea monster for whom she was fastened to a rock. 2. (astron.) Constellation, conspicuous for its great spiral nebula. **An·drom·e·des** (ăndrŏm´ĭdēz), **An·drom·e·dids** (ăndrŏm´ĭdĭdz) *ns. pl.* (astron.) System of meteors appearing to radiate from a point in Andromeda and usu. seen in November.

an·ec·dote (ăn´ĭkdōt) *n.* Short narrative of amusing or interesting incident. **an·ec·dot·age** (ăn´ĭkdō-tĭj) *n.* Anecdotes; (joc.) garrulous old age. **an·ec·dot·ist** *n.* **an·ec·do·tal, an·ec·dot·ic** (ănĭkdŏt´ĭk), **an·ec·dot·i·cal** *adjs.*

a·ne·mi·a (anē´mēa) *n.* Deficiency of red blood corpuscles or their hemoglobin, often causing paleness; **pernicious ~:** see PERNICIOUS. **a·ne·mic** (anē´mĭk) *adj.* (often fig.).

an·e·mom·e·ter (ănemŏm´ĭter) *n.* Instrument for measuring speed (sometimes also direction) of wind. **an·e·mo·met·ric** (ănemōmĕt´rĭk) *adj.* **an·e·mom´e·try** *n.*

a·nem·o·ne (anĕm´onē) *n.* Plant of the buttercup family of genus *A* ~ with flowers of various colors. [Gk., = "windflower"]

a·nent (anĕnt´) *prep.* (archaic) Concerning.

an·e·roid (ăn´eroid) *adj. & n.* (Barometer) that measures air pressure by its action on the flexible lid of a metal box nearly exhausted of air, not by height of fluid column.

an·es·the·sia, an·aes·the·sia (ănĭsthē´zha) *ns.* Loss of sensation; insensibility, esp. to pain, induced by certain drugs; **general ~,** anesthesia of the whole body; **local ~,** anesthesia induced in a limited area of the body. **an·es·the·si·ol·o·gy** (ănĭsthēzēŏl´ojē), **an·es·-**

*A small semi-independent State, **Andorra,** some 175 sq. miles, lies in the Pyrenees between France and Spain. It is a haven for smugglers of tobacco and cars especially.*

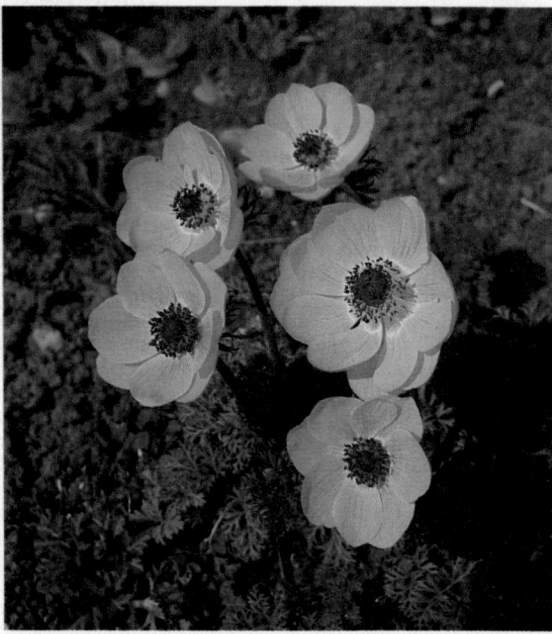

Anemones *are a group of mainly herbaceous and rock garden plants grown mostly from corms. The corms are able to survive all but the most severe winters.*

the·si·ol'o·gist *ns.*

an·es·thet·ic, an·aes·thet·ic (ănĭsthĕt´ĭk) *adjs. & ns.* (Drug) inducing local or general anesthesia, used esp. in surgical operations.

a·nes·the·tist, a·naes·the·tist (anĕs´thetĭst) *ns.* One who administers anesthetics during surgical operation.

a·nes·the·tize, a·naes·the·tize (anĕs´thetīz) *vbs.* (-tized, -tiz·ing). Render insensible; administer anesthetics to.

an·eu·rysm, an·eu·rism (ăn´yerĭzem) *ns.* (path.) Localized dilation of an artery caused by a weakening in its wall.

a·new (anōō´, anū´) *adv.* Again; in a different way.

an·gel (ān´jel) *n.* 1. Divine messenger; a celestial attendant of God; member of one of nine orders to which angels were held to belong in medieval theology, namely: seraphim, cherubim, thrones; dominations, virtues, powers; principalities, archangels, angels. 2. Lovely or innocent being; loving or obliging person. 3. Financial backer, esp. of theatrical production. 4. **an'gelfish**, (esp.) S. Amer. fresh water fish (various species of *Pterophyllum*), laterally flattened, with bars of black and silver; ~ **food cake**, very light sponge cake. [Gk. *aggelos* messenger]

An·gel (ān´jel) **Fall.** Highest uninterrupted waterfall in the world, over 3,000 feet (914 m); in SE. Venezuela.

An·ge·la Me·ri·ci (ăn´jela merē´-chē), **St.** (1474?–1540). Italian Roman Catholic nun; founder of the Ursuline Order.

an·gel·ic (ănjĕl´ĭk) *adj.* Like an angel.

an·gel·i·ca (ănjĕl´ĭka) *n.* Aromatic umbelliferous plant used in cooking and medicine; candied stalk of this.

An·ge·li·co (ănjĕl´ĭkō), **Fra.** Fra Giovanni da Fiesole (1387–1455), painter of religious subjects, active in Florence and Rome.

An·ge·lus (ăn´jelus) *n.* (R.C. Ch.) Devotional exercise (also **angelus**) (beginning *Angelus domini*; L., = "the angel of the Lord") commemorating the Incarnation, said morning, noon, and evening, at sound of bell; bell for this.

an·ger (ăng´ger) *n.* Hot displeasure, rage. ~ *v.t.* Make angry, enrage. [ON. *angr* affliction]

An·ge·vin (ăn´jevĭn) *adj.* Of Anjou or its ruling house; ~ **kings**, PLANTAGENET kings of England.

an·gi·na (ănjī´na) *n.* Constrictive sensation or pain, as in quinsy, croup, etc.; ~ **pectoris** (pĕk´terĭs), intense pain in chest, accompanied by sense of suffocation, caused by insufficient blood supply to heart.

an·gi·o·sperm (ăn´jēospĕrm) *n.* Flowering plant, i.e. one that has ovules enclosed in an ovary (opp. GYMNOSPERM).

Ang·kor (ăng´ker, -kōr). Group of ruins in NW. Kampuchea (formerly Cambodia), the most famous of which are the temple Angkor Wat and the ancient Khmer capital, Angkor Thom.

an·gle[1] (ăng´gel) *n.* Space between two meeting lines or planes; inclination of two lines to each other (**acute** ~, angle smaller than 90 ; **obtuse** ~, greater than 90 ; **right** ~, angle of 90 ; **reflex** ~, angle greater than 180); corner, sharp projection; (colloq.) point of view; aspect of a situation; **angle iron**, metal plate of L-shaped section. **an'gled** *adj.*

an·gle[2] (ăng´gel) *v.i.* (-gled, -gling). Fish with hook and bait; (fig.) use artifice, hints, etc., to obtain something. **an'gler** *n.* 1. Fisherman. 2. (zool.) Fish (esp. *Lophius piscatorius*) that preys on smaller fish, attracting them by filaments attached to its head and mouth. **an'gleworm** *n.* Earthworm used as bait in fishing.

An·gles (ăng´gelz) *n.pl.* One of the Germanic tribes that settled in Britain in the 5th c. A.D., where they formed the kingdoms of Northumbria, Mercia, and East Anglia, and finally gave their name to England and the English.

An·gli·can (ăng´glĭkan) *adj.* Of the reformed Church of England or any Church in the Anglican Communion, such as the Protestant Episcopal Church; ~ **Communion**, Churches in communion with, and recognizing the leadership of, the see of Canterbury. **Anglican** *n.* Member of Anglican Church. **An'gli·can·ism** *n.*

An·gli·cize (ăng´glĭsīz) *v.* (-cized, -ciz·ing). Make, become, English in form or character. **An'gli·cism** *n.* English idiom, Briticism; a typical English custom or trait.

An·glo (ăng´glō) *n.* (pl. **-glos**). (colloq.) English-speaking white American.

Anglo- *prefix.* English; English and—, as ~-American.

An·glo·phile (ăng´glofīl), **An'glo·phil** (ăng´glofīl) *ns.* One who loves the English. **An·glo·phil·i·a** (ănggloˈfīl´ēa) *n.* **An·glo·phil'i·ac** *adj.*

An·glo·phobe (ăng´glofōb) *n.* One who hates the English. **An·glo·pho·bi·a** (ănggloˈfō´bēa) *n.* **An·glo·pho·bic** (ănggloˈfō´bĭk) *adj.*

An·glo-Sax·on (ăng´glō săk´son) *adj. & n.* 1. (Member, language) of the Germanic tribes that settled in England in the 5th and 6th c. and remained dominant until 1066. 2. (Person) of English descent. 3. (colloq.) Plain English (language).

An·go·la (ănggō´la). Former Portuguese province of W. Africa, N. of SW. Africa and W. of Zambia; independent Nov. 1975.

An·go·ra (ănggōr´a, -gōr´a). Former name of ANKARA; fabric made from fleece of Angora goat or of sheep's wool mixed with hair of Angora rabbit; ~ **cat, goat, rabbit**, varieties of these animals with long silky hair.

An·gos·tu·ra (ănggostoor´a, -tūr´a). Former name of Ciudad Bolivar, town in Venezuela on Orinoco; **a** ~ (**bark**), aromatic bark formerly used as tonic and febrifuge, obtained from S. Amer. tree of family Rutaceae; ~ **bitters**, (trademark) tonic and flavoring made from this bark.

an·gry (ăng´grē) *adj.* (-gri·er, -gri·est). Enraged, resentful; irritable; (of wound etc.) inflamed, painful; ~ **young man**, (Brit.) one of a group of British writers of the 1950's noted for social protest; any similarly rebellious young person. **an'gri·ly** *adv.*

angst (ahngst) *n.* Anxiety; remorse. [Ger.]

Ang·ström (ăng´strom), **Anders Jonas** (1814–74). Swedish physicist and astronomer; **angstrom** (also **angstrom unit**), unit (abbrev. A) used for measuring electromagnetic wavelengths, one hundred millionth of a centimeter.

An·guil·la (ănggwĭl´a). Island in the West Indies, under British rule.

an·guish (ăng´gwĭsh) *n.* Severe mental or bodily pain.

an·gu·lar (ăng´gyuler) *adj.* Having angles; sharp cornered; placed in, at, an angle; bony, gaunt, awkward. ~ **momentum**, product of moment of inertia of a body moving about its axis and its angular velocity.

An·gus (ăng´gus). Former county of E. Scotland; a breed of hornless beef cattle originally raised there.

an·he·dral (ănhē´dral) *adj.* Of a rock that does not have its characteristic crystalline form.

an·hin·ga (ănhĭng´ga) *n.* Dark bird (*A* ~ *anhinga*) with long, snakelike neck living in tropical swamps; also called darter, water turkey, snakebird.

An·hui (ahn´hwā´) = ANHWEI.

An·hwei (ahn´hwā´). Province of China on the Yangtze Kiang.

an·hy·dride (ănhī´drīd) *n.* Substance formed by removal of water from a compound; substance that combines with water to form an acid or base.

an·hy·drous (ănhī´drus) *adj.* (chem.) Having no water; deprived of water of crystallization.

This picture was taken in Luanda on **Angola's** *'Independence Day' following the factional war. The child is a member of the M.P.L.A. pioneer youth wing, the 'lollipop army'.*

an·i·line (ăn′ilĭn, -līn) *n.* Phenylamine ($C_6H_5NH_2$), an oily liquid with characteristic smell, made by reduction of nitrobenzene and used in the manufacture of many chemicals, dyestuffs, drugs, etc. ~ *adj.* Derived from aniline; ~ **dye**, (pop.) any synthetic dyestuff. [formerly obtained from *anil*, the shrub indigo]

an·i·ma (ăn′ima) *n.* 1. The soul. 2. (psych.) Inner personality (opp. PERSONA); feminine part of a man's personality. [L., "breath," "soul"]

an·i·mad·ver·sion (ănimădvēr′zhon, -shon) *n.* Criticism, censure. **an·i·mad·vert** (ănimădvērt′) *v.i.* Pass criticism or censure *on.*

an·i·mal (ăn′imal) *n.* Organized being endowed with life, sensation, and voluntary motion; animal other than man; quadruped; brutish man. ~ *adj.* Pertaining to the functions of animals; pertaining to animals as opp. to vegetables; carnal; ~ **crackers**, small cookies baked in shapes of animals; ~ **kingdom**, all animals collectively; ~ **magnetism**, (hist.) mesmerism; magnetic personality, sensuality; ~ **spirits**, natural buoyancy. [L. *anima* breath]

an·i·mal·cule (ănimăl′kūl) *n.* Microscopic animal.

an·i·mal·ism (ăn′imalĭzem) *n.* Animal activity; sensuality; doctrine that men are mere animals.

an·i·mal·ize (ăn′imalĭz) *v.t.* (**-ized, -iz·ing**). 1. (art, religion) Represent as an animal, give animal features to. 2. Make coarse or brutal; sensualize.

an·i·mate (ăn′imĭt) *adj.* Living, lively. ~ (ăn′imāt) *v.t.* (**-mat·ed, -mat·ing**). Give life to; make lively; encourage; **animated cartoon**: see CARTOON. **an·i·ma·tion** (ănimā′shon) *n.* **an′i·mat·ed·ly** *adv.*

an·i·mism (ăn′imĭzem) *n.* Attribution of living soul to inanimate objects and natural phenomena. **an′i·mist** *n.* **an·i·mis·tic** (ănimĭs′tĭk) *adj.*

an·i·mos·i·ty (ănimŏs′ĭtē) *n.* (pl. **-ties**). Active enmity.

an·i·mus (ăn′imus) *n.* 1. Animating spirit; animosity. 2. (psych.) Masculine part of a woman's personality.

an·i·on (ăn′īon, -ŏn) *n.*: see ION. **an·i·on·ic** (ănīŏn′ĭk) *adj.* Of anions; having an active anion. [Gk. *ana* up, + ION]

an·ise (ăn′ĭs) *n.* Umbelliferous plant (*Pimpinella anisum*) with aromatic fruits and licorice-flavored seeds.

an·i·seed (an′īsēd) *n.* Seed of anise, used to flavor liqueurs, desserts, etc.

an·i·sette (ănĭsĕt′, -zĕt′, ăn′ĭsĕt, -zĕt) *n.* Colorless sweet liqueur flavored with aniseed.

An·ka·ra (ăng′kera). Capital city of Turkey since 1923.

ankh (ăngk) *n.* Keylike cross used in ancient Egypt as symbol of life. [Egypt., = "life, soul"]

an·kle (ăng′kel) *n.* Joint connecting foot with leg; slender part between this and calf. **an·klet** (ăng′klĭt) *n.* Fetter or ornamental band around ankle; short sock just covering ankle.

Ann (ăn), **Cape.** Peninsula near Gloucester in N. Massachusetts, projecting into the Atlantic Ocean.

an·nals (ăn′alz) *n.pl.* Narrative of events year by year; historical records. **an·nal·ist** (ăn′alĭst) *n.* Writer of annals.

An·nap·o·lis (anăp′olĭs). Capital of Maryland, site of the U.S. Naval Academy.

An·na·pur·na (ănapoor′na, -pēr′-). Part of the Himalayas in central Nepal; the highest elevation, Annapurna I, 26,502 feet (8,078 m).

Ann (ăn) **Arbor.** City in SE. Michigan.

Anne[1] (ăn) (1665–1714). Queen of Great Britain (1702–14); second daughter of James II; succeeded William, husband of her sister Mary, in 1702; **Queen** ~, (archit.) applied to a style of red brick and stone houses of *c*1660–*c*1720.

Anne[2] (ăn), **St.** Mother of the Virgin Mary; commemorated July 26.

an·neal (anēl′) *v.t.* Toughen (glass or metals) by heating and then cooling; temper.

Anne Boleyn: see BOLEYN.

an·ne·lid (ăn′elĭd) *n.* One of the phylum Annelida, segmented worms (including earthworms,

leeches, etc.).

Anne of Cleves (klēvz) (1515–1557). Daughter of John, Duke of Cleves, and fourth wife of Henry VIII of England; the marriage (1540) was annulled after a few months.

an·nex (anĕks′) *v.t.* Add as subordinate (part); append; take possession of (territory). **an·nex·a·tion** (ănĕksā′shon) *n.* **an·nex** (ăn′ĕks) *n.* Addition to document; building added to larger one, esp. to provide extra accommodation.

An·nie Oak·ley (ăn′ē ōk′lē) (1860–1926). Real name, Phoebe Anne Oakley Mozee. Famous American rider and markswoman; starred in Buffalo Bill's Wild West Show; hence a ticket (esp. a free ticket, meal ticket, etc.), so called from the similarity of a punched ticket to a bullet-riddled target.

an·ni·hi·late (anī′ilāt) *v.t.* (**-lat·ed, -lat·ing**). Demolish, destroy utterly. **an·ni·hi·la·tion** (anīilā′shon) *n.* Utter destruction.

an·ni·ver·sa·ry (ănivēr′serē) *n.* (pl. **-ries**). Yearly return of a date, celebration of this.

An·no Dom·i·ni (ă′nō dŏm′inē, -nī). In the year of our Lord, of the Christian era (abbrev. A.D.). [L.]

an·no·tate (ăn′ōtāt) *v.t.* (**-tat·ed, -tat·ing**). Furnish (a text) with notes. **an·no·ta·tion** (ănōtā′shon), **an′no·ta·tor** *ns.*

Ulus Square, **Ankara.** *Kemal Ataturk, founder of modern Turkey, chose Ankara as capital in 1923 because its 100-mile distance from the Black Sea made it easy to defend.*

Giant earthworms mating. Segmented worms, **annelids** include leeches. Anatomically an annelid is a tube (alimentary canal) within a tube (body wall) separated by the coelum.

Rockport on **Cape Ann,** north-eastern Massachusetts. Cape Ann, noted for its scenery, resorts, fishing villages and artists' colonies, was named after Queen Anne, wife of James I of Gt. Britain.

an·nounce (anowns´) *v.t.* **(-nounced, -nounc·ing).** Declare, make publicly known; intimate the approach of; serve as an announcement of. **an·nounce´ment** *n.* **an·nounc´er** *n.* (esp.) Person who announces program, reads news items, etc., over radio or television.

an·noy (anoi´) *v.t.* Irritate; molest, harass. **an·noy´ance** *n.* (Thing that causes) molestation; vexation; disgust.

an·nu·al (ăn´ūal) *adj.* Reckoned by the year; recurring yearly; lasting for one year; that lives only for a year; published yearly; ~ **ring,** ring in cross section of tree, fish, etc., from one year's growth. **annual** *n.* Plant that lives for one year; book etc. published yearly. **an´nu·al·ly** *adv.*

an·nu·i·ty (anoo´ĭte, anū´-) *n.* (pl. **-ties).** Sum payable in regard to a particular year; yearly grant; investment of money entitling investors to series of equal annual sums. **an·nu·i·tant** (anoo´itant, anū´-) *n.* One who holds an annuity.

an·nul (anŭl´) *v.t.* **(-nulled, -nul·ling).** Abolish, cancel; declare invalid, esp. of a marriage that was never consummated or was invalid to begin with. **an·nul´ment** *n.*

an·nu·lar (ăn´yuler) *adj.* Ringlike; ~ **eclipse,** partial eclipse of sun, during which a ring of the sun's surface can be seen surrounding the moon's disk.

an·nu·late (ăn´yulĭt, -lāt), **an·nu·lat·ed** (ăn´yulātĭd) *adjs.* Furnished, marked, with rings; formed of rings.

an·nu·lus (ăn´yulus) *n.* (pl. **-li** pr. -lī, **-lus·es).** Ring, ringlike body.

an·nun·ci·ate (anŭn´sēāt, -shē-) *v.t.* **(-at·ed, -at·ing).** Announce. **an·nun·ci·a·tion** (anŭnsēā´shon) *n.* Announcement; **the A~,** the announcement of the Incarnation made by the angel Gabriel to the Virgin Mary (Luke 1); festival commemorating this, March 25.

an·ode (ăn´ōd) *n.* (elect.) 1. Positively charged electrode. 2. Negative terminal of cell or storage battery. **an·od·ic** (ănŏd´ĭk) *adj.* **an·o·dize** (ăn´odīz) *v.t.* **(-dized, -diz·ing).** Cover (metal) with a protective film by electrolysis in which the metal acts as the anode. [Gk. *anodos* way up]

an·o·dyne (ăn´odīn) *adj. & n.* (Medicine, drug) able to assuage pain; (anything) mentally soothing.

a·noint (anoint´) *v.t.* Apply ointment, oil, to, esp. as religious ceremony at baptism or on consecration as priest or king.

a·nom·a·lous (anŏm´alus) *adj.* Irregular, abnormal. **a·nom´a·lous·ly** *adv.* **a·nom´a·lous·ness** *n.*

a·nom·a·ly (anŏm´alē) *n.* (pl. **-lies).** Irregularity; (astron.) angular distance of planet or satellite from its last perihelion or perigee.

a·non (anŏn´) *adv.* (archaic) Soon, presently; at another time.

anon. *abbrev.* Anonymous.

an·o·nym (ăn´onĭm) *n.* Person whose name is not revealed; pseudonym. **an·o·nym·i·ty** (ănonĭm´ĭte) *n.*

a·non·y·mous (anŏn´imus) *adj.* Not named; not bearing author's, painter's, etc., name; (fig.) lacking individuality. **a·non´y·mous·ly** *adv.*

a·noph·e·les (anŏf´elēz) *n.* Mosquito of genus *A~,* comprising numerous species, many of which are carriers of malaria. [Gk., = "hurtful"]

an·o·rex·i·a (ănerĕk´sēa) *n.* (path.) Loss of appetite; ~ **ner·vo·sa** (nervō´sa), syndrome in which chronic anorexia is induced by emotional disturbance.

an·oth·er (anŭdh´er) *adj.* Additional, different; a similar (one). ~ *pron.* Additional one; someone else, something else.

A·nouilh (ahnwē´), **Jean** (1910–). French dramatist, author of *le Bal des Voleurs, Antigone,* etc.

ans. *abbrev.* Answer.

An·schluss (ahn´shlōos) *n.* Annexation, esp. of Austria to Germany. [Ger., = "union"]

an·swer (ăn´ser) *v.* Give answer; reply to (charge); be responsible *for;* fulfill (purpose); suffice; correspond *to* (description etc.); act or operate in response (*to*); ~ **back,** reply impertinently. **an·swer** *n.* Something said or done in response to a question, accusation, etc.; defense; solution; (mus.) repetition of theme by another voice or instrument, esp. in fugue. **an'·swer·a·ble** *adj.* Responsible.

-ant *suffix.* Forms adjectives denoting existence of action (*repentant*) and nouns denoting agent (*applicant*).

ant (ănt) *n.* Small hymenopterous insect of superfamily Formicoidea, with complex instincts and social system, proverbial for industry; **ant'eater**, any of various tropical American mammals of the family Myrmecophagidae, feeding chiefly on ants and termites, esp. *Myrmecophaga tridactyla,* or giant anteater; also such mammals as ECHIDNA and PANGOLIN. **ant hill,** mound over ants' nest; (fig.) crowded dwelling(s) swarming with people.

ant. *abbrev.* Antenna; antonym.

ant- = ANTI-.

ant·ac·id (ăntăs'ĭd) *adj.* & *n.* (Agent) neutralizing acidity, esp. in stomach.

An·tae·us (ăntē'us). (Gk. myth.) Libyan giant, son of Poseidon and Ge; when Hercules wrestled with him, Antaeus was only overcome when lifted from the earth, from which he drew new strength whenever he touched it.

an·tag·o·nism (ăntăg'onĭzem) *n.* Active opposition; opposing principle.

an·tag·o·nist (ăntăg'onĭst) *n.* 1. Opponent. 2. (physiol.) Counteracting muscle. **an·tag·o·nis·tic** (ăntăgonĭs'tĭk) *adj.*

Australian green tree **ants.** *Ant species exceed 10,000. Most colonies have three castes (male, female, worker). A winged potential queen takes off coupled to a winged male. Workers cannot mate.* **Anteaters** *are mammals. Illustrated: The great anteater is more than 5 ft. long including its bushy tail. The scaly anteater. The echidna or spiny anteater is native to Australia and New Guinea and the marsupial banded anteater (numbat).*

an·tag·o·nize (ăntăg'onīz) *v.* (**-nized, -niz·ing**). Evoke hostility in, make into an enemy.

ant·arc·tic (ăntärk'tĭk, -är'tĭk) *adj.* Of the south polar regions. **A~ Circle,** parallel of 66 33'S., south of which the sun does not rise at midwinter or set at midsummer. **A~ Ocean,** southern extensions of the Atlantic, Pacific, and Indian Oceans which constitute the waters surrounding Antarctica. **Antarctic** *n.* Regions (both land and sea) around the S. Pole. [Gk. *anti* opposite + ARCTIC]

Ant·arc·ti·ca (ăntärk'tĭka, -är'-tĭ-). Continent mainly within the Antarctic Circle, almost entirely covered by ice sheet.

an·te (ăn'tē) *n.* (poker etc.) Stake put up before being dealt one's hand or drawing new cards; (slang) price, cost; one's share of the cost; **penny ~**: see PENNY.

ante- *prefix.* Before.

an·te·bel·lum (ăn'tēbĕl'um) *adj.* Before the war; specif., of the U.S. South before the Civil War. [L.]

an·te·ced·ent (ăntĭsē'dent) *adj.* Previous; presumptive. **~** *n.* Preceding thing or circumstance; (logic) part of conditional proposition on which other part depends; (gram.) noun, clause, etc., to which a following pronoun refers; (math.) first term of ratio; (pl.) ancestors.

an·te·cham·ber (ăn'tēchămbɛr) *n.* Room leading to chief apartment.

an·te·date (ăn'tĭdāt, ăntĭdāt') *v.t.* (**-dat·ed, -dat·ing**). Affix, assign, an earlier than the true date to; precede; anticipate.

an·te·di·lu·vi·an (ăntēdĭloo'-vēan) *adj.* Belonging, referring, appropriate, to the time before the Flood; very old, old-fashioned. **~** *n.* Antediluvian person.

an·te·lope (ăn'telōp) *n.* (pl. **-lopes,** collect. **-lope**). Any of several cloven-hoofed, horned ruminants of the family Bovidae

Great ant·eater

Scaly ant·eater

piny nt·eater

Banded ant-eater

*The flag flies 24 hours a day at the passenger terminal of Williams Field, the main airfield of **Antarctica**. The base lies on the 150 ft. thick edge of the Ross Ice Shelf in the Ross Sea.*

Brindled gnu

Eland

Grant's Gazelle

Antelopes *include chamois, gazelles and gnus, horned ruminants of the Bovidea family to which deer, sheep goats and cattle also belong. The brindled gnu ranges over central Africa. The eland is the largest antelope; adult bulls standing nearly 5 ft. at the shoulder. Grant's gazelle was named after a Scottish explorer.*

(related to deer, goats, and cattle) including the chamois, gazelle, and gnu.

an·te me·rid·i·em (ăn′tē merĭd′ēĕm, -em). (abbrev. a.m.) Between midnight and noon. **an·te·me·rid·i·an** *adj.* [L.]

an·ten·na (ăntĕn′a) *n.* 1. (pl. **-ten·nae** pr. -tĕn′ē). Sensory organ found in pairs on heads of insects and crustacea, usually long slender projections like horns, sometimes knobbed. 2. (pl. **-ten·nas**). Wire(s) or rod(s) used to transmit or receive radio waves; aerial. [L., = "sailyard"]

an·te·pe·nult (ăntĕpē′nŭlt, -pĭnŭlt′), **an·te·pe·nul·ti·mate** (ăntĭpĭnŭl′timĭt) *adjs.* & *ns.* (Syllable) last but two.

an·te·ri·or (ăntēr′ēer) *adj.* In or toward the front; prior *to*.

an·te·room (ăn′tēroom, -room) *n.* Room leading to another, antechamber; waiting room.

an·them (ăn′them) *n.* Hymn of praise or patriotism; nonmetrical musical setting of sacred words; religious composition sung antiphonally.

an·ther (ăn′ther) *n.* Terminal part of stamen containing pollen in pollen sacs.

an·thol·o·gy (ănthŏl′ojē) *n.* (pl. **-gies**). Collection of small choice literary pieces or extracts; literary collection; collection of songs etc. **an·thol′o·gize** *v.* (**-gized, -giz·-ing**). Make an anthology *from*. [Gk. *anthologia,* f. *anthos* flower, *-logia* collection (*legō* gather)]

An·tho·ny[1] (ăn′thonē), **St.** (*c*251–356). Born in Egypt, the first Christian monk; ′**St.** ~'s **cross**, T-shaped cross.

An·tho·ny[2] (ăn′thonē) **of Padua, St.** (1195–1231). Portuguese Franciscan monk, patron saint of Portugal.

An·tho·ny[3] (ăn′thonē), **Susan B(rownell)** (1820–1906). American leader of the women's suffrage movement; organized the National Woman Suffrage Association, 1869.

an·tho·zo·an (ănthozō′an) *adj.* & *n.* (Aquatic animal) of the class Anthozoa, including corals, sea anemones, etc. [Gk. *anthos* flower, *zōon* animal]

an·thra·cite (ăn′thrasīt) *n.* Glossy variety of coal containing much carbon and low percentage of volatile matter, burning with hot smokeless flame and leaving little ash. **an·thra·cit·ic** (ănthrasĭt′ĭk) *adj.*

an·thrax (ăn′thrăks) *n.* Disease of sheep and cattle, transmitted to man by infected wool, bristles, etc., and characterized by inflammatory skin lesions, caused by a bacillus (*B. anthracis*).

anthrop. *abbrev.* Anthropology.

an·thro·poid (ăn′thropoid) *adj.* Resembling man; ~ **ape**, one of the primates most nearly related to man, i.e., chimpanzees, gibbons, orangutans, and gorillas. ~ *n.* Anthropoid ape.

an·thro·pol·o·gy (ănthropŏl′ojē) *n.* Science of man, his origins, customs, etc.; study of man as an animal (**physical** ~) and of human, esp. primitive, societies (**social** ~). **an·thro·po·log·i·cal** (ănthropolŏj′ĭkal) *adj.* **an·thro·po·log′i·cal·ly** *adv.* **an·thro·pol′o·gist** *n.*

an·thro·po·mor·phism (ănthropomōr′fīzem) *n.* Ascription of human form and attributes to a god or to a thing not human. **an·thro·po·mor′phic** *adj.*

an·thro·po·mor·phous (ănthropomōr′fus) *adj.* Having human form. **an·thro·po·mor′phize** *v.* (**-phized, -phiz·ing**). Regard as anthropomorphous.

anti-, ant- *prefixes.* Opposite, against; (in the arts, literature, etc.) unlike the conventional form.

an·ti·air·craft (ăntēār′krăft, -kraft) *adj.* & *n.* (Force) for shooting down, or for defense against, hostile aircraft (abbrev. A.A.).

an·ti·bal·lis·tic (ăntēbalĭs′tĭk) **missile.** Defensive missile designed to intercept and destroy an attacking ballistic missile.

An·tibes (ăntēbz′; *Fr.* ahṅtēb′). Port and popular resort on the Riviera, in SE. France.

an·ti·bi·o·sis (ăntēbīō′sĭs, ăntī-) *n.* Condition of antagonism between organisms, esp. microorganisms (opp. SYMBIOSIS).

an·ti·bi·ot·ic (ăntĭbīŏt′ĭk, ăntī-, ăntē-) *adj.* & *n.* (Substance, drug, as penicillin, streptomycin) obtained from a mold, fungus, or other microorganism, or prepared synthetically, and having the power to inhibit the growth of other microorganisms; e.g. bacteria.

an·ti·bod·y (ăn′tĭbŏdē) *n.* (pl. **-bod·ies**). (physiol.) Protein formed within the body to inactivate compounds (esp. bacterial toxins and viruses) that are foreign to it.

an·tic (ăn′tĭk) *n.* (often pl.) Grotesque posture or gesture; playful prank.

An·ti·christ (ăn′tĭkrīst). Great personal opponent of Christ expected by early Christians to appear before the end of the world; person hostile to Christ and his teaching.

an·ti·chris·tian (ăntĭkrĭs′chan) *adj.* Opposed to Christianity.

an·tic·i·pate (ăntĭs′ipāt) *v.t.*

(**-pat·ed, -pat·ing**). Look forward to, expect; perform action before (another person or event), (of event) happen before (another event); satisfy (wish), obey (command), before it is expressed; use in advance. **an·tic·i·pa·tive** (ăntĭs′i-pātĭv, -patĭv), **an·tic·i·pa·to·ry** (ăntĭs′ipatōrē, -tōrē) *adjs.* **an·tic·i·pa·tion** (ăntĭsipā′shon) *n.*

an·ti·cler·i·cal (ăntēklĕr′ĭkal, ăntī-) *adj.* & *n.* (Person) opposed to undue influence of clergy or to existence of organized clerical hierarchy. **an·ti·cler′i·cal·ism** *n.*

an·ti·cli·max (ăntĭklī′măks) *n.* Lame end to anything promising a climax.

an·ti·cline (ăn′tĭklīn) *n.* (geol.) Archlike fold in bed(s) of rock (opp. SYNCLINE). **an·ti·cli·nal** (ăntĭklī′nal) *adj.*

an·ti·co·ag·u·lant (ăntēkōăg′yulant) *adj.* & *n.* (Drug) retarding or preventing the clotting of blood.

an·ti·cy·clone (ăntĭsī′klōn) *n.* Atmospheric system in which barometric pressure is high, and from center of which air tends to flow spirally outward (clockwise in N. hemisphere, counterclockwise in S. hemisphere).

Antiaircraft gun that was automatically loaded and aimed by radar and computer: the U.S. 3½ in. Gun M2. If the computer and electric power failed, manual operation was possible.

ramming rolls

round

fuse

fuse jaws

round is fired

breechblock closes

round is ejected

optical rangefinder

predictor computer

ammunition cylinders

case ejection shute

*English Harbor, former naval base at **Antigua** where Nelson met his future wife, Frances Nisbet. A British possession from 1632, Antigua became independent in 1967.*

an·ti·de·pres·sant (ăntēdĭprĕs´-ənt) *n*. Drug used in the treatment of mental depression to elevate spirits.

an·ti·dote (ăn´tĭdōt) *n*. Medicine etc. used to counteract disease or poison.

An·tie·tam (ăntē´tam). Creek near the town of Sharpsburg in W. Maryland; site of a major Civil War battle, 1862, in which the Confederates under Gen. Robert E. Lee were defeated by Union armies under Gen. McClellan.

an·ti·freeze (ăn´tĭfrēz) *n*. Chemical agent (usu. ethylene glycol) added to water to lower its freezing point, esp. in a car's radiator in winter.

an·ti·gen (ăn´tĭjen) *n*. Substance that stimulates production of an antibody when introduced into a living organism.

An·tig·o·ne (ăntĭg´onē). (Gk. legend) Daughter of Oedipus and Jocasta; she buried the body of her brother Polynices by night, against the order of her uncle King Creon; he condemned her to death but she took her own life.

an·ti·grav·i·ty (ăntēgrăv´ĭtē, ăntī-) *n*. Hypothetical force opposing gravity.

An·ti·gua (ăntē´gwa, -tĭg´wa). One of the Leeward Islands, in the West Indies, discovered in 1493 by Columbus; independent since 1967; capital, St. John's.

an·ti·he·ro (ăn´tē-hērō, ăntī-) *n*. (pl. **-roes**). Hero of unconventional type in novel etc.

an·ti·his·ta·mine (ăntĭhĭs´tamēn, -mĭn) *adj*. & *n*. (Drug) that counteracts the effect of histamine, used esp. in treatment of allergic conditions.

An·til·les (ăntĭl´ēz). Chain of West Indian islands separating the Caribbean Sea from the Atlantic Ocean; **Greater ~**, Cuba, Jamaica, Hispaniola (Haiti and the Dominican Republic), and Puerto Rico; **Lesser ~**, group of smaller islands to the SE.

an·ti·log (ăn´tĭlawg, -lŏg), **an·ti·log·a·rithm** (ăntĭlaw´gerĭdhem, -lŏg´e-) *ns*. Number to which a logarithm belongs (100 is the ~ of 2 to the base 10).

an·ti·ma·cas·sar (ăntĭmakăs´er) *n*. Covering on chair back to protect it from hair grease or as ornament. [f. *Macassar oil*, pop. as hair oil in 19th c.]

an·ti·mag·net·ic (ăntēmăgnĕt´-ik, ăntī-) *adj*. Resistant to magnetization, esp. of watch movements.

an·ti·mat·ter (ăn´tēmăter, ăn´tī-) *n*. (Hypothetical) matter composed solely of antiparticles.

ant·i·mo·ny (ăn´timōnē) *n*. (chem.) Brittle metallic element, bluish-white, of flaky crystalline texture, used in alloys, esp. with lead, and in medicine; symbol Sb, at. no. 51, at. wt. 121.75.

an·ti·no·mi·an (ăntĭnō´mēan) *adj*. & *n*. (Person) holding that the moral law is not binding on Christians on the ground that faith alone is sufficient to salvation. **an·ti·no´mi·an·ism** *n*.

an·tin·o·my (ăntĭn´omē) *n*. (pl. **-mies**). Contradiction in a law, or between laws, principles, etc.

An·ti·och (ăn´tēŏk). Name of several ancient cities of the Near East, esp. (1) the capital of Syria under the Seleucid kings (now Antakya in Turkey near the Syrian border); (2) "Antioch toward Pisidia" in the Roman province of Galatia (near the present Yalvac in SW. Anatolia, Turkey).

an·ti·par·ti·cle (ăn´tēpārtĭkel, ăn´tī-) *n*. (phys.) One of a pair of particles of equal mass but with opposite electrical charge (e.g. electron and positron) or direction of magnetic moment.

an·ti·pas·to (ăntĭpahs´tō, -păs´-) *n*. (pl. **-tos,** *It*. **-ti** pr. -tē). Assorted appetizers such as smoked meats, fish, olives, etc.; hors d'oeuvre.

an·tip·a·thy (ăntĭp´athē) *n*. (pl. **-thies**). Constitutional or settled aversion (*to*, *against*, *between*). **an·ti·pa·thet·ic** (ăntĭpathĕt´ĭk) *adj*.

an·ti·per·son·nel (ăntēpērso-nĕl´, ăntī-) *adj*. (of bombs, mines, etc.) Designed to kill or injure persons.

an·ti·per·spi·rant (ăntĭpēr´-sperant) *n*. Substance applied to the

Anzac Day commemoration, Sydney, Australia. Remembrance services are held each year on April 25th to honor the Australian and New Zealand forces who fought in the 1914–18 and 1939–45 wars.

skin to reduce perspiration.

an·tiph·o·nal (ăntĭf′onal) *adj.* Sung alternately.

an·tip·o·des (ăntĭp′odēz) *n.pl.* Places on opposite sides of the earth; **A~**, Australasia as region diametrically opposite to Europe. **an·tip′o·dal** *adj.* **an·tip·o·de·an** (ăntĭpodē′an) *adj. & n.* [Gk., = "having the feet opposite"]

an·ti·pope (ăn′tĭpōp) *n.* Pope in opposition to one (held to be) canonically chosen.

an·ti·py·ret·ic (ăntēpīrĕt′ĭk) *adj. & n.* (Drug) allaying or preventing fever.

an·ti·quar·y (ăn′tĭkwĕrē) *n.* (pl. **-quar·ies**). Student or collector of antiques or antiquities. **an·ti·quar·i·an** (ăntĭkwār′ēan) *adj. & n.* **an·ti·quar′i·an·ism** *n.*

an·ti·quat·ed (ăn′tĭkwātĭd) *adj.* Out of date; antique.

an·tique (ăntēk′) *adj.* Of or existing from old times; old-fashioned; of the ancients. **~** *n.* Relic of ancient art or of old times; piece of old furniture, work of art, etc., regarded as valuable esp. by collectors.

an·tiq·ui·ty (ăntĭk′wĭtē) *n.* (pl. **-ties**). Ancientness; ancient times, esp. (**classical ~**) the period of the ancient Greek and Roman civilizations; (pl.) customs, practices, etc., of ancient times, objects surviving from them.

an·ti·scor·bu·tic (ăntĭskŏrbū′tĭk, ăntī-) *adj. & n.* (Medicine etc.) preventing or curing scurvy.

an·ti·Sem·ite (ăntēsĕm′īt, ăntī-) *adj. & n.* (Person) hostile to Jews. **an·ti·Se·mit·ic** (ăntēsĕmīt′ĭk, ăntī-) *adj.* **an·ti·Sem·i·tism** (ăntē·sĕm′ĭtĭzem, antī-) *n.*

an·ti·sep·sis (ăntĭsĕp′sĭs) *n.* (med.) Antiseptic treatment or condition.

an·ti·sep·tic (ăntĭsĕp′tĭk) *adj. & n.* 1. (Agent) counteracting sepsis; germicide. 2. Clean, sterile. **an·ti·sep′ti·cal·ly** *adv.*

an·ti·so·cial (ăntēsō′shal, ăntī-) *adj.* Opposed to principles on which society is based; hostile, antagonistic to others. **an·ti·so′·cial·ly** *adv.*

an·ti·spas·mod·ic (ăntĭspăz·mŏd′ĭk, ăntī-) *adj. & n.* (Drug) that relieves spasms.

An·tis·the·nes (ăntĭs′thenēz) (5th c. B.C.). Athenian philosopher, pupil of Socrates and founder of the Cynic school of philosophy.

an·tith·e·sis (ăntĭth′ĭsĭs) *n.* (pl. **-ses** pr. **-sēz**). Contrast of ideas marked by parallelism of strongly contrasted words; direct opposite.

an·ti·thet·ic (ăntĭthĕt′ĭk), **an·ti·thet′i·cal** *adjs.*

an·ti·tox·in (ăntĭtŏk′sĭn) *n.* Substance serving to neutralize a toxin. **an·ti·tox′ic** *adj.*

an·ti·trust (ăntētrŭst′, ăntī-) *adj.* (of law) Opposed to or intended to regulate trusts and monopolies.

an·ti·ven·in (ăntēvĕn′ĭn, ăntī-) *n.* Antitoxin, esp. against snake poison.

ant·ler (ănt′ler) *n.* Whole or any branch of either horn of deer.

ant·li·on (ănt′līon) *n.* Any insect of the family Myrmeleontidae whose larva digs holes in sand to trap ants.

An·to·ni·nus Pi·us (ăntonī′nus pī′us) (A.D. 86–161). Roman emperor 138–161.

an·ton·o·ma·sia (ăntonomā′·zha) *n.* Substitution of epithet etc. for proper name; use of proper name to express general idea (e.g. *a Solomon*).

An·to·ny (ăn′tonē), **Mark.** Marcus Antonius (*c*83–30 B.C.), Roman general and consul; member of 2nd triumvirate; became enthralled by Cleopatra; was deprived of his powers (32 B.C.) by the senate and defeated at battle of Actium.

an·to·nym (ăn′tonĭm) *n.* Word of contrary meaning to another.

an·trum (ăn′trum) *n.* (pl. **-tra** pr. **-tra**). Cavity in the body, esp. one in the upper jawbone.

Ant·werp (ănt′twerp). (Fl. *Antwerpen*, Fr. *Anvers*) Belgian port city.

A·nu·bis (anoo′bĭs, anū′-). (Egyptian myth.) Jackal-headed deity, ruler of the dead, whom he conducts to the shades.

an·u·ran (anoor′an, anūr′-) *adj. & n.* (Member) of the Anura, an order of the Amphibia comprising frogs and toads, the adult forms of which have no tails or gills but have

strong hind legs for leaping and swimming.

a·nus (ā′nus) *n.* (pl. **a·nus·es**). Opening at end of alimentary canal through which solid matter is excreted.

an·vil (ăn′vĭl) *n.* Block (usu. of steel) on which metal is worked by smith; thing resembling this.

anx·i·e·ty (ăngzī′ĭtē) *n.* (pl. **-ties**). Uneasiness, concern; solicitous desire; neurotic fear. **anx·ious** (ăngk′shus, ăng′-) *adj.* Troubled, uneasy; earnestly desirous; causing anxiety. **anx′ious·ly** *adv.*

an·y (ĕn′ē) *adj. & pron.* One or some but no matter which; whichever is chosen. **~** *adv.* At all, in some degree.

an·y·bod·y (ĕn′ĕbŏdē, -bŭdē) *n. & pron.* Any person.

an·y·how (ĕn′ĕhow) *adv.* Anyway; in any case.

an·y·more (ĕnēmōr′, -mōr′) *adv.* (colloq.) Now, henceforth (in neg. and interrog. constructions).

an·y·one (ĕn′ēwŭn) *n. & pron.* Anybody.

an·y·place (ĕn′ēplās) *adv.* (colloq.) Anywhere.

an·y·thing (ĕn′ēthĭng) *n. & pron.* Whatever thing; a thing, no matter which.

an·y·time (ĕn′ētīm) *adv.* At any time.

an·y·way (ĕn′ēwā) *adv.* In any way whatever; anyhow; (colloq.) carelessly.

an·y·where (ĕn′ēhwār -wār) *adv. & pron.* (In to) any place; **get ~**, (colloq.) attain success, make progress.

An·zac (ăn′zăk) *adj. & n.* (Belonging to, member of) the Australian and New Zealand Army Corps (Anzacs) in World War I; also applied to any Austral. and N.Z. group, characteristic, etc. [initials of name]

*The **Apache** Indians, forced out of their tribal lands by white settlers live mainly on reservations in New Mexico and Arizona where they farm small plots of land.*

*Renaissance town hall in Grote Markt, **Antwerp,** Belgium's chief port on the Scheldt about 55 miles from North Sea, for centuries a center of commerce and the arts. Rubens lived there.*

A-O.K., A-OK, A-O·Kay (ā´ō kā´) *adjs.* Perfectly all right, excellent.

a·or·ta (āōr´ta) *n.* (pl. **-tas, -tae** or. -tē). Great artery issuing from left ventricle of heart, carrying blood through its branches to all other parts of body.

a·pace (apās´) *adv.* Swiftly.

A·pach·e (apăch´ē) *n.* (pl. **A·pach·es,** collect. **A·pach·e**) & *adj.* (Member) of tribe of southwestern U.S. Indians, fierce and skillful in raiding.

a·pache (apăsh´) *n.* Violent street ruffian in Paris; member of Parisian underworld; ~ **dance,** vigorous dance for two.

Ap·a·lach·i·co·la (ăpalăchĭkō´la) **River.** River in NW. Florida flowing from Georgia border 112 miles (180km) S. to the Gulf of Mexico.

a·part (apärt´) *adv.* Aside, separately; into pieces; to or at a

The **ape** *has manlike basic structure of head, neck, shoulder, girdle and arms. Illustrated: Orang-utan, a long-armed mainly arboreal ape up to 5½ ft. tall; gorilla, the largest anthropoid ape; the chimpanzee, most resembling man and allied to the gorilla; and the gibbon, arboreal and supremely agile.*

Orang-utan

Gorilla

Gibbon

Chimpanzee

distance; ~ **from**, not considering, with the exception of. ~ *adj.* Unique.

a·part·heid (apārt′hāt, -hīt) *n.* Policy of racial segregation in S. Africa; similar policy elsewhere. [Afrikaans]

a·part·ment (apārt′ment) *n.* Single room or set of rooms for use as a dwelling; ~ **house**, building divided into apartments.

ap·a·thy (ăp′athē) *n.* Insensibility to suffering; indifference; mental indolence. **ap·a·thet·ic** (ăpathĕt′ĭk) *adj.* **ap·a·thet·i·cal·ly** *adv.*

ape (āp) *n.* Anthropoid ape (see ANTHROPOID); (pop.) monkey; big, stupid, clumsy man; **great ~s**, gorilla, chimpanzee, orangutan; **ape-man**, pithecanthrope. **ape** *v.t.* (**aped, ap·ing**). Imitate, mimic.

Ap·en·nines (ăp′enīnz). Mountain range running down the length of Italy.

a·per·i·tif (apĕrĭtēf′) *n.* Alcoholic drink taken before meal to stimulate appetite.

ap·er·ture (ăp′ercher) *n.* Opening, gap; space through which light passes in camera or other optical instrument.

a·pet·al·ous (āpĕt′alus) *adj.* Without petals.

a·pex (ā′pĕks) *n.* (pl. **a·pex·es, a·pi·ces** pr. ā′pĭsēz, ăp′ĭ-). Tip, top; vertex (of cone, triangle).

a·pha·sia (afā′zha) *n.* Loss of speech, partial or total, or loss of power to understand written or spoken language as result of damage to the brain.

a·phe·li·on (afē′lēon) *n.* (pl. **-li·a** pr. -lēa). Point of planet's or comet's orbit farthest from sun.

a·phid (ā′fĭd, ăf′ĭd) *n.* Small, soft-bodied insect of family Aphididae, infesting leaves and stems of plants.

a·phis (ā′fĭs, ăf′ĭs) *n.* (pl. **aph·i·des** pr. ăf′ĭdēz) = APHID.

aph·o·rism (ăf′erĭzem) *n.* Short, pithy statement or maxim. **aph·o·ris·tic** (ăferĭstĭk) *adj.*

aph·ro·dis·i·ac (ăfrodĭz′ēăk) *adj.* & *n.* (Drug, food, etc.) provoking sexual desire. [f. APHRODITE]

Aph·ro·di·te (ăfrodī′tē). (Gk. myth.) Goddess of love (esp. sensual), beauty, and fertility, born of the sea foam; identified by the

Gran Sasso d'Italia, **Apennines,** *mountain backbone of Italy, ranging some 838 miles in length, 25–80 miles in width.*

Romans with Venus; her cult was of eastern origin, and she was identified with Astarte, Ishtar, etc.

A·pi·a (ah´pĭya). Capital of Western Samoa.

a·pi·ar·y (ā´pēērē) n. (pl. **-ar·ies**). Place where bees are kept.

a·pi·a·rist (ā´pēerĭst) n. Beekeeper.

ap·i·cal (ăp´ĭkal, ā´pĭ-) adj. Belonging to an apex; placed at the tip; (phon., of sound) articulated with tip of tongue.

a·pi·cul·ture (ā´pĭkŭlcher) n. Beekeeping.

a·piece (apēs´) adv. Severally, each.

A·pis (ā´pĭs). (Egyptian myth.) God, the incarnation as a bull of the sun-god Ptah, represented as a bull with the disk of the sun between his horns.

ap·ish (ā´pĭsh) adj. Like an ape.

a·plomb (aplŏm´, aplŭm´) n. Self-possession; poise.

A.P.O. abbrev. Army Post Office.

A·poc·a·lypse (apŏk´alĭps) n. Revelation, esp. that made to St. John in the island of Patmos; book of New Testament ("Revelation of St. John the Divine") recording this; cataclysmic event such as described in this book; end of the world. **a·poc·a·lyp·tic** (apŏkalĭp´- tĭk) adj. Of or pertaining to this revelation or to such violent events. **a·poc·a·lyp´ti·cal** adj. **a·poc·a· lyp´ti·cal·ly** adv.

a·poc·o·pe (apŏk´opē) n. Cutting off of last sound or syllable of word.

Apocr. abbrev. Apocrypha.

a·poc·ry·pha (apŏk´rifa) n.pl. 1. **the A ~**, books of Old Testament included in Septuagint and Vulgate, but not in Hebrew Bible and not in all modern Bibles. 2. Other writings of doubtful authenticity.

a·poc´ry·phal adj. 1. Of the Apocrypha; also applied to a number of early Christian writings in similar form to the canonical books of New Testament. 2. Of doubtful authenticity, spurious. [Gk. apokrupha hidden or secret (writings), i.e. those reserved for the initiated and often falsely ascribed]

ap·o·dal (ăp´odal) adj. & n. (zool.) Limbless (creature); (member) of the Apoda, an order of the Amphibia containing tropical legless wormlike animals, some of which have scales; (fish) with no ventral fin.

ap·o·gee (ăp´ojē) n. Point in orbit of moon, planet, or artificial satellite farthest from Earth; (fig.) highest point. **ap·o·ge·an** (ăpojē- an) adj.

a·po·lit·i·cal (āpolĭt´ĭkal) adj. Unconcerned with or detached from politics. **a·po·lit´i·cal·ly** adv.

A·pol·li·naire (ăpawlēnĕr´), **Guillaume** (1880–1918). Pen name of Wilhelm Apollinaris de Kostrowitzky, Polish-born French poet and man of letters.

A·pol·lo (apŏl´ō). (Gk. and Rom. myth.) God sometimes identified with the sun and called Phoebus (Apollo); son of Zeus and Leto and brother of Artemis; represented ideal type of manly beauty; associated esp. with music, poetry, and prophecy.

A·pol·lyon (apŏl´yon). "The destroyer," the angel of the bottomless pit (Rev. 9).

The **Temple of Apollo** at Delphi, the shrine of the most famous Greek oracle. Apollo, a God of prophecy, was consulted if trouble threatened. The reply was often cryptic.

a·pol·o·get·ic (apŏlojĕt´ĭk) adj. Regretfully acknowledging, excusing, fault or failure; of the nature of an apology. **a·pol·o·get´i·cal·ly** adv. **a·pol·o·get´ics** n.pl. (usu. considered sing.) Reasoned defense, esp. of Christianity. **a·pol· o·gist** (apŏl´ojĭst) n. One who defends by argument. **a·pol´o·gize** v.i. (**-gized, -giz·ing**). Make an apology.

ap·o·lo·gi·a (ăpolō´jēa) n. Defense or justification of conduct or opinions.

a·pol·o·gy (apŏl´ojē) n. (pl. **-gies**). Regretful acknowledgement of offense; statement of regret; apologia; ~ **for**, poor or scanty specimen of.

ap·o·phthegm (ăp´othĕm) n., **ap·o·phtheg·mat·ic** (ăpothĕg´- măt´ĭk) adj.: see APOTHEGM.

ap·o·plec·tic (ăpoplĕk´tĭk) adj. Pertaining to, causing, apoplexy; liable to, suffering from, apoplexy. **ap·o·plec´ti·cal·ly** adv.

ap·o·plex·y (ăp´oplĕksē) n. Seizure caused by blockage or rupture of an artery in the brain.

a·port (apōrt´, apōrt´) adv. (naut.) On or toward the port (left) side.

ap·o·si·o·pe·sis (ăposīopē´sĭs) n. (pl. **-ses** pr. -sēz). (rhet.) Breaking off short for effect.

a·pos·ta·sy (apŏs´tasē) n. (pl. **-sies**). Renunciation of religious vows, faith, party, etc.

a·pos·tate (apŏs´tāt, -tĭt) n. & adj. (One) guilty of apostasy. **a·pos·ta·tize** (apŏs´tatīz) v.i. (**-tized, -tiz·ing**). Become an apostate.

a pos·te·ri·o·ri (ā pŏstērēōr´ī, -ōr´ī, -ōr´ē, -ōr´ē). (Reasoning) from effects to causes. [L., = "from what comes after"]

a·pos·tle (apŏs´el) n. Messenger, esp. (**A ~**) any of the 12 disciples sent forth by Christ to preach Gospel (Matt. 10); first successful Christian missionary in a country; leader of reform; **Apostles' Creed**, simplest and prob. oldest of the Christian creeds, ascribed by tradition to the Apostles and beginning "I believe in God the Father Almighty." **ap·os·tol·ic** (ăpostŏl´- ĭk) adj. Of the Apostles; of the character of an Apostle; of the pope, esp. as successor of St. Peter.

a·pos·tro·phe (apŏs´trofē) n. The sign (') of omission of letter(s); also used in possessive case of nouns and to indicate plurals of numbers, omission of letters, etc.

a·poth·e·car·y (apŏth´ekērē) n. (pl. **-car·ies**). (obsolesc.) Pharmacist, druggist; pharmacy, drugstore. **apothecaries' measure, weight**, system of liquid measures, weights, used in pharmacy. [Gk. apothēkē storehouse]

ap·o·thegm, ap·o·phthegm (ăp´othĕm) ns. Terse or pithy

*The **Appalachian Mountains** extend for about 1,200 miles from Canada to Alabama. The Appalachian Trail offers spectacular hiking through 14 States and 8 national forests.*

saying. **ap·o·theg·mat·ic, ap·o·phtheg·mat·ic** (ăpothĕgmătˊĭk) *adjs.*

a·poth·e·o·sis (apŏthēōˊsĭs, ăpothēˊosĭs) *n.* (pl. **-ses** pr. -sēz). Deification; deified ideal. **a·poth·e·o·size** (apŏthˊēosīz, ăpothēˊosīz) *v.t.* (**-sized, -siz·ing**).

app. *abbrev.* Appendix; apparent(ly).

Ap·pa·la·chi·a (ăpalāˊchēa, -cha, -lăchˊēa, -lăchˊa, -lāˊkēa). Region in SE. U.S., in the area of the S. Appalachian Mountains, noted for scenery, coal mining, and poverty. **Ap·pa·laˊchi·an** *adj.* ~ **Mountains**, chief mountain chain of eastern N. America, from Ala. to S. Quebec; highest peak Mt. Mitchell (6,684 feet, 2,037m) in S.C.; ~ **Trail**, system of trails through the ~ **Mountains** extending 2,000 miles from Maine to Georgia.

ap·pall (apawlˊ) *v.t.* Dismay, terrify. **ap·pallˊing** *adj.* Horrifying; (colloq.) very bad.

Ap·pa·loo·sa (ăpaloōˊsa) *n.* Horse of western Amer. breed with dark spots on light background.

ap·pa·ra·tus (ăparătˊus, -rāˊtus) *n.* (pl. **-tus, -tus·es**). 1. Mechanical requisites, an appliance, for doing something, esp. for scientific experiment; a complex machine. 2. Organs effecting a natural process. 3. A political organization.

ap·par·el (apărˊel) *v.t.* (**-eled, (-elˊing**; *Brit.* **-elled, -elˊling**). (archaic) Dress, clothe. ~ *n.* Dress, clothing.

ap·par·ent (apărˊent, apārˊ-) *adj.* Manifest; seeming; **heir** ~, one who cannot be superseded by birth of nearer heir (cf. PRESUMPTIVE). **ap·parˊent·ly** *adv.*

ap·pa·ri·tion (ăparĭshˊon) *n.* Appearance, esp. of ghostly or startling kind; thing thought to be seen but having no material existence.

ap·peal (apēlˊ) *v.i.* Application *to* higher court for alteration of decision of lower; call (*to* witness) for corroboration, (*to* person) for assistance etc.; make earnest request; ~ **to**, be, prove, attractive to. ~ *n.* Act or right of appealing; earnest request, entreaty; quality that appeals; **Court of Appeals**, one hearing cases previously tried in a lower court.

ap·pear (apērˊ) *v.i.* Become visible; present oneself; seem; be manifest; come before the public; be present; (law) come before a court. **ap·pearˊance** (apērˊans) *n.* Appearing; look, aspect; (pl.) outward show (of prosperity etc.); apparition.

Stamen Style
Petal Sepal Ovule Ovary
Longitudinal sections
Carpel
Transverse sections
Vascular bundle
Endocarp
Outer limit of Carpel (Core line)
Seed

*Cutting away the stamens of **apple** blossom on an apple farm in Kent U.K. In the U.K. alone there are 2,000 varieties of apple; it is the most widely cultivated fruit of temperate climates. It thrives in any good, well-drained soil but is susceptible to frost and a large number of pests. The drawing shows successive stages in the apple from flower to fruit.*

ap·pease (apēz′) *v.t.* (**-peased, -peas·ing**). Pacify, soothe; make concessions to (an aggressor); satisfy. **ap·pease′ment** *n.*

ap·pel·lant (apĕl′ant) *n.* One who appeals to higher court. **ap·pel·late** (apĕl′ĭt) *adj.* Having authority to hear appeals and reverse decisions, as an ~ **court.**

ap·pel·la·tion (ăpela′shon) *n.* Identifying name, title.

ap·pend (apĕnd′) *v.t.* Attach to as an accessory; add, esp. in writing. **ap·pend·age** (apĕn′dĭj) *n.*

ap·pen·dec·to·my (ăpendĕk′- tomē) *n.* (pl. **-mies**). (surg.) Excision of appendix.

ap·pen·di·ci·tis (apĕndisī′tĭs) *n.* Inflammation of vermiform appendix.

ap·pen·dix (apĕn′dĭks) *n.* (pl. **-dix·es, -di·ces** pr. -dīsēz). 1. Subsidiary addition (*to* book etc.) 2. Small process developed from organ, esp. vermiform appendix of the intestine.

ap·per·tain (ăpertān′) *v.i.* Belong, be appropriate, relate *to.*

ap·pe·tite (ăp′ĭtīt) *n.* Desire, inclination (*for* food, pleasure, etc.); relish. **ap·pe·tiz·er** (ăp′ĭtīzer) *n.* Anything taken to give appetite for a meal. **ap·pe·tiz·ing** (ăp′etīzĭng) *adj.* Inducing appetite.

Ap·pi·an (ăp′ēan) **Way.** Roman highway running SE. from Rome to Brundisium (Brindisi), begun by the censor Appius Claudius Caecus, 312 B.C.

ap·plaud (aplawd′) *v.* Express approval (of), esp. by handclapping; praise.

ap·plause (aplawz′) *n.* Approval loudly expressed, esp. by handclapping.

ap·ple (ăp′el) *n.* Firm, fleshy, edible fruit of a rosaceous tree of genus *Malus;* ~ **butter,** jam made from apples; **upset person's applecart,** spoil plans; **ap′plejack** (*n.*), spirit distilled from cider; apple brandy; **apple of discord,** (Gk. myth.) golden apple, inscribed "For the fairest," contended for by Hera, Athene, and Aphrodite; see PARIS[2]; hence, cause, subject, of dispute; **apple of one's eye,** pupil, treasured person; **apple pan- dowd′y,** thick-crusted dessert of apples, sugar, and spices; **apple- pie order,** extreme neatness; **apple-polish** (*v.i.*), (colloq.) curry favor; **apple polisher** *n.*; **ap′ple- sauce** *n.*, apples sweetened and stewed to a pulp; (slang) nonsense.

Ap·ple·seed (ăp′elsēd), **Johnny** (1774–1845). Nickname of John Chapman, American pioneer and legendary hero; ranged over the Ohio River Valley planting and nurturing apple trees.

ap·pli·ance (aplī′ans) *n.* Any device or machine, esp. electrical or for household use.

ap·pli·ca·ble (ăp′lĭkabel, a-

plĭk′-) *adj.* Capable of being applied. **ap·pli·ca·bil·i·ty** (ăplĭka- bĭl′ĭtē) *n.*

ap·pli·cant (ăp′lĭkant) *n.* One who applies.

ap·pli·ca·tion (ăplĭkā′shon) *n.* Applying; thing applied; request; relevancy; diligence; printed form to make a request on (as for a job).

ap·pli·ca·tor (ap′lĭkāter) *n.* Device for applying a substance.

ap·pli·qué (ăplĭkā′) *n.* & *adj.* (Needlework) consisting of pieces of material cut out and sewn to the surface of other material of different color or texture; material so applied. ~ *v.t.* (**-quéd, -qué·ing**). Sew (material) to another as appliqué.

ap·ply (aplī′) *v.* (**-plied, -ply- ing**). Put in contact; administer (remedy); be relevant or suitable; devote (*to*); address oneself (*for* help etc.) *to*; make application (*for*); make use of; **applied** (*adj.*), put to practical use.

ap·point (apoint′) *v.t.* Fix (time etc.); assign *to* an office or position; **well appointed, badly appoint- ed,** so equipped. **ap·point·ee** (apointē′) *n.* Person appointed.

ap·point·ment (apoint′ment) *n.* Act of appointing; agreement to meet at specific time; office assigned; (pl.) furnishings, equipment.

Ap·po·mat·tox (ăpomăt′oks). Town in central Virginia; site of courthouse where Gen. Robert E. Lee surrendered to Gen. Ulysses S. Grant on April 9, 1865, ending the Civil War.

ap·por·tion (apōr′shon, -pôr′-) *v.t.* Give as due share; portion out. **ap·por′tion·ment** *n.*

ap·po·site (ăp′ozĭt) *adj.* Well put; appropriate. **ap·po·si·tion** (ăpozĭsh′on) *n.* Placing side by side; **in** ~, (gram.) syntactically parallel; in same case etc.

ap·praise (aprāz′) *v.t.* (**-praised, -prais·ing**). Fix or estimate value of; estimate. **ap- prais′al, ap·praise′ment** *ns.*

ap·pre·cia·ble (aprē′shabel) *adj.* Enough to be seen or estimated perceptible. **ap·pre′cia·bly** *adv*

ap·pre·ci·ate (aprē′shēāt) *v.* (**-at·ed, -at·ing**). Estimate rightly; recognize, understand; be thankful for; be sensitive to; esteem highly; raise, rise, in value. **ap·pre·ci·a- tion** (aprēshēā′shon) *n.* **ap·pre- cia·tive** (aprē′shatĭv, -shēā-) *adj.*

ap·pre·hend (ăprĭhĕnd′) *v.t.* Seize, arrest; understand; anticipate with fear.

ap·pre·hen·si·ble (ăprĭhĕn′si- bel) *adj.* Perceptible to senses.

ap·pre·hen·sion (ăprĭhĕn′shon) *n.* 1. Arrest; capture. 2. Understanding. 3. Uneasiness.

ap·pre·hen·sive (ăprĭhĕn′sĭv) *adj.* Relating to sensory perception, or intellectual understanding;

uneasy in mind. **ap·pre·hen′- sive·ly** *adv.* **ap·pre·hen′sive·ness** *n.*

ap·pren·tice (aprĕn′tĭs) *n.* Learner of a craft, formerly bound to serve, and entitled to instruction from, his employer for a specified term; a beginner. ~ *v.t.* (**-ticed, -tic·ing**). Bind or place as apprentice (*to*). **ap·pren′tice·ship** *n.*

ap·prise (aprīz′) *v.t.* (**-prised, -pris·ing**). Give notice *of*, inform.

ap·proach (aprōch′) *v.* Come near or nearer (to); set about (task); make overtures to. ~ *n.* Approaching; access, passage; (golf) shot that is intended to reach green. **ap·proach′a·ble** *adj.* Easy of access; welcoming, friendly to advances.

ap·pro·ba·tion (ăproba′shon) *n.* Sanction, approval.

ap·pro·pri·ate (aprō′preit) *adj.* Suitable, proper. **ap·pro′pri- ate·ly** *adv.* **ap·pro·pri·ate** (aprō′- preāt) *v.t.* (**-at·ed, -at·ing**). Take possession of; devote to special purposes. **ap·pro·pri·a·tion** (aprōprēā′shon) *n.* Funds set aside for a particular purpose.

ap·prove (aprōōv′) *v.* (**-proved, -prov·ing**). Confirm, sanction, commend; ~ **of,** pronounce or consider good. **ap·prov·al** (aprōō′val) *n.* Approving; **on** ~, (of goods supplied) to be returned if not satisfactory.

approx. *abbrev.* Approximate, approximately.

ap·prox·i·mate (aprŏk′simĭt) *adj.* Very near; fairly correct. **ap·prox′i·mate·ly** *adv.* **ap·prox- i·mate** (aprŏk′simāt) *v.* (**-mat·ed, -mat·ing**). Bring or come near (*to*). **ap·prox·i·ma·tion** (aprŏksi- mā′shon) *n.*

ap·pur·te·nance (apĕr′tenans) *n.* Appendage, accessory; belonging. **ap·pur′te·nant** *adj.* Belonging, appertaining.

Apr. *abbrev.* April.

a·près-ski (ăprăskē′, ah-) *n.* & *adj.* (Of, suitable for) time, period of relaxation, after skiing.

ap·ri·cot (ăp′rĭkŏt, ā′prĭ-) *n.* Succulent orange-pink fruit, with smooth stone, of the rosaceous tree *Prunus armeniaca;* this tree; color of the fruit.

A·pril (ā′prĭl). Fourth month of Gregorian (2nd of Julian) calendar, with 30 days; ~ **Fools' Day,** April 1 (the celebration of which is probably a survival of ancient festivities held at spring equinox), when the unsuspecting are made victims of practical jokes or sent on fools' errands.

a pri·o·ri (ā prīōr′ī, -ōr′ī, ā preōr′ē, -ōr′ē, ah prē-) *adv.* & *adj. phr.* (Reasoning) from cause to effect; deductive(ly); presumptive- (ly), without investigation; (of knowledge) obtained by deduction without sensory experience. [L., =

"from what is before"]

a·pron (ā'pron) *n.* 1. Garment worn in front of body to protect clothes; **tied to ~ strings of** (mother, wife, etc.), unduly dependent on. 2. Part of ceremonial dress (of bishops, freemasons, etc.). 3. (theatr.) Advanced strip of stage for playing scenes before proscenium arch. 4. Area near hangars of airfield for accommodation of aircraft maneuvering on ground.

ap·ro·pos (ăpropō') *adv.* To the purpose; in respect *of.* ~ *adj.* Pertinent.

apse (ăps) *n.* Semicircular or polygonal recess, usu. with vaulted roof, in church or other building.

ap·sis (ăp'sĭs) *n.* (pl. **ap·si·des** pr. ăp'sĭdēz). Aphelion or perihelion of planet; apogee or perigee of moon.

apt (ăpt) *adj.* Suitable, appropriate; quick, ready; inclined (*to*). **apt'ly** *adv.* **apt'ness** *n.*

ap·ter·ous (ăp'terus) *adj.* (zool.) Wingless.

ap·ti·tude (ăp'tĭtōod, -tūd) *n.* Fitness, natural propensity; ability; (psychol.) capacity to acquire skill in a particular field of bodily or mental performance.

Ap·u·le·ius (ăpyulē'us), **Lucius** (b. c123 A.D.). Platonic philosopher, of Madaura in N. Africa; author of the satire known as *The Golden Ass.*

A·pu·lia (apūl'ya). Ancient country and modern region (It. *Puglia*) forming the so-called heel of SE. Italy. **A·pu'lian** *adj.* & *n.*

A·qa·ba (ah'kahbah). Seaport in SW. Jordan; **Gulf of ~**, an extension of the Red Sea between Saudi Arabia and the Sinai Peninsula.

aq·ua (ăk'wa, ah'kwa) *n.* (pl. **aq·uae** pr. ăk'wē, ah'kwē, **aq·uas**). 1. Water. 2. Aquamarine. 3. (pharm.) Liquid; solution, esp. in water.

aq·ua (ăk'wa, ah'kwa) **for·tis** (fōr'tĭs). (obs.) Nitric acid. [L., = "strong water"]

Aq·ua-Lung (ăk'walŭng, ah'-kwa-) *n.* (trademark) Diver's portable breathing apparatus, consisting of cylinders of compressed air with valve and mouthpiece.

aq·ua·ma·rine (ăk'wamarēn', ahkwa-) *n.* Bluish-green transparent beryl; color of this. [L. *aqua marina* sea water]

aq·ua·naut (ăk'wanawt, -nŏt, ah'kwa-) *n.* Underwater explorer or swimmer, esp. one who lives in underwater installation for an extended time.

aq·ua·plane (ăk'waplān, ah'-kwa-) *n.* Board towed behind speed boat, carrying a rider. ~ *v.i.* (**-planed, -plan·ing**). 1. Ride on aquaplane. 2. (of vehicle traveling on wet surface) Lose contact with surface through build-up of water beneath tires.

aq·ua (ăk'wa, ah'kwa) **re·gia** (rē'ja, rē'jēa). Mixture of concentrated nitric and hydrochloric acids, able to dissolve gold and platinum, which are not attacked by the unmixed acids. [L., = "royal water"]

aq·ua·relle (ăkwarĕl', ahkwa-) *n.* (Painting in) transparent watercolor.

a·quar·i·um (akwār'eum) *n.* (pl. **a·quar·i·ums, a·quar·i·a** pr. akwār'ea). Artificial pond or tank for keeping live aquatic plants, fishes, or animals; park, building, or room, etc. containing such tanks.

A·quar·i·us (akwār'eus). The Water Carrier, a constellation; 11th sign (♒) of the zodiac, which the sun enters about Jan. 21. **A·quar'·i·an** *adj.* & *n.*

a·quat·ic (akwăt'ĭk, akwŏt'-) *adj.* Living in or frequenting water; (of sports) conducted in or on water. ~ *n.* Aquatic plant or animal; (pl.) aquatic sports.

aq·ua·vit (ah'kwavēt, ăk'wa-) *n.* Colorless or yellowish alcoholic liquor distilled from potatoes or other starch-containing plant; schnapps.

aq·ua (ăk'wa, ah'kwa) **vi·tae** (vī'tē). (obs.) Brandy or other alcoholic spirit; (alchemy) alcohol. [L., = "water of life"]

aq·ue·duct (ăk'wĭdŭkt) *n.* Artificial channel, esp. elevated structure of masonry across valley etc. for conveyance of water.

a·que·ous (ā'kwēus, ăk'wē-) *adj.* Of water, watery; (geol.) produced by the action of water.

aq·ui·cul·ture (ăk'wĭkŭlcher) *n.* Cultivation of plants or breeding of animals in water; hydroponics.

aq·ui·le·gia (ăkwĭlē'ja) *n.* Plant of genus *A* ~; columbine.

aq·ui·line (ăk'wĭlīn, -lĭn) *adj.* Of an eagle; eagle-like; curved like eagle's beak.

A·qui·nas (akwī'nas), **St. Thomas** (c1225–74). Italian theologian and philosopher, a Dominican friar, whose writings, notably his *Summa Totius Theologiae*, represent the culmination of scholastic philosophy.

AR *abbrev.* Arkansas.

Ar *symbol.* Argon.

Ar·ab (ăr'ab) *n.* 1. One of an orig. Semitic people inhabiting Saudi Arabia and neighboring countries. 2. = ARABIAN horse. 3. **street a ~**, homeless child. 4. **~ League**, confederation of Arab states established 1945 and augmented later; headquarters in Cairo; members Egypt, Saudi Arabia, Syria, etc. **Arab** *adj.*

ar·a·besque (ărabĕsk') *adj.* Arabian; Moorish, esp. in design; fantastic. ~ *n.* 1. Decoration of fancifully twisted scrollwork, leaves, etc., orig. devised by Muslim artists owing to ban on images. 2. Musical composition suggestive of this decoration. 3. (ballet) Pose in which dancer stands on one foot with one arm extended in front and the other arm and leg extended behind.

The Romans were the best if not the earliest builders of **aqueducts.** *Water from mountain springs was channelled through a duct. Below: The Pont du Gard, which supplied water to Nimes, southern France.*

The **Aqua-Lung** *(scuba) has been widely used since the 1939–45 war where it was developed by naval frogmen to facilitate underwater demolition work. Scuba diving has since become a popular sport.*

A·ra·bi·a (arā'bēa). Peninsula of SW. Asia, largely desert, lying between the Red Sea and the Persian Gulf and bounded on the north by Jordan and Iraq. See SAUDI ~. **A·ra·bi·an** (arā'bēan) adj. Of Arabia or the Arabs; ~ **camel** = DROMEDARY; ~ **Desert**, Egyptian desert area between the Nile and the Red Sea; ~ **horse**, orig. bred in Arabia, noted for its graceful build and speed; ~ **Nights'** (**Entertainments**), also called the *Thousand and One Nights*, a collection of Arabian fairy stories and fantastic romances linked together by a framework of Persian origin; the tales themselves were probably collected in Egypt during the 14th–16th centuries; ~ **Sea**, NW. part of Indian Ocean, between Arabia and India. **Arabian** n. Arab. **Ar·a·bic** (ăr'abĭk) adj. Arabian; **gum a~**, gum exuded from various kinds of acacia and used in the manufacture of adhesives, confectionery, and in textile printing, pharmacy, etc.; ~ **numerals**, those (1, 2, 3, etc.) now in common use in all western countries, most of which were first used in India and were introduced into the west by the Arabs. **Arabic** n. Semitic language, orig. that of the Arabs, but now spoken in a large part of N. Africa, Syria, and neighboring countries. **Ar·ab·ist** (ăr'abĭst) n. Student of Arabic or of Arab civilization etc. **ar·a·ble** (ăr'abel) adj. & n. (Land) suitable for plowing. **Ar·a·by** (ăr'abē). (poet.) Arabia. **a·ra·ceous** (arā'shus) adj. Of the Araceae or arum family of plants.

Left: Arabian Hall in Lord Leighton's house, London, U.K.: an example of **arabesque** *decoration. A successful 19th-century painter, Leighton toured the East in 1873 to collect objects for his house. Right: Map of* **Arabia,** *linked*

A·rach·ne (arăk'nē). (Gk. legend) Skillful weaver who challenged Athena to a contest; Athena tore the work up and when Arachne hanged herself changed her into a spider. **a·rach·nid** (arăk'nĭd) n. (zool.) Member of the Arachnida, a class of wingless arthropods including spiders, scorpions, mites, king crabs, and others, and distinguished from insects esp. by having eight or more legs and no antennae. **a·rach·noid** (arăk'noid) adj. 1. Of the arachnids. 2. (anat.) Of the three membranes surrounding the brain and supporting the blood-vessels. ~ n. Arachnoid membrane. **Ar·a·gon** (ăr'agŏn). Region of Spain, bounded on N. by the Pyrenees and on E. by Catalonia and Valencia. **Ar·al** (ăr'al) **Sea**. Inland sea of U.S.S.R., E. of Caspian Sea. **Ar·am** (ăr'am, ār'-). Biblical name of Syria. **Ar·a·mae·an** (ăramē'an) adj. & n. **Ar·a·ma·ic** (ăramā'ĭk) adj. & n. (Of) the NW. Semitic language, closely related to Hebrew, spoken in SW. Asia in the later Babylonian Empire and until c7th c. A.D. **Ar·an** (ăr'an) **Islands**. Group of three islands off W. coast of Ireland, lying across mouth of Galway Bay. **Ar'an** adj. **A·rap·a·ho** (arăp'ahō) n. (pl. **-hos**, collect. **-ho**). (Member,

to Africa by the Sinai Peninsula. The length of this vast region, from N.E. to S.W., is 1,800 miles; its maximum width from the Yemen to Oman 1,300 miles. Total area is about 1 million square miles.

language) of a tribe of N. Amer. Indians of Algonquian speech group, formerly living in Nebraska and Kansas, now in Wyoming and Oklahoma. **Ar·a·rat** (ăr'arăt). Either of two peaks of the Armenian plateau, in which region Noah's ark is said (Gen. 8) to have rested after the Flood (**Great** ~, 5,165 m, 16,945 ft.). **ar·bi·ter** (ār'bĭter) n. Judge; one appointed to settle dispute; one with entire control *of*. **ar·bi·trage** (ār'bĭtrahzh) n. Buying of stocks, etc., for immediate sale in other markets at higher prices. **ar'bi·trag·er** n. **ar·bi·trar·y** (ār'bĭtrĕrē) adj. Derived from mere opinion, capricious; despotic; (law) discretionary. **ar·bi·trar·i·ly** (ār'bĭtrĕrile, ārbĭtrār'-) adv. **ar·bi·trate** (ār'bĭtrāt) v. (**-trat·ed, -trat·ing**). Decide by arbitration. **ar·bi·tra·tion** (ārbĭtrā'shon) n. Settlement of dispute by an arbiter. **ar·bi·tra·tor** (ār'bĭtrāter) n. One chosen to settle dispute. **ar·bor** (ār'ber) n. Shady retreat with sides and roof of trees or climbing plants; bower; **A ~ Day**, day annually appointed in many states for public tree-planting. **ar·bo·ra·ceous** (ārberā'shus) adj. Tree-like; wooded. **ar·bo·re·al** (ārbōr'ēal, -bōr'-) adj. Of, living in, trees.

ar·bo·re·ous (ārbōr′ē*u*s, -bōr′-) *adj.* Wooded; arboreal; arborescent.

ar·bo·res·cent (ārberĕs′ent) *adj.* Treelike; branching. **ar·bo·res′cence** *n.*

ar·bo·re·tum (ārberē′t*u*m) *n.* (pl. **-tums, -ta** pr. -t*a*). Tree garden.

ar·bor·i·cul·ture (ār′ber*i*kŭl·cher) *n.* Cultivation of trees and shrubs. **ar·bor·i·cul·tu·ral** (ārber*i*kŭl′cher*a*l) *adj.* **ar·bor·i·cul′tur·ist** *n.*

ar·bor·vi·tae (ārbervī′tē) *n.* Coniferous evergreen shrub of genus *Thuja.*

ar·bu·tus (ārbū′t*u*s) *n.* (pl. **-tus·es**). Evergreen plant of genus *A* ~ of the heather family with red berries.

arc (ārk) *n.* 1. Part of circumference of circle or other curve. 2. (elect.) Intense electrical discharge in gas or vapor, a luminous bridge of conducting gas formed between two separate electrical poles; ~ **lamp**, ~ **light**, lamp using this; ~ **welding**: see WELD[2].

ar·cade (ārkād′) *n.* 1. Passage arched over; any covered walk, esp. one with shops etc. at side(s). 2. (archit.) Series of arches supported by columns.

Ar·ca·di·a (ārkā′dē*a*). Mountainous district in the Peloponnese, taken as an ideal region of rustic contentment (in this sense also **Ar·ca·dy** pr. ār′kadē). **Ar·ca′di·an** *adj.* & *n.* (Native, inhabitant) of Arcadia; ideal(ly) rustic.

ar·cane (ārkān′) *adj.* Mysterious, secret.

ar·ca·num (ārkā′n*u*m) *n.* (usu. in pl. **-na** pr. -n*a*). Mystery, secret.

arch[1] (ārch) *n.* Structure, usu. curved, consisting of wedge-shaped pieces so arranged as to support one another by mutual pressure, and used to carry weight of roof, wall, etc., or as ornament; any curved structure resembling this in form and function; curve; vault; (anat.) curve on inner side of foot; **arch′way** *n.,* arched passage or entrance. **arch** *v.* Furnish with, form into, form, an arch; span.

arch[2] (ārch) *adj.* Making hints or allusions in a jocose affected manner. **arch′ly** *adv.* **arch′ness** *n.*

arch. *abbrev.* Archaic; architect; architecture.

arch- *comb. form.* Chief; superior; leading; extreme; first.

ar·chae·ol·o·gy (ārkēŏl′ojē) *n.* Study of ancient peoples and cultures through their material remains. **ar·chae·o·log·i·cal** (ārkē-

Diagrams show various types of **arches** *and their construction. Key: 1. Voussoirs. 2. Keystone. 3. Extrados. 4. Intrados. 5. Springer. 6. Impost. 7. Orders. 8. Tympanum. 9. Hoodmold, dripstone or label. 10. Spandrel. The keystone is crucial, 'locking' the structure.*

The U.S. **archer**, John Williams, in action at the 1972 Olympics in Munich. The use of the bow in competitive sport may be traced back to the formation of Britain's Royal Company of Archers in 1676.

The 11th-century cliff-top citadel and cathedral, accessible by a stairway of 408 steps, at Dinant, Belgium. It lies in the **Ardennes** district which was the scene of fierce fighting in both the 1914–18 and 1939–45 wars.

Archimedes *was an early master of mechanics and hydrostatics. He invented the pulley and probably the hydrometer. His Archimedean screw (shown) is a method of raising water by turning a tube with a screw inside it.*

olŏj´ĭkal) *adj.* **ar·chae·o·log´i·cal·ly** *adv.* **ar·chae·ol´o·gist** *n.*

ar·chae·op·ter·yx (ärkēŏp´te-rĭks) *n.* Extinct primitive bird of the Jurassic period, transitional between reptile and bird.

ar·cha·ic (ärkā´ĭk) *adj.* Primitive, antiquated; no longer in common use. **ar·cha´i·cal·ly** *adv.*

ar·cha·ism (är´kēĭzem, -kā-) *n.* Obsolete word or phrase; retention or imitation of the old or obsolete (esp. in language and art).

arch·an·gel (ärk´ānjel) *n.* Angel of highest rank (see ANGEL).

arch·bish·op (ärchbĭsh´op) *n.* Chief bishop. **arch·bish´op·ric** *n.*

arch·dea·con (ärchdē´kon) *n.* Ecclesiastical dignitary next below bishop.

arch·di·o·cese (ärchdī´osĭs, -sēz) *n.* Archbishop's diocese.

arch·duke (ärch´dook´, -dūk´) *n.* Prince of former imperial house of Austria. **arch´du´cal** *adj.* **arch·duch·ess** (ärch´dŭch´ĭs) *n.*

ar·che·go·ni·um (ärkegō´nēum) *n.* (pl. **-ni·a** pr. -nēa). Female organ in cryptogams, corresponding to pistil in flowering plants.

arch·en·e·my (ärch´ĕn´emē) *n.* (pl. **-mies**). Chief enemy; **the ~**, Satan.

arch·er (är´cher) *n.* One who shoots with bow and arrows. **arch´er·y** *n.*

ar·che·type (är´kĭtīp) *n.* Original model, prototype.

arch·fiend (ärch´fēnd´) *n.* Satan.

ar·chi·e·pis·co·pal (ärkēĭpĭs´ko-pal) *adj.* Of an archbishop.

Ar·chi·me·des (ärkimē´dēz) (*c*287–212 B.C.). Greek mathematician of Syracuse; said to have made many mechanical inventions, including the **~ screw** for raising water; **~ principle**, (phys.) principle that when a body is partly or completely immersed in a fluid the apparent loss of weight is equal to the weight of the fluid displaced. **Ar·chi·me·de·an** (ärkimē´dēan, -mĭdē´an) *adj.*

ar·chi·pel·a·go (ärkipĕl´agō) *n.* (pl. **-gos, -goes**). Sea with many islands; group of islands.

ar·chi·tect (är´kĭtĕkt) *n.* 1. Designer of buildings who prepares plans and superintends execution; **marine ~**, designer of ship. 2. (fig.) Designer.

ar·chi·tec·ton·ics (ärkĭtĕktŏn´-ĭks) *n.* 1. Science of architecture.

2. Structural design, as in a work of art. 3. Systematization of knowledge. **ar·chi·tec·ton´ic** *adj.*

ar·chi·tec·ture (är´kĭtĕkcher) *n.* Art or science of building; profession of designing buildings; thing built; style of building; construction. **ar·chi·tec´tur·al** *adj.* **ar·chi·tec´tur·al·ly** *adv.*

ar·chive (är´kīv) *n.* (usu. pl.). Public records; place in which these are kept. **ar·chi·vist** (är´kivĭst) *n.* Keeper of archives.

arc·tic (ärk´tĭk, är´tĭk) *adj.* Of the North Pole; northern; intensely cold; **A ~ Circle**, parallel of 66° 32´ N., north of which the sun does not rise at midwinter or set at midsummer; **~ fox**, a fox (*Alopex lagopus*) of northern regions, white in winter and blue-gray or brown in summer; **A ~ Ocean**, ocean N. of the Arctic Circle. **Arc´tic** *n.* Regions (both land and sea) around the North Pole; **arctic**, (usu. pl.) thick waterproof overshoe; galosh. [Gk. *arktos* bear, Ursa Major]

Ar·dennes (ärdĕn´). Forest district including parts of Belgium, Luxemburg, and N. France, area of bitter fighting in World Wars I and II.

ar·dent (är´dent) *adj.* Eager, zealous, fervent; having strong feelings esp. of desire or devotion. **ar´dent·ly** *adv.*

ar·dor, Brit. **ar·dour** (är´der) *ns.*

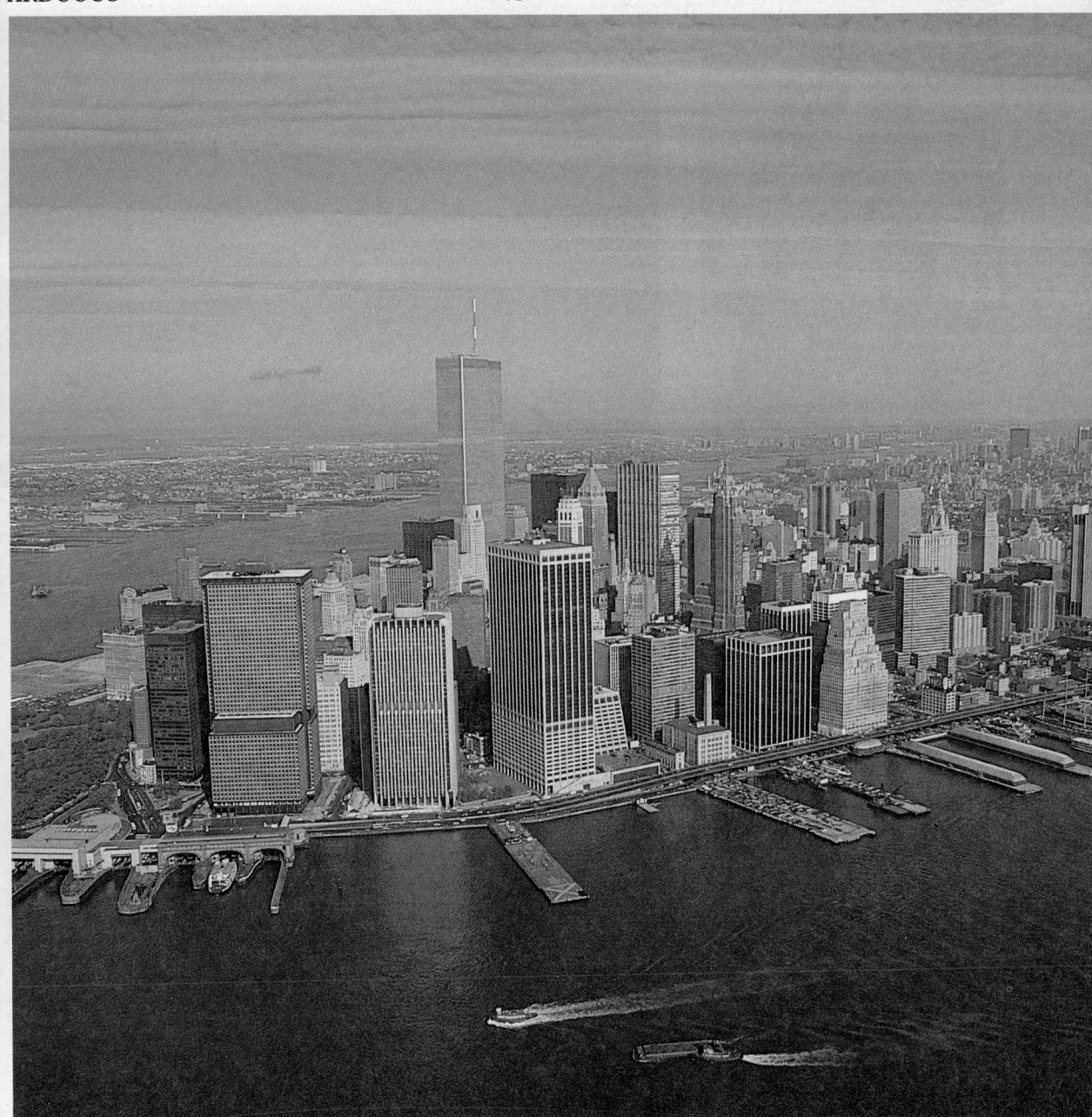

Zeal; ardent feelings.

ar·du·ous (är′jōōus) *adj.* Hard, laborious; strenuous. **ar′du·ous·ly** *adv.* **ar′du·ous·ness** *n.*

are[1] (är, ãr) *n.* Unit of square measure, = 100 square meters.

are[2] (är) *v.* Second pers. sing. and first, second, third pers. pl., pres. ind. of BE.

ar·e·a (är′ēa) *n.* Extent of space or surface; region; space intended for specific use, as *dining, parking,* ~; scope, range; field of study or competence; measure of a plane or of the surface of a solid; ~ **code**, 3-digit number identifying telephone area in U.S. and Canada, used in long-distance calls; **ar′e·a·way** *n.*, sunk court in front of house basement.

ar·e·ca (är′eka, arē′-) *n.* Tropical

*The Manhattan skyline, New York. The distinctive **architecture** of Manhattan reflects its reputation as one of the principal financial, commercial and industrial centers of the world. Its development began in 1626.*

Asiatic palm of genus *A* ~, bearing pungent astringent fruit.

A·re·ci·bo (ärĭsē′bō). Seaport in N. Puerto Rico.

a·re·na (arē′na) *n.* Central part of amphitheater, in which contests etc. took place; central part of stadium; scene of conflict or action.

aren't (ärnt, är′ent) *contr.* Are not.

a·re·o·la (arē′ola) *n.* (pl. **-lae** pr. -lē, **-las**). Interstice; small pigmented area, e.g. that surrounding nipple or pupil.

Ar·e·op·a·gus (ărēŏp′agus). Hill at Athens where (in antiquity) highest judicial court met; hence, this court. **Ar·e·op·a·gite** (ărēŏp′ajīt, -gīt) *n.* Member of court of Areopagus. [Gk. *Areios pagus* hill of Ares]

A·re·qui·pa (ärekē′pah). City in S. Peru founded by Pizarro on the site of an Incan town; now a major commercial center.

Ar·es (är′ēz). (Gk. myth.) God of war, son of Zeus and Hera; identified with the Roman MARS.

Ar·e·thu·sa (ărethōō′za). (Gk. legend) Water nymph who fled from Greece to Ortygia in Sicily, pursued by the river god Alpheus.

ar·gent (är′jent) *n.* & *adj.* Silver (color, esp. in heraldry).

The **Argentine** is a vast land of great contrasts—from the high Andes in the west to the lowland pampas in the center. Top left: Peon of the Salta Province in northern Argentine. Top right:

The Igassu Falls, Miseones Province, which marks the border between Argentine and Brazil. Above left: Map of the Argentine showing its narrow shape, over 2,000 miles long, and the

national flag. Above right: These two ice cream vendors in **Argentina** are typical of the young street workers who are forced into employment from a very early age due to family poverty.

Ar·gen·ti·na (ārjentē´na). Republic occupying most of S. part of S. America E. of the Andes; settled by Spaniards (1526 onward); remained a Spanish colony until 1816; capital, Buenos Aires. **Ar·gen·tine** (ār´jentēn, -tīn), **Ar·gen·tin·e·an** (ārjentĭn´ēan) adjs. & ns. [L. argentum silver, because the Rio de la Plata district exported it]

ar·gen·tine (ār´jentīn; -tēn) adj. Of silver; silvery.

Ar·go (ār´go) n.: see ARGONAUTS.

ar·gon (ārgŏn) n. (chem.) Inert gaseous element, present to extent of about 1% in the air, used in gas-filled electric light bulbs etc.; symbol Ar, at. no. 18, at. wt. 39.948.

Ar·go·nauts (ār´gonawts) n. pl. (Gk. legend) Heroes who accompanied Jason on board the ship Argo on the quest for the Golden Fleece.

Ar·gonne (ār´gŏn; Fr. ărgawn´) **Forest.** Wooded area in NE.

France; site of heavy fighting during World Wars I and II.

Ar·gos (ār´gŏs). Ancient Greek town of the E. Peloponnese.

ar·go·sy (ār´gosē) n. (pl. **-sies**). (hist., poet.) Large vessel (orig. of Ragusa or Venice) carrying rich merchandise. [prob. from It. Ragusea (nave) (ship) of Ragusa]

ar·got (ār´gō, -got) n. Jargon, slang, of a class or group, esp. of criminals.

ar·gue (ār´gū) v. (**-gued, -gu·ing**). Maintain by reasoning; reason; prove, indicate; raise objections, dispute. **ar´gu·a·ble** adj.

ar·gu·ment (ār´gyument) n. Reason advanced; verbal dispute, debate; summary of subject matter of book etc. **ar·gu·men·ta·tion** (ārgyumĕntā´shon) n. Methodical reasoning; debate.

ar·gu·men·ta·tive (ārgyumĕn´-tatĭv) adj. Logical; fond of arguing.

ar·gu·men·ta·tive·ly adv. **ar·gu·men´ta·tive·ness** n.

Ar·gus (ar´gus). 1. (Gk. myth.) Fabulous person with 100 eyes, slain by Hermes; after his death Hera transferred his eyes to the tail of the peacock. 2. (Gk. legend) Dog of Ulysses, who recognized his master on his return from Troy after an absence of 20 years.

ar·gyle (ār´gīl) n. Diamond-shaped varicolored knit pattern, esp. for socks; such a sock.

a·ri·a (ār´ēa) n. Long accompanied song for one voice in opera and oratorio; songlike movement in instrumental composition. [It.]

Ar·i·ad·ne (ărēăd´nē, ărēahd´-nĕ). (Gk. myth.) Daughter of Minos, king of Crete; gave Theseus the thread with which to find his way out of the labyrinth of the Minotaur; then became his wife, but he deserted her, and she

*Portrait of **Aristotle** (left) in 'The School of Athens', a painting by Raphael. The philosopher believed in three types of soul: 'rational' (man), 'sensitive' (animals), 'nutritive' (plants).*

*Cattle around a waterhole in **Arizona's** Painted Desert. The State is on the Mexican border. Its most spectacular feature is the Grand Canyon formed by the Colorado River.*

married Dionysus.

ar·id (ăr´ĭd) *adj.* Dry, parched; (geog., of climate or region) having insufficient water to support vegetation. **a·rid·i·ty** (arĭd´ĭtē) *n.*

Ar·i·el (ār´ēel). In Shakespeare's *The Tempest*, a spirit released by the magician Prospero from imprisonment by a witch, Sycorax.

Ar·ies (ār´ēz). The Ram, a constellation; 1st sign (♈) of the zodiac, which the sun enters at the vernal equinox.

a·right (arīt´) *adv.* Rightly.

Ar·i·ma·the·a (ărĭmathē´a): see JOSEPH[1], def. 3.

A·ri·on (arī´on) (7th c. B.C.). Greek poet and musician of Lesbos; said to have perfected the dithyramb; acc. to legend, sailors on a ship resolved to murder him, but he begged first to play a tune, did so, and leapt overboard; dolphins were attracted by the music, and one bore

him on its back to land.

A·ri·os·to (ārēŏs´tō), **Lodovico** (1474–1533). Italian poet, author of the romantic epic *Orlando Furioso*.

a·rise (arīz´) *v.i.* (**a·rose** pr. arōz´, **a·ris·en** pr. arĭz´en, **a·ris·ing**). Appear, spring up, occur, get up, rise.

Ar·is·tar·chus[1] (ărĭstär´kus) **of Samos** (3rd c. B.C.). Astronomer and mathematician; maintained that the Earth revolved around the sun.

Ar·is·tar·chus[2] (ărĭstär´kus) **of Samothrace** (c217–c145 B.C.). Librarian at Alexandria; edited the Greek classics.

Ar·is·ti·des (ărĭstī´dēz) (d. c466 B.C.). Athenian general and statesman, called "the Just"; commanded his tribe at the battle of Marathon.

Ar·is·tip·pus (ărĭstĭp´us). Name of two Greek philosophers; the elder (late 5th c. B.C.), a native of Cyrene and friend of Socrates, is freq. called the founder of the Cyrenaic school, prob. by confusion with the younger, his grandson (fl. c400–365), who taught that immediate pleasure is the only end of action.

ar·is·toc·ra·cy (ărĭstŏk´rasē) *n.* (pl. **-cies**). The nobility; government by nobles; best representatives (of intellect etc.); any class deemed superior.

a·ris·to·crat (arĭs´tokrăt, ăr´ĭs-) *n.* Member of aristocracy. **a·ris·to·crat·ic** (arĭstokrăt´ĭk) *adj.* Belonging to the aristocracy; having distinguished bearing and manners. **a·ris·to·crat´i·cal·ly** *adv.*

Ar·is·toph·a·nes (ărĭstŏf´anēz) (c445–c385 B.C.). Athenian comic dramatist; author of comedies (the

Birds, Frogs, Wasps, etc.) caricaturing his contemporaries and their attitude to public affairs.

Ar·is·tot·le (ăr´ĭstŏtel) (384–322 B.C.). Greek philosopher; pupil of Plato at Athens; tutor of Alexander the Great; conducted the PERIPATETIC school; wrote the *Ethics, Politics*, and *Poetics*, and works of zoology, physics, metaphysics, deductive logic, and rhetoric. **Ar·is·to·te·lian** (ărĭstotēl´yan) *adj.* & *n.*

arith. *abbrev.* Arithmetic.

a·rith·me·tic (arĭth´metĭk) *n.* Science of numbers; computation. ∼ (ărĭthmĕt´ĭk), **ar·ith·met·i·cal** (ărĭthmĕt´ĭkal) *adjs.* **arithmetic progression**, (series of numbers showing) increase or decrease by a constant quantity, as 2, 5, 8, 11, etc., or 26, 21, 16, 11, etc. **ar·ith·met´i·cal·ly** *adv.* **a·rith·me·ti·cian** (arĭthmetĭsh´an, ărĭth-) *n.*

Ar·i·us (ār´ēus, arī´us) (c250–c336). Priest of Alexandria; denied the true Divinity of Christ. **Ar·i·an** *adj.* & *n.* (Supporter) of Arius or his heresy. **Ar·i·an·ism** *n.*

Ariz. *abbrev.* Arizona.

Ar·i·zo·na (ărĭzō´na). State in southwestern U.S., admitted to the Union in 1912; capital, Phoenix.

ark (ärk) *n.* 1. Chest, box; **A ∼ of the Covenant**, wooden coffer containing tables of Jewish law, the most sacred religious symbol of early Israel (also ∼ **of the Law**), chest or cupboard in synagogue containing scrolls of the Law. 2. Covered floating vessel in which NOAH was saved at the time of the Flood.

Ark. *abbrev.* Arkansas.

Ar·kan·sas (är´kansaw). State in south-central U.S., admitted to the

Arlington National Cemetery. Monument to the cutter Tampa which sank in 1918. Some of the dead of each war fought by the U.S.A. are buried here at the nation's foremost military cemetery.

Union in 1836; capital, Little Rock. ~ **River**, river rising in the Rocky Mountains of central Colorado and flowing 1,460 miles (2,350 km) SE. to the Mississippi River.

Ark·wright (ārk′rīt), **Sir Richard** (1732–92). English engineer, inventor of the spinning jenny.

Ar·ling·ton (ār′lĭngtǒn). Suburban area in Virginia on the Potomac River, opposite Washington, D.C.; site of Arlington National Cemetery; ~ **National Cemetery**, U.S. military cemetery; former estate of Gen. Robert E. Lee; site of Tomb of the Unknown Soldier.

arm[1] (ārm) n. Upper limb of human body; sleeve; branch; armlike thing; support for arm on chair or sofa; (fig.) power, authority; **with open ~s**, cordially; **arm′-chair**, chair with supports for arms; (fig.) applied to persons who theorize without actively participating; **arm′hole**, (in garment) hole through which arm is put; **arm′pit**, hollow under arm at shoulder; **arm′rest**, support for arm on chair, car door, etc. **arm′-ful** n. (pl. **-fuls**). **arm′less** adj.

arm[2] (ārm) n. 1. Particular kind of weapon; (pl.) weapons, esp. firearms; branch of the military service; **up in ~s**, actively rebelling (against, lit. or fig.; about, fig.). 2. (pl.) Heraldic devices; **coat of ~s**: see COAT. **arm** v. Furnish with arms; take up arms; provide, furnish with; **armed forces, services**, military forces of a nation.

ar·ma·da (ārmah′dȧ). 1. (also **Spanish ~**) Fleet sent by Philip II of Spain against England in 1588; it was defeated in the English Channel and dispersed by the English fleet under Lord Howard of Effingham and such captains as Drake, Frobisher, and Hawkins. 2. Fleet of warships, planes, etc.

ar·ma·dil·lo (ārmadĭl′ō) n. (pl. **-los**). Burrowing, usu. nocturnal, mammal, protected by bony plates resembling armor. [Span. dim. of armado armed creature]

Ar·ma·ged·don (ārmageď′ŏn). (Scene of) supreme or large-scale conflict between nations. (Rev. 16).

ar·ma·ment (är′mament) n. Force equipped for war; military weapons and munitions; process of equipping for war; (pl.) all the forces and weapons of a nation.

ar·ma·ture (är′mȧcher) n. 1. Armor, defensive covering of animals or plants. 2. Piece of soft iron placed in contact with poles of

Fairy

Peludo (Hairy)

Nine Banded

Giant

The plates of the **armadillo** are articulated, allowing it to roll itself into a ball when danger threatens. It feeds on plants and insects, tearing open anthills with its claws and catching the insects with its long, sticky tongue. In Mexico armadillos are hunted for food.

a magnet to preserve the intensity of magnetization or to support a load; core of laminated iron wound with coils of insulated copper wire, that part of a dynamo which rotates in the magnetic field.

Ar·me·ni·a (ārmē′nēȧ, -mĕn′-yȧ). Constituent republic (properly *Armenian Soviet Socialist Republic*) of U.S.S.R., lying S. of the Caucasus, part of the former kingdom of Armenia, most of which was under Turkish rule from the 16th c.; capital, Erivan.

Ar·me·ni·an (ārmē′nēan, -mĕn′yan) adj. Of Armenia or its people or language. ~ *n.* Armenian person or language.

ar·mi·stice (ār´mĭstĭs) *n.* Cessation of hostilities by agreement between belligerents; short truce; **A ~ Day**, Nov 11, anniversary of the armistice that ended hostilities in World War I; since 1954 celebrated as VETERANS' DAY. [L. *arma* arms + *-stitium* stopping]

arm·let (ārm´lĭt) *n.* Band worn around arm.

ar·moire (armwār´) *n.* Ornate wardrobe cabinet.

ar·mor (ār´mer) *n.* 1. (hist.) Defensive covering for body worn in fighting. 2. (also ~ **plate**) Steel plates etc. protecting ship, tank, car, etc., from projectiles etc. (so ~ **plated**); tanks and other fighting vehicles equipped with such armor. ~ *v.t.* Furnish with such protective covering; **armored car, train,** one supplied with protective armor; **armored column, division,** etc., one equipped with armored cars, tanks, etc.

ar·mor·er (ār´merer) *n.* Maker of arms or armor; one in charge of small arms.

ar·mo·ri·al (ārmōr´ēal, môr´-) *adj.* Of heraldic arms.

ar·mor·y (ār´merē) *n.* (pl. **-mor·ies**). Place where arms are kept; arsenal; armorer's workshop.

Arm·strong[1] (ārm´strawng), **(Daniel) Louis "Satchmo"** (1900–71). American jazz musician and trumpet player.

Arm·strong[2] (ārm´strawng), **Edwin Howard** (1890–1954).

Israeli Centurion tanks form up during the six-day Arab–Israeli war, 1967. Mechanized **armor** *was introduced in 1898: a four-wheeled motor cycle with armored shield and machine-gun.*

American electrical engineer; developed FM radio.

Arm·strong[3] (ārm´strawng), **Neil Alden** (1930–). U.S. astronaut; first man to walk on moon, 1969.

ar·my (ār´mē) *n.* (pl. **-mies**). Organized force armed for fighting on land; the military profession; large number; organized body for a cause; (U.S. mil.) a military unit consisting of two or more army corps, a headquarters, and auxiliary

forces; ~ **ant,** any of the tropical Amer. ants that move in vast numbers.

ar·ni·ca (ār´nĭka) *n.* Composite plant of genus *A ~*, largely American, having yellow flowers; tincture, prepared from root and flowers of this and used for bruises, sprains, etc.

Ar·no (ār´nō). River of N. Italy, flowing through Florence and Pisa.

Ar·nold[1] (ār´nold), **Benedict** (1741–1801). American army officer in the Revolutionary War; while commander of West Point turned traitor and arranged its surrender to British; plot discovered; escaped to England where he later died.

Left: **Armor** *worn by Earl of Leicester, 1565 (Tower of London). 1. Armor of Greek hoplite (foot-soldier), 5th century B.C. 2. Suit of mail, 12th century. 3. Field armor, c. 1470. 4. Coat of plates, c. 1370. 5. Helm (helmet) for the tilt (joust), 15th century. 6. Sallet and beaver (c. 1480), a light head-piece with lower part curving outwards behind. Cloth uniforms took the place of steel armor towards the end of the 17th century.*

Crest
Helmet
Cuirass
Sword
Shield
Spear
Greave

1

2

3

4

5

6

Sage   Thyme   Peppermint   Mexican Orange Blue-gum eucalyptus Parsley

Ar·nold[2] (ār'nold), **Henry Hurley "Hap"** (1886–1950). American army general; chief of U.S. air forces during World War II.

Ar·nold[3] (ār'nold), **Matthew** (1822–88). English poet, critic, and educator.

a·ro·ma (arō'ma) n. Fragrance; subtle pervasive quality.

ar·o·mat·ic (ăromăt'ĭk) adj. 1. Fragrant, spicy. 2. (chem.) Of the group of organic compounds in which the carbon atoms are arranged in 6-membered rings (as in benzene).

a·rose (arōz'): see ARISE.

a·round (arownd') adv. On every side; round; nearby; here and there. ~ prep. All round; about; enveloping; near; at the edge of; approximately; ~ **the clock** = ROUND-THE-CLOCK (see ROUND[3]).

a·rouse (arowz') v.t. (**a·roused, a·rous·ing**). Awaken; stir up into activity, provoke, excite.

Arp (ārp), **Jean** (1887–1966). Original name Hans Arp. French abstract sculptor and artist; a founder of Dadaism.

ar·peg·gi·o (ārpĕj'ēō, -pĕj'ō) n. (pl. **-gi·os**). Chord of which notes are not played simultaneously but "harpwise," i.e. in succession. [It. arpa harp]

ar·que·bus (ār'kwebus) n. (pl. **-bus·es**) = HARQUEBUS.

arr. abbrev. Arrives, arriving, etc.

ar·rack (ăr'ak, arăk') n. Alcoholic spirit manufactured in the East, esp. from coconut palm or rice. [Arab. 'arak sweat, alcoholic spirit made from grapes or dates]

ar·raign (arān') v.t. Indict, accuse; (law) call before a court to answer an indictment. **ar·raign'·ment** n.

ar·range (arānj') v. (**-ranged, -rang·ing**). Put in order; settle; settle beforehand order etc. of; form plans, take steps; (mus.) adapt (a composition) for different medium, instrumental or vocal. **ar·range'·ment** n.

ar·rant (ăr'ant) adj. Downright, notorious.

Aromatic plants (from left): Sage, a hardy evergreen with leaves used as a culinary herb; thyme, the shoots of which give flavoring; peppermint, a herb yielding an oil which flavors confectionery and toothpaste; Mexican orange, which bears capsular fruit; blue-gum eucalyptus; parsley.

Ar·ras (arahs', ăr'as). Town in NE. France famous in 13th–16th centuries for tapestry weaving.

ar·ras (ăr'as) n. Rich tapestry; hangings of this around walls of room. [f. ARRAS]

ar·ray (arā') v.t. Dress, esp. with display; marshal (forces). ~ n. Dress; imposing series; martial order; orderly arrangement; (radio) assembly of antennas.

ar·rear (arēr') n. (usu. pl.) Outstanding debts; what remains undone; **in ~s**, behindhand, esp. in payment.

ar·rest (arĕst') v.t. Stop or slow; seize (person) esp. by legal authority; catch (attention); catch attention of. ~ n. Legal apprehension; stoppage; seizure. **ar·rest'a·ble** adj. (esp.) ~ **offense**, (law) offense for which person can be arrested

*The common **arrowhead** (Sagittaria sagittifolia) is a waterplant with arrow-shaped leaves that grows 3 or 4 ft. high. The giant arrowhead of South America grows to 6 ft.*

without a warrant.

ar·rive (arīv') v.i. (**-rived, -riv·ing**). Come to destination or end of journey; be brought; come; establish one's reputation or position. **ar·ri'val** n.

ar·ri·ve·der·ci (ahrēvĕdĕr'chē) int. Goodby, till we meet again. [It.]

ar·ro·gant (ăr'ogant) adj. Overbearing, presumptuous. **ar'ro·gant·ly** adv. **ar'ro·gance** n.

ar·ro·gate (ăr'ogāt) v.t.(**-gat·ed, -gat·ing**). Claim unduly. **ar·ro·ga·tion** (ărogāshon) n.

ar·row (ăr'ō) n. Missile shot from bow, usu. consisting of straight slender shaft with sharp point or head of stone or metal, and feathers fastened to the butt; figure or symbol like an arrow or arrowhead, often used as indication of direction etc.; **ar'rowhead**, pointed tip of an arrow; water plant (Sagittaria sagittifolia) with arrow-shaped leaves, growing in ponds and slow streams; **ar'rowroot**, tropical plant Maranta arundinacea; starch obtained from its rhizomes, used as food esp. for invalids.

ar·roy·o (aroi'ō) n. (pl. **-os**). Deep gully cut by a (usu. dry) stream; brook, stream. [Sp.]

ar·se·nal (ār'senal) n. Government establishment where weapons and ammunition are made or stored; supply of weapons. [Arab. dār aṣ-ṣinā'a factory, place where fighting ships are equipped]

ar·se·nic (ār'senĭk, ārs'nĭk) n. (chem.) Brittle steel-gray semimetallic element, symbol As, at. no. 33, at. wt. 74.9216; (pop.) white mineral substance (~ **trioxide**), a violent poison used as an insecticide and in the manufacture of paint, glass, etc. **ar·sen·ic** (ārsĕn'ĭk) adj. Of arsenic; (chem.) applied to compounds in which arsenic is pentavalent. **ar·sen'i·cal** adj. [Gk. arsenikon, f. Arab. az-zirnīk, orpiment, arsenic]

ar·son (ār'son) n. Willful setting on fire of houses or other property. **ar·son·ist** (ār'sonĭst) n. One who commits arson.

art[1] (ārt) n. Skill, esp. applied to

design, representation, or imaginative creation; human skill as opp. to nature; things embodying this, as paintings, statues, etc.; cunning, stratagem; subject in which skill may be exercised; (pl.) certain courses of study (**liberal** ~**s**) in school or college, esp. languages, history, philosophy, as distinct from sciences; **bachelor, master of** ~ **s**, degree denoting a standard of attainment in these studies; one who has received such degree; **decorative** ~ **s**, those concerned with the design and decoration of objects in practical use, handicrafts; **fine** ~ **s**, (usu.) paintings, architecture, sculpture, music, and poetry; **A** ~ **Deco** (ár′děko̅; árt′-), decorative art style of 1920's and 1930's; ~ **form**, established form of composition (e.g., novel, sonata, sonnet); medium of artistic expression; **A** ~ **Nouveau**: see ART NOUVEAU.

art² (árt) v. (archaic) Second pers. sing. pres. ind. of verb BE.

Ar·te·mis (ár′těmǐs). (Gk. myth.) Goddess of chastity and of hunting; daughter of Leto; twin sister of Apollo, identified with Selene and DIANA.

ar·te·ri·al (ártēr′ēal) adj. Belonging to, of the nature of, an artery. ~ n. Highway around a city, also ~ **highway.**

ar·te·ri·ole (ártēr′ēol) n. Small artery.

ar·te·ri·o·scle·ro·sis (ártērēo̅-skler̄o̅′sǐs) n. Hardening and thick-

ening of the walls of arteries.

ar·te·ry (ár′terē) n. (pl. **-ries**). 1. Muscular-walled blood vessel conveying the blood impelled by the heart to the small vessels which supply the tissues. 2. Something serving as channel of supplies, e.g. main road.

ar·te·sian (ártē′zhan) adj. ~ **well**, perpendicular bore into a curved or slanting water-saturated stratum, penetrating it at a level lower than the source of the water, which rises spontaneously to the surface in a continuous flow. [f. Artois, Fr. province]

art·ful (árt′ful) adj. Cunning, crafty.

ar·thri·tis (árthrí′tǐs) n. Inflammation of joint. **ar·thrit·ic** (árthrǐt′ǐk) adj.

ar·thro·pod (ár′thropŏd) n. One of the Arthropoda, the largest animal phylum, comprising insects, arachnids, myriapods, crustaceans, and trilobites, and characterized by jointed limbs and a hard jointed external skeleton.

Ar·thur¹ (ár′ther). King of Britain; historically perh. a 5th- or 6th-c. chieftain or general; acc. to legend he was the son of Uther Pendragon and Igerne; became king of Britain at age 15; married

*This tropical tree millipede, 4 ins. long, belongs to the **arthropod** phylum, which comprises three-quarters of all known animal species — from mites to the giant land-crab.*

Guinevere; held court at Caerleon-on-Usk and established there a company of knights whose seats were at a round table so that none had precedence; was mortally wounded at Camelford in battle against his usurping nephew Modred; was then borne off in a magic boat to Avalon, from which he will one day return. **Ar·thu·ri·an** (árthoor′ēan) adj.

Ar·thur² (ár′ther), **Chester Alan** (1830–86). American politician and lawyer; 21st president of U.S., 1881–5.

ar·ti·choke (ár′tǐchōk) n. 1. Plant, *Cynara scolymus* (of which bottom of flower and bases of its scales are edible), allied to thistle. 2. **Jerusalem** ~, species of sunflower with edible tuberous roots. [It. *articiocco*, f. Arab. *alkaršūfa*; Jerusalem, corrupt, of It. *girasole* sunflower]

ar·ti·cle (ár′tǐkel) n. Separate portion of anything written; separate clause, piece of nonfiction writing forming part of magazine etc.; particular; particular thing, as an ~ **of clothing**; (gram.) either of the adjectives "a, an" (**indefinite** ~) and "the" (**definite** ~), or their equivalents in other languages.

ar·tic·u·late (ártǐk′yulǐt) adj. Having joints; distinctly jointed, distinguishable; able to express oneself well; (of speech) clearly defined. ~ (ártǐk′yulāt) v. (**-lat·ed, -lat·ing**). Connect by joints; divide into words, pronounce distinctly; speak distinctly; express clearly; relate coherently the various parts (of a complex work of art, philosophy, etc.). **ar·tic·u·la·to·ry** (ártǐk′-yulatōrē, -tōrē) adj.

ar·tic·u·la·tion (ártǐkyulā′shon) n. Articulate utterance, speech; jointing.

ar·ti·fact (ár′tǐfăkt) n. Object, as paleolithic flint, made by human workmanship.

ar·ti·fice (ár′tǐfǐs) n. Cunning; skill; clever stratagem. **ar·tif·i·cer** (ártǐf′ǐser) n. Craftsman; ingenious person.

ar·ti·fi·cial (ártǐfǐsh′al) adj. Produced by art; not natural, made in imitation, as ~ *hand*; affected; not real; ~ **insemination**, injection of semen into uterus by artifical means; ~ **language**, invented language, esp. one designed for international use; ~ **respiration**: see RESPIRATION. **ar·ti·fi′cial·ly** adv. **ar·ti·fi·ci·al·i·ty** (ártǐfǐshěăl′ǐtē) n.

ar·til·ler·y (ártǐl′erē) n. Large mounted firearms or missile

*Curved rock strata with **artesian well** bore penetrating to a level lower than the water source. Water rises to the surface through resultant pressure. Artesian wells have reached depths of several hundred feet. In Europe they date from the 12th century.*

▨	Impermeable rock
▨	Permeable rock
▨	Saturated permeable rock
▨	Impermeable rock

Rain

launchers; cannon; branch of army that uses these; **artil′leryman**, one belonging to the artillery, gunner. **ar·til·ler·ist** (ärtĭl′erĭst) *n.* Artilleryman.

ar·ti·san (är′tĭzan) *n.* Mechanic; handicraftsman.

art·ist (är′tĭst) *n.* One who practices one of the fine arts, esp. painting; one who makes his craft a fine art; artiste. **ar·tis·tic** (ärtĭs′tĭk) *adj.* **ar·tis·try** (är′tĭstrē) *n.*

ar·tiste (ärtēst′) *n.* Professional singer, dancer, etc.

art·less (ärt′lĭs) *adj.* Guileless, simple; lacking art, crude. **art′·less·ly** *adv.* **art′less·ness** *n.*

Art Nou·veau (är nōōvō′, ärt). Decorative style (*c*1880–*c*1910) using flowing curves and naturalistic motifs. [Fr., = "new art"]

art·y (är′tē) *adj.* (**art·i·er**, **art·i·est**). Having artistic pretensions.

A·ru·ba (aroo′ba). Island resort in the Netherlands Antilles, in the Caribbean; site of huge oil refineries.

ar·um (är′um) *n.* Plant of genus *A* ∼, having arrow-shaped leaves and an inflorescence on a spadix enclosed within a spathe.

-ary *suffix.* Forming adjectives (*arbitrary, contrary, military*) and nouns (*dictionary, granary*).

Ar·y·an (är′ēan, är′-) *adj.* & *n.* 1. (archaic) Indo-European; (esp.)

The decorative **arum** lily belongs to a genus of tuberous-rooted herbs. There are some 20 species in Europe and the Mediterranean region. The water arum is a related plant.

Indo-Iranian. 2. (loosely) (Member) of a people speaking an Indo-European language; in Nazi Germany esp. contrasted with SEMITE. [Sansk. *ārya* noble (in earlier use a national name comprising worshippers of the gods of the Brahmans); the earlier *Arian* is f. L. *Arianus*, of Aria (f. Gk. *Areia* eastern Persia)]

as (ăz) *adv.* In the same degree; similarly; for example. ∼ *conj.* While, when; since, seeing that. ∼ *prep.* In the capacity or role of; ∼ **for, to**, with reference to; ∼ **if, though**, as it would be if; ∼ **is**, in the existing state; ∼ **of**, as from, as at (date).

A.S. *abbrev.* Anglo-Saxon.

as·a·fet·i·da (ăsafĕt′ĭda) *n.* Concreted resinous gum of various Persian plants of genus *Ferula* with strong smell of garlic and bitter taste, used in medicine. [Pers. *aza* mastic, L. *foetida* stinking]

A·sa·ma (ah′sah′mah′), **Mount.** Continuously active volcano on Honshu Island, Japan.

as·bes·tos (ăsbĕs′tos, ăz-) *n.* White or gray fibrous mineral (consisting largely of calcium and

Light **artillery** such as this howitzer are used as highly maneuverable support for close combat troops and anti-tank defense.

magnesium silicates) that can be woven into an incombustible fabric used for fireproof clothing, thermal insulation of pipes, etc., or formed into light sheet material for roofing. [Gk., = "unquenchable"]

as·cend (asĕnd´) v. Go or come up; rise, mount, climb; succeed to a throne, high office, etc.).

as·cend·an·cy, as·cend·en·cy (asĕn´densē) ns. Dominant control, powerful influence.

as·cend·ant, as·cend·ent (asĕn-dent) adjs. Rising; (astron.) rising toward zenith; (astrol.) just rising above eastern horizon; predomi-nant. ~ n. Dominant position, etc., as in the ascendant; (astrol.) ascendant point of ecliptic or degree of zodiac.

as·cen·sion (asĕn´shon) n. Ascent; A ~, bodily ascent of Christ into heaven on 40th day after resurrection; rising of a celestial body; A ~ Day, day commemorat-ing Christ's ascension, the 40th day after Easter.

As·cen·sion (asĕn´shon) **Island.** Small island in S. Atlantic, dis-covered by Portuguese on Ascen-sion Day 1501.

as·cent (asĕnt´) n. Ascending, rising; upward path or slope.

as·cer·tain (ăsertān´) v.t. Find out. **as·cer·tain´a·ble** adj. **as·-cer·tain´ment** n.

as·cet·ic (asĕt´ĭk) adj. Severely abstinent, austere. ~ n. One who practices severe self-discipline, esp. for religious reasons. **as·cet´-i·cal·ly** adv. **as·cet´i·cism** n.

Asch (ăsh), **Sholem** (1880–

1957). Polish-born American novelist and playwright; author of *Mottke the Thief, Uncle Moses, Song of the Valley*, etc.

As·cham (ăs´kam), **Roger** (1515–68). English scholar and prose writer, tutor to Elizabeth I, and author of *The Scholemaster*, a treatise on education.

as·cid·i·an (asĭd´ēan) n. Tuni-cate of the order Ascidiacea. [Gk. *askidion* dim. of *askos* wineskin]

As·cle·pi·us (asklē´pēus). (Gk. myth.) Hero and god of healing, freq. represented bearing staff with serpent coiled around it.

as·co·my·cete (ăskōmī´sēt, -mī-sēt´) n. Fungus, including the yeasts and mildews, producing spores in a sac-like structure.

a·scor·bic (askor´bĭk) adj. ~ **acid,** vitamin C, which occurs in fresh foods, esp. fruits and vege-tables, and is necessary to prevent scurvy.

as·cot (ăs´kot) n. Broad scarflike tie looped under chin.

as·cribe (askrīb´) v.t. (**-cribed, -crib·ing**). Attribute, impute; con-sider as belonging *to.* **as·crip·tion** (askrĭp´shon) n.

a·sep·sis (āsĕp´sĭs, a-) n. Ab-sence of putrefactive matter or harmful bacteria.

a·sep·tic (āsĕp´tĭk, a-) adj. Free from living disease germs.

a·sex·u·al (āsĕk´shooal) adj. Not sexual, without sex.

ash¹ (ăsh) n. Forest tree of genus *Fraxinus* with silver-gray bark, pinnate leaves, and close-grained wood; wood of this.

*Sea squirts or **ascidians,** a primitive group of marine animals found along the sea shore. They are hermaphrodites each producing both sperm and eggs.*

*Orange picking in California. Citrus fruit is an important source of **ascorbic acid,** or vitamin C, which prevents scurvy.*

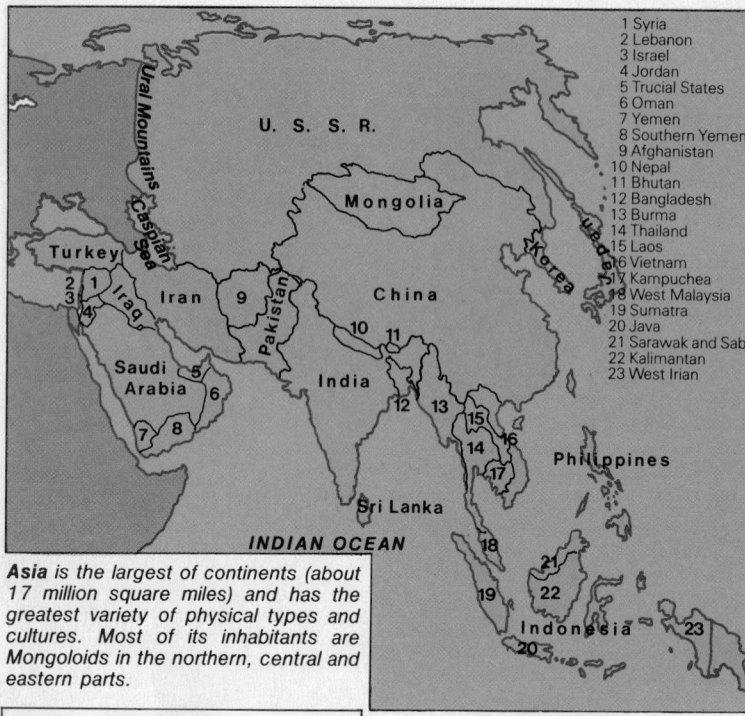

1 Syria
2 Lebanon
3 Israel
4 Jordan
5 Trucial States
6 Oman
7 Yemen
8 Southern Yemen
9 Afghanistan
10 Nepal
11 Bhutan
12 Bangladesh
13 Burma
14 Thailand
15 Laos
16 Vietnam
17 Kampuchea
18 West Malaysia
19 Sumatra
20 Java
21 Sarawak and Sabah
22 Kalimantan
23 West Irian

Asia is the largest of continents (about 17 million square miles) and has the greatest variety of physical types and cultures. Most of its inhabitants are Mongoloids in the northern, central and eastern parts.

*The **asp** is a venomous viper. 'Aspis' is the classical name for snake. A bite in the breast by a viper was held to be a quick and merciful death for a condemned prisoner.*

*The **aspen,** a deciduous tree of the poplar genus. The quaking, or golden, aspen is commonly found in the mountains of western U.S.A.*

ash[2] (ăsh) *n.* (freq. pl.) Powdery residue left after combustion of any substance; (pl.) mortal remains after cremation. ~ **blond(e)** *adj.* light blond; *n.* person with ash-blond hair; **A~ Wednesday**, first day of Lent (from custom of placing ashes on penitents' foreheads); **ash'tray**, receptacle for tobacco ash etc.

a·shamed (ashāmd´) *adj.* Abashed, upset by consciousness of guilt.

ash·en (ăsh'en) *adj.* Pale; of, resembling ashes.

Ash·er (ăsh'er). Hebrew patriarch, son of Jacob (Gen. 30); tribe of Israel, traditionally descended from him.

Ash·ke·naz·i (ahshkenah´zē) *n.* (pl. **-naz·im** pr. -nah´zĭm). Central or eastern European Jew, esp. a Yiddish-speaking one. (Cf. SEPHARDI) [Mod. Heb., f. *Ashke-*

naz, Gen. 10]

ash·ram (ahsh´ram) *n.* (in Indi Place of religious retreat, herm tage.

ash·y (ăsh'ē) *adj.* (**ash·i·e ash·i·est**). Of ashes; ash-colore pale.

A·sia (ā'zha, ā'sha). Contine of N. hemisphere, E. part of t great land mass formed by the O World; separated from Europe the Ural Mountains and t Caspian Sea; home of the olde known civilizations; ~ **Mino** westernmost part of Asia, a pe insula bounded by the Black Se the Aegean, and the Mediterranea and comprising most of Turke Anatolia. **A'sian, A·si·at·ic** (āzh ăt´ĭk) *adjs.* & *ns.*

a·side (asīd´) *adv.* To or on or side; away, apart. ~ *n.* Wor spoken by an actor and suppose not to be heard by other performer ~ **from**, in addition to, excludin except for.

as·i·nine (ăs'inīn) *adj.* Of asse stupid.

ask (ăsk) *v.* Call for an answe to; request information (about make a request (for); invit demand, require.

a·skance (askăns´) *adv.* Side ways; **look ~ at**, view suspiciously

a·skew (askū´) *adv.* Obliquel awry.

a·slant (aslănt´) *adv.* Obliquel

a·sleep (aslēp´) *adv.* In a stat of sleep. ~ *pred. adj.* (of limbs Benumbed.

As·ma·ra (ahsmār´ah). Ol Abyssinian town; now capital c Eritrea, N. Ethiopia.

A·so (ah'sō´). Volcano o Kyushu Island, Japan; one of th largest craters in the world.

a·so·cial (āsō´shal) *adj.* Antago nistic to or withdrawn from society

A·so·ka (asō´ka) (d. *c*232 B.C.) Emperor of India from *c*269 B.C. was converted to Buddhism, di much to propagate it, and is revere by Buddhists.

asp (ăsp) *n.* 1. Small viper of S Europe (*Vipera aspis*). 2. Viper o N. Africa and Arabia (species o *Cerastes*).

as·par·a·gus (aspăr´agus) *n* Liliaceous plant of genus *A~* wit many-branched fine stems, an leaves reduced to scales; species o this (*A. officinalis*) whose verna shoots are a table delicacy.

A.S.P.C.A. *abbrev.* American Society for the Prevention o Cruelty to Animals.

as·pect (ăs'pĕkt) *n.* Way a thing presents itself to eye or mind; side (of building etc.) looking, fronting in a given direction; appearance (philol.) form of the verb expressing duration, completion, etc., of an action.

as·pen (ăs'pen) *n.* Any of several varieties of poplar tree, esp. *Populus* *tremuloides*, with leaves tremulous on account of their long thin leaf stalks.

as·per·i·ty (*aspĕr´ĭtē*) *n*. Roughness; severity; harshness.

as·perse (*aspĕrs´*) *v.t.* (**-persed, -pers·ing**). Attack the reputation of, calumniate. **as·per·sion** (*aspĕr´zhon, -shon*) *n*. Defamatory statement, slander.

as·phalt (*ăs´fawlt*) *n*. 1. Solid or plastic pitch derived from petro-leum. 2. Mixture of this with sand etc. used for surfacing roads etc. ~ *v.t.* Pave (road) with asphalt.

as·pho·del (*ăs´fodĕl*) *n*. Any of various hardy liliaceous plants from the Mediterranean and India, including classical *Asphodeline lutea* in Greece; (poet.) immortal flower in Elysium.

as·phyx·i·a (*ăsfĭk´sēa*) *n*. Lack of oxygen and excess of carbon dioxide in the blood, causing loss of

A road construction gang shovels **asphalt** *onto the road surface from the hopper preparing it for the roller which will even the surface.*

consciousness or death. **as·phyx·i·ate** (*ăsfĭk´sēāt*) *v.* (**-at·ed, -at·ing**). Kill by asphyxia, suffocate. **as·phyx·i·a·tion** (*ăsfĭksēā´-shon*) *n*. [Gk. *a-* not, *sphuxis* pulse]

as·pic (*ăs´pĭk*) *n*. Gelatin used as a garnish or for making molds of cooked meat, fish, eggs, etc.

The common **ass** with foal. When an ass (donkey) is mated with a horse the offspring is a mule. The wild ass of Asia usually has stripes along its back and bands on its legs.

A favorite house plant in 19th-century England. The **aspidistra** is easy to grow indoors. It tolerates bad light and fluctuations in temperature. There are eight species.

as·pi·dis·tra (ăspĭdĭs′trα) n. Plant of the lily family, with broad tapering leaves, freq. grown as a house plant. [Gk. *aspis* shield]

as·pi·rant (ăs′perant, aspīr′ant) n. One who aspires.

as·pi·rate (ăs′perĭt) adj. Aspirated; begun with the sound of the letter h. ~ n. Aspirated consonant; the sound of *h*. ~ (ăs′perāt) v.t. (**-rat·ed, -rat·ing**). 1. Pronounce with a breathing, blended with the sound of *h*. 2. Draw out by suction.

as·pi·ra·tion (ăsperā′shon) n. Drawing of breath; strong desire; desired goal.

as·pi·ra·tor (ăs′perāter) n. Apparatus using suction to remove fluids or gases from a space, esp. one used in medicine to draw fluids from the body.

as·pire (aspīr′) v.i. (**-pired, -pir·ing**). Feel earnest desire or ambition; (fig.) reach high.

as·pi·rin (ăs′perĭn, -prĭn) n. (pl. **-rin, -rins**). Compound of acetylsalicylic acid, used to relieve pain and fever; tablet of this.

ass¹ (ăs) n. 1. Quadruped of the genus *Equus*, related to the horse, but smaller; esp. *E. asinus asinus* the domestic donkey descended from the African wild ass *E. asinus*, and *E. hemionus* the wild ass of Asia; donkey. 2. (slang) Ignorant or stupid person.

ass² (ăs) n. (vulg.) Buttocks, rump; anus.

as·sail (asāl′) v.t. Attack, assault. **as·sail′ant** n. One who assails.

as·sas·sin (asăs′ĭn) n. One who undertakes to kill for reasons of fanaticism or financial gain. [Arab. *hashshāshĭn*, oblique pl. of *hashshàsh* hashish addict]

as·sas·si·nate (asăs′ināt) v.t. (**-nat·ed, -nat·ing**). Kill (person) for political or sectarian reasons.

as·sas·si·na·tion (asăsinā′shon) n.

as·sault (asawlt′) n. Hostile attack; rush against walls of fortress etc.; (law) unlawful personal attack or threat of it. ~ **and battery**, (law) threat to make an unlawful personal attack followed by the attack itself. **assault** v.t. Make attack upon.

as·say¹ (ăs′ā, asā′) n. Testing of an alloy or ore to determine the proportion of a given metal.

as·say² (asā′) v. 1. Try, attempt; put to a test. 2. (metall.) Analyze (ore etc.) to determine the amount of gold or other valuable components in it. 3. Subject (a drug) to analysis in order to determine its strength. 4. Evaluate after examination or analysis.

as·sem·blage (asĕm′blĭj) n. Collection, assembly; (art) (also pr. ahsawnblahzh′) object made of unrelated things joined together.

as·sem·ble (asĕm′bel) v. (**-bled, -bling**). Bring or come together; collect; fit together parts of (machine etc.).

as·sem·bly (asĕm′blē) n. (pl. **-blies**). 1. Group of persons gathered together for discussion, worship, recreation, or other particular purpose. 2. Gathering of student body in auditorium for a special program. 3. **A~**, legislative body, esp. the lower house of the legislature in some states; **assem′blyman, assem′blywoman**,

member of a legislative assemb 4. Act of assembling; state of bei assembled. 5. Military call drum, bugle, etc. for troops to ma formation. 6. (eng.) Assembling those parts of a machine etc. th form a unit; parts so assemble **assembly line**, sequence machines and workers for assemb of product.

as·sent (asĕnt′) v.i. Agree (t defer (*to*); express agreement; s yes. ~ n. Concurrence; sanctio

as·sert (asĕrt′) v.t. Maintain claim to (rights); declare; ~ **on self**, put oneself forward insis ently, act confidently.

as·ser·tion (asĕr′shon) n. Insis ence upon a right; affirmatio positive statement.

as·ser·tive (asĕr′tĭv) adj. Give to assertion; positive, dogmati **as·ser′tive·ly** adv. **as·ser′tive ness** n.

as·sess (asĕs′) v.t. Fix amou of (taxes, fine); fine, tax; estima value of (esp. for taxation); evaluat **as·sess′ment** n.

as·ses·sor (asĕs′er) n. One wh assesses taxes or estimates value property for purpose of taxatio special adviser to judge.

as·set (ăs′ĕt) n. 1. (pl.) Tot resources of cash, property, etc (law) property available for pay ment of debts. 2. (loosely) An valuable possession; any usef quality. [med. L. *ad satis* suff ciently]

as·sev·er·ate (asĕv′erāt) v. (**-at·ed, -at·ing**). Solemnly de

*Basilica di San Francesco in **Assisi**, where St. Francis (1181?–1226) was born and died. He founded the Franciscans, friars who emphasize tending the sick and the poor.*

*This **assembly** of college students is just one of thousands of graduation ceremonies that take place at the end of each school year all over the U.S.A.*

clare. **as·sev·er·a·tion** (asĕverā´shon) n.

as·si·du·i·ty (ăsĭdoo͞´ĭtē, -dū´-) n. (pl. **-ties**). Close attention, persistent application.

as·sid·u·ous (asĭj´oous) adj. Persevering, diligent. **as·sid·u·ous·ly** adv. **as·sid·u·ous·ness** n.

as·sign (asīn´) v.t. Transfer (property, rights, etc.) formally; allot; appoint; ascribe. ~ n. One to whom a property, right, etc., is legally transferred.

as·sig·na·tion (ăsĭgnā´shon) n. Assigning; appointment (of time and place), esp. a tryst or rendez-vous of lovers.

as·sign·ee (asīnē´, ăsīnē´) n. One appointed to act for another; assign.

as·sign·ment (asīn´ment) n. Allotment; legal transference; task, commission.

as·sim·i·late (asĭm´ĭlāt) v. (**-lat·ed, -lat·ing**). Make or become like; absorb, be absorbed into the system. **as·sim·i·la·tion** (asĭmĭlā´shon) n. **as·sim·i·la·tive** (asĭm´ĭlātĭv, -latĭv), **as·sim·i·la·to·ry** (asĭm´ĭlatōrē; -tōrē) adjs.

As·si·si (asē´zē). Town of Umbria, central Italy; birthplace of St. Francis.

as·sist (asĭst´) v. Help; ~ n. Act of assisting (esp., as in sports, a play that leads to a teammate's scoring a goal etc.). **as·sis·tance** (asĭs´tans) n.

as·sis·tant (asĭs´tant) adj. Helping; subordinate, holding an auxiliary position, auxiliary. ~ n. Helper, subordinate worker; ~ **professor**, faculty member in a college or university ranking above an instructor and below an associate professor.

as·size (asīz´) n. (hist.) (usu. pl.) Periodic criminal and civil court sessions held in counties of England and Wales by circuit judges; their time or place.

assoc. abbrev. Association; associate.

as·so·ci·ate (asō´sēāt, -shē-) v. (**-at·ed, -at·ing**). Join; connect in idea; combine; have frequent dealings (with); ~ (asō´sēĭt, -shē-) adj. Joined, allied; subordinate. ~ n. Partner, colleague; subordinate member of an association; thing connected with another; ~ **professor**, faculty member in a college or university ranking above an assistant professor and below a professor. **as·so·ci·a·tive** adj.

as·so·ci·a·tion (asōsēā´shon; -shē-) n. Associating; organized body of persons; connection of ideas; intercourse; **free** ~: see FREE.

as·so·nance (ăs´onans) n. Resemblance of sound between two syllables; rhyming of one word with another in the accented vowel but not in the following consonants (e.g. *sonnet*, *porridge*). **as´so·nant** adj.

as·sort (asort´) v.t. Arrange or distribute according to kind, class, etc. **as·sort·ed** (asor´tĭd) adj. Of various sorts, mixed.

as·sort·ment (asort´ment) n. Assorting; mixed collection.

ASSR abbrev. Autonomous Soviet Socialist Republic.

asst. abbrev. Assistant.

as·suage (aswāj´) v.t. (**-suaged, -suag·ing**). Calm, soothe; appease; make milder or less severe. **as·suage´ment** n.

as·sume (asoom´) v.t. (**-sumed, -sum·ing**). Take upon oneself; undertake; take to be true or for granted for purpose of argument or action; pretend to be or have. **as·sum´ing** adj. Taking much upon oneself, arrogant.

as·sump·tion (asŭmp´shon) n. Assuming; thing assumed; arrogance; **the A~**, the bodily taking up of the Virgin Mary into heaven; feast in honor of this, Aug. 15.

as·sur·ance (ashoor´ans) n. Positive assertion, pledge; self-confidence, sureness; impudence; (Brit.) (life) insurance.

as·sure (ashoor´) v.t. (**-sured, -sur·ing**). Tell (person) confi-

*The **aster** is a genus of hardy herbaceous perennials. Its flowers can be
obtained in shades of blue, mauve,
pink, crimson, white and yellow.*

dently (*of* a thing, *of* its being so,
that it is so), reassure; make
(person) sure (of fact); make certain,
ensure the happening etc. of; make
safe or secure; (Brit.) insure, as
against loss. **as·sur·ed·ly** (ashoor´-
ĭdlē) *adv.*

As·syr·i·a (asĭr´ēa).   More
northerly of the two ancient empires
of Mesopotamia; capital, Assur;
supremacy ended soon after the
death of Assur-bani-pal (7th c.
B.C.), who had subdued rebellious
Egypt and Elam.

As·syr·i·an (asĭr´ēan) *adj. & n.*
(Member) of the Assyrian people,
a mixed Semitic race; (of) the
Assyrian language, a dialect of
Akkadian.

As·tar·te (ăstär´tē). Goddess of
love and fertility; Phoenician
equivalent of Aphrodite.

as·ta·tine (ăs´tatēn) *n.* (chem.)
Radioactive element of short life
(symbol At, at. no. 85, principal
isotope at. wt. 211), which does not
occur in nature but can be made
artificially; the heaviest element of
the halogen group. [Gk. *astatos*
unstable]

as·ter (ăs´ter) *n.* Herbaceous
plant of genus *A~* with showy
radiated flowers of various colors.
[Gk. *aster* star]

as·ter·isk (ăs´terĭsk) *n.* Star *
used to mark words for reference or
distinction, or fill up space in a line
where something is omitted. ~ *v.t.*
Mark with asterisk.

a·stern (astern´) *adv.* In, at, the
stern; behind.

as·ter·oid (ăs´teroid) *n.* 1.
(astron.) Any of the thousands of
small celestial bodies revolving
around the sun mainly between the
orbits of Mars and Jupiter. 2.
(zool.) One of the class of Asteroidea
or starfishes. **as·ter·oi·dal** (ăster-
oi´dal) *adj.* [Gk. *asteroeidēs* starlike]

asth·ma (ăz´ma) *n.* Disorder,
usu. of allergic origin, characterized
by paroxysms of difficult breathing.
asth·mat·ic (ăzmăt´ĭk) *adj. & n.*
(Person) suffering from asthma.
asth·mat´i·cal·ly *adv.*

As·ti (ah´stē). Town in Piedmont producing wines, including
the sweet white sparkling ~
spumante.

a·stig·ma·tism (astĭg´matĭzem)
n. Structural defect in eye or lens,
preventing rays of light from being
brought to a common focus, arising
from unequal refraction at different
points. **as·tig·mat·ic** (ăstĭgmăt´ĭk)
adj. **as·tig·mat´i·cal·ly** *adv.*

a·stir (aster´) *adv.* In motion;
out of bed.

as·ton·ish (astŏn´ĭsh) *v.* Amaze,
surprise. **as·ton´ish·ment** *n.*

*Front and back views of an **astrolabe**,
used by astronomers. 1. Ecliptic ring.
2. Index. 3. Star pointer. 4. Tropic of
Capricorn ring. 5. Zenith. 6. Horizon. 7.
Unequal hour line. 8. Equal hour scales.
9. Alidade. 10. Sight. 11. Scale of
degrees. 12. Zodiac calendar scales.
13. Shadow square.*

*The 150 in. (3.8 m.) Anglo-Australian reflecting telescope at Siding Springs, N.S.W. The larger the diameter (aperture) of an **astronomical** telescope, the greater the distance it can probe into space. The mirrors of the telescope shown are made of ceramic material which unlike glass prevents distortion due to changes in temperature.*

f15 Cassegrain secondary

Incoming light beam

Light baffle

Secondary mirror

Main horseshoe

Adjustable counterbalance

Light baffle

Mirror supports

Cassegrain focus

24 inch finder telescope

Image tube

Coude mirrors 3 and 4

Photographic plate holder

Prime focus end assembly

Corrector plate housing

as·tound (astownd') *v.t.* Shock with alarm or surprise; amaze.

as·tra·khan (ăs'trakan, -kăn) *n.* 1. Dark curly fleece of young lambs from Astrakhan, U.S.S.R. 2. Cloth imitating this.

as·tral (ăs'tral) *adj.* Connected with, consisting of, stars; ~ **body**, (theosophy) ethereal counterpart of the human body accompanying it in life, and surviving its death.

a·stray (astrā') *adv.* Out of the right way; (esp., fig.) in or into error or sin.

a·stride (astrīd') *adv. & prep.* With a leg on either side (*of*); extending across.

as·trin·gent (astrĭn'jent) *adj.* Causing to contract, styptic; severe; austere. ~ *n.* Astringent substance.

astro- *comb. form.* 1. Star, heavenly body, as *astronomy, astrophysics.* 2. Outer space, as *astronaut.*

as·tro·labe (ăs'trolāb) *n.* Instrument formerly used to take altitudes of celestial bodies and solve other problems of practical astronomy.

as·trol·o·gy (astrŏl'ojē) *n.* Art of understanding the reputed occult influence of the stars on human affairs. **as·trol'o·ger** *n.* **as·tro·log'i·cal** (ăstrolŏj'ĭkal) *adj.* **as·tro·log'i·cal·ly** *adv.*

as·tro·naut (ăs'tronawt) *n.* Person who travels in interplanetary space as pilot, navigator, etc. of a spacecraft.

as·tro·nau·tics (ăstronaw'tĭks) *n.* (considered sing.) Science and technology of space flight. **as·tro·nau'tic, as·tro·nau'ti·cal** *adjs.*

as·tro·nom·i·cal (ăstronŏm'-ĭkal) *adj.* Relating to, concerned with, astronomy; (of numbers, distances, etc.) very big, immense; ~ **unit**, (abbreviation a.u.) mean distance of the Earth from the sun as unit of measurement, approx. 150 million kilometers (93 million miles). **as·tro·nom'i·cal·ly** *adj.*

as·tron·o·my (astrŏn'omē) *n.* Science of the heavenly bodies. **as·tron'o·mer** *n.* One who studies astronomy.

as·tro·phys·ics (ăstrōfiz'ĭks) *n.* (considered sing.) That branch of physics which deals with the physical or chemical properties of heavenly bodies. **as·tro·phys'i·cal** *adj.* **as·tro·phys·i·cist** (ăstrōfĭz'-ĭsĭst) *n.*

as·tute (astōot', astūt') *adj.* Of great discernment or mental penetration; shrewd; crafty. **as·tute'ly** *adv.* **as·tute'ness** *n.*

A·sun·ción (ahs ōōnsēawn'). Capital city of Paraguay.

a·sun·der (asŭn'der) *adv.* Apart; to pieces.

A.S.V. *abbrev.* American Standard Version (of the Bible).

As·wan (ăs'wahn) **Dam.** Dam (1½ miles long) built on the Nile at Aswan in SE. Egypt 1902, enlarged 1933; **Aswan High Dam**, larger dam, about 4 miles upstream, completed 1969.

a·sy·lum (asī'lum) *n.* Sanctuary, place of refuge; (formerly) institution for the care of the insane or destitute; (also **political** ~) protection from arrest or extradition given by one nation to refugee from another.

a·sym·me·try (āsĭm′ĭtrē) n. Absence of symmetry. **a·sym·met·ric** (āsĭmĕ′trĭk), **a·sym·met′ri·cal** adjs. **a·sym·met′ri·cal·ly** adv.

as·ymp·tote (ăs′ĭmtōt) n. Line that continuously approaches a given curve, but does not meet it within a finite distance.

at (ăt) prep. Particle expressing exact, approximate, or vague position (at Chicago, at school, at dinner) or time of day (at one o'clock), amount (at 50 miles an hour), involvement (at work), condition (at peace), etc.; ~ that, at that estimate, moreover.

At·a·brine (ăt′abrĭn, -brēn) n. (trademark) Quinacrine hydrochloride.

At·a·ca·ma (ăt′akăm′a) Desert. Barren area of N. Chile; contains major nitrate deposits.

At·a·hual·pa (ahtawahl′pa) (1500?–33). Last emperor of the Incas; put to death by Pizarro for refusing to become a Christian.

At·a·lan·ta (ătalăn′ta). (Gk. legend) Huntress and athlete; she required all her suitors to run a race with her and killed them if they lost; but Milanion (or Hippomenes) won the race by throwing down three golden apples given to him by Aphrodite, which were so beautiful that Atalanta stopped to pick them up.

At·a·türk (ăt′atērk), **Kemal** (c1880–1938). Turkish nationalist

Dome of the New Metropolis, Athens, with the Acropolis in background. Capital of modern Greece, Athens was the leading city of ancient Greece and birthplace of democracy.

leader; first president of the republic 1923–38; known first as Mustapha Kemal, then as Kemal Pasha; took surname Atatürk in 1934. [Turk., = "father-Turk"]

at·a·vism (ăt′avĭzem) n. Resemblance to remote ancestors, reversion to earlier type. **at·a·vis·tic** (ătavĭs′tĭk) adj. **at·a·vis′ti·cal·ly** adv. [L. atavus great-grandfather's grandfather]

a·tax·i·a (atăk′sēa) n. Loss or lack of control of coordinated movement. **a·tax′ic** adj.

ate (āt): see EAT.

-ate suffix. Forming nouns denoting (1) office, state, function, group, or product (episcopate, magistrate, electorate, filtrate); adjectives (desolate, ornate); and verbs (fascinate, hyphenate); and (2) (chem.) a salt of an acid with corresponding name in -ic (chlorate, nitrate).

at·el·ier (ătelyā′) n. Artist's workshop, studio.

Ath·a·bas·ca (ăthabăs′ka). Lake in N. Alberta and Saskatchewan Provinces, Canada; over 3,000 square miles in area. **Ath·a·bas·can, Ath·a·pas·can** = ATHAPAS-KAN.

Ath·a·na·sius (ăthanā′shus), **St.** (c296–373). Bishop of Alexandria. Doctor of the church. **Ath·a·na·sian** (ăthanā′zhan) adj.

Ath·a·pas·kan (ăthapăs′kan adj. & n. (Member, language) of a American Indian people in wester North America from Alaska northern Mexico.

a·the·ism (ā′thēĭzem) n. Di belief in the existence of God gods; godlessness. **a′the·ist a·the·is·tic** (ātheĭs′tĭk) adj.

A·the·na (athē′na), **A·the·n** (athē′nē). (Gk. myth.) Goddess wisdom, industry, and war, identi fied with the Roman Minerva; sh sprang fully grown and armed fror the brain of her father, Zeus; he emblem was an owl.

ath·e·nae·um, ath·e·ne·un (ăthenē′um) ns. 1. Institution fo the promotion of learning. 2 Library or reading room. 3. A~ college of rhetoric and poetry founded at Rome c133 A.D. by th Emperor Hadrian. [L. f. Gk Athēnaion temple of ATHENA]

Ath·ens (ăth′ĭnz). (Gk. Athenai Leading city of ancient Greece capital of modern Greece. **A·the·ni·an** (athē′nēan) adj. & n.

a·thirst (athērst′) pred. adj Thirsty; eager (for).

ath·lete (ăth′lēt) n. One who competes or excels in sports or physical exercises; ~'s foot, contagious ringworm of the feet.

ath·let·ic (ăthlĕt′ĭk) adj. Pertaining to athletes; physically active or powerful. **ath·let′ics** n.pl Athletic sports (e.g. running, jumping, hurdling, etc.), games, or exercises. **at·let·i·cism** (ăthlĕt′-isĭzem) n.

a·thwart (athwōrt′) adv. Across

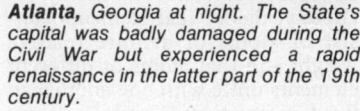

om side to side (usu. obliquely). *prep.* Across.

A·ti·tlan (ah´tĭtlahn).   Crater ke in SW. Guatemala; volcano S. the lake.

At·lan·ta (ătlăn´ta).   Commer- al and industrial city in NW. eorgia; the state capital.

At·lan·tic (ătlăn´tĭk) *adj.*   Of, djoining the Atlantic Ocean; ~ ·**cean**, great ocean lying between urope and Africa on E. and merica on W. ~ *n.* Atlantic ocean; **·attle of the** ~ , German offensive gainst Allied Atlantic shipping uring World War II. [f. ATLAS]

Atlantic City. Resort and con- ention city on the SE. coast of New ersey; famous for its 4-mile-long oardwalk.

At·lan·tis   (ătlăn´tĭs).   (Gk.

legend) Fabled island in the ocean W. of the Pillars of Hercules; it was beautiful and prosperous, the seat of an empire that dominated part of Europe and Africa, but was over- whelmed by the sea because of the impiety of its inhabitants.

At·las (ăt´las). (Gk. legend) One of the Titans, who was punished for revolting against Zeus by being made to support the heavens with his head and hands; acc. to another legend Perseus, with the aid of Medusa's head, turned him into a mountain (the ~ **Mountains** of N. Africa).

at·las (ăt´las) *n.*   1. Collection of maps in a volume, so called from the use of a figure of ATLAS supporting the heavens as a frontispiece.   2. Uppermost vertebra of backbone,

supporting the skull.

at·man (aht´man) *n.* (Hinduism) 1. The individual soul.   2. The principle of life.   3. **A**~, the supreme universal soul, source of all individual souls.

at·mos·phere (ăt´mosfēr) *n.* Gaseous envelope surrounding a heavenly body, esp. the envelope of air surrounding the Earth, which consists of gases (nitrogen, oxygen, argon, carbon dioxide, helium, and others) and water vapor, and is rarer as distance from the Earth increases; air (of a place); mental or moral environment or mood. **at·mos·- pher·ic** (ătmosfĕr´ĭk) *adj.* ~ **pres- sure**, pressure of the column of air above a given point, equivalent on the Earth's surface to about 14.7 pounds per square inch, but decreasing with increasing altitude above the Earth. **at·mos·pher´ics** *n.pl.* Atmospheric disturbances of electrical origin causing interfer- ence in telecommunications; crack- ling or other interference so caused.

at. no. *abbrev.* Atomic number.

at·oll (ăt´awl, -ŏl, -ōl, *a*tawl´, *a*tŏl´, *a*tōl´) *n.* Ring-shaped coral

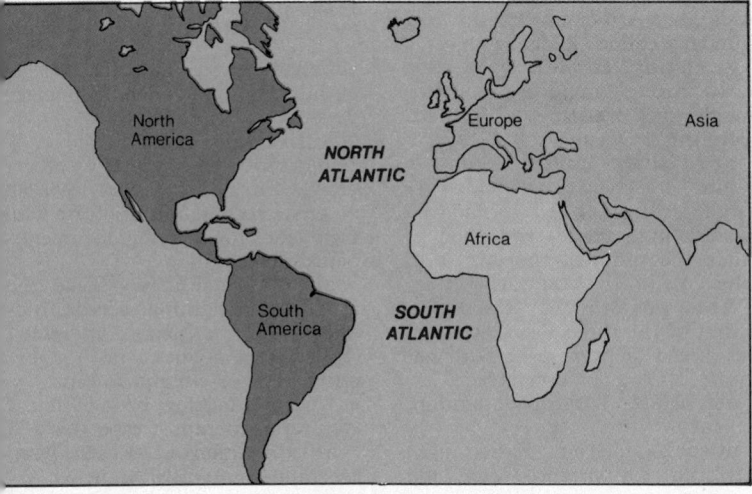

*The **Atlantic Ocean** dividing Europe and Africa from the Americas. In area about 32½ million square miles, it is second only to the Pacific Ocean in size.*

reef enclosing lagoon. [Malay]

at·om (ăt´om) *n.* 1. Body too small to be divided; minute portion, small thing. 2. (chem.) Smallest particle of an element that cannot be further subdivided without destroying its identity, regarded as consisting of a minute central positively charged nucleus in which almost all the mass is concentrated, and a number of negative electrons arranged around the nucleus; ~ **bomb** = ATOMIC bomb; ~ **smasher**: see ACCELERATOR.

a·tom·ic (atŏm´ĭk) *adj.* Of atoms; of, using, concerned with, atomic energy or weapons; ~ **bomb**, bomb deriving its destructive power from ~ **energy**, released by fission of atomic nuclei of certain heavy elements such as uranium 235 or plutonium or by the fusion of light nuclei; ~ **mass**, mass of an atom measured in units based on $\frac{1}{12}$ of the mass of the carbon-12 atom; ~ **number**, (abbreviated at. no.) number of unit positive charges carried by the nucleus of an atom or protons of an element, number determining the position of the element in the periodic table; ~ **pile** or ~ **reactor**: see REACTOR, def. 3; ~ **theory**, theory that elements consist of atoms of definite relative weight and that atoms of different elements unite with one another in fixed proportions; (philos.) atomism; ~ **weight**, (abbreviated at. wt.) = *atomic mass* (see above). **a·tom´i·cal·ly** *adv.*

at·om·ism (ăt´omĭzem) *n.* (philos.) Theory that all matter consists of minute indivisible particles. **a´om·ist** *n.* **at·om·is·tic** (ătomĭs´tĭk) *adj.*

at·om·ize (ăt´omīz) *v.t.* (**-ized, -iz·ing**). Reduce to atoms; reduce to fine particles or spray. **at´om·iz·er** *n.* Instrument for reducing liquids to a fine spray.

a·ton·al (ātō´nal) *adj.* (mus.) Not conforming to any system of key or mode. **a·to·nal·i·ty** (ātōnăl´ĭtē) *n.*

a·tone (atōn´) *v.i.* (**a·toned, a·ton·ing**). Make amends; ~ **for**, expiate. **a·tone´ment** *n.* **the A** ~, expiation of man's sin by Christ; **Day of A** ~: see YOM KIPPUR.

a·top (atŏp´) *adj. & adv.* At or on the top. ~ *prep.* On the top of.

A·tre·us (ā´trēus, ā´troōs). (Gk. legend) King of Argos, who set the flesh of his brother Thyestes' children before their father at a banquet in revenge because Thyestes had seduced his wife; he was himself murdered by Aegisthus.

a·tri·um (ā´trēum) *n.* (pl. **a·tri·a** pr. ā´trēa, **a·tri·ums**). 1. Central court of Roman house. 2. Either of the two upper cavities (*left* and *right* ~) of the heart into which the veins pour the blood.

a·tro·cious (atrō´shus) *adj.* Extremely wicked; very bad. **a·tro´cious·ly** *adv.*

a·troc·i·ty (atrŏs´ĭtē) *n.* (pl. **-ties**). Atrocious deed; bad blunder; (colloq.) hideous object.

at·ro·phy (ăt´rofē) *n.* Wasting away through imperfect nourishment or lack of use. ~ *v.* (**-phied, -phy·ing**). Waste away.

at·ro·pine (ăt´ropēn, -pĭn) *n.* White crystal-like alkaloid prepared from *Atropa belladonna* (deadly nightshade) and used to dilate the pupil of the eye or to relieve pain. [f. ATROPOS]

At·ro·pos (ăt´ropŏs). (Gk. myth.) Eldest of the three Fates, who cut the thread of human life with her shears. [Gk., = "inflexible"]

att. *abbrev.* Attached; attention; attorney.

at·tach (atăch´) *v.* Fasten, join; attribute (importance etc. *to*);

*Nuclear plant at Oyster Creek, Long Island. A nuclear or **atomic** reactor contains fissionable material arranged to keep up a controlled nuclear chain reaction.*

adhere, be incident *to*; seize by legal authority; bind in friendship, make devoted. **at·tach´ment** *n.*

at·ta·ché (ătashā´, ătă-) *n.* Diplomatic or military officer attached to an embassy or legation; ~ **case**, rectangular briefcase with rigid sides for carrying documents, papers, etc.

at·tack (atăk´) *v.* Take the initiative in fighting; act destructively on; criticize adversely; (colloq.) set about (a task) vigorously; rape or attempt to rape. ~ *n.* Act of attacking; bout of illness etc.; rape, attempted rape.

at·tain (atān´) *v.* Reach, gain, accomplish. **at·tain´ment** *n.* Attaining; thing attained; (pl.) personal accomplishments.

at·tar (ăt´er) *n.* Fragrant essential oil distilled from flowers, esp. roses. [ult. F, Arab. *'itr* perfume]

at·tempt (atĕmpt´) *v.t.* Try; try to master. ~ *n.* Attempting; endeavor.

at·tend (atĕnd´) *v.* 1. Turn the mind, apply oneself (*to*). 2. Be present (*at*); go regularly to (school, church, etc.). 3. Wait upon; serve; escort; accompany.

at·tend·ance (atĕn´dans) *n.* Attending (ATTEND *v.* defs 2, 3); number of persons present.

at·tend·ant (atĕn´dant) *n.* 1. One who attends or provides service. 2. One who is present. 3. Thing or circumstance that accompanies; concomitant or consequence. ~ *adj.* 1. Being present, accompanying. 2. Consequent, associated, related.

at·ten·tion (atĕn´shon) *n.* Act or faculty of attending (ATTEND *v.* def. 1); consideration, care; (pl.) ceremonious politeness; courtship; addresses; **at** ~, (mil.) formal attitude of troops standing in erect position as dist. from *at* EASE; (as command) order to stand thus.

at·ten·tive (atĕn´tĭv) *adj.* Giving or paying attention. **at·ten´tive·ly** *adv.* **at·ten´tive·ness** *n.*

at·ten·u·ate (atĕn´ūāt) *v.t.* (**-at·ed, -at·ing**). Make slender or thin; reduce in force or value. **at·ten·u·a·tion** (atĕnūā´shon) *n.* **attenuate** (atĕn´ūĭt) *adj.* Slender; rarefied.

at·test (atĕst´) *v.* Testify, certify; put on oath or solemn declaration. **at·tes·ta·tion** (ătestā´shon) *n.*

Att. Gen. *abbrev.* Attorney General.

At·tic (ăt´ĭk) *adj.* Of Attica; ~ **dialect,** Greek spoken by ancient Athenians; ~ **order,** square column of any of the five orders (see ORDER def. 6). **Attic** *n.* Attic dialect.

at·tic (ăt´ĭk) *n.* 1. (archit.) Structure consisting of small order placed above another of greater height. 2. (Room in) highest story of building, usu. immediately under the roof and not having a flat ceiling. [Fr. *attique* upper part of house, so called from Attic order of architecture.]

At·ti·ca (ăt´ĭka). District of ancient Greece of which Athens was the capital.

At·ti·la (atĭl´a, ăt´ĭla) (d. 453 A.D.). King of the Huns, known as the "scourge of God"; ravaged the Eastern Roman Empire (445–50); after making peace with Theodosius invaded the Western Empire and was defeated at Châlons by Aëtius in 451.

at·tire (atīr´) *v.t.* (**-tired, -tir·ing**) & *n.* Dress, array.

At·tis (ă´tĭs). (myth.) Youthful consort of CYBELE; his death was mourned for days in the spring, and his recovery (when his spirit passed into a pine tree and violets sprang up from his blood) then celebrated.

at·ti·tude (ăt´ĭtōōd, -tūd) *n.* 1. Posture of body; settled behavior, as indicating opinion. 2. Manner, feeling toward a person, idea, or thing. 3. Angular relation between aircraft's or spacecraft's axis and the wind, course, etc.

at·ti·tu·di·nize (ătĭtōō´dĭnīz, -tū´-) *v.i.* (**-nized, -niz·ing**). Practice attitudes; act, speak, etc. affectedly.

at·tor·ney (atēr´nē) *n.* (pl. **-neys**). Lawyer, esp. an attorney-at-law; **power of** ~, a legal document authorizing one person or party to act as attorney or agent for another; ~ **general** (pl. ~**s general** or ~ **generals**), chief law officer and legal counsel of a national or state government; the **A** ~ **General** of the United States is head of the Department of Justice and a member of the Cabinet.

at·tract (atrăkt´) *v.t.* Draw to itself or oneself; excite pleasurable emotions of; draw forth and fix on oneself (attention etc.). **at·trac·tion** (atrăk´shon) *n.* Attracting; thing that attracts; attractive qualities. **at·trac·tive** (atrăk´tĭv) *adj.* **at·trac´tive·ly** *adv.* **at·trac´tive·ness** *n.*

at·trib·ute (atrĭb´ūt) *v.t.* (**-ut·ed, -ut·ing**). ~ **to,** consider as caused by, resulting or originating from, made or composed by; consider as belonging or appropriate *to.* **at·tri·bu·tion** (ătrĭbū´shon) *n.* **attribute** (ăt´rĭbūt) *n.* Quality ascribed to anything; material object regarded as appropriate to person or office; characteristic quality; (gram.) attributive word, adjective.

at·trib·u·tive (atrĭb´yutĭv) *adj.* Assigning an attribute to a subject; (gram.) expressing an attribute, qualifying. ~ *n.* Word denoting an attribute. **at·trib´u·tive·ly** *adv.*

at·tri·tion (atrĭsh´on) *n.* Wearing down by friction; wearing out; gradual reduction of staff through retirement, resignation, etc.; weakening by harassment.

At·tucks (ăt´uks), **Crispus** (1723?–70). American patriot and leader of mob at Boston Massacre in which he was killed; may have been a runaway slave.

at·tune (atōōn´, atūn´) *v.t.* (**at·tuned, at·tun·ing**). Bring into (musical) accord; adapt.

Atty. Gen. *abbrev.* Attorney General.

ATV (ā´tē´vē´) *abbrev.* All-terrain vehicle, one capable of traveling on rough off-the-road terrain and going over water.

a·twit·ter (atwĭt´er) *adj.* Excited; nervous; agitated; twittering.

at. wt. *abbrev.* Atomic weight.

a·typ·i·cal (ātĭp´ĭkal) *adj.* Not typical.

a.u. *abbrev.* Astronomical unit.

au·brie·tia (ōbrē´sha) *n.* Spring-flowering dwarf perennial plant of genus *Aubrieta* of mustard family, with flowers of colors ranging through purple, red, and blue. [after Claude *Aubriet* (d. 1743), French painter of flowers and animals]

au·burn (aw´bern) *n.* & *adj.* Reddish brown (usu. of hair).

Au·bus·son (ōbüsawṅ´). Town in central France, famous since the 16th c. for the manufacture of tapestries and carpets.

Auck·land (awk´land). Largest city and chief seaport of New Zealand.

au cou·rant (ō kōōrahṅ´). Acquainted *with* what is going on, well informed; up-to-date. [Fr.]

auc·tion (awk´shon) *n.* 1. Public sale at which articles are sold to person making the highest bid. 2. (Also ~ **bridge**): see BRIDGE². ~ *v.t.* Sell (*off*) by auction.

auc·tion·eer (awkshonēr´) *n.* One who conducts auctions.

au·da·cious (awdā´shus) *adj.* Daring, bold; impudent. **au·da´-cious·ly** *adv.* **au·da´cious·ness, au·dac·i·ty** (awdăs´ĭtē) *ns.*

Au·den (aw´den), **Wystan Hugh** (1907–73). English-born poet and dramatist.

*The Temple of Zeus, built in 130 A.D., is in Athens, the chief city of **Attica**, a region of ancient Greece which was controlled and dominated by Athens from the 5th century B.C.*

A large **audience** gathered for a concert. At outdoor concerts and sporting events, the audience may total more than 100,000 people.

au·di·ble (aw′di̇bel) *adj.* That can be heard. **au′di·bly** *adv.*
au·di·bil·i·ty (awdi̇bil′īte) *n.*
au·di·ence (aw′dēens) *n.* Hearing; formal interview; persons within hearing; group of listeners or spectators.
au·di·o (aw′dēō) *adj.* Of (the reproduction of) sound; ~ **frequency**: see FREQUENCY. ~ *n.* 1. Reproduction of sound. 2. Audio element of television.
au·di·ol·o·gy (awdēŏl′ojē) *n.* Science of hearing. **au·di·ol′o·gist** *n.*
au·di·om·e·ter (awdēŏm′īter) *n.* Instrument for measuring the sensitivity of the ear to sounds.
au·di·o·phile (aw′dēofīl) *n.* Devotee of high-fidelity sound reproduction (on radios, record players, etc.).
au·di·o·vis·u·al (awdēōvĭzh′-ōōal) *adj.* Of or pertaining to both hearing and sight, esp. in educational materials such as movies, filmstrips, recordings, etc.
au·dit (aw′dĭt) *n.* Official examination of financial records or accounts. ~ *v.t.* 1. Examine (financial records) officially. 2. Register for and attend (class) without intending to obtain credits.
au·di·tion (awdĭsh′on) *n.* Hearing; trial hearing of actor, singer, etc., seeking employment. ~ *v.* Test, be tested, by an audition.
au·di·tor (aw′dĭter) *n.* 1. One who audits financial records. 2. College or university student who audits classes.
au·di·to·ri·um (awdĭtor′ēum, -tōr′-) *n.* 1. Room in a theater, school, or other building where audience sits. 2. Building for public meetings, concerts, theatrical performances, etc.
au·di·to·ry (aw′dĭtōrē, -tōrē) *adj.* Of hearing.
Au·du·bon (aw′dubŏn, -bon), **John James** (1785–1851). Amer. naturalist and painter; author of *Birds of America*, engraved in aquatint (1827–38).
auf Wie·der·seh·en (owf vē′der-zāen). (Goodby) till we meet again. [Ger.]
Aug. *abbrev.* August.
Au·ge·an (awjē′an) *adj.* Abominably filthy; resembling the stables of Augeas, legendary king of Elis, which went uncleaned for many years until Hercules, as one of his labors, accomplished the cleaning by diverting the river Alpheus through them.
au·ger (aw′ger) *n.* Tool for boring holes in wood, having a long shank with cutting edge and screw point, and handle at right angles.

aught¹, ought (awt) *ns.* Anything.
aught² (awt) = OUGHT¹.
aug·ment (awgmĕnt′) *v.* Increase, enlarge. **aug·ment′ed** *adj.* (esp., mus., of an interval) Widened by a semitone. **aug·men·ta·tion** (awgmĕntā′shon) *n.* Enlargement; addition; (mus.) repetition of a passage in notes longer than those of the original.
au gra·tin (ō grah′tin, ō grăt′in). Cooked with crisp brown crust usu. of bread crumbs or grated cheese.
au·gur (aw′ger) *n.* 1. (Rom. antiq.) Religious official who foretold future events by observing flight or notes of birds etc. 2. Soothsayer. ~ *v.* Forebode, anticipate; ~ **well, ill**, have good (bad) implications or expectations *of, for*.
au·gu·ry (aw′gyerē) *n.* (pl. **-ries**). Divination; omen.

*Illustration of an oriole, one of 435 plates from 'Birds of America'. The book is the masterpiece of **J. J. Audubon** (1785–1851), the American naturalist painter and author.*

Au·gust (aw′gust). Eighth month of Gregorian (5th of Julian) calendar, with 31 days. [named after Rom. emperor AUGUSTUS]
au·gust (awgŭst′) *adj.* Majestic, venerable. **au·gust′ly** *adv.* **au·gust′ness** *n.* [L. *augustus* consecrated, venerable]
Au·gus·ta¹ (awgŭs′ta). City in E. Georgia; the former state capital.
Au·gus·ta² (awgŭs′ta). Capital city of Maine, in the SW. on the Kennebec River.
Au·gus·tan (awgŭs′tan) *adj.* Of AUGUSTUS; ~ **Age**, period of literary eminence in the life of a nation, so called because Virgil, Horace, Ovid, etc., all flourished

The great **auk** (Pinguinus impennis), now extinct. Auks are short-winged sea-divers, ranging from 7 to 30 ins. in length. There are 22 species.

'St. Augustine in his Cell' by Botticelli. **St. Augustine** (354–430 A.D.). Bishop of Hippo in N. Africa, was in his day the dominant personality of the Western church.

uring Augustus' reign; in English terary history, the period of Pope nd Addison.

Au·gus·tine[1] (aw´gustĕn, aw-us´tĭn), **St.** (354–430). Doctor of ne church; son of a pagan father nd Christian mother (St. Monica); as for a time attracted by Manicheanism, but baptized as a Christian 387; became bishop of Hippo in N. Africa 391; defended Christianity in numerous writings, f which the best known are the City of God (Civitas Dei) and the utobiographical Confessions; commemorated Aug. 28.

Au·gus·tine[2] (aw´gustĕn, aw-us´tĭn), **St.** (d. 604). First archbishop of Canterbury; led mission o England from Rome and founded monastery at Canterbury; commemorated in England May 26, lsewhere May 28.

Au·gus·tin·i·an (awgustĭn´ēan) dj. Of St. AUGUSTINE[1] of Hippo; ~ **Friars**, mendicant order found-d c1250 and following Augustin-an principles.

Au·gus·tus (awgŭs´tus) (63 B.C.–4 A.D.). Gaius Octavius ("Octa-ian"), named Gaius Julius Caesar Octavianus after his adoption by ulius Caesar, his great-uncle; member of the 2nd triumvirate and irst Roman emperor; the title of Augustus was conferred on him by enate and people in 27 B.C. and was orne by all subsequent Roman

emperors.

au jus (ō zhoo´, ō joos´). (of meat) Served with the natural juices obtained during roasting.

auk (awk) n. Any of the Alcidae, a family of seabirds that includes the guillemot, puffin, razorbill, little auk (Plautus alle), and the great auk (Pinguinus impennis), formerly inhabiting N. Atlantic but extinct since mid-19th c.

auld lang syne (awld´ lăng zīn´, sīn´, ōld´). The days of long ago. [Sc., old long since]

Au·lis (aw´lis). Ancient Greek town on Boeotian coast, where (in legend) the Greek fleet was detained by contrary winds before the Trojan War, and where Iphigenia was offered for sacrifice.

au na·tu·rel (ō nătyürĕl´). (Cooked) in the simplest way; uncooked, in a natural state; nude. [Fr.]

aunt (ănt, ahnt) n. Father's or mother's sister; uncle's wife.

aunt·ie, aunt·y (ăn´tē, ahn´tē) ns. (pl. **aunt·ies**). (colloq.) Aunt.

au pair (ō pār´). (Person, esp. young girl) performing domestic duties in foreign country in return for room and board or a small salary. ~ adv. phr. [Fr.]

au·ra (ōr´a) n. Subtle emanation; atmosphere diffused by or attending a person etc. (esp. in mystical use as definite envelope

of body or spirit).

au·ral (ōr´al) adj. Of, received by, the ear. **au´ral·ly** adv.

Au·re·li·an (awrē´lēan, -rĕl´-yan). Lucius Domitius Aurelianus (c212–75 A.D.). Roman emperor, 270–5.

au·re·ole (ōr´ēōl), **au·re·o·la** (awrē´ola) ns. Celestial crown or halo worn by martyrs, saints, virgins, etc.; halo, esp. that of the sun seen in eclipses. [L. aureola (corona) golden crown]

Au·re·o·my·cin (ōrēōmī´sĭn) n. (trademark) Chlortetracycline.

au re·voir (ō revwār´). (Goodby) till we meet again. [Fr.]

au·ri·cle (ōr´ĭkel) n. 1. External ear of animals; earlike part. 2. Small appendage of the ATRIUM, def. 2.

au·ric·u·la (awrĭk´yula) n. Species of alpine primula with ear-shaped leaf. [L. auris ear]

au·ric·u·lar (awrĭk´yuler) adj. Pertaining to or like the ear; aural; pertaining to auricle of the heart.

au·rif·er·ous (awrĭf´erus) adj. Yielding gold.

Au·ri·gna·cian (ōrĭnyā´shan) adj. & n. (Of) a paleolithic culture believed to have existed in France c11,500–10,000 B.C. [f. Aurignac in Haute-Garonne, SW. France, where flint implements were found]

Au·ro·ra (awrōr´a, -rōr´a).

University of Texas at **Austin,** the capital of Texas, founded in 1840, originally named Waterloo.

(Rom. myth.) Goddess of the dawn, corresponding to the Greek Eos.

au·ro·ra (awrōr´*a*, -rôr´*a*) *n.* (poet.) Dawn; ~ **aus·tra·lis** (awstrā´lĭs), phenomenon similar to aurora borealis, seen in southern latitudes; ~ **bo·re·al·is** (bōrĕăl´ĭs, bōr-), luminous phenomenon, popularly called the *northern lights,* seen in northern latitudes esp. at night, usu. appearing as streamers of many colors ascending from above the northern horizon and supposed to be of electrical origin.

Ausch·witz (owsh´vĭts). City in S. Poland; site of an infamous Nazi concentration camp during World War II.

aus·cul·ta·tion (awskŭltā´shon) *n.* Act of listening, esp. (med.) to movement of heart, lungs, etc., as with a stethoscope. **aus·cul·ta·to·ry** (awskŭl´tatōrē, -tōrē) *adj.*

Map and flag of **Austria,** a republic in 1918 after break-up of the Austro-Hungarian Empire. It was annexed by Hitler in 1938, freed in 1945 and became a republic again in 1955.

aus·pice (aw´spĭs) *n.* (pl. **aus·pic·es** pr. aw´spĭsĭz, -sēz). Observation of birds for purpose taking omens; omen, sign; (p patronage; approving suppor **aus·pi·cious** (awspĭsh´*us*) *adj.* good omen; favorable; prosperou **aus·pi·cious·ly** *adv.* **aus·pi cious·ness** *n.*

Aus·sie (aw´sē) *n.* (slan Australian, orig. of Australia troops in World War I.

Aus·ten (aw´sten), **Jane** (1775 1817). English author of six novel *Pride and Prejudice, Northange Abbey, Sense and Sensibility, Mans field Park, Emma,* and *Persuasion.*

aus·tere (awstēr´) *adj.* Harsh stern; stringently moral; severel simple; frugal; thrifty. **aus·tere´l** *adv.* **aus·tere´ness** *n.* **aus·ter·i·t** (awstĕr´ĭtē) *n.* (pl. **-ties**). Qualit of being austere; severity, austere o ascetic practice.

Aus·ter·litz (aw´sterlĭts, ow´-) Town in Moravia, scene in 1805 o Napoleon's defeat of the Austrian and Russians.

Aus·tin[1] (aws´tĭn). Capital cit of Texas, in the central part on th Colorado River.

Aus·tin[2] (aws´tĭn), **Stephe Fuller** (1793–1836). America colonizer and political leader of th Texas Republic; worked towar Texas statehood.

aus·tral (aw´stral) *adj.* South ern. [L. *Auster,* the south wind]

Aus·tral·a·sia (awstralā´zha -sha). Term used loosely to includ Australia and the islands scattere over the SW. Pacific. **Aus·tral·a´ sian** *adj.* & *n.*

Aus·tral·ia (awstrāl´ya). Conti nent of S. hemisphere in the SW Pacific; federal commonwealth member nation of the British Commonwealth. The existence of a *Terra Australis* ("southern land" was known in Europe in the 16th c.; British colonization began in 1788; in 1901 the six colonies (New South Wales, Victoria, Queensland South Australia, Western Australia, and Tasmania) federated as sovereign states of the **Common wealth of** ~, which also adminis ters Northern Territory, Capita Territory (site of the federal capital. Canberra), and certain areas outside the continent.

Aus·tral·ian (awstrāl´yan) *adj* Of Australia; ~ **ballot,** ballot listing all the candidates, given to the voter at the polls and marked in secret; ~ **crawl,** form of crawl stroke in swimming originating in Australia. **Australian** *n.* Native or inhabitant of Australia.

Aus·tra·loid (aw´straloid), **Aus·tra·li·oid** (awstrā´lēoid) *adjs.* & *ns.* (Of) the ethnological types of Australian Aborigines.

Aus·tri·a (aw´strēa). German-speaking country of central Europe,

The island continent of **Australia** in the S.W. Pacific is rich in fauna and flora, and mineral resources. Its climate is diverse, hot and arid in much of the interior, temperate in the S.E. and S.W. British colonization began in 1788. Top: View across Sydney Harbor, showing the Opera House, originally controversial but now one of the most admired of modern buildings. Center: A view of Ayers Rock, the world's largest monolith rising 1,104 ft. above an open plain in S.W. Northern Territory. Bottom: Harvesting in progress at Humpty Doo, Northern Territory.

which became a republic in 1918; formerly it was the nucleus of the Austro-Hungarian Empire; it became a duchy in 1156 and later the seat of the Hapsburg emperors; in 1918 the empire was divided between Hungary, Poland, Czechoslovakia, Italy, Rumania, Yugoslavia, and Austria itself; in March 1938 Austria was forcibly annexed to the Third Reich; it was liberated from Nazi rule in 1945; capital, Vienna. **Aus′tri·an** *adj.* & *n.* (Native) of Austria.

Aus·tro·ne·sia (awstrōnē′zha, -sha). Islands of the central and south Pacific Ocean including Indonesia, Micronesia, Melanesia, and Polynesia.

au·tar·chy (aw′tārkē) *n.* (pl. **-chies**). Absolute sovereignty, despotism. [Gk. *autarkhia* (*arkhō* rule)]

auth. *abbrev.* Author; authorized.

au·then·tic (awthěn′tĭk) *adj.* Reliable, trustworthy; of undisputed origin. **au·then′ti·cal·ly** *adv.* **au·then·tic·i·ty** (awthěntĭs′ĭtē) *n.*

au·then·ti·cate (awthěn′tĭkāt) *v.t.* (**-cat·ed, -cat·ing**). Establish the truth or authorship of; make valid.

au·thor (aw′ther), fem. **au·thor·ess** (aw′therĭs) *ns.* Originator; writer of book etc. ~ *v.t.* Be the author or. **au′thor·ship** *n.*

au·thor·i·tar·i·an (awthŏrĭtār′ēan, -thār-) *adj.* Favoring obedience to authority as opp. to individual liberty; of, pertaining to, a dictatorship. ~ *n.* Authoritarian person.

au·thor·i·ta·tive (athŏr′ĭtātĭv, athār′-) *adj.* Possessing or claiming authority. **au·thor′i·ta·tive·ly** *adv.*

au·thor·i·ty (athŏr′ĭtē, athār′-) *n.* (pl. **-ties**). Power or right to act, command, or enforce obedience; delegated power; person etc. having authority; personal influence; expert.

au·thor·ize (aw′therīz) *v.t.* (**-ized, -iz·ing**). Sanction; give ground for; give authority to; **Authorized Version**, (of the Bible) the English translation of 1611, the *King James Bible*.

au·tism (aw′tĭzem) *n.* Morbid absorption in fantasy; condition, esp. in children, preventing proper response to environment. **au·tis·tic** (awtĭs′tĭk) *adj.*

au·to (aw′tō) *n.* (pl. **-tos**). Automobile.

auto-, aut- *prefixes.* Self, by one's or its own agency.

au·to·bahn (aw′tobahn) *n.* In Germany, an express highway. [Ger.]

au·to·bi·og·ra·phy (awtobĭŏg′rafē, -bē-) *n.* (pl. **-phies**). Writing the story of one's own life; the story

front sight   barrel   locking ribs   chamber   firing pin spring   rear sight
firing pin
hammer
hammer strut
grip safety
plug
recoil spring
barrel bushing
magazine
trigger
magazine catch
mainspring
mainspring housing
housing pin

M1911 A1 Colt .45 semi-automatic pistol. Pulling the trigger releases the hammer which the mainspring drives against the firing pin. Below Recoil action after firing. As the spent shell is ejected, the magazine spring pushes the next round up into the chamber, but the trigger must be squeezed again to fire the next bullet.

so written. **au·to·bi·o·graph·i·cal** (awtobīŏgrăf′ĭkal), **au·to·bi·o·graph′ic** adjs. **au·to·bi·og′ra·pher** n.

au·toch·thon (awtŏk′thon) n. (pl. **-thons, -tho·nes** pr. -thonēz). Original inhabitant. **au·toch·tho·nous** (awtŏk′thonus) adj.

au·to·clave (aw′toklāv) n. Vessel in which chemical reactions take place at high temperatures under pressure; apparatus for sterilizing by steam at high pressure. ~ v. (**-claved, -clav·ing**).

au·toc·ra·cy (awtŏk′rasē) n. (pl. **-cies**). Absolute government.

au·to·crat (aw′tokrăt) n. Absolute ruler; dictatorial overbearing person. **au·to·crat·ic** (awtokrăt′ĭk) adj. **au·to·crat′i·cal·ly** adv.

au·to·da·fé (awtōdafā′) n. (pl. **au·tos·da·fé**). Sentence of the Spanish Inquisition; execution of this, esp. burning of a heretic. [Port., = "act of faith"]

au·to·gi·ro (awtojīr′ō) n. (pl. **-ros**). Early form of helicopter with a conventional propeller for forward motion and freely rotating horizontal vanes that provide lift, keep the craft airborne, and permit slow and steep descent.

au·to·graph (aw′togrăf, -grahf) n. Person's own handwriting, esp. signature for keeping as a memento; document signed by its author, as dist. from HOLOGRAPH, one wholly written in his hand (freq. attrib., as ~ **letter**). ~ v.t. Write one's signature on or in; sign. **au·to·graph·ic** (awtogrăf′ĭk), **au·to·graph′i·cal** adjs. **au·to·graph′i·cal·ly** adv.

au·to·mat (aw′tomăt) n. Cafeteria in which meals etc. are provided from closed compartments into which customers deposit coins.

au·to·mate (aw′tomăt) v.

(**-mat·ed, -mat·ing**). Apply automation (to).

au·to·mat·ic (awtomăt′ĭk) adj. Working of itself, without direct human actuation; mechanical; unconscious; necessary, inevitable; ~ **control**, device enabling machine to maintain a predetermined temperature, pressure, speed, etc., without intervention of operator; ~ **pilot**, similar device in aircraft for maintaining a set course or altitude; ~ **pistol, rifle**, firearm which, after each shot is exploded, by gas pressure or force of recoil automatically ejects the empty case, loads another into the chamber, and fires, repeating this movement until

the ammunition in the mechanism is exhausted or pressure on the trigger is released; ~ **transmission**, system in motor vehicle in which gears engage automatically according to the speed of the vehicle or by means of a torque converter **automatic** n. Automatic pistol, machine, tool, etc. operated automatically. **au·to·mat′i·cal·ly** adv

au·to·ma·tion (awtomā′shon) n Completely automatic control of a

*A 1956 U.S. designed Thunderbird. The first true **automobile** was built in 1769 by Frenchman Nicolas-Joseph Cugnot, whose cumbersome steam-driven tricycle travelled at 2.25 m.p.h.*

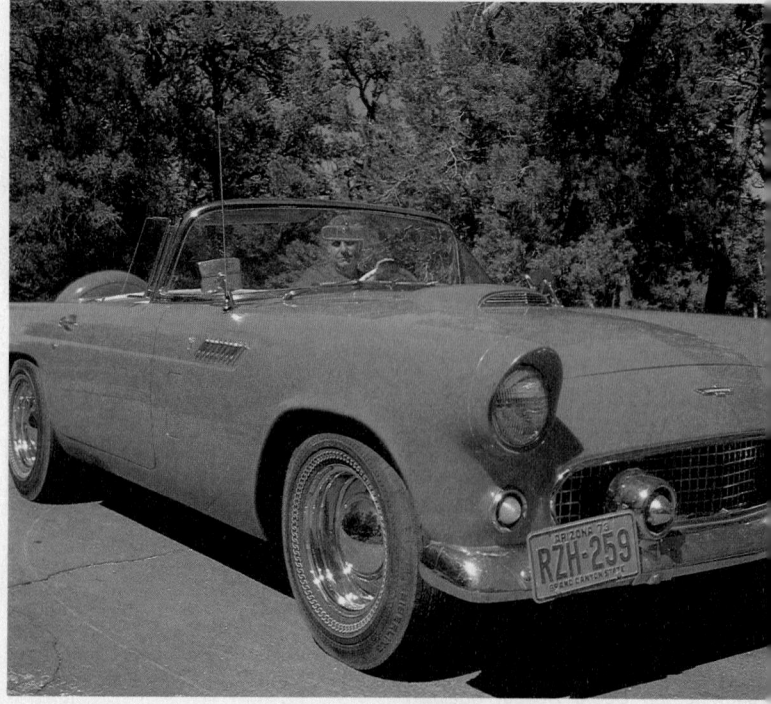

RZH-259

manufactured product through a number of successive stages; use of automatic mechanical or electronic devices.

au·tom·a·ton (awtŏm´atŏn, -ton) *n*. (pl. **-tons, -ta** pr. -ta). Robot; person whose actions are mechanical, following a customary routine.

au·to·mo·bile (awtomōbēl´, aw´tomobēl, awtomō´bēl, -bĭl) *n*. Motor-driven passenger road vehicle, usu. four-wheeled and propelled by an internal-combustion engine.

au·to·mo·tive (awtomō´tĭv) *adj*. Concerned with motor vehicles.

au·to·nom·ic (awtonŏm´ĭk) *adj*. (physiol.) Of that part of the nervous system (~ or *involuntary nervous system*) which functions more or less independently of the will, comprising the sympathetic and parasympathetic nervous systems.

au·ton·o·mous (awtŏn´omus) *adj*. 1. Self-governing. 2. (physiol., path.) Independent of the usual processes that regulate the growth of an organism. **au·ton´o·mous·ly** *adv*.

au·ton·o·my (awtŏn´omē) *n*. Right of self-government; freedom of the will.

au·to·pis·ta (aw´topĭsta) *n*. In Spain and Spanish-speaking countries, an express highway. [Span.]

au·top·sy (aw´tŏpsē, -top-) *n*. (pl. **-sies**). Examination of a corpse to determine the cause of death; post-mortem examination.

au·to·route (aw´tōrōot) *n*. In France, an express highway. [Fr.]

au·to·stra·da (awtōstrah´da) *n*. In Italy, an express highway. [It.]

au·tumn (aw´tum) *n*.: see FALL (*n*. def. 2); (fig.) season of incipient decay. **au·tum·nal** (awtŭm´nal) *adj*. Of autumn.

aux·il·ia·ry (awgzĭl´yerē, -zĭl´erē) *adj*. Helpful; supplemental; subsidiary; (gram., of verbs) serving to form tenses, moods, voices, of other verbs. ~ *n*. (pl. **-ries**). 1. Auxiliary person, group, theory. 2. (esp. pl.) Foreign troops serving with another country in war; (naval) vessel auxiliary to fighting vessels, as tanker, supply ship, etc.

av. *abbrev*. Average; avoirdupois.

A.V. *abbrev*. Authorized Version (of the Bible).

a·vail (avāl´) *v*. Be of use or assistance (to); help, benefit. ~ *n*. Use, profit.

a·vail·a·ble (avā´label) *adj*. At one's disposal, at hand; capable of being used. **a·vail·a·bil·i·ty** (avālabĭl´ītē) *n*.

av·a·lanche (ăv´alănch, -lahnch) *n*. Mass of snow, rock, and ice, sliding suddenly down mountain (also fig.).

Av·a·lon (ăv´alŏn). In the Arthurian legend, the place to which ARTHUR[1] was conveyed after death; (Welsh myth.) kingdom of the dead.

a·vant-garde (ăvahntgărd´, a-vănt-) *n*. Pioneers or innovators, esp. in any art in a particular period (freq. attrib.). [Fr.]

av·a·rice (ăv´erĭs) *n*. Greed for gain, cupidity. **av·a·ri·cious** (ăve-rĭsh´us) *adj*. **av·a·ri´cious·ly** *adv*.

a·vast (avăst´) *int*. (naut.) Stop, cease. [Du. *houd vast* hold fast]

av·a·tar (ăv´atär) *n*. (Hinduism) Descent to earth and incarnation of a deity.

a·vaunt (avawnt´) *int*. (archaic) Begone.

avdp. *abbrev*. Avoirdupois.

ave. *abbrev*. Avenue.

Ave·bur·y (āv´berē). Village in Wiltshire, England, site of a very large prehistoric stone circle.

A·ve Ma·ri·a (ah´vā marē´a), **A·ve Mar·y** (ah´vē mār´ē, ah´vā). (= Hail, Mary!), the angelic salutation to the Virgin (Luke 1:28), combined with that of Elizabeth (Luke 1:42), used as a devotional recitation, together with a prayer to the Virgin. ~ *n*. Utterance of this recitation and prayer. [L. *ave* hail]

a·venge (avĕnj´) *v.t.* (**a·venged, a·veng·ing**). Inflict retribution on behalf of; exact retribution for.

av·ens (ăv´enz) *n*. Small rose-aceous plant of genus *Jeum*.

Av·en·tine (ăv´entīn). Most southerly of the seven Hills of Rome.

a·ven·tu·rine (avĕn´cherĭn) *n*. Brownish glass with copper crystals, first manufactured near Venice; quartz, spangled with mica or hematite, resembling this. [It. *avventura* chance (from its accidental discovery)]

Avant-garde art challenges current and historical presumptions about the nature of art. Jackson Pollock's

'Alchemy', below, challenged concepts of orderly organization.

The **avocet**, *a wading bird about 18 ins. long which feeds in shallows by sifting water through its up-curved beak. There are four species distributed round the world.*

Avocado *with segment showing the large seed. In 1519 a Spanish explorer was the first European to discover the tree and fruit near Santa Marta, Colombia.*

av·e·nue (ăv′enū, -noō) *n.* Way of approach; approach to large house, bordered by trees; roadway with trees etc. at regular intervals; wide street, main thoroughfare.

a·ver (avēr′) *v.t.* (**a·verred, a·ver·ring**). Assert, affirm.

av·er·age (ăv′erĭj, ăv′rĭj) *n.* Arithmetical mean; generally prevailing amount, degree; **on the ~**, usually; typically; generally. **average** *adj.* Estimated by average; typical, ordinary. ~ *v.t.* (**-aged, -ag·ing**). Calculate an average value for; **~ out**, achieve or end with an average. [Arab. *'awārīya* damaged goods]

A·ver·ro·ës (avĕr′ōēz). Abul Walid Muhammad ben Ahmed ibn Rushd (1126–98), Muslim doctor born at Cordova, philosopher, and author of a famous commentary on Aristotle.

a·verse (avērs′) *adj.* Opposed, disciplined (*to, from*); unwilling.

a·ver·sion (avēr′zhon, -shon) *n.* Dislike, unwillingness; object of dislike.

a·vert (avērt′) *v.t.* Turn away; ward off.

A·ves·ta (avĕs′ta) *n.* Collection of sacred Zoroastrian writings. **A·ves′tan, A·ves′tic** *adjs. & ns.* (Of) the ancient E. Iranian language in which the Avesta is written.

a·vi·an (ā′vēan) *adj.* Of birds.

a·vi·ar·y (ā′vēĕrē) *n.* (pl. **-ar·ies**). Large cage or building for keeping birds.

a·vi·a·tion (āvēā′shon, ăvē-) *n.* 1. Method or practice of flying aircraft; operation of aircraft. 2. Design and manufacture of air-

craft.

a·vi·a·tor (ā′vēāter, ăvē-) *n.* (fem. **a·vi·a·trix** pr. āvēā′trĭks, ăvē-). Aircraft pilot.

av·id (ăv′ĭd) *adj.* Eager, greedy. **av′id·ly** *adv.* **a·vid·i·ty** (avĭd′ĭtē) *n.*

A·vi·gnon (ăvēnyawn′). City on river Rhône, in S. France, to which Clement V removed the papal seat in 1308; it remained there until 1377, and after the papal schism in 1378 two antipopes, Clement VII and Benedict XIII, resided there; the latter was expelled in 1408, but the city remained in papal possession until 1791.

a·vi·on·ics (āvēŏn′ĭks, ăvē-) *n.* Application of electronics in aviation. **a·vi·on′ic** *adj.*

av·o·ca·do (ăvokah′dō, ahvo-) *n.* (pl. **-dos**). Succulent pear-shaped fruit, a drupe with soft-coated seed, borne by the tropical Amer. and W. Indian tree *Persea gratissima.* [Span. *avocado* advocate, corrupt. of Mex. name]

av·o·ca·tion (ăvokā′shon) *n.* Minor occupation; hobby.

av·o·cet (ăv′osĕt) *n.* Wading bird with long upturned beak (*Recurvirostra americana*).

A·vo·ga·dro (ahvogah′drō), **Amadeo** (1776–1856). Italian physicist; **~'s law**, hypothesis that equal volumes of all gases at the same temperature and pressure contain equal numbers of molecules; **~'s number**, number of molecules in the gram-molecular weight of any gas; value, 6.02×10^{23}.

a·void (avoid′) *v.t.* Shun, refrain

from; evade, escape. **a·void′a·ble** *adj.* **a·void′a·bly** *adj.* **a·void′ance** *n.*

av·oir·du·pois (ăverdupoiz′) *n.* System of weights and measures based on ounces and pounds, a pound containing 16 ounces or 7,000 grains and equal to 453.59 grams. [corrupt. of Fr. *avoir de pois* goods of weight]

A·von[1] (ā′von, ăv′on). River, flowing through Warwickshire, England, a tributary of the Severn (**Bard of ~**, sobriquet for Shakespeare, who was born at Stratford-upon-Avon).

A·von[2] (ā′von, ăv′on). County of SW. England.

a·vow (avow′) *v.t.* Admit, confess. **a·vow′al** *n.* **a·vow′ed·ly** *adv.*

a·vun·cu·lar (avŭng′kyuler) *adj.* Of, resembling, an uncle.

aw (aw) *int.* Expression of mild remonstrance, commiseration, protest, etc.

a·wait (awāt′) *v.t.* Wait for.

a·wake (awāk′) *v.* (**a·woke** pr. awōk′ or **a·waked, a·wak·ing**). Cease to sleep; rouse from sleep. ~ *pred. adj.* Not asleep; vigilant. **a·wak′en** *v.* Awake. **a·wak′en·ing** *adj.* Rousing, stirring. ~ *n.* 1. Act of awaking from sleep. 2. Arousal of interest or attention. 3. Entering into state of awareness about something. 4. Revival of interest in religion.

a·ward (awōrd′) *v.t.* Give as payment, prize, etc.; grant, assign. ~ *n.* Judicial decision; payment, penalty, assigned by this; prize; grant.

a·ware (awār′) *pred. adj.* Conscious, not ignorant (*of, that*). **a·ware′ness** *n.*

a·wash (awŏsh′, awawsh′) *pred. adj.* Flush with or washed by the waves.

a·way (awā′) *adv.* To or at a distance; on opponent's ground; far, separate; aside, to a different place; **~ with**, go away, take away. **away** *adj.* Absent; distant; (of game) played on opponent's ground.

awe (aw) *n.* Reverential fear. ~ *v.t.* (**awed, aw·ing**). Inspire with awe. **awe·some** (aw′som) *adj.* **awe·strick·en** (aw′strĭken), **awe·struck** (aw′strŭk) *adjs.* Struck with awe.

a·weigh (awā′) *adv.* (of anchor) Just raised from bottom in weighing.

aw·ful (aw′ful) *adj.* Inspiring awe, fear, or dread; (colloq.) very bad, ugly, disliked, etc. **aw·ful·ly** (aw′fulē, aw′flē) *adv.* (esp. colloq.) Extremely. **aw′ful·ness** *n.*

a·while (ahwīl′, awīl′) *adv.* For a short time.

awk·ward (awk′werd) *adj.* Ill adapted for use; hard to deal with; clumsy; inconvenient, embarrass-

The **axolotl,** a salamander found in mountain lakes of Mexico and southwestern U.S.A. The name applies to any neotenic salamander i.e. one that matures sexually in the larval stage.

The **aye-aye** is a tree-climbing, nocturnal primate 31 to 41 ins. long, including the tail. It is now rare because most of its forest habitat in Madagascar has been destroyed.

ing. **awk·ward·ly** adv. **awk'-ward·ness** n.

awl (awl) n. Small pointed tool for piercing holes in leather, wood, etc., esp. that used by shoemakers.

awn·ing (aw´nĭng) n. Sheet of canvas etc. stretched on framework as protection from sun etc.

a·woke (awōk´) v.: see AWAKE.

A.W.O.L. abbrev. Absent without leave.

a·wry (arī´) adv. & pred. adj. Crookedly; amiss.

ax, axe (ăks) ns. (pl. **ax·es** pr. ăk´sĭz). Metal tool for chopping, cleaving, etc., with wooden handle; **get the** ~, (colloq.) to be dismissed from one's job. **ax, axe** vbs. t. (**axed, ax·ing**). Cut down (personnel, expenses, etc.); put an end to (project); **have an** ~ **to grind**, (colloq.) to have one's own special interest to promote.

ax·i·al (ăk´sēal) adj. Forming, belonging to, an axis. **ax´i·al·ly** adv.

ax·il (ăk´sĭl) n. Upper angle between leaf and stem it springs from, or between branch and trunk.

ax·i·om (ăk´sēom) n. Self-evident truth; established principle; maxim; (geom.) self-evident theorem. **ax·i·o·mat·ic** (ăksēomăt´ĭk) adj. **ax·i·o·mat´i·cal·ly** adv.

ax·is (ăk´sĭs) n. (pl. **ax·es** pr. ăk´sēz). 1. Line about which a body rotates; straight line from end to end of a body. 2. (math.) Line dividing a regular figure symmetrically; line by revolution about which a plane figure is conceived as generating a solid. 3. (bot.) Main stem or shoot; **floral** ~, that part of a shoot which bears the floral organs, receptacle. 4. (anat.) Second cervical vertebra, on which the head turns. 5. Alliance between two or more countries; **the A~**, alliance between Germany and Italy, and later Japan, during World War II.

ax·le (ăk´sel) n. Spindle on or with which wheel revolves; end of axletree; axletree; **ax´letree,** bar connecting wheels of carriage etc.

Ax·min·ster (ăks´mĭnster) n. Small town in Devon, England; ~ **carpet,** carpet of cut pile, first made at Axminster, orig. in imitation of hand-knotted oriental carpets.

ax·o·lotl (ăk´solŏtel) n. Salamander of genus *Ambystoma* of mountain lakes of Mexico and southwestern U.S., usu. retaining larval form throughout life. [Aztec]

ax·on (ăk´sŏn), **ax·one** (ăk´sōn) ns. That part of the nerve which is its conducting element or nerve fiber.

a·yah (ah´ya) n. Hindu nurse. [Port. *aia* fem. of *aio* tutor]

a·ya·tol·lah (ahyahtō´la) n. Chief spiritual leader of Shiite Muslims.

aye[1]**, ay**[1] (ī) advs. (esp. Sc. & dial.) Yes. ~ n. (pl. **ayes**). Affirmative answer or vote.

aye[2]**, ay**[2] (ā) advs. (literary) Always; **for** ~, for ever.

aye-aye (ī´ī) n. Small tree-climbing animal (genus *Daubentonia*) found in Madagascar, a primate related to the lemurs.

Ayr·shire (âr´shēr, -sher). Former county of SW. Scotland; hence, breed of dairy cattle, mostly white with reddish or black markings, orig. raised there; kind of bacon cured in Ayrshire.

AZ abbrev. Arizona.

a·zal·ea (azāl´ya) n. Flowering shrubby plant of the genus *Rhododendron*, chiefly native of N. America and China. [mod. L. f. Gk. *azaleos* parched, because Linnaeus believed them to grow in dry situations]

A·zer·bai·jan, A·zer·bai·dzhan (ahzerbījahn´, ăzer-). 1. One of the constituent republics (properly *Azerbaijan Soviet Socialist Republic*) of the U.S.S.R., lying between the Black and Caspian Seas; capital Baku. 2. Former province of NW. Iran, now divided into **Eastern** ~ and **Western** ~. **A·zer·bai·ja·ni** (ahzerbījah´nē, ăzer-) n. (pl. **-ja·nis,** collect. **-ja·ni**). (Native, inhabitant, language) of Azerbaijan.

az·i·muth (ăz´imuth) n. Arc of the heavens extending from the zenith to the horizon, which it cuts at right angles; (in full, **true** ~ of a heavenly body) arc of horizon intercepted between north (in S. hemisphere, south) point of horizon and the point where the vertical circle passing through the body cuts the horizon. [Arab. *al samt* the way, road, used in astron. for azimuth]

az·o (ăz´ō) adj. (chem.) Containing the **azo group,** —N = N—, where both bonds are attached to carbon atoms.

A·zores (azōrz´, azōrz´, ā´zōrz, ā´zōrz). Group of islands in N. Atlantic, some 800 miles W. of Portugal; in Portuguese possession.

Az·tec (ăz´tĕk) adj. & n. (Member, language) of an Indian people first known (c1100 A.D.) as inhabitants of the valley of Mexico; they built their capital (on the same site as modern Mexico City) in 1324 and extended their conquests in the 15th c., their most successful leader being Montezuma I (reigned 1440–1469); they were conquered by the invading Spaniards under Cortez, early in the 16th c.

A·zu·ma (ah´zoo´mah´). Volcano on Honshu Island, Japan.

az·ure (ăzh´er) adj. & n. Sky blue; blue of unclouded sky; lapis lazuli; (heraldry) blue. [Arab. *al lāzuward* lapis lazuli, cerulean blue, f. Pers. *lazhward*]

How (right) the written form of the letter *B, b* has evolved through the ages. Left: the classical grid on which the capital letter is constructed. The letter derives from the Greek beta and the Phoenician and Hebrew beth. It has, from the earliest times, been second letter of nearly all European alphabets.

Phoenician   Early Greek   Early Etruscan

Classical Latin   Anglo-Saxon   Italian (Roman)

B, b (bē) (pl. **B's, b's** or **Bs, bs**). 1. Second letter of modern English and ancient Roman alphabet, representing a voiced bilabial stop, and derived from the Greek *beta* (β) and Phoenician and Hebrew *beth* (ᗡ,ᗂ). 2. Second in series, order, or class. 3. **B**, (mus.) Seventh note in the natural scale (C major); scale or key with this note for tonic. 4. Grade or mark indicating good but not highest quality.

B. *abbrev. Beatus* (fem. -a) (L., = blessed); British; Bible; (music) bass, basso; book.

b. *abbrev.* Born; (baseball) base; brother.

B.A. *abbrev.* Bachelor of Arts.

baa (bă, bah) *n. & v.* (**baaed, baa·ing**). (of sheep) Bleat.

Ba·al (bā'al, bāl) (pl. **Ba·al·im** pr. bā'alĭm). God of the ancient Phoenicians and Canaanites; false god. **Ba'al·ism, Ba'al·ist, Ba'al·ite** *ns.* [Heb. *ba'al* lord, master]

Baal·bek (bahl'běk, bā'al-, bāl'-). Site in Lebanon of the Roman colony of Heliopolis (1st–3rd centuries A.D.), a center of worship of the sun-god Helios, identified with **Baal**.

ba·ba (bah'ba) *n.* (also **baba au rhum** pr. bah'ba ō rŭm'). Small

rich spongecake soaked in rum syrup.

Ba·bar (bah'ber) = **Baber**.

Bab·bitt (băb'ĭt). Hero of a novel (1922) by Sinclair Lewis; hence a materialistic complacent businessman. **Bab'bitt·ry** *n.*

bab·bitt (băb'ĭt) *n.* (also **Babbitt metal**). Soft alloy of tin, copper, and antimony, used for machine bearings. [I. *Babbitt* (1799–1862), Amer. inventor]

bab·ble (băb'el) *v.* (**-bled, -bling**). Talk half articulately, incoherently, foolishly, or excessively; murmur (of stream etc.). ~ *n.* Foolish or childish talk. **bab'ble·ment** *n.* **bab'bler** *n.* Chatterer; teller of secrets.

babe (bāb) *n.* Baby; (slang) an attractive young girl or woman.

Ba·bel (bā'bel, băb'el). (Heb. myth.) = **Babylon**; its people (Gen. 11) tried to build a tower that would reach heaven, but God prevented them by "confounding" their language (so that they could not understand one another) and scattering them abroad.

ba·bel (bā'bel, băb'el) *n.* Scene of confusion and uproar; confused mixture of voices or sounds. [f. **Babel**]

Ba·ber, Ba·bar, Bab·ur (bah'ber) (1483–1530). First Mogul

emperor, descended from Tamburlaine; he conquered most of India c1525.

bab·i·ru·sa, bab·i·rous·sa, bab·i·rus·sa (băbiroo'sa, bahbĭns). Wild hog (*Babirusa babyrussa*) male of which has long upper canine teeth which pierce the lip and grow upward like horns; found only in islands of Celebes and Buru. [Malagasy, = "hog deer"]

Ba·bi Yar (bah'bē yär'). Ravine outside Kiev, U.S.S.R., where the Jews of the city were slaughtered by German troops in 1941.

ba·boon (băboon') *n.* Medium-sized monkey (several species in genus *Papio*) of Arabia and Africa, S. and E. of Sahara, living in bands in open rocky country, occas. tree climbing, characterized by doglike snout, cheek prominences, and colored bare patches on the buttocks; (slang) brutish or ungentlemanly person.

Ba·bur (bah'ber) = **Baber**.

ba·bush·ka (baboosh'ka) *n.* Kerchief tied under chin. [Russ. = grandmother]

ba·by (bā'bē) *n.* (pl. **-bies**). Infant, very young child; childish person; very young animal; thing small of its kind; (fig.) one's responsibility; one's particular interest; (slang) an attractive young girl or woman; ~ **beef**, beef from a calf 12 to 20 months old; ~**blue**, pale blue; ~**'s-breath**, plant of the genus *Gypsophila* with branching clusters of small fragrant white flowers; ~ **buggy**, ~ **carriage**, carriage for one or two children usu. with four wheels, pushed by hand; ~ **face(d)**, (of an adult) having a smooth, plump babylike

The **babirusa**, a wandering wild pig, is a night hunter of the dense forests of Celebes and Buru, Indonesia. A peculiarity of the male is the exaggerated development of its canines.

Left: The **baboon** lives closely with a band or troop of other baboons under a dominant male leader jealous of his harem. Baboons can prove dangerous adversaries.

Facing page: The six preserved columns, 62 ft. high, 7½ ft. in diameter, of the Temple of Jupiter at **Baalbek**, Lebanon. The columns are notable for their carved entablature.

face; ~ **grand (piano)**, see PIANO²;
~ **talk**, the early speech of a very
young child or an adult's imitation
of it; infantile or mincing speech;
~ **tooth**, milk tooth. **ba·by·hood**
n. **ba′by·ish** *adj*. **ba′by·ish·ly**
adv. **ba′by·ish·ness** *n*. **ba′by·**
like *adj*. **baby** *v.t*. (**-bied,**
-by·ing). Treat like a baby.
ba′by-sit *v.i*. (**-sat, -sit′ting**). Act
as **baby-sitter**, person who looks
after child when its parents go out.
   Bab·y·lon (băb′ilon, -lŏn).
Capital city, on the Euphrates, of
the ancient Chaldean Empire; the
Jews were brought there in captivity by Nebuchadnezzar (597 and
586 B.C.); its **hanging** (i.e. terraced)
gardens were one of the Seven
Wonders of the ancient world; it
was sacked by Cyrus of Persia in
538 B.C. **Bab·y·lo·ni·a** (băbi-
lō′nēa). Empire of Babylon.
Bab·y·lo′ni·an *adj*. & *n*.
   bac·ca·lau·re·ate (băkalōr′ēit)
n. 1. Bachelor's degree. 2. Sermon
delivered at a commencement.
   bac·ca·rat, bac·ca·ra (bahka-
rah′, băka-, băh′karah, băk′a-) *ns*.
Gambling card game, played
against banker by players betting
that their hands will be closest to
totaling nine.
   bac·cha·nal (bahkanahl′, băka-
năl′, băk′anal) *adj*. Of Bacchus or
his rites. ~ *n*. Drunken revelry,
wild party.
   Bac·cha·na·lia (băkanāl′ya,
-nā′lēa) *n.pl*. Festival held in honor
of Bacchus; drunken revelry, orgy.
bac·cha·na′lian *adj*.
   bac·chic (băk′ĭk) *adj*. Of Bacchus or his worship; riotous,
drunken.
   Bac·chus (băk′us). (Gk. and
Rom. myth.) God of wine: see
DIONYSUS.
   bac·cif·er·ous (băksĭf′erus)
bac·ci·form (băk′sĭform), **bac-**
civ·or·ous (băksĭv′erus) *adjs*.
Berry-bearing, -shaped, -eating.
   bach (băch) *v*. ~ **it**, live alone
as a bachelor. [abbreviation of
bachelor]
   Bach (bahχ), **Johann Sebas-**
tian (1685–1750). German composer of many fugues and works for
organ and other keyboard instruments, a great Mass, and much
other choral church music.
   bach·e·lor (băch′eler, băch′ler)
n. Unmarried man; bachelor's
degree; **B~ of Arts** (B.A.), **of**
Science (B.Sc.), etc., holder of a
bachelor's degree, one awarded by
a college or university to a person
who successfully completes 4-year
undergraduate study program; the
degree itself; ~**'s button**, any of
various flowers of round or buttonlike form such as the cornflower,
orig. the double variety of *Ranun-*
culus acris; ~ **girl**, (archaic) young
unmarried woman living independently. **Bach′e·lor·dom, bach′e·-**

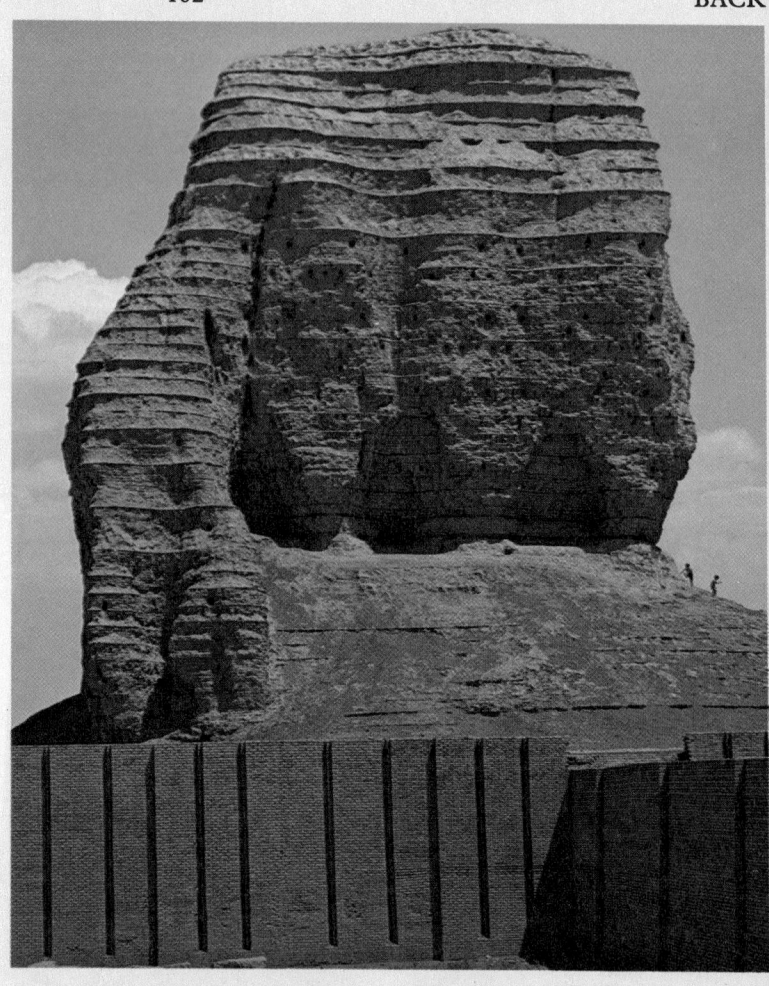

Ziggurat (temple) of Aqar Quf evokes
Babylon. *This famous city of antiquity*
with its hanging gardens lay just north of
the modern town of Hillah in southern
Iraq.

lor·hood, bach′e·lor·ship *ns*.
   ba·cil·lar (basĭl′er, băs′iler),
bac·il·lar·y (băs′ilĕrē) *adjs*. Consisting of little rods; connected
with bacilli.
   ba·cil·li·form (basĭl′iform) *adj*.
Rod-shaped.
   ba·cil·lus (basĭl′us) *n*. (pl. **-cil·li**
pr. -sĭl′ī). Any straight rod-shaped
bacterium; (loosely and usu. pl.)
disease-producing bacteria. [L.
dim. of *baculus* stick]
   back (băk) *n*. Rear surface of
human body, part of this between
shoulders and hips; corresponding
part of animal's body; side or part
away from or farther from spectator
or direction of motion; side of hand
opposite palm; part or area forming
rear of anything; backbone, spine;
(football) player stationed behind
scrimmage line; **behind (some-**
one's) ~, without his knowledge,
treacherously; **get (one's)** ~ **up**,
make (person) angry or stubborn;
turn (one's) ~ **on**, forsake. **back**
adj. Situated behind or at rear;
remote; of, pertaining to, the back;
in arrears, overdue; ~ **country**,

area away from settled districts.
back *adv*. To or at the rear; in(to)
an earlier position; to or in a
remote position. ~ *v*. Put, or be,
a back, lining, support, or background to; sponsor; support with
money, argument, etc. (also ~ **up**);
bet on; (cause to) move back; lay
(sail) against the wind; (of wind)
change counterclockwise (cf. VEER);
~ **down**, abandon claim; ~ **off**,
retreat; ~ **out** (*of*), withdraw
(from). **back′er** *n*. One who backs
or supports. **back′ing** *n*. Support,
assistance. **back-** combining form:
back′ache, pain in the back;
back′bite (*v*.) (**-bit, -bit** or **-bit-**
ten, -bit·ing), slander; **back′biter**
(*n*.); **back′board**, (basketball)
board to which basket is attached;
back′bone, spine, main support,
firmness of character; **back′break-**
ing, arduous; **(on the) back**
burner, deemed less important,
tabled; **back′court**, (as in tennis)
the area between service line and
baseline, or (as in basketball) area
near basket being defended; **back-**
date (*v*.) (**-dat·ed, -dat·ing**), affix
earlier date to (document etc.);
back′door (*adj*.), clandestine;
back′drop, painted curtain hung at
back of stage; setting; **back′field**,
(football) the backs, or the area they
play in; **back′fire** (*n*.), fire

1. Men 2. Points

Backgammon board. The game is one of the oldest known, possibly dating back to 3,000 B.C. The rules were codified in 1743 by Edmond Hoyle.

Action of the S-pull **backstroke,** *used by most world-class swimmers. The hand, forming a lengthened 's' shape, catches the water about 6 ins. below the surface (top) as the pull starts. The hand pulls back and the forearm rotates. The pull ends with a final thrust back and down. Normally the legs are kicked six times during every arm cycle.*

deliberately set to create burned area as protection against oncoming fire; (of internal combustion engine) premature explosion in cylinder or explosion in exhaust pipe; (v.) (**-fired, -fir·ing**), to explode thus; (fig. of plan etc.) go wrong, have adverse effect on instigator; **back formation,** the creation of a word by dropping an apparent affix in another word, as *burgle* from *burglar;* word so formed; **back′ground** (n.), back part of scene or picture; social surroundings, circumstances, origins, environment; (adj.), in, providing, a background; **back′hand,** (tennis etc.) (stroke) with back of hand turned in the direction of move-

ment; **back′handed,** of a similar stroke; (fig.) ambiguous, equivocal; **back′lash,** sudden or violent recoil; (fig.) hostile reaction esp. to real or fancied threat posed by social or racial reforms; **back′log,** large log at back of hearth to keep up fire; accumulation or reserve, of work, business, stock, etc.; **back number,** an out-of-date periodical; (colloq.) anything out of date; **back order** (n. & v.), (place) an order to be sent or filled at a future time; **back′pack,** knapsack usu. mounted on a light frame; (v.i.), hike while carrying a backpack; **back′packer** (n.); **back-pedal** (v.i.) (**-ped·aled** or **-ped·alled, -ped·al·ing** or **-ped·al·ling**), slow (a bicycle) by pedaling backwards; retreat; **back′rest,** a rest for one's back; **back road,** a relatively unused country road, often unpaved; **back seat,** humble or obscure position; **back-seat driver,** one who gives unwanted advice; **back′side,** buttocks; **back′slapper,** a noisy, overly effusive person; **back′slide** (v.i.) (**-slid, -slid** or **-slid·den, -slid·ing**), relapse into sin, error, etc.; **back′space** (v.i.) (**-spaced, -spac·ing**), move typewriter carriage backward by striking designated key; (n.), such a key; **back′spin,** reverse spin imparted to a ball to slow it or change its direction or bounce; **back′stage,** (part of theater) behind the scenes; also fig.; **back′stairs** (adj.), underhand, secret; **back′stitch** (v.), sew by inserting needle each time behind the place where it has just been brought out; (n.), stitch made thus; **back′stop,** a barrier to stop a ball from going too far out of playing area; (baseball, colloq.) the catcher; (colloq.) a substitute or support in case of need; (v.i.) (**-stopped, -stop·ping**), to act as backstop; **back′stroke,** stroke made by swimmer lying on his or her back; **back talk,** impudent repartee; **back′track** (v.), take the same route back; retreat; reverse policy; **back′up,** one who supports; a stoppage (as of traffic, plumbing, etc.); substitute mechanism or program ready if original fails; **back′wash,** motion of receding wave; motion of water caused by passage of vessel; **back′water,** stretch of still water parallel with a stream and fed from it at the lower end; (fig.) a stagnant place or condition; **backwoods′,** remote, only partially settled forest land;

backwoods′man (pl. **-men**), settler in backwoods; **back′yard′,** yard behind a house etc.; (fig.) a familiar or nearby place (esp. one's *own backyard*).

back·gam·mon (băk′găm*o*n, băkgăm′-) n. Game for two persons, played by moving pieces according to the throw of dice, on a board of two tables, each marked off into 12 spaces of alternating colors.

back·less (băk′lĭs) adj. Having no back; (of dress etc.) cut low at the back.

back·ward (băk′w*e*rd) adv. (also **back′wards**). Back foremost; back toward the starting point; the reverse way; toward the rear; ~ **and forward,** to and fro. **backward** adj. Directed to rear or starting point; reversed; slow in learning or developing; bashful, hesitant. **back′ward·ly** adv. **back′ward·ness** n.

ba·con (bā′kon) n. Cured meat from back and sides of a hog; **bring home the** ~, (colloq.) succeed.

Ba·con[1] (bā′kon), **Francis, Baron Verulam and Viscount St. Albans** (1561-1626). Lord Chancellor of England (1618-20), philosopher and essayist. **Ba·co·ni·an** (bākō′nēan) adj. & n. (Advocate) of the theory that Bacon wrote the plays of Shakespeare.

Ba·con[2] (bā′kon), **Roger** (1214?-94). English Franciscan, philosopher and student of experimental science (esp. optics) at Paris and Oxford; credited, then and later, with magical powers.

bac·te·ri·a (băktēr′ēa) n.pl. (sing. **-te·ri·um** pr. -tēr′ēum). Any of several types of microscopic or ultramicroscopic single-celled organisms occurring in enormous numbers everywhere in nature, not only in land, sea, and air, but also on or in many parts of the tissues of plants and animals, and forming one of the main biologically interdependent groups of organisms by virtue of the chemical changes that many of them bring about, e.g. many forms of decay, certain diseases, and the building up of nitrogen compounds in the soil. **bac·te′ri·al** adj. Of or caused by bacteria. **bac·te′ri·al·ly** adv. [Gk. dim. of *baktron* stick]

bac·te·ri·cide (băktēr′ĭsīd) n. Substance that destroys bacteria. **bac·te·ri·cid·al** (băktērĭsī′dal) adj.

bac·te·ri·ol·o·gy (băktērēŏl′ojē) n. Study of bacteria, esp. as a branch of medicine. **bac·te·ri·o·log·i·cal** (băktērēŏlŏj′ĭkal) adj. ~ **warfare,** use of bacteria to spread disease in the enemy. **bac·te·ri·o·log′i·cal·ly** adv. **bac·te·ri·ol′o·gist** n.

bac·te·ri·o·phage (băktēr′ēofāj) n. Virus capable of destroying bacteria. **bac·te·ri·o·phag′ic**

*A nocturnal mammal, the **badger** digs rapidly, far more quickly than a man with a shovel. For long periods it remains underground, where its young are usually born.*

(băktēreofăj´ĭk) *adj.*

Bac·tri·a (băk´trēa). Ancient country of central Asia (now *Balkh* in N. Afghanistan).

Bac·tri·an (băk´trēan) *adj.* Of Bactria or its people; ~ **camel**, two-humped camel of central Asia, *Camelus bactrianus*. **Bactrian** *n.* Native or inhabitant of Bactria.

bad (băd) *adj.* (**worse, worst**). 1. Worthless, inferior; defective, inefficient; not valid; unpleasant; (of coinage) counterfeit; rotten, spoiled; **go** ~, decay; **not** ~, (colloq.) rather good; ~ **debt**, one not recoverable; **bad´lands**, arid rocky region seamed with deep vertical gullies by erosion and thus uncultivable; see BAD LANDS; **bad-tempered**, ill-humored, surly. 2. Wicked, vicious; **bad egg, apple**, a dishonest or untrustworthy person; **bad´man** (pl. **-men**), desperado; **bad´mouth** (*v.*), slander, denigrate. 3. Painful; harmful; **bad blood**, ill feeling. 4. Ill, in pain. **bad** *n.* Ill fortune, ruin; **go to the** ~, go to ruin, degenerate. **bad´ly** *adv.* **bad´ness** *n.*

Ba·den-Ba·den (bah´den bah´-den). Health resort, with mineral springs, in Baden-Wurtemberg, the Federal Republic of Germany.

Ba·den-Pow·ell (bā´den pō´el, băd´en pow´el), **Robert Stephenson Smyth, 1st Baron Baden-Powell of Gilwell** (1857–1941). English soldier; defended Mafeking, 1900; founded the Boy Scout organization, 1908.

badge (băj) *n.* Distinctive emblem or mark as a sign of office, membership, etc.

badg·er (băj´er) *n.* Nocturnal plantigrade quadruped (*Taxidea taxus*) intermediate between weasel and bear, with coarse dark fur and a white blaze on the forehead, which digs a burrow, hibernates, and defends itself fiercely against attack; **badger game**, extortion scheme in which a man is lured into a compromising situation and then surprised and blackmailed. **badger** *v.* Pester as dogs worry a badger; tease, torment.

bad·i·nage (bădĭnahzh´) *n.* Banter.

Bad Lands. Extensive barren eroded region of SW. South Dakota and NW. Nebraska; ~ **National Monument**, tract of this region in South Dakota set aside to preserve fossils and rock formations.

bad·min·ton (băd´mĭnton) *n.* Game like tennis played with shuttlecocks and rackets over a high net. [name of the country seat of

*The dimensions and markings of a **badminton** court. This racket game is mostly played indoors either as singles or doubles. It derives from battledore and shuttlecock.*

Duke of Beaufort in Gloucestershire, Eng.]

Bae·de·ker (bā´dĭker) *n.* Any of the travel guidebooks issued by **Karl** ~ (1801–59), German publisher, and his successors; hence, any guidebook.

Baf·fin (băf´ĭn), **William** (1584?–1622). English navigator and explorer; discovered ~**Island**, large island off the NE. coast of Canada and ~ **Bay**, sea between it and Greenland.

baf·fle (băf´el) *v.t.* (**-fled, -fling**). Foil, frustrate, perplex. **baf´fler** *n.* **baf´fling** *adj.* Bewildering. **baffle** *n.* Shielding device or structure; esp. one checking or deflecting sound waves, improving tone of loudspeaker by hindering return of sound waves to back of speaker; one hindering or regulating passage of gases or fluids.

bag (băg) *n.* Receptacle of flexible material with an opening usu. at the top; suitcase, handbag, or purse; amount of game taken in hunting; pouch or pouch-like part; (baseball) a base; (slang) ugly girl or woman; (slang) one's special interest or avocation; (esp. pl.) folds of loose skin beneath the eyes; ~ **and baggage**, with all belongings, completely; **in the** ~, assured of success; **bag´man** (pl. **-men**), (slang) agent who collects or distributes money for illicit purposes. **bag** *v.* (**bagged, bag·ging**). Put in a bag; secure game; bulge, hang loosely, droop, swell.

ba·gasse (bagăs´) *n.* Residue of sugar cane after processing.

bag·a·telle (băgatĕl´) *n.* 1. Mere trifle; short unpretentious piece of music. 2. Game played on a table with a semicircular end, the object

The Bad Lands National Monument is in harsh, barren country in South Dakota. Opened in 1939, many fossils have been found in the area, such as the saber-toothed tiger and the three-toed horse.

being to strike balls into numbered holes with a cue.

ba·gel (bā′gel) *n.* Hard ring-shaped bread roll. [Yiddish]

bag·gage (băg′ĭj) *n.* Portable equipment of an army; luggage; (joc.) saucy girl; ~ **master**, person in charge of baggage in rail or bus terminal.

bag·gy (băg′ē) *adj.* (**bag·gi·er, bag·gi·est**). That bags or hangs loosely.

Bagh·dad, Bag·dad (băg′dăd, bahgdahd′). City on the Tigris, now the capital of Iraq.

bagn·io (băn′yō, bahn′-) *n.* (pl. **-ios**). Brothel.

bag·pipe (băg′pīp) *n.* (freq. pl.) Musical instrument consisting of several pipes, including drones and a chanter through which air is forced by pressure on a windbag held under the arm; now associated chiefly with Scotland.

ba·guette, ba·guet (băgĕt′) *ns.* Gem cut in long rectangular shape.

Ba·guio (bah′gyō). Summer capital of the Republic of the Phillippines on N. Luzon.

bah (bah, bă) *int.* Expression of contempt.

Ba·ha·mas (băhah′măz). (also

Bahama Islands) Archipelago of British W. Indies, the first land touched by Columbus in 1492; first colonized by Spaniards and later (in 17th c.) by the English; British colony 1783–1973; independent 1973; capital, Nassau. **Ba·ha·mi·an** (băhā′mēan; -hah′-) *adj.* & *n.*

Ba·hi·a (bah-ē′a). Atlantic coast state of E. Brazil; capital, Salvador.

Bah·rain, Bah·rein (bahrān′, -rīn′). Independent sheikdom consisting of a group of islands, the largest being Bahrain Island, in the Persian Gulf; capital, Manama.

Bai·kal (bīkahl′), **Lake.** Large lake in S. Siberia, U.S.S.R., containing largest volume of fresh water anywhere in the world.

bail¹ (bāl) *n.* 1. Security for a prisoner's appearance for trial; person providing this; release from prison granted in return for bail money; the privilege or right of

being so released. ~ *v.t.* Secure the liberation of on bail.

bail² (bāl) *n.* Bar separating horses in an open stable.

bail³ (bāl) *v.* Scoop water out of (boat etc.); ~ **out**, parachute from airplane; relieve or assist person in (esp. financial) crisis; (fig.) escape. **bail·er** *n.* Utensil for bailing.

bail⁴ (bāl) *n.* Handle of a bucket etc.

bail·iff (bā′lĭf) *n.* Court attendant entrusted with custody of prisoners under arraignment, protecting jurors, maintaining order in courtroom, etc.

bail·i·wick (bā′lĭwĭk) *n.* One's area of knowledge, skill, etc.

Bai·ram (bīrahm′, bī′rahm) *n.* Each of the two principal festivals of the Muslim year, **Lesser** ~ (lasting three days) following the fast of Ramadan, and **Greater** ~ (lasting four days) 70 days later.

bairn (bārn) *n.* (Sc.) Child.

bait (bāt) *v.* 1. Worry (animal) by setting dogs at it; worry (person) by jeers. 2. Put bait on or in (fishhook, trap, etc.). ~ *n.* Food etc. used to entice prey; allurement.

baize (bāz) *n.* Coarse woolen usu. green fabric used chiefly for coverings, linings, etc.

Ba·ja (bah′hah) **California.** State of Mexico and resort area in the N. part of the Lower California Peninsula; capital, Mexicali.

bake (bāk) *v.* (**baked, bak·ing**). Cook by dry heat, as in an oven; harden by heat; be or become baked; **baked Alaska**, dessert of cake, ice cream, and meringue browned quickly in oven; **baked beans**, beans so cooked (esp. as a canned food, in tomato sauce); **baking powder**, powder consisting of sodium bicarbonate and cream of tartar with a filling of starch or flour, used instead of yeast to make cakes etc. rise; **baking soda**, sodium bicarbonate.

bak·er (bā′ker) *n.* One who bakes and sells bread; ~**'s dozen**, 13 objects of any kind. **bak·er·y** *n.* (pl. **-er·ies**). Bakehouse; trade of baking.

Baker Street. Street in London where the fictional detective Sherlock Holmes resided.

ba·kla·va (bahklavah′, bah′klavah) *n.* Dessert of flaky pastry, honey, and nuts. [Turkish]

bak·sheesh, bak·shish (băk′shēsh, băkshēsh′) *ns.* Small gift of money. [Pers. *bakhshish* gift, munificence]

Ba·ku (bahkōō′). Capital of Azerbaijan, on the shore of the Caspian Sea; a center of the petroleum industry.

Beam balance or scales

2

3

Steelyard

Pallet
Hair-spring

Spring balance

5 Balance wheel

Above: The Scales of Justice on the roof of the Old Bailey, London, U.K. Above right: 1. Beam **balance.** *2. Spring balance. 3. Steelyard. 4. Escapement wheel. 5. Balance wheel.*

In a watch the pallet allows the escapement wheel to unwind one tooth at a time, rocking to and fro before letting it go. It is the movement that makes a watch tick.

Bal·a·kla·va (bălaklah′va, bahla-). Crimean village near Sevastopol, scene of battle (1854) of the Crimean War during which occurred the Charge of the Light Brigade.

bal·a·lai·ka (bălalī′ka) *n.* Russian stringed instrument played by plucking, resembling guitar but with triangular body and two, three, or four strings.

bal·ance (băl′ans) *n.* 1. Weighing apparatus consisting of a beam moving freely on a central pivot with a pan at either end; spring or lever substitute for this; scale; ~ **(wheel)**, regulating gear of a clock, watch, etc. 2. (State of) even distribution of weight or amount; state of stability, harmony, etc. 3. Preponderating weight or amount. 4. Excess of assets over liabilities or vice versa. 5. Remainder. 6. ~ **beam**, horizontal beam for gymnastic exercises; ~ **of payments**, difference of value between payments into and out of a country; ~ **of power**, equilibrium of military and political power between several nations; ~ **of trade**, difference between the value of total exports and total imports of a country, **favorable** if exports exceed imports; ~ **sheet**, statement of assets and liabilities, esp. of a business. **balance** *v.* (**-anced, -anc·ing**). 1. Weigh. 2. Equalize, match; bring or come into equilibrium. 3. Find the balance of assets and liabilities in (an account book). **bal′anced**

adj. (esp., of diet) Containing essential nutriments in suitable proportions.

Bal·an·chine (băl′anshēn, bălanshēn′), **George** (1904–). Russian-born American ballet dancer and choreographer.

bal·bo·a (bălbō′a) *n.* Principal monetary unit of Panama.

Bal·bo·a (bălbō′a), **Vasco Nuñez de** (1475–1517). Spanish explorer, esp. of Central America; first sighted the Pacific Ocean in 1513.

bal·brig·gan (bălbrĭg′an) *n.* Knitted cotton cloth; (esp. pl.) underclothes of this material. [from Balbriggan, Ireland]

bal·co·ny (băl′konē) *n.* (pl. **-nies**). 1. Balustraded or railed platform on the outside of a building with access from an upper-floor window. 2. In a theater, the seats above the dress or upper circle.

bald (bawld) *adj.* 1. Having the scalp wholly or partly hairless; (of animal, bird) without fur, feathers, etc.; (zool.) having white on head; ~ **eagle**, a N. Amer. eagle (*Haliaeetus leucocephalus*) with white head and tail, also called "American eagle," a symbol of the U.S. 2. Bare; meager; undisguised, obvious. **bald′ly** *adv.* **bald′ness** *n.*

bal·der·dash (bawl′derdăsh) *n.* Nonsense, rubbish.

bald·ing (bawl′dĭng) *adj.* Becoming bald.

bal·dric (bawl′drĭk) *n.* Belt for

supporting a sword, bugle, etc worn over shoulder and across bod to opposite hip.

Bald·win (bawld′wĭn), **Stanle** (1867–1947), **1st Earl Baldwin o Bewdley.** British Conservativ statesman; prime minister 1923–2 1924–9, 1935–7.

bale[1] (bāl) *n.* (archaic) Evi destruction, woe.

bale[2] (bāl) *n.* Large bundle o package, esp. of merchandise, usu wrapped and corded or looped. ~ *v.t.* (**baled, bal·ing**). Make up int bales. **bal′er** *n.*

Bal·e·ar·ic (bălēăr′ĭk) **Islands** Group of islands, includin Majorca and Minorca, off E. coas of Spain; a province of Spain.

ba·leen (balēn′) *n.* Whalebone

bale·ful (bāl′ful) *adj.* Perni cious, destructive, malignant **bale′ful·ly** *adv.* **bale′ful·ness** *n.*

Ba·li (bah′lē, băl′ē). Moun tainous island, area 2,146 squar miles, famous for its beautifu scenery, near the E. end of Java capital Singaradja. **Ba·li·nes·** (bahlinēz′, -nes′) *adj. & n.* (p **-nese**). (Native, language, people of the island of Bali.

balk (bawk) *v.* 1. Thwar hinder, discourage. 2. Shy. **3** (baseball) Commit a balk. ~ *n* (baseball) Illegal motion made b pitcher while preparing to pitc when there is a runner or runner on base. **balk′er** *n.*

Bal·kan (bawl′kan) *adj.* Of th Balkan Peninsula or States; ~ **Peninsula**, peninsula of Europ south of the Danube and Sav rivers; home of various people (Albanians, Vlachs, Greeks, Serbs Bulgars, and Turks) with differin cultures. From the 3rd to the 7t

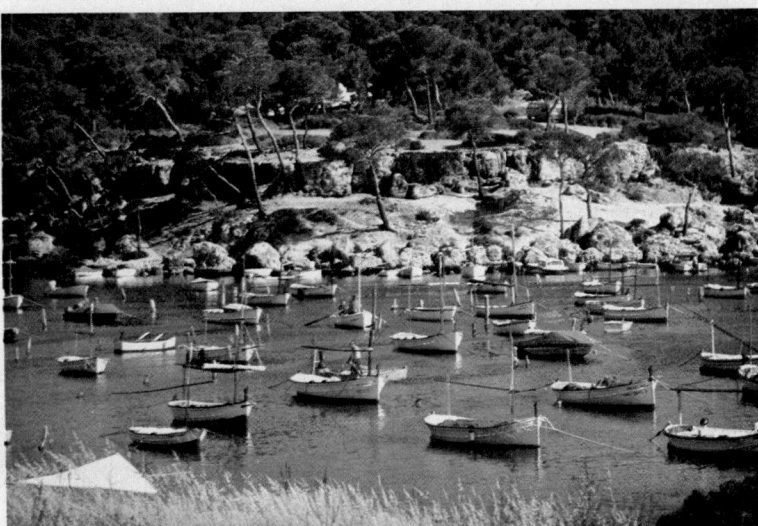

Fishing boats in the bay at Santa Ponsa, Majorca. Together with Minorca, Ibiza, Formentera and Cabrera, Majorca is one of the **Balearic Islands.**

centuries the peninsula was nomi-ally ruled by the Byzantine em-perors; in 1356 the Ottoman invasion began; Constantinople fell to the Turks in 1453, and by 1478 most of the peninsula was in their power; the subject nations did not recover independence until the 19th c.; in 1912–13 Turkey was attacked and defeated by other Balkan peoples in alliance; during World War I Turkey and Bulgaria sided with Austria and Germany and the other Balkan States with the Allies; after the war the peninsula was divided among Greece, Bulgaria, Albania, and Yugoslavia, with Tur-key retaining only Constantinople and the surrounding land; ~ **States**, countries of the Balkan Peninsula. **Bal′kans** *n.pl.* Balkan States.

Bal·khash (bahlxahsh′). Lake, area 7,100 square miles, in Kazakh-stan, central Asia.

ball[1] (bawl) *n.* 1. Solid or hol-low sphere, esp. one used in a game; rounded mass (as of snow, string, etc.); game played with a ball, as esp. baseball; (*pl.*, *vulg.*) testicles; ~ **of foot, thumb**, rounded base of big toe, thumb; **have a** ~, enjoy oneself; **on the** ~, (colloq.) alert; **play** ~, (colloq.) cooperate (with). 2. (baseball) Pitch outside the strike zone not swung at by the batter. 3. Missile for cannon, rifles, etc. 4. ~ **bearing**, bearing in which revolving parts of a machine turn upon a number of hard balls run-ning in grooves, which diminish friction; one of these balls; ~ **of fire**, very energetic, able person; ~ **park**, stadium for ball games; ~ **player**, professional player esp. of baseball; ~-**point (pen)**, writing instrument having for point a small ball bearing moistened from a reser-voir of semiliquid ink. **ball** *v.* (of snow etc.) Form lumps; (*vulg.*) have sexual intercourse (with); ~ **up**, (slang) confuse or bungle.

ball[2] (bawl) *n.* Social assembly for dancing; **ball′room**, large room suitable for this.

bal·lad (băl′ad) *n.* 1. Narrative poem (esp. traditional) designed to be sung, with the same melody for each verse. 2. Any poem in similar style; = BALLADE, def. 1. 3. Any light simple song. **bal·lad·eer** (băladēr′) *n.* **bal′lad·ry** *n.* Ballad poetry. [Provençal *ballada*, dancing song]

bal·lade (balahd′, bă-) *n.* 1. Poem of one or more triplets of seven or eight lined stanzas, each ending with the same line as refrain, followed by an envoi freq. of 4 lines. 2. Piece of esp. lyrical or romantic

Map showing the countries within the **Balkan Peninsula.** *The name derives from the Turkish word for 'mountain'. From the 15th century until 1912–13,* the Turks dominated the region through satrap governments and by setting one country against another.

instrumental music.

bal·last (băl′ast) *n.* 1. Heavy material, as sand or water, placed in a ship's hold or carried in a balloon or airship for stability. 2. Coarse stone, clinker, etc., forming bed of railway. ~ *v.t.* Furnish with bal-last.

bal·le·ri·na (bălerē′na) *n.* Female ballet dancer (strictly, dancer who takes one or more of certain classical roles).

bal·let (bălā′, băl′ā) *n.* Classical dance form demanding precision and grace; theatrical performance of dancing and mime to music; company performing this; musical score for this.

bal·lis·ta (balĭs′ta) *n.* (pl. -**tae** pr. -tē). Ancient military machine for hurling stones etc.

bal·lis·tic (balĭs′tĭk) *adj.* Of pro-jectiles; ~ **missile**, one that is powered and possibly guided during the initial stage of its flight, and then travels unpowered. **bal′-lis′tics** *n.* Science of projectiles.

bal·loon (baloon′) *n.* Large air-

*Hot-air **ballooning** near Bristol, U.K. The first manned balloon flights were made in France in 1756 in the Montgolfiers' experimental hot-air balloons.*

tight envelope of silk or other light material inflated with gas lighter than air so as to rise in the air, sometimes provided with a basket or car slung beneath from a net enclosing the envelope, used for making observations and as an anti-aircraft defense; small usu. rubber envelope inflated with air as toy; (colloq.) balloon-shaped outline enclosing speech or thought of character in strip cartoon etc. or added matter for printing etc.; ~ **tire**, low-pressure motor tire of large section. **balloon** *v.* Swell out like a balloon; ride in a balloon. **bal·loon′ist** *n.*

bal·lot (băl′ot) *n.* (Usu. secret) voting; the right to vote, franchise; paper used in voting; ~ **box**, receptacle for voters' ballots. **bal-lot** *v.* (**-lot·ed, -lot·ing**). Vote by ballot (*for*); cause to do this. [It. *ballotta* little ball]

bal·ly·hoo (băl′ēho͞o) *n.* (pl. **-hoos**). Sensational or clamorous publicity or advertising.

balm (bahm) *n.* 1. Aromatic substance consisting of resin mixed with volatile oils, exuding naturally from various trees; tree yielding this; ~ **of Gilead**, plant or tree of genus *Commiphora* yielding fragrant resinous substance; this substance. 2. Anything that soothes or heals.

Bal·mor·al (bălmŏr′al, -mär′-). Scottish residence in upper Deeside, Grampian, of the British sovereign.

balm·y (bah′mē) *adj.* (**balm·i·er, balm·i·est**). 1. Of or like balm; fragrant, mild, soothing. 2. (Brit. slang) Crazy, silly. **balm′i·ly** *adv.* **balm′i·ness** *n.*

ba·lo·ney, bo·lo·ney (balō′nē) *ns.* 1. (slang) Nonsense. 2. Bologna sausage.

bal·sa (bawl′sa) *n.* Tropical American tree, *Ochroma lagopus*; its wood (~ **wood**), used for life belts, model airplanes, etc., because of its extreme lightness.

bal·sam (bawl′sam) *n.* 1. = BALM 1; balm of Gilead. 2. Aromatic ointment, of various substances dissolved in oil or turpentine. 3. Tree yielding balm. 4. Flowering plant of genus *Impatiens*, with hooded and spurred colored sepals and thick succulent stem; ~ **fir**, N. Amer. evergreen (*Abies balsamea*) widely used as Christmas tree.

Balt (bawlt) *n.* Native or inhabitant of one of the Baltic States of Lithuania, Latvia, and Estonia, esp. a German inhabitant. ~ *adj.*

Bal·tha·zar (bălthā′zer, -thăz′-

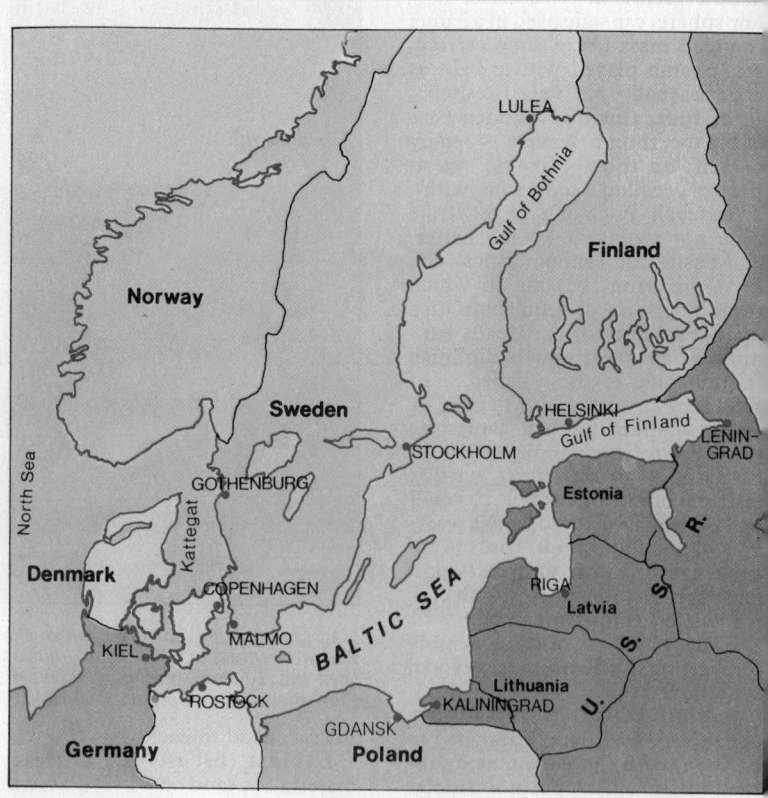

*Map of the almost land-locked **Baltic Sea**, connected to the North Sea by a channel between Denmark and Sweden. Its average width is about 124 miles. Low salinity leads to freezing of the surface in winter, and Baltic ports are frequently closed to ships.*

er, bawl′thaza̅r, băl′-). 1. = BEL-SHAZZAR. 2. Traditional name of one of the three Magi, represented as king of Chaldea.

Bal·tic (bawl′tĭk) *adj.* Of the Baltic Sea, States, or languages; ~

Facing page:
*Polling booths in the U.S.A. use the **ballot** system established in the 1880s which allows the voting public to register their vote in private without pressure or harassment from party supporters.*

language, branch of Indo-European languages containing Lithuanian, Lettish, and Old Prussian; ~ **Sea**, almost landlocked sea in N. Europe, bordered by Sweden, U.S.S.R., Germany, Denmark, etc.; ~ **States**, former independent republics of Estonia, Latvia, and Lithuania. **Baltic** *n.* Baltic Sea.

Bal·ti·more (bawl′timŏr, -mōr). Seaport in N. Maryland; ~ **oriole**, N. American bird (*Icterus galbula*), whose colors, black and orange, are like the coat of arms of Lord Baltimore. [Lord *Baltimore* (d. 1632), English proprietor of territory that later became Maryland]

Bal·to-Sla·vic (bawl′tō slah′vĭk, -slăv′ĭk) *adj. & n.* (Of) the group of languages including the Baltic and Slavic branches.

Ba·lu·chi (baloo′chē) *n.* (pl. **-chis**, collect. **-chi**). Native or inhabitant of, the Iranian language of, Baluchistan. **Ba·lu·chi·stan** (baloochĭstahn′, -stăn′). Mountainous region in West Pakistan.

bal·us·ter (băl′uster) *n.* Any of the closely spaced posts supporting a railing.

bal·us·trade (băl′ustrād) *n.* Row of balusters with a rail or coping as the parapet of a balcony or along a staircase.

Bal·zac (bawl′zăk, băl′-; *Fr.* bălzăk′), **Honoré de** (1799-1850). French realistic novelist, whose *Comédie Humaine* is a long series of novels intended to depict the whole of contemporary French society.

Ba·ma·ko (băm′akō). Largest city and capital of Mali, on the Niger River.

bam·boo (bămboo′) *n.* (pl. **-boos**). Tropical giant grass of genus *Bambusa*, with hollow jointed stem; stem of this as a stick, as material etc.; ~ **curtain**, ideological and political barrier to passage of persons and information at borders of China.

bam·boo·zle (bămboo′zel) *v.t.* (**-zled, -zling**). Hoax, mystify. **bam·boo′zle·ment, bam·boo′zler** *ns.*

ban (băn) *v.t.* (**banned, ban-ning**). Prohibit, interdict. ~ *n.* Curse, formal prohibition.

ba·nal (banăl′, -nahl′, bā′nal) *adj.* Commonplace, trite. **ba·nal·i·ty** (banăl′ĭtē, bā-) *n.* (pl. **-ties**). **ba·nal·ly** (bā′nalē) *adv.*

ba·nan·a (banăn′a) *n.* Tropical treelike plant (*Musa sapientum*); finger-shaped yellow pulpy fruit of this, growing in clusters or bunches; **ba·nan′as**, (slang) crazy, insane; **banana republic**, (esp. derog.) any small Latin American country whose economy depends on export of fruit; **banana split**, large sundae made of bananas, ice cream, etc. [Port. or Span., f. native name in Guinea]

band (bănd) *n.* 1. Thing that binds, bond (archaic). 2. Strip or hoop of material for supporting or holding things together or for decoration etc.; belt, strap; strip forming part of garment, esp. binding the neck or waist; (pl.). pair of white linen strips worn at neck as part of legal, ecclesiastical, or academic dress. 3. Body of musicians playing together, esp. wind instrument performers (**brass, dance, military** ~); organized company or group of persons. 4. (elect.) Range of frequencies or wavelengths falling between two limits (also **wave** ~). 5. (phys.) Group of closely spaced lines in a molecular spectrum. 6. **B~-Aid**, (trademark) a small adhesive bandage for minor wounds; (fig.) superficial or inadequate remedy for a major problem; **band′box**, box for hats (orig. for neckbands); (*adj.*) conspicuously neat and clean; **band′master**, conductor of a band of musicians; **band saw**, endless saw running over wheels; **bands′man** (pl. **-men**), member of a mili-

A row of balusters with a rail or coping form a **balustrade**. 1. Pier. 2. Baluster. During the Italian Renaissance, designers excelled in producing richly molded balusters.

Snow-covered Kholpur Bolan in **Baluchistan,** *the mountainous western province of Pakistan. Following Pakistan autonomy, 50,000 Hindus and Sikhs left for India.*

Statue of **Honoré de Balzac** *by his French compatriot, Auguste Rodin. One of the world's greatest novelists Balzac was attracted by the theme of the individual in conflict with society.*

A band of young musicians and singers at Disneyland attracts the crowds and adds to the holiday atmosphere during an open-air concert.

-dōr′a) *ns.* Wire-stringed musical instrument resembling the cittern. Also **pandora, pandore**.

ban·dy (băn′dē) *v.t.* (**-died, -dy·ing**). Throw or pass to and fro; discuss; exchange. ~ *adj.* (of legs) Curving outward at the knees; so ~ **-leg·ged** (-lĕgĭd, -lĕgd).

bane (bān) *n.* Ruin; poison. **bane′ful** *adj.* Poisonous; pernicious; injurious. **bane′ful·ly** *adv.* **bane′ful·ness** *n.*

bang[1] (băng) *v.* Strike or shut noisily; make sound as of a blow or explosion; thrash. ~ *n.* Sharp blow; loud noise; (slang) a thrill; **bang′tail**, (slang) a race horse. **bang** *adv.* (colloq.) Right, exactly; suddenly and loudly.

bang[2] (băng) = BHANG.

bang[3] (băng) *n. & v.t.* (Cut *hair* in) a fringe.

Bang·kok (băng′kŏk). Capital city of Thailand.

Bang·la·desh (băng′glädĕsh, bănggladĕsh′). Muslim country in SE. Asia, formerly East Pakistan; member nation of the British Commonwealth, independent since 1971; capital Dacca. [Bengali, = "land of Bengal"]

ban·gle (băng′gel) *n.* Ring bracelet or anklet.

Ban·gor (băng′gôr, -ger). Port city on the Penobscot River in E. Maine.

Ban·gui (bahṅggē′). Largest city and capital of the Central African Republic, in the SW., on the Ubangi River.

ban·ian (băn′yan) = BANYAN.

ban·ish (băn′ĭsh) *v.t.* Condemn to exile; drive away; dismiss from one's presence or mind. **ban′ish·er, ban′ish·ment** *ns.*

ban·is·ter, ban·nis·ter (băn′ister) *ns.* Post supporting handrail of a staircase; posts and handrail together. [corrupt. of BALUSTER]

ban·jo (băn′jō) *n.* (pl. **-jos, -joes**). Musical instrument having four, five, six, or seven strings, head and neck like guitar, and body like tambourine, played with fingers or with plectrum; ~ **clock**, pendulum clock shaped like a banjo. **ban′jo·ist** *n.* [Gk. *pandoura* three-stringed mus. instrument]

Ban·jul (bahnjool′). Capital of The Gambia, on the island of St. Mary at the mouth of the Gambia River.

bank[1] (băngk) *n.* 1. Raised shelf of ground; transverse slope of a road or curve, etc. 2. Ground at edge of river. 3. Mass of cloud. ~ *v.* 1. Contain or confine as or with bank(s). 2. Make (road, track) higher at outer edge of a bend to facilitate cornering at high speeds;

tary or brass band; **band′stand**, (covered, open-air) platform for musicians; **band′wagon**, wagon carrying the band at the head of a procession; **climb, jump, on the bandwagon**, join an enterprise that is likely to be successful. **band** *v.* Form into band or league; put a band on; **band′ed**, (bot., zool.) marked with colored bands or bars.

band·age (băn′dĭj) *n.* Strip or band of textile material used to bind a wound, sore, etc., or for blindfolding the eyes. ~ *v.t.* (**-aged, -ag·ing**). Bind up with a bandage.

ban·dan·na, ban·dan·a (băndăn′a) *ns.* Large brightly colored handkerchief esp. with yellow or white spots. [prob. from Hind. *bāndhnu*, a method of dyeing in different colors]

ban·deau (băndō′) *n.* (pl. **-deaux** pr.-dōz′). Band of ribbon etc. around the head; narrow hair band.

ban·de·ril·la (bănderē′a, -rēl′ya) *n.* Decorated dart thrust into bull's neck or shoulders in bullfight. **ban·de·ril·le·ro** (bănderēar′ō, -rēlyar′ō) *n.* (pl. **-ros**). Bullfighter or matador's assistant using banderillas.

ban·de·role, ban·de·rol (băn′derōl) *ns.* Long narrow flag or cleft end flying from a ship, lance, etc.; .ribbonlike scroll; (archit.) feature resembling this and bearing inscription.

ban·dit (băn′dĭt) *n.* (pl. **ban·dits, ban·dit·ti** pr. băndĭt′ē). Outlaw, brigand; lawless and violent robber, esp. member of an organized gang.

ban·do·leer, ban·do·lier (băndolēr′) *ns.* Shoulder belt with loops or pockets for cartridges.

ban·dore (băndōr′, -dôr′, ban′dōr, -dōr), **ban·do·ra** (băndōr′a, (aeronaut.) incline (aircraft) laterally in turning so as to avoid a sideslip; heap up; cover (a fire) with ashes, etc., to make it burn slowly. **bank²** (băngk) *n.* 1. Establishment for receiving, safeguarding, and lending money; building housing this; **central** ~: see CENTRAL; **savings** ~: see SAVINGS; **bank'-book**, book showing the state of a customer's account at a bank; **bank holiday**, weekday on which banks are legally closed, (Brit.) usu. kept as a general holiday; **bank'note**, authorized bank's promissory note circulating as money; **bank'roll** (*n.*), roll of banknotes, ready money; (*v.*), finance. 2. Money box; **piggy bank**: see PIGGY. 3. Money before keeper of a gaming

Below: Gold nuggets in a Sierra Nevada **bank.** *About 60 per cent of all gold mined is held in banks. Below right: The U.S. cent is made of copper with a zinc and tin alloy.*

table. 4. Store or storage place, reserve supply (of blood, organs, etc.). **bank** *v.* Deposit money in a bank; have an account with a bank; act as a bank or banker; handle funds; ~ **on**, count or rely on.

bank³ (băngk) *n.* Galley rowers' bench; tier (of oars) in galley; row of organ keys; group of similar objects in line or in tiers.

bank·er (băng'ker) *n.* 1. Proprietor or director of a BANK²; keeper of money. 2. Keeper of money staked at gaming table.

bank·ing (băng'kĭng) *n.* Business of a banker or BANK².

bank·rupt (băngk'rŭpt, -rupt) *n.* (law) Insolvent person whose property is administered and distributed for the benefit of all his or her creditors; (pop.) any insolvent person. ~ *adj.* Declared a bankrupt; insolvent; (fig.) bereft (of some quality). **bank'rupt·cy** *n.* (pl. **-cies**).

Banks (băngks) **Island.** Westernmost island of the Arctic Archipelago, about 25,000 square miles.

Ban·nek·er (băn'eker), **Benjamin** (1731–1806). American mathematician, astronomer, and black colonial leader; member of the group appointed to survey and lay out the site for Washington, D.C.

ban·ner (băn'er) *n.* Rectangular flag of a country, army, king, etc.; strip or piece of fabric bearing emblem or slogan etc.; (also ~ **headline**) newspaper headline in large type, esp. running across whole page. ~ *adj.* Preeminent (as in *banner year, crop*). **ban'-nered** *adj.*

ban·nis·ter (băn'ĭster) = BANISTER.

banns (bănz) *n.pl.* Notice of intended marriage, read three times in church, in order that any objec-

*Barrel-like trunk of a **baobab** tree. Some trees reach 30 ft. in diameter. The edible fruit pulp is called monkey bread and can be used in the preparation of cooling drinks.*

*Above: The **baptistery** of the cathedral at Pisa. Until the 11th century a baptistery, with its apse and font, was usually built separate from the main church.*

*Above left: Members of a **Bantu** tribe celebrating a festival in South Africa. Bantu-speaking peoples inhabit the equatorial and southern regions of the continent.*

tions may be lodged.

ban·quet (băng´kwĭt) *n*. Sumptuous feast; ceremonious dinner with speeches. ~ *v*. (**-quet·ed, -quet·ing**). Regale with, take part in, banquet. [Fr. f. It. *banchetto*, dim. of *banco* bench]

ban·quette (băngkĕt´) *n*. Firing step in trenches; upholstered seat along a wall.

ban·shee, ban·shie (băn´shē) *ns*. Spirit supposed by Irish and Highland superstition to wail under the windows of a house in which one of the inhabitants is about to die. [Ir., = "fairy woman"]

ban·tam (băn´tam) *n*. 1. Small variety of domestic fowl, of which the cock is a spirited fighter. 2. Small but spirited person. 3. **ban´- tamweight**, boxer of weight between 112 and 118 pounds. [f. *Bantam*, seaport in W. Java]

ban·ter (băn´ter) *n*. Humorous ridicule. **ban´ter·er** *n*. **ban´ter-ing·ly** *adv*. **banter** *v*. Make good-humored fun of, rally; jest.

Ban·tu (băn´tōō) *n*. (pl. **-tus**, collect. **-tu**). (Member of) an extensive group of black peoples inhabiting the equatorial and southern region of Africa; language(s) spoken by them.

Ban·tu·stan (băntōōstahn´, -stăn) *n*. Any of several segregated territories for Bantus in S. Africa.

ban·yan, banian (băn´yan) *ns*. (also ~ **tree**) E. Indian fig tree (*Ficus bengalensis*), whose branches root themselves like new trees over

a large area.

ban·zai (bahnzī´, bahn´zī) *int*. Japanese patriotic greeting or cheer. ~ *adj*. Suicidal, desperate (of an attack or charge). [Jap., = 10,000 years (of life to you)]

ba·o·bab (bā´ōbăb, bah´-) *n*. African tree (*Adansonia digitata*), naturalized also in Australia, India, and Ceylon, having extremely thick stem and large woody fruit with edible pulp, known as "monkey-bread."

bap·tism (băp´tĭzem) *n*. Religious rite of immersing in or sprinkling with water in sign of moral or spiritual purification or regeneration, and initiation into the (Christian) church; any initiation or initiation ceremony; ~ **of fire**, soldier's first experience of battle. **bap·tis·mal** (băptĭz´mal) *adj*. **bap·tis´mal·ly** *adv*. **baptismal name** = CHRISTIAN[1] name.

bap·tist (băp´tĭst) *n*. One who baptizes; **St. John the B~**: see JOHN[5]; **B~**, member of a Protestant Christian sect, founded early in the 17th c., which holds that baptism should be administered only to believers, not to infants, and by immersion.

bap·tis·ter·y, bap·tist·ry (băp-tĭstrē) *ns*. (pl. **-ries**). Part of church (or in early times separate building) used for baptism.

bap·tize (băp´tīz, băptīz´) *v.t*. (**-tized, -tiz·ing**). Administer baptism to; christen; name. **bap·-**

tiz′er *n.*

BAR *abbrev.* BROWNING[1] automatic rifle.

bar[1] (bār) *n.* 1. Long piece of rigid material; straight strip; **bar′bell**, iron bar with heavy ball at each end for weight lifting; **bar chart**, ~ **graph**, graph using parallel bars showing numbers, costs, etc. 2. Rectangular piece (of soap, chocolate, etc.). 3. Strip of silver below clasp of medal as additional distinction. 4. (mus.) Vertical line across stave dividing composition into sections of equal time value (also ~ **line**); such a section. 5. (her.) Stripe across shield; ~ **sinister**, erron. for BEND[1] sinister. 6. Rod or pole used to confine or obstruct; bolt or beam for fastening door etc. 7. Barrier of any shape; obstacle, hindrance; **sand ~**: see SAND. 8. Barrier limiting access etc.; place in court where prisoner stands; **the B~**, the legal profession. 9. Counter in tavern, restaurant, **bar and grill**, etc. across which drinks or food are served directly to customers; room or place containing this; ~ **car**, railroad car with a bar at which drinks etc. are served; **bar′fly** (pl. **-flies**), one who frequents bars; **bar′keep(er), bar′maid, bar′man** (pl. **-men**), **bar′tender**, attendant at bar serving alcoholic drinks; **bar′stool**, high stool for sitting at a bar. **bar** *v.t.* (**barred, bar′ring**). 1. Fasten with bars, keep in or out thus; obstruct, prevent. 2. Mark with stripes. ~ *prep.* Except, excluding.

bar[2] (bār) *n.* Unit of barometric pressure, = 10^5 newtons per square centimeter.

Bar·ab·bas (barăb′as). Robber released instead of Jesus Christ (Matt. 27).

barb (bärb) *n.* Secondary backward-projecting point of arrow, fishhook, etc.; sting, wounding remark; beardlike feelers of barbel etc.; lateral filament branching from shaft of feather. ~ *v.t.* Furnish with barb; **barb(ed) wire**, wire used in fencing and as an obstruction in war, with short pointed pieces of wire twisted in at intervals. [L. *barba* beard]

Bar·ba·dos (bärbā′dōs, -dŏz). Island in W. Indies settled by the British 1627, member nation of the British Commonwealth 1966; capital, Bridgetown. **Bar·ba·di·an** (bärbā′dēan) *adj. & n.*

bar·bar·i·an (bärbār′ēan, -bǎr′-) *n.* 1. Rough, wild, uncultured or uncivilized person, savage (orig. foreigner, one differing in language and customs). 2. (hist.) Non-Greek; person outside the Roman Empire; person outside the civilization of Christendom. ~ *adj.* Of or like a barbarian. **bar·bar′i·an·ism** *n.*

bar·bar·ic (bärbǎr′ĭk) *adj.* Rough, uncultured; of barbarians. **bar·bar′i·cal·ly** *adv.*

bar·bar·ism (bär′barĭzem) *n.* Savagery; absence of culture; ignorance; (use of) word or expression not in accordance with the established standard of a language.

bar·bar·i·ty (bärbǎr′ĭtē) *n.* (pl. **-ties**). Savage or barbarous cruelty.

bar·ba·rize (bär′barīz) *v.* (**-rized, -riz·ing**). Make, become, barbarous. **bar·ba·ri·za·tion** (bärbarīzā′shon) *n.*

Bar·ba·ros·sa (bärbarŏs′a): see FREDERICK[1].

bar·ba·rous (bär′barus) *adj.* Uncivilized, uncultured, savage. **bar′ba·rous·ly** *adv.* **bar′ba·rous·ness** *n.*

Norwegian bark (or barque). Now serving as training ships, barks had their heyday before the 1860s. The 5-masted bark 'France', 418 ft. long, was the largest sailing ship ever built.

Bar·ba·ry (bär′barē). Old name for the western part of N. Africa; ~ **ape**, large tailless ape of N. Africa and Gibraltar; ~ **Coast**, the Mediterranean coastal area of Barbary; a district of San Francisco notorious before 1906 for gambling and prostitution; ~ **sheep**, wild N. Afr. sheep with large horns.

bar·be·cue (bär′bekū) *n.* 1. Framework for cooking meat above an open fire. 2. Barbecued meat, fowl, or fish; animal roasted whole; ~ **sauce**, highly seasoned sauce of vinegar, spices, etc. 3. (Open-air) social gathering where barbecue is served. **barbecue** *v.t.* (**-cued, -cu·ing**). Cook on barbecue or with barbecue sauce. [Haitian *barbacòa* grate on posts]

bar·bel (bär′bel) *n.* Large European freshwater fish of genus *Barbus* with fleshy filaments hanging from mouth; such a filament.

bar·ber (bär′ber) *n.* One who cuts hair and shaves beards; **bar′**

ershop (adj.) (fig., colloq.) in the style of close-harmony male quartet; **~'s itch**, ringworm of face communicated by (unsterilized) shaving apparatus; **~'s pole**, pole painted spirally with red and white stripes, used as barber's sign.

Bar·ber (bär′ber), **Samuel** (1910–). American composer; winner of two Pulitzer Prizes, for the opera *Vanessa*, 1958, and for *Piano Concerto No. 1*, 1963.

bar·ber·ry (bär′bĕrē, -berē) *n.* (pl. **-ries**). Shrub, especially *Berberis vulgaris*, with spiny shoots and small yellow flowers; oblong, red, sharply acid berry of this.

bar·bi·tu·rate (bärbĭch′erĭt, -erāt) *n.* (chem.) Salt of barbituric acid; (pharmac.) any of various sedatives and hypnotic substances

The Church at Marisse' by Jean Corot, the 19th-century French landscape painter (Louvre, Paris). Corot influenced the Barbizon school of naturalistic landscape painting.

derived from barbituric acid. **bar·bi·tu·ric** (bärbĭtoor′ĭk, -tūr′-) *adj.* **~ acid**, white crystalline substance ($C_4H_3O_3N_2$) from which barbiturates are derived.

Bar·bi·zon (bär′bĭzŏn). Village near Fontainebleau, near Paris, frequented in mid-19th c. by the **~ School**, a colony of painters (T. Rousseau, Millet, Daubigny, and others) who produced naturalistic pictures of landscapes and peasant life.

Bar·bour (bär′ber), **John** (1316–1395). Author of "The Bruce" (c1375), a long historical poem; regarded as father of Scottish poetry.

bar·ca·role, bar·ca·rolle (bär′karōl) *ns.* Gondolier's song; imitation of this.

Bar·ce·lo·na (bärselō′na). City and province of Catalonia, NE. Spain.

bard (bärd) *n.* Celtic minstrel; poet; **~ of Avon**: see AVON[1]. **bard′ic** *adj.*

bare (bār) *adj.* (**bar·er, bar·est**). Unclothed, uncovered; exposed; unadorned; scanty; mere; unarmed; unconcealed; undisguised; with less than usual ornaments, furnishings; **bare′back**, (adj. & adv.) on unsaddled horse; **bare′faced**, shameless, impudent; **bare′foot**, (adj. & adv.) with bare feet; **bare′handed**, (adj. & adv.) without tools or weapons; **bare′headed**, with head uncovered. **bare′ly** adv. Scarcely, only just. **bare′ness** *n.* **bare** *v.t.* (**bared, bar·ing**). Make bare, strip, expose.

Bar·ents (băr′ents, bār′-), **Willem** (d. 1597). Dutch Arctic explorer, after whom is named the **~ Sea**, the extreme NE. part of the Atlantic Ocean.

bar·gain (bär′gĭn) *n.* Agreement on terms of transaction between two parties, compact; thing acquired by bargaining; something offered for sale cheaper than usual; advantageous purchase; **in(to) the ~**, moreover; **strike a ~**, come to terms. **~** v.i. Haggle over terms of transaction; stipulate; **~ for**, be prepared for, expect.

barge (bärj) *n.* Flat-bottomed freight boat for canals and rivers; ceremonial vessel used in pageants. **barge′man** *n.* (pl. **-men**). **barge** v.i. (**barged, barg·ing**). (colloq.) Lurch or rush heavily *into*.

bar·ite (bār′īt, băr′-) *n.* Barium sulfate, ore of barium.

bar·i·tone (băr′ĭtōn) *n.* Male voice between tenor and bass; singer with this voice. **~** *adj.*

bar·i·um (bār′ēum, băr′-) *n.* (chem.) White metallic element occurring chiefly as barite; symbol Ba, at. no. 56, at. wt. 137.34; **~ sulfate**, white, very insoluble heavy powder ($BaSO_4$), opaque to X-rays, used in a mixture in radiological examination of the alimentary tract and as a pigment in paints.

bark[1] (bärk) *n.* Rind or outer sheath of the trunk and branches of trees; bark used in tanning. **~** v. Strip bark from; rub the skin off, as of the shins. **bark′less** *adj.*

bark[2], barque (bärk) *ns.* Three-masted vessel with foremasts and mainmasts square-rigged, and mizen fore-and-aft rigged; (poet.) ship, boat.

bark[3] (bärk) v. (of dogs etc.) Utter sharp explosive cry; make sound like this; speak sharply or petulantly; (slang) cough; **~ up the wrong tree**, (fig.) be on the wrong track. **~** *n.* Sharp explosive cry of dogs, foxes, etc.; sound of gunfire; cough. **bark′er** *n.*, one who stands at entrance to a show soliciting customers with loud and extravagant shouts.

bar·ken·tine (bär′kentēn) *n.* Vessel with three or more masts, of which only the foremast is square-rigged.

Bark·ley (bärk'lē), **Alben (William)** (1877–1956). Congressman from Kentucky, 1913–49; Senate majority leader, 1937–47; Vice President of the U.S. under Harry Truman, 1949–53.

bar·ley (bär'lē) *n.* Cereal (*Hordeum distichon* and *H. vulgare*), used as food and in the preparation of malt; grain of this; **bar'leycorn**, grain of barley; **John Bar'leycorn**, personification of whiskey in general; malt liquor.

barm (bärm) *n.* Froth from fermenting malt liquor, used as leaven; yeast.

bar mitz·vah (bär mĭts'va; *Heb.* bär mĕtsvah'). (Religious initiation ceremony for) Jewish boy aged 13. [Heb., = "son of commandment"]

barn (bärn) *n.* Farm building for storing grain (or hay, straw, etc.) and housing livestock; ~ **door**, large door of this; target too big to be easily missed; ~ **owl**, owl (*Tyto alba*) often found in barns; **barn'storm**, act as **barn'stormer**, itinerant actor; **barn swallow**, fork-tailed swallow (*Hirundo rustica erythrogaster*) often nesting in barns; **barn'yard**, area surrounding a barn.

Bar·na·bas (bär'nabas), **St. Joseph**, surnamed Barnabas, an early leader of the Christian Church and companion of St. Paul on his missionary journeys (Acts 4, 9, 11, etc.).

bar·na·cle (bär'nakel) *n.* 1. Wild goose, *Branta leucopsis*, also called ~ **goose**, of N. Europe and Greenland. 2. Crustacean of the subclass Cirripedia; **goose** ~, one found attached to ships' bottoms etc.; **acorn** or **rock** ~, one found attached to rocks. **bar'na·cled** *adj.*

Bar·nard (bär'närd), **Christiaan N.** (1923–). South African surgeon; performed first human heart transplant, 1967.

bar·o·gram (bär'ogrăm) *n.* Record of variations in atmospheric pressure.

bar·o·graph (bär'ogrăf) *n.* Barometer with apparatus (usu. paper roll on drum rotated by clockwork) for making a barogram. **bar·o·graph'ic** *adj.*

ba·rom·e·ter (barŏm'ĭter) *n.* Instrument for measuring atmospheric pressure (and hence for predicting changes in the weather) by means of a tube containing a column of mercury (which rises and falls according to the weight of the atmosphere) or of a vacuum box (see ANEROID ~). **bar·o·met·ric** (băromĕt'rĭk), **bar·o·met'ri·cal** *adjs.* **bar·o·met'ri·cal·ly** *adv.* **ba·rom'e·try** *n.*

bar·on (băr'on) *n.* 1. (hist.) Great noble, noble holding directly from the king by military service. 2. Member of lowest order of

Gooseneck **barnacles,** stalked marine crustaceans that foul the hulls of ships in the open sea. Some barnacle species cling to almost any surface, e.g. rocks or shells of crabs.

nobility in British peerage; important financier or merchant (as **beef** ~). 3. ~ **of beef**, cut consisting of two sirloins left uncut at backbone. **bar·on·ess** (băr'onĭs) *n.* Wife, widow, of baron; woman with baronial title in her own right. **ba·ro·ni·al** (barō'nēal) *adj.* **bar'o·ny** *n.* (pl. **-nies**). Domain or rank of baron.

bar·on·age (băr'onĭj) *n.* Barons collectively.

bar·on·et (băr'onĭt, -nĕt) *n.* Member of the lowest hereditary titled British order, ranking as a commoner.

ba·roque (barōk') *adj.* 1. Irregularly shaped (of jewels, esp. pearls); grotesque, odd. 2. Of the style of art that evolved in Italy c1600 out of that of the Renaissance and prevailed in Europe (chiefly in Catholic countries) until c1720, being characterized by massive and complex design in which architecture was combined with painting, sculpture, etc., and esp. by vigorous, restless or violent movement; of the music or literature of this period. 3. Applied loosely to any style with similar characteristics. ~ *n.* Baroque style. [Fr. f. Span. *barrueco* rough pearl]

ba·rouche (barōosh') *n.* Four-wheeled horse-drawn carriage with a seat in front for the driver, and seats inside for two couples facing each other.

barque (bärk) = BARK².

bar·quen·tine (bär'kentēn) = BARKENTINE.

bar·racks (băr'aks) *n.pl.* Building(s) for lodging soldiers; large building of severely plain, dull, or dreary appearance.

bar·ra·cu·da (bărakōo'da) *n.* (pl. **-das**, collect. **-da**). Voracious fish, including great ~ and Pacific ~, of family Sphyraenidae found in warm seas.

bar·rage (barahzh'; *Brit.* bar'ij for def. 1, băr'ahzh for def. 2) *n.* 1. Artificial obstruction in river or watercourse. 2. (mil.) A barrier of artillery fire from a large number of guns (also fig.); ~ **balloon**, large balloon supporting steel cable in an almost vertical position, esp. as one of a series forming antiaircraft defense. **barrage** *v.* (**-raged**, **-rag·ing**). Subject to a barrage.

bar·ra·tor, **bar·ra·ter** (băr'ater) *ns.* One who vexatiously incites to litigation or raises discord.

bar·ra·try (băr'atrē) *n.* 1. Purchase or sale of ecclesiastical preferments or offices of state. 2. Vexatious persistence in or incitement to litigation. 3. Fraud or gross and criminal negligence of ship's master or crew at the expense of the owners. **bar'ra·trous** *adj.* **bar'ra·trous·ly** *adv.*

bar·rel (băr'el) *n.* 1. Wooden vessel of curved staves bound by hoops, with flat ends; contents or capacity of such a vessel. 2. Revolving cylinder in capstan, watch, etc. 3. Cylindrical body of object; belly and loins of horse. 4. Metal tube of firearm, through which the missile is projected. 5. ~ **organ**, musical instrument with pin-studded cylinder turned by a handle and operating a mechanism that opens the pipes, the handle also serving to work the bellows; piano organ; ~ **roll**, maneuver by an airplane that makes a complete rotation about its longitudinal axis.

bar·ren (băr'en) *adj.* Not bearing, incapable of bearing (children, fruit, etc.); waste; unprofitable. ~ *n.* (usu. pl.) Barren land; elevated plains on which grow small trees and shrubs, but no timber. **bar'ren·ly** *adv.* **bar'ren·ness** *n.*

Bar·rett (băr'ĭt), **Elizabeth**: see BROWNING².

bar·rette (barĕt') *n.* Bar-shaped clip for woman's hair.

bar·ri·cade (băr'ĭkād, bărĭkād') *n.* (Defensive) barrier, esp. one hastily erected across street etc. ~ *v.t.* (**-cad·ed**, **-cad·ing**). Block or defend with a barricade. **bar'ri·cad·er** *n.* [Span. *barrica* cask]

Bar·rie (băr'ē), **Sir James Matthew** (1860–1937). Scottish writer of comedies and short stories, author of *Peter Pan*, *Quality Street*, etc.

Facing page: A masterpiece of the **baroque** *style: the ceiling of the Banqueting Hall, Whitehall, London, U.K., painted by the great Flemish artist, Rubens, in 1634. His English contemporary, Inigo Jones, was architect of the building.*

Butch Hobson of the Red Sox **baseball** team. The rules of modern baseball were formulated by the Knickerbocker Baseball Club, established in 1845. The origins of the game are disputed. Some claim it's English, others all-American.

bar·ri·er (băr´ēer) *n.* Fence barring advance or preventing access; any obstacle, boundary, or agency that keeps apart, or prevents communication, success, etc.; ~ **reef**, high wall of coral rock separated from land by a broad deep channel and with a precipitous face on the seaward side.

bar·ri·o (băr´ēō, băr´-) *n.* (pl. **-ri·os**). Spanish-speaking quarter of a U.S. city. [Sp., = district of a town]

bar·ris·ter (băr´ĭster) *n.* (Brit.) Attorney who has the privilege of practicing as advocate in the superior courts of law.

bar·row[1] (băr´ō) *n.* Prehistoric grave mound.

bar·row[2] (băr´ō) *n.* Rectangular frame with short shafts for carrying loads; shallow box with two shafts and one wheel; small two-wheeled handcart; wheelbarrow.

bar·row[3] (băr´ō) *n.* A castrated pig.

Bar·row (băr´ō), **Point.** Northernmost point in Alaska, on the

Arctic Ocean.

Bar·ry·more (băr´imōr, -mōr). Family of American actors including: **Maurice** (real name Herbert Blythe) (1847–1905), English-born stage actor; his son, **Lionel** (1878–1954); his daughter, **Ethel** (1879–1959); and his son, **John** (1882–1942), known as "the great profile," and famous for his portrayal of Hamlet in Shakespeare's *Hamlet*.

bar·ter (bär´ter) *v.* Exchange (goods, rights, etc.) *for* things of like kind. ~ *n.* Act or practice of business involving exchange of goods or services rather than payment. **bar·ter·er** *n.*

Barth (bärt), **Karl** (1886–1968). Swiss Protestant theologian.

Bar·thol·di (bärthŏl´dē; *Fr.* băr-

tawldē´), **Frédéric Auguste** (1834–1904). French sculptor; creator of the Statue of Liberty in New York harbor.

Bar·thol·o·mew (bärthŏl´omū), **St.** One of the 12 Apostles, commemorated on Aug. 24.

Bart·lett (bärt´lĭt) *n.* Large, yellow juicy variety of pear. [f. Enoch *Bartlett* (1779–1860), U.S. merchant]

Bar·tók (bär´tŏk; *Hung.* bŭr´tawk), **Béla** (1881–1945). Hungarian composer and collector of Hungarian folk music.

Bar·ton (bär´ton), **Clara** (1821–1912). Founder of the American Red Cross, 1881.

bar·y·on (băr´ēŏn) *n.* (phys.) Elementary particle whose mass is equal to or greater than that of a proton.

bar·y·sphere (băr´isfēr) *n.* Core of the earth, consisting of a very heavy substance, prob. nickel iron.

ba·ry·ta (barī´ta) *n.* Barium monoxide, an alkaline earth distinguished by its great density.

bar·y·tone (băr′ĭtōn) = BARI-
ONE.

ba·sal (bā′sal, -zal) *adj.* Of or
the base; ~ **metabolism**,
hysiol.) minimum amount of
ergy needed by an organism at
est. **bas′al·ly** *adv.*

ba·salt (basawlt′, bā′sawlt, băs′-
wlt) *n.* 1. Dark fine-grained
ock occurring as a lava or as an
trusion, often showing columnar
ructure. 2. Black porcelain in-
ented by Wedgwood. **ba·sal′tic**
dj.

bas·cule (băs′kūl) *n.* Lever
pparatus often used in a draw-
ridge balanced by a counterpoise
at rises or falls as the bridge is
wered or raised.

base[1] (bās) *adj.* (**bas·er, bas·-
st**). Morally low, mean, ignoble,
ebased; menial; **base′born**, of low
irth; illegitimate; **base metals**,
ose that quickly corrode or tar-
ish (opp. NOBLE or PRECIOUS
etals). **base′ly** *adv.* **base′ness**

base[2] (bās) *n.* 1. That on which
anything stands or depends;
upport, foundation, principle,
roundwork, starting point, princi-
al element; substance used as first
yer (of paint, make-up, etc.). 2.
iol.) End at which an organ is
ttached to trunk. 3. (geom.) Line
r surface on which a plane or solid
gure is held to stand. 4. (surv.,
also ~ **line**) Known line used as geo-
etrical base for trigonometry. 5.
math.) Starting number for system
f numeration or logarithms (as 10
n decimal counting). 6. (chem.)
Antithesis of ACID, substance (in-
luding ALKALI) capable of com-
ining with an acid to form a salt. 7.
archit.) Part of column between
haft or pedestal and pavement;
ase′board, narrow board around
vall of room close to floor. 8. (mil.)
Town or other area in rear of an
rmy where supplies, hospital, etc.,

*A small all-purpose hunting dog of
African breed, the **basenji** seldom
barks. This dog was portrayed in
ancient Egyptian murals.*

are concentrated; military camp. 9.
(gram.) Form of a word to which
suffixes are attached. 10. One of
the four corners of the baseball
diamond, marked by a bag or home
plate; ~ **hit**, fair ball allowing
batter to reach first base without an
error or force play; ~ **line**, (surv.)
see sense 4; (tennis) line at end of
court; (baseball) line between successive bases; **base′man** (pl.
-men), fielder assigned to first,
second, or third base; **base on balls**
(pl. **bases on balls**), advancement
to first base of batter after four
balls; **base runner**, member of
baseball team at bat who is on or
running to a base; **off base** (baseball) not touching the base occupied; (fig.) mistaken, unprepared.
base *v.t.* (**based, bas·ing**). Found
or establish *on.*

base·ball (bās′bawl) *n.* Game
played between two teams of nine
(ten, counting the designated hitter)
players on a diamond-shaped field
with four bases around which the
batter runs in order to score; ball
used in this game.

base·less (bās′lĭs) *adj.* Groundless, unfounded.

base·ment (bās′ment) *n.*
Lowest part of a structure;

inhabited story partly or wholly
below ground level.

ba·sen·ji (basĕn′jē) *n.* Small
hunting dog of African breed that
rarely barks.

bash (băsh) *v.t.* Strike heavily
so as to smash *in.* ~ *n.* Heavy
blow; (slang) party.

bash·ful (băsh′ful) *adj.* Shy,
sheepish. **bash′ful·ly** *adv.* **bash′-
ful·ness** *n.*

ba·sic (bā′sĭk) *adj.* 1. Of,
forming or serving as a base or
basis, fundamental. 2. (chem.)
Having the chemical properties of
a base. 3. (min., of igneous rocks)
Having little silica in proportion to
the amount of lime, potash, etc. 4.
B ~ English, system of English
comprising a select vocabulary of
850 words, devised by C. K. Ogden
of Cambridge, England, as a
medium of international communication. **ba′si·cal·ly** *adv.*

ba·sic·i·ty (basĭs′ĭtē) *n.* (chem.)
Number of equivalents of a base
with which one molecule of an acid
can react.

ba·sid·i·um (basĭd′ēum) *n.* (pl.
-sid·i·a pr. -sĭd′ēa). Spore-bearing
structure in some fungi.

bas·il (băz′il, bā′zil) *n.* Aromatic
herb of the genus *Ocimum,* esp.
sweet ~ (*O. basilicum*) and the
dwarf **bush ~** (*O. minimum*), the
leaves of which are used for flavoring soups, salads, etc. [L. *basilisca*
the plant (supposed antidote to
basilisk's bite)]

Bas·il (băz′il, băs′-), St. (*c*330–
379). Doctor of the church, founder
of a monastic rule that is still the
basis of monasticism in the Orthodox Church.

ba·sil·i·ca (basĭl′ĭka, -zĭl′-) *n.*
1. (in ancient Rome) Large oblong
building used as exchange or law
court, having an apse at one or each
end and freq. side aisles; colon-
naded hall, resembling this, in
Roman house. 2. Church of similar

*To score runs in **baseball**, the batsmen
must hit the ball pitched to them and
complete the circuit of bases as many
times as possible.*

***Basil** is a hardy annual grown as a culi-
nary herb. Its leaves have a distinctive
flavor and can be used fresh or dried.*

*The object of **basketball** is to score points by throwing the ball into the opposing team's basket. The game is played by 2 teams of 5 players who are allowed to pass, throw, roll, bat, or dribble the ball.*

shape, having a wide nave with aisles, and an apse at one (orig. western) end. **ba·sil'i·can** *adj.* [Gk. *basilika* (*oikia*) royal (house), f. *basileus* king]

bas·i·lisk (băs′ĭlĭsk, băz′-) *n.* 1. Cockatrice, fabulous reptile hatched by a serpent from a cock's egg, said to kill by its breath or glance. 2. Small C. Amer. and S. Amer. lizard of the family Iguanidae, with a hollow crest that can be inflated at will. [L. *basilicus* kind of lizard, f. Gk. *basiliskos* little king]

ba·sin (bā′sĭn) *n.* 1. Circular or oval vessel of greater width than depth and with sloping or curving sides, for holding water etc.; contents of a basin. 2. Hollow depression; circular or oval valley; tract of country drained by river and its tributaries. 3. = DOCK³ defs. 1, 2; landlocked harbor. **ba′sined, ba′sin·like** *adjs.*

ba·sis (bā′sĭs) *n.* (pl. **-ses** pr. -sēz). Base; foundation, beginning, determining principle; main ingredient; common ground for negotiation etc.

bask (băsk) *v.i.* Revel in warmth and light (*in* the sun, firelight, etc.); **bask′ing shark**, one of the largest species of shark (*Cetorhinus maximus*), found in northern seas, so called from its habit of lying near surface of water.

bas·ket (băs′kĭt) *n.* Receptacle of plaited or interwoven canes, osiers, etc.; contents of this; (basketball) horizontal hoop attached to a raised backboard and suspending an open net through which a basketball is thrown; the score (one or two points) made by such a throw; **bas′ketball**, game played by two teams of five on a court at each end of which is a basket into which a ball is thrown; the inflated ball for this game; **basket case**, (slang) person whose four limbs have been amputated; completely ineffectual person; **Basket Maker**, member of an ancient Amer. Indian culture of southwestern U.S., preceding the Pueblo; **bas′ketwork**, interlaced osiers, twigs, etc. **bas′ket·like** *adj.*

Basle (bahl). (Ger. *Basel*, Fr. *Bâle*) Town and canton of Switzerland.

Basque (băsk, bahsk) *adj. & n.* (Member) of a people inhabiting both slopes of the W. Pyrenees and speaking a non-Indo-European language; (of) this language.

bas-re·lief (bah rĭlēf′, băs-, bah′rĭlēf, băs′-) *n.* Low relief, carving or modeling in which figures project less than one-half of rey-headed fruit **bat,** *Australia. Of the* rder *Chiroptera (meaning 'hand wings'* Greek), *bats are the only winged* ammals. *Nocturnal creatures, they*

heir true proportions from the ackground.

bass[1] (băs) *n.* (pl. **bass·es,** col- ·ct. **bass**). Any of a large group of shes in sea or fresh water, in- luding **sea ~** (family Serranidae), **triped ~** (*Roccus saxatilis*) etc.

bass[2] (bās) *adj.* Deep sounding; f, suited to, lowest part in armönized music; having a voice xtending 1 1/2 octaves or more elow middle C; **~ clef:** see CLEF; **~ drum:** see DRUM; **~ viol,** ouble bass, viola da gamba. **~** *n.* **ass** part; music for, singer with, ass voice; **bass'ist,** player of the OUBLE BASS.

bass[3] (băs) = BAST.

bas·set (băs'ĭt) *n.* (also **~ ound**) Short-legged dog of breed riginating in France, used in hunt- ng hares or badgers, followed on oot.

bas·set (băs'ĭt) **horn.** Tenor larinet, of somewhat greater range han the ordinary clarinet.

bas·si·net (băsĭnĕt', băs'ĭnĕt) *n.*

sleep hanging upside down in the dark. The hind feet, toes and sharply curved claws are modified for clinging without strain.

Hooded cradle for infants.

bas·so (băs'ō, bah'sō; *It.* bahs'- saw) *adj. & n.* (pl. **-sos,** *It.* **-si** pr. -sē). (mus.) Bass; **~ profundo,** (singer having) deep bass voice.

bas·soon (băsoon', ba-) *n.* Double-reed musical instrument, the bass of the woodwind family, having an 8-ft. pipe turned back so that the whole instrument measures only 4 ft. **bas·soon'ist** *n.*

bast (băst) *n.* (also **bass**[3], **bass'- wood**). Inner bark of linden tree (*Tilia americana*) which, cut into strips and coarsely woven, is used for matting etc.; similar fiber obtained from leaf bases or leaf stalks of certain palms and used for ropes, brooms, etc.; any flexible or fibrous bark.

bas·tard (băs'terd) *n.* Person born out of wedlock; hybrid, counterfeit thing; (slang) disliked person or thing. **bas'tard·ly** *adj.* **bas'tar·dy** *n.* (pl. **-dies**). **bas·tard·ize** (băs'terdīz) *v.t.* (**-ized, -iz·ing**). Declare or render

bastard; debase, corrupt. **bas'- tard·i·za·tion** (băsterdĭzā'shon) *n.*

baste[1] (bāst) *v.t.* (**bast·ed, bast·ing**). Sew together loosely, sew with long loose stitches, tack.

baste[2] (bāst) *v.t.* (**bast·ed, bast·ing**). 1. Moisten (roasting meat etc.) by pouring melted fat, gravy, etc. over (it). 2. (colloq.) Thrash, cudgel.

bas·tille, bas·tile (băstēl'; *Fr.* băstē'ye) *ns.* (pl. **bas·tilles** pr. băstēlz'; *Fr.* băstē'ye). 1. Prison. 2. **B ~,** 14th-c. prison fortress in Paris, used for political and other prisoners, stormed and destroyed by the revolutionary mob on July 14, 1789; the anniversary of its fall (**B ~ Day**), marking the end of absolute monarchy in France and the beginning of the French Revo- lution, the national holiday of republican France.

bas·ti·na·do (băstĭnā'dō) *n.* (pl. **-does**) **&** *v.t.* (**-doed, -do·ing**). (Punish with) caning or cudgeling on the soles of the feet.

bas·tion (băs'chon) *n.* Mass of masonry or brick- or stone-faced earthwork projecting from fortifi- cation in the form of an irregular pentagon; (fig.) stronghold. **bas'- tioned** *adj.*

Bas·togne (băstōn'; *Fr.* băs- tawn'ye). Town in SE. Belgium; a key point in the Allied line of defense during the Battle of the Bulge, 1944–5, in World War II.

Ba·su·to (basoo'tō) *n.* (pl. **-tos,** collect. **-to**). (Member of) a S. African people of Bantu stock; **Basutoland,** former name of LESOTHO.

bat[1] (băt) *n.* Small nocturnal mammal of the order Chiroptera, resembling a mouse, with leathery wings consisting of a membrane stretched from neck over forearms and elongated fingers, and along sides of body to hind limbs and (usu.) tail; (slang) a mean old woman; **have ~s in the belfry,** (slang) be insane, hence **bats** (slang) insane, crazy.

bat[2] (băt) *n.* Stout wooden stick used as cudgel; a blow, as from a bat; long, round stick with handle at one end used in baseball; similar stick used in other games; **at ~,** (baseball, cricket) taking one's turn as batter; **go to ~ for,** (colloq.) support or defend (someone); **right off the ~,** (colloq.) immediately; **bat'ter,** baseball player at bat. **bat** *v.* (**bat·ted, bat·ting**). 1. Hit, strike with a bat. 2. (esp. base- ball) Take one's turn at bat.

bat[3] (băt) *v.t.* (**bat·ted, bat·-**

The **bas-reliefs** *of Trajan's Column in Rome illustrate his victories over the Dacians (2nd century A.D.). The scenes wind around the shaft in marble spirals, a supreme example of continu- ous narration in classical art.*

ting). (colloq.) Blink; **not to ~ an eye(lid)**, (fig.) be unperturbed.

Ba·taan (batăn′, -tahn′). Peninsula of W. Luzon, Republic of the Philippines; surrendered and recaptured by American forces during World War II; famous as scene of Gen. MacArthur's promise: "I shall return."

Ba·ta·vi·a (batā′vēa). 1. Former name of DJAKARTA. 2. (hist.) Region between Rhine and Waal, inhabited in Roman times by a Celtic tribe, the Batavi.

batch (băch) n. Quantity of loaves etc. baked at one time; quantity, number, or set of people or things associated together, esp. in time.

bate (bāt) v.t. (**bat·ed, bat·ing**). Let down; restrain (breath); **with bated breath**, anxiously.

ba·teau (bătō′; Fr. bătō′) n. (pl. **-teaux** pr. -tōz′; Fr. -tō′). Light river boat, esp. the long, tapering, flat-bottomed boat used by French Canadians.

Bath (băth, bahth). City in SW.

England noted for its hot springs and mineral baths since its Roman days.

bath (băth, bahth) n. (pl. **baths** pr. bădhz, bahdhz, băths, bahths). Immersion or washing, esp. of the body, in water etc; water for this; room for this; bathtub; (usu. pl.) spa; **Order of the B ~**, high order of British knighthood, founded 1725 as revival of the "Knights of the Bath," first created 1399 at coronation of Henry IV and so named from the ceremonial bath that preceded installation; **bath′-house**, building with dressing room for bathers; **bath′robe**, dressing gown; **bath′room**, room with bathtub or shower and usu. washbasin and toilet; (euphem.) toilet; **bath′tub**, vessel for bathing in.

bathe (bādh) v. (**bathed, bath·ing**). Immerse in liquid (as for cleaning); wet thoroughly; envelop; go swimming; **bathing suit**, garment for bathing or swimming in; **bath′er** n.

bath·o·lith (băth′olĭth), **batholite** (băth′olīt) ns. Large body intrusive rock (e.g. granite) such is found esp. along Pacific coast America.

ba·thos (bā′thŏs) n. Fall fro sublime to ridiculous; anticlima insincere pathos. **ba·thet·** (bathĕt′ĭk) adj.

Bath·she·ba (băthshē′ba, băth she-). Wife of Uriah the Hittite Sam. 11); she became one of t wives of David and the mother Solomon.

bath·y·scaphe (băth′ĭskă -skăf), **bath·y·scaph** (băth′ĭskă **bath·y·scape** (băth′ĭskăp) ns. Ve sel for deep-sea diving and explor tion. [Fr., f. Gk. bathus deep skaphos ship; coined by A. Picca (1884–1962), Swiss physicist]

bath·y·sphere (băth′ĭsfēr) Spherical diving apparatus f deep-sea observation.

ba·tik (batēk′, bă-, băt′ĭk) Javanese method, practiced also the West, of executing designs textiles by painting parts of t

1	towing fairlead
2	observation lights
3	water entry/exit holes
4	forward air tanks
5	petrol buoyancy tanks
6	1hp electric motor
7	conning-tower
8	battery
9	battery skid
10	compass
11	vertical speed indicator
12	iron shot silos
13	electromagnets
14	silo discharge holes
15	stabilizing keel
16	air lock
17	crew ladder
18	petrol filler point
19	detachable petrol tanks
20	air-lock entrance hatch
21	command sphere
22	circuit board
23	shot levels
24	electromagnet panel
25	silver-zinc accumulators
26	pressure gauges
27	petroleum levels
28	sounding gauge
29	motor controls
30	junction box
31	pressure gauge
32	viewing port
33	power cables
34	sphere support strut
35	guide chain

*Cutaway illustration of a **bathyscaphe**, used for deep-sea exploration. Electric motors power the vessel. It is cast in two hemispheres designed so that watertightness increases with external pressure. Some compartments contain*

buoyant gasoline; others are open to the sea, equalizing pressure in the float with sea pressure. Ballast is provided by iron shot and detachable gasoline tanks, which can be jettisoned electromagnetically.

*Facing page: The Javanese craft of **batik** has been widely adopted by Western textile designers. Parts of the pattern are painted in wax. The parts which are left exposed are dyed. The wax is then removed.*

*Organized **battle** is as old as civilization.
Top: Tableaux of Custer's Last Stand at
Little Bighorn in 1876. Left: Battleship
U.S.S. Alabama at Mobile. Below: Baton
Rouge, capital of Louisiana and location
of 3 major battles between 1779 and
1863, is now the site of the U.S.'s
biggest oil refinery. Above: Battle-axes.
1. Poleax c. 1470. 2. Horseman's ax c.
1520. Ax remains dating back 30,000
years have been found.*

pattern in wax, dyeing the parts left
exposed, and then removing the
wax; material dyed thus. [Javanese,
= "drawing"]

Ba·tis·ta (bahtēs´tah), **Fulgen·
cio** (1901–73).   Cuban dictator,
1933–40, and president 1940–4,
1952–9; ousted by Fidel Castro.

ba·tiste (batēst´, bă-) *n.*   Fine
light cotton or other fine, smooth
fabric. [Fr., f. *Baptiste* of Cambrai,
first maker]

bat·man (bắt´man) *n.* (pl. **-men**
pr. -men) (fem. **-wom·an** pr.
-wŏŏman; pl. **-wom·en** pr.
-wĭmĭn). Member of British army
or air force acting as officer's serv-

t. [orig. man who carried
icer's baggage (Fr. *bât* pack-
idle)]

bat mitz·vah (baht mĭts′va;
·*b.* baht mĕtsvah′) (Religious
tiation ceremony for) Jewish girl
ed 12 to 14. [Heb., = "daughter
commandment"]

ba·ton (bătŏn′, ba-, băt′on) *n.* 1.
aff of office. 2. (mus.) Con-
ctor's wand for beating time. 3.
ort rod passed from one runner
another in a relay race.

Ba·ton Rouge (băt′on rōōzh′).
pital and important port of
uisiana, in the S., on the Missis-
pi River.

ba·tra·chi·an (batrā′kēan) *adj.*
, concerning, like tailless amphi-
ns, e.g., frogs and toads; ANURAN.
n. Tailless leaping amphibian.

bat·tal·ion (batăl′yon) *n.* Unit
infantry (*or* artillery) consisting
three or four companies (*or*
tteries).

bat·ten[1] (băt′en) *n.* Long, thin
rip of wood used in carpentry. ~
. Strengthen, fasten *down*, with
ttens.

bat·ten[2] (băt′en) *v.i.* (archaic)
ed gluttonously *on*; grow fat,
g.) thrive at another's expense.

bat·ter (băt′er) *v.* Strike re-
atedly so as to bruise or break;
at out of shape; handle severely;
at·tered child, young child with
juries inflicted by a parent; **bat-
red wife**, a woman habitually
aten by her husband; **bat′tering
am**, heavy beam used for batter-
g down walls or doors. **batter** *n.*
ixture of flour and eggs beaten
p with liquid for cooking.

bat·ter·y (băt′erē) *n.* (pl.
er·ies). 1. (law) Infliction of a

Globelight, 1927, a product of the
Bauhaus *movement. The aim of the
movement was to close the gap
between the creative artist and the
industrial craftsman.*

blow or blows on another person.
2. (mil.) Set of guns with their men,
and vehicles; group of guns on a
warship; the basic tactical artillery
unit. 3. Set of similar or connected
instruments, utensils, etc.; cell or
set of cells (**storage battery**)
generating electrical current by
chemical action. 4. (baseball)
Team's pitcher and catcher in a
game.

Bat·ter·y (băt′erē), **The.** (Park
on) the S. tip of Manhattan Island;
the site of defensive artillery during
the Colonial era.

bat·tle (băt′el) *n.* Combat, esp.
between large organized forces;
line of ~, troops or ships drawn up

to fight; **~-ax**, kind of long-
handled ax used as a medieval
weapon; (fig.) formidable or
domineering woman; ~ **cry**, war
cry, slogan; ~ **dress**, (formerly)
soldier's etc. fighting uniform; ~
fatigue, mental disorder due to
stress in wartime combat; **bat′tle-
field**, scene of battle; **bat′tle-
ship**, warship of the largest and
most powerfully armed class;
battle station(s), position(s) assigned for battle; **battle wagon**,
(slang) battleship. **battle** *v.* (**-tled,
-tling**). Struggle *with* or *against* or
for; fight against; fight (one's way
etc.). **bat′tler** *n.*

bat·tle·dore (băt′eldōr) *n.* An
early form of badminton (also called
~ **and shuttlecock**); the light
wooden paddle or racket used in
this game. [prob. f. Span. *batal-
lador* champion]

bat·tle·ment (băt′elment) *n.* Indented parapet at top of wall etc.,
orig. for purposes of defense against
assailants.

bat·ty (băt′ē) *adj.* (**-ti·er,
-ti·est**). (slang) Crazy.

bau·ble (baw′bel) *n.* 1. Showy
trinket. 2. Baton surmounted by
fantastic head with asses' ears carried by court fool or jester.

Bau·de·laire (bōdelār′, bō′de-
lār), **Charles Pierre** (1821–67).
French lyric poet, author of *Les
Fleurs du Mal* (1857).

Bau·douin I (bōdwăn′)
(1930–). King of Belgium since
1951.

Bau·haus (bow′hows). School
of design founded by Walter
Gropius (1883–1969) in Weimar,
Germany in 1919; closed in 1933.

baulk (bawk) = BALK.

Volta's first electric battery   A simple cell   Daniell cell   Leclanché cell

*An Italian, Alessandro Volta, described
the first electric **battery** in 1800. He
found he could cause a current to pass
through a wire by immersing 2 different
metals in a salt solution. Englishman*

*John Daniell developed the first cell free
of 'polarization' in 1836: a zinc negative
electrode dipped in a sulphuric acid
electrolyte, and a positive electrode of
copper dipped in copper sulfate sol-*

*ution. 'Dry' batteries with a depolarizer
derive from the Leclanché cell. In fact
the electrolyte is not dry but is made up
in the form of a paste or jelly.*

Baum (bahm, bawm), **L(yman) Frank** (1856–1919). American journalist and playwright; author of the children's classic, *Wonderful Wizard of Oz*.

baux·ite (bawk´sīt, bŏk´-) *n.* The principal ore of aluminum, containing aluminum hydroxide, ferric oxide, and silica. [originally found at *Les Baux* near Arles, France]

Ba·var·i·a (bavār´ēa). Former state of S. Germany, now a province of The Federal Republic; capital, Munich. **Ba·var´i·an** *adj.* & *n.*

bawd (bawd) *n.* (archaic) Procuress, brothel madam; prostitute.

bawd·y (baw´dē) *adj.* (**bawd·i·er, bawd·i·est**). Humorously vulgar or indecent; **baw´dy·house**, brothel. **bawd´i·ly** *adv.* **bawd´i·ness** *n.*

bawl (bawl) *v.* Shout or weep at the top of one's voice; ~ **out**, (slang) reprimand severely. **bawl´er** *n.*

bay¹ (bā) *n.* 1. Kind of laurel, esp. the sweet bay or bay laurel, (*Laurus nobilis*), with deep-green leaves (~ **leaf**) (used to flavor soups etc.) and many dark purple berries. 2. (also **bay´berry**) West Indian tree (*Pimenta acris*), bearing small green berries; the berry; **bay rum**, aromatic liquid made from its leaves, used as an astringent.

bay² (bā) *n.* Part of sea filling wide-mouthed opening of land.

bay³ (bā) *n.* 1. Division of wall between columns or buttresses. 2. Recess, alcove; compartment; **sick ~**, part of ship's deck used as hospital; part of building similarly used. 3. Space added to room by advancing window from wall line; **B~ State**, Massachusetts; ~ **window**, window in a bay; (slang) a protruding stomach.

bay⁴ (bā) *n.* Bark of large dog or of hounds in pursuit, esp. as they draw near the quarry; (**stand**) **at ~**, cornered and thus forced to show fight or turn against pursuers. ~ *v.* (of large dog) Bark, bark at.

bay⁵ (bā) *adj.* (of horse) Having body of light to dark brown, with

How ebb and flow of the tide acts on the shore to form a **beach**. The line of the shore, the water movement along it and the materials composing the beach influence the form the beach takes.

black mane and tail; reddish brown. ~ *n.* Bay horse.

Ba·yeux (bāyoo´, bah-; *Fr.* bahyö´) **tapestry.** An 11th- or 12th-c. embroidered linen tapestry 231 ft. long by 20 in. wide with scenes depicting the Norman Conquest of England and preserved in the cathedral of Bayeux, France.

Bayle (bāl), **Pierre** (1647–1706). French philosopher and skeptic, author of a *Dictionnaire historique et critique* (1695–7), which had great influence on Voltaire and other 18th-c. French skeptics.

bay·o·net (bā´onĭt, -nĕt, bāonĕt´) *n.* Stabbing blade that can be attached to rifle muzzle. ~ *v.t.* (**-net·ed** or **-net·ted, -net·ing** or **-net·ting**). Stab with bayonet.

bay·ou (bī´oo, -ō) *n.* (pl. **-ous**). Marshy inlet or stagnant creek, esp.

in southern U.S.

ba·zaar, ba·zar (bazār´) *n.* Oriental marketplace or shopping quarters; fancy shop, boutique; sale of goods for charities. [Pers. *bāzā* street of shops]

ba·zoo·ka (bazoo´ka) *n.* Crude trombone-like musical instrument. 2. Infantry's portable rocket launcher for firing armorpiercing (esp. antitank) rockets.

BB (bē´bē) *n.* A .18-inch diameter pellet shot by firing from an air rifle.

B.B.A. *abbrev.* Bachelor of Business Administration.

BBC *abbrev.* British Broadcasting Corporation.

B.C. *abbrev.* Before Christ; British Columbia.

bd. *abbrev.* Board.

B.D. *abbrev.* Bachelor of Divinity.

bdrm. *abbrev.* Bedroom.

Be *symbol.* Beryllium.

be (bē) *v.i.* [**am** (ăm), **are** (ār), **is** (ĭz), **was** (wŭz), **were** (wēr), **been** (bĭn, Brit. bēn), **being** (bē´ĭng), (archaic) **art** (ārt), **was**

Among birds the **beak** varies greatly in size, shape and strength, depending on the hunting and food-gathering role. The lorikeet has the short hooked beak common to parrots. The cormorant's

long bill aids the voracious fisher. The eagle's powerful beak equips it as a bird of prey. The woodpecker grubs out wood-boring insects with its chisel-like beak.

Ostrich   Golden Eagle   Ruby Throated Humming Bird

Tawny Owl

Rainbow Lorikeet   Cormorant   Green Woodpecker   Avocet

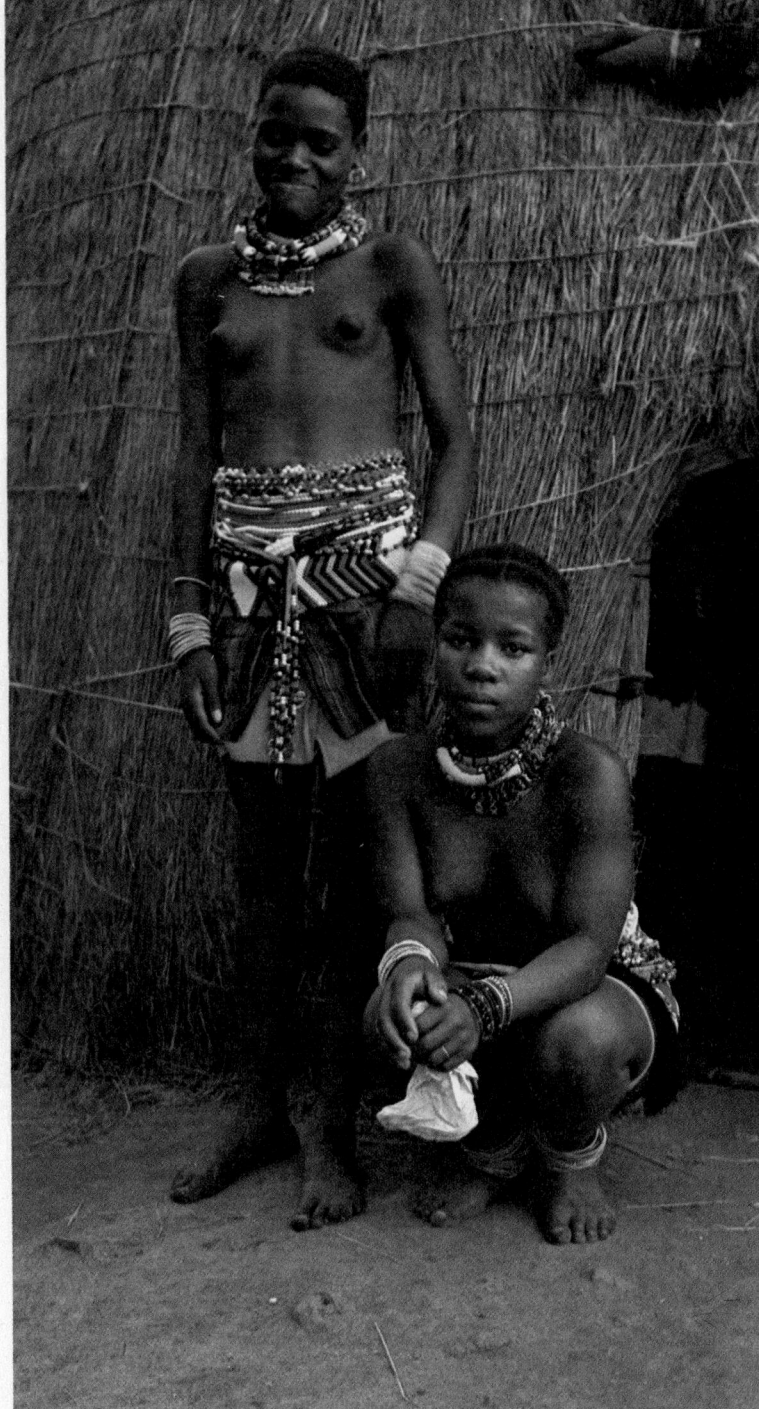

ulu girls at a gathering in Natal, South
frica. Many tribal peoples believe
eads have magical or talismanic
roperties as well as being decorative.
arly explorers used beads of metal or
lass to barter with native tribes.

vŭst), **wert** (wērt)] Exist, occur;
:cupy a position; remain, con-
nue; have a certain state or quality
pecified by following noun, adj.,
c.); **~-all and end-all**, abso-
tely everything, the whole *of*; ~
ff, go away.

beach (bēch) *n.* Sandy or
ebbly shore of the sea (or lake or
rge river); **~ ball**, large inflated
all for games on beach; **~ buggy**,
ghtweight or framework vehicle
ith oversized tires for driving on
nd beaches; **beach′comber**, long
ave rolling onto the beach; person
ho lives by gathering salable jet-
m or refuse from beaches; **beach
rass**, grass of the genus *Ammo-
hila* growing on sandy shores and
nes and having long clusters of
pikelets. **beach′head**, fortified
psition of troops landed on a
each; **beach plum**, (edible plum-
ke fruit of) New England coastal
rub (*Prunus maritima*) bearing
hite flowers. **beach** *v.t.* Run (ship
c.) ashore, haul up.

Beach-la-Mar (bēch la mar′) =
ÊCHE-DE-MER. [Port. *bicho do mar*
ea-worm]

bea·con (bē′kon) *n.* I. Guiding
r warning signal light or fire,
gnal fire on hill. 2. Conspicuous
ll or tower suitable for a beacon.
. Lighthouse; conspicuous object.
. Radio transmitter sending out
gnals enabling ship or aircraft to
x position.

bead (bēd) *n.* I. Small per-
orated ornamental ball etc. for
hreading with others on a string or
or sewing on to fabric; small bubble
r drop of liquid; (pl.) necklace;
osary; **tell (count, say) one's ~s**,
ay prayers with rosary beads. 2.
mall metal knob forming front
ight of gun (**draw a bead on**,
ake aim at). **bead** *v.* Furnish or
dorn with beads; form or grow into
eads. [OE, = "prayer," from the
se of strings of beads for keeping
ount of the number of prayers said]
ead′ed *adj.* **bead′ing** *n.*

bea·dle (bē′del) *n.* I. (hist.)
nferior parish officer appointed to
eep order in church, punish petty
ffenses, and carry messages, etc.
. Official who prepares and walks
efore procession, macebearer [in
he Engl. universities usu. spelled
edel(1)].

bead·y (bē′dē) *adj.* (**bead·i·er**,
ead·i·est**). (of eyes) Small and
right like beads, esp. as indicating
unning, greed, or meanness.

bea·gle (bē′gel) *n.* Small hound
ith long ears and short legs, orig.
red for hunting hares.

beak (bēk) *n.* Horny projecting
mandibles of bird; bill; extremities,
often horny in structure, of
mandibles of other animals (as
turtles); hooked nose; projection at
prow of ancient ships, esp. war
galleys. **beaked** (bēkt, bē′kĭd),
beak′less, **beak′like** *adjs.*

beak·er (bē′ker) *n.* I. Large
drinking cup. 2. Straight-sided
lipped glass for scientific experiments.

beam (bēm) *n.* I. Long piece of
squared timber such as is used in
building houses or ships; horizontal
support in building. 2. Transverse
bar of balance. 3. Transverse
horizontal timber of a ship; hence,
the greatest breadth of a ship;
broad in the ~, (colloq.) wide;
having wide hips or a wide rear end.
4. Ray or group of nearly parallel
rays of light, or of electric radiation,
etc.; (also **radio ~**) radio waves
sent as a beam (i.e. not dispersed or
broadcast); directional radio or
radar signal used to guide aircraft
or missiles; course indicated by this;

(phys.) directional flow of radiation or particles; **off the** ~, (colloq.) mistaken, on the wrong track; **on the** ~, (colloq.) correct, on the right track. 5. Radiance, bright look, smile. **beam** v. Emit (light, affection, etc.); direct, aim (radio signals etc.); shine, smile radiantly. **beamed, beam'ing, beam'less, beam'like** adjs. **beam'ing·ly** adv.

bean (bēn) n. 1. Edible kidney-shaped non-endospermic seed borne in pods of the family Leguminosae; plant producing such seeds; (slang) a person's head; **bean'pole**, tall, slender pole for supporting growing bean plants; (slang) tall, thin person. 2. Similar seed of other plants, as coffee. 3. **full of** ~**s**, (slang) in high spirits; **spill the** ~**s**, (slang) disclose a secret. **bean'er·y** n. (pl. **-er·ies**), (slang) cheap restaurant. 4. **beanbag**, small cloth bag filled with beans, used as a toy, ornament, etc.; **bean ball**, baseball pitch deliberately thrown at batter's head; **bean curd**, creamy white cake of soybean cheese used in oriental cooking; **bean'stalk**, stem of the bean plant. **bean** v.t. (slang) Hit on the head.

bear[1] (bâr) n. (pl. **bears**, collect. **bear**). 1. Heavily built, thick-furred plantigrade quadruped of family Ursidae. 2. Rough, gruff, or clumsy person. 3. (stock exch.) Person who believes price of stocks will decline; ~ **market**, one with falling prices. 4. **Great, Little B**~: see URSA. 5. ~ **baiting**, (hist.) setting dogs to attack captive bear; ~ **hug**, tight embrace; **bear'skin**, skin or pelt of a bear; garment, rug, etc., made from this. **bear'ish** adj. Rough mannered, surly; (of

stock market or prices) tending to fall.

bear[2] (bâr) v. (**bore, borne, bear·ing**). 1. Carry, bring; support; wear; ~ **out**, confirm. 2. Endure, tolerate; ~ **up**, endure, keep up one's courage; ~ **with**, be patient with. 3. (past. part. **born** in passive) Give birth to. 4. Produce, yield. 5. Apply weight; press or push against; tend, incline; move, tend in the direction of; ~ **down**, strive harder; ~ **down on**, move toward; ~ **hard on**, oppress; ~ **on**, relate to; **bring to** ~, apply. **bear'er** n.

Beard (bērd). Name of two American educators and historians: **Charles Austin** (1874–1948) and

his wife, **Mary Ritter** (1876*–* 1958); authors of *The Rise* *of* *American Civilization.*

beard (bērd) n. Hair on lowe*r* part of man's face (now usu. ex*-* cluding moustache and whiskers); chin tuft of animal. **beard'ed**, **beard'like** adjs. **beard'less** ad*j.* Youthful, immature. **beard** v. Oppose openly, defy.

Beard·sley (bērdz'lē), **Aubre***y* **Vincent** (1872–98). English artis*t* and illustrator, worked in style o*f* art nouveau.

bear·ing (bâr'ing) n. (esp.) *I.* Behavior. 2. Act, capability, o*r* period of birth or bringing forth*.* 3. Relation, reference, aspec*t*, tendency to exert influence on. *4.* Part of machine that supports an*d* guides a shaft, pivot, etc. *5.* Situation or direction of one point*,* object, etc., with respect to anothe*r*; determination of this; (pl.) relativ*e* position or direction (also fig.).

beast (bēst) n. 1. Anima*l,* quadruped as dist. from birds, man*,* insects, etc.; ~ **of burden**, anima*l* used for carrying heavy loads. *2.* Cruel, coarse person; brutal, savag*e* man. **beast'like** adj.

beast·ly (bēst'lē) adj. (**-li·er**, **-li·est**). Like a beast or its ways*;* (colloq.) unpleasant. **beast'li·nes***s* n.

Despite its massive body, a **bear** *can run at 30 m.p.h. Left to right: Grizzly bear, long-clawed and very fierce; Polar bear, which lives on Arctic ice-floes; Himalayan black bear has V-shaped blaze on its chest; Kodiak bear, a variety of Grizzly, is the largest land carnivore and often over 9 ft. tall.*

Kodiak

Polar

Grizzly

Himalayan black

beat (bēt) *v.* (**beat, beat·en** or **beat, beat·ing**). 1. Strike repeatedly; (of sun etc.) strike *upon*. 2. Thrash soundly; defeat, overcome, surpass; be too hard for, perplex. 3. (of wings etc.) Move up and down; (of heart etc.) pulsate, throb; ~ **it**, (slang) go away; ~ **time**, mark the time of music by the beat of a wand, tapping with the foot, etc. 4. Shift, drive, alter, deform, or shape by blows; make (a path) by repeated treading; (also ~ **up**) stir vigorously. 5. Strike bushes etc. to rouse game. 6. ~ (person) **up**, (colloq.) attack and injure person by blows and kicks. ~ *n.* 1. Stroke or blow; drum signal; movement of conductor's baton; measured sequence of strokes or sounds; marking of metrical divisions of music; accent or stress in music or poetry; a throb or throbbing. 2. Policeman's appointed course; newspaper reporter's habitual round. 3. (colloq.) = BEATNIK. ~ *adj.* (colloq.) Exhausted, worn out; ~-**up**, (colloq.) dilapidated.

beat·en (bē′ten) *adj.*: see BEAT; (esp.) ~ **gold** etc., gold etc. hammered into foil, shaped by the hammer; ~ **track, way**, well-trodden way (also fig.).

beat·er (bē′ter) *n.* (esp.) Man employed to rouse game; man who beats gold etc.; implement that beats, as **egg′beater** etc.

beat (bēt) **generation.** Young people (esp. after World War II) adopting unconventional dress, manners, habits, etc., as a means of self-expression and social protest and espousing mystical detachment. [Prob. f. *beat* = "exhausted"; perh. infl. by *beat* = "rhythm"; but coined by novelist J. Kerouac (b. 1922), connecting *beat* with *beatitude*]

be·a·tif·ic (bēatĭf′ĭk) *adj.* Bestowing bliss; blissful, saintly. **be·a·tif′i·cal·ly** *adv.*

be·at·i·fy (bēăt′ifī) *v.t.* (**-fied, -fy·ing**). Make supremely happy or blessed; (R.C. Ch.) declare to be in enjoyment of heavenly bliss (as the first step toward canonization). **be·a·ti·fi·ca·tion** (bēătĭfĭkā′shon) *n.* **be·at·i·tude** (bēăt′ĭtŏŏd, -tūd) *n.* Supreme blessedness; declaration of blessedness, esp. (pl.) those pronounced by Jesus Christ in the Sermon on the Mount (Matt. 5).

beat·nik (bēt′nĭk) *n.* Member and adherent of the beat generation.

beau (bō) *n.* Fop, dandy; suitor, lover; **B ~ Brummell**, like George Bryan Brummell (1778–1840). English dandy and fashion leader.

Beau·fort (bō′fert) **scale.** Series of numbers used by meteorologists to indicate force of wind (measured at 10 m above level ground), thus:

Force	m.p.h.		knots
0	less than 1	calm	less than 1
1	1–3	light air	1–3
2	4–7	light breeze	4–6
3	8–12	gentle breeze	7–10
4	13–18	moderate breeze	11–16
5	19–24	fresh breeze	17–21
6	25–31	strong breeze	22–27
7	32–38	near gale	28–33
8	39–46	gale	34–40
9	47–54	strong gale	41–47
10	55–63	storm	48–55
11	64–72	violent storm	56–63
12	73 or more	hurricane	64 or more

[devised by Admiral Sir F. *Beaufort* (1774–1857)]

beau geste (bō zhĕst′) (pl. **beaux gestes** pr. bō zhĕst′). Display of magnanimity. [Fr., = "beautiful (or splendid) gesture"]

Beau·jo·lais (bōzhola′) *n.* Red or (less freq.) white Burgundy from the Beaujolais district in the Rhône department of France.

Beau·mar·chais (bōmărsha′), **Pierre Augustin Caron de** (1732–90). French dramatist, author of famous comedies *Le Barbier de Seville* (1775), *Le Mariage de Figaro* (1778).

beau monde (bō mawṅd′). Fashionable society. [Fr., = "beautiful world"]

Beau·mont (bō′mŏnt). Industrial city and port on the Gulf of Mexico in E. Texas.

Beau·mont (bō′mŏnt), **Francis** (1584–1616). English playwright, collaborator with John Fletcher from *c*1606 to 1616.

Beau·re·gard (bō′regärd), **Pierre Gustave Toutant de** (1818–93). American Confederate army general; in command of bombardment of Fort Sumter.

beaut (būt) *n.* (slang abbreviation) Something beautiful or excellent.

beau·te·ous (bū′tēus, -tyus) *adj.* (archaic and poet.) Endowed with beauty. **beau′te·ous·ly** *adv.* **beau′te·ous·ness** *n.*

beau·ti·cian (būtĭsh′an) *n.* One skilled in giving beauty treatments, as in a beauty parlor.

beau·ti·ful (bū′tiful) *adj.* Having beauty; excellent; (colloq.) typical; ~ **people**, wealthy trendsetters, fashionable people; **the beautiful**, beauty in the abstract. **beau′ti·ful·ly** *adv.* **beau′ti·ful·ness** *n.*

beau·ti·fy (bū′tifī) *v.t.* (**-fied, -fy·ing**). Make beautiful.

beau·ty (bū′tē) *n.* (pl. **-ties**). Combination of qualities (as form, color, etc.) that delights the eye; combined qualities delighting the other senses, the moral sense, or the mind; beautiful trait or feature; person or thing possessing beauty; something excellent; (colloq.) a typical example; ~ **parlor**, (also ~ **shop**), establishment for hairdressing, manicuring, or other beauty treatment of women; ~ **sleep**, sleep obtained before midnight; (fig.) enough sleep to keep one beautiful; ~ **spot**, small patch placed on woman's face as foil to a beautiful complexion; beautiful place or scene; ~ **treatment**, use of massage, cosmetics, exercise,

*The vineyards that produce **Beaujolais** wine stretch from a little south of Anse to slightly north of Tournis in a narrow fertile strip along the west bank of the River Saône.*

etc., in an attempt to improve personal beauty.

beaux arts (bōzär´) *n.pl.* The fine arts. [Fr.]

bea·ver (bē´ver) *n.* (pl. **-vers,** collect. **-ver**). 1. Amphibious rodent of genus *Castor* with broad, oval, horizontally flattened tail, webbed hind feet, soft fur, and hard incisor teeth with which it cuts down trees: remarkable for its industry esp. in constructing dams of wood and mud; **bea´verboard,** a kind of fiberboard; **eager beaver,** (colloq.) zealous person. 2. Soft, short, rather wooly light brown fur of this animal; tall hat for men made from this.

be·bop (bē´bŏp) *n.* A style of jazz music.

be·calm (bĭkahm´) *v.t.* Deprive (a sailing ship) of wind necessary to move it.

became (bĭkām´): see BECOME.

be·cause (bĭkawz´) *adv.* By reason of. ~ *conj.* For the reason that.

bé·cha·mel (bā´shamĕl; *Fr.* bāshămĕl´) **sauce.** Rich white sauce of butter, flour, cream, and seasoning. [f. its inventor, Marquis de *Béchamel*, steward of Louis XIV]

bêche-de-mer (bĕsh *de* mär´) (also **beach-la-mar**) *n.* (pl. **bêches-de-mer,** collect. **bêche-**

de-mer for def. 1). 1. = TREPANG (sea cucumber). 2. Lingua franca of the SW. Pacific combining Malay and English.

Bech·u·an·a (bĕch ōoah´na, bĕkū-) *n.* (pl. **-nas,** collect. **-na**) = TSWANA.

beck (bĕk) *n.* Beckoning gesture, nod, etc.; **at the ~ and call of,** completely at the service of.

Beck·et (bĕk´ĭt), **St. Thomas à** (1117–70). Archbishop of Canterbury (1162) and Chancellor of England (1158) under Henry II; he successfully opposed Henry's policy in taxation and other matters, and was murdered by Henry's orders, in Canterbury Cathedral; he was canonized in 1173.

Beck·ett (bĕk´ĭt), **Samuel** (1906–). Irish novelist and dramatist, many of whose works are written first in French; author of the play *Waiting for Godot*; winner of the Nobel Prize for literature 1969.

beck·on (bĕk´on) *v.* Summon, call attention of, by gesture; make mute signal *to.*

be·cloud (bĭklowd´) *v.t.* Cover with clouds, obscure.

be·come (bĭkŭm´) *v.* (**be·came** pr. bĭkām´, **be·come, be·com·-ing**). 1. Come into being; begin to be; ~ **of,** (past t. and fut.) happen to, as in *what has, will,*

become of him? 2. Suit, befit, look well on. **be·com´ing** *adj.* Suitable; (of clothes etc.) giving pleasing appearance. **be·com´ing·ly** *adv.*

bed (bĕd) *n.* 1. Thing to sleep or rest on, esp. framework with mattress and coverings; animal's resting place or bedding; **go to ~ with,** (esp.) have sexual intercourse with. 2. Flat base on which anything rests; foundation of road or railroad; garden plot for plants; bottom of sea, river, etc.; stratum. 3. **~ and board,** sleeping accommodations and meals, as at a rooming house; **bed´board,** thin board placed under mattress to make bed firm; **bed´bug,** flat, evil-smelling, sucking insect (*Cimex lectularius*) infesting beds etc.; **bed´chamber,** (archaic) bedroom; **bed´clothes,** sheets, pillows, blankets, etc., of bed; **bed´fellow,** sharer of bed; (fig.) associate; **bed linen,** sheets and pillowcases; **bed´pan,** shallow TOILET pan for persons confined to bed; **bed´post,** upright support of bedstead; **bed´rid·den,** (*adj.*) confined to bed by infirmity; **bed´rock,** solid rock underlying soil etc., of earth's surface; **bed´roll,** bedding rolled into a bundle; **bed´room,** room for sleeping; **bed´side,** side of bed, esp. in **bedside manner,** of tactful doctor; **bed´sore,** sore developed by long

Beavers fell small trees which they roll into the water as building material for their lodges: covered islands of branches and twigs cemented together with mud. Here the beavers raise their young and hibernate in winter, living off small shoots and twigs stored away in the fall.

periods of lying in bed; **bed'-spread**, outer covering for a bed, coverlet; **bed'stead**, framework of bed; **bed'time**, hour for going to bed. **bed** *v.* (**bed·ded, bed·ding**). 1. Provide with a bed; put or go to bed; provide bedding for horses etc. 2. Plant *out* in a garden bed. 3. Cover up or fix firmly in something; embed. 4. Arrange as, be or form, a layer. **bed'less, bed'like** *adjs.*

be·daub (bǐdawb´) *v.t.* Smear or daub with paint, mud, etc.

be·daz·zle (bǐdǎz´el) *v.t.* (**-zled, -zling**). Completely dazzle; confuse (person).

bed·ding (bĕd´ĭng) *n.* (esp.) 1. Mattress and bedclothes; litter, straw, etc. for animals to sleep on.

The **Great Bed of Ware** *(top) stands 8 ft. 9 ins. high and is 10 ft. 8 ins. square. Made c. 1590 of oak, it is richly carved and inlaid. The novelist Charles Dickens was captivated by its grandeur and purchased it in 1864. The State Bed at Osterley Park, in Middlesex, U.K., was designed by the Scottish architect Robert Adam in 1776 in a style of the greatest elegance.*

Elizabethan Four-Poster

Late 17th Century Four-Poster

1 Ostrich feather plume   2 Cornice
3 Tester   4 Hangings   5 Valance
6 Headboard   7 Bedpost   8 Bedstead
9 Counterpane   10 Bolster

Honey bee

Drone   Queen   Worker

*A honey **bee** (top) collects pollen from a flower. The pollen adheres to hairs on its legs, and the bee brushes most of it to pollen baskets on its hind legs (right). Three types of bees live in a hive: one queen lays thousands of eggs after mating with drones; the worker bees gather pollen and maintain the hive.*

Hind wing   Front wing   Thorax   Compound eye

Head

Abdomen

Sting

Antennae

Front leg   Pollen Basket   Back leg

Tibia   Brush

Metatarsus

Claws

Tarsus

2. (geol.) Layered structure visible in some rocks resulting from their deposition in water in layers or beds.

Bede (bēd), **St.** (c673–735). English historian and scholar, a monk of Jarrow; author of a Latin history of the English Church and many other works in Latin; known since 9th c. as "the Venerable Bede."

be·deck (bǐděk′) *v.t.* Adorn.

be·dev·il (bǐděv′ǐl) *v.t.* (**-iled, -il·ing**; Brit. **-illed, -il·ling**). Torment diabolically, bewitch. **be·dev′il·ment** *n.*

be·dew (bǐdoo′, -dū′) *v.t.* Cover with drops of or like dew.

be·diz·en (bǐdī′zen, -dǐz′en) *v.t.* Deck out gaudily.

Bed·lam (běd′lam). (hist.)

Popular name for the hospital of St. Mary of Bethlehem, former asylum in London for the insane. **bed·lam** (běd′lam) *n.* 1. (hist.) Lunatic asylum. 2. Scene of uproar and confusion.

Bed·ling·ton (běd′lǐngton) *n.* (also ~ **terrier**) Curly-haired, gray English terrier with narrow head, short body and longish legs. [*Bedlington*, England]

Bed·ou·in (běd′ooǐn, běd′wǐn) *n.* (pl. **-ins**, collect. **-in**). Arab of the desert. [Arab. *badawiyyūn*, oblique case *badawiyyīn* desert dwellers]

be·drag·gle (bǐdrăg′el) *v.t.* (**-gled, -gling**). Wet (dress etc.) by trailing it, or so that it trails or hangs limp. **be·drag′gled** *adj.* **be·drag′gle·ment** *n.*

bee (bē) *n.* 1. Hymenopterous

four-winged stinging insect living in societies composed of one queen, a small number of drones, and a great number of workers, who produce wax and collect honey, which they store up in wax cells for winter food. 2. Any of a large group of allied insects. 3. Social gathering in order to perform together or compete, as for a competition in spelling (**spelling** ~). 4. ~ **in one's bonnet**, eccentric whim, craze on some point; **bee′bread**, honey and pollen eaten by nurse bees; **bee′hive**, HIVE; domed structure resembling one type of hive; **bee′keeper**, one who raises bees; **bee′line**, straight line or direct course between two points, such as a bee is supposed to make returning to the hive; **bees′wax**, *n. & v.t* polish with) wax secreted by bees (see WAX¹, 1).

beech (bēch) *n.* Tree of the genus *Fagus* (esp. *F. grandifolia* of eastern North America and *F. sylvatica* of Europe), with thin smooth light-colored bark, glossy oval leaves, and bearing a small, edible three-sided nut (**beech'nut**) in a rough or prickly involucre; its wood.

Bee·cham (bē'chɑm), **Sir Thomas, 2nd Bt.** (1879–1961). English conductor of opera and symphony orchestras.

Bee·cher (bē'chɛr), **Henry Ward** (1813–87). American Protestant clergyman, editor, and abolitionist leader; father of Harriet Beecher STOWE.

beef (bēf) *n.* (pl. **beeves** pr. bēvz, **beefs** for slang sense). Flesh of steer, bull, or cow used as food; adult steer, bull, or cow raised for its meat; (slang) complaint, ground for this; **beef'burger**, a hamburger; **beef'eaters**, a yeoman of the English royal guard or a warder of the Tower of London (both wear the same uniform); (slang) an Englishman; **beef'steak**, slice of beef cut from hind-quarters and suitable for broiling, frying, etc.; **beef tea**, broth made from beef extract or boiled beef juice. **beef'y** *adj.* (**beef·i·er, beef·i·est**). Solid, muscular; stolid. **beef** *v.i.* (slang) Complain, grumble; ~ **up**, (colloq.) to strengthen.

*In the forests of central and southern Europe the nuts of the **beech** tree, or mast, are harvested for their oil. They are also used in some countries as food for pigs.*

Be·el·ze·bub (bēĕl'zebŭb). Canaanite god, mentioned in 2 Kings as the "god of Ekron," and in the New Testament as "prince of demons"; the Devil. [Heb. *ba'al-zebûb* fly lord]

been (bĭn; *Brit.* bēn): see BE.

beep (bēp) *n.* Short high-pitched sound of various devices. ~ *v.* Emit beep. **beep'er** *n.* Device to indicate that telephone conversation is being recorded; pocket paging device; beeping alarm.

beer (bēr) *n.* Alcoholic beverage made from fermented malt flavored with hops; (in trade usage) any of the liquors brewed from malt, as ale, stout, porter, lager.

Beer·bohm (bēr'bōm), **Sir Max** (1872–1956). English author and caricaturist.

beer·y (bēr'ē) *adj.* (**beer·i·er, beer·i·est**). Of or like beer; betraying its influence.

beet (bēt) *n.* Any of several widely cultivated plants with edible roots and leaves sometimes eaten as greens (varieties of *Beta vulgaris*), including sugar beet, garden beet, etc.; the bulbous root of this plant, characteristically dark red in color.

Bee·tho·ven (bā'tōven; *Ger.* bāt'hōfen), **Ludwig van** (1770–1827). German composer of Flemish descent; worked mainly in Vienna; wrote nine symphonies, an opera, many piano sonatas, string quartets, and other orchestral and chamber music.

The first process in brewing **beer** is to malt the barley and produce enzymes. These maltings are crushed and mixed with water and additives such as cereals and sugars. The product, called wort, is separated from the used grain and boiled with hops. It is then filtered, cooled, and poured into fermentation tanks where yeast is added. After fermentation is complete, the beer is again filtered, after which it is ready to be drunk.

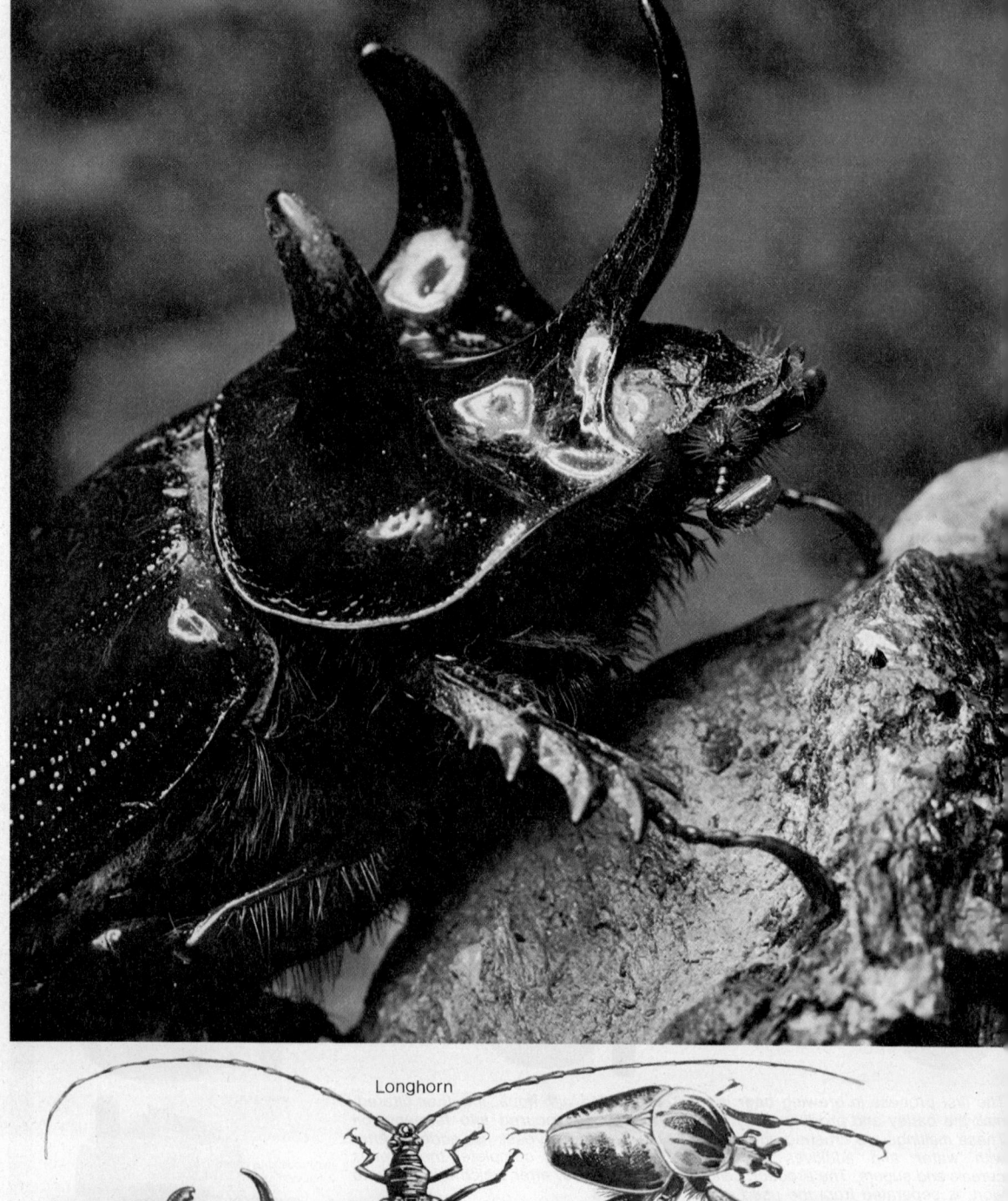

Longhorn

Goliath

Rhinoceros

Stag

Beetles are diverse insects. Some, like the rhinoceros (top), feed on decaying animal and plant matter. Others, like the Colorado beetle, on plants. Most beetles live on land, but some, such as the great silver water beetle, are aquatic. There are several beetles —such as the boll weevil, which lays its eggs in the cotton plant—which destroy crops that are valuable to man, but there are others that attack crop pests. The ladybird, for example, eats the destructive greenfly. All told, there are about 250,000 species of beetle.

bee·tle[1] (bē′tel) *n.* Tool with handle and heavy head for crushing, ramming, etc., mallet; machine for finishing cloth.

bee·tle[2] (bē′tel) *n.* Any coleopterous insect with front wings converted into hard sheaths or wing cases, which close over the back and protect the lower or true wings; (colloq.) insect resembling these.

bee·tle[3] (bē′tel) *v.i.* (**-tled, -tling**). Overhang, project. ~ *adj.* (in ~**brows**, ~**-browed**) Projecting, scowling.

B.E.F. *abbrev.* British Expeditionary Force.

be·fall (bĭfawl′) *v.* (**-fell, -fall·en, -fall·ing**). Happen, happen to.

be·fit (bĭfĭt′) *v.t.* (**-fit·ted, -fit·ting**). Be suited to, become.

be·fog (bĭfŏg′, fawg′) *v.t.* (**-fogged, -fog·ging**). Envelop in fog; confuse, obscure.

be·fore (bĭfōr′, -fôr′) *adv.* Ahead; in front; at an earlier time, already. ~ *prep.* In front of; ahead of; in the presence of; earlier than. ~ *conj.* Before the time when; rather than.

be·fore·hand (bĭfōr′hǎnd, -fôr′-) *adv.* In anticipation; in advance, early.

be·foul (bĭfowl′) *v.t.* Make foul or dirty.

be·friend (bĭfrĕnd′) *v.t.* Act as a friend to, help.

be·fud·dle (bĭfŭd′el) *v.t.* Make drunk; confuse. **be·fud′dler, be·fud′dle·ment** *ns.*

beg (bĕg) *v.* (**begged, beg·ging**). 1. Ask for (food, money, etc.) as alms or charity; live by alms. 2. Ask earnestly or humbly, entreat. 3. (of dog etc.) Sit up with forepaws raised expectantly. 4. ~ **the question**, take for granted the matter in dispute, assume by implication what one is trying to prove; (pop.) avoid, evade, an issue.

be·gan (bĭgăn′): see BEGIN.

be·get (bĭgĕt′) *v.t.* (**be·got** or archaic **be·gat, be·got·ten** or **be·got, be·get·ting**) Procreate, esp. be the father of; give rise to, occasion.

beg·gar (bĕg′er) *n.* One who begs, esp. one who lives by begging; poor person; (colloq.) fellow. ~ *v.t.* Reduce to poverty; exhaust resources of; go beyond, as description. **beg′gar·dom, beg′gar·hood** *ns.*

beg·gar·ly (bĕg′erlē) *adj.* Needy, poverty-stricken; mean, sordid, inadequate. **beg′gar·li·ness** *n.*

beg·gar·y (bĕg′erē) *n.* Extreme poverty.

Beg·hard (bĕg′erd, bĭgärd′) *n.* Member of lay brotherhoods which arose in the Low Countries in 13th c.; the name was soon adopted by many who were simply idle mendicants, and the brotherhoods were

The natural habitat of the **begonia** is in the American tropics, but it is cultivated widely as a bedding plant. Begonias may be grown from seed, or easily propagated from cuttings.

denounced by popes and councils and persecuted by the Inquisition.

be·gin (bĭgĭn′) *v.* (**be·gan, be·gun, be·gin·ning**). Start, perform first part of, set about; be the first; originate; come into being, arise. **be·gin′ner** *n.* (esp.) Tyro, learner. **be·gin′ning** *n.* (esp.) Time at which anything begins; source, origin; first part.

Begin (bā′gĭn), **Menachem** (1913–). Prime Minister of Israel, 1977– ; co-winner of the Nobel Peace Prize, 1978.

be·gird (bĭgerd′) *v.t.* (**-girt, -gird·ed, -gird·ing**). Gird, encircle.

be·gone (bĭgawn′, -gŏn′) *v.imp.* Be off, away with you.

be·gon·ia (bigōn′ya, -gō′nēa) *n.* Tropical plant of genus *B*~, having flowers with brightly colored perianths (but no petals) and often richly colored foliage; often cultivated as an ornamental plant. [Michel *Bégon*, Fr. patron of science (1638–1710)]

be·got·ten (bĭgŏt′en): see BEGET.

be·grime (bĭgrīm′) *v.t.* (**-grimed, -grim·ing**). Make grimy.

be·grudge (bĭgrŭj′) *v.t.* (**-grudged, -grudg·ing**). Envy the good fortune or pleasure of; be reluctant to give or permit.

be·guile (bĭgīl′) *v.t.* (**-guiled, -guil·ing**). Delude; cheat; charm, amuse; divert attention from (passage of time etc.). **be·guil′er** *n.* **be·guil′ing·ly** *adv.* **be·guile′ment** *n.*

Beg·uine (bĕg′ēn) *n.* Member of certain lay sisterhoods, small communities of which still exist esp. in Belgium, first founded in the Netherlands in the 12th c., who devoted themselves to a religious life but did not bind themselves by strict vows. [f. Lambert *Bègue* (or *le bègue* the stammerer), the

founder]

beg·uine (bĭgēn′) *n.* A W. Indian native dance; ballroom dance based on this; kind of syncopated bolero dance rhythm.

be·gum (bē′gum) *n.* Indian Muslim woman of high rank. [Turk. *bīgam*, fem. of *beg* lord]

be·gun (bĭgŭn′): see BEGIN.

be·half (bĭhăf′, -hahf′) *n.* **On** or **in the** ~ **of,** for, as a representative for.

be·have (bĭhāv′) *v.i.* & *refl.* (**-haved, -hav·ing**). Act in a particular way (~ **well, badly,** etc.); show good manners.

be·hav·ior, Brit. **be·hav·iour** (bĭhāv′yer) *ns.* Manners, conduct, way of behaving. **be·hav′ior·al** *adj.* ~ **science,** any of various sciences, as sociology or psychology, concerned with human behavior.

be·hav·ior·ism (bĭhāv′yerīzem) *n.* Psychological doctrine, based on the objective study of behavior, that all human actions admit of analysis into stimulus and response. **be·hav′ior·ist** *n.* & *adj.* **be·hav·ior·is·tic** (bĕhāvyerīs′tĭk) *adj.*

be·head (bĭhĕd′) *v.t.* Cut off the head of.

be·held (bĭhĕld′): see BEHOLD.

be·he·moth (bĭhē′moth, bē′e-) *n.* Enormous creature; in Job 40, prob. the hippopotamus.

be·hest (bĭhĕst′) *n.* Command; earnest request, entreaty.

be·hind (bĭhīnd′) *adv.* In or to the rear; past; too late; in concealment or unrevealed by; in arrears. ~ *prep.* In or to the rear of; hidden by; supporting. ~ *n.* (colloq.) The buttocks.

be·hind·hand (bĭhīnd′hănd) *adv.* & *pred. adj.* Late; backward, out of date.

Behn (bān), **Mrs. Aphra** (1640–1689). English dramatist and novelist, author of *Oroonoko.*

be·hold (bĭhōld′) *v.t.* (**-held, -hold·ing**). (archaic and rhet.) See; take notice, attend. **be·hold′er** *n.*

be·hold·en (bĭhōl′den) *pred. adj.* Under obligation *to.*

be·hoof (bĭhoof′) *n.* (pl. **-hooves** pr. -hoovz′). (archaic) Benefit, advantage.

be·hoove (bĭhoov′), **be·hove** (bĭhōv′) *vbs.t. impers.* (**-hooved, -hoov·ing**) (**-hoved, -hov·ing**). Be incumbent on; befit.

Behring = BERING.

beige (bāzh) *n.* Yellowish-gray or grayish-brown color of unbleached wool. ~ *adj.* Of color of beige.

Bei·jing (bā′jĭng′) = PEKING.

be·ing (bē′ĭng) *n.* (esp.) Existence; constitution, nature, essence, anything that exists; person.

Bei·rut (bāroot′, bā′root). Principal port and the capital of Lebanon, on the E. Mediterranean.

be·jew·el (bĭjoo′el) *v.t.* (**-eled,**

The **belay** (above) is one of the most widely used methods of securing a running rope to a belaying pin, cleat, single bollard or to a twin bollard.

Many of the principal cities of **Belgium**—map and flag (right)— are linked by waterways. Canals like the Speigelrei in Bruges (above right) serve the nation so well that Belgium has become one of the leading countries of Europe in the shipping and transit trade.

-el·ing, Brit. **-elled, -el·ling**). Adorn with jewels.

Bel (bāl, běl). (Babylonian and Assyrian myth.) = BAAL.

be·la·bor, Brit. **be·la·bour** (bǐlā′ber) vbs.t. Thrash, beat repeatedly; discuss at unreasonable length.

be·lat·ed (bǐlā′tǐd) adj. Coming late. **be·lat′ed·ly** adv. **be·lat′ed·ness** n.

be·lay (bǐlā′) v.t. (-layed, -lay·ing). Coil (running rope) around cleat etc., to secure it; imp. (naut.) stop!; **belaying pin**, fixed wooden or iron pin for belaying on.

bel can·to (běl′ kǎn′tō, kahn′-). Singing in the Italian manner, characterized by full rich tone and accomplished technique. [It.]

belch (bělch) v. Emit gas noisily from stomach through mouth; utter noisily or drunkenly; (of gun or volcano) emit (fire, smoke, etc.). ∼ n. Belching.

bel·dam (běl′dam), **bel·dame** (běl′dam, -dām) ns. Old woman, hag; virago.

be·lea·guer (bǐlē′ger) v.t. Besiege. **be·lea′guered** adj. **be·lea′guer·er** n.

Be·lém (bělěm′). Port city on the Para River in N. Brazil.

bel·em·nite (běl′emnīt) n. Common fossil, occurring in Mesozoic rocks, consisting of the hard part of

an extinct marine animal similar to the squid, freq. torpedo shaped. [Gk. belemnon dart]

Bel·fast (běl′fǎst, -fahst, běl-fǎst′, -fahst′). Seaport in Ulster, capital city of N. Ireland.

bel·fry (běl′frē) n. (pl -fries). Bell tower; room or story in which the bells are hung.

Bel·gian (běl′jan) adj. & n. (Native or inhabitant) of Belgium.

Bel·gium (běl′jum). Small kingdom of N.W. Europe, the S. part of the Low Countries (see NETHERLANDS, 2), inhabited by people of French and Flemish stock speaking both languages; established in 1831; capital, Brussels. [L. territory occupied by the Belgae]

Bel·grade (běl·grād′, běl′grād). (Serbo-Croatian Beograd) City on the Danube, capital of Yugoslavia.

Bel·gra·vi·a (běl·grā′vēa). Fashionable residential district of London. [f. Belgrave Square,

named after Belgrave, England]

Be·li·al (bē′lēal, běl′yal). 1. (Old Testament) Spirit of evil personified (as **sons of** ∼); (2 Cor.) the Devil. 2. (in Milton) Fallen angel representing impurity. [Heb. belīyya'al without use, without avail]

be·lie (bǐlī′) v.t. (-lied, -ly·ing). Show to be false; fail to justify or act up to; give false notion of.

be·lief (bǐlēf′) n. Trust, confidence (in); acceptance of any received theology; religious tenet; acceptance as true or existing; thing believed.

be·lieve (bǐlēv′) v. (-lieved, -liev·ing). Have faith (in), trust word of; accept as true; suppose, think; be of opinion that. **be·liev′a·ble** adj. **be·liev′er** n. **be·liev′ing·ly** adv.

be·lit·tle (bǐlǐt′el) v.t. (-tled, -tling). Disparage.

Be·lize (bělěz′). Formerly

British Honduras; a British Crown Colony in Central America on the Caribbean Sea; capital Belpoman.

bell (bĕl) *n.* 1. Hollow object of cast metal esp. in deep cup shape widening at lip, made to emit clear musical sound when struck by a tongue or a clapper suspended inside it or by a hammer impelled by a spring or by electricity etc. 2. Sound of this, esp. as signal; (naut.) one to **eight** ~**s**, half-hours of watch, indicated by strokes of bell. 3. Bell-shaped object or part. 4. **bell'bird**, any of several tropical American birds of the family Cotingidae having a bell-like call; **bell-bottomed**, (of trousers) widening from below knee to bottom of leg; **bell'boy**, man employed to carry luggage, run errands, etc., at a hotel; **bell buoy**, buoy with a bell rung by the motion of the sea; **bell glass**, bell jar; **bell'hop**, bell-boy; **bell jar**, bell-shaped glass used to protect instruments or contain gases etc. in a laboratory; **bell'-ringing**, ringing a peal of bells in a series of different sequences; **bell'-wether**, leading sheep of flock, with bell on neck (also fig.).

Bell[1] (bĕl), **Alexander Graham** (1847–1922). Scottish-born American inventor of the telephone.

Bell[2] (bĕl), **Currer, Ellis,** and **Acton.** Pen names of Charlotte, Emily, and Anne BRONTË.

bel·la·don·na (bĕladŏn'a) *n.* Specific name of the deadly nightshade (*Atropa belladonna*), with dark purple flowers and poisonous black berries; dried parts of this, containing atropine and related alkaloids, used as a drug to dilate the pupils; ~ **lily**, amaryllis. [It., = "fair lady"]

Bel·lay (bĕlā'), **Joachim du** (c1524–60). French poet and critic.

belle (bĕl) *n.* Handsome woman; reigning beauty.

Bel·leau (bĕl'ō; *Fr.* bĕlō') **Wood.** Forest near Chateau Thierry, N.E. France; site of 1918 World War I battle during which German drive to Paris was halted by U.S. troops.

Bel·ler·o·phon (belĕr'ofŏn). (Gk. legend) Hero who slew the Chimera with the help of Pegasus.

belles-let·tres (bĕl lĕ'tre) *n.pl.* Studies, writings, of a purely literary kind; essays, literary criticism, etc., as a division of literature. **bel·let·rist** (bĕllĕ'trĭst) *n.* **bel·let·ris·tic** (bĕletrĭs'tĭk) *adj.*

bel·li·cose (bĕl'ikōs) *adj.* Inclined to war or fighting. **bel'li·cose·ly** *adv.* **bel'li·cose·ness, bel·li·cos·i·ty** (bĕlikŏs'ĭtē) *ns.*

bel·lig·er·ent (belĭj'erent) *adj.* Waging war, bellicose. ~ *n.* Belligerent nation, party, or person. **bel·lig'er·en·cy** *n.* **bel·lig'er·ent·ly** *adv.*

1 Crown   4 Clapper
2 Waist   5 Headstock
3 Sound bow 6 Stay

*The **bell** (above) is turned through a full circle and produces a more resonant sound than a bell played by the carillon method, where the clapper strikes the bell while it is held steady.*

Bel·li·ni[1] (belē'nē; *It.* bĕlē'nē), **Giovanni** (c1435–1516). Italian painter of the Venetian School; his father **Jacopo** (c1400–70) and brother **Gentile** (1429?–1507) were also painters.

Bel·li·ni[2] (belē'nē; *It.* bĕlē'nē), **Vincenzo** (1801–35). Italian composer of operas.

Bel·loc (bĕl'ok, -ŏk), **Joseph Hilaire Pierre** (1870–1953). English essayist, novelist, and poet, born in France.

Bel·lo·na (belō'na). (Rom. myth.) Goddess of war.

bel·low (bĕl'ō) *v.* Roar as a bull; shout, roar, bawl with pain; shout loudly and angrily. ~ *n.* Bellowing sound. **bel'low·er** *n.*

Bel·low (bĕl'ō), **Saul** (1915–). American novelist; awarded Nobel Prize for literature, 1976; author of *Adventures of Augie March, Herzog,* etc.

bel·lows (bĕl'ōz) *n.pl.* 1. Instrument or machine for driving strong blast of air into fire, organ, etc., in its simplest form consisting of a pair of boards joined by flexible leather sides, with a valve through which air enters when the boards are moved apart, and a nozzle or tube through which air is forced as they are brought together. 2. Expandable portion of folding camera.

Bel·lows (bĕl'ōz), **George Wesley** (1882–1925). American realistic painter and lithographer; his most famous lithographs depict boxing scenes.

bel·ly (bĕl'ē) *n.* (pl. **-lies**). Abdomen; stomach; underpart of animal; underside, cavity, or bulging part of anything; **bel'lyache**, pain in abdomen or stomach, as from eating foods that disagree with one; (*v.i.*, slang) complain; **bel'ly-button**, (colloq.) navel; **belly dance**, erotic oriental dance involving movements of the abdominal muscles; so **belly dancer; belly flop**, (*n.*, colloq.) dive in which abdomen hits the water (also **belly flopper**); **bel'lyful**, (colloq.) as much as one can tolerate; **belly-landing**, (of aircraft) crash-landing on underside of fuselage; **belly laugh**, (colloq.) deep unrestrained laugh. **belly** *v.* (**-lied, -ly·ing**). Swell out.

Bel·mon·te (bĕlmawn'tĕ), **Juan** (1893–1962). Spanish bullfighter; known as the father of modern bullfighting.

be·long (bĭlawng', -lŏng') *v.i.* Have a rightful or appropriate place or position; fit an environment etc.; ~ **to**, (esp.) be a member or adherent etc. of; be a possession of. **be·long·ings** (bĭlawng'ĭngz, -lŏng'-) *n.pl.* Person's movable property etc.

Be·lo·rus·sia (byĕlorŭsh'a, bĕlo-) = BYELORUSSIA.

be·lov·ed (bĭlŭv'ĭd, -lŭvd') *adj.* Dearly loved; ~ *n.* Beloved person.

be·low (bĭlō') *adv.* At or to a lower level or part; in a lower position or rank; on earth (rather than up in heaven). ~ *prep.* Lower in position, amount, degree, rank, etc., than; unworthy of, beneath.

Bel·shaz·zar (bĕlshăz'er). (also **Balthazar**) Acc. to Old Testament (Dan. 5), son of Nebuchadnezzar and last king of Babylon, who was killed in the sack of the city by Cyrus (538 B.C.); but in inscriptions and documents from Ur, Belshazzar was the son of the last king of Babylon, Nabonidos, and did not himself reign.

belt (bĕlt) *n.* 1. Broadish flat strip of leather etc., used to gird or encircle the person, confine some part of the dress, or support various articles; such an article awarded to boxing champion or sash worn as a mark of rank, as by a knight or earl. 2. Strip of color etc., line of trees, around or on anything; zone or district; endless band to connect pulleys in machinery or to transmit motion, convey objects, etc.; flexible strip holding machine gun cartridges and carrying them to firing chamber. 3. (slang) A hard blow, hit; (slang) a drink of liquor; (slang) a thrill. ~ *v.* Put belt around, fasten with belt; (slang) give a hard blow (to); (slang) drink (liquor); (slang) sing (a song) loudly.

be·lu·ga (belōō'ga) *n.* White sturgeon, valued as a source of caviar; white whale.

bel·ve·dere (bĕl've de̅r) *n.* Raised turret or lantern, summer house, to view scenery from. [It. =

Monte Cassino, once a pagan shrine, was chosen by **St. Benedict of Nursia** for the site of his abbey. The building was destroyed in the 1939–45 war and subsequently rebuilt.

Above right: The Church's tradition of fine craftsmanship is maintained. The **Benedictine** monks of Prinknash Abbey, Gloucestershire (now Avon), England show vestments to visitors.

"fine view"]

Be·mel·mans (bē′melmanz, bĕm′el-), **Ludwig** (1898–1962). Austrian-born American painter, illustrator, and writer.

be·moan (bĭmōn′) *v.t.* Lament.

be·muse (bĭmūz′) *v.t.* (**-mused, -mus·ing**). Cause to be preoccupied, esp. to point of confusion; (pop.) amuse. **be·mused′** *adj.*

Be·nar·es (benär′ĭs, -ēz) = VARANASI.

bench (bĕnch) *n.* 1. Long seat for several persons. 2. Judge's or official's seat; office of judge, law court (**King's ~, Queen's ~**); **on the ~**, serving as judge; (sports) (team member) not participating in the game. 3. Working table in carpenter's shop, laboratory, etc., workbench; **~ mark**, surveyor's mark put on stone etc. to indicate a point of known elevation; **~ warrant**, one issued by a judge. ~ *v.t.* Exhibit (dog) at show; (sports) remove (player) from a game. **bench′less** *adj.*

Bench·ley (bĕnch′lē), **Robert Charles** (1889–1945). American humorist; wrote for *Vanity Fair, Life,* and *New Yorker* magazines.

bend[1] (bĕnd) *n.* 1. (naut.) Knot. 2. (her.) Diagonal band from upper right (dexter) to lower left (sinister) of shield; **~ sinister**, bend in the opposite direction, a mark of bastardy.

bend[2] (bĕnd) *v.* (**bent**, archaic **bend·ed, bend·ing**). 1. Force into, receive, curved or angular shape. 2. Attach (sail etc.) with bend or knot. 3. Turn in a particular direction. 4. Incline from perpendicular; bow, stoop, submit, force to submit. 5. Direct, apply (oneself) *to.*

6. Modify or interpret (law, rule, etc.) for one's own purposes. ~ *n.* 1. Bending, curve; bent part. 2. (pl.) Caisson disease. 3. **round the ~,** (Brit. slang) insane. **bend′-a·ble** *adj.*

bend·ed (bĕn′dĭd) *adj.* (of knee) Bent.

bend·er (bĕn′der) *n.* (slang) Drinking spree.

be·neath (bĭnēth′) *adv. & prep.* Below, under, underneath; **~ one's contempt**, not even worth despising.

ben·e·dict (bĕn′edĭkt) *n.* Newly married man, esp. one who has

The full economic union of the **Benelux** countries—map below— was gradually established by a series of treaties. The first was signed in 1922, followed by a customs union in 1947, and a final treaty in 1960.

long been a bachelor. [*Benedick,* Shakespeare's *Much Ado Abo Nothing*]

Ben·e·dict (bĕn′edĭkt), **S** (c480–543). Italian monk, found (529) of the first of the monast orders of the Western Church, f which he built the abbey of Mon Cassino.

Ben·e·dic·tine (bĕnedĭk′tĭ -tēn, -tīn for *adj.* & *n.* bĕnedĭk′tēn for *n.* 2) *adj.* Of t order of St. Benedict; **~ Rule,** ru written for it by St. Benedict, lat adopted by other monastic com munities. **Benedictine** *n.* Benedictine monk. 2. Liqueur brandy flavored with herbs etc made at Fécamp in Normand orig. by the monks of the Ben dictine abbey there.

ben·e·dic·tion (bĕnedĭk′shon) Utterance of blessing, at end religious service, or at tabl **ben·e·dic′tion·al, ben·e·dic to·ry** *adjs.*

ben·e·fac·tion (bĕnefăk′sho bĕn′efăk-) *n.* Doing good; char table gift.

ben·e·fac·tor (bĕn′efăkter, bĕne făk′-) *n.* Person who has give friendly aid; patron of, or donor t cause or charity.

ben·e·fice (bĕn′efĭs) *n.* (eccles Material livelihood of incumbent a parish; rectory, vicarage, or pe petual curacy. ~ *v.* (**-fice -fic·ing**). Provide with a benefic

be·nef·i·cent (bĕnĕf′ĭsent) *ad* Doing good, showing active kin ness. **be·nef′i·cence** *n.* **be·nef′i cent·ly** *adv.*

ben·e·fi·cial (bĕnefĭsh′al) *ad* 1. Advantageous. 2. (law) O having the right to receive proceed or other advantages, as from prop erty. **ben·e·fi′cial·ly** *adv.*

ben·e·fi·ci·ar·y (bĕnefĭsh′ēēr -fĭsh′erē) *n.* (pl. **-ar·ies**). Receive of benefits; recipient of funds etc. under a will, insurance policy, o

The view of **Ben Nevis**, Inverness-shire, (now part of Highland), Scotland, seen from the bank of the Caledonian Canal. It is the highest peak in the British Isles, 4,406 ft.

rust.

ben·e·fit (bĕn´efĭt) n.   I. Advantage. 2. Allowance, pension, tc. to which person is entitled; e.g. luring sickness, unemployment, tc. 3. Theater performance, game, tc., of which proceeds go to par- icular players or charity. ~ v. **-fit·ed, -fit·ing**). Do good to; eceive benefit. **ben´e·fit·er** n.

Ben·e·lux (bĕn´elŭks). Collec- ive name for *Bel*gium, the *Neth*er- ands, and *Lux*emburg, esp. with eference to their economic col- aboration.

Be·nét (benā´), **William Rose** 1886–1950). American editor and vriter; his brother, **Stephen Vin- cent** (1898–1943), poet and short tory writer; Pulitzer Prize winner, 1929; author of *The Devil and Daniel Webster*, *John Brown's Body*, ·tc.

be·nev·o·lent (benĕv´olent) adj. Desirous of doing good; charitable. **be·nev´o·lent·ly** adv. **be·nev´o- lence** n.

Ben·gal (bĕngawl´, bĕnggawl´, pĕn´gal, bĕng´-). District of the Ganges delta, formerly a province of British India, divided into **West ~**, a state of India (capital, Cal- cutta), and Bangladesh; **Bay of ~**, part of Indian Ocean lying between Indian peninsula and Burma; **Ben- gal tiger**, the tiger proper, so called from its abundance in lower Bengal.

Ben·gal·i (bĕngaw´lē, bĕng- gaw´lē) adj. & n. (Of) the Indo- European language spoken in Ben- gal; (native) of Bengal.

Ben-Gur·i·on (bĕngoor´ēon), **David** (1886–1973). Polish-born first Prime Minister of Israel, 1948– 1953 and 1955–63.

be·nign (benīn´) adj. Kind, gra- cious, gentle; beneficial, favorable; (path., of disease) mild, not malig- nant; (of tumor) not cancerous, dis- placing but not destroying sur- rounding tissue (opp. MALIGNANT).

be·nig·nant (benĭg´nant) adj. Kind, kindly, to inferiors; gracious; beneficial. **be·nig´nan·cy** (pl. **-cies**), **be·nig´ni·ty** (pl. **-ties**) ns. **be·nig´nant·ly** adv.

Be·nin (benēn´).   Formerly Dahomey, republic in W. Africa; independent since 1960; capital, Porto Novo.

ben·i·son (bĕn´ĭzon, -son) n. (archaic) Blessing.

Ben·ja·min (bĕn´jamĭn). He- brew patriarch, youngest and favor- ite son of Jacob (Gen. 35); smallest tribe of Israel, traditionally de- scended from him.

Ben·nett (bĕn´ĭt), **Enoch Ar- nold** (1867–1931). English novel- ist; author of *The Old Wives' Tale* etc.

Ben Ne·vis (bĕn nē´vĭs, nĕv´ĭs). Mountain in the Grampians, Scot- land, the highest peak (4,406 ft. 1,343 m) in the British Isles.

Ben·ning·ton   (bĕn´ĭngton). Town in S. Vermont, near site of Revolutionary War battle (1777) in which Americans defeated the British.

ben·ny (bĕn´ē) n. (pl. **-nies**). (slang) An amphetamine tablet.

bent[1] (bĕnt) n. Reedy or rushlike stiff-stemmed grass of various kinds; old stalk, of grasses; heath, unenclosed pasture.

bent[2] (bĕnt) n. Inclination, bias. **bent**[3] (bĕnt) adj.: see BEND[2] v. (esp.) curved, crooked; (slang) dis- honest, perverted.

Ben·tham (bĕn´tham, -tam), **Jeremy** (1748–1832). English Util- itarian philosopher, reformer, and writer on ethics, jurisprudence, and political economy; he believed that the highest morality is the pursuit

of the greatest happiness of the greatest number. **Ben´tham·ism, Ben´tham·ite** ns.

Ben·ton (bĕn´ton),   **Thomas Hart** (1889–   ). American paint- er and muralist; known for realistic paintings of ordinary people and scenes of life in the Midwest and South.

be·numb (bĭnŭm´) v.t. Make torpid; paralyze.

Benz (bĕnts), **Karl Friedrich** (1844–1929). German engineer and pioneer in the construction of motor-driven vehicles; built first gasoline-powered automobile, 1885.

Ben·ze·drine   (bĕn´zedrēn, -drĭn) n. (trademark) Ampheta- mine.

ben·zene (bĕn´zēn, bĕnzēn´) n. (chem.) Aromatic hydrocarbon (C_6H_6), a colorless, volatile, and highly inflammable liquid obtained from coal tar etc., used as a solvent and in the chemical industry; **~ ring**, ring-like hexagon arrange- ment of the six carbon atoms in the benzene molecule.

ben·zine (bĕn´zēn, bĕnzēn´) n. Mixture of hydrocarbons obtained from petroleum and used as a sol- vent, for removing grease stains etc.

ben·zo·caine (bĕn´zokān) n. White crystalline ester used as a local anesthetic.

ben·zo·in (bĕn´zōĭn,   -zoin, bĕnzō´ĭn) n. I. (also **gum ~**) Fragrant aromatic resin obtained from various trees of the genus *Styrax* from Sumatra and Thai- land, and used in perfumery, medi- cine, etc. 2. (chem.) Constituent of gum benzoin. **ben·zo·ic** (bĕnzō´ĭk) adj. (chem.) Of or derived from benzoin or benzoic acid; **benzoic acid**, benzene carboxylic acid (C_6H_5COOH). [Fr. *benzoin* f. Arab. *lubān jāwī* Java frankincense]

ben·zol (bĕn´zōl, -zawl, -zŏl) n. (obs.) Benzene.

Be·o·wulf (bā´owŏŏlf). Legend- ary Swedish hero celebrated in the Old English epic poem *Beowulf*, anonymous, believed to have been written in northern England be- tween 650 and 750 A.D.

be·queath (bĭkwēdh´, -kwēth´) v.t. Leave by will; hand down. **be·queath´a·ble** adj., **be- queath´al, be·queath´ment** ns.

be·quest (bĭkwĕst´) n. Bequeath- ing; thing bequeathed, legacy.

be·rate (bĭrāt´) v.t. (**-rat·ed, -rat·ing**). Scold.

Ber·ber (bĕr´ber) adj. & n. (Member) of a fair-skinned aboriginal people of N. Africa.

ber·ceuse (bĕrsöz´) n. (pl. **-ceuses** pr. Fr. -söz´). Lullaby; composition in style of this.

Berch·tes·ga·den   (bĕrx´tes- gah´den). Resort town in SE. West Germany, 10 miles S. of Salzburg, Austria: Adolf Hitler maintained a

The Kenyan child (above) has symptoms of **beriberi,** probably caused by a diet of highly refined grain. If left untreated, the condition may cause paralysis and death, but it can be cured with large doses of thiamine.

The Brandenburg Gate (above) was one of the few monuments of old **Berlin** to survive the devastation of the 1939–45 war. The Gate stands on the city's East/West boundary, established in 1945.

retreat here during World War II.

be·reave (bĭrēv′) *v.t.* (**-reaved** or **-reft, -reav·ing**). 1. Deprive *of* ruthlessly or by force. 2. Deprive by death of relation, wife, etc.; leave desolate. **be·reave′ment** *n.*

beret (berā′) *n.* (pl. **berets** pr. berāz′). Round flat visorless cloth cap, worn orig. by Basque farmers.

berg (bĕrg) *n.* Iceberg (see ICE, def. 3).

ber·ga·mot[1] (bĕr′gamŏt) *n.* 1. Small, spiny tree (*Citrus bergamia*) bearing sour pear-shaped fruit; fragrant oil (also called ~ **oil**) extracted from its fruit. 2. Any of various plants of the family Labiatae, esp. *Monarda* species. [f. *Bergamo* in Italy]

ber·ga·mot[2] (bĕr′gamŏt) *n.* Fine kind of pear. [Turk. *beg* prince, *armūdī* pear]

Ber·gen (bĕr′gen). Seaport and the second largest city in Norway, in the SW.

Ber·ge·rac (bĕr′zherăk), **Cyrano de** (1619–55). French soldier and author of comedies; said to have fought over 1,000 duels.

Berg·man (bĕrg′man), **Ingmar** (1918–). Swedish writer of screenplays and director of motion pictures.

berg·schrund (bĕrk′shro͞ont) *n.* Crevasse or gap at head of glacier, separating moving ice from stationary ice.

Berg·son (bĕrg′son; *Fr.* bĕrg-sawń′), **Henri** (1859–1941). French philosopher who regarded reality as change and movement, "becoming" rather than "being." **Berg·so·ni·an** (bĕrgsō′nēan) *adj.* & *n.*

ber·i·ber·i (bĕr′ēbĕr′e) *n.* Dis-ease of the peripheral nervous system caused by deficiency of vitamin B_1 in diet and characterized by emaciation, anemia, and partial paralysis of the extremities. [Sinhalese *beri* weakness]

Ber·ing, Behr·ing (bār′ĭng, bĕr′-, bēr′-), **Vitus Jonassen** (1680–1741). Danish navigator who explored Arctic seas on behalf of Russia; ~ **Sea**, northernmost part of Pacific between Alaska and Siberia; ~ **Strait**, strait between Asia and America, connecting Bering Sea with Arctic Ocean.

Berke·ley[1] (bĕrk′lē). City in N. California on San Francisco Bay across from San Francisco.

Berke·ley[2] (bĕrk′lē; *Brit.* bärk′-lē), **George** (1685–1753). Irish Protestant bishop and idealist philosopher, active in America (1728–31). **Berke·le′ian** *adj.* & *n.*

berke·li·um (bĕrk′lēum, be kē′-) *n.* (chem.) Metallic radioacti synthetic element; symbol Bk, a no. 97, principal isotope at. wt. 24 [*Berkeley,* Calif., where first mad

Ber·lin (berlĭn′; *Ger.* bĕrlēn′ Chief city of Germany; on riv Spree; capital of Germany fro 1871; since 1945 divided into **Ea** ~, capital of East Germany, an **West** ~, an isolated part of We Germany. ~ **wall**, Soviet- an East German-built wall dividin East and West Berlin. **Ber·lin′e** *n.* Native, inhabitant, of Berlin.

ber·lin (berlĭn, bĕr′lĭn) *n.* Fou wheeled covered carriage wit hooded seat behind, invented i Berlin in 17th c., popular in Franc and England in the 18th c.

Ber·li·oz (bĕr′lēoz), **Hecto** (1803–69). French composer c operas, symphonic works, etc.

The first journeys of **Vitus Bering** car ried him north to the straits sub sequently named after him. On his las voyage he crossed from the Siberian coast to Alaska.

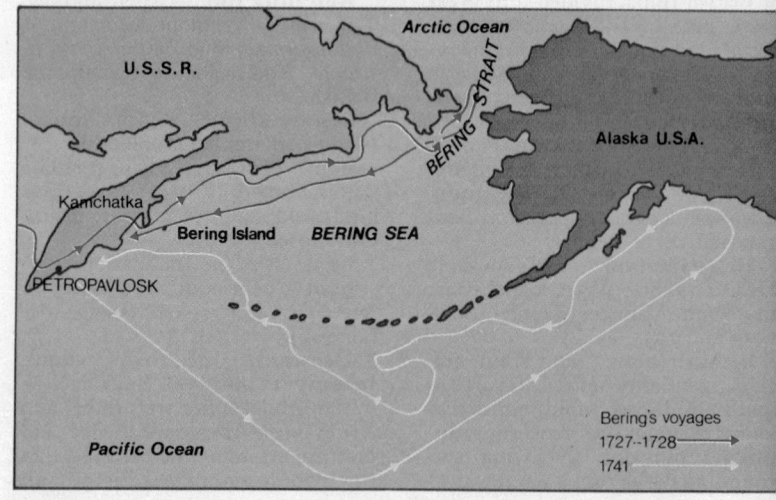

Arctic Ocean

U.S.S.R.

BERING STRAIT

Alaska U.S.A.

Kamchatka

Bering Island   **BERING SEA**

PETROPAVLOSK

Pacific Ocean

Bering's voyages
1727–1728 ——→
1741

The 'divine Sarah', as Oscar Wilde called **Sarah Bernhardt,** was the chief romantic and classical actress of the French stage from about 1870 to 1915. Mucha painted posters for her plays.

berm, berme (bẽrm) *ns.* Narrow space or ledge; (esp., fort.) space between ditch and parapet.

Ber·mu·da (bermū′da). (also ~ **Islands, Bermudas**) Group of over 350 small islands in W. Atlantic about 570 miles (917 km) SE. of North Carolina; a British colony with a total area of about 21 square miles; capital, Hamilton; ~ **grass,** wiry grass (*Cynodon dactylon*) used for lawns and pasturage in warm regions; ~ **onion,** large, mild, yellow-skinned variety of onion; ~ **rig,** fore-and-aft rig carrying a tall triangular mainsail, used on cruising and racing yachts; ~ **shorts,** (also **Bermudas**) knee-length shorts. **Ber·mu′di·an** *adj.* & *n.*

Bern (bẽrn; *Fr.* & *Ger.* bẽrn). (also **Berne**) Canton and capital city of Switzerland. **Ber·nese** (bẽrnēz′, -nēs′) *adj.* & *n.*

Ber·na·dette (bẽr′nadĕt, ber-nadĕt′), **St.** (1844–79). Original name, Marie Bérnarde Soubirous; French peasant girl of Lourdes, France, who claimed to have seen the Virgin Mary; a shrine was

Bernini *was the leading sculptor of the Italian baroque. He worked for most of his life for papal patrons, and like the 'Fountain of the Rivers' shown here almost all his sculpture is to be found in Rome.*

subsequently established at LOURDES.

Ber·na·dotte[1] (bẽr′nadŏt), **Count Folke** (1895–1948). Swedish humanitarian; assassinated while acting as United Nations mediator in Palestine.

Ber·na·dotte[2] (bẽr′nadŏt; *Fr.* bẽrnădawt′), **Jean Baptiste** (1763–1844). French soldier; one of Napoleon's marshals; was adopted by Charles XIII of Sweden in 1810 and himself became king (as Charles XIV) in 1818, thus founding the present royal house.

Ber·nard[1] (bernard′; *Fr.* bẽr-năr′), **St.** (923–1008). Priest of Menthon; founder of the Alpine hospices of the Great and Little St. Bernard; **St. ~ (dog),** dog of large and intelligent breed, of the mastiff type, usu. light brown and white, orig. bred by the monks of the St. Bernard hospices and trained to search for travelers lost in the snowdrifts of the Alpine passes.

Ber·nard[2] (bernard′; *Fr.* bẽr-năr′), **St.** (1090–1153). French churchman, first abbot of Clairvaux; he reformed the Cistercian Order and preached the 2nd Crusade.

Ber·nard[3] (bernard′; *Fr.* bẽr-năr′), **Claude** (1813–78). French physiologist; famous for his research on the pancreas and the glycogenic function of the liver, and his discovery of the vasomotor system.

Berne = BERN.

Bern·hardt (bẽrn′härt, bẽrn′-), **Sarah.** Name adopted by the French romantic and tragic actress Rosine Bernard (1845–1923).

Ber·ni·ni (bernē′nē; *It.* bẽrnē′-nē), **Giovanni Lorenzo** (1598–1680). Italian baroque architect and sculptor; designer of the colonnade of St. Peter's in Rome.

Ber·noul·li (bernoo′lē). Surname of Swiss family including several eminent mathematicians and scientists, including **Jacob** or **James** (1654–1705) and **Daniel** (1700–82); ~ **effect,** the decrease in pressure of a fluid as its velocity increases; ~**'s law,** statement of this relation, (essentially = CONSERVATION OF ENERGY). [from Daniel *Bernoulli*]

Bern·stein (bẽrn′stīn, -stēn), **Leonard** (1918–). American conductor, composer, and pianist.

ber·ry (bĕr′ē) *n.* (pl. **-ries**). 1. Any small round or oval juicy fruit without a stone; dry seed or kernel (of wheat etc.). 2. (bot.) Fruit of any size with seed(s) enclosed in pulp.

ber·serk (bersẽrk′, -zẽrk′) *adj.* & *adv.* Destructively or frenetically violent; deranged; **go ~,** behave thus. [Icel., prob. = "bearcoat" as worn by a *berserkr,* a fierce warrier]

berth (bẽrth) *n.* 1. Convenient searoom; room for ship to swing at anchor; ship's place at wharf; **give a wide ~ to,** avoid. 2. Sleeping place in ship, railroad car, etc. 3. Job, appointment. ~ *v.t.* Moor (ship).

ber·yl (bĕr′el) *n.* Transparent precious stone of pale green color or of light blue, yellow, or white, chemically beryllium aluminum silicate, the chief ore of beryllium.

be·ryl·li·um (berĭl′ēum) *n.* (chem.) Very light metallic element obtained from beryl; symbol Be, at. no. 4, at. wt. 9.01218.

bes·ant = BEZANT.

Bes·ant (bĕz′ant), **Mrs. Annie** (1847–1933). English writer, socialist and agnostic; became president of the Theosophical Society in 1907; active in the cause of Indian self-government.

be·seech (bĭsēch′)   *v.t.* (**-seeched** or **-sought** pr. -sawt′, **-seech·ing**). Ask earnestly for; entreat.

be·set (bĭsĕt′) *v.t.* (**-set, -set·-ting**). Hem in, surround; harass constantly.

be·side (bĭsīd′) *prep.* At the side of, close to; compared with; wide of; ~ **oneself**, strongly moved by emotion.

be·sides (bĭsīdz′) *adv.* In addition; otherwise, else. ~ *prep.* In addition to; except.

be·siege (bĭsēj′) *v.t.* (**-sieged, -sieg·ing**). Lay siege to; assail, crowd around. **be·sieg′er** *n.*

be·smear (bĭsmēr′) *v.t.* Smear, bedaub.

be·smirch (bĭsmẽrch′) *v.t.* Soil; sully. **be·smirch′er, be·smirch′-ment** *ns.*

be·som (bē′zom) *n.* Bundle of twigs tied around stick for sweeping.

be·sot·ted (bĭsŏt′ĭd) *adj.* Stupefied (esp. with drink).

be·sought (bĭsawt′): see BE-SEECH.

be·spat·ter (bĭspăt′er) *v.t.* Spatter; slander.

be·speak (bĭspēk′) *v.t.* (**-spoke, -spok·en, -speak·ing**). (Brit.) Engage beforehand; order; speak to (poet.); indicate, be evidence of. **be·spoke′** *v. & adj.* Ordered (now only in ~ **tailoring, footwear,** etc., opp. ready-made, or of tradesman making goods to order).

be·sprin·kle (bĭsprĭng′kel) *v.t.* (**-kled, -kling**). Sprinkle.

Bes·sa·ra·bi·a (bĕsarā′bēa).

Former Rumanian region now part of the Moldavian S.S.R.

Bes·se·mer (bĕs′emer), **Sir Henry** (1813–98). English engineer; inventor of ~ **process**, process for making steel (~ **steel**) in which iron is decarbonized by blowing a blast of air through the molten metal in a large pear-shaped metal container (~ **con-verter**).

best (bĕst) *adj.* (superl. of *good*). Of the most excellent kind; most advantageous, desirable, or serviceable; ~ **man,** bridegroom's chief attendant at wedding; the ~ **part,** most; ~ **seller,** book with large sale, esp. one that is among those having the largest sales during a given period. **best** *adv.* (superl. of *well*) In the most excellent way etc.; **had ~,** would find it wisest. ~ *n.* That which is best; (collect.) most excellent persons, (colloq.) kindest regards; **at ~,** under the most favorable circumstances; **for the ~,** with good intentions or outcome; **get the ~ of,** gain the advantage over, defeat; **make the ~ of,** manage as well as one can under adverse circumstances.

bes·tial (bĕs′chal, bĕst′yal) *adj.* Of, like a beast; brutish, barbarous; depraved, obscene. **bes·ti·al·i·ty** (bĕschĕăl′ĭtē, tĕăl′) *n.* (pl. **-ties**). (esp. law) Crime of person having sexual intercourse with animal. **bes′tial·ly** *adv.* **bes′tial·ize** *v.t.* (**-ized, -iz·ing**).

bes·ti·ar·y (bĕs′chēĕrē, -tē-) *n.* (pl. **-ar·ies**). Medieval moralizing treatise on beasts. **bes·ti·a·rist** (bĕs′chēĕrĭst, -tē-, -che-) *n.*

be·stir (bĭstẽr′) *v.refl.* (**-stirred, -stir·ring**). Exert, rouse.

be·stow (bĭstō′) *v.t.* Confer as gift. **be·stow′a·ble** *adj.* **be·stow′-al, be·stow′er, be·stow′ment** *ns.*

be·strew (bĭstrōō′)   *v.t.* (**-strewed, -strewn, -strew·ing**). Strew.

be·stride (bĭstrīd′) *v.t.* (**-strode** pr. -strōd, **-strid·den** pr. -strĭd′en, **-strid·ing**). Get or sit upon with legs astride; stand astride over.

bet (bĕt) *v.* (**bet, bet·ted, bet·ting**). Risk one's money etc. against another's on result of doubtful event; (loosely) think, reckon (something to be true etc.); ~ *n.* Act of betting; money etc. so risked; thing, event, etc. bet on.

be·ta (bā′ta; *Brit.* bē′ta) *n.* Second letter of Gk. alphabet (B, β), corresponding to *b*, used of the 2nd star in a constellation; and in other classifications; ~ **particles,** fast-moving electrons emitted by radioactive substances, orig. regarded as rays (~ **rays**) and having greater penetrating power than alpha particles and less than gamma rays.

be·take (bĭtāk′) *v.refl.* (**-took** pr. -tōōk, **-tak·en, -tak·ing**). (archaic) Commit (oneself) *to* some cause or means; go.

be·ta·tron (bā′tatrŏn) *n.* (phys.) Apparatus for accelerating electrons.

be·tel (bē′tel) *n.* Shrubby East Indian pepper plant (*Piper betle*); leaf of this plant, which is wrapped around parings of areca nut and chewed by people of India etc. for stimulating and narcotic effects; hence ~ **nut,** areca nut. [Malayalam *vettila*]

Be·tel·geuse, Be·tel·geux (bē′-teljōōz, bĕt′eljöz) *ns.* Yellowish-red variable star, the brightest in the

The conversion of iron to steel requires the burning of the iron's impurities or their absorption into slag. The Bessemer process achieves this by blasting a charge of pig-iron with a jet of heated air. The converter is swiveled to pour off first the molten steel and then the slag.

converter

slag

hollow trunnion

metal

tuyeres

wind box

teeming ladle

trunnion support

charging

blowing

pouring

constellation of Orion.

bête noire (bāt nwār´; *Fr.* bĕt nwär´) (pl. **bêtes noires** pr. bāt nwärz´; *Fr.* bĕt nwär´). Person or thing one particularly dislikes or dreads. [Fr.]

Beth·a·ny (bĕth´anē). Village near Jerusalem where Lazarus was raised from the dead by Christ (John 11).

Beth·el (bĕth´el, bĕthĕl´). Town near Jerusalem, considered a holy place after JACOB's dream there. [Heb., = "house of God"; Gen. 28]

beth·el (bĕth´el) *n.* Hallowed spot; seamen's church (ashore or floating).

be·think (bĭthĭngk´) *v.refl.* (**-thought** pr. -thawt´, **-think·-ing**). (archaic) Reflect, stop to think; remind oneself.

Beth·le·hem (bĕth´lĭhĕm, -lēem). Town near Jerusalem; birthplace of Jesus Christ.

Be·thune (bĕthūn´), **Mary McLeod** (1875–1955). American educator; president of Bethune-Cookman College from 1923.

be·tide (bĭtīd´) *v.* (**-tid·ed, -tid·ing**). (archaic) Happen, befall.

be·times (bĭt´mz´) *adv.* Early; in good time.

Bet·je·man (bĕch´eman), **Sir John** (1906–). English poet, poet laureate, 1972.

be·to·ken (bĭtō´ken) *v.t.* Be token of; presage; indicate. **be·to´ken·er** *n.*

bet·o·ny (bĕt´onē) *n.* (pl. **-nies**). Labiate plant (*Stachys officinalis*), with spike of reddish-purple flowers.

be·tray (bĭtrā´) *v.t.* Give up or reveal treacherously; be disloyal or unfaithful to; lead astray; (archaic) seduce and desert (a woman); reveal involuntarily; be evidence or symptom of. **be·tray´al, be·tray´er** *ns.*

be·troth (bĭtrōdh´, -trawth´) *v.t.* Bind with a promise to marry. **be·troth´al** *n.* **be·trothed´** *adj. & n.*

bet·ter (bĕt´er) *adj.* (comp. of *good*). Of a more excellent kind; superior use or value, etc.; larger, greater; ~ **half** (joc.) wife; ~ **part**, greater part. **better** *adv.* (comp. of *well*). In a more excellent way; more; (of person) (partially) recovered from illness; ~ **off**, in better circumstances; **had** ~, would find it wiser; **think** ~ **of**, reconsider, decide more wisely. **better** *n.* Person of higher rank (usu. pl.); that which has greater excellence; **for the** ~, in a way that is an improvement; **get the** ~ **of**, defeat, outwit. **better** *v.* Improve, surpass. **bet´ter·ment** *n.* Improvement.

bet·tor (bĕt´er) *n.* Person who bets.

be·tween (bĭtwēn´) *prep.* In, into, along, or across, a space or interval bounded by, *lies* ~ *Paris and Rouen; happened* ~ *Monday and Friday*; separating; connecting; intermediately in time, place, de-

Containing one of the world's great shrines, **Bethlehem** is situated on a slope overlooking the Dead Sea. Many of its inhabitants make a living from pilgrims to the shrine.

gree, quantity or order; shared by, confined to; to and from; reciprocally on the part of; ~ **ourselves,** ~ **you and me**, confidentially. **between** *adv.* Between two points or times.

be·twixt (bĭtwĭkst´) *prep. & adv.* 1. (archaic) Between. 2. ~ **and between**, in position intermediate between; neither one thing nor the other.

Beu·lah (bū´la). Biblical name for land of Israel (Isaiah 62); the land of peace described by Bunyan in *Pilgrim's Progress*.

bev·el (bĕv´el) *n.* 1. Carpenter's and mason's tool, a flat rule with movable tongue or arm stiffly connected to one end, for marking angles. 2. Slope from right angle, or from horizontal or vertical, surface so sloped; ~ **gear**, gear with toothed surface oblique with the axis usu. meshing with another set at right angles. ~ *v.* (**-eled, -el·ing**; *Brit.* **-elled, -el·ling**). Impart bevel to, slant.

bev·er·age (bĕv´erĭj, bĕv´rĭj) *n.* Any liquid for drinking, esp. other than water.

Bev·er·ly (bĕv´erlē) **Hills.** City in the Los Angeles area of S. California; known for its wealth and

Stories from the **Bible** inspired many of the early Christian artists. The 12th-century plaque (right) shows St. Paul escaping from Damascus, lowered from the walls in a basket and met below by his friends.

homes of movie celebrities.

bev·y (bĕv´ē) *n.* (pl. **bev·ies**). Flock (of birds, esp. quail); group (of girls or women).

be·wail (bĭwāl´) *v.t.* Wail over, mourn for. **be·wail´er** *n.*

be·ware (bĭwār´) *v.* (used without inflections). Be cautious (of), take heed (*of, lest, how*).

be·wil·der (bĭwĭl´der) *v.t.* Confuse, perplex. **be·wil´dered** *adj.* **be·wil´dered·ly** *adv.* **be·wil´der·ing** *adj.* **be·wil´der·ing·ly** *adv.* **be·wil´der·ment** *n.*

be·witch (bĭwĭch´) *v.t.* Affect by witchcraft; charm, enchant. **be·witch´er** *n.* **be·witch´ing** *adj.* **be·witch´ing·ly** *adv.*

bey (bā) *n.* (formerly) Turkish provincial governor; native ruler of former kingdom of Tunis or Tunisia; Turkish title of honor and respect. [Turk., = "lord"]

Beyle (bāl), **Henri**: see STENDHAL.

be·yond (bĭyŏnd´) *adv. & prep.* At, to, the farther side (of) past, besides; out of reach, comprehension or range (of). ~ *n.* Future life after death, the unknown.

bez·ant, bes·ant (bĕz´ant, bĭ-zănt´) *ns.* (hist.) Gold coin issued in Byzantium. [f. *Byzantium* where orig. struck]

bez·el (bĕz´el) *n.* Sloped edge or face of chisel etc.; oblique side or face of cut gem; groove holding gem or watch glass in setting.

be·zique (bezēk´) *n.* Card game similar to pinochle and played by two players using deck of 64 cards; combination of queen of spades and jack of diamonds in this game.

b.f. *abbrev.* Bold face (type); (accounting) brought forward.

B.F.A. *abbrev.* Bachelor of Fine Arts.

bhang, bang (băng) *ns.* Indian hemp plant; leaves of this mixed with resin used as intoxicant and narcotic.

b.h.p. *abbrev.* Brake horsepower.

Bhu·tan (bōōtahn´). Independent kingdom, a protectorate of the Republic of India, lying on the SE. of the Himalayas; capital, Thimphu.

Bi *symbol.* Bismuth.

bi- *prefix.* Twice, doubly, having two.

Bi·a·fra (bēah´fra). Region of E. Nigeria; an attempt to secede and set up the Republic of Biafra failed in 1970.

Bia·ly·stock (byăl´ĭstŏk; *Pol.* byah´wĭstawk). Industrial city and important railroad junction in NE. Poland.

Velocipede or 'bone shaker'   Penny-farthing

The racing **bicycle** of today has a lightweight tubular alloy frame, and is a highly geared machine capable of speeds in excess of 40 m.p.h. Early forms of bicycle, such as the velocipede of 1865 and the penny-farthing of 1875, had crude springs to support their saddles.

Bi·ar·ritz (bē´erĭts; *Fr.* byă-rēts´). Resort city on the Bay of Biscay in SW. France.

bi·as (bī´as) *n.* 1. Inclination, predisposition, prejudice, influence; (statistics) systematic distortion; (elect.) steady voltage or current applied to electronic device. 2. Diagonal line of direction, esp. across a fabric. ~ *v.t.* (**bi·ased, bi·as·ing**; *Brit.* **bi·assed, bi·as·sing**). Give bias to, influence, prejudice.

bib[1] (bĭb) *v.i.* (**bibbed, bib·bing**). (archaic) Drink much or often, tipple.

bib[2] (bĭb) *n.* Cloth, etc. placed under child's chin to protect its clothing from spilled food; apron top.

bib·cock (bĭb´kŏk) *n.* Faucet with bent down nozzle (dist. from (topcock).

Bi·ble (bī'bel) *n.* Sacred book of Christianity comprising the Old and New Testaments (and sometimes the Apocrypha); sacred writings of Judaism, comprising the Old Testament only; edition or copy of either of these; sacred book, (colloq.) authoritative work, set of rules, etc.; ~ **Belt**, those parts of the Southern and Midwestern U.S. that are strongly fundamentalist.

bib·li·cal (bīb'līkal) *adj.* Of, in, concerning, the Bible; (of language) of the Authorized Version. **bib'li·cal·ly** *adv.*

bib·li·og·ra·phy (bībleŏg'rafē) *n.* (pl. **-phies**). History of books, their publication, editions, etc.; list of books of any author, subject, etc. **bib·li·o·graph·ic** (bībleōgrăf'ĭk), **bib·li·o·graph'i·cal** *adjs.* **bib·li·o·graph'i·cal·ly** *adv.* **bib·li·og'ra·pher** *n.*

bib·li·o·ma·ni·a (bībleōmā'nēa, -mān'ya) *n.* Mania for collecting books. **bib·li·o·ma'ni·ac** *n. & adj.*

bib·li·o·phile (bīb'lēofīl) *n.* Book lover; book collector. **bib·li·oph'i·lism** (bībleŏf'ilīzem) *n.*

bib·u·lous (bīb'yulus) *adj.* Addicted to alcoholic drinking.

bi·cam·er·al (bīkăm'eral) *adj.* With two (legislative) branches.

bi·car·bon·ate (bīkär'bonĭt, -nāt) *n.* 1. Salt of carbonic acid in which only one hydrogen atom is replaced by a metal. 2. (pop., also ~ **of soda**) Sodium bicarbonate (NaHCO₃) used in medicine and as constituent of baking powder etc.

bi·cen·te·nar·y (bīsĕn'tenĕrē, -sĕntĕn'erē) *n.* (pl. **-nar·ies**). Bicentennial.

bi·cen·ten·ni·al (bīsĕntĕn'ēal, -yal) *adj.* Occurring every, lasting for, 200 years. ~ *n.* 200th anniversary.

bi·ceps (bī'sĕps) *n. & adj.* (pl. **-ceps·es, -ceps**). (Muscle) with two heads or attachments, esp. that on front of upper arm, which bends forearm.

bick·er (bīk'er) *v.i. & n.* Quarrel, wrangle.

bi·cus·pid (bīkŭs'pīd) *adj. & n.* (Tooth) with two cusps.

bi·cy·cle (bī'sīkel, -sikel) *n.* Vehicle having two wheels one behind the other and a seat on which the rider sits astride, driven by two pedals and having handlebars for steering. ~ *v.i.* (**-cled, -cling**). Ride bicycle. **bi'cy·cler, bi'cy·clist** *ns.*

bid (bīd) *v.* (**bade** pr. bād, băd, **bad** or **bid, bid·den** or **bid, bid·ding**). Command to; invite; salute with (greeting etc.); (past t. and past part. **bid**) offer (price) for a thing; (at bridge) made a bid. **bid'der** *n.* **bid** *n.* Offer of price, esp. at an auction; (at bridge) announcement of the number of tricks that a player will undertake to win at no trump or

with a specified suit as trump; attempt; invitation.

bid·da·ble (bīd'abel) *adj.* 1. (archaic) Obedient. 2. (Of a suit in a hand at bridge) on which a bid can reasonably be made.

bide (bīd) *v.* (**bid·ed** or **bode**, pr. bōd, **bid·ed** or archaic **bid, bid·ing**). Abide (archaic except in ~ **one's time**, wait for a favorable opportunity).

bi·det (bēdā', bĭdĕt') *n.* Bathroom fixture with low bowl-like basin and faucets, used for bathing the crotch.

bi·en·ni·al (bīĕn'ēal) *adj.* Lasting, recurring, or completing the normal term of life every two years. **bi·en'ni·al·ly** *adv.* **biennial** *n.* Plant that springs from seed one year and flowers, fructifies, and dies the next.

bier (bēr) *n.* Movable frame on which corpse or coffin is laid before burial.

Bierce (bērs), **Ambrose** (1842–1914?). American journalist and short story writer; known for caustic wit and cynicism; disappeared in Mexico, 1913.

biff (bĭf) *n.* (slang) Blow, whack. ~ *v.t.* Strike, hit.

bi·fid (bī'fĭd) *adj.* Divided by a deep cleft into two lobes.

bi·fo·cal (bīfō'kal, bī'fō-) *adj.* (of spectacle lenses) Having two segments of different focal lengths, the upper for distant, the lower for near, vision. **bi·fo'cals** *n.pl.* Bifocal spectacles.

bi·fo·li·ate (bīfō'lēĭt, -āt) *adj.* Of two leaves.

bi·fur·cate (bī'ferkāt, bīfer'-) *v.* (**-cat·ed, -cat·ing**). Divide into two branches, fork. ~ *adj.* (bīferkĭt, bīfer'-, -kāt). Forked. **bi·fur·ca·tion** (bīferkā'shon) *n.*

big (bĭg) *adj.* (**big·ger, big·gest**). Large; grown-up; important; successful; boastful; loud; (colloq.) major, outstanding; elder (as in ~ **brother,** ~ **sister**); (colloq.) magnanimous; ~ **with child,** advanced in pregnancy; B ~ **Apple,** (slang) any large city esp. New York City; **big bang theory,** theory that the universe was created from an explosion of compressed elementary particles and is still expanding; opp. STEADY STATE. **B ~ Ben,** great bell in clock tower of Houses of Parliament in London, England, hence the clock itself; **B ~ Bertha,** large cannon used by the Germans in World War I, esp. to bombard Paris in 1918 [Frau Berta Krupp, head of the Krupp steel manufacturing family in Germany]; **B ~ Brother,** head of state in George Orwell's novel *1984*, hence, head of authoritarian organization exercising dictatorial pseudobenevolent power; ~ **business,** commerce on grand scale; **Big'foot:** see SASQUATCH; **big'headed,** (colloq.) con-

ceited; **big game,** large wild animals hunted for sport, as deer, lions, etc.; **big gun,** (fig.) important person; **big-hearted,** kind, generous; **big'horn,** wild sheep (*Ovis canadenis*) of the Rocky Mountains, having massive curving horns; **big-league,** (adj.) of major league baseball, major, important; **big money,** large amount of money; **big'mouth,** (slang) loud, talkative person, esp. one who lacks discretion; ~ **shot,** (slang) important or influential person; **big three, four,** etc., predominant few; **big toe,** innermost, largest toe; **big top,** main circus tent, circus; **big'wig,** (colloq.) important person. **big** *adv.* **big'ness** *n.*

big·a·my (bĭg'amē) *n.* (pl. **-mies**). Crime of marrying while one has a legal spouse still living. **big'a·mist** *n.* **big'a·mous** *adj.* **big'a·mous·ly** *adv.*

Big Bend National Park. Mountain and desert area in W. Texas on the Mexican border.

Big Horn Mountains. Mountain range in N. Wyoming, part of the Rocky Mountains.

bight (bīt) *n.* Loop of a rope; curve or recess, of coast, river, etc., bay.

big·ot (bĭg'ot) *n.* Person obstinately and unreasonably holding some creed or view and intolerant toward others. **big'ot·ed** *adj.* **big'ot·ed·ly** *adv.* **big'ot·ry** *n.*

bi·jou (bē'zhoō, bēzhoō') *n.* Small, exquisite trinket. ~ *adj.* Small and elegant.

bike (bīke) *n. & v.i.* (**biked, bik·ing**). (colloq.) Bicycle; motorcycle; motorbike; **bike'way,** road, path, or lane especially for bicycle traffic.

Bi·ki·ni (bĭkē'nē). Atoll in the Marshall Islands of the W. Pacific Ocean; site of U.S. atomic bomb test, 1946.

bi·ki·ni (bĭkē'nē) *n.* Scanty two-piece bathing suit for women.

bi·la·bi·al (bīlā'bēal) *adj. & n.* (phon.) (Consonant) produced by the junction or apposition of both lips.

bi·lat·er·al (bīlăt'eral) *adj.* Of, on, with, two sides; affecting, between, two parties; ~ **symmetry,** symmetry about a plane, such that one half is a mirror image of the other (as left and right in general outward appearance of human body and in all other vertebrate and many invertebrate animals). **bi·lat'er·al·ism, bi·lat'er·al·ness** *ns.* **bi·lat'er·al·ly** *adv.*

Bil·ba·o (bĕlbah'aw). Commercial, manufacturing, and port city in N. Spain on an inlet of the Bay of Biscay.

bil·ber·ry (bĭl'bĕrē) *n.* (pl. **-ries**). Small blue-black edible berry of dwarf hardy shrub

(*Vaccinium myrtillus*) of N. Europe (also *whortleberry, blueberry*).

bil·bo (bĭl′bō) *n.* (pl. **-boes**). Iron bar with sliding shackles for prisoner's ankles.

bile (bīl) *n.* Bitter, brownish-yellow fluid secreted by the liver and poured into the duodenum in the process of digestion; (hist.) one of the four humors (see HUMOR, 4); (fig.) anger, peevishness.

bilge (bĭlj) *n.* Nearly horizontal part of ship's bottom; foulness that collects in the bilge; (slang) nonsense, rot; ~ **water**, foul water that collects in ship's bilge.

bil·har·zi·a·sis (bĭlhärzĭ′asĭs) *n.* Disease produced by trematode worm of genus *Bilharzia*, parasitic in veins of human pelvic region and urinary organs, esp. in Africa. [f. Theodor *Bilharz* (1825–62), German physician]

bil·i·ar·y (bĭl′ĕĕrē) *adj.* Of the bile.

bi·lin·gual (bīlĭng′gwal) *adj.* Having, written in, speaking, etc., two languages. **bi·lin′gual·ism** *n.* **bi·lin′gual·ly** *adv.* **bi·lin′guist** *n.*

bil·ious (bĭl′yus) *adj.* Arising from derangement of the bile; liable to, affected by, this; peevish, irritable. **bil′ious·ly** *adv.* **bil′-ious·ness** *n.*

bilk (bĭlk) *v.t.* Evade payment of (creditor or bill); cheat, defraud. **bilk′er** *n.*

bill[1] (bĭl) *n.* 1. Halberd or similar obsolete weapon with a hooked blade and long handle. 2. (also **bill′hook**) Implement used for pruning etc., having long blade with concave edge, and a wooden handle in line with blade.

bill[2] (bĭl) *n.* Bird's beak, esp. when slender or flattened; horny beak of platypus. ~ *v.i.* Stroke bill with bill (as doves); ~ **and coo**, exchange caresses, whisper endearments.

bill[3] (bĭl) *n.* 1. Draft of statute presented to legislature. 2. (law) Written statement of (plaintiff's) case; proposed indictment submitted to a court. 3. Statement of charges for goods delivered or services rendered. 4. Poster, placard; program of entertainment; **fill the** ~, (colloq.) suffice. 5. (also ~ **of exchange**) Written order to pay sum on given date to drawer or named payee. 6. Bank note. 7. **bill′board**, structure for the display of large advertisements; **bill′fold**, a wallet; **bill of fare**, list of dishes to be served, menu; **bill of health**, certificate regarding infectious disease on ship or in port at time of sailing; **bill of lading**, receipt given by a carrier for goods accepted for transportation; **bill of rights**, statement of rights and liberties of a nation or group of people; (cap. B & R) the first ten

amendments to the U.S. Constitution; (cap. B & R) English Statute of 1689; **bill of sale**, document transferring personal property from seller to buyer; **bill** *v.t.* Announce, put in the program; plaster with placards; send a bill to, enter as a charge on a bill. **bill′a·ble** *adj.* **bill′er** *n.*

bill·a·bong (bĭl′abŏng) *n.* (Austral.) Branch or effluent of river forming backwater or stagnant pool. [Ab. *Billibang*, old name of Bell River, f. *billa* water, *bang* of uncertain meaning]

bil·let (bĭl′ĭt) *n.* Order requiring householder to board and lodge soldier etc. bearing it; place where such a person is lodged; appointment, job. ~ *v.t.* (**-let·ed, -let·ing**). Quarter (soldiers etc.) *on* town, householder, etc., *in, at,* place.

bil·let-doux (bĭl′ēdoo′, -ā-; *Fr.* bēyĕdoo′) *n.* (pl. **bil·lets-doux** pr. bĭl′ēdooz′, -ā-; *Fr.* bēyĕdoo′). Love letter.

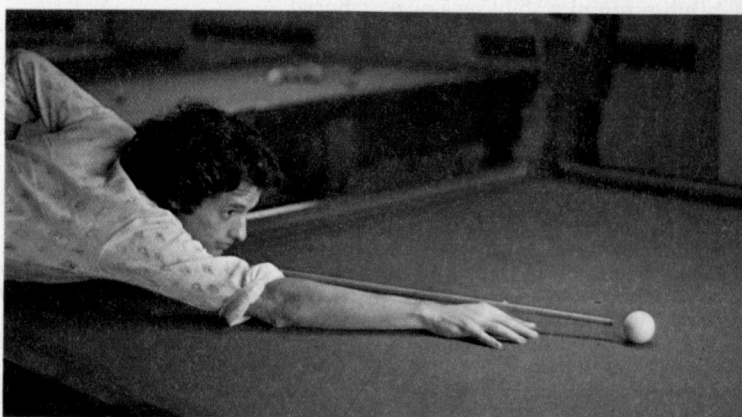

From the 16th century, the game of **billiards** and its variants has been popular in Europe. The table is generally 6 ft. by 12 ft., with a slate bed, ground perfectly flat, and covered in green baize. Above: the player makes a 'bridge' with his fingers to control the action of the cue.

bil·liards (bĭl′yerdz) *n.pl.* Gam played with three small solid ball driven about by cues on a hor zontal rectangular table covere with smooth green cloth, su rounded by a cushioned ledge; an of several similar games, such a one played on a similar table wit pockets at the corners and in th middle of the long sides; **billiar ball, cue, table**, etc., one used i billiards (cf. POOL[2]). **bil′liard·is** *n.*

Bil·lings·gate (bĭl′ĭngzgāt; *Bri* bĭl′ĭngzgĭt). Fish market estab lished at one of the old city gate of London; hence (also **b** ~), fou language (for which the market wa famous in 17th c.).

bil·lion (bĭl′yon) *n.* (pl. **-lions -lion** following a numeral). (U.S. One thousand millions; (Brit.) on million millions. **bil·lion·air** (bĭlyonār′) *n.* One whose wealth i a billion (dollars, pounds, etc.) o more.

bil·lon (bĭl′on) *n.* Alloy of gol

silver with a predominating
ⁿount of some base metal, used for
ᵢnage.

bil·low (bĭl'ō) *n.* Great wave;
ᵧthing that sweeps along, as
ₘoke, sound, etc. ~ *v.i.* Rise,
ₒve, in billows. **bil'low·y** *adj.*
ₒw·i·er, -low·i·est).

bil·ly¹ (bĭl'ē) *n.* (pl. **-lies**).
ᵤstral.) Tin can with (lid and)
ᵣe handle used as kettle etc. in
ₘping out and as container for
ₒdstuffs; so **bil'lycan**.

ᵢl·ly² (bĭl'ē) = BILLY GOAT.

ᵢl·ly·cock (bĭl'ĕkŏk), **billycock**
ₜt. (Brit.) Man's round, low-
ₒwned, hard felt hat; bowler.

bil·ly (bĭl'ē) **goat.** Male goat.

Bil·ly (bĭl'ē) **the Kid** (1859–81).
ₐl name, William H. Bonney;
ₜorious and legendary American
ₙdit of the Southwest; killed in
ₙbush.

bi·lobed (bī'lōbd) *adj.* Having,
divided into, two lobes.

Bi·lox·i (bĭlŏk'sē, -lŭk'-). Resort
ₗd commercial fishing city on the
ᵤlf of Mexico in S. Mississippi.

bi·me·tal·lic (bīmetăl'ĭk) *adj.* I.
ᶠ two metals. 2. Using both gold
ₗd silver at fixed ratio to each
ₕer, as a monetary standard.
·met·al·lism (bīmĕt'alizem),
·met'al·list *ns.*

Bim·i·ni (bĭm'inē). Two small
ₗands SE. of Florida in the
ₐhamas.

bi·month·ly (bīmŭnth'lē) *adj.* &
(pl. **-lies**). (Periodical) produced
ᵣ occurring every two months.

bin (bĭn) *n.* Receptacle or
ₐclosed place for corn, coal, etc.
ᵥ. (**binned, bin·ning**).

bi·na·ry (bī'nerē) *adj.* (pl. **-ries**).
ᵘal, of or involving pairs; ~

compound, (chem.) one consisting
of two elements; ~ **star**, system of
two stars revolving around their
common center of mass and often
appearing as a single visual object.

bind (bīnd) *v.* (**bound,
bind·ing**). Tie, fasten; put in
bonds, restrain; fasten, encircle, or
hold together; cause to cohere; (of
clothing) to restrict or chafe. 2. Be
obligatory, impose constraint or
duty upon; unite by legal or moral
tie; (pass.) be required by duty;
subject to legal obligation; indenture as apprentice; ~ **over**, (esp.)
put person under bond to appear in
court as required. 3. Bandage; edge
with braid, iron, etc.; fasten (sheets,
book) into cover. **bind** *n.* I.
Something that binds. 2. (mus.) =
TIE *n.* def. 4. 3. (slang) Predicament.

bind·ing (bīn'dĭng) *adj.* Obligatory (*on*). ~ *n.* (esp.) Book cover;
braid etc. for binding raw edges of
textiles. **bind'ing·ly** *adv.* **bind'-
ing·ness** *n.*

bin·dle (bĭn'del) **stiff.** (slang)
Itinerant worker who carries his
own bedroll. [*bindle*, alteration of
bundle]

bind·weed (bīnd'wēd) *n.* Convolvulus or other twining plant,
related to the morning glory.

bine (bīn) *n.* Flexible shoot; stem
of climbing plant, esp. the hop.

Bin·et (bīnā'), **Alfred** (1857–
1911). French psychologist; experimented in the measurement
of intelligence and was the first to

*A viewer sees images of greater depth
through* **binoculars** *than through a telescope. Binoculars are specified by two
numbers. The first indicates the magnification, the second the diameter of the
object lenses.*

devise intelligence tests; ~
(**-Simon**)**scale**, ~ (**-Simon**)**test**,
one for measuring relative mental
development, esp. in children, usu.
expressed in an intelligence
quotient (see INTELLIGENCE).

binge (bĭnj) *n.* (colloq.) Spree of
excessive indulgence, as in eating or
esp. drinking of alcoholic
beverages.

bin·go (bĭng'gō) *n.* Form of lotto
in which columns of numbered
squares are headed with the letters
B,I,N,G, and O. ~ *int.* Used to
express pleasurable surprise or
unexpected success.

bin·na·cle (bĭn'akel) *n.* Box for
compass on a ship.

bin·oc·u·lar (binŏk'yuler) *adj.*
Adapted for both eyes; ~ **vision**,
type of vision, peculiar to man and
some other primates, in which both
eyes cooperate in observing the
same object and receive a stereoscopic impression. ~ *n.* (usu. pl.)
Binocular instrument, as field or
opera glasses.

bi·no·mi·al (bīnō'mēal) *adj.*
Consisting of two terms or names;
~ **theorem**, general algebraic
formula, discovered by Newton, by
which any power of a binomial
quantity may be found without
performing the progressive multi-
plications. **binomial** *n.* I.
Algebraic expression consisting of
two terms joined by + or −, as
$3x + 2y$ and $x^2 − 3y$. 2. (zool. and
bot.) A taxonomic name consisting
of a generic and a specific term.

bio- *prefix.* (Course of) life of,
concerning, organic life; biological.

bi·o·chem·is·try (bīōkĕm'ĭstrē)
n. Science dealing with the
chemical properties of the parts of

ₒme species of the **bindweed** *family
ₐlled morning glory are cultivated as
ᵣnamental plants. They grow prolifi-
ₐlly and their blossoms often open
ₙly in the morning. The related
ₘoonflower blooms only at night.*

Field
of vision
diaphragm

Ocular

Reversing
prism

Objective

living organisms. **bi·o·chem·i·cal** (bīōkĕm′ĭkal), **bi·o·chem′ic** adjs. **bi·o·chem′i·cal·ly** adv. **bi·o·chem′ist** n.

bi·o·gen·e·sis (bīōjĕn′esĭs) n. Postulate that living matter arises only from living matter; synthesis of chemical substances by living matter; hypothetical development of living matter from complex inanimate substances. **bi·o·ge·net·ic** (bīōjenĕt′ĭk), **bi·o·ge·net′i·cal** adjs. **bi·o·ge·net′i·cal·ly** adv.

bi·o·ge·og·ra·phy (bīōjĕŏg′rafē) n. Study of the geographical distribution of animals and plants.

bi·og·ra·phy (bīŏg′rafē) n. (pl. **-phies**). Written account of another person's life; branch of literature dealing with such writing. **bi·og′ra·pher** n. **bi·o·graph·i·cal** (bīŏgrăf′ikal), **bi·o·graph′ic** adjs. **bi·o·graph′i·cal·ly** adv.

bi·ol·o·gy (bīŏl′ojē) n. Science of life, dealing with the morphology, physiology, behavior, origin, and distribution of animals and plants. **bi·ol′o·gist** n.

bi·o·log·i·cal (bīolŏj′ĭkal) adj. Of biology; ~ **control**, control of pests by the use of other organisms which devour or destroy them; ~ **warfare**, use of bacteria, viruses, etc., against an enemy or his animals or crops. **bi·o·log′i·cal·ly** adv.

bi·o·lu·mi·nes·cence (bīolōōmĭnĕs′ens) n. Emission of light by living organisms. **bi·o·lu·mi·nes′cent** adj.

bi·ome (bī′ōm) n. (ecol.) Biotic community of plants and animals.

bi·om·e·try (bīŏm′ĭtrē) n. Application of mathematics to biology, esp. the study of resemblances between living things by statistical methods. **bi·o·met·ri·cal** (bīōmĕt′rĭkal) adj. **bi·o·me·tri·cian** (bīōmetrĭsh′an, bīŏme-), **bi·o·met·ri·cist** (bīōmĕt′rĭsĭst) ns.

bi·o·phys·ics (bīōfĭz′ĭks) n. Science dealing with the mechanical and electrical properties of the parts of living organisms. **bi·o·phys′i·cal** adj. **bi·o·phys′i·cal·ly** adv. **bi·o·phys′i·cist** n.

bi·op·sy (bī′ŏpsē) n. (pl. **-sies**). (med.) Examination of tissue removed from the living body.

bi·o·sphere (bī′osfēr) n. Regions

There are many varieties of the **birch** *tree. Oil similar to oil of wintergreen is extracted from black birch; the bark of the others is used in tanning.*

of Earth's crust and atmosphere occupied by living organisms.

bi·ot·ic (bīŏt′ĭk) adj. (biol.) Relating to life; peculiar to living organisms.

bi·par·ti·san (bīpär′tĭzan, -san) adj. Of or including members from two (political) parties. **bi·par′ti·san·ship** n.

bi·par·tite (bīpär′tīt) adj. Divided into or consisting of two parts; (law, of agreement etc.) drawn up in two corresponding parts, each party delivering a counterpart to the other. **bi·par′tite·ly** adv. **bi·par·ti·tion** (bīpärtīsh′on) n.

bi·ped (bī′pĕd), **bi·ped·al** (bī′pĕdal, bīp′e-) ns. & adjs. Two-footed (animal).

bi·pin·nate (bīpĭn′āt) adj. (bot.)

Having leaflets arranged in tw rows on either side of leafstalk, th leaflets being themselves sub divided.

bi·plane (bī′plān) n. Airplan with two sets of wings, one abov the other.

bi·quad·rat·ic (bīkwŏdrăt′ĭk adj. Of, raised to, the square of square (or 4th power) of a number ~ **equation**, one in which th unknown quantity is biquadratic **biquadratic** n. Biquadrati equation; 4th power of a number.

birch (bẽrch) n. 1. Hardy northern forest tree of genus *Betul* with smooth tough bark and slende graceful branches; wood of this **birch′bark canoe**, one made of th bark of *B. papyrifera*. 2. Birch ro or bundle of birch twigs used fo flogging. **birch** v.t. Flog wit birch. **birch′en** adj. Made o birch.

bird (bẽrd) n. 1. Any feathere vertebrate animal, member of class nearly allied to reptiles bu distinguished by warm blood feathers, and adaptation of th forelimbs as wings. 2. Game bird 3. (slang) Young woman; (joc. person; ~**s of a feather**, peopl with opinions or interests i common; **for the** ~**s**, (slang contemptible or ridiculous. 4. **ge the** ~, (slang, esp. theatr.) be hissed, booed, etc.; so **give the** ~; **bird′bath**, dish of water, often on pedestal, set in garden for birds use; **bird′brain(ed)**, (person) with small brain, dolt, scatterbrain: **bird cage**, cage for bird(s), objec of similar design; **bird call**, note o bird; instrument imitating this; **bird cherry**, species of Eurasian cherry tree (*Prunus padus*) with white flowers and small black fruit; **bird dog**, dog used for hunting birds; (fig.) one who hunts out something for another; **bird′ lime**, sticky substance made from holly bark for catching small birds; **bird of paradise**, bird of family Paradiseidae native to New Guinea and notable for its brilliant colors and elegant plumes; **bird of**

The only creature in the world to have a covering of feathers, the **bird** *is ideally adapted to flight. Facing page: The male and female of the strikingly colored flamingo incubate their eggs in turn.*

Exterior		Internal
1	culmen	13 trachea
2	lore	14 syrinx
3	crest	15 lung
4	ear feathers	16 kidney
5	lesser wing coverts	17 testes
6	scapulars	18 rectum
7	greater wing coverts	19 cloaca
8	secondaries	20 intestines
9	upper tail coverts	21 gizzard
10	retrices	22 liver
11	primaries	23 lung
12	primary coverts	24 crop
		25 esophagus

The **bison** that roamed the North American prairies in great herds is now much reduced in numbers. The male stands about 5 ft. 10 ins. tall and weighs about 1,800 lb.

The Iron Chancellor, **Otto vo Bismarck**, was the architect of th German Empire. His success in unitin the German States into a nation wa matched by that of his diplomacy, as the Congress of Berlin (left), 1878.

passage, migratory bird (also fig. of sojourner); **bird of prey**, any of various predatory birds such as hawks and owls; **bird sanctuary**, area where birds are protected by law; **bird'seed**, any of various kinds of seed used for feeding birds; **bird's-eye**, any of several plants with small round bright flowers; **bird's-eye maple**, wood of the sugar maple when full of little knots; **bird's-eye view**, view of landscape from above; résumé of a subject; **bird's-nest soup**, Chinese soup made from edible nest of certain swallows found in the China Sea; **bird-watcher**, one who studies birds in their natural surroundings; **bird-watching**, this occupation. **bird'like** adj.

Birds·eye (bērdz´ī), **Clarence** (1886–1956). American inventor;

pioneered first practical method of freezing foods.

bi·reme (bī´rēm) n. Ancient galley with two banks of oars.

bi·ret·ta, bir·ret·ta, be·ret·ta, ber·ret·ta (berĕt´a) ns. Square cap with three projections worn by Roman Catholic and some Anglican clerics.

Bir·ming·ham[1] (bēr´mĭng-hăm). Industrial center and largest city in N. central Alabama.

·**Bir·ming·ham**[2] (bēr´mĭngam). Industrial midland city in England; 2nd largest city in England.

birth (bērth) n. 1. Emergence of child or animal from body of female parent; process of producing young; **give ~ to**, (of female parent) produce (young) from body (also fig.). 2. Origin, beginning. 3. Parentage, descent; noble lineage. 4. ~ **certificate**, form showing date and place etc. of birth; ~ **control**, regulation of the number of one's children through restriction of ovulation, intercourse, or

conception; **birth'day**, (annive sary of) day of one's birth **birthday suit**, (slang) state nakedness; **birth'mark**, congen tal mark on the body; **birth'plac** place at which one was born; **birt rate**, number of births per 1,0 of population per annum; **birth right**, rights, privilege, or positio to which one is entitled by birth.

Bis·cay (bĭs´kā, bĭskā´), **Bay o** Part of N. Atlantic between N. coa of Spain and W. coast of Franc notorious for storms.

Bis·cayne (bĭs´kān, bĭskān **Bay.** Inlet of the Atlantic Ocea along SE. coast of Florida; Miam is on NW. shore and Key Biscayn is on NE.

bis·cuit (bĭs´kĭt) n. 1. Small cak of shortened bread raised wit baking powder or soda. 2. (Brit Cracker or cookie. 3. Pottery afte firing but before glazing and paint ing.

bi·sect (bīsĕkt´, bī´sĕkt) v. Cut or divide into two (usu equal) parts. **bi·sec'tion** **bi·sec'tion·al** adj. **bi·sec' tion·al·ly** adv. **bi·sec'tor** Bisecting line.

bi·sex·u·al (bīsĕk´shōoal) adj Of both sexes; having both sexes i one individual, hermaphrodite sexually responsive to both sexes ~ n. Bisexual person. **bi·sex·u· al·i·ty** (bīsĕkshōoăl´ĭtē) n.

bish·op (bĭsh´op) n. 1. Clergy man consecrated as ecclesiastica governor of a diocese. 2. Miter shaped chessman moved diag onally. **bish'op·ric** n. Diocese o office of a bishop.

Bis·marck[1] (bĭz´mărk). Capita of North Dakota, in the SW. par on the Missouri River.

Bis·marck[2] (bĭz´mărk), **Prince Otto Eduard von Leopol** (1815–1898). Prussian and German statesman; first chancellor of th German Empire, 1871–90.

Bis·marck[3] (bĭz´mărk) **Archi pelago.** Group of small islands i the Pacific, NE. of New Guinea under Australian administration.

bis·muth (bĭz´muth) n. (chem. Reddish-white brittle metalli element melting at low tempera tures; symbol Bi, at. no. 83, at. wt 208. 9806. **bis'muth·al** adj.

bi·son (bī´son, -zon) n. (pl. **-son** 1. Species of wild ox (Bisor europaeus) of heavy build wit humped shoulders, formerly com mon in Europe and still existing ir the Caucasus. 2. N. Amer. wild ox (B. americanus) formerly roaming in vast herds over the continent now almost extinct except ir rotected areas.

bisque[1] (bĭsk) *n.* Advantage given to inferior player in certain games, esp. a free point or extra turn taken when desired.

bisque[2], **bisk** (bĭsk) *ns.* Thick, rich soup made with shellfish etc.

bis·sex·tile (bĭsĕks′tĭl, bĭ-) *adj. & n.* (Of or pertaining to) a leap year or its extra day. [L. *bis sextilis (annus)* (year) containing the doubled sixth day (because in the Julian calendar the day repeated, Feb. 24, was acc. to the Roman method of reckoning the sixth before the Calends of March)]

bis·tou·ry (bĭs′terē) *n.* (pl. -ries). Surgical knife for minor incisions.

bit[1] (bĭt) *n.* 1. Biting or cutting end or part of tool, as boring piece of drill; part of key that engages with levers of lock. 2. Mouthpiece of horse's bridle.

bit[2] (bĭt) *n.* 1. Morsel of food; something to eat. 2. Small piece of anything; small portion or quantity; a single character of computer language; a short time; (slang) an act, performance, or routine; **do one's** ~, play one's part; ~ **part**, **player**, (theatr.) (player of) very small part.

bit[3] (bĭt): see BITE.

bitch (bĭch) *n.* 1. Female of dog, fox, wolf. 2. (colloq.) Malicious, ill-tempered or lewd woman; (slang) difficult or unpleasant thing; (slang) complaint; ~ *v.* (slang) Complain. **bitch′y** *adj.* (**bitch·i·er**, **bitch·i·est**). **bitch′i·ness** *n.*

bite (bīt) *v.* (**bit** pr. bĭt, **bit·ten** or **bit, bit·ing**). 1. Cut into or off, nip or grip with teeth; (of insects etc.) sting, suck. ~ **the bullet**, accept, confront an unpleasant situation; ~ **the dust**, be killed, esp. in battle. 2. (of fish) Accept bait; accept, express interest in an offer, esp. one intended to deceive. 3. Cause glowing, smarting pain to. 4. Corrode. 5. (of wheels, screw, etc.) Grip. ~ *n.* Act of, wound made by, piece detached by, biting; a morsel or mouthful of food; small meal, snack; dental occlusion; taking of bait by fish; snack; grip, hold. **bit′er** *n.* **bit′ing·ly** *adv.* **bit′ing·ness** *n.*

Bi·thyn·i·a (bĭthĭn′ēa). Ancient region of NW. Asia Minor. **Bi·thyn′i·an** *adj. & n.*

bit·ing (bī′tĭng) *adj.* (esp.) Nipping, keen; pungent, stinging, sarcastic.

bit·ter (bĭt′er) *adj.* Tasting like wormwood, quinine, aloes, etc.; obnoxious, irritating, or unfavorably stimulating to the gustatory sense; unpalatable to the mind, full of affliction; resentful, hostile, or cynical; virulent, relentless; biting, harsh, piercingly cold; ~ **end**, (nautical) end of rope wound around a deck post (*bitt*) hence

(colloq.) final or unpleasant end; **bit′tersweet** *adj.*, both bitter and sweet to the taste; mingling pleasure with pain or regret; **bittersweet** *n.*, any of various climbing plants, such as *Solanum dulcamara*, with bright berries or seeds. **bit′ter·ish** *adj.* **bit′ter·ly** *adv.* **bit′ter·ness** *n.* **bitter** *n.* 1. Bitterness. 2. (Brit.) Bitter beer; (pl.) (usually alcoholic) liquor in which bitter herbs or roots have steeped, used to flavor mixed drinks or as a tonic.

bit·tern (bĭt′ern) *n.* Bird of genus *Botaurus*, allied to herons, but smaller; noted for booming cry; **American** ~, *B. lentiginosus.*

bi·tu·men (bĭtōō′men, -tū′-, bĭch′ōō-) *n.* Mineral pitch, asphalt; any of various kinds of native oxygenated hydrocarbon, as naphtha, petroleum. **bi·tu′mi·noid, bi·tu′mi·nous** *adjs.*

bi·va·lent (bīvā′lent, bĭv′a-) *adj.* (chem.). Having a valence of two.

bi·valve (bī′vălv) *adj.* Having two valves, having two shells hinged together. ~ *n.* Mollusk, as the clam, with shell consisting of two halves hinged together by elastic ligament.

biv·ou·ac (bĭv′ōōăk, bĭv′wăk) *n.* Temporary encampment made with tents or improvised shelter. ~ *v.i.* (**-acked, -ack·ing**). Remain, esp. during the night, in a bivouac.

bi·zarre (bĭzär′) *adj.* Eccentric, fantastic, grotesque, mixed in style. **bi·zarre′ly** *adv.* **bi·zarre′ness** *n.* [Span. *bizarro* brave, handsome]

Bi·zet (bēzā′), **Georges** (1838–1875). French composer of *Carmen* and other operas.

blab (blăb) *v.* (**blabbed, blab·bing**). Talk or tell foolishly or indiscreetly, reveal, let out; hence, **blab′bermouth**, one who cannot keep a secret. **blab′ber** *n.* **blab** *n.* Blabbing.

black (blăk) *adj.* 1. Opposite of white, colorless from the absence or complete absorption of all light; so near this as to have no distinguishable color; very dark colored; dark; dusky, gloomy; dirty. 2. (sometimes **B** ~) Of, belonging to, a dark-skinned ethnic group of African origin. 3. Deadly, sinister, wicked; dismal; angry, lowering; implying disgrace or condemnation (as ~ **mark** etc.); existing, bought, sold, in contravention of economic regulations. 4. ~ **-and-blue**, discolored with bruise(s); **B** ~ **and Tans**, (from their black and khaki uniform), the Royal Irish Constabulary, about 6,000 British soldiers specially recruited and sent to Ireland to suppress the Sinn Fein rebellion in 1919–21; ~ **and white**, written etc. in black ink on white paper; (of film etc.) not in color; (fig.) comprising opposite extremes; (**down in**) ~ **and white**, recorded in writing or print;

~ **art**, divination through alleged communication with the dead; sorcery; **black′ball**, (*v.t.*) exclude from club, society, etc. (orig. by putting black ball into urn or ballot box to express adverse vote); **black bear**, N. Amer. bear (*Ursus americanus*); **black belt**, (belt worn by) person who has attained a certain degree of proficiency in judo or karate; (colloq.) area, section predominantly inhabited by blacks; **black′berry**, bramble (*Rubus fruticosus*) or its fruit; **black′bird**, any of various birds of the family Icteridae, as grackles, redwings, etc.; European songbird (*Turdus merula*); **black′board**, large black or dark-colored board, panel, etc., used in schools and lecture rooms for writing or drawing on in chalk; **black box**, (esp.) device in aircraft recording details of flight or performing other functions electronically; **black coffee**, coffee without milk or cream; **black currant**, shrub *Ribes nigrum*; its small black fruit; **black′damp**, chokedamp of coal mines; **Black Death**, outbreak of plague, mostly in bubonic form, which spread into Europe from Asia in the 14th c., so called from the symptom of internal hemorrhages that blackened the skin of sufferers; **black earth**, dark soil rich in humus; **black eye**, eye with dark iris; discoloration around eye due to bruise; (colloq.) poor

*The superb camouflage of the **bittern** is demonstrated to good effect when the bird assumes an upright pose in keeping with the background of tall reeds.*

The white flowers of **blackthorn** are followed by small purple fruits. These may
be used to flavor gin and brandy. The
blackthorn can be trained to form a
strong hedge.

An inland sea of about 160,000 sq.
miles, the **Black Sea** is linked to the
Mediterranean by a narrow strait, called
the Bosphorus, which is overlooked by
the city of Istanbul.

reputation, dishonor; **black-eyed Susan**, flower with light usu. yellow petals and dark center, esp. *Thunbergia alata* and *Rudbeckia hirta*; **black′face**, make-up for minstrel show; **black′fish**, any of several saltwater and freshwater bass-like edible fish; **black fly**, any of the small, dark, biting gnats of the family Simuliidae; **Black Friar**, Dominican; **blackguard** (blăg′erd) (*adj. & n.*) scoundrel(ly); **Black Hand**, (hist.) secret terrorist society, composed largely of Sicilians, in U.S. in early 20th c.; any similar group; **black′head**, black-headed greasy plug in mouth of hair follicle; **black′hearted**, evil; **black hole**, (astron.) region from which no matter or radiation can escape; any dark hole or deep cell, esp. (hist.) punishment cell or guardroom in barracks; **Black Hole of Calcutta**, punishment cell of the barracks in Fort William, Calcutta, in which 146 Europeans were confined for a night (1756) by order of Suraj ud Daula and only 23 survived until the morning; **black′jack**, flexible loaded club; pirates' black flag; **black′leg**, strikebreaker; disease of sheep and cattle; **blacklist**, list of persons, groups, etc. under disfavor, esp. those to whom jobs are not to be given; **black′list** (*v.t.*); **black′mail**, payment extorted by threats or pressure, esp. by threatening to reveal discrediting secret; extortion of such payment; so **black′mail** (*v.t.*); **black′mailer** (*n.*); **Black Maria**, prison van; **black mark**: see sense 3; **black market**, illegitimate traffic in controlled goods, currencies, or commodities; hence **black marketeer**, (*n. & v.i.*); **black mass** (often **B~ Mass**), mass for the dead, at which vestments and drapings are black; travesty of this, used in the cult of Satanism; **black monk**, Bene-

dictine (from the color of his habit); **Black Muslim**, member of black organization advocating Islam; **black pepper**: see PEPPER; **Black Power**, U.S. movement of blacks in support of civil rights; the power of black Americans as a group; **Black Prince**, 16th-c. name given, for unknown reasons, to Edward (1330–76), the eldest son of Edward III; **Black Sea**, tideless sea between U.S.S.R. and Turkey; **black sheep**, scoundrel, unsatisfactory or disreputable member *of* (family etc.); **Black Shirt**, Fascist (from black shirt in uniform of Fascist militia); **black′smith**, smith working in iron, esp. one who makes horseshoes and shoes horses; **black′snake**, any of various dark non-venomous snakes of N. Amer., esp. *Coluber constrictor*; **black′strap** (**molasses**), dark, very thick molasses used to make alcohol and as cattle feed; **black-tailed deer**, also **Columbian black-tailed deer**, deer of the western slope of the Rocky Mountains (*Odocoileus hemionus columbianus*); **black tea**: see TEA; **black′thorn**, sloe (*Prunus spinosa*), a thorny shrub bearing white flowers before the leaves and small dark purple fruits; **black tie**, tie worn with tuxedo or dinner jacket; the jacket and attire as a whole; **black velvet**, mixture of stout and champagne; **black′water fever**, tropical fever, originating in malarial infection, characterized by brown or blue-black urine; **black widow**, small, jet-black spider (*Latrodectus mactans*), female of which is venomous. **black′ish** *adj.* **black′ly** *adv.* **black′ness** *n.* **black** *n.* 1. Black color, paint, etc.; **in**

the ~, (bookkeeping) operating a profit. 2. Black substance, as soo etc.; fungus, smut, in wheat etc. 3 Black variety of anything; blac cloth or clothing. 4. (sometime Black) Member of dark-skinne people of African descent. 5 (Player using) dark pieces in ches etc. **black** *v.t.* Make black, polis with blacking; obscure (window street, etc.) so that no light is visibl from outside or from the ai extinguish lights during stag performance; become unconscious **black′out** (*n.*) (1) (period of obscuration of artificial lights, esp in wartime; (2) failure or stoppag of electrical power, radio signal etc.; suspension or suppression o news; (3) temporary loss of vision and consciousness; (4) temporar loss of memory.

black·a·moor (blăk′amoor) *n* (archaic) Black person.

Black·beard (blăk′bērd) (d 1718). Real name Edward Teach or Thatch. British pirate along the Spanish Main, the Bahamas, and off the coasts of Virginia and Carolina; protected by corrup governor of N. Carolina; killed i attack by naval ships sent b governor of Virginia.

Black Canyon. Colorado Rive canyon between Arizona and Nevada; site of Hoover Dam.

black·en (blăk′en) *v.* Mak grow, black or dark; speak evil of **black′en·er** *n.*

Black Forest. Wooded moun tainous resort region in S.W. Wes Germany.

Black Hawk (1767–1838) American Indian leader of the Fo and Sauk during the Black Haw War, 1832.

Black Hills. Group of mountains rich in mineral deposits in W. South Dakota and N.E. Wyoming.

black·ing (blăk´ĭng) *n.* (esp.) paste or liquid for blacking or polishing boots.

Black·more (blăk´mōr), **Richard Dodridge** (1825–1900). English novelist, author of *Lorna Doone*.

Black·pool (blăk´pōōl). Seaside resort in N.W. England on the Irish Sea.

Black·stone (blăk´stōn), **Sir William** (1723–80). English jurist, author of *Commentaries on the Laws of England* (1765–9).

Black · well (blăk´wĕl), **Elizabeth** (1821–1910). American and British physician; resident of the U.S. 1832–69; first woman doctor in modern times; established private dispensary in New York, 1851, which became New York Infirmary and College for Women.

blad·der (blăd´er) *n.* 1. Membranous bag in human and other animal bodies, esp. urinary bladder; animal's bladder or part of prepared for various uses, inflated, etc. 2. Anything inflated and hollow, inflated pericarp or vesicle in plants and seaweeds. **blad´der·like, blad´der·y** *adjs.*

blade (blād) *n.* 1. Flat lanceolate leaf of grass and cereals; (bot.) broad thin expanded part of leaf as opp. to petiole or leafstalk. 2. Broad flattened leaflike part of instrument, as oar, paddle, spade, aircraft propeller, etc.; broad flattened bone, esp. shoulder blade. 3. Thin cutting part of edged tool or weapon; a sword; detachable usu. two-edged cutting part of safety razor; sharp part of ice skate in contact with the ice. 4. Swordsman; gallant, dashing fellow. **blade´-less, blade´like** *adjs.*

blain (blān) *n.* Inflamed swelling or sore on skin.

Blair (blār), **Eric Arthur**: see George ORWELL.

Blake (blāk), **William** (1757–1827). English poet, painter, and mystic; engraved, and sometimes colored by hand, many of his own works, which included the lyrical *Songs of Innocence* (1789) and *Songs of Experience* (1794), and the *Prophetic Books* (1793–1804).

blame (blām) *n.* Censure; responsibility for bad result. ~ *v.t.* (**blamed, blam·ing**). Find fault with; fix responsibility on. **blame´less** *adj.* Innocent. **blame´ful** *adj.* **blame´ful·ly** *adv.* **blame´ful·ness** *n.* **blame´less·ly** *adv.* **blame´less·ness** *n.* **blame´-wor·thy** *adj.*

blanch (blănch) *v.* Make white by withdrawing color, peeling (almonds), immersing in boiling water, or depriving of light (plants); make or grow pale with fear, cold, etc.

blanc · mange (blamahnj´, -mahn̊zh´) *n.* Flavored, sweetened milk pudding thickened with cornstarch.

bland (blănd) *adj.* Pleasantly agreeable, gentle; mild; (of food) nonspicy, soothing or nonirritating; unemotional, indifferent. **bland´ly** *adv.* **bland´ness** *n.*

blan·dish (blăn´dĭsh) *v.* Flatter, coax. **blan´dish·er, blan´dish·ment** *ns.*

blank (blăngk) *adj.* 1. Not written or printed on; with spaces left for signature or details. 2. Empty, not filled. 3. Void of interest, incident, result, or expression; unrelieved, sheer. 4. ~ **check**, check signed by drawer, with amount left for payee to fill in; hence, full discretionary power; ~ **verse**, unrhymed, metrical verse esp. of five-foot iambics; ~ **wall**, wall without opening; (fig.) impassable obstacle. **blank´ly** *adv.* **blank´ness** *n.* **blank** *n.* 1. Void; space left to be filled up in document; printed form containing such spaces; dash (—) written in place of omitted letter or word(s). 2. Gun cartridge containing powder but no bullet. 3. Piece of metal ready for stamping as coin, medal, etc. 4. Blank (losing) ticket in drawing; **draw (a)** ~, elicit no response, fail. **blank** *v.t.* 1. To keep (an opponent) from scoring in a game. 2. ~ **out**, cross out, obliterate, delete.

blan·ket (blăng´kĭt) *n.* Rectangular piece of woolen etc. material used for warmth esp. as bed covering; any covering, as a ~ **of snow**; (as *adj.*) covering or including all contingencies etc.; **wet** ~, (fig.) discouraging person. **blanket** *v.t.* Cover with blanket, stifle. **blan´ket·less** *adj.*

blan·ket·ing (blăng´kĭtĭng) *n.*

William Blake was a visionary poet and artist. His illustrations for other poets' works are imbued with his distinctive image of the world. Here, one of his illustrations for Dante's 'Commedia' shows the poet at hell's gates.

(esp.) Material for blankets.

blare (blār) *n.* & *v.* (**blared, blar·ing**). (Make) sound of trumpet; utter loudly.

Blar·ney (blār′nē). Village near Cork in S. Ireland; ~ **stone**, inscribed stone, very difficult to reach, in the Castle of Blarney, supposed to confer upon anyone who kisses it a cajoling tongue and the art of flattery or of telling lies with unblushing effrontery.

blar·ney (blār′nē) *n.* & *v.* (**-neyed, -ney·ing**). (Use, assail with) flattering or cajoling talk; nonsense.

bla·sé (blahzā′, blah′zā) *adj.* Bored, indifferent from an excess of worldliness.

blas·pheme (blăsfēm′, blăs′fēm) *v.* (**-phemed, -phem·ing**). Talk impiously; utter profanity about, revile. **blas·phem′er, blas·phe·my** (blăs′femē) *ns.* (pl. **-mies**). **blas′phe·mous** *adj.* **blas′phe·mous·ly** *adv.*

blast (blăst) *n.* Strong gust of wind; violent gust of air caused by explosion of bomb, etc.; explosion; blowing or sound of trumpet or other wind instruments; sudden loud noise; strong current of air used in smelting etc.; quantity of explosion used in blasting; (colloq.) violent reprimand; (slang) a party, esp. a wild one; (**at**) **full** ~, (colloq.) at maximum speed, capacity, etc.; ~ **furnace**, smelting furnace into which a blast of compressed heated air is driven by blower. **blast** *v.t.* 1. Blow up, break, dislodge, with explosives; criticize loudly or vigorously. 2. Wither, shrivel, blight. 3. (of rocket or spacecraft) ~**-off**, take off, be launched into space; use power in flight; **blast′off** (*n.*); **blast** *v.i.* Make a loud, blaring sound. **blast′ed** *adj.* (esp., colloq.) Damnable.

blas·to·derm (blăs′todĕrm) *n.* External layer of cells formed as a result of cleavage of a yolked egg, characteristic of eggs of reptiles, birds, and in a different form, insects.

blas·tu·la (blăs′chōōla) *n.* (pl. **-las, -lae** pr. **-lē**). (biol.) Early embryonic stage, usu. a hollow ball of cells, produced by cleavage of an egg. (cf. GASTRULA).

bla·tant (blā′tant) *adj.* Noisy, vulgarly clamorous; palpably obvious. **bla′tan·cy** *n.* **bla′tant·ly** *adv.*

blath·er (blădh′er) *n.* & *v.* (Utter) foolish talk; **blath′erskite**, a babbling, foolish person; foolish talk.

Bla·vat·sky (blavăt′skē), **Helena Petrovna** (1831–91). Russian spiritualist, founder (in New York) of the Theosophical Society.

blaze¹ (blāz) *v.i.* (**blazed, blaz·**

*A **blast furnace** is fueled with ore, coke, and a flux, usually limestone, at the top. Pre-heated air is pumped through the mixture from the base to ignite the coke which reduces the ore to molten iron and slag.*

ing). Burn with bright flame; be brilliantly lighted; burn with excitement etc.; show bright colors; emit light. ~ *n.* Bright flame or fire; glow of color, bright display; **go to** ~**s**, (slang) go to hell. **blaz′ing·ly** *adv.*

blaze² (blāz) *n.* White mark on face of horse or cow; white mark made on tree by chipping off bark, to indicate path, boundary, etc. ~ *v.t.* (**blazed, blaz·ing**). Mark (tree, path) with blaze; (fig.) ~ **a trail**, show a new way by pioneering activity.

blaze³ (blāz) *v.t.* (**blazed, blaz·ing**). Proclaim (news) as with trumpet.

blaz·er (blā′zer) *n.* Brightly colored sport jacket, usu. with badge on pocket, and often part of school uniform; solid color sport jacket, esp. one with metal buttons.

bla·zon (blā′zon) *n.* Heraldic shield, coat of arms, bearings, or banner; record, description, esp. of virtues etc. ~ *v.t.* Describe or paint (arms) heraldically; inscribe with arms etc. in colors; give luster to; set forth in fitting words; proclaim. **bla′zon·er, bla′zon·ment** *ns.* **bla′zon·ry** *n.* (Art of describing or painting) heraldic devices, armorial bearings; brightly colored display.

bleach (blēch) *v.* Whiten by exposure to sunlight or chemical process; **bleaching powder**, chemical, such as chloride of lime, used for bleaching. **bleach** *n.* Bleaching process or substance. **bleach′er** *n.* (usually ~**s**), roofless section of (cheapest) seats in base-

ball park (so called becau spectators there are exposed to su **bleach′erite**, a spectator who s in the bleachers, esp. an emotio fan of a team. **bleach′er, bleach er·y** *ns.*

bleak (blēk) *adj.* Bare vegetation; exposed, wind-swe cold, chilly, dreary; offering lit hope; (of person) depressed, lif less. **bleak′ly** *adv.* **bleak′ness**

blear (blēr) *adj.* Dim, film rheumy; misty, indistinct. ~ *v* Dim (eyes) with tears, rheum, et blur. **blear′y** *adj.* (**blear·i·e blear·i·est**). **blear′i·ly** *ad* **blear′i·ness** *n.*

bleat (blēt) *v.* (of sheep, go etc.) Utter characteristic tremulo cry; make sound resembling th speak feebly or foolishly. ~ *n.* C of sheep, goat, etc.; any simil sound. **bleat′er** *n.* **bleat′ing** *adv.*

bleed (blēd) *v.* (**bled** pr. blē **bleed·ing**). 1. Emit blood; suff wounds or violent death; feel pi sorrow, or anguish; (of plants) em sap; (of dyes) come out in wate 2. Draw blood surgically fro allow (liquid or gas) to escape fro (a container). 3. Part with mone suffer extortion; extort mon from. 4. (print.) Let illustration r to edge of page, without margin. **bleed′er** (blē′der) *n.* (esp Person suffering from hemophili

bleep (blēp) *n.* & *v.i.* (Em high-pitched intermittent soun censor word or words from tel vision or radio program by deleti them electronically.

blem·ish (blĕm′ĭsh) *v.t.* Ma spoil beauty or perfection of, sull ~ *n.* Physical or moral defec stain, flaw. **blem′ish·er** *n.*

blench (blĕnch) *v.i.* (archai Start aside, flinch, quail. **blench er** *n.*

blend (blĕnd) *v.* (**blend·ed blent, blend·ing**). Mix, ming (esp. sorts of tea, tobacco, whiske etc., to produce a certain quality mingle intimately *with*; mix so as be inseparable and indistinguish able; pass imperceptibly into eac other; fit, relate, or match. ~ Blending; mixture made by blend ing. **blend′er** *n.* (esp.) Kitche appliance for combining cookin ingredients.

blende (blĕnd) *n.* Zinc sulfide [Ger. *blenden* deceive, becaus although it often resembled galen it did not yield lead]

blen·ny (blĕn′ē) *n.* (pl. **-nies** Small spiny-finned fish of genu *Blennius* of family Blenniida

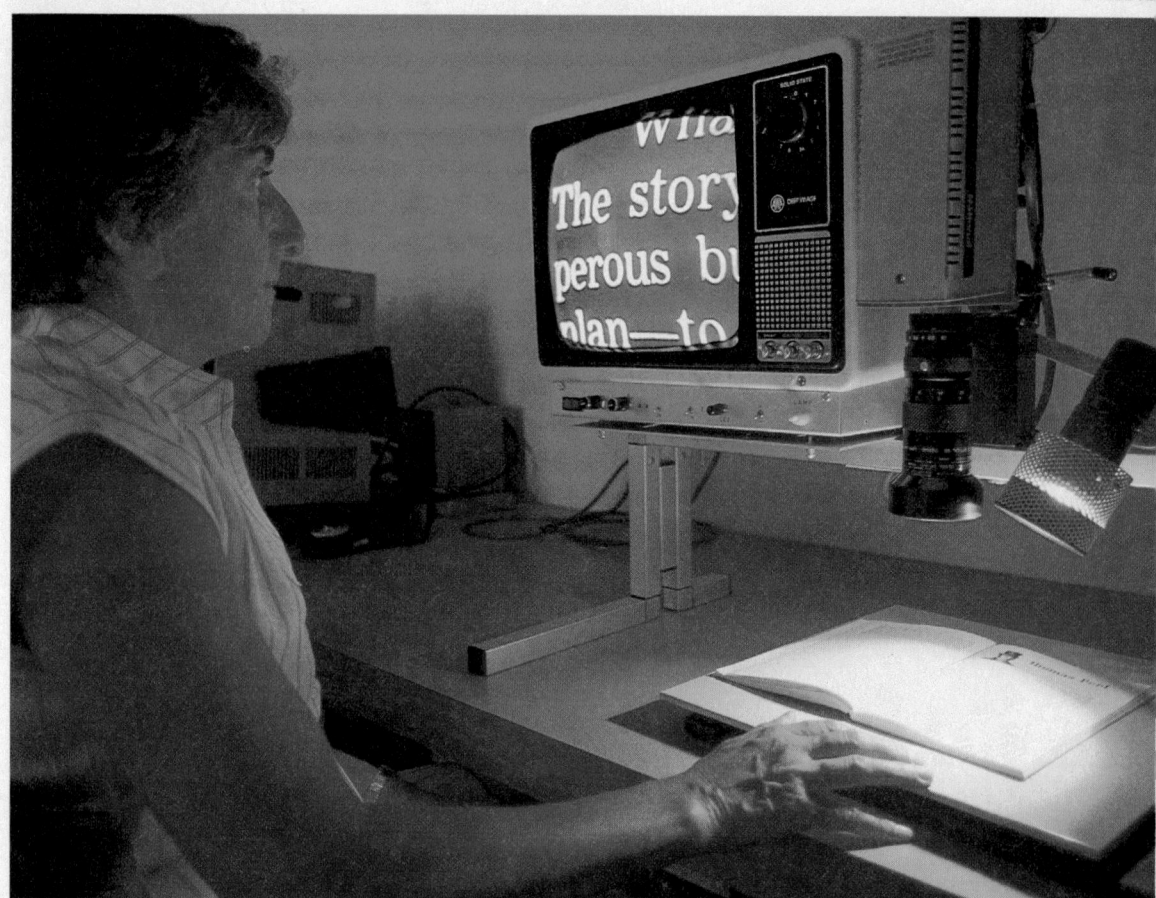

*A closed-circuit T.V. with lens attachment magnifies the text of an ordinary book. Technological advancements have made it possible for near **blind** and partially sighted people to lead more fulfilling lives.*

mostly shore fish found in shallow pools. **blen·ni·oid** (blĕn′ēoid) *adj.*

blent (blĕnt): see BLEND.

bleph·a·ri·tis (blĕƒerī′tĭs) *n.* Inflammation of the eyelids.

bless (blĕs) *v.t.* (**bless·ed** or **blest, bless·ing**). 1. Consecrate (esp. food); sanctify by making sign of cross. 2. Call holy, adore; glorify for benefits received. 3. Pronounce words (held) to confer supernatural favor and well-being upon; make happy or successful; make happy *with* some gift; *bless me! bless you!*, (**God**) **bless my soul!**, etc., exclamations of surprise or indignation.

bless·ed (blĕs′ĭd; sometimes blĕst) *adj.* 1. Consecrated; revered; fortunate; in paradise; beatified. 2. Blissful, bringing happiness. 3. (euphem.) Cursed etc. **bless′ed·ly** *adv.* **bless′ed·ness** *n.*

bless·ing (blĕs′ĭng) *n.* Declaration, invocation, or bestowal, of divine favor; grace before or after food; gift of God, nature, etc., that one is glad of; approval; **~ in disguise**, misfortune that works for eventual good.

blest (blĕst): see BLESS.

Bligh (blī), **William** (1754–1817). English vice-admiral, explorer, and colonial administrator; as a lieutenant he commanded the BOUNTY.

blight (blīt) *n.* 1. Disease of plants caused by fungoid parasites. 2. Any malignant withering influence. ~ *v.t.* Affect with blight; exert baleful influence on; nip in the bud, mar, frustrate.

blight·er (blī′ter) *n.* (Brit. slang) Contemptible or annoying person or thing; fellow, thing.

bli·mey (blī′mē) *int.* (Brit. slang) Exclamation of surprise or contempt. [f. *Gorblimey* = God blind me!]

blimp (blĭmp) *n.* Small, nonrigid type of airship.

Blimp (blĭmp), **Colonel.** Character invented by the English cartoonist David Low (1891–1963) representing a muddleheaded, obese, elderly gentleman, pop. interpreted as type of diehard or reactionary.

blind (blīnd) *adj.* 1. Without sight; (aeronaut.) without direct observation of objects etc., relying on instruments. 2. Without foresight, discernment, or moral or intellectual light; reckless; not ruled by purpose, reason, or control (as a ~ **chance**). 3. Secret, obscure, concealed (as a ~ **driveway**); with-

out windows or openings; walled up; closed at one end, not leading anywhere (as ~ **alley**). 4. (slang) Very drunk. 5. ~ **date**, social engagement between two persons of opposite sex who have not met before; either of these persons; **blind′man's buff**, game in which blindfolded player tries to catch and identify one of the others; **blind spot**, point in the retina not sensitive to light, where the optic nerve passes through the inner coat of the eyeball, hence (fig.) a subject, area, etc. about which one is ignorant, intolerant, or overly emotional; **blind-stamping** (bookbinding), stamping without the use of ink or gold leaf. **blind** *adv.* **blind′ing** *adj.* **blind′ing·ly, blind′ly** *advs.* **blind′ness** *n.* **blind** *v.t.* Deprive of sight permanently or temporarily; take away power of judgment, deceive. ~ *n.* Obstruction to sight or light; screen for windows etc., esp. on roller; pretext; shelter of canvas, leaves, etc. for concealing hunters, as a **duck ~**.

blind·fold (blīnd′fōld) *adj.* With eyes covered with cloth; without circumspection. ~ *v.t.* Deprive of sight by covering eyes with cloth. ~ *n.* A cloth covering the eyes to prevent seeing.

blink (blĭngk) *v.* 1. Shut one's eyelids momentarily, esp. in-

When a **block** is fitted with pulley wheels and linked by rope or belt to other pulleys it reduces the effort required to lift a weight. 1. A triple block with internal straps and side hook. Parts of the strap go through the block to form a becket. 2. A multiple block and tackle.

bloating.

bloat[2] (blōt) *v.* Inflate, swell. **bloat'ed** *adj.* Inflated, swollen; (fig.) swollen with pride, excessive wealth, etc.

blob (blŏb) *n.* Drop of liquid; small roundish mass; spot of color. ~ *v.* (**blobbed, blob·bing**).

bloc (blŏk) *n.* Combination of political parties, or of governments, groups, etc., formed to forward some interest.

block (blŏk) *n.* 1. Log of wood; large piece of wood for chopping or hammering on, mounting horse from, etc., (hist.) on which condemned persons were beheaded. 2. Compact usu. solid piece of any substance; unhewn lump of rock; prepared piece of building stone; mold or form on which something is shaped or displayed; piece of wood or metal engraved for printing; (mech.) pulley, system of pulleys mounted in case; (slang) head. 3. Section, compact set or group; group of buildings surrounded by (usu. four) streets. 4. Obstruction; (psychol.) mental obstruction preventing a particular thought or expression; (path.) obstruction of a nervous or muscular impulse. 5. **block'-buster**, (slang) large high-explosive bomb; overwhelmingly impressive object or idea, such as a novel or film; **block'busting**, inducing people to sell their homes at a low price by warning of change in racial patterns of a neighborhood; **block'head**, stupid person; **block'house**, detached fort (orig. one blocking passage), occas. one of connected chain of posts; one-storied timber building with loopholes; reinforced concrete shelter; **block letters, writing**, (writing with) detached letters, as in printing, usu. capitals; **block printing**, hand printing of fabrics with wooden blocks on which design is carved. **block** *v.t.* Obstruct (passage etc.); put obstacles in way of; restrict use or conversion of currency etc.; shape on block; ~ **in, out**, sketch roughly, plan.

Block (blŏk), **Adriaen.** Seventeenth c. Dutch navigator, discoverer of Block Island; ~ **Island**, island and summer resort off the coast of Rhode Island at the entrance to Long Island Sound.

block·ade (blŏkād') *n.* Surrounding of place, blocking of harbor, etc., by hostile forces to

voluntarily; (of eyes) shut thus. 2. (fig.) Shut one's eyes to, evade. . Send (tears etc.) away by blink-ng. 4. Shine suddenly or momentarily. ~ *n.* Blinking; momentary gleam or glimpse.

blink·er (blĭng'ker) *n.* 1. Either of two flaps on horse's bridle preventing it from seeing sideways. . A device for flashing light signals; blinking signal light, as for ignaling or warning motorists.

blip (blĭp) *n.* (radar) Image of bject as projected on screen.

bliss (blĭs) *n.* Gladness, enjoy-ment; the joy of heaven, perfect appiness, blessedness; being in eaven. **bliss'ful** *adj.* **bliss'ful·ly** dv. **bliss'ful·ness** *n.*

blis·ter (blĭs'ter) *n.* Thin vesicle n skin filled with serum, caused by riction, a burn, etc.; similar swel-ling on plant, metal, painted surface, etc.; rounded compartment protruding from body of airplane. ~ *v.* Raise blister on, be or become covered with blisters; (fig.) criticize scathingly. **blis'ter·y** *adj.*

blithe (blīdh) *adj.* (poet.) Gay, joyous. **blithe'ly** *adv.* **blithe'ness** *n.* **blithe'some** *adj.*

B.Litt. *abbrev.* *Baccalaureus Literarum.* (L., = Bachelor of Letters.)

blitz (blĭts) *n.* Quick, violent attack intended to bring speedy victory, intensive air attack. ~ *v.t.* Attack suddenly and violently. [Ger. *Blitzkrieg* lightning war]

bliz·zard (blĭz'erd) *n.* Heavy snowstorm with driving winds.

bloat[1] (blōt) *v.t.* Cure (herring) by salting and smoking. **bloat'er** *n.* (esp. Brit.) Herring cured by prevent goods etc. from reaching or leaving it; **raise, run the** ~, remove, evade, the blockading force. **blockade** *v.t.* (**-ad·ed, -ad·ing**). Subject to blockade. **block·ad′er** *n.*

block·age (blŏk′ĭj) *n.* Obstruction.

bloke (blōk) *n.* (Brit. slang) Man, fellow.

blond (blŏnd) *adj.* (of hair) Light colored, flaxen; (of complexion) fair. ~ *n.* Person with blond hair. **blonde** *n.* Woman with blond hair. **blond′ness** *n.*

blood (blŭd) *n.* 1. Liquid circulating in the veins and arteries of vertebrates, carrying nourishment and oxygen to all parts of the body and bringing away waste products to be excreted, consisting of a serum or plasma in which corpuscles are suspended and usu. red because of their hemoglobin content; (hist.) one of the four humors (see HUMOR, 4). 2. Analogous liquid in invertebrates performing (some of) the same functions. 3. Taking of life, guilt of bloodshed; passion, temperament, mettle. 4. Race, relationship, kin, descent, parentage. 5. Dandy, man of fashion. 6. ~ **bank**, place where supply of blood for transfusion is stored; ~ **bath**, massacre; ~ **brother**, brother by birth; one bound to another in solemn friendship by ceremonial mingling of blood; ~ **count**, (determination of) number of blood cells in a given volume of blood; ~ **donor**: see DONOR; ~ **group**, one of several types into which human blood may be divided on basis of its compatibility with that of other persons; **blood′hound**, large keen-scented dog used for tracking cattle, criminals, etc.; **blood′letting**, surgical removal of some of patient's blood; **blood′- mobile**, truck equipped for receiving and transporting blood donated for transfusions; **blood money**, that gained ruthlessly through others' suffering; that paid to a hired assassin; (hist.) that paid to next of kin for slaughter of relative; **blood poisoning**, condition caused by presence of pathogenic bacteria in the blood; **blood pressure**, pressure of blood against walls of arteries as it is impelled along them, freq. measured in diagnosis because in certain conditions it may be higher (hypertension) or lower (hypotension) than normal; **blood relation**, one related by virtue of common descent, not by marriage; **blood′shed**, spilling of blood, slaughter; **blood′shot**, (of eye) suffused, tinged, with blood; **blood sport**, sport involving killing of animals, esp. hunting; **blood′- stone**, green chalcedony with spots

About eight million **blood** cells in th body die every second in their figh against infection. They are constant, renewed. Above: Here, red and whit cells are seen under a microscope.

The human heart can, under stress pump up to 12 pints of blood every min ute. Oxygen-enriched blood is force round the arterial system (red) an returned through the veins (blue) f renewal. The blood is supplied to var ous parts of the body by blood vessel and capillaries.

Arterial System (red)
1 common carotid
2 right subclavian
3 ascending aorta
4 heart
5 brachial
6 coeliac artery
7 abdominal aorta
8 exterior iliac
9 femoral artery
Venous System (blue)
10 external jugular vein
11 innominate vein
12 vena azygos
13 brachial
14 common iliac
15 long saphenous vein
16 femoral vein

Veins have a series of valves that act a a check on the direction of flow. While the blood flows correctly (A), the valve remain open, but when the blood flow back in the wrong direction (B) it flicks the valve across the vein and closes it veins of red jasper; heliotrope; **lood′stream**, circulating blood human or animal system; **lood′sucker**, leech; extortioner; **lood′thirsty**, eager for blood-ed; **blood vessel**, vein, artery, or pillary conveying blood. **blood** *t.* Remove surgically some of the ood of; smear face of (novice at nting) with blood of fox after kill. **lood′less** *adj.* Without blood; feeling; pale; without bloodshed. **lood′like** *adj.*

blood·y (blŭd′ē) *adj.* (**blood·i-** , **blood·i·est**). 1. Of, like, run-ng or smeared with, blood. 2. volving, loving, resulting from, oodshed; cruel. 3. (Brit. slang) amned. ~ *adv.* (Brit. slang) onfoundedly, very. ~ *v.t.* **lood·ied, blood·y·ing**). Make oody; stain with blood. **blood′- y** *adv.* **blood′i·ness** *n.*

bloom (bloom) *n.* Flower, esp. f plants grown or admired chiefly r the flower, florescence. 2. rime, perfection; flush, glow; elicate powdery deposit on grapes, ums, etc.; cloudiness on a shiny rface; freshness. ~ *v.* Bear owers, be in flower; come into, be , full beauty; flourish.

Bloom·er (bloo′mer), **Mrs.** melia Jenks (1818–94). Ameri-an temperance leader, feminist, d popularizer of "rational dress" r women. **bloom′ers** *n.pl.* ostume with loose knee-length ousers formerly worn by women r gymnastics, cycling, etc.; under-arments of this shape.

Blooms·bur·y (bloomz′berē, rē). District of London con-ining British Museum and many uildings of London University, rmerly a fashionable and later a terary quarter.

blos·som (blŏs′om) *v.i.* Open to flower (lit. and fig.). ~ *n.*

*Its acute sense of smell and inborn skill in tracking makes the **bloodhound** valu-able to hunters. It pursues its quarry but does not kill. A hound stands 25–27 ins. at the shoulder.*

Flower, mass of flowers on fruit tree etc.; early stage of growth, promise. **blos′som·y** *adj.*

blot[1] (blŏt) *n.* Spot or stain of ink etc., dark patch; disfigurement, blemish, defect; disgraceful act or quality in good character. ~ *v.* (**blot·ted, blot·ting**). 1. Spot or stain with ink, etc.; make blots; smudge; sully, detract from; obliterate (writing etc.) with blot, destroy. 2. Dry with **blotting paper**, absorbent paper for soaking up wet ink. **blot′less** *adj.*

blot[2] (blŏt) *n.* Exposed piece in backgammon.

blotch (blŏch) *n.* Discolored or inflamed patch on skin; irregular patch of ink, color, etc. **blotch′y** *adj.* (**blotch·i·er, blotch·i·est**).

blot·ter (blŏt′er) *n.* Piece or pad of blotting paper; record book of daily occurrences or transactions; so **police ~**, book listing police arrests, calls answered, etc., each day.

blot·to (blŏt′ō) *adj.* (slang) Very drunk.

blouse (blows, blowz) *n.* 1. Woman's or child's loose garment for upper part of body, usu. worn tucked into skirt or trousers. 2. Upper part of battle dress, fitting closely at waist. ~ *v.* (**bloused, blous·ing**). Arrange (material, bodice), be arranged, in loose light folds like a blouse. **blouse′like** *adj.*

blow[1] (blō) *v.* (**blew** pr. bloo, **blown** pr. blōn, **blow·ing**). 1. Move as wind does, act as current of air; send current of air from mouth; pant, puff; (of whales etc.) eject water and air; cause to pant,

Bluebottles or blowflies are flies of metallic hue belonging to the family Calliphoridae. Some are a serious pest of sheep as they lay eggs in damp wool and the larvae cause wounds which become infected.

put out of breath. 2. Drive, be driven, by blowing; sound (wind instrument, or note *on* or *with* this); direct air current at; clear, empty, by air current; break *in* or send flying *off*, *out*, *up*, by explosion; (of instrument) sound; ~ **up** (*v.*), inflate, shatter or be shattered by explosion; (photog., colloq.) enlarge. 3. (of electric fuse or lamp filament) Melt when over-loaded. 4. (slang) Curse, confound; squander. 5. **blow′fly**, fly that lays its eggs on carrion etc.; **blow′gun**, pipe through which darts or pellets are blown by the breath; **blow′hard**, braggart; **blow′hole**, each of two holes (containing the nostrils) at top of head in whales etc. through which they blow; hole in ice through which seals etc. can breathe; **blow′out**, bursting (of automobile tire etc.); (slang) large meal, feast; **blow′pipe**, tube for heating flame by blowing air or other gas into it; **blow′torch**, apparatus for direct-ing very hot flame on a selected spot; apparatus for heating or cutting metals; **blow′up** (*n.*), explosion; (colloq.) enlargement; (colloq.) outburst of temper; **blow** *n.* Blowing; blowing of flute, one's nose, etc. **blow′er** *n.*

blow[2] (blō) *n.* Hard stroke with fist, hammer, etc.; disaster, shock; **~-by-~** *adj.*, (of narrative) giving all details in sequence.

blow·er (blō′er) *n.* (esp.) 1. Apparatus for increasing draft of fire. 2. (Brit. slang) Telephone.

blown (blōn): see BLOW[1].

blow·y (blō′ē) *adj.* (**blow·i·er**,

*Above: The black-crested **Steller's blue jay** is one of up to 35 species of the largely omnivorous jay found in the U.S.A.*

*Right: A typical farm building in the **Blue Ridge Mountains** which have a diverse farming community as well as tourist attractions.*

blow·i·est). Windy.

blowz·y (blow′zē) *adj.* (**blowz·i·er, blowz·i·est**). (of woman) Red-faced, coarse looking; slatternly.

blub·ber (blŭb′er) *n.* 1. Fatty tissue of aquatic mammals which keeps them warm, esp. **whale** ~, used as source of oil. 2. Weeping. **blubber** *adj.* (of lips) Swollen, protruding. ~ *v.* Utter with sobs, weep noisily. **blub′ber·er** *n.* **blub′ber·ing·ly** *adv.*

blu·cher (bloo′ker, -cher) *n.* (19th-c.) Strong leather half boot or high shoe. [f. BLÜCHER]

Blü·cher (bloo′ker, -cher; *Ger.* blü′χer), **Gebhard Leberecht von** (1742–1819). Prussian field marshal, led the Prussian army at the battle of WATERLOO.

bludg·eon (blŭj′on) *n.* Short heavy-headed stick. ~ *v.t.* Strike heavily or repeatedly with or as with bludgeon.

blue (bloo) *adj.* (**blu·er, blu·est**). 1. Colored like the cloudless sky, or with darker or paler shades of this color; livid, leaden colored. 2. Affected with fear, discomfort, anxiety, low spirits, etc. 3. Dressed in blue; (of talk etc.) indecent, obscene. 4. ~ **baby**, infant suffering from congenital cyanosis; **blue′bell**, any of various plants with blue, bell-shaped flowers, e.g. harebell, (*Scilla monscripta*, of Europe), lungwort (*Mertensia virginica*). **blue′berry**, (blue fruit of) one of

several plants of genus *Vaccinium*; **blue′bird**, any of three N. Amer. songbirds of genus *Sialis*, of mostly blue plumage, esp. *S. sialis*, the eastern bluebird; **blue blood**, high birth; **blue′bonnet**, round flat blue woolen cap formerly generally worn in Scotland; (hist.) Scottish soldier wearing this; wildflower with blue blossoms (*Lupinus subcarnosus*) common in SW. U.S.; **blue book**, student's examination booklet in blue paper cover; **blue′bottle**, dipterous insect with blue body of genus *Calliphora* (esp. *C. vomitoria* and *C. erythrocephala*), which deposits eggs on meat, carrion, etc.; **blue cheese**, cheese with veins of blue mold; **blue-chip**, (stock exch.) stock that is a fairly reliable investment, paying good dividends; (also attrib.); **blue-collar worker**, manual or industrial (opp. office) worker; **blue′fish**, voracious game fish (*Pomatomus saltatrix*); **blue′-grass**, species of *Poa* (esp. *P. pratensis*), as found in Kentucky and Virginia; hence, **the Blue′-grass**, region in central Kentucky famous for this grass and the breeding of race horses; **blue′-jacket**, seaman; **blue jay**, common crested jay (*Cyanocitta cristata*) of N. Amer.; **blue jeans**, blue denim trousers with reinforced seams and

seat; **blue law**, severely Puritanical law; **blue mold**, fungus of genus *Penicillium* forming on food; **once in a blue moon**, very rarely; **Blue Nile**: see NILE; **blue pencil**, pencil making blue mark, used chiefly in making corrections, obliterations, etc.; **blue-pencil** (*v.t.*) make marks, cuts, or alterations in; censor; **blue′point**, small, tasty oyster from south shore of Long Island [f. name of headland]; **blue′print**, photographic print of white lines on blue ground or blue lines on white ground, used in copying plans, machine drawings, etc.; (fig.) detailed plan, scheme; **blue ribbon**, first prize; greatest honor or distinction in any sphere; **blue-sky laws**, regulations forbidding sales to gullible investors; **blue′-stocking**, woman having or affecting literary tastes and learning [f. *Blue Stocking Society*, name given in 18th c. to meetings for literary conversation etc. at the houses of Mrs. Elizabeth Montagu (1720–1800) and her circle, from the fact that the men attending might wear the blue worsted stockings of ordinary daytime dress instead of the black silk of evening]; **blue water**, deep water, the open sea. **blu′ish** *adj.* **blue′ness** *n.*

ue *n.* 1. Blue color or pigment;
e cloth etc. 2. Sky, sea (**the ~**);
t of the ~, unexpectedly. 3.
.) Melancholy; (type of) mel-
choly song of U.S. black origin;
e blues. **blue** *v.t.* (**blued,**
u·ing). Make blue; treat with
ndering blue.

Blue·beard (blōō'bērd). Hero
a popular tale, who killed several
ves in turn because they showed
due curiosity about a locked
om.

Blue Ridge Mountains. SE.
nge of the Appalachian Moun-
ns from S. Pennsylvania to N.
orgia; contains many scenic and
ort areas.

bluff¹ (blŭf) *adj.* Having per-
ndicular broad front; abrupt,
nt, frank, hearty. **bluff'ly** *adv.*
uff'ness *n.* **bluff** *n.* Headland
th perpendicular broad face.

bluff² (blŭf) *v.* Make pretense
strength to gain advantage etc.
rig. in poker); mislead thus. ~
Bluffing; **call person's ~,**
allenge his attempted bluff.
uff'er *n.*

Blum (blŭm), **Léon** (1872–
50). French political leader;
emier of France, 1936–7 and
46–7.

blun·der (blŭn'der) *v.* Move
ndly, stumble; make gross mis-
ke. ~ *n.* Stupid or careless
stake. **blun'der·er** *n.* **blun'-
er·ing·ly** *adv.*

blun·der·buss (blŭn'derbŭs) *n.*
ort flintlock gun with large bore,
ing many balls or slugs, used esp.
17th and 18th centuries. [cor-
pt. of Du. *donderbus* lit. thunder
n]

blunt (blŭnt) *adj.* Dull, not
nsitive; without sharp edge or
int; outspoken. **blunt'ly** *adj.*
unt'ness *n.* **blunt** *v.t.* Make less
arp or sensitive.

A **blunderbuss** is a close-range flintlock of crude design. Some were made
with a butt that could be folded under
the barrel to enable the weapon to be
carried in a long pocket in the skirt of an
overcoat.

blur (blēr) *n.* Smear of ink etc.;
dimness, confused effect. ~ *v.*
(**blurred, blur·ring**). Smear with
ink etc.; sully, disfigure; make indistinct; efface; dim.

blurb (blērb) *n.* Publisher's
description of book printed on
jacket etc.; descriptive or com-
mendatory paragraph.

blurt (blērt) *v.t.* Burst *out* with,
utter abruptly.

blush (blŭsh) *v.i.* Become red
with shame or other emotion; be
ashamed; be red or pink. ~ *n.*
Glance, glimpse; reddening of face
in shame etc.; rosy glow, flush of
light. **blush'er** *n.* **blush'ful** *adj.*
blush'ing·ly *adv.*

blus·ter (blŭs'ter) *v.* Storm
boisterously; utter overbearingly.
blus'ter·er *n.* **blus'ter·ing·ly**
adv. **blus'ter·y, blus'ter·ous** *adjs.*
bluster *n.* Boisterous blowing,
noisy self-assertive talk, threats.

Bly (blī), **Nellie** (1867–1922).
Pseudonym of Elizabeth Cochrane
Seaman; American journalist,
famous for trip made around the
world in the record time of 72 days,
6 hours, 11 minutes; had herself
committed to New York City insane
ward to write *Ten Days in a Mad-
house;* also wrote *Around the World
in Seventy-Two Days.*

BM *abbrev.* Basal metabolism;
(colloq.) bowel movement.

BMR *abbrev.* Basal metabolic
rate.

bn. *abbrev.* Battalion.

B'nai B'rith (binä' brĭth').
Jewish organization promoting
welfare of Jews and social and
educational improvement. [He-
brew, = "sons of the covenant"]

B.O. *abbrev.* Body odor; box
office.

bo·a (bō'a) *n.* (pl. **bo·as**). 1. S.
Amer. tropical nonpoisonous snake
of family Boidae that kills its prey
by constriction or compression
(pop. extended to pythons); ~
constrictor, large Brazilian
species of boa; any great crushing
snake. 2. Long round fur or feather
wrap formerly worn around throat
by women.

Bo·ad·i·ce·a (bōădisē'a). (d. 62
A.D.). British queen, led revolt
against the Romans, took poison
when finally defeated by Suetonius
Paulinus. Also **Boudicca.**

boar (bōr, bōr) *n.* Uncastrated

*The African wild **boar** (below), like
those of Asia and Europe, is dangerous
when cornered. It feeds on roots and
berries and grows to about 3 ft. high at
the shoulder.*

constrictor snake (above) is of the
a family which includes the largest
ake in the world, the anaconda.
uth American constrictors rarely
ceed 12 ft. but the Central American
oe may be 15 ft. long.

Many racing yachts and other small **boats** have hulls built from molded glass-reinforced plastics. The method allows the forming of a strong, well-shaped, and smooth hull that enables the boat to slip unhindered through the water.

1 grip	17 breast hook
2 loom	18 apron
3 shaft	19 painter
4 blade	20 stem
5 transom	21 foresheets
6 gunwale	22 mast step
7 tiller	23 top strake
8 stretcher	24 rubbing piece
9 stern sheets	25 keelson
10 rowlock	26 garboard strake
11 rising	27 keel
12 bottom boards	28 rudder
13 knee	29 pintle
14 thwart	30 gudgeon
15 rib	31 plank
16 mast	

OAR
ROWLOCK
THOLE PINS
BOWS
STERN
DIAGONAL BUILD
CARVEL BUILD
CLINKER BUILD

thwart
knee
gunwale
knee
rib (exploded)
gunwale
rib
carvel planking
wedge
clinker planking
stern post knee
bow
forepost knee
stern
keel

male swine (wild or tame); flesh of this; **wild ~**, European wild swine (*Sus scrofa*), domesticated throughout the U.S.

board (bōrd, bôrd) *n.* 1. Thin piece of timber, usu. rectangular, and of greater length than breadth; one or more pieces of this or similar substance, used in games, for posting notices, etc.; (pl.) the stage; thick stiff paper used in bookbinding etc.; **across the ~**, embracing all categories. 2. Table spread for meals; food served, daily meals provided at contract price or in return for services; official group directing organization; **~ of directors; ~ of education**, body elected or appointed to provide and maintain colleges, public schools, etc. (also SCHOOLBOARD) in public school sense; **B ~ of Trade**, association of businessmen etc. to promote trade. 3. Ship's side (only in certain phrases); (naut.) tack; **on ~**, aboard, in or into ship, train, etc. 4. **board'walk**, footway of boards or planks. **board** *v.* 1. Cover with boards. 2. Provide with, receive, stated meals at fixed rate. 3. Go on board, enter (ship, train, etc.); (naut.) come alongside and force one's way on board (ship).

board·er (bôr'der, bōr'-) *n.* One who boards with someone; boy or girl at boarding school; one who boards a ship to capture it.

board·ing (bôr'ding, bōr'-) *n.* (esp.) **board'inghouse**, house in which persons are boarded and lodged for payment; **~ school**, school in which pupils live during term, as dist. from day school.

boast (bōst) *n.* Exceedingly proud statement; cause of pride. ~ *v.* Praise oneself, make boast(s) (*of, about*); possess as thing to be proud of. **boast'er** *n.* **boast'ful** *adj.* **boast'ful·ly** *adv.* **boast'ful·ness** *n.*

boat (bōt) *n.* 1. Small open vessel; fishing vessel, mail packet, small steamer; occas. large seagoing vessel; **in the same ~**, in the same predicament or circumstances. 2. Boat-shaped dish for gravy etc. 3. **~ hook**, long pole with hook and spike; **boat'house**, shed at water's edge for keeping boat; **boat'man**, hirer, or rower or sailer of boat for hire; **boat·swain** (bō'sun), **bo'sun**, (naut.) ship's officer in charge of sails, rigging, etc., and summoning men to duty with whistle; **boat train**, train having connection with a steamer at a port. **boat** *v.i.* Go in boat, esp. for pleasure.

boat·er (bō'ter) *n.* Straw hat with flat crown and brim.

Bo·az (bō'ăz): see RUTH[1].

bob[1] (bŏb) *n.* 1. Weight on pendulum, plumb line, or kite tail. 2.

*The **boardwalk** in Atlantic City, New Jersey was the first ever, built in 1870. It extends for 5 miles and is 60 ft. wide with amusement piers built out into the ocean which enhance the festive seaside atmosphere.*

Knot of hair, tassel-shaped curl; horses's docked tail; bobbed hair. ~ *v.t.* (**bobbed, bob·bing**). Cut (hair) to hang short of the shoulders.

bob[2] (bŏb) *n.* Jerk, bouncing movement; curtsy. ~ *v.i.* (**bobbed, bob·bing**). Move up and down, dance, rebound; curtsy; **~ for**, try to catch (floating apples, etc.) with the mouth.

bob[3] (bŏb) *n.* (pl. **bob**). (Brit. slang) Shilling.

bob·bin (bŏb'ĭn) *n.* 1. Cylinder on which thread, wire, etc., may be wound; reel, spool; **~ lace**: see LACE. 2. Rounded piece of wood attached to a string, for raising door latch.

bob·ble (bŏb'el) *v.* (**-bled, -bling**). 1. Bob up and down. 2. Fumble (a ball); blunder. ~ *n.* Fumble, blunder.

bob·by (bŏb'ē) *n.* (pl. **-bies**). (Brit. slang) Policeman. [Nickname for *Robert*, in allusion to Sir Robert Peel, who was British Home Secretary when the Metropolitan Police Act was passed in 1828]

bob·by·socks,   **bob·by·sox** (bŏb'ēsŏks) *ns.pl.* Socks reaching just above the ankle, once worn esp. by teenage girls. **bob'by·sox·er** *n.* (freq. derog.) Girl wearing bobbysocks.

bob·cat (bŏb'kăt) *n.* American wildcat (*Lynx rufus*), with stumpy tail, tufted ears, and spotted reddish-brown fur.

In the second **Boer War** one of the few clear successes for British forces was achieved when Lord Roberts forced Piet Cronge's surrender at Paardeberg in February, 1900, after the destruction of his laager.

The rapid firing capacity of the **Bofors** gun makes it ideal for an anti-aircraft role. It forms part of the armament of most ships in the navies of NATO. It is also effective against small ships.

bob·o·link (bŏb′olĭngk) n. N. Amer. songbird, also called ricebird (*Dolichonyx oryzivorus*). [orig. *Bob (o') Lincoln*; imit. of its call]

bob·sled (bŏb′slĕd) n. 1. Racing sled with two pairs of runners, brake, and steering mechanism. 2. Sled formed by two short sleds operating in tandem. ~ v.i. Ride on a bobsled.

bob·stay (bŏb′stā) n. (naut.) Rope or chain used to steady a bowsprit.

bob·tail (bŏb′tāl) n. (Horse or dog with) docked tail; **tag, rag, and** ~, rabble.

bob·white (bŏb′wīt′) n. Small chunky game bird, *Colinus virginianus*, of eastern U.S., named from its call.

Boc·cac·ci·o (bōkah′chēo), **Giovanni** (1313–75). Italian novelist, poet, and humanist, author of the *Decameron*.

Boc·che·ri·ni (bōkerē′nē), **Luigi** (1740–1805). Italian composer and cellist.

Boche (bŏsh, bawsh) n. & adj. (derog. slang, esp. in World War I) German.

bock (bŏk) n. (also ~ **beer**). Strong dark-colored German beer, usu. brewed for drinking in spring months. [Ger. f. *Einbockbier*, beer from *Einbeck*, in Hanover]

bode (bōd) v. (**bod·ed, bod·ing**). Foresee, foretell (evil); portend, foreshow; promise *well, ill*.

bo·de·ga (bōdē′ga; *Span.* bawdhĕ′gah) n. (pl. **-gas** pr. -gaz; *Span.* -gahs). Wine warehouse or wineshop; (esp. in Puerto Rican city neighborhoods) grocery store. [Sp., f. L., f. Gk. *apothēkē* store]

bo·dhi·satt·va (bōdĭsăt′wǎ) n. (Buddhism) Person who is entitled by his good deeds to enter Nirvana but who, out of compassion for human suffering, delays doing so in order to save others.

bod·ice (bŏd′ĭs) n. Upper part of woman's dress, down to waist; undergarment for same part of body. [orig. (pair of) *bodies*, stays, corset]

bod·i·less (bŏd′ēlĭs) adj. Incorporeal, separated from the body.

bod·i·ly (bŏd′ĭlē) adj. Of, affecting, the human body or physical nature (opp. *spiritual*). ~ adv. With the whole bulk, as a whole.

bod·kin (bŏd′kĭn) n. 1. Thic blunt needle with large eye f threading tape or ribbon through series of loops or a hem. 2. Sma pointed instrument for piercin holes in cloth or leather; long orn mental hairpin.

Bod·lei·an (bŏd′lēan, bŏdlē **Library.** (also **the Bodlei′a** Library of Oxford University, major scholarly and British cop right library.

bod·y (bŏd′ē) n. (pl. **bod·ies** 1. Material frame of man or anima corpse. 2. Trunk apart from hea and limbs; main portion of any thing; part of vehicle etc. fitted receive the load; shank of piece type. 3. Bulk, majority. 4. Perso 5. Aggregate of persons or thing collection; **in a** ~, in a group. Piece of matter (**heavenly** ~ mass of tissue forming a structur solidity, substance; (of wine) ri full flavor. 7. ~ **English**, twistin of the body by pool player an others as if to help a ball travel in the desired path; **bod'yguard**, guard for the person (esp. of dignitary), retinue, escort; **the body politic**, the nation; **body snatcher**, (hist.) one who secretly disinters corpses to sell them for dissection; **body stocking**, woman's undergarment covering trunk and legs.

Boehme (böm), **Jakob** (1575–1624). German mystic; held that will is the original force, that every manifestation involves opposition, and that existence is a process of conflict between pairs of contrasted principles, which are ultimately resolved into a new unity.

Boer (bōr, bōr; *Du.* boor) *n.* S. Afr. farmer of Dutch origin; ~ **War**, each of two wars fought by Great Britain: the first (1880–1) against Transvaal, which, annexed by Britain in 1877, had proclaimed its independence; the 2nd, and most important (1899–1902), against the Transvaal and Orange Free State, resulting in their annexation by Great Britain.

Bo·e·thi·us (bōē'thēus), **Anicius Manlius Severinus** (*c*475–525). Roman Christian philosopher, consul, and translator of Aristotle; he wrote *De Consolatione Philosophiae*, professing Neoplatonic and stoic ideas that had great influence throughout the Middle Ages.

Bo·fors (bō'fōrz, -fors) **gun.** Clip-fed, rapid-firing, double-barreled light anti-aircraft gun. [name of a munitions works in Örebro Län, Sweden]

bog (bŏg, bawg) *n.* (Piece of) wet spongy ground, consisting chiefly of decayed or decaying moss or other vegetable matter; **bog'gy** *adj.* **bog'gi·ness** *n.* **bog'gish** *adj.* **bog** *v.t.* (**bogged, bog·ging**). Submerge in bog; ~ **down** (fig.).

bo·gey (bō'gē) *n.* (pl. **-geys**). 1. Bogy. 2. (golf) One stroke over par for a hole. 3. (military slang) Unidentified flying aircraft; enemy aircraft. ~ *v.t.* (**-geyed, -gey·ing**). (golf) Make one stroke over par on a hole. [app. jocular application of *bogy*, "something to be afraid of"]

bog·gle (bŏg'el) *v.i.* (**-gled, -gling**). Start with fright, shy; hesitate, demur, *at*.

bo·gie (bō'gē) *n.* (pl. **-gies**). Undercarriage with two or more pairs of wheels, pivoted below front part of railroad engine or ends of long railroad car, streetcar, etc., to facilitate traveling around curves.

Bo·go·tá (bōgotah'). Capital and largest city of Colombia, South America.

bo·gus (bō'gus) *adj.* Sham, fictitious, spurious.

bo·gy, bo·gey, bo·gie (bō'gē, bōog'ē) *ns.* (pl. **-gies, -geys, -gies**). 1. (esp. **Old B**~) The Devil. 2. Goblin. 3. Bugbear.

Bo·hea (bōhē') *n.* Black tea of lowest quality, the last crop of the season (in 18th c., the finest kinds of black tea). [Chin. *Wu-i* district]

Bo·he·mi·a (bōhē'mēa, -hēm'ya). Slavonic kingdom of central Europe; came under Austrian rule, 1526; by the treaty of Versailles (1919) became a province of Czechoslovakia; now a region of Czechoslovakia. **Bo·he'mi·an** *adj.* & *n.* 1. (Native, inhabitant) of Bohemia. 2. (Person, esp. artist or writer) of free and easy habits, manners, and sometimes morals (from mistaken belief that gypsies came orig. from Bohemia).

Bohr (bōr, bōr), **Niels Henrik David** (1885–1962). Danish physicist; applied the quantum theory to the problem of atomic structure; won the Nobel Prize for physics in 1922.

boil[1] (boil *n.* Hard, inflamed suppurating tumor.

boil[2] (boil) *v.* (of a liquid) Reach or be at that temperature (**boiling point**) where the vapor pressure is equal to the pressure of the atmosphere above its surface and vapor is consequently evolved in bubbles from all parts of the liquid (also used of containing vessel); be agitated by the evolution, rising, and bursting of such bubbles; bring a liquid by the application of heat to this temperature; subject to heat of boiling water, cook, be cooked thus; (fig.) be agitated with anger etc.; ~ **down**, reduce by boiling; ~ **down to**, (fig.) mean basically; ~ **over**, bubble up so as to run over sides of vessel; said also of the vessel; **boiled shirt**, dress shirt. **boil** *n.* Boiling, boiling point.

*Above: The map and flag of **Bolivia**, a land-locked country of S. America. It is about 424,000 sq. miles in area and has a population of about 5½ millions, more than half being Indians. The photographs are of Lake Titicaca (upper right) and a market scene (right).*

boil·er (boi'ler) *n.* Vessel for boiling, esp. for making steam under pressure; tank for heating water for domestic use; metal tub in which laundry is boiled; **boil'er·maker**, one who builds or repairs boilers; (colloq.) whiskey with a beer chaser.

boil·ing (boi'ling) *n.* ~ **point**: see BOIL². ~ *adj.* (esp.) ~ **hot**, (colloq.) very hot.

Bois de Bou·logne (bwah de boolawn'ye). Park in Paris, France.

Boi·se (boi'zē). Capital and largest city of Idaho, in the SW.

bois·ter·ous (boi'sterus, -strus) *adj.* Violent, rough; noisily cheerful. **bois'ter·ous·ly** *adv.* **bois'ter·ous·ness** *n.*

bold (bōld) *adj.* Courageous, enterprising, confident; forward, immodest; vigorous, free, well-marked, clear; **bold'face(d)**, (type) having a thick face; **bold-faced**, impudent. **bold'ly** *adv.* **bold'ness** *n.*

bole¹ (bōl) *n.* Stem or trunk of tree.

bole² (bōl) *n.* Fine, compact earthy or unctuous clay, usu. reddish brown with iron oxide; reddish brown.

bo·lec·tion (bōlĕk'shon) *adj.* & *n.* (Molding) placed around a panel, which it holds in a groove.

bo·le·ro (bōlār'ō, bo-) *n.* (pl. **-ros**). 1. Lively Spanish dance, music for this. 2. Short jacket coming barely to the waist.

Bol·eyn (bōōl'ĭn, bolĭn'), **Anne** (c1507–36). Second wife of English King Henry VIII and mother of Elizabeth I; she was beheaded on a charge of unfaithfulness.

bol·i·var (bŏl'iver; *Span.* bawlē-vär') *n.* (pl. **-vars, -va·res** pr. *Span.* -vah'rĕs). Monetary unit of Venezuela.

Bol·i·var (bŏl'iver; *Span.* bawlē-vär'), **Simon** (1783–1830). Venezuelan patriot and statesman, called "the Liberator"; founded (1819) the Republic of Colombia, uniting Venezuela, New Granada (Colombia), and Ecuador; became dictator of Peru; formed the Republic of Bolivia.

Bo·liv·i·a (bōlĭv'ēa). S. Ame inland republic, formerly part of th Incan Empire, and subsequently the Spanish possession of Per capital, La Paz. **Bo·liv'i·an** *adj. n.*

boll (bōl) *n.* Rounded seed po as in flax or cotton; ~ **weevi** weevil (*Anthonomus grandis*), d structive to the cotton plant.

Bo·lo·gna (bawlawn'yah Manufacturing city and railroa center in N. Italy; site of olde European university, founde 1088.

bo·lo·gna (bolō'nē, -lōn'ya) Large sausage of veal, bacon, por etc. [orig. made at BOLOGNA]

bo·lom·e·ter (bōlŏm'eter, bo *n.* Electrical instrument f measuring radiant heat. **bo·lo met·ric** (bōlomĕt'rĭk) *adj.*

bo·lo·ney (bolō'nē) = BALONE

Bol·she·vik, bol·she·vik (bŏl shevĭk, bŏl'-; *Russ.* bawlshevēk') *n*

A replica of the atom **bomb** that destroyed Hiroshima on 6 August 1945 and killed or injured about 75,000 people. Many thousands died later as a result of exposure to radioactivity.

& *adjs.* (pl. **-viks, -vik·i** pr. -vĭkē, -vēkē; *Russ.* -vĭkē´). 1. (Member) of the Revolutionary party led by Lenin, which seized power in Russia in 1917 in the name of the proletariat and based its rule on the ideas of Karl Marx. 2. (loosely) (Of) a socialist or person suspected of subversive ideas. **Bol'she·vist, bol'she·vist** *ns.* & *adjs.* **Bol·she·vis'tic, bol·she·vis·tic** *adj.* **Bol'-she·vism** *n.* [Russ. *Bol'shevik* majority man (i.e. member of majority group in the Social-Democratic Party) f. *bol'shiv* more]

bol·ster (bōl'ster) *n.* Long, stuffed cushion for bed, sofa, etc. ~ *v.t.* (usu. with *up*) Support with bolster, prop; aid and abet, countenance; give fictitious support to (something unable to stand of itself); pad. **bol'ster·er** *n.*

bolt¹ (bōlt) *n.* 1. Short heavy arrow of crossbow. 2. Discharge of lightning; ~ **from the blue,** complete surprise. 3. Door fastening of sliding bar and staple; sliding part of mortise lock. 4. Sliding part of rifle that contains striker and mainspring and that locks the breech. 5. Metal pin with head, for holding things together, usu. secured by riveting or by a nut. 6. Length of fabric woven on a loom in one operation. ~ *adv.* ~ **upright,** stiffly upright.

bolt² (bōlt) *v.* 1. Dart off or away; (of horse) break from control, make violent dash. 2. Gulp down (food) hastily or unchewed. 3. Fasten (door etc.) with bolt; fasten together with bolts. ~ *n.* Sudden start; running away.

bolt³ (bōlt) *v.t.* Sift, pass through a sieve.

bo·lus (bō'lus) *n.* (pl. **-lus·es**) Large pill, esp. one administered to an animal; lump of food at moment of swallowing.

bomb (bŏm) *n.* Case filled with explosive, inflammable material, gas, etc., fired from a gun, dropped from aircraft, or thrown or deposited by hand; **the B~,** (esp.) nuclear bomb; ~ **bay,** compartment in aircraft for holding bombs; **bomb'proof,** strong enough to resist explosion of a bomb; **bomb'-shell,** artillery bomb; shell; (fig.) cause of great surprise. **bomb** *v.* Assail with bombs, throw bombs.

bom·bard (bŏm'bärd) *n.* Earliest kind of cannon, throwing stone ball or very large shot. ~ (bŏmbärd´) *v.t.* Batter with shot and shell; assail persistently with abuse, argument, etc.; (phys.) subject to a stream of (charged) atoms

The city of **Bombay** is built on low lying islands near the coast, where it forms the only deep-water harbor of western India. The city is a great commercial center and has a thriving cotton spinning industry.

or subatomic particles. **bom·-bard'er, bom·bard'ment** *ns.*

bom·bar·dier (bŏmberdēr´) *n.* Member of aircraft crew who aims and releases bombs from aircraft.

bom·bar·don (bŏm'berdon, bŏmbär´-) *n.* (mus.) Low-pitched brass instrument; organ stop imitating this.

bom·bast (bŏm'băst) *n.* Pompous language, tall talk. **bom·-bas·tic** (bŏmbăs'tĭk) *adj.* **bom·-bas'ti·cal·ly** *adv.* [orig. = cotton wool, used in 16th c. as padding for clothes; f. Gk. *bombux* silk, silkworm]

Bom·bay (bŏmbā´). Capital city of Maharashtra, on W. coast of

India; ~ **duck,** dried, salted fish used as a relish with curry.

bom·ba·zine (bŏmbazēn´, bŏm'bazēn) *n.* Twilled dress material of worsted formerly used for mourning.

bombe (bŏm, bŏmb; *Fr.* bawnb) *n.* Conical or cup-shaped frozen melon or mold dessert containing layers of ice cream.

bomb·er (bŏm'er) *n.* Aircraft designed to carry bombs.

bo·na fide (bō'na fīd, bŏn'a, bō'na fīdē). Genuine, authentic, sincere.

bo·nan·za (bonăn'za, bō-) *n.* Prosperity, large output (esp. of mines); run of luck, fine weather, good crops, etc. ~ *adj.* Yielding great wealth or a large output. [Sp., = "fair weather"]

Bo·na·parte (bō'napärt). Name of Corsican family including NAPOLEON I; **Joseph** ~, (1775–1844), brother of Napoleon I; king of Naples 1806; king of Spain 1808.

Bon·a·ven·ture (bŏn´avĕncher, bŏnavĕn´-), **St.** (1221–74). John of Fidanza, Italian Franciscan, scholastic theologian, and mystic; commemorated July 14.

bon·bon (bŏn´bŏn; *Fr.* bawn̄-bawn̄´) *n.* Piece of confectionery, sweet.

bond[1] (bŏnd) *n.* 1. (archaic, chiefly pl.) Thing restraining bodily freedom, shackle; restraining or uniting force; connection; adhesion between two surfaces etc.; (chem.) = VALENCE bond. 2. Binding agreement; document by which one binds oneself and one's heirs etc. to pay a sum to others; government's or public company's document undertaking to repay borrowed money, usu. with fixed rate of interest; any of various kinds of investment; **in ~**, (of goods) stored under charge of customs in bonded warehouse until importer pays duty; **bond´holder**, person holding bond(s) of another person or of company or government; **bond paper**, paper of superior quality as used for bonds. 3. Bond paper. **bond** *v.t.* Bind together; connect with a bond; put (goods) into bond; **bonded warehouse**, customs warehouse in which goods in bond are stored.

bond[2] (bŏnd) *adj.* (archaic) In serfdom or slavery; not free; so **bond´maid, bond´man, bond´ servant, bond´slave, bonds´-man**.

bond·age (bŏn´dĭj) *n.* Serfdom, slavery; subjection to some influence or obligation.

Bond (bŏnd) **Street.** London street noted for its fashionable shops. [named after Sir Thomas *Bond*, who began its construction c1688]

bone (bōn) *n.* One of the parts making up the skeleton of a human being or other vertebrate; substance (mainly calcium phosphate and fibrous protein) of which these consist; article made of this substance; strip of stiff substance in corset etc.; (pl.) skeleton, bodily frame, body, mortal remains; **~ to pick, ~ of contention**, subject of dispute; **make no ~s of** or **about**, make no attempt to hide; admit without hesitation; **~ china**, chinaware made of clay mixed with bonedust or phosphate of lime; **~-dry**, quite dry; **bone´head**, blockhead; **bone meal**, animal food, fertilizer, made from finely crushed bone. **bone** *v.t.* (**boned, bon·ing**). Take out bones from; stiffen with bone. **bone´less, bone´like** *adjs.*

bon·fire (bŏn´fīr) *n.* Large fire in the open air.

bong (bŏng) *n.* Deep, resonant sound as of a large bell. **~** *v.i.* Produce such a sound.

bon·go[1] (bŏng´gō, bawng´-) *n.*

(pl. **-gos**, collect. **-go**). Large striped African antelope (*Boocercus eurycerus*), related to bushbuck, living in dense forests.

bon·go[2] (bŏng´gō, bawng´-) *n.* (pl. **-gos, -goes**). (also **~ drum**) One of a pair of small drums played with the fingers.

bon·ho·mie, bon·hom·mie (bŏn´omē) *ns.* Good nature; geniality.

bon·i·face (bŏn´ifās) *n.* Jovial innkeeper. [name of the jovial innkeeper in Farquhar's *Beaux Stratagem* (1707)]

Bon·i·face (bŏn´ifās), **St.** (680–755). Winfrith, English Benedictine, apostle to the Germans under Pope Gregory II; commemorated June 5.

bon mot (bawn´ mō´; *Fr.* bawn̄ mō´) (pl. **bons mots** pr. bawn´mōz; *Fr.* bawn̄ mō´). Witty saying [Fr.]

Bonn (bŏn). Capital of the German Federal Republic, in the NW., on the Rhine River; site of

The greatest of the **Bonaparte** family was Napoleon I, whose portrait by Jacques Louis David is shown here. Napoleon established members of his family on various European thrones in the early 1800s.

famous 13th c. cathedral.

Bon·nard (bawnăr´), **Pierre** (1867–1947). French impressionist painter, lithographer, and etcher.

bon·net (bŏn´ĭt) *n.* 1. Woman's outdoor headdress with strings. 2. (Sc.) Man's cap. 3. (Brit.) Automobile hood.

Bon·ne·ville (bŏn´evĭl) **Salt Flats.** Stretch of barren land in NW. Utah; part of the bed of prehistoric Bonneville Lake; site where several world records were made in automobile speed tests.

bon·ny, bon·nie (bŏn´ē) *adjs.* (**-ni·er, -ni·est**). 1. (chiefly Sc.) Comely. 2. Healthy looking. **bon´ni·ly** *adv.* **bon´ni·ness** *n.*

bon·sai (bŏn´sī, bŏn´-) *n.* Potted plant or shrub artificially dwarfed

Cross-section of head of femur   Cross-section of joint   Articular surface

1	periosteum	11	simple fracture
2	compact bone	12	comminuted fracture
3	marrow	13	impacted fracture
4	bone	14	Pott's fracture
5	articular cartilage		
6	synovial membrane		
7	capsular ligament		
8	condyle		
9	cartilaginous head of child's femur		
10	epiphysis at head of child's ulna		

The body is supported and protected by **bone** of phenomenal strength. The cranium acts as a helmet to protect the brain. The skull (right) is of Australopithecus but the bone is like that of modern skulls. Limb bones, such as the femur, can accept stresses of over 2 tons per sq. inch.

Below: The 3-foot horns of the **bongo** make it a prized trophy for hunters. Found in equatorial Africa, the bongo is a large antelope, males standing about 4 ft. high at the shoulder.

as ornament; method of cultivating this. [Jap.]

bo·nus (bō′nus) n. Something to the good, into the bargain; (esp.) extra dividend to company's shareholders, distribution of profits to holders of insurance policies, gratuity to employees beyond their wages; ~ **army**, demonstration by war veterans in Washington, D.C., in 1932 demanding bonuses for their military service in World War I.

bon vi·vant (bawn vēvahn′) (pl. **bons vi·vants** pr. bawn vēvahn′). Gourmand. [Fr.]

bon voy·age (bŏn voiahzh′; Fr. bawn vwahyahzh′). Pleasant journey (used as expression of farewell to a traveler). [Fr.]

bon·y (bō′nē) adj. (**bon·i·er, bon·i·est**). Of, like, bone; bigboned; with little flesh; ~ **fishes**, those (including most of the common species) that have bones as opp. to cartilage. **bon′i·ness** n.

bonze (bŏnz) n. (European name for) Japanese or Chinese Buddhist priest.

boo (bōō) int., n. (pl. **boos**), & v. (**booed, boo·ing**). (Make) sound of disapproval or contempt (at); jeer (at); sound made to frighten, as by ghost or person wishing to startle or surprise another.

boo·by (bōō′bē) n. (pl. **-bies**). Stupid or babyish person; ~ **prize**, prize given in derision or fun to player with worst score; ~ **trap**, (mil.) harmless-looking object con-

cealing an explosive charge, designed to go off when disturbed.

boo·dle (bōō′del) n. (slang) Money, esp. for political bribery.

boo·gie-woo·gie (bōōg′ē wōōg′-ē, bōō′gē wōō′gē) n. (also **boogie**) Style of playing blues or jazz, usu. on the piano, marked by persistent bass rhythm.

book (bōōk) n. 1. Treatise written or printed on a number of sheets which are folded, fastened together in hinge-wise fashion at the folded edges, and protected by a binding or cover; in antiquity, set of written sheets pasted together to form a roll; literary composition that would fill

a book; main division of literary composition or of the Bible; libretto; anything from which one may learn; (colloq.) magazine. 2. Blank sheets of paper for keeping accounts, taking notes, etc., fastened together in the shape of a book; anything bound together in this shape, as checks, stamps, tickets, etc. 3. Betting book, record of bets made; (pl.) merchants' accounts. 4. **book′binder, book′-binding**, binder, binding, of books; **book′case**, case containing bookshelves; **book club**, business that sells books through the mails at reduced prices to its members;

Full Binding   Half Binding   Quarter Binding   Yapp Binding

Signature
Channelling
Spine liner
Gauze
Curved spine
Endpaper   Board
Cloth

In the 1st century A.D. books began to supersede scrolls, and throughout the Middle Ages they were copied and illuminated by monks. Top right: The copy of Matthew Paris's 'Chronica Majora' dates from the 13th century. Top left: The technique of printing was brought to England in 1476.

book'ends, pair of (ornamental) props used to keep row of books upright; **book'keeper, book'-keeping**, one who keeps, art of keeping, accounts of merchant etc.; **book learning**, knowledge gained from books not life; **book'maker**, (esp.) professional gambler who accepts bets on horse racing and other sports; **book'mobile**, mobile library; **book'plate**, label with owner's name for pasting into books; **book'shelf**, shelf for standing books on; **book value**, value of a commodity as entered in a firm's books (opp. *market value*); **book work**, study involving reading, opp. practical experiment etc.; paper work; **book'worm**, larva of various moths or beetles, that burrows into or destroys pages of books; (fig.) person who is always poring over books. **book** *v.* Enter in book or list; (esp. Brit.) secure seat etc. in advance; (Brit.) issue, obtain, ticket for journey etc.; enter (name) in police register etc. for alleged offense.
book·ie (book'ē) *n.* (slang) Bookmaker.
book·ish (book'ish) *adj.* Literary; addicted to reading books. **book'ish·ly** *adv.* **book'ish·ness** *n.*

book·let (book'lit) *n.* Small usu. paper-covered book, pamphlet.
Boole (bool), **George** (1815–1864). English mathematician and logician; **Bool'ean algebra**, abstract system of postulates and symbols applicable to logical problems.
boom[1] (boom) *n.* Long spar used to keep the bottom of a sail extended; floating barrier across mouth of a river, entrance to a harbor etc.; beam of derrick supporting weights; extendable arm carrying microphone or camera.
boom[2] (boom) *n. & v.i.* (Make, speak, etc., with) deep resonant sound.
boom[3] (boom) *v. & n.* (Show) sudden increase or development (esp. of prices, commercial ventures, etc.: opp. SLUMP).
boom·er·ang (boo'merăng) *n.* Australian missile of thin curved wood that can be thrown so as to return to the thrower; (fig.) scheme etc. that backfires on its originator. ~ *v.i.* Backfire on originator.
boon[1] (boon) *n.* Benefit, advantage.
boon[2] (boon) *adj.* ~ **companion**, congenial companion.
boon·docks (boon'dŏks) *n.pl.*

(slang) Rough or isolated country [Tagalog *bundok* = mountain]
boon·dog·gle (boon'dŏgel) *n. & v.* (**-gled, -gling**). (slang) (Engage in) trivial or unnecessary work.
Boone (boon), **Daniel** (1735–1820). American pioneer; explored and opened up Kentucky for settlement.
boor (boor) *n.* Ill-mannered fellow. **boor'ish** *adj.* **boor'ish·ly** *adv.* **boor'ish·ness** *n.*
boost (boost) *v.t.* 1. Push from below; advance the progress of by praise. 2. Raise power of electromotive force in (engine, circuit etc.). ~ *n.* Boosting. **boost'er** *n.* (esp.) Auxiliary rocket giving acceleration; one who praises, esp. an enthusiastic supporter; (med.) dose increasing or renewing effect of earlier one.
boot[1] (boot) *n.* Advantage (now only in **to** ~, as well). ~ *v.t.* (archaic; usu. impers. & abs.) Do good (*to*), avail. **boot'less** *adj* Unavailing.
boot[2] (boot) *n.* 1. Outer foot covering of leather etc., reaching above the ankle; **give (person) the** ~, dismiss; **boot'black**, shoeshine; see SHOE def. 3; **boot'jack**, contrivance for pulling off boots.

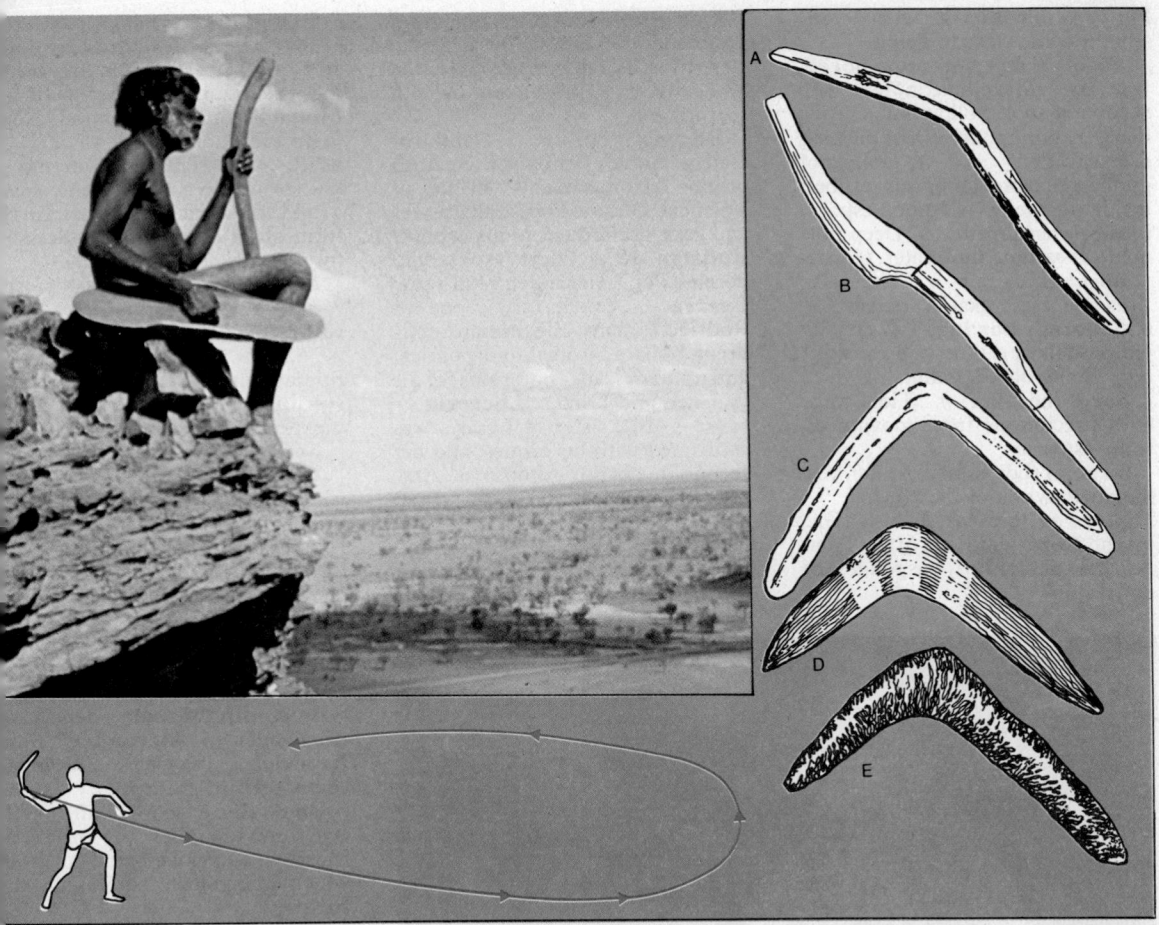

Top left: Australian Aboriginals can use the **boomerang** skillfully in hunting to stun small animals. There are two main types of this missile: straight fliers (A and B) and returners (C, D and E). The missile's aerodynamic shape, plano-convex in section, enables it to 'fly', giving it a range of about 200 yards in straight flight. Lower left: A simple return flight is useful if the hunter misses his quarry. Right: A and B are neolithic boomerangs found in East Jutland; C, D and E are Australian returning boomerangs.

boot′lace, lace fastening boots; **boot′leg**, smuggled, sold illicitly; **boot′legger, boot′legging**, smuggler, smuggling, of liquor (esp. during the prohibition period); **boot′licker**, (slang) toady. 2. (hist.) Instrument of torture encasing the foot. 3. (Brit.) Automobile trunk. **boot** v.t. Kick; (slang) kick (person) out (of the house, of employment, etc.). **boot′ed** adj. Wearing boots.

boot·ee (boo′tē) n. Infant's knitted or crocheted boot.

booth (booth, boodh) n. (pl. **booths** pr. boodhz, booths). Temporary shelter of canvas etc., covered stall in market, tent at fair, etc.; compartment, as **telephone ~**, one containing a telephone; **polling ~**, place where one votes at election.

Booth[1] (booth), **Edwin Thomas** (1833–93). American actor; his brother, **John Wilkes**, (1838–65), also an actor, assassinated President Abraham Lincoln, 1865.

Booth[2] (booth; Brit. boodh), **William** (1829–1912). English

revivalist preacher, founder and first general of the Salvation Army.

boo·ty (boo′tē) n. (pl. **-ties**). Plunder or profit acquired in common and to be divided; spoil, prize, plunder.

booze (booz) n. (colloq.) Alcoholic drink; a drinking bout. **~** v.i. (**boozed, booz·ing**). Drink deeply, go on drinking. **booz′er** n. Drinker. **booz′y** adj. (**booz·i·er, booz·i·est**).

Bo·phu·that·swa·na (bōfoo-thahtswah′nah). Republic in S. central Africa; achieved independence from Republic of South Africa, December 1977; capital Mmabatho.

bor·age (ber′ij, bor′-, bar′-) n. Blue-flowered, hairy-leaved plant (Borago officinalis).

bo·rate (bor′āt, bor′-, -ĭt) n. Salt of boric acid. **bo′rat·ed** adj.

bo·rax (bor′ăks, bor′-) n. (pl. **bo·rax·es, bo·ra·ces** pr. bor′-asēz, bor′-). Sodium borate ($Na_2B_4O_7.10H_2O$), a white crystalline substance giving a slightly alkaline solution, used in manufacture of glass and ceramics and as a

cleansing agent.

bor·a·zon (bor′azŏn, bor′-) n. Crystalline compound of boron nitride, extremely hard and resistant to oxidation at high temperatures.

Bor·deaux (bordō′). City and port of SW. France; any of the wines of the district about Bordeaux, including Graves, Sauternes, and Medoc.

Bor·den (bor′den), **Lizzie Andrew** (1860–1927). Central figure in famous American murder trial in Fall River, Massachusetts, 1892; tried for the ax murder of her father and stepmother, but acquitted.

bor·der (bor′der) n. Side, edge, boundary or part near it; frontier of country; continuous belt around garden or part of it, or along path, etc.; distinct edging for strength or ornament or definition around or along anything; **bor′derland**, land or district on or near a border (also fig.); **bor′derline**, strip of land along border; (adj.) near the margin of anything; uncertain or indefinite; marginal, as in **~** case. **border** v.

Put or be a border to; (also ~ **on**) adjoin; come close to being.

bore[1] (bōr, bor) v. (**bored, bor·ing**). Make hole in, usu. with revolving tool; hollow out evenly; make by boring, persistent pushing or excavation. ~ n. 1. Hollow of gunbarrel; diameter of this, caliber; inside diameter of tube, esp. in musical instrument. 2. Deep hole made in earth to find water, oil, etc.

bore[2] (bōr, bor) n. Nuisance; tiresome, esp. talkative, person. ~ v.t. (**bored, bor·ing**). Weary by tedious talk or dullness. **bore′dom** adj. Being bored, ennui.

bore[3] (bōr, bor) n. Tidal wave with precipitous front moving up some estuaries.

bo·re·al (bōr′ēal, bor′-) adj. Of the north wind; of the North.

Bo·re·as (bōr′ēas, bor′-). (Gk. myth.) North wind, son of the Titan Astraeus and of Eos, the goddess of dawn.

Bor·ghe·se (bōrgĕ′zĕ). Name of Italian noble family from Siena; noted for its famous art collection and active in politics from the 16th to 19th c.

Bor·gia (bōr′ja). Name of Italian noble family of Spanish origin: **Alfonso de** ~, bishop of Valencia, became Pope Calixtus III and gave preferment to his nephew **Rodrigo de** ~ (1431–1503), who became Pope Alexander VI in 1492; **Cesare** ~ (1475–1507), one of Rodrigo's many illegitimate children, Italian cardinal and political and military leader notorious for his violence and crimes; **Lucrezia** ~ (1480–1519), sister of Cesare, was associated with his crimes, and her second husband, Alfonso of Aragon, was murdered by his direction; she later married Alfonso d'Este, heir of the Duke of Ferrara, and her court became a center for artists, poets, and scholars.

Bor·glum (bōr′glum), **Gutzo** (1867–1941). American sculpt and painter best known for sculping the figures of presidents Mount Rushmore in South Dakot

bo·ric (bōr′ĭk, bor′-) adj. **acid,** acid (H_3BO_3) occurring hot springs in some volcanic area a mild antiseptic, widely used in t form of an ointment as a dressin for wounds and sores.

born (bōrn) adj.: see BEAR[2]; (esp ~ **of,** owing origin to; ~ **foo idiot,** etc., utter, hopeless, fool, et ~ **again,** regenerate, (esp. of fundamentalist Christian) rebor spiritually; ~ **yesterday,** naiv inexperienced, simple.

borne (bōrn, born): see BEAR[2].

Bor·ne·o (bōr′nēo). Larg island of Malay archipelago, com prising (1) Kalimantan, a region o Indonesia; (2) Sabah and Sarawal formerly British colonies, now part of Malaysia; (3) Brunei, a Britis protected State.

Born·holm (bōrn′hōm, -hŏlm) Danish island in the Baltic, 22 square miles in area.

Bo·ro·din (bōr′odĭn, -dēn; Russ bawrawdēn′), **Alexander Por firyevich** (1834–87). Russia composer and chemist.

Bo·ro·di·no (bŏrŏdē′nō). Vil lage some 120 miles (193 km) W. o Moscow; scene of a battle (1812) i which Napoleon defeated th Russians.

bo·ron (bōr′ŏn, bor′-) n. (chem. Dark-brown or greenish-brow nonmetallic solid element; symbo B, at. no. 5, at. wt. 10.81.

bor·ough (bĕr′ō, bŭr′ō) n. In corporated town or village; **pocke** ~, (Brit. hist.) borough in which election of member of parliamen was controlled by one perso **rotten** ~, (Brit. hist.) one that n longer had any real constituency.

bor·row (băr′ō, bor′ō) v.t Obtain or take temporary use of (something to be returned); adopt use without being the true or original owner or inventor, import from an alien source; **borrowed time,** unexpected extension o time, esp. of life. **bor′row·er** n.

borscht, borsht (bōrsht), **borsch** (bōrsh) ns. Beet soup served hot or cold, often with sour cream, made esp. in Russia and Poland.

Bor·stal (bōr′stal) n. One of a number of institutions in Great Britain to which young offenders may be sent for reformative train-

*The world's third largest island, **Borneo,** has about 287,000 sq. miles of dense jungle and rugged mountains that make communications difficult. The rivers are navigable and small boats carry trade to villages of the interior. The photograph shows a Dyak woman, with tattooed hands, and her children.*

*Established in 1630 by John Winthrop the elder, **Boston** has grown to be the largest city in New England. It is a busy port and a market for fish and wool. It has industries for food processing and for textile manufacture.*

ing; **~ boy**, a boy in or from such an institution. [f. *Borstal*, village in Kent where first experimental training was carried out]

bort (bôrt) *n.* Coarse diamonds; diamond fragments made in cutting.

bor·zoi (bôr′zoi) *n.* (pl. **-zois**). Dog of large high-standing breed, called also Russian or Siberian wolfhound, of greyhound type, but with thick silky coat, usu. white with yellow markings. [Russ. *bórziy* swift]

bos·cage (bŏs′kĭj) *n.* Mass of growing trees or shrubs; thicket, grove.

Bosch (bŏsh, bawsh), **Hieronymus** (1450–1516). Original name, van Aken; Dutch painter noted for caricatures and fantasy representations of monstrosities and gruesome subjects.

bosh (bŏsh) *n.* (slang) Contemptible nonsense. [Turk., = "empty," "worthless" (popularized by Morier's novel *Ayesha*, 1834)]

bosk·y (bŏs′kē) *adj.* (**bosk·i·er, bosk·i·est**). Wooded, bushy.

Bos·ni·a (bŏz′nēa). Federal unit of Yugoslavia, formerly a province of the Austro-Hungarian Empire.

Bos′ni·an *adj. & n.*

bos·om (bŏoz′om, bŏo′zom) *n.* Breast; enclosure formed by breast and arms; breast of dress, space between dress and breast; surface of sea, ground, etc.; heart, thoughts, desires, etc.; **~ friend**, especially intimate or beloved friend.

Bos·po·rus (bŏs′perus), **Bos·pho·rus** (bŏs′ferus). Strait connecting the Black Sea and the Sea of Marmara.

boss[1] (baws, bŏs) *n.* Protuberance; round metal knob or stud on center of shield or ornamental work; (archit.) projection, freq. carved, at intersecting point of vault ribs. **boss′y**[1] *adj.* (**boss·i·er, boss·i·est**).

boss[2] (baws, bŏs) *n.* Master, person in authority; employer, manager, supervisor; politician who controls a political organization. **~ v.t.** Be master or manager of. **boss′y**[2] *adj.* (**boss·i·er, boss·i·est**). Domineering. [orig. U.S., f. Du. *baas* master]

bos·sa no·va (bŏs′a nō′va). Brazilian dance like samba; music for it.

Bos·ton (baws′ton, bŏs′-). Capital city and seaport of Massachusetts, founded *c*1630 and named after Boston, town in Lincolnshire, England; **~ Tea Party**, throwing of a cargo of tea into Boston harbor by colonists, 1773, as a protest against the British tea tax, a prelude to the Revolutionary War. **Bos·to·ni·an** (bawstō′nēan, bŏs-) *adj. & n.*

bo·sun (bō′sun) *n.* (naut.) Boatswain (see BOAT).

Bos·well (bŏz′wĕl, -wel), **James** (1740–94). Scotsman, a lawyer who became a friend of Samuel Johnson and recorded his conversation in a biography published in 1791. **Bos·well·i·an** (bŏzwĕl′ēan) *adj.* **Bos·well·ize** *v.* (**-ized, -iz·ing**).

bot (bŏt) *n.* Parasitic larva of the **bot′fly**, an insect of genus *Oestrus;* **botts**, disease of horses, cattle, etc., caused by this.

bot·a·nize (bŏt′anīz) *v.i.* (**-nized, -niz·ing**). Study plants, esp. by seeking them as they grow.

bot·a·ny (bŏt′anē) *n.* (pl. **-nies**). Science of plants. **bo·tan·ic** (botăn′ĭk), **bo·tan′i·cal** *adjs.* (esp.) **~ garden**, garden for the display and study of plants. **bo·tan′i·cal·ly** *adv.* **bot·a·nist** (bŏt′anĭst) *n.*

Bot·a·ny (bŏt′anē) **Bay.** Bay on E. coast of New South Wales, Australia, (5 miles, 8 km, S. of modern Sydney) where Capt. Cook first landed in 1770, so named because of the variety of its plant life; site of an 18th-c. English penal settlement.

botch (bŏch) *n.* Bungled work. **~ v.t.** Spoil by unskillful work, bungle. **botch′er, botch′er·y** *ns.* **botch′y** *adj.* (**botch·i·er, botch·i·est**).

both (bōth) *adj. & pron.* The two (and not merely one of them); the pair (of). **~ adv.** **~ ... and**, not only ... but also.

both·er (bŏdh′er) *v.* Pester, worry; be troublesome; worry oneself, take trouble. **~ n.** Minor trouble, worry; fuss; worried state. **~ int.** Exclamation of impatience. **both·er·a·tion** (bŏdherā′shon) *n. & int.* Bother. **both·er·some** (bŏdh′ersom) *adj.* Annoying, troublesome.

Both·ni·a (bŏth′nēa), **Gulf of.** Northern arm of the Baltic Sea between Sweden and Finland.

Bot·swa·na (bŏtswah′nah). Republic of south central Africa; capital, Gaborone.

bott (bŏt): see BOT.

Bot·ti·cel·li (bŏtĭchĕl′ē), **Sandro** (1447–1510). Alessandro Filipepi, Florentine painter of the Renaissance.

bot·tle (bŏt′el) *n.* Narrow-necked vessel of glass or plastic

Madame de Pompadour was a pupil o.
her portrait painter, **Francois Boucher**
His elegant paintings made him the
most fashionable artist of his day and
brought him theater commissions too.

(orig. of leather) for storing liquid;
amount of liquid in it; feeding
bottle; ~-fed, (of infant or young
animal) fed on milk etc. from a
feeding bottle, not from breast; ~
glass, coarse dark-green glass; ~
green, dark green; **bot′tleneck**,
narrow stretch of road, narrow outlet, esp. one causing congestion of
traffic (freq. fig.); **bottle-nosed
dolphin, whale**, dolphin of genus
Tursiops, whale of genus *Hyper-
oödon*, with bottle-shaped snout;
bottle party, party to which guests
contribute drinks; **bottle washer**,
factotum, underling. **bottle** *v.t.*
(-tled, -tling). Store in bottles; ~
up, conceal, restrain for a time.
bot′tler *n.*

bot·tom (bŏt′om) *n.* 1. Lowest
part, part on which thing rests;
buttocks; seat (of chair). 2. Ground
under water of lake etc.; river basin
etc., low-lying land. 3. Less honorable end of table, class, etc., person
occupying this. 4. Keel, horizontal
part near keel, hull; ship, esp. as
cargo carrier. 5. Basis, origin;
essential character, reality; **at the
~ of**, causing, responsible for.
bottom *adj.* Lowest; last; ~ **line**,
line showing profit or loss in a
financial statement; final consideration. **bottom** *v.* Put bottom to;
base *on.*

bot·tom·less (bŏt′omlĭs) *adj.*
Unfathomable.

bot·u·lism (bŏch′ulĭzem) *n.*
Poisoning caused by eating food
that contains *botulinus* toxin, an
exceptionally powerful toxin
poisonous to nerve tissue, produced
by a bacillus (*Clostridium botu-*
linum) usu. in preserved foods that
have been imperfectly sterilized.

Bou·cher (booshā′), **François**
(1703–70). French rococo painter
of elegantly artificial pastorals.

bou·clé (booklā′) *n.* Yarn of
looped or curled ply; fabric of this.

Bou·dic·ca (boodĭk′a) =
BOADICEA.

bou·doir (bood′wār, -wōr) *n.*
Woman's private sitting room,
dressing room, or bedroom. [Fr.,
= "sulking place" (*bouder* sulk)]

bouf·fant (boofahn′) *adj.* Puffed
out.

Bou·gain·ville (boogănvēl′).
Largest of the Solomon Islands in
the SW. Pacific Ocean, part of the
trust territory of New Guinea.

Bou·gain·ville (boogănvēl′),
Louis Antoine de (1729–1811).
French navigator, military leader,
and scientist.

**bou·gain·vil·le·a, bou·gain·-
vil·lae·a** (boogĭnvĭl′ēa, -vĭl′ya) *ns.*
Tropical climbing plant of genus
B~, with large bright-colored
bracts. [named after L. A. de
BOUGANVILLE]

bough (bow) *n.* Tree branch.

bought (bawt): see BUY.

bou·gie (boo′jē, -zhē, boozhē′) *n.*
Wax candle; thin, flexible surgical
instrument for exploring, dilating,
etc., passages of the body. [*Bougie*,
Algerian town with wax trade]

bouil·la·baisse (bool′yabās,
boolyabās′; *Fr.* booyăbĕs′) *n.* Provençal dish of various kinds of
Mediterranean fish stewed in water
or spiced white wine; fish and shellfish stew.

bouil·lon (bool′yŏn, -yon; *Fr.*
booyawn′) *n.* Broth.

boul·der (bōl′der) *n.* Large
irregular water worn or weather
worn stone; (geol.) rounded rock
fragment about the size of a basketball or larger.

Boul·der (bōl′der) **Dam.** Former name of HOOVER DAM on the
Colorado River.

boul·e·vard (bool′evārd, boo′-
le-) *n.* Wide city street, often
lined with trees or landscaped.

Boulle (bool). Name of a French
family of cabinet makers (esp.
André Charles ~, 1642–1732),
noted for ebony furniture inlaid
with brass, tortoise shell, etc., and
mounted with gilt bronze.

boulle, buhl, boule (bool) *adjs.*
& *ns.* (Furniture, ornament) of the
type made by the BOULLE family.

bounce (bowns) *n.* Rebound.
~ *v.* (**bounced, bounc·ing**).
Rebound, bound like a ball; throw
oneself about; burst *into, out of*, etc.;
swagger; (of check) be returned
because the account has insufficient
funds to cover it. **bounc′ing** *adj.*
Big and lively; boisterous; **bouncing Bet**: see SOAPWORT. **bounc′y**
adj. (**bounc·i·er, bounc·i·est**).
That bounces; springy.

bound[1] (bownd) *n.* Limit of
territory etc.; (pl.) limitation,
restriction, limit beyond which
schoolchildren, students, soldiers,
etc., may not pass. ~ *v.t.* Set
bounds to, limit; be boundary of.
bound′less *adj.*

bound[2] (bownd) *n.* Springy
movement upward or forward;
recoil (of ball etc.). ~ *v.i.* (of ball
etc.) Recoil from wall or ground,
bounce; spring, leap, or advance
lightly.

bound[3] (bownd) *adj.* Ready to
start, having started (*for*).

bound[4] (bownd): see BIND.

bound·a·ry (bown′derē, -drē)
n. (pl. **-ries**). That which serves
to indicate bounds or limits of anything; bounds.

bound·en (bown′den) *adj.*
Obliged, beholden, indebted, esp.
~ **duty.**

bound·er (bown′der) *n.* (slang)
Cad.

boun·te·ous (bown′tēus) *adj.*
Beneficent, liberal; freely bestowed. **boun′te·ous·ly** *adv.*
boun′te·ous·ness *n.*

boun·ti·ful (bown′tiful) *adj.*
Bounteous; generous. **boun′ti-
ful·ly** *adv.* **boun′ti·ful·ness** *n.*

boun·ty (bown′tē) *n.* (pl. **-ties**).
Munificence, liberality in giving;
gift, gratuity; subsidy; prize money,
esp. that offered by a government.

Boun·ty (bown′tē), **Mutiny of**

The flowers of the **bougainvillea** have a flamboyance that attracts gardeners throughout the world. The plant is native to South America.

*Above: Replica of the **Bounty** at St. Petersburgh, Florida. This supply ship was made famous in 1789 by the mutiny of the crew, led by Fletcher Christian, on a voyage from Tahiti.*

*Below: **Boulder Dam** was completed in 1936 and renamed for President Herbert Hoover in 1947. Straddling the Arizona-Nevada border, it services the surrounding area.*

the. Mutiny (April 28, 1789) of the crew of H.M.S. *Bounty*, bound from Tahiti to the Cape of Good Hope, against their captain, Lieut. BLIGH. He and eighteen companions, set adrift in an open boat, succeeded in reaching Timor, nearly 4,000 miles away. Some of the mutineers eventually went on to Pitcairn Island, founding a settlement there which was not discovered until 1808.

bou·quet (bōkā′, bōō-) *n.* (pl. **-quets** pr. -kāz′). Bunch of flowers, esp. one presented as a compliment (also fig.); characteristic perfume of wine.

Bour·bon (boor′bon). Surname of branch of royal family of France; they became the ruling monarchs when Henry IV succeeded to the throne in 1589; members of this family also became kings of Spain (1700–1931) and of Naples.

bour·bon (ber′bon) *n.* (also ~ **whiskey**). Whiskey distilled from corn and rye, orig. made in Bourbon County, Kentucky.

bour·don (boor′don) *n.* Low-pitched (usu. 16-ft.) stop in organ; drone bass of bagpipe (ill. BAGPIPE). [Fr., = "drone bee, bass stop in organ"]

bour·geois[1] (boorzhwah′, boor′-zhwah) *n.* (pl. **-geois**) & *adj.* 1. (orig.) (Of) a French citizen or free-man of a small city or town. 2.

(Member) of shopkeeping or mercantile middle class; (person) of humdrum middle-class ideas (now freq. a rather vague term of abuse).

bour·geoi·sie (boorzhwahzē′) *n.* Middle class.

bour·geois² (berjois′) *n.* Size of type (approx. 9 point). [Perh. f. a French printer's name]

Bour·geois (boorzhwah′, boor′-zhwah), **Léon Victor Auguste** (1851–1925). French statesman; a founder and first chairman of the League of Nations; awarded the Nobel Peace Prize in 1920.

bour·rée (boorā′; *Fr.* boorā′) *n.* (pl. **-rées** pr. -rāz; *Fr.* -rā′). Lively dance, in duple time, of French or Spanish origin; music suitable for or derived from this, esp. as a movement in a suite.

bourse (boors) *n.* Money market, esp. (**B ~**) the Paris stock exchange.

bout (bowt) *n.* 1. Spell or turn of work, illness, exercise, etc.; fit of drinking. 2. Prizefight, contest, trial of strength.

bou·tique (bōōtēk′) *n.* Small shop or department selling fashionable clothes or accessories.

bo·vine (bō′vīn, -vēn, -vǐn) *adj.* Of, like, a cow; inert, dull.

bow¹ (bō) *n.* 1. Curve. 2. Weapon for shooting arrows, a strip of flexible wood or other material held in bent position, when in use, by a string stretched between its two ends. 3. Appliance for playing instruments of violin class, rod with a number of horsehairs stretched from end to end, for drawing across the strings. 4. Slipknot with double or single loop, ribbon etc. so tied. 5. **~ compass(es)**, drawing compass with jointed legs; **bowlegged** (bō′lěgǐd), having legs bowed or curved outward; bandylegged; **bow′man**, archer; **bow tie**, necktie tied in a bow. **bow** *v.* Play with bow (on violin etc.), use bow.

bow² (bow) *v.* Submit *to*; bend or kneel in sign of submission or reverence, incline head in greeting or assent; express by bowing, usher *in, out,* by bowing; cause to bend. **~** *n.* Bending of head or body in salutation, respect, content, etc.

bow³ (bow) *n.* Fore end of boat or ship from where it begins to arch inward (often pl.).

Bow (bō) **bells.** Peal of bells of St. Mary-le-Bow, a church in Cheapside near the center of London; hence, **within the sound of ~**, within the City of London.

Bow·ditch (bow′dǐch), **Nathaniel** (1773–1838). American astronomer, mathematician and navigational expert; prepared the American edition of *The Practical Navigator*, 1802.

Bowd·ler (bowd′ler, bōd′-), **Thomas** (1754–1825). M.D. of Edinburgh, editor of *Family Shakespeare* (1818), an edition "in which those words and expressions are omitted which cannot with propriety be read aloud in a family."

The bow was probably invented in the paleolithic period. Right: A New Guinea tribesman uses a light hunting bow. Below: Archer using a modern recurve bow fully-equipped for competitive archery.

The male **bowerbird** is sexually active during a long breeding season and, once it has made its arena or bower, will attract several females to mate. The plainer the species, the more elaborate is its courting bower. MacGregor's bowerbird makes a simple bower of twigs, but the plainer crestless bowerbird builds a roofed stage and garden. The female regent bowerbird is better camouflaged than her mate, a vital survival factor.

MacGregor's Bower Bird

Crestless Bower Bird

Regent's Bower B

bowd′ler·ize *v.t.* (**-ized, -iz·ing**). Expurgate.

bow·el (bow′el) *n.* Division of alimentary canal below stomach, intestine; (pl.) entrails, inside of body; pity, tender feeling; inside of anything, esp. in ~s **of the earth.** **bowel** (**-eled, -el·ing;** *Brit.* **-elled, -el·ling**). Disembowel.

bow·er¹ (bow′er) *n.* 1. (poet.) Dwelling, abode; inner room, boudoir. 2. Place closed in with foliage, arbor, summerhouse; **bow′erbird,** any of several Australian birds (e.g., **satin, regent, spotted** ~) of starling family, remarkable for their habit of building bowers or runs and adorning them with feathers, shells, etc., in courtship. **bow′er·like** *adj.*

bow·er² (bow′er) *n.* Each of the two highest cards at euchre, the jack of trumps (**right** ~) and the jack of the other suit of the same color (**left** ~). [Ger. *Bauer* peasant]

Bow·er·y (bow′erē, bow′rē), **The.** Street and section in lower part of Manhattan, formerly notorious as a haunt of criminals and, later, of derelicts. [Du. *bouwerij* husbandry, farm]

bow·ie (bō′ē) *n.* (also ~**knife**) Large hunting knife with long hollow-ground blade, curved and double-edged near the point and having a hilt and crosspiece. [Popularized by James *Bowie,* probably designed by his brother Retzin P. *Bowie*]

Bow·ie (bō′ē, boo′ē), **James** (1799–1836). Georgia-born Texas colonist and colonel in Texan army; became Mexican citizen, 1830; leader of opposition to Mexican control of Texas; killed at Battle of the Alamo, 1836.

bowl¹ (bōl) *n.* Deep, rounded basin for holding liquid or food; drinking vessel; contents of a bowl; bowl-shaped part of a tobacco pipe, spoon, etc.; bowl-shaped topographical depression; flat region noted for specific item, crop, etc.; bowl-shaped football stadium; ~ **game,** championship or important football game played by selected teams in such a bowl after regular season (as **Rose B** ~, **Cotton B** ~, **Super B** ~).

bowl² (bōl) *n.* 1. Wooden ball made slightly out of spherical shape (formerly spherical and weighted on one side) to make it run in a curved course; (pl.) game played on a bowling green with bowls, the object being to lay the bowls near a spike. ~ *v.* Play bowls; roll (bowl, hoop, etc.); roll like bowl or hoop, move on wheels; play a game of, r a bowl in, bowling; ~ **over,** kno down; disconcert, render helples

bowl·er¹ (bō′ler) *n.* One w bowls.

bowl·er² (bō′ler) *n.* (chief Brit.) (also ~ **hat**) Hard round fe hat; derby.

bow·line (bō′lĭn, -līn) *n.* Rope ship's rigging from weather side square sail to bow; (also **bow′kno** simple but very secure knot used fastening bowline to sail.

bowl·ing (bō′lĭng) *n.* Playi bowls; playing skittles; game playe by rolling a ~ **ball** down a woode

*Since the day early in the 19th century when a young woman first bowled over-arm in the game of cricket, the way was open for more complex **bowling** styles. Dennis Lillee, an Australian fast bowler, made great impact in the 1970s. The game of **bowls** may be played between two single players, pairs or fours, using wooden bowls weighing up to 3½ lb.*

Dennis Lillee

***Boxers** are placed in categories according to weight and here fight for the world championship.*

Table of Boxing Weights

Amateur		
Weight	Not more than	
light fly	48 kg	7st 8lb
fly	51 kg	8st
bantam	54 kg	8st 6lb
feather	57 kg	9st
light	60 kg	9st 7lb
light welter	63.5 kg	10st
welter	67 kg	10st 8lb
light middle	71 kg	11st 2lb
middle	75 kg	11st 11lb
light heavy	81 kg	12st 10lb
heavy	81 kg	12st 10lb
	and over	

Professional	
Weight	Not more than
fly	8st
bantam	8st 8lb
feather	9st
light	9st 9lb
welter	10st 7lb
middle	11st 6lb
light heavy	12st 7lb
heavy	12st 7lb
	and over

ley to knock down as many as ossible of a triangular group of ten ins; ~ **alley**, the wooden alley sed in bowling; building housing uch alleys; ~ **green**, lawn for laying bowls.

bow·sprit (bow′sprĭt, bō′-) *n.* par running out from ship's stem, o which forestays are fastened.

box[1] (bŏks) *n.* (pl. **box·es**). Ever-reen shrub or small tree of genus *Buxus* (esp. *B. sempervirens*), with mall dark-green leathery leaves, nuch used in garden borders and edges; (also **box′wood**), wood of his.

box[2] (bŏks) *n.* (pl. **box·es**). 1. Receptacle (usu. with lid, rectangu-ar or cylindrical, and for solids) of vood, cardboard, etc.; quantity ontained in this; receptacle at ewspaper office for replies to dvertisement; **post-office** ~: see post[2]. 2. Coachman's seat. 3. Small eparate compartment in theater tc., or for horse in stable or railroad ar; jury box; witness stand; hut for entry etc. 4. Protective case for iece of mechanism etc.; (typ.) pace enclosed by rules etc. 5. ~ amera, box-shaped camera; ~

kite, kite with light, rectangular frame at each end; ~ **office**, ticket office at a theater, stadium, etc.; (fig.) quality of entertainment etc. likely to attract audiences; ~ **pleat**: see PLEAT; ~ **spring**, one of a set of pocketed springs in a mattress etc.; hence ~**-spring mattress** or ~ **spring**, mattress containing such springs. **box** *v.t.* Provide with, put into, confine as in, box; partition *off* from other compartments; ~ **in**, block the movement of (a vehicle) so that it cannot maneuver; ~ **the compass**, (naut.) repeat compass points in correct order; (fig.) make complete revolution and end where one began; (Brit.) **Boxing Day**, first weekday after Christmas, observed as a holiday, traditional day for giving of Christmas gift boxes to servants and other service workers. **box′like** *adj.*

box[3] (bŏks) *v.* 1. Slap (person's) ears. 2. Fight with fists, usu. in padded leather gloves. **box′ing** *n.* (esp.) Act or sport of fighting with fists, usu. in padded leather gloves (~ **gloves**); ~ **match**, match between pugilists fighting in boxing gloves; **box** *n.* (pl. **box·es**). Slap

with hand *on the ear*.

Box·er (bŏk′ser) *n.* Member of a Chinese secret society that at-tempted to drive foreigners from China (1900) by violence and by besieging the legations at Peking, and tried to force Chinese Christians to renounce their religion. [transl. of Chinese word meaning "fist of harmony"]

box·er[1] (bŏk′ser) *n.* Person who fights in boxing match(es), pugilist.

box·er[2] (bŏk′ser) *n.* Dog of smooth-coated brown breed and having a short, square muzzle.

box·y (bŏk′sē) *adj.* (**box·i·er, box·i·est**). Resembling a box (BOX[2]) in shape.

boy (boi) *n.* Male child or youth, son; man retaining boy's character, tastes, etc.; (derog.) male servant or laborer; (derog.) familiarly as term of address; **boy′-friend**, woman's usual or preferred male companion; **Boy Scout**: see SCOUT. **boy** *int.* (colloq.; also **oh ~**) Exclamation of surprise, approval, etc.

boy·cott (boi′kŏt) *v.t.* Combine to punish or coerce by systematic refusal of social or commercial relations; abstain from (goods etc.) with this aim. **~** *n.* Boycotting. [f. Captain *Boycott*, an Irish landlord, victim of this treatment]

boy·hood (boi′hood) *n.* Boyish age; boys.

boy·ish (boi′ish) adj. Of or like boys. **boy′ish·ly** *adv.* **boy′ish·ness** *n.*

Boyle (boil), **Hon. Robert** (1627–91). English natural philosopher and chemist; **~′s law**, law, formulated by him, that the volume of a given quantity of gas varies inversely with the pressure when the temperature is constant.

Boz (bŏz). Pseudonym used by Charles DICKENS.

bp *abbrev.* Bishop.

B.P. *abbrev.* Bills payable; blood pressure.

b.p. *abbrev.* Bills payable; boiling point.

bpl. *abbrev.* Birthplace.

B.P.O.E. *abbrev.* Benevolent and Protective Order of Elks.

bra (brah) *n.* (colloq.) Brassiere.

Bra·bant (brabănt′, brah′bant). Former duchy in W. Europe, now divided into 2 provinces: **~** in Belgium and **N. ~** in the Netherlands.

brace (brās) *v.t.* (**braced, brac·ing**). Strengthen or tighten; make taut; give firmness to, invigorate. **~** *n.* 1. Thing that braces or connects; connecting mark in printing or writing ({); strengthening piece of iron or timber in buildings; (dentistry) wire device for straightening teeth; (naut.) rope attached to yard for trimming sail; (pl., Brit.) suspenders; **~ and bit**, tool for boring in which the bit is made to rotate by turning the brace etc. 2. Couple, pair, esp. of dogs or game.

brace·let (brās′lĭt) *n.* Ornamental band, chain, etc., for wrist or arm; (pl., slang) handcuffs.

brac·er (brā′ser) *n.* Stimulating drink; tonic.

bra·chi·al (brā′kēal) *adj.* Of the arm; like an arm.

brach·y·ce·phal·ic (brăkēse-făl′ĭk) *adj.* Short headed; with width of skull at least 4/5 of length. **brach·y·ceph·a·ly** (brăkēsĕf′alē), **brach·y·ceph′a·lism** *ns.*

brack·en (brăk′en) *n.* Kind of large fern (*Pteridium aquilinum*), abundant on heaths etc.; mass of this.

brack·et (brăk′ĭt) *n.* 1. Flat-

topped projection from wall servi as support; shelf with slantir underprop for hanging against wa wooden or metal angular suppor 2. (freq. pl.) Pair of marks [ ] use for enclosing words, figures, etc., as to separate them from the cor text. 3. (artillery) Specified dis tance between pair of shots fire beyond target and short of it, finding range. 4. Group bracketed together as of equal standing or fal ing between certain limits (a **income ~**). **~** *v.t.* Enclose i brackets; couple with brace, imp connection or equality betwee (artillery) fire shots beyond an short of target (see above).

brack·ish (brăk′ĭsh) *adj.* (water) Rather salty; unpalatable **brack′ish·ness** *n.*

bract (brăkt) *n.* (bot.) Modifie usu. small leaf or scale belov flower.

brac·te·ate (brăk′tēĭt, -āt) *adj* Bearing bracts.

brac·te·ole (brăk′tēōl) *n.* (bot. Small bract on flower stalk.

brad (brăd) *n.* Thin flattish na of same thickness throughout.

Brad·dock (brăd′ok), **Edward** (1695–1755). Commander in chie of British troops in America during the French and Indian War; wa defeated and died in surprise attac at Fort Duquesne, 1755.

Brad·ford (brăd′ferd), **William** (1590–1657). English Puritan colonist in America; signer of the Mayflower Compact; governor o

Boyle's Law states that the volume of a gas at constant temperature varies ir inverse proportion to pressure acting upon it. If the pressure is doubled the volume is halved; trebled the volume is reduced to one third.

The boxer, sometimes known as a German bulldog, stands 21–24 ins. at the shoulder and may be brindled or have white markings. Active and strong, it makes a good guard dog.

pressure

volume of gas

increased pressure

decreased volume of gas

LONGITUDINAL SECTION

*The greater the intelligence in mammals, the greater the complexity of the **brain** cerebrum which is the seat of reason. Anatomists believe that the active part of the cerebrum is in the cortex, the outer surface, and the more convoluted this is, the more intelligent the owner. The human cortex is corruscated into deep folds to give it great surface area.*

ymouth Colony five times.

Brad·ley (brăd′lē), **Omar Nelan** (1893–). American army neral; commander of the 12th my Group, largest American mbat force during World War II ropean campaign; first chairman, Joint Chiefs of Staff, 1949.

Brad·street (brăd′strēt), **Anne udley** (1612–72). Puritan colonist in America, 1630; first colonial merican woman poet, author of *he Tenth Muse*.

Bra·dy (brā′dē), **Matthew B.** 823?–96). American pioneer notographer; best known for notographing the Civil War.

brae (brā) *n.* (Sc.) Steep bank, llside.

brag (brăg) *v.* (**bragged, bragng**). Talk boastfully. ~ *n.* oastful talk. **brag′ger** *n.*

brag·ga·do·ci·o (brăgadō′shēō) (pl. **-ci·os**). Empty boasting. ormed by Spenser from *brag* as roper name of personification of ainglory]

brag·gart (brăg′ert) *n. & adj.* erson) given to bragging.

Brahe (brah, brah′hē), **Tycho** 546–1601). Danish astronomer; is observations of the sun pre- ared the way for the discoveries of epler (who worked under him) ut he did not accept the opernican system.

Brah·ma (brah′ma). (Hinduism) Supreme God, the divine reality, of which the entire universe is only a manifestation.

Brah·man, Brah·min (brah′man) *ns.* (pl. **-mans, -mins**). Member of the highest or priestly caste among Hindus; (colloq.) highly cultured or intellectual aloof person. **Brah·man·ic** (brahmăn′ĭk), **Brah·man′i·cal** *adjs.* **Brah′man·ism** *n.*

Brahms (brahmz), **Johannes** (1833–97). German composer of symphonies, chamber music, songs, etc.

braid (brād) *n.* 1. Entwined hair, plait; band, etc., entwined with the hair. 2. Woven fabric of silk, linen, etc., in the form of a band. ~ *v.t.* Plait, interweave, arrange in braids; trim, edge, with braid. **braid′er, braid′ing** *ns.*

Braille, braille (brāl) *ns.* System of printing for the blind consisting of embossed characters recognizable by touch, invented by Louis BRAILLE. ~ *v.t.* (**Brailled, Brail·ling**). Print in Braille.

Braille (brāl), **Louis** (1809–52). French educator and musician; blind from childhood; devised system of printing for the blind.

brain (brān) *n.* 1. Convoluted mass of nervous tissue, contained in the skull, which controls the processes of sensation, learning, and memory in vertebrates and is regarded as the center of thought and intellectual power in man; **fore′brain, mid′brain, hind′brain**, parts that develop from the three main parts of the primitive brain; **great** ~, cerebrum; **lesser** ~, cerebellum; ~ **stem**, medulla oblongata. 2. In many invertebrates, the part of the nervous system that corresponds to the vertebrate brain in function and position. 3. (colloq.) Very intelligent person; **the** ~**s**, cleverest person or major planner (of group, movement, etc.). 4. **brain′child**, invention, scheme; **brain drain**, (colloq.) emigration of highly qualified persons, esp. from England to U.S.; **brain fever**, (archaic) inflammation of the brain; **brain′pan**, part of skull containing the brain, cranium; **brain′storm**, sudden idea; **brain′storming**, spontaneous discussion in search for new ideas; **brain trust**, (hist.) group of advisers called in by President Franklin Roosevelt; group of experts advising a government; **brain′washing**, systematic elimination from person's mind of (esp. political) established ideas, esp. coercive conversion of dissidents in totalitarian state; so **brain′wash** (*v.t.*); **brain wave**,

1 cast iron disc
2 h.p. hose
3 friction pads
4 calliper
5 brake lining
6 leading shoe
7 half-shaft
8 trailing shoe
9 hydraulic feed-pipe
10 hand-brake cable
11 hydraulic piston
12 brake drum

Most large automobiles have drum **brakes** *fitted to the rear wheels but disk brakes on the front ones. Disk brakes have superior stopping power and were developed from brakes used in automobile racing.*

Brambles *of the genus* Rubus *grow wild throughout North America and are also cultivated for their fruit, the blackberry, which is a source of vitamin C.*

sudden inspiration, bright thought. **brain′less** *adj.* **brain** *v.t.* Dash out brains of.

brain·y (brā′nē) *adj.* (**brain·i·er, brain·i·est**). (colloq.) Intelligent.

braise (brāz) *v.t.* (**braised, brais·ing**). Cook by browning in fat and then simmering in small quantity of liquid in a covered container.

brake[1] (brāk) *n.* Bracken.

brake[2] (brāk) *n.* Thicket, brushwood.

brake[3] (brāk) *n.* Toothed instrument for braking flax and hemp; a heavy harrow. ∼ *v.t.* (**braked, brak·ing**). Crush (flax, hemp) by beating.

brake[4] (brāk) *n.* Frictional apparatus for checking motion of vehicle or machine by pressure, usu. applied to circumference of wheel or to special drum or hub on axle; (also ∼ **pedal**) pedal operating this; ∼ **horsepower,** (abbrev. b.h.p.) horsepower of an engine measured by an absorption dynamometer (orig. by resistance of an applied brake); **brake′man** (also Brit. **brakes′man**), trainman, assistant to conductor. **brake** *v.*

(**braked, brak·ing**). Apply brake; check with brake.

bram·ble (brăm′bel) *n.* Rough, prickly rambling shrub, esp. the blackberry. **bram′bly** *adj.* (**-bli·er, -bli·est**).

bran (brăn) *n.* Husks of grain separated from flour after grinding.

branch (brănch) *n.* Limb of tree etc. growing from stem or bough; lateral extension or subdivision of river, road, family, business, etc.; small stream. ∼ *v.i.* Put branches *out, forth,* spring *out;* spread *forth,* tend *away, off,* diverge *into.* **branch′ing** *adj.* & *n.* **branch′less** *adj.*

bran·chi·a (brăng′kēa) *n.* (pl. **-chi·ae** pr. -kēē). (zool.) Gill. **bran′chi·al,   bran·chi·ate** (brăng′kĕĭt, -āt) *adjs.*

Bran·cu·si (brahngkōo′zē), **Constantin** (1876–1957). Rumanian-born French sculptor, associated with modern school of art and symbolism.

brand (brănd) *n.* 1. Burning or charred piece of wood from hearth. 2. Mark made by burning with hot iron; stigma; trademark, goods of particular make or trademark; ∼**-new,** perfectly new. 3. Iron

instrument for branding. 4. (poet.) Sword. **brand** *v.t.* Burn with hot iron; impress on memory; stigmatize; **branding iron,** instrument for branding. **brand′er** *n.*

Bran·deis (brăn′dīs), **Louis Dembitz** (1856–1941). U.S lawyer and jurist; counsel in famous cases for limiting hours of the work week and against New England railroad monopoly; Supreme Court associate justice, 1916–39.

bran·dish (brăn′dĭsh) *v.t.* Wave about, flourish, in display or threat.

bran·dy (brăn′dē) *n.* (pl. **-dies**). Strong alcoholic spirit distilled from wine. **bran′died** *adj.* [Du. *brandewijn,* burnt, distilled wine]

Bran·dy·wine (brăn′dēwīn). Creek in SE. Pennsylvania and NW Delaware; site of victory of British over Americans during Revolutionary War, 1777.

brant (brănt) *n.* (pl. **brants,** collect. **brant**). (also Brit. *brent*) Any of several species of wild goose (esp. *Branta bernicla*); breeds in Arctic.

Braque (brahk), **Georges** (1882–1963). French Cubist painter and friend of Picasso.

brash (brăsh) *adj.* Vulgarly

sertive, impudent. **brash'ly** *adv.*
ash'ness *n.* **brash'y** *adj.*
rash·i·er, brash·i·est).
Bra·sil·ia (brahzēl'ya). City of
ntral Brazil, especially construct-
d as its capital; capital since 1960.
brass (brăs, brahs) *n.* 1. (hist.)
lloy of copper with tin or zinc,
onze; (now) yellow alloy of
pper and zinc, usu. with about 1/3
tal weight of zinc. 2. Monumental
sepulchral tablet of inscribed
rass or similar alloy; musical
struments of brass. 3. Effrontery,
amelessness. 4. (slang; also **top**
) Brass hats; senior officials.
rass *adj.* Made of brass; ∼ **band**,
nd of musicians with brass in-
ruments; ∼ **hat,** (slang) officer of
gh rank; ∼ **knuckles,** metal
evice worn to protect knuckles
om injury during fist-fighting and
increase effectiveness of punches;
tacks, (slang) actual details, real
usiness.
　bras·sard (brăs'ārd) *n.* Cloth
adge worn on arm; piece of armor
r protecting the arm.
　brass·ie (brăs'ē, brah'sē) *n.* (pl.
rass·ies). Wooden-headed golf
lub with brass plate under the
ead, for hitting long, low shots;
umber 2 wood.
　bras·siere (brazēr') *n.* Woman's
ndergarment supporting breasts.
　brass·y (brăs'ē, brah'sē) *adj.*
brass·i·er, brass·i·est). Yellow
ke brass; sounding like brass; im-
udent, shameless. **brass'i·ly** *adv.*
rass'i·ness *n.*
　brat (brăt) *n.* (contempt.) Child.
　Bra·ti·sla·va (brah'tĭslahvah).
Historic port and industrial city on
he Danube in S. central Czecho-
lovakia.
　brat·wurst (brăt'werst, -woorst,
raht'-; *Ger.* braht'voorsht) *n.*
piced pork sausage.
　Braun¹ (brown), **Eva** (1910–45).
German mistress and wife, just
efore their joint deaths, of Adolf
Hitler.
　Braun² (brown), **Karl Ferdi-
and** (1850–1918). German physi-
ist and pioneer in telegraphy;
nvented a cathode ray tube; co-
winner of the Nobel Prize in
hysics, 1909.
　Braun·schwei·ger (brown'-
shwīger; *Ger.* brown'shvīger) *n.*
also **braunschweiger**) Smoked
nd spiced liver sausage.
　bra·va·do (bravah'dō) *n.* (pl.
-does, -dos). Show of courage,
old front.
　brave (brāv) *adj.* (**brav·er,
brav·est**). 1. Ready to confront
nd steady in enduring danger or
ain. 2. Splendid, spectacular. ∼
n. N. Amer. Indian warrior.
brave'ly *adv.* **brave'ness** *n.*
brave *v.t.* (**braved, brav·ing**).
Defy, meet with courage.
　brav·er·y (brā'verē) *n.* (pl.
-er·ies). Brave conduct; splendor.

The development of valves for **brass** instruments in about 1815 brought about many improvements. By the middle of the 19th century most of the brass band instruments were established.

The largest country in South America,
Brazil *has an area of about 3,300,000
sq. miles. Top left: The old capital, Rio
de Janeiro, is dominated by the Sugar
Loaf Mountain. Right: The new capital
Brasilia, was planned in the late 1950s
to be the administrative center. The
cathedral in Brasilia serves the
predominantly Roman Catholic population.*

bra·vo (brah′vō, brahvō′) *int.* &
n. (pl. **-vos**). Cry of approval,
esp. to actors etc.

bra·vu·ra (br*a*vūr′*a*, -voor′*a*; *It.*
brahvōō′rah) *n.* (pl. **-ras**; *It.* **-re**
pr. -rĕ). Brilliant execution,
attempt at brilliant performance;
musical passage requiring great
skill and spirit in performance. [It.]

brawl (brawl) *n.* Squabble,
noisy quarrel or fight; (slang) a wild
party. ~ *v.i.* Engage in brawl.

brawn (brawn) *n.* Muscle;
muscular strength. **brawn′i·ness**
n.

brawn·y (braw′nē) *adj.*
(**brawn·i·er,** **brawn·i·est**).
Strong, muscular.

bray (brā) *n.* Peculiar cry of
some animals, esp. the donkey; loud
harsh jarring sound resembling
this. ~ *v.* Make bray; utter
harshly.

braze (brāz) *v.t.* (**brazed,
braz·ing**). Solder with hard, high-
melting-point solder, as with an
alloy of brass and zinc. **braz′er** *n.*

bra·zen (brā′zen) *adj.* Of brass;
strong, yellow, or harsh sounding,
as brass; shameless. **bra′zen·ly**
adv. **bra′zen·ness** *n.* **brazen** *v.t.*
Face shamelessly or defiantly under
charge or suspicion, esp. ~ **it out.**

bra·zier[1] (brā′zh*er*) *n.* Worker
in brass.

bra·zier[2] (brā′zh*er*) *n.* Large flat
pan for holding burning coals or

charcoal.

Bra·zil (br*a*zĭl′). S. Amer.
Portuguese-speaking republic;
colonized by Portugal in the early
16th c.; a republic since 1889; fifth
largest country in the world;
capital, Brasilia. **Bra·zil′ian** *adj.* &
n. [see BRAZIL]

bra·zil, bra·sil (br*a*zĭl′) *ns.* 1.
(usu. **brazil′wood**) The red wood
of any of several tropical trees of
the genus *Caesalpina* (esp. of the S.
Amer. *Caesalpina echinata*). 2. ~
nut, large three-sided edible nut,
the seed of a lofty tree (*Bertholletia
excelsa*), which forms large forests
in Brazil. [orig. the Span., Port.,
and Fr. name of the E. Indian
wood; transferred to the S. Amer.
species, and thence to the country
where this was found]

Braz·za·ville (brăz′*a*vĭl, brah-
zahvēl′). Capital and Congo River
port of the Republic of the Congo.

breach (brēch) *n.* 1. (archaic,

also ~ **of the sea**) Breaking o
waves. 2. Breaking or neglect (o
rule, duty, promise, etc.); breakin
of relations, alienation, quarrel; ~
of the peace, disturbance of publi
peace by brawl, riot, etc.; ~ o
promise, (esp.) breaking of prom
ise to marry. 3. Injury, broke
place, gap, esp. in wall or fortifica
tion; **breach** *v.t.* Break throug
make gap in.

bread (brĕd) *n.* Flour mois
tened, usu. leavened, kneaded int
dough, and baked in loaves; this a
staple article of food; livelihood
means of subsistence; ~ **an**
butter, livelihood, means of sup
port: ~**-and-butter letter,** lette
of thanks for hospitality; **bread′
board,** board to knead or cut brea
on; **bread′fruit,** starchy frui
about the size of a melon, and wit
whitish pulp like new bread, of th
bread′fruit tree (*Artocarp*
incisa) of the South Sea islands etc.

ead'winner, person supporting amily or household. **bread** *v.t.* at (food) with bread crumbs fore cooking.

breadth (brĕdth) *n.* 1. Broadss, measure from side to side; ce (of cloth etc.) of full standard eadth. 2. Wide extent or scope; geness, liberality, catholicity. **eadth'ways, breadth'wise** vs.

break (brāk) *v.* (**broke** or archaic **ake, bro·ken** or archaic **broke, eak·ing**). 1. Divide, disperse, lit, separate, otherwise than by tting; tame, subdue, crush; fall to ces; burst, issue, *forth*; solve pher etc.); (of voice) crack, ange tone (at puberty); (boxing) me out of clinch; ∼ **down**, (*v.i.*) llapse; lose control, become tear-l; **break'down**, (of machine etc.) ase to function; (trans.) itemize, alyze; **break even**, emerge with ither loss nor gain; **break in**, me, discipline; teach the rudi-ents; enter by force or stealth, as rob; hence, **break-in** (*n.*); **break** at, burst from restraint or con-alment; **break up**, disband; parate, obtain a legal separation f a married couple). 2. Ruin ancially, make bankrupt. 3. terrupt, change; put an end to; act ntrary to (agreement, law, etc.). Make a way through, with ddenness or violence; disclose; f news) be disclosed; (of day) wn; (of a storm) begin violently. (of baseball pitch) Curve. 6.

break'away, (*adj.*, esp.) seceding; **break'down,** collapse, stoppage; failure of health or (esp. mental) power(s); act of disintegrating or analyzing a substance; analysis of statistical figures etc.; **break'neck,** endangering the neck, headlong; **break'through,** (esp.) significant advance in knowledge, achievement, etc.; **break'up,** disintegra-tion, collapse, dispersal; **break'-water,** barrier built to break force of waves.   **break'a·ble** *adj.* **break'age** *n.* **break** *n.* Breaking; breach, gap, broken place; pause in work etc.; escape; curve of baseball after pitching; (billiards) the open-ing shot, points scored continu-ously; (slang) stroke of luck.

break·er[1] (brā'ker) *n.* (esp.) Heavy ocean wave breaking on coast or over reefs; (CB radio use) one wishing to transmit a message.

break·er[2] (brā'ker) *n.* (naut.) Small keg, esp. for a lifeboat.

break·fast (brĕk'fast) *n.* First meal of the day.   ∼ *v.i.* Take breakfast. **break'fast·er** *n.*

bream (brēm) *n.* (collect. **bream,** pl. **breams**). Any of several fresh-water fishes of genus *Abramis* with high-arched back; any of various porgies, such as the sea bream (*Archosargus rhomboid-alis*); also various fresh-water sun-fishes of genus *Lepomis*.

breast (brĕst) *n.* 1. Each of two soft protuberances on woman's thorax, secreting milk for feeding young; corresponding rudimentary

organ of man. 2. Upper front part of human body; corresponding part in animals, this as cut of meat; part of dress, coat, etc., covering this. 3. Heart, emotions, thoughts. 4. **breast'bone,** sternum; **breast-fed,** (of infant) fed at mother's breast; **breast'plate,** piece of embroidered fabric embellished with 12 precious stones, represent-ing the 12 tribes of Israel, worn on breast of Jewish high priest; (hist.) piece of armor covering breast; **breast'stroke,** stroke in swimming in which breast is squarely opposed to the water; **breast'work,** tem-porary defense or parapet a few feet high. **breast** *v.t.* Oppose breast to, face, contend with.

breath (brĕth) *n.* 1. Exhalation as perceptible to sight or smell; slight movement of air; whiff. 2. Air taken into and expelled from lungs; respiration; power of breath-ing; whisper, murmur; **take per-son's ∼ away,** dumbfound him or her; so **breath'taking** (*adj.*). 3. (phon.) Voiceless expiration of air, as in the articulation of *s* and *p*.

*The mass production of **bread** begins with a mixture in which all the ingredi-ents except sugar and salt are present. The mixture stands for two or three hours before sugar and salt are added. After standing until it is risen, the dough is divided and molded. The dough's elasticity is replaced by kneading, and a final molding leads to the ovens.*

1 coccyx
2 anus
3 cervix
4 pelvic floor
5 symphisis
6 bladder
7 peritoneum
8 abdominal wall
9 placenta
10 intestines
11 lumbar spine

Above: When a baby does not turn to present its head to the opening of the uterus, it may be born naturally but bottom first—a **breech birth.**

Below: Collies are trained as herding dogs for their capacity to learn and obey commands. **Breeding** *them as show dogs is also popular.*

breathe (brēdh) *v.* (**breathed** pr. brēdhd, **breath·ing**). Take air into and expel it from lungs or other respiratory organs; live; take breath, pause; sound, speak, blow, softly; take in (air etc.); utter softly or passionately, exhibit.

breath·er (brē'dher) *n.* (esp.) Short spell of exercise; spell of rest to recover one's breath after exertion.

breath·ing (brē'dhǐng) *n.* (esp. Gk. gram.) Mark indicating that initial vowel is or is not aspirated; ~ **space**, time to rest, pause.

breath·less (brĕth'lǐs) *adj.* Panting; holding the breath; unstirred by wind. **breath'less·ly** *adv.* **breath'less·ness** *n.*

breath·y (brĕth'ē) *adj.* (**breath·i·er, breath·i·est**). (of voice) With sound of emission of breath. **breath'i·ness** *n.*

brec·ci·a (brĕch'ēa, brĕsh'-) *n.* (geol.) Composite rock of angular fragments of stone etc. cemented

together by some matrix.

Brecht (brĕkt; *Ger.* brĕχt), **Bertolt** (1898–1956). German playwright.

Breck·in·ridge (brĕk'inrĭj), **John Cabell** (1821–75). American statesman; Vice President of the U.S. under James Buchanan, 1857–1861; a Confederate army general and Confederate Secretary of War.

bred (brĕd): see BREED.

breech (brēch) *n.* 1. Buttocks (archaic exc. physiol.); ~ **birth, delivery,** birth, delivery, of infant with breech presenting. 2. Part of cannon behind bore; back part of rifle or gun barrel; **breech'loader, breech'loading,** (gun) loaded at breech, not through muzzle. 3. **breeches** (brĭch'ĭz), (usu. considered pl.) Short trousers fastened above or (esp.) below knee, now used only for riding or in court costume etc.; (loosely) trousers; **breeches buoy,** life buoy, slung on a pulley, with canvas supports like

breeches for the legs.

breed (brēd) *v.* (**bred, bree·ing**). 1. Bear, generate; (ma propagate; yield, produce, resul arise, spread. 2. Train; fit for bei adapt *to*, bring up. 3. (phys.) Cre fissile material from nonfissile nuclear reaction. ~ *n.* 1. Strai animals etc. visibly resembling e other, esp. developed under con of man; similar group of plants. Stock, lineage. 3. Sort, kind.

breed·er (brē'der) *n.* One v breeds cattle etc.; animal t breeds; (phys., also ~ **react** reactor that can create more fis material than it consumes in chain reaction.

breed·ing (brē'dǐng) *n.* (es Result of training, (good) behav or manners.

breeze (brēz) *n.* 1. Gentle wi wind blowing in from sea dur day (**sea** ~), or from land to during night (**land** ~); (meteo see BEAUFORT scale. 2. (colloq.) easy task, sure thing. ~ (**breezed, breez·ing**). (collo Move *along* briskly; come **breeze'less** *adj.*

breez·y (brē'zē) *adj.* (**bree i·er, breez·i·est**). Wind-swe pleasantly windy; lively, jov **breez'i·ly** *adv.* **breez'i·ness** *n.*

Bre·men (brĕm'en; *G* brā'men). State in W. Germany; capital, a seaport on river Weser

Bren·ner (brĕn'er) **Pass.** Str tegic pass through the Alps betwe Austria and Italy.

brent (brĕnt) = BRANT.

br'er (brĕr, brär) *n.* (Southe dial.; as title prefixed to nam Brother.

Brest[1] (brĕst). Seaport in France on the Atlantic Ocean.

Brest[2] (brĕst). Former Poli town of Brest Litovsk (now U.S.S.R.), in which was signed t treaty of peace between Germa and Russia in March 1918.

breth·ren (brĕdh'rǐn) *n.pl.* (archaic) Brothers. 2. Members religious order etc. (see BROTHE 3).

Bre·ton (brĕt'on; *Fr.* bretawñ & *adj.* (Native, inhabitant, la guage) of Brittany.

Bret·ton (brĕt'on) **Wood** Resort in N. New Hampshire; si of 1944 United Nations conferen that established the Internation Monetary Fund and the Wor Bank.

Breu·er (broi'er), **Marcel Laje** (1902–). Hungarian-bo American architect and designer

Breu·ghel: see BRUEGHEL.

brev. *abbrev.* Brevet.

breve (brēv, brĕv) *n.* 1. (mus Note equal to two semibreves, no rarely used (‖O‖). 2. Mark placed over vowel to show that i short. 3. (hist.) Letter of authori from sovereign or pope.

ore·vet (brevĕt´; *Brit.* brĕv´ĭt) *n.*
cument, commission, often
nted as an honor, promoting
litary officer in rank without an
rease in authority or pay. ~
. **(-vet·ted, -vet·ting** or
·**t·ed, -vet·ing)**. Confer brevet
k on. **bre·vet´cy** *n.*

ore·vi·ar·y (brē´vēĕrē, brĕv´ē-)
(pl. **-ar·ies).** Book containing
yers, psalms, etc., for each
nonical hour, to be recited by
ose in (Roman Catholic or
glican) orders.

orev·i·ty (brĕv´ĭtē) *n.* Shortness,
efness.

brew (broō) *v.* 1. Make (beer
.) by steeping, boiling, and
mentation, or (tea, punch) by
eping or mixture. 2. Concoct,
. in motion; fester, gather force.
. *n.* Brewing; amount brewed;
verage etc. brewed.

brew·er (broō´er) *n.* (esp.) One
no brews beer. **brew´er·y** *n.* (pl.
r·ies).** Establishment where
ewing is carried out.

Brew·ster (broō´ster), **William**
567–1644). English Puritan
ionist in America; signer of May-
wer Compact; Pilgrim leader of
ymouth Colony.

Brezh·nev (brĕzh´nĕf; *Russ.*
ĕzhnyĕf´), **Leonid Ilyich** (1906–
). Soviet statesman; first sec-
tary of the Communist Party,
om 1964.

Bri·an Bo·ru (brī´an bōrōō´,
ĕn´) (926–1014). King of Mun-
r; defeated the Danes and in 1002
came high king of Ireland; was
led after a great victory over the
anes at Clontarf.

Bri·and (brēahnd´; *Fr.* brēahn´),

English bond Flemish bond

Dutch bond

Stretcher-bonded cavity wall
1. Course
2. Stretcher 5. Cavity
3. Header 6. Ventilating brick
4. Tie 7. Damp-course

Bricks were first used by the ancient Sumerians, and the technique of brick making was carried throughout Europe by the Romans. After a break, building in brick revived at the end of the Middle Ages.

Aristide (1862–1932). French
statesman; 11 times premier of
France.

bri·ar (brī´er): see BRIER[2]; ~
pipe, smoking pipe made of brierroot. **bri´ar·y** *adj.*

Bri·ar·e·us (brīār´ēus). (Gk.
myth.) Giant with 100 hands and
50 heads, confined under Mt. Etna
for fighting, with the other giants,
against the gods.

bribe (brīb) *n.* Money or other
inducement offered to procure
(often illegal or dishonest) action in
favor of the giver. ~ *v.t.* **(bribed,**

brib·ing). Persuade by bribe.
brib´a·ble *adj.* **brib´er, brib´er·y**
(pl. **-er·ies)** *ns.*

bric-a-brac (brĭk´abrăk) *n.*
(Collection of) miscellaneous old
ornaments, furniture, trinkets, etc.

brick (brĭk) *n.* 1. Clay kneaded,
molded, and baked by fire or sun,
used as a building material; rectangular block of this. 2. Brick-
shaped block; child's toy building
block. 3. (slang) Generous or loyal
person. 4. **brick´bat,** piece of
brick, esp. as missile (also fig.);
brick´layer, workman who lays
bricks in building; **brick red,** color
of red brick; **brick´work,** brick
construction. **brick** *v.t.* Block *up*
with brickwork. **brick´like,**
brick´y *adjs.*

brid·al (brī´dal) *adj.* Of bride or
wedding.

Brid·al·veil (brī´dalvāl). Waterfall in Yosemite National Park,
California, 620 feet (189 m) high.

bride (brīd) *n.* Woman on her
wedding day and shortly before or
after it.

Bride (brīd), **St.:** see BRIDGET.

bride·groom (brīd´groōm) *n.*
Man on his wedding day and
shortly before or after it.

brides·maid (brīdz´mād) *n.*
Woman, usu. young and unmarried
or girl, as flower girl, attending
bride at wedding.

bridge[1] (brĭj) *n.* 1. Structure

*The double-leaf bascule of **Tower Bridge**, London, U.K., allows the road bridge to be raised when a ship passes under it. Built between 1886 and 1894 the bridge has a center opening of 200 ft.*

Clapper

Arch

Suspension

Cantilever

Bascule

Swing

1. Anchorage   3. Anchor-plate   5 Suspended span
2. Chains   4 Cantilever-arm 6. Turntable

carrying road, path, etc., acr
stream, ravine, road, etc.; **B ~**
Sighs, 16th-c. bridge in Ven
between the Doges' Palace and
prison, crossed by prisoners on w
to execution. 2. (naut.) Platfo
amidships for officer in comma
3. Upper bony part of nose.
Movable piece over which strings
violin etc. are stretched.
(billiards) Support for cue form
with hand; contrivance consisti
of a long stick with device at e
to support cue. 6. (dentistry; a
bridge′work) Partial denture su
ported by teeth on each side.
bridge′head, (mil.) Fortificatie
post, at end of bridge or on side
a river nearest enemy; any positi
established in face of enemy, e.g.
landing force.   **bridge**
(bridged, bridg·ing). Fo
bridge; span as if with a bridge.

bridge² (brĭj) *n.* (orig.) Ca
game based on whist (now es
contract bridge; **auction**
variety of bridge in which the rig
to name trumps and play with t
dummy goes, with each deal, to t
player who makes the highest b
contract ~, the most usual for
of bridge, in which only the tric
the declarer has undertaken to ma
count toward the game.
   Bridg·et (brĭj′ĭt), **St.** (al
Brigid, in England **Bride)** Seco
patron saint of Ireland, traditic
ally held to have been born in Lou
in the time of St. Patrick; co
memorated Feb. 1.
   Bridge·town (brĭj′town). P
and capital on the SW. coast
Barbados, West Indies.
   bri·dle (brī′del) *n.* Headgear
harness, including headstall, b
and rein; restraint, curb; **~ pat**
trail for saddle horses. **~ v.** (**-dle**
-dling). Put bridle on, curb, co
trol; express resentment, vanit
etc., by throwing up head and dra
ing in chin. **bri′dler** *n.*
   Brie (brē) *n.* White, soft mol
ripened dessert cheese produced
Brie, a district of N. France.
   brief¹ (brēf) *n.* 1. Papal lett
on matter of discipline (less form
than BULL¹). 2. (law) Summary
facts and points of law of a case fil
by attorney before arguing the ca

*The size and type of obstacle to
crossed and the traffic that crosses
determine the type of **bridge** built. To
The **Verrazano-Narrows Bridge,** Ne
York City, which has the longest cent
span of any suspension bridge (4,2
ft.). Center: The development of bric
ing technology has produced a varie
of ways of supporting spans. Left: T
cantilevered structure of the old Fo.
Bridge, Scotland, has two 1,710
spans of steel, shown here before t
new bridge was built. Right: Brid
builders still use vines, as seen in th
suspension bridge in Papua Ne
Guinea.*

in court; abstract or condensation of document or series of documents; short or condensed statement or argument; **brief′case**, rectangular case for carrying documents etc. **brief** *v.t.* Instruct by brief; give instructions, necessary information, etc., to.

brief[2] (brēf) *adj.* Short, concise. **brief′ly** *adv.* **brief′ness** *n.*

briefs (brēfs) *n.pl.* Very short or legless tight-fitting underpants.

bri·er[1], **bri·ar**[1] (brī′er) *ns.* Prickly bush, esp. wild rose. **bri′er·y** *adj.*

bri·er[2], **bri·ar**[2] (brī′er) *ns.* White heath (*Erica arborea*) native to S. France, Corsica, etc.; smoking pipe made from brierroot.

brig[1] (brĭg) *n.* Two-masted square-rigged vessel having additional lower fore-and-aft sail with a gaff and boom on the mainmast.

brig[2] (brĭg) *n.* Ship's prison; (slang) military prison, guardhouse.

Brig. *abbrev.* Brigadier, brigade.

bri·gade (brĭgād′) *n.* Major military unit, usually consisting of several regiments or battalions; organized or uniformed band of workers.

brig·a·dier (brĭgadēr′) *n.* (~ **general**) Officer ranking immediately above colonel and below major general in the U.S. Army, Air Force, and Marine Corps.

brig·and (brĭg′and) *n.* Bandit, robber. **brig′and·ish** *adj.* **brig′and·age, brig′and·ism** *ns.*

brig·an·tine (brĭg′antēn, -tīn) *n.* Two-masted vessel with square-rigged foremast and fore-and-aft rigged mainmast.

bright (brīt) *adj.* Emitting or reflecting much light, shining; lit up with joy etc.; vivid; illustrious; vivacious; quick-witted. **bright′ly** *adv.* **bright′ness** *n.* **bright′en** *v.t. & v.i.* **bright** *adv.* Brightly.

Bright's (brīts) **disease.** Granular degeneration of the kidneys. [Dr. Richard *Bright*, English physician (1789–1858)]

Brig·id (brĭj′ĭd, brē′ĭd): see BRIDGET.

Bril·lat-Sa·va·rin (brēyă′săvă-răn′), **Anthelme** (1755–1826). French statesman, writer, and journalist; author of a literary work on gastronomy, *The Physiology of Taste.*

bril·liant (brĭl′yant) *adj.* Bright, sparkling; illustrious; highly talented; showy. **bril′liant·ly** *adv.* **bril′liance, bril′lian·cy** *ns.* **brilliant** *n.* 1. Diamond or other gem of faceted cut; ~-**cut**, faceted; (in diamond) cut designed to give maximum brilliance, usu. consisting of 58 facets. 2. (print.) Very small size of type, approx. 3 1/2 point.

bril·lian·tine (brĭl′yantēn) *n.* Oily preparation for keeping hair smooth and glossy.

Brig

Brigantine

During the 18th and 19th centuries, **brigantines** were found in all the world's oceans as trading vessels and as naval ships. Being small a maneuverable, they were ideal for r trading, scouting and chasing.

brim (brĭm) *n.* Edge or lip of cup, bowl, or hollow; projecting edge of hat; **brim′ful**, full to the brim. **brim** *v.* (**brimmed, brim′ming**). Fill, be full, to the brim. **brim′less** *adj.*

brim·stone (brĭm′stōn) *n.* (obs.) Sulfur fuel of hellfire.

brin·dled (brĭn′deld) *adj.* Brownish or tawny with streaks of other color; **brin′dle** *adj.* **brindle** *n.* A brindled color or animal.

brine (brīn) *n.* Water saturate or strongly impregnated, with s the sea. ~ *v.t.* (**brined, brin·in** Steep or pickle in brine.

bring (brĭng) *v.* (**brought** brawt, **bring·ing**). Cause to con come with or convey in any fashio cause, result in; prefer (charg adduce (argument); cause to b come; persuade; ~ **about**, cause pen; **~ around**, convince; ...ve, restore to consciousness; ~ ...vn, kill or wound, cause to fall, ...se (penalty) to alight *on*, abase, ...er, continue (record) *to* a point; **down the house**, (colloq.) ...eive loud applause; **~ forth**, ...r, produce; cause; **~ in**, pro-...ce, introduce; pronounce (ver-...t); **~ off**, conduct with success; ...to, restore to consciousness; ~ **mind**, cause (oneself) to remem-...; **~ to pass**, cause to happen; **up**, rear, educate, come to a ...p, call attention (*again*) to.

...**rink** (brĭngk) *n.* Edge of steep ...ce; border of water, esp. when ...ep; verge (also fig.). **brink·-...an·ship** (brĭngk′mănshĭp) *n.* ...nk of advancing to the very ...nk of war but not engaging in it.

...**brin·y** (brī′nē) *adj.* (**brin·i·er, ...in·i·est**). Very salty. **~** *n.* ...ang) The sea.

...**bri·o** (brē′ō) *n.* Vivacity, vigor, ...sh. [It.]

bri·quette, bri·quet (brĭkĕt′) *ns.* Block of compressed coal dust or charcoal, usu. with addition of binding substance such as pitch.

Bris·bane (brĭz′bān, -bĭn). Capital, chief port, and main industrial center of Queensland, in SE. Australia.

brisk (brĭsk) *adj.* Active, lively; enlivening, keen. **brisk′ly** *adv.* **brisk′ness** *n.*

bris·ket (brĭs′kĭt) *n.* Chest of animals; meat from this part.

bris·ling (brĭs′lĭng) *n.* Young herring or sprat.

bris·tle (brĭs′el) *n.* Stiff hair (esp. of hog's back and sides), used for brushes; anything resembling this. **bris′tly** *adj.* (**-tli·er, -tli·est**).

*The ancient port of **Bristol**, in Gloucestershire (now Avon), U.K., received its first charter in 1155. St. Mary Redcliffe shown here is one of several fine buildings in the city. It is one of England's largest parish churches.*

bristle *v.i.* (**-tled, -tling**). (Cause to) stand on end, raise, rise, like bristles; show temper, prepare for fight; be thickly set (*with* difficulties etc.).

Bris·tol (brĭs′tol). City and port on river Avon, in SW. England; ~

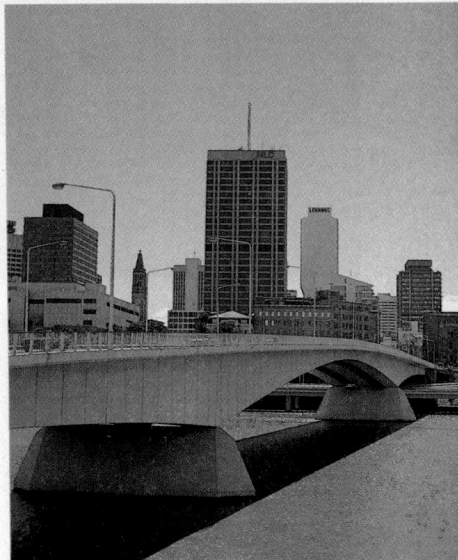

Brisbane, *capital and principal port of Queensland, is Australia's 3rd-largest city. Founded in 1824 as a penal colony, it was proclaimed a city in 1902.*

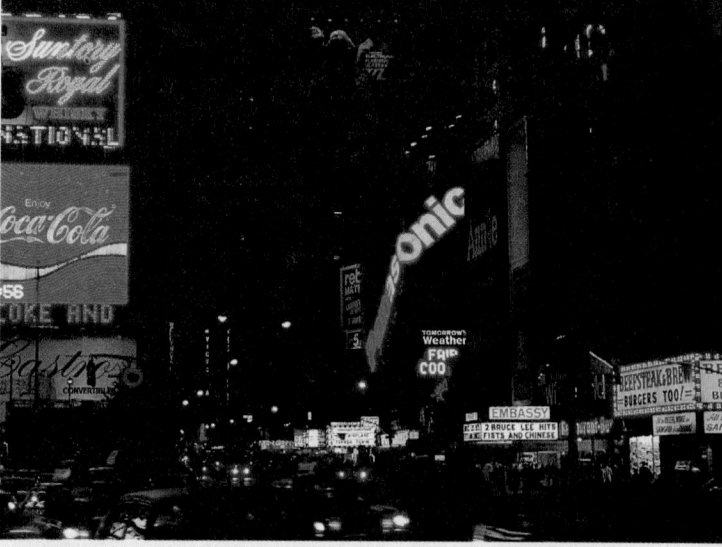

*The peoples who have contributed to the history of **Britain** have left behind them many traces of their cultures. Top: Stonehenge, Wiltshire, is a mysterious ruin raised in various stages from about*

2100 to 1400 B.C. Above left: The sculptor of this Anglo-Saxon cross at Irton, Cumbria, belonged to one of the peoples that invaded Britain during the Dark Ages.

*Above: **Broadway,** the New York City thoroughfare which runs throug Manhattan is most famed as the theate district.*

board, fine cardboard for drawing; **~ Channel**, arm of the Atlantic between Wales and SW. England.

Brit. *abbrev.* Britain; British.

Brit·ain (brĭt´in). (also **Great ~**) Island containing England, Wales, and Scotland, with their dependencies; **Battle of ~**, series of air battles (Aug.–Sept. 1940) over London and SE. England between British and German air forces in which British victory ended the threat of German invasion.

Bri·tan·ni·a (brĭtăn´ēa, -tăn´ya). 1. (poet.) Great Britain. 2. Britain personified, usu. represented (e.g. on coins) as a woman with shield, helmet, and trident. 3. **~ metal**, an alloy of tin with copper, antimony, and sometimes bismuth, used for tableware etc. [L.]

Bri·tan·nic (brĭtăn´ĭk) *adj.* (now chiefly in **His, Her ~ Majesty**) Of

Britain. **Brit·i·cism** (brĭt´ĭsĭzem) *n.* Word or idiom used in Great Britain but not in U.S. etc. Also **Britishism**.

Brit·ish (brĭt´ĭsh) *adj.* 1. Of Great Britain; (loosely) of the United Kingdom, or the British Empire or Commonwealth; **~ Broadcasting Corporation**, (abbreviation B.B.C.) public corporation responsible for all radio and noncommercial television broadcasting in the United Kingdom; **~ Commonwealth of Nations**: see COMMONWEALTH; **~ Empire**, (formerly) territories under leadership or control of Great Britain; **~ Library**, national library of Britain, one of the COPYRIGHT libraries; **Order of the ~ Empire**, military and civil award (instituted 1917) for services rendered to the British Empire; **~ Museum**, British national museum

of antiquities etc. in Bloomsbu London; **~ thermal unit**: s THERMAL. **British** *n.* People Britain.

Brit·ish (brĭt´ĭsh) **Columbi** Westernmost province of Canad bordering on the Pacific Ocea capital, Victoria.

Brit·ish·er (brĭt´ĭsher) *n.* Nati or inhabitant of Great Britain.

Brit·ish (brĭt´ĭsh) **Isles**. Brita and Ireland, with the islands ne their coasts.

Brit·ish·ism (brĭt´ĭshĭzer (Brit.) = BRITICISM.

Bri·ton (brĭt´on) *n.* 1. Inhabita of Great Britain. 2. (also **ancie ~**) Celtic inhabitant of the S. pa of ancient Britain at the time of t Roman invasion.

Brit·ta·ny (brĭt´anē). (Bretagne) NW. district of Franc an ancient province and duch largely inhabited by a Celtic sto lated to that of Britain.

Brit·ten (brĭt´en), **Edward Benjamin** (1913–). British composer of operas (*Peter Grimes* &c.) and other music.

brit·tle (brĭt´el) *adj.* (**-tler, -tlest**). Apt to break, fragile. ~ *n.* Brittle candy made from melted sugar, usu. containing nuts, as peanut ~.

broach[1] (brōch) *n.* 1. Spit for roasting. 2. Tool for shaping and enlarging holes. ~ *v.t.* Pierce (cask) to draw liquor, begin drawing (liquor), open (bale, box, etc.); begin discussion of (subject). **broach'er** *n.*

broach[2] (brōch) *v.* (usu. ~ **to**) veer, cause (ship) to veer and present side to wind and waves.

broad (brawd) *adj.* 1. Large across, wide, not narrow; in width, *is 20 ft.* ~; extensive. 2. Full, clear, plain, explicit; general; tolerant; bold in effect or style; (of humor) coarse; (of speech) strongly dialectal. 3. ~ **bean**, (seed of) a variety of edible bean (*Vicia faba*); **broad'cloth**, fine twilled woolen cloth, (also) plainly woven cotton cloth (the name refers rather to quality than width); **broad'loom**, (carpet) woven in width greater than 54 in.; loom weaving this; **broad-minded**, tolerant or liberal in thought or opinion; **broad'side**, ship's side above water between bow and quarter; (discharge of) all guns on one side of ship; (fig.) direct attack; large sheet of paper printed on one side as an advertisement; **broad'sword**, broadbladed cutting sword; **broad'tail**, [transl. Ger. *breitschwanz*] karacul fur. **broad** *n.* Broad part; (slang) a woman. **broad'ish** *adj.* **broad'ly** *adv.* **broad'ness** *n.* **broad** *adv.* Broadly.

broad·cast (brawd´kăst) *adj.* 1. (of seed) Scattered freely, not in drills or rows. 2. (of information, news, music, etc.) Sent or received by broadcasting. ~ *adv.* (Sown, disseminated) in this manner. ~ *n.* Action of broadcasting; broadcast program etc. ~ *v.* (**-cast** or **-cast·ed, -cast·ing**). 1. Sow (seed) broadcast. 2. Disseminate (news, musical performances, etc.) from a radio or television transmitting station; said also of performer etc. **broad'cast·er** *n.* **broad'cast·ing** *n. & adj.*

broad·en (braw´den) *v.* Make, grow, broader.

Broad·way (brawd´wā). Street in New York City extending the entire length of Manhattan and famous for its commerce and theaters; (colloq.) the professional New York City theater.

Brob·ding·nag (brŏb´dĭngnăg). In Swift's *Gulliver's Travels*, a country inhabited by giants. **Brob·ding·nag'i·an** *adj. & n.*

bro·cade (brōkād´) *n.* 1. Fabric, of any weave or yarn, enriched by a design that is formed by additional weft threads, often of metal, running back and forth across each motif only (not from selvage to selvage). 2. Fabric superficially resembling this, produced by Jacquard loom. ~ *v.t.* (**-cad·ed, -cad·ing**). Enrich (fabric) with design by these means. **bro·cad'ed** *adj.*

broc·co·li (brŏk´ōlē) *n.* Cultivated plant of genus *Brassica* resembling cauliflower, eaten as

vegetable before the green buds open.

bro·chure (brōshoor´) *n.* Booklet, pamphlet.

brogue[1] (brōg) *n.* Rough Irish and Scottish Highland shoe of untanned leather; strong outdoor shoe with bands of ornamental perforations.

brogue[2] (brōg) *n.* Dialectal, esp. Irish, accent.

broil[1] (broil) *n.* Quarrel, tumult.

broil[2] (broil) *v.* Cook (meat), be cooked, by exposure to radiant heat; scorch, make or be very hot.

broil·er (broi´ler) *n.* (esp.) 1. Tender young chicken suitable for broiling. 2. Part of stove used for broiling; small electric appliance used for broiling.

broke (brōk) *adj.* (colloq.)

*The people of **Brittany**, in France, maintain many old customs and styles of dress. The coif is worn daily by older women, and the young women wear it for festivals.*

Ruined, penniless.

bro·ken (brō′ken) *adj.*: see BREAK; ~ **English** etc., imperfect English spoken often with a strong foreign accent; ~ **ground**, uneven ground; ~**-hearted**, crushed by grief. **bro′ken·ly** *adv.* Spasmodically, by jerks, with breaks. **bro′ken·ness** *n.*

bro·ker (brō′ker) *n.* Middleman, agent; stockbroker. **bro′ker·age** *n.* Broker's fees or commission, esp. on stock exchange transactions. [OF. *brocheor* "broacher," retailer of wine]

bro·me·li·ad (brōmē′lĕăd) *n.* Any of various Amer. chiefly epiphytic plants of the family Bromeliaceae, including the pineapple, Spanish moss, and many ornamental species.

bro·mide (brō′mīd) *n.* 1. Compound of bromine with an element of organic radical. 2. Potassium bromide, KBr, taken as a sedative; (fig., colloq.) conventional and commonplace person or remark.

bro·mine (brō′mēn) *n.* (chem.) Non-metallic element, closely resembling chlorine in its properties and compounds; dark reddish-black heavy liquid with a strong irritating smell; symbol Br, at. no. 35, at. wt. 79.904. [Gk. *brōmos* stink]

bron·chi·a (brŏng′kēa) *n.pl.* Ramifications of bronchi in lungs.

bron·chi·al (brŏng′kēal) *adj.* Of the bronchi or bronchia.

bron·chi·tis (brŏngkī′tĭs) *n.* Inflammation of bronchial mucous membrane.

bron·cho·scope (brŏng′koskōp) *n.* Instrument for inspecting interior of bronchi.

bron·chus (brŏng′kus) *n.* (pl. **-chi** pr. -kī). Either of the two main divisions of the windpipe.

bron·co, bron·cho (brŏng′kō) *ns.* (pl. **-cos, -chos**). Wild or half-tamed horse or pony of Western U.S.; **bron′cobuster**, cowboy who breaks in broncos.

Bron·të (brŏn′të), **Charlotte** (1816–55), **Emily** (1818–48), and **Anne** (1820–49). Novelists, daughters of a Yorkshire clergyman of Irish descent; wrote under pseudonyms of Currer, Ellis, and Acton Bell; Charlotte is famous esp. for *Jane Eyre* (1847), Emily for *Wuthering Heights* (1848).

bron·to·saur (brŏn′tosōr) *n.* Herbivorous dinosaur of genus *Brontosaurus* from the Jurassic and Cretaceous periods, one of the largest terrestrial vertebrates. [Gk. *brontë* thunder, *sauros* lizard]

Bronx (brŏngks), **The.** One of the five boroughs of New York City.

bronze (brŏnz) *n.* Brown alloy chiefly of copper and tin; work of art made of bronze; color of bronze; **B~ Age**, that stage of a people's culture, between the Stone Age and Iron Age, during which its weapons etc. were made of bronze. **bronze** *adj.* Made of, colored, like, bronze. ~ *v.* (**bronzed, bronz·ing**). Give bronze-like surface to; make or become brown, tan. **bronz′y** *adj.* (**bronz·i·er, bronz·i·est**). [L. (*aes*) *Brundisinum* (brass) from Brundisium (Brindisi)]

brooch (brōch, brōoch) *n.* Ornamental clasp worn on dress etc., secured by hinged pin and catch.

brood (brōod) *n.* Young birds etc. produced at one hatch; (usu. joc.) human family, children. ~ *adj.* For breeding. ~ *v.i.* 1. (of bird) Sit on eggs to be hatched. 2. Hang close *over, on*; meditate, often sullenly or with resentment (*on, over*, etc.). **brood′ing·ly** *adv.*

brood·y (brōo′dē) *adj.* (**brood·i·er, brood·i·est**). (of hen) Wanting to remain on nest to hatch eggs; (of person) moody, gloomy.

brook[1] (brōok) *n.* Small stream.

brook[2] (brōok) *v.t.* Put up with, tolerate.

Brooke (brōok), **Rupert** (1887–1915). English poet famous for his poems on World War I, in which he died.

Brook (brōok) **Farm.** Utopian socialist community in West Roxbury, Mass., 1841–7; noted for its association with Emerson and other literary figures.

Brook·lyn (brōok′lĭn). One of the five boroughs of New York City.

Brooks (brōoks), **Van Wyck** (1886–1963). American essayist, critic, and translator; author of *America's Coming-of-Age*, *The Flowering of New England*, etc.

broom (brōom) *n.* 1. Yellow flowered shrub of the genus *Cytisus*, growing on sandy banks, heaths, etc.; shrub of related genus *Genista*; **broom′rape**, brown leafless fleshy-stemmed parasitic plant

*A typical tenement in the largely-residential area of the **Bronx**, New York City, also renowned for its zoo, refurbished in the 1960s, and the Yankee Stadium.*

Above: The suppleness of the human form was expressed in **bronze** *by Indian sculptors in this image of Siva. Above right: Bronze beaten into a sheet and ornamented with repoussé motifs and enamel bosses shows the skills of Celtic workmanship. Above: African smiths in Benin, now south-west Nigeria, produced beautiful cast figures and heads in bronze.*

genus *Orobranche*, growing on ~~~ots of brooms and other plants.

Implement for sweeping, orig. ~~~ broom twigs fixed to long stick ~~~ handle, now of any material; **room'stick**, handle of broom (on ~~~hich witches were said to fly ~~~hrough the air).

bros. *abbrev.* Brothers.

broth (brawth, brŏth) *n.* Un~~~leared meat or fish stock used for ~~~aking soup; thin, clear soup.

broth·el (brŏth'el, brŏdh'-, ~~~aw'thel, -dhel) *n.* House where ~~~rostitutes are available.

broth·er (brŭdh'er) *n.* 1. Male ~~~ith the same parents as another ~~~erson. 2. Fellow, companion, ~~~qual. 3. (with pl. **breth·ren** pr. ~~~rĕdh'ren) Member of religious ~~~rder, fellow member of church, ~~~uild, order, etc. 4. **~-in-law**, brother of one's husband or wife, husband of one's sister. **broth'er·ly** *adj.* Of, like, a brother('s), fraternal. **broth'er·li·ness** *n.*

broth·er·hood (brŭdh'erhood) *n.* Fraternal tie; companionship; (members of) association for mutual help etc.

brougham (brŏom, brŏo'em, brŏm, brŏ'em) *n.* One-horse, four-wheeled closed carriage with an open driver's seat in front; closed electrically-driven carriage for four or five passengers; limousine with open seat for driver. [f. Lord *Brougham* (1778–1868), lawyer,

politician, and Lord Chancellor of England]

brought (brawt): see BRING.

brow (brow) *n.* Arch of hair over eye (usu. in pl.); forehead; edge, projection, of cliff etc., top of hill in road.

brow·beat (brow'bēt) *v.t.* (**-beat, -beat·en, -beat·ing**). Bully, bear down, with looks and words. **brow'beat·er** *n.*

brown (brown) *adj.* 1. Of the color produced by a mixture of orange and black pigments, or by partial charring of starch or woody fiber, as in toasted bread, etc. 2.

Dark, dark skinned; tanned. 3. ~
bread, bread of dark flour; ~
paper, unbleached paper used for
packing, etc.; **brown'shirt**, Nazi
storm trooper; **brown'stone**, dark
brown sandstone used in building;
a building made of this; ~ **study**,
reverie; ~ **sugar**, unrefined or
partially refined sugar. **brown** *n.*
Brown color or pigment; (ellipt.)
brown clothes, etc. ~ *v.* Make or
become brown by roasting, chemical process, etc.

Brown (brown), **John** (1800–
1859). Abolitionist leader who with
only 18 men seized the Federal
arsenal at Harper's Ferry, Virginia
(1859); pursued and caught by army
troops under Robert E. Lee; hanged
at Charlestown, Virginia; hero of
popular songs, poems, etc.

Browne (brown), **Sir Thomas**
(1605–82). English physician,
author of *Religio Medici* (1642).

Brown·i·an (brow'nĕan) **movement.** Irregular oscillatory movement of microscopic particles in
fluids, due to molecular bombardment. [discovered by Robert
Brown (1773–1858), Scottish
botanist]

brown·ie (brow'nē) *n.* 1.
Benevolent shaggy goblin (a "wee
brown man") said to haunt houses
and do household work secretly. 2.
B ~, member of junior branch of
Girl Scouts at ages seven and eight.
3. A square, moist cake-like chocolate cookie.

Brown·ing[1] (brow'nĭng) *n.* (also
~ **automatic rifle**). A .30 caliber
air-cooled automatic and semiauto-
matic gas-operated magazine rifle
used in World Wars I and II; ~
machine gun, .30 caliber automatic machine gun; .50 caliber
automatic machine gun. [J.M.
Browning (1885–1926), Amer. firearms designer]

Brown·ing[2] (brow'nĭng), **Elizabeth Barrett** (1806–61). English
poet, wife of Robert Browning.

Brown·ing[3] (brow'nĭng),
Robert (1812–89). English poet,
author of numerous philosophical
and dramatic lyrics and of several
dramas.

browse (browz) *v.* (**browsed,
brows·ing**). Feed *on*, crop (leaves,
twigs, scanty vegetation); feed thus;
(fig.) read desultorily for enjoyment. ~ *n.* Browsing. **brows'er**
n.

Bruce (brōōs), **Robert de**
(1274–1329). Robert I, king of
Scotland (1306–29), which he

*The Dome of Florence Cathederal (Il
Duomo) seen by night from Piazza
Michelangelo.* ***Filippo Bruneleschi*** *was
responsible for the design of the dome,
and the machines that were required to
carry out the work, from 1420 until 1446.*

erated from the English.

bru·cel·lo·sis (brōōselō´sĭs) *n.* ... sease caused by bacteria of genus *ucella*, causing abortion in cattle; man) undulant fever.

bru·cine (brōō´sēn, -sĭn) *n.* ...ghly poisonous vegetable alka-...d found in false Angostura bark d in nux vomica.

Bruck·ner (brŭk´ner; *Ger.* ōōk´ner), **Anton** (1824–96). ...strian composer of church music d symphonies.

Brue·ghel, Breu·ghel, Brue-...l (broi´gel, brōō´-; *Flem.* brö´gel). ...rname of a large family of ...emish painters, the most famous ... whom is **Pieter Bruegel the** ...der (*c*1520–69), painter of lively ...asant scenes.

Bru·ges (brōōzh; *Fr.* brüzh). ...l. Brugge) City in Belgium, ...pital of West Flanders, famous ...r its bells and canals.

bru·in (brōō´ĭn) *n.* Bear. [Name ... bear in fable of Reynard the Fox, ...Du., = BROWN]

bruise (brōōz) *n.* Injury by blow ... body, fruit, etc., discoloring skin. ...*v.* (**bruised, bruis·ing**). Injure ...blow that discolors skin without ...eaking it; batter; pound, grind ...hall; show effects of blow. ...ruis´er *n.* (esp.) Big strong man.

bruit (brōōt) *v.t.* Spread (a ...mor) *abroad, about.*

Bru·maire (brōōmār´; *Fr.* ...ümĕr´) *n.* Second month in

The city of **Bruges,** capital of the West Flanders province of Belgium, retains some of its old street trades. Here a woman is seen making bobbin lace.

French Revolutionary calendar, Oct. 22–Nov. 20; **18** ~, Nov. 9, 1799, day on which Napoleon Bonaparte became First Consul. [Fr. *brume* mist]

Bru·nei (brōōnī´). British protected state on NW. coast of Borneo; its capital.

Bru·nel·les·chi (brōōneĕs´kē), **Bru·nel·les·co** (brōōneĕs´kō), **Filippo** (1377–1446). Florentine architect and engineer; designed dome of Cathedral of Florence.

'Children Playing' by **Pieter Brueghel** *the Elder, is typical of the lively and humorous paintings made early in his life. Later, many of his works show a more satirical view of the world.*

bru·nette (brōōnĕt´) *n.* & *adj.* Dark-skinned and brown-haired (woman); **brunet,** such a person.

Brun·hild, Bryn·hild (brōōn´-hĭld). In the *Nibelungenlied,* wife of Gunther, who instigated the murder of Siegfried; in Norse versions, a Valkyrie whom Sigurd wins by penetrating the wall of fire behind which she lies in an enchanted sleep.

Bru·no[1] (brōō´nō), **Giordano** (*c*1548–*c*99). Italian philosopher; regarded God as the unity reconciling spirit and matter; was condemned to death by the Inquisition.

Bruno[2] (bro͞onō), **St.** (c1035–1101). Founder of the Carthusian order.

brunt (brŭnt) n. Chief stress of shock or attack etc.

brush (brŭsh) n. 1. Thicket, brushwood, growing or cut in faggots; land covered with thicket; backwoods; dense forests, undergrowth and thickets of small trees. 2. Implement of bristles, hair, wire, etc., set in wood etc. for sweeping or scrubbing dust and dirt from a surface, usu. named acc. to its use, as **clothes′brush, hair′brush**; bunch of hairs etc. in straight handle for painting etc.; application of brush, brushing; (mus.) one of a pair of devices with wire bristles for striking drums etc. 3. Tail, esp. of

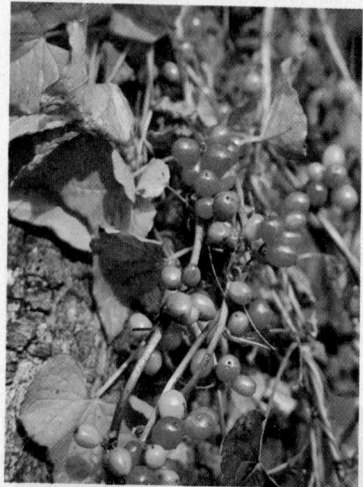

fox; brushlike tuft. 4. (elect.) Brushlike discharge of sparks; strip of conducting material (usu. hardened carbon) for making or breaking contact; fixed contact that bears on slip ring of dynamo. 5. Short sharp encounter, skirmish. 6. **brush′wood**, cut or broken twigs etc.; undergrowth, thicket; **brush′-work**, painter's (style of) manipulation. **brush** v. Sweep or scrub, put in order, remove, with brush; graze or touch in passing; ~ **aside**, **away**, (fig.) ignore, pass over; ~ **off**, dismiss, rebuff; ~**-off** (n.) curt dismissal; ~ **up**, furbish, renew one's memory of; **brush′up** (n.). **brushed** (adj.) (esp. of fabric) With nap raised by brushing. **brush′y** adj. (**brush·i·er, brush·-i·est**).

brusque (brŭsk) adj. Blunt, offhand, abrupt.

Brus·sels (brŭs′elz). (Fr. *Bruxelles*) Capital city of Belgium; ~ **carpet**, carpet with back of strong linen thread and pile of wool; ~ **lace**, rich lace with appliqué design, as first made in Brussels in 18th c.; ~ **sprouts**, edible bud-bearing cabbage (*Brassica oleracea*

Left: Tamus communis, called black bryony, carries elliptical scarlet berries in the Fall. These are poisonous and larger than the berries of white bryony which is of another genus.

Below: The Grande Place, Brussels, has many noble buildings. The 13th-century meeting place of the Estates General and several guildhalls border the square, which is nowadays the site of a bird market.

gemmifera), producing buds l small cabbages in the axils of leaves; its buds.

brut (bro͞ot) adj. (of wine) D unsweetened. [Fr.]

bru·tal (bro͞o′tal) adj. Savage cruel, coarse, sensual. **bru′tal** adv. **bru·tal·i·ty** (bro͞otăl′ītē) (pl. **-ties**). **bru′tal·ize** v.t. & v (**-ized, -iz·ing**).

brute (bro͞ot) adj. 1. (of bea Not possessing the capacity reason. 2. Stupid, sensual, beas like, cruel, or passionate; ~ **forc** unreasoning force. **brute** n. Bru beast, lower animal; brutal, brut like person; lower nature in ma **brut′ish** adj. **brut′ish·ly** ad **brut′ish·ness** n.

Bru·tus[1] (bro͞o′tus). Legendar founder of the British peopl according to myth a great-grandso of AENEAS; brought a group of t Trojans to England, founde Troynovant or New Troy (lat called London), and was a pr genitor of a line of kings.

Bru·tus[2] (bro͞o′tus), **Luciu Junius** (d. 508 B.C.). Legendar First Consul of Rome, and leade in the expulsion of the Tarquins

Bru·tus[3] (boo′tus), **Marcu Junius** (85–42 B.C.). Roma soldier; joined the conspirators wh assassinated Julius Caesar in hop of restoring republican governi ment.

Bry·an (brī′an), **William Jenn ings** (1860–1925). America lawyer and political leader; thre times a candidate for the presi dency; advocate of free coinage c silver; a prosecuting attorney in th famous trial of John Scopes fo teaching evolution.

Bry·ant (brī′ant), **Willian Cullen** (1794–1878). America poet, newspaper owner, and editor author of the poems "Thanatop sis," "To a Waterfowl," etc.

Bryce (brīs) **Canyon Nationa Park.** National park in S. Utal noted for its colorful rock pinnacle and canyons.

Bryn·hild (bro͞on′hild) = BRUNHILD.

bry·o·ny (brī′onē) n. (pl. **-nies**) Either of two European climbing plants: **black** ~ (*Tamus communis*) dark shining green, without ten drils; **white** ~ (*Bryonia dioica*) rough textured and light colored with conspicuous coiled tendrils.

bry·o·phyte (brī′ofīt) n. Mem ber of the Bryophyta, a group of plants comprising the liverworts and mosses. **bry·o·phyt·ic** (brīofīt′ĭk) adj.

bry·o·zo·an (brīozō′an) adj. & n. (Member) of the Bryozoa, a phylum

Bryce Canyon National Park, Utah, established as a national monument and a sanctuary for many species of anima and bird life.

James Buchanan, 15th President of
the U.S.A. (1857–61), whose attempts
to avert the conflict between North and
South over slavery dominated his term
in office.

Cowboys ride **bucking** broncos into
submission, a test of courage and
horsemanship. The taming of wild
horses is a traditional activity in the
western states of the U.S.A.

of aquatic animals that form
colonies of small polyps.

B.S. *abbrev.* Bachelor of Science.

B.S.A. *abbrev.* Boy Scouts of
America.

B.Sc. *abbrev.* Bachelor of
Science.

bsh. *abbrev.* Bushel, bushels.

bskt. *abbrev.* Basket.

Bt. *abbrev.* Baronet.

Btu, B.T.U., B.t.u. *abbrevs.*
British thermal unit(s).

bub·ble (bŭb′el) *n.* 1. Spherical
or hemispherical envelope of liquid
(or solidified liquid, as glass)
enclosing air etc. 2. Unsubstantial
or visionary project, enterprise, etc.
3. Sound or appearance of boiling;
~ **chamber,** (phys.) container of
superheated liquid for detection of
ionizing particles; ~ **gum,** chewing gum that can be blown into
bubbles. **bubble** *v.i.* (**-bled,**
-bling). Send up, rise in, make the
sound of, bubbles.

bub·bly (bŭb′lē) *adj.* (**-bli·er,**
-bli·est). Full of bubbles. ~ *n.*
(slang) Champagne.

bu·bo (bū′bō) *n.* (pl. **-boes**).
Inflamed swelling in glandular part
esp. groin or armpit.

bu·bon·ic (būbŏn′ĭk, bōō-) *adj.*
Characterized by buboes; ~
plague, disease characterized by

these and by fever and prostration,
carried by rats and transmitted to
man by fleas.

buc·ca·neer (bŭkanēr′) *n.*
Pirate, esp. one who preyed upon
Spanish shipping in the West
Indies in 17th c.; unscrupulous
adventurer. ~ *v.i.* Act as buc-
caneer. [Fr. *boucanier* f. *boucaner*
to cure meat on a *boucan* (i.e.
barbecue), a Tupi wd.]

Bu·ceph·a·lus (būsĕf′alus).
Favorite war horse of Alexander the
Great.

Bu·chan·an (būkăn′an), **James**
(1791–1868). Fifteenth president
of U.S., 1857–61.

Bu·cha·rest (būkerĕst′, bōō -,
bū′kerĕst, bōō′-). (Rumanian
Bucuresti) Capital city of Rumania.

Bu·chen·wald (bōōk′enwawld;
Ger. bōō′χenvahlt). Village in E.
Germany; site of notorious Nazi
concentration camp during World
War II.

buck¹ (bŭk) *n.* (pl. **bucks,**
collect. **buck**). Male of fallow deer,
reindeer, chamois, hare, rabbit;
dandy; ~ **fever,** nervousness of

inexperienced hunter at first chanc
to shoot; **buck′shot,** large lead sho
for shotgun shells; **buck′skin**
(leather made of) buck's skin; (pl.
breeches of this; **buck′thorn**
thorny shrub esp. of genu
Rhamnus; **buck′tooth**(**ed**), (hav
ing) projecting tooth. ~ *adj*
(slang) Male. **buck′er** *n.*

buck² (bŭk) *v.* (of horse) Jum
vertically with back arched and fee
drawn together.

buck³ (bŭk) *v.* (slang) Oppose
~ **up,** become or make vigorous o
cheerful.

buck⁴ (bŭk) *n.* Body of cart
chiefly in combination, as **buck′-
board,** plank slung upon wheels
light vehicle with body consisting of
this.

buck⁵ (bŭk) *n.* (slang) Dollar.

buck⁶ (bŭk) *n.* Sawbuck; padded
block in gymnasium for vaulting;
buck′saw, saw for cutting firewood, with blade set across wooden
frame.

buck⁷ (bŭk) *n.* Counter placed
before a poker player to mark him
as the next dealer; **pass the ~,**

*The **Great Buddha**, Kamakura, Japan. Wherever Buddhism has spread in Asia, temples house the dominating images of various Buddhas, Bodhisattvas and saints.*

Buckingham Palace, London residence of the British Royal Family, was bought in 1762 by George III. It was rebuilt by John Nash. Queen Victoria was first sovereign to live there.

ang) shift responsibility (*to*).

Buck (bŭk), **Pearl** (1892–1973). American novelist; awarded Nobel ize for literature, 1938; author of *e Good Earth*, which won the litzer Prize, 1932, and *Dragon ed*, etc.

buck·et (bŭk′ĭt) *n.* 1. Vessel for llecting, holding, or carrying ter etc.; amount contained in this so **buck′etful**); ~ **brigade**, line persons passing buckets of water m pond etc. to put out a fire so fig.). 2. Anything resembling is; (esp.) compartment of water eel; scoop of dredger. 3. ~ at, seat with high rounded or olded back, as in sports cars; ~ op, fraudulent firm of stock-okers that speculates on its own count without regard for its ents' interests.

Buck·ing·ham (bŭk′ĭngam, ăm), **George Villiers, 1st Duke** f (1592–1628). Favorite of James of England.

Buck·ing·ham (bŭk′ĭngam, ăm) **Palace.** Official London sidence of the British sovereign.

buck·le (bŭk′el) *n.* Clasp usu. ith hinged tongue for securing rap, belt, etc.; ornament for shoe c. resembling this. ~ *v.* (**-led, ling**). Fasten with buckle; (cause) give way, crumple up, under ressure; ~ **down** (**to**), set about, t to work, start vigorously.

buck·ram (bŭk′ram) *n.* Coarse nen or cotton fabric stiffened with lue, used in linings and for binding ooks.

buck·wheat (bŭk′hwēt, -wēt) *n.* Cereal plant (*Polygonum fago-yrum*), with seed used for fodder nd flour; ~ **cake**, pancake made of his flour.

bu·col·ic (būkŏl′ĭk) *adj.* Of hepherds, pastoral, rustic; a pas-oral poem.

bud¹ (bŭd) *n.* 1. Projection at nd of shoot or axil of leaf, pro-ected by scales which are altered

leaves, forming rudiment of shoot, foliage, or flower; leaf or flower not fully open; ~ **scale**, altered leaf protecting a bud. 2. (zool.) Asexual reproductive growth attached to parent and developing into new individual esp. in coelenterates. 3. **nip in the** ~, (fig.) stop (some-thing) before it is fully developed. **bud** *v.* (**bud·ded, bud·ding**). 1. Put forth buds; begin to grow or develop. 2. Graft a bud on to another plant.

bud² (colloq.) = BUDDY.

Bu·da·pest (bōō′dapĕst, bū′-; *Hung.* bōō′dapĕsht). Capital city of Hungary, orig. consisting of two towns, Buda on right bank of river Danube and Pest on left.

Bud·dha (bōō′da, bōōd′a). "Enlightened one," name applied esp. to Siddartha Gautama (*c*560–*c*480 B.C.), son of the rajah of the Sakya tribe (hence also called *Sakyamuni*, "sage of the Sakyas"; as a young man he abandoned his home in Nepal and renounced the world; practiced an extreme as-ceticism, preached, and became the founder of Buddhism.

Bud·dhism (bōō′dĭzem, bōōd′-ĭz-) *n.* System founded by the Buddha, orig. practiced chiefly in India; it was in decline there by the 4th c. A.D. but was diffused over China, Japan, and central and SE. Asia; there are two principal schools, MAHAYANA and THERA-VADA (Hinayana); chief doctrines: the principal cause of suffering is desire; and the suppression of desire and consequently of suffer-ing can be obtained by discipline and ultimately rewarded by NIRVANA. **Bud′dhist** *n.* & *adj.* **Bud·dhis′tic** *adj.*

bud·dle·ia (bŭd′lēa, bŭdlē′a) *n.* Shrub or tree of genus *B*~, often having honey-scented flowers. [Adam *Buddle* (d. 1715), Engl. botanist]

bud·dy (bŭd′ē) *n.* (pl. **-dies**). (colloq.) Brother; companion, friend (freq. as form of address). [Childish pronunciation of *brother*]

budge (bŭj) *v.* (**budged, budg·ing**). Move in the slightest degree, stir.

budg·er·i·gar (bŭj′erēgar) *n.* A parakeet (*Melopsittacus undulatus*), native to Australia and having green, yellow, or blue plumage, req. kept as pet; abbrev. **bu′dgie** (′bŭj′ē).

budg·et (bŭj′ĭt) *n.* 1. (archaic) Contents of a bag or bundle (chiefly fig. of news etc.). 2. Annual estimate of revenue and expenditure. 3. Amount of money required or available. 4. *attrib.* Inexpensive. **budg′et·ar·y** *adj.* **budget** *v.* (**-et·ed, -et·ing**). ~ **for**, allow or arrange for in budget. **budg′et·er** *n.*

Bue·na Vis·ta (bwā′na vēs′ta). Historic battlefield near Saltillo, NE. Mexico, where U.S. troops under Zachary Taylor defeated the Mexicans under Santa Anna, 1847, ending the northern campaign in the Mexican War.

Bue·nos Ai·res (bwā′nos ār′ēz, īr′ĭs; *Sp.* bwĕ′naws ī′rĕs). Capital city and chief port of Argentina.

buff (bŭf) *n.* 1. Stout velvety dull-yellow leather of buffalo, elk, or ox hide; **in (the)** ~, naked. 2. Dull-yellow color of buff. **buff** *adj.* Made of, colored like, buff. ~ *v.t.* Polish (metal) with buff, make (leather) velvety like buff. **buf′fer** *n.*

Buf·fa·lo (bŭf′alō). Port city on Lake Erie in W. New York State; site of 1901 Pan-American Exposition, at which President McKinley was assassinated.

buf·fa·lo (bŭf′alō) *n.* (pl. **-loes**, **-los**, collect. **-lo**). Ox, esp. of one of three species: *Bison bison* of N. Amer., *Bubalus bubalis* of Asia, and *Syncerus caffer*, of S. Africa; ~ **chips**, dried dung of buffalo etc. as fuel; ~ **grass**, prairie grass (*Sesleria dactyloides*).

Buf·fa·lo (bŭf′alō) **Bill.** Popular nickname of William Frederick Cody (1846–1917), Amer. frontiersman, scout, and showman, credited with legendary exploits against Indians and bandits and with killing buffalo to provide meat to workmen building the transcontinental railroad.

buff·er (bŭf′er) *n.* 1. Apparatus for deadening by springs or pad-ding, or sustaining by strength of beams etc.; a heavy impact esp. of railroad cars or engines. 2. Shield or device preventing contact or interaction (also fig.); ~ **state**, small country lying between two larger possible belligerents. 3. (chem.) Substance or mixture that in solution resists change in acidity on addition of a small amount of acid or alkali. ~ *v.t.* Protect with a buffer; cushion; (chem.) treat with a buffer.

buf·fet[1] (bŭf′ĭt) *n.* Blow with the hand; blow of fate etc. ~ *v.* (**-fet·ed, -fet·ing**). Strike with the hand; force, struggle, contend (*with*

In Asia the **buffalo** has long been domesticated for draft work and milk, but the wild Cape buffalo of South Africa is described by many hunters as the most unpredictable and dangerous of wild animals.

waves etc.); strike against repea edly. **buf′fet·er** *n.*

buf·fet[2] (bufă′, boo-; *Br* boo′fă, bŭf′ĭt) *n.* (pl. **-fets** pr. -fa Brit. -făz, -fĭts). 1. Sideboard wit drawers and cupboard, for china glass, etc. 2. Table or counte from which food or refreshmen are served; service from this or fro sideboard where guests help them selves; party in which food is serve in this way.

Buf·fet (bufā′), **Bernar** (1928–). French artist, painte and lithographer.

buf·fle·head (bŭf′elhĕd) *n.* (als ~ **duck**) Small N. Amer. duc (*Bucephala albeola*).

buf·foon (bŭfoon′) *n.* (usu contempt.) Wag, clumsy jeste mocker. **buf·foon′er·y** *n.* **buf foon′ish** *adj.*

bug (bŭg) *n.* 1. Hemipterou insect; any small insect. 2. (colloq. Microorganism, (esp.) virus; (fig craze. 3. (slang) Defect in machin etc. 4. (slang) Concealed micro phone. ~ *v.t.* (**bugged, bug ging**). (slang) 1. Equip wit alarm or concealed microphone. 2 Annoy.

bug·a·boo (bŭg′aboo) *n.* (pl **-boos**) = BUGBEAR.

bug·bear (bŭg′bār) *n.* Fancie object of fear; imaginary terror (archaic) hobgoblin.

bug·gy (bŭg′ē) *n.* (pl. **-gies**) Light two-wheeled vehicle; four wheeled vehicle, often hooded drawn by one or two horses.

bu·gle (bū′gel) *n.* Brass in strument like small trumpet used for military signals. ~ *v.* (**-gled, -gling**). Sound bugle, sound (call) on a bugle. **bu′gler** *n.*

bu·gloss (bū′glŏs) *n.* Any of several plants related to borage, esp. species of *Echium*, as **viper's** ~ (*E. vulgare*).

buhl (bool) = BOULLE.

build (bĭld) *v.* (**built, build·ing**). Construct by putting parts of material together; make one's house or nest; make gradually; base *on*, rely *on*; ~ **up**, establish, make, or accumulate gradually; strengthen; praise; surround or cover with houses etc.; ~**-up** (*n.*) (colloq.) publicity (campaign); preparation; extravagant praise. **build** *n.* Proportions of human body.

build·er (bĭl′der) *n.* (esp.) Master builder, contractor for building houses.

build·ing (bĭl′dĭng) *n.* (esp.) House, edifice; ~ **blocks**, small solid shapes, as child's toy for building; interrelated pieces, ideas, etc.

built (bĭlt) *adj.*: see BUILD; (esp.) ~**-in**, forming integral part of structure, as in *built-in furniture;* ~**-up**, increased in height, thickness, etc., by addition of parts; (of area) covered with houses etc.

Bed-bug Capsid-bug Shield-bug Frog-hopper Mealy-bug Pond-skater Assassin-bug

3

5

Only those insects in the order Hemiptera are properly called **bugs** but the name is widely used for any small insect. A bug has a jointed beak for piercing and sucking blood or plant juices. Typically it has a smooth body, 2 pairs of wings, long legs and many have a repulsive smell. 1. A red assassin preys on insects and bites man. 2. Left to right are bed-bug, capsid, shield-bug, frog-hopper, pond-skater, mealy-bug, and assassin. 3. The bed-bug cannot fly, having wing pads only. 4. The stink-bug. 5. The shield-bug.

Bu·jum·bu·ra (bōōjōōmboor´-a). Capital of Burundi at the northern end of Lake Tanganyika.

bulb (bŭlb) n. 1. Globular base of the stem of certain plants, such as lily, onion, etc., consisting of thick fleshy scales and sending roots downward and leaves etc. upward; leaf bud detaching itself from stem and becoming separate plant; (anat.) roundish swelling of any cylindrical organ, as of hair root. 2. Dilated part of glass tube; electric lamp; bulb-shaped swelling of rubber tube. ~ v.i. Swell into bulb(s). **bulb·ar** (bŭl´ber, -bār), **bulbed** adjs.

bulb·ous (bŭl´bus) adj. Of, having, like, springing from, a bulb.

bul·bul (bōōl´bōōl) n. Any of several Asian songbirds of the family Pycnonotidae.

Bul·finch (bōōl´fĭnch), **Thom-as** (1796–1867). American mythologist and author of *The Age of Fable*, better known as "Bulfinch's Mythology."

Bul·gar (bŭl´ger, bōōl´gār) adj. & n. (Native, inhabitant) of Bulgaria.

Bul·gar·i·a (bŭlgār´ēa, bōōl-). Balkan republic (until 1946 a kingdom), with a population largely descended from a people related to the Huns and Avars and speaking a Slavonic language; capital, Sofia.

Bul·gar·i·an (bŭlgār´ēan, bōōl-) adj. Of Bulgaria or its people or language. ~ n. Bulgarian person or language.

bulge (bŭlj) n. Convex part, irregular swelling, tendency to swell out, on surface; outward swell

on ship's hull below waterline; (fig.) temporary increase in volume or numbers. ~ v. (**bulged, bulg·ing**). Swell outward irregularly; extend (bag etc.) by stuffing it. **bulg´y** adj. **bulg´i·ness** n. [L. *bulga* knapsack]

Bulge (bŭlj), **Battle of the.** Last German counteroffensive of World War II, during December 1944 and January 1945, in which the Allies were victorious; so named because the combat line formed a large bulge into Belgium.

bulk (bŭlk) n. 1. Cargo; in ~, loose, not in packages; in large quantities (so ~ **buying** etc.). 2. Large shape, body, person. 3. Size, magnitude; great size; mass, large mass; greater part or number *of*. ~ v.i. Seem in respect of size or importance.

bulk·head (bŭlk´hĕd) n. Upright partition dividing watertight compartments of ship; such a compartment in ship, aircraft, or train; partition dividing engine from body in motor vehicle.

bulk·y (bŭl´kē) adj. (**bulk·i·er, bulk·i·est**). Large, voluminous. **bulk´i·ly** adv. **bulk´i·ness** n.

bull¹ (bōōl) n. Papal edict. [L. *bulla* seal]

bull² (bōōl) n. 1. Uncastrated male bovine animal; male of elephant, whale, seal, and other large animals. 2. (astron.) the **B~**: see TAURUS. 3. (stock exch.) Speculator who buys low in expectation of a rise in prices or in order to effect such a rise; ~ **market**, one with rising prices. 4. (slang) Lies, nonsense, baloney. 5. **bull´dog**

(v.t.) throw (a steer) by graspi the horns and twisting the hea (adj. & n.) tenacious a courageous (person); dog of pow ful and courageous large-head smooth-haired breed; **bull´doz** clear (ground etc.) with bulldoz make *way* forcibly (also fig.); inti idate, coerce; **bull´dozer**, powe ful tractor with broad vertical bla in front for clearing ground et **bull´fight**, Spanish spectacle baiting a bull with horseme (picadors), footmen (banderilleros and a swordsman (matador) w finally kills it; similar sport Mexico, Portugal, and S. Franc in which bull is not killed; **bull fighter, bull´fighting** ns.; **bull finch**, strong-beaked, handsom plumaged songbird (*Pyrrhu pyrrhula*); **bull´frog**, large frog es of genus *Rana* with loud bellowin note; **bull´head**, small fish wit large head, esp. any of severa catfish (genus *Ictalurus*) and fresh water sculpins (genus *Cottus* **bull´headed**, stubborn; **bull´pen** (baseball) area where relief pitche warm up; **bull´ring**, arena fo bullfight; ~'**s-eye**, boss of glas formed at center of sheet of blow glass; hemispherical piece or thic disk of glass; hemispherical len lantern with such a lens; sma circular window; central area o target; hit on this part; ~ **terrie** dog of heavily built, smooth-haire usu. white breed. **bull´ish** ad Like a bull; (of stock market o prices) tending to rise. **bull´ish·l** adv. **bull´ish·ness** n. **bull´-lik** adj.

Bull (bōōl), **John:** see JOHN Bull.

bul·let (bōōl´ĭt) n. Missile o lead etc., spherical or conical, used in small arms.

Sections of the tulip **bulb** and the lily bulb. A bulb is a compound organ of certain plants and may also be described as an underground bud from which a new plant will emerge and grow.

1. A **bull** of good pedigree and championship quality is of great value as a progenitor of stock. 2. The British **bulldog** was bred from a strain that was admired for its courage in seizing the muzzle of a bull in a fight and hanging on however much it was hurt. The bulldog was aided in this by the way its jaws 'lock', making it difficult for it to let go. 3. The **bullfinch** has a thicker head and neck than other finches. 4. The **bullfrog** grows slowly through the tadpole stage, taking 3 years to mature.

bul·le·tin (bōōl′etĭn) n. Short official statement of news or on a matter of public interest; special broadcast report of news, weather, etc.; periodical published by an organization or society; ~ **board**, board mounted on a wall on which notices may be posted.

bul·lion (bōōl′yon) n. Gold and silver before (or as valued apart from) coining or manufacturing.

bull·ock (bōōl′ok) n. Castrated bull, ox.

Bull (bōōl) **Run.** Creek in NE. Virginia near Manassas, scene of two important Civil War battles 1861 and 1862) in which the Confederates defeated the Union forces.

bul·ly[1] (bōōl′ē) n. (pl. **-lies**). One who oppresses or dominates by threat of) superior force. ~ v.t. **-lied, -ly·ing**). Persecute, oppress, tease, physically or morally; frighten *into* or *out of*; play he bully. ~ adj. & int. (colloq.) Excellent, splendid.

bul·ly[2] (bōōl′ē) **beef.** Canned or pickled beef.

bul·rush (bōōl′rŭsh) n. Kind of tall rush (*Scirpus lacustris*); reed mace; (in the Bible) papyrus of Egypt.

bul·wark (bōōl′werk) n. 1. Rampart, earthwork, etc.; breakwater; person, principle, etc., that acts as a defense. 2. Ship's side above deck.

bum[1] (bŭm) n. (chiefly Brit. slang) Buttocks; **bum′boat**, boat, plying to ships in port or off shore with fresh provisions.

bum[2] (bŭm) n. (colloq.) 1. Lazy and dissolute person; loafer, tramp. 2. Enthusiast of a particular recreational activity, as a **beach** ~. **bum** adj. Worthless, poor, wretched. ~ v. (**bummed, bum·ming**). Loaf or wander (*around*); lead life of a bum; cadge. **bum′mer** n.

bum·ble (bŭm′bel) v.i. (**-bled, -bling**). Make buzzing or humming sound, as a bee; **bum′blebee**, large bee of genus *Bombus*, with a loud hum.

bum·bling (bŭm′blĭng) adj. 1. Buzzing. 2. Bungling, incompetent.

bum·mer (bŭm′er) n. (slang) 1. Error, failure. 2. Unpleasant experience, esp. with a drug.

bump (bŭmp) v. 1. Push, throw down, impinge violently, strike solidly (*against, into, on*). 2. ~ **into**, (colloq.) meet by chance; ~ **off**, (slang) murder. **bump** n. 1. Dull-sounding blow, knock, collision; swelling caused by this. 2. Protuberance; (phrenol.) prominence on skull, faculty supposed to be indicated by it. 3. Irregularity in aircraft's motion; rising current of air causing this. **bump′y** adj. (**bump·i·er, bump·i·est**).

bump·er (bŭm′per) *n.* 1. Full glass of wine etc. 2. (slang) Anything (as harvest, theater audience) unusually large or abundant. 3. Horizontal bar attached to front and back of a vehicle to take the first shock of collision.

bump·kin (bŭmp′kĭn) *n.* Country lout, awkward or bashful fellow.

bump·tious (bŭmp′shus) *adj.* Self-assertive, offensively conceited.

bun (bun) *n.* 1. Small soft bread roll, often sweetened or spiced, or with raisins, currants, etc; **hot cross ~**, spiced bun marked with icing in form of cross and eaten (esp. hot) on Good Friday. 2. Hair coiled at back of head in shape of bun.

bunch (bŭnch) *n.* Cluster of things growing or fastened together; lot, collection; company, band. **bunch′y** *adj.* (**bunch·i·er**, **bunch·i·est**). **bunch** *v.* Make into bunch(es), gather (fabric) thickly into folds, come, cling, crowd, together.

bunch·ber·ry (bŭnch′bĕrē) *n.* (pl. **-ries**). Dwarf cornel (*Cornus canadensis*), which bears densely clustered red berries.

Bunche (bŭnch), **Ralph Johnson** (1904–71). American statesman and undersecretary of the United Nations, 1954–71.

bun·dle (bŭn′del) *n.* Collection of things fastened together; sets of sticks, rods, etc., bound up; set of parallel fibers, nerves, etc. ~ *v.* (**-dled, -dling**). Tie in, make *up* into, bundle; throw confusedly *in* any receptacle; go, put, or send hurriedly or unceremoniously *out, off*, etc.; ~ **up**, dress warmly. **bundle** *v.i.* Sleep or lie in one bed

aerated flame (lighter blue)

mixed gas and air

from tap

air hole

Mixing air and gas in a ratio of approximately 2½:1, a **bunsen** burner completely burns the gas to produce a hot smokeless flame that gives little light. Robert von Bunsen invented the burner in 1855.

while clothed (a form of courting early New England, with **bundling board** between t| sweethearts).

bung (bŭng) *n.* Stopper, es large cork stopping hole in cas **bung′hole**, hole in cask closed wi| bung. **bung** *v.t.* Stop (cask wi| bung); stop, close, shut up.

bun·ga·low (bŭng′galō) *n.* Small one-storied house. [Hin| *bangla* of Bengal]

bun·gle (bŭng′gel) *n.* Clums| work, confusion, blunder. ~ | (**-gled, -gling**). Make bungl| blunder over, fail to accomplish.

bun·ion (bŭn′yon) *n.* Swellin| on foot, esp. at first joint of big to|

bunk[1] (bŭngk) *n.* Sleepin| berth, platform bed, freq. one | two or more in tiers; **bunk′house** house in which miners, lumbermer etc., are lodged. **bunk** *v.i.* Slee| in bunk.

bunk[2] (bŭngk) *n.* Humbug| nonsense. [abbreviation of BUN| KUM]

bunk·er (bŭng′ker) *n.* 1. Larg| compartment in a ship for storin| coal or oil; bin for storing domesti| fuel. 2. Sand trap forming a| obstacle on golf course. 3. Under ground shelter or fortified earth work, esp. of reinforced concrete ~ *v.* 1. Fill bunkers of (ship etc.| fuel. 2. (golf) Hit into bunker.

Bun·ker (bŭn′ker) **Hill.** Hill in Charleston, Mass., near Boston, scene of the first major battle (June 17, 1775) of the American Revolu-

The **bunker** remains one of the more irritating obstacles on a golf course. It is usually constructed as a sand-filled hol low.

tion; the British captured the hill but suffered heavy losses.

bun·kum (bŭng′kum) *n.* Humbug, clap-trap. [*Buncombe* county in N. Carolina; around 1820 Felix Walker, Congressman for this district, insisted on making an unnecessary speech in Congress "for Buncombe"]

bun·ny (bŭn′ē) *n.* (pl. **-nies**). Childish or pet name for rabbit.

Bun·sen (bŭn′sen), **Robert Wilhelm von** (1811–99). German chemist, credited with the invention of the ~(gas) **burner**, which produces a very hot, nonluminous flame by the mixture of air with the stream of gas before it is lighted.

bunt[1] (bŭnt) *v.* (baseball) Tap or push (a pitched ball), with hands apart on bat, so that ball does not roll far. ~ *n.* Such a hit; a ball so hit.

bunt[2] (bŭnt) *n.* Cavity, baggy part, of fishing net, sail, etc.

bunt·ing[1] (bŭn′tĭng) *n.* Bird of subfamily Emberizinae, allied to finches.

bunt·ing[2] (bŭn′tĭng) *n.* Worsted or cotton material of open weave used for flags; flags (esp. of ship) collectively; streamers etc. used as festive decorations.

Bun·yan[1] (bŭn′yan), **John** (1628–88). English Nonconformist preacher; author of the allegory *Pilgrim's Progress.*

Bun·yan[2] (bŭn′yan), **Paul.** Legendary American lumberjack of the NW. forests; of gigantic size and appetites, he is the subject of many comic "tall tales."

buoy (boo′ē, boi) *n.* (pl. **buoys**). Anchored float marking a channel or indicating position of something, e.g., wreck, reefs; **life** ~, float that can support person in water. **buoy** *v.t.* 1. (usu. with *up*) Keep afloat; bring to surface of water; sustain, uplift. 2. Mark with buoy(s).

buoy·an·cy (boi′ansē, boo′yan-) *n.* Capacity for floating, tendency to float in water or air; (fig.) elasticity, recuperative power.

buoy·ant (boi′ant, boo′yant) *adj.* Apt to float, rise, keep up, or recover; able to keep things up; light-hearted.

bur, burr (bēr) *ns.* 1. Clinging hooked fruit or flower head; hence, person hard to shake off. 2. Knob or knot in wood. 3. Rotary cutting tool for attaching to a drill. 4. See BURR def. 3.

Bur·bage (bēr′bĭj), **Richard** (c1567–1619). English actor and theater manager, part owner of the Globe Theatre; acted principal parts in plays by Shakespeare, Jonson, and Beaumont and Fletcher.

Bur·bank (bēr′băngk), **Luther** (1849–1926). American horticulturist; developed new and improved varieties of plants.

A **buoy** may be designed as an aid to navigation, as a mooring for a boat or as a marker for an underwater hazard. Top: A small permanent navigation buoy near Manacles Rocks off the Lizard, Cornwall, U.K. 1. A mooring buoy. 2. A light buoy. 3. A light buoy equipped with a bell. 4. A whistle buoy. 5. A light buoy powered by an atomic generator.

Atomic generator

bur·ble (bėr´bel) *n.* Murmurous noise. ~ *v.* (**-bled, -bling**). Speak or say murmurously.

bur·bot (bėr´bot) *n.* (pl. **-bots**, collect. **-bot**). Eel-like flat-headed bearded fresh-water fish (*Lota lota*).

bur·den[1] (bėr´den) *n.* 1. Load; obligation; bearing of loads; obligatory expense. 2. (archaic **bur·then** pr. bėr´dhen) Ship's carrying capacity, tonnage. ~ *v.t.* Load; encumber; oppress.

bur·den[2] (bėr´den) *n.* Refrain, chorus of song; drone of a bagpipe. [var. of BOURDON]

bur·den·some (bėr´densom) *adj.* Oppressive, wearying. **bur´den·some·ly** *adv.* **bur´den·some·ness** *n.*

bur·dock (bėr´dŏk) *n.* Coarse weedy plant (*Arctium lappa*), with prickly flower heads and dock-like leaves.

bu·reau (būr´ō) *n.* (pl. **-reaus, -reaux**). 1. Chest of drawers; (chiefly Brit.) writing desk or table with drawers. 2. Office, esp. of government department.

bu·reauc·ra·cy (byurŏk´rasē) *n.* (pl. **-cies**). Government by bureaus, centralization; body of officials. **bu·reau·crat** (būr´akrăt) *n.* **bu·reau·crat·ic** (būrakrăt´ĭk) *adj.* **bu·reau·crat´i·cal·ly** *adv.*

bu·rette, bu·ret (byurĕt´) *ns.* Graduated glass tube with tap at lower end for delivering measured small quantities of liquid in chemical analysis.

burg (bėrg) *n.* (colloq.) Town.

bur·gee (berjē´, bėr´jē) *n.* Small swallow-tailed pendant used by yachts etc., usu. as distinguishing flag.

bur·geon (bėr´jon) *v.i.* Put forth, spring forth as, young shoots, bud, begin to grow.

bur·gess (bėr´jĭs) *n.* 1. (hist.) Member of lower house of colonial legislature of Virginia or Maryland. 2. (hist.) Member of English Parliament representing a town, borough, or university.

burgh·er (bėr´ger) *n.* 1. (hist.) Member of merchant class of a medieval city. 2. Solid middle-class citizen.

bur·glar (bėrg´ler) *n.* One who enters building as trespasser and commits or intends to commit a theft. **bur·glar·i·ous** (berglar´ēus) *adj.* **bur´gla·ry** *n.*

bur·gle (bėr´gel) *v.* (**-gled, -gling**). (colloq.) Commit burglary; rob by burglary.

bur·go·mas·ter (bėr´gōmăster, -mahs-) *n.* Mayor of Dutch, Flemish, Austrian, or German town.

bur·goo (bėr´gōō, bergōō´) *n.* (southern U.S.) Thick, spicy stew of mixed meats and vegetables.

Bur·gun·dy (bėr´gundē). (Fr. *Bourgogne*) Region, formerly an ancient kingdom, later duchy and province, of SE. France; any of the wines produced there, including Beaune, Chambertin, Pommard (red), and Chablis and Montrachet (white); similar wine made elsewhere.

bur·i·al (bėr´ēal) *n.* Burying, esp. of dead body.

Burke[1] (bėrk), **Edmund** (1729–1797). English statesman and political and philosophical writer.

Burke[2] (bėrk), **John** (1787–1848). Irish-born genealogical and heraldic writer, first compiler of *Burke's Peerage*, officially entitled *Peerage and Baronetage* (1826), issued annually since 1847.

burl (bėrl) *n.* Knot in wool, cloth, or wood; overgrown knot in walnut etc., used in veneering.

bur·lap (bėr´lăp) *n.* Coarse canvas of jute, used for sacks.

bur·lesque (berlĕsk´) *adj.* Imitating derisively; bombastic, mock serious; caricaturing, parodying (esp. literary or dramatic work). ~ *n.* Literary or dramatic burlesque work or performance; bombast, mock seriousness; derisive imitation; vaudeville frequently featuring striptease. ~ *v.* Make or perform burlesque (of), caricature, travesty.

bur·ley, Bur·ley (bėr´lē) *ns.* Light tobacco grown esp. in Kentucky.

bur·ly (bėr´lē) *adj.* (**-li·er, -li·est**). Large and sturdy. **bur´li·ness** *n.*

Bur·ma (bėr´ma). Republic, established in 1948, occupying the NW. portion of the peninsula pro- jecting south from Asia betwe‹ India and China; capital, Rangoo‹

Bur·mese (bermēz´, -mēs´) *adj.* *n.* (pl. **-mese**).

Bur·ma (bėr´ma) **Road.** Sever‹ hundred-mile road between Chi‹ and Burma used as a supply rou‹ by the Allies during World War I‹

burn (bėrn) *v.* (**burned ‹ burnt, burn·ing**). Consume, b‹ consumed, waste, by fire; blaze ‹ smolder; injure by burning; bran‹ utilize the nuclear energy ‹ (uranium etc.); feel intense heat ‹ emotion; ~ **off**, burn vegetation o‹ land to clear it for cultivation. **bur‹** *n.* Sore, mark, made by burning burned area in forest etc. **burn´e‹** *n.*, device for burning; part of stov‹ or apparatus that shapes the flam‹ or emits the heat.

bur·net (bėr´nĭt) *n.* Brown‹ flowered plant of genus *Sanguisorb‹* or genus *Poterium*.

Bur·ney (bėr´nē), **Frances** *o‹* **Fanny** (*Madame D'Arblay*) (1752‹ 1840). English novelist, originato‹ of the simple novel of home life.

burn·ing (bėr´nĭng) *adj.* Tha‹ burns; flagrant; hotly discussed exciting; ~**-bush**, "the bush tha‹ burned and was not consumed" (Exod. 3); any of various shrubs o‹ plants with scarlet berries or foliage‹ turning red in autumn etc.

bur·nish (bėr´nĭsh) *v.* Polish by‹ friction; take a polish.

bur·noose, bur·nous (bernōōs´, bėr´nōōs) *ns.* Arab or Moorish‹ hooded cloak.

Burns (bėrnz), **Robert** (1759‹ 1796). Scottish poet, many of

Hinayana Buddhism was introduced to **Burma** in 1044 by her ruler, Anawratha, who ran an immense program of temple building. Temples such as this (facing page) are found in mos‹ Burmese towns. Below: In Rangoon a‹ child, dressed for a festival, prays.

whose poems are written in Low-land Scots.

Burn·side (bern′sīd), **Ambrose Everett** (1824–81). Union general during Civil War; relieved of command and resigned commission after being blamed for failure to lead aggressively; became governor of and senator from Rhode Island after the war; **burnsides**, full side whiskers worn with a mustache but with the chin kept clean shaven, as worn by General Burnside.

burnt (bernt) *adj.*: see BURN; (esp., of pigment) calcined to a deeper color *e.g.,* ~ **sienna,** ~ **umber**; (of color) of a deeper shade; ~ **offering**, sacrifice offered by burning.

burp (berp) *n. & v.* (colloq.) (Cause to) belch.

burr (ber) *n.* 1. Rough edge left on cut metal etc. 2. Small drill for cutting into tooth or bone. 3. (also **bur**) Rough sounding of letter *r.* ~ *v.* 1. Pronounce with burr; speak with rough or indistinct articulation. 2. Make burring sound.

Burr (ber), **Aaron** (1756–1836).

From this cottage in Alloway, Strathclyde, Scotland, **Robert Burns** used to go to work on his father's farm. Burns's use of Lowland dialect brought a lively freshness to his poems.

A Navajo cemetery in Arizona where a man has been **buried** with the bones of his horse and his saddle placed on top of the grave. Originally semi-nomadic, the Navajo have become farmers and weavers.

Vice President of the U.S. under Thomas Jefferson, 1801–5; killed Alexander Hamilton in a duel, 1804; tried for conspiring to seize territory from Spanish America and create a republic in the Southwest; acquitted, 1807.

bur·ro (bĕr´ō, boor´ō, bŭr´ō) n. (pl. **-ros**). Small donkey, esp. one used as pack animal.

bur·row (bĕr´ō, bŭr´ō) n. Hole or excavation in ground in which rabbits, foxes, etc., live. ~ v. Make, live in, burrow; make by excavating; hide oneself, move, into, under. **bur´row·er** n.

bur·sa (bĕr´sa) n. (pl. **-sae** pr. -sē, **-sas**). (physiol.) Synovial sac between joints or between muscles, skin, etc., and bones, for lessening friction. **bur´sal** adj.

bur·sar (bĕr´ser, -sär) n. Treasurer, esp. of a college or university. **bur·sar·i·al** (bersär´ēal) adj. **bur´sar·ship** n.

bur·si·tis (bersī´tĭs) n. Inflammation of a bursa.

burst (bĕrst) v. (**burst, burst·ing**). Fly violently asunder, give way suddenly; explode; rush, move, appear, violently or suddenly; speak, utter, be uttered, explosively. ~ n. Bursting, split; explosion, outbreak; spurt; continuous gallop. **burst´ing** adj. (esp.) Full to overflowing.

bur·then (bĕr´dhen): see BURDEN[1], 2.

Bur·ton[1] (bĕr´ton), **Sir Richard Francis** (1821–90). English adventurer, Orientalist, and Arabic scholar; the first Englishman to reach Mecca; translator of the Arabian Nights.

Bur·ton[2] (bĕr´ton), **Robert** (1577–1640). English clergyman, scholar, and writer; author of the Anatomy of Melancholy.

Bu·run·di (berŭn´dē, booroon´dē). Republic on E. side of Lake Tanganyika; established 1962; capital Bujumbura.

bur·y (bĕr´ē) v.t. (**bur·ied, bur·y·ing**). 1. Deposit in, commit to, earth, tomb, or sea; perform burial rites over; put under ground. 2. Put away, forget; consign to obscurity; hide in earth, cover up, submerge; plunge (head in hands etc.).

bus (bŭs) n. (pl. **bus·es, bus·ses**). Long motor vehicle for carrying passengers; **bus´boy**, waiter's assistant; **bus stop**, place at which bus, following a fixed route, makes a regular or scheduled stop.

bus·by (bŭz´bē) n. (pl. **-bies**). Tall fur cap of hussars and guardsmen in British army.

bush (boŏsh) n. Woody plant with numerous stems of moderate length; clump of shrubs; woodland, unsettled or remote area; luxuriant growth of hair etc.; **bush´buck**,

Near a village in **Burundi,** east central Africa, a girl bears on her head a traditional decorative gift of split leaves in a basket. The map shows the relationship of Burundi (formerly called Urundi), an independent republic since 1962, to its much larger neighbors, Zaire and Tanzania. The area of the country is 10,700 sq. miles and its population about 3 million.

Large areas of semi-desert, the **bush** is characterized by coarse scrub vegetation in Australia, where this type of land is also called the outback. In South Africa it is described as veldt.

This traditional samurai dress embodies the spirit of **bushido,** the Japanese code of ethics which demands absolute obedience from the samurai warriors.

Mostly found in the arid wester regions of the U.S.A., the flat–toppe **butte** is formed by erosion of the su rounding plains and is a striking featur of this desert area.

all African antelope of genus *agelaphus*, dwelling in forests and amps, esp. common bushbuck *. scriptus*); **bush league**, (base-ll) minor league; **bush'man**, ember, language, of aboriginal be of S. Africa; (chiefly Austral-) dweller in Australian bush; **ash'master**, very large venom-s viper (*Lachesis mutus*) of pical America; **bush'whacker**, ckwoodsman. **bush** *v.i.* Grow, anch like a bush. **bushed** *adj.* olloq.) Exhausted.

bush·el (boosh'el) *n.* U.S. dry easure = 4 pecks = 2,150.42 bic inches.

Bu·shi·do, bu·shi·do (boo-ēdaw') *ns.* Code of honor and orals evolved by the samurai of pan. [Jap., = "military knight ay"]

bush·ing (boosh'ing) *n.* Metal ing for axle hole etc.; box or aring in which shaft revolves; rforated plug.

bush·y (boosh'e) *adj.* (**bush·i·er**, ush·i·est**). Abounding in bushes; owing thickly.

busi·ness (biz'nis) *n.* 1. Task, ty, province; errand; agenda. 2. rious occupation, work; habitual cupation, profession; trade, mmercial transactions; com-ercial house, firm; ~ **end**, (col-q.) working end of object, opp. ndle; **busi'nesslike**, systematic, actical; **busi'nessman**, fem. usi'nesswoman**, one engaged in usiness or commerce. 3. (theatr.) ction, dumb show. 4. (contempt.) rocess, concern, affair, thing.

bus·kin (bus'kin) *n.* 1. Boot aching to calf or knee. 2. Thick-led boot lending height to ancient thenian tragic actor; (fig.) tragedy.

bust[1] (bust) *n.* 1. Sculpture of rson's head and upper portion of dy. 2. Upper front of body, esp. oman's bosom.

bust[2] (bust) *v.* (slang) Burst. ~ dj.* (slang) Broke, without money. *n.* (slang) Burst, (esp.) spree; -up**, quarrel.

bus·tard (bus'terd) *n.* Large vift-running bird of genus *Otis*.

bus·tle[1] (bus'el) *v.* (-tled, ling**). Bestir oneself, make show activity, hurry *about*; make thers) hurry or work hard. *n.* Excited activity, fuss.

bus·tle[2] (bus'el) *n.* Pad or frame-ork puffing out top of woman's irt at the back.

bus·y (biz'e) *adj.* (**bus·i·er**, us·i·est**). Occupied, working, ngaged, with intention concen-ated; unresting, always employed, irring; fussy, meddlesome, pry-g; (excessively) full of detail; us'ybody**, meddlesome person, ischief maker. **bus'i·ly** *adv.* us'y *v.t.* (**bus·ied, bus·y·ing**). Occupy, keep busy.

but (but) *prep.* Without, apart

from. ~ *adv.* Merely. ~ *conj.* On the other hand; except; unless; yet.

bu·ta·di·ene (butadi'en, -dien') *n.* Highly unsaturated carbon (C_4H_6), gaseous at ordinary temperatures, used in manufacture of synthetic rubber.

bu·tane (bu'tan) *n.* Colorless hydrocarbon gas (C_4H_{10}), used compressed in cylinders as a fuel, refrigerant, etc.

butch (booch) *n.* (slang) Tough youth or man; mannish lesbian; short haircut, crew cut.

butch·er (booch'er) *n.* One who slaughters animals for food, dealer in meat; person who causes or delights in bloodshed; **butch'-erbird**, kind of shrike. **butcher** *v.t.* Slaughter in the manner of a butcher (lit. and fig.).

butch·er·y (booch'ere) *n.* (pl. -er·ies). Butcher's trade; needless or cruel slaughter.

but·ler (but'ler) *n.* Male servant in charge of plate, table, wine cellar, etc., head servant.

But·ler[1] (but'ler), **Samuel** (1612–80). English poet and satirist; author of *Hudibras*.

But·ler[2] (but'ler), **Samuel** (1835–1902). English critic and novelist; author of the Utopian novel *Erewhon* and an auto-biographical novel, *The Way of All Flesh*.

butt[1] (but) *n.* Wine or ale cask (holding 108–40 gallons); a unit of volume equal to 126 gallons; any barrel.

butt[2] (but) *n.* 1. Thicker end, esp. of tool or weapon. 2. Stub of cigar or cigarette; (slang) cigarette.

*Women wore the **bustle** around 1870. It was a modification of the hooped crin-oline and comprised a pad or framework that pulled out a woman's skirt at the back.*

3. (slang) Buttocks, rear end.

butt[3] (but) *n.* 1. Mound behind target; shooting range; target. 2. End, aim, object *of* (ridicule etc.); object of teasing and ridicule.

butt[4] (but) *v.* Push with the head; ~ **in**, intervene, meddle. **butt** *n.* Butting, push with the head. **butt'er** *n.*

Butte (but). Mining city in SW. Montana; situated over extremely large mineral deposits, especially copper.

butte (but) *n.* Isolated abrupt flat-topped hill.

but·ter (but'er) *n.* Fatty pale yellow substance made from cream by churning, used for spreading on bread and in cooking; substance of similar consistency or look (as **peanut** ~); ~ **and eggs, toadflax**, ~ **bean**, dried seed of white varieties of lima bean, used as vege-table; **but'tercup**, any of various kinds of ranunculus with yellow cup-shaped flowers; **but'ter-fingers**, **but'terfingered**, (per-son) inclined to drop things; **but'-terfish**, GUNNEL[1]; also any of several related fishes; **but'termilk**, sour milk remaining after butter has been churned out. **but'ternut**, (large oily fruit of) N. Amer. white walnut tree (*Juglans cinerea*); **but'terscotch**, syrup, sauce, flavoring, or candy made chiefly of brown sugar and butter; **but'ter-wort**, violet-flowered fleshy-leaved, bog plant (*Pinguicula vulgaris*). **butter** *v.t.* Spread, cook, with butter; ~ **up**, flatter.

but·ter·fly (but'erflī) *n.* (pl. -flies). 1. Diurnal lepidopterous insect (cf. MOTH) with knobbed

*The **bustard**, extinct in Great Britain, is now found only in southern Europe, North Africa and Australia. A male has a wingspan of up to 8 ft. and may be about 4 ft. from beak to tail.*

antennae, carrying the wings erect when at rest. 2. Vain or frivolous person; trifler, esp. social ~. 3. (swimming) Stroke in which the arms are lifted out of the water simultaneously.

but·ter·y (bŭt'erē) *adj.* Of, resembling, containing, covered in, butter.

but·tock (bŭt'ok) *n.* One of the two protuberances of the rump; (usu. pl.) rump.

but·ton (bŭt'on) *n.* Knob or disk attached to garment etc. to serve as fastening when pressed through loop or buttonhole, or for ornament; bud; unopened mushroom; small rounded body; terminal knob (on foil etc.), knob, handle, catch, as on electric bell; **but'tonhole**, slit through which button passes; flower(s) for wearing in buttonhole in lapel of coat; (*v.t.*) sew with buttonhole stitch; seize, detain (reluctant listener); **but'tonhole**

stitch, looped stitch used for edging buttonholes; **but'tonhook**, small hook for pulling button through buttonhole in boots etc. **but'tonwood**: see SYCAMORE. **button** *v.* Furnish with button(s); fasten (often *up*) with button(s). **but'ton·er** *n.* **but'ton·less, but'ton·like** *adjs.*

but·tress (bŭt'rĭs) *n.* Support built against wall etc., prop; buttress-like projection of hill. ~ *v.* Support with buttress, by argument etc.

bux·om (bŭk'som) *adj.* (of woman) Plump of figure; full-bosomed. **bux'om·ness** *n.*

buy (bī) *v.t.* (**bought, buy·ing**). Obtain in exchange for money or other consideration; gain over by bribery; ~ **in**, purchase stock or interest in; buy back for the original owner at auction by naming higher price than the highest offered; ~ **off**, get rid of by

payment, bribe; ~ **up**, buy as mu as possible of. **buy** *n.* Purcha **good** ~, bargain; useful purcha **buy'er** *n.* (esp.) Purchasing ag for a retail store.

buzz (bŭz) *n.* Hum of bee e confused low sound like this; **saw**, circular saw; **buzz'wo** pseudo-technical catchword slogan. **buzz** *v.* Make buzz; mo *about* busily; (of aircraft) wa annoy, etc., by flying fast and cl to; ~ **off**, (slang) go away.

buz·zard (bŭz'erd) *n.* I. Na of various kinds of hawk of gen *Buteo* and family Cathartidae. Turkey buzzard.

Buz·zards (bŭz'erdz) **Bay.** Inlet of the Atlantic Ocean in S Massachusetts. 2. Resort town ne the entrance to the inlet.

buz·zer (bŭz'er) *n.* (esp.) A electric signaling device that mak a buzzing sound.

B.V. *abbrev.* Blessed Virgin.

B.W.I. *abbrev.* British We Indies.

by (bī) *prep.* I. Near to, besid (of compass point) slightly inclini to (as *N. by E.*, between N. a NNE.); ~ **oneself**, alone. 2. Alor

*Generally speaking, **butterflies** are distinguished from moths by the butterfly's clubbed antennae and its diurnal habit. Below: An Australian big greasy butterfly (Cressida cressida). The male is more colorful than the female. Bottom left: A black-veined white butterfly (Aporia crataegi). Below: A male diadem butterfly (Hypolimnas misipus).*

Below right: the rough-legged **buzzard** migrates from the Arctic, where it preys on ptarmigan and other small birds, to N. Europe and N. America. Both the rough-legged buzzard and the lizard buzzard (above) sight their prey, including fledgling birds and small rodents, while hovering.

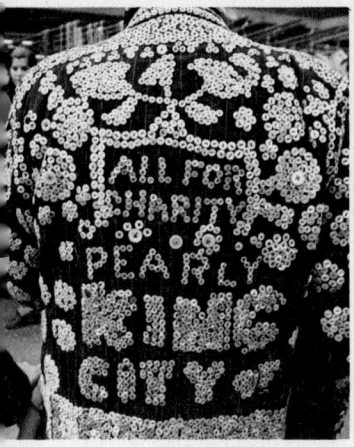

Pearly **buttons** adorn the suits of the pearly kings and queens of London, U.K. The tradition and some of the costumes have been handed down by cosermongers since the 1880s.

...ia, past. 3. During. 4. Through ...he agency, means, etc., of; (of ...nimals) having as sire. 5. As soon ...s, not later than. 6. According to. ... After, succeeding. 8. To the ...xtent of. 9. In respect of. 10. ...in oaths etc.) In the belief of. ~ *adj.* 1. Side, out of the way, ...evious, as **by′path, by′road, ...y′way**. 2. Collateral, side; **by′- ...lay**, action, usu. dumb show, ...arried on aside, esp. on stage; **by- ...roduct**, substance etc. produced ...ncidentally in making something ...lse. 3. Additional, subsidiary; **by′- ...vord**, proverb. **by** *adv.* Near; ...side, in reverse; past; ~ **and** ~, ...efore long; ~ **and large**, on the

whole; **by′stander**, spectator.

bye (bī) *n.* Position of player in round of a tournament not paired with an opponent and thus advanced to the next round; hence, **draw a** ~.

bye-bye (bī′bī′) *int.* (colloq. and nursery var. of) GOODBYE.

Bye·lo·rus′sia, Be·lo·rus′sia (byĕlōrŭsh′a, bĕl-). White Russia, one of the constituent republics

(properly *Byelorussian, Belorussian Soviet Socialist Republic*) of the U.S.S.R., including former provinces of Minsk, Vitebsk, and Mogilov; capital, Minsk. **Bye·lo·rus′sian, Be·lo·rus′sian** *adjs.* & *ns.* (Native, language) of Byelorussia; White Russian.

by·gone (bī′gawn, -gŏn) *adj.* Past, departed; antiquated. **by′-gones** *n.pl.* Past, past offenses.

by·law (bī′law) *n.* Regulation made by local government, corporation, etc.

by·pass (bī′păs) *n.* 1. Secondary pipe or channel conveying gas or

Espousal by the English Romantic poet,
Lord Byron, *of the Greek nationalist*
cause led him to adopt their national
costume in which he was shown in this
portrait by T. Phillips.

Under Justinian, who reigned
527–565, the **Byzantine Empire,**
(green areas in map at right) was at its
most productive phase. The Empire's
characteristic art reached its zenith
shortly after Justinian's reign. Above
right and facing page: The Basilica of
St. Mark's, Venice, shows the force of
this style.

Istanbul, Turkey, formerly called
Byzantium *and Constantinople, the*
capital of the Byzantine Empire to which
it gave its name. The city is famed for its
works of art of the period.

BYZANTINE EMPIRE circa 540 AD

liquid around fixture etc.; alternative passage for blood during surgical operation on heart; (elect.) shunt. 2. Road designed to relieve congestion by providing an alternative route for through traffic, esp. around a city. ~ *v.t.* (**-passed** or **-past, -passing**). Furnish with a bypass; make detour around (town etc.) (also fig.). **by'passed** *adj.*

Byrd (bērd), **Richard Evelyn** (1888–1957). Amer. polar explorer; made first flight over N. Pole (1926) and over S. Pole (1929).

By·ron (bīʹon), **George Gordon, 6th Baron** (1788–1824). English Romantic poet, whose poetry exerted great influence on the Romantic movement; he joined the Greek insurgents in 1823, and died of fever at Missolonghi,

Greece. **By·ron·ic** (bīrŏnʹĭk) *a* **By·ron'i·cal·ly** *adv.*

Byz·an·tine (bĭzʹantēn, -tĭ bĭzănʹtĭn) *adj.* Of Byzantium or t Byzantine Empire; of the style of and architecture typical of th characterized esp. by use of t round arch, circle, dome, and cro and by rich mosaic ornament; **Empire,** eastern part of Rom Empire, esp. after collapse Western Empire in 476, with capital at Constantinople until th city was captured by the Turks 1453. **Byzantine** *n.* Nativ inhabitant, of Byzantium or t Byzantine Empire. ~ *adj.* Co plicated, underhand.

By·zan·ti·um (bĭzănʹtēu -shēum). Original name of Co STANTINOPLE.

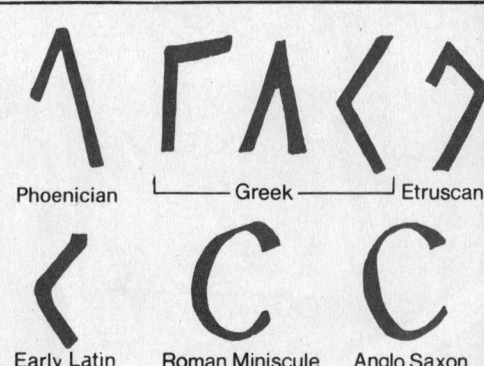

How the form of the letter **C, c** has evolved through the ages—from the Phoenician to the Anglo-Saxon. The letter corresponds to the Semitic 'gimel', probably derived from an early sign for camel, and the Greek gamma.

Phoenician   Greek   Etruscan

Early Latin   Roman Miniscule   Anglo Saxon

C, c (sē) (pl. **C's, c's** or **Cs, cs**). 1. Third letter of modern English and ancient Roman alphabet, deriving its form from Gk. *gamma* (Γ). 2. Third in series, order, or class. 3. **C**, (mus.) name of the keynote in the natural major scale and the corresponding minor scales; name of these scales. 4. Roman numeral symbol for 100.

C *abbrev*. Celsius; centigrade; coulomb(s).

c. *abbrev*. Carat; cent(s); century; chapter; circa (also *c, ca.*); cubic.

CA *abbrev*. California.

Ca *symbol*. Calcium.

ca. *abbrev*. Circa.

Caa·ba (kah′ba) = KAABA.

CAB, C.A.B. *abbrevs*. Civil Aeronautics Board.

cab (kăb) *n*. 1. Hackney carriage, esp. of brougham or hansom shape; taxicab; **cab′stand**, place where cabs are authorized to wait. 2. Driver's compartment in locomotive, truck, etc.

ca·bal (kabăl′) *n*. Secret intrigue; conspiratorial group of plotters; clique, faction. ~ *v.i.* (**-balled, -bal·ling**). Combine in cabal, intrigue privately. [f. CABALA]

cab·a·la (kăb′ala, kabah′-) *n*. 1. Jewish oral tradition handed down from Moses to the rabbis of the Mishna and Talmud, or the pretended tradition of the mystical interpretation of the Old Testament. 2. Mystery; esoteric doctrine. **cab′a·lism, cab′a·list** *ns*. **cab·a·lis·tic** (kăbalĭs′tĭk), **cab·a·lis′ti·cal** *adjs*. **cab·a·lis′ti·cal·ly** *adv*. [Heb. *ḳabbālāh* traditional law]

ca·bal·le·ro (kăbalyār′ō, -lār′ō; *Sp*. kahvahlyě′raw) *n*. (pl. **-le·ros** pr. -lyār′ōz, -lār′ōz; *Sp*. -lyě′raws). Spanish gentleman; (southwest) horseman, lady's escort or admirer.

cab·a·ret (kăbarā′) *n*. 1. Small night club; restaurant with entertainment provided by live performers. 2. Entertainment provided in restaurant etc. while guests are at table.

cab·bage (kăb′ĭj) *n*. Any of various kinds of green vegetable (esp. of *Brassica oleracea*), with compact globular heart or head of unexpanded leaves; ~ **butterfly**, one of several white butterflies of the family Pieridae whose green larvae feed on cabbage; ~ **palm, tree**, any of various trees with edible cabbagelike terminal buds (esp. the W. Ind. *Roystonea oleracea*); ~ **rose**, double rose with large round compact flowers (esp. *Rosa centifolia*).

cab·ba·la (kăb′ala, kabah′-) = CABALA.

cab·by (kăb′ē) *n*. (pl. **-bies**). (colloq.) Cab driver.

Cab·ell (kăb′el), **James Branch** (1879–1958). Amer. essayist and novelist; best known for his novel *Jurgen*.

ca·ber (kā′ber) *n*. Roughly trimmed young pine trunk used in Sc. Highland sport of **tossing the** ~. [Gael. *cabar* pole]

cab·in (kăb′ĭn) *n*. 1. Small rude dwelling. 2. Room or compartment in ship for sleeping or eating in; officer's or passenger's room; compartment in aircraft; ~ **boy**, boy waiting on officers or passengers on ship; ~ **cruiser**, power-driven pleasure boat with cabin for living in.

Ca·bin·da (kabēn′da). Ter tory of Angola on the Atlantic Co of Africa, between Zaire and t Congo Republic.

cab·i·net (kăb′inĭt) *n*. (archaic) Small private roo closet. 2. Case with drawe shelves, etc., for keeping valuab or displaying objects. 3. (Group persons appointed by preside prime minister, etc., to act as his her council of advisers and serve executives of various departme of government. 4. **cab′inetmak** craftsman skilled in making fi furniture of wood; **cab′ine making, cab′inetwork**.

ca·ble (kā′bel) *n*. 1. Strong thi rope of hemp or wire; (nau studded link chain attached to anchor; measurement of distance sea, = 720 feet (262.8 m). 2. A insulated conductor of electrici orig. the conductor of a submari

The **cabbage butterfly** *Pierisrap regarded throughout North America a serious pest attacking cabbage crop was introduced in about 1860.*

*Born in Genoa, **John Cabot** is shown here embarking from Bristol in search of the North West Passage to India. He and his son failed to find it but discovered Newfoundland.*

legraph. 3. = CABLEGRAM. 4. -**stitch**, any of various twisted pelike stitches in knitting and broidery. 5. ~ **car**, car on ~ ailway worked by cable and ationary engine; car hanging from d traveling along an overhead ble; **ca′blelaid**, (of rope) made of ree hawser-laid ropes laid up left-nded; **cable TV**, television pro-ams broadcast via coaxial cable or air to a community antenna. ble *v.* (**-bled, -bling**). 1. urnish, fasten with cable. 2. ransmit (message), communicate cable.

ca·ble·gram (kā′belgrăm) *n.* elegraph message transmitted by bmarine cable.

cab·o·chon (kăb′oshŏn) *n.* Gem, lished, not cut into facets, cular or elliptical in shape with med top.

ca·boo·dle (kaboo′del) *n.* lloq.) **the whole** (**kit and**) ~, e whole lot.

ca·boose (kaboos′) *n.* 1. Galley ship's deck. 2. Last car on ight train, containing crew's chen and sleeping quarters.

Cab·ot (kăb′ot), **John** (c1450–98). Venetian navigator in the rvice of England; discovered brador in 1497 with his son

Sebastian (1477–1557); ~ **Strait**, channel connecting the Gulf of St. Lawrence with the Atlantic Ocean.

Ca·bral (kabrahl′), **Pedro Alvares** (1460–1526?). Portuguese navigator; discovered Brazil, 1500, and claimed it for Portugal.

Ca·bri·ni (kabrē′nē), **Saint Frances Xavier** ("Mother Cabrini") (1850–1917). Founder of Missionary Sisters of the Sacred Heart; first American canonized, 1946.

cab·ri·ole (kăb′rēōl) *n.* Kind of curved leg in 17th- and 18th-c. furniture, esp. that of Chippendale style.

cab·ri·o·let (kăbrēolā′) *n.* Light two-wheeled hooded one-horse carriage. [Fr., f. *cabriole* goat's leap]

ca·ca·o (kakā′ō, -kah′ō) *n.* (pl. **-ca·os**). Seed of a tropical Amer. tree (*Theobroma cacao*), from which cocoa and chocolate are prepared; the tree itself (also ~ **tree**).

cac·cia·to·re (kächatōr′ē, -tōr′ē) *adj.* Stewed with herbs, tomatoes, and other seasonings.

cach·a·lot (kăsh′alŏt, -lō) *n.*

Sperm whale.

cache (kăsh) *n.* Hiding place for treasures, ammunition, provisions, etc., esp. as used by explorers; the stores hidden. ~ *v.t.* (**cached, cach·ing**). Place in cache.

ca·chet (kăshā′, kăsh′ā) *n.* Stamp, seal, distinguishing mark, commemorative design; prestige.

cach·in·nate (kăk′ināt) *v.i.* (**-nat·ed, -nat·ing**). Laugh loudly. **cach·in·na·tion** (kăkinā′shon) *n.*

ca·cique (kasēk′) *n.* W. Ind. and Latin Amer. Indian chief; Spanish or Latin Amer. local political boss.

cack·le (kăk′el) *n.* Clucking of hen after laying; noisy, inconsequent talk; shrill laugh. ~ *v.i.* (**-led, -ling**). Make cackle; talk glibly and noisily.

cac·o·dyl (kăk′odĭl) *n.* (chem.) The radical dimethyl arsenic ($As(CH_3)_2$). [Gk. *kakōdēs* stinking]

cac·o·e·thes (kăkōē′thēz) *n.* Mania or incurable itch (for doing something unwise); ~ **scribendi**, compulsion to write (books, poetry, etc.). [L., f. Gk. *kakos* bad, ugly; *ēthos* disposition]

ca·cog·ra·phy (kakŏg′rafē) *n.* Bad handwriting or spelling. **ca·cog′ra·pher** *n.* **cac·o·graph·ic** (kăkogrăf′ĭk), **cac·o·graph′i·cal** *adjs.* **cac·o·graph′i·cal·ly** *adv.*

cac·o·mis·tle (kăk'omĭsel) *n.* Small raccoon-like carnivore of Mexico and SW. U.S. (*Bassariscus astutus*), with bushy black-and-white ringed tail, also called ring-tailed cat.

ca·coph·o·ny (kakŏf'onē) *n.* (pl. **-nies**). Ugly sound, dissonance, discord. **ca·coph'o·nous** *adj.* **ca·coph'o·nous·ly** *adv.*

cac·tus (kăk'tus) *n.* (pl. **-tus·es, -ti** pr. -tī). Plant of the family Cactaceae, flourishing in arid districts of the Western Hemisphere, having a thick fleshy stem adapted for retaining moisture (usu. with spines, rarely with leaves) and bearing brilliantly colored flowers. **cac·toid** (kăk'toid) *adj.*

cad (kăd) *n.* Ungentlemanly man, esp. in behavior toward women. **cad'dish** *adj.*

ca·dav·er (kadăv'er) *n.* Corpse. **ca·dav'er·ic, ca·dav'er·ous** *adjs.* [L.]

cad·die, cad·dy¹ (kăd'ē) *ns.* (pl. **-dies**). Attendant who carries golfer's clubs etc. ~ *v.i.* (**-died, -dy·ing**). Act as caddie. [f. CADET]

cad·dis (kăd'ĭs) *n.* **cad'disfly**, feebly flying freq. nocturnal insect of order Trichoptera, with membranous or hairy wings, living near water; **cad'disworm**, larva of caddisfly etc., living in water and making cylindrical case of sticks, stone, shells, etc., used as bait for fishing.

cad·dy² (kăd'ē) *n.* (pl. **-dies**). Small box or other container, esp. one for holding tea. [Malay *kati*, weight of 1⅓ lb. (603 g)]

ca·dence (kā'dens) *n.* Rhythm; measured movement, esp. of sound; falling tone, esp. of voice at end of period; intonation; (mus.) close of musical movement or phrase. **ca'denced** *adj.*

ca·den·za (kadĕn'za) *n.* (mus.) Elaborate passage for solo instrument (or, less freq., voice) at close of movement or between two parts of movement, sometimes improvised by performer.

ca·det (kadĕt') *n.* 1. (archaic) Younger son or brother. 2. Student in a military school, training to be an officer.

cadge (kăj) *v.* (**cadged, cadg·ing**). Get by begging.

Cad·il·lac (kăd'ĭlăk), **Sieur Antoine de la Mothe** (1658–1730). French army officer and administrator in America; founder of French settlement in Detroit, 1701; governor of Louisiana, 1713–1716.

Cá·diz (kā'dĭz, kadēz'). Seaport in SW. Spain, on the Atlantic Ocean near Gibraltar.

cad·mi·um (kăd'mēum) *n.* (chem.) Soft bluish-white metallic element resembling tin, used in various alloys and as a protective coating on iron and steel; symbol Cd, at. no. 48, at. wt. 112.40; ~ **yellow**, cadmium sulfide, an intense yellow pigment.

Cad·mus (kăd'mus). (Gk. legend) Founder of Thebes in Boeotia, reputed to have introduced the alphabet into Greece; slew a dragon and sowed its teeth in the earth, from which armed men sprang up and slew one another until only five survived, with whom he founded Thebes. **Cad·me·an** (kădmē'an) *adj.*

ca·dre (kăd're, kah'dre) *n.* Framework, scheme; (mil.) permanent nucleus of regiment; in Communist countries, = CELL, def. 6.

ca·du·ce·us (kadōō'sēus, -dū'-, -shus) *n.* (pl. **-ce·i** pr. -sēī, -shī). Ancient Greek or Roman herald's wand; esp. the wand of Mercury, usu. represented with two serpents twined around it; similar staff used as a symbol of the medical profession.

ca·du·cous (kadōō'kus, -dū) *adj.* Fleeting, perishable; (biol., organs and parts) shed when the work is done. **ca·du·ci·ty** (kadōō'sĭtē, -dū'-) *n.*

cae·cil·i·an (sēsĭl'ēan) *adj.* & (zool.) (Member) of the Apoda (s APODAL).

cae·cum (sē'kum) = CECUM.

Caed·mon (kăd'mon) (7th c English monk; said by Bede to ha received in a vision the power song and put into English ver passages from the Scriptures.

Cae·li·an (sē'lēan). One of tl seven Hills of Rome.

Cae·no·zo·ic (sēnozō'ĭk) CENOZOIC.

Cae·sar (sē'zer). Cognomen the Roman dictator Caius JULI CAESAR, used as title by the Rom; emperors from Augustus Hadrian, and subsequently by tl emperor's heir presumptive. **Cae**

Few of the cactus family are useful to man, but they are cultivated for their beauty and curious shapes. 1. The Saguabo cactus in Tucson Mountain Park, Arizona. 2. The orchid epiphyllum cactus. 3. The golden b (Echinocactus grusonii) growing ne the Mediterranean.

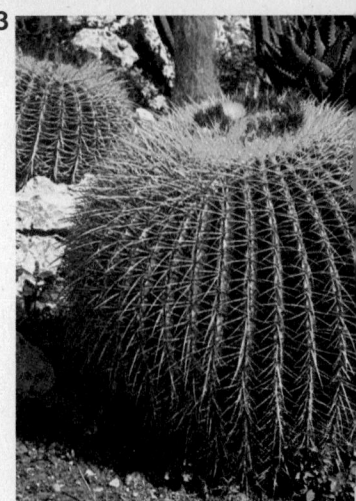

ar·e·an, Cae·sar·i·an (sĭzār´ēan)
adjs. Of Caesar or the Caesars; ~
ection, operation of cutting
through walls of the mother's
abdomen to deliver a child, as was
done, acc. to Pliny, at the birth of
Julius Caesar.

Cae·sa·re·a (sēzarē´a, sĕs-).
Ancient seaport built by Herod the
Great; capital of Roman Palestine.

cae·si·um (sē´zēum) = CESIUM.

cae·su·ra, ce·su·ra (sĭzhoor´a,
-zoor´a, -zūr´a) *ns.* (pl. **-su·ras,
-su·rae** pr. -zhoor´ē, -zoor´ē,
-zūr´ē). (Gk. and Rom. pros.)
Break between words within a
metrical foot; (modern pros.) pause
about the middle of metrical line.
cae·su´ral *adj.*

ca·fé (kăfā´, ka-) *n.* Coffeehouse,
restaurant, bar; ~ **au lait**, coffee
mixed with about an equal quantity
of hot milk; the brownish-cream
color of this.

caf·e·te·ri·a (kăfetēr´ēa) *n.* Restaurant in which customers take
their food from a counter and carry
it to a table for eating.

caf·feine, caf·fein (kăfēn´,
kăf´ēn) *ns.* Vegetable alkaloid
crystallizing in white silky needles,
found in leaves and seeds of coffee
and tea plants etc. (and hence in
these beverages); used in medicine
as a cardiac stimulant and as a
diuretic.

caf·tan (kăf´tan, kăftăn´) *n.*
Long girdled tunic worn in eastern
countries; woman's long loose
dress.

cage (kāj) *n.* 1. Fixed or portable
enclosure, of wire or with bars, esp.
for confining birds or beasts. 2.
Any cagelike frame or device;
elevator car. ~ *v.t.* (**caged,
cag·ing**). Place or keep in cage.

cag·ey (kā´jē) *adj.* (**cag·i·er,
cag·i·est**). (colloq.) Wary, noncommittal.

Ca·glios·tro (kălyaws´trō),
Count Alessandro (1743–95).
Name assumed by Giuseppe
Balsamo, a notorious adventurer,
magician, and charlatan born at
Palermo.

Ca·ho·ki·a (kahō´kēa) **Mounds.**
Archaeological site of a group of
pre-Colombian Indian mounds in
SE. Illinois.

ca·hoots (kah ōōts´) *n.pl.*
(colloq.) **in** ~ (**with**), in collusion,
league, questionable company
(with).

Cai·a·phas (kā´afas, kī´-),
Joseph. Jewish high priest from
18(?) to 36 A.D., president of the
council that condemned Jesus
Christ (Matt. 26).

cai·man, cay·man (kā´man) *ns.*
(pl. **-mans**). Any of several tropical
Amer. saurians (most of genus
Caiman) resembling alligators and
crocodiles.

Cain (kān). Eldest son of Adam
and Eve, who became the first
murderer when he killed his brother
Abel out of jealousy (Gen. 4);
murderer, fratricide; **raise** ~,
(colloq.) make a disturbance, create
trouble.

Cai·no·zo·ic (kīnozō´ĭk) =
CENOZOIC.

ca·ique, ca·ïque (kah-ēk´) *ns.*
Light narrow rowboat used in the
Middle East; small Levantine sail-
ing vessel.

cairn, carn (kārn) *ns.* 1.
Pyramid of stones as memorial,
landmark, etc. 2. (also **Cairn
terrier**) Small terrier (named from
being used to hunt among cairns)
with longish body, short legs, and

shaggy coat, developed in Scotland.

Cai·ro (kī´rō). Capital city of
Egypt, situated on the Nile about
100 miles (160 km) from its mouths.
[Arab. *alkāhira* the victorious (conjuncture)]

cais·son (kā´son, -sŏn) *n.* 1.
Ammunition chest or wagon. 2.
Large watertight chamber used in
laying foundations under water;
buoyant chamber attached to side of
ship engaged in raising wreck; boat-
shaped vessel used as dock gate; ~
disease, disorder caused by working under high atmospheric pressure, in which bubbles of nitrogen
released from body fluids if pressure is reduced too rapidly collect
in joints and blood vessels; the
bends.

cai·tiff (kā´tĭf) *n. & adj.* (archaic)
Base, despicable (person);
coward(ly).

caj·e·put, caj·u·put (kăj´eput,
-pŏot) *ns.* E. Ind. tree of genus
Melaleuca; (also ~ **oil**) aromatic oil
obtained from this, used as stimulant, antispasmodic, and sudorific.
[Malay *kayu* wood, *puteh* white]

ca·jole (kajōl´) *v.t.* (**-joled,
-jol·ing**). Persuade or soothe by
flattery, deceit, etc. **ca·jol´er·y** *n.*
(pl. **-er·ies**).

Ca·jun, Cai·jan (kā´jun) *ns.*
(sometimes taken to be offensive)
Louisiana native descended from
French exiles from Acadia; their
patois or dialect. [alteration of
Acadian]

cake (kāk) *n.* 1. Flat, thin mass
of fried or baked batter or dough.
2. Baked sweetened mixture of flour
and other ingredients, as butter,

*Hunters of the spectacled **cayman** in
the Amazon region have reduced its
numbers to a point where the reptile is
in danger of extinction. Its powerful
jaws are equipped with conical teeth.*

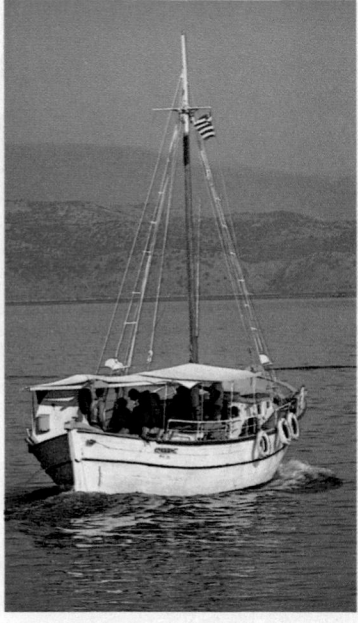

*It is still possible to see a few **caiques**
rigged for sail in the Levant, but many
are now equipped with diesel engines
and are in everyday service as ferries.*

eggs, spices, currants, raisins, etc. 3. Flattish compact mass of other food (as fish etc.) or of any compressed substance, as soap, wax, tobacco. 4. **cake′walk**, (orig.) a promenade of black American origin in which a prize of a cake was given for the most graceful and intricate steps; popular stage dance developed from these steps. **cake** *v.* (**caked, cak·ing**). Form into compact flattish mass.

Cal. *abbrev.* California.

cal. *abbrev.* Calorie, caliber, calendar.

cal·a·bash (kăl′abăsh) *n.* Any of various gourds or pumpkins, the shells of which are used for holding liquids etc.; the vessel made from such a shell; ∼ **tree,** tropical Amer. and W. Ind. tree *Crescentia*, bearing a large oval or globular fruit with a hard shell.

cal·a·boose (kăl′aboos, kăla-boos′) *n.* (colloq.) Prison.

Ca·la·bri·a (kalā′brēa). Region in SW. Italy.

ca·la·di·um (kalā′dēum) *n.* Any of various widely cultivated tropical Amer. plants of the genus *Cala-dium,* esteemed for their ornamental leaves.

Ca·lais (kălā′, kăl′ā). Seaport in N. France, opposite Dover, England.

cal·a·man·co (kălamăng′kō) *n.* (pl. **-cos**). Glossy Flemish woolen cloth, checkered on one side, much used in 18th c.

cal·a·man·der (kăl′amănder) *n.* Extremely hard cabinet wood of Ceylon and India, from the tree (related to ebony) *Diospyros quaesita.*

cal·a·mine (kăl′amīn, -mǐn) *n.* 1. Carbonate of zinc (ZnCO₃). 2. Pink powder containing zinc carbonate and ferric oxide, used in skin

The South American **calceolaria** is grouped in the Scrofulariaceae family and is native to Central and South America. C. arachnoidea is illustrated.

lotions and ointments.

ca·lam·i·ty (kalăm′itē) *n.* (pl. **-ties**). Adversity, deep distress; grievous disaster; **C∼ Jane,** nickname of Martha Jane Burke (*née* Canary, ?1852–1903), Amer. frontierswoman and markswoman; applied to a prophet of disaster. **ca·lam′i·tous** *adj.* **ca·lam′i·tous·ly** *adv.*

cal·car·e·ous (kălkār′eus) *adj.* Of, containing, calcium carbonate or limestone.

This Jain temple is one of the glories of **Calcutta,** capital of W. Bengal and its most important manufacturing city and port. It stands on the Hooghly River 86 miles inland.

cal·ce·o·lar·i·a (kălsēolār′ēa) Widely cultivated S. Amer. plant genus *C∼,* with yellow flowe somewhat resembling a broad-toe slipper; the pocketbook plant.

cal·ce·o·late (kăl′sēolāt) *aa* (bot.) Slipper-shaped.

cal·ci·cole (kăl′sikōl) *n.* Plant animal inhabiting a soil with fr calcium carbonate (or, in wide sense, soils rich in calcium **cal·cic·o·lous** (kălsĭk′olus) *adj.*

cal·cif·er·ous (kălsĭf′erus) *ad* Yielding or containing chalk calcium carbonate.

cal·ci·fy (kăl′sĭfī) *v.* (**-fied -fy·ing**). Convert, be converted into chalk or calcium carbonate harden by deposit of calcium salt petrify. **cal·ci·fi·ca·tion** (kălsĭf kā′shon) *n.*

cal·cine (kăl′sīn, -sĭn) *v* (**-cined, -cin·ing**). Reduce quicklime or friable substance b heating strongly; desiccate; refin by consuming grosser part; burn ashes. **cal·ci·na·tion** (kălsĭnā shon) *n.* Process of calcining.

cal·cite (kăl′sīt) *n.* (min. Crystalline calcium carbonate widely distributed in nature a marble, limestone, etc.

cal·ci·um (kăl′sēum) *n.* (chem. Silver-white malleable light meta an element in the alkaline eart group (symbol Ca, at. no. 20, at. w 40.08), widely distributed in natur as limestone or chalk (∼ **carbon ate,** CaCO₃); ∼ **carbide,** com pound of calcium and carbo (CaC₂), produced by intense heatin of limestone and coke in an electri

American sculptor **Alexander Calde** created the first mobiles. He also mad stationary forms that he called stabiles In this sculpture the two themes ar mixed.

rnace and yielding acetylene gas
treatment with water; ~ **hypo-**
lorite, chloride of lime or
eaching powder (CaOCl$_2$), used
disinfectant; ~ **oxide**, (CaO)
uicklime.

calc·spar (kălk′spär) n. (min.)
rystalline from of calcium carbon-
e (limestone).

cal·cu·la·ble (kăl′kyulabel)
dj. That may be reckoned,
easured, computed, or relied
on. **cal·cu·la·bil·i·ty** (kălkyula-
l′itē) n.

cal·cu·late (kăl′kyulāt) v. (-lat-
l, -lat·ing). Compute by figures;
certain beforehand by exact
ckoning; plan deliberately; (dial.)
ppose, believe; (usu. pass.)
range, adapt, for, to; **calculating**
achine, machine that performs
ithmetical processes. **cal′cu-**
t·ed adj. (esp.) Fit, suitable to do.
cal·cu·la·tion (kălkyulā′shon) n.
Result got by) calculation; forecast.
cal·cu·la·tor (kăl′kyulāter) n.
sp.) Set of tables for use in
lculating; calculating machine.
cal·cu·lous (kăl′kyulus) adj. Of,
ffering from, calculus or stone.
..., = small stone used in reckon-
g on abacus]

cal·cu·lus (kăl′kyulus) n. (pl. **-li**
r. -lī, **-lus·es**). 1. (med.) Stone,
ncretion in some part of the body.
(math.) Particular method of
lculation, esp. DIFFERENTIAL and
TEGRAL calculus.

Cal·cut·ta (kălkŭt′a). City and
port in India, capital of W. Bengal;
Black Hole of ~: see BLACK adj.

Cal·der (kawl′der), **Alexander**
(1898–1976). Amer. sculptor,
famous for mobiles.

Cal·de·rón de la Bar·ca (kahl′-
derŏn dĕla bär′ka), **Pedro** (1600–
1681). Spanish dramatist and poet,
author of over 120 plays.

cal·dron (kawl′dron) = CAUL-
DRON.

Cal·e·do·ni·a (kăledō′nēa).
(poet. and rhet.) Scotland, the
Scottish Highlands.

Cal·e·do·ni·an (kăledō′nēan)
adj. Of Scotland; ~ **Canal**, 60-
mile-long (96.6 km) ship canal from
Inverness on the E. coast of Scotland to Fort William on the W.
coast, connecting the North Sea
with the Atlantic Ocean. **Caledo-**
nian n. Native, inhabitant, of
Scotland.

cal·en·dar (kăl′ender) n. 1.
System by which the beginning,
length, and subdivision of civil year
is fixed, esp. the GREGORIAN ~; ~
month, one of the 12 months into
which year is divided by calendar,
as opp. to lunar MONTH; **Jewish** ~;
see JEWISH. 2. Table(s) showing
months, weeks and festivals, etc., of
a given year or years. 3. Register,
list, esp. of canonized saints,
prisoners for trial, or documents
chronologically arranged with sum-
maries. **calendar** v.t. Register,
enter in list; arrange, analyze, and
index (documents).

cal·en·der (kăl′ender) n. Machine in which cloth, paper, etc., is
pressed under rollers to glaze or
smooth it. ~ v.t. Press in calender.
cal·ends (kăl′endz) n. pl. First
day of month in Roman calendar.
cal·en·ture (kăl′encher, -choor)
n. Tropical fever or delirium.
calf[1] (kăf, kahf) n. (pl. **calves** pr.
kăvz, kahvz). 1. Young of bovine
animal, esp. domestic cow, for first
year; young of elephant, whale, etc.;
golden ~: see Exod. 32; wealth as
an object of worship; ~ **love**,
immature romantic affection,
puppy love. 2. Leather made from
skin of domestic calf. 3. (naut.)
Floating piece of ice detached from
glacier, iceberg, or floe.
calf[2] (kăf, kahf) n. (pl. **calves** pr.
kăvz, kahvz). Fleshy back part of
shank of leg; part of stocking
covering this.
Cal·gar·y (kăl′gerē). City in
Alberta, Canada; center of cattle-
raising region; site of annual ~
stampede, or rodeo.
Cal·houn (kălhoōn′), **John**
Caldwell (1782–1850). Vice president of the U.S. under John Quincy
Adams and Andrew Johnson, 1825–
1832; as S. Carolina member of
Congress, was a champion of
slavery; U.S. Secretary of War,
1817–25, Secretary of State, 1844–
1845.
Cal·i·ban (kăl′ibăn). Character
in Shakespeare's *Tempest*, a "savage
and deformed slave."
cal·i·ber, esp. Brit. **cal·i·bre**
(kăl′iber) ns. 1. Internal diameter
of gun or any tube; diameter of
bullet or shell. 2. Degree of
personal capacity or ability, or of
merit or importance. [Arab. *qalib*
mold]
cal·i·brate (kăl′ibrāt) v.t.
(-brat·ed, -brat·ing). Find
caliber of; calculate irregularities of
(tube, gauge) before graduating;
graduate (a gauge) make allowance
for irregularities. **cal·i·bra·tion**
(kălibrā′shon), **cal·i·bra·tor** ns.
cal·i·bre (kăl′iber) = CALIBER.
cal·i·co (kăl′ikō) n. (pl. **-coes**,
-cos). Coarse cotton cloth usually
printed with bright designs; (Brit.)
plain white unprinted bleached or
unbleached cotton cloth. ~ adj.
Of, like calico; variegated, piebald,
esp. ~ **cat**. [*Calicut*, town on
Malabar coast]
Calif. abbrev. California.
Cal·i·for·nia (kălifōr′nya, -nēa).
State on Pacific coast of U.S.,
admitted to the Union in 1850;
capital, Sacramento; **Gulf of** ~,
inlet of the Pacific Ocean between
the Lower California peninsula and
Mexico, also called the Sea of

Cortez. **Cal·i·for′nian** *adj.* & *n.*

cal·i·for′ni·um (kălĭfōr′nēum) *n.* (chem.) Transuranic element; symbol Cf. at. no. 98, principal isotope at. wt. 244.

Ca·lig·u·la (kalĭg′yula), **Gaius Caesar.** Roman emperor 37–41 A.D.; notorious for his cruelty and vices.

cal·i·pash (kăl′ĭpăsh, kălĭpăsh′) *n.* Dull green gelatinous substance beneath a turtle's upper shell.

cal·i·pee (kăl′ĭpē, kălĭpē′) *n.* Light yellow gelatinous substance inside a turtle's lower shell.

cal·i·per (kăl′ĭper) *n.* (usu. pl.) 1. Compasses with bowed legs for measuring diameter of convex bodies, or with turned out points for measuring cavities. 2. (also ~ **brake**) Brake, esp. on bicycle, of two blocks worked through pivot to grip rim of wheel; brake of similar principle on automobile, in which two pads grip revolving disk. ~ *v.t.* Measure with calipers.

ca·liph (kā′lĭf, kăl′ĭf) *n.* (in certain Muslim countries) Chief civil and religious ruler, as successor of Muhammad. **ca·liph·ate** (kă′lĭfāt, -fĭt, kăl′i-) *n.* [Arab. *ḳalīfa* successor]

cal·is·then·ics (kălĭsthĕn′ĭks) *n.pl.* Simple gymnastic exercises for health and general physical well-being.

calk (kawk) *n.* Sharp iron piece to prevent horseshoe or boot from slipping. ~ *v.t.* Provide with calk.

call (kawl) *v.* 1. Cry, shout, speak loudly; utter characteristic note; cry *out, to;* read *out* (names of those on list); name (suit as trumps, at cards); pay brief visit (*at* house, *on* person) in order to speak, deal, etc.; communicate by radio or telephone. 2. Summon; summon or nominate by divine authority into the Church. 3. Name, describe as; consider, regard as. 4. ~ **down**, reprimand; ~ **for**, order; demand; need; go and fetch; ~ **forth**, elicit; ~ **off** (a project), cancel it; ~ **on**, invoke, appeal to; ~ **out**, summon (troops) esp. to aid civil authorities; summon (workers) to strike; shout or utter loudly; ~ **up**, imagine; ring (on telephone); summon to serve in army etc. **call** *n.* 1. Shout, cry; special cry of bird etc., imitation of, instrument for imitating, this; signal on bugle etc. 2. Short formal or business visit. 3. Invitation, summons; duty, need, occasion; demand, claim. 4. Telephone conversation. 5. Demand for money, esp. for unpaid capital from company shareholders; (Stock Exch.) option of claiming stock at given date. 6. ~ **girl**, prostitute accepting appointments by telephone; ~ **name**, name adopted by a citizens' band radio operator for use in transmissions; ~ **sign**, identifying signal of a radio station.

Calipers, for measuring the width of an object, are of various designs. 1. Calipers for outside measurement. 2. Calipers for inside measurement. 3. Calibrated calipers for both measurements.

cal·la (kăl′a) *n.* 1. (also ~ **lily**) Tropical plant (*Zantedeschia aethiopica*), widely cultivated indoors for its pure white showy spathe and yellow spadix. 2. Aquatic plant (genus *C~*) of N. Europe and eastern N. America.

call·er (kaw′ler) *n.* (esp.) Person paying a call or visit; person who initiates telephone call.

cal·lig·ra·phy (kalĭg′rafē) *n.* (Art of) beautiful handwriting. **cal·lig′ra·pher, cal·lig′ra·phist** *ns.* **cal·li·graph·ic** (kălĭgrăf′ĭk) *adj.*

call·ing (kaw′lĭng) *n.* (esp.) Occupation, profession, trade; persons following a particular occupation; ~ **card**, small card bearing a person's name, address, etc., used for social or business purposes.

Cal·li·o·pe (kalī′ope). (Gk. and Rom. myth.) Muse of eloquence and epic poetry. [Gk. *kalliope* beautiful voiced]

cal·li·o·pe (kalī′ope, kăl′ēōp) *n.* Set of steam whistles producing musical notes, played by a keyboard like that of an organ.

cal·li·per (kăl′ĭper) = CALIPER.

Cal·lis·the·nes (kalĭs′thenēz). 4th c. B.C. Greek philosopher and chronicler of Alexander the Great.

Cal·lis·to (kalĭs′tō). 1. (Gk. myth.) Daughter of Lycaon, loved by Zeus and punished for her unchastity by being turned into a bear; she and her son were transformed into constellations. 2. (astron.) Constellation URSA Major.

cal·los·i·ty (kalŏs′ĭtē) *n.* (pl. -ties). Abnormal hardness and thickness of skin; hardened insensible part, lump.

cal·lous (kăl′us) *adj.* 1. Hard-

ened, hard (of parts of skin). 2. Unfeeling, insensible. **cal′lous ly** *adv.* **cal′lous·ness** *n.*

cal·low (kăl′ō) *adj.* 1. Unfledged; downy like young birds. 2. Raw, inexperienced. **cal′low ness** *n.*

cal·lus (kăl′us) *n.* (pl. **-lus·es**) Thickened part of skin or soft tissue; bony material formed while bone fracture heals; (bot.) new tissue, usu. more or less corky, covering a wound.

calm (kahm) *n.* Stillness, serenity; windless period. ~ *adj.* Tranquil, quiet; windless; undisturbed; unabashed, impudent. **calm′ly** *adv.* **calm′ness** *n.* **calm** *v.* Make calm; pacify; ~ **down** become calm.

cal·o·mel (kăl′omĕl, -mel) *n.* Mercurous chloride (HgCl), heavy white powder used as purgative and fungicide.

cal·o·rie (kăl′orē) *n.* 1. (also **kilogram** or **large ~**) Standard unit of heat, amount required to raise the temperature of one kilogram (one liter) of water one degree centigrade; unit for measuring the heat and other energy produced by the metabolism of food. 2. (also **gram** or **small ~**) Amount of heat required to raise one gram (one cubic cm) of water one degree centigrade. **ca·lor·ic** (kalōr′ĭk, -lăr′-) *adj.* Of calories; of heat.

cal·o·rif·ic (kălorĭf′ĭk) *adj.* Of producing heat.

cal·o·rim·e·ter (kălorĭm′eter) *n.* Apparatus for measuring heat. **cal·o·ri·met·ric** (kălorĭmĕt′rĭk) **cal·o·ri·met′ri·cal** *adjs.* **cal·o·ri·met′ri·cal·ly** *adv.*

cal·trop (kăl′trop) *n.* 1. (hist.) 4-spiked iron ball thrown on ground to impede cavalry horses. 2. of various plants that have spiny burs or bracts.

cal·u·met (kăl′yumĕt, kălyumĕt′) *n.* Long-stemmed ornamental pipe used by N. American Indians for ceremonial purposes, esp. used as symbol of peace or friendship (the *peace pipe*).

ca·lum·ni·ate (kalŭm′nēāt) *v.t.* (-at·ed, -at·ing). Slander. **ca·lum·ni·a·tion** (kalŭmnēā′shon) *n.*

cal·um·ny (kăl′umnē) *n.* (pl. -nies). Malicious misrepresentation; false report; slander.

Cal·va·ry (kăl′verē). Hill near Jerusalem on which Jesus Christ was crucified. [L. *calvaria* skull, transl. of GOLGOTHA in Matt. 27]

calve (kăv, kahv) *v.i.* (**calved, calv·ing**). Give birth to calf; (of glacier, iceberg, etc.) throw off masses of ice.

*The site of **Calvary** is uncertain, but the scholar Charles Gordon in the 19th century proposed a low hill outside the Damascus Gate of Jerusalem. The painting of Jesus crucified on Calvary is by Bramantino.*

The leaf-like protective parts of a flower are collectively a *calyx*. This consists of modified petals, usually green but in lilies the same color as the flower itself.

A few Bactrian came (foreground) are found w in Turkestan and Mongol Bactrian camels are supe beasts for the desert. Eac can carry about 800 lbs f nearly 30 miles in a da The Arabian camel (bac ground) is a riding came valued for its speed an endurance.

Cal·vin (kăl′vĭn), **John** (1509–1564). French theologian and reformer; settled in Geneva, 1536; wrote *Institutes of the Christian Religion* (1535), in which he expounded his doctrine of original sin, of predestination and election; his dogma is held by the continental Reformed Churches and forms the basis of Scottish Presbyterianism.

Cal·vin·ism (kăl′vĭnĭzem) *n.* Tenets and doctrines of CALVIN and his followers and of the Calvinistic Churches, whose distinguishing doctrines, usu. called **the five points of** ∼, are election or predestination, limited atonement, total depravity, irresistibility of grace, and the perseverance of the saints. **Cal′vin·ist** *n. & adj.* Follower of Calvin, adherent of Calvinism. **Cal·vin·is·tic** (kălvĭnĭs′tĭk), **Cal·vin·is′ti·cal** *adjs.* Pertaining to, characteristic of, Calvinism.

Ca·lyp·so (kalĭp′sō). (Gk. legend) In the *Odyssey*, a nymph who kept ODYSSEUS seven years on her island, Ogygia.

ca·lyp·so (kalĭp′sō) *n.* (pl. **-sos**). Spontaneous topical, often humorous, W. Ind. song or chant with African rhythm.

ca·lyp·tra (kalĭp′tra) *n.* (bot.) Hood or cover, esp. hood of spore case in mosses. [Gk. *kaluptra* veil]

ca·lyx (kālĭks, kăl′ĭks) *n.* (pl. **ca·lyx·es, cal·y·ces** pr. kăl′ĭsēz, kā′lĭ-). (bot.) Whorl of floral parts, often leaflike, forming outer protective envelope of flower.

cam (kăm) *n.* Portion of revolving shaft or wheel bearing against, and shaped so as to impart a particular type of motion to, a lever or other movable part of a machine; **cam′shaft**, shaft bearing cam(s).

ca·ma·ra·de·rie (kahmarah′-derē) *n.* Intimacy, mutual trust, and sociability of comrades. [Fr.]

cam·ber (kăm′ber) *n.* Slight convexity of upper surface, arched form (of road, ship's deck, airplane wing, etc.); setting of automobile wheels closer together at the bottom than at the top. ∼ *v.* Have, construct with, camber.

Cam·ber·well (kăm′berwĕl, -wel) **beauty.** Species of butterfly (*Nymphalis antiopa*). [*Camberwell*, borough of London]

cam·bi·um (kăm′bēum) *n.* (bot.) Layer of cells from which annual growth of woody tissue and bark takes place.

Cam·bo·di·a (kămbō′dēa, -bŏd′ya): see KAMPUCHEA.

Cam·bri·a (kăm′brēa). Ancient or poetic name for Wales. **Cam′bri·an** *adj. & n.* 1. Welsh(man). 2. (geol.) (Of) the earliest period or system of the Paleozoic era. [Latinized f. *Cymry* Welshman]

cam·bric (kăm′brĭk) *n.* Fine white linen or cotton fabric of plain weave. [*Kamerijk*, Fl. name of *Cambrai*, where linen cambric was made]

Cam·bridge[1] (kăm′brĭj). City in Cambridgeshire on River Cam, England, about 50 miles (80.5 km) NE. of London; site of Cambridge University, which was first organized in 1209 and recognized by a royal writ in 1230.

Cam·bridge[2] (kăm′brĭj). City in Massachusetts on the Charles River opposite Boston; site of Harvard University, founded in 1636.

cam·el (kăm′el) *n.* 1. Large ruminant quadruped of genus *Camelus* with long neck, cushioned feet, and either two humps (**Bactrian** ∼) or one (**dromedary** ∼) which store food, closely related to the llama and alpaca, used as beast of burden in arid regions; ∼**'s hair, cam′elhair,** hair of this animal, woven into a soft, warm,

lightweight, usu. long-piled fabr imitation of this fabric, usu. fav or light tan. **camel's-hair brus** artist's paintbrush usu. made squirrel hair. 2. Float for increasi buoyancy of ship or raising sunk ship. 3. Shade of fawn.

ca·mel·lia (kamēl′ya, -mē′lē *n.* Flowering evergreen shrub genus *C*∼ of the tea family, chie native of China and Japan; al called japonica. [Joseph *Kam* (1661–1706), Moravian Jesuit w described botany of island of Luz in the Philippines]

ca·mel·o·pard (kamĕl′opärd) (archaic) Giraffe.

Cam·e·lot (kăm′elŏt). Arthurian legend, the place whe King Arthur held his court, stat by Malory to be Winchester.

Cam·em·bert (kăm′embār) Rich soft dessert cheese made ne the village of Camembert Normandy; cheese of similar typ

cam·e·o (kăm′ēō) *n.* (pl. **cam e·os**). 1. Small piece of reli carving in stone (onyx, agate, etc freq. with two layers of differe colors, the lower of which serves background. 2. (fig.) Short litera sketch etc., small well-define acting part.

cam·er·a (kăm′era, kăm′ra) Apparatus for taking photograph consisting essentially of a box hol ing at one end a plate or film whic is sensitized so as to retain the imag projected through a lens at th other; (television) apparatus whic forms the image and converts it in electrical impulses. **cam′erama** *n.* (esp.) One who operates motion-picture camera. [L., "vaulted room"]

cam·er·lin·go (kămerlĭng′gō) (pl. **-gos**). The cardinal who serv as the Pope's chamberlain an financial secretary, highest offic

The numbered labels on the main cutaway diagram appear throughout the image.

1. rewind lever
2. shutter release button
3. frame counter
4. depth of field preview button
5. shutter speed dial
6. eyepiece optics
7. viewfinder
8. pentaprism
9. rewind lever
10. strap lug
11. main spring
12. film transport gear train
13. shutter release axle
14. return spring
15. shutter speed ratchet
16. meter
17. meter inputs
18. meter inputs
19. field lens
20. focusing screen
21. diaphragm variable resistance
22. coupling prong
23. max. aperture setting (here f.2)
24. synchronization coupling
25. film take-up spool
26. filmtransport sprocket
27. self timer movement
28. self timer escape lever
29. shutter release lever
30. self timer lever
31. self timer release button
32. diaphragm stop-down linkage
33. diaphragm stop-down linkage
34. diaphragm stop-down pin
35. mallory cell
36. cadmium disulphide (CDS) cell
37. lens mounting ring
38. CDS incident light 45 mirror
39. main reflex mirror
40. main reflex mirror axle
41. diaphragm coupling
42. diaphragm ring
43. lens mounting
44. focusing ring
45. rear lens group (4 elements, 3 groups)
46. front lens group (3 elements, 3 groups)
47. iris diaphragm

e highly developed mechanism of a
dern *camera* offers great advan-
es of speed and variety of adjust-
nt over the ponderous cameras of
 early days of photography. But
tographers still depend on delicate
ntrol of the effects of light on silver
mpounds to produce a picture. The
nera has proved its worth in record-
 memorable events.

In this film transport and shutter sys-
m the film is shown dark green, the
nsport in light green, and the shutter
nds in dark blue and brown. 1.
hutter-cocking lever and film wind in
ound-on position. 2. Film take-up
pool. 3. Transport sprocket. 4. Film.
Film cassette. 6. First shutter blind.
Second shutter blind.
 On an SLR, a 'match needle' through

the lens light-metering system. 1.
Meter. 2. Setting for the meter in
relation to the film speed scale. 3.
Photocell reacts to light to move the
needle. 4. Mirror reflecting light to the
photocell. 5. A semi-opaque mirror
through which light reaches 4. 6. The
same as 5 but shown retracted. 7. The
indicator needle seen through the
viewfinder. 8. Shutter speed dial con-

trols the centering of the needle in a
claw, and modifies the aperture of the
lens. 9. Variable resistor transmits the
adjustment of 8 to the lens. 10. Mercury battery to power the system.
C. The reflex viewing system. 1. The
parts of the camera lens. 2. Reflex mirror. 3. Focusing screen. 4. Field lens.
5. Pentaprism. 6. Eyepiece.

in the papal household.

Cam·e·roun, Cam·e·roon
(kămerōon′, kămrōon′). Republic
on W. coast of Africa between
Nigeria and Congo; from 1884 to
1916 a German protectorate; after
World War I administered under
League of Nations (later U.N.)
trusteeship by France (*French
Cameroons*) and Great Britain
(*British Cameroons*); became a
Federal Republic in 1960–1, and a
United Republic in 1972; capital,
Yaoundé.

cam·i·sole (kăm′ĭsōl) *n.*
Woman's underbodice, often embroidered or trimmed with lace.

Cam·o·ëns (kăm′ōĕns), **Luiz
Vaz de** (1524–80). Portuguese
poet, author of the "Lusiads," an
epic poem on the descendants of
Lusus, the legendary hero of Portugal, and on the exploits of Vasco da
GAMA.

cam·o·mile, cham·o·mile
(kăm′omĭl, -mĕl) *ns.* Aromatic
creeping herb (*Anthemis nobilis*)
with downy leaves and yellow or

white daisy-like flowers of which a
tea is made and used as a tonic,
shampoo, etc.; ~ **tea**, brew of
camomile flowers.

Ca·mor·ra (kamōr′a, -mār′a).
In the 19th c., a secret society
practicing violence and extortion in
Naples and Neapolitan cities.
Ca·mor′rist *n.*

cam·ou·flage (kăm′oflahzh) *n.*
Disguising, disguise, of objects
used in war, as guns, ships,
factories, etc., by means of boughs,
obscuring outlines by netting and
paint of various colors, etc.; deception of any kind whereby an object
is concealed or made to look like
something else. ~ *v.t.* (**-flaged,
-flag·ing**). Conceal by or as by
camouflage.

camp[1] (kămp) *n.* 1. Place where
troops are lodged in tents etc. or
received for training. 2. Temporary
quarters of nomads, gypsies, travelers; (persons) camping out. 3.
(fig.) Body of adherents. 4. ~
chair, portable folding chair;
camp′fire, fire in camp or en-

campment, open-air fire; **ca**
follower, nonmilitary follower
hanger-on of camp or army (a
fig.); **camp′ground**, place fo
camp or camp meeting; **ca**
meeting, religious meeting held
open air or in a tent and usu. last
several days. **camp** *v.* Encam
lodge in camp; (also ~ **out**) lod
in tent or in the open, take
quarters; station (troops) in cam

camp[2] (kămp) *adj.* (slang)
Affected, outlandish. 2. Hom
sexual, effeminate. ~ *v.* (slan
(also ~ **it up**) Behave, do, in a can
way.

Cam·pa·gna (kahmpahn′y
Rich level district of Italy SE.
river Tiber, extending from the s
on the W. to the Sabine Hills.

cam·paign (kămpān′) *n.*
Series of military operations in
definite theater or with one obje
tive or constituting the whole or
distinct part of a war. 2. Organiz
course of action, esp. in politics,
before an election etc. ~*v.i.* Ser
in a campaign. **cam·paign′er**

*Below: The stick insect in naturally
camouflaged by its color, that matches
the privet leaves on which it feeds, and
by its shape that imitates the privet
stems.*

*Bottom: The ruins of Pompeii, an
ancient city of Italy, in the **Campania**
region, a few miles south of Mt.
Vesuvius. The ruins are important for
the study of Roman architecture.*

*Below: In St. Mark's Square in Ven
stands the great **campanile** that is t
focal point of the old city. Rebuilt ea
this century after it had collapsed,
stands 320 ft. high.*

Cam·pa·ni·a (kămpā′nēa). SW. gion of Italy. **Cam·pa′ni·an** *adj. n.*

cam·pa·ni·le (kămpanē′lē) *n.* l. **-ni·les, -ni·li** pr. -nē′lē). Bell wer, esp. one detached from main uilding.

cam·pa·nol·o·gy (kămpanŏl′- ē) *n.* The subject of bells (casting, nging, etc.). **cam·pa·nol′o·gist, am·pa·nol′o·ger** *ns.*

cam·pan·u·la (kămpăn′yula) *n.* ⁀erbaceous plant of genus *C~*, ith bell-shaped, usu. blue or hite, flowers.

Camp·bell (kăm′bel), **Mrs. atrick** (1867–1940). Original ame, Beatrice Stella Tanner; nglish stage actress; appeared in ⁀he Second Mrs. Tanqueray, Hedda abler, Pygmalion; famous for her orrespondence with George Ber- ⁀rd Shaw.

camp·er (kăm′per) *n.* Trucklike ⁀ehicle outfitted as living quarters ⁀r camping or long excursions.

cam·phor (kăm′fer) *n.* Trans- ⁀cent waxy crystalline substance ⁀ith strong characteristic smell and ⁀tter taste, obtained from a species ⁀ laurel growing in Japan, China, ⁀c., also made synthetically from ⁀rpentine; used in pharmacy, as ⁀sect repellent, and in manufacture ⁀ film, plastics, explosives, etc.

am·phor·ic (kămfŏr′ĭk, -fār′-) ⁀dj. **cam·phor·ate** (kăm′forāt) *v.t.* ⁀rat·ed, -rat·ing). Impregnate or ⁀eat with camphor.

cam·pi·on (kăm′pēon) *n.* Any of ⁀arious plants of genus *Lychnis*, ⁀ith red, pink, or white flowers.

Cam·pi·on (kăm′pēon), ⁀homas (1567–1620). English ⁀hysician, poet, and musician.

Cam·po·bel·lo (kămpobĕl′ō). ⁀sland off the SW. coast of New ⁀runswick, Canada; summer home ⁀f President Franklin D. Roosevelt.

cam·pus (kăm′pus) *n.* Grounds ⁀f a college or university, open ⁀pace between or around the ⁀uildings; (transf.) college or ⁀niversity life or people. [L., = ⁀field"]

Cam·ranh (kăm′rahn) **Bay.** ⁀rm of the South China Sea off the ⁀E. coast of Vietnam.

Ca·mus (kămü′), **Albert** (1913– ⁀960). French Existentialist novel- ⁀st and playwright; one of the ⁀aders of the French Resistance in ⁀orld War II; author of *The ⁀lague, The Stranger*, etc.; won ⁀obel Prize for literature, 1957.

can¹ (kăn) *n.* Small sealed metal ⁀ontainer, usu. tin-clad steel or ⁀luminum, in which food or drink ⁀s preserved; **~ of worms**, com- ⁀lex situation or problem. **can** *v.t.* ⁀canned, can·ning**). Preserve in a ⁀an; (slang) dismiss from a job. ⁀anned** *adj.* Preserved in a can; ⁀ slang, of music etc.) recorded; ⁀slang) dismissed from one's job.

can² (kăn, unstressed kan) *v. auxil.* (neg. **can·not** contraction **can't** (kănt, kahnt); past t. and conditional **could** (kŏŏd); defective parts supplied from *be able to*). Be able to; have the right to; (colloq.) be permitted to, may.

Can. *abbrev.* Canada.

Ca·naan (kā′nan). Biblical name of esp. western part of region later called Palestine, promised by God to Abraham (Gen. 12). **Ca′naan·ite** *adj. & n.*

Can·a·da (kăn′ada). Member State of the British Common- wealth, occupying the N. half of the N. Amer. continent (with the ex- ception of Alaska); the second largest country in the world; dis- covered by Cabot in 1497, occupied by the French in 1534, and ceded to Gt. Britain in 1763; the provinces of Canada were united as the Dominion of Canada in 1867; capital, Ottawa; **~ balsam**, oleo- resin obtained from a pine (*Abies balsamea*), used for mounting microscope slides; **~ goose**, wild goose (*Branta canadensis*) of N. America; **~ jay**, bold, noisy, gray jay (*Perisoreus canadensis*) of north-

The **camphor** tree (Cinnamomum cam- phor) is native to Japan. Natural cam- phor can be produced by using the wood in a special distillation process.

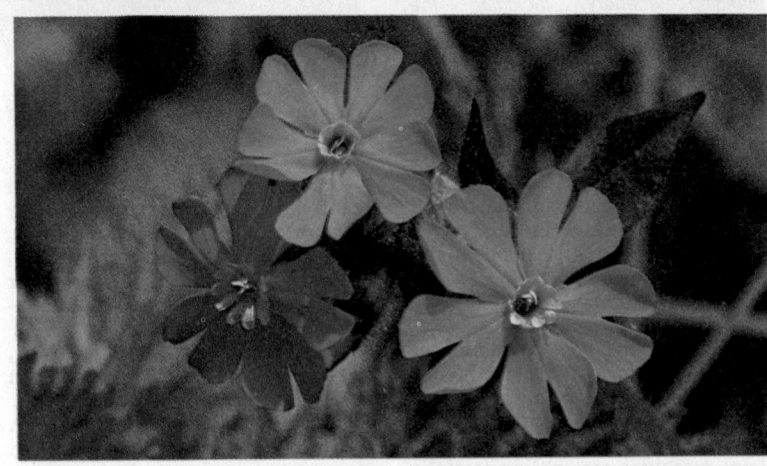

Above: There are several species of **campion.** *One of the same family is the gillyflower with which the Elizabethans used to flavor their wine and beer.*

Top: Named after their resemblance to bells, the flowers of the Campanu- laceae family include the bluebell and **Campanula** *portenschlagiana, illus- trated here.*

Canada covers an area of about 3,850,000 sq. miles. Top right: The map and the maple leaf flag. Top left: The City Hall, Toronto. The St. Lawrence Seaway, linking the Great Lakes with the sea, has increased Toronto's importance as a commercial and wholesale center of Canada. Above: The province of Ontario has outstanding scenery, including the Kakabeka Falls. Right: Combines harvest Canada's prairie wheat.

ern N. America. **Ca·na·di·an** (kanā′dēan) *adj.* & *n.*

Ca·na·di·an (kanā′dēan) **Falls.** Part of Niagara Falls separated from the American Falls by Goat Island; also called "Horseshoe Falls"; **Canadian River**, river flowing from N. New Mexico to the Arkansas River.

ca·naille (kanāl′, -nī′) *n.* Rabble. [Fr.]

ca·nal (kanăl′) *n.* 1. Duct in plant or animal body for food, liquid, air, etc. 2. Artificial waterway for inland navigation or for irrigation. 3. (astron.) One of the faint markings resembling straight lines observed on the surface of the planet Mars.

Ca·na·let·to (kănalĕt′ō), **Giovanni Antonio Canal** (1697–1768). Venetian painter and etcher, known esp. for his paintings of buildings and views of Venice.

ca·nal·ize (kanăl′īz, kăn′alīz) *v.t.* (**-ized, -iz·ing**). 1. Furnish with canals; convert (river) into canal by straightening course, making locks, etc. 2. Direct (energies, wealth, etc.) into a particular course or channel. **ca·nal·i·za·tion** (kănălīzā′shon) *n.*

Can·an·dai·gua (kănandā′gwa), **Lake.** One of the Finger Lakes in W. New York State.

can·a·pé (kăn′apē, -pā) *n.* A cracker or small piece of bread, toast, or pastry on which food is served as an appetizer. [Fr.]

ca·nard (kanärd′, -när′) *n.* False or unfounded story, slanderous rumor. [Fr., = "duck," "false report"]

Ca·nar·y (kanār′ē). Islan (**Grand** ~, *Gran Canaria*) off NW coast of Africa; ~ **Island Canaries**, the group to which belongs, in Spanish possession. [I *canaria* (*insula*) (isle) of dogs]

ca·nar·y (kanār′ē) *n.* (pl. **-naries**). 1. Sweet white wine from th Canary Islands, resembling sherry 2. Songbird (*Serinus canarius*) brought from the Canary Island and commonly kept in captivity; th wild canary, or serin, is greenis above and yellow below, but th cage breed is mainly yellow (~ **yellow**).

ca·nas·ta (kanăs′ta) *n.* Car game for two to six persons, playe with two standard 52-card pack and four jokers, related to rummy eld of seven cards. [prob. f. Span. *canastra* "basket" (from the many cards, or "basketful" of cards, used) t. f. Gk. *kanastron*]

Ca·nav·er·al (kanăv′eral), **ape**. Cape on E. central coast of Florida, location of John F. Kennedy Space Center and Patrick Air Force Base.

Can·ber·ra (kăn′bĕra, -bera). Capital of the Commonwealth of Australia, in SE. New South Wales.

can·can (kăn′kăn) *n.* High-kicking dance performed by women. [Fr.]

can·cel (kăn′sel) *v.* (**-celed, -cel·ing; -celled, -cel·ling**). Obliterate, annul, make void, counter-mand; neutralize, balance, make up for; (print.) delete, omit; (arith. etc.) strike out (same factor) from numerator and denominator, from two sides of equation, etc.; (of terms) neutralize or balance each other (also ~ **out**). **can·cel·la·tion** (kănsela′shon) *n.* (print.) Deletion, omission.

Can·cer (kăn′ser). The Crab, a constellation; 4th sign (♋) of the zodiac, which the sun enters at the summer solstice; **Tropic of ~**, northern TROPIC.

can·cer (kăn′ser) *n.* Malignant tumor; (fig.) a continuously increasing or spreading evil. **can′-er·ous** *adj.* [L., = "crab," f. resemblance of swollen veins round tumor to crab's limbs]

can·croid (kang′kroid) *adj.* Crablike; like cancer. **~** *n.* A skin cancer.

can·de·la (kăndē′la) *n.* (abbr. cd) Unit of luminous intensity, = CANDLE, def. 2.

can·de·la·brum (kăndelah′-brum, -lăb′rum, -lā′brum) *n.* (pl. **-bra** pr. **-bra, -brums**). Large, branched candlestick.

can·des·cence (kăndĕs′ens) *n.* Bright glow, as of white-hot metal. **can·des′cent** *adj.* Glowing (as) with white heat.

can·did (kăn′dĭd) *adj.* Unbiased; not censorious; frank; (photog.) not posed; **~ camera**, small camera for taking unposed or informal snapshots. **can′did·ly** *adv.* **can′-did·ness** *n.* [L. *candidus* white]

can·di·date (kăn′dĭdāt, -dĭt) *n.* One who seeks or is put forward for election or for appointment to an office or honor; one who undergoes a test or examination; one thought likely to gain any position. **can·di-da·cy** (kăn′dĭdase) *n.* [L. *candi-datus* one aspiring to an office (who was clothed in white toga)]

Can·dide (kăndēd′). Hero of a satirical novel by Voltaire, whose travels and misadventures mock the optimistic philosophy that "all is for the best in this best of all possible worlds"; hence, any innocent optimist.

can·died (kăn′dēd) *adj.*: see CANDY; (esp.) preserved by impregnating and coating with sugar.

can·dle (kăn′del) *n.* 1. Cylinder of wax, tallow, etc., enclosing wick, for giving light. 2. Unit of luminous intensity equal to $\frac{1}{60}$ of the luminous intensity of one sq. cm. of a black body heated to 1773.5°C; candlepower; **can′dlelight**, light of candles; any artificial light; **can′-dlepower**, illuminating power of electric light etc., formerly measured in terms of the light of a standard candle; **can′dlestick**, holder for candle(s); **can′dlewick**, wick of a candle; (material with raised usu. tufted pattern in) thick soft yarn.

Can·dle·mas (kăn′delmas, -măs) *n.* The religious festival in honor of the presentation of the infant Jesus in the temple, Feb. 2. [Mass at which candles for the coming year are blessed]

can·dor, Brit. **can·dour** (kăn′-der) *ns.* Fairness, impartiality; openness, frankness.

can·dy (kăn′dē) *n.* (pl. **-dies**). Confection or food with sugar or other sweeteners, flavored or filled with or partly composed of chocolate, fruit, peppermint, etc.; a small shaped piece of this; **~ stripe**,

Venetian scene, one of many of the city painted by Giovanni Antonio Canal (1677–1768), commonly known as **Canaletto.** *English visitors to Venice were his foremost patrons.*

Planned by Walter Burley Griffin of Chicago, **Canberra,** *Australia's capital city, was founded in 1913. The Australian parliament first met there in 1927. Previously, the Australian capital had been Melbourne.*

-striped, pattern(ed) in alternate stripes of white and color; ~ **striper**, (slang) volunteer hospital worker, usu. young girl (from striped uniforms worn by these volunteers). **candy** v. (**-died, -dy·ing**). Preserve, cook, coat with sugar or syrup; form into crystals. [Fr. *sucre candi*, f. Arab.-Pers. *qand* crystallized sugar cane juice, ult. f. Sansk. *khaṇḍ* broken crystallized sugar]

can·dy·tuft (kăn′dētŭft) n. Herbaceous cruciferous plant of genus *Iberis*, with white, pink, or purple flowers in flat corymbs or tufts. [*Candia* the island of Crete]

cane (kān) n. Hollow, jointed stem of reeds and grasses, or solid stem of slender palms; walking stick; rod for flogging; stem of raspberry and similar plants; **cane′brake**, tract of land thickly overgrown with canes; **cane sugar**, sugar obtained from the sugar cane as contrasted with beet sugar. **cane** v.t. (**caned, can·ing**). Beat with cane; fit (seat of chair) with (braided) cane. **can′ing** n.

ca·nine (kā′nīn) adj. Of, as of, a dog or dogs; ~ **tooth**, one of the four strong pointed teeth between incisors and molars, eyetooth. **canine** n. Canine tooth.

can·is·ter (kăn′ĭster) n. Small case or box, usu. of metal, for keeping dry foods, shot, etc. [Gk. *kanastron* wicker basket]

can·ker (kăng′ker) n. 1. Ulcerous sore (also ~ **sore**) of the mouth and lips; ulcerous disease of animals; disease of fruit trees; (also **can′kerworm**) caterpillar of a moth destroying leaves or buds. 2. Corrupting influence. **can′ker·ous** adj. **canker** v.t. Consume with canker; infect, corrupt. [as CANCER]

can·na (kăn′a) n. Tropical plant of genus *C*~ now cultivated widely, with bright yellow, red, or orange flowers and ornamental foliage.

can·na·bis (kăn′abĭs, kanah′-) n. Hemp. esp. *C*~ *sativa* or *C. indica*; preparation of hemp plant as drug; see MARIJUANA, HASHISH.

Can·nae (kăn′ē). (It. *Canne*) Ancient town in SE. Italy, scene of a defeat of the Romans by Hannibal in the Second Punic War, in 216 B.C.

can·nel (kăn′el) n. (also ~ **coal**) Coal with high gas content which burns with smoky flame and can be lit by a match.

Cannes (kăn, kănz). Mediterranean seaport and resort town in SE. France; site of annual film festival.

can·ni·bal (kăn′ĭbal) n. Person who eats human flesh; animal that eats its own species. ~ adj. Of, having, these habits. **can′ni·bal·ism** n. **can·ni·bal·is·tic** (kănĭbalĭs′tĭk) adj. [Span. *Canibales*, variant form of *Caribs*]

can·ni·bal·ize (kăn′ĭbalīz) v.t. (**-ized, -iz·ing**). Take parts from (machine) as spares for others.

can·ni·kin (kăn′ĭkĭn) n. Small can or cup; wooden bucket.

can·non (kăn′on) n. Piece of ordnance; mounted gun for firing heavy projectiles; aircraft's automatic shell-firing gun; **can′non·ball**, round projectile fired by cannon; **cannon fodder**, (fig.) men regarded merely as material to be consumed in war. **cannon** v. Fire, bombard (with) cannon; cannonade.

can·non·ade (kănonād′) n. Continuous gunfire. ~ v. (**-ad·ed, -ad·ing**). Fire continuously, bombard.

can·not (kăn′ŏt, -ot, kănŏt′, ka-) see CAN[2].

can·ny (kăn′ē) adj. (**-ni·er, -ni·est**). Shrewd; worldly-wise; thrifty; circumspect; sly. **can′ni·ly** adv. **can′ni·ness** n.

ca·noe (kanoo′) n. Small light keelless boat propelled by paddle(s). ~ v.i. (**-noed, -noe·ing**). Paddle or propel canoe; travel by canoe.

can·on[1] (kăn′on) n. 1. Church decree; ~ **law**, official body of law governing a Christian church (R.C.) ecclesiastical law as set down by the pope and the councils. 2. General rule, fundamental principle, axiom; standard of judgment or authority, test, criterion. 3. Collection or list of books of the Bible accepted by the Christian churches as genuine and inspired. 4. Portion of the Mass between the Sanctus and the Lord's Prayer containing the words of consecration. 5. List of recognized genuine works of a particular author, e.g. the *Hawthorne canon*.

These **cannon** were used at the Battle of Gettysburg which was fought in 3 days in July 1863 and is regarded as the major turning point of the American Civil War.

Below: A member of the mustard family, **candytuft** is a popular border plant in gardens. It is low growing and comes in a range of several colors.

Canoeing on the Guadalupe River in Texas. The modern lightweight canoes and kayaks were developed in the 1930s and the sport has been increasing in popularity since then.

ca·non² (kăn′on) n. 1. Member of a religious community bound by vows and living under common rules. 2. One of a chapter of priests serving in a cathedral or collegiate church.

cañ·on (kăn′yon): see CANYON.

ca·non·i·cal (kanŏn′ĭkal) adj. 1. Of, required or abiding by canon law; ~ **hours**, (R.C. and some Episcopal Churches) special prayers and psalms appointed to be read by priests etc. at certain hours of the day: matins and lauds, prime, tierce, sext, nones, vespers, and compline. 2. Included in the canon of Scripture. 3. Authoritative, standard, accepted. 4. Of a cathedral chapter or a member of it. **ca·non·i·cal·ly** adv. **ca·non·i·cals** n.pl. Canonical dress.

can·on·ist (kăn′onĭst) n. Canon lawyer.

can·on·ize (kăn′onīz) v.t. (**-ized**, **-iz·ing**). Admit formally to calendar of saints; regard as a saint; sanction by authority of Church. **can·on·i·za·tion** (kănonīzā′shon) n.

can·on·ry (kăn′onrē) n. (pl. **-ries**). Benefice, status, etc., of a canon.

Ca·no·pic (kanō′pĭk) adj. Of the town of Canopus; ~ **vase**, Egyptian vase with a lid in the form of a human head, used for holding the entrails of embalmed bodies.

Ca·no·pus (kanō′pus). 1. (Gk. myth.) Helmsman of Menelaus who

died in Egypt on the return from Troy. 2. Town in ancient Egypt named after him. 3. (astron.) Bright star Alpha in the southern constellation Argo, the second brightest star in the sky.

can·o·py (kăn′opē) n. (pl. **-pies**). Covering suspended or held over throne, bed, person, etc.; part of parachute that fills with air when released from its packing; (fig.) any overhanging shelter; the sky etc. ~ v.t. (**-pied**, **-py·ing**). Supply, be, a canopy to. [Gk. *kōnōpeion* mosquito net (*kōnōps* gnat)]

Ca·nos·sa (kanŏs′a). Castle and village in Tuscany where in 1077 the Holy Roman Emperor Henry IV submitted to the penance and humiliation imposed on him by Pope Gregory VII.

cant¹ (kănt) n. Bevel, oblique face, slope, slant; sloping or tilted position. ~ v. 1. Bevel; slope, slant, tilt. 2. Throw, jerk. 3. (naut.) Swing around.

cant² (kănt) n. Jargon of class, profession, sect, etc.; temporary catchwords; words used for fashion without being meant; unreal use of words implying piety; hypocrisy. ~ v.i. Use cant.

can't: see CAN².

can·ta·bi·le (kahntah′bĭlā) adj. & n. (Music) in a smooth flowing style, songlike, melodious. [It.]

can·ta·loupe, can·ta·loup (kăn′talōp) ns. Small, round, ribbed, delicate-flavored variety of melon with reddish-orange flesh, developed in Italy; a similar variety of muskmelon. [*Cantalupo*, castle near Rome]

can·tan·ker·ous (kăntăng′kerus) adj. Ill-tempered, quarrelsome. **can·tan′ker·ous·ly** adv. **can·tan′ker·ous·ness** n.

can·ta·ta (kantah′ta) n. Choral work, either a short oratorio or a short lyric drama set to music but not intended for acting.

can·teen (kăntēn′) n. 1. Provision and liquor shop in barracks, camp, post exchange; place of relaxation and entertainment maintained by civilian group for armed forces personnel; refreshment room in factory or office building. 2. Soldiers', campers', hikers' water flask.

can·ter (kăn′ter) n. Easy gallop. ~ v. Go, make (horse) go, at this pace. [shortened f. CANTERBURY gallop]

Can·ter·bur·y (kăn′terbĕrē). Cathedral city in SE. England, see of the archbishop and primate of all England; the shrine of Thomas à Becket (St. Thomas of Canterbury), who was murdered in the cathedral, was in pre-Reformation times a favorite object of pilgrimage; ~ **bell**, kind of campanula (f. bells of pilgrims' horses); (Brit.) ~ **gallop, pace, trot**, etc., the easy pace of the mounted pilgrims to Canterbury.

can·thar·i·des (kănthăr′ĭdēz) *n.pl.* (sing. **-thar·is** pr. -thăr′ĭs). Dried Spanish flies (*Lytta* (*Cantharis*) *vesicatoria*), formerly used in medicine and as an aphrodisiac, usu. SPANISH fly.

can·ti·cle (kăn′tĭkel) *n.* Hymn; one of the hymns, mostly taken from the Scriptures, used in church services, as the *Benedicite, Nunc Dimittis, Te Deum;* **Canticles,** Song of Solomon.

can·ti·le·ver (kăn′tĭlĕver, -lēver) *n.* (archit., eng.) Beam or girder fixed at one end to a pier or wall and free at the other, long bracket; ~ **bridge**, bridge composed of girders projecting from piers and meeting midway between them or carrying intermediate sections. **can·ti·le·vered** *adj.* Projecting like, supported by, a cantilever.

can·tle (kăn′tel) *n.* Rear portion of saddle.

can·to (kăn′tō) *n.* (pl. **-tos**). Division of long poem.

Can·ton (kăntŏn′, kăn′tŏn). City of S. China on the Chu-Kiang River; the capital of Kwangtung Province. **Can·ton·ese** (kăntonēz′, -nēs′, kăn′tonēz, -nēs) *adj. & n.* (Native, inhabitant, dialect) of Canton.

can·ton (kăn′ton, -tŏn, kăntŏn′) *n.* Subdivision of a country; one of the sovereign states of the Swiss federation. **can′ton·al** *adj.* **canton** *v.t.* 1. Divide into cantons. 2. Quarter (troops).

can·ton·ment (kăntŏn′ment, -tōn′-; *Brit.* kăntōon′ment) *n.* Temporary lodging assigned to troops; temporary military station.

can·tor (kăn′ter, -tōr) *n.* 1. Synagogue official, the chief singer of the liturgy. 2. Leader or chief singer of a church choir.

Ca·nuck (kanŭk′) *n.* (offensive slang) Canadian, esp. French Canadian.

Ca·nute, Cnut (kanōot′, -nūt′). Danish king of England, 1016–35.

can·vas (kăn′vas) *n.* 1. Strong unbleached plain-woven cloth of hemp, flax, or other coarse yarn, for sails, tents, etc.; open kind of this, usu. flax or cotton, for tapestry, embroidery, etc.; **under** ~, in tent(s); with sails spread. 2. (also **artists'** ~) Canvas prepared for painting on by coating with size, white lead, etc.; hence, a painting, picture (lit. and fig.). 3. Sail, sails collectively. 4. **can′vasback,** N.

Amer. duck (*Aythya valisineria*) (from the color of its gray-and-white mottled back feathers).

can·vass (kăn′vas) *v.* 1. Discuss thoroughly. 2. Solicit votes, solicit votes from; ascertain sentiments or opinion of; ask custom of. **can′vass·er** *n.* **canvass** *n.* Solicitation of votes, opinions, etc. [f. CANVAS, the original sense being "toss in a sheet etc.," and hence "shake up, agitate," etc.]

can·yon (kăn′yon) *n.* Deep gorge or ravine with steep sides formed by river cutting through soft rock.

[Span. *cañon* tube, f. L. *canna* reed

Can·yon de Chel·ly (kăn′yon (shā′) **National Park.** An area NE. Arizona reserved to prote ruins of ancient Indian cl dwellings.

caou·tchouc (kow′chŏok, kow chŏok′) *n.* Natural rubber (s RUBBER[1] *n.* def. 3). [Fr., f. Carib

cap (kăp) *n.* 1. Covering for th

The ancient town of **Canterbury,** *U.K is dominated by the 235-ft. 15th century tower of the cathedral. Th illustration shows the church as see from the south-west.*

One of the most impressive of all **canyons,** *the Grand Canyon, N.W. Arizona, was gouged nearly one mile deep by the Colorado River. The canyon is about 217 miles long.*

ad, esp. close-fitting and usu. soft d brimless; **~ in hand**, (fig.) mbly, in supplication. 2. Special address denoting rank, occupa-n, membership in a particular oup, etc.; **~ and bells**, jester's signia; **~ and gown**, mortar-ard and cassocklike gown worn at ademic processions, college com-encement, etc. 3. Mortarboard. Caplike covering, as of mush-om, toe of shoe, etc. 5. (also ercussion **~**) Cap-shaped piece copper lined with explosive, for niting explosive in firearms etc.; per percussion cap of toy pistol. **ap'ful** n. **cap** v.t. (**capped, p·ping**). 1. Put cap upon. 2. orm or serve as cap of; overlie, ver; complete, supply finishing uches. 3. (colloq.) Surpass; llow with another (story etc.).

cap. abbrev. Capital (city); pital (letter).

ca·bil·i·ty (kāpabĭl´ĭtē) n. (pl. **ies**). Power of, for, to; un-veloped faculty.

ca·pa·ble (kā´pabel) adj. 1. Sus-eptible. 2. **~ of**, having the power fitness for; wicked enough for. Able, gifted, competent. **ca'pa-ly** adv.

ca·pa·cious (kapā´shus) adj. oomy. **ca·pa´cious·ly** adv. **a·pa´cious·ness** n.

ca·pac·i·tance (kapăs´ĭtans) n. (elect.) Ratio of change in electric charge to corresp. change in poten-tial; ability to store an electric charge. **ca·pac'i·tive** adj.

ca·pac·i·tate (kapăs´ĭtāt) v.t. (**-tat·ed, -tat·ing**). Render capable; make legally competent.

ca·pac·i·tor (kapăs´ĭter) n. Device that stores electricity during part of an operation, usu. consisting of conductors separated by insula-tor; formerly called CONDENSER.

ca·pac·i·ty (kapăs´ĭtē) n. (pl. **-ties**). 1. Ability to contain or receive; cubic content, volume. 2. (fig.) Mental power; faculty, talent; capability, opportunity, to, of, etc.; relative character (as in his **~** as critic); legal competency. 3. Maxi-mum number or amount that can be contained, produced, etc.; **to ~**, to the limit.

cap-a-pie, cap-à-pie (kăpapē´) advs. From head to foot.

ca·par·i·son (kapăr´ĭson) n. Horses' trappings; equipment, out-fit. **~** v.t. Put caparison upon.

cape¹ (kāp) n. Short sleeveless cloak, either as separate garment or as fixed or detachable part of longer cloak or coat. **caped** adj.

cape² (kāp) n. Promontory. **Cape** (kāp), **The.** Cape Cod; the Cape of Good Hope; **C~ Cod**,

peninsula in SE. Massachusetts famous as a summer resort. **~ Dutch**, early form of Afrikaans; **~ gooseberry**, tropical Amer. plant (Physalis peruviana) with yellow flowers and berries; **~ of Good Hope**, promontory near southern extremity of Africa; **~ Hatteras**, promontory of Hatteras Island off the coast of North Carolina; **cape'-skin**, soft leather made from sheep-skin (orig. from S. Afr. sheepskin).

Cape Bret·on (kāp´ brĭt´on, brĕt´-) **Island.** Island off NE. Nova Scotia, Canada.

Ca·pek (chah´pĕk), **Karel** (1890–1938); Czech novelist and playwright; author of the play R.U.R., the novel War with the Newts, etc.

Ca·pel·la (kapĕl´a). Star of first magnitude in the constellation Auriga.

ca·per¹ (kā´per) n. Bramblelike S. European shrub (Capparis spin-osa); (pl.) its flower buds, pickled for use in sauces.

ca·per² (kā´per) n. Capering

*The city of **Cape Town**, founded by Jan van Riebeeck in 1652, spreads from the shore of Table Bay to the foot of Table Mountain. The wisp of cloud on the plateau is called the 'tablecloth'.*

The flower buds of the **caper** briar are pickled and used in piquant sauces, generally served with meat dishes. The plant is cultivated in Southern Europe and the U.S.

The largest game bird in Europe, the **capercaillie** became extinct in Scotland, where it had been a native but was reintroduced there from Scandinavia.

The **Capitol** in Washington, D.C. where the U.S. Congress meets, was begun in 1793 and completed 70 years later when the statue 'Freedom' was mounted on the cupola.

movement; wild escapade; (slang) criminal or illegal act. ~ *v.i.* Dance or leap merrily or fantastically; prance as a horse.

cap·er·cail·lie (kăperkāl′yē) *n.* Wood grouse (*Tetrao urogallus*), the largest European gallinaceous bird. [Gael. *capull coille* horse of the wood]

Ca·pet (kăp′ĭt, kā′pĭt). French dynasty founded by Hugo Capet in 987, which ruled until 1328, when it was succeeded by the House of Valois.

Cape (kāp) **Town.** Legislative capital of the Republic of S. Africa.

Cape Ver·de (kāp vēr′dē) **Islands.** Two groups of islands, Windward and Leeward, about 400 miles W. of Senegal, formerly a Portuguese possession; independent 1975.

cap·il·lar·y (kăp′ĭlĕrē) *adj.* 1. Of, or resembling, hair. 2. Having very minute or hairlike internal diameter. 3. Of capillaries. 4. ~ **attraction**, effect of surface tension of liquid that wets material of fine tube in raising liquid inside tube to a level higher than that outside; ~ **repulsion**, corresponding effect of surface tension of liquid that does not wet tube in depressing level inside tube. **capillary** *n.* (pl. **-lar·ies**). One of the hairlike vessels joining arteries and veins in

which the blood is brought into effective contact with the tissues.

cap·i·tal[1] (kăp′ĭtal) *n.* Head of pillar or pilaster, wider than the shaft and usu. ornamented.

cap·i·tal[2] (kăp′ĭtal) *adj.* 1. Involving loss of life; punishable by death; ~ **punishment**, punishment by death for a crime. 2. Chief; important, leading, first-class. 3. (chiefly Brit. colloq.) Excellent, first-rate. 4. Original, principal, of money capital. 5. ~ **letter**, one of the form and size used at beginning

of name, sentence, etc., majuscul

capital *n.* 1. Chief town of countr state, etc., usu. the seat of gover ment. 2. Stock of company wit which it enters business and o which dividends are paid; (econ accumulated wealth of individua community, etc., used as fund fo starting fresh production; wealth o any kind used in producing mor wealth; ~ **gain**, profit from sale o investments or property; hence ~ **gains tax;** ~ **goods**, goods for us in producing commodities, opp

Greek Doric

Greek Ionic

Greek Corinthian

Composite

Venetian

The capping member of a column, the **capital,** *is at the point where the weight of the roof is transferred to the column; therefore it must be strong. Left: The temple of Olympian Zeus, in Athens, has capitals of the Corinthian order.*

consumer goods. 3. Capitalists or employers of labor collectively. 4. Capital letter.

cap·i·tal·ism (kăp′ĭtalĭzem) *n.* Economic system by which ownership of capital or wealth, the production and distribution of goods, and the reward of labor are entrusted to private enterprise. **cap′i·tal·ist** *n.* Private owner or holder of capital, esp. in large amounts; one who has capital available for employment in finance or industry. **cap·i·tal·is·tic** (kăpĭ-talĭs′tĭk) *adj.* **cap′i·tal·ize** *v.t.* **(-ized, -iz·ing).** Convert into, use as, capital; compute or realize present value of (income). **cap·i·tal·i·za·tion** (kăpĭtalĭză′shon) *n.*

cap·i·ta·tion (kăpĭtā′shon) *n.*

(Levying of) tax or fee of so much a head; a per capita or poll tax.

Cap·i·tol (kăp′ĭtol). 1. Great national temple of ancient Rome, dedicated to Jupiter Optimus Maximus, on the Saturnian or Tarpeian (afterward called Capitoline) Hill; the hill itself, one of the seven Hills of ancient Rome. 2. Building in Washington, D.C., occupied by the U.S. Congress; the building in which a state legislature meets.

ca·pit·u·late (kapĭch′ulāt) *v.i.* **(-lat·ed, -lat·ing).** Surrender on terms; (loosely) give up, acquiesce.

ca·pit·u·la·tion (kapĭchulā′-shon) *n.* 1. Summary, outline. 2. Agreement, conditions. 3. Surrender on terms, agreement con-

taining such terms.

ca·pit·u·lum (kapĭch′ulum) *n.* (pl. **-la** pr. -la). 1. (physiol.) Protuberance of bone received into a hollow portion of another bone. 2. (bot.) Close head of sessile flowers.

ca·pon (kā′pŏn, -pon) *n.* Castrated rooster. **ca·pon·ize** (kāponĭz) *v.t.* **(-ized, -iz·ing).**

Ca·po·te (kapō′tē), **Truman** (1924–). American novelist and short story writer; author of *Other Voices, Other Rooms; The Grass Harp; Breakfast at Tiffany's; In Cold Blood,* etc.

Cap·pa·do·cia (kăpadō′sha). Ancient region of eastern Asia Minor, now central Turkey. **Cap·pa·do′cian** *adj.* & *n.*

Ca·pri (kaprē´, kah´prē). Island and resort area in the Bay of Naples, Italy.

ca·pric·ci·o (kaprē´chēō, -chō) *n.* (pl. **-ci·os**). Lively, usu. short, musical composition.

ca·price (kaprēs´) *n.* Unaccountable change of mind or conduct; fancy, freak; inclination to these; (mus.) capriccio. [It. *capriccio* suddenly start, app. f. *capra* goat]

ca·pri·cious (kaprĭsh´us) *adj.* Guided by whim; inconstant, irregular. **ca·pri´cious·ly** *adv.* **ca·pri´cious·ness** *n.*

Cap·ri·corn (kăp´rĭkōrn). The Goat, a constellation; 10th sign (♑) of the zodiac, which the sun enters at the winter solstice; **Tropic of ~,** southern TROPIC. [L. *caper* goat, *cornu* horn]

cap·ri·ole (kăp´rēōl) *n.* 1. Leap or caper. 2. (in manège) Horse's high leap and kick, with all four feet off the ground, without advancing. **~** *v.i.* (**-oled, -ol·ing**). Make a capriole.

caps. *abbrev.* Capital letters.

Cap·si·an (kăp´sēan) *adj. & n.* (Of) a Stone Age culture of N. Africa. [f. *Capsa* (gafsa), Tunisia]

cap·si·cum (kăp´sĭkum) *n.* Plant of genus *C~*, the common garden pepper, with very pungent capsule and seeds; fruit of these, used as condiment and as a digestive stimulant and counterirritant.

cap·size (kăp´sīz, kăpsīz´) *v.* (**-sized, -siz·ing**). Upset, overturn, esp. on water.

cap·stan (kăp´stan) *n.* Revolving vertical cylinder rotated manually or by motor, for winding in cable, hoisting sails, etc.

cap·sule (kăp´sul, -sūl) *n.* 1. (physiol.) Membranous envelope. 2. (bot.) Dry seedcase opening when ripe by parting of valves. 3. (med.) Gelatine envelope enclosing drug or other medicinal substance.

Characteristic of multicarpel plants, a **capsule** *opens by one of several means to scatter its seeds. In the campion, the apical teeth part. The iris capsule splits along its longitudinal valves.*

4. Airtight cap or seal for bottle etc. 5. Detachable nose cone of rocket or cabin of spacecraft for carrying instruments or astronauts. **~** *adj.* Compact, consise; summary. **cap·su·lar** (kăp´suler, -syu-), **cap·su·late** (kăp´sulāt, -syu-), **cap´su·lat·ed** *adjs.* **cap·sul·ize** (kăp´sulīz, -syu-) *v.t.* (**-ized, -iz·ing**). Condense (information etc.).

Capt. *abbrev.* Captain.

cap·tain (kăp´tĭn) *n.* 1. Chief, leader; great soldier, strategist, experienced commander. 2. (mil.) Army, Air Force, or Marine Corps officer, of rank just below major and above first lieutenant, normally commanding company or troop; (nav.) officer of rank between commander and commodore (or rear admiral), officer commanding warship; master of merchant ship; pilot of civil aircraft. 3. Leader of team in game or sport. **cap´tain·cy, cap´tain·ship** *ns.* **captain** *v.t.* B captain of; lead.

cap·tion (kăp´shon) *n.* Heading of chapter, section, newspaper article, etc.; wording under illustration; title, descriptive passage dialogue, etc., inserted in (silent motion picture. **~** *v.t.* Provide with caption.

cap·tious (kăp´shus) *adj.* Disposed to finding fault or criticizing perplexing; deceptive. **cap´tious·ly** *adv.* **cap´tious·ness** *n.*

cap·ti·vate (kăp´tĭvāt) *v.t.* (**-vat·ed, -vat·ing**). Fascinate charm. **cap·ti·va·tion** (kăptĭvā´shon) *n.* **cap´ti·vat·ing** *adj.* **cap´ti·vat·ing·ly** *adv.*

cap·tive (kăp´tĭv) *adj. & n.* (Person, animal) taken prisoner, kept in confinement, unable to escape; (of, like) prisoner. **cap·tiv·i·ty** (kăptĭv´ĭtē) *n.*

cap·tor (kăp´ter) *n.* One who takes a captive.

cap·ture (kăp´cher) *n.* Capturing; thing or person captured. **~** *v.t.* (**-tured, -tur·ing**). Take prisoner; seize as prize; (phys., of atomic particle, atom, or nucleus) acquire an additional particle; (astron., of star or planet) bring (object) within its gravitational field.

Cap·u·chin (kăp´yuchĭn, -shĭn) *n.* 1. Franciscan friar of the new rule of 1528. 2. Woman's garment of cloak and hood. 3. **~** monkey, Central and S. Amer. monkey of genus *Cebus*, with black hair like a cowl at back of head.

cap·y·ba·ra (kăpĭbăr´a) *n.* Large tailless semiaquatic rodent (*Hydrochoerus capybara*), allied to guinea pig, of tropical S. America.

car (kär) *n.* Wheeled vehicle, (poet.) chariot; automobile; any wheeled vehicle running on tracks

About 1 yard long, the **capybara** *lives in South America. It is at home in water, where it is prey to the cayman, and on land it can run swiftly. It has a horse-like gait.*

The typical organ-grinder's monkey, the **capuchin monkey** *thrives in captivity. In its wild state it lives in large groups in the trees of tropical South America.*

Cappadocia *extended across the high plateau region of Turkey, from the Black Sea to the Taurus Mountains. Right: A villager descends a ladder from his house in a rock village.*

petrol tank under seat

water tank

tanks for lubricating oil

belt drive

fixed

handbrake

brake block

fly whee

iron tyre

carburettor

chain

The dream of a machine-driven car became a practical reality when Karl Benz (1844–1929) developed a gasoline engine and fitted it to a car in 1885. The model illustrated here was built 4 years later. Its single-cylinder 4-stroke engine was mounted in the rear of the vehicle. The lack of a radiator meant that the water boiled away rapidly.

or cables, as **cable ~, railroad ~, street′car**; special type of railroad car, as **dining car, sleeping car**, etc.; part of airship or balloon holding passengers; enclosure for passengers, as an **elevator car; car coat**, short coat designed esp. for car drivers; **car′hop**, (colloq.) waiter at drive-in restaurant; **car pool**, (arrangement by) group of commuters who take turns driving group to work or share expenses of car; **car′port**, roofed open shelter for automobile; **car′sick**, nauseated from motion of automobile; **car′- sickness** (n.).

ca·ra·ba·o (kārabah′ō) n. (pl. **-ba·os**). (Philippines) Water BUFFALO.

car·a·bin (kăr′abĭn), **car·a·bine** (kăr′abĭn, -bēn) = CARBINE.

car·a·bi·neer, car·a·bi·nier (kărabinēr′) = CARBINEER.

car·a·cal (kăr′akal) n. Kind of lynx (*Felis caracal*) of N. Africa and SW. Asia, with reddish fur and

black-tipped ears and tail; pelt of this animal. [Turk. *kara* black *kulak* ear]

Car·a·cal·la (kărakăl′a). Marcus Aurelius Antoninus Bassianus (188–217), Roman emperor 211–17.

ca·ra·ca·ra (kārakār′a) n. Any of various long-legged carrion hawks of southern U.S. and Central and S. Amer., (esp. *Caracara cheriway*) called **Audubon′s ~**.

Ca·ra·cas (karah′kas). Capital of Venezuela, 8 (13 km) miles south of the Caribbean.

car·a·cole (kăr′akōl) n. Horseman's half-wheel to right or left, succession of such turns to right and left alternately. ~ *v.i.* (-**coled, -col·ing**). Execute caracole(s).

car·a·cul (kăr′akul) = KARAKUL.

ca·rafe (karăf′, -rahf′) n. Glass bottle for water or wine at table. [Fr., ult. f. Arab. *ġarrāfa* drinking vessel]

car·a·mel (kăr′amel, -mĕl, kăr′- mel) n. Brown substance obtained

by heating sugar or syrup and used for coloring spirits etc.; brown color of this; candy made of or flavored with this.

car·a·mel·ize (kăr′amelīz, kăr′- me-) *v.* (-**ized, -iz·ing**). Make (sugar) into caramel; (of sugar) turn brown when heated.

car·a·pace (kăr′apās) n. Upper body shell of tortoises and crustaceans.

car·at (kăr′at) n. 1. Measure of weight, about 200 milligrams, for precious stones. 2. See KARAT.

Ca·ra·vag·gio (kăravah′jō), **Michelangelo da** (1573–1610). Italian painter noted for his realistic treatment of traditional themes.

car·a·van (kăr′avăn) n. 1. Company of merchants, pilgrims, etc., in the East or in N. Africa, traveling together for security, esp. through desert; group of vehicles traveling together. 2. Covered cart or carriage, as house on wheels of gypsy, traveling showman, etc. 3.

e Sacrifice of Isaac'. (Uffizi,
rence) by **Michelangelo da
ravaggio** (1573–1610), who revo-
ionized Italian painting with his realism
d conception of color.

rit.) Trailer. ~ *v.i.* (**-vaned** or
-anned, -van·ing or **-van·ning**).
avel, live, in a caravan. [Pers.
rwān]

car·a·van·sa·ry (kăr·avăn′serē),
r·a·van·sa·rai (kăr·avăn′serī,
·) *ns.* (pl. **-sa·ries**). Eastern inn
th large courtyard where
ravans put up.

car·a·vel, car·a·velle (kăr′avĕl)
· (hist., also **carvel**) Small, light,
st sailing ship, chiefly Spanish or
rtuguese, of 15th-17th centuries.

car·a·way (kăr′awā) *n.* Umbel-
erous plant (*Carum carvi*) with
all aromatic seedlike fruits, ~
eds, used in cooking, etc.

car·bide (kār′bīd) *n.* Compound
carbon with a metal; esp.
lcium ~ : see CALCIUM, and **iron**
, (Fe₃C) an important constituent
steel.

car·bine (kār′bīn, -bēn) *n.* Kind
short rifle orig. introduced for
valry use; also **carabin,
arabine.**

car·bi·neer (kārbinēr′) *n.* Soler armed with a carbine; also
arabineer, carabinier.

car·bo·hy·drate (kārbōhī′drāt)
One of a group of compounds
carbon, hydrogen, and oxygen in
hich the last two elements are
esent in the same proportions as
water; including sugars, starches,
d cellulose and forming an
nportant part of the structure of
ant material and of the food of
an and other animals.

car·bol·ic (kārbŏl′ĭk) *adj.* ~
cid: see PHENOL.

car·bon (kār′bon) *n.* 1. (chem.)
lement occurring in two crystal-
ne forms (diamond and graphite)
d an amorphous form (charcoal),
d in combination in all organic
ompounds; symbol C, at. no. 6, at.
t. 12.011. 2. (elect.) Rod of carbon
sed in arc lamps. 3. Carbon paper;
arbon copy. 4. ~ **copy**, copy
ade with carbon paper; (fig.) exact
opy; ~ **cycle**, (biol.) cycle in
hich carbon dioxide is absorbed
om the atmosphere by plants and
eplaced mainly by respiration of
ants and animals and by decay of
rganic matter; (astron.) cycle of
hermonuclear reactions in which
arbon acts as a catalyst in the con-
ersion of hydrogen into helium,
he energy released being held to be
he source of that radiated by sun
nd stars; ~ **dioxide**, compound
CO₂) of carbon with oxygen, a
olorless odorless gas formed by
ombustion of carbon, breathed out
y animals, formed during fermen-
ation, etc.; ~ **14**, long-living radio-
ctive isotope of mass number 14,
he regular decay rate of which

The principal coal measures were laid
down in the **carboniferous** period
which lasted from about 345 million to
280 million years ago. Ferns such as
this Alcthopeteris lanchitica, shown
here fossilized, were prolific.

makes RADIOCARBON dating possible; ~ **monoxide**, highly poisonous inflammable colorless odorless
gas (CO), formed by the incomplete
combustion of carbon or carbon
compounds, as in charcoal stoves,
gasoline engines, etc; ~ **paper**,
thin paper, coated on one side with
a colored wax preparation, which
when it is inserted between two
sheets of paper causes anything
written on the upper sheet to appear
also on the lower one; ~ **tetra-
chloride**, poisonous, noninflam-

mable, volatile liquid used as fire
extinguisher, solvent, or cleaning
fluid.

car·bo·na·ceous (kārbonā′shus)
adj. Of, like, coal or charcoal;
consisting of or containing carbon.

car·bo·na·do (kārbonā′dō,
-nah′dō) *n.* (pl. **-does, -dos**). Dark
opaque variety of diamond found in
Brazil, used as an abrasive etc.

car·bon·ate (kār′bonāt, -nĭt) *n.*
Salt of carbonic acid. **car·bon·ate**
(kār′bonāt) *v.t.* (**-at·ed, -at·ing**).
Form into a carbonate; charge with
carbon dioxide gas.

car·bon·ic (kārbŏn′ĭk) *adj.* Of
carbon; ~ **acid**, compound
(H₂CO₃) of carbon dioxide and
water.

car·bon·if·er·ous (kārbonĭf′-
erus) *adj.* Producing, containing

carbon or coal; **C~**, (geol.) of the period or system of the Upper Paleozoic between Devonian and Permian, containing workable coal on at least three continents. **Car·bon·if·er·ous** *n.* Carboniferous period or system.

car·bon·ize (kär′bonīz) *v.t.* (**-ized, -iz·ing**). Reduce to charcoal or coke by burning off superfluous material. **car·bon·i·za·tion** (kärbonīzā′shon) *n.*

Car·bo·run·dum (kärborŭn′-dum) *n.* (trademark) SILICON carbide.

car·box·yl (kärbŏk′sil) *n.* (chem.) Univalent radical, COOH, characteristic of most organic acids.

car·boy (kär′boi) *n.* Large globular wicker-covered glass bottle for holding acids or other corrosive liquids. [Pers. *karāba* large flagon]

car·bun·cle (kär′bŭngkel) *n.* 1. (archaic) Deep red cabochon garnet. 2. Painful, pus-producing localized inflammation of the skin and subcutaneous tissue. **car·bun·cu·lar** (kärbŭng′kyuler), **car′-bun·cled** *adjs.*

car·bu·ret (kär′burāt, -byu-, -rĕt) *v.t.* (**-ret·ed, -ret·ing**, Brit. **-ret·ted, -ret·ting**). Combine chemically with carbon or hydrocarbons.

car·bu·re·tor (kär′burāter, -byu-) *n.* (in gasoline engines) Apparatus for impregnating air with fine particles of fuel and thus preparing the explosive mixture for the cylinders.

car·bu·rize (kär′burīz, -byu-) *v.t.* (**-rized, -riz·ing**). Cause carbon to penetrate (surface of solid steel) in order to harden it.

car·cass (kär′kas) *n.* 1. Dead body (of human body now only in contempt or ridicule); (butchering, cooking) dead body of beast or bird without head, limbs, or organs. 2. Worthless remains; skeleton, framework (of house, ship, tire, etc.).

Car·cas·sonne (kärkäsawn′). City in S. France; site of ancient fortifications, medieval castle, and 12-arch bridge.

car·cin·o·gen (kärsĭn′ojen) *n.* Cancer-producing substance or agent. **car·cin·o·gen·ic** (kärsinō-jĕn′ĭk) *adj.*

car·ci·no·ma (kärsinō′ma) *n.* (pl. **-mas, -ma·ta** pr. -mata). (path.) Cancer, esp. of epithelial origin.

card[1] (kärd) *n.* Toothed instrument or wire brush for combing wool, flax, cotton, hemp, etc., raising nap on cloth etc. **~** *v.t.* Prepare (wool etc.) for spinning by combing out impurities and straightening the fibers with cards.

card[2] (kärd) *n.* 1. Thin, flat, usu. rectangular, piece of stiff paper or pasteboard used for various pur-

As the throttle is opened, suction in t **carburetor** increases, drawing up th piston, and the tapered needle is lift out of the jet, allowing greater flow of and fuel to the engine. The float in th chamber beside the carburetor contro the supply of gasoline.

incoming fuel

section through float chamber

float lever closed

screw top

float

piston suction chamber

piston damper

air intake

float chamber

throttle butterfly valve

tapered needle

poses, as for greetings, invitation, identity, membership, credit, program, etc. 2. (also **playing ~**) One of a pack of small oblong pieces of pasteboard used in playing games, consisting (except in some special games) of 52 cards divided into 4 suits; (pl.) card-playing, game(s) with cards; **in the ~s**, (fig.) likely, possible. 3. (colloq.) Amusing person, jokester. 4. **card′board**, pasteboard for cutting cards from, making boxes, etc.; **card case**, case for carrying calling or credit cards; **card catalog**, catalog, usu. library catalog, with items entered on separate cards; **card′shark**, a professional card player who cheats; also **card′sharp, card′sharper.**

car·da·mom (kär′damom), **car·da·mon** (kär′damon) *ns.* Spice consisting of seed capsules of various species of the E. Ind. and Chinese genera *Amomum* and *Elettaria*, used as a medicine, in curries etc.

car·di·ac (kär′dēăk) *adj.* 1. O the heart. 2. (anat.) Of, adjoining the upper orifice of the stomach.

Car·diff (kär′dĭf). Seaport and capital city of Wales.

car·di·gan (kär′digan) *n* Sweater or knitted woolen jacke opening down the front. [f. 7th Earl of *Cardigan*, distinguished in the Crimean War]

car·di·nal (kär′dinal) *adj.* 1. On which something hinges; fundamental, important; **~ number**, number that answers the question "how many" (*one, two, three,* etc.); **~ point**, any of the four chief points of the compass; **~ virtue**, one of the four "natural" virtues, justice, prudence, temperance, and fortitude. 2. Of the color of a cardinal's robes, scarlet. **car·di-nal·ly** *adv.* **cardinal** *n.* 1. (**C~**) One of the ecclesiastical princes of the R.C. Church who constitute the Sacred College or College of Cardinals and whose duty it is to ct the Pope. 2. (hist.) Woman's oak, orig. of scarlet cloth with ood. 3. (also ~ **grosbeak**) N. mer. crested grosbeak (*Richmonna cardinalis*), with scarlet umage. 4. ~ **flower**, N. Amer. ower, the scarlet lobelia; ~ **red**, right scarlet-red color, from the lor of a cardinal's robes. **car·di-al·ate** (kär′dinalāt, -lĭt) *n.* The ollege of Cardinals; the position, nk, title, etc. of a Roman Catholic rdinal.

cardio- *prefix.* Of the heart.

CARE (kār) *abbrev.* Cooperative r American Relief Everywhere, rivate organization established ter World War II to assist needy ople in foreign countries.

care (kār) *n.* (Occasion for) olicitude, anxiety; serious attenon; heed, caution, pains; charge,

protection; things to be done or seen to; **care′free**, free from anxiety; **care′taker**, person hired to take charge, as of house during owner's absence, of school or factory buildings, etc.; **caretaker government**, temporary government; **care′worn**, worn by anxiety and trouble. **care** *v.i.* (**cared, car·ing**). Feel concern or interest *for, about*; feel regard, deference, affection *for*, be concerned *whether*, etc.; be willing or desire *to*; ~ **for**, look after.

ca·reen (karēn′) *v.* 1. Turn (ship) on one side for cleaning, caulking, etc.; (cause to) heel over.

The map shows the area of the Atlantic Ocean called the **Caribbean.** *Its islands, the West Indies, consist of a chain of young mountain tops formed by recent geological activity.*

2. Move rapidly and in uncontrolled manner; lurch; swerve.

ca·reer (karēr′) *n.* 1. Swift course; impetus. 2. Course or progress through life, esp. when publicly conspicuous or successful; development and success of party, principle, etc.; course of professional life or employment, way of making livelihood. **career** *v.i.* Go swiftly or wildly.

ca·reer·ist (karēr′ĭst) *n.* Person (esp. holder of public office, government employee, etc.) who is mainly intent on personal advancement. **ca·reer′ism** *n.*

care·ful (kār′ful) *adj.* Painstaking, watchful, cautious; done with, showing, care. **care′ful·ly** *adv.*

care·less (kār′lĭs) *adj.* Unconcerned, light-hearted; inattentive, negligent, thoughtless; inaccurate. **care′less·ly** *adv.* **care′less·ness** *n.*

ca·ress (karĕs′) *n.* Fondling touch. ~ *v.t.* Bestow caress(es) on; pet.

car·et (kăr′ĭt) *n.* Mark (∧) placed below line in writing to indicate where something is to be inserted. [L., = "is wanting"]

car·go (kär′gō) *n.* (pl. **-goes, -gos**). Freight carried on ship, plane, etc.

Car·ib (kăr′ĭb) *n.* (pl. **-ibs**, collect. **-ib**). One of the native Amer. Indian peoples of northern S. America and the W. Indies; their language.

Car·ib·be·an (kărĭbē′an, karĭb′ē-) *adj.* ~ **Sea**, sea lying between the W. Indies and the mainland of Central and S. America. ~ *n.* Caribbean Sea.

Car·i·boo (kăr′ibōō) **Mountains.** Part of the Rocky Mountain range in E. British Columbia, Canada.

car·i·bou (kăr′ibōō) *n.* (pl.

One of the finch family, the **cardinal grosbeak** *or redbird is a North American song-bird. Varieties in the north are scarlet, farther south they may be gray and red.*

Non-migratory woodland **caribou** *are found throughout the boreal forest of N. America. Barren-ground caribou range the Arctic tundra.*

-bous, collect. **-bou**). Any of several large arctic Amer. deer of the genus *Rangifer*, related to the reindeer, both sexes having antlers.

car·i·ca·ture (kăr'ĭkacher, -choor) *n.* Grotesque or ludicrous representation of person or thing by emphasis on characteristic or striking features. ~ *v.t.* (**-tured**, **-tur·ing**). Represent in caricature. **car'i·ca·tur·ist** *n.*

car·ies (kār'ēz, -ēēz, kăr'-) *n.* (pl. **-ies**). Decay (of teeth or bones). **car·i·ous** (kār'ēus, kăr'-) *adj.* Decayed.

car·il·lon (kăr'ĭlŏn, -lon) *n.* Set of bells sounded either from keyboard or mechanically.

ca·ri·na (karī'na, -rē'-) *n.* (pl. **-nas, -nae** pr. -nē). (bot., zool.) Structure in form of keel or ridge. **car·i·nat·ed** (kăr'ĭnātĭd) *adj.* Having a keellike part. **car·i·na·tion** (kărĭnā'shon) *n.*

Car·lisle (kārlīl', kār'līl). Scottish border town in NW. England; once an important Roman town; place of imprisonment of Mary, Queen of Scots, 1568.

Car·lo·ta (kārlō'ta, -lŏt'a) (1840–1927). Original name, Marie Charlotte Amelie; wife of Archduke Maximilian of Austria; empress of Mexico, 1864–67.

Car·lo·vin·gi·an (kārlovĭn'-jēan): see CAROLINGIAN.

Carls·bad (kārlz'băd) **Caverns National Park.** Region in SE. New Mexico containing a series of limestone caves.

Carls·ru·he (kārlz'rōōe): = KARLSRUHE.

Car·lyle (kārlīl'), **Thomas** (1795–1881). Scottish literary critic, historian, and writer on social and political problems.

Car·mel (kārměl'), **Mount.** Ridge across NW. Israel to the Mediterranean.

Car·mel·ite (kār'melīt) *adj. & n.* (Member) of order of mendicant friars (White Friars) originating in a colony founded in the 12th c. on Mount Carmel by Berthold, a Calabrian; (member) of a community of nuns of this order.

car·min·a·tive (kārmĭn'atĭv, kār'mĭnā-) *adj. & n.* (Drug) curing flatulence.

car·mine (kār'mĭn, -mīn) *n. & adj.* (Colored like, color of) a crimson red pigment obtained from cochineal.

car·nage (kār'nĭj) *n.* Great slaughter.

car·nal (kār'nal) *adj.* Sensual; sexual; worldly. **car·nal·i·ty** (kārnăl'ĭtē) *n.* **car'nal·ly** *adv.*

Car·nar·von (kārnār'von), **George Edward Stanhope Molyneux Herbert, 5th Earl of,** (1866–1923). English Egyptologist and collaborator with Howard Carter in excavating near Thebes; co-discoverer of tomb of Tut-

ankhamen.

car·na·tion[1] (kārnā'shon) *n.* 1. Light rosy pink or bright red color. 2. Flesh tints in a painting; the representation of naked flesh. ~ *adj.* Deep red.

car·na·tion[2] (kārnā'shon) *n.* Widely cultivated Eurasian plant (*Dianthus caryophyllus*) having fragrant white, pink, or red flowers with fringed petals; its flower.

car·nau·ba (kārnaw'ba, -now'-) *n.* Brazilian wax palm; its yellowish wax.

Car·ne·gie (kārnā'gē, kār'ne-), **Andrew** (1835–1919). Scottish-born American owner of iron and steel works etc., famous for his philanthropy.

car·nel·ian (kārnēl'yan) *n.* (also **cornelian**) Red or reddish variety of chalcedony used in jewelry.

car·ni·val (kār'nĭval) *n.* 1. Last three days or last week before Lent; festivities during this season. 2. Riotous revelry, feasting, merry-making. 3. Traveling amusement show having side shows, game booths, and merry-go-round, Ferris wheel, or other rides. [Fr., f. It. *carnevale* Lenten season, f. L. *caro carn–* flesh and *levare* put away]

car·ni·vore (kār'nĭvŏr, -vōr) *n.* Member of the Carnivora, a large order of mammals including many (cats, dogs, seals, etc.) that feed on other animals, having usu. sharp incisors and well-developed canine teeth; animal that feeds on other animals. **car·niv·o·rous** (kārnĭv'-erus) *adj.*

car·ob (kăr'ob) *n.* Mediterranean evergreen tree (*Ceratonia siliqua*) bearing edible seed pods whose seeds are said to have been the original karat weight used by goldsmiths.

car·ol (kăr'ol) *n.* Joyous song, esp. Christmas hymn. ~ *v.* (**-oled, -ol·ing**, Brit. **-olled, -ol·ling**). Sing joyfully, sing carols. **Car·o·le·an** (kărolē'an) *adj.* = CAROLINE.

Car·o·li·na (kărolī'na). (hist.) English colony in N. Amer., first settled in 1653, named after Charles II of England; divided into what became the present NORTH and SOUTH CAROLINA in 1729; (also **the** ~s) North and South Carolina.

Car·o·line (kăr'olĭn) *adj.* Of, pertaining to, Charles I or Charles II of England. **Car·o·lin·i·an** (kărolĭn'ēan) *adj. & n.*

Car·o·line (kăr'olĭn, -lĭn) **Islands.** Archipelago in the W. Pacific Ocean, part of the present (United Nations') Trust Territory of the Pacific Islands, under U.S. administration; scene of several World War II battles.

Car·o·lin·gi·an (kărolĭn'jēan) *adj.* Of CHARLEMAGNE; of the line of French kings descended from

him; ~ **Empire**, empire acquir by Charlemagne early in 9th c. a regarded by him as a revival of t Roman Empire; at its greate extent it comprised France (exce Brittany), Germany, the Lo Countries, N. and central Ita Bohemia, and Croatia, its capita being Aix-la-Chapelle (Aache and Rome; ~ **Renaissance**, r vival of art and letters, imitation classical antiquity, fostered l Charlemagne; ~ **script**, rounde script adopted in Carolingia period. Also **Carlovingian**.

car·o·tene (kăr'otēn) *n.* (chem Red or orange-yellow crystallin hydrocarbon ($C_{40}H_{56}$) contained carrots, tomatoes, and many oth vegetables, important source o vitamin A. **ca·rot·e·noid** (karŏt enoid) *adj. & n.* (Of) a pigmen resembling carotene, found i plants and animals.

ca·rot·id (karŏt'ĭd) *adj. & n.* (O near) one of the two main arterie in the neck, which in mamma carry blood to the face and cerebr hemispheres.

Facing page: The king of **carnivoro** *beasts that feed on other animals, a lio in a game reserve in Mozambiqu Africa, relishes the zebra he has kille In plant life, the counterparts of th carnivors are insectivorous plants lik the Venus's fly-trap (below), structure to trap and digest insects.*

ca·rouse (karowz´) *n.* Drinking bout. ~ *v.i.* (**-roused, -rous·ing**). Engage in carouse, drink deep. **ca·rous·al** *n.* [Ger. *gar aus* (*trinken*) drink to the bottom]

car·ou·sel, car·rou·sel (kărusĕl´, -zĕl´, kăr´usĕl, -zĕl) *ns.* Merry-go-round.

carp[1] (kärp) *n.* (pl. **carps,** collect. **carp**). Fresh-water fish (*Cyprinus carpio*) commonly bred in ponds; other fish of genus *Cyprinus* or *Carassius*, which includes gold-fish, silverfish, etc.

carp[2] (kärp) *v.i.* Talk queru-lously, find fault. **carp´ing** *adj.* (esp.) Captious.

Car·pa·thi·an (kärpā´thēan) **Mountains.** (also **Carpathians**) Mountain system between Poland and Czechoslovakia.

car·pel (kär´pel) *n.* (bot.) One of the units of which a compound ovary is composed. **car·pel·lar·y** (kär´pelĕrē) *adj.*

car·pen·ter (kär´penter) *n.* Worker who builds or repairs wooden structures, esp. houses and ships; ~ **ant,** ant of the genus *Camponotus,* nesting and boring in decaying trees and dead wood; ~ **bee,** solitary bee of the genus *Xylocopidae,* nesting in wood. **car·penter** *v.* Do, make by, carpenter's work. **car·pen·try** (kär´pentrē) *n.*

car·pet (kär´pĭt) *n.* Thick fabric for spreading on floor or stair, freq. patterned in colors, and made by knotting short lengths of yarn on to the warp threads of a fabric during weaving, or by same means as tapestry, or by various mechanical weaving processes; covering or expanse of grass, flowers, etc., resembling a carpet; **on the car·-pet,** being reprimanded; under discussion; **car´petbag,** traveling bag, made of carpet fabric; **car´pet-bagger,** after the Civil War, a Northerner who went into the South to make money or gain political power; a meddler in the politics of a locality with which he has no genuine connection; **carpet sweeper,** household implement with revolving brush for sweeping carpets. **car´pet·ing** *n.* **car´pet-less** *adj.* **carpet** *v.t.* Cover with, as with a carpet.

car·pus (kär´pus) *n.* (pl. **-pi** pr. -pī). (anat.) Set of bones (eight in man) connecting forearm to hand; wrist. **car·pal** (kär´pal) *adj. & n.* (Bone) of the carpus.

car·ra·geen (kăr´agēn, -jēn) *n.* (also ~ **moss**) Seaweed (*Chondrus crispus*) yielding, when dried and boiled, a jelly used for food and in medicine. [*Carragheen* near Water-ford in Ireland]

car·rel (kăr´el) *n.* Small alcove in or near library stacks for use by individual reader.

car·riage (kăr´ĭj) *n.* 1. Convey-ing, transport; cost of conveying. 2. Manner of carrying; bearing, deportment. 3. Wheeled vehicle for persons; esp. four-wheeled private vehicle with two or more horses. 4. Wheeled support of gun; wheeled framework of vehicle apart from body; (mech.) sliding etc. part of machinery for shifting position of

Situated near Tunis, N. Africa, Carthage stood near the ruins of Utica, a Phoenician city. The prosperity of Carthage lay in the energy of her sea-going merchants.

other parts. 5. (Brit.) Rail passenger car.

car·ri·er (kăr´ēer) *n.* 1. One or that which carries; person ply for hire with cart, truck, etc., carrying goods, packages, etc. Person or animal carrying dise germs. 3. (colloq.) Aircraft carr 4. ~ **pigeon:** see PIGEON; ~ **wa** radio wave whose modulati carry communication signals.

car·ri·on (kăr´ēon) *n.* D putrefying flesh.

Car·roll (kăr´ol), **Lewis.** Ps donym of Charles Lutwi Dodgson (1832–98); Engl mathematician; author of *Ali Adventures in Wonderland* (186 *Through the Looking-Glass* (187 *The Hunting of the Snark* (187 etc.

car·rot (kăr´ot) *n.* Umbelli ous plant (*Daucus carota*) with la tapering root; orange-red, flesl sweet root of cultivated varieties this, used as vegetable; ~ **t** (slang) person with red ha **car´rot·y** *adj.*

car·ry (kăr´ē) *v.* (**-ri -ry·ing**). 1. Convey, transpo bear; conduct; be the bearer push (process, principle, etc.) specified point. 2. Support, h up; hold (oneself etc.) in specifi way; have about the person rea for use. 3. Have specified range; sound) penetrate, travel; (golf, et cross, pass over. 4. Succeed establishing, passing, electing, 5. Capture, take by storm. (arith.) Transfer (figure) to colun of higher notation. 7. Have as res or corollary, involve. 8. ~ **awa** inspire, transport, deprive of se ntrol; **carrying charge**, interest unpaid balance of charge acunt or installment payments; **rry forward**, (arith.) transfer gure) to top of new page or lumn; **carry off**, remove from e; win; make brave show of (event c.); **carry on**, advance (process) stage; continue; manage; go on th what one is doing; (colloq.) have strangely, flirt, have morous intrigue; **carry-on**, (luge) bag, suitcase, small enough be kept by airplane passenger ring flight; **carry out**, put in actice; **carry over**, carry forard; **carry-over**, a sum so transrred; goods kept over for later use; **rry through**, bring safely out of fficulties; complete. **carry** n. 1. olf) Ball's flight. 2. Portage tween rivers etc. 3. Range (of n, sound, etc.).

Car·son (kär′son), (**Christoher**) "Kit" (1809–1868). Amer. ontiersman, Indian agent, and out; **Carson City**, capital o evada, in the SW.

cart (kärt) n. Two- or fourheeled vehicle used in farming d for carrying heavy goods; twoheeled one-horse vehicle for riving in; **put the ~ before the orse**, reverse proper order, conse effect with its cause; **cart′- heel**, wheel of a cart; (slang) silver ollar or other large coin; lateral omersault, with arms and legs xtended like spokes of a wheel. **art** v. Carry in a cart; convey,

Principles of **cartography** *were understood as early as 2500 B.C., when Babylonians drew maps on clay tablets. Later map-makers made more accurate charts to which they added figurative embellishments.*

transport. **cart′er** n.

Car·ta·ge·na (kärtajē′na; *Span.* kärtahä′na). Seaport in SE. Spain, on the Mediterranean.

carte blanche (kärt′ blänch′, blahnch′; *Fr.* kärt blahñsh′) n. (pl. **cartes blanches**, pr. kärts′ blänch′, blahnch′; *Fr.* kärt blahñsh′). Full discretionary power. [Fr., = "blank card"]

car·tel (kärtĕl′, kär′tel) n. 1. Written challenge, as for duel. 2. Manufacturers' combine to control production, marketing, and price.

Car·ter[1] (kär′ter), **Howard** (1873–1939). English archaeologist; co-discoverer with Lord Carnarvon of tomb of Tutankhamen, 1922.

Car·ter[2] (kär′ter), (**James Earl, Jr.**) "Jimmy" (1924–). Thirtyninth president of the U.S., 1977–81.

Car·te·sian (kärtē′zhan) adj. & n. (Follower) of DESCARTES or his philosophy or mathematical methods; ~ **coordinates**, system of locating a point in a plane by its distance from each of two perpendicularly intersecting axes, or in space by its distance from three mutually perpendicular axes.

Car·thage (kär′thĭj). Ancient city near Tunis on N. coast of

Africa, founded by the Phoenicians; destroyed during the PUNIC Wars, and rebuilt by Augustus.

Car·tha·gin·i·an (kärthajĭn′-ēan) adj. Of Carthage. ~ n. Native, inhabitant, of Carthage.

Car·thu·sian (kärthōō′zhan) adj. & n. (Member) of order of monks founded in Dauphiné, France, in 1086 by St. Bruno, and remarkable for the severity of their rule. [*Chatrousse*, place of the first monastery]

Car·tier (kärtyä′), **Jacques** (1491–1557). French explorer of Canada; claimed the St. Lawrence River valley for France in 1534.

car·ti·lage (kär′tĭlĭj) n. Elastic flexible tissue that forms the skeleton of young vertebrates and (except for some parts near the joints) changes later into bone; structure composed of this; flexible connecting tissue. **car·ti·lag·i-nous** (kärtĭlăj′inus) adj.

car·tog·ra·phy (kärtŏg′rafē) n. Map drawing. **car·tog′ra·pher** n. **car·to·graph·ic** (kärtográf′ĭk) adj.

car·ton (kär′ton) n. 1. Small white disk in bull's-eye of target. 2. Cardboard box; its contents.

car·toon (kärtōōn′) n. 1. Preliminary drawing on stout paper as design for painting of same size or for tapestry, mosaic, etc. 2. Humorous or topical drawing in newspaper etc.; ~ **strip**, series of small drawings depicting events usu. concerning some central character, freq. serial. 3. (in motion

Carving an image from a solid piece of material requires skill of a high order. Above: A good carver can work accurately even with a fairly crude tool such as an adze.

The Sisters' Peaks in the **Cascade Range** *of Oregon. First explored in 1806 by Lewis and Clark, the range is a major tourist attraction with its magnificent scenery.*

pictures, also **animated** ~) Drawings photographed in series to give illusion of movement.

car·touche (kär̄ōōsh') *n.* (archit.) Scroll ornament, e.g. volute of Ionic capital; tablet imitating, drawing of, scroll with rolled up ends, usu. bearing inscription; (archaeol.) oval containing hieroglyphic names and titles of Egyptian kings etc.

car·tridge (kär̄'trĭj) *n.* 1. Case containing explosive charge and (for small arms) bullet or shot; ~ **belt**, belt with pockets for cartridges; ~ **clip**, device for holding cartridges conveniently for use in automatic rifle, pistol, etc. 2. Small container.

car·un·cle (kăr̄'ŭngkel, ka-rŭng'-) *n.* 1. Fleshy excrescence, as turkey's wattles. 2. Small hard outgrowth formed on seeds of certain plants, e.g. castor-oil plant.

Ca·ru·so (karōō'sō), **Enrico** (1873–1921). Italian operatic tenor.

carve (kärv) *v.* (**carved, carv·-ing**). Cut; produce by cutting; change by cutting *into*; cover or adorn *with* cut figures, designs, etc.; slice (meat, fowl) into portions at or for table; subdivide; **carving** *n.*, carved work, carved figure or design; **carving knife**, long knife for carving meat.

car·vel (kär̄'vel) *n.* 1. (hist.) = CARAVEL. 2. ~-**built**, (of boat) with planks flush with the side.

Car·ver[1] (kär̄'ver), **George Washington** (1864–1943). Amer. educator and agriculturist; born of slave parents; Teacher at Tuskegee Institute from 1896; best known for his agricultural research, esp. on industrial use of the peanut.

Car·ver[2] (kär̄'ver), **John** (1576–1621). First governor of Plymouth Colony in America, 1620–1.

car·y·at·id (kăreăt'ĭd) *n.* (pl. **-at·ids, -at·i·des** pr. -ăt'ĭdēz). Female figure used as column to support entablature. [Gk. *Caryatis*, a priestess of Artemis at Caryae in Laconia]

car·y·op·sis (kăreŏp'sĭs) *n.* (pl. **-ses**, pr. -sēz, **-si·des** pr. -sĭdēz). (bot.) One-seeded indehiscent fruit with pericarp fused to seed coat, as in wheat and barley.

Cas·a·blan·ca (kăsablăng'ka). Seaport of NW. Morocco on the Atlantic; site of World War II conference between Winston Churchill and Franklin D. Roosevelt, 1943.

Ca·sals (kasălz', -sahlz'), **Pablo** (1876–1973). Spanish cellist, in Puerto Rico from 1956.

Cas·a·no·va (kăsanō'va, kăz-). Giovanni Jacopo Casanova de Seingalt (1725–98). Italian adventurer, author of memoirs, in French, describing his escapades and amours throughout Europe.

Cas·bah (kăz'ba, -bah, kahz'-), **The.** Native quarter of several north African cities, especially Algiers.

cas·cade (kăskād') *n.* Waterfall, one section of large broken waterfall; wavy fall of lace etc. ~ *v.i.* (**-cad·ed, -cad·ing**). Fall in or like cascade.

Cas·cade (kăskād') **Range**. Northern part of the Sierra Nevada mountains from northern California through western Washington.

cas·car·a (kăskăr̄'a) *n.* [also ~ **sa·gra·da** (sagrah'da, -grā-)] (Extract of) bark of a California buckthorn, *Rhamnus purshiana*, used as a laxative or cathartic [Span., = "sacred bark"]

case[1] (kās) *n.* 1. Instance of thing's occurring; state of affairs, circumstances; **in** ~, if (something should happen); **in any** ~, no matter what happens. 2. (med.) Condition of disease in a person, instance of disease; (fig. slang) a (*someone's*) a (*mental*) ~. 3. (law) Cause, suit, for trial; statement of facts drawn up for consideration of higher court; cause that has been decided. 4. (gram.) In inflected languages, form of substantive, pronoun, or adjective expressing its relation to other words in sentence; in uninflected languages, this relation apart from form. 5. ~ **history**, (record of) information about patient etc.; ~ **law**, law based on judicial decision and precedent rather than on statute. **case'work**, social work done by personal study, handling of cases (individuals or families), hence **case'worker**.

case[2] (kās) *n.* Thing to contain or hold something else; box, chest, sheath, etc.; outer protective and covering part; box or chest with its contents; (print.) shallow wooden tray for holding type, divided into compartments to take the various letters of the alphabet; **lower** ~ case usu. holding letters other than capitals; hence (in) small letters; **upper** ~, case holding large or

*Below: There are several standard sizes of **casks**. Most are made to store wine, spirits or beer. A cooper shapes oak staves so that they are wider in the middle than at their ends. He fits them into a truss at each end and heats the wood so that it will bend. Then he hammers hoops into place. Left: A butt is tapped in a wine cellar.*

charge of cash of bank or other business firm, paying and receiving money etc.; one in retail store etc. who receives customers' payments.

cash·ier² (kăshēr´) *v.t.* Dismiss from service; fire.

cash·mere (kăzh´mēr, kăsh´-) *n.* Material woven from fine soft wool found beneath the hair of goats of Kashmir and Tibet; woolen fabric imitating this.

cas·ing (kā´sĭng) *n.* (esp.) = CASE²; framework; outer covering of a tire for car, bicycle, etc.

ca·si·no (kasē´nō) *n.* (pl. **-nos**). 1. Public room or house for entertainment, esp. gambling. 2. (also **cassino**) Card game in which each player tries to win cards by matching those exposed on the table, points being scored for winning the greatest number of cards, one for the greatest number of spades, two for ten of diamonds (**big** ~), and one for two of spades (**little** ~). [It., = "little house"]

cask (kăsk, kahsk) *n.* Barrel used esp. for beer, wine, and cider; contents or capacity of cask.

cas·ket (kăs´kĭt, kahs´-) *n.* 1. (archaic) Small, often ornamental, box for holding jewels or other valuables. 2. Coffin.

Cas·lon (kăz´lon), **William** (1692–1766). English type founder; hence, applied to style of type orig. cut at his foundry.

Cas·par (kăs´per). One of the three Magi.

*The **cashew** nut of the S. American tree Anacardium occidentale has several uses. It is a nourishing food in itself when roasted and its oil is excellent for cooking.*

ital letters etc., hence, (in) ital letters; **case′harden** den surface of, esp. give steel face to (iron etc.) by carbon- ng; (fig.) make callous; **case-** ife, knife worn in sheath. **case** , (**cased, cas·ing**). 1. Put into, otect with a case. 2. (slang) amine (house etc.) in planning a me.

ca·sein (kā´sēn, -sēin, kāsēn´) *n.* protein, one of the constituents milk, coagulated by acids, and ming the basis of cheese.

case·ment (kās´ment) *n.* Metal wooden hinged frame with glass, ming window or part of one; et.) window.

Case·ment (kās´ment), **Sir ger David** (1846–1916). British lomat and Irish nationalist; ecuted for treason after seeking rman aid for Irish independence ring World War I.

Ca·ser·ta (kazĕr´ta). City near ples, Italy; Mediterranean head- arters of the Allies during World ar II; site of surrender in 1945 of rman forces that fought in Italy d Yugoslavia.

cash (kăsh) *n.* Ready money; ins and banknotes; ~ **crop**, crop own for sale; ~ **flow**, movement money as affecting liquidity of m etc., or as a measure of ofitability; ~ **register**, till for ording and adding amounts put o it. **cash** *v.t.* Give or obtain sh for (check, money order, etc.); **in one's chips**, settle accounts game of poker; (slang) die.

cash·ew (kăsh´oo, kashoo´) *n.* rge tree (*Anacardium occidentale*) W. Indies etc., cultivated for its lney shaped edible nut (~ **nut**). ort. *caju*, f. Tupi (*a*) *caju*]

cash·ier¹ (kăshēr´) *n.* One in

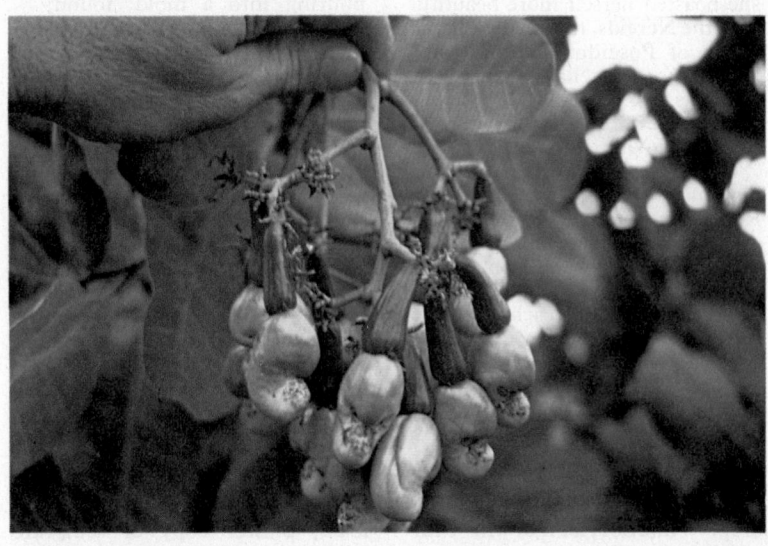

Labels on cask diagram: bung-hole, hoop, stave, tap hole, brandy puncheon, butt, hogshead, barrel, kilderkin, firkin

Cas·pi·an (kăs′pēan) **Sea.** Inland sea between Europe and Asia; the largest inland body of water in the world, often classified as a salt lake.

casque (kăsk) *n.* (hist., poet.) Helmet.

Cas·san·dra (kasăn′drạ). (Gk. myth.) Daughter of Priam, king of Troy; she was loved by Apollo, who gave her the gift of prophecy and when she deceived him ordained that her prophecies, though true, should not be believed.

Cas·satt (kasăt′), **Mary** (1845–1926). Amer. impressionist painter in France; best known for paintings of mothers and children.

cas·sa·va (kasah′va) *n.* 1. Plant of genus *Manihot*, widely cultivated in tropical America and Africa for its fleshy tuberous roots. 2. Nutritious starch obtained from its roots, used to make tapioca and as a staple in the tropics.

cas·se·role (kăs′erōl) *n.* Heatproof vessel in which food is baked and served; food cooked in this. [Fr., = "stew pan"]

cas·sette (kasĕt′, kă-) *n.* Light-proof container for photographic film; closed container of magnetic tape for tape recorder; ~ **player**, machine for playing this; **video** ~, for recording television program.

cas·sia (kăsh′a, kă′sēa) *n.* 1. Coarse kind of cinnamon, esp. the bark of *Cinnamonum cassia*; this tree. 2. Plant of genus *C~* of warm climates, yielding senna leaves; any medicinal preparation from these.

Cas·si·no (kasē′nō). Town in central Italy near Naples; Benedictine monastery stands above the town, on Monte Cassino; site of World War II battles in which Allies gained victory in push toward Rome.

Cas·si·o·pe·ia (kăsēopē′a). 1. (Gk. myth.) Wife of Cepheus, king of Ethiopia, mother of Andromeda; she boasted herself more beautiful than the Nereids, thus incurring the wrath of Poseidon. 2. (astron.) Northern constellation between Cepheus and Perseus.

cas·sit·er·ite (kasĭt′erīt) *n.* Stannic dioxide, TINstone.

Cas·sius Lon·gi·nus (kăsh′us lŏnjī′nus), **Gaius** (d. 42 B.C.). Roman general; conspired with others to assassinate Julius Caesar.

cas·sock (kăs′ok) *n.* Long closefitting tunic, usu. black, buttoning up to the neck and reaching to the feet, worn by clergy.

cas·so·war·y (kăs′owĕrē) *n.* (pl. **-war·ies**). Large flightless running bird of genus *Casuarius*, related to ostrich, found in Australia, New Guinea, etc. [Malay *kasuari*]

cast (kăst, kahst) *v.* (**cast, cast·ing**). 1. Throw, cause to fall or drop; ~ **anchor**, let it down; ~ **an**

The world's largest body of inland water, the **Caspian Sea** has an area of 163,800 sq. miles. Its waters are salty and its surface lies 92 ft. below sea level. Its greatest known depth is about 3,200 ft.

eye, glance. 2. Throw off, shed, esp. in process of growth; (of horse) lose (a shoe). 3. Form (metal etc.) into desired shape by melting and pouring into a mold; found; ~ **iron**: see IRON; ~**-iron** (*adj.*), made of cast iron; hard, very strong, unadaptable. 4. Arrange (facts *into* a shape, actors *for* parts in play). 5. ~ **about**, look about, search here and there, *for*; ~ **adrift**, leave to drift; ~ **ashore**, leave behind on seashore; ~ **away**, reject; (pass., of ship, sailor, etc.) be wrecked; **cast′away**, person shipwrecked or cast adrift or rejected; **cast down**, depress; **cast off**, throw away, abandon; (print.) estimate printed length or size of (MS.); **cast′off** (*n.*) thing discarded; (print.) estimated length. **cast** *n.* 1. Throw of missile, fishing line, sounding lead, etc.; throw of dice, number thrown. 2. Model, shape, made by running molten metal or pressing soft substance into a mold; the mold itself; plaster copy of sculpture

Top: The **cassowary** bird is aggress[ive] if provoked and it is a formidable fight[er]. Above: Its neck is unfeathered and [its] head carries a horny casque.

made thus. 3. Earth excreted [by] earthworm; undigested fo[od] thrown up by bird. 4. Set of acto[rs] taking the parts in a play. 5. Twi[st,] inclination; slight squint. 6. Tin[ge,] hue. **cast′er**[1] *n.*

Cas·ta·gno (kahstahn′yō), **A[n-]drea del** (1423–1457). Itali[an] Florentine realistic painter.

cas·ta·net (kăstanĕt′) *n.* Sm[all] concave shell of ivory or hard wo[od] used to make rattling sound[s as] accompaniment to dancing, a pa[ir] being held in the palm of the ha[nd] and clapped together with t[he]

*Since he rose to power in Cuba in 1959, **Fidel Castro** has worked towards close ties with Communist nations in Europe. He is seen here inspecting machines in Czechoslovakia.*

castles were generally built on sites *against* which it would be hard to launch *an* attack, and many dominated a fea-*ture* of importance. *Top: The castle of San Angelo in Rome commands the bridge over the River Tiber. Above: Dover Castle dominates the town.*

...agers.

caste (kăst, kahst) *n.* One of the ...ur major hereditary classes (...RAHMAN, KSHATRIYA, VAISYA, and ...DRA) into which Hindu society is ...vided, each separated from the ...hers by restrictions on occupa-...on, marriage, and social inter-...urse; any social class rigidly ...parated from others by occupa-...on, heredity, etc.; social status ...nferred by class (**lose ~**, lose ...estige); **~ system**, social system ...sed on caste. **caste′less** *adj.*

cas·tel·lat·ed (kăs′tĕlātĭd) *adj.*

Built like a castle, having battle-ments; castlelike. **cas·tel·la·tion** (kăstĕlā′shon) *n.*

cast·er², **cas·tor²** (kas′ter, kahs′-) *ns.* 1. Small solid wheel and swivel on leg of piece of furniture for moving it without lifting. 2. Small vessel with perforated top for sprinkling pepper, sugar, flour, etc.

cas·ti·gate (kăs′tĭgāt) *v.t.* (**-gat·ed**, **-gat·ing**). Chastise, punish. **cas·ti·ga·tion** (kăstĭgā′-shon), **cas·ti·ga·tor** *ns.*

Cas·tile (kăstēl′). Central part of Spain, an ancient kingdom; **~ soap**, fine hard white or mottled soap made with olive oil and soda. **Cas·til·i·an** (kăstĭl′yan) *adj. & n.* (Native, inhabitant) of Castile; (of) the language of Castile, literary Spanish.

cast·ing (kăs′tĭng, kahs′-) *adj.* **~ vote**, (f. obs. sense of cast =

"turn the scale") vote that decides between two equal parties. **casting** *n.* (esp.) 1. Piece of metal or other substance shaped by melting and pouring into a mold; this process of manufacture; DIE-¹ def. 3, SAND-, PRESSURE **~**: see these words. 2. = CAST *n.* def. 2.

cas·tle (kăs′el, kah′sel) *n.* 1. Large fortified building or set of buildings; dwelling that was once fortified; (colloq.) palace. 2. (hist.) Small wooden tower used in war etc. and borne on elephant's back or ship's deck. 3. (chess) = ROOK². 4. **~(s) in the air, in Spain**, daydream(s), visionary project or scheme. **castle** *v.i.* (**-tled, -tling**). (chess) Move king two squares toward one of the rooks and (in the same move) this rook to the square next past the king.

Cas·tor (kăs′ter, kahs′-). (Gk. myth.) One of the twin sons (**~ and Pollux**) of Tyndareus and Leda, and half brother of Helen. 2. (astron.) More northerly of the two bright stars in the constellation Gemini.

cas·tor¹ (kăs′ter, kahs′-) *n.* 1. Reddish-brown unctuous bitter substance obtained from anal glands of beaver and used in perfumery and formerly in medi-cine. 2. (archaic) Hat (orig. one of beaver or imitation beaver).

cas·tor² (kăs′ter, kahs′-) = CASTER².

cas·tor (kăs′ter, kahs′-) **oil.** Pale yellow nauseous acrid oil obtained from seeds of **Castor-oil plant** (*Ricinus communis*), used as purga-tive and lubricant.

cas·trate (kăs′trāt) *v.t.* (**-trat-ed, -trat·ing**). Remove testicles of, geld; deprive of vigor; expurgate (book). **cas·tra·tion** (kăstrā′shon) *n.*

cas·tra·to (kăstrah′tō, ka-) *n.* (pl. **-ti** pr. **-tē**). Adult male singer retaining boy's voice as a result of castration. [It.]

Cas·tro (kăs′trō), **Fidel** (1927–). Cuban revolutionary and premier (since 1959).

cas·u·al (kăzh′ōoal) *adj.* Accidental; irregular; undesigned, coming by chance or accident; unmethodical, careless; unconcerned, uninterested; (of clothes) informal. **cas′u·al·ly** *adv.* **cas′u·al·ness** *n.*

cas·u·al·ty (kăzh′ōoaltē, kăzh′-al-) *n.* (pl. **-ties**). Accident, mishap, disaster; killed, wounded, or injured person; (pl.) list or number of such persons.

cas·u·ist (kăzh′ōoĭst) *n.* Person (orig. a theologian) who reasons subtly in matters of conscience and conduct; hence, disparagingly, a disingenuous hairsplitter. **cas·u·ist·ry** (kăzh′ōoĭstrē) *n.*

ca·sus bel·li (kā′sus bĕl′ī, kăs′us; *Lat.* kah′sōos bĕl′ē) (pl. **ca·sus bel·li**). Cause of war, act justifying or regarded as reason for war. [L.]

CAT *abbrev.* Clear-air turbulence.

cat (kăt) *n.* 1. Small domesticated furry carnivorous quadruped (*Felis domesticus*), kept to destroy mice and as pet; **wild′cat**: see WILD. 2. Any member of the genus *Felis*, which includes lions, tigers, panthers, etc. 3. Catlike animal of other species, as *civet cat*, *polecat*, etc. 4. (colloq.) Spiteful or gossiping woman. 5. (naut.) Cathead, beam projecting from bows of ship, for raising the anchor, or carrying it suspended, so called because in early times the ring to which the anchor was drawn commonly hung from an ornament, often an animal mask. 6. Cat-o'-nine-tails (see below). 7. Caterpillar tractor. 8. (slang) Jazz musician or devotee; a man. 9. ~**-and-dog**, very quarrelsome (life etc.); **cat′bird**, N. Amer. songbird (*Dumetella carolinensis*) having gray plumage; **cat burglar**, one who enters house by climbing to upper story; **cat′call**, shrill call or whistle expressing disapproval; (*v.*) make catcalls, receive with catcalls; **cat′fish**, any fish of the group Siluridae, including the bullhead, most of which live in fresh water and have barbels around the mouth; **cat′head**: see sense 5 above; **cat′mint**, (archaic) catnip, esp. as a tea; **cat′nap**, short light sleep taken sitting in chair etc.; **cat′nip**, aromatic labiate plant with pale-blue flowers (*Nepeta cataria*) to which cats are strongly attracted; small bag of this for cats to play with; **cat-o′-nine-tails**, whip of nine knotted cords formerly used in military and naval punishments; **cat's-cradle**, child's game with players lifting intertwined string from fingers in such a way as to form new patterns; **cat's-eye**,

*The domestic **cat** evolved from a civet-like creature that lived in the Miocene period some 20 million years ago. 1. The European wild cat has tabby markings, and some people believe that it*

precious stone resembling cat's eye with contracted pupil, a hard chalcedonic quartz from Ceylon, Malabar, etc.; playing marble made of or resembling this; small round reflector on vehicles, along roads, etc., to aid in night driving; **cat's-paw**, (colloq.) person used as tool by another; **cat('s) whisker**, fine usu. copper wire placed in contact with sensitive spot in crystal wireless receiver; **cat′tail**, reedlike marsh plant (*Typha latifolia*) with flowers in tall cylindrical spikes; **cat′walk**, narrow bridge or footway giving access to machinery etc. **cat** *v.* (**cat·ted, cat·ting**). (naut.) Raise (anchor) to cathead.

cat. *abbrev.* Catalog.

cata- *prefix.* Down from, down to, against, in opposition to, mis-.

ca·tab·o·lism (katăb′olĭzem) *n.*

mated with an African cat to produ[ce] the domestic variety. The wild cat has [a] rather bigger and flatter head than t[he] domestic cat. 2. The Russian Blue [cat] has a remarkably thick double coat. It [...]

Phase of metabolism in whic[h] complex compounds break in[to] simpler ones. **cat·a·bol·i[c]** (kătabŏl′ĭk) *adj.*

cat·a·chre·sis (kătakrē′sĭs) [n.] Perversion, improper use, of word[s] either for rhetorical effect or fro[m] ignorance.

cat·a·clysm (kăt′aklĭzem) [n.] Deluge, esp. the Flood; sudde[n] convulsion or alteration of con[...]ditions, political, social, etc., up[...] heaval. **cat·a·clys·mal** (kătaklĭz[′-]mal), **cat·a·clys′mic** *adjs.*

cat·a·comb (kăt′akōm) *n.* Sub[...]terranean cemetery (orig. tha[t] under the basilica of St. Sebastia[n] near Rome, supposed burying plac[e] of Peter and Paul); (pl.) subter[...]ranean galleries made by Jews an[d] early Christians in and near Rom[e] with recesses in the sides for tomb[s].

5

6

ensively bred in the U.S. 3. The grey
by cat almost died out in Great
tain during the 1939–45 war but the
ed was revived by importing a good
ain. 4. The Siamese cat was bred
m a strain said to have been brought

to Europe from Bangkok in 1884. It has
a raucous call. 5. The Australian wild
cat, carnivorous marsupial unrelated to
true cats. 6. The Manx cat, sometimes
called a rumpie, has no tail. The breed
is reputed to come from the Isle of Man,

but tailless breeds are found in many
countries, including China and the
U.S.S.R.

hilar works elsewhere. [LL.
acumbas, name given to the
acomb under St. Sebastian;
gin unknown]

ca·tad·ro·mous (katăd′romŭs)
i. (of fish) Descending to lower
aches of river, or to sea, to spawn.

cat·a·falque (kăt′afălk, -fawk,
wlk) *n.* Platform or base upon
ich a deceased person lies in
te; open hearse.

Cat·a·lan (kăt′alăn, kătalän′)
i. & n. (Native, inhabitant) of
talonia; (of) the dialect of Pro-
nçal (or langue d′oc) spoken in
talonia.

cat·a·lep·sy (kăt′alĕpsē) *n.*
uscular rigidity and lack of sensa-
n and awareness, often associated
th epilepsy, hysteria, or schizo-
renia. **cat·a·lep·tic** (kătalĕp′tĭk)

adj.

Cat·a·li·na (kătalē′na) **Island.**
Island and resort area off the coast
of California near Los Angeles.

cat·a·log, cat·a·logue (kăt′-
alawg, -lŏg) *ns.* Complete list, usu.
alphabetical or arranged under
headings, and often with descriptive or other particulars. ~ *v.*
(**-loged, -log·ing, -logued,
-logu·ing**). Enumerate, enter, in a
catalog.

Cat·a·lo·ni·a (kătalō′nēa, -nya).
(Span. *Cataluña*) NE. part of
Spain, formerly a province.

ca·tal·pa (katăl′pa, -tawl′-) *n.*
Tree of genus *C~* with large
simple leaves and trumpet-shaped
flowers, native to N. America, W.
Indies, Japan, and China.

ca·tal·y·sis (katăl′ĭsĭs) *n.* (pl.

-ses pr. -sēz). Facilitation of a
chemical reaction by the presence
of an added substance that is itself
not consumed in the reaction.
cat·a·lyze (kăt′alīz) *v.t.* (**-lyzed,
-lyz·ing**). **cat·a·lyt·ic** (kătalĭt′ĭk)
adj. & n.

cat·a·lyst (kăt′alĭst) *n.* Substance causing catalysis.

cat·a·ma·ran (kătamarăn′) *n.*
Raft or float of logs tied together,
with longest one in middle; sailing
boat with twin hulls. [Tamil
katta-maram tied tree]

cat·a·mite (kăt′amīt) *n.* Boy
kept by a pederast. [L. *Catamitus*,
corrupt form of *Ganymēdes*
Ganymede]

cat·a·mount (kăt′amownt) *n.*:
see MOUNTAIN lion.

cat·a·pult (kăt′apŭlt, -pŏŏlt) *n.*

The principle of the **catamaran** has long been known, but not until modern materials, light and strong enough to withstand heavy seas, were available, could an ocean catamaran be built.

The mobile **catapult** was one of many siege engines designed for commanders who encountered the problems of capturing walled cities and strong fortresses.

The **caterpillar** tractor performs more efficiently on heavy ground or light soil where ordinary tractor tir either bog or cannot grip.

1. Ancient military engine worked with lever and ropes for hurling stones etc. 2. (chiefly Brit.) Slingshot. 3. Mechanism for launching aircraft from deck of ship. ~ v. Shoot with catapult; hurl as from catapult; launch with catapult.

cat·a·ract (kăt′arăkt) n. 1. Waterfall, esp. large precipitous fall or series of falls; downpour, rush of water. 2. Progressive opacity of lens of eye, resulting, unless treated, in impairment of vision and eventual blindness.

ca·tarrh (katär′) n. Inflammation of mucous membrane, esp. of nose, throat, and bronchial tubes, causing increased flow of mucus. **ca·tarrh′al, ca·tarrh′ous** adjs.

cat·ar·rhine (kăt′arīn) adj. & n. (Animal) of one of the two divisions of the suborder Anthropoidea, distinguished from the PLATYRRHINE by having the nostrils close together and directed downward, and including the Old World monkeys, the anthropoid apes, and man.

ca·tas·tro·phe (katăs′trofē) n. Dénouement of dramatic piece; disastrous end, overthrow, calamitous fate; event subverting order or system of things. **cat·a·stroph·ic** (kătastrŏf′ĭk) adj. **cat·a·stroph′i·cal·ly** adv.

cat·a·to·ni·a (kătatō′nēa) n. (path.) Schizophrenia marked by negativism and mutism with intervals of catalepsy and occas. violence. **cat·a·ton·ic** (kătatŏn′ĭk) adj. & n.

cat·boat (kăt′bōt) n. Broadbeamed sailboat with mast well forward and rigged with one sail.

catch (kăch) v. (**caught, catch·ing**). 1. Capture, lay hold of, seize; be entangled, take hold; hit; come level with, make up arrears (also ~ **up**); intercept (ball etc.) in motion, esp. take hold of (ball thrown) before it reaches ground; be in time for (train etc.); check suddenly. 2. Surprise, detect. 3. Ignite, be ignited (also ~ **fire**). 4. Receive, incur, be infected with. 5. Grasp with senses or mind; arrest, captivate, arrest attention of; take by surprise, trick, deceive. **catch′-all**, receptacle to catch or include various items (also fig.); **catch′penny**, got up merely to sell, without concern for quality, cheap; **catch-22**, (colloq.) conflicting or self-contradictory regulations producing frustration [f. *Catch-22*, novel (1961) by Joseph Heller, Amer. author b. 1923]; **catch′word**, word so placed as to attract attention, as word at head of entry in dictionary etc.; word caught up and repeated, esp. in politics etc. **catch** n. 1. Act of catching; amount or number of fish caught; device for fastening or restraining something; chance of, success in, catching ball, as in baseball; thing or person caught or worth catching. 2. Something designed to deceive or trip up; unforeseen difficulty or awkwardness; hidden trap; surprise. 3. (mus.) Round, sometimes devised to produce punning or other humorous verbal combinations. **catch·er** (kăch′er) n. (esp.) Baseball player behind home plate who directs pitcher, catches pitches that

go past batter, etc.

catch·ing (kăch′ĭng) adj. (es Infectious; captivating.

catch·ment (kăch′ment) Catching and collection of rain over a natural drainage area; bas reservoir for collecting or drain water; the water so collected.

catch·y (kăch′ē) adj. (**catch·i catch·i·est**). (colloq.) Attracti (of tune etc.) easily remembered

cat·e·chism (kăt′ekĭzem) Treatise for instruction by quest and answer, esp. on religious d trine.

cat·e·chize (kăt′ekīz) (**-chized, -chiz·ing**). Instruct question and answer, or by the of a catechism; put questions examine. **cat·e·chist** (kăt′ekĭst) *n.*

cat·e·chu·men (kătekū′men) *n.* Christian convert under instruction before baptism; neophyte.

cat·e·gor·i·cal (kătegŏr′ĭkal, -gär′-) *adj.* Unconditional, absolute; explicit, direct; ~ **imperative**, (Kantian ethics) an absolute and universally binding moral law. **cat·e·gor′i·cal·ly** *adv.*

cat·e·go·ry (kăt′egōrē, -gōrē) *n.* (pl. **-ries**). 1. Class, division. 2. In Aristotle, one of a possibly exhaustive set of classes among which all things might be distributed.

cat·e·nar·y (kăt′enĕrē; *Brit.* katē′nerē) *adj. & n.* (pl. **-nar·ies**). (Like) curve formed by uniform chain hanging freely from two points not in one vertical line.

cat·e·nate (kăt′enāt) *v.t.* (**-nat·ed, -nat·ing**). Connect like links of chain. **cat·e·na·tion** (kătenā′shon) *n.*

ca·ter (kā′ter) *v.i.* Purvey food; provide amusement etc. *for*; provide anything desired *to*. **ca′ter·er** *n.*

cat·er·pil·lar (kăt′epĭler, kăt′er-) *n.* 1. Larva of butterfly, moth, sawfly, resembling a worm but possessing several pairs of legs, strong jaws, and short antennae and feeding on leaves, fruit, or other succulent parts of plants. 2. **C~** (trademark) Tractor equipped with endless articulated steel bands carrying treads passing around two or more wheels. [OF. *chatepelose* hairy cat]

cat·er·waul (kăt′erwawl) *n.* Cry of cat in heat, similar squalling sound. ~ *v.i.* Make caterwaul.

cat·gut (kăt′gŭt) *n.* Dried and twisted intestines of sheep, horse, etc. (not cat), used for strings of musical instruments, tennis rackets, etc., and for sutures in surgical operations.

ca·thar·sis (kathär′sĭs) *n.* (pl. **-ses** pr. -sēz). 1. (med.) Purgation. 2. (with ref. to Aristotle's *Poetics*) Purification of emotions by vicarious experience, esp. through the drama. 3. (psychotherapy) Relieving of neurotic state by reenacting or relating an experience of strong emotional character that has undergone repression.

ca·thar·tic (kathär′tĭk) *adj.* Effecting catharsis; purgative; cleansing. ~ *n.* Purgative medicine.

Ca·thay (kăthā′). (archaic and poet.) CHINA.

*The larval stage of the life of a butterfly is called a **caterpillar**. In many cases the caterpillar has a body larger than that of the moth or butterfly it will become. The energy built up during this stage, by a tremendous rate of eating, is required to sustain the insect during the great changes it will experience at the pupal stage.*

ca·the·dral (kathē'dral) *n.*
Principal church of diocese, containing bishop's *cathedra* or throne.
~ *adj.* Ranking as a cathedral,
containing or belonging to a
cathedral.

Cath·er (kăth'*er*), **Willa Sibert**
(1873–1947). Amer. novelist,
author of *My Antonia, One of Ours,
Death Comes for the Archbishop,*
etc.; awarded Pulitzer Prize, 1922.

Cath·er·ine[1] (kăth'erĭn, kăth'-
rĭn) "the Great" (1729–96).
Empress of Russia 1762–96; by
birth a German, Princess Sophia of
Anhalt-Zerbst; married the Russian heir; six months after his
accession (as Peter III) he was
forced to abdicate and was
murdered, whereupon Catherine
became Empress.

Cath·er·ine[2] (kăth'erĭn, kăth'-
rĭn), **St.** (d. 307). Legendary saint
and martyr of Alexandria; she was
beheaded, after other methods of
putting her to death, including that
of the wheel, had failed; ~ **wheel**,
(orig.) instrument of torture consisting of four wheels armed with
knives and teeth turning different
ways; now, a kind of firework that
rotates while burning.

Ca·the·rine[3] **de Mé·di·cis**
(kăth'erĭn d*e* měd'ĭsēz, kăth'rĭn,
měd'ĭchēz) (1519–89). Wife of
Henry II of France; regent of
France (1547–59) during the
minority of her son, Charles IX.

Cath·erine[4] **of Ar·a·gon** (kăth'-
erĭn *ov* ăr'*a*gon, -gŏn, kăth'rĭn)
(1483–1536). Daughter of Ferdinand and Isabella of Spain;
married Arthur, prince of Wales
1501, and, after his death, became
the first wife of his younger brother
Henry VIII 1509; divorced by
Henry 1526, on ground that her
first marriage made her second invalid.

cath·e·ter (kăth'ĭter) *n.* Slender,
flexible tube for introducing into
a body channel to withdraw excess
fluid or sample for analysis, esp.
urine from the bladder. **cath·e·-
ter·ize** (kăth'ĭterīz) *v.t.* (-ized,
-iz·ing). Use a catheter on.

cath·ode (kăth'ōd) *n.* (elect.)
Negatively charged electrode; ~
ray, beam of electrons issuing from
cathode of electrical discharge tube
(~ **ray tube**).

cath·o·lic (kăth'olĭk, kăth'lĭk)
adj. 1. Universal, of universal interest or use; all-embracing, of wide
sympathies. 2. **C~ Church,** (*a*)
the whole body of Christians; (*b*)
after the separation of Eastern and
Western Churches, the Western or
Latin Church; (*c*) after the Reformation, claimed as its exclusive
title by that part of the Western
Church that remained under
Roman obedience, but (*d*) held by
Anglicans to include the Church of
England. 3. Of or belonging to any

of these churches, esp. = Roman
Catholic (see ROMAN def. 6). 4.
His C~ Majesty, title of former
kings of Spain. **C~** *n.* Member
of a Catholic church, esp. Roman
Catholic. **ca·thol·i·cal·ly** (kathŏl'-
ĭklē) *adv.* **ca·thol·i·cism** (kathŏl'-
ĭsĭzem), **cath·o·lic·i·ty** (kathŏ-
lĭs'ĭtē) *ns.* **ca·thol·i·cize** (kathŏl'-

*The late Middle Ages produced a sp.
of **cathedral** building through*
Europe. Top: the cathedral at We
Somerset U.K., is one of the finest
these. Its style shows the progress
of changes in Gothic taste from the l
12th to the 15th centuries. Above:
Patrick's Cathedral, New York, w
designed by James Renwick and de
cated in 1879.

sīz) *v.t.* & *v.i.* (**-cized, -ciz·ing**).
cat·i·on (kăt' īon) *n.*: see ION.
at·i·on·ic (kătīŏn'ĭk) *adj.* [Gk., = "going down"]
cat·kin (kăt'kĭn) *n.* Deciduous pike, usu. of unisexual apetalous lowers, of willow, birch, etc.
Ca·to (kā'tō), **Marcus Porcius.** Name of two Romans: (1) "Cato the Elder" or "Cato the Censor" (239–49 B.C.), famous for his opposition o the lax morals and luxury of the Romans and for his insistence that "Carthage must be destroyed"; uthor of a treatise *De Agri Cultura*, the oldest extant literary prose vork in Latin; (2) his great-randson "Cato the Younger" (95–6 B.C.), also a man of unbending haracter; chief political antagonist f Julius Caesar.
Cats·kill (kăt'skĭl) **Mountains.** Low mountain range and resort rea in SE. New York State.
cat·sup (kăt'sup, kăch'up, kĕch'-) *n.* Var. of KETCHUP.
cat·tle (kăt'el) *n.* Bovine domestic animals (steers, cows, etc.) raised or meat, milk, etc.; ~ **prod**, prod to drive cattle, now esp. n electric one; ~ **rustler**, marauder who steals cattle.
cat·tley·a (kăt'lēa, kătlē'a, -lā'a) *n.* Orchidaceous Central Amer. and Brazilian plant of genus *C*~ with violet, pink, or yellow flowers. [William *Cattley* (d. 1832), English patron of botany]
cat·ty (kăt'ē) *adj.* (**-ti·er, -ti·est**). Spiteful, malicious; gos-

sipy. **cat'ti·ly** *adv.* **cat'ti·ness** *n.*
Ca·tul·lus (katŭl'us), **Gaius Valerius** (87–54? B.C.). Roman poet.
Cau·ca·sian (kawkā'zhan, -shan, -kăzh'an, -kăsh'an) *adj.* & *n.* 1. (Native, inhabitant, language) of the Caucasus. 2. Caucasoid.
Cau·ca·soid (kaw'kasoid) *adj.* & *n.* (Member) of the light-skinned

*Several trees produce **catkins**. They are flowers borne by deciduous trees such as the beech, hazel and willow.*

division of mankind found esp. in Europe, N. Africa, and SW. Asia; Caucasian.
Cau·ca·sus (kaw'kasus). Mountain range between Black Sea and Caspian Sea; region of the U.S.S.R. between these two seas.
cau·cus (kaw'kus) *n.* (pl. **-cus·es**). Political party meeting to decide policy or select candidates; policy meeting.
cau·dal (kaw'dal) *adj.* Of, at, like, tail. **cau·date** (kaw'dāt) *adj.* Tailed; of the order Caudata. **cau'·dat·ed** *adj.*
cau·dil·lo (kawdēl'yō, -dē'ō; *Sp.* kowdhēl'yaw, -dhē'yaw) *n.* (pl. **-dil·los** pr. -dēl'yōz, -dē'ōz; *Sp.* -dhēl'yaws, -dhē'yaws). (in Spanish-speaking countries) Military dictator. [Span., = "leader"]
caught (kawt): see CATCH.
caul (kawl) *n.* Amnion or inner membrane enclosing fetus; part of this enclosing child's head at birth.
caul·dron (kawl'dron) *n.* Large kettle (usu.) with hoop handle and removable lid.
cau·li·flow·er (kaw'lĭflowₑr, kŏl'ĭ-) *n.* Cultivated plant of genus *Brassica* with young inflorescence forming close white fleshy edible head; ~ **ear**, (prize fighter's) ear

thickened and distorted by blows.

cau·line (kaw´lĭn, -līn) *adj.* (bot.) Of, growing on, a stem.

caulk (kawk) *v.t.* Stop up seams of (ship etc.), as with oakum and melted tar.

caus·al (kaw´zal) *adj.* Of, acting as, expressing, due to, a cause or causes; of the nature of cause and effect. **cau·sal·i·ty** (kawzăl´ĭtē) *n.* (pl. **-ties**). Being, having, a cause; relation of cause and effect, doctrine that everything has cause(s).

cau·sa·tion (kawzā´shon) *n.* Causing; relation of cause and effect. **caus·a·tive** (kaw´zatĭv) *adj.* Acting as cause (*of*); (gram.) expressing a cause or causation.

cause (kawz) *v.t.* (**caused, caus·ing**). Be the cause of, make (something) happen; induce, make (person *to* do, thing to be done). ~ *n.* 1. What produces an effect, what gives rise to any action, phenomenon, or condition; person or other agent bringing something about; ground or reason for action; motive; **First C~**, original cause or creator of the universe. 2. (law etc.) Ground for legal action; lawsuit; side of question or controversy expressed by a person or party; goal, or principle pursued with dedication; subject of concern.

cause cé·lè·bre (kawz selĕb´re, -lĕb´; *Fr.* kōz sālĕb´re) (pl. **causes cé·lè·bres** pr. kawz selĕb´rez, -lĕbz´; *Fr.* kōz sālĕb´re). Lawsuit or scandal exciting much public interest. [Fr.]

cause·way (kawz´wā) *n.* Raised road across low or wet place or piece of water.

caus·tic (kaw´stĭk) *adj.* 1. Burning, corrosive, destroying organic tissue; ~ **soda**, sodium hydroxide. 2. Bitter, cutting, sarcastic. 3. (optics) Formed by intersection of rays from one point reflected or refracted from a curved surface. **caustic** *n.* Caustic substance. **caus·ti·cal·ly** *adv.* **caus·tic·i·ty** (kawstĭs´ĭtē) *n.*

cau·ter·ize (kaw´terīz) *v.t.* (**-ized, -iz·ing**). Sear with hot iron or caustic, esp. in treatment of wounds etc. **cau·ter·i·za·tion** (kawterĭzā´shon) *n.*

cau·tion (kaw´shon) *n.* 1. Warning; (colloq.) extraordinary, strange person or thing. 2. Avoidance of rashness, attention to safety. ~ *v.t.* Warn; admonish.

cau·tion·ar·y (kaw´shonĕrē) *adj.* Conveying a warning or admonition.

cau·tious (kaw´shus) *adj.* Disposed to or exhibiting caution. **cau´tious·ly** *adv.* **cau´tious·ness** *n.*

cav·al·cade (kăvalkād´, kăv´alkād) *n.* Ceremonial procession, esp. on horseback; colorful procession or pageant.

cav·a·lier (kăvalēr´, kăv´alēr) *n.*

Top: 'The Laughing Cavalier' by Franz Hals, painted in 1624, captures the spirit of élan that most people associate with **cavaliers** of the 17th century. Their taste for luxury is reflected in their rich dress.

Above: The **cavalry's** dash later fou: expression in the splendor of formal u: forms. These often copied the fashio of admired opponents, as with t British Lancers' adoption of Polis Lancers' caps.

1. Horseman. 2. Courtly gentleman, gallant, esp. as escorting a lady. 3. (**C~**) Adherent of Charles I of England; Royalist. ~ *adj.* 1. Careless in manner, offhand; haughty, supercilious. 2. Royalist. **cav·a·lier·ly** *adj.* & *adv.*

cav·al·ry (kăv´alrē) *n.* (pl. **-ries**). Horse soldiers, mounted troops troops formerly mounted but no equipped with tanks or armore cars; ~ **twill**, strong material i double twill used for clothing. **cav·al·ry·man** *n.* (pl. **-men**).

cave (kāv) *n.* Hollow place opening more or less horizontally under the ground or into side of hill; ~ **man**, prehistoric man living in cave; person resembling prehistoric man in behavior, crude, rough man; ~ **in**, collapse (of earth etc. over hollow place), yield to pressure from outside or above; (fig.) yield to pressure, submit, give in; smash in; also **cave-in** (*n.*).

ca·ve·at (kā′vēăt, kăv′ē-, kah′-ēaht) *n.* 1. (law) Formal notice by interested party to court requesting postponement of proceedings until he is heard. 2. Warning, caution. [L., = "let him beware"]

ca·ve·at emp·tor (kā′vēăt ĕmp′-ōr, kăv′ē-, kah′vēaht). "Let the buyer beware," legal principle that the seller is not responsible for the quality of his merchandise unless he supplies a written warranty. [L.]

Cav·ell (kăv′el), **Edith Louisa** (1865–1915). English nurse; shot by the Germans during World War I for aiding the escape of Allied soldiers from Belgium to Holland.

cav·en·dish (kăv′endĭsh) *n.* Tobacco softened, sweetened with molasses, and pressed into cakes.

Cav·en·dish (kăv′endĭsh), **Henry** (1731–1810). English natural philosopher; discovered the composition of water and air and the density of the earth; experimented in electricity.

cav·ern (kăv′ern) *n.* (Vast) underground cave, hollow place. **cav·ern·ous** (kăv′ernus) *adj.*

cav·i·ar, cav·i·are (kăv′ēăr, kăvēăr′) *ns.* Roe of sturgeon and other large fish, pressed and salted, and eaten as a delicacy or a relish.

cav·il (kăv′il) *v.i.* (**-iled, -il·ing,** Brit. **-illed, -il·ling**). Raise trivial

objection. ~ *n.* Quibbling objection; caviling.

cav·i·ta·tion (kăvĭtā′shon) *n.* Successive formation and collapse of bubbles in liquids by mechanical forces, as from a ship's propeller.

cav·i·ty (kăv′ĭtē) *n.* (pl. **-ties**). Empty space within solid body, hollow place; pitted or decayed area in tooth.

ca·vort (kavōrt′) *v.i.* Prance, caper, frolic.

Ca·vy (kā′vē) *n.* (pl. **-vies**). Large rodent of S. Amer. genus *Cavia*, including guinea pigs. [*cabiai*, native name in Fr. Guiana]

caw (kaw) *n.* Cry of crow, raven, etc.; sound resembling this. ~ *v.i.* Utter caw.

Cax·ton (kăks′ton), **William** (1422?–91). First English printer; published first book printed in English; established a press at Westminster, 1477–91, from which he issued about 80 books, many of them his own translations of French romances.

cay (kā, kē) *n.* Small, low islet or reef of sand, rocks, etc., esp. off coast of Latin America.

Cay·enne (kīĕn′, kā-). Capital of French Guiana, on ~ **Island**.

cay·enne (kīĕn′, kā-) *n.* (also ~ **pepper**) Very hot pungent reddish powder obtained from seeds of plants of genus *Capsicum*, used as a condiment.

cay·man (kā′man) = CAIMAN.

Cay·man (kā′man) **Islands.**

Spelunking, the exploration of **caves** *as a sport, can involve various skills including climbing and diving and is becoming increasingly popular. The scientific study of caves is called speleology.*

British dependency of three islands in the Caribbean; capital, Georgetown on Grand Cayman.

Ca·yu·ga (kāū′ga, kī-), **Lake.** One of the Finger Lakes in W. New York State.

cay·use (kī′ōōs, kīūs′) *n.* Amer. Ind. pony; (dial.) horse. [Name of Amer. Ind. tribe]

C.B. *abbrev.* Citizen's band (radio).

CBC *abbrev.* Canadian Broadcasting Company.

cc, c.c. *abbrevs.* Cubic centimeter.

CCC *abbrev.* Civilian Conservation Corps.

C.D., CD *abbrevs. Corps diplomatique* (diplomatic corps); Civil Defense.

Cd *symbol.* Cadium.

Cdr., CDR *abbrevs.* Commander.

Ce *symbol.* Cerium.

C.E. *abbrev.* Church of England; civil engineer; chemical engineer; Common Era.

cease (sēs) *v.* (**ceased, ceas·-ing**). Abstain *from* continuing (action etc.); stop; come, bring, to an end; ~ **-fire,** (mil.) signal to cease firing; cessation of shooting or fighting. **cease** *n.* Ceasing (now only in **without** ~, incessantly). **cease′less** *adj.* Not ceasing. **cease′less·ly** *adv.*

Ce·cil·ia (sĭsēl′ya) **St.** (d. 230 A.D.). Roman martyr; patron saint of music and musicians; commemorated Nov. 22.

ce·cum, cae·cum (sē′kum) *ns.* (pl. **-ca** pr. **-ka**). Any tube with one closed end in the structure of an animal, esp. that arising from the colon and ending at the vermiform appendix in mammals.

cell wall | cytoplasm | nucleus | zona pellucida

1. A single cell develops into millions to build a child's body. The fertilized egg is in one cell, its wall, holding cytoplasm and nucleus, is protected by a zona pellucida membrane.

2. The cell divides into 2 exactly similar cells after a life of some 30 hours.

3. By the third day there are a few score cells in the zona pellucida.

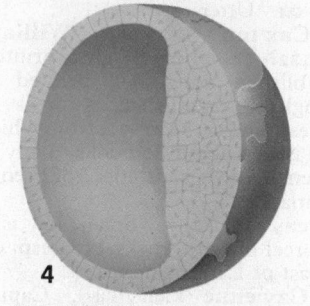

4. On the fifth day some cells congregate to start embryo and others to become the placenta. The zona pellucida disintegrates.

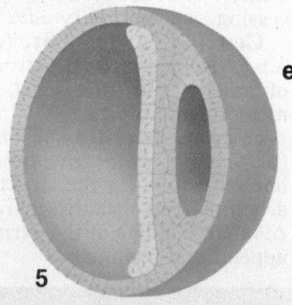

5. 14 days after fertilization a double disk begins to develop.

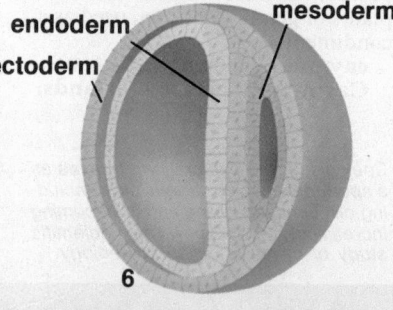

endoderm | ectoderm | mesoderm

6. At about 20 days, another layer is added, this time of different cells. The ectoderm becomes the embryo's skin and brain, the endoderm its digestive tract, liver and lungs, and the mesoderm its heart, blood, bones, kidneys and muscles.

Above: The growth of the cedar is always fairly slow in height, up to 14 ins. a year; but after 2 years, growth in girth is quick. Many huge and apparently ancient cedars were planted in the past 150 years.

Above: One of the earliest of spring flowers seen in Great Britain is the lesser celandine. Very common, it is found blooming in shady places from March to May. Its fruit is of massed carpels.

ce·dar (sē′der) n. Coniferous evergreen Old World tree of genus *Cedrus*; similar tree of genus *Juniperus* or *Thuja*; their aromatic wood highly resistant to insect and rot.

Ce·dar (sē′der) **Rapids.** Industrial city in E. Iowa on the Cedar River.

cede (sēd) v.t. (**ced·ed, ced·ing**). Give up, grant, admit; surrender (territory).

ce·dil·la (sĭdĭl′a) n. Mark written under letter c thus (ç) to show that it is sibilant.

ceil·ing (sē′lĭng) n. 1. Interior upper surface of a room. 2. (aeron.) Altitude beyond which a given aircraft cannot climb and at which

only one speed of flight is possible; (meteor.) height of the lowest cloud or fog layer obscuring sky. 3. Upper limit of prices, wages, etc.

cel·an·dine (sĕl′andīn, -dēn) n. Either of two Old World yellow-flowered plants, the **greater** ~ (*Chelidonium majus*) and the **lesser** ~ (*Ranunculus ficaria*), also known as pilewort; a N. Amer. jewelweed (*Impatiens capensis*) with crimson-spotted orange flowers.

Cel·e·bes (sĕl′ebēz). Island of Indonesia, now Sulawesi. **C~ Sea**, the part of the western Pacific Ocean between Sulawesi and Mindanao Islands.

cel·e·brant (sĕl′ebrant) n. Officiating priest, esp. at Eucharist;

participant in any celebration.

cel·e·brate (sĕl′ebrāt) (**-brat·ed, -brat·ing**). 1. Perform (religious ceremony etc.) publicly and duly; officiate at Eucharist. Observe, honor (festival, event with rites, festivities, etc. 3. Publish abroad, praise, extol. **cel′e·brat·ed** adj. Famed, renowned. **cel·e·bra·tion** (sĕlebrā′shon) n.

ce·leb·ri·ty (selĕb′rĭtē) n. (p **-ties**). 1. Being famous. Celebrated person.

ce·ler·i·ty (selĕr′ĭtē) n. Swiftness.

cel·er·y (sĕl′erē) n. Umbelliferous plant (*Apium graveolen* cultivated for its blanched edib stalks.

2

ce·les·ta (seles′ta) *n.* Musical instrument consisting of metal plates struck with hammers played from a keyboard.

ce·les·tial (seles′chal) *adj.* 1. Of the sky; ~ **equator**, great circle of celestial sphere, formed by plane cutting through Earth's center at right angles to its axis (so called because when sun is at the equator, day and night are of equal length); ~ **guidance**, guidance system for spacecraft or missile that navigates automatically by reference to celestial bodies; ~ **sphere**, imaginary sphere on which the heavenly bodies appear to lie, having its center at the center of the Earth (or at the point where the observer stands) and an infinite radius. 2.

Ceilings may reflect the structure or the style of a building. Top left: The 17th-century ceilings of Sudbury Hall, Derbyshire, U.K., are of the Caroline period. The ceiling paintings were commissioned from the Frenchman, Louis Laguerre. Top right: In the vaulting of the roof of Norwich Cathederal, U.K.

Heavenly, divine; divinely good, beautiful, etc. 3. Chinese; **C~ Empire**, (transl. of native title) the former Chinese Empire. **ce·les′-tial·ly** *adv.*

cel·i·bate (sel′ibit, -bāt) *n. & adj.* (Person) remaining unmarried, abstaining from sexual relations, esp. by religious vow. **cel·i·ba·cy** (sel′i-basē) *n.*

cell (sel) *n.* 1. Hermit's one-roomed dwelling. 2. Single per-

the builders achieved a sublime decorative effect with the revealed structural members. Left: The lead ceiling of Wolsey's closet at Hampton Court, London, is an heraldic expression of Tudor ambition. Right: Ceilings at Badminton House, Gloucestershire (now Avon), are the work of Robert Adam.

son's small room in monastery etc.; similar small, confining room in prison or other place of detention. 3. (biol.) Unit of structure of living matter, mass of protoplasm bounded by a membrane (~ **wall**) and usu. containing a nucleus. 4. (zool.) Small container of earth, silk, wax, etc., in which larva or pupa develops, esp. in comb of social insects, e.g. bees. 5. (elect.) Voltaic apparatus with only one pair of metallic elements, unit of battery. 6. (fig.) Small group or single person working in factory, particular district, etc., as nucleus of political, esp. revolutionary, activity; headquarters of such group etc.

cel·la (sĕl´*a*) *n.* (pl. **cel·lae** pr. sĕl´ē). (Gk. and Rom. antiq.) Principal chamber of temple.

cel·lar (sĕl´*er*) *n.* Underground room or vault, used for storage, etc; wine cellar, stock of wines. **cel·lar·age** (sĕl´*er*ĭj) *n.* Fee for storage in cellar; cellar space.

cel·lar·et (sĕlerĕt´) *n.* Case or sideboard for holding bottles of wine etc.

Cel·li·ni (chelē´nē), **Benvenuto** (1500–71). Florentine goldsmith and sculptor, famous also for his *Autobiography*.

cel·lo, 'cel·lo (chĕl´ō) *ns.* (pl. **-los**). Instrument of the violin family, four-stringed and held upright on floor by seated player, lower in tone than viola and higher than double bass, having very wide range. **cel'list, 'cel'list** *ns.*

cel·lo·phane (sĕl´*o*fān) *n.* Thin transparent material made of cellulose and used as wrapping etc.

cel·lu·lar (sĕl´*y*uler) *adj.* Of, having, consisting of, cells; porous.

cel·lule (sĕl´ūl) *n.* Small cell.

Cel·lu·loid (sĕl´*y*uloid) *n.* (trademark) Solid inflammable material consisting essentially of soluble cellulose nitrate and camphor, used in the manufacture of photographic film and many other items.

cel·lu·lose (sĕl´*y*ulōs) *n.* (chem.) Carbohydrate that forms chief constituent of cell walls of all plants and of textiles such as cotton and linen. ~ **acetate**, acetic ester of cellulose, used to make rayon, plastics, etc.; ~ **nitrate**, nitric ester of cellulose, a constituent of smokeless gunpowders and of cordite, celluloid, etc. **cel·lu·lo·sic** (sĕl*y*ulōsĭk) *adj.*

Cels. *abbrev.* Celsius.

Cel·si·us (sĕl´sē*u*s, -shē-, -sh*u*s), **Anders** (1701–44). Swedish astronomer; inventor of the centigrade scale for measuring temperature; hence = CENTIGRADE (abbreviated C).

Celt (sĕlt, kĕlt) *n.* 1. Member of one of the ancient peoples of W. Europe; Gaul. 2. One of the peoples speaking languages related to those of the ancient Gauls, including Bretons, Cornish, Welsh, Irish, Manx, and Gaels.

celt (sĕlt) *n.* Prehistoric bronze, stone, or iron ax.

Cel·tic (sĕl´tĭk, kĕl´-) *adj.* Of the Celts; of the branch of the Indo-European family of languages spoken by the ancient Celts or their modern representatives; ~ *n.* Celtic language. **Cel·ti·cism** (sĕl´tĭsĭz*e*m, kĕl´-) *n.*

The salt-cellar by **Benvenuto Cellini** shows the figures of Neptune and Earth worked in gold and enamels. The piece was made for Francis I, King of France, who became Cellini's patron in 1540.

The Christian **Celts** of Ireland adopted Gallic drystone walling techniques and the oversailing vault when they built small churches, such as the Oratory of Gallus at Dingle in County Kerry.

ce·ment (sĭmĕnt´) *n.* Any compound substance, esp. of lime or other stone, ground to powder and mixed with water, which hardens rapidly into stony consistency, used for binding together stones or bricks, covering floors, walls, etc.; similar substance mixed with sand and gravel etc. to form concrete; plastic material for filling tooth cavities; any adhesive material used to mend small articles of glass, china, etc.; (fig.) link or bond of union. ~ *v.t.* Unite firmly with

or as with cement; coat or line wit cement. **ce·men·ta·tion** (sēmĕn tā´shon) *n.*

cem·e·ter·y (sĕm´ĭtĕrē) *n.* (p -ter·ies). Place for burying th dead, graveyard.

cen·o·taph (sĕn´*o*tăf) *n.* Sepul chral monument to person whos body is buried elsewhere.

Ce·no·zo·ic (sēnozō´ĭk, sĕn*o* *adj.* & *n.* (geol.) (Of) the era o group of systems following th Mesozoic and including the presen era, characterized by the firs appearance of birds and mammals sometimes = TERTIARY.

cen·ser (sĕn´ser) *n.* Vessel i which incense is burned.

cen·sor (sĕnser) *n.* 1. (Rom antiq.) Either of two magistrate

From the Parthenon, Athens, this figure of a **centaur** triumphing over a dead Lapith portrays the violence embodied in the fabulous creature. The Lapiths of Thessaly suffered attacks by savage mountain tribes, represented here by the centaur.

cent (sĕnt) *n.* 1. **percent'**, (often written $^0/_0$), for (in, to) every 100, esp. in stating rates of interest etc. 2. $\frac{1}{100}$ of various monetary units, esp. the dollar, Netherlands florin, etc; coin worth one cent, penny.

cent. *abbrev.* Century.

cen·taur (sĕn'tôr) *n.* 1. (Gk. myth.) Fabulous creature with head, trunk, and arms of man joined to body and legs of horse. 2. **the C~**, (astron.) the southern constellation Centaurus.

cen·tau·ry (sĕn'tôrē) *n.* (pl. **-ries**). Any of various plants of the genus *Centaurium* (including *C. pulchellum* and *C. umbellatum*), whose medicinal properties were supposed to have been discovered by Chiron the Centaur; American knapweed (*Centaurea americana*).

cen·ta·vo (sĕntah'vō) *n.* (pl. **-vos** pr. -vŏz, -vōs). $\frac{1}{100}$ of a peso or similar unit of currency in various republics of S. America and elsewhere; a coin of this denomination.

cen·te·nar·i·an (sĕntenār'ēan) *adj. & n.* (Person) 100 years old or more.

cen·te·nar·y (sĕn'tenĕrē; *Brit.* sĕntēn'erē, -tē'nerē) *adj. & n.* (pl. **-nar·ies**). (Of) 100 years; (celebration of) 100th anniversary.

cen·ten·ni·al (sĕntĕn'ēal) *adj.* Of, having lived or lasted, completing, 100 years; of the 100th anniversary. **~** *n.* 100th anniversary.

cen·ter, *Brit.* **cen·tre** (sĕn'ter) *ns.* 1. Middle point of circle, sphere, line, etc.; middle point or part of anything; point, line, upon which a body turns or revolves. 2. Point of concentration, attraction, or dispersion, nucleus, source; place, building(s), etc., forming central point or main area (as **civic ~, health ~**). 3. Person, thing, occupying central position; (football etc.) player in middle of line or field of players; (pol.) persons of moderate opinions. 4. **~ of attraction**, (phys. etc.) point to which bodies tend by gravity etc.; point or object drawing general interest; **~ of gravity**, point about which all parts of a body exactly balance each other, so that if this point is supported the body remains at rest. 5. **cen'terboard**, plate lowered through slot in keel of sailboat to increase stability and check leeway; **cen'terfold**, two-page spread at middle of magazine; **cen'terpiece**, flower arrangement or other ornament for center of dining table. **cen'ter·less, cen'tric, cen·tri·cal** (sĕn'trĭkal) *adjs.*

The use of incense to promote a sense of worship has a long history. The **censer** in which the incense smoulders is often of intricate pierced metal to allow smoke to escape.

Growing in open, dry ground, the common **centaury** bears clusters of pink flowers in late summer. It grows to a height of 12–18 ins., and may have tonic properties.

who drew up the register or census of citizens and supervised public morals; hence, any person supervising or criticizing the morals and conduct of others. 2. Official inspecting books, letters, newspapers, etc., to ensure that they contain nothing immoral, seditious, or unacceptable to military or other authorities. **cen'sor·ship** *n.* **cen'sor** *v.t.* Act as censor to; make excisions or changes in for reasons of morality, national security, politics, etc. **cen'sor·a·ble** *adj.*

cen·so·ri·al (sĕnsōr'ēal, -sôr'-) *adj.* Of a censor; censorious.

cen·so·ri·ous (sĕnsōr'ēus, -sôr'-) *adj.* Severely critical, faultfinding. **cen·so'ri·ous·ly** *adv.* **cen·so'ri·ous·ness** *n.*

cen·sure (sĕn'sher) *n.* Expression of disapproval or blame, reprimand. **~** *v.t.* (**-sured, -sur·ing**). Criticize harshly and unfavorably. **cen'sur·a·ble** *adj.*

cen·sus (sĕn'sus) *n.* (pl. **-sus·es**). 1. Official counting of population with various statistics. 2. (Rom. antiq.) Registration of citizens and property for taxation.

center *v.* (**-ered, -er·ing**). Be concentrated, have center *in, on, at,* etc.; place in or as in center; (football etc.) pass (ball) to or from center.

cen·tes·i·mal (sĕntĕs´imal) *adj.* Reckoning, reckoned, by $\frac{1}{100}$.

cen·ti- *prefix.* $\frac{1}{100}$ of.

cen·ti·grade (sĕn´tigrād) *adj.* Divided into 100 degrees; (abbreviated C) of, measured by, **C ~ scale**, temperature scale, invented by CELSIUS, in which the freezing point and the boiling point of water are taken as 0 degrees and 100 degrees respectively (Celsius is now the preferred term in technical use).

cen·ti·gram, *Brit.* **cen·ti·gramme** (sĕn´tigrăm) *ns.* (abbreviated cg) $\frac{1}{100}$ of a gram.

cen·ti·li·ter, Brit. **cen·ti·li·tre** (sĕn´tilēter) *ns.* (abbreviated cl) $\frac{1}{100}$ of a liter.

cen·time (sahntēm´) *n.* $\frac{1}{100}$ of a franc or similar unit of currency; a coin of this denomination.

cen·ti·me·ter, Brit. **cen·ti·me·tre** (sĕn´timēter) *ns.* (abbreviated cm) $\frac{1}{100}$ of a meter, or 0.3937 (nearly $\frac{2}{5}$) of an inch; **~ -gram-second**, (abbreviated CGS, cgs) applied to a system of units of measurement based on the centimeter, gram, and second as units of length, mass, and time.

cen·ti·pede (sĕn´tipēd) *n.* Wingless wormlike animal of the class Chilopoda, having many segments and a pair of legs attached to each segment.

cen·tral (sĕn´tral) *adj.* Of, in, at, from, containing, the center; leading, principal, dominant; **~ bank**, main bank of a country, responsible for influencing the conduct of all other banks and financial institutions in pursuance of the government's monetary policy; **~ heating**, heating of building from a central source, as by circulating hot water, steam, or air through

Centrifugal force is utilized by industry, sciences, and also in the entertainment industry. Here, patrons on this ride feel themselves flung outwards by the force.

pipes or vents; **C ~ Powers**, (before 1914) Germany and Austria-Hungary; (during World War I) these two countries plus Bulgaria and Turkey. **cen·tral·i·ty** (sĕn·trăl´ītē) *n.* (pl. **-ties**). **cen´tral·ly** *adv.*

Cen·tral (sĕn´tral) **African Republic.** Republic between Cameroon Republic and Sudan, formerly a French colony; capital, Bangui.

Cen·tral (sĕn´tral) **America.** Region of the Western Hemisphere between Mexico and Colombia.

The **centipede** *(below) lives under a stone or in the bark of a tree. It preys on earthworms and insects. In the tropics some varieties may grow to nearly 8 ins. long.*

cen·tral·ism (sĕn´tralĭzem) *n* Centralizing system. **cen´tral·is** *adj. & n.*

cen·tral·ize (sĕn´tralīz) *v* (**-ized, -iz·ing**). 1. Come, bring, t a center. 2. Concentrate (administrative powers) in single center in stead of distributing them amon local departments; bring (countr etc.) under this system. **cen·tral·i·za·tion** (sĕntralīza´shon) *n.*

cen·tre (sĕn´ter) *n. & v.* (**-tred -tring**) (Brit.). Center.

cen·trif·u·gal (sĕntrĭf´yugal -trĭf´u-) *adj.* Flying, tending to fly from center; **~ force**, force i direction away from center. **cen·trif´u·gal·ly** *adv.*

cen·tri·fuge (sĕn´trifūj) *n.* Cen

The **Central African Republic** *covers an area of over 238,000 sq. miles. I has a mainly agricultural economy although there is some gold and dia mond mining.*

Lower left: A **cephalopod** (Verania sigula) uses its powerful arms to attack another mollusk. Top left: The Octopus vulgaris is found in the Mediterranean Sea and the Atlantic. It has 8 arms with rows of suckers on each, and grows to about 10 ft. in diameter. Below right: the nautilus has survived 200 million years in this form. Its shell has many chambers or septa, the largest of which is inhabited by the animal.

trifugal machine, esp. one for separating cream from milk, or for drying objects, by rotary motion. ~ *v.t.* (**-fuged, -fug·ing**). Subject to action of a centrifuge. **cen·trif·u·ga·tion** (sĕntrĭfyugā′shon, -trĭfu-) *n.*

cen·trip·e·tal (sĕntrĭp′etal) *adj.* Tending toward the center.

cen·tu·ri·on (sĕntoor′ēon, -tūr′-) *n.* (Rom. antiq.) Commander of a century.

cen·tu·ry (sĕn′churē) *n.* (pl. **-ries**). 1. (Rom. antiq.) Company in army, orig. of 100 men; each of the 193 political divisions by which the Roman people voted. 2. 100 years, esp. each successive period of 100 years reckoning from a fixed date, e.g. the assumed date of Christ's birth; ~ **plant**, plant of the genus *Agave*, esp. *A. americana*, supposed to flower once in 100 years, but often flowering after only five.

ce·phal·ic (sefăl′ĭk) *adj.* Of, in, the head; ~ **index**, number indicating the ratio of transverse to longitudinal diameter of skull.

ceph·a·lo·pod (sĕf′alopŏd) *n.* Animal of the class Cephalopoda, the most highly organized class of Mollusca, characterized by head with tentacles attached and including octopus, squid, etc.

ceph·a·lo·tho·rax (sĕfalōthŏr′-ăks, -thŏr′-) *n.* (pl. **-tho·rax·es, -tho·ra·ces** pr. -thŏr′asēz, -thŏr′-). (zool.) In some arthropods, part of body formed by fusion of head and thorax.

Left: Grain being loaded on ship. Above: Cereal crops were developed from grasses, the first probably being wheat. This was not grown in America where maize predominated. Barley was used for bread until the 16th century. Rye was grown on land too poor for wheat.

ce·ram·ic (serăm'ĭk) *adj.* Of (the art of) pottery; of (making of) substances etc. produced by firing of minerals, esp. clay, at very high temperatures. **ceramic** *n.*; product produced by ceramics. **ce·ram'ics** *n.* Ceramic art. **cer·a·mist** (sĕr'amĭst) *n.*

Cer·ber·us (sĕr'berus). (Gk. myth.) The three-headed (acc. to Hesiod, 50-headed) dog guarding the entrance to Hades.

cere (sēr) *n.* Naked waxlike membrane at base of beak in some birds.

ce·re·al (sēr'ēal) *adj.* Of an edible grain, as wheat, oats, or corn. ~ *n.* (freq. pl.) (Any) grain or grassy plants cultivated for their seed as human food; an article of food (esp. as breakfast dish) made from cereal. [f. CERES]

cer·e·bel·lum (sĕrebĕl'um) *n.* (pl. **-bel·lums, -bel·la** pr. -bĕl'a). Little brain, posterior part of brain, highly developed in mammals and concerned in coordination of movement and maintenance of equilibrium; see BRAIN.

cer·e·bral (sĕr'ebral, serē'-) *adj.* 1. Of the brain or cerebrum; ~ **hemisphere**, either of the two halves into which the cerebrum is divided longitudinally by a deep fissure; ~ **palsy**: see PALSY. 2. Intellectual.

cer·e·bra·tion (sĕrebrā'shon) *n.* Working of the brain. **cer·e·brate** (ser'ebrāt) *v.i.* (**-brat·ed, -brat·ing**). Think (about).

cerebro- *prefix.* Of the cerebrum; **cerebrospi'nal**, of the brain

and spinal cord; **cerebrospi'nal fluid**, solution of salts and protein filling cavities of brain and spinal cord; **cerebrospi'nal meningitis**, inflammation of the meninges of brain and spinal cord.

cer·e·brum (sĕr'ebrum) *n.* (pl. **-brums, -bra** pr. -bra). Great brain, convoluted mass of tissue forming the anterior and, in the higher vertebrates, largest part of the brain, in man filling nearly the whole skull; see BRAIN.

cere·cloth (sēr'klawth, -klŏth) *n.* (pl. **-cloths** pr. -klawdhz, -klŏdhz, -klawths, -klŏths). Waxed cloth, esp. for wrapping the dead.

cere·ment (sēr'ment, sĕr'ement) *n.* (usu. pl.). Cerecloth.

cer·e·mo·ni·al (sĕremō'nēal) *adj.* With or of ritual or ceremony, formal. ~ *n.* System of rites; formalities proper to any occasion; observance of convention. **cer·e·mo'ni·al·ly** *adv.*

cer·e·mo·ni·ous (sĕremō'nēus) *adj.* Accompanied with rites; according to prescribed or customary formalities; punctilious in observing formalities. **cer·e·mo'·ni·ous·ly** *adv.* **cer·e·mo'ni·ous·ness** *n.*

cer·e·mo·ny (sĕr'emōnē) *n.* (pl. **-nies**). 1. Outward rite or observance; solemnity; empty form. 2. Usage of courtesy, politeness, or civility; formalities, observance of conventions; **stand on** ~, insist on punctilious observance of formalities.

Ce·res (sēr'ēz). 1. (Rom. myth.) Goddess of agriculture, identified

by the Romans with DEMETER an in this later cult worshipped as cor and earth goddess. 2. (astron Largest of the asteroids.

ce·rise (serēs', -rēz') *n. & adj,* Moderate to deep red, cherry rec

ce·ri·um (sēr'eum) *n.* (chem. Element of rare-earth group, re sembling iron in color and luster symbol Ce, at. no. 85, at. w 140.12.

cer·met (sĕr'mĕt) *n.* Alloy o ceramic substance with metal.

cert. *abbrev.* Certificate; certi fied.

cer·tain (sĕr'tin) *adj.* 1. Settled fixed, unfailing; unerring, reliable sure to happen; sure *to* do; in dubitable, indisputable. 2. Con vinced, confident (*of, that*); sure. 3 That might but need not be speci fied; occas., that it would not b polite to specify; of positive ye restricted amount, degree, etc.; a particular, a definite (person etc.) 4. **for** ~, for a certainty.

cer·tain·ly (sĕr'tinlē) *adv.* 1 Indubitably; infallibly; confidently admittedly. 2. (in answers) I admi it; of course; no doubt, yes.

cer·tain·ty (sĕr'tintē) *n.* (pl **-ties**). Thing certain or sure; being certain.

cer·tif·i·cate (sertĭf'ikĭt) *n* Document formally attesting a fact esp. the bearer's status, acquire ments, fulfillment of conditions right to company shares, etc. **cer·tif·i·cate** (sertĭf'ikāt) *v.t.* (**-cat·ed, -cat·ing**). Furnish with, license by, certificate. **cer·ti·fi·ca·tion** (sĕrtĭfikā'shon) *n.*

cer·ti·fy (sĕr'tifī) *v.t.* (**-fied, -fy·ing**). 1. Attest formally, declare by certificate; (chiefly Brit.) declare by certificate (of doctor etc.) to be insane; **certified public account·ant**, accountant holding legal certificate of professional competence. 2. Inform certainly, assure. **cer·ti·fi·a·ble** *adj.* (esp. of lunatic or lunacy). **cer·ti·fi·a·bly** *adv.*

cer·ti·o·ra·ri (sĕrsheorār'ī) *n.* Writ from higher court calling for records of case tried in lower court. [LL., = "to be informed," occurring in original writ]

cer·ti·tude (sĕr'tĭtood, -tūd) *n.* Feeling certain, conviction; freedom from doubt.

ce·ru·le·an (serōō'lēan) *adj.* Deep blue; sky blue; ~ **blue**, pigment of this color prepared from cobalt.

ce·ru·men (serōō'men) *n.* Yellow waxy secretion in the external canal of the ear. **ce·ru'mi·nous** *adj.*

Cer·van·tes (servăn'tēz; *Sp.* thĕrvahn'tĕs), **Miguel de** (1547–1616). Spanish novelist and dramatist, author of *Don Quixote* (1605–15).

cer·vi·cal (sĕr'vĭkal) *adj.* (anat.)

The rich variety of **ceramics** is the product of local materials, skills and tastes. Left: A ram-shaped aquamanile of buffware with a green glaze is decorated with pellets. It was found near Scarborough, Yorkshire, U.K., where it was made in the late 13th century. Below: This painted Ancient Greek vase was probably produced in the 6th century BC.

Above: Greek potters produced work of great variety. These storage jars may have been used for keeping grain or olives. The wide necks of the jars would leave the contents accessible to a scoop or ladle. Left: A Chinese neolithic jar painted in a monochrome design, part of which is linear, dark on a light ground, and part in reverse, light on a dark ground, showing an advanced grasp of decorative techniques with simple color. Right: A porcelain figure made in England at the Chelsea works, c. 1765. Underneath, it bears the gold anchor mark of the maker. Its modeling and many colored glazes make it a fine quality piece.

'A Man with a Pipe' was painted by **Paul Cézanne** a Neo-Impressionist of genius. While he was no theorist, his remark that painters should look for the cone, sphere and cube in Nature was taken as law by Cubists.

In common with many of the Fringilla genus, the **chaffinch** is useful as an eater of weed seeds. Chaffinches of northern areas migrate to the Mediterranean in fall.

The republic of **Chad** covers an area of about 496,000 sq. miles. In the sou the terrain is of savanna and woodlar types, and in the north the land is de ert. The photograph shows a nativ horn player.

Of the neck; of the cervix of an organ.

cer·vine (sĕr'vīn) adj. Of, like, deer.

cer·vix (sĕr'vĭks) n. (pl. **cer·-vix·es, cer·vi·ces** pr. sĕr'visēz, servī'-). (anat.) Neck; necklike structure, esp. neck of the uterus.

ce·si·um, cae·si·um (sē'zēum) ns. (chem.) Rare alkali metal element discovered spectroscopically by Bunsen in 1861; symbol Cs, at. no. 55, at. wt. 132.9054. [L. caesius bluish-gray, f. the distinctive lines in its spectrum]

ces·sa·tion (sĕsā'shon) n. Ceasing, pause.

ces·sion (sĕsh'on) n. Ceding, giving up.

cess·pool (sĕs'pōol) n. Well sunk to receive sewage etc., retaining solid matter and allowing liquid to escape; (fig.) any filthy or morally corrupt place.

ce·ta·cean (sĭta'shon) adj. & n. (Member) of the Cetacea, an order of marine mammals, including whales, dolphins, porpoises, etc.

ce·ta'ceous adj. [Gk. kētos whale]

Cey·lon (sĭlŏn'). Name until 1972 of SRI LANKA. **Cey·lo·nese** (sēlonēz', -nēs') adj. & n. (pl. **-nese**).

Cé·zanne (sĕzăn'), **Paul** (1839–1906). French painter, central figure of the movements known as Impressionism and Post-Impressionism.

Cf. symbol. Californium.

cf. abbrev. Compare. [L. confer compare]

C.G. abbrev. Coast Guard; commanding general; consul general.

Cg. abbrev. Centigram(s).

c.g. abbrev. Center of gravity.

cgs, c.g.s., CGS abbrevs. Centimeter-gram-second.

Ch. abbrev. Chaplain; chapter China; Chinese; Church.

Chab·lis (shăblē') n. Dry whit wine produced near Chablis, in N Burgundy, France.

cha·conne (shăkŭn', -kŏn') n Old stately Spanish dance; instru mental composition in ¾ time wit an unchanging harmonic patter against which the upper parts ar varied (cf. PASSACAGLIA, which i resembles).

Chad (chăd). Republic of N central Africa extending from Lak Chad across the E. Sudan; capita Ndjaména (formerly Fort Lamy) **Lake C~**, lake in N. centra Africa bordered by Chad, Niger and Nigeria, from 5,000 to 10,000 square miles (12,500 to 25,000 sq km) in area, depending on rainfall **Chad'i·an** adj. & n.

Chad·wick (chăd'wĭk), **Si James** (1891–). English physi cist; discovered the neutron, carried on research on radioactivity and nuclear fission; Nobel Prize for physics 1935.

chafe (chāf) v. (**chafed, chaf·ing**). 1. Rub (skin etc.) to restore warmth or sensation; rub so as to abrade or injure the surface. 2. Irritate; show irritation, fume, fret. ~ n. Rubbing; chafing.

chaf·er (chā'fer) n. Large slow-moving beetle, esp. COCKCHAFER.

chaff (chăf, chahf) n. 1. Husks of grain separated by threshing or winnowing; chopped hay and straw for feeding cattle. 2. Refuse, worthless stuff. 3. Teasing; banter. ~ v. Tease, make fun of.

chaf·fer (chăf'er) n. & v. Haggle, bargain.

chaf·finch (chăf'ĭnch) n. European songbird (Fringilla coelebs)

The fiercest of the **cetaceans**, the killer whale hunts in packs of up to 50 strong. Top right: A common dolphin. Below: A common porpoise.

Common Dolphin

Killer Whale

Common Porpoise

*The **chair** in various forms has evolved over a period of at least 5,000 years. Left to right: Early 19th-century English chair with fruitwood back and elm seat and legs; the 'Shaker', an early American slat-backed armchair; the ornate chair in Japanese beech,*

1730 (Temple Newsam House, Leeds), bearing the label of Giles Grendey of London, was part of a suite made for a Spanish nobleman. Left: An ancient Egyptian child's chair and footstool. Furniture was sometimes entombed with its illustrious owner on his death.

with blue crown in male and white wing patches.

chaf·ing (chā'fĭng) **dish.** Dish set above a heating device to cook or keep food warm at table.

Cha·gall (shahgahl'), **Marc** (1887–). Russian impressionist and cubist artist who has lived mostly in France and U.S.

cha·grin (shagrĭn') *n.* Acute disappointment, mortification. ~ *v.t.* (**-grined** or **-grinned, -grin·ing** or **-grin·ning**). Vex acutely, mortify, by thwarting or disappointment.

chain (chān) *n.* 1. Flexible string of connected metal links. 2. (pl.) Fetters, bonds; confinement, restraint. 3. Personal ornament in form of chain around neck. 4. Connected course, train, or series (of events, objects, mountains, etc.); series of branch businesses. 5. Surveyor's measuring rod of 100 jointed iron rods called links; the length of this, 66 ft. (24.1 m). 6. (chem.) Atoms (usu. of carbon) joined in series in a molecule. 7. ~ **armor**, armor of interlaced links or rings, mail; ~ **gang**, gang of convicts chained together at work etc.; ~ **letter**, letter of which the recipient is asked to make copies to be sent to a specified number of others, these being asked to do the like in their turn; ~ **link fence**, fence of linked thick steel wires; ~ **mail**, chain armor; ~ **reaction**, chemical reaction forming intermediate products that react with the original substance and are repeatedly renewed; (phys.) self-sustaining nuclear reaction, as a

series of fissions; ~ **saw**, power saw with teeth on endless chain; ~ **smoker**, one who lights another cigarette etc. from the stump of the last smoked; ~ **-smoke** (*v.*); ~ **smoking**; ~ **stitch**, embroidery or crochet stitch resembling links of a chain; ~ **store**, one of a series of retail stores belonging to one firm and selling the same goods. **chain** *v.t.* Secure, confine, with chain.

chair (chār) *n.* 1. Seat for one person; movable, usu. four-legged, seat with rest for the back. 2. Seat, position, of authority, state, or dignity; seat occupied by person presiding at meeting etc.; seat, office, of mayor, university professor, etc. 3. (hist.) Sedan. 4. (slang) Electric chair. 5. ~ **lift**, series of chairs on endless cable for carrying passengers up mountain etc. **chair** *v.t.* Act as chairman of, preside over, (meeting).

chair·man (chār'man) *n.* (pl. **-men** pr. -men). (fem. formerly **chair·wom·an**, pr. chār'woŏmĭn; pl. **-wom·en** pr. -wĭmĭn) Person chosen to preside over meeting, permanent president of committee, board, etc. **chair'man·ship** *n.* Office etc. of chairman.

chair·per·son (chār'pér̄son) *n* Chairman or chairwoman.

chaise (shāz, shĕz) *n.* 1. Ligh open carriage for one or two persons, esp. a two-wheeled one drawn by one horse. 2. Chaise longue.

chaise longue (shāz lawng', chāz, shĕz) (pl. **chaise longues,** *Fr.* **chaises longues**). Kind of long low chair with seat long enough to support sitter's outstretched legs. [Fr.]

chal·ced·o·ny (kălsĕd'onē, kăl'sedōnē) *n.* (pl. **-nies**). Precious or semiprecious stone, a cryptocrystalline form of silica with waxlike luster; including agate, cornelian, onyx, etc.

Chal·cis (kăl'sĭs). Ancient Greek city on Euboea Island; invasion point for campaign against Greece by Persians; scene of death of Aristotle.

Chal·de·a (kăldē'a). Country of the Chaldeans, freq. identified in the Old Testament with Babylonia.

Chal·de·an (kăldē'an) *adj. & n.* (Member) of a Semitic people originating from Arabia, who settled in the neighborhood of Ur and were later merged with the Babylonians; (of) their language.

cha·let (shălā', shăl'ā; *Fr.* shălā') *n.* (pl. **cha·lets** pr. shălāz', shăl'āz; *Fr.* shălā'). Swiss peasant's wooden house or cottage; villa or vacation cottage built in this style.

Cha·lia·pin (shahlyah'pĭn), **Fyodor Ivanovich** (1873–1938). Russian-born French operatic basso and concert singer.

chal·ice (chăl'ĭs) *n.* Goblet,

Marc Chagall is famous for his paintings such as 'L'Anniversaire' (The Birthday) shown above. He was also an accomplished stage designer.

eucharistic wine cup; cup-shaped blossom.

chalk (chawk) *n.* Opaque white soft earthy limestone, consisting largely of calcium carbonate; used for burning into lime, making cement, and for writing etc. on blackboards or other **chalk′-boards**; colored preparation of similar texture used for drawing etc.; **chalk stripe, -striped**, (with) pattern of thin white stripes on dark ground; **chalk talk**, (slang) lecture, talk, illustrated by drawings or diagrams on blackboard. **chalk** *v.t.* Rub, mark, draw, write, etc., with chalk; ~ **it up (to)**, charge it (to) (person etc.); ~ **up**, score, register (success). **chalk′y** *adj.* (**chalk·i·er, chalk·i·est**). Abounding in, white as, chalk. **chalk′i·ness** *n.*

chal·lah (χah′la; *Heb.* χahlah′) *n.* (pl. **chal·lahs**; *Heb.* **chal·loth** pr. χahlawt′). Loaf of bread, usu. braided before baking, specially prepared for the Jewish Sabbath. [Heb.]

chal·lenge (chăl′ĭnj) *n.* I. Demand to respond, explain, justify, esp. sentry's demand for password etc. 2. (law etc.) Exception taken (to a prospective juror, a vote, etc.). 3. Summons to trial or contest, esp. duel; defiance. 4. Stimulating problem, demanding task. ~ *v.t.* (**-lenged, -leng·ing**). I. Call to account. 2. Take exception to; dispute, deny. 3. Claim (attention, admiration, etc.). 4. Invite to play against, fight duel, etc.; defy. **chal′lenge·a·ble** *adj.* **chal′-leng·er** *n.*

chal·lis, chal·lie (shăl′ē) *ns.* Lightweight soft clothing fabric.

Châ·lons (shălawṅ′). Place on the Marne, France, scene of the defeat of the Huns under Attila in 451 A.D. by the Romans and Visigoths.

cham·ber (chām′ber) *n.* I. Room, esp. bedroom (poet. or archaic); (also **burial** ~) compartment or cavity used for burial; (pl.) judge's room for hearing cases etc. not needing to be taken in court. 2. (Hall used by) deliberative or judicial body, one of the houses of a legislature; ~ **of commerce**, association to promote and protect business and commercial interests locally. 3. (also ~ **pot**) Toilet pan or pot used in bedroom etc. for urination and defecation. 4. Cavity in animal body; enclosed space in mechanism, esp. part of gun bore in which charge is placed; in a revolver, each compartment of a cylinder holding a cartridge. 5. **cham′bermaid**, housemaid who cleans and straightens up bed-rooms, now chiefly in hotels; **chamber music**, classical music for small instrumental groups; chamber orchestra, small orchestra.

cham·ber·lain (chām′berlĭn) *n.* Officer managing household of sovereign or nobleman; chief steward; high-ranking officer of a royal court; (Brit.) officer receiving rents and revenues of a municipality; treasurer.

Cham·ber·lain (chām′berlĭn), **(Arthur) Neville** (1869–1940). British prime minister 1937–40; followed policy of appeasement toward Germany and Italy until 1939.

Cham·ber·tin (shahṅbĕrtăṅ) *n.* Dry red wine produced near Chambertin in Burgundy, France.

Cham·bord (shahṅbōr′). Village in the Loire valley in N. central France, famous for its Renaissance chateau built by Francis I.

cha·me·le·on (kamē′lēon, -mēl′yon) *n.* Saurian reptile of the genus *Chamaeleo*, small lizardlike creature with power of changing color of skin to suit surroundings;

The sure-footed **chamois** ascends mountains to the snow-line in summer and returns to wooded regions in the winter.

(fig.) variable or inconstant person. [Gk. *khamaileōn*, lit. = "ground lion"]

cham·fer (chăm´fer) *n.* Oblique surface produced by beveling square edge or corner. ~ *v.t.* Give chamfer to; make oblique; flute.

cham·ois (shăm´ē) *n.* (pl. **cham·ois, cham·oix** pr. shăm´ēz). 1. Capriform antelope (*Rupicapra rupicapra*) found in mountain ranges of Europe and Asia. 2. Soft pliable washable leather from skin of goats, sheep, deer, and split hides of other animals.

cham·o·mile (kăm´omīl, -mēl) = CAMOMILE.

Cha·mo·nix (shămawnē´). Valley and ski-resort area in E. France near Mont Blanc.

champ[1] (chămp), **chomp** (chŏmp) *vbs.* Munch (fodder) noisily; bite hard upon (bit); making chewing action or noise; ~ **at the bit**, be impatient.

champ[2] (chămp) *n.* (colloq.) Champion.

cham·pagne (shămpān´) *n.* Sparkling white wine bottled before fermentation has ceased, made in region of Champagne, France; similar wine made elsewhere.

cham·pi·on (chăm´pēon) *n.* 1. Fighting man, combatant; person who fights, argues, etc., for another or for a cause. 2. Person (esp. boxer, athlete), animal, plant, etc., that has defeated, or been judged superior to, all competitors. **cham´pi·on·ship** *n.* **cham´pi·on** *adj.* That is a champion. **champion** *v.t.* Fight for, maintain the cause of.

Cham·plain (shămplăn´), **Samuel de** (1567?-1635). French explorer of the St. Lawrence River and of the area from Great Lakes to E. Canada; founded Quebec, 1608;

governor of New France, 1633-5; **Lake Champlain**, lake and resort area between the borders of New York and Vermont.

champ·le·vé (shahṅlevā´) *adj.* & *n.* (Enamelwork) of which the metal ground is hollowed out and the spaces filled with enamel (cf. CLOISONNÉ). [Fr., = "field removed"]

Cham·pol·lion (shahṅpawlyawṅ´), **Jean François** (1790-1832). French Egyptologist; found key to deciphering hieroglyphics from study of Rosetta Stone.

Chanc. *abbrev.* Chancellor; chancery.

chance (chăns, chahns) *n.* 1. Unpredictable way in which things occur; fortune; casual or fortuitous circumstance or occurrence, accident. 2. Possibility, probability, of anything happening. 3. Absence of design or assignable cause, fortuity. 4. **by** ~, as it happens or happened; without design; **the main** ~: see MAIN[1]; **take one's chances**, take what may befall one; seize one's opportunity. **chance** *adj.* Happening by chance, fortuitous. ~ *v.*

Temperature, light and emotional stimuli govern the color changing facility of the **chameleon.** *Below (from top): Jackson's chameleon, flap-necked chameleon and the common chameleon.*

(**chanced, chanc·ing**). Happen by chance; take the risk of, hazard; ~ **on, upon**, meet or find by accident.

chan·cel (chăn´sel, chahn´-) *n.* Part of church near altar, reserved for clergy, choir, etc., and freq. enclosed by a railing or lattice [L. *cancelli* lattice bars]

chan·cel·ler·y (chăn´selerē -slerē, chahn´-) *n.* (pl. **-ler·ies**) Position, staff, department, official residence, of chancellor; office or building of embassy, consulate, or legation.

chan·cel·lor (chăn´seler, -sler chahn´-) *n.* 1. **Lord (High) C~ C~ of England**, highest officer of the British Crown, presiding in House of Lords, a member of the Cabinet, and the highest judicial functionary in England. 2. **C~ of the Exchequer**, highest finance minister of British Government and a member of the Cabinet. 3. Judge of a court of equity in some U.S. states. 4. Head of certain universities. 5. In Germany, Austria, etc., chief minister of state. **chan´cel·lor·ship** *n.*

Facing page: a chameleon shoots out its long, sticky-tipped tongue to catch a grasshopper; the tongue will rapidly retreat with the victim trapped on it.

Jackson's

Flap-necked

Common

*Renaissance artists and founders contributed a variety of forms and materials for the perfection of the **chandelier**, derived from the simple suspended candleholder in early churches.*

Chan·cel·lors·ville (chăn′sel-erzvĭl, -slerz-, chahn′-). Town in NE. Virginia; site of a Civil War Confederate victory in which the Union's Gen. Hooker failed to break through Lee's lines; Gen. "Stonewall" Jackson was killed during this battle.

chan·cer·y (chăn′serē, chahn′-) *n.* (pl. **-cer·ies**). 1. (Brit.) Lord Chancellor's court. 2. A court in equity. 3. Office attached to embassy or consulate.

chan·cre (shăng′ker) *n.* Syphilitic ulcer. **chan′crous** *adj.*

chanc·y (chăn′sē, chahn′-) *adj.* (**chanc·i·er, chanc·i·est**). Uncertain, risky.

chan·de·lier (shăndelēr′) *n.* Ornamental branched hanging support for a number of light bulbs, candles, etc.

chan·dler (chănd′ler, chahnd′-) *n.* Dealer in candles, oil, soap, paint, and groceries; maker or seller of candles; **ship('s)** ~: see SHIP. **chan′dler·y** *n.*

change (chānj) *n.* 1. Alteration; substitution of one for another; variation, variety. 2. What may be substituted for another of the same kind, esp. in ~ **of clothes** etc. 3. Lower coins or bills given for equal value of higher ones; money returned as balance of that given in payment. 4. Any of the various orders in which a peal of bells is or may be rung; **ring the** ~**s**, go through all the changes in ringing a peal of bells; vary ways of putting or doing thing. 5. ~ **of life**, menopause. **change** *v.* (**changed, chang·ing**). 1. Take another instead of; resign, get rid of, *for*; give or get smaller or foreign coins or bills for; put on different clothes; put fresh clothes or coverings on (e.g., ~ **a baby**, replace used diaper with clean one); go from one to another; change trains; give and receive, exchange. 2. Make or become different; ~ **one's mind**, change one's purpose or opinion. 3. ~ **off**, take turns, alternate. **change′ful, change′less** *adjs.*

change·a·ble (chān′jabel) *adj.* Irregular, inconstant. **change·a·bil·i·ty** (chānjabĭl′ĭtē) *n.*

change·o·ver (chānj′ōver) *n.* Change from one system or situation to another.

chan·nel (chăn′el) *n.* 1. Natural or artificial bed of running water; comparatively narrow body of water joining two large bodies; **the C**~, the English Channel. 2. Tube or tubular passage for fluids. 3. (fig.) Course in which anything moves, direction; medium of trans-

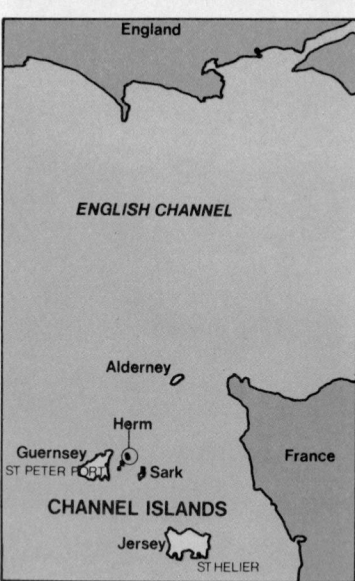

*The **Channel Islands** are known to the French as 'Iles Normandes'. The 4 main islands, Jersey, Guernsey, Alderney and Sark, total 75 sq. miles in area.*

mission, communication, etc. 4. Band of frequencies sufficiently wide for transmission of radio or television signal. 5. Groove; flute. ~ *v.t.* (**-neled, -nel·ing**, Brit. **-nelled, -nel·ling**). Form channel(s) in, groove; cut out (way etc.); (fig.) direct, as in ~ **one's energies**.

Chan·nel (chăn′el) **Islands.** Group of nine small British islands in the English Channel off the coast of Normandy, of which the largest

Charlie Chaplin in one of his earlie films, 'The Champion' (1915). began his career when only seven in clog-dancing act.

are Jersey, Guernsey, and Alde ney.

chan·nel·ize (chăn′elīz) (**-ized, -iz·ing**). Channel.

chan·son de geste (shahnsaw de zhĕst′) (pl. **chan·sons de ges** pr. shahnsawn de zhĕst′). One a group of French historical ver romances, mostly connected wi Charlemagne, composed in th 11th–13th centuries; this genre medieval French epic poem.

chant (chănt, chahnt) *n.* 1. Son

Short musical passage in two or more phrases each beginning with reciting note, for singing to unmetrical words (psalms, canticles).

Measured monotonous song, musical recitation of words; singing intonation. ~ v. Sing; utter musically; intone, sing to a chant. **chant'er** n.

chan·teuse (shäntooz′, -tooz′; *r.* shahntöz′) n. (pl. **-teuses** pr. oo′sĭz, -zĭz; *Fr.* -töz′). Female singer of popular songs, esp. in night clubs.

chant·ey (shän′tē, chän′-) n. (pl. **-eys**). Sailors' song, esp. one sung in rhythm to hauling up sails, turning capstan, etc.

chan·ti·cleer (chăn′tĭklēr, -ăn′-) n. Domestic rooster, used as proper name in medieval fables.

chan·try (chăn′trē, chahn′-) n. (pl. **-tries**). Endowment for priest(s) to say masses for founder's soul; altar or chapel so endowed.

Cha·nu·kah (χah′nookah, χnuka, hah′-; *Heb.* χahnookah′) = HANUKKAH.

cha·os (kā′ŏs) n. 1. Formless void, abyss from which cosmos was created. 2. Utter confusion. **cha·ot·ic** (kāŏt′ĭk) adj. **cha·ot′i·cal·ly** adv.

chap¹ (chăp) n. Fissure in skin caused by exposure to cold, dampness, wind, etc. ~ v. (**chapped, chap'ping**). Crack, cause to crack, in fissures.

chap² (chăp, chŏp) = CHOP².

chap³ (chăp) n. (colloq.) Man, boy, fellow.

chap·ar·ral (shăpərăl′) n. Dense tangled shrubs, esp. such as abounds on poor soil in the SW. U.S. and Mexico.

chap·book (chăp′book) n. Small pamphlet of popular tales, ballads, poems, or religious tracts of the kind formerly sold by peddlers (chapmen).

cha·peau (shăpō′) n. (pl. **-peaux, -peaus** pr. -pōz′). (colloq.) Hat. [Fr.]

chap·el (chăp′el) n. 1. Place of Christian worship smaller than and subordinate to a church, as one attached to a college, hospital, home, etc.; compartment or cell of cathedral etc. separately dedicated and with its own altar. 2. Private place of worship. 3. Chapel service. 4. Print shop, printing house; body of printers. [L. *cappella* dim. of *cappa* cape; first chapel was sanctuary in which St. Martin's sacred cloak was kept]

chap·er·on, chap·er·one (shăp′erōn) ns. Married or mature woman accompanying young unmarried woman for sake of propriety on public occasions etc. ~ v.t. Act as chaperon to. **chap′er·on·age** n. [Fr., orig. sense "hood"]

chap·fall·en (chăp′fawlen) adj. With jaw hanging down, dejected.

chap·lain (chăp′lĭn) n. Priest of chapel, clergyman officiating in private chapel or institution, on board ship, or for military unit, etc. **chap·lain·cy** n.

chap·let (chăp′lĭt) n. 1. Wreath of flowers, leaves, gems, etc., for head. 2. String of prayer beads one-third of length of rosary; string of beads as necklace. 3. Anything resembling string of beads.

Chap·lin (chăp′lĭn), **Charles Spencer ("Charlie")** (1889–1977). English-born motion picture actor, producer, director, and writer, in America 1913–52, best known for his comic roles in silent films, esp. portraying "the little tramp."

chap·man (chăp′man) n. (pl. **-men** pr. -men). (Brit. hist.) Peddler, hawker.

chaps (chăps, shăps) n.pl. Stout leather trousers without seat worn over regular trousers by cowboys as protection against thorns and bushes. [Short for Mex. Span. *chaparreras*]

chap·ter (chăp′ter) n. 1. Main division of a book or treatise (abbreviated *c.*, *cap.*, *ch.*, or *chap.*); (fig.) limited subject, piece of narrative, etc.; ~ **and verse**, exact reference. 2. General meeting or assembly of canons of cathedral or members of religious or knightly order for consultation and transaction of affairs; body of persons constituting this, esp. canons of cathedral; local branch of an organization, as of a society or fraternity.

char¹ (chär) n. (Brit. colloq.) Charwoman. ~ v.i. (**charred, char′ring**). Act as charwoman.

char² (chär) v. (**charred, char′ring**). Burn to charcoal; scorch; blacken with fire.

char³, charr (chär) ns. (pl. **chars, charrs**, collect. **char, charr**). Trout of genus *Salvelinus*, found in mountain lakes.

char·ac·ter (kăr′ĭkter) n. 1. Distinctive mark, brand; graphic sign or symbol, esp. graphic symbol standing for sound, syllable, or notion, used in writing or printing; handwriting, printing; cabalistic sign or emblem. 2. Characteristic, esp. (pl.) distinguishing features of species or genus; sum of distinguishing features of individual etc., mental and moral qualities; such qualities strongly developed or strikingly displayed; reputation, (good) repute. 3. Personage, personality; imaginary person created by novelist or dramatist or played by actor; (colloq.) odd or eccentric person; ~ **actor**, one who plays pronounced or eccentric characters. **char·ac·ter·less** adj.

char·ac·ter·is·tic (kărĭkterĭs′tĭk) adj. Distinctive, displaying the character of. ~ n. 1. Characteristic trait, mark, or quality. 2. (math.) Whole number in logarithm. **char·ac·ter·is′ti·cal·ly** adv.

char·ac·ter·ize (kăr′ĭkterīz) v.t. (**-ized, -iz·ing**). Describe character of; describe *as*; be characteristic of, impart character to. **char·ac·ter·i·za·tion** (kărĭkterĭzā′shon) n.

cha·rade (sharād′; *Brit.* sharahd′) n. Game of guessing word, phrase, or book, song, motion picture, etc. title from written or

Chaparral country provides food for an abundance of wildlife during the brief wet season. In late summer, sudden fires create the right climate for germinating this typically dense scrub.

The **Charge of the Light Brigade** in the Battle of Balaclava, Crimean War, 1854, depicted by R. Caton Woodville. The cavalry charge cost the British 40 per cent casualties.

acted clue given for each syllable, or word, or the whole; (fig.) absurd pretense. [Provençal *charrado* chatter]

char·coal (chär′kōl) *n.* Product of destructive DISTILLATION of wood or black residue of partly burned wood, bones, coal, etc.; porous, capable of reduction to powder, and (when pure) consisting wholly of carbon; ~ **gray**, a dark gray color.

chard (chärd, shärd) *n.* (also **Swiss** ~) Variety of beet with large succulent leaves used as a vegetable.

charge (chärj) *n.* 1. Quantity of anything that receptacle, piece of mechanism, etc. receives at one time; quantity of explosive for a gun or for one firing in blasting. 2. Electrical energy present in a proton or electron; such energy imparted to an object; accumulation of chemical energy in storage battery etc. available for conversion into electrical energy; NEGATIVE, POSITIVE ~: see these words; (slang) thrill, pleasure. 3. Responsibility, care, custody; task, duty; thing or person entrusted to another. 4. Price for services or goods; expenses; liability to pay money laid upon person; ~ **account**, credit account at store etc., permitting customer to receive goods in advance of billing; ~ **card** or **plate**, small metal or plastic CREDIT card, usu. valid for only one store or chain. 5. Precept, mandate, order; official instruction by judge to jury, bishop to clergy, etc. 6. Accusation, esp. that upon which prisoner is brought up for trial. 7. Impetuous attack; (mil.) signal for charge. **charge** *v.* (**charged, charg·ing**). 1. Fill to full or proper extent; fill *with*; impart electrical energy to (object), generate charge in (battery etc.). 2. Burden, entrust, *with*; command, order, enjoin, ex-

hort or instruct formally or officially. 3. Bring accusation against. 4. Subject or make liable to financial obligation or liability; demand as price or sum (*for*). 5. Make violent onset, attack or assail impetuously. **charge′a·ble** *adj.*

char·gé d'af·faires (shärzhā′-dafär′, shär′zhā; *Fr.* shärzhā dăfĕr′) *n.* (pl. **char·gés d'af·faires** pr. shärzhāz′ dafär′, shär′zhāz; *Fr.* shärzhā dăfĕr′). 1. Ambassador's deputy. 2. Low-ranking diplomatic officer or envoy serving in a country to which an ambassador or other high-ranking diplomat is not sent.

charg·er (chär′jer) *n.* (esp.) Horse ridden in charging enemy; horse ridden by officer in the field.

char·i·ot (chăr′ēot) *n.* Light two-wheeled horse-drawn vehicle used in ancient warfare and racing. **char·i·ot·eer** (chărēotēr′) *n.* Chariot driver.

cha·ris·ma (karĭz′ma) *n.* Divine gift or talent; capacity to inspire followers with devotion and enthusiasm. **char·is·mat·ic** (kărĭzmăt′-ĭk) *adj.*

char·i·ta·ble (chăr′itabel) *adj.* Liberal in giving to the poor; connected with such giving; inclined to judge favorably of persons, acts, etc. **char′i·ta·bly** *adv.* **char′i·ta·ble·ness** *n.*

char·i·ty (chăr′itē) *n.* (pl. **-ties**). 1. Christian love of fellow men; kindness, affection. 2. Disposition to judge leniently of character, acts, etc., of others. 3. Beneficence, liberality to the poor, almsgiving, alms; bequest, foundation or institution for the benefit of others, esp. the poor or helpless.

char·la·tan (shär′latan) *n.* I poster in medicine, quack; p tender to knowledge or sk pretentious imposter. **char′l tan·ism, char′la·tan·ry** *ns. ciarlare* patter]

Char·le·magne (shär′lemä Charles the Great (742–814), k of the Franks 768–814; crowned the Pope as Holy Roman Empe (as Charles I), 800.

Char·le·roi (shärlerwah′). C in S. central Belgium; site of fi battle of World War I, 1914.

Charles[1] (chärlz), "**the Grea** see CHARLEMAGNE.

Charles[2] (chärlz) (1500–5 King of Spain (as Charles I) 151 1556 and Holy Roman Emperor Charles V) 1519–56 during t Reformation; abdicated the I perial crown in favor of his brotl Ferdinand and the crown of Sp in favor of his son Philip II.

Charles[3] (chärlz). Name of t kings of Gt. Britain: **Charles** (1600–49), succeeded his fath James I in 1625; his conflict w Parliament led to the English Ci War; beheaded in 1649; **Charles** (1630–85) son of Charles I, becai king at the Restoration, 1660; **River**, short river flowing ir Boston harbor and separating B ton and Cambridge, Massachuset named after Charles I of Englan

Charles[4] (chärlz) (1948– Prince of Wales; eldest son Queen Elizabeth II of the Unit Kingdom.

Charles[5] (chärlz) (1682–171 King of Sweden (as Charles X 1697–1718; a great military co mander; defeated Peter the Great Narva, 1700, but was in tu totally defeated at Poltava, 1709.

Charles[6] (chärlz) (1403–6 King of France (as Charles VI 1422–61; defeated English Orleans, 1429, with help of Joan Arc.

Charles Mar·tel (chärlz' mär-ʹ) (689?–741). Ruler of Frankish empire; defeated the Muslims at Tours, 732; grandfather of CHARLE-MGNE.

Charles's Law (chärlz'ez). (phys.) Law that volume of gas at constant pressure expands in proportion to absolute temperature. [Jacques *Charles*, Fr. physicist (1746–1823)]

Charles·ton[1] (chärlz'ton, ärls'ton). Capital of West Virginia, in the W. central part.

Charles·ton[2] (chärlz'ton, ärls'ton). Seaport in SE. South Carolina. ~ *n.* Fast dance characterized by side kicks from the knee, popular in the 1920's; ~ *v.i.* dance this.

char·ley (chär'lē) **horse.** Stiffness or cramp of muscles, esp. in the thigh, from overexertion or injury.

char·lock (chär'lok) *n.* Wild mustard (*Brassica kaber*), a yellow-flowered annual weed.

Char·lotte (shär'lot). Industrial city in SW. North Carolina.

char·lotte (shär'lot) *n.* Dessert pudding of sponge cake or bread with filling of stewed fruits, custard, whipped cream, etc.; ~ **russe**, mold of whipped cream or custard surrounded by ladyfingers.

Char·lotte A·ma·lie (shär'lot mahl'yĕ). Formerly, St. Thomas; the capital of the U.S. Virgin Islands on the S. part of St. Thomas island.

Char·lottes·ville (shär'lotsvĭl). City in central Virginia; site of Monticello, the home of Thomas Jefferson, and Ash Lawn, home of James Monroe.

charm (chärm) *n.* 1. Word(s), act, or object having or supposed to have magic or occult power or influence; talisman; amulet; trinket worn on bracelet etc. 2. Quality, attribute, feature, etc., exciting love or admiration; (pl.) beauty. ~ *v.t.* bewitch, influence, by or as by charm or magic; endow with magic power or virtue; captivate, delight. **charmed** *adj.* (esp.) Bewitched; possessed of magic power or influence; protected, fortified, by a spell or charm. **charm'er** *n.* **charm'ing** *adj.* Fascinating; very pleasing, delightful. **charm'-ing·ly** *adv.*

char·nel (chär'nel) **house.** House or vault in which dead bodies or bones are piled.

Cha·rol·lais, Cha·ro·lais (shă-rolä') *ns.* Kind of beef cattle. [name of hills near Charolles, NW. of Lyons, France]

Char·on (kăr'on, kār'-). (Gk.

myth.) Ferryman who conveyed the souls of the dead across the Styx to Hades.

charr (chär) = CHAR.[3]

chart (chärt) *n.* 1. Map, esp. one for navigators, showing depth of sea, rocks, channels, coasts, anchorages, etc. 2. Record (by means of curves etc. on graph) of fluctuations of temperature, prices, population, etc.; any sheet with information arranged in tabular form. ~ *v.t.* Make chart of, map.

char·ter (chär'ter) *n.* 1. Written grant of privileges, rights, etc., by sovereign or legislature, esp. creating or incorporating city, college, bank, or other public or private corporation. 2. Written instrument, contract, deed, etc. 3. Privilege; publicly conceded right; **Great C~:** see MAGNA CHARTA; **People's C~:** see CHARTIST. 4. ~ **flight,** flight in which entire plane or block of seats thereon is booked by an organized group of passengers. **charter** *v.t.* 1. Grant charter to; privilege, license. 2. Hire or lease (a vehicle, ship, or plane).

Chart·ist (chär'tĭst) *n.* Member of English political reforming body, chiefly of working classes, active 1837–48, whose aims were embodied in the People's Charter, demanding adult male suffrage, annual parliaments, and equal electoral districts. **Chart'ism** *n.*

Char·tres (shär'tre, shärt; *Fr.* shär'tr). City in N. central France famous for its 13th c. Gothic cathedral.

char·treuse (shärtrōōz'; for def. 2 sometimes shärtrōōs') *n.* 1. Green or yellow liqueur of brandy and aromatic herbs, made by monks of Grande Chartreuse, the chief Carthusian monastery, near Grenoble, France. 2. Color of green chartruese, pale apple green.

char·wom·an (chär'wŏŏman) *n.* (pl. **-wom·en** pr. -wĭmĭn). (Brit.) Woman hired by the day or hour for cleaning.

char·y (chār'ē) *adj.* (**char·i·er, char·i·est**). Cautious, wary; fastidious, shy; careful (*of*); frugal, sparing (*of*).

Cha·ryb·dis (karĭb'dĭs). (Gk. legend) Dangerous whirlpool in a narrow channel (later identified with the Strait of Messina, where there is no whirlpool), opposite the cave of SCYLLA.

chase[1] (chās) *n.* 1. Pursuit; **the ~,** (the sport of) hunting. 2. Hunting ground; unenclosed park (now mainly in place-names). 3. Hunted animal; quarry. ~ *v.t.* (**chased, chas·ing**). Pursue; drive *from, out of*, etc.; (colloq.) try to obtain. **chas'er** *n.* (esp.) 1. Hunter, pursuer. 2. Small drink of water, beer, etc. taken after hard liquor.

chase[2] (chās) *n.* (print.) Frame holding composed type for page or sheet.

chase[3] (chās) *v.t.* (**chased, chas·ing**). Engrave (metal), esp. with ornament.

Chase (chās), **Salmon P(ort-land)** (1808–73). Amer. statesman and lawyer; gained prominence for defending fugitive slaves; U.S.

Three impressions of Charles I in a painting by Sir Anthony Van Dyck. The king was beheaded outside the Banqueting Hall in Whitehall in 1649. He said he was 'a martyr of the people'.

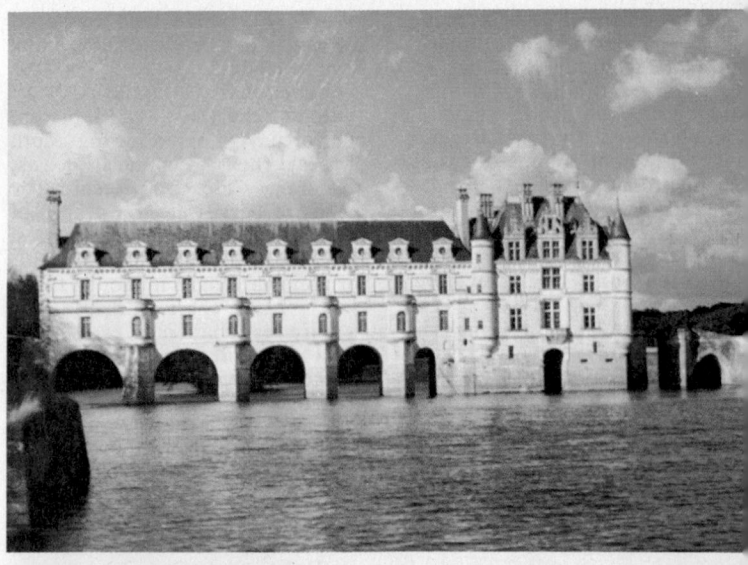

The 16th-century **Château Chenonceaux** in the Loire, France, is an example of the 'château de plaisance', a stately home, evolving from the 'château fort', a strongly fortified medieval castle.

senator, 1849–55, 1860; governor of Ohio, 1855–9; as secretary of the Treasury, 1861–4, he originated national banking system; chief justice of the U.S. Supreme Court, 1864–73.

chasm (kăz′em) *n.* Deep fissure, cleft, or gap; break, hiatus; wide and profound difference of feelings, interests, etc.

chas·sis (shăs′ē, chăs′ē, -ĭs) *n.* (pl. **chas·is** pr. shăs′ēz, chăs′ēz). Frame of gun carriage; frame of motor vehicle, aircraft, etc., with its engine, as dist. from the body; body or cabinet of machine, electronic device, etc.

chaste (chāst) *adj.* (**chast·er, chast·est**). Not having had pre-marital or extramarital sexual intercourse, virtuous, continent; undefiled, pure; decent; modest, free from excess. **chaste′ly** *adv.* **chaste′ness** *n.* **chas·ti·ty** (chăs′-tĭtē) *n.* State or quality of being chaste; ~ **belt**, device designed to prevent a woman from having sexual intercourse.

chas·ten (chā′sen) *v.t.* 1. Discipline, correct by suffering. 2. Make chaste in style etc., refine; temper, subdue.

chas·tise (chăs′tīz, chăstīz′) *v.t.* (**-tised, -tis·ing**). Punish; beat. **chas·tise′ment** *n.*

chas·u·ble (chăz′yubel, -ubel, chăs′-) *n.* Sleeveless vestment worn over all by priest at Mass.

chat¹ (chăt) *n. & v.i.* (Indulge in) familiar and easy talk. **chat′ty** *adj.* **chat′ti·ly** *adv.* **chat′ti·ness** *n.*

chat² (chăt) *n.* Any of various birds known for their chattering call, as the N. Amer. *Icteria virens* (also called **yellow-breasted** ~).

châ·teau (shătō′) *n.* (pl. **-teaus, -teaux** pr. -tōz). Castle, large mansion or country house, in France.

Cha·teau·bri·and (shătōbrē-ahn′), François René, Vicomte de (1768–1848). French author, diplomat, and political leader; one of the pioneers of the French romantic movement; author of *Le Génie du Christianisme* (1802) and several romances; **Chateaubriand** *n.* A thick slice of broiled tenderloin with sauce, named in his honor.

Châ·teau-Thier·ry (shăt′ō-tēr′ē; *Fr.* shătō tyĕr′ē). Town on the Marne in N. France; site of heavy fighting during World War I, 1918.

chat·e·laine (shăt′elān) *n.* 1. Mistress of castle or country house. 2. Chain(s) holding keys, watch, scissors, etc., formerly worn hang-

'Death of Chatterton' (Tate, London) by Henry Wallace. When only 17, the poet **Thomas Chatterton** killed himself with arsenic in a London attic in 1770.

ing from woman's girdle or belt.

Chat·ta·hoo·chee (chătahōō′-chē). River in NE. Georgia flowing 436 miles (696 km) to the Flint River at the Florida border.

Chat·ta·noo·ga (chăt′anōō′ga). Industrial city on the Tennessee River in SE. Tennessee; site of several Civil War battles.

chat·tel (chăt′el) *n.* (law) Property of every kind except real estate; (pl.) goods, possessions; (rhet.) slave.

chat·ter (chăt′er) *v.i.* 1. (of birds) Utter rapid series of short notes, esp. of sounds approaching those of human voice. 2. (of persons) Talk quickly, incessantly, foolishly, or inopportunely. 3. (of teeth etc.) Rattle together. ~ *n.* Sound of chattering; incessant trivial talk; **chat′terbox**, talkative person, esp. child. **chat′ter·er** *n.*

Chat·ter·ton (chăt′erton) **Thomas** (1752–70). English po who fabricated a number of poe purporting to be the work of imaginary 15th-c. Bristol po Thomas Rowley.

Chau·cer (chaw′ser), Geoffr (1340?–1400). English poet, auth of the *Canterbury Tales*. **Cha ce·ri·an** (chawsēr′ēan) *adj.* Af the manner of Chaucer. *n.* Schol specializing in the writings Chaucer.

chauf·feur (shō′fer, shōfer′) Paid driver of private automobil

Chau·tau·qua (shataw′kw Town in SW. New York; site o popular adult summer recreati and educational program i augurated in 1874.

chau·vin·ism (shō′vĭnĭzem) Militant and boastful patriotis MALE chauvinism. **chau′vin·i** *adj. & n.* **chau·vin·is·tic** (sh vĭnĭs′tĭk) *adj.* [f. Nicolas *Chauv* French veteran soldier of Fir Republic and Empire who demonstrative loyalty was cel

haw (chaw) *n.* & *v.* (dial.) ew.

heap (chēp) *adj.* 1. Not costly; ting less than the usual price, e etc.; worth more than its cost; money) obtainable at low rate of erest. 2. Costing little trouble, or, etc. 3. Worthless; made light brought into contempt by being de too familiar; common, vulgar, noral. 4. ~ **shot,** (slang) un-, unkind, remark or action; **ap'skate,** (slang) stingy per-, penny pincher; **cheap, ap'ly** *advs.* **cheap'ness** *n.*

heap·en (chē'pen) *v.* Make or ome cheap, depreciate.

heat (chēt) *n.* 1. Fraud, decep-n, imposition. 2. Swindler; eiver, impostor. ~ *v.* Deceive, k (*out of* something); deal udulently; beguile (time, fatigue, .) **cheat'er** *n.*

check[1] (chĕk) *int.* (chess) Call ifying opponent that his or her g is exposed. ~ *n.* 1. (chess) sition of king when exposed to ect attack. 2. Sudden arrest in eer or onward course; rebuff, ulse; sudden stoppage or pause. Restraint on action or conduct. Control securing accuracy, eement, etc.; token, ticket, of ntification for baggage, coat left baggage room, coatroom, etc.; taurant bill; counter used in card nes, chip. 5. Symbol (✓) to in-ate verification, enumeration, agreement. ~ *v.* 1. (chess) ce in check. 2. Suddenly est motion of; stop. 3. Restrain, rb. 4. Test (figures etc.) by nparison etc., examine accuracy correspond, agree upon com-rison; ~ **in, out,** record arrival departure (of). 5. ~ **list,** list of ms to be compared, scheduled, rchased, supervised, etc.; ~ **off,** eck items in such a list; **check'-**f, deduction of union dues by an ployer from a worker's pay-eck; **check'out,** counter or desk ere payment is made in self-vice store; **check'point,** point re traffic and travelers are ecked, as at national border; eck'up,** examination (esp. medi-), scrutiny. **check'er** *n.* [OF. hec, f. Arab., f. Pers. *shāh* king]

check[2] (chĕk) *n.* Pattern of osslines forming) small squares, e chessboard; fabric woven or nted with this. **checked** *adj.*

check[3] (chĕk), Brit. **cheque** *ns.* itten order to bank to pay sum money to bearer or named per-; form on which this is written; eck'book,** book of such forms ued to customer of bank; eck'ing account,** bank account meeting current expenditure, wn on by check.

check·ers (chĕk'erz) *n.pl.* (usu. nsidered sing.) Game played by two persons on checkerboard with 24 pieces that are moved diagonally; **check'erboard,** game board with 64 squares of alternating colors, on which chess and checkers are played. **check'er** *v.* Mark like checkerboard; **check'ered,** (fig.) undergoing varied fortunes.

check·mate (chĕk'māt) *n.* 1. (chess) Position in which king can-not be extricated from check, move which brings this about. 2. Final defeat; deadlock. ~ *v.t.* (**-mat·ed, -mat·ing**). Give checkmate to; foil, stop, or defeat utterly. [OF. *eschec mat* (see CHECK[1]) f. Arab. *shāh māt* (the chess) king is dead]

Ched·dar, ched·dar (chĕd'er) *ns.* (also ~ **cheese**) Any of several types of smooth, hard yellow cheese varying from mild to sharp in flavor, orig. made near Cheddar, a village in England.

cheek (chēk) *n.* 1. Side wall of mouth, side of face below eye; **cheek'bone,** bone forming lower boundary of eye orbit. 2. (colloq.) Impudence; cool confidence, ef-frontery.

cheek·y (chē'kē) *adj.* (**cheek·i·er, cheek·i·est**). (colloq.) Impu-dent. **cheek'i·ly** *adv.* **cheek'i·ness** *n.*

cheep (chēp) *v.i.* & *n.* (Utter) shrill feeble sound as of young bird.

Painting of **Geoffrey Chaucer,** *whose 'Canterbury Tales' vividly portrayed pil-grims from London to the shrine of St. Thomas à Becket in Canterbury.*

cheer (chēr) *n.* 1. Shout of encouragement or applause; **three ~s**, successive united hurrahs. 2. Frame of mind (only in phrases, as **be of good ~**). 3. (archaic) Food. **cheer** *v.* 1. Comfort, gladden; **~ up**, comfort, be comforted. 2. Incite, urge *on*, by shouts etc.; **cheer′leader**, one who leads organized cheering, esp. at games; also fig. 3. Applaud; shout for joy. **cheers** (chērz) *int.* Exclamation used as toast.

cheer·ful (chēr′ful) *adj.* In good spirits; pleasant; willing, not reluctant. **cheer′ful·ly** *adv.* **cheer′- ful·ness** *n.*

cheer·i·o (chēr′ēō, chērēō′) *int.* & *n.* (pl. **cheer·i·os**). (chiefly Brit. colloq.) Goodby.

cheer·less (chēr′lĭs) *adj.* Gloomy, dreary. **cheer′less·ly** *adv.* **cheer′less·ness** *n.*

cheer·y (chēr′ē) *adj.* (**cheer·- i·er, cheer·i·est**). Lively, genial.

cheer′i·ly *adv.* **cheer′i·ness** *n.*

cheese[1] (chēz) *n.* 1. Food made of the curd of milk, separated from the whey and pressed into a close mass; mass of this, usu. wheel-shaped, cylindrical, or globular, with a hardened outer layer or rind. 2. **cheese′burger**, hamburger with cheese on it; **cheese′cake**, cake made of cottage or cream cheese, etc., with eggs, sugar, milk, flavoring; (slang) display of scantily clad shapely female body in photographs, advertisements, etc.; **cheese′cloth**, thin cotton cloth (of the kind) in which curds are pressed for cheese. **chees′y** *adj.*

cheese[2] (chēz) *v.imp.* (slang) Stop. **~ it**, look out; run away.

chee·tah, che·tah (chē′ta) *ns.* Large, tawny, spotted member of cat family (*Acinonyx jubatus*), of Africa and S. Asia, with non-retractile claws; the fastest four-legged animal. [Hindi *chītā*, f.

Sansk. *chitraka*]

chef (shĕf) *n.* Cook, esp. h cook.

chef-d'oeu·vre (shĕdö′vre (pl. **chefs-d'oeuvre** pr. s dö′vre). Masterpiece. [Fr.]

Che·khov (chĕk′awf, -ŏf; *R* chĕ′χŏf), **Anton Pavlov** 1860–1904). Russian dramatist novelist, author of *The Seag Uncle Vanya, The Cherry Orcha* and other plays, and of numer short stories.

che·la[1] (chā′lah) *n.* (Buddhi Novice qualifying for initiati pupil of a guru.

che·la[2] (kē′la) *n.* (pl. **-lae** -lē). Prehensile claw of cra lobsters, scorpions, etc.

che·late (kē′lāt) *adj.* & *n.* (che (Compound) with cyclic struct looping around central metal and attached at two or more poi **~ v.i.** (**-lat·ed, -lat·ing**). Comb with (substance) to form che

Displayed is a variety of **cheeses**. Cheeses are in general cla fied according to consistency (soft to hard), manufactu method (acid or rennet curd) and degree of ripening.

1 Cheshire
2 Double Gloucester
3 Stilton
4 Gruyere
5 Provolone
6 Emmental
7 Sage Derby
8 Edam
9 Bel Paese
10 Cut of Emmental
11 Tom Savoie
12 Gouda
13 Caerphilly
14 Port Salut
15 Provolone (unwrapped)
16 Smoked Cheese (Austrian)
17 Roquefort
18 Camembert
19 English Cheddar
20 Farmhouse Cheddar
21 Cut of Coloured Cheshire
22 Leicester
23 Mozzarella
24 Whole Brie
25 Nucatall

*Left: On Founders Day at the Royal Hospital, **Chelsea,** London, U.K., Chelsea Pensioners parade for inspection. The home for 'worthy old soldiers broken in the wars' was founded by Charles II and completed in 1692. The bemedaled scarlet-uniformed military veterans remain a conspicuous part of the London scene. A fine gold Chelsea plate (above) made in Chelsea in 1770.*

g. **che·la·tion** (kēlā′shon) *n.*
Chel·le·an, Chel·li·an (shĕl′-ă): see ABBEVILLIAN.
Chel·sea (chĕl′sē). Borough th Kensington) of London, ociated with artists and writers.
chem·i·cal (kĕm′ĭkal) *adj.* Of, de by, relating to, chemistry; ~ **gineering,** industrial applica- n of chemistry; ~ **warfare,** use war of chemical substances other n explosives, esp. poison gases, purpose of injuring the enemy. **emical** *n.* Substance obtained or used in chemical processes. **em′i·cal·ly** *adv.*
chem·i·lum·i·nes·cence (kĕmĭ- mĭnĕs′ens) *n.* Emission of light chemical reaction. **chem·i- mi·nes′cent** *adj.*
che·min de fer (shemăn de fār′; shmăn de fĕr′). Form of bac- at. [Fr., = "railroad," so called m the speed of the game]
che·mise (shemēz′) *n.* Woman's rtlike undergarment; dress aging straight from shoulders.
chem·ist (kĕm′ĭst) *n.* I. entist specializing in chemistry. Brit.) Pharmacist.
chem·is·try (kĕm′ĭstrē) *n.* (pl. ies). Science of the composition ubstances and their combination I change under various condi- s; **inorganic** ~, chemistry of elements other than carbon; ganic ~, formerly, chemistry of stances found in organic ictures; now, chemistry of com- nds of carbon, whether natural ynthetic; **physical** ~, study of physical aspects of chemistry.
hem·nitz (kĕm′nĭts) = KARL RX STADT.
he·mo·ther·a·py (kĕmō- ′apē, kĕme-) *n.* Treatment of

disease by chemical substances that act on microorganisms or malignant tissue. **che·mo·ther·a·peu·tics** (kĕmōthĕrapū′tĭks, kĕme-), **che- mo·ther′a·pist** *ns.*
che·nille (shenēl′) *n.* Yarn with pile protruding all around it; fabric of this or of tufted fabric, used for bedspreads, rugs, etc. [Fr., = "caterpillar"]
Chen·nault (shenawlt′), **Claire Lee** (1890–1958). U.S. Air Force general during World War II; air adviser to Chiang Kai-shek, 1937; formed the "Flying Tigers," a volunteer air corps, to help defend China and protect the Burma Road in World War II.
Che·ops (kē′ŏps) (2900?–2877 B.C.). Fourth dynasty Egyptian king; constructed Great Pyramid.
cheque (chĕk) *n.* (Brit.) Var. of CHECK[3].
Cher·bourg (shār′boorg; *Fr.* shĕrboor′). Seaport and naval base in NW. France.
cher·chez la femme (shĕrshā′ lă făm′). Look for the woman (freq. facet., implying that the key to a problem etc. is a woman). [Fr.]
cher·ish (chĕr′ĭsh) *v.t.* Foster, nurse; value, keep in the memory or heart, cling to.
Cher·o·kee (chĕr′okē, chĕrokē′) *adj. & n.* (pl. **-kees,** collect. **-kee**). (Member) of an Iroquoian- speaking tribe of N. Amer. Indians formerly occupying North Carolina and N. Georgia, now settled primarily in Oklahoma.
che·root (sheroot′) *n.* Thin, un- tapered, dark cigar open at both ends.
cher·ry (chĕr′ē) *n.* (pl. **-ries**). Pulpy fruit of certain species of *Prunus,* esp. of the cultivated tree,

Cherry tree with its blossom and fruit. Cherries belong to the large group of trees with a single seed enclosed in a stone, in turn enclosed in an edible fruity tissue.

P. cerasus; (wood of) tree bearing this; ~ **picker,** (esp.) type of crane, usu. mobile, for raising and lower- ing worker by means of a maneuver- able boom; **cher′rystone (clam),** small clam, a half-grown quahog. **cherry** *adj.* Red.
chert (chĕrt) *n.* (geol.) Form of amorphous silica found in several varieties, e.g. flint.
cher·ub (chĕr′ub) *n.* (pl. for I **cher·u·bim** pr. chĕr′ubĭm,

Above: Late 17th-century carved oak **chest** with arcaded front and gad-rooned (convex-fluted) drawer at the base. Right: Highboy chest of draws, c. 1770.

-yŭbĭm; for 2 **cher·ubs**). 1. Order of angels (see ANGEL), gifted esp. with knowledge. 2. Representation of one of the cherubim in art, usu. as a winged child, or child's head with wings and no body; beautiful child. **che·ru·bic** (cherōō'bĭk, chĕr'u-) adj. [Heb. kᵉrŭb]

cher·vil (chēr'vĭl) n. Garden herb (*Anthriscus cerefolium*) with aromatic leaves used in salads, soups, etc.

Ches·a·peake (chĕs'apēk) **Bay.** Large inlet of the Atlantic Ocean about 200 miles (321.9 km) long, between Maryland and Virginia.

Chesh·ire (chĕsh'er, -ēr). English county of N. Midlands, bordering on Wales; **grin like a ~ cat**, grin broadly (explained as ref. to Cheshire cheeses made in shape of cat, or to lion rampant on Cheshire inn signs); **~ cheese**, kind of hard, yellow cheese made orig. in Cheshire.

chess (chĕs) n. Game played by two persons on board divided into 64 squares, each player having 16 pieces or "men" (a king, a queen, two bishops, two knights, two rooks, and eight pawns), the object being to CHECKMATE the opponent's king; **chess'board**, board on which chess is played, the same as a checkerboard: **chess'man**, one of the pieces used in the game.

chest (chĕst) n. 1. Large strong box; box for sailor's belongings. 2. Treasury of institution; fund kept in this. 3. Case of some commodity, esp. tea. 4. **~ of drawers**, piece of furniture with set of drawers. 5. Part of human or animal's body enclosed by ribs and breastbone, and containing heart and lungs.

ches·ter·field (chĕs'terfēld) n. Kind of overcoat, usually with a velvet collar. [f. a 19th-c. earl of *Chesterfield*]

Ches·ter·field (chĕs'terfēld), **Philip Dormer Stanhope, 4th**

Earl of (1694–1773). British statesman and diplomat, chiefly remembered for his *Letters* to his son.

Ches·ter·ton (chĕs'terton), **G(ilbert) K(eith)** (1874–1936). English author of essays, novels, verse, etc.

chest·nut (chĕs'nŭt) n. 1. Tree of the genus *Castanea* of the N. Hemisphere, bearing a large edible nut enclosed in a prickly pericarp or burr; this nut; the American chestnut, *C. dentata*, has been almost exterminated by a blight caused by a parasitic fungus. 2. = horsechestnut: see HORSE. 3. (colloq.) Stale anecdote or joke. 4. Chestnut color; chestnut-colored horse. **~** adj. Of chestnut color, varying from bright to dark reddish brown.

chest·y (chĕs'tē) adj. (**chest·i·er, chest·i·est**). (colloq.) Having a large chest; (colloq.) proud, conceited; (of voice) have a low register.

chev·a·lier (shĕvalēr', shevăl'-

'The Calling of St. Peter and Andrew' (National Gallery, London) Caravaggio is an example of **chia** **curo**, the disposition of light and sh in a painting, from the Italian 'chi (light) and 'oscuro' (shade).

yā) n. Horseman, knight (h or archaic); member of cert orders of knighthood, or of Frer Legion of Honor; soldier cadet old French nobility.

chev·i·ot (shĕv'ēot, chĕv'-) (One of) a breed of sheep w short, thick wool originally rais in the Cheviot Hills on the bor between England and Scotlar fabric made from its wool.

chev·ron (shĕv'ron) n. Bent of inverted **V** shape as heral device, architectural orname etc.; distinguishing mark of t shape on sleeve of noncomm sioned officers, policemen, e stripe.

Chev·y (chĕv'ē) **Chase.** Skirmish, celebrated in a ballad

General view of **Chicago,** Illinois, located at the south-west corner of Lake Michigan. It is the third most populous city in the U.S.A.

A ruin similar to those found at **Chichén-Itzá,** the ancient Mayan city founded by the Mayan people who were later invaded by the Itzá. By the mid 15th century the city was virtually uninhabited.

th-c. origin, beteen Percy, Earl Northumberland, and his cottish neighbor "the doughty ouglas"; both were killed in the ght. 2. Town in Maryland, sidential suburb of Washington, .C.

chew (choo) v. Work about be-een teeth, grind to pulp or indent ith repeated biting; chew tobacco; rn over in mind, meditate on or ver; ~ **the cud,** (of ruminant nimals) bring back half-digested od into mouth for further chew-g; ~ **the fat,** (slang) talk in-rmally; **chewing gum,** prepara-on of flavored hardened secretion f spruce tree, or similar insoluble ubstance, used for chewing (see so CHICLE). **chew** n. Act of hewing; quid of tobacco.

Chey·enne (shīĕn′, -ăn′) n. (pl. ennes, collect. -enne). (Member f) an Algonquin tribe of N. Amer. ndians formerly inhabiting central Minnesota and North and South Dakota, now settled mainly in Montana and Oklahoma; ~, capital f Wyoming, in the SE. part.

chi (kī) n. Twenty-second letter f Greek alphabet (X, χ), = ch; ~-rho, monogram of chi and rho, rst two letters of Gk. Christos = Christ), ✗, used on altar cloths, estments, etc., as monogram and ymbol for Christ.

Chiang Kai-shek (chyahng′

kī shĕk′, chăng′). Chiang Chung-cheng (1887–1975), Chinese general and statesman; president of the Republic of China from 1943; withdrew government to Taiwan, 1949.

Chi·an·ti (kēahn′tē) n. Dry red wine produced in or near the Chianti Mountains in Tuscany, Italy.

chi·a·ro·scu·ro (kēāroskūr′ō, -skoor′ō), **chi·a·ro·o·scu·ro** (kēārōōskūr′ō, -skoor′ō) ns. (pl. -ros). Treatment of light and shade in painting, esp. when strongly con-trasted. [It., = "bright dark"]

chi·as·mus (kīăz′mus) n. (pl. -mi pr. -mī). (rhet. etc.) Inversion in a second phrase of the order followed in first, e.g. He saved others; himself he cannot save. [Gk. chiasmos arrangement like letter chi, χ]

chic (shēk, shĭk) n. Sophistica-tion in dress and manner; stylish-ness. ~ adj. Stylish, in fashion.

Chi·ca·go (shĭkah′gō, -kaw′-). The second largest city in the U.S., on Lake Michigan in N. Illinois; important port and distribution

center; commercial and financial center of the midwest; known for large grain and livestock market and meat-packing plants.

chi·cane (shĭkān′) n. Chicanery. ~ v. (-caned, -can·ing). Use chicanery; cheat.

chi·can·er·y (shĭkā′nerē) n. (pl. -er·ies). Trickery, deception; underhand dealing; sophistry.

Chi·chén-It·zá (chēchĕn′ētsah′, chē′chĕnēt′sa). Village in Yucatan, Mexico; famous as site of Mayan ruins.

chi·chi (shē′shē, shēshē′) n. & adj. Fussily ornamented, showy, (thing); affected (manner).

chick (chĭk) n. Chicken; young bird before or after hatching; (slang) young woman; **chick′-weed,** weed of genus Stellaria.

chick·a·dee (chĭk′adē) n. Any of several small gray N. Amer. tit-mice of the genus Parus (esp. P. atricapillus), the common black-capped chickadee of northeastern U.S. and Canada.

Chick·a·mau·ga (chĭkamaw′-ga). Town near Chickamauga Creek in NW. Georgia; site of a defeat of Union troops under Gen.

Rosecrans by Confederate troops under Gen. Bragg during Civil War.

chick·en (chĭk′en) *n.* 1. Young bird, esp. of domestic fowl; flesh of domestic fowl as food. 2. (colloq.) Youthful person. 3. (slang, as adjective) Cowardly. 4. ~ **feed**, (colloq.) something trivial, esp. small amount of money; ~-**hearted**, (slang) timorous, cowardly; ~ **pox**, mild eruptive disease with some resemblance to smallpox, chiefly affecting children. **chicken** *v.i.* (slang) Abstain through cowardice (also ~ **out**).

chick·pea (chĭk′pē) *n.* Dwarf pea (*Cicer arietinum*), widely esteemed as food, esp. in S. European and Latin American cuisine.

chic·le (chĭk′el) *n.* Gumlike substance obtained from the sapodilla (*Sapota zapotilla*) used for making chewing gum. [Nahuatl *tzictli*]

chic·o·ry (chĭk′erē) *n.* 1. (bot.) Any plant of the genus *Cichorium*. 2. Species of this (*C. intybus*) with long smooth blanched leaves eaten as salad; its root, ground and roasted as addition to or substitute for coffee.

chide (chīd) *v.* (**chid·ed, chid, chid·den, chid·ing**). Scold. **chid′er** *n.* **chid′ing·ly** *adv.*

chief (chēf) *n.* 1. Head, leader, ruler, of body of people, esp. of clan, tribe, etc.; superior officer, head of department. 2. **C~ Executive**, President of the U.S.; ~ **justice**, presiding judge over a

Chicory plant in flower. The two main species of the plant, native to Europe, are relished as salads. The root of *Cichorium intybus* is ground as a coffee additive or substitute.

court with several judges, esp. the Supreme Court of the U.S.; **C~ of Staff**, senior officer of a service, as of U.S. Army; (l.c.) senior officer in command of a general staff; senior staff officer at or higher than division level; ~ **petty officer**, (U.S. Navy and Coast Guard) noncommissioned officer above petty officer first class and below senior petty officer. **chief** *adj.* Formally the chief or head; first in importance, influence, etc.; prominent, leading. **chief·dom** (chēf′dom) *n.* **chief′ly** *adv. & adj.* Above all; mainly but not exclusively.

chief·tain (chēf′tĭn) *n.* Military leader (poet.); chief of clan or tribe.

chif·fon (shĭfŏn′, shĭf′ŏn) *n.* Diaphanous fabric of fine hard-twisted yarn (silk, nylon, etc.). ~ *adj.* (cooking) Having a light, fluffy consistency, esp. as made with beaten egg whites (~ **pie**).

chif·fo·nier, chif·fon·nier (shĭfonēr′) *ns.* High chest of drawers, usu. with a mirror.

chig·ger (chĭg′er) *n.* Larva of a parasitic mite of the family Trombidiidae, which causes violent itching in human skin.

chi·gnon (shēn′yŏn, shēnyŏn′) *n.* Coil of hair worn at back of head by women.

chig·oe, chig·o (chĭg′ō) *ns.* Small tropical flea (*Tunga penetrans*), the fertile female of which burrows under human skin.

Chi·hua·hua (chĭwah′wah, -wa) *n.* Very small smooth-haired dog of Mexican breed. [*Chihuahua*, city and State of Mexico]

Above: A girl in **Chile** *with her pet chinchilla. Left: Map of Chile, S. American republic on the Pacific coast. The country is narrow, averaging only 1... miles in width, but it extends ab... 2,650 miles in length.*

chil·blain (chĭl′blān) *n.* Inflammatory itching swelling on han... foot, etc., caused by exposure... cold and poor circulation.

child (chīld) *n.* (pl. **chil·dren** ... chĭl′drĭn). Young human bein... immature person; offsprin... descendant, follower, product (*of*... **child′birth**, parturition; **child**... **play**, easy task; **with child**, pre... nant; **child′less** *adj.* **child′less**... **ness** *n.*

child·hood (chīld′hŏŏd)... Time from birth to puberty... **second** ~, dotage.

child·ish (chīl′dĭsh) *adj.* O... proper to, a child; not befitting a... adult. **child′ish·ly** *adv.* **child**... **ish·ness** *n.*

child·like (chīld′līk) *ad*... Having the good qualities of a chil... as innocence, frankness, etc.

Chil·e (chĭl′ē; *Sp.* chē′lĕ). S... Amer. Republic lying between th... Andes and the Pacific; discovere... by Spanish adventurers in the 16t... c. and remained under Spanish ru... until 1818; capital, Santiag... **Chil·e·an** *adj. & n.*

chil·i (chĭl′ē) *n.* (pl. **chil·ies**... **chil·li** (chĭl′ē) *n.* (pl. **-lies**), **chil**... (chĭl′ē) *n.* Dried pod of kinds c... capsicum, acrid, pungent and o... deep red color, used to mak... cayenne pepper; chili con carne... chili sauce; ~ **con carne**, Mexica...

Above right: Former **Chief Executive** *... the U.S.A. Gerald Ford who replace... Richard Nixon after Watergate force... his resignation. Ford remained in offic... for 2 years.*

Right: Sorting and drying green **chilli**... *in Sri Lanka. This pungent spice gradu... ally changes color as it dries in the ho... sun.*

stew of chili-flavored minced beef, beans, onions, etc.; ~ **sauce**, sauce made from tomatoes with chilies and other spices. [Nahuatl]

chill (chǐl) n. 1. Cold sensation, lowered temperature of body, feverish cold. 2. Unpleasant coldness of air, water, etc. 3. Depressing influence; coldness of manner. ~ adj. Lacking warmth. ~v. 1. Make, become, cold; deaden, blast, with cold; keep (meat or other food) at low temperature but without freezing. 2. Depress, dispirit.

chil·ly (chǐl´ē) adj. (**-li·er, -li·est**). Rather cold; not genial, cold-mannered. **chill´i·ness** n.

chime (chīm) n. Set of tuned bells, series of sounds given by this; harmony, melody, rhythm; agreement, correspondence. ~ v. (**chimed, chim·ing**). 1. Make (bell) sound; ring chimes, ring chimes on; show (hour) by chiming. 2. Harmonize, agree (with); ~ **in**, join in harmoniously; break into a conversation.

Chi·me·ra, Chi·mae·ra (kī-mēr´a, kǐ-). (Gk. myth.) Fire-breathing monster with lion's head, goat's body, and serpent's tail, killed by Bellerophon.

chi·me·ra, chi·mae·ra (kī-mēr´a, kǐ-) ns. (pl. **-ras**). Grotesque monster; thing of hybrid character, fanciful conception; organism formed by grafting etc. from tissues of different genetic origin. **chi·mer·i·cal** (kīmĕr´ĭkal, -mēr´-, kǐ-) adj. **chi·mer´i·cal·ly** adv.

chim·ney (chǐm´nē) n. (pl. **-neys**). Flue carrying off smoke or steam of fire, furnance, etc.; part of flue above roof; glass tube enclosing flame of a lamp; natural vent of volcano etc.; narrow cleft by which cliff may be climbed; ~ **corner**, warm seat within old-fashioned fireplace; ~ **piece**, mantel; decoration over a fireplace; ~ **pot**, earthenware or metal pipe at top of chimney; ~ **sweep**, person whose trade it is to clean soot from chimneys.

chimp (chǐmp) n. (colloq.) Chimpanzee.

chim·pan·zee (chǐmpǎnzē´, chǐmpǎn´zē) n. African ape of genus *Pan*, allied to gorilla, bearing the closest resemblance to man of any of the surviving anthropoids. [native W. African name]

chin (chǐn) n. Front of lower jaw. ~ v. (**chinned, chin·ning**). Lift (oneself), while hanging by the hands from a horizontal bar above, until chin is at height of bar; (colloq.) chatter, gossip.

Chi·na (chī´na). Large country of E. Asia with a civilization dating from the 3rd millennium B.C., governed during most of its history by emperors of numerous (often rival) dynasties; after a revolution (in 1911) a republic was proclaimed

Of surviving anthropoids the **chimpanzee** *is most like man and endowed with considerable intelligence. In trees the chimpanzee swings from branch to branch with great agility.*

A small rodent resembling a rabbit but with smaller ears, the **chinchilla** *is about 14 ins. long. Chinchilla fur, particularly that of the Peruvian or royal chinchilla, is highly valued.*

The **chipmunk,** *the striped squirrel of N. America, is 4 to 6 ins. long, it is a good swimmer as well as climber. The chipmunk's call is a shrill 'chip-chip' sound.*

(1912); Communist forces obtain control 1949, and Chiang Kai-sh withdrew the government of **Republic of China** to TAIWA leaving mainland China to Communists who proclaimed t **People's Republic of Chir** capital, Peking; **Chi´nama** (usually derog.) Chinese; **Chi syndrome**, theoretical conditi in which uncontrollable radioact material, as from a damaged aton reactor, would burn a hole throu Earth, as from the U.S. to Chir [ult. origin unknown; not the nati name; found in Sansk. c 1st c.]

chi·na (chī´na) n. Very hard fi semitransparent porcelain of hard paste kind, orig. manufactur in China; ~ **clay**, kaolin. ~ a Of china. [orig. *China-ware*, wa from China]

Chi·na·town (chī´natown). Pa of an Occidental city inhabit chiefly by Chinese people.

chinch (chǐnch) n. (dial.) Be bug.

chin·chil·la (chǐnchǐl´a) Small S. Amer. squirrellike rode of genus *C*~; fine soft grayish f of one species, *C. laniger* of Pe and Chile.

chine (chīn) n. Backbon animal's backbone or cut of me from it; ridge or crest.

Chi·nese (chīnēz´, -nes´) adj. C China or its people or language; **checkers**, game in which marbl are moved from hole to hole acro a board; ~ **lantern**, collapsib lantern of thin colored paper; ~ **restaurant syndrome**, gastr discomfort and faintness fro reaction to monosodium glutama often used in Chinese cooking; **Wall**: see GREAT Wall of Chin ~ **white**, pigment, zinc oxid **Chinese** n. (pl. same) Chine person or language.

Ch'ing (chǐng). Manch dynasty that ruled in China 1644 1912.

Chink (chǐngk) n. (derog Chinese.

chink[1] (chǐngk) n. Narro opening, esp. one that lets ligh air, etc., through.

chink[2] (chǐngk) v. (Cause t make sound as of glasses or coin striking together. ~ n. Chinkin sound.

chin·ka·pin (chǐng´kapǐn): CHINQUAPIN.

chi·no (chē´nō) n. (pl. **-nos** Cotton twill cloth, usu. khak colored; (pl.) trousers made of it.

chi·noi·se·rie (shēnwŏzerē -wŏz´erē) n. Imitation of Chines motifs in furniture etc.

Chi·nook (shǐnŏōk´, -nŏōk chǐ-) n. (pl. **-nooks**, collect **-nook**). 1. (Member of) N. Ame Ind. tribe orig. inhabiting regio around Columbus river in Oregon their language. 2. (also ~ **jargon**

Above: The Great Wall of **China,** thought by many to be the most ambitious building project in history, stands as a reminder of China's past. It was built from the 3rd century B.C. as a defensive fortification against northern barbarians and extends about 1500 miles from the Gulf of Chihli on the Yellow Sea to central Asia. Left: Map and flag of China. Communist forces won control in 1949 and proclaimed the country the People's Republic of China. The country has the world's largest population and covers a vast area exceeding 3½ million sq. miles. Below left: a principal street in Peking, the capital, with cyclists predominating. Below: Joe Fei, a 12th-century hero.

Jargon of English, French, and Indian words, formerly used by traders and Indians from Oregon to Alaska. 3. Warm, moist wind blowing from the sea on the Washington and Oregon coasts; warm, dry wind from the Rocky Mountains.

chin·qua·pin (chǐng′kapǐn) n. Shrubby chestnut (*Castanea pumila*) of U.S., bearing small edible nuts; evergreen (*Castanopsis chrysophylla*) of Pacific coast; the nut of either of these.

chintz (chǐnts) n. Orig., painted or stained calico from India; now cotton cloth printed with bright-colored designs. **chintz′y** *adj.* (**chintz·i·er, chintz·i·est**). (esp.) Cheap; gaudy. [Hind. *chīnt*, f. Sansk. *chitra* variegated]

chi·o·no·dox·a (kīonōdŏk′sa) n. Blue-flowered liliaceous plant of genus *C~* from Crete and Asia Minor, blooming in early spring; glory of the snow. [Gk. *khiōn* snow + *doxa* glory]

chip (chǐp) n. 1. Thin piece cut from wood or broken from stone etc.; in gem cutting, piece chipped off weighing less than ¾ carat. 2. (pl.) (Brit.) French fried potatoes; **potato** ~s, thin fried slices of potato sold in packages. 3. Counter used in games of chance; **let the ~s fall where they may**, no matter what the cost (or incidental damage); no matter who is offended; **when the chips are down**, at a critical point. 4. Flaw or slight fracture caused by chipping. 5. Small square of semiconductor used to make integrated circuit. 6. ~ **off the (old) block**, child resembling father; ~ **on one's shoulder**, grievance; belligerent mood; ~ **shot**, (golf) short, slightly lofted approach shot. **chip** *v.* (**chipped, chip·ping**). Cut (wood), break (stone, crockery), at surface or edge; cut or break *off*; be susceptible to breakage at edge; make chip shot; ~ **in**, (colloq.) interrupt; contribute.

chip·munk (chǐp′mŭngk) n. Small striped rodent (*Tamias striatus*) of eastern N. Amer., resembling a squirrel but living on the ground; any similar rodent of genus *Eutamias* of western N. Amer. or N. Asia. [Amer. Ind.]

Chip·pen·dale (chǐp′endāl), **Thomas** (1718–79). London cabinetmaker; his business was carried on by his son **Thomas** (1749–1822); hence (as *n.*) style of furniture, characterized by flowing lines and rococo ornamentation, made by Chippendale.

chi·rop·o·dy (kĭrŏp′odē, shǐ-, kī-) n. Treatment of feet. **chi·rop′o·dist** n.

chi·ro·prac·tic (kīr′oprăktĭk, kīroprăk′-) n. & *adj.* (Of) manipulation of the spinal column as method of treating disease. **chi·ro·prac-**

*The style established by **Thomas Chippendale** in his 'Gentleman and Cabinet-Maker's Director' lasted 150 years. His designs were a fusion of Queen Anne and Georgian tastes. Above: A Chippendale chair c. 1760. Top: A dressing table, also c. 1760.*

The cacao bean is the source of chocolate. The bean is the fruit of the Theobroma cacao tree which grows in the tropics. The bean is fermented, cured, roasted and ground to a paste.

tor (kīr′oprăkter) n.

chirp (chĕrp) n. Short sha[r] thin note as of small bird. ~ Utter chirp.

chis·el (chĭz′el) n. Cutting to[ol] with square beveled metal en[d] worked by pressure or by blows [of] a mallet or hammer. ~ *v.t.* (**-ele[d], -el·ing**). Cut, shape, with chise[l]; (slang) defraud, cheat *out o*[f]. **chis′eled** *adj.* (esp., of feature[s]) Sharply defined. **chis′el·er** n.

Chis·holm (chĭz′om) **Trai**[l]. Former trail (1867–*c*1887) f[or] driving cattle from San Antoni[o], Texas, to the railhead at Abilen[e], Kansas; the first major trail of th[is] kind and the subject of cowbo[y] songs and legend.

chit[1] (chĭt) n. Young child, es[p]. a girl.

chit[2] (chĭt) n. Check, bill, as fo[r] food or drink. [Anglo-Ind.]

chit·chat (chĭt′chăt) n. Lig[ht] conversation; gossip.

chi·tin (kī′tĭn) n. Organic sub[stance] forming part of exoskeleto[n] of arthropods. **chi′tin·ous** *adj.*

chit·ling (chĭt′lĭn, -lĭng), **chit[-] lin** (chĭt′lĭn), **chit·ter·ling** (chĭt[′] erlĭng, chĭt′lĭn) *ns.* Small intestine[s] of pigs, cooked for food.

chiv·al·ry (shĭv′alrē) n. Knighthood; knightly system [of] feudal times with its religious, moral, and social code and usages; **Age of C~**, period of this. 2[.] Brave, honorable, and courteou[s] character attributed to the idea[l] knight. **chiv′al·rous** *adj.* **chiv′al·rous·ly** *adv.* **chiv′al·rous·ness** n. [OF. *chevalerie* knighthood (*cheva*[l] horse)]

chive (chīv) n. Small cultivate[d] herb (*Allium schoenoprasum*); ~s, its leaves, used as a seasoning i[n] salads.

chlo·ral (klōr′al, klōr′-) n[.] Trichloroacetaldehyde, an oil[y] liquid with pungent odor, used t[o] manufacture DDT and **chlora[l] hydrate**, a hypnotic and anesthet[ic].

chlo·rate (klōr′āt, klōr′-) n. Sa[lt] of chloric acid ($HClO_3$).

chlo·ride (klōr′īd, klōr′-) n. Simple compound of chlorine with a metal or organic radical.

chlo·rine (klōr′ēn, klōr′-) n. (chem.) Nonmetallic element, [a] yellowish-green, heavy, chemically active gas with irritating smell an[d] powerful bleaching and disinfecting qualities; symbol Cl, at. no. 17, at. wt. 35.453. **chlo·rin·ate** (klōr′ ĭnāt, klōr′-) *v.t.* (**-at·ed, -at·ing**) Treat or act upon with chlorine; sterilize (drinking water) thus. **chlo·rin·a·tion** (klōrĭnā′shon, klōr-) n.

chlo·rite (klōr′ĭt, klōr′-) n. Hydrous silicate mineral, usu. green, often found with and resembling mica.

chlo·ro·form (klōr′of ōrm

-ōr´-) *n.* Colorless liquid with
etherlike odor and pungent sweetish taste; formerly used as a general
anesthetic. ~ *v.t.* Administer
chloroform to.

chlo·ro·phyll, chlo·ro·phyl
(klōr´ofĭl, klŏr´-) *ns.* Coloring
matter of leaves and other green
parts of plants etc.

chlo·ro·plast (klŏr´oplăst,
klōr´-) *n.* Plastid containing chlorophyll, in cells of algae and higher
plants.

chlo·ro·sis (klōrō´sĭs, klŏr-) *n.*
Greensickness, anemic disease of
girls about age of puberty.

chlor·prom·a·zine (klŏrprō´-
mazēn, klōr-) *n.* Bitter drug used
as sedative and against vomiting.

chlor·tet·ra·cy·cline (klŏr´tĕt-
rasī´klēn, klōr´-) *n.* Yellow crystalline antibiotic trademarked as
aureomycin and used to treat a
variety of infections.

chock (chŏk) *n.* Block of wood,
wedge. ~ *v.t.* Make fast, wedge,
with chocks. ~ *adv.* Closely,
tightly; **~-a-block, ~-full,**
stuffed, crammed.

choc·o·late (chŏk´olĭt, chaw´ko-,
chŏk´lĭt, chawk´-) *n.* Paste or cake
of seeds of cacao roasted, ground,

sweetened, and flavored with
vanilla etc.; drink made with this;
candy covered with or made of
chocolate; chocolate color. ~ *adj.*
Covered with or made of or with
chocolate; brown. [Nahautl *choco-
latl* (not f. *cacao* or *cocoa*)]

Choc·taw (chŏk´taw) *n.* (pl.
-taws, collect. -taw). (Member of)
a tribe of N. Amer. Indians
formerly living in S. Mississippi
and Alabama, now chiefly settled
in Oklahoma; language of this tribe.

choice (chois) *n.* Act, power,
right, etc., of choosing; what is
chosen; variety to choose from;
elite. ~ *adj.* (**choic·er, choic·est**).
Of picked quality, exquisite; carefully chosen.

choir (kwīr) *n.* 1. Group of
singers performing or leading in
musical parts of church service;
choral society, company of singers.
2. Chancel; part of church assigned
to choir (**choir loft**); **choir'-
master**, director, trainer, of a

*The Mormon Tabernacle Choir in
rehearsal at the Mormon Tabernacle in
Salt Lake City, Utah, an imposing building with 6 spires. The 375 trained choir
members are standing below the great
organ in the temple.*

choir.

choke (chōk) *n.* 1. Narrowed
or constricted part of mechanism.
2. (Device operating) valve that
partly closes air inlet of gasoline
engine. 3. (elect.) Coil having low
resistance and large inductance
inserted in circuit to impede and
smooth out changes in, or change
phase of, current. **choke'cherry**,
(astringent fruit of) N. Amer.
cherry (esp. *Prunus virginiana*);
choke'damp, carbon dioxide in
coal mines etc. **choke** *v.* (**choked,
chok·ing**). Suffocate; stop breath
of; suffer temporary stoppage of
breath; become speechless from
anger etc.; smother, stifle; block up
wholly or partly; ~ **back**, suppress
(tears); ~ **off**, deter, dissuade;
~ (**up**), (colloq.) become in-
capacitated, perform ineptly
(through fear etc.). **chok·er** *n.*
(esp.) High stand-up collar;
woman's close-fitting necklace etc.

chol·er (kŏl´er) *n.* 1. (hist.) One
of the four cardinal humors, bile.
2. (poet., archaic) Anger.

chol·er·a (kŏl´era) *n.* (also
Asiatic ~) Infectious and freq.
fatal disease with violent vomiting
and diarrhea, cramps, and collapse.

chol·er·ic (kŏl′erĭk, kolĕr′-) *adj.* Irascible, hot-tempered; (archaic) characterized by choler, or bile.

cho·les·ter·ol (kolĕs′terōl, -rawl, -rōl) *n.* Steroid alcohol ($C_{27}H_{45}OH$) present in animal cells and body fluids.

chomp (chŏmp) *v.* Var. of CHAMP[1].

Chong·qing (chawng′chŏng′) = CHUNGKING.

choose (chōoz) *v.* (**chose, cho-sen** pr. chō′zen, **choos·ing**). Select out of greater number; make choice *between*; select as; decide, think fit, be determined *to* do; (theol.) destine to be saved. **choos′y, choos′ey** *adjs.* (**choos·i·er, choos·i·est**). Fastidious, fussy. **choos′i·ness** *n.*

chop[1] (chŏp) *v.* (**chopped, chop·ping**). Cut by a blow or blows, as with hatchet or ax; cut small; cut short (words etc.); (tennis etc.) make short heavy edgewise blow, strike (ball) thus. ~ *n.* Chopping; chopping stroke; slice of meat, esp. lamb or pork, usu. including a rib; short broken motion (of waves etc.); **chop′house**, restaurant specializing in steaks and chops. **chop′per** *n.* 1. Person or thing that chops. 2. (slang) Helicopter. **chop′py** *adj.* (**chop·pi·er, chop·pi·est**). (of waves, their motion, etc.) Short and broken.

chop[2] (chŏp), **chap**[2] (chăp, chŏp) *ns.* (usu. pl.) Jaws of animal etc.; **lick one's** ~**s**, show relish or anticipation; **chop′fallen**, var. of chapfallen.

chop[3] (chŏp) *v.i.* (**chopped, chop·ping**). Change direction suddenly, swerve, as a ship in the wind.

Cho·pin (shō′păn; *Fr.* shaw-păṅ′), **Frédéric François** (1810–1849). Polish pianist; lived in France from 1829; composer of a large number of piano compositions.

chop·stick (chŏp′stĭk) *n.* One of

Originating in China, the **chow** has a double-layer coat of soft underhair and straight outer fur. The dog stands 18-20 ins. high at the shoulder.

The **Christmas Cactus**, native to Brazil, has become a popular house plant for its striking red flowers. In its natural habitat it grows on trees and shrubs in shady positions.

a pair of small sticks of ivory, bone, wood, etc., held between thumb and fingers of one hand and used by Chinese, Japanese, and Koreans in eating. [Pidgin English (*chop* = quick + *stick*) equivalent of Chin. *k'wai-tsze* "nimble ones"]

chop su·ey (chŏp′ sōo′ē). Chinese-American dish of meat or chicken, bean sprouts, etc. served with rice. [Chin. *tsa-sui* = "mixed bits"]

cho·ral[1] (kōr′al, kōr′-) *adj.* Of, sung by, a choir or chorus; spoken by group of voices. **cho·ral·ly** *adv.*

cho·ral[2], **cho·rale** (korăl′, -rahl′) *ns.* (Metrical hymn set to) simple tune, usu. sung in unison.

chord[1] (kōrd) *n.* 1. String of musical instrument (poet.); also fig. of mind, emotions, etc. 2. (math.) Straight line joining extremities of arc.

chord[2] (kōrd) *n.* (mus.) Group of notes sounded together, combined according to a harmonic system.

chor·date (kōr′dāt) *adj. & n.* (zool.) (Member) of the phylum Chordata; (organism) possessing at some stage of its life history a

notochord, i.e. a rod of tissue lying along the back below the nerv cord.

chore (chōr, chŏr) *n.* Routin minor, or unpleasant task; dai domestic or farming task, such washing dishes, feeding livestoc etc.

cho·re·a (korē′a, kō-, kaw-) Disease, esp. of children, charac terized by involuntary movemen of muscles; St. Vitus's dance. [I *chorea Sancti Viti* dance of S

A cry of 'k'chuf' gives the **chough** i name. It is an insectivor capable c acrobatic flight. Other than at the matin season, choughs congregate in flock of about 100.

ho·re·og·ra·phy (kōrĕŏg′rafē, -) n. Arrangement of the cing in a ballet; art of dancing. **or·e·og′ra·pher** n. Designer of dancing in a ballet. **chor·e·o-** **·ph·ic** (kōrēŏgrăf′ĭk, kŏr-) adj. **ho·ric** (kŏr′ĭk, kōr′-) adj. Of, , CHORUS, def. 1.

ho·rine (kŏr′ēn, kōr′-) n. ng) Chorus girl.

ho·ri·on (kŏr′ēŏn, kōr′-) n. termost membrane enveloping is before birth; membrane und egg of certain insects.

hor·is·ter (kŏr′ĭster, kōr′- ′-) n. Member of (usu. male) ir, esp. boy.

ho·roid (kŏr′oid, kōr′-) n. & . (Of) the vascular membrane ng the eyeball between sclerotic t and retina.

hor·tle (chŏr′tel) v.i. (-tled, ing) & n. Chuckle. [portman-u word invented by Lewis rroll, perh. f. chuckle + snort]

cho·rus (kōr′us), kōr′-) n. (pl. us·es). (Gk. antiq.) Organized nd of singers and dancers in igious festivals and dramatic per-mances, in Attic tragedy presenting interested spectators d employed to explain the action, press sympathy with characters, d draw morals; song(s) sung by ese. 2. Adaptation of this in other ama. 3. Band of singers, choir; up of singers or dancers in musi-l comedy etc. 4. Thing sung by any at once, simultaneous utter-ce; refrain of song, in which dience joins; main part of popular ng as dist. from introductory rse; musical composition, usu. in ur parts, for a considerable mber of voices; **in ~**, in unison. **~ girl**, female member of chorus musical comedy etc. **chorus** v. **rused, -rus·ing**). Sing, speak, y, in chorus.

cho·sen (chō′zen): see CHOOSE.

Chou En-lai (jō′ĕnlī′) (1898–76). Chinese Communist states-an; prime minister of Chinese ople's Republic, 1949–76.

chough (chǔf) n. Old World rd (Pyrrhocorax pyrrhocorax) of ow family, with red feet and bill.

chow (chow) n. 1. (slang) Food. Dog of Chinese breed, with short ick coat and black tongue.

chow·chow (chow′chow) n. elish of chopped vegetables ckled in mustard.

chow·der (chow′der) n. Thick up of clams or fish and vegetables, ually in a milk base. [app. orig. Brittany, France, in phr. faire la audière = to supply a pot etc. for oking a stew]

chow mein (chow mān′, show). hinese-American dish of stewed getables and meat, chicken, or rimp served with fried noodles. hin. ch'ao mein = "fried flour"]

Holman Hunt (1827–1910) painted **Christ** as 'The Light of the World'. The picture became an extremely popular devotional work, intended to portray Christ offering his light to man.
The tradition of sending **Christmas cards** began in the mid-19th century, one of the most recent accretions to

the ancient festival. Illustrated is a 19th century card showing a scene enacted by children's peg dolls.
Helleborous niger or **Christmas rose** is an evergreen plant of the Ranun-culaceae family. It is used medicinally but has some highly poisonous sub-stances.

chres·tom·a·thy (krĕstŏm′athē) n. (pl. **-thies**). Collection of choice passages.

Christ (krīst). Messiah or Lord's Anointed of Jewish proph-ecy; (title, now treated as proper name, given to) JESUS, regarded by Christians as fulfilling this proph-ecy. [L. Christus f. Gk. khristos anointed one (khriō anoint) transl. of Heb.; see MESSIAH]

chris·ten (krĭs′en) v. 1. Admit or initiate into Christian Church by baptism; give name to at baptism. 2. Name, dedicate (ship etc.) with ceremony like baptism; name, give name to.

Chris·ten·dom (krĭs′endom) n. Christians collectively; the Chris-tian world.

Chris·tian¹ (krĭs′chan) adj. Believing, professing, or belonging to, religion of Christ; resembling Christ or following or exemplifying his teaching; **~ era**: see ERA; **~ name**, name given at christening; first name; **~ Science, Scientist**, (person believing in) principles formulated by Mrs. EDDY, esp. that matter is an illusion and bodily disease an error of the mind, to be cured by teaching the patient the truth as revealed in the teaching and healing of Christ. **Christian** n. Christian person.

Chris·tian² (krĭs′chan), **Fletch-**

er (fl. 1789). Leader of mutiny against Captain Bligh of the Bounty, 1789; with other mutineers fled to and founded colony on Pit-cairn Island.

Chris·tia·ni·a (krĭschĕăn′ēa, -tē-, -ah′nēa) n. (skiing) Turn made from a crouching position to change direction or stop short. [former name of OSLO]

Chris·ti·an·i·ty (krĭschĕăn′ĭtē) n. 1. Christian faith, doctrines of Christ and his apostles; Christian spirit or character. 2. Christendom.

Chris·tie¹ = CHRISTIANIA.

Chris·tie² (krĭs′tē), **Agatha Mary Clarissa** (née Miller; Lady Mallowan) (1891–1976). English author of mystery novels and plays.

Christ·mas (krĭs′mas). Festival of nativity of Christ, observed Dec. 25, as time of festivity and re-joicing; **Father ~**, (Brit.) Santa Claus or a similar personification of Christmas as a benevolent old man bringing gifts to children; **~ cac-tus**, spineless cactus (Zygocactus truncatus) of Brazilian rain forests, used as a house plant for its bril-liant red flowers; crab cactus; **~ card**, card sent with greetings at Christmas; **~ Day**, Dec. 25; **~ Eve**, the night of Dec. 24; **~ pudding**, (Brit.) plum pudding eaten at Christmas; **~ rose**, white-flowered winter-blooming Euro-

The first accurate **chronometer** was made by Robert Hooke and became an essential instrument in navigation. He made it possible by improving the design of watch mechanisms. Today chronometers are driven by electricity.

pean species of hellebore (*Helleborus niger*); ~ **stocking**, one hung up by children on Christmas Eve for Santa Claus to fill with candy and presents; ~**tree**, small evergreen or artificial tree decorated with ornaments, lights, etc., during the Christmas season.

Chris·tophe (krēstawf′), **Henri** (1767–1820). Haitian revolutionary leader; proclaimed King Henry I, 1811; his cruelty caused rebellion and he killed himself with a silver bullet.

Chris·to·pher (krĭs′tofer), **Saint**. Third c. legendary Christian martyr; according to tradition, devoted himself to charitable work of carrying wayfarers across a river where there was no bridge; patron saint of travelers, ferrymen, etc.

Chris·ty (krĭs′te) *n.* (pl. **-ties**) = CHRISTIANIA.

chro·mate (krō′māt) *n.* Salt of chromic acid.

chro·mat·ic (krōmăt′ĭk) *adj.* 1. Of, produced by, color; full of bright color; ~ **aberration**, failure of different colors to come to same focus after refraction. 2. (mus.) Including notes that do not belong to the diatonic scale of the prevailing key; ~ **scale**, full series of notes (12 to an octave, each note differing by a semitone from the next) on which Western music is normally based. **chro·mat′i·cal·ly** *adv.*

chro·ma·tic·i·ty (krōmatĭs′ĭte) *n.* Quality of a color measured optically.

chro·ma·tin (krō′matĭn) *n.* (biol.) Part of cell tissue containing DNA, which can be stained readily when immersed in dye.

chro·ma·tog·ra·phy (krōmatŏg′rafē) *n.* (chem.) Process of separating components of a mixed

The resting stage in the metamorphos of a butterfly and some other insec occurs while the creature is protecte by a **chrysalis**. Illustrated here is a b terfly emerging into adult life.

solution by slow passage through a tube or over adsorbing material, making use of differences of partition, adsorption, ion exchange, etc.; **gas** ~, analogous process using carrier gas as moving phase to carry gaseous or vaporized sample. **chro·ma·to·graph·ic** (krōmatogrăf′ĭk), **chro·ma·to·graph′i·cal** *adjs.* **chro·ma·to·graph′i·cal·ly** *adv.*

chrome (krōm) *n.* 1. Chromium. 2. (also ~ **yellow**) Yellow pigment and color obtained from lead chromate ($PbCrO_4$). 3. Chromium compound used in dyeing and tanning. ~ *v.t.* (**chromed, chrom·ing**). Treat with chromium solution.

chro·mic (krō′mĭk) *adj.* Applied to compounds of chromium in which this element is trivalent; ~ **acid**, acid (CrO_3), strictly the anhydride of the acid) known only in solution and in form of its salts; ~ **oxide**, chromium sesquioxide (Cr_2O_3), a green powder used in metallurgy and as a pigment.

chro·mi·um (krō′mēum) *n.* (chem.) Metallic element remarkable for the brilliant red, yellow, or green color of its compounds; symbol Cr, at. no. 24, at. wt. 51.996; widely applied in electroplating and in a variety of alloys, the chief being

with iron and steel, to which imparts hardness and stainlessnes

chro·mo·some (krō′mosōm) (biol.) One of the rodlike structur that occur in pairs in the ce nucleus of an animal or plant an hence, in every developed cell; the carry genes in linear order and a usu. constant in number for eac species (the human cell nucleus h 23 pairs); **X** ~, one of the se chromosomes, usu. occurring pairs in the female, singly in th male; **Y** ~, sex chromosome occu ring only in the male. **chro·mo·so·mal** (krōmosō′mal) *adj.*

chro·mo·sphere (krō′mosfēr) Red gaseous envelope around a sta **chro·mo·spher·ic** (krōmosfĕr′ĭk *adj.*

chro·mous (krō′mus) *ad* Applied to compounds of chr mium in which this element divalent.

Chron. *abbrev.* Chronicles (Ol Testament).

chron·ic (krŏn′ĭk) *adj.* (of dis eases etc.) Lasting a long time; (o invalid) having such disease ansf.) continuous, constant; (loq.) bad, intense, severe. ~on'i·cal·ly *adv.*

chron·i·cle (krŏn'ĭkel) *n.* De-led and continuous register of ents in order of time; record, ister; (*1st* and *2nd Book of the*) ronicles, two historical books of d Testament. ~ *v.t.* (-cled, ling). Enter or record in a ronicle. chron'i·cler *n.*

chron·o·graph (krŏn'ŏgräf, rahf) *n.* Instrument recording ne with extreme accuracy; stop-atch.

chro·nol·o·gy (krŏnŏl'ojē) *n.* l. -gies). Computation of time, signment of events, etc., to their rrect date, arrangement in order time; chronological table or list. ron·o·log·i·cal (krŏnŏlŏj'ĭkal) j. chron·o·log·i·cal·ly *adv.*

chro·nom·e·ter (krŏnŏm'eter) Timepiece adjusted to keep curate time in all variations of mperature, used for determining osition at sea or in the air and for her exact observations. chron·met·ric (krŏnomĕt'rĭk), chron·met'ri·cal *adjs.* Of chro-ometry. chro·nom'e·try *n.* ccurate time measurement.

chrys·a·lis (krĭs'alĭs) *n.* (pl. -es or chrysalides pr. krĭsăl'idēz). Inactive state into which larva of most insects passes before be-coming imago or perfect insect; hard sheath or case enclosing larva at this stage.

chrys·an·the·mum (krĭsăn'-themum) *n.* Composite plant of genus *C~*; cultivated species of this, having showy flowers and blooming in autumn.

Chrys·os·tom (krĭs'ostom, krĭ-sŏs'tom), **St. John** (*c*345–407). Patriarch of Constantinople (398–404); commemorated Jan. 27.

chtho·nic (thŏn'ĭk) *adj.* (of deities etc.) Dwelling in or beneath surface of the earth.

chub (chŭb) *n.* Thick fat coarse-fleshed European and Caspian river fish of carp family (*Leuciscus cephalus*); any of various other fishes, such as the American ~ and whitefish (*Coregonus*).

chub·by (chŭb'ē) *adj.* (-bi·er, -bi·est). Plump, round-faced.

Found in south-west North America the **chuckwalla** *grows up to 20 inches in length. When threatened it moves into a rock crevice and inflates its body size which makes it difficult to dislodge.*

chub'bi·ness *n.* [f. CHUB]

chuck¹ (chŭk) *v.* 1. Tap lightly *under the chin.* 2. Fling, throw, toss, carelessly or easily (*away*); ~ it, (colloq.) cease, give up; ~ out, discard, throw out; force out, eject. chuck *n.* Act of chucking; jerk, toss, bump.

chuck² (chŭk) *n.* 1. Cut of beef extending from neck to ribs, incl. shoulder piece. 2. Part of lathe etc. that holds rotating workpiece or tool.

chuck³ (chŭk) *n.* (colloq.) Wood-chuck.

chuck·le (chŭk'el) *v.i.* (-led, -ling) & *n.* (Make) suppressed and inarticulate sound(s) expres-sing mirth, exultation, etc.

chuck·le·head·ed (chŭk'el-hĕdĭd) *adj.* (colloq.) Stupid.

chuck (chŭk) wagon. Wagon equipped with cooking utensils and food for serving meals to workers at a ranch, lumber camp, etc.

chuck·wal·la (chŭk'wahla) *n.* Lizard (*Sauromelus ohesus*) resem-bling the iguana, found in arid areas of SW. U.S. and Mexico.

chug (chŭg) *n.* & *v.i.* (chugged, chug·ging). (Make) repeated plunging or explosive sound (esp.

A. Plan of Winchester Cathedral

Nave · Aisle · Transept · Crossing · Choir Screen · East End · Lady Chapel · Retrochoir · Presbytery or Sanctuary · Slype · Chapter House

B. Clerestory · Triforium · Nave Arcade

C. Chevet · Ambulatory · East End · Transept · Nave · Aisle

D. Chancel · Finial · Pinnacle · Clerestory · Spire · Tower · Vestry · Transept · Aisle · Nave · Porch

1. The **church** of St. Lawrence, Bradford-on-Avon, Wiltshire, U.K., is a rare building dating from before the Norman Conquest. 2. This church sits on a cliff at the entrance to Roosevelt National Forest, Colorado. 3. Some representative layouts of cathedrals and churches. A. Plan of Winchester Cathedral. B. Bay of the nave, Salisbury Cathedral. C. Plan of Rheims Cathedral N. France. D. Typical large English parish church. 4. A stave church built in Oslo, Norway. 5. White spired church in Lexington, Massachusetts. 6. A modern church in St. Louis, Missouri.

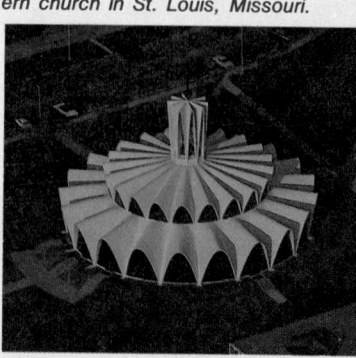

machine).

chuk·ka (chŭk´a) **boot.** Ankle-
h leather boot, as originally worn
polo.

chuk·ker, chuk·kar (chŭk´er)
Each of the 7½-minute
riods into which a game of polo is
vided. [Hind. *chakkar*, f. Sansk.
akra wheel]

chum[1] (chŭm) n. (colloq.) Innate friend or companion. ~ *v.i.*
hummed, **chum·ming**). Be
se friends *with*; share the same
om.

chum[2] (chŭm) n. Chopped or
ound bait thrown into the water
bring fish to the place where one
fishing. ~ *v.i.* To fish with such
it.

chum·my (chŭm´ē) *adj.*
mi·er, -mi·est). (colloq.) Innate, sociable.

chump (chŭmp) n. (colloq.)
lockhead; dupe.

Chung·king (chŏong´kĭng´,
ŏng´gĭng´). City in SE. Szechwan
rovince, SW. China, on the
angtze River.

chunk (chŭngk) n. Thick lump
it or broken off anything.

church (chêrch) n. 1. Building
r public Christian worship. 2.
e C~, the Christian community;
y branch or distinct part of this.
Clergy and officers of the
hurch; clerical order or profes-
on. 4. Congregation of Christians
cally organized for religious
orship etc.; **church´man,
hurch´woman,** member of a
hurch; clergyman. 5. **Church of
ngland,** English branch of the

Western Church, which at the
Reformation repudiated the Pope's
authority and asserted that of the
sovereign over ecclesiastical as well
as temporal matters in his
dominions; **Church of Jesus
Christ of Latter-day Saints,**
official name of the MORMON
Church; **church´warden,** (Anglican and Episcopalian) one of the
(usu. two) lay officers of a church
elected annually to manage various
parochial offices, etc.; clay pipe
with very long stem; **church´-
yard,** enclosed area around a
church, esp. as used for burials.

Church·ill (chêr´chĭl), **Sir
Winston Leonard Spencer**
(1874–1965). British statesman,
orator, and historian; prime minister 1940–5; 1951–5; rallied and led
the United Kingdom during World
War II.

churl (chêrl) n. Rude, boorish
person; peasant; niggardly person.
churl´ish *adj.* **churl´ish·ly** *adv.*
churl´ish·ness n.

churn (chêrn) n. Vessel or
machine for making butter, in
which milk or cream is shaken,
beaten, or otherwise agitated so as
to separate the globules of fat from
the serous parts. ~ *v.* Shake
(milk, cream) in churn into butter;
make (butter) thus; stir (liquid)

*Sir Winston Churchill photographed at
his desk in 10 Downing Street after the
announcement of the Allies' Victory in
Europe in the 1939–45 war. Later in
1945, Sir Winston and the Conservatives lost to Labour in the general election.*

about, make it froth; (of sea etc.)
wash to and fro, seethe; ~ **out,**
(fig.) produce in quantity.

chute[1] (shōot) n. 1. Smooth
rapid descent of water over slope.
2. Sloping channel, slide, for conveying things to lower level, for
sliding down into water, etc.

chute[2] (shōot) n. (colloq.) Parachute.

chut·ney (chŭt´nē) n. (pl.
-neys). Strong pungent relish of
fruits, vinegar, sugar, spices, etc.
[Hind. *chatnī*]

chutz·pa (χōot´spa) n. (slang)
Shameless audacity. [Yiddish]

CIA, C.I.A. *abbrevs.* Central
Intelligence Agency.

ciao (chow) *int.* (informal)
Goodby; hello. [It.]

ci·bo·ri·um (sĭbôr´ēum, -bōr´-)
n. (pl. **-bo·ri·a** pr. -bôr´ēa, -bōr´-).
1. (eccles. archit.) Canopy,
canopied shrine. 2. Covered chalice
for holding consecrated wafers of
the Eucharist.

ci·ca·da (sĭkā´da, -kah´-) n. (pl.
-das, -dae pr. -dē). Plant-sucking
insect, usu. large, the male of which
makes shrill sound from two tympanic structures on the abdomen.

cic·a·trix (sĭk´atrĭks, sĭkā´-) n.
(pl. **cic·a·tri·ces** pr. sĭkatrī´sēz,
sĭkā´tri-). 1. Scar of healed wound.
2. (bot.) Mark left where leaf or
branch has been detached.

Cic·er·o (sĭs´erō), **Marcus Tullius** (106–43 B.C.). Roman republican statesman and orator.
Cic·er·o´ni·an (sĭserō´nēan) *adj.*

ci·ce·ro·ne (sĭserō´nē, chĭch-) n.
(pl. **-nes, -ni** pr. -nē). Guide who

*Found throughout tropical and temperate regions, the **cicada** makes its characteristic shrill call by vibrating membranes on the forepart of the abdomen. Only males make the sound, the females are mute.*

understands and explains antiquities etc.

Cid (sĭd; *Sp*. thēd), **El.** Title in Spanish literature of Ruy Diaz, count of Bivar, 11th-c. champion of Christianity against the Moors. [Arab. *sayyid* lord]

-cide *suffix*. Forming nouns meaning (1) person or substance that kills (*regicide, insecticide*); (2) killing of (*homicide, suicide*).

ci·der (sī′der) *n*. Juice pressed from apples; a beverage of this, which may be either unfermented (**sweet ~**) or fermented (**hard ~**); **~ press**, press for crushing apples and extracting juice. [Heb. *šēkār* strong drink]

ci·gar (sĭgär′) *n*. Compact roll of tobacco leaves for smoking.

cig·a·rette, cig·a·ret (sĭgarĕt′, sĭg′arĕt) *ns*. Small cylinder of finely cut tobacco rolled in thin paper for smoking; similar cylinder of other finely cut plant leaves etc. for smoking, as a **marijuana ~**; **~ holder**, mouthpiece holding cigarette.

cil·i·a (sĭl′ēa) *n.pl.* (sing. **cil·i·um** pr. sĭl′ēum). 1. Eyelashes; delicate hairs resembling eyelashes on edge of leaf, insect's wing, etc. 2. Hairlike vibrating organs on animal and some vegetable tissues, serving as chief means of locomotion for many lower animals living in water. **cil·i·ar·y** (sĭl′ēĕrē), **cil·i·ate** (sĭl′ēĭt, -āt) *adjs*. Of the Ciliata, a class of protozoa that move by means of cilia.

Cim·ar·ron (sĭm′arŏn). River flowing from NE. New Mexico to the Arkansas River in NE. Oklahoma.

Cim·me·ri·an (sĭmēr′ēan) *adj*. Of the Cimmerii, a people fabled by the ancients (and mentioned in Homer) as living in perpetual darkness; gloomy, dark. **~ n.** One of the Cimmerii.

C. in C. *abbrev*. Commander in Chief.

cinch (sĭnch) *n*. 1. Girth for a saddle or pack. 2. (slang) Safe or easy thing; dead certainty. **~ v.** 1. Fix saddle securely with girth. 2. Bind, grip securely; (slang) make sure of, be deciding factor of.

cin·cho·na (sĭnkō′na) *n*. S. Amer. tree or shrub of genus *C*~ with fragrant white or pink flowers; **~ bark**, bark of certain species of this containing quinine and other related alkaloids and used as tonic and febrifuge; drug prepared from it. [named by Linnaeus in honor of countess of *Chinchon* (Spain), who when vice-queen of Peru was cured of a fever by cinchona bark in 1638 and brought a supply to Europe in 1640]

Cin·cin·nat·i (sĭnsinăt′ē). Industrial city on the Ohio River in SW. Ohio.

Cin·cin·na·tus (sĭnsinā′tus), **Lucius Quinctius.** Roman who, acc. to tradition, was called in 458 B.C. from farming to deliver the

Roman army from the peril which it stood in its conflict with Aequians; often referred to as model of simple virtue.

cinc·ture (sĭngk′cher) *n*. Gird belt, border; ring at top and bott of column dividing shaft fr capital and base. **~ v.t.** (**-ture -tur·ing**). Girdle, gird.

cin·der (sĭn′der) *n*. Residue burned material; (pl.) ashes; **block**, concrete building blo made with cement and cinders; **path, track**, footpath, runni track, of fine cinders. **cin′der** *adj*.

Cin·der·el·la (sĭnderĕl′ Heroine of a fairy tale who, treat as a drudge by her mean ste mother and stepsisters, was tran formed by her fairy godmother in a richly dressed guest at the cou ball, where she met the handson prince whom she eventually ma ried; hence, girl who achiev sudden recognition or wealth. *adj*. Achieving sudden wealt fame, etc.; going from rags to riche

cin·e·ma (sĭn′ema) *n*. Motic picture; motion-picture theate (also **the ~**) films collectively, es as an art form. [abbreviation c *cinematograph*]

cin·e·mat·ic (sĭnemăt′ĭk) *ad* Appropriate to the cinema.

cin·e·ma·tog·ra·phy (sĭnema tŏg′rafē) *n*. Art, technique c motion-picture photography **cin·e·ma·tog′ra·pher** *n*. **cin·e mat·o·graph·ic** (sĭnemătogrăf′ĭk *adj*. **cin·e·mat·o·graph′ic·al·l** *adv*. [Gk. *kinēma* movement

One of the forerunners of the **cinema,** the zoöpraxiscope projected animated pictures on to a screen. Eadweard Muybridge (1830–1904), who changed his name to James Muggeridge, invented the machine in 1881. He specialised in studies of movement, taking many photographs of the gaits, walking or running, of both humans and animals.

Above left: In the market at Kano, Nigeria, cigarette sellers make their wares in sight of their customers, using mounds of home-grown tobacco blended to local tastes. Above: Machines that make filter-tip cigarettes roll a double cigarette with a large filter in the center. A rotary knife cuts it in two. In this way the machine produces 2,500 cigarettes per minute.

graphō write, record]

cin·é·ma vé·ri·té (sĭn′ema vĕrĭtā′). Documentary style films using realistic techniques to avoid artificiality and present the appearance of real life. [Fr.]

cin·er·ar·i·a (sĭnerār′ēa) *n.* Any of several potted plants derived from a perennial herb (*Senecio cruentus*) of the Canary Islands, with white, red, blue, or purple flowers. [L. *cinerarius* of ashes, from the ash-colored down on the leaves]

cin·na·bar (sĭn′abār) *n.* Red crystalline form of mercuric sulphide (HgS), esp. as pigment; vermilion.

cin·na·mon (sĭn′amon) *n.* Yellowish-brown, aromatic inner bark of an E. Ind. tree (*Cinnamomum zeylanicum*), dried in the sun and used as a spice; the tree itself. ~ *adj.* Cinnamon-colored.

cin·que·cen·to (chĭngkwĭchĕn′tō) *n.* (Style of art and architecture of) the 16th c. in Italy.

cinque·foil (sĭngk′foil) *n.* 1. Plant of genus *Potentilla*, with compound leaves each of five leaflets. 2. (archit.) 5-cusped ornament in an arch or circle.

Cinque (sĭngk) **Ports.** Five ports of SE. England, orig. Hastings, Sandwich, Dover, Romney, and Hythe, to which were added Winchelsea and Rye, on the Strait of Dover and the North Sea, which defended the coast and furnished the chief part of the English navy in the 13th c. and in return were granted special privileges by Edward the Confessor, most of which they kept until the 1830's.

CIO, C.I.O. *abbrevs.* Congress of Industrial Organizations.

ci·pher (sī'fer) *n.* 1. Arithmetical symbol or character (o) of no value by itself, which when placed after any figure (or series of figures) in a whole number increases its value tenfold, and when placed before a figure in decimal fractions decreases its value in the same proportion. 2. Person or thing of no importance or worth, nonentity. 3. (rare) Any Arabic numeral. 4. Secret or disguised manner of writing; anything so written; key to this. 5. Device of intertwined initials or other letters, monogram. ~ *v.* 1. Do arithmetic; calculate. 2. Put into secret writing. [Arab. *ṣifr* zero]

cir·ca (sẽr'ka) *prep.* About. [L.]

cir·ca·di·an (serkā'dēan, sẽrkadē'-) *adj.* Of physiological activity occurring approximately every twenty-four hours.

Cir·cas·sian (serkăsh'an, -kăs'-ēan) *adj. & n.* (Member, language) of a group of tribes of the Caucasus, some of whom moved into Turkish territory in 19th c., whose women were remarkable for their beauty. [Russ. *Cherkés*, tribe calling themselves Adighe]

Cir·ce (sẽr'sē). (Gk. legend) Enchantress dwelling on island of Aeaea, who transformed all who drank of her cup into swine; in the *Odyssey* she detained Odysseus and his men for a year. **Cir·ce·an, Cir·cae·an** (sersẽ'an) *adjs.* Of, pertaining to, Circe; bewitching.

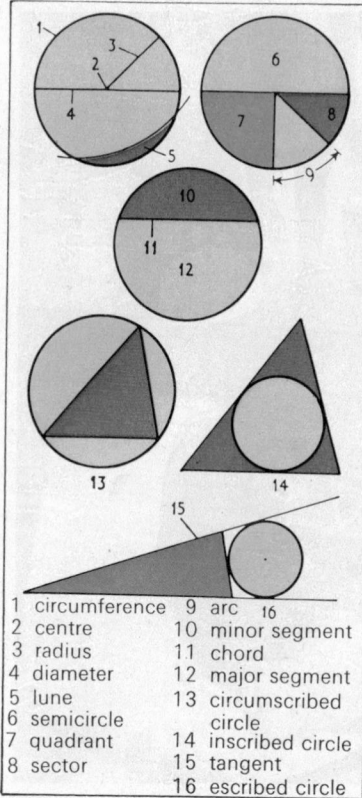

1	circumference	9	arc
2	centre	10	minor segment
3	radius	11	chord
4	diameter	12	major segment
5	lune	13	circumscribed circle
6	semicircle	14	inscribed circle
7	quadrant	15	tangent
8	sector	16	escribed circle

The geometry of the Ancient Greeks examined the properties of the **circle**, some of which are illustrated here. The circle has posed for mathematicians many of their hardest problems.

cir·cle (sẽr'kel) *n.* 1. (Line enclosing) plane figure with circumference everywhere equidistant from center; **great ~ (of a sphere)**, circle on surface of sphere, whose plane passes through center of sphere. 2. Anything shaped like a circle, ring; curved tier of seats at theater etc.; **dress ~**, lowest (and most expensive) of these in a theater, in which evening dress was once required; **upper ~**, circle next above dress circle. 3. Period, cycle, round; completed chain or sequence of events, parts,

etc., esp. of consequences that re upon and intensify their cau (often **vicious ~**); (logic) fallacio reasoning, by which a propositi is used to establish a conclusion a is itself proved by means of t conclusion it has established (a **vicious ~**). 4. Persons group around center of interest; s coterie, class; society. **circle** (**-cled, -cling**). 1. (poet.) E compass. 2. Make circuit of; mo in a circle.

cir·clet (sẽr'klĭt) *n.* Small circ circular band, esp. of gold, jewe etc., worn on head, arm, etc.

cir·cuit (sẽr'kĭt) *n.* 1. Li enclosing an area, distance aroun area enclosed; journey aroun roundabout way or journey. Journey of judges, preachers (call **~ riders**), etc. through certa areas for purpose of holding cour of justice, preaching and perform ing religious ceremonies, etc. various places in succession. Number of theaters etc. under or control. 4. (elect.) Course or pat of an electric current; **~ breake** device for interrupting electric ci cuit to prevent excessive curre from causing damage or fire. **cir cuit·ry** *n.* Plan, components electric circuit; system of suc circuits.

cir·cu·i·tous (serkū'itus) *ad* Going a long way around, indirec **cir·cu·i·tous·ly** *adv.* **cir cu'i·tous·ness, cir·cu'i·ty** *ns.*

cir·cu·lar (sẽr'kyuler) *adj.* O the form of, pertaining to, movin in, passing over, a circle; **~ saw** power saw in form of revolvin toothed disk. **cir·cu·lar·i·t** (sẽrkyulăr'ĭtē) *n.* **cir·cu·lar·ly** *ad* **circular** *n.* Advertisement, notice etc. for mass distribution. **cir cu·lar·ize** *v.t.* (**-ized, -iz·ing** Advertise, notify by circulars.

cir·cu·late (sẽr'kyulāt) *v* (**-lat·ed, -lat·ing**). 1. Move, pas through a circuit, circuitous course system of pipes, etc.; (of blood) flov from heart through arteries an

1. When an electrical **circuit** is wired in parallel, current is divided among its parts. 2. When the circuit is in series, current passes through its parts one after another. 3. A circuit-breaker is a switch that makes and breaks the current in an electric circuit.

cum·nav·i·ga·tor *ns.*

cir·cum·po·lar (sērkumpō'ler) *adj.* Around, about, near, a (terrestrial or celestial) pole; (astron., of star etc.) describing its whole diurnal circle above the horizon.

cir·cum·scribe (sēr'kumskrīb) *v.t.* (**-scribed, -scrib·ing**). 1. Draw line around; encompass. 2. Mark out or define limits of; confine, restrict. 3. (geom.) Describe (figure) about another so as to touch it at certain points without cutting it. **cir·cum·scrip·tion** (sērkumskrĭp'shon) *n.* Circumscribing; circular inscription around coin, seal etc.

cir·cum·so·lar (sērkumsō'ler) *adj.* Situated near, moving around, the sun.

cir·cum·spect (sēr'kumspĕkt) *adj.* Cautious, wary; taking everything into account. **cir'cum·spect·ly** *adv.* **cir·cum·spec'tion** *n.*

cir·cum·stance (sēr'kumstăns, -stans) *n.* 1. (pl.) Time, place, manner, cause, occasion, etc., surroundings, of an act; external conditions affecting or that might affect an agent. 2. (pl.) Material welfare, means. 3. Detail in narrative. 4. Formality, ceremony. 5. Incident, occurrence, fact. 6. Comparable or important thing or fact. ~ *v.t.* (**-stanced, -stanc·ing**). Place in particular circumstance or relation.

cir·cum·stan·tial (sērkumstăn'shal) *adj.* 1. Of or dependent on circumstances; ~ **evidence**, indirect evidence from circumstances affording a certain presumption or capable of only one explanation. 2. Adventitious, accidental; incidental. 3. Full of, particular as to, details. **cir·cum·stan'tial·ly** *adv.*

cir·cum·vent (sērkumvĕnt', sēr'kumvĕnt) *v.t.* Entrap; outwit; avoid, evade. **cir·cum·ven'tion** *n.*

cir·cus (sēr'kus) *n.* (pl. **-cus·es**). 1. Rounded or oval arena lined with tiers of seats, and often covered by a tent (~ **tent**), for equestrian and other exhibitions; entertainment given in this, consisting usu. of acrobatics, clown acts, feats of horsemanship, and performances by animals; traveling show of riders, acrobats, etc., and their equipment. 2. (Rom. antiq.) Large

---

apillaries and back through veins o heart. 2. Pass from place to place, from person to person, etc.; of newspaper etc.) pass into hands of readers. 3. Put into circulation, cause to circulate; **circulating library**, library from which books are circulated among subscribers.

cir·cu·la·tion (sērkyulā'shon) *n.* 1. Movement of blood from and back to heart; movement to and fro. 2. Transmission, distribution (of news, books, money, etc.); number of copies sold, esp. of newspapers.

cir·cu·la·to·ry (sēr'kyulatōrē, -tōrē) *adj.* Of circulation of the blood etc.

circum- *prefix.* Around, about.

cir·cum·am·bi·ent (sērkumăm'bēent) *adj.* Surrounding (esp. of air or other fluids). **cir·cum·am'bi·ence** *n.*

cir·cum·cise (sēr'kumsīz) *v.t.* (**-cised, -cis·ing**). Cut off foreskin of (as Jewish or Muslim rite, or surgically), remove clitoris of. **cir·cum·ci·sion** (sērkumsĭzh'on) *n.*

cir·cum·fer·ence (serkŭm'ferens) *n.* Encompassing boundary, esp. of figure enclosed by curve, as circle; distance around. **cir·cum·fer·en·tial** (serkŭmferĕn'shal) *adj.*

cir·cum·flex (sēr'kumflĕks) *n.* A mark (^, in Greek ˆ) placed over vowel to indicate contraction, length, or special quality; also circumflex accent.

cir·cum·fuse (sērkumfūz') *v.t.* (**-fused, -fus·ing**). Pour or diffuse around; surround *with*, bathe. **cir·cum·fu·sion** (sērkumfū'zhon) *n.*

cir·cum·lo·cu·tion (sērkumlōkū'shon) *n.* Use of many words where few would do; evasive talk; roundabout expression. **cir·cum·loc·u·to·ry** (sērkumlŏk'yutōrē, -tōrē) *adj.*

cir·cum·nav·i·gate (sērkumnăv'ĭgāt) *v.t.* (**-gat·ed, -gat·ing**). Sail around. **cir·cum·nav·i·ga·tion** (sērkumnăvĭgā'shon), **cir-**

LUNGS

HEART

BODY

*The citron was the first of the **citrus** fruits to be introduced into the Mediterranean. During the crusades others were adopted from the Arabs and grown in Europe. Later, they were introduced to the New World.*

oval or oblong building surrounded with rising tiers of seats for public spectacles and horse or chariot races. 3. (Brit.) Open usu. circular space in town with streets converging on it, traffic circle. 4. (colloq.) Excitement, fun, uproar.

cirque (sẽrk) *n.* (geol.) Bowl-shaped hollow at head of valley or on mountain slope, partly enclosed by steep walls and formed orig. by glacier.

cir·rho·sis (sĭrō'sĭs) *n.* Disease of liver, most frequent among heavy drinkers, marked by progressive destruction and regeneration of liver cells and increased connective tissue, causing portal blockage and hypertension, and eventual liver failure. **cir·rhot·ic** (sĭrŏt'ĭk) *adj.*

cir·ri·ped (sĭr'ĭpĕd) *n.* (zool.) Member of the Cirripedia, subclass of Crustacea comprising marine animals esp. the barnacles, usu. with shelly plates strengthening the carapace and feathery legs that protrude from the shell valves to collect food. ~ *adj.*

cir·ro·cu·mu·lus (sĭrōkū'myu-lus) *n.* (meteor.) Form of usu. high cloud consisting of roundish fleecy cloudlets in contact with one another, mackerel sky.

cir·ro·stra·tus (sĭrōstrā'tus, -străt'us) *n.* (meteor.) Thin usu. high cloud consisting of horizontal or inclined sheets attenuated upward into light cirri.

cir·rus (sĭr'us) *n.* (pl. **cir·ri** pr. sĭr'ī, **cir·rus**). 1. (zool.) Slender filamentary process or appendage. 2. (meteor.) Form of cloud, usu. high, with diverging filaments or wisps, often resembling curl or lock of hair or wool.

cis- *prefix.* On this side of.

cis·al·pine (sĭsăl'pīn, -pĭn) *adj.* On this (usu. = the Roman) side of the Alps; ~ **Gaul**, the part of ancient Gaul S. of the Alps, northern Italy.

cis·lu·nar (sĭslōō'ner) *adj.* Between Earth and moon.

Cis·ter·cian (sĭstẽr'shan) *n.* & *adj.* (Member) of the contemplative monastic order founded by reformist Benedictines at Cîteaux near Dijon, France, in 1098. [L. *Cistercium* Cîteaux]

cis·tern (sĭs'tern) *n.* Artificial reservoir for storing water, usu. tank for catching and holding rain water.

cit·a·del (sĭt'adĕl, -del) *n.* Fortress, esp. one guarding or commanding a city; any strongly protected place.

cite (sīt) *v.t.* (**cit·ed, cit·ing**). 1. Summon to appear in court. 2.

Quote in support of a position; mention as example. **ci·ta·tion** (sītā'shon) *n.* Act or instance of citing or quoting; mention in an official dispatch, recommendation for a decoration or honor; summons, esp. to appear in court.

cith·er, cith·ern = CITTERN.

cit·i·zen (sĭt'īzen, -sen) *n.* 1. Burgess, freeman, inhabitant, of city or town; enfranchised member of a state; ~ **of the world**, cosmopolitan; **citizens' band**, radio frequencies reserved for communications among licensed operators. 2. (hist., as title; fem. **cit·i·zen·ess** pr. sĭt'īzenĭs) Representing Fr. *citoyen, citoyenne*, which at the Revolution took the place of *Monsieur, Madame*. **cit'i·zen·ship** *n.*

cit·rate (sĭt'rāt) *n.* Salt of citric acid.

cit·ric (sĭt'rĭk) *adj.* ~ **acid**, colorless, sharp-tasting crystalline acid ($C_6H_8O_7$) found in the juice of citrus fruits.

cit·ron (sĭt'ron) *n.* Ovate acid fruit with pale yellow rind, larger,

*The nocturnal **civet** is catlike but no related to the cat family. There are many species of civet in the Old World. Near their genitals they have scent glands which produce a powerfu musky odor. Derivatives of this substance are used as fixatives for certain perfumes.*

ss acid, and thicker skinned than
mon; tree (*Citrus medica*) bearing
is.

cit·ron·el·la (sĭtronĕl′a) *n.*
ragrant grass (*Cymbopogon
rdus*) of S. Asia yielding a fra-
ant oil used in insect repellents
d perfumery; this oil.

cit·rus (sĭt′rus) *n.* Fruit of genus
~ including citron, orange, lime,
mon, and grapefruit. ~ *adj.*

cit·tern (sĭt′ern), **cith·er** (sĭth′-
), **cith·ern** (sĭth′ern) *ns.* Stringed
usical instrument somewhat like
te but with flat back, usu. played
ith plectrum, common in times of
haucer and Shakespeare.

cit·y (sĭt′ē) *n.* (pl. **cit·ies**). 1.
oosely) Important town; (in
ngland) town created city by
harter, in early times esp. one
ontaining a cathedral; town of
reater importance, or size, or with
ider municipal powers, than those
alled simply towns; **Celestial
C~, Holy C~, C~ of God,**
aradise; **Eternal C~, C~ of the
even Hills,** Rome; **Holy C~,**
sp.) Jerusalem; ~**-state,** one of
he small autonomous republics of

ancient Greece; any small sovereign
state consisting of an autonomous
city and its dependencies. 2. (in
England) **the C~ (of London),**
that part of London within the
ancient boundaries under the jurisdiction of the Lord Mayor and
Corporation; esp. the part of this
near the Stock Exchange and Bank
of England, the center of financial
and commercial activity; ~ **editor,**
one who deals with local news; ~
hall, municipal offices or (fig.)
municipal officials; ~ **manager,**
official directing administration of
a city.

Ci·u·dad Juá·rez (syōōdahd′
hwah′rĕs): see JUAREZ.

Ci·u·dad Tru·ji·llo (syōōdahd′
trōōhē′yō): see SANTO DOMINGO.

civ·et (sĭv′ĭt) *n.* 1. Yellowish or
brownish substance, unctuous and

Founded in 1718 New Orleans is the
largest **city** in Louisiana. Famous as the
home of jazz and for its annual Mardi
Gras, it is of economic importance to
the U.S.A. as the main port trading with
Latin America.

smelling strongly of musk, obtained
from anal glands of civet cat or
related species. 2. Carnivorous
quadruped of family Viverridae
yielding this, esp. the central
African ~ **cat** (*Civettictis civetta*),
between fox and weasel in appearance.

civ·ic (sĭv′ĭk) *adj.* Of, proper to,
citizens; of a city, municipal; of
citizenship, civil. **civ′ics** *n.*
Science of civic affairs.

civ·il (sĭv′ĭl) *adj.* 1. Of citizens
or citizen community. 2. Of,
becoming, befitting, a citizen;
polite, obliging. 3. Nonmilitary;
nonecclesiastical, secular; (law) not
criminal or political. 4. ~ **defense,**
protection of civil population
against air raids or other enemy
action; ~ **disobedience,** refusal to
obey the laws as part of a political
campaign; ~ **engineering**: see
engineer; ~ **law,** law pertaining to
the private rights and remedies of
a citizen (cf. CRIMINAL law); law of
Roman citizens; Roman law as a
whole, esp. as received in Western
Christendom in and after Middle
Ages; ~ **liberty,** freedom

Early in the 18th century J. C. Denner invented the clarinet in Nuremburg, Germany. Some authorities believe his clarinet is an improved version of the chalumeau, a stopped pipe only 8 ins. long.

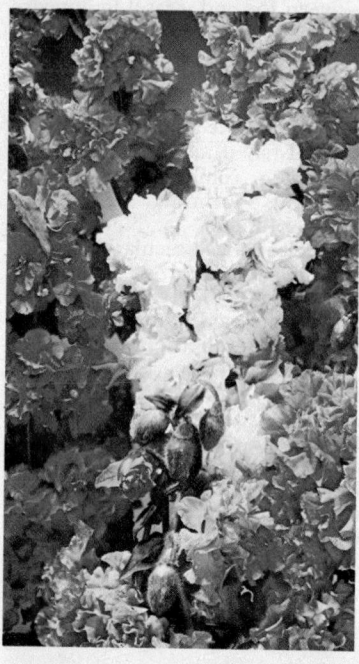

*In cultivating **clarkia**, various reds can be obtained, from pale pink to dark red. The effect of the double-flowered variety is more colorful in masses but the individual flowers are less delicate.*

*The memorial at Gettysburg commemorates the death of over 40,000 men who died in what proved to be one of the bloodiest battles of the U.S. **Civil War.***

guaranteed by the laws of a nation to its citizens to exercise the rights of free speech, thought, and action; ~ **list**, in Gt. Britain and other countries, the yearly funds provided by the legislature for the household and personal expenses of the monarch, royal family, etc.; ~ **proceedings**, legal proceedings aimed at the redress of wrong; ~ **rights**, rights to personal liberty; rights of all to equality as citizens; ~ **servant**, official or employee in civil service; ~ **service**, administrative service of state, including all government departments and public offices (excluding armed forces); persons employed in this; **C~ War**, (i) (U.S. hist.) war between the Union (the North) and the CONFEDERACY (the South) from 1861–5, also called War of the Secession and War Between the States; the conflict grew out of sectional disputes over slavery in the South, the introduction of slavery into new states and territories, and the claim that states had the right to secede from the Union; when eleven southern states seceded (1860–1) and formed the Confederacy, war began, ending in complete defeat for the South, re-admission of the eleven states into the Union, and the abolition of slavery. (ii) (Engl. hist.) Struggle

between Royalists and Parliament, 1642–51. (iii) (Span. hist.) Struggle between Fascist and Republican factions, 1936–9. ~ **war**, war between factions or regions of a country. **civ·il·ly** *adv.* **ci·vil·i·ty** (sĭvĭl´ĭtē) *n.* (pl. **-ties**). Politeness.

ci·vil·ian (sĭvĭl´yan) *adj.* & *n.* (Person) not of one of the armed services.

civ·i·li·za·tion (sĭvĭlĭzā´shon) *n.* Making or becoming civilized; stage, esp. advanced stage, in social development. **civ·i·lize** (sĭv´ĭlīz) *v.t.* (**-lized, -liz·ing**). Bring out of barbarism; instruct in the arts of life; refine, enlighten.

civ·vies (sĭv´ēz) *n.pl.* (colloq.) Civilian clothes.

CJ *abbrev.* Chief Justice.

cl *abbrev.* Centiliter(s).

cl. *abbrev.* 1. Centiliter(s). 2. Class; classification. 3. Clause.

clack (klăk) *n.* Sharp sound as of boards struck together; noise or clatter of human tongues. ~ *v.i.* Chatter, prate; make clack.

clad (klăd): see CLOTHE. **clad´-ding** *n.* Coating or covering applied to surface of object, building, etc.; application of this.

claim (klām) *v.t.* Demand as one's due; represent oneself as having; demand recognition of the fact that; profess; deserve, assert. ~ *n.* 1. Demand for something as

due; right, title, *to*; right to ma demand *on*. 2. Piece of la allotted, esp. for mining. **claim ant** *n.* One who makes or ente a claim.

clair·voy·ance (klārvoi´ans) Supposed supernatural faculty seeing what is removed in time space from natural sight. **clair voy´ant** *adj.* & *n.* (Person) havin clairvoyance.

clam (klăm) *n.* Any of variou bivalve shellfish, esp. the N. Ame hard or round clam (*Ven mercenaria*), and soft or long cla (*Mya arenaria*), found abundantl on sandy or muddy shores an esteemed as food; (slang) silen uncommunicative person. **clam´ bake** *n.* Social gathering for eatin esp. clams and other shellfish, ou doors. **clam** *v.i.* (**clamme clam·ming**). Dig for clams; ~ **u** (slang) become silent, cease talkin [orig. *clamshell*; ult. f. Ger. *klar press* or *squeeze together*]

clam·ber (klăm´ber) *v.i.* Clim with hands and feet; climb wit difficulty or labor. ~ *n.* Climbin thus.

clam·my (klăm´ē) *adj.* (**-mi·er -mi·est**). Moist and cold **clam´mi·ly** *adv.* **clam´mi·ness** n

clam·or (klăm´er) *n.* Shoutin loud appeal, complaint, or deman confused noise. ~ *v.i.* Mak clamor *for, against*, etc. **clam´or ous** *adj.* **clam´or·ous·ly** *adv* **clam´or·ous·ness** *n.*

clamp (klămp) *n.* Brace, clasp or band for strengthening othe aterials or holding things to-ther; appliance or tool with posite sides connected by screw r holding or compressing. ~ Strengthen, fasten, with amp(s); ~ **down** (**on**), (fig.) come (more) strict (about), put a op to.

clam·shell (klăm'shĕl) n. 1. ell of a clam. 2. Bucket for edging, made of two scoops nged together at the top and ening at the bottom.

clan (klăn) n. 1. Group of rsons descended from same cestor and associated together, p. in Scottish Highlands; **clans'-an**, (fellow) member of a clan. Family holding together; coterie, t. **clan'nish** adj. **clan'nish·ly** v. **clan'nish·ness** n.

clan·des·tine (klăndĕs'tĭn) adj. urreptitious, secret, underhand. **an·des'tine·ly** adv.

clang (klăng) n. Loud resonant etallic sound. ~ v. Make, cause make, this sound.

clang·or (klăng'er, klăng'ger) n. uccession of loud metallic ringing oises. **clan'gor·ous** adj.

clank (klăngk) n. Sharp abrupt und, as of heavy pieces of metal ruck together. ~ v. Make, cause make, this sound.

clap[1] (klăp) n. 1. Loud explosive oise as of thunder; peal. 2. ound made by striking palms of ands together; act of doing this as pplause. ~ v. (**clapped, lap·ping**). 1. Make clap; signify pplause, delight, etc., with clap; pplaud with claps. 2. Slap with alm of hand, in approval or ncouragement; apply, place, set, uickly or energetically; put (in rison); ~ **eyes on**, catch sight of; ~ **into** (jail), put swiftly into.

clap[2] (klăp) n. (vulg. slang) Gonorrhea.

clap·board (klăb'erd, klăp'bōrd,

-bōrd) n. Long narrow board with one edge thicker than the other, used to cover outside walls of houses by nailing horizontally so that the thick edge overlaps the narrow edge of the board beneath it. ~ v.t. Cover with clapboards.

clap·per (klăp'er) n. (esp.) Tongue or striker of bell.

clap·trap (klăp'trăp) n. Language used or sentiments expressed only to gain applause; pretentious but empty assertions; nonsense.

claque (klăk) n. Body of hired applauders in theater etc.; group of fawning admirers.

Clar·en·don (klăr'endon), **Edward Hyde, Earl of** (1609–74). English statesman and historian; lord chancellor under Charles II; author of *The True Historical Narrative of the Rebellion and Civil Wars in England*, from the profits of which a new printing house, which bore his name, was built for the Oxford University Press.

clar·et (klăr'ĭt) n. Red wine from Bordeaux; color of this, dark reddish purple; (slang) blood; ~ adj. Claret-colored.

clar·i·fy (klăr'ĭfī) v. (**-fied, -fy·ing**). Make clear; free from impurities, make transparent (liquid, butter, etc.); become or be made clear or pure. **clar·i·fi·ca·tion** (klărĭfīkā'shon) n.

clar·i·net (klărĭnĕt') n. Wood-wind single-reed instrument with range of about 3½ octaves from C♯ or D below middle C, having cylindrical tube with bell-shaped end, and played with fingers on holes and keys.

Chemistry class in progress. Many educationalists consider a critical factor to be the average number of pupils per school class; an excessive number may thwart the individual child.

clar·i·on (klăr'ēon) n. Shrill narrow-tubed trumpet formerly used in war; sound of trumpet, any similar rousing sound. ~ adj. Loud and clear, like a clarion.

clar·i·ty (klăr'ĭtē) n. 1. Clearness to the eye. 2. Clearness and freedom from ambiguity in verbal expression.

Clark (klärk), **George Rogers** (1752–1818). Amer. frontiersman; led many raids against Indians in Indiana, Kentucky, Illinois area; frontier military leader during Revolutionary War; his brother, **William** (1770–1838), Amer. military officer and explorer; co-leader with Meriwether Lewis of the Lewis and Clark Expedition (see LEWIS[3]).

clark·i·a (klär'kēa) n. Annual plant of genus C~ of western N. America with white, pink, or purple flowers. [W. *Clark*, see prec.]

clar·y (klär'ē) n. (pl. **clar·ies**). Aromatic herb (*Salvia sclarea*), native to S. Europe, Syria, etc., and having bluish-white flowers; other species of same genus.

clash (klăsh) n. 1. Loud broken sound as of collision, striking weapons or cymbals, bells rung together. 2. Encounter, conflict; disagreement. ~ v. 1. Make clash. 2. Conflict, disagree, be at variance *with*; (of colors) be discordant.

clasp (klăsp, klahsp) n. 1. Contrivance of two interlocking parts for fastening; **tie** ~, ornament for neatly holding a necktie against shirt front. 2. Embrace; grasp or joining of hands. **clasp** v. 1. Fasten with or as clasp. 2. Encircle, hold closely, embrace; grasp (another's hand); join (hands) by interlocking fingers.

class (klăs, klahs) n. 1. Rank, order, of society; class system. 2. (slang) Elegance, excellence. 3. Division of students taught together or considered of same standing; their time or place of meeting, the instruction given to them; (colleges) all students of the same standing, who enter together, graduate together, etc., *class of 1978*, those who were graduated in that year. 4. Division grouping, according to merit or quality. 5. Number of individuals having some character or feature in common; (biol.) division of animals or plants below phylum, subdivided into orders, families, genera, species. 6. ~-**action suit**, legal action against a single party taken on behalf of a group of individuals with the same complaint; ~ **conscious**, conscious of belonging to a particular class, often with impli-cation of hostility to other classes; ~ **consciousness**; ~ **struggle**, in Marxism, the struggle for economic and political power between the bourgeoisie, or capitalists, and the proletariat, or workers; ~ **syst** division of society into clas **class** *v.t.* Assign to class. **clas less** *adj.* (of a society) N recognizing, not having, cl distinctions.

clas·sic (klăs′ĭk) *adj.* 1. avowed excellence. 2. Of ancient Greek and Latin authors Greek and Roman antiquity. (opp. ROMANTIC) In the clas style, simple, harmonious, p portioned, and finished. 4. Havi literary or historic associations. Of simple style that endures desp changes of fashion. ~ *n.* Writer or artist, work, acknowledged excellence. Ancient Greek or Latin writer; (p studies of these.

clas·si·cal (klăs′ĭkal) *adj.* 1. CLASSIC *adj.*; constituting a mod 2. Of ancient Greek or La standard authors or art; learned studying, or based on these. 3. I following, the restrained style classical antiquity; (in the art traditional. 4. (of physics etc Based on theories etc. establishe before the discovery of quantu theory, relativity, etc. **clas·si·cal ly** *adv.*

clas·si·cism (klăs′ĭsĭzem) Following of classic(al) styl classical scholarship. **clas·si·cist**

clas·si·fy (klăs′ĭfĭ) *v.t.* (**-fie -fy·ing**). Arrange in classes, assig to a class; **classified**, (of offici documents) belonging to a clas e.g. secret or confidential, that on specified persons may see. **clas·si fi·ca·tion** (klăsĭfĭkā′shon) *n.*

class·y (klăs′ē) *adj.* (**class·i·e class·i·est**). (slang) Stylish elegant; superior, excellent.

clat·ter (klăt′er) *n.* Rattlin sound, as of many plates struc together; noisy talk, confused din o voices. ~ *v.* Make clatter, cause t rattle.

Clau·di·us (klaw′dēus) (10 B.C.- 54 A.D.). Tiberius Claudius Drusu Nero Germanicus, Roman empero 41–54 A.D.

clause (klawz) *n.* 1. (gram. Subordinate part of sentence including subject and predicate and forming part of a compound o complex sentence. 2. Single proviso in treaty, law, contract, o other document. **claus′al** *adj.*

Clau·se·witz (klow′zevĭtz), Karl von (1780–1831). Prussian army officer; writer on military science.

claus·tro·pho·bi·a (klawstrofō′- bēa) *n.* Pathological fear of confined places. **claus·tro·pho·- bic** *adj.* 1. Suffering from

A mechanically valuable adjunct to the paws of many animals, **claws** may be used to rend, scrape or pare. Illustrated here, the mole's claws, curved outwards on the forepaws, are ideal for digging.

Above: The plasticity of **clay** allows a potter to 'throw' a pot on a wheel turned by treadle or electric motor. Potters have used a wheel for their work since c. 4,000 B.C.

laustrophobia. 2. Inducing claus-
rophobia.

clav·i·chord (klăv´ĭkord) *n.*
Musical instrument resembling
square piano, with keyboard and
strings struck by tangents, the
earliest keyboard instrument with
strings, appearing in mid-14th c.

clav·i·cle (klăv´ĭkel) *n.* Collarbone. **cla·vic·u·lar** (klavĭk´-
yuler) *adj.*

clav·ier, klav·ier (klavēr´) *ns.*
Instrument with) keyboard, esp.
before introduction of piano.

claw (klaw) *n.* Pointed horny
nail of beast's or bird's foot; foot so
armed; pincers of shellfish; (contempt.) hand; mechanical or other
contrivance for grappling, tearing,
etc.; ~ **hammer**, hammer with
one end bent and split, for
extracting nails. **claw** *v.* Scratch,
tear, seize, pull toward one, with
claws or nails.

clay (klā) *n.* 1. Stiff viscous
earth consisting chiefly of
aluminum silicate and forming with
water a tenacious paste, which can
be molded, or dried and baked into
bricks, pottery, tiles, etc.; **feet of**
~, (fig.) fundamental weakness in
person of supposed merit (cf. Dan.
2); ~ **pigeon**, clay disk thrown or
ejected from trap as a flying target
for trapshooting. 2. Earth; earth as
the material of the human body,
hence, the body. **clay′ey** *adj.*

Clay (klā), **Henry** (1777–1852).
Amer. lawyer, statesman, and U.S.
senator; Secretary of State, 1825–
1829; sought to avert the Civil War
by the Compromise of 1850; known
as the "Great Pacificator" and
"Great Compromiser."

clay·more (klā´mōr, -mŏr) *n.*
Two-edged broadsword formerly
used by Scottish Highlanders.
[Gael. *claidheamb mòr* great sword]

clean (klēn) *adj.* 1. Free from
anything contaminating or from
dirt; free from weeds, barnacles,
etc.; free from defects; (of paper)
blank; (of typescript, printer's
proof, etc.) free from corrections;
not smudged; (of nuclear devices)
producing relatively little fallout;
(of fuel) not polluting the air; ~
room, any enclosed area where air
is kept free of all contaminants, as
for carrying on certain scientific
experiments, medical treatments,
etc.; **come** ~, (colloq.) confess. 2.
Free from moral stain, as in ~
record; free from ceremonial
defilement or of disease; (of beasts
etc.) fit for food. 3. Neatly made,
not unwieldy, trim; neat; unencum-
bered, unobstructed. 4. Entire,
complete, total; ~ **sweep**, complete victory over all other contestants or in all contests. **clean·ly¹**
(klēn´lē) *adv.* **clean′ness** *n.* **clean**
adv. Completely; absolutely. ~ *v.*
Make clean; make oneself clean; ~
out, empty, strip; ~ **up**, clean,

make tidy, clear up; (slang) earn or
win large amount. **clean** *n.* Cleaning.

clean·er (klē´ner) *n.* (esp.) Person employed to clean house etc.;
(freq. pl.) drycleaner.

clean·ly² (klĕn´lē) *adj.* Habitually neat and clean, attentive to
cleanness. **clean′li·ness** *n.*

cleanse (klĕnz) *v.t.* (**cleansed,
cleans·ing**). 1. Make clean. 2.
Purify; free from guilt.

clear (klēr) *adj.* 1. Unclouded,
transparent, not turbid; lustrous;
unspotted; (of soup) strained to
remove particles. 2. Distinct,
intelligible; manifest. 3. Discerning, penetrating; confident, certain.
4. Easily audible. 5. Without
reduction, net; free *of*, whole,
complete; open, unobstructed;
unengaged, free; not encumbered
by debt; ~-**cut** (*adj.*) defined or
formed sharply; evident, distinct.
clear *adv.* Clearly; quite; apart,
without contact. ~ *n.* (esp.) **in the**
~, free, esp. from imputation of
guilt. **clear** *v.* 1. Make, become,
clear. 2. Free from imputation of
guilt, from suspicion, etc. 3. Free
or rid *of*; remove; depart; (become)
empty. 4. Free from contact or
entanglement; pass without entanglement, contact, or collision. 5.
Settle (debt etc.); free from debt;
satisfy requirements, obligations,
examination, etc.; (naut.) free (ship)
by paying all dues; (of ship) sail. 6.
Make (sum of money) as net gain.
7. Get approval of (proposal etc.).
8. ~ **away**, remove, remove
remains of meal from table, (of mist
etc.) disappear; ~ **off**, get rid of,
melt away, (of intruders) go away;

*The sensitive 'touch' of the **clavichord's** keyboard and the delicacy of
its tone won it a place high in the affections of composers of the 15th to 18th
centuries.*

~ **out**, empty, make off; ~ **up**,
solve (mystery), make tidy, (of
weather etc.) grow clear.

clear·ance (klēr´ans) *n.* 1.
Clearing; removal of obstructions;
passing of checks through clearing
house; (certificate of) clearing of
ship at custom house. 2. Clear
space; room to pass. 3. ~ **sale**,
store's sale of merchandise at
reduced prices in order to get rid of
superfluous stock.

clear·ing (klēr´ĭng) *n.* (esp.)
Piece of land cleared for cultivation;
~ **house**, institution or office
where banks exchange checks and
drafts and settle accounts; agency
for collecting and distributing information etc.

clear·ly (klēr´lē) *adv.* Distinctly;
manifestly; undoubtedly.

clear·ness (klēr´nĭs) *n.* Transparency; distinctness; freedom
from obstruction.

cleat (klēt) *n.* Wedge; projecting
piece bolted on spar, gangway, etc.,
to give footing or prevent rope from
slipping; piece of metal, rubber,
etc., fastened to sole of shoe to
prevent slipping; wedge-shaped or
other projecting piece of wood or
metal for fastening ropes to, etc.

cleav·age (klē´vĭj) *n.* Cleaving;
being cleft; way or line in which
anything tends to split; property (of
minerals and rocks) of splitting
readily in certain directions;
(colloq.) cleft between woman's

*Above: A favorite climbing plant in gardens, **clematis** is of a large genus with many varieties. Shown here is a popular clematis called Nellie Moser.*

breasts, revealed by low-cut dress.

cleave[1] (klēv) *v.* (**cleft** pr. klĕft or **cleaved** or **clove** pr. klōv, **cleft** or **cleaved** or **clo·ven** pr. klō′ven, **cleav·ing**). Split; chop, break, or come apart, esp. along grain or line of cleavage; make way through (water, air, etc.). **cleav′er** *n.* (esp.) Butcher's heavy axlike knife or hatchet.

cleave[2] (klēv) *v.i.* (**cleaved** or archaic **clave** pr. klāv, **cleaved, cleav·ing**). Stick fast, adhere *to* (archaic); be faithful.

clef (klĕf) *n.* Symbol on musical staff to indicate pitch of notes; **bass** ~, symbol that locates the F next below middle C; **treble** ~, symbol that locates the G above middle C.

cleft[1] (klĕft) *n.* Space or division made by cleaving; fissure, split.

cleft[2] (klĕft) *adj.*: see CLEAVE[1]; (esp.) ~ **palate**, malformation of palate with longitudinal gap in middle or on either side of roof of mouth.

clem·a·tis (klĕm′atĭs, klemah′-tĭs, -măt′ĭs) *n.* Twining shrub of genus *C*~ having flowers with showy calyx and no corolla.

Cle·men·ceau (klĕmensō′), **Georges** (1841–1929). French statesman; premier 1906–9 and 1917–20; chairman of the Versailles Peace Conference.

clem·en·cy (klĕm′ensē) *n.* (pl. **-cies**). Mildness of temper or weather; mercy.

Clem·ens (klĕm′enz), **Samuel Langhorne**: see Mark TWAIN.

Clem·ent (klĕm′ent). Name of several popes and bishops of Rome including ~ **I**, bishop of Rome during the late 1st c. and reputedly third successor to Saint Peter; ~ **V** (1264–1314), Pope (1305–14), he removed the seat of papacy from Rome to Avignon, France, in 1309; ~ **VII** (1478–1534), Pope (1523–1534), a Medici and cousin of Pope Leo X; he refused to sanction the divorce of Henry VIII of England in 1534.

cle·ment (klĕm′ent) *adj.* Mild, showing mercy.

clench (klĕnch) *v.* Fix securely, make fast, as with nails; clinch (a nail etc.); close (teeth, fingers) tightly; grasp firmly. ~ *n.* Clenching, being clenched.

Cle·o·pa·tra (klēopăt′ra, -pah′-tra, -pā′-) (68–30 B.C.). Queen of Egypt; daughter of Ptolemy Auletes, king of Egypt; wife of Ptolemy III, her brother; mistress of Julius Caesar, who restored her to her throne in 47 B.C. after her expulsion by Pothinus; mistress of Mark Antony; in the war between Antony and Augustus, the defection of her fleet at the battle of Actium (31 B.C.) hastened Antony's defeat; to escape being carried captive to Rome, she took her own life. The granite obelisks known as ~'s **Needles** have no connection with the queen, but were originally

erected at Heliopolis by Thothm III *c*1475 B.C.

clep·sy·dra (klĕp′sĭdra) *n.* (p -dras, -drae pr. -drē). Ancien time-measuring device worked b flow of water, also called "wat clock." [Gk. *kleptō* steal *hud* water]

clere·sto·ry (klēr′stōrē, -stō n. (pl. **-ries**). Upper part of wa of nave, choir, and transepts cathedral or large church, an containing windows.

cler·gy (klĕr′jē) *n.* (pl. **-gie** collect. **-gy**). 1. The clerical orde all persons ordained for religio service; clergymen. 2. **withou benefit of** ~, (colloq.) withou being married; **cler′gyman**, men ber of the clergy.

cler·ic (klĕr′ĭk) *n.* Clerical ma clergyman. [Gk. *klērikos* f. *klēr* lot, inheritance, as used (e.g.) Acts I:17]

cler·i·cal (klĕr′ĭkal) *adj.* 1. the clergy, a clergyman, or clergy men. 2. Of, made by, a clerk office worker; ~ **error**, error writing anything out. **clerical** Clergyman.

cler·i·cal·ism (klĕr′ĭkalĭzem) (esp.) Clerical rule or influenc **cler′i·cal·ist** *n.*

clerk (klĕrk; *Brit.* klärk) *n.* (archaic) Clergyman. 2. Officer charge of records, accounts, etc., o any department, court, corpora tion, etc. 3. Office worker wh makes written records, keep accounts, attends to correspon ence, files, etc. 4. Salesperson

The ambition and charm of **Cleopatra** quickly became legendary, capturing the imagination of writers over many centuries. Left: Cleopatra and the Roman, Antony, are in love in Shakespeare's play about them.

Erosion of a shore can produce a **cliff**. The sea undercuts the rock. It then dashes fallen boulders against the base of the cliff, continuing the work of erosion.

store. **clerk'ship** n. **clerk** v.i. colloq.) Act as clerk.

Cleve·land¹ (klēv′land). Indusrial city and port on Lake Erie in NE. Ohio.

Cleve·land² (klēv′land), (**Stehen**) **Grover** (1837–1908). 'wenty-second and 24th president f U.S., 1885–9 and 1893–7.

clev·er (klĕv′er) adj. Adroit, eat in movement; talented; ngenious. **clev·er·ly** adv. **clev′rness** n.

clev·is (klĕv′ĭs) n. U-shaped iece of metal with holes at the ends hrough which a bolt or pin is run, sed to attach a whiffletree, plow, tc.

clew (kloo) n. 1. Ball of thread or arn; such a ball used as guide hrough maze or labyrinth (in many nythological or legendary stories). . (naut.) Small cords suspending ammock; lower corner of square ail, after corner of fore-and-aft sail, o which are fastened tacks and heets for extending and securing it. . Clue. ~ v.t. (naut.) Draw lower nds of (sails) up to upper yard or nast for furling.

cli·ché (klēshā′, klĭ-) n. Stereo-

typed or hackneyed phrase or expression.

click (klĭk) n. 1. Slight sharp hard nonringing sound as of dropping latch etc.; ~ **beetle**, adult wireworm or other beetle of family Elateridae, which when turned over rights itself by jumping with a click. 2. (phon.) Class of sharp nonvocal sounds occurring in certain African languages, formed by suction, with sudden withdrawal of tongue from contact with part of mouth. **click** v. Make click; (slang) secure one's object; be a great success; get on friendly terms (with person of opposite sex).

cli·ent (klī′ent) n. 1. (Rom. antiq.) Plebeian under protection of noble; (archaic) dependent, hangeron. 2. One employing services of lawyer; employer of services of any professional or business man; customer.

cli·en·tele (klīentĕl′, klē-, klēahn-) n. Body of clients, customers, or patrons.

cliff (klĭf) n. Steep rock face; **cliff'hanger**, story, contest, etc. with outcome in suspense.

cli·mac·ter·ic (klīmăk′terĭk,

klīmăktĕr′ĭk) n. & adj. (Constituting) a crisis, critical; esp. (occurring at) period of life (45–60) at which vital forces begin to decline; menopause.

cli·mate (klī′mĭt) n. (Region with specified) prevailing conditions of temperature, rainfall, humidity, wind, etc.; (fig.) prevailing mental or moral attitude etc. **cli·mat·ic** (klīmăt′ĭk) adj. **cli·mat′i·cal·ly** adv.

cli·ma·tol·o·gy (klīmatŏl′ojē) n. Study of climates. **cli·ma·to·log·i·cal** (klīmatolŏj′ĭkal) adj.

cli·max (klī′măks) n. 1. Culmination, apex. 2. Orgasm. 3. (ecol.) State of equilibrium reached by plant and animal community. **cli·mac·tic** (klīmăk′tĭk) adj.

climb (klīm) v. 1. Ascend, mount, go up, esp. with help of hands; ~ **down**, descend similarly; (fig.) retreat from position taken up, give in. 2. (of sun, aircraft, etc.) Gain height. 3. (of plants) Creep up by aid of tendrils or by twining. 4. Slope upward. 5. Rise by effort in social rank, intellectual or moral power, etc. **climb** n. Climbing; place climbed or to be climbed.

Robert Clive *went to India for the East India Company in 1743. He joined the Company's army in 1744. His victories at Pondicherry (1748), Arcot (1751) and Plassey (1757) consolidated British power in India.*

climb·er (klī′mer) *n.* (esp.) Mountaineer; climbing plant; one who attempts to rise to higher social standing.

clime (klīm) *n.* (poet.) Region; climate.

clinch (klĭnch) *n.* 1. (naut.) Way of fastening large ropes with half hitch; clinched part of rope; anything that grips. 2. Struggle or scuffle at close quarters; (boxing) grappling at close quarters. 3. (slang) Close embrace. ~ *v.* 1. Clench. 2. Drive home, make conclusive, confirm, establish. 3. Embrace closely.

clinch·er (klĭn′cher) *n.* (esp.) Remark, argument, reason that settles a matter.

cling (klĭng) *v.i.* (**clung** pr. klŭng, **cling·ing**). Adhere *together*, remain in one body or in contact, resist separation; adhere *to*; remain faithful *to*; **cling′stone** (**peach**), variety in which flesh adheres to stone.

clin·ic (klĭn′ĭk) *n.* 1. Teaching of medicine or surgery at the bedside; class, institution, so taught or conducted. 2. Institution or center for giving medical advice or treatment; medical offices of several specialists working cooperatively. 3. Center that offers counsel or instruction in fields other than medicine. **cli·ni·cian** (klĭnĭsh′an) *n.*

clin·i·cal (klĭn′ĭkal) *adj.* Of, at, the sickbed (esp. of lectures, teach-ing); dispassionate; ~ **medicine**, observation and treatment of patients as distinct from theoretical study of medical science; ~ **ther-mometer**, one for taking patient's temperature. **clin′i·cal·ly** *adv.*

clink[1] (klĭngk) *n.* Sharp, abrupt, clear ringing sound, as of small metallic objects or glasses struck together. ~ *v.* Make clink.

clink[2] (klĭngk) *n.* (slang) Prison, jail. [proper name of a former prison in London]

clink·er[1] (klĭng′ker) *n.* (colloq.) Mistake, error.

clink·er[2] (klĭng′ker) *n.* 1. Very hard pale-yellow paving brick; brick with surface vitrified by great heat. 2. Mass of bricks fused by excessive heat; hardened mass formed by fusion of earthy impurities of burned coal, limestone, etc., slag; mass of hardened volcanic lava.

Clin·ton (klĭn′ton), **George** (1739–1812). First governor of New York State, 1777–95, 1801–4; vice president of the U.S. under Thomas Jefferson and James Madison, 1805–12; his nephew, **De Witt**, (1769–1828), Amer. lawyer and statesman, U.S. senator 1802–1803; governor of New York State, 1817–21, 1825–28.

Cli·o (clī′ō). (Gk. and Ro[m] myth.) Muse of epic poetry a[nd] history. [Gk. *kleiō* celebrate]

clip[1] (klĭp) *n.* Appliance f[or] holding things together, or f[or] attachment to objects; set of ca[r]tridges held together at base packed in special container [for] insertion into magazine of repeati[ng] firearm; piece of jewelry f[or] clipping on; **clip′board**, boa[rd] with spring clip for holding pape[r] etc. **clip** *v.t.* (**clipped, clip·ping**) Grip tightly, grasp; fasten wi[th] clip(s).

clip[2] (klĭp) *n.* Clipping, shearin[g]; quantity of wool clipped fro[m] sheep, flock, etc.; (colloq.) rate [of] speed, rapid pace; (colloq.) sma[ll] blow; ~ **joint**, (slang) bar, club, et[c.] charging exorbitant prices. **clip** (**clipped, clipped** or **clipt, clip·ping**). 1. Cut with shears [or] scissors; trim, make tidy, thus; c[ut] off part of (hair, wool) thus; remo[ve] hair or wool of (sheep etc.) thu[s]; pare edge of (coin); remove sma[ll] piece of (ticket) to show that it ha[s] been used; cut short. 2. (colloq.) Move quickly, run. 3. (colloq.) H[it] smartly. 4. (slang) Overcharge.

clip·per (klĭp′er) *n.* (esp.) Instrument for clipping hair. [2.] Ship with forward-raking bows a[nd] aft-raking masts. 3. Aircraft es[p.] for transoceanic flights.

clip·ping (klĭp′ing) *n.* (esp.) Small piece clipped off, as shred [of] cloth; (also **press** ~) item clippe[d] from newspaper etc.

clique (klēk, klĭk) *n.* Sma[ll] exclusive party, set, coteri[e]. **cliqu′ish, cliqu′ey, cliqu′y** *adj*[s.]

clit·o·ris (klĭt′orĭs, klī′to-) *n.* Rudimentary erectile organ [of] female genitals, homologue [of] penis.

Clive (klīv), **Robert, Baro[n]** **Clive of Plassey** (1725–74). English soldier and statesman in th[e] service of the East India Compan[y]; avenged the Black Hole of Calcut[ta] at the battle of Plassey, 175[7]; became governor of Bengal, 1758.

clo·a·ca (klōā′ka) *n.* (pl. **-cae** -sē). 1. Sewer. 2. Commo[n] excretory cavity at end of intestina[l] canal in birds, reptiles, et[c.] **clo·a′cal** *adj.*

cloak (klōk) *n.* Loose us[ually] sleeveless outer garment; (fig[.]) covering, pretense, pretext; ~ **and-dagger**, involving es[p.] dramatic events of intrigue an[d] espionage; **cloak′room**, room [in] which coats, hats, etc., may be le[ft] temporarily, as in a theater, schoo[l] etc. **cloak** *v.t.* Cover with, wrap i[n] cloak; conceal, disguise.

clob·ber (klŏb′er) *v.t.* (slang[.]) Thrash; defeat decisively; critici[ze] severely.

cloche (klōsh, klawsh, klŏsh) [n.] 1. Bell-shaped glass vessel f[or]

The urge to **climb** to the top of natural obstacles, such as mountains, is one experienced by adventurous people of many ages, but it was not until the 19th century that the urge developed into a sport of international dimensions.

Before the mid-17th century the **clock** was an inaccurate instrument for measuring time. This highly wrought silver and gilt case is by Hans Conrad Breghtel, c. 1600 (left).

As the skills of the clock-makers grew, some produced elaborate astrological timekeepers (above left) showing the relationship of the planets, as in this clock in Prague in Czechoslovakia. The invention of the pendulum by Galileo was adopted by clock-makers after the mid-17th century. This winged lantern clock has a pendulum with a bob shaped like an anchor (far left).

By the late 17th century, cabinet-makers and clock-makers joined their crafts to make fine long-case clocks. This one is by A. C. Cooper, and was made c. 1850 (above).

vering plants, food, etc. 2. oman's close-fitting, bell-shaped t.

clock¹ (klŏk) *n.* 1. Time-easuring instrument consisting of ain of wheels set in motion by eights, spring, electricity, etc., tuating and regulated by a ndulum, balance wheel, quartz ystal, etc., and recording hours, inutes, etc., usu. by movement of nds on a dial or displayed figures; ocklike device showing readings a dial; **against the ~**, against ime limit; **put the ~ back**, move nds of clock to earlier position; g.) revert to earlier state of affairs. Downy seed head of dandelion c. 3. **~ watcher**, employee who atches assiduously for time of end working day; **clock'wise**, oving like hands of a clock, in rve from left to right as seen from nter; **clock'work**, mechanism of ock, mechanism similar to this for riving toys etc.; (attrib.) regular, echanical, driven by clockwork; ke clockwork, regularly, auto-atically. **clock** *v.* Time by the ock; attain (time or speed) in a ce; register on clock or dial; **~ in**, ut, register arrival, departure at ctory, office, etc. by means of a me clock.

clock² (klŏk) *n.* Ornamental attern on side of stocking or sock ear the ankle.

clod (klŏd) *n.* Lump of earth c.; blockhead; **clod'hopper**, umpkin, lout. **clod'dish** *adj.* lod'dish·ly *adv.* **clod'dish·ness** clod'dy *adj.* (**-di·er**, **-di·est**).

clog (klŏg) *n.* 1. Block of wood

fastened to animal's leg to impede motion; encumbrance, hindrance. 2. Heavy wooden-soled shoe. ~ *v.* (**clogged, clog·ging**). 1. Fetter or confine with clog; be encumbrance to, burden, impede, hamper. 2. Stop up; fill up with impeding matter; cease to function or function badly from being stopped up.

cloi·son·né (kloizonā', klaw-) *adj. & n.* (Enamel) of which different colors have been applied between thin metal plates laid on edge on foundation (cf. CHAMPLEVÉ).

clois·ter (kloi'stər) *n.* 1. Convent, monastery. 2. Covered walk or arcade of monastery, college, large church, often running around open court of quadrangle with plain wall on outer side and colonnade or windows on inner. **clois'tered** *adj.* Monastic; sheltered; secluded. **clois·tral** (kloi'-strəl) *adj.*

clone (klōn) *n.* 1. (bot.) Group of cultivated plants the individuals of which are transplanted parts of one original seedling or stock. 2. (biol.) Individual or group of individuals produced asexually from and genetically identical with one ancestor. ~ *v.t.* (**cloned, clon·ing**). Propagate as clone.

close¹ (klōs) *adj.* 1. Narrow, confined, contracted; covered, con-

cealed; secret; niggardly; restricted. 2. Near; dense, compact; in or nearly in contact; fitting exactly; intimate; nearly equal; concentrated. 3. Sultry; ill-ventilated. 4. (of vowel) Pronounced with tongue near the palate. 5. **~ call**, (colloq.) narrow escape from death; **close'fisted**, niggardly; **close harmony**, singing of parts within octave or twelfth; **close-hauled**, (naut.) with sails hauled close, so as to sail as near the wind as possible; **close-mouthed**, reticent; **close order**, (mil.) arrangement of men in line with only slight gaps between them; **close quarters**, immediate contact with opponent or enemy; uncomfortable proximity; **close shave**, (fig.) narrow escape from accident; **close-up**, (phot.) picture taken at close range or with a telephoto lens so as to show persons etc. on large scale. **close'ly** *adv.* **close'ness** *n.* **close** *adv.* So as to be close. ~ *n.* Enclosed space; precincts of cathedral; (Scottish) narrow lane or alley.

close² (klōz) *v.* (**closed, clos·ing**). 1. Shut; (of place of business etc.) declare, be declared, not open; **closed circuit**, (elect.) circuit providing uninterrupted endless path for the flow of current; (television) circuit transmitting signal to restricted set of receivers;

*The Chinese produced **cloisonné** enameled work, such as this early Ming twin-cylinder case, of outstanding craftsmanship. The reservoirs of enamel are on a copper base.*

*By the 11th century the **cloister** had become an established part of the monastery. This fine Romanesque cloister is in St. Trophine's Church at Arles in France.*

*Examining the phenomenon of **cloud** the English scientist Luke Howard established in 1803 a classification that was adopted in 1929 by the International Meteorological Commission.*

Top: Cirrus is a high cloud of feathery, delicate plumes. It often portends fine weather. Left: Altocumulus is a low cloud formation arranged in thick rolling masses. Above: Nimbus is a low, rain-bearing cloud. In its towering development cumulonimbus may assume an anvil shape and produce thunderstorms.

closed season, period during which it is unlawful to take certain specified game or fish; **closed shop**, industrial or other concern in which the employees are obliged to belong to one particular trade union. 2. Be boundary of, conclude; bring or come to an end; complete, settle. 3. Bring or come into contact; close gap(s) in rank, series, etc.; come within striking distance, grapple *with*; (naut.) approach, come alongside of. 4. ~ **down**, close finally, end business etc.; (of transmitting) cease to broadcast; ~ **in**, enclose, come nearer; **close'out**, sale of goods when a firm is going out of business or discontinuing certain kinds of merchandise; **close up**, block, fill, fill gaps (in), coalesce; move closer to; shut (place of business, etc.). **close** *n*. Conclusion, end.

clos·et (klŏz'ĭt) *n*. Small room (archaic); small storage room, cabinet; toilet. ~ *adj*. Not public, secret. ~ *v.t.* Shut up or detain in private room as for conference etc.

clo·sure (klō'zher) *n*. 1. Closing, closed condition. 2. Var. of CLOTURE.

clot (klŏt) *n*. Mass of material stuck together; semisolid lump of coagulated liquid, esp. blood. ~ *v*. (**clot·ted, clot·ting**). Form into clots; **clotted cream**, thick cream obtained by scalding milk.

cloth (klawth, klŏth) *n*. (pl. **cloths** pr. klawdhz, klawths, klŏdhz, klŏths). (Piece, used for any purpose, of) woven or felted stuff; covering for table, esp. at meals; woolen woven fabric as used for clothes; ~ **of gold**, **silver**, tissue of gold or silver threads interwoven

with silk or wool; **the** ~, the clergy.

clothe (klōdh) *v.t.* (**clothed** or **clad, cloth·ing**). Provide with clothes, put clothes upon; cover like or as with clothes or a cloth.

clothes (klōz, klōdhz) *n.p.* Wearing apparel, dress; **clothes' bag, clothes'basket**, bag, basket for dirty or newly washed linen; **clothes'horse**, frame on which laundry is hung for drying; person overly concerned with dressing fashionably; **clothes'line**, rope, wire, etc. for hanging wash up to dry; **clothes'pin**, forked peg or clip for fastening wash to clothesline.

cloth·ier (klōdh'yer, -ēer) *n*. One who makes or sells clothing or cloth.

cloth·ing (klō'dhĭng) *n*. (esp.) Clothes collectively.

Clo·tho (klō'thō). (Gk. myth.) One of the three Fates, who spun he thread of life.

clo·ture (klō´cher) *n.* In legislative bodies, decision by vote or under rules to end debate and vote on the question. ~ *v.t.* (**-tured, -tur·ing**). Apply cloture to motion, speakers, etc.).

cloud (klowd) *n.* 1. Visible mass of condensed water vapor floating in air at some distance above general surface of ground; **in the ~s**, deep in reverie, dreamy, impractical; **on ~ nine**, (slang) extremely happy. 2. Unsubstantial or fleeting thing; mass of smoke or dust; local dimness or obscurity in otherwise clear or transparent thing; innumerable body of insects, birds, horsemen, crows, moving together; obscurity, anything obscuring or concealing; anything causing) state of gloom, trouble, suspicion, etc.; darkening of countenance; **under a ~**, under suspicion; out of favor; deep in reverie, dreamy, impractical. 3. **cloud´burst**, violent rainstorm; **cloud chamber**, (phys.) apparatus containing water vapor, esp. one through which charged particles are passed and become identifiable after condensation of vapor. **cloud**

The **clown** often combines the skills of juggler, acrobat and knockabout comedian. Above: The traditional white-faced make-up derives from the clown's origins in the harlequinade.

v. Overspread, darken, with clouds, gloom, or trouble; variegate with vague patches of color or opacity; become overcast or gloomy. **cloud´less** *adj.* **cloud´less·ly** *adv.* **cloud´y** *adj.* (**cloud·i·er, cloud·i·est**). **cloud´i·ly** *adv.* **cloud´i·ness** *n.*

clout (klowt) *n.* 1. (archaic and dial.) Patch; cloth; rap, knock, blow. 2. (colloq.) Influence (esp. political). ~ *v.t.* (archaic and dial.) Mend, patch; cuff heavily.

clove¹ (klōv) *n.* One of the small bulbs making up compound bulb of garlic, shallot, etc.

clove² (klōv) *n.* Dried flower bud of a tropical tree (*Eugenia aromatica*), used as a pungent aromatic spice; the tree itself; ~ **pink**, clove-scented species of pink (*Dianthus caryophyllus*), the original of the carnation and other cultivated forms. [Fr. *clou de girofle*; *girofle* was orig. name of the spice; *clou* (L. *clavus* nail) was used of it with ref. to its shape]

clove (klōv) **hitch.** Way of fastening rope around spar etc., formed by passing rope around twice in such a way that both ends pass under center part of loop in front. [old past part. of CLEAVE¹]

clo·ven (klŏ´ven) *adj.*: see CLEAVE¹; (esp.) ~ **hoof**, divided hoof of ruminant quadrupeds, ascribed in pagan mythology to Pan, and thence in Christian mythology to the Devil.

clo·ver (klō´ver) *n.* Any plant of the genus *Trifolium*, having compound leaves with usu. three leaflets and tight heads of small flowers; largely cultivated for fodder; **in ~**, in ease and luxury; **clo´verleaf**, highway interchange resembling four-leaf clover.

Clo·vis I (klō´vĭs) (466?–511). King of the Franks, 481–511; overthrew Romans; endeavored to unite all Franks into one kingdom.

clown (klown) *n.* 1. Rustic, lout. 2. Jester, esp. in pantomime or circus with loose baggy garments and painted face. ~ *v.* Play the clown, act like a clown, perform farcically.

clown·ish (klow´nĭsh) *adj.* Of or like a clown; rustic, boorish. **clown´ish·ly** *adv.* **clown´ish·ness** *n.*

cloy (kloi) *v.t.* Satiate, weary, by richness, sweetness, or excess.

club (klŭb) *n.* 1. Heavy stick with one thick end, esp. as weapon; stick with crooked (and usu. thickened) end used in various games, esp. golf. 2. (Playing card with) black trefoil(s); (pl.) suit of these cards. 3. Association of

*Originating in Europe, with over 300 known species, **clover** is now grown as fodder throughout the temperate regions of the world.*

*The River **Clyde** flows for about 100 miles to pour into the sea through the Firth of Clyde. On its north bank lies Clydebank, an area important for shipbuilding.*

*It is common practice to use a **clutch** to connect the drive wheels of a vehicle with the engine. The operation of a clutch allows the driver to apply the engine power to the wheels gradually.*

DOG CLUTCH

Driving Shaft

Driven Shaft

Fly-wheel

Driven plate

Release lever plate

Pressure plate

Carbo thrust ring

Drive Shaft to gear-bo

MOTOR VEHICLE CLUTCH

persons with some common interest meeting periodically; body of persons combined for social purposes and having premises for meals, temporary residence, etc.; **club′house**, premises used by club. 4. **club′foot**, any of various (usu. congenital) distortions giving foot a stunted lumpy appearance; **club moss**, herb (*Lycopodium clavatum*) with clublike upright fertile spikes of spore cases; any species of evergreen plant *Lycopodium*; **club sandwich**, one containing three layers of bread (often toasted) with two fillings; **club soda**: see SODA. **club** *v.* (**clubbed, club·bing**). 1. Beat with club; use butt of (gun) as club. 2. (archaic) Bring, come, into a mass. 3. Combine *together*, or *with* others, in joint action.

cluck (klŭk) *n.* 1. Abrupt hollow guttural sound made by hen desiring to sit or calling her brood together; any similar sound. 2. Dull-witted person. ~ *v.i.* Make cluck.

clue (kloo) *n.* Anything that

points the way, indicates a solution, or puts one on track of a discovery; sentence or phrase indicating word(s) to be inserted in crossword puzzle; clew.

clump (klŭmp) *n.* Cluster *of* trees or shrubs; cluttered mass; lump. ~ *v.* Tread or move heavily and clumsily; plant in clump; keep or mass together. **clump′y** *adj.* (**clump·i·er, clump·i·est**).

clum·sy (klŭm′zē) *adj.* (**-si·er, -si·est**). Awkward in movement or shape, ungainly; ill-contrived; tactless. **clum′si·ly** *adv.* **clum′si·ness** *n.*

clus·ter (klŭs′ter) *n.* Group of similar things, esp. such as grow together, bunch; swarm, group, of persons, stars, etc. ~ *v.* Bring, come, into cluster; be in cluster.

clutch[1] (klŭch) *v.* Seize eagerly,

grasp tightly; snatch *at.* ~ *n.* Tight grasp; (pl.) grasping han cruel grasp. 2. (mech.) Dev enabling engine or driving parts machine to be connected to disconnected from the driven pa (also ~ **pedal**) pedal operati this. 3. Small purse or handb without a strap or handle. 4. (e sports) Critical moment or situ tion.

clutch[2] (klŭch) *n.* Set of eg brood of chickens.

clut·ter (klŭt′er) *n.* Crowd confusion, confused mass. ~ Litter, strew untidily *with*, cro with disorderly assemblage things.

Clyde (klīd). River in S Scotland flowing north to the Fi of Clyde; **Firth of** ~, an inlet the Atlantic Ocean in S

ove: The **coach** and harness collec-
n kept in the Royal Mews at
ckingham Palace, London, is one of
e finest. It includes this so-called
ss coach.

e stage coach was much used as a
m of public transport in 18th and
th century England. Right: The
ctorian Royal Mail coach had space
r passengers and baggage on top.

otland.

Clydes·dale (klīdz′dāl) n. One
a breed of large, powerful draft
rses orig. bred in the Clyde River
lley, Scotland.

clys·ter (klĭs′ter) n. (archaic)
ema.

Cly·tem·nes·tra (klītemnĕs′-
a). (Gk. legend) Daughter of
yndareus, king of Sparta, and
da; wife of AGAMEMNON.

Cm symbol. Curium.

cm, cm. abbrevs. Centimeter(s).

Cmdr. abbrev. Commander.

CNO abbrev. Chief of Naval
erations.

Cnut (kenoōt′, -nŭt′) = CANUTE.

CO abbrev. Commanding
icer; conscientious objector;
lorado.

Co symbol. Cobalt.

Co. abbrev. Company; county.

co- prefix. 1. Jointly, mutually;
nt, mutual. 2. (math.) Of the
mplement; complement of.

c/o abbrev. Care of.

coach (kōch) n. 1. Large closed
rriage with four wheels. 2. Rail-
d passenger car. 3. Low-priced
ss of passenger accommodation
on train or plane. 4. Bus, esp. a
long-distance one. 5. Private tutor
preparing candidate for examination; instructor or trainer of athletic
team; trainer of singers, actors, etc.
6. **coach'man**, driver of coach or
carriage; **coach'work**, (Brit.)
bodywork. **coach** v. Train, tutor;
study with a tutor.

co·ad·ju·tor (kōăj′uter, kōajōō′-
ter) n. Helper, assistant, esp. one
assisting a bishop.

co·ag·u·late (kōăg′yulāt) v.t.
(-lat·ed, -lat·ing). Convert, be
converted, from fluid to more or
less solid state; clot, curdle, set.
co·ag'u·lant n. Coagulating agent.
co·ag·u·la·tion (kōăgyulā′shon) n.
co·ag'u·la·ble adj.

coal (kōl) n. Black or blackish
sedimentary rock consisting mainly
of carbonized plant tissue, found in
seams or beds and used as fuel;
(pl.) pieces of coal; pieces of glowing, burned, or charred coal, wood,
etc; **carry** ~s **to Newcastle**,
bring superfluous goods etc.; **haul
over the** ~s, reprimand; ~-
black, completely black; ~ **dust**,
powdered coal; ~ **field**, district
with series of coal strata; ~ **gas**,
mixture of gases (mainly hydrogen

and methane) produced by destructive distillation of coal and used for lighting and heating; ~ **mine**, mine in which coal is dug; ~ **oil**, kerosene; ~ **tar**, thick black viscous liquid, a product of destructive distillation of coal, used to make dyes, drugs, paint, roofing, organic chemicals, etc.

coal·er (kō'ler) *n.* Ship, train, truck carrying or supplying coal.

co·a·lesce (kōales') *v.i.* (**-lesced, -lesc·ing**). Come together and form one; combine in coalition. **co·a·les'cence** *n.* **co·a·les'cent** *adj.*

co·a·li·tion (kōalish'on) *n.* Union, fusion; (government by) temporary combination of political parties. **co·a·li'tion·ist** *n.* & *adj.*

coam·ing (kō'ming) *n.* (naut.) Raised border around hatches and scuttles etc. to keep out water.

coarse (kōrs, kôrs) *adj.* Common, inferior; rough, loose, or large in texture, grain, or features; not delicate, unrefined; vulgar, obscene. **coarse'ly** *adv.* **coarse'ness** *n.* **coars'en** (kôr'sen, kôr'-) *v.t.* & *v.i.* Make, become, coarse.

coast (kōst) *n.* 1. Border of land near sea, seashore; **the ~ is clear**, the danger is over, the way is open; **C~ Guard**, military service under the Dept. of Transportation in peacetime, when it is responsible for protecting lives and property at sea, enforcing revenue, immigration, and navigation laws, and maintaining aids to navigation; in wartime it may aid the U.S. Navy with convoy duty, amphibious landing operations, etc.; (~ **guard**) any similar naval or military organization or (also **coast'-guardsman**) member of such an organization; **coast'line**, configuration of coast. 2. Downhill ride on bicycle etc. without pedaling, or in car etc. with engine idling or not running. **coast'ward, coast'wards** *advs.* **coast'wise** *adj.* & *adv.* **coast** *v.i.* 1. Sail along coast, trade between ports on same coast. 2. Slide downhill on sled etc.; ride downhill on bicycle without pedaling, or in car with engine idle or off.

coast·al (kōs'tal) *adj.* Of, on, pertaining to, the coast.

coast·er (kōs'ter) *n.* 1. (esp.) Vessel employed in coasting. 2. Small dish or mat placed under a glass to protect table top. 3. Person who coasts.

coat (kōt) *n.* 1. Sleeved outer garment opening at the front and covering the body from the shoulders to the waist or below. 2. Natural covering compared to garment; beast's hair, fur, etc.; covering membrane etc. of organ; skin, rind, husk; layer of bulb etc.; covering of paint etc. laid on at one time. 3. ~ **hanger**, shaped frame,

hanging by central hook, on which coat etc. is draped; ~ **of arms**, tabard or surcoat blazoned with heraldic arms; heraldic insigne; **coat'tail**, hanging part of back of a man's jacket or coat; **on someone's coattails**, undeservedly benefiting from another's progress etc. **coat'less** *adj.* **coat** *v.t.* Provide with coat; cover with surface layer or coating.

co·a·ti (kōah'tē) *n.* (pl. **-tis**). (also **co·a·ti-mun·di** pr. kōah'tēmun'-dē) Amer. plantigrade carnivorous mammal of the genus *Nasua*, resembling civet and raccoon, with long flexible snout and long tail.

coat·ing (kō'ting) *n.* (esp.) Layer of paint etc.; material for coats.

co·au·thor (kōaw'ther, kō'aw-) *n.* & *v.t.* (Be) joint author (of).

coax (kōks) *v.* Persuade by blandishments, wheedle; manipulate (tool etc.) gently.

The intelligent and lively **coati** *is found in the forests of Central and South America. Its partly prehensile tail helps it to keep its balance when climbing trees.*

co·ax·i·al (kōak'sēal), **co·ax·a** (kōak'sal) *adjs.* (math.) Having common axis; ~ **cable**, high frequency television, telephone and telegraph cable comprising a enclosed and insulated conductin tube surrounding a centra insulated conducting core.

Below: Air circulates around a **coal mine** *by means of a large fan which sucks used air out, drawing fresh air down another shaft. In this mine the roof is held up by 'posts' of coal left standing.*

Opposite: Self-propelling roof-suppo systems are applied in the 'short wa mining technique at Corrimal mine New South Wales, Australia, and els where.

winding tower

ventilation shaft

winding shaft

cage with coal cars

cage for miners

longwall face

coal train

room and pillar mining

conve for co

*Found in Africa and Asia, the **cobra** is a highly poisonous snake. The king cobra may grow to 18 ft. in length. It is the smaller Egyptian cobra that is used by snake charmers.*

cob (kŏb) *n.* 1. Male swan. 2. Stout short-legged riding horse. 3. Roundish lump of coal etc. 4. Corncob.

co·balt (kō'bawlt) *n.* 1. (chem.) Silver-white malleable slightly magnetic metallic element; symbol Co, at. no. 27, at. wt. 58.9332; radioactive form of this, extensively used in radiotherapy. 2. Deep blue pigment (~ **blue**), a mixed oxide of cobalt and aluminum. [Ger. *kobold* goblin haunting mines]

co·bal·tite (kō'bawltīt, kōbawl'- tīt) *n.* Silver-white mineral with brilliant metallic luster.

Cobb (kŏb), **Ty(rus) Raymond** (1886–1961), "the Georgia Peach." Baseball player for Detroit and Philadelphia; established many batting, scoring, and base-stealing records.

cob·ble[1] (kŏb'el) *n.* (also **cob'- blestone**) Water-worn rounded stone, esp. of suitable size for paving. **cobble** *v.t.* (**-bled, -bling**). Pave with cobblestones.

cob·ble[2] (kŏb'el) *v.t.* (**-bled, -bling**). Make or mend (shoes or boots); make clumsily, bungle.

cob·bler (kŏb'ler). 1. One whose business is mending shoes. 2. (archaic) Clumsy workman or mender, botcher. 3. Iced drink or punch of wine or liquor, sugar, and lemon. 4. Deep-dish fruit pie with thick top crust.

co·bel·lig·er·ent (kōbelĭj'erent) *adj.* & *n.* (Nation) waging war along with another.

Co·blenz (kō'blĕnts). City at the junction of the Rhine and Moselle Rivers in West Germany.

COBOL (kō'bōl, -bawl) *n.* Computer language for writing programs, esp. in business operations that process large amounts of uniformly related data. [*co*(mmon) *b*(usiness) *o*(riented) *l*(anguage)]

co·bra (kō'bra) *n.* Venomous snake of genus *Naja*, found in S. Asia and Africa, able to dilate its neck into a hoodlike shape when excited; esp. the **king** ~ or HAMADRYAD of India (*N. hannah*), largest of all venomous snakes, which may attain a length of more than 15 feet (5.5 m). [Port. *cobra de capello* snake with hood (L. *colubra* snake)]

cob·web (kŏb'wĕb) *n.* 1. Web or fine network spun by spider for capture of its prey; single thread of this. 2. Anything frail or flimsy; any musty accumulation, obstruction, etc., which ought to be swept away, like dusty cobwebs in a neglected room. **cob'web·by** *adj.*

co·ca (kō'ka) *n.* S. Amer. shrub (*Erythroxylon coca*) with leaves containing cocaine and related alkaloids; dried leaves of this chewed by people of the Andes as a stimulant.

co·caine, co·cain (kōkān', kō'kān) *ns.* Alkaloid obtained from coca leaves and young twigs, used as local anesthetic, stimulant, etc.

co·cain·ism (kōkā'nĭzem, kō'ka-) *n.* (Chronic condition produced by) habitual use of cocaine.

coc·cus (kŏk'us) *n.* (pl. **coc·ci** pr. kŏk'sī). Spherical bacterium.

coc·cyx (kŏk'sĭks) *n.* (pl. **coc·cy·ges** pr. kŏk'sĭjēz, **coc·cix·- es**). Small triangular bone ending spinal column in man and some apes; analogous part in birds etc. **coc·cyg·e·al** (kŏksĭj'ēal) *adj.* [Gk. *kokkux* cuckoo (f. resemblance to cuckoo's bill)]

Co·chin (kō'chĭn'). City in SW. India on the Malabar coast; founded by Vasco de Gama, 1502, first European settlement in India.

Co·chin-Chi·na (kō'chĭn-chī'- na, kŏch'ĭn). Former French colony, part of Indochina; now part of Vietnam.

coch·i·neal (kŏchĭnēl', kŏch'- ĭnēl) *n.* Red dye prepared from dried bodies of the female of the insect *Dactylopius coccus*, found on cactuses in Mexico etc.; this insect.

Co·chise (kōchēs', -chēz') (1815?–1874). Amer. Apache chief and Indian leader.

coch·le·a (kŏk'lēa, kō'klēa) *n.* Spiral cavity of internal ear. [L., = "snail"]

cock[1] (kŏk) *n.* 1. Male of common domestic fowl (*Gallus domesticus*); male of other birds. 2. Spout, short pipe, with device for controlling flow of liquid or gas; lever in firearm raised ready to be released by trigger; cocked position or state; way of cocking hat to side; **at full** ~, with cock raised ready for firing. 3. **~-and-bull story**, incredible tale; **cock'fighting**, setting cocks to fight as sport; **cock of the walk**, (fig.) leader, head, chief person; **cocks'comb**, cock's

*The **cockatoo** is a crested parrot fou~~n~~ in Australia. There are several varietie~~s~~ their plumage ranging from white, y~~el~~ lows and pinks to black.*

crest. **cock** *v.* 1. Raise cock ~~or~~ hammer of (gun) in readiness f~~or~~ firing. 2. Erect, stick, or tilt ~~up~~ jauntily or defiantly; ~ **one's ear~~s~~**, listen attentively; ~ **one's hat**, s~~et~~ it jauntily on one side; turn up bri~~m~~ of hat.

cock[2] (kŏk) *n.* Small conical hea~~p~~ of hay or straw in field. ~ *v.* Heap (hay or straw) in cocks.

cock·ade (kŏkād') *n.* Roset~~te~~ etc. worn in hat as badg~~e~~. **cock·ad'ed** *adj.*

cock·a·leek·ie (kŏkalē'kē) *n.* Scotch cream soup of chicken an~~d~~ leeks.

cock·a·ma·mie (kŏkamā'm~~ē,~~ kŏk'amā-) *adj.* (slang). 1. Wort~~h~~less, fake. 2. Nonsensical, absur~~d.~~

cock·a·too (kŏk'atoo, kŏkatoo~~'~~) *n.* (pl. **-toos**). Any of vario~~us~~ parrots of the genus *Kakatoe*, ~~of~~ Australia and E. Ind. islands, wi~~th~~ movable crest or tuft of feathers ~~on~~ head. [Malay *kakatua*]

cock·a·trice (kŏk'atrĭs) *n.* Mythical monster, half cock an~~d~~ half serpent, supposedly able to k~~ill~~ with a glance.

cock·chaf·er (kŏk'chāfer) *n.* Large European pale-brown beet~~le~~ (*Melolontha melolontha*), flying b~~y~~ night with loud whirring sound.

Cock·croft (kŏk'krawft, -krŏft~~)~~ **Sir John Douglas** (1897–196~~7~~) British physicist; joint winner ~~of~~ Nobel Prize for physics, 1951, f~~or~~ pioneer work on transmutation ~~of~~ atomic nuclei by artificially a~~c~~celerated atomic particles.

cocked (kŏkt) *adj.*: see COCK[1] *v.* ~ **hat**, hat with very wide bri~~m~~ permanently turned up at two ~~or~~ three places, esp. a three-cornere~~d~~ hat; tricorn.

cock·er·el (kŏk'erel, kŏk'rel) *n.* Young rooster.

cock·er (kŏk'er) **spaniel.** (Bree~~d~~ of) small dog with drooping ea~~rs~~ and long, silky, slightly wave~~d~~

ick coat.

cock·eyed (kŏk´īd) *adj.* (slang) cross-eyed; askew, crooked; (fig.) absurd; drunk.

cock·horse (kŏk´hôrs) *n.* Anything a child rides astride upon; rocking horse.

cock·le[1] (kŏk´el) *n.* Plant (*Lychnis* or *Agrostemma githago*) with reddish-purple flowers and capsules of numerous black seeds, growing as weed in grain fields.

cock·le[2] (kŏk´el) *n.* Bivalve mollusk of genus *C~*, esp. *C. edule*, common on sandy coasts and used for food; the shell or a valve of the shell, of this; (**warm**) **the ~s of the heart**, (delight) one's feelings; **cock´leshell**, shell of cockle; small sail boat. **cockle** *v.* (**-led, -ling**). Wrinkle, pucker.

cock·ney (kŏk´nē) *n.* (pl. **-neys**). (often **C~**) Native of the East End of London (strictly, one born within the sound of Bow Bells); London East End dialect. **~** *adj.* Of, characteristic of, cockneys. [orig. meaning "cock's egg," prob. small or misshapen egg; later, "townsman"]

cock·pit (kŏk´pĭt) *n.* 1. Pit or enclosed area for cockfights; arena of any struggle. 2. (naut.) Open space or well in after part of small vessel, for helmsman, crew, etc. 3. Place for pilot etc. in fuselage of aircraft; place for driver in racing car.

cock·roach (kŏk´rōch) *n.* Nocturnal voracious dark-brown beetle-like insect of the order

Blattaria, esp. of genus *Blatta* or *Periplaneta*, infesting kitchens etc.

cock·sure (kŏk´shoor´) *adj.* Absolutely certain *of, about*; self-confident, dogmatic, presumptuous. **cock´sure´ness** *n.*

cock·tail (kŏk´tāl) *n.* 1. Any of various chilled mixed drinks of liquor with fruit juice, bitters, or other flavorings; **~ party**, party, usu. in the late afternoon or early evening before dinner, at which alcoholic drinks and canapés are served; **~ shaker**, tall cuplike shaker with top, in which cocktails are vigorously shaken to mix them. 2. Appetizer such as cold seafood, fruit pieces, juice, etc. **cocktail**

The tricorne or **cocked hat** *was first worn in Europe in the mid-18th century and taken up by American settlers until replaced by the top hat in the 19th century.*

adj. Of, for a cocktail party, as **~ dress**.

cock·y (kŏk´ē) *adj.* (**cock·i·er, cock·i·est**). Cheerfully self-confident; conceited. **cock´i·ly** *adv.* **cock´i·ness** *n.*

co·co (kō´kō) *n.* (pl. **-cos**). (also **coconut palm**) Tropical palm tree (*Cocos nucifera*) producing the coconut.

co·coa (kō´kō) *n.* Powder produced by crushing and grinding

The **cockchafer** *is a large beetle often found on the leaves of European oaks in the day, and flying noisily at dusk. Left: the male is at the top of the illustration, the female below. Below: There are about 1,200 species of* **cockroach**, *an orthopterous insect found in most parts of the world and especially abundant in the tropics.*

cacao seeds; beverage made by combining this powder with milk or water and sugar; ~ **bean**, cacao seed; ~ **butter**, fatty matter obtained from cacao seed. [corruption of CACAO, confused with COCO]

co·co·nut (kō'kŏnŭt) *n.* Large ovate brown hard-shelled fruit of the coconut palm, with edible white lining and milky fluid (~ **milk**) filling the hollow center; ~ **fiber**, fiber of outer husk of coconut; ~ **palm** = COCO.

co·coon (kŏkoon') *n.* Case of silky thread spun by larvae of many insects to protect them in chrysalis state, esp. that spun by silkworm and used as source of silk; (fig.) protective covering. [Fr. *cocon*, f. mod. Provençal *coucoun* eggshell, cocoon, dim. of *coca* shell]

Co·cos (kō'kōs, -kŏs) **Islands.** Group of 27 small coral islands in the Indian Ocean, about 700 miles (1127 km) SW. of Sumatra; administered by Australia.

co·cotte (kŏkŏt'; *Fr.* kawkawt') *n.* (pl. **-cottes** pr. -kŏts'; *Fr.* -kawt'). (archaic) Fashionable prostitute.

Coc·teau (kŏktō'), **Jean** (1891–1963). French avant-garde poet, novelist, and playwright.

cod (kŏd) *n.* (pl. **cods**, collect. **cod**). Large fish of the family Gadidae of N. Atlantic and connected seas; ~**-liver oil**, oil extracted from cod's liver, rich in vitamins A and D.

C.O.D., COD *abbrevs.* Cash on delivery.

co·da (kō'dɑ) *n.* (mus.) More or less independent passage concluding movement or piece of music; (ballet) concluding section. [It., f. L. *cauda* tail]

cod·dle (kŏd'el) *v.t.* (**-dled,**

Most spiders have 3 pairs of spinnerets on their abdomens. With one pair they spin a special silk for their **cocoons**. Their eggs are protected in the cocoon until hatched.

-dling). 1. Treat indulgently, baby. 2. Cook in water just below boiling point.

code (kōd) *n.* 1. Systematic collection or digest of laws, rules and regulations, etc. 2. Set of conventional symbols used in transmitting messages by flags, telegraph, etc.; system, set, of words, figures, groups of letters, etc., used for other words or phrases, to ensure secrecy or brevity in messages or as system of reference; system of symbols used in computer etc.; also transf.; ~ **book**, list of signals, symbols, etc. used in a code; ~ **name**, ~ **number**, word or symbol, number, used for secrecy or convenience instead or ordinary name; **genetic** ~: see GENETIC. **code** *v.t.* (**cod·ed, cod·ing**). Convert into a code. **cod'er** *n.*

co·deine (kō'dēn) *n.* Alkaloid narcotic derived from opium, used as an analgesic, to relieve coughing, etc. [Gr. *kōdeia* poppy head]

co·dex (kō'dĕks) *n.* (pl. **co·di·ces** pr. kō'dĭsēz, kŏd'ĭ-). Manuscript volume, esp. of ancient texts.

codg·er (kŏj'er) *n.* (colloq.) Old man.

cod·i·cil (kŏd'ĭsĭl) *n.* Supplement to will or agreement, altering, explaining, or revoking original contents. **cod·i·cil·la·ry** (kŏdĭsĭl'erē) *adj.*

cod·i·fy (kŏd'ĭfī, kō'dĭ-) *ı* (**-fied, -fy·ing**). Reduce to a co or system. **cod·i·fi·ca·tic** (kŏdĭfĭkā'shon, kōdi-) *n.*

Co·dy (kō'dē), **Willia Frederick**: see BUFFALO BILL.

co·ed, co-ed (kō'ĕd, kōĕd') *aɑ* Coeducational. ~ *n.* (colloq.) G or woman student in coeducatior institution.

co·ed·u·ca·tion (kōĕjŏōkā'shɑ *n.* Education of both sex together. **co·ed·u·ca'tion·al** *adj*

co·ef·fi·cient (kōefĭsh'ent) (algebra) Number placed befo and multiplying known or u known quantity; (phys.) numb expressing amount of some chan or effect under certain conditions temperature, pressure, etc. as ~ *expansion*.

coe·la·canth (sē'lɑkănth) Fish of family Coelacanthidae wi fleshy fin bases and narro symmetrical tail, believed extin since Cretaceous period un specimens (*Latimeria chalumna* were found in SE. Afr. seas in 19 and later.

coe·len·ter·ate (sēlĕn'terāt, -rɩ *adj. & n.* (Member) of phylu Coelenterata, comprising aquat animals (mostly marine, includin jellyfish, sea anemones, and coral that have an intestinal canal but r separate true body cavity, usu. wi

*The abundant **cod** is one of the for most food fish of the seas. Cod are bo tom feeders, eating mollusks, squid an small fish. Illustrated below, is an Aus tralian reef cod.*

coelenterates *are the lowest form of animal life that has definite tissue. The phylum includes polyps, corals and jellyfish such as the one—catylerhiza tuberculata—illustrated here.*

inging cells and showing radial symmetry.

coe·lom (sē´lom) *n.* (pl. **coe·-oms, coe·lo·ma·ta** pr. sēlō´mata, lŏm´ata). (zool.) Body cavity or pace between intestinal canal and ody wall.

co·e·qual (kōē´kwal) *adj.* & *n.* Equal. **co·e´qual·ly** *adv.*

co·erce (kōērs´) *v.* (**-erced, erc·ing**). Constrain into obedi-nce etc.; use, secure by, force. **o·er·cion** (kōēr´shon) *n.* Con-raint, compulsion, government by rce. **co·er·cive** (kōēr´sĭv) *adj.*

co·es·sen·tial (kōĭsĕn´shal) *adj.* Of the same substance or essence.

Coeur d'Alene (kēr dalān´). Lake and resort area in N. Idaho.

Coeur de Lion (kēr de lēawṅ´). Lionhearted, epithet of RICHARD I.

co·e·val (kōē´val) *adj.* & *n.* (Person) of equal antiquity, of same ge; contemporary. **co·e´val·ly** dv.

co·ex·ist (kōĭgzĭst´) *v.i.* Exist together or *with*. **co·ex·ist´ence** *n.* (esp. pol.) Peaceful existence side by side of nations professing different ideologies.

co·ex·ten·sive (kōĭkstĕn´sĭv) *adj.* Extending over same space, time, or scope.

C. of C. *abbrev.* Chamber of Commerce.

cof·fee (kaw´fē, kŏf´ē) *n.* Dark brown, slightly stimulating drink made from the shrub *Coffea arabica* by roasting and grinding its seeds and brewing them in boiling water;

Specimens of the **coelacanth,** *for long believed extinct, have been caught since a 5-ft. specimen was discovered in 1938. About 40 coelacanths have been found near Madagascar. The fish thrived in the Devonian period.*

these seeds, the powder made by grinding them; the shrub itself, a native of eastern Asia and Africa, bearing fragrant white flowers and red fleshy berries each containing two seeds (~ **beans**); cup of coffee; light brown color; **cof´feecake,** cake or sweetened bread to be eaten with coffee, often containing raisins, nuts, or bits of candied fruit and covered with sugar or icing; **coffee grounds**, granular sediment in coffee after brewing; **cof'feehouse**, restaurant selling coffee etc., esp. in 17th and 18th c. when they were frequented for political and literary conversation etc.; **coffee klatsch, coffee klatch** (also **kaffee klatsch**), informal social gathering for coffee and conversation; **coffee mill**, contrivance for grinding roasted coffee beans; **cof'feepot**, percolator; pot in which coffee is made or served; **coffee shop**, small restaurant, esp. at a motel or hotel; **coffee table**, small low table. [Arab. *ḳahwa* the drink]

cof·fer (kaw'fer, kŏf'er) *n.* 1. Box, esp. strongbox for valuables etc.; funds; treasury. 2. (archit.) Sunk panel in ceiling or soffit. 3. (also **cof'ferdam**) Caisson. **coffer** *v.t.* Ornament with coffers.

cof·fin (kaw'fĭn, kŏf'ĭn) *n.* 1. Oblong box in which corpse is buried or cremated. 2. Horse's hoof; ~ **bone**, small spongy bone in horse's hoof, last phalangeal bone of foot. **coffin** *v.t.* Enclose in or as in coffin.

C. of S. *abbrev.* Chief of Staff.

cog (kŏg, kawg) *n.* One of a series of projections on wheel, bar, etc., transmitting or receiving motion by engaging with corresponding projections on another wheel etc.; ~ **railway**, (also **rack railway**) railway with a cogged center rail that engages with center cogwheel on locomotive, which thereby has enough traction to climb steep grades; **cog'wheel**, toothed wheel, wheel with cogs.

co·gent (kō'jent) *adj.* Forcibly convincing. **co'gen·cy** *n.* **co'gent·ly** *adv.*

cog·i·tate (kŏj'ĭtāt) *v.* (**-tat·ed, -tat·ing**). Ponder, meditate. **cog'i·ta·tor** *n.* **cog·i·ta·tion** (kŏjĭtā'shon) *n.* **cog'i·ta·tive** *adj.*

co·gnac (kōn'yăk, kŏn'-) *n.* Brandy produced in the vicinity of Cognac in western France. [*Cognac*, town in Charente]

cog·nate (kŏg'nāt) *adj.* 1. Descended from a common ancestor, esp., in Roman law; akin in origin, allied, related. 2. (of languages) Of the same linguistic stock; (of words) having the same root or origin, representing the same original word. ~ *n.* Cognate person; cognate word. **cog'na·tion** (kŏgnā'shon) *n.* Cognate relationship.

cog·ni·tion (kŏgnĭsh'on) *n.* Action or faculty of knowing or acquiring knowledge (including sensation, conception, etc.) as dist. from feeling and volition. **cog'ni·tive** (kŏg'nĭtĭv) *adj.*

cog·ni·za·ble (kŏg'nĭzabel, kŏgnī'za-) *adj.* Perceptible, knowable; within jurisdiction of a court etc.

cog·ni·zance (kŏg'nĭzans) *n.* 1. Being aware; notice. 2. (Right of) dealing with a matter legally or judicially. 3. Distinguishing device or mark. **cog'ni·zant** *adj.* Having or taking cognizance; (philos.) having cognition.

cog·no·men (kŏgnō'men) *n.* (pl. **-no·mens, -nom·i·na** pr. -nŏm'-ina). 1. Third or family name of Roman citizen, as Caius Julius *Caesar*; additional name or epithet

bestowed on individual; nicknam 2. Family name; surname; name.

co·gno·scen·ti (kŏnyoshĕn't kŏgno, kŏno-) *n.pl.* (sing. **-te** -tē). Persons of superior taste knowledge, connoisseurs. [It.]

co·hab·it (kōhăb'ĭt) *v.i.* Li together as husband and wife (fre of persons not legally marrie **co·hab'it·ant, co·hab·i·ta·tio** (kōhăbĭtā'shon) *ns.*

Co·han (kō'hăn), Georg M(ichael) (1878–1942). Ame vaudeville performer, actor, son writer, playwright, and produce best known for his songs "I'm Yankee Doodle Dandy," "You're Grand Old Flag," "Give M Regards to Broadway," "Ov There," etc.

co·heir (kō'âr'), **co·heir·e** (kō'âr'ĭs) *ns.* Joint heir, masculi and feminine.

co·here (kōhēr') *v.i.* (**-here -her·ing**). Stick together, rema united; be consistent, well-knit.

co·her·ent (kōhēr'ent) *a* Cohering; consistent, not ramblin or inconsequent. **co·her'ent·l** *adv.* **co·her'ence, co·her'en·c** *ns.*

co·he·sion (kōhē'zhon) *n.* C hering; tendency to remain unite (chem.) molecular force of attra tion between similar kinds molecules (opp. ADHESION **co·he·sive** (kōhē'sĭv) *adj.*

co·hort (kō'hôrt) *n.* One of th ten divisions of a Roman legio consisting of 300 to 600 men; ban of warriors; group; (collo associate, companion.

coif (koif) *n.* (hist.) Close ca covering top, back, and sides,

*A **cog railway** carries tourists to the summit of Mt. Washington in New Hampshire's White Mountains. The center cog provides additional traction for the train.*

*Below: The evergreen bush that bears the **coffee** bean was probably native to Ethiopia. It grows well on well-drained volcanic soils that have over 15 ins. rainfall.*

Facing page: The husk of the coffe bean is chaffed in a simple machin The beans are roasted before use s that the oil may be released an imparted to the eventual brew.

head.

coif·feur (kwahfer´) *n.* (fem. **coif·feuse** pr. kwahföz´) Hair-dresser. [Fr.]

coif·fure (kwahfūr´) *n.* Way hair is dressed; hair style.

coil (koil) *n.* Length of rope etc. wound continuously around one point; anything arranged thus; such arrangement; one turn of anything coiled; (elect.) helically-wound wire serving as conductor. ~ *v.* Dispose, wind, into circular or spiral shape.

coin (koin) *n.* Piece of metal of definite weight and value, made into money by being stamped with official device; coined money, money in circulation. ~ *v.t.* 1. Make (money) by stamping metal; make (metal) into coin. 2. Turn into money; ~ **money**, (colloq.) make or gain money quickly. 3. Fabricate, invent (esp. new word or phrase).

coin·age (koi´nĭj) *n.* (Right of) coining; coins collectively, currency; invention, fabrication; coined word.

co·in·cide (kōĭnsīd´) *v.i.* (-cid·ed, -cid·ing). Fall together and agree in position; (geom.) occupy same portion of space; occur at, occupy, same space of time; be identical, agree exactly.

co·in·ci·dence (kōĭn´sĭdens) *n.* (Instance of) coinciding; notable concurrence of events or circumstances without apparent causal connection. **co·in·ci·dent, co·in·ci·den·tal** (kōĭnsĭdĕn´tal) *adjs.* **co·in·ci·den·tal·ly** *adv.*

co·i·tus (kō´ĭtus, kōē´-) *n.* Insertion of penis into vagina and (usu.) ejaculation of semen. [L.]

coke[1] (kōk) *n.* Compact form of impure carbon obtained from coal by heating out of contact with air, used for smelting metals, for foundry work, as a fuel, etc. ~ *v.t.* (**coked, cok·ing**). Convert (coal) into coke.

coke[2] (kōk) *n.* (slang) Cocaine.

Coke (kook), **Sir Edward** (1552–1634). English jurist and adherent of common law; first Lord Chief Justice of England; prosecuted Essex and Raleigh, and Gunpowder Plot conspirators.

Col. *abbrev.* Colonel; Colorado.

col. *abbrev.* College; collegiate; colony; color; column.

co·la[1] (kō´la) = KOLA.

co·la[2] (kō´la) *n.* Any carbonated soft drink flavored with a syrup made from kola nuts or seeds.

col·an·der (kŭl´ander, kŏl´-) *n.* Perforated container for straining water from foods after washing or cooking.

Col·bert (kawlber´), **Jea Baptiste** (1619–83). Frenc statesman; economic adviser t Louis XIV; founded the Frenc

*The **Colchicum** autumnale (autumn cro cus) is one of several species o crocus-like plants cultivated for pink white or purple tube-shaped flowers The stem contains a substance used t treat rheumatism and gout.*

*The oldest British footguards regiment, the **Coldstream Guards** was founded in 1659 at Coldstream in Scotland. The Coldstreams, prominent ceremonial troops, are highly trained infantrymen.*

*Works by the English Romantic poet **Samuel Taylor Coleridge** include 'The Rime of the Ancient Mariner' and 'Kubla Khan'. The latter was written under the influence of opium, to which he became addicted.*

Academies of Literature, Science, and the Fine Arts.

col·chi·cine (kŏl′chĭsēn, -sĭn, kŏl′kĭ-) *n.* Alkaloid ($C_{22}H_{25}O_6N$) derived from colchicum, used in plant breeding etc.

col·chi·cum (kŏl′chĭkum, kŏl′-ĭ-) *n.* Liliaceous plant of genus C~ including autumn crocus; dried corm or seed of this, containing colchicine.

Col·chis (kŏl′kĭs). Ancient region on the Black Sea S. of the Caucasus Mountains; famous in Greek legend as the land of the Golden Fleece and the home of MEDEA.

cold (kōld) *adj.* 1. Of low temperature, esp. when compared with human body or with usual temperature; relatively without heat, not heated, having been allowed to cool; feeling cold. 2. Without ardor, friendliness, or affection; undemonstrative; apathetic; chilling, depressing; **leave (person) ~**, fail to excite him. 3. (of colors) Suggesting a cold or sunless day, esp. containing blue or gray. 4. (of hunting scent) Not strong, faint. 5. (in children's games) Far from the object sought, or from finding or guessing. 6. (colloq.) Unconscious. 7. ~-**blooded**, (of fish and reptiles as dist. from other vertebrates) having blood whose temperature varies with that of the external air or water; (of persons, actions) unimpassioned, cool; unfeeling, callous; deliberately cruel; **in ~ blood**, without human feelings, deliberate and cruel; ~ **cream**, cosmetic for skin; ~ **cuts**, sliced cold cooked meats; ~ **duck**, drink made by combining sparkling burgundy and champagne; **have, get, ~ feet**, (slang) become afraid; (**give the**) ~ **shoulder**, (treat with) intentional coldness or indifference, snub; ~-**shoulder** (*v.t.*); ~ **sore**, sore caused by virus infection around the mouth, usu. accompanying a fever or head cold; ~ **sweat**, simultaneous chill and perspiring as a result of shock, pain, fear, nervousness, etc.; ~ **turkey**, (slang) abrupt withdrawal of narcotics from an addict; ~ **war**, unfriendly relations between nations characterized by hostile propaganda etc. and threat of actual war; ~ **water**, unheated water; chilled water; **throw ~ water on**, disparage, discourage. **cold′ly** *adv.* **cold′ness** *n.* **cold** *n.* 1. Prevalence of low temperature in the atmosphere; cold weather; sensation produced by loss of heat from the body. 2. Inflammatory condition of mucous membrane of nose and throat, with catarrh and freq. hoarseness and cough (freq. **head ~, ~ in the head**).

Cold·stream (kōld′strēm) **Guards.** British regiment of guards of the royal household; formed in 1659 at Coldstream on the Tweed, a river in Scotland.

cole (kōl) *n.* (rare exc. in comb.) Cabbage; see RAPE[2]; **cole′slaw**, salad of shredded raw cabbage with dressing.

co·le·op·ter·ous (kōlēŏp′terus, kŏlē-) *adj.* Of the Coleoptera or beetles, a large order of insects having the front pair of wings converted into hard sheaths that cover the other pair when not in use.

co·le·op·tile (kōlēŏp′tĭl, kŏlē-) *n.* (bot.) Hollow organ produced by germinating grasses, inside which the first leaf makes its way to the ground surface.

Cole·ridge (kōl′rĭj), **Samuel Taylor** (1772–1834). English romantic poet and literary critic, one of the Lake poets (see LAKE[1]); author of "The Ancient Mariner," "Kubla Khan," "Christabel," etc.

Co·lette (kōlĕt′, kŏ-), **Sidonie Gabrielle** (1873–1954). French music hall performer and novelist; author of *Chéri, Gigi,* etc.

Col·fax (kōl′făks), **Schuyler** (1823–85). Vice president of the U.S. under Ulysses S. Grant, 1869–73.

col·ic (kŏl′ĭk) *n.* Severe spasmodic pain in belly and bowels. **col′ick·y** *adj.*

Col·i·se·um, Col·os·se·um (kŏlĭsē′um). 1. Amphitheater in Rome, begun by Vespasian in 72 A.D.; scene of gladiatorial combats and the martyrdom of many Christians. 2. (c~) Amphitheater for public entertainment, sports, etc.

co·li·tis (kōlī′tĭs) *n.* Inflammation of membrane of large intestine.

coll. *abbrev.* College; colloquial.

col·lab·o·rate (kōlăb′ōrāt) *v.i.* (**-rat·ed, -rat·ing**). Work in combination (*with*) esp. on literary or artistic production; cooperate treasonably with the enemy (esp. in countries occupied by the Germans in World War II). **col·lab·o·ra·tion** (kōlăbōrā′shon) *n.* **col·lab·o·ra′tion·ist** *n.* Treacherous collaborator. **col·lab′o·ra·tor** *n.*

col·lage (kolahzh′, kō-) *n*. Art form in which pieces of paper and other materials and objects are glued to the pictorial surface; such a work of art.

col·la·gen (kŏl′ajen) *n*. Protein found in animal tissue and bone, which yields gelatin on boiling. **col·la·gen·ic** (kŏlajĕn′ĭk) *adj*.

col·lapse (kolăps′) *n*. 1. Falling in, sudden shrinking together, giving way; failure, breakdown. 2. Prostration by loss of nervous or muscular power; breakdown of mental energy, sudden loss of courage, spirits, etc. ~ *v*. (-lapsed, -laps·ing). 1. Fall together, give way, by external pressure, cave in; contract. 2. (Cause to) fail, break down, or come to nothing. **col·laps·i·bil·i·ty** (kolăpsĭbĭl′ĭtē) *n*. **col·laps′i·ble** *adj*. Made to collapse or fold together.

col·lar (kŏl′er) *n*. 1. Part of garment encircling neck or forming turned-back upper border near the neck; band (often separate) of linen, lace, etc., worn around neck and completing upper part of costume. 2. Ornamental chain forming part of insigne of order of knighthood; band around neck of dog or other animal for identification or ornament; part of harness of draft animal, fitting over lower part of neck. 3. Restraining or connecting band, ring, pipe, etc., in machines etc. 4. **col′larbone**, bone connecting breastbone with shoulder blade, clavicle. **collar** *v.t*. Seize (person) by the collar, capture;

Schools such as Eton in Berkshire were called **colleges.** This indicated that the establishment provided secondary education — a social privilege in the U.K. until the 19th century.

(slang) lay hold of, seize, arrest (felon).

col·late (kŏlāt′, kō-, kŏl′āt, kō′lāt) *v.t*. (-lat·ed, -lat·ing). 1. Compare carefully and exactly (esp. copy of text *with* other or the original); (bookbinding) verify order of sheets of printed book by signatures; assemble in proper numerical or logical sequence. 2. Admit (a cleric) *to* a benefice.

col·lat·er·al (kolăt′eral) *adj*. 1. Situated or running side by side, parallel; subordinate but from same source; contributory; connected but aside from main subject, course, etc. 2. (opp. LINEAL) Descended from same stock but in a different line. ~ *n*. Collateral kinsman; security pledged as guarantee of repayment of loan. **col·lat′er·al·ly** *adv*.

col·la·tion (kŏlā′shon, kō-) *n*. 1. Collating; comparison; description of book or manuscript by signatures, list of contents, etc. 2. Light meal permitted on fast days; any light meal.

col·league (kŏl′ēg) *n*. Fellow member of a profession, faculty, staff, etc.; associate.

col·lect¹ (kŏl′ĕkt) *n*. Short prayer before the epistle in a communion service as appointed for particular day or season.

col·lect² (kolĕkt′) *v*. Bring or

The **collie,** a sheep-dog which renowned for its loyalty and inte gence, has been used to herd she for over 300 years.

come together, accumulate; gath (money) from a number of peop for charity, as taxes, etc.; ma collection of (curiosities, ra books, etc.); regain control concentrate, recover (one's facult etc., also oneself); (colloq.) call f and take away. **col·lect′ed** *a* (esp.) Bound together or similar and sold as a single book or set, ~ works of an author; n distracted, cool. **col·lect′ed** *adv*. **col·lect′ed·ness** *n*.

col·lec·tion (kolĕk′shon) *n*. Collecting; money collected. 2. S of things gathered together.

col·lec·tive (kolĕk′tĭv) *a* Constituting a collection, gather into one or into a whole, aggregat of, from, a number of individua taken or acting together, as *people's* ~; common; ~ **bargain ing**, negotiation between employ and union representatives determine wages, hours, benefi working conditions, etc.; ~ **farr** in U.S.S.R., farm or group of farr organized as a unit and worked b a community under state supe vision; ~ **noun**, singular nov (such as *class, jury*) used to deno a collection or number of ind viduals; ~ **security**, security f nations, obtained by trusting united strength of an internation organization for peace or of a grou f allied nations; ~ **unconscious**: see UNCONSCIOUS. **col·lec′tive·ly** *adv.* **col·lec′tive** *n.* Collective noun; collective farm. **col·lec′-tiv·ism** *n.* Theory or practice of collective ownership or control of all means of production, esp. of land, by the whole community or nation. **col·lec′tiv·ist** *adj. & n.* **col·lec′tiv·ize** *v.t.* (**-ized, -iz·ing**). **col·lec·ti·vi·za·tion** (kŏlĕktĭvĭzā′shon) *n.*

col·lec·tor (kolĕk′ter) *n.* One who collects, esp. scientific specimens, curiosities, works of art, etc.; one who collects money for overdue bills, taxes, etc.

col·leen (kŏl′ēn, kŏlēn′) *n.* (colloq.) Irish girl. [Ir. *caile countrywoman*]

col·lege (kŏl′ĭj) *n.* 1. Organized body of persons performing certain functions and sometimes possessing special rights and privileges; **Electoral C~**: see ELECTOR; **C~ of Cardinals**, body of all cardinals of the Roman Catholic Church, who constitute the pope's council and elect to the papacy. 2. Independent corporation of scholars within, or in connection with, a university (Brit.); similar organization outside a university; university; any school of higher education granting the bachelor's degree in liberal arts or science. 3. Building of a college. **col·le·gian** (kolē′jan -jēan) *n.* Member of a college. **col·le·giate** (kolē′jĭt) *adj.* Of, constituted as, a college; ~ **church**, church endowed for a body corporate or chapter but with no bishop's see; (Scotland) church under joint pastorate.

col·len·chy·ma (kolĕng′kima) *n.* (bot.) Tissue consisting of cells with local cellulose thickening on their walls, usu. developed near surface of young stems and leaves and strengthening these.

col·lide (kolīd′) *v.i.* (**-lid·ed, -lid·ing**). Come forcibly into contact (*with*), strike or dash together; be in conflict, clash.

col·lie (kŏl′ē) *n.* Sheep dog of a Scotch breed, with long hair, pointed nose, and bushy tail.

col·lier (kŏl′yer) *n.* 1. Coal miner. 2. Coal ship. **col′lier·y** *n.* (Brit.) (pl. **-lier·ies**). Coal mine.

col·li·mate (kŏl′imāt) *v.t.* (**-mat·ed, -mat·ing**). Adjust (telescope) so that line of sight is in correct position; place (telescopes, lenses, etc.) with optical axes in same line; (of lens etc.) make (rays of light) parallel. **col·li·ma·tor** (kŏl′imāter) *n.* Small telescope with cross hairs at its focus, used for adjusting line of sight of larger instrument, such as surveyor's transit. **col·li·ma·tion** (kŏlimā′shon) *n.*

Col·lins[1] (kŏl′ĭnz), **Michael** (1890–1922). Irish revolutionary leader, active in Sinn Fein move-

ment and Irish Volunteers military group; minister of finance and commander of military forces of Irish Free State; mortally wounded in repelling an attack of irregulars.

Col·lins[2] (kŏl′ĭnz), (**William**) **Wilkie** (1824–89). English novelist; author of *The Moonstone* (1868), considered by many to be one of the first English detective novels.

col·li·sion (kolĭzh′on) *n.* Colliding; violent encounter of moving body, esp. car, ship, or train, with another; clash, clashing; ~ **course**, course bound to end in collision.

col·lo·cate (kŏl′okāt) *v.t.* (**-cat·ed, -cat·ing**). Place together, arrange. **col·lo·ca·tion** (kŏlokā′shon) *n.*

col·lo·di·on (kolō′dēon) *n.* Colorless syrupy liquid, a solution of pyroxylin in ether and alcohol, drying rapidly in air, and used for covering photographic plates, wounds, burns, etc.

col·logue (kolōg′) *v.i.* (**-logued, -logu·ing**). Talk confidentially; (dial.) conspire.

col·loid (kŏl′oid) *adj.* Gluey; ~ **substance, tissue**, etc., (path.) gelatinous substance produced in certain forms of tissue degeneration. **colloid** *n.* (chem.) Suspension of finely divided solid in a liquid, etc. forming a system that does not separate on standing.

col·loi·dal (kŏloi′dal) *adj.*

colloq. *abbrev.* Colloquial.

col·lo·qui·al (kolō′kwēal) *adj.* Of or in talk, conversational; belonging to familiar, not formal or elevated, speech. **col·lo′qui·al·ism** *n.* **col·lo′qui·al·ly** *adv.*

col·lo·quy (kŏl′okwē) *n.* (pl. **-quies**). Conversation, esp. a formal one; conference.

col·lo·type (kŏl′otīp) *n.* Planographic printing process used mainly for fine reproduction work; print so made.

col·lu·sion (kolōō′zhon) *n.* Fraudulent secret understanding. **col·lu·sive** (kolōō′sĭv) *adj.* **col·lu′sive·ly** *adv.*

Colo. *abbrev.* Colorado.

col·o·cynth (kŏl′osĭnth) *n.* Bitter apple (*Citrullus colocynthis*), a plant of the gourd family, bearing fruit about size of orange with light spongy extremely bitter pulp; purgative drug prepared from this.

Co·logne (kolōn′). (Ger. *Köln*) Industrial city on the lower Rhine in West Germany; famous since the Middle Ages for its cathedral; (also **eau de ~, c~**) toilet water made of aromatic oils and alcohol, first

*The magnificent Gothic cathedral in **Cologne** is one of the finest of its type in the world. The city, now the cultural and economic center of the Rhineland, was founded by the Romans.*

Co·lom·bi·a (kolŭm´bēa). Republic in NW. South America; under Spanish rule until 1819, when a republic was established by Simon BOLIVAR, consisting of the territories now known as Colombia, Panama, Venezuela, and Ecuador; Venezuela and Ecuador seceded in 1830 and Panama in 1903; capital, Bogotá. **Co·lom´bi·an** adj. & n.

Co·lom·bo (kolŭm´bō). Capital city of Sri Lanka.

Co·lon (kōlŏn´). Port city of Panama on the Caribbean.

co·lon[1] (kō´lon) n. (pl. **-lons, -la** pr. **-la**). Greater part of large intestine, extending from cecum to rectum. **co·lon·ic** (kōlŏn´ĭk) adj.

co·lon[2] (kō´lon) n. (pl. **-lons**). Punctuation mark (:), used esp. before illustration or quotation.

Co·lón (kawlawn´) **Archipel·ago**: see GALAPAGOS ISLANDS.

colo·nel (kēr´nel) n. 1. Officer in command of a regiment, ranking above lieutenant colonel and below brigadier general. 2. Honorary state title, as a **Kentucky ~. colo´nel·cy** n.

co·lo·ni·al (kolō´nēal) adj. Of a colony; (hist.) of the thirteen British colonies of America that became the original thirteen states of the United States; (of architecture, etc.) of the period during which these states were still colonies; **C~ Office**, department of British

The state of Colorado has its western half in the Rocky Mountains. Its most famous feature is the Grand Canyon. Seen here is a cliff palace of the Pueblo Indians in the Mesa Verde.

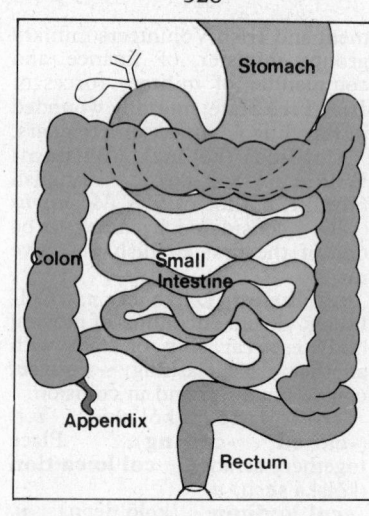

One of the functions of the colon is to store waste products until they are ready to be passed from the body. The various medical problems associated with the colon include colitis and cancer.

Government in charge of colonies, now merged with Commonwealth Relations Office. **colonial** n. Native, inhabitant, of a colony. **co·lo·ni·al·ism** n.

col·o·nist (kŏl´onĭst) n. Settler in, founder, or inhabitant of, a colony.

col·o·nize (kŏl´onĭz) v. (**-nized, -niz·ing**). Establish colony in; establish in a colony; form or establish a colony or settlement. **col·o·ni·za·tion** (kŏlonĭzā´shon) n.

col·on·nade (kŏlonād´) n. Row of columns at regular intervals supporting a roof.

col·o·ny (kŏl´onē) n. (pl. **-nies**). 1. (Gk. hist.) Independent city

founded by emigrants; (Rom. hi settlement of Roman citizens (u veteran soldiers) in conquer territory, where they acted as garrison. 2. Settlement, settlers, new country remaining subject to connected with parent nati territory so peopled or belonging a nation by conquest or annexati 3. Number of people of o nationality or occupation formin community in a city. 4. (bio Aggregate of individual animals plants forming physiologica connected structure or (m loosely) living close together. **C~**, one of the 13 original colon that became U.S. states.

col·o·phon (kŏl´ofŏn) n. Inscription or device at end of bo or manuscript, containing tit scribe's or printer's name, da place of printing. 2. Publishe emblem or trademark plac usually on title page of book.

col·or (kŭl´er), Brit. **col·o** (kŭl´er) ns. 1. Quality or waveleng of light emitted or reflected from object, determined by the physic configuration of the emitting reflecting surface and the quality the incident light (if any); sensatio produced by stimulation of opt nerve by particular light vibration 2. Particular hue, one of t constituents into which white colorless light can be decompose mixture of these, including black (which rays of light are whol absorbed) and white (in which th are wholly reflected); **primary** (physiol.) one of the three colo (red, green, and violet), con binations of which give rise sensations of all others; (in pain

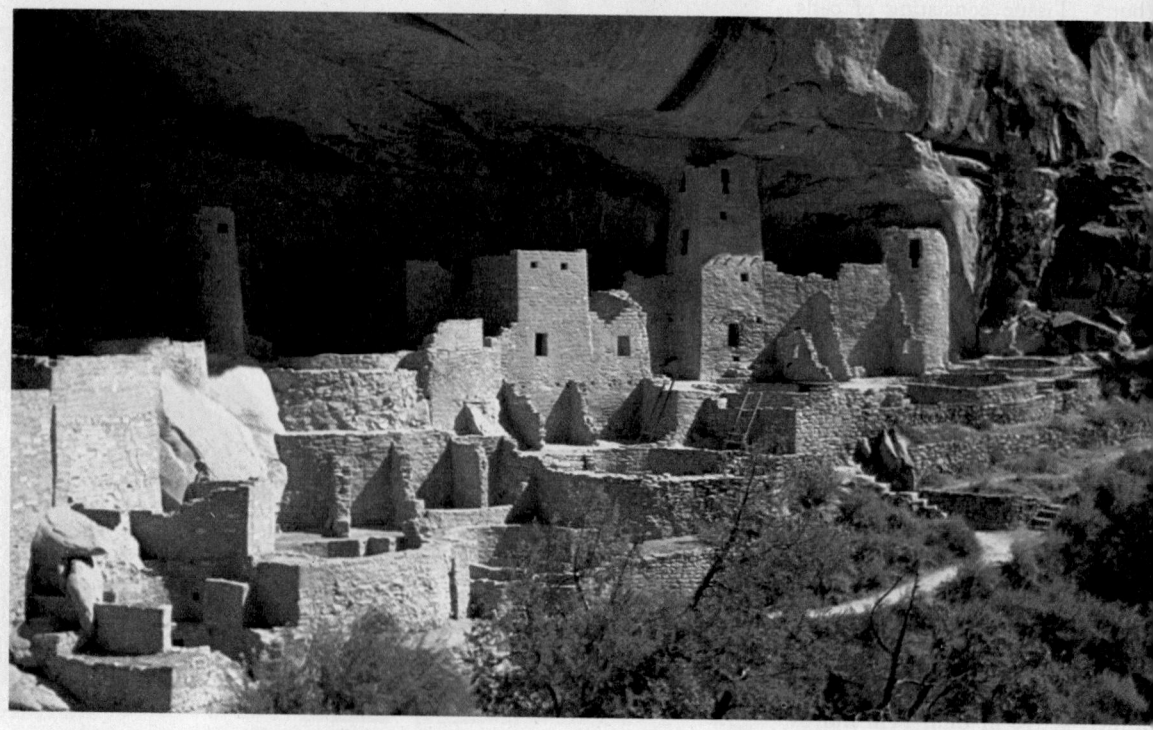

g) red, blue, or yellow, which may mixed to produce all other lors; **secondary** ~, one oduced (as green, purple) by ixing two primary colors. 3. omplexion of a member of a black ce. 4. Complexion, ruddy hue of eeks, etc. 5. Representation of lor in painting; coloring. 6. (pl.) olored ribbon, emblem, badge, c. worn as symbol of party, ganization, athletic team, etc.; g, ensign, or standard of giment or ship. 7. Pigment, int; colored material etc. 8. utward appearance, semblance; etext, show of reason; tone, aracter, kind, shade of meaning; us. 9. **local** ~, see LOCAL; **bar**, legal or social distinction tween white and other races; **blind**, unable to see, or to istinguish between, certain colors; so fig., of races; ~ **line**, social emarcation between white and onwhite persons; ~ **scheme**, stematic arrangement of colors or olored items. **color** v. Give

color to; paint, stain, dye; give a distinctive character or quality to; influence; modify; distort; misrepresent; take on color; blush. **col′ored** adj. (of persons) Not white, wholly or partly of black descent.

Col·o·rad·o (kŏlɵrăd′ō, -rah′dō). Rocky Mountain state in W. central U.S., admitted to the Union in 1876, named after the ~ **River**, which rises there and flows into the Gulf of California; capital, Denver; ~ **beetle**, potato beetle; **C**~ **Desert**, arid region in SE. California and NW. Mexico; **C**~ **Springs**, resort city in central Colorado and site of U.S. Air Force Academy.

col·or·a·tion (kŭlɵrā′shɵn) n. Coloring; arrangement of colors; natural, esp. variegated, color of living things.

col·o·ra·tu·ra (kŭlɵrɵtoor′ɵ, -tūr′ɵ, kŏl-, kōl-) n. Florid ornament, freq. extempore, in singing; (also ~ **soprano**) (singer with) high flexible voice capable of this. [It., = "colored (music)"]

*The **Colorado Beetle** (above) is found in western N. America and attacks the leaves of potato plants. By the 1870s it had become a widespread pest. It is orange-red in color with black stripes and is ⅜ ins. long.*

col·or·ful (kŭlɵrful) adj. Full of color; vivid. **col·or·ful·ly** adv. **col·or·ful·ness** n.

col·or·im·e·ter (kŭlɵrĭm′eter) n. Instrument for determining, specifying, or measuring (intensity of) color.

col·or·ing (kŭl′erĭng) n. (esp.) Style in which a thing is colored, or in which artist uses color; complexion.

col·or·ist (kŭl′ erĭst) *n.* Painter skillful in coloring.

col·or·less (kŭl′erlis) *adj.* Without color; pale; dull; wanting in character or vividness; neutral, indifferent. **col′or·less·ly** *adv.* **col′or·less·ness** *n.*

co·los·sal (kolŏs′al) *adj.* Of, like a colossus; gigantic; (colloq.) magnificent. **co·los′sal·ly** *adv.*

Col·os·se·um (kŏlosē′um) = COLISEUM.

co·los·sus (kolŏs′us) *n.* (pl. **-los·si** pr. -lŏs′ī, **-los·sus·es**). Gigantic statue; huge dominating figure, thing, person, like the statue at Rhodes which was thought to have stood astride the harbor; **C ~ of Rhodes**, bronze statue of the god Apollo, said to have been 120 ft. (36.5 m) high; erected in 280 B.C.; it was shattered by an earthquake in 224 B.C. and the fragments, which lay about the harbor for centuries, were regarded as one of the Seven Wonders of the World.

co·los·to·my (kolŏs′tomē) *n.* (pl. **-mies**). (surg.) (Formation of) an artificial excretory opening from the colon through the abdominal wall.

co·los·trum (kolŏs′trum) *n.* First milk secreted by mammal after parturition and lasting for a few days.

Colt (kōlt) *n.* (trademark) Kind of revolver. [f. Samuel Colt (1814–1862), Amer. inventor]

colt (kōlt) *n.* Young male of horse; (colloq.) inexperienced or frisky youth; **colts′foot**, common Old World weed (*Tussilago farfara*) with yellow flowers appearing before the heart-shaped leaves. **colt′ish** *adj.*

Co·lum·ba (kolŭm′ba), **St.** (521–97). Irish monk and missionary to northern Picts; founded the monastery of Iona, Scotland.

Co·lum·bi·a¹ (kolŭm′bēa). Poetic name for America; ~, capital of South Carolina, in the central part. [f. COLUMBUS]

Co·lum·bi·a² (kolŭm′bēa) **River.** River flowing from SE. British Columbia, Canada, and through the NW. U.S. 1,200 (1931 km) miles to the Pacific Ocean; it forms most of the border between Washington and Oregon.

Col·um·bine (kŏl′umbīn). Character in Italian comedy, the mistress of Harlequin.

col·um·bine (kŏl′umbīn) *n.* Plant (*Aquilegia canadensis*), the inverted flower of which, with its horned nectaries, resembles five pigeons clustered together. [L. *columba* dove]

co·lum·bi·um (kolŭm′bēum) *n.* (formerly) Niobium.

Co·lum·bus, Christopher (c1451–1506). Genoese navigator who prevailed upon Ferdinand and Isabella of Spain to bear the expenses of an expedition

This double-action **Colt** revolver of 1892 was a version of that patented by Samuel Colt in 1835–6. It contained several bored chambers, each designed to receive cartridges which successively moved into position behind the barrel.

The **columbine**, a flowering plant of the buttercup family, is found in temperate regions in the northern hemisphere. The common European variety flowers from May to July.

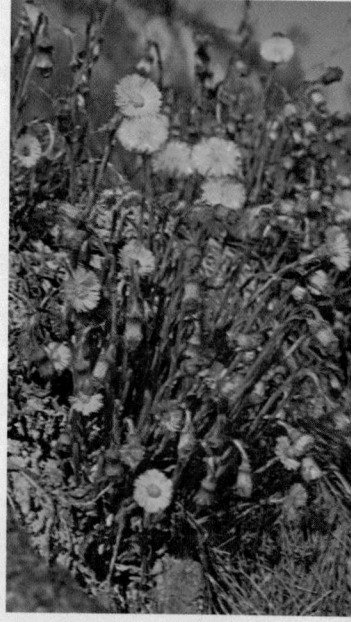

The **coltsfoot**, a prolific weed of Britain and Europe, has leaves that were used in herbal tobacco and cigarettes, and smoked as a remedy for asthma and coughs.

of discovery and set out on his first voyage in 1492; generally credited with discovery of New World; first discovered the Bahamas (Oct. 12, 1492) and Cuba, and on his third voyage (1498) landed near the mouth of the Orinoco in S. America; ~, industrial city and the capital of Ohio, in the central part; ~ **Day**, once Oct. 12, now the second Monday in October, a legal holiday in U.S. celebrating the discovery of the New World by Columbus.

col·umn (kŏl′um) *n.* 1. (archit.) Long cylindrical of slightly tapering body usu. supporting roof or arch or standing alone as monument. 2. Natural column-shaped formation, esp. of igneous rock; anything resembling a column in shape or function; upright mass of air, liquid, smoke, etc. 3. One of the narrow vertical divisions of a sheet of paper, page of book, etc., used for lists of figures, names, etc., or for convenience in arranging printed matter on a wide page; esp such a division of a newspaper, the printed matter filling it, a newspaper article. 4. Formation of troops, armored vehicles, etc., in which the elements are placed one behind the other as dist. from *line* in which they are abreast. **col′umned** *adj.*

co·lum·nar (kolŭm′ner) *adj.* Like a column; in columns.

col·um·nist (kŏl′umnĭst, -mĭst) *n.* Writer who regularly writes a newspaper or magazine column.

col·za (kŏl′za) *n.* Plant of the mustard family; RAPE².

com- *prefix.* With.

co·ma¹ (kō′ma) *n.* (pl. **-mas**). (path.) Deep unconsciousness;

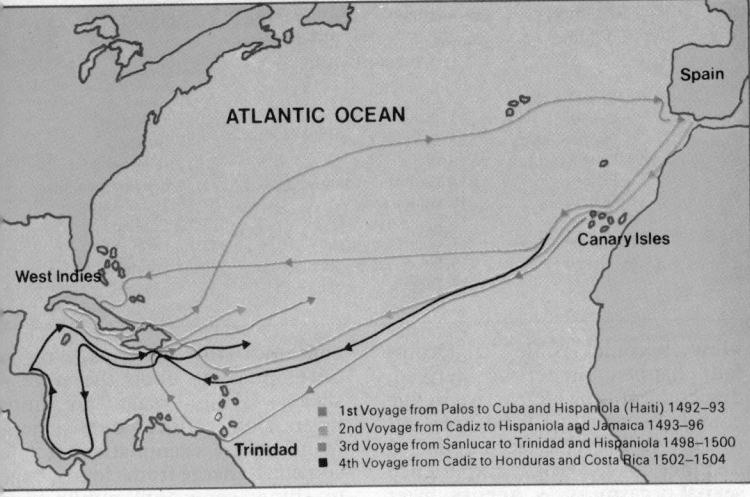

1st Voyage from Palos to Cuba and Hispaniola (Haiti) 1492–93
2nd Voyage from Cadiz to Hispaniola and Jamaica 1493–96
3rd Voyage from Sanlucar to Trinidad and Hispaniola 1498–1500
4th Voyage from Cadiz to Honduras and Costa Rica 1502–1504

ATLANTIC OCEAN

Spain

Canary Isles

West Indies

Trinidad

*Nelson's **Column** in London's Trafalgar Square reaches a height of nearly 185 ft. including the 17 ft.-high statue of the admiral at the top. At its base are four bronze lions by Sir Edwin Landseer.*

*Christopher **Columbus**, the discoverer of the New World, believed that by sailing west he could reach the Orient. After much difficulty he obtained the patronage of the Spanish king and queen and set out in 1492 on the first of four voyages (left) in the 'Santa Maria', seen here in replica (above left).*

(loosely) stupor, lethargy. **co·ma·-tose** (kō′matōs, kŏm′a-) *adj.* In a state of coma; drowsy, lethargic.

co·ma² (kō′ma) *n.* (pl. **-mae** pr. -mē). (astron.) Nebulous envelope surrounding nucleus of comet. [Gk. *komē* hair]

Co·man·che (komăn′chē) *adj.* & *n.* (pl. **-ches**, collect. **-che**). (Member, language) of a N. Amer. Indian people formerly ranging from Wyoming to Texas, now chiefly in Oklahoma.

comb (kōm) *n.* 1. Strip of bone, metal, etc., with indentations forming series of teeth, or with teeth inserted, used for disentangling, cleaning, and arranging hair, or to keep it in place. 2. Any of various things of similar appearance or function: instrument with several rows of teeth for carding wool or flax. 3. Red fleshy indented or serrated crest or caruncle on head of domestic fowl, esp. male. 4. Honeycomb. ~ *v.* Draw comb through (hair), dress (wool, flax) with comb; (of wave) curl over; search or examine closely.

com·bat (kŏm′băt, kŭm′-) *n.* Battle, fight; struggle; conflict; ~ **fatigue** = BATTLE fatigue. **combat** (kombăt′, kŏm-) *v.* (**-bat·ted, -bat·ting**). Do battle; fight with; oppose.

com·bat·ant (kombăt′ant, kŏm′batant, kŭm′-) *n.* One who fights. ~ *adj.* Fighting.

com·bat·ive (kombăt′ĭv, kŏm′-batĭv, kŭm′-) *adj.* Pugnacious.

com·bat′ive·ly *adv.* **com·bat′-ive·ness** *n.*

com·bi·na·tion (kŏmbĭnā′shon) *n.* 1. Combining; combined state; group or set of things combined; sequence of letters or numbers that open a combination lock. 2. ~ **lock**, lock that can be opened only by specific sequence of movements.

com·bi·na·tive (kŏm′binātĭv, kombī′na-) *adj.* Combining; of combination.

com·bine (kombīn′) *v.* (**-bined, -bin·ing**). 1. Join together, unite; come together; unite for common purpose, cooperate; **combined operations**, operations in which army, naval, and air forces are combined; **combining form**, (gram.) special form of word used in compounds or derivatives. 2. Enter into chemical union (*with*); **combining weight**: see EQUIVALENT. **combine** (kŏm′bīn) *n.* Combination of persons in business, politics, etc., esp. to control prices or obstruct course of trade; harvesting

A. STROKES OF FOUR-STROKE ENGINE.

B. FOUR-CYLINDER FOUR-STROKE ENGINE.

INDUCTION   COMPRESSION

FIRING   EXHAUST

A

B

COMPRESSION-INDUCTION   EXHAUST-TRANSFER

C. TWO-STROKE ENGINE.

INDUCTION OF AIR   COMPRESSION   OIL INJECTION AND FIRING   EXHAUST

C

D

D. DIESEL ENGINE

*The **internal combustion engine** burns its fuel inside the cylinders of an engine. The four-stroke gasoline engine is the commonest type, used for most autos and some motor-cycles. The two-stroke gasoline engine gives nearly twice the power of the four-stroke engine but is wasteful of fuel. The diesel engine is used in heavy machinery, locomotives and trucks.*

A. 1. Sparking plug
2. Cylinder.
3. Poppet-valve.
4. Exhaust port.
5. Piston.
6. Connecting rod.
7. Fly-wheel.
8. Crankshaft.
9. Inlet port.

B. 10. Fan.
11. Dynamo.
12. Fan belt.
13. Water jacket.
14. Little end of connecting rod.
15. Gudgeon pin.
16. Journal.
17. Main bearings.
18. Big end of connecting rod.
19. Tappet.

20. Cam.
21. Camshaft.
22. Sump.
23. Inlet manifold.
24. Exhaust manifold.
C. 25. Transfer port.
26. Cooling fins.
D. 27. Oil injector.
28. Air inlet port.

machine reaping and threshing in one operation. **com·bin'a·ble** *adj.*

comb·ings (kō'mĭngz) *n.pl.* (esp.) Hairs, wool, etc. combed off.

com·bo (kŏm'bō) *n.* (slang) 1. Small jazz band. 2. Sandwich with combination of fillings. 3. Any combination, as of clothes, colors, etc.

com·bus·ti·ble (kombŭs'tĭbel) *adj. & n.* (Matter, thing) capable of burning; excitable, inflammable.

com·bus·tion (kombŭs'chon) *n.* Consumption or destruction by fire; development of light and heat accompanying chemical combination; oxidation of organic material; **internal ~ engine**, engine in which the motive power is produced by the combustion and expansion of a mixture of gasoline or oil vapor and air inside the cylinders.

come (kŭm) *v.i.* (**came, come, com·ing**). 1. Move or start toward, arrive at, a point, time, or result; be brought; fall, land (*on*); **~ into**

view, become visible. 2. Occur, fall; happen; issue; be derived, descend; (of time etc.) arrive in due course; become, get to be; turn out to be. 3. Traverse, accomplish (a distance). 4. (vulg.) Experience sexual orgasm. 5. **~ across**, meet with; **~ across** (**with**), hand over; **~ along**, make haste; **~ around**, revive, regain consciousness, become agreeable; **~ at**, reach, discover, get access to; **~ back**, return; recur to memory; **come'-back** (*n.*), retaliation, retort; return, recovery, reinstatement; **come by**, obtain; **come down**, extend downward *to*; be handed down; fall, be humbled; **come forward**, present oneself before the public etc.; **come in**, enter building or room; finish in a specified place (in race etc.); come into power or office; be received as income; become seasonable or fashionable; serve a purpose, find a place; **come into**, receive, esp. as heir; **come off**, become detached; occur; succeed; **come on**, advance;

continue to progress, thrive develop; come upon the stage o scene; (slang) make an initia impression; **come out**, emerg from contest, examination, etc.; (o sun etc.) emerge from clouds, begi to shine; come into public view become public, be published appear or be found by computatio etc.; develop, display itself; mak debut on stage or in society; **com out with**, utter; **come to**, revive **come to pass**, happen; **come up** come to higher situation in life come close *to*; arise as subject o attention, discussion, etc.; rise t level or height of; **come up with** catch up; produce. **come in** Expression of annoyance, as in **~ now. come'down** *n.* Fall from dignity, prosperity, etc. **come-o** *n.* (slang) Inducement, lure; in viting look.

co·me·di·an (komē'dēan) *n* Comic actor or entertainer (archaic) writer of comedies; perso who always jokes or tries to amuse

o·me·di·enne (komēdēĕn´) *n. fem.*
o·me´dic *adj.*

com·e·do (kŏm´edō) *n.* (pl. **-dos,**
om·e·do·nes pr. kŏmedō´nēz).
med.) Skin blemish, blackhead.

com·e·dy (kŏm´edē) *n.* (pl.
dies). Drama of light, amusing,
nd often satirical character, with a
appy conclusion to its plot; branch
f drama that adopts a humorous or
amiliar style and depicts laughable
haracters and incidents; life, or an
ncident in it, regarded as a comic
pectacle.

come·ly (kŭm´lē) *adj.* (**-li·er,**
-li·est). Pleasant to look at. **come´-**
i·ness *n.*

Co·me·ni·us (komē´nēus), **John**
Amos (1592–1670). Czech theo-
ogian and educator; known for innovations in teaching methods, esp.
or languages.

com·er (kŭm´er) *n.* 1. One who
arrives (as **late ~**, etc.); **all ~s**, any
who apply, take up challenge, etc.
2. (colloq.) Promising person or
hing.

co·mes·ti·ble (komĕs´tĭbel) *n.*
usu. pl.) Thing to eat.

com·et (kŏm´ĭt) *n.* Celestial
body with starlike nucleus and a
rain or tail of light moving about
un in elliptical or parabolic orbit.
com´et·ar·y, co·met·ic (komĕt´ĭk)
adjs.* [Gk. *kométēs* long-haired
star)]

com·fit (kŭm´fĭt, kŏm´-) *n.*
Piece of candy containing nut or
piece of fruit.

com·fort (kŭm´fert) *n.* 1. Relief
in affliction, consolation; person
who consoles one or saves one
trouble; cause of satisfaction. 2.
Well-being, being comfortable;
thing that produces or ministers to
enjoyment and content. **~** *v.t.*
Soothe in grief, console; make

comfortable. **com´fort·ing,**
com´fort·less *adjs.* **com´fort·-**
ing·ly *adv.*

com·fort·a·ble (kŭmf´tabel,
kŭm´fertabel) *adj.* Affording consolation; attended with or ministering to comfort or physical well-
being; in a state of tranquil enjoyment and content, at ease. **com´-**
fort·a·bly *adv.* **com´fort·er** *n.* 1.
One who comforts; **the C~**, the
Holy Spirit. 2. Quilted coverlet.

com·frey (kŭm´frē) *n.* (pl.
-freys). Any of several bristly Old
World plants of the genus
Symphytum, with rough leaves and
bell-shaped flowers.

com·fy (kŭm´fē) *adj.* (**-fi·er,**
-fi·est). (colloq.) Comfortable.

com·ic (kŏm´ĭk) *adj.* Of comedy;
mirth provoking, laughable or
meant to be so, facetious, burlesque, funny; **~ strip,** set of
drawings, usu. broadly humorous,
forming part of a series appearing
regularly in a **~ section** of a
newspaper. **comic** *n.* Comic actor,
performer, strip, or magazine; **~**
book, children's magazine consisting of stories in comic-strip form.

com·i·cal (kŏm´ĭkal) *adj.* Mirth
provoking, laughable; odd, queer.
com·i·cal·i·ty (kŏmĭkăl´ĭtē) *n.*
com´i·cal·ly *adv.*

Com·in·form (kŏm´ĭnfôrm). International communist information
bureau established 1947 and dissolved 1956.

com·ing (kŭm´ĭng) *adj.* 1. Next,
approaching. 2. Promising success

*The first **commando** troops fought during the Boer War in South Africa. The
commandos below are U.S. Marines
surveying a map before a survival
course.*

or fame in the future. **~** *n.*
Approach, advent, arrival.

Com·in·tern (kŏm´ĭntērn).
Third Communist International,
founded at Moscow in March 1919;
formally dissolved June 1943.

com·i·ty (kŏm´ĭtē) *n.* (pl. **-ties**).
Courtesy; civility; **~ of nations,**
friendly and courteous recognition
by nations of laws and usages of
other nations; (loosely) nations
observing this.

com·ma (kŏm´a) *n.* 1. Punctuation mark (,) used to separate
smallest parts of a sentence, also
used to separate figures etc.; (mus.)
minute interval or difference of
pitch; caesura. 2. (also **~ butter-**
fly) Butterfly (*Polygonia comma*)
with white comma-shaped mark on
underside of wings.

com·mand (komănd´, -mahnd´)
n. 1. Order, bidding. 2. Exercise
or tenure of authority, esp. military;
body of troops, district, ship, etc.
under commander; **high ~,**
highest military leadership during
military operations. 3. Control,
mastery, possession; **~ perfor-**
mance, performance given at the
request of a head of state; (joc.) any
performance given on request of
person in authority. **command** *v.*
1. Order, bid. 2. Have authority
over or control of, be supreme; be
in command (of). 3. Restrain,
master; have at disposal or within
reach; demand and obtain; dominate (position etc.) from superior
height, look down over.

com·man·dant (kŏm´andănt,
-dahnt, kŏmandănt´, -dahnt´) *n.*
Commanding officer, esp. one
holding special command, of depot,
particular force, etc.

com·man·deer (kŏmandēr´) *v.*
Force (men) into, seize (stores) for,
military service; take arbitrary
possession of.

com·mand·er (komăn´der,
-mahn´-) *n.* One who commands;
one who has command of a ship,
naval officer ranking next below
captain; **c~ in chief,** chief
commander of all military forces of
a nation (in the U.S. the president);
officer commanding a major armed
force.

com·mand·ing (komăn´dĭng,
-mahn´-) *adj.* Ruling, controlling;
nobly dignified; **~ officer,** officer
in command.

com·mand·ment (komănd´-
ment, -mahnd´-) *n.* Divine
command, esp. (**C~**) one of the
Ten Commandments, precepts
delivered by God to Moses (Exod.
20).

com·man·do (komăn´dō,
-mahn´-) *n.* (pl. **-dos, -does**).
Small fighting unit for quick raids
on enemy-held territory; member
of such a unit.

comme il faut (kŭm ēl fō´) *adj.*
phr. According to etiquette,

proper. [Fr.]

com·mem·o·rate (koměm'erāt) *v.t.* (**-rat·ed, -rat·ing**). Celebrate in speech or writing; preserve in memory by some celebration; by a memorial of. **com·mem·o·ra·tion** (koměmerā'shon) *n*. **com·mem·o·ra·tive** (koměm'erativ) *adj*.

com·mence (koměns') *v.* (**-menced, -menc·ing**). Begin; come into existence. **com·mence'ment** *n*. Beginning; ceremony of conferring academic degrees or diplomas; ~ **day**, day on which such a ceremony takes place.

com·mend (koměnd') *v.t.* Entrust, commit (archaic exc. in, e.g., ~ **one's soul to God**); praise, extol; recommend (a person). **com·mend·a·ble** (koměn'dabel) *adj*. Praiseworthy. **com·mend'a·bly** *adv*.

com·men·da·tion (kŏmendā'shon) *n*. Praise; act of commending person to another's favor.

com·mend·a·to·ry (koměn'datōrē, -tōrē) *adj*. Serving to praise or recommend.

com·men·su·ra·ble (koměn'serabel, -she-) *adj*. Measurable by the same standard; properly proportioned; fitting; divisible without remainder by the same quantity. **com·men·su·ra·bil·i·ty** (koměn-serabĭl'ĭtē, -she-) *n*. **com·men'su·ra·bly** *adv*.

com·men·su·rate (koměn'serĭt, -she-) *adj*. Coextensive; proportionate; corresponding in extent or degree, as in ~ **with one's ability**. **com·men'su·rate·ly** *adv*.

com·ment (kŏm'ĕnt) *n*. Explanatory or critical note or remark; expository or critical matter; criticism. ~ *v.i.* Write explanatory or critical notes *on*; make comments or remarks (*on*).

com·men·ta·ry (kŏm'entĕrē) *n*. (pl. **-tar·ies**). Expository treatise; series of running comments on book, speech, performance, public event, etc.; comment, remark.

com·men·ta·tor (kŏm'entāter) *n*. Writer or speaker of commentary; one who analyzes news events on radio or television.

com·merce (kŏm'ers) *n*. I. Buying and selling of merchandise, esp. on a large scale between different countries or districts, comprising all forms of trade and ancillary services such as banking, insurance, and transportation. 2. Social intercourse.

*The **Common Market** or European Economic Community has its headquarters in Brussels. It was founded in 1958 with the aim to increase trade among its members.*

com·mer·cial (komēr'shal) *a* Of, engaged in, bearing commerce; ~ **traveler**, traveli salesperson. **commercial** Advertisement broadcast on rad or television. **com·mer'cial·is** *n*. **com·mer'cial·ize** *v.t.* (**-ize -iz·ing**). **com·mer'cial·ly** *adv*.

com·mie (kŏm'ē) *n*. (slan (freq. **C**~) Communist.

com·mi·na·tion (kŏmĭnā'sho *n*. Formal denunciation; threate ing, esp. of divine punishment.

com·min·gle (komĭng'gel) *v* (**-gled, -gling**). Mingle or m together.

com·mi·nute (kŏm'inōot) *v.* (**-nut·ed, -nut·ing**). Reduce minute particles; divide into sma portions; **comminuted frac ture**, fracture producing multip fragments. **com·mi·nu·tio** (kŏminōo'shon) *n*.

com·mis·er·ate (komĭz'erāt) (**-at·ed, -at·ing**). Feel, sho express pity for; condole *wit* **com·mis·er·a·tion** (komĭzerā shon) *n*. **com·mis'er·a·tive** *adj*.

com·mis·sar (kŏm'īsār, kŏm sār') *n*. (until 1946) Head government department (commi sariat) of U.S.S.R. or its constitue republics.

com·mis·sar·i·at (kŏmĭsār'ēa *n*. I. Department (esp. military) f

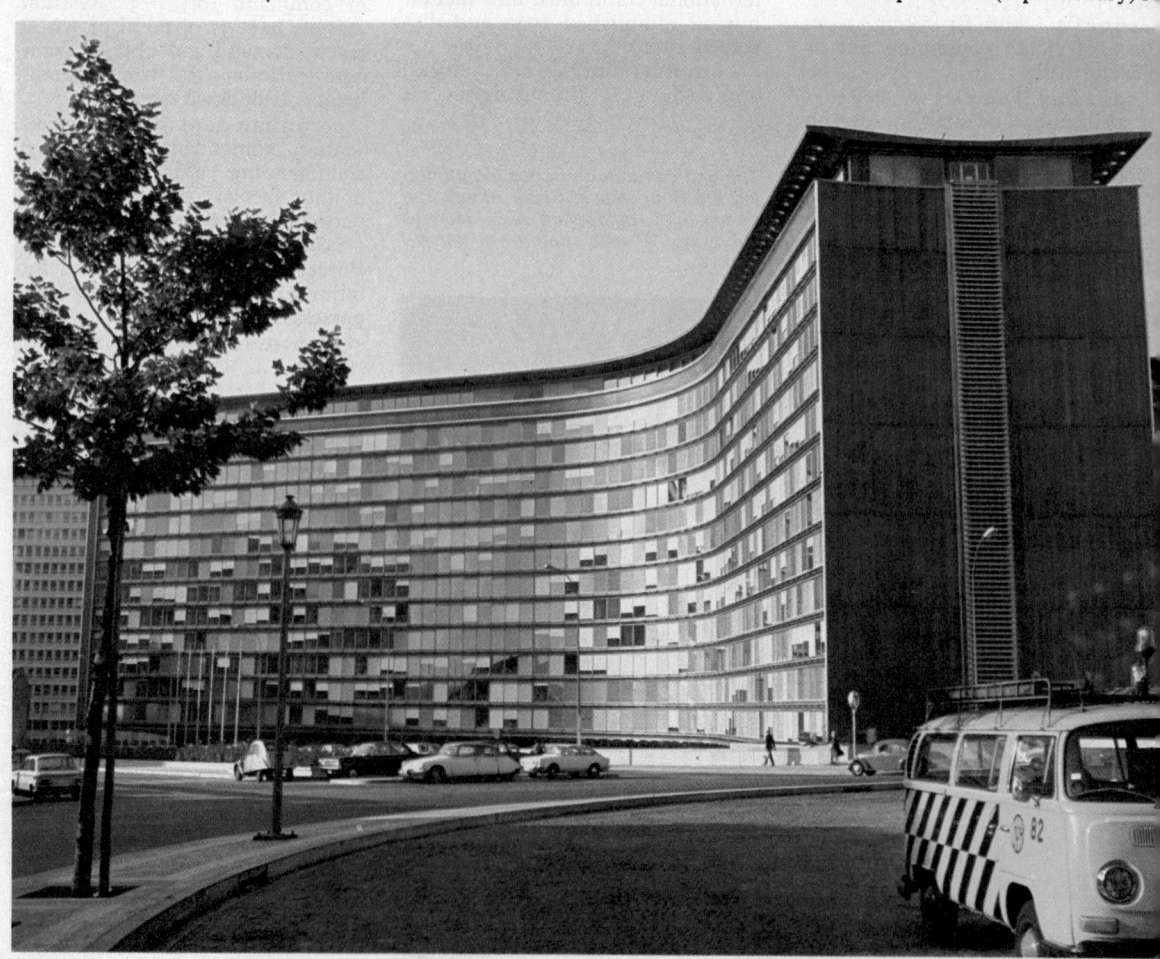

pply of food etc. 2. (until 1946) epartment of Civil Service of .S.S.R.

com·mis·sar·y (kŏm´ĭsĕrē) *n.* l. **-sar·ies**). 1. Deputy, delegate. Officer charged with supply of ood etc. for body of soldiers. 3. upermarket and department store r personnel on military base. 4. mployees' lunchroom, cafeteria at actory, office, etc.

com·mis·sion (komĭsh´on) *n.* 1. .uthoritative charge or direction; uthority, esp. delegated authority, ody of persons having authority, p act in some specified capacity, nvestigate some specified question, tc. 2. Warrant conferring author-ty, warrant by which officer in rmed services exercises command; ffice conferred by such a warrant. 3. Being authoritatively entrusted or given in charge; **in ~**, (of a ship f war) manned, armed, and ready or sea; in working order; ready; in ervice; **out of ~**, not in service; not in working order. 4. Charge ntrusted to anyone to perform; order given to artist, writer, etc. for a particular piece of work. 5. Authority to act as agent for another n trade or business; system of trading in which dealer (**~ merchant**) acts as agent for another, receiving a percentage as remuneration; the percentage of the amount involved paid to the agent. **commission** *v.t.* Empower by commission; give (officer) com-mand of ship; order (ship) prepared for active service; assume command of (ship); give (artist etc.) a com-mission; order (work of art etc.) as a commission. **com·mis´sioned** *adj.* (esp.) (of officer) Holding rank by commission.

com·mis·sion·er (komĭsh´oner) *n.* One appointed by or a member of a commission; representative of supreme authority in district, department, etc.; official at head of government department etc.; **High C ~**, chief officer of British colonial territory; chief representative of British Commonwealth country.

com·mis·sure (kŏm´ĭshoor) *n.* Joining, seam; joint between two bones; line where lips, eyelids, meet; band or bundle of white or gray nerve substance connecting hemispheres of brain, parts of cere-brum and cerebellum, two sides of spinal cord, etc.

com·mit (komĭt´) *v.t.* (**-mit·ted, -mit·ting**). 1. Entrust, consign, for treatment or safe keeping, consign officially *to*, place in, custody, prison, etc.; refer (bill etc.) to committee. 2. Perpetrate (crime, blunder). 3. Involve, compromise; engage or pledge by implication (*to*). 4. **~ to memory**, memorize; **~ to writing** or **paper**, write down. **com·mit´ment** *n.* (esp.) Engagement; thing undertaken,

responsibility. **com·mit´tal** *n.* Committing, consigning, esp. com-mitting to prison; committing of body to grave at burial; reference to committee; committing of oneself.

com·mit·tee (komĭt´ē) *n.* Body of persons appointed for special function by (and usu. out of) larger body; **joint ~**, one composed of members nominated by two or more distinct bodies; **standing ~**, one that is permanent during the existence of the appointing body; **in ~**, (of a bill) under consideration by a legislative committee.

com·mode (komŏd´) *n.* Chest of drawers, chiffonier; chair or box containing chamber pot; toilet; stand or cupboard containing wash basin.

com·mo·di·ous (komō´dēus) *adj.* Roomy. **com·mo´di·ous·ly** *adv.* **com·mo´di·ous·ness** *n.*

com·mod·i·ty (komŏd´ĭtē) *n.* (pl. **-ties**). Useful thing; article of trade, esp. product as opp. to service, often a grain traded on a **commodities market.**

com·mo·dore (kŏm´odōr, -dŏr) *n.* Naval officer ranking above cap-tain and below rear admiral; as courtesy title, senior captain when three or more ships cruise together; president of yacht club etc.

com·mon (kŏm´on) *adj.* 1. Possessed or shared alike by both or all; belonging to more than one; belonging to all mankind alike; general; public. 2. Of ordinary occurrence and quality; usual, frequent, undistinguished, ordi-nary; of little value, inferior; low class, vulgar. 3. (math.) Of a number or quantity, belonging

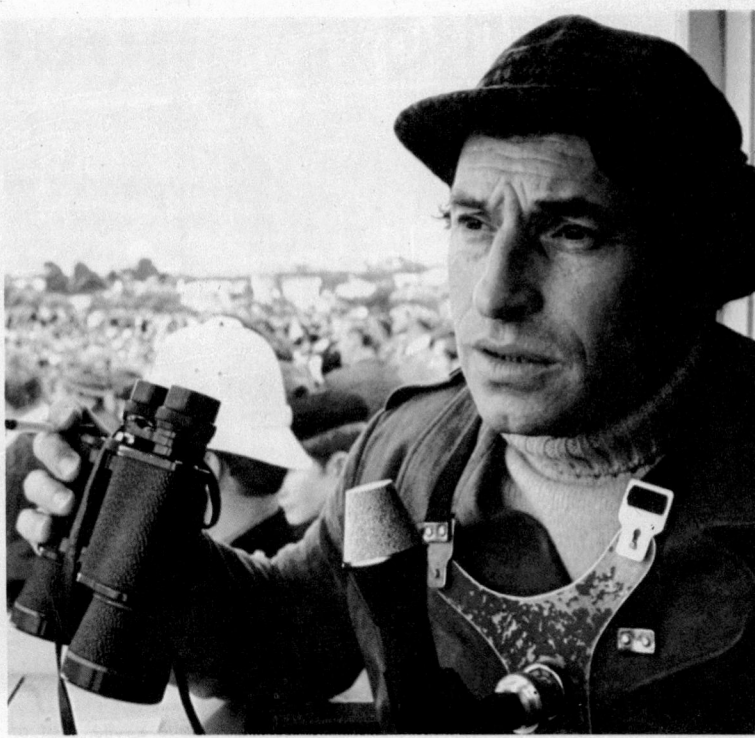

*In radio and television the **commentator** on sporting or other events is usually an expert in his field. Here Milton Berle and a commentator discuss the finer points of golf.*

equally to two or more quantities. 4. (gram., logic) Of a noun, name, etc., applicable to every individual or species of a class or genus; of either gender or sex. 5. (mus. etc.) (of time, measure) Consisting of two or four beats in a bar. 6. **~ carrier**, transportation company recognized by law as bound to serve the public; **~ denominator**, (math.) common multiple of denominators of several fractions; (colloq.) common feature of members of a group; **C~ Era**, Christian Era; **~ ground**, basis for argument etc. accepted by both sides; **~ law**, body of unwritten law originating in England, based on court decisions, custom, or usage in contrast to statutory law; **~-law husband, wife**, one established by common law, usu. as a result of couple living as man and wife for a specified length of time without a recognized marriage ceremony; **C~ Market**, European Economic Community; **C~ Prayer**, liturgy or form of public service prescribed by Church of England and first set forth in the Book of Common Prayer of 1549; **~ sense**, normal understanding, good prac-tical sense in everyday affairs; **~ stock**, shares in capital of corporation or company that have exclusive claim on all income and assets after all other obligations are paid; cf. preferred stock (see

The Chamber of the U.K. parliament, the **House of Commons** was originally a chapel with the altar at the end where the Speaker now sits. Government and Opposition sit facing each other on the benches.

Communication forms a vital part of our lives. The rapid technological progress made this century enables us to receive information as it is happening. Sophisticated video cameras greatly improve news coverage today.

PREFER). **com′monweal**, (archai commonwealth; public welfar **common** *n.* 1. Land belonging t or used by local community as whole; (often) ~**s** (pl. used as sin or pl.). 2. **in** ~, in joint use, share **in** ~ **with**, in the same way as, lik

com·mon·al·ty (kŏm′*onal*tē) (pl. **-ties**). General body of th community, the common people a dist. from those of rank or i authority; general or universa body.

com·mon·er (kŏm′*oner*) *n.* On of the common people, one belov the rank of a noble.

com·mon·ly (kŏm′*on*lē) *adv* Usually, frequently.

com·mon·place (kŏm′*on*plās *n.* Opinion or statement generally accepted; ordinary topic; anything common and trite; ~ **book** personal journal in which quotable passages, comments, and literary excerpts are written. **common· place** *adj.* Lacking originality trivial, hackneyed.

com·mons (kŏm′*onz*) *n.pl.* 1 Common people; **House of C** ~ representatives of counties boroughs, etc., forming the lowe house of Parliament of the United Kingdom and of Canada; building where these meet. 2. Provisions shared in common, esp. in monastic house, college, etc.

com·mon·wealth (kŏm′*on* wělth) *n.* 1. Body politic, independ ent community; republican or democratic nation. 2. **the C** ~, (also **C** ~ **of Nations**, formerly **British C** ~ **of Nations**), the association of the United Kingdom and its dependencies and certain former colonies that are now self governing sovereign nations; **C** ~

The opening of CHOGM (**Common-wealth** Heads of Government Meeting) in September 1981. Forty-four member countries (most were former British colonies) participated. CHOGM is held biennially in a Commonwealth capital.

Day, (formerly Empire Day) a day celebrating the British Commonwealth, now celebrated on the Queen's official birthday. 3. **the C~**, (Engl. hist.) the parliamentary government between the execution of Charles I in 1649 and the Restoration in 1660; under Oliver CROMWELL until 1658, then under his son, Richard. See Lord PROTECTOR. 4. **C~ of Australia**, title of the federated states of AUSTRALIA.

com·mo·tion (komō'shon) n. Physical disturbance; bustle, confusion; public disorder.

com·mu·nal (komū'nal, kŏm'u-) adj. Of or for a commune or community; for common use.

com·mu·nal·ism (komū'na-ĭzem, kŏm'yu-) n. Principle of communal organization of society; theory of government by local autonomy. **com·mu'nal·ist** n. **com·mu·nal·is·tic** (komūnalĭs'tĭk, ŏmyu-) adj.

com·mune¹ (kŏm'ūn) n. 1. Smallest local political division for administrative purposes in France, Belgium, etc. 2. **C~**, revolutionary committee that governed Paris from 1789–95 and played a leading part in the Reign of Terror; (also) revolutionary government set up in Paris from March 18 to May 28,

1871. 3. Small group of persons (not all of one family) sharing living accommodations and goods, often composed of members who adhere to a distinct social or religious ideology. 4. KIBBUTZ.

com·mune² (komūn') v.i. (-muned, -mun·ing). Converse intimately, exchange thoughts and feelings *with*; receive Holy Communion.

com·mu·ni·cant (komū'nĭkant) n. 1. One who receives or is entitled to receive Holy Communion. 2. One who communicates.

com·mu·ni·cate (komū'nĭkāt) v. (-cat·ed, -cat·ing). 1. Impart, transmit (*to*). 2. Receive, administer, Holy Communion (*to*). 3. Exchange, express thoughts, feelings, etc; transmit (by speech, writing, etc.). 4. (of spaces, rooms, etc.) Have common door or opening (*with*).

com·mu·ni·ca·tion (komūni-kā'shon) n. Imparting (esp. news); information given; exchange of messages etc.; access or means of

Students hold an anti-Iran rally in Washington. The **commotion** of public demonstration has become a traditional way for people to express political views.

access, passage, connection by railroad, road, telegraph, etc., between places; (mil., pl.) connection between base and front.

com·mu·ni·ca·tive (komū'ni-katĭv) adj. Ready to impart; open; talkative.

Conductor Brush & Holder Armature winding soldered to Commutator

Shaft   Insulation   Copper segments

The **commutator,** a component of e‹
tric motors, consists of a drum of c‹
per segments, insulated from e‹
other, which is in contact with car‹
brushes.

ment or contract between partie‹

com·pact[2] (kompăkt´) a‹
Closely or neatly packed togeth‹
dense, solid; condensed, ter‹
com·pact'ly adv. **com·pact'ne**‹
n. **compact** (kŏm´păkt) n. Sm‹
case containing mirror and f‹
powder, for carrying in handb‹
compact (kompăkt´) v.t. J‹
firmly together; consolidate; co‹
press, condense; devise, compos‹

com·pan·ion[1] (kompăn´yon)
1. One who accompanies ‹
associates with another; associa‹
in, sharer of. 2. Person paid to l‹
with another as a friend or eq‹
rather than as a servant. 3. Thi‹
that matches another; one of a pa‹
~ v. Accompany; associate wit‹
com·pan'ion·a·ble adj. Sociab‹
com·pan'ion·a·bly adv. **com**‹
pan'ion·a·ble·ness n.

com·pan·ion[2] (kompăn´yon)
(naut.) Raised frame on quarte‹
deck for lighting cabins etc. belo‹
compan'ionway, stairway fro‹
ship's deck to area, cabins belo‹
[Du. kompanje quarter-dec‹
corresp. to It. (camera dell‹
compagna pantry, caboose]

com·pan·ion·ship (kompăn‹
yonshĭp) n. Fellowship.

com·pa·ny (kŭm´panē) n. (p‹
-nies). 1. Companionship; t‹
society of others. 2. Number ‹
individuals assembled togethe‹
person(s) with whom one usual‹
associates; guests. 3. Body ‹
persons combined or incorporate‹
for a common (esp. commercia‹
object; medieval trade guild, or ‹
corporation historically represen‹
ing this. 4. Association formed ‹
carry on some commercial ‹
industrial undertaking; partner ‹
partners not named in title of fir‹
(abbreviated Co.). 5. Troupe ‹
actors or other performers. ‹
(mil.) Subdivision of a regiment ‹
battalion, usu. commanded ‹
captain. 7. (naut.) Entire crew ‹
ship. 8. ~ **union,** workers' unio‹
within a given company, uncor‹
nected with a trade union, an‹
closely associated with th‹
employers; **keep** ~ **(with),** be ‹
friend (of); carry on courtshi‹
part ~, cease associating (with).

com·pa·ra·ble (kŏm´perabe‹
kŏm´pra-) adj. That may b‹
compared (with), worthy to be ‹
compared (to). **com·pa·ra·bil·i·t**‹

com·mu·ni·ca·tor (komū´ni-kāter) n. Person, thing, that communicates.

com·mun·ion (komūn´yon) n. Sharing, participation; fellowship (esp. between branches of Catholic Church); body professing one faith; **(Holy) C**~, Eucharist; elements of the Eucharist, as in **receive C**~.

com·mu·ni·qué (komūnikā´, komū´nĭkā) n. Official announcement or report.

com·mu·nism (kŏm´yunĭzem) n. 1. Order of society in which property is owned in common. 2. (usu. **C**~) Order of society in which the means of production, distribution, and exchange are owned in common and each member is to work according to his capacity and be paid according to his needs; this as the professed aim of political parties that derive their doctrines from MARX, ENGELS, and LENIN. 3. Doctrines and activities of these parties regarded as an international movement (**international** ~ or **C**~). 4. Social order established in Russia by the Bolshevik party under Lenin after the revolution of 1917 (**Soviet** ~); similar social order established elsewhere. **com'mu·nist** adj. & n. (Advocate) of communism. **com·mu·nis·tic** (kŏmyunĭs´tĭk) adj.

Com·mu·nism (kŏm´yunĭzem), **Mount.** Formerly Stalin Peak, 24,500 ft. (8,942 m), in the Pamir Range; the highest mountain in the Soviet Union.

com·mu·ni·ty (komū´nĭtē) n. (pl. **-ties**). 1. Joint or common ownership, liability, etc. 2. Identity of character, quality in common. 3. Social intercourse; life in association with others; body of people organized into political, municipal, or social unity; body of persons living (amid larger group) in same locality, or with common race, religion, pursuits, etc. 4. Body of persons living together and practicing community of goods. 5. (ecol.)

Association of organisms in a given area. 6. ~ **college,** public college serving residents of local area; ~ **property,** property of wife and/ or husband deemed by law of some states to be jointly owned.

com·mu·nize (kŏm´yunīz) v.t. (**-nized, -niz·ing**). Make common property; make communistic.

com·mut·a·ble (komū´tabel) adj. 1. Exchangeable, convertible into money value. 2. (of a prison sentence) Subject to reduction of severity of punishment. **com·mut·a·bil·i·ty** (komūtabĭl´ĭtē) n.

com·mu·ta·tion (kŏmyutā´-shon) n. Commuting; ~ **ticket,** reduced-rate ticket for commuter.

com·mu·ta·tive (komū´tatĭv) adj. Relating to or involving substitution or interchange.

com·mu·ta·tor (kŏm´yutāter) n. Device for changing course of electric current; ring-shaped fitting on dynamo or electric motor providing the brushes with a series of separate connections with different parts of the armature during each revolution and so enabling a dynamo to generate, or a motor to utilize, a direct current.

com·mute (komūt´) v. (**-mut·ed, -mut·ing**). 1. Exchange, change, interchange; redeem obligation by money payment; change (punishment etc.) for (to, into) less severe one, or a fine; change (one kind of payment) into, for, another. 2. Travel daily to and from work by any means of conveyance. **com·mut'er** n.

Co·mo (kō´mō). Lake and resort city in N. Italy, on the Swiss border.

Com·o·ro (kŏm´orō) **Islands.** Group of islands off the E. coast of Africa between Mozambique and Madagascar; under French rule 1886–1975; became independent July 6, 1975; capital, Moroni. **Co·mo·ran** (komō´ran) adj. & n.

comp. abbrev. Comparative; complete; compound.

com·pact[1] (kŏm´păkt) n. Agree-

Communism, a form of governmer‹
which is based on the abolition of cap‹
talism in favor of state ownership an‹
the power of the worker. Facing page‹
Chinese Army Guardsman on duty at ‹
state visit to Peking.

Quadrantal corrector

Permanent magnets inside

(kŏmp*e*rabĭl´ĭtē, kŏmpr*a*-), **com´-pa·ra·ble·ness** *ns.* **com´pa·ra·bly** *adv.*

com·par·a·tive (kompăr´atĭv) *adj.* 1. Of or involving comparison, esp. of different branches of a study, as ~ **anatomy.** 2. (gram., of an inflectional form of adjective or adverb, as *higher, faster*) Expressing a higher degree of the quality etc. denoted by the positive form (e.g. *high, fast*) of the word. 3. Estimated by comparison. **com·par´a·tive·ly** *adv.* **comparative** *n.* (gram.) (Word in) the comparative degree.

com·pare (kompār´) *v.* (**-pared, -par·ing**). Liken, pronounce similar (*to*); estimate the similarity of (one thing *with, to,* another; two things together); bear comparison (*with*). ~ *n.* Comparison (chiefly in **beyond, without,** ~).

com·par·i·son (kompăr´ĭson) *n.* Comparing; simile, illustration by comparing; (gram.) **degrees of** ~, positive, comparative, and superlative of adjectives or adverbs (as *fast, faster, fastest*).

com·part·ment(kompārt´ment) *n.* Space separated by partitions; watertight division of ship. **com·part·men·tal** (kompārtmĕn´tal, kŏm-) *adj.* **com·part·men´tal·ize**

*This 16th century Italian **compass** is typical of the type used by European mariners from the 12th century. The compass was invented by the Chinese.*

v.t. (**-ized, -iz·ing**). Separate into compartments (esp. fig.) **com·-part·men·tal·i·za·tion** (kompārt-mĕntalĭzā´shon, kŏm-) *n.*

com·pass (kŭm´p*a*s, kŏm´-) *n.* 1. (often pl., also **pair of compasses**) Instrument for taking measurements and describing circles, consisting of two legs connected at one end by movable joint. 2. Circumference, boundary; area, extent; range. 3. Instrument for determining magnetic meridian, or one's direction or position with respect to it, consisting of a magnetized needle turning freely on a pivot; **box the** ~: see BOX[2]; GYRO, PRISMATIC, ~: see these words; **point of the** ~, any of the 32 equidistant points marked in a circle on the ~ **card,** (also ~ **rose**) disk to which the magnetized needle (usu.) is attached with its pivot at the center of the circle. **compass** *v.t.* 1. Go around; hem in. 2. Contrive, devise; accomplish, achieve.

com·pas·sion (kompăsh´on) *n.* Pity accompanied by a desire to spare or succor.

The binnacle, in which the ship's co pass stands, is fitted with compens ing magnets and pieces of iron reduce deviation from Magnetic No

com·pas·sion·ate (kompăsh onĭt) *adj.* Feeling or showing co passion; granted out of compassio **com·pas´sion·ate·ly** *adv.* **com pas´sion·ate·ness** *n.*

com·pat·i·ble (kompăt´ĭbel) *a* Mutually tolerant; accordant, co sistent, congruous. **com·pat·i bil·i·ty** (kompătĭbĭl´ĭtē), **com pat´i·ble·ness** *ns.* **com·pat´i·b** *adv.*

com·pa·tri·ot (kompā´trēot) Fellow citizen of a country. **com pa´tri·ot·ism** *n.*

com·peer (kŏm´pēr, kompēr´) (literary) Equal, peer; comrade.

com·pel (kompĕl´) *v.t.* (**-pelle -pel·ling**). Constrain, force; bri about by force. **com·pel´ling** *a* (esp.) Arousing strong interes respect, etc. **com·pel´la·ble** *a* **com·pel´la·bly** *adv.*

com·pen·di·ous (kompĕn´dē*a adj.* Brief but comprehensiv **com·pen´di·ous·ly** *adv.* **com pen´di·ous·ness** *n.*

com·pen·di·um (kompĕn dēum) *n.* (pl. **-di·ums, -di·a** p -dēa) (also **com·pend** pr. kŏm pĕnd). Abridgement; summar ncise and comprehensive account treatise.

com·pen·sate (kŏm′pensāt) *v.* **-sat·ed, -sat·ing**). Counter-lance; make amends; recom-nse; provide with mechanical mpensation, make up for (varia-ns in a pendulum etc.); eutralize; (psychol.) counter-alance defect by development of me other characteristic. **com-en·sa′tion** (kŏmpensā′shon) *n.* ompensating; recompense, mends. **com·pen·sa·tive** (kŏm′-ensātĭv, kŏmpĕn′sa-), **com·pen-a·to·ry** (kŏmpĕn′satōrē, -tōrē) djs. **compensatory damages**, aw) sum awarded to plaintiff as ecompense for injury. **com′pen-a·tor** *n.*

com·pete (kŏmpēt′) *v.i.* **-pet·ed, -pet·ing**). Strive (*with* nother, *for* or *in* something), vie *with*), contend (*for*). **com·pet·i-ive** (kŏmpĕt′itĭv) *adj.* **com·pet′i-ive·ly** *adv.* **com·pet′i·tive·ness** . **com·pet′i·to·ry** *adj.* **com-et′i·tor** *n.*

com·pe·tence (kŏm′petens), **om·pe·ten·cy** (kŏm′petensē) *ns.* l. **-cies**). Sufficiency of means r living; ability (*to do, for* a task); f court, magistrate, etc.) legal apacity, right to take cognizance. **com·pe·tent** (kŏm′petent) *adj.* dequate, sufficient; properly or egally qualified; belonging *to*, per-issible, admissible. **com′pe-ent·ly** *adv.*

com·pe·ti·tion (kŏmpetĭsh′on) . Act of competing (*for*) by xamination etc.; rivalry in market-lace; striving for business; contest sp. for supremacy or prize.

Com·piègne (kawṅpyĕn′ye). City in N. France near Paris, on he Oise River; site of capture of oan of Arc by English; World War armistice, 1918, and armistice etween France and Germany, 940, signed nearby.

com·pi·la·tion (kŏmpilā′shon) . Compiling; thing compiled.

com·pile (kŏmpīl′) *v.t.* **-piled, pil·ing**). Collect (materials) into volume; make up (volume) of such materials. **com·pil′er** *n.*

com·pla·cen·cy (kŏmplā′sensē), om·pla·cence (kŏmplā′sens) *ns.* l. **-cies**). Tranquil pleasure; self-atisfaction. **com·pla′cent** *adj.* om·pla′cent·ly *adv.*

com·plain (kŏmplān′) *v.i.* Ex-ress dissatisfaction or discontent; et it be known that one is suffering from illness etc.); make formal omplaint of grievance *to* or *before* ompetent authority. **com-plain′er** *n.* **com·plain′ant** *n.* One who complains; plaintiff; one who nakes a formal charge in a court. om·plain′ing·ly *adv.*

com·plaint (kŏmplānt′) *n.* 1. Utterance of grievance. 2. Formal accusation; plaintiff's case in civil

action. 3. Subject, ground, of complaint. 4. Bodily ailment.

com·plai·sance (komplā′sans, -zans, kŏm′plazans) *n.* Obliging-ness; deference. **com·plai′sant** *adj.*

com·ple·ment (kŏm′plement) *n.* 1. What completes; (gram.) word or words that complete a predicate; (math.) angular amount that, with another angle, adds up to 90°. 2. Full quantity or number required, esp. full number of ship officers and crew. ~ *v.t.* Complete; form complement to.

com·ple·men·tal (kŏmplemĕn′-tal) *adj.* Forming a complement, completing. **com·ple·men′tal·ly** *adv.*

com·ple·men·ta·ry (kŏmple-mĕn′terē, -trē) *adj.* Forming a complement, completing; (of two or more things) mutually com-plementing each other; ~ **angle**, either of two angles that together make 90°.

com·plete (komplēt′) *adj.* Having all its parts; entire; finished, thorough, unqualified; (archaic, of persons) accomplished. **com-plete′ly** *adv.* **com·plete′ness** *n.* **complete** *v.t.* (**-plet·ed, -plet-ing**). Finish; make whole or perfect; make up the amount of. **com·ple′tion** *n.*

com·plex (kŏm′plĕks) *n.* 1. Whole consisting of several parts. 2. (psychol.) Group of related ideas or memories of strongly emotional character that have undergone re-pression; (loosely) fixed mental tendency or obsession; inferiority ~; see INFERIOR; Oedipus ~: see OEDIPUS. **complex** (komplĕks′, kŏm′plĕks) *adj.* Consisting of parts, composite; complicated; ~ **number**, (math.) an expression

$(a + bi)$ in which a and b are real numbers and $i^2 = -1$; (gram.) ~ **sentence**, one containing sub-ordinate clause(s). **com·plex′ly** *adv.* **com·plex′ness** *n.* **com-plex′i·ty** *n.* (pl. **-ties**).

com·plex·ion (komplĕk′shon) *n.* Natural color, texture, and appearance of skin (esp. of face); character, aspect. **com·plex′-ioned** *adj.* Having a (specified) complexion (as *fair-complexioned*).

com·pli·ance (komplī′ans) *n.* Action in accordance with request, demand, etc.; submission; **in** ~ **with**, in recognition of; according to. **com·pli′an·cy** *n.*

com·pli·ant (komplī′ant) *adj.* Disposed to comply, yielding. **com·pli′ant·ly** *adv.*

com·pli·cate (kŏm′plĭkāt) *v.t.* (**-cat·ed, -cat·ing**). Mix up *with* in intricate or involved way; make complex or intricate. **com′pli-cat·ed·ly** *adv.* **com′pli·cat·ed-ness** *n.* **com·pli·ca′tion** (kŏmplĭ-kā′shon). Involved condition; entangled state of affairs; compli-cating circumstance.

com·plic·i·ty (komplĭs′ĭtē) *n.* (pl. **-ties**). Partnership in an evil action.

com·pli·ment (kŏm′pliment) *n.* Polite expression of praise, act equivalent to this; (pl.) formal greetings. ~ (kŏm′plimĕnt, -ment) *v.t.* Pay compliment to (person *or* something); present *with* as mark of courtesy. **com·pli·men·ta·ry** (kŏmplimĕn′terē) *adj.* Expressive of, conveying, compliment; (of

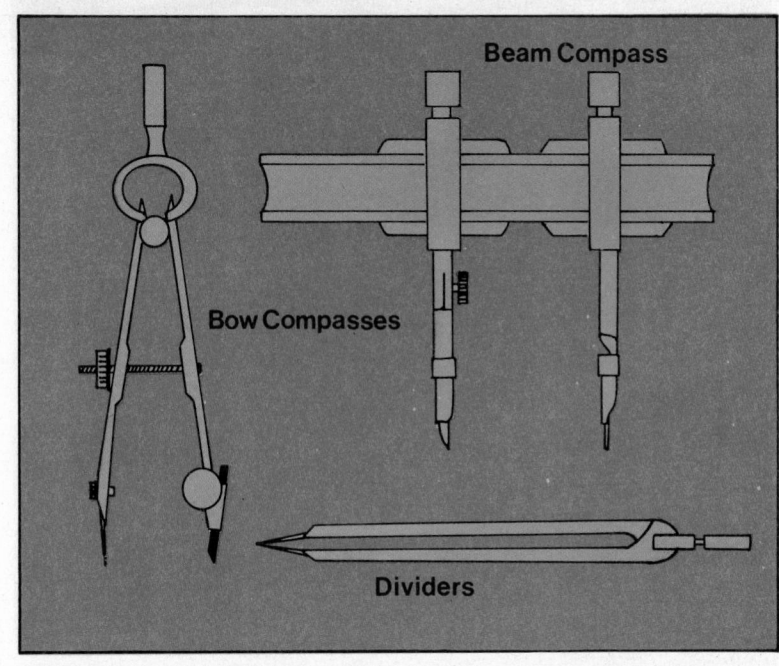

Beam Compass

Bow Compasses

Dividers

tickets etc.) presented without charge as a courtesy. **com·pli-men·tar·i·ly** (kŏmplĭmĕn′terĭlē) *adv.*

com·ply (komplī′) *v.i.* (**-plied, -ply·ing**). Act in accordance (*with*). **com·pli′er** *n.*

com·po·nent (kompō′nent) *adj.* Contributing to the composition of a whole. ~ *n.* Component part.

com·port (kompōrt′) *v.* Conduct, behave (oneself); (literary) agree, correspond *with*. **com·port′ment** *n.*

com·pose (kompōz′) *v.t.* (**-posed, -pos·ing**). 1. Make up, constitute. 2. Construct in words; produce in literary form; (mus.) invent and put into proper form; set to music. 3. (print.) Set up (type); set up in type; **composing room**, room in which type is set up; **composing stick**, compositor's metal or wooden tray of adjustable width in which type is set. 4. Put together so as to form a whole; arrange artistically. 5. Settle, arrange; adjust (oneself, one's features, etc.) in specified or understood manner, or for specified purpose; tranquilize. **com·posed′** *adj.*

com·pos·er (kompō′zer) *n.* One who composes (usu. music).

com·pos·ite (kompŏz′ĭt) *adj.* 1. Made up of various parts, com-

pound; ~ **material**, material made of constituents that remain recognizable. 2. (archit., **C**~) Of the 5th classical order, of Ionic and Corinthian mixed. 3. (bot.) Of the natural order Compositae, in which what is pop. called the flower is a close head of many small flowers sessile on a common receptacle and surrounded by a common involucre of bracts, as daisy, dandelion, etc. **com·pos′ite·ly** *adv.* **com·pos′-ite·ness** *n.* **composite** *n.* Composite thing or plant.

com·po·si·tion (kŏmpozĭsh′on) *n.* 1. Putting together; formation, construction. 2. Art of literary production; composing of music. 3. Setting up of type. 4. Arrangement (of the parts of a picture etc.); thing composed; piece of music or writing. 5. Compromise; agreement for paying, payment, esp. agreement by which creditor accepts portion of debt from debtor; sum of money paid thus.

com·pos·i·tor (kompŏz′ĭter) *n.* (see COMPOSE *v.* def. 3) Typesetter.

com·post (kŏm′pōst) *n.* Mixture of decaying organic material, such as leaves and dung, for fertilizer. ~ *v.t.* Treat with, make into, compost.

com·po·sure (kompō′zher) *n.* Tranquil demeanor, calmness.

com·pote (kŏm′pōt) *n.* Fruit

stewed or cooked in syrup; lo stemmed dish for serving can nuts, etc.

com·pound[1] (kompownd′) *v.* Mix; combine (verbal elemer into word; make up (a compos whole). 2. Settle (matter) by mut concession, (debt) by partial pa ment or lump sum etc.; condo (liability, offense) for money et come to terms *with* (person). Compute (interest) on bc principal and accrued intere **compound** (kŏm′pownd, kŏm pownd′) *adj.* Make up of sever ingredients, consisting of sever parts, combined, collective; (zoc bot.) consisting of a combination organisms or simple parts; ~ ey (in insects and crustaceans), e consisting of numerous minu simple eyes bound together; **fracture**, fracture of bone assoc ated with skin wound; ~ **interes** see INTEREST; ~ **leaf**, leaf in whic blade is divided to form two more leaflets on a single stalk; **number**, quantity involving di ferent units of measure, as 2 pec and 3 quarts; ~ **sentence**, or containing two or more independ ent clauses but no dependen clause. **compound** (kŏm′pown *n.* 1. (mainly fig.) Mixture elements; compound thing, es word. 2. (chem.) Substance th

The sunflower is a **composite** flower o the order *Asterales* which contains some 20,000 species. The plant is shown here in cross-section in various stages of flowering and in full bloom. Other *Compositae* are chrysanthemums and marigolds.

cloth applied to relieve inflammation.

com·pres·sion (kŏmprĕsh′on) n. Act of compressing or state of being compressed; in internal combustion engines, act of compressing the explosive mixture after admission to the engine and before combustion. ∼ **ratio**, (in internal combustion engines) ratio of volume of fuel mixture when compressed by engine to its volume at entry.

com·pres·sor (kŏmprĕs′er) n. Mechanical device for reducing the volume taken up by a quantity of gas.

com·prise, comprize (kŏmprīz′) vbs.t. (-prised, -pris·ing; -prized, -priz·ing). Include, consist of; contain.

com·pro·mise (kŏm′promīz) n. Settlement of dispute by mutual concession; adjustment of conflicting opinions, courses, etc., by modification of each. ∼ v. (-mised, -mis·ing). Settle (dispute) by mutual concession; make compromise; bring under suspicion, into danger, by indiscreet action. **com′pro·mis·er** n.

comp·trol·ler (kontrō′ler) n. Var. of controller (see CONTROL), retained in some official titles.

com·pul·sion (kompŭl′shon) n. Constraint, obligation; (psychol.) strong, usu. irresistible urge to act in a certain way, esp. against one's better judgment.

com·pul·sive (kompŭl′siv) adj. Tending to compel; (psychol.) done under stress of compulsion, as in ∼ **behavior. com·pul′sive·ly** adv.

com·pul·so·ry (kompŭl′serē) adj. Enforced, obligatory; compelling, coercive. **com·pul′so·ri·ly** adv.

com·punc·tion (kompŭngk′shon) n. Pricking of conscience; uneasiness caused by regret or guilt. **com·punc′tious** adj. **com·punc′tious·ly** adv.

com·pute (kompūt′) v. (-put·ed, -put·ing). Reckon; determine (an amount or number) by mathematics. **com·put′a·ble** adj. **com·put·a·bil·i·ty** (kompūtabĭl′ĭtē), **com·pu·ta·tion** (kŏmpyutā′shon) ns.

com·put·er (kompū′ter) n. Person who computes; electronic apparatus for performing high-speed mathematical and logical operations, storing, processing, retrieving, and transmitting coded data, etc.; **analog** ∼, one using physical quantities (voltage,

consists of elements chemically united in fixed proportions and has properties different from those of its components.

com·pound² (kŏm′pownd) n. Houses, huts, etc., enclosed by a barrier for protection, segregation, or imprisonment. [perh. f. Malay *kampong*]

com·pre·hend (kŏm′prĭhĕnd) v.t. Grasp mentally, understand; include, take in. **com·pre·hend·i·ble** (kŏmprĭhĕn′dĭbel) adj. **com·pre·hend′ing·ly** adv.

com·pre·hen·si·ble (kŏmprĭhĕn′sĭbel) adj. That may be understood, or comprised. **com·pre·hen·si·bil·i·ty** (kŏmprĭhĕnsĭbĭl′ĭtē)

n. **com·pre·hen′si·bly** adv.

com·pre·hen·sion (kŏmprĭhĕn′shon) n. Understanding; inclusion.

com·pre·hen·sive (kŏmprĭhĕn′sĭv) adj. 1. Of understanding. 2. Including much, as in ∼ **education,** ∼ **treatment. com·pre·hen′sive·ly** adv. **com·pre·hen′sive·ness** n.

com·press (komprĕs′) v.t. Squeeze together; force into smaller volume, condense. **com·pressed′** adj. **com·pres′sive, com·pres′si·ble** adjs. **com·pres·si·bil·i·ty** (komprĕsĭbĭl′ĭtē) n. **compress** (kŏm′prĕs) n. Soft pad of gauze etc. for compressing artery etc.; wet

*The **conch** shell is broadly triangular in shape and has a wide lip. The spider conch (right) with its underside (below right) belongs to the genus Lambis and is found in tropical seas of the eastern hemisphere.*

weight, length) to represent data; **digital** ~, one operating with data represented by digits, usu. in binary system; ~ **program**, plan or set of coded instructions for processing data by computer; ~ **programmer**, person trained to write computer programs. **com·pu′ter·ize** *v.t.* (**-ized, -iz·ing**). Equip with, perform by, produce by computer. **com·pu·ter·i·za·tion** (kǫmpūterĭzā′shǫn) *n.*

com·rade (kŏm′răd) *n.* Friend, companion, associate in work or play or fighting, equal with whom one is on familiar terms; (as title) used by socialists, communists, etc., before surname. **com′rade·li·ness** *n.* **com′rade·ly** *adv.* **com′rade·ship** *n.*

Com·sat, COM·SAT (kŏm′săt) *abbrev.* Communications satellite; corporation set up by U.S. government to manage such satellites.

Com·stock[1] (kŭm′stŏk, kŏm′-), **Anthony** (1844–1915). Amer. reformer; secretary of militant Society for the Suppression of Vice, 1873–1915.

Com·stock[2] (kŭm′stŏk, kŏm′-) **Lode.** Gold and silver lode discovered by Amer. prospector, Henry Comstock, 1859, in W. Nevada, site of Virginia City.

Comte (kawṅt), **Auguste** (1798–1857). French mathematician and philosopher, founder of the positivist system (see POSITIVISM). **Comt′ism, Comt′ist** *ns.* **Com′ti·an** *adj.*

con[1] (kŏn) *v.t.* (**conned, con·ning**). Peruse, scrutinize, learn (by heart).

con[2] (kŏn) *v.t.* (**conned, con·ning**). Direct steering of (ship) from commanding position on shipboard.

con[3] (kŏn) *n.* (attrib.) Confidence, esp. in ~ **game, man**: see CONFIDENCE. **con** *v.t.* (**conned, con·ning**). Swindle by confidence trick.

con[4] (kŏn) *adv. & n.* (Argument) against a proposition etc.; **pros and** ~**s**, arguments for and against.

con[5] (kŏn) *n.* (slang) Convict; ex-convict.

con-[6] *prefix.* With.

Con·a·kry (kŏnakrē′). Capital and Atlantic seaport of the Republic of Guinea, in the SW.

con bri·o (kŏn brē′ō, kōn). (mus.) With spirit. [It.]

con·cat·e·nate (kǫnkăt′enāt) *v.t.* (**-nat·ed, -nat·ing**). Link together (fig.) ~ *adj.* **con·cat·e·na·tion** (kǫnkătenā′shǫn) *n.*

con·cave (kŏnkāv′, kŏn′kāv) *adj.* Having outline or surface curved like interior of circle or sphere (cf. CONVEX); hollow. **con·cave′ly** *adv.* **concave** (kŏn′kāv) *n.* Concave surface or line. **con·cave′ness** *n.* **con·cave′ly** *adv.* **con·cav·i·ty** (kǫnkăv′ĭtē) *n.* (pl. **-ties**). Being concave; concave surface; hollow, cavity.

concavo- *prefix.* Concavely, concave and ..., as ~**-concave**, concave on both surfaces, as certain lenses; ~**-convex**, concave on one side, convex on the other.

con·ceal (kǫnsēl′) *v.t.* Keep secret; hide. **con·ceal′er, con·ceal′ment** *ns.* **con·ceal′a·ble** *adj.*

con·cede (kǫnsēd′) *v.t.* (**-ced·ed, -ced·ing**). Admit, allow, grant.

con·ced′er *n.*

con·ceit (kǫnsēt′) *n.* 1. Person vanity. 2. Fanciful notion, fa fetched comparison, etc. **con ceit′ed** *adj.* Vain. **con·ceit′ed·** *adv.* **con·ceit′ed·ness** *n.*

con·ceiv·a·ble (kǫnsē′vabel) *ac* That can be (mentally) conceive **con·ceiv′a·bly** *adv.* **con·ceiv·a· bil·i·ty** (kǫnsēvabĭl′ĭtē), **con·ceiv a·ble·ness** *ns.*

con·ceive (kǫnsēv′) *v.* (**-ceived -ceiv·ing**). 1. Become pregnan (with). 2. Form in the min imagine; fancy, think. 3. Formu late, express in words, etc. **con ceiv′er** *n.*

con·cen·trate (kŏn′sentrāt)

trat·ed, -trat·ing). Bring to or ward a common center; focus attention), keep mind or attention atently fixed (on); increase rength of (solution etc.) esp. by vaporation of solvent etc.; con-entrated, (fig.) intense. concen-ate n. Concentrated substance. on·cen·tra·tion (kŏnsentrā'shon) n.

~ camp, camp in which large umbers of people, esp. political risoners, are detained by force, sp. any of the camps established by ne Nazis in World War II for the etention, persecution, and mass xecution of Jews and other non-.ryans, civilian war prisoners, rc.

con·cen·tric (konsĕn'trĭk) adj. Having a common center. con-en'tri·cal adj. con·cen'tri·cal·ly dv. con·cen·tric·i·ty (kŏnsĕn-·is'ĭtē) n.

con·cept (kŏn'sĕpt) n. Idea of a lass of objects, general notion.

con·cep·ta·cle (kŏnsĕp'takel) n. oot.) Hollow organ of some algae nd fungi within which sexual rgans are formed.

con·cep·tion (konsĕp'shon) n. Conceiving; thing conceived; idea. on·cep'tion·al adj. Of, like, a onception or idea.

con·cep·tive (konsĕp'tĭv) adj. Conceiving; of conception.

con·cep·tu·al (konsĕp'chōōal) dj. Of mental conceptions. on·cep'tu·al·ly adv.

con·cep·tu·al·ism (konsĕp'-hōōalĭzem) n. 1. (philos.) Doc-rine that universals have reality nly as mental concepts. 2. psychol.) Doctrine that the mind is apable of forming ideas corre-ponding to abstract and general erms. con·cep'tu·al·ist n. con-ep·tu·al·is·tic (konsĕpchōōalĭs-ĭk) adj.

con·cern (konsĕrn') v.t. Relate o, affect; interest (oneself). on·cerned' adj. (esp.) Involved; roubled. con·cern'ing prep. Regarding, relating to. concern n. Relation, reference; interest, solici-ous regard, anxiety; matter that affects one; business establishment, irm.

con·cert (kŏn'sert) n. 1. Agree-ment; union by mutual agreement. 2. Combination of voices or sounds. 3. Musical entertainment; ~ grand, grand piano of largest size or concerts. 4. in ~, acting ogether. concert (konsĕrt') v.t. Arrange, plan by mutual agree-ment. con·cert'ed adj. Contrived, prearranged; done in concert. con·cert'ed·ly adv.

con·cer·ti·na (kŏnsertē'na, -cher-) n. Small, hexagonal accordion with bellows and buttons or keys.

con·cer·to (konchĕr'tō, -chĕr'-) n. (pl. -tos, -ti pr. -tē). Musical composition, usu. in sonata form

with three or four movements, for a solo instrument (or, rarely, more than one) accompanied by orchestra.

con·ces·sion (konsĕsh'on) n. 1. Conceding; thing conceded; esp. grant of land or franchise by a government, company, or person for a special use or purpose. 2. Space within premises, e.g., carnival ~, for a subsidiary business. con·ces·sion·ar·y (kon-sĕsh'onĕrē) adj. & n. (pl. -ar·ies). con·ces·sion·aire (konsĕsho-nār'), con·ces·sion·er (konsĕsh'o-ner) ns. Holder or operator of con-cession.

con·ces·sive (konsĕs'ĭv) adj. Of, tending to, concession.

conch (kŏngk, kŏnch) n. (pl. conchs pr. kŏngks, con·ches pr. kŏn'chĭz). 1. Shellfish; (now usu.) large gastropod, esp. Strombidae; the Queen Conch (strombus gigas); shell of mollusk, esp. spiral shell of any large gastropod; such a shell used as a trumpet, esp. (Rom. myth.) of Triton. 2. External ear, its central concavity.

con·chif·er·ous (kŏngkĭf'erus) adj. Shell-bearing.

con·chol·o·gy (kŏngkŏl'ojē) n. Study of shells and shellfish. con·chol'o·gist n.

con·cierge (kŏnsyĕrzh') n. In France etc., doorkeeper, porter, of apartment house, hotel, etc.

con·cil·i·ar (konsĭl'ēer) adj. Of a council. con·cil'i·ar·ly adv.

con·cil·i·ate (konsĭl'ēāt) v.t. (-at·ed, -at·ing). Gain (goodwill, esteem, etc.) by acts that pacify, soothe, etc.; gain over, overcome distrust or hostility of. con·cil·i·a·tion (konsĭlēā'shon) n. Reconcile-ment; use of conciliatory measures. con·cil·i·a·to·ri·ness, con·cil'-i·a·tor ns. con·cil·i·a·tive, con-cil·i·a·to·ry, con·cil·i·a·ble adjs. con·cil·i·a·to·ri·ly adv.

con·cise (konsīs') adj. Brief and comprehensive in expression. con·cise'ly adv. con·cise'ness n.

con·clave (kŏn'klāv, kŏng'-) n. Meeting place, assembly, of cardinals for election of pope; private assembly.

con·clude (konklōōd') v. (-clud·ed, -clud·ing). Bring to an end, make an end; come to an end; settle, arrange (treaty etc.); infer; come to a conclusion; resolve. con·clud'er n.

con·clu·sion (konklōō'zhon) n. Termination; final result; infer-ence; decision; (logic) proposition deduced from previous ones, esp. last of three forming a syllogism; settling, arrangement (of peace etc.).

con·clu·sive (konklōō'sĭv) adj. Decisive, convincing. con·clu'-sive·ly adv. con·clu'sive·ness n.

con·coct (konkŏkt') v.t. Make up by mixing variety of ingredients;

fabricate. con·coc·tion (konkŏk'-shon), con·coct'er ns. con·coc'-tive adj.

con·com·i·tance (konkŏm'-ĭtans), con·com·i·tan·cy (kon-kŏm'ĭtansē) ns. (pl. -cies). Being concomitant, coexistence, esp. of body and blood of Christ in each of Eucharistic elements.

con·com·i·tant (konkŏm'ĭtant) adj. Going together, accompany-ing. ~ n. Accompanying state, quality, thing, etc. con·com'-i·tant·ly adv.

Con·cord[1] (kŏng'kerd). Capital of New Hampshire, in the S. central part.

Con·cord[2] (kŏng'kerd). Town in E. Massachusetts, near Boston; site of an early Revolutionary War battle, 1775.

con·cord (kŏn'kord, kŏng'-) n. Agreement, harmony, between persons or things; treaty.

con·cord·ance (konkōr'dans) n. 1. Agreement, harmony. 2. Alpha-betical arrangement of chief words or subjects occurring in a book (esp. the Bible) or in an author's works, with citations of passages con-cerned.

con·cord·ant (konkōr'dant) adj. Agreeing, harmonious. con·cord'-ant·ly adv.

con·cor·dat (konkōr'dăt) n. Formal agreement, esp. between pope and secular government for settlement and control of ec-clesiastical affairs.

con·course (kŏn'kōrs, -kōrs, kŏng'-) n. 1. Flocking together; crowd, confluence; assemblage. 2. Large main hall, or central open area, as at a railroad station; broad thoroughfare, avenue.

con·crete (kŏn'krēt, konkrēt') adj. 1. (gram., of noun) Denoting a thing as opp. to a quality, state, or action; not abstract. 2. Existing in material form, real. 3. Made of concrete. con·crete'ly adv. con·crete'ness n. concrete n. 1. Concrete thing. 2. Composition of broken stone, sand, gravel, etc., formed into a mass with cement and used for building, paving, etc. concrete (konkrēt') v. (-cret·ed, -cret·ing). 1. Form into a mass, solidify. 2. Treat, build, pave, etc., with concrete.

con·cre·tion (konkrē'shon) n. Coalescence; concrete mass, esp. (path.) hard morbid formation in body, stone; (geol.) mass formed by aggregation of solid particles, usu. around a nucleus. con·cre'-tion·ar·y adj.

con·cu·bi·nage (konkū'binĭj) n. Cohabiting of man and woman not legally married; being, having, a concubine.

con·cu·bine (kŏng'kyubīn, kŏn'-) n. Woman who cohabits with man to whom she is not married; (among polygamous

The Andean **condor** is the world's largest flying bird and the Californian species (above) is one of the rarest. It feeds near open coastland. Each female lays a single egg in a year. It is now a protected species in the U.S.A.

con·den·sa·tion (kŏndĕnsā shon, -den-) n. Condensin condensed mass; liquid formed condensed gas or vapor.

con·dense (kŏndĕns′) (-densed, -dens·ing). 1. Increa density of, reduce in volum compress, thicken, concentrat **condensed milk**, milk thicken by evaporation and sweetened. Compress into few words. Reduce, be reduced, from form gas or vapor to liquid.

con·dens·er (kŏndĕn′ser) (esp.) 1. (elect.) Capacitor. 2. Len system of lenses, for concentrati light.

con·de·scend (kŏndĭsĕnd′) v Deign, stoop; be condescendin waive one's superiority. **con·de scend′ing** adj. (esp.) Making show of condescension, patroni ing. **con·de·scend′ing·ly** ad **con·de·scend′ence** n.

con·de·scen·sion (kŏndĭsĕn shon) n. Affability to inferior patronizing manner.

con·dign (kŏndīn′) adj. (punishment) Adequate, appropr ate, deserved. **con·dign′ly** adv.

con·di·ment (kŏn′diment) Something used to give addition flavor to food, as ketchup, mustar or spice.

con·di·tion (kŏndĭsh′on) n. Stipulation; thing upon fulfil ment of which depends that something else. 2. (pl.) Circun stances, esp. those essential to thing's existence. 3. State of bein in ~, out of ~, in good, ba training and health. **condition** v. 1. Stipulate; agree by stipulatio (to). 2. Subject to as a condition 3. Bring into (good) condition (for 4. Train to adopt certain habits et **con·di′tioned** adj. (esp.) **reflex**, reflex or reflex actio which through habit or training ha been induced to follow a stimulu that is not naturally associated wit it.

con·di·tion·al (kŏndĭsh′ona adj. 1. Not absolute; dependen 2. (gram.) Of a clause, mood, con junction, phrase, expressing c introducing a condition. **con·di tion·al·ly** adv.

con·dole (kŏndōl′) v.i. (-dole -dol·ing). Express sympathy (wit person upon loss etc.). **con·dol′e con·do·lence** (kŏndō′lens), **con dole′ment** ns. **con·do·la·to·r** (kŏndō′latōrē, -tōrē) adj.

con·dom (kŏn′dom, kŭn′-) ɴ Contraceptive or prophylacti sheath worn on penis during sexu intercourse.

con·do·min·i·um (kŏndomĭn′ ēum) n. Apartment house etc. i which each dwelling unit i individually owned; apartment s owned.

con·done (kŏndōn′) v.t (-doned, -don·ing). Forgive

peoples) secondary wife, usu. of inferior status.

con·cu·pis·cence (konkū′- pĭsens) n. Sexual appetite. **con·cu′pis·cent** adj. Lustful, eagerly desirous.

con·cur (konkēr′) v.i. (-curred, -cur·ring). Coincide; cooperate; agree, express agreement, (with). **con·cur′rence, con·cur′ren·cy** ns. (pl. -cies).

con·cur·rent (konkēr′ent, -kŭr′-) adj. 1. Running together, going on side by side, occurring together; meeting in or tending to same point. 2. Cooperating; agree ing. **con·cur′rent·ly** adv.

con·cus·sion (konkŭsh′on) n. 1. Violent shaking; shock. 2. Injury caused, esp. to brain, by shock of

heavy blow, fall, etc. **con·cus·sive** (konkŭs′ĭv) adj.

con·demn (kondĕm′) v.t. 1. Censure, blame; bring about conviction of. 2. Give judicial sentence against, find guilty; sentence (to death etc.); (fig., esp. pass.) doom to some (unkind) fate or condition. 3. Pronounce unfit for use or consumption. 4. Take title to (property) for public use. **con·demn·er** (kondĕm′er) n. **con·dem·na·ble** (kondĕm′nabel) adj. **con·demn′ing·ly** adv.

con·dem·na·tion (kŏndĕmnā′- shon, -dem-) n. Censure; con demning; state of being con demned; ground for condemning. **con·dem·na·to·ry** (kondĕm′- natōrē, -tōrē) adj.

verlook (offense) with forgiveness;
ive tacit approval to. **con·do·na-
·ion** (kŏndōnā′shon), **con·don′er**
s.

con·dor (kŏnder, -dôr) n. Large
. Amer. vulture (*Vultur gryphus*)
ith blackish plumage and fleshy
xcrescence falling over bill;
:alifornia ~, great Californian
ulture (*Gymnogyps californianus*)
omewhat resembling this.

con·duce (kondōōs′, -dūs′) *v.i.*
-**duced, -duc·ing**). (usu. of
vents) Lead, contribute, *to*.
on·duc′er, con·du′cive·ness *ns*.
on·du·cive (kondōō′sĭv, -dū′-)
dj.

con·duct (kondŭkt′) *v.* 1. Lead,
:uide *to*. 2. Direct (orchestra,
oncert, etc.); manage (business
tc.). 3. Behave (*oneself*). 4. (phys.;
f a body) Convey (some form of
nergy, as heat, electricity, etc.)
hrough its particles, transmit.
on·duct (kŏn′dŭkt) n. Manner of
onducting (any business etc., or
neself), behavior. **con·duct′i·ble**
dj. **con·duct·i·bil·i·ty** (kondŭk-
·bĭl′ĭtē, kŏn-) n.

con·duct·ance (kondŭk′tans) n.
elect.) Conducting power of a
;iven conductor.

con·duc·tion (kondŭk′shon) n.
:onducting (of liquid through a
)ipe etc.); transmission (of heat,
:lectricity, etc.).

con·duc·tive (kondŭk′tĭv) *adj*.
-Iaving the property of conducting
iome form of energy, esp.
:lectricity. **con·duc·tiv·i·ty**
kŏndŭktĭv′ĭtē) n. (pl. **-ties**).

con·duc·tor (kondŭk′ter) n.
fem. **-tress** pr. **-trĭs**). 1. Leader,
;uide; manager. 2. Director of
)rchestra or chorus, who indicates
:o the performers the rhythm,
:xpression, etc., by motions of a
)aton or the hands. 3. Person in
:harge of a train or bus. 4. Thing
:hat conducts or transmits (some
orm of energy).

con·duit (kŏn′dōōĭt, -dū-, -dĭt)
n. Channel or pipe for conveying
water or other liquids; tube or duct
for enclosing electric wires and
:able.

con·dyle (kŏn′dīl, -dĭl) n. (anat.)
Rounded process at end of bone,
orming articulation with another
bone. **con·dy·loid** (kŏn′dĭloid) *adj*.

cone (kōn) n. 1. Solid of which
:he base is a circle (or other curved
figure) and the summit a point,
and every point in the intervening
surface is in a straight line between
the vertex and the circumference of
the base; any conical mass. 2. Fruit
of pine or fir, a dry, scaly multiple
fruit, more or less cone-shaped,
formed by hard persistent
imbricated scales covering naked
seeds. 3. Cone-shaped object;
marine shell of genus *Conus* of
gastropods; cone-shaped volcanic
peak; (physiol.) one of the minute

The **cone** shellfish feeds on worms and mollusks. Its shell is conical in shape. At one time sea-cone shells were much sought by collectors, particularly that of the rare glory-of-the-sea cone.

cone-shaped bodies that form, with
rods, one of the layers of nerve
elements in the retina. 4. **cone′-
flower**, garden plant of genus
Rudbeckia, esp. the black-eyed
Susan (*R. hirta*), native to N.
America. **cone** *v.t.* (**coned,
con·ing**). Shape into a cone.

Con·es·to·ga (kŏnestō′ga) n.
(Member of) tribe of N. Amer.
Indians formerly inhabiting parts
of Pennsylvania and Maryland;
Huron Indian name for the
Susquehanna river; ~ **Valley**,
Susquehanna river valley; ~
wagon, heavy, broad-wheeled,
Pennsylvania Dutch freight wagon,
later adapted by pioneers for west-
ward travel. [*Conestoga* (= "place
of muddy water"), Pennsylvania]

co·ney (kō′nē, kŭn′ē) n. (pl.

This **cone-flower** of the genus *Rudbeckia* is one of 25 annual, biennial and perennial species. Many have segmented leaves and yellow flowers with brown or black disks, and are native to N. America.

-neys) = CONY.

Co·ney (kō′nē) **Island**. Amusement resort on the Atlantic Ocean
in S. Brooklyn, New York City.

con·fab (kŏn′făb) n. (slang)
Confabulation. ~ *v.i.* (**-fabbed,
-fab·bing**). (slang) Confabulate.

con·fab·u·late (konfăb′yulāt)
v.i. (**-lat·ed, -lat·ing**). Converse,
chat. **con·fab·u·la·tion** (konfăb-
yulā′shon) n.

con·fec·tion (konfĕk′shon) n. 1.
Mixing, compounding. 2.
Medicinal preparation com-
pounded with sweetening; sweet

The **Conestoga Wagon** was the prototype of those used by the American
pioneers to transport their possessions
to the West. The floor was curved to
prevent any movement as they travelled
the rough trails.

preparation, as a bonbon. **con·-fec·tion·ar·y** (konfĕk'shonĕrē) *adj.*

con·fec·tion·er (konfĕk'shoner) *n.* Maker or seller of candy, pastry, etc. **con·fec·tion·er·y** (konfĕk'-shonĕrē) *n.* (pl. **-er·ies**). Things made or sold by a confectioner; confectioner's shop; confectioner's art.

con·fed·er·a·cy (konfĕd'erasē, -fĕd'ra-) *n.* (pl. **-cies**). 1. League, alliance; league for unlawful or evil purpose; conspiracy. 2. Body of allies, esp. union of states; (**Southern**) **C~**, Confederate States of America.

con·fed·er·ate (konfĕd'erĭt, -fĕd'rĭt) *adj.* Allied; **C~ States** (of America), confederacy of 11 Southern states that seceded from the U.S. in 1860–1 and fought the Civil War against the Union: Alabama, Arkansas, Florida, Georgia, Louisiana, Mississippi, North Carolina, South Carolina, Tennessee, Texas, Virginia. **con·federate** *n.* 1. Accomplice. 2. **C~**, supporter of the Confederate States of America. **confederate** (konfĕd'erāt) *v.* (**-at·ed, -at·ing**). Bring, come, into alliance (*with*). **con·fed·er·a·tion** (konfĕderā'-shon) *n.* (Union formed by) confederating.

con·fer (konfēr') *v.* (**-ferred, -fer·ring**). 1. Grant, bestow (title, degree, favor, etc., *on*). 2. Converse, take counsel (*with*) **con·fer'ment** *n.* Bestowing, granting. **con·fer'ra·ble** *adj.*

con·fer·ence (kŏn'ferens, -frens) *n.* 1. Consultation; meeting, for consultation or discussion. 2. Association of athletic teams, schools, or churches.

con·fess (konfĕs') *v.* Acknowledge, own, admit; make formal confession of guilt (to police, court, etc.) or of sins, esp. to a priest; (of priest) hear confession of (a penitent). **con·fess·ed·ly** (konfĕs'-ĭdlē) *adv.*

con·fes·sion (konfĕsh'on) *n.* Acknowledgment, admission (of fact, guilt, etc.); acknowledgment of sin (as by individual penitent to a priest); thing confessed; **C~ (of Faith)**, formulary in which Church or body of Christians sets forth religious doctrines that it considers essential; creed.

con·fes·sion·al (konfĕsh'onal) *adj.* Of confession. **~** *n.* Cabinet or stall in which priest hears confession.

con·fes·sor (konfĕs'er) *n.* 1. One who makes confession. 2. One who avows his religion in the face of persecution but does not suffer martyrdom. 3. Priest who hears confession.

con·fet·ti (konfĕt'ē) *n.pl.* (usu. considered sing.) Small pieces of colored paper tossed into the air at celebrations, at bride and groom at

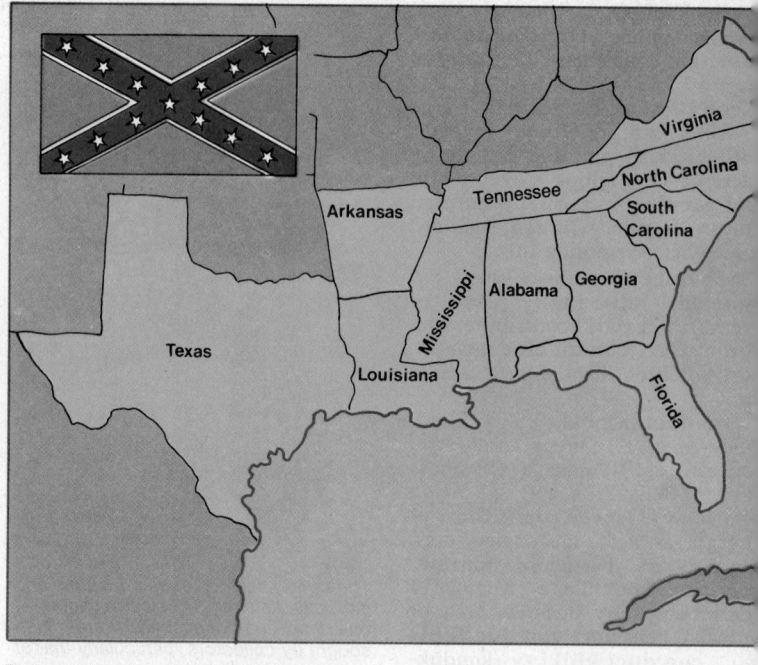

*During the American Civil War 11 southern states banded together to form the **Confederate States**. They wanted to retain state rights, as against a centralized authority in Washington. confederation is usually a league form of union between independent states.*

weddings, etc. [It., = "sweet-meats"]

con·fi·dant (kŏn'fīdănt, -dahnt, kŏnfīdănt', -dahnt') *n.* (fem. **-dante**). One to whom private matters or secrets are entrusted or confided.

con·fide (konfīd') *v.* (**-fid·ed, -fid·ing**). Repose confidence *in*; impart (secret *to*); entrust (*to*); **~ in**, talk confidentially to.

con·fi·dence (kŏn'fīdens) *n.* 1. Firm trust; assured expectation. 2. Boldness, fearlessness; impudence, presumption. 3. Imparting of private matters; thing so imparted. 4. **~ game**, (also **con game**) swindle worked by gaining the confidence or trust of a credulous person; **~ man**, (also **con man**) one who practices this.

con·fi·dent (kŏn'fīdent) *adj.* Trusting, fully assured; bold; impudent. **con·fi·dent·ly** *adv.*

con·fi·den·tial (kŏnfīdĕn'shal) *adj.* Spoken, written, in confidence; entrusted with secrets or private matters. **con·fi·den·tial·ly** *adv.*

con·fig·u·ra·tion (konfĭgyurā'-shon) *n.* Mode of arrangement, conformation, outline; (astron.) relative position of planet or other celestial bodies. **con·fig·u·ra'-tion·al** *adj.*

con·fine (kŏn'fīn) *n.* (usu. pl.) Border, boundaries, limit. **confine** (konfīn') *v.t.* (**-fined, -fin·ing**). Keep *within*, *to*, limits; imprison, immure; (pass.) be in childbirth. **con·fine·ment** (konfīn'ment) *n.* Imprisonment; restriction, limitation; childbirth. **con·fin'a·ble** *adj.*

con·firm (konfĕrm') *v.t.* 1. Establish more firmly; ratify corroborate; establish, encourag (person *in* opinion etc.). Administer religious rite confirmation to. **con·firm'a·ble con·firm·a·to·ry** (konfĕr'matōr -tōrē-), **con·firm'a·tive** *adjs.*

con·fir·ma·tion (kŏnfermā'-shon) *n.* 1. Confirming, cor roboration. 2. Rite administered t baptized persons esp. at age o discretion in various Christia Churches. 3. Rite by which Jewis child, after a prescribed course o study, is admitted to adult statu in some sections of the Jewis community; see BAR MITZVAH, BA MITZVAH.

con·fis·cate (kŏn'fīskāt) *v.t* (**-cat·ed, -cat·ing**). Appropriat to the public treasury by way o penalty; seize as by authority appropriate summarily. **con·fis·ca·tion** (kŏnfīskā'shon), **con·fis·ca·tor** (kŏn'fīskāter) *ns* **con·fis·ca·to·ry** (konfīs'katōre -tōre) *adj.*

con·fla·gra·tion (kŏnflagrā'-shon) *n.* Great and destructive fire

con·flict (kŏn'flĭkt) *n.* Fight struggle; collision; clashing (o opposed principles etc.). **~** (konflĭkt') *v.i.* Struggle; clash, b incompatible.

con·flu·ence (kŏn'flōoens) *n* Flocking or flowing together, esp joining of two or more streams etc **con·flu·ent** (kŏn'flōoent) *adj* Flowing together, uniting. **~** *n* Stream uniting with another. **con'-flu·ent·ly** *adv.*

con·form (konfôrm') *v.* Form according to, agree with, a pattern

Traffic congestion, both human and vehicular, is becoming an increasing headache for town planners as urban populations continue to grow and people go on buying cars.

secular matters. **Con·fu·cian** (konfū′shan) *adj.* & *n.* (Follower) of Confucius. **Con·fu′cian·ism** *n.* Ethical system based on teachings of Confucius, emphasizing virtue, justice, and devotion to family and the spirits of one's ancestors; political and cosmological system that evolved in China during the Han dynasty (206 B.C.–220 A.D.), which regarded the emperor and hierarchy of officials as divinely appointed, and social relations as governed by the rules of Confucius. [Latinized f. Chin. *K'ung-fu-tzŭ* or *K'ung-fu-tse* K'ung the master (or philosopher)]

con fuo·co (kŏn fwō′kō, kōn). (mus.) With fire. [It.]

con·fuse (konfūz′) *v.t.* (-fused, -fus·ing). Throw into disorder; mix up in the mind; abash, perplex. **con·fus·ed·ly** (konfū′zĭdlē, -fūzd′-) *adv.* **con·fus′ed·ness** *n.* **con·fus′ing·ly** *adv.*

con·fu·sion (konfū′zhon) *n.* Confusing; confused state; tumult.

con·fute (konfūt′) *v.t.* (-fut·ed, -fut·ing). Convict (person) of error by proof, refute (argument). **con·fu·ta·tion** (kŏnfyōōtā′shon) *n.*

con·ga (kŏng′ga) *n.* (pl. -gas). Latin-Amer. dance in which dancers form a long winding line (~ **line**) behind a leader.

con·geal (konjēl′) *v.* Solidify, as by freezing or cooling; coagulate. **con·geal′a·ble** *adj.* **con·geal′-ment** *n.*

con·gen·ial (konjēn′yal) *adj.* Kindred, sympathetic (*with, to*); suited, agreeable (*to*). **con·ge·ni·al·i·ty** (konjēnēăl′ĭtē) *n.* **con·gen′ial·ly** *adv.*

con·gen·i·tal (konjĕn′ĭtal) *adj.* Existing before or at birth; dating from birth (esp. of defects, diseases, etc.). **con·gen′i·tal·ly** *adv.*

con·ger (kŏng′ger) *n.* (also ~ **eel**) Large species of eel of the family Congridae, esp. *Conger oceanicus* of Atlantic waters.

con·ge·ries (kŏnjēr′ez, kŏn′je-) *n.* (considered sing. or pl.). Collection; mass, heap.

con·gest (konjĕst′) *v.* Accumulate to excess; affect with congestion. **con·ges′ted** *adj.* Overcrowded; filled. **con·ges′tive** *adj.* (med.) Overcharged with blood.

con·ges·tion (konjĕs′chon) *n.* 1. Congested or overcrowded condition, as of population, traffic, etc. 2. (med.) Abnormal accumulation of blood in an organ etc.

con·glom·er·ate (konglŏm′erĭt) *adj.* Gathered together into more or less rounded mass, clustered; (geol., of rock) formed of pebbles or gravel cemented together. ~ *n.*

make similar (*to*); adapt *oneself to*; omply with, be conformable (*to*). **on·form′er** *n.*

con·form·a·ble (konfôr′mabel) *dj.* Similar (*to*); consistent, dapted (*to*); tractable. **con·form′-·bil·i·ty** (konfôrmabĭl′ĭtē) *n.* **on·form′a·bly**, *adv.*

con·for·ma·tion (kŏnformā′-hon) *n.* 1. Conforming, adaptation. . Manner in which thing is formed, tructure.

con·form·ist (konfôr′mĭst) *n.* One who conforms to practices of group, society, etc.

con·form·i·ty (konfôr′mĭtē) *n.* pl. -ties). Likeness (*to, with*); ompliance (*with, to*).

con·found (konfownd′) *v.t.* 1. Defeat utterly, discomfit (archaic);

overthrow, defeat (plan, hope); (bibl.) put to shame. 2. Throw into perplexity; throw into disorder; mix up; confuse (in idea). 3. Damn, esp. in mild oath (as ~ *it*). **con·found′ed·ly** *adv.* Damnably.

con·frere (kŏn′frār) *n.* Fellow member of profession etc.

con·front (konfrŭnt′) *v.t.* Meet face to face, stand facing; be opposite to; face in hostility or defiance; oppose; bring (person) face to face *with* (accusers etc.); compare. **con·fron·ta·tion** (kŏnfrontā′shon), **con·front′ment** *ns.*

Con·fu·cius (konfū′shus) (*c*550–478 B.C.). Chinese philosopher and teacher; famous for his sayings relating mainly to temporal and

1. Conglomerate rock. 2. Company consisting of number of subsidiary units in unrelated industries. ~ (konglŏm'erāt) v. (-at·ed, -at·ing). Collect into a coherent mass. **con·glom·er·a·tion** (konglŏmerā'shon) n.

Con·go (kŏng'gō). Second largest river of Africa, 2,900 mi. (4,640 km), flowing from Zambia in central Africa into Atlantic; area surrounding it; **Belgian ~**, former name of ZAIRE; **People's Republic of the C~**, country in W. Africa bordering on the Atlantic; the former French Congo; member of the French Community; capital, Brazzaville. **Con·go·lese** (kŏnggolēz', -lēs') adj. & n.

con·gou (kŏng'gōō) n. Kind of black China tea. [Chin. kung-fu (ch'a) labor (tea)]

con·grat·u·late (kongrăch'ulāt) v.t. (-lat·ed, -lat·ing). Address (person) with expression of sympathetic joy (on something); ~ **oneself**, think oneself fortunate. **con·grat·u·lant** adj. & n. **con·grat·u·la·tor** n. **con·grat·u·la·tion** (kongrăchulā'shon) n. Congratulating; (pl.) congratulatory expressions (also as int.) **con·grat·u·la·to·ry** (kongrăch'ulatōrē, -tōre) adj.

con·gre·gate (kŏng'gregāt) v. (-gat·ed, -gat·ing). Collect, gather, into a crowd or mass. **con·gre·ga·tion** (kŏnggregā'shon) n. 1. Collection into a body or mass; assemblage. 2. General assembly of a group; body of assembled people. 3. Body of persons assembled for religious worship or habitually attending a particular place of worship. **con·gre·gant** (kŏng'gregant), **con·gre·ga·tor** ns.

con·gre·ga·tion·al (kŏnggregā'shonal) adj. 1. Of a congregation. 2. **C~**, of or adhering to Congregationalism. **Con·gre·ga·tion·al·ism** (kŏnggregā'shonalĭzem) n. System of ecclesiastical polity regarding all legislative, disciplinary, and judicial functions as vested in the individual church or local congregation of believers; referring to doctrine of Congregational Christian Church. **Con·gre·ga·tion·al·ist** n.

con·gress (kŏng'grĭs) n. Coming together, meeting. 2. Formal meeting of delegates for discussion, esp. of envoys or persons engaged in special studies. 3. **C~**, national legislative body of U.S. consisting of the Senate and the House of Representatives; legislative body of certain other republics; session of this; **con'gressman, con'gresswoman**, member of U.S. Congress, esp. of the House of Representatives; **Congress of Racial Equality**, organization founded in 1942 in U.S., dedicated to ending racial segregation, improving social conditions, etc.; abbrev. CORE. **con·gres·sion·al** (kongrĕsh'onal) adj. Of a congress or of Congress.

Con·greve (kŏn'grēv, kŏng'), **William** (1670–1729). Engli[sh] writer of Restoration comedie[s]; author of Love for Love, The Wa[y] of the World, etc.

con·gru·ence (kŏng'grōoens) n. Agreement, consistency. **con·gru·en·cy** n. (pl. -cies). Co[n]gruence; (math.) relation betwe[en] two numbers which, when divide[d] by a third (the modulus), give th[e] same remainder.

con·gru·ent (kŏng'grōoent) ad[j.] Suitable; accordant (with); (math[.]) having congruency; (of triangle[s,] etc.) equal in all respects, capab[le] of exact superposition. **con·gru·ent·ly** adv.

con·gru·ous (kŏng'grōous) ad[j.] Accordant, conformable (with[,]) fitting. **con·gru·i·ty** (kongrōō'ĭt[y,] kŏn-) n. (pl. -ties).

con·ic (kŏn'ĭk) adj. Con[e-] shaped; of a cone; ~ **section**, figu[re] (circle, ellipse, parabola, or hype[r-] bola) formed by intersection of [a]

*The river **Congo** (facing page) is th[e] second largest in Africa and contain[s] over 4,000 islands and some 8,00[0] miles of natural waterways. Cong[o] (Brazzaville) (below) is a relatively po[or] country with most of its populatio[n] engaged in subsistence agriculture. [It] has a hot and humid climate. Fishing [is] carried out in primitive boats by tribe[s] living along the river (left).*

The **conifer** is mostly an evergreen tree
or shrub, native to the northern hemisphere, whose seeds form a cone. The
Norway spruce (above) and Scots Pine
(right) are common in parts of western
Europe with long winters and a high
rainfall.

plane and a right circular cone.
con·ics n. Branch of geometry
dealing with cones and conic
sections.

con·i·cal (kŏn′ĭkal) adj. Cone-
shaped; of or relating to a cone.

co·ni·fer (kŏn′ĭfer, kō′nĭ-) n.
Cone-bearing tree or shrub.
co·nif·er·ous (konĭf′erus, kō-) adj.

con·jec·tur·al (konjĕk′cheral)
adj. Involving, given to, conjecture.
con·jec′tur·al·ly adv.

con·jec·ture (konjĕk′cher) n.
Inference based on evidence that is
not complete, guessing. ~ v.
(-tured, -tur·ing). Guess; make
a guess. **con·jec′tur·a·ble** adj.
con·jec′tur·er n.

con·join (konjoin′) v. Join;
combine. **con·joint′** adj.
con·joint′ly adv.

con·ju·gal (kŏn′jugal) adj. Of
marriage; of husband or wife in
their relation to each other.
con·ju·gal·ly adv. **con·ju·gal·i·ty**
(kŏnjugăl′ĭtē) n.

con·ju·gate (kŏn′jugāt) v.
(-gat·ed, -gat·ing). 1. (gram.)
Inflect (verb) in voice, mood, tense,
number, person. 2. Unite; join in
conjugation. **conjugate** (kŏn′jugĭt,
-gāt) adj. Joined together; coupled;
(gram.) derived from same root;
(math.) joined in a reciprocal
relation; (bot. etc.) fused. ~ n.
Conjugate word or thing.

con′ju·ga·tive adj. **con′ju·ga·tor**
n.

con·ju·ga·tion (kŏnjugā′shon) n.
1. Joining together; (biol.) fusion
of two (apparently) similar cells for
reproduction. 2. (gram.) Scheme
of verbal inflection. **con·ju·ga′-
tion·al** adj.

con·junct (konjŭngkt′, kŏn′-
jŭngkt) adj. Joined together;
associated. **con·junct′ly** adv.

con·junc·tion (konjŭngk′shon)
n. 1. Union, connection; **in ~,
together** (with). 2. (astron.)
Apparent proximity of two heavenly
bodies. 3. Combination of events
or circumstances. 4. (gram.) One
of the parts of speech; an uninflected word used to connect
other words, phrases, clauses, or
sentences. **con·junc′tion·al** adj.
con·junc′tion·al·ly adv.

con·junc·ti·va (kŏnjŭngktī′va)
n. (pl. **-vas, -vae** pr. -vē). Mucous
membrane lining inner eyelid and
reflected over front of eyeball.
con·junc·ti·vi·tis (konjŭngktĭvī′-
tĭs) n. (med.) Inflammation of
conjunctiva.

con·junc·tive (konjŭngk′tĭv)
adj. 1. Serving to join or unite.
2. (gram.) Of the nature of, acting
as, a conjunction; uniting sense as
well as construction (cf. DIS-
JUNCTIVE). ~ n. Conjunctive word.
con·junc′tive·ly adv.

con·junc·ture (konjŭngk′che
n. Combination of events, postu
of affairs.

con·ju·ra·tion (kŏnjerā′shon)
Solemn appeal, incantation, co
juring.

con·jure (kŏn′jer, konjoo
kŭn′jer) v. **(-jured, -jur·ing**
1. Constrain (spirit) to appear
invocation. 2. Effect, bring ou
convey away, by juggling; jugg
produce magical effects by natur
means, perform marvels; ~ u
cause to appear to the mind
fancy.

con·jur·er, con·jur·or (kŏn
jurer, kŭn′-) ns. One who practic
legerdemain.

conk (kŏngk, kawngk) v.t. (slan
Hit on the head. ~ **out** (slan
Break or fail (of a machine); fai
go to sleep, be drained of energy

con mo·to (kŏn mō′tō, kōn
(mus.) With spirited movemen
[It.]

Conn. abbrev. Connecticut.

con·nect (konĕkt′) v. Join; lir
together in sequence or orde
associate in occurrence or actio
(pass.) have to do with; associa
mentally; unite with others
family relationship, common aim
etc.; join on (with); run
connection (with); **connectin
rod,** rod connecting rotating wi
reciprocating parts of an engin

p. rod connecting piston with ankshaft in automobile. **con·ec′tor, con·nect′er** *ns.* **con·ect′ed·ly** *adv.* **con·nect′ed·ness**

Con·nect·i·cut (konět′ikut). ew England state of U.S., one of e original 13 states of the Union 788); capital, Hartford; ~ **River**, rgest river in New England, wing 345 mi. (555.2 km) S. from e Canadian border of New ampshire, forming the New ampshire-Vermont boundary, d then flowing through Masschusetts and Connecticut into ong Island Sound at New Haven.

con·nec·tion, (Brit.) **con·nex-n** (konĕk′shon) *ns.* 1. Connecting, eing connected; connecting part or ning; (mech.) joint between embers. 2. Relation of thought c.; personal relation or interourse; business relationship. 3. erson related by family or arriage; influential friend or cquaintance. 4. Meeting of one eans of transport (as railroad ain) by another at appointed time nd place to take on the passengers;

train etc. meeting another thus. 5. Means of communication, as in *telephone* ~. 6. (slang) Narcotics dealer or purchase. **con·nec′-tion·al** *adj.*

con·nec·tive (konĕk′tĭv) *adj.* Serving, tending, to connect; ~ **tissue**, fibrous tissue connecting and supporting organs of the body. **con·nec′tive·ly** *adv.* **con·nec′-tiv·i·ty** (konĕktĭv′ĭtē) *n.*

conn·ing (kŏn′ĭng) **tower.** Pilothouse of warship; superstructure on submarine in which periscope is mounted and from which steering, firing, etc. are directed when the submarine is on or near the surface. [CON² v.]

con·niv·ance (konī′vans) *n.* Conniving; tacit permission.

con·nive (konīv′) *v.i.* (**-nived, -niv·ing**). Wink *at* (what one ought to oppose); cooperate secretly, conspire. **con·niv′er** *n.*

con·nois·seur (konoseī′, -soor′) *n.* Critical judge (*of*, *in*, matters of taste). **con·nois·seur′ship** *n.*

con·note (konōt′) *v.t.* (**-not·ed, -not·ing**). (of words) Imply in addition to the primary meaning;

(of facts etc.) imply as a consequence or condition. **con·no·ta-tion** (kŏnotā′shon) *n.* **con·no·ta-tive** (kŏn′otātĭv, konō′ta-) *adj.* **con·no·ta·tive·ly** *adv.*

con·nu·bi·al (konoō′bēal, -nū′-) *adj.* Of marriage; of husband or wife; married. **con·nu′bi·al·ly** *adv.* **con·nu·bi·al·i·ty** (konoō-bēăl′itē, -nū-) *n.* (pl. **-ties**).

con·quer (kŏng′ker) *v.* Overcome by force; get the better of; acquire, subjugate. **con′quer·or** *n.* **con′quer·ing, con′quer·a·ble** *adjs.* **con′quer·ing·ly** *adv.*

con·quest (kŏn′kwĕst, kŏng′-) *n.* Subjugation, conquering; conquered territory; person whose affections have been won.

Con·rad (kŏn′răd), **Joseph** (1857–1924). Pen name of Teodor Josef Konrad Korzeniowski, English writer born in Poland; wrote novels and short stories about seafaring life; author of *Lord Jim*, *The Heart of Darkness*, etc.

Con·rail (kŏn′rāl) *abbrev.* Consolidated Rail Corporation, a U.S. government-sponsored railroad network.

Cons. *abbrev.* Constable; consul.

con·san·guin·e·ous (kŏnsăng-gwĭn′ēus) *adj.* Of the same blood, akin. **con·san·guin·i·ty** (kŏnsăng-gwĭn′ĭtē) *n.* Blood relationship. **con·san·guine** (kŏnsăng′gwĭn) *adj.* **con·san·guin·e·ous·ly** *adv.*

con·science (kŏn′shens) *n.* Moral sense of right and wrong as regards things for which one is responsible; faculty or principle pronouncing upon moral quality of one's own actions or motives; **in all** ~, in reason or fairness; ~ **money**, money paid or used to relieve conscience; ~**-stricken**, overcome with remorse. **con′science·less** *adj.*

con·sci·en·tious (kŏnshēĕn′-shus) *adj.* Obedient to conscience, scrupulous; ~ **objector**, one who for moral or religious reasons, refuses participation in military service. **con·sci·en′tious·ly** *adv.* **con·sci·en′tious·ness** *n.*

con·scious (kŏn′shus) *adj.* Aware, knowing; with mental faculties awake or active; self-conscious; (of actions etc.) realized by the performer thereof. **con′scious·ly** *adv.* **con′-scious·ness** *n.* State of being conscious; totality of person's thoughts and feelings, or of a class of these; perception (*of*, *that*).

con·script¹ (kŏn′skrĭpt) *adj.* ~ **fathers**, (Rom. hist.) collective title of Roman senators.

con·script² (kŏn′skrĭpt) *n.*

*The **conning tower** is designed to house sophisticated radio and radar antennae. The nuclear powered submarine U.S.S. Finback can stay submerged indefinitely.*

Recruit enrolled by conscription; draftee. **conscript** (konskrĭpt´) v.t. Enroll by conscription, draft. **con·scrip·tion** (konskrĭp´shon) n. Compulsory enrollment of soldiers into military service.

con·se·crate (kŏn´sekrāt) v.t. (**-crat·ed, -crat·ing**). Set apart as sacred (to); devote to (purpose); sanctify. **con´se·cra·tor, con´-se·crat·er** ns.

con·se·cra·tion (kŏnsekrā´shon) n. Act of consecrating, dedication, esp. of church, churchyard, etc.; ordination to sacred office, esp. of bishop; devotion to (purpose). **con·se·cra·to·ry** (kŏn´sekratōrē, -tōrē) adj.

con·sec·u·tive (konsĕk´yutĭv) adj. Following in succession without interruption. **con·sec´-u·tive·ly** adv. **con·sec´u·tive·ness** n.

con·sen·su·al (konsĕn´shōōal) adj. Relating to or involving consent. **con·sen´su·al·ly** adv.

con·sen·sus (konsĕn´sus) n. (pl. **-sus·es**). General agreement (of opinions etc.).

con·sent (konsĕnt´) v.i. Express willingness (to), agree (to, that, etc.). ~ n. Voluntary agreement, compliance; permission; **con´-sent´er** n.

con·se·quence (kŏn´sekwĕns, -kwens) n. 1. Thing or circumstance that follows as a result (of something preceding); logical inference. 2. Importance, moment;

social distinction, rank, as a person of ~.

con·se·quent (kŏn´sekwĕnt, -kwent) n. Event etc. following another (without implication of causal connection); (logic) second part of conditional proposition, dependent on antecedent; (math.) second term of a ratio. ~ adj. Following (on) as a result; following logically; logically consistent.

con·se·quen·tial (kŏnsekwĕn´-shal) adj. 1. Following as a result or inference. 2. Having consequence, important. **con·se·quen´tial·ly** adv. **con·se·quen·ti·al·i·ty** (kŏnsekwĕnshēăl´ĭtē) n.

con·se·quent·ly (kŏn´sekwĕntlē, -kwent-) adv. & conj. As a result; therefore.

con·ser·van·cy (konsĕr´vansē) n. (pl. **-cies**). Careful use of natural resources.

con·ser·va·tion (kŏnservā´shon) n. Preservation, esp. of natural resources; ~ **of energy**, principle that energy is never consumed, that the total quantity of energy in the universe remains constant even though energy may change form. **con·ser·va·tion·ist** n. One who advocates conservation, esp. of

*The present day need for **conservation** of natural resources has led to a number of experiments using wind power for the generation of electricity. There has so far been little significant commercial success.*

natural resources. **con·serv** **tion·al** adj.

con·ser·va·tive (konsĕr´va adj. 1. Preservative, keeping tending to keep intact or changed. 2. Disliking great cha (pol.) favoring maintenance existing institutions; **C~ par** one of the main parties in Britain. 3. (of estimate et Moderate, cautious, low. **co servative** n. Conservative pers person who holds conservat political views. **con·ser´va·tive** adv. **con·ser´va·tism, con·se va·tive·ness** ns.

con·ser·va·tor (kŏn´servat konsĕr´va-) n. Preserver, guardi (law) guardian; keeper.

con·ser·va·to·ry (konsĕr´vatō -tōrē) n. (pl. **-ries**). 1. Mu school. 2. Small greenhouse.

con·serve (kŏn´serv, konsĕrv´) (usu. pl.) Jam made from two more fruits stewed in sug ~ (konsĕrv´) v.t. (**-serve -serv·ing**). Keep from har protect; preserve. **con·serv´a·b** adj. **con·serv´er** n.

con·sid·er (konsĭd´er) v. C template mentally; weigh the mer of; reflect, reckon with, ma allowance for; be of opinion; rega as.

con·sid·er·a·ble (konsĭd´erab adj. Worth considering; notab important; much, not sma **con·sid´er·a·bly** adv.

con·sid·er·ate (konsĭd´erĭt) a Thoughtful for others. **con·sid er·ate·ly** adv. **con·sid´er·ate ness** n.

con·sid·er·a·tion (konsĭderā shon) n. 1. Considering; medit tion; **take into** ~, consider. Fact, thing, regarded as a reaso **in** ~ **of**, in return for, on accou of. 3. Compensation, reward; (la thing given, done, as equivalent person to whom a promise is mad 4. Thoughtfulness for others.

con·sid·er·ing (konsĭd´erĭn prep. Taking into account, in vie of; (ellipt., colloq.) considering th circumstances.

con·sign (konsīn´) v.t. Han over, deliver, to; transmit, send b rail etc., to; entrust to another care; set apart for special us commit irrevocably. **con·sign´ a·ble** adj. **con·sign·ee** (kŏnsīnē -sĭ-, konsī-), **con·sign·or** (konsī ner, kŏnsīnōr´) ns.

con·sign·ment (konsīn´ment) Consigning; goods consigned to a agent for sale; **on** ~, (sent to retailer) to be paid for when sold or returned if not sold.

*Episcopal **consecration** by Pope Pa VI in St. Peter's, Rome. The conse cration of bishops in the Roman Cath olic Church necessitates an elaborat ceremony.*

*The frigate **U.S.S. Constitution** was launched in 1797 and had an illustrious career until condemned as unseaworthy in 1828. Nicknamed 'Old Ironsides', it is open to the public in Boston.*

con·sist (kŏnsĭst′) *v.i.* Be composed *of*; be comprised or contained *in*; agree, harmonize, *with*.

con·sis·ten·cy (kŏnsĭs′tensē), **con·sis·tence** (kŏnsĭs′tens) *ns.* (pl. **-cies**). 1. Degree of density, esp. of thick liquids; firmness, solidity. 2. Being consistent.

con·sis·tent (kŏnsĭs′tent) *adj.* 1. Compatible (*with*), not contradictory. 2. Constant to same principles of thought or action. **con·sis′·tent·ly** *adv.*

con·sis·to·ry (kŏnsĭs′torē) *n.* (pl. **-ries**). 1. Senate in which pope, presiding over whole body of cardinals, deliberates on affairs of the Church. 2. Religious court or governing body of clergy or lay members. **con·sis·to·ri·al** (kŏnsĭstōr′ēal, -tōr′-), **con·sis·to′·ri·an** *adjs.*

con·so·la·tion (kŏnsolā′shon) *n.* Alleviation of grief or disappointment; consoling circumstance; ~ **prize**, one given to competitor who has not won a main prize.

con·sol·a·to·ry (kŏnsŏl′atōrē, -tōrē, -sō′la-) *adj.* Tending or designed to console.

con·sole[1] (konsōl′) *v.t.* (**-soled, -sol·ing**). Bring consolation to. **con·sol′ing·ly** *adv.* **con·sol′a·ble** *adj.* **con·sol′er** *n.*

con·sole[2] (kŏn′sōl) *n.* 1. Decorative bracket supporting a cornice, shelf, art object, etc; ~ **table**, table supported by bracket

against a wall. 2. Cabinet for radio, television set, etc. 3. Ensemble of keyboards, stops, etc., of organ, esp. when separate from body of instrument, as in electric organ. 4. Control panel for electrical or mechanical equipment.

con·sol·i·date (kŏnsŏl′ĭdāt) *v.* (**-dat·ed, -dat·ing**). 1. Solidify, strengthen. 2. Combine (territories, companies, debts, statutes, etc.) into one whole. **con·sol·i·da·tion** (kŏnsŏlĭdā′shon), **con·sol′i·da·tor** *ns.*

con·som·mé (kŏnsomā′) *n.* Clear soup made from meat, poultry, or vegetable stock.

con·so·nance (kŏn′sonans), **con·so·nan·cy** (kŏn′sonansē) *ns.* (pl. **-cies**). Recurrence of same or similar consonant sounds in words or syllables, assonance; (mus.) sounding together of notes in harmony; consonant interval; agreement, harmony.

con·so·nant[1] (kŏn′sonant) *adj.* Agreeable *to*, consistent *with*; harmonious; agreeing in sound; (mus.) making concord. **con′·so·nant·ly** *adv.*

con·so·nant[2] (kŏn′sonant) *n.*

Sound in speech, other than a vowel, produced by a complete momentary stoppage or by partial stoppage or constriction of the air stream in some part of the mouth cavity or by the lips as it passes from the lungs; letter or symbol representing such a sound. **con·so·nan·tal** (kŏnsonăn′tal) *adj.* [L *consonantem* (*litteram*); the name is due to the erroneous view that a consonant can only be sounded along with a vowel]

con sor·di·no (kŏn sōrdē′nō, kōn). (mus.) With the mute or damper. [It.]

con·sort (kŏn′sōrt) *n.* 1. Husband or wife; **king, prince** ~, (titles sometimes given to) husband of reigning queen; **queen** ~, king's wife. 2. Ship sailing in company with another. 3. Companion; partner. 4. (mus.) Group of performers or instruments. **consort** (konsōrt′) *v.* Associate; keep company, (*with*); agree, harmonize, (*with*).

con·sor·ti·um (konsōr′shēum, -tēum) *n.* (pl. **-ti·a** pr. -shēa -tēa, **-ti·ums**). Association of business, banking, or manufacturing organizations for an activity requiring large amounts of capital or other resources.

con·spec·tus (konspĕk′tus) *n.* (pl. **-tus·es**). General or comprehensive survey; summary.

con·spic·u·ous (konspĭk′ūus) *adj.* Clearly visible, striking to the

; attracting notice, remarkable. **·spic′u·ous·ness** *n.* **con·spic′-us·ly** *adv.*

·on·spir′a·cy (konspĭr′asē) *n.* **-cies**). Conspiring; combina-1 for unlawful, treacherous, or l purpose; plot. **con·spir′a·tor** nspĭr′ater) *n.* **con·spir·a·to·al** (konspĭrator′ēal, -tōr′-) *adj.* **n·spir·a·to′ri·al·ly** *adv.*

·on·spire (konspĭr′) *v.* (**-spired, ·ir′ing**). Combine for unlawful, acherous, or evil purpose, esp. ason, murder, sedition; combine, ncur (*to* do); plot, devise. **n·spir′er** *n.*

·on·sta·ble (kon′stabel, kŭn′-) 1. Chief officer or governor of val household, administration, or litary forces. 2. Officer of the ace in rural area; (*Brit.*) police-n or policewoman. **con′-·ble·ship** *n.* [L. *comes stabuli* unt of the stable]

Con·sta·ble (kŭn′stabel, kon′-), hn (1776–1837). English land-pe painter.

con·stab·u·lar·y (konstăb′-lērē) *adj.* Of constables. ~ *n.* . -lar·ies). Body of constables; trict under a constable. **n·stab·u·lar** (konstăb′yuler) *n.*

Con·stance (kon′stans). City in V. West Germany on Lake onstance, 1414–18, which ended e Great Schism; **Lake ~**, erman name, *Bodensee*) lake unded by West Germany, vitzerland, and Austria.

con·stan·cy (kon′stansē) *n.* rmness, endurance; faithfulness; changingness.

con·stant (kon′stant) *adj.* Un-oved, resolute; faithful; unchang-g; unremitting. ~ *n.* (math. etc.) uantity that does not vary; merical quantity expressing lation, property, etc., that mains the same for the same bstance under all conditions.

con·stant·an (kon′stantăn) *n.* loy of copper and nickel.

Con·stan·tine I (kon′stantēn, in) (274–337), **"the Great."** oman emperor (306–37); con-rted to Christianity, which he ade the state religion; in 328 ansferred the capital of the npire to Byzantium, which he re-med Constantinople.

Con·stan·ti·no·ple (konstăn-nō′pel). Former name of TANBUL, capital of Turkey until 923; the Roman city of Byzantium nder CONSTANTINE I.

con·stant·ly (kon′stantlē) *adv.* lways; often.

con·stel·la·tion (konstelā′shon) 1. Number of fixed stars grouped ithin outline of an imaginary gure as viewed from the Earth; olloq.) group of distinguished ersons. 2. (astrology) Relative osition of stars, esp. at time of a

person's birth, considered as influencing future events.

con·ster·na·tion (konsternā′-shon) *n.* Amazement and terror such as to prostrate one's faculties, dismay.

con·sti·pa·tion (konstĭpā′shon) *n.* Condition of bowels in which defecation is irregular and difficult. **con·sti·pate** (kon′stĭpāt) *v.t.* (**-pat·ed, -pat·ing**). Affect with constipation.

con·stit·u·en·cy (konstĭch′-ōoensē) *n.* (pl. **-cies**). Body of voters who elect a representative member; place, residents in place, so represented.

con·stit·u·ent (konstĭch′ōoent) *adj.* Composing, making up, a whole; appointing, electing; able to form or alter a (political) consti-tution. ~ *n.* 1. Component part. 2. One represented by an agent, elected official, etc.

con·sti·tute (kon′stĭtōot, -tūt) *v.t.* (**-tut·ed, -tut·ing**). 1. Appoint (person) to office, dignity, etc., of; establish, found, give legal form to (assembly, institution, etc.). 2. Frame, form (by combination of elements); make up, be components of.

con·sti·tu·tion (konstĭtōo′shon, -tū′-) *n.* 1. Act, mode, of constituting; way in which thing is constituted; esp. character of body in regard to health, strength, vitality, etc.; condition of mind, disposition. 2. Mode in which nation etc. is organized; body of fundamental principles according to which a nation etc. is governed; **the C~**, Constitution of the U.S.

framed at Philadelphia in 1787 and ratified 1788, together with subsequent amendments. 3. **U.S.S. C~**, 44-gun frigate used by Amer. navy in War of 1812, popularly known as "Old Ironsides."

con·sti·tu·tion·al (konstĭtōo′-shonal, -tū′-) *adj.* 1. Of, inherent in, affecting, the bodily or mental constitution. 2. Belonging to the very constitution of anything; essential. 3. Of, in harmony with, authorized by, the political consti-tution; adhering to the political constitution; ~ **monarchy**, monarchy limited by constitutional forms. **constitutional** *n.* (colloq.) Walk taken for health's sake. **con·sti·tu·tion·al·ism, con·sti·tu′tion·al·ist, con·sti·tu·tion·al·i·ty** (konstĭtōoshonăl′ītē, -tū-) *ns.* **con·sti·tu′tion·al·ly** *adv.*

con·strain (konstrān′) *v.t.* Compel; bring about by compul-sion; confine forcibly, imprison. **constrained′** *adj.* Forced, embarrassed. **con·strain′ed·ly** (konstrā′nĭdlē), **con·strain′ing·ly** *advs.* **con·strain′a·ble** *adj.* **con-strain′er** *n.*

con·straint (konstrānt′) *n.* Compulsion; confinement; restraint of natural feelings, constrained manner.

con·strict (konstrĭkt′) *v.t.* Contract, compress; cause (organic tissue) to contract. **con·stric′tion** *n.* **con·stric′tive** *adj.*

The Roman emperor, **Constantine,** *under whose reign the empire became Christian, was commemorated by this arch in Rome which was completed in A.D. 312.*

con·stric·tor (konstrĭk′ter) *n.* 1. Muscle that draws together or narrows a part. 2. Snake, such as boa or python, that coils around and crushes its prey.

con·struct (konstrŭkt′) *v.t.* Fit together, frame, build; (gram.) combine (words) syntactically; (geom.) draw, delineate. ~ (kŏn′strŭkt) *n.* Anything constructed. **con·struc′tor, con·-struct′er** *ns.*

con·struc·tion (konstrŭk′shon) *n.* 1. Act, mode, of constructing; thing constructed. 2. (gram.) Syntactical connection betweeen verbs and their objects or complements, prepositions and their objects, etc. 3. Construing, explanation (of words); interpretation. 4. ~ **gang**, workers engaged in construction project. **con·-struc′tion·al** *adj.* Of, engaged in, construction; structual.

con·struc·tion·ist (konstrŭk′-shonĭst) *n.* One who interprets a law or body of laws in a specified way.

con·struc·tive (konstrŭk′tĭv) *adj.* 1. Intending to be helpful (esp. as opp. to DESTRUCTIVE). 2. Of construction, structural. 3. (law) Inferred, based on interpretation. **con·struc′tive·ly** *adv.* **con·-struc′tive·ness** *n.*

con·strue (konstrōō′) *v.* (-strued, -stru·ing). Combine

A **container** *ship, like this converted C-2 'Warrior' at San Juan, Puerto Rico, is designed to receive containers prepacked with cargo. This has proved an economical method of marine transportation.*

(words) grammatically; interpret; analyze grammatically and/or translate literally.

con·sub·stan·tial (kŏnsubstăn′-shal) *adj.* Of the same substance, esp. of the three Persons of the Trinity. **con·sub·stan·ti·al·i·ty** (kŏnsubstănshēăl′ĭtē) *n.* **con·sub·-stan′tial·ly** *adv.*

con·sub·stan·ti·ate (kŏnsub-stăn′shēāt) *v.* (-at·ed, -at·ing). Unite in one substance. **con·sub·-stan·ti·a·tion** (kŏnsubstănshēā′-shon) *n.* Lutheran doctrine that body and blood of Christ exist together with bread and wine in Eucharist (dist. from TRANSUB-STANTIATION).

con·sul (kŏn′sul) *n.* 1. (Rom. hist.) Either of two annually elected magistrates exercising supreme authority under the Republic. 2. One of three chief magistrates of French Republic (1799–1804), and of whom the **First C**~, Napoleon Bonaparte, had all the real power. 3. Foreign service officer stationed in a country abroad to promote trade, protect rights of fellow citizens in residence there, etc.; ~ **general**, consular officer of highest

rank. **con′sul·ar** *adj.*

con·sul·ate (kŏn′sulĭt) *n.* Of of consul and consular staff.

con·sult (konsŭlt′) *v.* T counsel (*with*); seek information advice from; take into c sideration; **consulting chemi engineer, firm**, etc., person concern whose business is giv professional advice. **consulti physician** etc., physician etc. whom others may refer th patients for advice. **con·sult·a** (konsŭl′tant) *n.* **con·sul·ta·ti** (kŏnsultā′shon) *n.* Act of consu ing; deliberation; conference. **co sul·ta·tive** (konsŭl′tatĭv) *a* **con·sul·ta·to·ry** (konsŭl′tatō -tōrē) *adj.* **con·sult′er** *n.*

con·sume (konsōōm′) (-sumed, -sum·ing). Use up; e drink, up; burn up; spend, was waste away; **con·sumed′**, eaten *with.* **con·sum′a·ble** *adj.*

con·sum·er (konsōō′mer) One who consumes; one who b goods or services; customer; buy ~ **goods**, goods that direc satisfy human wants through th consumption or use, such as fo and clothing; ~ **price index**, ind of changes in cost of goods a services to a typical consumer bas on their cost at an arbitrarily chos period; also called "cost-of-livi index."

con·sum·mate (konsŭm′

(´sumĭt) *adj.* Complete, perfect.
nsummate (kŏn´sumāt) *v.t.*
nat·ed, -mat·ing. Accom-
sh, complete (esp. marriage by
tual intercourse). **con·sum·ma·-
n** (kŏnsumā´shon) *n.* Com-
tion; desired end, goal;
rfection; perfected thing;
ysical completion of marriage.

con·sump·tion (konsŭmp´shon)
1. Consuming; destruction;
ste; amount consumed. 2.
asting disease, esp. pulmonary
perculosis.

con·sump·tive (konsŭmp´tĭv)
j. 1. Tending to consume. 2.
aving a tendency to, affected with,
lmonary tuberculosis. ~ *n.*
nsumptive person. **con·sump´-
ve·ly** *adv.*

con·tact (kŏn´tăkt) *n.* State,
ndition, of touching; (math.)
eeting of curves or surfaces so as
have tangents or tangent planes
common; (elect.) junction or
uching surface of two conductors
ends of conducting wire through
hich a current passes; (usu. pl.)
iendly or business relationships,
rsons with whom one comes into
uch; acquaintance, esp. one useful
business; (med.) person who has
en exposed to contagious disease;
ome into ~ with, come across,
eet; **make, break ~**, complete,
terrupt electric circuit; **~ lens**,
nall lens worn on eyeball. **contact**
.t. Get into touch with (person).

con·ta·gion (kontā´jon) *n.* Com-
unication of disease by direct or
direct contact; contagious disease;
oral corruption; contagious
nfluence.

con·ta·gious (kontā´jus) *adj.*
Communicating disease or corrup-
ion by contact; (of diseases)
ommunicable by contact; (fig.)
atching, infectious. **con·ta´-
gious·ly** *adv.* **con·ta´gious·ness**
.

con·tain (kontān´) *v.t.* 1. Have,
old, as contents; comprise,
nclude; (of a measure) be equal to;
geom.) enclose, form boundary of;
of numbers) be divisible by
number) without remainder. 2.
Restrain; (mil.) hold (enemy force)
n position so that it cannot operate
lsewhere; (fig.) keep within limits.
con·tain´ment *n.* esp. ~
building, that housing nuclear
eactor and associated equipment in
nuclear power station. **con·tain´er**
n. (esp.) Receptacle of standardized
design for transportation of freight;
so ~ **ship**, etc., one carrying freight
in containers. **con·tain´a·ble** *adj.*
con·tain·er·ize (kontā´nerīz) *v.t.*
(-ized, -iz·ing). Pack into,
transport in, sealed, reusable
containers. **con·tain·er·i·za·tion**
(kontānerĭzā´shon) *n.*

con·tam·i·nate (kontăm´ināt)
v.t. **(-nat·ed, -nat·ing)**. Pollute,
infect. **con·tam·i·na·tion** (kon-

*The world's **continents** — Europe, Asia, Africa, North and South America, Australia and Antarctica — vary enormously in size. Two-thirds of the continental land surface is in the northern hemisphere.*

tămĭnā´shon) *n.*

con·temn (kontĕm´) *v.t.*
Despise, treat with disregard.
con·temn·er (kontĕm´er, -tĕm´-
ner), **con·tem·nor** (kontĕm´ner) *ns.*

con·tem·plate (kŏn´templāt) *v.*
(-plat·ed, -plat·ing). Gaze upon;
view mentally; expect; intend,
purpose; meditate. **con·tem·pla·
tion** (kŏntemplā´shon), **con´tem·
pla·tor** *ns.*

con·tem·pla·tive (kontĕm´-
platĭv, kŏn´templā-) *adj.* Medita-
tive, thoughtful; (of life or monastic
order) devoted to meditation. ~ *n.*
Contemplative person. **con·tem´-
pla·tive·ly** *adv.* **con·tem´pla·
tive·ness** *n.*

con·tem·po·ra·ne·ous (kon-
tĕmporā´nēus) *adj.* Existing, occurring, at the same time (*with*); of the
same period. **con·tem·po·ra´ne·
ous·ly** *adv.* **con·tem·po·ra·
ne·i·ty** (kontĕmperanē´ĭtē), **con·
tem·po·ra´ne·ous·ness** *ns.*

con·tem·po·rar·y (kontĕm´-
porĕrē) *adj.* Belonging to the same
time; equal in age; modern, esp. of
art, furniture, etc. ~ *n.* (pl.
-rar·ies). Contemporary person or
thing.

con·tempt (kontĕmpt´) *n.* Act,
mental attitude, of despising; condition of being despised; willful
disobedience to or disrespect for
legislative body or court of law.
con·tempt´i·ble *adj.* Deserving
contempt, despicable. **con·
tempt´i·bil·i·ty** (kontĕmptĭbĭl´ĭtē),
con·tempt´i·ble·ness *ns.* **con·
tempt´i·bly** *adv.*

con·temp·tu·ous (kontĕmp´-
chōous) *adj.* Showing contempt

(*of*); scornful; insolent. **con·
temp´tu·ous·ly** *adv.* **con·temp´-
tu·ous·ness** *n.*

con·tend (kontĕnd´) *v.* Strive;
fight; struggle *with*; compete, be in
rivalry; argue (*with*); maintain
(*that*). **con·tend´er** *n.*

con·tent[1] (kŏn´tĕnt) *n.* 1. Containing capacity; volume; amount
contained or yielded. 2. (often pl.)
What is contained; esp. things
contained or treated of in writing or
document; **table of ~s**, listing of
chapters, subjects, etc. included in
a book or document. 3. Constituent
elements of a conception; substance
(of art etc., as opp. to *form*).

con·tent[2] (kontĕnt´) *n.* State or
feeling of being satisfied. ~ *adj.*
Satisfied; willing (*to* do). ~ *v.t.*
Satisfy; ~ **oneself**, be satisfied
(*with*). **con·tent´ed** *adj.* **con·
tent´ed·ly** *adv.* **con·tent´ed·ness,
con·tent´ment** *ns.*

con·ten·tion (kontĕn´shon) *n.*
Strife, controversy; rivalry; assertion made in arguing; point disputed.

con·ten·tious (kontĕn´shus) *adj.*
Quarrelsome; involving contention.
con·ten´tious·ly *adv.* **con·ten´-
tious·ness** *n.*

con·ter·mi·nous (kontēr´minus)
adj. Having a common boundary
(*with*); coextensive. **con·ter´mi·
nous·ly** *adv.*

con·test (kŏn´tĕst) *n.* Contending; competition. **contest** (kon-
tĕst´) *v.* Dispute; contend or
compete for. **con·test´a·ble** *adj.*
con·test´ant *n.* One who contests.
con·test´er, con·tes·ta·tion (kŏn·
tĕstā´shon) *ns.*

con·text (kŏn´tĕkst) *n.* Whole
structure of connected passage in
relation to any of its parts; parts that
immediately precede or follow a
written or spoken passage and
determine its meaning. **con·tex·-**

tu·al (kontĕks'chooal) adj. con·-tex'tu·al·ly adv.

con·tig·u·ous (kontĭg'ūus) adj. Touching, adjoining; neighboring. con·tig'u·ous·ly adv. con·tig'u-ous·ness n. con·ti·gu·i·ty (kŏntĭgū'ĭtē) n. (pl. -ties).

con·ti·nent[1] (kŏn'tĭnent) adj. Temperate, characterized by sexual restraint; able to control bladder and bowel functions. con'ti-nent·ly adv. con·ti·nence (kŏn'-tĭnens) n.

con·ti·nent[2] (kŏn'tĭnent) n. One of the main continuous bodies of land on Earth's surface (now usu. reckoned as Europe, Asia, Africa, N. and S. America, Australia, and Antarctica); the C~, the mainland of Europe.

con·ti·nen·tal (kŏntĭnĕn'tal) adj. Of or pertaining to a continent; (hist.) of the Amer. colonies or states (during and immediately after the War of Independence); C~ Congress, either of two assemblies of representatives from the Amer. colonies during the Revolutionary era: the first, meeting in 1774, voiced grievances against the British Crown; the second, convened first in 1775, established the Continental army, issued the Declaration of Independence, and served as the government until 1789, when the U.S. Constitution came into effect; ~ divide (also C~ Divide in N. Amer.), divide separating river systems that flow to opposite sides of a continent; ~ drift, (geol.) slow movement of the continents away from a single land mass to their present positions; ~ shelf, sloping platform around continent, outside which the ocean bed descends steeply. continental n. 1. Native or inhabitant of a continent, esp. Europe. 2. (hist.) Soldier of the Continental army in Revolutionary War.

con·tin·gen·cy (kontĭn'jensē) n. (pl. -cies). 1. Being contingent; contingent event etc., chance occurrence; thing incident to another. 2. Emergency, as in ~ plan.

con·tin·gent (kontĭn'jent) adj. 1. Of uncertain occurrence. 2. True only under existing conditions; nonessential; conditional, dependent on some prior occurrence or condition. con·tin'gent·ly adv. contingent n. 1. Contingent thing. 2. Troops contributed to form part of military or naval force (also fig.).

con·tin·u·al (kontĭn'ūal) adj. Always continuing, incessant; very frequent. con·tin'u·al·ly adv.

con·tin·u·ance (kontĭn'ūans) n. Continuing in existence or operation, duration.

con·tin·u·a·tion (kontĭnūā'-shon) n. 1. Carrying on, resumption. 2. That by which anything is continued, continuing addition.

The members of the **Continental Congress** in the U.S. War of Independence (1774–83) met in this hall in Philadelphia as representatives of the people of the colony states, later the United States of America.

con·tin·u·a·tive (kontĭn'ūātĭv, -atĭv) adj.

con·tin·ue (kontĭn'ū) v. (-ued, -u·ing). 1. Go or keep on with; not cease; maintain. 2. Remain in existence. 3. Resume. con·tin'u-a·ble adj. con·tin'u·er n.

con·ti·nu·i·ty (kŏntĭnoo'ĭtē, -nū'-) n. (pl. -ties). 1. Being continuous; unbroken series, succession; close relationship, logical sequence, of ideas. 2. Script or scenario for motion picture, or for television or radio program.

con·tin·u·ous (kontĭn'ūus) adj. Connected, unbroken, in time or sequence; ~ wave, (phys.) electromagnetic wave of constant amplitude; (esp. of lasers) not pulsed. con·tin'u·ous·ly adv.

con·tin·u·um (kontĭn'ūum) n. (pl. -tin·u·a pr. -tĭn'ūa, -tin·-u·ums). Continuous series or whole, as space-time ~.

con·tort (kontort') v.t. Twist, distort.

con·tor·tion (kontor'shon) n. Twisting; twisted state. con·tor'-tion·ist n. Person who performs gymnastic exercises involving contorted postures.

con·tour (kŏn'toor) n. Outline of figure, object, coast, etc.; (also ~ line) line representing horizontal contour of Earth's surface at given elevation; ~ map, one containing ~ lines; ~ plowing, plowing along lines of constant elevation to minimize erosion; con-tour v.t. Mark with contour lines.

con·tra (kŏn'tra) prep. Against. ~ adv. Against (a proposition, etc.); on the contrary. [CON⁴]

contra- prefix. Against; in names of mus. instruments and

organ stops, denoting a pitch of an octave below.

con·tra·band (kŏn'traband) Prohibited traffic, smugglin, smuggled goods. ~ adj. Forbidde to be imported or exported; co cerned with contraband. con'tra band·ist n.

con·tra·bass (kŏn'trabās) (mus.) Double bass. con'tra bass·ist n.

con·tra·cep·tion (kŏntrasĕp shon) n. Prevention of conceptio or impregnation. con·tra·cep'tiv adj. & n.

con·tract (kŏn'trăkt) n. Mutual agreement between partie: nations, etc., esp. business agree ment for supplying goods o performing work at specified price 2. Agreement enforceable by law department of law relating t contracts; formal agreement fo marriage. 3. (in game of bridge Undertaking by declarer to make s many tricks; ~ bridge: se BRIDGE². contract (kontrăkt') v. 1 Enter into business or lega arrangement. 2. Form (friendship habit); incur (disease, liability). 3 Draw together; make or become smaller; (gram.) shorten (word) by combination or elision. con-tract·i·bil·i·ty (kontrăktabĭl'ĭtē) n con·tract'i·ble adj.

con·trac·tile (kontrăk'til, -tīl) adj. Capable of, producing, contraction. con·trac·til·i·ty (kŏn-trăktĭl'ĭtē) n.

con·trac·tion (kontrăk'shon) n. Contracting; contracted word. con·trac'tion·al, con·trac'tive adjs.

con·trac·tor (kŏn'trăkter, kon-trăk'-) n. 1. One who undertakes a contract, esp. in building and related trades. 2. Contracting muscle.

con·trac·tu·al (kontrăk'chooal) adj. Of (the nature of) a contract. con·trac'tu·al·ly adv.

con·tra·dict (kŏntradĭkt') v.t. Deny (statement); deny words of (person); be contrary to; imply a denial of. con·tra·dict'a·ble adj. con·tra·dic'tor, con·tra·dict'er ns.

con·tra·dic·tion (kŏntradĭk'-shon) n. Verbal denial; direct opposition; statement contradicting another; inconsistency; ~ in terms, plainly self-contradictory statement or words.

con·tra·dic·to·ry (kŏntradĭk'-terē) adj. Making denial; mutually opposed or inconsistent. con·tra-dic'to·ri·ly adv. con·tra·dic'-to·ri·ness, con·tra·dic'to·ry ns.

con·tra·dis·tinc·tion (kŏntra-dĭstĭngk'shon) n. Distinction by contrast.

con·tral·to (kontrăl'tō, -trahl'-) n. (pl. -tos, -ti pr. -tē). Lowest female voice; singer with such voice; musical part for this.

con·trap·tion (kontrăp′shon) *n.* (olloq.) Contrivance or device.

con·tra·pun·tal (kŏntrapŭn′tal) *dj.* Of, in, counterpoint. **con′-a·pun′tal·ly** *adv.* **con·tra-un′tist** *n.* One skilled in ounterpoint.

.n·tra·ri·e·ty (kŏntrarī′itē) *n.* l. **-ties**). Opposition in nature, uality, or action; disagreement, inconsistency.

con·tra·ri·wise (kŏn′trĕrēwīz, ontrar′-) *adv.* On the other hand; a the opposite way; perversely.

con·tra·ry (kŏn′trĕrē) *adj.* 1. pposed in nature or tendency (*to*); f wind) impeding, unfavorable. 2. erverse, self-willed. 3. Opposite i position or direction. **con′-rar·i·ly** *adv.* **contrary** *adv.* In pposition (*to*). **con′tra·ri·ness** *n.* ontrary *n.* (pl. **-ries**). Opposite; bject, fact, or quality that is the ery opposite of something else; **on he ~**, (corroborating a denial xpressed or understood); **to the ~**, to the opposite effect (contra-licting something that has been aid or assumed).

con·trast (kŏn′trăst) *n.* Juxta-osition showing striking differ-nces; comparison clearly revealing lifferences or opposing qualities; erson or thing of most opposite jualities; (photog. etc.) differentia-ion between tones. **contrast** kontrăst′) *v.* Set (two things, one vith another) in opposition, so as :o show their differences; show striking difference on comparison vith. **con·trast′a·ble, con·trast′-ive** *adjs.*

con·tra·vene (kŏntravēn′) *v.t.* -vened, -ven·ing). Infringe law); dispute (statement); conflict with. **con·tra·ven·tion** (kŏntra-vĕn′shon), **con·tra·ven′er** *ns.*

con·tre·temps (kŏn′tretahṅ) *n.* kpl. **-temps** pr. -tahṅz). Unlucky accident; embarrassing or inoppor-tune occurrence.

con·trib·ute (kontrĭb′ūt, -yut) *v.* (**-ut·ed, -ut·ing**). Pay, furnish (*to* common fund etc.), give or pay jointly with others; **~ to**, have a part or share in producing; provide (literary work). **con·trib·u·tor** (kontrĭb′yuter) *n.* **con·trib·u·tor·y** (kontrĭb′yutōrē, -tōrē) *adj.* **con-tributory negligence**, negligence on the part of a person injured that has helped to bring about the injury.

con·tri·bu·tion (kŏntribū′shon) *n.* Contributing; something con-tributed; payment in aid of common fund or collection.

con·trite (kontrīt′, kŏn′trīt) *adj.* Crushed in spirit by a sense of sin, completely penitent; (of action) arising from contrition. **con·trite′ly** *adv.* **con·trite′ness** *n.*

con·tri·tion (kontrĭsh′on) *n.* Being contrite, penitence.

con·triv·ance (kontrī′vans) *n.* 1. Contriving. 2. Deceitful practice. 3. Invention; inventive capacity; thing contrived; mechanical device. **con·trive** (kontrīv′) *v.t.* (**-trived, -triv·ing**). Devise, plan, skillfully; bring to pass, manage (thing, *to* do etc.). **con·triv′er** *n.* **con·triv′a·ble** *adj.*

con·trol (kontrōl′) *n.* 1. Control-ling; function or power of directing and regulating. 2. Restraint; check; standard of comparison for check-ing inferences from experiment etc. 3. Controller; (spiritualism) per-sonality or spirit alleged to control medium's words and actions. **~** *v.t.* (**-trolled, -trol·ling**). Exer-

The **Continental Divide** *in North America runs along the top of the Rocky Mountain range providing drain-age to the east and west of the conti-nent. In South America the Andes per-form the same function.*

cise restraint or direction over; command, dominate, regulate; hold in check; check, verify; **~ tower**, tower at an airport from which air traffic is directed by radar and radio. **con·trol′ler** *n.* One who controls, esp. one who checks expenditures, as of a public office or business; **air traffic con-trol(ler)**, system, person(s), that direct(s) air traffic over a wide area. **con·trol′ler·ship** *n.*

con·tro·ver·sial (kŏntrovēr′-shal, -sēal) *adj.* Of, open to, given to, controversy. **con·tro·ver′sial-ist** *n.* **con·tro·ver′sial·ly** *adv.*

con·tro·ver·sy (kŏn′troversē) *n.* (pl. **-sies**). Disputation, quarrel, esp. prolonged public debate or argument.

con·tro·vert (kŏn′trovērt, kŏn-trovērt′) *v.t.* Call in question, dispute truth of. **con·tro·vert′-i·ble** *adj.* **con·tro·vert′i·bly** *adv.*

con·tu·ma·cious (kŏntoōmā′-shus, -tyoō-) *adj.* Insubordinate, disobedient. **con·tu·ma′cious·ly** *adv.* **con·tu·ma′cious·ness** *n.* **con·tu·ma·cy** (kŏn′toōmasē, -tyoō-) *n.* (pl. **-cies**).

con·tu·me·ly (kŏn′toōmelē, -tyoō, kontoō′-, -tŭ′, kŏn′tumlē) *n.* (pl. **-lies**). Rudeness, insolence; insulting remark or act. **con-tu·me·li·ous** (kŏntoōmē′lēus, -tyoō-) *adj.* **con·tu·me′li·ous·ly** *adv.*

con·tuse (kontoōz′, -tūz′) *v.t.* (**-tused, -tus·ing**). Bruise. **con-tu·sion** (kontoō′zhon, -tū′-) *n.*

co·nun·drum (konŭn′drum) *n.* Riddle, puzzle.

con·va·lesce (kŏnvalĕs′) *v.i.* (**-lesced, -lesc·ing**). Regain health. **con·va·les·cence** (kŏn-valĕs′ens) *n.* Gradual recovery of health after illness.

con·va·les·cent (kŏnvalĕs′ent) *adj.* Recovering from illness. **~** *n.* Convalescent person; **~ home**,

*The **convent**, the communal establishment in which nuns live after they have taken their religious vows, traditionally provides seclusion from the outside world. Some enclosed communities receive no visitors.*

hospital, nursing home, hospital, for such persons.

con·vec·tion (konvĕk'shon) *n.* (phys.) Conveyance of heat by movement of gas or fluid; ~ **heater**, appliance that warms room by convection. **con·vec'tor** *n.* **con·vec'tion·al** *adj.*

con·vene (konvēn') *v.* (**-vened, -ven·ing**). Assemble; convoke; summon (person *before* tribunal). **con·ven'er** *n.*

con·ven·ience (konvēn'yens) *n.* 1. Suitableness; commodiousness; material advantage; personal comfort or ease; advantage. 2. Useful appliance; (Brit.) lavatory; (pl.) material comforts. **con·ven·ient** (konvēn'yent) *adj.* Fit, suitable; not troublesome; (colloq.) conveniently near. **con·ven'ient·ly** *adv.*

con·vent (kŏn'vĕnt) *n.* Religious community (usu. of women, cf. MONASTERY) living together; building occupied by this.

con·ven·ti·cle (konvĕn'tĭkel) *n.* (hist.) Clandestine religious meeting, esp. of nonconformists or dissenters.

con·ven·tion (konvĕn'shon) *n.* 1. Convening. 2. Formal assembly for deliberation or legislation on important matters; esp. **political ~s**, which meet to nominate candidates for public office and to establish party platforms. 3. Assembly of delegates or representatives, conference. 4. Agreement; in diplomacy, less formal or less important agreement than treaty, such as the GENEVA Convention. 5. General agreement or consent (often implicit) as foundation of usage etc., rule or practice based on this; accepted usage that has become artificial and formal; (pl., in game of bridge etc.) standard methods of bidding, leading, etc.

con·ven·tion·al (konvĕn'shonal) *adj.* Depending on convention(s), not natural, not spontaneous; usual, expected; (of weapons) other than nuclear. **con·ven'tion·al·ly** *adv.* **con·ven'tion·al·ism, con·ven'tion·al·ist** *ns.* **con·ven·tion·al·i·ty** (konvĕnshonăl'ĭtē) *n.* (pl. **-ties**).

con·verge (konvērj') *v.i.* (**-verged, -verg·ing**). (of lines etc.) Tend to meet in a point or line; approach nearer together; (math., of series) approximate in sum of its terms toward a definite limit. **con·ver·gence** (konvēr'jens)

*This vintage automobile is one of the earliest **convertibles**, with a top that may be folded back, lowered or removed. The soft top, however, gives little protection in an accident.*

con·ver'gen·cy n. (pl. **-cies**). **n·ver'gent** adj.

·con·ver·sant (konvēr'sant) adj. ·ell acquainted (with). **con·ver'-** ·nce n. **con·ver'san·cy** n. (pl. ·ies). **con·ver'sant·ly** adv.

·con·ver·sa·tion (kŏnversā'shon) 1. Talk, interchange of thoughts ·d words. 2. ~ **piece**, something ·at serves as a topic of conversation ·cause of its unusualness etc.

·con·ver·sa·tion·al (kŏnversā'- ·onal) adj. In the manner of, ·rtaining to, conversation. **con·-** ·r'sa'tion·al·ly adv. **con·ver·** ·'tion·al·ist n.

·con·verse¹ (konvērs') v.i. ·versed, -vers·ing). Talk.

·con·verse² (kŏn'vērs) adj. Op- ·osite, contrary. ~ n. Opposite; ·gic) converted proposition; state- ·ent etc. derived from another by ·ansposition of two important ·titithetical members, e.g. he is ·ave but not good is the converse of ·e is good but not brave. **con·-** ·erse·ly (konvērs'lē, kŏn'vērs-) ·lv.

·con·ver·sion (konvēr'zhon, ·hon) n. Converting; being con- ·rted; (football) play for points ·ter touchdown; point made by ·ck or two points made by pass on ·is play. **con·ver'sion·al, con·-** ·er·sion·ar·y** (konvēr'zhonĕrē, ·ho-) adjs.

·he **convolvulus** *or morning glory ·rows in both tropical and temperate ·reas and has colorful trumpet-shaped ·owers. The seeds of two of its species ·re the source of an hallucinogenic ·drug.*

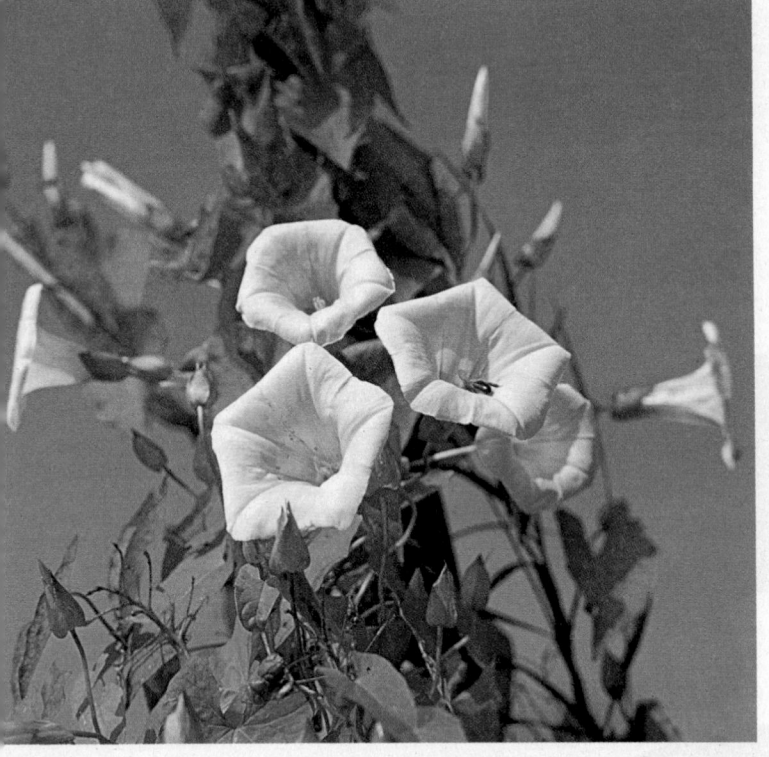

con·vert (konvērt') v. 1. Change (into). 2. Cause to turn (to opinion, faith, etc.); turn to god- liness; (logic) transpose (subject and predicate). 3. (football) Make point after touchdown. ~ (kŏn'- vērt) n. Person converted, esp. to religious faith or life.

con·vert·i·ble (konvēr'tibel) adj. That may be converted; (econ., of a currency) that may be freely con- verted into gold or another currency. **con·vert·i·bil·i·ty** (kon- vērtibil'itē) n. **con·vert'i·ble** n. Automobile having folding roof.

con·vex (kŏnvěks', kŏn'věks) adj. Curved like outside of circle or sphere, reverse of CONCAVE. **con·vex·i·ty** (konvěk'sĭtē) n. (pl. -ties). **con·vex'ly** adv.

con·vey (konvā') v.t. Transport, carry; transmit; impart, communi- cate (idea, meaning); (law) transfer, make over (property) by deed or legal process. **con·vey'a·ble** adj.

con·vey·ance (konvā'ens) n. 1. Carrying; transmission; communi- cation. 2. (Document effecting) transference of property. 3. Means of conveying, esp. a vehicle.

con·vey·or, con·vey·er (kon- vā'er) ns. (esp.) Mechanical device (usu. in form of endless belt or band) for conveying materials or items, esp. those in process of manufacture (also ~ **belt**).

con·vict (konvĭkt') v.t. Prove guilty (of offense); declare guilty by verdict of jury or decision of judge; (theol.) impress (person) with sense of error. ~ (kŏn'vĭkt) n. Con- demned criminal serving prison sentence. **con·vic'tive** adj. **con·-**

vic'tive·ly adv.

con·vic·tion (konvĭk'shon) n. Convicting; being convicted; ver- dict of guilty; being convinced, firm belief.

con·vince (konvĭns') v.t. (-vinced, -vinc·ing). Firmly persuade (of, that). **con·vin'ci·ble** adj. **con·vinc'ing·ly** adv. **con· vinc'ing·ness** n. Open to conviction.

con·viv·i·al (konvĭv'ēal) adj. Sociable, jovial; of, befitting, a feast; festive. **con·viv'i·al·ly** adv. **con·viv·i·al·i·ty** (konvĭvēăl'ĭtē) n.

con·vo·ca·tion (kŏnvokā'shon) n. Calling together; assembly, esp. ecclesiastical or academic assembly. **con·vo·ca'tion·al** adj.

con·voke (konvōk') v.t. (-voked, -vok·ing). Call together; summon to assemble.

con·vo·lute (kŏn'volōot) adj. Rolled up together, coiled, twisted; complicated or involved. ~ n. Coil. **convolute** v. (-lut·ed, -lut·ing). **con'vo·lut·ed** adj. **con·vo·lu·tion** (kŏnvolōo'shon) n.

con·vol·vu·lus (konvŏl'vyulus) n. (pl. -lus·es, -li pr. -lī). Plant of genus C~ with twining stem and trumpet-shaped flowers, bind- weed.

con·voy (kŏn'voi, konvoi') v.t. (of warship or aircraft) Escort (usu. merchant or passenger vessel); escort with armed force. **con'voy** n. 1. Convoying. 2. Company, supply of provisions, etc., under escort; number of merchant ships under escort or sail- ing in company; number of vehicles traveling in company, esp. with military or police protection.

con·vulse (konvŭls') v.t. (-vulsed, -vuls·ing). Shake violently; throw into convulsions (usu. pass.); cause to be violently seized with laughter (usu. pass.).

con·vul·sion (konvŭl'shon) n. 1. (usu. pl.) Violent irregular motion of limb or body due to involuntary contraction of muscles (esp. as disorder of infants); (pl.) violent fit of laughter. 2. Violent social or political agitation; violent physical disturbance, esp. earthquake etc.

con·vul·sive (konvŭl'sĭv) adj. Attended or affected with, pro- ducing, resembling, convulsions. **con·vul'sive·ly** adv.

co·ny, co·ney (kō'nē) ns. (pl. **co·nies, co·neys**). 1. Rabbit (now retained mainly as name for the fur). 2. = PIKA.

coo (kōo) v. Make soft murmur- ing sound of, or as of, doves; say cooingly. ~ n. Cooing sound. **coo'ing·ly** adv.

cook (kōok) v. Prepare food, prepare (food) by application of heat; undergo cooking; concoct (a dish or meal); (slang) tamper with, falsify (accounts etc.), esp. in ~ **the books; cook'book**, book of recipes

The barrel **cooper**, above, is seen shaping the sides of barrel staves. Making barrels is a skilled job. They are durable and easy to use, but heavy and costly. They are mostly used for whiskey and beer.

and directions for cooking; **cook'-house**, building or place for cooking, esp. for camp, ranch, etc. **cook one's goose**, ruin one's chances; **cook'out**, party, picnic, at which cooking is done outdoors; **cook up** (colloq.) plan (scheme), contrive. **cook'stove**, stove for cooking. **cook** n. One who cooks food.

Cook (kook), **James** (1728–79). ("**Captain Cook**"). English navigator and explorer esp. of the Pacific and Australasia; first European discoverer of Hawaiian Islands, 1778; **Cook Islands**, group of islands in the S. Pacific Ocean, self-governing in association with New Zealand; **Cook Strait**, strait separating North and South Islands, New Zealand.

cook·er (kook'er) n. Appliance or vessel for cooking; **pressure** ~: see PRESSURE. **cook'er·y** n. Art, practice, of cooking.

cook·ie, cook·y (kook'ē) ns. (pl. **cook·ies**). 1. Small thin crisp cake made from sweet stiff dough. 2.

(slang) Person, e.g. *tough, smart* ~, etc.

cool (kool) adj. 1. Moderately cold. 2. Unexcited, calm; lacking zeal, lukewarm; wanting cordiality. 3. Calmly audacious or impudent. 4. (colloq.) Applied complacently or emphatically to a large sum of money, e.g. *it cost me a* ~ *thousand*. 5. (of jazz music) Restrained or relaxed in style. **cool'ly** adv. **cool'ness** n. **cool** n. Cool place or state; (slang) composure, calm.   ~ v.   Make or become cool; ~ **one's heels**, be kept waiting. **cool'ish** adj.

cool·ant (kool'ant) n. Cooling agent; (esp.) fluid applied to edge of a cutting tool to lessen friction; cooling medium in internal combustion engine, nuclear reactor, etc.

The **coot**, a duck-like water-dwelling bird, is found in larger inland waters and streams. This African species, the crested coot (Fulica cristata), is distinguished by two red knobs on its forehead.

cool·er (kool'er) n. Device container in which anything cooled or kept cool; portable chest; (slang) jail.

Coo·lidge (kool'ĭj), (**Joh Calvin** (1872–1933). Governor Massachusetts, 1919–20; vice president under Harding, 1921–3; 30 president of the U.S., 1923– succeeded to presidency on Harding's death, then elected to a ful term.

coo·lie (kool'lē) n. Unskilled Oriental laborer.

coon (koon) n. 1. (colloq.) RACCOON. 2. (derog.) Black person

coop (koop) n. Cage or enclosure for poultry or small animals; place of confinement; **fly the** ~, escape from confinement, flee. **coop** 1. Put in coop; confine narrowly (also ~ **up**). 2. (slang, esp. said police) Sleep while on duty.

co-op (kō'ŏp) n. (colloq.) Co operative.

coop·er (koo'per) n. Maker casks and other wooden vessel formed of staves and hoops. ~ v. Make or repair (casks). **coop'er·age** n. Cooper's work or workshop.

Coo·per (koo'per), **Jame Fenimore** (1789–1851). Amer novelist; author of *The Last of th Mohicans, The Pathfinder, Th Deerslayer*, etc.

co·op·er·ate (kŏŏp'erāt) v.i (**-at·ed, -at·ing**). Work togethe (*with* person *in* a work, *to* an end) concur in producing an effect **co·op·er·a·tor** n. **co·op·er·a·tion** (kŏŏperā'shon) n. Working together to same end; cooperative.

co·op·er·a·tive (kŏŏp'erativ) adj. Of cooperation, cooperating willing to cooperate; ~ **apartment**, apartment house jointly owned by owners of its individual apartments; apartment in such a building; ~ **farm, society, store** one in which profits are shared (often in form of dividends on purchases) by all contributing members. **cooperative** n. Cooperative store, apartment, or other enterprise.

co-opt (kŏŏpt') v.t. 1. Elect into body by votes of existing members. 2. Preempt; appropriate. **co·op·ta·tion** (kŏŏptā'shon), **co-op'tion** ns. **co-op·ta·tive** (kŏŏp'tativ), **co-op'tive** (kŏŏp'tĭv) adjs.

co-or·di·nate (kŏŏr'dinĭt, -nāt) adj. Equal in rank, degree, or importance; (gram.) of equal value, as ~ *phrases, clauses*. **co·or·di·nate·ly** adv. **co·or·di·nate** (kŏŏr'dinĭt, -nāt) n. Coordinate thing, esp. (math.) each of a system of two or more magnitudes used to define position of point, line, or plane, by reference to fixed system of lines, points, etc. **co·or·di·nate** (kŏŏr'dināt) v.t. (**-nat·ed, -nat·ing**). Make coordinate; bring (parts) into proper relation.

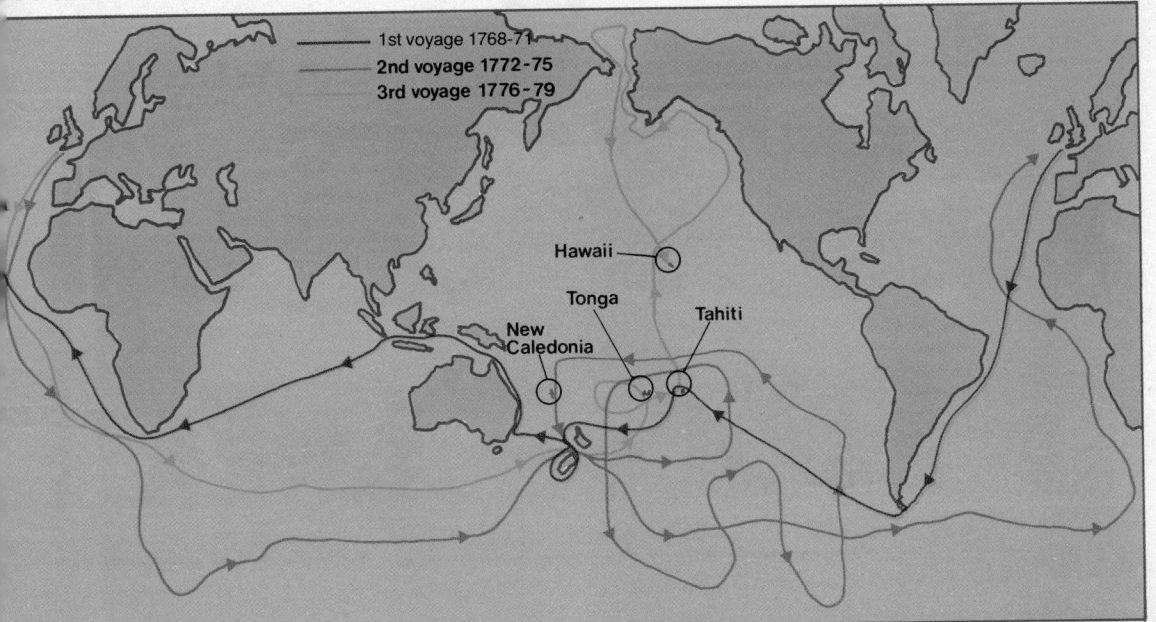

1st voyage 1768-71
2nd voyage 1772-75
3rd voyage 1776-79

Hawaii

Tonga

Tahiti

New
Caledonia

Captain James **Cook** *(above) was a great English maritime explorer who discovered the east coast of Australia. The first of his three voyages (top) began in 1768. Cook was killed by natives in Hawaii in 1779 during a voyage with the aim of discovering a north-west passage between the Pacific and Atlantic oceans.*

Calvin **Coolidge** *was the 30th president of the U.S.A. President Harding's sudden death thrust him into office and he was elected in his own right in 1924.*

co·or·di·na·tion (kōȯrdinā′shon), **co·or′di·na·tor** ns. **co·or·di·na·tive** (kōȯr′dinativ, -nātiv) adj.

Coos (koos) **Bay.** Inlet of the Pacific Ocean in SW. Oregon; port city on this inlet.

coot (koot) n. Any of various swimming and diving birds of genus *Fulica*, esp. *F. americana* of the New World and *F. atra* of the Old World, inhabiting edges of lakes and rivers; **old** ~, (colloq.) foolish or stubborn old man.

cop¹ (kŏp) n. (spinning) Roll of yarn wound upon spindle in such a way that it needs no support.

cop² (kŏp) n. (slang) Policeman. ~ v.t. (**copped, cop·ping**). (slang) Catch, capture; steal; ~ **a plea**: see PLEA; ~ **out** (slang) back out (of obligation). **cop′out** n. (slang) Act of copping out.

co·pal (kō′pal, -păl) n. Hard translucent odoriferous resin obtained from various tropical trees and used to make a fine transparent varnish. [Mex. Spanish from Nahuatl *copalli* incense]

Co·pán (kawpahn′). Site of a ruined Mayan city in W. Honduras.

co·part·ner (kōpärt′ner, kō′-pärt-) n. Partner, sharer, associate. **co·part′ner·ship** n.

cope¹ (kōp) n. Long semi-circular cloak without sleeves or armholes worn by clergy in procession. ~ v.t. (**coped, cop·ing**). Furnish with cope; cover (wall etc.) with coping.

cope² (kōp) v.i. (**coped, cop·ing**). Contend in well-matched struggle *with*; grapple successfully; deal competently (*with*), esp. in everyday affairs.

co·peck (kō′pĕk) n. Var. of

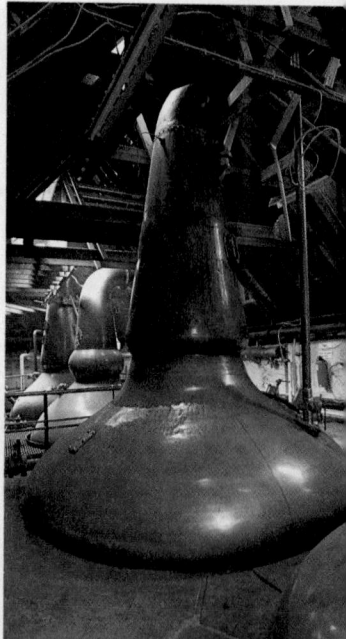

Copper *is found in a free metallic sta in nature and was first used by neolith man. Later it was extracted from ore The ancient Egyptians and Sumeria made utensils, jewelry and decorati objects of copper, such as this pan from Sumeria (top). Copper is used whisky distillers (above) to resi corrosion.*

KOPECK.

Co·pen·ha·gen (kōpenhā′gen, -hah′-, kō′penhā-, -hah-). (Dan. *Köbenhavn*) Capital city of Denmark.

Co·per·ni·cus (kopēr′n*i*kus, ko-), **Nicolaus** (1473–1543). Latinized name of Mikolaj Kopernik, Polish astronomer, who demonstrated that the planets revolve on their own axes and move in orbits around the sun. **Co·per′-**

ni·can *adj.* & *n.*

Co·pia·pó (kawpyahpaw′). Volcano, 19,950 ft. (6,081 m) in N. central Chile.

co·pi·lot (kō′pīlot) *n.* Second pilot in airplane; (fig.) right-hand man.

cop·ing (kō′pĭng) *n.* Top course of masonry or brickwork in wall or roof, usu. sloping.

co·pi·ous (kō′pēus) *adj.* Plentiful; full of matter, thoughts, or

words. **co′pi·ous·ly** *adv.* **co′pi·ous·ness** *n.*

Cop·land (kōp′land), **Aaro** (1900–). Amer. composer symphonies, chamber music, etc.

Co·pley (kŏp′lē), **John Single ton** (1738–1815). Amer. artis known for his portraits; settled England, 1775.

co·pol·y·mer (kōpŏl′imer) Polymer of two or more differen monomers. **co·pol·y·mer·iz**

pŏl'imerīz) v. (-ized, -iz·ing).
pol·y·mer·i·za·tion (kōpŏli-
rīza'shon) n.
cop·per[1] (kŏp'er) n. 1. (chem.)
alleable ductile metallic element
yellowish-red color having high
ctrical conductivity; symbol Cu,
no. 29, at. wt. 63.546. 2.
in made of copper or copper
oy. ~ **beech**, variety of Euro-
an beech (*Fagus sylvatica cuprea*)
th copper-colored leaves;
p'perhead, venomous snake
nkistrodon contortrix) of eastern
S., so called from reddish-brown
lor of top of head; (fig., usu.
opperhead) Northern sympa-
izer with the South during the
vil War; **cop'perplate**, polished
ate of copper on which design is
graved or etched for printing;
int from this; (of handwriting)
at, careful; **cop'persmith**,
orker in copper. **copper** v.t.
over or coat with copper.
p'per·y adj. (esp.) Copper-
lored. [L. *cuprum*, f. *Cyprium*
es) Cyprian (metal)]
cop·per[2] (kŏp'er) n. (slang)
oliceman; law enforcement
ficer.
cop·ra (kŏp'ra, kō'pra) n. Dried
rnels of coconut from which
oconut oil is extracted, used in
anufacture of margarine, candles,
c.
cop·roph·a·gous (kŏprŏf'agus)
dj. (of beetles) Dung-eating.
copse (kŏps) n. Thicket of low
ees and shrubs.
Copt (kŏpt) n. 1. Native
gyptian descendant of ancient
gyptians. 2. Member of the
optic Church. [Arab. *al-kibt* f.
optic *gyptios*, f. Gk *Aiguptios*
gyptian]
Cop·tic (kŏp'tĭk) adj. Of Coptic
r the Copts. ~ n. Language of
he Copts, surviving only in the
turgy of the ~ **Church**, the native
Christian church of Ethiopia and
gypt.
cop·u·la (kŏp'yula) n. (pl. -las,
lae pr. -lē). (logic, gram.) Verb
e or verb with similar function
employed merely as sign of predica-
ion. **cop'u·lar** adj.
cop·u·late (kŏp'yulāt) v.i.
-lat·ed, -lat·ing). Unite in
copulation. **cop·u·la·tion** (kŏpyu-
lā'shon) n. Physical union between
male and female animals, as in act
of procreation.
cop·u·la·tive (kŏp'yulatĭv, -lā-)
adj. Serving as copula, connecting
subject and predicate; relating to
sexual intercourse. **cop'u·la·**
tive·ly adv. **copulative** n.
Copulative conjunction or particle.
cop·y (kŏp'ē) n. (pl. cop·ies). 1.
Reproduction (of writing, picture,
etc.); imitation; specimen of penmanship written after a model. 2.
One of the written or printed
specimens of the same writing or

work. 3. (archaic) Original from
which a copy is made; esp. specimen
of penmanship to be copied. 4.
Manuscript or other matter prepared for printing; material for a
story; text of advertisement. 5.
cop'ybook, book, containing
copies for learners to imitate;
(*attrib.*) conventional, commonplace; **cop'yboy**, office boy in
newspaper office; **cop'ycat**, (colloq.) one who copies another; **copy
desk**, desk, office, where newspaper is edited and prepared for
printing; **copy editor, cop'y-
reader**, one who prepares a
manuscript for publication esp.
correcting spelling, punctuation,
etc.; **cop'ywriter**, one who writes
advertisements. **copy** v. (cop·ied,
cop·y·ing). Transcribe (*from
original*); make copy of; imitate.
cop'y·ist n. One who makes

written copies.
cop·y·right (kŏp'ērīt) n. Sole
legal right to produce or reproduce
a literary, dramatic, musical, or
artistic work, by making copies or
performance or any other means;
~ **library**, national or major
library entitled to receive copies of
all or specific collections of books
copyrighted in a country, as the
Library of Congress in the U.S.;
~ **union**, international union
established by the Berne Convention of 1886, whereby each member
country undertakes to give to
foreign authors the same rights and

*Coptic art shows a variety of influences
from India, Syria, Mesopotamia,
Byzantium and Egypt. It is highly
stylized but with a remarkable sense of
color. This brightly colored mural with
its flat figures is from Ethiopia.*

*The **coracle** is still used in Wales as a river fishing boat. Its frame was originally made of woven canes and reeds, but it now has a canvas and tar covering.*

copyright protection its own authors receive. **copyright** *adj.* Protected by copyright. ~ *v.t.* Protect (book etc.) by copyright; secure copyright for.

co·quet (kōkĕt′) *v.i.* (**-quet·ted, -quet·ting**). Play the coquette; flirt (*with*); dally, trifle, *with*. **co·quet·ry** (kō′kĭtrē, kōkĕt′rē) *n.* (pl. **-ries**). Coquettish behavior or act; coquetting, trifling. **co·quette′** *n.* Woman who (habitually) trifles with the affections of men, flirt. **co·quet′tish** *adj.* **co·quet′tish·ly** *adv.*

Cor. *abbrev.* Corinthians (New Testament).

cor·a·cle (kōr′akel, kăr′-) *n.* Small boat of wickerwork covered with waterproof canvas. [Welsh *corwgl* f. *cwrwg* = Ir. *curach* boat]

cor·a·coid (kōr′akoid, kăr′-) *adj.* Beaked like a crow. ~ *n.* Short projection of the scapula in vertebrates.

cor·al (kōr′al, kăr′-) *n.* 1. Hard calcareous substance consisting of the continuous skeleton secreted by many kinds of submarine coelenterate polyps for their support and habitation, found growing on sea bottom or in extensive accumulation (~ **reef**). 2. Piece of coral as ornament etc. 3. Unimpregnated roe of lobster (so called from color when boiled). 4. One of the individual animals that secrete ~. 5. **C~ Gables**, city on Biscayne Bay in SE. Florida; ~ **reef**, see sense 1; **C~ Sea**, area of Pacific Ocean with many coral reefs between New Guinea and N.E. Australia; site of an important U.S. naval victory (1942) over the Japanese in World War II. ~ **snake**, any of several venomous snakes of southern U.S. and tropical America of the genus *Micrurus*, having brilliant red, black, and yellow colors. **coral** *adj.* Of (the color of) coral, reddish-pink. **cor·al·loid** (kōr′a-loid, kăr′-) *adj.* Like or akin to coral.

cor·al·line (kōr′alĭn, -līn, kăr′-) *adj.* Coral red; corallike. ~ *n.*

Seaweed of genus *Corallina* with calcareous jointed stem; any of various plantlike compound animals.

cor·bel (kōr′bel) *n.* Projection of stone, timber, etc., jutting out from wall to support weight; short timber laid longitudinally under beam or girder to shorten its unsupported span. ~ *v.t.*(**-beled, -bel·ing**, Brit. **-belled, -bel·ling**). **cor′beled** *adj.* [OF. *corbel* raven]

Cor·cy·ra (kōrsī′ra): see CORFU.

cord (kōrd) *n.* 1. (Piece of) string made from several twisted strands. 2. (anat.) Flexible cord-shaped structure of tissue fiber; SPINAL ~, VOCAL ~; see these words. 3. Raised cordlike rib on

cloth, ribbed fabric, esp. cordur (pl.) clothing made of this fab 4. Measure of cut wood for fu usu. 128 cu. ft. (3.63 cu. m). **co** *v.t.* Bind or fasten with cord(s).

cord·age (kōr′dĭj) *n.* Cord ropes collectively, esp. in rigging a ship.

cor·date (kōr′dāt) *adj.* Hea shaped.

cord·ed (kōr′dĭd) *adj.* Boun furnished, with cords; ribbe twilled.

cor·dial (kōr′jal; Brit. kōr′dĕ *adj.* 1. That stimulates the hea 2. Hearty, sincere; warm, friendl ~ *n.* Liqueur. **cor·dial·i·** (kōrjăl′ĭtē) *n.* **cor′dial·ly** *adv.*

cor·dil·le·ra (kōrdĭlyar′a, kō dĭl′era) *n.* One of a parall series of mountain ridges, esp. i the Andes and Mexico; chain mountains, esp. a principal rang **C~s**, name given to many range the entire complex of ranges western America from Alaska t Cape Horn.

cord·ite (kōr′dīt) *n.* Smokeles explosive powder of nitrocellulos nitroglycerine, and petrolatum usu. pressed into rods of varyin length and thickness.

Cór·do·ba (kōr′doba, kōrdō′- *Sp.* kōr′dawvah). City of S. Spai on river Guadalquivir; Moorisl capital 756–1236.

cor·do·ba (kōr′doba, -va) *n* Principal monetary unit o

*Reef-forming **coral** (facing page) car only thrive in the clear waters of tropica seas where the temperature never falls below 70°F. The Great Barrier Reef (below) off the east coast of Australia, is the largest single system of cora reefs in the world.*

Nicaragua, = 100 centavos.

cor·don (kōr´don) *n.* 1. (archit.) String-course, projecting (usu. flat) band of stone on face of wall. 2. Line of troops consisting of men placed at intervals to prevent passage; line or circle of police or other persons. 3. Ornamental cord or braid worn as badge of honor; ~ **bleu** (kōrdawṅ blö´), blue ribbon worn formerly by Knights of the Holy Ghost, the highest order under the Bourbons; hence, person of eminence, (esp.) first-class cook.

cor·do·van (kōr´dovan) *n.* Kind of soft leather, hence ~ **shoes**.

cor·du·roy (kōr´duroi, kōrduroi´) *n.* 1. Cotton fabric with ridges in the pile; (pl.) corduroy trousers. 2. Corduroy road. ~ *adj.* Made of corduroy, ribbed like corduroy; ~ **road**, road of tree trunks or logs laid transversely across swamp or miry ground.

CORE (kōr, kōr) *abbrev.* Congress of Racial Equality.

core (kōr, kōr) *n.* 1. Dry horny capsule embedded in pulp and containing seeds of apple, pear, etc. 2. Central portion cut out, as of rock in boring. 3. Central part of different character from what surrounds it; (esp.) assemblage of soft iron layers in center of electromagnet or induction coil; central cord of conducting wires in telegraph etc. cable; part of center of

nuclear reactor that contains fissionable fuel; unit of magnetic material in a computer. 4. Innermost part, center, heart, of anything. **core** *v.t.* (**cored, cor·ing**). Remove core from.

co·re·li·gion·ist (kōrĭlĭj´onĭst) *n.* Adherent of same religion.

co·re·op·sis (kōrēŏp´sĭs, kōr-) *n.* Composite plant of genus *C*~ cultivated for its handsome daisy-like yellow or variegated flowers.

co·re·spond·ent (kōrĭspŏn´dent, kōr-, kär-) *n.* (law) Man or woman proceeded against together with RESPONDENT in a divorce suit.

Cor·fu (kōr´foo, -fū). One of the Ionian islands off the W. coast of Greece, anciently called Corcyra.

cor·gi (kōr´gē) *n.* (also **Welsh** ~) Dog of short-legged breed with foxlike head.

co·ri·an·der (kōrēăn´der, kōr-, kär-) *n.* Herb (*Coriandrum sativum*) of S. Europe, Levant, etc., with compound leaves and globose aromatic fruit (~ **seed**) used as flavoring and condiment.

Cor·inth (kōr´ĭnth, kär´-). City of Greece in the NE. Peloponnesus on an inlet (**the Gulf of** ~) of the Ionian Sea; notorious in ancient

*The **Corinth Canal** crosses the isthmus of Corinth and joins the Gulf of Corinth with the Saronic Gulf. Opened in 1893, it has cut the distance between the Adriatic and Piraeus by 200 miles.*

times for luxury and profligacy.

Co·rin·thi·an (korĭn´thēan) *a* 1. Of Corinth or its people. (archit.) Of the Corinthian ord 3. (archaic) Given to elegant d sipation, profligate. 4. ~ **ord** (archit.) most ornate of the Gr orders, with bell-shaped capi adorned with rows of acanth leaves giving rise to volutes a helices. **Corinthian** *n.* 1. Nati inhabitant, of Corinth; (**Epistle the**) ~**s**, either of two books New Testament, epistles of St. P. to the Church at Corinth. (archaic) Profligate.

Co·ri·o·la·nus (kōrēolā´n, kär-), **Gaius Marcius.** Legenda Roman patrician and general of t first half of the 5th c. B. prosecuted for aspiring to becon tyrant, and exiled; whereupon joined the Volscians and led th against Rome, but on the entreat of his mother, Veturia, he spar the town and withdrew to Antiu where he was murdered by t Volscians.

Cork (kōrk). Largest county Republic of Ireland; county seat this county.

cork (kōrk) *n.* 1. Bark of t cork oak (*Quercus suber*), whi grows to a thickness of 1 to 2 in. (2 to 5.1 cm) and is very light, toug and elastic; the tree itself. 2. Pie of cork used as float for fishing lir

The **cork** tree (left), although native to the Mediterranean area is now cultivated in India and the west of the U.S.A. The outer bark is removed, boiled and stacked in strips (above).

c. 3. Cylindrical or tapering piece
cork used as stopper for a bottle,
sk, etc.; similar stopper of other
bstance. 4. (bot.) Tissue forming
ter division of bark in higher
ants and consisting of closely
acked air-containing cells nearly
pervious to air and water. 5. ~
ak, tree (*Quercus suber*); **cork′-
rew**, instrument for drawing
rks from bottles, usu. consisting
a piece of steel twisted into a
iral with sharp point and trans-
rse handle; (*adj.*) spirally twisted;
.) twist spirally, (cause to) pro-
ed spirally; **cork-tipped**, (ciga-
tte) with band of corklike sub-
ance at one end; **cork** *adj.* Made
cork. ~ *v.t.* Stop, stop *up*,
ith or as with cork; blacken with
urnt cork.

cork·age (kôr′kĭj) *n.* Corking,
ncorking, of bottles; restaurant's

charge for opening and serving each
bottle of wine or liquor not bought
on the premises.

corked (kôrkt) *adj.* 1. (of wine)
Tasting of the cork, spoiled by an
unsound cork into which the wine
penetrates. 2. (of face and hands)
Blackened with burnt cork as part
of theatrical make-up. 3. Sealed in
(bottle).

cork·er (kôr′ker) *n.* (slang)
Something that precludes further
discussion; excellent person or
thing. **cork′ing** *adj. & adv.*
(slang) Excellent.

corm (kôrm) *n.* (bot.) Swollen
base of stem containing food
reserves, occurring in some monocotyledonous plants, such as
crocus.

cor·mo·rant (kôr′merant, -rănt)
n. Large, lustrous, black, voracious
sea bird, e.g. *Phalacrocorax auritus*;
(pl.) family to which this belongs.
[med. L. *corvus marinus* sea raven]

corn[1] (kôrn) *n.* 1. Any of several
varieties of a tall cereal plant (*Zea
mays*) widely cultivated for food
and oil, with seeds or kernels on
large ears, some varieties of which
are also called maize or Indian corn;
ears of this plant; the kernels. 2.
(Brit.) Any of several cereal plants,
esp. wheat or (in Scotland) oats. 3.
(slang) Anything old-fashioned,

trite, or sentimental. **corn′y**, *adj.*
(**corn·i·er, corn·i·est**). 4. **corn′-
ball**, (slang) corny; **C ~ Belt**, area
in U.S. Middle West noted for
raising corn and corn-fed livestock,
esp. Indiana, Illinois, and Iowa;
corn bread, bread made from
cornmeal; **corn′cob**, woody core of
ear of corn; **corncob pipe**, tobacco
pipe made from corncob; **corn′-
crib**, building for storing ears of
corn, with ventilated sides; **corn′-
fed**, fed on corn; (fig.) husky,
innocent, and provincial; **corn′-
flakes**, breakfast cereal made of
toasted flaked and flavored corn;
corn′flower, name of various
plants, esp. the blue-flowered
Centaurea cyanus, or bachelor's
button; **Corn Laws**, (Brit. hist.)
series of British laws restricting the
importation of grain, repealed
1846; **corn′meal**, meal made of
corn; **corn pone** (Southern U.S.)
corn bread made without milk or
eggs; **corn silk**, silky fibers in corn
husk; **corn′stalk**, stalk of corn;
corn syrup, sweet syrup made
from corn; **corn whiskey**, whiskey
distilled from corn.

corn[2] (kôrn) *n.* Horny
induration of cuticle with hard
center and root sometimes
penetrating deep into subjacent
tissue, caused by undue pressure,
chiefly of shoes on feet.

corn[3] (kôrn) *v.* Sprinkle,
preserve (meat) with salt; **corned
beef**, beef so preserved.

cor·ne·a (kôr′nēa) *n.* Transparent horny part of anterior
covering of eyeball. **cor′ne·al** *adj.*

Cor·neille (kōrnā′), **Pierre** (1606–84). French dramatist, author of classical tragedies *Le Cid*, *Horace*, etc.

cor·nel (kōr′nel) *n.* Any tree, shrub, or plant of the genus *Cornus*, including the dogwood and bunch-berry.

cor·nel·ian (kōrnēl′yan) *n.* Var. of CARNELIAN.

cor·ne·ous (kōr′nēus) *adj.* Made of horn, hornlike.

cor·ner (kōr′ner) *n.* 1. Angular meeting place of converging sides or edges, projecting angle, esp. where two streets meet; hollow angle enclosed by meeting walls etc.; **drive into a** ~, force into difficult position from which there is no escape. 2. Secluded, secret, or remote place; region, quarter; extremity or end of the earth. 3. Buying up all or most of any stock or commodity, in order to profit by raising its price. 4. **cor′nerstone**, one of those forming corner angle of wall; (fig.) indispensable thing or part. **corner** *v.* 1. Furnish with corners. 2. Set in corner; drive into corner (esp. fig.). 3. (of vehicle etc.) Go around a corner. 4. Force (dealers) or control (commodity) by means of corner (sense 3); form corner *in* (stock or commodity). **cor′nered** *adj.*

cor·net (kōrnĕt′ for def. 1; kōr′-nĭt for def. 2) *n.* 1. Brass musical instrument of trumpet class with valves operated by pistons for producing additional notes; cornet player. 2. Conically rolled piece of paper for candy, nuts, etc. **cor′net·ist, cor′net′tist** *ns.*

cor·nice (kōr′nĭs) *n.* (archit.) Horizontal molded projection crowning or finishing (part of)

building etc., esp. uppermost member of entablature, surmount-ing the frieze; ornamental molding around wall of room just below ceiling.

Cor·nish (kōr′nĭsh) *adj.* Of Cornwall. ~ *n.* Ancient Celtic language of Cornwall.

cor·nu·co·pi·a (kōrnukō′pēa) *n.* Horn of plenty, represented as a goat's horn overflowing with flowers, fruit, corn, etc. **cor·nu-co′pi·an** *adj.* Overflowingly abundant. [L. *cornu copiae* = "horn of plenty," the horn of the goat Amalthea by which the infant Zeus was suckled]

Corn·wall (kōrn′wawl; *Brit.* kōrn′wal). County in the extreme SW. of England.

Corn·wal·lis (kōrnwaw′lĭs, -wŏl′ĭs), **Charles** (1738–1805). First Marquis Cornwallis, 1792; English major general; commanded British troops in America during the Revolutionary War; sur-rendered to George Washington at Yorktown, 1781, ending the war; later became successful British governor general and commander in chief in India, then Viceroy of Ireland.

co·rol·la (kōrŏl′a) *n.* (bot.) Whorl of floral leaves (petals) forming inner envelope of flower, and usu. its most conspicuous part.

cor·ol·lar·y (kōr′olĕrē, kar′-) *n.* (pl. **-lar·ies**). Proposition appended to one already demon-

strated, as self-evident inferenc from it; immediate deduction natural consequence, result. [*corollarium* money paid for chaplet, gratuity]

co·ro·na (kōrō′na) *n.* (pl. **-na -nae** pr. -nē). 1. Circle of ligh seen around and close to luminou body, esp. sun or moon, caused b diffraction by water droplets in thi cloud (cf. HALO); **solar** ~, rarefie gaseous envelope of sun, visible a radiating white light during tota solar eclipse; (elect.) luminou appearance around conducte accompanying ionization o surrounding gas. 2. Circula candleholder hung from ceiling. (archit.) Member of cornice, wit broad vertical face, usu. of con siderable projection. 4. (anat zool.) Any of various crownlik parts of body. 5. (bot.) Crownlik appendage on inner side of coroll in daffodil and other flowers. Long cigar with blunt tip.

Co·ro·na·do (kōronah′dō, kōr-**Francesco Vasquez de** (1510 1554). Spanish explorer of th southwestern U.S. and Centra America; discovered the Gran Canyon, explored Californi Peninsula, and followed course o Rio Grande River.

cor·o·nal (kōr′onal, kar′-, koro′ nal) *adj.* 1. (anat.) ~ **suture** transverse suture of skull betwee frontal bone and parietal bones. 2 (bot.) Of a corona.

cor·o·nar·y (kōr′onĕrē, kar′-) *adj.* 1. (of vessels, ligaments nerves, etc.) Encircling parts lik a crown; (of parts) connected wit these. 2. (of arteries, veins) Supply ing blood to the heart; ~ **occlusion, thrombosis**, throm

*The **cornet** has been superseded by the trumpet in modern usage although it is still popular with military and brass bands as a solo instrument. It first appeared in Europe in the 1820s.*

*The county of **Cornwall** in the south-west extremity of England has an attractive coastal landscape and a mild climate. It is a popular tourist area, with long stretches of its coast unspoilt.*

...osis occurring in a coronary artery. **cor·o·nary** *n.* (pl. **-nar·ies**). (esp.) Coronary thrombosis; (loosely) heart attack.

cor·o·na·tion (kŏrŏnā′shon, kăr-) *n.* Ceremony of crowning sovereign or sovereign's consort.

cor·o·ner (kŏr′oner, kăr′-) *n.* Public official whose chief duty is to investigate deaths thought to be caused by other than natural causes.

cor·o·net (kŏr′onĭt, kăr′-, kŏro-

nĕt, kăr-) *n.* 1. Small crown, esp. crown denoting dignity inferior to sovereign's, worn by nobility and varying in form according to rank. 2. Decorative fillet or wreath, esp. as part of woman's headdress; garland for the head. **cor′o·net·ed, cor′o·net·ted** *adjs.* Wearing a coronet; esp., belonging to the peerage.

Co·rot (kawrō′, ko-), **Jean Baptiste Camille** (1796–1875). French landscape painter.

corp. *abbrev.* Corporal, corporation.

cor·po·ral[1] (kŏr′peral, -pral) *adj.* Of the human body; personal, bodily; as in ~ **punishment**, that

cor·po·ral·i·ty (kōrperăl'ĭtē) *n.* Material existence; body.

cor·po·ral[2] (kōr'peral, -pral) *n.* Fine linen cloth on which consecrated elements are placed during Mass.

cor·po·ral[3] (kōr'peral, -pral) *n.* Noncommissioned officer ranking below sergeant; **the little C~**, nickname of Napoleon I.

cor·po·rate (kōr'perĭt, -prĭt) *adj.* Forming a body politic or corporation; forming one body of many individuals; of, belonging to, a body politic. **cor'po·rate·ly** *adv.*

cor·po·ra·tion (kōrperā'shon) *n.* 1. Body corporate legally authorized to act as a single individual; business so organized. 2. Body created for governmental purposes; agency of government. **cor·po·ra·tive** (kōr'porātĭv, -poratĭv, -pratĭv) *adj.*

cor·po·re·al (kōrpōr'ēal, -pōr'-) *adj.* Bodily; material; tangible. **cor·po're·al·ly** *adv.*

cor·po·sant (kōr'pozănt) *n.* St. Elmo's fire; see ELMO, ST.

corps (kōr, kōr) *n.* (pl. **corps** pr. kōrz, kōrz). 1. Army corps; body of troops for special service. 2. Body of persons in common organization; **corps de ballet**, members of ballet company who perform as a group and do not have solo rôles.

corpse (kōrps) *n.* Dead (usu. human) body.

cor·pu·lent (kōr'pyulent) *adj.* Bulky (of body); fat. **cor'pu·lence, cor'pu·len·cy** *ns.*

cor·pus (kōr'pus) *n.* (pl. **-po·ra** pr. -pora). 1. Body, collection, of writings. 2. (physiol.) Structure of special character or function in animal body. 3. ~ **callosum**, band of tissue connecting hemispheres of brain; ~ **delicti** (L., = "body of the crime"), material evidence that a crime has been committed; (pop.) body of murdered person; ~ **juris**, body of law; ~ **luteum**, structure formed in ovary of mammals after ovulation.

Cor·pus Chris·ti[1] (kōr'pus krĭs'tē). Feast of the Blessed Sacrament or body of Christ, the Thursday after Trinity Sunday.

Cor·pus Chris·ti[2] (kōr'pus krĭs'tē, -tī). Seaport and industrial city in SW. Texas, on the Gulf of Mexico.

cor·pus·cle (kōr'pusel, -pŭs-), **cor·pus·cule** (kōrpŭs'kūl) *ns.* 1. Minute body forming distinct part of organism; (esp.) one of the minute rounded or disklike bodies constituting a large part of the blood of vertebrates. 2. (phys. chemistry) Discrete particle, such as a proton, electron, or atom. **cor·pus·cu·lar** (kōrpŭs'kyuler) *adj.*

cor·ral (korăl') *n.* Enclosure for horses, cattle, etc; defensive enclosure of wagons in encampment; enclosure for capturing wild animals. **corral** *v.t.* (**-ralled, -ral·ling**). Drive (animals) into and confine in corral; (slang) capture, obtain.

cor·rect (korĕkt') *adj.* True, accurate; right, proper (of conduct, manners, etc.), in accordance with a good standard (of taste etc.). **cor·rect'ly** *adv.* **cor·rect'ness** *n.* **correct** *v.t.* 1. Set right, amend; substitute right for (wrong); mark errors on (student's paper, printer's proof-sheet, etc.) for amendment. 2. Admonish (person); cure (person) of fault; punish (person, fault). 3. Counteract, neutralize, (hurtful qualities). 4. Bring (result of mathematical or physical observation or calculation) into accordance with certain standard conditions; eliminate aberration etc. from lens etc. **cor·rect'a·ble**

adj. **cor·rec'tor** *n.*

cor·rec·tion (korĕk'shon) *n.* Correcting. 2. Thing substitute for what is wrong. 3. Punishmen **cor·rec'tion·al** *adj.*

cor·rec·tive (korĕk'tĭv) *adj. &* (Thing) serving, tending, to corre or counteract what is harmfu **cor·rec'tive·ly** *adv.*

Cor·reg·gio (korĕj'ēō). Antoni Allegri (1494–1534), called " Correggio" from the place of hi birth in Lombardy, an Italia painter famous for his chiaroscuro

Cor·reg·i·dor (korĕg'ĭdō -dōr). Island in the Philippines the entrance to Manila Bay; site o World War II battle, 1942, in whic Amer. forces under Gen MacArthur surrendered t Japanese; in 1945 Amer. force under MacArthur invaded islan and overcame Japanese.

cor·re·late (kōr'elāt, kăr'-) *n* Each of two things so related tha one implies or is complementary t the other; each of two related thing viewed in reference to the other **correlate** *v.* (**-lat·ed, -lat·ing** Have a mutual relation (*with, to* bring (thing) into such relatio

Corsica, the fourth largest island in the Mediterranean, is a 'département' of France. It is 100 miles south-east of France and 50 miles west of Italy. Left: View of Calvi, a favorite tourist resort. Above: Map of Corsica.

ith another). **cor·re·la·tion** (ŏrelā′shon, kār-) *n.*

cor·rel·a·tive (korĕl′atĭv) *adj.* 1. aving a mutual relation (*with, to*); alogous. 2. (gram., of words) rresponding with each other and gularly used together each in one ember of compound or complex ntence (e.g. *either—or; so—as*). ~ Correlative word or thing. **r·rel′a·tive·ly** *adv.* **cor·rel·a· vi·ty** (korĕlativ′ĭtē) *n.*

cor·re·spond (korĕspŏnd′, kār-) . 1. Be congruous, in harmony *ith, to*); be similar, analogous (*to*); ree in amount, position, etc. (*to*). Communicate by interchange of ters (*with*). **cor·re·spond′ing·ly** *v.*

cor·re·spond·ence (korĕspŏn′- ns, kār-) *n.* 1. Agreement, rmony. 2. Communication by ters; letters; ~ **course, school,** e instructing by correspondence. **cor·re·spond·ent** (korĕspŏn′- nt, kār-) *n.* One who writes ter(s) to another; person ployed to contribute news, icles, etc., to newspaper etc., esp. m a distant place or on a rticular subject; person etc. with gular business relations with other (esp. in foreign country). *adj.* Corresponding.

cor·ri·dor (kor′ider, -dor, kār′-) 1. Main passage in large build- g, on which many rooms open; tside passage connecting parts of ilding; hallway; aisle. 2. Strip territory of one country running rough another territory to give cess e.g. to the sea; **air** ~, route which aircraft are restricted; **lish C** ~, strip that ran through ussia from Poland to the Baltic Danzig, created by the Treaty Versailles (1919).

cor·ri·gen·dum (korĭjĕn′dum, kār-) *n.* (pl. **-da** pr. -da). Thing to be corrected (esp. mistake in printed book); (pl.) list of items to be corrected.

cor·ri·gi·ble (kor′ĭjibel, kār′-) *n.* Capable of being corrected; open or receptive to correction.

cor·rob·o·rate (korŏb′erāt) *v.t.* (**-rat·ed, -rat·ing**). Confirm, support, or strengthen (other evidence, a statement, etc.); attest the truth of. **cor·rob·o·ra·tive** (korŏb′orātĭv, -erativ), **cor·rob·o·ra·to·ry** (korŏb′oratōre, -tōrē) *adjs.* **cor·rob·o·ra·tion** (korŏborā′- shon), **cor·rob·o·ra·tor** (korŏb′- orāter) *ns.*

cor·rode (korōd′) *v.* (**-rod·ed, -rod·ing**). (of rust, chemical agents, etc.) Wear away, destroy gradually; become destroyed thus; decay. **cor·rod′i·ble** *adj.* **cor·ro·sion** (korō′zhon), **cor·ro·sive·ness** *ns.* **cor·ro·sive** (korō′sĭv) *adj.* & *n.* **cor·ro′sive·ly** *adv.*

cor·ru·gate (kor′ugāt, kār′-) *v.* (**-gat·ed, -gat·ing**). Contract into wrinkles or folds; mark with, bend into, parallel folds or ridges. **cor′ru·gat·ed** *adj.* (esp.) ~ **iron,** galvanized sheet iron or steel bent into a series of parallel ridges and grooves, used for roofing etc.; ~ **cardboard,** type of ridged card-board used for packing. **cor·ru·ga·tion** (korugā′shon, kār-) *n.*

cor·rupt (korŭpt′) *adj.* Rotten, decomposed (archaic); debased in character, depraved, wicked; perverted or influenced by bribery; (of language, texts, etc.) vitiated by errors or alterations. **cor·rupt′ly** *adv.* **cor·rupt′ness** *n.* **corrupt** *v.* Infect, taint; bribe; destroy purity of (text, language); make, become, corrupt. **cor·rup′tive** *adj.*

cor·rupt·i·ble (korŭp′tibel) *adj.* Liable to corruption, perishable; capable of moral corruption. **cor·rupt·i·bil·i·ty** (korŭptibĭl′ĭte) *n.* **cor·rupt′i·bly** *adv.*

cor·rup·tion (korŭp′shon) *n.* Decomposition; moral deteriora-tion; use of corrupt practices; bribery etc.; perversion (of language etc.) from original state.

cor·sage (korsahzh′) *n.* Bodice of woman's dress; fresh flower(s) worn by a woman on bodice, shoulder, or wrist.

cor·sair (kor′sār) *n.* Mediter-ranean privateer, esp. of Barbary; corsair's ship.

cor·set (kor′sĭt) *n.* Closely fitting foundation garment, usu. stiffened and freq. laced to give support around waist and hips, worn esp. by women; stays. ~ *v.t.* Fit with corset; (fig.) constrict.

cor·se·tier, cor·se·tière (korsetēr′) *ns.* Corset maker or fitter.

Cor·si·ca (kor′sĭka). Island off the W. coast of Italy, belonging to France; capital, Ajaccio.

Cor·si·can (kor′sĭkan) *adj.* Of Corsica or its people. ~ *n.* Native, inhabitant, of Corsica; **the** ~, Napoleon I, born at Ajaccio in Corsica.

cor·tege, cor·tège (kortĕzh′, -tāzh′) *ns.* Train of attendants; procession, esp. a funeral proces-sion.

Cor·tés (kortĕz′), **Hernando** (1485–1547). Spanish explorer and conquistador, conqueror of the Aztecs and colonial administrator of New Spain.

cor·tex (kor′tĕks) *n.* (pl. **-ti·ces** pr. -tĭsĕz, **-tex·es**). 1. (bot.) Inner bark. 2. (anat.) Layer of gray matter on surface of brain; outer part of kidney; outer portion of suprarenal gland. **cor'ti·cal** *adj.*

cor·ti·cate (kôr'tĭkĭt, -kāt), **cor·ti·cat·ed** (kôr'tĭkātĭd) *adjs.* Having bark or a cortex. **cor·ti·cose** (kôr'tĭkōs) *adj.*

cor·ti·sone (kôr'tĭsōn, -zōn) *n.* Steroid hormone ($C_{21}H_{28}O_5$) found in adrenal cortex; similar substance prepared synthetically, used in treatment of diseases.

co·run·dum (kǒrŭn'dum) *n.* Crystallized alumina (Al_2O_3), translucent mineral used as an abrasive in the form of emery. [Tamil *kurundum* ruby]

cor·us·cate (kôr'uskāt, kär'-) *v.i.* (**-cat·ed, -cat·ing**). Sparkle, flash. **cor·us·ca·tion** (kôruskā'shon, kär'-) *n.* **co·rus·cant** (korŭs'kant, kôr'us-, kär'-) *adj.*

cor·vette (kôrvĕt') *n.* 1. (hist.) Flush-decked warship with one tier of guns. 2. Fast, lightly armed warship, smaller than a destroyer, used esp. for convoy work.

cor·vine (kôr'vĭn, -vīn) *adj.* Of, akin to, raven or crow.

Cor·y·don (kôr'ĭdon, -dŏn, kär'-). Name given by Theocritus and Virgil to a shepherd; hence, shepherd or rustic in pastoral poetry.

cor·ymb (kôr'ĭmb, -ĭm, kär'-) *n.* (bot.) Inflorescence; raceme in which lower flower stalks are longer than upper ones, so that flowers form a flat or slightly convex head.

cor·y·phée (kôr'ĭfā, kär'-) *n.* Leader of *corps de ballet.*

co·ry·za (kŏrī'za) *n.* (path.) Inflammation of nasal mucous membrane and sinuses; cold in the head.

cos[1] (kŏs, kaws) *n.* (also ~ **lettuce**): see ROMAINE. [introduced from *Cos*, island in Aegean]

cos[2] *abbrev.* Cosine.

co·sec *abbrev.* Cosecant.

co·se·cant (kōsē'kant, -kănt) *n.* (trig., function of angle in right-angled triangle) Secant of complement of given angle (abbrev. cosec).

cosh (kŏsh) *n.* (chiefly Brit.) Blackjack. ~ *v.t.* Strike with cosh.

co·sig·na·to·ry (kōsĭg'natōrē, -tōrē) *n.* (pl. **-ries**) & *adj.* (Person) signing jointly with others.

co·sine (kō'sīn) *n.* (trig., function of angle in right-angled triangle) Sine of complement of given angle (abbrev. cos).

cos·met·ic (kŏzmĕt'ĭk) *adj.* Designed to beautify hair, skin, or complexion; (of surgery etc.) improving or modifying the appearance. ~ *n.* Cosmetic preparation. **cos·me·ti·cian** (kŏzmetĭsh'an) *n.* Cosmetic specialist. **cos·met'i·cal·ly** *adv.*

cos·mic (kŏz'mĭk) *adj.* Of the universe or cosmos; ~ **dust**, minute particles of matter in or from outer space; ~ **rays**, high-energy radiation originating in outer space. **cos'mi·cal·ly** *adv.*

cos·mog·o·ny (kŏzmŏg'onē) *n.* (pl. **-nies**). (Theory of) the origin of the universe. **cos·mo·gon·ic** (kŏzmogŏn'ĭk), **cos·mo·gon'i·cal** *adjs.* **cos·mog'o·nist** *n.*

cos·mog·ra·phy (kŏzmŏg'rafē) *n.* (pl. **-phies**). Description, mapping, study of general features of universe or Earth. **cos·mog'ra·pher** *n.* **cos·mo·graph·ic** (kŏzmogrăf'ĭk), **cos·mo·graph'i·cal** *adjs.*

cos·mol·o·gy (kŏzmŏl'ojē) *n.* Study, philosophy, of the universe as an ordered whole. **cos·mo·log'i·cal** *adj.* **cos·mol'o·gist** *n.*

cos·mo·naut (kŏz'monawt, -nŏt) *n.* (Russian) astronaut.

cos·mo·pol·i·tan (kŏzmopŏl'ĭtan) *adj.* 1. Belonging to all parts of the world; free from local, provincial, or national limitations or prejudices. 2. (of a city) Containing people from many parts of the world. ~ *n.* Citizen of the world, one without national attachments or prejudices. **cos·mo·pol'i·tan·ism** *n.*

cos·mop·o·lite (kŏzmŏp'olīt) *n.* Cosmopolitan.

cos·mos[1] (kŏz'mos, -mōs) *n.* Universe as an ordered whole; ordered system of ideas etc., sum total of experience; (astron.) all stars in existence, all the galaxies.

cos·mos[2] (kŏz'mos, -mōs) *n.* (pl. **-mos, -mos·es**). Composite tropical Amer. plant of genus *C* ~, cultivated for its rose, scarlet, and purple flowers.

Cos·sack (kŏs'ăk, -ak, kaw'săk) *n.* Member of a tribe in imperial Russia who were allowed privileg by the Czars, including autonor for their settlements in S. Rus (esp. Ukraine) and Siberia in retu for service in protecting t frontiers; one of the descendants these, noted for warlike qualitie and horsemanship. ~ *adj.* Of t. Cossacks. [Turk. *quzzāq*, secede adventurer (first used of an u related non-Russian nomad people of S. Siberia, the Kazakhs

cost (kawst, kŏst) *n.* Price (to b paid for thing; expenditure of tim labor, etc.; loss, penalty, detrimen (pl.) law expenses, esp. tho allowed by court etc. against losir party; ~ **accounting**, accountir system indicating costs and (esp overhead expenses in a busines ~ **of living**, cost of basic necess ties of life; ~**-of-living index**: se CONSUMER PRICE INDEX. **cost** (cost, cost'ing). 1. Be acquirab at, involve expenditure of; result the loss of. 2. Estimate or fix co of production.

co-star (kō'stär) *n.* Motic picture, stage, or television sta appearing with other star(s). ~ (kō'stär') *v.* (**-starred, -star ring**). Perform with, includ co-star(s).

Cos·ta Ri·ca (kŏs'ta rē'k. kaws'ta, kōs'ta). Republic

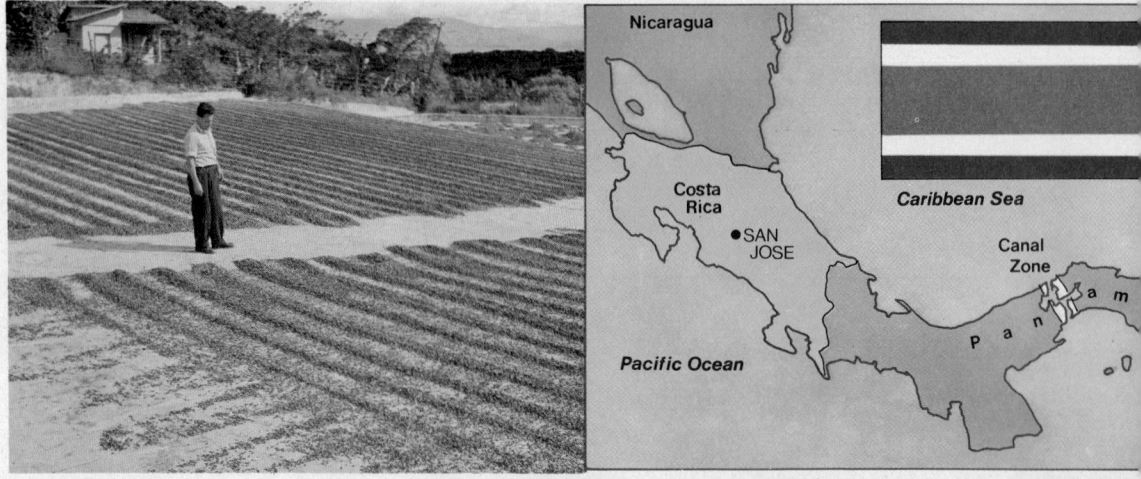

Costa Rica *is a republic in Central America on the narrow isthmus joining North and South America. Coffee, drying in the sun (above), is the country's largest export. Above right: Map and flag of Costa Rica.*

southern Central America between Panama and Nicaragua; until 1821 part of Spanish-American dominions; capital, San José.

cos·tate (kŏs′tāt) *adj.* Ribbed, having ribs.

cos·ter (kŏs′ter, kaws′-), **cos·ter·mon·ger** (kŏs′termŭngger, -mŏng-, kaws′-) *ns.* (Brit.) Man who sells fruit, fish, etc., from barrow, cart, or stand in street (esp. in London).

cos·tive (kŏs′tĭv, kaws′-) *adj.* Constipated; causing constipation. **cos′tive·ly** *adv.* **cos′tive·ness** *n.*

cost·ly (kawst′lē, kŏst′-) *adj.* (-li·er, -li·est). High-priced; resulting in great loss or sacrifice. **cost′li·ness** *n.*

cos·tume (kŏs′tōōm, -tūm) *n.* 1. Mode or fashion of personal attire and dress of a particular nation, class, or period; this as worn on the stage, to a ~ **ball** or ~ **party**, etc.; ~ **drama, play**, dramatic piece in which actors wear costume of some past period. 2. Complete set of outer garments; garments suitable for a special occasion or season. 3. ~ **jewelry**, artificial or semiprecious jewelry worn as fashion accessory. **costume** (kŏstōōm′, -tūm′, kŏs′tōōm, -tūm) *v.t.* (-tumed, -tum·ing). Provide with costume.

cos·tum·er (kŏstōō′mer, -tū′-) *n.* Maker of, dealer in, costumes.

co·sy (kō′zē): see COZY.

cot¹ (kŏt) *n.* Small shelter; (poet.) little cottage.

cot² (kŏt) *n.* Lightweight, narrow bed of canvas stretched on a collapsible frame. [f. Hind. *khāṭ* bedstead, bier]

co·tan·gent (kōtăn′jent, kō′tăn-) *n.* (trig., function of angle in right-angle triangle) Tangent of complement of given angle.

cote (kōt) *n.* Shed, stall, shelter, esp. for animals or birds.

Côte d'A·zur (kawt d'ăzür′). Mediterranean coast of France, esp. the eastern end, famous as a summer resort area.

co·te·rie (kō′terē) *n.* Circle, set, of persons associated by exclusive interests; select circle in society. [Fr., orig. association of country people, f. *cotier* cottager]

co·ter·mi·nous (kōter′minus), **co·ter·mi·nal** (kōter′minal) *adjs.* = CONTERMINOUS. **co·ter′mi·nous·ly** *adv.*

co·til·lion (kōtĭl′yon, ko-) *n.* Dance with elaborate series of steps and figures, with giving of favors and changes of partner; coming-out party. [Fr. *cotillon* petticoat]

co·to·ne·as·ter (kotō′nēăster, kŏt′onēster) *n.* Deciduous or evergreen shrub or small tree of genus *C~* with white or pinkish flowers and usu. red or orange berries.

Co·to·pax·i (kōtopäk′sē). Active volcano in the Cordillera Real, Ecuador; probably the highest active volcano in the world.

Cots·wold (kŏts′wōld, -wold) *adj.* Of the Cotswold Hills. ~ *n.* (Breed of) long-wooled sheep originally developed in the Cotswolds. ~ **Hills**, (also ~s) area, range of hills in SW. England.

History enthusiasts wearing the co̸ tume of the Minutemen re-enact th̸ roles as ever-ready militia defend̸ Concord, Massachusetts, from ̸ depredations of the British army.

cot·tage (kŏt′ĭj) *n.* 1. Sma̸ simple dwelling in village or ru̸ area; one-story house. 2. Sm̸ house used for vacations. 3. ̸ **cheese**, soft white cheese ma̸ from curds; ~ **industry**, indus̸ carried on by workers in th̸ homes. **cot′tag·er** *n.* One w̸ lives in a cottage.

cot·ter (kŏt′er) *n.* Key, wed̸ bolt, for inserting through a slot ̸ hold parts of machinery, e̸ together; (also ~ **pin**) a split cot̸ that opens at one end to fast̸ securely.

cot·ton¹ (kŏt′on) *n.* Wh̸ downy fibrous substance coveri̸ seeds of cotton plant, used ̸ making thread, cloth, etc.; cott̸ plant; thread spun, cloth ma̸ from cotton; ~ **candy**, mass ̸ fluffy spun sugar for eating; ~ g̸ machine for separating cotton fr̸ its seeds; ~ **grass**, species of gra̸ like bogplants of the gen̸ *Eriophorum*, with heads of lo̸ white silky hairs; **cot′tonmou̸** venomous snake (*Ankistroa̸ piscivorus*), about 6 ft. (1.83 m) lo̸ of low-lying swampy areas in sout̸ eastern U.S.; water moccasin; **cotton plant**, plant of genus *Gossypium*, yielding cotton; **cot′tonseed**, seed of cotton plant, furnishing oil (**cottonseed oil**) and cattle fodder; **cot′tontail**, any of several N. Amer. rabbits of genus *Sylvilagus*, with a white fluffy tail; **cot′tonwood**, any of various N. Amer. species of poplar, with seeds surround by cottonlike tufts. **cot′ton·y** *adj.* [Arab. *kutkn*]

cot·ton² (kŏt′on) *v.i.* (colloq.) Be drawn *to*; ~ **(on) to**, understand, agree to, like (idea etc.).

cot·y·le·don (kŏtɪlē′don) *n.* Primary leaf in embryo of higher plants, seed leaf. **cot·y·le′don·ous** *adj.* Having cotyledons.

couch¹ (kowch) *n.* Long upholstered seat with a back and freq. with raised ends, sofa. ~ *v.* 1. Lie, esp. in lair (of animals); crouch; lie in wait. 2. Lower (spear) to position of attack. 3. (embroidery) Stitch thick thread on surface of material by means of fine thread. 4. Express *in* language, words, terms, etc.

couch² (kowch, kōōch) *n.* (usu. ~ **grass**) Species of grass (*Agropyron repens*) with long creeping underground stems, a common and troublesome weed, also called *twitch grass*. [var. of QUITCH]

couch·ant (kow′chant) *adj.* (her., of animals) Lying with body resting on legs and head lifted.

Cou·é (kōōā′), **Émile** (1857–1926). French psychotherapist, advocate of a system of autosuggestion. **Cou·é·ism** (kōōā′ɪzem, kōō′ā-) *n.*

Cottonfields in Alabama (above left) are usually planted and harvested annually. The plant is then processed and the **cotton** *fibers separated from the seed (below left). Next, the fiber is baled, usually in packages, ready for transportation (below right). The principal cotton-growing countries are U.S.A., U.S.S.R., China, India and Brazil.*

A boxer may deliver a **counter-pur**
while parrying his opponent's blow. 7
match for the world heavyweight title
New York was won by Joe Fra:
against Jimmy Ellis.

cou·gar (kōo'ger) *n.* (pl. **-gars**, collect. **-gar**). Mountain lion (cf. LION). [Fr., repr. Guarani *guaçu ara*]

cough (kawf, kŏf) *v.* Expel air from lungs with violent effort and characteristic noise produced by abrupt opening of glottis, in order to remove obstruction or relieve irritation in air passages; ∼ **out, up**, eject by, say with, cough; ∼ **up**, (slang) bring out, produce (esp. money). **cough** *n.* Act of coughing; tendency to cough; condition of respiratory organs resulting in coughing.

could (kŏod): see CAN[2].

cou·loir (kōolwăr') *n.* Deep mountain gorge or gully. [Fr., *couler*, flow, f. L. *colare*, strain, filter]

cou·lomb (kōo'lŏm, kōolŏm') *n.* Quantity of electricity conveyed in 1 second by current of 1 ampere (abbrev. C). [f. COULOMB].

Cou·lomb (kōo'lŏm, kōolŏm'; Fr. kōolawṅ'), **Charles Augustin de** (1736–1806). French physicist, experimented with electricity, magnetism, etc.; inventor of method of measuring the quantity of electricity.

coun·cil (kown'sil) *n.* 1. Ecclesiastical assembly for regulating doctrine or discipline in church; (New Testament) Jewish Sanhedrin. 2. Advisory or deliberative assembly. 3. (Governmental) assembly or group acting in deliberative, advisory, or supervisory capacity. 4. ∼ **of war**, assembly of military or naval officers called to consult with general etc., usu. in special emergency (freq. fig.). 5.

coun'cilman, coun'cilwoman, member of town or city council. **coun·ci·lor** (kown'siler, -sler) *n.* Official member of a council.

coun·sel (kown'sel) *n.* 1. Consultation; advice; **keep one's (own)** ∼, be reticent about one's intention or opinions. 2. Lawyer or legal advisers in cause, esp. a court case. **counsel** *v.t.* (**-seled, -sel·ing**, Brit. **-selled, -sel·ling**). Advise; recommend. **coun·se·lor** (kown'seler, -sler) *n.* Adviser in school, college, camp, or other institution; (also ∼**-at-law**) attorney.

count[1] (kownt) *v.* 1. Enumerate, reckon (*up*); repeat numerals in order; include, be included, in reckoning; ∼ **down** (**count'down** *n.*) count in reverse from a given number to zero, usu. in seconds, to mark lapse of time before an event, esp. firing of explosive or missile, launching of spacecraft etc. 2. ∼ **out**, count while taking from a stock; declare (boxer) to have lost fight by counting ten seconds before he rises to resume fight; (colloq.) remove from consideration, exclude. 3. Esteem, account, consider; be reckoned; enter into account or reckoning; ∼ **on**, depend or rely on, expect with assurance. **count** *n.* 1. Counting; sum total. 2. (boxing) Counting of ten seconds (time allowed for boxer who has been knocked down to rise and resume fighting or be declared loser). 3. (textiles) Number indicating the fineness of yarn, usu. based on the length of yarn that amounts to a given weight. 4. (law) Each charge in an indictment.

count'a·ble *adj.*

count[2] (kownt) *n.* (in so European countries) Noblem corresp. to English *earl*.

coun·te·nance (kown'tenans Expression of face; face; comp sure; moral support. ∼ (**-nanced, -nanc·ing**). Sanct encourage.

count·er[1] (kown'ter) *n.* (esp.) Small usu. round piece of me ivory, etc., used for keeping co in games of chance, esp. car imitation coin. 2. Banker's merchant's table; table or surface on which money is count business is transacted, or food a drink are served; **under the** clandestinely (esp. illegally).

count·er[2] (kown'ter) *n.* 1. P of horse's chest between should and under neck. 2. (naut.) Curv part of stern of ship. 3. Depress part of face of printing type, co or medal. 4. (fencing) Circu parry, parry in which hand reta same position while point describ circle. 5. (boxing) Blow deliver while receiving or parrying anoth 6. (shoemaking) Stiff mater forming back part of shoe or b around the heel. ∼ *adj.* Oppos opposite. ∼ *adv.* In the oppos direction; contrary. ∼ *v.* Oppo contradict, controvert; meet w counter move; (boxing) give retu blow while receiving or deflecti opponent's blow.

counter- *prefix.* 1. Agair opposite. 2. In reversal. 3. reciprocation or reply. 4. opposite member or constituent. With contrary action etc. 6. (mu = CONTRA-.

coun·ter·act (kownterăk kown'terăkt) *v.t.* Hinder, defeat, contrary action; neutralize. **cou ter·ac·tion** *n.* **coun·ter·ac·ti** *adj.*

coun·ter·at·tack (*v.* kownte tăk'; *n.* kown'teratăk). Attack reply to enemy's attack.

coun·ter·bal·ance (kown't bălans) *n.* Weight balanc another. **counterbal'ance** (**-anced, -anc·ing**). Act counterbalance to.

coun·ter·claim (kown'terklā *n.* Claim set up against anoth claim by defendant in su **counterclaim'** *v.* Claim agai plaintiff or prior claim.

coun·ter·clock·wise (kownt klŏk'wīz) *adv.* & *adj.* Moving curve from right to left as se from center, i.e. opposite to t hands of a clock.

coun·ter·cul·ture (kown't kŭlcher) *n.* Mode of life of persc

iberately rejecting established
ial values and practices.

coun·ter·es·pi·o·nage (kown-
ĕs´pēonahzh, -nĭj) n. Espionage
detect and frustrate an enemy spy
stem.

coun·ter·feit (kown´terfĭt) adj.
n. (Thing) made in imitation,
t genuine (esp. money bill or
n). ~ v.t. Make a counterfeit
(esp. bill or coin); imitate
udulently; resemble closely.
un´ter·feit·er n.

coun·ter·in·tel·li·gence (kown-
ĭntĕl´ĭjens) n. = COUNTER-
PIONAGE.

coun·ter·ir·ri·tant (kownter-
tant) n. (med.) Thing used to
oduce surface irritation and thus
unteract symptoms of disease
so fig.).

coun·ter·mand (kownter-
nd´, -mahnd´, kown´termănd,
ahnd) v.t. Revoke (command);
all by contrary order; cancel
ler for. **coun´termand** n.
der revoking previous one.

coun·ter·march (n. kown´ter-
rch; v. kowntermārch´, kown´-
märch). (Cause to) march in
trary direction.

coun·ter·pane kown´terpān) n.
verlet, bedspread.

coun·ter·part (kown´terpärt) n.
plicate; person, thing, forming
ural complement to another.

coun·ter·plot (kown´terplŏt) n.
t contrived to defeat another.
unterplot (kownterplŏt´, kown´-
plŏt) v. (-**plot·ted, -plot·ting**).
ustrate by, devise, counterplot.

coun·ter·point (kown´terpoint)
(mus.) Melody added as

accompaniment to given melody;
art of adding one or more melodies
as accompaniment to given melody
according to certain fixed rules; this
style of composition.

 coun·ter·poise (kown´terpoiz)

*Launch pad 39–A at the John F.
Kennedy Space Center, Cape Canav-
eral, Florida. The space shuttle awaits
the **countdown** which will activate the
vast propulsion turbines to thrust the
shuttle into space.*

*the Christian church an ecumenical
general **council** is a meeting of the
hops of the entire church. The
cond Vatican Council was convened
Pope John XXIII in 1962 and con-
ued by Pope Paul VI.*

1 Highland
2 Grampian
3 Tayside
4 Central
5 Fife
6 Strathclyde
7 Lothian
8 Borders
9 Dumfries and Galloway
10 Londonderry
11 Antrim
12 Tyrone
13 Fermanagh
14 Armargh
15 Down
16 Cumbria
17 Northumberland
18 Durham
19 Tyne and Wear
20 Cleveland
21 North Yorkshire
22 Lancashire
23 West Yorkshire
24 Humberside
25 Merseyside
26 Greater Manchester
27 South Yorkshire

28 Lincolnshire
29 Nottinghamshire
30 Derbyshire
31 Cheshire
32 Clwyd
33 Gwynedd
34 Powys
35 Salop
36 Staffordshire
37 Leicestershire
38 Cambridgeshire
39 Norfolk
40 Suffolk
41 Essex
42 Hertfordshire
43 Bedfordshire
44 Northampton
45 Warwickshire
46 West Midlands
47 Hereford and Worcester
48 Gwent

49 South Glamorg
50 Mid Glamorgan
51 West Glamorga
52 Dyfed
53 Avon
54 Gloucestershire
55 Oxfordshire
56 Buckinghamshir
57 Greater London
58 Kent
59 East Sussex
60 West Sussex
61 Surrey
62 Berkshire
63 Hampshire
64 Wiltshire
65 Dorset
66 Somerset
67 Devon
68 Cornwall

The present day **counties** *of Great Britain evolved from the ancient shires of the 10th century, which remained virtually unchanged until the 19th century when the Local Government Act of 1888 established county councils, each with an administrative area. The function of county councils is to provide local services.*

n. Counterbalancing weight; thing of equivalent force etc. on opposite side; equilibrium. ~ *v.t.* (**-poised, -pois·ing**). Counterbalance; compensate; bring into, keep in, equilibrium.

coun · ter · ref · or · ma · tion (kownterrĕfermāˊshon) *n.* Reformation running counter to another; C~ R~, (hist.) reformation in the R. C. Ch. during the latter part of the 16th c, after the Protestant Reformation, initiated by the Council of TRENT[2].

coun·ter·rev·o·lu·tion (kownˊterrĕvolooˊshon) *n.* Revolution reversing results of previous revolution. **coun′ter·rev·o·lu·tion·ar·y** *adj.* & *n.* (pl. **-aries**).

coun·ter·sign[1] (kownˊtersīn) *n.*

Watchword, password, given to person on guard.

coun · ter · sign[2] (kownˊtersīn, kowntersīnˊ) *v.t.* Add signature to (document already signed); ratify. **coun·ter·sig·na·ture** (kownter-sigˊnacher, kownˊtersig-) *n.*

coun·ter·sink (kownˊtersingk, kowntersingkˊ) *v.t.* (**-sank, -sunk, -sink·ing**). Bevel off (top of hole) to receive head of screw or bolt; sink (screwhead) in such hole, so as to lie flush with surface. **coun′ter-sunk** *adj.* (esp., of screw) With head beveled for this purpose.

coun·ter·spy (kownˊterspī) *n.* (pl. **-spies**). Spy engaged in counterespionage.

coun·ter·ten·or (kownˊtertĕner) *n.* (mus.) (Part for, singer with)

male voice above that of tenor.

coun·ter·vail (kowntervālˊ) *v.* Counterbalance; avail against.

count·ess (kownˊtĭs) *n.* Wif widow, of count or (in Gt. Britai earl; lady ranking with count or ea in her own right.

count·ing (kownˊtĭng) **house** Building, room, devoted to keepin accounts.

count·less (kowntˊlĭs) *adj.* To many to count.

coun·tri·fied (kŭnˊtrĭfīd) *ad* Rural, rustic; unsophisticated.

coun·try (kŭnˊtrē) *n.* (pl. **-tries** 1. Region; territory of nation; lan of person's birth, citizenship, etc fatherland. 2. Rural districts a opp. to towns; rest of a land a opp. to capital; ~ **club**, suburba

b for golf, tennis, other sports,
ial activities, etc.; ~ **cousin**,
ation of countrified manners or
earance; ~ **gentleman**, owner
an estate in the country; ~
use, house in country, esp.
idence of country gentleman; ~
usic, simple music, usu. with
timental lyrics, originating in
southern U.S., based on folk
d cowboy songs, spirituals and
spel music, and blues, usu. sung
the accompaniment of such
truments as guitar, banjo, man-
lin, and fiddle; **coun'tryside**,
ral district, its inhabitants.

coun·try·man (kŭn'trĭman) *n.*
. **-men** pr. -men). (fem.
un·try·wom·an pr. kŭn'trĭwōō-
an, pl. **-wom·en** pr. -wĭmĭn) 1.
rson of one's own (or a specified)
untry. 2. Person living in rural
rts.

coun·ty (kown'tē) *n.* (pl. **-ties**).
Administrative division of a state.
Territorial division of Gt. Britain
d Ireland exercising administra-
e, judicial, and political func-
ns. 3. People of county. 4. ~
ent, official who represents
deral and state governments in
vising residents of rural regions
farming practices, agricultural
arketing, home economics, etc.;
court, county judicial court; ~
at, town in which business of
unty is transacted.

coup (koō) *n.* (pl. **coups** pr.
ōz). Notable or successful stroke
move; a coup d'état; ~ **d'état**,
dden and decisive political stroke,
p. violent or illegal change of
vernment; ~ **de grâce**, finishing
oke; deathblow administered to
ing person.

coupe (koōp), **cou·pé** (koōpā')
Four-wheeled closed carriage
th inside seat for two and outside
at for driver; closed two-door
tomobile with a sloping back.

cou·ple (kŭp'el) *n.* Pair; wedded
engaged pair; pair of partners in
nce; two. ~ *v.* (**-pled, -pling**).
sten, link, together; connect
evice) to other mechanism; con-
ct (railroad cars) by a coupling;
ite, bring together, in pair(s);
sociate in thought or speech;
pulate. **cou·pler** (kŭp'ler) *n.*
sp.) Device for coupling two rail-
ad cars; contrivance for connect-
g two keyboards in an organ etc.
they both sound when one is
ayed.

cou·plet (kŭp'lĭt) *n.* 1. Pair of
ccessive lines of verse, esp. when
yming together and of same
ngth. 2. Two similar things; pair.

cou·pling (kŭp'lĭng) *n.* (esp.)
ain or link connecting two rail-
ad cars, etc.; act of coupling.

cou·pon (koō'pŏn, kū'-) *n.* De-
chable part of ticket, advertise-
ent, or other certificate entitling
lder to some refund, gift, bond

interest, service, etc., or as inquiry
form, entry form for a competition,
etc.

cour·age (kĕr'ĭj, kŭr'-) *n.*
Bravery, boldness; fortitude.

cou·ra·geous (kurā'jus) *adj.*
Brave, fearless. **cou·ra'geous·ly**
adv. **cou·ra'geous·ness** *n.*

Cour·bet (koorbĕ'), **Gustave**
(1819–77). French painter associated with realist school.

cou·ri·er (kĕr'ēer, koor'-) *n.*
Special messenger.

course (kōrs, kôrs) *n.* 1.
Onward movement; line or direction taken or planned; career;
habitual or ordinary manner of
procedure. 2. Ground on which
race is run etc.; golf links; line to
be taken in race. 3. Watercourse.
4. Planned or prescribed series of
actions or proceedings, as of
lectures, study, diet, etc. 5. Each
of successive divisions of meal,
consisting of one dish or several.
6. (building) Single continuous
layer of bricks, stones, etc., of same
height throughout; row of slates,
tiles, etc. 7. (naut.) Sail attached to
lower yards of ship. 8. **in due** ~,
in the natural order; **in the ~ of**,
during; **of** ~, naturally, inevitably.
course *v.* (**coursed, cours·ing**).
Pursue (game, esp. hares) with
hounds; run about, run. **cours'er**
n. (poet). Swift horse.

court[1] (kōrt, kôrt) *n.* 1. Open
area surrounded by walls of buildings; confined yard opening off
street; enclosed quadrangle, open
or covered, plot of ground marked
off for games (as for basketball,
tennis, etc.). 2. Sovereign's
residence; his establishment and
retinue; the body of courtiers;
sovereign and his counselors as
ruling power. 3. Formal assembly

held by sovereign at his residence.
4. Assembly of judges or other
persons acting as tribunal, e.g.
Court of Appeals, to hear and determine any cause; place in which
justice is administered; session of
judicial assembly; **out of** ~, without a legal trial. 5. Attention paid
to one whose favor, affection, or
interest is sought. 6. **court'house**,
building in which courts of law are
held; seat of government of a
county; **court-martial** (pl. ~**s-
martial**), trial of military personnel of any rank, conducted by
officers, for offenses against
military law; **court-martial** (*v.t.*)
(**-tialed, -tial·ing**), try by court
martial; **court'room**, room where
sessions of a law court are held;
court'yard, open space surrounded by walls or buildings.

court[2] (kōrt, kôrt) *v.* Pay court
(to); try to win favor or affection
(of); try to attract sexually; seek to
win (applause etc.); invite, tempt.

cour·te·ous (kĕr'tēus) *adj.*
Polite, kind, considerate, in manner
or address. **cour'te·ous·ly** *adv.*
cour'te·ous·ness *n.*

cour·te·san, cour·te·zan (kôr'-
tezan, kĕr', -zăn) *ns.* Prostitute or
kept woman, esp. one associating
with men of rank or wealth. [It.
cortigiana, orig. woman attached to
the court]

cour·te·sy (kĕr'tesē) *n.* (pl.
-sies). Courteous behavior or disposition; courteous act.

cour·ti·er (kōr'tēer, kôr'-) *n.*

*The **courtyard** was a common feature
of the grand houses of Tudor and Stuart
England, such as Lacock Abbey in
Wiltshire. In ancient times both the
Greeks and Romans built their villas
around a courtyard.*

Attendant at, frequenter of, sovereign's court.

court·ly (kōrt'lē) *adj.* (**-li·er, -li·est**). Polished, refined, in manners; obsequious, flattering. **court'li·ness** *n.*

court·ship (kōrt'shĭp, kôrt'-) *n.* (Period of) courting.

cous·cous (kōōs'kōōs) *n.* N. Afr. dish of crushed grain steamed with meat and vegetables. [Arab. *kuskus*, f. *kaskasa* bruise, pound small]

cous·in (kŭz'ĭn) *n.* 1. Child of one's uncle or aunt (also **first** ~); **second** ~, one's parent's first cousin's child. 2. Member of kindred group. **cous'in·ly** *adv.* & *adj.*

Cous·teau (kōōstō'), **Jacques** (1910–). French undersea explorer; developer of scuba-diving apparatus.

cou·ture (kōōtoor', -tūr') *n.* Fashionable dressmaking or designing; clothes made thus. **cou·tu·ri·er** (kōōtoor'ēā, -ēer, -toor'yā) *n.* (fem. **-tu·ri·ère** pr. -toor'ēer, -ēār) Fashion designer.

co·va·lence (kōvā'lens) *n.* (chem.) Covalent bond (see VALENCE); electrons forming this; number of covalent bonds an atom can form. **co·va'lent** *adj.* **co·va'lent·ly** *adv.*

cove[1] (kōv) *n.* Small bay; sheltered recess; (archit.) concave arch, curved junction of wall with ceiling. ~ *v.t.* (**coved, cov·ing**). Arch; slope inward.

cove[2] (kōv) *n.* (Brit. slang) Fellow, chap.

cov·en (kŭv'en, kō'ven) *n.* Assembly of witches.

cov·e·nant (kŭv'enant) *n.* Compact, bargain; (law) formal, sealed contract, clause of this; (bibl.) compact between God and the Israelites. ~ *v.* Make covenant (with). **cov·e·nan·tal** (kŭvenăn'tal) *adj.* **cov'e·nan·ter** *n.*

Cov·en·try (kŭv'entrē). City in central England noted for its modern cathedral; **send (person) to** ~, (chiefly Brit.) refuse to associate with or speak to him or her.

cov·er (kŭv'er) *v.t.* 1. Put or lay something over; put covering on. 2. Be over whole top of. 3. (of stallion etc.) Copulate with. 4. Conceal or shield; have gun, pistol, etc., trained on. 5. Include, provide for. 6. Extend or stretch over; traverse (distance). 7. Defray (expense etc.); protect by insurance; report for newspaper etc. 8. **covered wagon**, large wagon with

Couture houses, where clothes are specially designed and tailored for wealthy and fashion-conscious clients. New fashions originate in spring and fall 'collections' where models show the clothes to the press and public (above). In this painting (right) clients are seen ordering clothes at the house of Paquin, Paris, in 1907.

...ched canvas top, used by Amer. ...oneers going west during the 19th ...; **covering letter**, one sent along ...ith another document to explain

cov·er·ing *n.* (esp.) Cover. ...ver *n.* 1. Thing that covers; lid; ...nding of book, either board of ...is; wrapper, envelope, of letter. ... Protection; shelter. 3. Screen, ...etense, esp. for a spy. 4. Woods ... undergrowth sheltering game, ...vert. 5. ~ **charge**, fixed charge ...r entertainment added to cost of ...od and drink at a night club; ~ **...op**, crop grown to protect soil ...om leaching or eroding or to ...rich soil. **cov·er·age** (kŭv′erĭj, ...ĭv′rĭj) *n.*

Cov·er·dale (kō′verdāl, kŭv′-), **...iles** (1488–1568). English ...rotestant bishop; made first ...nglish translation of the entire ...ible and Apocrypha (from ...erman and Latin versions).

cov·er·let (kŭv′erlĭt) *n.* Bed-...read.

cov·ert[1] (kŭv′ert, kō′vert) *n.* 1. ...helter, esp. thicket hiding game; ~ **cloth**, twilled cloth of cotton, ...oolen, or worsted material having ...speckled appearance and used for ...oats and suits. 2. One of the ...eathers covering the bases of a ...ird's wing and tail feathers.

cov·ert[2] (kō′vert, kŭv′ert) *adj.* ...oncealed, hidden, secret, dis-...uised. **cov·ert·ly** *adv.* **cov·ert·...ess** *n.*

cov·er·ture (kŭv′ercher) *n.* ...overing; condition of married ...oman under husband's protec-...on.

The **covert** feathers on the wings of a bird cover the base of the primary and secondary flight feathers and the tail feathers. They are small and soft, and have a protective function.

cov·et (kŭv′ĭt) *v.t.* Desire eagerly and wrongfully (usu. what belongs to another), as in Tenth Commandment: "Thou shalt not covet...." **cov·et·a·ble** *adj.*

cov·et·ous (kŭv′ĭtus) *adj.* Eager-ly desirous (*of*); grasping, avaricious. **cov′et·ous·ly** *adv.* **cov′et·ous·ness** *n.*

cov·ey (kŭv′ē) *n.* (pl. **-eys**). Brood of partridges; family, party, set.

cow[1] (kow) *n.* Female of any bovine animal, esp. of the domestic species (*Bos taurus*); female of elephant, moose, whale, seal, etc.; (slang) fat, slovenly woman; **cow′-bird**, any of various American blackbirds, esp. *Molothrus ater*, that lay their eggs in other birds' nests; **cow′boy**, man, formerly on horse-back, who drives and tends cattle on a ranch, esp. in the western U.S.; man who demonstrates at rodeos the skills of cowboys, including feats of horsemanship, cattle

A **cowboy** *shows his bulldogging style at a rodeo as he tackles a writhing steer. Rodeos test the individual skills of cowboys to the limit.*

roping, etc.; (slang) reckless auto-mobile driver; **cow'catcher**, frame fixed in front of locomotive or streetcar to remove cattle and other obstructions from tracks; **cow'-hand**, cowboy; **cow'herd**, one who herds or tends cattle; **cow'hide**, (leather, whip, made of) cow's hide; **cow'lick**, habitually protruding lock of hair; **cow'poke**, (colloq.) cowboy; **cow'pox**, vaccine disease appearing as bluish or livid vesicles on teats of cows; **cow'puncher**, (colloq.) cowboy.

cow² (kow) *v.t.* Intimidate.

cow·ard (kow′erd) *adj. & n.* Fainthearted, pusillanimous (person). **cow'ard·ly** *adv.* **cow'ard·li·ness** *n.* [OF. *coard*, f. L. *cauda* tail]

Cow·ard (kow′erd), **Noël** (1899–1973). English playwright, actor, composer of light music, and librettist.

cow·ard·ice (kow′erdĭs) *n.* Faintheartedness.

cow·er (kow′er) *v.i.* Crouch, esp. in fear. **cow'er·ing·ly** *adv.*

cowl (kowl) *n.* 1. Monk's hooded garment; hood of this. 2. Hood-shaped covering (freq. turning with wind) of top of chimney or ventilating shaft to assist ventilation. **cowled** *adj.*

cowl·ing (kow′lĭng) *n.* Metal housing or cover for an airplane engine.

Cow·per (kōō′per, kou′-), **William** (1731–1800). English lyric poet and hymn writer.

cow·rie, cow·ry (kow′rē) *ns.* (pl. **-ries**). Porcelainlike shell of small gastropod (*Cyprea moneta*) of Indian Ocean, used as money in parts of Africa and southern Asia; this animal, or any gastropod (or shell) of genus *Cyprea*, of oval shape, with undeveloped spine and narrow aperture as long as shell. [Hind. *kauri*]

In the milk of the **cow,** *sugar, cream and protein content are about equal. It is less creamy than goat's milk and less sweet than ass's milk. With cows bred for milk, efforts are made to increase cream content.*

cow·slip (kow′slĭp) *n.* 1. Wild plant (*Primula veris*) growing in pastures etc. and flowering in spring, with drooping umbels of fragrant yellow flowers. 2. MARSH marigold.

cox (kŏks) *n.* (pl. **cox·es**) & *v.* (Act as) coxswain.

cox·a (kŏk′sa) *n.* (pl. **cox·ae** pr. kŏk′sē). Hip; (zool.) similar joint in insects etc.

cox·comb (kŏks′kōm) *n.* Conceited dandy; fop. **cox'comb·ry** *n.* (pl. **-ries**). Foppery; pretension of manner. [= *cock's comb*]

cox·swain (kŏk′sin, -swān) *n.* Helmsman of boat; person on board ship in charge of ship's boat and crew. [f. *cock* = cockboat + *swain*]

coy (koi) *adj.* Shy, esp. affectedly or archly so. **coy'ly** *adv.* **coy'ness** *n.*

coy·o·te (kīō′tē, kī′ōt) *n.* (pl. **-o·tes** pr. -ō′tēz, -ōts; collect. **-o·te**). Wolflike animal (*Canis latrans*) of western N. Amer.; (slang) sneaky, contemptible person. [Mex. Sp. f. Nahautl *coyotl*]

coy·pu (koi′pōō) *n.* (pl. **-pus**, collect. **-pu**) = NUTRIA.

coz·en (kŭz′in) *v.t.* (archaic) Cheat, swindle (*out of*); beguile (*into*). **coz'en·age** *n.*

co·zy, co·sy (kō′zē) *adjs.* (**-zi·er**, **-zi·est**, **-si·er**, **-si·est**). Comfortable, snug. ~ *n.* (pl. **-zies**, **-sies**). Covering of (padded) material to retain heat in a teapot. **co'zi·ly** *adv.* **co'zi·ness** *n.*

cp. *abbrev.* Compare.

C.P. *abbrev.* Communist Party; Common Prayer; command post.

c.p. *abbrev.* Candlepower.

The **cowslip** *is a primrose with fragra yellow flowers, which blooms in ea spring. The marsh marigold, whi grows in swamps, is called a cowslip N. America.*

C.P.A. *abbrev.* Certified pub accountant.

CPFF *abbrev.* Cost plus fix fee.

Cpl *abbrev.* Corporal.

CPO *abbrev.* Chief petty office

cps *abbrev.* Cycles per secon

Cr *symbol.* Chromium.

crab (krăb) *n.* 1. Any of vario decapod crustaceans, mostly of t group Brachyura, with abdom short and bent under thorax, t first legs being pincers, esp. edib species found on or near seacoas 2. **the C**~: see CANCER. 3. Cro peevish person. 4. Machine (or with claws) for hoisting hea weights. 5. (pl.) Lowest throw a pair of dice, in most games, tw 6. (rowing) **catch a** ~, make fau stroke by which oar becom jammed under water. 7. ~ **gras** annual creeping grass infesti lawns; ~ **louse**, parasitical inse (*Phthirus pubis*) infesting hum body. **crab** *v.* (**crabbed, crab ing**). 1. Catch or hunt crabs. (Cause to) move sideways or oblique course. 3. (colloq.) Crit cize adversely; complain; interfe with. **crab'ber** *n.* **crab'by** ac (**-bi·er, -bi·est**). Morose; irritab **crab'bi·ly** *adv.* **crab'bi·ness** *n.*

crab (krăb) **apple.** Wild app (*Malus coronaria*), or a cultivat variety having similar sour, hars astringent quality.

crab·bed (krăb′ĭd) *adj.* I tempered; perverse; complicate difficult to interpret; (of han writing) hard to decipher. **crab bed·ly** *adv.* **crab'bed·ness** *n.*

crack (krăk) *v.* 1. (Cause t

The **coyote,** which is noted for its mournful howls, is found on the plains of N. America. It is an intelligent animal with a reputation for cunning and swiftness.

The **cowrie** shell, usually found in warm waters, has been used as currency for many centuries. The dowry for a bride in West Africa was once set at 100,000 cowries.

make sharp or explosive noise; utter (joke). 2. Break with sudden sharp report; break without complete separation of parts; collapse, break down; break open (a safe) in order to steal the contents. 3. Render (voice) dissonant; (of voice) become dissonant. 4. Split up (petroleum etc.) by heat and catalysts to produce lighter hydrocarbons (as gasoline). 5. (slang) **get cracking,** start; **crack up,** suffer breakdown; have a fit of laughing; crash automobile. 6. **crack'brained,** crazy. **crack** n. 1. Sudden sharp noise, as of whip, rifle, thunder; sharp blow; **have a ~ at,** (colloq.) make an attempt at. 2. Instant; break (of dawn, day). 3. Fissure formed by breakage; partial fracture (the parts still cohering); narrow opening formed by breaking; = CHINK[1]. 4. (slang) Sharp, cutting, or witty remark, also **wise'crack; crack'-pot,** eccentric or impractical person). **crack** adj. (colloq.) First-rate.

cracked (krăkt) adj. (esp., slang) Crazy.

crack·er (krăk'er) n. (esp.) 1. Instrument for cracking, esp. nutcracker. 2. Thin crisp biscuit or wafer, usu. made of unleavened dough. 3. (southern U.S. derog.) Poor white, esp. in Georgia and Florida. 4. (pl., as pred. adj.; slang) Crazy.

crack·er·jack (krăk'erjăk) n. & adj. (slang) Exceptionally fine or splendid (person or thing).

crack·le (krăk'el) v.i. (**-led, -ling**). Emit slight continuous cracking sound. ~ n. 1. Crackling. 2. China or pottery glaze with minute cracks all over surface. **crack·ly** (krăk'lē) adj. (**-li·er, -li·est**).

crack·ling (krăk'lĭng) n. (esp.) Crisp skin of roast pork.

Appetizing cooked **crab,** Fisherman's Wharf, San Francisco. Crabs range from species the size of a pea to the giant crab with legs spanning over 8 ft. The fiddler crab has an enormous claw which it waves to attract females. Hermit crabs can withdraw inside the discarded shells of univalves.

Cra·cow (kră'kow, krah'kow): see KRAKOW.

-cracy comb. form. Government, ruling body, influential class, etc. (bureaucracy, aristocracy).

cra·dle (krā'del) n. 1. Small, low bed for infant, esp. one on rockers; (fig.) place in which thing is nurtured in earliest stage; ~ **song,** lullaby. 2. Framework resembling cradle, esp. stage suspended from scaffolding for manual workers; framework on which ship rests during construction or repairs; light wooden frame attached to scythe to catch grain and lay it flat as it is cut; protective or supporting framework for injured limb etc.; support for telephone receiver not in use; (mining) trough on rockers in which gold-bearing material is shaken in water to separate the gold. **cradle** v.t. (**-dled, -dling**). Place in cradle; contain or shelter as cradle; reap (grain) with scythe fitted with cradle.

craft (krăft, krahft) n. 1. Skill; cunning, deceit. 2. Art, trade; members of a trade. 3. (pl. same) Boat, vessel; aircraft, spacecraft. **crafts'man** n. (pl. **-men**) (also **craftsperson**). One who practices a craft, artisan; skilled person. **crafts'man·ship** n.

craft·y (krăf'tē, krahf'-) adj. (**craft·i·er, craft·i·est**). Cunning, artful, wily. **craft'i·ly** adv. **craft'-i·ness** n.

crag (krăg) n. Steep projecting rock forming part of cliff or headland. **crag'gy** adj. (**-gi·er, -gi·est**). **crag'gi·ness** n.

cram (krăm) v. (**crammed, cram·ming**). 1. Fill overfull; force (into, down); stuff (with food); eat greedily. 2. (colloq.) Prepare intensively for examination; learn (subject) by intensive study. **cram'mer** n.

cramp[1] (krămp) n. Sudden painful involuntary contraction of muscles from chill, slight strain, etc.; **writer's** ~: see WRITER. **cramp** v.t. 1. Affect with cramp. 2. Confine narrowly; restrict.

cramp[2] (krămp) n. Metal bar with bent ends for holding masonry etc. together; frame with movable part (also ~ **iron**) that can be fixed for pressing pieces of wood etc. together for joining; restraint. **cramp** v.t. Fasten with cramp.

cram·pon (krăm'pŏn), **cram·-poon** (krămpoon') ns. Iron spike attached to boot for climbing over ice etc.; grappling iron.

Cra·nach (krah'nahx), **Lucas** (1472–1553). German painter and engraver during the Renaissance.

cran·ber·ry (krăn'bĕrē, -berē) n. (pl. **-ries**). Small bright-red tart berry, fruit of N. Amer. dwarf shrub (Vaccinium macrocarpon); ~ **sauce**, sauce made from this berry.

crane (krān) n. 1. Large wading bird with very long legs, neck, and bill, esp. the ashy-gray common European crane (Grus cinerea), the whooping crane (G. americana), and the sandhill crane (G. canadensis). 2. Machine for raising and lowering heavy weights, usu. post rotating on vertical axis with projecting arm or jib over the end of which runs a cable on which the

Cramps are used for holding together parts of a brick wall, masonry or lengths of timber. The G cramp for smaller work has an adjustable screw. The sash cramp moves on a metal bar.

Cranberry vines are flooded to preve[nt] crops being blighted by frost. The bu[lk] of the harvest is canned for sauce to b[e] added as a relish to meat dishes, especially turkey.

An electric transporter **crane**. Transporter cranes are used for shifting bulk cargoes on a large scale; those shown (at Birkenhead, U.K.) are designed for unloading.

Crafts are still carried out in man[y] countries without the aid of sophisti[-]cated machinery. These copper pots displayed here in a market at Bahrain are made by individual craftsmen employing traditional methods.

An Australian brolga (left) and the ra
American whooping **crane**, now almo
extinct. The common crane (Grus gru
is over 3½ ft. from beak to tail,
migratory and inhabits marshland.

crap·u·lent (krăp′yulent) ad
Given to, suffering from effect o
resulting from, overdrinking o
overeating.   **crap′u·lence** n
crap′u·lous adj.

crash[1] (krăsh) n. Loud noise a
of hard body or bodies broken b
violent percussion, or of thunde
loud music, etc.; violent percussio
or breakage; crashing of aircraf
car, etc.; (fig.) sudden ruin o
collapse, esp. financial; (attrib. or a
adj.) rapid, intensive (course, pro
gram, etc.); ~ **dive** (n.), ~**-div**
(v.i.) (**-dived, -div·ing**), (of sub
marine) (make) sudden and stee
dive; ~ **helmet**, helmet worn a
protection in case of crashing; ~
landing, emergency aircraft land
ing that damages aircraft; s
~**-land** (v.i.); ~ **pad**, (slang) plac
to sleep, esp. in emergency. **crash**
v. Make a crash; move, go, drive
throw, with a crash; (of aircraft) fall
cause to fall, violently to earth
(cause car etc. to) come violentl
into collision with vehicle o
obstacle; (fig.) fail, esp. financially
(colloq.) attend (a party) withou
invitation.

crash[2] (krăsh) n. Coarse wover
fabric of linen or cotton. [Russ
krashenína colored linen (krásk
color, dye)]

crass (krăs) adj. Thick, gross

weight may be suspended. 3. ~ **fly**,
two-winged long-legged fly of
genus *Tipula*, daddy-longlegs;
cranesbill, species of wild geranium (from the long slender beak of
the fruit). **crane** v. (**craned,
cran·ing**). Stretch (neck), stretch
neck like crane.

Crane[1] (krān), (**Harold**) **Hart**
(1899–1932). Amer. poet, author of
"The Bridge" etc.

Crane[2] (krān), **Stephen** (1871–
1900). Amer. novelist, short-story
writer, and war correspondent in
Cuba and Greece, 1896–8; best
known for his novel *The Red Badge
of Courage*, a realistic account of the
common man under fire in the Civil
War, and his short stories "The
Open Boat," "The Bride Comes to
Yellow Sky," and "The Blue
Hotel."

cra·ni·al (krā′nēal) adj. Of the
cranium; ~ **index**, ratio of length
of skull to its width, multiplied by
100; ~ **nerve**, any member of 12
pairs of nerves attached to brain and
serving regions of head and neck.

cra·ni·um (krā′nēum) n. Skull.

crank[1] (krăngk) n. Part of axis
bent at right angles for converting
reciprocal into circular motion, or
vice versa; **crank′case**, case covering crankshaft of reciprocating

engine; **crank′shaft**, shaft driven
by crank. **crank** v. 1. Bend in
shape of crank; attach crank to. 2.
(also ~ **up**) Start (engine) by
turning crank.

crank[2] (krăngk) n. Eccentric
person, esp. one enthusiastically
possessed by idea etc; grouchy
person. **crank′y** adj. (**crank·i·er,
crank·i·est**). (esp.) Ill-tempered.
crank′i·ly adv. **crank′i·ness** n.

cran·ny (krăn′ē) n. (pl. **-nies**).
Chink, crevice. **cran′nied** adj.

crap[1] (krăp) n. (vulgar) 1. Feces.
2. Nonsense; junk, rubbish. ~ v.i.
(**crapped, crap′ping**). (vulgar)
Defecate. **crap′py** adj. (**-pi·er,
-pi·est**).

crap[2] (krăp) v.i. (**crapped,
crap′ping**). Make losing throw of
2, 3, or 12 in craps. ~ n. Such
a throw; ~ **game**, game of craps;
~ **out**, be unsuccessful, withdraw
from game etc.

crap·pie (krăp′ē) n. Either of
two sunfishes, **black** ~ (*Pomoxis
nigromaculatis*) and **white** ~ (*P.
annularis*) good game and eating
fishes.

craps (krăps) n. (usu. considered
sing.) Game of chance played with
two dice; **shoot** ~, play this game;
crap′shooter, one who plays
craps.

*The bright blue meadow **crane's-bill**
which grows 1 to 2 ft. high is one of
numerous types of crane's-bill. The
multi-flowered varieties (geraniums) are
often cultivated.*

ater Lake, formed in the collapsed
ter of the extinct volcano Mt.
zama. It is notable for its vivid blue
ter and Wizard Island, a volcanic
ne rising from its depths.

g.) gross; grossly stupid; un-
eling, unsensitive. **crass′ly** *adv.*
ass′ness *n.*

Cras·sus (krăs′us), **Marcus
cinius** (*c*112–53 B.C.). Roman
neral, member of 1st TRIUM-
ʀATE.

crate (krāt) *n.* Large wooden or
icker container for shipping or
oring, esp. fragile goods; (slang)
rcraft, vehicle (esp. old one). ~
t. (**crat·ed, crat·ing**). Pack in
ate.

cra·ter (krā′ter) *n.* I. Bowl- or
nnel-shaped hollow at top or side
volcano from which eruption
kes place; bowl-shaped cavity,
p. that formed by exploding shell
bomb, meteor, etc.

Cra·ter (krā′ter) **Lake.** Lake,
ooo ft. (610 m) deep, in the center
extinct volcano in SW. Oregon.

cra·vat (kravăt′) *n.* I. (archaic)
rnamental band with long flowing
ads, or handkerchief tied, with
ow in front, around neck outside
irt collar. 2. Scarf or necktie.
ʼr. *cravaté* f. Croatian *Hrvat*
roat]

crave (krāv) *v.* (**craved,
rav·ing**). Long for; beg, long, *for.*
rav′er *n.* **crav′ing** *n.* Strong
esire, intense longing.

cra·ven (krā′ven) *adj.* & *n.*
owardly, abject (person). **cra′-
en·ly** *adv.* **cra′ven·ness** *n.*

craw (kraw) *n.* Crop of bird or
asect; stomach of animal; **stick in
ne's** ~, be objectionable, be
nacceptable.

craw·fish (kraw′fish) *n.* (pl.
fish·es, collect. **-fish**): see
ʀAYFISH.

crawl[1] (krawl) *n.* Pen or
nclosure in shallow water for fish,
irtles, etc. [Dutch KRAAL]

crawl[2] (krawl) *v.* Move slowly
ith body on or close to ground,

op: Inside the **crater** of a volcano on
ulcano, the southernmost of the Lipari
les off Sicily. These islands were, with
tna, the first to which the word 'vol-
ano' was applied and were said to be
he seat of Vulcan, the Roman god of
re. Right: Mt. Kilimanjaro, the highest
ountain in Africa, now extinct as
volcano.

or on hands and knees; walk, move, slowly; creep abjectly; swim with crawl; swarm *with* crawling things; feel creepy sensation. ~ *n.* Crawling; (also **Australian** ~), fast swimming stroke in which arms execute alternate overarm movements and legs are kicked rapidly; ~ **space**, shallow space in a building, too low for person to stand in, but useful for storage, access to ducts etc. **crawl′er** *n.*

cray·fish (krā′fish) *n.* (pl. **-fish·es**, collect. **-fish**). Any small lobsterlike freshwater crustacean of the genera *Astacus* and *Cambarus*; similar crustacean, esp. the spiny lobster.

cray·on (krā′ŏn, -*on*) *n.* Stick of colored wax, charcoal, or chalk for drawing; drawing in crayons. ~ *v.t.* Draw with crayon(s).

craze (krāz) *v.* (**crazed, craz·ing**). 1. Drive, become insane or obsessed (usu. in past part.). 2. Produce small cracks in (glaze of pottery); have such cracks. ~ *n.* Mania; fad.

cra·zy (krā′zē) *adj.* (**-zi·er, -zi·est**). Mad, demented; insane; uncontrolled; extremely eager; (colloq.) foolish, wild, incredible, etc.; (colloq.) infatuated, enthusiastic (*about, for*). ~ **quilt**, patchwork quilt. **cra′zi·ly** *adv.* **cra′zi·ness** *n.*

Cra·zy (krā′zē) **Horse** (1849?–1877). Indian name, Tashunca-Uitco; Oglala Sioux chief and leader at the battle of Little Big Horn in which Gen. Custer was killed; surrendered and killed resisting imprisonment.

creak (krēk) *v.i.* & *n.* (Make) harsh shrill grating noise as of ungreased hinge etc. **creak′y** *adj.* (**creak·i·er, creak·i·est**). Tending to creak, full of creaks; frail; dilapidated; decrepit. **creak′i·ly** *adv.*

cream (krēm) *n.* 1. Fatty part of milk, which gathers on top, and by churning is made into butter. 2. Food like or made of cream; attrib., (of soup or sauce) containing milk or cream; (of candy, cookie, etc.) with creamy filling. 3. Creamlike substance, esp. cosmetic. 4. Best or choicest part of anything. 5. Part of liquid that gathers on top. 6. Cream color, yellowish-white. 7. ~ **of tartar**: see TARTAR. 8. ~ **pie, puff**, etc., pie, pastry, cake, etc. filled with cream or creamy custard etc.; ~ **cheese**, soft rich cheese made of unskimmed milk and cream; ~ **sherry**, full-bodied mellow sherry. **cream′y** *adj.* (**cream·i·er, cream·i·est**). **cream′i·ly** *adv.* **cream** *v.* Form cream or scum; cause (milk) to cream; take cream from (milk); take best part of; add cream to; treat (skin) with cosmetic cream; work (butter etc.) into creamy con-

The **crawl** style in swimming was dev oped by the Australian champion swi mer, Richard Cavill, who broke t world record for 100 yards in 19 using this stroke. He combined an alte nating over-arm movement with t rapid vertical action of the legs kno as the flutter kick. The style was furth refined by American swimming coache who slightly altered the leg action.

sistency; (slang) beat throughl defeat decisively.

cream·er (krē′mer) *n.* Machin for separating cream from mil small pitcher for cream. **cream er·y** (krē′merē) *n.* (pl. **-er·ies** Butter (and cheese) factory; stor where milk, cream, etc., are sold.

crease (krēs) *n.* 1. Line cause by folding; fold; wrinkle. (hockey) Area in front of goal. *v.* (**creased, creas·ing**). Mak creases in; fall into creases **creas′er** *n.*

cre·ate (krēāt′) *v.* (**-at·e -at·ing**). 1. Bring into existence give rise to; originate; design. Constitute, invest (person) wit rank. **cre·a·tive** (krēā′tĭv) *ad* **cre·a′tive·ly** *adv.* **cre·a′tive·ness cre·a·tiv·i·ty** (krēātĭv′ĭtē) *ns.*

cre·a·tine (krē′atēn, -tĭn) *n* Amino acid found in muscles o vertebrates.

cre·a·tion (krēā′shon) *n.* 1 Creating; **the C~**, God's prima act of bringing the world or uni verse into existence. 2. All create things. 3. Production of huma intelligence or power, esp. of the imagination.

cre·a·tor (krēā′ter) *n.* One wh creates; **the C~**, God.

crea·ture (krē′cher) *n.* Create thing; animate being; animal (ofte as distinct from man); huma being, person.

crèche (krĕsh, krāsh) *n.* 1 Tableau of the Nativity scene. 2 Foundling home.

cre·dence (krē′dens) *n.* 1. Belief. 2. (also ~ **table**) Small table or shelf on which Eucharistic elements are placed before consecration.

cre·den·tial (krĭdĕn′shal) *n.* (usu. pl.) Letter(s) of introduction; evidence of qualifications or authority, usu. in written form, as a diploma or certificate; (colloq.) experience.

cred·i·ble (krĕd′ibel) *adj.* Believable, worthy of belief. **cred·i· bil·i·ty** (krĕdibĭl′ĭtē), **cred′i·ble· ness** *ns.* **cred′i·bly** *adv.*

cred·it (krĕd′ĭt) *n.* 1. Belief, trust. 2. Good reputation; power derived from this; acknowledgment of merit; source of commendation or honor. 3. Trust in person's ability and intention to pay at some

There are two families of **crayfish**, the Astacidae and the Parastacidae, the former found in the northern, the latter in the southern, hemisphere. Some species are edible.

Wistaria, a quick-growing and hardy deciduous shrub, is among the most popular and decorative ***creepers.*** *It is named after an American anatomist, Caspar Wistar.*

ıture time; reputation of solvency nd probity in business; (book-eeping) acknowledgment of pay-ıent by entry in account, sum ntered on credit side of account; **etter of ~**, banker's etc. ocument authorizing person to raw money from writer's corre-pondent in another place; ~ **card**, ard authorizing purchase of goods r services on credit; ~ **rating**, stimate of person's or firm's ability ɔ pay; ~ **union**, cooperative rganization that makes small loans ɔ its members at low interest rates. . Value of course of study in school r college in reckoning progress oward diploma or degree; certifi-ate or record of successful com-letion of course of study. 5. (usu. l.) List of acknowledgments giving ame(s) of person(s) responsible for vork on film etc. **credit** *v.t.* 1. Believe. 2. Carry to credit side of ccount; give credit or acknowledg-nent to; ~ **with**, give credit for.

cred·it·a·ble (krĕd′ĭtabel) *adj.* That brings credit or honor. **cred′it·a·bly** *adv.* **cred·it·a·bil·i·ty** (krĕdĭtabĭl′ĭtē), **cred′it·a·ble·ness** *ns.*

cred·it·or (krĕd′ĭter) *n.* One who gives credit for money or goods; one to whom debt is owing.

cre·do (krē′dō, krā′-) *n.* (pl. **-dos**). Creed, esp. Apostles' Creed and Nicene Creed, which begin in Latin *credo* (= "I believe"); musical setting for these.

cred·u·lous (krĕj′*ulus*) *adj.* Too ready to believe; characterized by or arising from readiness to believe. **cre·du·li·ty** (kredōō′lĭtē, -dū′-), **cred′u·lous·ness** *ns.* **cred′u·lous·ly** *adv.*

creed (krēd) *n.* Brief formal summary of Christian doctrine, esp. Apostles' Creed and Nicene Creed; confession of faith; system of belief.

Creek (krēk) *n.* (pl. **Creeks**, collect. **Creek**). (Member of) a N. Amer. Ind. tribe formerly inhabiting parts of Georgia, Alabama, and northern Florida, now mainly settled in Oklahoma. [transl. Algonkin *maskoki* creeks]

creek (krēk, krĭk) *n.* 1. Brook, stream. 2. (Brit.) Narrow inlet of seacoast or tidal estuary.

creel (krēl) *n.* Large wicker basket for fish; angler's fishing basket.

creep (krēp) *v.i.* (**crept, creep·ing**). 1. Crawl; move timidly, slowly, or stealthily; proceed, exist, abjectly. 2. (of plants) Grow along ground, wall, etc.; **creeping Jenny** = moneywort (see MONEY). 3. (of flesh) Have a tingling sensation creeping over it (as result of fear, repugnance, etc.). 4. (of metal rails etc.) Move gradually forward under recurrent pressure; (of hot metal) extend slowly under tension; (of liquid) spread upward in crystals on side of vessel. **creep** *n.* 1. Creeping; creeping action of metal etc. 2. **the ~s**, (colloq.) nervous shrinking or shiver of dread or horror. 3. (slang) Obnoxious person.

creep·er (krē′per) *n.* (esp.) Plant that creeps along ground or up wall etc.; person, animal that creeps; kind of grapnel for dragging ground under water; bird that creeps on trees, esp. **brown ~** (*Certhia familiaris*).

creep·y (krē′pē) *adj.* (**creep·i·er, creep·i·est**). Having or producing a creeping of the flesh, frightening, repugnant; given to creeping. **creep·y-crawl·y** (krē′pē kraw′lē) *adj.* & *n.* (Insect, worm, etc.) producing creeping sensation. **creep′i·ly** *adv.* **creep′i·ness** *n.*

cre·mate (krē′māt, krĭmāt′) *v.t.* (**-mat·ed, -mat·ing**). 1. Consume (esp. corpse) by fire. 2. (slang) Beat thoroughly; defeat decisively. **cre·ma·tion** (krĭmā′shon), **cre′ma·tor** *ns.*

cre·ma·to·ri·um (krēmatōr′-ē*u*m, -tōr′-, krĕm*a*-) *n.* (pl. **-to·ri·ums, -to·ri·a** pr. -tōr′ē*a*, -tōr′-). Establishment for cremation.

cre·ma·to·ry (krē′matōtē, -tōrē, krĕm′*a*-) *n.* (pl. **-ries**). Crematorium. ~ *adj.* Of cremation.

crème (krĕm, krēm, krām) *n.* Syrupy liqueur; ~ **de cacao**, sweet chocolate-flavored liqueur; ~ **de menthe**, sweet green liqueur flavored with mint; ~ **de la ~**, (fig.) the best of anything.

Cre·mo·na (krĭmō′n*a*). Town in Lombardy, Italy, where the craft of violin-making reached its height in 17th and early 18th centuries; hence, violin made there.

cre·nate (krē′năt), **cre·nat·ed** (krē′nātĭd) *adjs.* (bot., zool.) With notched or scalloped edge. **cre·na·tion** (krĭnā′shon) *n.*

cre·na·ture (krē′n*a*cher, krĕ-n′*a*-) *n.* Notch or scalloped projection on edge of leaf etc.

cren·el·at·ed, *Brit.* **cren·el·lat·ed** (krĕn′elātĭd) *adjs.* Having battlements. **cren·el·a·tion** (krĕnelā′shon) *n.*

Cre·ole (krē′ōl) *n.* 1. Descendant of European settlers or slaves in W. Indies. 2. Descendant of early French or Spanish settlers in Louisiana etc.; (hist.) American-born black as dist. from an imported African slave. ~ *adj.* Born and naturalized in W. Indies etc., but of European or black descent.

Cre·on (krē′ŏn). (Gk. myth.) 1. King of Thebes and successor to Oedipus. 2. King of Corinth, father of CREUSA.

cre·o·sote (krē′*o*sōt) *n.* Brown oily liquid, a mixture of phenols obtained from coal tar (formerly from wood tar) having antiseptic properties and used esp. for preservation of timber and as a disinfectant; ~ **bush**, evergreen shrub (*Larrea tridentata*) found in N. Mexico and S. Texas. **creosote** *v.t.* (**-sot·ed, -sot·ing**). Coat with creosote.

crepe (krāp) *n.* Light, thin textile fabric with crinkled surface produced chemically or by twisting the yarn; black band of this displayed or worn on the sleeve or hat as sign of mourning; rubber rolled into thin sheets with crinkled surface; ~ **de Chine** (shēn), fine

silk crepe; ~ **paper**, thin crinkled paper; ~ **sole**, shoe sole of rubber crepe; **crêpe** (pr. also krĕp) **Su·zette** (sōōzĕt'), small dessert pancake served flambé.

crep·i·tate (krĕp'ĭtāt) *v.i.* (-tat·ed, -tat·ing). Make crackling sound. **crep·i·ta·tion** (krĕpĭtā'-shon) *n.* (med.) Grating sound made by ends of bone rubbing together; rattle of breath as heard in pneumonia etc.

crept (krĕpt): see CREEP.

cre·pus·cu·lar (krĭpŭs'kyuler) *adj.* Of twilight; (zool.) appearing, active, at twilight.

cres., cresc. *abbrevs.* Crescendo.

cre·scen·do (krĭshĕn'dō) *adv., n.* (pl. -dos, *It.* -di pr. -dē) & *adj.* (mus.) (Passage performed) with gradually increasing volume, indicated thus <; also fig. [It.]

cres·cent (krĕs'ent) *n.* 1. Waxing moon, between new moon and full; concavo-convex figure of moon during first or last quarter, esp. when very new or very old. 2. Representation of this shape, esp. as badge of Turkish sultans; Turkish power (hist.); Muslim religion. 3. Anything crescent-shaped. ~ *adj.* 1. Increasing;

waxing. 2. Crescent-shaped.

cre·sol (krē'sŏl, -sawl, -sŏl) *n.* Any of three isomeric methyl phenols present in wood and coal tar and forming chief constituents of creosote.

cress (krĕs) *n.* Any of various cruciferous plants, usu. with pungent edible leaves, esp. WATER-CRESS.

Cres·si·da (krĕs'ĭda). In medieval legends of the Trojan War, the daughter of Calchas, a priest; she was faithless to her lover Troilus, a son of Priam.

crest (krĕst) *n.* 1. Comb, tuft, on bird's or animal's head; erect plume or other ornament on top of helmet or headdress. 2. (her.) Device (orig. borne by knight on his helmet) above shield and helmet in coat of arms, or used separately, as on seal, notepaper, etc. 3. Top of helmet; helmet, headpiece; summit, top, esp. of hill or mountain. 4. Ridge forming top of anything, esp. of roof or wave; surface line of neck in animals, mane; (anat.) ridge along surface of bone. 5. **crest'-fallen**, with drooping crest; abashed, disheartened. **crest** *v.* 1. Form into crest. 2. Reach crest or summit of. **crest'ed** *adj.*

cre·ta·ceous (krĭtā'shus) *adj.* O (the nature of) chalk; **C~** (geo of the last period of the Mesozoi **Cre·ta'ceous** *n.* Cretaceous peric or system.

Crete (krēt). Aegean islan belonging to Greece. **Cre'tan** *ad* & *n.* (Native, inhabitant) of Crete **cre·tin** (krē'tĭn) *n.* One sufferin from cretinism; idiot. **cre'tin·isn** *n.* Idiocy combined with arreste and deformed physical develop ment, and caused by thyroi deficiency. **cre'tin·ous** *ad* [Swiss Fr. *crestin* Christian, i sense of "(barely) human creature"]

cre·tonne (krĭtŏn', krē'tŏn) *n.* Strong unglazed cotton or linen fabric with printed pattern.

Cre·u·sa (krēōō'sa). (Gk legend) 1. Daughter of Creon, kin of Corinth; when she was about t marry Jason, she put on a garmen given her by Medea which wa poisoned and set her body on fire 2. Daughter of Priam king of Troy and wife of Aeneas.

cre·vasse (krevăs') *n.* Deep fis sure in a glacier; crack in a levee or dike.

crev·ice (krĕv'ĭs) *n.* Narrow opening, fissure, esp. in rock, build ing, etc.

*The **Cretaceous** period was between 65 and 136 million years ago. Reptiles predominated. Towards the end of this era, the reptile population declined, and smaller mammals began to develop. The forms of Cretaceous reptiles are* *known from fossil remains: the tyrannosaurus and triceratops are both dinosaurs; the pteranodon was a giant winged lizard or pterodactyl (a toothed bird), the ichthyornis was a smaller toothed bird; the ornithomimus was a* *small ostrich-like animal; and the triconodont was a hairy primitive mammal, which was two feet long and probably carnivorous.*

Pteranodon

Triceratops

Tyrannosaurus Rex

Triconodont

Ichthyornis

Ornithomimus

crew (krōo) *n.* Group of people
rking together; group of people
nning ship, aircraft, train, etc.;
metimes, men manning ship, ex-
ding officers; associated body,
mpany, of persons; set, gang,
b; ~ **cut**, man's closely cropped
ircut. **crew'man** *n.* (pl. **-men**).
ew *v.* Supply or act as crew (for).

crew'el (krōo'el) *n.* Thin,
osely twisted worsted yarn used
embroidery; ~ **work**, decora-
e embroidery employing this
rn.

crib (krĭb) *n.* 1. Barred recep-
:le for fodder etc. 2. Cabin, hovel;
ang) living quarters. 3. Child's
d with barred or latticed sides. 4.
amework lining shaft of mine;
avy crossed timbers used in
undations in loose soil etc. 5. Set
cards in cribbage made up from
scards from players' hands. 6.
olloq.) Plagiarism; translation. 7.
lso ~ **sheet**) Set of answers for
egitimate use by students. **crib**
t. (**cribbed, crib·bing**). 1. Con-
e in small space. 2. Furnish
owshed etc.) with cribs. 3. Pilfer;
lagiarize; cheat (on student ex-
mination).

crib·bage (krĭb'ĭj) *n.* Card game
r two, three, or four persons,
layed with pack of 52 cards and a
oard of 61 holes on which points
e scored with pegs, five or six
rds being dealt to each player and
e dealer having in addition the
RIB (see def. 5).

crib·ri·form (krĭb'ri fōrm) *adj.*
nat., bot.) Perforated with
umerous small holes.

Crich·ton (krī'ton), **James**
560–85). Scottish intellectual
rodigy said to have disputed on
cientific questions in 12 languages;
dmirable ~, nickname given to
im; hence, any very versatile per-
n.

crick[1] (krĭk) *n.* Painful spasm of
uscles of neck, back, etc., sudden
iffness.

crick[2] (krĭk) *n.* (dial.) Creek.

The Australian crested pigeon, also
known as the 'top-knot' pigeon. **Crests**
are used, by the male birds particularly,
in amorous and aggressive display.
Combs and wattles have the same function.

Crick (krĭk), **Francis Harry
Compton** (1916–). British bio-
chemist; co-discoverer (with J. D.
WATSON) of DNA molecular structure; awarded Nobel Prize for
medicine, 1962.

crick·et[1] (krĭk'ĭt) *n.* Orthop-
terous jumping insect of genus
Acheta or related genera, esp. the
common American **field** or **black**
~ (*A. assimilis*) and the **house** ~
(*A. domestica*) living in hearths and

Crete is the 5th largest island in the
Mediterranean. During the Bronze-Age
rule of Minos, the palaces of Knossos
and Phaistos were built. Crete is rich in
minerals as well as archeological relics.

other warm places, and producing
a characteristic shrill noise by
rubbing parts of forewings together.

crick·et[2] (krĭk'ĭt) *n.* Outdoor
game, popular in Gt. Britain,
played with bats, ball, and two
wickets by two sides of 11 players
each, in which the batsman (one at
each wicket) defends his wicket
against the ball and scores by runs
made between the wickets after the

Greece

Turkey

Aegean Sea

IRAKLION

CRETE

*The derivation of the word **cricket** and the evolution of the game in England are not known with certainty, but cricket has been played since at least the 16th century. Top right: The Marylebone Cricket Club (M.C.C.), seen in this early 19th century color lithograph, was founded in 1788. Top left: A test match between Australia and the West Indies.*

*About 700 species of **crinoid** are known. The feathery tentacles are lined with tiny hairs to sweep food to the mouth.*

ball has been struck by the bat; **not** ~, (chiefly Brit., colloq.) unsporting, unfair. **cricket** *v.i.* Play cricket. **crick'et·er** *n.*

cri·coid (krī'koid) *adj.* Ring-shaped. ~ *n.* (anat.) Cartilage of this shape forming lower and back part of larynx.

cri·er (krī'er) *n.* (esp.) (hist.) (also **town** ~) Person employed to shout out public announcements in the street.

crime (krīm) *n.* Act punishable by law; evil act, sin; unjust, senseless act or condition; ~ **of passion**, crime (esp. murder) resulting from sexual jealousy; ~ **wave**, sudden brief increase in number of crimes committed.

Cri·me·a (krīmē'a). Peninsula of U.S.S.R. lying between Sea of Azov and Black Sea. **Cri·me'an** *adj.* ~ **War**, war fought chiefly in the Crimea, 1854–6, in which Russia was defeated by Turkey, France, and Gt. Britain, both sides sustaining heavy losses.

crim·i·nal (krĭm'ĭnal) *adj.* Of (the nature of) crime; concerned with crime or its punishment; guilty of crime; ~ **conversation**, (archaic) adultery; ~ **law, proceedings**, those involving crime and its punishment (cf. CIVIL law). **crim'i·nal·ly** *adv.* **criminal** *n.* Person guilty or convicted of crime. **crim·i·nal·i·ty** (krĭmĭnăl'ĭtē) *n.* (pl. **-ties**).

crim·i·nate (krĭm´ĭnāt) *v.t.* **·at·ed, -nat·ing**). Charge with me; prove guilty of crime; in-minate. **crim·i·na·tion** (krĭmĭ-´shon) *n.* **crim·i·na·tive** (krĭm´ĭnātĭv), **crim·i·na·to·ry** (krĭm´ĭnatōrē, -tōrē) *adjs.*

crim·i·nol·o·gy (krĭmĭnŏl´ojē) *n.* ientific study of crime. **crim·i-·l´o·gist** *n.* **crim·i·no·log·i·cal** (krĭmĭnolŏj´ĭkal) *adj.*

crimp (krĭmp) *v.t.* 1. Compress to pleats or folds, frill; wrinkle crumple minutely. Cause (flesh newly caught fish) to contract d become firm by gashing. ~ *n.* ld, crease; (fig.) **put a ~ in**, terfere with.

crim·son (krĭm´zon, -son) *adj.* & (Of) deep red color inclining ward purple. ~ *v.* Make, be-me, crimson.

cringe (krĭnj) *v.i.* (**cringed, ·ing·ing**). Cower; bow servilely; have obsequiously. ~ *n.* Fawn-g obeisance.

cri·nite (krī´nīt) *adj.* (bot., zool.) airy.

crin·kle (krĭng´kel) *v.* (**-kled, kling**) & *n.* Wrinkle. **crin´kly** *dj.* (**-kli·er, -kli·est**).

cri·noid (krī´noid, krĭn´oid) *adj.* *n.* (Echinoderm) usu. with alked and rooted calyxlike body; a lily.

crin·o·line (krĭn´olĭn, -lēn) *n.* tiff fabric of horsehair etc. rmerly used for skirts; petticoat f this, or hooped petticoat, used to xpand skirt of woman's dress.

crip·ple (krĭp´el) *n.* Lame per-n. ~ *v.t.* (**-pled, -pling**). Lame; sable, impair.

cri·sis (krī´sĭs) *n.* (pl. **-ses** pr. -sēz). Turning point, esp. of disease; moment or brief period of danger or suspense.

crisp (krĭsp) *adj.* Hard or firm but fragile, brittle; bracing; brisk, decisive; (of hair etc.) closely curl-ing. **crisp´ly** *adv.* **crisp´ness** *n.* **crisp** *n.* Anything dried or shriveled by frying, roasting, etc. ~ *v.* Make or become crisp. **crisp´y** *adj.* (**crisp·i·er, crisp-·i·est**). **crisp´i·ness** *n.*

cris·pa·tion (krĭspā´shon) *n.* Crisping, curling, undulation; slight contraction (esp. of skin in "goose flesh").

criss·cross (krĭs´kraws, -krŏs) *n.* Crossing lines, currents, etc.; network of intersecting lines. ~ *adj.* In crossing lines. ~ *adv.* Crosswise. ~ *v.* Mark with criss-cross lines; cross repeatedly. [orig. *Christ's cross*]

cris·tate (krĭs´tāt), **cris·tat·ed** (krĭs´tātĭd) *adjs.* Crested, like a crest.

cri·te·ri·on (krītēr´ēon) *n.* (pl. **-te·ri·a** pr. -tēr´ēa, **-te·ri·ons**). Principle, rule, standard, by which thing is judged.

crit·ic (krĭt´ĭk) *n.* One who pronounces judgment; censurer; judge of literary, dramatic, or artis-tic works; one skilled in textual criticism.

crit·i·cal (krĭt´ĭkal) *adj.* 1. Censorious, faultfinding; skillful, engaged, in criticism; belonging to criticism; providing textual criti-cism. 2. Relating to crisis; involving risk or suspense. 3. (math., phys.) Marking transition from one state, property, condition, etc., to an-other; (of nuclear reactor) main-taining self-sustaining chain re-action; ~ **angle**, (optics) largest angle at which light rays passing through a dense medium can strike the face of a rarer medium and pass into it (i.e. be refracted; if the angle exceeds this, they will be totally reflected); ~ **mass**, amount of fissile material required to sus-tain chain reaction; ~ **point**, temperature for any gas above which it cannot be liquefied by compression (also ~ **tempera-ture**). **crit´i·cal·ly** *adv.* **crit´i·cal·ness** *n.*

crit·i·cism (krĭt´ĭsĭzem) *n.* Criticizing; work of a critic; critical essay or remark; science dealing with text, character, composition, and origin of literary documents; **higher ~**, criticism, other than verbal or textual (**lower ~**), of the Bible; **textual ~**, criticism that seeks to ascertain the genuine text and meaning of a literary work.

crit·i·cize (krĭt´ĭsīz) *v.* (**-cized, -ciz·ing**). Discuss critically; cen-sure, find fault (with). **crit´i·ciz-a·ble** *adj.* **crit´i·ciz·er** *n.*

cri·tique (krĭtēk´) *n.* Critical essay or notice; criticism.

croak (krōk) *n.* Deep hoarse sound made by frog or crow; sound resembling this. **croak´y** *adj.* (**croak·i·er, croak·i·est**). **croak** *v.* 1. Utter croak; utter dismally; forebode evil. 2. (slang) Die.

croak·er (krō´ker) *n.* Any of N.

The **cricket** *of the insect family Gryllidae is best recognized by its sound. There are about 1,400 known species. Their adaptations range from soil-burrowing to arboreal.*

Amer. marine fishes of the family Sciaendae that make drumming sounds.

Croat (krōt, krō'ăt) n. Native, inhabitant, of Croatia; descendant of Slavonic tribe which occupied that country in 7th c.; their language; Serbo-Croatian. **Cro·a·tia** (krōā'sha). District of Yugoslavia. **Cro·a'tian** adj. Of Croatia or the Croats. ~ n. Croat; language of the Croats.

Cro·ce (krō'chĕ), **Benedetto** (1866–1952). Italian philosopher and historian.

cro·chet (krōshā'; Brit. krō'shā, -shē) n. Kind of knitting done with a hooked needle (~ **hook**); material so made. ~ v.t. (**-cheted** pr. -shād'; Brit. -shād, -shēd; **-chet·ing** pr. -shā'ĭng; Brit. -shāĭng, -shēĭng). Do crochet work; make of crochet.

crock[1] (krŏk) n. Earthen pot or jar; broken piece of earthenware, potsherd; (slang, fig.) pot full of lies, rubbish, or nonsense.

crock[2] (krŏk) n. (chiefly Brit. slang) Broken down or disabled person or thing.

crocked (krŏkt) adj. (slang) Drunk.

crock·er·y (krŏk'erē) n. Earthenware vessels, esp. for domestic use.

Crock·ett (krŏk'ĭt), **(David) "Davy"** (1786–1836). Amer. frontiersman; member of U.S. House of representatives from Tennessee, 1827–31, 1833–5; joined Texan forces and was killed at the Alamo, 1836.

croc·o·dile (krŏk'odīl) n. 1. Large amphibious thick-skinned long-tailed saurian reptile of Crocodilus or related genera, esp. C. acutus, the American crocodile, and C. niloticus, the crocodile of the Nile; tanned skin of this. 2. ~ **bird**, Egyptian black-headed plover (Pluvianus aegyptius), a small bird with lavender and cream plumage and black-and-white markings, which eats crocodile's insect parasites; ~ **tears**, (from the

ancient belief that the crocodile wept while devouring its victim) hypocritical tears or sympathy. **croc·o·dil·i·an** (krŏkodĭl'ēan) adj. & n.

cro·cus (krō'kus) n. (pl. **-cus·es, -ci** pr. -kē, -kī, -sī). Hardy dwarf plant with corm (genus C~), cultivated for its brilliant, usu. yellow or purple, flowers, appearing in early spring or in autumn.

Croe·sus (krē'sus) (6th c. B.C.). King of Lydia, famous for his riches; hence, a very rich man.

croft (krawft, krŏft) n. Enclosed piece of (usu. arable) land; small agricultural holding worked by peasant tenant, esp. in Scottish Highlands. **croft'er** n.

crois·sant (krwahsahn') n. (pl. **-sants** pr. -sahn'). Buttery, flaky, crescent-shaped bread roll. [Fr.]

Cro-Mag·non (krōmăg'non, -măn'yon). Cave in Dordogne, France, where remains of Homo sapiens were found in 1868 among deposits of upper paleolithic age; applied to a group of mankind (persisting in mesolithic and neolithic times) with long heads, low foreheads, very broad faces, deep-set eyes, and tall stature.

Crom·well[1] (krŏm'wel, -wĕl,

krŭm'-), **Oliver** (1599–165 Leader of the parliamentary troo in the English Civil War; Lo PROTECTOR of England, 1653–8.

Crom·well[2] (krŏm'wel, -w krŭm'-), **Thomas, Earl of Ess** (1485?–1540). Adviser and age of Henry VIII and Cardinal Wols in Protestantizing England, pol cal matters, etc.; executed treason.

crone (krōn) n. Withered woman; old ewe.

Cro·nus (krō'nus, krŏn'u (Gk. myth.) One of the Tita and father of Zeus, by whom he w dethroned as ruler of the univers

cro·ny (krō'nē) n. (pl. **-nie** Intimate friend.

crook (krook) n. 1. Shepherd staff, with one end curved hooked, for catching sheep's le bishop's or abbot's pastoral sta anything hooked; hook; curv bend. 2. (colloq.) Dishone person, esp. swindler or thief. ~ Bend, curve.

crook·ed (krook'ĭd) adj. N straight, bent, angled, twisted; d formed; bent with age; not straigh foward, dishonest. **crook'ed** adv. **crook'ed·ness** n.

croon (kroon) n. Low monot

rochet first became popular in the 9th century and was perfected as a raft in Ireland, where it was introduced s relief work during the potato famine. he exquisite quality compares with enetian lace.

Oliver Cromwell *and his New Model Army at Dunbar in a painting by A. C. Gow. The execution of Charles I in 1649 brought unrest in Scotland. Cromwell won the battle of Dunbar on 3 September 1650.*

Thomas Cromwell *in a portrait by Holbein. His role in negotiating the necessary Reformation legislation for Henry VIII has been disputed; he has been both credited as author and dismissed as mere instrument.*

nous singing. ~ *v.* Utter croon; hum or sing softly. **croon′er** *n.* Singer of popular songs in a soft sentimental voice.

crop (krŏp) *n.* 1. Pouchlike enlargement of gullet in birds, where food is prepared for digestion. 2. Stock, handle, of whip; (also **hunting** ~) short whip with loop instead of lash. 3. Produce of cultivated plants, esp. cereals; agricultural produce; season's total yield (of cereal etc.). 4. Cropping

of hair; style of wearing hair cut short; piece cropped or cut off anything. ~ *v.* (**cropped, crop·ping**). 1. Cut off; cut short; (of animals) bite off (tops of plants). 2. Gather, reap. 3. Trim, cut off unwanted part(s), esp. of photograph. 4. Raise crop on; bear a crop. 5. ~ **up**, turn up unexpectedly; come to surface; ~ **out**, appear.

crop·per (krŏp′er) *n.* (esp.) 1. (slang) Sharecropper. 2. (slang) Heavy fall (**come a** ~; also fig.).

cro·quet (krōkā′; *Brit.* krō′kā, -kē) *n.* 1. Game played on lawn, in which wooden balls are driven with wooden mallets through hoops fixed in the ground. 2. Croqueting a ball in this game. ~ *v.t.* (**-queted** pr. -kād′; *Brit.* -kād, -kēd;

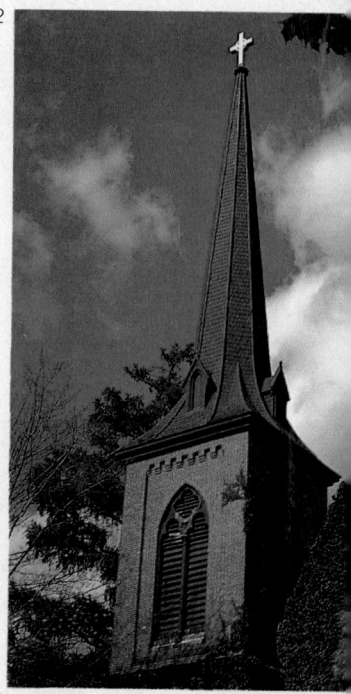

The **cross** has developed complex symbolic meanings, combining religious and non-religious ideas of love and comfort with more militant connotations. Stone crosses marked routes as on Bodmin Moor, Cornwall, U.K. (1) and others were symbols of peace and security. (2) Spire of St. Peter's Episcopal Church, Concord, New Hampshire.

-quet·ing pr. -kā´ĭng; *Brit.* -kāĭng, -kēĭng). Drive away (another ball) by striking one's own ball placed in contact with it.

cro·quette (krōkĕt´) *n.* Fried patty, usu. breaded, of minced fish, meat, potatoes, etc.

cro·sier, cro·zier (krō´zher) *ns.* Pastoral staff or crook of bishop or abbot.

cross (kraws, krŏs) *n.* 1. Stake (usu. with transverse bar) used by the ancients for crucifixion, esp. (**the C~**) that on which Christ was crucified; model of this as religious emblem; sign of cross made with right hand as religious act; staff surmounted with cross and borne before archbishop or in processions. 2. Trial, affliction; annoyance. 3. Cross-shaped thing or mark; southern constellation (**Southern C~**) within Antarctic Circle, with four bright stars roughly in shape of cross; cross-shaped decoration; **fiery ~**: see FIERY. 4. Intermixture of breeds; animal etc. resulting from this; mixture, compromise, *between* two things. 5. Thing that crosses. **cross´wise, cross´ways** *advs.* **cross** *v.* 1. Place crosswise. 2. Make sign of cross on or over. 3. Draw line across; write across (what is already written, a letter). 4. Go across; bestride; carry, move, across; meet and pass. 5. Thwart; defy. 6. Crossbreed; cross-fertilize. **~** *adj.* 1. Passing from side to side, transverse; intersecting; **~ reference**, reference from one part of book etc. to another; **~ section**, cutting across; section made by plane cutting any solid transversely; typical representation of constituents of a thing or group. 2. Con-

trary, opposed. 3. (colloq.) Peevish, out of humor. **cross´ly** *adv.* In a cross or peevish way. **cross´ness** *n.*

cross- *comb. form.* **cross´bill**, bird of genus *Loxia* (one of the finches), with mandibles curved so as to cross each other when bill is closed; **cross´bones**, figure of two thighbones laid across each other, usu. under skull as emblem of death; **cross´bow**, bow fixed across wooden stock, with groove for missile (arrow, stone, etc.) and mechanism for drawing back and releasing string; **cross´bowman** (*n.*); **cross´bred**, hybrid (animal etc.); **cross´breed**, (cause to) produce hybrid; **cross-check**, verify, verification, by alternative method; **cross-country**, across fields etc. instead of following roads; **cross´cut**, diagonal cut; **cross´cut saw**, saw for making crosscut; **cross-examine**, examine by questions designed to check answers of previous questions; esp. so examine (witness who has already given evidence for other side) in court of law; **cross-examination, cross-examiner** (*ns.*); **cross-eyed**, having squint in which eyes are turned inward; **cross-fertilize**, fertilize (plant) with gamete from another; **cross-grained**, (of wood) with grain running irregularly or in crossing directions; (fig.) perverse, intractable; **cross´hatch**, shade (drawing, engraving, etc.) with intersecting series of parallel lines; **cross-legged**, with legs crossed; with one leg laid across the other; **cross´patch**, ill-tempered person; **cross-pollinate**, pollinate from one plant to another; (**be at**) **cross-purposes**, (having) contrary or conflicting purposes; **cross´roads**,

intersection of two roads; (fig critical turning point; **cross stitch**, needlework stitch of tw straight stitches crossing each othe **cross´tie**, (esp. railroads) trans verse connecting piece (of timbe etc.); **cross´town** (*adj.*), lyin leading, going, across a tow **cross´tree**, one of the horizont. transverse timbers bolted to mast ship; **cross´word** (**puzzle**), puz zle that is solved by filling in word indicated by verbal clues down an across a pattern of numbere squares.

crosse (kraws, krŏs) *n.* Imple ment used in lacrosse for catchin and throwing ball, consisting o long shank curved around at en with net stretched across part. [Fr see LACROSSE]

cross·ing (kraw´sĭng, krŏs´ĭng *n.* (esp.) Intersection of two roads railroads, etc.; place where street crossed.

crotch (krŏch) *n.* Fork of tree o bough; fork of human body wher legs join trunk; corresponding par of garment.

crotch·et (krŏch´ĭt) *n.* 1. (mus. Quarter note. 2. Whimsical fancy **crotch´et·y** *adj.* Peevish **crotch´et·i·ness** *n.*

cro·ton (krō´ton) *n.* Plant, usu tropical, of genus *C~*, the seeds o one species of which, the Asian *C tiglium*, yield **~ oil**, a drastic purga tive. [Gk. *kroton* sheep tick, croton so called from shape of seeds]

crouch (krowch) *v.i.* Stoop bend, esp. timidly or servilely; (o animals) lie close on ground, wher about to pounce on prey, or from fear. **~** *n.* Action or position o crouching.

croup[1] (krōōp) *n.* Inflammatory

---

crowns have consisted of oak leaves and acorns and of the world's most precious gems and metals. Two regal crowns are shown here. Above: A crown of the former Shah of Persia. Above Right: The English Imperial State crown made for Queen Victoria in 1838.

disease in larynx and trachea of children, marked by hard cough and difficulty in breathing.

croup² (krōōp) n. Rump, hind-quarters, esp. of horse.

crou·pi·er (krōō′pēer, -pēā) n. One who rakes in (with a ~'s stick) and pays out money at gambling table. [Fr., orig. = "one who rides behind on the croup"]

crou·ton (krōō′tŏn, krōōtŏn′) n. Small piece of fried or toasted bread used for garnishing or served with soup. [Fr.]

Crow (krō) n. Member, language, of tribe of N. Amer. Indians formerly inhabiting region between Platte and Yellowstone rivers; now settled mainly in Montana.

crow¹ (krō) n. 1. Bird of genus *Corvus* with glossy black feathers and raucous call. 2. (also **crow′-bar**) Metal bar, usu. with beaklike end, used as lever. 3. ~'s-foot, wrinkle at outer corner of human eye; ~'s-nest, barrel or protected platform fixed at masthead of sailing vessel for lookout; **as the ~ flies**, in a straight line; **eat ~**, submit to humiliation, be forced to admit that one is wrong.

An Australian **crow** (Corvus cecilae), usually seen in large numbers except when breeding. Like the raven (C. coronides), from which it can be distinguished by its call, it consumes enormous quantities of insects.

crow² (krō) n. Crowing of cock; joyful cry. ~ v.i. Utter crow; exult loudly; boast.

crowd (krowd) n. Throng, dense multitude; (colloq.) clique, set, lot; large number (of things). ~ v. 1. Collect in a crowd; fill, occupy, cram (*with*); fill (places etc.) as crowd does; force one's way *into*, *through*, etc. (confined space etc.); ~ **out**, exclude by crowding. 2. (naut.) Press or hasten on; ~ **(on) sail**, hoist large amount of sail to increase speed.

crown (krown) n. 1. Wreath of flowers etc. worn on head, esp. as emblem of victory. 2. Sovereign's head-covering of gold etc. and jewels; (also the **C** ~; fig.) king or queen, regal power, supreme governing power in a monarchy. 3. Crown-shaped ornament. 4. Any of various coins orig. stamped with a crown; former silver coin of Gt. Britain worth five shillings. 5. Top part, esp. of skull; whole head. 6. Upper part of cut gem above girdle; highest or central part of arch or arched structure; top part of hat; part of tooth projecting from gum, artificial replacement of this. 7. ~ **colony**, colony with legislation

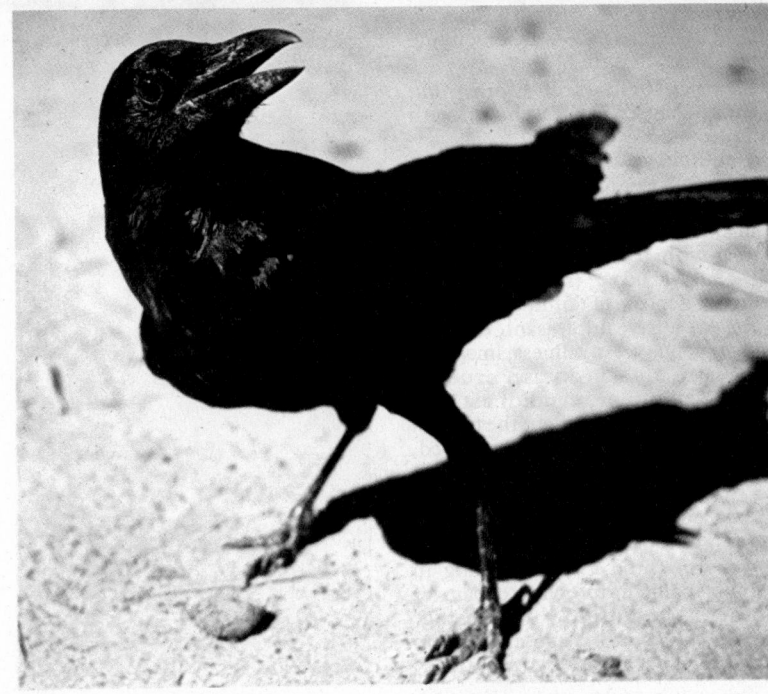

under control of sovereign, usu. administered by an appointed governor; ~ **glass**, kind of thick glass without lead or iron, made in circular sheets by blowing and whirling; formerly used for window panes; kind of optical glass with low refractive index; ~ **jewels**, jewels forming part of the emblems and symbols of a sovereign or royal family; ~ **prince**, heir apparent or designate to throne; ~ **princess**, wife of crown prince; female heir presumptive; ~ **vetch**, Old World plant (*Coronilla varia*) with compound leaves and pink flowers, naturalized in the U.S. **crown** *v.t.* 1. Place crown on; invest with regal crown or dignity; (fig.) reward; (slang) hit on the head. 2. Occupy the head of, form chief ornament to; put finishing touch to; bring (efforts) to happy issue. 3. (checkers) Make (piece) king, by putting another piece on top; (dentistry) fit crown to (tooth).

cro·zier (krō′zher) = CROSIER.

CRT *abbrev.* Cathode ray tube.

cru·cial (krōō′shəl) *adj.* 1. Decisive, critical. 2. Cross-shaped.

cru·ci·ate (krōō′shēāt, -ĭt) *adj.* (zool., bot.) Cross-shaped; overlapping.

cru·ci·ble (krōō′sĭbel) *n.* Vessel (usu. of earthenware) withstanding great heat, and used for fusing metals etc.; hollow at bottom of furnace to collect molten metal; (fig.) severe test or trial.

cru·cif·er·ous (krōōsĭf′erus) *adj.* 1. Wearing, adorned with, a cross. 2. (bot.) Of the family Cruciferae, having flowers with four equal petals arranged crosswise.

cru·ci·fix (krōō′sĭfĭks) *n.* Figure of Christ on the Cross; (erron.) cross.

cru·ci·fix·ion (krōōsĭfĭk′shon) *n.* Crucifying; **the C~**, the crucifying of Christ; picture of this.

cru·ci·form (krōō′sĭfôrm) *adj.* Cross-shaped, esp. of church with transepts.

cru·ci·fy (krōō′sĭfī) *v.t.* (-**fied**, -**fy·ing**). Put to death by fastening to a cross; (fig.) mortify (passions, sins, flesh); (colloq.) persecute, treat with gross injustice.

crud (krŭd) *n.* (slang) 1. (Coating or deposit of) filth, impurities, etc. 2. Dirty, unpleasant, disgusting person. 3. Any illness, imagined or real, esp. a skin disease. **crud′dy** *adj.* (**crud·di·er, crud·di·est**).

crude (krōōd) *adj.* In the natural or raw state; unripe; unpolished; lacking refinement; rude, blunt. ~ *n.* (also ~ **oil**) Unrefined petroleum. **crude′ly** *adv.* **crude′- ness, cru·di·ty** (krōō′dĭtē) *ns.*

cru·el (krōō′el) *adj.* Liking to inflict pain; indifferent to pain of others; painful, distressing. **cru·el′ly** *adv.* **cru·el·ness** *n.* **cru·el·ty** (krōō′eltē) *n.* (pl. **-ties**).

Many of the **cruciferous** flowering plants commonly referred to as the 'cabbage' family, are sweet-scented, and a large number, like sea-kale, radishes, and cress, are edible and highly nutritious. They are found mainly in temperate regions.

The **crucifix**, as a central emblem of the Christian religion, has developed elaborate forms in the hands of craftsmen. That shown is silver and enamel, early 20th century.

cru·et (krōō′ĭt) *n.* Small gla bottle with stopper for vinegar, o etc., for use at table.

cruise (krōōz) *v.* (**cruise cruis·ing**). 1. Sail about, makin for no particular port or calling series of ports; sail for pleasure; (naval vessel) sail in specified are for protection of shipping etc. Travel at cruising speed. 3. Driv at random, esp. slowly, as patrollin car, taxi looking for fare, etc. Cruise in (specified area). 5. **missile**, low-flying jet-powere radar-controlled guided missil **cruis′ing speed**, normal, eco nomical traveling speed of vehic or aircraft. **cruise** *n.* Cruisin voyage.

cruis·er (krōō′zer) *n.* 1. Warshi adapted for cruising, faster and le heavily armored and having le firepower than battleship. 2. (als **cabin** ~) Motorboat with cabin.

crul·ler (krŭl′er) *n.* Cris doughnut, often in a twisted shape

crumb (krŭm) *n.* Small frag ment, esp. of bread, such as break or falls off by rubbing etc.; (fig small particle. ~ *v.t.* Cover, pre pare with bread crumbs; break int crumbs. **crumb·y** (krŭm′ē) ad (**crumb·i·er, crumb·i·est**).

crum·ble (krŭm′bel) *v.* (-**bled -bling**). Break, fall, into crumb or fragments. ~ *n.* Crumbly c crumbled substance. **crum·bl** (krŭm′blē) *adj.* (-**bli·er, -bli·est** Apt to crumble.

crum·my (krŭm′ē) *adj.* (-**mi·er -mi·est**). (slang) Shabby; cheap inferior, worthless; inadequate nasty.

crum·pet (krŭm′pĭt) *n.* (chiefl Brit.) Soft muffinlike brea cooked on griddle and eate toasted.

crum·ple (krŭm′pel) *v.* (-**pled -pling**). Crush together or *up* int creased state; ruffle, wrinkle; be come creased; give way, collapse.

crunch (krŭnch) *v.* Crush wit teeth, esp. noisily; grind under foo (gravel etc.); make one's way thus ~ *n.* Crunching (noise); (colloq. crisis. **crunch′y** *adj.* (**crunch·i·er crunch·i·est**). Making a crunch ing sound.

crup·per (krŭp′er, krōōp′-) *n.* Strap buckled to back of saddle an passing under horse's tail; hind quarters of horse.

cru·sade (krōōsād′) *n.* 1. (freq **C~**) One of several military ex peditions undertaken by the Chris tians of Europe in the 11th, 12th and 13th centuries to recover the Holy Land from the Muslims; ir the **First C~** (1096–9) the crusaders captured Jerusalem and set up a kingdom there; the **Third C~** (1189–91), in which Richard I of England, the Holy Roman Emperor Frederick Barbarossa, and Philip Augustus of France took

1st Crusade 1096-99
2nd Crusade 1147-49
3rd Crusade 1189 92
4th Crusade 1202-04
5th Crusade 1217-21
6th Crusade 1228 29
7th Crusade 1248-54
8th Crusade 1270

*The **crusades** had public and private purposes, the former in terms of the Christian church's aim to recover the Holy Land from the Muslims; the latter in that the individual could atone for his sins by making the pilgrimage to the Holy Land.*

*Seen here is US **cruiser**, California. Cruisers are warships built for high speed, long range travel. They are smaller than aircraft carriers, bigger than destroyers.*

by application of pressure; (fig.) subdue, overwhelm. ~ *n.* 1. Act of crushing. 2. Crowded mass (esp. of persons). 3. Drink, dish prepared by crushing berries or fruit. 4. (colloq.) (Object of) infatuation; **have, get, a ~ on,** (slang) form a passionate attachment to (a person).

Cru·soe (krōō′sō), **Robinson**: see ROBINSON CRUSOE.

crust (krŭst) *n.* Hard outer part of bread; similar casing of anything, e.g., harder layer over soft snow; hard dry scrap of bread; pastry shell, pastry under (**bottom ~**) or covering (**top ~**) pie; hard dry formation, scab, on skin; (geol.) outer portion of earth; coating, deposit, on surface of anything; deposit of tartar etc., on inside of wine bottle; hard external covering of animal or plant, such as crustaceans and lichens; (slang) insolence, gall. **crust** *v.* Cover with, form into, crust; become covered with crust. **crust′ed** *adj.* Having a

art, resulted in the capture of Acre nd the establishment of a Latin ingdom in the East; in the **Sixth** : ~ (1228–9) Jerusalem was reaptured but finally lost; the other rusades were all unsuccessful; **Children's C~**, crusade of about 00,000 unarmed children who set ut in 1212 from France and

Germany to recover Jerusalem. 2. Any holy war undertaken with papal sanction; (fig.) aggressive movement against public evil etc. **crusade** *v.i.* (**-sad·ed, -sad·ing**). Engage in crusade. **cru·sad′er** *n.*

crush (krŭsh) *v.* Compress, be compressed, with violence, so as to break, bruise, etc.; crease; pulverize crust; (of wine) having deposited a crust, as old port etc.

crus·ta·cean (krŭstā'shan) *adj.* & *n.* (Arthropod) of the class Crustacea, including crabs, lobsters, shrimps, etc., mostly aquatic, freq. with hard shell and many legs.

crus·ta·ceous (krŭstā'shus) *adj.* Crustlike; having a hard covering; crustacean.

crust·y (krŭs'tē) *adj.* (**crust·i·er, crust·i·est**). Crustlike, hard; irritable, curt. **crust'i·ly** *adv.* **crust'i·ness** *n.*

crutch (krŭch) *n.* 1. Staff (now usu. with crosspiece at top fitting under armpit) for lame person; support, prop, esp. with forked top; any of various forked supports or contrivances. 2. Anything that gives support.

crux (krŭks) *n.* (pl. **crux·es, cru·ces** pr. krōō'sēz). Difficult matter, puzzle; point at issue; critical point, vital moment.

cru·zei·ro (krōōzār'ō) *n.* (pl. **-ros**). Principal monetary unit of Brazil, = 100 centavos.

cry (krī) *n.* (pl. **cries**). 1. Loud inarticulate utterance of grief, pain, fear, joy, etc.; loud excited utterance of words; appeal, entreaty. 2. Proclamation of wares sold in streets. 3. Public voice, generally expressed opinion; watchword. 4. Fit of weeping; **cry'baby**, one who cries frequently with little cause. 5. Yelping of hounds, pack of hounds; **in full cry**, in full pursuit.

cry *v.* (**cried, cry·ing**). 1. Utter cry or cries; utter loudly; exclaim. 2. Announce for sale; make public announcement of. 3. Weep. 4. (colloq.) Complain. 5. **a far ~**, a very different matter. **cry'ing** *adj.* (esp., of evils) Calling for notice, flagrant, as *a crying shame.*

cry·o·gen (krī'ojen) *n.* Refrigerant for achieving very low temperatures. [Gr. *kruos* frost]

cry·o·gen·ics (krīojĕn'ĭks) *n.* (usu. considered sing.) Branch of physics dealing with very low temperatures and their effects. **cry·o·gen'ic** *adj.* **cry·o·gen'i·cal·ly** *adv.*

cry·o·lite (krī'olīt) *n.* Fluoride of sodium and aluminum (Na_3AlF_6) used in aluminum refining and electrical insulation. [Gk. *kruos* frost]

cry·o·stat (krī'ostăt) *n.* Apparatus for maintaining constant low temperature.

cry·o·sur·ger·y (krīōsēr'jerē) *n.* Surgery using local or general application of intense cold for anesthesia or therapy.

crypt (krĭpt) *n.* Underground cell, vault, esp. one beneath church,

*The **crypt** of Mottisfont Abbey, Hampshire, U.K. founded c. 1200 by the Austin Canons, an austere order originating in Northern Italy and Southern France in the 11th century.*

used as burial place.

cryp·tic (krĭp'tĭk) *adj.* Secr mystical; obscure in meanin (zool.) adapted for concealment, **~ coloring**, animal's resemblan in color, markings, etc., to environment or to another anim

crypto- *prefix.* Hidden; secr **cryp·to·gam** (krĭp'togăm) (bot.) Plant of the class Cryp gamia having no stamens or pis and therefore no flowers or see and reproducing by spores, such ferns, mosses, algae, lichens, a fungi. **cryp·to·gam·ic** (krĭp găm'ĭk), **cryp·tog·a·mous** (krĭ tŏg'amus) *adjs.*

cryp·to·gram (krĭp'togrăm **cryp·to·graph** (krĭp'togră -grahf) *ns.* Anything written code or cipher. **cryp·tog·ra·ph** (krĭptŏg'rafer) *n.* **cryp·te graph·ic** (krĭptogrăf'ĭk) *a* **cryp·tog·ra·phy** *n.* Art of writi in, or solving, ciphers.

cryp·to·mer·i·a (krĭptomēr'ē *n.* Evergreen coniferous tree (*japonica*) of N. China and Japa Japanese cedar.

crys·tal (krĭs'tal) *n.* 1. Cle transparent icelike mineral, es pure quartz (**rock ~**); piece of th piece of natural or artificial miner used in contact with another or wi a thin wire as a simple rad detector. 2. Glass of very tran parent quality, usu. with high pr portion of lead oxide; fine cut glas anything made of this; watch glas 3. (chem. etc.) Form in which ator and molecules of many elemen and compounds regularly aggr gate, with definite internal stru ture and external form of soli enclosed by a number of symmetr cally arranged plane faces. 4. **gazing**, concentrating the gaze o ball of rock crystal or glass for pu pose of inducing a hallucinator vision of distant or future event (fig.) trying to predict the futur **crystal** *adj.* Made of, like, clea as, crystal. **crys·tal·line** (krĭs'talĭ -lĭn) *adj.* Made of, like, clear a crystal; having crystal form; **lens**, transparent body in eye en closed in membranous capsul behind iris, acting as princip agent in focusing rays of light o retina. **crys·tal·lize** (krĭs'talīz) (**-lized, -liz·ing**). 1. Form int crystals or (fig.) definite or perma nent state. 2. Coat with, melt or sugar.

crys·tal·log·ra·phy (krĭstalŏg rafē) *n.* Branch of science dealin with structure, classification, an

Crystal or *cut-glass making evolved from about 1600 when a glass-maker in Prague used crystal and jewel cutting techniques on glass.*

*Picasso's 'Girl with a Mandolin' (191 The **Cubist** structuring of the subj does not prevent identification. emphasis by some Cubists was on li and shade rather than on color as e dent in this reproduction.*

properties of crystals. **crys·tal·-log′ra·pher** *n.* **crys·tal·lo-graph·ic** (krĭstalogrăf′ĭk) *adj.*

crys·tal·loid (krĭs′taloid) *adj.* & *n.* (Substance) of crystalline structure, esp. substance capable, in solution, of passing through membranes (as dist. from COLLOID).

Crys·tal (krĭs′tal) **Palace.** Large building of iron frames and glass walls built to house exhibition in London in 1851; similar building that housed exhibition of New York City World's Fair of 1853.

C.S. *abbrev.* Chief of Staff; Christian Science; Christian Scientist; Civil Service.

Cs *symbol.* Cesium.

C/S *abbrev.* Cycles per second.

C.S.A. *abbrev.* Confederate States of America.

CST *abbrev.* Central Standard Time.

CT *abbrev.* Connecticut.

C.T. *abbrev.* Central Time.

Ct. *abbrev.* Connecticut.

ct. *abbrev.* Carat; cent; county.

ctr. *abbrev.* Center.

cu. *abbrev.* Cubic.

cub (kŭb) *n.* 1. Young of fox; young of bear or other wild beast. 2. Inexperienced youth; ~ **re-porter,** apprentice newspaper reporter. 3. **C~ Scout,** member of junior division of the Boy Scouts.

Cu·ba (kū′ba). Largest of the W. Ind. islands, discovered by Columbus in 1492; formerly a part of the Span.-Amer. dominions; freed from Spanish rule by U.S. forces in Spanish American War (1898) and proclaimed an independent republic in 1902; dictatorship government of Fulgencio Batista overthrown by coup led by Fidel Castro, 1959, who established communistic government in alliance with U.S.S.R.; capital, Havana; ~ **li·bre** (lē′bre). Drink of rum, cola, and lemon or lime juice. **Cu′ban** *adj.* & *n.* (Native, inhabitant) of Cuba.

cub·by·hole (kŭb′ēhōl) *n.* Small or snug room, compartment, niche, cupboard, etc.

cube (kūb) *n.* 1. Regular solid figure contained by six equal squares; anything of this shape. 2. (math.) Third power of a quantity; ~ **root,** number or quantity which when cubed produces given number or quantity. **cube** *v.t.* (**cubed, cub·ing**). 1. Find cube of (number), find cubic content of. 2. Cut into small cubes. 3. Tenderize (meat) by slashing the fibers in a pattern of squares; ~ **steak,** thin slice of cubed beef, usu. broiled in a pan.

cu·beb (kū′bĕb) *n.* Pungent spicy berry of Javanese climbi shrub (*Piper cubeba*), formerly us in medicinal cigarettes.

cu·bic (kū′bĭk) *adj.* Cub shaped; of three dimensions, sol involving cube of a quantity; **content,** volume (of solid) e pressed in cubic feet, meters, et ~ **foot, inch,** etc., volume of a cu whose edge is one foot, inch, e **cu′bi·cal** *adj.* **cu′bi·cal·ly** *adv.*

cu·bi·cle (kū′bĭkel) *n.* Sm sleeping compartment; any sm partitioned space, esp. for study work purposes.

cu·bi·form (kū′bĭfōrm) *a* Cube-shaped.

Cub·ism (kū′bĭzem) *n.* Phase Post-Impressionist art, initiat *c*1907 by Picasso and Braque, which objects were reduced to cu and other geometrical forms. **cub ist** *n.* & *adj.* **cu·bis·tic** (kūbĭs′t *adj.*

cu·bit (kū′bĭt) *n.* Ancie measure of length, 17 to 21 i **cu′bi·tal** *adj.* 1. Of the leng of a cubit. 2. Of the for arm or corresponding part

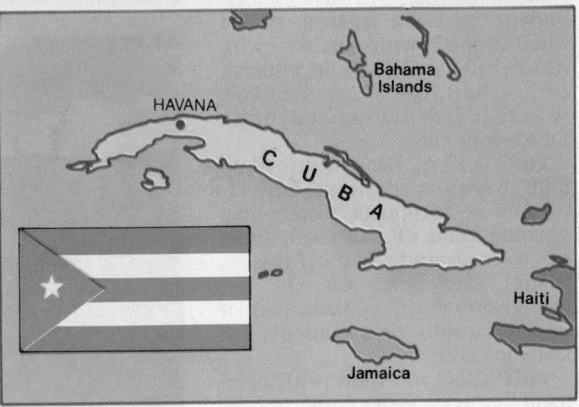

Cuba's population is multi-racial but wholly Spanish-speaking. The mainly agricultural economy is based on sugar, tobacco, coffee, fruit, and cattle. Cuba has rich mineral reserves, particularly of iron ore. Cuba is important as the closest Communist country to the U.S.A.

*The cultivation of the **cucumber** is believed to have started in S. Asia and its use certainly spread to the Ancient Greeks and Romans from India. The plant trails or climbs.*

animals. [L. *cubitum* length of forearm (*cubitus* elbow)]

cu·boid (kū′boid) *adj.* Cubeshaped, like a cube; of the ~ **bone.** **cuboid** *n.* Solid resembling cube, with rectangular faces not all equal; (also ~ **bone**) one of the bones of the foot, between heel bone and fourth and fifth metatarsal bones.

cuck·ing (kŭk′ĭng) **stool.** (hist.) Chair in which nagging women, dishonest tradesmen, etc. were tied and exposed to public ridicule or ducked in water.

cuck·old (kŭk′old) *n.* Husband of unfaithful wife. ~ *v.t.* Make a cuckold of. [OF. *cucu* cuckoo]

cuck·oo (kōō′kōō, kŏŏk′ōō) *n.* (pl. **-oos**). Migratory bird of family Cuculidae with characteristic note or cry, esp. yellow-billed cuckoo (*Coccyzus americanus*) and blackbilled cuckoo (*C. erythrophthalmus*); characteristic two-note call or cry of this bird; ~ **clock,** clock in which hours are sounded by imitation of cuckoo's call; **cuck′oo-flower,** lady's smock (*Cardamine pratensis*), plant with pale lilac flower, blooming in spring. **cuckoo** *adj.* (slang) Crazy; foolish. [OF. *cuca* imit. of bird's cry]

cu·cum·ber (kū′kŭmber) *n.* 1. Creeping plant (*Cucumis sativus*) widely cultivated for its long fleshy fruit; the fruit of this, commonly eaten as salad. 2. (also ~ **tree**), N. Amer. tree (*Magnolia acuminata*), also called cucumber magnolia, with fruit resembling small cucumbers.

cud (kŭd) *n.* Food that ruminating animal brings back from first stomach into mouth and chews at leisure; a quid of chewing tobacco; **chew one's ~,** ruminate, ponder.

cud·dle (kŭd′el) *v.* (**-dled,**

The early history of **cultivation** and how suitable kinds of seed were developed and propagated is little known. Today advanced techniques are used to evolve crops resistant to pests, adapted to particular conditions and high-yielding. 1. Flax drying near Foxton, New Zealand. 2. Sugar beet on peatland in Lancashire, U.K.

-dling). Hug gently, fondle; lie close and snug; nestle together; curl oneself *up*. ~ *n*. Act of cuddling. **cud·dle·some** (kŭd′elsom), **cud·dly** (kŭd′lē) *adjs*. (**-dli·er, -dli·est**). Pleasant to cuddle.

cudg·el (kŭj′el) *n*. Short thick stick used as weapon. ~ *v.t.* Beat with cudgel; (fig.) rack (one's brains).

cue[1] (kū) *n*. Last word or words of a speech in a play, serving as signal to another actor to enter or speak; similar guide to musical performer; sign or intimation when or how to speak or act etc. ~ *v.t.* (**cued, cu·ing, cue·ing**). Give cue to; ~ **in**, insert cue for; (slang) inform.

cue[2] (kū) *n*. 1. (usu. *queue*) Pigtail. 2. Long tapering rod of wood tipped with leather, with which balls are struck in billiards etc.; ~ **ball**, ball struck with cue. ~ *v.t.* (**cued, cu·ing, cue·ing**). Strike with cue.

cuff[1] (kŭf) *n*. Band or turned up fold at bottom of sleeve; turned-up fold at bottom of trouser leg; separate band of (stiffened) linen etc. worn around wrist; **off the** ~, (slang) extempore; **on the** ~, (slang) on credit; ~ **link**, pair of linked buttons or ornaments for fastening shirt cuff.

cuff[2] (kŭf) *n*. Blow with open hand. ~ *v.t.* Strike thus.

cui·rass (kwĭrăs′) *n*. Body armor, breastplate and backplate fastened together. **cui·ras·sier** (kwĭrasēr′) *n*. Cavalryman wearing cuirass.

cui·sine (kwĭzēn′) *n*. Style of cooking; food cooked (in a given style).

cuisse (kwĭs) *n*. (hist., usu. pl.) Thigh armor.

cul-de-sac (kŭl′desăk, kool′-kŭldesăk′, kool-) *n*. Dead-end street. [Fr., "bottom of the sack"]

cu·let (kū′lĭt, kŭl′ĭt) *n*. Horizontal face forming bottom of brilliant cut gem.

cu·li·nar·y (kū′lĭnĕrē, kŭl′ĭ-) *adj*. Pertaining to, fit for a kitchen or cooking.

cull (kŭl) *v.t.* Pick out from others; select; gather; kill surplus (animals, as deer, seals, etc.). ~ *n*. Act of culling; something picked out from others, usu. as inferior.

culm[1] (kŭlm) *n*. Waste and coal dust from anthracite mines; inferior anthracite coal.

culm[2] (kŭlm) *n*. (bot.) Stem of

Cultivators

trip cord

depth control lever

draw bar

harrow attachment

spring tine

tine		loop spring

plant, esp. jointed, usu. hollow, stem of grasses.

cul·mi·nant (kŭl′mĭnant) *adj*. At, forming, the top; culminating; highest. **cul·mi·nate** (kŭl′mĭnāt) *v.t.* (**-nat·ed, -nat·ing**). Reach its highest point; (astron.) be on the meridian. **cul·mi·na·tion** (kŭlmĭnā′shon) *n*.

cu·lottes (koo′lŏts, kū′-, koo-lŏts′, kū-) *n.pl.* Women's trousers cut to resemble skirt; divided skir

cul·pa·ble (kŭl′pabel) *ad* Criminal, blameworthy. **cul·pa bil·i·ty** (kŭlpabĭl′ĭtē) *n*. **cul′pa·bl** *adv*.

cul·prit (kŭl′prĭt) *n*. Perso charged with a crime or offens guilty person; wrongdoer. [orig. 17th c. legal phrase to prisone pleading "Not Guilty"; prol abbreviation of Anglo-Fr. *Cu* *able: prest d'averrer* etc. (You are) guilty: (I am) ready to prove etc.]

cult (kŭlt) *n.* System or community of religious worship and ritual, esp. one with rites centering round sacred symbols; devotion, homage, to person or thing; object of such devotion; group bound together by devotion to an idea, interest, object, etc.

cul·ti·vate (kŭl'tĭvāt) *v.t.* (-vat·ed, -vat·ing). 1. Till; break up (ground) with cultivator to prepare for planting; grow, tend (crops, flowers, etc.). 2. Improve, develop (person, mind, etc., esp. in last part.); pay attention to, cherish; seek the acceptance or good will of. **cul·ti·va·ble** (kŭl'tĭvabel) *adj.* Capable of being cultivated. **cul·ti·va·tion** (kŭltĭvā'shon) *n.* Cultivating, cultivated state. **cul·ti·va·tor** (kŭl'tĭvāter) *n.* 1. Tiller, farmer. 2. Agricultural implement for breaking up ground and uprooting weeds between growing plants.

cul·ture (kŭl'cher) *n.* 1. Tillage; rearing, production (of trees, crops, animals, etc.); (biol.) artificial development of bacteria etc. in specially prepared media; bacteria etc. so produced. 2. Improvement or refinement of mind, manners, etc., by education and training; condition of being thus trained and refined, esp. in the arts. 3. Particular form or type of intellectual development or civilization; ~ **shock**, state of confusion in people who abruptly come into contact with a cultural environment completely different from that to which they are accustomed. **cul·tur·al** (kŭl'chural) *adj.* (esp.) ~ **revolu·tion**, movement and vast purge in People's Republic of China, begun in 1965, seeking to restore original purity of Maoist doctrine. **cul'·tur·al·ly** *adv.* **culture** *v.t.* (-tured, -tur·ing). Cultivate (esp. fig.); (biol.) make a culture of bacteria etc.); **cultured pearl,**

Cumberland Gap was of strategic importance during the U.S. Civil War and was alternately held by Federal and Confederate troops.

pearl formed by oyster after artificial insertion of foreign body.

cul·vert (kŭl'vert) *n.* Channel, conduit, carrying water across, under road, canal, etc.

cum (kŭm, kōōm) *prep.* With; plus; ~ *gra·no sa·lis* (kŭm grā'nō sā'lĭs; *Lat.* kōōm grah'nō sah'lĭs), with skepticism (L., = "with a grain of salt"); **cum lau·de** (kōōm low'dā, -dē, -de, kŭm law'dē) with honor; used on diplomas to indicate graduation with high rank. Cf. MAGNA CUM LAUDE; SUMMA CUM LAUDE. [L.]

cum. *abbrev.* Cumulative.

cum·ber (kŭm'ber) *v.t.* Hamper, hinder; burden. **cum'ber·some** *adj.* Unwieldly, clumsy.

cum'ber·some·ly *adv.* **cum'ber·some·ness** *n.*

Cum·ber·land (kŭm'berland). River flowing from E. Kentucky through Tennessee and Kentucky to the Ohio River; **C~ Gap,** pass through the Cumberland Mountains at the border of Kentucky, Tennessee, and Virginia, used by Daniel Boone and early settlers; **C~ Road,** first national highway in the U.S., started 1811, from Cumberland, Md., to Vandalia, Ill.

cum·brous (kŭm'brus) *adj.* Cumbersome. **cum'brous·ly** *adv.* **cum'brous·ness** *n.*

cum·in, cum·min (kŭm'ĭn) *ns.* Umbelliferous plant (*Cuminum cyminum*) of the parsley family; aromatic seeds of this plant, used as a condiment.

cum·mer·bund (kŭm'erbŭnd) *n.* Broad, pleated waist sash worn as part of men's formal dress. [Hind. *kamar-band* loin band]

Cum·mings (kŭm'ĭngz), **Ed·ward Estin** (until the 1930s preferred the lower-case **e. e. cum·mings**) (1894–1962). Amer. poet; used unique typography and punctuation to indicate rhythmic pattern and meaning in his poetry.

cu·mu·late (kū'myulāt) *v.* (-lat·ed, -lat·ing). Accumulate. **cu·mu·la·tion** (kūmyulā'shon) *n.*

cu·mu·la·tive (kū'myulatĭv) *adj.* Tending to accumulate; increasing in force etc. by successive additions. **cu'mu·la·tive·ly** *adv.* **cu'mu·la·tive·ness** *n.*

Cultivators take many forms, and may be simple hand-held hoes, or mechanized ploughs driven by tractors.

Cuneiform *lettering is the earliest known form of writing and was used by the Mesopotamians in the 4th and 3rd millennia BC. Many of the characters are purely pictorial.*

Tulips in Augusta, Maine, U.S.A. The colorful **cup**-*shaped blossom of the tulip makes it a world-wide favorite with horticulturists.*

cu·mu·lo·nim·bus (kūmyulō-nĭm′bus) *n.* (pl. **-bus**). (meteor.) Type of ~ dense cloud, a tall voluminous mass, present in thunderstorms.

cu·mu·lus (kū′myulus) *n.* (pl. **-lus**). (meteor.) Form of CLOUD, usu. low, consisting of rounded masses heaped up on nearly horizontal base, frequent in summer skies.

cu·ne·ate (kū′nēĭt, -āt) *adj.* Wedge-shaped.

cu·ne·i·form (kūnē′ĭfōrm, kū′nē-) *adj.* Wedge-shaped; composed of wedge-shaped or arrow-head marks used in ancient inscriptions of Assyria, Babylonia, Persia; ~ **bone,** wedge-shaped bone. **cuneiform** *n.* Cuneiform characters or writing impressed in clay in ancient times.

cun·ning (kŭn′ĭng) *n.* Skill, dexterity; skill in deceit or evasion. ~ *adj.* Possessed of or displaying cunning; (colloq.) quaintly pretty. **cun′ning·ly** *adv.* **cun′ning·ness** *n.*

cunt (kŭnt) *n.* (vulg.) 1. Female pudendum. 2. Applied abusively to woman.

cup (kŭp) *n.* 1. Any drinking vessel with or without handle and stem; (esp. in modern use) a small drinking vessel with a handle and having a flat bottom; ornamental cup or other vessel as prize for race or other contest. 2. Rounded cavity, as socket of certain bones, cup-shaped hardened involucre of an acorn, calyx of flower, cup-shaped blossom, etc. 3. Cupful; (as measure in recipes) half pint, 8 fluid ounces; (fig.) something to be partaken of, experience, portion, lot; (pl.) potations; **in one's ~s,** drunk; **one's ~ of tea,** (colloq.) what interests or suits one. 4. Beverage of wine, cider, fruit juice, etc., sweetened and flavored, and usu. iced; **cup′-bearer,** one who serves wine, esp. officer of royal or noble household; **cup′cake,** small cake baked in cup-shaped container and serving one person. **cup** *v.* (**cupped, cup·-**

There are several species of **curass** *These game birds live in trees in s flocks and build nests of deli branches interwoven with grass. T are sometimes semi-tamed.*

ping). Take or contain as in a cup, make or be cup-shaped. **cup′ful** *n.*

cup·board (kŭb′erd) *n.* Recess or structure, usu. with shelves and door, for storage of dishes and food.

Cu·pid (kū′pĭd). (Rom. myth.) God of love, son of Venus; identified with the Greek Eros; often represented as a beautiful naked boy with wings, carrying bow and arrows. ~**'s bow,** (line or shape resembling) the double-curved bow of Cupid. [L. *cupido* desire, love]

cu·pid·i·ty (kūpĭd′ĭtē) *n.* Gr of gain, avarice.

cu·po·la (kū′pola) *n.* 1. Do forming the roof of a building part of a building; diminutive do above a roof; ceiling of dome. Furnace for melting metals for ca ing (formerly with dome leading chimney, now often without dom

cu·pric (kū′prĭk, kōō′-) a (chem.) Containing copper in bi lent state.

cu·prous (kū′prus, kōō′-) (chem.) Containing copper in u

cu·pule (kū′pūl) *n.* (bot., zool.) up-shaped organ, receptacle, etc.

cur (ker) *n.* Worthless, lowbred, snappish dog; mongrel; surly, -bred, or cowardly fellow.

Cu·ra·çao (kūr′asō, koor′asow). Dutch island in Caribbean off the NW. coast of Venezuela; main sland of the Netherlands Antilles; apital: Willemstad; **curaçao** *n.* iqueur flavored with peel of bitter ranges, first produced in Curaçao.

cu·ra·cy (kūr′asē) *n.* (pl. **-cies**). Curate's office, duties, or term of ffice.

cu·ra·re, cu·ra·ri (kyurār′ē, u-) *ns.* Blackish-brown resinous itter poisonous substance ex-racted from S. Amer. tropical lants (esp. *Strychnos toxifera*), sed by Indians to poison their rrows, and consisting of various lkaloids that block the action of the notor nerves on skeletal muscle. corrupt. of *wurali*, native Carib ame]

cu·ras·sow (kūr′asō, kyurăs′ō). Any of several long-tailed tropi-al Amer. game birds of the family Cracidae, related to domestic fowl and pheasants.

cu·rate (kūr′ĭt) *n.* 1. (chiefly Brit.) Clergyman who assists or is deputy of a vicar or rector. 2. (archaic) Clergyman in charge of a parish; parish priest.

cu·ra·tive (kūr′ativ) *adj. & n.* (Thing) tending to cure (esp. disease).

cu·ra·tor (kyurā′ter, kūr′ā-) *n.* Person in charge, manager, of museum, library, etc. **cu·ra·to·ri·al** (kūrator′ēal, -tōr′-) *adj.* **cu·ra′tor·ship** *n.*

curb (kerb) *n.* 1. Chain, strap, passing under lower jaw of horse, used as check; (fig.) check, re-straint. 2. Hard swelling on back of horse's hind leg. 3. Concrete or stone edging along the side of a street and forming part of the gutter. ~ *v.t.* Apply curb to; restrain.

cur·cu·ma (ker′kyuma) *n.* Tuberous plant of genus *C~* yield-ing arrowroot, turmeric, etc. [Arab. *kurkum* saffron, turmeric]

curd (kerd) *n.* (often pl.) Co-agulated substance formed (natur-ally or artificially) by action of acids on milk, made into cheese or eaten as food; anything resembling this. **curd′y** *adj.* (**curd·i·er, curd·i-est**).

cur·dle (ker′del) *v.* (**-dled, -dling**). Congeal, form into curd; ~ **the blood**, horrify, terrify.

cure (kūr) *n.* 1. Remedy; course of medical or other treatment (esp. of specified kind); successful medi-cal treatment, restoration to health; ~**all** (*n.*) panacea. 2. Spiritual charge or care of parishioners etc.; parish etc. **cure** *v.* (**cured, cur-ing**). Restore to health; remedy (an evil). 2. Preserve (meat, fruit, hides) by salting, drying, smoking, etc. 3. Render (substance) harder or more durable. **cur′a·ble** *adj.* **cur·a·bil·i·ty** (kūrabĭl′ĭtē) *n.*

cu·ré (kyurā′, kūr′ā) *n.* Parish priest in France etc.

cu·ret, cu·rette (kyurĕt′) *ns.* Sugeon's small scoop-like instru-ment. **curet** *v.t.* Scrape with curet. **cu·ret·tage** (kūretahzh′, kūr′etahzh) *n.* Process of curetting, esp. tissue from the uterus.

cur·few (ker′fū) *n.* 1. Medieval regulation for extinction of fires at fixed hour in evening (orig. for pre-vention of conflagrations); hour for this, bell announcing it. 2. Signal or time after which all inhabitants, or specified groups (as young people), must be indoors.

cu·ri·a (kūr′ēa, koor′-) *n.* (pl. **cu·ri·ae** pr. kūr′ēē, -ī, koor′ēī). 1. (Rom. hist.) One of the ten divisions of each of the three ancient Roman tribes; building belonging to such division, serving primarily for wor-ship. 2. Senate house at Rome; senate of ancient Italian towns. 3. Court of justice, esp. under feudal organization. 4. (**C~**) Papal court, government departments of the Vatican. **cu′ri·al** *adj.*

cu·rie (kūr′ē) *n.* Unit of radio-activity equal to 3.7×10^{10} dis-integrations per second. [f. CURIE]

Cu·rie (kūr′ē, kyoorē′), **Marie** (1867–1934). Original name, Marja Sklodowska; Polish-born French physical chemist; discovered polo-nium and radium, isolated radium from pitchblende, and investigated radioactivity; was awarded Nobel Prize for physics, with her husband, Pierre, 1903, and Nobel Prize for chemistry, 1911; died of leukemia caused by radiation; her husband, **Pierre Curie** (1859–1906), French chemist, conducted research on magnetism; worked on radio-activity with his wife Marie and was awarded Nobel Prize for physics with her, 1903; their daughter,

*The **cupola** is the small dome most usually seen at the top of a large domed structure. In the Italian town of Alverobella in Apulia, however, all the houses are built with cupolas in stone and without cement.*

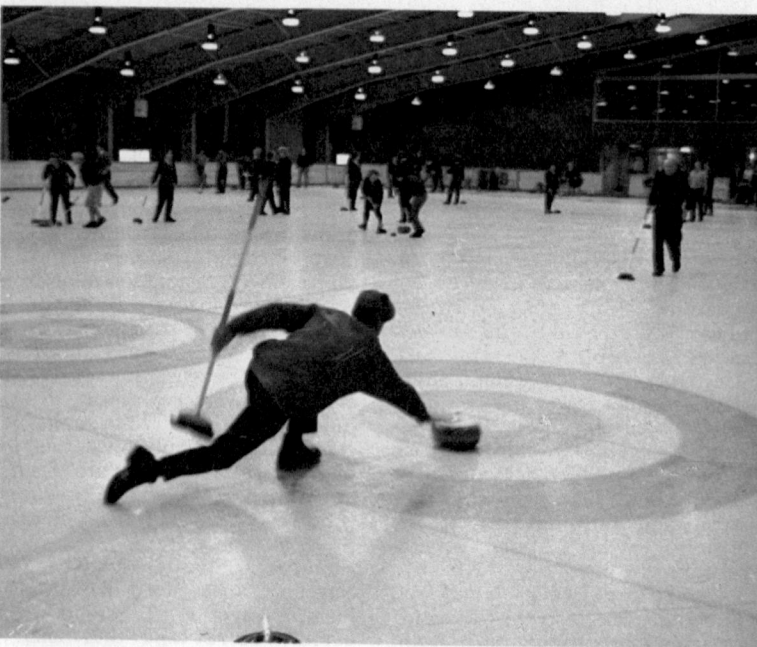

Irene Curie (1897–1956), physicist, shared Nobel Prize with her husband, Frederic Joliot (later Joliot-Curie), 1935, in chemistry, for synthesis of new radioactive elements.

cu·ri·o (kūr′ēō′) n. (pl. **-os**). Curious object of art or piece of bric-a-brac.

cu·ri·o·sa (kūrēō′sa) n.pl. Curiosities, esp. books, pamphlets, etc. dealing with unusual subjects; erotica.

cu·ri·os·i·ty (kūrēŏs′ĭtē) n. (pl. **-ties**). 1. Inquisitiveness; desire to know. 2. Strangeness; strange or rare object.

cu·ri·ous (kūr′ēus) adj. 1. Inquisitive; eager to learn. 2. Strange, surprising. **cu′ri·ous·ly** adv. **cu′ri·ous·ness** n.

cu·ri·um (kūr′ēum) n. (chem.) Radioactive metallic transuranic element; symbol Cm, at. no. 96, principal isotope at. wt. 242. [f. CURIE]

curl (kĕrl) n. Spiral or convolute lock of hair; anything spiral or incurved; act of curling; state of being curled. ~ v. 1. Bend, coil, into spiral or curved shape; move in spiral or curved form. 2. Play at CURLING. **curl′er** n. (esp.) Pin, clip, etc., for curling the hair. **curl′y** adj. (**curl·i·er, curl·i·est**). **curl′i·ness** n.

cur·lew (kĕr′lōō) n. (pl. **-lews**, collect. **-lew**). Wading shore bird of the genus Numenius, esp. the long-billed curlew (N. americanus), with long slender curved bill.

curl·i·cue (kĕr′lĭkū) n. Decorative curl or twist.

curl·ing (kĕr′lĭng) n. (esp.) 1. Scottish game played on ice with large stones that are hurled along a rink toward a tee; ~ **stone**,

Two Bruegel paintings have been used as evidence that **curling**, *a Scottish game, originated in Holland. But, Holland has no granite curling-stones.*

oblate stone used in this, of polished granite, and not more than 36 in. in circumference or 50 lb. in weight, with an iron or wooden handle on the upper surface. 2. ~ **iron**, tongs for curling the hair.

cur·mudg·eon (kermŭj′on) n. Churlish or miserly fellow. **cur·mudg′eon·ly** adv.

cur·rant (kĕr′ant, kŭr′-) n. 1. Small seedless raisin grown in California and eastern Mediterranean regions, used in cooking. 2. Small red, black, or greenish fruit of any of various prickly shrubs of genus Ribes having a sour taste and used for making jelly. 3. Shrub bearing such fruit. [orig. raisins of Corauntz (Corinth)]

cur·ren·cy (kĕr′ensē, kŭr′-) n. (pl. **-cies**). 1. Time during which thing is current; (of money) circulation; (of words, ideas, etc.) prevalence. 2. Money in actual use in a country; **hard, soft,** ~: see HARD, SOFT.

cur·rent (kĕr′ent, kŭr′-) adj. In general circulation or use; popular, in vogue; (of time) now passing; belonging to, of the current time. **cur′rent·ly** adv. **current** n. 1. Running stream; water, air, etc., moving in given direction. 2. Course, tendency (of events, opinions, etc.). 3. Transmission of electricity, electricity transmitted, through a body.

cur·ri·cle (kĕr′ĭkel, kŭr′-) n. Light open two-wheeled carriage drawn by two horses abreast.

cur·ric·u·lum (kurĭk′yulum) n. (pl. **-lums, -la** pr. **-la**). 1. Course

(of study); all courses offered school or college; series of cou leading to a particular degree certificate. 2. ~ **vitae**, account of one's career; resu **cur·ric′u·lar** adj. [L.]

cur·ri·er (kĕr′ēer, kŭr′-) n. who dresses and colors tan leather.

Cur·ri·er (kĕr′ēer, kŭr′-) **Ives** (īvz). **Nathaniel Curr** (1813–88) and **James Merritt I** (1824–95). Partners in an Ar lithographing company famous vivid prints depicting An events, life, and people.

cur·ry[1] (kĕr′ē, kŭr′ē) n. **-ries**). Curry powder; dish meat, fish, fruit, or vegetab cooked with curry powder and served with rice; ~ **powder**, pi aration of turmeric and st spices for making curries. **cu** v.t. (**-ried, -ry·ing**). Make curry; season with curry pow [Tamil kari sauce]

cur·ry[2] (kĕr′ē, kŭr′ē) v.t. (**-ri -ry·ing**). 1. Rub down or d (horse etc.) with comb; d (tanned leather) by soaki scraping, beating, coloring, etc. **favor** (orig. favel, f. OF. fau chestnut horse), ingratiate one (with person) by officious court etc.; **cur′rycomb**, comb for cur ing horses etc.; (v.t.) curry.

The **curlew** *(Numenius arquata)* 1½–2 ft long with a bill 5–7 *Species are found in Europe, Amer Africa, and Australia. They perfe strange dances and have odd courts rites.*

Horse's leap from rearing position, with hind legs outstretched before forelegs reach ground. ~ *v.i.* (**-vet·ted, -vet·ed, -vet·ting, -vet·ing**). (of horse or rider) Make curvet.

cur·vi·lin·e·ar (kẽrvĭlĭn'ēer) *adj.* Contained by, consisting of, curved line(s). **cur·vi·lin'e·ar·ly** *adv.*

cu·sec (kū'sĕk) *n.* Unit of flow of liquids, one cubic foot per second.

Cush (kŭsh). Oldest son of Ham; **land of C~**, ancient legendary region in Africa, identified with Ethiopia, settled by descendants of Cush.

Cush·ing (kōōsh'ĭng), **Harvey William** (1869–1939). Amer. physician specializing in brain surgery; awarded Pulitzer Prize, 1925.

cush·ion (kōōsh'on) *n.* 1. Case of cloth etc. filled with soft material or air, for sitting, kneeling, or reclining on or against. 2. Elastic lining or rim of inner side of billiard table, from which the balls rebound; soft buffer; body of air or stream as buffer or support. ~ *v.* Furnish, protect, with cushions; (fig.) protect against shock, mitigate effects of.

cush·y (kōōsh'ē) *adj.* (**cush·i·er, cush·i·est**). (slang; of job, task, etc.) Easy, pleasant, well paid. [Hind. *khush* pleasant]

cusp (kŭsp) *n.* Apex, peak; (geom.) point at which two branches of curve meet and stop; (archit.) projecting point between small arcs in tracery; (astrol.) initial point of house; (bot.) pointed end, esp. of leaf. **cus·pate** (kŭs'pĭt, -pāt), **cusped** (kŭspt), **cus·pi·date** (kŭs'pĭdāt), **cus·pi·dat·ed** (kŭs'pĭdātĕd) *adjs.*

cus·pi·dor (kŭs'pĭdōr) *n.* Spittoon.

cuss (kŭs) *v.* (colloq.) Curse. ~ *n.* (colloq.) Curse; person (esp. an odd or perverse one). **cuss'ed·ness** *n.* Peversity.

cus·tard (kŭs'terd) *n.* Dish of beaten eggs and milk, baked or cooked; ~ **apple**, fruit of S. Amer. and W. Ind. tree (*Anona reticulata*) with dark brown rind and yellowish pulp like custard in appearance and flavor.

Cus·ter (kŭs'ter), **William Armstrong** (1839–76). Amer. army officer; Union general and cavalry hero during Civil War; active on western patrol duty and in Indian fighting; killed with all of his troops by Sioux Indians led by Sitting Bull and Crazy Horse at battle of Little Big Horn, 1876, famous as "Custer's Last Stand."

cus·to·di·al (kŭstō'dēal) *adj.* Relating to custody.

cus·to·di·an (kŭstō'dēan) *n.* Guardian, keeper, esp. of public building etc.

cus·to·dy (kŭs'todē) *n.* (pl. **-dies**). Guardianship, care; im-

---

curse (kẽrs) *n.* 1. Utterance (by deity or person invoking deity) supposed or intended to consign person thing to destruction, divine vengeance, etc.; formal ecclesiastical censure, sentence of excommunication. 2. Profane oath, imprecation. 3. Evil inflicted in response to curse; great evil, bane. ~ *v.* (**cursed, curst, curs·ing**). Utter curse against; excommunicate; afflict *with*; utter curses; swear profanely.

curs·ed (kẽr'sĭd) *adj.* (esp.) damnable, abominable. **curs'·ly** *adv.* **curs'ed·ness** *n.*

cur·sive (kẽr'sĭv) *adj.* & *n.* (Writing) done in a flowing style, with the characters joined together.

cur·so·ri·al (kersōr'ēal, -sōr'-) *adj.* (zool.) of birds etc.). Having limbs adapted for running.

cur·so·ry (kẽr'serē) *adj.* Hasty, superficial. **cur·so·ri·ly** *adv.* **cur'so·ri·ness** *n.*

curt (kẽrt) *adj.* Discourteously brief; terse, concise. **curt'ly** *adv.* **curt'ness** *n.*

cur·tail (kertāl') *v.t.* Cut short. **cur·tail'ment** *n.*

cur·tain (kẽr'tĭn) *n.* 1. Suspended cloth used as screen esp. at window; screen separating state of theater from auditorium; (fig.) = IRON curtain. 2. Partition, cover, in various technical senses; (mil.) barrage. 3. (pl., colloq.) The end. ~ **call**, call for actor to appear before curtain after play or scene of play to take bow and receive applause; ~ **raiser**, short opening piece performed before principal play in theater; ~ **rod**, horizontal rod from which curtain is hung. **curtain** *v.t.* Furish, cover, shut off, with curtains.

Cur·tis (kẽr'tĭs), **Charles**

The custard apple is the name used for the fruit of some trees in the genus Anona. Other varieties may be called sweetsops and bullock's hearts.

(1860–1936). Vice president of the U.S. under Herbert Hoover, 1929–1933.

Cur·tiss (kẽr'tĭs), **Glen Hammond** (1878–1930). Amer. aviation pioneer; designer and manufacturer of engines, motorcycles, speedboats, and airplanes; accomplished first U.S. airplane flight of 1 mi. distance, 1908; held early airplane speed records; developed hydroplane and flying boat.

curt·sy, curt·sey (kẽrt'sē) *ns.* (pl. **-sies, -seys**). Feminine bow of respect or salutation, made by placing one foot behind the other and bending the knees so that trunk is lowered (usu. **make a ~**). ~ *v.i.* (**-sied, -sy·ing, -sey·ing**). Make curtsy (*to* person).

cur·va·ture (kẽr'vacher) *n.* Curving; curved form; (geom.) amount or rate of deviation (of curve) from straight line or curved surface from plane.

curve (kẽrv) *n.* 1. Line of which no part is straight, locus traced by moving point, the direction of whose motion continuously changes or deviates from a straight line; curved form or thing; (on graph or diagram) line drawn from point to point so as to represent diagrammatically a continuous variation of quantity, force, etc. 2. (baseball) (also ~ **ball**) pitched ball that curves as it approaches the batter. ~ *v.* (**curved, curv·ing**). Bend or shape so as to form curve; make, travel in a curve; (baseball) pitch a curve ball to.

cur·vet (kervĕt', kẽr'vĭt) *n.*

prisonment, legal detention.

cus·tom (kŭs′tom) *n.* 1. Usual practice; (law) established usage having the force of law. 2. (pl.) Duty levied on imports from foreign countries; **Customs,** government agency collecting such duties; **custom(s) house,** office (esp. in seaport) at which customs are collected. 3. Business patronage, as of a store; **custom-made clothes,** clothes made to measure (so ∼**-made suit** etc.). 4. ∼**built,** (*adj.*) built to customer's order.

cus·tom·ar·y (kŭs′tomĕrē) *adj.* Usual; (law) subject to, held by, custom (of a property etc.). **cus·tom·ar·i·ly** (kŭstomĕr′ĭlē, kŭs′tomĕr-) *adv.*

cus·tom·er (kŭs′tomer) *n.* Buyer, purchaser; patron, shopper; (slang) (**cool, tough, ugly,** etc. ∼), person to be dealt with.

cut (kŭt) *v.* (**cut, cut·ting**). 1. Penetrate, wound, with edged instrument (also fig.); divide with knife etc. (*in, into,* pieces etc.); detach by cutting; carve (meat). 2. Cross, intersect; pass *across, through,* etc.; (slang) leave, go quickly. 3. Reduce by cutting (hair etc.); reduce (wages, price, time, etc.); shape, fashion, by cutting; edit (film); (motion pictures) make quick transition *to* next shot. 4. Perform, execute, make, as ∼ **a caper, figure,** etc. 5. Divide (pack of cards) into two or more parts and combine them into new order to prevent cheating or before drawing cards to select dealer or partners, etc. 6. (tennis) Strike ball across its line of flight so as to impart spin etc; (baseball) swing (*at* a pitched ball). 7. Renounce acquaintance of (person), decline to recognize him or her; absent oneself from, avoid, renounce. 8. Have (tooth) appear through gum. 9. ∼ **corners,** pass around corner(s) closely or go over them; (fig.) take unorthodox course, omit details to save time; act illegally; ∼ **down,** bring or throw down by cutting; reduce (expenses etc.); ∼ **in,** enter abruptly, interpose, supersede a partner during a dance; obstruct path of vehicle by moving sharply in front of it after overtaking; ∼ **it out** (slang) stop, cease; ∼ **off,** remove by cutting; bring to an end; intercept, interrupt (supplies, communications); exclude (*from*); obstruct path of oncoming vehicle by moving out from one's own side of the road; ∼ **out,** remove by cutting; outdo or supplant (rival); shape by cutting (out of a piece); form, fashion (esp. fig. in past part.); disconnect; (slang) leave, depart; separate (cattle) from herd, select; **have one's work** ∼ **out,** have a difficult task; ∼ **up,** cut in pieces; (slang) criticize severely; (boxing) lacerate

The **cuttlefish** is a salt-water invertebrate related to the octopus and sometimes confused with the squid; its distinguishing feature is the cuttlebone. There are about 100 species inhabiting mainly shallow coastal waters. The eggs of the common cuttlefish (above) are laid on pieces of coral, plants or on the tubes of marine worms.

(opponent's face); play pranks; behave in a silly manner. 10. ∼ **and dried,** (of opinions etc.) readymade, lacking freshness; **cut′away,** man's formal coat cut to taper toward the tails; **cut′back** (*n.*), reduction of expenditures etc., pruning; **cut′off,** shorter channel or route cutting off bend etc., bypass; **cut′out,** device for automatically disconnecting (electric circuit etc.); **cut′purse** (archaic) thief; **cut′throat** (*n.*) murderer; bloodthirsty ruffian; (*adj.*) intensive, merciless; **cut′worm,** caterpillar that cuts off young plants level with ground. **cut** *n.* 1. Act of cutting; stroke, blow, with knife, sword, whip; act, speech, deeply wounding the feelings; excision of a part; reduction in wages, prices, time, etc. 2. Particular stroke in tennis or baseball (see *v.* def. 6). 3. Avoiding, renouncing of acquaintance. 4. Passage or way across, esp. as opposed to going round about (**short′cut**). 5. Way something is cut. 6. Wound made by cutting; incision, slash. 7. Passage, channel, opening. 8. Engraved plate or wood block used for printing. 9. Piece, esp. of meat, cut off. 10. (slang) Share (of profit etc.). 11. Unexcused absence from school or a particular class. 12. ∼ **above,** (colloq.) Slightly better than.

cu·ta·ne·ous (kūtā′nēus) *adj.* Of the skin.

cute (kūt) *adj.* (**cut·er, cut·est**). Affectedly clever or pretty, precious; (colloq.) pleasingly personable and pert; shrewd. **cute′ly** *adv.* **cute′ness** *n.*

cu·ti·cle (kū′tĭkel) *n.* Epidermis or other superficial skin; dead skin at base of fingernail or toenail; (bot.) continuous layer of impervious material secreted by cells of epidermis. **cu·tic·u·lar** (kūtĭk′yuler) *adj.*

cut·ie (kū′tē) *n.* (slang) Attrac

Several kinds of small vessel are referred to as **cutters**. That shown, a gaff cutter, was quite fast and used as an auxiliary to a war fleet or in the prevention of smuggling.

e **cyclamen** originated in the editerranean region. Of the 15 or so ecies, **Cyclamen Indicum** has come the most popular as a hardy door plant.

ve young woman; cute person.

cu·tis (kū´tĭs) n. (pl. **-tes** pr. -tēz, **is·es**). (anat.) True skin or ermis.

cut·lass, cut·las (kŭt´las) ns. hort sword with slightly curved lade, esp. that formerly used by ilors.

cut·ler (kŭt´ler) n. One who akes or deals in knives and similar tensils. **cut·ler·y** (kŭt´lerē) n. rade of cutler; things made or sold y cutlers; household knives, forks, d spoons.

cut·let (kŭt´lĭt) n. 1. Thinly iced meat, esp. lamb or veal, itable for frying or broiling. 2. mall flat croquette of minced eat, fish, or fowl.

cut·ter (kŭt´er) n. 1. Person, ing, that cuts; cutting part of machine. 2. Boat belonging to ship of war, fitted for rowing and sailing; small single–masted vessel rigged like sloop but with running bowsprit; fast armed motorboat used by the Coast Guard; small light sleigh, usu. drawn by one horse.

cut·ting (kŭt´ĭng) n. (esp.) 1. Excavation, as of high ground for railroad, road, etc. 2. Piece cut from plant for propagation. ~ adj. (esp.) That wounds the mind or feelings. **cut´ting·ly** adv.

cut·tle·fish (kŭt´elfĭsh) n. (pl. ~**fishes**, collect. ~**fish**). Squidlike cephalopod of genus *Sepia*, esp. *S. officinalis*, which when pursued ejects black fluid from a sac and darkens water.

Cu·vi·er (kōō´vēā, kōōvyā´), **Georges Léopold Chrétien Fréderic Dagobert** (1769–1832). French naturalist; a founder of comparative anatomy and paleontology.

CWO abbrev. Chief warrant officer.

cwt. abbrev. Hundredweight.

-cy suffix. Forming nouns indicating: condition or quality (*vagrancy, idiocy*); rank or office (*presidency*).

cy·an (sī´ăn, -an) adj. & n. (Greenish blue) color.

cy·an·ic (sīăn´ĭk) adj. 1. Blue. 2. ~ **acid**, colorless poisonous pungent volatile unstable liquid (HCNO).

cy·a·nide (sī´anīd) n. Salt of hydrocyanic acid (HCN), compound of cyanide group CN with organic radical, as **potassium** ~ (KCN); ~ **process**, extraction of gold and silver from ore with dilute solution of sodium cyanide.

cy·an·o·gen (sīăn´ojen) n. Colorless inflammable highly poisonous gas (C_2N_2).

cy·a·no·sis (sīanō´sĭs) n. (path.) Blueness of skin caused by presence of large quantities of deoxygenated blood in its minute vessels. **cy·a·not·ic** (sīanŏt´ĭk) adj.

Cyb·e·le (sĭb´elē). (myth.) Anatolian mother-goddess, worshipped esp. in Phrygia and later in Greece with her consort Attis.

cy·ber·na·tion (sībernā´shon) n. Control by machines.

cy·ber·net·ics (sībernĕt´ĭks) n. Theory, study, of communication and control in living organisms and machines.

cy·cad (sī´kăd) n. (bot.) Plant of family Cycadaceae, related to conifers, but resembling palms, the trunk of which yields sago. **cyc·a·da·ceous** (sīkadā´shus) adj.

Cyc·la·des (sĭk´ladēz). Circular group of Greek islands in the S. Aegean. **Cy·clad·ic** (sĭklăd´ĭk, sī-) adj.

cy·cla·mate (sī´klamāt, sĭk´la-) n. Salt of cyclohexylsulphamic acid ($C_6H_{11} \cdot NH \cdot SO_3H$), with sweetening properties.

cy·cla·men (sī´klamen, sĭk´la-) n. Primulaceous plant of genus C ~ with fleshy rootstocks, cultivated for its early-blooming flowers; pinkish red color.

cy·cle (sī´kel) n. 1. Recurrent period (of events, phenomena, etc.); period of a thing's completion; (phys. etc.) recurring series of operations or states; one complete oscillation; esp. (elect.) short form for ~ **per second**, frequently of an alternating current or potential (abbrev. c/s and cps). 2. Complete set or series; series of poems or songs dealing with central event, character, or idea. 3. (colloq.) Motorcycle, bicycle, or tricycle. ~ v.i. (**-cled, -cling**). 1. Move in cycles. 2. Ride cycle.

cy·clic (sī´klĭk, sĭk´lĭk), **cy·cli-**

cal (sī′klĭkal, sĭk′lĭ-) *adjs.* 1. Recurring in cycles; belonging to a definite chronological cycle. 2. Of a cycle of mythic and heroic stories. 3. (bot., of flower) With its parts arranged in whorls. 4. (math.) Of a circle or cycle. 5. (chem., -*ic*) With the constituent atoms in a ring formation.

cy·clist (sī′klĭst) *n.* Rider of a cycle.

cy·cloid (sī′kloid) *n.* Curve traced in space by point in circumference or on radius of a circle as the circle rolls along a straight line. **cy·cloi′dal** *adj.*

cy·clom·e·ter (sīklŏm′eter) *n.* 1. Instrument for measuring circular arcs. 2. Apparatus attached to wheel of bicycle etc. for measuring distance traversed.

cy·clone (sī′klōn) *n.* 1. System of winds rotating rapidly around region of low barometric pressure, usu. accompanied by heavy rain and severe storm conditions. 2. Loosely, any severe storm, such as TORNADO. **cy·clon·ic** (sīklŏn′ĭk) *adj.*

Cy·clo·pe·an (sīklopē′an, sīklō′pē-) *adj.* 1. Of, like, a Cyclops; huge. 2. Applied to an ancient style of masonry of immense irregular stones, found in Greece, Italy, etc., and anciently supposed to be the work of the Cyclops.

cy·clo·pe·di·a, **cy·clo·pae·di·a** (sīklopē′dēa) *ns.* = ENCYCLOPEDIA. **cy·clo·pe′dic, cy·clo·pae′dic** *adjs.*

Cy·clops (sī′klŏps) *n.* (pl. **Cy·clo·pes** pr. sīklō′pēz, **Cy·clops, Cy·clop·ses** pr. sī′klŏpsĭz). (Gk. myth.) One of a race of one-eyed giants who inhabited an island and forged thunderbolts for Zeus.

cy·clo·ra·ma (sīklorăm′a, -rah′-ma) *n.* Circular panorama; curved back of stage.

cy·clo·tron (sī′klotrŏn, sĭk′lo-) *n.* (phys.) Apparatus for accelerating charged atomic particles, moving in a widening spiral, by passing them repeatedly through the same electromagnetic field.

cyg·net (sĭg′nĭt) *n.* Young swan.

cyl·in·der (sĭl′ĭnder) *n.* 1. (geom.) Solid or surface generated by straight line moving parallel to a fixed straight line and tracing a closed curve, esp. a circle, with one of its points. 2. Roller-shaped body, hollow or solid. 3. Cylindrical part of various machines, esp. chamber in which liquids or gases can exert pressure on a moving piston; roller used in printing to receive impression, carrying printing plates, etc.; ~ **lock**, one

Tropical **cyclones** *usually occur towards the end of the hot season. The winds spiral inwards and attain speeds of 100 m.p.h. or more and are accompanied by torrential rains. This type of storm may also be called a typhoon or hurricane.*

operated by revolving one barrel inside another.

cy·lin·dri·cal (sĭlĭn′drĭkal) *adj.* Cylinder-shaped.

cy·ma (sī′ma) *n.* (pl. **-mae** pr. -mē, **-mas**). (archit.) Molding with double continuous curve.

cym·bal (sĭm′bal) *n.* One of a pair of concave brass or bronze plates, stuck together to make ringing sound or singly with drumstick etc.

cyme (sīm) *n.* (bot.) Inflorescence in which primary axis bears single terminal flower that develops first, system being continued by axes of secondary and higher orders. **cy·mose** (sī′mōs, sīmōs′) *adj.*

Cym·ric (kĭm′rĭk, sĭm′r **Kym·ric** (kĭm′rĭk) *adj.* Of pertaining to the Cymry. ~ The Celtic languages of the We Cornish, and Bretons. [We *Cymru* Wales, *Cymry* the Wels

Cym·ry, Cym·ri (kĭm sĭm′rē), **Kym·ry** (kĭm′rē) Branch of the Celtic people, cc prising the Welsh, Cornish, Bretons.

Cyn·e·wulf (kĭn′ewŏolf). An Saxon poet of the latter part of 8th c.

This mobile home has been wrecke the force of a **cyclone** *passing thro the area. Millions of dollars wortl damage occurs each year in cyc areas.*

□ Cyclone areas

The various evergreen trees known as **cypresses** are indigenous to southern Europe, Asia, and North America. Right: The Italian cypress (Cupressus sempervirens) Left: Louisiana cypress trees on the Grant Canal.

cyn·ic (sĭn′ĭk) *n.* 1. (**C~**) Philosopher of an ancient Greek sect, founded by Antisthenes, whose teachings showed contempt for ease, wealth, and the enjoyments of life. 2. One who sarcastically discredits the sincerity or goodness of human motives and actions. ~ *adj.* 1. (**C~**) Of, characteristic of, Cynic philosophers. 2. Cynical. **cyn′i·cal** *adj.* Incredulous of human goodness; sneering. **cyn′i·cal·ly** *adv.* **cyn·i·cism** (sĭn′ĭsĭzem) *n.* [Gk. *kuōn kunos* dog, nickname for cynic]

cy·no·sure (sī′noshoor, sĭn′o-) *n.* Center of attraction or admiration. [Gk. *Kunosoura* (lit., = "dog's tail") constellation Ursa Minor, containing polestar]

Cyn·thi·a (sĭn′thēa). (Gk. and Rom. myth.) Artemis, said to have been born on Mt. Cynthus. [L. *Cynthia* (*dea*) the Cynthian goddess]

cy·pher (sī′fer) (Brit.) = CIPHER.

cy·press (sī′prĭs) *n.* Coniferous tree of genus *Cupressus*, esp. the Monterey cypress (*C. macrocarpa*) of the Southwest, with hard durable wood and dense dark foliage; its wood; the bold cypress (*Taxodium distichum*) of southeastern U.S. and Mexico is not a true cypress.

Cyp·ri·an (sĭp′rēan) *adj. & n.* 1. Cypriote. 2. (archaic) Licentious (person).

cyp·ri·noid (sĭp′rĭnoid, sĭprī′noid) *adj. & n.* (Fish) resembling or allied to carp, of the division Cyprinoidea.

Cyp·ri·ote (sĭp′rēot, -ot), **Cyp·ri·ot** (sĭp′rēot) *adjs. & ns.* (Native, inhabitant, Greek dialect) of Cyprus.

Cy·prus (sī′prus). Island in E. Mediterranean famous in ancient times for worship of Aphrodite; captured by the Turks 1570; from 1878 administered by Gt. Britain; taken over as British colony 1914; republic since 1960; member State of the British Commonwealth; ethnically divided into 82% Greek and 18% Turkish population; capital, Nicosia.

Cyr·e·na·ic (sĭrenā′ĭk, sīre-) *adj. & n.* (Philosopher) of the hedonistic school of Aristippus of Cyrene.

Cyr·e·na·i·ca (sĭrenā′ĭka, sīre-). District of NE. Libya.

Cy·re·ne (sĭrē′nē). Ancient

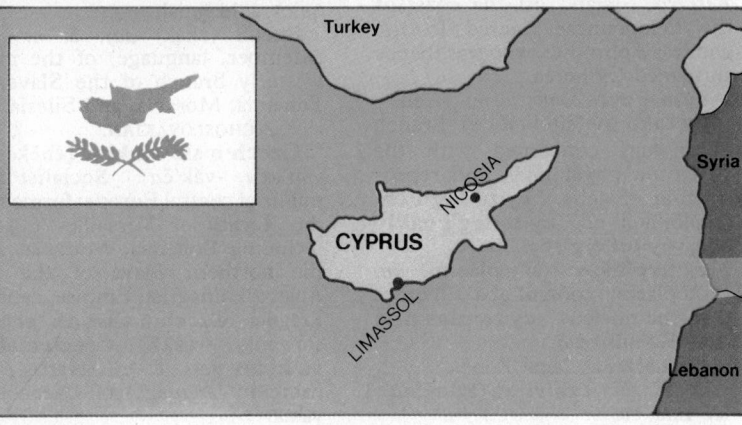

The Mediterranean island of **Cyprus** has a mixed community of both Greek and Turkish 'Cypriots', each with differing religions. Above left: A woman basket-weaver at Mesoyi.

Above: Prague, Old Town Square.
Czechoslovakia *is rich in its historical associations, particularly in its architecture. Its mineral resources include silver-mines. Both industry and agriculture are important.*

Greek colony in what is now Libya.

Cyr·il (sĭr′ĭl), **Saint** (827–69). Greek Christian theologian; apostle to Slavs; reputed inventor of Cyrillic alphabet in which he and his brother, Methodius, translated the Gospels.

Cy·ril·lic (sĭrĭl′ĭk) *adj. & n.* (Of) the alphabet, based on Greek uncials, used by Slavonic peoples of the Eastern Church, attributed to St. CYRIL (who in fact devised the GLAGOLITIC alphabet); now used with modifications for Russian, Bulgarian, some other Slavic languages, and other languages in the U.S.S.R.

Cy·rus (sīr′us), "the Great," d. 529 B.C. Founder of the Persian Empire; subdued the Greek cities of Asia Minor and conquered the Babylonians.

cyst (sĭst) *n.* (biol.) Hollow organ, bladder, etc., in animal or plant, containing liquid secretion; (path.) sac containing morbid matter, parasitic larva, etc.; cell containing embryo etc. **cyst′ic** *adj.* Of the urinary bladder; of the gall bladder; of the nature of a cyst; ~ **fibrosis**, hereditary disease affecting mucous glands, usu. appearing in young children and interfering with digestion and respiration.

cys·ti·tis (sĭstī′tĭs) *n.* Inflam-

mation of the bladder.

Cyth·er·a (sĭth′era). (mod. Gk. *Kithira*) Island off the coast of the Peloponnese, sacred to the goddess Aphrodite, who was thence surnamed Cytherea.

cyto-, cyt- *comb. forms.* Cell.

cy·tol·o·gy (sītŏl′ojē) *n.* Branch of biology concerned with the structure, physiology, and reproduction of cells. **cy·to·log·i·cal** (sītolŏj′ĭkal) *adj.* **cy·to·log·i·cal·ly** *adv.* **cy·tol′o·gist** *n.*

cy·to·plasm (sī′toplăzem) *n.* Protoplasmic content of a cell other than the nucleus. **cy·to·plas·mic** (sītoplăz′mĭk) *adj.*

CZ *abbrev.* Canal Zone.

czar, (zär), **cza·ri·na** (zahrē′na): see TSAR etc.

czar·das (chär′dahsh) *n.* Hu garian dance with slow start a quick wild finish.

Czech (chĕk) *adj. & n.* (Member, language) of the m westerly branch of the Slavs, Bohemia, Moravia, and Silesia. = CZECHOSLOVAKIAN.

Czech·o·slo·va·ki·a (chĕkos vah′kēa, -văk′ēa). Socialist F public of central Europe; formed the Treaty of Versailles (191 including Bohemia, Moravia, a the northern Slavs of the Austro-Hungarian Empire; capit Prague. **Czech·o·slo·vak** (chĕk slō′vahk, -văk), **Czech·o·sle va·ki·an** *adjs. & ns.* (Native, habitant, language) of Czechos vakia.

The present form of the letter **D** is a direct derivation of the north Semitic daleth and the Greek delta. In Greece the letter was also used as a geographical term for the delta of a river. In Latin the D took on its present rounded form. Left: Dürer's drawing of the letter D.

Phoenician   Early Greek   Early Etruscan

Ionic   Roman Colonial   Classical Latin

D, d (dē) (pl. **D's, d's** or **Ds, ds**). Fourth letter of modern English and ancient Roman alphabet, corresponding to Greek *delta* (*Δ*, δ), and Phoenician and Hebrew *daleth* (ד), representing a voiced dental (or in English rather alveolar) stop consonant. 2. Fourth in serial order; classification indicating a low grade; **D-layer**, lowest stratum of the ionosphere. 3. **D**, (mus.) second note of natural scale (C major); scale or key with this note as tonic. 4. Roman numeral for 500. 5. **D**, symbol for day on which a military operation is timed to begin (= *day*, used before date is divulged, preceding days being designated as D-1, D-2, etc.); hence, **D-day**, applied esp. to June 1944, day on which British, Canadian, and American forces landed in N. France. 6. **3 D**, three-dimensional. 7. Deuterium.

D. *abbrev.* December; Democrat; Doctor; Dutch.

d. *abbrev.* Date; daughter; day; dead.

D.A. *abbrev.* Department of Agriculture; District Attorney.

DAB *abbrev.* Dictionary of American Biography.

dab¹ (dăb) *n.* Slight or uncided but sudden blow; brief application of soft or moist thing to surface without rubbing; moisture, color, etc., so applied. ~ *v.* (**dabbed, dab·bing**). Make dab(s) on; make dab (*at*); apply briefly without rubbing.

dab² (dăb) *n.* Small flatfish (*Limanda limanda*), like flounder.

dab·ble (dăb'el) *v.* (**-bled, -ling**). 1. Wet intermittently, lightly, or partly; soil, splash; move (with hands, bill, etc.) in shallow water, liquid, mud, etc., with splashing. 2. Engage in desultory or dilettante way (*in*). **dab'bler** *n.*

da ca·po (dah kah'pō). (mus.) repeat from beginning. [It.]

Dac·ca (dăk'a). Capital of Bangladesh, situated in the E. central part of the country.

dace (dās) *n.* (pl. **daces**, collect. **dace**). Any of several freshwater minnows of the family Cyprinidae, the redside ~ (*Clinostomus*

elongatus) and the redbellied ~ (*Chiosomus erythrogaster*).

Da·chau (dah'kow; *Ger.* dah'xow). City near Munich, West Germany; site during World War II of infamous Nazi concentration camp.

dachs·hund (dŏks'ho͞ont, -ho͞ond, dăk'sund, dăsh'und) *n.* Small dog of German breed with short crooked legs and very long body. [Ger., = "badger-dog"]

Da·cron (dā'krŏn, -kron, dăk'rŏn, -ron) *n.* (trademark) Synthetic textile fiber resistant to stretching and wrinkling.

dac·tyl (dăk'til) *n.* Metrical foot of one long and two short, or one accented and two unaccented syllables (– ⌣ ⌣); (zool.) finger; toe; digit. **dac·tyl·ic** (dăktĭl'ĭk) *adj.* & *n.* (Verse consisting) of dactyl(s). [Gk. *daktulos* finger (f. resemblance

The **dace** (also called the dare or dart) is found in Europe and Siberia, inhabiting fairly fast-flowing rivers. It is a quick and elegant swimmer rarely more than 12 ins. long.

to its three bones)]

dad (dăd), **da·da** (dă'dă), **dad·dy** (dăd'ē) *ns.* (pls. **dads, da·das, dad·dies**). (colloq.; childish or familiar) Father (esp. as vocative); **daddy-longlegs**, arachnid having a compact body and long, slender legs.

Da·da (dah'dah) *n.* International movement in painting and literature initiated 1916 in Zurich, repudiating tradition, culture, and reason. **Da'da·ism** *n.* Dada move-

*Man Ray's 'Pisces', **Dada** emerged as a reaction to the horror of the 1914–18 war and was founded on the absurd and random. It began in Zurich, while a similar movement started in New York.*

ment; its doctrine. **Da′da·ist** n. [Fr. *être sur son dada*, ride one's hobby horse]

da·do (dā′dō) n. (pl. **-does, -dos**). 1. Block forming body of pedestal, between base and crown. 2. Lower part of interior wall, of different material or color from upper part.

Daed·a·lus (dĕd′alus; Brit. dē′da-). (Gk. myth.) Skillful artisan who constructed the Cretan labyrinth; he was imprisoned in Crete with his son ICARUS but escaped to Sicily on wings that he made. **Dae·da·li·an, Dae·da·le·an** (dĭdā′lēan, -dāl′yan) adjs. Intricate, labyrinthine. [Gk. *daidalos* cunning one]

dae·mon (dē′mon) = DEMON 1.

daf·fo·dil (dăf′odĭl) n. Yellow-flowered bulbous plant (*Narcissus pseudo-narcissus*) blooming in early spring; pale yellow color. ∼ adj. Pale yellow.

daf·fy (dăf′ē) adj. (**-fi·er, -fi·est**) (colloq.) Silly, foolish; daft.

daft (dăft, dahft) adj. Foolish, reckless, wild, crazy, daffy.

dag·ger (dăg′er) n. Short two-edged pointed weapon, like small sword, for thrusting and stabbing; (print.) mark like dagger, obelisk (†); **double** ∼ (‡).

da·go (dā′gō) n. (pl. **-gos, -goes**). (contempt.) Spaniard, Portuguese, or esp. Italian. [app. f. Span. *Diego* = James]

da·guerre·o·type (dagĕr′otīp, -ēotīp) n. (Photograph taken by)

early photographic process in which image was taken on silvered copper plate sensitized by iodine, and developed by exposure to mercury vapor. ∼ v.t. Photograph by this process. [name of inventor, Louis *Daguerre* (1787–1851)]

dahl·ia (dăl′ya, dahl′-; Brit. dāl′ya) n. Plant of genus D∼, native to Mexico and Central America, widely cultivated for its many-colored single and double flowers. [f. A. *Dahl* (d. 1789), Swedish botanist]

Da·ho·mey (dahō′mē; Fr. dăawmā′). Former name of BENIN.

Dail Eire·ann (doil ār′an). House of Representatives of the Republic of Ireland. [Ir., = "assembly of Ireland"]

dai·ly (dā′lē) adv. Every day or weekday; from day to day, constant(ly). ∼ adj. Done, occurring, published, etc., daily; ∼ **bread**, one's necessary food or livelihood; ∼ **double**, in horse racing, system of betting whereby a bet on the results of two consecutive races is placed in a special pool; ∼ **dozen**, series of physical exercises to be done every day. **daily** n. (pl. **-lies**). Daily newspaper.

Daim·ler (dīm′ler), **Gottlieb** (1834–1900). German engineer and

automotive pioneer; invented ea internal combustion engine.

dain·ty (dān′tē) n. (pl. **-tie** Choice morsel, delicacy. ∼ a (**-ti·er, -ti·est**). Choice; prett neat; fastidious, of delicate tas and sensibility. **dain′ti·ly** a **dain′ti·ness** n.

dai·qui·ri (dī′kerē, dăk′erē) Iced cocktail of rum, lime jui lemon, and sugar.

dair·y (dār′ē) n. (pl. **dair·ie** Room or building for keeping m and cream and making butter et store in which milk, cream, etc., sold; department of farm or farmi concerned with production of mi butter, and cheese; dairy farm; **farm**, farm producing chie milk, butter, etc.; **dair′ymai** woman employed at dai **dair′yman** (pl. **-men**), dealer milk etc.

da·is (dā′ĭs, dī′ĭs, dās) n. Rais platform, esp. at one end of hall, speaker's lectern, high tab throne, etc.

dai·sy (dā′zē) n. (pl. **-sies**). Any of various related plants w rayed flowers, esp. *Chrysanthem leucanthemum*, native of Eurasia b naturalized throughout N. Ame whose flowers have yellow rays a a yellow disk at the center; al called "oxeye daisy." 2. Sm European wild and garden flow *Bellis perennis*, with yellow disk a white rays; ∼ **chain**, chain daisies threaded together. 3. **pu up the daisies**, (slang) be dead a

Dahlias when first introduced to Europe were 7–8 ft. high with yellow centers, and red rays. Since then numerous varieties have been developed, double and single, and some a mere 18 ins. tall.

buried.

Da·kar (dahkär´). Capital and largest city of Senegal, on the Atlantic.

Da·ko·ta (dakō´ta). Former territory of U.S., organized in 1889 into the states of NORTH DAKOTA and SOUTH DAKOTA. ~ *adj.* & *n.* (Member, language) of a Siouan-speaking group of N. Amer. plains Indians, generally called Sioux and formerly living in the area of North and South Dakota; **Dakota River**: see JAMES RIVER 1.

Da·la·dier (dälädyä´), **Edouard** (1884–1970). French statesman; premier 1933–4, 1938–40.

Da·lai La·ma (dah´lī lah´ma). Grand Lama, chief lama of Tibet.

dale (dāl) *n.* Valley.

Da·li (dah´lē), **Salvador** (1904–). Spanish surrealist artist; settled in U.S. 1940.

Dal·las¹ (dăl´as). Second largest city in Texas, in the NE part.

Dal·las² (dăl´as), **George Mifflin** (1792–1864). Vice president of U.S. under James Knox Polk, 1845–9.

dal·ly (dăl´ē) *v.* (**-lied, -ly·ing**). Be evasive *with* person or business; idle, loiter, delay; flirt, play, esp. amorously. **dal·li·ance** (dăl´ēans, dăl´yans) *n.*

Dal·ma·tia (dălmā´sha). Province of Yugoslavia on the Adriatic coast; formerly (until 1918) province of the Austro-Hungarian Empire.

Dal·ma·tian (dălmā´shan) *adj.* Of Dalmatia or its people. ~ *n.* 1. Native, inhabitant, of Dalmatia. 2. Dog with short-haired white coat with black or brown spots, of a breed supposed to have originated in Dalmatia.

Dal·ton (dawl´ton), **John** (1776–1844). English physicist and chemist, who formulated the atomic theory and table of atomic weights. **dal´ton·ism** (sometimes **D** ~) *n.* Congenital color blindness, esp. inability to distinguish green from red, so called after John Dalton, who was so affected. **dal·ton·ic** (dawltŏn´ĭk) *adj.*

dam¹ (dăm) *n.* Barrier constructed across stream etc. to hold back water and raise its level, form

*Many animals provide milk suitable for human consumption, but modern **dairy** farming is based on the cow as source of milk, butter, cream, and cheese. Advanced mechanization has made a naturally self-sufficient branch of farming highly productive and hygienic. Top: Herring-bone milking sheds in New Zealand. Left: Collective butter-making.*

a reservoir, or prevent flooding; barrier constructed in stream by beavers. ~ *v.t.* (**dammed, dam·ming**). Furnish or confine with dam; block *up*, obstruct.

dam² (dăm) *n.* Mother (usu. of quadruped).

dam·age (dăm´ĭj) *n.* 1. Harm; injury impairing value or useful-

ness. 2. (law, pl.) Sum of money claimed or adjudged in compensation for loss or injury; (slang) cost. ~ *v.t.* (**-aged, -ag·ing**). Injure (usu. thing) so as to diminish value; detract from reputation of (person etc.). **dam´age·a·ble** *adj.*

dam·a·scene (dăm´asēn, dăma-sēn´) *v.t.* (**-scened, -scen·ing**). 1.

Produce watered or striped patt in (sword, armor, etc.) by hamm ing on steel in which the iron carbon particles have separated i patches or bands during cooli 2. Inlay (steel or iron surface) w designs in gold or silver. DAMASCUS]

Da·mas·cus (damăs´kr (Arab. *Esh Sham*) Capital city Syria in the SW. part; an anci city, famous in the Middle Ages its silks and steel, esp. for sw blades, hence ~ **steel**.

dam·ask (dăm´ask) *n.* 1. Reve ible figured fabric in which design is executed in a differe weave from the background in su a way that the two weaves appear the face and on the back exchanged positions, orig. of si

high earth banks retain moisture

corroded masonry

moisture from 'under-floor area

moisture from the ground

rising damp

Various methods of combating ris damp have been developed. A spe problem has been to devise ways protecting old buildings with no buil damp course. Strips of impermea material are inserted between layers bricks, silicone solutions are injec into the bricks, water is syphoned of pipes, and copper strips, embedded the walls and earthed, prevent wa rising by inhibiting osmotic pressure

airbrick

felt or sheeting   silicone penetration   syphonage

electro-osmosis   vertical damp proofing course   vertical damp proof course weather-boarding

*Above: The **Kariba Dam** in Zimbabwe under construction. Right: The [Euc]umbene Dam in New South Wales, [A]ustralia. The building of dams has [be]en practiced for many thousands of [y]ears. More recently dams have been [u]sed for large scale irrigation and for [hy]dro-electricity generation.*

[mat]ter of linen, cotton, etc. 2. Steel [m]anufactured at Damascus; com-[bi]nation of iron and steel with wavy [p]attern on surface (see DAMASCENE). [~] **rose**, species of rose native to [A]sia (*Rosa damascena*), to which [m]any garden varieties belong. [d]**amask** *adj.* Made of or resem-[bl]ing damask fabric or steel. ~ *v.t.* [1.] Weave with figured designs. 2. [D]amascene; ornament with pat-[te]rn. [f. DAMASCUS]

dame (dām) *n.* 1. Woman [(a]rchaic or poet.; also slang). 2. [T]itle formerly given to the mistress [of] a household, woman in authority, [et]c.; (Brit.) D~, title of woman of [ra]nk of Knight (used as prefix [co]rresp. to *Sir*).

Da·mi·en (dā′mēen), **Father** [(1]840–89). Orig. name, Joseph de [V]euster; Belgian R.C. missionary; [d]evoted his life to care of lepers on [M]olokai Island, Hawaii, and died of [th]e disease.

damn (dăm) *v.* (**damned, damn·ing**). 1. Condemn, censure; condemn (play etc.) as a failure; bring condemnation on, be the ruin of. 2. Doom to hell; cause damnation of; curse. ~ *n.* Uttered curse; negligible amount (**not worth a** ~, worthless). ~ *int.* Exclamation of annoyance.

dam·na·ble (dăm′nəbel) *adj.* Deserving damnation; hateful, annoying. **dam′na·bly** *adv.*

dam·na·tion (dămnā′shon) *n.*

Damning; (condemnation to) eternal punishment in hell.

dam·na·to·ry (dăm′natōrē, -tōrē) *adj.* Conveying, causing, censure or damnation.

damned (dămd) *adj.* (esp.) Damnable, detestable; **the D~**, souls in hell. **damned** *adv.* Damnably. **damned·est** (dăm′dĭst) *n.* **one's** ~, one's utmost.

dam·ni·fy (dăm′nĭfī) *v.t.* (**-fied, -fy·ing**). (law) Cause damage or loss to.

Dam·o·cles (dăm′oklēz). (Gk. legend) Flatterer who extolled the happiness of Dionysius, tyrant of Syracuse; but Dionysius, to show how precarious a ruler's happiness was, seated him at a banquet with a sword suspended over his head by a hair; hence, **sword of** ~, imminent danger, esp. in midst of prosperity. **Dam·o·cle·an** (dămo-klē′an) adj.

Da·mon (dā′mon). (Gk. and Rom. legend) Syracusan whose friend Phintias was sentenced to death; Damon posted his life as bail for Phintias, who came back at the last moment and saved him; hence, ~ **and Pythias** (erron. for Phintias), faithful friends.

damp (dămp) n. 1. Moisture in air, on surface, or diffused through solid. 2. Dejection, chill, discouragement. ~ adj. Slightly wet; moist, humid; ~**-dry** (v.t.), dry (laundry) partially, leaving slightly moist. **damp′ly** adv. **damp′ness** n. **damp** v.t. 1. Stifle, choke, dull; extinguish; (mus. etc.) stop vibrations of (string etc.), furnish (piano strings) with dampers; (phys.) cause decrease in amplitude of radio waves etc. 2. Dampen. 3. Moisten, make damp.

damp·en (dăm′pen) v. 1. Make or become damp, moisten. 2. Stifle, choke, extinguish. 3. Discourage, depress (hopes etc.).

damp·er (dăm′per) n. 1. Person or thing that depresses. 2. Small cloth- or felt-covered pad in piano resting against string to prevent it from vibrating except when key is struck or pedal depressed. 3. Adjustable plate in flue controlling combustion by regulating or stopping draft.

Dam·rosch (dăm′rŏsh), **Walter Johnson** (1862–1950). German-born Amer. conductor and composer.

dam·sel (dăm′zel) n. (archaic and literary) Young unmarried woman; **dam′selfly**, insect of order Odonata resembling dragonfly but with wings usu. held together over the body while resting.

dam·son (dăm′zon, -son) n. Small dark purple plum (Prunus insititia) introduced in very early times into Italy and Greece from Syria; tree bearing this. [L. (prunum) Damascenum (plum) of Damascus]

Dan (dăn). 1. Hebrew patriarch, son of Jacob and Bilhah (Gen. 30); tribe of Israel traditionally descended from him. 2. City in the extreme north of Canaan.

Dan. abbrev. Danish.

Da·na (dā′na), **Richard Henry** (1815–82). Amer. lawyer, sailor, and author; wrote Two Years Before the Mast.

Dan·a·ë (dăn′aē) (Gk. myth.) Daughter of Acrisius, king of Argos; an oracle foretold that she would bear a son who would kill her father; he therefore imprisoned her in a tower, but Zeus visited her there in the form of a shower of gold and she conceived PERSEUS, who after many adventures killed Acrisius by accident.

Dan·a·id (dăn′aĭd) n. (Gk. myth.) Any of the 50 daughters of Danaus, king of Argos; all exc one, Hypermnestra, murdered t husbands on the wedding night were condemned in Hades to ca water in sieves or bottom vessels.

Da·nang (dahnahng′, danăn Port city in Vietnam on So China Sea.

dance (dăns, dahns) v. (**danc danc·ing**). Move rhythmic with glides, leaps, etc., usu. music, alone or with partner or set; perform (dance); jump abo skip, move in lively way; bob up a down on water etc. ~ n. Dancing motion; definite succ sion or arrangement of steps rhythmical movements in danci music for this. 2. Dancing pa 3. ~ **of death**, allegorical repres tation (common in Middle Ages Death leading all sorts and c ditions of men in a dance to grave; **St. Vitus'** ~, chor **danc′er** n. (esp.) One who dan professionally in public.

dan·de·li·on (dăn′delīon) Common composite plant (Tara cum officinale), abundant as a we with widely toothed leaves a large yellow flower on naked holl stalk, succeeded by globular head seeds. [Fr. dent de lion lion's too

dan·der (dăn′der) n. (collo Temper, anger, indignation; g **one's** ~ **up**, become or ma angry.

Dan·die Din·mont (dăn dĭn′mŏnt). Terrier of short-legg long-bodied, rough-coated bre

As a means of expression, the **dance** is universal, although its types and styles are infinitely diverse, some having religious or tribal significance. Below: In

the Western world ballroom danc developed from the less sedate fo of peasant dances. Facing pa Bhutanese folk dancers.

There are many species of **dandelion** and they are found in many parts of the world. Unpopular with gardeners as lawn 'weeds', they are nevertheless useful plants; the leaves serve for salads, the roots for medicinal purposes.

This 17th or 18th century painting, probably French, shows **Daphne**, daughter of the river god Ladon, escaping from Apollo. Another suitor, Leucippus, was slain by her nymphs.

from Scottish borders. [name of a character in Sir W. Scott's *Guy Mannering*, who kept a special breed of terriers]

dan·druff (dăn'drŭf) n. Dead skin in small scales among the hair, scurf.

dan·dy (dăn'dē) n. (pl. **-dies**). 1. Man paying excessive attention to elegance in dress etc. 2. Anything superlatively fine, neat, or dainty. 3. (naut.) Sloop with mizzen lugsail on jiggermast aft. ~ adj. (**-di·er, -di·est**). Foppish; (colloq.) splendid, first-rate. **dan'dy·ish** adj. **dan'dy·ism** n. [orig. Sc., perh. f. name *Andrew*]

Dane (dān) n. 1. Native of Denmark. 2. (hist.) Viking. 3. **Great** ~, dog of large powerful short-haired breed, of type between mastiff and greyhound.

Dane·law, Dane·lagh (dān'law) ns. (hist.) Part of NE. England occupied by the Danes in the 9th and 10th centuries; (erron.) body of laws established by these Danish invaders and settlers.

dan·ger (dān'jer) n. Liability or exposure to harm, risk, peril (*of*); thing that causes peril. **dan'ger·ous** adj. **dan'ger·ous·ly** adv.

dan·gle (dăng'gel) v. (**-gled, -gling**). Hang loosely, swaying to and fro; hold or carry (thing) swaying loosely; keep (hopes, expectations, etc.) hanging uncertainly (*before* person); hang *after* or *about* a person; **dan'gling participle**, participle or participial phrase, usu. at the opening of a sentence, that is not clearly connected with the sentence element that it was supposed to modify, as *sleeping deeply* in the sentence *Sleeping deeply, the tiger's skin was singed by the fire.*

Dan·iel (dăn'yel). Hebrew prophet, captive at Babylon, who interpreted the dreams of Nebuchadnezzar and was delivered by God from the lions' den into which he had been thrown by Darius; book of Old Testament bearing his name.

Dan·ish (dā'nĭsh) adj. & n. (Language) of Denmark or the Danes; ~ **pastry**, piece of light pastry topped with icing, bits of dried fruit, nuts, etc.

dank (dăngk) adj. Unpleasantly damp; wet and chilly. **dank'ness** n.

D'An·nun·zio (danŭn'zēō; *It.* dahnōōn'tsyō), **Gabriele** (1863–1938). Italian poet, author, aviator, and politician.

dan·seur (*Fr.* dahṅsör') n. (pl. **-seurs** pr. *Fr.* -sör'). Male ballet dancer.

dan·seuse (*Fr.* dahṅsöz') n. (pl. **-seuses** pr. *Fr.* -söz'). Female

ballet dancer.

Dan·te Al·i·ghie·ri (dahn'tĕ ahlēgyär'ē) (1265–1321). Italian poet, probably born at Florence, author of *Divina Commedia*, a philosophical poem comprising the "Inferno," "Purgatorio," and "Paradiso"; in his visit to Hell and Purgatory Dante has the poet Virgil for a guide; there he sees and converses with his former friends or foes; in "Paradiso" the poet encounters the lady whom he once loved, Beatrice, now an angel. **Dan·tesque** (dăntĕsk') adj. Of, after the manner of, Dante.

Dan·ton (dăn'ton; *Fr.* dahṅtawṅ'), **Georges Jacques** (1759–1794). French statesman of the Revolution; member of the Convention and the first (Dantonist) Committee of Public Safety; he came into conflict with ROBESPIERRE and was guillotined.

Dan·ube (dăn'ūb) (Ger. *Donau*). European river about 1,700 miles (2,736 km) long, rising in Black

*The **Dardanelles** was the setting of t legend of Hero and Leander. In mode times, as the only access between t Black Sea and the Mediterranean, t Dardanelles has great strategic a commercial importance.*

Forest of SW. West Germany ar flowing into the Black Sea at th SE. coast of Rumania.

Dan·zig (dăn'sĭg; *Ger.* dahn'tsĭ (Polish *Gdansk*). Baltic city ar port of Poland, near mouth Vistula.

Daph·ne (dăf'nē). (Gk. myth Nymph who was turned into laurel bush to save her from th pursuit of Apollo.

daph·ne (dăf'nē) n. Flowerin shrub of genus *D*~.

dap·per (dăp'er) adj. Nea smart, in appearance or movemen

dap·ple (dăp'el) v. (**-plee -pling**). Variegate, becon variegated, with rounded spots patches of color or shade. ~ ac Dappled; ~**-gray**, (horse) of gra dappled with darker spots. **dappl**

Dappled effect; dappled horse c. **dap′pled** *adj.*

D.A.R. *abbrev.* Daughters of the merican Revolution.

Dar·da·nelles (därdanĕlz′). arrow strait between Europe and siatic Turkey, anciently called the ellespont; scene of unsuccessful tack on Turkey by British and rench troops in 1915.

dare (dār) *v.* (**dared, dar·ing**). Venture (to), have boldness or ourage or impudence (to); attempt, ke the risks of. 2. Defy, challenge erson) *to* thing, *to* do. 3. **dare′- evil**, reckless (person). **dar′ing** , (esp.) Adventurous courage. **ar′ing** *adj.* (esp.) Adventurous, old. **dar′ing·ly** *adv.*

Dare (dār), **Virginia** (1587?–?). irst child born in America of English parentage at the colony of *Roanoke Island*, all traces of which lisappeared.

Dar es Sa·laam (där ĕs alahm′). Capital and largest city of Tanzania, on the NE. coast.

Dar·i·en (där′ēĕn, -ēen). Region f eastern Panama; **Gulf of ~**, bay n the Caribbean between NE. Panama and NW. Colombia; **sthmus of ~**, former name of sthmus of PANAMA.

Da·ri·us (darī′us), "the Great" 558?–486 B.C.). King of Persia, 521–486 B.C.; extended the Persian Empire and began the great war etween the Persians and the Greeks; his army was defeated at MARATHON (490 B.C.).

Dar·jee·ling (därjē′lĭng). Resort city in NE. India, in the foothills of the Himalayas. **~ tea**, fine black tea grown there.

dark (därk) *adj.* 1. Characterized by (absolute or relative) absence of

light; unilluminated; gloomy, somber. 2. (of color) Approaching black in hue; deep in shade; (of complexion etc.) brown, not fair. 3. Evil, wicked; dismal; sullen; obscure; secret; unenlightened. 4. **D~ Ages**, (formerly =) Middle Ages; (now usu.) approx. 5th–8th centuries A.D., or from fall of Rome to coronation of Charlemagne. **D~ Continent**, Africa; **~ horse**, horse about whose racing powers little is known; person of unknown capacities; relatively unknown political candidate who may receive more votes than originally expected; **dark′room**, room from which daylight is excluded and which is lighted when desired by a type of colored light that does not appreciably affect sensitive photographic materials. **dark** *n.* Absence of light; nightfall; dark color; **~ adaptation**, reflex adjustment of eyes to low light intensity; **be in the ~**, lack knowledge. **dark′ish** *adj.*

*Many small towns dot the **Darjeeling** area of north east India (left). High mountain ranges and deep-cut river valleys characterize the area, which is noted for its fine teas.*

*The **darter** lives on lakes and large rivers, feeding on fish which it often spears with its bill. It is an agile swimmer, carrying only its head above the water surface.*

dark′ly *adv.* **dark′ness** *n.*

dark·en (där′ken) *v.* Make or become dark.

dar·ling (där′lĭng) *n. & adj.* Loved, best loved, lovable (person or animal).

Darm·stadt (därm′stăt; *Ger.* därm′shtaht). City in W. central West Germany.

darn¹ (därn) *v.t.* Mend (esp. knitted fabric) by interweaving yarn with needle across hole; embroider with darning stitch. **~ n.** Darned place in cloth. **darn′er** *n.* **darn′ing** *n.* (esp.) **~ needle**, long, large-eyed needle for darning.

darn² (därn) *n. & v.t.* Damn (as mild imprecation). **darned** *adj. & n.* Damned.

*A young **danseuse**, or ballerina, in classic pose (right). They are often seen as the embodiment of elegance, conveying human experience and emotion in a tangible form.*

Dar·row (dăr′ō), **Clarence Seward** (1857–1938). Amer. lawyer and social reformer; defense counsel in many celebrated cases, including the SCOPES case.

dart (därt) *n.* 1. Pointed missile thrown by hand, esp. light javelin; arrow; light pointed missile thrown at target; (*pl.*) game played with darts of this kind. 2. Tapering stitched fold in garment. 3. Sudden rapid motion. ∼ *v.* 1. Throw (missile). 2. Emit suddenly and sharply, shoot out; spring or start with sudden rapid motion, shoot. **dart′er** *n.* (esp.) 1. = ANHINGA. 2. Any of various small, brightly colored freshwater fishes, esp. of the subfamily Etheostominae, including the **johnny** ∼ (*Etheostoma nigrum*) and **rainbow** ∼ (*E. caeruleum*), any of various perch of the family Percidae.

Dart·moor (därt′moor). Barren heath district in Devon, England; prison located there.

Dart·mouth (därt′mŭth) **College.** Private, orig. men's, now coed, college at Hanover, N.H., dating from 1769.

Dar·von (där′vŏn) *n.* (trademark) Dextropropoxyphene, a nonnarcotic compound, $C_{22}H_{29}NO_2$, used as an analgesic.

Dar·win[1] (där′wĭn), **Charles Robert** (1809–82). English naturalist; author of *On the Origin of Species by means of Natural Selection* (1859), in which he propounded the theory of evolution by mutation and natural selection of those organisms best adapted to their environment. **Dar·win·i·an** (därwĭn′ēan) *adj. & n.* **Dar·win·ism** *n.*

Dar·win[2] (där′wĭn). Capital city of Northern Territory of Australia on the Timor Sea; named after Charles DARWIN[1]

dash (dăsh) *v.* 1. Shatter *to pieces*; knock, drive, throw, thrust, *away, off,* etc.; fling, drive, splash, *against, into, upon.* 2. Bespatter *with* water etc. 3. Frustrate; discourage. 4. Put *down* on paper, throw *off* (drawing, composition) hastily and vigorously. 5. Damn (as mild imprecation, esp. in ∼ **it all**). 6. Fall, move, throw oneself, with violence; come into collision *against, upon*; ride, run, drive, *up,* move about, behave, with spirit or display. 7. **dash′board**, orig. board in front of wagon to protect driver etc. from being splashed by mud and water from road; now board or panel in front of driver of car or of airplane pilot carrying indicators, gauges, etc. **dash** *n.* 1. Violent blow, impact, or collision;

Date palms from Majorca, Spain. The tree grows to a height of 100 ft. and is native between North Africa and Asia Minor. It was first introduced to America by the Spanish.

violent throwing and breaking of water etc., upon anything; sound of dashing. 2. Splash of color; infusion, touch, tinge. 3. Hasty pen stroke; punctuation mark used to indicate break in sense, parenthesis, omitted letters or words, etc., or in Morse code. 4. Rush, onset, sudden advance; (capacity for) vigorous action; showy appearance or behavior. 5. (colloq.) Dashboard.

dash·er (dăsh′er) *n.* (esp.) Contrivance for agitating cream in churn or ice cream freezer.

da·shi·ki (dashē′kē) *n.* Loose,

Bowerman's Nose, a rock outcrop on **Dartmoor,** *U.K., a high granite plateau of heath and woodland, in Devon. Dartmoor has tin, iron, and copper mines and china clay quarries.*

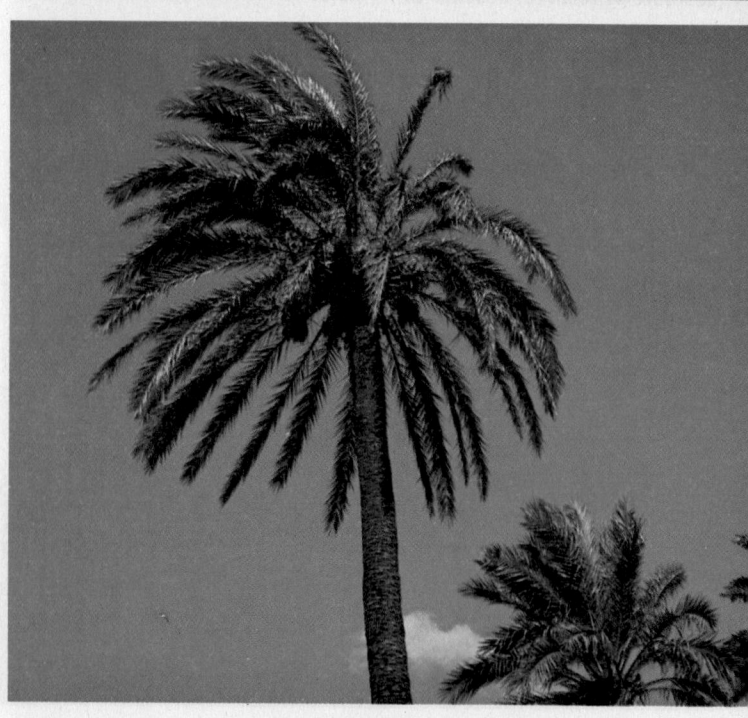

brightly colored shirt for men, or from western Africa.

dash·ing (dăsh′ĭng) *adj.* (es Spirited, lively; showy. **das ing·ly** *adv.*

Dasht-i-Ka·vir (dahsht′ē ka vēr′). (also called Kavir Dese Great salt desert in central Iran

Dasht-i-Lut (dahsht′ē loo (also called Lut Desert) La stone and sand desert in E. Iran

das·tard (dăs′terd) *n.* Base despicable coward, esp. one w commits malicious or brutal a **das′tard·ly** *adj.* **das′tard·li·ne** *n.*

dat. *abbrev.* Dative.

da·ta (dā′ta, dăt′a, dah′ta) *n.* (*sing.* **da·tum** *pr.* dā′tum, dăt′u dah′tum). (often construed as sin 1. Things known or grante

sumptions or premises from
which inferences may be drawn. 2.
cts, statistics, etc. arranged for
alysis or computation. 3. ~
nk, place where organized data
e stored in large amounts, avail-
le for use or computer analysis;
processing, automatic, high-
eed performance of operations on
ta by computer.

date[1] (dāt) n. Fruit of the ~
lm, (*Phoenix dactylifera*) an
blong berry, growing in large
usters, with single hard seed or
one and sweet pulp, an important
ticle of food in W. Asia and N.
frica; the tree itself. [Gk. *daktulos*
nger]

date[2] (dāt) n. Specification in
ocument, letter, book, inscription,
time (and often place) of execu-

tion, writing, publication, etc.;
specified time (month, day of
month, year) at which anything
takes place or is to take place;
season, period; (colloq.) engagement, person with whom one has
social engagement; period to which
something ancient belongs; duration, term of life or existence; **out of
date**, obsolete, antiquated; **up to
date**, up to the knowledge,
standard, requirements, of the time;
in fashion; **date'line**, line in newspaper at head of dispatch, special
article, etc., giving date and place of

Michelangelo's **'David'** *(1501–4)
expresses the Florentine Republic's
self-confidence. The sculpture's classical proportions are in the tradition of
Giotto.*

writing; **International Date
Line**, line in Pacific Ocean (approx.
meridian of 180° from Greenwich,
England) at which calendar day is
reckoned to begin and end, so that
at places east and west of it the date
differs by a day. **date** v. (**dat·ed,
dat·ing**). Mark (letter etc.) with
date; refer (event) to a time; count
time, reckon (*from*); bear date, be
dated; have origin *from*; be or
become or make recognizable as of a
past or particular period; (colloq.)
make, have, social engagement
with. **date'less** adj. Undated.

da·tive (dā'tĭv) adj. (gram.) Of
the case chiefly denoting the indirect object. ~ n. (Word in)
dative case.

da·tum (dā'tum, dăt'um, dah'-
tum) n. Sing. of DATA. [L., =
"(thing) given"]

da·tu·ra (datoor'a, -tūr'a) n.
Poisonous plant of genus D ~.

daub (dawb) v. 1. Coat (wall
etc.) *with* plaster, clay, etc.; smear
(surface); lay *on* (greasy or sticky
stuff); soil, bedaub. 2. Paint
coarsely and inartistically, apply
(paint) crudely and clumsily. ~ n.
1. Material for daubing walls etc.;
clay or mud mixed with stubble or
chaff, daubed on laths to make walls
etc. 2. Patch or smear of paint,
grease, etc. 3. Clumsy coarse
painting. **daub'er** n. Soft rounded
mass used to apply ink, color, etc.,
to a surface in printing, painting on
china, etc.

Dau·det (dōdā'), **Alphonse**
(1840–97). French novelist, author
of *Tartarin de Tarascon*.

daugh·ter (daw'ter) n. Female
child in relation to her parent(s);
female descendant, female member
of family, race, etc.; woman as
spiritual or intellectual descendant
of some person or thing; also
transf.; ~**-in-law**, son's wife, (pl.
~ **s-in-law**); **D ~ s of the American Revolution**, patriotic society
formed 1890. **daugh'ter·ly** adj.

Dau·mier (dōmyā'), **Honoré**
(1808–79). French painter and
caricaturist.

daunt (dawnt) v.t. Discourage,
intimidate. **daunt'less** adj. In-
trepid; persevering. **daunt'less·ly**
adv. **daunt'less·ness** n.

dau·phin (daw'fĭn) n. (hist.)
Orig. title of lords of Viennois,
France, whose coat of arms bore
three dolphins; (from 1349 to 1830)
title of the eldest son of the king
of France.

Da·vao (dahvow'). Seaport on
Mindanao in the Philippines; **D ~
Gulf**, inlet on the SE. coast of
Mindanao.

dav·en·port (dăv'enpōrt, -pŏrt)
n. 1. (Brit.) Small ornamental
writing desk. 2. Large sofa. [prob.
from desk maker's name].

Da·vid[1] (dā'vĭd). Second king of
Judah; slayer of a Philistine,

traditionally GOLIATH; on the death of Saul became king of Judah and later of the whole of Israel; father of King Solomon and reputed author of many of the Psalms.

Da·vid² (dahvĕd´), **Jacques Louis** (1748–1825). French painter of classical and historical subjects.

da Vin·ci: see LEONARDO DA VINCI.

Da·vis¹ (dā´vĭs), **Jefferson** (1808–89). Amer. Army officer and political leader; U.S. secretary of war, 1853–7; U.S. senator from Mississippi, 1847–51, 1857–61; president of the Confederate States of America, 1861–5; arrested for treason after Civil War but prosecution proceedings dropped; retired to his estate, Beauvoir, near Biloxi, Mississippi.

Da·vis² (dā´vĭs), **Richard Harding** (1864–1916). Amer. war correspondent, novelist, and editor.

Da·vis (dā´vĭs) **Cup.** Trophy awarded to the nation whose team is the winner of the annual International Lawn Tennis Championship competition; it was donated in 1900 by Dwight F. Davis (1879–1945), Amer. politician.

Da·vis·son (dā´vĭson), **Clinton Joseph** (1881–1958). Amer. physicist; worked on electricity, magnetism, radiant energy, and discovered diffraction of electrons; shared Nobel Prize for physics, 1937.

dav·it (dăv´ĭt, dā´vĭt) *n.* Crane at ship's bow for hoisting anchor clear of side; one of pair of uprights curved at top for suspending or lowering ship's boat.

Da·vos (dah´vōs). Resort center in E. Switzerland.

Da·vy (dā´vē), **Sir Humphry** (1778–1829). English chemist, discoverer of 12 chemical elements and inventor of an early safety lamp (~ **lamp**) for miners.

Da·vy Jones (dā´vē jōnz´). Spirit of the sea, sailors' devil; **~'s locker**, bottom of the sea, esp. as grave of those who are drowned or die at sea.

daw (daw) jackdaw: see JACK.

daw·dle (daw´del) *v.* (**-dled, -dling**). Idle, dally; **~ away**, waste (time). **dawdle** *n.* Act of dawdling.

Dawes (dawz), **Charles Gates** (1865–1951). Amer. statesman; vice president of the U.S. under Calvin Coolidge, 1925–9; shared Nobel Prize for peace, 1925.

dawn (dawn) *n.* First light, daybreak; rise or incipent gleam of anything. **~** *v.i.* Begin to appear or to grow light; **~ on**, begin to be perceptible to.

Daw·son (daw´son) **Creek.** Starting point of Alaska Highway in E. British Columbia, Canada.

day (dā) *n.* 1. Time during which sun is above horizon, interval of light between successive periods of darkness or night; dawn; daylight. 2. Time occupied by Earth in one revolution on its axis, 24 hours; 24 hours reckoned from midnight to midnight; **sidereal ~**, actual mean solar time required for complete rotation of the Earth; 2 hours, 56 minutes, 4.09 seconds. 3. Specified or appointed day; **carry the ~**, be victorious. 4. Period of time, era; lifetime, span of existence; period of power or influence. 5. Part of day allotted for work. 6. **~ by ~, ~ after ~, from ~ to ~, every ~**, with daily repetition or progress. 7. **~ bed**, couch convertible into or used as a bed; **day´book**, book in which daily business transactions are recorded; (business) diary or memo book; appointment book; **day´break**, dawn; **day-care center**, place where infants and preschool children are looked after while their parents work; **day coach**, ordinary railroad passenger car with no sleeping or other special accommodations; **day´dream**, dream (indulged in) while awake; **day labor**, labor hired by the day (**day laborer**); **day´light (saving) time**, time one or more hours later than STANDARD time for a country or region, usu. adopted for summer months to add hours of daylight to the working day. **day lily**, any of several liliaceous plants of genus *Hemerocallis* with large yellow or orange flowers lasting only for a day; **day nursery**, nursery where pre-school children are cared for during day; **day school**, private school for pupils (**day students**) living at home; **day'time**, time of daylight.

Day (dā), **Benjamin Harrison** (1810–89). Amer. newspaperman; founded *New York Sun*, 1833, first one-cent newspaper; his grandson, **Clarence Shepard, Jr.**, (1874–1935), Amer. writer, best known for *Life With Mother* and *Life with Father*.

Day·ak (dī′ăk, -ak) *n.* Var. of DYAK.

Day-Lew·is (dā′lōṓĭs), **Cecil** (1904–72). English poet (also detective novelist, pseudonym, *Nicholas Blake*); poet laureate 1968–72.

day'light (dā′līt) *n.* Light of day; dawn; openness, publicity; visible interval, as between boats in race; clear understanding (**see** ~); ~- **saving time**, one hour or more later than the standard time for a region or locality, usu. used during summer to give working day more daylight; **beat the daylights out of**, (colloq.) beat (someone) into a state of unconsciousness.

Day·to·na (dātō′na) **Beach.** Resort city in E. Florida noted for its beautiful beach; site of International Speedway.

daze (dāz) *v.t.* (**dazed, daz·ing**). Stupefy, bewilder. ~ *n.* Dazed state. **daz'ed·ly** *adv.*

daz·zle (dăz′el) *v.t.* (**-zled, -zling**). Confuse, dim sight of (eye, person) with excess of light, intricate motion, incalculable number, etc.; confound, surprise, by brilliant display. ~ *n.* Glitter; bright confusing light. **daz'zler** *n.* **daz'zling·ly** *adv.*

dB *abbrev.* Decibel(s).

DC, D.C., dc, d-c, d.c. *abbrevs.* 1. (**DC, D.C.**) District of Columbia. 2. Direct current.

D.C.M. *abbrev.* (Brit.) Distinguished Conduct Medal.

D.D. *abbrev.* Doctor of Divinity.

D.D.S. *abbrev.* Doctor of Dental Science; Doctor of Dental Surgery.

DDT *abbrev.* Colorless, crystalline, and water-insoluble solid $(ClC_6H_4)_2\ CHCCl_3$, used as a contact insecticide. [*D*(ichlor) *d*(iphenyl) *t*(richlorethane)]

DE *abbrev.* Delaware.

de- *prefix.* 1. Down; away; completely. 2. Un- (in this sense a living prefix in English).

de·ac·ces·sion (dēăksĕsh′on) *v.t.* Remove (artifact, art, books, etc.) from the collection of a museum, library, etc. to sell, exchange, or make space for new acquisitions, etc.

dea·con (dē′kon) *n.* 1. Kind of minister or officer of early church; in the Roman Catholic, Greek Orthodox, and Anglican churches, member of the clergy ranking just below priest. 2. In Protestant churches, lay official who assists minister in various duties. **dea·· con·ess** (kē′konĭs) *n.fem.* Woman with functions analogous to deacon's.

dead (dĕd) *adj.* 1. That has ceased to live. 2. Benumbed, insensible; without spiritual life; ~ **to**, unconscious or inappreciative of, hardened against. 3. Obsolete; past; not effective. 4. Inanimate. 5. Extinct; dull, lusterless; without force; muffled, inactive, idle. 6. Unconnected to source of electrical power. 7. Abrupt; complete, unrelieved, exact; absolute. 8. (slang) Exhausted, tired out; ~ **to the world**, fast asleep. 9. ~ **ball**, (sports) ball out of play; ~ **end**, closed end of any passage road etc., through which there is no way (also fig.); **dead'eye**, (naut.) round flat three-holed block for extending shrouds; (slang) expert marksman; **dead'fall**, trap for large game with weighted board or heavy log that falls on the quarry; **dead'head**, (colloq.) nonpaying theatergoer, passenger, etc.; streetcar, railroad car, etc. carrying no passengers or freight; dull, sluggish, or stupid person; **dead heat**, race in which two or more competitors cross finish line at same time; **dead letter**, unclaimed or undelivered

A one-handed deaf-and-dumb alphabet is used in the U.S.A. and Ireland, and with some variations in parts of Europe. The U.K. and Australia use the two-handed system shown here.

letter at post office; **dead'line**, time limit etc. for finishing a piece of work; **dead'lock**, complete stoppage, standstill; state of affairs from which further progress is impossible; **dead man's throttle, brake**, etc. (on locomotives etc.) throttle that must be pressed down for engine to work, so that train etc. stops if engineer or operator loses grasp of it; **dead march**, march-like funeral music; **dead nettle**, nonstinging plant of genus *Lamium* with leaves like nettle's; **dead'pan**, (slang) expressionless; **dead reckoning**, (naut. and aeronaut.) estimation of ship's or aircraft's position from log, compass courses, etc., and not from observations; **dead shot**, unerring marksman; **dead soldier**, (slang) empty whiskey or beer bottle; **dead weight**, heavy inert weight, weight of dead body or lifeless matter; **dead'wood**, wood no longer alive; useless person(s) or thing(s). **dead** *n.* 1. **the** ~, dead person or persons; all who have ever died. 2. Dead period or time; time of intensest stillness, darkness, cold, etc. (*of* night, winter). ~ *adv.* Profoundly; absolutely, completely; ~ **against**, directly opposite or opposed to; **dead'beat** (*n.*) person who does not pay his or her just debts.

dead·en (dĕd′en) *v.* Deprive of, lose, vitality, force, brightness, feeling, etc.; make insensible *to*.

dead·ly (dĕd′lē) *adj.* (**-li·er, -li·est**). 1. Causing fatal injury; of poisonous nature; implacable, mortal, to the death. 2. (of sin) Entailing spiritual death, mortal; ~ **sins**, the seven sins of pride, lust, covetousness, envy, gluttony, anger, and sloth. 3. Resembling death; intense. **dead'li·ness** *n.* **dead'ly** *adv.* As if dead; extremely.

Dead (dĕd) **Sea.** Salt lake or inland sea between Israel and Jordan with intensely bitter water, into which river Jordan flows; ~ **Scrolls**, large collection of Hebrew and Aramaic parchment scrolls, including parts of most books of Old Testament, found (1947–) in caves NW. of Dead Sea, apparently stored there by a community that lived at Qumran *c*135 B.C.–70 A.D.

deaf (dĕf) *adj.* 1. Wholly or partly without hearing. 2. Insensible *to*; not giving ear *to*; uncompliant. 3. ~**-mute**, person unable to hear or speak, often communicating by ~**-and-dumb alphabet**, a system of signs made with the hands. **deaf'ly** *adv.* **deaf'ness** *n.*

deaf·en (def′en) *v.t.* Deprive of hearing by noise, stun with noise.

deal[1] (dēl) *n.* **a great** (or **good**) ~, a large (or fairly large) amount; (adverbially) by much, considerably.

deal² (dēl) *n.* Sawn fir or pine wood (11 in. wide, 2½ in. thick, and 12 ft. long); wood in this form; fir or pine wood.

deal³ (dēl) *n.* 1. Distribution, sharing; dealing of cards; turn to deal cards. 2. Business transaction, bargain; secret agreement in business or politics; **Fair D~**, policy of social improvement introduced by the presidential administration of Harry S. TRUMAN; **New D~**, program of social and economic reform of the presidential administration of Franklin D. Roosevelt from 1932 on. **deal** (dēl) *v.* (**dealt** pr. dĕlt, **deal·ing**). 1. Distribute, give *out*, among several. 2. Distribute cards to players for a game or round; give (card, hand, etc.) to player. 3. Associate *with*; do business (*with* person, *in* goods); occupy oneself, grapple by way of discussion or refutation, take measures, *with*; behave (*well, honorably, cruelly,* etc., *with* or *by* person). 4. (slang) Buy and sell drugs, as hallucinogens, narcotics, etc., without legal authorization. **deal'er** *n.* 1. Trader in a particular class of goods. 2. Player dealing at cards. 3. (slang) One who engages in illegal buying and selling of drugs. **deal'ing** *n.*

dean (dēn) *n.* 1. Official in charge of a university or college faculty or with specified administrative responsibilities; **~'s list**, listing by a school or college of students with high academic standing. 2. Head of chapter of collegiate or cathedral church. 3. Senior member of a particular group, profession, etc.; doyen. [L. *decanus* one set over ten (monks)]

dear (dēr) *adj.* 1. Beloved, loved (now often merely polite and part of ordinary formula at beginning of most letters); precious in one's regard, to which one is attached; **D~ John letter**, (slang) letter received by a man from his girlfriend or fiancée informing him that she is discontinuing their relationship. 2. Costly. **dear** *n.* Dear one, charming person or thing. **~** *adv.* At a high price; fondly. **dear'ly** *adv.* **dear'ness** *n.* **dear** *int.* Exclamation expressing surprise, distress, sympathy, etc. (**~ ~!, oh ~!, ~ me!**).

dearth (dērth) *n.* Scanty supply of.

death (dĕth) *n.* 1. Dying; final cessation of vital functions; being dead; cause or occasion of death; **put to ~**, execute; **talk to ~**, (colloq.) overdo discussion of a subject so that it becomes tiresome and boring. 2. Being or becoming spiritually dead; end, extinction, destruction. 3. **death'bed**, bed on which person dies; **deathbed statement** or **confession**, one made during the last hours of life; **death'blow**, blow that causes death; **death mask**, cast taken from person's face after death; **death penalty**, capital punishment; **death rate**, proportion of deaths usu. estimated per 1,000 of population per annum; **death rattle**, rattling sound in throat of dying person, caused by partial stoppage of air passage by mucus; **death's-head**, (figure or representation of) human skull, esp. as

emblem of mortality; **death'**·**head moth**, large Old World haw· moth (*Acherontia atropos*) wi· markings resembling skull · thorax; **death'trap**, place etc. th· is unwholesome or dangerou· **death warrant**, warrant f· execution of death sentence (al· fig.); **death'watch**, vigil ke· beside dying, condemned, or dea· person; **deathwatch beetle**, sma· beetle (*Xestobium rufovillosum* which makes noise like watc· ticking, formerly supposed to po· tend death, the larva of which bor· in old wood; insect making simila· sound; **death wish**, (psychol· alleged inborn tendency of organ· isms to seek death, capable of bein· directed against the self or others· **death·less** (dĕth'lĭs) *adj.* Im· mortal.   **death'less·ly** *ad·* **death'less·ness** *n.*

death·ly (dĕth'lē) *adj.* Deadl· gloomy, pale, etc., as death. · *adv.* To a degree resemblin· death.

Death Valley, California, the lowest point of the American continent (282 ft. below sea level), has almost no rain and temperatures reach 130°F. It was named after gold seekers who died there in 1849.

The furniture beetle, the **deathwatch** beetle, destroys hardwood timber in old houses, particularly oak and chestnut. It has a characteristic tapping noise which is heard particularly during the mating season in April and May.

v.t.

de·bris (debrē′, dā′brē) *n.* Scattered fragments, wreckage, drifted accumulation.

Debs (dĕbz), **Eugene Victor** (1855–1926). Amer. labor leader; organized Social Democratic Party of America, 1879, and was 5 times Socialist candidate for president; indicted and convicted of violation of Espionage Act, 1918, but released from prison, 1921, by order of President Harding.

debt (dĕt) *n.* Money, goods, or service, owing; being under obligation to pay something; **national** ~, total financial obligations of a country; ~ **of honor**, debt, usu. of sum lost in gambling, not legally enforceable.

debt·or (dĕt′er) *n.* One who owes money, or an obligation or duty.

de·bunk (dĭbŭngk′) *v.t.* Remove the false sentiment from (person, cult, etc.); expose (false claim etc.).

De·bus·sy (dĕbūsē′, dā′būsē, debū′sē), **Claude** (1862–1918). French composer of symphonic poems, piano compositions, and the opera *Pelléas et Mélisande.*

de·but (dābū′, dĭ-, dā′bū, dĕb′ū) *n.* First appearance, on stage etc. as performer, or in society.

deb·u·tante, déb·u·tante (dĕb′yutahnt) *ns.* Young woman making first appearance in society.

De·bye (dĕbī′), **Peter Joseph Wilhelm** (1884–1966). Dutch-born Amer. physicist; researched molecular structure and developed theory of specific heat; awarded Nobel Prize for chemistry, 1936.

Dec. *abbrev.* December.

dec. *abbrev.* Deceased; decimeter.

dec-, deca- *comb. forms.* Ten, ten times.

dec·ade (dĕk′ād) *n.* Set, series, of ten; period of ten years.

dec·a·dence (dĕk′adens) *n.* Falling away, declining (from former excellence, vitality, prosperity, etc.), esp. of morals or period of art or literature after a culmination.

dec·a·dent (dĕk′adent) *adj.* In a state of decay or decline; of morals, literature, art, etc., belonging to a decadent age. ~ *n.* Decadent writer or artist. **dec′a·dent·ly** *adv.*

de·caf·fein·ate (dēkăf′ināt, -ēināt) *v.t.* (**-at·ed, -at·ing**). Remove caffeine from or reduce quantity of caffeine in (coffee).

dec·a·gon (dĕk′agŏn) *n.* Plane figure with ten sides and ten angles. **de·cag·o·nal** (dekăg′onal) *adj.*

dec·a·gram (dĕk′agrăm) *n.*

Death (dĕth) **Valley.** Desert in California and W. Nevada that ⸗cludes the point with the lowest ⸗itude (280 ft., 85 m, below sea ⸗el) in the Western Hemisphere; **National Monument,** tourist ⸗d resort area of Death Valley, ⸗ted for ancient pictographs and ⸗ique geological formations.

deb (dĕb) *n.* (colloq.) Debutante.

de·ba·cle (debah′kel, -băk′el) *n.* (geol.) Sudden deluge of water, ⸗eaking down barriers and carry-⸗g stones and other debris with it, ⸗p. the breakup of ice on northern ⸗vers. 2. Sudden and overwhelm-⸗g collapse, rout, ruin. [Fr., = ⸗reakup of ice in river"]

De Ba·key (debā′kē), **Michael ⸗llis** (1908–). Amer. surgeon ⸗d educator; pioneer in heart ⸗rgery.

de·bar (dĭbār′) *v.t.* (**-barred, ⸗ar·ring**). Exclude *from* ad-⸗ission or right, esp. of lawyer; ⸗nder or prohibit. **de·bar′ment**

de·bark (dĭbārk′) *v.* Disembark. **⸗·bar·ka·tion** (dēbārkā′shon) *n.*

de·base (dĭbās′) *v.t.* (**-based, ⸗as·ing**). Lower in quality, value, character; depreciate (coin) by ⸗ixture of alloy or otherwise. **⸗·base′ment** *n.*

de·bat·a·ble (dĭbā′tabel) *adj.* ⸗uestionable, subject to dispute or ⸗bate.

de·bate (dĭbāt′) *v.* (**-bat·ed, ⸗at·ing**). Contest, fight for ⸗rchaic); dispute about, discuss, ⸗uestion); engage in (formal) ⸗gument or discussion (of), esp. in ⸗gislative or other assembly; con-⸗er, ponder; **debating society,** ⸗ciety whose members meet for ⸗actice in debating. **de·bat′er** *n.* ⸗ebate *n.* Controversy; discussion; ⸗blic argument.

de·bauch (dĭbawch′) *v.t.* Pervert from virtue or morality; make intemperate or sensual; seduce; vitiate (taste, judgment). ~ *n.* Bout or habit of sensual indulgence. **de·bauch·ee** (dĭbawchē′, -shē′), **de·bauch·er·y** (dĭbaw′cherē) *ns.*

de Beau·voir (de bōvwār′), **Simone** (1908–). French writer and one of the founders of the existentialist movement.

de·ben·ture (dĭbĕn′cher) *n.* 1. Voucher or certificate acknowledging indebtedness by the signer. 2. Certificate issued by a custom house providing for refund of a tariff or other tax. 3. (also ~ **bond**) Fixed-interest bond of a private business or governmental agency or corporation, secured only by the credit of the issuer.

de·bil·i·tate (dĭbĭl′ĭtāt) *v.t.* (**-tat·ed, -tat·ing**). Enfeeble (constitution etc.). **de·bil·i·ta·tion** (dĭbĭlĭtā′shon) *n.* **de·bil·i·ta·tive** (dĭbĭl′ĭtātĭv) *adj.*

de·bil·i·ty (dĭbĭl′ĭtē) *n.* (pl. **-ties**). Feebleness (of health, purpose, etc.).

deb·it (dĕb′ĭt) *n.* Item of debt; entry in account of sum owing; side of account (left-hand) in which these entries are made; ~ **card,** credit card by which bills are paid by direct deduction from the payer's bank account. **debit** *v.t.* Charge (person) *with* sum; enter (sum) *against* or *to* person.

deb·o·nair, deb·o·naire (dĕbo-nār′) *adjs.* Suave, urbane; genial, pleasant. **deb·o·nair′ly** *adv.*

de·bouch (dĭbōōsh′, -bowch′) *v.i.* Issue from ravine, wood, etc., into open ground. **de·bouch′ment** *n.*

de·brief·ing (dēbrē′fĭng) *n.* Interrogation, discussion, after completion of mission etc. **de·brief′**

(abbrev. dkg) Unit of grams.

dec·a·he·dron (dĕkahē'drŏn) n. (pl. **-drons, -dra** pr. -dra). Ten-sided solid. **dec·a·he'dral** adj.

de·cal·ci·fy (dēkăl'sĭfī) v.t. (-fied, -fy·ing). Deprive of lime or calcareous matter. **de·cal·ci·fi·ca·tion** (dēkălsĭfĭkā'shŏn) n.

dec·a·li·ter (dĕk'aletēr) n. (abbrev. dkl) Ten liters.

Dec·a·logue, Dec·a·log (dĕk'a-lawg, -lŏg) ns. (also d~) The Ten Commandments (Exod. 20).

De·cam·er·on (dĭkăm'erŏn), **The.** Work by BOCCACCIO, written between 1348 and 1358, containing 100 tales told in ten days by a party of seven young ladies and three young men who had fled from the plague in Florence.

dec·a·me·ter (dĕk'amētēr) n. (abbrev. dkm) Ten meters.

de·camp (dĭkămp') v.i. Break up or leave camp; go away suddenly, abscond. **de·camp'·ment** n.

de·cant (dĭkănt') v.t. Pour off (clear liquid of solution) by gently inclining vessel without disturbing sediment; pour (wine) similarly from bottle into decanter; pour or empty out. **de·cant'er** n. Stoppered glass vessel in which decanted wine etc. is brought to table.

de·cap·i·tate (dĭkăp'ĭtāt) v.t. (-tat·ed, -tat·ing). Behead. **de·cap·i·ta·tion** (dĭkăpĭtā'shŏn) n.

dec·a·pod (dĕk'apŏd) n. Ten-footed crustacean.

de·car·bon·ize (dēkār'bonīz), **de·car·bu·rize** (dēkār'burīz) vbs.t. (-ized, -iz·ing, -rized, -riz·ing). Remove carbon from, esp. carbon deposit from (internal combustion engine). **de·car·bon·i·za·tion** (dēkārbonĭzā'shŏn) n.

dec·a·syl·la·ble (dĕk'asĭlabel) n. (Metrical line) of ten syllables.

de·cath·lon (dĭkăth'lŏn) n. Athletic contest comprising ten different track and field events.

De·ca·tur (dĭkā'ter), **Stephen** (1779–1820). Amer. naval officer; victorious in battles against Tripoli, 1803–4, and during War of 1812; famous for his toast, "——our country right or wrong."

de·cay (dĭkā') v. 1. Deteriorate; lose quality; decline in power, wealth, beauty, etc.; (phys.) diminish in intensity; (of radioactive particles etc.) disintegrate *into* different particles etc. ~ **heat**, heat produced by radioactive decay. 2. Rot, cause to deteriorate. ~ n. Act, process of decaying.

Dec·can (dĕk'an) **Plateau.** Triangular plateau of most of peninsula of India.

de·cease (dĭsēs') n. (legal or formal) Death. ~ v.i. (-ceased, -ceas·ing). Die. **de·ceased'** adj. & n. Dead (person).

de·ce·dent (dĭsē'dent) n. (legal) Deceased person.

de·ceit (dĭsēt') n. Trick or ploy to mislead or to persuade of what is false; falseness. **de·ceit'ful** adj. **de·ceit'ful·ly** adv. **de·ceit'ful·ness** n.

de·ceive (dĭsēv') v. (-ceived, -ceiv·ing). Persuade of what is false, mislead; disappoint (hopes etc.). **de·ceiv'er** n. **de·ceiv'ing·ly** adv.

de·cel·er·ate (dēsĕl'erāt) v. (-at·ed, -at·ing). Decrease speed or velocity (of). **de·cel·er·a·tion** (dēsĕlerā'shŏn), **de·cel'er·a·tor** ns.

De·cem·ber (dĭsĕm'ber). Twelfth month of Gregorian (tenth of Julian) calendar, with 31 days. [L. *decem* ten]

De·cem·brist (dĭsĕm'brĭst) n. (hist.) One of those who in Dec. 1825 tried to raise revolt against Tsar Nicholas I of Russia.

de·cen·cy (dē'sensē) n. (pl. -cies). Propriety of behavior or demeanor; compliance with recognized notions of modesty or delicacy, freedom from impropriety; respectability; (pl.) decent or becoming acts or observances, outward conditions of decent life.

de·cen·ni·al (dĕsĕn'ēal) adj. Of ten-year period; recurring in ten years. **de·cen'ni·al·ly** adv. **de·cen·ni·um** (dĭsĕn'ēum) n. (pl. -cen·ni·ums, -cen·ni·a pr. -sĕn'ēa). Period of ten years.

de·cent (dē'sent) adj. 1. Seemly, not immodest, obscene, or indelicate; respectable. 2. Fair, tolerable, passable; (colloq.) kind, not severe or censorious. **de'cent·ly** adv.

de·cen·tral·ize (dēsĕn'tralīz) v.t. (-ized, -iz·ing). Divide and distribute (government, organization, etc.) among local centers. **de·cen·tral·i·za·tion** (dēsĕntralĭzā'shŏn) n.

de·cep·tion (dĭsĕp'shŏn) n. Deceiving, being deceived; trick, sham.

de·cep·tive (dĭsĕp'tĭv) adj. Apt to deceive, easily mistaken. **de·cep'tive·ly** adv. **de·cep'tive·ness** n.

deci- *prefix.* One-tenth of.

dec·i·bar (dĕs'ibār) n. (meteor.) One-tenth of a BAR[2].

dec·i·bel (dĕs'ibĕl) n. Unit (= $\frac{1}{10}$ of a bel) used in comparison of levels of power in electrical communications circuit(s) or of intensities of sounds (abbrev. dB).

de·cide (dĭsīd') v. (-cid·ed, -cid·ing). Settle (question, issue, dispute) by giving victory to one side; give judgment (*between, for, against*, etc.); bring, come, to a resolution or decision. **de·cid'a·ble** adj. **de·cid'ed** adj. (esp.) Definite, unquestionable; (of persons) of clear opinions or vigorous initiative; not vacillating. **de·cid'er** n. **de·cid'ed·ly** adv.

de·cid·u·ous (dĭsĭj'ōos) adj.

Shed periodically or normally; plant) shedding its leaves annual

dec·i·gram (dĕs'igrăm) (abbrev. dg) One-tenth of a gra

dec·i·li·ter (dĕs'ilētēr) (abbrev. dl) One-tenth of a lite

de·cil·lion (dĭsĭl'yon) n. Eleventh power of a thousand followed by 33 zeros). 2. (Bri Tenth power of a million followed by 60 zeros).

dec·i·mal (dĕs'imal) adj. 10th parts, of the number te proceeding by tens; ~ **fracti** fraction whose denominator is som power of 10, esp. such a fracti written to right of the units figu after the ~ *point*, and denoti tenths, hundredths, thousandth etc.; ~ **point**, period at the left a decimal fraction; ~ **syster** system of weights and measures which each denomination is t times the value of that immediate below it. **decimal** n. Decim fraction. **dec'i·mal·ly** adv. **dec·i·mal·ize** (dĕs'imalīz) v.t. (-ize -iz·ing). Express as decima convert to decimal system. **dec·i· mal·i·za·tion** (dĕsimalĭzā'shŏn)

dec·i·mate (dĕs'imāt) v. (-mat·ed, -mat·ing). Put to dea one in ten of; destroy $\frac{1}{10}$ of; kill destroy large part of. **dec·i·ma tion** (dĕsimā'shŏn) n.

dec·i·me·ter (dĕs'imētēr) (abbrev. dm) One-tenth of a mete

de·ci·pher (dĭsī'fer) v.t. Conve (what is written in cipher) in ordinary writing; make out, in terpret, by means of key; make o meaning of. **de·ci'pher·a·ble** a **de·ci'pher·ment** n.

de·ci·sion (dĭsĭzh'on) n. Settle ment (*of*), conclusion, forma judgment; making up one's min resolve; resoluteness, decide character.

de·ci·sive (dĭsī'sĭv) adj. De ciding, conclusive; decided; di playing ability to make decision unmistakable, unquestionable **de·ci'sive·ly** adv. **de·ci'sive·nes** n.

deck[1] (dĕk) n. 1. Platform planks or wood-covered iro extending from side to side of shi or part of it (in large ships **mai middle, lower** ~s, also **upper** above main); planking of bridg etc.; one of several floors or level **clear the** ~s, make ready to figh as by getting rid of unneeded gea make ready for some activity work, as by eliminating obstacle ~ **chair**, folding canvas chair of th kind used on passenger ships; ~ **hand**, sailor who works on deck

deck'house, room erected on upper deck of ship; **hit the deck**, (slang) get out of bed; fall, be pushed, or drop (oneself) to the ground or floor; **on deck**, (colloq.) ready for action; on hand; (baseball) next in order. 2. Pack of playing cards.

deck² (děk) v.t. 1. Array, adorn. 2. Cover as or with deck, furnish with deck. 3. (colloq.) Knock down (person, beast) with blow of fist etc.

deck·le (děk'el) n. Frame in papermaking machine for limiting size or width of sheet; ~ **edge**, rough uncut edge of paper formed by deckle; ~**-edged** (adj.) having such an edge, as handmade paper.

de·claim (dĭklām') v. Speak or utter rhetorically; recite; deliver impassioned rather than reasoned speech.

dec·la·ma·tion (děklamā'shon) n. Act or art of declaiming; rhetorical exercise, set speech; impassioned speech, harangue. **de·claim'er** n. **de·clam·a·to·ry** (dĭklăm'atōrē, -tōrē) adj.

de·clar·ant (dĭklār'ant) n. One who makes legal declaration, esp. of becoming citizen of a country.

dec·la·ra·tion (děklarā'shon) n. Stating, announcing, openly, explicitly, or formally; emphatic, solemn or legal assertion or proclamation; public statement as embodied in document, instrument, or public act; (law) plaintiff's statement of claim; simple affirmation sometimes allowed in lieu of oath or solemn affirmation; creation or acknowledgment of trust or use in writing; (cards) in bridge, a bid, esp. final bid naming trump suit; **D~ of Independence:** see INDEPENDENCE; ~ **of war**, formal announcement by one nation of commencement of hostilities against another.

de·clare (dĭklār') v. (-clared, -clar·ing). 1. Make known, proclaim publicly, formally, or explicitly; pronounce to be; acknowledge possession of (dutiable goods); ~ **war**, formally proclaim beginning of hostilities. 2. (law) Make declaration. 3. (cards) In bridge, name trump suit or "no-trump" with final bid. **de·clar'a·ble, de·clar·a·tive** (dĭklăr'atĭv), adjs. **de·clar·a·to·ry** (dĭklăr'atōrē, -tōrē) adj. **de·clar'er** n.

dé·clas·sé (dāklăsā', -kla-) (fem. -sée) adj. Having sunk in the social scale.

de·clas·si·fy (dēklăs'ifī) v.t. (-fied, -fy·ing). Cease to designate (information etc.) as secret.

de·clen·sion (dĭklěn'shon) n. 1. Declining or deviating from vertical or horizontal position. 2. Decrease; decline, deterioration, decay. 3. (gram.) Variation of form of noun, adjective, or pronoun, constituting its cases; class in which noun etc. is grouped according to its inflections; declining. **de·clen'sion·al** adj.

dec·li·na·tion (děklinā'shon) n. 1. Slope, inclination, from vertical or horizontal position; decline; deviation. 2. (astron.) Angular distance of heavenly body from celestial equator. 3. (also **magnetic ~**) Deviation of magnetic needle from true north-and-south line, variation. 4. Declining, refusal.

de·cline (dĭklīn') n. 1. Sinking; gradual loss of vigor or excellence; decay; deterioration; wasting disease; downward movement in price or value. 2. Setting, last part of course, of sun, (fig.) of life, etc. ~ v. (-clined, -clin·ing). 1. Have downward inclination; bend down, bow down, droop. 2. (of sun, day, life, etc.) Draw to end of its course. 3. Fall off, decay, decrease, deteriorate. 4. Turn away from, refuse, withhold oneself from (discussion, challenge, etc.); not accept, refuse politely. 5. (gram.) Inflect, recite cases of. **de·clin'er** n.

de·clin'a·ble adj. (gram.) That c be declined.

de·cliv·i·ty (dĭklĭv'ĭtē) n. (-ties). Downward slope; hollow

de·coct (dĭkŏkt') v.t. Ma decoction of. **de·coc·tion** (dĭkŏ shon) n. (Liquor obtained b boiling substance in liquid so as extract soluble parts.

de·code (dĭkōd') v.t. (-cod·e -cod·ing). Decipher (cod message).

dé·colle·tage (dākoltahzh', dě ole-) n. (Exposure of neck a shoulders by) low-cut neck of dres **dé·colle·té** (dākoltā', děkole-) ac (of dress) Low-necked; (of perso wearing low-necked dress. [Fr.

de·com·mis·sion (dēkomĭsh'o v.t. Withdraw (ship etc.) fro tive service.

de·com·pose (dēkompōz') v. posed, -pos·ing). 1. Separate or solve into constituent parts or ements. 2. Disintegrate, break); rot. **de·com·po·si·tion** ēkŏmpozĭsh'on) n.

de·com·press (dēkomprĕs') v.t. Relieve pressure on (person who as been in compressed air) by eans of air lock. 2. Reduce ompression in (vehicle engine) us making engine easier to start. e·com·pres·sion (dēkomprĕsh'- n.; ~ sickness, caisson disease.

de·con·gest·ant (dēkonjĕs'tant) dj. & n. (Drug etc.) that lieves congestion.

de·con·tam·i·nate (dēkontăm'- āt) v.t. (-nat·ed, -nat·ing). Rid erson, area, etc.) of con- mination, esp. from poison gas, dioactivity; etc. **de·con·tam·i- a·tion** (dēkontămĭnā'shon) n.

de·con·trol (dēkontrōl') v.t. trolled, -trol·ling) & n. Release om (esp. government) control.

dé·cor, de·cor (dākōr', dĭ-, ā'kōr) ns. Scenery and furnish- gs, decorative style, of home, om, stage set, etc.

dec·o·rate (dĕk'erāt) v.t. rat·ed, -rat·ing). 1. Furnish ith ornamental accessories; hang streets etc.) with flags etc.; paint, aper, etc. (room, house); serve as dornment to. 2. Confer medal, onor, etc. upon. **dec·o·ra·tive** ĕk'erativ, dĕk'ra-, -erā-) adj. ec·o·ra·tive·ly adv. **dec·o·ra- ve·ness** n.

dec·o·ra·tion (dĕkorā'shon) n. sp.) 1. Decorating. 2. (pl.) Flags

etc. put up on festive occasion. 3. Medal etc., conferred and worn as mark of honor; **D~ Day =** MEMORIAL Day.

dec·o·ra·tor (dĕk'orāter) n. Interior decorator.

dec·o·rous (dĕk'orus, -kōr'-) adj. Not violating good taste or propriety, dignified and decent. **dec'o·rous·ly** adv.

de·co·rum (dĭkōr'um, -kōr'-) n. Seemliness, propriety, etiquette; particular usage required by polite- ness or decency.

de·cou·page, dé·cou·page (dākōōpahzh') ns. Decoration of surfaces with paper cutouts.

de·coy (dē'koi, dĭkoi') n. 1. Enclosed place, pond, etc., into which wildfowl may be lured and caught. 2. Living or artificial bird or other animal used to entice game, esp. wild ducks, into shooting range or a trap; (fig.) person or thing used to decoy others. **de·coy** (dĭkoi') v.t. Entice into place of capture, esp. with decoy; allure *into, out of, away,* etc., ensnare.

de·crease (dĭkrēs') v. (-creased, -creas·ing). Lessen, diminish. **decrease** (dē'krēs; dĭkrēs') n. Diminution, lessening.

de·cree (dĭkrē') n. 1. Ordinance or edict set forth by authority; edict or law of ecclesiastical council; one of eternal purposes, will, of God, Providence, Nature, etc. 2. Judgment of court of equity, admiralty, probate, or divorce; in divorce cases, order of court declaring nullity or dissolution of marriage; ~ nisi: see NISI. **decree** v.t. (-creed, -cree·ing). Ordain

by decree.

dec·re·ment (dĕk'rement) n. Decrease, amount lost by diminution or waste (opp. *increment*).

de·crep·it (dĭkrĕp'ĭt) adj. Wasted, worn out, enfeebled with age and infirmities. **de·crep·i·tude** (dĭkrĕp'ĭtood, -tūd) n.

de·cres·cent (dĭkrĕs'ent) adj. Waning, decreasing (usu. of moon).

de·cre·tal (dĭkrē'tal) n. Papal decree; **D~s**, collection of such decrees, forming part of canon law.

de·crim·i·nal·ize (dēkrĭm'- ĭnalĭz) v.t. (-ized, -iz·ing). Abolish or reduce criminal penalties for (specific crime, esp. use or possession of marijuana).

de·cry (dĭkrī') v.t. (-cried, -cry·ing). Disparage, cry down.

de·cum·bent (dĭkŭm'bent) adj. Reclining; prostrate; (bot., zool.) lying along ground, lying flat on surface. **de·cum'bent·ly** adv.

de·cus·sate (dĭkŭs'āt, -ĭt) adj. X-shaped; (bot.) with pairs of opposite leaves etc. each at right angles to pair below. **decussate** (dĭkŭs'āt, dĕk'usāt) v. (-sat·ed, -sat·ing). Arrange, be arranged thus, intersect. **de·cus·sa·tion** (dēkusā'shon, dĕku-) n.

ded·i·cate (dĕd'ĭkāt) v.t. (-cat·ed, -cat·ing). Devote (*to* God etc.) with solemn rites; give up, devote (*to* person, purpose); inscribe (book, music, etc.) *to* patron or friend. **ded·i·ca·to·ry** (dĕd'ĭkatōrē, -tōrē) adj. **ded·i·ca·tion** (dĕdĭkā'shon) n. (esp.) Dedica- tory inscription. **ded·i·ca·tor** n.

de·duce (dĭdoos', -dūs') v.t.

(-duced, -duc·ing). 1. Trace course of, bring down (record etc.) *from* or *to* particular period; trace derivation or descent of. 2. Derive as conclusion *from* something already known; infer. **de·duc'i·ble** *adj.*

de·duct (dǐdŭkt') *v.t.* Take away, put aside (amount etc.) *from*. **de·duct'i·ble** *adj.*

de·duc·tion (dǐdŭk'shon) *n.* 1. Deducting; amount deducted, as in *income tax* ~. 2. Deducing; inference by reasoning from generals to particulars (opp. IN-DUCTION); thing deduced.

de·duc·tive (dǐdŭk'tǐv) *adj.* Of, reasoning by, deduction. **de·duc'-tive·ly** *adv.*

deed (dēd) *n.* 1. Thing done by intelligent or responsible agent; act of bravery, skill, etc., feat, performance, doing. 2. (law) Written instrument purporting to effect some legal disposition, and sealed and delivered by disposing party (in practice now always signed also but not always delivered). ~ *v.t.* Convey or transfer by deed.

dee·jay (dē'jā) (slang) = DISC jockey.

deem (dēm) *v.t.* Believe, consider, judge, count.

de-em·pha·size (dēĕm'fasīz) *v.t.* **(-sized, -siz·ing).** Remove emphasis from. **de-em·pha·sis** (dēĕm'fasǐs) *n.* (pl. **-ses** pr. -sēz).

deep (dēp) *adj.* 1. Extending far down from top, or far in from

surface or edge. 2. (fig.) Hard to fathom; profound, not superficial, penetrating. 3. Heartfelt; absorbing; absorbed; intense, vivid, extreme. 4. Not shrill; low-pitched, full-toned. 5. ~ **freeze**, refrigerator in which food can be quickly frozen and stored for long periods (**Deep'freeze**, trademark); **~-sea** (*adj.*), of the deeper part of the sea, some way from shore; ~ **set** (*adj.*), deeply placed; well established; ~ **space**, regions beyond solar system. **deep'ly** *adv.* **deep'ness** *n.* **deep** *n.* 1. (poet.) **the** ~, the sea. 2. Deep part of the sea; abyss, pit, cavity; mysterious region of thought or feeling. ~ *adv.* Deeply; far down or in; **~-freeze** (*v.t.*), freeze food quickly; (colloq.) store away (damaging information) to prevent discovery; **~-fry** (*v.t.*), fry by immersion in a deep pan of hot oil or fat; **~-rooted**, having deep roots; (fig.) not easily eradicated; **~-seated**, having its seat far below surface; not superficial; ~ **-six** (*v.t.*), (slang) discard, throw away, jettison. **deep'en** *v.* Make, become, deep or deeper.

Above left: Red **deer.** *Below left: Fallow deer. Above right: Reindeer. Below right: Roe deer. Deer are woodland creatures found in Europe, Asia, America, and northern Africa. Speed and highly developed senses protect them from danger. The species differ in their habits.*

Deep (dēp) **South.** South eastern states of the U.S., particu larly the former Confederate stat of South Carolina, Georgi Alabama, Mississippi, and (ofte Louisiana.

deer (dēr) *n.* (pl. **deer**, some times **deers**). Ruminant quad ruped of family Cervidae, most the males of which have deciduou branching antlers; Amer. specie include **white-tailed** ~, **black tailed** ~, ELK, MOOSE, and CARIBO Old World species include **fallow red, roe** ~ (see FALLOW[2]; REE ROE[1]); ~ **fly**, any of severa blood-sucking flies of the genu *Chrysops* with dark wing marking **deer'hound**, large rough grey hound of Scottish breed; **dee park**, park where deer are kep **deer'skin**, (made of) deer's ski **deer'stalker**, one who stalks dee cloth cap with peak before an behind.

de·face (dǐfās') *v.t.* **(-faced -fac·ing).** Disfigure; mar, spo appearance of; make illegible **de·face'ment** *n.*

de fac·to (dē făk'tō, dā) *adj.* & *adv. phr.* In fact, whether by righ or not. [L.]

de·fal·cate (dǐfăl'kāt, -fawl'- *v.i.* **(-cat·ed, -cat·ing).** Embezzl or misuse funds; misappropriat property in one's charge. **de· fal·ca·tion** (dēfălkā'shon, -fawl-) *n*

de·fame (dǐfām') *v.t.* **(-famed -fam·ing).** Attack the goo

...utation of, speak ill of. **def·a·ma·tion** (dĕfamā´shon) *n.* **de·fam·a·to·ry** (dĭfăm´atōrē, -tôrē) . **de·fam´er** *n.*

de·fault (dĭfawlt´) *n.* Want, ...ence; failure to act or appear; ...glect; failure to pay. ~ *v.* 1. ...ke, be guilty of, default; fail to ...pear in court; fail to pay money ...e. 2. Declare (party) in default ...d give judgment against him or ...: **de·fault´er** *n.*

de·feat (dĭfēt´) *v.t.* Win victory ...er, conquer, in battle or other ...test; frustrate, baffle; (law) ...nul. ~ *n.* Act or instance of ...eating or being defeated; frustra...n.

de·feat·ism (dĭfē´tĭzem) *n.* Dis...sition, conduct, of one who ...cepts defeat as inevitable. **·feat´ist** *n.* & *adj.*

de·fe·cate (dĕf´ekāt) *v.* (-**cat·ed,** ...at·ing). Clear of dregs, refine, ...rify; get rid of, purge away, ...egs, excrement, sin); void feces. **f·e·ca·tion** (dĕfekā´shon) *n.*

de·fect (dē´fĕkt, dĭfĕkt´) *n.* Lack ...something essential to complete...ss; shortcoming, failing; blemish; ...ount by which thing falls short. **·fect** (dĭfĕkt´) *v.i.* Desert, esp. ...another cause, country, etc. **·fec·tion** (dĭfĕk´shon), **de·fec´·** ...r *ns.*

de·fec·tive (dĭfĕk´tĭv) *adj.* ...aving defect(s); incomplete; ...alty; wanting or deficient *in*; ...ram.) not having all usual ...flected forms. ~ *n.* (esp.) ...ental ~, mentally defective ...rson. **de·fec´tive·ly** *adv.* **·fec´tive·ness** *n.*

de·fend (dĭfĕnd´) *v.* 1. Ward off ...ack from; keep safe; protect ...gainst, from). 2. Uphold by ...gument, speak or write in favor ...(law) make defense in court; (of

counsel) appear for defendant, conduct defense of. **de·fend´a·ble** *adj.* **de·fend´er** *n.*

de·fend·ant (dĭfĕn´dant) *n.* Person sued in court of law. ~ *adj.* That is a defendant.

de·fend·er (dĭfĕn´der) *n.* One who defends; holder of championship etc. defending the title; **D ~ of the Faith** (L. *Fidei Defensor*), title borne by English sovereigns since Henry VIII, on whom it was conferred in 1521 by Pope Leo X as reward for writing against Luther.

de·fen·es·tra·tion (dēfĕnestrā´shon) *n.* Throwing out of a window.

de·fense (dĭfĕns´) *n.* 1. Defending from, resistance against, attack. 2. Thing that defends; means of resisting or warding off attack; military resources of a country; (pl.) fortifications. 3. Justification, vindication; speech or writing used to this end; (law) denial or charge by accused party, defendant's pleading or proceedings. 4. ~ **mechanism,** (psychol.) dynamic mental system serving to protect the conscious personality against disruptive unconscious impulses. **de·fense´less** *adj.* **de·fense´less·ly** *adv.*

de·fen·si·ble (dĭfĕn´sĭbel) *adj.* Easily defended (in war or argument); justifiable. **de·fen·si·bil·i·ty** (dĭfĕnsĭbĭl´ĭtē) *n.* **de·fen´si·bly** *adv.*

de·fen·sive (dĭfĕn´sĭv) *adj.* Serving, used, done, for defense; protective; not aggressive. **de·fen´sive·ly** *adv.* **defensive** *n.* State or position of defense.

de·fer¹ (dĭfĕr´) *v.* (-**ferred, -fer·ring**). 1. Put off, postpone; procrastinate, be dilatory. 2. Exempt from military service

temporarily. 3. **deferred payment,** payment by installments; with payments or benefits withheld until a future date. **de·fer´ral** (dĭfĕr´al), **de·fer´ment, de·fer´rer** *ns.*

de·fer² (dĭfĕr´) *v.t.* (-**ferred, -fer·ring**). Submit or make concessions in opinion or action *to* (person etc.).

def·er·ence (dĕf´erens) *n.* Compliance with advice etc. of one superior in wisdom or position; respect, manifestation of desire to comply, courteous regard; **in ~ to,** out of respect for. **def·er·en·tial** (dĕferĕn´shal) *adj.* **def·er·en´tial·ly** *adv.*

def·er·ent (dĕf´erent) *adj.* Conveying away.

de·fi·ance (dĭfī´ans) *n.* Challenge to fight or maintain cause, assertion, etc.; open disobedience or disregard.

de·fi·ant (dĭfī´ant) *adj.* Expressing defiance. **de·fi´ant·ly** *adv.*

de·fi·cien·cy (dĭfĭsh´ensē) *n.* (pl. -**cies**). Being deficient; want, lack; thing wanting; amount by which thing, esp. revenue, falls short; ~ **disease,** disease caused by lack in diet of necessary elements, esp. vitamins. **de·fi·cient** (dĭfĭsh´ent) *adj.* Incomplete, defective, wanting *in*; insufficient in quantity, force, etc. **de·fi´cient·ly** *adv.*

def·i·cit (dĕf´ĭsĭt) *n.* Amount by which anything, esp. sum of money, is too small; excess of liabilities over assets or of expenditure over income.

def·i·lade (dĕfĭlād´) *v.t.* (-**lad·ed, -lad·ing**). Secure (fortress) against enfilading fire. ~ *n.* Act or operation of defilading.

de·file¹ (dĭfīl´, dē´fīl) *n.* Narrow way along which troops can march only in file; narrow pass or gorge. ~ *v.i.* (-**filed, -fil·ing**). March in files, by files.

de·file² (dĭfīl´) *v.t.* (-**filed, -fil·ing**). Make dirty, befoul; pollute, corrupt; desecrate, profane; make ceremonially unclean. **de·file´ment** *n.*

de·fine (dĭfīn´) *v.t.* (-**fined, -fin·ing**). Settle limits of; make clear, esp. in outline; set forth essence of, declare exact meaning of; characterize, constitute definition of. **de·fin´a·ble** *adj.* **de·fin´a·bly** *adv.*

def·i·nite (dĕf´ĭnĭt) *adj.* With exact limits; determinate, distinct, precise, not vague; ~ **article**: see ARTICLE. **def´i·nite·ly** *adv.* Clearly, plainly; yes indeed; without fail. **def´i·nite·ness** *n.*

def·i·ni·tion (dĕfĭnĭsh´on) *n.* 1.

The Ballet Scene from Meyerbeer's 'Roberto il Diavolo' by **Edgar Degas.** *The Impressionist painter's compositions were influenced by the then new techniques of photography. Degas excelled in ballet and circus portrayal.*

Defining; statement of precise nature of thing or meaning of word. 2. Making or being distinct, degree of distinctness of details in a photograph, film, television picture, etc.

de·fin·i·tive (dĭfĭn′ĭtĭv) *adj*. Decisive, unconditional, final; authoritative (~ **edition**). **de·fin′i·tive·ly** *adv*. **de·fin′i·tive·ness** *n*.

de·flate (dĭflāt′) *v*. (**-flat·ed, -flat·ing**). 1. Let air etc. out of (tire, balloon, etc.). 2. Reduce (inflated currency); practice deflation. 3. Lower (person's spirits, confidence, etc.).

de·fla·tion (dĭflā′shon) *n*. 1. Deflating, esp. situation in any country where prices generally are falling relatively to costs of production, giving rise to losses and unemployment. 2. Lowering (person's spirits, confidence, etc.). **de·fla′tor** *n*. **de·fla′tion·ar·y** *adj*.

de·flect (dĭflĕkt′) *v*. Bend or turn aside; bend (ray of light) from straight line. **de·flec′tive, de·flect′a·ble** *adjs*. **de·flec′tor** *n*.

de·flec·tion (dĭflĕk′shon) *n*. Deflecting; (esp.) turning of magnetic needle or recording needle of galvanometer away from its zero.

def·lo·ra·tion (dĕflŏrā′shon, dĕflō-) *n*. Deflowering.

de·flow·er (dĭflow′er) *v.t*. Deprive of virginity; ravage, spoil; strip of flowers.

De·foe (dĕfō′), **Daniel** (1660?– 1731). English journalist and novelist; author of *Robinson Crusoe, Moll Flanders,* etc.

de·fog (dēfawg′, -fŏg′) *v.t*. (**-fogged, -fog·ging**). Eliminate condensation, fog, etc. from (mirror, car window, etc.). **de·fog′ger** *n*.

de·fo·li·ant (dĭfō′lēant) *n*. Spray or dust to defoliate plants.

de·fo·li·ate (dĭfō′lēāt) *v.t*. (**-at·ed, -at·ing**). Remove leaves from, esp. as military tactic. **de·fo·li·a·tion** (dēfōlēā′shon), **de·fo·li·a·tor** *ns*.

de·for·est (dēfôr′ĭst, -fär′-) *v.t*. Clear of forest. **de·for·est·a·tion** (dēfôrĭstā′shon, -fär-) *n*.

De For·est (dĭ fôr′ĭst, fär′-), **Lee** (1873–1961). Amer. inventor; called "the father of radio"; worked on wireless telegraphy, radiotelephony, sound-on-film, television, etc.

de·form (dĭfôrm′) *v.t*. Deface; put out of shape, misshape (esp. in past part.). **de·form′a·ble** *adj*.

de·for·ma·tion (dēfôrmā′shon, dĕfer-) *n*. Disfigurement; change for the worse; perverted form.

de·form·i·ty (dĭfôr′mĭtē) *n*. (pl. **-ties**). Being deformed, ugliness,

disfigurement; malformation (e of body or limb).

de·fraud (dĭfrawd′) *v.t*. Che **de·fraud′er** *n*.

de·fray (dĭfrā′) *v.t*. Sett satisfy by payment; bear or p (costs etc.). **de·fray′ment de·fray′a·ble** *adj*. **de·fray′al** *n*

de·frock (dĭfrŏk′) = UNFROCK

de·frost (dĭfrawst′, -frŏst′) Remove frost from; thaw, e frozen food.

defs. *abbrev*. Definitions.

deft (dĕft) *adj*. Dextrous, esp. manual skill. **deft′ly** *adv*. **def ness** *n*.

de·funct (dĭfŭngkt′) *adj*. De no longer existing.

de·fuse (dēfūz′) *v.t*. (**-fuse -fus·ing**). 1. Remove fuse fr (explosive). 2. Reduce likeliho of trouble arising from (crisis etc

de·fy (dĭfī′) *v.t*. (**-fied, -fy·in** 1. Challenge to combat (archai challenge *to* contest or trial skill. 2. Resist boldly or openly, at naught; (of things) be beyo power of.

deg. *abbrev*. Degree.

De·gas (dāgah′, dā′gah), **Hilai Germain Edgar** (1834–191 French Impressionist painter a sculptor, known especially for paintings of the ballet and of hors

De Gaulle (de gōl′, gawl **Charles** (1890–1970). Fren general and statesman; head of t "Free French" movement after t occupation of France by Germa

1940 and of the French Pro-
ional Government, 1944–5;
emier of France, 1958–9;
sident 1945–6 and 1959–69.

de·gauss (dēgows´) *v.t.* De-
gnetize; esp. render (ship)
mune to magnetic mines or
evision receiver) to magnetic
erference. [see GAUSS]

de·gen·er·ate (dĭjĕn´erĭt) *adj.*
ving lost qualities proper to race
kind, sunk from former
cellence, debased, degraded;
ol.) having reverted to lower
e. **de·gen·er·a·cy** (dĭjĕn´erasē)
degenerate *n.* Degenerate
rson or animal. **degenerate**
jĕn´erāt) *v.i.* (**-at·ed, -at·ing**).
come degenerate. **de·gen´er-**
·ly *adv.* **de·gen´er·ate·ness** *n.*
·**gen·er·a·tive** (dĭjĕn´erātĭv,
a-) *adj.*

de·gen·er·a·tion (dĭjĕnerā´shon)
Becoming degenerate; (path.)
rbid disintegration of tissue or
ange in its structure.

de·glu·ti·nate (dēgloo´tĭnāt) *v.t.*
at·ed, -nat·ing). Extract
uten from (flour etc.). **de·glu-**
na·tion (dēglootĭnā´shon) *n.*

de·grade (dĭgrād´) *v.* (**-grad·ed,**
rad·ing). 1. Reduce to lower
nk or office. 2. Bring into
honor or contempt; lower in
aracter or quality, debase. 3.
em.) Break down (molecule);
hys.) reduce (energy) to a form
s capable of transformation. 4.
ol.) Wear down (rocks etc.) by
rface abrasion or disintegration.
·**grad´a·ble** *adj.* **deg·ra·da-**
n (dĕgradā´shon) *n.* **de-**
ad´ed·ly *adv.* **de·grad´ed·ness,**
·**grad´er** *ns.*

de·gree (dĭgrē´) *n.* 1. Thing
aced like step in series; stage in
cending or descending scale or
ocess; **by ∼s,** gradually. 2. Stage
direct line of descent. 3. Relative
cial or official rank; relative con-
tion or state. 4. Stage in intensity
amount; (criminal law) dis-
active grade of crime (**murder in**
e **first** ∼, homicide premedi-
ted or resulting from commission
grave crime; **in the second** ∼,
apremeditated, or resulting from
mmission of lesser crime); **third**
: see THIRD. 5. Academic title
nferred by college or university to
udent who has completed course
study or (**honorary** ∼) on
rson of distinction as honor;
eemasonry) each step of profi-
ency in order, conferring success-
ely higher rank. 6. (gram.) Stage
ositive, comparative, superlative)
comparison of adjective or
lverb. 7. (geom. etc.) Unit of
gular measurement (symbol °),
gle equal to $\frac{1}{90}$ right angle, arc
$\frac{1}{360}$ circumference of circle; esp.
of Earth's circumference, = 60
inutes; (thermometry) unit of
mperature, varying according to

*Detail from 'Dante and Virgil in the
Underworld' (Louvre, Paris) painted by
Ferdinand Delacroix (1799–1863),
notable for his symbolic use of color.*

scale employed; (mus.) (interval
between) successive notes forming
a scale.

de·hisce (dĭhĭs´) *v.i.* (**-hisced,
-hisc·ing**). Gape; (bot., of seed
vessel etc.) burst open. **de·his´-
cence** *n.* **de·his´cent** *adj.*

de·hu·man·ize (dēhū´manīz,
dēū´-) *v.t.* (**-ized, -iz·ing**). Divest
of human characteristics. **de·hu-
man·i·za·tion** (dēhūmanĭzā´shon,
dēū-) *n.*

de·hu·mid·i·fy (dēhūmĭd´ĭfī,
dēū-) *v.t.* (**-fied, fy·ing**). Remove

moisture from. **de·hu·mid·i·fi-
ca·tion** (dēhūmĭdĭfĭkā´shon, dēū-)
de·hu·mid´i·fi·er *ns.*

de·hy·drate (dēhī´drāt) *v.*
(**-drat·ed, -drat·ing**). (chem.)
Deprive of, lose, water or its
constituent elements; dry completely, desiccate (foods). **de·hy-
dra·tion** (dēhīdrā´shon) *n.*

de·ice (dēīs´) *v.t.* (**-iced,
-ic·ing**). Remove, prevent formation of, ice on (airplane, windshield,
etc.). **de·ic´er** *n.* Device or
substance for deicing.

de·i·fy (dē´ĭfī) *v.t.* (**-fied,
-fy·ing**). Make a god of; make
godlike; regard as a god, worship.
de·if·i·ca·tion (dēĭfĭkā´shon) *n.*

deign (dān) *v.* Think fit,

condescend (*to*); condescend to give, vouchsafe.

de·i·on·ize (dēī'onīz) *v.t.* (**-ized, -iz·ing**). Remove ions or ionic constituents from (water etc.). **de·i·on·i·za·tion** (dēīonīzā'shon) *n.*

de·ism (dē'īzem) *n.* Belief in the existence of a god without accepting revelation; natural religion. **de'ist** *n.* **de·is·tic** (dēīs'tĭk) *adj.* **de·is'ti·cal·ly** *adv.*

de·i·ty (dē'ĭtē) *n.* (pl. **-ties**). 1. Divine status, quality, or nature; a god. 2. (**the**) **Deity**, God.

dé·jà vu (dāzhah voo'; *Fr.* dĕzhăvū'). Feeling of having previously experienced what is happening but has not actually been experienced before. [Fr., = "already seen"]

de·ject (dĭjĕkt') *v.t.* Dispirit, depress. **de·ject'ed·ly** *adv.* **de·jec·tion** (dĭjĕk'shon) *n.*

de jure (dē joor'ē) *adj. & adv. phr.* Rightful, by right. [L.]

Dek·ker (dĕk'er), **Thomas** (1570?–1632). (also **Deck·er**) English Elizabethan dramatist, author of *The Honest Whore, The Shoemaker's Holiday*, etc.

Del. *abbrev.* Delaware.

del. *abbrev.* Delegate.

De·la·croix (delăkrwah'), **Ferdinand Victor Eugène** (1799–1863). French Romantic painter.

Del·a·ware[1] (dĕl'awār) *n.* (Member, language) of an Algonquian-speaking group of N. Amer. Ind. tribes living in the Delaware River Valley and the New Jersey area.

Del·a·ware[2] (dĕl'awār). Mid-Atlantic state of U.S.; one of original 13 states and second smallest; capital, Dover; ~ **Bay**, inlet of Atlantic between Delaware and New Jersey; ~ **River**, river flowing S. from Catskill Mts. to Delaware Bay, forming several state borders along its course; ~ **Water Gap**, gorge in E. Pennsylvania formed by this river.

De La Warr (dĕl'awār), **Baron** (1577–1618). (**Thomas West**) Lord Delaware; English colonial administrator in Amer.; governor and captain general of Virginia colony, 1610; arrived in time to prevent abandonment of Jamestown by settlers.

de·lay (dĭlā') *n.* Delaying; procrastination; hindrance to progress. ~ *v.* 1. Postpone, defer, put off; hinder. 2. Loiter, be tardy; wait. 3. **delayed-action**, (attrib.) of a device etc. that operates after a lapse of time. **de·lay'er** *n.*

The 16th-century observatory, Jantar Mantar, Delhi. Once the capital of the Mogul empire, Delhi is rich in historical monuments. The city is the 7th on the site, built between 1638 and 1658 during the reign of Shah Jahan.

de·le (dē'lē) *v.t.* (**-led, -le·in** (print.) Delete indicated lett word, etc. (usu. written ᵭ).

de·lec·ta·ble (dĭlĕk'tabel) *a* Delightful, pleasant. **de·lec·ta tion** (dēlĕktā'shon) *n.* Enjoyme **de·lec'ta·bly** *adv.*

del·e·gate (dĕl'egāt, -gĭt) Deputy, commissioner; elect representative sent to conferen **del·e·gate** (dĕl'egāt) *v.t.* (**-gat·e -gat·ing**). Depute, send representative; commit (author etc.) to agent. **del·e·ga·tie** (dĕlegā'shon) *n.* Entrusting authority to deputy; body delegates; members of legislatu representing particular politi unit. **del·e·ga·cy** (dĕl'egasē) *n.* (**-cies**).

de Les·seps (de lĕs'eps), **Fe dinand Marie, Vicomte** (180 94). French diplomat; promot building of Suez Canal; preside of French construction compa that worked on it, 1881–8, but ga up because of financial and politic difficulties.

de·lete (dĭlēt') *v.t.* (**-let· -let·ing**). Strike out, oblitera (letter, word, passage, etc **de·le·tion** (dĭlē'shon) *n.*

del·e·te·ri·ous (dĕleter'ēus) *a* Noxious, harmful. **del·e·te'ri ous·ly** *adv.* **del·e·te'ri·ous·ne** *n.*

Delft (dĕlft). Town in Nethe

Delicatessens sell fine food and delicacies for the table. Usually one finds gourmet treats and specialized ethnic foods.

n. (pl. **-cies**). Being a delinquent; neglect or violation of duty; guilt; act of delinquency, offense, misdeed. **de·lin·quent** (dĭlĭng'-kwent) *adj.* Defaulting, guilty. ~ *n.* Delinquent person. **de·lin'-quent·ly** *adv.*

del·i·quesce (dĕlĭkwĕs') *v.i.* (**-quesced, -quesc·ing**). Become liquid, dissolve in moisture absorbed from the air; (fig.) melt away. **del·i·ques'cence** *n.* **del·i·ques'cent** *adj.*

de·lir·i·ous (dĭlēr'ēus) *adj.* Affected with delirium, temporarily or apparently mad, raving; wildly excited, ecstatic; betraying delirium or ecstasy. **de·lir'i·ous·ly** *adv.* **de·lir'i·ous·ness** *n.*

de·lir·i·um (dĭlēr'ēum) *n.* (pl. **-i·ums, -i·a** pr. **-ēa**). Disordered state of mind with incoherent speech, hallucinations, and frenzied excitement; great excitement, ecstasy; ~ **tremens** (trē'mĕnz), form of delirium with terrifying delusions, to which heavy drinkers are liable.

De·li·us (dē'lēus, dĕl'yus), **Frederick** (1862–1934). English composer of songs, concertos, choral works, etc.

de·liv·er (dĭlĭv'er) *v.t.* 1. Rescue, save, set free (*from*). 2. Assist (female) in giving birth; assist in the birth of; (also **be delivered of**) give birth to. 3. Unburden *oneself of* opinion, thought, etc., in discourse. 4. Give *up, over,* abandon, resign, hand on *to* another; distribute (letters, packages, etc.) to addressee or purchaser; present, render, (account); (law) hand over formally (esp. deed to grantee or third party). 5. Launch, aim (blow, ball, attack). 6. Utter, pronounce openly or formally (speech, judgment, etc.).

de·liv·er·ance (dĭlĭv'erans) *n.* Rescue, esp. from bondage or danger; emphatically or formally delivered opinion, esp. jury's verdict.

de·liv·er·y (dĭlĭv'erē, -lĭv'rē) *n.* (pl. **-er·ies**). 1. Childbirth. 2. Surrender (*of*); handing over (esp. of letters or goods). 3. (law) Formal handing over of property; formal transfer of deed to grantee or third party. 4. Delivering (blow, ball, etc.); action shown in doing this. 5. Uttering of speech etc.; manner of doing this.

dell (dĕl) *n.* Small hollow or valley, usu. wooded.

del·la Rob·bia (dĕla rō'bēa, rŏb'ēa), **Luca** (1400–82). Florentine sculptor famous for his work in terracotta; his terracotta process, which was inherited by the della Robbia family, is characterized by

---

ands; hence, kind of pottery (also **Delft ware**) produced there, usu. with white glaze on which a decoration is painted in blue.

Del·hi (dĕl'ē, -hī). Third largest city in India, located in N. part, capital from 1912–31; a union territory of N. India, see NEW DELHI.

del·i (dĕl'ē) *n.* (pl. **del·is** pr. dĕl'ēz). (colloq.) Delicatessen.

de·lib·er·ate (dĭlĭb'erĭt) *adj.* Intentional; considered, not impulsive; slow in deciding, cautious; leisurely, not hurried. **de·lib'er·ate·ly** *adv.* **de·lib'er·ate·ness** *n.* **deliberate** (dĭlĭb'erāt) *v.* (**-at·ed, -at·ing**). Consider, think carefully; take counsel, consult, hold debate.

de·lib·er·a·tion (dĭlĭbe-rā'shon) *n.* Careful consideration; discussion, debate; care, avoidance of impulsiveness, slowness of movement.

de·lib·er·a·tive (dĭlĭb'erātĭv, -era-) *adj.* Of, appointed for purpose of, deliberation or debate. **de·lib'er·a·tive·ly** *adv.*

del·i·ca·cy (dĕl'ĭkasē) *n.* (pl. **-cies**). 1. Fineness of texture, substance, outline, etc., or of feeling or observation. 2. Frailty; susceptibility to injury or disease; need of care in handling. 3. Refinement, sense of what is becoming or modest; regard for feelings of others. 4. Choice or dainty item of food. 5. Delicate trait; nicety.

del·i·cate (dĕl'ĭkĭt) *adj.* 1. Palatable, dainty (of food);

---

sheltered, luxurious, (of life, upbringing, etc.). 2. Fine of texture, soft, slender, slight; of exquisite quality of workmanship; (of color) subdued. 3. Subtle. 4. Easily injured; liable to illness. 5. Requiring careful handling (lit. and fig.). 6. Subtly sensitive; finely skillful; avoiding the offensive or immodest, considerate. **del'i·cate·ly** *adv.* **del'i·cate·ness** *n.*

del·i·ca·tes·sen (dĕlĭkatĕs'en) *n.* (Store selling) foods ready for serving or nearly so, such as salads, cooked meats, sandwiches, etc.

de·li·cious (dĭlĭsh'us) *adj.* Highly delightful, esp. to taste, smell, or sense of humor. **de·li'cious·ly** *adv.* **de·li'cious·ness** *n.*

de·light (dĭlīt') *n.* Being delighted; thing affording delight. ~ *v.* Give great pleasure or enjoyment to; rejoice, be highly pleased. **de·light'ful** *adj.* **de·light'ful·ly** *adv.* **de·light'ful·ness** *n.*

De·li·lah (dĭlī'la). Woman who betrayed Samson, her lover, to the Philistines by having his hair shorn as he was sleeping (Judges 16); hence, seductive treacherous woman.

de·lim·it (dĭlĭm'ĭt) *v.t.* Determine limits or boundary of. **de·lim·i·ta·tion** (dĭlĭmĭtā'shon) *n.*

de·lin·e·ate (dĭlĭn'ēāt) *v.t.* (**-at·ed, -at·ing**). Show by drawing or description, portray. **de·lin·e·a·tion** (dĭlĭnēā'shon), **de·lin'e·a·tor** *ns.*

de·lin·quen·cy (dĭlĭng'kwensē)

the use of white figures against a usu. blue background.

De·los (dē′lŏs, dĕl′ŏs). Island in the Aegean, one of the Cyclades; supposed to have been raised from the sea by Poseidon and anchored to the bottom of the sea by Zeus; an important center of the worship of Apollo. **De·li·an** (dē′lēan, dēl′yan) *adj.*

de·louse (dēlows′) *v.t.* (-loused, -lous·ing). Clear of lice.

Del·phi (dĕl′fī). Greek town on slopes of Mt. Parnassus, with ancient sanctuary and oracle of Apollo. **Del·phi·an** (dĕl′fēan), **Del·phic** (dĕl′fĭk) *adjs.* Of Delphi or the Delphic Apollo or oracle; obscure and ambiguous like the oracle's responses.

del·phin·i·um (dĕlfĭn′ēum) *n.* Ranunculaceous plant of genus *D* ~ including larkspur, with handsome irregular-shaped blue or pink flowers, (esp.) cultivated species or variety of this. [Gk. *delphinion* larkspur, dim. of *delphin* dolphin]

del·ta (dĕl′ta) *n.* 1. Fourth letter of Greek alphabet *Δ, δ* (corresponding to *d*). 2. Triangular tract of sand, gravel, and silt enclosed and traversed by the diverging mouths of a river. 3. ~ **ray**, one of the rays of low penetrative power produced by particles emitted by radium, polonium, uranium, etc., consisting of low-velocity electrons

*The excavations at **Delphi**, begun in 1892, uncovered temples, treasuries, sculptures and fragmented frescoes of the 6th–4th centuries B.C. Inscriptions give praise to Apollo.*

knocked from an atom during a collision with some other particle; ~ **wing**, triangular sweptback wing of highspeed aircraft; airplane with such a wing.

del·toid (dĕl′toid) *adj.* Triangular; like river delta; ~ **muscle**, large triangular muscle forming prominence of shoulder and serving to lift upper arm. **deltoid** *n.* Deltoid muscle.

de·lude (dĭlood′) *v.t.* (-lud·ed, -lud·ing). Mislead, deceive; cause to believe what is not true.

del·uge (dĕl′ūj) *n.* Great flood, inundation; heavy fall of rain; flood of words etc.; **the D** ~, the great flood in the time of Noah. **deluge** *v.t.* (-uged, -ug·ing). Flood, inundate. [L. *diluvium* flood]

de·lu·sion (dĭlōō′zhon) *n.* False impression or opinion, esp. as symptom or form of madness. **de·lu·sion·al, de·lu·sive** (dĭlōō′-sĭv), **de·lu·so·ry** (dĭlōō′serē) *adjs.* **de·lu·sive·ly** *adv.* **de·lu·sive·ness** *n.*

de·luxe (delōōks′, -lŭks′) *adj.phr.* Luxurious, sumptuous; of superior kind. ~ *adv.phr.* [Fr.]

delve (dĕlv) *v.* (**delved,**

delv·ing). Dig (archaic or dial (fig.) make laborious research documents etc.

Dem. *abbrev.* Democrat.

de·mag·net·ize (dēmăg′netī *v.t.* (-ized, -iz·ing). Deprive magnetic quality. **de·mag·net·i za·tion** (dēmăgnetīzā′shon) *n.*

dem·a·gogue, dem·a·go (dĕm′agawg, -gŏg) *ns.* Leader popular faction, or of mob; agitat appealing to passions and preju dices of mob; (hist.) popular leade orator who espoused people's caus against other parties in countr **dem·a·gog·ic** (dĕmagŏj′ĭk, -gŏg′ *adj.* **dem·a·gog·y** (dĕm′agōjē -gawjē, -gŏjē), **dem·a·gog·uer** (dĕm′agawgerē, -gŏgerē) *ns.*

de·mand (dĭmănd′, -mahnd′) 1. Authoritative or peremptor request or claim; what is demanded legal claim. 2. Call for commodit by consumers; urgent or pressin claim or requirement; **on** ~, as soo as the demand is made, esp. fo payment of a bill. **demand** *v.* 1. Ask for with legal right o authority; (law) make formal clain to; ask for peremptorily or urgentl require, have need of. 2. Ask t know, authoritatively or formally.

de·mand·ing (dĭmăn′dĭng) *ad* 1. Trying or exacting in demands 2. Requiring great skill, care, effort etc.

de·mar·ca·tion, de·mar·ka· tion (dēmärkā′shon) *ns.* Markin of boundary or limits of anything **de·mar·cate** (dĭmär′kāt, dē′mär *v.t.* (-cat·ed, -cat·ing).

dé·marche (dāmärsh′, dĭ-) *n* (diplomacy) Political step o proceeding, esp. one involving change in a course of policy o action. [Fr.]

de·ma·te·ri·al·ize (dēmatēr′ēa līz) *v.* (-ized, -iz·ing). Make become, nonmaterial or spiritual.

de·mean[1] (dĭmēn′) *v.refl.* Be have, conduct, *oneself* (in specifie way). **de·mean′or** *n.* Bearing outward behavior.

de·mean[2] (dĭmēn′) *v.t.* Lowe in dignity, reputation, etc.; lower o humble *oneself.*

de·ment·ed (dĭmĕn′tĭd) *adj* Crazed, mad; affected wit dementia. **de·ment·ed·ly** *adv.*

de·men·tia (dĭmĕn′sha, -shēa *n.* Insanity characterized by failure or loss of mental powers and cause by disease in or injury to the brain ~ **praecox** (prē′kŏks), schizo phrenia.

de·mer·it (dĭmĕr′ĭt) *n.* Qualit deserving blame or punishment censurable conduct; want of merit fault, defect.

de·mesne (dĭmān′, -mēn′) *n.* 1. (law) Possession and use of one's own land. 2. Domain; landed property, estate; grounds belonging to estate or mansion.

De·me·ter (dĭmē′ter). (Gk.

h.) Goddess of agriculture, the
ghter of Cronus and mother of
ephone; identified by the
nans with CERES.

emi- *prefix.* Half, semi-.

em·i·god (dĕm´ēgŏd) *n.* Partly
ne being, son of god and mortal,
eified man.

em·i·john (dĕm´ējŏn) *n.* Large
tle with bulging body and
row neck and usu. cased in
kerwork. [corrupt. of Fr.
e-Jeanne Dame Jane]

e·mil·i·ta·rize (dēmĭl´ĭtarīz)
(**-rized, -riz·ing**). Do away
h military organization or
trol of; **demilitarized**, (of area)
taining no armed forces. **de·
·li·ta·ri·za·tion** (dēmĭlĭtarĭzā´-
n) *n.*

e Mille[1] (de mĭl´), **Agnes**
09–). Amer. choreographer;
atly influenced style of Amer.
sical comedy.

e Mille[2] (de mĭl´), **Cecil
.ount)** (1881–1959). Amer.
vie producer and director esp.
ed for films on historic subjects.

em·i·mon·daine (dĕmēmŏn-
a´, -mŏn´dān) *n.* Woman of the
nimonde.

em·i·monde (dĕm´ēmŏnd) *n.*
ass of women on outskirts of
iety, of doubtful reputation and
nding, esp. because of sexual
miscuity.

e·min·er·al·ize (dēmĭn´eralīz)
(**-ized, -iz·ing**). Remove
neral content from.

e·mise (dĭmīz´) *v.* (**-mised,
is·ing**). 1. Convey, grant,
tate) by will or lease; transmit
le etc.) by death or abdication.
Die, decease. ~ *n.* 1.
nveyance or transfer of estate by
ll or lease; transference of
vereignty, as by death or deposi-
n of sovereign. 2. Decease,
ath.

dem·i·sem·i·qua·ver (dĕmē-
n´ēkwāver) (stress variable) *n.*
us., chiefly Brit.) Note half as
ng (♬ ♭) as semiquaver.

dem·i·tasse (dĕm´ĭtăs, -tahs) *n.*
mall cup of) strong black coffee
ved after dinner.

dem·i·urge (dĕm´ēērj) *n.* (often
~) (in Platonic philosophy)
eator of material world; (in
nostic and other systems) a being
bordinate to Supreme Being;
cas., author of evil. **dem·i·ur·gic**
ēmēēr´jĭk) *adj.* [Gk. dēmiourgos
aftsman (dēmios of the people,
gos working)]

de·mo·bi·lize (dēmō´bilīz) *v.t.*
lized, -liz·ing**). Release from
obilized condition; disband
oops, ships, etc.). **de·mo·bi·li·
·tion** (dēmōbilīzā´shon) *n.*

chniques of **demolition** and preser-
tion of buildings have improved dur-
‣ the 20th century, but the disappear-
ce of landmarks has brought public
position.

de·moc·ra·cy (dĭmŏk´rasē) *n.*
(pl. **-cies**). 1. Form of government in which power resides in the
people as a whole, and is exercised
either directly by them or by their
elected representatives; nation
having this form of government. 2.
Society, condition of individual
equality and respect.

dem·o·crat (dĕm´okrăt) *n.* 1.
Advocate of democracy. 2. **D~**,
member of DEMOCRATIC Party.

dem·o·crat·ic (dĕmokrăt´ĭk) *adj.*
1. Of, like, practicing, advocating,
democracy. 2. Of the Democratic
Party; **D~ Party**, political party
that claims JEFFERSON[1] for its
founder and opposes the (present-
day) REPUBLICAN Party, so called
since c1828, but previously known,
at various times, as Anti-Federalist,
Republican, and Democratic-
Republican. **dem·o·crat´i·cal·ly**
adv. **de·moc·ra·tize** (dĭmŏk´ratīz)
v. (**-tized, -tiz·ing**). **de·moc·ra·
ti·za·tion** (dĭmŏkrĭtĭzā´shon) *n.*

De·moc·ri·tus (dĭmŏk´rĭtus)
(5th c. B.C.). Greek philosopher
("the laughing philosopher"),
regarded, with Leucippus, as
founder of ATOMISM. **De·moc´·
ri·te·an** (dĭmŏkrĭtē´an) *adj.*

de·mod·u·late (dēmŏj´ulāt,
-mŏd´yu-) *v.t.* (**-lat·ed, -lat·ing**).
(radio) Extract modulating signal
from (modulated wave). **de·
mod·u·la·tion** (dēmŏjulā´shon,
-mŏdyu-) *n.*

de·mog·ra·phy (dĭmŏg´rafē) *n.*
Study of statistics of births, deaths,
disease, etc., as illustrating conditions of life in communities.
de·mog´raph·er *n.* **de·mo·
graph·ic** (dēmogrăf´ĭk, dĕmo-)
adj. **de·mo·graph´i·cal·ly** *adv.*

dem·oi·selle (dĕmwahzĕl´,
-wa-) *n.* 1. Young lady. 2. (zool.)
Numidian crane (*Anthropoides
virgo*) with long feathers and white
plumes behind the eyes [Fr., =
"damsel"]

de·mol·ish (dĭmŏl´ĭsh) *v.t.* Pull
or throw down (building); destroy,
make an end of; consume, eat up.
dem·o·li·tion (dĕmolĭsh´on) *n.*

de·mon, dae·mon (dē´mon) *ns.*
1. (esp. in Gk. myth.) Supernatural
being, intermediate between gods
and man; spirit, genius. 2. Evil
spirit, devil; cruel, malignant,
destructive, or terrible person; evil
passion or agency personified. 3.
Person exhibiting great energy,
zeal, etc. **de·mon·ic** (dĭmŏn´ĭk),
de·mon´i·cal *adjs.*

de·mon·e·tize (dēmŏn´etīz,
-mŭn´-) *v.t.* (**-tized, -tiz·ing**).
Withdraw from use as money;
deprive of its status as money.
de·mon·e·ti·za·tion (dēmŏnetĭ-
zā´shon, -mŭn-) *n.*

de·mo·ni·ac (dĭmō´nēăk, dē-
monī´ăk) *adj.* Possessed by a demon
or evil spirit; of demoniacal possession; of or like demons; devilish;
frenzied. ~ *n.* One possessed by
a demon. **de·mo·ni·a·cal** (dē-
monī´akal) *adj.* Demoniac.

de·mon·ic (dĭmŏn´ĭk) *adj.*
Demoniac; fiendish.

de·mon·ism (dē´monĭzem) *n.*
Belief in the power of demons.

de·mon·ol·o·gy (dēmonŏl´ojē) *n.*
Study of beliefs about demons.

de·mon·stra·ble (dĭmŏn´stra-
bel) *adj.* Capable of being shown
or logically proved. **de·mon´-
stra·bly** *adv.* **de·mon·stra·
bil·i·ty** (dĭmŏnstrabĭl´ītē) *n.*

dem·on·strate (dĕm´onstrāt) *v.*

Denmark is strategically positioned between the Baltic and North Seas.

(**-strat·ed, -strat·ing**). 1. Show, display (feelings etc.). 2. Describe and explain by help of specimens or experiments; act as demonstrator. 3. Establish truth of by argument or deduction; prove. 4. Make, take part in, public demonstration.

dem·on·stra·tion (dĕmonstrā'shon) *n.* 1. Outward exhibition, display *of*; (mil.) show of military force or offensive movement; public manifestation (usu. mass meeting or march) of interest or sympathy with some cause etc. 2. Demonstrating, clear or indubitable proof, argument(s) proving an assertion etc.; exhibition and explanation of specimens or experiments as method of instruction in science or art.

de·mon·stra·tive (dĭmŏn'strativ) *adj.* 1. Serving to point out or exhibit, esp. (gram.) of certain adjectives and pronouns. 2. Demonstrating logically or conclusively; serving as proof *of*; evident or provable by demonstration. 3. Given to or marked by outward exhibition or expression of feelings etc. **de·mon'stra·tive·ly** *adv.* **de·mon'stra·tive·ness** *n.*

dem·on·stra·tor (dĕm'onstrāter) *n.* One who demonstrates; sample used in a demonstration; one who takes part in public demonstration.

de · mor · al · ize (dĭmŏr'alīz, -mär'-) *v.t.* (**-ized, -iz·ing**). Corrupt morals of, deprave; destroy discipline, courage, powers of endurance, etc., of (esp. troops). **de·mor·al·i·za·tion** (dĭmŏralīzā'shon, -mär-), **de·mor'al·i·zer** *ns.*

De·mos (dē'mŏs) *n.* Personification of the populace, esp. in a democracy.

De·mos·the·nes (dĭmŏs'thenēz) (384–322 B.C.). Athenian orator, who roused the Athenians to the danger of the subjugation of Greece by Philip of Macedon.

de·mote (dĭmōt') *v.t.* (**-mot·ed, -mot·ing**). Reduce to lower rank or class. **de·mo·tion** (dĭmō'shon) *n.*

de·mot·ic (dĭmŏt'ĭk) *adj.* Of the common people; esp. as epithet of popular simplified form of writing used in ancient Egypt from *c*700 B.C. until 5th c. A.D. (as dist. from *hieratic*); of the popular form of modern Greek. ~ *n.* Demotic writing; demotic Greek.

de·mul·cent (dĭmŭl'sent) *adj.* & *n.* Soothing (medicine).

de·mur (dĭmèr') *v.i.* (**-murred, -mur·ring**). Make difficulties, raise scruples or objections *to, at*; (law) put in a demurrer. ~ *n.* Objecting, objection. **de·mur'ral** *n.* Act of demurring.

de · mure (dĭmūr') *adj.* (**-mur·er, -mur·est**). Sober, serious, composed; affectedly or constrainedly modest or decorous. **de·mure'ly** *adv.* **de·mure'ness** *n.*

de·mur·rage (dĭmèr'ĭj) *n.* (Compensation for) detention of ship, railroad freight car, etc., by loader or unloader beyond time agreed upon.

de·mur·rer (dĭmèr'er) *n.* 1. Person who demurs; objector. 2. (law) Pleading that allegedly true statements of the opposition in a lawsuit fail to sustain claim on which they are based. 3. Objection; exception taken to anything.

de·my·thol·o·gize (dēmĭthŏl'ojīz) *v.* (**-gized, -giz·ing**). Remove mythical elements (from); reinterpret mythological elements in the Bible.

den (dĕn) *n.* Wild beast's lair; hiding place of thieves etc.; small room in which person secludes himself or herself to work etc.

Den. *abbrev.* Denmark.

de·nar·i·us (dĭnâr'ēus) *n.* (pl. **-nar·i·i** pr. -nâr'ēī). Ancient Roman silver coin.

de·na·tion·al·ize (dēnăsh'onalīz) *v.t.* (**-ized, -iz·ing**). Deprive of nationality; destroy independent or distinct nationality of; make (institution etc.) no longer national; transfer (enterprise, industry) from national to private ownership. **de·na·tion·al·i·za·tion** (dēnăshonalīzā'shon) *n.*

de·nat·ur·al·ize (dēnăch'eralīz) *v.t.* (**-ized, -iz·ing**). Alter or pervert the nature of, make unnatural; deprive of status and rights of natural subject or citizen. **de·nat·ur·al·i·za·tion** (dēnăcheralīzā'shon) *n.*

de·na·ture (dēnā'cher) *v.t.* (**-tured, -tur·ing**). Change nature or properties of; render unfit to drink or eat, esp. by adding methanol to ethyl alcohol so it

cannot be drunk. **de·na'tu·ra** *n.* Substance used as denatur agent. **de·na·tu·ra·tion** (năcherā'shon) *n.*

de·na·zi·fi·ca·tion (dēnahts kā'shon, -nătsi-) *n.* (after Wo War II) Eradication of N influence in Germany; removal Nazis from positions of respor bility in German public l **de·na·zi·fy** (dēnah'tsĭfī, -năt' *v.t.* (**-fied, -fy·ing**).

den·drite (dĕn'drīt) *n.* 1. (Sto or mineral with) natural treel marking. 2. Branching process nerve cell. **den·drit·ic** (dĕndrĭt' *adj.*

den·dro·chro·nol·o·gy (dĕ drŏkronŏl'ojē) *n.* Study chronology from evidence of ann growth rings in (ancient) trees a timber. **den·dro·chron·o·log cal** (dĕndrōkrŏnolŏj'ĭkal) *adj.*

den·drol·o·gy (dĕndrŏl'ojē) *n.* Study of trees. **den·drol'o·g** *n.* **den·dro·log·ic** (dĕndrolŏj'ĭ **den·dro·log'i·cal** *adjs.*

den·gue (dĕng'gā, -gē) *n.* Vir lent tropical and subtropi epidemic infectious disease chara terized by fever, rash, excruciati pains in joints, and great prost tion and debility. [prob. or Swahili *dinga*, associated w Span. *dengue* prudery, with ref. stiffness in patient's neck a shoulders]

de·ni·a·ble (dĭnī'abel) *adj.* Th can be denied.

de·ni·al (dĭnī'al) *n.* Refusal request; self-denial; contradicti statement that thing is not tr or existent; disowning, disavov (*of* person).

de·nier (denēr') *n.* Unit weight used to estimate the finene of silk or synthetic yarn (based a length of 450 meters of ya weighing 50 milligrams).

den·i·grate (dĕn'igrāt) *v* (**-grat·ed, -grat·ing**). Blacke defame. **den·i·gra·tion** (dĕnigra

n) *n.*

den·im (děn´ĭm) *n.* Twill cotton ~ric used for overalls, work ~hes, etc.; (pl.) overalls, trousers, ~ made of this. [f. Fr. (*serge*) *de* ~*nes* (serge) of Nîmes in S. ~nce]

den·i·zen (děn´ĭzen) *n.* Inhabit~, occupant (*of place*); (Brit.) ~eigner admitted to residence and ~tain rights; naturalized foreign ~mal or plant. **den´i·zen·ship** *n.*

Den·mark (děn´märk). King~n of N. Europe, consisting of the ~nds of Zealand, Funen, Lolland, ~, between the North and Baltic ~s, the peninsula of Jutland, and ~ outlying Baltic island of ~rnholm; capital, Copenhagen; ~ **Strait**, channel between Green~d and Iceland connecting Arctic ~1 Atlantic.

de·nom·i·nate (dĭnŏm´ĭnāt) *v.t.* ~**at·ed, -nat·ing**). Give name to, ~l or describe as.

de·nom·i·na·tion (dĭnŏminā´~n) *n.* 1. Name, designation; ~. characteristic or class name; ~ss, kind, with specific name. 2. ~ss of units in numbers, weights, ~ney, etc. 3. Religious sect. ~**nom·i·na´tion·al** *adj.* Of, like, ~eligious denomination; sectarian. ~**nom·i·na´tion·al·ly** *adv.*

de·nom·i·na·tive (dĭnŏm´ĭnā~, -ĭnatĭv) *adj.* Serving as, giving, ~ame.

de·nom·i·na·tor (dĭnŏm´ĭnātɇr) ~ (arith. etc.) Number written below line in fraction, giving quantity that divides the numerator; parts into which integer is divided; **common ~**, denominator common to a number of fractions; (freq. fig.) common feature of members of a group.

de·no·ta·tion (děnōtā´shon) *n.* 1. Denoting; expression by marks or symbols; mark by which thing is made known or indicated; designation. 2. Meaning, signification a word or expression usually elicits; (logic) what word denotes, as dist. from *connotation*, aggregate of objects of which word may be predicated.

de·no·ta·tive (dē´nōtātĭv, dĭnō´ta-) *adj.* Denoting. **de´no·ta·tive·ly** *adv.*

de·note (dĭnōt´) *v.t.* (**-not·ed, -not·ing**). 1. Mark out, distinguish, be the sign of; indicate, give to understand; signify, stand as name for (cf. CONNOTE); (logic) designate, be a name of, be predicated of.

de·noue·ment, dé·noue·ment (dānōōmahń´) *ns.* Unraveling of plot or complications, final solution, in play, novel, etc. [Fr.]

de·nounce (dĭnowns´) *v.t.* (**-nounced, -nounc·ing**). 1. Prophesy (woe, vengeance), proclaim as threat or warning. 2. Inform against, accuse. 3. Inveigh against. 4. Give notice of termination of (armistice, treaty, etc.). **de·nounce´ment, de·nounc´er** *ns.*

dense (děns) *adj.* (**dens·er, dens·est**). 1. Closely compacted in substance; crowded together. 2. Crass, stupid. **dense´ly** *adv.* **dense´ness** *n.*

den·si·ty (děn´sĭtē) *n.* (pl. **-ties**). 1. Closeness of substance; crowded state; (photog.) opaqueness of developed film in negative. 2. Stupidity, crassness. 3. (phys.) Degree of consistency of body etc. expressed as weight per unit of volume.

dent (děnt) *n.* Hollow or impression in surface such as is made by blow with blunt instrument. **~ v.** Make dent in; receive dent in.

den·tal (děn´tal) *adj.* Of tooth, teeth, or dentistry; (of consonant) pronounced with tip of tongue against front upper teeth; **~ floss**, soft thread, waxed or unwaxed, used to clean between teeth; **~ hygienist**, assistant to a dentist,

Tooth-filling and plate-making in modern **dentistry.** *The top diagrams show a drill cleaning out the cavity and surrounding area; the hole is then lined and plugged with a mixture of dental amalgam. Below: The construction of dentures.*

Plastic teeth are set in wax on a plaster model of the palate. After pressing, the teeth and model are held in the plaster while acrylic resin is pressed in and heated to 'cure' the plate.

cavity · air turbine · lining · plugger · excavator

~late · impression material · ridge · dental plaster mix · plastic teeth · wax · set impression (model)

flask press · ~del) · denture flask

esp. in cleaning patients' teeth; ~ **surgeon**, dentist specializing in surgery involving the teeth and associated oral areas. **dental** *n*. Dental consonant.

den·tate (dĕn´tāt) *adj*. Toothed; edged with toothlike projections. **den·ta·tion** (dĕntā´shon) *n*.

den·ti·cle (dĕn´tĭkal) *n*. Small tooth, or toothlike projection. **den·tic·u·lar** (dĕntĭk´yuler), **den·tic´u·late** *adjs*. **den·tic·u·la·tion** (dĕntĭkyulā´shon) *n*.

den·ti·frice (dĕn´tĭfrĭs) *n*. Preparation for cleaning teeth.

den·tine (dĕn´tēn, dĕntēn´), **den·tin** (dĕn´tĭn) *ns*. Hard dense tissue forming main part of teeth. **den·tin·al** *adj*.

den·tist (dĕn´tĭst) *n*. One who treats diseases and malformations of teeth and repairs, extracts, or replaces defective teeth. **den´tist·ry** *n*.

den·ti·tion (dĕntĭsh´on) *n*. Teething; characteristic arrangement of teeth in animal.

den·ture (dĕn´cher) *n*. One or more artificial teeth.

de·nude (dĭnōōd´, -nūd´) *v.t.* (-nud·ed, -nud·ing). Make naked; strip *of*; (geol.) lay (rock etc.) bare by removal of what lies above. **de·nu·da·tion** (dēnōōdā´shon, -nū, dĕnyu-) *n*.

de·nun·ci·a·tion (dĭnŭnsēā´shon) *n*. Denouncing; invective. **de·nun·ci·a·tive** (dĭnŭn´sēātĭv), **de·nun·ci·a·to·ry** (dĭnŭn´sēatōrē, -tōrē) *adjs*.

Den·ver (dĕn´ver). Capital and largest city in Colorado in the N. central part; known as the "mile high" city because of its altitude, 5,280 ft (1,609 m).

de·ny (dĭnī´) *v.t.* (-nied, -ny·ing). Declare untrue or nonexistent; disavow, repudiate; refuse; ~ **oneself**, be abstinent.

de·o·dar (dē´odār) *n*. Large cedar (*Cedrus deodara*), native of Himalayas. [Hind. f. Sansk. *deva-dāru* divine tree]

de·o·dor·ant (dēō´derant) *adj*. & *n*. (Substance) that removes or conceals unwanted odors.

de·o·dor·ize (dēō´derīz) *v.t.* (-ized, -iz·ing). Remove odor from. **de·o·dor·i·za·tion** (dēōderīzā´shon), **de·o·dor·iz·er** *ns*.

de·on·tol·o·gy (dēŏntŏl´ojē) *n*. Science of duty, ethics. **de·on·to·log·i·cal** (dēŏntolŏj´ĭkal) *adj*. **de·on·tol´o·gist** *n*. [Gk. *deon* duty]

de·ox·i·dize (dēŏk´sĭdīz) *v.t.* (-dized, -diz·ing). Remove oxygen from. **de·ox´i·diz·er** *n*.

de·ox·y·ri·bo·nu·cle·ic (dēŏxĭrī´bōnōōklē´ĭk, -nū-) **acid**: see DNA.

dep. *abbrev*. Depart; department; deposit; deputy.

de·part (dĭpärt´) *v*. 1. Go away (*from*), take one's leave (chiefly literary); (esp. in timetables) start,

The **deodar** or 'god tree' is found in large forests at altitudes over 7,000 ft. The wood is of great value. Light red and durable, it is used in cabinet work; it polishes very highly.

leave; diverge, deviate (*from*). 2. Die; leave by death. **de·part´ed** *adj*. Bygone; deceased. ~ *n*. Deceased person.

de·part·ment (dĭpärt´ment) *n*. 1. Separate division or part of complex whole or organized system; (esp.) division of state or municipal administration; one of the major executive divisions of the U.S. government, headed by a member of the cabinet. 2. In France, one of the administrative districts substituted for the old provinces in 1790. 3. ~ **store**, large store selling a variety of articles, organized in departments. **de·part·men·tal** (dēpärtmĕn´tal) *adj*. **de·part·men´tal·ly** *adv*. **de·part·men´tal·ize** *v.t.* (-ized, -iz·ing). **de·part·men·tal·i·za·tion** (dēpärtmĕntalīzā´shon) *n*.

de·par·ture (dĭpär´cher) *n*. 1.

Departing; deviation (*from* tr etc.). 2. Starting, esp. of tr etc.; setting out on course of act or thought. 3. (navigation) D tance moved due east or west a ship etc. on its course.

de·pend (dĭpĕnd´) *v.i.* 1. contingent *on* or conditioned **that depends**, (colloq.) t depends on circumstances. 2. dependent; rely for maintenan support, etc. (*on*); rely, reck confidently (*on*). 3. Hang do *from*.

de·pend·a·ble (dĭpĕn´dabel) *a* That may be relied on. **de·pen a·ble·ness, de·pend·a·bil·i·ty** (dĭpĕndabĭl´ĭtē) *ns*. **de·pend´a·b** *adv*.

de·pend·ence, de·pend·an (dĭpĕn´dens) *ns*. 1. Depending (o being conditioned, subordina subject. 2. Living at another's co 3. Reliance, confident trust; thi relied on.

de·pend·en·cy (dĭpĕn´densē) (pl. **-cies**). Something subordin. or dependent, esp. country province controlled by another.

de·pend·ent, de·pend·ant (dĭ-n'dent) *adjs.* Depending (*on*); ntingent, subordinate, subject; aintained at another's cost; ram., of clause etc.) in sub-dinate relation to sentence or ord. ~ *n.* One who depends another for support; retainer, vant. **de·pend'ent·ly, de·nd'ant·ly** *advs.*

de·per·son·al·ize (dēpĕr'sona-) *v.t.* (**-ized, -iz·ing**). Deprive personality; make impersonal. **·per·son·al·i·za·tion** (dēpĕr-nalĭza'shon) *n.*

de·pict (dĭpĭkt') *v.t.* Represent picture, sculpture, words; ortray, describe. **de·pic·tion** ĭpĭk'shon) *n.*

dep·i·late (dĕp'ĭlāt)*v.t.* (**-lat·ed, at·ing**). Remove hair from. **·ep·i·la·tion** (dĕpĭlā'shon) *n.* **·pil·a·to·ry** (dĭpĭl'ătōrē, -tōrē) *dj.* & *n.* (*pl.* **-ries**) (Substance) pable of removing hair.

de·plane (dēplān') *v.* (**-planed, ·lan·ing**). Disembark from an rplane.

de·plete (dĭplēt') *v.t.* (**-plet·ed, ·let·ing**). Empty out; exhaust. **·ple·tion** (dĭplē'shon) *n.*

de·plore (dĭplōr', -plōr') *v.t.* plored, -plor·ing). Bewail, ieve over, regret; be scandalized . **de·plor'a·ble** *adj.* **de·plor'a-** y *adv.* **de·plor·a·bil·i·ty** (dĭ-ōrabĭl'ĭtē, -plōr-), **de·plor'a-** ·e·ness *ns.*

de·ploy (dĭploi') *v.* (mil.) Spread t from column into line; arrange , take up, battle formation; move rategically. **de·ploy'ment** *n.*

de·plume (dēploom') *v.t.* plumed, -plum·ing). Pluck, rip of feathers.

de·po·lar·ize (dēpō'lerīz) *v.t.* (**-ized, -iz·ing**). Deprive of polarity, reverse or destroy effect of polarization. **de·po·lar·i·za·tion** (dēpōlerĭza'shon) *n.*

de·po·lit·i·cize (dēpolĭt'ĭsīz) *v.t.* (**-cized, -ciz·ing**). Make non-political; remove from political activity or influence.

de·po·nent (dĭpō'nent) *adj.* (of Latin or Gk. verb) Passive in form but active in meaning (so called from idea that these verbs had laid aside their passive meaning). ~ *n.* 1. Deponent verb. 2. Person making deposition on oath or giving written testimony for use in court etc.

de·pop·u·late (dēpŏp'yulāt) *v.t.* (**-lat·ed, -lat·ing**). Reduce population of. **de·pop·u·la·tion** (dē-pŏpyulā'shon), **de·pop'u·la·tor** *ns.*

de·port (dĭpōrt', -pōrt') *v.t.* 1. Bear, conduct, *oneself*; behave. 2. Carry away, remove; esp. expel, banish (alien), hence **de·por·ta·tion** (dēpōrtā'shon, -pōr-), **de·por·tee** (dēpōrtē', -pōr-) *ns.*

de·port·ment (dĭpōrt'ment, -pōrt'-) *n.* Bearing, demeanor, manners.

de·pose (dĭpōz') *v.* (**-posed, -pos·ing**). 1. Remove from office; dethrone. 2. Bear witness under oath *that*, testify, esp. in writing. **de·pos'a·ble** *adj.* **de·pos'er** *n.*

de·pos·it (dĭpŏz'ĭt) *n.* 1. Thing stored or entrusted for safekeeping; sum placed in bank; sum required and paid as pledge for performance

Known as St. Charles until 1858, Denver, Colorado, was an early stopping place for traders and explorers. The surrounding high mountains are popular with skiers.

of contract, part payment of price etc. 2. Layer of precipitated or deposited matter, natural accumulation. ~ *v.t.* 1. Lay or set down, place in more or less permanent position of rest; lay (eggs); (of water or other natural agencies) leave (matter) lying, form as natural deposit. 2. Store or entrust for keeping (esp. sum of money in bank); pay as pledge for fulfillment of contract or further payment.

de·pos·i·tar·y (dĭpŏz'ĭtĕrē) *n.* (*pl.* **-tar·ies**). Person to whom thing is entrusted; depository, sense 1.

dep·o·si·tion (dĕpozĭsh'on) *n.* 1. D~, taking down of the body of Christ from the cross; representation of this in art. 2. Deposing from office. 3. (Giving of) sworn evidence, esp. written statement. 4. Depositing.

de·pos·i·tor (dĭpŏz'ĭter) *n.* Person who deposits money etc.

de·pos·i·to·ry (dĭpŏz'ĭtōrē, -tōrē) *n.* (*pl.* **-ries**). 1. Storehouse; repository. 2. = DEPOSITARY.

de·pot (dē'pō; *mil.* & *Brit.* dĕp'ō) *n.* 1. (mil.) Place for stores; headquarters of regiment; station for assembling and drilling recruits. 2. Place where goods are deposited or stored; warehouse. 3. Railroad or bus station.

de·prave (dĭprāv') *v.t.* (**-praved, -prav·ing**). Make bad, deteriorate, pervert, corrupt, esp. in moral character or habits. **dep·ra·va·tion** (dĕpravā'shon) *n.* **de·praved'** *adj.*

de·prav·i·ty (dĭprăv'ĭtē) *n.* (*pl.* **-ties**). Moral corruption, viciousness, abandoned wickedness.

dep·re·cate (dĕp´rekāt) *v.t.* (**-cat·ed, -cat·ing**). Plead against, express earnest disapproval of. **dep·re·ca·tion** (dĕpreka´shon), **dep´re·ca·tor** *ns.* **dep·re·ca·tive** (dĕp´rekātĭv, -kativ), **dep·re·ca·to·ry** (dĕp´rekatōrē, tōrē) *adjs.*

de·pre·ci·ate (dĭprē´shāt) *v.* (**-at·ed, -at·ing**). 1. Diminish in value; lower market price of; reduce purchasing power of (money). 2. Disparage, belittle. **de·pre´ci·a·tor** *n.*

de·pre·ci·a·tion (dĭprēshēā´shon) *n.* Depreciating, being depreciated; (allowance made in accounting and taxation valuations, etc., for) wear and tear.

dep·re·da·tion (dĕpredā´shon) *n.* (usu. *pl.*) Spoliation, ravages.

de·press (dĭprĕs´) *v.t.* Press down, lower; bring low, humble; reduce activity of (esp. trade); dispirit, deject; **depressed area**, area of economic depression.

de·pres·sant (dĭprĕs´ant) *adj.* & *n.* (med.) Lowering, sedative (drug etc.).

de·pres·sion (dĭprĕsh´on) *n.* 1. Lowering, sinking; depressed or sunken formation or surface, hollow, low place. 2. (astron. etc.) Angular distance of star or other object below horizon (as opp. to *elevation* above it). 3. Lowering in quality, vigor, value, or amount, esp. of business activity; **Great D~**, economic crisis marked by low industrial and business activity and severe unemployment in the U.S.

and abroad, dating from about Oct. 1929, when stock prices plummeted, through the 1930s. 4. Lowering of barometric or atmospheric pressure; (meteorol.) center of minimum pressure, or system of winds around it. 5. Being depressed in spirits, dejection; (path.) state of reduced vitality.

de·pres·sive (dĭprĕs´ĭv) *adj.* That depresses; involving (esp. mental) depression. **de·pres´sive·ly** *adv.*

de·pres·sor (dĭprĕs´er) *n.* (esp.) Muscle depressing or pulling down part to which it is attached; (med.) instrument for pressing down some part of organ, esp. a **tongue ~**.

dep·ri·va·tion (dĕprivā´shon) *n.* Loss, being deprived (*of*); taking away of rank or office.

de·prive (dĭprīv´) *v.t.* (**-prived, -priv·ing**). 1. Strip, bereave, debar from enjoyment, *of*; **deprived child**, one lacking due parental care. 2. Depose from office.

de pro·fun·dis (dā prōfoon´dĭs). Psalm 130, beginning thus in Latin (= "Out of the depths (have I cried)"); cry from depths of suffering or sin.

de·pro·gram (dēprō´grăm, -gram) *v.t.* Induce (person) by strong argument to leave cult whose

The Derby, one of the world's most prestigious horse races, has been run at Epsom, U.K. since 1780 and is for three-year-old colts and fillies. Here, the horses round Tattenham Corner.

doctrines he or she has accep **de·pro´gram·mer** *n.* **de·pr gram·ming** *adj.* & *n.*

dept. *abbrev.* Departm deputy.

depth (dĕpth) *n.* 1. Being de measurement from top down, fr front to back, or from surf inward. 2. Profundity, abstru ness; sagacity; intensity (of feelin colors, silence, etc.). 3. Deep of sea or any body of water (u *pl.*); (*pl.*) lowest part of pit, cav etc.; abyss (usu. *pl.*), lowest inmost part; low moral conditi middle (of winter, night); d region of thought, feeling, or bei 4. **in ~**, comprehensive(thorough(ly); **out of one's ~**, water too deep to stand in; (f engaged in a matter beyond or understanding; **~ charge**, explosive device designed for against underwater targets, e submarines.

dep·u·ta·tion (dĕpyutā´shon) Body of persons appointed to go mission on behalf of othe delegation.

de·pute (dĭpūt´) *v.t.* (**-put -put·ing**). Commit (task, auth ity) to substitute; appoint as or substitute.

dep·u·tize (dĕp´yutīz) *v.* (**-tiz -tiz·ing**). Appoint, serve deputy.

dep·u·ty (dĕp´yutē) *n.* (*pl.* **-ti** 1. Person appointed to act another or others, substi lieutenant; deputy sheriff. 2. Me

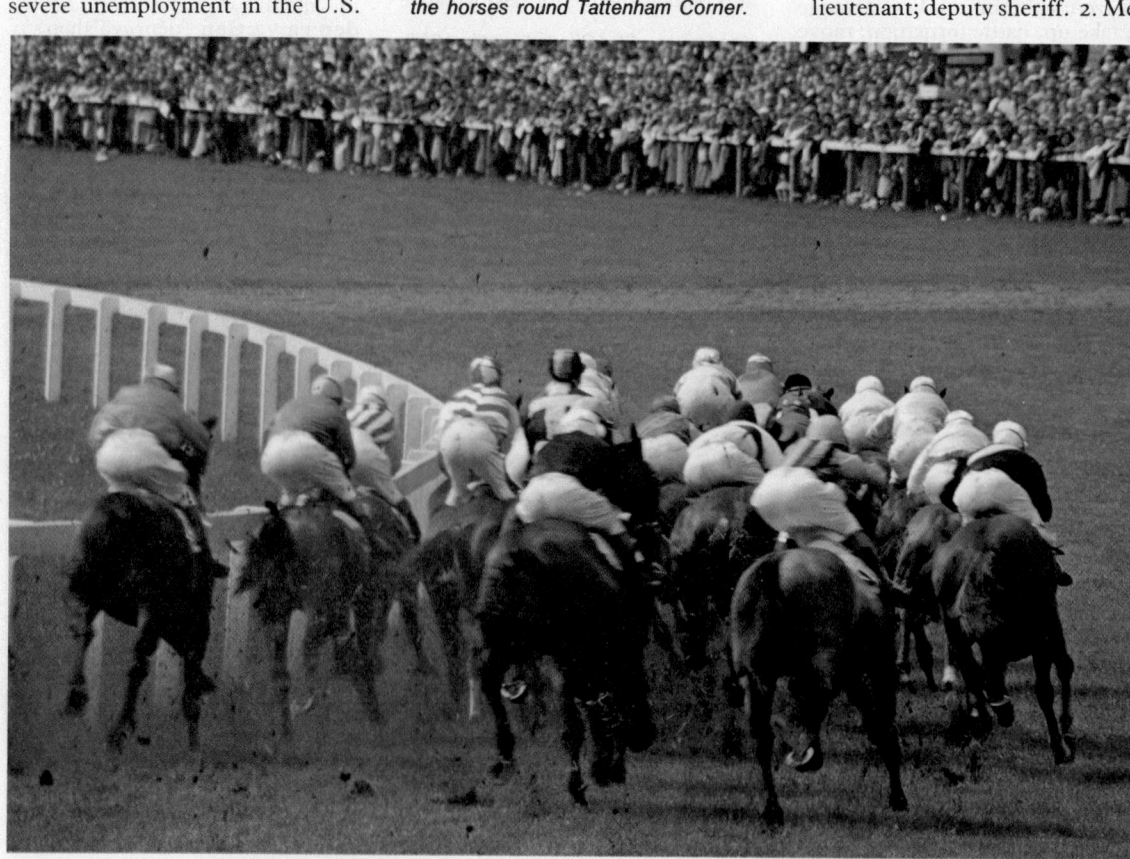

r of certain legislative assemblies; **hamber of Deputies**, lower ouse in some countries' legisla-ures. **deputy** *adj.* Deputed; cting instead of, or as subordinate , as in ~ *sheriff*.

De Quin·cey (dǐ kwǐn′sē) homas (1785–1859). English ssayist etc., author of *Confessions* ʻ *an English Opium Eater* (1822).

de·rac·i·nate (dǐrăs′ǐnāt) *v.t.* ·nat·ed, -nat·ing). Tear up by e roots.

de·rail (dǐrāl′) *v.t.* Cause (train tc.) to leave rails. **de·rail′ment**

de·range (dǐrānj′) *v.t.* (**-ranged,** **rang·ing**). Throw into confusion; isorganize; cause to act irregularly; nake insane. **de·range′ment** *n.*

Der·by (dẽr′bē; *Brit.* dãr′bē). 1. City and county seat of Derbyshire, England; **the ~**, annual horse race, ʻor 3-year-olds, founded 1780 by 2th earl of Derby, at Epsom Downs, in Surrey, England; **The** **Kentucky ~**, annual horse race for ʻ-year-olds, founded 1875, at Churchill Downs, in Louisville, Kentucky; any of various other aces or contests such as a **roller** l ~, in which two teams of roller skaters compete on a circular track.

der·by (dẽr′bē; *Brit.* dãr′bē) *n.* pl. **-bies.**) Stiff felt hat with ʻounded crown and narrow brim, ʻowler.

der·e·lict (dẽr′elǐkt) *adj. & n.* 1. Abandoned, ownerless (thing, esp. hip at sea). 2. (Person) abandoned ʻy society.

der·e·lic·tion (dẽr′elǐk′shon) *n.* ʻ. Forsaking, abandonment; being ʻbandoned; retreat of sea exposing ʻew land. 2. Morally wrong or ʻreprehensible abandonment or ʻeglect (*of* duty etc.); failure in ʻduty, delinquency.

de·ride (dǐrīd′) *v.t.* (**-rid·ed,** **-rid·ing**). Laugh to scorn. **de·-** **ris·i·ble** (dǐrǐz′ǐbel) *adj.*

de ri·gueur (de rēgẽr′). Re-quired by etiquette. [Fr.]

de·ri·sion (dǐrǐzh′on) *n.* Ridi-cule, mockery.

de·ri·sive (dǐrī′sǐv) *adj.* Scoff-ing; mocking; provoking derision. **de·ri′sive·ly** *adv.*

deriv. *abbrev.* Derivation, deriv-ative.

der·i·va·tion (dẽr′ivā′shon) *n.* Obtaining from a source; extrac-tion, descent; formation of word from word or root, tracing or statement of this.

de·riv·a·tive (dǐrǐv′atǐv) *adj. &* *n.* (Thing, word, etc.) of derived character or nature, derived from another or from a source, not primitive or original. **de·riv′a-** **tive·ly** *adv.*

de·rive (dǐrīv′) *v.* (**-rived,** **-riv·ing**). Get, obtain (*from* a source); have one's or its origin etc. *from*; gather, deduce, *from*; (pass.,

refl.) be descended or have one's origin *from*; (pass., of words) be formed *from*; trace, show, assert, descent or origin or formation of (person, thing, word) *from*.

der·ma¹ (dẽr′ma) = DERMIS.

der·ma² (dẽr′ma) *n.* Fowl or beef intestine used as a casing for certain dishes, esp. **stuffed ~**, or kishke, consisting of a seasoned mixture of flour, onion, and suet stuffed into the casing and then roasted.

der·ma·ti·tis (dẽrmatī′tǐs) *n.* Inflammation of the dermis.

der·ma·tol·o·gy (dẽrmatŏl′ojē) *n.* Science of the skin, its nature, diseases, etc. **der·ma·to·log·i·cal** (dẽrmatolŏj′ǐkal) *adj.* **der·ma·-** **tol′o·gist** *n.*

der·mis (dẽr′mǐs) *n.* (anat.) True skin, layer of tissue beneath epidermis. **der′mal** *adj.*

der·o·gate (dẽr′ogāt) *v.i.* (**-gat·ed, -gat·ing**). 1. Detract, make improper or injurious abate-ment, *from*. 2. Do something unsuited to one's rank or position.

der·o·ga·tion (dẽrogā′shon) *n.* Lessening or impairment *of* law, position, dignity, etc.; deteriora-tion, debasement.

de·rog·a·to·ry (dǐrŏg′atōrē, -tōrē), **de·rog·a·tive** (dǐrŏg′atǐv) *adjs.* Tending to detract *from*, involving impairment, disparage-ment, or discredit, *to*; lowering, unsuited to one's dignity or position. **de·rog·a·to·ri·ly** (dǐrŏg-

*Three Frenchmen on 11 March 1962 set a new world record for highland parachute-dropping by their **descent** into the crater of Mt. Kilimanjaro in Tanzania (over 19,000 ft).*

ator′ǐlē, -tōr′-) *adv.*

der·rick (dẽr′ǐk) *n.* Contrivance for hoisting or moving heavy weights; spar or boom set up obliquely on shipboard, with foot lashed, pivoted, or socketed to deck; kind of crane with jib pivoted to foot of central post, so as to take various angles with perpendicular; any outstanding jib or arm with pulley at end; framework over deep bore, as that of an oil well, for supporting drilling equipment and for hoisting or lowering. [orig. = hangman, the gallows, f. surname of hangman at Tyburn c1600]

der·ri·ère (dẽrēãr′) *n.* Buttocks; rump; rear.

der·rin·ger (dẽr′ǐnjer) *n.* Short-barreled pocket pistol. [named after its inventor, gunsmith Henry *Deringer* (1786–1868)]

der·vish (dẽr′vǐsh) *n.* Member of any of various orders of Muslim ascetics, some of whom dance, whirl, chant, or sing as part of their religious devotions. [f. Pers. *darwīsh* poor]

de·sal·i·nate (dēsăl′ināt) *v.t.* (**-nat·ed, -nat·ing**). Desalinize. **de·sal·i·na·tion** (dēsălinā′shon) *n.*

de·sa·lin·ize (dēsăl′inīz) *v.t.* (**-ized, -iz·ing**). Remove salt from (esp. sea water).

des·cant (dĕs′kănt) *n.* 1. Song
ontaining a fixed melody and a
ubordinate melody added above;
e added melody. 2. (fig.)
mplification of a subject, dis-
ursive comment on it. **descant**
(dĕskănt′, dĭs-) *v.i.* 1. Talk at
rge, dwell freely, *upon.* 2. Sing a
escant.

Des·cartes (dākārt′), **René**
(1596–1650). French mathema-
ician, physicist, and philosopher;
uthor of *Le Discours de la*
Méthode (1637), in which he
xpounded a quasimechanical con-
eption of the universe, which he
educed to space, matter, and
notion, operating under mathe-
natical laws. **Car·te·sian** (kär-
ē′zhən) *adj.*

de·scend (dĭsĕnd′) *v.* 1. Come or
go down, fall, sink; have downward
xtension, direction, or slope; come
r go down (hill, steps, etc.). 2.
Make excursion or attack, fall

violently *on* (also transf.). 3. Come
down ideally, mentally, or morally;
proceed to something subsequent in
time or order, or from general to
particular; stoop. 4. Be transmitted
by inheritance *from*, pass; **be
descended from**, be derived by
generation from (person, family,
etc.).

de·scend·ant (dĭsĕn′dənt) *n.* ~
(**of**), person or thing descended
(from).

de·scend·ent (dĭsĕn′dent) *adj.*
1. Moving down. 2. Proceeding
from a source or ancestor.

de·scent (dĭsĕnt′) *n.* 1. Descending, downward motion; downward
slope; a way down. 2. Sudden
attack. 3. Decline, sinking in scale,
fall. 4. Being descended, lineage;
transmission of property, title, or
quality, by inheritance.

de·scribe (dĭskrīb′) *v.t.*
(**-scribed, -scrib·ing**). 1. Set
forth in words; recite characteristics
of; qualify *as.* 2. Mark out, draw
(esp. geom. figure); move in, pass or
travel over (a certain course or
distance). **de·scrib′a·ble** *adj.*

de·scrip·tion (dĭskrĭp′shən) *n.*
Describing, verbal portrait or
portraiture of person, object, or
event, more or less complete

definition; sort, kind.

de·scrip·tive (dĭskrĭp′tĭv) *adj.*
Serving to describe; consisting
chiefly of description. **de·scrip′-
tive·ly** *adv.*

de·scry (dĭskrī′) *v.t.* (**-scried,
-scry·ing**). Catch sight of, succeed
in discerning.

des·e·crate (dĕs′ĕkrāt) *v.t.*
(**-crat·ed, -crat·ing**). Deprive of
sacred character; outrage, profane
(something sacred). **des·e·cra·
tion** (dĕsĕkrā′shon), **des′e·crat·er,
des′e·cra·tor** *ns.*

de·seg·re·gate (dēsĕg′regāt) *v.t.*
(**-gat·ed, -gat·ing**). Reunite
(persons, classes, etc.) hitherto
segregated; esp. abolish racial
segregation in (schools etc.). **de·-
seg·re·ga·tion** (dēsĕgregā′shon) *n.*

de·sen·si·tize (dēsĕn′sĭtīz) *v.t.*
(**-tized, -tiz·ing**). Reduce
sensitiveness of (esp. sensitized
photographic material). **de·sen·-
si·ti·za·tion** (dēsĕnsĭtīzā′shon),
de·sen′si·tiz·er *ns.*

de·sert¹ (dezĕrt′) *n.* 1. Deserving, being worthy of reward or
punishment; (usu. pl.) that in
conduct or character which
deserves recompense; merit, worth.
2. (usu. pl.) Due reward or recompense (good or evil).

des·ert[2] (dĕz′ert) *n.* Desolate, barren, waterless and treeless region; ~ **rat**: see JERBOA; **D ~ Rats**, (colloq.) soldiers of 7th (British) armored division, whose divisional sign was a jerboa, and who took part in World War II desert campaign in N. Africa (1941–1942). **desert** *adj.* Uninhabited, desolate; uncultivated; barren.

de·sert[3] (dĭzērt′) *v.* 1. Abandon, give up (thing); depart from (place, haunt); forsake (person or thing having claims on one). 2. Forsake one's post or duty, esp. leave service in the armed forces without official approval and with the intention of never returning. **de·sert′er, de·ser′tion** *ns.*

de·serve (dĭzērv′) *v.* (**-served, -serv·ing**). Be entitled by conduct or qualities to (good or bad); have established claim to be *well* or *ill* treated at the hands *of.* **de·serv′ing** *adj.* 1. Meritorious. 2. Worthy (*of* praise, censure, etc.). **de·served′** *adj.* **de·serv′ed·ly, de·serv′ing·ly** *advs.*

des·ha·bille (dĕzabēl′, dĕs-) = DISHABILLE. [Fr.]

des·ic·cant (dĕs′ikant) *adj. & n.* (Substance) capable of drying.

des·ic·cate (dĕs′ikāt) *v.t.* (**-cat·ed, cat·ing**). Exhaust of all moisture, dry, dry up (esp. articles of food for preservation). **des·ic·ca·tion** (dĕsikā′shon), **des·ic·ca·tor** *ns.* **des·ic·ca·tive** (dĕs′ikātĭv) *adj.*

de·sid·er·ate (dĭsĭd′erāt) *v.t.* (**-at·ed, -at·ing**). Long for; feel the want of. **de·sid·er·a·tion** (dĭsĭderā′shon) *n.*

de·sid·er·a·tive (dĭsĭd′erātĭv, -erativ) *adj.* 1. Of desire. 2. (gram.) Formed from another verb to express desire of doing act thereby denoted.

de·sid·er·a·tum (dĭsĭderah′tum,

Left: *A late 18th or early 19th century* **desk** *by Thomas Chippendale the Younger, at Stourhead, Wiltshire, U.K. Chippendale's work provides an excellent example of Regency furniture.* Right: *An 18th century English desk and stand of beechwood, lacquered in*

-rā′-) *n.* (pl. **-ta** pr. -ta). Something wanting and required or desired.

de·sign (dĭzīn′) *n.* 1. Plan or scheme to be carried out; end in view; purpose, intention; contrivance in accordance with a preconceived plan; scheme of attack *upon.* 2. Preliminary sketch for a work of art; plan for a building, machine, or any composite structure; combination of parts in a whole; general idea, construction, plot, etc.; faculty of evolving these; pattern, outline of decoration etc.; **industrial** ~, art of making designs for objects that are to be produced by machine. **design** *v.* 1. Form plan or scheme for; contrive; purpose, intend, have in view. 2. Set apart in thought for use *as,* or *for* advantage of. 3. Make preliminary sketch for (work of art etc.); plan construction of. **de·sign′ed·ly** *adv.* On purpose, intentionally. **de·sign′er** *n.* **de·sign′ing** *adj.* (esp.) Crafty, artful, scheming.

des·ig·nate (dĕz′ĭgnĭt, -nāt) *adj.* (placed after noun) Appointed or nominated but not yet installed. **des·ig·nate** (dĕz′ĭgnāt) *v.t.* (**-nat·ed, -nat·ing**). Specify, particularize; serve as name or distinctive mark of; style, describe as; appoint to office. **~d hitter**, 10th player on a team, who bats in regular rotation but does not field, replacing at bat one who fields but does not bat. **des·ig·na·tion** (dĕzĭgnā′shon) *n.* Appointing to office; name, description, title.

China. The two desks shown here a pointers to the multiplicity of desk for developed.

de·sir·a·ble (dĭzīr′abel) *a* Worthy of, arousing, desire; adv able. ~ *n.* Desirable thing person. **de·sir·a·bil·i·ty** (dĭz abĭl′ĭtē), **de·sir′a·ble·ness** **de·sir′a·bly** *adv.*

de·sire (dĭzīr′) *n.* 1. Feeling emotion directed to attainment possession of something expect to give pleasure or satisfactio sensual appetite, lust. 2. Expre sion of desire, request. 3. Obje of desire. ~ *v.t.* (**-sired, -sir·ing** Long for, crave, wish; ask for; pra entreat, command.

de·sir·ous (dĭzīr′us) *pred. a* Wishful, desiring, (*to* do); amb tious, having the desire, (*of*).

de·sist (dĭzĭst′, -sĭst′) *v.i.* Cea (*from*).

desk (dĕsk) *n.* 1. Piece of furn ture for reading or writing a having as its essential feature board etc. that serves as a rest f books and papers, and ofte drawers etc. for writing materia 2. Section responsible for particul subject or operation within a organization, such as *the Midea desk* of the U.S. Department State; editorial subdivision of new paper office, e.g. *the city desk.*

Des Moines (de moin′). Capit of Iowa in the S. central part the **Des Moines River**, whic flows from SW. Minnesota an joins the Mississippi in Iowa.

des·o·late (dĕs′olĭt) *adj.* Le alone, solitary; uninhabite deserted; dreary, dismal, forlor **des′o·late·ness** *n.* **des·o·lat** (dĕs′olāt) *v.t.* (**-lat·ed, -lat·ing**

Depopulate, devastate; render wretched and comfortless.

des·o·la·tion (dĕsolā'shon) *n.* Devastation; dreary barrenness; desolate place, dreary waste or ruin; solitariness; grief, wretchedness.

des·ox·y·ri·bo·nu·cle·ic (dĕs-ŏksīrībōnōōklē'ĭk, -nū-) **acid**: see DNA.

de·spair (dĭspār') *n.* Loss, utter want, of hope; what causes despair. ~ *v.i.* Lose, be without, hope. **de·spair'ing** *n.* **de·spair'ing·ly** *adv.*

des·patch = DISPATCH.

des·per·a·do (dĕsperah'dō, -rā'-) *n.* (pl. **-does, -dos**). Desperate, dangerous criminal, esp. of the old West.

des·per·ate (dĕs'perĭt) *adj.* 1. Leaving little or no room for hope; extremely dangerous or serious; hopelessly or extremely bad, extreme. 2. Reckless from despair; staking all on a small chance. **des'per·ate·ly** *adv.* **des'per·ate·ness, des·per·a·tion** (dĕsperā'shon) *ns.*

des·pi·ca·ble (dĕs'pĭkabel, dĭs-pĭk'a-) *adj.* Vile, contemptible. **des'pi·ca·bly** *adv.*

de·spise (dĭspīz') *v.t.* (**-spised, -spis·ing**). Look down on, think scornfully or slightingly of.

de·spite (dĭspīt') *prep.* In spite of. **de·spite'ful** *adj.* **de·spite'ful·ly** *adv.* (archaic).

de·spoil (dĭspoil') *v.t.* Plunder, spoil, rob, deprive. **de·spoil'er, de·spoil'ment** *ns.*

de·spo·li·a·tion (dĭspōlēā'shon) *n.* 1. Act of despoiling or plundering. 2. Condition of being despoiled or plundered.

de·spond (dĭspŏnd') *v.i.* Lose heart, be dejected. ~ *n.* Despondency (archaic; only in **slough of D** ~ in John Bunyan's allegory *Pilgrim's Progress*, 1678). **de·spond·en·cy** (dĭspŏn'densē), **de·spond'ence** *ns.* Condition of having lost heart, dejection. **de·spond'ent** *adj.* **de·spond'ent·ly, de·spond'ing·ly** *advs.*

des·pot (dĕs'pot, -pŏt) *n.* Absolute or tyrannical ruler; tyrant, oppressor. **des·pot·ic** (dĕspŏt'ĭk) *adj.* **des·pot'i·cal·ly** *adv.*

des·pot·ism (dĕs'potĭzem) *n.* Arbitrary rule; despotic state.

des·sert (dezért') *n.* Last course of lunch or dinner, usu. a sweet food as fruit, pie, cake, ice cream, etc.; (Brit.) course of fruit, nuts, etc., served after sweet course at end of dinner; ~ **fork**, ~ **spoon**, etc., those used for dessert. [Fr., f. *desservir* clear the table]

des·ti·na·tion (dĕstĭnā'shon) *n.* Place to which person or thing is bound.

des·tine (dĕs'tĭn) *v.t.* (**-tined, -tin·ing**). Appoint, foreordain, devote, set apart (*to, for*).

des·ti·ny (dĕs'tĭnē) *n.* (pl. **-nies**). 1. What is destined to happen, fate. 2. Power that foreordains, overruling or invincible necessity.

des·ti·tute (dĕs'tĭtoot, -tūt) *adj.* Without resources, in want of necessaries; devoid *of.* **des·ti·tu·tion** (dĕstĭtoo'shon, -tū'-) *n.*

de·stroy (dĭstroi') *v.t.* Pull down, demolish; make useless, spoil utterly; kill.

de·stroy·er (dĭstroi'er) *n.* (esp.) One of a class of small fast warships armed with guns, torpedoes, depth charges, etc., used for escort work, attacking submarines, etc.; ~ **escort**, warship smaller than a destroyer, used to convoy merchant ships and in submarine warfare.

de·struct·i·ble (dĭstrŭk'tibel) *adj.* Able to be destroyed. **de·struct·i·bil·i·ty** (dĭstrŭktĭbĭl'ĭtē) *n.*

de·struc·tion (dĭstrŭk'shon) *n.* Destroying, being destroyed; what destroys, cause of ruin.

de·struc·tive (dĭstrŭk'tĭv) *adj.* Destroying, causing destruction; (of criticism etc.) negative, not constructive. **de·struc'tive·ly** *adv.* **de·struc'tive·ness, de·struc'tor** *ns.*

des·ue·tude (dĕs'wĭtood, -tūd) *n.* Passing into, state of, disuse.

des·ul·to·ry (dĕs'ultōrē, -tōrē) *adj.* Skipping from one thing to another, disconnected, unmethodical. **des'ul·to·ri·ly** *adv.* **des'ul·to·ri·ness** *n.* [L. *desultor* circus rider]

de·tach (dĭtăch') *v.t.* Unfasten and separate (*from*); (mil., nav.) separate and send off (part from

A starboard quarterbow view of the Spruance class destroyer U.S.S. Elliott. Launched in 1974, it was built by Ingells Shipbuilding Co.

main body) for special purpose or mission. **de·tach'a·ble** *adj.* **de·tach·a·bil·i·ty** (dĭtăchabĭl'ĭtē) *n.*

de·tached (dĭtăcht') *adj.* 1. Separate; unattached, standing apart. 2. Disinterested, feeling no personal involvement. **de·tach'-ed·ly** *adv.* **de·tach'ed·ness** *n.*

de·tach·ment (dĭtăch'ment) *n.* 1. Detaching. 2. Number of troops, ships, etc., detached from main body for employment on separate service etc. 3. Standing aloof from objects or circumstances, withdrawal from association with surroundings; aloofness from worldly concerns etc.

de·tail (dĭtāl', dē'tāl) *n.* 1. Dealing with things item by item; minute account, number of particulars. 2. Item, small or subordinate particular; minor decoration in building, picture, etc., way of treating this. 3. (mil.) Distribution of orders of the day; selecting and dispatching; small party selected and dispatched for particular service or duty. **detail** (dĭtāl') *v.t.* 1. Give particulars of, relate or enumerate in detail. 2. (mil.) Select and dispatch for special duty. **de·tailed** (dĭtāld', dē'tāld) *adj.* (esp.) Related or described in detail.

de·tain (dĭtān') *v.t.* 1. Keep in confinement or under restraint. 2. Withhold (esp. what is due); keep from proceeding, keep waiting. **de·tain'ment** *n.*

de·tain·ee (dĭtānē', dē-) *n.* Person detained.

de·tain·er (dĭtā'ner) *n.* (law) (Wrongful) withholding of another's property; writ by which person already arrested may be detained pending action.

de·tect (dĭtĕkt') *v.t.* Find out, discover (person) in possession of some quality or performance of some act; discover presence, existence, or fact of (something apt to elude observation). **de·tect'-a·ble** *adj.* **de·tec'tion** *n.* Detecting, esp. of criminals.

de·tec·tive (dĭtĕk'tĭv) *n.* Person, esp. policeman, employed in investigating criminal etc. activities; **~ story**, story in which interest is centered in a crime and the detection of the criminal. **detective** *adj.* Employed in, relating to, serving for, detection.

de·tec·tor (dĭtĕk'ter) *n.* (esp.) Instrument for detecting any thing or action liable to escape observation.

de·tent (dĭtĕnt') *n.* Pawl; mechanism acting as a checking or detaining device.

dé·tente, de·tente (dātahnt') *ns.* (diplomacy) Relaxing of strained relations between two nations. [Fr.]

de·ten·tion (dĭtĕn'shon) *n.* Detaining, being detained; arrest, con-

'St. Michael and Satan' by John Flaxman, an 18th-century English sculptor. The personification of the **devil** as half-man, half-serpent is unusual.

finement, esp. temporary custody while awaiting trial; **~ center, house**, disciplinary institution for juvenile offenders.

de·ter (dĭter') *v.t.* (**-terred, -ter·ring**). Discourage or restrain by fear or by consideration of danger or trouble. **de·ter'ment** *n.*

de·ter·gent (dĭter'jent) *n.* Water-soluble cleansing substance, a wetting agent and emulsifier, prepared from chemical compounds instead of the fats and oils used to make soap.

de·te·ri·o·rate (dĭter'ēorāt) *v.* (**-rated, -rat·ing**). Make, grow, worse. **de·te·ri·o·ra·tion** (dĭterēorā'shon) *n.* **de·te'ri·o·ra·tive** *adj.*

de·ter·mi·na·ble (dĭter'min-abel) *adj.* Capable of being determined; liable to be terminated. **de·ter'mi·na·bly** *adv.*

de·ter·mi·nant (dĭter'minant) *adj. & n.* Determining, decisive, conditioning, defining (agent, element, word, etc.); (math.) square array of quantities representing the sum of the products of all possible sets of factors taking one from each row and one from each column, the signs of these products being determined by the direction of the diagonals joining at their factors.

de·ter·mi·nate (dĭter'minĭt) *adj.* Limited, definite, distinct, finite, definitive. **de·ter'mi·nate·ly** *adv.* **de·ter'mi·nate·ness** *n.*

de·ter·mi·na·tion (dĭtermĭnā'shon) *n.* 1. Decision, settlement (of controversy, suit, etc.); conclusion, opinion, sentence. 2. Fixing, delimitation, definition settlement, (of anything); exac ascertainment. 3. Fixed direction decisive bias; settling of purpose fixed purpose or intention; resoluteness.

de·ter·mi·na·tive (dĭter'minā tĭv, -natĭv) *adj. & n.* (Thing serving to determine. **de·ter'mi·na·tive·ly** *adv.* **de·ter'mi·na·tive·ness** *n.*

de·ter·mine (dĭter'mĭn) *v* (**-mined, -min·ing**). 1. (esp. law Bring, come, to an end. 2. Settle decide, as judge or arbiter; come t conclusion, give decision; be decisive factor in regard to. 3. Ascertain precisely, fix. 4. Give an aim to direct, impel *to*; decide (person) t do; resolve. **de·ter'mined** *adj* (esp.) Resolute, unflinching.

de·ter·min·ism (dĭter'minĭzem *n.* Philosophical doctrine that human action is not free but necessarily determined by motives, regarded as external forces acting on the will. **de·ter'min·ist** *n.* **de·ter·min·is·tic** (dĭterminĭs'tĭk) *adj.*

de·ter·rent (dĭter'ent, -tŭr'-, -tĕr'-) *adj.* That deters. **~** *n.* Something that deters; (sep.) nuclear weapon(s), deterring enemy from attacking, hence, **nuclear ~**. **de·ter'rence** *n.*

de·test (dĭtĕst') *v.t.* Abhor, dislike intensely. **de·test'a·ble** *adj.* **de·test'a·ble·ness** *n.* **de·test'-a·bly** *adv.* **de·tes·ta·tion** (dētĕs-tā'shon) *n.* Abhorrence; detested person or thing.

de·throne (dēthrōn') *v.t.* (**-throned, -thron·ing**). Depose. **de·throne'ment** *n.*

det·o·nate (dĕt'onāt) *v.* (**-nat·ed, -nat·ing**). (Cause to) explode with loud report. **det·o·na·tion** (dĕto-nā'shon) *n.*

det·o·na·tor (dĕt'onāter) *n.* Detonating contrivance, esp. fuse, percussion cap, etc., as part of bomb or shell.

de·tour (dē'toor, dĭtoor') *n.* Deviation, roundabout way, digression; byroad used temporarily while main route is unusable, being repaired, etc.

de·tox·i·fy (dĕtŏk'sifī) *v.t.* (**-fied, -fy·ing**). Remove poison or effects of poison from. **de·tox·i·fi·ca·tion** (dĕtŏksifīkā'shon) *n.*

de·tract (dĭtrăkt') *v.* Take away (*much, something*, etc.) *from*; **~ from**, diminish, lessen in value, depreciate. **de·trac'tion, de·trac'tor** *ns.* **de·trac'tive** *adj.*

de·train (dētrān') *v.* Discharge (troops etc.), alight, from railroad train.

det·ri·ment (dĕt'riment) *n.* Harm, damage. **det·ri·men·tal**

dĕtrimĕn′tal) *adj.* Harmful, causing loss or damage. **det·ri·-men′tal·ly** *adv.*

de·tri·tion (dĭtrĭsh′on) *n.* Wearing away by rubbing.

de·tri·tus (dĭtrī′tus) *n.* Matter produced by detrition, esp. gravel, sand, clay, etc., eroded and washed away by action of water.

De·troit (dĭtroit′). City in SE. Michigan, on the ~ **River**; a center of automobile production.

de trop (de trō′). Not wanted, unwelcome, superfluous. [Fr.]

de·tu·mes·cence (dētoōmĕs′-ns, -tū-) *n.* Subsidence from swelling, esp. contraction of swollen organ or part to normal size.

deuce¹ (doōs, dūs) *n.* 1. The two at dice or cards. 2. (tennis) State of score when the two sides or players each have 40 points in a game (or 5 or more games) and either must gain 2 points (or games) in succession to win.

deuce² (doōs, dūs) *n.* Plague, mischief; the Devil; **play the ~ with**, spoil, ruin.

deu·ced (doō′sĭd, dū′-, doōst, dūst) *adj.* & *adv.* Confounded(ly); extreme(ly). **deu′ced·ly** *adv.*

de·us ex ma·chi·na (dē′oōs ĕks mah′kĭnah). Power, event, that comes in nick of time to solve difficulty, providential interposition, esp. in novel or play. [L., = "god from the machinery" (by which in ancient theater gods were shown in the air)]

Deut. *abbrev.* Deuteronomy.

deu·te·ri·um (doōtēr′ēum, dū-) *n.* Isotope of hydrogen, present to extent of about 1 part in 6000 in ordinary hydrogen; symbol D, at. no. 1, at. wt. 2.013; ~ **oxide** (D₂O), heavy water (see HEAVY *adj.*). [Gk. *deuteros* second]

deu·ter·on (doō′terŏn, dū′-) *n.* Nucleus of DEUTERIUM atom.

Deu·ter·on·o·my (doōterŏn′-omē, dū-). Fifth book of the Old Testament, stating the law of Moses completely for the second time. [Gk. *deuteronomiom* 2nd book of law, from a mistranslation of Hebrew words (Deut. 17 : 18) meaning "a copy or duplicate of this law"]

Deut·sche (doi′che) **mark** (pl. **mark**, Eng. **marks**). Monetary unit of West Germany, = 100 pfennig.

dev. *abbrev.* Deviation.

De·va (dā′va). (Hindu myth.) Divinity, one of the good spirits. [Sansk., = "god"]

De Va·le·ra (dĕ valār′a, -lēr′a), **Ea·mon** (1882–1975). American-born prime minister of Republic of Ireland 1937–48, 1951–4, 1957–9, president 1959–73.

de·val·ue (dĕvăl′ū), **de·val·u·-ate** (dĕvăl′ūat) *vbs.t.* (**-val·ued, -val·u·ing**; **-at·ed, -at·ing**). Deprive of value; effect devaluation of (currency). **de·val·u·a·tion** (dē-

vălūā′shon) *n.* (esp.) Reduction of official value of currency in terms of gold or another currency.

De·va·na·ga·ri (dāvanah′gerē). Formal alphabet in which Sanskrit, Hindi, and other languages of India are written. [Sansk.]

dev·as·tate (dĕv′astāt) *v.t.* (**-tat·ed, -tat·ing**). Lay waste, ravage. **dev·as·ta·tion** (dĕvastā′-shon), **dev·as·ta·tor** *ns.* **dev′as·-ta·ting** *adj.* (esp., fig.) Very effective; astounding. **dev′as·tat·ing·ly** *adv.*

de Ve·ga (de vā′ga), **Lope** (1562–1635). Spanish poet and playwright; founder of Spanish national drama.

de·vel·op (dĭvĕl′op) *v.* 1. Unfold, bring out all that is potentially contained in; bring or come forth from latent or elementary condition, make or become manifest; realize potentialities of (land), esp. by converting it for residential or industrial purposes. 2. (mus.) Elaborate (a theme), unfold its qualities, reveal its possibilities by modification of melody, harmony, rhythm, etc. 3. (photog.) Render visible (latent image produced by actinic action on sensitive surface) by chemical treatment. 4. Make or become fuller, more elaborate or systematic, more active, bigger; make progress; come or bring into maturity. 5. Bring or come to light; make, become known.

de·vel·op·er (dĭvĕl′oper) *n.* 1. (esp.) Chemical agent for developing photographs. 2. (real estate) Subdivider of tracts for new home building.

de·vel·op·ment (dĭvĕl′opment) *n.* Act or process of developing, as the development of an organism etc.; developed product etc.; (mus.) in sonata or similar composition, the second section of a movement, containing elaborations on the theme(s) stated in the first section; housing subdivision. **de·vel·op·-men′tal** *adj.* **de·vel·op·men′-tal·ly** *adv.*

de·vi·ant (dē′vēant) *adj.* & *n.* (Thing or person) that deviates from what is considered normal state or behavior. **de′vi·ance, de′vi·an·cy** *ns.*

de·vi·ate (dē′vēāt) *v.i.* (**-at·ed, -at·ing**). Turn aside (*from*); digress.

de·vi·a·tion (dēvēā′shon) *n.* (esp.) Deflection of ship's compass needle by iron in ship etc.; divergence. **de·vi·a′tion·ism** *n.* **de·vi·a′tion·ist** *adj.* & *n.*

de·vice (dĭvīs′) *n.* 1. (pl.) Fancy, will, desire (only in **leave, left, to one's own devices**). 2. Arrangement, contrivance, expedient; something designed to perform special (esp. mechanical or electrical) function. 3. Design, figure; emblematic or heraldic design;

motto.

dev·il (dĕv′il) *n.* 1. **the D~**, Satan; in Jewish and Christian theology, the supreme spirit of evil, tempter and spiritual enemy of man, represented as a person, usu. with cloven hoofs, horns, and a tail. 2. Demon; heathen god, esp. malignant or evil deity, unclean spirit by which demoniacs were supposed to be possessed; one of the host of Satan, supposed to have their abode in hell. 3. Malignantly wicked or cruel person; energetic, clever, knavish, etc., person; poor wretch, luckless person (usu. **poor ~**). 4. Printer's apprentice (hist.). 5. Personified evil quality; temper, fighting spirit. 6. **Tasmanian ~**: see TASMANIAN. 7. Any of various instruments or machines, esp. with sharp teeth or spikes, for destructive use. 8. **a ~ of a**, a confounded, very violent; **like the ~**, with the violence, energy, etc., attributed to the devil; **between the ~ and the deep sea**, in an unpleasant dilemma; **go to the ~**, go to ruin or perdition; **the ~ to pay**, much trouble, violence. 9. **dev′ilfish**, any of several rays of the family Mobulidae, esp. of the genus *Manta*, e.g. the **devil ray**, inhabiting warm seas and having winglike pectoral fins spreading to about 20 feet and hornlike fleshy protuberances on the head; **devil-may-care** (*adj.*), wildly reckless; careless and rol-

Sandy beaches, where coins are easily lost, provide a profitable hunting ground for some-one with patience and a metal detector.

licking; **devil's advocate** = PRO-
MOTER FIDEI; one who advocates an
opposing cause, esp. for argument;
devil's bit, applied to several
American plants, including the
blazing-stars (*Liatris*), because of
their bitter taste; esp. the devil's
bit, *Chamaelirium luteum*. **devil's
food cake**, rich chocolate cake.
Devil's Island, former French
penal colony; one of the Safety
Islands, off the coast of French
Guiana; **devil** v. (-iled, -il·ing,
-illed, -il·ling). 1. Work as
printer's apprentice. 2. Prepare
(food) by chopping finely and adding mustard, pepper, and other
strong seasoning; hence ~ed eggs.
dev·il·ish (dĕv′ĭlĭsh) *adj*. Like,
worthy of, the devil, fiendish; extreme, excessive. **dev′il·ish·ly** *adv*.
dev′il·ish·ness *n*.
    dev·il·ment (dĕv′ĭlment) *n*.
Mischief, wild spirits.
    dev·il·try (dĕv′ĭltrē) *n*. (pl.
-tries). Diabolical art, magic; the
devil and his works; wickedness,
cruelty; reckless mischief, daring,
or hilarity.
    de·vi·ous (dē′vēus) *adj*. Winding
or straying, circuitous, erratic; err-

*Dhows are used in trading voyages in
the Arabian Sea and on the east coast
of Africa. The most common type has a
single mast and is a small, although sea-
worthy, vessel.*

ing. **de′vi·ous·ly** *adv*. **de′vi·ous·-
ness** *n*.
    de·vise (dĭvīz′) *v.t.* (-vised,
-vis·ing). 1. Plan, invent; plot,
scheme. 2. (law) Assign or give
(now only real property) by will. ~
n. (law) Testamentary disposition
of real property, clause in will conveying this. **de·vi·see** (dĭvīzē′,
dĕvĭ-) *n*. Person to whom property
is devised.
    de·vi·tal·ize (dēvī′talīz) *v.t.*
(-ized, -iz·ing). Make lifeless or
effete. **de·vi·tal·i·za·tion** (dē-
vītalĭzā′shon) *n*.
    de·void (dĭvoid′) *adj*. Destitute,
empty, *of*.
    dev·o·lu·tion (dĕvoloo̅′shon) *n*.
1. Descent through a series of
changes; descent of property by
natural or due succession. 2. (biol.)
Degeneration (now rare). 3. Delegation of work or power.
    de·volve (dĭvŏlv′) *v*. (-volved,
-volv·ing). Pass on, delegate

(duty, work), fall, descend, up
(deputy, or one who must act f
want of others).
    Dev·on (dĕv′on) *n*. County
SW. England; (one of) a breed
reddish cattle developed there; ~
island in Northwest Territorie
Canada, S. of Ellesmere Island.
    De·vo·ni·an (dĭvō′nēan) *adj*.
n. 1. (Native, inhabitant) of Devon
2. (geol.) (Of) the period or syste
of the Paleozoic era, occurring fro
350,000,000 to 400,000,000 yea
ago, between Silurian and Ca
boniferous.
    Dev·on·shire (dĕv′onshē
-sher) = DEVON; ~ **cream**, thic
clotted cream prepared by slo
scalding.
    de·vote (dĭvōt′) *v.t.* (-vot·ed
-vot·ing). Consecrate, dedicat
give up exclusively *to*. **de·vot′e
adj. (esp.) Zealously attached, loya
or faithful. **de·vot′ed·ly** *adv*.
    dev·o·tee (dĕvotē′, -tā′, dĭvō-) *n*
Votary *of*, one devoted *to*; zealousl
or fanatically pious person.
    de·vo·tion (dĭvō′shon) *n*.
Devoutness; religious worship o
observance; (pl.) prayers, worship
2. Enthusiastic addiction, attach

t, or loyalty (*to*). **de·vo'-** **al** *adj.* **de·vo'tion·al·ly** *adv.*
e·vour (dĭvowr') *v.t.* 1. Eat up aciously, as a beast of prey, prey n; eat greedily; eat ravenously arbarously. 2. Consume reckly; waste, destroy. 3. Engulf; e in greedily with eyes, ears, ; engross the attention of. **vour'er** *n.* **de·vour'ing·ly** *adv.*
e·vout (dĭvowt') *adj.* Earnestly gious, reverent; earnest, sincere. **vout'ly** *adv.* **de·vout'ness** *n.*
lew (dōō, dū) *n.* 1. Vapor densed in small drops on cool faces on or near the ground, en nocturnal radiation has led the lower layer of the atmosere. 2. Anything resembling this, something refreshing, moist, or re. 3. Any beaded or glistening isture, esp. tears, sweat. 4. **w'berry**, trailing plant of genus *bus*, which includes the black-ries; fruit of this plant; **dew'** w, rudimentary inner toe on ide of dog's leg, higher than er toes and not touching the und; **dew'drop**, drop of isture condensed in form of dew; **w point**, temperature at which nosphere becomes saturated with ter vapor by cooling. **dew'y** *adj.* **ew·i·er, dew·i·est**). **dew'i·ly** *v.* **dew'i·ness** *n.* **dew** *v.t.* dew, moisten.
Dew·ey¹ (dōō'ē, dū'ē), **George** 837–1917). Amer. naval officer; stroyed Spanish ships in Manila ay, 1898, during Spanish-merican War.
Dew·ey² (dōō'ē, dū'ē), **John** 859–1952). Amer. pragmatic ilosopher, author, and educator.
Dew·ey³ (dōō'ē, dū'ē), **Melvil** 851–1931). Amer. librarian; vised decimal system (~ ecimal System) of classifying ooks for library indexing and splay.
dew·lap (dōō'lăp, dū'-) *n.* Fold loose skin hanging from throat p. in cattle. **dew'lapped** *adj.*
DEW line. Distant early warng line (see DISTANT).
dex·ter (dĕk'ster) *adj.* Of, on, e right-hand side (but in heraldry = on right side of shield from earer's point of view, i.e. on pectator's left); opp. SINISTER.
dex·ter·i·ty (dĕkster'ĭtē) *n.* Manual or mental adroitness, skill.
dex·ter·ous (dĕk'strus, -sterus), **ex·trous** (dĕk'strus) *adjs.* 1. Handling things neatly; skillful. 2. Mentally adroit; clever. 3. Right-anded. **dex'ter·ous·ly** *adv.* **ex'ter·ous·ness** *n.*
dex·trin (dĕk'strĭn) *n.* (chem.) Gummy substance, used as adesive, into which starch is converted by dilute acids or alkalis, eat, etc.
dex·trose (dĕk'strōs) *n.* Glucose n animal and vegetable tissue,

synthesized from starch.
dex·trous: see DEXTEROUS.
D.F.C. *abbrev.* Distinguished Flying Cross.
dg *abbrev.* Decigram(s).
dho·ti (dō'tē) *n.* (pl. **-tis**). Loin cloth worn by Hindus.
dhow (dow) *n.* Lateen-rigged Arab vessel.
di-¹ *prefix.* Two-, twice-, double-.
di-², **dia-** *prefixes.* Through, throughout, thorough(ly), apart, across.
di·a·be·tes (dīabē'tĭs, -tēz) *n.* Disease (in medicine called **diabetes mellitus**) characterized by excessive discharge of glucose-containing urine, with thirst and emaciation, caused by failure of the pancreas to secrete an adequate amount of insulin and the consequent excessive accumulation of glucose in the blood; ~ **insipidus**, disease characterized by discharge of large quantities of urine, but not involving sugar metabolism, caused by disorder of pituitary gland.
di·a·bet·ic (dīabĕt'ĭk) *adj.* Of, suffering from, diabetes. ~ *n.* Diabetic person.
di·a·bol·ic (dīabŏl'ĭk), **di·a·bol·i·cal** (dīabŏl'ĭkal) *adjs.* Of, having to do with, under the influence of, the devil; devilish,

Devonshire's mild, wet climate and large areas of highland have encouraged farming. Dairy cattle, as here at Exmoor, U.K. are important; Devonshire clotted cream is famous.

inhumanly wicked. **di·a·bol'i-cal·ly** *adv.*
di·a·bo·lism (dīăb'olĭzem) *n.* Sorcery, witchcraft; devilry; worship of the devil.
di·a·crit·i·cal (dīakrĭt'ĭkal) *adj.* Distinguishing, distinctive; ~ **sign, mark**, one used to indicate different sounds of a letter, as accent, dieresis, etc.
di·a·dem (dī'adĕm) *n.* Crown; jeweled or plain band worn around head as badge of royalty; sovereignty. **di·a·demed** (dī'adĕmd) *adj.*
di·aer·e·sis (dīĕr'esĭs) *n.* (pl. **-ses** pr. -sēz). Var. of DIERESIS.
Dia·ghi·lev (dyah'gĭlĕf), **Sergei Pavlovich** (1872–1929). Russian ballet impresario; founder (1909) of the Russian ballet company that revived the art of ballet in W. Europe.
di·ag·nose (dī'agnōs, -nōz, dīagnōs', -nōz') *v.t.* (**-nosed, -nos·ing**). Form a diagnosis of (a disease).
di·ag·no·sis (dīagnō'sĭs) *n.* (pl. **-ses** pr. -sēz). Identification of disease by investigation of symptoms and history; formal statement of this.
di·ag·nos·tic (dīagnŏs'tĭk) *adj.* Of, assisting, diagnosis. ~ *n.* Diagnosis; symptom. **di·ag·nos'ti·cal·ly** *adv.* **di·ag·nos·ti·cian** (dīagnŏstĭsh'an) *n.*
di·ag·o·nal (dīăg'onal) *adj.* Extending, as a line etc., from one angle to a nonadjacent angle of a

DIAGRAM 460 DIAMETE

rectilineal figure or solid, or from one corner of anything to the opposite corner; having an oblique direction; marked with diagonal lines. **di·ag'o·nal·ly** *adv.* **diagonal** *n.* Diagonal line, part, row, etc.

di·a·gram (dī'agrăm) *n.* 1. (geom.) Figure composed of lines, illustrating definition or aiding in proof etc. 2. Illustrative figure giving the general scheme or outline of an object and its parts. 3. Graphic representation of the course or results of an action or process. ~ *v.* (**-gramed, -gram·ing, -grammed, -gram·ming**). Make a diagram of. **di·a·gram·mat·ic** (dīagramăt'ĭk) *adj.* **di·a·gram·mat'i·cal·ly** *adv.*

di·al (dī'al) *n.* 1. Sundial. 2. Surface of clock or watch bearing graduations and figures marking hours etc.; circular plate marked with figures etc. and fitted with movable index finger; rotatable ring of numbers and letters on telephone (~ **telephone**) used to make calls; ~ **tone**, steady humming sound given over telephone to show that caller may start to dial. **dial** *v.t.* (**-aled, -al·ing, -alled, -al·ling**). Measure, indicate (as) with dial; make telephone call by rotating a dial.

dial. *abbrev.* Dialect; dialectal; dialectic; dialectical.

di·a·lect (dī'alĕkt) *n.* Form of speech peculiar to a district, class, etc.; subordinate variety of a language with distinguishing vocabulary, pronunciation, or idioms. **di·a·lec'tal** *adj.* **di·a·lec'tal·ly** *adv.* **di·a·lec·tol·o·gy** (dīalĕktŏl'ojē) *n.*

di·a·lec·tic (dīalĕk'tĭk) *adj.* Logical; of disputation. ~ *n.* 1. (freq. pl.) Art of critical examination into truth of opinion; investigation of truth by discussion; logical disputation. 2. Criticism dealing with metaphysical contradictions and their solutions, esp., in Hegelian philosophy, the stages of thesis, antithesis, and synthesis representing the process of thought developing toward completion. **di·a·lec·ti·cian** (dīalĕktĭsh'an) *n.* **di·a·lec·ti·cal** (dīalĕk'tĭkal) *adj.* 1. = DIALECTIC *adj.* 2. Of DIALECTIC *n.* (def. 2); ~ **materialism,** theory propagated by Karl Marx and Friedrich Engels, acc. to which political events are regarded as arising from a conflict of social forces (the "class struggle") produced by people's material needs, and history as a series of contradictions and their solutions (the thesis, antithesis, and synthesis of Hegelian philosophy). 3. = dialectal: see DIALECT. **di·a·lec'ti·cal·ly** *adv.*

di·a·logue (dī'alawg, -lŏg) *n.* 1. Conversation; literary work in form

*Hardest of all minerals, the **diamond** is cut by craftsmen. Low-grade diamonds have industrial uses. It was not until the mid-18th century that the art of cutting*

of conversation between two or more persons; conversational part of novel or play. 2. Exchange of ideas, esp. on political or diplomatic issue.

di·al·y·sis (dīăl'ĭsĭs) *n.* (pl. **-ses** pr. -sēz). (chem.) Separation of soluble crystalloid substances in mixture from colloid by diffusion through semipermeable membrane; (med.) similar process used in purifying blood. **di·a·lyze** (dī'alīz) *v.t.* (**-lyzed, -lyz·ing**).

diam. *abbrev.* Diameter.

di·a·mag·net·ic (dīamăgnĕt'ĭk)

was developed to the standard seen i this ruby and diamond set (above) completed in 1816 for Louis XVIII c France. Top: A cutter at work.

adj. (of substance, as bismuth, zinc copper, lead, or tin) Tending t become magnetized in the presence of a magnetic field so that it lie with its long axis at right angles to the field. **di·a·mag·net·ism** (dīamăg'netĭzem) *n.*

di·am·e·ter (dīăm'eter) *n.* 1 (geom.) Straight line passing through center of circle or sphere and terminated at each end by its circumference or surface, or through center of any conic section or through middle points of system of parallel chords in curve of any der; line passing from side to side any body through center. 2. ransverse measurement, width, ickness; unit of measurement of neal magnification of an object.

di·a·met·ri·cal (dīamĕt′rĭkal), **i·a·met·ric** (dīamĕt′rĭk) adjs. 1. f, along, a diameter. 2. (of pposition, difference, etc.) Direct, omplete, like that between pposite ends of diameter. **di·a-et′ri·cal·ly** adv.

dia·mond (dī′mond, dī′a-) n. 1. ery hard and brilliant precious one, colorless or variously tinted, onsisting of pure carbon crystal-zed in regular octahedrons and llied forms. 2. Glittering particle r point. 3. Glass cutting tool of nall diamond set in handle. 4. Diamond-shaped figure, rhombus, r square, placed with diagonals ertical and horizontal; (playing ard with) red diamond-shaped gure(s); (pl.) suit of these cards. . (baseball) Figure formed by the bases; infield. 6. (print.) Size of ype (4½ point). 7. **black ~**, variety f dark-colored diamond; (pl.) coal; **lia′mondback**, any of several arge, venomous rattlesnakes with iamond-shaped markings on he back, including the **liamondback-terrapin** (Malalemys), Crotalus adamanteus of SE. J.S., and C. atrox of SW. U.S. and Mexico; **diamond cut**, cut with acets like a diamond; **Diamond Head**, promontory on SE. coast of Oahu, Hawaii; **diamond wed-ling**, 60th anniversary of wedding. **liamond** adj. Made of, set with, liamond(s); rhombus-shaped. ~ o.t. Adorn with or as with liamonds.

Di·an·a (dīăn′a). (Rom. myth.) Goddess of hunting, chastity, and he moon; later regarded as identi-cal with ARTEMIS; hence, huntress; poetic) the moon.

di·an·thus (dīăn′thus) n. (pl. -thus·es). Flowering plant of genus D~ of the order Caryophyl-aceae, including pinks and carnations.

di·a·pa·son (dīapā′zon, -son) n. 1. Fixed standard of musical pitch; **~ normal**, pitch in which the A above middle C is set at 435 vibra-ions per second. 2. One of the chief foundation stops in an organ open ~ and stopped ~) extend-ing through whole compass of the instrument.

dia·per (dī′per, dī′a-) n. 1. Fabric woven with small simple diamond pattern; towel etc. of this, esp. absorbent cloth folded and worn around a baby's waist and bottom. 2. Ornamental design of diamond reticulations. ~ v.t. 1. Weave, decorate with diamond-shaped pattern. 2. Put diaper on a baby.

di·aph·a·nous (dīăf′anus) adj. Transparent or translucent; vague, indistinct.

di·a·pho·ret·ic (dīaforĕt′ĭk) adj. & n. (Drug, treatment) inducing perspiration.

di·a·phragm (dī′afrăm) n. 1. Muscular partition, convex toward thorax, separating thorax from abdomen in mammals, which contracts and becomes flatter when air is breathed in, thus increasing the capacity of the thorax; (zool., bot.) partition in certain shells, gastropods, plant tissues, etc. 2. Thin lamina or plate used as parti-tion etc.; thin rubber or plastic contraceptive cap fitted over cervix; vibrating membrane or disk in acoustic instrument (telephone, loudspeaker, etc.); mechanism con-sisting of set of plates for varying effective aperture of lens of camera etc. **di·a·phrag·mat·ic** (dīafrăg-măt′ĭk) adj.

di·ar·rhe·a (dīarē′a) n. Ex-cessive looseness of bowels. **di·ar·rhe′al, di·ar·rhe′ic** adjs.

di·a·ry (dī′arē) n. (pl. -ries). Daily record of events etc.; book etc. prepared for this or for noting future engagements. **di′a·rist** n. One who keeps a diary.

Di·as·po·ra (dīăs′pera) n. Dis-persion of the Jews, after the Exile, among Gentile nations; Jews so dispersed.

di·a·stase (dī′astās) n. (chem.)

Enzyme formed in germinating seeds and having property of con-verting starch into sugar.

di·as·to·le (dīăs′tolē) n. Dilation or relaxation of heart, rhythmically alternating with systole. **di·a-stol·ic** (dīastŏl′ĭk) adj.

di·as·tro·phism (dīăs′trofĭzem) n. Geological process that deforms the Earth's crust, thereby creating continents, mountains, faults etc. **di·a·stroph·ic** (dīastrŏf′ĭk) adj. **di·a·ther·mic** (dīather′mĭk) adj. Of diathermy.

di·a·ther·my (dī′athermē), **di·a·ther·mi·a** (dīather′mēa) ns. Therapeutic use of low-voltage alternating electric currents of very high frequency to produce heat in parts of body below surface.

di·a·tom (dī′atŏm, -tom) n. Microscopic unicellular alga with silicified cell wall, existing in great numbers in sea and fresh water, and often forming extensive fossil deposits. **di·a·to·ma·ceous** (dīa-tomā′shus) adj. Containing or consisting of diatoms or their siliceous remains.

di·a·tom·ic (dīatŏm′ĭk) adj. (chem.) Consisting of two atoms;

Dice were used in the 2nd millenium B.C. and have been used ever since in games of chance. This painting of dice players is by a French painter, Georges de la Tour.

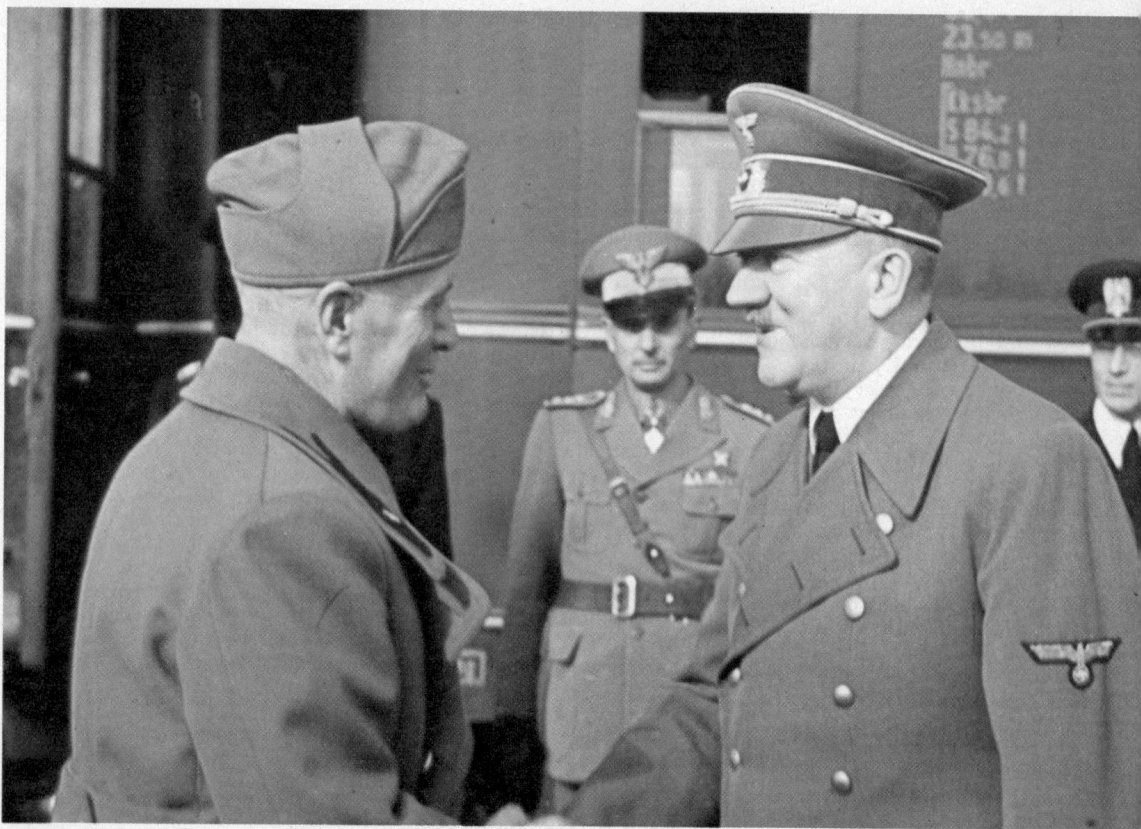

In Roman times the **dictator** was an official who was given extraordinary powers in times of crisis. Here two 20th-century dictators, Mussolini and Hitler, meet at Florence Railway Station in October 1940.

containing two replaceable atoms of hydrogen.

di·a·ton·ic (dīatŏn´ĭk) *adj.* (mus., of scale) Proceeding by notes proper to its key without chromatic alteration; (of melody etc.) constructed from such a scale.

di·a·tribe (dī´atrīb) *n.* Piece of bitter criticism, invective, denunciation. [Gk. *diatribē* wearing away (of time), discourse]

Di·az (dē´az; *Port.* dē´azh), **Bartholomeu** (1450?–1500). Portuguese navigator and explorer; sailed around Africa; discovered Cape of Good Hope.

di·az·o (dīăz´ō) **compound.** Organic compound, esp. one of those derived from aromatic hydrocarbons containing the characteristic group $-N=N-$, and forming the basis of a large group of dyestuffs (*azo dyes*).

di·bas·ic (dībā´sĭk) *adj.* Containing two replaceable hydrogen atoms.

dice (dīs) *n.pl.*: see DIE[1]; any game of chance using dice, esp. craps. **no** ~, (slang) no use, success, or luck. **dice** *v.* (**diced, dic·ing**). 1. Gamble, win or lose (money), with dice. 2. Cut (food) into small cubes.

di·ceph·a·lous (dīsĕf´alus) *adj.* Having two heads.

di·chot·o·my (dīkŏt´omē) *n.* (pl. **-mies**). 1. Division into two; classification into two groups; something paradoxical or ambivalent. 2. (bot., zool.) Form of

branching in which each successive axis divides into two. **di·chot´o·mous** *adj.* **di·chot´o·mize** *v.* (**-mized, -miz·ing**).

di·chro·ic (dīkrō´ĭk), **di·chro·it·ic** (dīkrōĭt´ĭk) *adjs.* Having two colors; esp. (of doubly refracting crystals) showing different colors when viewed in different directions, (of solutions) showing essentially different colors at different concentrations. **di·chro·ism** (dī´krōĭzem) *n.*

di·chro·mat·ic (dīkrōmăt´ĭk) *adj.* Having two colors, esp. (zool.) having two color phases in the adult stage.

di·chro·mic (dīkrō´mĭk) *adj.* Of, including, (only) two colors; esp., of vision of color-blind persons, including only two of the three primary colors.

dick (dĭk) *n.* (slang) Detective.

dick·cis·sel (dĭksĭs´el) *n.* A bunting (*Spiza americana*), U.S. bird with brownish back, yellowish breast, and black-patched throat.

dick·ens (dĭk´ĭnz) *n.* **the** ~, (colloq.) the deuce. [app. alliterative substitute for *devil*]

Dick·ens (dĭk´ĭnz), **Charles John Huffam** (1812–70). English novelist (pseudonym *Boz*), some of whose work, e.g. *Oliver Twist* and

Bleak House, exposed social evi creator, esp. in *Pickwick Papers*, many humorous characters. **Dick en·si·an** (dĭkĕn´zēan) *adj.*

dick·er (dĭk´er) *v.i.* Trade l barter; haggle; vacillate.

dick·ey (dĭk´ē) *n.* (pl. **-eys**). Small bird (also **dick´eybird**). False shirt front.

Dick·in·son (dĭk´ĭnson), **Emi (Elizabeth)** (1830–86). Ame poet; all six volumes of her poet were published posthumously.

di·cot·y·le·don (dīkŏtɪlē´don) Flowering plant with two cot ledons; see COTYLEDON. **di·cot·y le´don·ous** *adj.*

dict. *abbrev.* Dictatio dictionary.

Dic·ta·phone (dĭk´tafōn) (trademark) Machine that recore words spoken into it and subse quently reproduces them for trar scription.

dic·tate (dĭk´tāt, diktāt´) (**-tat·ed, -tat·ing**). 1. Say or rea aloud (matter to be written down 2. Prescribe, lay down authorita tively (terms, thing to be done); la down the law, give orders. **dic·ta tion** (dĭktā´shon) *n.* **dictate** (dĭk tāt) *n.* Directive, command authoritative direction (usu. reason, conscience, nature, etc.).

dic·ta·tor (dĭk´tāter, dĭktā´-) 1. Absolute ruler of a nation person with absolute authority i any sphere. 2. One who dictate for transcription. **dic·ta·tor·shi** *n.* Rule of dictator.

The 19th-century English novelist **Charles Dickens** achieved fame and fortune at the early age of 24 when his comic masterpiece 'The Pickwick Papers' was published.

dic·ta·to·ri·al (dĭktɑtŏr´ēal, -ŏr´-) *adj.* Of a dictator; imperious, overbearing. **dic·ta·to´ri·al·ly** *adv.* **dic·ta·to´ri·al·ness** *n.*

dic·tion (dĭk´shon) *n.* 1. Choice of words and phrases, verbal style, in speech or writing. 2. Manner of speaking, elocution; enunciation of words.

dic·tion·ar·y (dĭk´shonĕrē) *n.* (pl. **-ar·ies**). Book dealing, usu. in alphabetical order, with the individual words of a language or some specified subject etc., setting forth their spelling, pronunciation, meaning, inflections, history, etymology, equivalents in another language, etc., or some of these; also, book of reference on any subject with items arranged in alphabetical order.

dic·tum (dĭk´tum) *n.* (pl. **-tums, -ta** pr. **-ta**). 1. Formal saying, pronouncement; (law) expression of judge's opinion on matter of law, not being the formal resolution or determination of a court. 2. Current saying; maxim.

did (dĭd): see DO.

di·dac·tic (dīdăk´tĭk) *adj.* Meant to instruct; (of persons) too much inclined to instruct, tending to lay down the law. **di·dac´ti·cal·ly** *adv.* **di·dac´ti·cism** *n.*

did·dle (dĭd´el) *v.* (**-dled, -dling**). 1. (Brit. slang) Cheat, swindle. 2. Waste time. **did´dler** *n.*

Di·de·rot (dē´derō), **Denis** (1713–84). French philosopher, dramatist, and critic; one of the founders of the *Encyclopédie*.

did·n't (dĭd´ent). Contraction of *did not.*

Di·do (dī´dō). Legendary daughter of a Tyrian king; fled to Africa after the death of her husband Sycheaus and is reputed to have founded the city of Carthage.

di·do (dī´dō) *n.* (pl. **-does, -dos**). (colloq.) Antic, caper, prank.

di·dym·i·um (dīdĭm´ēum, dĭ-) *n.* Rare metal, formerly supposed to be an element and given symbol Di and subsequently separated into the elements neodymium and praseodymium. [Gk. *didumos* twin, from its being always found with lanthanum]

die[1] (dī) *n.* 1. (pl. **dice** pr. dīs, freq. used as sing.) Small cube with faces marked with 1–6 spots, thrown from box or hand in games of chance; (pl.) game played with

A **dicotyledon** is a plant whose seed holds two seed-leaves or embryos. Ranunculus, above, is a typical dicotyledon.

these; **the ~ is cast**, the irrevocable decision has been made. 2. Small cubical piece of anything. 3. Engraved stamp for impressing design etc. upon softer material, as in coining etc.; **~ casting**, casting obtained from metal mold(s); process of making such castings. 4. (mech.) Cutting device in a press or stamping machine.

die² (dī) *v.i.* (**died, dy·ing**). 1. Cease to live, expire. 2. Suffer spiritual death. 3. Suffer as in death; **be dying for, to**, desire keenly or excessively; **die laughing**, be exhausted by laughing. 4. Lose vital force, decay; come to an end, cease to exist; (of fire etc.) go out; (also **~ out**) disappear, be forgotten. 5. **~ away**, languish; **die'hard**, stubbornly conservative person.

Die·fen·bak·er (dē'fenbāker), **John George** (1895–). Canadian prime minister, 1957–63.

diel·drin (dēl'drĭn) *n.* Crystalline, water-insoluble insecticide.

di·e·lec·tric (dīĭlěk'trĭk) *adj.* & *n.* Insulating, nonconducting

(medium or substance).

Dien Bien Phu (dyěn'byěn'-foo'). Village in NW. Vietnam near border of Laos; site of victory of Vietminh forces over French army, 1954, during war between France and Indochina.

di·er·e·sis, di·aer·e·sis (dīĕr'esĭs) *ns.* (pl. **-ses** pr. -sēz). Sign (¨) placed over vowel indicating that it is to be pronounced separately, as in *naïve*.

die·sel (dē'zel) *n.* (also **~ engine**) Internal combustion engine in which air is first drawn into the cylinder and compressed so highly that the heat generated is sufficient to ignite the oil subsequently injected; vehicle driven by this; **~ fuel**, petroleum fraction used as fuel in diesel engines. [f. inventor, Rudolf *Diesel* (1858–1913), German engineer]

Diet differs from country to country because of the varying foodstuffs available. In India and many other eastern countries rice is the staple food, and lack of animal protein often results in under-nourishment.

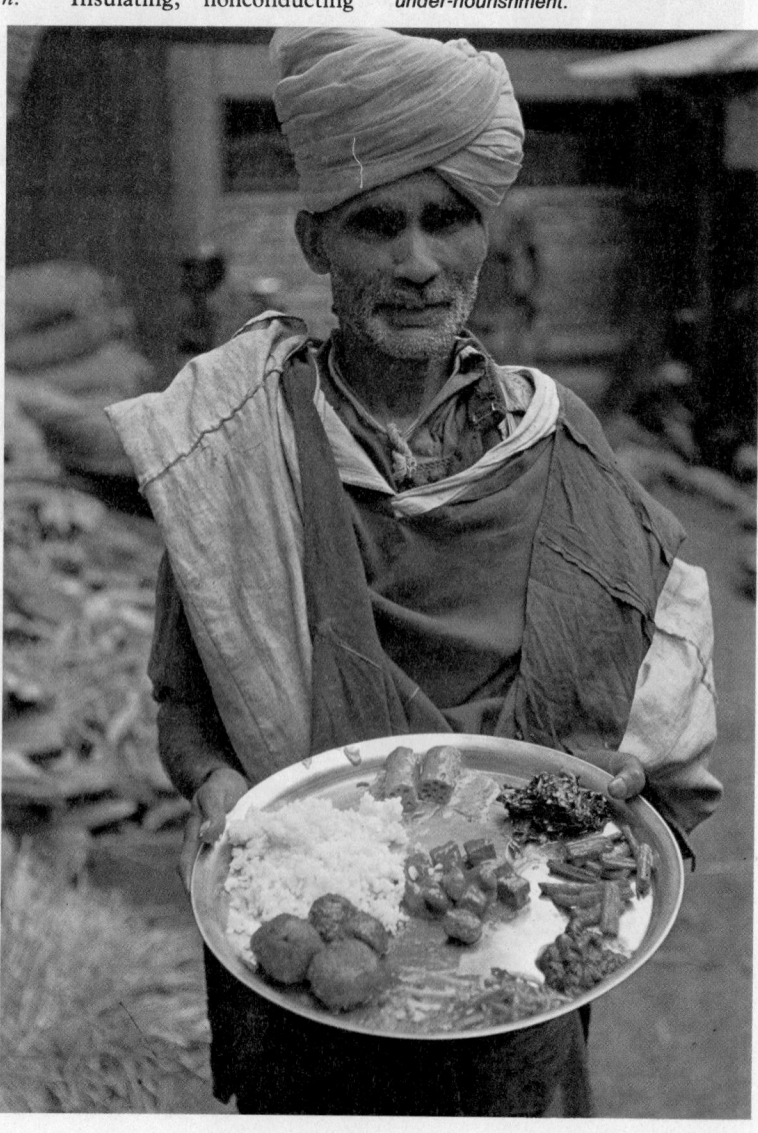

di·et¹ (dī'ĭt) *n.* Conference congress, on national or international business; legislature; **D of Worms**, that convened in 15 at Worms, Germany, at whi Luther was condemned as a heret

di·et² (dī'ĭt) *n.* Way of feedin prescribed type, quantity, etc. food, regimen; one's habitual foo **~ v.** (**di·et·ed, di·et·ing**). Ke to special diet; attempt to lo weight by special diet.

di·e·tar·y (dī'etěrē) *n.* (-**tar·ies**). Allowance or charact of food. **~ adj.** Of diet or dietary.

di·e·tet·ic (dīetĕt'ĭk), **di·e·tet·i cal** (dīetĕt'ĭkal) *adjs.* Of diet, of th regulation of kind and quantity food; specially prepared or pro cessed for restrictive diets; contain ing little sugar, starch, et **di·e·tet'ics** *n.pl.* (usu. considere sing.). Part of medicine dealin with regulation of diet.

di·eth·yl·stil·bes·trol (dīĕth ĭlstĭlběs'trōl, -trawl, -trŏl) White, crystalline solid almo insoluble in water, a synthet estrogen.

di·e·ti·tian, di·e·ti·cian (dī tĭsh'an) *ns.* Person versed dietetics.

dif·fer (dĭf'er) *v.i.* Be unlike, b distinguishable *from*; be at varianc disagree (*with, from*).

dif·fer·ence (dĭf'erens, dĭf'rens *n.* 1. Being different, dissimilarit point in which things differ quantity by which amounts differ remainder after subtraction; **spli the ~**, come to compromise **what's the ~?** (colloq.) Is important? What does it matter 2. Disagreement in opinion dispute, quarrel.

dif·fer·ent (dĭf'erent, dĭf'rent *adj.* Differing; distinct; out of th ordinary. **dif'fer·ent·ly** *adv.*

dif·fer·en·tial (dĭferĕn'shal) *ad* 1. Of, exhibiting, depending on, difference; differing according t circumstances; constituting specific difference, relating t specific differences. 2. (math. Relating to differentiation or t infinitesimal differences. 3. **~ calculus**, (math.) method of calcu lation devised by Leibniz (1677) treating of infinitesimal difference between consecutive values o continuously varying quantities; **~ gear**, arrangement of gears con necting two shafts or axles in th same line and enabling one shaft t revolve faster than the other whe required (e.g. in an automotiv vehicle when turning a corner)

Diesel engines are used where econ omy and durability are more importan than high performance. Locomotives tractors, taxis, cargo ships, and con struction plants have used diese engines increasingly since th 1939–45 war.

1 oil filter	10 cam follower	17 air inlet duct
2 dipstick	11 piston	18 water galleries
3 oil scavenge pipe	12 oil scraper and	19 cylinder bore
4 oil pump	compression rings	20 inlet valve
5 crankshaft	13 turbocharger	21 injector
6 connecting rod	exhaust duct	22 rocker shaft
7 crankshaft web	14 turbocharger spindle	23 rocker
8 oil pump drive	15 turbocharger turbine	
9 camshaft	16 compressor	

dif·fer·en'tial·ly *adv.* **differential** *n.* 1. (math.) Each of the infinitesimal differences of which the differential calculus treats. 2. Differential gear. 3. Difference or amount of difference between things that are comparable.

dif·fer·en·ti·ate (dĭferĕn'shēāt) *v.* (**-at·ed, -at·ing**). 1. Constitute difference between; make or become different in process of growth or development, esp. by modification for special function or purpose. 2. Discriminate between, distinguish. **dif·fer·en·ti·a·tion** (dĭferĕnshēā'shon) *n.*

dif·fi·cult (dĭf'ikŭlt, -kult) *adj.* Hard to do, troublesome; obscure, perplexing; unaccommodating, stubborn.

dif·fi·cul·ty (dĭf'ikŭltē, -kul-) *n.* (pl. **-ties**). Being difficult to accomplish, understand, etc.; difficult thing or question; (usu. pl.) embarrassment of affairs, financial trouble.

dif·fi·dence (dĭf'idens) *n.* Self-distrust, excessive modesty, shyness. **dif·fi·dent** *adj.* **dif'fi·dent·ly** *adv.*

dif·fract (dĭfrăkt') *v.t.* (optics) Deflect and break up (beam of light) at edge of opaque body or through narrow aperture or slit. **dif·frac·tion** (dĭfrăk'shon) *n.* Breaking up thus of beam of monochromatic light into series of light and dark spaces or bands, or of white or composite light into series of spectra; ~ **grating**: see GRATING. **dif·frac'tive** *adj.* **dif·frac'tive·ly** *adv.*

dif·fuse (dĭfūs') *adj.* Spread out, not concentrated; not concise, wordy. **dif·fuse'ly** *adv.* **dif·fuse'·ness** *n.* **diffuse** (dĭfūz') *v.* (**-fused, -fus·ing**). Disperse or be dispersed from a center; spread widely, disseminate. **dif·fu·sion** (dĭfū'zhon) *n.* **dif·fu'sive** *adj.* **dif·fu'sive·ly** *adv.* **dif·fu'sive·ness** *n.*

Digger wasps, such as the Crabro hunt flies and Lepidoptera ammonphila, crush the head or neck of their prey and carry it off either in flight or by dragging it over the ground.

*The **digitalis** or common foxglove is found in Europe and in the Mediterranean region. It is used to produce a drug of the same name which stimulates the heart and slows the heartbeat.*

dig (dĭg) *v.* (**dug, dig·ging**). Turn up (ground) with spade or other tool, or with snout or claws; break up and turn over (soil); excavate; thrust or plunge (something) *in, into,* stab, prod; give (person) sharp nudge (*in ribs* etc.); (slang) understand, appreciate, experience; ~ **in,** (esp.) entrench; (colloq.) begin hard work; ~ **out,** get, find, make, by digging, discover by research; ~ **up,** get out of ground etc. by digging; excavate; break up and loosen soil of; find. **dig** *n.* 1. Piece of digging;

archaeological excavation. Thrust, poke; (fig.) gibe. 3. (pl Brit. colloq.) Lodgings.

di·gam·ma (dīgăm'a) *n.* Sixt letter of original Greek alphabe (F, ϝ, prob. pronounced lik English *w*), later disused bu important in philology.

di·gas·tric (dīgăs'trĭk) *n.* (anat Muscle having two bellies wit intervening tendon. ~ *adj.* Of th digastric muscle of the neck.

di·gest (dī'jĕst) *n.* 1. Methodica compendium or summary, esp. o body of law. 2. Periodical contain ing condensed versions of article etc. **digest** (dĭjĕst', dī-) *v.* 1 Reduce into systematic (and usu condensed) form, classify; arrang methodically in mind, ponder over 2. Reduce (food) in stomach an intestines to assimilable form; (o food) undergo digestion. **di·gest·i·bil·i·ty** (dĭjĕstɪbĭl'ĭtē, dī-) *n* **di·gest'i·ble** *adj.*

di·ges·tion (dĭjĕs'chon, -jĕsh-, dī-) *n.* Digesting of food; power o digesting.

di·ges·tive (dĭjĕs'tĭv, dī-) *adj* Of, promoting, digestion. ~ *n* Substance promoting digestion **di·ges'tive·ly** *adv.*

dig·ger (dĭg'er) *n.* (esp.) 1. On who digs; (colloq.) Australian o N.Z. soldier. 2. ~ **wasp,** wasp o family Sphecidae, most of whic build their nests in burrows.

dig·gings (dĭg'ĭngz) *n.pl.* 1 (often construed as sing.) Plac where digging is done. 2. Materia taken out of an excavation. 3 (chiefly Brit., also **digs**) Lodgings living quarters.

dig·it (dĭj'ĭt) *n.* 1. (zool., anat. or joc.) Finger or toe. 2. Each numeral below 10 (orig. counted or fingers); each Arabic numeral from 0 to 9. **dig·it·al** *adj.* Using digits ~ **clock,** ~ **watch,** one that shows time by displayed digits, not by hands; ~ **computer:** see COMPUTER.

dig·i·tal·is (dĭjĭtăl'ĭs, -tā'lĭs) *n.* 1. Plant of genus *D*~, including foxglove, of the order Scrophulariaceae. 2. Drug prepared from dried leaves of foxglove, used as heart stimulant, causing heart to beat more strongly and regularly, thus increasing flow of blood and resting heart muscles. [mod. L. transl. of Ger. *Fingerhut* thimble, foxglove]

dig·i·tate (dĭj'ĭtāt), **dig·i·tat·ed** (dĭj'ĭtātĭd) *adjs.* (zool., bot.) Having separate fingers or toes; with deep radiating divisions. **dig·i·ta·tion** (dĭjĭtā'shon) *n.*

dig·ni·fy (dĭg'nĭfī) *v.t.* (**-fied, -fy·ing**). Make worthy or illustrious; confer dignity on. **dig'ni·fied** *adj.* Stately, marked by dignity, majestic.

dig·ni·tar·y (dĭg'nĭtĕrē) *n.* (pl. **-tar·ies**). Person holding high rank office.

dig·ni·ty (dĭg′nĭtē) *n.* (pl. **-ties**). . Worth, nobleness, excellence; gh estate, position, or estimation; gh or honorable office, rank, or tle. 2. Proper stateliness, elevation f aspect, manner, or style; gravity.

di·graph (dī′grăf, -grahf) *n.* Pair f letters expressing one sound, as .

di·gress (dĭgrĕs′, dī-) *v.i.* iverge from the track, stray; epart from main subject tempo- rily. **di·gres·sion** (dĭgrĕsh′on, ī-) *n.* **di·gres·sive** (dĭgrĕs′ĭv, dī-) *dj.*

di·he·dral (dīhē′dral) *adj.* aving two plane faces; ~ **angle**, ngle formed by intersecting planes r surfaces. **dihedral** *n.* Dihedral ngle; upward (**positive** ~) or ownward (**negative** ~, also called nhedral) inclination of aircraft ing from true horizontal.

di·hy·dric (dīhī′drĭk) *adj.* aving two hydroxyl groups.

dike, dyke (dīk) *ns.* 1. Ditch; ny water course or channel. 2. ow wall, esp. of earth; embank- ent, long ridge, dam, against ooding by sea, rivers, etc.; raised auseway. ~ *v.t.* (**diked, dik·ing,** yked, dyk·ing**). Provide, protect ith dike(s).

Di·lan·tin (dĭlăn′tĭn, dī-) *n.* (trademark) Drug that arrests epileptic convulsions.

di·lap·i·date (dĭlăp′ĭdāt) *v.* (**-dat·ed, -dat·ing**). Bring, come, into disrepair or decay. **di·lap·i- da·tion** (dĭlăpĭdā′shon) *n.*

di·late (dīlāt′, dī′lāt) *v.* (**-lat·ed, -lat·ing**). Make or become wider or larger; expand, widen, enlarge; expatiate, speak or write at length. **di·la·tion** (dīlā′- shon), **dil·a·ta·tion** (dĭlatā′shon, dīla-) *ns.*

dil·a·to·ry (dĭl′atōrē, -tōrē) *adj.* Tending to, designed to cause, given to, delay. **dil′a·to·ri·ly** *adv.* **dil′a·to·ri·ness** *n.*

di·lem·ma (dĭlĕm′a) *n.* Argu- ment forcing opponent to choose one of two alternatives (the *horns* of the dilemma), both unfavorable to him or her; position involving choice between two evils.

dil·et·tante (dĭletănt′, -tahnt′, dĭl′etănt, -tahnt, dĭletăn′tē, -tahn′tē) *n.* (pl. **-tantes, -tan·ti** pr. -tăn′tē, -tahn′tē). Lover of the fine arts; (now usu.) one who is interested in an art or science

*The raised causeway or **dike** is most common in areas of flat land surrounded by water where there is particular danger of flooding. This dike and high- way in Holland also serves as a dam and crosses the Ijsselmeer.*

merely as a pastime and without serious study. ~ *adj.* Of, like, a dilettante. **dil·et·tan′tish** *adj.* **dil·et·tant′ism** *n.*

dil·i·gence (dĭl′ījens) *n.* Persist- ent effort or work; industrious character.

dil·i·gent (dĭl′ījent) *adj.* Hard working, steady in application, industrious; attentive to duties. **dil′i·gent·ly** *adv.*

dill (dĭl) *n.* Umbelliferous annual yellow-flowered herb (*Anethum graveolens*); its leaves or seed; ~ **pickle**, cucumber pickled with dill.

dil·ly·dal·ly (dĭl′ēdălē) *v.i.* (**-lied, -ly·ing**). (colloq.) Vacillate; loiter; waste time.

dil·u·ent (dĭl′ūent) *adj.* Dilut- ing. ~ *n.* Diluting agent.

di·lute (dīloōt′, dī-) *v.t.* (**-lut·ed, -lut·ing**). Reduce strength of (fluid) by adding water or other solvent; water down. **di·lute** (dīloōt′, dī-, dī′loōt) *adj.* Weakened by addition of water; watery, watered down.

di·lu·tion (dīloō′shon, dī-) *n.* Act of diluting; state of being diluted; diluted substance.

dim (dĭm) *adj.* (**dim·mer, dim·mest**). Deficient in bright- ness or clearness; obscure; in- distinct; (of person) mentally dull.

Top: sexual **dimorphism** in animals is the difference in appearance between male and female of one species, shown here in Mearn's quail.

Left: The Australian **dingo** shuns human settlements and hunts mostly at night.

dim′ly *adv.* **dim′ness** *n.* **dim** *v.* (**dimmed, dim·ming**). 1. Become, make, dim; becloud; outshine. 2. Lower automobile headlight beams, using a **dimmer**, a rheostat for dimming; **dim-out**, reduced artificial lighting in streets etc. during wartime (as dist. from *blackout*) or as result of reduced power.

dim., dimin. *abbrevs.* Diminuendo; diminutive.

dime (dīm) *n.* U.S. coin of value of one-tenth of a dollar, or 10 cents; **a ~ a dozen**, commonplace; **~ novel**, melodramatic novel of adventure or romance of a kind that formerly sold for 10 cents; **~ store**: see FIVE-AND-TEN.

di·men·sion (dĭmĕn′shon) *n.* 1. Measurable extent of any kind; (usu. pl.) measurement, measure, size. 2. Magnitude, or extension, in a particular direction; **fourth ~**, imaginary direction in which matter is supposed to extend in addition to the three dimensions (length, breadth, and thickness) of Euclidean geometry. 3. (alg.) Each of the (unknown or variable) qualities contained in a product as factors of it. **di·men′sion·al** *adj.*

dim·e·ter (dĭm′īter) *n.* Verse of two measures (a measure having one foot in some meters and two in others).

di·min·ish (dĭmĭn′ĭsh) *v.* Make, cause to appear, grow, less or

smaller; lessen in importance, estimation, or power; **law of diminishing returns**, (econ. principle that expenditure of labor or capital beyond a certain point does not produce proportionate return. **di·min′ished** *adj.* (esp. mus., of an interval) Less by semitone.

di·min·u·en·do (dĭmĭnūĕn′dō *adv., n.* (pl. **-dos**), & *adj.* (mus. (Passage played) with gradually decreasing volume, indicated thu >.

di·min·u·tion (dĭmĭnoo′shon -nū′-) *n.* Diminishing, reduction (mus.) repetition of a passage in shorter notes than those previously used.

di·min·u·tive (dĭmĭn′yutĭv) *adj* 1. Minute, tiny. 2. (gram.) Indicating smallness, familiarity lovableness, etc. (used of such affixes as *-let, -kin, -ling* and of words formed with them, e.g. *ringlet, lambkin, duckling*). **di·min′u·tive·ly** *adv.* **di·min′u·tive·ness** *n.* **diminutive** *n* Diminutive word or term; small person or thing.

dim·mer (dĭm′er): see DIM.

di·mor·phic (dĭmor′fĭk) *adj.* (bot., zool.) Occurring in two distinct forms in same species, individual, etc. **di·mor′phism** *n.* **di·mor′phous** *adj.*

dim·ple (dĭm′pel) *n.* Small hollow or dent in body, esp. in cheek or chin; slight surface depression or indentation resembling this. **~** *v.* (**-pled, -pling**). Mark with dimples, break into dimples or ripples.

din (dĭn) *n.* Continued confused loud noise. **~** *v.* (**dinned, din·ning**). Make din; utter continuously so as to deafen or weary; **~ into**, make (person) understand by continuous repetition.

di·nar (dĭnär′) *n.* Principal monetary unit of various countries in Middle East and N. Africa.

dine (dīn) *v.* (**dined, din·ing**). Take dinner; entertain at dinner; **dining car**, railroad car in which complete meals are served; **dining room**, room in which principal meals are taken.

din·er (dī′ner) *n.* 1. One who dines. 2. Dining car; inexpensive restaurant with long counter and booths built from or shaped like railroad car.

Din·e·sen (dĭn′ĭsen), **Isak** (1885–1962). Pen name of Baroness Karen Dinesen Blixen; Danish writer residing for many years in Kenya.

din·ette (dĭnĕt′) *n.* Small room or alcove for informal meals; set of table and chairs used there.

din·ghy (dĭng′gē) *n.* (pl. **-ghies**). Small rowboat, inflatable rubber boat. [Hind. *dĭngī* small boat]

din·gle (dĭng′gel) *n.* Deep dell or

ollow, usu. shaded with trees.

din·go (dĭng′gō) *n.* (pl. **-goes**). Wild or semidomesticated dog of Australia (*Canis dingo*), usu. reddish brown and with bushy tail. [Native name]

din·gy (dĭn′jē) *adj.* (**-gi·er, gi·est**). Dull-colored, grimy, dirty; shabby; worn. **din′gi·ly** *adv.* **in′gi·ness** *n.*

din·ky (dĭng′kē) *adj.* (**-ki·er, ki·est**). (colloq.) Small; insignificant.

din·ner (dĭn′er) *n.* Chief meal of day, eaten at midday or in the evening; formal meal or banquet in honor of some person, event, etc.; ~ **jacket**, man's short jacket for formal or semiformal evening wear; ~ **pail**, vessel in which worker carries his or her, usu. hot, dinner or lunch; **din′nerware**, china, glasses, etc. for use at **dinner table. din′ner·less** *adj.*

di·no·saur (dī′nosôr) *n.* Any of the extinct saurian reptiles (orders Saurischia and Ornithischia) of the Mesozoic era, some of which were of gigantic size; **D~ National Monument**, area in NE. Utah reserved to protect fossil remains of prehistoric animals. [Gk. *deinos* terrible, *sauros* lizard]

dint (dĭnt) *n.* 1. **by ~ of**, by force of, through the persistence or vigor of. 2. Dent. ~ *v.t.* Make dent or dents in.

di·oc·e·san (dīŏs′esan, -zan) *adj.* Of a diocese. ~ *n.* Bishop of diocese.

di·o·cese (dī′osĭs, -sēz, -sēs) *n.* District under pastoral care of a bishop.

Dinosaurs of species as small as chickens and others that were the largest known land beasts lived for 100 million years before they became extinct for unknown reasons at the end of the Cretaceous period about 80 million years ago.

Di·o·cle·tian (dīoklē′shan) (245–313). Caius Aurelius Valerius Diocletianus, Roman emperor 284–305; during his reign the Christians were severely persecuted.

di·ode (dī′ōd) *n.* Any electronic device that limits current flow to one direction.

di·oe·cious (dīē′shus) *adj.* (bot.) Having the male and female flowers on separate plants.

Di·og·e·nes (dīŏj′enēz) (*c*400–*c*325 B.C.). Greek Cynic philosopher; exponent of asceticism.

Di·o·ny·si·us (dīonĭs′ēus, -nĭsh′-) **of Hal·i·car·nas·sus** (hălĭkärnăs′us). First c. B.C. Greek historian; wrote history of Rome.

Di·o·ny·sus, Di·o·ny·sos (dīonī′sus). (Gk. myth.) Son of Zeus and Semele; god of wine and of orgiastic religion celebrating the fertility of nature; identified by the Romans with Bacchus. **Di·o·ny·sian** (dīonĭsh′an, -nĭs′ē) *adj.*

Brachiosaurus

Brontosaurus

Diplodocus

Tyrannosaurus

Trachodon

Triceratops

Ankylosaurus

Stegosaurus

di·op·ter (dīŏp′ter) *n.* Unit for expressing the power of a lens, equal to the reciprocal of its focal length in meters.

di·op·tric (dīŏp′trĭk), **di·op·tri·cal** (dīŏp′trĭkal) *adjs.* Of refraction, refractive; of dioptrics. **di·op′tri·cal·ly** *adv.* **di·op′trics** *n.* Branch of optics dealing with refraction.

di·o·ra·ma (dīorăm′a, -rah′ma) *n.* Small-scale representation of scene with objects etc. in front of painted background, viewed through aperture at the front; hence, small-scale model. **di·o·ram′ic** *adj.*

Di·os·cu·ri (dīoskūr′ī, -ŏs′kyurī) (Gk. myth.) Twin sons of Zeus, CASTOR and POLLUX.

di·ox·ide (dīŏk′sīd) *n.* (chem.) Oxide of an element in which two atoms of oxygen are united to one of the element.

dip (dĭp) *v.* (**dipped, dip·ping**). 1. Put or let down temporarily or partially into liquid or the like; dye thus; make (candle) by dipping wick in melted tallow or wax; wash (sheep, cattle, etc.) in vermin-killing liquid. 2. Obtain or take *up* by dipping. 3. Lower (flag etc.) for an instant. 4. Go under water and emerge quickly. 5. Put hand, ladle, etc., *into* to take something out. 6. Sink or drop down through small space, or below particular level, as if dipping into water; have downward inclination. 7. Look cursorily or skippingly *into.* ~ *n.* 1. Dipping; quantity dipped up; brief swim; plunge or immersion. 2. (astron. etc.) Apparent depression of horizon because of observer's elevation; MAGNETIC inclination; downward slope of surface, esp. of stratum or vein. 3. Hollow depression. 4. Candle made by dipping. 5. Sheep-dip. 6. Creamy mixture for scooping with crackers etc. 7. **dip′stick**, rod for measuring depth of liquid, esp. of oil in crankcase.

diph·the·ri·a (dĭfthēr′ēa, dĭp-) *n.* Acute, highly infectious disease characterized by inflammation of a mucous surface (usu. that of the throat), and by an exudation forming a firm pellicle or false membrane. **diph·ther·ic** (dĭfthĕr′ĭk, dĭp-), **diph·the·rit·ic** (dĭftherĭt′ĭk, dĭp-), **diph·the′ri·al** *adjs.*

diph·thong (dĭf′thawng, -thŏng) *n.* 1. Union of two vowels pronounced as one syllable. 2. (pop.) Ligature, as æ.

diph·thong·ize (dĭf′thawngīz, -thŏng-, dĭp′-) *v.t.* (**-ized, -iz·ing**). Develop diphthong from single vowel. **diph·thong·i·za·tion** (dĭfthawngĭzā′shon, -thŏng-, dĭp-) *n.*

dipl. *abbrev.* Diplomat(ic).
diplo- *comb. form.* Double.

The big-horned sheep in this **diorama** feature above the snow-covered peaks in the background, but the viewer still gains an impression of the area that these animals inhabit

dip·loid (dĭp′loid) *adj. & n.* (biol.) (Organism, cell, nucleus) with chromosomes in homologous pairs.

di·plo·ma (dĭplō′ma) *n.* 1. Document issued by school or university conferring a degree or attesting to satisfactory completion of a course of study. 2. Document conferring honor or privilege. [Gk., = "folded paper," "letter of recommendation"]

di·plo·ma·cy (dĭplō′masē) *n.* Management of international relations by negotiation; skill in conduct of international intercourse; adroitness, skill, in dealing with others.

dip·lo·mat (dĭp′lomăt) *n.* One officially engaged in diplomacy; adroit negotiator; extremely tactful person.

dip·lo·mate (dĭp′lomāt) *n.* Holder of diploma, esp. a physician who has been certified in a medical specialty.

dip·lo·mat·ic (dĭplomăt′ĭk) *adj.* Of the management of international relations; tactful, discreet; ~ **corps**, group of diplomats accredited to a government; ~ **immunity**, exemption of diplo-

matic staff etc. abroad from arres taxation, etc. **dip·lo·mat′i·cal·l** *adv.* **diplomatic** *n.*

di·pole (dī′pōl) *n.* 1. (phys. chem.) Object oppositely charge at two points or poles. 2 (electronics) (also ~ **antenna** Radio or television antenna consist ing of two parallel rods extendin straight outward in different direc tions. **di·po·lar** (dīpō′ler) *adj* Having two poles, as a magnet.

dip·per (dĭp′er) *n.* 1. Any o various birds that dip or dive i water, esp. the water ouzel (*Cinclu mexicanus*) of western N. Amer 2. Utensil for dipping up water, esp long-handled ladle. 3. (**Big**) **D** ~ constellation of 7 bright stars i Ursa Major; **Little D** ~, simila group of 7 stars in Ursa Minor.

dip·so·ma·ni·a (dĭpsomā′nēa) *n* Morbid craving for alcoho **dip·so·ma′ni·ac** *n.* **dip·so·ma· ni·a·cal** (dĭpsomanī′akal) *adj.*

dip·ter·an (dĭp′teran) *adj. & n* (Two-winged fly) of the orde Diptera.

dip·ter·ous (dĭp′terus) *adj* (entom.) Two-winged; (bot. having two winglike appendages o processes, as some seeds.

dip·tych (dĭp′tĭk) *n.* 1. Ancien hinged two-leaved writing table with inner sides waxed. 2. Paint ing, esp. altarpiece, on two panel hinged together.

dir. *abbrev.* Director.

dire (dīr) *adj.* (**dir·er, dir·est**). dreadful, calamitous; indicating disaster; urgent. **dire'ly** *adv.*

di·rect (dĭrĕkt', dī-) *v.* 1. address (letter etc. *to* person or place); utter, write, *to* or to be conveyed *to.* 2. Control; govern the movements of. 3. Turn straight *to* something; tell (person) the way *to.* (of adviser or principle) Guide. Order (person) *to* do, (thing) *to* be done; give orders; be director of film etc.). ~ *adj.* 1. Straight, not devious or crooked; (of light etc.) coming straight from the source, without reflection, refraction, etc.; moving, proceeding, situated, at right angles to given surface etc.; straightforward, uninterrupted; (of succession) in an unbroken line from father to son. Going straight to the point, unambiguous, straightforward; upright, downright. 3. Immediate, without intermediation; (of speech etc.) in form in which it was uttered, not reported in third person. 4. ~ **action**, action taking effect without intermediate instrumentality; esp., exertion of pressure in community by strikes, demonstrations, etc.; ~ **current**, abbreviated DC, D.C., dc, d.c.) electric current flowing through circuit in one direction only; ~ **hit**, one right on the target (esp. of

bombing); ~ **mail**, mail, generally made up of advertising, requests for contributions, etc., sent directly to those who are expected to buy, contribute, etc. ~ **object**: see OBJECT; ~ **opposite**, exact opposite; ~ **tax(ation)**, tax(ation) levied directly on a person's income or property (rather than on commodities). **di·rect'ness** *n.* **direct** *adv.* By direct route; without intermediaries.

di·rec·tion (dĭrĕk'shon, dī-) *n.* 1. Directing; esp., management, administration; directorate. 2. Instruction how to proceed or act, or how to find some person etc. 3. Course pursued by moving body; point to or from which person or thing moves or looks; scope, sphere, subject; ~ **finder**, radio receiving apparatus so constructed as to indicate direction from which signals are coming.

di·rec·tion·al (dĭrĕk'shonal, dī-) *adj.* (esp., radio) Sending signals in one direction only.

di·rec·tive (dĭrĕk'tĭv, dī-) *adj.* Giving guidance. ~ *n.* Statement setting forth policy etc. for guidance of others, esp. subordinates.

*The common European **dipper** resembles the wren in shape and stance but is much larger. It is a solitary bird and keeps to the same stretch of mountain stream.*

di·rect·ly (dĭrĕkt'lē, dī-) *adv.* In a direct manner; at once, without delay.

Di·rec·toire (dĭrĕktwär'). Executive body in France during part of the revolutionary period (Oct. 1795–Nov. 1799), consisting of five members called directors. ~ *adj.* Of, imitating, the dress, furniture, etc., of this period in France, characterized by extravagance of design and imitation of Greek and Roman styles.

di·rec·tor (dĭrĕk'ter, dī-) *n.* (esp.) Superintendent, manager, esp. member of board of directors of company; person responsible for directing cast and supervising a play or making of a film; conductor of an orchestra or chorus. **di·rec·to·ri·al** (dĭrĕktōr'ēal, -tōr'-, dī-) *adj.*

di·rec·tor·ate (dĭrĕk'terĭt, dī-) *n.* Office of director; group of directors.

di·rec·to·ry (dĭrĕk'terē, -trē, dī-) *n.* (pl. **-ries**). Book containing lists of inhabitants of districts, telephone subscribers, members of professions, etc., with various details.

dirge (dĕrj) *n.* 1. (obs.) Traditional ecclesiastical name (orig. *dirige*) for the Office of the Dead. 2. Song of mourning or lament for the dead; funeral hymn. [orig. *dirige*, first word of L. antiphon *Dirige, Domine, Deus meus, in conspectu tuo viam meam,* "Direct, O Lord, my God, my way in thy sight," taken from Ps. 5]

dir·i·gi·ble (dĭr'ĭjĭbel, dĭrĭj'ĭ-) *n.* Steerable balloon or airship.

dirk (dĕrk) *n.* Kind of dagger, esp. that worn by a Scottish Highlander. ~ *v.t.* Stab with dirk.

dirn·dl (dĕrn'del) *n.* Dress with tight bodice and full skirt; full skirt with tight waistband.

dirt (dĕrt) *n.* 1. Unclean matter such as soils things by adhering to them; mud; anything worthless or unclean. 2. Earth, soil; material from which metallic ore etc. is separated, esp. alluvial deposit, hence **pay** ~, gravel containing gold, (fig.) profit. 3. Foul talk or action. 4. **eat** ~, submit to degrading treatment; ~ **-cheap**, as cheap as dirt, exceedingly cheap; ~ **road**, road, one with natural earth surface; ~ **track**, race track with dirt surface; track of cinders etc. for motorcycle racing.

dirt·y (dĕr'tē) *adj.* (**dirt·i·er, dirt·i·est**). 1. Soiled with dirt, muddied; mixed with dirt; that soils or befouls; **wash one's** ~ **linen in public**, talk openly about quarrels at home etc.; (of nuclear device) producing relatively large amount of fallout. 2. Morally unclean; obscene, as in ~ **joke**; dishonorably sordid, base, or corrupt; repulsive, despicable; ~ **pool**,

deny, contradict; repudiate (agre
ment etc.).

dis·a·gree (dĭsagrē´) v
(**-greed, -gree·ing**). 1. Differ,
unlike, not correspond; differ
opinion, dissent, quarrel. 2. (
food etc.) Be unsuitable, have b
effects. **dis·a·gree´ment** n.

dis·a·gree·a·ble (dĭsagrē´abe
adj. 1. Not to one's tast
unpleasant. 2. Unamiable, ba
tempered. **dis·a·gree´a·bly** adv

dis·al·low (dĭsalow´) v.t. Refu
to sanction, accept as reasonable,
admit; prohibit. **dis·al·low´an**
n.

dis·ap·pear (dĭsaper´) v.i. Cea
to be visible; cease to exist or
known; die away gradually. **dis**
ap·pear´ance n.

dis·ap·point (dĭsapoint´) v.
Not fulfill desire or expectation o
frustrate, thwart. **dis·ap·point**
ing·ly adv. **dis·ap·point´ment**
Disappointing; being disappointe
person or thing that disappoints.

dis·ap·pro·ba·tion (dĭsăprobā
shon) n. Disapproval.

dis·ap·prove (dĭsaproov´)
(**-proved, -prov·ing**). Hav
express, unfavorable opinion (of
dis·ap·prov´al n. **dis·ap·prov**
ing·ly adv.

dis·arm (dĭsärm´) v. 1. Depriv
of weapons or means of defens
reduce (armed service), be reduce
to peace footing; abandon or cu
down military establishment. 2
Deprive of power to injure; pacif
hostility or suspicions of, conciliate
dis·arm´ing adj. **dis·arm´ing·l**
adv.

dis·ar·ma·ment (dĭsär´ma
ment) n. Reduction or abolition c
a country's military forces an
weapons of war.

dis·ar·range (dĭsaranj´) v.
(**-ranged, -rang·ing**). Put int
disorder, disorganize. **dis·ar**
range´ment n.

dis·ar·ray (dĭsarā´) n. & v.
(Throw into) disorder, confusion.

dis·ar·tic·u·late (dĭsärtĭk´yulā
v. (**-lat·ed, -lat·ing**). Disjoint.

dis·as·sem·ble (dĭsasĕm´be
v.t. (**-bled, -bling**). Tak
(machine etc.) to pieces.

dis·as·ter (dĭzăs´ter, -zahs´-) n
Sudden or great misfortune. **dis**
as·trous (dĭzăs´trus, -zahs´-) ad
dis·as´trous·ly adv.

dis·a·vow (dĭsavow´) v.t. Refus
to avow, own, or acknowledge
repudiate, disown. **dis·a·vow´al** n

dis·band (dĭsbănd´) v. Break up
disperse. **dis·band´ment** n.

dis·bar (dĭsbär´) v.t. (**-barred**
-bar·ring). Expel (lawyer) fron
the legal profession. **dis·bar´men**
n.

dis·be·lieve (dĭsbĭlēv´) v
(**-lieved, -liev·ing**). Refus
credence to; not believe in. **dis**
be·lief (dĭsbĭlēf´) n.

dis·bur·den (dĭsber´den) v.t

Physical handicaps impose some limitations upon the lives of the **disabled**.
Imaginative training, such as teaching
this child archery, creates new fields of
choice.

(slang) unfair or unsportsmanlike
behavior; ~ **shame**, very unfortunate or disappointing event. 3.
(of weather) Foul, (at sea) wet and
squally. 4. (of color) Inclining to,
with some tinge of, black, brown, or
dark gray. **dirt´i·ly** adv. **dirt´i-**
ness n. **dirt´y** v. (**dirt·ied,**
dirt·y·ing). Make, become, dirty.

dis- prefix. Asunder, away,
apart or between; un-, not, the
reverse of.

dis·a·bil·i·ty (dĭsabĭl´ĭte) n. (pl.
-ties). Thing, want, that prevents
one's doing something, esp. legal
disqualification; physical incapacity caused by injury or disease.

dis·a·ble (dĭsā´bel) v.t. (**-bled,**
-bling). 1. Incapacitate; cripple.
2. Disqualify legally.

dis·a·buse (dĭsabūz´) v.t.
(**-bused, -bus·ing**). Undeceive,
disillusion.

di·sac·cha·ride (dĭsăk´arīd) n.
Carbohydrate, such as sucrose, that
yields two monosaccharide molecules when hydrolyzed.

dis·ad·van·tage (dĭsadvăn´tĭj,
-vahn´-) n. Unfavorable condition
or circumstance; loss or injury to
interest, credit, reputation. **dis-**
ad·van·ta·geous (dĭsădvantā´jus)
adj. **dis·ad·van·ta´geous·ly** adv.

dis·ad·van·taged (dĭsadvăn´-
tĭjd, -vahn´-) adj. Placed in
unfavorable social and economic
conditions.

dis·af·fect·ed (dĭsafĕk´tĭd) adj.
Estranged, unfriendly, alienated.
dis·af·fect´ v.t. **dis·af·fec´tion** n.

dis·af·firm (dĭsafĕrm´) v.t.
(law) Annul, reverse (decision etc.);

*Jesus Christ's 12 **disciples** at 'The Last Supper': a painting by Leonardo da Vinci. They received Christ's training and teaching. Peter was recognized as their leader and the founder of the Christian church.*

lieve of a burden; get rid of
urden).

dis·burse (dĭsbẽrs´) *v.*
ursed, -burs·ing). Expend;
ray; pay out money. **dis·-
rse'ment** *n.* Money expended.

disc (dĭsk) *n.* 1. see DISK. 2.
onograph record; ~ **jockey**,
·son who selects and introduces
onograph records for radio show,
cotheque, etc.

dis·card (dĭskärd´) *v.* 1. Throw
, reject (card) from hand at
ds; esp. play (card not of trump
t) when unable to follow suit. 2.
st aside, give up. ~ (dĭs´kärd)
Discarding at cards; thing (esp.
d) discarded.

dis·cern (dĭsẽrn´, -zẽrn´) *v.*
cognize, perceive distinctly (with
nd or senses). **dis·cern'ing** *adj.*
ving quick or true insight,
netrating. **dis·cern'ment** *n.*

dis·charge (dĭschärj´) *v.*
harged, -charg·ing). 1. Un-
d; rid of charge or load; fire off
earm); rid, rid itself, of electric
arge. 2. Relieve *of*, release *from*,
ligation etc.; dismiss from
vice; release from custody; send
ay, let go. 3. Send forth, emit;
fly, fire off; give, find, vent;
ed.) emit (fluid etc.). 4. Cancel
der of court); pay, perform (debt,
ty, vow). ~ (dĭs´chärj, dĭschärj´)
Discharging or being dis-
arged; certificate of this; (med.)
id etc. discharged.

dis·ci·ple (dĭsī´pel) *n.* 1. One of
arist's personal followers, esp.
e of the 12 Apostles; any early
liever in Christ. 2. Follower,
herent, of any leader of thought,
, etc. **dis·ci'ple·ship** *n.*

dis·ci·pli·nar·i·an (dĭsiplinär´-
n) *n.* Maintainer of (esp. strict)
scipline.

dis·ci·pli·nar·y (dĭs´iplinĕrē)
j. Of, promoting, discipline.

dis·ci·pline (dĭs´iplĭn) *n.* 1.

Branch of instruction; mental and
moral training. 2. Trained condition; order maintained among
persons under control or command,
as pupils, soldiers, etc.; system for
maintenance of order. 3. Control
exercised over members of church
and their conduct, as by censure,
excommunication, etc. 4. Correction, chastisement; mortification of
flesh by penance; whip, scourge. ~
v.t. (**-plined, -plin·ing**). Bring
under control, train to obedience
and order.

dis·claim (dĭsklām´) *v.* 1. Renounce legal claim to; renounce
claim. 2. Disown, disavow; deny,
repudiate. **dis·claim'er** *n.* Act of
disclaiming, renunciation, dis-
avowal.

dis·close (dĭsklōz´) *v.t.* (**-closed,
-clos·ing**). Uncover, expose to
view; make known, reveal. **dis·-
clo·sure** (dĭsklō´zher) *n.* Disclosing; thing disclosed.

dis·co (dĭs´kō) *n.* (pl. **-cos**)
(colloq.) DISCOTHEQUE. ~ *adj.* Of
or pertaining to amplified music,
strobe lights, dancing, style of
dress, etc. at a discotheque.

dis·cob·o·lus (dĭskŏb´olus) *n.*
(pl. **-li** pr. -lī, -lē). Thrower of
discus.

dis·coid (dĭs´koid) *adj.* Disk-
shaped; (bot., of composite flowers)
having disk only, with no ray.

dis·col·or (dĭskŭl´er) *v.* Change
or spoil the color of, stain, tarnish;
become stained, tarnished, etc.
dis·col·or·a·tion (dĭskŭlerā´shon)
n.

dis·com·bob·u·late (dĭskom-
bŏb´yulāt) *v.t.* (**-lat·ed, -lat·ing**).
(colloq.) Disturb, disconcert.

dis·com·fit (dĭskŭm´fĭt) *v.t.* 1.
(archaic) Defeat in battle. 2.
Thwart, disconcert; make uneasy,
embarrass. **dis·com·fi·ture** (dĭs-
kŭm´fĭcher) *n.*

dis·com·fort (dĭskŭm´fert) *n.*

Uneasiness of body or mind; want
of comfort. ~ *v.t.* Make uneasy.

dis·com·pose (dĭskompōz´) *v.t.*
(**-posed, -pos·ing**). Disturb
composure of, ruffle, agitate. **dis·-
com·po·sure** (dĭskompō´zher) *n.*

dis·con·cert (dĭskonsẽrt´) *v.t.*
Perturb, upset; embarrass.

dis·con·nect (dĭskonĕkt´) *v.t.*
Sever the connection of or between.
dis·con·nect'ed *adj.* (esp., of
speech or writing) Incoherent,
jerky. **dis·con·nect'ed·ly** *adv.*
dis·con·nect'ed·ness *n.*

dis·con·so·late (dĭskŏn´solĭt)
adj. Forlorn, inconsolable, unhappy, disappointed. **dis·con'so·-
late·ly** *adv.* **dis·con'so·late·ness**
n.

dis·con·tent (dĭskontĕnt´) *n.*
Dissatisfaction, want of contentment; grievance. ~ *v.t.* (usu. in
past part.) Make dissatisfied.
dis·con·tent'ed *adj.*

dis·con·tin·ue (dĭskontĭn´ū) *v.*
(**-tin·ued, -tin·u·ing**). Cause to
cease, break off; give up, leave off.
dis·con·tin'u·ance *n.*

dis·con·tin·u·ous (dĭskontĭn´-
ūus) *adj.* Not continuous.
dis·con·tin'u·ous·ly *adv.* **dis·-
con·ti·nu·i·ty** (dĭskŏntĭnoō´itē,
-nū´-) *n.* (pl. **-ties**)

dis·cord (dĭs´kôrd) *n.* 1. Disagreement, variance, strife. 2.
Harsh noise, clashing sounds. 3.
(mus.) Want of harmony between
notes sounded together. **dis·cord'-
ant** *adj.* **dis·cord'ant·ly** *adv.*
dis·cord'ance *n.* **discord** (dĭs-
kôrd´) *v.i.* Disagree; be different,
inconsistent, or discordant.

dis·co·theque, dis·co·thèque

(dĭs'kotĕk, dĭskotĕk', -kō-) *ns.* Night club where amplified recorded music is played for dancing.

dis·count (dĭs'kownt) *n.* Deduction from nominal value or price; deduction from amount of bill etc.; discounting; **at a ~**, below the usual price; **~ house**, store selling goods below list price. **discount** (dĭs'kownt, dĭskownt') *v.t.* 1. Give or receive value (after deduction of discount) of bill of exchange before it is due. 2. Leave out of account; lessen, detract from; allow for exaggeration in; take (news, event) into account beforehand, thus lessening its effect or interest.

dis·coun·te·nance (dĭskown'tenans) *v.t.* (**-nanced, -nanc·ing**). Refuse to countenance, discourage, show disapproval of.

dis·cour·age (dĭskĕr'ĭj, -kŭr'-) *v.t.* (**-aged, -ag·ing**). Deprive of courage, confidence, or energy; deter *from*; discountenance. **dis·cour·age·ment** *n.* **dis·cour·ag·ing·ly** *adv.*

dis·course (dĭs'kōrs, -kŏrs) *n.* Talk, conversation; dissertation, treatise, sermon. **~** (dĭskōrs', -kŏrs') *v.* (**-coursed, -cours·ing**). Talk, converse; hold forth in formal speech or writing on a subject.

dis·cour·te·ous (dĭskĕr'tēus) *adj.* Rude, uncivil. **dis·cour·te·ous·ly** *adv.* **dis·cour·te·sy** (dĭskĕr'tesē) *n.* (pl. **-sies**).

dis·cov·er (dĭskŭv'er) *v.t.* 1.

(archaic) Disclose. 2. (chess) Give (check) by removing one's own obstructing man. 3. Find out; obtain sight or knowledge of for first time; notice. **dis·cov'er·er** *n.*

dis·cov·er·y (dĭskŭv'erē) *n.* (pl. **-er·ies**). Discovering; thing discovered.

dis·cred·it (dĭskrĕd'ĭt) *n.* Loss of repute, thing involving this; doubt, distrust. **~** *v.t.* Refuse to believe; bring disrepute or disbelief upon.

dis·cred·it·a·ble (dĭskrĕd'ĭtabel) *adj.* Bringing discredit, shameful. **dis·cred'it·a·bly** *adv.*

dis·creet (dĭskrēt') *adj.* Prudent; cautious in speech or action. **dis·creet'ly** *adv.*

dis·crep·an·cy (dĭskrĕp'ansē) *n.* (pl. **-cies**). Want of agreement, variance, inconsistency. **dis·crep'ant** *adj.* **dis·crep'ant·ly** *adv.*

dis·crete (dĕskrēt') *adj.* Separate, individually distinct, discontinuous. **dis·crete'ly** *adv.* **dis·crete'ness** *n.*

dis·cre·tion (dĭskrĕsh'on) *n.* 1. Liberty or power of deciding or acting as one thinks fit. 2. Discernment, prudence, judgment. **dis·cre'tion·ar·y** *adj.*

dis·crim·i·nate (dĭskrĭm'ĭnāt)

The **discus** *was thrown in the ancient Olympics and has been in the modern Olympic Games since 1896. Here, Faina Melinki competes in the 1972 women's discus at Munich.*

v. (**-nat·ed, -nat·ing**). Constit set up, observe, a differe between, distinguish *from, betw* make a distinction; observe dist tions carefully; give unfair tre ment on the basis of prejudice. **~ against**, be prejudiced agai (esp. people of other ra religions, nationalities, etc.). **d crim'i·nat·ing** *adj.* Discerni acute. **dis·crim·i·na'tion** (dĭskrĭminā'shon) *n.* **dis·crim'i·n tive** *adj.* **dis·crim'i·na·tive** *adv.*

dis·cur·sive (dĭskĕr'sĭv) *adj.* Rambling, digressive, expatiati 2. Proceeding by reasoning argument, not intuitive. **dis·cu sive·ly** *adv.* **dis·cur'sive·ness**

dis·cus (dĭs'kus) *n.* Heavy d now usu. weighing about 4½ pou (2 kg), thrown for distance athletic competitions; field even throwing this.

dis·cuss (dĭskŭs') *v.t.* Exam by argument, debate; speak, wr or treat of; talk over. **dis·cus·si** (dĭskŭsh'on), **dis·cus'sant** *ns.*

dis·dain (dĭsdān') *v.t.* Sco regard with contempt; consi beneath oneself or one's notice. *n.* Scorn, contempt. **dis·dain'** *adj.* **dis·dain'ful·ly** *adv.*

dis·ease (dĭzēz') *n.* Mor condition of body or plant, or so part of it; (specific) disorder, illne deranged, depraved, or mor condition of mind etc. **dis·eas** *adj.*

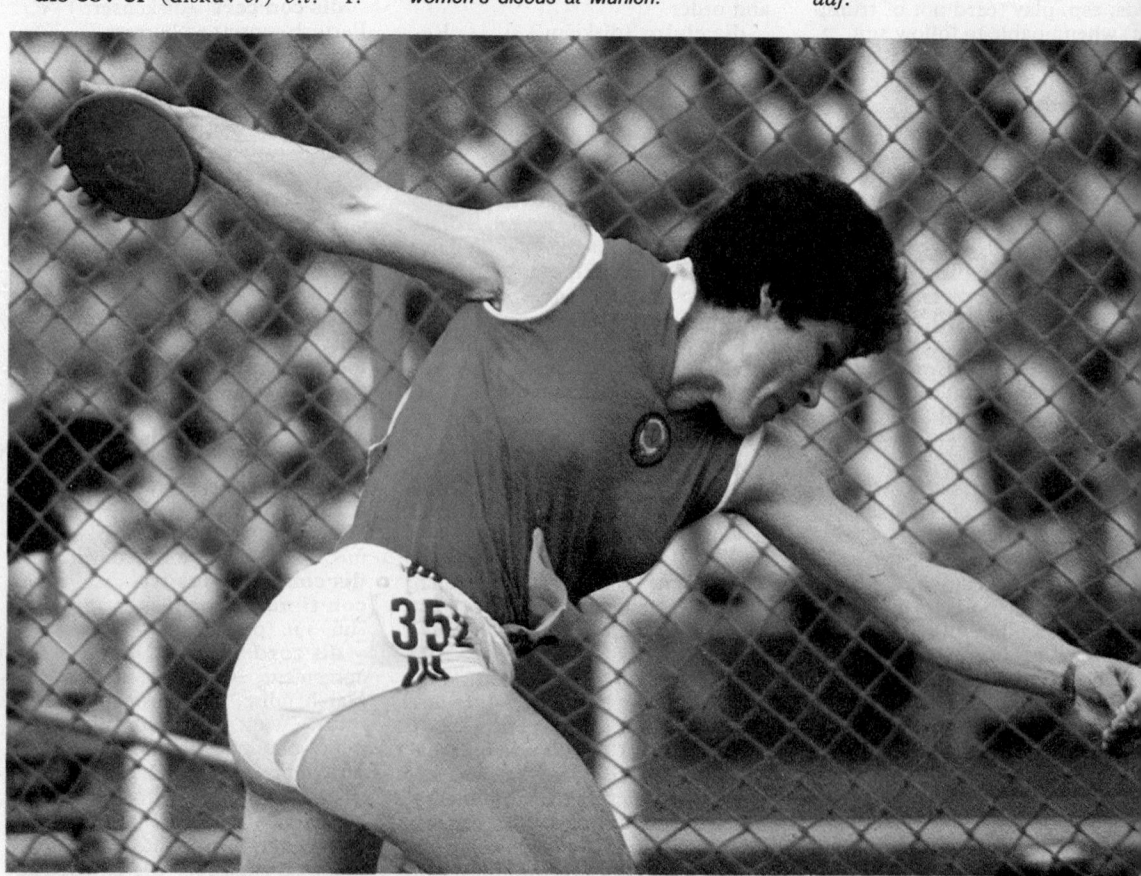

dis·em·bark (dĭsĕmbărk´) v. ut, go, ashore. **dis·em·bar·ka-on** (dĭsĕmbărkā´shon) n.

dis·em·bar·rass (dĭsĕmbăr´as) t. Free from embarrassment, rid relieve (of). **dis·em·bar·rass-ent** n.

dis·em·bod·y (dĭsĕmbŏd´ē) v.t. **bod·ied, -bod·y·ing**). Separate, ee (soul from body, or idea from rm in which it is embodied).

dis·em·bow·el (dĭsĕmbow´el) t. (**-eled** or **-elled, -el·ing** or **-l·ling**). Remove entrails of.

dis·em·broil (dĭsĕmbroil´) v.t. xtricate from confusion or atanglement.

dis·en·chant (dĭsĕnchănt´, hahnt´) v.t. Free from enchant-ent or illusion. **dis·en·chant´-ent** n.

dis·en·cum·ber (dĭsĕnkŭm´ber) t. Free from encumbrance.

dis·en·fran·chise (dĭsĕnfrăn´-hīz) v.t. (**-chised, -chis·ing**) = ISFRANCHISE.

dis·en·gage (dĭsĕngāj´) v.t. **gaged, -gag·ing**). 1. Detach, berate, loosen; come apart, break ntact. 2. Release from engage-ent, obligation, friendship, etc. **is·en·gaged´** adj. (esp.) Un-ccupied; at liberty. **dis·en·gage´-ent** n.

dis·en·tan·gle (dĭsĕntăng´gel) v. gled, -gling**). Extricate, free om complications; unravel, ntwist. **dis·en·tan´gle·ment** n.

dis·es·tab·lish (dĭsĕstăb´lĭsh) .t. Deprive of established haracter; esp. deprive (church) of ate connection and support. **is·es·tab´lish·ment** n.

dis·es·teem (dĭsĕstēm´) n. Lack f esteem.

di·seur (dēzör´) n. [fem. **di·-euse** (dēzöz´)] Person (usu. pro-ssional entertainer) who recites onologues. [Fr.]

dis·fa·vor (dĭsfā´ver) n. Dislike, isapproval; being disliked.

dis·fig·ure (dĭsfĭg´yer) v.t. **-ured, -ur·ing**). Mar appearance f; deform. **dis·fig´ure·ment** n.

dis·fran·chise (dĭsfrăn´chīz) v.t. **-chised, -chis·ing**). Deprive of ights and privileges of citizenship, sp. the right to vote, or of some ranchise or privilege previously njoyed. **dis·fran´chise·ment** n.

dis·gorge (dĭsgôrj´) v. (**-gorged, gorg·ing**). Vomit forth (what has een swallowed, lit. and fig.); ischarge, spew, pour forth.

dis·grace (dĭsgrās´) n. 1. Loss f favor, downfall from position of onor; shame. 2. Cause of eproach. ~ v.t. (**-graced, grac·ing**). Dismiss from favor, egrade from position; bring shame r discredit upon, be a disgrace to. **is·grace´ful** adj. **dis·grace´-ul·ly** adv. **dis·grace´ful·ness** n.

dis·grun·tled (dĭsgrŭn´teld) adj. Discontented, displeased.

*Leprosy is a **disease** which is most prevalent in low-lying tropical or sub-tropical areas. Today, the use of sulphone drugs arrests the infection and produces improvement in the patient in most cases.*

dis·guise (dĭsgīz´) v.t. (**-guised, -guis·ing**). Conceal identity of by changing personal appearance or dress; dress *as* someone, *in* some garb; alter appearance of (anything) so as to mislead or deceive; conceal or cloak real character, state, or identity of. ~ n. Use of changed dress or appearance for sake of concealment; disguised condition; garb used to deceive; pretense.

dis·gust (dĭsgŭst´) n. Loathing, nausea, repugnance, strong aver-sion, or indignation in. **dis·gust´-ing** adj. **dis·gust´ing·ly** adv.

dish (dĭsh) n. 1. Shallow flat-bottomed vessel for holding food. 2. Food served on or contained in dish; variety or article of food; (slang) attractive woman. 3. Any-thing dish-shaped or concave, esp. as receptacle. 4. **dish´cloth, dish´-rag**, cloth for washing dishes and plates; **dish´pan**, basin to wash dishes in; **dish´washer**, person who washes dishes, esp. one hired to do so in restaurant; machine for washing dishes etc. automatically; **dish´water**, water in which dishes have been washed. **dish** v. Put (food) into dish ready for serving; ~ **out**, distribute, esp. indiscrimi-nately; ~ **up**, serve, serve meal; (fig.) present (facts, arguments, etc.).

dis·ha·bille (dĭsabĕl´) n. Being negligently or partly dressed; undress; lounging attire.

dis·har·mo·ny (dĭs-här´monē) n. (pl. **-nies**). Discord, dissonance. **dis·har·mo·ni·ous** (dĭs-härmō´-nēus) adj.

dis·heart·en (dĭs-här´ten) v.t. Make despondent, rob of courage. **dis·heart´en·ing** adj.

di·shev·eled (dĭshĕv´eld) adj. With disordered hair; (of hair) loose, disordered; untidy, unkempt. **di·shev´el·ment** n. **di·shev·el** v.t. (**-eled** or **-elled, -el·ing** or **-el·ling**).

dis·hon·est (dĭsŏn´ĭst) adj. Not honest; fraudulent; insincere. **dis·hon´est·ly** adv. **dis·hon´es·ty** n. (pl. **-ties**).

dis·hon·or (dĭsŏn´er) n. Dis-

Scrubbing up before surgery prevents infection during or after it. Modern techniques of **disinfection** stem from the discovery of the germ theory of disease.

grace. ~ *v.t.* 1. Treat with indignity; violate honor or chastity of. 2. Bring dishonor upon. 3. Fail to pay (bill or other obligation). **dis·hon′or·a·ble** *adj.* Involving disgrace, ignominious, as in ~ **discharge** from military service; unprincipled, base; against dictates of honor. **dis·hon′or·a·ble·ness** *n.* **dis·hon′or·a·bly** *adv.*

dis·il·lu·sion (dĭsĭlōō′zhon) *v.t.* Free from illusion, disenchant. ~ *n.* Freedom from illusion, disenchantment. **dis·il·lu′sion·ment** *n.*

dis·in·cli·na·tion (dĭsĭnklĭnā′shon) *n.* Want of inclination, willingness, or liking.

dis·in·cline (dĭsĭnklīn′) *v.t.* (**-clined, -clin·ing**). Make averse or unwilling.

dis·in·fect (dĭsĭnfĕkt′) *v.t.* Cleanse from infection, destroy germs of disease in. **dis·in·fect′ant** *adj. & n.* Disinfecting (agent).

dis·in·gen·u·ous (dĭsĭnjĕn′ūus) *adj.* Insincere, not candid or frank. **dis·in·gen′u·ous·ly** *adv.* **dis·in·gen′u·ous·ness** *n.*

dis·in·her·it (dĭsĭnhĕr′ĭt) *v.t.* Deprive or dispossess of right to inherit. **dis·in·her′i·tance** *n.*

dis·in·te·grate (dĭsĭn′tegrāt) *v.* (**-grat·ed, -grat·ing**). Separate into component parts; deprive of, lose, cohesion. **dis·in·te·gra·tion** (dĭsĭntegrā′shon) *n.*

dis·in·ter (dĭsĭntēr′) *v.t.* (**-terred, -ter·ring**). Exhume, esp. a corpse from place of burial; unearth. **dis·in·ter′ment** *n.*

dis·in·ter·est (dĭsĭn′terĭst, -trĭst) *n.* Impartiality, disinterestedness; absence of interest. **dis·in·ter·est·ed** (dĭsĭn′terĕstĭd, -trĭstĭd) *adj.* Not influenced by self-interest or partiality; (colloq.) not interested. **dis·in′ter·est·ed·ly** *adv.* **dis·in′ter·est·ed·ness** *n.*

dis·in·tox·i·ca·tion (dĭsĭntŏksĭkā′shon) *n.* (med.) Freeing a person from effects of poison in his or her body, as an addict from a drug.

dis·join (dĭsjoin′) *v.t.* Separate, disunite.

dis·joint (dĭsjoint′) *v.t.* Dislocate; disturb working or connection of; separate at the joints. **dis·joint′ed** *adj.* (esp. of speech etc.) Incoherent, desultory. **dis·joint′ed·ly** *adv.* **dis·joint′ed·ness** *n.*

dis·junc·tive (dĭsjŭngk′tĭv) *adj.* Disjoining, involving separation; (logic) alternative; involving choice between two propositions etc.; (gram., of conjunction) expressing an alternative, contrast, or opposition between the clauses it connects. **dis·junc′tive·ly** *adv.* **disjunctive**

n. Disjunctive proposition or conjunction.

disk, disc (dĭsk) *ns.* Thin circular plate; round, flat (or apparently flat) object, as **sun's** ~; round flattened part in body, plant, etc.; ~ **brake**, automobile etc. brake using disk-shaped friction surfaces; ~ **harrow**, harrow with concave disks set at an angle; ~ **jockey:** see DISC jockey.

dis·like (dĭslīk′) *v.t.* (**-liked, -lik·ing**) Not like; have aversion or objection to. ~ *n.* Aversion.

dis·lo·cate (dĭs′lōkāt, dĭslō′-) *v.t.* (**-cat·ed, -cat·ing**). Put out of joint; displace, shift, disturb. **dis·lo·ca·tion** (dĭslōkā′shon) *n.*

dis·lodge (dĭslŏj′) *v.t.* (**-lodged, -lodg·ing**). Remove, turn out, from position. **dis·lodg′ment** *n.*

dis·loy·al (dĭsloi′al) *adj.* Unfaithful; untrue to allegiance. **dis·loy′al·ly** *adv.* **dis·loy′al·ty** *n.* (pl. **-ties**).

dis·mal (dĭz′mal) *adj.* Depressing, miserable, somber, dreary. **Dismal Swamp**, swamp in SE. Virginia and NE. North Carolina, about 600 sq. miles. **dis′mal·ly** *adv.* **dis′mal·ness** *n.* [orig. noun, = "unlucky days"; OF. *dis mal* f. L. *dies mali* ill days (the medieval calendar recognized two of these in each month)]

dis·man·tle (dĭsmăn′tel) *v.t.* (**-tled, -tling**). Strip of equipment, furniture, etc.; take apart, tear down; deprive of defense. **dis·man′tle·ment** *n.*

dis·may (dĭsmā′) *n.* Consternation; utter loss of moral courage or resolution in prospect of danger or difficulty. ~ *v.t.* Rouse dismay in;

reduce to despair.

dis·mem·ber (dĭsmĕm′ber) *v.* Tear or cut limb from limb; divid into parts or sections so as t destroy integrity. **dis·mem′ber·ment** *n.*

dis·miss (dĭsmĭs′) *v.t.* 1. Sen away, disperse, disband; allow t go; send away from one's presence 2. Discharge from employment service, school, etc. 3. Put out o one's thoughts. 4. Have done with bring to an end. 5. (law) Send ou of court, refuse further hearing t (case etc.). **dis·miss′al** *n.*

dis·mount (dĭsmownt′) *v* Alight, cause to alight, from horse back, etc.; unseat, unhorse; remove (thing) from its mount.

Dis·ney (dĭz′nē), **Walt(er** **Elias** (1901–66). Amer. cartoonist film director and producer; creator of animated cartoons, esp. Mickey Mouse. **Dis′neyland**, an amusement park (California); (fig.) any land of make-believe. **Dis′ney·world**, an amusement park (Florida); (fig.) any land of make-believe.

dis·o·be·di·ence (dĭsobē′dēens *n.* Being disobedient, withholding of obedience. **dis·o·be′di·ent** *adj* Refusing or failing to obey stubborn, intractable. **dis·o·be′di·ent·ly** *adv.*

dis·o·bey (dĭsobā′) *v.* Disregard orders, break rules; fail or refuse t obey.

Disneyland amusement park i Anaheim, south-west California, wa planned by **Walt Disney** and opened i 1955. It is dominated by Sleeping Beauty's castle. Along the drawbridge are Snow White and the Seven Dwarfs.

dis·o·blige (dĭsoblīj´) *v.t.*
(**-bliged, -blig·ing**). Refuse,
neglect, to act in accord with the
wishes of; (regional) inconvenience.
dis·o·blig´ing *adj.* **dis·o·blig´-**
ing·ly *adv.*

dis·or·der (dĭsōr´der) *n.* 1. Want
of order, confusion. 2. Tumult,
riot, commotion. 3. Ailment,
disease. ~ *v.t.* Disarrange, throw
into confusion; put out of health,
upset. **dis·or´der·ly** *adj.* 1.
Untidy, confused. 2. Irregular,
unruly, riotous; violating public
order or morality; ~ **house**,
brothel; place used illegally for
gambling. **dis·or´der·li·ness** *n.*

dis·or·gan·ize (dĭsōr´ganīz) *v.t.*
(**-ized, -iz·ing**). Destroy system
etc. of; throw into confusion.
dis·or·gan·i·za·tion (dĭsōrganĭ-
zā´shon) *n.*

dis·o·ri·ent (dĭsōr´ēent, -ōr´-),
dis·o·ri·en·tate (dĭsōr´ēentāt,
-ōr´-) *vbs.t.* (**-tat·ed, -tat·ing**).
Confuse (person) as to his or her
bearings (also fig.). **dis·o·ri·en·-**
ta·tion (dĭsōrēentā´shon, -ōr-) *n.*

dis·own (dĭsōn´) *v.t.* Refuse to
recognize, repudiate, disclaim;
renounce allegiance to.

*Many birds, like the peacock, **display**
their plumage in courtship or sometimes
as a gesture of aggression. Here a cock
fans his tail before the hen, strutting,
quivering and uttering loud screams.*

dis·par·age (dĭspăr´ĭj) *v.t.*
(**-aged, -ag·ing**). Bring discredit
on, lower; speak slightingly of,
depreciate. **dis·par´age·ment** *n.*
dis·par´ag·ing·ly *adv.*

dis·pa·rate (dĭs´perĭt, dĭspăr´-)
adj. Essentially different, diverse
in kind, incommensurable, without
relation. **dis´pa·rate·ly** *adv.* **dis´-**
pa·rate·ness *n.*

dis·par·i·ty (dĭspăr´ĭtē) *n.* (pl.
-ties). Inequality, difference,
incongruity.

dis·pas·sion·ate (dĭspăsh´onĭt)
adj. Free from emotion, calm,
impartial. **dis·pas´sion·ate·ly** *adv.*
dis·pas´sion·ate·ness, dis·-
pas´sion *ns.*

dis·patch, des·patch (dĭspăch´)
vbs. 1. Send off to destination or
for purpose. 2. Give death blow
to, kill. 3. Get (task, business)
promptly done; settle, finish off; eat
(food, meal) quickly. ~ *n.* 1.
Sending off. 2. Putting to death.

3. Prompt settlement of busine
promptitude, efficiency, rapidi
4. Written message; official co
munication, esp. military
diplomatic. 5. News story sent
newspaper by reporter or cor
spondent.

dis·pel (dĭspĕl´) *v.t.* (**-pell**
-pel·ling). Dissipate, disperse.

dis·pen·sa·ble (dĭspĕn´sab
adj. That which may be d
without, unimportant; that wh
can be dispensed or administere

dis·pen·sa·ry (dĭspĕn´serē)
(pl. **-ries**). 1. Place where son
thing (esp. medicine) is dispense
2. Public or charitable instituti
where medicines are dispensed a
medical advice is given.

dis·pen·sa·tion (dĭspensā´sho
-pĕn-) *n.* 1. Distributing, deali
out. 2. Ordering, management, e
the divine ordering of world
affairs; special dealing of Prov
dence with community or perso
(theol.) religious order or system
part of a progressive revelati
adapted to particular nation
age, as **Mosaic** ~. 3. Exempti
from penalty or duty laid down
ecclesiastical etc. law; granting

dis·please (dĭsplēz′) v.t. (**-pleased, -pleas·ing**). Offend, annoy, make indignant or angry; be disagreeable to; **be displeased** (*at, with*), disapprove, be indignant or dissatisfied. **dis·pleas′ing·ly** *adv.*

dis·pleas·ure (dĭsplĕzh′er) *n.* Displeased feeling, dissatisfaction, disapproval, anger.

dis·pos·a·ble (dĭspō′zabel) *adj.* That can be disposed of or dis-posed, (of article) designed to be thrown away after use.

dis·pos·al (dĭspō′zal) *n.* Dis-posing of, getting rid of; settling, dealing with; bestowal, assignment; sale; control, management (usu. **at one's** ~); placing, disposition, arrangement.

dis·pose (dĭspōz′) v. (**-posed, -pos·ing**). 1. Place suitably, in particular order, in proper posi-tions. 2. Bring (person, mind) into certain state; incline, make willing or desirous, *to;* give (thing) tendency *to.* 3. Determine course of events. 4. ~ **of,** do what one will with, regulate; get off one's hands, stow away, settle, finish, kill, demolish; sell.

dis·po·si·tion (dĭspozĭsh′on) *n.* 1. Setting in order, arrangement, relative position of parts. 2. Plan; stationing of troops for attack, defense, etc. 3. Ordinance, dis-pensation. 4. Bestowal by deed or will. 5. Control, disposal. 6. Temperament, natural tendency; inclination *to.*

dis·pos·sess (dĭspozĕs′) v.t. Oust, dislodge; deprive *of.* **dis·-pos·ses·sion** (dĭspozĕsh′on) *n.*

dis·proof (dĭsproof′) *n.* Refuta-tion, thing that disproves.

dis·pro·por·tion (dĭspropōr′-shon, -pōr′-) *n.* Want of propor-tion. **dis·pro·por′tion·ate** *adj.* Wanting proportion; relatively too large or too small. **dis·pro·por′-tion·ate·ly** *adv.*

dis·prove (dĭsproov′) v.t. (**-proved, -prov·ing**). Prove false, show fallacy of, refute.

dis·pu·ta·ble (dĭspū′tabel) *adj.* Open to question, uncertain. **dis·pu′ta·bly** *adv.*

dis·pu·tant (dĭspū′tant, dĭs′-pyu-) *adj. & n.* (Person) who disputes or engages in controversy.

dis·pu·ta·tion (dĭspyutā′shon) *n.* Debate, discussion; academic exercise in which parties formally sustain, attack, and defend a question or thesis. **dis·pu·ta′tious** *adj.* **dis·pu·ta′tious·ly** *adv.* **dis·pu·ta′tious·ness** *n.*

dis·pute (dĭspūt′) v. (**-put·ed, -put·ing**). Argue, hold disputa-tion; have altercation; controvert, call in question; contend for. ~

...ense by pope, archbishop, or ...shop, to a person to do what is ...rbidden by ecclesiastical law.

dis·pense (dĭspĕns′) v. (**...pensed, -pens·ing**). 1. Distrib-...e, deal out; administer (sacra-...ent, justice). 2. Make up (medi-...ne) according to prescription or ...rmula. 3. Grant dispensations; ...lease *from* obligation. 4. ~ **with,** ...lax, give exemption from (rule); ...nul binding force of (oath); ren-...r needless; do without. **dis·-...n′ser** *n.*

dis·perse (dĭspērs′) v. (**-persed, ...ers·ing**). Scatter; drive, go, ...row, send, in different directions; ...ut, dispel, be dispelled; send to, ...tion at, different points; put in ...culation, disseminate; (of gases ...liquids) diffuse; (optics) spread ...eam of light) so as to produce ...ectrum. **dis·per′sal** *n.* **dis·per′-...ve** *adj.* **dis·per·sion** (dĭspēr′-...on, -shon) *n.* (esp. chem.) ...spension of particles in a ...edium, as in homogenized milk, ...og, or emulsions; **The D** ~: see ...ASPORA.

dis·pir·it (dĭspĭr′ĭt) v.t. Make ...spondent, depress. **dis·pir′it-**

ed·ly *adv.*

dis·place (dĭsplās′) v.t. (**-placed, -plac·ing**). 1. Shift from proper position; remove from office. 2. Oust, take the place of; put something else in the place of; replace. 3. **displaced person,** one removed from his home country by military or political pressure; orig., civilian deported from a German-occupied country to work in Germany during World War II and thereafter homeless.

dis·place·ment (dĭsplās′ment) *n.* 1. Displacing, being displaced; amount by which thing is shifted from its place; ousting, replace-ment. 2. Amount or weight of fluid displaced by body floating or immersed in it.

dis·play (dĭsplā′) v.t. Exhibit, expose to view, show; show osten-tatiously; reveal, betray, allow to appear. ~ *n.* Displaying; exhibition, show; ostentation; specialized pattern of behavior by which birds communicate with each other; (print.) selection and arrangement of types to attract attention; (also ~ **type**) large, attention-attracting type.

n. Controversy, debate; heated contention, quarrel.

dis·qual·i·fy (dĭskwŏl´ĭfī) *v.t.* (**-fied, -fy·ing**). Make unfit, disable; declare unqualified or ineligible (esp. to hold place or prize won in contest). **dis·qual·i·fi·ca·tion** (dĭskwŏlĭfĭkā´shon) *n.* (esp.) Thing that disqualifies.

dis·qui·et (dĭskwī´ĭt) *v.t.* Deprive of peace, worry. **dis·qui·e·tude** (dĭskwī´ĭtood, -tūd) *n.* Anxiety, unrest.

dis·qui·si·tion (dĭskwĭzĭsh´on) *n.* Formal discourse, treatise, or dissertation.

Dis·rae·li (dĭzrā´lē), **Benjamin, 1st Earl of Beaconsfield** (1804–1881). British statesman, prime minister 1868 and 1874–80; author of *Coningsby* (1844) and other novels.

dis·re·gard (dĭsrĭgärd´) *v.t.* Pay no attention to; ignore; treat as of no importance. ~ *n.* Indifference, neglect.

dis·re·pair (dĭsrĭpār´) *n.* Bad condition for want of repairs.

dis·rep·u·ta·ble (dĭsrĕp´yutabel) *adj.* Discreditable; of bad repute, not respectable in character or appearance. **dis·rep·u·ta·ble·ness** *n.* **dis·rep·u·ta·bly** *adv.*

dis·re·pute (dĭsrĭpūt´) *n.* Disgrace, discredit.

dis·re·spect (dĭsrĭspĕkt´) *n.* Want of respect, rudeness. **dis·re·spect´ful** *adj.* **dis·re·spect´ful·ly** *adv.* **dis·re·spect´ful·ness** *n.*

dis·robe (dĭsrōb´) *v.* (**-robed, -rob·ing**). Divest of robe or garment; undress.

dis·rupt (dĭsrŭpt´) *v.t.* 1. Interrupt flow, continuity, procedure of. 2. Cause disorder in, throw into confusion. 3. Shatter, separate forcibly. **dis·rup´tion** *n.* **dis·rup´tive** *adj.* **dis·rup´tive·ly** *adv.*

dis·sat·is·fy (dĭssăt´ĭsfī) *v.t.* (**-fied, -fy·ing**). Fail to satisfy, make discontented. **dis·sat·is·fac·tion** (dĭssătĭsfăk´shon) *n.*

dis·sect (dĭsĕkt´, dī-) *v.t.* Cut up, esp., cut up (animal body, plant, etc.) to display position, structure, and relation of internal parts; analyze, examine or criticize minutely. **dis·sec´tion** *n.*

dis·sem·ble (dĭsĕm´bel) *v.* (**-bled, -bling**). Feign, pretend; disguise, conceal one's opinions, intentions, etc., under feigned guise. **dis·sem´bler** *n.*

dis·sem·i·nate (dĭsĕm´ināt) *v.t.* (**-nat·ed, -nat·ing**). Scatter abroad, sow in various places; (pass., of disease) dispersed or spread throughout organ, tissue, or whole body. **dis·sem·i·na·tion** (dĭsĕminā´shon), **dis·sem·i·na·tor** *ns.*

dis·sen·sion (dĭsĕn´shon) *n.* Discord arising from difference in opinion.

dis·sent (dĭsĕnt´) *v.i.* Refuse to assent; disagree; think differently, express different opinion (*from*); differ in religious opinion, differ from doctrine or worship of established church. ~ *n.* (Expression of) difference of opinion; refusal to accept doctrines of estab-

lished church; nonconformit **dis·sent´er** *n.* (esp.) Member dissenting church or sect. **dis· sen·tient** (dĭsĕn´shent) *adj.* & *n.*

dis·ser·ta·tion (dĭsertā´shon) Spoken or written discourse trea ing a subject at length, esp. sub stantial written treatise by unive sity doctoral candidate.

dis·serv·ice (dĭssēr´vĭs) Rendering of ill service or ill tur injury, detriment.

dis·sev·er (dĭsĕv´er) *v.* Seve divide.

dis·si·dence (dĭs´ĭdens) *n.* Dis agreement, dissent.

dis·si·dent (dĭs´ĭdent) *adj.* Dis agreeing, dissenting. ~ *n.* On who disagrees; dissenter.

dis·sim·i·lar (dĭsĭm´iler) *ad* Unlike (*to*). **dis·sim·i·lar·i·t** (dĭsĭmilăr´ĭtē) *n.* (pl. **-ties**). **dis· sim´i·lar·ly** *adv.*

dis·si·mil·i·tude (dĭssĭmĭl´ tood, -tūd) *n.* Unlikeness.

dis·sim·u·late (dĭsĭm´yulāt) *v.* (**-lat·ed, -lat·ing**). Dissembl (feelings etc.); be hypocritica **dis·sim·u·la·tion** (dĭsĭmyulā shon), **dis·sim´u·la·tor** *ns.*

dis·si·pate (dĭs´ipāt) *v.* (**-pat·ed -pat·ing**). Dispense, dispel (clou vapor, etc.); bring or come t nothing; squander, fritter awa (money, time, etc.). **dis´si·pat·e** *adj.* (esp.) Given to dissipation dissolute.

dis·si·pa·tion (dĭsipā´shon) 1. Dissipating; wasteful expendi ture *of.* 2. (Frivolous) amusemen 3. Dissolute indulgence in pleasur or vice; intemperance.

dis·so·ci·ate (dĭsō´sēāt, -shē *v.t.* (**-at·ed, -at·ing**). Disunite sunder, cut off from association o society; (chem.) decompose, esp. b at. **dis·so·ci·a·tion** (dĭsōsēā´-n, -shē-) *n.* (esp.) Disintegration personality or consciousness; th.) state of mind in which two more personalities exist in the ne person. **dis·so´ci·a·tive** *adj.*

lis·so·lute (dĭs´olōot) *adj.* Lax morals, licentious. **dis´so-te·ly** *adv.* **dis´so·lute·ness** *n.*

dis·so·lu·tion (dĭsolōo´shon) *n.* Disintegration, decomposition. Undoing or relaxation of any tie bond; formal dismissal of embly or legislature. 3. Death; ning, being brought, to an end; integration, disorganization.

dis·solve (dĭzŏlv´, -zawlv´) *v.* olved, -solv·ing). I. Liquefy; g.) lose composure (∼ in(to) ughter, tears); (phys., of liquid) x with (a solid, another liquid, a gas) without chemical action as to form a homogeneous liquid solution; (of substance) mix thus a liquid. 2. Bring to naught, stroy; become faint, melt *away*.

Disperse; bring (meeting, embly, legislature), come, to an d. 4. (motion pict., television) ange (picture) gradually by ling out one scene while next ene fades in over it. ∼ *n.* otion pict., television) Scene nsition made by dissolving.

dis·so·nant (dĭs´onant) *adj.* Dis-rdant, harsh toned, incongruous. s´so·nant·ly *adv.* **dis´so·nance**

dis·suade (dĭswād´) *v.t.* suad·ed, -suad·ing). Advise erson) against; divert *from* course persuasion or influence. **dis-ua·sion** (dĭswā´zhon) *n.* s·sua·sive (dĭswā´sĭv) *adj.* **dis-ua´sive·ly** *adv.*

dis·syl·la·ble = DISYLLABLE.
dist. *abbrev.* District; distance; stant.

dis·taff (dĭs´tăf, -tahf) *n.* I. left staff about 3 ft. long on which ool or flax was wound for spinning hand; corresponding part of nd-turned spinning wheel. 2. oman's work. 3. Female sex. ∼ de, female branch of family.

dis·tance (dĭs´tans) *n.* I. Being r off, remoteness; extent of space tween, interval. 2. Aloofness; eep one's ∼, avoid familiarity. 3. stant point; remote field of sion; distant part of landscape. 4. ing apart in time; extent of this terval. **distance** *v.t.* (-tanced, anc·ing). Place, make seem, far f; leave far behind in race or mpetition.

dis·tant (dĭs´tant) *adj.* I. Far vay; specified distance away *rom*); remote, far apart, in posi-on, time, resemblance, etc.; ∼ rly warning line, also DEW ne, radar system in N. Amer. for lvance detection of aircraft or issile attack. 2. Reserved, cool, t intimate. **dis´tant·ly** *adv.*

The most important industrial applications of **distillation** *concern petroleum and the production of alcohol and alcoholic 'spirits'. However, aromatic plants, such as lavender being distilled here, and other flowers and herbs are evaporated and condensed to produce perfumed essence. Distillation of the most simple kind occurs in a Liebig condenser.*

dis·taste (dĭstāst´) *n.* Dislike, repugnance, slight aversion (*for*). **dis·taste´ful** *adj.* Disagreeable, repellent (*to*). **dis·taste´ful·ly** *adv.* **dis·taste´ful·ness** *n.*

dis·tem·per (dĭstĕm´per) *n.* I. Derangement, ailment, of body or mind. 2. Disease of dogs characterized by vomiting, fever, cough, and loss of strength; any of various diseases of other animals.

dis·tend (dĭstĕnd´) *v.* Swell out by pressure from within. **dis·ten-si·ble** (dĭstĕn´sĭbel) *adj.* **dis·ten-sion, dis·ten·tion** (dĭstĕn´shon) *ns.*

dis·till (dĭstĭl´) *v.* I. Trickle down; issue, give forth, in drops, exude. 2. Vaporize substance by means of heat, and then condense the vapor by cooling it, so as to obtain the substance or part of it in concentrated or purified state; extract essence of, transform or convert, make or produce, drive *off*, by distillation; undergo distillation.

dis·til·la·tion (dĭstĭlā´shon) *n.* (esp.) Extraction of spirit or essence of any substance by first converting into vapor and then condensing the vapor; **destructive** ∼, decomposition of substance by strong heat in a retort, and collection of volatile matters evolved; **fractional** ∼, separation by distillation of two or more liquids having different boiling points, utilizing the fact that the first portion or fraction of the distillate has a higher proportion of the more volatile liquid than later

*The angle from which this photograph was taken has produced a **distortion** of both man and oars, so that they seem out of proportion. This gives the composition greater impact.*

fractions.

dis·till·er (dĭstĭl´er) n. (esp.) One who distills, esp. alcoholic liquors. **dis·till'er·y** n. (pl. **-er·ies**). Business, plant for distilling alcoholic liquors.

dis·tinct (dĭstĭngkt´) adj. 1. Not identical, separate, individual; different in quality or kind, unlike. 2. Clearly perceptible, plain, definite; unmistakable, decided, positive. 3. Unusual or notable. **dis·tinct'ly** adv. **dis·tinct'ness** n.

dis·tinc·tion (dĭstĭngk´shon) n. 1. Making of a difference; discrimination; difference made. 2. Being different. 3. Thing that differentiates; mark, name, title. 4. Showing of special consideration, mark of honor. 5. Distinguished character, excellence, eminence; individuality.

dis·tinc·tive (dĭstĭngk´tĭv) adj. Distinguishing, characteristic. **dis·tinc'tive·ly** adv. **dis·tinc'tive·ness** n.

dis·tin·gué (dĭstănggā´, dĭstăng´gā) adj. Having distinguished air, features, manners, etc.

dis·tin·guish (dĭstĭng´gwĭsh) v. 1. Class, classify. 2. Mark as different or distinct, differentiate, characterize. 3. Recognize as distinct or different; perceive difference, make or draw distinction, *between*. 4. Perceive distinctly, recognize. 5. Notice specially, honor with special attention; make prominent, remarkable, or eminent in some respect (usu. pass. or refl.). **dis·tin'guish·a·ble** adj.

dis·tin·guished (dĭstĭng´gwĭsht) adj. (esp.) Remarkable (*for, by*); eminent, famous, of high standing; **D~ Flying Cross**, (abbrev. D.F.C.) U.S. military decoration for distinguished heroism or achievement in aerial combat; **D~ Service Cross**, (abbrev. D.S.C.) U.S. Army decoration for exceptional heroism in combat; **D~ Service Medal**, (abbrev. D.S.M.) U.S. military decoration for distinguished performance in carrying out great responsibility.

dis·tort (dĭstôrt´) v.t. Put out of shape, make crooked or unshapely; misrepresent; give a false meaning to. **dis·tort'ed·ly** adv.

dis·tor·tion (dĭstôr´shon) n. Distorting, being distorted; faulty transmission or reproduction of sound.

dis·tract (dĭstrăkt´) v.t. Divert, draw away (mind, attention); draw in different directions, divide or confuse the attention of; bewilder, perplex; drive mad, infuriate. **dis·tract'ed·ly, dis·tract'ing·ly** advs.

dis·trac·tion (dĭstrăk´shon) n. 1. Diversion of mind or attention; something that distracts or diverts; amusement. 2. Lack of concentration. 3. Confusion, perplexity, dissension; frenzy, madness; **to ~**, to degree approaching madness.

dis·trait (dĭstrā´) adj. [fem. **dis·traite** (dĭstrāt´)] Worriedly inattentive, absent-minded, anxiously preoccupied.

dis·traught (dĭstrawt´) adj. Violently agitated; emotionally upset to point of derangement.

dis·tress (dĭstrĕs´) n. 1. Severe pressure or strain of pain, sorrow, etc., anguish, affliction; damage or danger to ship; exhausted or distressed condition; misfortune, calamity; **~ signal**, signal of ship in distress. 2. (law) Legal seizure

*The **District of Columbia** is the seat the U.S. national government and territory is the City of Washington. T Capitol building is seen here fr Pennsylvania Avenue.*

and detention of property agai payment of debt. **dis·tress'ful** a **dis·tress'ful·ly** adv. **distress** ı Subject to severe strain, exhau afflict; vex, make anxious unhappy. **dis·tress'ing** adj. **di tress'ing·ly** adv.

dis·trib·ute (dĭstrĭb´ūt) ı (**-ut·ed, -ut·ing**). 1. Deal out, g share of to each of a numb spread abroad, scatter, put different points; divide into par arrange, classify; (logic) use (ter in its full extension, so that includes every individual of t

ss. 2. Promote, sell, and ship
erchandise). **dis·trib'u·tor** *n.*
.) 1. Device distributing
ctric current in proper sequence
spark plugs. 2. Business firm or
son engaged in distribution.
dis·tri·bu·tion (dĭstrĭbū´shon)
1. Distributing, being distrib-
d. 2. (esp., econ.) Dispersal
ong consumers effected by
mmerce; extent to which indi-
luals or classes share in aggregate
oducts of community. 3. Way in
ich a particular character is
ead over members of a class,
ually represented graphically by a
curve. dis·tri·bu·tion·al *adj.*
dis·trib·u·tive (dĭstrĭb´yutĭv)
j. 1. Of, concerned with,
oduced by, distribution. 2.
gic, gram.) Referring to each
dividual of a class, not to the
ass collectively. ~ *n.* (gram.)
istributive word. **dis·trib'u·-**
ve·ly *adv.*

dis·trict (dĭs´trĭkt) *n.* Territory
arked off for special administra-
·e or judicial purpose; assigned
here of operations; tract of
untry with common characteris-
·s, region; ~ **attorney,** (abbrev.
.A.) public prosecutor of a
dicial district. **district** *v.t.*
ivide into districts.
Dis·trict (dĭs´trĭkt) **of Colum-**
ia. (abbrev. D.C.) Federal
istrict of the U.S., coextensive
ith the capital city of Washington.
dis·trust (dĭstrŭst´) *n.* Want of
ust; doubt, suspicion. ~ *v.t.*
ave no confidence in, doubt,
spect. **dis·trust'ful** *adj.* **dis-**
ust'ful·ly *adv.* **dis·trust'ful·-**
ess *n.*
dis·turb (dĭstûrb´) *v.t.* Agitate,
ouble, disquiet, unsettle; perplex.
dis·turb·ance (dĭstûr´bans) *n.*
terruption of tranquility, agita-
on; tumult, uproar, outbreak.
dis·turbed (dĭstûrbd´) *adj.* (esp.)
motionally or mentally unstable.
dis·sul·fide (dĭsŭl´fīd) *n.* Sulfide
ntaining two atoms of sulfur.
dis·un·ion (dĭsūn´yon) *n.*
eparation, want of union, dis-
ension. **dis·u·nite** (dĭsūnīt´) *v.t.*
·nit·ed, -nit·ing). **dis·u·ni·ty**
(dĭsū´nĭtē) *n.* (pl. **-ties**).
dis·use (dĭsūs´) *n.* State of not
eing used or of being no longer
use. **dis·used** (dĭsūzd´) *adj.*
di·syl·la·ble, dis·syl·la·ble (dĭ´-
label, dĭsĭl´-) *ns.* Word, metrical
ot, of two syllables. **di·syl·la·bic,**
is·syl·la·bic (dĭsĭlăb´ĭk, dĭsĭ-)
djs.
ditch (dĭch) *n.* Long narrow
xcavation, esp. to hold or conduct
vater or serve as boundary; water-
ourse. ~ *v.* Make or repair
itches; provide with ditches; run,
rive (vehicle) into ditch or off track
r road; (slang) bring (aircraft)
own into sea in emergency; (slang)
t rid of; leave in the lurch.

dith·er (dĭdh´er) *n.* State of
agitation or indecision. ~ *v.* Be
in a dither.
dith·y·ramb (dĭth´irăm, -rămb)
n. 1. (Gk. antiq.) Wild choric
hymn (orig. in honor of Dionysus)
from which Greek tragedy is
believed to have evolved. 2.
Vehement or inflated poem, speech,
or writing. **dith·y·ram·bic**
(dĭthirăm´bĭk) *adj.* & *n.*
dit·to (dĭt´ō) *n.* (pl. **-tos**).
(abbrev. do, symbol ″, known as
~ **mark**) The aforesaid, the same
thing (used in accounts and lists,
or colloq.); duplicate, similar thing.
ditto *v.t.* (**-toed, -to·ing**). Agree
with, endorse opinion of; make
copies. ~ *adv.* As before, likewise. [It. *ditto* (now *detto*) said,
aforesaid]
dit·ty (dĭt´ē) *n.* (pl. **-ties**). Short
simple song.
dit·ty (dĭt´ē) **bag, ditty box.**
Sailor's bag for holding odds and
ends; box for same purpose.
di·u·re·sis (dīyurē´sĭs) *n.* Passing of urine in large amounts.
di·u·ret·ic (dīyurĕt´ĭk) *adj.* & *n.*
(Substance) stimulating kidneys to
secrete urine.
di·ur·nal (dīûr´nal) *adj.* Occupying one day (chiefly of apparent
motion of heavenly bodies);

performed, happening, recurring,
every day; of the day as dist. from
the night; (zool.) active in daytime.
di·ur'nal·ly *adv.*
Div. *abbrev.* Divine; Divinity.
div. *abbrev.* Divided; dividend;
division; divisor; divorced.
di·va (dē´va) *n.* (pl. **-vas, -ve** pr.
-vě). Great woman singer; prima
donna.
di·va·lent (dīvā´lent) = BIVA-
LENT.
di·van (dĭvăn´, -vahn´, also for
def. 2 dī´văn) *n.* 1. (in Muslim
countries) Council chamber; seat
used by Sultan or administrator,
when holding audience. 2. Long
backless couch, usu. against wall of
room, and furnished with cushions.
[Pers. *dīwān* account book, court,
council, couch]
dive (dīv) *v.i.* (**dived, dove,**
div·ing). Plunge, esp. head foremost, into water etc.; go down or
out of sight suddenly, dart; plunge
hand *into* water, vessel, pocket;
plunge *into* subject; (of aircraft etc.)
descend steeply and fast; (of

*Political **disturbance** and demonstrations have become a familiar feature
of modern life in most countries of the
world. Here, Cambodian students
protest in 1970.*

The **diver** has an awkward gait on land but can slide below the water with barely a ripple. It is noted for its eerie cries during the breeding season.

Competition swimmers always begin their races by **diving** into the water (above) while high diving is an Olympic competition. Top: Skin-diving has become a popular pastime for amateurs who spear fish, and for professional and amateur photographers.

submarine) submerge; ~**-bomb** (*v.*) attack from aircraft with bombs released at end of steep dive; ~ **bomber**, aircraft performing in this manner; **div′ing bell**, open-bottomed bell-like vessel, supplied with air under pressure, in which person can be let down into deep water; **diving helmet**, headgear of diving suit; **diving suit**, air- and water-tight garment (esp. with lead-soled boots and glass-fronted helmet, and apparatus for pumping in air) in which person can go down into deep water and remain there for some time. **dive** *n.* 1. Diving; plunge, precipitate fall. 2. (slang) Disreputable or cheap night-club, bar, etc. 3. (slang) Deliberate attempt by boxer to lose by feigned knockout, esp. in **take a** ~.

div·er (dī′ver) *n.* (esp.) who dives for pearls, to exam and repair sunken vessels or recover valuable cargo.

di·verge (dīvērj′, dī-) (**-verged, -verg·ing**). Procee different directions from poin from each other; deviate; ca (lines, rays) to diverge; (math. a series, approach in its sum to indefinitely great amount whe large number of terms is tak **di·ver′gence** *n.* **di·ver′gent di·ver′gent·ly** *adv.*

di·vers (dī′verz) *adj.* (litera Sundry, several, various.

di·verse (dīvērs′, dī-, dī′ve *adj.* Unlike in nature or qualit varied, changeful. **di·verse′ly** *a* **di·verse′ness** *n.*

di·vers·i·fy (dīvēr′sīfī, dī-) (**-fied, -fy·ing**). Make dive vary, modify, variegate; ext (activity of a business) into vari fields; spread (investment) o several products or enterprises, e to guard against loss. **di·ver·si· ca·tion** (dīvērsīfīkā′shon, dī-) n.

di·ver·sion (dīvēr′zhon, -sh dī-) *n.* 1. Deflecting, deviation. Diverting of attention; maneuve secure this; feint. 3. Recreati pleasant distraction, pastime.

di·ver·si·ty (dīvēr′sītē, dī-) (pl. **-ties**). Being diverse, unli ness; different kind; variety.

di·vert (dīvērt′, dī) *v.t.* T aside from (proper) direction course; ward off; draw off atte tion of, distract; entertain, amu **di·vert′ing** *adj.* **di·vert′ing** *adv.*

di·ver·tic·u·li·tis (dīvertīky lī′tīs) *n.* Inflammation of DIVERTICULUM, esp. in the colon

di·ver·tic·u·lum (dīvertīk′ lum) *n.* (pl. **-la** pr. -la). (ana Blind tubular side branch of cav or passage.

di·ver·tisse·ment (dīvēr′t ment; *Fr.* dēvērtēsmahṅ′) *n.* (**-ments** pr. -ments; *Fr.* -mahṅ Short ballet; performance giv between acts or longer pieces.

di·vest (dīvĕst′, dī-) *v.t.* U clothe; strip *of* garment etc.; prive, rid, *of* (property). **di·ves ment, di·ves′ture** *ns.*

di·vide (dīvīd′) *v.* (**-vid -vid·ing**). 1. Separate into parts smaller groups, split, break u mark out actually or mentally ir parts; make classification in, d tinguish kinds of; sunder, part. Cause to disagree; set at varian 3. Distribute, deal out, (*among, tween*); share *with* others. 4. (mat Find how many times a number contained in another; (of number quantity) be contained exact nu ber of times in (another). ~ Ridge separating 2 watershe **Great D** ~, in the Rocky Mou tains, the divide of Continen

.; (fig.) dividing line, esp. be-
-en life and death.

div·i·dend (dĭv´ĭdĕnd) *n.* 1.
th.) Number to be divided by
ther (the *divisor*). 2. Share of
fits for stockholder, etc.; (col-
.) something extra, bonus.

di·vid·er (dĭvī´der) *n.* (esp., pl.,
pair of ~s) Compasses
ing a screw fastened to one leg
passing through the other, used
measuring small intervals, and
dividing straight lines etc. into
desired number of equal parts;
ple pair of compasses with steel
nts.

div·i·na·tion (dĭvĭnā´shon) *n.*
vining; insight into or discovery
unknown or future by super-
ural means; skillful forecast,
d guess.

di·vine¹ (dĭvīn´) *v.* (-vined,
n·ing). Make out by inspira-
n, magic, intuition, or guessing;
esee, predict, conjecture; prac-
e divination; **divining rod**,
wsing rod. **di·vin´er** *n.*

di·vine² (dĭvīn´) *adj.* 1. Of, from,
e, God or a god; ~ **right of**
gs, that claimed according to
ctrine that kings derive their
wer from God, unlimited by any
hts of their subjects. 2. De-
ted or addressed to God; sacred;
service, public worship of God.
Superhumanly excellent, gifted,
beautiful. **di·vine´ly** *adv.*

divine *n.* Person (usu. cleric)
skilled in divinity, theologian.

di·vin·i·ty (dĭvĭn´ĭtē) *n.* (-ties).
1. Being divine; deity; **D** ~, God;
godhead. 2. Object of adoration,
adorable being. 3. Theology.

di·vis·i·ble (dĭvĭz´ĭbel) *adj.*
Capable of being divided; (math.)
~ **by**, containing (a number) some
number of times without remain-
der. **di·vis·i·bil·i·ty** (dĭvĭzĭbĭl´ĭtē)
n.

di·vi·sion (dĭvĭzh´on) *n.* 1.
Dividing, being divided; severance,
separation; distribution, sharing;
~ **of labor**, division of work into
(types of) tasks, each performed by
particular person or group. 2.
Disagreement, discord. 3. (math.)
Process of dividing number by
another; **long** ~, method in which
each stage of the process is written
down (adopted esp. when divisor is
greater than 12), opp **short** ~ in
which the quotient is set down
directly. 4. Dividing line, boundary. 5. Part, section; administrative, judicial, political, or other,
division of country, territory, district, etc. 6. Definite part, under
single command, of army, fleet, or
air force; unit of an army intended
to be capable of independent
operations, varying in size and
composition, but usually consisting
of three infantry regiments and an
artillery regiment, as well as various

supporting units; (also) specialized
arm of military force, as **armored**
~. 7. (bot.) Major classificatory
grouping = PHYLUM; (zool.) subsidiary category between major
groups, e.g. between phylum and
class. **di·vi´sion·al** *adj.*

di·vi·sor (dĭvī´zer) *n.* Number
by which another (the *dividend*) is
to be divided; number that divides
another without remainder, factor.

di·vorce (dĭvōrs´, -vōrs´) *n.*
Legal dissolution of marriage; (fig.)
complete separation, disunion of
things closely connected. ~ *v.t.*
(-vorced, -vorc·ing). Legally dissolve marriage between; separate
by, obtain divorce *from* (spouse);
put away, repudiate; dissolve
(union); sever. **di·vor·cé** (dĭvōrsā´,
-vōr-, -vōr´sā, -vōr´-) *n.* (fem.
di·vor·cee, di·vor·cée pr. dĭvōrsē´,
-sā´, -vōr-, -vōr´sē, -sā, -vōr´-)
Divorced person. **di·vorce´ment**
n.

div·ot (dĭv´ot) *n.* (golf) Piece of
turf cut out by player's club when
striking the ball.

di·vulge (dĭvŭlj´) *v.t.* (-vulged,
-vulg·ing). Let out, reveal.
di·vulge´ment, di·vul´gence *ns.*

*The **Great Divide** in North America is
the continuous range of mountains that
divides the continent's principal drainage into eastward and westward flowing
patterns.*

Dix·ie (dĭk′sē). 1. Southern U.S., the South; **Dix′iecrat** (*n.*) Member of dissenting group of southern Democratic politicians during 1940s who opposed racial integration and formed States' Rights Party in 1948; **Dix′ieland** (*n.*), style of instrumental jazz with strong 2-beat rhythm and group and solo improvisation. 2. (**"Dixie"**) Popular marching song (prob. composed by Dan Emmett, 1859) sung by Confederate soldiers in the Amer. Civil War. [origin doubtful; perh. f. *dixie* (Fr. *dix* ten), a 10-dollar note issued in Louisiana before the Civil War]

diz·zy (dĭz′ē) *adj.* (**-zi·er, -zi·est**). Giddy, dazed, unsteady, tottering, confused; making giddy; whirling rapidly. **diz′zi·ly** *adv.* **diz′zi·ness** *n.* **dizzy** *v.t.* (**-zied, -zy·ing**). Make dizzy, bewilder.

D.J., DJ *abbrevs.* Disc jockey.

Dja·kar·ta (jakär′ta). City and seaport of NW. Java, capital of Indonesia.

Dji·bou·ti (jĭboo′tē). Republic in NE. Africa on Gulf of Aden, formerly French territory of Afars and Issas; capital and port city of this republic.

djin, djinn: see JINN.

dkg *abbrev.* Decagram(s).

dkl *abbrev.* Decaliter(s).

dkm *abbrev.* Decameter(s).

dl *abbrev.* Deciliter(s).

D.Lit. *abbrev.* Doctor of Literature.

D.Litt. *abbrev.* Doctor of Letters.

DM, Dm *abbrevs.* Deutsche mark.

dm *abbrev.* Decimeter(s).

DNA *abbrev.* Deoxyribonucleic or desoxyribonucleic acid, any of the class of nucleic acids present in the chromosomes of higher organisms and storing genetic information.

D.N.B. *abbrev.* (Brit.) Dictionary of National Biography.

do (doo) *v.* (**did, done, do·ing**). 1. (*v.t.*) Perform, effect, execute; complete; produce, make; operate on, deal with; put forth, exert; (colloq.) provide (food etc.) for; tour, visit as a tourist; swindle. 2. (*v.i.*) Act, proceed; perform deeds; fare, get on; be suitable, suffice. 3. Used as auxiliary verb esp. in questions, as *do you know?*, negative or emphatic statements, as *I did not know*; *I do know*, and urgent requests, as *do come!* 4. Used as substitute for verb just used, to avoid repetition, as *I wanted to see him, and I did* (i.e. saw him). 5. With noun of action as object; = cognate verb of action; e.g. **do re·pairs**, repair things; **do battle**, fight. 6. **done!**, I accept (offer, bet, etc.); **have to do with**, be concerned or connected with, have

The **dock** is a common weed or pasture plant of the family that includes the common sorrel and the sheep's sorrel; both have a characteristic acidic taste. It has large leaves and is wind-pollinated.

Floating docks are used to repair larg ships where there are no suitable d docks. They are submerged when th ship docks and are raised as the wate is pumped out.

dealings with; **it isn't done**, it is forbidden by custom or propriety; **nothing** etc. **doing**, nothing etc. happening or going on; (colloq.) announcement of refusal, failure, etc.; **do away (with)**, abolish; **do by**, treat, deal with, in specified way; **do for**, (colloq.) do house-cleaning for; ruin, destroy; exhaust; **do in**, (slang) kill; exhaust; **do or die**, be undeterred by danger; **do time, do** (10 etc.) **years**, undergo imprisonment; **do to, unto**, do by; **do up**, restore, repair; wrap up (package); **do with**, find sufficient; (colloq.) be pleased to have, need; **do without**, dispense with. 7. **do-gooder**, (usu. derog.) well-meaning but unrealistic social reformer etc.; **do-it-yourselfer**, amateur craftsman or home handyman etc. **do** *n.* (slang) Party, entertainment; **dos and don'ts**, rules. **do′a·ble** *adj.* **do′er** *n.*

do *abbrev.* Ditto.

D.O. *abbrev.* Doctor of Optometry; Doctor of Osteopathy.

D.O.A. *abbrev.* Dead on arriva

dob·bin (dŏb′ĭn) *n.* Draft farm horse. [pet form of *Robert*]

Do·ber·man pin·scher (dc berman pĭn′sher). German houn with smooth, short, usu. black coa [*Dobermann*, name of breeder; Ge *pinscher* terrier]

doc (dŏk) *n.* (slang) 1. Docto 2. Word of address to person who name is unknown to speaker.

do·cent (dō′sent) *n.* Universi lecturer not a regular faculty men ber; lecturer or guide in a museun

do·cile (dŏs′ĭl) *adj.* Teachabl submissive; easily managed. **do cil·i·ty** (dŏsĭl′ĭtē, dō-) *n.*

dock[1] (dŏk) *n.* Species of *Rume* coarse weedy herbs with clusters inconspicuous greenish flower and large leaves.

Djakarta, the largest city and capital Indonesia, lies at the mouth of the Chiliwong River and has a population nearly 4 million. One of its mo impressive structures is this freedo statue.

The first London docks were built early in the 19th century to relieve congestion at the port of London. They were dug out of the marshes of the Isle of Dogs.

dock² (dŏk) *n.* Solid fleshy part of animal's tail. ~ *v.t.* Cut short (animal's tail, person's hair, etc.); withhold part of (the wages) of (an employee).

dock³ (dŏk) *n.* 1. Pier, wharf; platform for loading or unloading ships, trucks, etc.; usu. artificial enclosure for ships with means for regulating depth of water; **dry** ~, dock from which water can be pumped out, leaving vessel dry for repairs; **floating dry** ~, floating structure usable as dry dock. 2. (pl.) Range of docks with wharves, warehouses, offices, etc.; dockyard. 3. **dock'yard**, enclosure for building and repairing ships, preparing and collecting ships' stores, etc. **dock** *v.* 1. Bring (ship), come, into dock. 2. Join (spacecraft) to another, become joined, in space.

dock⁴ (dŏk) *n.* Enclosure in criminal court where defendant stands or sits.

dock·et (dŏk´ĭt) *n.* 1. Abstract, summary (hist.). 2. (law) Memorandum or register of legal judgments; list of cases for trial or of persons with cases pending. 3. Label, ticket affixed to package listing contents, directions, etc. ~ *v.t.* (**-et·ed, -et·ing**). Make abstract of and enter in docket; enter (case) in docket.

doc·tor (dŏk´ter) *n.* 1. (archaic) Teacher, eminently learned man. 2. (used as prefix to name, usu. abbrev. Dr.) Holder of highest academic degree awarded by college or university in any discipline; esp., doctor of medicine; (pop.) any medical practitioner. 3. Any of various mechanical appliances for removing defects, regulating, adjusting, etc. **doc'tor·al** *adj.* **doctor** *v.t.* Give, receive medical treatment; adulterate, falsify.

doc·tor·ate (dŏk´terĭt) *n.* Doctor's degree.

doc·tri·naire (dŏktrĭnār´) *n.* One who holds some doctrine or theory and tries to apply it without allowing for circumstances; pedantic theorist. ~ *adj.* Of, like, a doctrinaire; theoretical, impractical. **doc'tri·nair'ism** *n.* [*Doctrinaire,* name of a Fr. political party, 1815]

doc·trine (dŏk´trĭn) *n.* What is taught, body of instruction; religious, political, scientific, etc., belief, dogma, or tenet; **Monroe D** ~: see MONROE.

Dry docks are essential for repairing areas below the waterline of boats and ships. This huge cargo ship has recently had its rudder and stern painted.

doc·u·ment (dŏk′yum*ent*) *n.* something written, inscribed, etc., that furnishes evidence or information on any subject, as manuscript, ...ed to property, etc. ~ *v.t.* ...ove or support by documentary ...idence; furnish or provide with ...cuments or evidence. **doc·u·en·ta·tion** (dŏky*u*mĕntā′sh*on*) *n.*

doc·u·men·ta·ry (dŏky*u*mĕn′-...ē) *adj.* Of documents; (of film) ...aling with real happenings or ...rcumstances, not fiction. ~ *n.* ...l. **-ries**). Documentary film.

dod·der[1] (dŏd′*er*) *n.* Slender ...afless parasitic vine of genus ...uscuta with twining threadlike ...ems.

dod·der[2] (dŏd′*er*) *v.i.* Tremble, ...ake, with frailty. **dod′der·er** *n.* **...od′der·ing** *adj.* Mentally feeble ...inept, futile.

dodeca- *prefix.* Twelve-.

do·dec·a·gon (dōdĕk′*a*gŏn) *n.* ...ane figure of 12 angles and sides.

do·dec·a·he·dron (dōdĕkahē′-...*on*) *n.* (pl. **-drons, -dra** pr. -dr*a*). ...olid figure of 12 faces.

Do·dec·a·nese (dōdĕkanēs′, ...ēz′, dōd*e*-). Group of 12 Greek ...lands in SE. Aegean between ...urkey and Crete.

do·dec·a·syl·la·ble (dōdĕkasĭl′-

The **flying doctor** service is used in the sparsely populated areas of the Australian outback for bringing medical aid to outlying farms. Most homesteads are in radio contact with the service's headquarters.

Howard Chandler Christy's 'Signing of Constitution' shows the importance, practical and symbolic, that is attached to **documents.** Most documents receive less ceremony, but to individuals they can be very important.

abel) n. (pros.) Line of 12 syllables.

dodge (dŏj) v. (**dodged, dodg·-ing**). Move to and fro, change position, shuffle; move quickly *around, about, behind,* obstacle so as to elude pursuer, blow, etc.; avoid, elude, by change of position, shifts, etc. ~ **n.** Dodging, quick side movement; trick, artifice; (colloq.). clever expedient, contrivance, etc. **dodg′er** n.

Dodg·son (dŏj′son), **Charles Lutwidge:** see CARROLL.

do·do (dō′dō) n. (pl. **-dos, -does**). 1. Extinct bird (*Raphus cucullatus*) with massive clumsy body and wings too small for flight, formerly inhabiting Mauritius. 2. Hopelessly old-fashioned person; dullard. [Port. *doudo* simpleton]

DOE abbrev. Department of Energy.

doe (dō) n. (pl. **does**, collect. **doe**). Female of deer; female of certain other animals, as hare, kangaroo, etc.; **doe′skin**, skin of doe, kind of leather made from this.

does (dŭz) v. Third pers. sing. pres. tense of DO. **does′n't**, contraction of *does not.*

doff (dŏf, dawf) v.t. Take off (hat, clothing); lift, tip (hat) in salutation.

dog (dawg, dŏg) n. 1. Carnivorous quadruped of the genus *Canis*, found wild in various parts of the world, and domesticated or semidomesticated in almost all countries, in numerous races or

Dogs have been used since the Neolithic period, in hunting and tracking, as herders of sheep and cattle, as guards, guides and domestic pets and companions. Dogs have been used as pack animals and are here being trained in the Antarctic to carry loaded sleds. In Crufts famous dog show, held in London, U.K., a whippet wins an important prize in 1973.

Points

1	muzzle
2	forehead
3	occiput
4	withers
5	saddle
6	loins
7	croup
8	stern
9	hock
10	pastern
11	stifle
12	knee
13	brisket

Skeleton

Internal organs

14	skull
15	scapula
16	ribs
17	vertebral column
18	pelvis
19	femur
20	fibula
21	tibia
22	metatarsus
23	ulna
24	radius
25	humerus
26	brain
27	oesophagus
28	liver
29	stomach
30	spleen
31	kidney
32	intestine
33	rectum
34	testicles
35	heart
36	lungs
37	trachea

*The **dodo** was exterminated by man in the 17th century. Its large clumsy body and friendly disposition were thought to denote stupidity and it was easily captured and killed.*

...reeds varying greatly in shape, ...ze, and color. 2. Male of this ...imal, or of fox or wolf. 3. (slang) ...nattractive woman; (also **gay ~**) ...ay or jovial fellow; **dirty ~**, ...lang) despicable person. 4. Any ...f various mechanical devices, usu. ...aving a tooth or claw for gripping ...r holding. 5. Firedog, andiron. 6. ...ie like a ~, die miserably or ...hamefully; **~ in the manger**, one ...ho prevents others from enjoying ...hat is useless to him or her; **a ...~'s life**, a life of misery, or of ...iserable subserviency; **a hair of ...he ~ that bit you**, more drink ...o take off effects of drunkenness; ...o the ~s, to destruction or ruin. ...; **dog′bane**, any plant of family ...pocynaceae, with milky juice and ...bitter root; **dog biscuit**, hard ...iscuit for feeding dogs; **dog′cart**, ...wo-wheeled cart drawn by a horse ...nd having two transverse seats ...ack to back (the rear one orig. ...made to shut so as to form a box for ...ogs); small cart drawn by dog; **...og′catcher**, person appointed to ...ound up stray dogs or cats for the ...municipal pound; **dog collar**, col...ar for dog's neck; (slang) clergy...man's stiff white collar fastening at ...ack of neck; straight high close...itting collar, esp. jeweled one; **dog ...days**, period during part of July ...nd August about time when Sirius, ...the dog star, rises and sets with the ...sun; considered from ancient times ...he hottest and most unwholesome ...period of the year; **dog-eared**, (of

book) having leaves turned down at corner, or crumpled; **dog′fight**, fight between dogs; general melee; melee between aircraft; **dog′fish**, any of several small sharks, esp. genus *Mustelus* or *Squalus*, found in Atlantic and Pacific waters; **dog′house**, dog's kennel; **in the doghouse**, (slang) in disgrace; **dog′leg**, something bent or angled like a dog's hind leg; **dog paddle**, swimming stroke like dog's, with all four limbs submerged and paddling alternately; **Dog Star**, Sirius; **dog tag**, metal identification disk for dog or (esp. military) person; **dog-tired**, tired out, extremely tired; **dog′tooth**, canine tooth; **dog′-tooth violet**, N. Amer. spring-flowering plant of genus *Erythronium*, esp. *E. americanum*, with yellow flowers with reddish spots; also called *adder's tongue* and *trout lily*; **dog′trot**, easy steady trot like a dog's; **dog′watch**, (naut.) each of the two short watches between 4 and 8 p.m. (of two, instead of four, hours each); **dog′wood**, (also **flowering dogwood**) eastern N. Amer. tree (*Cornus florida*) with very small greenish flowers surrounded by large white (occas. pink) bracts, and with bright red berries and colorful leaves in autumn; any of several other trees and shrubs of genus *Cornus*; **dog′-gish, dog′like** *adjs*. **dog** *v.t.* (**dogged, dog′ging**). Follow closely, pursue, track; (mech.) grip with dog; **~ it**, (slang) pretend to work, slight duty.

doge (dōj) *n*. (hist.) Chief magistrate of republics of Venice

*The **dog-tooth violet** is not, in fact, a violet but belongs to the lily family. It grows in temperate regions of the northern hemisphere and has lily-like flowers on long stems.*

*Flowering **dogwood** (Cornus florida), a North American species, is widely grown as an ornamental for its showy bracts (modified leaves) under the tiny flowers.*

and Genoa.

dog·ged (daw′gĭd, dŏg′ĭd) *adj*. Obstinate, tenacious, persistent, unyielding. **dog′ged·ly** *adv*. **dog′-ged·ness** *n*.

dog·ger·el (daw′gerel, dŏg′er-) *adj. & n*. Trivial or irregular (verse).

dog·gone (dawg′gŏn′, dŏg′-) *adj., adv., v.t. & int*. Mild expletive; pesky, annoying. [euphemism for Goddamn]

dog·gy, dog·gie (daw′gē, dŏg′-) *ns*. (pl. **-gies**). (nursery) Dog; **~ bag**, (colloq.) small bag offered by restaurant for taking home uneaten food. **dog′gy** *adj*. (**-gi·er, -gi·est**). Of dogs; devoted to dogs.

do·gie, do·gy (dō′gē) *ns*. (Western U.S.) Stray or motherless calf.

dog·ma (dawg′ma, dŏg′-) *n*. (pl. **-mas, -ma·ta** pr. -mata). Principle, tenet, doctrinal system, esp. as laid down by authority of church; principle, belief, statement of ideas considered as absolute truth.

dog·mat·ic (dawgmăt′ĭk, dŏg-), **dog·mat·i·cal** (dawgmăt′ĭkal, (dŏg-) *adjs*. 1. Of, based on, dogmas; **~ theology**: see THEOLOGY. 2. Asserting dogmas or opinions, esp. arrogantly. **dog·mat′i·cal·ly** *adv*. **dog·mat′ics** *n. pl*. (usu. considered sing.). Study of arrangement and statement of religious doctrines.

dog·ma·tize (dawg′matīz, dŏg′-) *v*. (**-tized, -tiz·ing**). Make positive unsupported assertions, speak authoritatively; express (principle etc.) as a dogma. **dog′-ma·tism, dog′ma·tist** *ns*.

Do·ha (dō′ha). Capital of Qatar on Persian Gulf.

doi·ly (doi′lē) *n.* (pl. **-lies**). 1. (archaic) Small napkin used at dessert. 2. Small decorative mat of lace etc. to protect or adorn furniture. [fabric named f. 17th-c. inventor]

do·ing (dōo̅′ĭng) *n.* Action, responsibility, conduct; (pl.) events, activities.

do-it-your·self (dōo̅′ĭtyersĕlf′) *adj.* Intended to be built or operated by a person without professional experience.

dol. *abbrev.* Dollar(s)

dol·ce (dōl′chā) *adv.* (mus.) Sweetly, softly. [It.]

dol·drums (dōl′drumz, -dŏl′) *n. pl.* 1. Dullness, dumps, depression; **in the ~**, (of ship) becalmed. 2. Region near equator where meeting of trade winds produces light baffling winds, sudden storms, and calms. [prob. f. *dull*, the geog. sense being prob. due to misunderstanding of phrase **in the ~**]

The **doll** *may be the oldest toy in the world. In Ancient Greek and Roman periods dolls were made of wood, ivory and burnt clay. By the end of the 18th century wax and porcelain dolls became popular and were often magnificently dressed in the fashions of the day. Today dolls are made in a variety of materials, including cloth, plastics, and rubber.*

dole (dōl) *n.* 1. (archaic) Lot, destiny. 2. Charitable distribution; charitable gift; portion sparingly dealt out; (chiefly Brit. colloq.) unemployment benefit; **on the ~**, receiving this. **dole** *v.t.* (**doled, dol·ing**). Deal *out* sparingly.

dole·ful (dōl′fŭl) *adj.* Dreary, dismal; sad, discontented, melancholy. **dole′ful·ly** *adv.* **dole′ful·ness** *n.*

dol·i·cho·ce·phal·ic (dŏlıkōse-făl′ĭk) *adj.* Long-headed; with breadth of skull less than ⅘ of length.

doll (dŏl) *n.* Small model of human figure, esp. as toy; pretty child; (slang) pretty but vacuous woman; (slang) very attractive person; **~** *v.* **~ up**, dress finely. [shortened pet form of *Dorothy*]

dol·lar (dŏl′er) *n.* 1. (orig.) Name for the German thaler and also for the Spanish piece of eight

(peso) current in Spanish Ameri and used in British N. Ame colonies. 2. Principal moneta unit (symbol $) of U.S., Canac Australia, and other countrie equals 100 cents. [orig. *daler*, *Joachimstaler*, coin from silver mi in Joachimstal, Bohemia (Ger. *t* valley); symbol $ a modification P^s, Mex. abbreviation for pesos piastres]

dol·lop (dŏl′op) *n.* (colloc Large clumsy or shapeless lum serving, or portion.

dol·ly (dŏl′ē) *n.* (pl. **-lies**). (Pet name for) doll. 2. Mobi platform on casters or wheels f moving heavy loads, a motio picture or television camera abo a set, etc.

Dol·ly Var·den (dŏl′ē vär′den Trout (*Salvelinus malma*) of north western N. Amer.; (also **~ ha** woman's large hat with brim loop

at one side, trimmed with
wers etc. [name of character in
ckens's *Barnaby Rudge*]

dol·man (dŏl'man, dawl'-, dŏl'-)
(pl. **-mans**). 1. Long Turkish
be open in front. 2. Hussar's
iform, elaborately decorated
pelike jacket. 3. Woman's cloak
coat with capelike sleeves; ~
eeve, loose sleeve like that of
lman, cut in one piece with body
garment.

dol·men (dŏl'men, dawl'-, dŏl'-)
Megalithic burial chamber, large
t stone laid horizontally upon up-
ght ones. [Fr., prob. f. Cornish
mên, lit. "hole of stone"]

do·lo·mite (dō'lomīt, dŏl'o) *n.*
(chem.) Double carbonate of
lcium and magnesium occurring
crystal or in white or colored
anular masses; rock of this. 2.
olomite mountain, esp. (**Dolo-
ites**) those of the southern Tyrol.
Dieudonné Gratet de *Dolomieu*
750–1801), French mineralogist]

do·lor·ous (dō'lorus, dŏl'-) *adj.*
su. poet.) Distressing, painful;
oleful; distressed. **do'lor·ous·ly**
dv.

dol·phin (dŏl'fĭn, dawl'-) *n.* 1.
Cetaceous mammal of many
pecies all of family Delphinidae,
he best-known of which are the
ommon dolphin (*Delphinus del-
his*), resembling a porpoise but
ith longer and more slender snout,
nd the bottlenosed dolphin (*Tur-
iops truncatus*). 2. Either of two
ridescent fishes of the genus *Cory-
haena*, found in tropical waters.

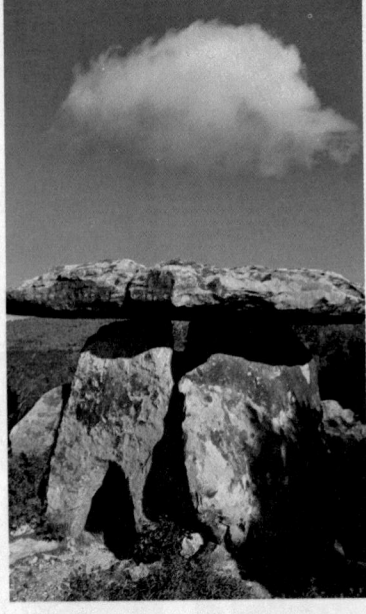

*Dolmens, megalithic tombs found in
Europe, were built chiefly in the Neolithic and Chalcolithic periods. This one
is at Grandmont, near Lodève in
Hérault, France.*

dolt (dōlt) *n.* Stupid person.
dolt'ish *adj.*   **dolt'ish·ly** *adv.*
dolt'ish·ness *n.*

Dom. *abbrev.* Dominican.

dom. *abbrev.* Dominion; domestic.

-dom *suffix.* Forming nouns,
denoting rank, condition, domain,
as *earldom, freedom, kingdom* or
collective nouns as *officialdom.*

do·main (dōmān') *n.* 1. Estate,
lands, dominions; district under
rule; realm, sphere of influence;
scope, field, province, of thought or
action; **eminent** ~, government's
power of controlling or confiscating
private property for public use,
subject to compensation. 2. (phys.,
in ferromagnetic materials) Aggregation of atoms or ions that
behaves as an elementary magnet,
all the ions in a domain having the
axes of their permanent magnetic
moment aligned in the same direction.

dome (dōm) *n.* 1. (poet.)
Stately building, mansion. 2.
Rounded vault forming roof, with
circular, elliptical, or polygonal
base; natural vault, canopy (of trees,
sky, etc.); rounded summit of hill
etc.; (slang) the head. ~ *v.t.*
(**domed, dom·ing**). Cover with,
shape as, dome. **domed** *adj.*
Vaulted, domelike; having a dome
or domes. [Fr., f. It. *duomo* cathedral, dome, f. L. *domus* house]

Domes·day (dōomz'dā, dōmz'-)
Book. Written record of census
and survey of lands of England,
their extent, value, ownership, etc.,
made by order of William the Conqueror in 1086. [pop. name
(= Doomsday) given to the book as
final authority]

*The many varieties of **dolphin** are found
in tropical and temperate seas. They
have a reputation for intelligence and
are gregarious mammals that move
about in schools.*

The **dome** spans a large open area within a building, uncluttered by roof supports. The Romans established its popularity as an architectural feature and it was their example that influenced architects from the Renaissance onwards. Top left: The dome of St. Peter's, Rome, designed by Michelangelo. Top right: Part of the interior of the dome at St. Peter's.

do·mes·tic (dɔmĕs′tĭk) *adj.* 1. Of the home, household, or family affairs; of one's own country, not foreign; native, homemade; ~ **science**, study of household management. 2. (of animals) Tame, kept by or living with people. 3. Housekeeping; fond of home, domesticated. **domestic** *n.* Household servant. **do·mes′ti·cal·ly** *adv.*

do·mes·ti·cate (dɔmĕs′tĭkāt) *v.t.* (**-cat·ed, -cat·ing**). Naturalize; attach to home and its duties (esp. in the past part.); tame and bring under control (animals), accustom to live near people; civilize. **do·mes′ti·ca·ble** *adj.* **do·mes·ti·ca-** tion (dɔmĕstĭkā′shɔn) *n.*

do·mes·tic·i·ty (dōmĕstĭs′ĭtē) *n.* (pl. **-ties**). Domestic character; home life or devotion to it; (pl.) domestic affairs.

dom·i·cile (dŏm′ĭsĭl, dō′mĭ-) *n.* Residence; home; (law) place of permanent or legal residence. ~ *v.* (**-ciled, -cil·ing**). Establish, settle, in a place.

dom·i·nant (dŏm′inant) *adj.* 1. Ruling, prevailing, most influential; occupying commanding position. 2. (mus.) Of the dominant; (of chord) having dominant for its root. 3. (biol., of inherited character) That is apparent in offspring when an opposite character is also inherited (opp. RECESSIVE). ~ *n.* Dominant thing or constituen (esp., mus.) 5th note of ascendin scale; reciting note in ecclesiastica modes, usu. 5th from final; (biol. dominant character. **dom′i·nance dom′i·nan·cy** *ns.* **dom′i·nant·l** *adv.*

dom·i·nate (dŏm′ināt) *v* (**-nat·ed, -nat·ing**). Have com manding influence over; be th most influential or conspicuous; (o height) overlook; occupy com manding position. **dom·i·na·tio** (dŏminā′shon) *n.* 1. Ascendancy sway, control. 2. (pl.) Fourth orde of angels (see ANGEL). **dom′i·na tor** *n.*

dom·i·neer (dŏminēr′) *v.i.* Ac imperiously, tyrannize (*over*), be overbearing. **dom·i·neer′ing** *adj* **dom·i·neer′ing·ly** *adv.*

Dom·i·nic (dŏm′inĭk), **St.** Domingo de Guzman (1170–1221),

anish-born priest active in
ance; founder (in 1215) of an
der of preaching friars (Domini-
as).

Dom·i·ni·ca (domĭn′ika, dŏmĭ-
′-). Island in the West Indies,
merly in British possession,
ember of the West Indies As-
ciated States; capital, Roseau.

Do·min·i·can[1] (domĭn′ĭkan) *adj.*
St. Dominic or the order of
ars founded by him. ~ *n.*
ominican friar, black friar.

Do·min·i·can[2] (domĭn′ĭkan) *n.*
adj. (Native, inhabitant) of the
ominican Republic.

Do·min·i·can[3] (domĭn′ĭkan)
epublic. Republic (since 1844)
cupying the E. two-thirds of the
. Indian island of Hispaniola,
rmerly part of the Spanish
mpire; capital, Santo Domingo.

do·min·ion (domĭn′yon) *n.* 1.

*The **Dominican Republic**, an indepen-*
ent state in the West Indies, has a
opulation of over 4 million. Below (bot-
om): Its capital, Santo Domingo, has
ry winters, wet summers and frequent
arthquakes.

Rule, sovereignty, control; (law)
right of possession, ownership. 2.
Domains of feudal lord; territory
of sovereign or government. 3.
D ~, former title of any of the self-
governing nations within the
British Commonwealth.

dom·i·no (dŏm′inō) *n.* (pl.
-noes, nos). 1. Loose hooded
cloak, app. of Venetian origin, worn
at masquerades with small mask
over upper part of face; person
wearing this. 2. One of a number
(usu. 28) of rectangular pieces of
ivory, wood, etc., usu. black, and
with upper side equally divided into
two squares, each either blank or
marked with pips, so as to present
all possible combinations from
double blank to double 6; (pl.) game
played with these (usu.) by placing
corresponding ends in contact; ~
theory, theory that political event
etc. in one place will cause similar
events in others, like row of falling
dominoes.

don[1] (dŏn) *n.* 1. Spanish title
prefixed to Christian names;
Spanish gentleman, Spaniard; distinguished person. 2. (Brit. colloq.)

Head, fellow, or tutor of college,
esp. at Oxford or Cambridge.
[Span., f. L. *dominus* lord]

don[2] (dŏn) *v.t.* (**donned, don**-
ning). Put on (garment).

Do·na·tel·lo (dŏnatĕl′ō) (1386–
1466). Italian sculptor, famous esp.
for his bronze *David* in Florence.

do·na·tion (dōnā′shon) *n.* Bestowal, presenting; thing presented,
gift (esp. money given to institution). **do·nate** (dō′nāt, dōnāt′) *v.t.*
(**-nat·ed, -nat·ing**). Make donation of; give, grant. **do′na·tor** *n.*

done (dŭn) *v.* Past part. of DO;
~ **for**, doomed, ruined, exhausted,
dying; ~ **in**, very tired.

do·nee (dōnē′) *n.* Recipient of
gift.

dong (dŏng) *n.* (pl. **dong**). Principal monetary unit of Vietnam.

Don·i·zet·ti (dŏnĭzĕt′ē), **Gae-
tano** (1797–1848). Italian composer of operas.

Don Ju·an (dŏn wahn′; *Brit.* dŏn
jōō′an). Legendary Spanish nobleman of dissolute life; hence, rake,
libertine.

don·key (dŏng′kē, dŭng′-) *n.* (pl.
-keys). Domesticated ass, descended from the wild *Equus asinus*;
stupid person; ~ **engine**, small
steam engine, usu. for subsidiary
operations on board ship; ~ **-work**,
(colloq.) drudgery.

Donne (dŭn), **John** (1573–1631).
Dean of St. Paul's; preacher and
metaphysical poet; author of
satires, epistles, and elegies.

Don·ner (dŏn′er) **Pass**, in the
Sierra Nevada, named for a party of
westward migrants (including
families named Donner) who, in
1846, were driven to cannibalism
when they became stalled by winter
snows.

Donatello was the greatest Florentine
sculptor before Michelangelo and a
most influential artist of the Re-
naissance. This gilt terracotta is of the
'Virgin and Child'.

don·nish (dŏn´ĭsh) *adj.* Like a university don; pedantic, erudite, bookish.

Don·ny·brook (dŏn´ĕbrook). Town near Dublin, Ireland; ~ **Fair**, annual fair formerly held there; hence, **d~**, uproar, brawl, free-for-all.

do·nor (dō´ner) *n.* 1. Giver; contributor of money, work of art, etc. 2. (med.) Person, animal, from whose body biological material is removed, as blood for transfusion (**blood** ~), organ (**heart** ~), or tissue (**tissue** ~), for transplantation to another person, etc.

Don Qui·xo·te: see QUIXOTE.

don't (dōnt). Contraction of do not.

do·nut = doughnut: see DOUGH.

doo·dad (doo´dăd) *n.* (colloq.) Fancy article; trivial ornament; gadget.

doo·dle (doo´del) *n.* Aimless scrawl made by a person while his attention is otherwise engaged;

quick, inartistic sketch. ~ *v.t.* (**-dled, -dling**). Make a doodle.

doom (doom) *n.* 1. Fate, lot, (usu. evil) destiny; ruin, death. 2. Unfavorable sentence or judgment. 3. Last Judgment (chiefly in **day of** ~); **dooms´day**, day of judgment; **till doomsday**, to the end of the world, forever. **doom** *v.* Pronounce sentence against; condemn *to* some fate, *to* do; consign to misfortune or destruction (esp. in past part.).

door (dōr, dôr) *n.* 1. Movable barrier of wood or other material, turning on hinges or sliding in groove etc., and serving to close or open passage into building, room, etc.; doorway; means of entrance or exit; **at death's** ~, on the point of dying; **lay, lie, at the** ~ **of**, impute, be imputable, to. 2. **door´-bell**, bell to be rung from outside to gain admission; **door´jamb**, one of two vertical members framing a door and supporting the lintel;

door´keeper, person who gua[rds] door, porter, janitor; **door´kno[b]** knob for turning to release latch [of] door; **door´man**, doorkeeper, e[tc.] of apartment building; **door´ma[t]** mat placed at door for wiping sh[oes] on entering; **door´nail**, large n[ail] driven through door and clinch[ed] so as to be not reusable; hence d[ead] **as a** ~; **door´step**, step [or] threshold of door; **door´wa[y]** opening or passage that door serv[es] to close or open; **door´yard**, ya[rd] in front of door or house.

dop·ant (dō´pant) *n.* Substan[ce] added to a semiconductor to chan[ge] its electrical properties.

dope (dōp) *n.* 1. Thick liqu[id] used as lubricant etc; varnish, es[p.] that applied to cloth parts of mo[del] planes and (formerly) airplanes [to] keep them taut and airtight. [2.] (slang) Narcotic; drug administer[ed] to horse etc. before race to impro[ve] or spoil its performance; ~ **fien[d]** (slang) drug addict; (slang) i[n]formation, esp. **inside** ~. 3. (slan[g]) Stupid person. **dope** *v.t.* (**dope[d],** **dop´ing**). Drug; doctor; app[ly] dope to (airplane fabric etc[.]) **dop´ey, dop´y** *adj.* (**dop·i·e[r]**

*The first **doors** made of rigid and permanent materials were often of bronze or stone, but the wooden door is the oldest and most common in antiquity. Since earliest times doors and door-ways have been decorative features. Below left: Front door, Ham House, London, U.K. Bottom left: Chinese door at Claydon House. Below: St. Patrick's Cathedral, N.Y.*

*The **dormouse**, which resembles a small squirrel in appearance and way of life, hibernates from mid-October to mid-April. It feeds on insects and forages only at night.*

•p·i·est). (slang) Heavy or stuped, as if drugged; stupid. [app. Du. *doop* sauce]

Dop·pel·gäng·er (dŏp´elgäng-), **dou·ble·gang·er** (dŭb´elgäng-) *ns*. Wraith, ghostly double at haunts the living person. ·er.]

Dop·pler (dŏp´ler), **Johann** ·803–53). Austrian physicist; ~ ·fect, apparent increase (or de·ease) in frequency of electro·agnetic and sound waves when ·urce and observer move closer to ·ch other (or farther apart).

Do·ré (dawrā´), **Paul Gustave** ·833–83). French artist; famous ·r his scriptural paintings and ·ustrations of Dante, Milton, etc.

Do·ri·an (dōr´ēan, dŏr´-) *adj.* Of ·ORIS or the Dorians; ~ **mode**, ·us.) ancient Greek mode, re·tedly simple and solemn in ·aracter; first of ecclesiastical ·odes. **Dorian** *n.* Native, in·bitant, of Doris.

Dor·ic (dŏr´ĭk, dŏr´-) *adj.* I. ·orian. 2. (archit.) Of the Doric ·der, oldest, strongest, and

simplest of the Greek orders of architecture, characterized by heavy fluted columns, having saucer-shaped capitals and no base. ~ *n.* I. Doric dialect of ancient Greece. 2. Doric architecture.

Do·ris (dōr´ĭs, dŏr´-). Small country in ancient Greece, S. of Thessaly, the home of the Dorians.

dor·mant (dōr´mant) *adj.* Sleeping; inactive as in sleep; with animation or development suspended; not active, in abeyance; (bot., esp. of seeds and buds) in state of suspended growth; (her., of beast) with head resting on paws. **dor´man·cy** *n.*

dor·mer (dōr´mer) *n.* (also ~ **window**) Projecting vertical window in sloping roof.

dor·mi·to·ry (dōr´mĭtōrē, -tōrē) *n.* (pl. **-ries**). I. Residence hall or hostel esp. at college or university. 2. Sleeping room with several

beds and sometimes cubicles.

dor·mouse (dōr´mows) *n.* (pl. **-mice** pr. -mīs). Small Old World hibernating rodent akin to mouse but resembling squirrel in form and habit.

dor·sal (dōr´sal) *adj.* (anat., bot., zool.) Of, on, near, the back; ~ **fin**, main fin on dorsal surface of fishes etc. **dor´sal·ly** *adv.*

do·ry[1] (dōr´ē, dŏr´ē) *n.* (pl. **-ries**). (also **John D** ~) European sea fish (*Zeus faber*) used as food. [Fr. *dorée* gilded]

do·ry[2] (dōr´ē, dŏr´ē) *n.* (pl. **-ries**). Small flat-bottomed fishing boat with high sides.

dos·age (dō´sĭj) *n.* Giving of medicine in doses; size of dose; amount of x-rays etc. applied at one time.

dose (dōs) *n.* I. Amount of medicine etc. given or prescribed to be given at one time. 2. (phys.) Amount of radiation received by person or thing exposed to it. ~ *v.t.* (**dosed, dos·ing**). Give medicine to (person). **dos´er** *n.*

do·sim·e·ter (dōsĭm´eter) *n.* De-

Dots *take on many forms: in morse code (top) a dot is a short audible signal; in braille (above) it is a raised area that may be felt by the reader.*

The **double bass,** *which measures about 6 ft. in height, was largely ignored by early composers. It was brought to prominence by Beethoven and later composers who recognized its unique qualities.*

vice to measure amount of radiation absorbed. **do·sim′e·try** *n.*

Dos Pas·sos (dōs păs′ŏs), **John Roderigo** (1896–1970). Amer. novelist; author of the trilogy *U.S.A.* etc.

dos·si·er (daws′yā, dŏs′-, -ēā) *n.* Set or file of documents relating to a particular person or happening.

Dos·to·ev·sky, Dos·to·ev·ski (dŏstoyĕf′skē, dŭs′-, -toiĕf′-), **Feodor Mikhailovich** (1821–81). Russian novelist; author of *Crime and Punishment, The Idiot, The Brothers Karamazov,* etc.

DOT *abbrev.* Department of Transportation.

dot[1] (dŏt) *n.* Small spot, speck, roundish pen mark; period, point over *i* or *j*, point used as diacritical mark; (in Morse code) small mark or signal shorter than dash; (mus.) point placed after note or rest, lengthening it by half its value; point over or under note indicating that it is *staccato*; **on the ~**, punctually; **dot** *v.t.* (**dot·ted, dot·ting**). Mark with dot(s); place dot over (letter *i*, note in music) or after (musical note). **dotted line**, line of

dots or dashes to follow in drawing etc., or on document to receive signature; hence, **sign on the dotted line**, agree formally. **dot′-ter** *n.*

dot[2] (dŏt) *n.* Woman's marriage portion; dowry. [Fr.]

dot·age (dō′tĭj) *n.* Impaired intellect, esp. through old age; second childhood, senility.

dot·ard (dō′terd) *n.* Senile person.

dote (dōt) *v.i.* (**dot·ed, dot·ing**). 1. Be silly, infatuated, or feeble-minded, esp. from age. 2. Concentrate one's affections, bestow excessive fondness, *on.* **dot′er** *n.* **dot′ing·ly** *adv.*

dot·tle, dot·tel (dŏt′el) *ns.* Plug of tobacco left unsmoked in pipe.

dot·ty (dŏt′ē) *adj.* (**-ti·er, -ti·est**). Feeble-minded, half idiotic. **dot′ti·ness** *n.*

Dou·ai (dōōā′). Town in N.

France; ~ (usu. **Douay**) **Bible version**, English translation of th Latin Vulgate Bible used in R.C Church; the New Testament wa published at Rheims in 1582 an the Old Testament at Douai i 1609–10.

dou·ble (dŭb′el) *adj.* 1. Cor sisting of two members, things, (sets combined; twofold; forming pair; folded, bent; stooping much having some part double; (c flowers) having number of peta multiplied by conversion of sta mens and carpels into petals. 2 Having twofold relation or applica tion; dual; ambiguous. 3. Twice a much or as many (*of*); of twofol or extra size, strength, value, etc (mus., of instruments etc.) a octave lower in pitch (from the fac that a pipe, string, etc., of doubl length gives a note an octave lower **~** *adv.* To twice the amount etc two together. **~** *adj.* or *adv.* i comb.: **~-acting**, acting in tw ways, directions, etc., **~ agent**, on spying for two rival parties; **~ barreled**, (of gun) with two bar rels; **~ bass**, largest and lowest ched instrument of violin class, h four strings usu. tuned a fourth rt; **~ bed**, bed for two people; **boiler**, saucepan with detach- e upper compartment in which d is slowly cooked by water ling in the lower; **~-breasted**, coat etc.) having the two fronts erlapping across the breast; **~ in**, chin with fold of flesh under- ath; **~ cross**, (slang) treachery both parties, esp. by pretended lusion with each, betrayal by ing in contradiction to agree- nt; **~-cross** (*v.t.*) betray thus; **-dealing**, duplicity, deceit; *j.*) deceitful; **~-dealer**; **~- cker**, bus with two decks; sand- ch with three slices of bread and o layers of filling; **~-dipper**, ired soldier, airman, etc., work- on salary from federal govern- nt while also drawing pension; **eagle**, (hist.) 20-dollar gold ce; **~-edged**, with two cutting ges; (fig., of argument etc.) tell- against as well as for one; **~ ures**, number between nine and o; **dou'bleheader**, two games in ccession on same day between the ne teams; **double helix**, pair of rallel helices with common axis, . in structure of DNA molecule; **uble-jointed**, having joints that ow unusual bending movements limb etc.; **double-knit**, jersey- e fabric knitted double with the o surfaces locked together; **uble-park**, park (vehicle) ngside another already parked rallel to curb; **double play** aseball) play in which two run- rs are put out; **double pneu- onia**, pneumonia affecting both ngs; **double-quick**, very

quick(ly); **double standard**, rule etc. applied more strictly to some persons than to others; esp. one applied more strictly to women than to men in sexual morals; **double star** = BINARY STAR; **double-stopping**, (mus.) simultaneous sounding of notes on two strings of instrument of violin class; **double take**, delayed reaction to situation etc. immediately after one's first reaction; **double-talk**, language (usu. deliberately) ambiguous; gibberish; **double-talk** (*v.i.*); **dou'blethink**, conscious belief in contradictory ideas at the same time [word coined by George Orwell in *1984*]; **double time**, (mil.) marching pace of 180 steps per minute; **double-tonguing**, rapid vibratory motion of tongue in producing staccato or rapidly repeated notes on flute, clarinet, etc. **dou'bly** *adv*. **double** *n*. 1. Double quantity; twice as much or as many; **on the ~**, quickly; (mil.) running. 2. (bridge) Call by declarer's opponent involving doubling of score for tricks and a bonus to the declarer if he or she wins. 3. Counterpart or duplicate of thing or person. 4. (pl.) Game (tennis, handball, etc.) with two players on each side. 5. Lodging with double bed. 6. Double shot of whiskey etc. **double** *v*. (**-bled, -bling**). 1. Make or become double, increase twofold, multiply by two; amount to twice as much as; (mus.) add same note in lower or higher octave to; call a double (at bridge). 2. Bend, turn, over upon itself; clench (fist); **~ up**, (cause to) bend into stooping or curled up position; become folded;

share living, sleeping quarters with. 3. (naut.) Get around (headland). 4. Turn sharply, reverse.

dou·ble en·ten·dre (dŭb'el ahn-tahn'dre, -tahnd'). Ambiguous expression, phrase with two meanings, one usu. risqué; use of such phrases. [Fr., obs. (now *double entente*)]

dou·blet (dŭb'lĭt) *n*. 1. (hist.) Man's close-fitting jacket with or without sleeves (14th–18th centuries). 2. Pair; one of a pair; one of two words of same derivation but different form or sense.

dou·ble·ton (dŭb'elton) *n*. (cards) Two cards only of a suit, in one hand.

dou·bloon (dŭblōon') *n*. (hist.) Spanish gold coin (orig. two pistoles).

doubt (dowt) *n*. Feeling of uncertainty (*about*), undecided frame of mind, inclination to disbelieve; uncertain state of things; **give** (person) **benefit of the ~**, assume innocence rather than guilt when evidence is contradictory or inconclusive; **no ~**, certainly, admittedly; **without ~**, certainly. **doubt** *v*. Be in doubt or uncertainty (about); call in question; mistrust. **doubt'a·ble** *adj*. **doubt'er** *n*. **doubt'ing·ly** *adv*.

doubt·ful (dowt'fŭl) *adj*. Of uncertain meaning, character, truth, or issue; undecided, ambiguous, questionable; uncertain, hesitating. **doubt'ful·ly** *adv*. **doubt'ful·ness** *n*.

doubt·less (dowt'lĭs) *adv*. Certainly; no doubt. **doubt'less·ly** *adv*.

douche (doosh) *n*. Jet of liquid applied to body externally or internally for cleansing or for medicinal purpose; application of liquid in this manner; instrument for such application. **~** *v*. (**douched, douch·ing**). Administer douche to, take douche.

*amblers, such as the rose **Dorothy rkins,** flower mainly on new canes, e previous year's cane having been t down in the Fall after flowering.*

*The design of London's famous red **double-decker** omnibuses has evolved from the early 1900s. Originally they were roofless with an uncovered stairway to the upper deck.*

Dover is famous for its high chalk cliffs and owes its importance to its nearness to the French coast. Dover Castle is one of England's best-preserved medieval fortresses.

dough (dō) *n.* Mass of flour or meal kneaded into paste ready to be baked into bread etc.; any soft pasty mass; (slang) money; **dough'boy**, (esp. in World War I) infantry soldier; **dough'nut**, small, usu. ring-shaped, cake of dough fried in deep fat. **dough'y** *adj.* (**dough·i·er, dough·i·est**).

dough·ty (dow'tē) *adj.* (**-ti·er, -ti·est**). (usu. joc.) Valiant, stouthearted. **dough'ti·ly** *adv.* **dough'ti·ness** *n.*

Doug·las[1] (dŭg'las), **Stephen Arnold** (1813–61). Amer. political leader; U.S. senator from Illinois, 1847–61; best known for his series of debates with Abraham Lincoln, 1858; defeated for presidency by Lincoln, 1860.

Doug·las[2] (dŭg'las) **fir.** Very tall evergreen tree of northwestern N. Amer., *Pseudotsuga taxifolia* or *P. menziesii*, grown for lumber. [named f. David *Douglas* (1798–1834) Scottish botanist in Amer.]

Doug·lass (dŭg'las), **Frederick** (1817?–95). Original name, Frederick Augustus Washington Bailey; Amer. black abolitionist, lecturer, editor, and statesman.

Dou·kho·bors (doo'kōbōrz): see DUKHOBORS.

dour (dowr, door) *adj.* Stern, forbidding; gloomy. **dour'ly** *adv.* **dour'ness** *n.*

douse (dows) *v.t.* (**doused, dous·ing**). 1. Extinguish (fire, light). 2. Immerse; drench, soak.

dove (dŭv) *n.* Bird of family Columbidae (see PIGEON), esp. the **tur'tledove** (*Streptopelia turtur*) of Europe and the MOURNING ~ of N. Amer.; symbol of gentleness or innocence; messenger of peace and deliverance (Gen. 8); darling; ~- (**color**), warm gray with tinge of pink or lavender; **dove'cot(e)**, structure for housing pigeons. **dov'ish** *adj.*

Do·ver (dō'ver). Seaport on E. coast of Kent in England on **Strait(s) of** ~, strait at E. end of English Channel between SE. coast of England and N. France; **White Cliffs of** ~, chalk cliffs lining Dover coast; **Dover**, capital of Delaware in E. central part.

dove·tail (dŭv'tāl) *n.* Tenon

Newly hatched chickens are cove with fine soft down. Later this will replaced by the adult feathers, some down will remain in underplumage.

shaped like dove's spread tail reversed wedge, fitting into c responding mortise and form joint; such joint. ~ *v.* together with dovetails; fit toget compactly.

dow·a·ger (dow'ajer) *n.* Won with title or property derived fr her late husband; matron of h social standing.

dow·dy (dow'dē) *adj.* (**-di -di·est**). (of clothes) Shabby, fashionable; (of woman) shabt or unfashionably dressed. **do di·ly** *adv.* **dow'di·ness** *n.* **dow** *n.* (pl. **-dies**). Dowdy woman.

dow·el (dow'el) *n.* Headless of wood, metal, etc., fastening gether two pieces of wood, sto etc. ~ *v.t.* (**-eled, -el·ing** or **-ell -el·ling**). Fasten with dowel(s)

dow·er (dow'er) *n.* Wido share for life of husband's est property or money brought by v to husband, dowry; endowme gift of nature, talent. ~ Give dowry to; endow *with* ta etc.

Dow-Jones (dow' jōn **average.** Index of the relat price of stocks based on the curr average price of certain indust and other stocks, published Dow-Jones & Co., publishers of *Wall Street Journal*.

down[1] (down) *n.* Open high l (often pl.); treeless undulat chalk upland of S. England.

down[2] (down) *n.* First fine covering of young birds; bi underplumage, used for stuff pillows, jackets, etc.; fine soft h esp. first hair on face; soft hair fruit etc.; any feathery or fl substance. **down'y** *adj.* (**dow i·er, down·i·est**).

Diamond

Emerald

Mourning

*above: The **dove** has been semi-domesticated in Europe since the Middle Ages and reared as a source of food. The hundreds of species include the turtledove (top). All doves pair for life and both sexes share in rearing their young.*

down³ (down) *adv.* 1. From above, to lower place, to ground; to place regarded as lower; into helpless position; with current or wind; as initial cash payment at time of purchase (so ~ **payment**). 2. In lower place; in fallen posture, prostrate; at low level, in depression, humiliation, etc.; lower in price. 3. From higher to lower point in series or order; from earlier to later time; into quiescence. 4. **be ~ on**, be opposed to, disapprove of; **come ~ on**, pounce on; treat severely; **go ~**, be swallowed; find acceptance; (of ship) sink; (of sun etc.) set. 5. ~ **and out**, (boxing) unable to resume the fight; (transf.) defeated; destitute (person); ~ **east**, New England, esp. Maine; **down'hearted, down in the mouth**, dispirited; **down south**, in, into, the southern states; **down-to-earth**, practical, realistic; **down'trodden**, (fig.) oppressed; **down under**, at or to the Antipodes, in Australia etc. **down** *prep.* Downward along, through or into; from top to bottom of; at a lower part of; with (the wind, current, etc.); **down'stage**, at, toward, front of stage; **downstream'**, in direction of current, toward mouth, of river; **downtown'**, into the (business part of) town; (situated) in more central part of town. **down** *adj.* Directed downward; **down'beat** (mus.) (1) accented beat; downward stroke of conductor's baton to indicate the first beat of a measure; (2) depressed, gloomy; **on the down'grade**, (fig.) deteriorating; **down'grade** (*v.t.*), lower in status etc.; **down payment**: see *adv.*, sense 1; **down'range**, (of a missile) away from the launch pad and toward the target; **down'shift**, (of automobile transmission) shift into a lower gear. **down** *v.t.* (colloq.) Put, throw, knock, gulp, etc., down. ~ *n.* Reverse of fortune; throw in wrestling etc.; (football) one of a series of four plays in which the team must advance the ball at least ten yards.

down·cast (down'kăst, -kahst) *adj.* (of looks) Directed downward; dejected.

down·fall (down'fawl) *n.* Fall (of rain etc.); fall from prosperity, ruin.

down·hill (down'hǐl') *adj.* Sloping down; declining. ~ *adv.* In descending direction; on a decline.

Down·ing (dow'nǐng) **Street.** Street in London containing official residence of Prime Minister (no. 10), hence, the British Government. [Sir George *Downing* (c1624–1684), British diplomat]

down·pour (down'pōr, -pŏr) *n.* Heavy fall of rain etc.

down·right (down'rīt) *adj.* Plain, definite, straightforward, blunt; out-and-out. ~ *adv.*

Thoroughly, positively, quite.

Down's (downz) **syndrome**: see MONGOLISM.

down·stairs (down'stārz') adv. Down the stairs. **down'stairs** adj. & n. (Of, in) lower floor of house etc.

down·trod·den (down'trŏden) adj. Crushed by oppression or tyranny.

down·ward (down'werd) adj. & adv. Toward what is lower or inferior. **down'wards** adv.

dow·ry (dow'rē) n. (pl. **-ries**). Portion woman brings to her husband on marriage.

dows·er (dow'zer) n. Person who attempts to locate underground water or minerals by holding in both hands a forked stick etc., which is supposed to dip abruptly when it is over the right spot. **dows'ing** n. Searching for water etc., thus ~ **rod**, forked stick etc. used by dowser, divining rod.

dox·ol·o·gy (dŏksŏl'ojē) n. (pl. **-gies**). Hymn of praise to God, esp. short hymn used at conclusion of psalm, canticle, etc. **dox·o·log·i·cal** (dŏksolŏj'ĭkal) adj.

dox·y (dŏk'sē) n. (pl. **dox·ies**). (archaic) Beggar's wench, paramour; prostitute.

doy·en (doi'en, doiěn') n. (fem. **doy·enne** pr. doiěn'). (chiefly Brit.) Senior member of a body, esp. senior ambassador at a court.

Doyle (doil), **Sir Arthur Conan** (1859–1930). British physician and novelist, famous for his "Sherlock Holmes" detective stories.

doz. abbrev. Dozen.

doze (dōz) v.i. (**dozed, doz·ing**). Sleep lightly, be half asleep; ~ **off**, fall lightly asleep. **doze** n. Short light sleep. **doz'er** n. **doz·y** adj. (**doz·i·er, doz·i·est**).

doz·en (dŭz'en) n. (pl. **-ens**, following a numeral **-en**). Twelve; set of twelve: **baker's** ~, thirteen.

D.P., DP abbrevs. Displaced person.

dpt. abbrev. Department

Dr. abbrev. Doctor; drive (of street names).

dr. abbrev. Debit; debtor; drachma(s); dram(s).

drab (drăb) adj. (**drab·ber, drab·best**) & n. (Of) dull light brown color; dull, monotonous. **drab'ly** adv. **drab'ness** n.

drach·ma (drăk'ma) n. (pl. **-mas, -mae** pr. **-mē, -mai** pr. mī). 1. Principal monetary unit of Greece. 2. Coin and weight of ancient Greece.

Dra·co (drā'kō), **Dra·con** (drā'kon). Chief magistrate (archon) at Athens in 621 B.C., said to have established a severe code of laws. **Dra·co·ni·an** (drākō'nēan), **Dra·con·ic** (drākŏn'ĭk) adjs. Of Draco or his code of laws; rigorous, harsh, cruel.

In Christian Europe **dragons** symbolized sin and paganism. One of the legendary saints who fought them was St. Michael, seen here in a painting by Fouquet.

draft (drăft, drahft) n. 1. (Selection of) detachment of men from larger body for special duty; contingent; reinforcement; member of such detachment; conscription for military service; men conscripted for military service; ~ **dodger**, one evading conscription. 2. Drawing of money by written order; bill or check drawn, esp. by one branch of bank on another. 3. Sketch of work to be executed. 4. Rough copy of document. 5. Current of air in room etc. 6. Drawing, traction; drawing of net for fish; catch of fish at one drawing. 7. Single act of drinking, amount so drunk; dose of liquid medicine. 8. Depth of water ship draws or requires to float her. 9. Drawing of liquor from vessel; ~ **beer**, beer drawn from cask, not bottled; **beer on** ~, beer in tapped cask. **draft** v.t. 1. Draw off (part of larger body, esp. of troops) for special purpose: conscript. 2. Prepare, make rough copy of (document, report, etc). **draft·ee'**, **draft'er** ns. **draft'·a·ble** adj.

drafts·man (drăfts'man, drahfts'-) n. (pl. **-men** pr. -men). One employed to make drawings, plans, or sketches: one skilled in drawing or designing. **drafts'·man·ship** n.

drag (drăg) v. (**dragged, drag·ging**). 1. Pull along with force, difficulty, or friction; allow (feet, tail, etc.) to trail; ~ **anchor**, trail anchor along the bottom, owing to force of wind or current. 2. Extend (conversation etc.) tediously. 3. Trail, go heavily; ~ **on**, continue tediously. 4. Search bottom of (water) with grapnels, nets etc. (for). 5. Retard (wheel, vehicle) by applying a drag to it (see n. def. 3 below). **drag** n. 1. Rough sledge;

large four-horse coach like stag coach. 2. Net drawn over botto of water to enclose all fish; (al **drag'net**, which also has fig. sen of systematic large-scale round of criminals); apparatus for dred ing bottom of rivers or pools. Iron brake for retarding vehic downhill; obstruction to progres 4. Strong smelling lure for houn in lieu of fox; hunt with houn following this. 5. Slow motio impeded progress; (aeron.) atmo pheric resistance. 6. (slang) Tran vestite clothing; puff on a cigarett boring thing or person; influence get special privilege. 7. ~ **rac** race to determine car with faste acceleration from a standstill; **strip**, straight, short paved road strip for drag races; **main** ~, ma street.

drag·gle (drăg'el) v. (**-gle -gling**). Make wet, limp, and dirt by trailing; hang trailing.

drag·o·man (drăg'oman) n. (p **-mans, -men**). Interpreter (ar guide), esp. in Arabic, Turkish, Persian. [Arab. tarjumān inte preter]

drag·on (drăg'on) n. 1. Myth cal monster like crocodile or snak with large claws, usu. winged, an often breathing fire. 2. (archai Large serpent. 3. Lizard of genu Draco, with broad winglike mem brane on each flank. 4. **drag'on fly** (pl. **-flies**), insect of orde Odonata with long body, prominer eyes, and elaborately veined mem branous wings usu. spread whil resting, freq. brightly colored, an capable of rapid darting flight (als called "(devil's) darning needle")

dra·goon (dragōōn') n. Cavalry man, orig. of mounted 17th an 18th c. infantry armed with a ki of carbine called a dragoon, now certain European cavalry regiment historically representing these. v.t. Persecute, oppress; force int course by persecution. [Fr. drago carbine, so named as breathing fir

drain (drān) v. Draw (liquic off, away, by conduit, drainpipe etc.; drink (liquid), empty (vessel to the dregs; dry (land etc.) b providing channels for the escape the water in it; (of river) carry o superfluous water of (district trickle through, flow graduall away; become rid of moisture by it gradual flowing away; **drain'pip** large pipe used for draining. **drai** n. Channel carrying off liquic artificial conduit for water, sewage etc.; (surg.) tube for drawing of discharge from abscess etc.; con stant outlet, withdrawal, demand or expenditure. **drain'er** n.

The **drawbridge** over the Wilamette River in Portland, Oregon. The raising and lowering requires immense power and equally strong stability from the supporting structure.

English **drama** reached its height Elizabethan times in the works Shakespeare. Here Australian acto are taking part in a production Richard II.

drain·age (drā′nĭj) n. Draining; system of drains; what is drained off, sewage.

drake[1] (drāk) n. Mayfly of genus *Ephemera* used in fishing.

drake[2] (drāk) n. Male duck.

Drake (drāk), **Sir Francis** (1540?-96). English navigator, privateer, and admiral; plundered West Indies and W. coast of South Amer.; first Englishman to circumnavigate globe in his ship, *Golden Hind*; brought home first unsuccessful colonists from Virginia with potatoes and tobacco; commanded a division of English fleet which decisively defeated the Spanish Armada, 1588; **Drake Passage**, strait between Cape Horn and South Shetland Island connecting S. Atlantic and S. Pacific oceans.

dram (drăm) n. 1. One-sixteenth of an ounce. 2. (abbrev. dr.) Apothecaries' weight of 60 grains. 3. Small draft of liquor; bit.

dra·ma (drah′ma, drăm′a) n. Stage play, motion picture, or television program presenting story in dialogue; dramatic art, composition and presentation of plays; series of events having the unity and progress of a play and leading to final catastrophe or consummation.

Dram·a·mine (drăm′amēn) n. (trademark) Antihistamine used to counteract motion sickness.

dra·mat·ic (dramăt′ĭk) adj. Of, like, drama; theatrical; sudden, striking, impressive. **dra·mat′i·cal·ly** adv.

dram·a·tis per·so·nae (drăm′atĭs persō′nē, drah′ma-). (List of) characters in a play.

dram·a·tist (drăm′atĭst, drah′ma-) n. Writer of dramas or dramatic poetry.

dram·a·tize (drăm′atīz, drah′ma-) v. (**-tized, -tiz·ing**). Convert (novel etc.) into play; admit of such conversion; impart dramatic character to. **dram·a·ti·za·tion** (drămatĭzā′shon, drahma-) n.

dram·a·turge (drăm′aterj, drah′ma-), **dram·a·tur·gist** (drăm′aterjĭst, drah′ma-) ns. Dramatist. **dram·a·tur·gic** (drămater′jĭk, drahma-) adj. **dram·a·tur·gy** (drăm′aterjē, drah′ma-) n.

drape (drāp) v. (**draped, drap**-ing). Cover, hang, adorn, wi cloth etc.; (of clothes, hangings et arrange; hang in graceful folds. n. Curtain; way in which clot clothes, etc. fall or hang. **drap a·ble, drape′a·ble** adjs.

drap·er (drā′per) n. (Brit.) R tailer of cloth and piece good **dra′per·y** n. (pl. **-per·ies**). Cloth, textile fabrics. 2. Arrang ment of clothing in sculpture et clothing or hangings disposed folds.

dras·tic (drăs′tĭk) adj. Acti strongly, vigorous, violent. **dras ti·cal·ly** adv.

drat (drăt) int. Curse. **dra ted** adj.

draught (drăft) (chiefly Brit.) DRAFT.

Dra·vid·i·an (dravĭd′ēan) a & n. (Member) of a people of India and Ceylon (including Tam and Kanarese); (of) any of t languages spoken by these peopl **Dra·vid·ic** adj. [f. *Dravida*, o province of S. India]

draw (draw) v. (**drew, draw draw·ing**). 1. Pull; pull after on contract, distort (features etc.); ha *in* (net); bend (bow); pull at; pu (curtain, drapes, blind) open shut. 2. Attract, bring to one; ta in; attract attention or custom; i duce *to* do; be attracted, assembl *around, together*, etc. 3. Extra pull out (sword, handgun, or oth weapon from sheath or holster take out sword, handgun, etc.; pu or take one from a number things so as to decide something chance (esp. in ~ **lots** etc.); obta by lot; haul up (water) from we bring out (liquid, blood) fro vessel, body; take, get, from source; (also ~ **out**) encoura (person) to talk, reveal informatio

*The principal element of **drawing** is the line. In recent times the line has been conceived of as an autonomous element of form, independent of representation, as in this study for the dirt cart by William Dobell, left. Below left, a Michelangelo drawing.*

etc.; deduce, ınter; extract something from, empty, drain; disembowel; (cards) cause (trumps etc.) to be played. 4. Protract, stretch, elongate; make (wire) by pulling piece of metal through successively smaller holes; (naut., of sail) swell out with wind. 5. Trace, delineate, make (picture), represent (object), by drawing lines; use pencil, pen, etc. thus; describe in words; practice delineation; frame (document) in due form, compose; formulate, institute (comparisons, distinctions); write out (bill, check, draft, *on* bank etc.); make call *on* person, his faith, memory, etc., *for* money or service. 6. Make way, move, *toward*, *near*, *off*, etc.; (racing) get farther *away* to the front, come *level*, gain *on*. 7. (of ship) Require (a depth of water) to float. 8. End (game, battle) as a tie; (abs.) succeed in doing this. 9. ~ **back**, withdraw from undertaking; ~ **in**, entice, persuade to join; (of train or vehicle) = PULL in; ~ **off**, withdraw; ~ **on**, allure; approach, draw near; ~ **out**, lead out, detach, or array (as troops); prolong; elicit; induce to talk, reveal talent etc.; elongate; (of train or vehicle) = PULL out; ~ **up**, come up *with*, *to*; stop before finish line; bring (troops), come, into regular order; compose (documents etc.); ~ **oneself up**, assume stiff attitude. 10. **draw'string**, string that can be pulled to tighten mouth of bag, waist of garment, etc. **draw** *n*. Act of drawing, esp. pull; thing that draws business, attention, etc.; drawing of lots; raffle; drawn game; act of drawing a handgun from holster etc.

draw·back (draw'băk) *n*. 1. Refund, esp. as discount on taxes, duties, or price of goods or services for large or favored users. 2. Thing that qualifies satisfaction; disadvantage.

draw·bridge (draw'brĭj) *n*. Bridge across moat, river, etc., made to be raised, lowered, or moved to one side to prevent passage over it, or to be raised to permit passage of boat or ship.

draw·er (draw'er, drôr) *n*. 1. One who draws. 2. Box-shaped receptacle sliding in and out of special frame, or of table etc.; (pl.) chest of drawers. 3. (pl.) Underpants.

draw·ing (draw'ĭng) *n*. (esp.) Art of representing by line; delineation by means of pen or pencil or other pointed instrument; product of this, sketch; ~ **board**, board for

stretching drawing paper on; **on the
~ board**, undergoing preparation;
incompletely designed; **~ card**,
entertainer etc. attracting large
audience or many clients.

draw·ing (draw´ĭng) **room**. 1.
Room for reception of company. 2.
Private room on railroad train.
[earlier *withdrawing room*]

drawl (drawl) *v*. Speak slowly,
with prolonged or diphthongized
vowels. **~** *n*. Regional accent of
one who drawls; drawling, slow
utterance. **drawl'ing·ly** *adv.*

drawn (drawn) *adj.*: see DRAW
v.; (esp.) **~ butter**, butter melted
and clarified, often with herbs.

dray (drā) *n*. Low cart without
sides for heavy loads; **~ horse**,
draft horse; **dray'man** (pl. **-men**),
driver of dray.

dread (drĕd) *v*. Be in great fear
of; shrink from, look forward to
with terror; fear greatly; be afraid
(*to* do). **~** *n*. Great fear; object of
fear or awe. **~** *adj.* Greatly
feared, dreadful.

dread·ful (drĕd´fŭl) *adj.* Terrible, awe-inspiring; troublesome,
disagreeable; very bad; **penny ~**,
(chiefly Brit.), cheap sensational
story of crime and horror. **dread'-
ful·ly** *adv.* **dread'ful·ness** *n*.

dread·nought, dread·naught
(drĕd´nawt) *ns*. Heavily armed
battleship. [f. *D~*, name of first

*Nowadays, the wooden ox **dray** is more
an historical piece than a useful farm
implement. This dray can be seen in
San Fernando de Espana Mission,
California.*

such Brit. battleship, launched
1906]

dream (drēm) *n*. Train of
thoughts, images, or fancies passing
through mind during sleep; conscious indulgence of fancy, reverie;
thing of dreamlike beauty, charm,
goodness, etc. **dream'less,
dream'like** *adjs.* **dream** *v*.
(**dreamed** or **dreamt** pr. drĕmt,
dream·ing). 1. Have visions etc.
in sleep; see hear, etc., in sleep. 2.
Imagine as in a dream; think possible; (with negative) so much as
contemplate possibility *of*, have any
conception *of*; **~ up**, (colloq.) conceive, devise (idea or plan). 3. Fall
into reverie; form imaginary visions
of; be inactive or unpractical.
dream'er *n*. (esp.) Impractical
person.

dream·land (drēm´lănd) *n*.
Ideal or imaginary land; utopia.

dream (drēm) **world**. 1.
World of fantasy or illusion. 2.
Condition of preoccupation with
unworldly pursuits.

dream·y (drē´mē) *adj.*
(**dream·i·er, dream·i·est**). 1.
Full of dreams; given to reverie,

fanciful, impractical; dreamli
vague, misty. 2. (colloq.) M
velous, wonderful. **dream'i**
adv. **dream'i·ness** *n*.

drear·y (drēr´ē) *adj.* (**drea
i·er, drear·i·est**). Dismal, gloo
dull. **drear'i·ly** *adv.* **drear'
ness** *n*.

dredge[1] (drĕj) *n*. Apparatus
bringing up oysters, specimer
etc., clearing out mud etc., fro
river or sea bottom, or obtaini
ores from alluvial deposits. **~**
(**dredged, dredg·ing**). Bring
clear *away, out*, with dredge; cle
out (harbor, river) with dredge; u
dredge. **dredg'er**[1] *n*.

dredge[2] (drĕj) *v.t.* (**dredge
dredg·ing**). Sprinkle with flour
other powder; sprinkle (flour et
over. **dredg'er**[2] *n*. Box with pe
forated lid for sprinkling flour e

dreg (drĕg) *n*. (usu. pl.) Se
ment, grounds, lees; worthless pa
refuse.

Drei·ser (drī´zer, -ser), **The
dore (Herman Albert)** (187
1945). Amer. novelist and edito
author of *An American Trage*
etc.

drench (drĕnch) *n*. 1. Dose
medicine, esp. for animal. 2. Soa
ing; downpour. **~** *v.t.* 1. For
(animal) to take dose of medicine.
Steep, soak. 3. Wet all over w
falling liquid.

Spud Frame

Boom

Floating pipe

Floats

Main pump

Earth sucked through

Cutter

Dres·den (drĕz'den). City in East Germany on the Elbe; famous for Baroque architecture, art, and museums; almost totally destroyed by Allied air raids during World War II; ~ **china**, porcelain made near Dresden.

dress (drĕs) *n.* Clothing, esp. the visible part of it, costume; woman's gown; frock; external covering, outward form; **full ~**, that worn on formal occasions; **evening ~**, that worn at dinners or evening parties; **morning ~**, men's formal daytime wear; ~ **circle**: see CIRCLE *n.*; ~ **coat**, swallow-tailed coat for evening dress; **dress'maker**, woman who makes women's dresses, **dress'-making**, (*n*); **dress rehearsal**, final rehearsal, in costume, of play etc. **dress** *v.* 1. (mil.) Correct alignment of (companies etc. or men in line); come into correct place in line etc. 2. Array, clothe; provide oneself with clothes; put on one's clothes; put on evening dress; ~ **up**, clothe oneself, clothe elaborately or in masquerade. 3. Deck, adorn (ship with flags, store window with items for sale, etc.). 4. Treat (wound), apply dressing to. 5. Subject to cleansing, trimming, smoothing, etc; brush, comb, do up (hair); curry (horse, leather); finish surface of (textile fabrics, stone for building); prepare, cook (food); manure (ground), esp. in **top dressing**.

dres·sage (drĕsahzh', dre-) *n.* Training of horse in obedience and deportment; execution by horse of precise movements in response to its rider.

dress·er[1] (drĕs'er) *n.* (esp.) Person who helps actor or actress to dress for part.

dress·er[2] (drĕs'er) *n.* Chest of drawers, esp, with mirror, in bedroom.

dress·ing (drĕs'ĭng) *n.* (esp.) 1. Seasoning, sauce, etc. used in cooking. 2. Stuffing for poultry etc. 3. Manure etc. spread over land. 4. Remedies, bandages, etc., with which wound is dressed. 5. ~ **down**, scolding; ~ **gown**, garment worn while making toilet or in dishabille; ~ **room**, room for dressing, applying make-up, etc., in home or theater; ~ **table**, table with mirror, drawers, etc., for use while dressing.

Dresden, the most beautiful baroque city in Germany, was destroyed by air raids during the 1939–45 war. Much has been rebuilt, including this wooden bridge leading to the Crown Gate.

drink *n.* Liquid drunk; beverag
intoxicating liquor; excessive in
dulgence in this, intemperance
glass or portion of liquor; **the** ~
(slang) the sea. **drink'er** *n.*
drink·a·ble (drĭng'kabel) *ad*
Fit to drink.
drip (drĭp) *v.* (**dripped** o
dript, drip·ping). Fall, let fall, i
drops; let drops fall, be so wet a
to shed drops; ~ **coffee**, coffe
made by allowing boiling water t
drip slowly through finely groun
coffee beans; ~-**dry**, (of fabri
clothes) that will dry when hun
up to drip, without wringing o
ironing; ~ **grind**, fine-groun
coffee beans for drip coffee. **dri**
n. 1. Act of dripping; drippin
liquid; (med.) continuous slow in
troduction of fluid into vein etc
2. (slang) Dull or unpleasant per
son.
drip·ping (drĭp'ĭng) *n.* (usu
plural) Juice and fat melted fron
roasting meat and used for grav
etc.
drive (drīv) *v.* (**drove, driv·en**
driv·ing). 1. Urge in som
direction, esp. by blows, threats
violence, etc.; chase or frighter
(game, wild beasts, etc.) from larg
area into small in order to kill o
capture. 2. Direct course o
(animal drawing vehicle, vehicle
locomotive, etc.); convey in vehicle
act as driver of vehicle; travel i
car at one's disposal; ~-**in**, (bank
restaurant, etc.) that can be usec
without alighting from car. 3
Impel forcibly, compel. 4. Caus
to move, carry along, throw, propel
send, (thing) in some direction
(golf) strike (ball), strike ball wit
driver; force (stake, nail, etc.) *int*
ground etc. with blow. 5. Bor
(tunnel, horizontal cavity). 6. Ain
blow or missile (*at*). 7. (of stean
or other power) Set or keep
(machinery) going. 8. Striv
energetically toward objective
work hard. 9. Move along impellec
by current, wind, etc.; ~ **at**
have for one's aim; allude to. **driv**
n. 1. Excursion in vehicle. 2
Driving of game, enemy, etc. 3
Forcible blow, stroke, or hit at base
ball etc. (in baseball also **line** ~)
(golf) hit made with a driver. 4
Energy, push; energetic campaign
5. (psychol.) Inner urge, motiv
principle. 6. Driving part o
machinery; transmission of powe
to wheels of vehicle esp. througr
~ **shaft.** 7. (also **drive'way**
Private road to house, garage, etc.
driv·el (drĭv'el) *n.* Silly non
sense, twaddle. ~ *v.i.* (-**eled**
-**el·ing** or -**elled, -el·ling**). Run a
mouth or nose like child; talk
childishly or idiotically. **driv'el·er**
driv'el·ler *ns.*
driv·er (drī'ver) *n.* 1. One whc
drives; ~'**s seat**, seat for driver

dress·y (drĕs'ē) *adj.* (**dress·i·er,
dress·i·est**). Fond of, smart in,
dress; (of clothes) stylish; elaborate.
dress'i·ness *n.*
drib·ble (drĭb'el) *v.* (**-bled,
-bling**). 1. Flow, let flow, in drops
or trickling stream; drool, slobber.
2. (basketball, soccer, etc.) Work
(ball) forward with series of short
bounces, kicks, etc. ~ *n.* Small
trickling or barely continuous
stream; act of dribbling.
drib·let (drĭb'lĭt) *n.* Small
amount or portion.
dried (drīd) *adj.*: see DRY *v.*;
(esp., of food) with moisture removed as method of preservation.
dri·er (drī'er) *n.* Substance
mixed with oil paints to expedite
drying; dryer.
drift (drĭft) *n.* 1. Being driven
by current; slow course or current;
ship's deviation from course due to
currents; aircraft's deviation due to
wind etc. 2. Natural or unperceived
progress, tendency. 3. Purpose,
meaning (as in the ~ **of an argument** etc.), tenor, scope. 4.
Shower, driving mass; accumulation of snow, sand, etc. heaped up
by wind. 5. (geol.) Anything
transported and deposited by wind,
water, or ice, esp. rock debris left
by a glacier. 6. (mining) Horizontal
passage following vein of mineral.
7. ~ **anchor**, floating frame keeping ship's head to wind in gale or
when dismasted; ~ **ice**, detached
drifting pieces of ice; ~ **net**, large
net for catching fish, extended by
weights at bottom and floats at top
and allowed to drift with tide;
drift'wood, wood drifting on, or
cast ashore by, water. **drift** *v.* Be
carried by or as by current of air
or water; (of current) carry; go pas-

Dave Twardzik in action, showing his deft
dribbling skills as he tries to outwit his
opponent. Years of hard work go into
acquiring dribbling, a ball skill essential
in many sports.

sively or aimlessly; pile, be piled by
wind, into drifts, cover with drifts.
drift·er (drĭf'ter) *n.* 1. (esp.)
Vagabond, vagrant; person who
drifts from place to place, job to
job, etc. 2. Boat used in fishing
with drift net.
drill[1] (drĭl) *n.* 1. Contrivance
(steel tool, machine, etc.) for boring
holes in metal, stone, sinking oil-
wells, etc; ~ **press**, drilling
machine used primarily on metals.
2. Shellfish that bores into shells of
oysters. 3. Military exercise or
training, hence, **drill'master**;
rigorous discipline, exact routine.
drill *v.* 1. Bore with drill etc.
2. Train in, perform, military
movements and exercise; train rigorously and exactly; impart (knowledge etc.) by training in memoriz-
ing, repetition, etc. **drill'er** *n.*
drill[2] (drĭl) *n.* 1. Small furrow,
ridge, for sowing seed in; row of
plants sown in it. 2. Machine for
sowing seed in drills. ~ *v.t.* Sow
(seed) in rows; plant (ground) in
drills.
dri·ly (drī'lē) *adv.* Var. of
DRYLY.
drink (drĭngk) *v.* (**drank, drunk**
or **drank, drink·ing**). 1. Take
(liquid) through mouth and throat
into stomach, swallow; swallow
contents of (cup etc.); swallow
liquid; (of plants, porous substances, etc.) absorb (moisture). 2.
Take *in*, esp. with eyes or ears,
with eager delight. 3. Drink alcoholic liquor; indulge in alcohol to
excess, tipple; honor (toast etc.) by

.) position of power. 2. (golf) ooden-headed club (also called nber 1 wood) used to send ball ong distance, esp. from tee.

rive (drīv) **wheel.** Wheel nmunicating motion to other eels in machinery; large wheel of omotive, to which power is nsmitted through connecting rod crank; wheel of vehicle to which ving power is applied.

driz·zle (drĭz'el) *v.i.* (**-zled, ing**) & *n.* Rain in fine, dense, aylike drops. **driz'zly** *adj.*

drogue (drōg) *n.* 1. Canvas cone n at both ends with a hoop at ger end, used as sea anchor; ter form of this towed by air- ft to serve for target practice. 2. achute or cone used to reduce ed of aircraft etc.

droll (drōl) *adj.* Whimsically using; amusingly odd. **drol'ly** . **droll'ness** *n.* **droll'er·y** *n.* oll action(s) or humor.

drom·e·dar·y (drŏm'edĕrē, ĭm'-) *n.* (pl. **-dar·ies**). One- mped domesticated camel, used beast of burden in N. Africa .; also called "Arabian camel."

drone (drōn) *n.* 1. Male of honey , which does not work; lazy er, sluggard. 2. Continued deep notonous sound, as of humming buzzing. 3. Open bass pipe of gpipe, emitting one continuous e; tone emitted by this. ~ *v.* **roned, dron·ing**). Buzz like bee bagpipe; talk, utter, monot- ously.

drool (drool) *v.i.* & *n.* Drivel; ow) excessive pleasure; water at e mouth, as in expectation of asure.

droop (droop) *v.* Hang down, cline, as from weariness or ex- ustion; (of eyes) be turned down, th lowered eyelids; languish, flag;

Hand drills *with bits are used by carpenters and workers in light materials. The small electric-powered hand drill has largely replaced the type rotated by hand.*

become dejected, lose heart; let (head, eyes, etc.) droop. ~ *n.* Drooping attitude; loss of spirit, fall of tone. **droop'y** *adj.* (**droop'- i·er, droop·i·est**). **droop'i·ness** *n.*

drop (drŏp) *n.* 1. Small quantity of liquid that falls, hangs, trickles down, or detaches itself in spherical or pear-shaped form; teardrop, drop of rain, blood, dew, etc.; very small quantity, esp. small quantity of drink; (pl.) medicinal prepara- tion to be administered in drops. 2. Candy lozenge. 3. Fall, drop- ping, descent; abrupt fall in level

Dromedary with its young. It is a one- humped variety of camel used in the African and Arabian deserts to carry burdens or for riding. It is a swift traveller.

of surface; depth to which anything sinks; distance through which any- thing falls; ~**-off**, steep descent, cliff; a decline; ~**-off charge**, extra fee for returning (esp.) a rented car at a depot other than that at which it was rented. 4. Curtain let down before stage between acts or scenes of play etc. (also ~ **cur- tain**). 5. Trapdoor on gallows, which is let fall from under feet of person to be hanged. 6. Slot through which something is de- posited, as mail; repository. 7. Material, persons, etc., dropped by parachute. **drop** *v.* (**dropped** or **dropt, drop·ping**). 1. Fall in drops; give off drops, drip; fall vertically, like a single drop; descend abruptly; fall, sink to ground. 2. Cease, lapse, fall through; fall in direction, amount, degree, etc. 3. Allow oneself to fall *behind, to the rear,* etc. 4. Come down *on* forcibly. 5. Let fall, shed, in drops; let fall like a drop or drops; let fall (words etc.) casually; send (letter etc.); (of animals) give birth to (young); (slang) lose, part with (money). 6. Fell, bring down, with blow, shot, etc. 7. Set down, from ship or vehicle. 8. Omit (esp., letter etc. in pronunciation). 9. Let droop; lower (voice). 10. Break off acquaintance or association with; ~ **in**, (esp.) pay casual visit; ~ **off**, (esp.) fall asleep; become less numerous etc.; ~ **out**, (esp.) with- draw. 11. ~ **kick**, (football) kick made by dropping ball and kicking it as it begins to bounce; **drop'- out**, one who withdraws from course of study, conventional way of life, etc.

drop·let (drŏp'lĭt) *n.* Little drop.

drop·per (drŏp'er) *n.* Device for administering liquid in drops; also

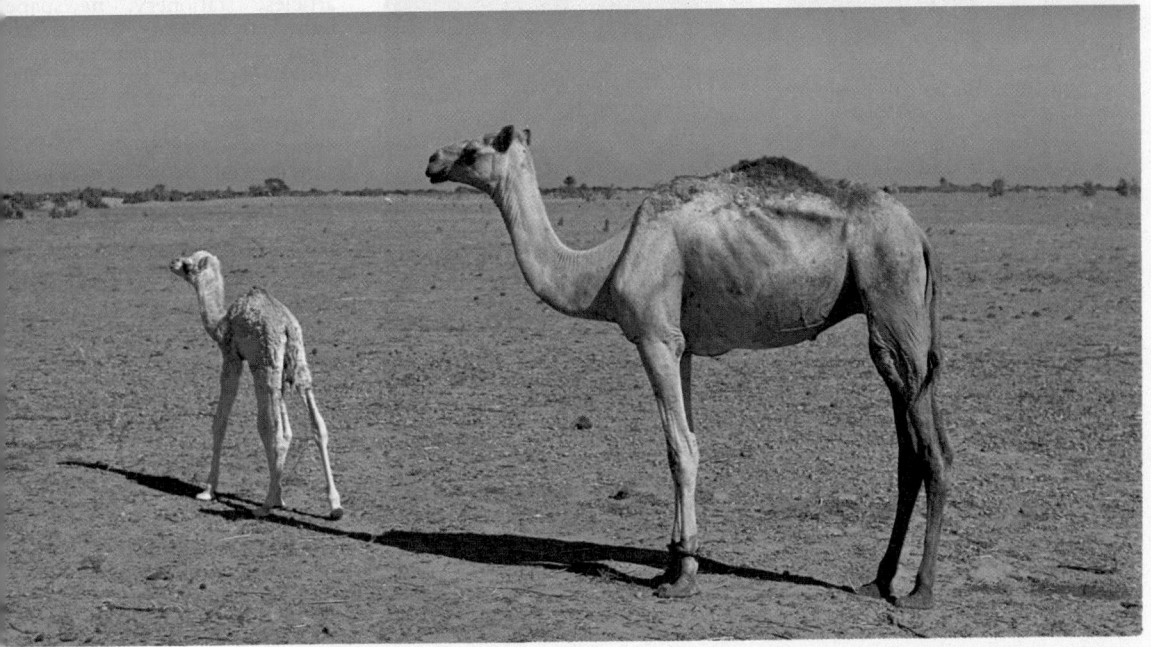

called **eye'dropper, medicine dropper**.

drop·ping (drŏp′ĭng) *n.* That which drops or falls in drops, as melted wax, etc.; (pl.) dung of animals or birds.

drop·sy (drŏp′sē) *n.* Accumulation of watery fluid in serous cavities or connective tissues of body. **drop′si·cal, drop′sied** *adjs.*

drosh·ky (drŏsh′kē, drawsh′-) *n.* (pl. **-kies**). Russian low four-wheeled open carriage.

dro·soph·i·la (drŏsŏf′ila) *n.* (pl. **-las, -lae** pr. -lē). Fruit fly of genus *D~*, much used in genetic research.

dross (draws, drŏs) *n.* Scum thrown off from metal in melting; foreign matter mixed with any substance; worthless stuff, refuse, rubbish. **dross′y** *adj.* (**dross·i·er, dross·i·est**). **dross′i·ness** *n.*

drought (drowt), **drouth** (drowth) *ns.* Continuous dry weather, lack of rain; dearth, scarcity.

drove (drōv) *n.* 1. Herd, flock, being driven or moving together; crowd, multitude, large number. 2. Mason's broad-faced chisel.

drov·er (drō′ver) *n.* One who drives cattle or sheep in droves to market; cattle dealer.

drown (drown) *v.* Suffocate by submersion, flood, drench; overcome (grief etc.) with or in drink;

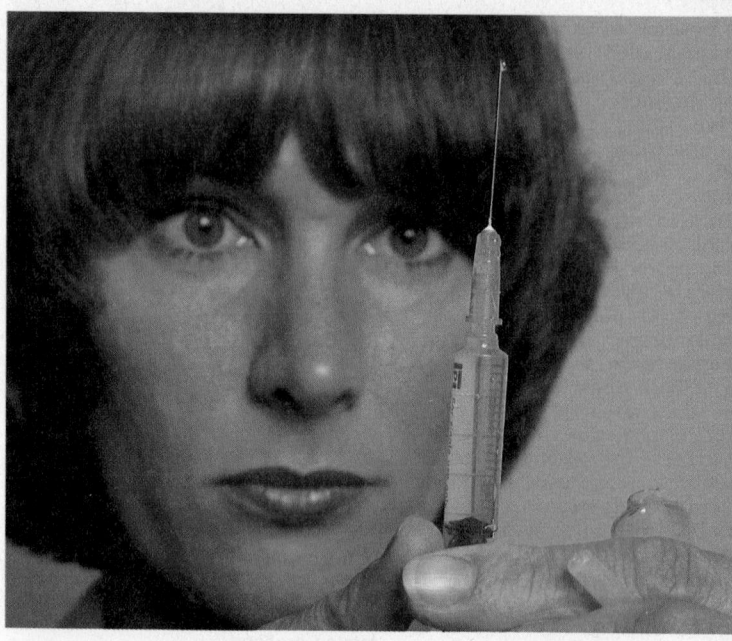

The **drosophila** *or fruit-fly is often used in scientific experiments on breeding because of its speed of reproduction and its four large paired chromosomes.*

overpower (sound) by greater loudness.

drowse (drowz) *v.* (**drowsed, drows·ing**). Doze; be half asleep; pass *away* (time etc.) in drowsing. *~ n.* Half-asleep condition.

drow·sy (drow′zē) *adj.* (**-si·er, -si·est**). Heavy with sleepiness; half asleep; soporific; sluggish, lethargic. **drow′si·ly** *adv.* **drow′si·ness** *n.*

drub (drŭb) *v.t.* (**drubbed, drub·bing**). Cudgel, thrash, belabor; defeat decisively. **drub′bing, drub′ber** *ns.*

drudge (drŭj) *n.* Servile worker,

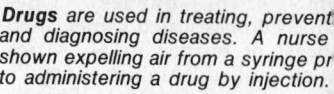

Drugs are used in treating, prevent and diagnosing diseases. A nurse shown expelling air from a syringe pr to administering a drug by injection.

slave, hack; hard toiler. *~* (**drudged, drudg·ing**). Perfo mean or servile tasks; work hard laboriously, toil. **drudg′er·y** *n.* (**-er·ies**).

drug (drŭg) *n.* Medicinal su stance; (esp.) narcotic; (a **dangerous ~, hard ~**) one t causes euphoria in the taker a predisposes him to addiction, e preparation or extract of opium coca; *~* **addict**, person addicted one of these; *~* **on the mark** commodity no longer in demar unsalable thing; **drug′store**, st where prescribed drugs are d pensed and where medicines, toi articles, stationery, newspape light refreshments, etc. are so. **drug traffic**, commercial sale drugs, forbidden by law. **dr** *v.t.* (**drugged, drug·ging**). A minister drug, esp. narcotic, to; a drug to (food or drink).

drug·gist (drŭg′ĭst) *n.* Pharm cist.

dru·id, Dru·id (droo′ĭd) (fem. **-id·ess** pr. -ĭdĭs). One of order of priests among the Celts ancient Gaul and Britain w appear in Irish and Welsh lege as magicians. **dru·id·ic** (drooĭd′ *adj.* **dru′id·ism** *n.* Religio system of Druids.

drum (drŭm) *n.* 1. Percussi musical instrument consisting hollow cylindrical or hemispheri frame with tightly stretched mer

Drought is the most serious phys hazard to agriculture in most parts the world. This skull is of an ani killed by drought. Efforts to make r by seeding clouds have had only limit success.

The **drum,** *essential to most orchestras and jazz bands (right), is still widely associated with magic in some societies. Above: The Embu tribesmen from Mount Kenya use it as an accompaniment to ritualistic dances. The drum is also associated with military music.*

brane at one or both ends, which is struck to produce sound; sound of this; **bass** ~, large drum with 2 heads struck sideways simultaneously to make a loud, low sound; **ket′tledrum**, cauldron-shaped drum that can be tuned to produce note of definite pitch. 2. Drum-shaped thing, as cylinder wound with cable, wire, etc; barrel-like metal receptacle for oil etc.; (archit.) solid part of Corinthian and composite capitals; block of stone forming one section of shaft of column; cylindrical structure supporting dome. 3. = *drumfish* (see def. 4 below). 4. **drum′-beat,** sound of a drum; **drum′fire,** rapid heavy gunfire; **drum′fish,** any of various Amer. fishes (*Sciaenops ocellata, Pogonias cromis,* etc.) making a drumming noise; see CROAKER. **drum′head,** stretched skin or membrane of drum; circular top of capstan, into which capstan bars are fixed; **drumhead court-martial,** court-martial (hist. held around an upturned drum) for summary treatment of offenses during military operations; **drum major,**

person who leads marching band; **drum majorette,** girl or woman accompanying marching band and twirling baton etc.; **drum′stick,** stick often with padded knob at one end for beating drum; lower part of leg of cooked poultry, so called from its shape. **drum** *v.* (**drummed, drum·ming**). 1. Play the drum; beat, tap, or thump, continuously on something; (of bird, insect) make loud hollow noise with quivering wings. 2. Summon, beat *up,* as by drumming; (colloq.) obtain (custom, customers) by canvassing etc.; solicit orders; drive *out* of regiment etc. publicly by beat of drum, so as to heighten disgrace; din *into* (person). **drum′mer** *n.* 1. Player of drum. 2. Traveling salesman.

drunk (drŭngk) *adj.:* see DRINK *v.*; (esp.) intoxicated. ~ *n.* Drinking bout; drunken person; alcoholic. **drunk′ard** *n.* Sot; habitually drunken person. **drunk′en** *adj.* Often drunk; caused by or exhibiting drunkenness. **drunk′-en·ly** *adv.* **drunk′en·ness** *n.*

drupe (drōōp) *n.* Fleshy or

pulpy fruit having single ha stone, as peach, plum, cher **dru·pa·ceous** (drōōpā′shus) *a* Bearing drupes.

Druse (drōōz) *n.* Member Muslim political and religious s in Syria and Lebanon, believing transmigration, and holding the C Fatimate Caliph, Hakim Biam lahi, to be a divine incarnatio [Arab *durūz,* prob. f. *Ismā′īl Darazī* (the tailor), their founde

dry (drī) *adj.* (**dri·er, dri·es** 1. Free from moisture, not wet st; deficient in rain, not rainy; d, desiccated, parched; thirsty, ing thirst; not yielding water (of cows etc.) not yielding milk. Not under, in, or on water; not merged. 3. (of bread etc.) With-butter or the like. 4. Solid, liquid; (of measures etc.) re-ng to non-liquids. 5. (of wines Not sweet or fruity. 6. oring or enforcing prohibition lcoholic liquor. 7. Feeling or wing no emotion; stiff, cold; stically witty; uttered in, using, ter-of-fact tones without air of santry. 8. ~ **battery**, battery sisting of dry cells; ~-**bulb** rmometer, one of a pair of mometers in hygrometer of ch one has dry and other wet o; ~ **cell**, (electr.) voltaic cell se contents are made non-lable by use of some absorbent stance or having electrolyte in n of moist paste; ~-**clean** (v.t.) n (clothes etc.) with chemical vent having no or little water; **cleaner**, shop that dry-cleans; **dock**: see DOCK³; ~ **farming**, ous methods of arable farming igned to conserve moisture in areas: ~ **fly**, (angling) artificial resting lightly on water; ~ **ods**, clothing, textiles, and re-d articles of trade; **D** ~ **Ice**, demark) solid carbon dioxide, ch passes directly from a solid a gas at −78.5°C., absorbing a at amount of heat, making it use- as refrigerant; ~ **measure**, em of units for measuring dry ntities, esp. for grain, fruits, ; ~ **plate**, (photog.) sensitized te that does not require immer-n before exposure; **dry'point**, ong pointed tool for scratching ign (without use of acid) on per plate from which prints are en; process of engraving thus, nt so produced; ~ **rot**, decayed dition, caused by various fungi, unventilated timber, in which it comes dry, light, and friable; ~ n, (colloq.) rehearsal; (mil.) ctice exercise without ammuni-n; ~ **spell**, period of little or no n; ~ **wall**, (stone) wall without rtar; **dry'wall** (n. & adj.), (of) l construction with plaster-ard, plywood, etc., without ster; **dry well**, drainage hole ed with loose stones, for collect-g and dispersing rainwater etc. y·a·ble adj. dry'ly, dri'ly advs. y'ness n. dry v. (dried, dry·-g). Make or become dry by ping, evaporation, draining, etc.; **up**, make, become, utterly dry; se to yield water or milk; (slang)

cease talking.

dry·ad (drī'ăd) n. (pl. **-ads, -a·des** pr. -adēz). Wood-nymph.

Dry·den (drī'den), **John** (1631–1700). English poet, dramatist, critic; translator of Virgil, Horace, Ovid, etc.

dry·er (drī'er) n. Thing, person that dries, esp. appliance to dry clothers, hair, etc.; drier.

D.S.C., DSC abbrevs. Distinguished Service Cross.

D.S.M., DSM abbrevs. Distinguished Service Medal.

DST abbrev. Daylight-saving time.

d.t., d.t.'s abbrevs. Delirium tremens.

Du. abbrev. Dutch.

du·al (dōō'al, dū'-) adj. Of two; twofold, divided in two; double; having a double nature or character. **du·al·i·ty** (dōōăl'itē, dū-) n. **du·al·ism** (dōō'alizem, dū'-) n.

1. Being dual. 2. Theory or system of thought recognizing two independent principles; (philos.) doctrine that mind and matter exist as distinct entities (opp. MONISM and PLURALISM); doctrine that there are two independent principles, good and evil. **du·al·ist** n. & adj. **du·al·is·tic** (dōōalĭs'tĭk, dū-) adj.

dub¹ (dŭb) v.t. (**dubbed, dub·-bing**). 1. Make (person) into a knight by striking shoulder with sword. 2. Invest with (new title); name, nickname. 3. Smear leather with grease. 4. (golf) Hit a ball ineffectually. ~ n. (esp.) Poor golfer; clumsy person.

dub² (dŭb) v.t. (**dubbed, dub·-ing**). Add sound effects or new

*Typical **drupes**, or fleshy fruits with one or more seeds each surrounded by a hard layer, are cherries and walnuts. In raspberries small drupes are clustered together.*

Apricot   Peach   Cherry

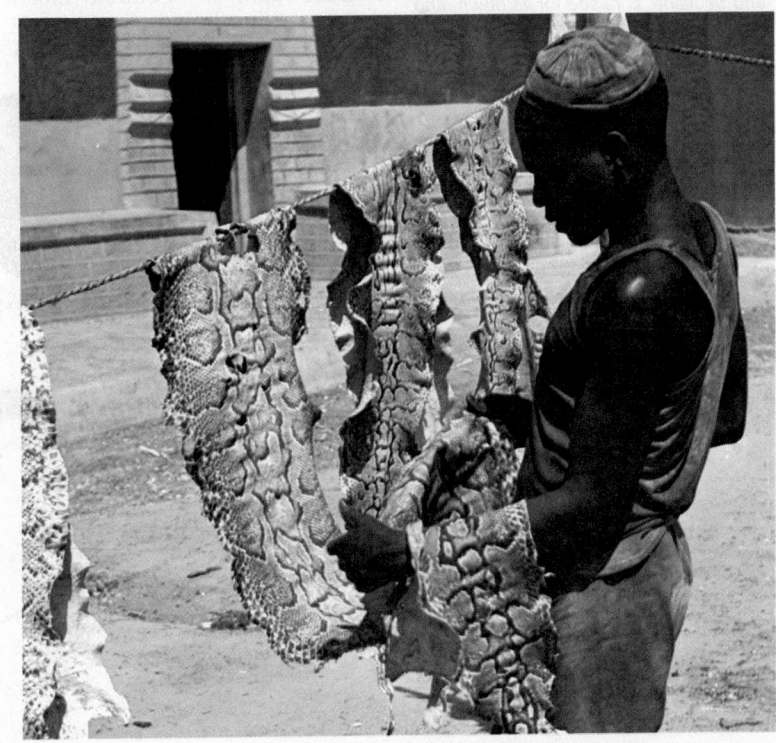

e **drying** of snake or crocodile skins Nigeria is achieved by simply expos-the skin to the sun's heat. The dried ns are then despatched for manufac-e into handbags, shoes etc.

sound track, esp. in a different language, to (film); insert (sound effects) *in* film or radio or television production.

du·bi·e·ty (dōobī′etē, dū-) *n.* (pl. **-ties**). Feeling of doubt.

du·bi·ous (dōo′bēus, dū′-) *adj.* Doubtful; of questionable or suspected character. **du′bi·ous·ly** *adv.* **du′bi·ous·ness** *n.*

Dub·lin (dŭb′lĭn). Capital of the Republic of Ireland, port on the Irish Sea; formerly capital of all Ireland.

Du Bois (dōo bois′), **W(illiam) E(dward) B(urghardt)** (1868–1963). Amer. sociologist, educator and writer; a founder of the NAACP, 1910.

Du·brov·nik (dōobrawv′nĭk). Port city and resort on Dalmatian coast of Yugoslavia.

Du·buf·fet (dübüfē′), **Jean** (1901–). French sculptor and painter.

du·cal (dōo′kal, dū′-) *adj.* Of, like, bearing title of, duke.

duc·at (dŭk′ĭt) *n.* (hist.) Gold coin of varying value formerly current in most European countries; (hist.) Italian silver coin; (colloq.) coin, (pl.) cash.

Duc·cio di Buo·nin·se·gna (dōot′chaw dē bwawnēnsĕ′nyah) (1255?–1319). Ital. painter and founder of the Sienese school.

duch·ess (dŭch′ĭs) *n.* Wife or widow of duke; lady holding title to a duchy in her own right.

duch·y (dŭch′ē) *n.* (pl. **duch·-**

Some of the many species of duck have considerable commercial value. The eider duck, which breeds in Iceland and Scotland, is raised for its down, and ducks have been reared for food for hundreds of years.

ies). Territory of reigning duke or duchess.

duck[1] (dŭk) *n.* (pl. **ducks**, collect. **duck**). 1. Any of several kinds of swimming bird of the family Anatidae found all over the world, esp. domesticated form of mallard or wild duck; female of this (male being DRAKE[2]); flesh of this bird. 2. **dead** ~, person or cause certain to fail; **lame** ~, elected official completing remaining term after an election in which he was not reelected; ~**s and drakes**, game of making flat stone skip over surface of water; **duck′bill**, ~-**billed platypus**: see PLATYPUS; **duck′board**, narrow path of wooden slats laid on muddy ground; **duck′pin**, short bowling pin; **duck soup**, (slang) easy task; **duck′weed**, any plant of genus *Lemna*, floating on still water and covering surface like a green carpet.

duck[2] (dŭk) *n.* Strong untwilled linen or cotton fabric for clothing, sails, etc.; (pl.) clothing, esp. trousers of this.

duck[3] (dŭk) *v.* Plunge, dive, dip head, under water and emerge; bend quickly, bob, to avoid blow etc; plunge (person) momentarily *in, under* water; lower (head) suddenly. ~ *n.* Quick dip below water in bathing; lowering of head.

duck·ing (dŭk′ĭng) *n.* Immersion in water, or wetting by submersion; ~ **stool**, chair in which scolds, dishonest tradesmen, etc., were tied and ducked in water as a punishment.

duck·ling (dŭk′lĭng) *n.* Young duck; **ugly** ~: see UGLY.

duct (dŭkt) *n.* Conduit, tube, for conveying liquid; conduit for electric cable; (physiol.) tube or

canal conveying secretions [...] lymph in animal body; (bot.) ves [...] of plant's vascular tissue hold [...] air, water, etc. **duct′less** [...] (of gland) Having no ducts, c [...] taining secretion that pas [...] directly from cells to blood; en [...] crine. **duct** *v.t.* Convey throu [...] a duct.

duc·tile (dŭk′tĭl, -tīl) *adj.* 1. [...] metal) Malleable, flexible, [...] brittle; (tech.) capable of bei [...] drawn into wire, tough. 2. Plast [...] pliable, pliant. **duc·til·i·ty** (dŭ [...] tĭl′ĭtē) *n.*

dud (dŭd) *n.* 1. (slang) ([...] Clothes. 2. Shell etc. that fails [...] explode; futile plan or person.

dude (dōod, dūd) *n.* (slar [...] Exaggeratedly fastidious or foppi [...] person; dandy, swell; (also) a [...] male; ~ **ranch**, cattle ranch co [...] verted into resort for visitors, w [...] facilities for riding etc.

dudg·eon (dŭj′on) *n.* (usu. **hig** [...] ~) Resentment, feeling of offens [...]

due (dōo, dū) *adj.* 1. Owin [...] payable, as a debt or obligation; th [...] ought to be given or rendered (t [...] fitting, proper, rightful. 2. To [...] ascribed or attributed *to* (caus [...] agent, etc.). 3. Under engageme [...] or contract to be ready, be preser [...] or arrive (at defined time). ~ *aa* [...] (with ref. to points of compas [...] Straight, exactly, directly. ~ [...] 1. Person's right, what is owed hi [...] what one owes. 2. (usu. pl.) F [...] or charge for membership, as in [...] club, etc.; **pay one's** ~**s**, (slan [...] gain experience through trouble. [...]

du·el (dōo′el, dū′-) *n.* Fight wi [...] deadly weapons between two pe [...] sons, in presence of two observe [...] (*seconds*), to settle quarrel; any co [...] test between two parties, person [...]

Long-tailed · Tufted · Mallard · Shelduck · Mandarin · Eider

The Carolina **wood duck** is one of the most brilliantly colored of all ducks. The white markings highlight and accentuate the duck's lines and features.

mals, causes. ~ *v.i.* (**-eled, -ing** or **-elled, -el·ling**). Fight el. **du'el·ist, du'el·er** *ns.*

du·en·na (dōōĕn'a, dū-) *n.* der woman acting as governess d chaperon to girl(s) (orig. and . in Spanish family); chaperon.

du·et (dōōĕt', dū-) *n.* (mus.) omposition for) two voices or truments.

duf·fel, duf·fle (dŭf'el) *ns.* arse woolen cloth with thick nap; nper's change of clothes or rsonal effects; ~ **bag**, cylindrical vas bag; ~ **coat**, coat made of ffel, esp. one with hood and gle fastenings. [f. *Duffel* in Bra-nt]

duf·fer (dŭf'er) *n.* (colloq.) In-icient or stupid person, novice, ginner.

dug (dŭg) *n.* Udder, breast, or t of female mammal.

du·gong (dōō'gŏng) *n.* Large uatic herbivorous mammal, *D~ gon*, of tropical Asian coasts. lalay *duyong*]

dug·out (dŭg'owt) *adj.* Hol-wed out by digging. ~ *n.* 1. noe made of hollowed out tree ink. 2. Underground shelter esp. troops in trenches. 3. Roofed, nken shelter at side of baseball ld for players not on the field.

dui·ker (dī'ker) *n.* (pl. **-kers**, llect. **-ker**). Small African telope (genus *Cephalophus*) with ort backward-pointing horns; so lled from its habit of diving sud-nly into the bush. [Du. *duiker* ver]

duke (dōōk, dūk) *n.* 1. In Gt. itain and some other countries, reditary noble ranking next low prince; **royal** ~, duke who

is a member of royal family, taking precedence of other dukes. 2. In some parts of Europe, sovereign prince, ruler of duchy. 3. (slang) Hand, fist. **duke'dom** *n.* Duchy; office or dignity of duke.

Du·kho·bors (dōō'kōbōrz), **Du·kho·bor·tsy** (dōōkōbōrt'sē) *ns.pl.* Members of a Russian Christian sect who rejected author-ity of church and state, were perse-cuted for refusing to pay taxes or perform military service, and migrated to Saskatchewan and British Columbia, Canada, in 1899.

*The **duiker** or duikerbok is a small ante-lope that inhabits forest and brush country in Africa. It has a habit of diving into and threading its way through thick bush.*

[Russ., = "spirit wrestler"]

dul·cet (dŭl'sĭt) *adj.* Sweet, soothing (esp. of sounds).

dul·ci·mer (dŭl'simer) *n.* Musi-cal instrument in which metallic strings of graduated length are stretched over a trapezoidal sound-ing board and struck with hammers held in the hands; similar folk in-strument played by plucking strings.

dull (dŭl) *adj.* 1. Slow of understanding, stupid; lacking sensibility or keenness of percep-tion; (of pain etc.) not keen or intense. 2. Slow, heavy, drowsy; stagnant, sluggish; listless, not lively or cheerful, depressed; causing depression or boredom. 3. Not sharp or keen; not clear, vivid, or intense; obscure, muffled, flat, insipid; (of weather) overcast, gloomy. ~ *v.* Make or become dull, sluggish, inert, etc.; blunt; make or become dim or indistinct. **dull'ard** *n.* Dull or stupid person, dunce. **dul'ly** *adv.* **dull'ness, dul'ness** *ns.*

dulse (dŭls) *n.* Edible species of reddish-brown seaweed (*Rhody-menia palmata*).

du·ly (dōō'lē, dū'-) *adv.* Rightly, properly, fitly; sufficiently; punc-tually.

Du·mas (dōōmah', dū-), **Alex-andre**. (1) "Dumas *père*" (1802–70), French dramatist and prolific writer of swashbuckling historical novels including *The Three Musketeers*, *The Count of Monte Cristo*; (2) "Dumas *fils*," his natural son **Alexandre** (1824–95), French dramatist, author of *La Dame aux Camélias* etc.

dumb (dŭm) *adj.* 1. Destitute

Sand **dunes** *are most commonly found in deserts and on sea coasts. They may range in height from a few feet to more than 300 feet, particularly, as here, in the Sahara Desert.*

Some species of **dung** *beetle knead animal dung into balls which they roll along the ground and into a hollow. The dung is for their own consumption or is collected for their brood.*

of faculty of speech. 2. Temporarily bereft of speech from astonishment, shock, etc.; remaining persistently silent; refusing to speak. 3. (of actions) Not attended with speech. 4. Not emitting or attended with sound; silent, mute; not having some quality, property, etc., usual in things of the name. 5. Foolish, stupid (prob. after Ger. *dumm*). 6. **dumb′bell**, short bar with heavy knob at each end, used in pairs for exercising muscles; object of this shape; **dumb cluck**, (slang) stupid person; **dumb show**, pantomime; communication by gestures; **dumb′waiter**, small elevator for conveying food etc. between floors. **dumb′ly** *adv.* **dumb′ness** *n.*

dum·dum (dŭm′dŭm) *n.* (also ~ **bullet**) Soft-nosed bullet that expands on impact. [*Dum-Dum*, town and arsenal near Calcutta]

dum·found, dumb·found (dŭm′fownd′) *vbs.t.* Strike dumb, confound, nonplus.

dum·my (dŭm′ē) *n.* (pl. **-mies**). 1. (bridge) Hand turned up and played by declarer; person holding this hand. 2. Person taking no real part, or present only for show, figurehead, mere tool; ~ **corporation**, corporation set up to mask real aims (usu. illegal or unethical) of its promoters. 3. Counterfeit object, sham package, etc. 4. Man's figure used as target; manikin; imitation ammunition used in train-

ing. 5. (colloq.) Stupid person. ~ *adj.* That is a dummy, sham.

dump (dŭmp) *n.* Rubbish heap, place where garbage or refuse is deposited; temporary depot, pile, of ammunition, equipment, etc.; (colloq.) unpleasant or dreary place; (pl. colloq.) low spirits. ~ *v.* Deposit, unload, put down (rubbish); let fall with a bump; send (goods unsalable at high price in home market) to foreign market for sale at low price; sell or otherwise dispose of unwanted merchandise

or possessions at a loss; (collo abandon.

dump·ling (dŭm′plĭng) *n.* of dough cooked in stew, boi with beef, etc., or sweetened a baked with fruit inside.

dump·y (dŭm′pē) *adj.* (**dum i·er, dump·i·est**). Short and sto

dun¹ (dŭn) *adj.* Of dull grayis brown color; (of horse) of gold sand-colored body with black ma and tail; (poet.) dark, dusky. ~ Dun color; dun horse.

dun² (dŭn) *v.t.* (**dunned, du ning**). Importune for payment debt; pester.

dunce (dŭns) *n.* One slow learning, dullard; ~'s **cap**, co shaped paper cup formerly put head of dunce at school. [Jo Duns Scotus, whose followers we ridiculed by 16th-c. reformers a humanists as enemies of learning

dun·der·head (dŭn′derhĕd) Blockhead; dunce. **dun′der head·ed** *adj.*

dune (dōōn, dūn) *n.* Mound ridge of drifted sand; ~ **buggy** BEACH buggy.

dung (dŭng) *n.* Manure; excr ment of animals (rarely of ma moral filth; ~ **beetle**, any various beetles that breed in dun **dung′hill**, heap of dung; foul infamous place. **dung** *v.t.* Manu (field).

dun·ga·ree (dŭnggarē′, dŭng garē′) *n.* Sturdy, usu. blue, deni

ric; (pl.) trousers or overalls of
is.

dun·geon (dŭn′jon) *n.* Strong
rk cell; subterranean place of con-
ement.

dunk (dŭngk) *v.t.* 1. Dip (bread,
ke, doughnut, etc.) into soup,
ffee, etc. while eating. 2. (colloq.)
oot (basketball) through basket
om above, hence ~ **shot.** 3. Sub-
erge in water or other liquid.

Dun·kirk (dŭn′kĕrk), *Fr.* **Dun-·
rque** (dônkĕrk′). Seaport in
E. France on North Sea; scene of
roic British troop evacuation
ay 29–June 3, 1940, during
orld War II; any similar with-
awal, crisis, etc.

dun·lin (dŭn′lĭn) *n.* Small
ddish-backed migratory wading
rd (*Erolia alpina*), allied to sand-
per, abundant on sea coasts of
urope and northern N. Amer.;
so called red-backed sandpiper.

dun·nage (dŭn′ĭj) *n.* Light
aterial, as brushwood, mats, etc.,
owed under or among cargo to
revent damage; miscellaneous
aggage.

ummies stored in a factory (below)
ok rather like merchandise in a human
are parts store. These dummies will
hish up in a store window, displaying
e latest clothes.

The evacuation of British forces from
the beaches and harbor of **Dunkirk** in
1940 during the 1939–45 war
involved the use of naval ships and
many small civilian craft.

The small **dunlin**, about 8 ins. long,
breeds around the North Pole and
northern Europe, and winters further
south towards the Equator. The curved
beak probes for food.

du·o (dōō′ō, dū′ō) *n.* (pl. **du·os**).
1. (mus.) Duet. 2. Couple or pair.

du·o·dec·i·mal (dōōōdĕs′imal,
dū-) *adj.* Of 12 or twelfths, proceeding by twelves.

du·o·dec·i·mo (dōōōdĕs′imō,
dū) *n.* (abbreviated 12mo) Page or
book size (5 × 7¾ in.; 12.7 × 19.7
cm) of a book formed by folding a
single printed sheet into 12 leaves;
book composed of pages of this size.

du·o·de·num (dōōōdē′num,
-ŏd′e-, dū-) *n.* (pl. **du·o·de·na** pr.
dōōōdē′na, -ŏd′e, dū-, **du·o·de-·
nums**). (anat.) First portion of
small intestine immediately below
stomach. **du·o·de′nal** *adj.* [L.
duodeni 12 at once (f. its being about
12 in. long)]

dup. *abbrev.* Duplicate.

dupe (dōōp, dūp) *n.* Victim of
deception; person easily fooled,
gull. **dup′er·y** *n.* (pl. **-er·ies**).
dupe *v.t.* (**duped, dup·ing**).
Cheat, make a fool of.

du·ple (dōō′pel, dū′-) *adj.* (mus.,
of time) Having two beats in
bar; (math., of proportion) in which
one quantity is double the other.

du·plex (dōō′plĕks, dū′-) *adj.* Of
two elements; twofold; (also ~
apartment) One on two connected
floors; house for two families.

du·pli·cate (dōō′plĭkĭt, dū′-)
adj. 1. With two corresponding
parts; existing in two examples. 2.
Doubled; twice as large or as many.
3. Exactly like thing already existing. ~ *n.* One of two things
exactly alike; exact copy; second
copy, with equal legal force, of
letter or document; **in** ~, in two
exactly corresponding copies or
parts. ~ (dōō′plĭkāt, dū′-) *v.t.*
(**-cat·ed, -cat·ing**). 1. Double,
multiply by two. 2. Make in
duplicate; make exact copy of; produce copies of; repeat. **du·pli·ca·-
tion** (dōōplĭkā′shon, dū-) *n.*

du·pli·ca·tor   (dōō′plĭkāter,

dū´-) *n.* Machine (mimeograph etc.) for producing copies of documents.

du·plic·i·ty (dōoplĭs´ĭtē, dū-) *n.* (pl. **-ties**). Double-dealing, deceitfulness; deception.

dur·a·ble (door´abel, dūr´-) *adj.* Lasting, not transitory; resisting wear, decay, etc.; ~ **goods**, manufactured products, as cars, appliances, etc., that can be used over a period of time; ~ **press** = PERMANENT press. **du·ra·bil·i·ty** (doorabĭl´ĭtē, dūr-) *n.*

du·ra ma·ter (door´a mā´ter). (anat.) Dense tough membrane enveloping brain and spinal cord. [med. L. transl. of Arab anatomical term, = "hard mother," so called because it was supposed to give rise to all membranes of body]

du·ra·men (durā´men, dyu-) *n.* Dense inner part of tree trunk, heartwood.

dur·ance (door´ans, dūr´-) *n.* Forced confinement, imprisonment, esp. (literary) **in ~ vile**.

Du·rant (durănt´), **Will(iam) James** (1885–). Amer. educator; with his wife, **Ariel** (1898–), wrote popular works on philosophy and history, notably the multivolume *Story of Civilization*.

du·ra·tion (durā´shon, dyu-) *n.* Continuance in time; time during which thing, action, or state continues.

Dur·ban (dẽr´ban). Port city on E. coast of Republic of South Africa.

Dü·rer (door´er, dūr´-), **Albrecht** (1471–1528). German Renaissance engraver and painter; famous for his line engravings and woodcuts.

du·ress (durĕs´, dyu-, door´ĭs, dūr´-) *n.* Forcible restraint, imprisonment; constraint illegally exercised to force person to perform some act, compulsion.

Dur·ham (dẽr´am). 1. County in NE. England; its county seat; (one of) a breed of Shorthorn beef cattle orig. developed in this county. 2. City in North Carolina, site of Duke University.

dur·ing (door´ĭng, dūr´-) *prep.* Throughout, at some point in, the continuance of.

Dürr·en·matt (door´enmaht), **Friedrich** (1921–). Swiss novelist and playwright.

durst (dẽrst) *v.* (archaic) Past tense of DARE, before expressed or implied infinitive without *to*.

du·rum (door´um, dūr´-) *n.* Species of wheat (*Triticum durum*) with hard seeds, used chiefly for pasta.

dusk (dŭsk) *n.* Shade, gloom; darker stage of twilight. ~ *adj.* (poet.) Dusky.

dusk·y (dŭs´kē) *adj.* (**dusk·i·er, dusk·i·est**). Shadowy, dim; darkcolored. **dusk'i·ly** *adv.* **dusk'i·ness** *n.*

Düs·sel·dorf (dōos´eldorf; *Ger.* düs´eldorf). Industrial city on Rhine River in West Germany.

dust (dŭst) *n.* 1. Earth or other solid matter in minute and fine state of subdivision, in particles small and light enough to be easily raised and carried in cloud by wind; cloud

of dust; **bite the ~**, fall to t ground killed or wounded; **dry ~**, extremely boring, pedan **throw ~ in person's ey** deceive him. 2. What anything reduced to by disintegration decay, esp. remains of dead bo person's mortal remains. 3. **dus bin,** (Brit.) trash can, garbage c **dust bowl,** area made desert

*Top: **Dusk** in Yellowstone National Park sees a young deer make its way to water. Above: In strong winds, dunes of sand can easily be transformed into **dust** storms, sometimes erasing all visibility.*

deforestation, drought, and dust storms; **dust devil**, small column-like whirlwind of dust; **dust jacket**, paper jacket covering hardcover book; **dust'man**, (Brit.) person who collects and carts away refuse etc.; **dust'pan**, utensil into which dust is swept from floor etc.; **dust storm**, severe dust-filled wind-storm, esp. in arid region, during drought; **dust'up**, (colloq.) quar-rel, fight. **dust** *v.* 1. Sprinkle with dust or powder, (cooking) flour, sugar, etc.; make dusty; sprinkle (powder etc.). 2. Clear of dust by brushing, wiping, etc.; clear away (dust etc.); clear furniture etc. of dust.

dust·er (dŭs'ter) *n.* 1. Cloth or brush for dusting furniture etc. 2. Smock; woman's loose-fitting dresslike housecoat.

dust·y (dŭs'tē) *adj.* (**dust·i·er, dust·i·est**). Full of dust, strewn with dust; finely powdered like dust; ~ **miller**, any of several plants with gray or white leaves covered with dustlike down, esp. the beach wormwood (*Artemisia stelleriana*) and *Lychnis coronaria*, or mullein pink. **dust'i·ly** *adv.* **dust'i·ness** *n.*

Dutch (dŭch) *adj.* 1. Of the Netherlands or its language or people; coming from the Netherlands; characteristic of the Dutch. 2. (hist.) Of Germany, German; Teutonic; **High ~**, of the southern Germans, High German; **Low ~**, of the northern Germans, of the northern and northwest parts, including the Netherlands and Flanders. 3. **go ~**, have each person pay his or her own expenses; **in ~**, (colloq.) in trouble, out of favor; **~ courage**, (colloq.) courage from intoxicants and therefore not lasting; **~ door**, door with upper and lower halves that can be opened independently; **~ elm disease**, fatal disease of elm trees, caused by a fungus *Ceratocystis ulmi*, first found in the Netherlands; **~ metal**, alloy of copper and zinc made in leaf form in imitation of gold leaf; **~ oven**, (1) metal box of which open side is turned toward fireplace, for roasting meat etc.; (2) large, heavy, usu. cast-iron pot with close-fitting lid, for cooking roasts, etc.; **~ treat**, party, date, etc. in which each person pays for or contributes his or her own share; **~ uncle**, (colloq.) severe and candid critic. **Dutch** *n.* 1. (collect.) People of the Netherlands. 2. Language of the Netherlands, a Germanic dialect that has not undergone the High German consonant mutation (second sound shift). 3. (obs.) German language; **High ~** = HIGH GERMAN; **Low ~** = LOW GERMAN; **Pennsylvania ~**, (German as spoken by) descendants of 17th · and 18th c. German and Swiss immigrants into Pennsylvania. **Dutch'man** *n.* (pl. **-men**). 1. Native, inhabitant, of the Netherlands. 2. Dutch ship;

Dutch customs, culture and landscape have been magnificently recorded by such artists as Rembrandt, Vermeer and Van Gogh. This painting, 'The Lacemaker', is by Jan Vermeer.

Flying ~, legendary spectral s condemned with all her crew to the seas for ever, and suppose be seen near the Cape of G Hope. 3. (hist.) German. **Dutchman's breeches**, a w flower (*Dicentra cucullaria*) called from the shape of its flow which resembles breeches hang upside down.

du·te·ous (dōo'tēus, dū'-) (poet.) Dutiful, obedient. **d te·ous·ly** *adv.* **du'te·ous·ness** *n*

du·ti·a·ble (dōo'tēabel, di *adj.* Subject to import tax.

du·ti·ful (dōo'tĭful, dū'-) c Regular or willing in obedience a service. **du'ti·ful·ly** *adv.* **du' ful·ness** *n.*

du·ty (dōo'tē, dū'-) *n.* (pl. **-ti** 1. Action and conduct owed deference, respect, custom, etc. Payment to public revenue lev on imports. 3. Action, act, due way of moral or legal obligation. Business, office, function, perf mance of or engagement in th

The **Dyaks** of the Borneo forests, once headhunters and cannibals, are extremely fond of ornaments, as can be seen in the large metal earrings worn by the womenfolk.

on, off, ~, actually so engaged or
ot);(eccles.)performance of church
ervices; ~ **officer,** (mil. etc.) per-
on left in charge when others are
bsent. 5. Measure of engine's
ffectiveness in units of work done
er unit of fuel.

du·um·vir (dooŏŭm´ver, dū-) *n.*
Rom. hist.) One of a pair of
oequal magistrates and function-
ries in Rome and her colonies.
du·um´vir·ate *n.*

Du·va·lier (dooōvahlyā´; *Fr.*
lüvălyā´), **François** (1907–71).
Commonly called "Papa Doc";
resident and dictator of Haiti,
957–71.

D.V.M. *abbrev.* Doctor of
Veterinary Medicine.

Dvo·rak (dvor´zhahk, -zhăk),

Anton(in) (1841–1904). Czech
composer of symphonies, Slavic
dances, operas, etc.

dwarf (dwôrf) *n.* (pl. **dwarfs,
dwarves** pr. dwôrvz). 1. Person,
animal, or plant, much below
ordinary size of species. 2. (also
~ **star**) One of the class of smaller
stars of greater density as dist. from
the larger diffuse stars or "giants."
3. (Teutonic, esp. Scand., myth.)
Small manlike, often ugly, creature
living underground. **dwarf** *adj.*
Undersized; puny, stunted. ~
cornel: see BUNCHBERRY. **dwarf´-**

ish adj. **dwarf´ish·ness** *n.*
dwarf´ism *n.* (med.) Condition of
being considerably undersized.
dwarf *v.t.* Stunt in growth, intellect, etc.; make to look small by
contrast or distance.

dwell (dwĕl) *v.i.* (**dwelt,
dwelled, dwell·ing**). 1. Continue,
remain, for a time (archaic); have
one's abode, live (in house, country,
etc.). 2. ~ **on,** spend time upon,
linger over in thought; treat at
length. **dwell´er** *n.* Inhabitant,
resident.

dwell·ing (dwĕl´ĭng) *n.* (esp.)
Place of residence, house; ~ **place,**
dwelling.

dwin·dle (dwĭn´del) *v.i.* (**-dled,
-dling**). Become smaller, shrink,
waste away; lose importance, de-

cline; degenerate.

dwt. *abbrev.* Pennyweight.

Dy *symbol.* Dysprosium.

dy·ad (dī′ăd) *n.* The number two; group of two, couple, pair.

Dy·ak (dī′ăk) *n.* Member, language, of an aboriginal tribe of Borneo.

dyb·buk (dĭb′uk) *n.* (pl. **dyb·-buks**, *Heb.* **dyb·bu·kim** pr. dĭ-bōōkĕm′). (Jewish folklore) Malevolent spirit (of dead person) that enters living person's body and controls it until exorcised.

dye (dī) *v.* (**dyed, dye·ing**). Color, stain, tinge; impregnate with color, fix a color in the substance of; make (thing) specified color; **dyed in the wool**: see WOOL. **dy′er** *n.* One who dyes clothes etc. **dye** *n.* Color produced by or as by dyeing; tinge, hue; matter used for dyeing, coloring matter in solution. **dye′stuff**, material used as or producing a dye.

dy·ing: see DIE[2]

dyke: see DIKE.

dy·nam·ic (dīnăm′ĭk) *adj.* Of force producing motion; of force in action or operation, active; potent, energetic; of dynamics; (philos.) relating to the reason of existence of an object of experience; accounting for matter, or mind, as merely the action of forces. **dy·nam′ics** *n.pl.* Branch of physics treating of the behavior of matter under the action of force; branch of any science considering force or forces; moving forces, physical or moral, in any sphere. **dy·nam′i·cal·ly** *adv.*

dy·na·mism (dī′namĭzem) *n.* Philosophical system or theory explaining phenomena of universe by some immanent force or energy. **dy·na·mis·tic** (dīnamĭs′tĭk) *adj.*

The constituents of a **dynamo**: an alternator (above) and a generator (below). A dynamo is used to convert mechanical energy into electrical energy.

dy·na·mite (dī′namīt) *n.* High explosive of nitroglycerine contained in some absorbent substance. ~ *v.t.* (**-mit·ed, -mit·ing**). Set charge of dynamite to, blow up with dynamite. **dy′na·mit·er** *n.* [named by Alfred Nobel (1833–96), the inventor, f. Gk. *dunamis* force]

dy·na·mo (dī′namō) *n.* (pl. **-mos**). Machine converting mechanical into electrical energy by rotating coils of copper wire in a magnetic field. [short for *dynamo-electric machine*]

dy·na·mom·e·ter (dīnamŏm′-eter) *n.* Instrument for measuring energy.

dy·nast (dī′năst, -nast; *Brit.* dĭn′ăst) *n.* Ruler, member dynasty. **dy·nas·ty** (dī′nastē; *B* also dĭn′astē) *n.* (pl. **-ties**). L of hereditary rulers. **dy·nas** (dīnăs′tĭk; *Brit.* also dĭnăs′tĭk) **dy·nas′ti·cal·ly** *adv.*

dyne (dīn) *n.* (phys.) Absol unit of force in the cgs system, fo that, acting on a mass of 1 gra will make it move 1 cm per seco faster in every second.

dys- *prefix.* Bad; difficult.

dys·en·ter·y (dĭs′entĕr′ē) Disease with inflammation of n cous membrane and glands of la intestine, and mucous and bloc evacuations.

dys·lex·i·a (dĭslĕk′sēa) *n.* Par word blindness, impairment ability to read due to impair neural function. **dys·lex′ic** *adj.*

dys·pep·si·a (dĭspĕp′sea) *n.* digestion. **dys·pep·tic** (dĭspĕp′t *adj. & n.*

dysp·ne·a (dĭspnē′a) *n.* (me Difficult or labored breathing.

dys·pro·si·um (dĭsprō′zēu -zhē-) *n.* (chem.) Element of ra earth group; highly magnetic; sy bol Dy, at. no. 66, at. wt. 162. [mod. L., f. Gk. *dusprositos* hard get at]

dys·tro·phy (dĭs′trofē) *n.* (pat Imperfect nutrition; disord characterized by weakness a wasting esp. of muscles (**muscul** ~).

dz. *abbrev.* Dozen, dozens.

Dyeing fabric involves primit methods in some parts of Africa. Belc Pits are used for indigo dyeing Nigeria. Facing page: In the dyewo in Fez, Morocco, more up-to-d methods are used.

How the form of the letter **E, e** 5th letter of the modern English and ancient Roman alphabet, has developed through the ages. The letter has Semitic, Greek and Latin derivations.

Phoenician   Greek   Corinthian

Early Latin   Classical Latin   Italian

E, e (ē) (pl. **E's, e's** or **Es, es**). 1. Fifth letter of modern English and ancient Roman alphabet, representing Semitic ⱻ, which orig. expressed a sound like that of *h* but was adopted by the Greeks as a vowel. 2. Fifth in a series or row. 3. **E**, (mus.) third note of natural scale (C major); scale or key with this for tonic. 4. **E-layer**, stratum of ionosphere some 60 mi. (100 km) above the Earth, transparent to shortwave radio waves and reflecting back long wave ones. **E** *abbrev*. 1. East(ern). 2. (physics) Energy. 3. English. **e** *abbrev*. 1. East(ern). 2. Electron. 3. (baseball) Error. 4. (math.) Number having value of approximately 2.7182818 ..., used as base of natural system logarithms.

E. *abbrev*. 1. Earl. 2. Ear 3. East(ern). 4. Easter. 5. En neer(ing). 6. English. **e.** *abbrev*. 1. Engineer(ing). Eldest. 3. (baseball) Error. **ea.** *abbrev*. Each. **each** (ēch) *adj*. Every (one) tak separately; ~ **other**, (used as compound reciprocal pronoun) o another. ~ *adv*. To, from, or each. ~ *pron*. Each one. **ea·ger** (ē′ger) *adj*. Strong desirous; keen, impatient. **ea′ger ly** *adv*. **ea′ger·ness** *n*. **ea·gle** (ē′gel) *n*. 1. Any of number of large birds of prey family Accipitridae, noted for ke vision and powerful flight, incl. t 2 N. Amer. species *Aquila chry aëtos*, the bald eagle, and *Haliaeet leucocephalus*, the golden eagle. Representation or figure of t eagle, esp. as symbol of the U. (astron.) Northern constellati *Aquila*. 3. (hist.) Coin bearir

Left: The **golden eagle,** *the best-known of these large birds of prey, inhabits mountainous or rocky regions of N. America, Europe, and Asia. Below: The huge wing-span of a wedge-tailed eagle from Australia.*

semi-circular canals
vestibule
stirrup-bone
temporal bone
anvil
malleus
pinna
cochlea
conch
internal
auditory
meatus
eustachian tube
ear drum
lobe
cochlea
endolymph
perilymph
organ of Corti

The human **ear** has three parts: the outer ear or auricle; the middle ear, joined to the outer ear by a canal and containing three bones, the malleus (hammer), incus (anvil), and stapes (stirrup), and the eustachian tube which allows air to pass from the nose, and finally the inner ear, vital for balance as well as sound perception, the cochlea being concerned with the latter.

image of eagle; 10-dollar gold coin (**double** ~, 20-dollar). 4. (golf) Score of two under par on any hole. 5. ~**-eyed**, keen-sighted.

ea·glet (ē′glĭt) *n.* Young eagle.

Ea·kins (ā′kĭnz), **Thomas** (1844–1916). Amer. painter and sculptor.

ear[1] (ēr) *n.* 1. Organ of hearing in man and animals, esp. the external part of this. 2. Sense of hearing; faculty of discriminating sounds, esp. that of recognizing musical intervals; listening, attention. 3. Earlike object; handle of pitcher etc.; projection on side of anything serving as handle, support, etc. 4. **be all** ~**s**, listen attentively; **turn a deaf** ~, disregard request etc. 5. **ear′ache**, pain in internal ear; **ear′drum**, tympanum; **ear′mark**, mark, usu. a notch, in ear of sheep etc. as sign of ownership; (*v.t.*) mark (animals) thus, mark (anything) as one's own, assign (fund etc.) for some purpose; **ear′muff**, either of a pair of coverings for the ears worn as protection against the cold; **ear′-phone**, one of pair of telephone or radio receivers attachable to listener's ears; **ear′ring**, ornament worn in or on lobe of ear; **ear′-shot**, hearing distance; **ear′-splitting**, very loud; **ear trumpet**, trumpet-shaped tube held to ear by partly deaf persons to enable them to hear better; **ear′wax**, cerumen.

ear[2] (ēr) *n.* Grain-bearing spike, head, of corn, containing its flowers or seeds.

Ear·hart (âr′härt), **Amelia** (1898–1937?). Amer. aviator; first woman to fly across Atlantic, 1928; lost on flight over Pacific, 1937.

earl (ērl) *n.* British nobleman ranking between marquis and viscount. **earl′dom** *n.*

ear·ly (ēr′lē) *adj.* (**-li·er, -li·est**). Absolutely or relatively near the beginning of a portion of time; of, in, the first part of the morning, the year, etc.; ~ **bird**, (joc.) person who is early or arises early in the morning; ~ **on**, at an early stage. ~ *adv.* At an early time.

earn (ērn) *v.t.* Obtain as reward of labor or merit. **earn′ings** *n.pl.* Money earned.

ear·nest[1] (ēr′nĭst) *n.* Money

There are 1,200 species of **earwig**, and modern communications are spreading them throughout the world. They are characterized by a pair of horny forceps.

The **earth,** taken from 'Apollo II', July 1969. The earth's movement round the sun is dictated by the forces of the solar system. The attraction of the earth for the sun is mirrored by the moon's attraction for the earth.

1. North Pole. 2. North Magnetic Po[le]
3. Arctic Circle. 4. Tropic of Canc[er]
5. Equator. 6. Tropic of Caprico[rn]
7. Antarctic Circle. 8. South Po[le]
9. South Frigid Zone. 10. Meridian [of]
Greenwich. 11. South Tempera[te]
Zone. 12. Torrid Zone. 13. North Te[m]perate Zone. 14. North Frigid Zone.

paid as part payment to confirm contract etc.; foretaste, presage, token (of what is to come).

ear·nest² (ẽr´nĭst) adj. Serious, zealous, not trifling; ardent. **ear´-nest·ly** adv. **ear´nest·ness** n. **ear´nest** n. Complete seriousness; **in ∼,** serious(ly), not jesting(ly).

Earp (ẽrp), **Wyatt** (1849–1929). Amer. frontier law officer.

earth (ẽrth) n. 1. Ground; soil, esp. as suited for cultivation; dry land; (also **E ∼**) planet on which we dwell, the world; the present abode of man, as dist. from heaven or hell. 2. Hole or hiding place of fox, badger, etc.; **run to ∼,** (fig.) find by searching. 3. (Brit. elect.) GROUND¹. 4. (chem.) Any of certain naturally occurring metallic oxides. 5. **earth´ling,** inhabitant of Earth; **earth mother,** (myth.) spirit symbolizing earth; (fig.) sensual and maternal woman;

earth´nut, (plant having) edible roundish tubers, roots, or pods; **earth science,** any of several sciences, including geology, physical geography, and others that deal with the earth and any of its phenomena; **earth´shaking,** having great impact on basic beliefs, theories, attitudes, etc.; **earth´work,** bank or mound of earth as rampart or

fortification; **earth´worm,** anne[lid] worm (of various genera) that su[b]sists on soil. **earth** v. Cover (roo[ts] of plants *up*) with heaped-up ear[th]. **earth·en** (ẽr´then, -dhen) a[dj.] Made of earth; made of baked cla[y]. **earth´enware** n. (Vessels e[tc.] made of) baked clay, esp. coar[se] porous kinds fired at relatively l[ow] temperature as dist. from porcela[in] (also attrib.).

earth·ly (ẽrth´lē) adj. (-li·e[r,] -li·est). Of the earth, terrestri[al;] **no ∼ use** etc., (colloq.) no use et[c.] at all. **earth´li·ness** n.

earth·quake (ẽrth´kwāk) [n.] Convulsion of earth's surfa[ce] caused by volcanic activity or fau[lt] in the earth's crust; (fig.) any di[s]turbance or upheaval.

earth·y (ẽr´thē, -dhē) a[dj.] (**earth·i·er, earth·i·est**). Like, [of] earth or soil; grossly materia[l;]

rse. **earth'i·ness** n.

ar·wig (ēr'wǐg) n. Insect of the
er Dermaptera and, in the U.S.,
ily Labiidae with about 20
cies, having large terminal for-
s, formerly held to penetrate
head through ear; kind of small
tipede.

ase (ēz) n. Freedom from pain
trouble; freedom from con-
nt; relief from pain; facility; **at**
(mil. etc.) stand in relaxed atti-
e, with hands behind back and
apart. ~ v.t. (**eased, eas·ing**).
lieve from pain, trouble, etc.;
e mental ease to; relax, adjust
at is too tight); (naut.) slacken
pe, sail, speed, etc.); move gently
gradually; relax or cease one's
orts; ~ **off, up**, become less
rdensome, take things easy.

ea·sel (ē'zel) n. Frame to sup-
rt picture (esp. while artist is at
rk on it) etc. [Du. ezel = Ger.
ass]

ease·ment (ēz'ment) n.   1.
chaic) Advantage, convenience;
nething serving as convenience,
shed, farm building, etc., accom-
odation in house.   2. (law)
quired right or privilege of using
nething not one's own (e.g. right
way).

east (ēst) adv. Toward, in, the
st. ~ n. 1. Point of horizon
ere sun rises at equinox; this
ection. 2. Cardinal point of the
mpass 90° to the right of north.
(usu. **the E** ~) That part of a
untry, district, etc. which lies to
e east; part of world lying east of
Europe, the Orient; Communist
countries of Asia and eastern
Europe; states of U.S. bordering on
the Atlantic esp. N. of Maryland;
New England. ~ adj. Toward, in,
the east; (of wind) blowing from
the east; **E** ~ **Berlin**: see BERLIN;
E ~ **Cape**, easternmost point of
Papua New Guinea; easternmost
point of New Zealand; former name
of Cape Dezhnev; **E** ~ **China Sea**,
arm of Pacific between E. coast of
China and Ryukyu Islands; **E** ~
Germany, German Democratic
Republic: see GERMANY; **E** ~ **India
Company**, company of British
merchants trading with the East
Indies, incorporated in 1600; **E** ~
Pakistan, former name of BANGLA-
DESH; **E** ~ **River**, strait connecting
Upper New York Bay and Long
Island Sound, separating Man-
hattan and Long Island; **E** ~ **Side**,
part of Manhattan, N.Y.C., E. of
Fifth Ave. **east·ward** (ēst'werd)
adj., adv., & n. **east'ward·ly** adj.
& adv. **east'wards** adv.

East·er (ēs'ter) n.   Christian
festival commemorating the resurrection of Christ, and observed by
the Western Churches on the first
Sunday after the calendar full
moon falling on or next after Mar.
21; (also **Eastertide**) week commencing with this day; ~ **egg**,
colored egg or egg-shaped candy
used as Easter gift or ornament.

Eas·ter (ēs'ter) **Island.** Pacific
island west of Chile, discovered by
the Dutch navigator Roggeveen on
Easter Day, 1722, noted esp. for
its monolithic statues.

east·er·ly (ēs'terlē) adj.   In
the east; (of wind) blowing from the
east. ~ adv. Toward the east.
~ n. East wind.

east·ern (ēs'tern) adj. Of the
east; oriental; lying or directed
toward the east; (poet.) in, coming
from, the east; **E** ~, of the East i.e.
of Communist countries; **E** ~
Church, ORTHODOX Church; **E** ~
Empire: see ROMAN Empire;
E ~ **Hemisphere**: see HEMISPHERE;
E ~ **Shore**, parts of Maryland and
Virginia E. of Chesapeake Bay.
east·ern·most (ēs'ternmōst) adj.
east'ern·er n. (also **E** ~) Native,
inhabitant, of the east, esp. of
eastern U.S.

East (ēst) **Indies.** Islands off the
SE. coast of Asia, formerly in-
cluding India and the Malay
peninsula. **East Indian** adj. & n.
(Native, inhabitant) of the East
Indies.

eas·y (ē'zē) adj. (**eas·i·er, eas·-
i·est**). 1. Free from pain, worry,
or constraint. 2. Conducive to ease
or comfort. 3. Causing little discomfort, difficulty, or obstruction;
compliant; easily obtained; loosely
fitting; **of** ~ **virtue**, (of woman)
sexually promiscuous. 4. ~ **chair**,
padded or stuffed chair with arms;
~ **does it**, go carefully; **ea'sy·
going**, relaxed and casual; tolerant;

*These statues on **Easter Island** are
made from compressed volcanic ash.
Those found have varied in height from
3 to 36 ft.*

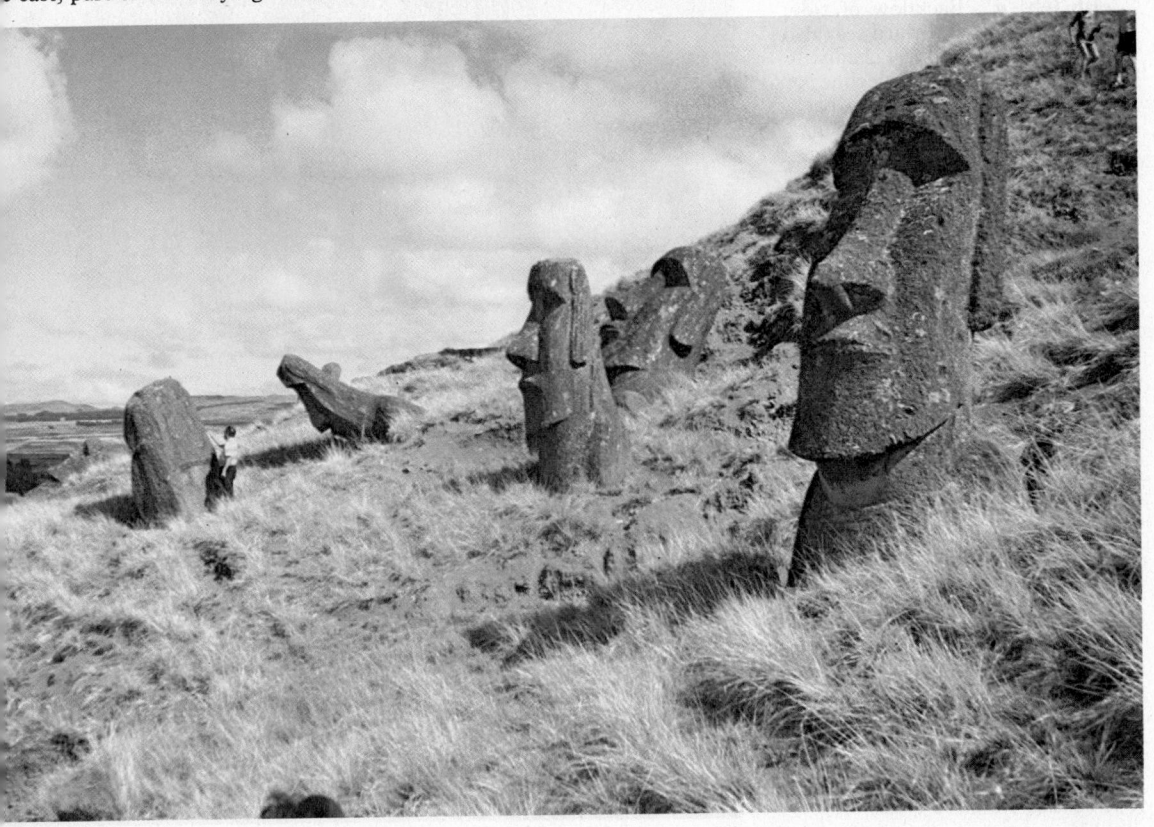

easy mark, (colloq.) person or thing easily overcome, persuaded, etc.; **easy money,** money obtained or obtainable without hard work or difficulty. **eas'i·ly** *adv.* **eas'i·ness** *n.* **easy** *adv.* In an easy manner, at leisurely pace; ~!, (move) gently!; **take it** ~, proceed comfortably, do no more than one must.

eat (ēt) *v.* (**ate, eat·en, eat·ing**). 1. Take into mouth, masticate, and swallow as food, swallow (soup etc.); consume food, take a meal; ~ **one's words,** retract them in humiliating manner; ~ **out,** take a meal elsewhere than at home; ~ **out of person's hand,** be tamely or completely submissive to him. 2. Devour, consume, prey upon; (of frost, rust, etc.) destroy slowly and gradually; make (hole, passage), make a way, by fretting or corrosion; **what's eat'ing you?,** (colloq.) why are you angry, worried, etc.?; **eat away** or ~ **into,** destroy gradually. **eats** *n.* (slang) Food. **eat'a·ble** *adj.* **eat'a·bles** *n.pl.* Articles of food. **eat·er·y** (ē'terē) *n.* (pl. **-er·ies**). (slang) Restaurant, diner, etc.

eau de Cologne (ō de kolōn'): see COLOGNE.

eaves (ēvz) *n.pl.* (orig. sing.) Overhanging edge of roof. **eaves·drop** (ēvz'drŏp) *v.i.* (**-dropped, -drop·ping**). Stand close to walls of house under eaves to listen to secrets; listen secretly to private conversation. **eaves'-drop·per** *n.*

ebb (ĕb) *n.* Backflow of tide, return of tidewater toward sea (also ~ **tide**); decline, decay, change to worse state, point of decline or depression. **ebb** *v.i.* Flow back, recede; flow away; decay, decline.

eb·on (ĕb'on) *adj.* & *n.* (poet.) (Made of, black as) ebony.

eb·on·ite (ĕb'onīt) *n.* Vulcanite.

eb·on·y (ĕb'onē) *n.* (pl. **-on·ies**). Hard heavy black wood obtained from various tropical trees, esp. various species of *Diospyros* of Ceylon, Madagascar, and Coromandel; tree yielding this. ~ *adj.* Made of, black as, ebony; intensely black.

E·bro (ē'brō). Longest river in Spain, 575 mi. (920 km), flowing SE. from Cantabrian Mountains in N. to Mediterranean.

e·bul·lient (ĭbŭl'yent, ĭbōōl'-) *adj.* Boiling; exuberant, enthusiastic. **e·bul'lience, e·bul'lien·cy** *ns.* **e·bul'lient·ly** *adv.*

e·bul·li·tion (ĕbŭlĭsh'on) *n.* Boiling; effervescence; sudden outburst (*of* violence, passion, etc.).

Ebony wood has been highly va since classical times for actual legendary properties. Left: Tree fruit of one of the species Diospy from which ebony is obtained.

EC *abbrev.* ·European C munity.

ec·ce ho·mo (ĕch'ā hō'mō, ĕ ĕk'ā). Representation of Cl wearing crown of thorns. [L. "behold the man," words usec Pontius Pilate to present Ch crowned with thorns, to accusers. (John 19)]

ec·cen·tric (ĭksĕn'trĭk, ĕk 1. Not concentric to, with a point of support, etc., otherw than centrally placed; not centr placed or passing through cen (of orbital motion, curve, etc.) circular, deviating from a cir moving in eccentric orbit. 2. regular, capricious, odd, whimsi **ec·cen'tri·cal·ly** *adv.* **ec·ce tric·i·ty** (ĕksĕntrĭs'ĭtē) *n.* **-ties**). **eccentric** *n.* 1. Eccen disk on revolving shaft, with c necting rods etc., for chang rotating into backward and forw motion. 2. Eccentric person.

Eccl., Eccles. *abbrevs.* Eccl astes (Old Testament).

Ec·cle·si·as·tes (ĭklēzĭăs't Book of Old Testament traditi ally ascribed to Solomon.

ec·cle·si·as·tic (ĭklēzĕăs'tĭk) Clergyman, priest.

ec·cle·si·as·ti·cal (ĭklēzĕăs kal) *adj.* Of Church or cler

*Carved **ebony** table and candlestands, Ham House, London, U.K. The wood is hard, deep in colour and easy to polish: such things as black piano keys and knife handles are made of it.*

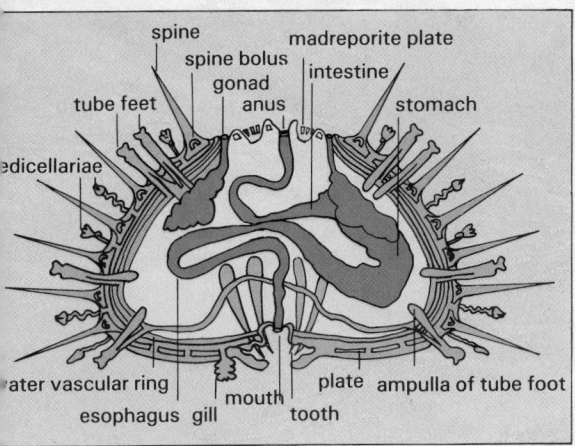

Labels on diagram: spine, spine bolus, madreporite plate, gonad, intestine, tube feet, anus, stomach, pedicellariae, water vascular ring, esophagus, gill, mouth, plate, tooth, ampulla of tube foot

ec·cle·si·as'ti·cal·ly *adv.*

Ec·cle·si·as·ti·cus (ĭklēzēăs'-kŭs). Book of the Apocrypha, otherwise known as "The Wisdom of Jesus the son of Sirach," containing moral and practical maxims.

ec·dys·i·ast (ĕkdĭz'ēăst, -ast) . Stripteaser.

ec·dy·sis (ĕk'dĭsĭs) *n.* (pl. **-ses** r. -sēz). (zool.) Casting of outer skin or shell.

ECG *abbrev.* Electrocardiogram.

ech·e·lon (ĕsh'elŏn) *n.* 1. Step-like formation of troops or airplanes n parallel units, each with its front lear of that in advance; any similar ormation. 2. Grade, rank. [Fr. *chelle* ladder]

e·chid·na (ĭkĭd'na) *n.* Spiny ant-ater (*Tachyglossus aculeatus*), an gg-laying burrowing nocturnal mammal, with long extensile ongue for eating ants, native to

Echinoderm comes from a Greek word meaning 'prickle-skinned', and is used for a large group of sea-dwelling creatures. The five extant forms are the sea-urchin (see top, above left, and above right), the starfish or sea-star (see top), the brittle-star, the feather-star and sea-lily, and the sea-cucumber. Their symmetry is striking.

Australia, N.Z., etc.: see ANT.

e·chi·no·derm (ĭkī'nodĕrm, ĕk'-ĭno-) *n.* Member of the class Echinodermata (sea urchins, starfish, etc.), some species of which have skin studded with spines or hard plates.

e·chi·noid (ĭkī'noid, ĕk'ĭ-) *adj.* Resembling the *Echinus*, a genus of sea urchins. ~ *n.* Any of the sea urchins (Echinoidea), a large group of marine animals with usu. globular or heart-shaped calcareous skeleton of interlocking plates; fossilized member of this group.

ech·o (ĕk'ō) *n.* (pl. **ech·oes**). Repetition of sound produced by reflection of sound waves from something denser than air, usu. from a rigid and approx. vertical surface; secondary sound constituted by reflected waves; reflection of radar wave; (fig.) repetition or close imitation, enfeebled reproduction; close or obsequious imitator or adherent; **echoloca'tion**, location of objects by reflected sound. **echo** *v.* (**ech·oed, ech·o·ing**). (of place) Resound with echo; (of sounds) be repeated by echoes, reverberate, resound; repeat (sound) by or like echo; repeat (another's words), imitate words or opinions of.

e·cho·ic (ĕkō'ĭk) *adj.* (of word etc.) Echoing the sound that it denotes; onomatopoeic.

é·clair (āklār', ĭ-, ā'klār) *n.* Small finger-shaped pastry filled with cream or custard and usu.

Despite rich mineral and agricultural resources, the majority of the people of **Ecuador** remain poor, many continue to wash their clothes in the rivers (right). Map and flag (below).

iced.

é·clat (āklah´) *n.* Conspicuous success, acclaim; brilliance of achievement.

ec·lec·tic (ĭklĕk´tĭk, ĕ-) *adj.* & *n.* 1. (Philosopher, esp. of antiquity) not belonging to any recognized school but selecting such doctrines as pleased him in every school. 2. (Person) borrowing freely from various sources, not exclusive in opinion, taste, etc. **ec·lec´ti·cal·ly** *adv.* **ec·lec·ti·cism** (ĭklĕk´tĭsĭzem, ĕ-) *n.*

e·clipse (ĭklĭps´) *n.* 1. Partial or total interception of light of sun by passage of moon between it and the earth (∼ **of the sun, solar** ∼); partial or total obscuration of moon by the Earth's shadow (∼ **of the moon, lunar** ∼); similar obscuration of a satellite by another planet. 2. Obscuration, obscurity, loss of brilliance or splendor. **eclipse** *v.t.* (**e·clipsed, e·clips·ing**). (of moon) Cause eclipse of the sun from a portion of the Earth; usu. pass., (of sun) have light so intercepted, (of moon) be obscured by Earth's shadow; deprive of luster, outshine, surpass.

e·clip·tic (ĭklĭp´tĭk) *n.* Great circle of celestial sphere, apparent orbit of sun (so called because eclipses happen only when moon is on or very near this line).

ec·logue (ĕk´lawg, -lŏg) *n.* Short poem, esp. pastoral dialogue.

E.C.M. *abbrev.* European Common Market.

e·co·cide (ē´kosīd, ĕk´o-) *n.* Destruction of the natural environment, as by discharge of pollutants etc.

ecol. *abbrev.* Ecological; ecology.

e·col·o·gy (ĭkŏl´ojē) *n.* Branch of biology dealing with relations of living organisms to their surroundings, their habits, modes of life, populations, etc. **ec·o·log·i·cal** (ĕkolŏj´ĭkal, ēko-) *adj.* **ec·o·log´i·cal·ly** *adv.* **e·col´o·gist** *n.*

econ. *abbrev.* Economic(s); economy.

e·con·o·met·rics (ĭkŏnomĕt´-rĭks) *n.* Branch of economics concerned with application of mathematical economics by use of statistics. **e·con·o·met´ric, e·con·o·met´ri·cal** *adjs.* **e·con·o·me·tri·cian** (ĭkŏnometrĭsh´an), **e·con·o·met´rist** *ns.*

e·co·nom·ic (ēkonŏm´ĭk, ĕko-) *adj.* Of economics, maintained for profit; practical, utilitarian. **e·co·nom´i·cal** *adj.* 1. Saving, thrifty; not wasteful (of). 2. Economic. **e·co·nom´i·cal·ly** *adv.* **e·co·-**

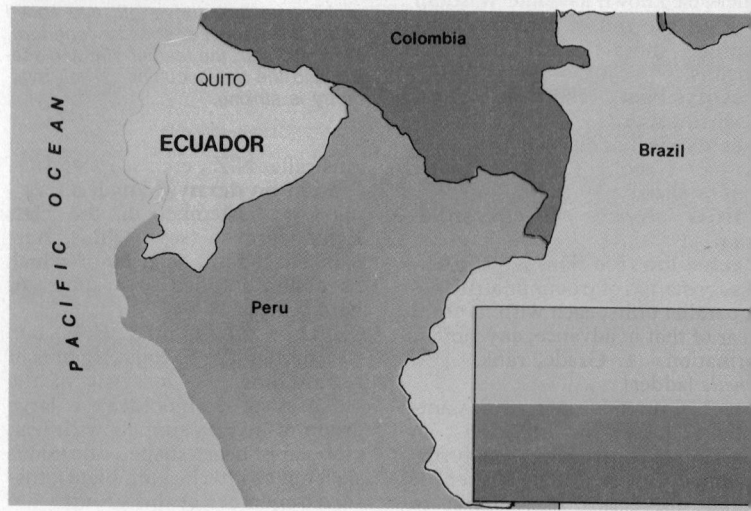

om'ics *n.pl.* Science relating to the production and distribution of material wealth; condition of country with regard to material prosperity.

e·con·o·mist (ĭkŏn´omĭst) *n.* One expert in economics or political economy.

e·con·o·mize (ĭkŏn´omīz) *v.* (**-mized, -miz·ing**). Use economically; practice economy; reduce expenditure.

e·con·o·my (ĭkŏn´ome) *n.* (pl. **-mies**). I. Administration of concerns and resources of any community; art or science of such administration; **political** ~, former name for ECONOMICS, now applied esp. to analysis of problems of economic policy of governments. 2. Careful management of resources, so as to make them go as far as possible; frugality, thrift; saving. ~ *adj.* Economical, thrifty.

e·co·sys·tem (ē´kōsĭstem, ĕk´ō-) *n.* System comprising living organisms together with their physical environment.

ec·ru (ĕk´rōō, ā´krōō) *adj.* & *n.* Of) grayish to pale yellow, light tan color.

ec·sta·sy (ĕk´stasē) *n.* (pl. **-sies**). Exalted state of feeling, rapture, transport, esp. of delight; state of rapture in contemplation of divine things; poetic frenzy.

ec·stat·ic (ĕkstăt´ĭk, ĭk-) *adj.* Of, producing, subject to, ecstasy. ~ *n.* One subject to ecstasy.

ecto- *prefix.* Outer, external.

ec·to·blast (ĕk´toblăst) *n.* physiol.) Outer membrane of a cell.

ec·to·derm (ĕk´todērm) *n.* embryol.) Outermost of three layers of cells formed by embryo at early stage, layer from which skin and nervous system are developed.

-ectomy *comb. form.* Removal of a part by surgery, as in *appendectomy, hysterectomy*.

ec·top·ic (ĕktŏp´ĭk) *adj.* (path.) In an abnormal place, as an ~ **pregnancy**, one in which the fertilized ovum develops outside the uterus.

ec·to·plasm (ĕk´toplăzem) *n.* I. (biol.) Clear viscid outer layer of cytoplasm in an animal cell. 2. (spiritualism) Supposed emanation from body of medium.

Ec·ua·dor (ĕk´wadōr). Republic in northwest S. Amer.; capital, Quito.

ec·u·men·i·cal (ĕkyumĕn´ĭkal) *adj.* Of or representing the whole Christian world; seeking worldwide Christian unity, as an ~ **council**; worldwide. **ec·u·men´i·cal·ism, ec·u·me·nic·i·ty** (ekyumenĭs´ĭtē), **ec´u·me·nism, ec·u·men´i·cism** *ns.* **ec·u·men´i·cal·ly** *adv.*

ec·ze·ma (ĕk´sema, ĕg´ze-, ĭgzē´-) *n.* (path.) Inflammation of skin, with redness, itching, and lesions that discharge serous matter. **ec´-zem·a·tous** (ĭgzĕm´atus) *adj.*

-ed¹ *suffix.* Forming past tense and past participle of most verbs (*borrowed, moaned, slipped*).

-ed² *suffix.* Forming adjectives from nouns indicating having, characterized by, provided with, wearing, etc. (*striped, whiskered*).

ed. *abbrev.* Edited (by), edition, editor.

EDC *abbrev.* European Defense Community.

Ed.D. *abbrev.* Doctor of Education.

Ed·da (ĕd´a). I. (also **Elder, Poetic,** ~) Collection (c1200) of ancient Old Norse poems on mythical or traditional subjects. 2. (also **Younger, Prose,** ~) Miscellaneous manual of Icelandic poetry with quotations and prose paraphrases, partly by the Icelandic historian Snorri Sturlason (c1230).

ed·dy (ĕd´ē) *n.* (pl. **-dies**). Circular current in water, small whirlpool; similar unsteady or swirling motion of air, wind, fog, dust, etc. ~ *v.i.* (**-died, -dy·ing**). Whirl around, move, in eddies.

Ed·dy (ĕd´ē), **Mrs. Mary Baker Glover** (1821–1910). American founder of the Church of Christ, Scientist (the Christian Science movement).

e·del·weiss (ā´delvīs, -wīs) *n.* Alpine plant (*Leontopodium alpinum*) with white flower, growing in rocky places. [Ger. *edel* noble, *weiss* white]

e·de·ma (ĭdē´ma) *n.* Abnormal accumulation of fluid in tissue; dropsy.

E·den¹ (ē´den). (also **Garden of** ~) Abode of Adam and Eve at their creation, Paradise; (transf.) delightful abode, state of supreme happiness. [Heb. *éden*, orig. = "delight"]

E·den² (ē´den), **(Robert) Anthony, 1st Earl of Avon** (1897–1977). British statesman; prime minister 1955–7.

*An **eddy**, known in the region as the 'Dust Devil', funnels dust up to great heights in Tanzania, Africa. Such swirling motions can be caused either on land or water.*

e·den·tate (ĭdĕn´tāt) *adj.* & *n.* (Animal) belonging to mammalian order Edentata, having no teeth or very simple teeth without enamel (sloths, great anteaters, armadillos, aardvarks, etc.); lacking teeth.

edge (ĕj) *n.* I. Thin sharpened side of cutting instrument or weapon; sharpness given to blade by whetting; (fig.) effectiveness, trenchancy (of speech etc.); **be on** ~, be excited or irritable; **set person's teeth on** ~, jar his or her nerves or sensibilities. 2. Crest of ridge; line at which 2 surfaces

Eclipses have been watched and recorded since ancient times. Modern astronomers can predict precisely future eclipses and calculate the dates of past ones. A total eclipse of the sun allows observation of stars near the sun and of its outer layers.

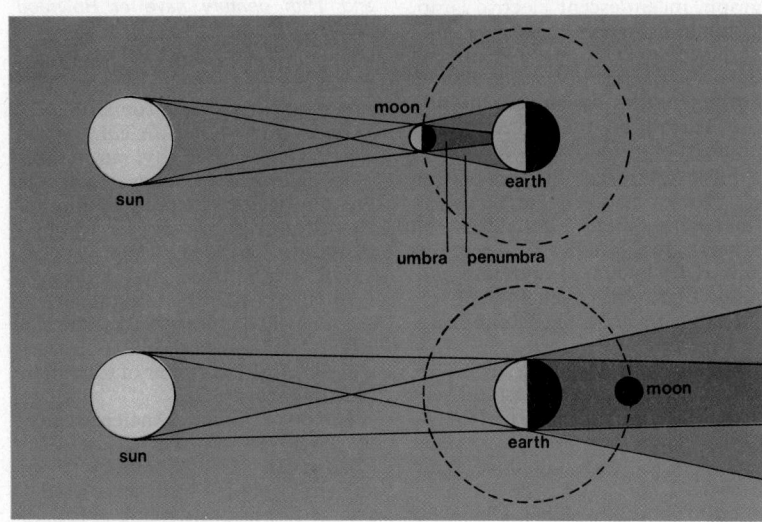

meet abruptly; (fig.) perilous or critical position or moment. 3. One of narrow surfaces of thin flat object; rim (of vessel); one of the 3 surfaces of book left uncovered by binding. 4. Boundary of any surface, border, brink (of precipice). 5. (colloq.) Advantage, superiority. ~ *v.* (**edged, edg·ing**). 1. Give an edge to, sharpen. 2. Border; furnish with edging. 3. Move edgewise; advance (esp. obliquely) by repeated almost imperceptible degrees; move (thing, oneself) thus, nudge on.

edge·wise (ĕj′wīz), **edge·ways** (ĕj′wāz) *advs.* With edge foremost or turned toward spectator; edge to edge; (moving) with edge foremost; **get (word) in ~**, manage to speak in interval of loquacious person's talk.

edg·ing (ĕj′ĭng) *n.* (esp.) Border, fringe, etc., on garment, border (of grass etc.) around flower beds or lawn; lace etc. made to be sewn to edge of garment.

edg·y (ĕj′ē) *adj.* (**edg·i·er, edg·i·est**). Sharp-edged; tense, nervous; irritable.

ed·i·ble (ĕd′ĭbel) *adj. & n.* (Thing) fit to be eaten, eatable. **ed·i·bil·i·ty** (ĕdĭbĭl′ĭtē), **ed′i·ble·ness** *ns.*

e·dict (ē′dĭkt) *n.* What is proclaimed by authority; order issued by sovereign to subjects; **E~ of Nantes**: see NANTES.

ed·i·fice (ĕd′ĭfĭs) *n.* Building, esp. large and stately one.

ed·i·fy (ĕd′ĭfī) *v.t.* (**-fied, -fy·ing**). Benefit spiritually, strengthen, support; instruct, improve. **ed·i·fi·ca·tion** (ĕdĭfĭkā′shon) *n.*

Ed·in·burgh (ĕd′ĭnberō, -bŭrō; *Brit.* ĕd′ĭnbru). Capital of Scotland, situated on the Firth of Forth; capital of Scottish kingdom, 1436–1707.

Ed·i·son (ĕd′ĭson), **Thomas Alva** (1847–1931). American inventor of the microphone, phonograph, incandescent electric lamp, alkaline storage battery, etc.; obtained over 1,000 patents on these and on improvements, devices dealing with dynamos, motors, the telegraph, the mimeograph, photography, motion pictures, etc.

ed·it (ĕd′ĭt) *v.t.* Prepare edition of (book, article, etc.); collate (material chiefly provided by others) for publication; act as editor of; assemble and integrate final (film, sound track, tape recording) by cutting, combining, and splicing.

e·di·tion (ĭdĭsh′on) *n.* Form in which literary work is published; whole number of copies of book, newspaper, etc., printed from same set of types and issued at same time.

ed·i·tor (ĕd′ĭter) *n.* One who edits; one who supervises newspaper or periodical, or section of newspaper etc. **ed′i·tor·ship** *n.*

ed·i·to·ri·al (ĕdĭtōr′ēal, -tōr′-) *adj.* Of, written by, an editor. ~ *n.* Newspaper, magazine article written by or expressing opinion of its editor or publisher. **ed·i·to′ri·al·ly** *adv.*

Ed·mon·ton (ĕd′monton). Capital of Alberta, Canada, in S. central part on North Saskatchewan River; important transportation and distribution center of Canadian Northwest.

E·dom (ē′dom). Ancient region of Asia S. of the Dead Sea. **E′dom·ite** *n.* (Member) of an ancient people traditionally descended from Esau, living in Edom.

Edinburgh Castle and Princes Street Gardens. From the castle the Royal Mile runs down to the Palace of Holyrood House and ruins of the 12th and 13th century nave of Holyrood Abbey.

*Downtown **Edmonton**, in Alberta, Canada. Edmonton is the commercial hub of the Canadian northwest, particularly for agricultural and oil-based industries.*

EDP *abbrev.* Electronic data processing.

EDT, E.D.T. *abbrevs.* Eastern Daylight Time.

educ. *abbrev.* Education(al).

ed·u·ca·ble (ĕj′ukabel, ĕd′yu-) *adj.* Capable of being educated or trained. **ed·u·ca·bil·i·ty** (ĕjuka-bĭl′ĭtē, ĕdyu-) *n.*

ed·u·cate (ĕj′ukāt, ĕd′yu-) *v.t.* **cat·ed, -cat·ing**). Bring up from childhood, so as to form habits, manners, intellectual aptitudes, etc.; instruct, provide schooling for; train, discipline, so as to develop some special aptitude, taste, or disposition. **ed′u·ca·tor** *n.*

ed·u·ca·tion (ĕjukā′shon, ĕdyu-) *n.* Systematic instruction, schooling, or training in preparation for life or some particular task; scholastic instruction; bringing up. **ed·u·ca·tion·al** *adj.* ~ **television**, television program(s) produced for educational purposes. **ed·u·ca′-tion·al·ly** *adv.* **ed·u·ca′tion·al·ist** One who studies the science and methods of education.

ed·u·ca·tive (ĕj′ukātiv, ĕd′yu-) *adj.* Of education; educating; bearing on, conducive to, education.

e·duce (ĭdoōs′, ĭdūs′) *v.t.* **duced, e·duc·ing**). Bring out, elicit, develop, from latent, rudimentary, or potential condition; infer; extract. **e·duc′i·ble** *adj.*

1877 Thomas Alva Edison applied for a U.S. patent for his phonograph (below), which consisted of a tin-foil covered cylinder and a hand crank. He later produced a motor-driven cylinder player. Right: The original Edison light bulb. Left: The first commercial light bulb.

Education today still concerns itself with the basic lessons, despite having moved very much into the computer age. Audio-visual aids and computers are now an integral part of education.

e·duc·tion (ĭdŭk′shon) *n.*

Ed·ward[1] (ĕd′werd). Name of two kings of the English before the Norman Conquest; ~ **the Con-fessor**, son of Ethelred the Unready, reigned 1042–66; last Anglo-Saxon king of England; ~ **the Martyr**, reigned 975–9, assassinated by order of his step-mother.

Ed·ward[2] (ĕd′werd). Name of six kings of England since the Norman Conquest and two of the United Kingdom: **Edward I** (1239–1307), son of Henry III; king of England 1272–1307; conquered Wales and attempted the conquest of Scotland; **Edward II** (1284–1327), succeeded his father Edward I in 1307; continued the attempted conquest of Scotland but was

Edward VI, *when he was 13, painted by a follower of Hans Holbein, c. 1550. His reign as King of England (1547–53) was rife with faction fights.*

Edward VII *in a painting by Sir Luke Fildes. After the long reign of his mother, Queen Victoria, he succeeded to the U.K. throne in 1901 aged 60.*

defeated by Robert Bruce at Bannockburn (1314); murdered in 1327; **Edward III** (1312–77), son of Edward II, reigned 1327–77; the Hundred Years War against France began in his reign, and he gained temporarily the duchy of Aquitaine by the Treaty of Bretigny (1360); **Edward IV** (1442–83), the first Yorkist king; descended from Edward III; reigned 1461–83; defeated the Lancastrians in the Wars of the Roses; **Edward V** (1470–83), son of Edward IV; king in 1483, in which year he was deposed; **Edward VI** (1537–53), son of Henry VIII and Jane Seymour; reigned 1547–53; **Edward VII** (1841–1910), son of Queen Victoria; king of the United Kingdom 1901–10; **Edward VIII** (1894–1972); succeeded his father, George V, 1936; abdicated same year to marry Amer. divorcée Wallis Warfield Simpson.

Ed·ward·i·an (ĕdwōr′dēan, -wãr′-) *adj.* & *n.* (Person) belonging to, characteristic of, or following styles and views of reign of Edward VII of the United Kingdom.

Ed·wards (ĕd′werdz), **Jonathan** (1703–58). Amer. Congregational clergyman and Calvinist theologian; known for powerful emotional sermons such as "Sinners in the Hands of an Angry God."

E.E. *abbrev.* Electrical engineer-(ing).

EEC *abbrev.* European Economic Community.

EEG *abbrev.* Electroencephalogram.

eel (ēl) *n.* (pl. **eels**, collect. **eel**).

1. Any of numerous small-finned and soft-finned snakelike fishes of the order Anguilliformes (or Apodes), the fresh-water forms of which migrate to the Sargasso Sea to spawn. 2. Any of various other fishes resembling eels in shape. 3. **electric** ~: see ELECTRIC; **eel′grass**, any of several submerged aquatic plants of genus *Zostera* of coastal areas, with grasslike leaves; **eel′worm**, any of various wormlike often microscopic animals of the phylum Nematoda, some of which are parasitic on crops.

e'er (ãr) *adv.* (poet.) = EVER.

ee·rie, **ee·ry** (ēr′ē) *adjs.* (**ee·ri·er**, **ee·ri·est**). Gloomy, strange, weird. **ee′ri·ly** *adv.* **ee′ri·ness** *n.*

ef·face (ĭfās′) *v.t.* (**-faced, -fac·ing**). Rub out; obliterate, wipe out; reduce *oneself* to insignificance, be humble. **ef·face′a·ble** *adj.* **ef·face′ment** *n.*

ef·fect (ĭfĕkt′) *n.* 1. Resu consequence; efficacy; combinati of color or form in picture, lar scape, etc.; (pl.) lighting, approp ate sounds, etc., in play e phenomenon. 2. (pl.) Proper goods. 3. Being operative; ope tive influence; **take** ~, beco operative, come into force. Impression produced on spectat hearer, etc. 5. **in** ~, virtually, practical purposes. **effect** Bring about, accomplish. **ef·fe tive** *adj.* 1. Having an effect; t is actually brought to bear on object; coming into effe becoming operative. 2. Power in effect; striking. 3. Functi ing, operative. 4. Actual, exi ing. **ef·fec′tive** *n.* Combat-rea soldier. **ef·fec′tive·ly** *a* **ef·fec′tive·ness** *n.*

ef·fec·tu·al (ĭfĕk′chooal) *a* Answering its purpose; val **ef·fec′tu·al·ly** *adv.*

ef·fec·tu·ate (ĭfĕk´chŏŏāt) *v.t.* **-at·ed, -at·ing**). Bring to pass, accomplish. **ef·fec·tu·a·tion** (ĭfĕk-ŏŏā´shon) *n.*

ef·fem·i·nate (ĭfĕm´ĭnĭt) *adj.* womanish, unmanly. **ef·fem´i-nate·ly** *adv.* **ef·fem·i·na·cy** (ĕm´ĭnasē) *n.*

ef·fen·di (ĭfĕn´dē) *n.* (pl. **-dis**). former Turkish title of respect for officials etc.

ef·fer·ent (ĕf´erent) *adj.* (physiol.)) Conveying outward; (of nerves) conveying impulses from central nervous system to muscles and glands.

ef·fer·vesce (ĕfervĕs´) *v.i.* vesced, -vesc·ing**). Give off bubbles of gas, esp. as result of chemical action; bubble. **ef·fer-ves´cence** *n.* **ef·fer·ves´cent** *adj.*

ef·fete (ĭfēt´) *adj.* Exhausted, worn out; feeble, incapable; decadent. **ef·fete´ness** *n.*

ef·fi·ca·cious (ĕfĭkā´shus) *adj.* (of instrument, method, action) producing, sure to produce, intended or appropriate effect. **ef·fi·ca´cious·ly** *adv.* **ef·fi·ca´-cious·ness, ef·fi·ca·cy** (ĕf´ĭkasē) (pl. **-cies**) *ns.*

ef·fi·cient (ĭfĭsh´ent) *adj.* Making, causing to be; productive of effects; effective, operative; skilled, capable. **ef·fi´cient·ly** *adv.* **ef·fi´cien·cy** (ĭfĭsh´ensē) *n.* (pl. **-cies**). State or quality of being efficient; (phys.) ratio of energy or work produced to that expended.

ef·fi·gy (ĕf´ĭjē) *n.* (pl. **-gies**). portrait, image; rough representation of hated person; **burn (hang) a ~**, burn (or hang) image of hated person as expression of anger, disdain, ridicule.

ef·flo·resce (ĕflorĕs´) *v.i.* resced, -resc·ing**). I. Blossom, flower (lit. and fig.). 2. (chem., of crystals or salts) (Come to surface and) turn to fine powder on exposure to air; (of surface) become covered with powdery saline crust. **ef·flo·res´cence** *n.* **ef·flo·res´-ent** *adj.*

ef·flu·ence (ĕf´lōŏens, ĕflōŏ´-) *n.* flowing out; what flows out; emanation.

ef·flu·ent (ĕf´lōŏent, ĕflōŏ´-) *adj.* flowing forth. **~** *n.* Stream flowing from larger stream, reservoir, lake, etc.; outflow from septic tank etc.

ef·flu·vi·um (ĭflōŏ´vēum) *n.* (pl. via** pr. **-vēa**). Barely visible or invisible outflow of gas or particulate matter, esp. one that is offensive or noxious. **ef·flu´vi·al** *adj.*

ef·flux (ĕf´lŭks) *n.* Flowing out (of liquid, air, gas); that which flows out.

ef·fort (ĕf´ert) *n.* Strenuous exertion; display of power, achievement.

ef·fort·less (ĕf´ertlĭs) *adj.* Requiring, making little or no effort;

easy. **ef·fort·less·ly** *adv.* **ef·fort-less·ness** *n.*

ef·fron·ter·y (ĭfrŭn´terē, ĕ-) *n.* (pl. **-ter·ies**). Shameless audacity; impudent boldness.

ef·ful·gent (ĭfŭl´jent) *adj.* Radiant. **ef·ful´gent·ly** *adv.* **ef·ful´gence** *n.*

ef·fuse (ĭfūz´) *v.t.* (**-fused, -fus·ing**). Pour forth; spread out.

ef·fu·sion (ĭfū´zhon) *n.* Pouring forth; outpouring, as of emotions, words, etc.

ef·fu·sive (ĭfū´sĭv) *adj.* Exuberant, unduly demonstrative. **ef·fu´sive·ly** *adv.* **ef·fu´sive·ness** *n.*

eft (ĕft) *n.* Newt.

Eg. *abbrev.* Egypt(ian).

e.g. *abbrev. Exempli gratia* (L., = "for example").

e·gal·i·tar·i·an (ĭgălĭtār´ēan) *adj. & n.* (Person) asserting equality of mankind, esp. in political or social life.

egg[1] (ĕg) *n.* I. (pop.) More or less spheroidal body, containing germ of new individual within a shell or membrane, deposited externally (laid) by female of some animals esp. birds, reptiles, fishes, and insects; esp., domestic fowl's egg as article of food. 2. (zool.) Non-motile cell produced by female, capable, usu. after fertilization by a sperm, of developing into a new individual; ovum. 3. (**have** or **put**) **all one's ~s in one basket**, (risk) all on a single venture; **bad ~**, person who comes to no good; **good ~**, (slang) nice person. 4. **egg´beater**, device for beating eggs, mixing cake batter, etc.; (slang) helicopter; **egg´cup**, cup-shaped vessel to hold boiled egg in shell for eating; **egg foo yong** (or **young**), Chinese dish of eggs beaten and cooked with bean sprouts, onions, celery, and ginger-root, combined with minced meat, fish, or poultry; **egg´head**, (slang) intellectual, highbrow; **egg´nog**, drink of milk or cream, beaten eggs, sugar, and nutmeg, usu. mixed with

*Below: Easter **eggs** by Fabergé (1846–1920); the turn-of-the-century work of this Russian jeweller and goldsmith is highly valued. Bottom: Two* *blackbird's eggs. The colored shells serve to camouflage the eggs from predators.*

The **egret** *is found in N. America, Asia, and Australia. The popularity of the dorsal plumes (ospreys) that the egret sports when breeding brought one species close to extinction.*

liquor; **egg′plant**, perennial plant (*Solanum melongena*) cultivated for its edible fruit, served as a vegetable; ovoid fruit of this plant, aubergine; **egg roll**, Chinese dish of egg pastry rolled into oblong casings that are stuffed with minced meat or seafood and chopped vegetables and browned in deep fat; **eggs Benedict**, poached eggs on toasted English muffins and ham, topped with hollandaise sauce; **egg′shell**, shell of egg; freq. as type of anything frail or fragile; **egg tooth**, protuberance on bill sheath of embryo bird, reptile, etc., for cracking its shell.

egg² (ĕg) *v.t.* Incite, encourage, urge (*on*).

eg·lan·tine (ĕg′lantĭn, -tēn): see SWEETbrier.

e·go (ē′gō, ĕg′ō) *n.* (pl. **e·gos**). 1. (metaphys.) Conscious thinking subject as opp. to *non-ego* or object; the self. 2. (psychol.) That part of the mind which is organized and has a sense of individuality (thus used by Freud to distinguish it from the primitive, impersonal, unconscious part which he called the *id*); ~ **trip**, (colloq.) activity etc. devoted entirely to one's own interests or feelings. [L., = "I"]

e·go·cen·tric (ēgōsĕn′trĭk, ĕgō-) *adj.* Centered in the ego; self-centered, egoistic. **e·go·cen·tric·i·ty** (ēgōsĕntrĭs′ĭtē, ĕgō-) *n.*

e·go·ism (ē′gōĭzem, ĕg′ō-) *n.* 1. (ethics) Theory that regards self-interest as foundation of morality.

2. Regard to one's own interest, systematic selfishness; selfish aims or purposes; self-opinionatedness. **e′go·ist** *n.* **e·go·is·tic** (ēgōĭs′tĭk, ĕgō-), **e·go·is′ti·cal** *adjs.* **e·go·is′ti·cal·ly** *adv.*

e·go·ma·ni·a (ēgōmā′nēa, -mān′ya, ĕgō-) *n.* Morbid egotism. **e·go·ma′ni·ac** *n.*

e·go·tism (ē′gotĭzem, ĕg′o-) *n.* Practice of talking about oneself excessively; boasting; self-conceit. **e′go·tist** *n.* **e·go·tis·tic** (ēgotĭs′tĭk, ĕgo-), **e·go·tis′ti·cal** *adjs.* **e·go·tis′ti·cal·ly** *adv.*

e·gre·gious (ĭgrē′jus) *adj.* Glaringly bad, blatant, **e·gre′gious·ly** *adv.* **e·gre′gious·ness** *n.* [L. *egregius*, lit. "towering above the flock" (*grex* flock)]

e·gress (ē′grĕs) *n.* (Right or liberty of) going out; (astron.) end of eclipse or occultation; exit.

e·gret (ē′grĭt, ĭgrĕt′, ĕg′rĭt) *n.* Any of several herons having long ornamental drooping plumes during breeding season, esp. the American egret (*Casmerodius albus egretta*), the snowy egret (*Leucophoyx thula*), and the reddish egret (*Dichromanassa rufescens*).

E·gypt (ē′jĭpt). Arab Republic of Egypt, a country in NE. Africa bounded on N. by the Mediterranean and on E. by the Red Sea; capital Cairo; **Ancient** ~, civilization in the Nile valley from the Stone Age until the Roman period; ruled by successive dynasties until conquest by Alexander the Great in 332 B.C.; after periods of Greek and Roman domination it passed to the Byzantine Empire (395–642); the ancient culture died out after the Arab conquest, and Egypt became a province of the Ottoman Empire 1517–1879, then a British protectorate 1914–22.

Built when France led the world in t development of iron and steel building and initially a subject of protest, t **Eiffel Tower** *remains a prominent fe ture of Paris. It now serves also as T.V. transmitter.*

E·gyp·tian (ĭjĭp′shan) *adj.* Egypt or its people or languag ~ *n.* 1. Egyptian person. Language of the ancient Egyptia together with its descendan Coptic, which is still used in t liturgies of the Coptic Church; o of the Hamitic group of languag

E·gyp·tol·o·gy (ējĭptŏl′ojē) Study of Egyptian antiquiti **E·gyp·tol′o·gist** *n.*

eh (ā) *int.* Ejaculation of inqui or surprise, or inviting assent.

EHF *abbrev.* Extremely hi frequency.

Ehr·lich (ār′lĭx), **Paul** (185 1915). German bacteriologi

The Republic of Ireland or É constitutes the major part of the seco largest of the British Isles. The histo of this mainly agricultural island h been turbulent.

Above: sculpture of man with harpoon.

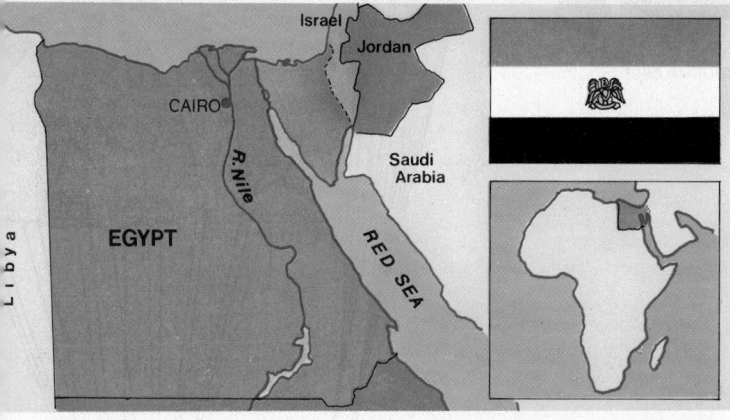

e central geographical feature of ypt is the Nile whose fertile valley ms the most populous area of the untry and whose seasonal flooding tated the patterns of agriculture until dern systems of irrigation were developed. The chief cash crop is cotton. Egypt's rich and ancient history has been extensively preserved in monuments and artifacts thanks to the dry climate. *Top left: The Sphinx of Hatshepsut at Memphis.*

oneer in bacteriology, immunol-
,y, and chemotherapy; discoverer
salvarsan; shared Nobel Prize for
edicine and physiology 1908.

ei·der (ī′der) *n.* Any of several
a ducks of N. hemisphere, esp. of
nus *Somateria*, having valuable
wn; **ei′derdown**, small soft
athers from breast of eider duck;
ft quilt, orig. one stuffed with
lerdown.

ei·det·ic (īdĕt′ĭk) *adj.* (psychol.,
mental image) Vivid or lifelike,
often unreal, esp. of images experienced in childhood. **ei·det′i·cal·ly**
adv.

Eif·fel (ī′fel) **Tower.** Iron
tower, 984 ft. (300 m) high,
originally built for the Exposition
of 1889 by A. G. Eiffel in Paris,
France.

eight (āt) *adj.* One more than
seven ~ *n.* One more than seven;
symbol for this (8, viii, or VIII);
anything in the form 8, esp. skating
figure; card with eight pips; eight

o'clock; size etc. indicated by 8; set
of eight things or persons, esp. a
rowing crew; **eight′ball**, black pool
ball bearing the number 8; (slang)
clumsy person, bungler; **behind
the eightball**, (slang) at a disadvantage; in trouble; ~**-track**
(*n.*), magnetic tape cartridge, esp.
one having eight parallel tracks of
prerecorded music or sound.

eight·een (ā′tēn′) *adj.* & *n.* One
more than 17 (18, xviii, or XVIII).
eight·eenth (ā′tēnth′) *adj.* & *n.*

eighth (ātth) *adj.* Next after
seventh. ~ *n.* Eighth part (see
PART[1] def 1); eighth thing etc.

eight·y (ā′tē) *adj.* Eight times
10 in number. ~ *n.* (pl. **eight·ies**).
Cardinal number 8 times 10 (80,
lxxx, or LXXX); set of 80 things or
persons; **eight′ies**, numbers etc.
from 80 to 89; these years of century
or life. **eight·i·eth** (ā′tēĭth) *adj.* &
n.

Ein·stein (īn′stīn; *Ger.* īn′shtīn),
Albert (1879–1955). German-
born Amer. theoretical physicist;
explained Brownian motion and the
photoelectric effect, investigated
atomic spectra; most famous for his
revolutionary theory of the nature
of space and time, known as the
theory of RELATIVITY, which upset
the Newtonian conception of the
universe.

ein·stein·i·um (īnstī′nēum) *n.*
(chem.) Transuranic element,
symbol E, at. no. 99, principal
isotope at. wt. 253.

Eir·e (ār′e, īr′e). Former and
Gaelic name for the Republic of
IRELAND.

Ei·sen·how·er (ī′zenhower),

Sequence of events in the operation of an ejection seat.

1 face screen pulled down

2 ejection mechanism triggered

3 cockpit canopy ejected

4 seat begins to eject

8 main parachute released

9 face screen released

10 pilot freed from seat

11 drogues pull pilot clear of seat

7 drogues stabilize seat

5 seat ejected   6 drogues out

12 parachute opens for normal desc

Dwight David (1890–1969). Amer. general and president; commander in chief of Allied forces in N. Africa 1942–3; supreme commander of Allied Expeditionary Forces in W. Europe 1943–5; North Atlantic supreme commander 1950–2; 34th president of the U.S. 1953–61.

ei·ther (ē′dh*er*, ī′-) *adj.* & *pron.* Each of two; one or the other of two. ~ *adv.* Introducing first of alternatives (**either ... or ...**); (in neg. or interrog. sentences) any more than the other, as *if you do not go, I shall not* ~.

e·jac·u·late (ĭjăk′yulāt) *v.t.* (**-lat·ed, -lat·ing**). 1. Utter suddenly. 2. Eject (fluids, esp. semen) from body. **e·jac·u·la·tion** (ĭjăkyulā′shon) *n.* **e·jac·u·la·to·ry** (ĭjăk′yulatōrē, -tōrē) *adj.*

e·ject (ĭjĕkt′) *v.t.* 1. Expel, evict (*from* place, office, etc.). 2. Throw out from within; emit. **e·jec′tion** *n.* ~ **seat**, escape seat designed to eject with its occupant from an aircraft in emergencies and parachute to earth. **e·jec′tor** *n.*

eke[1] (ēk) *v.t.* (**eked, ek·ing**). ~ **out**, supplement with great effort,

Ejection seats equipped with parachutes to control their rate of fall, were first considered by Leonardo da Vinci about 1500. In the 18th century, balloonists made jumps using something like an umbrella; the first folding parachute was used in America in 1880. A modern ejection seat with a parachute which opens automatically was not perfected until after the development of high-speed aircraft.

ain to supply deficiencies of; ntrive to make (livelihood) or pport (existence) by various keshift means.

eke² (ēk) *adv.* (archaic) Also.

EKG *abbrev.* Electrocardio- am.

e·kis·tics (ĭkĭs′tĭks) *n.pl.* (usu. nsidered sing.). Study of human tlements and their planning and velopment. **e·kis′tic, e·kis′ti- l** *adjs.* **e·kis·ti′cian** *n.*

el. *abbrev.* Elevation.

e·lab·o·rate (ĭlăb′ŏrĭt) *adj.* refully or minutely worked out; ghly finished. **e·lab′o·rate·ly** *v.* **e·lab′o·rate·ness** *n.* **elab- ate** (ĭlăb′ŏrāt) *v.t.* (**-rat·ed,** at·ing). Work out with care in tail; develop thoroughly; create; d details in writing or speech. **lab·o·ra·tion** (ĭlăbŏrā′shon) *n.*

E·laine (ĭlān′). In Arthurian gend, the name of two women no loved Lancelot; one died of requited love, the other was the other of Galahad by him.

E·lam·ite (ē′lamīt) *adj. & n.* lative, inhabitant, language) of am, an ancient country of esopotamia with its capital at sa (now Shush, in Iran).

é·lan (ālahn′) *n.* Vivacity, dash; yle, flair.

e·land (ē′land) *n.* (pl. **e·lands,** llect. **e·land**). Either of two rge heavily built African ante- pes of genus *Taurotragus*, with irally twisted horns.

élan vi·tal (*Fr.* ālahn vētăl′). In e philosophy of Henri Bergson, e life force or mysterious vital inciple, basis of an organism's ysical form, growth, and velopment.

e·lapse (ĭlăps′) *v.i.* (**e·lapsed,** laps·ing**). (of time) Pass, slip vay.

e·las·mo·branch (ĭlăz′mo- ăngk) *n.* (pl. **-branchs** pr. răngks). (zool.) Any cartilagi- us fish (shark, ray, skate, etc.).

e·las·tic (ĭlăs′tĭk) *adj.* 1. pontaneously resuming its normal ılk or shape after having been ntracted, dilated, or distorted; uoyant, springy; flexible, accom- odating. 2. (of fabric etc.) ontaining, made of, thin strips or reads of rubber usu. covered with oven material, or made of elasti- zed material. ~ *n.* Elastic fabric, astic cord or string. **e·las′ti- l·ly** *adv.* **e·las·tic·i·ty** (ĭlăstĭs′- reat or weave (yarn or cloth) to ve it elastic properties.

e·las·to·mer (ĭlăs′tomer) *n.* ynthetic rubber or plastic resem- ing rubber. **e·las·to·mer·ic** ăstomēr′ĭk) *adj.*

e·late (ĭlāt′) *v.t.* (**-lat·ed,** at·ing). Raise spirits of, courage, excite. **e·la′tion** *n.*

El·ba (ĕl′ba). Italian island off e W. coast of Italy, the place of

Top: 'The **Election**; Chairing the Mem- ber', by William Hogarth (1697–1764), a satirical comment on political elec- tions. Above: Delegates demonstrate at a Republican Party national convention during the U.S. presidential election campaign, 1968. The basis of the fran- chise and electoral traditions and methods vary from country to country.

Napoleon's first exile (1814–15).

el·bow (ĕl′bō) *n.* Outer part of joint between fore- and upper arm; elbow-shaped bend or corner in river, road, etc.; short piece of pipe bent at an angle to join two straight pieces; **out at the** ~**s,** ragged, poor; **up to the** ~**s,** busily, fully engaged *in*; ~ **grease,** vigorous rubbing, hard work; ~ **macaroni,** short-cut tubular macaroni, dried in small, curved pieces; **el′bowroom,** sufficient space to move or work in. **elbow** *v.* Thrust, jostle, (as) with the elbows.

El·brus (ĕl′brŏos), **Mount.** (also **El·bo·rus**) Highest mountain in Europe, 18,480 ft. (5,636 m), in the Caucasus range of Georgian U.S.S.R.

El Cap·i·tan (ĕl kăpĭtăn′, kahpētahn′). Peak, 7,564 ft. (2,307 m), in Yosemite National Park in the Sierra Nevadas, California.

eld·er¹ (ĕl′der) *n.* Low tree or shrub of genus *Sambucus*, with clusters of small white flowers and red, purple, or black berries; **el′- derberry,** elder; its fruit, used esp. to make **elderberry wine.**

eld·er² (ĕl′der) *adj.* Senior (of relations, or of 2 indicated persons); ~ **statesman,** retired statesman etc. whose advice is available. **elder** *n.* 1. (pl.) Persons of greater age. 2. (chiefly hist.) Member of senate, governing body, or class, of men venerable for age. 3. (eccles.) One of a body of laymen assisting in the management of church affairs, having pastoral or teaching functions etc.

eld·er·ly (ĕl′derlē) *adj.* Some- what old; past middle age.

eld·est (ĕl′dĭst) *adj.* Oldest, esp. first-born or oldest surviving (member of family, son, daughter, etc.).

El Do·ra·do, El·do·ra·do (ĕldorah′dō, -rä′-). Legendary country or city abounding in gold, jewels, etc., believed by 16th-c. explorers to exist in Spanish Amer.; hence, any place of fabulous wealth, opportunity, etc., esp. California during the gold rush. [Span., = "the gilded"]

El·e·at·ic (ĕlēăt′ĭk) *adj.* Of, per- taining to, a school of Greek philosophers of the 6th C. B.C. founded by PARMENIDES and his successor Zeno at Elea in Lucania.

el·e·cam·pane (ĕlekămpān´) *n.* Perennial Eurasian plant (*Inula helenium*) with large yellow flowers and bitter aromatic leaves and root, formerly used as tonic etc.

e·lect (ĭlĕkt´) *adj.* 1. Chosen; choice. 2. (theol.) Chosen by God, esp. for salvation or eternal life. 3. (usu. following n.) Elected but not yet installed in office, as *president-elect.* ~ *v.t.* Choose, choose (person) by vote; (of God) choose (persons) for salvation etc.; choose to study (a course).

e·lec·tion (ĭlĕk´shon) *n.* Choosing, esp. by vote; public vote.

e·lec·tion·eer (ĭlĕkshonēr´) *v.i.* Work on behalf of a political candidate, party, etc. in an election.

e·lec·tive (ĭlĕk´tĭv) *adj.* 1. Appointed or filled by, (of authority) derived from, election; having power of electing by vote; pertaining to, based on, system or principle of election. 2. (of courses in university etc.) Optional. ~ *n.* Elective course.

e·lec·tor (ĭlĕk´ter) *n.* Person with right to vote in election; member of **Electoral College**, elected by the voters of the 50 states and the District of Columbia and responsible for election of the president and vice president of the U.S.; **Elector**, one of the German princes of the Holy Roman Empire entitled to take part in electing the emperor. **e·lec·tor·al** *adj.*

e·lec·tor·ate (ĭlĕk´terĭt) *n.* 1. (hist.) Territory of German elector. 2. Whole body of qualified voters.

E·lec·tra (ĭlĕk´tra). (Gk. myth.) Daughter of Agamemnon and Clytemnestra; urged her brother Orestes to kill Clytemnestra and Aegisthus in revenge for murder of Agamemnon; ~ **complex**, (psychol.) counterpart in females of OEDIPUS complex, daughter's feeling of attraction toward father and hostility toward mother.

e·lec·tric (ĭlĕk´trĭk) *adj.* Of, charged with, worked by, capable of developing, electricity; electrifying, thrilling; ~ **blue**, brilliant light blue; ~ **chair**, chair in which persons condemned to death are executed by electrocution; ~ **circuit**, system of conductors through which electric energy is conveyed; ~ **current**, flow of electricity through conducting body from positive to negative pole, or from high to low potential; ~ **eel**, large S. Amer. fresh-water eellike fish (*Electrophorus electricus*), capable of giving electric shock; ~ **eye**: see PHOTOELECTRIC; ~ **ray**, RAY[2] of family Torpedinidae that emits electric discharges to numb or kill its prey; ~ **shock**, effect on animal body of sudden discharge of electricity; ~ **spark**, luminous discharge over gap in electric circuit. **e·lec·tri·cal** *adj.* Relating to, connected with, of nature of, electricity; electric. **e·lec·tri·cal·ly** *adv.*

e·lec·tri·cian (ĭlĕktrĭsh´an, ē-)

n. Person who makes, inst[...] repairs, or operates electr[...] apparatus or wiring.

e·lec·tric·i·ty (ĭlĕktrĭs´ĭtē, ē-[...] Form of energy present in PRO[...] or ELECTRON, energy associa[...] with the displacement or movem[...] of CHARGE.

e·lec·tri·fy (ĭlĕk´trĭfī) *v.t.* (**-fi[...] -fy·ing**). 1. Charge with electric[...] pass electric current through; s[...] ject to electric shock; con[...] (railroad, factory, etc.) to use[...] electric power. 2. Startle, ro[...] excite, as with electric sh[...] **e·lec·tri·fi·ca·tion** (ĭlĕktrĭfĭ[...] shon) *n.* **e·lec·tri·fi·er** *n.*

electro- *comb. form.* Of, pert[...] ing to, caused by electricity (*elec[...] dynamic, electrolysis, electrotype[...]*

e·lec·tro·car·di·o·gram (ĭ[...] trōkär´dēogrăm) *n.* (abbrev. E[...] or EKG) Record of sequence[...] electrical waves generated at e[...] beat of heart, used in diagnosi[...] heart disorders. **e·lec·tro·car[...] o·graph** *n.* Instrument applie[...] body for taking such records.

e·lec·tro·chem·is·try (ĭlĕk[...] kĕm´ĭstrē) *n.* Branch of chemi[...] concerned with relation betw[...] chemical changes and electr[...] phenomena. **e·lec·tro·chem´i[...]** *adj.* **e·lec·tro·chem´i·cal·ly** *a[...]*

e·lec·tro·cute (ĭlĕk´trokūt) (**-cut·ed, -cut·ing**). Put to de[...] execute, by powerful elec[...] current; kill by electricity. **e·le[...] tro·cu·tion** (ĭlĕktrokū´shon) *n.*

e·lec·trode (ĭlĕk´trōd) *n.* C[...] ductor or semiconductor by wh[...]

---

*An **electric** bell: An electromagnet pulls an iron armature so that an attached bob strikes a gong. The armature's movement breaks the current; the armature is forced back by a spring, thus reconnecting the circuit.*

*An **electrolyte** solution is used in electroplating, a method of giving objects a thin coating of metal. A bath in the electrolyte, with an electric current passed through, plates the immersed article.*

1. Alternating current. 2. Earth. 3. C[...] 4. Switch. 5. Wires joining. 6. Wires[...] pass without joining. 7. Fuse. [...] Resistor. 9. Variable resistor. 10. C[...] 11. Ammeter. 12. Voltmeter. [...] Amplifier. 14 Capacitor. 15. Ano[...] 16. Diode. 17. Transistor. 18. Tra[...] former.

A selection of electronic symbols

tron Microscope

exposure meter

70mm camera

phosphor coated screen

camera retraction lever

hera shutter

vacuum chassis

ond projector lens

t projector lens

cimen
ation control

objective lens

ling jackets

ecimen holder

ndenser control

t condenser lens

specimen stage

el frame

60 KV electron gun

*An optical microscope and an **electron** microscope both use a lens to illuminate the object to be magnified, but while the former uses light rays and curved glass lenses to produce enlargement, the latter uses electron rays and electro-magnet lenses.*

electricity enters or leaves an electrolyte, gas, or vacuum.

e·lec·tro·dy·nam·ics (ĭlĕktrō-dīnăm'ĭks) *n.* (usu. considered sing.) Branch of physics dealing with relationships among electric currents, magnets, and mechanical phenomena. **e·lec·tro·dy·nam'ic** *adj.*

e·lec·tro·en·ceph·a·lo·gram (ĭlĕktrōĕnsĕf'alogrăm) *n.* (abbrev. EEG) Record of minute electrical impulses inside the brain. **e·lec·tro·en·ceph'a·lo·graph** *n.* Instrument for producing an electro-encephalogram.

e·lec·trol·y·sis (ĭlĕktrŏl'ĭsĭs, ē-) *n.* Chemical decomposition by action of electric current; method of obtaining a purified deposit of a metal on the cathode, as in electro-plating, and hence of purifying certain metals.

e·lec·tro·lyte (ĭlĕk'trolīt) *n.* Substance that dissociates into ions when in solution or when fused, thus becoming an electrical conductor. **e·lec·tro·lyt·ic** (ĭlĕktro-lĭt'ĭk) *adj.* **e·lec·tro·lyt'i·cal·ly** *adv.*

e·lec·tro·lyze (ĭlĕk'trolīz) *v.t.* (**-lyzed, -lyz·ing**). Decompose (a liquid) by electricity.

e·lec·tro·mag·net (ĭlĕktrōmăg'-nĭt) *n.* Magnet consisting of soft iron core wound with current-carrying coil of wire, the current in which produces magnetization of the core. **e·lec·tro·mag·net·ic** (ĭlĕktrōmăgnĕt'ĭk) *adj.* Having both electrical and magnetic character or effects; applied esp. to those waves or radiations that travel with the same velocity as light and whose special character seems to depend entirely on their frequency or wavelength, and which include X-rays, ultraviolet visible, and infrared light, radiant heat, radio waves, and other types of radiation.

e·lec·tro·mag·net·ism (ĭlĕktrō-măg'netĭzem) *n.* (Study of) magnetic force produced by means of electricity.

e·lec·trom·e·ter (ĭlĕktrŏm'ĭter, ē-) *n.* Instrument for detecting and measuring the magnitude of an electric charge, current, or voltage.

e·lec·tro·mo·tive (ĭlĕktrōmō'-tĭv) *adj.* Of, pertaining to, producing electric current; **~ force**, (abbrev. emf) force set up by difference of potential in an electric circuit, usu. measured in volts.

e·lec·tron (ĭlĕk'trŏn) *n.* (phys.) Elementary particle with an indivisible charge of negative electricity, one or more of which surround the nucleus of each atom and give it its chemical properties and the movement of which, when free, constitutes an electric current; **free ~**, electron freed from its bound state within the atom; **~ lens**, device producing system of electric and magnetic fields capable of focusing a stream of electrons; **~ microscope**, microscope with extremely high magnification, using electrons focused by magnetic lenses rather than visible light to form a magnified image; **~ tube**, sealed glass tube, either completely evacuated or containing gas under low pressure, used to control flow of current between one or more pairs of electrodes; **~-volt**, (abbrev. eV) unit of energy equal to that acquired by an electron accelerated through a potential difference of 1 volt.

e·lec·tron·ic (ĭlĕktrŏn'ĭk, ē-) *adj.* 1. Of or relating to electrons or

*The African **elephant** (left) and the Indian elephant. The former has been much hunted for its tusks, which may reach 10 ft. long and 220 lbs in weight. The latter is used as a working animal in India, Burma, and Thailand.*

electronics; **~ surveillance**, use o electronic devices to gathe information secretly, as in espio nage, crime detection, etc. 2. (c musical instruments) Producin sound electronically, without pipe strings, etc., esp. **~ organ**. **e·lec tron'i·cal·ly** *adv.* **e·lec·tron'ics** 1. Science, technology of electroni phenomena. 2. Electronic device industry or business.

e·lec·tro·pho·re·sis (ĭlĕktro forē'sĭs) *n.* (phys.) Movement o particles in a fluid under th influence of an electric field.

e·lec·tro·plate (ĭlĕk'troplāt) *v.* (**-plat·ed, -plat·ing**). Coat (usu. metallic surface) with a film o another metal (e.g. chromiun silver, or nickel) by electrolysis.

e·lec·tro·scope (ĭlĕk'troskōp) Instrument formerly used fo detecting presence of electricity freq. consisting of two pieces o gold leaf or two pith balls suspende together from the end of a conduc tor, now used for detecting an measuring radioactivity, the ioniza tion of air produced by this havin the effect of discharging a charge electroscope.

e·lec·tro·stat·ics (ĭlĕktro stăt'ĭks) *n.* Branch of physic dealing with electric charges at res **e·lec·tro·stat'ic** *adj.*

e·lec·tro·ther·a·py (ĭlĕktrō thĕr'apē) *n.* Medical treatment b means of electricity.

e·lec·tro·type (ĭlĕk'trotīp) *n* Printing plate made by electro lytically depositing copper onto mold of wax or lead. **~** *v.* (**-typed, -typ·ing**). Copy b electrotype.

e·lec·tro·va·lence (ĭlĕktrōvā' lens), **e·lec·tro·va·len·cy** (ĭlĕktrō vā'lensē) *ns.* 1. Valenc characterized by the transfer o electrons between atoms of tw different elements accompanied b ormation of ions. 2. Number of harges an atom acquires or loses s the result of such a transfer of lectrons. **e·lec·tro·va′lent** *adj.*

el·ee·mos·y·nar·y (ĕlemŏs′-něrē, -mŏz′-, ĕlēe-) *adj.* Of, lependent on, charity; charitable.

el·e·gant (ĕl′egant) *adj.* 1. Tastefully ornate in dress; graceful; asteful, refined; of refined luxury. . Excellent, first-rate. **el′e·gance** . **el′e·gant·ly** *adv.*

el·e·gi·ac (ĕlejī′ak, -ăk, ĭlē′jēăk) *dj.* Appropriate to elegies; mournul; (of meter, couplet) consisting f dactylic hexameter and pentamter.

el·e·gy (ĕl′ejē) *n.* (pl. **-gies**). Song of lamentation, esp. for the lead; poem, poetry, in elegiac neter. **el·e·gize** (ĕl′ejīz) *v.* **-gized, -giz·ing**). Write elegy, write elegy upon.

el·e·ment (ĕl′ement) *n.* 1. Component part; constituent; esistance wire carrying the current n an electric heater etc. 2. In ncient and medieval philosophy, ne of the four substances (earth, vater, air, fire) of which all material oodies were held to be com-ounded; now, (pl.) atmospheric gencies or powers; (fig.) person's tc. ordinary range of activity, urroundings in which one feels at nome. 3. (chem.) Any of over oo different substances that have never been separated into simpler ubstances by chemical means and hat alone or in combination con-titute all matter; they are dis-inguished from each other by the number of electrons in their atoms outside the atomic nucleus (see PERIODIC law). 4. (pl.) Rudiments f learning; first principles of an rt or science.

el·e·men·tal (ĕlemĕn′tal) *adj.* 1. Of all or any of the four elements see ELEMENT def. 2); of the powers or agencies of nature. 2. Of the nature of an ultimate constituent, imple, uncompounded; basic, constituent.

el·e·men·ta·ry (ĕlemĕn′terē, -trē) *adj.* 1. Rudimentary, intro-luctory; simple. 2. Fundamental, essential, irreducible; **~ particle**, phys.) one smaller than an atom; **~ school**, the first six to eight grades of school, where young children receive basic education. **el·e·men′ta·ri·ly** *adv.* **el·e·men′-ta·ri·ness** *n.*

e·len·chus (ĭlĕng′kus) *n.* (pl. -chi pr. -kī, -kē). Logical refuta-ion; **Socratic ~**, Socratic method f eliciting truth by short question nd answer.

el·e·phant (ĕl′efant) *n.* (pl. -phants, collect. -phant). 1. Huge our-footed thick-skinned mammal f the order Proboscidea, with long curving ivory tusks and a prehensile runk or proboscis (only two

'The Burial of Count Orgaz', a painting by **El Greco** (1541–1614). El Greco used color in his works to heighten emotional impact. His output was large and his way of life, when he settled in a Spanish castle, luxurious.

species, the Indian and the African, now exist). 2. **~ seal** or **sea ~**, either of 2 species of seal of genus *Mirounga* (the large *M. leonina* of S. hemisphere and the smaller *M. angustirostris* of N. Amer. Pacific coast) with prolonged snout in male.

el·e·phan·ti·a·sis (ĕlefantī′asĭs) *n.* Tropical disease, caused by a nematode parasite, resulting in gross enlargement of legs etc. and thickening of skin.

el·e·phan·tine (ĕlefăn′tĭn, -tīn, -tēn) *adj.* Of elephants; elephant-like; clumsy, ponderous.

elev. *abbrev.* Elevation.

el·e·vate (ĕl′evāt) *v.t.* (**-vat·ed, -vat·ing**). Lift up; hold up; raise (eyes etc.), direct upward; exalt in rank etc.; raise morally or intellec-tually; (gunnery) raise axis of (gun etc.). **el′e·vat·ed** *adj.* (esp.) 1. Elated, exhilarated. 2. (also **~ railroad**) Railroad supported on pillars or arches above street level; (also **~ train**) train on such rail-road.

el·e·va·tion (ĕlevā′shon) *n.* 1. Elevating, being elevated. 2. Swelling; rising ground, eminence. 3. Angle with horizon (esp. of gun); (astron.) angular distance of heavenly body above horizontal plane (as opp. to *depression*, below it). 4. Height above a given level, esp. that of sea; height, loftiness, grandeur, dignity. 5. Drawing of building made in projection on vertical plane, as dist. from ground plan.

el·e·va·tor (ĕl′evā′ter) *n.* (esp.) 1. Muscle that raises limb etc. 2. Machine for hoisting grain, usu. a bucket conveyor; large building (containing such machines) for storing grain. 3. Apparatus for

raising and lowering people or things to other floor of building. 4. (aeron.) Movable stabilizing surface on an airplane, usu. hinged to tail, where it functions like a horizontal rudder and makes the craft go up or down.

e·lev·en (ĭlĕv′en) *adj.* Amount-ing to 11. **~ n.** One more than 10; symbol for this (11, xi, or XI); 11 o'clock; size etc. indicated by 11; set of 11 things or persons, esp. forming football team.

e·lev·enth (ĭlĕv′enth) *adj.* Next after 10th; **~ hour**, latest possible time (Matt. 20). **eleventh** *n.* Eleventh part (see PART[1]); 11th thing etc.

elf (ĕlf) *n.* (pl. **elves** pr. ĕlvz). One of a class of supernatural beings, in early Teutonic belief supposed to be of dwarfish form and to have magic powers; mis-chievous creature; dwarf, little creature. **elf·in** (ĕl′fĭn) *adj.* Of elves, elflike; diminutive; fairy-like, full of strange charm. **elf′ish** *adj.* **elf′ish·ly** *adv.* **elf′ish·ness** *n.*

El Fai·yum (ĕl fīyōom′). City in N. Egypt, in bed of ancient lake noted for abundant archaeological objects.

El·gin (ĕl′gĭn, -jĭn) **Marbles.** Collection of Greek sculptures chiefly of the school of Phidias and from the Parthenon, acquired by the 7th Earl of Elgin and sold by him to the British Government in 1816; now in the British Museum.

El Grec·o (ĕl grĕk′ō), **Domeni-**

kos Theotokopoulos (1541–1614). Crete-born Spanish painter, esp. of religious pictures and portraits. [Span., = "the Greek"]

e·lic·it (ĭlĭs'ĭt) *v.t.* Draw forth (what is latent or potential); educe (truths etc.) *from* data; extract, (information, response, etc.) *from* person. **e·lic·i·ta·tion** (ĭlĭsĭtā'shon), **e·lic'i·tor** *ns.*

e·lide (ĭlīd') *v.t.* (**e·lid·ed, e·lid·ing**). Omit, slur over (vowel, syllable) in pronunciation.

el·i·gi·ble (ĕl'ĭjĭbel) *adj.* Fit to be chosen, qualified (*for* office etc.); acceptable, suitable (esp. as husband or wife). **el·i·gi·bil·i·ty** (ĕlĭjĭbĭl'ĭtē) *n.* **el'i·gi·bly** *adv.*

E·li·jah (ĭlī'ja). Hebrew prophet of 9th c. B.C.; raised the dead son of the widow of Zarephath; was carried to heaven in a chariot of fire (1 Kings 17–2 Kings 2).

e·lim·i·nate (ĭlĭm'ĭnāt) *v.t.* (**-nat·ed, -nat·ing**). Remove, get rid of (esp. waste matter from body or tissues by excretion); expel, exclude; (alg.) get rid of (quantities) from equation; get rid of (unknown quantities) in simultaneous equations by combining equations. **e·lim·i·na·tion** (ĭlĭminā'shon), **e·lim'i·na·tor** *ns.*

El·i·ot[1] (ĕl'ēot, ĕl'yot), **George.** Pen name of Mary Ann Cross (1819–80), *née* Evans; English novelist; author of *Adam Bede, The Mill on the Floss, Silas Marner, Middlemarch*, etc.

El·i·ot[2] (ĕl'ēot, ĕl'yot) **T(hom-**

Elizabeth I by Gheeraerts the Younger, c 1592. Her reign was complicated by religious conflict and lack of an heir but British influence increased with victory over the Spanish.

as) S(tearns) (1888–1965). American-born Brit. poet, critic, and playwright; author of the poems "The Waste Land," "Four Quartets," etc.; Nobel Prize for literature 1948.

E·li·sha (ĭlī'sha). Hebrew prophet; disciple and successor of Elijah.

e·li·sion (ĭlĭzh'on) *n.* Suppression or slurring of letter (esp. vowel) or syllable in pronouncing.

e·lite, é·lite (ĭlēt', ā-) *ns.* Choice part, best (*of*); select group or class; typewriter type with 12 characters to the inch. **e·lit'ism** *n.* Advocacy of or reliance on leadership or dominance of a select group. **e·lit'ist** *n. & adj.*

e·lix·ir (ĭlĭk'ser) *n.* 1. (alchemy) Preparation designed to change base metals into gold or to prolong life indefinitely; universal remedy for disease. 2. Sweetened aromatic solution of water and alcohol used as flavoring for medicine. [Arab. *al-iksīr*, prob. f. late Gk. *xērion* desiccative powder for wounds]

E·liz·a·beth (ĭlĭz'abeth). Name of two English queens: **Elizabeth I** (1533–1603), daughter of Henry VIII and Anne Boleyn; queen of England 1558–1603; **Elizabeth II** (1926–), daughter of George VI,

Elizabeth II in 1953, the year of he[r] coronation in the U.K. As a const[i]tutional monarch, she has few of th[e] direct powers enjoyed by Elizabeth [I] she is detached from political factions

Elm *trees, found chiefly in the N. Hem[i]sphere, are popular as ornamental a[nd] shade trees. American or white elm a[nd] English or Wych elm are both susce[p]tible to attack by fungus known [as] Dutch elm disease. Few elms no[w] remain in U.K.*

een of the United Kingdom 52– . **E·liz·a·be·than** (ĭlĭzạ-ʹthan, -bĕthʹan) *adj. & n.* (Person, writer) of the time of Queen izabeth I or (occas.) II.

elk (ĕlk) *n.* (pl. **elks**, collect. **elk**). Either of two large N. Amer. deer *ervus canadensis,* also called piti, or *Cervus nannodes,* the tule), both of western U.S. and nada, having basically brown ir and a nearly black mane and, mature males, widely branched tlers of six or seven points. 2. rit.) = MOOSE. 3. **elk'hound,** nting dog of Scandinavian breed th thick gray coat and tail curled er back. 4. **E~,** *n.* Member of ternal organization, Benevolent d Protective Order of Elks.

ell (ĕl) *n.* L-shaped room; wing building at right angle to main ructure.

el·lipse (ĭlĭpsʹ) *n.* Plane closed rve in which the sum of the stances of any point from the two ci is a constant quantity; figure oduced when a cone is cut liquely by a plane making a naller angle with the base than the de of the cone makes with the se. **el·lip·tic** (ĭlĭpʹtĭk), **el·lip·ti·-** **al** (ĭlĭpʹtĭkal) *adjs.* **el·lip'ti·cal·ly** v.

el·lip·sis (ĭlĭpʹsĭs) *n.* (pl. **-ses** pr. ēz). 1. (gram.) Omission from ntence of word(s) needed to com-ete grammatical construction but ot necessary for understanding (as *oming?* for *Are you coming?*). 2. ries of marks (... or ***) used printing and writing to indicate nission of word(s), as in a long uotation.

el·lip·soid (ĭlĭpʹsoid) *n.* Solid rmed by rotating an ellipse about axis through its foci or the rpendicular bisector of this. ·lip·soi'dal *adj.*

El·lis (ĕlʹĭs) **Island.** Island in ew York harbor, belonging to .S. Government, major U.S. nmigration center (1892–1943), ow part of the Statue of Liberty ational Monument.

El·li·son (ĕlʹĭson), **Ralph** Waldo) (1914–). Amer. writer; est known for his novel, *Invisible Man.*

elm (ĕlm) *n.* Large tree of genus *lmus,* usually with doubly errated leaves, rough bark, and rching branches, widely planted as shade tree; wood of such trees.

El·mo (ĕlʹmō), **St.** (pop.) St. eter González (c1190–1246), panish Dominican preacher who ecame patron saint of seamen; **St.** ·'s fire, luminous electrical dis-harge sometimes seen on ship uring storm, interpreted as sign of t. Elmo's protection, or sometimes f impending disaster, also called orposant.

El Mor·ro (ĕl morʹō) **National**

Monument. Area in W. New Mexico reserved for protection of cliff-dweller ruins and sandstone rock bearing inscriptions of Spanish explorers.

el·o·cu·tion (ĕlokūʹshon) *n.* Manner, style, art, of vocal produc-tion and delivery, esp. of public speaking. **el·o·cu'tion·ar·y** *adj.* **el·o·cu'tion·ist** *n.*

E·lo·him (ĕlōhĭmʹ, ĕlōʹhĭm; Heb. ĕlawhēmʹ). Hebrew name for God.

E·lo·hist (ĕlōʹhĭst) *n.* Author(s) of those parts of the Hexateuch where God is referred to as *Elohim* rather than *Yahweh.* **E·lo·his·tic** (ĕlōhĭsʹtĭk) *adj.*

e·lon·gate (ĭlawngʹgāt, -lŏngʹ-, ēʹlawng-, -lŏng-) *v.* (**-gat·ed, -gat·ing**). Lengthen, prolong; have slender or tapering form. ~ *adj.* (bot., zool.) Long in propor-tion to its breadth; slender, tapering.

e·lon·ga·tion (ĭlawnggāʹshon, -lŏng-, ē-) *n.* Lengthening; exten-sion.

e·lope (ĭlōpʹ) *v.i.* (**e·loped, e·lop·ing**). Run away from home for secret marriage, (*with* lover); (of couple) run away together to get married. **e·lope'ment** *n.*

el·o·quence (ĕlʹokwens) *n.* Fluent, forcible, and apt use of language; rhetoric. **el'o·quent** *adj.* **el'o·quent·ly** *adv.*

El Pas·o (ĕl păsʹō). City in W. Texas on Rio Grande opposite Ciudad Juarez, Mexico.

El Sal·va·dor (ĕl sălʹvadŏr). Republic in W. Central America, on Pacific; capital, San Salvador.

else (ĕls) *adv.* (following indef. or interrog. pron.) Besides, as *any-thing ~, who ~?*; instead, as *what ~ could I say?*; otherwise, if not, as *run, or ~ you will be late.* **else·where** (ĕlsʹhwār, ĕlsʹwār) *adv.* In, to, some other place, at some

other point.

El·si·nore (ĕlsĭnōrʹ). Seaport in Denmark; setting of Shakespeare's play, *Hamlet.*

e·lu·ci·date (ĭlooʹsĭdāt) *v.t.* (**-dat·ed, -dat·ing**). Throw light upon, clear up, explain. **e·lu·ci·-** **da·tion** (ĭloosĭdāʹshon) *n.*

e·lude (ĭloodʹ) *v.t.* (**e·lud·ed, e·lud·ing**). Escape by dexterity or stratagem (blow, danger, etc.); slip away from (person, pursuit, etc.); evade. **e·lu·sion** (ĭlooʹzhon) *n.* **e·lu·sive** (ĭlooʹsĭv) *adj.* **e·lu'sive·ly** *adv.* **e·lu'sive·ness** *n.*

el·ver (ĕlʹver) *n.* Young eel.

E·ly·sée (ālēzāʹ). Official resi-dence of French president, on the Champs Elysées, Paris.

E·ly·si·um (ĭlĭzʹēum, ĭlĭzhʹ-, ĭlēʹzhē-). (Gk. myth.) Abode of the blessed after death; hence, place, state, of ideal or perfect happiness. **E·ly·sian** (ĭlĭzhʹan, ĭlēʹzhan) *adj.* ~ **fields,** Elysium.

el·y·tron (ĕlʹĭtrŏn) *n.* Outer hard wing case of coleopterous insect.

em (ĕm) *n.* 1. Letter M, m. 2. (print.) Measure equivalent to 12 points; also, the square of the body size of any type used as a unit of measure, as of the length of a dash.

em- = EN-.

e·ma·ci·ate (ĭmāʹshēat) *v.t.* (**-at·ed, -at·ing**). Make thin, as by starvation or illness. **e·ma·ci·a·-** **tion** (ĭmāshēāʹshon) *n.*

em·a·nate (ĕmʹanāt) *v.i.* (**-nat·ed, -nat·ing**). Issue, originate (*from* source, person, etc.); proceed, issue, flow forth (*from*). **em·a·na·tive** (ĕmʹanātĭv) *adj.*

em·a·na·tion (ĕmanāʹshon) *n.*

Ellis Island, in Upper New York Bay, was reopened to the public in 1976 after a checkered history in which it was used as a ballast dump and deten-tion center.

(esp.) 1. Something emitted or radiated (*from*). 2. (chem.) Radioactive gas produced by radioactive decay of a solid, e.g. radon.

e·man·ci·pate (ĭmăn'sĭpāt) *v.t.* (-pat·ed, -pat·ing). 1. Set free from control, or from legal, social, or political restraint; esp., set free (slave). 2. (Rom. law) Release (child, wife) from power of *pater familias*. **e·man'ci·pa·tor** *n.*

e·man·ci·pa·tion (ĭmănsĭpā'-shon) *n.* Setting free, esp. from slavery, intellectual or moral fetters, or legal disabilities; **E~ Proclamation**, (U.S. hist.) proclamation issued by President Lincoln on Jan. 1, 1863, freeing slaves in all areas still in rebellion against the Union.

e·mas·cu·late (ĭmăs'kyulāt) *v.t.* (-lat·ed, -lat·ing). Castrate; weaken, make effeminate; enfeeble, impoverish (language); weaken (literary composition) by removing what is supposed to be indecorous or offensive. **e·mas·cu·la·tion** (ĭmăskyulā'shon) *n.* **e·mas·cu·la·tive, e·mas·cu·la·to·ry** (ĭmăs'kyulātōrē, -tōrē) *adjs.* **emasculate** (ĭmăs'kyulĭt) *adj.* Castrated; effeminate.

em·balm (ĕmbahm') *v.t.* Preserve (corpse) from decay by treatment with preservatives; preserve, cherish the memory of; endow with balmy fragrance. **em·balm'er, em·balm'ment** *ns.*

em·bank (ĕmbăngk') *v.t.* Shut in, confine (river etc.) by banks, raised stone structure, etc. **em·bank'ment** *n.* 1. Mound, bank, etc., for confining river etc. 2. Long earthen bank or mound supporting roadway.

em·bar·go (ĕmbär'gō) *n.* (pl. -goes). Order forbidding ships of foreign power to enter, or any ships to leave, ports of a country, usu. issued in anticipation of war; suspension of (branch of) commerce; stoppage, prohibition. ~ *v.t.* (-goed, -go·ing). Lay (vessel, trade) under embargo.

em·bark (ĕmbärk') *v.* 1. Put, go, on board ship (*for* destination). 2. Set out (*on, upon*, undertaking etc.). **em·bar·ka·tion** (ĕmbärkā'shon) *n.*

em·bar·rass (ĕmbăr'as) *v.t.* 1. Encumber, hamper, impede; (pass.) be in difficulties from want of money, encumbered with debts. 2. Perplex, throw into doubt or difficulty; cause to feel self-conscious or ashamed; complicate (question etc.). **em·bar·rassed·ly** (ĕmbăr'astlē, -asĭdlē), **em·bar'-rass·ing·ly** *advs.* **em·bar'rass·ment** *n.* Embarrassed state or condition.

em·bas·sy (ĕm'basē) *n.* (pl. -sies). Ambassador's function or office; ambassador's residence; mission to foreign government headed by ambassador.

em·bat·tle (ĕmbăt'el) *v.t.* (-tled, -tling). 1. Arrange in battle order; prepare for battle. 2. Fortify against attack. **em·bat'tled** *adj.* Arranged or ready for battle.

em·bed (ĕmbĕd') *v.t.* (-bed·ded, -bed·ding). Fix firmly in surrounding mass; (of mass) surround thus.

em·bel·lish (ĕmbĕl'ĭsh) *v.t.* Beautify, adorn; add to, heighten (narrative) with fictitious additions. **em·bel'lish·ment** *n.*

em·ber (ĕm'ber) *n.* (usu. pl.) Small piece of live coal or wood in dying fire; smoldering ash.

em·bez·zle (ĕmbĕz'el) *v.t.* (-zled, -zling). Divert to one's own use (money etc.) in violation of trust or official duty. **em·bez'zle·ment** *n.*

em·bit·ter (ĕmbĭt'er) *v.t.* Make bitter (now usu. fig.); exasperate (person, feeling). **em·bit'ter·ment** *n.*

em·bla·zon (ĕmblā'zon) *v.t.* Inscribe or portray conspicuously, as on heraldic shield; adorn *with* heraldic devices etc.; celebrate, extol. **em·bla'zon·ment** *n.* **em·bla'zon·ry** *n.* = BLAZONRY.

em·blem (ĕm'blem) *n.* Symbol, typical representation; type, personification (*of* a quality); heraldic device, or other figured object as distinctive badge of person, family, etc.

em·blem·at·ic (ĕmblemăt'ĭk), **em·blem·at·i·cal** (ĕmblemăt'ĭkal) *adjs.* Serving as type or emblem (*of*). **em·blem·at'i·cal·ly** *adv.*

em·bod·y (ĕmbŏd'ē) *v.t.* (-bod·ied, -bod·y·ing). 1. Invest or clothe (spirit) with body; give concrete form to (what is abstract or ideal); be embodiment or expression of. 2. Unite into one body; incorporate; include, comprise (various elements). **em·-**

*An **embryo** develops from the fusion of 2 cells, the male spermatozoon and the female ovum or egg, each of which has equal influence on the resulting individual, although these influences are far from fully understood.*

bod'i·ment *n.*

em·bold·en (ĕmbōl'den) *v* Make bold, encourage (*to* do).

em·bo·lism (ĕm'bolĭzem) Blockage of blood vessel by bloo clot, air bubble, fat globule, etc.

em·bon·point (ahṅbawṅpwăṅ *n.* (Fr.) Plumpness; stoutness.

em·boss (ĕmbaws', -bŏs') *v.* Carve, mold, in relief; cause figur etc. to stand out on (surface **em·boss'ment** *n.*

em·bou·chure (ahmbushoon ahm'bushoor) *n.* 1. Mouth of rive 2. Mouthpiece of wind instrumen 3. Manner of applying the lips an tongue to wind instrument mouthpiece.

em·brace (ĕmbrās') *v.* (-braced, -brac·ing). 1. Clas (person) in arms, usu. as sign fondness or friendship (also abs. clasp, enclose. 2. Accept eagerl avail oneself of (offer, opportunit etc.); adopt (course of action, part opinion, etc.). 3. Include, com prise; take in with eye or mind. *n.* Folding in the arms. **em brace'ment** *n.*

em·bra·sure (ĕmbrā'zher) Beveling off of wall at sides of do or window, so that inside profile window is larger than that outside; opening in wall or parap for gun, widening from within.

em·broi·der (ĕmbroi'der) *v.* Ornament (cloth etc.; or abs.) wit needlework; work in needlewor embellish (narrative) with rhetor cal ornament or fictitious addition **em·broi·der·y** (ĕmbroi'derĭ -drē) *n.* (pl. -der·ies).

em·broil (ĕmbroil') *v.t.* Brin (affairs, narrative, etc.) into state confusion; involve (person) hostility (*with* another). **em broil'ment** *n.*

em·bry·o (ĕm'brēō) *n.* (pl. -os 1. (biol.) Organism in its earl stages of development, as the youn before birth or emergence from egg 2. (bot.) Rudimentary plant con tained in seed. 3. Thing rudimentary stage. ~ *adj.* Un developed, immature. **em·bry on·ic** (ĕmbrēŏn'ĭk) *adj.*

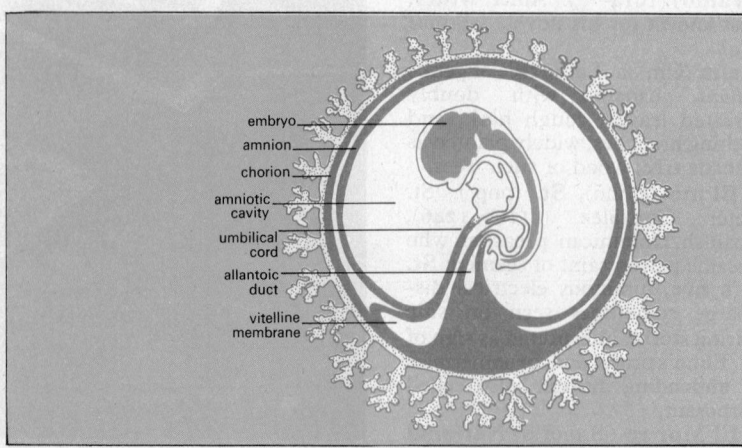

embryo
amnion
chorion
amniotic cavity
umbilical cord
allantoic duct
vitelline membrane

The structure of a human **embryo.** In modern research on transmission of hereditary characteristics, the sciences of genetics and embryology are closely linked.

The **emperor** penguin, near Li
America, Antarctica. The penguin is
flightless seabird. It uses its wings
paddles, to walk, and to fight. It bree
in large 'rookeries'.

em·bry·ol·o·gy (ĕmbrēŏl′ojē) *n.*
Branch of biology dealing with the
formation, early stages, and
development of embryos. **em·
bry·ol′o·gist** *n.* **em·bry·o·log·i·
cal** (ĕmbrēolŏj′ĭkal) *adj.*

em·cee (ĕm′sē) *n.* Master of
ceremonies. ~ *v.* (**-ceed, -cee··
ing**). Act as master of ceremonies
(for).

e·mend (ĭmĕnd′) *v.t.* Correct;
esp., remove errors from (text of
book etc.). **e·men·da·tion**
(ēmĕndā′shon, ĕmen-), **e·men·da·
tor** (ē′mendāter) *ns.* **e·mend·a··
to·ry** (ĭmĕn′datŏrē, -tōrē) *adj.*

em·er·ald (ĕm′erald) *n.* 1.
Bright green precious stone, variety
of beryl found chiefly in S. Amer.,
Siberia, and India. 2. ~ **cut**, (of
gem) type of step cut with beveled
corners; ~ **green**, vivid green; **E ~
Isle**, island of Ireland (from its
greenness).

e·merge (ĭmērj′) *v.i.*
(**e·merged, e·merg·ing**). Come
up out of liquid; come into view,
issue (*from* enclosed space, state of
suffering, etc.); rise into notice
(*from* obscurity etc.); (of fact etc.)
come out as a result of investigation
or discussion. **e·mer′gence** *n.*
e·mer′gent *adj.*

e·mer·gen·cy (ĭmēr′jensē) *n.* (pl.
-cies). Situation or sudden occurrence demanding immediate action;
(attrib.) used, arising, etc., in an
emergency.

e·mer·i·tus (ĭmĕr′ĭtus) *adj.*
Retired with honorary title
corresponding to that held before
retirement, as **professor** ~. [L.,
= "that has served his time"]

Em·er·son (ĕm′erson), **Ralph
Waldo** (1803–82). Amer. poet and
essayist; leader of transcendentalist
philosophy; called "The Sage of
Concord"; wrote *Essays First and
Second Series, Nature,* etc.

em·er·y (ĕm′erē, ĕm′rē) *n.*
Coarse corundum, used for polishing metals, stones, glass, etc.; ~
board, emery-coated nail file; ~
cloth, paper, wheel, cloth,
paper, wheel, coated with emery
powder; ~ **powder**, ground
emery.

e·met·ic (ĭmĕt′ĭk) *adj. & n.*
(Medicine) that causes vomiting.

emf, EMF *abbrevs.* Electromotive force.

em·i·grate (ĕm′ĭgrāt) *v.i.*
(**-grat·ed, -grat·ing**). Leave one's
country to settle in another. **em·i·
grant** (ĕm′ĭgrant) *adj. & n.*
em·i·gra·tion (ĕmĭgrā′shon) *n.*

é·mi·gré (ĕm′ĭgrā) *n.* Emigrant,
esp. one who fled his or her
country during a revolution. [Fr.]

em·i·nence (ĕm′ĭnens) *n.* 1.

Rising ground. 2. Distinguish
superiority. 3. **E ~**, in R.
Church, title of honor borne
cardinals.

em·i·nent (ĕm′ĭnent) *a.*
Exalted, distinguished; (of qua
ties) remarkable in degree; sign
noteworthy; ~ **domain**: s
DOMAIN. **em′i·nent·ly** *adv.*

e·mir (ĕmēr′) *n.* 1. Arab chie
tain prince, or governor. 2. Ti
given to descendants of Muha
mad; title of Muslim rule
e·mir·ate (ĕmēr′āt, -ĭt) *n.* Ran
office, or domain of an emir. [Ara
'*amīr* commander]

em·is·sar·y (ĕm′ĭsĕrē) *n.* (p
-sar·ies). Person sent on missio
to gain information, adherents, e

e·mis·sion (ĭmĭsh′on) *n.* Givi
of or out; what is emitted; di
charge. **e·mis·sive** (ĭmĭs′ĭv) *a*
em·is·siv·i·ty (ĕmĭsĭv′ĭtē)
(phys.) Power of a surface
radiate heat, light, etc.

e·mit (ĭmĭt′) *v.t.* (**e·mit·te
e·mit·ting**). Give out, send for
(light, heat, sound, opinion, etc.)

Em·man·u·el (ĭmăn′ūel): s
IMMANUEL.

e·mol·li·ent (ĭmŏl′yent) *adj.
n.* (Substance) having power
softening or relaxing living anim
tissues.

e·mol·u·ment (ĭmŏl′yument) *
Fee from office or employmen
salary.

e·mo·tion (ĭmō′shon) *n.* Agita
tion or disturbance of min
vehement or excited mental stat
feeling. **e·mo′tion·less** *adj.*

e·mo·tion·al (ĭmō′shonal) *ad*
Of the emotions; liable to emotio
e·mo′tion·al·ism *n.* **e·mo′tion
al·ly** *adv.*

e·mo·tive (ĭmō′tĭv) *adj.* O
tending to excite, emotion. **e·mo
tive·ly** *adv.*

Emp. *abbrev.* Emperor; empire
empress.

em·pan·el (ĕmpăn′el): s
IMPANEL.

em·pa·thy (ĕm′pathē) *n.* Abilit
to identify oneself mentally with
person or thing and so understan
his feelings or its meanin
em·path·ic (ĕmpăth′ĭk) *ad*
[transl. of Ger. *Einfühlung* (ein- i
fühlen feel)]

em·pen·nage (ahmpenahzh′) *
Arrangement of stabilizing surface
in the tail assembly of an airplan

em·per·or (ĕm′perer) *n.* Rule
of an empire (title); (hist., esp
sovereign of Roman or Byzantin
Empire or head of Holy Roma
Empire; ~ **butterfly**, any c
several richly colored butterflies c
the family Nymphalidae, such a
the tawny emperor (*Asterocamp*

The **Empire State Building** rising above the New York skyline. Completed in 1931, it was the first skyscraper to be so high (1,250 ft.). The Roman **Empire**. Numerous empires have risen and fallen, encouraging cyclical theories of history. Their organization has differed considerably.

ton), having orange-tawny wings with dark brown markings; ~ **nguin**, largest known species of nguin of the Antarctic.

em·pha·sis (ĕm′fasĭs) *n.* (pl. es pr. -sez). Stress on word or rase to indicate special significance or importance; vigor, ensity, of expression, feeling, ion, etc.; importance assigned to t, idea, etc.; prominence.

em·pha·size (ĕm′fasīz) *v.t.* ized, -siz·ing). Lay stress on ord, fact, etc.).

em·phat·ic (ĕmfăt′ĭk) *adj.* (of aguage, tone, gesture) Forcibly pressive; (of words etc.) bearing ess; (of person) expressing onef with emphasis; (of actions) cible, significant. **em·phat′i-l·ly** *adv.*

em·phy·se·ma (ĕmfīsē′ma) *n.* ath.) Abnormal distention of the cells of the lungs, causing pairment in breathing.

em·pire (ĕm′pīr) *n.* Political it consisting of several territories, ates, peoples, etc., ruled by an peror or empress. 2. Powerful ganization under control of one dividual, family, corporation, .; the **E**~, (esp.) (i) the Holy oman Empire (see ROMAN); (ii) e British Empire; (iii) (period of) ign of Napoleon I as Emperor of

the French, 1804–15, also called **First E**~ to distinguish it from the **Second E**~ of Napoleon III, 1852–70. 3. (attrib.) **E**~ (ahṅpēr′), of, in the style of, the First French Empire, (of furniture) having long straight lines and details from classical and ancient Egyptian art, (of women's dress) having very high waist, low neck, and flowing skirt; (less freq.) of the Second Empire; **E**~ **State**, nickname for state of New York; **E**~ **State Building**, one of the world's tallest buildings, 1,250 ft. (381 m), located on Fifth Ave. in New York City.

em·pir·ic (ĕmpĭr′ĭk) *adj.* Empirical. ~ *n.* 1. Person believing

practical experience is sole source of knowledge, as scientist relying solely on observation and experiment. 2. Untrained practitioner, quack.

em·pir·i·cal (ĕmpĭr′ĭkal) *adj.* 1. Based, acting, on observation and experiment, not on theory. 2. (chem.) ~ **formula**, simplest formula of a compound, indicating only the numerical ratios of the atoms present in the molecule of the compound but not necessarily their actual number and not implying its molecular structure. **em·pir′i·cal·ly** *adv.*

em·pir·i·cism (ĕmpĭr′ĭsĭzem) *n.* 1. Use of empirical methods. 2.

(philos.) Belief that experience is the sole source of knowledge. 3. Practice of medicine without regard for scientific knowledge; quackery. **em·pir'i·cist** n.

em·place·ment (ĕmplās'ment) n. Situation; placing; platform for mounting heavy guns.

em·ploy (ĕmploi') v.t. Apply (thing) to definite purpose, devote (effort, thought, etc.) to object; make use of (time etc.); use services of (person) in professional capacity or for some special work or business; find work or occupation for (person, his or her bodily or mental powers). ~ n. Being employed, esp. for wages; employment, occupation, profession, business.

em·ploy·ee, em·ploy·e (ĕmploi'ē, ĕmploiē') ns. Person employed for wages.

em·ploy·er (ĕmploi'er) n. (esp.) One who employs servants, work-

The **emu** is, apart from the ostrich, the largest living bird. It inhabits open country, nesting in shallow pits in the ground. Numerous eggs are incubated by the cock. Its diet consists of fruits, roots, and herbage.

men, etc., for wages; company th employs workers.

em·ploy·ment (ĕmploi'mei n. (esp.) Regular occupation business, trade, profession; state being employed; number of peop gainfully employed; ~ **agenc** business that finds employers employees for those seeking the

em·po·ri·um (ĕmpōr'ēu -pŏr'-) n. (pl. **-po·ri·un -po·ri·a** pr. -pōr'ēa, -pōr'ēa). Center of trade; marketplace. Large store; department store.

em·pow·er (ĕmpow'er) z Authorize, license (to do); enabl

em·press (ĕm'prĭs) n. Wi widow of emperor; woman ruli an empire.

emp·ty (ĕmp'tē) adj. (**-ti·e -ti·est**). 1. Containing nothin void, devoid, (of); vacant, u occupied; without anything carry; (colloq.) hungry. Frivolous, foolish; unsatisfactor vain; ~**-handed**, bringing no gi carrying nothing away; ~**-heade** frivolous, witless; ~**-neste** (colloq.) married person who children have grown and left hon or who never had childre **emp'ti·ly** adv. **emp'ti·ness** empty n. (pl. **-ties**). Empty truc freight car, etc.; empty box, bott etc., that has contained somethin ~ v. Remove contents of; transf (contents of one thing into another (of river etc.) discharge itself (int become empty.

em·py·re·an (ĕmpirē'an, -pī ĕmpĭr'ēan) adj. & n. (Of) th highest reaches of heaven, as (: ancient cosmology) the sphere fire, or as the abode of Go **em·py·re'al** adj.

EMU abbrev. Electromagnet unit.

e·mu (ē'mū) n. Large flightle Australian bird (Dromaius nova hollandiae), allied to cassowar with long drooping feathers.

em·u·late (ĕm'yulāt) v. (**-lat·ed, -lat·ing**). Try to equal excel; rival; imitate zealousl **em·u·la·tion** (ĕmyulā'shon), **em u·la·tor** ns. **em·u·la·tive** adj.

em·u·lous (ĕm'yulus) ad Zealously or jealously imitativ (of); desirous (of renown etc. actuated by spirit of rivalry **em'u·lous·ly** adv.

e·mul·si·fy (ĭmŭl'sĭfī) v. (**-fied, -fy·ing**). Convert int emulsion. **e·mul'si·fi·er** n.

e·mul·sion (ĭmŭl'shon) n. Sus pension of small globules of on liquid in another with which th first will not mix; this as pharma ceutical preparation, cosmeti lubricant, paint, etc.; (photog light-sensitive coating on film **e·mul'sive** adj.

en (ĕn) n. 1. Letter N, n. 2 (print.) Measure equivalent to ha an em.

namelled and jewelled boxes, c.
820, Swiss. Placed against a ground
f precious metal, **enamel** has great
rilliance of color and it has been used
 enrich such work.

ncaging an animal generally means
omething far more humane than it did
ome years ago. Zoos and animal parks
ave realized contact between viewer
nd animal is of prime importance.

en-, em- *prefixes.* In, into, on.
-en *suffix.* Forming: (1) verbs
rom adjectives to indicate being,
ecoming, or causing to be (*deepen,*
horten, weaken) or verbs from
ouns to indicate coming to have,
ausing to have (*lengthen, heighten*);
2) adjectives from nouns to
ndicate consisting of, made of, or
ke (*golden, wooden*); (3) past
articiples of strong verbs (*frozen*);
4) pl. nouns (*brethren*); (5) diminu-
ives (*children, chicken*).
   en·a·ble (ĕnā´bel) *v.t.* (**-bled,**
bling). Authorize, empower (*to*
o); supply with means *to* (do).
   en·act (ĕnăkt´) *v.t.* 1. Make
bill) into legislative act, pass (bill)
n legislature. 2. Act out (a play,
he part of, etc.). **en·act´ment,**
n·ac´tor** *ns.*
   en·nam·el (ĭnăm´el) *n.* 1. Colored
lass, powdered and fused, used as
ecoration for gold, silver, or
opper, or for painting. 2. Hard oil
aint, freq. containing varnish,
which renders it glossy; any smooth
nd lustrous surface coloring. 3.
Calcified substance forming glossy
oating of teeth. ~ *v.t.* Inlay,
ncrust, cover, with enamel;

variegate like enamel work.
   en·am·or, Brit. **en·am·our**
(ĕnăm´er) *vbs.t.* Inspire with love,
make fond (*of*; usu. pass.).
   en·cage (ĕnkāj´) *v.t.* (**-caged,**
-cag·ing). Confine (as) in cage.
   en·camp (ĕnkămp´) *v.* Set up or
live in camp; lodge in open in tents
etc. **en·camp´ment** *n.* (esp.)
Place where troops are encamped;
temporary quarters of nomads etc.
   en·case (ĕnkās´) *v.t.* (**-cased,**
-cas·ing). Put into case; surround

as with case.
   -ence *suffix.* Forming nouns
from adjectives ending in -*ent* to indicate action or quality (*reminis-
cence, congruence*).
   en·ceinte (ahṅsăṅt´) *adj.* (of
woman) Pregnant.
   en·ceph·a·li·tis (ĕnsĕfalī´tĭs) *n.*
(path.) Inflammation of the brain;
lethargic ~ (or ~ **lethargica**),
infectious form of this due to a
virus, usu. accompanied by extreme
drowsiness; sleeping sickness.

en·chain (ĕnchān´) v.t. Chain up, fetter.

en·chant (ĕnchănt´, -chahnt´) v.t. Bewitch; charm, delight. **en·chant´er, en·chant´ress, en·chant´ment** ns. **en·chant´ing·ly** adv.

en·chi·la·da (ĕnchĭlah´da) n. Tortilla with meat etc. and chili sauce.

en·ci·pher (ĕnsī´fer) v.t. Write (message etc.) in cipher.

en·cir·cle (ĕnsēr´kel) v.t. (-cled, -cling). Surround, encompass; form a circle around.

encl. abbrev. Enclosed; enclosure.

en·clave (ĕn´klāv) n. Territory surrounded by territory of another country; minority culture or other group existing within a group.

en·close (ĕnklōz´) v.t. (-closed, -clos·ing). 1. Surround (with walls, forces, etc.) so as to prevent free access; fence in; shut up in. 2. Shut up in receptacle (esp. something along with letter in envelope); bound on all sides, contain; surround, hem in on all sides.

en·clo·sure (ĕnklō´zher) n. Enclosing; enclosing fence etc.; enclosed place; document etc. enclosed with letter in envelope.

en·code (ĕnkōd´) v.t. (-cod·ed, -cod·ing). Put (message) into code or cipher; encipher. **en·cod´er** n.

en·co·mi·um (ĕnkō´mēum) n. (pl. **-mi·ums, -mi·a** pr. -mēa). Formal or high-flown expression of praise; eulogy, panegyric.

en·com·pass (ĕnkŭm´pas) v.t. Surround, form circle about; comprise; include. **en·com´pass·ment** n.

en·core (ahng´kōr, -kōr, ahn´-) n. & int. (Call for performance to be repeated) again, once more; repetition or additional item given in response. ~ v.t. Demand encore of (song, performer, etc.).

en·coun·ter (ĕnkown´ter) v.t. 1. Meet as adversary, confront in battle. 2. Meet, fall in with, esp. casually; experience (opposition etc.). ~ n. Meeting in combat or casually; ~ **group**, small group of persons who meet to improve their self-awareness and responsiveness through therapy that involves open expression of emotions.

en·cour·age (ĕnkēr´ĭj, -kŭr´-) v.t. (-aged, -ag·ing). Inspire with courage, embolden; stimulate by assistance, reward, approval, etc.; allow or promote continuance or progress of. **en·cour´age·ment** n. **en·cour´ag·ing** adj. **en·cour´ag·ing·ly** adv.

en·croach (ĕnkrōch´) v.i. Intrude usurpingly (on). **en·croach´ment** n.

en·crust (ĕnkrŭst´) = INCRUST.

en·cum·ber (ĕnkŭm´ber) v.t. Hamper with burden; burden with obligations, debts, etc.

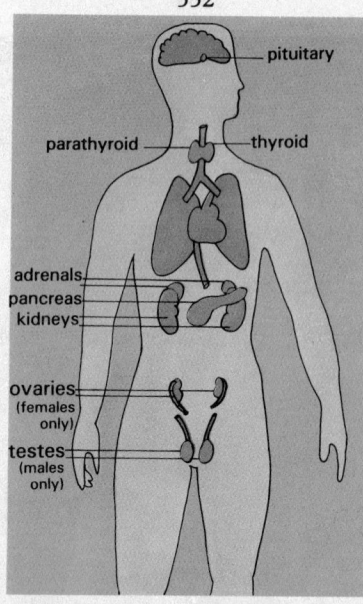

Endocrine glands, with the exception of the pancreas which secretes insulin, release hormones into the bloodstream. The pituitary gland controls other glands shown in the diagram.

en·cum·brance (ĕnkŭm´brans) n. 1. Burden; impediment. 2. Claim or lien upon property.

-ency suffix. Forming nouns indicating quality (efficiency) or state (presidency), but not action (cf. -ENCE).

ency., encyc., encycl. abbrevs. Encyclopedia.

en·cyc·li·cal (ĕnsĭk´lĭkal, -sī´klĭ-) adj. & n. (Letter, esp. issued by pope) intended for extensive circulation and dealing with matters of doctrine.

en·cy·clo·pe·di·a (ĕnsīklopē´dēa) n. Reference work containing extensive information on all branches or one particular branch of knowledge, usu. in alphabetical or topical order. **en·cy·clo·pe´dic** adj. **en·cy·clo·pe´dist** n. [pseudo-Gk. egkuklopaideia, spurious f.

egkuklios paideia all-around education, the arts and sciences considered essential to a liberal education]

en·cyst (ĕnsĭst´) v.t. Enclose or become a cyst.

end (ĕnd) n. 1. Extreme point, outermost part, utmost limit; o of the extremities of line or greatest dimension of obje surface bounding thing at eith extremity; piece broken off et remnant; (naut.) last length, sho length, of rope or cable. 2. Lim close, conclusion, of period of tin action, process, series, discours book, etc.; latter or concluding pa termination of existence, destru tion; death; ultimate state condition. 3. Event, issue; intend result, aim, purpose; object f which thing exists or is designe 4. **be at, come to, an ~**, b become, exhausted; be complete end; **be at the ~ of**, have no mo of; **bring to an ~**, exhaus complete, end; **keep one's ~ u** (colloq.) bear one's part, acqu oneself well; **make both ~s mee** live within one's income; **no ~** (colloq.) vast quantity or numbe of; immensely; **on ~**, resting on i end, upright; consecutively; pu **an ~ to**, put a stop to; ~ **to ~** with ends in contact, lengthwise. ~ **game**, (chess) last stage in gam when few pieces are left; ~ **ma** man at either end of row minstrels, playing bones tambourine and contributing com effects; ~ **organ**, any specialize structure forming the periphera terminus of nerve fibers havin either motor or sensory function ~ **papers**, blank leaves at begin ning and end of book, esp. the fir

The *endoplasm* is the central granula fluid in the protoplasm of an amoeba which consists also of an outer plasma membrane and a layer of clear ecto plasm just beneath that.

1 ectoplasm
2 endoplasm

d last, which are pasted to the
ding; **~ product**, finished
icle as opposed to raw material;
table, small table to be placed at
e end of a sofa or beside a chair.

d *v.* Bring to an end; put an end
destroy; come to an end; result
~ by (**doing**), come ultimately
(doing); **~ up**, conclude, finish.

en·dan·ger (ĕndān′jer) *v.t.*
use danger to. **en·dan′gered**
j. In danger of extinction, esp.
species, plant, animal, bird,
:., threatened with extinction
cause of destruction of environ-
nt etc.

en·dear (ĕndēr′) *v.t.* Render
ar (*to*). **en·dear′ing·ly** *adv.*
·dear′ment *n.* (esp.) Action or
terance expressing affection.

en·deav·or (ĕndĕv′er) *v.* Try (*to*
·); strive. **~** *n.* Attempt, effort.

en·dem·ic (ĕndĕm′ĭk) *adj.* Reg-
arly found among (specified)
ople or in (specified) country or
strict as a disease. **en·dem′-**
al·ly *adv.* **en·dem′ic** *n.* En-
mic plant or animal; endemic
sease.

d·ing (ĕn′dĭng) *n.* (esp.)
oncluding part (of book, story,
c.); (gram.) inflectional or forma-
e suffix.

en·dive (ĕn′dīv) *n.* 1. Plant
Cichorium endivia), the lacy leaves
 which are used in salads; variety
 this, ESCAROLE. 2. Variety of
ommon chicory, (*Cichorium
ybus*), whose long, narrow leaves
e bleached in cultivation and used
r salads.

end·less (ĕnd′lĭs) *adj.* Infinite;
ernal; incessant. **end′less·ly** *adv.*
d′less·ness *n.*

endo- *prefix.* Within.

en·do·car·di·um (ĕndōkär′-
ēum) *n.* (pl. **-di·a** pr. **-dēa**).
hysiol.) Smooth membrane lining
vities of heart. **en·do·car·di·tis**
ndōkärdī′tĭs) *n.* Inflammation of
e endocardium.

en·do·carp (ĕn′dōkärp) *n.* (bot.)
ner layer of pericarp, lining seed
amber, fleshy (as in orange),
embranous (as in apple), or hard
s in peach).

en·do·crine (ĕn′dōkrĭn, -krīn,
krēn) *adj. & n.* (Gland) pouring its
cretions into the blood or lymph;
uctless (gland).

en·do·cri·nol·o·gy (ĕndōkrin-
′ojē) *n.* Branch of medicine
ealing with the endocrine glands
d their secretions. **en·do·cri-**
ol′o·gist *n.*

en·do·derm (ĕn′dōdĕrm) *n.*
hysiol.) Innermost layer of cells
f embryo, from which alimentary
ystem is developed.

en·do·der·mis (ĕndōdĕr′mĭs) *n.*
ot.) Cylinder of tissue 1 cell thick
ing between cortex and conduct-
g tissues.

en·dog·a·my (ĕndŏg′amē) *n.*
Custom of marrying only within

Endive was supposedly introduced to
Europe from the East Indies or Egypt. It
is cultivated for culinary purposes and
bleached while growing to prevent the
leaves from tasting bitter.

one's own clan, tribe, caste, etc.
en·dog′a·mous *adj.*

en·dog·e·nous (ĕndŏj′enus) *adj.*
Growing or originating from
within.

en·do·plasm (ĕn′dōplăzem) *n.*
(biol.) Granular fluid cytoplasm
contained within ectoplasm in an
animal cell. **en·do·plas·mic**
(ĕndōplăz′mĭk) *adj.*

en·dorse (ĕndōrs′) *v.t.* (**-dorsed,**
-dors·ing). 1. Write on back

of (document), esp. sign one's name
(as payee etc.) on (bill, check, etc.);
make (check etc.) payable *to* another
by endorsement. 2. Confirm,
vouch for (statement, opinion);
express approval of (thing, person,
etc.). **en·dorse′ment** *n.*

en·do·sperm (ĕn′dōspĕrm) *n.*
(bot.) Albumen enclosed with
embryo in many seeds. **en·do-**
sper·mic (ĕndōspĕr′mĭk) *adj.*

en·do·the·li·um (ĕndōthē′lēum)
n. (pl. **-li·a** pr. **-lēa**). Layer of cells
lining blood vessels etc.

en·do·ther·mic (ĕndōthĕr′mĭk)
adj. (chem.) Occurring or formed
with absorption of heat.

en·dow (ĕndow′) *v.t.* Give,
bequeath, permanent income to
(person, institution, etc.); enrich
with (privileges etc.); furnish *with*
(quality, ability, etc.). **en·dow′-**
ment *n.*

en·dur·ance (ĕndoor′ans,
-dūr′-) *n.* 1. Act, power, or quality
of withstanding fatigue, stress,
pain, etc. 2. Fact or state of
persevering; lasting or continuing.

en·dure (ĕndoor′, -dūr′) *v.*
(**-dured, -dur·ing**). 1. Undergo
(pain etc.); submit to; bear (*to* do);
tolerate (thing, person). 2. Last.

Types of **energy:** Top left: Muscular energy; Alan Pascoe jumping hurdles. Bottom left: Nuclear energy; research workers handle isotopes, using mechanical hands from behind protective barriers. Top right: Potential kinetic energy — the Victoria Falls, between Zambia and Zimbabwe. Bottom, far right: A drainage windmill at Horsey, Norfolk, U.K. Bottom, near right: Two of the many large generators in the Foster Dam, Oregon.

end·ways (ĕnd'wāz), **end·wise** (ĕnd'wīz) *advs.* With end toward spectator or uppermost or foremost; end to end.

En·dym·i·on (ĕndĭm'ēon). (Gk. myth.) Shepherd, the most beautiful of men, of whom Selene (he Moon) became enamored.

ENE, E.N.E., e.n.e. *abbrevs.* ast-northeast.

-ene *comb. form.* (chem.) Used to form names of unsaturated hydrocarbons (*benzene, ethylene*).

en·e·ma (ĕn'ema) *n.* (med.) njection of fluid into the rectum, sp. as laxative; fluid injected in this manner.

en·e·my (ĕn'emē) *n.* (pl. **-mies**). . Hostile person; opponent, antagonist; opposing person, influence, etc. 2. (Member of) hostile army or nation; hostile force; nation at war with another. ∼ *adj.* Of a hostile force or nation; hostile.

en·er·get·ic (ĕnerjĕt'ĭk) *adj.* strenuously active; forcible, vigorous; powerfully operative. **en·er·get'i·cal·ly** *adv.*

en·er·gize (ĕn'erjīz) *v.t.* (**-gized, -giz·ing**). Supply with energy; activate; charge. **en'er·giz·er** *n.*

en·er·gy (ĕn'erjē) *n.* (pl. **-gies**). . Force, vigor (of speech, action, person, etc.); active operation; power actively exerted, (pl.) individual capacity to produce effect. 2. (phys.) Power of doing work possessed at any instant by a body or system of bodies; **conservation of** ∼: see CONSERVATION; **kinetic** ∼, power of doing work possessed by moving body by virtue of its motion; **potential** ∼, body's power of doing work by virtue of stresses resulting from its relation to other bodies; **mass-**∼, energy that all bodies possess in virtue of their mass, and of which a small portion is released (as radiations etc.) in radioactivity and other types of atomic disintegration. 3.

Fuel and other sources of such energy used for the operation of machinery etc.

en·er·vate (ĕn'ervāt) *v.t.* (**-vat·ed, -vat·ing**). Weaken physically, debilitate; deprive of strength or vitality. **en·er·va·tion** (ĕnervā'shon) *n.*

en·fant ter·ri·ble (ahṅfahṅ tĕrē'ble). Child who embarrasses his or her elders by untimely remarks (also transf.). [Fr.]

en·fee·ble (ĕnfē'bel) *v.t.* (**-bled, -bling**). Make feeble. **en·fee'ble·ment** *n.*

en·fi·lade (ĕn'filād, -lahd, ĕnfilād', -lahd') *n.* Fire from guns etc. sweeping line from end to end. ∼ *v.t.* (**-lad·ed, -lad·ing**). Subject (troops etc.) to enfilade.

en·fold (ĕnfōld') *v.t.* Wrap up (*in, with*); clasp, embrace.

en·force (ĕnfōrs', -fōrs') *v.t.* (**-forced, -forc·ing**). Compel (performance of action, observance of law, etc.). **en·force'ment** *n.* **en·force'a·ble** *adj.*

en·fran·chise (ĕnfrăn'chīz) *v.t.* (**-chised, -chis·ing**). 1. Set free as from bondage. 2. Admit to full rights of citizenship, esp. voting rights. **en·fran·chise·ment** (ĕnfrăn'chīzment, -chĭz-) *n.*

Eng. *abbrev.* England; English.

eng. *abbrev.* Engine; engineer(ing).

en·gage (ĕngāj') *v.* (**-gaged, -gag·ing**). 1. Bind by contract or promise (esp. of marriage); pledge oneself. 2. Hire (employee); contract beforehand to occupy (position, office, etc.). 3. Attract, charm. 4. Fasten, attach; (mech.) mesh or interlock (*with*), fit into

corresponding part. 5. Hold fast, attract (attention etc.); employ, occupy (person, his powers, thought, etc.); embark *in*, enter upon, action, business, etc. 6. Bring, come, into conflict *with* enemy; attack, enter into combat with. **en·gaged'** *adj.* (esp.) Betrothed; occupied; in use. **en·gage'ment** *n.*

en·gag·ing (ĕngā'jĭng) *adj.* (esp.) Winning, attractive. **en·gag'ing·ly** *adv.*

En·gels (ĕng'elz), **Friedrich** (1820–95). German socialist leader and writer; settled in England 1849; collaborated with Karl Marx in producing the *Communist Manifesto*, 1848.

en·gen·der (ĕnjĕn'der) *v.* Beget (now only fig.); give rise to, bring about.

en·gine (ĕn'jin) *n.* 1. Machine consisting of several parts working together to produce given physical effect; esp., machine consisting of oscillating or reciprocating parts that converts the chemical energy of fuel into mechanical power in a useful form; locomotive; ∼ **room**, room containing (esp. ship's) engine. 2. (hist.) Machine used in warfare, esp. of large size (e.g. catapult, battering ram).

en·gi·neer (ĕnjinēr') *n.* 1. One skilled in the construction and maintenance of works of public utility such as roads and bridges (**civil** ∼), or in the design, construction, and maintenance of machines (**mechanical** ∼), or in the production and transmission of electrical energy and the manufacture of electrical apparatus

*The **steam engine** was developed from the first inefficient pumping machine of 1700. James Watt improved on this model in the 18th century but only in the 19th was a way found of using steam to provide locomotive power.*

*A surveyor at work during the construction of a main road in Australia. **Engineering** requires wide-ranging technical knowledge that enables the engineer to communicate and work with other specialists.*

England is the largest, richest, and most populous unit of the United Kingdom. Its countryside is varied. Above: Coniston Water in the Lake District. Right: The West Gate, Canterbury, an ancient entrance to one of England's most historic cities.

(**electrical** ~). 2. One who designs and constructs military works for attack or defense. 3. One who has charge of steam engine (also **stationary** ~); operator of locomotive. **engineer** *v.* 1. Act as engineer; construct, manage (work), as engineer. 2. Contrive, arrange, bring about. **en·gi·neer'-ing** *n.* Science, profession, of engineer; work done by engineer.

Eng·land (ĭng'glănd). Kingdom occupying, together with Wales, the southern part of Gt. Britain; capital, London; (pop.) Gt. Britain; the United Kingdom of Gt. Britain and Northern Ireland.

Eng·lish (ĭng'glĭsh) *adj.* Of England or its people or language; ~ **Channel**, channel between S. coast of England and N. coast of France; ~ **horn**, double-reed woodwind musical instrument, similar to the oboe but larger and pitched ½ lower; **Eng'lishman, Eng'lishwoman**, English person; ~ **sonnet**: see SONNET. **English** *n.* 1. (collect.) English people. 2. Language of the English, member of the western branch of the Germanic family of languages, orig. the dialect of the Angles, later including all dialects of the vernacular whether Anglian or Saxon, and including **Old** ~, Anglo-Saxon, *c*5th c. to *c*1100, **Middle** ~, *c*1100 to *c*1500, and **Modern** ~, *c*1500– ;

American ~, the variety of English spoken in U.S.; **Canadian** ~, English language as spoken and written in Canada, having elements of English pronunciation and vocabulary and showing strong U.S. influence; **King's (Queen's)** ~, correct grammatical English; (**in**) **plain** ~, (in) plain intelligible words. 3. (print.) Size of type (14 point). 4. (sometimes **e** ~) (billiards, bowling, etc.) Spinning motion given to a ball by striking it on the side or letting it go with a quick twist. 5. ~ **muffin**, round, rather flat yeast roll, baked on a griddle, and toasted after being split with fork; ~ **setter**, any of a breed

of setter of medium size and havi[ng] flat, silky white coat with black [or] brownish markings and feathe[ry] hair on the tail and backs of leg[s]; ~ **sparrow**: see HOUSE sparrow; ~ **walnut**, walnut tree (*Jugla[ns] reglia*) of Asia, cultivated in [S.] Europe and California on a com[-] mercial basis for its large edib[le] nuts.

en·gorge (ĕngôrj') *v.* (**-gorged, -gorg·ing**). 1. Devou[r] greedily. 2. (pass.) Be crammed (path.) be congested with bloo[d.] **en·gorge'ment** *n.*

engr. *abbrev.* Engineer(ing) engraved; engraver; engraving.

en·grave (ĕngrāv') *v.*

-graved, -grav·ing). Inscribe, ornament (hard surface) *with* incised marks; carve (design, letters, etc.) *upon* surface; cut design etc.) on metal plate or wood block for printing; (fig.) impress deeply (*upon* memory etc.). **n·grav'er** *n.*

en·grav·ing (ĕngrā'vĭng) *n.* esp.) Print made from engraved plate; copy of painting etc. made by his means; art of imparting designs to plates or blocks in such a way that prints may be taken from them, esp. by incising lines (**line ~**); this and numerous other hand and mechanical processes collectively.

en·gross (ĕngrōs') *v.t.* Occupy entirely or exclusively, monopolize person, his attention, etc.). **en·gross'ment** *n.*

en·gulf (ĕngŭlf') *v.t.* Plunge into, swallow up (as) in, gulf; surround. **en·gulf'ment** *n.*

en·hance (ĕnhăns', -hahns') *v.* (-hanced, -hanc·ing). Heighten, intensify (qualities, powers, etc.); exaggerate; increase in price or value. **en·hance'ment** *n.*

e·nig·ma (enĭg'ma) *n.* (pl. **-mas**, **-ma·ta** pr. -mata). Riddle; puzzling person or thing. **en·ig·mat·ic** (ĕnĭgmăt'ĭk), **en·ig·mat'i·cal** *adjs.* **en·ig·mat'i·cal·ly** *adv.*

en·join (ĕnjoin') *v.t.* 1. Prescribe, impose (action, conduct, *on* person); command. 2. Prohibit, restrain (esp. by legal injunction).

en·joy (ĕnjoi') *v.t.* 1. Find pleasure in; **~ oneself**, experience pleasure, be happy. 2. Use, possess, or experience with delight, take delight in; have use or benefit of. **en·joy'a·ble** *adj.* **en·joy'a·bly** *adv.* **en·joy'ment** *n.*

en·kin·dle (ĕnkĭn'del) *v.t.* (-dled, -dling). Cause (flame, passions, war, etc.) to blaze up.

en·lace (ĕnlās') *v.t.* (-laced, -lac·ing). Encircle tightly; enfold; entwine. **en·lace'ment** *n.*

en·large (ĕnlärj') *v.* (-larged, -larg·ing). 1. Make, become larger, extend limits of, increase size, amount, or number of; (phot.) make picture larger than original negative. 2. Extend range or scope of, widen (ideas, sympathies, etc.); expatiate *upon.* **en·large'ment** *n.* **en·larg'er** *n.* Photographic apparatus for enlarging or reducing negatives or positives.

en·light·en (ĕnlī'ten) *v.t.* Instruct, inform (*on* subject); free from prejudice or superstition. **en·light'en·ment** *n.* **the E~**, (after Ger. *Aufklärung*) an 18th c. philosophical movement characterized by a reliance on reason and directed to freeing religion and morals from tradition and prejudice.

en·list (ĕnlĭst') *v.* 1. (Persuade to) enter military service voluntarily; enroll (volunteer); hence

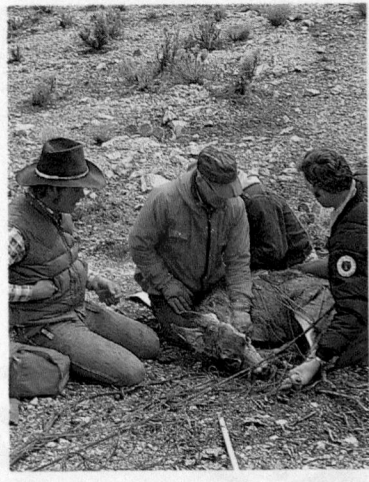

This mule deer, **ensnared** in a rope net, will be released by its captors, trained wildlife officers, at a location better suited to its longterm survival. This particular operation involved many mule deer.

enlistee' *n.* and **enlisted man** or **woman**, as opp. to *draftee.* 2. Secure cooperation or support of (*in* enterprise etc.). **en·list'ment** *n.*

en·liv·en (ĕnlī'ven) *v.t.* Animate, make lively; brighten. **en·liv'en·ment** *n.*

en masse (ahn măs', ĕn; *Fr.* ahn măs'). In a mass; in one body, all together. [Fr.]

en·mesh (ĕnmĕsh') *v.t.* Entangle (as) in net; involve. **en·mesh'ment** *n.*

en·mi·ty (ĕn'mĭtē) *n.* (pl. **-ties**). Hatred; state of hostility.

en·no·ble (ĕnnō'bel) *v.t.* Invest with nobility; add to the honor of. **en·no'ble·ment** *n.*

en·nui (ahnwē', ahn'wē) *n.* Boredom.

e·nor·mi·ty (īnōr'mĭtē) *n.* (pl. **-ties**). Monstrous wickedness; crime, monstrous offense.

e·nor·mous (īnōr'mus) *adj.* Very large. **e·nor'mous·ly** *adv.* **e·nor'mous·ness** *n.*

e·nough (īnŭf') *adj., n., & adv.* Adequate or sufficient (in quantity, number, or degree).

e·now (īnow') *adj., n., & adv.* (poet.) Enough.

en·plane (ĕnplān') *v.i.* (-planed, -plan·ing). Go on board an airplane.

en·quire (ĕnkwīr'), **en·quir·y** (ĕnkwīr'ē, ĭn'kwerē): see INQUIRE, INQUIRY.

en·rage (ĕnrāj') *v.t.* (-raged, -rag·ing). Make furious.

en·rap·ture (ĕnrăp'cher) *v.t.* (-tured, -tur·ing). Delight intensely.

en·rich (ĕnrĭch') *v.t.* Make rich; make better or finer. **en·rich'ment** *n.*

en·roll, **en·rol** (ĕnrōl') *vbs.* (-rolled, -roll·ing). Write (name), inscribe name of (person) on roll or list, esp. of school etc.; incorporate (person) as member (*in* club etc.); record; enlist. **en·roll'ment**, **en·rol'ment** *ns.*

en route (ahn rōōt', ĕn; *Fr.* ahn rōōt'). On or along the way. [Fr.]

Ens. *abbrev.* Ensign.

en·sconce (ĕnskŏns') *v.t.* (-sconced, -sconc·ing). Establish (*in* concealed, secure, comfortable, etc., position).

en·sem·ble (ahnsahm'bel, -sahmb') *n.* Thing viewed as whole; woman's outfit of harmonizing items; = CHORUS *n.* def. 3; (mus.) united performance of group of voices or instruments in concert. [Fr.]

en·shrine (ĕnshrīn') *v.t.* (-shrined, -shrin·ing). Enclose (relic etc.) in or as in shrine; cherish as sacred. **en·shrine'ment** *n.*

en·shroud (ĕnshrowd') *v.t.* Cover completely, hide from view.

en·sign (ĕn'sīn; *naut.* ĕn'sin) *n.* 1. Conventional sign, emblem; esp., badge or symbol of dignity or office. 2. (chiefly naut.) Standard, banner, flag. 3. (U.S. Navy and Coast Guard) Commissioned officer of lowest rank, below a lieutenant, junior grade.

en·si·lage (ĕn'sĭlĭj) = SILAGE.

en·sile (ĕnsīl', ĕn'sīl) *v.t.* (-siled, -sil·ing). Put (fodder) into silo; preserve (fodder) in silo.

en·slave (ĕnslāv') *v.t.* (-slaved, -slav·ing). Make slave of, reduce to slavery. **en·slave'ment** *n.*

en·snare (ĕnsnār') *v.t.* (-snared, -snar·ing). Entrap.

en·sue (ĕnsōō') *v.* (-sued, -su·ing). Happen afterward; result (*from, on*).

en·sure (ĕnshoor') *v.t.* (-sured, -sur·ing). 1. Make certain; secure, guarantee (thing *to, for,* person, etc.). 2. Insure.

-ent *suffix.* Forming adjectives denoting existence of action (*consequent, effluent*) and nouns denoting agent (*coefficient, president*), usu. from verbs.

en·tab·la·ture (ĕntăb'lacher) *n.* (archit.) Part of classical order above column, including architrave, frieze, and cornice.

en·tail (ĕntāl') *n.* Act of entailing property; entailed estate. **~ *v.t.*** 1. Limit the inheritance (of property) to a specific, unalterable succession of heirs, so that inherited property cannot be bequeathed at pleasure by any succeeding one; bestow (thing) as inalienable possession. 2. Impose (expense, duty, *on* person); necessitate. **en·tail'ment** *n.*

en·tan·gle (ĕntăng'gel) *v.t.* (-gled, -gling). Catch in snare or among obstacles; involve in difficulties; make tangled or intricate. **en·tan'gle·ment** *n.*

En·teb·be (ĕntĕb'ĕ). Former capital of Uganda from 1896–1962,

en·tice (ĕntīs′) v.t. (**-tice-
-tic·ing**). Attract, esp. insidious
or adroitly, by offer of pleasure
advantage. **en·tice′ment** n.

en·tire (ĕntīr′, ĕn′tīr) a
Whole, complete; not broken; n
castrated; all of one piec
continuous; pure, unmixed.
en·tire·ly (ĕntīr′lē) adv. Wholl·
solely. **en·tire·ty** (ĕntīr′tē) n. (p
-ties). Completeness; whole, su
total; **in its ~**, in its complete form
as a whole.

en·ti·tle (ĕntī′tel) v.t. (**-tle
-tling**). 1. Give (person, book
etc.) the title of. 2. Give (perso
etc.) a right (to a thing, to do,
en·ti′tle·ment n.

en·ti·ty (ĕn′tĭtē) n. (pl. **-ties**
1. A thing's existence, as dist. fror
its qualities or relations. 2
Something that has a real existence

en·tomb (ĕntoōm′) v.t. Place ir
tomb; serve as tomb for. **en
tomb′ment** n.

en·to·mol·o·gy (ĕntomŏl′ojē) n
Branch of zoology dealing with
insects. **en·to·mo·log·i·cal** (ĕnto
molŏj′ĭkal) adj. **en·to·mol·o·gis**
n.

en·tou·rage (ahntoōrahzh′) n
Persons surrounding or attendin
on a superior; surroundings. [Fr.

en·tr'acte (ahn′ trăkt, -trahk
ahntrăkt, -trahkt′) n. (Performanc
in) interval between acts of play
music etc. for this. [Fr.]

en·trails (ĕn′trālz, -tralz) n.pl
Internal organs, esp. the intestines
viscera; inner parts (of the Earth
etc.).

en·train (ĕntrān′) v. 1. Put, go
on a train. 2. (of a liquid) Trap
bubbles.

en·trance[1] (ĕn′trans) n. 1
Coming or going in; coming of acto:
upon stage; entering into, upon
(office etc.). 2. Right of admission
fee paid on admission. 3. Door
passage, etc., one enters by.

en·trance[2] (ĕntrăns′, -trahns
v.t. (**-tranced, -tranc·ing**)
Throw into trance; overwhelm
(with joy, fear); fascinate, enchant

en·trant (ĕn′trant) n. One who
enters room, profession, etc., or fo
(race etc.).

en·trap (ĕntrăp′) v.t. (**-trapped
-trap·ping**). Catch in or as in trap
beguile (into doing).

en·treat (ĕntrēt′) v.t. 1. Ask
earnestly (to do). 2. (archaic) Treat
deal with, in specified manner
en·treat·y (ĕntrē′tē) n. (pl
-treat·ies). Earnest request.

en·tre·chat (ahn′treshah; Fr
ahntreshă′) n. (ballet) Leap during
which dancer crosses the feet a

in the S. part on Lake Victoria.
en·tente (ahntahnt′; Fr. ahn-
tahnt′) n. (pl. **-tentes** pr. -tahnts′;
Fr. -tahnt′). (diplom.) Friendly
understanding or, usu. informal,
agreement between nations for
cooperative policy or action; group
of nations; **Triple E~**, that
between England, France, and
Russia (1908); **E~ Cordiale**, that
formed between Gt. Britain and
France in 1904. [Fr.]

en·ter (ĕn′ter) v. 1. Go, come,
in; come upon stage; **~ for**, undertake to compete in (race etc.); **~
into**, engage in, form part of, bind
oneself by (contract, treaty, etc.).
2. Go, come, into; penetrate; begin
(period of time). 3. Become
member of (society or organized
body). 4. Put (name) on list, (fact
etc.) into description or record,
etc.; admit, procure admission for,
as pupil, member of club etc.; **~ a
judgment, writ, protest**, present
or submit a judgment etc. for
consideration, esp. officially.

en·ter·ic (ĕntĕr′ĭk) adj. Of the
intestines; **~ fever**, typhoid.
enteric n. Enteric fever. **en·ter-
i·tis** (ĕnterī′tĭs) n. (Acute) inflammation of intestinal tract.

en·ter·prise (ĕn′terprīz) n.
Undertaking, esp. bold or difficult
one; courage, readiness to engage in
enterprises; initiative; business
venture; **private ~**, economic
activity under private control.
en′ter·pris·ing adj. Energetic,

full of initiative.
en·ter·tain (ĕntertān′) v.t. 1.
Occupy (person etc.) agreeably,
amuse. 2. Receive as guest, show
hospitality to (also abs.). 3. Admit
to consideration, harbor, cherish
(idea, opinion, proposal, etc.).
en·ter·tain′er n. Person who
entertains, esp. comedian, popular
singer, etc. **en·ter·tain′ing** adj.
en·ter·tain′ing·ly adv.
en·ter·tain·ment (ĕntertān′-
ment) n. (esp.) Amusement; public
performance.

en·thrall, en·thral (ĕnthrawl′)
vbs.t. (**-thralled,-thrall·ing**). En-
slave; charm. **en·thrall′ment,
en·thral′ment** ns.

en·throne (ĕnthrōn′) v.t.
(**-throned, -thron·ing**). Place
(king etc.) on throne, esp. as formal
induction; exalt, revere. **en-
throne′ment** n.

en·thuse (ĕnthooz′) v. (**-thused,
-thus·ing**). Show, evoke enthusiasm in.

en·thu·si·asm (ĕnthoō′zēăzem)
n. 1. (archaic) Poorly regulated or
misdirected religious emotion; extravagant or false confidence in
divine inspiration or favor. 2.
Rapturous intensity of feeling for a
person, cause, pursuit, etc.;
passionate eagerness; object of this.

en·thu·si·ast (ĕnthoō′zēăst) n.
One who is full of enthusiasm;
follower, fan. **en·thu·si·as·tic**
(ĕnthoōzēăs′tĭk) adj. **en·thu·si·-
as′ti·cal·ly** adv.

umber of times, often with a eating motion. [Fr.]

en·tree, en·trée (ahn′trā) *ns.* I. Right or privilege of admission. 2. usu.) Main course; dish served before main course, esp. between ish and meat courses (in formal lining).

en·trench (entrĕnch′) *v.t.* I. surround, fortify, with trench freq. fig.). 2. Establish firmly in lefensible position. **en·trench′-ment** *n.*

en·tre nous (ahntre̯ noo′). Between ourselves; in private. [Fr.]

en·tre·pre·neur (ahntreprener̯′, noor′) *n.* I. Organizer, manager, of (esp. musical) entertainments; manager. 2. One who undertakes an enterprise. **en·tre·pre·neur′i·al** *adj.*

en·tro·py (en′trope̯) *n.* (phys.) Measure of the degree of molecular lisorder existing in a system, also letermining how much of the system's thermal energy is unavailable for conversion into mechanical work, expressed as a thermodynamic function.

en·trust (entrŭst′) *v.t.* Charge (person) *with* (duty, object of care); confide (duty etc. *to* person etc.).

en·try (en′tre̯) *n.* (pl. **-tries**). I. Coming or going in; coming (of actor) upon stage; ceremonial entrance; ~**-level (job)**, generally low paying (work for beginners in a factory etc.), but offering opportunity to acquire skills and earn promotion. 2. Place of entrance; door, gate, entrance hall, etc. 3. Entering or registering in list, record, ledger, etc. or in dictionary, encyclopedia, etc.; **double** ~, of bookkeeping in which every credit item of one account in ledger is entered to debit of another. 4. One item so entered; registered as competitor, participant (in race etc.).

en·twine (entwīn′) *v.t.* (**-twined, -twin·ing**). Twine or twist together, with, or around.

e·nu·mer·ate (īnoo̅′merāt, inū′-) *v.t.* (**-at·ed, -at·ing**). Count; mention (number of things or persons) separately; specify. **e·nu·mer·a·tion** (īnoo̅omerā′shon, inū-) *n.* **e·nu·mer·a·tive** (īnoo̅′merātiv, -mera-, inū′-) *adj.*

e·nun·ci·ate (inŭn′sēāt) *v.t.* (**-at·ed, -at·ing**). Express (proposition, theory) definitely; proclaim; pronounce (articulate sounds). **e·nun·ci·a·tion** (inŭn-sēā′shon), **e·nun′ci·a·tor** *ns.*

en·u·re·sis (enyure̯′sis) *n.* (path.) Involuntary passing of urine.

en·vel·op (envĕl′op) *v.t.* Wrap up; cover; enclose; (mil.) surround. **en·vel′op·ment, en·vel′op·er** *ns.*

en·ve·lope (en′velop, ahn′-) *n.* I. Wrapper, covering; folded and gummed cover for letter; fabric enclosing gasbag of airship. 2.

(bot.) Calyx or corolla, or both together. 3. (math.) Line or curve tangent to each line or curve of a given family.

en·vi·a·ble (en′veabel) *adj.* Likely to arouse envy; highly desirable. **en′vi·a·bly** *adv.*

en·vi·ous (en′veus) *adj.* Full of envy; feeling envy *of.* **en′vi·ous·ly** *adv.*

en·vi·ron·ment (envī′ronment, -vī′ern-) *n.* Surroundings, surrounding objects, region, conditions, or influences. **en·vi·ron·men·tal** (envīronmen′tal, -vīern-) *adj.*

en·vi·ron·men·tal·ist (envī′ronment′alist) *n.* Person working for protection of the environment

from pollution, exhaustion of natural resources, adverse effects of rapid population growth, etc. **en·vi·ron·men′tal·ism** *n.*

en·vi·rons (envī′ronz, -vī′ernz, en′veronz) *n.pl.* Outskirts, surrounding districts, of town etc.

en·vis·age (envĭz′ij) *v.t.* (**-aged, -ag·ing**). Think of as likely in the future; imagine; visualize.

en·vi·sion (envĭzh′on) *v.t.* Picture in one's mind; foresee.

en·voi, en·voy[1] (en′voi, ahn′-)

*Always popular with both children and adults, Mickey Mouse and his friends at Disneyland seem to know what **entertainment** is all about. The unique Disney characters have seen many forms of entertainment come and go.*

The final scene from 'The Fall of the Roman Empire' (1964). The cinema has developed a modern form of epic, a large-scale narrative film of heroic or semi-legendary events and people.

ns. Concluding stanza, esp. of ballade dedicating poem to a patron, serving as a summation etc.

en·voy[2] (ĕn´voi, ahn´-) *n.* Public minister, now esp., diplomatic minister ranking below ambassador and above chargé d'affaires; messenger, representative.

en·vy (ĕn´vē) *n.* (pl. **-vies**). Mortification, ill will, or longing occasioned by another's good fortune; object of this. ~ *v.t.* (**-vied, -vy·ing**). Feel envy of (person, his advantages). **en´vy·ing·ly** *adv.*

en·zyme (ĕn´zīm) *n.* Protein catalyst of a specific biochemical reaction. **en·zy·mic** (ĕnzī´mĭk, -zĭm´ĭk) *adj.*

E·o·cene (ē´osēn) *adj.* & *n.* (geol.) (Of) the 2nd epoch or system of the Tertiary period.

e.o.m. *abbrev.* End of the month.

e·on (ē´on, ē´ŏn) *n.* Immeasurably long period; an age of the universe; longest division of geologic time, including 2 or more eras.

-eous *suffix.* Forming adjectives meaning "of the nature of" (*ligneous* like wood, *vitreous* like glass).

EPA *abbrev.* Environmental Protection Agency.

ep·arch (ĕp´ärk) *n.* Governor or bishop of eparchy. **ep´ar·chy** *n.* 1. Subdivision of modern Greece. 2. Diocese of Greek Orthodox Church.

ep·au·let, ep·au·lette (ĕp´ulĕt, -lĭt, ĕpulĕt´) *ns.* Ornamental shoulder piece of uniform.

e·pee, é·pée (āpā´, ā´pā) *ns.* Fencing sword with bowl-shaped guard and long, thin, blunt-tipped, 3-sided blade having no cuttin edge. **é·pée´ist** *n.*

e·pergne (ĭpĕrn´, āpärn´) Large (esp. branched) ornament dish (for fruit, flowers, etc.) fo centerpiece of dining table.

Eph. *abbrev.* Ephesians (Ne Testament).

e·phah, e·pha (ē´fa) *ns.* Unit o dry measure used by ancien Hebrews, equal to slightly mor than a bushel.

e·phed·rine (ĭfĕd´rĭn, ĕf´edrēn -drĭn) *n.* Alkaloid drug used t relieve asthma, allergies, etc.

e·phem·er·a (ĭfĕm´era) (p **-er·as, -er·ae** pr. -erē), **e·phem er·on** (ĭfĕm´erŏn) (pl. **-er·ons** er·a pr. -era) *ns.* Short-lived insec of order Ephemeroptera; common est of the mayflies, insect wit delicate lacy wings and three lon tail filaments, found near water hence, short-lived thing; thing o transitory usefulness.

e·phem·er·al (ĭfĕm´erəl) adj. 1. (of insects etc.) Living for a day or a few days. 2. Short-lived, transitory.

e·phem·er·is (ĭfĕm´erĭs) n. (pl. **phe·mer·i·des** pr. ĕfemĕr´idēz). Table showing predicted positions of heavenly body for every day during given period; astronomical almanac.

E·phe·sian (ĭfē´zhən) adj. Of Ephesus. ~ n. Native, inhabitant, of Ephesus; (**Epistle to the**) ~s, book of New Testament ascribed to St. Paul, an epistle to the Christians of Ephesus.

Eph·e·sus (ĕf´esus). One of the principal Ionian cities on the Aegean coast of Asia Minor (now several miles inland); site of the Temple of Artemis.

epi- prefix. Upon, at, on the ground or occasion of, in addition.

ep·ic (ĕp´ĭk) adj. Of, in, that species of poetical composition celebrating in continuous narrative achievements of heroic personage(s) of history or tradition; such as is described in epic poetry, of heroic type or scale; heroic or majestic; ~ **dialect**, dialect in which Greek epic poems were written. **epic** n. Epic poem; composition comparable to epic poem; subject worthy of epic treatment.

ep·i·carp (ĕp´ĭkärp) n. (bot.) Outermost layer, skin, of fleshy fruit.

ep·i·cene (ĕp´ĭsēn) adj. 1. (L. and Gk. gram.) Denoting either sex without change of gender. 2. For, used by, both sexes; having characteristics of both sexes; effeminate or unmanly. ~ n. Epicene person.

ep·i·cen·ter (ĕp´ĭsĕnter), **ep·i·cen·trum** (ĕp´ĭsĕn´trum) ns. (pl. **-trums, -tra** pr. -trə). Point on earth's surface directly above place where earthquake originates. **ep·i·cen´tral** adj.

ep·i·cure (ĕp´ĭkūr) n. One who cultivates discriminating taste in food and drink. **ep´i·cur·ism** n. [f. EPICURUS].

Ep·i·cu·re·an (ĕpĭkyurē´ən, -kūr´ē-) adj. & n. 1. (Follower) of Epicurus. 2. (**e**~) (Person) devoted to pleasures, esp. refined sensuous enjoyment. **Ep·i·cu·re´an·ism, ep·i·cu·re´an·ism** ns.

Ep·i·cu·rus (ĕpĭkūr´us) (341–270 B.C.). Athenian philosopher who held that the highest good was calmness of mind and freedom from pain, and rejected the idea of an afterlife and of the influence of gods in human affairs.

ep·i·cy·cle (ĕp´ĭsīkel) n. 1. (geom.) Small circle rolling on the circumference of a greater one. 2. (hist., in ancient astronomy) Circle having its center on the circumference of a greater circle, used in the Ptolemaic system to represent

An **epigraph**, inscription, on a tombstone. Although perhaps a sombre study, the scrutiny of memorial inscriptions has yielded much historical information.

the revolutions of the planets.
ep·i·cy·clic (ĕpĭsī´klĭk, -sĭk´lĭk) adj.

Ep·i·dau·rus (ĕpĭdôr´us). Ancient Greek town on E. coast of Argolis; site of well-preserved ancient theater.

ep·i·dem·ic (ĕpĭdĕm´ĭk) adj. & n. (Disease) spreading rapidly through a community for a period (cf. ENDEMIC). **ep·i·dem´i·cal** n. **ep·i·dem´i·cal·ly** adv.

ep·i·de·mi·ol·o·gy (ĕpĭdēmēŏl´ojē) n. Science of epidemics.

ep·i·der·mis (ĕpĭdēr´mĭs) n. 1.

An **epergne** — a branched, ornamental centre-piece for the table — was used to hold desserts. The name may derive from the French word 'épargne' which means saving.

(physiol.) Outer nonvascular layer of skin of animals, cuticle; outer animal integument of shell. 2. (bot.) Outermost cell layer in plants before secondary growth begins. **ep·i·der´mal, ep·i·der´mic, ep·i·der´moid** adjs.

ep·i·gas·tri·um (ĕpĭgăs´trium) n. (pl. **-tri·a** pr. -trēə). Part of abdomen immediately over stomach. **ep·i·gas´tric** adj.

ep·i·glot·tis (ĕpĭglŏt´ĭs) n. (pl. **-glot·tis·es, -glot·i·des** pr. -glŏt´idēz). Erect cartilage at root of tongue, depressed in act of swallowing to cover glottis.

ep·i·gram (ĕp´ĭgrăm) n. Short poem ending in witty or ingenious turn of thought; pointed saying or mode of expression. **ep·i·gram·mat·ic** (ĕpĭgramăt´ĭk) adj. **ep·i·gram·mat´i·cal·ly** adv. **ep·i·gram·ma·tist** (ĕpĭgrăm´atĭst) n.

ep·i·graph (ĕp´ĭgrăf, -grahf) n. Inscription on stone, statue, coin, etc.; motto. **ep·i·graph·ic** (ĕpĭgrăf´ĭk) adj.

ep·i·lep·sy (ĕp´ĭlĕpsē) n. Symptom of nervous disorder generally involving recurrent temporary loss of consciousness with or without convulsions, automatic movements, muscular spasms, etc. **ep·i·lep·tic** (ĕpĭlĕp´tĭk) adj. Of, subject to, epilepsy. ~ n. Epileptic person.

ep·i·logue, ep·i·log (ĕp´ĭlawg, -lŏg) ns. Concluding part of, short addition to, literary work; speech, short poem, addressed by actor to spectators at end of play.

ep·i·neph·rine (ĕpĭnĕf´rĭn, -rēn) n. 1. Adrenal hormone that raises blood pressure. 2. Isolated or synthesized preparation of this for heart stimulant, treatment of asthma, etc.

E·piph·a·ny (ĭpĭf´anē) n. (pl. **-nies**). Christian festival commemorating the manifestation of Christ to the Gentiles in the persons of the Magi, observed on Jan. 6.

e·piph·a·ny (ĭpĭf´anē) n. 1. Revelation or manifestation of a divine being. 2. Sudden revelation or recognition of the essential nature of something.

ep·i·phyte (ĕp´ĭfīt) n. Plant growing on another (usu. deriving only support, not nutrition, from it); vegetable parasite on animal body. **ep·i·phyt·ic** (ĕpĭfĭt´ĭk) adj.

Epis. abbrev. Epistle; Episcopal(ian).

Episc. abbrev. Episcopal(ian).

e·pis·co·pa·cy (ĭpĭs´kopasē) n. (pl. **-cies**). Government of church by bishops; the bishops collectively.

e·pis·co·pal (ĭpĭs´kopal) adj. Of bishop(s); **E**~ **Church** (also Protestant Episcopal Church) church body in the U.S. separate since 1789 but orig. part of Church of England and still in communion with it and close to it in practices and doctrine. **e·pis′co·pal·ly** *adv.*

e·pis·co·pa·lian (ĭpĭskopāl′yan, -pā′lēan) *adj.* & *n.* (Adherent) of episcopacy; **E~**, (member) of Episcopal Church. **e·pis·co·pa′-lian·ism, E·pis·co·pa′lian·ism** *ns.*

e·pis·co·pate (ĭpĭs′kopĭt, -pāt) *n.* Office, see, tenure, of bishop; the bishops collectively.

ep·i·si·ot·o·my (ĭpēzēŏt′omē) *n.* (pl. **-mies**). (surg.) Incision of the vulva to facilitate childbirth.

ep·i·sode (ĕp′ĭsōd, -zōd) *n.* 1. Incidental narrative, digression, in poem, story, etc.; incidental happening or series of events in history of a country or in person's life, as in **psychotic ~**, temporary insanity; separately presented section of a serial novel, radio or television drama, etc. 2. In Gk. tragedy, interlocutory (orig. interpolated) parts between 2 choric songs. 3. (mus.) Intervening passage. **ep·i·sod·ic** (ĕpĭsŏd′ĭk, -zŏd′-) *adj.*

Epist. *abbrev.* Epistle.

e·pis·te·mol·o·gy (ĭpĭstemŏl′ojē) *n.* (pl. **-gies**). Theory of method or grounds of knowledge. **e·pis·te-mo·log·i·cal** (ĭpĭstemolŏj′ĭkal) *adj.*

e·pis·tle (ĭpĭs′el) *n.* 1. Letter; (esp.) letter from apostle, forming part of canon of Scripture; **E~**, extract from one of these read as part of Communion service. 2. Literary work, usu. in verse, in form of letter.

e·pis·to·lar·y (ĭpĭs′tolĕrē) *adj.* Of, carried on by, suited to, letters.

ep·i·style (ĕp′ĭstīl) *n.* (archit.) Architrave.

ep·i·taph (ĕp′ĭtăf, -tahf) *n.* Inscription upon tomb; brief composition expressed as if for inscribing on tombstone.

ep·i·tha·la·mi·on (ĕpĭthalā′-mēon) (pl. **-mi·a** pr. -mēa), **ep·i·tha·la·mi·um** (ĕpĭthalā′mēum) (pl. **-mi·ums, -mi·a** pr. -mēa) *ns.* Nuptial song or poem.

ep·i·the·li·um (ĕpĭthē′lēum) *n.* (pl. **-li·ums, -li·a** pr. -lēa). (biol.) Layer of cells that covers the body surface or lines a cavity that communicates with it. **ep·i·the′-li·al** *adj.*

ep·i·thet (ĕp′ĭthĕt) *n.* Adjective expressing quality or attribute; this as term of abuse or profanity; significant appellation or characterization that comes to substitute for name of person, as *Honest Abe* for Abraham Lincoln, or *The Melancholy Dane* for Hamlet. **ep·i·thet·ic** (ĕpĭthĕt′ĭk), **ep·i·thet′i·cal** *adjs.*

e·pit·o·me (ĭpĭt′omē) *n.* Summary, abstract, of book; condensed account; (fig.) thing representing entire class or type; embodiment. **e·pit′o·mize** *v.t.*

The Owen Stanley Range, New Guinea. **Equatorial** *rain forests, large, dense, richly diverse forests dependent on heavy rainfall and high temperatures, are found in central Africa, Malaysia, Indonesia, and the Amazon Basin.*

(**-mized, -miz·ing**).

e plu·ri·bus u·num (ē ploor′ĭ-bus ū′num, ōō′num). Out of many, one; the motto of the U.S. [L.]

ep·och (ĕp′ok; *Brit.* ē′pok) *n.* (Beginning of) era in history, science, life, etc.; division of a geological period. **ep′och·al** *adj.* **ep′och·al·ly** *adv.*

ep·o·nym (ĕp′onĭm) *n.* Person, real or mythical, who gives his name to a people, place, institution, etc., as *Romulus* for *Rome*, Captain *Boycott* to *boycott*, *Saturn* to *Saturday*, etc. **e·pon·y·mous** (ĕpŏn′imus), **ep·o·nym·ic** (ĕpo-nĭm′ĭk) *adjs.*

ep·ox·y (ĕpŏk′sē, ĭ-) *n.* (pl. **-ox·ies**). Any of various thermosetting resins used for strong glues or tough surface finishes.

ep·si·lon (ĕp′sĭlŏn, -lon; *Brit.* ĕpsī′lon) *n.* Fifth letter of Greek alphabet (E, ε), corresponding to short *e*.

Ep·som (ĕp′som). Town in Surrey, England, famous for nearby race track, **~ Downs**, where the English Derby is run; **~ salt(s)**, bitter crystalline salt,

magnesium sulphate, used as cathartic, orig. prepared from Epsom mineral waters.

eq. *abbrev.* Equal; equation; equivalent.

eq·ua·ble (ĕk′wabel, ē′kwa-) *adj.* Uniform, even, not easil disturbed. **eq·ua·bil·i·ty** (ĕkwa bĭl′ĭtē, ēkwa-) *n.* **eq′ua·bly** *adv.*

e·qual (ē′kwal) *adj.* The same in number, size, value, degree, etc. having strength, courage, ability etc., adequate *to* (occasion etc.) uniform in operation, action, etc. evenly balanced; **~ sign**, symbo (=) used, esp. in equations, t indicate that the terms it separate are logically or mathematicall equal; **~ time**, (pol.) principle tha different points of view should b allowed equal time in debate; (esp radio and television) principle tha station must give equal broadcas time to all political candidates o parties if it gives to one. **equal** *n* Person equal to another in rank etc (pl.) equal things. **~** *v.t* (**e·qualed, e·qualled, e·qual·ing e·qual·ling**). Be equal to.

e·qual·i·tar·i·an (ēkwŏlĭtār′ēan *adj.* & *n.* Egalitarian.

e·qual·i·ty (ĭkwŏl′ĭtē) *n.* (pl **-ties**). Condition of being equa equal footing.

e·qual·ize (ē′kwalīz) *v.t.* (**-ized -iz·ing**). Make (thing etc.) equa (to, with). **e·qual·i·za·tion**

Show-jumping is an exhilarating form of **equestrian** skill, requiring close co-operation between horse and rider and a certain amount of natural talent in both.

(ēkwalĭzā′shon) *n.* **e′qual·iz·er** *n.* (slang) Pistol.

e·qual·ly (ē′kwalē) *adv.* In an equal degree; in equal shares; uniformly.

e·qua·nim·i·ty (ēkwanĭm′ĭtē, ĕkwa-) *n.* Evenness of mind or temper; composure; resignation.

e·quate (ĭkwāt′) *v.t.* (**e·quat·ed, e·quat·ing**). State equality of (thing *to*, *with*, another); treat as equivalent.

e·qua·tion (ĭkwā′zhon, -shon) *n.* 1. Make equal, balancing; equilibrium, equality. 2. (math.) Formula affirming equivalence of 2 quantitative expressions, which are connected by the sign =. 3. (chem.) Expression representing chemical reaction quantitatively by means of symbols.

e·qua·tor (ĭkwā′ter) *n.* (astron., also **celestial** ∼): see CELESTIAL; (geog.) great circle of the earth equidistant from poles; similar circle on any spherical body; **magnetic** ∼, irregular line around earth near equator on which the angle of magnetic dip is zero.

e·qua·to·ri·al (ēkwatōr′ēal, -tōr′-, ĕkwa-) *adj.* Of, near, the equator. **e·qua·to′ri·al·ly** *adv.*

E·qua·to·ri·al (ēkwatōr′ēal, -tōr′-, ĕkwa-) **Guinea.** Republic in W. Central Africa, on the Atlantic; established 1959; capital, Malabo.

e·ques·tri·an (ĭkwĕs′trēan) *adj.* 1. Of, skilled in, horseback riding; mounted on horse; (of statue) representing person on horseback. 2. (Rom. antiq.) Of the order of *Equites* or knights. ∼ *n.* Rider, performer, on horseback.

e·ques·tri·enne (ĭkwĕstrēĕn′) *n.* Horsewoman.

equi- *comb. form.* Equal.

e·qui·an·gu·lar (ēkwēăng′-gyuler) *adj.* Having equal angles.

e·qui·dis·tant (ēkwĭdĭs′tant) *adj.* Separated by equal distance(s); parallel.

e·qui·lat·er·al (ēkwĭlăt′eral) *adj.* Having all the sides equal, as in ∼ **triangle.**

e·quil·i·brate (ĭkwĭl′ĭbrāt) *v.* (**-brat·ed, -brat·ing**). Cause (2 things) to balance; balance; be or keep in equilibrium; counterpoise.

e·qui·li·bra·tion (ēkwĭlĭbrā′shon) *n.*

e·quil·i·brist (ĭkwĭl′ĭbrĭst) *n.* Tightrope walker, acrobat.

e·qui·lib·ri·um (ēkwĭlĭb′rēum) *n.* (pl. **-ri·ums, -ri·a** pr. -rēa). State of equal balance between opposing forces or powers; balance, stability; mental or emotional balance or stability.

inese **equilibrists** (balance artists) rforming at a Chinese fair exhibition. e Chinese are noted for their balanc- skills.

e·quine (ē′kwīn) *adj.* Of, like, a horse.

e·qui·noc·tial (ēkwĭnŏk′shal) *adj.* 1. Of, at, or near time of equinox, as ~ **winds;** ~ **line,** celestial equator. 2. At, near, the equator. **equinoctial** *n.* Equinoctial line; (pl.) equinoctial gales.

e·qui·nox (ē′kwĭnŏks, ĕk′wĭ-) *n.* Time when the sun crosses the equator and day and night are equal, occurring twice yearly, on March 20 or 21 (**vernal** ~) and Sept. 22 or 23 (**autumnal** ~); either of the two points at which the sun's path crosses the equator.

e·quip (ĭkwĭp′) *v.t.* (**e·quipped, e·quip·ping**). Furnish (ship, army, person, *with* requisites); provide (*oneself* etc.) for journey etc.

equip. *abbrev.* Equipment.

eq·ui·page (ĕk′wĭpĭj) *n.* Requisites for undertaking; outfit for journey etc.; carriage and horses with attendants. **e·quip·ment** (ĭkwĭp′ment) *n.* Equipping, being equipped, manner in which person or thing is equipped; outfit, warlike apparatus, necessaries for expedition, voyage, etc.

e·qui·poise (ē′kwĭpoiz, ĕk′wĭ-) *n.* Equilibrium; counterpoise, balancing force or thing.

e·qui·po·ten·tial (ēkwĭpotĕn′shal) *adj. & n.* (phys.) (Surface, line, etc.) such that the potential of a force is the same or constant at all its points.

eq·ui·ta·ble (ĕk′wĭtabel) *adj.* Fair, just; (of claims etc.) valid in equity as dist. from law. **eq′ui·ta·bly** *adv.* **eq′ui·ta·ble·ness** *n.*

eq·ui·ta·tion (ĕkwĭtā′shon) *n.* Riding on horseback; horsemanship.

eq·ui·ty (ĕk′wĭtē) *n.* (pl. **-ties**). 1. Fairness, impartiality. 2. Recourse to general principle of justice to correct or supplement provisions of law; system of law existing side by side with common and statute law, and superseding these when they conflict with it. 3. Equitable right, right recognizable by court of equity. 4. Value of business, property, etc. after all mortgages, liabilities, charges, etc. are satisfied.

equiv. *abbrev.* Equivalent.

e·quiv·a·lent (ĭkwĭv′alent) *adj.* 1. Equal in value; having equal or corresponding import or meaning; that is virtually the same thing, tantamount; corresponding. 2. (chem.) ~ **weight** (also **combining weight**), that amount of an element, by weight, that will combine with or replace 1 unit weight of hydrogen. **equivalent** *n.* Equivalent thing, amount, word, etc.; (chem.) see *adj.* above. **e·quiv′a·lence, e·quiv′a·len·cy** *ns.*

e·quiv·o·cal (ĭkwĭv′okal) *adj.* Of

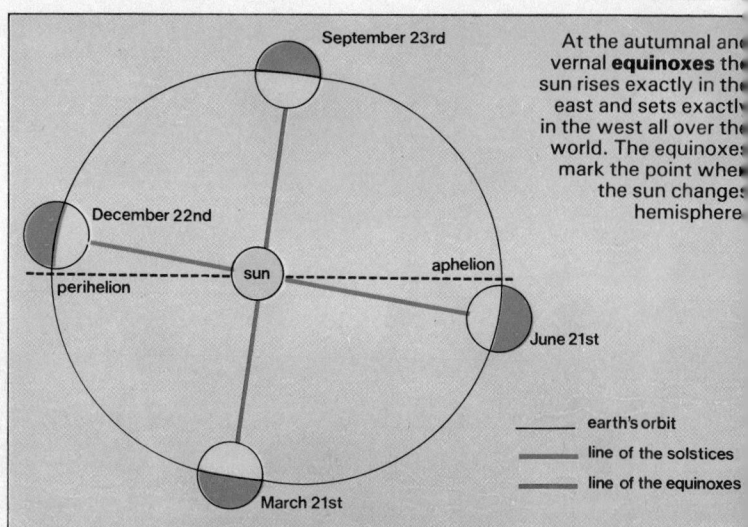

September 23rd

December 22nd

sun

perihelion   aphelion

June 21st

March 21st

At the autumnal and vernal **equinoxes** the sun rises exactly in the east and sets exactly in the west all over the world. The equinoxes mark the point where the sun changes hemisphere.

earth's orbit
line of the solstices
line of the equinoxes

'Erasmus Writing' (1523), one of Hans Holbein's most notable portraits. A leading critic of the Catholic Church, **Erasmus** *never shared Luther's extreme views, but their public disagreement did credit to neither position.*

double meaning, ambiguous; of uncertain nature; undecided; questionable, suspicious. **e·quiv′o·cal·ly** *adv.* **e·quiv′o·cal·ness** *n.* **e·quiv·o·cate** (ĭkwĭv′okāt) *v.i.*

(**-cat·ed, -cat·ing**). Use ambiguous words to conceal truth, hedge. **e·quiv·o·ca·tion** (ĭkwĭv·kā′shon), **e·quiv′o·ca·tor** *ns.*

Er *symbol.* Erbium.

-er [1] *suffix.* Forming nouns from nouns, adjectives, and verbs meaning: (1) person or animal that does (*lover, maker*) or person or thing that is or has (*foreigner, fiver, four-wheeler*); (2) instrument

The stoat or **ermine,** the latter name strictly applicable only to the animal in its winter coat. In more southern latitudes the coat does not become entirely white. The fur is valued.

nachine, occurrence, action, etc. ~oker, computer, eye-opener, ~eader); person concerned with hing (geographer, outfielder); (3) ~erson belonging to a place etc. ~New Yorker, Vermonter).

-er² suffix. Forming comparatives of adjectives and adverbs (wider, faster).

ERA abbrev. Equal Rights ~mendment (proposed for U.S. ~onstitution, prohibiting discrimination based on sex).

e·ra (ēr′a, ĕr′a) n. 1. System of chronology starting from some ~articular point of time (as the **Christian** ~, from the date of the ~irth of Jesus Christ; the **Muslim** ~, from the year of Muhammad's ~ight from Mecca (622), etc.); ~nitial point in such system. 2. Historical period; period in ~ndividual's life, in some continu~us process, etc.; major division of ~eological time, usu. comprising ~everal periods.

e·rad·i·cate (ĭrăd′ĭkāt) v.t. **-cat·ed, -cat·ing**). Remove all ~races of; annihilate; erase. **e·rad′-~ca·ble** adj. **e·rad·i·ca·tion** (ĭrădĭkā′shon) n.

e·rase (ĭrās′) v.t. (**e·rased, ~ras·ing**). Rub out; obliterate. ~**ras′er** n. That which erases, esp., ~reparation of rubber or similar ~ubstance for rubbing out writing ~tc. **e·ra·sure** (ĭrā′sher, -zher) n. ~rocess of erasing; word etc. ~ubbed out.

E·ras·mus (ĭrăz′mus), **Desider-~us** (1466–1536), orig. name Geert ~eerts. Dutch theologian, scholar, ~nd humanist; prepared the way for ~he Reformation by his version of ~he New Testament and his con~emnation of Church abuses in ~Moriae Encomium (The Praise of ~olly).

E·ra·to (ĕr′atō). (Gk. and Rom. ~nyth.) Muse of love, erotic poetry, ~nd mime.

er·bi·um (ēr′bēum) n. (chem.) ~Metallic element of rare-earth ~roup, occurring in gadolinite etc.; ~ymbol Er, at. no. 68, at. wt. ~67.26. [f. Ytterby in Sweden, ~here found].

ere (ār) prep. & conj. (poet., ~rchaic). Before (in time).

Er·e·bus (ĕr′ebus). (Gk. myth.) Place of darkness between earth and Hades; ~ **Mount**, active volcano, 13,202 ft. (4,027 m), on Ross Island, Antarctica.

E·rech·the·um (ĭrĕk′thēum). Temple of Erechtheus, legendary founder and king of Athens, on the Acropolis, erected 421–407 B.C.

e·rect (ĭrĕkt′) adj. Upright, not stooping; vertical; (of hair etc.) rigid and upright, bristling; (of part of the body) enlarged and rigid, esp. from sexual excitement. **e·rect′ly** adv. **e·rect′vness** n. **erect** v.t. Raise, set upright; build; assemble or form into; establish.

e·rec·tile (ĭrĕk′tĭl, -tīl) adj. Capable of being erected; ~ **tissue**, tissue in various parts of animals capable of being distended with blood and becoming rigid under excitement.

e·rec·tion (ĭrĕk′shon) n. Erecting; building, structure; erect state of penis or clitoris.

e·rec·tor (ĭrĕk′ter) n. Person, thing, that erects; muscle that holds up or causes erection of a body part.

er·e·mite (ĕr′emīt) n. Recluse, hermit.

erg (ērg) n. (phys.) Amount of work done when a force of 1 dyne acts over a distance of 1 centimeter.

er·go (ēr′gō, ĕr′-) adv. Therefore. [L.]

er·gos·ter·ol (ērgŏs′terōl, -rawl, -rŏl) n. Sterol that, when exposed to ultraviolet radiation, gives a mixture of compounds including vitamin D, found in yeasts and fungi and present in small quantities in the fats of plants and animals.

er·got (ēr′got, -gŏt) n. Diseased condition of seed of rye and other grasses; dark violet hardened mycelium of the fungus (Claviceps purpurea) causing this, used medically to control hemorrhage or contract uterus. **er′got·ism** n. Disease of grasses consisting in formation of ergot; diseased condition of man or animals caused by eating grain or grasses infected with ergot and characterized by lameness and gangrene.

Er·ics·son (ēr′ĭkson), **Leif** (lēf; Icel. lāv). Son of ERIC THE RED, first European discoverer of N. Amer., c1000 A.D., founded settlement in VINLAND, prob. Newfoundland.

Er·ic (ĕr′ĭk) **the Red.** Tenth c. Icelandic explorer; discovered, settled, and named Greenland.

Er·ie (ēr′ē) n. 1. (Member of) an Iroquoian tribe of N. Amer. Indians formerly inhabiting the region around Lake Erie; **Lake** ~, fourth largest of the Great Lakes, on the boundary between the U.S. and Canada; ~ **Canal,** canal extending 363 mi. from Albany to Buffalo, N.Y., connecting the Hudson River to Lake Erie, now part of N.Y. State Barge Canal system. 2. Shipping and industrial city in NW. Pennsylvania, on Lake Erie.

Er·in (ĕr′ĭn, ēr′-, ār′-). Ancient name or Ireland, now only poetical.

Er·i·tre·a (ĕrĭtrē′a). Province of Ethiopia, on the Red Sea; formerly an Italian colony.

er·mine (ēr′mĭn) n. (pl. **-mines**, collect. **-mine**). 1. (in U.S.) Any of various weasels. 2. Carnivorous mammal of weasel family (Mustela erminea), inhabiting northern European countries, with reddish-brown fur above and white beneath in summer and (in northern regions) white in winter, except for black tip of tail; stoat. 3. Fur of the ermine.

e·rode (ĭrōd′) v.t. (**e·rod·ed, e·rod·ing**). (of acids, water currents, etc.) Eat away, destroy surface of.

e·rog·e·nous (ĭrŏj′enus) adj. Of, giving rise to, sexual desire.

E·ros (ĕr′ŏs, ēr′-). (Gk. myth.) God of love, son of Aphrodite; identified by the Romans with Cupid.

e·ros (ĕr′ŏs, ēr′-) n. Earthly or sexual love. (opp. AGAPE¹).

e·ro·sion (ĭrō′zhon) n. Eroding; (geol.) wearing away of earth's surface by wind, water, or ice (cf. ABRASION). **e·ro·sive** (ĭrō′sĭv) adj.

e·rot·ic (ĭrŏt′ĭk) adj. Of sexual love. **e·rot·i·ca** (ĭrŏt′ĭka) n.pl. Erotic writings, pictures, etc. **e·rot·i·cism** (ĭrŏt′ĭsĭzem), **er·o·tism** (ĕr′otĭzem) ns. **e·rot·i·cal·ly** adv.

err (ēr, ĕr) v.i. Make mistakes; be incorrect; sin.

er·rand (ĕr′and) n. Short journey on which person is sent to carry message etc.; business on which one is sent, object of journey.

er·rant (ĕr′ant) adj. Roaming in quest of adventure (esp. in **knight** ~); wandering; straying from the proper course, opinion, conduct, etc. **er′ran·cy** n.

Erosion in areas altered by man, such as this farmland in Wyoming, is usually the result of overgrazing or removal of surface vegetation.

er·ra·tic (ĭrăt´ĭk) *adj.* Wandering; (of diseases, pains, etc.) moving from one part to another; irregular or uncertain in movement, having no fixed course, eccentric in conduct, habit, or opinion. **er·rat´i·cal·ly** *adv.*

er·ra·tum (ĭrah´tum, ĭrăt´um) *n.* (pl. **-ta** pr. -ta). Error in printing or writing, esp. (usu. pl.) list of errors and corrections attached to book.

er·ro·ne·ous (ĭrō´nēus) *adj.* Mistaken, incorrect. **er·ro·ne·ous·ly** *adv.*

er·ror (ĕr´er) *n.* Mistake; condition of erring in opinion, wrong opinion; transgression; (math. etc.) quantity of deviation from correct or accurate result, determination, etc.; (baseball) any mistaken play by a fielder in catching or throwing that permits a runner to be safe when he could have been put out.

Erse (ērs) *adj.* & *n.* Irish Gaelic, formerly applied also to the Gaelic of Scotland. [var. of *Irish*]

erst (ērst) *adv.* (archaic) Formerly, of old; first. **erst·while** (ērst´hwīl, -wīl) *adv.* & *adj.* Erst, former.

e·ruc·ta·tion (ĭrŭktā´shon) *n.* Belching; eruptive action of volcano; emission of gas from stomach. **eruct** *v.i.*

er·u·dite (ĕr´yudĭt, ĕr´u-) *adj.* Learned. **er·u·dite·ly** *adv.* **er·u·di·tion** (ĕryudĭsh´on, ĕru-) *n.*

e·rupt (ĭrŭpt´) *v.* Break out or through; (of volcano) emit rocks, lava, ash, or gases, (of geyser) spurt water; (of teeth) break through gums; (of rash) appear on skin.

e·rup·tion (ĭrŭp´shon) *n.* Erupting; outbreak of volcano, ejection of hot water from geyser, etc.; breaking out of rash etc.; also (fig.) of war, passion, mirth, etc.

e·rup·tive (ĭrŭp´tĭv) *adj.* Bursting forth; tending to burst forth; of, formed by, forced up by, volcanic eruption. **e·rup´tive·ly** *adv.*

-ery *suffix.* Forming nouns meaning class of persons or things (*citizenry, greenery*); condition (*slavery*); place or occupation (*brewery, eatery*); derogation (*trumpery, popery, foolery*).

er·y·sip·e·las (ĕrĭsĭp´elas) *n.* Acute inflammation of lymphatic vessels of the skin, caused by streptococcal infection.

er·y·the·ma (ĕrĭthē´ma) *n.* Superficial blotchy redness of skin, as caused by sunburn or chemical poisoning.

e·ryth·ro·cyte (ĭrĭth´rosĭt) *n.*

*The **eruption** of a volcano at Vestmannaeyjar, Iceland, 24 January 1973. Eruptions are produced by gases. The lava, which solidifies when it cools, is a compound, differing between volcanoes, but the rock is usually basalt.*

Red blood cell.

Es *symbol.* Einsteinium.

-es[1] Plural ending for nouns ending with a sibilant.

-es[2] Ending, third person sing. pres. ind., for verbs ending with a sibilant or -*o*.

E·sau (ē´saw). Elder son of Isaac and Rebecca; sold his birthright to his brother Jacob for a mess of pottage (Gen. 25).

es·ca·late (ĕs´kalāt) *v.* (**-late** -lat·ing**). Increase or develop degrees; intensify (esp. a wa **es·ca·la·tion** (ĕskalā´shon) *n.*

es·ca·la·tor (ĕs´kalāter) Moving stairway (with stairs link to an endless belt).

es·cal·lop, es·cal·op (ĕskŏl´ -kăl´-) *ns.* 1. = SCALLOP *n.* def. 2. Thin slice of meat for frying baking.

es·ca·pade (ĕs´kapād, ĕskapāc *n.* Breaking loose from restrair carefree, reckless adventure; flir caper.

es·cape (ĕskāp´) *v.* (**-cape -cap·ing**). 1. Gain liberty fleeing, get free from detention *schscholtzia,* or *Californian poppy. veral varieties of different colors of s sun-loving poppy are cultivated in y spots. There is a dwarf species (E. espitosa).*

This **escarpment,** in the Zion National Park, Utah, is a sheer drop of several hundred feet, clearly dividing mountain and valley.

ontrol, oppression, etc.; (of fluids c.) issue, find a way out; (of words c.) issue unawares from (person, s lips). 2. Get off safely, go nhurt or unpunished; get clear way from (person, his grasp, etc.); void; elude notice or recollection f. **escape** *n.* Act of escaping; ct of having escaped; leakage (of as etc.); outlet; FIRE escape; ~ lause, clause in a contract solving a contracting party from particular obligation in specified rcumstances; ~ **chute,** slide pening automatically from air- lane for emergency exit; ~ **hatch,** leans of emergency exit (from sub- arine etc. or fig.); ~ **velocity,** inimum velocity needed for an bject to escape from a gravitational eld, as that of a spacecraft from arth's gravity; ~ **wheel,** toothed heel in escapement.

es·cap·ee (ĕskāpē′) *n.* One who as escaped.

es·cape·ment (ĕskāp′ment) *n.*)utlet; mechanism in watch or lock or other timing device, ntervening between motive power nd regulator, and alternately hecking and releasing the train, ausing intermittent impulse to be iven to regulator.

es·cap·ism (ĕskā′pĭzem) *n.* Tendency to escape from realities f life into fantasy, amusements, tc. **es·cap′ist** *adj.* & *n.*

es·ca·role (ĕs′karōl) *n.* Variety f ENDIVE, *Cichorium endivia,* used n salads.

es·carp·ment (ĕskärp′ment) *n.* Steep bank immediately in front of

and below rampart; similar natural formation.

-escence *suffix.* Forming nouns corresponding to adjectives ending in *-escent* (*deliquescence, effervescence*).

-escent *suffix.* Forming adjectives denoting beginning of a state or variation of color etc. (*deliquescent, iridescent*).

es·cha·tol·o·gy (ĕskatŏl′ojē) *n.* Branch of theology concerned with death, judgment, heaven, and hell. **es·cha·to·log·i·cal** (ĕskatolŏj′ĭkal) *adj.*

es·cheat (ĕschēt′) *n.* (law) Reversion of fief to feudal lord when tenant died without leaving qualified successor; lapsing of land to crown, nation, or lord of manor on owner's dying intestate without heirs; property so lapsing or reverting. ~ *v.* Confiscate; hand over (property) as an escheat; revert by escheat.

es·chew (ĕschōō′) *v.t.* Avoid, abstain from (particular kind of conduct, food, etc.). **es·chew′al, es·chew′er** *ns.*

esch·scholt·zi·a (ĕshōlt′sēa) *n.* Californian herbaceous plant of genus **E**~ of the poppy family, the best known species being *E. californica,* California poppy, which has finely divided glaucous leaves and large bright yellow flowers with saffron-colored center. [J. F.

von *Eschscholtz* (1793–1831), Ger. botanist]

es·cort (ĕs′kôrt) *n.* Body of armed men or women acting as guard to persons, baggage, etc.; person(s) accompanying another on journey for protection or guidance, or for courtesy's sake; ship(s), aircraft, etc., so employed. ~ (ĕskôrt′) *v.t.* Act as escort to.

es·cri·toire (ĕskrētwär′) *n.* Writing desk with drawers etc.

es·cu·do (ĕskōō′dō) *n.* (pl. **-dos**). 1. Principal monetary unit of Portugal, = 100 centavos. 2. Principal monetary unit of Chile, = 100 centesimos.

es·cutch·eon (ĕskŭch′on) *n.* 1. Shield or shieldlike emblem bearing a coat of arms. 2. Plate on ship's stern bearing its name and home port.

Es·dras (ĕz′dras). Name of first two of the books of the Apocrypha; the first is mainly a compilation from Chronicles, Nehemiah, and Ezra, and the second is a record of angelic revelations.

ESE, E.S.E., e.s.e. *abbrevs.* East-southeast.

-ese *suffix.* Forming adjectives and nouns (pl. same) f. names of foreign countries and cities (*Japanese, Viennese*), meaning (inhabitant or language) of; or f. nouns or names of writers (*officialese, Dreiserese*), meaning style of writing.

Es·ki·mo, Es·qui·mau (ĕs′kimō) *ns.* (pl. **-mos,** collect. **-mo**; pl. **-maux** pr. **-mōz,** collect. **-mau**). (Member of a) people inhabiting

Arctic coastal regions from Green-land to Alaska and NE. Siberia; their language; ~ **dog**, breed of powerful dog with long hair, used by the Eskimos as sled dog.

e·soph·a·gus (ĭsŏf′agus) *n.* (pl. **-gi** pr. -gī, -jī). Canal leading from mouth to stomach; gullet.

es·o·ter·ic (ĕsŏtĕr′ĭk) *adj.* (of philosophical doctrine etc.) Meant for, intelligible to, the initiated only; (of disciples) initiated; pri-vate, confidential. **es·o·ter′i·cal·ly** *adv.*

ESP *abbrev.* Extrasensory per-ception.

esp. *abbrev.* Especially.

es·pa·drille (ĕs′padrĭl) *n.* Rope-soled canvas shoe.

es·pal·ier (ĕspăl′yer, -yā) *n.* Framework on which fruit trees or ornamental shrubs are trained; tree so trained.

es·pe·cial (ĕspĕsh′al) *adj.* Pre-eminent, exceptional; particular; belonging chiefly to one person, thing, etc. **es·pe′cial·ly** *adv.*

Es·pe·ran·to (ĕsperahn′tō, -răn′-) *n. & adj.* (Of) an artificial language invented (1887) for uni-versal use by a Polish physician, Dr. Ludovik Lazarus Zamenhof, with vocabulary consisting of roots com-mon to the chief European languages with endings normalized. **Es·pe·ran′tist** *n.* [pen name, Dr. *Esperanto* (= "hopeful one"), of

A team of **Eskimo dogs** pull a sled across the Antarctic ice to the runway at McMurdo Station. In Arctic regions also these dogs are invaluable. They travel in areas that would be impassable for motor transport.

its inventor, f. L. *spero* hope]

es·pi·o·nage (ĕs′pēonahzh, -nĭj, -nahj, ĕspēonahzh′) *n.* Practice of spying or using spies.

es·pla·nade (ĕsplenahd′, -nād′) *n.* Level piece of ground or pavement used for public prom-enade, esp. along a shore.

es·pouse (ĕspowz′) *v.t.* (**-poused, -pous·ing**). 1. (usu. of man) Marry; give (woman) in mar-riage (to). 2. Adopt, support (cause, opinion, etc.) **es·pou·sal** (ĕspow′-zal) *n.*

es·pres·so (ĕsprĕs′ō) *n.* Coffee made under steam pressure; device for making this.

es·prit (ĕsprē′) *n.* Sprightliness, wit; ~ **de corps**, spirit of devotion to and enthusiasm for group one belongs to. [Fr.]

es·py (ĕspī′) *v.t.* (**-pied, -py·-ing**). Catch sight of; detect.

Esq., Esqr. *abbrevs.* Esquire.

-esque *suffix.* Forming adjec-tives meaning "in the manner of" (*picturesque, arabesque, Giottesque*).

Es·qui·line (ĕs′kwĭlīn). One of the Seven Hills of Rome.

Es·qui·mau: see ESKIMO.

es·quire (ĕs′kwīr, ĕskwīr′) *n.* (hist. archaic) Young man of gent birth attending on knight; squir 2. Man belonging to higher order English gentry, ranking immed ately below knight. 3. Courtes title appended to a man's name formal use (esp. of a lawyer) an (abbreviated Esq.) in addressin letters etc. where no prefixed tit is used. [L. *scutarius* shield beare

-ess *suffix.* Forming nouns d noting females (*lioness, goddes actress*).

es·say (ĕs′ā; for def. 1. also ĕsā *n.* 1. Attempt (at). 2. Litera composition of moderate length o any subject. ~ (ĕsā) *v.t.* Tr test (person, thing); attempt. **es say·ist** *n.* Writer of essays.

es·sence (ĕs′ens) *n.* 1. Existenc entity (now usu. spiritual or in material). 2. Absolute bein reality underlying phenomena; th by which anything subsists, four dation of being. 3. All that make a thing what it is; intrinsic natu as a thing in itself; (loosely) mo important indispensable quality constituent element of anything. Extract obtained by distillation et from plant, medicinal, odoriferou or nutritious substance, etc.; alco holic solution containing volati elements to which perfume, flavo etc., are due; perfume.

Es·sene (ĕs´ēn, ĕsēn´) *n.* Member of an ascetic Jewish sect living in a community in Palestine from 2nd c. B.C. to 2nd c. A.D.

es·sen·tial (ĭsĕn´shəl) *adj.* 1. Of, constituting, a thing's essence; that is such in essence; indispensable; necessarily implied; absolutely necessary. 2. That is or is like, an essence or extract; ~ **oil**, volatile oil obtained by distillation and marked by characteristic odor etc.; substance from which it is extracted. **essential** *n.* Indispensable element. **es·sen·ti·a·li·ty** (ĕnshĕăl´ĭtē) *n.* **es·sen´tial·ly** *adv.*

-est[1] *suffix.* Forming superlatives of adjectives and adverbs (*widest, fastest*).

-est[2] *suffix.* Forming archaic 2nd person sing. of verbs (*knowest*).

est. *abbrev.* Estimate(d); estate; established.

estab. *abbrev.* Established.

es·tab·lish (ĕstăb´lĭsh) *v.t.* Set up on permanent basis; settle; secure permanent acceptance for; place beyond dispute; make state institution of (particular religion or church).

es·tab·lish·ment (ĕstăb´lĭshment) *n.* Establishing; Church system established by law, established Church; organized body of men maintained for a purpose, as army, navy, civil service; staff of servants, etc.; public institution, house of business; household; **the E~**, those with (official or unofficial) authority or influence, regarded as having joint interest in resisting change.

es·tate (ĕstāt´) *n.* 1. (chiefly archaic) State, condition; worldly standing, fortune, etc.; status, degree of rank; **man's, woman's ~**, manhood, womanhood. 2. Order, class of citizens as part of body politic and as sharing directly or indirectly in government; **fourth ~**, politically powerful group other than the three estates in Britain or pre-revolutionary France (bishops, nobles, and commons), hence, the public press. 3. Whole of one's wealth, property, possessions, etc., esp. left by a deceased person; large piece of rural or residential land, usu. with a large house; **real ~**, property in land and buildings; **real ~ agent**, person, company, conducting business in sale of buildings and land.

es·teem (ĕstēm´) *v.t.* Think highly of; consider. **~** *n.* Favorable opinion, regard, respect.

es·ter (ĕs´ter) *n.* Any of a class

*'Bathers', an **etching** by Rembrandt (1606–69). As in line-engraving, the lines to be printed are incised, rather than left in relief, as in wood-engraving. Etching has been practiced in N. Europe since at least the 15th century.*

Rembrandt. f 163?

of organic compounds formed by the interaction of an acid and an alcohol with the elimination of water; used as solvents, flavoring essences, etc., and in many chemical processes.

Es·ther (ĕs´ter). Beautiful Jewish queen of Persia who saved her people from massacre; book of Old Testament containing the story of Esther.

es·thete = AESTHETE.

es·thet·ic = AESTHETIC.

es·ti·ma·ble (ĕs´timabel) *adj.* Worthy of esteem.

es·ti·mate (ĕs´timĭt, -māt) *n.* Approximate judgment (of number, amount, etc.); quantity assigned by this; statement of sum for which one offers to undertake specified work; judgment of character or qualities. **~** (ĕs´timāt) *v.t.* (**-mat·ed, -mat·ing**). Form estimate of; fix by estimate *at* (so much); form an opinion of. **es·ti·ma·tor** *n.*

es·ti·ma·tion (ĕstimā´shon) *n.* Judgment of worth; opinion, judgment; esteem.

es·ti·val: see AESTIVAL.

Es·to·ni·a (ĕstō´nēa). Former country in NE. Europe along Baltic Sea; once part of the Russian Empire; proclaimed an independent republic 1918; incorporated in the Soviet Union 1940 as a constituent republic (properly *Estonian Soviet Socialist Republic*); capital, Tallinn. **Es·to´ni·an** *adj. & n.* (Native, inhabitant, language) of Estonia.

es·top (ĕstŏp´) *v.t* (**-topped, -top·ping**). (law) Stop, bar, hinder; (refl. and pass.) be precluded by one's own previous act or declaration from doing etc. **es·top·pel** (ĕstŏp´el) *n.* Being estopped.

es·trange (ĕstrānj´) *v.t.* (**-tranged, -trang·ing**). Cause (person) to turn away in feeling or affection; make hostile or indifferent. **es·trange´ment** *n.*

es·tro·gen (ĕs´trojen) *n.* Any of several hormones produced esp. by the ovary, capable of developing and maintaining female characteristics of body.

es·trus (ĕs´trus) *n.* Periodic sexual excitement and readiness for mating in female animals; rut.

es·tu·ar·y (ĕs´chōoĕrē) *n.* (pl. **-ar·ies**). Tidal mouth of river; inlet of sea extending inland to a river. **es·tu·ar·ine** (ĕs´chōoarīn, -rĭn) *adj.*

ETA *abbrev.* Estimated time of arrival.

e·ta (ā´ta, ē´-) *n.* Eighth (later seventh) letter of Greek alphabet (*H*, η), transliterated in English by long *e* (ē).

é·ta·gère (ātăzhâr´) *n.* Vertical series of open shelves, supported by legs at the corners, for knicknacks, plants, etc.

et al. *abbrev. Et alii* (L., = "and others").

etc. *abbrev.* Et cetera.

et·cet·er·a (ĕt sĕt´era, sĕt´ra). And the rest, and so on. **et·cet´er·as** *n.pl.* Extras, additional odds and ends. [L.]

etch (ĕch) *v.* Portray by drawing with an **etching needle** on a metal plate previously coated with a wax and resin mixture (the *ground*) and immersing in acid, which corrodes the parts laid bare by the needle; make (print) from plate thus prepared; copy (picture) by this process; practice this craft. **etch´er** *n.* **etch´ing** *n.* Print made from an etched plate; art, process, of etching.

ETD *abbrev.* Estimated time of departure.

e·ter·nal (ĭtẽr´nal) *adj.* Without beginning or end, that always (has existed and always) will exist; (colloq.) incessant, too frequent; **E~ City**, Rome; **~ triangle**, (emotional relationships in) group of two women and a man or two men and a woman. **e·ter´nal·ize** *v.t.* (-ized, -iz·ing). **e·ter´nal·ly** *adv.*

e·ter·ni·ty (ĭtẽr´nĭtē) *n.* (pl. **-ties**). Being eternal; infinite (esp. future) time; the future life; tediously long time.

-eth[1] *suffix*: see -TH.

-eth[2] *suffix.* Forming archaic 3rd pers. pres. sing. of verbs (*findeth, doeth*).

eth·ane (ĕth´ān) *n.* Colorless odorless gas (C_2H_6), a constituent of natural gas used as a fuel, refrigerant, etc.

eth·a·nol (ĕth´anōl, -nawl, -nŏl) *n.* = ETHYL alcohol.

Eth·el·red (ĕth´elrĕd) (*c*968–1016), "the Unready" (= "without

counsel"). King of the English 979–1016; son of Edgar and father of Edward the Confessor.

e·ther (ē´ther) *n.* 1. Clear sky, upper regions of space beyond Earth's atmosphere. 2. Hypothetical substance of great elasticity and subtlety formerly postulated by the wave theory of light as permeating the whole of space, esp. as medium of propagation of radio waves etc. 3. (chem.) Colorless volatile liquid ($(C_2H_5)_2O$) with a characteristic aromatic odor obtained by distillation of alcohol with sulfuric acid and used as a solvent for the extraction of oils, fats, waxes, etc., and as an anesthetic; any of a large class of compounds of similar composition.

e·the·re·al (ĭthēr´ēal) *adj.* 1. Light, airy; heavenly; of unearthly delicacy of substance, character, or appearance. 2. Of, like, ether. **e·the·re·al·i·ty** (ĭthērēăl´ĭtē) *n.* **e·the´re·al·ly** *adv.*

eth·ic (ĕth´ĭk) *n.* Principle or body of principles of right or good conduct. **eth·i·cal** (ĕth´ĭkal) *adj.* Relating to, treating of, morals or ethics; moral, honorable; (of drug etc.) available only on doctor's prescription. **eth´i·cal·ly** *adv.*

eth·ics (ĕth´ĭks) *n.pl.* 1. (as sing.) Science of morals, study of principles of human duty; treatise on this. 2. (as pl.) Moral principles; rules of conduct.

E·thi·o·pi·a (ēthēō´pēa). (hist.) Region on the upper Nile; (in modern usage) a country in NE. Africa SW. of Red Sea and Gulf of Aden; capital, Addis Ababa; after

Ethiopia is a huge mountain plateau divided by the Great Rift Valley, through which runs a chain of lakes. The population is of diverse ethnic origin: the Amhara and Tigreans are of Hamitic-

being converted to Christianity 4th c., the country was cut off fro European influences by Musli dominion; rediscovered by Po tuguese in 16th c.; Italians invade and annexed the country in 193 but were driven out in 1941 an Emperor Haile Selassie I was r instated; he was deposed in 197 **E·thi·o´pi·an** *adj.* Of, pertainin to, Ethiopia. **~** *n.* Native, ir habitant, of Ethiopia; (hist.) Afr can.

E·thi·op·ic (ēthēŏp´ĭk, -ō´pĭ *adj. & n.* (Of) an ancient Semit language (Ge´ez) of Ethiopia su viving in the liturgical language the Christian Church of Ethiopia

eth·nic (ĕth´nĭk) *adj.* Origina ing from a national, linguistic racial, etc., group sharing distinc tive cultural characteristics. **~** Member of ethnic group.

eth·nic·i·ty (ĕthnĭs´ĭtē) *n.* Con dition of belonging to a particula ethnic group; ethnic feeling, pride

eth·nog·ra·phy (ĕthnŏg´rafē) *n* Scientific description of races o men. **eth·nog´ra·pher** *n.* **eth·no graph·ic** (ĕthnogrăf´ĭk), **eth·no graph´i·cal** *adjs.* **eth·no·graph´ i·cal·ly** *adv.*

eth·nol·o·gy (ĕthnŏl´ojē) *n* Science of races and peoples, thei relations to one another, distinctiv physical and other characteristics etc. **eth·no·log·i·cal** (ĕthnolŏj´ĭ kal) *adj.* **eth·no·log´i·cal·ly** *adv* **eth·nol´o·gist** *n.*

e·thol·o·gy (ēthŏl´ojē) *n.* Study of animal behavior. **e·tho·log·i·ca** (ētholŏj´ĭkal) *adj.* **e·thol´o·gist** *n.*

Semitic origin and are Coptic Christians the Galla (right: Galla child) are o Hamitic origin, and may be Christians o Muslims; the Falashas are Jews.

Left: An **Etruscan** *skyphos or cup c. 300 B.C. The origin of the Etruscans is not known — possibly they came from Asia Minor. Etruria was rich, thanks to fertile soil and iron- and copper-mines. The three periods of its art were influenced by Asia, Greece, and Rome.*

e·thos (ē′thŏs) *n.* 1. Characteristic sentiment, attitude, etc. of community, people, or system. 2. Underlying principle of a literary or other movement, statement, work of art, etc.

eth·yl (ĕth′il) *n.* 1. (chem.) Alkyl radical having two carbon atoms (C_2H_5). 2. (**E** ~) (trademark) lead tetraethyl, $Pb(C_2H_5)_4$, a substance added to gasoline to improve combustion, thereby increasing its antiknock properties. 3. ~ **alcohol**, ordinary alcohol or **ethanol** (C_2H_5OH), an inflammable volatile liquid produced by the fermentation of sugars by yeast, used in intoxicating beverages, as a fuel, as a solvent, and in the chemical industry; ~ **chloride**, volatile liquid (C_2H_5Cl), with ethereal odor, used as solvent, refrigerant, etc.

eth·yl·ene (ĕth′ilēn) *n.* Inflammable gas (C_2H_4) with faint sweet smell used as an anesth'etic and as a color enhancer for citrus fruits; ~ **glycol**, colorless slightly viscous liquid used as antifreeze in car engines, for deicing aircraft, etc.

e·ti·o·late (ē′tēolāt) *v.t.* (**-lat·ed, -lat·ing**). Render (plant etc.) pale and colorless by excluding light; blanch; give sickly hue to (person). **e·ti·o·la·tion** (ētēolā′shon) *n.*

e·ti·ol·o·gy (ētēŏl′ojē) *n.* Assignment of a cause; philosophy of causation; (med.) science of the cause of disease. **e·ti·o·log'i·cal** (ētēŏlŏj′ĭkal) *adj.* **e·ti·o·log'i·cal·ly** *adv.*

et·i·quette (ĕt′ĭkĭt, -kĕt) *n.* Conventional rules of personal behavior in polite society; ceremonial of

court; unwritten professional code of behavior.

Et·na (ĕt′na), **Mount.** Highest active volcano in Europe (altitude 10,758 ft., 3,279 m), in E. Sicily.

E·ton (ē′ton). ~ **College**, English private school for boys near Windsor, founded 1440; ~ **collar**, broad stiff white collar overlapping the lapels, worn with an ~ **jacket**, short black waist-length jacket (formerly worn by younger boys at Eton), worn open in front. **E·to·ni·an** (ētō′nēan) *adj. & n.*

E·trus·can (ĭtrŭs′kan) *adj. & n.* (Member, language) of the earliest historical inhabitants of Etruria, an ancient country between the Arno and Tiber rivers (approximately modern Tuscany), who there developed a system of powerful city-states and a flourishing civilization.

et seq. *abbrev.* (pl. **et seqq.**, **et sqq.**). *Et sequentia* (L., = "and what follows").

-ette *suffix.* Forming nouns meaning small (*kitchenette*), imitation (*leatherette*), or female (*suffragette, usherette*).

é·tude (ā′tōōd, -tūd) *n.* Short musical composition or exercise.

ETV *abbrev.* Educational television.

et·y·mol·o·gy (ĕtĭmŏl′ojē) *n.* (pl. **-gies**). Account of, facts relating

to, origin and development word(s); branch of linguist science concerned with this; part grammar treating of individu words and their formation and i flections; abbrev. *etym.* **et·y·mo log·i·cal** (ĕtĭmolŏj′ĭkal) *adj.* **et·y mo·log'i·cal·ly** *adv.* **et·y·mol'o gist** *n.*

Eu *symbol.* Europium.

eu- *prefix.* Well; beneficial, in *eugenics, eulogy.*

eu·ca·lyp·tus (ūkalĭp′tus) *n.* (p -ti pr. -tī, -tus·es). Plant of gen **E** ~ including gum tree of Austral and the neighboring island (pop.) = ~ **oil**, essential o obtained from the leaves of a speci of eucalyptus with strong chara teristic odor, used in treatment respiratory diseases. [Gk. *eu kalu tos* well covered, the flower before opens being protected by a cap]

Eu·cha·rist (ū′kerĭst) *n.* Chri tian sacrament of body and bloo of Christ, in which bread and wi are partaken of; consecrated el ments, esp. bread. **Eu·cha·ris·ti** (ūkerĭs′tĭk), **Eu·cha·ris'ti·cal** *ad* [Gk. *eukharistia* thanksgivi (*kharizomai* offer willingly)]

eu·chre (ū′ker) *n.* Card game fo two, three, or four persons, play with pack of 32 cards (the 2, 3, 5, 6, of each suit being rejecte in which, if a player fails to ta three tricks, he or his side is sa to be "euchred," and the other si gains two points. ~ *v.t.* (**-chre -chring**). Gain advantage ov (opponent) by his failure to ta three tricks; (fig.) outwit.

Eu·clid (ū′klĭd) (*c*300 B.C

thematician of Alexandria,
.hor of the first systematic
.tise on geometry (the *Ele-*
.ts). **Eu·clid·e·an, Eu·clid·i·an**
.lĭd´ēan) *adj.* Of Euclid; ~
.metry, geometry based on his
.tulates; ~ **space**, kind of space
which his postulates are valid (in
.ich, e.g., a straight line may be
.duced to infinity).

.u·gen·ics (ūjĕn´ĭks) *n.pl.* (usu.
.sidered sing.) (Study, science,
. improving (esp. human) species
. selective breeding.

.u·gé·nie (üzhănē´) (1826–
.o). Full name, Eugénie Marie
. Montijo de Guzmán; wife of
.poleon III, and empress of
.nce, 1853–71.

.u·lo·gize (ū´lojīz) *v.t.* (**-gized,**
.z·ing**). Extol, praise. **eu´lo·gist**
.eu·lo·gis·tic (ūlojĭs´tĭk) *adj.*
.u·lo·gy (ū´lojē) *n.* (pl. **-gies**).
.eech, writing, in commendation
.praise.

.u·men·i·des (ūmĕn´ĭdēz). (Gk.
.th.) (Euphemistic name for) the
.ries. [Gk., = "kindly ones"]

.u·nuch (ū´nŭk) *n.* Castrated
.n, esp. one employed in harem
. (in Oriental courts and under
.man Empire) in affairs of state.

.u·on·y·mus (ūŏn´imus) *n.*
.rub, tree, or vine of genus **E**~,
. which many species are
.tivated for decorative foliage or

.orge of the **Euphrates** *near Malatya,*
.key. The river rises in the Turkish
.menian highlands and its course is
.ut 1,700 miles. It is not generally
.igable.

The **euonymus** *may be deciduous or evergreen and its many species grow throughout the northern temperate zone. The flowering of the euonymus was said to foreshadow the arrival of the plague.*

berries. [Gk. *euonumos* well-named, lucky (*onoma* name)]

eu·phe·mism (ū´femĭzem) *n.* Substitution of mild or vague expression for harsher or more offensive one; expression thus substituted. **eu·phe·mis·tic** (ūfemĭs´tĭk) *adj.* **eu·phe·mis´ti·cal·ly** *adv.*

eu·pho·ny (ū´fonē) *n.* (pl. **-nies**). Pleasing sound; quality of having this. **eu·phon·ic** (ūfŏn´ĭk),

eu·pho·ni·ous (ūfō´nēus) *adjs.* **eu·pho´ni·ous·ly** *adv.*

eu·pho·ri·a (ūfōr´ēa, ūfôr´-) *n.* Sense, feeling, of well-being; bliss; exaggerated sense of well-being with no basis in reality. **eu·phor´ic** *adj.*

Eu·phra·tes (ūfrā´tēz). River of SW. Asia, flowing 1,739 mi., (2,799 km) through E. Turkey and Iraq to join the Tigris and then the Persian Gulf.

Eu·phros·y·ne (ūfrŏs´ĭnē). (Gk. myth.) One of the Graces.

eu·phu·ism (ū´fūĭzem) *n.* Affectedly elegant style of language, originally the literary style used by imitators of John Lyly, known for its elaborate alliteration, antitheses, and long strings of similes. **eu´phu·ist** *n.* **eu·phu·is·tic** (ūfūĭs´tĭk), **eu·phu·is´ti·cal** *adjs.* [f. *Euphuēs* (Gk., = "well-endowed"), chief character in two of Lyly's works]

Eur. *abbrev.* Europe(an).

Eur·a·sian (yŏorā´zhan) *adj.* Of mixed European and Asian parentage; of Europe and Asia. ~ *n.* Eurasian person.

Eur·at·om (yŏorăt´om) *n.* Organization formed by France, the Netherlands, West Germany, Belgium, and Luxembourg in 1957 to coordinate development of atomic energy.

eu·re·ka (yŏorē´ka) *int.* & *n.* Exclamation of exultation, "I have found it!" [Gk. *heurēka* (*heuriskein* find) uttered by Archimedes when, while bathing, he discovered means

Members of the E.E.C.
Communist countries

ICELAND

ATLANTIC OCEAN

NORWAY

SWEDEN

FINLAND

U.S.S.R.

EIRE

GREAT BRITAIN

NETHERLANDS

DENMARK

BELGIUM

LUX.

WEST GERMANY

EAST GERMANY

POLAND

CZECHOSLOVAKIA

FRANCE

SWITZ.

AUSTRIA

HUNGARY

RUMANIA

Bay of Biscay

Black Sea

PORTUGAL

SPAIN

I T A L Y

Adriatic Sea

YUGOSLAVIA

ALBANIA

BULGARIA

Turkey

GREECE

Mediterranean Sea

North Africa

of determining volume of irregular
solid by measuring its displacement
of water; he was thus able to
determine the proportion of base
metal in Hiero's golden crown]

eu·rhyth·mics (yo͞orĭdh´mĭks)
n. (considered sing. or pl.) System
(founded by Swiss composer Émile
Jaques-Dalcroze, 1865–1950) of
expressing musical rhythm in
bodily movement.

Eu·rip·i·des (yo͞orĭp´ĭdēz)
(*c*485–*c*406 B.C.). Greek tragedian;
author of *Alcestis, Medea, The
Trojan Women,* etc.

Euro- *comb. form.* Europe;
European.

Eu·ro·com·mu·nism (ūrō-
cŏm´yunĭzem) *n.* (Policies of)
Communist parties in W. Europe
alleged to differ significantly from
policies of the Soviet Union.

Eu·ro·dol·lars (ūr´odŏlerz) *n.pl.*
Dollars held in bank in Europe etc.,
not in U.S.

Eu·ro·pa (yo͞orō´pa). (Gk.
myth.) Daughter of Agenor, king
of Phoenicia; was wooed and
abducted to Crete by Zeus, who
took the form of a beautiful white

*Europe is the smallest continent except
for Australia. The distinction between
Asia and Europe was made in the 5th
century B.C., apparently first by the
Assyrians, when Asia was regarded as
the land of the rising sun and Europe as
that of the setting sun.*

bull.

Eu·rope (ūr´op). Continent of
N. hemisphere, western part of the
Eurasian or Old World land mass,
bordering on the Atlantic Ocean;
about 3,700,000 sq. mi.

Eu·ro·pe·an (ūropē´an) *adj.* Of
Europe or its people; ~ **Economic
Community**, economic association established in 1957, consisting
of Belgium, France, Italy, Luxembourg, the Netherlands, West
Germany, and (1973) Denmark, the
Republic of Ireland, and the United
Kingdom; also called "Common
Market," "Euromarket," "Euro-
mart"; ~ **plan**, hotel rate covering
room and service but not meals
(opp. AMERICAN plan). **European**
n. European person.

eu·ro·pi·um (yo͞orō´pēum) *n.*
(chem.) Rare-earth element;
symbol Eu, at. no. 63, at. wt.

151.96. [f. EUROPE]

Eu·rus (ūr´us). (Gk. and Ro
myth.) God of E. or SE. wind.

Eu·ryd·i·ce (yo͞orĭd´ĭsē). (G
myth.) Wife of ORPHEUS.

Eu·sta·chi·us (ūstā´kēus), Ba
tolommeo (d. 1574).   Itali
anatomist.   **Eu·sta·chian** (ūst
shan, -kēan) *adj.*   ~ **tu**
pharyngo-tympanic tube, passa
communicating between the mid
ear (tympanic cavity) and the ba
of the throat (larynx), and servi
to equalize air pressure on bo
sides of the eardrum.

eu·tec·tic (ūtĕk´tĭk) *adj.* &
(Of) a mixture whose constitue
are in such proportions as to m
and solidify at one temperature l
a pure substance.

Eu·ter·pe (ūtēr´pē). (Gk. a
Rom. myth.) Muse of music a
lyric poetry.

eu·tha·na·sia (ūthanā´z
-zhēa, -zēa) *n.* Gentle and ea
death; bringing about of this
merciful reasons, esp. in case
incurable and painful disease.

eu·troph·ic (ūtrŏf´ĭk, ūtrō´f
adj. Designating a pond, lake, et

which nutrients accumulate in
~ndance, supporting heavy
~wth of plant life that causes
~gen deficiency and hence ex-
~ction of animal life in the water.
troph·i·ca·tion (ūtrofīkā´shon),
tro·phy (ū´trofē) ns.
V, Ev abbrevs. Electron volt.
EVA abbrev. (astronautics)
~travehicular activity.
e·vac·u·ate (ĭvăk´ūāt) v.t.
t·ed, -at·ing). 1. Empty (esp.
~mach or other bodily organ of
~tents); discharge excrement etc.
~Withdraw troops, inhabitants,
~m (place); remove (person) esp.
~m a place considered dangerous.
ac·u·a·tion (ĭvăkūā´shon) n.
e·vac·u·ee (ĭvăkūē´) n. Person
~cuated from place of danger etc.
e·vade (ĭvād´) v.t. (**e·vad·ed,
~ad·ing**). Escape, avoid, elude
~ack, pursuit, etc.); avoid doing
~ty etc.), answering (question),
~lding to (argument etc.), esp. by
~ckiness or cleverness while com-
~ing with rules, laws, etc.; baffle.
ad´er n.
e·val·u·ate (ĭvăl´ūāt) v.t.
t·ed, -at·ing). Ascertain
~ount or value of; appraise;
~imate. **e·val·u·a·tion** (ĭvălūā´-
~on) n.
ev·a·nesce (ĕvanĕs´) v.i.
~esced, -nesc·ing). Fade out of
~ht; disappear.
ev·a·nes·cent (ĕvanĕs´ent) adj.
~ickly fading or vanishing away;
~nsitory; fleeting. **ev·a·nes´-
~ce** n. **ev·a·nes´cent·ly** adv.
e·van·gel (ĭvăn´jel) n. (archaic)
~ristian gospel; one of the four
~spels of the New Testament.
~k. euaggelion (reward for

Painted porcelain plate: 'The Temptation of Adam'. The Biblical story of the
world's genesis neatly explains the hard
lot of woman as the result of **Eve's**
weakness towards the serpent.

bringing) good news]
e·van·gel·i·cal (ēvănjĕl´ĭkal,
ĕvan-) adj. 1. Of, according to, the
teaching of the Christian gospel. 2.
(often **E~**) Protestant, (esp.) of the
school of Protestants maintaining
that the essence of the gospel
consists in the doctrine of salvation
by faith and grace and denying that
either sacraments or good works
have any saving efficacy. **~** n.
Member of evangelical Church.

Lake Everard, a salt lake in South Australia. The **evaporation** of water is so
fast that only salt is left. The water
vapor produced by evaporation from all
over the world's surface is vital to the
earth's atmosphere.

e·van·gel´i·cal·ism n. **e·van-
gel´i·cal·ly** adv.
e·van·gel·ism (ĭvăn´jelĭzem) n.
Zealous preaching or promulgation
of the gospel.
e·van·ge·list (ĭvăn´jelĭst) n. 1.
(usu. cap.) One of the writers of
the 4 Gospels of the New Testament: Matthew, Mark, Luke, or
John. 2. Preacher of the gospel;
now usu., layman doing home
missionary work. **e·van·ge·lis·tic**
(ĭvănjelĭs´tĭk) adj.
e·van·gel·ize (ĭvăn´jelīz) v.t.
(**-ized, -iz·ing**). Preach gospel to,
win over to Christian faith.
e·van·gel·i·za·tion (ĭvănjelĭzā´-
shon) n.
Ev·ans (ĕv´anz), **Mary Ann.**
Real name of George ELIOT[1].
e·vap·o·rate (ĭvăp´orāt) v.
(**-rat·ed, -rat·ing**). Turn from
solid or liquid into vapor; pass away
like vapor; remove liquid part of by
heating or drying; lose liquid by
evaporation; **evaporated milk**,
concentrated unsweetened milk
prepared by evaporation. **e·vap·o-
ra·tion** (ĭvăporā´shon), **e·vap´-
o·ra·tor** ns.
e·va·sion (ĭvā´zhon) n. Act,
means, of evading; subterfuge.
e·va·sive (ĭvā´sĭv) adj. Seeking to
evade, addicted to evasion; tending
to evasion. **e·va´sive·ly** adv.
e·va´sive·ness n.
Eve (ēv). Name given by Adam
to his wife (Gen. 3), the first
woman; hence, woman.
eve (ēv) n. 1. (poet. and archaic)
Evening. 2. Evening or day before
saint's day, holiday, etc., or before
any date or event; time immediately
preceding.

e·ven¹ (ē´ven) *n.* (poet. and archaic) Evening; **e'vensong,** Evening Prayer; **e'ventide,** (archaic) evening.

e·ven² (ē´ven) *adj.* 1. Level; smooth; uniform in quality; in same plane or line *with*. 2. Equally balanced, impartial; equal in number or amount; **get ~ (with),** take one's revenge (on). 3. (of temper etc.) Equable, unruffled; **e'venhanded,** equitable; fair; impartial. 4. (of numbers) Integrally divisible by 2; (of sums of money etc.) expressible in integers, tens, etc. (opp. ODD); **~ money,** equal stakes in betting. **even** *v.t.* Make even. **e'ven·ly** *adv.* **e'ven·ness** *n.*

e·ven³ (ē´ven) *adv.* Inviting comparison of an assertion, negation, etc., with a less strong one that might have been made, as *I never ~ opened the book* (much less read it), *does he ~ suspect* (not to say realize) *the danger?, she sings ~ better than he does* (though he sings very well), etc.; (archaic) exactly, just.

eve·ning (ēv´nĭng) *n.* Close of day, esp. time between sunset and bedtime; closing or declining period of life etc.; **~ dress:** see DRESS; **~ gown,** woman's formal dress, usu. floor-length, for wear in the evening; **E~ Prayer,** (Anglican Ch.) evening service that is read or sung; **~ primrose:** see PRIMROSE; **~ star,** Venus (occas. also Jupiter or Mercury) when seen in the west after sunset.

e·vent (ĭvĕnt´) *n.* 1. (Actual or contemplated) fact of a thing's happening; thing that happens, esp. important thing. 2. Any of several possible mutually exclusive occurrences, one of which will happen under stated conditions; something on issue of which money is staked; one of the items in a sports program. 3. Result, outcome; **in any ~, at all ~s,** in any case. **e·vent'ful** *adj.* 1. Having many events. 2. Significant; important.

e·ven·tu·al (ĭvĕn´chooal) *adj.* That will happen in certain circumstances; ultimately resulting.

For 70 years, **Mount Everest,** 29,028 ft. the world's highest mou tain, has challenged climbers. For m of the time, it is swathed in the clou that rise from the plains of India.

e·ven'tu·al·ly *adv.* **e·ven'tu al·i·ty** (ĭvĕnchooăl´ĭtē) *n.* (**-ties**). Possible event.

e·ven·tu·ate (ĭvĕn´chooāt) *v* (**-at·ed, -at·ing**). Turn out; res (*in*); happen, come to pass.

ev·er (ĕv´er) *adv.* 1. Always, all times, as in **~ after, ~ sin forev'er,** for all future tin incessantly. 2. (with negatives, in interrogative, hypothetical, conditional sentences) At any tin by any chance, at all. 3. Add for emphasis to *before* etc., following interrogative pronou adverbs, etc., to intimate that speaker has no notion what answer will be. 4. **~ so,** (collo very.

Ev·er·est (ĕv´erĭst), **Mou** Highest mountain of the wo (29,028 ft., 8,848 m), in

alayas on the border of Nepal
Tibet. [f. Sir George *Everest*
90–1866), surveyor general of
ia]

v·er·glade (ĕv′erglād) *n.*
shy tract of land mostly under
er and covered in places with tall
ss; **The Everglades**, large
mpy region of S. Florida
uding the Everglades National
k, abundant in tropical and
tropical wildlife and plants.

v·er·green (ĕv′ergrēn) *adj.*
ays green or fresh; (of trees
) having green leaves all year
nd and in some cases for several
rs (the leaves of one season
aining on the tree until those of
next are completely formed). ~
Evergreen tree or shrub.

v·er·last·ing (ĕverlăs′tĭng,
h′stĭng) *adj.* Lasting forever;
ing long; lasting too long,
eated too often; (of plants)
ping their shape and color when
ed. ~ *n.* 1. Eternity; **the**
~, God. 2. Everlasting flower.

v·er·more (ĕvermōr′, -mōr′)
. Constantly; always in future.

eve·ry (ĕv′rē) *adj.* 1. Each; all
en separately. 2. **eve′rybody**,
ry person; **everybody else**,
ry other person; **eve′ryday**,

occurring daily, worn or used on
ordinary days, commonplace;
eve′ryone, each (*of*), each person,
everybody; **eve′rything**, all things,
thing of first importance; **eve′ry-
way**, in every way, in every respect;
eve′rywhere, in every place.

Eve·ry·man (ĕv′rēmăn) *n.*
Ordinary or typical person. [Name
of leading character in 15th c.
morality play]

e·vict (ĭvĭkt′) *v.t.* Expel (tenant)
by legal process. **e·vic′tion** *n.*

ev·i·dence (ĕv′ĭdens) *n.* 1. Being
evident, clearness; **in** ~, present;
prominent, conspicuous. 2. Indication, mark, sign, (*of* something);
ground for belief, testimony or facts
tending to prove or disprove something. 3. Information (personal
testimony, production of material
objects, etc.) given in legal investigation to establish a fact or point in
question; statements etc. admissible
as testimony in court of law; **turn
state's** ~, (Brit.) **turn Queen's
(King's)** ~, (of accomplice or

*The devil personified during Indepen-
dence Day celebrations in Liberia,
Africa. In Jewish and Christian theology, the Devil, Satan, is the supreme
spirit of **evil** that tempts man.*

sharer in crime) offer himself as
witness for prosecution against
other persons implicated. **evidence** *v.t.* (**-denced, -denc·ing**).
Serve to indicate; attest; show
clearly. **ev·i·dent** (ĕv′ĭdent) *adj.*
Obvious to eyes or mind, clear,
plain. **ev′i·dent·ly** *adv.* **ev·i·den·-
tial** (ĕvĭdĕn′shal) *adj.*

e·vil (ē′vĭl) *adj.* Bad, harmful,
wicked; boding ill; **the E~ One**,
the Devil; **e′vildoer**, person who
does evil; **evil eye**, malicious or
envious look, superstitiously
believed to do material harm;
supposed faculty of inflicting injury
by a look; **evil-minded**, having
evil ideas, thoughts, plans, etc. **evil**
n. Evil thing; sin; harm, mischief.
e′vil·ly *adv.*

e·vince (ĭvĭns′) *v.t.* (**e·vinced,
e·vinc·ing**). Show, indicate
(quality etc.); exhibit, demonstrate
(quality). **e·vin′ci·ble** *adj.*

e·vis·cer·ate (ĭvĭs′erāt) *v.t.*
(**-at·ed, -at·ing**). Disembowel;
remove entrails of; (fig.) remove a
vital part. **e·vis·cer·a′tion**
(ĭvĭserā′shon) *n.*

e·voke (ĭvōk′) *v.t.* (**e·voked,
e·vok·ing**). Call up, elicit (spirit,
feeling, memory, etc.). **ev·o·ca-
tion** (ĕvokā′shon) *n.* **e·voc·a·tive**

(ĭvŏk´atĭv, ĭvō´ka-) *adj.* **e·vok´er** *n.*

ev·o·lu·tion (ĕvoloo´shon, ēvo-) *n.* 1. Appearance (of events etc.) in due succession. 2. Development, detailed working out, of what is implicitly or potentially contained in an idea or principle; development from rudimentary to mature or complete state. 3. Origination of species of animals and plants by process of development from earlier forms; the theory of this origination. **ev·o·lu´tion·al, ev·o·lu´tion·ar·y** *adjs.* **ev·o·lu´tion·ism, ev·o·lu´tion·ist** *ns.*

e·volve (ĭvŏlv´) *v.* (**e·volved, e·volv·ing**). 1. Unfold, open out; set forth in due sequence; develop, deduce (theory, facts, etc.). 2. Produce, give off (heat etc.). 3. Develop by natural process from rudimentary to more highly organized condition; produce or modify by evolution.

ev·zone (ĕv´zōn) *n.* Member of select Greek infantry regiment.

EW *abbrev.* Enlisted woman; enlisted women.

ewe (ū) *n.* Female sheep.

ew·er (ū´er) *n.* Large wide-mouthed pitcher or water jug.

ex[1] (ĕks) *prep.* 1. Without. 2. Out of. 3. Of particular college class without having graduated with it.

ex[2] (ĕks) *n.* (colloq.) Former occupant of specific position etc., esp. former spouse.

Ex. *abbrev.* Exodus (Old Testament).

ex- *prefix.* 1. (with verbs) Out of; thoroughly. 2. (with adjectives) Without, deprived of. 3. (with nouns) Former (as *ex-president*).

ex·ac·er·bate (ĭgzăs´erbāt) *v.t.*

(**-bat·ed, -bat·ing**). Aggravate (pain, anger, etc.); irritate. **ex·ac·er·ba·tion** (ĭgzăserbā´shon) *n.*

ex·act[1] (ĭgzăkt´) *adj.* Precise, rigorous; accurate, strictly correct; ~ **sciences**, those that admit of absolute precision in results, e.g., physics and chemistry. **ex·act´-ness, ex·ac·ti·tude** (ĭgzăk´tĭtood, -tūd) *ns.*

ex·act[2] (ĭgzăkt´) *v.t.* Demand and enforce payment of (money etc.); insist upon (act, conduct); require urgently. **ex·ac´tion** *n.* Exacting; thing etc. exacted.

ex·act·ing (ĭgzăk´tĭng) *adj.* 1. Making very severe demands; stringent. 2. Requiring great attention, effort, or care.

ex·act·ly (ĭgzăkt´lē) *adv.* (esp., as answer or confirmation) Quite so, just as you say.

ex·ag·ger·ate (ĭgzăj´erāt) *v.t.* (**-at·ed, -at·ing**). Magnify beyond limits of truth; intensify, aggravate; make (physical features etc.) of abnormal size. **ex·ag´ger·at·ed·ly** *adv.* **ex·ag·ger·a·tion** (ĭgzăjerā´-shon), **ex·ag´ger·a·tor** *ns.* **ex·ag·ger·a·tive** (ĭgzăj´erātĭv, -erātĭv) *adj.*

ex·alt (ĭgzawlt´) *v.t.* Raise, place high in rank, power, etc.; praise, extol; dignify, ennoble. **ex·al·ta·tion** (ĕgzawltā´shon, -zal-) *n.* Raising, lifting up; elation, rapturous emotion.

ex·am (ĭgzăm´) *n.* (colloq.) Examination.

ex·am·i·na·tion (ĭgzămĭnā´-shon) *n.* 1. Investigation by inspection or experiment, minute inspection; investigation; scrutiny. 2. Testing of knowledge or ability of

pupils etc. by oral or writt questions; ~ **paper**, paper questions to be answered; writt answers to these questions. Formal interrogation, esp. witness or accused person; cros ~: see CROSS-. **ex·am·i·na´tion** *adj.*

ex·am·ine (ĭgzăm´ĭn) *v.* (**-ine -in·ing**). Investigate; scrutiniz test, esp. test knowledge or capaci of, by questions; interroga formally, esp. witness or accuse person in court of law; inquire in **ex·am·i·nee** (ĭgzămĭnē´), **ex·am in·er** *ns.*

ex·am·ple (ĭgzăm´pel, -zahm *n.* 1. Typical instance, fact, thin person, illustrating or formin particular case of general princip rule, state of things, etc.; specime of workmanship etc. 2. Warning others. 3. Precedent. 4. Action conduct as object of imitation.

ex·arch (ĕk´särk) *n.* 1. Govern of province in Byzantine Empir 2. (Eastern Orthodox Churc) Bishop ranking between patriar and metropolitan; patriarch deputy. **ex·ar·chate** (ĕk´särkā ĕksär´-) *n.*

ex·as·per·ate (ĭgzăs´perāt) *v* (**-at·ed, -at·ing**). Irritate; provol (person). **ex·as·per·a·tion** (ĭgză perā´shon) *n.*

exc. *abbrev.* Except; *excudit* (L = engraved this).

Ex·cal·i·bur (ĕkskăl´ĭber (Arthurian legend) Name of Kir ARTHUR'S[1] magic sword, which drew easily from a rock where it wa held fast, and which was returne on his death to the Lady of th Lake.

ex ca·the·dra (ĕks kathē´dr

*Forms of man during his **evolution**. T earth is believed to be 5,000–6,00 million years old, while man's traces g back 1–3 million years. During the la 2 stages of the Tertiary period a gro of apes, called Australopithecine emerged; these may have been direc tool-making ancestors of Homo erect Human fossils are usually named aft their place of discovery, e.g.,*

late Australopithecus

Homo erectus

early Australopithecus

Steinheim man

giant **excavator** for opencast lignite
~ing. In the late 19th century steam
~vels were used to move earth. The
~sel engine has made possible the
~ of a wide number of specialized
~es of machine.

th´ĭdr*a*). Authoritative(ly),
~icial(ly), said esp. of papal
~nouncements; **speak** ~, (of the
~pe) pronounce an infallible
~gment on matter of faith or
~rals. [L., = "from the chair"]
~**ex·ca·vate** (ĕks´kavāt) *v.t.*
~vat·ed, -vat·ing). Make hollow;
~ake (hole etc.) by digging; dig out
~oil) leaving a hole; unearth, get
~t, uncover, by digging. **ex·ca·**
~**tion** (ĕkskavā´sh*o*n), **ex´ca·va·**
~*r* *ns.*

~**ex·ceed** (ĭksēd´) *v.* Do more than
~ warranted by (one's authority,
~ghts, etc.); be greater than
~uantity, thing, *by* so much);
~rpass; be preeminent. **ex·ceed´-**
~g *adj.* **ex·ceed´ing·ly** *adv.*

~**ex·cel** (ĭksĕl´) *v.* (**-celled,**
~**el·ling**). Surpass; be preemi-
~nt.

~**ex·cel·lence** (ĕk´sel*e*ns) *n.* Sur-
~assing merit; thing in which
~rson etc. excels.

~**Ex·cel·len·cy** (ĕk´sel*e*nsē) *n.* (pl.
~**ies**). Title of ambassadors,
~shops, archbishops, governors,
~d some other high officers.

~**ex·cel·lent** (ĕk´sel*e*nt) *adj.* Pre-
~minent; very good. **ex´cel·lent·ly**
~*dv.*

~einheim and Neanderthal. The latter
~as living at the beginning of the last
~ Age; at the same time Modern Man,
~omo sapiens, Cro-Magnon, was
~olving, seemingly independently.
~esolithic and Neolithic are types of
~odern Man.

Neanderthal man   Cro Magnon   Mesolithic   Neolithic

*A painting of the **execution** of Charles I outside the Banqueting Hall, Whitehall, in 1649. He was the only English king to have been tried and sentenced to death by his subjects.*

ex·cel·si·or (ĭksĕl'sēer) *n.* Short thin shavings of soft wood for stuffing, packing, etc. ~ *adj.* (L.) Always upward; higher; used as motto on the New York State seal.

ex·cept[1] (ĭksĕpt') *v.* Exclude (thing) from enumeration, statement, etc.

ex·cept[2] (ĭksĕpt'), **ex·cept·ing** (ĭksĕp'tĭng) *preps. & conjs.* Not including; but, save, with the exception of; (archaic) unless.

ex·cep·tion (ĭksĕp'shon) *n.* Excepting; thing excepted, thing that does not follow the rule; (law) objection to ruling of court; **the ~ proves the rule**, the excepting of some cases shows that the rule exists, or that it applies to those not excepted; **take ~**, object *to.*

ex·cep·tion·al (ĭksĕp'shonal) *adj.* Forming an exception; unusual. **ex·cep'tion·al·ly** *adv.*

ex·cerpt (ĕk'serpt) *n.* Extract from book etc. ~ (ĭksĕrpt') *v.t.* Extract, quote, (passage *from* book etc.)

ex·cess (ĭksĕs', ĕk'sĕs) *n.* 1. (usu. pl.) Overstepping limits of moderation; (esp.) intemperance in eating or drinking. 2. Fact of exceeding; amount by which one quantity exceeds another; exceeding of proper amount or degree; ~ **baggage,** luggage over the weight or total dimensions ordinarily carried free and for which a passenger must pay an extra charge; ~ **profits tax,** tax levied on business profits in excess of average profits of a standard period.

ex·ces·sive (ĭksĕs'ĭv) *adj.* **ex·ces'sive·ly** *adv.*

ex·change (ĭkschānj') *v.* (**-changed, -chang·ing**). Give, receive, (thing) in place of (*for*) another; interchange (blows, words, glances, etc.). ~ *n.* 1. Act, process, of exchanging; exchanging of coin, notes, bank deposits, etc., for their equivalent in another country's money; (also ~ **rate, rate of** ~) price at which another country's money may be bought; difference between this and par. 2. Building where merchants, stockbrokers, etc., assemble to transact business. 3. (also **telephone** ~) Center to which local telephone lines are connected and through which communication between individual telephones is effected.

ex·change·a·ble (ĭkschān'jable) *adj.* That may be exchanged (*for*). **ex·change·a·bil'i·ty** *n.*

ex·cheq·uer (ĕks'chĕker, chĕk'-) *n.* 1. Brit. government department of public service charged with the collection and care of revenue. 2. Formerly a Brit. court dealing with matters of revenue etc. 3. Royal or national treasury (esp. Brit.); money of private person, society, etc. [f. *eschequier* f. med. L. *scaccarium* chessboard, from use of table with checkered cloth for accounts]

ex·cise[1] (ĕk'sīz, -sīs) *n.* Duty or tax levied on goods and commodities produced or sold within the country and on various licenses etc.

ex·cise[2] (ĭksīz') *v.t.* (**-cised, -cis·ing**). Cut out or away (passage of book, limb, organ, etc.). **ex·ci·sion** (ĭksĭzh'on) *n.*

ex·cite (ĭksīt') *v.t* (**-cit·ed, -cit·ing**). Set in motion, stir up, rouse

eelings, faculties, etc.); provoke,
ing about, stimulate (action,
tive condition); arouse (a person)
xually; move (person) to strong
notion, stir up to eager tumul-
ous feeling. **ex·cit′a·ble** *adj.*
sp., of persons) Easily excited.
x·cit·a·bil·i·ty (ĭksītabĭl′ĭtē), **ex-**
·ta·tion (ĕksītā′shon) *ns.* **ex-**
·t′ed·ly *adv.* **ex·cite·ment**
ksīt′ment) *n.*

excl. *abbrev.* Exclamation; exuding; exclusive.

ex·claim (ĭksklām′) *v.* Cry out,
p. from pain, anger, delight, etc.;
tter thus.

ex·cla·ma·tion (ĕksklamā′shon)
Exclaiming; words exclaimed;
iterjection; **~ mark, ~ point,**
unctuation mark (!) used after ex-
amation. **ex·clam·a·to·ry** (ĭk-
klăm′atōrē, -tōrē) *adj.*

ex·clude (ĭksklōōd′) *v.t.* **(-clud·**
d, -clud·ing). Shut out (*from*
lace, society, privilege, etc.); pre-
ent the occurrence of, make
npossible; leave out, not include.
x·clu·sion (ĭksklōō′zhon) *n.*

ex·clu·sive (ĭksklōō′sĭv) *adj.* 1.
hutting out; not admitting *of*;
esirous of excluding others, (of
ocial group etc.) chary of admitting
thers, select; (of news, goods, etc.)
ot to be had, not published, else-
here; (of terms etc.) excluding all
ut what is specified; employed,
ollowed, to the exclusion of all else.
. (quasi-*adv.*) **~ of,** not including,
ot counting. **ex·clu′sive·ly** *adv.*
x·clu′sive·ness *n.*

ex·com·mu·ni·cate (ĕkskomū′-
īkāt) *v.t.* **(-cat·ed, -cat·ing).**
eccles.) Cut off (person) from
participation in sacrament, or from
ll communication with Church.
x·com·mu·ni·ca·tion (ĕkskomū-
īkā′shon), **ex·com·mu′ni·ca·tor**
s. **ex·com·mu′ni·ca·tive, ex-**
om·mu′ni·ca·to·ry** *adjs.*

ex·co·ri·ate (ĭkskōr′ēāt, -skōr′-)
·t. **(-at·ed, -at·ing).** 1. Remove
part of skin of (person etc.) by
brasion etc.; strip, peel off (skin).
. Denounce; upbraid; berate
arshly. **ex·co·ri·a·tion** (ĭkskōr-
ā′shon, -skōr-) *n.*

ex·cre·ment (ĕk′skrement) *n.*
Waste matter discharged from the
ody, esp. feces. **ex·cre·men·tal**
ĕkskremĕn′tal) *adj.*

ex·cres·cence (ĭkskrĕs′ens) *n.*
Abnormal or morbid outgrowth on
animal or vegetable body (also fig.).
ex·cres·cent (ĭkskrĕs′ent) *adj.*
Growing abnormally, redundant.

ex·cre·ta (ĭkskrē′ta) *n.pl.* Waste
expelled from body, esp. feces and
urine.

ex·crete (ĭkskrēt′) *v.t.* **(-cret·ed,**
-cret·ing). (of animals, plants, etc.)
Separate and expel (waste matters)
from system. **ex·cre′tion** *n.*
ex·cre′tive, ex·cre·to·ry (ĕk′-
skretōrē, -tōrē) *adjs.*

ex·cru·ci·ate (ĭkskrōō′shēāt) *v.t.*

(-at·ed, -at·ing). Torture physically or mentally. **ex·cru′ci·at-**
ing·ly *adv.* **ex·cru·ci·a·tion** (ĭk-
skrōōshēā′shon) *n.*

ex·cul·pate (ĕk′skŭlpāt, ĭk-
skŭl′-) *v.t.* **(-pat·ed, -pat·ing).**
Free from blame; clear (*from* charge
etc.). **ex·cul·pa·tion** (ĕkskŭlpā′-
shon) *n.* **ex·cul·pa·to·ry**
(ĭkskŭl′patōrē, -tōrē) *adj.*

ex·cur·sion (ĭkskĕr′zhon, -shon)
n. 1. Journey or ramble from any
place with intention of returning to
it; pleasure trip, esp. one taken by
a number of persons; **~ fare,** reduced rate for a round-trip ticket on
a train, bus, etc., usu. with time
limits for departure and return; **~**
flight, trip by airplane to specified
place(s), for which limited group of
individuals pay excursion fare. 2.
Sortie, military raid (obs. exc. in
alar(u)ms and ~s). 3. (astron.)
Deviation from regular path or
course. **ex·cur′sion·ist** *n.* One
who makes pleasure excursion.

ex·cur·sive (ĭkskĕr′sĭv) *adj.*
Desultory; erratic, digressive, in
writing or speech. **ex·cur′sive·ly**
adv. **ex·cur′sive·ness** *n.*

ex·cuse (ĭkskūz′) *v.t.* **(-cused,**
-cus·ing). 1. Attempt to clear
(person) from blame without denying or justifying his imputed action;
seek to remove or extenuate blame
of (acknowledged fault); serve as
excuse for. 2. Obtain exemption or
release for, set free, (person) from
task, duty, obligation. 3. Accept
apology for, overlook, condone;

pardon faults of, regard indulgently; dispense with. 4. **~ me,**
used as apology for lack of ceremony, interruption, etc., or as
polite way of disputing statement;
~ oneself, ask permission to leave.
ex·cus′a·ble *adj.* **excuse** (ĭkskūs′)
n. Apology offered, exculpation;
ground of this; plea for release from
duty etc.

ex·e·cra·ble (ĕk′sekrabel) *adj.*
Abominable. **ex′e·cra·bly** *adv.*

ex·e·crate (ĕk′sekrāt) *v.* **(-crat·**
ed, -crat·ing). Express, feel,
abhorrence for; utter curses. **ex·e-**
cra·tion (ĕksekrā′shon), **ex′e·cra-**
tor *ns.*

ex·ec·u·tant (ĭgzĕk′yutant) *n.*
One who executes, performer (esp.
of music).

ex·e·cute (ĕk′sekūt) *v.t.* **(-cut-**
ed, -cut·ing). 1. Carry (plan,
command, law, will, judicial sentence) into effect; perform (action,
operation, etc.); make (legal instrument) valid by signing, sealing, etc.;
discharge (office, function). 2.
Carry out design for (product of art
or skill); perform (musical composition). 3. Inflict capital punishment
on.

ex·e·cu·tion (ĕksekū′shon) *n.*
Executing; manner of executing;
effective action; infliction of capital

The ornate New York **Stock Exchange,**
*commercial and financial focal point of
the western world, dominates Wall
Street.*

punishment. **ex·e·cu′tion·er** *n.* One who carries out a capital sentence.

ex·ec·u·tive (ĭgzĕk′yutĭv) *adj.* Pertaining to, having function of, executing; concerned with executing laws, decrees, and sentences; ~ **order**, president's order on administrative matter not requiring legislation; ~ **session**, private legislative session to deal with executive business; hence, private meeting. **executive** *n.* 1. Executive branch of government. 2. Person holding executive position in business etc.; executive official.

ex·ec·u·tor (ĭgzĕk′yuter) *n.* 1. One who carries out or performs. 2. Person appointed by testator to execute his will; **literary** ~, person entrusted with papers and unpublished works of writer. **ex·ec·u·to·ri·al** (ĭgzĕkyutōr′ēal, -tōr′-) *adj.* **ex·ec′u·tor·ship** *n.*

ex·ec·u·trix (ĭgzĕk′yutrĭks) *n.* (pl. **ex·ec·u·tri·ces** pr. ĭgzĕkyutrī′sēz, **ex·ec·u·trix·es**). Female executor.

ex·e·ge·sis (ĕksejē′sĭs) *n.* (pl. **-ses** pr. -sēz). Critical exposition, interpretation, esp. of Scripture. **ex·e·get·ic** (ĕksejĕt′ĭk), **ex·e·get′i·cal** *adjs.* **ex·e·get′i·cal·ly** *adv.*

ex·e·gete (ĕk′sejēt) *n.* Person skilled in exegesis.

ex·em·plar (ĭgzĕm′pler, -plär) *n.* Worthy model; pattern; typical example.

ex·em·pla·ry (ĭgzĕm′plerē) *adj.* Fit to be imitated; illustrative; (of penalty, damages) serving as a warning. **ex·em′pla·ri·ly** *adv.* **ex·em′pla·ri·ness** *n.*

ex·em·pli·fy (ĭgzĕm′plĭfī) *v.t.* (**-fied, -fy·ing**). Illustrate by example; be example of. 2. Make official copy of; make attested copy of (public document).

ex·empt (ĭgzĕmpt′) *adj.* Freed *from* allegiance or liability to; ~ **from**, not liable, exposed, or subject to (charge, duty, etc.). ~ *n.* Exempted person. ~ *v.t.* Grant to (person) immunity or freedom *from.* **ex·emp′tion** *n.*

ex·e·quies (ĕk′sekwēz) *n.pl.* Funeral rites.

ex·er·cise (ĕk′sersīz) *n.* 1. Employment (of organ, faculty, power, right); practice (of virtues, profession, functions, religious rites). 2. Exertion of muscles, limbs, etc., esp. for health's sake; (pl.) military drill, athletics, etc. 3. Bodily, mental, or spiritual training; task set for this purpose; composition etc. assigned to pupils at school; piece of music etc. designed to afford practice to learners. 4. Ceremony on some special occasion. ~ *v.* (**-cised, -cis·ing**). Employ (faculty, right, etc.); train (person etc.); tax the powers of; discharge (functions); take, give (dog etc.), exercise.

ex·ert (ĭgzĕrt′) *v.t.* Exercise, bring to bear (quality, force, influence); ~ **oneself**, use efforts or endeavors, strive. **ex·er·tion** (ĭgzĕr′shon) *n.* Exerting; vigorous action, effort.

ex·e·unt (ĕk′sēunt). (stage direction) They (2 or more actors) leave the stage. [L., = "they go out"]

ex·ha·la·tion (ĕks-halā′shon) *n.* Exhaling; what is exhaled.

ex·hale (ĕks-hāl′, ĕks′hāl) *v.* (**-haled, -hal·ing**). Give off, be given off, in vapor, evaporate; breathe out.

ex·haust (ĭgzawst′) *v.* 1. Draw off (air); empty (vessel) of contents. 2. Consume entirely; use, account for, the whole of; treat or study (subject etc.) so as to leave nothing further to be explained or discovered. 3. Drain (person etc.) of strength, resources, etc.; tire out. **ex·haust′i·ble** *adj.* **ex·haust·i·bil·i·ty** (ĭgzawstĭbĭl′ĭtē) *n.* **exhaust** *n.* Expulsion or exit of vaporous waste material from an engine; fumes or gases expelled thus; (also ~ **pipe**) pipe by which they escape.

ex·haus·tion (ĭgzaws′chon) *n.* (esp.) Total loss of energy.

ex·haus·tive (ĭgzaws′tĭv) *adj.* (esp.) Comprehensive, exhausting a subject. **ex·haus′tive·ly** *adv.* **ex·haus′tive·ness** *n.*

ex·hib·it (ĭgzĭb′ĭt) *v.t.* Show,

Exercise takes many forms. It can be passive and relaxing, or strenuous and exhausting. Modern man seem[s] obsessed with fitness, evidenced b[y] the many gyms and fitness record[s] available.

display; submit (document) for inspection; manifest (quality); show publicly. ~ *n.* 1. (law) Document or thing formally introduced as evidence in court. 2. Thing, collection of things, sent by person, firm, etc. to exhibition, or on permanent show in museum etc. **ex·hib′it·er**, **ex·hib′i·tor** *ns.*

ex·hi·bi·tion (ĕksĭbĭsh′on) *n.* Showing, exhibiting, display; public display (of works of art, manufactured articles, etc.), place where this is held.

ex·hi·bi·tion·ism (ĕksĭbĭsh′onĭzem) *n.* Tendency toward display, extravagant behavior; (psychol.) compulsive indecent exposure. **ex·hi·bi′tion·ist** *n.*

ex·hil·a·rate (ĭgzĭl′erāt) *v.t.* (**-rat·ed, -rat·ing**). Enliven, invigorate, gladden (person, spirits). **ex·hil·a·ra·tion** (ĭgzĭlerā′shon) *n.*

ex·hort (ĭgzōrt′) *v.t.* Admonish earnestly; urge (*to*). **ex·hor·ta·tion** (ĕgzōrtā′shon, ĕksōr-) *n.* **ex·hor′ta·tive** *adj.*

ex·hume (ĭgzōom′, -zūm′, ĕks·hūm′) *v.t.* (**-humed, -hum·ing**)

ig out (something buried), un-
rth. **ex·hu·ma·tion** (ĕks-hūmā´-
ion) n.

ex·i·gen·cy (ĕk´sĭjensē), **ex·i-
ence** (ĕk´sĭjens) ns. (pls. **-cies,
gences**). 1. Quality or state of
eing urgent. 2. (usu. ~**cies**)
emand or need that is an essen-
al of a situation, condition, etc.
x´i·gent adj. Urgent, pressing;
xacting.

ex·ig·u·ous (ĭgzĭg´ūus, ĭksĭ´-) adj.
canty, small. **ex·ig·u·i·ty**
ksĭgū´ĭtē), **ex·ig´u·ous·ness** ns.

ex·ile (ĕg´zīl, ĕk´sīl) n. 1.
anishment; long absence from
ne's country; **the E~**, esp.,
aptivity of Jews in Babylon in 6th
B.C. 2. Exiled person; one
ving in a foreign country. **exile**
.t. (**-iled, -il·ing**). Banish (from).

ex·ist (ĭgzĭst´) v.i. Have objective
eing; have being in specified place
r under specified conditions;
ccur, be found; live; continue in
eing. **ex·ist·ence** (ĭgzĭs´tens) n. Being,
xisting; life; mode of existing; all
at exists; existing thing.

ex·ist·ent (ĭgzĭs´tent) adj. Exist-
ng, actual, current.

ex·is·ten·tial (ĕgzĭstĕn´shal,
ksĭs-) adj. Of or relating to
xistence; (logic, of a proposition)
redicating existence; of existen-
alism. **ex·is·ten´tial·ism** n.
hilosophic theory emphasizing
xistence of the individual as free
nd responsible agent determining
is own development. **ex·is·ten´-
ial·ist** adj. & n.

ex·it[1] (ĕg´zĭt, ĕk´sĭt) n. Depar-
ure of actor from stage (also fig.);
eath; going out or forth, liberty
o do this; way out.

ex·it[2] (ĕg´zĭt, ĕk´sĭt) v.i. (stage
irection) Goes off stage. [L., =
goes out"]

ex li·bris (ĕks lē´brĭs, lĭb´rĭs).
rom the library of (person whose
ame follows); as used on book-
lates. [L.]

exo- prefix. Outside; external.

ex·o·crine (ĕk´sokrĭn, -krēn,
krīn) adj. & n. (Gland) secreting
xternally, through a duct.

Exod. abbrev. Exodus (Old
Testament).

ex·o·der·mis (ĕksōdĕr´mĭs) n.
Outer layer of blastoderm.

Ex·o·dus (ĕk´sodus). Second
book of Old Testament, relating
eparture of Israelites from Egypt.

ex·o·dus (ĕk´sodus) n. Depar-
ure, esp. in considerable numbers;
he **E~**, departure of Israelites
rom Egypt under the leadership of
Moses.

ex of·fi·ci·o (ĕks ofĭsh´ēō). By
virtue of one's office. [L.]

ex·og·a·mous (ĕksŏg´amus) adj.
Following the custom compelling
man to marry outside his own tribe
or group. **ex·og´a·my** n.

ex·og·e·nous (ĕksŏj´enus) adj.
Growing or originating externally.

ex·on·er·ate (ĭgzŏn´erāt) v.t.
(**-at·ed, -at·ing**). Exculpate; free
(person) from (blame etc.); release
(person from duty etc.). **ex·on·er-
a·tion** (ĭgzŏnerā´shon) n.

**ex·oph·thal·mos, ex·oph-
thal·mus** (ĕksŏfthăl´mos) ns. Abnormal protrusion of eyeball,
caused by injury or disease. **ex-
oph·thal´mic** adj.

ex·or·bi·tant (ĭgzŏr´bĭtant) adj.
Grossly excessive (of price, demand, ambition, person). **ex·or´-
bi·tance** n. **ex·or´bi·tant·ly** adv.

ex·or·cise, ex·or·cize (ĕk´sŏrsīz,
-ser-) vbs.t. (**-cised, -cis·ing,
-cized, -ciz·ing**). Expel (evil spirit
from, out of, person or place) by
invocation or use of holy name; clear
(person, place, of evil spirits).
ex·or·cism (ĕk´sŏrsīzem, -ser-),
ex·or·cist ns.

ex·o·skel·e·ton (ĕksōskĕl´eton)
n. External skeleton, as of insect,
crustacean, etc.

ex·o·sphere (ĕk´sōsfēr) n.
Outermost layer of atmosphere,
beginning at 300–600 mi. above the
Earth.

ex·o·ter·ic (ĕksotĕr´ĭk) adj. (of
doctrines, mode of speech, etc.)
Intelligible to outsiders; (of disciples) not admitted to esoteric
teaching; commonplace, ordinary,
popular. **ex·o·ter´i·cal·ly** adv.

ex·o·ther·mic (ĕksōthēr´mĭk),
ex·o·ther·mal (ĕksōthēr´mal) adjs.
(chem.) Liberating, as opposed to
absorbing, heat.

ex·ot·ic (ĭgzŏt´ĭk) adj. (of plants,
words, fashions) Introduced from
abroad; strange, bizarre; ~ **dancer**, striptease, belly dancer, nude
or partially clothed dancer, etc.
exotic n. Exotic plant (also fig.).

exp. abbrev. Expenses; experi-
ment(al); export; express.

ex·pand (ĭkspănd´) v. 1. Spread
out flat or smooth; unfold, open
out; swell, increase in bulk. 2.
Expound, write out, in full (what
is condensed or abbreviated, algebraic expression, etc.). 3. Become
genial or talkative, throw off
reserve. **ex·pand´a·ble** adj. & n.
ex·pan·si·ble (ĭkspăn´sĭbel) adj.

ex·panse (ĭkspăns´) n. Wide area
or extent; expansion.

*Expo 70, Japan, the U.S.S.R. Pavilion.
Large international industrial **exhibitions** with ancillary attractions stem
largely from The Great Exhibition held in
London, U.K. in 1851.*

*Ra II, a papyrus-reed vessel in which Thor Heyerdahl crossed the Atlantic in 1970 from Safi, Morocco, to Bridgetown, Barbados, to show that the early Egyptians could have made such an **expedition** to the New World.*

ex·pan·sile (ĭkspăn′sĭl, -sīl) *adj.* (Capable) of expansion.

ex·pan·sion (ĭkspăn′shon) *n.* Expanding; increasing, increase, extension (of trade, territory, etc.); increase in bulk. **ex·pan′sion·ism** *n.* **ex·pan′sion·ist** *adj. & n.* (Advocate of) policy or theory of expansion, esp. of territory.

ex·pan·sive (ĭkspăn′sĭv) *adj.* Able, tending, to expand; extensive; comprehensive; (of persons, feelings, speech) effusive. **ex·pan′sive·ly** *adv.* **ex·pan′sive·ness** *n.*

ex par·te (ĕks pär′tē). (law) On, in interests of, one side only; made or said thus.

ex·pa·ti·ate (ĭkspā′shēāt) *v.i.* (**-at·ed, -at·ing**). Speak, write, copiously (*on* subject). **ex·pa·ti·a·tion** (ĭkspāshēā′shon) *n.*

ex·pa·tri·ate (ĕkspā′trēāt) *v.t.* (**-at·ed, -at·ing**). Banish; (*refl.*) withdraw from one's country, renounce one's citizenship. **ex·pa·tri·a·tion** (ĕkspātrēā′shon) *n.* **ex·pa·tri·ate** (ĕkspā′trĕĭt, -āt) *adj. & n.* Expatriated (person); (person) living in a foreign country.

ex·pect (ĭkspĕkt′) *v.t.* Look forward to, regard as likely; look for, anticipate coming of (person or thing); (colloq.) think, suppose. **ex·pect′er** *n.*

ex·pect·an·cy (ĭkspĕk′tănsē) *n.* (pl. **-cies**). State of expectation; prospect, esp. of future possession;

prospective chance (*of*).

ex·pect·ant (ĭkspĕk′tant) *adj.* Expecting; having the prospect, in normal course, of possession, office, etc.; (law) reversionary; ~ **mother**, pregnant woman. **ex·pect′ant·ly** *adv.* **ex·pec′tant** *adj. & n.*

ex·pec·ta·tion (ĕkspĕktā′shon) *n.* Awaiting; anticipation; ground for expecting; (pl.) prospects, esp. of inheritance; being expected; thing expected.

ex·pec·to·rate (ĭkspĕk′terāt) *v.t.* (**-rat·ed, -rat·ing**). Eject (phlegm or other material) from lung airways by coughing; spit. **ex·pec·to·ra·tion** (ĭkspĕk′terāshon) *n.* **ex·pec·to·rant** (ĭkspĕk′terant) *adj. & n.* (Medicine) promoting expectoration.

ex·pe·di·ent (ĭkspē′dēent) *adj.* Advantageous, suitable; politic rather than just. **ex·pe′di·ent·ly** *adv.* **ex·pe′di·ence, ex·pe′di·en·cy** *ns.* **expedient** *n.* Contrivance, device; means to an end.

ex·pe·dite (ĕk′spedīt) *v.t.* (**-dit·ed, -dit·ing**). Speed up, facilitate progress of (measure, process, etc.); dispatch (business).

ex·pe·di·tion (ĕkspedĭsh′on) *n.* 1. Warlike enterprise; journey voyage, excursion, for definite pur pose; body of persons, fleet, etc sent out for warlike or other definit purpose. 2. Promptness, speed **ex·pe·di′tion·ar·y** *adj.*

ex·pe·di·tious (ĕkspedĭsh′us adj. Doing, done, speedily; suite to speedy performance. **ex·pe·di′tious·ly** *adv.* **ex·pe·di′tious·nes** *n.*

ex·pel (ĭkspĕl′) *v.t.* (**-pelled -pel·ling**). Eject (*from*) by force turn out (person *from* community school, etc.).

ex·pend (ĭkspĕnd′) *v.t.* Spend (money, time, care, etc.); use up consume. **ex·pend′a·ble** *adj.* Tha can be expended or spared; (mil. that may be sacrificed in order t accomplish an objective.

ex·pend·i·ture (ĭkspĕn′dĭcher *n.* Laying out, spending; con suming; amount expended.

ex·pense (ĭkspĕns′) *n.* Expendi ture cost; (pl.) outlay in perform ing one's job etc.; reimbursemen of this.

ex·pen·sive (ĭkspĕn′sĭv) *adj* Costly. **ex·pen′sive·ly** *adv.*

ex·pe·ri·ence (ĭkspēr′ēens) *n.* 1. Actual observation of facts o events; knowledge resulting from this. 2. Event that affects one fact, process, of being so affected ~ *v.t.* (**-enced, -enc·ing**). Mee

th, feel, undergo (pleasure, treat-
nt, fate, etc.); learn, find.
·pe′ri·enced adj. (esp.) Having
perience, wise or skillful through
perience. **ex·pe·ri·en′tial** (ĭk-
ērēēn′shăl) adj. **ex·pe·ri·en′-**
·al·ly adv.

ex·per·i·ment (ĭkspĕr′ĭmĕnt,
pēr′-) n. Action or operation
dertaken in order to discover
mething unknown, test hypoth-
s, illustrate known fact, etc.;
thod etc. adopted in un-
rtainty whether it will answer the
rpose. ~ (ĭkspĕr′ĭmĕnt, -spēr′-)
. Conduct experiment (on, with).
ex·per·i·men·tal (ĭkspĕrĭmĕn′-
, -spēr′-) adj. 1. Based on, derived
m, experience; empirical. 2.
sed on experiment; of, used in,
periments. **ex·per·i·men′tal·ly**
v.

ex·pert (ĕk′spērt, ĭkspērt′) adj.
ained by practice, skillful (at, in).
·pert′ly adv. **ex·pert′ness** n.
pert (ĕk′spērt) n. Person having
ecial skill or knowledge (freq.
trib.).

ex·pert·ise (ĕkspērtēz′) n. Ex-
rt skill or knowledge.

ex·pi·ate (ĕk′spēāt) v.t. (-at·ed,
t·ing). Pay penalty of, make
ends or atonement for (sin).
·pi·a·ble (ĕk′spēabel), **ex·pi·a-**
·ry (ĕk′spēatōrē, -tōrē) adjs.
·pi·a·tion (ĕkspēā′shon), **ex′-**
·a·tor ns.

ex·pi·ra·tion (ĕkspērā′shon) n.
. Breathing out. 2. Termination
f period of time, something made
last a certain time); ending.
·pir·a·to·ry (ĕkspīr′atōrē, -tōrē)
j.

ex·pire (ĭkspīr′) v. (-pired,
ir·ing). 1. Breathe out. 2. Die;
f fire etc.) die out. 3. (of period)
ome to an end; (of law, patent,
c.) become void, reach its term.

ex·plain (ĭksplān′) v. Give de-
ils of; make plain or intelligible;
ve explanation; interpret; make
ear cause, origin, or reason of,
count for; ~ **away**, modify, do
vay with, by explanation; ~ **one-**
·lf, make one's meaning clear, give
count of one's motives or in-
ntions.

ex·pla·na·tion (ĕksplanā′shon)
Explaining, esp. with view to
utual understanding or recon-
liation; statement, circumstance,
at explains.

ex·plan·a·to·ry (ĭksplăn′atōrē,
ōrē) adj. Serving, meant, to ex-
ain. **ex·plan·a·to′ri·ly** adv.

ex·ple·tive (ĕk′spletĭv) adj.
rving to fill out; (of words etc.)
rving to fill out sentence, metrical
ne, etc. ~ n. Expletive word or
rase, esp. exclamation; oath, esp.

an obscene or profane one.
ex·pli·ca·ble (ĕk′splĭkabel, ĭk-
splĭk′-) adj. That may be explained.
ex·pli·cate (ĕk′splĭkāt) v.t.
(-cat·ed, -cat·ing). 1. Develop
(notion, principle, proposition). 2.
Explain; interpret (text). **ex′pli-**
ca·tive, ex′pli·ca·to·ry adjs.
ex·plic·it (ĭksplĭs′ĭt) adj. Stated
in detail, leaving nothing merely
implied; definite; (of persons) outspoken. **ex·plic′it·ly** adv. **ex-**

plic′it·ness n.
ex·plode (ĭksplōd′) v. (-plod·ed,
-plod·ing). 1. Bring into disrepute, expose hollowness of
(theory, belief, etc.). 2. (Cause to)
go off with loud noise; (of gunpowder etc.) expand violently with
loud report under influence of
suddenly developed internal
energy; (of shell, etc.) burst from
similar cause; (of boiler etc.) burst
from excessive pressure of steam
inside it. 3. Give vent suddenly to

bove right: Miners **explode** copper
posits at Bougainville Island so that
e ore can be easily removed. Right:
n explosion during a military exercise.

Discoveries 1400–1600

Spanish discoveries   Portuguese discoveries   English discoveries   French discoveries
——— Magellan   ——— Dias   ——— Cabot   ——— Cartier
• • • Columbus   - - - Vasco da Gama   → Drake
· · · · Vespucci   known lands

emotion. 4. (of population etc.) Increase suddenly or rapidly.

ex·plod·ed (ĭksplō′dĭd) *adj.* (esp., of diagram etc.) Showing components of a machine etc. separately but retaining their relative positions (as in ~ **view**).

ex·ploit[1] (ĕk′sploit, ĭksploit′) *n.* Heroic or spectacular feat.

ex·ploit[2] (ĭksploit′) *v.t.* Work, turn to account (mine etc.); make use of (person etc.), esp. unfairly or selfishly. **ex·ploit′a·ble** *adj.* **ex·ploi·ta·tion** (ĕksploitā′shon) *n.*

ex·plore (ĭksplōr′, -splôr′-) *v.t.* (**-plored, -plor·ing**). 1. Investigate (condition, fact); examine, pry into; probe, examine by touch (wound etc.). 2. Search into, examine region, place, etc. by going through it; go into, range over, for purpose of discovery. **ex·plo·ra·tion** (ĕksplorā′shon), **ex·plor′er** *ns.* **ex·plor′a·tive, ex·plor′a·to·ry** *adjs.*

ex·plo·sion (ĭksplō′zhon) *n.* Exploding; resulting noise, detonation; sudden marked increase, esp. **population** ~; outburst (of anger etc.).

ex·plo·sive (ĭksplō′sĭv) *adj.* Tending to drive something forth with violence and noise; tending to explode or cause explosion; of, like, explosion; (of consonant) produced by explosion of breath, stopped. **ex·plo′sive·ly** *adv.* **ex·plo′sive·ness** *n.* **explosive** *n.* 1. Explosive

Map of routes of **exploration.** *The motives for exploration include economic necessity and pure curiosity, personal ambition and the desire of a country for expansion. It is from Europe that the history of exploration emanates, for it was Europeans who stretched the world map consistently by sea and land.*

agent or compound; **high** ~, kind having violent and shattering effect and used not as propellant but in shells, bombs, etc. 2. Explosive consonant.

ex·po·nent (ĭkspō′nent; for def. 2 also ĕk′spōnent) *n.* 1. Person or thing that sets forth or interprets; type, representative. 2. (alg.) Index; symbol denoting number of times particular quantity is to be taken as factor to produce the power indicated. **ex·po·nen·tial** (ĕkspōnĕn′shal) *adj.* (esp., math.) Involving the unknown quantity as (part of) an exponent. ~ *n.* Exponential quantity or function.

ex·port (ĭkspōrt′, -spôrt′, ĕk′spōrt, -spôrt) *v.t.* Send out (goods) to another country. **ex·port′a·ble** *adj.* **ex·por·ta·tion** (ĕkspōrtā′shon, -spôr-) *n.* **export** (ĕk′spōrt, -spôrt) *n.* Exported article; (usu. pl.) (amount exported); exportation.

ex·pose (ĭkspōz′) *v.t.* (**-posed, -pos·ing**). 1. Leave, place, in unsheltered or unprotected position; (fig.) lay open, subject (*to* risk etc.). 2. Exhibit, display; disclose (secret,

project, etc.); unmask, show (fault, guilty person, etc.). (photog.) Subject (sensitized surface of film etc.) to action of actinic rays.

ex·po·sé (ĕkspōzā′) *n.* Statement of facts; showing up (of discreditable thing). [Fr.]

ex·po·si·tion (ĕkspozĭsh′on) *n.* 1. Exposure; exhibition. 2. Setting forth, description; explanation, commentary. 3. (mus.) Presentation of principal theme(s).

ex·pos·i·to·ry (ĭkspŏz′ĭtō, -tōrē) *adj.* Descriptive; explanatory.

ex post fac·to (ĕks′ pōst făk′tō) Acting retrospectively or retroactively. [L., = "from what is made (i.e. enacted) afterward"]

ex·pos·tu·late (ĭkspŏs′chulāt) *v.i.* (**-lat·ed, -lat·ing**). Reason earnestly against something; make (esp. friendly) remonstrance. **ex·pos·tu·la·tion** (ĭkspŏschulā′shon) *n.* **ex·pos′tu·la·to·ry** *adj.*

ex·po·sure (ĭkspō′zher) *n.* 1. Exposing, being exposed; (time taken in) exposing of photographic film etc.; area of film exposed for single photograph. 2. (of building etc.) Aspect. 3. Frequent public appearance, as on television. Condition of being exposed in helpless state to natural elements; **indecent** ~, intentional act publicly and indecently exposing one's body; ~ **meter**, phot-

'Madonna', a lithograph by Edvard Munch (1863–1944). Munch was a leading exponent of **Expressionism**, a movement in art which set out to express human emotions rather than to portray the physical world.

ectric device indicating correct ength of time for film etc. to be xposed.

ex·pound (ĭkspownd´) v.t. Set orth in detail (doctrine etc.); ex-lain, interpret.

ex·press[1] (ĭkspres´) adj. 1. (of ikeness) Exact; definitely stated, ot merely implied. 2. Done, made, ent, for special purpose; ~ **high-vay**, major highway of four or nore traffic lanes with limited ccess and no or very few cross-oads, traffic lights, etc., esp. for igh-speed travel over long dis-ances; ~ **train**, fast train stopping nly at a few important stations orig., train run expressly to convey passengers to a particular place); so ~ **bus** etc. 3. (to be delivered) By fastest means (so ~ **letter, air** ~, etc.). **ex·press´ly** adv. **ex·press** adv. With speed; by express messenger, train, etc. **ex·press** n. Express train or bus etc.; company for transporting packages etc.; ~ **agent**, agent of express company. **express** v.t. Send by express (delivery).

ex·press[2] (ĭkspres´) v.t. 1. Press, squeeze, or wring out; emit, exude, as if by pressure. 2. Represent by drawing etc. or by figures or other symbols; represent in language, put into words; (refl.) put one's thought into words; manifest, reveal, communicate (feelings, personal qualities, etc.).

ex·pres·sion (ĭkspresh´on) n. Expressing; wording, diction, word, phrase; (alg.) collection of symbols together expressing algebraical quantity; expressive quality; aspect (of face), intonation (of voice), etc.; manner of musical performance suited to bringing out feeling of passage; (painting etc.)

mode of expressing character. **ex·pres'sion·less** *adj.* Lacking expression; impassive.

ex·pres·sion·ism (ĭkspresh'on-ĭzem) *n.* (freq. cap.) Movement in art, literature, and music in late 19th and early 20th centuries seeking to express emotional experience rather than impressions of the physical world. **ex·pres'sion·ist** *adj.* & *n.* **ex·pres·sion·is·tic** (ĭkspreshonĭs'tĭk) *adj.* **ex·pres·sion·is·ti·cal·ly** *adv.*

ex·pres·sive (ĭkspres'ĭv) *adj.* Of expression, serving to express; full of, emphatic in, expression; significant. **ex·pres'sive·ly** *adv.* **ex·pres'sive·ness** *n.*

ex·press·way (ĭkspres'wā) *n.* Express highway; see EXPRESS[1].

ex·pro·pri·ate (ĕkspro'prēāt) *v.t.* (**-at·ed, -at·ing**). Deprive of, take away (property), esp. for public use; take and use (another's work, idea, etc.) as one's own. **ex·pro·pri·a·tion** (ĕksprōprēā'-shon) *n.*

ex·pul·sion (ĭkspŭl'shon) *n.* Expelling.

ex·punge (ĭkspŭnj') *v.t.* (**-punged, -pung·ing**). Erase, omit, strike out.

ex·pur·gate (ĕk'spergāt) *v.t.* (**-gated, -gat·ing**). Purify (book etc.) by removing objectionable matter; clear away (such matter). **ex·pur·ga·tion** (ĕkspergā'shon), **ex'pur·ga·tor** *ns.*

ex·qui·site (ĕkskwĭz'ĭt, ĕk'-skwĭzĭt) *adj.* Of consummate excellence or beauty; acute; keen. **ex·qui'site·ly** *adv.* **ex·qui'site·ness** *n.*

ext. *abbrev.* Extension; external; extra; extract.

ex·tant (ĕk'stant, ĭkstănt') *adj.* Still existing (esp. of documents etc.).

ex·tem·po·re (ĭkstĕm'perē) *adv.* & *adj.* (Spoken, done) without preparation; offhand. **ex·tem·po·ra·ne·ous** (ĭkstĕmperā'nēus) *adj.* **ex·tem·po·ra·ne·ous·ly** *adv.* **ex·tem·po·rar·y** (ĭkstĕm'perĕrē) *adj.*

ex·tem·po·rize (ĭkstĕm'perīz) *v.* (**-rized, -riz·ing**). Compose, produce, speak extemporaneously. **ex·tem·po·ri·za·tion** (ĭkstĕmperī-zā'shon) *n.*

ex·tend (ĭkstĕnd') *v.* 1. Place (esp. body, limbs, etc.) at full length. 2. Reach, cause to reach (*to* point, *over*, *across*, etc., space). 3. Prolong (period); enlarge (scope, meaning, of word, etc.). 4. (mil.) Spread out, cause (line etc.) to spread out, into open order with regular intervals between men. 5. Tax powers of (horse, athlete, etc.) to the utmost. 6. Stretch forth (hand, arm); accord (kindness, patronage, *to*). 7. (law) Seize (land etc.) for debt. **ex·tend'ed** *adj.* ~ **care**, nursing care given at home or

in nursing homes to persons unable to care for themselves; ~ **family**, family unit consisting of parents, children, and other near relatives, all living in close proximity. **ex·tend'i·ble, ex·tend'a·ble, ex·ten'si·ble** *adjs.* **ex·tend·i·bil·i·ty** (ĭkstĕndĭbĭl'ĭtē), **ex·tend'er** *ns.*

ex·ten·sile (ĭkstĕn'sĭl, -sīl) *adj.* Capable of being stretched out or protruded.

ex·ten·sion (ĭkstĕn'shon) *n.* Extending; extent, range; prolongation, enlargement; additional part, building, line, etc. (of railroad, plan, theory, etc.); subsidiary telephone; (**university**) ~ **course**, one offered away from the campus.

ex·ten·sive (ĭkstĕn'sĭv) *adj.* Large; far-reaching, comprehensive; (of agricultural production) cultivating vast areas with a minimum of labor and expense. **ex·ten'sive·ly** *adv.* **ex·ten'sive·ness** *n.*

ex·ten·sor (ĭkstĕn'ser, -sōr) *n.* Muscle serving to extend or straighten out any part of body (opp. FLEXOR).

ex·tent (ĭkstĕnt') *n.* 1. Space over which thing extends; width of application, scope. 2. (law) Writ for creditor's temporary seizure, (of lands etc.).

ex·ten·u·ate (ĭkstĕn'ūāt) *v.t.* (**-at·ed, -at·ing**). Lessen seeming magnitude of (guilt, offense) by partial excuse, as in **extenuating circumstances. ex·ten·u·a·tion** (ĭkstĕnūā'shon) *n.*

ex·te·ri·or (ĭkstēr'ēer) *adj.* Outer, situated or coming from without; ~ **angle**, that between any side of a polygon and adjacent side produced. **ex·te'ri·or·ly** *adv.* **exterior** *n.* Outward aspect or demeanor; (film) outdoor scene.

ex·ter·mi·nate (ĭkstēr'mĭnāt) *v.t.* (**-nat·ed, -nat·ing**). Destroy utterly, root out (species, race, etc.).

ex·ter·mi·na·tion (ĭkstērmĭna-shon), **ex·ter'mi·na·tor** *ns.*

ex·tern (ĕk'stĕrn) *n.* Pers having some association with institution but not living in it, es a nonresident physician in hospital.

ex·ter·nal (ĭkstĕr'nal) *adj.* Sit ated outside; (of remedies et applied to outside of body; consis ing in outward acts or appearance belonging to external world things or phenomena, considered outside the perceiving min arising, acting, from without, co nected with, referring to, what outside; ~ **evidence**, eviden derived from source independe of the thing discussed. **ex·ter nal·i·ty** (ĕkstērnăl'ĭtē) *n.* (pl. **-ties ex·ter'nal·ly** *adv.* **ex·ter'na** *n.pl.* Outward features or aspec external circumstances; no essentials.

ex·ter·nal·ize (ĭkstĕr'nalīz) *v.* (**-ized, -iz·ing**). Give, attribut external existence to. **ex·ter·nal i·za·tion** (ĭkstērnalīzā'shon) *n.*

ex·tinct (ĭkstĭngkt') *adj.* (of fi etc.) No longer burning; (volcano) that has ceased eruptio (of life, hope, etc.) quenched; (family, class, species) that has die out.

ex·tinc·tion (ĭkstĭngk'shon) Extinguishing; making, being, b coming, extinct. **ex·tinc'tive** *adj*

ex·tin·guish (ĭkstĭng'gwĭsh) *v.* Put out, quench (light, hope, lif etc.); eclipse, obscure (person) b superior brilliance.; wipe ou (debt). **ex·tin'guish·a·ble** *adj.*

ex·tin·guish·er (ĭkstĭng'gwĭsh er) *n.* (esp.) Hollow conical cap fo

---

After the hard work of training, and th tensions of competition, the winner ha the right to **exult** *and be jubilant. Below an exultant marathon runner (Robert d Castella) holds up his medal.*

tinguishing light of candle etc.; RE extinguisher.

ex·tir·pate (ĕk′sterpāt, ĭkstēr′-) t. (**-pat·ed, -pat·ing**). Root out, estroy. **ex·tir·pa·tion** (ĕksterpā′-on), **ex′tir·pa·tor** ns.

ex·tol, ex·toll (ĭkstōl′) vbs.t. **tolled, -tol·ling**). Praise en-usiastically. **ex·tol′ler** n.

ex·tort (ĭkstōrt′) v.t. Obtain money, promise, etc.) by violence, timidation, abuse, etc. (from).

ex·tor·tion (ĭkstōr′shon) n. Ex-rting, esp. of money; illegal xaction. **ex·tor·tion·ate** (ĭkstōr′-onĭt) adj. Using, given to, xtortion; (of prices etc.) exorbi-nt. **ex·tor′tion·ist** n.

ex·tra (ĕk′stra) adj. Additional; rger than its name indicates; eyond what is anticipated; of uperior quality. ~ adv. More than sually; additionally. ~ n. Extra ning, one for which extra charge is nade; special or additional issue of ewspaper; (film) actor hired to lay a very minor part, as in crowd cene.

extra- prefix. Situated outside f a thing, not coming within its cope.

ex·tract (ĕk′străkt) n. 1. (chem.) reparation containing active prin-iple of substance in concentrated orm obtained by treatment with a olvent (usu. followed by evapora-ion of solvent). 2. Passage copied rom book etc., excerpt, quotation. ~ (ĭkstrăkt′) v.t. 1. Copy out passage in book etc.); make extracts rom (book etc.) 2. Take out by orce (tooth, anything firmly fixed); lraw forth (money, admission, etc.) gainst person's will. 3. Obtain juices etc.) by suction, pressure, listillation, etc.; derive (pleasure tc. from); deduce (principle etc. rom). 4. (math.) Find (root of a number). **ex·trac′tive** adj. & n. **ex·trac′tor** n.

ex·trac·tion (ĭkstrăk′shon) n. 1. Extracting. 2. Lineage; origin; descent, as of Indian ~.

ex·tra·cur·ric·u·lar (ĕkstraku-rĭk′yuler) adj. Not included in the curriculum.

ex·tra·dite (ĕk′strad ĭt) v.t. (**-dit·ed, -dit·ing**). Give up (fugitive, criminal) to the proper authorities in another jurisdiction (state or country).

ex·tra·di·tion (ĕkstradĭsh′on) n. Delivery of fugitive or criminal to authorities of country, state, etc. in which crime was committed.

ex·tra·ga·lac·tic (ĕkstragalăk′-tĭk) adj. Situated outside the galaxy.

ex·tra·ju·di·cial (ĕkstrajōō-dĭsh′al) adj. Not belonging to the case before the court; (of opinion, confession, etc.) not made in court; outside ordinary course of law or justice. **ex·tra·ju·di′cial·ly** adv.

ex·tra·le·gal (ĕkstralē′gal) adj.

Beyond legal authority; unregu-lated by law.

ex·tra·mar·i·tal (ĕkstramăr′ĭ-tal) adj. (of a sexual relationship) Outside marriage, adulterous.

ex·tra·mu·ral (ĕkstramūr′al) adj. Outside the walls or boundaries of a school, city, etc.

ex·tra·ne·ous (ĭkstrā′nēus) adj. Of external origin; foreign to (object to which it is attached etc.); not belonging (to matter in hand, class); unessential; irrelevant. **ex·tra′ne-ous·ly** adv. **ex·tra′ne·ous·ness** n.

ex·traor·di·nary (ĭkstrōr′di-nĕrē, ĕkstraor′-) adj. Out of the usual course; exceptional, surpris-ing; unusually great; (of officials etc.) additional, specially em-ployed. **ex·traor·di·nar′i·ly** adv.

ex·trap·o·late (ĭkstrăp′olāt) v. (**-lat·ed, -lat·ing**). (math.) Calcu-late, from known terms, a series of other terms that lie outside the range of the known terms (also fig.). **ex·trap·o·la·tion** (ĭkstrăpolā′shon) n.

ex·tra·sen·so·ry (ĕkstrasĕn′-serē) adj. (of perception) Made otherwise than by the known sense organs.

ex·tra·ter·res·tri·al (ĕkstra-terĕs′trēal) adj. (Originating) out-side the Earth or its atmosphere.

ex·tra·ter·ri·to·ri·al (ĕkstra-tĕrĭtōr′ēal, -tōr′-) adj. Located outside of territorial boundaries; of the privilege extended to ambas-sadors of being regarded as outside the territory, and therefore free from the jurisdiction, of the power to which they are sent; of a country's rights of jurisdiction over all its subjects abroad. **ex·tra·ter·ri·to·ri·al·i·ty** (ĕkstratĕrĭ-tōrĕăl′ĭtē, -tōr-) n.

ex·trav·a·gance (ĭkstrăv′agans) n. Being extravagant; absurd state-ment or action; unreasonably costly item.

ex·trav·a·gant (ĭkstrăv′agant) adj. Immoderate; exceeding the bounds of reason; profuse, waste-ful; (of price etc.) exorbitant. **ex·trav′a·gant·ly** adv.

ex·trav·a·gan·za (ĭkstrăvagăn′-za) n. Extravagant or fantastic entertainment.

ex·tra·ve·hic·u·lar (ĕkstravē-hĭk′yuler) adj. Outside a vehicle, esp. (also ~ **activity**) of an astronaut's activity (exploration, repair, etc.) conducted outside a space vehicle while in flight.

ex·tra·vert (ĕk′stravērt) n. Var. of EXTROVERT.

ex·treme (ĭkstrēm′) adj. (**-trem·er, -trem·est**). 1. Outer-most; farthest from center; situated at either end. 2. Utmost. 3. ~ **unction**, (R.C. Ch.) sacrament in which a priest anoints and prays for the recovery and salvation of a person who is critically ill or injured. 4. (of actions, measures,

etc.) Severe, stringent; (of opinions, persons, etc.) going to great lengths, not moderate. **ex·treme′ly** adv. **ex·treme′ness** n. **extreme** n. 1. **in the** ~, extremely. 2. Thing at either end of anything; esp. (pl.) things as remote or as different as possible; excessive degree. 3. (logic) Major or minor term in syllogism; (math.) first or last term of ratio or series.

ex·treme·ly (ĭkstrēm′lē) **high frequency**. Any radio frequency in the highest range, between 30,000 and 300,000 megahertz.

ex·trem·ist (ĭkstrē′mĭst) n. One who holds extreme views or advocates extreme measures. **ex·trem′ism** n.

ex·trem·i·ty (ĭkstrēm′ĭtē) n. (pl. **-ties**). 1. Extreme point; very end; (pl.) hands and feet. 2. Extreme adversity, embarrassment, etc.; (usu. pl.) extreme measure(s).

ex·tri·cate (ĕk′strĭkāt) v.t. (**-cat·ed, -cat·ing**). Disentangle, release (from confinement, diffi-culty, etc.). **ex·tri·ca·ble** (ĕk′stri-kabel, ĭkstrĭk′-) adj. **ex·tri·ca·tion** (ĕkstrĭkā′shon) n.

ex·trin·sic (ĭkstrĭn′zĭk, -sĭk) adj. Lying outside, not belonging, (to); operating from without; not in-herent or essential. **ex·trin′si-cal·ly** adv.

ex·tro·vert (ĕk′strovērt, -strō-) n. (psychol.) One whose thoughts and activities are directed to things outside the self (opp. INTROVERT). **ex·tro·ver·sion** (ĕkstrovēr′zhon, -shon, ĕk′strōvēr-, -strō-) n. **ex·tro·ver′sive** adj.

ex·trude (ĭkstrōōd′) v. (**-trud·ed, -trud·ing**). 1. Thrust out (from). 2. Shape (metal, plastics, etc.) by forcing through die. 3. Protrude. **ex·trus′ive** adj. 1. Tending to extrude. 2. (geol.) Forced out as molten matter through the Earth's crust. **ex·tru·sion** (ĭkstrōō′zhon) n.

ex·u·ber·ant (ĭgzōō′berant) adj. Luxuriant, prolific; effusive; copious; full of high spirits or joyous abandon. **ex·u′ber·ant·ly** adv. **ex·u′ber·ance** n.

ex·ude (ĭgzōōd′) v. (**-ud·ed, -ud·ing**). Ooze out, give off (moisture etc.) like sweat. **ex·u·da·tive** (ĭgzōō′datĭv, ĕk′sūdā-) adj. **ex·u·da·tion** (ĕksūdā′shon, ĕksu-, ĕgzu-), **ex·u·date** (ĕk′sūdāt, -su-, ĕg′zu-) ns.

ex·ult (ĭgzŭlt′) v.i. Rejoice exceedingly; triumph (over). **ex·ul·ta·tion** (ĕgzŭltā′shon, ĕksŭl-) n. **ex·ult′ant** adj. **ex·ult′ant·ly** adv.

ex·urb (ĕk′sērb, ĕg′zērb) n. Community outside city or town, esp. prosperous and fashionable area beyond suburbs.

ex·ur·ban·ite (ĕksēr′banĭt, ĕg-zēr′-) n. Person who lives in an exurb.

ex·ur·bi·a (ĕksēr′bēa, ĕgzēr′-) n.

Exurbs collectively, region beyond suburbs.

eye (ī) *n.* 1. Organ of sight; iris of this; region of the eyes; eye as possessing power of vision; sense of seeing; look, glance, gaze; attention, regard; estimation, opinion, judgment; **have an ~ for**, be capable of perceiving or appreciating; **in the ~ of**, in the direction of (the wind); **keep an ~ on**, direct one's attention (lit. or fig.) to; **make ~s at**, look amorously at, ogle; **see ~ to ~**, agree entirely (*with*); **set ~s on**, catch sight of; **with an ~ to**, with a view to. 2. Thing like eye; spot on peacock's tail, wing of insect etc.; one of three spots at end of coconut; hole in needle for thread etc., hole in tool or implement for insertion of some other object; metal loop used with hook for fastening dress etc.; loop of cord or rope; undeveloped bud of plant; center of flower; leafbud of potato etc. 3. **eye'ball**, eye within lids and socket; **eye'bolt**, bolt, bar, with circular hole through head; **eye'brow**, fringe of hair along upper orbit of eye; **eye catcher**, (colloq.) something that particularly attracts one's attention; **eye'dropper**, dropper for administering medicines to the eye; **eye'ful**, (slang) remarkable or attractive sight, esp. attractive woman; **eye'glass**, lens for assisting defective sight; monocle; (pl.) pair of these lenses worn in frame that passes over nose and over or around the ears; **eye'hole**, cavity or socket of eye; hole to look through; **eye'lash**, hair, row of hairs, on edge of eyelid; **eye'lid**, one of movable folds of skin with which eyes are covered or

horizontal section of eyeball

*In order to see properly, not only a functioning **eye** is required but an intact nervous system to convey the impulses from the eye to the right part of the brain for interpretation.*

uncovered; **eye'liner**, cosmetic applied as line around eye; **eye'opener**, enlightening or surprising circumstance etc.; alcoholic drink, esp. in morning; **eye'piece**, lens(es) at eye end of telescope etc.; **eye'shade**, device to protect eyes from strong light; **eye shadow**, cosmetic applied to eyelids or around the eyes; **eye'sight**, power, faculty, of seeing; **eye'sore**, ugly object, thing that offends the sight; **eye'strain**, weariness of eyes from excessive or incorrect use; **eye'tooth**, pointed tooth just under eye,

*In Zaire, an African fishing-eagle nests in his remote **eyrie**. Eagle species build their large nests of twigs at high altitudes on ledges of mountains or cliffs.*

in upper or lower jaw, upper can tooth; **eye'wash**, lotion for e (slang) humbug, blarney; **eye'wi ness**, one who can bear witne from his own observation. **eye** (**eyed, ey·ing**). Observe, watch.

eye·let (ī'lĭt) *n.* Small hole cloth, sail, etc., for lace, ring, rop etc.; loophole; small eye.

ey·rie, ey·ry (ār'ē, ēr'ē, īr'ē) (pl. **-ries**). Var. of AERIE.

E·ze·ki·el (ĭzē'kēel, -kyel). H brew major prophet of 6th c. B. book of Old Testament contain his prophecies.

Ez·ra (ĕz'ra). Hebrew scribe a priest of 5th c. B.C.; book of C Testament dealing with the retu of the Jews from Babylon and t rebuilding of the Temple.

*Model Jane Seeney shows how impe ant the **eyes** are to appearance, a how **eye shadow** can enhance th effect on the viewer, creating a st ning impression.*

The illustrations show how the written forms of the letter **F, f** have developed through the ages. It is the 6th letter of the Modern English and ancient Roman alphabet. In the earliest Latin, the two letters w h were used to signify the f sound. The elongated small f probably first came into use when early scribes, writing at speed, joined it to the preceding and following letters.

Phoenician   Early Greek   Early Etruscan

Classical Latin   Anglo-Saxon   Italian (italic)

F, f (ĕf) (pl. **F's, f's** or **Fs, fs**). 1. Sixth letter of modern English and ancient Roman alphabet, representing Semitic *waw* (= *w, u*) and preclassical Greek digamma (F) and pronounced in English as a voiceless labiodental spirant. 2. **F**, (mus.) fourth note of natural scale (C major); scale or key with this note for tonic. 3. **F-layer**, highest stratum of the ionosphere, approximately 120–250 mi. (190–400 km) above the Earth.

F *abbrev.* Fahrenheit; farad(s).

f *abbrev.* (photog.) Focal length (used with numbers to indicate ratio of focal length of lens to diameter of stop); frequency; farad; (music) forte.

f. *abbrev.* Feminine, female; farad; following; foot; folio; (music) forte; franc(s); from.

FAA *abbrev.* Federal Aviation Agency.

Fa·bi·an (fā′bēan) *adj.* 1. Of, like, Quintus Fabius Maximus (d. 203 B.C.), Roman general who harassed Hannibal in the second Punic War by avoiding major battles while weakening the enemy by cutting off supplies; hence, cautious in strategy, avoiding direct confrontation. 2. Of the ~ **Society**, society of English socialists advocating Fabian policy rather than immediate revolutionary action, founded 1884. **Fabian** *n.* Member of the Fabian Society. **Fa·bi·an·ism** *n.*

fa·ble (fā′bel) *n.* 1. Story, esp. of supernatural character, not founded on fact; (collect.) myths, legendary tales. 2. Short story, esp. with animals for characters, conveying a moral. ~ *v.* (**-bled, -bling**). (archaic and poet.) Tell fictitious tales; state fictitiously; **fabled** *adj.* celebrated in fable, fictitious; unreal.

fab·ric (făb′rĭk) *n.* Thing put together; edifice, building; frame, structure; construction, texture, tissue; woven material.

fab·ri·cate (făb′rĭkāt) *v.t.* (**-cat·ed, -cat·ing**). 1. Construct, manufacture, esp. by joining components together. 2. Invent (fact), forge (document). **fab·ri·ca·tion**

(făbrĭkā′shon), **fab′ri·ca·tor** *ns.*

fab·u·list (făb′yulĭst) *n.* Composer of fables; liar.

fab·u·lous (făb′yulus) *adj.* Celebrated in fable; incredible; (colloq.) wonderful. **fab′u·lous·ly** *adv.* **fab′u·lous·ness** *n.*

fac. *abbrev.* Facsimile; faculty; factory.

fa·çade, fa·cade (fasahd′, fă-)

The origins of fable are lost in the mists of time. Aesop's **fable** *of the 'Fox and the Grapes', depicted here on an 18th century French tapestry, was one of those included in the 'Fables' of La Fontaine.*

ns. Face of building, esp. principal front; hence, from appearance of anything (also fig.).

face (fās) *n.* 1. Front of head, from forehead to chin; ~ **to** confronted; ~ **to** ~ **with**, confronting; **fly in the** ~ **of**, openly disobey. 2. Expression of countenance; grimace. 3. Composure, coolness, effrontery. 4. Outward show; aspect; surface; front, façade; right side, obverse; dial of clock etc.; working surface of implement etc.; each surface of solid; (also **type** ~) part of type or plate that takes the ink; style or design of this; **lose** ~, be humiliated; lose one's good name; **on the** ~ **of it**, to judge by appearance; obviously, plainly; **put a new** ~ **on**, alter aspect of; **save** ~, save one's good name. 5. **card**, one of a pack of playing cards on which a human face is represented; the king, queen, or knave. **face′cloth**, cloth for washing the face; **face-lift**, face lifting; (fig.) improvement in appearance; **face lifting**, operation for tightening the skin of the face to remove wrinkles etc.; **face-saving**, serving to keep one from being humiliated; **face value**, nominal value as stated on coin, note, etc.; (fig.) apparent value. **face** *v.* (**faced, facing**). 1. Meet confidently or defiantly; not shrink from, stand fronting; ~ **the music**, not quail at moment of trial or punishment. 2. Present itself to; look, have face or front, in special direction; front toward, be opposite to; (mil.) turn in special direction. 3. Cover part of (garment) with another material, esp. at edge, trim, turn up with; cover (surface) with layer of other material; dress surface of. 4. (in hockey etc.) Start play by dropping (puck, etc.) between sticks of two opposing players (also ~ **off**). **faced** *adj.*

face·less (fās′lĭs) *adj.* (esp.) Anonymous, characterless, without identity. **face′less·ness** *n.*

fac·et (făs′ĭt) *n.* One side of many-sided body, esp. of cut gem; one segment of compound eye. ~ *v.t.* (**-et·ed, -et·ing**, Brit. **-et·ted, -et·ting**). Cut facets on.

*magnificent Gothic **façade** of vieto cathedral in Italy shows the nted arches, stone lace-work and ned-glass windows characteristic of Gothic style. The cathedral was gun in 1290 A.D.*

'a·ce·tious (fasē'shus) *adj.* ing, esp. in forced or trivial way. **ce'tious·ly** *adv.* **fa·ce'tious·ss** *n.*

'a·cial (fā'shal) *adj.* Of the face. *n.* Beauty treatment for the face, en including a facial massage.

ac·ile (făs'ĭl; *Brit.* also făs'īl) . Easily done or won; working ily, ready, fluent; of easy temper, ible. **fac'ile·ly** *adv.*

a·cil·i·tate (fasĭl'ĭtāt) *v.t.* **at·ed, -tat·ing**). Make easy, omote, help forward (action or ult). **fa·cil·i·ta·tion** (fasĭlĭtā'-on) *n.*

a·cil·i·ty (fasĭl'ĭtē) *n.* (pl. **-ties**). ing easy, absence of difficulty; impeded opportunity; ease or adiness of speech etc.; pliancy; ang) toilet; (pl.) amenities, vices.

fac·ing (fā'sĭng) *n.* (esp.) Some-ng with which garment is faced, cuffs and collar of jacket; coating different material, esp. of stone ., on wall.

fac·sim·i·le (făksĭm'ĭlē) *n.* Exact py, esp. of writing, printing, cture, etc. ~ *v.t.* (**-led, -le·ing**). ake facsimile of.

fact (făkt) *n.* 1. Thing certainly own to have occurred or be true; tum of experience; thing assumed basis for inference; what is true existent; reality; **~s of life,** olloq.) facts of sex and reproduc-on. 2. Evil deed, crime (in **before, ter, the ~**). **fact'ful** *adj.*

fac·tion (făk'shon) *n.* Self-terested, turbulent, or unscru-ilous party, esp. in politics; inority group within a larger oup. **fac'tion·al, fac'tious** *adjs.* **c'tious·ly** *adv.* **fac'tious·ness** *n.*

fac·ti·tious (făktĭsh'us) *adj.* oduced artificially; contrived; ot natural. **fac·ti'tious·ly** *adv.* **c·ti'tious·ness** *n.*

fac·tor (făk'ter) *n.* 1. Agent; m, person granting short-term isiness loans accepting accounts ceivable as security. 2. (math.) ne of two or more numbers etc. at, when multiplied together, give given number, expression, etc. Circumstance, fact, influence, ntributing to result. 4. (biol.) ene or other agent transmitted om parent to offspring and fluencing or determining a ereditary character. ~ *v.t.* esolve into factors or components.

fac·to·ri·al (făktōr'ēal, -tōr'ē-)

*he Melanesian tribal dancer in New aledonia, W. Pacific, has a traditional attern painted on his **face.** Decoration r masking of the face is customary in ibal ritual throughout the world.*

The Krupp **factory** *at Essen, West Germany, was the center of the German munitions industry from the late 19th century to the end of the 1939–45 war.*

adj. Of a factor or a factorial. ~ *n.* (math.) Product of series of factors in arithmetical progression; product of integer multiplied by all lower integers.

fac·to·ry (făk´terē, -trē) *n.* (pl. **-ries**). Building or group of buildings with equipment for manufacturing goods.

fac·to·tum (făktō´tum) *n.* Man of all work.

fac·tu·al (făk´chōōal) *adj.* Concerned with, of the nature of, facts. **fac´tu·al·ly** *adv.*

fac·ul·ty (făk´ultē) *n.* (pl. **-ties**). 1. Aptitude for any special kind of action; power inherent in the body or an organ; a mental power (e.g. will, reason). 2. One of the departments or divisions of learning at a university or college; teaching staff of any of these; entire teaching staff of a school, body of teachers; members of a learned profession, esp. medicine. 3. Liberty to do something given by law or a superior; authorization.

fad (făd) *n.* Fashion that has wide but brief popularity, craze. **fad´dish** *adj.* **fad´dist** *n.*

fade (fād) *v.* (**fad·ed, fad·ing**). Droop, wither; (cause to) lose freshness or color; disappear gradually; (of sound) grow faint, die *away, out*; (of brake) gradually lose power; ~ **in, out, up**, gradually increase or decrease brightness, intensity, or distinctness of (motion picture, sound, etc.).

fae·ces (fē´sēz) = FECES.

Fa·en·za (fahĕn´za). City in N. Italy, 19 mi. (30.5 km), SW. of Ravenna; gained renown in 15th and 16th centuries for production of ceramic Faenza ware or faïence.

Faer·oe (fār´ō) **Islands.** Group of self-governing Danish islands in the N. Atlantic between the Shetland Islands and Iceland; capital, Thorshaven.

fag (făg) *v.* (**fagged, fag·ging**). 1. (of occupation) Tire, make weary. 2. (in certain British boys' schools, of seniors) Require menial tasks of (juniors); (of juniors) do menial tasks for seniors. 3. (slang) Faggot. ~ *n.* 1. Drudgery; unwelcome task; exhaustion. 2. (in certain British boys' schools) Junior who has to fag. 3. (slang) Cigarette; ~ **end**, inferior or useless remnant of anything, esp. of cigar or cigarette; extreme end.

fag·got (făg´ot) *n.* (slang) Male homosexual (freq. **fag**).

Fa·gin (fā´gin). Corrupt old man who teaches young children to steal. [from a character in Dickens's *Oliver Twist*]

fag·ot (făg´ot) *n.* Bundle of sticks or twigs bound together as fuel; bundle of iron or steel rods bound together for reheating or welding.

~ *v.* Bind in fagot(s); make fago

Fahr·en·heit (făr´enhīt), **G brn el Daniel** (1686–1736). Pru sian physicist; popularized use mercurial thermometer and d vised temperature scale; hence *adj.*, (abbreviated F, Fahr., Fa according to the Fahrenheit sca ~ **thermometer, scale**, etc., o with 32° and 212° as freezing a boiling points of water.

fa·ïence (fāahns´, fī-) *n.* Paint and glazed earthenware, majolic [Fr., = *Faenza*, Italy, site factory]

fail (fāl) *n.* **without** (emphasizing injunction or pron ise), for certain, irrespective hindrances. ~ *v.* 1. Be or becom deficient; die away; flag, bre down; disappoint hopes of, be of help; ~ **-safe**, (of mechanis nuclear devices, etc.) revert, event of breakdown, to conditic involving no danger. 2. Be wantin or deficient *in*. 3. Fall short performance or attainment; n succeed (*in* doing, *to* do); come nothing; become bankrupt; rejected, reject, as candidate; unsuccessful in (examinatio course, etc.).

fail·ing (fā´ling) *n.* (esp.) Foib shortcoming, weakness. ~ *pre* In default of.

faille (fīl, fāl) *n.* Delicate ribbed cloth woven of silk, cotto or rayon.

fail·ure (fāl´yer) *n.* Nonoccu

irs have traditionally been held at tablished times and places for the xchange of goods. Top: Nowadays ernational exhibitions, such as the ussels Fair of 1958, are often called

fairs although no selling takes place. Above: Sideshows and amusements, such as the roundabout accompany the business of buying and selling at a fun fair.

nce, nonperformance; running ort; breaking down; ill success; solvency; unsuccessful person, ing, or attempt.

fain (fān) *pred. adj.* (archaic) Villing, ready *to*; obliged *to*. ~ *dv.* Gladly, willingly (as in **would**).

faint (fānt) *adj.* 1. Sluggish; mid; feeble; dim, indistinct, pale. Giddy or languid with fear, unger, etc., inclined to faint; dizzy nd weak; **faint′hearted**, timid, owardly; **faint′heartedly** (*adv.*), aint′heartedness (*n.*) **faint′ly** *dv.* **faint′ness** *n.* **faint** *v.i.* , (archaic) Lose heart or courage, ag. 2. Lose consciousness. ~ *n.* ainting fit.

fair[1] (fār) *n.* Periodical gathering for sale of goods, often with shows and entertainments, at fixed place and time; trade show; (also **country** ~) exhibition of farm products, farm animals, etc. in competition at **fair′ground.**

fair[2] (fār) *adj.* 1. Beautiful; pleasing at first sight or hearing. 2. (of complexion etc.) Light, not dark; ~**-haired**, blond; ~**-haired boy**, (colloq.) young man who is looked upon with favor by superior, or who tries to gain favor. 3. Free from blemish; clear, clean; just, equitable. 4. Of moderate quality; not bad, pretty good. 5. Favorable, promising; gentle; unobstructed; ~**-spoken**, speaking or spoken

politely or in a convincing way. 6. ~ **ball,** (baseball) ball batted inside the foul lines; ~ **copy,** copy of document etc. made from corrected rough copy or after final correction; ~ **play,** equal conditions for all; ~ **shake,** (slang) honest or just treatment; equal chance; ~**-trade law,** federal or state law permitting manufacturer and retailer to set minimum prices on trademarked products; **the ~ sex,** women; **fair′way,** navigable channel, usual course of vessel(s); (golf) short-grassed part of course between tee and green; **fair- weather,** fit only for fine weather (freq. fig. of inconstant friends). **fair** *n.* What is fair. **fair′ish** *adj.* **fair′ness** *n.* **fair** *adv.* In a fair manner; **bid ~ to do,** show promise of doing.

Fair·banks (fār′băngks). Chief city of central Alaska at the junction of Tanana and Chena Rivers, 250 mi. (402 km) N. of Anchorage; northern terminus of railroad to Seward and Alaska Highway.

fair·ing (fār′ĭng) *n.* (eng.) Shielding around struts of aircraft, supports of bridge, etc., reducing resistance to air or water; stream- lining.

fair·ly (fār′lē) *adv.* In a fair manner; utterly, completely; rather, tolerably.

Fair (fār) **Oaks.** Site of Civil War battle of 1862, also called "Seven Pines," 6 mi. E. of Rich- mond, Va.; Union troops led by George B. McClellan repulsed Confederate forces under Joseph E. Johnston.

fair·y (fār′ē) *n.* (pl. **fair·ies**). 1. Small supernatural being with magical powers; **fair′yland,** country of fairies, enchanted land of fancy; **fairy ring** (on grass), circular band of darker grass caused by fungi or a ring of mushrooms growing in grass, pop. attributed to fairy dancing; **fairy tale,** story about fairies; unreal or incredible story; falsehood. 2. (slang) Male homosexual. **fairy** *adj.* Of fairies; imaginary, fictitious; fairylike, beautiful and delicate or small.

fait ac·com·pli (fāt *a*kōmplē′; *Fr.* fĕt ăkawṅplē′) (pl. **faits ac·com·plis** pr. fāt *a*kōmplēz′; *Fr.* fĕz ăkawṅplē′). Accomplished fact. [Fr.]

faith (fāth) *n.* 1. Reliance, trust, *in*; belief founded on authority; (theol.) belief in religious doctrines, esp. such as affects character and conduct, spiritual apprehension of divine truth apart from proof. 2. System of religious belief; things (to be) believed. 3. Duty of fulfill- ing trust, promise, etc.; observance of this; loyalty, fidelity; **good ~,** honesty of intention; **bad ~,** intent to deceive. 4. ~ **cure, healing,** cure, healing, by power of faith, not drugs etc.

faith·ful (fāth´ful) *adj.* Showing faith; loyal, constant (*to*); conscientious; trustworthy; true to fact, the original, etc., accurate. ~ *n.* (collect., **the** ~) True believers; practicing members of a religious faith, esp. Christians or Muslims. **faith´ful·ly** *adv.* **faith´ful·ness** *n.*

faith·less (fāth´lĭs) *adj.* (esp.) Perfidious, false to promises; unreliable. **faith´less·ly** *adv.* **faith´less·ness** *n.*

fake (fāk) *v.t.* (**faked, fak·ing**). Counterfeit; feign; make presentable or specious; contrive out of poor material; tamper with, contrive, in order to deceive. ~ *n.* (freq. attrib.) Piece of faking; faked thing.

fa·kir (fāker´, fah-, fā´ker) *n.* Muslim (or Hindu) religious mendicant, devotee. [Arab. *fakir* poor man]

Fa·lang·ist (fälän´jĭst) *n.* & *adj.* (Member) of the ruling party in Spain under General Franco, orig. founded (1933) as a Fascist movement. [Span. *falange* phalanx]

fal·cate (făl´kāt) *adj.* (anat., bot., zool.) Sickle-shaped.

fal·con (fawl´kon, făl´-, faw´kon) *n.* Small diurnal bird of prey of genus *Falco*, with short hooked beak and powerful claws; one of these trained to hunt other birds or game, usu. the peregrine falcon (*F. peregrinus*). **fal´con·er** *n.* Keeper and trainer of hawks; one who hunts with hawks. **fal´con·ry** *n.* Hawking; breeding and training of hawks.

Falk·land (fawk´land) **Islands.** Group of British islands in the S. Atlantic, off the SE. coast of Argentina.

fall (fawl) *v.i.* (**fell, fall·en, fall·ing**). 1. Descend freely, drop, lose high position; become detached and drop off; hang down; (of speech etc.) issue from; (of the young of animals) be born. 2. Sink, descend to lower level; decline; slope; subside, diminish; (of river etc.) discharge itself *into*; (of face) show sudden dismay; (of eyes) be lowered. 3. Cease to stand; come, be brought, (suddenly) to the ground; prostrate oneself; succumb to attack or opposing force; yield to temptation; drop down wounded or dead, die by violence; stumble, be drawn or forced, *into* (danger etc.). 4. (of missile, sight, light, etc.) Take direction, be directed; settle; have its situation *in* certain place, *on* certain object etc.; (of choice, lot, etc.) light *upon*; be allotted or apportioned; come as burden or duty. 5. Come by chance into certain position etc.; come naturally. 6. Pass suddenly, accidentally, or in the course of events, into a certain condition, become (as ~ **asleep, silent**, etc.). 7. Come to pass, befall; come in due course; (of season etc.) occur at stated time,

Fairies, as imaginary creatures with powers of good and evil, have formed part of the folk-lore of all civilizations. This watercolor by Edmund Dulac shows popular fairytale characters.

within certain limits etc. 8. W preps.: ~ **all over oneself**, sh great enthusiasm; ~ **behind**, outstripped by; ~ **for**, (colloq. captivated by, be enamored of; into, take one's place in (line e engage, enter upon (talk etc.); d into (habit); ~ **on**, make hos descent or attack on; ~ **to**, take begin; ~ **under**, be classi among; be subjected to (observat etc.). 9. With advs.: ~ **aw** desert, revolt, apostatize; dec vanish; ~ **back**, retreat, give w ~ **back on**, have recourse to; **behind**, lag; ~ **flat**, (colloq.) fai create the desired impression; ~ (mil.) take, cause to take, places line; give way inward; ~ **in w** happen to meet; accede to, ag with (views etc.); ~ **off**, withdra decrease, degenerate; ~ o quarrel; (mil.) leave the ranks; **short**, be or become insufficie (of missile) not go far enough; **through**, miscarry, fail; ~ begin eating or fighting. 10. **guy**, (slang) person who is ea deceived, dupe; person to blam scapegoat; **fall´out**, airborne rad active refuse of a nuclear explosi **falling star**: see STAR. **fall** *n.* Falling; what falls, esp. amount rain etc. 2. Autumn; season of y

*The **falcon** is one of the most wid distributed of all bird species, some which are called hawks, kestrels merlins. The hooded Saker falc (below) is specially bred for hunti Other common species are shown the facing page.*

merlin

gyr

rock dove

hobby

peregrine swooping on rock-dove

caracara

prairie falcon

lanner

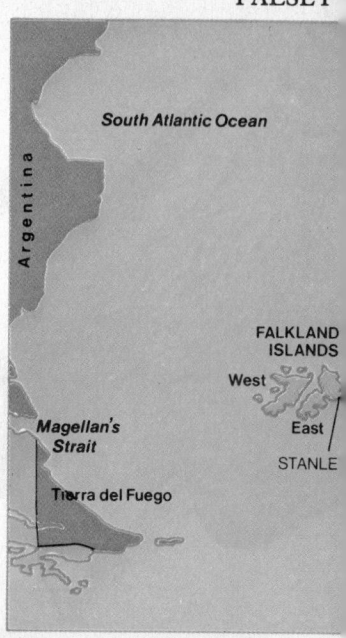

*The **Falkland Islands,** off the southern tip of South America, have a population of 2,100. The people are of British origin and their principal occupation is sheep-farming. Above: General view and map of the islands.*

*One of the most spectacular ways to break a **fall** is with parachutes. These three parachutes control the fall of Apollo 16, 27 April 1972, carrying three astronauts.*

between summer and winter, popularly reckoned in N. hemisphere as comprising the months September, October, and November, but astronomically as lasting from autumnal equinox (Sept. 22 or 23) to winter solstice (Dec. 21 or 22); (fig.) season of incipient decay. 3. (freq. pl.) Cataract, cascade; ~ **line**, line joining waterfalls on parallel rivers, usu. demarking mountains from a coastal plain. 4. Downward trend, amount of descent. 5. Thow in a wrestling bout. 6. (naut.) Hoisting tackle. 7. Succumbing to temptation; **the F ~ (of man)**, Adam's sin of eating the forbidden fruit and the consequent loss of man's innocence and of grace.

Fal·la (fah′ya), **Manuel de** (1876–1946). Spanish composer, noted esp. for instrumental music; his works include the opera *La Vida Breve* and the ballets *Wedded by Witchcraft* and *The Three-Cornered Hat.*

fal·la·cy (făl′asē) *n.* (pl. **-cies**). Misleading argument, sophism; (logic) material or formal flaw that vitiates a syllogism; delusion, error; unsoundness, delusiveness. **fal·la·cious** (fală′shus) *adj.* **fal·la′cious·ly** *adv.* **fal·la′cious·ness** *n.*

fall·en (faw′len) *adj.* see FALL; (esp., of woman) unchaste (archaic).

fal·li·ble (făl′ibel) *adj.* Liable to error or be erroneous. **fal·li·bil·i·ty** (făl*i*bĭl′ĭtē) *n.* **fal′li·bly** *adv.*

Fal·lo·pi·an (falō′pēan) **tube.** Either of the pair of oviducts in humans and other mammals. [discovered by G. *Falloppio*, Italian physician (1523–62)].

fal·low[1] (făl′ō) *adj.* (of ground) Ploughed and tilled but left unseeded during a growing season. ~ *v.t.* Plough and break up (land) for sowing or to destroy weeds.

fal·low[2] (făl′ō) *adj.* Of pale brownish or reddish yellow (now only in ~ **deer**, species of Eurasian deer (*Dama dama*) smaller than the red deer and usu. dappled).

Fal·mouth (făl′muth). Resort town in SE. Massachusetts near E. shore of Buzzards Bay; former whaling town; site of Woods Hole Oceanographic Institute.

false (fawls) *adj.* (**fals·er, fals·est**). 1. Erroneous; not true or correct. 2. Lying, deceitful; treacherous, unfaithful *to*; dece tive; spurious, sham, artificial. Improperly so called, pseud substituted for, supplementing. ~ **alarm**, alarm given witho good cause, either to deceive under misapprehension of dang **under ~ colors**, under a flag o has no right to (freq. fig.); ~ **daw** transient light in east, freq. p ceding true dawn by about an ho ~ **Solomon's-seal**, any of seve wildflowers of the genus *Smilaci* esp. *S. racemosa* of eastern America; ~ **start**, wrong start (es in racing); ~ **step**, stumble; tra gression. **false′ly** *adv.* **false′ne fal·si·ty** (fawl′sĭtē) (pl. **-ties**) **false** *adv.* **play ~**, cheat or betr

false·hood (fawls′hood) Falsity; something untrue; co trariety to fact; lying, lie(s).

fal·set·to (fawlsĕt′ō) *n.* Voice register above the natural range e in men, singer with such voice.

j. & adv.

fal·si·fy (fawl'sĭfĭ) *v.t.* (**-fied, -y·ing**). Fraudulently alter (document); misrepresent; counterfeit, rge. **fal·si·fi·ca·tion** (fawlsĭfĭ-'shon) *n.*

Fal·staff (fawl'stăf, -stahf), **Sir** hn. Fat convivial good-humored aggart in Shakespeare's *Henry IV* d *Merry Wives of Windsor.* **al·staff·i·an** (fawlstăf'ēan) *adj.*

fal·ter (fawl'ter) *v.* Stumble, agger, go unsteadily; stammer, eak hesitatingly; waver, lose urage, flinch. **fal'ter·ing·ly** *adv.*

fame (fām) *n.* Public recognin, renown; reputation, good putation; renown, celebrity. ~ *t.* (**famed, fam·ing**). (pass.) Be nowned. **famed** *adj.* Famous, uch spoken of.

fa·mil·ial (famĭl'yal, -ēal) *adj.* f, occurring in, characteristic of nembers of) a family.

fa·mil·iar (famĭl'yer) *adj.* 1. xtremely friendly, intimate (*with*); osely acquainted *with* (some bject). 2. Well-known, no longer vel, (*to*); common, current, usual. Unceremonious, free, overfree; norously or sexually intimate *vith*). **fa·mil'iar·ly** *adv.* **fa·mil'·ar** *n.* 1. (R.C. Ch.) Person render-ing domestic services in household of pope or bishop; (hist.) officer of Inquisition, chiefly employed in arresting and imprisoning accused. 2. Intimate friend or associate.

fa·mil·i·ar·i·ty (famĭlĕăr'ĭtē) *n.* (pl. **-ties**). Close intercourse, intimacy *with* (person, subject); amorous intimacy, (pl.) caresses etc.; unceremoniousness, treating of inferiors or superiors as equals.

fa·mil·iar·ize (famĭl'yerĭz) *v.t.* (**-ized, -iz·ing**). Make (thing) well known; make well acquainted or at home *with.* **fa·mil·iar·i·za·tion** (famĭlyerĭzā'shon) *n.*

fam·i·ly (făm'ĭlē, făm'lē) *n.* (pl. **-lies**). 1. Members of household, parents, children, etc.; set of parents and children, or of relations, whether living together or not; person's children. 2. All descendants of common ancestor, house, lineage; group of peoples from common stock. 3. Group of objects, languages, etc., distinguished by common features; (biol.) grouping above *genus* and below *order*. 4. ~ **man**, man with family, domestic person; ~ **planning**, birth control; ~ **tree**, genealogical chart; **in the ~ way**, pregnant.

fam·ine (făm'ĭn) *n.* Extreme scarcity of food in district etc.; dearth of something specified; hunger, starvation.

fam·ish (făm'ĭsh) *v.* Reduce, be reduced, to extreme hunger.

fa·mous (fā'mus) *adj.* Celebrated (*for*); well-known. **fa'mous·ly** *adv.*

fan¹ (făn) *n.* 1. Winnowing machine. 2. Instrument, usu. folding and sector-shaped when spread out, on radiating ribs, for agitating air to cool face; anything so spread out, as bird's tail, wing, leaf, kind of ornamental vaulting; rotating apparatus giving current of air for ventilation, etc.; (in windmill) small rudderlike vane for keeping sails at right angles to the wind; ~ **belt**, belt driving radiator fan on car engine; **fan'jet**, jet engine with additional thrust from cold air drawn in by fan; **fan'light**, fan-shaped window; **fan'tail**, fan-shaped tail or end; kind of pigeon, goldfish, etc. with fan-shaped tail; overhang at stern of ship. **fan** *v.* (**fanned, fan·ning**). 1. Winnow (grain); winnow away (chaff). 2. Sweep *away* (as) by wind from fan; move (air) with fan; drive current of air (as) with fan upon, to cool (face etc.) or to kindle (flame); (of breeze) blow gently on, cool. 3. Spread *out* in fan shape. 4. Increase (love, interest, etc.).

fan² (făn) *n.* Devotee of specified amusement, or of a particular person or thing; **fan'dom** (*n.*), fans collectively; **fan mail**, letters from fans. [abbrev. of *fanatic*]

fa·nat·ic (fanăt'ĭk) *n. & adj.* (Person) filled with excessive or unreasoning enthusiasm, esp. in religion. **fa·nat'i·cal** *adj.* **fa·nat'·i·cal·ly** *adv.* **fa·nat·i·cism** (fanăt'ĭsĭzem) *n.*

fan·ci·er (făn'sēer) *n.* Connoisseur of some article or animal (as **bird-~, rose-~**).

fan·ci·ful (făn'sĭful) *adj.* Indulging in fancies, whimsical, capricious; fantastically designed, ornamented, etc.; imaginary, unreal. **fan'ci·ful·ly** *adv.* **fan'ci·ful·ness** *n.*

fan·cy (făn'sē) *n.* (pl. **-cies**). 1. Delusion; unfounded belief. 2. Faculty of calling up things not present, of inventing imagery; mental image; supposition resting on no solid grounds, arbitrary notion. 3. Caprice, whim; individual taste, inclination; **take a ~ to**, have a passing liking or taste for; **~-free**, carefree, without commitment or (esp. romantic) attachment. 4. **fancy** *adj.* (**-ci·er, -ci·est**). Ornamental, not plain; parti-

*The **fallow deer** is commonly kept on estates and in parks and zoos, but is still found wild in Europe and elsewhere. The males remain apart from females and young except during the breeding season.*

colored (of flowers etc.); capricious, whimsical, extravagant; based on imagination, not fact; (of animal) bred for particular points or qualities; ~ **dress**, fanciful costume, esp. representing historical or fictitious character etc., worn for party or ball; **fan'cywork**, ornamental needlework etc. **fancy** *v.t.* (**-cied, -cy·ing**). 1. Picture to oneself; conceive, imagine; be inclined to suppose, rather think. 2. (colloq.) Have good conceit of (*oneself* etc.); take a fancy to, like. 3. Breed, grow (animals, plants) in order to develop particular points or qualities.

fan·dan·go (făndăng'gō) *n.* (pl. **-gos**). Lively Spanish dance in ¾ time; tune for this.

fan·fare (făn'fār) *n.* Short showy or ceremonious sounding of trumpets, bugles, etc.

fang (făng) *n.* Canine tooth, esp. of dogs and wolves; serpent's venom tooth.

fan·ny (făn'ē) *n.* (pl. **-nies**). (colloq.) Buttocks.

fan·ta·si·a (făntā'zha, -zhēa, făntazē'a) *n.* Musical composition in which form is subservient to fancy.

fan·ta·size (făn'tasīz) *v.* (**-sized, -siz·ing**). Have fantasy or fanciful vision (of). **fan·ta·sist** (făn'tasĭst,

-zĭst, făntā'zhĭst) *n.*

fan·tas·tic (făntăs'tĭk) *adj.* Extravagantly fanciful; grotesque or quaint in design etc.; (colloq.) very great; remarkable. **fan·tas'ti·cal** *adj.* **fan·tas'ti·cal·ly** *adv.* **fan·tas'ti·cal·ness** *n.*

fan·ta·sy (făn'tasē, -zē) *n.* (pl. **-sies**). Image-making faculty, esp. when extravagant or visionary; mental image; fantastic design; fantasia; whimsical speculation.

FAO *abbrev.* Food and Agriculture Organization (of the United Nations).

far (fär) *adv.* At a great distance, a long way off; to a great distance or advanced point; by a great interval, by much; **as ~ as**, right to, not short of; **as ~ as, so ~ as, in so ~ as**, to whatever extent; **by ~**, by a large amount; **how ~**, to what extent; **so ~**, to such a distance, up to now; **far'away**, remote, long past; (of look etc.) absent, dreamy; **far between**, infrequent; **far-fetched**, (of simile, illustration, etc.) studiously sought out, strained; **far-flung**,

*In Western society nowadays the **family** usually means a husband and wife and their children. It has gradually excluded other relatives. One such 'nuclear' family is depicted in this painting by Picasso of the Soler family.*

widely extended; widely distri ted; **far-gone**, advanced; very very drunk, much in debt, e **far-off**, remote, (sla unusual, different; avant ga extreme; **far-reaching**, wid applicable; carrying many con quences; **far'seeing**, presci prudent; **far'sighted**, farsee seeing distant things more cle than near ones. **far** *adj.* (**far·t** or **fur·ther, far·thest** or **fu thest**). Distant, remote; **F ~ E** Asia, esp. China and Japan; **West**, regions in Rocky Mounta and along Pacific coast.

far·ad (făr'ad, -ăd) *n.* Unit capacitance, capacitance of a pacitor in which a charge o coulomb raises the potential c ference between the plates by 1 v (abbreviated f or f.). [f. FARADA

Far·a·day (făr'adā, -d **Michael** (1791–1867). Engl physicist and chemist; famous his discovery of electric a magnetoelectric induction and his work on electrolysis.

farce (färs) *n.* Dramatic wo with sole object of excitii laughter; this species of dran absurdly futile proceeding, p tense, mockery. **far'ci·cal** *a* **far'ci·cal·ly** *adv.*

fare (fār) *v.i.* (**fared, far·in**

Michael Faraday, *the 19th-century English scientist, was early in his career an assistant to Sir Humphrey Davy. His important work on electrical and magnetic phenomena was carried out in this laboratory at the Royal Institute.*

Farmers *in long-settled districts generally take a pragmatic view of environment and land use, striving to reach a balance between the two. Leaving vegetation along streams is one way of maintaining a balance.*

journey, go, travel (poet.). 2. open, turn out; get on *well, ill,* , have specified luck. 3. Be rtained, be fed, feed oneself, , etc. ~ *n.* 1. Cost of senger's transportation; passen- transported for a fee. 2. Food vided.

are·well (fārwĕl´) *int.* Goodby. *n.* Leave-taking, parting good hes.

a·ri·na (farē´na) *n.* Fine meal de from grain and other starchy nt products, used as a cereal, in king, etc. **far·i·na′ceous** *adj.* de from, resembling starch; ly, powdery.

arm (fārm) *n.* Tract of land d for cultivation; also tract of er used for breeding oysters ; ~ **hand,** worker on farm; **m′house,** house of farm; **m′stead,** farm with buildings t; **farm team,** (baseball) minor ue team associated with major ue team, used to train players; **m′yard,** enclosure attached to nhouse. **farm** *v.* 1. Cultivate, till the soil, be a farmer. 2. Take ceeds of (tax, office, etc.) on ment of fixed sum; let (*out*) ceeds of (tax etc.) to person for d sum; arrange for (work) to be formed by other than principal tractor. 3. (baseball) Assign

1

2

3

The **farming** of land and the breeding of livestock are as old as history. Both provide man with essential foods which he either uses himself or trades in return for other necessary commodities. 1.

The cultivated fields in the Cotswolds in England are devoted to mixed farming. 2. The farmhouse is occupied by either the farmer himself or his tenant. Farm workers live in other cottages on the

farm or in houses in nearby villages. Traditional **farming** methods in the U.S.A. still see some farmers shepherding their flocks.

A sow and her piglets, soon after **farrowing**. The piglets are born blind, covered with soft white fur. In a few days the eyes open and the fur largely disappears. Many religious taboos cover pigs.

player) to farm team (used with *ut*).

farm·er (fär´mer) *n.* One who arms (esp. land); ~ **cheese**, ressed cheese of a consistency like ry cottage cheese.

far·o (fär´ō, făr´ō) *n.* Gambling ame in which players bet on the rder in which certain cards will ppear when taken singly from top f pack. [f. PHARAOH]

Far·oe Islands: see FAEROE SLANDS.

far·ra·go (farah´gō, -rā´-) *n.* (pl. **goes**). Medley, confused mixture. L., = "mixed fodder" (*far* corn)]

Far·ra·gut (făr´agut), **David Glasgow** (1801–70). American dmiral for Union forces during Civil War; captured New Orleans 1862) and Forts Morgan and Gaines (1864) on Mobile Bay.

far·ri·er (făr´ēer) *n.* One who hoes horses. **far´ri·er·y** *n.* (pl. er·ies).

far·row (făr´ō) *n.* Giving birth o, litter of, pigs. ~ *v.* Produce pigs).

fart (färt) *v.i.* (vulg.) Emit wind rom anus. ~ *n.* (vulg.) Such mission.

far·ther (fär´dher) *adv.* & *adj.* To or at a point that is) more istant; further. **far´ther·most**

adj. **far´thest** *adj.* & *adv.*

far·thing (fär´dhĭng) *n.* Former British coin, one quarter of an old penny; very small amount.

F.A.S. *abbrev.* Free alongside ship.

fas·ces (făs´ēz) *n.pl.* (usu. considered sing.) Bundle of wooden symbol of official authority in ancient Rome, carried before Roman consul or other high official; this as emblem of Italian fascists. [L. pl. of *fascis* bundle]

fas·ci·a (făsh´ēa) *n.* (pl. **fas·ci·ae** pr. făsh´ēē). 1. (archit.) Long flat surface of wood or stone under eaves or cornice. 2. (anat.) Thin sheet of connective tissue separating muscle layers and ensheathing muscle bundles. 3. Stripe, band. **fas´ci·al** *adj.*

fas·ci·cle (făs´ĭkel) *n.* 1. One part of book published in installments. 2. (bot. etc.) Bunch, bundle. **fas·cic·u·lar** (fasĭk´yuler), **fas·cic·u·late** (fasĭk´yulĭt, -lāt), **fas-**

cic´u·lat·ed *adjs.* **fas·cic·u·la·tion** (fasĭkyulā´shon) *n.*

fas·ci·nate (făs´ĭnāt) *v.t.* (-**nat·ed, -nat·ing**). Deprive (victim) of power of escape or resistance by one's look or presence (esp. of serpents); attract irresistibly, enchant, charm. **fas´ci·nat·ing** *adj.* **fas´ci·nat·ing·ly** *adv.* **fas·ci·na·tion** (făsĭnā´shon), **fas´ci·na·tor** *ns.*

fas·cism (făsh´ĭzem) *n.* (often F ~) Principles and organization of Italian nationalist anticommunist dictatorship (1922–43); system of extreme right wing or authoritarian views. **fas´cist** *adj.* & *n.* (freq. **Fas´cist**). [see FASCES]

fash·ion (făsh´on) *n.* 1. Make, shape; style, pattern, manner; **after, in, a** ~, tolerably, somehow or other, not too well. 2. Prevailing custom, esp. in dress; **the** ~, mode of dress, speech, etc., adopted in society for time being; person, thing, temporarily admired or discussed; **man** etc. **of** ~, person of social standing, moving in and conforming with upper-class society; ~ **plate**, (obs.) engraved, often colored picture of person(s) wearing clothes of latest designs; (fig.) person wearing such clothes. **fashion** *v.t.* Give shape to, form, mold.

3

*Women's **fashions** have often reflected the social climate of their particular age. The soft diaphanous garments of the 1820s (1) reflected the spirit of post-revolutionary Europe and the slender gowns of the 1900s (2) a reaction against stiff Victorian clothes. The emphasis throughout the 1930s was on slim hips (3) while during the 1939–45 war a broad-shouldered, short skirted look prevailed (4).*

4

fash·ion·a·ble (făsh′onabel) *adj.* Following, suited to, the fashion; characteristic of, treating of, patronized by, persons of fashion. **fash′ion·a·ble·ness** *n.* **fash′ion·a·bly** *adv.*

fast[1] (făst, fahst) *v.i.* 1. Abstain from all or some kinds of food as religious observance, a sign of mourning, protest, etc. 2. Go without food. ~ *n.* Act of fasting; season or day appointed for fasting; going without food; ~ **day**, day appointed for fasting.

fast[2] (făst, fahst) *adj.* 1. Firmly fixed or attached; (of friends) steadfast; (of color etc.) not fading or washing out. 2. Rapid, quick-moving; producing quick movement; (of watch etc.) more advanced than the true time; (photog., of lens) transmitting a large amount of light; (of flim) very sensitive to light; (of persons) dissipated (see below); **fast′back**, automobile with back sloping in continuous line; such a back; **fast-food**, (of restaurants, sandwich shops, etc.) where food is quickly prepared and served; **fast one**, (colloq.) shrewd

or unscrupulous action; **fast-talk**, (colloq.) persuade by rapid or deceitful talk. **fast** *adv.* 1. Firmly; fixedly; tightly; securely. 2. (archaic and poet.) Close *beside*, *upon*, etc. 3. Quickly; in quick succession; **live** ~, live in a dissipated way; expend much energy in short time.

fas·ten (făs′en, fah′sen) *v.* 1. Make fast, attach, fix; secure by some tie or bond; become fast. 2. Direct (look, thoughts, etc.) keenly *on*; fix (nickname etc.) *on*; ~ **on**, lay hold of, single out for attack, seize on (pretext). **fas′ten·er**, **fas′ten·ing** *ns.*

fas·tid·i·ous (făstĭd′ēus) *adj.* Easily disgusted, exacting in taste, hard to please. **fas·tid′i·ous·ly** *adv.* **fas·tid′i·ous·ness** *n.*

fast·ness (făst′nĭs, fahst′-) *n.* (esp.) Stronghold, fortress.

fat (făt) *adj.* (**fat·ter**, **fat·test**). 1. Fed up for slaughter, fatted; well-fed, plump; corpulent; thick, substantial. 2. Greasy, oily, unctuous. 3. Fertile, rich; abundant; (slang, of actor's part) offering abundant opportunity for skill, dis-

play, etc. 4. **fat′back**, fat off t back of a hog, usu. dried a cured with salt; **fat cat**, (slan wealthy person, esp. as contribut of money; **fat chance**, (slang) ve little chance; **fat farm**, (collo place where people undergo spec regimens of exercise and diet to lc weight; **fat′head**, (slang) stup person; **fatheaded**, (*adj.*) stup **fat** *n.* 1. Fat part of anythir (colloq.) best or richest part; **li off the ~ of the land**, have t best of everything. 2. Oily su stance composing fat parts animal bodies; (chem.) one of t organic compounds of whi animal fats are composed, glycer ester of a fatty acid. **fat** (**fat·ted**, **fat·ting**). Fatten; **k the fatted calf** (Luke 15), recei returned prodigal with joy; (e tended) celebrate. **fat′ly** *adv.* **fa ness** *n.*

fa·tal (fā′tal) *adj.* 1. Like fa inevitable, necessary; of, appoint by, destiny. 2. Fateful, importa decisive. 3. Destructive, ruino ending in death; deadly, sure to ki **fa′tal·ly** *adv.*

...st-war **fashion** has ventured into a ...de variety of styles, some of them ...arre and highly impractical. 1. Hot ...nts, usually worn with boots, had a ...ort life in the early 1970s. 2. ...lmain's evening dress of 1972 was ...ditionally feminine. 3. The space-age ...stic 'garments' produced in Paris ...re part of the fashion revolution. **3**

fa·tal·ism (fā′talĭzem) n. Belief ...at all events are predetermined by ...bitrary decree; submission to all ...at happens as inevitable. **fa′tal-** ...: n. **fa·tal·is·tic** (fātalĭs′tĭk) adj. ...·tal·is′ti·cal·ly adv.

fa·tal·i·ty (fătăl′ĭtĕ, fa-) n. (pl. ...ies). 1. Subjection to, supremacy ..., fate; predestined liability to ...saster; fatal influence. 2. Mis- ...rtune, calamity; death by ...cident, in war, etc.

fate (fāt) n. 1. Power predeter- ...ining events unalterably from ...ernity; (myth.) goddess of ...stiny; **the Fates**, (Gk. myth.) the ...Greek goddesses of destiny, ...otho, Lachesis, and Atropos; ...cand. myth.) Norns. 2. What is ...stined to happen; appointed lot of ...rson etc.; ultimate condition, ...stiny; death, destruction, ruin. ...v.t. (**fat·ed, fat·ing**). (usu. pass.) ...eordain; **fated**, doomed to ...lamity.

fate·ful (fāt′ful) adj. Prophetic; ...ught with destiny, important, ...cisive; controlled by, showing ...wer of, fate. **fate′ful·ly** adv.

fate′ful·ness n.

fa·ther (fah′dher) n. 1. Male parent; father-in-law; stepfather; man who has adopted a child; progenitor, forefather. 2. Origi-nator, designer, early leader; one who deserves filial reverence; religious teacher or counselor; **Fathers (of the Church)**, Chris-tian writers of first 5 centuries. 3. **the F ~**, God; (theol.) first person of the Trinity. 4. (eccles.) Confessor, spiritual director; priest belonging to religious order or congregation; superior of monastic house; **the Holy F ~**, the Pope. 5. Venerable person, god; oldest member, doyen; (pl.) leading men, elders. 6. **~-in-law** (pl. **~s-in-law**), father of one's wife or husband; **fa′therland**, one's native country; **the Fatherland**, Ger-many. **fa′ther·less**, **fa′ther·ly** adjs. **fa′ther·hood** n. **father** v.t. Beget, be the father of; originate (statement etc.); be the author, of; govern paternally; fix paternity of (child, book, etc.) on.

fath·om (fădh′om) n. (pl. **-oms**, collect. **-om**). Measure of 6 ft. (1.83 m) chiefly used in marine soundings. **~ v.t.** Measure with fathom line, sound (depth of water); (fig.) get to the bottom of, compre-hend. **fath′om·less** adj. That cannot be fathomed, of measureless depth; that cannot be understood.

fa·tigue (fatēg′) n. 1. Weariness after exertion. 2. Weakness in metals etc. caused by cyclic varia-tions in stress. 3. Task etc. that wearies; (also **~ duty**) soldier's menial or manual duty, sometimes allotted as punishment; **fatigues** (fatēgz′) (n.pl.), (mil.) uniform worn by soldiers while engaged in non-military duties. **fatigue** v.t. (**-tigued, -tigu·ing**). Cause fatigue to, exhaust.

Fat·i·ma (făt′ĭma, fah′tēmah) (606?–632). Daughter of Muham-mad by his first wife. **Fat·i·mid** (făt′ĭmĭd), **Fat·i·mite** (făt′ĭmīt) ns. (Person) descended from Fatima and her husband Ali; (member) of Muslim dynasty ruling part of N. Africa, Egypt, and Syria, 908–1171.

fat·ten (făt′en) v. Make fat (esp.

animals for slaughter); grow fat; enrich (purse).

fat·ty (făt´ē) *adj.* (**-ti·er, -ti·est**). 1. Like fat, greasy. 2. Consisting of fat, adipose; with morbid deposition of fat; ~ **degeneration**, morbid condition that begins in individual cells and results in deposits of fat in the tissues. 3. (chem.) ~ **acid**, one of a series of acids of the general formula CnH_2nO_2, of which some members occur in or are derived from natural fats. **fatty** *n.* (pl. **-ties**). Fat person.

fat·u·ous (făch´ōous) *adj.* Vacantly silly, purposeless, idiotic. **fat´u·ous·ly** *adv.* **fat´u·ous·ness, fa·tu·i·ty** (fatōō´ĭtē, -tū´-) *ns.* (pl. **-ties**).

fau·bourg (fō´boor, -boorg) *n.* Suburb, esp. of Paris. [Fr.]

fau·cet (faw´sĭt) *n.* Device for letting liquid flow from a pipe, barrel, cask, etc.

Faulk·ner (fawk´ner), **William** (**Cuthbert**) (1879–1962). American novelist and short-story writer; famous for *Sartoris, The Sound and the Fury, Absalom, Absalom!, Light in August,* etc.; awarded Nobel Prize for literature (1949) and Pulitzer Prize (1955, and 1963 posthumously).

fault (fawlt) *n.* 1. Defect, imperfection, blemish, of character, structure, appearance, etc.; **to a** ~, excessively. 2. Transgression, offense; thing wrongly done; (tennis, etc.) ball wrongly served; **double** ~, two consecutive faults; **find** ~ **with**, criticize unfavorably, complain of, hence **fault´find·er, fault´find·ing** (*ns.*). 3. Culpability,

responsibility for something wrong; defect causing specified evil. 4. (hunting) Loss of the scent by dogs; **at** ~, at a loss, in the wrong. 5. Flaw in ice; (geol.) place or line where rocklayers have fractured and moved out of alignment; ~ **plane**, plane of a fault, surface along which rocks on one side of a fault have moved relatively to those on the other. **fault** *v.* Cause fault in (strata etc.); show fault; find fault with. **fault´less** *adj.* **fault´less·ly** *adv.* **fault´y** *adj.* (**fault·i·er, fault·i·est**). **fault´i·ly** *adv.* **fault´i·ness** *n.*

faun (fawn) *n.* (Rom. myth.) One of the rural deities represented with horns, pointed ears, and tail of goat, and later also with goat's legs like satyrs, with whom they were associated. [f. FAUNUS]

fau·na (faw´na) *n.* (pl. **-nas, -nae** pr. -nē). Animals or animal life of a region or period. [L. *Fauna,* rural goddess, sister of FAUNUS]

Fau·nus (faw´nus). (Rom. myth.) God or demigod of nature and fertility worshiped by shepherds and farmers and identified with the Greek PAN.

Faust (fowst), **Johann.** Wandering astrologer and magician who lived in Germany *c*1488–1541 and was reputed to have sold his soul to the Devil; hero of dramas by Marlowe and Goethe. **Faust´i** *adj.*

Fauve (fōv) *adj.* & *n.* (sometin f~) (Member) of group of Fren painters in early 1900s who u vivid colors and distorted image their works. **Fauv´ism, Fauv** *ns.*

faux pas (fō pah´) (pl. **faux p** pr. fō pahz´). Error in mann breach of etiquette; indiscreti [Fr.]

fa·vor (fā´ver) *n.* 1. Frien regard, goodwill; approval; g graces; kindness beyond what due, partiality, too lenient generous treatment; aid, furth ance; **in** ~ **of**, on behalf or support of; on the side of; to advantage or account of. 2. Th given or worn as mark of fav small gift distributed at a par e.g., knickknack, paper hat; kno ribbons, rosette, badge. 3. (arch Looks, countenance. 4. (Permission for sexual intima **favor** *v.t.* 1. Look kindly up approve; treat kindly, countenan indulge, oblige, *with.* 2. Treat w partiality; be propitious or adv tageous to; aid, support. 3. (collo Resemble in face or feature. (journalese) Choose to wear. f **vored** *adj.* **most favored nati clause,** clause in trade agreem giving special advantages w regard to import duties, permiss to trade, etc., to a particular nati hence, **most** ~ **nation; well-, i favored,** having handsome, ug features.

fa·vor·a·ble (fā´vorabel) *a* Propitious; encouraging, appr ing; promising, auspicious; help suitable (*to*). **fa´vor·a·bly** *a* **fa´vor·a·ble·ness** *n.*

fa·vor·ite (fā´verĭt) *adj.* P ferred above others; ~ **son,** pers preferred as political candidate delegates from his own sta chosen as intimate by king superior and unduly favored. ~ Favorite person or thing; **the** (racing, sports) competitor gen ally favored as being most likely win. **fa´vor·it·ism** *n.* (es Favoring one person or gro unfairly.

Fawkes (fawks), **Guy** (157 1606). English Roman Cathol who, with other conspirato planned to blow up the Houses Parliament and assassinate the ki on Nov. 5, 1605 (Gunpowder Pl in retaliation for increasing repre sion of Roman Catholics; he w arrested on Nov. 4 and hang **Guy** ~ **day,** (in Britain) Nov. anniversary of this plot, celebrat with fireworks and burning Fawkes in effigy.

fawn[1] (fawn) *n.* 1. Young de esp. one less than 1 year old. Color of this, light yellowish brov ~ *adj.* Fawn-colored.

*The **FBI** division of the U.S. Department of Justice investigates violations of Federal law including espionage, kidnapping and fraud against the government. Some of their medical and scientific equipment is shown below.*

The **feathers** of many birds, such as this red-sided parrot (above), are brilliantly colored, and have often been used by women as a fashion accessory. The different parts of a feather are shown on the right.

Vane

Shaft

Vane

Quill

Barb interlocking with adjacent barb

fawn [2] (fawn) *v.i.* (of animal, esp. dog) Show affection by tail-wagging, groveling, etc.; (of persons) behave servilely, cringe. fawn'er *n.* fawn'ing·ly *adv.*

fay (fā) *n.* Fairy; sprite or elf.

faze (fāz) *v.t.* (**fazed, faz·ing**). (also **feaze**) (colloq.) Disconcert, perturb.

FBI, F.B.I. *abbrevs.* Federal Bureau of Investigation.

FCC, F.C.C. *abbrevs.* Federal Communications Commission.

F.D. *abbrev.* Fire department; DEI DEFENSOR.

FDA, F.D.A. *abbrevs.* Food and Drug Administration.

FDIC, F.D.I.C. *abbrevs.* Federal Deposit Insurance Corporation.

Fe. *symbol.* Iron.

fe·al·ty (fē'altē) *n.* (pl. **-ties**). Feudal tenant's or vassal's fidelity to his lord; acknowledgment or obligation of this.

fear (fēr) *n.* Emotion caused by

impending danger or evil; state of alarm; dread *of, that*; dread and reverence; anxiety for the safety *of*; **for ~ of**, in order to avoid or prevent; **no fear!**, it is not likely; **without ~ or favor**, impartially. **fear** *v.* Be afraid; be afraid of; hesitate *to* do, shrink from *doing*; revere (God); apprehend, expect uneasily; be afraid *that.* **fear'less** *adj.* Feeling no fear, brave. **fear'less·ly** *adv.* **fear'less·ness** *n.*

fear·ful (fēr'ful) *adj.* 1. Terrible,

awful; (by exaggeration) annoying etc. 2. Frightened, timid; apprehensive *of*; reverential. **fear'ful·ly** *adv.* **fear'ful·ness** *n.*

fear·some (fēr'som) *adj.* Appalling; awesome. **fear'some·ly** *adv.* **fear'some·ness** *n.*

fea·si·ble (fē'zibel) *adj.* Practicable, possible; capable of being done or accomplished; (loosely) likely, probable. **fea·si·bil·i·ty** (fēzibil'itē) *n.* (pl. **-ties**).

feast (fēst) *n.* 1. Religious anniversary appointed to be observed with rejoicing; **movable ~**, feast (as Easter etc.) of which date varies from year to year. 2. Sumptuous meal, esp. one given to number of guests and of public nature; (fig.) gratification, rich treat, to senses or mind. **feast** *v.* Partake of feast, fare sumptuously; regale.

feat (fēt) *n.* Noteworthy act, esp. deed of valor; act of dexterity or strength, surprising trick.

feath·er (fĕdh'er) *n.* 1. One of the appendages growing from a bird's skin, usu. consisting of a central horny shaft fringed on either side with a vane of barbs forming rounded outline at end; (collect.) plumage; **birds of a ~**, people of the same kind or character; **~ duster**, brush for light dusting, made of feathers. 2. Piece(s) of feather attached to base of arrow or dart to direct flight; plume worn in hat etc.; very light object; **a ~ in one's cap**, something one may be proud of. 3. Tuft or ridge of upright hair, as on leg or tail of some dogs; featherlike flaw in gem. 4. (rowing) Action of feathering (see *v.* sense 2). 5. **~ bed**, mattress stuffed with feathers; **feath'er·bedding**, keeping people on payroll to do unnecessary jobs or restricting production; **feath'er·brain**, silly person; **feath'er·brained**, silly; **feath'erstitch**, zigzag embroidery stitch; **feath'er·weight**, very light or insignificant thing or person; boxer of weight between bantamweight and lightweight. **feath'ered, feath'er·less, feath'er·y** *adjs.* **feather** *v.* 1. Furnish, adorn, line, coat etc. with feathers; form featherlike covering or adornment for; **~ one's nest**, enrich oneself. 2. Float, move, wave, like feathers; turn (oar), turn oar as it leaves water, so that it passes through air horizontally edgeways; rotate (blades of propeller) so that they are parallel to direction of motion.

feath·er·ing (fĕdh'ering) *n.* (esp.) Plumage; feathers of arrow; feathery structure or marking.

fea·ture (fē'cher) *n.* 1. (usu. pl.) Part(s) of the face, esp. with regard to shape and visible effect. 2. Distinctive or characteristic part of a thing, part that arrests attention;

distinctive or prominent article in newspaper; feature film or program; **fea′ture·less** *adj.* **feature** *v.t.* (**-tured, -tur·ing**). Stand as distinctive mark upon; portray, sketch prominent points of; make attraction or special feature of; (of film) give prominence to (actor etc.), as **featured player** etc.

feaze (fēz, fāz) = FAZE.

Feb. *abbrev.* February.

feb·ri·fuge (fĕb′rĭfūj) *n.* & *adj.* (Medicine) that reduces fever.

fe·brile (fē′brĭl, fĕb′rĭl) *adj.* Of fever, feverish.

Feb·ru·ar·y (fĕb′rŏōĕrē) *n.* (pl. **-ar·ies**). Second month of Gregorian (12th of Julian) calendar, with 28 days except in leap year, when it has 29; ~ **revolution**: see Russian REVOLUTION. [L. *februa*, Roman festival of purification held on 15th of this month]

fe·ces, fae·ces (fē′sēz) *ns.pl.* Excrement; waste matter discharged from bowels. **fe′cal** *adj.*

feck·less (fĕk′lĭs) *adj.* Feeble, futile, inefficient. **feck′less·ly** *adv.* **feck′less·ness** *n.*

fe·cund (fē′kund, -kŭnd, fĕk′-und, -ŭnd) *adj.* Prolific, fertile; productive. **fe·cun·di·ty** (fĭkŭn′-dĭtē) *n.*

fe·cun·date (fē′kundāt, fĕk′un-) *v.t.* (**-dat·ed, -dat·ing**). Make fruitful.

fed¹ (fĕd) *adj.* see FEED; (esp.) ~ **up**, (slang) surfeited, disgusted

(*with*), bored.

fed² (fĕd) *n.* (freq. **Fed**) (colloq.) Official of the federal government, esp. a law enforcement officer.

Fed. *abbrev.* Federal.

fed·a·yeen (fĕdahyēn′) *n.pl.* 1. Arab guerrillas operating against Israel. 2. Iranian guerrillas, having left-wing political sympathies, active from about 1970 and important in the 1979 revolution.

fed·er·al (fĕd′eral, fĕd′ral) *adj.* 1. Of the form of government in which two or more states form a political unity but remain independent in internal affairs; of such political unity, as dist. from the separate states composing it; **F ~ district**, area in some countries reserved for national capital, such as the District of Columbia; **F ~ Republic of Germany**: see GERMANY. 2. Favoring strong central government; of the Union or its troops, in the U.S. Civil War. **fed′er·al·ism** *n.* 1. Federal system of government or organization. 2. Support or advocacy of such a system. 3. (**F ~**) Principles of the Federalist Party. **fed′er·al·ist** *adj.* & *n.* **Federalist Party**, (hist.) group that advocated adoption of U.S. Constitution; later, a

political party favoring stro[ng] centralized U.S. governme[nt] **fed·er·al·is·tic** (fĕderalĭs′tĭk, fĕ′ral-) *adj.* **fed′er·al·ize** *v.t.* (**-ize[d], -iz·ing**). 1. Bring (states) togeth[er] in a federal union. 2. Put und[er] jurisdiction of a federal gover[n]ment. **fed·er·al·i·za·tion** (fĕder′līzā′shon, fĕdra-) *n.*

fed·er·ate (fĕd′erāt) *v.* (**-at·e[d], -at·ing**). Bind together in leag[ue] for some common object; organi[ze] on federal basis. ~ (fĕd′eri[t]) **fed·er·a·tive** (fĕd′erātĭv, -erati[v]) *adjs.*

fed·er·a·tion (fĕderā′shon) [n.] Federating; federated society, es[p.] federal group of states.

fe·do·ra (fĭdōr′a, -dōr′a) *n.* L[ow] soft felt hat with curled brim a[nd] crown creased lengthways. [*Fédor[a]*, title of 1882 play (pop. in U.S. 1883) by Fr. playwright Victori[en] Sardou]

fee (fē) *n.* 1. (hist.) Fi[ef,] feudal benefice. 2. (law) Estate [of] inheritance in land; estate held [in] fee, lordship; **in ~**, as one[′s] absolute and rightful possessio[n;] ~ **simple**, estate in land in whi[ch] the inheritor has unqualifi[ed] ownership and right of dispositio[n;] **in ~ simple**, in absolute posse[s]sion; ~ **tail**, estate in land limit[ed] to some particular class of heirs [or] person to whom it is granted. [3.] Sum payable to public officer f[or] performing his or her function; su[m] id or due to professional, per-ormer, etc., for service or rformance; entrance money for ntest, school, society, etc. **fee** v.t. y fee to.

fee·ble (fē′bel) adj. (**-bler**, **lest**). Weak, infirm; wanting in ergy, force, or effect; dim, distinct. **fee′ble·ness** n. **fee′bly** v.

fee·ble·mind·ed (fē′belmĭn′dĭd) i. Lacking normal mental ability; lower than average intelligence; pid. **fee′ble·mind′ed·ness** n.

feed (fēd) v. (**fed, feed·ing**). Supply with food; put food into outh of; graze (cattle); deal out odder) to animals; take food, eat; rve as food for. 2. Gratify anity, eyes, etc.), comfort erson) with hope, etc. 3. Nourish, ake grow. 4. Keep (reservoir, fire, c.) supplied; supply (machine) th material to work on; supply aterial) to machine; (basketball, ckey, etc.) give (ball, puck, etc.) ; (theatr. slang) give (actor) cues, portunities for jokes, etc. 5. **ed′back**, (electr.) return of a action of the output signal from e stage of a circuit, amplifier, c., to the input of the same or a eceding stage; (transf.) modifica-on of a process etc. by its own fects; information; **feed′pipe**, pe conveying material, water, etc. where it is needed. **feed** n. 1.

Act of feeding; giving of food; **off one's ~**, with no appetite. 2. Pasturage, grain crops; horse's allowance of oats etc.; fodder; **feed′lot**, place where cattle etc. are fattened with extra food before slaughtering. 3. (colloq.) Meal, feast.

feed·er (fē′der) n. (esp.) 1. Tributary stream. 2. Hopper or feeding apparatus in machine. 3. (freq. attrib.) Railroad line, air service, etc. linking outlying districts with main line or service.

feel (fēl) v. (**felt, feel·ing**). 1. Explore by touch; search (about) with hand for; try to ascertain by touch whether, if, how; **~ one's way**, find one's way by groping, (also fig.); **~ out**, try to get information from or about by devious means. 2. Perceive by touch; have sensation of touch. 3. Be conscious of (sensation, emotion, conviction); be con-sciously; experience, undergo con-sciously; be affected by, behave as if conscious of; **~ like**, (colloq.) have inclination for; **~ up to**, (colloq.) be ready for, capable of, or ready to. 4. Be emotionally affected by; have sympathy with,

*The **feelers** on this American cock-roach (Periplaneta americana), act as sensory organs that aid in the detection of food, especially when the cockroach is active at night.*

compassion for; have vague or emotional conviction (that). 5. Be realized as; seem, produce impres-sion of being. **feel** n. Sense of touch; testing by touch; sensation characterizing something; **have a ~ for**, be endowed with inborn ability or awareness.

feel·er (fē′ler) n. (esp.) 1. (pop.) Organ in certain animals for testing things by touch or searching for food. 2. (fig.) Tentative pro-posal or hint designed to test probable response.

feel·ing (fē′lĭng) n. (esp.) 1. Sense of touch; physical sensation. 2. Emotion; (pl.) susceptibilities, sympathies; readiness to feel, tenderness for others' sufferings. 3. Consciousness of; conviction not based solely on reason; sentiment. 4. (art etc.) General emotional effect produced. **~** adj. (esp.) Sensitive, sympathetic; showing emotion. **feel′ing·ly** adv.

feet (fēt): see FOOT.

feign (fān) v. 1. Fabricate (excuse, story, accusation). · 2. Represent falsely; imitate decep-tively; pretend.

feint (fānt) n. Sham attack (blow, cut, thrust, etc.) to divert attention or deceive opponent; pretense. **~** v.i. Make feint.

feist·y (fīs′tē) adj. (**feist·i·er, feist·i·est**). Aggressive, exuberant; touchy.

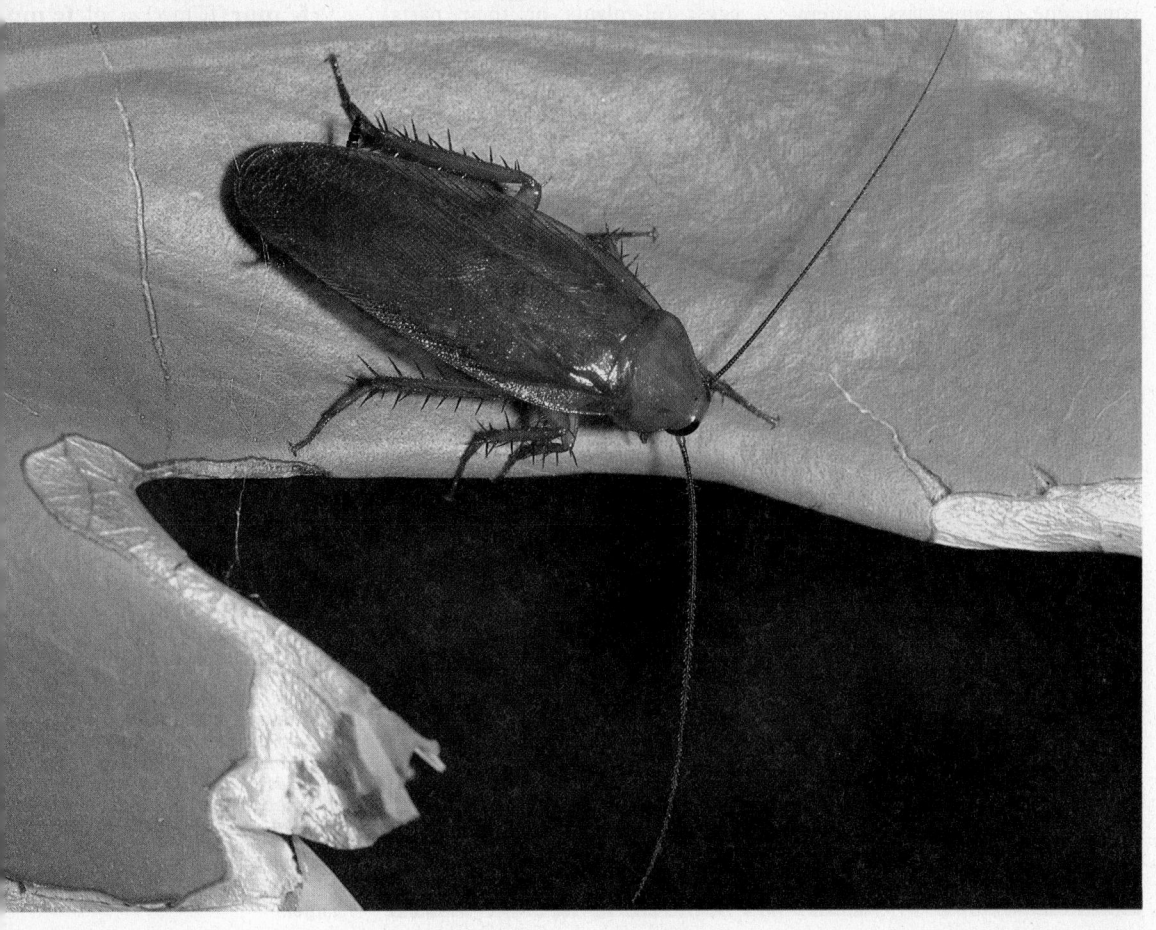

feld·spar (fĕld′spär, fĕl′-), **fel′-spar** (fĕl′spär) *ns.* Any of a group of minerals, esp. aluminosilicates of potassium, sodium, and calcium, usu. white or flesh colored, occurring in crystals and in granite and other primary rocks; used in ceramic and enameling processes.

fe·lic·i·tate (fĭlĭs′ĭtāt) *v.t.* (-tat·ed, -tat·ing). Congratulate (*on*). **fe·lic·i·ta′tion** *n.*

fe·lic·i·tous (fĭlĭs′ĭtus) *adj.* Strikingly apt in expression or manner (of words, action, etc., or of person). **fe·lic′i·tous·ly** *adv.*

fe·lic·i·ty (fĭlĭs′ĭtē) *n.* (pl. **-ties**). 1. Being happy, intense happiness. 2. Happy faculty in expression, appropriateness.

fe·line (fē′līn) *adj.* 1. Of cats; catlike. 2. Stealthy, sly. ~ *n.* Member of Felidae or cat family. **fe·lin·i·ty** (fĭlĭn′ĭtē) *n.*

fell[1] (fĕl) *adj.* Fierce, ruthless, terrible, destructive.

fell[2] (fĕl) *v.* 1. Strike (person, animal) down by blow or cut. 2. Cut down (tree). 3. Stitch (edge of seam) so that it lies flat. ~ *n.* Amount of timber cut in a season.

fel·lah (fĕl′a) *n.* (pl. **fel·lahs, fel·la·hin, fel·la·heen** pr. fĕlah-hēn′). Egyptian peasant. [Arab. *fellāḥ* = "husbandman"]

fel·low (fĕl′ō) *n.* 1. One associated with another, comrade. 2. Counterpart, match; other of equal, one of same class, contemporary. 3. (Brit.) Incorporated member of college or collegiate foundation; graduate student holding grant on condition of pursuing specified branch of study. 4. Member of learned society. 5. Man;

boy. 6. (attrib.) Belonging to same class; associated in joint action; in same relation to same object; ~ **creature**, person or animal also created by God; ~ **traveler**, (esp.) noncommunist who sympathizes with aims and general policy of Communist Party.

fel·low·ship (fĕl′ōshĭp) *n.* 1. Participation, sharing, community of interest. 2. (also **good** ~) Companionship, friendliness. 3. Body of associates, company; fraternity; brotherhood. 4. Graduate scholarship or grant at a college or university.

fe·lon (fĕl′on) *n.* One who has committed felony. ~ *adj.* (poet.) Cruel, wicked, murderous. **fe·lo·ni·ous** (felō′nēus) *adj.* Criminal; (law) of, involving, of the nature of felony. **fe·lo′ni·ous·ly** *adv.*

fel·o·ny (fĕl′onē) *n.* (pl. **-nies**). Grave indictable offense, such as murder, rape, larceny.

fel·spar: see FELDSPAR.

felt[1] (fĕlt) *n.* Fabric made by shrinking and rolling wool, fur, etc. so that the fibers interlock; ~ **(tip[ped]) pen**, pen with felt point. **felt** *v.* Make into felt; mat together, become matted; cover with felt.

felt[2] (fĕlt): see FEEL.

fem. *abbrev.* Female, feminine.

fe·male (fē′māl) *adj.* 1. Of the sex that bears offspring or produces eggs; (of plants or their parts)

The crystalline minerals of the **feldspar** *group are usually white or pink in color. They are used in the manufacture of porcelain and glass and as a source of semi-precious stones.*

fruit-bearing. 2. Of women; female animals or plants. 3. part of machinery etc.) Designed receive corresponding male pa ~ *n.* Female person or anim woman, girl. **fe′male·ness** *n.*

fem·i·nine (fĕm′ĭnĭn) *adj.* 1. women; womanly; womanish. (gram.) Of gender to which appe tions of females belong; (of endi proper to this gender. 3. Gen delicate. 4. (pros.) ~ **endi** ending of line of verse with stress on penult; ~ **rhyme**, in verse, one ending in mute *e* common feminine suffix); her rhyme of two syllables of wh second is unstressed. **fem′ nine·ly** *adv.* **feminine** *n.* (gra (Word having) feminine gend **fem′i·nine·ness, fem·i·nin·i** (fĕmĭnĭn′ĭtē) *ns.*

fem·i·nism (fĕm′ĭnĭzem) Advocacy of extended recognit of claims and achievement women; advocacy of wome rights. **fem′i·nist** *adj.* & **fem·i·nis·tic** (fĕmĭnĭs′tĭk) *adj.*

fem·i·nize (fĕm′ĭnĭz) *v.* (-nize -niz·ing). Make, become, fer nine. **fem·i·ni·za·tion** (fĕmĭnĭ shon) *n.*

femme fa·tale (fĕm fat -tahl′, fahm). Woman who seductive charms lead men on a cause dangerous situations. [Fr. "fatal woman"]

fe·mur (fē′mer) *n.* (pl. **fe·mu fem·o·ra** pr. fĕm′era). 1. Thi bone. 2. One of upper portions an insect leg. **fem·o·ral** (fĕm′er *adj.*

fen (fĕn) *n.* Low marshy flooded tract of land.

fence (fĕns) *n.* 1. Bulwa (archaic); hedge, wall, railing, et keeping out intruders from fie etc.; **sit on the** ~, remain neut in contest, be undecided in opinio 2. Guard, guide, or gauge, regula ing movements of tool or machin 3. Receiver, then seller, of stol goods. **fence** *v.* (**fenced, fen ing**). 1. Practice swordplay or of fencing; use sword scientifica ~ **with**, parry, try to eva (question, questioner). 2. Scree shield, protect (*from, against*); ke *off* or *out*; surround (as with fen enclose. 3. Deal in stolen goo **fenc′er** *n.* (esp.) One who fenc with a foil.

fenc·ing (fĕn′sĭng) *n.* 1. Railir fences; material for fences. 2. Spo or art of attack and defense with t

The art of **fencing** *was developed the Italians in the 16th century wh they produced the rapier. It was pe fected in the 17th century at the co of Louis XIV of France. Modern fenci is based on the movements worked c then. 1. U.S.S.R. and Hungary co pete in the Munich Olympics. 2. T lunge and return to guard. 3. The eic defensive positions. 4. The parts of t target.*

prime   seconde   tierce   quarte

quinte   sixte   septime   octave

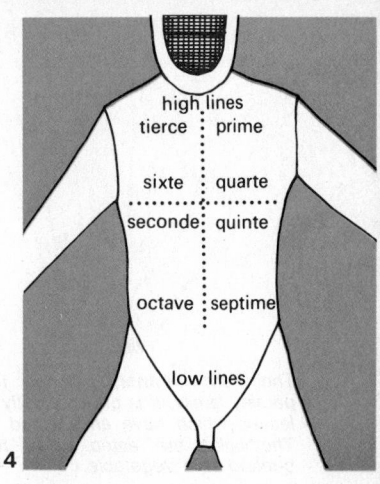

high lines
tierce : prime

sixte : quarte

seconde : quinte

octave : septime

low lines

4

épée, foil, or saber.

fend (fĕnd) v. Ward *off*; provide *for* (usu. *oneself*).

fend·er (fĕn´der) n. Thing used to keep something off, prevent collision, etc.; guard; metal frame around hearth to prevent falling coals from rolling into room; (naut.) piece of old cable, matting, old tires, etc., hung over vessel's side; part of automobile body over, framing, or near each wheel to protect body from mud etc.

fe·nes·trate (fenĕs´trāt, fĕn´es-trāt) *adj.* Having small perforations or openings like windows. **fe·nes·trat·ed** (fenĕs´trātĭd, fĕn´estrā-) *adj.*

fen·es·tra·tion (fĕnestrā´shon) n. (esp.) 1. Arrangement of windows in building. 2. (surg.) Perforation esp. of bony labyrinth of ear to restore hearing.

Fe·ni·an (fē´nēan, fēn´yan) *adj.* & n. (hist.) 1. (pl.) Legendary group of heroic Irish warriors of the 2nd and 3rd centuries. 2. (Member) of secret organization formed by Irish in New York City in the middle of the 19th c. to overthrow British rule in Ireland. **Fe´ni·an·ism** n. [OIr. *féne* the ancient Irish people, confused with *fiann* warriors defending Ireland under Finn and other legendary kings]

fen·nel (fĕn´el) n. Fragrant yellow-flowered perennial umbellifer (*Foeniculum vulgare*) native to Europe whose seeds are used as flavoring; the seeds of this; the stalks of this.

fen·u·greek (fĕn´yugrēk) n. Leguminous plant (*Trigonella foenum-graecum*) with seeds used as flavoring; the seeds of this.

feoff (fĕf): see FIEF.

feoff·ee (fĕfē´) n. Person to whom feoffment is granted.

The herb, **fennel,** belongs to the parsley family. It is grown chiefly for its leaves which have an aniseed flavor. The bulbs are eaten either raw or cooked as a vegetable.

feoff'ment n. Grant of land(s) as a fee. **feof'for** n. **feoff'er** n. One who grants a feoffment.

FEPC *abbrev.* Fair Employment Practices Committee.

fe·ral (fēr´al, fĕr´-) *adj.* Wild, untamed, uncultivated; brutal; (zool.) escaped from captivity and reverted to wild state.

Fer·di·nand (fĕr´dinănd) (1452–1516). Ferdinand V of Castile and II of Aragon, known as "The Catholic"; king of Sicily (1468–1516), of Aragon (1479–1516), and of Naples (1504–16); joint sovereign with wife Isabella of Castile (1474–1504); conquered Granada (1492), Spain's last Moorish kingdom; funded Columbus's expedition to New World; established Spanish Inquisition (1478).

fer·ment (fĕr´ment) n. 1. Leaven; any fermentative agent, such as yeast. 2. Fermenting, fermentation; agitation, excitement, tumult. ~ (fĕrmĕnt´) v. Undergo, subject to, fermentation; (make) effervesce; excite, stir up, foment.

fer·men·ta·tion (fĕrmĕntā´-

shon) n. Process like that induce by yeast on dough or suga solutions, with effervescenc evolution of heat, and change properties; agitation, excitemen **fer·ment·a·tive** (fĕrmĕn´tatĭv) a

Fer·mi (fĕr´mē; *It.* fĕr´mē **Enrico** (1901–54). Italian atom and nuclear physicist, living U.S. from 1939; he helped develop first self-sustaining cha reaction; Nobel Prize for physi 1938.

fer·mi·um (fĕr´mēum) (chem.) Transuranic elemen symbol Fm, at. no. 100, princip isotope at. wt. 256. [f. FERMI]

fern (fĕrn) n. Any of variou flowerless, seedless plants, fre with feathery fronds, of the orde Filicales; ~ **seed,** supposed see (actually spores) of the fern, on pop. believed to be invisible an to render invisible those wh

At Dover harbor one **ferry** backs in while another loads cars on deck. Ferries are used extensively in the English Channel to carry, not only goods and passengers, but also cars, to ports on the European continent.

carried it. **fern·y** *adj.* (**fern·i·er, fern·i·est**). **fern·er·y** *n.* (pl. **-er·ies**). Place where ferns are grown; collection of ferns.

fe·ro·cious (ferō'shus) *adj.* Fierce, savage, cruel. **fe·ro'·cious·ly** *adv.*

fe·roc·i·ty (ferŏs'itē) *n.* Ferocious character or act.

-ferous *suffix.* Forming adjectives (usu. with intermediate -i-) with sense bearing, having, as in *coniferous.*

fer·ret[1] (fĕr'it) *n.* Half-tamed variety of Old World polecat (*Mustela putorius*), kept for driving rabbits from burrows, killing rats, etc.; also, **black-footed** ~ (*Mustela nigripes*), a rare and endangered animal of Western N. Amer. ~ *v.* 1. Hunt with ferrets; clear out (holes, ground), take or drive away (rabbits etc.), with ferrets. 2. Rummage; search *out.*

fer·ret[2] (fĕr'it) *n.* Stout cotton or silk tape for edging or binding fabric. [It. *fioretti* floss silk (L. *flos* flower)]

ferri- *prefix.* (chem.) Containing iron in the ferric or trivalent state.

fer·ric (fĕr'ik) *adj.* 1. Of iron. 2. (chem.) Applied to compounds of trivalent iron, e.g. ~ **oxide** (Fe_2O_3).

Fer·ris (fĕr'is) **wheel.** Giant revolving vertical wheel suspending passenger seats on its rim, an amusement ride at fairs etc. [G. W. G. *Ferris* (1859–96), Amer. engineer]

fer·rite (fĕr'īt) *n.* 1. (chem.) Compound formed from ferric oxide and a basic oxide or from ferric hydroxide and a base, esp. magnetic substance used in high-frequency electrical components. 2. (metall.) Soft allotrope of pure iron; solid solution based on this allotrope.

ferro- *comb. form.* 1. Of, containing, iron. 2. (chem., in names of compounds) Containing iron in the ferrous or bivalent state.

fer·ro·mag·net·ic (fĕrōmăg-nĕt'ik) *adj.* Possessing the property shown by iron, cobalt, nickel, and their alloys, of having a large magnetic permeability and retaining magnetization in the absence of an external magnetic field. **fer·ro·mag'net·ism** *n.*

fer·ro·man·ga·nese (fĕrō-măng'ganēs, -nēz) *n.* Alloy of manganese and iron used in making alloy steels.

fer·ro·type (fĕr'otīp) *n.* Photographic process producing print on thin iron plate; such photograph;

The **ferret** is said to have been bro[ught] to Europe from North Africa by [the] Romans and has been used for hun[ting] since that time. It is a domestic[ated] form of the polecat.

Fertilizers, either natural or chemical, are used where soil is either poor or impoverished. Where large areas of land are under cultivation, as here in Australia, aerial crop-dusting is employed.

tintype.

fer·rous (fĕr′us) *adj.* (chem.) Of or containing iron, esp. in the bivalent state, e.g. ~ **oxide** (FeO).

fer·rule (fĕr′ul, -ōol) *n.* Metal ring or cap strengthening end of stick or tube; ring or band holding parts together; one of several small rings through which line runs on fishing rod.

fer·ry (fĕr′ē) *n.* (pl. **-ries**). Place where boats pass to and fro over river etc., to transport passengers, cars, or freight; ferryboat; ferryboat landing; short-distance transportation service, esp. one connecting main-line services; **fer′ryboat,** boat used for ferrying; **fer′ryman,** man who owns or operates a ferry. **ferry** *v.* (**-ried, -ry·ing**). Transport (person, car, freight, etc.) across a body of water; (of boat) pass to and fro, over river, lake, etc.; transport from place to place, esp. on regular service; deliver, transport (vehicle) under its own power.

fer·tile (fĕr′til; *Brit.* fĕr′tīl) *adj.* Bearing abundantly, fruitful; (of seed or egg etc.) capable of developing into a new individual; **F ~ Crescent,** semicircle of formerly fertile land from Israel to the Tigris River and the Persian Gulf. **fer·til·i·ty** (fĕrtil′itē) *n.*

fer·til·ize (fĕr′tilīz) *v.t.* (**-ized, -iz·ing**). 1. Make fertile, enrich (esp. soil); make productive. 2. (biol.) Make (ovum etc., female individual or organ) fruitful by introduction of sperm, pollen, etc. **fer·til·i·za·tion** (fĕrtilīzā′shon) *n.* Fertilizing; (biol.) fusion of male reproductive cell with female one. **fer′til·iz·er** *n.* (esp.) Manure; chemical compound, usu. containing nitrogen, phosphorus, or potassium, used to increase fertility of soil.

fer·ule (fĕr′ul, -ōol) *n.* Cane, rod, or stick used for punishing children.

fer·vent (fĕr′vent) *adj.* 1. Hot, glowing. 2. Ardent, intense. **fer′ven·cy** *n.* **fer′vent·ly** *adv.*

fer·vid (fĕr′vĭd) *adj.* 1. Hot, glowing. 2. Fervent; impassioned. **fer′vid·ly** *adv.* **fer′vid·ness** *n.*

fer·vor (fĕr′ver) *n.* 1. Intense heat. 2. Vehemence, passion, zeal.

fes·cue (fĕs′kū) *n.* Grass of genus *Festuca,* valuable as pasturage.

fes·tal (fĕs′tal) *adj.* Of a feast; festive; joyous. **fes′tal·ly** *adv.*

The **Edinburgh Festival** offers a variety of cultural events, mostly in music and drama, for a period of 3 weeks in the Fall. Here a tattoo is performed in front of Edinburgh Castle.

fes·ter (fĕs´ter) v. (of wound or sore) Generate matter, ulcerate; (of poison, disease, grief) cause suppuration, rankle; putrefy, rot; cause festering in. ~ n. Festering condition.

fes·ti·val (fĕs´tĭval) adj. Of, befitting, a feast or feast day. ~ n. Time of festive celebration; merry-making; (periodic) series of performances (of music, drama, films, etc.).

fes·tive (fĕs´tĭv) adj. Of a feast or festival; joyous. **fes´tive·ly** adv.

fes·tiv·i·ty (fĕstĭv´ĭtē) n. (pl. **-ties**). Gaiety, rejoicing; festive celebration; (pl.) festive proceedings.

fes·toon (fĕstōon´) n. Chain of flowers or leaves, or ribbons etc., hung in curve between 2 points; carved or molded representation of this. ~ v. Adorn (as) with, form into, festoons. **fes·toon´er·y** n.

Fest·schrift (fĕst´shrĭft) n. (pl. **-schrift·en** pr. **-shrĭften, -schrifts**). (also l.c.) Collection of writings in honor of eminent scholar. [Ger., = "festival writing"]

F.E.T. abbrev. Federal Excise Tax.

fe·tal (fē´tal) adj. Of, pertaining to, or like a fetus.

fetch (fĕch) v. 1. (Go for and) bring back (person or thing); (now rare) cause to come, draw forth (blood, tears, etc.). 2. Bring in, realize, sell for (a price). 3. Heave (sigh); draw (breath); deal (blow). **fetch´ing** adj. Attractive, taking. **fetch** n. Act of fetching.

fete, fête (fāt, fĕt) ns. Festival; elaborate party, dinner, or entertainment; bazaar or fair. ~ v.t. (**fet·ed, fet·ing, fêt·ed, fêt·ing**). Entertain, honor, or celebrate with a fete.

fet·id, Brit. **foet·id** (fĕt´ĭd, fē´tĭd) adjs. Stinking. **fet´id·ly** adv. **fet´id·ness** n.

fet·ish (fĕt´ĭsh, fē´tĭsh) n. 1. Inanimate object worshipped by primitive peoples for its supposed inherent magical powers or as being inhabited by a spirit; anything irrationally reverenced. 2. (psych.) Abnormal stimulus, or object, of sexual desire. **fet´ish·ism, fet´ish·ist** ns. **fet·ish·is·tic** (fĕtĭshĭs´tĭk) adj. [Port. feitiço charm. f. L. facticius factitious]

fet·lock (fĕt´lŏk) n. Part of horse's leg where tuft of hair grows behind pastern joint; this tuft of hair.

fe·tor (fē´ter) n. Stench.

fet·ter (fĕt´er) n. Shackle for feet; bond; (pl.) captivity; check, restraint. ~ v.t. Bind (as) with fetters; impede, restrain.

fet·tle (fĕt´el) n. Condition, trim (only in **in fine** etc. ~).

fet·tu·ci·ni (fĕtuchē´nē) n. (considered sing. or pl.). Pasta in

This **fetish** is from Rarotonga, in the Cook Islands in the south-west Pacific Ocean. It is an ironwood image of the god, Te Rango, and his 3 sons.

The **feverfew** thrives in ordinary soil and in open positions. It was formerly used for medicinal purposes, but can also be a troublesome weed.

narrow strips, cooked and serv with a sauce.

fe·tus, foe·tus (fē´tus) ns. (**-tus·es**). Unborn or unhatch offspring, esp. human embryo mo than eight weeks after conceptio

feud (fūd) n. Lasting mut hostility, esp. between two clans families, with murderous assaults revenge for previous injury. ~ v Engage in feud.

feu·dal (fū´dal) adj. Of a fief; resembling, according to, the feuc system; ~ **system**, medieval Eur pean economic and social syste based on relation of superior a vassal arising from holding of lan in feud; system by which land w held in return for services, inclu ing military service, homage, etc. a superior. **feu´dal·ly** adv. **feu dal·ism, feu´dal·ist** ns. **feu·dal is·tic** (fūdalĭs´tĭk) adj.

fe·ver (fē´ver) n. 1. Abnormal high body temperature; reaction the body to a general infectio characterized by raised temper ture, restlessness, panting, thirs and wasting; any of a group diseases, each caused by a specif agent, in which this reaction occur ~ **therapy**, artificial production state of fever in order to raise bo temperature to a point lethal certain organisms of disease. Nervous excitement, agitation.

fe·ver·few (fē´verfū) n. Feath ery-leaved perennial plant (Chr santhemum parthenium) allied to t camomile, formerly used as febrifuge. [L. febris fever, fuga drive away]

fe·ver·ish (fē´verĭsh) adj. Havir symptoms of fever; excited, fitfu restless; of or like fever; causin infected by, fever. **fe´ver·ish·l adv. fe´ver·ish·ness** n.

few (fū) adj. Not many but mo than one; ~ **and far betwee** infrequent; **have a** ~, (colloq.) tak several alcoholic drinks; **quite a** ~ a fair number (of); **some** ~, n great number (of). **few** n. Fev persons or things; **the** ~, th minority, the elect, etc. **few´nes** n.

fey (fā) adj. 1. (Sc.) Fated to di at point of death; having visionar power, like person about to die. 2 Affected; whimsical.

fez (fĕz) n. Muslim man's red fel cap like truncated cone, with lon black tassel from top, formerl Turkish national headdress [Turk., perh. f. Fez, town i Morocco.]

ff abbrev. (music) Fortissimo.

ff. abbrev. Folios; followin pages etc.

FHA abbrev. Federal Housin Administration.

fi·an·cé, fem. **fi·an·cée** (fēahn sā´, -ahn´sā) ns. One's betrothed.

fi·as·co (fēăs´kō, -ah´skō) n. (pl **-coes, -cos**). Complete failure o

Another name for violin is fiddle. Though most violins are played in an orchestra, occasionally a fiddler will entertain drinkers in a restaurant or bar.

reakdown; ignominious result. It., = "bottle" (unexplained llusion)]

fi·at (fī′at, fē′-, -ăt) *n*. Authoriation; decree, order; **~ money**, aper money made legal tender by overnment fiat and not backed by old or silver. [L. *fiat* be it done]

fib (fĭb) *n. & v.i.* (**fibbed, ib·bing**). (Tell) venial or trivial alsehood; lie. **fib′ber** *n*.

fi·ber, Brit. **fi·bre** (fī′ber) *ns*. Threadlike cell or filament formng, with others, animal or egetable tissue or textile subtance; substance consisting of ibers; fibrous structure; fibrous ubstance fit for textile fabrics; mall root or twig; **fi′berboard**, tiff board of wood fibers; i′berglass (also **Fiberglas** [tradenark]), glass in fibrous form woven nto textiles or used for packing, nsulation, etc.; plastic reinforced with this; **~ optics**, transmission of mages through glass etc. fibers by otal internal reflection. **fi·briform** (fī′brifōrm, fĭb′ri-) *adj*.

fi·bril (fī′brĭl, fĭb′rĭl) *n*. 1. Small fiber; subdivision of fiber. 2. Ultimate subdivision of root.

fi·bril·la·tion (fībrĭlā′shon, ĭbri-) *n*. Formation of fibers or ibrils; (path.) quivering movement

in fibrils of muscle or nerve.

fi·brin (fī′brĭn) *n*. Insoluble protein formed from fibrinogen during blood clotting, and polymerizing to form the network of the clot. **fi′brin·ous** *adj*.

fi·brin·o·gen (fībrĭn′ojen) *n*. Soluble protein in blood plasma, precursor of fibrin.

fibro- *comb. form*. Fiber.

fi·broid (fī′broid) *adj*. (chiefly path.) Resembling fiber or fibrous tissue; (of disease) characterized by formation or inflammation of connective tissue. **~** *n*. Fibroid uterine tumor.

fi·bro·sis (fībrō′sĭs) *n*. (path.) Fibroid degeneration; development of fibrous tissue in organ.

fi·brous (fī′brus) *adj*. Of, resembling, fiber(s).

fib·u·la (fĭb′yula) *n*. (pl. **-lae** pr. -lē, **-las**). (anat.) Slender bone on outer side of leg between knee and ankle. **fib′u·lar** *adj*.

-fic *suffix*. Forming (usu. with intermediate -i-) adjectives with sense of producing, making (*beatific, pacific, scientific*).

F.I.C.A. *abbrev*. Federal Insurance Contributions Act.

fiche (fēsh, fĭsh) *n*. Microfiche.

fick·le (fĭk′el) *adj*. Inconstant, changeable. **fick′le·ness** *n*.

fic·tion (fĭk′shon) *n*. 1. Feigning, invention; thing feigned or imagined, invented statement or narrative; literature consisting of such narrative, esp. novels. 2. Conventionally accepted falsehood; **legal ~**: see LEGAL. **fic′tion·al** *adj*. **fic′tion·al·ly** *adv*. **fic′tion·al·ize** (fĭk′shonalīz) *v.t.* (**-ized, -iz·ing**). Make into fiction.

fic·ti·tious (fĭktĭsh′us) *adj*. Counterfeit, not genuine; (of name or character) feigned, assumed; imaginary, unreal; of fiction; constituted or regarded as such by (legal or conventional) fiction. **fic·ti′tious·ly** *adv*. **fic·ti′tious·ness** *n*.

fic·tive (fĭk′tĭv) *adj*. Creating, created, by imagination; of fiction or its creation.

fid·dle (fĭd′el) *n*. 1. (colloq.) Violin; **play first, second, ~**, take leading, subordinate, position. 2. (naut.) Rack, guardrail, etc. to keep things from rolling off table. 3. **fiddlededee′!**, nonsense!; **fiddlefaddle**, trifling talk or action, trivial matters; (*int.*) nonsense! (*v.i.*) fuss, trifle; **fid′dlestick**, violin bow; **fiddlesticks!**, nonsense!; **~** *int*. nonsense! **fiddle** *v*. (**-dled, -dling**). 1. Play the fiddle; play (tune) on fiddle. 2. Be idle or frivolous; make aimless movements or changes (*with*); fritter *away*. 3. Cheat, swindle; falsify (accounts).

fid·dler (fĭd′ler) *n*. (esp.) 1. Player on fiddle. 2. **~ crab**, any of several small, burrowing crabs of the genus *Uca*, in coastal regions, the male of which has one of its claws much enlarged.

Fi·de·i De·fen·sor (fī′dēī dĭfen′sōr). Defender of the Faith; title of English sovereigns since Henry VIII, who received it from Pope Leo X in 1521 as a reward for writing against Luther. [L.]

fi·del·i·ty (fĭdĕl′ĭtē, fī-) *n*. (pl. **-ties**). Faithfulness, loyalty (*to*); strict conformity to truth or fact, exact correspondence to the original.

fidg·et (fĭj′ĭt) *n*. 1. Bodily uneasiness seeking relief in spasmodic movements (freq. **the ~s**); restless mood. 2. Person who fidgets. 3. Fidgeting. **~** *v*. Move restlessly (*about*); be uneasy, worry; make (person) uncomfortable, worry. **fidg′et·y** *adj*. **fidg′et·i·ness** *n*.

fi·du·cial (fĭdoo′shal, -dū′-) *adj*. 1. Of, of the nature of, trust or reliance. 2. (surveying etc.) of line, point, etc.) Assumed as fixed basis of comparison.

fi·du·ci·ar·y (fĭd oo′shēērē, -dū′-, -sherē) *adj*. Of trust or trustee(ship); held or given in trust; **~ bond**, bond posted as surety by a fiduciary as administrator of an estate. **fiduciary** *n.* (pl. **-ar·ies**). Trustee of property, securities, etc.

fief (fēf) *n.* Feudal estate; fee.

field (fēld) *n.* 1. (Piece of) ground, esp. one used for tillage or pasture; tract abounding in some natural product, as coal, oil, diamonds. 2. Ground on which battle is fought; scene of campaign or military operations; **in the ~**, (esp.) engaged in military operations; working with agents, customers, etc. away from home office; **leave the ~ open**, abstain from interference or competition; **play the ~,** (colloq.) avoid exclusive commitment to one person etc. 3. Ground for playing football, cricket, etc.; (baseball) outfield. 4. Those who take part in outdoor contest or sport; all competitors in race etc., or all except the favorite; in horse races, those entries that are treated as a single entry in pari-mutuel betting. 5. Large stretch, expanse, of sea, ice, snow, etc. (also fig.). 6. Surface on which something is portrayed; (her.) surface of escutcheon or of one of its divisions; ground of flag, picture, etc. 7. Area

or sphere of action, operation, investigation, etc.; space or range within which objects are visible through optical instrument; **magnetic ~**, region in which magnetic properties can be detected. 8. (attrib.) (of animals, plants, etc.) Growing or living in a field or fields; wild; (of investigation, study, etc.) carried out on the spot, not in laboratory, classroom, or office; **~ artillery**, light and mobile artillery for use in the field, so **~ gun; ~ day**, day devoted to outdoor games, sports, activities, athletic competitions, etc.; **~ events**, throwing

and jumping events of a track me as opp. to the running events; **glasses**, portable lightweig binocular telescope for outdoor u **~ goal**, (basketball) score of tw points, made by tossing b through basket during regular pla (football) score of three poin made by kicking the ball fro field; **~ hand**, hired farm work **~ hockey**, game played on fie between goals, using ball a curved sticks; **~ hospita** temporary hospital near battlefie **~ marshal**: see MARSHAL; **officer**, army officer above rank captain and below that of gener **field'stone**, stone as it natura occurs in fields, esp. when used f building; **field test**, test of product, process, etc., by subjec ing it to actual working conditior **field work**, field investigatio study, etc. (see above). **field** Act as a fielder in baseball, cricke etc.; stop (and return) ball; p (team) into field. **field'er** *n.*

Field glasses or binoculars are used many outdoor activities. In sports l horse racing and baseball where t spectator may be some distance fro the action, they are essential.

armored shield

sight port to enable telescope to be used

anti-tank telescope

range scale

elevation handwheel

traverse handwheel (4° left and right of center line

gunners seat

spade digs into so ground to counter

heavy duty tires for cross country towing

This 25-pounder field gun was used by the British Army as an anti-tank weapon during the 1939–45 war and continued in use until the late 1960s. Its range was about 12,500 yards.

Field¹ (fēld), **Cyrus West** (1819–92). Amer. financier who promoted and backed construction of first underwater transatlantic cable (1854); first message was transmitted between England and U.S. on Aug. 16, 1858.

Field² (fēld), **Eugene** (1850–95). Amer. journalist and poet noted for children's verse; wrote "Wynken, Blynken, and Nod," "Little Boy Blue," "The Little Peach," etc.

field·fare (fēld′fār) *n.* Species of Old World thrush (*Turdus pilaris*) having brown and gray plumage.

Field·ing (fēl′dĭng), **Henry** (1707–54). English novelist; author of *Joseph Andrews, Tom Jones*, etc.

Fields (fēldz), **W(illiam) C(laude) Dunkenfield** (1880–1946). Amer. vaudeville and motion picture actor.

fiend (fēnd) *n.* (usu. cap.) The Devil; evil spirit, demon; person of superhuman wickedness (esp. cruelty or malignity); one addicted (esp. to drugs); one obsessed with a hobby, job, etc. **fiend′ish** *adj.* **fiend′ish·ly** *adv.* **fiend′ish·ness** *n.*

fierce (fērs) *adj.* Violent in hostility, angrily combative; of formidably violent and intractable temper; raging, vehement; ardent, eager. **fierce′ly** *adv.* **fierce′ness** *n.*

fi·er·y (fī′ērē, fīr′ē) *adj.* **-er·i·er, -er·i·est.** 1. Consisting of or flaming with fire. 2. Looking like fire, blazing red; (of eyes) flashing, ardent. 3. Hot as fire; acting like fire, producing burning sensation. 4. ~ **cross**, wooden

Field events, particularly throwing contests, were a part of the original Olympic Games as played in Greece. Jumping events include high jump, broad jump and triple jump.

cross with arms charred or dipped in blood, formerly sent among Scottish Highland clans as a call to arms; burning cross used by Ku Klux Klan as symbol or emblem. 5. Eager, pugnacious, spirited; excitable; tempestuous. **fi′er·i·ly** *adv.* **fi′er·i·ness** *n.*

fi·es·ta (fēĕs′ta) *n.* (in Spain etc.) Religious or other festival.

fife (fīf) *n.* Small shrill-toned instrument of flute kind, used chiefly to accompany drum in military music. ~ *v.* (**fifed, fif·ing**). Play fife; play (air etc.) on fife. **fif′er** *n.*

FIFO *abbrev.* First in first out (method of inventory valuation under which the price of merchandise sold and used is based on the cost of the earliest acquisitions and the value of the remaining merchandise is based on the cost of the most recent acquisition).

fif·teen (fĭf′tēn′) *adj.* Amounting to 15. ~ *n.* One more than 14 (15, xv, or XV). **fif′teenth′** *adj.* & *n.*

fifth (fĭfth *adj.* Next after fourth; **F ~ Amendment**, amendment to the U.S. Constitution providing that no one may be held for a serious crime unless indicted, nor be tried twice for the same offense, nor be forced to testify against himself or herself, nor deprived of life, liberty, or property without due process of law; **F ~ Avenue**, one of the

principal streets of New York, noted for its fine stores; ~ **column**, orig. the column of supporters that Gen. Mola declared himself to have in Madrid, when he was besieging it in the Spanish Civil War, in addition to the 4 columns of his army outside the city; hence, organized body sympathizing with and working for enemy within a country at war; ~ **columnist**, member of such a body; **taking the F ~,** refusing to testify on the grounds that to do so might incriminate oneself; ~ **wheel,** superfluous person or thing. **fifth** *n.* Fifth part; fifth thing etc.; fifth grade in school; (mus.) interval of which the span involves five alphabetical names of notes, harmonic combination of notes thus separated. **fifth′ly** *adv.* In the fifth place.

fif·ty (fĭf′tē) *adj.* Amounting to 50. ~ *n.* (pl. **-ties**). Cardinal number, 5 times 10 (50, l, or L); **fifties,** numbers etc. from 50 to 59; these years of century or life; **fifty-fifty,** (colloq.) half-and-half (i.e. 50% each), equally; equal. **fif′ti·eth** *adj.*

fig¹ (fĭg) *n.* 1. (usu. ~ **tree**) Broad-leaved tree (esp. *Ficus carica*) bearing soft pear-shaped multiple fruit eaten fresh or dried; this fruit. 2. Anything valueless, as in *I don't care a* ~. 3. ~ **leaf,** leaf of a fig tree; stylized representation of such a leaf, esp. as used on statues to conceal the genitals; something designed to hide whatever might be thought in questionable taste (see Gen. 3); ~ **marigold,** any of

FIG 620 FIGUI

various South African plants of the genus *Mesembryanthemum* having fleshy leaves and brilliant blooms of various colors; **fig·wort** (fĭg′wert, -wȯrt), herb of genus *Scrophularia* (esp. *S. lanceolata*).

fig² (fĭg) *n.* Dress, array; condition, form.

fig. *abbrev.* Figure(s); figurative(ly).

fight (fīt) *v.* (**fought** pr. fawt, **fight·ing**). Contend in battle or single combat (*against, with*); strive to overcome (disease, fire, fear, etc.); maintain (cause, suit at law, quarrel) against opponent; contend over (question), win one's way by fighting; contend with in battle or duel, or with the fists; set on (cocks, dogs) to fight; ~ **back**, resist; ~ **for**, fight on behalf of (person, beliefs, etc.) or to secure (thing); ~ **off**, repel with effort; ~ **it out**, settle by fighting; ~ **shy of**, keep aloof from; **fighting chance**, chance of succeeding by great effort; **fighting cock**, gamecock trained to fight; **fighting fish**, Siamese fish of genus *Betta* (esp. *B. splendens*). **fight** *n.* Action of fighting; battle; combat, esp. pugilistic or unpremeditated, between two or more persons, animals or parties; strife, conflict; appetite or ability for fighting, as in *he has* ~ *in him yet*; **running** ~, fight kept up while one party flees and one pursues; **show** ~, not yield tamely.

fight·er (fī′ter) *n.* One who fights; fast warplane designed for aerial combat rather than for bombing; ~**-bomber**, military aircraft combining functions of a fighter and a bomber.

fig·ment (fĭg′ment) *n.* Invented statement; thing with no existence except in imagination.

fig·ur·al (fĭg′yeral) *adj.* Of human or animal figures or their pictorial representation.

fig·ur·a·tion (fĭgyurā′shon) *n.* 1. Determination to a certain form; the resulting form. 2. Allegorical or figurative representation. 3. (mus.) Use of florid counterpoint.

fig·ur·a·tive (fĭg′yerativ) *adj.* 1. Representing by a figure or emblem; of pictorial or plastic representation. 2. (of speech etc.) Using metaphors, metaphorical, not literal; metaphorically so called; abounding in, addicted to, figures of speech. **fig·ur·a·tive·ly** *adv.* **fig·ur·a·tive·ness** *n.*

fig·ure (fĭg′yer; *Brit.* fĭg′er) *n.* 1. External form, shape; (geom.) definite form constituted by line or lines enclosing superficial space, or by surface or surfaces enclosing space of three dimensions; bodily shape; person considered with regard to visible form or appearance; person as contemplated mentally. 2. Conspicuous appear-

The **fig** tree is cultivated for its fruits and is grown commercially in all Mediterranean countries. The fruit contains a large amount of sugar and is eaten either dried or fresh.

ance, as in *cut a fine* ~; (archaic) importance, distinction. 3. Image, likeness; representation of human form in sculpture, painting, etc. 4. Diagram, illustration; pattern, design; (dancing) evolution or movement of dance or dancer, division of set dance; (skating) movement, series of movements, beginning and ending at center. 5. Numerical system, esp. one of the ten Arabic numerals; amount, number, sum, expressed in figures. 6. (rhet.) Form of expression deviating from normal order or use of words used to give variety, force, etc., e.g., hyperbole, metaphor, etc. (also ~ **of speech**); (logic) particular form of syllogism according to position of middle term; (mus.)

*Animals rarely **fight** or attack their ow species. They display aggression, ho ever, when guarding their territory their young, and when competing for mate. In many instances such displa follow a ritualistic pattern.*

brief melodic or rhythmic formu out of which longer passages a developed. 7. **fig′urehead**, orn mental carving, usu. bust or ful length figure, over ship's pro nominal leader, president, etc without real authority or influenc **figure** *v.* (**-ured, -ur·ing**). Represent in diagram or pictur picture mentally, imagine; en bellish with design or pattern, es (mus.) with accompaniment quicker time. 2. Mark wi (numerical) figures; (mus.) wri

Porcelain **figurines,** which were both delicate and durable, were produced in England and Europe from the early 1700s. This was because of the addition of bone to the china clay. This Derby figurine was made about 1755.

This flamboyant **figurehead,** (left) the Ajax, is from a ship of the early 19th century. Figureheads originally had religious or military significance and were lavishly painted and decorated.

Filigree metalwork, with its open, lace-like effect, has an ancient and wide-spread history. There are numerous examples from ancient Greece, Egypt, and Rome. This dagger is of Italian origin.

figures over or under (bass) to indicate harmony. 3. Use figures in arithmetic; work out (sum); (colloq.) calculate, reckon, estimate; ~ **on,** rely on, count on.

fig·ur·ine (fĭgyurēn′) n. Small modeled or sculpted figure, statuette.

Fi·ji (fē′jē). 1. Principal island of ~ **Islands,** an archipelago of about 250 islands in the S. Pacific; in British possession from 1874; republic, member of Brit. Commonwealth, 1970; capital, Suva. 2. Native, language, of Fiji or the Fiji Islands. **Fi·ji·an** (fē′jēan, fījē′-) adj. & n.

fil·a·gree (fĭl′agrē) = FILIGREE.

fil·a·ment (fĭl′ament) n. Slender threadlike body (esp., in animal and vegetable structures, one consisting of a row of cells); (bot.) part of stamen supporting anther; fine, not easily fusible metallic conductor in electric light bulb, vacuum tube, etc., heated or made incandescent by current. **fil·a·men·ta·ry** (fĭlamĕn′terē), **fil·a·men′tous** adjs.

fi·lar·i·a (fĭlār′ēa) n. (pl. **-lar·i·ae** pr. -lār′ēē). Parasitic nematode worm esp. of genus Filaria, infesting vertebrates, including man. **fi·lar′i·al, fi·lar′i·an** adjs.

fil·a·ri·a·sis (fĭlarī′asĭs) n. Disease caused by filarial worms when they infest lymph tissue.

fil·bert (fĭl′bert) n. (Nut of) cultivated hazel (Corylus maxima). [Fr. noix de filbert, from being ripe near St. Philibert's day, Aug. 20]

filch (fĭlch) v.t. Steal, pilfer.

file[1] (fīl) n. Instrument usu. of steel with one or more surfaces covered with numerous small raised cutting edges or teeth, for abrading, reducing, or smoothing surfaces. ~ v.t. (**filed, fil·ing**). Smooth, reduce surface of, with file; ~ **away, off,** remove with file.

file[2] (fīl) n. Receptacle, etc. that keeps documents for preservation and reference; folder or other device for holding papers for reference; set of papers so kept; series of issues of newspaper in order. ~ v.t. (**filed, fil·ing**). Place (papers) on file or among public records.

file[3] (fīl) n. (mil.) Line of soldiers or vehicles one behind the other; row of persons or things one behind the other; (chess) one of the 8 lines of squares extending across board from player to player; **in** ~, one behind the other; **rank and** ~: see RANK[1]; **on** ~, stored in file. **file** v. (**filed, fil·ing**). March in file.

fi·let (fīlā′, fĭl′ā; Brit. fĭl′ĭt) n. (pl. **fi·lets** pr. fĭlāz′, fĭl′āz; Brit. fĭl′ĭts). 1. Net with square mesh, used for curtains etc. 2. = FILLET def. 2.

fi·let mi·gnon (fīlā′mĭnyŏn′) (pl. **fi·lets mi·gnons** pr. fīlā′mĭnyŏnz′). Small round cut of beef tenderloin.

fil·i·al (fĭl´ēal) *adj.* Of, befitting, a son or daughter.

fil·i·bus·ter (fĭl´ĭbŭster) *n.* 1. Adventurer who engages in a private military action against a foreign country; (hist.) piratical adventurer pillaging Spanish W. Indian colonies in 17th c.; member of bands of adventurers organizing revolutionary expeditions from U.S. to Central America and Spanish W. Indies, 1850–60. 2. Obstructionist, obstruction, in legislative assembly, esp. one who or that which employs prolonged speeches; long obstructive speech or series of speeches in a legislature. ~ *v.* Conduct a legislative fili-buster. [Du. *vrijbuiter* freebooter]

fil·i·gree (fĭl´ĭgrē) *n.* Ornamental work of fine gold or silver wire formed into delicate tracery; fine metal openwork; anything delicate resembling this. ~ *v.t.* (**-greed, -gree·ing**). Decorate or form into filigree.

fil·ing (fī´lĭng) *n.* (esp., usu. pl.) Particle(s) rubbed off by file.

Fil·i·pi·no (fĭlĭpē´nō) *n.* (pl. **-nos**). Native, inhabitant, of Philippine Islands.

fill (fĭl) *v.* 1. Make or become full (*with*); stock abundantly, occupy whole capacity or extent of, pervade; satisfy, satiate; (of wind) cause (sails) to swell; (of sail) become full of wind; (of dentist) block up (cavity) with cement etc.; (poker) complete (flush, full house, etc.) by drawing card(s). 2. Hold (position), discharge duties of (office); occupy (vacant time); appoint holder of (vacant post). 3. Adulterate; add a foreign substance. 4. ~ **in**, complete (outline); act as substitute; add what is wanted to complete (unfinished document, blank check, etc.); (slang) inform (person) more fully; ~**-in** (*n.*), person or thing that substitutes or replaces, usu. temporarily; (colloq.) short summary of basic facts; ~ **out**, enlarge, become enlarged; ~ **up**, fill completely; fill tank of vehicle with gasoline; supply vacant parts or places or deficiencies in; grow full. **fill´er** *n.* Trivial news item designed primarily to fill space in newspapers; substance used to fill spaces left in construction; person or substance that fills. **fill** *n.* Full supply of drink or food (only in **drink, eat, have**, etc., **one's** ~); enough to fill something.

fil·let (fĭl´ĭt; for def. 2 of *n.* & *v.* also fīlā´, fĭl´ā) *n.* 1. String, narrow band of any material, bound around head to confine hair, for ornament, etc.; band, bandage; thin narrow strip of anything. 2. (also **filet**) Piece of boneless meat or fish. 3. (archit.) Narrow flat band separat-

Filberts fruit best in well-drained soil and in full sun. These hazelnut plantations are in Turkey which, with Italy and Spain, is a leading commercial producer of the hazelnut.

ing two moldings; small ba between flutes of column; rais rim or edge on any surface; (boo binding) plain line impressed w cover, tool for making this. ~ *v* 1. Bind (hair etc.) with fille encircle with ornamental band. Divide (fish or meat) into fillet remove bones from.

fill·ing (fĭl´ĭng) *adj. & n.* (esp Cement etc. inserted into cavity tooth; ~ **station**, retail establis ment selling gasoline to motorist

fil·lip (fĭl´ĭp) *n.* Sudden relea of finger or thumb when it has be bent and checked by thumb finger; slight smart stroke th given; stimulus, incentive. ~ Propel (coin, marble, etc.) with fillip; stimulate; strike slightly ar smartly; make a fillip.

Fill·more (fĭl´mōr, -mŏr Millard (1800–74). Vice preside of U.S., 1849–50; 13th president U.S., 1850–3.

fil·ly (fĭl´ē) *n.* (pl. **-lies**). Fema colt; (slang) lively young woman.

film (fĭlm) *n.* 1. Thin skin, plat coating, or layer; slight veil o covering of haze, mist, etc.; fi thread or filament; morbid growt on eye; growing dimness in eyes o dying person. 2. (phot.) Thin stri of material (esp. cellulose acetat coated with light-sensitive emu sion for exposure in camera; piec of this for one exposure, or ro sufficient for a series. 3. Story incident, etc., recorded on film motion pictures; (pl.) cinem industry. 4. **film´dom**, motio picture business or the people wh work in it; **film´goer**, one who goe to the cinema; **film pack**, cu photographic films arranged in pil in case or holder for dayligh loading or changing; **film´stri** series of transparencies for projec tion. **film´y** *adj.* (**film·i·er, film i·est**). 1. Of or resembling a film transparent, gauzy. 2. Covered b or as if by a film; hazy, blurred **film´i·ness** *n.* **film** *v.* 1. Cove become covered, (as) with film. 2 Photograph (scene, story, etc.) for movie; make a movie.

fil·ter (fĭl´ter) *n.* Contrivance fo freeing liquid from suspende impurities by passing it throug stratum of sand, fiber, charcoa etc.; porous substance used for thi purpose; combination of electri circuits designed to suppress un wanted frequencies; (phot.) screer (usu. of colored glass or gelatine for absorbing light of certain colors ~ **paper**, unsized paper for filter ing liquids; ~ **tip, -tipped**, (ciga rette or cigar) with mouthpiece tha filters the smoke. **filter** *v.* Pass (liquid etc.), flow, through filter make way *through, into*, etc.; (o news etc.) leak *out*, come *through* obtain by filtering. **fil´ter·a·ble fil´tra·ble** *adjs.*

filth (filth) *n.* Foul or dirty matter; corruption, pollution, obscenity; foul language. **filth′y** *adj.* **filth·i·er, filth·i·est**). ~ **lucre**, dishonorable gain; money. **filth′-ly** *adv.* **filth′i·ness** *n.*

fil·trate (fil′trāt) *n.* Filtered liquid. ~ *v.* **(-trat·ed, -trat·ing)**. Filter. **fil·tra·tion** (filtrā′shon) *n.*

fin (fin) *n.* 1. Membranous appendage extending from body of fish, cetaceans, etc. for propelling and steering; (slang) hand. 2. Small projecting surface on various parts of aircraft etc. for ensuring stability. . (slang) Five-dollar bill.

Fin. *abbrev.* Finland; Finnish.

fin. *abbrev.* Financial; finance.

fi·na·gle (finā′gel) *v.* **(-gled, gling)**. (colloq.) Use, get by, trickery; wangle. **fi·na′gler** *n.*

fi·nal (fī′nal) *adj.* 1. At the end, coming last, ultimate; putting an end to doubt etc., conclusive, definitive, unalterable. 2. Concerned with end or purpose. **fi′nal·ly** *adv.* **final** *n.* (sing. or pl.) Last or deciding heat, game, or series; last examination in academic course; last edition of newspaper in a given day. **fi′nal·ist** *n.* Competitor in final.

fi·na·le (finăl′ē, -nah′lē) *n.* (mus.) Last movement of instrumental composition; music bringing act of opera to a close; last scene, closing part, of drama etc., conclusion, end.

fi·nal·i·ty (finăl′ītē) *n.* (pl. **-ties**). Being final; conclusiveness; final act, state, or utterance.

fi·nal·ize (fī′nalīz) *v.t.* **(-ized, -iz·ing)**. Put in final form; approve final form of; complete (agreement etc.).

fi·nance (finăns′, fī′năns) *n.* 1. (pl.) Pecuniary resources of nation, company, person, etc. 2. Management of (esp. public) revenue; money management; ~ **company**, company that makes loans to businesses and consumers. **finance** *v.t.* **(-nanced, -nanc·ing)**. Furnish with finances, or money; find capital for.

fi·nan·cial (finăn′shal, fī-) *adj.* Of finance(s). **fi·nan′cial·ly** *adv.*

fin·an·cier (finansēr′, fī-, -năn-) *n.* One skilled in raising and controlling capital for investment; one skilled in or conducting financial operations.

finch (finch) *n.* Any of numerous small birds of the family Fringillidae, including the bullfinch, bunting, canary, cardinal, and grosbeak, having short conical beak used for cracking seeds.

find (fīnd) *v.t.* **(found** pr. fownd, **find·ing)**. 1. Come across, fall in with, light upon; meet with, obtain, get (usu. something desirable or needful); gain, recover, use of; perceive, recognize; acknowledge or discover to be. 2. Discover

by search; recover (something lost); succeed in obtaining; summon up (courage, resolution, etc.); reach, obtain, attain, as if by effort; ascertain, discover, by mental effort, calculation, study, etc.; ~ **one's bearings**, discover one's location, esp. point or (fig.) condition from which to continue; ~ **one's way**, contrive to reach one's destination; go, be brought, to place, position, etc., in spite of difficulties, inexperience, etc.; ~ **oneself**, discover one's vocation or true self. 3. (law) Determine and declare (person) *guilty* or *innocent*; agree upon (verdict); ascertain validity of (indictment etc.). 4. Supply, provide, furnish. 5. ~ **out**, discover; devise; solve. **find** *n.* Finding, discovery; what is found.

find·er (fīn′der) *n.* Person, thing, that finds; small telescope attached to large one to find object; (photog.) viewfinder.

fin de siè·cle (făn de syě′kle). Characteristic of end of 19th c.; decadent. [Fr.]

find·ing (fīn′dĭng) *n.* (esp.) Verdict, decision (of court, jury, etc.); conclusion after examining; (pl.), small articles, tools, etc., supplied by workmen; verdict or decision reached after judicial proceeding.

fine¹ (fīn) *n.* 1. End (now only in **in** ~, to sum up, finally). 2.

The true **finch** *is restricted to 125 species. The name, however, is often used to refer to any small, seed-eating bird, including waxbills, buntings, and weavers. This one is the Bicheno or banded finch.*

Sum of money fixed as penalty for offense. ~ *v.* **(fined, fin·ing)**. Punish by a fine.

fine² (fīn) *adj.* **(fin·er, fin·est)**. 1. Of high quality; clear, pure, refined; (of gold or silver) containing specified proportion of pure metal. 2. Delicate, subtle; exquisitely fashioned; (of feelings) elevated. 3. Of slender thread; in small particles; thin; sharp. 4. Capable of delicate perception or discrimination; perceptible only with difficulty. 5. Excellent, of striking merit, good, satisfactory, fortunate, of good effect (often iron.); well-conceived or expressed; of handsome appearance or size, dignified; refined; (of weather) bright, free from rain; ornate, showy, smart; fastidious, dainty, flattering, complimentary. 6. ~ **arts**: see ART¹; ~**-drawn**, subtle; extremely thin; ~ **hand**, devious method of manipulating people or events; cunning; subtle; **fine′spun**, delicate, flimsy; excessively subtle; **go over** (or **through**) **with a fine-tooth(ed) comb**, make detailed search or investigation. **fine′ly** *adv.* **fine′ness** *n.* **fine** *adv.*

With only a small margin of time or space, as **to cut** ~. **fine** *v.* (**fined, fin·ing**). Make, become clearer, finer, etc.

fin·er·y (fī′nerē) *n.* (pl. **-er·ies**). Showy dress or decoration.

fi·nesse (fĭnĕs′) *n.* 1. Delicate manipulation, subtle discrimination; artfulness, cunning strategy. 2. (bridge) Playing lower card in hope of taking trick, while holding higher card of same suit (not in sequence). ~ *v.* (**-nessed, -ness·ing**). Use finesse; trick *into* etc. by finesse; make finesse, play (card) by way of finesse, in bridge.

fin·ger (fĭng′ger) *n.* 1. One of five terminal members of hand, or four excluding thumb (usu. numbered first to fourth, starting from that next to thumb); **have a finger in**, be concerned in; **lay, keep one's fingers crossed**, wish for good luck etc. or hope that nothing bad may occur; **put one's finger on**, point with precision to; **turn, twist, around one's (little) finger**, cajole; persuade easily. 2. Part of glove made to receive a finger. 3. Measure, breadth of a finger; small quantity of liquor. 4. Fingerlike object or projection. 5. **fin′gerboard**, part of neck of violin, guitar, etc., on to which strings are pressed when stopped by fingers; **finger bowl**, bowl for rinsing fingers at table after a meal; **Finger Lakes**, group of long, narrow glacial lakes in central and W. New York resort region; **fin′gernail**, horny covering of upper surface of tip of finger; **finger paint**, paint of jellylike consistency, used esp. by children and applied to damp paper with fingers or entire hand; **finger painting**, (1) creation of a painting

The republic of **Finland** in northern Europe has a population of 4½ million, most of whom live in southern areas near the Gulf of Finland, although there are some Lapps in the Arctic north. Seventy per cent of the land is forest. Above left: Floating logs and timber stacks on Lake Saimaa. Above right: Map and flag of Finland.

with finger paints; (2) painting created with finger paints; **fingerpaint** (*v.t.*); **fin′gerprint**, impression of tip of finger, esp. as means of identification; **fin′gertip**, end of finger; **have at one's fingertips**, be versed in, know familiarly; **finger wave**, hair wave made by dampening the hair and shaping with comb and fingers. **finger** *v.t.* 1. Touch with, turn about in, the fingers. 2. Play upon (musical instrument) with fingers; (mus.) mark (music) with figures indicating finger with which note is to be played. 3. (slang) Indicate (victim or criminal to police).

fin·ger·ing (fĭng′gerĭng) *n.* (esp.) Proper method of using fingers in playing music; marks on music indicating this.

fin·ger·ling (fĭng′gerlĭng) *n.* Fish of about 1 finger's length or any young fish less than 1 year old.

fin·i·al (fĭn′ēal) *n.* Ornament finishing off apex of roof, gable, spire, etc.; similar ornament used on top of cabinet etc.

fin·i·cal (fĭn′ĭkal) = FINICKY. **fin′i·cal·ly** *adv.* **fin′i·cal·ness** *n.*

fin·ick·y (fĭn′ĭkē) *adj.* Overnice, precise, fastidious; difficult to please; fussy.

fi·nis (fĭn′ĭs, fēnē′, fī′nĭs) *n.* (at end of book or motion picture). End; end of anything.

fin·ish (fĭn′ĭsh) *n.* Last stage, termination; what serves to give completeness; accomplished or completed state; style of finishing (esp. furniture); surface coating or texture; final coat of paint etc. (**fight) to a** ~, (fight) till one party is completely worsted. **finish** *v.* Bring to an end, come to the end omplete; consume, get through, whole or remainder of; **~ off**, dispatch, overcome com-ely; perfect, put final or finish-touches on; complete education reach the end, cease, leave *off*; *in* something or *by* doing; 1, complete one's use of or ociation with; **fin'ishing ch(es)**, step(s) that complete or fect the making of something. **ish·er** *n*. (esp.) Workman or :hine doing last operation in ufacture.

·nite (fī'nīt) *adj*. Bounded, ited; not infinite; (gram., of >) limited by number and son, not infinitive. **fi'nite·ly** . **fi'nite·ness** *n*.

ink (fingk) *n*. 1. Strikebreaker, . a professional one. 2. ormer. 3. Unpleasant person.

'in·land (fin'land). Country of . Europe situated on the gulfs of 1land and Bothnia; captured by ssia from Sweden in 1809; since .7 an independent republic;

capital, Helsinki.

Finn[1] (fin) *n*. Native of Finland. **Finn'ish** *adj*. & *n*. (Language) of Finland.

Finn[2] (fin). Principal hero of a cycle of Irish legends; son of Cumal and father of Ossian; supposed to have lived in the 3rd c. A.D.

Finn. *abbrev*. Finnish.

fin·nan had·die (fin'an hăd'ē). Haddock cured with smoke. [app. f. name of river *Findhorn*, confused with *Findon*, village in Kincardine-shire, Scotland]

Finno- *prefix*. Finnish; **~-Ugrian, -Ugric**, (of) a subfamily of the Uralic languages spoken in Hungary, Lapland, Finland, and some adjacent parts of U.S.S.R.

fiord = FJORD.

fir (fēr) *n*. 1. (also **~ tree**) Evergreen coniferous tree of genus *Abies*, esp. **balsam ~** (*Abies balsamea*), the common eastern Christmas tree; various other genera of evergreen trees with needles arranged singly on the

shoots.

fire (fīr, fī'er) *n*. 1. Natural agency or active principle operative in combustion; flame, incandes-cence; volcanic heat; state of ignition; **catch, take, ~**, begin to burn; **on ~**, burning; **set ~ to, set on ~**, cause to burn, kindle. 2. Burning fuel in grate, furnace, etc. 3. Destructive burning, esp. of building, forest, etc., conflagration. 4. Luminosity, glow, like that of fire; **St. Elmo's ~**: see ELMO. 5. Burning heat, fever. 6. Burning passion; fervor, enthusiasm; live-liness and warmth of imagination, poetic inspiration. 7. Discharge of firearms; **line of ~**, path of bullet etc.; **open ~**, begin firing; **under**

Fiords *are formed by the sinking of the land or the rise of sea-level leading to the flooding of mountainous coastal val-leys. Fiords, like this one in New Zealand, are found also in Scotland, Alaska, Iceland, and Norway.*

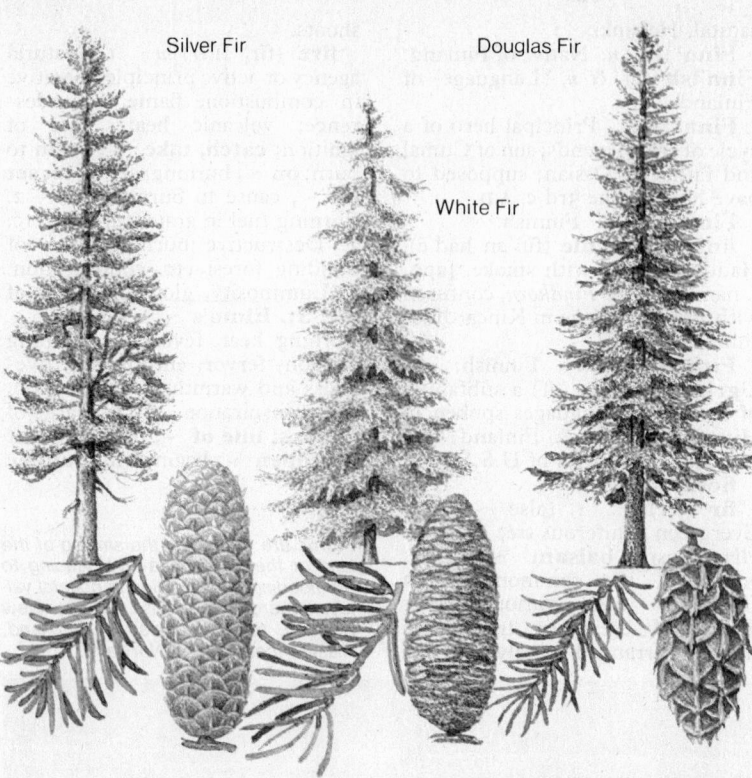

Silver Fir   Douglas Fir

White Fir

*The **fir** tree differs from the pine in that its leaves are short and are borne separately along the twigs. The silver fir is found in Britain and central Europe where it forms large forests. The*

Colorado (white) fir is often used for planting in parks. The Douglas fir and some spruces are mistakenly called firs.

~, being shot at. 8. ~ **alarm**, automatic arrangement for giving notice of outbreak of fire; **fire′-arm**, (usu. pl.) weapon from which missiles are propelled by gunpowder or other explosive; **fire′-ball**, large luminous meteor, lightning in globular form; **fire′base**, military base near front line, giving support to advancing troops with artillery, rockets, etc.; **fire′boat**, boat with fire-fighting equipment, used in waterfront areas; **fire′-bomb**, incendiary bomb; **fire′box**, fuel chamber of steam boiler; **fire′brand**, piece of burning wood; person who stirs up strife or mischief; **fire′break**, strip of land cleared, burned, or plowed to stop the advance of a fire through a forest, across a prairie, etc.; **fire′brick**, brick capable of withstanding great heat, used in furnaces etc.; **fire′bug**, (colloq.) incendiary, pyromaniac, arsonist; **fire′cracker**, cylinder of paper or cardboard containing an explosive and having a fuse that can be lit to cause an explosion (usu. for fun); **fire′damp**, explosive mixture of methane and air formed in coal mines; **fire′dog**, andiron; **fire door**, fire-resistant door, usu. metal, designed to check spreading of fire; **fire-eater**, entertainer who pretends to eat flames; vigorous or combative person; (colloq.) fire-

man; **fire engine**, vehicle carrying apparatus and firemen for extinguishing fires; **fire escape**, metal stairway on outside of building, movable ladder, or other apparatus for emergency exit to escape from fire; **fire extinguisher**, portable container from which a chemical can be discharged to extinguish fire; **fire fight**, (mil.) preliminary encounter or skirmish before a major battle; **fire fighter**, person employed by fire department to fight fires; **fire′fly**, beetle capable of emitting light (any of about 2,000 species); **fire′guard**, protective screen placed in front of fireplace to catch sparks and to prevent injury to people; **fire hose**, hose for extinguishing fire; **fire′-house**, headquarters where on-duty firemen stay and fire-fighting equipment is stored; **fire insurance**, insurance against loss by fire; **fire irons**, implements for tending fireplace, usu. shovel, tongs, and poker; **Fire Island**, 30-mi.-long barrier beach and summer resort off S. central Long Island, N.Y., between Great South Bay and Atlantic Ocean; **fire′light**, light given by fire; **fire′lock**, flintlock; **fire′man**, firefighter; tender of furnace or fire of steam engine; stoker; **fire′place**, grate or hearth for fire in room etc.; **fire′plug**, hydrant for drawing water from a

water main to extinguish fi **fire′power**, (mil.) amount accurate fire that a weapon military unit is capable of deli ing; **fire′proof**, capable of w standing fire or preventing dan by fire; not inflammable; **fi resistant**, able to resist but completely to prevent destruc by fire; less than fireproof; **screen**, fireguard; **fire′side**, s around fireplace; home life; **storm**, large and intense fire, o following atomic explosion, which mass of rising hot air cre strong rush of winds that feed spread the flames; **fire′trap**, str ture that is dangerous in case of because of inflammable mater and inadequate escape routes; **truck**, fire engine; **fire w** ceremony of walking barefoot c hot stones, ashes, etc., as religi rite or ordeal; hence, **fire walk fire watcher**, person detailed detect and report fires; **fire′wat** (slang) strong whiskey; **fire′we** any of various plants springing in newly burned areas, *Epilobium angustifolium*, also ca willow herb, with showy purpli pink flowers; **fire′wood**, wood fuel; **fire′work**, contrivance apparatus for producing specta lar colored lights, smoke, and n by use of combustibles, explosiv etc.; (pl.) pyrotechnic display. *v.* (**fired, fir·ing**). 1. Set fire with intention of destroying; kin (explosives). 2. Catch fire; beco heated or excited; redden; internal combustion engine) h gaseous mixture ignite. 3. B (pottery, bricks) in a kiln. 4. Sup (furnace, engine) with fuel. Cause (explosive) to explode; sh discharge gun, etc.; (of gun etc.) off; propel (missile) from gun 6. (slang) Discharge from a j dismiss (person). 7. ~ **aw** begin, go ahead; ~ **up**, sh sudden anger; **firing line**, line guns, men engaged in firing enemy or at a target; **firing squ** squad of soldiers detailed to sh condemned person.

firm[1] (fērm) *n.* Company, u not a corporation, for carrying business, commercial house.

firm[2] (fērm) *adj.* Of solid compact structure; fixed, stab steady, not shaking; establishe immutable; (of offer etc.) not lia to cancellation after acceptan steadfast, unflinching, resolu constant *to*; (of prices, goo maintaining their level or valu **firm′ly** *adv.* **firm′ness** *n.* **f** *adv.* Firmly (chiefly in **hold stand ~**). **firm** *v.* Solidi compact; make, become firm.

fir·ma·ment (fēr′mament) Vault or expanse of the heavens.

first (fērst) *adj.* 1. Earliest time or order; foremost in positi

2

4

re is particular danger of **fire** where
ly inflammable liquids such as oil
involved. Despite stringent safety
autions, explosions do occur, such
his one on an oil rig in the Gulf of

Mexico in 1970 (1). The most devastating fires, however, have been bushfires where the spread of flames can be uncontrollably fast and where fire will leap hundreds of yards at a time. This

bushfire was in Zambia (2). Fireworks displays show how fire can be harnessed (3) but often controls are needed, such as here in the Bronx (4).

k, or importance; coming next
r specified or implied time;
s., of part) highest or chief part
a certain voice or instrument in
certed music; that performs
h a part; **in the ~ place**, to
in with; first; **(the) ~ thing**, as
first thing that is done.   2.
aid, assistance given to injured
ore medical treatment is avail-
e; **~ class**, set of persons or
gs grouped together as better
n others; best level of accom-
dations on train, plane, ship, in
el, etc.; **~-class** (adj.) being

first class, of best quality, very
good; (adv.) by first class; with best
accommodations, care, etc.; **~
cousin**, child of one's uncle or aunt;
~-day cover, envelope bearing
stamp(s) postmarked on day of first
issue; **~ floor**, ground floor;
(chiefly Brit.) floor above ground
floor; **~ form**, lowest class in Brit.
school; **~ fruit**, (usu. pl.) first
products of agriculture for season,
esp. as offered to God; first products
of work etc.; **first'hand**, direct,
without intermediate agency; **first
lady**, wife of the president; wife

of governor, mayor, etc.; foremost
woman in any art or profession;
first lieutenant, commissioned
officer next above a second lieutenant and below a captain; **first
mate**, ship's officer next in rank
beneath the captain; **first name**
(n.), **first-name** (adj.), given
name, Christian name; **first-
night(er)**, (habitual frequenter of)
first performance of play etc.; **first
offender**, offender against whom
no previous conviction is recorded;
first person, (gram.) form of pronoun (I, we) or verb (am, are)

referring to the speaker or speakers; **first-rate**, of the highest quality; excellent; **first sergeant**, noncommissioned officer in the U.S. Army and Marine Corps, next in rank beneath sergeant major; **first-string**, (colloq.) made up of regular players on a team, as in baseball; **first** *n*. First day (*of* month); first or lowest gear of an automotive vehicle or bicycle; (pl.) best quality (of certain articles of commerce); **the ~**, person or thing first mentioned; **at ~**, at the beginning; **from ~ to last**, throughout; **from**

the **~**, from the beginning. **first** *adv*. Before anyone or anything else; before some specified or implied event, time, etc., in preference, rather; for the first time; **~ and last**, taking one thing with another, on the whole; **first'born**, eldest (child).

first·ling (ferst'lĭng) *n*. (usu. pl.). First result of anything; first offspring.

first·ly (ferst'lē) *adv*. (only in enumerating) In the first place, first.

firth (ferth) *n*. Arm of sea;

estuary.

fis·cal (fĭs'kal) *adj*. Of pu revenue; financial. **fis'cal·ly** *a*

fish[1] (fĭsh) *n*. (pl. **fish·es**, coll **fish**). 1. (pop.) Animal liv exclusively in water; (strictly) of class of vertebrate aqu animals having gills throughout and usu. fins. 2. Flesh of fish food; **other ~ to fry**, (collo more important business to atte to; **~ and chips**, fried fish fried chipped potatoes; **fish ca** small cake of shredded fish mashed potato. 3. (colloq.) Pers fellow, of specified kind, as p **~, queer ~**. 4. **the Fishes**: PISCES. 5. **fish'bowl**, glass bow which live fish are kept; **~ ha** osprey; **fish'hook**, barbed h used for catching fish; **fis monger**, (chiefly Brit.) dealer fish; **fish'pond**, pond in which are kept; **fish story**, (collo exaggerated or unbelievable sto **fish'tail**, shaped like tail of a fi **fish'wife**, woman selling fish; l abusive woman, termagant. **fish** Catch or try to catch fish; search something in or under water; coll (pearls, coral) from bottom of s try to catch fish in (pool etc.); dr *out of* water, pocket, etc., draw seek by indirect means or artifice (secrets, compliments, etc.); (fact, opinion, secret) *out*; **fish troubled waters**, make on profit out of disturbances; **fishi rod**, long tapering usu. jointed to which line is attached catching fish.

fish[2] *n*. 1. (naut.) Piece of curv wood, used to strengthen mast yard. 2. (also **fish'plate**) Flat pl of steel, wood, etc., strengthen beam or joint; one of two pla bolted together through ends of t rails on railroad to cover a strengthen joint.

fish·er (fĭsh'er) *n*. 1. Fisherm (archaic). 2. Carnivorous mamm (*Martes pennanti*) of northern Amer., like a weasel but larger a having dark brown-black f **fish'er·man** *n*. (pl. **-men**). M who lives by fishing; angl fishing boat. **fish'er·y** *n*. (**-er·ies**). Business or occupation catching fish etc.; fishing grou fish hatchery; right of fishing.

fish·y (fĭsh'ē) *adj*. (**fish·i· fish·i·est**). 1. Like fish; smelling tasting like fish. 2. (slang) dubious character, questionab **fish'i·ly** *adv*. **fish'i·ness** *n*.

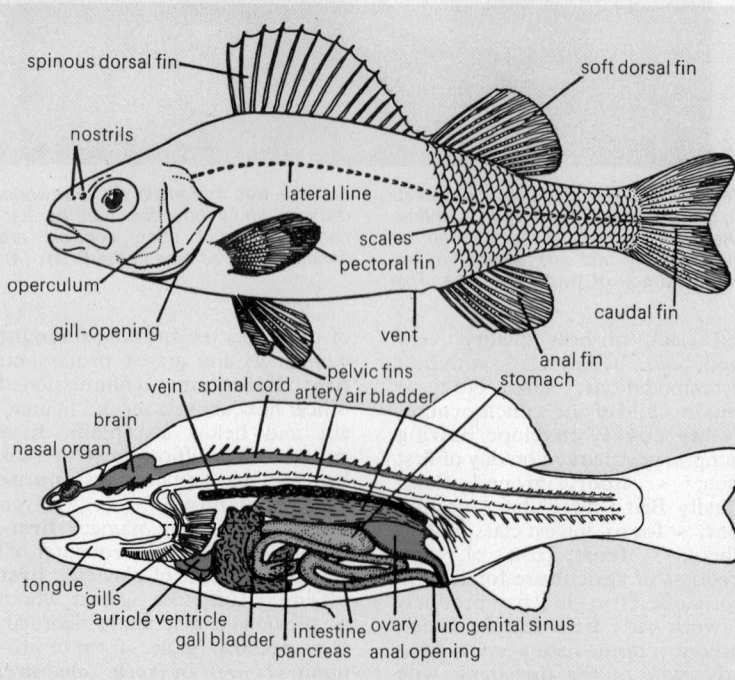

*The decorative **firefish** (Pter volitans) (above left) has venomous spines which can produce painful pu ture wounds. Left: The external a internal organs of a **fish**. The grou (facing page) lives mainly in tropi waters and is one of the prime fo fishes. The jewfish is one of the large and best known of the species, as the Nassau grouper which chang color.*

*Many **flags** have undergone changes as their nations have altered in structure and makeup. The American flag is no exception. Left: an early version of the stars and stripes. Right: A giant colonial stars and stripes flying over Fort McHenry in Marylands takes viewers back many years.*

Fisk (fĭsk), **James** (1834–72). Amer. financier and stock market speculator; became wealthy in Erie Railroad and gold price fixing dealings; tried to corner gold market (Black Friday, Sept. 1869) but failed when government intervened.

Fiske (fĭsk), **Minnie Maddern Davey** (1865–1932). Amer. actress; appeared in many Ibsen plays.

fissi- *prefix.* Cleft, divided.

fis·sile (fĭs′ĭl, -īl) *adj.* 1. Cleavable, tending to split. 2. Capable of undergoing NUCLEAR fission. **fis′·sil·i·ty** (fĭsĭl′ĭtē) *n.*

fis·sion (fĭsh′on) *n.* 1. (biol.) Division of cell or organism into new cells or organisms, as mode of asexual reproduction. 2. NUCLEAR fission. **fis′sion·a·ble** *adj.* Capable of undergoing nuclear fission.

fis·sure (fĭsh′er) *n.* Opening, usu. long and narrow, made by splitting or separation of parts; (anat.) groove, furrow dividing an organ into lobes etc., esp. in the brain. ~ *v.* (-**sured**, -**sur·ing**). Split.

fist (fĭst) *n.* Clenched hand, esp. as used in boxing. **fist′ful** *n.* Handful. **fist′ic** *adj.* Pugilistic.

fis·ti·cuffs (fĭs′tĭkŭfs) *n.pl.* Fighting with the fists; boxing.

fis·tu·la (fĭs′chu̇la) *n.* (pl. **-las**, **-lae** pr. -lē). Long pipe-like ulcer with narrow mouth; suppurating canal; passage made surgically. Pipelike. **fis′tu·lar, fis′tu·lous** *adjs.*

fit[1] (fĭt) *n.* Paroxysm, or one of recurrent attacks, of periodic or constitutional ailment; sudden transitory attack of some illness;

sudden seizure, with loss of consciousness or convulsions, of hysteria, apoplexy, fainting, paralysis, or epilepsy; violent outburst (of laughter, rage, etc.), capricious impulse, mood; **by ~ s and starts**, spasmodically; **have ~ s, throw a ~**, (colloq.) become very angry or excited.

fit[2] (fĭt) *adj.* (**fit·ter, fit·test**). Well adapted or suited (*for, to*); good enough *for*; becoming, proper, right; qualified, competent, worthy (*to*); in suitable condition, ready, *to* do, *for*; in good athletic condition or health, as in **~ as a fiddle. fit** *v.* (**fit, fit·ted, fit·ting**). Be in harmony with, become, befit; be of right measure, shape, and size for (esp. of dress); fill up, exactly correspond to, make to do this; make suitable, adapt, *for, to*: make competent *for, to*; supply, furnish (ship etc.) *with*; **~ out, up**, equip. **fit** *n.* Way thing fits.

fit·ful (fĭt′ful) *adj.* Characterized by irregular fits of activity or strength; spasmodic, changing, capricious. **fit′ful·ly** *adv.* **fit′ful·ness** *n.*

fit·ness (fĭt′nĭs) *n.* Being fit; moral worthiness; propriety.

fit·ter (fĭt′er) *n.* (esp.) 1. Mechanic who installs or adjusts parts of machine or other equip-

ment. 2. Tailor or dressmake who alters garments.

fit·ting (fĭt′ĭng) *n.* (esp., usu. pl. Fixtures; furniture; apparatus. ~ *adj.* (esp.) Becoming, proper, right **fit′ting·ly** *adv.* **fit′ting·ness** *n.*

Fitz·ger·ald[1] (fĭtsjĕr′ald), **Edward** (1809–83). English scholar famous for his poetic translation o the *Rubáiyát of Omar Khayyám*.

Fitz·ger·ald[2] (fĭtsjĕr′ald) **F(rancis) Scott (Key)** (1896 1940). Amer. novelist and short-story writer; author of the novel *The Great Gatsby, The Last Tycoon Tender Is the Night*, etc. and many stories of the jazz age.

five (fīv) *adj.* Amounting to five **~ -finger exercise**, piano exercis for practicing all fingers, keeping them on same five notes all the time **F ~ Nations**, powerful confeder acy of five Iroquoian Indian tribe in western New York, first formed *c*1570 and consisting of the Senecas Cayugas, Onondagas, Oneidas, and Mohawks; **F ~ -year plan**, scheme for economic development over period of five years, orig. that begun in U.S.S.R. in 1928. **five** *n.* One more than four; symbol for this (5 v, or V); card, die face, or domino with five pips; five o'clock; size etc indicated by five; set of five things or persons. **five′fold** *adj. & adv.*

five-and-ten(-cent store) five-and-dime, dime (ten-cent store. Store selling variety of inexpensive articles, orig. priced a 5 or 10 cents.

fiv·er (fī′ver) *n.* (slang) Five-dollar bill.

fix (fĭks) *v.* 1. Make firm or stable, fasten, secure, implant; direct steadily, set (eyes, attention, etc.) *on*; (of object) attract and hold (attention etc.); make (eyes, features), or become, rigid; deprive of, lose, volatility or fluidity, congeal; make (color, photographic image) fast; **~ with one's eyes**, direct steady gaze upon. 2. Place definitely or permanently, station, establish; settle one's choice, decide

; assign precise position of; refer
ming, person) to definite place or
me; determine incidence of
ability etc.); settle, determine,
ecify (price, date, place); arrest
anges or development in, settle
rmanent form of (language etc.);
range, get ready, put in order
lso ~ **up**); ~ **it**, arrange matters.
x *n.* Dilemma, position hard to
cape from; position determined
bearings or astronomical obser-
tions; (slang) addict's dose of
ug; (slang) correction. **fix'er** *n.*
One who or that which fixes. 2.
olloq.) Person who exerts influ-
ce or pays bribes to affect results,
in arranging outcome of sports
ents. 3. (slang) Person who
ranges illegal sale of narcotics to
ers.

fix·a·tion (fĭksā'shon) *n.* 1.
xing, being fixed. 2. (psycho.)
rsistent attachment to a person or
ject, esp. when developed early
life in association with great

pleasure, sorrow, fear, etc., and
continuing as neurotic or immature
behavior.

fix·a·tive (fĭk'sătĭv) *adj.* Tending to fix. ~ *n.* Fixative substance,
esp. with which drawing or watercolor, film, etc. is coated to prevent
blurring or evaporation.

fixed (fĭkst) *adj.* 1. Immovable;
stationary; ~ **satellite**, earth
satellite that remains over a specific
location on Earth's surface; ~ **star**:
see STAR. 2. Steady; unyielding;
resolute. 3. (chem.) Nonvolatile,
used of oils. 4. Not affected by
fluctuation or change; unvarying.
5. (colloq.) Situated as regards
money etc. 6. (slang) With results
dishonestly planned beforehand.
fix·ed·ly (fĭk'sĭdlē) *adv.* In fixed
manner, intently. **fix'ed·ness** *n.*

fix·ings (fĭk'sĭngz) *n.pl.* Necessary apparatus or equipment;
accessories, adjuncts, trimmings.

fix·i·ty (fĭk'sĭtē) *n.* (pl. **-ties**).
Fixed state; stability, permanence.

fix·ture (fĭks'cher) *n.* Thing
fixed or fastened in position; (law)
article of accessory character
annexed to houses or lands; person
or thing confined to or established
in one place.

fizz (fĭz) *n.* Hissing or spluttering sound; effervescence; (colloq.)
champagne; any effervescing drink.
fizz'y *adj.* (**fizz·i·er, fizz·i·est**).
fizz *v.i.* Make hissing or spluttering sound; effervesce.

fiz·zle (fĭz'el) *v.i.* (**-zled,
-zling**). Hiss or splutter feebly;
~ **out**, come to lame conclusion,
fail. **fizzle** *n.* Hissing, spluttering;
(colloq.) failure, fiasco.

fjord (fyôrd) *n.* Long narrow
arm of sea between high cliffs, as
in Norway.

FL *abbrev.* Florida.
fl. *abbrev.* Florin(s); floruit.
Fla. *abbrev.* Florida.
flab (flăb) *n.* (colloq.) Flabby, fat
flesh.

flab·ber·gast (flăb'ergăst) *v.t.*
Dumbfound, overwhelm with
astonishment.

flab·by (flăb'ē) *adj.* (**-bi·er,
-bi·est**). Lacking firmness; flaccid,
soft; feeble; ineffectual; fat. **flab'-
bi·ly** *adv.* **flab'bi·ness** *n.*

flac·cid (flăk'sĭd) *adj.* Hanging
or lying loose or wrinkled, limp,
flabby; drooping. **flac·cid·i·ty**
(flăksĭd'ĭtē) *n.* **flac'cid·ly** *adv.*

flag[1] (flăg) *n.* Any of various
monocotyledonous plants with
bladed or sword-shaped leaves, esp.
of the genus *Iris*, mostly growing
in moist places; **blue** ~ (*Iris
versicolor*) of N. Amer. **sweet** ~,
(*Acorus calamus*) plant with aromatic rhizome.

flag[2] (flăg) *n.* Flat slab of any
fine-grained rock that can be split
into flagstones; (also **flag'stone**)
flat stone suitable for paving.
flag *v.t.* (**flagged, flag·ging**).
Pave with flags.

flag[3] (flăg) *n.* Piece of bunting
or other material attached by one
edge to staff or halyard and used as
standard, ensign, or signal; (naut.)
flag carried by flagship as emblem
of admiral's rank afloat; plate
attached to taxicab meter and
lowered to start meter when vehicle
is engaged; flag used to indicate
start or finish of race; distinctly
colored or shaped tail of deer, dog,
etc.; **black** ~, flag used as ensign
by pirates; also, that formerly
hoisted at prison to announce
execution of criminal; **quarantine**
~, yellow flag (see below); **white**
~, plain white flag used in token of
truce or surrender; **yellow** ~, flag
displayed by ship with infectious

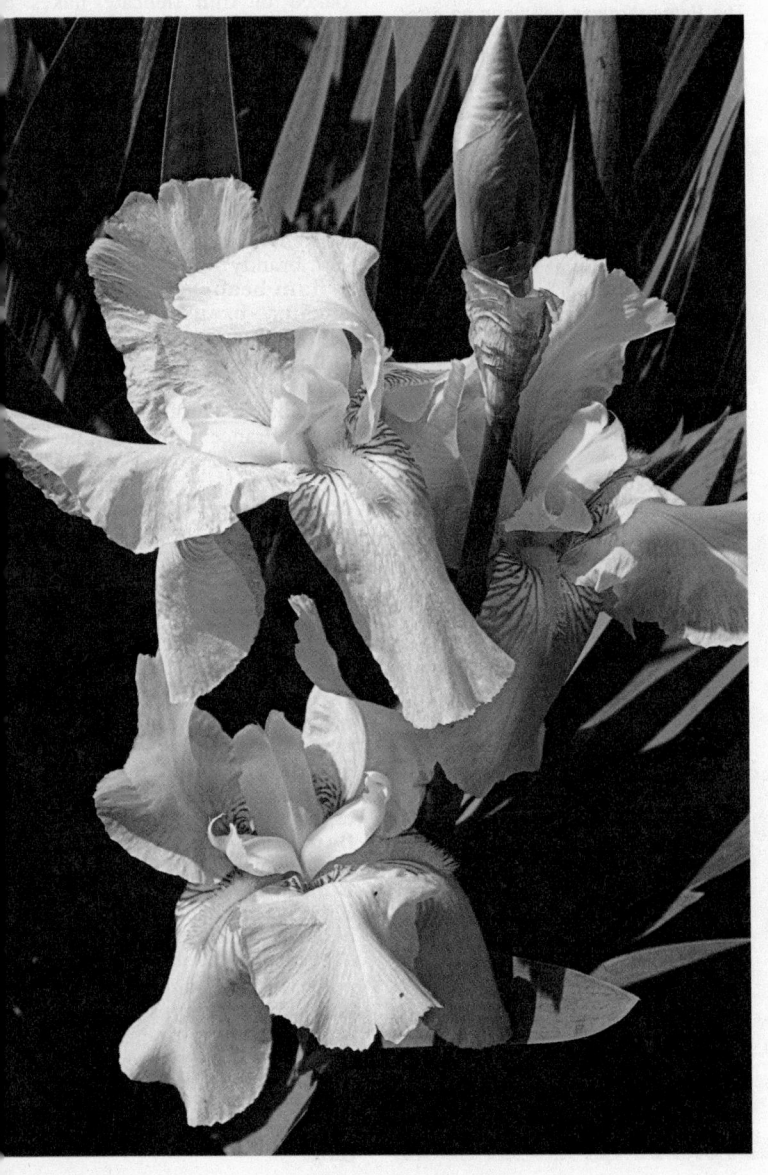

*The **flag** or iris is one of the world's
most popular and varied garden
flowers. The yellow or water flag is a
swamp plant found in Eurasia and North
Africa; the blue flag occupies similar
areas in North America.*

disease on board, hospital ship, or ship in quarantine; ~ **of convenience**, foreign flag under which ship is registered to avoid certain taxes, duties, etc.; ~ **captain**, captain of flagship; **F ~ Day**, June 14, annual holiday celebrating the adoption by Congress of the official U.S. flag (1777); **flag′man** (pl. **-men**), signaler at races etc.; **flag officer**, admiral, vice-admiral, or rear admiral; **flag′pole**, pole on which flag is hoisted; **flag′ship**, ship having fleet or squadron commander on board and flying that officer's flag; **flag′staff**, flagpole. **flag** v.t. (**flagged, flag·ging**). Place flag on or over; mark out with flags; inform, warn, communicate, by flag signals; ~ **down**, bring to a stop thus.

flag[4] (flăg) v.i. (**flagged, flag·ging**). Hang down, flap loosely; droop, fade, become limp; lag, lose vigor, grow languid; fall off in interest.

flag·el·lant (flăj′elant, flajĕl′-) n. & adj. (One) who scourges himself, esp. as religious discipline or penance.

flag·el·late[1] (flăj′elāt) v.t. (**-lat·ed, -lat·ing**). Scourge, whip. **flag·el·la·tion** (flăjelā′shon), **flag′el·la·tor** ns.

fla·gel·lum (flajĕl′um) n. (pl. **-gel·la** pr. -jĕl′a, **-gel·lums**). (zool., bot.) Microscopic lashlike appendage, esp. one used for locomotion. **flag·el·late**[2] (flăj′elĭt, -lāt, flajĕl′ĭt) adj. & n. (Protozoan) having one or more flagella. **fla·gel·li·form** (flajĕl′ifôrm) adj.

flag·eo·let (flăjolĕt′, -lā′) n. Small flute blown at end.

flag·on (flăg′on) n. Large vessel, usu. with handle, spout, and lid, to hold wine or liquor; large bottle for wine etc., often of flattened globular shape, usu. holding about twice as much as ordinary bottle.

fla·grant (flā′grant) adj. (of offense or offender) Glaring, notorious, scandalous. **fla′gran·cy** n. **fla′grant·ly** adv.

fla·gran·te de·lic·to (flagrăn′tē dĭlĭk′tō) = in flagrante delicto.

flail (flāl) n. Threshing imple-

The **flame-thrower** *has been an effective weapon in war since 1915 and is used mainly to force the enemy out of cover. Here, British troops use a pack-type flame-thrower.*

ment, wooden staff at end of whic a heavy stick hangs swinging. v. Beat or strike (as) with fla wave wildly or erratically.

flair (flâr) n. Instinctive discerr ment, selective instinct for what good, paying, etc.

flak (flăk) n. Antiaircraft fir (fig. slang) barrage of criticisn opposition, abuse, etc. [Ger., initial letters of *Fl*iegerabwehr*kan* one A.A. gun]

flake[1] (flāk) n. Frame or rac for drying fish etc.; small platforn hung over ship's side for workme to stand on.

flake[2] (flāk) n. Small light fleec mass, esp. of snow; thin broad piec peeled off surface; natural divisio of fish flesh; (archaeol.) piece o hard stone chipped off core for us as tool. ~ v. (**flaked, flak·ing** Fall like, sprinkle as with, snow take, come, *away, off*, in flakes **flak′y** adj. (**flak·i·er, flak·i·est** 1. (esp., of pastry) Consisting whe baked of thin delicate flakes o layers. 2. (slang) Very unconven tional or odd; eccentric. **flak′i·nes** n.

flam[1] (flăm) n. Hoax, trick deception; FLIMFLAM.

flam[2] (flăm) n. Drumbeat mad by hitting the drumhead with botl sticks in rapid succession.

flam·bé (flahmbā′) adj. (of food Served flaming in ignited liquor esp. brandy.

flam·beau (flăm′bō) n. (pl **-beaux, -beaus** pr. -bōz). Torch esp. of several thick waxed wicks.

flam·boy·ant (flămboi′ant) adj 1. (archit.) Characterized by wavy flamelike lines: of the style preva lent in France in 15th and first hal of 16th centuries. 2. Florid, floridly decorated; gorgeously colored ornate. **flam·boy′ance** n.

flame (flām) n. 1. Vapor heated to point of combustion, ignited gas: portion of this, often spire-like or tonguelike; (pl.) fire; visible com bustion; **flame′out**, failure of jet engine because of poor combustion or failure in fuel supply; **flame′-thrower**, (Ger. *flammenwerfer*), machine of war with reservoir from which long spray of flame can be ejected. 2. Bright light; brilliant coloring; flame-red. 3. Passion, esp. of love; (slang) sweetheart. **flame** v. (**flamed, flam·ing**). 1. Emit flames, blaze. 2. (of passion) Burst out; (of persons) break *out*, blaze *up*, into anger. 3. Glow like or as with flame; shine brightly. 4. Move as or like flame.

fla·men·co (flamĕng′kō) n. (pl. **-cos**). Spanish gypsy style of singing or dancing; song or dance in this style.

flam·ing (flā′mĭng) adj. Very hot; bright-colored; very bright; highly colored, exaggerated, startling.

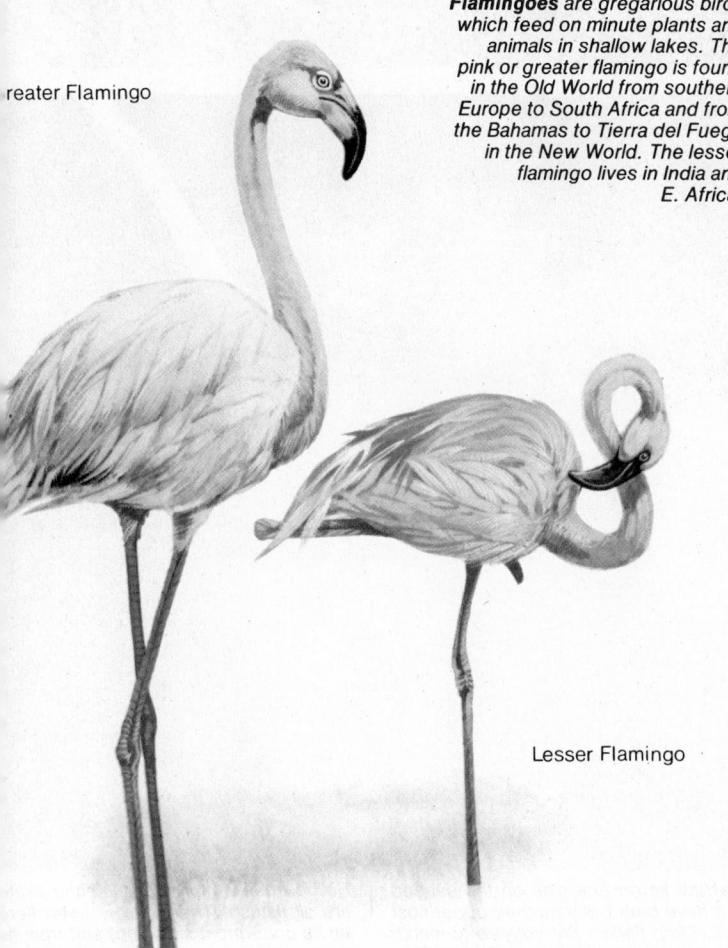

Flamingoes are gregarious birds which feed on minute plants and animals in shallow lakes. The pink or greater flamingo is found in the Old World from southern Europe to South Africa and from the Bahamas to Tierra del Fuego in the New World. The lesser flamingo lives in India and E. Africa.

reater Flamingo

Lesser Flamingo

fla·min·go (flamĭng′gō) *n.* (pl. **-gos, -goes**). Wading bird of the widely distributed family Phoeni-copteridae with reddish-orange plumage, extremely long legs and neck, and heavy bent bill.

flam·ma·ble (flăm′abel) *adj.* Easily set on fire, inflammable. **flam·ma·bil·i·ty** (flămabĭl′ĭtē) *n.*

flan (flăn, flahn) *n.* Molded custard with burnt caramel topping.

Flan·ders (flăn′derz). Ancient countship now a region divided between Belgium, France, and Holland; also, the area of Belgium comprising the provinces of **East** ~ and **West** ~.

flange (flănj) *n.* Projecting flat rim, collar, or rib, used to strengthen an object, attach it to another, etc. ~ *v.t.* (**flanged, flang·ing**).

flank (flăngk) *n.* 1. Fleshy or muscular part of side between ribs and hip. 2. Side of building, mountain, etc.; (mil.) extreme left or right side of army or body of troops. 3. Slice of meat from animal flank, often ~ **steak. flank** *v.t.* Guard, protect, strengthen, on flank; menace or attack flank of; be posted or situated at flank of; (pass.) have at flanks or sides.

flan·nel (flăn′el) *n.* Light soft woolen fabric, usu. without nap; (pl.) underclothing of flannel; (pl.) garments, esp. trousers, of flannel. ~ *v.t.* Wrap in flannel; polish with flannel.

flap (flăp) *v.* (**flapped, flap·-**

ping). 1. Strike with something broad and flexible. 2. Swing or sway about, flutter, oscillate; move (wings), (of wings) move, up and down; beat the wings. ~ *n.* 1. Light blow with something broad; motion of something broad and loose, as wing, etc. 2. Broad hanging piece hinged or attached by one side only, as leaf of table, piece of cloth covering opening of pocket, etc.; movable section on wing or tail of aircraft, used to modify lift or drag. 3. (slang) State of agitation or fuss.

flap·jack (flăp′jăk) *n.* Pancake.

flap·per (flăp′*er*) *n.* (esp.) 1. Broad fin; flipper. 2. (colloq.) Young woman of the 1920s, esp. one having bold manners and dressing unconventionally.

flare (flâr) *v.* (**flared, flar·ing**). 1. (Cause to) widen or spread (gradually) outward, as the sides of a ship, a skirt, etc.; **flared** (*adj.*) widening thus. 2. Burn with spreading unsteady flame; shine like such flame; glow as with flame; **flare up**, burst into sudden blaze or anger. **flare** *n.* 1. Dazzling irregular light; unshaded flame in open air; sudden outburst of flame; combustible material burned as signal or guide in fog, at night, etc.; bright light dropped from aircraft to illuminate target etc.; (photog.) fogging caused by internal reflection within a lens; **flare′-up** (*n.*) (1) sudden blaze of flame; (2) sudden outburst of rage, violence, illness, etc. 2. Gradual widening or spreading of ship's sides, skirt, etc.

flash (flăsh) *n.* 1. Sudden quick transitory blaze; time occupied by this, instant; brief outburst, transitory display; superficial brilliance, ostentation; (photog.) artificial light illuminating subject briefly during exposure; ~ **in the pan**, ignition of gunpowder in pan of old gun without discharge of missile; (fig.) abortive effort or outburst. 2. Flashlight. 3. (also **news** ~) Very brief, important news report. 4. **flash′back**, (motion pictures, novels, etc.) Recapitulation of earlier scene, episode beginning with sudden change to an earlier point of time; **flash′bulb**, electric bulb that briefly emits dazzling light when ignited, for taking photographs; **flash card**, any of a group of cards having words, numbers, or pictures flashed individually by teacher in front of class for quick answers during a drill; **flash′cube**, small cube containing four flashbulbs and rotating automatically when a photograph is taken with the camera into which it is plugged; **flash flood**, sudden localized flooding occurring after heavy rain in the immediate area; **flash gun**, synchronized photographic apparatus that simul-

Flatfish lie on one side on the seabed and have both eyes on their uppermost side. Most flatfish are colored to match the ground on which they lie and they are found in warm and temperate seas.

Halibut, plaice, turbot, sole, and skate are all flatfish. The skate is seen here on its uppermost side (top) and from its underside (bottom).

neously discharges a flashbulb and works camera shutter; **flash'-ght**, small, portable electric light operated by dry batteries; (photog.) rief burst of dazzling light from a motographic lamp; **flash'over**, ectric spark or arc appearing uddenly across surface of insu-ating material; **flash point**, emperature at which vapor given f by oil etc. will ignite; **flash'-ube**, gaseous discharge tube used an electronic flash and producing hort, intense bursts of light. **flash** *dj*. 1. (archaic) Connected with hieves, tramps, etc., or their rgon. 2. Showy; sudden, brief. **ash** *v*. 1. Break suddenly into ame or light; give out flame or parks; emit or reflect light, gleam; end, reflect, like a flash or in ashes; cause to flash. 2. Burst uddenly into view or perception; ove swiftly. 3. Express or ommunicate quickly. 4. (colloq.) Make ostentatious show (of ossessions). 5. (slang) Show (a un, badge, etc.). 6. Protect joints f roofing etc. with flashing. 7. slang) Expose part(s) of body to ublic view. **flash'er** *n*.

flash·ing (flăsh'ĭng) *n*. Strip of metal to prevent flooding or leakage t joint of roofing etc.

flash·y (flăsh'ē) *adj*. (**flash·i·er, ash·i·est**). Brilliant but shallow r transitory; cheaply attractive; howy, gaudy; given to display. **lash'i·ly** *adv*. **flash'i·ness** *n*.

flask (flăsk, flahsk) *n*. 1. (hist., su. **powder** ~) Leather or metal ase for carrying hunter's etc. upply of gunpowder. 2. Narrow-ecked bulbous bottle. 3. Pocket ottle of metal or glass.

flat¹ (flăt) *n*. (chiefly Brit.) Apartment.

flat² (flăt) *adj*. (**flat·ter, lat·test**). 1. Horizontal, level; pread out, lying at full length. 2. ven, smooth, unbroken, without rojection; with broad level surface nd little depth. 3. Unqualified, lain, downright. 4. Dull, lifeless, monotonous; dejected; without nergy; (of drink) that has lost its ffervescence or flavor, insipid, tale; (of paint) without luster; photog.) wanting in contrast. 5. Below the true pitch; **B ~, E ~**, tc. (written B♭ etc.; see *n*. below, ense 5), a semitone lower than B, , etc. 6. (of price, rate, etc.) Unvarying, fixed, uniform; not arying with changed conditions. . **flat'bed**, truck or trailer with ody in the form of a platform or hallow box; **flat'boat**, flat-ottomed boat for transport in hallow water; **flat'car**, railroad reight car without sides or top; **lat'fish**, any of numerous fishes, ncluding halibut, flounder, turbot, nd sole, having a compressed body nd both eyes on the uppermost

side; **flat'foot(ed)**, (having) foot not normally arched at instep; hence, (fig.) heavy, clumsy; (slang) police officer; **Flat'head**, (member of) one of several N. Amer. Ind. tribes of the NW. coast thought to flatten their children's heads; (member of) the Salishan tribe of Montana; **flat'iron**, iron for pressing clothes (now usu. of one heated from below, not within); **flat-out** (*adj*.) (colloq.) thorough, absolute; **flat race**, horse race over clear and level dirt track (opp. to STEEPLECHASE); **flat'ware**, table utensils such as knives, forks, and spoons; **flat'worm**, any of the tapeworms, flukes, etc. **flat'ly** *adv*. **flat'ness** *n*. **flat** *adv*. Downright, positively, plainly; fully, quite; ~ **out, ~-out,** = ALL out. **flat** *n*. 1. What is flat; flat surface or part, esp. broad surface of blade as opp. to edge; inside of open hand; (often pl.) level country; low lying marshy land, swamp; (usu. pl., also **mud** ~ **s**) level ground over which tide flows, or which is covered by shallow water. 2. (theatr.) Section of scenery mounted on frame. 3. Shallow box for plant seedlings. 4. Deflated automobile tire. 5. (mus.) Note lowered by a semitone below usual pitch; sign (♭) indicating this lowering, placed before note that is to be flattened or forming part of key signature; **double ~** (♭♭), sign indicating that note must be lowered two semitones; **two ~ s, three ~ s**, etc., key indicated by two, three, etc., flats in key

signature. **flat** *v*. (**flat·ted, flat·ting**). Make flat.

flat·ten (flăt'en) *v.t.* Make flat; ~ **out**, (esp.) bring (flight of air-craft) parallel with ground after diving.

flat·ter (flăt'er) *v.t.* Court, fawn upon; praise or compliment unduly or insincerely; gratify vanity or self-esteem of, make feel honored or distinguished; please (usu. **oneself**) with belief, idea, suggestion, *that;* exaggerate good points of, repre-sent too favorably. **flat'ter·er, flat'ter·y** *ns*. **flat'ter·ing·ly** *adv*.

flat·u·lent (flăch'ulent) *adj*. Generating gas or air in the alimentary canal; caused by, attended with, troubled with, accumulation of this; (fig.) inflated, puffed up, windy, pretentious. **flat'u·lence** *n*. **flat'u·lent·ly** *adv*.

fla·tus (flā'tus) *n*. Gas, air, in stomach or bowel.

Flau·bert (flōbār'), **Gustave** (1821–80). French realistic novel-ist; author of *Madame Bovary, Salammbô*, etc.

flaunt (flawnt) *v*. Wave proudly; display oneself or one's finery; show off, parade. **flaunt'ing·ly** *adv*.

flau·tist (flow'ĭst, flaw'-) *n*. Flute player; flutist.

fla·vin (flā'vĭn) *n*. Any of a group of yellow pigments found in

Flatworms like this beef tapeworm, are small slender parasites which dwell in or on the bodies of other animals or plants. This tapeworm is parasitic in man.

Flax produces two kinds of yarn. One is very fine and is used for high-quality linen and lace. The coarser kind is mainly used for making rope. Linseed oil, from the seed, is used in paint and varnishes.

Fleabane plants are characterized by their white or purplish flower heads and orange centers; all are reputed to repel fleas.

plants and animals and used as dyes and antiseptics.

fla·vor (flā′ver) *n.* Distinctive taste; undefinable characteristic quality. **fla′vor·ful, fla′vor·less, fla′vor·some** *adjs.* **flavor** *v.t.* Give flavor to. **fla′vor·ing** *n.* Something used for flavoring food or drink.

flaw¹ (flaw) *n.* Crack, breach, rent; imperfection, blemish; invalidating defect in legal document etc. ~ *v.* Crack, damage, mar. **flaw′less** *adj.* **flaw′less·ly** *adv.* **flaw′less·ness** *n.*

flaw² (flaw) *n.* Squall of wind; short storm.

flax (flăks) *n.* Blue-flowered plant (*Linum usitatissimum*) cultivated for its seeds (linseed) and for textile fiber obtained from the stem of the plant; dressed or undressed flax fibers; cloth made from these, linen; **flax′seed,** linseed. **flax′en** *adj.* Of flax; (of hair) colored like dressed flax, pale yellow.

flay (flā) *v.t.* Strip off skin or hide of; (fig.) criticize severely; fleece, charge extortionately; peel off (skin, bark, peel).

flea (flē) *n.* Small wingless insect of order Siphonapter, well known for its biting propensities and powers of jumping, feeding on human and other blood; **flea′bag,** (joc.) old worn-out horse; cheap hotel; **flea′bane,** any of various plants of the genus *Erigeron,* having daisylike flowers of several colors, reputed to repel fleas; **~-bitten,**

bitten by or infested with fleas; (colloq.) showing wear or heavy use; seedy, disreputable; ~ **market,** shop or market, usu. having numerous separate tables, stalls, etc., selling antiques, second-hand merchandise, etc.

fleck (flĕk) *n.* Spot in the skin, freckle; patch of color or light; small particle, speck. ~ *v.t.* Mark with flecks, dapple, variegate.

fled (flĕd): see FLEE.

The fleece of sheep bred mainly for wool yields about 15 lbs per animal; in Britain, where the emphasis is on mutton, woolly breeds only give about 10 lbs. Shearing (facing page) takes place

fledge (flĕj) *v.t.* (**fledged fledg·ing**). Provide with feather or plumage, wing for flight; cove as with feathers or down; feathe (arrow).

fledg·ling (flĕj′lĭng) *n.* Youn bird just fledged.

flee (flē) *v.* (**fled, flee·ing**). Ru away, seek safety in flight; vanish cease, pass away; run away from leave abruptly; shun.

fleece (flēs) *n.* Woolly coverin of sheep or similar animal; quantit of wool shorn from sheep at on time; thing like a fleece, whit cloud, falling snow, etc.; **Golde**

once a year, and the fleece, whic should come off in one piece, is rolle up and graded (below). In Australia an New Zealand it takes about 5 minutes t shear a sheep.

Alexander Fleming *accidentally dis-covered the antibiotic, penicillin, when he was cultivating bacteria responsible for boils, and found his culture spoilt by a blue-green mold. Fleming was awarded the Nobel Prize in 1945.*

The major **Flemish** *artist of the century was Jan van Eyck who ...fected the use of oil as a mediu... painting. His brilliant use of color ... realistic detailing are evident in ... painting, 'Arnolfini Marriage'.*

F~: see GOLDEN. **fleec'y** *adj.* (**fleec·i·er, fleec·i·est**). **fleece** *v.t.* (**fleeced, fleec·ing**). 1. (rare) Shear (sheep). 2. Strip of money, property, etc.; plunder, rob heart-lessly. 3. Overspread as with fleece.

fleet[1] (flēt) *n.* Navy, number of warships under one command; number of ships or boats sailing in company; number of boats, vehicles, etc. forming, owned, or operated as a group or unit; **~ admiral**, highest ranking officer of U.S. Navy, next above admiral, and wearing five stars.

fleet[2] (flēt) *n.* (Brit. archaic or dial.) Inlet.

fleet[3] (flēt) *adj.* Swift, nimble. **fleet'ly** *adv.* **fleet'ness** *n.*

fleet[4] (flēt) *v.i.* Glide away, vanish, be transitory; pass rapidly, slip *away*; move swiftly, fly. **fleet'-ing** *adj.* **fleet'ing·ly** *adv.* **fleet'-ing·ness** *n.*

Flem, Flem. *abbrevs.* Flemish.

Flem·ing[1] (flĕm'ĭng) *n.* Native, inhabitant, of Flanders.

Flem·ing[2] (flĕm'ĭng), **Sir Alexander** (1881–1955). Brit. bacteriologist; the chief discoverer of PENICILLIN.

Flem·ish (flĕm'ĭsh) *adj.* Of Flanders or its people or language. **~** *n.* 1. (collect.) People of Flanders. 2. Language of Flanders.

flense (flĕns) *v.t.* (**flensed, flens·ing**), also **flench** (flĕnch). Strip (blubber) from (whale, seal).

flesh (flĕsh) *n.* 1. Soft substance, esp. muscular parts, of animal body between skin and bones; **~ and blood**, human body or its material; mankind; human nature with its emotions and infirmities; (as *adj.*) actually living, not supernatural or imaginary; **one's own ~ and blood**, near relations, descendants. 2. Pulpy substance of fruit or plant. 3. Plumpness, fat; **lose, put on, ~**, grow thin, fat. 4. Tissue of animal bodies (sometimes excluding fish and fowl) as food; meat. 5. Visible surface of human body, with ref. to color or appearance. 6. Whatever has corporeal life; the body (now only in biblical allusions); man's physical nature; the sensual appetites; **in the ~**, in bodily form, in life; in person; **sins of the ~**, unchastity. 7. **~-color(ed)**, (of the) color of Caucasian skin, yellowish-pink; **~ fly**, insect of family Sarcophagidae, which deposits eggs in dead flesh; **flesh'-pots**, (with ref. to Exod. 16) places offering licentious high living, luxuries; **flesh wound**, wound not reaching bone or vital organ. **flesh** *v.t.* Incite (hound etc.) by taste of blood; initiate in bloodshed.

flesh·ly (flĕsh'lē) *adj.* (**-li·er, -li·est**). 1. Carnal, lasciv... sensual. 2. Mortal, material; ... divine or spiritual; worldly. **fle... li·ness** *n.*

flesh·y (flĕsh'ē) *adj.* (**flesh-... flesh·i·est**). Plump, fat; (of ... etc.) pulpy; like flesh. **flesh'i·... *n.*

fleur-de-lis, fleur-de-lys de lē', floor, lēs'; *Fr.* flör delēs' (pl. **fleurs-de-lys** pr. flēr de ... floor; *Fr.* flör de lēs'). Iris flo... heraldic lily; royal arms of Fra... resembling three petals of an ... tied together.

flew (floo): see FLY[2].

flex (flĕks) *v.t.* Bend; esp. b... (joint or limb) by action of fl... muscles.

flex·i·ble (flĕk'sĭbel) *adj.* ... will bend without breaking, plia... pliant; easily led, managea... adaptable, versatile; supple, c... plaisant. **flex·i·bil·i·ty** (flĕksi... ĭtē) *n.* **flex'i·bly** *adv.*

flex·ion (flĕk'shon) *n.* Bend... bent state (esp. of limb or join...

flex·or (flĕk'ser) *n.* Mu... producing flexion in any par... body (opp. EXTENSOR).

flex·ure (flĕk'sher) *n.* Bend... curvature, bent state.

flick (flĭk) *n.* 1. Light sharp blow with whiplash etc. shot out and withdrawn, or with fingernail; sudden movement, jerk; quick turn of wrist, as in bowling or batting; light sharp cracking sound. 2. (fig. Brit. slang) Motion picture. — *v.* Strike with a flick; dash or flick *away, off*; give a flick with; throw (ball etc.) with a flick of the wrist; flutter, twitch.

flick·er[1] (flĭk′er) *v.i.* Quiver, vibrate; wave to and fro, flutter; flash up and die away alternately; burn fitfully or unsteadily. — *n.* Flickering movement; wavering or rapidly fluctuating light or flame.

flick·er[2] (flĭk′er) *n.* Large N. amer. woodpecker of genus *Colaptes* with spotted breast and brown back.

fli·er, fly·er (flī′er) *ns.* Bird etc. that flies; animal, vehicle, etc., moving with exceptional speed; (usu. *flyer*) airplane pilot; (colloq.) speculation, business risk; handbill.

flight[1] (flīt) *n.* 1. (Manner of) flying; swift movement, esp. through the air; swift passage (of time); soaring, excursion, sally (of wit, fancy, ambition, etc.). 2. Migration, migrating body, flock, of birds or insects; number of airplanes forming a subdivision of a squadron; volley *of* arrows etc. 3. Distance that bird, aircraft, or missile can fly. 4. Airplane trip; scheduled airplane; (mil.) planes flying in formation. 5. Series (*of* stairs etc.) mounting between landings, or without change of direction. 6. Feather etc. on arrow or dart. 7. ~ **bag**, small lightweight bag in which airline passengers carry personal items; ~ **deck**, deck of aircraft carrier for taking off and landing of aircraft; ~ **line**, section of airfield where planes are parked and serviced; ~ **path**, locus of center of gravity of airplane while airborne; ~ **recorder**, device in aircraft recording details of flight; ~ **strip**, landing strip for emergency use by airplanes; ~ **-test**, (*v.*), test (airplane) when in the air.

flight[2] (flīt) *n.* Running away, fleeing; hasty retreat; absconding; **put to** ~, rout; **take (to)** ~, run away.

flight·less (flīt′lĭs) *adj.* (of bird etc.) Unable to fly.

flight·y (flī′tē) *adj.* (**flight·i·er, flight·i·est**). Guided by whim or fancy, fickle; unstable, irresponsible; dim-witted. **flight′i·ly** *adv.* **flight′i·ness** *n.*

flim·flam (flĭm′flăm) *n.* Nonsense; humbug; deception, swindle, confidence game.

flim·sy (flĭm′zē) *adj.* (**-si·er, -si·est**). Easily destroyed, frail, slightly put together; paltry, trivial; frivolous, superficial. **flim′si·ly** *adv.* **flim′si·ness** *n.* **flim′sy** *n.* Thin kind of paper, esp. that used for carbon copies; carbon copy.

flinch (flĭnch) *v.i.* Give way, draw back, shrink (*from something* as dangerous, painful, or difficult); wince.

fling (flĭng) *v.* (**flung, fling·ing**). 1. Rush, go angrily or violently. 2. Throw, cast, hurl; throw with violence, or hostile intent, hurl as missile; extend (arms) with sudden movement; cast (glance etc.); throw *into* (prison etc.); (of wrestler or ridden horse) throw to the ground; launch (troops etc.) *on* enemy, *against* fortress, etc. — *n.* 1. Throw, cast. 2. Vigorous dance in which arms and legs are flung about (esp. **Highland** ~). 3. Spell of indulgence in pleasure; esp. in **have a** ~. 4. Attempt, esp. in **take a** ~ **at.**

flint (flĭnt) *n.* Hard stone of nearly pure silica found in roundish nodules, usu. steely gray and encrusted with white, and having the property of giving off sparks when struck with steel; piece of this used with steel to kindle flame, fire powder in flintlock gun, etc.; piece of hard alloy used to produce spark in cigarette lighter etc.; pebble or

*This **flight recorder,** known as the 'red egg', converts information on an aircraft's flight into digital form and records it on stainless steel wire. Its case can withstand extremes of pressure and temperature.*

stainless steel recording wire — inner reel — outer reel — feed pulleys — spring — brake arm — gearing — erase — replay — pivot — bridge — record — record — erase — replay — drive motor — oscillating platform — outer casing — input leads — cam and spherical roller for feed mechanism — recording heads for 2nd cycle (off) (rewinding) — recording heads for 1st cycle (on) (recording) nodule of flint flaked or chipped by prehistoric man to form a tool or weapon; ~ **glass**, pure lustrous glass, orig. made with ground flint; **flint'lock**, (gun with) lock in which flint struck against hammer produces sparks which ignite priming. **flint'y** *adj.* (**flint·i·er, flint·i·est**). **flint'i·ly** *adv.* **flint'i·ness** *n.*

flip[1] (flĭp) *n.* Mixture of beer, or usu. liquor, sweetened and heated with hot iron rod; mixed drink with wine or liquor, egg, etc.

flip[2] (flĭp) *v.* (**flipped, flip·ping**). Propel, strike, with fillip or flick; make, move with, flip; (slang) react strongly or enthusiastically; ~ **one's lid**, ~ **out**, lose self-control. **flip** *n.* Fillip, flick; ~ **side**, (colloq.) reverse side of phonograph record.

flip[3] (flĭp) *adj.* (**flip·per, flip·pest**). Flippant, glib.

flip·pant (flĭp'ant) *adj.* Lacking in gravity; treating serious subjects with unbecoming levity, disrespectful. **flip'pan·cy** *n.* **flip'pant·ly** *adv.*

flip·per (flĭp'er) *n.* Limb used to swim with, e.g., forelimb of cetacean, any limb of seal, walrus, turtle; wing of penguin; (pl.) rubber etc. devices attached to the feet for underwater swimming.

flirt (flĕrt) *v.* 1. Flit, dart. 2. Play at courtship *with*; trifle, toy *with*. ~ *n.* 1. Sudden jerk; quick motion quickly checked. 2. Man who pays, or usu. woman who invites or accepts, amorous attentions merely for amusement. **flir·ta·tion** (flĕrtā'shon) *n.* **flir'·ta'tious** *adj.* **flir·ta'tious·ly** *adv.*

flit (flĭt) *v.i.* (**flit·ted, flit·ting**). 1. Move, dart about rapidly. 2. Fly lightly and swiftly; make short and swift flights. ~ *n.*

flitch (flĭch) *n.* 1. Salted or cured side of bacon. 2. Slice cut lengthwise from tree trunk; strengthening plate on beam, girder, etc. ~ *v.t.* Cut into flitches.

flit·ter (flĭt'er) *v.i.* Flit about, flutter.

fliv·ver (flĭv'er) *n.* (slang) Old or cheap automobile, usu. a Model-T Ford.

float (flōt) *v.* 1. Rest, drift, on surface of liquid; (of stranded vessel) get afloat; be suspended freely *in* liquid; move or be suspended in air as if buoyed up; hover *before* eye or mind; (of currency) (allow to) fluctuate in regard to exchange rate. 2. Launch (scheme, enterprise, etc.), be launched. 3. Cover with liquid, inundate; (of water etc.) support, bear along (object); set afloat; waft through air. ~ *n.* 1. Floating object; raft; cork supporting fishing line and dipping when fish bites; cork etc. supporting edge of fishing net; hollow metallic ball regulating water level in boiler or tank; watertight structure attached to seaplane to give it buoyancy when resting on surface of water. 2. Cold soft drink with ball of ice cream floating on top. 3. Large flat vehicle or platform on wheels carrying an

*A well-preserved **flintlock** pistol and powderhorn. The combustion achieved by igniting the powder propelled metal shot.*

exhibit in parade etc. 4. Tool f smoothing plaster. 5. (commer Sum representing outstandi checks in process of collection.

float·er (flō'ter) *n.* 1. One w floats. 2. One who drifts from pla to place, job to job, etc.

float·ing (flō'tĭng) *adj.* (esp.) Having little attachment, d connected; (of kidney etc.) d placed, out of the normal positic ~ **rib**, rib (in man, one of the tw lower pairs) not attached to brea bone in front. 2. (commerc.) circulation; (of capital) available f use; (of debt) short-term. Fluctuating; variable; not settled definite state or place. 4. ~ (dr **dock**: see DOCK[3].

floc·cu·lant (flŏk'yu̇lant) Chemical agent for causing su pended particles to form floccule masses.

floc·cu·lent (flŏk'yu̇lent) ac Like tufts of wool; in, showin tufts. **floc'cu·lence** *n.*

flock[1] (flŏk) *n.* Lock, tuft, wool, cotton, etc.; material f quilting and stuffing made of wo refuse or shredded cloth; powder wool or felt applied to paper, clot etc. to produce a pattern or textur

flock[2] (flŏk) *n.* 1. Large assemb of people. 2. Number of animals one kind (now esp. birds) feedi or traveling in company; number domestic animals (now only she or goats) kept together. 3. Co gregation, esp. in relation to minister; (occas.) any body persons under charge or guidan of another person. ~ *v.i.* Co gregate, go in great numbers, troo e lobster trap **float** (above) is used to ovide buoyancy to the trap. There is multitude of fishing floats. The inderland flying boat (right) floats on e water when at rest. Flying boats are ainly used where there are few con- ntional landing strips, but plenty of lm water.

loe (flō) *n.* Sheet of floating ice.
log (flŏg) *v.t.* (**flogged, flog·- g**). 1. Beat with stick, whip, 2. (slang) Sell. **flog′ger** *n.*
lood (flŭd) *n.* Flowing in of tide; wing water, river, stream, sea et.); irruption of water over d, inundation (**the F ~**, the great uge recorded in Genesis as curring in time of Noah); out- uring of water; torrent, down- ir (also fig. as **~ of abuse, ~ tears**); **flood′gate**, gate that can

be opened or closed to admit or exclude water, esp. floodwater; lower gate of lock; sluice; **flood′- light**, artificial light flooding surface of building etc. more or less uniformly; (*v.t.*) light thus; **flood plain**, plain near a river, subject to flooding; **flood tide**, high tide; (fig.) peak, climax.   **flood** *v.* Inundate, cover with a flood; irrigate; deluge with water; (of rain) fill (river) to overflowing; become flooded; come in floods or great quantities; drive *out* by floods.

floor (flōr, flor) *n.* 1. Layer of boards, brick, etc., on which people tread in room, lower surface of interior of room; bottom of sea, cave, etc.; lowest boundary or part. 2. (in legislative assemblies etc.) Part of house where members sit and from which they speak; hence, in parliamentary proceedings, the right of speaking. 3. Set of rooms etc. on same level in building, story. 4. Level area; platform or leveled space for threshing etc. 5. Bottom price or limit, in law, at an auction, etc; 6. **floor′board**, one of the boards of a floor, esp. in a boat; (often pl.) the floor of a car; **floor leader**, person appointed by a political party to direct its activities on the floor of legislative body; person at convention who directs campaign of candidate seeking nomination; **floor manager**, stage manager of television production; **floor′shift**, automobile gearshift lever set in floor; **floor show**, entertainment presented in night club etc.; **floor′walker**, (formerly) department store sales supervisor. **floor** *v.t.* 1. Furnish with floor; pave; serve as floor of. 2. Bring to floor or ground, knock down; confound, nonplus; get the better of.

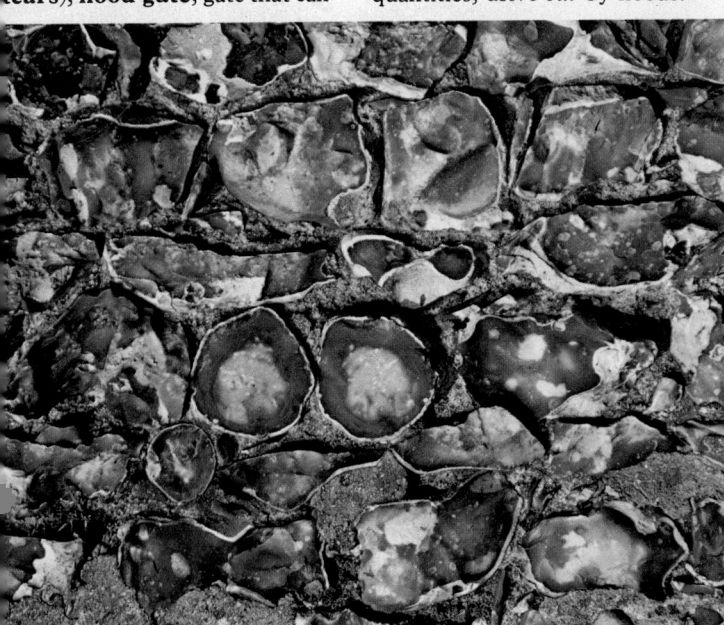

Flint was first used by primitive man for making knives, spearheads and other tools and weapons since it broke easily into flakes and fragments. It is an excel- lent building material because of its durability.

Floods have always been a part of the natural order, and in many ancient civilizations were put to good use as a means of supplying nutrients to the land. Modern man, however, sees floods in a destructive light. Right: Floodwaters spilling across roads in Bonsale, California. Middle: Farmland submerged under water at least 10 ft. deep. Bottom: Floods tore through these grain elevators in the Mid-West, ruining the crop. Flood control is a problem that has confronted man for many years, and still no real solution is in sight.

loo·zy (floo′zē) *n.* (pl. **-zies**). eaply and flashily dressed man of loose morals; a prostitute.

lop (flŏp) *v.* (**flopped, flop·-ag**). Sway about heavily and sely, flap; move clumsily or vily, or with sudden bump or d; (slang) fail. ~ *n.* Flopping tion, sound made by it; (slang) lure. **flop′py** *adj.* (**-pi·er, i·est**). Inclined to flop.

flop·house (flŏp′hows) *n.* Low-de rooming house or hotel efly for indigent men.

flop·o·ver (flŏp′ōvər) *n.* Con-uous vertical motion on tele-ion screen, caused by poor ception.

Flo·ra (flōr′a, flôr′a). (Rom. th.) Goddess of flowers and ring.

flo·ra (flōr′a, flôr′a) *n.* (pl. **·ras, flo·rae** pr. flōr′ē, flôr′ē). ist of) plants of particular region epoch. **flo′ral** *adj.* Of flora(s); flower(s). **flo′ral·ly** *adv.* [f. ORA]

Flo·ré·al (flawrāahl′). Eighth nth (Apr. 20–May 19) in French volutionary calendar.

Flor·ence (flōr′ens, flär′-). Cen-al Italian city in Tuscany on the no River at the foot of the ennines; major cultural and tistic center in W. Europe during th–16th centuries, esp. in velopment of Italian Renais-nce.

Flor·en·tine (flōr′entēn, -tīn, r′-) *adj.* Of Florence. ~ *n.*

15th century **Florence** was the center of Italian art and culture and the birth-place of the Renaissance. The city con-tains some of the finest works of that period, many of them housed in the Palazzo Pitti.

Native, inhabitant, of Florence.

flo·res·cence (flōrĕs′ens) *n.* Period or state of blossoming. **flo·res′cent** *adj.*

flo·ret (flōr′ĭt, flôr′-, flōrĕt′) *n.* (bot.) One of the small flowers making up a composite flower; small flower.

flo·ri·bun·da (flōrĭbŭn′da, flôr-) *n.* Plant (esp. kind of rose) bearing flowers in dense clusters.

flo·ri·cul·ture (flōr′ĭkŭlchər, flôr′-) *n.* Cultivation of flowers. **flo·ri·cul·tur·ist** (flōrĭkŭl′cherĭst, flôr′-) *n.*

flor·id (flōr′ĭd, flär′-) *adj.* (obs.) Profusely adorned as with flowers; elaborately ornate; ostentatious, showy; ruddy, flushed, high-colored. **flor′id·ly** *adv.*

Flor·i·da (flōr′ĭda, flär′-). Southeasternmost U.S. state, extending as a peninsula between the Atlantic and the Gulf of Mexico; 27th state to join Union (1845); capital Tallahassee; ~ **Keys,** chain of small islands extend-ing from S. tip of Florida 150 mi. (242 km) SW. to Key West; ~ **Straits,** straits between the Florida Keys and Cuba connecting the Gulf of Mexico with the Atlantic Ocean. **Flo·rid′i·an, Flor′i·dan** *adjs. & ns.*

flor·in (flōr′ĭn, flär′-) *n.* 1. Brit. coin, former 2-shilling piece. 2. Monetary unit of various European and South African countries. 3. (hist.) Gold coin first issued at Florence in 1252; any of various other gold coins formerly current in Europe. [OF. f. L. *flos flor-* flower, because the orig. florin was stamped with a lily]

flo·rist (flōr′ĭst, flär′-) *n.* One who (raises and) sells flowers and ornamental plants.

flo·ru·it (flōr′ūĭt, flôr′-, -ōōĭt) *n.* Period (failing exact dates of birth and death) at which person was alive or worked (abbrev. fl.). [L., = "flourished"]

floss (flaws, flŏs) *n.* Rough silk enveloping silkworm cocoon; un-twisted or loosely twisted filaments of silk used for needlework. **floss′y** *adj.* (**floss·i·er, floss·i·est**).

flo·ta·tion (flōtā′shon) *n.* Float-ing; launching of a company or enterprise; ~ **collar,** circular inflated tube attached to space vehicle after landing in water.

flo·til·la (flōtĭl′a) *n.* Small fleet; fleet of boats or small ships; (U.S. Navy) unit of two or more squadrons of small warships.

flot·sam (flŏt′sam) *n.* Wreckage found floating (cf. JETSAM).

flounce¹ (flowns) *v.i.* (**flounced, flounc·ing**). Go with agitated or violent motion, flop, plunge, throw the body about. ~ *n.* Fling, jerk, of body or limb.

flounce² (flowns) *n.* Ornamental

strip gathered and sewn by upper edge around woman's skirt etc. and with lower edge hanging. ~ *v.t.* Trim with flounces.

floun·der[1] (flown'der) *n.* (pl. **-ders**, collect. **-der**). Small edible flatfish, esp. the **winter** ~ (*Pseudopleuronectes americanus*) of N. Atlantic waters.

floun·der[2] (flown'der) *v.i.* Struggle or plunge (as) in mud or wading; make mistakes, manage affair badly or with difficulty.

flour (flowr, flow'er) *n.* Finer part of meal (of wheat or other grain) obtained by grinding and sifting; wheat meal as dist. from that of other grain; fine soft powder, esp. that obtained by grinding seeds, farinaceous roots, etc. ~ *v.t.* Sprinkle with flour; grind into flour; **flour mill**, mill for making flour (dist. from *gristmill*). **flour'y** *adj.* [form of FLOWER; orig. sense "finest part"]

flour·ish (flĕr'ish, flŭr'-) *v.* 1. Grow vigorously; thrive, prosper, be successful; be in one's prime. 2. Embellish with flourishes. 3. Show ostentatiously; wave (weapon) about; throw (limbs) about. ~ *n.* Ornament of flowing curves about letter or word in handwriting; rhetorical embellishment, florid expression; ostentatious waving of weapon etc.; (mus.) fanfare of brass instruments, esp. to announce distinguished person's approach; florid passage, profuse ornamentation; short extemporized sequence of notes as prelude.

flout (flowt) *v.* Mock, insult, express contempt for by word or act; scoff *at.* **flout'er** *n.*

flow (flō) *v.i.* 1. Glide along as a stream; (of blood etc.) circulate; (of persons, things) come, go, in numbers; (of talk, literary style, etc.) move easily; (of garment, hair, etc.) hang easily, undulate; result *from.* 2. Gush out, spring; (of blood) be spilled; run full, be in flood; (of wine etc.) be poured out without stint. ~ *n.* Flowing movement in stream; amount that flows; flowing liquid; outpouring, stream, continuous supply; rise of tide; ~ **chart,** ~ **diagram,** schematic representation of a sequence of operations, procedures, etc., in manufacturing, computer use, etc.

flow·er (flow'er) *n.* 1. (bot.) Reproductive organ in plant containing one or more pistils or stamens or both, and usu. a corolla and calyx; (pop.) colored (i.e. not green) part of plant from which seed or fruit is later developed; blossom; flowering plant. 2. (pl., chem. etc.) Pulverulent form of substance, esp. powder formed by sublimation. 3. Pick or choice *of*; best part, choicest embodiment *of.* 4. State of blooming; prime. 5. ~ **children,**

young people of 1960s living a Bohemian life and carrying flowers as symbols of peace and love; ~ **girl,** very young girl in wedding procession walking in front of bride and carrying flowers; ~ **head,** cluster of florets giving effect of single flower; **flow'erpot,** pot holding soil in which plant may be set; **flower show,** competitive or other exhibition of flowers etc. **flow'ered, flow'er·less, flow'er-**

The **flower** *of a plant is responsible for the production of seeds. Certain parts of the flower, like the stamens and the carpels, are concerned only with reproduction. Other parts, like the petals and* *sepals, are protective or serve to attra insects to the flowers. Flowering plar of many different kinds have been c tivated by man because of their beau and their decorative qualities.*

ing *adjs.* **flower** *v.* Produ flowers; be in full bloom; bring in flower; decorate with flowers floral design; develop fully, rea maturity or peak, flourish.

flow·er·y (flow'erē) *ac* Abounding in flowers; full of fi words, compliments, figures speech, etc. **flow'er·i·ness** *n.*

flow·ing (flō'ing) *adj.* (esp., style) Fluent, easy; (of line smoothly continuous. **flow'ing|**

v.

flown (flōn): see FLY[2].

fl. oz. *abbrev.* Fluid ounce.

flu (flōō) *n.* Influenza.

flub (flŭb) *v.* (**flubbed, flub-ing**). Botch, bungle. ~ *n.* Something flubbed.

fluc·tu·ate (flŭk'chōōāt) *v.i.* (**-at·ed, -at·ing**). Vary irregularly, rise and fall, be unstable; vacillate, waver. **fluc·tu·a·tion** (flŭkchōōā'shon) *n.*

flue (flōō) *n.* Smoke duct in chimney; channel for conveying heat.

flu·en·cy (flōō'ensē) *n.* Smooth easy flow, esp. in speech; ready utterance.

flu·ent (flōō'ent) *adj.* 1. Flowing (easily); liable to change. 2. (of motion, curves, etc.) Graceful, easy; (of speech, style) copious, coming easily, ready; expressing oneself quickly and easily. **flu·ent·ly** *adv.*

fluff (flŭf) *n.* Light feathery stuff such as separates from dressed wool etc.; soft fur; soft downy mass or bunch; (slang) mistake, blunder, esp. by actor in speech. ~ *v.t.* Make into fluff; shake *up* or *out* into fluffy mass; (slang) make mistake, blunder; bungle. **fluff'y** *adj.* (**fluff·i·er, fluff·i·est**).

flu·id (flōō'id) *adj.* Consisting of particles that move freely among themselves and yield to the slightest pressure; moving readily, not solid or rigid, not stable; ~ **dram**, ⅛ fluid ounce; ~ **drive**, transmission of automobile power between two rotors with vanes operating in oil, permitting smooth starts; ~ **ounce**: see OUNCE[1]. **fluid** *n.* Fluid substance (gas or liquid); liquid constituent or secretion. **flu·id·i·ty** (flōōid'itē), **flu·id·ness** *ns.*

flu·id·ics (flōōid'iks) *n.pl.* (usu. considered sing.) Technique of using small interacting flows and fluid jets for amplification, switching, etc.

fluke[1] (flōōk) *n.* 1. Flatfish, esp. the common FLOUNDER. 2. One of the class Trematoda of parasitic flatworms infesting the liver of sheep and cattle (so called from resemblance to flounder).

fluke[2] (flōōk) *n.* Broad flattened barbed extremity of the arm of an anchor; barbed head of lance, harpoon, etc.; either of the two sections of a whale's large triangular tail.

fluke[3] (flōōk) *n.* Unexpected or undeserved success. ~ *v.* (**fluked, fluk·ing**). Make a fluke; get by a fluke. **fluk'y** *adj.* (**fluk·i·er, fluk·i·est**). **fluk'i·ness** *n.*

flume (flōōm) *n.* Artificial channel conveying water for industrial use, to carry logs, etc.; ravine with stream. ~ *v.* Convey down a flume.

flum·mer·y (flŭm'erē) *n.* (pl. **-mer·ies**). Orig. a jellylike food made by straining boiled, slightly fermented oatmeal; any of various soft, bland foods, e.g. custard; empty compliments, trifles, nonsense. [Welsh *llymru*]

flum·mox (flŭm'oks) *v.t.* (slang) Confound, bewilder, disconcert.

flung (flŭng): see FLING.

flunk (flŭngk) *v.* (colloq.) Fail, esp. in an examination; reject or fail (a student or candidate); ~ **out**, be dismissed from school etc. because of academic failure.

flun·ky (flŭng'kē) *n.* (pl. **-kies**). (orig. Sc.) Liveried servant, footman (usu. contempt.); lackey; servile aide; toady.

fluo·res·cence (flōōrĕs'ens, flo-; *Brit.* flŏŏōrĕs'ens) *n.* Colored luminosity produced in some materials by direct action of (esp. violet and ultraviolet) light rays, X-rays, and other invisible radiations; property of converting ultraviolet light and other invisible radiations into visible light by absorption and reemission. **fluo·resce** *v.i.* (**-resced, -resc·ing**). **fluo·res'cent** *adj.*

fluor·i·da·tion (flōōrĭdā'shon, flōr-, flôr-) *n.* (esp.) Addition of traces of fluoride to water supply with the object of reducing the incidence of dental caries. **fluor·i·date** (flōōr'ĭdāt, flōr'-, flôr'-) *v.t.* (**-dat·ed, -dat·ing**).

fluo·ride (flōōr'īd, flōr'-, flôr'-; *Brit.* flŏŏō'orīd) *n.* Salt of hydrofluoric acid, compound of fluorine with another element or organic radical.

fluo·rine (flōōr'ēn, -ĭn, flōr'-, flôr'-; *Brit.* flŏŏō'orēn, -rĭn) *n.*

(chem.) Pungent corrosive gaseous element of pale greenish-yellow color, extremely active chemically; symbol F, at. no. 9, at. wt. 18.99840.

fluor·o·scope (floor'oskōp, flōr'-, flôr'-; *Brit.* flŏŏō'oroskōp) *n.* Apparatus incorporating a fluorescent screen, used for viewing objects by means of X-rays.

flur·ry (flĕr'ē, flŭr'ē) *n.* (pl. **-ries**). 1. Gust, squall; light snowfall, not enough to cover ground; snow shower. 2. Commotion, excitement; nervous hurry, agitation. ~ *v.t.* (**-ried, -ry·ing**). Confuse by haste or noise, agitate.

flush[1] (flŭsh) *v.* Take wing and fly away; cause (birds) to do this, put up; (fig.) bring into the open. ~ *n.* Bird or flock of birds suddenly taking flight.

flush[2] (flŭsh) *v.* 1. Spurt, rush out; cleanse (drain etc.) by flow of water; flood. 2. (Cause to) glow with warm color; (of blood) rush into and redden face; (of face) become red or hot, blush; inflame with pride or passion. ~ *n.* 1. Rush of water; sudden abundance; cleansing of drain by flushing. 2. Rush of emotion, elation produced by it or by victory etc. 3. Freshness, vigor. 4. Rush of blood to face, reddening caused by this or by fever.

flush[3] (flŭsh) *adj.* 1. Full to overflowing, in flood. 2. (usu. pred.) Having plentiful supply of

Flowers are typically bright colored in an effort to attract insects — often essential in pollination. Masses of flowers, as on this dogwood, increase the chance of success.

ocelli (simple eyes)

compound eye

antenna

salivary d

pseudo-trachea

phary

maxillary palp

probos

superior lip

labellum

inferior

*The best known and most widespread of flies is the common **house fly,** the head of which appears above right. It is prolific and the female deposits from 500 to 2,000 eggs after copulation. It is an offensive pest which is capable of transmitting diseases to man and domestic animals. Other species of flies include the robber fly (top), consuming a moth it has captured in mid-air. Flies differ from all other insects in possessing only one pair of functiona wings. The others are reduced to clublike balances.*

money etc. 3. Even, in same plane; level *with*; without projections or raised edges. ~ *v.t.* Level; fill in (joint) level with surface.

flush[4] (flŭsh) *n.* (cards) Hand of cards all of one suit, or including prescribed number of one suit.

flus·ter (flŭs´ter) *v.* Confuse; make nervous; be agitated, bustle. ~ *n.* Flurry, flutter, agitation.

flute (flōot) *n.* 1. Musical instrument of woodwind family, a wooden or silver tube without a reed; the modern type is played horizontally and has a mouth hole at the side and holes stopped by keys, and its range is 3 octaves above middle C. 2. Organ stop with flutelike tone. 3. Semicylindrical vertical groove in pillar; similar groove or channel elsewhere, e.g., in frills. ~ *v.* (**flut·ed, flut·ing**). 1. Play flute; play on flute. 2. Make flutes or grooves in. **flut´ing** *n.* **flut´ist** *n.* Player of flute.

flut·ter (flŭt´er) *v.* 1. Flap wings, flap (wings), without flying or in short flights; come or go with quivering motion; go about restlessly, flit, hover; quiver, vibrate; (of pulse) beat feebly and irregularly; move (flag, fan, etc.) irregularly. 2. Tremble with excitement, be agitated; agitate, ruffle; throw into confusion or agitation. ~ *n.* Fluttering; tremulous excitement; stir, sensation; (colloq.) small bet (on horse etc.).

flu·vi·al (flōo´vēal) *adj.* (found in, river(s).

flux (flŭks) *n.* 1. Flowi continued flow or flood. Continuous succession of chang of condition, composition, etc. (phys.) Rate of flow of matter energy; amount of light incident a given area in a given time; to amount of magnetic or electric fie passing through a given area. (archaic) Morbid or excessive d charge of blood or excrement, as **bloody** ~, dysentery. 5. Substan mixed with metal etc. to facilita soldering and to remove oxid substance used to make colo fusible in enameling etc. ~ 1. Issue in a flux; flow copious

...catchers of the Old ...rld, such as the ...adise flycatcher, have ...upright stance and make ...rt erratic flights to catch ...sing insects. New ...rld or 'tyrant' flycatchers ...the most aggressive of ...erican perching birds.

paradise flycatcher   Old World

vermilion flycatcher   New World

*The limbs of **flying lemurs** have gliding membranes which enable the animal to glide through the air for several yards. The flying lemur resembles a squirrel.*

***Flying fish** execute a rapid glide, rather than a true flight, and take to the air in shoals, often to escape a pursuing enemy. Their take-off speed is about 40 m.p.h.*

spot; **fly′weight**, boxer of lightest weight.

fly[2] (flī) v. (**flew**, for baseball def. **flied, flown, fly·ing**). 1. Move through air with wings; travel, convey, by aircraft etc., (of aircraft etc.) travel through air or space; pilot (aircraft); make (pigeon, hawk) fly; make (kite) rise and stay aloft; pass or rise quickly through air; jump clear over or *over* fence, etc.; ~ **high**, be ambitious; be successful for the moment; **high-flown**, exalted; turgid, bombastic. 2. (of flag, hair, garment, etc.) Flutter, wave; set or keep (flag) flying. 3. Travel swiftly, rush along, pass rapidly; hasten; be driven or forced off suddenly; (baseball) hit a fly ball; **let** ~, discharge (missile); shoot, use strong language, *at*; ~ **at**, attack violently. 4. Run away, flee, flee from. 5. **fly′by**, (often ceremonial) flight by aircraft past a given point, usu. at low altitude; (of a spacecraft) close approach to a planet etc. for observation; **fly-by-night**, transitory, unstable, of dubious c...racter; **fly-by-wire** (of model air.raft), controlled electrically by a wire tether; **fly the coop**, (colloq.) escape, depart suddenly. **fly** n. (pl. **flies**). 1. Fold on garment, esp. on front of trousers, to contain or cover fastening; tent fly. 2. Part of flag farthest from staff; breadth of flag from staff to

2. Make fluid, melt; fuse; treat with flux.

flux·ion (flŭk′shon) n. Flowing; continuous change. **flux′ion·al, flux′ion·ar·y** *adjs.*

fly[1] (flī) n. (pl. **flies**). Two-winged insect, esp. of the order Diptera; winged insect, as caddis fly; natural or artificial fly used as bait in fishing; ~ **in the ointment**, disturbing condition in otherwise workable scheme; **fly′blow**, (*n.*) egg or larva of blowfly, esp. as maggot in meat etc.; (*v.t.*) deposit eggs in, taint; **fly′blown**, so tainted; **fly book**, case for keeping angler's flies in; **fly′catcher**, any of various birds of the New World family Tyrannidae or the Old World family Muscicapidae that characteristically dart out from a perch to catch flying insects; **fly fishing, fly casting**, technique of angling with fly as lure; **fly′paper**, paper treated with preparation for catching or poisoning flies; **fly′speck**, tiny spot made by excrement of a fly; any insignificant

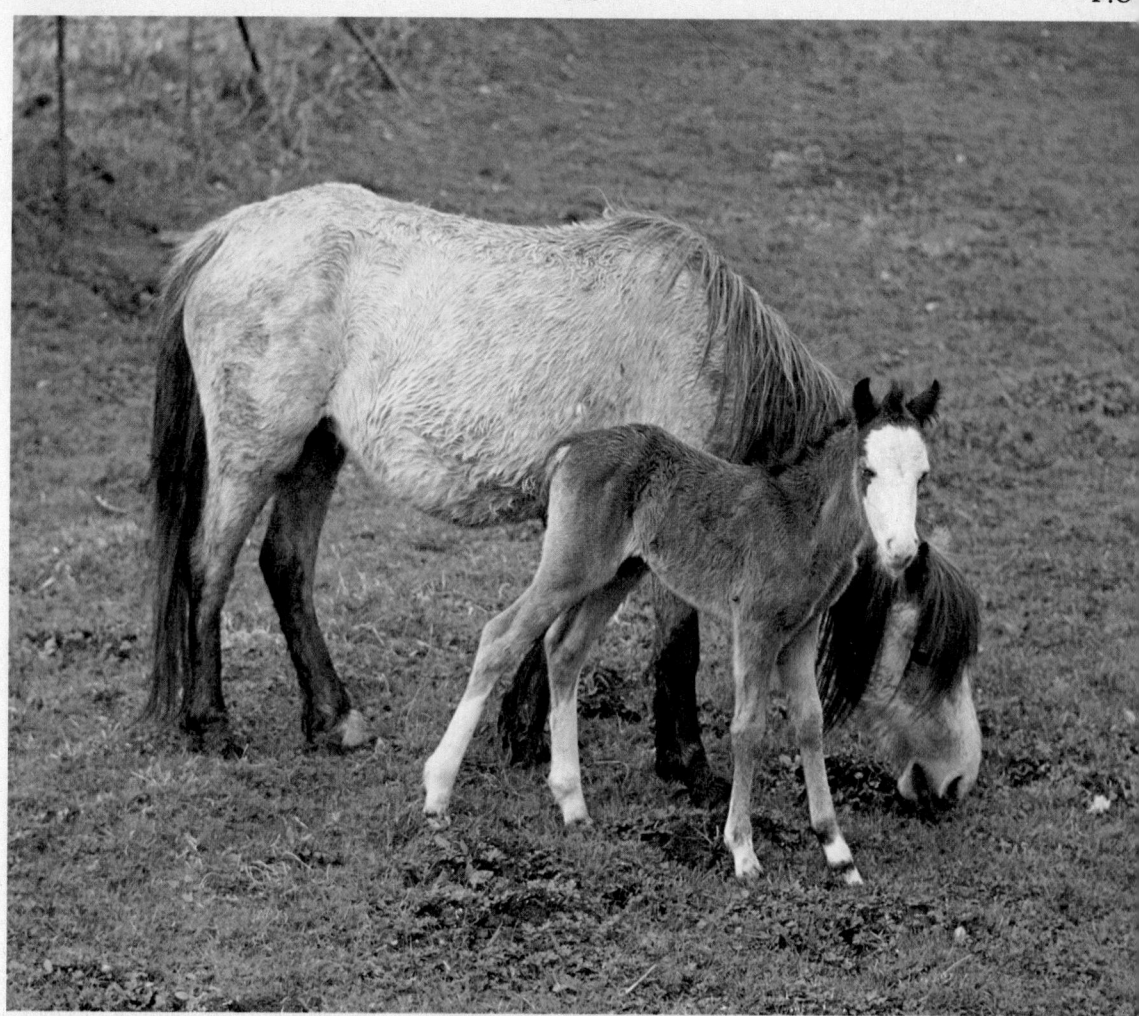

end. 3. (theatr., pl.) Space over proscenium, including upper mechanism and galleries on each side from which it is worked. 4. Speed-regulating device, usu. of vanes on rotating shaft, for regulating striking mechanism of clock etc. flywheel etc. for regulating speed of machinery. 5. ~ **ball**, (baseball) ball batted high in air, esp. to the outfield; **fly'leaf** (pl. **-leaves**), blank leaf at beginning or end of book; **fly'wheel**, wheel with heavy rim on revolving shaft, for regulating motion of machinery or accumulating power.

fly·er: see FLIER.

fly·ing (flī′ĭng) *adj.* 1. That flies. 2. Floating loosely, fluttering, waving; hanging loose. 3. Traveling or passing swiftly; ~ **start**, start of a race in which starting point is passed at full speed. 4. ~ **buttress**, (archit.) buttress slanting from pier etc. to wall and usu. carried on arch for taking thrust of roof or vault; ~ **colors**, high success, triumph; ~ **doctor**, doctor who visits patients in remote areas, esp. Australian outback, by aerial ambulance; F ~ **Dutchman**: see DUTCH; ~ **fish**, fish of two

A mare is generally mated to a stallion in spring or early summer and gives birth to a **foal** *about 11 months later. The foal gets to its legs about half an hour after birth.*

genera (*Dactylopterus* and *Exocetus*), found in warm seas, which can rise into air by means of enlarged winglike pectoral fins; ~ **fox**, fruit-eating bat of genus *Pteropus*, found in tropical Africa, Asia, and Australia; ~ **jib**, light sail set before jib on the jib boom; ~ **saucer**, unidentified disk- or saucer-shaped object reported as appearing in the sky; ~ **squirrel**, any of several squirrels, esp. of genera *Pteromys* and *Glaucomys*, which can glide through air by means of extension of skin connecting fore and hind limbs. **flying** *n.* Act or process of moving through the air; flight; ~ **boat**, seaplane with boatlike hull; ~ **machine**, airplane, esp. an early type or model.

FM *abbrev.* Frequency modulation.

Fm *symbol.* Fermium.

F number. Ratio of focal length to the aperture diameter of a

camera lens.

foal (fōl) *n.* Young of hors ass, etc., colt or filly. ~ Give birth to (foal).

foam (fōm) *n.* 1. Collection small bubbles formed in liquid agitation, fermentation, etc.; fro of saliva or perspiration. 2. (poe Sea. 3. Rubber or plastic mater in form of cellular mass; ~ **rubbe** light, firm rubber with high conte of air, used for cushions, ma tresses, etc. **foam** *v.i.* Emit foa froth at the mouth; (of water etc froth, gather foam, run foami along, down, over, etc.; (of cup, et be filled with foaming liqui **foam′y** *adj.* (**foam·i·er, foam·i est**)

fob[1] (fŏb) *n.* 1. Small pocket f watch etc. formerly made in wais band of trousers. 2. Short chain ribbon attached to watch, to worn outside pocket for display. Ornament attached to watch cha for display.

fob[2] (fŏb) *v.t.* (**fobbed, fob bing**). Cheat, take in; palm (som thing inferior) *off on* person; p (person) *off with* somethi inferior.

f.o.b., F.O.B. *abbrevs.* Free

...rd (i.e., price quoted includes ...very onto a carrier at a specified ...nt but not the carrier's charges).

...o·cal (fō'kᵊl) *adj.* Of, situated ...ollected at, a focus; ~ **distance** ...**ength**, distance between center ...ens or mirror and its focus; ~ ...**ne**, plane parallel with that of ..., passing through the focus; ~ ...**nt**, center of action or attention; ...us.

...o'c's'le (fōk'sᵊl): see FORE-...TLE.

...o·cus (fō'kᵘs) *n.* (pl. **-cus·es, -ci** ...-sī). 1. (geom.) One of the ...nts from which the distances to ... point of a given curve are ...nnected by a linear relation. 2. ...tics etc.) Point at which rays ...et after being refracted or ...lected; point from which rays ...pear to proceed; point at which ...ject must be situated in order ...t image produced by lens may be ...ar and well defined; adjustment ... eye or eyeglass) necessary to ...oduce a clear image. 3. Principal ...t of disease; center of activity. ...*v.t.* Converge, make converge, ...a focus; adjust focus of (lens, eye); ...ng into focus.

...fod·der (fŏd'er) *n.* Feed for ...estock, esp. hay, straw, corn-...lks, etc. ~ *v.t.* Give fodder to.

...foe (fō) *n.* Enemy, adversary, ...ponent.

...foe·tid = FETID.

...foe·tus = FETUS.

...fog (fŏg, fawg) *n.* 1. Thick mist ... cloud of minute water droplets ...spended in atmosphere at or near ...rth's surface; obscurity caused by ...is; **fog'horn**, sounding instru-...ent for warning ships in fog. 2. ...hotog.) Opaque cloudy patch on ...veloped negative. **fog** *v.* ...**ogged, fog'ging**). Envelop (as) ...ith fog; bewilder, perplex; ...hotog.) cause fog on (negative); ...come enveloped in fog.

...fog·gy (fŏg'ē, faw'gē) *adj.* ...**gi·er, -gi·est**). Thick, murky; of, ...ke, infested with, fog; obscure, ...ull, confused; beclouded, in-...istinct. **fog'gi·ly** *adv.* **fog'gi-**...**ess** *n.*

...fo·gy, fo·gey (fō'gē) *ns.* (pl. ...**gies, -geys**). (usu. **old** ~) Person ...ith antiquated ideas.

...foi·ble (foi'bᵊl) *n.* 1. Weak point; ...eakness of character; quality on ...hich one mistakenly prides one-...elf. 2. (fencing) Pliant part of ...word blade from middle to point.

...foil¹ (foil) *n.* 1. Metal hammered ...r rolled into thin sheet; sheet of ...his formerly placed behind glass of ...irror to produce reflection; thin ...eaf of metal placed under precious ...tone to increase its brilliance, or ...nder transparent substance to ...ake it look like precious stone. 2. ...nything serving to set off another ...hing by contrast, esp. a person. ...~ *v.t.* Set off by contrast.

foil² (foil) *v.* Beat off, repulse; frustrate, parry, baffle.

foil³ (foil) *n.* Blunt-edged fencing sword with flat guard and blunt-tipped point.

foist (foist) *v.t.* Introduce surreptitiously or unwarrantably *into* or *in*; palm (*off*) *on*.

fol. *abbrev.* Folio, following.

fold¹ (fōld) *n.* Enclosure for sheep; flock of sheep; (fig.) Church, body of believers. ~ *v.t.* Shut up (sheep etc.) in fold.

fold² (fōld) *n.* Doubling of folded object; hollow between two thicknesses, in mountain, etc.; coil of serpent etc.; folding; line made by folding; (geol.) bend in strata. ~ *v.* 1. Double (flexible thing) over upon itself; ~ **over, together**; bend portion or (thing) *back, down*; become, be able to be, folded; ~ **up**, make more compact by folding; (colloq.) fail; **fold'away**, designed to be folded and stored out of the way when not in use, as *foldaway cot;* **folding door**, door in two parts (often themselves consisting of hinged leaves that fold up when door is open) hung on opposite jambs, so that edges meet when door is closed; **fold'out**, large insert in book or magazine folded so as to fit within the pages. 2. Wind, clasp (arms etc.) *around*; interlace (arms), clasp (one's) hands; swathe, envelop; embrace *in* arms, *to* breast. **fold'er** *n.* (esp.) Folded circular etc.; cover or holder for loose papers.

*These dancers in South Korea perform a traditional **folk dance**. Such dances reveal something of the life and culture of a country, and of how war and other events have influenced it. Some such dances are purely recreational.*

-fold *suffix*. Multiplied by, as *sevenfold*.

fo·li·age (fō'lēᵢj) *n.* Leaves, leafage.

fo·li·ate (fō'lēᵢt, -āt) *adj.* Leaf-like; having leaves; having specified number of leaflets. ~ (fō'lēāt) *v.* (**-at·ed, -at·ing**). Split into laminae; decorate with foils; number leaves (not pages) of (volume) consecutively. **fo·li·a·tion** (fōlēā'shᵊn) *n.*

fo·lic (fō'lĭk, fŏl'ĭk) *adj.* Of, involving, folic acid; ~ **acid**, vitamin of the B group, deficiency of which in people is associated with anemia.

fo·li·o (fō'lēō) *n.* (pl. **-li·os**). 1. Leaf of paper, parchment, etc., numbered only on front; two opposite pages of ledger etc. used concurrently in bookkeeping; page of ledger etc. used for both sides of account; page number of printed book; number of words (in U.S. usu. 100, in England usu. 72 or 90) taken as unit in reckoning length of document. 2. Sheet of paper folded once; volume of the largest common size, made up of sheets of paper folded once. ~ *adj.* Formed of sheets or a sheet folded once; folio size.

folk (fōk) *n.* (pl. **folks**, sometimes **folk**). 1. People; ethnic group; race. 2. (usu. pl.) People in general; people of specified class; relatives. 3. (attrib.) Of the people; ~ **dance**, (music for) traditional dance of popular origin in a nation or region; ~ **etymology**, popular perversion of a word to make it seem derived from familiar elements, as *cole slaw* into *cold slaw*, *chaise longue* into *chaise lounge*, or *foxglove* into *folk's-glove*; **folk'lore**,

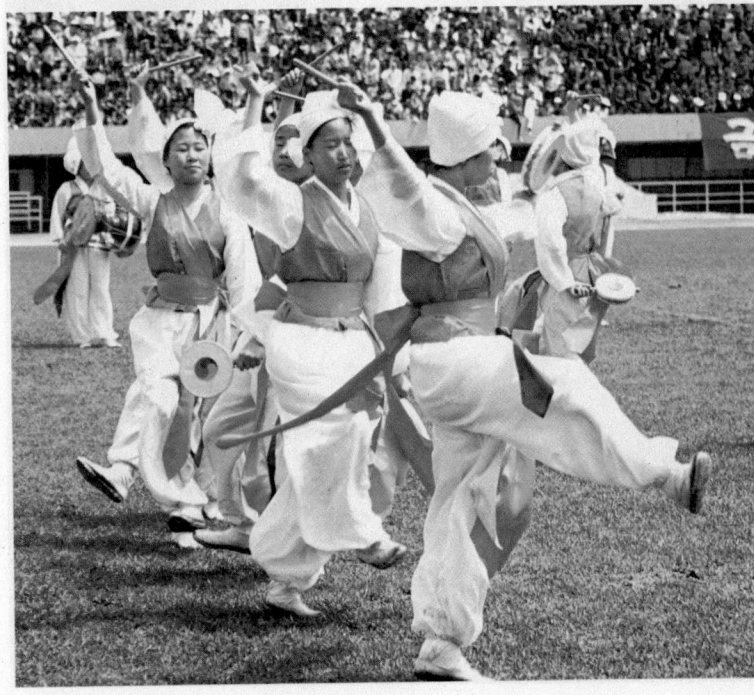

traditional beliefs, customs, etc., of the people; study of these; hence **folk′lorist; folk mass**, liturgical mass with folk music instead of conventional church music; **folk medicine**, traditional medicine developed by people isolated from modern practices, relying esp. on vegetable remedies; **folk music**, music arising from common people of a nation or region, usu. orally transmitted and anonymous; **folk rock**, style of music combining elements of rock-‘n’-roll and folk music; **folk singer**, singer of either kind of folk song; **folk song**, song belonging to the folk music of a people, or one composed in deliberate imitation of such a song; **folk′ways**, (sociol. etc.) traditional patterns of behavior common to members of a particular culture or society. **folk·sy** (fōk′sē) *adj.* (-si·er, -si·est). Sociable, friendly, informal; resembling folk art.

foll. *abbrev.* Following.

fol·li·cle (fŏl′ikel) *n.* 1. (anat.) Small sac; secretory gland of this shape; minute pit in which hair root grows; **Graafian ~**: see GRAAF. 2. (bot.) Fruit that consists of a single carpel and splits open along ventral suture only. **fol·li·cu·lar** (folĭk′yuler), **fol·lic′u·lat·ed** *adjs.*

fol·low (fŏl′ō) *v.* 1. Go or come after (moving thing or person); pursue; go along (path); come after, come next, in order or time; **~ the leader**, game in which each player must move as leader does; **~ one’s**

nose, go straight on; be guided by instinct; **~ one’s star(s)**, pursue what one believes is one’s destined success. 2. Accompany, serve, attend upon; go as person’s attendant; go after as admirer; be consequence of; result (from). 3. Strive after, aim at. 4. Take as guide or leader; take as rule; conform to; practice (profession etc.); **~ the sea**, be a sailor. 5. Keep up with mentally; grasp the meaning of; grasp argument, meaning, etc. 6. **~ through**, (golf, baseball, etc.) carry stroke through to fullest possible extent after striking ball; **~-through** (*n.*); **~ up**, pursue steadily; add another blow etc. to (previous blow etc.); (fig.) prosecute (suggestion etc.) to a conclusion; **~-up** (*n.*).

fol·low·er (fŏl′ōer) *n.* (esp.) Adherent, disciple.

fol·low·ing (fŏl′ōĭng) *n.* (esp.) Body of adherents, followers. **~** *adj.* (esp.) Now to be mentioned; coming next. **~** *prep.* After.

fol·ly (fŏl′ē) *n.* (pl. **-lies**). 1. Foolishness; foolish act, idea, etc. 2. (pl. considered as sing.) Theatrical revue featuring glamorous female performers. 3. Costly enterprise deemed useless or foolish; **Seward’s ~**, U.S. purchase of Alaska from Russia for $7 million, arranged by Secretary of State William SEWARD in 1867.

fo·ment (fōmĕnt′) *v.t.* 1. Bathe with warm or medicated lotions; apply warmth to. 2. Foster,

stimulate, instigate (sentimen conduct, sedition, etc.). **fo·men ta·tion** (fōmĕntā′shon) *n.* (App cation of) warm or medicat substance for fomenting purpose

fond (fŏnd) *adj.* Tender, lovin doting; (archaic) foolishly cred lous; **~ of**, full of love for, mu inclined to. **fond′ly** *adv.* **fond ness** *n.*

fon·dle (fŏn′del) *v.* (**-dle -dling**). Touch or stroke loving toy amorously.

fon·due (fŏndōō′, fŏn′dōō; *F* fawndü′) *n.* (cookery) Hot melt cheese flavored with wine, bee etc., into which pieces of bre are dipped.

font (fŏnt) *n.* 1. Receptacle, us of stone, for baptismal wate receptacle for holy water; oil rese voir of lamp. 2. (of type) Comple assortment of one size and style.

Fon · taine · bleau (fŏn′tĭnbl *Fr.* fawn̈těnblō′). French town Seine River, 35 mi. SSE. of Pa in Fontainebleau Forest; chate there was former residence French monarchs, now a summ home of country’s presidents; Edi of NANTES revoked there (1685).

fon·ta·nel, fon·ta·nelle (fŏnt nĕl′) *ns.* Membrane-covered spa in bony vault of skull where unic of the bones is incomplete at birt normally closing in infancy.

fon·ti·na (fŏntē′na) *n.* Type Italian cheese made from ewe milk.

Foo·chow (fōo′chow′; *Chi* fōo′jō′). Province of SE. China.

food (fōod) *n.* Substance take into the body to maintain life an growth; solid substance used th (opp. drink); (particular kind o edibles (also transf. and fig.); **~ chain**, (ecol.) series of organisms i which each eats a smaller and is i turn eaten by a larger; **~ proc essor**, kitchen appliance fc preparing foods by grinding, shrec ding, etc.; **~ stamps**, stamps give or sold below face value by feder government to poor persons an redeemed at face value for food **food′stuff**, material for food; (pl articles of food in bulk.

fool (fōol) *n.* Silly person simpleton; dupe; professional jeste in medieval great household; **pla the ~**, blunder, trifle; indulge i buffoonery; **fool′proof**, so plai that even a fool cannot mis understand; (of machines etc.) no apt to be injured by misuse; **fool cap**, fantastic cap, usu. with bells worn by medieval jester; dunce’ conical paper cap; **fools′cap**, lon sheet of writing or printing pape

The baptismal **font** *is normally placed near the west end of the church. It name comes from the Latin word fo ‘stream’. This magnificent Norman fon is at Torpenhow church, near Wigton Cumbria, U.K.*

nes of **foot**
d ankle

phalanges	6 fibula
metatarsus	7 lateral malleolus
navicular	8 heel bone
talus	9 cuboid bone
tibia	(3, 4, 5, 9, 10 – tarsus)

One of the earliest and most practical forms of **footwear** was the wooden shoe or clog which is still worn in rural France, Belgium, the Netherlands, and Germany. It was particularly suitable for walking over wet or muddy ground.

× 16 inches (381–432 × 305–343 m) (from watermark of fool's cap some old paper); **fool's errand**, uitless errand; **fool's gold**, iron yrites, sometimes mistaken for old; also fig.; **fool's paradise**, lusory happiness. **fool·er·y** ōō´ler·ē) n. **fool·ish** (fōo´lĭsh) adj. ool'ish·ly adv. **fool'ish·ness** n. ol adj. That is a fool. **fool** v. lay the fool; cheat (person) out of; row away foolishly; make a fool f, dupe, play tricks on; ~ **around**, pend time aimlessly; flirt, hilander; ~ **with**, play aimlessly ith, meddle with. [OF. fol mad L. follis bellows, empty-headed erson]

fool·har·dy (fōol´härdē) adj. -di·er, -di·est). Foolishly enturesome, delighting in needless isks. **fool'har·di·ness** n.

foot (fŏŏt) n. (pl. **feet**). 1. Lowest part of leg beyond ankle; this as organ of locomotion; **on ~**, walking, not riding; **put one's ~ down**, take up firm position (fig.); **put one's ~ in it, put one's ~ in one's mouth**, blunder; **under ~**, beneath the foot or feet; in the way; into state of subjection or inferiority. 2. End of bed, grave, etc., toward which feet are placed; part of stocking etc. covering foot. 3. Metrical unit, division of line, with varying number of syllables, one of which is accented. 4. Linear measure of 12 inches. 5. Lower (usu. projecting) part of object, base. 6. (zool.) Organ of locomotion or attachment of some invertebrates, e.g., mussels. 7. Bottom (of hill, stairs, page, etc.). 8. **~-and-mouth (disease)**, contagious fever, caused by a filtrable virus, of horned cattle and other animals, with ulcerating vesicles in mouth, near hoof, etc.; **foot'ball**, Amer. game played with an ellipsoid ball on a field 100 yards long by two teams of 11 players, who seek to get and hold the ball and by running and passing advance over the others' goal line; the ball used in this game; see also SOCCER; **foot'-bridge**, bridge for foot passengers; **foot-candle**, unit of illumination,

equal to the illumination of a surface at a uniform distance of 1 ft. from a symmetrical point source of 1 candela; **foot'fall**, sound of footsteps; **foot'hill**, lower hill at foot of mountain or mountain range; **foot'hold**, place just wide enough for a foot to be placed on when climbing etc.; small but secure position gained in a business etc.; **foot'lights**, row of lights along front of stage on level with actors' feet; **foot'locker**, small trunk for personal belongings, esp. for a soldier to keep at the foot of bunk; **foot-loose**, free, unhampered by ties or obligations; **foot'man**, liveried servant attending carriage, waiting at table, and answering door; **foot'note**, note inserted at foot of page; **foot'pad**, (hist.) unmounted highwayman or street robber; **foot'path**, path for pedestrians; **foot-pound**, work done when a force of 1 pound moves its point of application 1 foot in the line of action of the force; **foot'print**, impression left by foot; **foot'race**, race between persons on foot; ~ **soldier**, infantryman; **foot'sore**, having sore feet, esp. from walking; **foot'step**, tread; noise made by treading; **foot'stool**, low stool for resting feet on; **foot'wear**, shoes, boots, slippers, etc., collectively; **foot'work**, manner of using feet in sports, dancing, etc.; agility. **foot'less** adj. **foot'age** n. Number of linear feet of material, motion picture film, etc. **foot** v. (**foot·ed, foot·ing**). Traverse on foot (rare); put foot to (stocking); add up or up (account); pay (bill).

foot·ing (fŏŏt´ĭng) n. Foothold; secure position; conditions, relations, position, status, in which person is toward others.

foot·sie, foot·sy (fŏŏt´sē) ns. (pl. **-sies**). Amorous play with the feet; **play ~ with**, carry this on; cooperate secretly.

fop (fŏp) n. Dandy. **fop'per·y** n. **fop'pish** adj. **fop'pish·ly** adv. **fop'pish·ness** n.

for (fôr, unstressed fer) prep. In place of, as in b. stands ~ born; in exchange against, sold ~ $2; in defense or favor of; in the interest of, to reach, obtain, etc., went ~ a taxi, sailed ~ Bermuda; as regards (esp. with words implying fitness), as fit ~ nothing; because of, on account of; corresponding to, ~ every enemy he has 50 friends; considering the nature of, cool ~ a summer day; during, to the extent of, wait ~ years, walk ~ 3 miles. **for** conj. (introducing new sentence etc. containing reason for believing what has been previously stated) Seeing that, since; because.

fo·ra: see FORUM.

for·age (fôr´ĭj, fär´-) n. Food for horses and cattle, fodder. ~ v.

Henry Ford's famous 'Model T' car, seen here in a 4-seater tourer version of 1915, was designed for the mass market. Between 1908 and 1927, 15 million were produced.

The French **Foreign Legion** was set in 1831 as a means of organizing mer soldiers and political refugees help to conquer Algeria. It acce recruits without proof of identity.

(-aged, -ag·ing). Collect forage from, ravage; search for forage or (fig.) *for* anything, rummage; supply with forage; get by foraging. **for′ag·er** *n.*

fo·ra·men (forā′men) *n.* (pl. -ram·i·na pr. -răm′ina, -ra·mens). Orifice, hole, passage in a bone or anatomical structure.

for·ay (for′ā, fай′-) *n.* Incursion, raid. ~ *v.i.* Go on, make, foray.

for·bear[1] = FOREBEAR.

for·bear[2] (forbār′) *v.* (-bore, -borne, -bear·ing). Abstain or refrain from or *from*; not use or mention; be patient. **for·bear′ance, for·bear′er** *ns.*

for·bid (ferbĭd′, for-) *v.t.* (-bade or -bad, -bid·den or -bid, -bid·ding). Command not *to* do, not *to* go to (place); not allow (person etc. something; person or thing to exist or happen); prevent; **Forbidden City**, Lhasa in Tibet, which foreigners were forbidden to enter; also walled area of Peking containing the imperial palace of the former Chinese Empire. **for·bid′ding** *adj.* Repellent, of un-inviting appearance. **for·bid′ding·ly** *adv.*

force (fors, fôrs) *n.* 1. Strength, violence, intense effort; strength exerted on an object, coercion; ~ **play**, (baseball) put out a base-runner by touching foot to base or home plate. 2. Military strength; body of armed men, army; body of police; **in** ~, in great numbers; (pl.) troops. 3. Mental or moral strength; power to convince, vividness of effect; binding power, validity; real import, precise meaning; **in** ~, in operation, valid.

4. (phys.) Measurable and determinable influence inclining body to motion, intensity of this; (formerly) cause of any class of physical phenomena (e.g. of heat or motion) conceived as inherent in matter; (fig.) agency likened to these. **force** *v.t.* 1. Constrain, compel; put strained sense upon (words); (cards) compel (player) to trump or reveal his or her strength, compel player to play (certain card); compel (person) *to* do, *into* doing, *into* specified action; strain to the utmost; (baseball) compel base runner (by a hit) to vacate base only to be put out at the next base; ~ **out**, (make) such a hit; ~ **play**, putting out such a runner; ~ **(in)**, cause a run to be scored by passing the batter when bases are full; ~ **person's hand**, compel him to act prematurely or adopt policy unwillingly; ~ **the pace**, adopt high speed in race to tire adversary out quickly. 2. Overpower, capture, make way through, break open (stronghold, defenses, pass, lock, door) by force; drive by force; propel against resistance; effect, produce, by effort; take by force, extort, wring; impose, press, (thing) *on* person. 3. Artificially hasten maturity of (plant etc.). **forced** *adj.* (esp.) ~ **landing**, unavoidable landing of aircraft in an emergency; ~ **march**, march requiring special effort by troops etc. **forc′ed·ly** *adv.*

force·ful (fors′ful, fôrs′-) *a* Full of force; effective; persuasi **force′ful·ly** *adv.* **force′ful·ne** *n.*

force·meat (fors′mēt, fôrs′-) Meat chopped, spiced, a seasoned for stuffing etc.; stuffin

for·ceps (for′seps, -seps) *n.* (-ceps, -ci·pes pr. -sipēz). Instr ment like pincers, for seizing a holding objects (esp. in surger (zool. etc.) clasping organ rese bling forceps (esp. in insects).

for·ci·ble (for′sibel, fôr′-) *a* Done by, involving, force; powe ful; convincing. **for′ci·ble·ne** *n.* **for′ci·bly** *adv.*

ford (ford, fôrd) *n.* Shallo place where river etc. can crossed by wading or in wheel vehicle. ~ *v.t.* Wade or dri across (river etc.). **ford′a·ble** *a*

Ford[1] (ford, fôrd), **Gera R(andolph)** (born Leslie Lyn King, later renamed after ste father) (1913–). Appointed vi president of U.S. (1973–4) aft resignation of Spiro Agnev became 38th president of U. (1974–7) upon resignation Richard Nixon.

Ford[2] (ford, fôrd), **Henr** (1863–1947). Amer. founder an president (1903–19, 1943–5) of on of world's largest automobil manufacturing plants, Ford Moto Co. in Detroit, Mich.; emphasize the economy of mass productio introduced profit sharing in com ny (1914).

fore[1] (fōr, fŏr) *adj.* Situated in
)nt. ~ *n.* Fore part, bow of
ip; **to the ~**, ready at hand,
nspicuous; into, toward promi-
nce.

fore[2] (fōr, fŏr) *adv.* **~ and aft**,
bow and stern; lengthwise in
ip; **~-and-aft** (*adj.*) (of rigging)
ith sails set lengthwise as in a
hooner.

fore[3] (fōr, fŏr) *int.* (golf) Warn-
g cry to person in line of flight
the ball.

fore- *prefix.* In front; before-
and, in advance; anticipatory,
recedent.

fore·arm[1] (fōr'ärm, fŏr'-) *n.*
rm from elbow to wrist or
ngertips.

fore·arm[2] (fōrärm', fŏr-) *v.t.*
rm beforehand.

fore·bear (fōr'bār, fŏr'-) *n.*
orefather; ancestor.

fore·bode (fōrbōd', fŏr-) *v.t.*
-bod·ed, -bod·ing). Betoken,
ortend; have presentiment of (a
misfortune). **fore·bod'ing** *adj.* &
. Presage, omen, presentiment
esp. of evil or misfortune). **fore-**
od'ing·ly *adv.*

fore·brain (fōr'brān, fŏr'-): see
RAIN.

fore·cast (fōr'kăst, -kahst, fŏr'-)
.t. (**-cast** or **-cast·ed, -cast·ing**).
stimate, conjecture, calculate
oeforehand. ~ *n.* Conjectural
stimate, calculation of future
hing, esp. of coming weather.

fore·cas·tle (fōk'sel, fōr'kăsel,
-kahsel, fŏr'-), **fo'c's'le** (fōk'sel) *ns.*
forward part of upper deck of a
hip; crew's quarters in this or in
special superstructure at bow of a
merchant ship; (hist.) short raised
deck at ship's bow.

fore·close (fōrklōz', fŏr-) *v.*
-closed, -clos·ing). 1. Bar, preclude, prevent; shut out from
enjoyment of. 2. (mortgage law)
Bar (person entitled to redeem)
upon nonpayment of money due;
bar (right of redemption); take away
power of redeeming (mortgage).
fore·clo·sure (fōrklō'zher, fŏr-) *n.*

fore·court (fōr'kōrt, fōr'kôrt) *n.*
Enclosed space, courtyard before
building; (tennis, handball, etc.)
part of court nearest net or wall.

fore·doom (fōrdoom', fŏr-) *v.t.*
Doom beforehand; condemn
beforehand *to*; foreordain, predestine.

fore·fa·ther (fōr'fahdher, fŏr'-)
n. (chiefly pl.) Ancestor, progenitor.

fore·fin·ger (fōr'fingger, fŏr'-)
n. Finger next to thumb, index
finger.

fore·foot (fōr'fŏŏt, fŏr'-) *n.* (pl.
-feet). 1. One of animal's front
feet. 2. (naut.) Foremost part of
keel.

fore·front (fōr'frŭnt, fŏr'-) *n.*
Very front, foremost part; foremost

position.

fore·go (fōrgō', fŏr-) *v.* (**-went,
-gone, -go·ing**). Precede in place
or time; **foregoing**, previously
mentioned; **foregone conclusion**,
decision or opinion formed before
case is argued or full evidence
known; result that can be or could
have been foreseen.

fore·ground (fōr'grownd, fŏr'-)
n. Part of view, esp. in picture,
nearest observer; most conspicuous
position.

fore·hand (fōr'hănd, fŏr'-) *n.*
Part of horse in front of rider;
(tennis etc.) forehand stroke. ~
adj. (tennis etc.) (of stroke) Made
with palm of hand turned forward;
foremost, leading; prior (Cf. BACK-
HAND).

fore·head (fōr'id, făr'-, -hĕd) *n.*
Part of face above eyebrows and
between temples.

for·eign (fōr'in, făr'-) *adj.* 1.
Belonging to, proceeding from,
other persons or things; alien *from*
or *to*; irrelevant, dissimilar, inappropriate, *to*; introduced from
outside (esp. **~ body** in the eye,
tissues, etc.); situated outside,
coming from another culture, area,
etc. 2. Outside the country, not in
one's own land; of, in, characteristic of, coming from, dealing with,
some country not one's own. 3.
F ~ Legion: see LEGION. **for'-
eign·er, for'eign·ness** *ns.*

fore·knowl·edge (fōr'nŏlĭdj,
fōr'-, fōrnŏl'-, fŏr'-) *n.* Prior
knowledge; prescience.

fore·leg (fōr'lĕg, fŏr'-) *n.*
Animal's front leg.

fore·limb (fōr'lĭm, fŏr'-) *n.*
Front limb of animal.

fore·lock[1] (fōr'lŏk, fŏr'-) *n.*
Lock of hair growing just above
forehead.

fore·lock[2] (fōr'lŏk, fŏr'-) *n.*
(chiefly naut.) Wedge put through
hole in bolt to keep it in place;
linchpin.

fore·man (fō'man, fŏr'-) *n.* (pl.
-men). Chairman and spokesman
of jury; principal workman superintending others.

fore·mast (fōr'măst, -mahst,
fŏr'-) *n.* Forward lower mast of
ship.

fore·most (fōr'mōst, fŏr'-) *adj.*
Most advanced in position, front;
most notable, best, chief. ~ *adv.*
Before anything else in position; in
the first place.

fore·noon (fōr'nŏŏn, fŏr'-) *n.*
Part of day between sunrise and
noon.

fo·ren·sic (fŏrĕn'sĭk) *adj.* 1. Of,
used in, legal proceedings; **~
medicine**, application of medical
knowledge to legal, esp. criminal,
problems. 2. Of, used in, debate
or argument; rhetorical. **fo·ren'-
sics** *n.* (pl. considered as sing.)
Study, art, of formal debate and
argument. **fo·ren'si·cal·ly** *adv.*

fore·or·dain (fōr ōrdān', fŏr-)
v.t. Predestinate, appoint beforehand. **fore·or·di·na·tion** (fōr-
ōrdinā'shon, fŏr-) *n.*

fore·play (fōr'plā, fŏr'-) *n.*
Stimulation preceding sexual intercourse.

fore·run (fōrrŭn', fŏr-) *v.t.*
(**-ran, -run, -run·ning**). Be precursor of, foreshadow. **fore·run'-
ner** *n.*

fore·sail (fōr'sāl, fŏr'-; naut.
fōr'sel, fŏr'-) *n.* Principal sail on
foremast; in square-rigged vessel,
lowest square sail; in fore-and-aft
rigged, triangular sail before mast.

fore·see (fōrsē', fŏr-) *v.t.* (**-saw,
-seen, -see·ing**). See or realize
beforehand.

fore·shad·ow (fōrshăd'ō, fŏr-)
v.t. Prefigure, serve as type or
presage of; warn of beforehand.

fore·short·en (fōrshôr'ten, fŏr-)
v.t. Show, portray, (object) with
the apparent shortening due to
visual perspective; (of visual perspective) cause (object) to appear
shorter in directions not lying in
plane perpendicular to line of sight.

fore·sight (fōr'sīt, fŏr'-) *n.*
Foreseeing, prevision; care for the
future.

fore·skin (fōr'skĭn, fŏr'-) *n.*
Prepuce.

for·est (fōr'ist, făr'-) *n.* Large
tract covered with trees and undergrowth; **~ ranger**, person caring
for or supervising (esp. public or
national) forest.

fore·stall (fōrstawl', fŏr-) *v.t.*
1. (hist.) Buy up (goods) in order
to profit by enhanced price; prevent sales at (fair, market) thus.

*Most temperate **forests** in Europe and
North America have been reduced by
agriculture over the centuries. In
Rumania, however, forests occupy 27
per cent of the land.*

*This **forge** at Brandeston, U.K. with furnace, anvil and bellows, was once the workshop of a blacksmith. Forging metals into a desired shape is now done with sophisticated machinery.*

2. Anticipate in action; take precautionary measures.

for·est·er (fŏr′ester, fär′-) *n.* 1. Person in charge of forest, or of growing timber; person trained in forestry. 2. Dweller in forest; bird or beast of forest.

for·es·try (fŏr′estrē, fär′-) *n.* Wooded country, forests; science and art of managing forests.

fore·taste (fōr′tāst, fōr′-) *n.* Partial enjoyment or suffering (*of*) in advance. ~ *v.t.* (**-tast·ed, -tast·ing**). Taste beforehand, anticipate enjoyment etc. of.

fore·tell (fōrtĕl′, fōr-) *v.t.* (**-told, -tell·ing**). Predict, prophesy; presage, be precursor of.

fore·thought (fōr′thawt, fōr′-) *n.* Previous contriving, deliberate intention; provident care.

fore·to·ken (fōrtō′ken, fōr-) *v.t.* Portend, point to. ~ (fōr′tōken, fōr′-) *n.*

for·ev·er (forĕv′er) *adv.* For all (future) time, incessantly; (colloq.) for a very long time.

for·ev·er·more (forĕvermōr′, -mōr′) *adv.* For all future time.

fore·warn (fōrwōrn′, fōr-) *v.t.* Warn beforehand.

fore·word (fōr′wĕrd, fōr′-, -werd) *n.* Preface; introduction, esp. to a book.

for·feit (fōr′fĭt) *n.* Thing lost owing to crime or fault; penalty for breach of contract or neglect, fine; trivial fine for breach of rules in games etc.; article surrendered by player in game of **forfeits** to be redeemed by performing ludicrous task; forfeiture. **forfeit** *adj.* That has been lost or given up as penalty. ~ *v.t.* Lose right to, be deprived of, have to pay, as penalty of crime, neglect, etc., or as necessary consequence of something. **for·fei·ture** (fōr′fĭcher) *n.*

for·fend (fōrfĕnd′) *v.t.* (archaic) Avert, keep away, prevent; defend; forbid.

for·gath·er (fōrgădh′er, fōr-) *v.i.* Assemble, meet together, associate; meet accidentally *with*.

forge[1] (fōrj, fōrj) *n.* Blacksmith's hearth or fireplace with bellows, smithy; furnace or hearth for melting or refining metal, workshop containing this. ~ *v.* 1. Shape by heating in forge and hammering. 2. Fabricate, invent (tale, lie); make in fraudulent imitation, esp. imitate (signature etc.) in writing in order to pass it off as genuine; commit forgery. **forg·er** *n.*

forge[2] (fōrj, fōrj) *v.i.* (**forged, forg·ing**). Make way, advance, gradually or with difficulty; ~ **ahead**, take lead in race etc., get start; make good progress.

for·ger·y (fōr′jerē, fōr′-) *n.* (pl. **-ger·ies**). Forging, counterfeiting, or falsifying, of document; spurious thing, esp. document or signature.

for·get (fergĕt′) *v.* (**-got, -gotten, -get·ting**). Lose remembrance of or *about*; neglect; inadvertently omit to bring, mention, attend to, etc.; put out of mind, cease to think of; disregard, overlook, slight; ~ **oneself**, neglect one's own interests; act unbecomingly, presumptuously, or unworthily; ~ **-me-not**, plant of genus *Myosotis* (esp. *M. scorpioides*) with small yellow-eyed blue flowers. **for·get·ful** *adj.* **for·get·ful·ly** *adv.* **for·get·ful·ness** *n.*

for·give (fergĭv′) *v.t.* (**-gave, -giv·en, -giv·ing**). Absolve, excuse from payment of (debt etc.); give up resentment against, pardon (offender). **for·giv·a·ble** *adj.* **for·give·ness** *n.* **for·giv·ing** *adj.* **for·giv·er** *n.*

for·go (fōrgō′, fōr-) *v.t.* (**-went, -gone, -go·ing**). Abstain from, go without, let go, omit to take or use, relinquish.

*The **forget-me-not** is native to temperate regions and common in Europe northern Asia, North America, Australia and New Zealand. The five-petalled flowers are usually sky-blue.*

fork (fōrk) *n.* 1. Pronged agricultural instrument for digging, lifting, carrying, or throwing. Two-, three-, or four-pronged instrument used to hold food while it is cut, convey it to mouth etc., and in cooking. 3. Two-pronged steel instrument giving musical note when struck, tuning fork. 4. Stake with forked end; forking, bifurcation, e.g., that of diverging roads, rivers, etc.; forked part of bicycle frame in which wheel revolves. 5. **fork'lift**, vehicle with fork in front for lifting and carrying loads. **fork** *v.* Form fork, have or develop branches; lift, carry, dig, throw, with fork; ~ **over**, (slang) hand over, pay. **forked** *adj.* Having a fork or forked like branches.

for·lorn (fōrlōrn′) *adj.* Desperate, hopeless; abandoned, forsaken; (poet.) deprived *of*; in pitiful

ndition, of wretched appearance.
r·lorn'ly *adv.* **for·lorn'ness** *n.*

form (fōrm) *n.* 1. Shape, rangement of parts, visible aspect sp. apart from color); shape of)dy; body in respect to outward hape and appearance. 2. Mode in hich thing exists or manifests self; species, kind, variety; (gram.) ne of various modes of spelling, flection, etc., under which word ay appear, external characteristics f words, as dist. from their mean-g. 3. One of the numbered asses or grades in British schools d some U.S. private schools. 4. rrangement and style in literary or usical composition; orderly ar-ngement of parts. 5. Set or ustomary method or procedure; t or fixed order of words etc.; ocument with blanks to be filled p. 6. Formality, mere piece of eremony, as a ~ **letter**, one rinted in many copies to be sent a number of people; behavior ccording to rule or custom; **good,** ad, ~, behavior satisfying or ffending current ideals. 7. Con-ition of health and training; good pirits. 8. (print.) Body of type ecured in chase for printing at ne impression; film material rranged for making plate, etc. 9. air or nest in which hare rests. **orm** *v.* Fashion, mold; assume hape, become solid; mold by dis-ipline, train, instruct; embody, rganize, *into* company etc.; frame, nake, produce; articulate (word); onceive (idea, judgment); develop habit); contract (alliance); be naterial of, make up, make *one* or *art of*; (mil.) draw up in order, ssume specified formation.

-form *suffix.* Forming adjec-ives (1) having the form of (*cruci-orm, cuneiform*); (2) indicating number of forms (*uniform, multi-'orm*).

for·mal (fōr'mal) *adj.* 1. Of the orm or constitutive essence of a thing, essential; of the outward orm, shape, appearance, or ex-ternal qualities; (logic) concerned with the form, not the matter, of reasoning. 2. That is such in form; that is according to recognized forms, or the rules of art or law; valid by virtue of its form, ex-plicit and definite, not merely tacit. 3. Ceremonial, required by conven-tion; perfunctory, having the form without the spirit; observant of forms, precise; excessively regular or symmetrical, stiff, methodical. **for'mal·ly** *adv.*

form·al·de·hyde (fōrmăl'dehīd, fer-) *n.* Colorless gas (CH$_2$O) with a characteristic pungent odor, used in solution as preservative, disin-fectant etc.

for·mal·ism (fōr'malĭzem) *n.* Strict observance of forms; exces-sive regularity or symmetry. **for'-**

Forsythias, also called 'golden bells', flourish in gardens of all temperate regions. Their bright yellow flowers appear in early spring, often before the leaves unfold.

mal·ist *n.* **for·mal·is'tic** *adj.*

for·mal·i·ty (fōrmăl'ĭtē) *n.* (pl. **-ties**). Conformity to rules, pro-priety; ceremony, elaborate pro-cedure; formal or ceremonial act, requirement of etiquette or custom; being formal, precision of manners, stiffness of design.

for·mal·ize (fōr'malīz) *v.t.* (**-ized, -iz·ing**). Give definite shape or legal formality to; make ceremonious, precise, or rigid; imbue with formalism.

for·mat (fōr'măt) *n.* Shape and size (of book etc.); style of arrange-ment etc.

for·ma·tion (fōrmā'shon) *n.* Forming, being formed; thing formed; arrangement of parts, structure; (mil.) disposition of troops, formal stationing or ar-rangement of number of ships, air-craft, etc.; (geol.) assemblage of rocks or series of strata having some common characteristic.

form·a·tive (fōr'mătĭv) *adj.* Serving to form, of formation; (gram., of suffixes etc.) used in forming words. ~ *n.* Formative element of a word.

for·mer (fōr'mer) *adj.* Of the past or an earlier period; **the ~**, the first or first mentioned of two (freq. with ellipsis of *n.*; opp. LATTER). **for'mer·ly** *adv.*

form·fit·ting (fōrm'fītĭng) *adj.* Adhering closely to the body; de-signed to reveal or suggest rather than conceal.

For·mi·ca (fōrmī'ka, fer-) *n.* (trademark) Hard durable plastic laminate used esp. as decorative

surfacing material.

for·mi·da·ble (fōr'mĭdabel, formĭd'-) *adj.* To be dreaded; likely to be hard to overcome, resist, or deal with. **for'mi·da·ble·ness** *n.* **for'mi·da·bly** *adv.*

form·less (fōrm'lĭs) *adj.* Shape-less, without determinate or regular form.

For·mo·sa (fōrmō'sa). Former name of TAIWAN; ~ **Strait**, strait of the China Sea between Taiwan and the People's Republic of China. [Port. name, f. L. *formosus* beauti-ful]

for·mu·la (fōr'myula) *n.* (pl. **-las, -lae** pr. -lē, -lī). 1. Set form of words in which something is defined, stated, etc., or which is prescribed for use on ceremonial occasion etc.; conventional usage or belief. 2. Recipe; prescription; (math.) rule or principle expressed in algebraic symbols; (chem.) ex-pression of constituents of com-pound in symbols and figures; tabulation of facts etc. in symbols and figures. 3. Class or specifica-tion of a racing car. **for·mu·lar·ize** (fōr'myulerīz) *v.t.* (**-ized, -iz·ing**).

for·mu·late (fōr'myulāt) *v.t.* (**-lated, -lat·ing**). Reduce to, express in, a formula; set forth systematically. **for·mu·la·tion** (fōrmyulā'shon) *n.*

for·ni·cate (fōr'nĭkāt) *v.i.* (**-cat·ed, -cat·ing**). Commit fornication. **for·ni·ca·tion** (fōrni-kā'shon) *n.* Voluntary sexual inter-course between a man and a woman not married to each other. **for'-ni·ca·tor** *n.*

for·sake (fōrsāk') *v.t.* (**-sook** pr. -sŏŏk, **-sak·en, -sak·ing**). Give up, break off from, renounce; with-draw one's help etc. from: desert, abandon.

for·swear (fōrswār') *v.* (**-swore, -sworn, -swear·ing**). Abjure, re-nounce on oath; ~ **oneself**, swear falsely, perjure oneself; commit perjury; **forsworn'**, perjured.

for·syth·i·a (fōrsĭth'ēa, fer-) *n.* Ornamental spring-flowering shrub of genus *F~* with bright yellow bell-shaped flowers. [f. W. *Forsyth* (1737–1804), English botanist]

fort (fōrt, fôrt) *n.* Fortified place, usu. single building or set of connected military buildings; trading station (hist., orig. forti-fied); **hold the ~**, act as temporary substitute; cope with emergency.

fort. *abbrev.* Fortification.

forte[1] (fōrt, fôrt, fōr'tā, -tē; fencing fōrt, fôrt) *n.* Person's stong point; (fencing) strong part of sword blade, from hilt to middle.

for·te[2] (fōr'tā) *adv.* (mus.) Loudly; **double ~**, very loudly; ~ **piano**, loudly then immediately softly. **forte** *adj.* & *n.* Loud (passage). [It.]

The silent guns of Fort McHenry, in Maryland guard its perimeters. Other U.S. fortifications are much more active.

The Roman forum, of which only the ruins remain, was located between the Capitoline and Palatine hills. It was the center of life in ancient Rome.

forth (fōrth, fôrth) *adv.* Forward (now only in **back and** ~, to and fro); onward in time (now only in **from this time** ~ etc.); forward into view; out, away, from home, etc.; **and so** ~, and so on, and the like.

forth·com·ing (fōrth´kŭm´ĭng, fôrth´-) *adj.* About or likely to come forth; approaching; available when wanted.

forth·right (fōrth´rīt, fôrth´-) *adj.* Proceeding straight ahead; straightforward, frank, candid, outspoken, unswerving; decisive. **forth·right´** *adv.* Straight ahead.

forth·with (fōrthwĭth´, -wĭdh´, fôrth-) *adv.* Immediately, without delay.

for·ti·fi·ca·tion (fôrtĭfĭkā´shɒn) *n.* 1. Fortifying. 2. Defensive work, wall, earthwork, tower, etc.

for·ti·fy (fôr´tĭfī) *v.* (**-fied, -fy·ing**). Strengthen structure of; impart vigor or strength or endurance to, encourage; provide with defensive works; erect fortifications; strengthen (wine etc.) with alcohol; add nutrients to (food).

for·tis·si·mo (fôrtĭs´ĭmō) *adv., n.* (pl. **-mos, -mi** pr. -mē) & *adj.* (mus.) (Passage performed) very loud(ly).

for·ti·tude (fôr´tĭtōod, -tūd) *n.* Courage in pain or adversity.

Fort Knox (nŏks). Military reservation in N. central Kentucky, SSW. of Louisville; site of U.S. gold bullion depository since 1936.

Fort Mc·Hen·ry (mɒkhĕn´rē) **National Monument.** Harbor fort and surrounding 43 acres in Baltimore, Md., established as national monument in 1925; attack on fort by British (1814) inspired Francis Scott Key to compose "The Star Spangled Banner."

fort·night (fôrt´nīt, -nĭt) *n.* (chiefly Brit.) Period of two weeks. **fort´night·ly** *adj. & adv.* (Happening, appearing) once every two weeks.

FOR·TRAN (fôr´trăn) *n.* Computer programming language used chiefly for scientific and mathematical calculations. [*for*mula *tran*slation]

for·tress (fôr´trĭs) *n.* Military stronghold, esp. strongly fortified town fit for large garrison.

Fort Sum·ter (sŭm´ter)

National Monument. Fort i[n] Charleston harbor, SE. Sout[h] Carolina, attacked and conquere[d] by Confederate forces on Apr. 1[?], 1861, in opening battle of Civ[il] War.

for·tu·i·tous (fôrtōo´ĭtu̇s, -tū´-) *adj.* Due to or characterized b[y] chance, accidental, casual. **for·tu´i·tous·ly** *adv.* **for·tu´i·tous·ness** *n.* **for·tu´i·ty** *n.* For[-] tuitousness; a chance occurrence[;] accident.

for·tu·nate (fôr´chu̇nĭt) *adj.* Favored by fortune, lucky, pros[-] perous. **for´tu·nate·ly** *adv.* Luckily, successfully.

for·tune (fôr´chu̇n) *n.* 1. Chanc[e] as a power in people's affairs; freq[.] personified as goddess with wheel[.]

betokening vicissitude, as emblem; **soldier of** ~ : see SOLDIER. 2. Luck, good or bad, falling to anyone in life or particular affair; destiny; what is to befall in future (chiefly **in tell person his** ~); **for'tune-eller**, one who professes to fore-tell the future. 3. Good luck; prosperity, prosperous condition, wealth; large sum of money; **make (one's)** ~, become rich, prosper; ~ **hunter**, person seeking rich spouse.

for·ty (fôr'tē) *adj*. Amounting to forty; ~ **-five** (*n.*) .45-caliber revolver; ~ **-niner**, one who went to California in the gold rush of 1849; ~ **winks**, nap. **forty** *n*. (pl. **-ties**). Cardinal number, four times ten (40, xl, or XL); **for'ties**, numbers etc. from 40 to 49; these years of century or life. **for'-i·eth** *adj. & n.*

fo·rum (fôr'um, fŏr'-) *n*. (pl. **o·rums; fo·ra** pr. fôr'a, fŏr'a). Rom. antiq.) Public place or marketplace of city; in ancient Rome, place of assembly for judicial and other public business; place of public discussion; court, tribunal freq. fig.).

for·ward (fôr'werd) *adj*. 1. naut.) Belonging to fore part of hip. 2. Lying in front, or in direc-ion of movement; onward or oward the front; ~ **pass**, (foot-all) pass thrown forward toward or over line of scrimmage; opp. LATERAL pass. 3. Advanced, pro-ressing to maturity or completion. 4. Precocious, presumptuous, pert.

for'ward·ly *adv*. **for'ward·ness** *n*. **forward, for'wards** *advs*. 1. Toward the future, continuously onward; toward the front, in the direction one is facing; with con-tinuous forward motion; in advance, ahead; to the front, into prominence; onward so as to make progress; **bring forward**, draw attention to; **bring, carry for-ward**, (bookkeeping) transfer entry to next page or column; **come forward**, offer oneself for task, position, etc.; **put forward**, sug-gest, allege; **put oneself forward**, make oneself conspicuous. 2. (naut.) To, at, in, fore part of ship. **forward** *n*. (basketball, soccer, hockey, etc.) Player in the front line usu. for offense. **forward** *v.t.* Help forward, promote; send (letter etc.) on to another stipulated destination; (loosely) dispatch (goods etc.). **for'ward·er** *n*. (usu. **freight** ~) Person or agency that forwards; esp. one handling freight or getting goods to their destina-tion.

fosse, foss (fŏs, faws) *ns*. Ditch; moat.

fos·sil (fŏs'il) *adj*. Of the nature of a fossil. ~ *n*. Thing found in strata of earth recognizable as remains of plant or animal of former geological period or as showing vestiges of animal or vegetable life

A fossil may be in the form of the actual remains of a creature or plant or it may be the impression left by that object in rock, as with this brachiopod found in limestone.

of such period; (person or thing) belonging to the past, antiquated, incapable of further growth or pro-gress. **fos·sil·ize** (fŏs'ilīz) *v.t.* (**-ized, -iz·ing**). **fos·sil·i·za·tion** (fŏsilīzā'shon) *n*.

fos·ter (faw'ster, fŏs'ter) *v.t.* Bring up, rear, tend with affec-tionate care; encourage or harbor (feeling); (of circumstances) be favorable to. ~ *adj*. Having a specified relation, not by blood but in virtue of nursing or bringing up (~ *brother, child, daughter, father, mother,* etc.); concerning care of orphans etc. (~ *care,* ~ *home*). **fos'ter·ling** *n*. Foster child.

Fos·ter (faw'ster, fŏs'ter), **Stephen (Collins)** (1826–64). Amer. songwriter best known for contributions to music of black minstrel troupes; wrote "My Old Kentucky Home," "Massa's in the Cold, Cold Ground," "O Susanna," "Old Black Joe," etc.; elected to American Hall of Fame (1940).

fought: see FIGHT.

foul (fowl) *adj*. 1. Offensive to the senses, loathsome, stinking; dirty, soiled; charged with noxious matter. 2. Clogged, choked; (of ship's bottom etc.) overgrown with weeds, barnacles, etc. (hence **foul'-ing** (*n.*), such an incrustation). 3. Morally polluted, obscene, dis-gustingly abusive; unfair, against rules of game etc.; (of weather) wet, rough, stormy; (of wind) contrary; (naut.) embarrassed, entangled, in collision, etc. 4. ~ **ball**, (base-

ball) any batted ball going outside
foul lines; ~ **line**, (baseball) either
of the lines between home plate and
1st base and home plate and 3rd
base and prolonged into the outfield; (basketball) line from which
free throws are made; **foul'-
mouthed'**, given to obscene or
abusive speech; **foul play**, unfair
play in games; unfair or treacherous
dealing, esp. involving murder.
foul'ly *adv.* **foul'ness** *n.* **foul** *n.*
Something foul; (sports) action
contrary to rules, usu. against
opponent's body; (boxing) blow
struck low or otherwise illegally;
(baseball) foul ball. **foul** *adv.* In
a foul or irregular way. ~ *v.* Make
or become foul; entangle, become
entangled; collide with; hit foul
ball, commit foul (blow) against;
~ **out**, (baseball) hit foul fly ball
that is caught; ~ **up**, (colloq.)
botch, bungle, mess up; **~-up**,
(colloq.) confusion arising from in-
eptitude or mechanical breakdown.

fou·lard (foolärd') *n.* Thin soft
smooth material, usu. silk, cotton,
or rayon and with a small printed
design; a necktie, scarf, etc. of this.

found[1] (fownd) *v.* Lay base of
(building etc.); be original builder,
begin building, of (town, edifice);
set up, establish (esp. with endowment), originate, initiate, (institution); construct, base (tale, one's
fortunes, rule, etc.) *on* some
ground, support, principle, etc.;
rely, base oneself, (of argument etc.)
be based, *on.* **found'er**[1] *n.*

found[2] (fownd) *v.t.* Melt and
mold (metal), fuse (materials and
glass); make (thing of molten metal,
glass) by melting. **found'er**[2] *n.*

found[3]: see FIND.

foun·da·tion (fowndā'shon) *n.*
1. Establishing, constituting on
permanent basis, esp. of endowed
institution; funds given for permanent support of hospital, school,
etc.; organization established by
endowment to promote arts,
science, education, etc. 2. Solid
ground or base, natural or artificial,
on which building rests; lowest part
of building, usu. below ground
level; basis, groundwork, underlying principle; body or ground on
which other parts are overlaid. 3.
(cosmetics) Base. 4. ~ **garment**,
woman's supporting undergarment, e.g., corset or girdle.

found·er[1, 2] (fownd'er): see
FOUND[1, 2].

found·er[3] (fownd'er) *v.* 1. (of
earth, building, etc.) Fall down or
in, give way; (of horse) collapse,
fall lame, stumble etc.; (of ship)
fill with water and sink. 2.
Cause (horse, ship) to founder. ~
n. Inflammation of horse's hoof
from overwork.

found·ling (fownd'ling) *n.* Deserted infant of unknown parents.

found (fownd) **object.** Object

*Builders of early artificial **fountains** may
have been symbolizing their belief in the
sanctity of springs of water. The 18th
century fountain illustrated is one of
Rome's many public fountains.*

picked up by chance and kept as
or as part of a work of art.

found·ry (fown'drē) *n.* (pl.
-ries). Factory in which molten
metal castings are produced.

fount[1] (fownt) *n.* (poet. or rhet.)
Spring, source, fountain.

fount[2] (fownt, fŏnt) *n.* (chiefly
Brit.) = FONT def. 2.

foun·tain (fown'tin) *n.* Spring,
esp. as the source of a river etc.;
jet of water made to spout, structure provided for it; structure for
constant supply of drinking water;
soda fountain; **foun'tainhead**,
original source; **fountain pen**, pen
containing reservoir of ink.

four (fōr, fôr) *adj.* Amounting
to four; ~ **figures**, 1,000 (dollars
etc.) or over; **~-flush**, (poker)
flush containing only four (instead
of five) cards; **four'flusher**, (slang)
pretender, humbug; **Four Freedoms**: see FREEDOM; **Four-H club**,
4-H club, club sponsored by U.S.
Department of Agriculture to instruct young people in agriculture
and citizenship (improving head,
hearts, hands, and health); **~-
handed**, (of games) played by,
requiring four players; (of piano
music) composed, arranged for,
four hands, as a duet; **the F ~
Hundred**, most exclusive social

set, orig. that of New York (wh
*c*1890 was supposed to consist
about this number of people);
in-hand, vehicle with four hor
driven by one person; necktie t
in a slipknot with long ends ha
ing and overlapping; **~-let**
word, any of several monosylla
English words dealing with sex
excrement and generally regard
as vulgar or obscene; **~-o'-clo**
plant (*Mirabilis jalapa*) native
tropical Amer. and with flow
opening about four p.m.; a
prairie wildflower (*M. nyctagine*
four'poster, bed having four
corner posts (to support canopy a
curtains); **four'score**, 80; **fou**
square, square-shaped; soli
based, steady, forthright, hone
four-wheel, (vehicle) with fo
wheels, esp. **four-wheel dri**
(vehicle) with power transmitted
all four wheels. **four** *n.* One m
than three; symbol for this (4,
or IV); card, die face, or dom
with four pips; four o'clock; s
etc. indicated by 4; **on all fou**
crawling on hands and kne
four'fold *adj. & adv.* In fo
parts; four times as much.

Fou·rier[1] (foor'ēä, fooryä
(François Marie) Charl
(1772–1837). French Utopi
socialist writer. **Fou·ri·er·is**
(foor'ēerīzem) *n.* Communi
system for the reorganization
society devised by Fourier und
which the population was to

ouped in *phalansteries*, socialistic
roups of about 1,800 persons hold-
g property in common.

Fou·rier[2] (foor´ēā, fooryā´),
aron Jean Baptiste Joseph
768–1830). French mathemati-
an and physicist; received title of
aron from Napoleon Bonaparte
808).

four·some (fōr´som, fōr´-) *adj.*
onsisting of, involving four per-
ns together. ~ *n.* Golf match
other game between two pairs
players; company or party of four
rsons.

four·teen (fōr´tēn´, fōr´-) *adj.* &
. One more than thirteen (14,
iv, or XIV). **four´teenth´** *adj.*
n. ~ **of July**, French annual
oliday in celebration of fall of
astille, 1789.

fourth (fōrth, fōrth) *adj.* Next
fter third. ~ *n.* 1. Fourth part
see PART¹ def. 1), quarter. 2.
nus.) Interval of which the span
volves four alphabetical names of
otes; harmonic combination of two
otes thus separated. 3. Fourth
ning etc.; **the F~**, the 4th of
uly, annual holiday celebrating the
gning of the Declaration of In-
ependence (1776), also called In-
ependence Day; ~ **class**, class of
ail consisting of merchandise or
ertain printed matter and sent at
owest rate; ~ **dimension**: see
IMENSION; ~ **estate**: see ESTATE.
. Fourth grade in school. 5. (in
otor vehicle) Fourth gear.

fo·ve·a (fō´vēa) *n.* (pl. **-ve·ae**

pr. -vēē). (anat.) Small pit or
cuplike depression in bone or
organ; ~ **centralis**, small depression in macula lutea of retina, spot
where vision is most acute.

fowl (fowl) *n.* (pl. **fowls**, collect.
fowl). 1. Any bird(s) used as food
or hunted as game; birds (rare exc.
in **wild´fowl**); flesh of birds as
food. 2. (also **domestic** ~)
Domestic chicken of genus *Gallus*;
its flesh as food. ~ *v.i.* Catch,
hunt, shoot, or snare wildfowl;
fowl´ing piece, light shotgun for
shooting birds. **fow´ler** *n.*

Fow·ler (fow´ler), **Henry Watson** (1858–1933). English lexicographer; with his brother F. G.
Fowler, wrote *The King's English*

*The wide demand for the eggs and
meat of the domestic **fowl** led to the
development of new breeds to meet the
conditions of intensive production after
the 1939–45 war.*

(1906) and compiled *The Concise
Oxford Dictionary of Current
English* (1911); author of *A Diction-
ary of Modern English Usage* (1926).

fox (fŏks) *n.* (pl. **fox·es**, collect.
fox). 1. Flesh-eating quadruped
of the dog family, esp. the red
foxes (Vulpes) and the gray foxes
(Urocyon) having elongated
pointed muzzle, upright ears, and
long bushy tail; proverbial for
cunning; crafty person. 2. **Fox**,
tribe of N. Amer. Indians; member
of this tribe. 3. **fox´fire**, phos-
phorescence from decaying wood;
fox´glove, tall plant of genus
Digitalis, esp. European *Digitalis
purpurea*, the leaves of which yield
digitalis, with drooping, tubular

*he canny **fox** is a skillful hunter and
akes a difficult prey for those who
unt it. The red fox, found in much of
urasia, North Africa, and North
merica, is hunted for pleasure. Silver*

*and black foxes are color phases
occasionally found in a red fox's litter. In
North America they are bred for the
value of their fine quality pelts.*

arctic

red

grey

bat-eared

fennec

purple or white flowers; also, the N. Amer. **false** ~**s** (Geradia) with bright yellow flowers. **fox'hole**, (mil.) small pit in ground used by soldier as shelter on battlefield; (fig.) place of refuge or concealment; **fox'hound**, kind of hound bred and trained to hunt foxes; **fox hunt**, chase, hunting of, fox with hounds; **fox'tail**, species of grass with soft brushlike spikes of flowers, esp. *Alopecurus pratensis*; **fox terrier**, small terrier with smooth or rough (wire-haired) short hair, usu. white with black markings, of a kind bred for unearthing foxes, but kept chiefly as pets; **fox trot**, ballroom dance in $\frac{1}{4}$ time based on slow or quick steps. **fox** *v.* Trick, outwit; be sly and crafty; outfox; (loosely) impede, ruin plans of, etc.

fox·y (fŏk´sē) *adj.* (**fox·i·er, fox·i·est**). 1. Crafty, cunning. 2. Fox-colored, reddish brown.

foy·er (foi´er) *n.* Lobby or entrance hall of a theater, hotel, etc; vestibule or entrance hall of a home or apartment.

f.p., fp *abbrevs.* Forward pass, freezing point.

FPC *abbrev.* Federal Power Commission.

fpm *abbrev.* Feet per minute.

FPO *abbrev.* Fleet post office.

fps *abbrev.* Foot-pound-second.

f.p.s. *abbrev.* Feet per second.

Fr *symbol.* Francium.

Fr. *abbrev.* Father (priest), French, franc(s).

fr. *abbrev.* Fragment, franc(s), from.

Fra (frah) *n.* Brother (title of a friar). [It.]

fra·cas (frā´ḳas; *Brit.* frăk´as) *n.* (pl. same). Noisy quarrel, row, brawl.

frac·tion (frăk´shon) *n.* 1. Numerical quantity that is not an integer, one or more aliquot parts of unit or whole number; small piece or amount, scrap; **proper (improper)** ~, fraction in which numerator is less than (greater than or equal to) denominator. 2. Portion separable by fractionation. **frac·tion·al** *adj.* **frac·tion·al·ly** *adv.*

frac·tion·ate (frăk´shonāt) *v.t.* (**-at·ed, -at·ing**). Separate (mixture) by distillation or otherwise into portions of differing properties. **frac·tion·a·tion** (frăk-shonā´shon) *n.*

frac·tious (frăk´shus) *adj.* Unruly, cross, peevish. **frac'tious·ly** *adv.* **frac'tious·ness** *n.*

frac·ture (frăk´cher) *n.* 1. Breaking, breakage or crack, esp. of bone or cartilage; **compound** ~, fracture of bone with breaking of skin; **simple** ~, breaking of bone but not of skin. 2. Characteristic appearance of fresh surface of mineral broken with hammer. ~ *v.* (**-tured, -tur·ing**). Cause fracture in, be fractured; break continuity of.

frag (frăg) *v.t.* (**fragged, frag- ging**). Attack (esp. unpopular commander) with a grenade.

frag·ile (frăj´il) *adj.* Easily snapped or shattered; weak, perishable; of delicate frame or constitution. **fra·gil·i·ty** (frajĭl´ītē) *n.*

frag·ment (frăg´ment) *n.* Part broken off, detached piece; isolated or incomplete part, remainder or lost or destroyed whole; esp. extant remains or unfinished portion of writing or work of art. **frag·men·tar·y** (frăg´mentĕrē) *adj.* **frag·men·ta·tion** (frăgmentā´shon) *n.* Separation into fragments; ~ **bomb**, one designed to disintegrate into small fragments on explosion. **fragment** (frăg´ment) *v.* Break or separate into fragments.

Fra·go·nard (frăgonār´), **Jean Honoré** (1732–1806). French engraver and painter.

fra·grant (frā´grant) *adj.* Sweet smelling. **fra´grance** *n.* Quality of being fragrant; perfume.

frail[1] (frāl´) *n.* Rush basket for holding fruit, esp. dried fruit as figs, raisins, etc.; quantity of fruit contained in a frail, usu. 50–75 lbs.

frail[2] (frāl) *adj.* Fragile; morally weak, unable to resist temptation. **frail·ty** (frāl´tē) *n.* (pl. **-ties**). Liability to err or yield to temptation; fault, weakness, foible.

frame (frām) *n.* 1. Construction, constitution, build; established order, plan, system. 2. Temporary state (*of* mind). 3. Framed work or structure; human or animal body, skeleton of building; underlying support or essential substructure of

---

The growing use of steel and other alloys in the building industry has led to an examination of new ways of constructing **frames** to provide great strength and rigidity with lightness so that few interior supports are needed. The geodesic dome, built of triangular sections, and double grids offers solutions to the problem of strength versus weight.

geodesic dome

one unit of geodesic dome

one unit of double layer grid

top layer

bottom layer

double layer grid

diagonal members

top layer

bottom layer

anything. 4. Case or border enclosing picture, pane of glass, etc. . (gardening) Glazed structure protecting plants from cold. 6. Rigid part of bicycle; skeleton of motor vehicle etc. supporting machinery and body. 7. (bowling) Any of ten divisions of game. 8. Each separate picture on a motion-picture film. 9. Single complete picture transmitted in series of lines by television. 10. (pool, etc.) Triangular rack in which balls are set up; the balls as set up; round of play required to pocket them all. 11. ~ **house**, house of wooden framework covered with boards etc; ~ **of reference**, characteristic of perception whereby objects are

correctly localized in space; standard governing perceptual or logical evaluation; ~**-up**, (colloq.) conspiracy, trumped-up case or charge; **frame'work**, frame, sub-structure, upon or into which anything may be put. **frame** v. (**framed, fram·ing**). 1. Shape, direct, dispose, to a purpose; adapt, fit, *to*, or *into*. 2. Construct by combination of parts or adaptation to design; contrive, devise, invent, compose, express; articulate (words); conceive, imagine. 3. Set in frame; serve as frame for. 4. (slang) Concoct false charge or rig evidence against, make victim of frame-up.

franc (frăngk) *n.* Principal

monetary unit of France, Belgium, Switzerland, and certain other countries, usu. = 100 centimes; (hist.) any of various gold and silver coins. [Fr., perh. f. *Francorum Rex* king of the Franks, legend on earliest coin so called]

France[1] (frăns, frahns). Repub-lic of W. Europe; the monarchial system of government was overthrown during the French Revolution (1789–93), and the First Republic lasted until Napoleon founded the First Empire in 1804; the monarchy was restored in 1814 and lasted until 1848 when the Second Republic was formed, which became the Second Empire under Napoleon III in 1852; Napoleon was deposed in 1870 and the Third Republic established; this lasted until the occupation of France by the Germans (1940) during World War II; after the liberation of France (1945) the republic was restored and the Constitution of the Fourth Republic was in force from 1945 until Oct. 1958, when a new constitution established the Fifth Republic; capital, Paris.

France[2] (frăns, frahns), **Ana-tole.** Pseudonym of Jacques Anatole Thibault (1844–1924), French satirical writer.

fran·chise (frăn'chīz) *n.* 1. (chiefly hist.) Legal immunity or exemption from some burden or jurisdiction; privilege or excep-tional right, granted to person,

The large area covered by **France,** *about 212,660 sq miles, includes a wide variety of landforms. Upper Left: The Alps in the south east, photo-graphed through a glaciated valley to Col D'Iseran, form a border with Italy. Lower left: Avignon, a town in the Rhône Valley, was first established in Roman times. Below: Map of France.*

corporation, etc.; right to distribute, sell company's products or services in particular area, often under the company's name and with its advice and direction. 2. Full membership of corporation or nation, citizenship. 3. Right of voting at public elections, esp. for member of legislative body; principle of qualification for this. ~ *v.t.* (**-chised, -chis·ing**). Give franchise to.

Fran·cis of As·si·si (frăn'sĭs *ov* asē'zē, frahn'-) **St.** Giovanni Francesco Bernardone (1181?–1226). Italian friar; founded *c*1209 an order of friars, whose rules require chastity, poverty, and obedience, and lay special stress on preaching and ministration to the sick. **Fran·cis·can** (frănsĭs'kan) *adj.* & *n.* (Member) of the order founded by St. Francis (also called *Minorites, Gray Friars*).

fran·ci·um (frăn'sēum) *n.* (chem.) Radioactive metallic element of short life, the heaviest member of the alkali metal series; symbol Fr, at. no. 87, principal isotope at. wt. 223. [f. *France*, because its existence was first reported by a Frenchwoman, Mlle. M. Perey]

Fran·co (frăng'kō), **Generalissimo.** Francisco Franco Bahamonde (1892–1975), Spanish political leader; leader (caudillo) of the Empire, chief of the State, and head of the Falangist party 1939–75.

Franco- *prefix.* French and —, as ~ *-German.*

Fran·co·phile (frăng'kofĭl), **Fran·co·phobe** (frăng'kofōb) *ns.* One who loves, hates, the French.

fran·gi·pan·i (frănjĭpăn'ē, -pah'nē) *n.* (pl. **-pan·is, -pan·i**) [also **fran·gi·pane** (frăn'jĭpān)] 1. Kind of filling for pastry made with almonds, sugar, and cream. 2. Perfume made from flowers of red jasmine or imitation of this. 3. Tropical Amer. tree, the red jasmine (*Plumeria rubra*), with showy fragrant flowers. [family name *Frangipani*]

Frank (frăngk) *n.* (Member of) one of the Germanic tribes of the Rhine region in the early Christian era, esp. the tribe that conquered Gaul in 6th c. and established a vast empire by the 9th c. **Frank'ish** *adj.*

frank[1] (frăngk) *adj.* Ingenuous, open, candid, outspoken; undisguised, avowed. **frank'ly** *adv.* **frank'ness** *n.* [med. L. *francus* free, f. *Francus* Frank]

frank[2] (frăngk) *v.t.* Superscribe (letter etc.) with signature or official mark to ensure its being carried without charge, send free of charge; **frank'ing privilege**, perquisite granted to members of Congress of franking and sending mail free.

The rich white and yellow flowers of the Hawaiian **frangipani** fill the long summer days and nights with a scent that pervades every nook and cranny. It is even packaged into aerosol cans.

frank *n.* (hist.) Franking signature, franked cover.

frank[3] (frăngk) *n.* (colloq.) Frankfurter.

Frank·en·stein (frăng'kenstīn). Hero of the novel *Frankenstein* (1818) by Mary Wollstonecraft Shelley; he is a medical student who constructs a human monster that eventually destroys him, whence ~ **'s monster**, thing that becomes formidable to or destroys its creator.

frank·furt·er (frăngk'ferter) *n.* (also **frank'furt**). Smoked beef or beef and pork sausage made in long, reddish links, orig. associated with Frankfurt, Germany; hot dog.

frank·in·cense (frăng'kĭnsĕns) *n.* Aromatic gum resin obtained from trees, chiefly E. African, of genus *Boswellia* and burned as incense.

frank·lin (frăngk'lĭn) *n.* (Brit. hist.) Landowner of free but not noble birth in 14th–15th centuries.

Frank·lin (frăngk'lĭn), **Benjamin** (1706–90). Amer. writer, publisher, inventor, scientist, and statesman; publisher of *The Penn-*

sylvania Gazette (1730–48) and collection of wit and morality, *P Richard's Almanack* (1732–5 author of *Autobiography*, publish with inaccuracies in 1791 and 18 corrected and reissued in 18 colonial emissary to Europe; me ber of the Second Continen Congress (1775); drafter and sig of the Declaration of Indeper ence; signer of the Treaty of Pa (Sept. 3, 1783) with Great Brita ending the Revolutionary W ambassador to France (1776–8 member of the Constitutional Cc vention (1787); experimenter w electricity and optics; inventor the lightning rod, bifocal glass improved cast-iron heating sto etc.

fran·tic (frăn'tĭk) *a* Wildly excited, beside oneself w rage, pain, grief, etc.; show frenzy, uncontrolled. **fran't cal·ly, fran'tic·ly** *advs.*

Franz Jo·sef (frahns' jō' fränz' jōzĭf; *Ger.* frănts' yō'z (1830–1916). Emperor of Aust (1848–1916); king of Hunga (1867–1916); concluded Tri Alliance with Germany and It (1883); assassination of his nepl and heir Archduke Francis F dinand at Sarajevo (June 28, 19 precipitated World War I.

frap·pé (frăpā´), **frappe** (frăp). n. 1. Milk shake. 2. Frozen fruit-flavored dessert. 3. Liqueur poured over crushed ice.

frat (frăt) n. (slang) College or high school fraternity.

fra·ter (frā´ter) n. Comrade, brother, esp. in a religious order.

fra·ter·nal (frater´nal) adj. (As) of brothers, brotherly; ~ **order**, friendly or charitable society, brotherhood; ~ **twins**, twins not necessarily of same sex and freq. bearing merely fraternal resemblance, resulting from fertilization of two ova, not one (opp. IDENTICAL).

fra·ter·ni·ty (frater´nĭtē) n. (pl. **ties**). 1. Being fraternal, brotherness; brotherhood. 2. Body or order of men organized for religious or devout purposes; body of men associated by some tie or common interest, or of same class, occupation, etc.; social association of male students of school, college, or university.

fra·ter·nize (frăt´ernīz) v.t. **-nized, -niz·ing**). Associate with, together, etc.), make friends, behave as intimates; cultivate friendly relations with (troops or inhabitants of enemy country). **frat·er·ni·za·tion** (frăternĭzā´shon) n.

frat·ri·cide (frăt´rĭsīd) n. Killing of one's brother; one who commits fratricide. **frat·ri·cid·al** (frătrĭsī´dal) adj.

fraud (frawd) n. Criminal deception, using of false representations to obtain unjust advantage or injure another; dishonest trick or stratagem; dishonest contrivance or person; impostor, humbug.

fraud·u·lent (fraw´julent) adj. Guilty of, of the nature of, characterized or effected by, fraud. **fraud·u·lence** n. **fraud·u·lent·ly** adv.

fraught (frawt) adj. Stored, equipped, with (poet.); ~ **with**, (fig.) involving, attended with, threatening (danger, woe, etc.); full of (meaning etc.).

fray[1] (frā) n. Noisy quarrel, brawl; fight, conflict.

fray[2] (frā) v. Wear away by rubbing; unravel edge or end of; become ragged at edge (also fig.).

Fra·zer (frā´zer), **Sir James George** (1854–1941). Scottish anthropologist, author of *The Golden Bough*.

fraz·zle (frăz´el) n. Worn or exhausted state. ~ v. (**-zled, -zling**). To fray; become frayed or worn out.

FRB abbrev. Federal Reserve Board.

freak (frēk) n. 1. Caprice, vagary; capriciousness. 2. Product of sportive fancy; eccentric person; (also ~ **of nature**) monstrosity, abnormally developed individual; very unusual or irregular thing or occurrence. 3. (slang) Narcotics user; fanatical devotee (of music, food, etc.). ~ v. (usu. ~ **out**) (slang) (Cause to) undergo narcotic etc. hallucinations or wild excitement, adopt unconventional life style. **freak´out** n. Such experience. **freak´ish, freak´y** adjs. **freak´ish·ly** adv. **freak´ish·ness** n.

freck·le (frĕk´el) n. Spotted pigmentation of skin, produced esp. by ultraviolet light, and probably serving as a protection to the tissues; (pl.) number of such spots on various parts of the body, caused by exposure to sun. ~ v. (**-led, -ling**). Spot, be spotted, with freckles. **freck´ly** adv.

Fred·er·ick[1] (frĕd´rĭk, -erĭk). (Ger. **Friedrich**) Name of 3 Holy Roman Emperors; **Frederick I** (1121?–90), "Barbarossa" (= "Redbeard"); emperor 1155–90; king of Germany 1152–90; king of Italy 1155–90; **Frederick II** (1194–1250), emperor 1220–50; **Frederick III** (1415–93), emperor 1440–1493.

Fred·er·ick[2] (frĕd´rĭk, -erĭk). (Ger. **Friedrich**) Name of 3 kings of Prussia: **Frederick I** (1657–1713), reigned 1701–13; **Frederick II** (1712–86), "the Great"; engaged in wars against Austria and France and raised Prussia to the rank of a powerful state; **Frederick III** (1831–88), German emperor 1888.

Fred·er·icks·burg (frĕd´rĭksbĕrg). Industrial city in NE. Virginia on Rappahannock River, 41 mi. SW. of Alexandria, where Confederate army under Robert E.

The austerity of the rule imposed by St. Francis of Assisi on himself and members of his order, the Franciscans, is symbolized in the devotional picture by Francisco de Zurbaran.

As Caudillo of Spain, Generalissimo Franco ruled his nation as a dictator. In 1937 Franco reduced his country's political parties to one, the Falangist party.

664

Lee defeated Union forces led by Burnside (Dec. 11–15, 1862) during Civil War.

free (frē) *adj.* (**fre·er, fre·est**). 1. Not in bondage to another, having personal rights and social and political liberty; (of nation, its citizens, etc.) subject neither to foreign dominion nor to despotic government, having national and civil liberty. 2. At liberty, not in custody or confinement; without ties, obligations, or constraint upon one's action; released or exempt from work or duty; not constrained or timid; not fettered in judgment; (of literary composition etc.) not observing strict laws of form; (of translation) not adhering strictly to original. 3. Allowable or allowed (*to* do); unobstructed; clear *of, from*; not fixed or fastened; not in contact; (chem.) uncombined. 4. Spontaneous, gratuitous, willing; lavish, frank, unreserved; forward, familiar. 5. Released or exempt *from*; possessed of certain exclusive rights or privileges; not subject to tax, toll, duty, trade restrictions, fees, etc.; provided without payment. 6. ~**-and-easy**, unconstrained, unaffected, unconventional; ~ **association**, undirected mental activity like that of reverie or dreams; this as a method of psychoanalysis; **free'board**, part of ship's side between line of flotation and deck level; **free'-born**, born a free person (not a slave); born to the conditions and privileges of citizenship; **free city**, independent city-state under international protection; (hist.) medieval independent city-state in Germany and Italy; **free enterprise**, (system, doctrine, of) competitive private businesses operating for profit with a minimum of governmental interference; **free fall**, part of fall in parachute descent before parachute opens; fall of a body due entirely to the pull of gravity; **free flight**, flight of aircraft or rocket without power or control; **free-for-all**, fight in which all and sundry engage promiscuously; **free'hand**, (of drawing) done without guiding instruments, measures, or other artificial aid; **free-handed**, open-handed, generous; **free'hold**, (estate held by) tenure in fee simple or for term of life; held by freehold, **free'holder**, possessor of freehold estate; **free kick**, (soccer) kick allowed without interference, as penalty for infraction of rules by the other side; **free lance**, writer or artist who sells his or her work or services to a variety of employers or for short periods of time; person working for himself and not for an employer; **free-living**, given to self-indulgence; **free'load** (*v.*) (**-load·ed, -load·ing**), (slang) sponge; eat, drink, be

The development of parachute design has encouraged the daring practice of **free fall** *parachuting. Here a team of free fallers glide into position for a linked-hands formation high above Geneva.*

entertained, etc., at others' expense; **free'loader** (*n.*) person who habitually freeloads; **free love**, sexual relations irrespective of marriage; **free'man**, one who is not a slave or serf, or not subject to tyranny or usurped dominion; one who has full rights and privileges of citizenship; **free'mason**, member of secret international fraternity for mutual help and brotherly feeling, called **Free and Accepted Masons**, having elaborate ritual and system of secret signs (the original **freemasons** were probably skilled masons emancipated and moving from place to place for erection of important buildings in and after 14th c., the *accepted masons* being

honorary members (orig. suppos to be eminent for architectural antiquarian learning) who began be admitted early in 17th c.); **fre masonry**, system and institutio of Freemasons; secret or ta brotherhood, instinctive sympath **free on board**, (abbrev. f.o.b.) goods) with all charges paid delivery when put on board ship other means of conveyance; **fr port**, port open to all commerc vessels to load and unload in, (als port, or zone within a port, whe imports and exports are exem from customs duty; **free scho** school charging no fees; (196 school organized as alternative public and private schools, wi unconventional teaching metho and curriculum; **free silver**, fr coinage of silver usu. at fixed ra with gold; political theory favori this; **free'standing**, (of sculptu column, etc.) not supported structural framework; **Free Sta** state prohibiting slavery before t

vil War; **free'stone**, fine-grained
ndstone or limestone that can
sily be cut or sawn; kind of peach
c. in which when ripe the stone
loose; **free'thinker**, one who
fuses to submit his reason to con-
ol of authority in matters of
ligious belief; rationalist, deist,
c.; so **free thought**; **free trade**,
ade left to its natural course with-
t customs duties to restrict
ports or protect home industries;
ee **university**, (1960s) informal
ganization of college students
fering unconventional courses
d methods, analogous to free
hool; **free verse**, verse without
etrical pattern or fixed or predict-
le rhythm; **free'way**, express-
y; **free'wheeling**, (of) device
at permits vehicle to coast with
heels disengaged from driving
echanism; (fig., colloq.) irrespon-
le, independent, heedless; **free
ll**, unconstrained choice; (belief
) power of directing one's own
tions without constraint by
cessity or fate; **free world**, non-
mmunist countries' collective
me for themselves. **free'ly** adv.
ee adv. Freely; without cost or
yment. ~ v.t. (**freed, free·ing**).
Make free, set at liberty. 2.
elieve *from*, rid or ease *of*; clear,
sengage, disentangle; **freed'-
an**, emancipated slave.

free·boot·er (frē'boōter) n. (lit.
d fig.) Pirate, piratical adven-
rer.

free·dom (frē'dom) n. 1. Per-
nal liberty, exemption or release
om slavery or imprisonment; civil
erty, independence; liberty of
action; power of self-determina-
tion, independence of fate or necessity; **Four Freedoms**, those propounded by President F. D.
Roosevelt in 1941 (freedom of
speech and worship, freedom from
want and fear). 2. Frankness, out-
spokenness; undue familiarity;
facility, ease, in action; boldness of
conception. 3. Exemption *from*
defect, disadvantage, burden, etc.

free·si·a (frē'zhēa, -zēa, -zha) n.
Iridaceous bulbous plant of genus
F~, of S. Africa, allied to gladiolus and cultivated for its ornamental
and perfumed flowers. [F. H. T.
Freese (d. 1876), German physi-
cian]

freeze (frēz) v. (**froze, fro·zen,
freez·ing**). 1. (impers.) To have
the temperature such that water
becomes ice. 2. Be converted into
or covered with ice; become hard or
rigid as result of cold; become
fastened *to, together*, by freezing or
action of frost; ~ **on to**, (colloq.)
take or keep tight hold of. 3. Be
affected by, feel, extreme cold; die
by frost; be devoid of heat; be
chilled or immobilized by fear etc.
4. Cause to congeal, change (fluid)
to solid by diminution of heat,
cause ice to form on; congeal (the
blood) as if by frost, with terror
etc.; chill (feelings etc.), paralyze
(powers etc.): stiffen, harden, injure, kill, etc., by chilling; preserve
(meat etc.) by freezing; make (assets

etc.) unrealizable, peg or stabilize
(prices, wages, etc.); (fig.) become
stuck or fixed (by heat, friction,
etc.); ~**-dry** (v.t.) freeze material
and dry it by evaporation of ice
under high vacuum; **freezing
point**, temperature at which water
freezes, temperature at which given
liquid freezes; **freeze out**, exclude
from business, society, etc., by
competition, boycotting, etc.;
freeze over, cover or (esp. of
pond, river, etc.) become covered
with ice (colloq., **till hell freezes
over** = forever). **freeze** n. State,
coming, period, of frost; freezing of
assets etc. **freez'er** n. Person or
thing that freezes, esp. refrigerated
room or compartment for keeping
food frozen; deep-freeze.

freez·ing (frē'zĭng) adj. (esp.)
Very cold; (of manner) chilling;
distant. **freez'ing·ly** adv.

freight (frāt) n. Cargo transported by a vessel or vehicle, esp.
by a commercial carrier; commercial transportation of goods; charge
for this; load, burden, freight train;
~ **car**, railroad car for carrying
freight, esp. a boxlike car for this;
~ **train**, railroad train made up of
freight cars. **freight** v.t. Load
with goods for transport; transport,
convey commercial cargo.

freight·age (frā'tĭj) n. Commercial transportation of goods; the
charge for this; cargo.

freight·er (frā'ter) n. Shipper

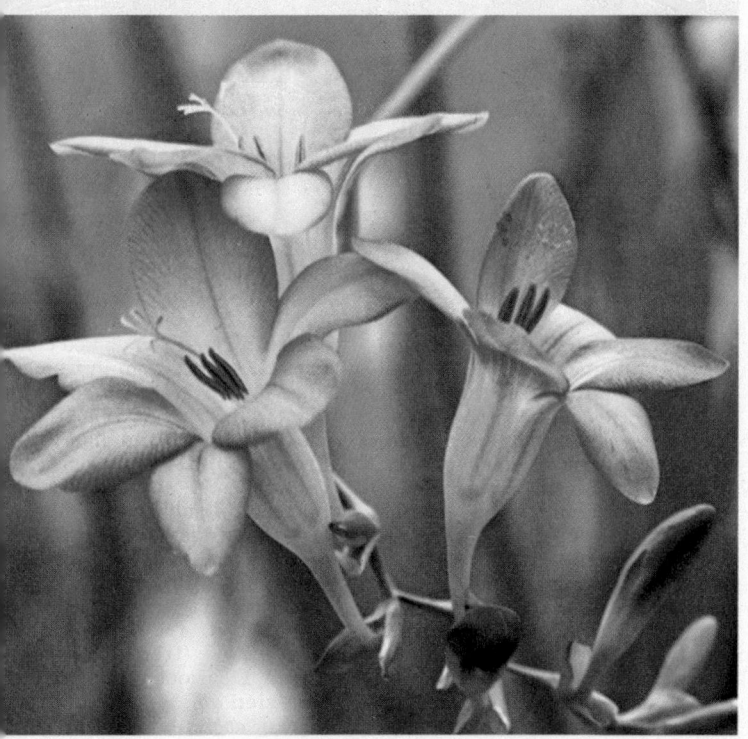

*The purple of the **freesia** illustrated
here is only one of the wide variety of
colors commonly found in this fragrant
flower, which is a hybrid.*

*The shipment of **freight** overland and
by sea is now frequently organized in a
system using modular containers which
are moved by purpose-built trucks,
cranes and ships.*

One of the key events of the **French Revolution** was the storming of the Tuileries Palace on 10 August 1792, here depicted dramatically by the painter Bertaux. For a time, the palace became a prison for Louis XVI.

The **French bean** grows well in soils of most kinds, provided they are not too heavy or too acid. The plant requires warm soil for germination.

of cargo; cargo ship, freight-carrying aircraft.

French (frĕnch) *adj.* Of France or its people or language; ∼ **and Indian War**, 1754–60, war in America in which French and their Indian allies opposed the English; ∼ **bean**, (chiefly Brit.) kidney or haricot bean (*Phaseolus vulgaris*) used as culinary vegetable both in unripe sliced pods and in ripe seeds; ∼ **bread**, bread of flour, water, and yeast baked in long crusty loaves; ∼ **Community**, association formed in 1958 of France, her departments and territories overseas, and former French territories that chose to maintain association after achieving independence; ∼ **cuff**, shirt cuff of double thickness and fastened with a cuff link; ∼ **door**, door having glass panes from top to bottom, usu. hung in pairs; ∼ **dressing**, salad dressing of vinegar and oil usu. seasoned; ∼ **fries**, French-fried slices of potato; ∼ **fry** (*v.*) (**fried, fry·ing**) fry in deep fat; ∼ **Guiana**, French overseas department in NE. South

Amer., bounded by Brazil on E. and S. and Surinam on W.; capital Cayenne; ∼ **horn**: see HORN[1] def. 3; **take ∼ leave**, depart, go away without notice; **French′man, French′woman**, French person; **French Polynesia**, French overseas territory in the S. Pacific Ocean, encompassing the Marquesa, Society, Gambier, Tuamotu, and other island groups; capital Papeete on Tahiti, Society Islands; **French Revolution**, revolution in which the French monarchy was overthrown and the First Republic established; the First Republic lasted from 1789–

99, when Napoleon gained contr● **French seam**, seam in which r edges of cloth are enclosed; **Fren● toast**, sliced bread dipped in e● and-milk batter and lightly fri● **French window** = French do● **French** *n.* 1. (collect.) People ● France. 2. Language of France, ● of the descendants of Latin; **Old** French from *c*9th to *c*13th ● sometimes 16th) century.

fre·net·ic (frĕnĕt′ĭk) *adj.* Fr● tic; frenzied. **fre·net′i·cal·ly** *a●* **fren·zy** (frĕn′zē) *n.* ● **-zies**). Delirious fury or agitati● **fren′zied** *adj.*

freq. *abbrev.* Frequent(ly).

Italian artists of the Renaissance carried **fresco** *painting to its highest stage of achievement. 'The Creation of Adam', a detail from Michelangelo's frescos in the Sistine chapel in the Vatican is considered a masterpiece.*

kwěnt′, frē′kwěnt) *v.t.* Go often or habitually to. **fre·quent′er** *n.*

fres·co (frěs′kō) *n.* (pl. **-coes, -cos**). Method of painting with powdered pigments by mixing them with water and applying them to wall or ceiling before plaster is dry; picture painted thus. ∼ *v.t.* (**-coed, -co·ing**). Paint in fresco. [It., = "fresh"]

fresh (frěsh) *adj.* 1. New, novel; not previously known, met with, used, etc.; different; recent, newly made or arrived; newly come or taken *from*; raw, inexperienced; **fresh′man**, high school, college, or university student in first year. 2. (of food) Not artificially preserved, not salted, pickled, smoked, etc., not frozen or canned; (of butter) not salted; (of water) not salt or bitter, fit for drinking; (of air etc.) pure, untainted, refreshing; **fresh·wat·er**, (*adj.*) of fresh water, not of the sea. 3. Not stale, musty, or vapid; not faded; unsullied, bright and pure in color; looking healthy or young. 4. Not weary, vigorous. 5. (slang, prob. infl. by Ger. *frech* impertinent) Presumptuous, forward. **fresh′ness** *n.* **fresh′en** *v.* **fresh** *adv.* Freshly, recently, newly. ∼ *n.* 1. Fresh or early part of day etc. 2. Freshet. **fresh′ness** *n.*

fresh·et (frěsh′ĭt) *n.* Rush of fresh water flowing into sea; overflow of river from heavy rain or melted snow.

fresh·ly (frěsh′lē) *adv.* Recently; with unabated vigor; with fresh appearance, odor, etc.

Fres·nel (frĕnĕl′), **Augustin Jean** (1788–1827). French physicist; supported wave theory of light; initiated use of compound lenses in lighthouses.

fret¹ (frĕt) *n.* Ornamental pattern of continuous combinations of straight lines joined usu. at right angles; ∼ **saw**, very thin saw stretched on frame for cutting thin wood in ornamental patterns; **fret′work**, (archit.) carved work in decorative patterns, esp. of intersecting lines; wood cut with fret saw into ornamental patterns. **fret** *v.t.* (**fret·ted, fret·ting**). Adorn with fretwork.

fret² (frĕt) *v.* (**fret·ted, fret·ting**). 1. Gnaw; wear away; eat *away*; form or make by wearing away. 2. Chafe, worry; distress oneself with regret or discontent. ∼ *n.* Irritation, vexation, worry. **fret′ful** *adj.* **fret′ful·ly** *adv.* **fret′ful·ness** *n.*

fret³ (frĕt) *n.* Bar or ridge on fingerboard of certain stringed in-

fre·quen·cy (frē′kwensē) *n.* (pl. **-cies**). 1. Frequent occurrence; being repeated at short intervals. 2. (physiol.) Number of pulsebeats per minute. 3. (phys., acoustics, etc.) Rate of recurrence of a repeated event, e.g., a vibration; (elect.) number of complete cycles per second of an alternating current or potential; such currents are classified as: **audio** ∼ (AF) frequency within the audible range, 30 Hz–20 kHz; **high** ∼, (HF) used of frequencies above the audible range, esp. those used for radio communication; **low** ∼, (LF) used of audio frequencies as dist. from radio (and see below); **radio** ∼, (RF) frequency suitable for radio transmission, above 10^4 Hz and below 3×10^{12} Hz approx., subdivided into **low** ∼ (LF) 30–300 kHz, **medium** ∼ (MF) 3×10^5–3×10^6 Hz, **very high** ∼ (VHF) 30–300 MHz, **ultra-high** ∼ (UHF) 3×10^8–3×10^9 Hz; ∼ **modulation**: see MODULATE. 4. (statistics) Ratio of number of actual to number of possible occurrences of an event.

fre·quent (frē′kwent) *adj.* Often occurring or appearing; happening in close succession, constant. **fre′quent·ly** *adv.* **frequent** (frē-struments fixing positions of fingers to produce required notes.

Freud (froid), **Sigmund** (1856–1939). Austrian neurologist and founder of psychoanalysis; advocated free association of ideas as a method of treatment; stressed importance of dreams as manifestations of repressed, particularly sexual, desires. **Freud·i·an** (froi′-dēan) *adj.* & *n.*

Fri. *abbrev.* Friday.

fri·a·ble (frī′abel) *adj.* Easily crumbled. **fri·a·bil·i·ty** (frī-abīl′ītē), **fri′a·ble·ness** *ns.*

fri·ar (frī′er) *n.* Brother or member of certain religious orders, esp. of the 4 mendicant orders, Franciscans (**Gray Friars**), Augustines (**Austin Friars**), Dominicans (**Black Friars**), and Carmelites (**White Friars**). **fri′ar·y** *n.* Monastery, fraternity, of friars.

fric·as·see (frĭkasē′, -zē′, frĭk′-asē, -zē) *n.* Dish of meat, poultry, etc., cut up, braised lightly, then stewed, and served in sauce. ~ *v.t.* (**-seed, -see·ing**). Make fricassee of.

fric·a·tive (frĭk′atĭv) *adj.* & *n.* (phonet.) (Consonant) produced by friction of breath through narrow opening formed in the mouth with the tongue or lips, as *s*, *f*.

Frick (frĭk), **Henry Clay** (1849–1919). Amer. industrialist and philanthropist; instrumental in formation of U.S. Steel Corporation (1901).

fric·tion (frĭk′shon) *n.* Rubbing of one object or surface against another; (phys. etc.) resistance

body meets with in moving over another; (fig.) clash of wills, temperaments, opinions, etc.; ~ **coupling**, device to transmit motion by frictional contact; ~ **tape**, strong cloth adhesive tape used esp. to insulate electrical conductors. **fric′tion·al** *adj.* **fric′-tion·al·ly** *adv.*

Fri·day (frī′dē, -dā) *n.* Sixth day of the week; **Good ~**, Friday before Easter, observed by Christians in commemoration of the Crucifixion of Jesus; **man ~**, once Robinson Crusoe's devoted companion in Defoe's story, now male assistant with diverse duties (so **girl ~**). [= "day of (the goddess) Frig" (i.e. FRIGG), transl. of L. *dies Veneris* day of (the planet) Venus]

fried (frīd). Past t. and past part. of FRY².

friend (frĕnd) *n.* 1. Person one knows well, likes, and trusts; acquaintance or associate; stranger toward whom one wishes to express goodwill or kindly condescension. 2. Sympathizer, helper, patron; ~ **at court**, one who will use his or her influence in high places to help another. 3. One who is not an enemy, who is on same side. 4. **F ~**, member of Society of Friends, Quaker; ordinary mode of address among Quakers; (**Society of**) **Friends**, the QUAKERS as a communion. **friend′less** *adj.*

friend·ly (frĕnd′lē) *adj.* Acting, disposed to act, as friend; characteristic of friends, expressing, showing, prompted by, kindness; opportune. **friend′li·ness** *n.*

friend·ship (frĕnd′shĭp) *n.* Be[ing] friends, relation betwee[n] friends; friendly disposition felt o[r] shown.

frieze¹ (frēz) *n.* Coarse woole[n] cloth with nap usu. on one side only[.]

frieze² (frēz) *n.* Member of en[-] tablature above architrave an[d] below cornice; horizontal broa[d] band of sculpture filling this; an[y] horizontal band of painted o[r] sculptured decoration etc. along th[e] upper part of a wall. [Fr. *frise* [fr.] L. *Phrygium* (*opus*) Phrygia[n] (work)]

frig·ate (frĭg′ĭt) *n.* 1. Fas[t,] medium-sized sailing warship o[f] the 17th c.–19th c., usu. wit[h] raised quarterdeck and forecastl[e.] 2. (U.S. Navy) Warship between [a] cruiser and destroyer in size an[d] used mainly for escort duty. 3. ~ **bird**, large swift brown seabir[d] (genus *Fregata*) of tropical region[s] with habit of cruising near othe[r] species and snatching food fro[m] them; esp. **magnificent ~** (*[F.] magnificens*) of the Florida Key[s;] also man-o'-war-bird.

Frig·ga (frĭg′a), **Frigg** (frĭg) [.] (Scand. myth.) Wife of Odin an[d] goddess of married love, the hearth[,] and heaven.

fright (frīt) *n.* Sudden fea[r,] violent terror, alarm; grotesqu[e] person or thing. ~ *v.t.* (poet[.)] Frighten.

fright·en (frī′ten) *v.t.* Thro[w] into a fright, terrify; drive (*awa[y] out of*, *into*, etc.) by frigh[t.] **frightened at**, affected with frigh[t] of.

fright·ful (frīt′ful) *adj.* Drea[d-] ful, shocking, revolting; ugl[y,] hideous; (slang) very great. **fright[·]ful·ly** *adv.* **fright′ful·ness** *n.*

frig·id (frĭj′ĭd) *adj.* 1. Intense[ly] cold; **F ~ Zone**, region lying withi[n] either polar circle. 2. Withou[t] ardor, apathetic; (of a woma[n)] sexually unresponsive. 3. Forma[l,] forced. **frig′id·ly** *adv.* **frig′id[·]ness, fri·gid·i·ty** (frijĭd′ītē) *ns.*

frill (frĭl) *n.* Ornamental edgin[g] of strip of material with one edg[e]

*Left: The aggressive **frigate bir[d]** sometimes called the man o' war bir[d] forces other sea birds to disgorge the[ir] catches. Right: The bird's distinctiv[e] orange pouch turns bright red durin[g] courtship.*

gathered and the other left loose so as to give wavy or fluted appearance; natural fringe of feathers, hair etc., on bird, animal, or plant; unnecessary or superfluous ornament or convenience. ~ *v.* Furnish or decorate with frill; form frill. **frill'y** *adv.* (**frill·i·er, frill·i·est**).

fringe (frĭnj) *n.* Ornamental bordering of threads of silk, cotton, etc., either loose or formed into tassels, twists, etc.; anything resembling this, border, edging; margin, outer edge; ~ **area**, area where television reception is unsatisfactory because of distance from station, blockage, etc.; ~ **benefit**, benefit, in addition to salary, received by employee, as medical insurance, pension, etc. **fringe** *v.t.* (**fringed, fring·ing**). Adorn or encircle with fringe; serve as fringe to; **fringed gentian**: see GENTIAN.

frip·per·y (frĭp' erē) *n.* (pl. **-per·ies**). Pretentious finery, needless or tawdry adornment, esp. in dress; trifles.

frisk (frĭsk) *v.* 1. Move sportively; caper. 2. (slang) Search (person, clothing) for concealed weapon etc. ~ *n.* 1. Frolic, caper. 2. (slang) Act of frisking for weapons. **frisk'y** *adj.* (**frisk·i·er, frisk·i·est**). **frisk'i·ly** *adv.* **frisk'i·ness** *n.*

frit (frĭt) *n.* Calcined mixture of sand and fluxes prepared for melting to form glass; vitreous composition from which soft porcelain is made. ~ *v.t.* (**frit·ted, frit·ting**). Make into frit; partially fuse, calcine.

Fritch·ie (frĭch'ē), **Barbara.** Patriotic old woman who re-

portedly waved a Union flag from her window as Stonewall Jackson and Confederate troops marched through Frederick, Md.; subject of poem (1864) by John Greenleaf Whittier.

frit·il·lar·y (frĭt'ilĕrē) *n.* (pl. **-lar·ies**). 1. Bulbous plant of the liliaceous genus *Fritillaria*. 2. Any of various butterflies of family Nymphalidae, esp. of genus *Speyeria* and *Boloria*, with spotted markings. [L. *fritillus* dicebox, with ref. to checked markings of corolla]

frit·ter[1] (frĭt'er) *n.* Portion [of] deep-fried batter, usu. containin[g] pieces of corn, fruit, etc.

frit·ter[2] (frĭt'er) *v.t.* Thro[w] *away* (time, money, energy, etc.) [in] trifling and wasteful way on variou[s] aims.

friv·ol (frĭv'ol) *v.i.* (**-oled, -ol[ing], -olled, -ol·ling**). Be a trifle [or] trifle.

friv·o·lous (frĭv'olus) *ad[j.]* Paltry, trifling, futile; given [to] trifling, silly. **friv'o·lous·ly** *ad[v.]* **friv'o·lous·ness, fri·vol·i·ty** (fr[i] vŏl'ĭtē) *ns.* (pl. **-ties**).

friz (frĭz) *v.* (**frizzed, friz[zed,]** **zing**). Curl, crisp, form into mas[s] of small curls. ~ *n.* (pl. **friz·zes**). Frizzed state; frizzed hair, mass [of] curls. **friz'zy** *adj.* (**-zi·er, -zi·est**).

friz·zle (frĭz'el) *v.* (**-zle[d,]** **-zling**). 1. Curl (*up*) in sma[ll] crisp curls. 2. Make sputterin[g] noise in frying. **friz'zly** *aa[j.]* (**-zli·er, -zli·est**).

fro (frō) *adv.* Away (only in t[o] **and** ~: see TO *adv.*).

frock (frŏk) *n.* 1. Long hab[it] with large open sleeves, the oute[r] and characteristic dress of a mon[k] (fig.) priestly character. 2. Woman's or girl's dress. 3. Froc[k] coat; man's double-breasted co[at] with long square tails or skirts n[ot] cut away in front.

frog[1] (frŏg, frawg) *n.* Tailless chiefly aquatic amphibious animal of order Salientia, esp. the common frog (genus *Rana*) with smooth shiny skin and long powerful web-footed hind legs with which it swims and leaps; (**F** ~, contempt.) Frenchman (as eating frogs; also **frog-eater**); **frog'fish**, any of various fishes of the family Antennariidae, esp. the angler; **frog in one's throat**, hoarseness; **frog'-man**, underwater swimmer and demolition expert equipped with long rubber foot flippers like frog's hind feet.

frog[2] (frŏg, frawg) *n.* Elastic horny substance in middle of sole of horse's hoof.

frog[3] (frŏg, frawg) *n.* Attachment to or loop on belt to support or hold sword, bayonet, etc.; ornamental looped braid with a spindle-shaped knot or covered button for decoration or fastening front of garment.

frog[4] (frŏg, frawg) *n.* Grooved piece of steel on intersecting railroad tracks permitting train wheels to cross the junction.

frol·ic (frŏl'ĭk) *adj.* (archaic) Joyous, sportive. ~ *v.i.* (**-icked, -ick·ing**). Play pranks; gambol. ~ *n.* Outburst of gaiety; prank; merriment; party. **frol'ic·some** *adj.*

from (frŭm, frŏm; unstressed from) *prep.* Out of, indicating place etc. whence motion or action proceeds (*walked* ~ *the town; called* ~ *the window*), starting point (~ *the beginning;* ~ *July*), first-named limit (~ *10 to 20 men*), object etc. whereby distance or remoteness is reckoned (*10 miles* ~ *the station; am far* ~ *saying*), source (*water* ~ *the well*), giver, sender (*a present* ~ *Ann*), thing or person got rid of, avoided, etc. (*dissuade* ~ *folly; release* ~ *engagement*), state changed for another (~ *being*

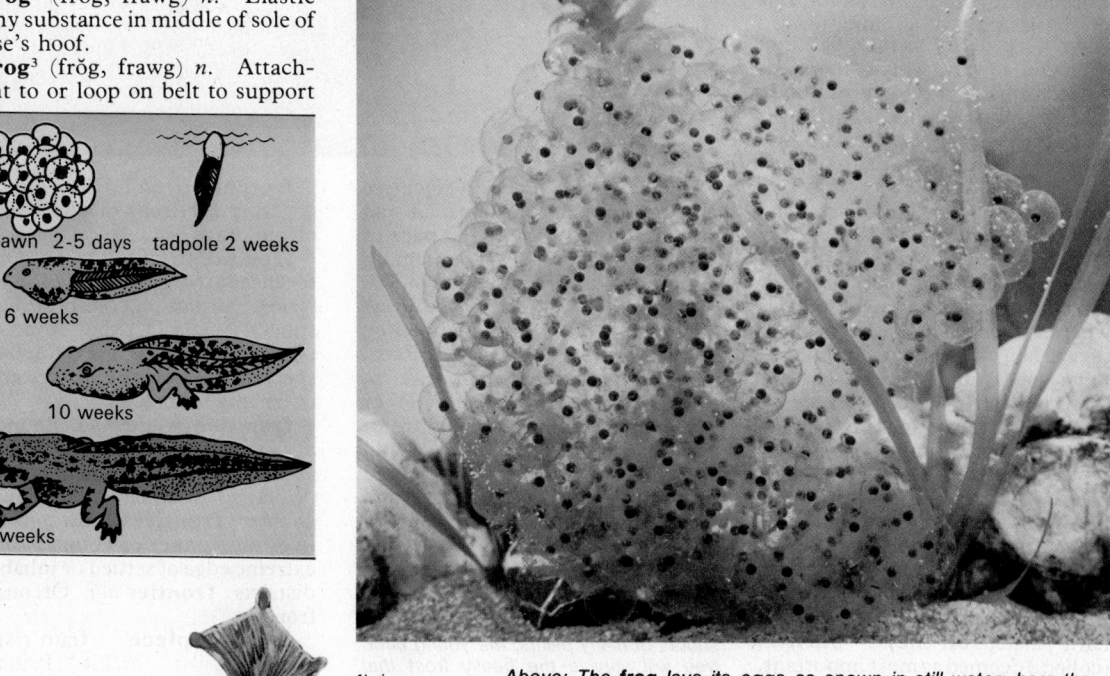

*Above: The **frog** lays its eggs as spawn in still water; here the spawn is of Rana dalmatina. Top left: The frog metamorphoses through a tadpole stage before adulthood. Below: Some of the species of frog adapted to various environments.*

spawn 2-5 days   tadpole 2 weeks

6 weeks

10 weeks

2 weeks

flying

giant

arrow poison

common

*The American **Frontier** was slowly extended thanks to these hardy souls who pushed into largely virgin land, regardless of the many risks.*

attacked became the aggressor), thing distinguished (*know good ~ bad*), origin in place or time, with adverbs or adverbial phrases or prepositions (*~ long ago; ~ under the bed*).

frond (frŏnd) *n.* (bot.) Leaf of certain flowerless plants, esp. ferns; (zool.) leaflike expansion in certain seaweeds, lichens, etc.

front (frŭnt) *n.* 1. Forehead (poet.); face (archaic). 2. (mil.) Foremost line of military unit; line of battle; part of ground toward enemy; scene of actual fighting; direction toward which line faces when formed. 3. Organized body of (esp. leftist) political forces, as **popular** ~ etc. 4. (archit.) Any face of building, esp. that containing main entrance. 5. (meteor.) Forward edge of an advancing mass of warm air meeting cold, or vice versa. 6. Side or part normally nearer or toward spectator or direction of motion; part of theater where audience sits (i.e. in front of the curtain); of land area, property, town, etc. fronting ocean, lake, or river (**ocean ~, water ~, river ~, lake** ~); organization etc. serving as cover for criminal activities; breast of man's shirt. 7. (with prep.) Forward position or situation; **in ~ of**, before, in advance of; confronting. **front** *adj.* Of the front; situated in front; (phonet., of sound) in which forepart of tongue touches or is raised toward front of hard palate; **(on the) ~ burner**, (colloq.) deemed as most important, for immediate attention; **~ door**, principal entrance door of house; ~

office, main office, executive officers, policy makers, of an organization; ~ **page**, first page of a newspaper, esp. as containing important or remarkable news; hence **front'-page** (*adj.*), sensational; **front runner**, competitor in the lead. **front** *v.* 1. Face, look out upon; stand opposite to, confront; have front on side of (street etc.). 2. Furnish with front.

front·age (frŭn′tĭj) *n.* 1. Land abutting on street or water; land between front of building and street; extent of front; front of building. 2. Fronting in certain direction; exposure, outlook.

*While **frost** will kill the young buds and shoots of many plants, the young birch tree will survive the heavy frost that coats its branches if the buds have not yet opened.*

fron·tal[1] (frŭn′tal) *n.* Movab covering for front of altar; facac of building.

fron·tal[2] (frŭn′tal) *adj.* 1. Of th forehead; ~ **bone**; ~ **lobe**, ar terior portion of cerebral hem sphere. 2. Of the front; (portrait, painted figure, etc.) facin spectator; ~ **attack**, direct attac on enemy's front.

fron·tier (frŭntēr′) *n.* Boundar of a country where its territor abuts on that of another; borde of settled or inhabited regions country; **frontiers'man**, one wh lives on frontier of country, or extreme edge of settled or inhabite districts. **frontier** *adj.* Of, on, th frontier.

fron·tis·piece (frŭn′tĭspē frŏn′-) *n.* 1. (archit.) Princip face of building; decorated er trance; pediment over door etc. Illustration facing title page of boc or one of its divisions.

front·let (frŭnt′lĭt) *n.* Bar worn on forehead; phylacter animal's forehead; cloth hangir over upper part of altar frontal.

fron·ton (frŏn′tŏn, frŏntŏn′): s JAI ALAI.

frost (frawst, frŏst) *n.* 1. Free ing temperature of atmosphe when it is below freezing point water; frozen dew or vapor; **frost bite**, inflamed or gangrenous sta of skin and adjacent parts produce by exposure to severe cold; **frost bitten**, affected with this. **fro** *v.t.* 1. Kill, injure (plants etc with frost. 2. Cover (as) with fros cover (cake) with icing, ice. 3. Gi roughened or finely granulated su face to (glass, metal). 4. Tur tint strands of (hair) white or lig blond. **frost'ing** *n.* (esp.) Icing f cakes.

Frost (frawst, frŏst), **Robe (Lee)** (1875–1963). American po and winner of Pulitzer Prize (192 1930, 1936, 1942); author of "

The edible parts of a **fruit** may be its seed, juicy envelope or skin, or all of these. 1. The banana is eaten either unripe and green or ripe and yellow. 2. Oranges and blossom on the same tree in Florida. 3. Italians of the Chianti district grow purple grapes for making red wine. 4. Peaches require a warm, temperate climate to ripen. 5. The pineapple is low growing. 6. A pomegranate.

Boy's Will," "North of Boston," "A Further Range," etc.

frost·y (fraws'tē, frŏs'-) *adj.* (**frost·i·er, frost·i·est**). Affected with frost, ice-cold; chilling, frigid, lacking in warmth of feeling; covered, looking as if covered, with frost.

froth (frawth, frŏth) *n.* Aggregation of small bubbles in liquid, caused by agitation, fermentation, effervescence, etc.; insubstantial or worthless thing, triviality. ~ *v.* Emit, cover with, froth; ~ **at the mouth**, emit foam of saliva, as in convulsive seizures etc.; (fig.) be enraged. **froth'y** *adj.* (**froth·i·er, froth·i·est**). **froth'i·ly** *adv.* **froth'i·ness** *n.*

frown (frown) *n.* Vertically furrowed state of brow; look expressing severity, disapproval, or deep thought. ~ *v.* Knit brows, esp. to express displeasure or concentrate attention; (of future, fate, etc.) present gloomy aspect; express disapprobation (*at, on*); express (defiance etc.) with frown.

frow·zy (frow'zē) *adj.* (**-zi·er, -zi·est**). Ill-smelling, musty; unkempt, slovenly, shabby. **frow'-zi·ly** *adv.* **frow'zi·ness** *n.*

fro·zen (frō'zen) *adj.:* see FREEZE; (esp., of food) preserved by freezing; (of assets etc.) not realizable.

FRS *abbrev.* Federal Reserve System.

fruc·ti·fi·ca·tion (frŭktifikā'-shon, frook-) *n.* 1. Production of fruit. 2. (bot.) Reproductive parts of plant, esp. of ferns and mosses.

fruc·ti·fy (frŭk'tifī, frook'-) *v.* (**-fied, -fy·ing**). Bear fruit; make fruitful or productive.

fruc·tose (frŭk'tōs, frook'-) *n.* (chem.) Fruit sugar, levulose, occurring in sweet fruits and honey.

fru·gal (froo'gal) *adj.* Careful, sparing (*of*); economical, thrifty; sparingly used or supplied; costing little. **fru·gal·i·ty** (froogal'itē) *n.* (pl. **-ties**). **fru'gal·ly** *adv.*

fruit (froot) *n.* (pl. **fruits**, collect. **fruit**). 1. (now usu. pl.) Vegetable products fit for food. 2. Edible product of plant or tree, consisting of seed and its envelope, esp. when this is juicy or pulpy; (bot.) ripe seeds and structure surrounding them. 3. (chiefly bibl.) Offspring. 4. What results from action, effort, cause, etc.; issue, consequence; advantage, profit; (pl.) products, revenues. 5. ~ **bat,**

tropical fruit-eating bat of suborder Megachiroptera, esp. flying fox; **fruitcake**, cake containing raisins, nuts, preserved fruits, etc.; **fruit fly**, any of numerous small flies of the family Drosophilidae whose larvae feed on fruit; **fruit salad**, mixture of various sliced or diced fruits served in their juices, syrup, etc.; **fruit tree**, tree cultivated for its fruit. **fruit** v. Bear, make bear, fruit.

fruit·ar·i·an (frōōtār′ēan) n. & adj. (Of) one who lives on fruit.

fruit·er (frōō′ter) n. 1. Tree producing fruit. 2. Ship carrying fruit.

fruit·ful (frōōt′ful) adj. Productive, fertile, causing fertility; productive of offspring, prolific; beneficial, remunerative. **fruit′ful·ly** adv. **fruit′ful·ness** n.

fru·i·tion (frōōish′on) n. Enjoyment, attainment of thing desired, realization of hopes, etc.

fruit·less (frōōt′lĭs) adj. Not bearing fruit; yielding no profit; useless, vain. **fruit′less·ly** adv. **fruit′less·ness** n.

fruit·y (frōō′tē) adj. (**fruit·i·er, fruit·i·est**). Of or like fruit; (of wine) tasting of the grape.

frump (frŭmp) n. Plain, dull, dowdy woman. **frump′ish** adj. **frump′y** adj. (**frump·i·er, frump·i·est**).

frus·trate (frŭs′trāt; Brit. frŭs-trāt′) v.t. (**-trat·ed, -trat·ing**). Balk, baffle; counteract; defeat, foil. **frus·tra·tion** (frŭstrā′shon) n. **frus′trat·ed** adj.

frus·tum (frŭs′tum) n. (pl. **-tums, -ta** pr. -ta). Portion of regular solid left after cutting off upper part by plane parallel to base; portion between two planes either parallel or inclined to each other.

fru·ti·cose (frōō′tĭkōs) adj. Shrublike.

fry¹ (frī) n. (pl. **fry**). Young fishes, esp. just produced from spawn; young of other creatures produced in large numbers; **small ~**, young or insignificant beings, children, etc.

fry² (frī) v. (**fried, fry·ing**). Cook in hot fat or oil in frying pan; **deep-~**, cook by completely immersing in hot fat or oil in deep pan; **frying pan, fry pan**, skillet, shallow pan with long handle for frying. **fry** n. (pl. **fries**). Dish of fried food; social gathering at which fried food is served, as a **fish-~**.

FSLIC abbrev. Federal Savings and Loan Insurance Corporation.

f-stop (ĕf′stŏp) n. Camera lens aperture setting indicated by an f-number.

ft abbrev. Foot, feet.

ft. abbrev. Fort, fortification; foot, feet.

FTC abbrev. Federal Trade Commission.

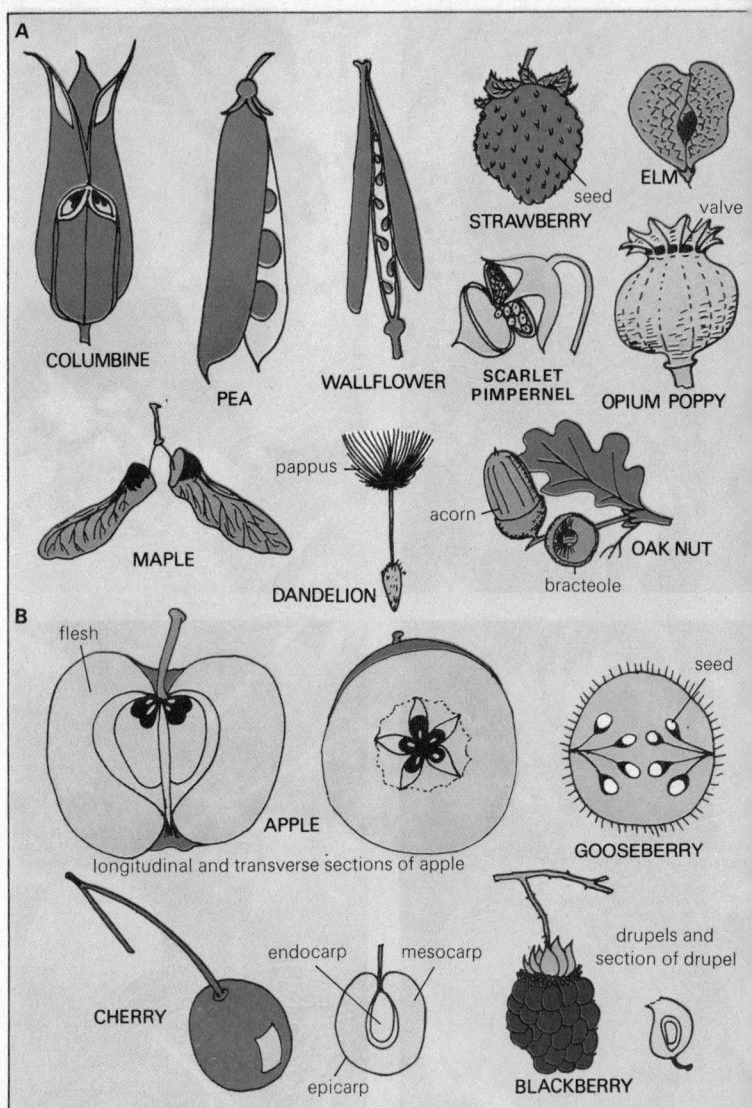

A

COLUMBINE   PEA   WALLFLOWER   SCARLET PIMPERNEL   STRAWBERRY   seed   ELM   valve   OPIUM POPPY   MAPLE   pappus   DANDELION   acorn   OAK NUT   bracteole

B

flesh   APPLE   longitudinal and transverse sections of apple   seed   GOOSEBERRY   CHERRY   endocarp   mesocarp   epicarp   drupels and section of drupel   BLACKBERRY

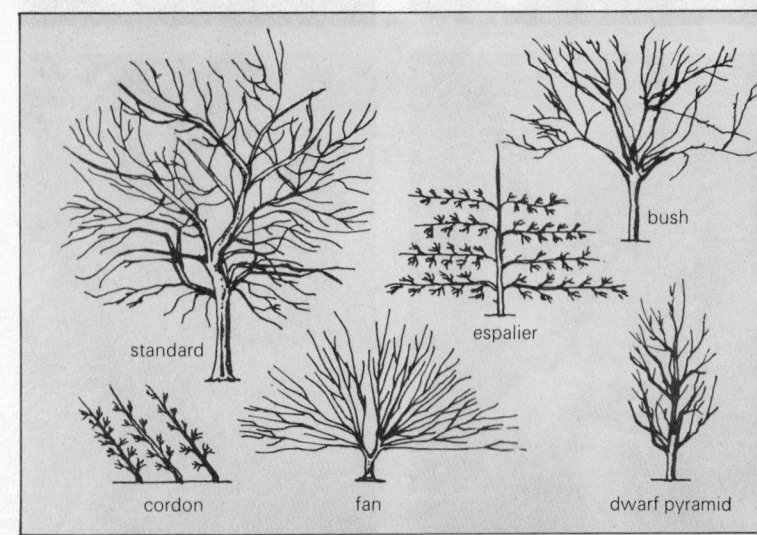

standard   espalier   bush   cordon   fan   dwarf pyramid

*Top: The base of a blossom develops into a **fruit** that will be of either a dry (A) or succulent (B) type. For distributing their seeds, fruits have a variety of mechanisms, those of the dry fruits being perhaps more varied. Bottom:*

Trees are cultivated in shapes that a convenient to the grower and that ta best advantage of the tree's charact istics and of its position in the garden orchard in relation to the sun and wir

*Above: Most **fuchsias** seen in gardens are hybrids. Native to S. America, their pendulous crimson and purple flowers have made them popular ornamentals. Left: Native fuchsia of Australia.*

't-lb *abbrev.* Foot-pound(s).
'uch·sia (fū′sha) *n.* Ornamental ub of genus *F*~ with drooping, . red, flowers; color of vivid rplish red. [L. *Fuchs*, 16th-c. rman botanist]

uck (fŭk) *v.* (vulg.) 1. Copulate th). 2. Used in exclamations . **fuck′ing** *adj.* & *adv.* (vulg.) ed abusively or as intensive. **ck** *n.* (vulg.) Act of copulation.

fu·cus (fū′kus) *n.* (pl. **-ci** pr. -sī, us·es). Brown seaweed of genus ~ with flat leathery fronds.

fud·dle (fŭd′el) *v.* (**-dled, ling**). Intoxicate; stupefy, con-se. ~ *n.* Fuddled state.

fud·dy-dud·dy (fŭd′ē dŭd′ē) *n.* . **-dud·dies**) & *adj.* Excessively -fashioned or fussy (person).

fudge (fŭj) *int.* Nonsense! ~ *n.* Nonsense. 2. Soft, rich candy, de by boiling together sugar, tter, milk, chocolate, and flavor-. ~ *v.* (**fudged, fudg·ing**). 1. ake up, in a makeshift or dis-nest way, fake, falsify. 2. Avoid ing reality (of a situation).

fueh·rer (fūr′er; *Ger.* für′er): = HRER.

fu·el (fū′el, fūl) *n.* Material for es, combustible matter; material ed as source of nuclear energy; g.) something that feeds passion, citement, etc; ~ **cell**, primary l producing electricity direct m chemical reaction; ~ **injec-on**, direct introduction of fuel der pressure into combustion it of internal combustion engine; **oil**, heavy petroleum oil having a sh point higher than that of kero-

sene, used esp. in furnaces, diesels, etc; ~ **pellet**, segmented form of uranium used to create and maintain fission in nuclear power plant. **fuel** *v.* (**-eled, -el·ing, -elled, -el·ling**). Provide (ship etc.) with fuel; (of ship etc.) take in fuel; **fueling station**, port where this is done.

fu·ga·cious (fūgā′shus) *adj.* Fleeting, evanescent. **fu·gac·i·ty** (fūgăs′ītē) *n.* (pl. **-ties**).

fu·gi·tive (fū′jĭtĭv) *adj.* 1. Fleeing; that has taken flight (from duty, an enemy, master, etc.). 2. Fleeting, transient; (of literature) of passing interest, ephemeral, as ~ **verse**. ~ *n.* One who flees (*from*).

fugue (fūg) *n.* 1. (mus.) Polyphonic composition in which a short melodic theme is introduced by one of the parts and successively taken up by others, thereafter forming the main material of the texture. 2. (psychol.) Loss of awareness of one's identity, often coupled with disappearance from one's usual environment, and amnesia of all actions during the period.

füh·rer (fūr′er; *Ger.* für′er) *n.* 1. Leader, esp. one with the powers of a tyrant. 2. **der F**~, title assumed by Adolf HITLER as head of the German Reich. [Ger., = "leader"]

Fu·ji (fōō′jē). [also known as **Fu·ji·ya·ma** (fōōjēyah′ma)] Extinct volcano and Japan's highest mountain peak (12,388 ft., 3,776 m) in S. central Honshu Island, 70 mi. (113 km) WSW. of Tokyo; con-

sidered sacred by Buddhists.
Fu·jian (fōō′jahn′) = FUKIEN.
Fu·kien (fōō′kyĕn′). Maritime province of SE. China; capital Foochow.

-ful *suffix.* Forming adjectives with sense full of (*beautiful*), suggesting (*masterful, direful*), or accustomed to (*forgetful*); forming nouns with sense amount needed to fill (*spoonful, handful*).

ful·crum (fōōl′krum, fŭl′-) *n.* (pl. **-crums, -cra** pr. -kra). 1. (mech.) Point against which lever is placed to get purchase or on which it turns or is supported. 2. Any means of exerting influence. [L. = "post of couch"]

ful·fill, ful·fil (fōōlfĭl′) *vbs.t.* (**-filled, -fill·ing**). Bring to consummation, carry out (prophecy, promise), satisfy (desire, prayer); perform, execute (command, law); answer (purpose), comply with (conditions); bring to an end, complete (period, work). **ful·fill′ment** *n.*

ful·gent (fŭl′jent) *adj.* Shining, brilliant.

full[1] (fōōl) *adj.* 1. Containing all it will hold, having no space empty, replete; containing abundance *of*, charged, crowded; abounding (in); replete with food. 2. ~ **of**, engrossed with, absorbed in. 3. Copious, satisfying. 4. Complete; answering in every respect to a name or description; reaching the specified or usual limit; (of moon) having disk completely illuminated; (of face etc.) entirely visible to spectator; ~ **brother, sister**, one born of same father and mother. 5. (of light) Intense; (of color) deep; (of motion etc.) vigorous. 6. Swelling, plump, protuberant; (of dress) containing superfluity of material arranged in gathers or folds. 7. **full′back**, (football) position, player, behind the quarterback; **full-blooded**, vigorous, hearty, sensual; **full-blown**, completely developed, in full bloom; **full-bodied**, esp. of wine, with much body; **full dress**: see DRESS; **full house**, (poker) hand containg three of a kind and a pair; **full nelson**: see NELSON; **full-scale**, of the same size as the original, complete; not limited, using all resources; **full tilt**, at full speed, with full force; **full time**, total normal duration of work etc. **full** *n.* Whole; point or state of greatest fullness; entire amount or range; **in ~**, without abridgement; with no more owing. **full** *adv.* Very (chiefly poet.); quite, fully; exactly; more than sufficiently; **full-fledged**, having fully developed adult plumage; (fig.) mature, having full status or position; **~-grown**, having reached maturity. **full′ness, ful′ness** *ns.*

full² (fŏŏl) *v.t.* Tread or beat (cloth) to cleanse and thicken it; cleanse and thicken (cloth etc.). **full·er** (fŏŏl′er) *n.* One who fulls cloth; **~'s earth**, absorbent clay containing hydrated silica and alumina, used in fulling cloth and purifying oils and fats.

full·y (fŏŏl′ē) *adv.* Completely, without deficiency.

ful·mar (fŏŏl′mer) *n.* Arctic sea bird (*Fulmarus glacialis*) about size of gull, noted for its easy gliding flight by sea cliffs.

ful·mi·nant (fŭl′minant) *adj.* Fulminating; (path., of diseases or pain) developing suddenly and intensely.

ful·mi·nate (fŭl′mināt) *v.* (**-nat·ed, -nat·ing**). 1. Flash like lightning; explode, detonate. 2. Thunder forth, utter or publish (censure); issue (usu. official) censures *against*. **ful·mi·na·tion** (fŭlminā′shon) *n.* **ful·mi·na·to·ry** (fŭl′minatōrē, -tōrē) *adj.* **fulminate** *n.* (also **~ of mercury**) Very sensitive explosive, $Hg(ONC)_2$, used in detonators.

ful·ness = FULLness.

ful·some (fŏŏl′som) *adj.* (of flattery, servility, etc.) Cloying, excessive, disgusting by excess. **ful′some·ly** *adv.* **ful′some·ness** *n.*

Ful·ton (fŏŏl′ton), **Robert** (1765–1815). Amer. engineer; invented first financially profitable U.S. steamboat (1807).

fu·ma·role (fū′marōl) *n.* Hole in earth's crust near a volcano, through which gases and vapor issue.

fum·ble (fŭm′bel) *v* (**-bled, -bling**). 1. Use the hands awkwardly, grope about; handle or deal with awkwardly or nervously. 2. (sports) Fail to catch or field (ball) clearly. **~** *n.* Bungling attempt. **fum′bler** *n.*

fume (fūm) *n.* (esp. pl.) Odorous smoke, vapor, or exhalation; fit of anger. **~** *v.* (**fumed, fum·ing**). 1. Treat with, emit, fumes. 2. Be pettish; chafe, fret. **fum′y** *adj.* (**fum·i·er, fum·i·est**).

fu·mi·gate (fū′migāt) *v.t.* (**-gat·ed, -gat·ing**). Apply fumes to, esp. to exterminate insects, vermin, etc.; disinfect or purify with fumes. **fu·mi·ga·tion** (fūmigā′shon), **fu′·mi·ga·tor** *ns.*

fun (fŭn) *n.* Sport, amusement; jocularity, drollery; **make ~ of, poke ~ at**, ridicule.

func·tion (fŭngk′shon) *n.* 1. Activity proper to person or institution; mode of action by which thing fulfills its purpose. 2. Social meeting of formal or important kind. 3. (math.) Variable quantity regarded in relation to other(s) in terms of which it may be expressed or on whose value its own depends. 4. **~ word**, (gram. jargon) word expressing chiefly grammatical relation, as preposition, conjunction,

The gliding flight of the **fulmar** charac-terizes it as one of the 35 species o the shearwater family. Above: Fulmaru glacialis of the Arctic with its new hatched chick was photographed in th Farne Islands.

auxiliary verb, etc. **function** *v.* Fulfill a function, operate, act.

func·tion·al (fŭngk′shonal) *ad* 1. Of a function or functions. (physiol.) Of, affecting, only th functions of an organ etc., n structural or organic (esp. diseases). 3. (math.) Of a functior 4. (of building etc.) Shaped, cor structed, with regard only to i function, not to traditional or othe theories of design. **func′tion·al ism** *n.* **func′tion·al·ist** *adj.* & **func′tion·al·ly** *adv.*

func·tion·ar·y (fŭngk′shonĕrĕ *n.* (pl. **-ar·ies**). One with certai functions or duties to perform official.

fund (fŭnd) *n.* Permanent stoc of something ready to be draw upon; sum of money, esp. one se apart for a purpose; (pl.) financi resources; **mutual ~**: see MUTUAI **fund** *v.t.* Convert (debt) int more or less permanent debt a fixed interest; furnish a fund for pay for.

fun·da·ment (fŭn′dament) *r* Buttocks; anus.

fun·da·men·tal (fŭndamĕn′tal *adj.* 1. Of the groundwork, goin to the root of the matter, servin as base or foundation; essential primary, original; from whicl others are derived. 2. (mus., c a note) That is the lowest note of chord in its original form; (of chord) with the root as the lowes e; (of a tone) that is produced by vibration of the whole of a orous body (as dist. from *har-ics*). **fun·da·men′tal, fun-·men·tal·i·ty** (fŭndəmĕntăl′ĭtē) (pl. **-ties**). Principle, rule, cle, serving as groundwork of em (often pl.). **fun·da·men′-ly** *adv.*

un·da·men·tal·ism (fŭndə-′talĭzem) *n.* Strict adherence raditional orthodox (Protestant) ets (e.g. the literal infallibility Scripture), held to be funda-ntal to Christianity; adherence raditional beliefs of any kind. **·da·men′tal·ist** *adj. & n.*

′un·dy (fŭn′dē), **Bay of.** Atlan-Ocean inlet approx. 100 mi. km) long, in SE. Canada be-en New Brunswick and Nova tia, noted for treacherous cur-ts and high tides (reaching up o ft. (22 m) at head of bay).

u·ner·al (fū′nerəl) *adj.* Of, d, carried, etc., at burial or nation of the dead; ~ **pyre**, pile wood etc. on which corpse is ned. **funeral** *n.* Burial of the d with its ceremonies etc; eral procession; funeral service; **director**, person who is in rge of funeral service or funeral ne; undertaker; ~ **home**, blishment where bodies are

prepared for burial or cremation and funerals are conducted.

fu·ner·ar·y (fū′nerĕrē) *adj.* Of funeral or burial.

fu·ne·re·al (fūnēr′ēal) *adj.* Appropriate to funeral, gloomy, dark, mournful. **fu·ne′re·al·ly** *adv.*

fun·gi·cide (fŭn′jĭsīd) *n.* Fungus-destroying substance. **fun·gi·ci·dal** (fŭnjĭsī′dal) *adj.*

fun·goid (fŭng′goid) *adj.* Fun-guslike.

fun·gous (fŭng′gus) *adj.* Of, caused by, fungi; having nature of a fungus.

fun·gus (fŭng′gus) *n.* (pl. **fun·gi** pr. fŭn′jī, -jē, **fun·gus·es**). Mush-room, toadstool, or one of the allied plants, including the various molds; (bot.) cryptogamous plant without chlorophyll deriving its substance from organic matter. **fun·gal** (fŭng′gal) *adj.*

fu·nic·u·lar (fūnĭk′yuler) *adj.* Of a rope or its tension; depend-ing on or worked by a rope or cable; ~ *n.* cable railroad in which ascending and descending cars are counterbalanced.

funk (fŭngk) *n.* (colloq.) Fear, panic; dejection; coward; **blue ~**, terror. **funk** *v.* Flinch, shrink, show cowardice, fight shy of, (try to) evade; be afraid of.

fun·ky (fŭng′kē) *adj.* (**-ki·er, -ki·est**). (slang) 1. (jazz) Uncom-plicated, pulsating, based on blues. 2. Strong smelling. 3. Fashionably unconventional, offbeat.

fun·nel (fŭn′el) *n.* 1. Narrow-ing tube, cone-shaped vessel with tube at apex, for conducting liquid, powder, etc., into small opening. Ventilating etc. shaft; smokestack of locomotive, ship, etc.

fun·ny (fŭn′ē) *adj.* (**-ni·er, -ni·est**). Causing laughter or amuse-ment, affording fun, comical; queer, perplexing; ~ **bone**, part of elbow over which ulnar nerve passes (from peculiar sensation ex-perienced when it is struck); ~ **farm**, (slang) mental hospital; ~ **money**, counterfeit money; money from concealed or dishonest sources. **fun′ni·ly** *adv.* **fun′ni·ness** *n.*

fur (fẽr) *n.* 1. Coat of certain animals (as ermine, beaver, fox,

Capable of reproducing asexually, fungus is generally parasitic and has neither roots nor flowers. Fungi are useful in the preparation of enzymes, alcohol, antibiotics, and vitamins, and are vital to the renewal of soil by assist-ing in the decomposition of humus. Below left: Hypholoma fasciculare. Below: Dictyophol. sp. Bottom: Amanita muscaria.

etc.); dressed coat of such animals or imitation of this, used for garments, trimming, lining, etc.; a coat, stole, etc., of this; (usu. pl.) garment(s) of or trimmed with fur. 2. Short fine soft hair of certain animals as distinct from the longer and coarser hair; (pl.) skins of such animals with the fur. **fur·ry** (fẽr´ē, fŭr´ē) *adj*. (**-ri·er, -ri·est**).

fur *v*. (**furred, fur·ring**). 1. Trim, line, cover, with fur. 2. (carpentry) Line, level (floor timbers, rafters, etc.), with FURRING.

fur. *abbrev*. Furlong.

fur·be·low (fẽr´belō) *n*. Gathered strip, as a ruffle or flounce, or other trimming, esp. on 17th–18th c. dress; showy ornament. ~ *v.t*. Adorn with furbelows.

fur·bish (fẽr´bĭsh) *v.t*. Polish, burnish; give new look to, renovate, revive.

fur·cate (fẽr´kāt, -kĭt) *adj*. Forked, branched. ~ (fẽr´kāt) *v.i*. (**-cat·ed, -cat·ing**). Branch, divide.

fu·ri·ous (fūr´ēus) *adj*. Full of fury, raging, frantic, violent; **fast and ~**, very fast, uproarious(ly), in great numbers, with rapid repetition. **fu´ri·ous·ly** *adv*.

furl (fẽrl) *v*. Roll up and tie (sail, flag, etc.) on yard, boom, or pole; roll or gather up, close, fold up; become furled; roll away like clouds.

fur·long (fẽr´lawng, -lŏng) *n*. Measure of length, ⅛ mile or 220 yards. [OE. *furlang*, f. *furh* furrow and *lang* long]

fur·lough (fẽr´lō) *n*. Leave of absence, esp. one longer than a weekend to member of armed forces; leave. ~ *v.t*. Grant furlough to.

fur·nace (fẽr´nĭs) *n*. Apparatus containing chamber for combustibles in which minerals, metals, etc., may be subjected to continuous action of intense heat; device with combustion chamber for furnishing heat to a building, etc.; (fig.) hot place.

Fur·neaux (fẽr´nō) **Islands.** Group of islands in Bass Strait off coast of NE. Tasmania, Australia, encompassing 900 sq. mi. (2,331 sq. kl); Flinders Island and Cape Barren Island are the largest.

fur·nish (fẽr´nĭsh) *v.t*. Provide *with*; fit (house, room) with all necessary appliances, esp. movable furniture; provide, afford, yield; **fur´nishing**, (*n*., esp. pl.) articles of furniture or other things required to furnish a house etc.

fur·ni·ture (fẽr´nĭcher) *n*. Movable articles (as tables, chairs) for use or ornament in house or room; necessary equipment, as for a ship, factory, etc.

fu·ror (fūr´ŏr) *n*. 1. Outburst of enthusiasm. 2. Uproar.

When a crucible of molten metal leaves a **furnace** it has slag on its surface. The slag can be skimmed off and used elsewhere in cement-making.

fur·ri·er (fẽr´ēer, fŭr´-) *n*. Dealer in, dresser of, furs.

fur·ring (fẽr´ĭng, fŭr´-) *n*. Fixing strips of wood or metal to floor timbers, rafters, etc. to form a level surface or space above which a new surface may be applied; strips of wood used for this.

fur·row (fẽr´ō, fŭr´ō) *n*. Narrow trench made in earth with plow; rut, track, groove, long indentation; deep wrinkle. ~ *v.t*. Plow; make furrows, grooves, etc., in; mark with wrinkles.

fur·ther (fẽr´dher) *adv*. To a greater extent, more (also **fur´thermore**); in addition; to a more advanced point in time; farther. ~ *adj*. Going beyond what exists or has been dealt with, additional; more distant. ~ *v.t*. Help on, promote, favor. **fur´ther·ance** *n*. **fur´ther·most** *adj*.

fur·thest (fẽr´dhest) *adj*. & *adv*. Most distant in time or degree; farthest.

fur·tive (fẽr´tĭv) *adj*. Stealthy, sly; taken secretly. **fur´tive·ly** *a* **fur´tive·ness** *n*.

fu·ry (fūr´ē) *n*. (pl. **-ries**). Fierce passion, wild anger; fie impetuosity or violence. 2. F (Gk. myth.) one of the snake-hair goddesses (esp. Alecto, Megae Tisiphone) sent from Tartarus avenge wrong and punish crin (fig.) avenging or tormenting spir 3. Virago, angry or maligna woman.

furze (fẽrz) *n*. Gorse.

fuse[1] (fūz) *v*. (**fused, fus·in** Melt with intense heat; bler amalgamate, into whole (as) melting. ~ *n*. Strip or wire easily fused metal in electric circ which melts and so interrupts t circuit if current increases beyo a certain limit. **fu´si·ble** *a* **fu·si·bil·i·ty** (fūzibĭl´ĭtē) *n*.

fuse[2], **fuze** (fūz) *ns*. (usu. *fu* Tube, casing, cord, etc., filled saturated with combustible mat for igniting blasting charge, bon etc.; (usu. *fuze*) component screw into shell, mine, etc., designed detonate explosive charge eit after an interval (**time ~**) or impact, or when subjected magnetic, vibratory, or oth

mulation. **fuse** v.t. (**fused, fus·-**
g). Fit fuse to.

fu·see (fūzē´) n. 1. Conical pulley
wheel, esp. wheel in watch or
ock on which chain is wound and
nich equalizes power of main-
ring. 2. Large-headed match
r use in wind; raiiroad warning
re.

fu·se·lage (fū´selĭj, -ze-, -lahzh)
Body or framework of air-
ane.

fu·sel (fū´zel, -sel,) **oil.** Mix-
'e of several alcohols, chiefly
ayl, sometimes produced, usu. in
aall amounts, during fermenta-
n of alcoholic liquor and making
armful or poisonous. [Ger. *fusel*
Du. *foezel* bad spirit]

fu·sil (fū´zĭl, -sĭl) n. (hist.)
ght musket or firelock.

fu·sil·ier, fu·sil·eer (fūzĭlēr´) ns.
st.) Soldier armed with a fusil;
siliers (soldiers of) certain Brit.
antry regiments formerly armed
h fusils.

fu·sil·lade (fū´sĭlād, -lahd, -zi-)
(Wholesale execution by) con-
ous discharge of firearms.

fu·sion (fū´zhon) n. Fusing;
sed mass; blending of different
ngs into one; coalition; (phys.)
ergy-releasing union of atomic
clei in thermonuclear reaction to
m heavier nucleus.

e ambition of artists who embraced
urism was to employ all aspects of
dern life in their work. This philos-
hy is seen in the use of newspapers
d textures in St. Etienne's 'Still Life
h Lacerba'.

fuss (fŭs) n. Bustle, excessive
commotion, ostentatious or nervous activity; treatment of trifles as
important; (colloq.) person who is
always making a fuss (also **~-
budget, ~ pot**). **fuss** v. Make
fuss; busy oneself restlessly with
trifles; move fussily *about*, etc.,
agitate, worry (person). **fuss'y** adj.
(**fuss·i·er, fuss·i·est**). (esp.) Fastidious; meticulous.

fus·tian (fŭs´chan) n. 1. Thick
twilled cotton cloth with short nap,
usu. dyed in dark dull colors. 2.
Pompous language, bombast. **~**
adj. Made of fustian; bombastic.

fus·tic (fŭs´tĭk) n. Small tropical
Amer. tree (*Chlorophora tinctoria*),
having wood yielding a yellow dyestuff; the wood of this tree; the dye.
[Arab. *fustuq* f. Gk. *pistakē* pis-
tachio]

fus·ty (fŭs´tē) adj. (**-ti·er,
-ti·est**). Stale-smelling, musty;
stuffy; old-fashioned. **fus'ti·ness**
n.

fut. abbrev. Future.

fu·tile (fū´tĭl; Brit. fū´tīl) adj.
Useless, ineffectual, vain, frivolous.
fu'tile·ly adv. **fu·til·i·ty** (fūtĭl´ĭtē)
n. (pl. **-ties**).

fu·ture (fū´cher) adj. That will
be hereafter; of time to come;
(gram., of tense) relating to time to
come. **~** n. Time to come; what
will happen in the future; person's,
country's, etc., prospective condition; (gram.) future tense;
(commerc., pl.) commodities and
stocks sold for future delivery,
contracts for these; **~ perfect**,

(gram.) tense designating action
completed at a certain time in the
future (*will have done*); **~ shock**,
disorientation and demoralization
caused by too swift social and
technological changes. [title of
book (1970) by Alvin Toffler,
Amer. author] **fu·tu·rol·o·gy**
(fūcherŏl´ojē) n.

fu·tur·ist (fū´cherĭst) n. Adherent of futurism. **fu·tur·is·tic**
(fūcherĭs´tĭk) adj. **fu'tur·ism** n.
Artistic and literary movement
begun *c*1909 in Italy, marked by
violent departure from traditional
methods and attempting to represent nature not in a static but
in a dynamic state.

fu·tu·ri·ty (fūtoor´ĭtē, -tūr´-,
-choor´-) n. (pl. **-ties**). Future
time; future events; future condition, extent, or possibility; (also **~
race**) horse race in which horses
must be entered far in advance of
the running, e.g. at birth.

Fu·zhou (fōō´jō´) = FOOCHOW.

fuzz[1] (fŭz) n. Mass of fine light
fluff; fibers, hairs, etc.; down,
as of a peach. **fuzz'y** adj.
(**fuzz·i·er, fuzz·i·est**). Of, covered
with fuzz; frayed, fluffy; blurred,
indistinct; frizzled; confused.

fuzz[2] (fŭz) n. (slang) Policeman;
(collect.) the police.

fwd. abbrev. Four-wheel drive.
FY abbrev. Fiscal year.
-fy suffix. Forming verbs with
sense of make, produce, or cause
(*satisfy, solidify, stupefy*).

FYI abbrev. For your information.

*Although some **furniture** is still made
by individual craftsmen, most is mass-
produced, one group of workers
completing part of the manufacture and
the item being finished and assembled
by hand at the end of the process.*

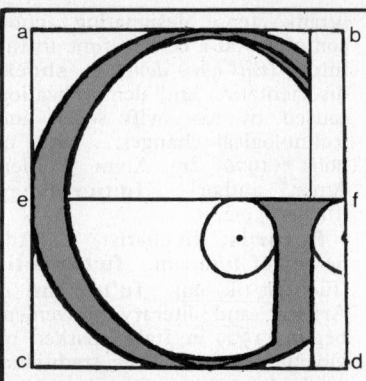

How the written form of the letter **G, g** has developed over the centuries from the apparently unrelated early Phoenician version to the Latin version in use today. Left: The G in Albrecht Durer's design of the Alphabet.

Phoenician   Early Greek   Etruscan

(G) > G

Archaic Latin   Corinthian   Latin

G, g (jē) (pl. **G's, g's** or **Gs, gs**). 1. Seventh letter of modern English and ancient Roman alphabet, orig. differentiated form of C, representing in English a voiced postpalatal stop (*hard g*) except in some words, chiefly of French, Latin, or Greek origin, before *e* or *i*, where it is equivalent to the composite sound (*j*). 2. **G**, (mus.) fifth note of natural scale (C major); scale or key with this note for tonic.

G *abbrev.* Gauss; giga-; (slang) $1,000.

g *abbrev.* Gram(s); acceleration due to gravity.

G. *abbrev.* German; gulf.

g. *abbrev.* Gauge; gender.

Ga *symbol.* Gallium.

Ga., GA *abbrevs.* Georgia.

G.A. *abbrev.* General Assembly.

gab (găb) *n.* (colloq.) Talk, prattle, twaddle; **gift of** ~, talent for speaking; loquacity. **gab** *v.i.* (**gabbed, gab·bing**).

gab·ar·dine (găb´erdēn, găberdēn´) *n.* Twill woven cloth of worsted, cotton, or rayon.

gab·ble (găb´el) *v.* (**-bled, -bling**). Talk volubly or inarticulately; utter too fast. ~ *n.* Rapid esp. unintelligible talk. **gab´bler** *n.*

ga·ble (gā´bel) *n.* Vertical triangular upper part of wall at end of ridged roof, from level of eaves upward; triangular section over a window, door, etc. **ga´bled** *adj.*

Ga·bon (găbŏn´; *Fr.* găbawṅ´). Republic in W. Africa; formerly a territory of French Equatorial Africa; independent since 1960; capital, Libreville. **Gab·on·ese** (găbonēz´, -nēs´) *adj. & n.*

Gab·o·ro·ne (găborō´ne). Capital of Botswana, in the SE. part.

Ga·bri·el (gā´brēel). One of the seven archangels enumerated in the "Book of Enoch," a messenger of God (Dan. 8, Luke I); in Muslim religion, one of the 4 principal angels.

Gad (găd). Hebrew patriarch, son of Jacob and Zilpah (Gen. 30); tribe of Israel, traditionally descended from him.

gad (găd) *v.i.* (**gad·ded, gad·ding**). (usu. ~ **about**) Go *about* seeking entertainment; rove, wander.

half-timbered gable   finial   dutch gable   gable with corbie stones or crow steps

barge-board

pendant

The ornamentation of the **gables** of houses has long been practiced and the feature reached a new level of importance in 17th-century Dutch town houses. Here the gables rise in regular

waves along the terraces of a Amsterdam street. Hooks were commonly built into the gables for the convenience of hoisting furniture in and out of windows.

gad·a·bout (găd´abowt) *adj. & n.* (Person) given to gadding about.

gad·fly (găd´flī) *n.* (pl. **-flies**). Fly that bites and goads cattle, esp. one of the family Tabanidae; irritating or harassing person.

gadg·et (găj´ĭt) *n.* (orig. naut.) Small fitting, contrivance, or piece of mechanism; device.

ga·doid (gā´doid) *adj. & n.* (Fish) of the cod family (Gadidae).

gad·o·lin·i·um (gădolĭn´ēum) *n.* (chem.) Metallic element of rare-

earth group; symbol Gd, at. no. 6. at. wt. 157.25. [J. *Gadolin* (1760 1852), Finnish mineralogist]

Gads·den (gădz´den), **Jame** (1788–1858). Amer. railroa promoter and statesman; U.S minister to Mexico, 1853–54; i 1853 he negotiated the $10,000,00 purchase (**Gadsden Purchas** from Mexico of 29,640 sq. m (76,767 sq. km), in what is now Ne Mexico and Arizona.

Gae·a (jē´a). (Gk. myth

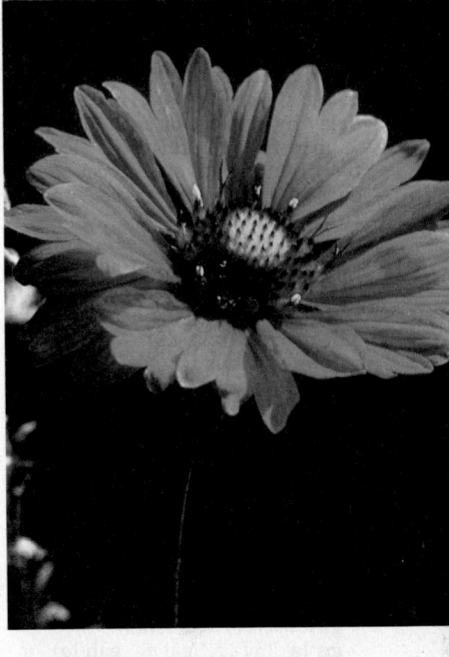

The red, yellow or purple flowers of the **gaillardia** make a brilliant display. In the U.S. they grow in such profusion as to warrant the name of blanket flower.

A swarm of **gadflies** can distress cattle with their stinging bites to the point where the cattle stampede. Here two gadflies feed on an animal.

republic of approximately 520,000 people, **Gabon** has an area of 102,000 sq. miles. Until 1815, it was an infamous center of the slave trade. The late Dr. Albert Schweitzer's leper hospital was at Lambarene in western Gabon.

Personification of the earth.

Gael (gāl) n. Scottish or Irish Celt. **Gael'ic** adj. & n. (Language) of the Celtic inhabitants of Scottish highlands, or of the branch of Celts including Scottish, Irish, and Manx Celts.

Gael. abbrev. Gaelic.

gaff (găf) n. 1. Barbed fishing spear; stick with iron hook for landing large fish. 2. (naut.) Spar used to extend fore-and-aft sails not set on stays; **stand the ~**, (slang) endure difficulties. **gaff** v.t. Seize (fish) with gaff.

gaffe (găf) n. Blunder, indiscreet act or remark, faux pas. [Fr.]

gaf·fer (găf'er) n. Elderly rustic, old fellow. [contr. of godfather, gaby assoc. w. grandfather]

gag (găg) n. 1. Thing thrust into mouth to prevent speech or outcry; obstacle to or censorship of free speech; closure. 2. Joke. ~ v. (**gagged, gag·ging**). 1. Apply gag to; silence, deprive of free speech. 2. Joke. 3. Retch; choke.

ga·ga (gah'gah) n. Senile, doting; silly, inane, fatuous.

Ga·ga·rin (gagar'ĭn), **Yuri** **Alekseyevich** (1934–68). Russian cosmonaut and first man to orbit Earth, 1961.

gage[1] (gāj) n. Pledge, thing deposited as security; (glove thrown down as, any symbol of) challenge to fight; challenge, test. ~ v. (**gaged, gag·ing**).

gage[2] = GAUGE.

gage[3] (gāj) = greengage: see GREEN.

gag·gle (găg'el) n. Flock (of geese). ~ v.i. (**-gled, -gling**). (of geese) Make clucking sound.

gai·e·ty (gā'etē) n. (pl. **-ties**). Being gay or merry; mirth; merry-making, festivity; bright or showy appearance.

gail·lar·di·a (gālär'dēa) n. Showy-flowered composite plant of genus G~ of western N. Amer., with yellow- or red-rayed flowers. [Gaillard de Marentonneau, Fr. botanist]

gai·ly (gā'lē): see GAY.

gain (gān) n. Increase of possessions, advantage, etc., of any kind; profit, improvement; acquisition of wealth; increase in amount; (pl.) sums acquired by trade etc., emoluments, winnings. ~ v. Obtain, secure (desired or advantageous thing); win (sum) as profits etc.; earn; make a profit, be benefited, improve or advance in some respect; be enhanced by comparison or contrast; win (battle, victory); bring over to one's interests or views; reach, arrive at (desired place); (of clock etc.) become fast; ~ **the ear of**, get favorable hearing from; ~ **on**, get closer to (person or thing pursued); ~ **time**, obtain delay by pretexts or slow methods.

gain·ful (gān′fŭl) *adj.* Lucrative, remunerative; (of occupation etc.) paid. **gain′ful·ness** *n.* **gain′-ful·ly** *adv.*

gain·say (gān′sā) *v.t.* (**-said, -say·ing**). Deny, contradict.

Gains·bor·ough (gānz′bēr̄ō, -bŭrō; *Brit.* gānz′bero, -bro), **Thomas** (1727–88). English painter; famous for portraits.

gait (gāt) *n.* Manner of walking; bearing or carriage as one walks. **gait′ed** *adj.*

gai·ter (gā′ter) *n.* Covering of cloth, leather, etc., for ankle, or ankle and lower leg.

gal (găl) *n.* (colloq.) Woman or girl.

Gal. *abbrev.* Galatians (New Testament).

gal. *abbrev.* Gallon(s).

ga·la (gā′la, găl′a, gah′la) *n.* Festive occasion, fête.

ga·lac·tic (galăk′tĭk) *adj.* (astron.) Of a galaxy; of the Milky Way.

Gal·a·had (găl′ahăd), **Sir.** In Arthurian legend, knight of immaculate purity, destined to retrieve the Holy Grail.

gal·an·tine (găl′antēn, gălan-tēn′) *n.* Dish of meat or fish, boned, stuffed, boiled, and served cold in aspic.

Ga·lá·pa·gos (galah′pagōs) **Islands (Colón Archipelago).** Pacific Ocean island group, a province of Ecuador, encompassing 2,966 sq. mi. (7,681 sq. km), located 650 mi. (1,046 km) W. of mainland on the equator; capital San Cristobal; famous for species of almost extinct giant tortoise; site of study of species and fossils conducted by Charles Darwin in his research on evolution.

Gal·a·te·a (gălatē′a). (Gk. myth.) Statue of a woman brought to life by Aphrodite in answer to the prayers of its sculptor, Pygmalion, who had fallen in love with it.

Ga·la·tia (galā′sha). Ancient region of central Asia Minor, centered about modern-day Ankara, Turkey.

Ga·la·tian (galā′shan) *adj.* Of Galatia. ~ *n.* One of its inhabitants, believed to have been Gauls who settled there in the 3rd c. B.C.; (**Epistle to the**) ~**s**, book of New Testament, epistle of St. Paul to the Christians of Galatia about 58 A.D.

gal·ax·y (găl′aksē) *n.* (pl. **-ax·ies**). 1. One of the independent systems of stars and other matter existing in space, esp. (**G**~) group containing the solar system. 2. **G**~, Milky Way. 3. (fig.) Brilliant

The Edge-on **Galaxy** *is one of many elliptical galaxies in the universe. They are generally the largest galaxies, and seem to contain no young stars, or interstellar dust from which stars could form.*

company or assemblage (of). [Gk. *gala* milk]

gale¹ (gāl) *n.* (also **sweet** ~). Bog myrtle.

gale² (gāl) *n.* 1. Strong wind; (naut.) storm; (meteor.) wind of speed between 32 and 63 mi. per hour; ~ **warning**, notice of probability of gales issued by the weather bureau. 2. Gust, outburst, esp. of laughter.

Ga·len (gā′len). Claudius Galenus (*c*130–*c*201 A.D.), Greek physician and writer on medicine; practiced in Rome; physician to emperor Marcus Aurelius. **Ga·len·ic** (gālĕn′ĭk, ga-), **Ga·len′i·cal** *adjs.* Of, according to, Galen; (of remedies) made of vegetable, not chemical, components.

ga·le·na (galē′na), **ga·le·nite** (galē′nīt) *ns.* (min.) Lead sulfide, the common ore of lead (PbS).

Ga·li·cia¹ (galĭsh′a, -lē′shēa Span. gahlē′thyah). Region and ancient kingdom of NW. Spain **Ga·li′cian** *adj. & n.*

Ga·li·cia² (galĭsh′a; *Yid.* galĭt′-sēa). Former Austrian crown land. now divided between Poland and U.S.S.R.; includes the city o Kraków.

Gal·i·lee (găl′ilē). Northern hilly part of ancient Palestine, W. of the Jordan (now in Israel); **Sea of** ~ (also called Sea of Tiberias and Lake of Gennesaret), freshwater lake in NE. Israel on Syrian border, fed by Jordan River; 696 ft. (212 m) below sea level. **Gal·i·le·an¹** (gălĭlē′an) *adj. & n.*

Gal·i·le·o (gălĭlā′ō, -lē′ō). Galileo Galilei (1564–1642), Italian astronomer and physicist; discovered the four most prominent satellites of Jupiter, the libration of the moon, etc.; his observations brought him into conflict with the Inquisition and he was compelled to repudiate the Copernican theory. **Gal·i·le·an²** (gălĭlē′an) *adj.* (of telescope) Of the form invented by Galileo, a refracting telescope with *center of Judaism after the fall of ~rusalem in A.D. 70,* **Galilee** *became ~e center for Zionism in the 19th cen-~ry. The Sea of Galilee is a freshwater ~ke.*

The Metropolitan Museum of Art, a highly respected **gallery** *on the corner of 5th and 82nd Streets, New York, draws viewers from many parts of the world.*

A **gall** *can be formed by the larvae of various insects including flies and wasps. They remain within this plant tissue for most of their life cycle and emerge when mature.*

~ncave eyepiece.

gall[1] (gawl) *n.* Bitter greenish ~cretion of the liver, bile (now only ~ lower animals); gallbladder and ~s contents; (fig.) anything bitter; ~perity, rancor; impudence; **gall'-~ladder,** vessel containing the gall ~ bile; **gall'stone,** calculus or ~one in gallbladder.

gall[2] (gawl) *n.* Painful swelling, ~ustule, blister, esp. in horse; sore ~roduced by chafing; mental sore-~ess or irritation; something galling ~ exasperating; place rubbed bare. ~ *v.* Rub sore, injure by rubbing; ~ex, humiliate. **gall'ing** *adj.* ~all'ing·ly *adv.*

gall[3] (gawl) *n.* Excrescence ~roduced on trees by deposition of

the eggs of mites or insects; **gall'fly** *n.* (pl. **-flies**), insect causing galls.

Gal·la (găl'a) *n.* (pl. **-las**, collect. **-la**). One of a group of largely pastoral Hamitic tribes of S. Ethiopia and the Somali Republic, allied to Ethiopians in language and origin.

gal·lant (găl'ant; esp. for def. 3 galănt', -lahnt') *adj.* 1. Fine, stately (esp. of ship, horse, etc.). 2. Brave, chivalrous. 3. Markedly attentive to women; amatory. **gal'lant·ly** *adv.* **gallant** (galănt', -lahnt', găl'ant) *n.* Man of fashion; ladies' man; paramour. ~ (galănt', -lahnt') *v.* Play the gallant, flirt (with); escort.

gal·lant·ry (găl'antrē) *n.* (pl. **-ries**). 1. Bravery, dashing courage. 2. Courtliness, devotion to women; polite or amorous act or speech; conduct of a gallant.

gal·le·on (găl'ēon, găl'yon) *n.* (hist.) Large three-masted, multi-decked sailing ship of the 15th and 16th centuries, used as a trading ship and warship, esp. by Spain.

gal·ler·y (găl'erē, găl'rē) *n.* (pl. **-ries**). 1. Covered space for walking, partly open at side; portico, colonnade; balcony; long narrow passage in thickness of wall or supported on corbels, open toward interior of building. 2. Platform projecting from inner wall of church, hall, etc., providing extra

*The **galley** of a ship is equipped to enable the cook to produce meals even when the ship is rolling. Top: The galley of a reconstruction of the 17th century barque, 'Mayflower'.*

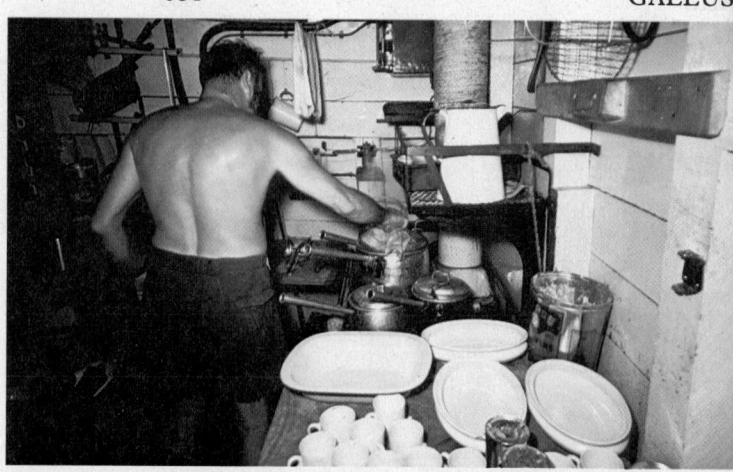

room for spectators etc. or reserved for musicians etc.; highest of such balconies in theater, containing cheapest seats; persons seated there, least refined part of audience; group of spectators at golf match etc.; **play to the ~**, appeal to lower taste. 3. Long narrow room, passage, corridor; room or building used for showing works of art. 4. (mil., mining) Underground horizontal or nearly horizontal passage. 5. Ornamental parapet or railing along edge of table, shelf, etc. **gallery** v. (**-ler·ied, -ler·y·ing**). Provide, pierce, etc., with gallery or galleries.

gal·ley (găl′ē) n. (pl. **-leys**). 1. (chiefly hist.) Low flat single-decked seagoing vessel using sails and oars, and usu. rowed by slaves or criminals (**~ slaves**). 2. Greek or Roman warship with one or more banks of oars. 3. Kitchen on ship or aircraft. 4. (print.) Oblong tray for holding type that has been set; corresponding part of composing machine. 5. (also **~ proof**) Printer's proof taken from type in galley.

Gal·lic (găl′ĭk) adj. 1. Of the Gauls or Gaul, Gaulish. 2. French. **Gal·li·cism, gallicism** (găl′ĭsĭz-em) ns. 1. French idiom or phrase used in another language. 2. French characteristic, custom, etc. **gal·li·cize** (găl′ĭsīz) v. (**-cized, -ciz·ing**).

Gal·li·can (găl′ĭkan) adj. & n. Of the French R. C. Ch.; (member) of the French Roman Catholics who maintained the right of the French Church to be in certain respects free from papal control (opp. ULTRAMONTANE). **Gal′li·can·ism** n.

gal·li·mau·fry (găl*i*maw′frē) n. (pl. **-fries**). Heterogeneous mixture, jumble, medley; hash.

gal·li·na·ceous (găl*i*nā′sh*u*s) adj. (zool.) Of the order Galliformes, including domestic poultry, pheasants, partridges, turkeys, etc.

Ga·lli·nas (gahyē′nahs), **Point.** Cape in N. central Colombia, northermost point of S. Amer.

gal·li·nule (găl′*i*nool, -nūl) n. Any of various wading birds of genera *Gallinula* and *Porphyrula*, with long webless toes and glossy plumage.

Gal·lip·o·li (gal*i*p′olē). Peninsula of European Turkey, 63 mi. (101 km) long, between the Dardanelles and the Aegean.

gal·li·um (găl′ēum) n. (chem.) Rare bluish-white metallic element found in some zinc and aluminum minerals, remarkable for its extremely low melting point (29° C); symbol Ga, at. no. 31, at. wt. 69.72. [L. *gallus* cock, transl. of *Lecoq* de

Boisbaudran, its discoverer, 1875]

gal·li·vant, gal·a·vant (găl′ivănt) vbs.i. Gad about.

gal·lon (găl′on) n. Unit of liquid capacity equal to 4 quarts or 3.785 liters.

gal·lop (găl′op) n. Horse's or other quadruped's fastest pace (though slower than a run) with all feet off ground together in each stride; a ride at this pace; (fig.) any speedy action. **~** v. Go at a gallop; make (horse etc.) gallop; read, speak, very fast; move or progress rapidly. **gal′lop·er** n.

Gal·lo-Ro·man (găl′ō rō′man) adj. & n. (Inhabitant) of Gaul when it formed part of Roman Empire.

gal·lows (găl′ōz) n.pl. (pl. **-lows·es, -lows**). (usu. considered

*Above: 'Nonsuch II', a reconstruction of a **galleon**, undergoing sea trials off Falmouth, Cornwall, U.K. Galleons were formidable gun ships but could be outmaneuvered by smaller ships.*

sing.) Structure, usu. of two uprights and crosspiece, on which criminals may be hanged; similar structure for other uses; punishment of hanging; **~ bird**, person fit to be hanged; **~ humor**, grim and ironical humor.

Gal·lup (găl′up) **poll.** Poll taken from a cross section of the inhabitants of a country or region in order to ascertain public opinion on a topic. [after G. H. *Gallup* (1901–), Amer. statistician]

gal·lus·es (găl′usĭz) n.pl. (colloq.) Trouser suspenders.

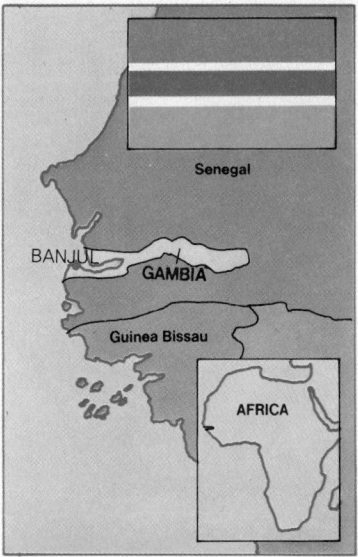

The republic of **Gambia** has a population of 510,000. Most of the people are engaged in agriculture and produce the main export crops of peanuts and palm kernels. Above: Map and flag of Gambia. Left: A shark cleaned on the beach.

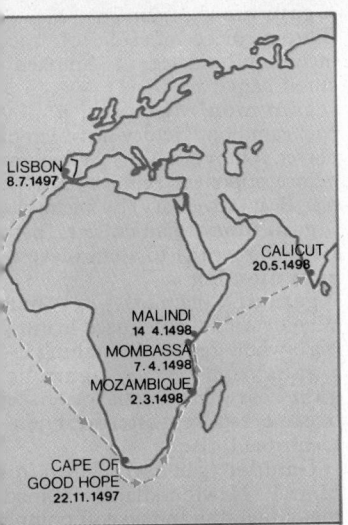

The map of the voyages of **Vasco da Gama** indicates the enormous range of his achievement. He was the first European to reach India by sea when he arrived at Calicut in 1498 and again in 1503.

(-**nized, -niz·ing**). 1. Stimulate to activity by or as by electricity, rouse by shock or excitement. 2. Coat iron or steel with rust-resistant zinc (usu. without the use of electricity) to protect it from rust. **gal·va·ni·za·tion** (gălvănĭzā'shon) *n.*

gal·va·nom·e·ter (gălvanŏm'-eter) *n.* Apparatus for detecting and measuring small electric currents.

Gal·ves·ton (găl'veston). Port on E. end of Galveston Island at mouth of Galveston Bay off SE. Texas.

Gal·way (gawl'wā). County of W. central Ireland; ~ **Bay**, Atlantic Ocean inlet extending 20 mi. (32 km) inland between counties Galway and Clare in W. central Ireland.

gam (găm) *n.* (slang) Person's leg, esp. a woman's attractive leg.

Ga·ma (gah'ma, găm'a), **Vasco da** (*c*1469–1524). Portuguese navigator; he was the first European to sail around the Cape of Good Hope (1497) and to reach India by sea.

Gam·bi·a (găm'bēa). (also **The** ~) W. African republic on river Gambia; former Brit. colony; independent, 1965; capital, Banjul. **Gam'bi·an** *adj. & n.*

gam·bir, gam·bier (găm'bēr) *ns.* Astringent extract of Asiatic plant (*Uncaria gambir*) used in tanning etc. [Malay *gambir*, the plant]

gam·bit (găm'bĭt) *n.* Chess opening in which player sacrifices pawn or pieces to obtain some advantage over opponent; opening move in discussion etc. [It. *gambetto* tripping up (*gamba* leg)]

and playwright; author of *The Forsyte Saga* etc.

Gal·ton (gawl'ton), **Sir Francis** (1822–1911). British meteorologist and anthropologist; founded science of eugenics; his work on the markings of fingertips led to the adoption of fingerprint identification of criminals.

ga·lumph (galŭmf') *v.i.* Go prancing exultantly. [coined by Lewis Carroll, perh. f. *gallop, triumph*]

galv. *abbrev.* Galvanized.

Gal·va·ni (gahlvah'nē), **Luigi** (1737–98). Italian scientist; discoverer of electricity produced by chemical action.

gal·van·ic (gălvăn'ĭk) *adj.* Of, produced by, suggestive of, galvanism; ~ **battery**, battery of primary cells used in galvanism.

gal·va·nism (găl'vanĭzem) *n.* Direct-current electricity, usu. from a primary battery or other chemical source.

gal·va·nize (găl'vanĭz) *v.t.*

gal·op (găl'op) *n.* Lively 19th c. dance in ¾ time. ~ *v.i.* Dance a galop.

ga·lore (galōr', -lór') *adv. & n.* (n) abundance. [Ir. *go leór* to sufficiency]

ga·losh, ga·loshe (galŏsh') *ns.* Waterproof overshoe usu. of rubber.

Gals·wor·thy (gawlz'wērdhē), John (1867–1933). English novelist

'Mahatma' Gandhi, Indian political and spiritual leader. His frail figure and advocacy of passive resistance belied his political strength and determination to liberate India from British rule.

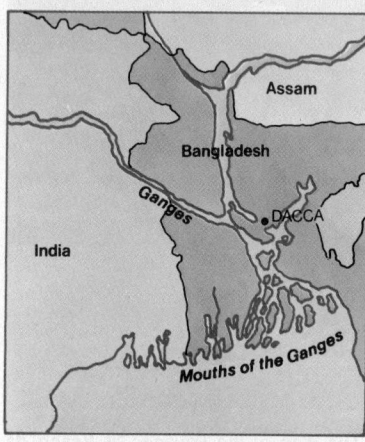

The sacred river of the Hindus, t Ganges flows through the sacred c of Benares. Above: A funeral py burns on the river bank before t ashes are cast into the river. Left: T map of the Ganges shows its de where it flows into the Bay of Beng

gam·ble (găm′bel) v. (**-bled, -bling**). Play games of chance for money; risk, chance, take a chance on (freq. fig.); ~ **away**, lose by gambling. **gamble** n. Gambling; risky undertaking or attempt. **gam′bler** n.

gam·boge (gămbōj′, -boozh′) n. Gum resin from various Asiatic trees of genus *Garcinia*, used as pigment giving bright yellow color. [f. *Cambodia*]

gam·bol (găm′bol) n. & v.i. (**-boled, -bol·ing, -bolled, -bol′-ling**). Caper; skip(ping) about.

game¹ (găm) n. 1. Diversion, pastime; bit of fun. 2. Contest played according to rules and decided by skill, strength, or luck; (pl., Gk. and Rom. antiq.) athletic, dramatic, and musical contests, gladiatorial etc. shows; (pl.) organized athletics in school etc. 3. Scheme, undertaking, etc., followed up like a game; (also ~ **plan**) policy, plan of action; (pl.) dodges, tricks. 4. Single round in some contests, e.g. tennis; winning score in game. 5. Person's normal standard of play; **on, off, one's** ~, playing well, badly. 6. Object of chase, animal(s) hunted; object of pursuit; (collect.) wild animals or birds hunted for sport or food, flesh of these. 7. **game′bag**, bag for holding game killed by sportsman; **game′cock**, cock bred and trained for fighting, or of breed suitable for cockfighting; ~ **fish**, any edible fish caught by anglers for sport; **game′keeper**, man employed to take care of game, prevent poaching etc; **games′manship**, art of winning unfairly but without breaking rules; **game point**, point that enables scorer to win game, as in

tennis; **game theory**, mathematical analysis of conflicts in war, economics, games of skill, etc. **game** adj. (**gam·er, gam·est**). Pertaining to animals hunted for sport; like a gamecock, spirited; having the spirit *for*. **game′ly** adv. **game′ness** n. **game** v. (**gamed, gam·ing**). Play at games of chance for money, gamble; throw *away* in gambling; **gaming house**, house frequented for gambling; so **gaming table**.

game² (găm) adj. (of limb) Lame, crippled.

game·some (găm′som) adj. Sportive. **game′some·ly** adv. **game′some·ness** n.

game·ster (găm′ster) n. Gambler.

gam·ete (găm′ēt, gamēt′) n. Protoplasmic body capable of uniting with another to form new individual; mature sexual cell, **ga·met·ic** (gamĕt′ĭk) adj.

gam·in (găm′ĭn) n. (fem. **gam·-ine** pr. gămēn′). Street urchin; waif; mischievous child. [Fr.]

gam·ma (găm′a) n. 1. Third letter of Greek alphabet (Γ, γ) corresponding to g, used in enumerations etc. 2. ~ **globulin**,

globulin fraction containing ma antibodies present in the origir serum; ~ **rays**, electromagne radiations of very short waveleng emitted by radioactive substance orig. regarded as the 3rd and mo penetrating kind of rays emitted radium (see ALPHA, BETA) but no known to be identical with ve short X-rays.

gam·mon¹ (găm′on) n. Bottom piece of side of baco including hind leg. 2. Smoked cured ham.

gam·mon² (găm′on) n. backgammon, victory in which o player removes all his or her m before opponent removes any. v.t. Beat (adversary) by a gammor

gam·mon³ (găm′on) v.t. (naut Lash (bowsprit) to stem of vesse **gam′mon·ing** n.

gam·ut (găm′ut) n. (mus Whole series of notes used in musi (fig.) whole range of anything.

gam·y (gā′mē) adj. (**gam·i·e gam·i·est**). Having flavor or scen of game, esp. kept after freshness lost; ribald, risqué.

Gan·der (găn′der). Town in central Newfoundland, Canad major fuel stop and takeoff point fe transatlantic flights to Europe, ar site of U.S. air base.

gan·der (găn′der) n. Male goos

Gan·dhi (gahn′dē, găn′-**Indira Nehru** (1917–). Prim minister of India, 1966–77; 1979 daughter of Jawaharlal Nehr Congress Party leader.

Gan·dhi (gahn′dē), **Mohanda Karamchand**, called "Mahatma (1869–1948). Indian nationali and spiritual leader; originator

Below: the **gannet** dives on to fish that are its prey and pursues them underwater. Tropical and sub-tropical gannets are called boobies. Left: Gannets lay their eggs on ledges and their chicks are well camouflaged.

ssive resistance as a form of political action.

gang (găng) *n.* 1. Group of workers working together; group of aves or prisoners; band of persons ting or going about together, esp. r criminal purpose or one disproved of by speaker. 2. Set of ols etc. arranged to work multaneously; **chain** ~: see HAIN; **gang'land**, domain of ngsters. **gang** *v.i.* ~ **up (on)**, olloq.) combine (against).

Gan·ges (găn'jēz). River in NE. dia flowing SE. 1,557 mi. (2,506 n) from the Himalaya Mountains the Bay of Bengal, held sacred by indus.

gan·gling (găng'glĭng) *adj.* Tall, in, and ungraceful; lanky.

gan·gli·on (găng'glēon) *n.* (pl. li·a pr. -glēa, **-gli·ons**). 1. nlargement or knot on nerve rming center for reception and ansmission of impulses. 2. (path.) yst-like swelling on tendon. **an'gli·on·at·ed, gan·gli·on·ic** ănggleŏn'ĭk) *adjs.*

gang·plank (găng'plăngk) *n.* Movable plank usu. with cleats ailed on it for walking into or out f boat etc.

gan·grene (găng'grēn, găng-rēn') *n.* Local death and decay of ody tissue caused by obstruction f the blood circulation. ~ *v.* **-grened, -gren·ing**). Become ffected, affect, with gangrene. **an·gre·nous** (găng'grenus) *adj.*

gang·ster (găng'ster) *n.* Member f gang of criminals. **gang'ster·-sm** *n.*

gang·way (găng'wā) *n.* Passage, sp. between rows of seats; passage tc. on ship, esp. platform con-ecting quarterdeck and forecastle; pening in bulwarks by which ship entered or left, bridge laid across om this to shore etc.

gan·net (găn'ĭt) *n.* (pl. **-nets**, ollect. **-net**). Any of several large hite seabirds of family Sulidae, ith black-tipped wings and edge-shaped tail, esp. *Monus*

bassanus of N. Atlantic coastal waters.

gan·oid (găn'oid) *adj.* (of fish scales) Armorlike, covered with layers of dentine and enamel and therefore shiny; (of fish) having such scales. ~ *n.* Fish with ganoid scales, as the sturgeon, gar, etc.

Gan·su (gahn'sōō') = KANSU.

gant·let (gănt'lĭt, gawnt'-) = GAUNTLET[2].

gan·try (găn'trē) *n.* (pl. **-tries**). Four-footed wooden stand for barrels; structure supporting traveling crane, railroad signals, equipment to prepare rocket for launching, etc.

Gan·y·mede (găn'ĭmēd). 1. (Gk. myth.) Trojan youth, so beautiful that Zeus caused an eagle to carry him up to heaven and made him his cupbearer. 2. (astron.) Fourth and largest moon of the planet Jupiter. 3. (usu. **g** ~) Young barman or waiter who serves alcoholic drinks.

GAO *abbrev.* General Accounting Office.

gaol (jāl) *n.* (Brit.) JAIL. **gaol'er** *n.*

gap (găp) *n.* Breach in hedge or wall; gorge, pass; unfilled space or interval, blank; break in continuity; wide divergence in views, sympathies, etc. **gapped'** *adj.*

gape (gāp) *v.i.* (**gaped, gap'-**

ing). Open mouth wide; open or be open wide, split, part asunder; stare, gaze curiously, *at*; yawn. ~ *n.* Yawn; open-mouthed stare; expanse of open mouth or beak, part of beak that opens; ~**s**, disease of poultry and some wild birds constituted by the presence of **gape'worm** (*Syngamus trachea*) in the trachea, the obstruction caused by which makes the birds gape or gasp for breath. **gap'er** *n.* **gap'ing·ly** *adv.*

gar (gär) *n.* (pl. **gars**, collect. **gar**). (also **gar'fish, gar'pike**) 1. Fish of family Belonidae, allied to flying fish; needlefish. 2. N. and Central Amer. fresh-water fish of the ganoid genus *Lepisosteus* with lozenge-shaped scales, bony pike; **alligator** ~, large species of this living in rivers of southern U.S. with head resembling alligator's.

G.A.R. *abbrev.* Grand Army of the Republic.

ga·rage (garahzh', -rahj'; *Brit.* găr'ĭj, -ahzh) *n.* Building or establishment for storing or repair of motor vehicles; ~ **sale**, sale, usu. in garage, of one's unwanted

*The **gar** or gar pike is a primitive fish found in lakes and rivers of N. America. Lurking in weeds much of the time, it rushes from cover to capture smaller fish.*

The formal **garden** at Hampton Court, London, U.K. laid out geometrically with flower beds, gravelled or paved walks and topiary, is typical of those gardens conceived as natural cloisters for conversation.

furniture, kitchen utensils, clothing, etc. **garage** *v.t.* (**-raged, -rag·ing**). Put (car etc.) into a garage.

garb (gārb) *n.* Dress, costume, esp. distinctive attire of one's occupation or calling; appearance. ~ *v.t.* Attire, put (esp. distinctive) clothes upon.

gar·bage (gār′bĭj) *n.* Kitchen waste; refuse; rubbish (also fig.)

gar·ban·zo (gārbăn′zō, -bahn′-) *n.* (pl. **-zos**): see CHICKPEA.

gar·ble (gār′bel) *v.t.* (**-bled, -bling**). Make (usu. unfair or malicious) selections from (facts, statements, etc.); distort; scramble. [Arab. *ḡarbala* sift, select]

Gar·ci·a Lor·ca (gārsē′*a* lōr′ka), **Federico** (1899–1936). Spanish poet and playwright; considered the greatest 20-c. Spanish poet, murdered by Falangists during the Spanish Civil War.

gar·çon (gărsawṅ′) *n.* (pl. **-çons** pr. -sawṅ′). Waiter in French restaurant, hotel, etc. [Fr.]

Gar·da (gār′da) **Lake.** Italy's largest lake, 143 sq. mi. (370 sq. km), in the N. part.

gar·dant = GUARDANT.

gar·den (gār′den) *n.* Piece of ground devoted to growing flowers, fruit, or vegetables; (pl.) ornamental grounds for public resort; ~ **party**, outdoor party or social gathering on lawn or in garden. **garden** *adj.* Of, pertaining to, or grown in a garden; ~ **variety**, (colloq.) ordinary, common. **garden** *v.i.* Cultivate, work in, a garden. **gar′den·er** *n.* One who gardens; person employed to tend garden.

gar·de·nia (gārdēn′ya) *n.* Tree or shrub of genus *G*~ of tropical Asia and Africa, bearing large white or yellow, usu. fragrant, flowers; flower of one of these. [Dr. Alexander *Garden* (1731–90), Scottish naturalist]

Gar·field (gār′fēld), **James Abram** (1831–81). Twentieth president of U.S., 1881; shot by Charles J. Guiteau on July 2, 1881, and died Sept. 19, 1881.

gar·fish (gār′fĭsh) *n.* (pl. **-fish·es**, collect. **-fish**) = GAR.

gar·gan·tu·an (gārgăn′chōoan) *adj.* Enormous, gigantic. [*Gargantua*, giant king with enormous physical and intellectual appetites, the hero of Rabelais' satirical romance *Gargantua and Pantagruel*]

gar·gle (gār′gel) *v.* (**-gled, -gling**). Wash (throat or mouth) with liquid held suspended in throat and kept in motion by breath; wash mouth or throat thus. ~ *n.*

Liquid used for gargling.

gar·goyle (gār′goil) *n.* Grotesque waterspout usu. with human or animal mouth, head, or body, projecting from gutter of (esp. Gothic) building to carry water clear of wall.

Gar·i·bal·di (gărɪbawl′dē, -băl′-), **Giuseppe** (1807–82). Italian general and nationalist leader; hero of the RISORGIMENTO; commanded a volunteer force for Sardinia against Austria, 1859; organized expeditions by which he conquered Sicily; expelled Francis II from Naples; and finally marched (unsuccessfully) against Rome, 1860–2.

gar·ish (găr′ish, gār′-) *adj.* Obtrusively bright, gaudy. **gar′ish·ly** *adv.* **gar′ish·ness** *n.*

gar·land (gār′land) *n.* Wreath of

The use of **gargoyles** to carry wate spouts clear of the sides of mediev churches may have had the dual pu pose of avoiding damp penetrating th walls and scaring demons, as at th church of Notre Dame, Paris.

flowers, leaves, etc., worn on hea or hung on something as decora tion; distinction, prize, for victor etc.; representation of garland i metal etc.; (archaic) anthology miscellany. ~ *v.t.* Crown wit garland; deck with garlands; serv as garland to.

gar·lic (gār′lĭk) *n.* Plant of genu *Allium* (usu. *A. sativum*) wit strong-smelling pungent-tastin bulbs used as a seasoning. **gar′ lick·y** *adj.*

gar·ment (gār′ment) *n.* Articl of dress; (pl.) clothes.

gar·ner (gār′ner) *n.* Granary

v.t. Gather and store; acquire, ollect (usu. fig.).

Gar·ner (gär´ner), **John Nance** 868–1967). Amer. politician; peaker of the House of Representatives, 1931–3; vice president nder Franklin D. Roosevelt, 933–41.

gar·net (gär´nĭt) *n.* Vitreous ineral, occurring as a 12-sided rystal of which the deep red ansparent variety is used as a gem. ned. L. *granatum* pomegranate (f. esemblance to its seeds)]

gar·nish (gär´nĭsh) *v.t.* Decoate, embellish (esp. dish for table). *n.* Decorative or savory ddition to dish for table. **gar´ ish·er, gar´nish·ment** *ns.*

gar·nish·ee (gär´nĭshē´) *v.t.* nish·eed, -nish·ee·ing). Serve otice on (person) for purpose of ttaching money, such as pay, elonging to debtor; attach (money, ay) thus. ~ *n.* Person in whose ands money belonging to debtor attached.

gar·ret (găr´ĭt) = ATTIC, def. 2.

Gar·rick (găr´ĭk), **David** (1717– 779). Actor-manager of Drury ane Theatre, London.

gar·ri·son (găr´ĭson) *n.* Troops ationed in fortress, town, etc., to efend it; military post. ~ *v.t.* urnish with, occupy as, garrison; lace (troops, soldier) on garrison uty.

Gar·ri·son (găr´ĭson), **William** loyd (1805–79). Amer. abolitiont leader and editor; founder of *The iberator*, a weekly newspaper ublished from 1831–65, denouncg slavery; founder, 1833, and resident, 1843–65, of the Amerian Anti-Slavery Society; editor of *ation*, 1865–1906.

gar·rote, ga·rotte, gar·rotte garōt´, -rŏt´) *ns.* Spanish method f capital punishment by strangulaon; instrument used in it with pparatus for strangling, later with rass collar fitted with a sharp point at pierces the spinal cord; robbery erformed by throttling victim. **arrote** *v.t.* (-rot·ed, -rot·ing, rot·ted, -rot·ting). Execute or ill by strangulation; throttle in rder to rob. **gar·rot´er** *n.*

gar·ru·lous (găr´ulus, -yulus) dj. Talkative, wordy. **gar´ru· ous·ly** *adv.* **gar´ru·lous·ness, ar·ru·li·ty** (garōo´lĭtē) *ns.*

gar·ter (gär´ter) *n.* Band worn bove or below knee to keep tocking up or as ornament; **the** ĭ ~, badge (dark blue velvet ribbon dged and buckled with gold, worn elow knee) of highest order of nglish knighthood, instituted 1344; membership of this order, he order itself. ~ *v.t.* Fasten stocking), encircle (leg), with arter.

garter (gär´ter) **snake.** Any f numerous small harmless N.

*The flowers of the **garlic** (Allium sativum) emerge from clustered bulbils. The bulb of the plant is used as a flavoring. When eaten by cattle, wild garlic (Allium vineale) spoils their milk.*

Amer. snakes of the genus *Thamnophis*, often having longitudinal stripes along the back.

Gar·vey (gär´vē), **Marcus** (1887–1940). Jamaican-born Amer. black leader; founder of Universal Negro Improvement Association, 1914; advocate of racial separatism.

gas[1] (găs) *n.* (pl. **gas·es**). 1. Substance that is neither solid nor liquid, capable of expanding indefinitely when subjected to temperature and pressure changes and completely filling its container. 2. Substance(s) in gaseous state, (i) suitable to be burned for lighting, heating, or cooking, esp. natural gas; (ii) used as anesthetic, esp. in surgery; (iii) (esp. hydrogen or helium) used to inflate balloon etc.; (iv) producing asphyxiating, poisonous, or irritant atmosphere, esp. in warfare; **poison** ~, (coal mining) explosive mixture of firedamp with air. 3. (colloq.) Empty talk, boasting. 4. ~ **bag**, bag for holding gas; empty talker; airship's gas container; ~ **chamber**, place of execution by gas poisoning; ~ **fitter**, one who installs and repairs gas pipes or fixtures and appliances; **gashouse**: see GASWORKS; **gas´ light**, light from an incandescent mantle; **gas mantle**: see MANTLE; **gas mask**, device including respirator, worn over the face as protection against poison gas; **gas turbine**, gas-driven turbine, esp. one used to drive air compressor in jet-propelled aircraft; **gas´works, gas´house**, factory producing gas for lighting and heating. **gas** *v.* (**gassed, gas·sing**). 1. Supply, treat, with gas. 2. Project poison gas upon (enemy, place); (pass.) be poisoned with gas. 3. Talk emptily or boastfully. **gas·e·ous** (găs´ēus, găsh´us) *adj.* [wd invented by Van Helmont, Du. chemist, after Gk. *khaos* chaos]

gas[2] (găs) *n.* Gasoline; ~ **pedal**,

*The discovery of large deposits of natural **gas**, most of which lie in areas remote from the industries that use it, has necessitated the building of long pipelines. Here sections of pipe are being welded together.*

Heart
Pericardium
Hermaphroditic gland
Shell
Stomach
Gills
Gills
Eye
Intestine
Mouth
Pedal Gland

Gastropods *represent the most numerous class in the mollusk phyllum. Top: Brown-lipped snail (Cepaea nemoralis) has the typical helical shell and broad muscular foot of most gastropods.*

Center: Cross section of a gastropod showing the unsegmented body protected by a strong shell. Bottom, right to left: the abalone inside its shell, outer shell and pearly lining.

pedal that controls supply of g oline to internal combusti engine; ~ **station**, place whe gasoline, oil, and other supplies f motor vehicles are sold a automotive maintenance servic provided; filling station; servi station; **step on the** ~, accelera car by pressing harder on gas ped (fig.) put on speed, hurry.

Gas·con (găs′kon) *adj.* & (Native, inhabitant) of Gascon former province of SW. Franc braggart.

gas·con·ade (găskonād′) *n.* & *v* **(-ad·ed, -ad·ing).** Boast.

gash (găsh) *n.* Long and de slash, cut, or wound; cleft such might be made by slashing cut; a of making such cut. ~ *v.t.* Ma gash in; cut.

Gas·kell (găs′kel), **Mrs. Eliz beth Cleghorn** (1810–65). Engli novelist; author of *Cranford* etc.

gas·ket (găs′kĭt) *n.* Small co for securing furled sail to yar strip of hemp, asbestos, rubb metal, etc., used for packing pisto forming water- or gas-tight joint pipe, internal combustion engir etc.

gas·kin (găs′kĭn) *n.* Hind thi of horse.

gas·o·hol (găs′ohawl, -hŏl) Fuel for automobile engines, cor bining 90% gasoline and 10 alcohol.

gas·o·line, gas·o·lene (găsolē găs′olēn) *ns.* Volatile, inflammal liquid mixture of hydrocarbo obtained by fractional distillation petroleum and used mainly as a fu for internal-combustion engines.

gas·om·e·ter (găsŏm′ĭter) *n.* (Brit.) Fuel-gas storage containe esp. a large cylindrical tank. Gas-measuring apparatus.

gasp (găsp, gahsp) *v.* Cat breath, strain *for* air or breath, wi open mouth as in exhaustion astonishment; utter with gasps. *n.* Convulsive catching of breat **at one's last** ~, at point of dea (also fig.). **gasp′ing·ly** *adv.*

Gas·pé (găspā′) **Peninsul** Peninsula of SE. Quebec, Canad between Chaleur Bay N. of Ne Brunswick and the mouth of the S Lawrence River.

gas·sy (găs′ē) *adj.* **(-si·e -si·est).** Of, full of, like, gas; talk etc.) empty, verbose.

gas·tric (găs′trĭk) *adj.* Of t stomach; ~ **juice**, thin clear ac nearly colorless fluid secreted certain stomach glands and actir as agent of digestion.

gas·tri·tis (găstrī′tĭs) *n.* Inflar mation of the stomach.

gastro-, gastr- *comb. forms.* the stomach; **gastroenteri′tis**, i flammation affecting both stoma and intestines; **gastrointes′tin** of or pertaining to the stoma and intestines.

The **gauchos** of South America have pursued an independent, robust and politically active style of life. Here a gaucho, aided by companions, ropes a steer.

gas·tro·nome (găs′trɒnōm) n. nnoisseur of cookery; gourmet. s·tron·o·my (găstrŏn′omē) n. : and science of good eating. s·tron′o·mer, gas·tron′o·mist gas·tro·nom·ic (găstronŏm′-, gas·tro·nom′i·cal adjs. gas·-·nom′i·cal·ly adv.

gas·tro·pod (găs′tropŏd) n. One the Gastropoda, a class of llusks having the locomotive an placed ventrally (snails, elks, limpets, etc.).

gas·tru·la (găs′trula) n. (pl. -la). ol.) Stage in development of bryo (typically a double-layered) produced by migration of cells BLASTULA into new positions.

gat (găt) n. (slang.) Revolver or tol. [short for GATLING GUN]

gate (gāt) n. 1. Opening in wall city or enclosure, made for rance and exit and capable of ng closed with barrier; means of rance or exit. 2. Barrier closing ening of wall, wooden or metal . framework, solid or of bars or tings, hung on hinges, turning pivots, or sliding; contrivance gulating passage of water or gas ough a dam or conduit; (photog.) chanism controlling passage of n behind lens; (in computers) ctronic device, signal, etc., con-lling passage of current, select-g signals, etc. 3. Number enter-g by payment at gates to see sports test, public entertainment, etc.; ount of money thus taken. 4. crash (v.) (slang) gain entrance party, reception, etc.) without

invitation or ticket of admission; ~ **crasher** (n.); **gate′house** (pl. -houses), lodge of park etc.; (hist.) room over city gate often used as prison; room over gate of castle; **gate-leg(ged) table**, folding table with leaves supported on gate-shaped structure, which can be swung back to allow them to hang down; **gate′post**, post on which gate is hung or on which it shuts; **gate′way**, frame of or structure built over gate; any passage by which a region can be entered.

gath·er (gădh′er) v. 1. Bring or come together. 2. Pick or harvest (flowers, grain, etc.); pick up from ground; infer, deduce (that); ~ **way**, (of ship) begin to move. 3. Summon up (energies); gain or recover (breath); summon up (thoughts, strength, etc.) for an effort. 4. Draw (garment, brow) together in folds or wrinkles; pucker (part of dress) by running thread through; draw up (limbs, person) into smaller compass. 5. Come to a head, develop purulent swelling. **gather** n. (usu. pl.) Gathered part of dress. **gath′er·er** n. **gath′er·ing** n. 1. Assembly; meeting, collection, accumulation. 2. Gather in cloth or a garment.

Gat·ling (găt′lĭng) **gun.** Machine gun with cluster of barrels.

[R. J. *Gatling* (1818–1903), inventor]

GATT abbrev. General Agreement on Tariffs and Trade (treaty to which 85 countries are parties to promote trade and economic development).

Ga·tun (gahtōon′). Artificial lake, 164 sq. mi. (425 sq. km), created by the Gatun Dam in the northern Canal Zone, Panama.

gauche (gōsh) adj. Tactless; without ease or grace, socially awkward. **gauche′ly** adv. **gauche′ness** n. **gau·che·rie** (gōsheré′) n. Gauche manners; a gauche action.

gau·cho (gow′chō) n. (pl. -chos). Cowboy of South Amer. pampas.

gaud (gawd) n. Showy ornament.

gaud·y (gaw′dē) adj. (gaud·i·er, gaud·i·est). Tastelessly or inappropriately showy. **gaud′i·ly** adv. **gaud′i·ness** n.

gauge (gāj) n. 1. Standard measure to which things must conform, as measure of capacity or contents of barrel, diameter of bullet, thickness of sheet metal, etc.; distance between rails of railroad etc. 2. Graduated instrument measuring force or quantity of rainfall, stream, tide, wind, etc.; instrument for testing and verifying dimensions of tools, wire, etc.; carpenter's adjustable tool for marking parallel lines; (print.) strip regulating depth of margin etc.; means of estimating, criterion, test.

While President of France, **General de Gaulle** pursued a foreign policy that was often at variance with the wishes of his NATO allies. Here he is shown with a characteristic expression.

There are many species of **gazelle.** Most stand between two and three ft high at the shoulder. Grant's gazelle, seen here with its superb ribbed horns, was photographed in Nairobi National Park, Kenya.

'The Girl with a Fan' by **Paul Gau**(gin) shows a lingering influence of the s(ymbolism) he adopted in 1888, requiring the (use) of non-naturalistic color and flat pla(nes.) His paintings were always power(fully) designed.

~ *v.t.* (**gauged, gaug·ing**). Measure exactly (esp. objects of standard size, as wire, bolts; depth of liquid content; fluctuating quantities or forces, as rainfall, wind); find capacity or content of (cask etc.) by measurement and calculation; estimate, take measure of (person, character); make uniform, bring to standard size or shape. **gaug′er** *n.*

Gau·guin (gōgăn′), (**Eugène Henri**) **Paul** (1848–1903). French painter; spent the latter part of his life in the South Sea Islands.

Gaul (gawl). 1. Roman province of W. Europe. 2. Native or inhabitant of ancient Gaul; Frenchman.

Gaul·ish (gaw′lĭsh) *adj.* Of Gaul; French. ~ *n.* Celtic language of Gaul.

gaunt (gawnt) *adj.* Lean, haggard; grim or desolate looking. **gaunt′ly** *adv.* **gaunt′ness** *n.*

gaunt·let[1] (gawnt′lĭt) *n.* 1. (hist.) Glove worn as part of armor, usu. of leather covered with steel plates; **fling, throw, down the ~**, issue challenge; **pick, take, up the ~**, accept challenge. 2. Protective glove with long wrist or flaring cuff. **gaunt′let·ed** *adj.*

gaunt·let[2] (gawnt′lĭt, gahnt′-) *n.* **run the ~**, (orig. mil.) undergo punishment of passing between two rows of men who strike one with sticks etc.; (fig.) be subjected to criticism. [Swed. *gatlopp* (*gata* lane, *lopp* course)]

Gauss (gows), **Karl Friedrich** (1777–1855). German mathematician, astronomer, and physicist.

gauss (gows) *n.* Unit of magnetic induction in cgs system, equal to the induction that exerts a force of 1 dyne on each centimeter of a straight wire carrying 1 electromagnetic unit of current when the induction is perpendicular to the wire (abbreviated G). [f. GAUSS]

Gau·ta·ma, Go·ta·ma (gaw′tama, gow′-). Family name of the BUDDHA.

gauze (gawz) *n.* Thin transparent fabric of silk, cotton, wire, etc.; slight haze. **gauz′y** *adj.* (**gauz·i·er, gauz·i·est**). **gauz′i·ly** *adv.* **gauz′i·ness** *n.*

gav·el (găv′el) *n.* Auctioneer's or judge's mallet or hammer.

ga·vi·al (gā′vēal) *n.* Long-snouted fish-eating crocodilian inhabiting S. Asia.

ga·votte, ga·vot (gavŏt′) *ns.* French 18th c. peasant dance, like minuet but more lively; music for this, in common time.

G.A.W. *abbrev.* Guaranteed annual wage.

gawk (gawk) *n.* Awkward or bashful person. **gawk′i·ly** *adv.* **gawk·y** *adj.* (**gawk·i·er, gawk·i·est**). **gawk** *v.i.* Stare stupidly.

gay (gā) *adj.* 1. Mirthful, light-hearted. 2. Showy, bright-colo(red). 3. Dissolute, immoral. 4. (sla(ng)) Homosexual; ~ **bar**, one freque(nt)ed primarily by homosexu(als); ~ **rights**, claim for equal le(gal) treatment of homosexuals in reg(ard) to employment etc. **gai′ly** (adv.) **gay′ness** *n.*

Gay (gā), **John** (1685–17(32).) English playwright; author of (The) *Beggar's Opera.*

Gay-Lus·sac (gālusăk′), **Jos**(eph) **Louis** (1778–1850). Fre(nch) chemist; ~ **'s Law**, (i) or law (of) combining volumes, statement (that) when gases react together the(re is) always a simple numerical relati(on)ship between their volumes and (those) of the products, if gaseous (also) called "law of combining vol(umes"); (ii) = CHARLES'S LAW.

gaz. *abbrev.* Gazette; gazette(er).

Ga·za (gah′za, găz′a). Medi(ter)ranean seaport in the Gaza S(trip) near SW. Israel; ~ **Strip**, Mediterranean coastal area bord(er)ing Israel; administered by (the) United Arab Republic but subject of territorial dispute.

gaze (gāz) *v.i.* (**gazed, gaz·in**(g)). Look fixedly. ~ *n.* Intent lo(ok.) **gaz′er** *n.*

ga·ze·bo (gazē′bō) *n.* (pl. **-b**(os,) **-boes**). Structure from which (an) attractive view may be se(en;) belvedere, pavilion, etc.

ga·zelle (gazĕl′) *n.* (pl. **-zell**(es,) collect. **-zelle**). Small grace(ful)

soft-eyed delicately formed antelope esp. of genus *Gazella*, found in Asia and Africa. [Arab. *ḡazāl*]

ga·zette (gazĕt´) *n.* Newspaper; official journal; used often in names of newspapers.

gaz·et·teer (găzetēr´) *n.* Geographical index or dictionary. [f. an early work of this kind, *The Gazetteer's or Newsman's Interpreter*]

G.B. *abbrev.* Great Britain.

G.C.M. *abbrev.* Good Conduct Medal.

G.C.T. *abbrev.* Greenwich Civil Time.

Gd *symbol.* Gadolinium.

Gdansk (gdahnsk, gdănsk). (or German, Danzig) Port city on the Gulf of Danzig in N. Poland.

Ge *symbol.* Germanium.

gear (gēr) *n.* 1. Equipment, apparel, etc.; harness of draft animals; apparatus, appliances, tackle, tools. 2. Combination of wheels, levers, etc.; wheels working on one another by teeth etc.; mechanical arrangement connecting motor with its work, usu. effecting a change of relative speed of revolution between driving and driven parts; **in, out of,** ~, in, out of, connection with motor; working, not working; **high, low,** ~, gear by which driven part of vehicle etc. revolves faster, slower, relatively to driving part (so *first, second, third, reverse,* etc. ~). 3. Rigging. 4. **gear´box**, in motor vehicle, the part containing the gear-changing mechanism; transmission; **gear´shift**, mechanism for changing gears in a power transmission unit, esp. in motor vehicle; **gear´wheel**, cogwheel, esp. that in bicycles, that is driven

directly by pedals. **gear** *v.* Put (machinery) in gear; provide with gear; (of cogwheel) fit exactly *into*, be in gear *with*; ~ **up**, modify (production, organization) to meet more demanding requirements.

gear´ing *n.* Manner in which a machine is geared; apparatus for transmission of motion or power from one part of a machine to another, esp. a train of toothed wheels.

geck·o (gĕk´ō) *n.* (**-os, -oes**). Any of numerous species of small lizard (family Gekkonidae), found in warm climates, with peculiar cry and (in some species) adhesive disks on the feet enabling them to climb vertical surfaces. [Malay *gēkoq*,

Performing a sleeve dance: **geisha** *girls of the Geisha Theatre, Kyoto, Japan, keep alive the arts practiced by past geishas, many of whom were influential courtesans.*

The use of **gears** *is one of the old means of transferring motion from o part of a machine to another where distance of transfer is short. Where s ping must be avoided, gears are p ferred to belt drive.*

imitating its cry]

gee[1] (jē) *int.* Word of comma to horse etc. to go on, go fast (also ~ **up**), or turn to right. ~ (**geed, gee·ing**).

gee[2] (jē) *int.* (slang) Exclamati of surprise, discovery, etc., **gee·whil·li·kens** (jē´hwĭl´ĭkĭn **gee-whiz** (jē´hwĭz´).

geese: see GOOSE.

Ge·ez, Ge´ez (gēĕz´, gā-): ETHIOPIC.

gee·zer (gē´zer) *n.* (slang) O man, esp. an eccentric one.

ge·fil·te (gefĭl´te) **fish**. (Jewi cookery) Balls of boneless fi mixed with bread crumbs, egg, a seasoning, cooked in broth, ar usu. served chilled.

Ge·hen·na (gehĕn´a). He place of burning, torment, misery. [Heb. *gê-hinnōm* valley ne Jerusalem where children we burned in sacrifice to Baal Moloch]

Gei·ger (gī´ger) **counter**. I strument for detecting and coun ing ionizing radiation; used esp. f measuring radioactivity. [Ha Geiger (1882–1945), Germa physicist]

gei·sha (gā´sha, gē´-) *n.* (-sha, -shas). Japanese girl train as traditional singer, dancer, a entertainer, esp. for men.

gel (jĕl) *n.* Semisolid colloid solution. ~ *v.i.* (**gelled, gel·ling** Form or become a gel.

gel·a·tin, gel·a·tine (jĕl´atĭn) *r* Amorphous brittle yellowish tran parent substance consisting esse tially of protein, extracted fro animal skins and bones, used making soups, jellies, etc., in ma photographic processes, and as t principal constituent of glu **ge·lat·i·nize** (jelăt´inīz, jĕl´ati-) *v*

...re are about 670 species of **gecko** ...nd in warm climates in many parts of ...world. They are small lizards with ...gues that they extend to catch ...cts. All species have eyes without ...vable lids. Below: A variegated ...ko with her eggs.

(-nized, -niz·ing). **ge·lat′i·nous** *adj.* Jellylike in consistency etc.; of gelatin.

geld (gĕld) *v.t.* (**geld·ed** or **gelt, geld·ing**). Deprive (usu. male animal) of generative power, castrate, excise testicles of. **geld′-ing** *n.* Gelded horse or other animal.

gel·id (jĕl′ĭd) *adj.* Ice-cold; cool. **gel′id·ly** *adv.*

gem (jĕm) *n.* Precious stone, esp. when cut and polished (also **gem′-stone**); object of great beauty or worth, choicest part *of*, prized possession. ~ *v.t.* (**gemmed, gem·ming**). Adorn (as) with gems.

Ge·ma·ra (gemär′a, -mōr′a). Later (5th c. A.D.) part of the Talmud, Aramaic commentary paragraph by paragraph on the oldest part (Mishnah). [Aram. *gemārā* completion]

Gem·i·ni (jĕm′inī, -nē). The Twins, a constellation also called "Castor and Pollux"; 3rd sign [♊] of the zodiac, which the sun enters about May 21. [L., = "twins"]

gem·ma (jĕm′a) *n.* (pl. **gem·-mae** pr. jĕm′ē). 1. (bot.) Small cellular body that separates from mother plant and starts new one, esp. in mosses, liverworts, etc. 2. (zool.) = BUD[1] def. 2.

gem·mate (jĕm′āt) *adj.* Having buds, reproducing by gemmation. ~ *v.i.* (-mat·ed, -mat·ing). Put forth buds, propagate by gemmation. **gem·ma·tion** (jĕmā′shon) *n.* Act, manner, of budding; arrangement of buds; reproduction by gemmae.

gem·ol·o·gy, gem·mol·o·gy (jĕmŏl′ojē) *ns.* Science or study of gems. **gem·ol′o·gist, gem·mol′-o·gist** *ns.*

ge·müt·lich (gemüt′lĭx) *adj.* Cheerful; cozy; genial.

Gen. *abbrev.* General; Genesis.

gen., genit. *abbrevs.* Genitive.

-gen *suffix.* Forming nouns with sense "that which produces" (*oxygen, hydrogen, antigen*).

gen·darme (zhahn′därm) *n.* Soldier employed in police duties, esp. in France. **gen·dar·me·rie, gen·dar·mer·y** (zhahndär′merē) *ns.* Force of gendarmes.

gen·der (jĕn′der) *n.* Each of the three (or in some languages two) grammatical kinds, corresponding more or less to distinctions of sex and absence of sex (*masculine, feminine, neuter*), into which nouns are divided according to the modification they may require in words syntactically connected with them; property (in a noun) of belonging to or (in other parts of speech) of having the appropriate form to concord with a specified one of these kinds; division of words into genders as principle of grammatical classification; classification of or by sex; sex.

gene (jēn) *n.* Member of any of the pairs of factors, usu. forming segments of a chromosome at fixed positions relative to each other, that cause the development in offspring of certain characters, one member of each pair being transmitted from each parent, the pairs of genes being on pairs of chromosomes.

ge·ne·a·log·i·cal (jēnēalŏj´ĭkal, jĕnē-) *adj.* Of genealogy; tracing family descent; ~ **chart**, **tree**, chart like branching tree showing descent of family or of animal species. **ge·ne·a·log´i·cal·ly** *adv.*

ge·ne·al·o·gy (jēnēŏl´ojē, -ăl´-, jĕnē-) *n.* (pl. **-gies**). Account of descent from ancestor by enumeration of intermediate persons; pedigree; investigation of pedigrees; plants' or animals' line of development from earlier forms. **ge·ne·al´o·gist** *n.*

gen·er·a: see GENUS.

gen·er·al (jĕn´eral) *adj.* Completely or approximately universal, not partial or particular; of a whole territory or organization etc.; prevalent, usual; not restricted, not specialized; dealing with main elements, features, etc., with neglect of unimportant details; vague, indefinite; (mil., of officer) above rank of colonel; (appended to titles) chief, head, with unrestricted authority or sphere; **in ~**, generally; in all ordinary cases, barring special exceptions, for the most part; **G~ Assembly**, deliberative and legislative council of certain religious denominations; legislative body of various organizations, states, etc.; deliberative body of the United Nations, consisting of delegations from all members; ~ **delivery**, postal service that delivers mail to the post office, where addressee goes to collect it; ~ **election**, one in which representatives are elected by every state, constituency, etc.; **G~ headquarters**, (abbrev. GHQ) headquarters of commander in chief; ~ **hospital**, hospital for all patients, with full range of services; ~ **post office**, (loosely) chief post office in town etc. (abbreviated G.P.O.); ~ **practice**, **practitioner**, (work of) doctor who treats cases of all kinds; ~ **semantics**, study of how words and symbols may be used to improve human behavior; ~ **staff**, (mil.) group of officers who assist military commander in planning and administration; ~ **store**, store that retails a variety of merchandise but is not organized in separate departments; ~ **strike**, strike by workers of all or most important trades or industries; strike of working citizens as political protest etc. **general** *n.* 1. (pl.; now rare) General principles, notions, or rules. 2. Chief of certain religious orders, fraternal and charitable

The Swiss city of **Geneva,** a canton capital, stands on the shores of a lake of the same name. The lake is part of the River Rhône and flows out near the city. The language spoken in this area is mainly French.

organizations, political groups, etc. 3. (mil.) Officer holding a rank above colonel in U.S. Army, Air Force, and Marine Corps, including **brigadier ~**, **lieutenant ~**, and **major ~**; commander of army; tactician, strategist.

gen·er·al·is·si·mo (jĕneralĭs´imō) *n.* (pl. **-mos**). Commander in chief of the armed forces in certain countries; commander of combined forces.

gen·er·al·i·ty (jĕnerăl´ĭtē) *n.* (pl. **-ties**). 1. Being general, applicability to whole class of instances. 2. Vagueness. 3. General point, principle, law, or statement. 4. Main body, bulk, majority, *of.*

gen·er·al·i·za·tion (jĕneralĭzā´shon) *n.* (esp.) (Forming of) general notion or proposition obtained by induction.

gen·er·al·ize (jĕn´eralīz) *v.* (**-ized, -iz·ing**). 1. Reduce to general laws, form into a general notion, give a general character to, call by a general name; infer (law,

conclusion) by induction; general statement upon (facts e (math., philos.) throw into gen form, extend application of; f general notions by abstraction. Make vague or indefinite; generalities, speak vaguely. Bring into general use. 4. **gener ized**, (zool., of organ or struct suitable for general use, not spec ized (e.g. reptile's forelimb distinct from bird's wing); animal) having generalized org etc.

gen·er·al·ly (jĕn´eralē) *adv.* the most part, extensively; i general sense, without regard particulars; not specially; a general rule, commonly.

gen·er·al·ship (jĕn´eralshĭp Office of a general; strate military skill; leadership, ski management, tact, diplomacy.

gen·er·ate (jĕn´erāt) *v.t.* (**-at -at·ing**). Bring into existe produce, evolve; (math., of po line, surface, conceived as mov make (line, surface, solid).

gen·er·a·tion (jĕnerā´shon) *n*

*The camouflage of the **genet** is adapted to the dappled light that fi through the leaves of the tropical ests in which it lives.*

creation, propagation of species, getting or being begotten; production by natural or artificial process. 2. Offspring of same rent or parents, regarded as gle step in descent or pedigree; ole body of persons born about ne time; time covered by lives of se; in reckoning historically, erval of time between birth of rents and that of their children; **gap**, differences of opinion ween those of different generas. **gen·er·a′tion·al** adj.

gen·er·a·tive (jĕn′erativ, -ātĭv) . Of procreation; able to duce, productive. **gen′er·a·e·ly** adv.

gen·er·a·tor (jĕn′erāter) n. Beter; apparatus for producing es, steam, etc.; machine for conting mechanical into electrical rgy, dynamo.

ge·ne·ric (jenĕr′ĭk) adj. Characistic of a genus or class; applied (any individual of) a large group class; general, not specific or cial; not protected by trademark, . ~ **drug** (cf. PROPRIETARY); **name**, (biol.) Latin name ritten with capital) indicating the us to which an animal or plant longs and preceding the *specific me*, which indicates the species. **ner′i·cal·ly** adv.

gen·er·ous (jĕn′erus) adj. Magnimous, noble-minded, not mean prejudiced; free in giving, inificent; ample, abundant, ious; (of wine, color, etc.) rich d full. **gen′er·ous·ly** adv. **n·er·os·i·ty** (jĕnerŏs′ĭtē) n. (pl. es).

Gen·e·sis (jĕn′esĭs). First book Old Testament containing count of creation of the world. **gen·e·sis** (jĕn′esĭs) n. (pl. -ses pr. z). Origin; mode of formation or neration. [Gk., = "origin,"

"creation"]

gen·et (jĕn′ĭt) n. (Fur of) kind of civet cat (*Genetta vulgaris*), native of S. Europe, Africa, and W. Asia.

Gen·et (zhenā′), **Jean** (1910–). French dramatist, poet and novelist; author of the novel *The Thief's Journal* and the plays *The Maids*, *The Blacks*, etc.

ge·net·ic (jenĕt′ĭk) adj. Of, in, concerning, origin; of genetics. **ge·net′i·cal·ly** adv. **ge·net′ics** n.pl. Branch of biology concerned with natural development; study of heredity and variation; **genetic code**, system of storage of genetic information in chromosomes. **ge·net′i·cist** n.

Ge·ne·va (jenē′va). City of SW. Switzerland on the Lake of Geneva and the Rhône River; ~ **bands**, strips of white cloth suspended from the front of the collar, worn esp. by the Calvinist and Presbyterian clergy; ~ **Convention**, convention of 1864 and later, governing status of wounded, hospitals, ambulances, etc., in war; ~ **cross**, red Greek cross on a white ground used as a symbol of the Red Cross Society, as a sign of neutrality, and as identification for hospitals etc. in time of war; more commonly called the red cross; ~ **gown**, loose black, wide-sleeved clerical or academic gown, orig. worn by Calvinist clergymen in Geneva; **Lake of** ~ (also called Lake Léman), lake in SW. Switzerland covering 225 sq. mi. (583 sq. km) with southern shore in E. France. **Ge·ne·van** (jenē′van) adj. Of Geneva; (esp.) Calvinistic.

*In the 17th century Flemish artists brought to **genre** painting a fresh intimacy and sensitiveness. Jan Vermeer's 'A Woman Reading a Letter' is typical of this rich vein of domestic art.*

Gen·e·vese (jĕnevēz′) adj. & n. (pl. -vese). (Native, inhabitant) of Geneva.

Gen·ghis Khan (jĕng′gĭs kahn′) (1162–1227). Mongol conqueror whose empire extended from the shores of the Pacific to the northern shores of the Black Sea.

ge·nial[1] (jē′nyal, -nēal) adj. 1. Conducive to life or growth; pleasantly warm, mild. 2. Cheering, kindly, sociable. **ge′ni·al·ly** adv. **ge·ni·al·i·ty** (jēnĕāl′ĭtē) n. **ge·ni·al**[2] (jenī′al) adj. (anat.) Of the chin.

ge·nie (jē′nē) n. (pl. -nies, -ni·i pr. -nēī). Sprite or goblin of Arabian tales, esp. sprite who does one's bidding; jinnee.

gen·i·tal (jĕn′ītal) adj. Of animal generation; ~ **stage**, (psychoanalysis) (i) of or pertaining to the focusing of sexual interest on the genitals; (ii) of or pertaining to the adult or final stage of psychosexual development, in which the individual finds satisfaction in the sexual relationship (cf. ANAL; ORAL). **gen′i·tals**, **gen·i·ta·lia** (jĕnĭtāl′ya, -tā′lēa) ns. pl. Organs of generation, esp. external.

gen·i·tive (jĕn′ĭtĭv) adj. (gram.) Of the case (also **possessive**) chiefly denoting relation as source, possessor, etc. ~ n. (Word in) genitive case. **gen·i·ti·val** (jĕnĭtī′val) adj.

gen·i·to·u·ri·nar·y (jĕnĭtōur′inĕrē) adj. Of the genital and urinary organs.

gen·ius (jēn′yus) n. (pl. **gen·ius·es** for defs. 1, 3, 4; **gen·i·i** pr. jē′nēī for defs. 1 & 2). 1. (Rom. myth.) Tutelary spirit of person, place, or institution; **good**, **evil**, ~, mutually opposed spirits by whom every person was supposed to be attended; hence, person powerfully influencing another for good or evil. 2. (Muslim myth.) Demon, supernatural being. 3. Prevalent feeling, opinions, taste, of nation, age, etc.; character, spirit, drift, method, of language, law, etc.; associations, inspirations, *of* a place. 4. Natural ability, special mental endowments; exalted intellectual power, instinctive and extraordinary imaginative, creative, or inventive capacity; person having this.

Gen·nes·a·ret (jenĕs′arĕt), **Lake of**: see GALILEE, Sea of.

Gen·o·a (jĕn′ōa). (Ital. *Genova*) City and seaport of NW. Italy on the Ligurian Sea. **Gen·o·ese** (jĕnōēz′, -ēs′) adj. & n. (Native, inhabitant) of Genoa.

gen·o·cide (jĕn′osīd) n. Planned, systematic extermination of a race, ethnic group, population, etc. **gen·o·ci·dal** (jĕnosī′dal) adj.

gen·o·type (jĕn′otĭp) n. (biol.) Genetic constitution of an organism (cf. PHENOTYPE).

-genous *suffix.* Forming adjectives with sense "produced" (*nitrogenous*).

gen·re (zhahn´re) *n.* Kind, esp. of art or literature; (also ~ **painting**) portrayal of scenes from ordinary life, esp. that of a particular class, e.g. peasants.

gens (jĕnz) *n.* (pl. **gen·tes** pr. jĕn´tēz). 1. (Rom. antiq.) Clan. 2. (anthrop.) Line of descent through father. [L.]

gent (jĕnt) *n.* (colloq.) Gentleman; (slang) **G ~ s**, public toilet for men.

gen·teel (jĕntēl´) *adj.* 1. Wellbred; elegant; refined in manners etc. 2. Affectedly refined. **gen·teel´ly** *adv.*

gen·tian (jĕn´shan) *n.* Plant of the genus *Gentiana*, usu. with conspicuous blue flowers, esp. the **fringed** ~ (*G. crinita*) of eastern N. Amer., with fringed petals; and the **bottle** or **closed** ~ (*G. andrewsii*), with deep-blue blossoms that remain closed; (also ~ **root**) (pharm.) dried rhizome and roots of *G. lutea*, sometimes used as a tonic; ~ **violet**, dye, used as antiseptic. [L. f. *Gentius* king of Illyria]

gen·tile (jĕn´tīl) *adj. & n.* (also **G ~**) (Person) not of Jewish faith, esp. a Christian as distinguished from a Jew; (in Mormon use) non-Mormon; heathen, pagan.

gen·til·i·ty (jĕntĭl´ĭtē) *n.* (pl. **-ties**). 1. (now rare) Gentle birth, status of gentleman or lady. 2. Being genteel, esp. affectedly so.

gen·tle (jĕn´tel) *adj.* (**-tler, -tlest**). 1. Wellborn; (her.) having right to bear arms; (of birth, blood,

etc.) honorable. 2. (archaic) Generous, noble, courteous. 3. Tame, quiet; easily managed; not stormy, rough, or violent; mild; moderate, gradual; kind, tender. ~ *n.* (f. obs. sense *soft* of *adj.*) Larva of bluebottle fly, used as bait by anglers. ~ *v.t.* (**-tled, -tling**). Break in or handle (horse) gently.

gen·tle·folk, gen´tle·folks *ns.pl.* Persons of good position and family.

gen·tle·man (jĕn´telman) *n.* (pl. **-men**). 1. (Brit.) Man of gentle birth or entitled to bear arms but not included in nobility (chiefly hist.); man of gentle birth attached to household of sovereign or great person; ~ **-at-arms**, one of Brit. sovereign's ceremonial bodyguards. 2. Man of chivalrous instincts, fine feelings, and good breeding; man of good social position, man of wealth and leisure; (courteous synonym for) man; **gentleman's** ~, valet; ~ **'s agreement**, unwritten agreement binding only as a matter of honor; (ironic) illegal or unethical unwritten agreement, as to exclude minority groups from membership in clubs, to inflate prices, etc.

gen´tle·man·like *adj.* Appropriate to, resembling, a gentleman.

gen´tle·man·ly *adv.* Feeling, behaving, or looking like a gentleman; befitting a gentleman.

gen·tle·ness (jĕn´telnĭs) *n.* Kindliness, mildness; freedom from severity, violence, suddenness, etc.

gen·tle·wom·an (jĕn´telwōoman) *n.* (pl. **-wom·en** pr. -wĭmĭn). Woman of good birth or breeding,

lady.

gen·tly (jĕnt´lē) *adv.* Quie moderately, softly, slowly; mil kindly.

gen·try (jĕn´trē) *n.* 1. (Br People next below nobility position and birth, esp. the up middle class. 2. Well-bred peo

gen·u·flect (jĕn´yuflĕkt) Bend the knee, kneel or halfv kneel, esp. in worship or adorati **gen·u·flec·tion** (jĕnyuflĕk´shon)

gen·u·ine (jĕn´ūĭn) *adj.* Of original stock, purebred; re proceeding from its reputed sou or author; having the suppo character, not counterfeit, prope so called. **gen·u·ine·ly** *a* **gen´u·ine·ness** *n.*

ge·nus (jē´nus) *n.* (pl. **gen·e** pr. jĕn´era, **ge·nus·es**). (log Class of things including s ordinate kinds or species; (bi taxonomic category smaller tha family and larger than a species (a usu. containing several species) animals or plants having comm structural characteristics distir from those of all other grou (loosely) kind, class, order, tribe

-geny *comb. form.* Formi nouns with sense of "mode production or development ((*ontogeny*).

Geo. *abbrev.* George.

geo- *prefix.* Of Earth (*geoch nology, geophysics*).

ge·o·cen·tric (jēōsĕn´trĭk) *a* Considered as viewed from Eart center; having or representi Earth as center. **ge·o·cen´tr cal·ly** *adv.*

ge·o·chem·is·try (jēōkĕm´ĭst

A map, drawn in 1617 by Pieter van der Keere, of the Provinces of United Netherlands. Map-making has been to the science of **geography** what printing has been to the realm of literature.

Science of the chemical composition of and changes in earth's crust. **ge·o·chem·i·cal** (jē'ōkĕm'ĭkal) adj.

ge·ode (jē'ōd) n. Cavity in an igneous rock that has been partly filled with minerals in well-shaped crystals. **ge·od·ic** (jēŏd'ĭk) adj.

ge·od·es·y (jēŏd'ĭsē) n. Branch of mathematics dealing with size and shape of Earth or large portions of it. **ge·o·des·ic** (jēodĕs'ĭk) adj. of geodesy; **geodesic dome**, light-weight domelike structure framed with short struts that form a network of polygons; **geodesic line**, shortest possible line joining points on a curved surface. **geodesic** n. Geodesic line. **ge·o·det·ic** (jēodĕt'ĭk), **ge·o·det'i·cal** adjs. **ge·o·det'i·cal·ly** adv.

ge·o·graph·ic (jēogrăf'ĭk), **ge·o·graph·i·cal** (jēogrăf'ĭkal) adjs. of geography; ~ **mile**, 1 minute of longitude measured along the equator, equal to 1,852 m (about 6,076 ft.). **ge·o·graph'i·cal·ly** adv.

ge·og·ra·phy (jēŏg'rafē) n. (pl. -phies). Science of Earth's surface, form, physical features, natural and political divisions, climate, productions, population, etc.; subject matter of geography; treatise or manual of geography; features, arrangements, of place. **ge·og'ra·pher** n.

ge·o·log·i·cal (jēolŏj'ĭkal), **ge·o·log·ic** (jēolŏj'ĭk) adjs. Of geology; ~ **map**, map showing the formations of rock exposed at, or underlying, the surface of a region; ~ **survey**, survey that reports on the geological aspects of a country or area, as water supply, mineral deposits, etc. **ge·o·log'i·cal·ly** adv.

ge·ol·o·gy (jēŏl'ojē) n. (pl. **-gies**). Science of the formation of Earth, the strata of its crust, and their relations and changes; geological features of a district. **ge·ol'o·gist** n.

ge·o·man·cy (jē'omănsē) n. Divination from figure given by handful of earth thrown down, and hence from figures given by dots made at random. **ge'o·man·cer** n. **ge·o·man·tic** (jēomăn'tĭk) adj.

ge·o·met·ric (jēomĕt'rĭk), **ge·o·met·ri·cal** (jēomĕt'rĭkal) adjs. Of, according to, geometry; (of patterns) rectilinear or curvilinear; ~ **mean**, the nth root, generally positive, of the product of n factors; ~ **progression**, progression in which each term is a fixed multiple of the preceding one, as 1, 3, 9, 27. **ge·o·met'ri·cal·ly** adv.

ge·om·e·trid (jĕŏm′etrĭd) *adj*. & *n*. (Member) of the family Geometridae of moths whose larvae move with a looping movement as if measuring the ground, hence called "loopers," "inchworms," or "measuring worms."

ge·om·e·try (jĕŏm′etrē) *n*. (pl. **-tries**). Science of properties and relations of magnitudes in space, as lines, surfaces, solids.

ge·o·mor·phol·o·gy (jēōmōr̄-fŏl′ojē) *n*. Branch of geology dealing with the origin, evolution, and configuration of the natural features of Earth's surface. **ge·o·mor·pho·log·i·cal** (jēōmōrfolŏj′ĭkal) *adj*. **ge·o·mor·phol′o·gist** *n*.

*The study of **geophysics** encompasses astronomy, geology, oceanography, seismology, meteorology and several other sciences. Here a technician examines meteorological instruments in a laboratory.*

ge·o·phys·ics (jēōfĭz′ĭks) *n*. Study of the physics of Earth and geological phenomena, including oceanography, seismology, meteorology, etc.; application of methods of physics to the study of Earth. **ge·o·phys′i·cal** *adj*. **ge·o·phys·i·cist** (jēōfĭz′ĭsĭst) *n*.

ge·o·pol·i·tics (jēōpŏl′ĭtĭks) *n. pl*. (treated as sing.) 1. Study of the interrelationship between geography and politics, esp. the effect of geography on a nation's domestic and foreign policies. 2. National policy based on such an interrelationship, esp. Nazi program of expansion aimed at domination of the world by Germany. **ge·o·po·lit·i·cal** (jēōpolĭt′ĭkal) *adj*.

George[1] (jôrj). Name of 6 kings of Gt. Britain: (**the four ~s**, George I–IV, of the House of Hanover, who ruled Gt. Britain from 1714–1830): **George I** (1660–

For long the patron saint of England, George was portrayed slaying evi devotional paintings. Lack of histor substance in the legends surround his name led the Vatican to de-canon him.

1727), son of the first Elector Hanover and great-grandson James I, reigned 1714–27; **Geor II** (1683–1760), his son, reigr 1727–60; **George III** (1738–182 grandson of George II, reigr 1760–1820; **George IV** (176 1830), son of George III; Prin Regent 1811–20; reigned 1820– **George V** (1865–1936), son Edward VII, reigned 1910– **George VI** (1895–1952), son George V and brother of Edwa VIII, reigned 1936–52.

George[2] (jôrj), **St.** (d. 30 Christian martyr; legendary sla of a dragon; patron saint of Engla from 14th c.; **St. ~'s cross**, verti and horizontal bars crossing center; (her.) red cross on wh ground, the national cross England.

George·town (jôrj′town). Ch seaport and capital of Guyana.

Geor·gia[1] (jôr′ja). S. Atlan state of U.S., founded as English colony in 1733; one of t original 13 states of the Uni (1788); capital, Atlanta. [f. name George II of England]

Geor·gia[2] (jôr′ja) (Ru Gruziya) District of the Caucas an ancient kingdom now a constit ent republic (properly Georgi Soviet Socialist Republic) of t U.S.S.R.; capital, Tbilisi (Tiflis)

Geor·gia[3] (jôr′ja), **Strait** Pacific Ocean inlet 150 mi. (241 k

*By the beginning of the Iron A Mediterranean cultures understo some **geometry**. Craftsmen of t period incorporated geometrical p terns in their work, as in this Cypr bowl of c. 1000–759 B.C.*

Two Hanoverian British monarchs. Top left: **George II,** *painted by John Shackleton, the king's painter. Top right:* **George III,** *painted by the German, Johann Zoffany, who worked mostly in England.* **George V** *(of the House of Windsor) is portrayed by F. O. Salisbury at a thanksgiving service. The king is with Queen Mary and followed by his sons, Prince Edward and Prince Albert.*

between Canada and U.S., unded by Vancouver Island on ., mainland British Columbia on and NE., and the state of ashington on the SE.

Geor·gian[1] (jôr′jan) *adj.* Of the ne of the four Georges of Gt. itain, who ruled from 1714 to 30.

Geor·gian[2] (jôr′jan) *adj. & n.* 1. nhabitant) of the U.S. state of orgia. 2. (Inhabitant, language) Georgia in the Caucasus.

ge·ot·ro·pism (jēŏt′ropĭzem) *n.* lation of plant growth to gravity; sitive ~, tendency (of roots etc.) grow towards center of Earth; gative ~, tendency (of stems .) to grow away from center of rth. **ge·o·trop·ic** (jēotrŏp′ĭk, ō′pĭk) *adj.* **ge·o·trop′i·cal·ly** *v.*

Ger. *abbrev.* German; Germany.

ge·ra·ni·um (jerā′nēum) *n.* Herceous plant or shrub of genus ~ of temperate regions, with red, nk, or purple, or white flowers. k. *geranos* crane because the it resembles a crane's bill]

ger·bil, ger·bille (jer′bĭl) *ns.* Small burrowing rodent of Africa and Asia with long hind legs, now a popular household pet.

ger·fal·con = GYRFALCON.

ger·i·at·ric (jĕrĕăt′rĭk) *adj.* Of, concerning, the health and welfare of old people. **ger·i·at′rics** *n.pl.* Branch of medicine, or of social science, dealing with geriatric problems.

germ (jĕrm) *n.* 1. Portion of organism capable of developing into a new one; embryo of seed; (fig.) seed, rudiment, elementary principle. 2. Microorganism or microbe, esp. one of those capable of causing disease. 3. ~ **cell**, cell in body of an organism that is specialized for the purpose of reproduction, and, when united to one of the opposite sex, forms a new individual; gamete; ~ **plasm**, nuclear part of germ cell containing hereditary material, genes and chromosomes.

Ger·man (jer′man) *adj.* Of Germany or its people or language; ~ **Democratic Republic**: see GERMANY; ~ **measles**, mild contagious disease (*rubella*) resembling measles; ~ **shepherd** (**dog**) or ~ **police dog**, large dog of a breed developed in Germany to herd sheep, wolflike in appearance and having a thick coat that may be black, brownish, black and tan, gray, or brindled, used in police work and as a guide for the blind. **German** *n.* 1. German person. 2. German language, one of the Germanic or Teutonic group, subdivided into **High** ~, group of dialects spoken in south and part of central Germany, and **Low** ~, dialects of N. Germany; **Old High** ~, High German from *c*750 to *c*1100. **Ger′man·ism, Ger′-**

Above right: After the 1939–45
Germany was divided into the Fed
Republic of Germany, covering 95,
sq. miles (excluding W. Berlin), and
German Democratic Republic
41,500 sq. miles (excluding E. Be
Above left: A fairy-tale ca
Neuschwanstein, in Bavaria. Left:
Moselle River, Germany.

man·ist *ns*.

ger·man (jĕr'man) *adj*. In the fullest sense of parental relationship; **brother-**~, brother having the same parents, own brother; similarly **sister-**~; **cousin-**~, child of one's father's or mother's own brother or sister; first cousin.

ger·man·der (jermăn'der) *n*. Any plant of the genus *Teucrium*, usu. aromatic and with reddish or purplish flowers.

ger·mane (jermān') *adj*. Relevant, pertinent, *to* the matter or subject. [var. of GERMAN]

Ger·man·ic (jermăn'ĭk) *adj*. Of, pertaining to, the Teutons or their language; German. ~ *n*. Language of the Teutons, esp. in its earliest form, a branch of the Indo-European language family divided into **East** ~, Gothic and some almost lost languages as Burgundian and Vandal; **North** ~,

Danish, Norwegian, Swedish, and Icelandic; **West** ~, German, English, Frisian, and Dutch.

ger·ma·ni·um (jermā'nēum) *n*. (chem.) Rare metallic element of grayish-white color; symbol Ge, at. no. 32, at. wt. 72.59. [L. *Germania* Germany]

Ger·man·y (jĕr'manē). Former state of central Europe between the Baltic Sea and the North Sea; in 1871 a confederation of German-speaking states united under the king of Prussia, who became German emperor; this Second Empire (regarded as the successor to the Holy Roman Empire) lasted until the end of World War I; it was followed by the Weimar Republic, then by the Third Empire (Third Reich) under Adolf Hitler, 1933–1945; since World War II the region has been divided between the **Federal Republic of** ~ (also

called West ~; capital, Bonn) and the **German Democra Republic** (also called **E. Germany**; capital, East Berlin)

ger·mi·cide (jĕr'mĭsīd) *n*. & (Substance) having power destroy (esp. disease) ger **ger·mi·ci·dal** (jĕrmĭsī'dal) *adj*.

Ger·mi·nal (jĕr'mĭnal; zhĕrmēnăl') *n*. Month from Ma 21 to April 19 in the Fren Revolutionary calendar.

ger·mi·nal (jĕr'mĭnal) *adj*. germs, of the nature of a germ; the earliest stage of developme **ger'mi·nal·ly** *adv*.

ger·mi·nate (jĕr'mĭnāt) (**-nat·ed, -nat·ing**). Sprout, b cause to shoot, produce. **ger·m na·tion** (jĕrmĭnā'shon), **ger'm na·tor** *ns*. **ger'mi·na·tive** *adj*.

Ge·ron·i·mo (jerŏn'imō) (182 1909). (Indian name Goyathl Amer. Apache Indian chief a leader against whites, 1885–6, Arizona.

ger·on·toc·ra·cy (jĕrontŏk'ra *n*. (pl. **-cies**). Government b governing body of, elders.

ger·on·tol·o·gy (jĕrontŏl'ojē) Study of old age, esp. conditi affecting the health of the age **ger·on·tol'o·gist** *n*. **ge·ron·te log·i·cal** (jerŏntolŏj'ĭkal) *adj*.

ger·ry·man·der (jĕr'imănd *v*. Divide (a state, county, etc.) ir voting districts in such a way as give unfair advantage to c political party in elections. ~ Such manipulation. [orig.

bridge *Gerry*, governor of Mas-
chusetts, + (sala)*mander*, from
e shape of an election district
rmed to his advantage in 1812]

Gersh·win (gĕrsh′wĭn), **George**
898–1937). Amer. composer of
pular songs, musical comedies,
mphonic jazz and orchestral
rks; famous for the symphony
Rhapsody in Blue," the folk opera
rgy and Bess, etc.; Pulitzer Prize,
32, for musical comedy *Of Thee
Sing.*

ger·und (jĕr′und) *n.* 1. Form of
tin verb capable of being con-
ued as noun but able to govern
e verb. 2. English word with
rbal ending -*ing* functioning as
un.

ge·run·dive (jerŭn′dĭv) *adj.* Of,
e, the gerund. — *n.* Latin
rbal adjective, with same suffix
gerund, expressing idea of fitness
necessity.

Ge·sell (gezĕl′), **Arnold Lucius**
880–1961). Amer. psychologist,
diatrician and author; founder,
11, of Yale Clinic of Child
evelopment.

ges·so (jĕs′ō) *n.* Plaster of Paris
d glue prepared for use in
odeling or as ground for painting.

ge·stalt (geshtahlt′, -shtawlt′) *n.*
l. -**stal·ten** pr. -shtahl′ten,
htawl′-, -**stalts**). (psychol.)
ape or structure that as an object
perception forms a specific whole
d has properties that cannot be
mpletely deduced from a knowl-
ge of the properties of its parts;
iefly attrib. as ~ or **G**~
ychology, theory that percep-
ons, reactions, etc. are gestalts.
Ger., = "form," "shape"]

Ge·sta·po (gestah′pō; *Ger.* ge-
tah′pō) *n.* (pl. -**pos**). Nazi secret
lice. [Ger., initial letters of
eheime *Sta*atspolizei secret state
lice]

ges·ta·tion (jĕstā′shon) *n.*
arrying or being carried in womb
tween conception and birth; this
riod. **ges·tate** (jĕs′tāt) *v.t.*
tat·ed, -tat·ing).

ges·tic·u·late (jĕstĭk′yulāt) *v.*
lat·ed, -lat·ing). Use expressive
otion of limbs or body with or
stead of speech; express thus.
es·tic·u·la·tion (jĕstĭkyulā′shon),
s·tic·u·la·tor *ns.* **ges·tic·u·la·**
ve, ges·tic·u·la·to·ry *adjs.*

ges·ture (jĕs′cher) *n.* 1. Signifi-
nt movement of limb or body; use
such movements as expression of
eling or rhetorical device. 2. (after
r. *geste*) Step or move calculated to
oke response from another or
nvey (esp. friendly) intention. ~
(-tured, -tur·ing). Gesticulate.

get (gĕt) *v.* (**got** pr. gŏt or **got·ten**
. gŏt′en, **get·ting**). 1. Obtain,
oduce, by effort or contrivance;
rn, gain, win; learn *by heart* or *rote*;
otain as result of calculation; reive as gift, wages, etc.; extract by

plea, demand, inquiry, etc.; come to
have; contract; have inflicted on
one; receive as one's lot or penalty;
procure, provide; catch (fish etc.);
bring in, carry home (crop); communicate with by telephone; obtain
radio signal from; succeed in
bringing, placing, etc.; bring into
some state; suffer injury etc.;
induce, prevail upon (person) *to* do;
(of animals) beget; (colloq.) puzzle,
catch in argument; understand;
enthrall; (in perf.) have; *have got to*,
must; ~ **the best** or **worst of it**,
be victorious, be defeated; ~ **it**,
be punished or reprimanded; understand (something); ~ **on the
brain**, be obsessed by; ~ **on one's
nerves**, be irritated by; ~ **religion**, become (esp. suddenly)
zealous about religion. 2. (intrans.)
Succeed in coming or going *to*,
from, *over*, *here*, etc.; (slang) be off,
clear out; (with infin.) acquire
habit; come to be (doing); become.
3. (with preps.): ~ **around**, cajole;
evade; ~ **at**, get hold of, ascertain;
(slang) tamper with, bribe, etc.;
(slang) attack; ~ **into**, (colloq.) put
on (shoes, clothes); ~ **off**, dismount from; obtain release from
(engagement etc.); not remain on;

~ **on**, mount (horse etc.); ~ **over**,
surmount (difficulty); recover from
(illness, disappointment, or from
surprise at); ~ **through**, bring to
an end; (of bill etc.) be passed by
(legislature); ~ **to**, begin (business
etc.). 4. (with advs.): ~ **about**, go
from place to place; begin to walk
(after illness etc.); ~ **across**,
(slang) reach audience, be understood or effective; ~ **along**,
advance, meet with success, fare
well, etc.; move along; manage
without something; live harmoniously *together*, *with*; ~ **along with
you!**, (colloq.) be off!; nonsense!;
~ **away**, escape; start; (imper.)
leave!; ~ **back**, come home etc.;
recover (lost thing); ~ **one's own
back**, have one's revenge; ~
better, **well**, recover from illness;
~ **down**, dismount; depress, weary
(person); ~ **in**, be elected; enter
car, house, etc.; bring home (crop);
fit (work etc.) into given time;
succeed in placing (blow); ~

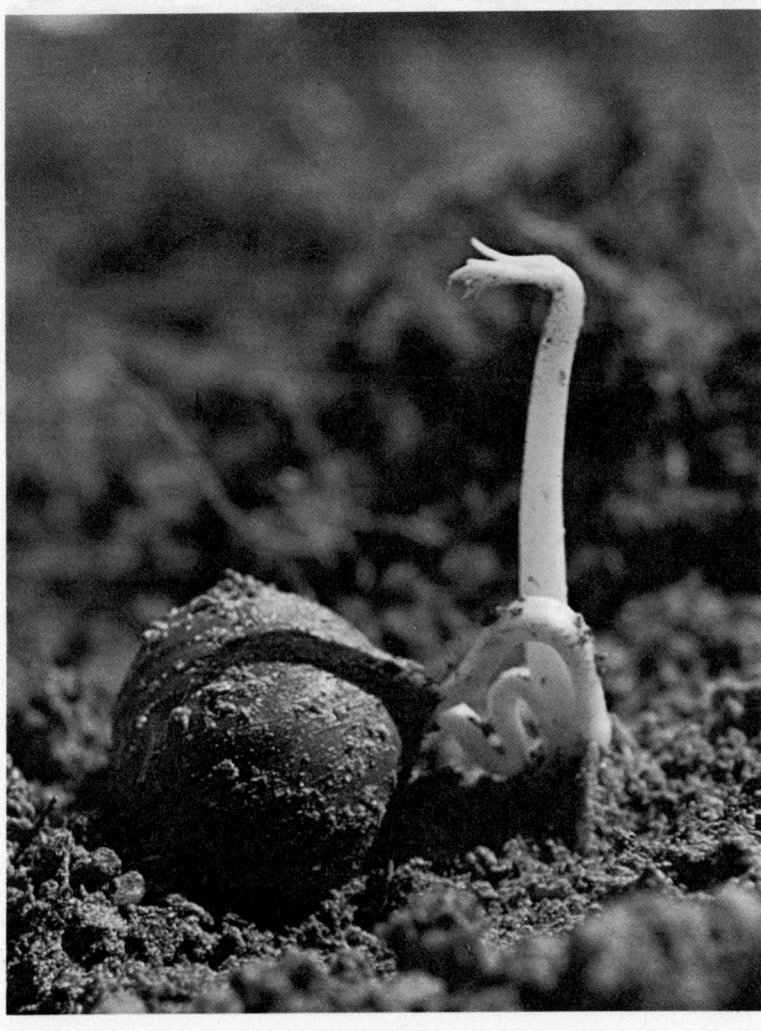

*After a period of dormancy a sweet
chestnut will* **germinate** *and the seedling shoot towards light, fed by the
energy stored in the endosperm or in
the cotyledons. The seedling then
obtains food from the soil.*

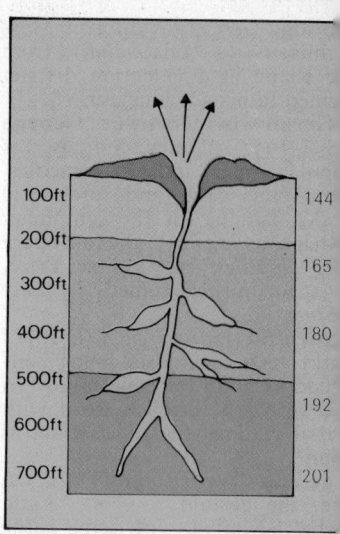

A **geyser** *may send a fountain of water and mud as high as 200 ft. is followed by a jet of steam, after wh it is dormant for a while. Above: Wa flows down the vent, is heated, releases dissolved gases which fo the water out again.*

nowhere, achieve nothing; make no progress; ~ **off**, escape; start; be acquitted or pardoned, be let off *with* or *for* specified penalty; procure pardon, acquittal, or slight penalty for (person); ~ **on**, don; advance, make progress; prosper, fare; advance in time or age; ~ **out!** (imper.) leave!; nonsense!; succeed in uttering, publishing, etc.; ~ **out of**, issue or escape from; abandon (habit) gradually; evade doing; elicit (information), obtain (money) from (person); ~ **over**, bring (troublesome task etc.) to an end; get across; ~ **there**, (colloq.) succeed; reach one's goal; ~ **through**, bring to, reach, destination, establish communication, esp. by telephone or radio; (of bill etc.) be passed in a legislature; ~ **together**, collect; meet; ~ **up**, rise, esp. from bed; arrange the appearance of; make rise; produce; work up (emotion etc.); ~ **up steam**, produce enough to work engine etc.; (fig.) work oneself up into action or energy; ~ **wind of**,

learn of. 5. (comb.) **get'away**, (esp.) escape of criminals; **get-together**, meeting, social gathering; **get'up**, costume; style; **get-up-and-go**, initiative; ambition. **get'ta·ble, get'a·ble** *adjs.* (esp.) Obtainable; reachable. **get** *n.* (male) animal.

Geth·sem·a·ne (gěthsěm'anē). Garden on the Mount of Olives E. of Jerusalem, scene of the agony, betrayal, and arrest of Jesus (Matt. 26).

get·ter (gět'er) *n.* (esp.) Substance inserted into vacuum to absorb stray gases exuded into it after sealing.

Get·tys·burg (gět'ēzbērg). Town in S. Pennsylvania, site of a decisive battle (1863) in the Civil War, in which Union forces under Meade defeated the Confederates under Lee; site of ~ **National Military Park**, national cemetery for those killed in the battle; ~ **Address**, speech by Abraham LINCOLN[2] at dedication of the cemetery, containing the phrase

"government of the people, by people, for the people."

GeV *abbrev.* Gigaelectron v

gew·gaw (gū'gaw, goo'-) Gaudy plaything or orname bauble; paltry showy trifle.

gey·ser (gī'zer) *n.* Hot spr (usu. in volcanic area) that spo water at more or less regu intervals. [*Geysir*, name of a spring in Iceland]

Gha·na (gah'na, găn'a). (hist.) Medieval African kingdo in W. Sudan. 2. W. African coun comprising the former Gold Co colony, Ashanti, the Northe Territories (of the Gold Co region), and Transvolta-Togola member of the British Comm wealth; independent 1957; capit Accra. **Gha·na·ian** (gah'nē· găn'ē-) *adj. & n.*

ghast·ly (găst'lē, gahst'-) *a* (**-li·er, -li·est**). Horrible, frightf deathlike, pallid; unpleasant, b ~ *adv.* (chiefly with adjective **ghast'li·ness** *n.*

ghat (gawt) *n.* 1. Either of mountain ranges of S. India, t **Eastern G**~ along the Bay Bengal or the **Western G**~ alo the Arabian Sea. 2. Mountain pa defile. 3. Passage or flight of ste leading to riverside. 4. (a **burning** ~) Hindu funeral pyr

ghee (gē) *n.* Indian buffalo m butter clarified to resemble oil.

Ghent (gěnt). Manufacturi and commercial city in NW. cent Belgium; Treaty of Ghent, Dec. 1814, signed here ending War 1812 between U.S. and Gr Britain.

gher·kin (gēr'kǐn) *n.* Young small cucumber, used for picklir

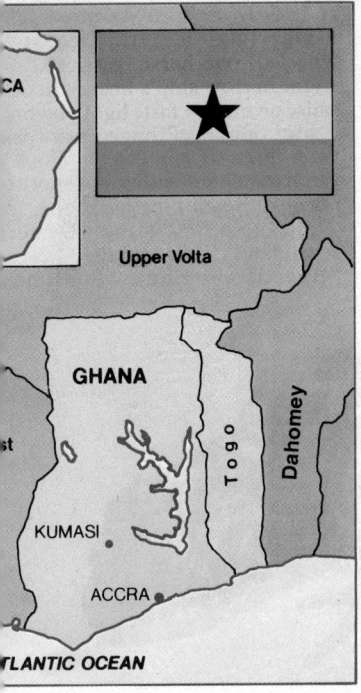

*Left: The republic of **Ghana**, populated by 9,600,000, has a land area of about 92,000 sq. miles. The country has rich resources of minerals and hardwoods. Above: The Ashanti, once part of an independent kingdom, are now subjects of Ghana.*

ghet·to (gĕt′ō) *n.* (pl. **-tos, -toes**). Quarter of a European city to which Jews were restricted (hist.); (esp. slum) quarter inhabited predominantly by minority group(s).

Ghi·ber·ti (gēbĕr′tē), **Lorenzo** (1378–1455). Florentine sculptor, painter and goldsmith, noted for his use of perspective and gilt bronze relief, especially in the N. and E. doors of the baptistry of Florence.

ghost (gōst) *n.* 1. Soul or spirit, as principle of life (now only in **give up the ~**, die); Spirit (of God), Holy Ghost. 2. Soul of dead person appearing to living; apparition, specter; emaciated person; shadowy outline or semblance. 3. (optics) Bright spot or secondary image in field of telescope due to defect of lens; (television) faint duplicated image not coinciding with the intended one. 4. (also **ghost-writer**) Person who writes for and gives credit of authorship to employer; **ghost′write** *v.* (**-wrote, -writ·ten, -writ·ing**). 5. **~ town**, town with few or no remaining inhabitants. **ghost** *v.i.* Act, write, as ghost (sense 4). **ghost′ly** *adj.* 1. (archaic) Spiritual; incorporeal; concerned with incorporeal matters. 2. (As) of a ghost, spectral. **ghost′li·ness** *n.*

ghoul (gōol) *n.* Spirit supposed in Muslim superstition to prey on corpses; person enjoying what is gruesome. **ghoul′ish** *adj.* **ghoul′-ish·ly** *adv.*

GHQ *abbrev.* General Headquarters.

GI (jē′ī′) *n. & adj.* (pl. **GI's, GIs**). (colloq.) (Pertaining to) enlisted man in or veteran of U.S. Army (esp. one serving in World War II). [abbrev. of *government* (or *general*) *issue*]

G.I., GI, g.i. *abbrevs.* 1. Galvanized iron. 2. Government issue. 3. General issue. 4.

Gastrointestinal.

gi·ant (jī′ant) *n.* 1. Being of human form but superhuman stature; (Gk. myth.) one of the race of beings, sons of Gaea (Earth) and Uranus (Heaven) or Tartarus (Hell) who warred against and were destroyed by the gods. 2. Agency of enormous power; abnormally tall or large person, animal, or plant; person of extraordinary ability, courage, strength, etc. 3. Large diffuse star, as dist. from DWARF. 4. **Giant's Causeway**, group of basaltic columns formed in Tertiary period on N. coast of Antrim, N. Ireland.

gi·ant·ism (jī′antĭzem) *n.* Growth (esp. of bones) to abnormally large size.

Gib. *abbrev.* (colloq.) Gibraltar.

gib·ber (jĭb′er, gĭb′-) *v.i.* Speak fast and inarticulately, chatter like an ape. ~ *n.* Gibbering speech.

gib·ber·ish (jĭb′erĭsh, gĭb′-) *n.* Unintelligible speech, meaningless sounds; blundering or ungrammatical talk.

gib·bet (jĭb′ĭt) *n.* (orig.) Gallows; (later) upright post with arm on which bodies of executed criminals were hung up. ~ *v.t.* (**-bet·ed, -bet·ing**). Put to death by hanging; expose on gibbet; hand up as on gibbet; hold up to infamy or contempt.

gib·bon (gĭb′on) *n.* Long-armed, arboreal tailless ape of genus *Hylobates*, found in SE. Asia.

Gib·bon (gĭb′on), **Edward** (1737–94). English historian; author of *History of the Decline and Fall of the Roman Empire*.

gib·bous (gĭb′us) *adj.* 1. Convex, protuberant; (of moon or planet) having bright part greater than semicircle and less than circle. 2. Humped, hunchbacked. **gib′-bous·ly** *adv.* **gib·bos·i·ty** (gĭbŏs′-ĭtē) *n.*

gibe (jīb) *v.* (**gibed, gib·ing**). Flout, jeer, mock (*at*). ~ *n.* Taunting remark. **gib′er** *n.* **gib′ing·ly** *adv.*

gib·let (jĭb′lĭt) *n.* usu. *pl.* Heart,

liver, gizzard of fowl, as removed before cooking; gizzard.

Gi·bral·tar (jĭbrawl′ter). British self-governing dependency covering 2¼ sq. mi (5.8 sq. km), and town on peninsula of S. Spain on the Strait of Gibraltar at W. entrance to Mediterranean; site of British naval and air base; **Rock of** ~, peninsular headland on the S. central coast of Spain; **Strait of** ~, 36-mi.-long strait connecting the Mediterranean Sea with the Atlantic Ocean and separating Spain and N. Africa. [Arab. *gebel-el-Tarik* hill of Tarik (a Saracen commander of the 8th c.)]

Gib·son¹ (gĭb′son) *n.* Dry martini having a small pickled onion instead of an olive or twisted lemon peel.

Gib·son² (gĭb′son), **Charles Dana** (1867–1944). Amer. illustrator; originator of the **Gibson girl**, idealized 1890s Amer. girl dressed in tailored blouse with puffed sleeves and long skirt.

gid·dy (gĭd′ē) *adj.* (**-di·er, -di·est**). Dizzy, disposed to fall, stagger, or spin around; making dizzy; excitable, flighty. **gid′di·ly** *adv.* **gid′di·ness** *n.* **gid′dy** *v.* (**-died, -dy·ing**). Make or become giddy.

Gide (zhēd), **André** (1869–1951). French novelist, critic, and

*The name **gillyflower** is in so[me] countries applied to stocks and pinks [as] well as to wallflowers. Here are pink [gil]lyflowers (dianthus).*

essayist; author of *The Immoral[ist]* etc.; Nobel Prize for literature 194[7].

Giel·gud (gĭl′good, gēl′-), **S[ir] (Arthur) John** (1904–), Engli[sh] actor and director of plays, film[s] etc.

gift (gĭft) *n.* 1. Giving; vo[l]untary transference of proper[ty] without recompense. 2. Thi[ng] given, present, donation; facul[ty] looked upon as given by heaven et[c.] natural endowment, talent; ~ **[of] gab**, loquacity; ~ **of tongues**: s[ee] GLOSSOLALIA. ~**-wrap** (*v.* (**-wrapped** or **wrapt, -wrap[-] ping**), wrap (gift etc.) decorative[ly.] **gift** *v.t.* Endow with gifts; prese[nt] *with* as a gift; bestow as gi[ft.] **gift′ed** *adj.* (esp.) Natura[lly] endowed with gifts, talented.

gig¹ (gĭg) *n.* 1. Light tw[o-] wheeled one-horse carriage. [2.] Light narrow ship's boat with oa[rs,] sails, or motor; fast, light rowbo[at.]

gig² (gĭg) *n.* Pronged fish spe[ar.] ~ *v.* (**gigged, gig·ging**). Hook [or] catch (fish etc.) with gig. [short f[or] *fizgig*, f. Span. *fisga* harpoon]

gig³ (gĭg) *n.* (slang) Demer[it,] reprimand for a soldier. ~ *[v.]* (**gigged, gig·ging**). Reprima[nd.]

with a gig; give gig to.

gig[4] (gĭg) *n.* (slang) 1. Engagement for jazz musician(s). 2. Any job or task.

giga- *prefix.* One billion (abbrev.).

gi·gan·tic (jīgăn′tĭk) *adj.* Giant-like in size, stature, etc.; abnormally large, huge. **gi·gan′ti·cal·ly** *adv.* **·gan·tism** (jīgăn′tĭzem, jī′găn-) . Giantism.

gig·gle (gĭg′el) *v.i.* (**-gled,** **-gling**). Laugh continuously, not uproariously but in manner suggesting foolish levity or uncontrollable amusement. ~ *n.* Giggling laugh. **gig′gler** *n.* **gig′gly** *adj.* (**-gli·er, -gli·est**). **gig′gling·-** *adv.*

gig·o·lo (jĭg′olō, zhĭg′-) *n.* (pl. os). Man supported by mistress, esp. an older woman; professional dancing partner of woman client.

gigue (zhēg) *n.* (mus.) = JIG.

Gi·la (hē′la) **monster.** Large venomous lizard (*Heloderma sus- ectum*) of southwestern U.S. and . Mexico.

gil·bert (gĭl′bert) *n.* (phys.) Unit magnetomotive force in the cgs stem, equivalent to 10 ÷ 4π mpere turns. [William *Gilbert* 540–1603), English physicist]

Gil·bert[1] (gĭl′bert), **Sir Humphrey** (1539?–83). English navigator and discoverer; founded (1583) at St. John's, Newfoundland, the first British colony in N. Amer.

Gil·bert[2] (gĭl′bert), **William** (1540–1603). English physician and physicist, known as the "father of electricity"; originated the terms "electric force," "electric attraction," and "magnetic pole."

Gil·bert[3] (gĭl′bert), **William Schwenck** (1836–1911). English librettist of light satiric operas written in collaboration with Arthur Sullivan (Gilbert composed the libretto and Sullivan the music); famous for *H.M.S. Pinafore, The Pirates of Penzance, The Mikado,* etc.

Gil·bert (gĭl′bert) **Islands:** see KIRIBATI.

gild[1] (gĭld) *v.t.* (**gild·ed** or **gilt,** **gild·ing**). Cover with thin layer of gold laid on as gold leaf or otherwise; give, esp. deceptive, attractive appearance to; ~ **the lily,** try to

improve what is already quite satisfactory. **gild′ing** *n.*

gild[2] = GUILD.

Gil·e·ad (gĭl′ĕăd). Mountainous region in ancient Palestine, now NW. Jordan, E. of Jordan River between the Sea of Galilee and the Dead Sea.

gill[1] (gĭl) *n.* (usu. pl.) 1. Respiratory organ(s) in fishes and other water-breathing animals, so arranged that venous blood is exposed to aerating influence of water. 2. Wattles or dewlap of fowl. 3. Vertical radial plates on underside of mushrooms etc. 4. Flesh below person's jaws and ears. ~ *v.t.* Gut (fish); catch (fish) in a ~ **net,** fishnet set vertically in the water to entangle fish by the gills.

gill[2] (jĭl) *n.* Liquid measure = ½ pint.

gil·ly·flow·er, **gil·li·flow·er** (jĭl′ĕflower) *ns.* 1. Any of several plants of the genus *Dianthus,* as the carnation. 2. Any of various other plants having fragrant blooms, including stock and wallflower. [OF. *girofle,* ult. f. Gk. *karuophullon* (*karuon* nut, *phullon* leaf)]

gilt[2] (gĭlt) *adj.:* see GILD[1]. ~ *n.* Gilding; ~**-edged,** having gilded

Giorgione, an innovator and leader of Venetian 16th-century painters, used warm colors to create expressive atmosphere in 'The Tempest', in which a nursing woman forms a foreground to the summer storm.

edges, as the pages of a book; (of securities etc.) reliable, safe (not touched by market fluctuations), orig. Brit. Government stock (from being printed on gilt-edged paper).

gim·bals (jǐm′balz, gǐm′-) *n.pl.* (usu. **gimbal** in comb.) Contrivance, usu. of rings and pivots, for keeping objects such as compass or chronometer horizontal at sea.

gim·crack (jǐm′krǎk) *n.* Useless article, knickknack. ~ *adj.* Showy and flimsy, worthless. **gim′-crack·er·y** *n.* (pl. **-er·ies**).

gim·let (gǐm′lǐt) *n.* Small boring tool usu. with wooden crosspiece as handle and screw at pointed end; cocktail of vodka or gin, sugar, and lime juice.

gim·mick (gǐm′ǐk) *n.* (slang) Tricky device; device adopted in order to attract attention or pub-

licity. **gim′mick·er·y, gim′-mick·ry** *ns.* **gim′mick·y** *adj.*

gimp (gǐmp) *n.* Silk, worsted, or cotton twist with cord or wire running through it; trimming made of this; (slang) limp; (slang) cripple.

gin¹ (jǐn) *n.* 1. Snare, net, trap. 2. Hoisting apparatus, crane; (now usu.) tripod with winch for winding rope; (mining) windlass, drum, etc., for hoisting, pumping, etc. 3. Machine (**cotton** ~) for separating seeds from cotton fibers, esp. type invented by Eli Whitney in 1793. ~ *v.t.* (**ginned, gin·ning**). Remove (seeds from cotton) with a gin.

gin² (jǐn) *n.* 1. Strong alcoho[l] liquor obtained by distilling gra[in] and flavoring with juniper berri[es]. 2. Similar liquor flavored w[ith] coriander, aniseed, or oth[er] aromatic agent; ~ **mill**, che[ap] disreputable tavern; ~ **rumm[y]** form of rummy in which play[ers] with cards totaling less than t[en] points may end a game.

gin·ger (jǐn′jer) *n.* 1. (Tropi[cal] plant, *Zingiber officinale*, with) [its] spicy root used as a flavoring a[nd] medicine, and preserved in syr[up] or candied as dessert. 2. Mett[le,] spirit; liveliness; vigor. 3. Lig[ht] reddish-yellow color. 4. ~ **a[le,]** ginger-flavored effervescent s[oft] drink; ~ **beer**, strong ginger [ale] flavored with fermented ging[er,] popular in England; **gin′gerbrea[d,]** cake made with molasses a[nd]

A male giraffe may have a height of 18 ft. Its neck has the same seven vertebrae as other mammals, but those on the giraffe are each 15 inches long. The height is to enable these animals to obtain shoots from trees. Above: To drink from a water-hole a giraffe must spread its forelegs.

plant (*Panax*) found in N. China, Nepal, Canada, and eastern U.S., having a forked root and believed by some to have medicinal or mystic properties. [Chin. *jên shên* image of man (from forked shape of root)]

Gior·gio·ne (jōrjō'nē). **Giorgio da Castelfranco** (1477–1510), Venetian painter.

Giot·to (jŏt'ō). **Giotto di Bondone** (1266?–1337), Florentine painter, architect, and sculptor.

gip = GYP.

gip·sy = GYPSY.

gi·raffe (jirăf', -rahf') *n.* (pl. **-raffes**, collect. **-raffe**). African ruminant quadruped with remarkably long neck and forelegs, and tan skin spotted like panther's.

gir·an·dole (jīr'andōl), **gi·ran·do·la** (jirăn'dola) *ns.* 1. Revolving display, esp. of firework. 2. Branched candleholder or other support for lights. 3. Earring or pendant with large central stone surrounded by smaller ones.

gird (gėrd) *v.t.* (**gird·ed** or **girt**, **gird·ing**). Encircle (waist, person as to waist) with belt etc., esp. to confine clothes; equip *with* sword in belt; fasten (sword etc.) on with belt; secure (clothes) on body with girdle or belt; put (cord etc.) *around*; encircle; ~ **(up) one's loins**, prepare for action.

gird·er (gėr'der) *n.* Beam supporting joists of floor; iron or steel beam for like use; latticed or other compound structure of steel etc. forming span of bridge, roof, etc.

inger, often cut into shapes, as of a boy or girl, and decorated with colored icing; **gin'gersnap**, thin brittle cookie flavored with ginger and molasses. **ginger** *v.t.* Flavor with ginger. **gin'ger·y** *adj.*

gin·ger·ly (jĭn'jerlē) *adv. & adj.* With, showing, extreme caution so as to avoid making a noise or injuring oneself or what is touched or stepped on.

ging·ham (gĭng'am) *n.* Plain-woven cotton fabric of dyed yarns, often striped or checked. [Malay *inggang* striped]

gin·gi·val (jĭnjī'val, jĭn'ji-) *adj.* Of the gums.

gin·gi·vi·tis (jĭnjivī'tĭs) *n.* Inflammation of the gums.

gink·go (gĭng'kō) *n.* (pl. **-goes**). Maidenhair tree (*G ~ biloba*) with wedge-shaped leaves and yellow seeds, native to China and cultivated elsewhere esp. because of its resistance to air pollution; the only living species of the order Ginkgoales, which flourished in the Mesozoic era. [Jap., f. Chin. *yin-hing* silver apricot]

gin·seng (jĭn'sĕng) *n.* (Root of)

gir·dle (gẽr'del) *n.* 1. Belt or cord worn around waist; elasticized corset. 2. Something that surrounds like girdle; part of cut gem dividing crown from base and held by the setting; (anat:) bony support for upper and lower limbs (**pelvic ~, pectoral ~**); ring around tree made by removal of bark. ~ *v.t.* (**-dled, -dling**). Surround with girdle; remove ring of bark from (tree), usu. to kill it.

girl (gẽrl) *n.* Female child; young unmarried woman; maidservant; (colloq.) man's sweetheart (also **best ~**); ~ **Friday**: see FRIDAY; **girl'friend**, female friend, esp. boy's or man's usual or preferred female companion; ~ **scout**, member of the **Girl Scouts**, organization founded by Juliette Low in Savannah, Ga., in 1912 to teach girls citizenship and homemaking skills, good personal habits, etc. **girl'hood** *n.* **girl'ish** *adj.* **girl'ish·ly** *adv.* **girl'ish·ness** *n.*

girt (gẽrt): see GIRD.

girth (gẽrth) *n.* 1. Leather or cloth band tightened around body of horse etc. to secure saddle etc. 2. Measurement around any more or less cylindrical thing. ~ *v.t.* Secure (saddle etc.) with girth.

Gis·card d'Es·taing (zhēskär' dĕstăn') **Valéry** (1926–). President of France 1974– .

gis·mo = GIZMO.

gist (jĭst) *n.* Real idea or point, substance or pith of a matter.

give (gĭv) *v.* (**gave, giv·en, giv·ing**). 1. Bestow gratuitously, hand over as present or donation; confer, grant; accord (affection, confi-

The role of gladiator (below) probably derives from the Etruscan custom of holding fights to the death at funerals, though it is mainly associated with such contests in Rome (circa 200 B.C.–400 A.D.)

dence, etc.); sanction marriage of (daughter etc.). 2. Deliver, hand over, without reference to ownership; put (food etc.) before one; administer (medicine); deliver (message etc.); consign, entrust; pledge, assign as guarantee (*one's word* etc.). 3. Make over in exchange or payment, pay, sell *for* price. 4. Devote, dedicate; addict. 5. Put forth (some action or effort) to affect another; deliver (judgment etc.) authoritatively; provide (party, dinner, etc.) as host. 6. Present, offer (one's hand, arm, etc.); perform or produce (play etc.). 7. Make partaker of; impart, be source of. 8. Allot; grant; assume. 9. Yield as product or result. 10. Cause or allow to have. 11. Collapse; lose firmness, yield to pressure, become relaxed; make room, shrink. 12. (of window etc.) Look, lead, *on, into.* 13. ~ **chase**, start in pursuit; ~ **ear**, listen; ~ **rise to**, occasion; ~ **way**, retire; collapse; be superseded; be dislodged; allow precedence *to*; abandon oneself *to* grief etc. 14. (with adverbs) ~ **away**, transfer by gift; hand over (bride) to bridegroom; betray or expose to ridicule or detection; distribute (prizes); ~ **back**, give (thing) again to its previous owner; ~ **forth**, emit; ~ **in**, yield, cease fighting or arguing; ~ **off**, emit (vapor etc.); ~ **out**, announce; distribute; cease or break down from exhaustion etc.; run short; ~ **over**, hand over; ~ **up**, resign, surrender, part with; deliver (fugitive etc.) into hands of pursuers etc.; abandon *oneself to* a feeling etc.; cease to have to do with; cease from effort; divulge (names of accomplices etc.); pronounce insoluble, renounce hope of. **giv'en** *adj.* ~ **name**, name given to person, hence first name, opp. surname. **giv'er** *n.* **give** *n.* Yielding to pressure, elasticity; springiness, bending, resiliency; **~-and-take**, mutual concession, compromise, exchange of talk; **give'away**, telltale disclosure; sales premium; gift; television program offering prizes to contestants.

Gi·za (gē'za). City in N. Egypt on W. bank of Nile River near Cairo; the Great Pyramids and the Sphinx are 5 mi. to the W.

giz·mo, gis·mo (gĭz'mō) *ns.* (slang) Device; gadget, esp. one without a name.

giz·zard (gĭz'erd) *n.* Bird's second, or muscular, stomach for grinding food after it has been mixed in the first with gastric juice; thickened muscular stomach of some mollusks; (colloq.) stomach; **stick in one's ~**, be unwelcome or unpalatable.

Gk. *abbrev.* Greek.

gla·brous (glā'brŭs) *adj.* (anat. etc.) Free of hair or down,

smooth-skinned.

gla·cé (glăsā') *adj.* 1. Crusted with a glaze of sugar; candied. 2. Having a glossy, smooth surface. ~ *v.* (**-céed, -cé·ing**).

gla·cial (glā'shal) *adj.* 1. (geol. Characterized, produced, by th presence or agency of ice; of a period during which the greate part of the N. hemisphere wa covered with an ice sheet; ~ **deposit**, formation laid down by the action of ice (e.g. boulder clay moraine, kame). 2. Resembling ice bitterly cold. **gla'cial·ly** *adv.*

gla·ci·ate (glā'shēāt) *v.t.* Subject to, mark, polish by, glacia action; cover with a glacier. **gla·ci·a·tion** (glāshēā'shon) *n.*

gla·cier (glā'sher) *n.* Slowl moving mass of ice in high mountain valley formed by accu mulation and gradual consolidatio of snow on higher ground; **G~ National Park**, region in NW Montana covering 1,560 sq. mi (4,040 sq. km) of forests, moun tains, glaciers, and lakes designatec a national park in 1910.

gla·ci·ol·o·gy (glāshēŏl'ojē) *n* Science of geological action of ice **gla·ci·ol'o·gist** *n.*

glad (glăd) *adj.* (**glad·der glad·dest**). Pleased; marked by filled with, expressing, joy; givin joy; (of nature etc.) bright, beauti ful; ~ **eye**, (slang) amorous glance ogle; ~ **hand**, (colloq.) heart welcome, esp. if overdone o insincere; ~ **rags**, (slang) bes clothes, esp. evening dress. **glad'ly** *adv.* **glad'ness** *n.* **glad** *v.t.* (**glad·ded, glad·ding**). (archaic Make glad. **glad'den** *v.t.* **glad' some** *adj.* (poet.) **glad'some·l** *adv.* **glad'some·ness** *n.*

glade (glād) *n.* Clear open spac in forest.

glad·i·a·tor (glăd'ēāter) *n.* 1. I ancient Rome, man armed wit sword, club, etc., and forced to figh other men or animals in an arena fo the entertainment of spectators. 2 Any person taking part in a publi dispute or controversy. **glad·i·a· to·ri·al** (glădēatōr'ēal, -tōr'-) *adj.*

glad·i·o·lus (glădēō'lus) *n.* (pl -li pr. -lī, -lē, **-lus, -lus·es**). Plan of iris family with sword-shape leaves and spikes of brillian flowers; many varieties are native t S. Africa. [L. = "little sword"]

Glad·stone (glăd'stōn), **Wil liam Ewart** (1809–98). Britis

*Facing page: Peaking at over 10,00 ft., the **Tasman Glacier**, the longest New Zealand, flows from the easter slopes of Mount Cook. Its rate of move ment is as high as 20 ins. a day. Th area is a popular skiing center.
Below: Three successive phases in th development of a glacier. When period of cold climate is prolonged, th snow line gets lower and lower and th glacial elements finally merge, flowin into a single basin.*

statesman; 4 times prime minister, 1868–74, 1880–5, 1886, and 1892–1894; ~ **bag**, light leather piece of hand luggage, hinged so as to open flat into 2 approx. equal compartments.

Glag·o·lit·ic (glăgolĭt'ĭk) *adj.* & *n.* (Of) the alphabet, based on Greek minuscules, devised by St. CYRIL² and still used in liturgical books of the Uniats in Dalmatia. [Slav. *glagol* word]

glam·our, glam·or (glăm'er) *ns.* Alluring beauty or charm; attractive and exciting qualities that arouse envy; (archaic) magic, enchantment. **glam'or·ous, glam'our·ous** *adjs.* **glam'or·ize** *v.t.* (**-ized, -iz·ing**). Make glamorous. **glam·or·i·za·tion** (glămerĭză'shon) *n.* [var. of *grammar* in old sense of magic or necromancy]

glance (glăns, glahns) *v.* (**glanced, glanc·ing**). 1. (of weapon) Glide off object instead of striking it full; (of talk etc.) pass quickly *over*, glide *off* or *from*, subject. 2. (of bright object or light) Flash, dart, gleam; (of eye etc.) cast momentary look, give brief look *at*; ~ **at, over**, read cursorily. **glance** *n.* 1. Swift oblique movement or impact. 2. (Sudden movement producing) flash or gleam; brief look.

gland¹ (glănd) *n.* Organ in animal body secreting the chemical compounds required for a particular function and discharging them (usu. through a duct, but cf. ENDO-CRINE ~) into the body or outside it; similar organ in plant. **glan'-du·lar** (glăn'juler), **gland'less** *adjs.*

gland² (glănd) *n.* (mech.) Sleeve

*The craft of the **glass blower**, who collects a ball of molten glass on the end of a tube and blows into it to fashion a hollow vessel, survives. Below: A glass blower at work in Mexico City. Below*

used to press a packing tight on a piston rod.

glare (glār) *v.* (**glared, glar·ing**). 1. Shine dazzlingly or disagreeably; be overly conspicuous or obtrusive. 2. Look fixedly or fiercely (*at*); express (hate etc.) by look. **glar'ing** *adj.* **glar'ing·ly** *adv.* **glare** *n.* Strong fierce light, oppressive unrelieved sunshine;

right: Most glassware is now made in automated factories. Right: The Portland Vase is a 1st-century masterpiece of Roman cameo glass. The vase was made in two layers; the outer one

The **gladiolus** receives its name f the resemblance of its leaves to sw blades. It is a cultivated variety of iris family and is grown in many col

tawdry brilliance; fierce or fi look. **glar'y** *adj.* (**glar·i·** **glar·i·est**).

Glas·gow (glăz'gō, glăs' Largest city in Scotland, situate the SW. on the banks of the Clyc

glass (glăs, glahs) *n.* 1. Nc crystalline solid substance, us transparent, lustrous, hard, a brittle, made by fusing sand (silic with soda or potash, or both, a usu. with other ingredients, as le oxide; ornaments, utensils, wi dows, etc., made of this. 2. Gl vessel esp. for drinking, amount liquid contained in this, drir sandglass, hourglass; window; pl of glass; looking glass; eyegla (pl.) spectacles; glass disk coverir watch face; barometer; lens, es one that magnifies; (pl.) field opera glasses. 3. ~ **blower**, o who fashions hollow and oth glassware by blowing molten gla ~ **cutter**, tool for cutting glas glazier's diamond; ~ **eye**, false e made of glass; **glass'ware**, artic made of glass; **glass wool**, glass form of fine fibers for insulatio filters, etc.; **glass'wort**, any various plants (esp. *Salicorn herbacea* and *Salsola kali*) contai ing large quantity of alkali, former burned to provide potash for glas making. **glass** *v.t.* Fit or cover wi glass; mirror, reflect. **glass'ful** (pl. **-fuls**). Amount of fluid he in a glass.

glass·y (glăs'ē, glah'sē) *ac* (**glass·i·er, glass·i·est**). Havi

was delicately cut away to leave wh images on a dark blue ground. It w smashed in 1845 but brillian restored.

John Glenn was the first U.S. astronaut to orbit the Earth, in space capsule 'Friendship', 1962. Glenn made three orbits in just under five hours, travelling at 17,545 mph.

properties of, resembling, glass; (of eye etc.) lacking fire, dull, fixed. **glass'i·ly** *adv.* **glass'i·ness** *n.*

Glas·we·gian (glăswē´jạn, -jēạn) *adj. & n.* (Native, inhabitant) of Glasgow.

Glau·ber (glow´bẹr), **Johann Rudolf** (1604–68). German chemist and physician; ~**'s salt(s)**, sodium sulfate, used in paper and glass manufacturing and as a cathartic.

glau·co·ma (glawkō´mạ, glow-) *n.* Eye disease characterized by increased tension and hardness of eyeball causing gradual impairment or loss of sight. **glau·co´ma·tous** *adj.*

glau·cous (glaw´kụs) *adj.* Of dull grayish green or blue; (bot.) covered with bloom as of grapes.

glaze (glāz) *v.* (**glazed, glaz·ing**). 1. Fit (window, picture) with glass. 2. Cover (pottery etc.) with vitreous substance fixed by fusion; overlay (cloth, leather, pastry, etc.) with smooth lustrous coating; cover (eye) with a film; cover (painted surface) with thin coat of transparent color to modify tone; give glassy surface to; become glassy. ~ *n.* Vitreous composition for glazing pottery etc.; anything used to produce glazed or lustrous surface; smooth and glossy surface; thin transparent coat of color laid over another color. **glaz'ing, glaz'er** *ns.*

gla·zier (glā´zhẹr) *n.* One whose trade is to glaze windows.

gleam (glēm) *n.* Subdued or transient light; faint, temporary, or intermittent show *of* some quality etc. ~ *v.i.* Emit gleams, shine with subdued or interrupted brightness.

glean (glēn) *v.* Gather grain left by reapers; collect in small quantities; scrape together (news, facts, etc.). **glean'er, glean'ing** *ns.*

glee (glē) *n.* 1. Unaccompanied part song for three or more male voices, popular in 18th c.; ~ **club**, singing group that performs choral music. 2. Mirth; lively and manifest delight. **glee'ful** *adj.* **glee'ful·ly** *adv.*

glen (glĕn) *n.* (chiefly Sc.) Narrow valley.

Glenn (glĕn), **John H(erschel), Jr.** (1921–). First Amer. astronaut to orbit the Earth, 1962; U.S. senator from Ohio, 1975– .

glib (glĭb) *adj.* (**glib·ber, glib·best**). (of speaker, speech,

*Mexican pottery in Calexico, California, showing the diverse and colorful applications of **glaze**. Glazing serves both aesthetic and practical purposes in pottery.*

*The man-powered launches of **gliders** in the 1890s have been superseded. Gliders now may be launched by towing them behind an aeroplane or catapulting them from the ground using an elastic rope.*

c.) Fluent, more talkative than ncere or thoughtful. **glib′ly** *adv.* **ib′ness** *n.*

glide (glīd) *v.* (**glid·ed, glid·-g**). Pass, proceed, by smooth ontinuous motion; go quietly or ealthily; pass gently or gradually; ause to glide; (aeron.) fly without ngine power, fly in glider. ~ *n.* ct of gliding; (mus., phonet., etc.) accession of sounds, sound, made passing from one note to another, from one speech sound to nother. **glid′er** *n.* 1. Person or ning that glides. 2. Aircraft like an rplane, but not having an engine nd depending upon air currents for ight. 3. Swinging couch, generally sed on porches, hung from a ertical framework with springs on nks.

glim·mer (glĭm′er) *v.i.* Shine intly or intermittently. ~ *n.* eeble or wavering light; faint leam *of* hope etc.; glimpse, half iew. **glim′mer·ing** *n.*

glimpse (glĭmps) *n.* Faint and ransient appearance; momentary r imperfect view of. ~ *v.t.* **glimpsed, glimps·ing**). Catch limpse of, see faintly or partly.

glint (glĭnt) *v.* & *n.* (Make) ash, glitter, sparkle.

glis·sade (glĭsahd′, -sād′) *n.* Controlled sliding down steep slope esp. of ice or snow); dance step onsisting of glide to right or left. ~ *v.i.* (**-sad·ed, -sad·ing**). Perorm glissade.

glis·san·do (glĭsahn′dō) *adv.*, *n.* (pl. **-di** pr. -dē, **-dos**), & *adj.* (music) Effect produced by blending one tone into the next, as by sliding tip or back of finger over piano keys or harp strings. [Italianized form of Fr. *glissant*, f. *glisser* slide]

glis·ten (glĭs′en) *v.i.* Shine fitfully; glitter, sparkle. ~ *n.*

glit·ter (glĭt′er) *v.i.* Shine with brilliant tremulous light, gleam, sparkle; be showy or splendid (*with* jewels etc.). ~ *n.*

gloam·ing (glō′mĭng) *n.* (chiefly Sc. or poet.) Evening twilight.

gloat (glōt) *v.i.* Feast eyes or mind lustfully, avariciously, malignantly, etc., *on* or *over*. **gloat′-ing·ly** *adv.*

glob (glŏb) *n.* 1. Small drop or globule of something. 2. Rather rounded lump or mass, as of grease, clay, pudding, etc.

glob·al (glō′bal) *adj.* Of the whole of a group of items, categories, etc.; of, extending over, the whole world; spherical. **glob′-al·ism** *n.* Policy, attitude, etc. that encompasses the needs of the whole world rather than those of single nations. **glob′al·ist** *n.* **glob′al·ly** *adv.*

globe (glŏb) *n.* Spherical body; Earth; spherical chart of Earth (**terrestrial** ~) or the constellations (**celestial** ~); golden orb as emblem of sovereignty; approximately spherical glass vessel, esp. electric light bulb or fishbowl; **globe′fish**, tropical fish (species of Tetraodontidae) able to inflate itself into globular shape; **globe′-flower**, plant (*Trollius laxus*) of family Ranunculaceae with round yellow flowers; **G~ Theatre**, London theater where many of Shakespeare's plays were originally produced; **~-trotting**, traveling through foreign countries for sightseeing; hence, **globetrotter**. **globe** *v.* (**globed, glob·ing**). Make, become, globular. **glo·boid** (glō′boid) *adj.* & *n.* **glo·bose** (glō′bōs, glōbōs′) *adj.* **glo·bos·i·ty** (glōbŏs′ĭtē) *n.*

glob·u·lar (glŏb′yuler) *adj.* Globe-shaped, spherical; composed of globules. **glob′u·lar·ly** *adv.*

glob·ule (glŏb′ūl) *n.* Small spherical body, esp. of liquid; drop.

glob·u·lin (glŏb′yulĭn) *n.* Protein found in animal or plant tissue.

glock·en·spiel (glŏk′enshpēl, -spēl) *n.* Musical instrument, series of tuned metal bars played with hammers. [Ger., = "bell play"]

gloom (glōōm) *n.* Darkness, obscurity; melancholy, despondency. **gloom′y** *adj.* (**gloom·i·er, gloom·i·est**). **gloom′i·ly** *adv.*

The **globe-flower** grows wild in the meadows and marshes of northern temperate lands, and the species (Trollius europaeus) is cultivated in European and American gardens.

Native to the West Indies and tropical America, the **gloxinia** is cultivated as a pot plant for the beauty of its dark foliage as well as its richly coloured flowers. Above right: (Sinningia speciosa).

gloom'i·ness n. **gloom** v.i. (**gloomed, gloom·ing**) Look or be gloomy.

glop (glŏp) n. (colloq.) Liquid or viscous substance, esp. unattractive food.

glo·ri·a (glōr'ēa, glōr'ēa) n. 1. (short for **G ~ Patri**) Doxology beginning "Glory be to the Father"; **G ~ in excelsis Deo**, doxology beginning "Glory be to God on high." 2. Aureole, halo. [L.]

glo·ri·fy (glōr'ĭfī, glōr'-) v.t. (**-fied, -fy·ing**). 1. Make glorious, exalt to the glory of heaven; invest with radiance; transform into something more splendid, invest (common or inferior thing) with charm or beauty. 2. Extol, laud. **glo·ri·fi·ca·tion** (glōrĭfĭkā'shon, glōr-) n.

glo·ri·ous (glōr'ēus, glōr'-) adj. Possessing glory, illustrious; conferring glory, honorable; splendid, excellent. **glo·ri·ous·ly** adv.

glo·ry (glōr'ē, glōr'ē) n. (pl. -ries). 1. Exalted renown, honorable fame; subject for boasting, special distinction, ornament, pride. 2. Adoring praise and thanksgiving. 3. Resplendent majesty, beauty, or magnificence; effulgence of heavenly light; imagined unearthly beauty; bliss and splendor of heaven. 4. State of

exultation, prosperity, etc. 5. Circle of light around head or figure of deity or saint, aureole, halo. ~ v.i. (**-ried, -ry·ing**). Exult, pride oneself, in.

gloss[1] (glŏs, glaws) n. Word inserted between lines or in margin to explain word in text; comment, explanation, interpretation, paraphrase; misrepresentation of another's words; glossary, interlinear translation, or set of notes. ~ v. Insert glosses in (text etc.); write glosses; make comments, esp. unfavorable ones; read different sense into, explain away.

gloss[2] (glŏs, glaws) n. Surface shininess or luster; deceptive appearance, fair outside. ~ v.t. Make glossy; give specious appearance to (freq. over). **gloss'y** adj. (**gloss·i·er, gloss·i·est**). **gloss'i·ly** adv. **gloss'i·ness** n.

glos·sa·ry (glŏs'erē, glaw'serē) n. (pl. -ries). Collection of glosses; list and explanations of abstruse, obsolete, dialectal, or technical terms, partial dictionary. **glos·sar·i·al** (glŏsār'ēal, glaw-) adj. **glos'sar·ist** n.

glos·so·la·li·a (glŏsolā'lēa, glaw-) n. 1. Gift of tongues: see TONGUE. 2. Nonsense speech, esp. in some kinds of schizophrenia.

glot·tal (glŏt'al) adj. Of, produced in, the glottis; ~ **stop**, speech sound produced by sudden explosive release of breath from behind the closed glottis.

glot·tis (glŏt'ĭs) n. (pl. **glot·-**

tis·es, glot·ti·des pr. glŏt'ĭdē: Opening at upper part of windpi and between vocal cords, affecti modulation of voice by contracti or dilating.

Glouces·ter (glŏs'ter, glaws'- Fishing port and summer resort mi. (43 km) NE. of Boston coast of Cape Ann, NE. Mass chusetts.

glove (glŭv) n. Covering leather, cotton, silk, wool, etc., f the hand, usu. with separate fingers; padded glove for boxin ~ v.t. (**gloved, glov·ing**) Provic with gloves. **glov'er** n. Maker seller of gloves.

glow (glō) v.i. Be heated incandescence, throw out light an heat without flame; shine like thin intensely heated; show warm colo burn with bodily heat or emotion fervor. ~ n. Glowing stat brightness and warmth of colo ardor, passion. **glow'ing·ly** adv.

glow·er (glow'er) v.i. Star scowl (at). **glow'er·ing·ly** adv.

glow·worm (glō'wẽrm) n. An of various wingless insects or larva of the Lampyridae family that em greenish luminescence, esp. th female or larva of the firefly.

glox·in·i·a (glŏksĭn'ēa) n. Trop ical S. Amer. plant with large bel shaped flowers. [Benjamin Pete Gloxin, 18th-c. Ger. botanist]

Gluck (glook), **Christoph Wil libald von** (1714–87). Bavaria composer of operas, of whic Orpheus and Eurydice is the mo:

famous.

glu·cose (gloo´kōs) *n*. Dextrose, grape sugar ($C_6H_{12}O_6$), occurring in many plant and fruit juices, in animal tissue fluids, and in blood.

glue (gloo) *n*. Viscous adhesive substance obtained from the hides, bones, and other waste parts of animals by boiling with suitable solvents; any similar adhesive substance; ~ **sniffing**, inhalation of fumes of plastic cement as narcotic. **glue** *v.t*. (**glued, glu·ing**). Fasten or join (as) with glue; attach tightly or closely. **glue´y** *adj*. **glu·i·er, glu·i·est**).

glum (glŭm) *adj*. (**glum·mer, glum·mest**). Sullen, looking dejected or displeased. **glum´ly** *adv*. **glum´ness** *n*.

glut (glŭt) *v.t*. (**glut·ted, glut·ting**). Feed (person, stomach) or indulge (appetite, desire) to the full, overload with food; satiate, cloy; choke up, fill to excess; over-stock (market) with goods. ~ *n*. Full indulgence; one's fill, surfeit; supply in excess of demand.

glu·te·al (gloo´tēal, glootē´-) *adj*. ~ **muscle**, one of the three large muscles (*gluteus maximus, medius, minimus*) forming buttock and serving to move thigh in man.

glu·ten (gloo´ten) *n*. Nitrogenous part of flour, remaining as viscid substance when starch is washed out.   **glu·ti·nos·i·ty** (glootinŏs´ĭtē) *n*. **glu´ti·nous** *adj*. Viscid, sticky. **glu´ti·nous·ly** *adv*.

The wolverine (Gulo gulo) is a **glutton** and its zoological name is derived from its voracious habits. These animals are related to the weasels but are much larger.

glu´ti·nous·ness *n*.

glut·ton (glŭt´en) *n*. 1. Excessive eater, gormandizer; (fig.) person with excessive appetite *for* some activity etc.   2. (Brit.) = WOLVERINE.   **glut´ton·ize** *v.i*. (**-ized, -iz·ing**). **glut´ton·ous** *adj*. **glut´ton·ous·ly** *adv*. **glut´ton·y** *n*. (pl. **-ton·ies**).

glyc·er·ide (glĭs´erīd) *n*. (chem.) Ester of glycerin.

glyc·er·in (glĭs´erĭn), **glyc·er·ine** (glĭs´erĭn, -erēn) *ns*. Colorless sweet viscous liquid obtained as a by-product in the conversion of animal and vegetable oils and fats into soap; used as ointment, as vehicle for drugs, in manufacture of explosives, etc.

gly·co·gen (glī´kojen) *n*. Reserve carbohydrate ($C_6H_{10}O_5)_n$ of the animal cell, into which sugar is converted by insulin. **gly·co·gen·ic** (glīkojĕn´ĭk) *adj*.

gly·col (glī´kōl, -kawl, -kŏl) *n*. Any aliphatic dihydric alcohol, esp. ethylene glycol (see ETHYLENE). **gly·col·ic** (glīkŏl´ĭk) *adj*.

gm. *abbrev*. Gram(s).

G-man (jē´măn) *n*. (pl. **-men** pr. -měn). Agent of the Federal Bureau of Investigation. ["G" = "government"]

GMT, G.M.T. *abbrevs*. Greenwich mean time.

gnarled (närld) *adj*. (of tree) Covered with protuberances; twisted, rugged, knotted, like an old tree.

gnash (năsh) *v*. Grind, grind teeth; (of teeth) strike together.

gnat (năt) *n*. Any of various

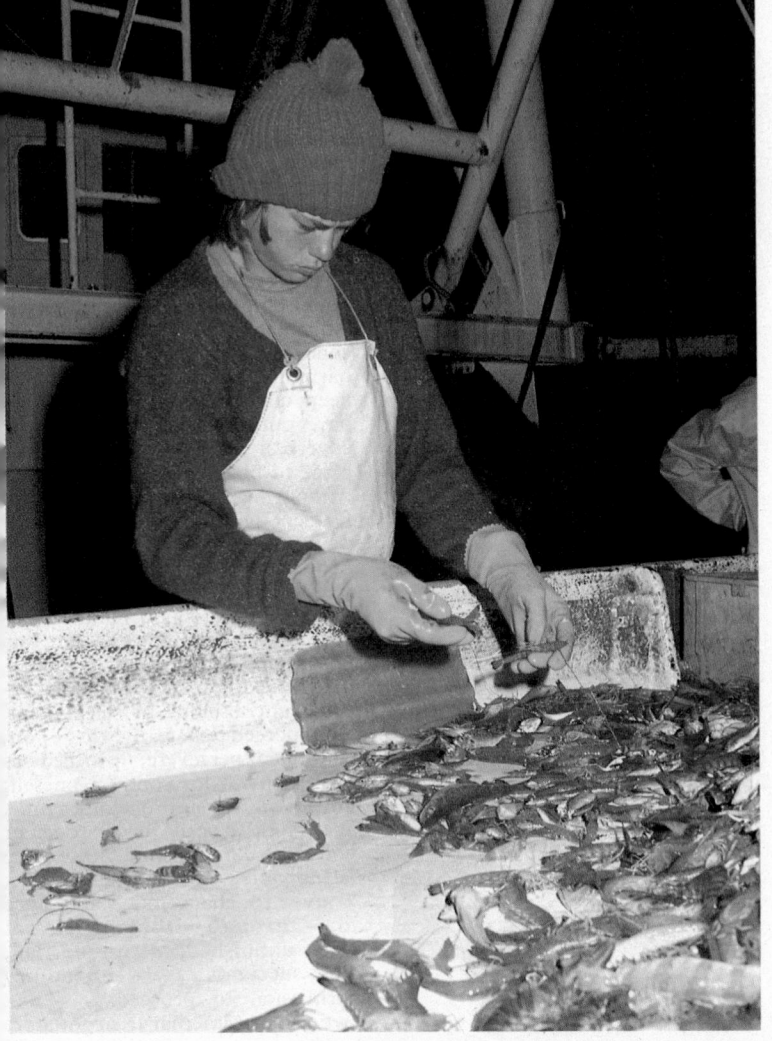

Gloves come in a wide variety of styles, and each is better suited to one job than another. Some are purely for dress; some serve to keep the hands warm; and here they provide protection from cuts.

The mountain **goat** is known for its hardiness and great agility. Like most goats it prefers an arid climate but will live in wet temperate regions quite happily.

small 2-winged insects, esp. those that bite.

gnaw (naw) v. Bite persistently, wear away thus; (of pain etc.) corrode, waste away, consume, torture. **gnaw′er** n. **gnaw′ing·ly** adv.

gneiss (nīs) n. (geol.) Coarse-grained metamorphic rock in which the mineral grains are arranged in roughly parallel bands, usu. containing feldspar and a dark mineral and sometimes quartz.

gnome[1] (nōm) n.   Maxim, aphorism.   **gno′mic** adj.   Of, consisting of, using, aphorisms.

gnome[2] (nōm) n.   1. (myth.) Supernatural dwarfish being of subterranean race guarding treasures of the earth; goblin, dwarf. 2. (colloq.) International (esp. Swiss) financier, esp. in ~s of Zurich (with implication of sinister influence). **gnomish** (nō′mĭsh) adj. [f. mod. L. gnomus invented by Paracelsus]

gno·sis (nō′sĭs) n.   Special knowledge of spiritual mysteries; Gnosticism.

-gnosis comb. form. Knowledge, recognition (diagnosis, prognosis).

gnos·tic (nŏs′tĭk), **gnos·ti·cal** (nŏs′tĭkal) adjs. Relating to intellectual or spiritual knowledge; **G~**, of the Gnostics, occult, mystic. **Gnos′tic** n. (hist.) Member of heretical sects of early Christians claiming to have superior knowledge of spiritual things, and interpreting sacred writings by a mystic philosophy. **Gnos·ti·cism** (nŏs′tĭsĭzem) n.

GNP abbrev.   Gross national product.

gnu (nōō, nū) n. (pl. **gnus**, collect. **gnu**). African quadruped of genus Connochaetes, of antelope family but resembling ox or buffalo; wildebeest.

go[1] (gō) v. (**went** pr. wĕnt, **gone** pr. gawn, gŏn, **go·ing**). 1. Start, depart, move, continue moving, from some place, position, time,

etc. (often not specified if obvious); begin motion; travel, proceed. 2. (of line etc.) Lie, point, in certain direction. 3. Be moving, acting, in working order. 4. Make specified motion. 5. (of time) Pass, elapse. 6. (of document etc.) Have specified tenor. 7. (of verse etc.) Be adaptable to a tune. 8. (of events) Turn out well, badly, etc.; (colloq.) be permitted. 9. Get away free, unpunished, etc. 10. Be sold for sum. 11. (of money) Be spent for goods. 12. Be relinquished, abolished, or lost; die (esp. in past part.). 13. Be kept or put in certain place. 14. Reach, extend, penetrate. 15. Be allotted; tend. 16. (of number) Be capable of being contained in another either without

The **goblet** has long been the object of elaborate workmanship. The two-handled example illustrated here was fashioned in silver gilt by Jules Barbe in the late 19th century.

remainder or simply. 17. Pass int a (esp. undesirable) condition. 18 Bid, offer. 19. (phrases): **going to** preparing or intending to; about tc **gone**, dead, lost, undone; **gone on** (colloq.) infatuated with; **far gone** in advanced stage (of disease etc.) deeply engaged or entangled. 20 (with prepositions): ~ **about**, se to work at; ~ **at**, attack, take in hand energetically; ~ **behind**, seel out, examine grounds of (decision etc.); ~ **by**, be guided by; ~ **for** fetch; be accounted as; strive to attain; be applicable to; (colloq.) be infatuated with; show interest in (colloq.) attack; ~ **into**, enter (profession etc.); take part in investigate; ~ **over**, inspect details of; rehearse, retouch; ~ **through** discuss in detail; scrutinize; per form (ceremony etc.); undergo; (o book) be published successively in (so many editions); ~ **with**, be concomitant of, be associated with harmonize with, match; (colloq. keep company; ~ **without**, no have, put up with want of. 21. (with adverbs): ~ **about**, move from place to place; ~ **ahead**, proceed without hesitation; ~ **around**, be long enough to encompass; (of food etc.) suffice for whole party etc.; ~ **around with**, (colloq.) date frequently; ~ **by**, pass; ~ **down** (of ship) sink; (colloq.) find acceptance with; ~ **in**, enter; ~ **in for** take as one's pursuit, style, etc.; ~ **off**, leave the stage; explode; become unconscious in sleep, faint etc.; succeed well, badly, etc.; ~ **on**, continue, persevere; proceed as next step to do; conduct oneself; **going on to**, approaching (time, age, etc.); ~ **out**, leave room or house; be extinguished; cease to be fashionable; (of workmen) strike; ~ **over to**, change one's allegiance to; ~ **through with**, complete, not leave unfinished; ~ **under**, fail, sink, succumb. 22. **~-ahead** (n.) permission to proceed; **~- between**, intermediary, negotiator;

The **go-cart** is a popular hobby for children and, in its simplest form, is quite easy to make. Races add to the pleasure. Modified, motor-driven versions are also available.

*he once numerous herds of **gnu** have eclined greatly. The smaller white-ailed species is now domesticated but e slightly larger brindled gnu is found wild herds.*

-cart, small wagon for children ride in or to pull; light framework casters for helping children learn walk; handcart; small, low, racing d recreational vehicle, consisting f a framework on wheels with a river's seat, motor, and steering heel; **~-getter**, active, ambitious erson. **go** *n.* (pl. **goes**). 1. Act f going. 2. Mettle, dash, anima- on. 3. Turn at doing something; ttempt *at.* 4. **it's no ~**, nothing an be done; **on the ~**, in motion. **go²** (gō) *n.* (also **I-go**) Japanese ame of territorial possession, using board of 19 parallel lines inter- ecting 19 others at right angles, reating 361 points of intersection n which the players' pieces, 361 tones, are placed and on which the ame is played.

Go·a (gō´a). District on W. coast f India, administered (with)aman and Diu) by India; capital,

Panaji. **Go·a·nese** (gōanēz´, -nēs´) *adj. & n.*

goad (gōd) *n.* Spiked stick used for prodding cattle; thing that torments, incites, or stimulates. ~ *v.t.* Urge with goad; irritate; instigate, drive (*on*), by annoyance.

goal (gōl) *n.* 1. Finish line of race; object of effort or ambition; destination. 2. Posts between which ball is to be driven, kicked, etc. at soccer, football, and other games; points won by doing this; **goal´keeper, goal´tender, goal´-ie**, (soccer etc.) player stationed to protect goal; **goal line**, line (at either end of playing field) in center of which goal posts are placed.

goat (gōt) *n.* Hardy usu. horned and bearded ruminant quadruped (genus *Capra*); licentious person; fool; scapegoat; **get one's ~**, irritate a person; **the G~**: see CAPRICORN; **goat´herd**, one who tends goats; **goats´beard**, plant (*Tragopogon pratensis*), with yellow flowers; (*Aruncus dioicus*) tall plant with small white flowers; **goat´-skin**, (garment, bottle, made of)

skin of goat; **goat´sucker**, any of several birds of the family Caprimulgidae, including the nighthawk and whippoorwill (formerly believed to suck the milk of goats).

goat·ee (gōtē´) *n.* Small beard on chin resembling goat's beard.

gob¹ (gŏb) *n.* (colloq.) Small lump.

gob² (gŏb) *n.* (colloq.) Sailor in the U.S. Navy.

gob·ble¹ (gŏb´el) *v.* (**-bled, -bling**). Eat hurriedly and noisily. **gob´bler¹** *n.*

gob·ble² (gŏb´el) *v.i.* (**-bled, -bling**). (of male turkey) Make characteristic sound in throat. **gob´bler²** *n.* Male turkey.

gob·ble·dy·gook, gob·ble·de-gook (gŏb´eldēgōōk) *ns.* Pretentious and unintelligible jargon and circumlocution, esp. in bureaucratic writing.

Gob·e·lin (gŏb´elĭn, gō´be-) *adj.* Of, made at, the French government-owned tapestry factory of the Gobelins in Paris, orig. workshops owned by a 15th-c. family of dyers named Gobelin. ~ *n.* Tapestry of a kind woven there.

Go·bi (gō´bē) **Desert.** Desert in E. central Asia covering 500,000 sq. mi. (1,295,000 sq. km), mostly in Mongolian People's Republic.

gob·let (gŏb´lĭt) *n.* (archaic) Bowl-shaped drinking cup without handles; drinking vessel with a stem and base, dist. from TUMBLER.

gob·lin (gŏb´lĭn) *n.* Mischievous and ugly demon.

go·by (gō´bē) *n.* (pl. **-bies**, collect. **-by**). Small fish (esp. *Gobius*) with ventral fins joined into disk or sucker.

god (gŏd) *n.* 1. Any superhuman being worshipped as having power over nature and human fortunes, deity; **~ of fire**, Vulcan; **~ of love**, Cupid; **~ of war**, Mars; **~ of wine**, Bacchus. 2. Image, animal, or other object, worshipped as symbolizing, being the visible habitation of, or itself possessing, divine power; an idol; adored, admired, or influential person. 3. **God**, supreme being, creator and ruler of universe; **God the Father, Son, Holy Spirit**, persons of the Trinity; **God knows**, it is beyond mortal or my knowledge, I don't know; **play G~**, attempt to direct the destiny of others; **in the lap of the gods**, beyond human control at the moment; **god willing**, if circumstances allow. 4. **god´-father, god´mother, god´-parent**, sponsor, as at baptism; so **god´child, -son, -daughter**; **god´father**, (colloq.) feared and revered absolute leader, esp. of the Mafia; **God-fearing**, sincerely religious; **Godforsaken**, devoid of all merit; forlorn, dismal; **god'-send**, unexpected welcome event or acquisition; **God'speed**, usu. in **wish** or **bid person Godspeed**, wish him success in journey, undertaking, etc. **god'hood** *n*. **god'like** *adj*.

god·dess (gŏd´ĭs) *n*. Female deity; ~ **of love**, Venus; ~ **of wisdom**, Minerva.

Go·dey (gō´dē), **Louis Antoine** (1804–78). Amer. publisher; founded first U.S. periodical for women, *Godey's Lady's Book*, 1830. ,

god·head (gŏd´hĕd) *n*. Being God or a god, divine nature, deity; **the G ~**, God.

Go·di·va (godī´va). Wife of Leofric, earl of Mercia; acc. to legend, her husband had imposed a tax on the inhabitants of Coventry, England, which he jestingly promised to remit if she would ride naked through the streets at noonday; taking him at his word, she did this, having told the people to stay indoors with closed windows.

god·less (gŏd´lĭs) *adj*. Without a god; not recognizing God; impious, wicked. **god'less·ness** *n*.

god·ly (gŏd´lē) *adj*. (**-li·er**, **-li·est**). Religious, pious, devout. **god'li·ness** *n*.

Go·du·nov (gŏd´unawf, gōōd´-), **Boris Fyodorovich** (1552–1605). Tsar of Russia, 1598–1605; his career was theme of opera by Russian composer Mussorgski, based on play by Pushkin.

God·win Aus·ten (gŏd´wĭn aws´ten) = K2.

god·wit (gŏd´wĭt) *n*. One of several species of large wading birds of genus *Limosa*, like curlew but with bill slightly curved upward.

Goe·thals (gō´thalz), **George Washington** (1858–1928). U.S. army officer and engineer; chief engineer in Panama Canal construction, 1907–14; governor of Canal Zone, 1914–16.

Goe·the (gö´te), **Johann Wolfgang von** (1749–1832). German novelist, poet, and dramatist; *Faust*, a dramatic poem, and the novels *The Sorrows of Young Werther* and *Wilhelm Meister* are the most famous of his works.

Gog and Ma·gog (gŏg´ an mā´gŏg). 1. Names of various people and lands in Old Testament. 2. Nations under dominion of Satan (Rev. 20) opposed to the people of God. 3. (in medieval legend) Opponents of Alexander the Great, living north of the Caucasus. 4. Names given to two giant statues standing in the Guildhall, London, from the time of Henry V (destroyed in 1666 and 1940; replaced in 1953), either (acc. to Caxton) the last two survivors of a

*Completed in 1937, the **Golden Gate Bridge,** spanning the Golden Gate Strait, is unmatched for the beauty of its setting. The main span is 4,200 ft. in length.*

race of giants inhabiting Britain before Roman times, or (in another account) Gogmagog, chief of the giants, and Corineus, a Roman invader.

gog·gle (gŏg´el) *v*. (**-gled, -gling**). Squint, roll eyes about; (of eyes) project, roll about; turn (eyes) sideways or from side to side. ~ *adj*. (of eyes) Protuberant, full and rolling. **gog'gles** *n.pl*. Large spectacles with shielding sidepieces for protecting eyes from glare, dust, etc.

go-go (gō´gō) *adj*. (slang) Energetic, modern, full of pep; (of a young woman) dancing solo, often partially undressed, at a discotheque.

Go·gol (gō´gol), **Nikolai Vasilievich** (1809–52). Russian novelist and dramatist best known for his picaresque romance *Dead Souls* satirizing provincial Russian society.

go·ing (gō´ĭng) *n*. (esp.) Condition of ground for walking, riding, etc.; **goings-on**, behavior.

going *adj*. ~ **concern**, business in actual, esp. successful, operation.

goi·ter, goi·tre (goi´ter) *ns*. Morbid enlargement of thyroid gland, often visible as swelling in neck. **goi'trous** *adj*.

Gol·con·da (gŏlkŏn´da). Old name of Hyderabad, formerly celebrated for diamonds; hence, mine of wealth, source of great riches.

gold (gōld) *n*. 1. (chem.) Metallic element, malleable, ductile, of yellow color and high specific gravity, occurring in the free state, not attacked by most acids, but dissolved by aqua regia, regarded as a precious metal, and used as a standard of value and as the international medium of exchange; symbol Au, at. no. 79, at. wt. 196.9665. 2. Coins made of gold, money in large sums, wealth; metal used for coating surface or as pigment, gilding; color of the metal; (fig.) brilliant, beautiful, or precious things, stuff, etc. 3. **gold'brick**, something worthless that appears valuable; a fraud; **gold'brick** (*v*.), (slang) swindle; seek out sinecures; shirk work; **gold'brick(er)**, (slang) one who goldbricks; **gold bug**, N. Amer.

*The ore in which **gold** is present is broken down mechanically and separated chemically. It may be refined by a smelting process after which it is poured into molds where it cools into ingots of standard size.*

etle (*Metriora bicolor*) with lden luster; (slang) advocate of e gold standard, or of gold as an vestment; **gold digger**, one who gs for gold; (slang) woman attaching herself to man merely for gain; ld dust, gold in fine particles, as ten found; **gold field**, area in hich gold is found; **gold foil**, gold aten into thin sheet; **gold leaf**, eet of beaten gold, thinner than ld foil; **gold mine**, place where ld is mined; source of wealth; ld-plate (*v.t.*), plate with gold; ld rush, rush to new gold field; ld'smith, worker in gold; **gold andard**, financial system of a untry in which paper, silver oney, etc., is redeemable on mand in gold at a fixed weight d fineness. **gold** *adj*. Wholly or iefly of, colored like, gold; **gold'-**

finch, bright yellow Amer. songbird (*Spinus tristis*) with black cap and wings; also green-backed or black-backed Western species (*S. psaltria*), or the European goldfinch (*Carduelis carduelis*); **gold'fish**, golden-red Asiatic fresh-water fish (*Carrasius auratus*) of carp family.

Gold (gōld) **Coast**: see GHANA.

gold·en (gōl′dɛn) *adj*. Made, consisting, of gold; colored, shining, like gold; precious, excellent, important; ~ **age**, (i) (Gk. and Rom. myth.) first and best age of world, in which mankind was

ideally prosperous and happy; (ii) most flourishing period (of literature etc.); ~ **ager**, (colloq., often ironic) elderly retired person; ~ **chain**, laburnum; ~ **eagle**, large eagle of Northern hemisphere with golden yellow feathers on head and neck; **gold'eneye**, either of two species of duck of genus *Bucephala* with dark-and-white plumage in male and gold-colored iris of the eye; **Golden Fleece**, (Gk. legend) fleece of gold taken from the ram that bore Phrixus through the air to Colchis; it was placed in a sacred grove by Aeëtes, king of Colchis, where it was guarded by a sleepless dragon, until it was won by JASON; **Golden Gate**, entrance strait of San Francisco Bay; **Golden Horde**, (trans. of Tartar name, from richness of Batu Khan's

1. Alluvial **gold** scoured into rivers is washed from lighter sand and mud in a pan. 2. Gold is smelted and cast into ingots which are then weighed. 3. Gold's malleability allows craftsmen to beat it into extremely thin sheets. They may then be laid down on any surface that requires decoration. The initial is enriched with gold leaf laid down by the limner of the Book of Kells which dates from the 8th or 9th century. 4. Gold bullion supports much currency and here a bank counts in a new deposit. The workmanship of a pre-Columbi gold vase worked in the shape of head demonstrates the malleability gold.

tent) Tartar horde that overran Eastern Europe in 13th c. under Batu Khan, grandson of Genghiz, and kept Russia in subjection until 1486; **G ~ Horn**, curved inlet of Bosporus, forming harbor of Istanbul, Turkey; **golden mean**, moderation; course between extremes; **gold'enrod**, composite chiefly N. Amer. plant of genus *Solidago* with rodlike stem and spike of bright yellow flowers; **golden rule**, rule, *do unto others as you would have them do unto you,* from the precept in Matt. 7; **golden section**, division of a straight line into 2 parts so that the ratio of the whole line to the larger part is the same as the ratio of the larger part to the smaller; **golden wedding**, 50th anniversary of wedding.

Gold·smith (gōld´smĭth), **Oliver** (1728–74). Irish writer; author of the novel *The Vicar of Wakefield* and the comic play *She Stoops to Conquer.*

go·lem (gō´lĕm, -lem) *n.* (Jewish legend) Clay figure supernaturally brought to life; automaton, robo

golf (gŏlf, gawlf) *n.* Game which small hard rubber-cored b is struck with clubs over surface course into series of small holes smooth greens, the aim being to the ball with the fewest possib strokes into any hole or all 9 or holes successively; **~ clu** (premises of) association for playi golf; one of the sticks with whi golf is played; **~ course, link** tract of land on which the game played, usu. of 9 or 18 hol ranged at intervals freq. with artificial obstacles (bunkers etc.) added; **~ widow**, woman whose husband spends much time at golf. **golf** *v.i.* Play golf. **golf'er** *n.*

Gol·gi (gawl'jē) **apparatus, Golgi body.** (biol.) Intracellular system of membranes and vacuoles near the nucleus in cells of most animals and some plants, usu. concerned with intracellular secretion. [Camillo *Golgi* (1844–1926), Ital. physician]

Gol·go·tha (gŏl'gotha). Aramaic name of CALVARY (Mark 15); hence, burial place, cemetery. [Heb. *gulgōleth* skull]

Go·li·ath (goli'ath). Philistine giant, acc. to legend slain by DAVID[1] (1 Sam. 17), with a stone and sling. **gol·ly** (gŏl'ē) *int.* (colloq. euphemism) By God (used as mild expletive).

go·losh (golŏsh'): see GALOSH.

Go·mor·rah, Go·mor·rha (gomor'a, -mär'-). Town of ancient Palestine that, along with Sodom, was destroyed by God because of the godlessness of its inhabitants (Gen. 18, 19); hence, (type of) wicked town.

Gom·pers (gŏm'perz), **Samuel** (1850–1924). British-born U.S. labor leader; president and one of organizers of American Federation of Labor, 1886–94, 1896–1924.

go·nad (gō'năd) *n.* (biol.) Organ (as testis or ovary) producing gametes. **go·nad·al** (gōnăd'al) *adj.*

gon·do·la (gŏn'dola) *n.* Light flat-bottomed boat with cabin amidships and high point at each end, worked by one oar at stern, used on Venetian canals; basket or car suspended from balloon or airship; (also **~ car**) flat, open railroad freight car with low sides. **gon·do·lier** (gŏndolēr') *n.* Rower or poler of gondola.

Gond·wa·na·land (gŏndwah'naländ). Ancient land mass supposed to have existed in the southern hemisphere until late Paleozoic times, including Africa, India, Australia, and South America.

gone: see GO[1].

gon·er (gaw'ner, gŏn'er) *n.* (slang) Person or thing doomed, irrevocably lost, etc.

gong (gawng, gŏng) *n.* Metal disk with turned rim giving resonant note when struck with padded mallet. [Malay]

go·ni·om·e·ter (gōnēŏm'eter) *n.* 1. Optical instrument for measuring angles in crystals etc. 2. Apparatus for detecting direction of radio waves without the need for a rotating aerial.

gon·o·coc·cus (gŏnokŏk'us) *n.* pl. **-coc·ci** pr. **-kŏk'sī**). Microorganism causing gonorrhea.

gon·or·rhe·a (gŏnorē'a) *n.* Venereal disease characterized by

inflammatory discharge of mucus from urethra or vagina. **gon·or·rhe'al** *adj.*

goo (goō) *n.* (slang) Viscous or sticky substance; (fig.) sickly sentiment.

goo·ber (goō'ber) *n.* (southern U.S.) Peanut.

good (goōd) *adj.* (**bet·ter, best**). Having the right qualities, adequate; expedient; morally excellent, virtuous; benevolent; well-behaved (esp. of child), not giving trouble; agreeable, advantageous; wholesome; suitable; efficient; reliable, safe; valid, sound; considerable; not less than (as in *a ~ 3 miles* etc.); **as ~ as**, practically, almost; **have a ~ mind to**, be much inclined to; **have a ~ time**, enjoy oneself; **make ~**: see MAKE[1]; **say a ~ word for**, commend, defend; **~ afternoon, day, morning, night**, forms of salutation at meeting or parting; **~ breeding**, good character as revealed in manners and sensitivity to others; **~ fellow**, sociable person, agreeable companion; **~-fellowship**, conviviality, sociability; **~ for**, beneficial to; having good effect on; in condition to undertake or pay; (of a check) drawn for (so much); **~-for-nothing**, worthless, useless (person); **G~ Friday**: see FRIDAY;

*The canal system of the lagoon city of Venice has a unique form of transport in the **gondolas**. These fragile, light craft are maneuvered with great skill along the narrow canals.*

~-hearted, kindly, willing to please; **~ humor**, cheerful mood or disposition, amiability; **~-humored** (*adj.*), **~-humoredly** (*adv.*); **~-looking**, handsome; **~ luck**, being fortunate, happy chance; **~ nature**, kindly disposition, willingness to humor others or permit encroachment on one's rights; **~-natured** (*adj.*), **~-naturedly** (*adv.*); **~ Samaritan**, genuinely charitable person who goes out of his way to help others (Luke 10); **~ sense**, practical wisdom; **~ temper**, freedom from irritability; **~-tempered** (*adj.*), **~-temperedly** (*adv.*); **good** *n.* 1. What is good or beneficial, well-being, profit, advantage; desirable end or object; **be any ~**, be of any use (similarly **some ~, no ~**); **do ~**, act philanthropically, show kindness *to*, benefit; **for ~**, finally, permanently; **to the ~**, as balance on right side, something extra etc.; **up to no ~**, bent on mischief. 2. (pl.) Movable property, merchandise, wares; (Brit.) freight.

good·by, good·bye (goōdbī') *ints. & ns.* (pl. **-bys, -byes**). Expression used conventionally at parting. [contraction of *God be with you!* with *good* substituted on analogy of *good night* etc.]

Good (goōd) **Hope, Cape of.** Promontory in Republic of South Africa, S. of Cape Town at tip of Africa, the foot of the continent; Vasco da Gama rounded cape in 1497 journey to India.

good·ly (goōd'lē) *adj.* (**-li·er,**

-li·est). Comely, handsome; of considerable size etc. **good'li·ness** *n.*

good·ness (good'nĭs) *n.* Virtue; excellence; benevolence, kindness, generosity, what is good in a thing, its essence or strength; (in exclamations substituted for) God.

good·will (good'wil') *n.* Kindly feeling toward person; cheerful acquiescence, willingness; good relationship of a business to its customers (esp. when considered an intangible asset).

good·y[1] (good'ē) *n.* (pl. **good·-ies**). (usu. pl.) Something good to eat, esp. a sweet.

good·y[2] (good'ē), **good·y-good·y** (good'ē good'ē) *adjs. & ns.* (pl. **-good·ies**). Ostentatiously virtuous (person); (person) good in a weak or sentimental way. ~ *ints.* Exclamations of delight used by children.

Good·year (good'yēr), **Charles** (1800–60). Amer. inventor of vulcanization process for rubber.

goof (goof) *n.* (slang) Silly or stupid person; mistake; ~-**ball**, (slang) (1) pill containing barbiturate or other drug; (2) very stupid person. **goof'y** *adj.* (**goof·i·er, goof·i·est**). **goof** *v.* Bungle, make a mistake; loaf, waste time (usu. ~ off); ~-**off** (*n.*), one who goofs off.

goo·gol (goo'gŏl, -gol) *n.* (math.) Number 1 followed by 100 zeros

(10[100]); **goo'gol·plex'**, number 10 raised to the googol power; 1 followed by 10[100] zeros. [word coined by the young daughter of Edward Kasner (1878–1955), Amer. mathematician]

gook (gook) *n.* (slang) 1. Grimy goo. 2. (offensive) Oriental.

goon (goon) *n.* 1. (slang) Hired thug. 2. Dull or stupid person.

goose (goos) *n.* (pl. **geese** pr. gēs). 1. Large web-footed bird (of

Canada

Red-breasted

Egyptian

Snow

Chinese

genus *Anser* or subfamily Anserinae), usu. between duck and swa in size; female of this; its flesh a food. 2. Simpleton. 3. Tailor pressing iron (with handle like nec of goose). 4. **barnacle** ~: se BARNACLE; **cook one's** ~, (colloq ruin one's chances; ~ **egg**, (colloq score of zero in a game or innin ~ **flesh, bumps, pimples**, roug bristling state of skin produced b cold or fright; **goose'foot**, plant o genus *Chenopodium* (from shape o leaves); **goose'neck**, pipe, lamp etc., curved like neck of goose **goose step**, balance step, used b some armies in marching o ceremonial parades, in which th legs are alternately advanced with out bending the knees; **goose-step** (*v.i.*) (**-stepped, -step·ping**) march thus. **goose** *v.t.* (**goosed goos·ing**). (slang) Poke (person in sensitive part of the body, esp the buttocks.

goose·ber·ry (goos'bĕrē, -berǐ gooz'-) *n.* (pl. **-ries**). (Edible berr of) any thorny species of *Ribes*.

G.O.P. *abbrev.* Grand Old Part (U.S. Republican Party).

go·pher (gō'fer) *n.* 1. Short tailed burrowing rodent of famil Geomyidae of N. Amer. havin external cheek pouches. 2 Nocturnal burrowing land tortois of southern U.S. 3. ~ **snake** non-venomous snake (*Pituoph catenifer*) of western N. Ame preying on gophers. 4. Groun squirrel; ~ **ball**, (baseball slang

*Above: The Indian **goral** is sometimes called the Indian antelope. It is a goat-antelope rather like a chamois and lives between 8,000 and 12,000 ft. high on mountain slopes. Below: The goral lies in an intermediate evolutionary stage between true antelopes and goats.*

tch easy to hit or *go for*; HOME n ball.

go·pher·wood (gō′ferwood) *n.* nidentified wood used in con- ruction of Noah's ark (Gen. 6), pposed to be cypress.

go·ral (gōr′al, gōr′-) *n.* Goatlike ntelope (*Naemorhedus goral*) of E. sia, having short backward- rving horns.

Gor·di·an (gōr′dēan) *adj.* ~ ot, intricate knot tied by ordius, king of Gordium in nrygia; an oracle declared that hoever loosened it should rule sia, and Alexander the Great, nable to undo it, cut it with his vord; hence, a difficult problem or sk; **cut the ~ knot,** solve roblem by bold direct action.

gore[1] (gōr, gōr) *n.* Blood shed d thickened or clotted. **gor′y** *adj.* or·i·er, gor·i·est). Covered with ood; involving bloodshed. **gor′- ly** *adv.*

gore[2] (gōr, gōr) *n.* Wedge- aped piece in garment, umbrella, il, etc.; wedge-shaped strip of nd. ~ *v.t.* (**gored, gor·ing**). hape, provide, with gore.

gore[3] (gōr, gōr) *v.t.* (**gored, or·ing**). Pierce with the horn or arely) tusk.

Gor·gas (gōr′gas), **William**

Crawford (1854–1920). U.S. army surgeon general, 1914–18; rid Havana, Cuba, of yellow fever while chief sanitary officer there, 1898–1902, after Spanish-American War; made digging of Panama Canal possible by controlling yellow fever while chief sanitary officer, Panama Canal Commission, 1904–13.

gorge (gōrj) *n.* 1. (rhet.) Internal throat. 2. What has been swallowed, contents of stomach; act of gorging; surfeit; **one's ~ rises at,** one is disgusted or angered by. 3. (fort.) Neck of bastion or other outwork; rear entrance to a work. 4. Narrow opening between hills, rocky ravine, usu. with stream. ~ *v.* (**gorged, gorg·ing**). Feed greedily; satiate, glut; swallow, devour greedily; fill, distend, choke up.

gor·geous (gōr′jus) *adj.* Richly colored, sumptuous, magnificent. **gor′geous·ly** *adv.* **gor′geous·ness** *n.*

Gor·gon (gōr′gon). (Gk. myth.) One of three sisters, Stheno, Euryale, and MEDUSA (the only mortal one), with snakes for hair, whose look turned the beholder to stone; hence (**g** ~), repulsive or terrifying woman.

Using its power and strength of its talons and beak, the **goshawk** seizes its prey — birds, reptiles and small mammals. Goshawks of all varieties hunt by day using to advantage their phenomenal binocular vision to discover their victims.

black-mantled goshawk

gabor goshawk

white throat

northern goshaw

stock dove

Gor·gon·zo·la (gorgonzō'la) *n.* [Ri]ch strong cheese, with veinings [of] bluish mold, orig. made at [G]orgonzola, a village near Milan, [It]aly.

go·ril·la (goril'a) *n.* 1. Large [p]owerful anthropoid ape, *Gorilla [go]rilla*, of western equatorial Africa. 2. (slang) Brutish man; gangster.

Gor·ki, Gor·ky (gôr'kē), **[M]axim** (1868–1936). Pseudonym [of] Alexei Maximovich Pyeshkov, [R]ussian writer and revolutionary; [fa]mous for his realistic short stories, [de]aling principally with thieves, [tr]amps, and other outcasts.

gor·mand·ize (gôr'mandīz) *v.* [(-]ized, -iz·ing). Eat voraciously [or] gluttonously. **gor'mand·iz·er**

gorse (gôrs) *n.* Prickly yellow-[fl]owered European shrub (*Ulex [e]uropaeus*).

gosh (gŏsh) *int.* (colloq. [e]uphemism) By God (used as mild [e]xpletive).

gos·hawk (gŏs'hawk) *n.* Long-[ta]iled hawk (*Accipiter gentilis*), [la]rgest of its genus, of N. N. Amer. [an]d N. Europe.

Go·shen (gō'shen). Prosperous [r]egion of ancient Egypt on E. delta [o]f the Nile, inhabited by Israelites [fr]om the time of Joseph until the [E]xodus; hence, a place of plenty [(G]en. 45, Exod. 8, 9).

gos·ling (gŏz'ling) *n.* Young [g]oose.

gos·pel (gŏs'pel) *n.* 1. Glad [ti]dings (of kingdom of God) [p]reached by Christ; religious [d]octrine of Christ and his apostles, [C]hristian revelation. 2. (usu. **G ~**) [R]ecord of Christ's life and teaching [i]n first 4 books of New Testament [(M]atthew, Mark, Luke, John); any [o]f these books. 3. Thing that may [s]afely be believed; principle that [o]ne acts upon, believes in, or [p]reaches. 4. **~ singing**, fervent or [e]vangelical singing, esp. as a style of [ja]zz; **~ singer**; **~ truth**, truth [c]ontained in gospel; something as [tr]ue as gospel. [OE. *god-spel* (*god* [g]ood, *spell* tidings)]

gos·sa·mer (gŏs'amer) *n.* Light [fi]lmy substance, spiderwebs or [c]obwebs floating in calm air or [s]pread over grass; thread of this; [s]omething flimsy; delicate gauze. **~** *adj.* Light and flimsy as [g]ossamer. [ME. *gossomer* = "goose [s]ummer," St. Martin's summer, [i.]e. early November, when geese [w]ere customarily eaten and gossa-[m]er is abundant]

gos·sip (gŏs'ip) *n.* 1. (archaic) [F]amiliar acquaintance; (esp. [w]oman) friend. 2. Idle talker, [ta]ttler (esp. of woman). 3. Idle [t]alk, groundless rumors, tittle-[ta]ttle; easy unconstrained talk or [w]riting, esp. about persons or social [in]cidents; hence **~ column**, [c]olumn devoted to this in news-paper. **gos'sip·y** *adj.* **gos'sip** *v.i.* (**-siped, -sip·ing**). Talk idly or lightly, tattle; write in gossipy style. [orig. = sponsor at baptism, f. *God* + *sib* akin, related]

got: see GET.

Gö·te·borg (gaw'teborg; *Swed.* yöteboŕ'ye), **Goth·en·burg** (gŏth'-enberg, gŏt'-). Second largest city in Sweden, in the SW.; seaport and shipbuilding center.

Goth (gŏth) *n.* One of a Germanic tribe who in 3rd, 4th, and 5th centuries invaded both the Eastern and Western Roman Empires and founded kingdoms in Italy, France, and Spain; hence, barbarian or rude or ignorant person.

*The **gorilla** is the largest of the anthropoid apes, a group that also includes the chimpanzee. Only one species exists, but this is divided into three races.*

Goth. *abbrev.* Gothic.

Goth·am (def. 1 gŏ'tham, -tam; def. 2 gŏth'am, gō'tham). 1. Village (perh. the one of this name in Nottinghamshire, England) proverbial for folly of its inhabitants. 2. (joc.) New York City, a name first given to it in *Salmagundi*, a humorous work by Washington Irving, William Irving, and J. K. Paulding, because its inhabitants were reputed to be wiseacres. **Goth'am·ite** *n.* New Yorker.

Goth·ic (gŏth'ĭk) *adj.* 1. Of, like, the Goths; hence (fig.) barbarous, rude. 2. (archit.) Of the style of architecture prevalent in W. Europe from the 12th to the 16th c., characterized by ribbed vaults, pointed arches, clustered pillars, etc.; of the art of this period; (of script) of style used by Ulfilas (see *n.* 2 below). 3. **~ Revival**, revival in England and U.S. of Gothic architecture in the mid-18th and esp. the 19th c.; ~ **novel**, (hist.) novel, fashionable in late 18th c., featuring mystery, horror, and sentimental romance; 20th c. popular novels resembling these.

Gothic *n.* 1. Gothic architecture. 2. Extinct language of the Goths, one of the E. GERMANIC group of languages, known from the 4th-c. translation of parts of the Bible made by Bishop Ulfilas and from other scattered remnants.

Goths (gŏths): see OSTROGOTH and VISIGOTH.

Got·land (gŏt′land). Island in Baltic Sea off SE. coast of Sweden; early Roman and Byzantine trade center.

got·ten: see GET.

Göt·ter·däm·mer·ung (göter- dĕm′erōong) *n.* (Ger. myth.) Twilight of the gods (see TWILIGHT).

gouache (gwahsh; *Brit.* gōō′- ahsh) *n.* (Painting in) opaque watercolor.

Gou·da (gōō′da) *n.* Flat, round, mild, pale-yellow cheese, usu. in red wax coating, and orig. made at Gouda in the W. Netherlands.

gouge (gowj) *n.* Concave- bladed chisel. ~ *v.t.* 1. Cut with gouge; cut *out* (as) with gouge; force (out, esp. person's eye with thumb) (as) with gouge; force out eye of. 2. (colloq.) Swindle. **goug′er** *n.*

gou·lash (gōō′lahsh) *n.* Hun- garian stew of meat and vegetables seasoned with paprika, also **Hungarian** ~. [Magyar *gulyás- hús* (*gulyás* herdsman, *hús* meat)]

gourd (gōrd, gōrd, goord) *n.* (Large fleshy fruit of) trailing or climbing plant of family Cucurbi- taceae, related to the squash and pumpkin; shell of the fruit dried and used as vessel.

gour·mand (goor′mahnd, -mand, goormahnd′) *n.* Lover of food in both quality and quantity; glutton.

gour·met (goormā′, goor′mā) *n.* Connoisseur of fine food and wine.

gout (gowt) *n.* 1. Metabolic disease characterized by painful inflammation of smaller joints, esp. that of big toe, and excessive amount of uric acid in blood. 2. Blob, clot, mass of something fluid or sticky, drop, esp. of blood. **gout′y** *adj.* (**gout·i·er, gout·i·est**). **gout′i·ness** *n.*

Gov., gov. *abbrevs.* Governor, government.

gov·ern (gŭv′ern) *v.* 1. Rule with authority; conduct policy and affairs of (nation etc.); curb, control; sway, influence; constitute law, rule, principle, etc., for, serve to decide (case); **governing board, body**, managers of hospital, school, etc. 2. (gram., esp. of verb or preposition) Have (noun, case) depending on it; be necessarily

The **Gothic** *style of architecture emerged in the ambulatory of the Abbey of St. Denis, Paris, c. 1140. Its pointed arch and ribbed vaults crossed the English Channel where they found* expression *(top) in Gloucester C thedral. The style was revived in t 18th century and (above) was used architects of the British Houses of P liament in the 19th century.*

followed by (a certain case).

gov·ern·ance (gŭv′ernans) *n.* Act, manner, fact, or function, of governing.

gov·ern·ess (gŭv′ernĭs) *n.* Woman employed to educate, train, and look after children of a house- hold.

gov·ern·ment (gŭv′ernment, -erment) *n.* 1. Act, manner, fact, of governing; area under a single rule; system of governing, form of polity. 2. Body or successive bodies of persons governing a state; the state as an agent; administration or

ministry; **G~ House**, offic residence of governor of Br colony; **government issue**, (oft cap.) (of) equipment issued soldiers etc. by governmen **gov·ern·men·tal** (gŭvernmĕn′ta **gov·ern·men′tal·ly** *adv.*

gov·er·nor (gŭv′erner) *n.* 1. O who governs, ruler; offic appointed to govern province, tov etc.; chief executive of a U.S. sta officer commanding fortress garrison; head, or member governing body, of institution; **general** (pl. **governors gener**

governor generals). 2. (chiefly Brit. slang) One's employer; one's father; sir. 3. (mech.) Automatic regulator of supply of gas, steam, etc., to machine, ensuring an even motion; device for keeping clockwork or similar machine at constant speed. **gov′er·nor·ship** n.

gown (gown) n. Loose flowing outer garment, esp. woman's dress, frock; ancient Roman toga; official or uniform robe of various types worn by judges, clergymen, members of university, etc.; **cap and ~**: see CAP[1]; **town and ~**: see TOWN. **~** v.t. (chiefly in past part.) attire in gown.

Go·ya (goi′a), **Francisco José de Goya y Lucientes** (1746–1828). Spanish painter, esp. of portraits; etcher of the "Disasters of War" and other series of macabre and satirical prints.

G.P. abbrev. General practitioner (doctor).

GPO, G.P.O. abbrevs. General post office; Government Printing Office.

G.P.U. (also O.G.P.U.; hist.) Soviet secret police organization (1922–34) that superseded the Cheka. [f. initials of Russ. Obedinennoe) Gosudarstvennoe Politicheskoe Upravlenie (United State Political Directorate]

gr. abbrev. Grain(s); grade; grammar; gross; group.

Early paintings by **Goya** *express a fresh delight in life through scenes of common life. At Court he painted portraits that might be honest to the point of cruelty but in this one of Countess de Gondomar he is tender.*

Below: The State Department building in Washington D.C. **Government** *is typically divided into departments to facilitate smooth operation and strategic differentiation of labor.*

Above: Tourists passing through the main street of Lima, Peru, are offered an amazing variety of **gourds.** *They range from the practical and simple to the ornate and decorative.*

Right: The jaws of a **grab** are held apart until they surround their load; then the jaws are closed on the load by another rope. On some the jaws are operated by means of an electric motor. Left above: A grab may be used to load harvests such as sugar cane.

Graaf (grahf), **Regnier de** (1641–73). Dutch anatomist. **Graafian** (grah′fēan) **follicle**, one of the small sacs in the ovary of mammals in which the ova are matured.

grab (grăb) v. (**grabbed, grab·bing**). 1. Seize suddenly, appropriate rapaciously; capture, arrest; make snatch *at*. 2. (slang) Attract, arouse interest. ~ n. 1. Sudden clutch, grasp, seizure, or attempt to seize; practice of grabbing, rapacious proceedings, esp. in politics or commerce. 2. (mech.) Device for clutching or gripping. 3. ~ **bag**, at bazaar, party, etc., container of articles of more or less value to be drawn blindly; any miscellaneous collection; **up for** ~s, (colloq.) readily available to first comer, or to anyone willing to work for it. **grab′ber** n. (esp. colloq.) One who grabs without scruple or consideration.

grace (grās) n. 1. Pleasing quality, attractiveness, charm, esp. that belonging to elegant proportions or ease and refinement of movement, manner, etc.; attractive feature; **with good** ~, as if willing. 2. (mus.) Embellishment of additional note(s) (~ **note**) not essential to harmony or melody. 3. (Gk. myth.) **the (three) Graces**, beautiful sister-goddesses (Aglaia, Thalia, Euphrosyne), bestowers of beauty and charm. 4. Benign regard or its manifestation on part of superior; unconstrained goodwill as ground of concession; boon; dispensation from statutes; **be in person's good** ~s, enjoy his or her favor or liking. 5. (theol.) Unmerited favor of God; divine

regenerating, inspiring, and strengthening influence; condition (also **state of** ~) of being so influenced; divinely given virtue or excellence, etc.; (archaic) **year of** ~, year as reckoned from birth of Christ. 6. Favor shown by granting delay; mercy, clemency; ~ **period, days of** ~, time allowed for payment without penalty of a premium, note, etc., after it is due. 7. Short blessing or prayer of thanksgiving before or after meal. 8. **his, her, your, G**~, forms of address or description for duke, duchess, or archbishop. **grace** v.t. (**graced, grac·ing**). Add grace to, adorn, set off *with*; confer honor or dignity on, honor *with* title etc.; do credit to. **grace′ful** adj. Full of grace (sense 1). **grace′ful·ly** adv. **grace′ful·ness** n.

grace·less (grās′lĭs) adj. Without sense of decency; without charm or elegance. **grace′less·ly** adv. **grace′less·ness** n.

grac·ile (grăs′īl) adj. Slender, thin, lean.

gra·cious (grā′shus) adj. (archaic) Agreeable, pleasing; kindly, benevolent, courteous; (of God) dispensing grace, merciful, benignant. **gra′cious·ly** adv. **gra′cious·ness** n. **gracious** int. (ellipt. for ~ **God**, as) **good** ~!, ~ **me!**, exclamations of surprise.

grack·le (grăk′el) n. Either of 2 N. Amer. blackbirds, the **common** ~ (*Quiscalus quiscula*), or the very

large **boat-tailed** ~ (*Cassi mexicanus*).

grad (grăd) n. (colloq.) Gra ate. ~ adj. (colloq.) Gradua usu. in ~ **student**.

gra·date (grā′dāt) v. (**-dat -dat·ing**). (Cause to) pass imperceptible degrees from shade of color to another; arra in steps or grades.

gra·da·tion (grādā′shon) Stage(s) of transition or adva (usu. pl.); series of degrees rank, merit, divergence, etc.; such degrees; arrangement in su degrees; (fine arts) gradual pass from one shade, tone, etc., another. **gra·da′tion·al** a **gra·da′tion·al·ly** adv.

grade (grād) n. 1. Degree rank, proficiency, value, etc.; cl of persons or things alike in de (pupils constituting) an elementa school class; ~ **school**: see ELEME TARY school 2. (cattle breedi Variety produced by crossi ordinary stock with superior bre 3. Gradient, slope; rate of asc or descent; ~ **crossing**, pl where railroad and road or t railroads cross at same level; **ma the** ~, reach the proper standa be up to the mark. 4. Rating school assignment, examination, course of study. **grade** v (**grad·ed, grad·ing**). Arrange grades, class, sort; gradate; redu (road etc.) to easy gradients; (cat breeding) cross with better bre **grad′er** n.

gra·di·ent (grā′dēent) Amount of slope, inclination horizontal, in road etc., measur as the ratio of the difference elevation between two points to t horizontal distance between the that a slope rising 1 ft. per ft. of horizontal distance has a adient of 1 in 10).

grad·u·al[1] (grăj'ōoal) *n.* Re- onse sung in the service of the ass between Epistle and Gospel; ok containing this and other usic for the Mass. [so called cause sung at altar steps; f. L. *adus* steps]

grad·u·al[2] (grăj'ōoal) *adj.* aking place by degrees, slowly ogressive; not rapid, steep, or rupt. **grad'u·al·ly** *adv.* **ad'u·al·ness** *n.*

grad·u·ate (grăj'ōoĭt, -āt) *n.* ne who holds an academic degree; e who has been graduated from gh school, elementary school, etc. (grăj'ōoāt) *v.* (**-at·ed, -at·ing**). Take academic degree; receive ploma for completing high school ucation or work at other educa- nal institution; certify (students) having completed education or aining. 2. Mark out in degrees; range in gradations, apportion cidence of (tax) according to a ale; hence, **graduated income x** etc. **grad·u·a'tion** (grăjōoā'- on), **grad'u·a·tor** *ns.*

Grae·cism (grē'sĭzem): see RECISM.

graf·fi·to (grafē'tō) *n.* (pl. **-ti** pr.). Drawing or writing scratched wall etc., esp. on ancient walls at Pompeii; (pl.) scribblings or awings made on walls in public aces; messages or slogans in- ribed there, usu. of obscene or litical nature.

graft[1] (grăft, grahft) *n.* Plant nsisting of shoot or scion inserted to a stock, from which it receives p; (surg.) piece of transplanted ing tissue; process of grafting; ace where graft is inserted. ~ *v.* sert (scion) as graft; insert graft(s) on (stock); insert graft(s); (surg.) nsplant (living tissue); insert or in or upon so as to produce vital

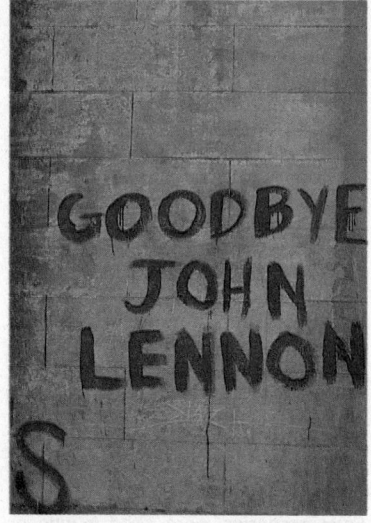

Graffiti, irreverent inscriptions painted on walls in public places, deal with many subjects. Graffito originally referred to a method of decoration.

or indissoluble union.

graft[2] (grăft, grahft) *n.* Obtain- ing of profit or advantage by dishonest means; profits so ob- tained. ~ *v.i.* Seek, make, graft. **graft'er** *n.*

Gra·ham[1] (grā'em), **Martha** (1894–). Amer. dancer and choreographer, a pioneer developer of modern dance.

Gra·ham[2] (grā'am), **Sylvester** (1794–1851). Amer. advocate of vegetarianism; **graham cracker**, cracker made from unbolted wheat flour (~ **flour**).

Grail (grāl) *n.* (also **holy** ~) In medieval legend, the cup or chalice that Christ used at the Last Supper

One of the common ways of propagat- ing a shrub or tree is by grafting. A cut is made in the root stock and a new plant material, a scion, is inserted and bound in place. This may be done sev-

and in which Joseph of Arimathaea received Christ's blood at the Cross; medieval romances tell how it was sought for by Arthur's knights.

grain (grān) *n.* 1. Fruit or seed of a cereal; (collect. sing.) wheat or the allied food grasses or their seeds after harvesting; ~ **alcohol**, ETHYL alcohol; ~ **elevator**, building in which grain is stored and handled by elevators and conveyors. 2. Small hard usu. roundish particle of sand, salt, gunpowder, etc. 3. Smallest unit of weight, 0.002285 ounce; smallest possible quantity, hence ~ **of truth** (in something). 4. (poet.) Dye, color; **in** ~, fast dyed, genuine, thorough. 5. Granular texture, roughness of surface, mottling, texture, arrange- ment and size of constituent particles, in flesh, skin, wood, stone, etc.; lines of rays in wood, often giving a pattern; (fig.) nature, temper, tendency. 6. **against the** ~, contrary to inclination. **grain** *v.* Form into grains; give granular surface to; remove hair from (hides); paint in imitation of grain of wood or marble. **grain'y** *adj.* (**grain·i·er, grain·i·est**).

gram[1] (grăm) *n.* Chickpea; any legume used as horse fodder.

gram[2] (grăm) *n.* $\frac{1}{1000}$ of a kilo- gram (abbrev. g).

Gram (grahm), **Hans Chris- tian Joachim** (1853–1938). Danish biologist; ~-**positive**, ~- **negative**, (of organism) that does, does not, stain by Gram's method of staining bacteria for microscopic examination.

-gram[1] *suffix.* Forming nouns, indicating something written or pictured, as *telegram, diagram.*

eral ways. A cleft may be cut in the stock and a scion inserted. A cut may be mortised in a tongue shape. A bud may be grafted into stock by binding it into a slit in the bark.

Scion   Bud grafting

Cleft graft   Tongue graft   1   2   3

-gram[2] *suffix.* Comb. form of GRAM[2], as in *kilogram*.

gram·mar (grăm'er) *n.* 1. Language study dealing with inflectional forms or other means of indicating relation of words within sentence, and with rules for employing these (in early English use *grammar* meant only *Latin grammar*); treatise or book on grammar; person's manner of using grammatical forms; speech or writing regarded as good or bad by the rules of grammar, what is correct according to those rules; body of forms and usages in a language; elements, rudiments, of an art or science; **comparative ~**, study of relation between grammars of two or more languages; **historical ~**, study of historical development of the grammar of a language. 2. **~ school**, grade school; (hist.) school stressing the study of classical languages. **gram·mar·i·an** (gramār'ēan) *n.*

gram·mat·i·cal (gramăt'ĭkal) *adj.* Of grammar; conforming to rules of grammar; **~ gender**, gender (in most Indo-European and Semitic languages) not determined by real or attributed sex. **gram·mat'i·cal·ly** *adv.*

gramme (grăm) *n.* Brit. var. of GRAM[2].

Gram·o·phone (grăm'ofōn) *n.* (trademark) Phonograph, esp. of an early type.

gram·pus (grăm'pus) *n.* (pl. **-pus·es**). Dolphinlike marine mammal (*Grampus griseus*); also (sometimes) KILLER whale.

Gra·na·da (granah'da; *Sp.* grahnah'dhah). Province of S. Spain on Mediterranean coast; former Moorish kingdom, 8th–15th centuries; captured in 1492 by Ferdinand and Isabella of Castile, ending Moorish power in Spain; city in S. Spain and former capital of Moorish Granada province.

gran·a·dil·la (grănadĭl'a) *n.* Tropical Amer. species of passionflower, esp. *Passiflora quadrangularis* or its edible fruit.

gran·a·ry (grā'nerē, grăn'erē) *n.* (pl. **-ries**). Storehouse for threshed grain; region producing, and esp. exporting, much wheat.

grand (grănd) *adj.* 1. (in official titles) Chief over others, of highest rank; **G~ Army of the Republic**, organization of U.S. Civil War veterans founded in 1866; **G~ Duke, Duchess**, ruler of certain European countries (**G~ Duchies**); (also, hist.) child of Tsar of Russia; **G~ Master**, head of various orders, as of knighthood,

Freemasons, Oddfellows, etc.; **~ vizier**, chief minister of a Muslim country, esp. formerly of Turkish empire. 2. (law) Great, principal, chief, (opp. petty); **~ jury**: see JURY; **~ larceny**, larceny involving goods whose value is above a certain amount (see PETTY larceny;) 3. Of most or great importance; main; (mus.) full, of full dimensions, for full orchestra, in full classical form; (in Fr. phrases or imitations) great; **~ opera**: see OPERA. 4. Conducted with solemnity, splendor, etc.; fine, splendid; belonging to high society, distinguished; imposing, great and handsome; dignified, lofty in conception, treatment, or expression; morally imposing, noble, admirable; (colloq.) very satisfactory;

Early **granaries** were sited in pits or buildings. The disadvantages of this arrangement (vulnerability to damp and rodents) were overcome by building huge concrete containers for above-ground storage.

~ manner, style, style a manner fitted for great subjec **G~ Old Party** (G.O.P.), Reput can Party. 5. (in names of relatio ships) In the second degree ascent or descent, as **gran daughter, grand'son**, on child's daughter, son; **grand father, grand'mother**, on parent's father, mother; so **gran child, grand'parent**, etc. 6. combinations: **grand'fath clock**, eight-day clock of ki formerly in common use, w weight-and-pendulum moveme and tall wooden case; **grand pian** see PIANO[2]; **grand'sire**, (archa grandfather; forefather; **Gra Prix**: see separate entry; **gra slam**: see SLAM[2]; **grand'stan** principal stand for spectators stadium, race track, etc.; **Gra Teton**: see separate entry; **gra tour**: see TOUR. **grand'ly** *ad* **grand'ness** *n.* **grand** *n.* Grand piano; **baby ~**, small gra piano. 2. (slang) 1,000 dollars.

Grand prix motor races are driven over specially built circuits in many countries. Here the cars compete for the Dutch Grand Prix in 1971. The cars must conform to rules governing size and power.

Grand (grănd) **Banks.** Shoal in tlantic Ocean off S. and E. ewfoundland, Canada; world's eatest cod fishing area.

Grand (grănd) **Canal.** 1. Canal NE. China extending 1,000 mi. ,609 km) from Tientsin (Tianjin) to Hangchow (Hangzhou); also lled "Imperial River" or "Transrt River" by the Chinese. 2. lain waterway of Venice, Italy, 80 175 ft. (24 to 53 m) wide.

Grand (grănd) **Canyon.** NW. rizona gorge, formed by the olorado River, extending W. from e mouth of the Little Colorado iver to Lake Mead on the Arizonaevada boundary; about 280 mi. 51 km) long, 4 to 18 mi. (6 29 km) wide, and up to 1 mi. .6 km) deep; ~ **National ark**, park in NW. Arizona, tablished in 1919, covering 1,009 . mi. (2,613 sq. km), including rt of the Grand Canyon.

Grand Cou·lee (grănd kōō′lē) **am.** Dam at the N. end of the olumbia River in the state of ashington.

gran·dee (grăndē′) n. Spanish or ortuguese nobleman of highest nk; person of high rank or ninence.

gran·deur (grăn′jer, -dyer) n. reatness; great nobility of characr; sublimity, majesty; conscious gnity; splendor.

Grand Gui·gnol (grahń ĕnyawl′). Paris theater specializg in short sensational plays with emes of violence and bloodshed; nce, sensational, violent enterinment, incidents, etc. [f. assoc. ith *Guignol*, pop. hero of Fr. uppet theaters, and perh. f. finity with *guignon* evil]

gran·dil·o·quent (grăndĭl′oɰent) adj. Pompous or bombastic language. **gran·dil·o·quent·ly** dv. **gran·dil·o·quence** n.

gran·di·ose (grăn′dēōs) adj.

Producing, intended or trying to produce, an impression of greatness; planned on a magnificent scale; pompous. **gran′di·ose·ly** adv. **gran·di·os′i·ty** n.

grand mal (grahn′mahl′, grăn′măl; Fr. grahń măl′). Severe form of epilepsy (opp. PETIT MAL). [Fr.]

Grand·ma Mo·ses (grănd′mah mō zĭz). (full name, Anna Mary Robertson Moses) (1860–1961); U.S. primitive painter who began career late in life.

Grand Prix (grahń prē′) (pl. **Grands Prix** pr. grahń prē′). International horse race for threeyear-olds, run annually at Longchamps, near Paris; any of various international road races for sport cars of specific engine size.

Grand Te·ton (grănd tē′tŏn). Highest peak (13,766 ft., 4,196 m) in Teton Range, NW. Wyoming; ~ ~ **National Park**, NW. Wyoming national park covering 310,358 acres (125,601 hectares) and including **Grand Teton Mountain.**

grange (grānj) n. 1. (Brit.) Country house with farm buildings attached. 2. (cap.) U.S. farmers' association founded in 1867; one of its lodges.

gran·ite (grăn′ĭt) n. Granular crystalline rock of quartz, feldspar, and mica, very abundant and used in building because of its hardness and durability; ~ **ware**, kind of pottery speckled like granite; kind of speckled enameled ironware.

gran·ny, gran·nie (grăn′ē) ns. (pl. **-nies**). 1. (colloq.) Grandmother; old woman; (fig.) fussy person. 2. (also **granny knot**)

*The spectacular **Grand Canyon,** carved by the erosive powers of the Colorado River, takes on many different colors depending on the time of day and the prevailing weather. Right: Mule trains carry weary tourists along the winding slopes of the canyon.*

Granite is formed by cooling magma. It is high in quartz and feldspar, and is the most common plutonic rock of the Earth's crust.

Square knot crossed the wrong way. **granny** adj. Old-fashioned, as in *granny glasses.*

gra·no·la (granō′la) n. Dry breakfast food, a mixture of grains, nuts, fruit, etc.

grant (grănt, grahnt) v.t. Consent to fulfill (request etc.); concede as indulgence; allow (person) to have; give formally, transfer (property) legally; concede (proposition) as basis for argument; **take for granted**, assume. ~ n. Granting; formal conferment, legal assignment; thing, esp. sum of money, granted; conveyance by written instrument; ~**-in-aid** (pl. **grants-in-aid**), sum granted to individual to finance university studies; **grants′manship**, (colloq.) art of gaining government grants, usu. for projects enriching the grantee more than enhancing public welfare or world of intellect; art of parlaying one grant to more, as a way of life. **gran·tee** (grăntē′, grahn-), **gran·tor** (grăn′ter, grahn′-, grăntōr′, grahn-) ns.

Starch from the bulbs of the grape hyacinth was once used to stiffen linen and won it the name of starch lily. The flower grows to a height of 7 ins. and blooms in spring. It is often grown as a border plant.

The grape harvest at Limogne, in France, is gathered in baskets to be taken from the vineyards to the presses where the juice is extracted for winemaking. Grapes were introduced into France by the Romans.

Ulysses Grant ruled the U.S.A. President from 1869–77, during wh time he advocated amnesty for Confe erate leaders, and protection of c rights of Negroes. Much of his rule w clouded by scandal.

Grant (grănt), **Ulysses S(impson)** (1822–85). (original name, Hiram Ulysses); 18th president of U.S., 1869–77; West Point graduate, 1843; entered Civil War as a colonel, appointed major general after several victories; won battle at Vicksburg, July, 1863, shattering Confederate control of the Mississippi and dividing the Confederacy in half; promoted to lieutenant general; received surrender of Robert E. Lee at Appomattox courthouse, Apr. 9, 1865, ending the Civil War; promoted to rank of general, 1866.

gran·u·lar (grăn´yuler) *adj.* Of, like, grains; with granulated surface or structure. **gran'u·lar·ly** *adv.* **gran·u·lar·i·ty** (grănyulăr´ĭtē) *n.*

gran·u·late (grăn´yulāt) *v.* (**-lat·ed, -lat·ing**). Form into grains; roughen surface of. **gran'-u·lat·ed** *adj.* (of sugar etc.) Formed into or consisting of granules or grainlike bodies. **gran·u·la·tion** (grănyulā´shon), **gran'u·la·tor** *ns.*

gran·ule (grăn´ūl) *n.* Small grain or particle.

grape (grāp) *n.* Green or purple berry growing in clusters on vine, eaten as fruit or used in making wine; **the ~**, wine; **grape'fruit**, globular fruit of tree *Citrus paradisi*, with a bitter yellow rind and acid juicy pulp, so called as growing in clusters; **grape hyacinth**, plant of genus *Muscari* with a raceme of small blue flowers; **grape'shot**, cluster of small iron balls formerly used as charge for cannon; **grape**

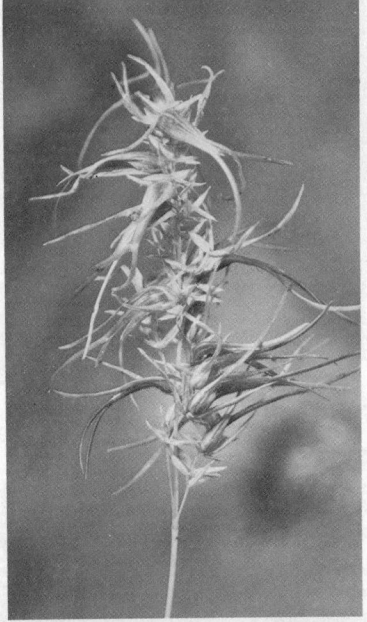

2

3

*more than 10,000 species, **grass** the widest distribution of the vasculants and is one of the plant world's t adaptable groups. 1: Couch-grass ts from long rhizomes. 2: Poa ara grass. 3: Rye-grass grows two tall. 4: Lesser quaking grass grows oadsides and arable land. 5: The le plumes of pampas grass are to ornament houses and gardens.*

4

5

ar, dextrose; **grape′vine**, vine ring grapes; (colloq.) route by ch rumors pass.

raph (grăf, grahf) *n.* Diagram esenting the relation between or more variable quantities by distance of a series of points (or rve or other line joining these) n axes of reference, which are at right angles to each other; cissa of any point corresponding he value of one variable and the inate to that of the other. ~ Represent (information) in a ph. [abbrev. of *graphic formula*] **graph** *suffix.* Forming nouns, oting something written, wn, or recorded, as *photograph, nograph.*

raph·ic (grăf′ĭk) *adj.* Of drawpainting, engraving, etching, ; vividly descriptive, lifelike; of ting; of diagrams, linear figures, ymbolic curves; ~ **arts**, reprotive arts of engraving, etching, dcut, lithography, etc. **graph′l** *adj.* **graph′i·cal·ly** *adv.*

raph·ics (grăf′ĭks) *n.pl.* (conred sing. or pl.) Design and oration involving or accomying printed work; use of grams in calculation and design; duction of diagrams etc. by mputer.

raph·ite (grăf′īt) *n.* Crystalline tropic form of carbon, used in cils, as solid lubricant, etc.

gra·phit·ic (grafĭt′ĭk) *adj.*
graph·ol·o·gy (grăfŏl′ojē) *n.* Study of character deduced from handwriting. **graph·ol′o·gist** *n.* **graph·o·log·i·cal** (grăfolŏj′ĭkal) *adj.*

grap·nel (grăp′nel) *n.* Metalclawed instrument thrown with rope to seize object, esp. enemy's ship; small anchor with several flukes, used for boats and balloons.

grap·ple (grăp′el) *n.* Grapnel; hold or grip (as) of wrestlers. ~ *v.* (**grap′pled, grap′pling**). Seize, fasten, (as) with grapnel; take hold of, grip, with the hands, come to close quarters with; contend in

close fight, struggle *with*; ~ **with**, try to overcome, accomplish, or deal with; **grappling iron** = GRAPNEL.

grasp (grăsp, grahsp) *v.* Clutch *at*, try to seize; seize and hold firmly with hand; get mental hold of, comprehend. ~ *n.* Fast hold, grip; control, mastery; mental hold, comprehensiveness of mind. **grasp′a·ble** *adj.* **grasp′ing** *adj.* (esp.) Greedy, avaricious. **grasp′ing·ly** *adv.*

grass (grăs, grahs) *n.* Herbage in general, blades or leaves and stalks of which are eaten by horses, cattle, etc.; plant belonging to the

Grasshoppers have various defenses. They have remarkable powers of jumping and many are well camouflaged. Top: 5 per cent of greenleaf long-horned grasshoppers have wings. They exude a noxious smell from glands near their hind legs to repel predators. Their brilliant green color ensures the aggressors remember the results of an attack. Below; left: A bladder grasshopper looks like a leaf; right: A mating pair of green leaf grasshoppers.

order Gramineae (in bot. use including, in popular use excluding, the cereals, reeds, and bamboos); grazing, pasture; pasture land; grass-covered ground, lawn, grass border; (slang) marijuana (as drug); **grass′hopper**, orthopterous insect (of families Tettigoniidae and Locustidae) with remarkable powers of leaping and producing a shrill chirping noise by rubbing the forewings together or with the hind legs; **grass′land**, area of grass or grasslike vegetation; prairie; ∼-of-**Parnassus**, any plant of the genus

Parnassia, with wide leaves and a single pale flower; ∼ **roots**, (fig.) source; rank and file of political party etc. ∼-**roots** (*adj*.); ∼ **snake**, harmless common ringed snake (*Natrix natrix*) of Europe, and common green snake (*Ophiodrys vernalis*) of U.S.; ∼ **widow**, married woman whose husband is absent for a period. **grass′less**; **grass′y** *adjs*. (**grass·i·er, grass·i-est**). **grass** *v.t.* Cover with grass, grow grass on; feed grass to (animals).

grate[1] (grāt) *n.* Frame of metal bars for holding fuel in firepla stove, or furnace; fireplace.

grate[2] (grāt) *v.* (**grat·** **grat·ing**). Reduce to small p ticles by rubbing on rough surfa have irritating effect *on*; gr (teeth); rub with harsh scrap noise *against, on* something el sound harshly or discordant **grat′er** *n.* Utensil for grat cheese, vegetables, etc. **grat′ing** *adv.*

grate·ful (grāt′ful) *adj.* Co forting, refreshing, agreeable; fe ing or showing gratitude. **grat ful·ly** *adv.* **grate′ful·ness** *n.*

grat·i·fy (grăt′ĭfī) *v.t.* (**-fi -fy·ing**). Please, satisfy, delig give free course to, indulge (desire, feeling, impulse). **grat fi·ca·tion** (grătĭfĭkā′shon)

grat·i·fy·ing *adj.* **grat′i·fy·ing·ly** *adv.*

grat·ing (grā′tǐng) *n.* Framework of parallel or crossed wooden or metal bars; (optics) (also **diffraction** ~,) arrangement of parallel wires, surface of glass, etc., ruled with parallel lines, for producing spectra by diffraction.

gra·tis (grăt′ĭs, grah′tĭs, grā′-) *adv. & adj.* Gratuitous(ly); free(ly); without charge.

grat·i·tude (grăt′ĭtōod, -tūd) *n.* Being thankful, appreciation of and inclination to return kindness.

gra·tu·i·tous (gratōo′ĭtus, -tū′-) *adj.* Received or given free, not earned or paid for; uncalled for, unwarranted, motiveless, done or acting without good or assignable reason. **gra·tu′i·tous·ly** *adv.* **gra·tu′i·tous·ness** *n.*

gra·tu·i·ty (gratōo′ĭtē, -tū′-) *n.* (pl. **-ties**). Money present, in addition to payment due, given in recognition of services, tip.

gra·va·men (gravā′men) *n.* (pl. **-am·i·na** pr. -văm′ina). (law) Essence, worst part, *of* accusation or charge.

grave[1] (grāv) *n.* Excavation to receive corpse, mound or monument over it; death; receptacle of or for what is dead; **grave′clothes**, clothes or shroud in which corpse is buried; **grave′stone** (also *head-stone*), stone over grave, inscribed one at head or foot of grave; **grave′yard**, burial ground; **graveyard shift**, (colloq.) work shift beginning at midnight; workers on this shift.

grave[2] (grāv) *adj.* (**grav·er, grav·est**). 1. Important, weighty, needing serious thought; (of faults, responsibilities, charges, etc.) serious, formidable; dignified, solemn, slow-moving, not gay; somber, plain, not showy. 2. (of sounds) Low in pitch, deep in tone; ~ **accent**, (*grave* usu. pr. grahv) accent, orig. indicating a low or falling pitch on vowel so marked; (usu. in English verse) indicating a pronounced *e* in verb ending *-ed*. **grave′ly** *adv.* **grave** *n.* Grave accent.

grave[3] (grāv) *v.t.* (**graved, grav·en** or **graved, grav·ing**). Clean (ship's wooden bottom) by burning off accretions and tarring while aground or in dry dock.

grav·el (grăv′el) *n.* 1. Coarse sand and small water-worn stones, freq. with slight intermixture of clay. 2. (path.) (Disease with) aggregations of urinary crystals recognizable as masses by naked eye. **grav′el·ly** *adj.* **gravel** *v.t.* (**-eled, -el·ing, -elled, -el·ling**). 1. Pave, strew, with gravel. 2. Perplex, puzzle, nonplus.

Graves (grāvz), **Robert (Ranke)** (1895–). English poet, novelist, scholar; author of histori-cal novels *I, Claudius, The Golden Fleece*, etc.

Graves′ (grāvz) **disease.** (med.) Exophthalmic goiter. [Robert James *Graves* (1796–1853), Irish physician]

grav·id (grăv′ĭd) *adj.* Pregnant; full of, distended by, ripe eggs.

grav·i·tate (grăv′ĭtāt) *v.* (**-tat·ed, -tat·ing**). Move or tend by force of gravity *toward* a body; sink (as) by gravity, tend to low level, settle down; cause to sink by gravitation; (transf.) be strongly attracted *to(ward)* some center of influence.

grav·i·ta·tion (grăvĭtā′shon) *n.* Falling of bodies to earth, or sinking to lowest level, moving or tending to center of attraction; tendency of every particle of matter toward every other particle, of which fall of bodies to earth is an instance; **law of** ~, law (formulated by Sir Isaac Newton) according to which the attractive force of bodies varies directly as their masses and inversely as the square of the distance between them. **grav·i·ta′tion·al** *adj.*

grav·i·ty (grăv′ĭtē) *n.* (pl. **-ties**). 1. Being grave, solemnity; importance, seriousness; staidness, sobriety, serious demeanor. 2. Weight; **specific** ~, relative weight of any kind of matter, expressed by ratio of weight of given volume to weight of equal volume of some substance taken as standard (usu. water for liquids and solids, hydrogen or air for gases). 3. Attractive force by which all bodies tend to move toward center of earth,

The **grave** *of an admired person is usually commemorated with elaborate display but Sir Ernest Shackleton's grave in the Whaler's Cemetery on St. Georgia Island is austerely simple.*

degree of intensity with which body in given position is affected by this, measured by amount of acceleration produced (abbrev. g); degree of intensity with which any body is similarly attracted by any other.

gra·vure (gravūr′, grāv′yer) *n.* Photogravure; rotogravure.

gra·vy (grā′vē) *n.* (pl. **-vies**). Fat and juices exuding from meat during and after cooking; sauce for meat etc. made from these with condiments etc.; ~ **boat**, boat-shaped vessel for gravy. 2. (slang) Unearned or unexpected money or benefit; excess money; ~ **train**, (slang) sinecure; source of easy money.

gray, Brit. **grey** (grā) *adjs.* Intermediate between black and white, colored like ashes or lead, between light and dark; dull, clouded, depressing, dismal; (of horse) of dark metallic color, iron gray; (of person, hair, etc.) turning white with age etc.; ancient, immemorial; belonging to old age, experienced, mature; ~ **area**, undecided or ambiguous aspects of a matter or parts of a controversy; **gray′beard**, old man; **Gray Friar**, Franciscan, from the color of the habit; **gray matter**: see MATTER; **gray power**, political pressure of organized old or retired persons; **gray squirrel**, common squirrel (*Sciurus carolinensis*), gray or black, arboreal, with bushy tail. **gray** *n.* Gray clothes; cold sunless light; gray color, pigment, horse. ~ *v.* Become, make, gray. **gray′ish** *adj.* **gray′ly** *adv.* **gray′ness** *n.*

Gray (grā), **Thomas** (1716–71). English poet; author of "Elegy in a Country Churchyard" etc.

gray·lag (grā′lăg) *n.* Common European wild goose (*Anser anser*).

gray·ling (grā′lǐng) *n.* (pl. **-lings**, collect. **-ling**). 1. Silver-gray freshwater fish (*Thymallus*) of salmon family, with long high dorsal fin, used for food. 2. Common butterfly.

graze[1] (grāz) *v.* (**grazed, graz·ing**). Feed (esp. cattle, or *v.i.* of cattle) on growing grass etc.; feed on (grass etc.); tend grazing cattle; pasture cattle.

graze[2] (grāz) *v.* (**grazed, graz·ing**). Touch lightly in passing; abrade (skin etc.) in rubbing past; suffer slight abrasion of (part of body). ~ *n.* Grazing; abrasion caused by grazing.

Gr. Br. *abbrev.* Great Britain.

grease (grēs) *n.* Melted fat of dead animals, esp. when soft; oily or fatty matter, esp. as lubricant; oily matter in wool, uncleansed wool; ~ **gun**, kind of pump for lubricating parts of machinery with grease; ~ **monkey** (slang) mechanic who lubricates machines; garage worker; ~ **paint**, make-up for painting actors' faces etc.; **greasewood**: = CREOSOTE BUSH. **grease** (grēs, grēz) *v.t.* (**greased, greas·ing**). Anoint or lubricate with grease; ~ **person's palm**: see PALM²; **like greased lightning**, (slang) very fast.

greas·er (grē′ser, -zer) *n.* (derog.) Native Mexican, Spanish-American.

greas·y (grē′sē, -zē) *adj.* (**greas·i·er, greas·i·est**). 1. Smeared or covered with, containing, made of, like, with too much, grease; (of wool) uncleansed; ~ **spoon**, (slang) cheap and dirty restaurant. 2. Slimy or slippery with mud, moisture, etc. 3. (of manners or expression) Disagreeably unctuous. **greas′i·ly** *adv.* **greas′i·ness** *n.*

great (grāt) *adj.* 1. Large, big (freq. preceding partly synonymous adjective, as ~ **big**, ~ **thick**, etc.); (of animal etc., species or variety) larger than others; (of part of building etc.) main, principal; (of qualities, emotions, etc.) beyond the ordinary in degree or extent; **the ~ majority**, much the larger part; **Greater**, (of cities) including adjoining areas etc. 2. Important,

elevated, distinguished, *the* chief, preeminent; **the G~** (following proper name), the most famous of the name, one of the great figures of history. 3. Of remarkable ability, genius, intellectual or practical qualities, loftiness or integrity of character; fully deserving the name of, (with agent nouns) doing the act much or on a large scale, as **a ~ fiasco, a ~ scoundrel**; (colloq.) highly satisfactory, fine, magnificent; (predic.) having much skill *at* or information *on*; **great′hearted** (*adj.*), noble, magnanimous, generous, courageous. 4. (with terms denoting kinship, esp. with compounds of *grand*) One degree farther removed in ascending or descending relationship; as ~ **-aunt, -uncle**, one's parent's aunt, uncle, ~ **-grandfather, -grandmother**, one's parent's grandfather, grandmother; so ~ **-grandchild** etc.; ~ **-~-grandfather** etc., one's parent's great-grandfather etc. 5. **G~ Australian Bight**, wide bay of the Indian Ocean stretching from S. to W. Australia; **G~ Barrier Reef**, largest coral formation in the world, a series of reefs extending for

more than 1,250 miles (2,012.5 k off the coast of Queensland, N Australia; **G~ Britain**: BRITAIN; ~ **circle**: see CIRC **great′coat**, large heavy overc **the Great Fire of London**, that in Sept. 1666 destroyed mos London; **great horned owl**: OWL; **Great Lakes**: see separ entry; **Great Powers**, nati having great political and milit influence and international i portance; **great primer**: PRIMER²; **Great Russian**, Russ language excluding Ukrainian a Byelorussian; **Great Spir** supreme deity of many N. Am Indians; **great unwashed**: UNWASHED; **Great War**, Wo War I (see WORLD). **great′ness great** *n.* (pl. **greats**, colle **great**). (pl.) Great persons.

Great (grāt) **Basin**. Eleva region in the W. United Sta covering 189,000 sq. mi. (489, sq. km); it includes most of Nev and parts of Utah, Californ Oregon, Idaho, and Wyoming; a includes the Great Salt Lake a Mojave Deserts, Carson Sink a Death Valley; area has no drain to the ocean, the Great Salt L serving as the primary inter drainage center.

Great·er An·til·les (grā ăntĭl′ēz). Caribbean island gr forming part of the West Ind consisting of Cuba, Hispani Jamaica, and Puerto Rico.

great crested grebe

black-necked grebe

slavonian grebe

Diving birds renowned for their cou ship displays, species of **grebe** *a found in N. and S. America, Euras Africa, Asia and Australia. Parents sha in nest building and care of young.*

*ove left: A map of **Greece** and the*
tional flag. The nation occupies
,000 sq. miles of territory and has a
opulation of 9 million, half of whom
rk in agriculture. Above right:
men hoe the parched earth of a co-
erative farm. Right: The Academy in
hens, the capital. The nation is work-
to industrialize and many factories
being built.

great (grāt) **horned owl.** Large
. Amer. owl (*Bubo virginianus*)
th feathery projections on either
le of its head.

Great (grāt) **Lakes.** Five lakes,
e largest group of freshwater lakes
the world, covering almost
,000 square mi. (152,950 km) on
her side of the U.S.-Canadian
rder, and consisting of lakes
perior, Michigan, Huron, Erie,
d Ontario.

great·ly (grāt′lē) *adv.* 1. Much,
much. 2. Nobly, loftily.

Great (grāt) **Plains.** Region of
lleys and plains in central N.
ner., bounded by the base of the
cky Mountains in the W.,
nada's Laurentian Highlands in
e N., and the margins of the
ntral Plains in the U.S.

Great (grāt) **Salt Lake.** Shal-
v, strongly saline lake occupying
000 sq. km) of N.
ah near Salt Lake City in the
eat Basin of the U.S.; **Great**
lt Lake Desert**, flat, arid area
out 110 mi. by 50 mi., (177 km
80 km) SW. of the Great Salt
ke in N. Utah.

Great (grāt) **Smoky Moun-
ins.** (also called **Great Smokies**)
palachian mountain range ex-
ding along North Carolina-
nnessee boundary; highest peak,
ngmans Dome (6,643 ft., 2,025
.

Great (grāt) **Wall of China.**
(also known as *Chinese* Wall *or*
Chin. *Chang-chêng*) Defensive wall
in N. China, 20 to 50 ft. (6 to 15 m)
high, 15 to 25 ft. (4.5 to 7 m) thick,
extending 2,000 mi. (3,219 km)
from Kansu province E. to the
Yellow Sea; it was constructed in
3rd c. to prevent incursions from
what is now called Manchuria and
Mongolia.

greaves (grēvz) *n.pl.* (considered
sing. or pl.) Fibrous matter or skin
found in animal fat after rendering;
cracklings.

grebe (grēb) *n.* (pl. **grebes**,
collect. **grebe**). Any of various
short-bodied almost tailless diving
birds of family Podicipedidae with
flattened and lobed feet set far
behind.

Gre·cian (grē′shan) *adj.* Greek,
Hellenic (rare exc. of architecture
and facial outline); ~ **nose, pro-**

file, nose straight in profile,
continuing forehead line without a
dip. ~ *n.* (rare) Native of Greece;
(archaic) Greek scholar.

Gre·cism (grē′sĭzem) *n.* Greek
idiom, esp. as imitated in another
language; Greek spirit, style, etc.,
imitation of these. **Gre′cize** *v.t.*
(**-cized, -ciz·ing**). Make Greek in
form or character.

Gre·co-Ro·man (grĕk′ō rō′-
man, grē′kō-) *adj.* Of or relating
to both ancient Greece and ancient
Rome; of the later ancient world
dominated by Rome.

Greece (grēs). Maritime
country (a republic since 1973) in
SE. Europe, bounded on the N. by
Albania, Yugoslavia, and Bulgaria,
on the S. and W. by the Ionian
Sea, and on the E. by the Aegean
and Turkey; capital, Athens;
Ancient or **classical** ~, earliest
great civilization of Europe, which

...about 6,000 ft. the monastery of ...nt Athos stands above a scene ...aracteristic of north-eastern **Greece**. ...estone mountains stretch into three ...insulas of the Chalcidice, the ...ernmost being Mount Athos.

...eloped around the shores of the ...ean, reached its peak in 5th c. ..., and consisted of a number of ... states of which Athens and ...rta became the most powerful; ...46 B.C. Greece became part of ... Roman Empire; remained ...er the Eastern (Byzantine) ...pire until overrun by Serbia ...ing the 13th c.; was conquered ... Turkey in the 14th–15th ...turies and remained under ...rkish rule until independence in ...1; was overrun by Germans in ...rld War II, liberated in 1945.

...**reed** (grēd) n. Insatiate long-..., esp. for food or wealth. ...**ed′y** adj. (**greed·i·er, greed·i-**...). **greed′i·ly** adv. **greed′i·ness**

...**reek** (grēk) adj. Of, pertaining ...Greece, its inhabitants or their ...guage; ~ **Church**, ~ **Ortho-**...**Church**: see ORTHODOX: ~ ...ss, upright cross with limbs of ...al length; ~ **god**, (fig.) paragon ...ale beauty. **Greek** n. 1. Greek ...son. 2. Language of the Greeks, ...that of the classical period, a ...nber of the Indo-Germanic ...ily of languages, represented in ...sical times by four main dia-..., Ionic, Attic, Aeolic, and

...ow: A map of **Greenland,** the ...d's largest island after Australia. Its ...a of 840,000 sq. miles is mainly ...in the Arctic Circle and the popula-...is 49,000. Most of these people ...k in the fish industry on the west ...st. Below right: Houses of the capi-...Godthaab, are wooden and have ...p roofs.

GREENLAND

Greenland Sea

Arctic circle

Iceland

...OTHAAB

Atlantic Ocean

Doric; (ii) the modern form, dating from 15th c.

Gree·ley (grē′lē), **Horace** (1811–72). Amer. journalist and politician; co-founder of the *New Yorker*, 1834, a weekly journal that later merged and became the New York *Tribune*, 1841; Republican presidential nominee, 1872, defeated by Ulysses S. Grant.

green (grēn) adj. 1. Of the color between blue and yellow in the spectrum, colored like grass, emerald, etc.; covered with herbage, verdant, in leaf; (of complexion) pale, sickly-hued, as in jealousy, sickness, etc.; (fig.) jealous, envious. 2. (of fruit etc.) Unripe; not withered or worn out; (of persons) immature, inexperienced, gullible; (of wood) not dried or seasoned; (of hide) not tanned. 3. **green′back**, U.S. currency note; **Greenback Party**, former U.S. political party, organized 1874, advocating greenbacks as the sole U.S. paper currency; **green bean**: see STRING bean; **green belt**, strip of land around a built-up area, kept free from building development etc.; **green cheese**, unripened cheese; very strong green-colored cheese; **green corn**: see SWEET CORN; **green-eyed**, (esp.) jealous; **green-eyed monster**, jealousy; **green flash**, rarely seen, dazzling momentary green appearance of top of sun's disk caused by refraction as sun dips below or rises above horizon; **green′gage**, green plum (f. name of Sir W. *Gage*); **green′grocer**, (Brit.) retail dealer in fruit and vegetables; so **green′grocery**; **green′heart**, tropical Amer. tree (*Ocotea rodiaei*), with dark, greenish, very hard wood; **green′horn**, (colloq.) inexperienced, immature person; newcomer, recent immigrant; gullible person; **green′house**, glass house for rearing delicate or tropical plants; **green**

light, (fig.) permission to proceed; **green pepper**: see PEPPER def. 2; **green′room**, room in theater or television studio accommodating performers when off stage; **green salad**, salad composed wholly or almost wholly of greens; **green sickness**, chlorosis; **green′stick (fracture)**, bone fracture, esp. in children, in which one side of bone is broken and one only bent; **green′stone**, any of various eruptive rocks containing feldspar and hornblende; **green′sward**, turf; **green tea**: see TEA; **green thumb**, (colloq.) aptitude for making plants grow; **green′wood**, woodlands in summer. **green′ly** adv. **green′ness** n. **green′ish** adj. **green** n. 1. What is green; green part of anything; green color; green dye. 2. Vegetation, greenery; (pl.) leafy plants eaten as vegetables; cut leaves and branches used as decoration, esp. for Christmas. 3. (hist.) Piece of public or common grassy land; grass plot used for special purpose. 4. (golf) Area of closely mown turf around hole. ~ v. Become green.

Green (grēn), **William** (1873–1952). Amer. labor leader; president of American Federation of Labor, 1924–52.

green·er·y (grē′nerē) n. (pl. **-er·ies**). Verdure; green branches or leaves as decoration.

green·ing (grē′nĭng) n. Kind of cooking apple, green when ripe.

Green·land (grēn′land). Largest island in the world, 839,999 sq. mi. (2,175,597 sq. km), with only about 135,000 sq. mi. (349,650 sq. km) ice-free, in N. Atlantic NE. of N. Amer.; first colonized by Eric the Red in 985; now in Danish possession; capital, Godthaab; the only known source of cryolite, necessary in aluminum production.

Green·wich (grĕn′ĭj, -ĭch; grĭn′-; for def. 2 also grĕn′wĭch).

1. Borough of London, original site of the British Royal Astronomical Observatory, founded 1675 for the purpose of calculating longitude; ~ **Mean Time**, (abbrev. GMT or G.M.T.; also ~ **Time**) mean solar time of the meridian of Greenwich, England, used as a basis for calculating time, and in navigation, throughout most of the world. 2. Town in SW. Connecticut, 35 mi. (56 km) from New York City; ~ **Village**, section of lower Manhattan, New York City, frequented by artists, writers, and students.

greet (grēt) *v.t.* Accost with salutation; salute *with* words or gestures, receive on meeting or arrival *with* speech or action; (of sight etc.) meet (eye, ear). **greet′er, greet′ing** *ns.*

gre·gar·i·ous (gregār′ēus, -găr′-) *adj.* Living in flocks or communities; fond of company; of flocks or crowds. **gre·gar′i·ous·ly** *adv.* **gre·gar′i·ous·ness** *n.*

Gre·go·ri·an (grĭgōr′ēan, -gōr′-) *adj.* Pertaining to, originated by, some person named Gregory, esp. one of the popes of that name; ~ **calendar**, modified calendar, also known as the "New Style," introduced by Pope Gregory XIII in 1582 and now in use throughout most of the world; ordinary year has 365 days, and leap year of 366 days occurs when year is divisible by 4, except centenary years e.g. 2000, 2100; ~ **chant**, monodic liturgical plainsong of the R.C. Ch., founded on the "Antiphonarium," of which Pope Gregory I is presumed to have been the compiler.

Greg·o·ry[1] (grĕg′erē). Name of 16 popes: **Gregory I**, saint, pope 590–604, a zealous propagator of Christianity; sent AUGUSTINE to

England; is presumed to have originated the GREGORIAN chant; **Gregory VII**, saint, pope 1073–85, a Benedictine monk, called Hildebrand; before his election attempted to extend the temporal power of the papacy; **Gregory XIII**, pope 1572–85, introduced the GREGORIAN calendar.

Greg·o·ry[2] (grĕg′erē), **Lady** (Isabella) Augusta (Persse) (1859?–1932). Irish dramatist; helped establish the Irish National Theater Society with W. B. Yeats and others and the Abbey Theatre in Dublin, which she directed.

The Marriage Room at **Gretna Green,** *Dumfries, Scotland, is now a place visited for the sake of its romantic associations with eloping couples in the past.*

The modern hand **grenade** is prim with a detonator. When the safety pi pulled free the handle is released a triggers the grenade. Its fuse delays explosion for a fixed period of secon

greige (grā, grāzh) *n. & adj.* (color between beige and gray. [*grège* raw (silk)]

grem·lin (grĕm′lĭn) *n.* M chievous sprite to whom mecha cal defects of military airpla were humorously attributed dur World War II; mechanical trou or its cause.

Gre·na·da (grenä′da, -nah Island in the West Indies, 120 mi. (193 sq. km), southernmost the Windward Islands; with adjacent islands, the south Grenadines, it is an independ member (since 1974) of Commonwealth of Nations; capi St. George's.

gre·nade (grenād′) *n.* Sm explosive shell thrown by ha (**hand** ~) or shot from rifle; g receptacle thrown to dispe chemicals for extinguishing fi etc. [Span. *granada* pomegrana

gren·a·dier (grĕnadēr′) *n.* (orig.) Soldier who threw grena (orig. four or five men in ea company); later, in England, company of the tallest and fin men in each regiment, hence C **Guards**, or **Grenadiers**, fi regiment of British royal househ infantry. 2. Deep-sea fish of fam Macrouridae, related to cod, w long tapering tail; rat-tail.

gren·a·dine[1] (grĕnadēn′, grĕ adēn) *n.* Loosely-woven silk silk-and-wool dress fabric.

gren·a·dine[2] (grĕn′adēn, grĕ dēn′) *n.* French cordial syrup pomegranates.

Gren·a·dines (grĕnadēn grĕn′adēnz). Chain of about 6

Originating as a fabulous beast legends from the eastern Mediterra ean the **griffin** *may have symboliz strength and attentiveness, quȧlit carried into heraldic usage.*

islands in the central Windward group in the E. Caribbean, between Grenada and St. Vincent.

Gresh·am's (grĕsh'amz) **Law.** (econ.) Tendency, when two or more kinds of money of equal nominal value but different intrinsic value are in circulation, for the one having the least intrinsic value to remain in circulation and for the other to be hoarded; expressed (colloq.) as "bad money drives out good." [Sir Thomas Gresham (1519?–1579), English financier, founder of the Royal Exchange]

Gret·na (grĕt'na) **Green.** Village in Scotland, near English border, noted as a place where eloping English couples could be quickly married (between 1754 and 1857, after which Scottish marriage laws became stricter).

grey adj. (chiefly Brit.) = GRAY.

Grey[1] (grā), **Lady Jane** (1537–1554). Great-granddaughter of Henry VII; proclaimed queen of England after death of Edward VI, 1553, in unsuccessful plot to alter succession to throne; she was imprisoned, refused to renounce Protestantism, and was beheaded; succeeded by Catholic queen Mary Tudor.

Grey[2] (grā), **Zane** (1875–1939). Amer. writer of adventure stories, freq. with western backgrounds; author of *Riders of the Purple Sage*, *The Vanishing American*, *West of the Pecos*, etc.

grey·hound (grā'hownd) n. Slender long-legged keen-sighted swift dog, now used primarily in dog racing.

grid (grĭd) n. 1. Grating, frame of parallel bars; gridiron. 2. Network of lines, esp. system of numbered squares printed on map and forming basis of map reference. 3. Network of wires for distributing electric current, of pipes for distributing gas, etc. 4. (elect.) Electrode in a vacuum tube that controls the flow of electrons in the tube.

grid·dle (grĭd'el) n. Flat pan or metal surface for cooking by dry heat; frying pan or surface; ~ **cake**, thin flat cake of batter cooked on griddle; PANCAKE.

grid·i·ron (grĭd'īern) n. Metal utensil with bars for supporting food to be broiled or grilled; (theatr.) structure high over stage supporting lights, mechanism for raising and lowering backdrops, etc.; football field (from the parallel yard lines).

grief (grēf) n. Deep or violent sorrow, keen regret; **come to ~**, meet with disaster, fail, fall.

Grieg (grēg), **Edvard Hagerup** 1843–1907). Norwegian composer noted for folk songs, Norwegian dances, and compositions for piano,

orchestra and chorus.

griev·ance (grē'vans) n. Real or fancied ground of complaint; complaint or resentment against unjust act; hence, ~ **committee**, esp. of a labor union.

grieve (grēv) v. (**grieved, griev·ing**). Give deep sorrow to; feel grief. **griev·er** n.

griev·ous (grē'vus) adj. 1. Causing grief or suffering; (of pain, problems, etc.) serious, grave, dire. 2. Flagrant, heinous. **griev·ous·ly** adv. **griev·ous·ness** n.

grif·fin, grif·fon[1] (grĭf'in) ns. Fabulous creature with eagle's head and wings and lion's body; (her.) representation of this creature as charge or crest.

Grif·fith (grĭf'ĭth), **D. W. (David Lewelyn Wark)** (1875–1948). Amer. motion picture producer and director; famous for such cinematography innovations as the close-up shot, etc.; among his works, *The Birth of a Nation*, *Intolerance*, *Broken Blossoms*.

grif·fon[2] (grĭf'on) n. Kind of coarse-haired terrier-like dog of Belgian breed.

grill[1] (grĭl) v. Broil under grill or on gridiron; (colloq.) subject to severe questioning. ~ n. 1. Grilled dish; cooking surface or flame for broiling or frying; restaurant serving grilled food; **bar and ~**: see BAR[1]. **grilled** adj.

grille, grill[2] (grĭl) ns. Grating, latticed screen, esp. in window or gateway.

grim (grĭm) adj. (**grim·mer, grim·mest**). Stern, unrelenting,

merciless, severe; of forbidding or harsh aspect; sinister, ghastly, unmirthful. **grim·ly** adv. **grim·ness** n.

gri·mace (grĭm'ĭs, grĭmās') n. Wry face expressing annoyance etc. or meant to raise a laugh; affected look. ~ v.i. (**-maced, -mac·ing**). Make wry face.

grime (grīm) n. Soot, dirt, ingrained in some surface, esp. the skin. ~ v.t. (**grimed, grim·ing**). Blacken, befoul. **grim'y** adj. (**grim·i·er, grim·i·est**).

Grimm (grĭm), **Jacob Ludwig Carl** (1785–1863) and **Wilhelm Carl** (1786–1859). Brothers, famous for their research into German language, literature, and antiquities and for their collection of German folk tales (*Grimm's Fairy Tales*); ~**'s Law**, statement, formulated by Jacob Grimm in 1822, of the regular changes that certain consonants of the primitive Indo-Germanic consonant system have undergone in the Germanic languages.

grin (grĭn) v. (**grinned, grin·ning**). Show teeth in cheerful or unrestrained or forced smile, or in sign of pain or fatuity; express (contempt, satisfaction) by grinning. ~ n. Act of grinning. **grin·ner** n.

grind (grīnd) v. (**ground, grind·ing**). 1. Reduce to small

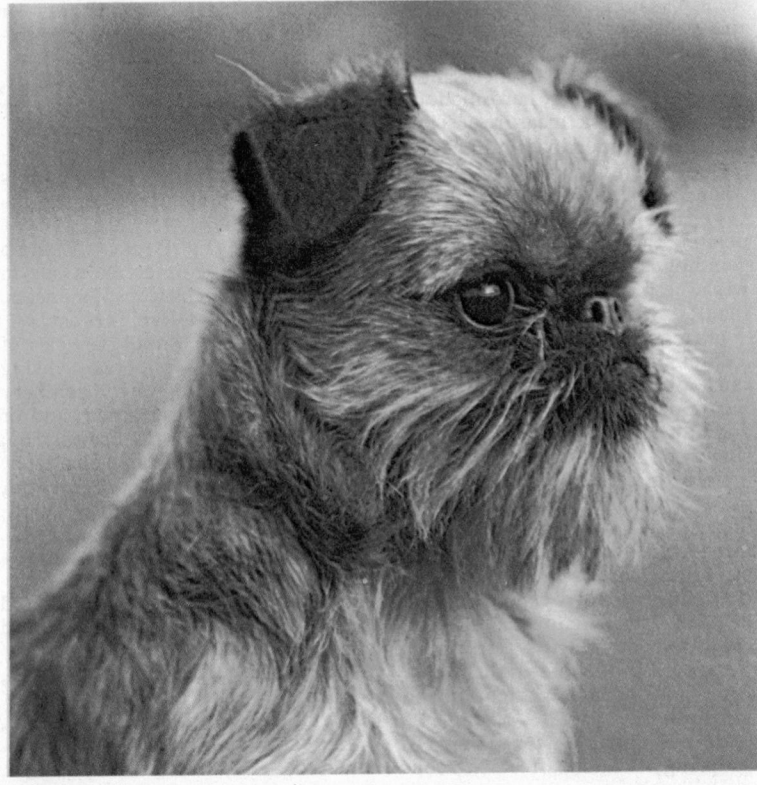

*Accepted as a show breed from 1886, the **Brussels griffon** is a popular dog. It should weigh between 6 and 9 lbs. and its color may be red, black or black and tan.*

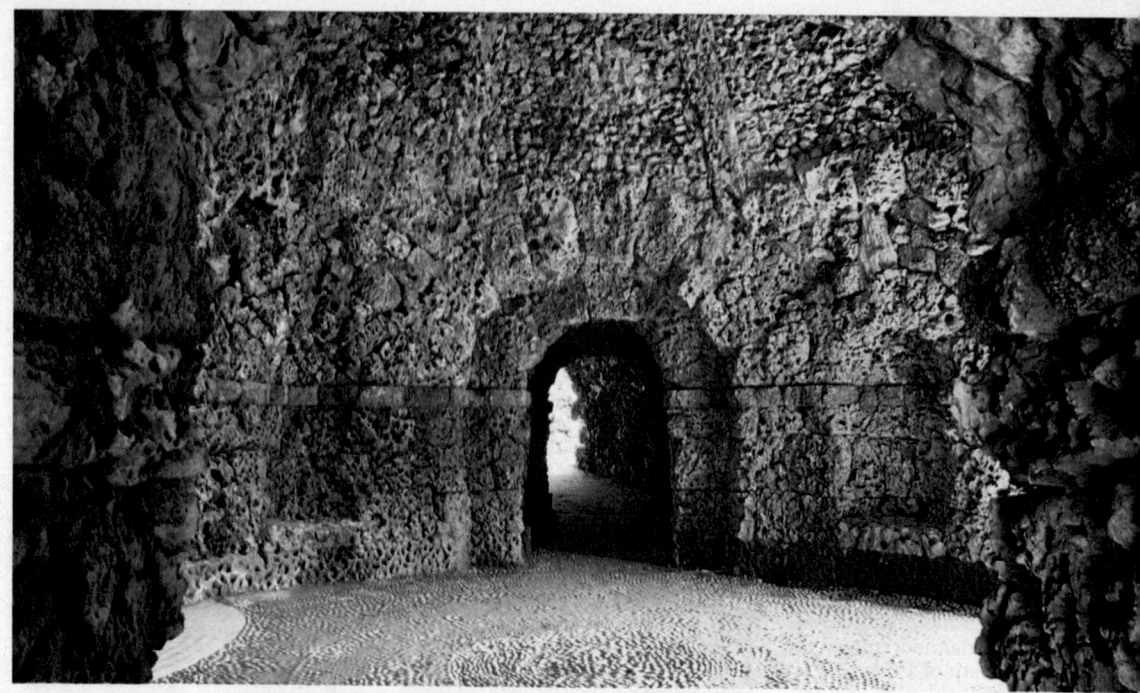

*To the new style of 'natural' landscape gardens of the 18th century a **grotto**, temple or picturesque ruin was added to lend a romantic air to the gardens. This one is at Stourhead, Wiltshire, U.K.*

particles or powder by crushing between millstones, teeth, etc.; produce (flour) by grinding; work (handmill); turn handle of (hurdy-gurdy), produce (music) from hurdy-gurdy etc.; (quasi-pass.) admit of being ground. 2. Sharpen, smooth, or fit by abrasion as in ~ **in** (valves etc.). 3. Oppress, harass with exactions; toil monotonously, study hard. 4. Rub gratingly *against*; rub (teeth) hard together. 5. **grind'stone**, thick revolving stone disk for grinding, sharpening, and polishing; kind of stone used for these; **keep one's nose to the grindstone**, work incessantly. **grind** *n.* Grinding; hard monotonous work or task; measure of size of particles obtained by grinding, as of coffee beans, *percolator grind*; (slang) student who works hard. **grind·er** (grīn'der) *n.* Thing, person, that grinds; molar tooth; grinding machine; (slang) sandwich, esp. hero sandwich (see HERO).

grin·go (grĭng'gō) *n.* (pl. **-gos**). (contempt.) Among Latin Americans, a U.S. citizen, esp. of Anglo-Saxon descent; any foreigner. **gri·ot** (grē'ot) *n.* Tribal bard, singer, historian, of W. Africa. **grip** (grĭp) *n.* Firm hold, tight grasp or clasp, grasping power; way of clasping hands; control, mastery, intellectual hold; power of arresting attention; part in machinery etc. that clips, part of weapon etc. that is held; small suitcase. ~ *v.* (**gripped** or **gript, grip'ping**). Seize, grasp, or hold, tightly; take firm hold; compel attention of. **grip'per** *n.*

gripe (grīp) *v.* (**griped, grip'ing**). Clutch; affect with colic pains; annoy, irritate; (slang) complain. ~ *n.* 1. Act of griping; handle of implement or weapon; (slang) complaint. 2. (pl.) Colic pains. **grippe** (grĭp) *n.* Influenza. **gri·saille** (grĭzī', -zāl') *n.* Method of painting in gray or grayish monochrome, freq. representing figures in relief. **gris·ly** (grĭz'lē) *adj.* (**-li·er, -li·est**). Causing horror, terror, or superstitious dread. **gris'li·ness** *n.* **grist** (grĭst) *n.* Grain for grinding; ground grain; ~ **for one's mill**, something useful or profitable. **gris·tle** (grĭs'el) *n.* Whitish tough flexible connective tissue in vertebrates; cartilage, esp. in meats. **gris'tly** *adj.* (**-tli·er, -tli·est**). **grit** (grĭt) *n.* Small particles of stone or sand, esp. as causing discomfort or clogging machinery etc.; (geol.) coarse-grained sand or sandstone; grain or texture of stone; (colloq.) strength of character, pluck, endurance. ~ *v.* (**grit·ted, grit·ting**). Produce, move with, grating sound; grind (teeth). **grit'ty** *adj.* (**-ti·er, -ti·est**). **grit'ti·ness** *n.* **grits** (grĭts) *n.pl.* (considered sing. or pl.). Coarsely ground grain, esp. corn; HOMINY. **griz·zle** (grĭz'el) *v.* (**-zled, -zling**). Make, become gray. **griz·zly** (grĭz'lē) *adj.* (**-zli·er, -zli·est**). Gray, grayish, gray-haired; ~ **bear**, very large,

fierce, yellowish-brown or gray ("silvertip") bear (*Ursus horribi* of western N. America. ~ *n.* (**-zlies**). Grizzly bear. **groan** (grōn) *n.* Deep inarti late sound expressing pain, grief, disapproval. ~ *v.* Utter gro; utter with groans; creak, as boar furniture, etc., with impos weight. **groan'ing·ly** *adv.* **groat** (grōt) *n.* (hist.) Engl silver coin worth four pence, f; coined in 1351–2 and current un 1662. [MDu. *groot* great, th (penny)] **groats** (grōts) *n.pl.* (consider sing. or pl.) Hulled (sometin also crushed) grain, esp. o; KASHA. **gro·cer** (grō'ser) *n.* Merch; selling foodstuffs and househc supplies. **gro'cer·y** *n.* (**-cer·ies**). Grocer's store; (pl.) fc sold there. **grog** (grŏg) *n.* Drink of ru and water. [reputedly f. *grogra* nickname (from his cloak) of B; Admiral Edward Vernon (168 1757) who first had grog served navy instead of straight rum] **grog·gy** (grŏg'ē) *adj.* (**-gi· -gi·est**). Drunk(en); totterii unsteady, shaky. **grog'gi·ly** a **grog'gi·ness** *n.* **groin** (groin) *n.* 1. Depressi between belly and thigh. 2. (arch; Edge formed by intersecting vaul fillet covering this. ~ *v.t.* (arch: Build with groins. **groin'ing** *n.* **grom·met** (grŏm'ĭt) *n.* Rei forced eyelet in cloth etc. to recei cord, fastener, etc.; (naut.) ring secure edge of sail. **grom·well** (grŏm'wel) *n.* A plant of genus *Lithospermum*, w; hard stony seeds formerly used medicine.

groom (grōōm) *n.* 1. One of certain officers of English Royal household, chiefly in Lord Chamberlain's department. 2. servant having care of horses. 3. bridegroom; **grooms'man** (pl. **men**), (archaic) best man or usher at wedding. **groom** *v.t.* Curry etc. (horse); give neat or attractive appearance to; train, prepare (person) for a specific role, position, etc.

groove (grōōv) *n.* Channel or hollow, esp. one made to direct motion or receive corresponding ridge; satisfactory niche; routine, undeviating course, rut; **in the ~**, (slang) performing excellently. ~ *v.t.* (**grooved, groov·ing**). Make groove(s) in; (slang) get along wel' with (person), be in the groove. **groov'y** *adj.* (**groov·i·er, groov·-est**). (slang) In the groove, exciting, deeply satisfying.

grope (grōp) *v.i.* (**groped, rop·ing**). Feel about as in dark (for); search blindly; ~ **one's way**, find way by feeling, proceed tentatively. **grop'ing·ly** *adv.*

Gro·pi·us (grō'pēus), **Walter** 1883–1969). German-born Amer. architect; founded BAUHAUS school of design in Weimar in 1919.

gros·beak (grōs'bēk) *n.* Any of various finches with large strong beak, esp. those of genera *Pinicola* and *Hesperiphona*.

gros·grain (grō'grān) *n.* Corded fabric or ribbon of silk etc.; ribbon of this.

gros point (grōs'point) (pl. **gros points**). 1. Needlepoint lace with design in high relief. 2. Large embroidery cross-stitch covering two or more threads of canvas.

gross[1] (grōs) *n.* (pl. **gross**). Twelve dozen.

gross[2] (grōs) *adj.* 1. Repulsively fat; flagrant, glaring. 2. Total, without deductions, not net; ~ **national product**, total market value of goods produced and services provided in a country in one year. 3. Dense, thick; coarse, dull; coarse in manners or morals, unrefined, indecent; disgusting. ~ *v.t.* Earn a total of. **gross'ly** *adv.* **gross'ness** *n.*

gro·tesque (grōtĕsk') *n.* Decoration with fantastic interweaving of human and animal forms with foliage; (pop.) comically distorted figure or design. ~ *adj.* (archit.) In the style of a grotesque; distorted, bizarre; ludicrous from incongruity, absurd. **gro·tesque'-ly** *adv.* **gro·tesque'ness** *n.* [It. *grottesca* antique work, prob. *grotta* (grotto) of ancient Roman houses, where such paintings were found]

Gro·ti·us (grō'shēus, -shus), **Hugo** (1583–1645). Dutch statesman and jurist; famous for his

purple gromwell   common gromwell

treatise codifying international law, the *De jure Belli et Pacis*, published in 1625.

grot·to (grŏt'ō) *n.* (pl. **-toes, -tos**). Picturesque cave; artificial ornamental cave; (geog.) cave formed by underground stream.

grouch (growch) *n.* Grumbling; complaint; sulky, grumbling mood; grumbler. **grouch'y** *adj.* (**grouch·i·er, grouch·i·est**). **grouch'i·ly** *adv.* **grouch'i·ness** *n.* **grouch** *v.i.* Grumble; be sulky.

ground[1] (grownd) *n.* 1. Bottom of sea; (pl.) dregs, esp. of coffee. 2. Base, foundation; motive, valid reason. 3. Substratum, underlying part; surface worked upon in embroidery, painting, etc.; undecorated part; prevailing color or tone; (painting) preparation spread

*Commonly called the **blue gromwell**, Lithospermum purpurocaeruleum is normally found in soil rich in calcium carbonate such as chalk.*

Ground ivy (Nepeta hederacea) is not related to common ivy and is a ground dweller. Its flowers are blue to purple and bloom from mid- to late summer.

over canvas, panel, etc., to isolate it from paint layer. 4. Surface of Earth; position, area, etc. on Earth's surface; area of special kind or use; portion of land forming person's property; space on which person etc. takes a stand (freq. fig.); (pl.) enclosed land for ornament or recreation attached to house; **above ~**, alive; **down to the ~**, (colloq.) in all respects; thoroughly; **be dashed to the ~**, (of scheme, hope) be abandoned, fail; **forbidden ~**, subject that must be avoided; **gain ~**, advance; **lose, give, ~**, retreat, decline; **run into the ~**, explain at unreasonable length; overdo; **stand, shift, one's ~**, maintain, change, one's argument or intention. 5. (elect.) Connection to earth (or some other large conducting body) as completion of circuit. 6. attrib.: (in names of birds) terrestrial, (of beasts) burrowing in or lying on ground, (of plants) dwarfish or trailing. 7. ~ **ball** (also **grounder**), (baseball) batted ball that rolls or bounces (opp. FLY ball); ~ **bass**, (mus.) theme in bass constantly repeated with varied melody or harmony above; ~ **cover**, low-growing plants used in place of grass or to control erosion; ~ **crew**, workers, mechanics, etc., who service and maintain aircraft on the ground; ~ **floor**, floor of a building at or nearly at level of outside ground; **get in on the ~ floor**, be admitted to company, scheme, etc. at its inception; **ground'hog**, woodchuck; **ground ice**, ice formed at bottom of water; **ground ivy**, common labiate plant (*Glechoma hederacea*) with bluish-purple flowers; **ground'nut**, edible tuber or underground nut of a plant, as the peanut. **ground pine**, European herbaceous plant (*Ajuga chamaepitys*) with resinous smell; club moss; **ground plan**, plane drawing of divisions of building on the ground level or ground floor; outline, general design, of anything; **ground rule**, (usu. pl.) basic principle(s) of a situation; (baseball etc.) rule(s) arising from nature of playing field or location of spectators; **ground'sheet**, waterproof sheet for spreading on ground as protection against damp, as under sleeping bag etc.; **ground speed**, horizontal component of aircraft velocity relative to the earth; **ground squirrel**, gopher; **ground swell**, heavy sea swell as result of distant storm; unexpected gathering or increase of public opinion; **ground water**, water lying below Earth's surface in springs and in pores of rock; **ground'work**, foundation or basis (usu. fig.). **ground** *v.* Base, establish, *on* some fact or authority; instruct thoroughly (*in* elements of subject); prepare ground of (canvas etc. for painting); keep on the ground, prevent (aircraft pilot) from taking off or flying; run ashore, strand; (elect.) connect an electric circuit, appliance, etc. to a ground.

ground² (grownd): see GRIND; (esp.) ~ **glass**, glass made non-transparent by grinding or etching. **ground·ing** (grown'dĭng) *n.* (esp.) Instruction in, understanding of elements of subject.

ground·less (grownd'lĭs) *adj.* Without foundation, authority, or support, unfounded. **ground'-less·ly** *adv.* **ground'less·ness** *n.*

ground·sel (grownd'sel) *n.* Plant of genus *Senecio*, esp. *S. vulgaris*, common European weed with small yellow flowers.

The term **grouse** *may refer to a particular British game bird, or to a wider group in the northern hemisphere, also hunted for food. 1: The spruce grouse. 2: The red grouse found in Great Britain. 3: The black grouse. 4: The sage grouse of the U.S.A., so called because its sage diet flavors its flesh.*

Groundsel (Senecio vulgaris) grows abundantly on cultivated ground, and flowers throughout the year. It is a common weed which contains a substance poisonous to birds.

group (grōōp) *n.* In fine arts, 2 or more figures or objects forming complete design or distinct part of one; number of persons or things standing near together, knot, cluster; number of persons or things belonging or classed together; **Oxford G**~: see MORAL Rearmament; ~ **captain**, officer of Brit. Royal Air Force, ranking above wing commander; ~ **insurance**, insurance covering all members of a group, usu. at lower premium rates; ~ **practice**, medical practice run by several doctors in cooperation; ~ **therapy** (psych.) therapy in which patient are brought together to discus their problems and assist on another. **group** *v.* Form into group, place in a group (*with*); form into well-arranged and harmoniou whole; classify. **group'ie** *n.* (slang Young girl devotee of rock group team, etc.; hanger-on; member of group sharing a vacation house.

group·er (grōō'per) *n.* (pl. **-ers** collect. **-er**). Any of various, ofte very large, marine food fishes of th family Serranidae, found esp. in tropical seas.

grouse¹ (grows) *n.* (pl. **grouse**) Name of many species of gallina ceous birds of the family Tetraoni dae esp. (in Amer.) **ruffed** ~ (*Bonasa umbellus*), medium-sized with feathered feet, the males usu staging elaborate courtship display

grouse² (grows) *v.i.* (**groused grous·ing**) & *n.* (colloq.) Grumble complain. **grous'er** *n.*

grout (growt) *n.* Thin fluid mortar for filling masonry joint etc. ~ *v.t.* Fill up or finish with grout or cement.

grove (grōv) *n.* Small wood group of trees.

grov·el (grŏv'el, grŭv'-) *v.i.* (**-eled, -el·ing, -elled, -el·ling**) Lie prone, humble oneself **grov'el·ing** *adj.* Abject, low, base **grov'el·ing·ly**, **grov'el·ling·ly** *advs.*

grow (grō) *v.* (**grew** pr. grōō **grown, grow·ing**). 1. Develop or exist as living plant; germinate, sprout, spring up, be produced come naturally into existence, arise 2. Increase in size, height, quantity degree, power, etc.; become gradually; **growing pains**, children's pains prob. of a rheumatic character popularly attributed to growing;

owing season, season (longest ar equator) when rainfall and mperature permit plants to grow; **ow on**, gain more and more of rson's etc.) liking or admiration; **ow up**, advance to maturity; ich full size; (of custom) arise, come common. 3. Produce by ltivation; bring forth; let (beard .) grow; (pass.) be covered (over) th some growth. **grow'er** n. sp.) Person growing produce; int that grows in specified way.

growl (growl) n. Guttural sound anger; rumble; angry murmur, mplaint. ~ v. Utter growl, imble, murmur angrily; utter with growl. **growl'ing·ly** adv.

grown (grōn) adj.: see GROW; sp.) ~-**up**, (adj. & n.) adult.

growth (grōth) n. Growing, evelopment, increase; what has own or is growing; (path.) morbid rmation.

grub (grŭb) n. 1. Larva of insect, iterpillar, maggot. 2. (slang) ood. ~ v. (**grubbed, grub'-ing**). 1. Dig superficially; clear round) of roots and stumps; clear vay (roots etc.); fetch up or out y digging; search, rummage. 2. lod, toil, on, along, away. 3. (slang) eed; **grub'stake** (n.), supplies or ioney advanced (orig. to mining rospector) with agreement that rofits will be shared; **grub'stake**).) (**-staked, -stak·ing**), supply a rubstake. **grub'ber** n.

grub·by (grŭb'ē) adj. (**-bi·er, bi·est**). 1. Of, infested with, rubs. 2. Dirty, grimy, slovenly. rub'bi·ness n.

Grub (grŭb) **Street.** London treet (now Milton Street) inhab-:ed in 17th c. by impoverished uthors and literary hacks; hence, uch writers (also attrib.).

grudge (grŭj) v.t. (**grudged, rudg·ing**). Be unwilling to give, rant, or allow (to); be unwilling o do. **grudg'ing·ly** adv. **grudge** . Feeling of resentment or ill will.

gru·el (grōō'el) n. Thin, watery orridge.

gru·el·ing, gru·el·ling (grōō'e-ing) adjs. & ns. Exhausting or unishing (experience).

grue·some (grōō'som) adj. Grisly, disgusting. **grue'some·ly** idv. **grue'some·ness** n.

gruff (grŭf) adj. Surly, laconic, ough-mannered, rough-voiced. gruff'ly adv. **gruff'ness** n.

grum·ble (grŭm'bel) n. Dull narticulate sound, murmur, com-plaint. ~ v. (**-bled, -bling**). Utter grumble, murmur, growl faintly; rumble; complain; utter complain-ingly. **grum'bler** n. **grum'-bling·ly** adv.

grump·y (grŭm'pē) adj. (**grump·i·er, grump·i·est**). Ill-tempered, surly. **grump'i·ly** adv. grump'i·ness n.

Grun·dy (grŭn'dē), **Mrs.** In

Thomas Morton's English play *Speed the Plough* (1798), a neighbor who never appears but is constantly referred to ("What will Mrs. Grundy say?"); hence, symbol of conventional propriety or prudery. **Grun'dy·ism** n.

grun·ion (grŭn'yon) n. Small California sea fish that comes ashore to spawn.

grunt (grŭnt) n. 1. Low gruff sound characteristic of hogs, any similar sound. 2. Any of several tropical marine fishes of family Pomadasyidae, which make grunt-ing noise. ~ v. Utter grunt; express discontent, dissent, assent, fatigue, etc., by this; utter with grunt.

Gru·yère (grōōyār', grē-) n. Pale, firm, yellow cow's-milk cheese, often with small cavities, orig. made at Gruyère, Switzer-land.

GSA abbrev. General Services Administration; Girl Scouts of America.

G-string (jē'string) n. Narrow strip of cloth etc. covering the genitals, esp. as worn by strip teasers.

G-suit (jē'sōōt) n. Garment to enable flier or astronaut to with-stand high acceleration.

*The stage between the egg and the pupa of an insect is the **grub** or larval stage. Aborigines of Australia search for bardies or witchety grubs which they eat, raw or cooked.*

Gt. Br. abbrev. Great Britain.
GU abbrev. Guam.

gua·ca·mo·le (gwahkamō'lē) n. 1. Mexican sauce of mashed avocado, hot peppers, etc. 2. Latin Amer. salad with avocado.

Gua·da·la·ja·ra (gwahdala-hār'a). City in W. central Mexico; noted for its cathedral, university, and pottery and handicrafts.

Gua·dal·ca·nal (gwahdalka-năl'). Island of the Solomon group in W. Pacific; occupied by Japanese in World War II and scene of several major battles with U.S. forces, Aug. 7–Nov. 13, 1942, before Japanese evacuated, Feb., 1943.

Gua·de·loupe (gwahdelōōp'). Pair of islands in the E. West Indies, which, together with their five adjacent dependencies, consti-tute a French overseas department; discovered by Columbus, 1493; capital Basse-Terre.

guai·a·col (gwī'akōl, -kawl, -kŏl) n. Colorless or yellowish liquid or white crystalline solid with strong smell, obtained by distilling guaiacum resin or wood tar creosote, and used in medicine.

guai·a·cum (gwī'akum): see LIGNUM VITAE.

Guam (gwahm). Largest and southernmost of the Mariana Islands in the W. Pacific; ceded to U.S. by Spain in 1898; capital, Agaña.

guan (gwahn) n. Any of several S. Amer. gallinaceous birds allied

The **guan** is a gregarious bird. The blue throated guan (above) lives in areas between Texas and Argentina and feeds on insects, fruit and vegetation of many kinds. Attempts have been made to domesticate the guan but they have not succeeded.

The **guanaco** grazes the mountain slopes of the Andes. It is related to the camel and grows to a height of some 3½ ft. at the shoulder. Its hide is used to make warm clothing. The guanaco is able to drink salty water as well as fresh water when necessary.

to curassows.

gua·na·co (gwahnah′kō) n. (pl. **-cos**, collect. **-co**). S. Amer. wild llama (*Lama huanacus*) with reddish-brown wool.

Gua·na·jua·to (gwahnahhwah′-tō). City in central Mexico famous for its gold and silver mines and catacombs.

Guang·dong (gwahn′dŏŏng′) = KWANGTUNG.

Guang·xi Zhuang (gwahng′shē jwahng′) = KWANGSI-CHUANG.

Guang·zhou (gwahng′zhŏō′) = CANTON.

gua·no (gwah′nō) n. Excrement of sea birds or bats accumulated along certain coastal or island areas and in caves, rich in phosphates and ammonia and used as manure; artificial manure, esp. that made from fish.

Guan·ta·na·mo (gwahntah′na-mō). Town in SE. Cuba on ~ **Bay**, a Caribbean Sea inlet; site of U.S. naval base; Amer. forces landed here during Spanish-American War, June, 1898.

Gua·ra·ní (gwãranē′) n. (pl. **-nís**, **-níes**, collect. **-ní**). One of the two main divisions of the Tupi-Guaraní Indians of Bolivia, Paraguay, and S. Brazil; language of this people.

guar·an·tee (gărantē′) n. Person making guaranty or giving security; guaranty; thing given or existing as security for fulfillment of conditions or permanence etc. of something; ~ v.t. (**-teed, -tee·ing**). Be guarantee for, answer for due fulfillment of (contract etc.) or genuineness etc. of (article); engage *that* something has happened or will happen; secure possession of *to* person; secure *against* or *from* (risk etc.). **guar·an·tor** (găr′antōr, -ter) n.

guar·an·ty (găr′antē) n. (pl. **-ties**). Undertaking, esp. written, to answer for payment of debt or performance of obligation by another person; ground or basis of security; act of giving security; guarantor. ~ v.t. (**-tied, -ty·ing**).

guard (gărd) n. 1. Defensive posture or motion in fencing, boxing, etc.; watch, vigilant state; **be on ~**, act as sentry etc.; **on, off, one's ~**, prepared, unprepared, against attack, surprise, etc. 2. Protector, defender, sentry; one who supervises prisoners. 3. Body of soldiers etc. serving as protectors of place or person, escort etc.; **Guards**, selected bodies of troops normally for escort or ceremonial duties, e.g. in British Army the *Royal Horse Guards*, the *Coldstream Guards*, etc. 4. Contrivance to prevent injury or accident; e.g. part of sword hilt protecting hand from injury, trigger guard, etc. 5. (sports) One who guards an

opponent; (football) (one of t players having) a position on eit side of the center; (basketball) (of two players having) a positi defending in back court or pl making in mid-court. 6. **~ cha** chain securing watch, brooch, e **guard′house** (pl. **-hous·e** building for accommodation military guard or keeping prisoners under guard; **guard′ra** hand- or other rail to preve falling, etc.; extra inner rail to ke wheel on line at railroad switch crossings, etc.; **guard′room**, roc for keeping prisoners under gua or for military guard; **guards′m** (pl. **-men**), guard; member of U. National Guard; (Brit.) member the Guards. **guard** v. Keep sa stand guard over, keep (door et so as to control passage; prote defend; secure by explanations stipulations etc. from misunde standing or abuse; keep (though speech) in check; take precautio *against*; (sports) block or frustra (an opponent). **guard′ed** a Cautious. **guard′ed·ly** aa Cautiously.

guard·ant, gard·ant (gār′dar adjs. (her.) (of a beast) Havi the full face toward the viewer.

guard·i·an (gār′dēan) Keeper, defender, protector; (la one having custody of person property, or both, of minor, etc.; **angel**, spirit watching over pers or place. **guard′i·an·ship** n.

Guar·ne·ri, Guar·nie·ri (gwä nār′ē) n. Name of a 17th- ar 18th-c. family of Italian violi makers of Cremona; henc **Guar·ne·ri·us** (gwārnār′ēus), vio rowing in damp woodlands and in arshy ditches the **guelder rose** ooms in the middle summer months. ater it bears clusters of attractive, arlet globose fruits.

n made by one of this family.

Gua·te·ma·la (gwahtemah′la). Most northerly republic of Central America, bordering on Mexico; capital, Guatemala City. **Gua·te-ma′lan** adj. & n.

gua·va (gwah′va) n. Tree of ropical Amer. genus *Psidium* of amily Myrtaceae, esp. *P. guajava;* cid fruit of this, used for making elly etc. [Span. *guayaba*, prob. f. ative Amer. name]

Gua·ya·quil (gwahyahkēl′). Largest city of Ecuador, in the SW., seaport on mouth of Guayas River.

gu·ber·na·to·ri·al (gooberna-tōr′eal, -tōr′-, gū-) adj. Of a overnor; of the office of governor.

gudg·eon[1] (gŭj′on) n. Small European freshwater fish (*Gobio obio*) used as bait; gullible person.

gudg·eon[2] (gŭj′on) n. Pivot at nd of beam, axle, etc., on which ell, wheel, etc., works; socket in vhich rudder works; pin holding wo blocks of stone etc. together.

guel·der (gĕl′der) **rose.** Small ree or shrub (*Viburnum opulus*), ative to Eurasia bearing round unches of white flowers and small ed fruit. [f. *Guelders*, town in Prussia, or *Guelderland*, province of he Netherlands]

Guelph, Guelf (gwĕlf) ns. 1. Member of medieval Italian party supporting the pope and the Italian city-states against the German

emperor. 2. Member of a ducal family of Swabian origin established in the 9th c. [It. *Guelfo* f. MHG. *Welf*, name of the founder of the family]

guer·don (gĕr′don) n. & v.t. (poet.) Reward, recompense.

Guer·ni·ca (gwĕr′nĭka; *Sp.* gĕrnē′kah) (also ~ **y Lu·na** pr. -ēloō′nah). Basque town in N. central Spain; destroyed by the Condor Legion, the German air force supporting Franco's forces, in mass bombing, 1937, during

The most densely populated country of S. America, **Guatemala** *has a population of 5.5 million occupying its 42,000 sq. miles of land. Above: Some of the citizens carry firewood to sell in Guatemala City, the nation's capital. Center: A map of Guatemala and the national flag.*

Spanish civil war; the bombing is the subject of Picasso's famous mural "Guernica."

Guern·sey (gĕrn′zē). Second largest of the English Channel Islands; capital, St. Peter Port.

guern·sey (gĕrn′zē) n. 1. Thick knitted closely fitting wool shirt as worn by seamen. 2. **G~** (pl. **-seys**), (one of) a breed of usu. fawn-and-white dairy cattle, orig. raised in Guernsey.

guer·ril·la, gue·ril·la (gerĭl′a) ns. Person engaged in irregular fighting [~ **war(fare)**] carried out by small bodies of men and women serving a patriotic or revolutionary movement; ~ **theater**, crude, quasi-impromptu playlets (on war, peace, justice, revolution, etc.) produced in the streets. [Span. *guerrilla* little war]

guess (gĕs) *v.* Estimate; think likely; form hypothesis as to, conjecture, hazard opinion about; conjecture (answer to riddle etc.) rightly; **I ~**, I feel sure, I know well. **~** *n.* Rough estimate, conjecture, hypothesis; **guess'-work**, (procedure based on) guessing. **guess'er** *n.*

guess·ti·mate (*v.* gĕs'tĭmāt; *n.* gĕs'tĭmĭt, -māt) *v.* (**-mat·ed, -mat·ing**) & *n.* (slang) (Make a) rough, uninformed estimate.

guest (gĕst) *n.* Person given food or lodging at another's house etc.; person lodging at hotel, boarding-house, etc.; **paying ~**, boarder; **guest'house**, (1) separate house for guests on an estate; (2) small, informal hotel, sometimes inexpensive, sometimes luxurious.

guf·faw (gŭfaw', gu-) *n.* Loud, boisterous laugh. **~** *v.* Make, say with, guffaw.

Gug·gen·heim (goog'enhīm, goo'gen-), **Daniel** (1856–1930). Amer. industrialist and philanthropist; leading figure in copper industry; established the Guggenheim Foundation, 1924, to promote "the well-being of mankind."

Gui·a·na (gēăn'a, -ah'na, gī-). Region in NE. South Amer., including Guyana, French Guiana, and Surinam. **Gui·a·nese** (gēanēz', -nēs', gī-) *adj.* & *n.*

gui·dance (gī'dans) *n.* Guiding, direction; psychological or vocational counseling in a school or social service agency, hence **~ counselor; inertial ~ (system)**, (computer and devices for) keeping missile, aircraft, etc., on course by responding to inertial forces.

guide (gīd) *n.* 1. One who shows the way; hired conductor of traveler, tourist, or climber; adviser; directing principle or standard; **G ~** (formerly **Girl G ~**) member of the Girl Guides Association, a Brit. organization for girls somewhat similar to the Girl Scouts. 2. Book of rudiments, manual; (also **guide'book**), book to inform tourists about country, city, museum, etc. 3. (mech.) Bar, rod, etc., directing motion of something; gauge etc.; controlling tool; thing marking a position or guiding the eye. 4. **~ dog**, dog trained to guide blind person; **guide'line**, (usu. pl., often bureaucratic jargon) suggestion or indication of future action; statement of policy by some authority; directions to be followed, but without the clarity or sanction of law; **guide'post**, signpost. **guide** *v.t.* (**guid·ed, guid·ing**). Act as guide to, go before, lead,

direct course of; arrange course of (events); be principle, motive, or ground, of; conduct affairs of (state etc.); **guided missile** etc., missile etc. steered by remote control or internal mechanism. **guid'er** *n.*

gui·don (gī'don; *Brit.* gē'don) *n.* Small flag or pennant, often with forked end; this as a military unit's standard; the soldier carrying such a standard.

guild (gĭld) *n.* Society for mutual aid or prosecution of common object, esp. medieval trade

or craft association, acting benefit society, promoting comm— trade interests of members et— **guild'hall**, hall in which mediev— guild met; town hall; **Guildha**— meeting hall of the Corporation the City of London, used for sta— banquets etc.

guil·der (gĭl'der) *n.* Princip— monetary unit of the Netherland— the Netherlands Antilles an— Surinam, = 100 cents; Netherland— florin.

guile (gīl) *n.* Treachery, decei—

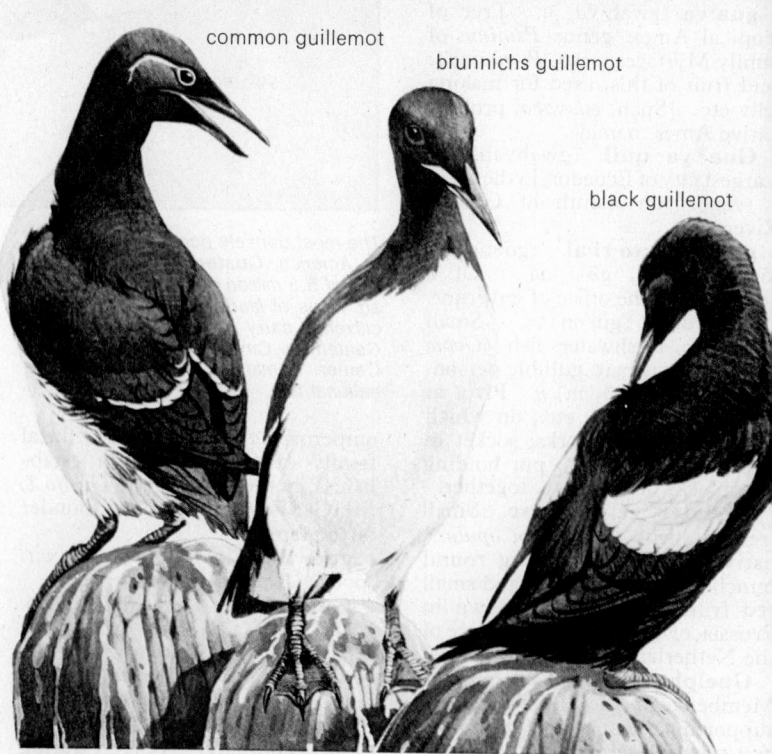

common guillemot

brunnichs guillemot

black guillemot

A member of the auk family, the common **guillemot** *is about 16 ins. in length. It is one of the most skilful diving birds. Above right: It nests on inaccessible cliffs. The black guillemot is a smaller bird with white wing covers.*

e West African republic of **Guinea**
s a population of 4.3 million inhabiting
,000 sq. miles. The nation has the
est bauxite deposits in the world but
st of the people work in agriculture.

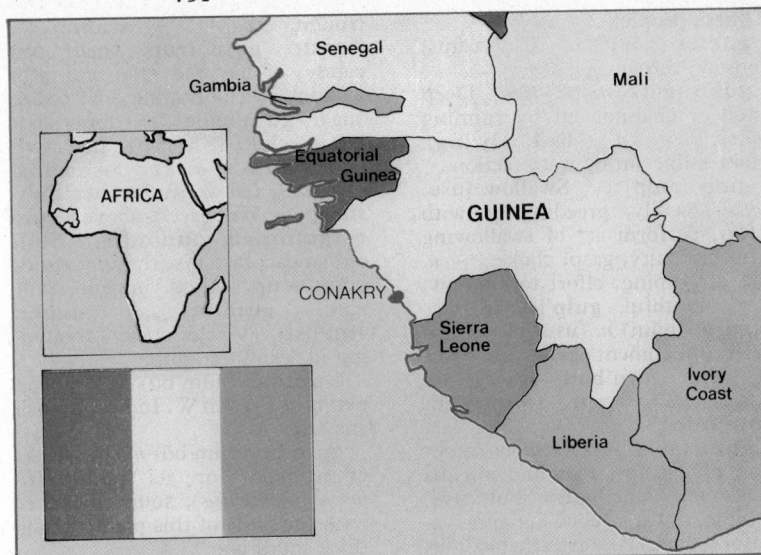

The helmeted **guinea fowl** is native to
Africa and Madagascar though long
domesticated in Europe and the U.S.A.
The **guinea pig** grows to 10 ins. in
length. It is part of the diet in many S.
American countries.

nning devices. **guile′ful** adj.
ile′ful·ly adv. **guile′ful·ness**
guile′less adj. **guile′less·ly**
. **guile′less·ness** n.

guil·le·mot (gĭl′emŏt) n. Small
thern sea bird of genus Cepphus
h white markings on black
mage.

guil·lo·tine (gĭl′otēn, gē′o-) n.
Instrument used in France (esp.
ring the Revolution) and else-
ere for beheading, consisting of
avy, sharp blade sliding between
oved posts. 2. Surgical instru-
nt for excising tonsils etc. ~
′otēn, gē′o-, gĭlotēn′, gēo-) v.t.
ined, -tin·ing). Behead with a
llotine. [J. I. Guillotin (1738–
14), French physician, who
vocated its use in 1789]

guilt (gĭlt) n. Fact of having
mmitted a specified or implied
ense; criminality, culpability.
ilt′less adj. Innocent (of).
ilt′less·ly adv. **guilt′less·ness**

guilt·y (gĭl′tē) adj. (guilt·i·er,
ilt·i·est). Criminal, culpable;
nscious of, prompted by, guilt;
ving committed a particular
ense; ~, not ~, pleas, verdicts,
criminal trials. **guilt′i·ly** adv.
ilt′i·ness n.

Guin·ea (gĭn′ē). Republic on
ast of W. Africa, formerly part of
ench West Africa; capital,
onakry. **Guin′e·an** adj. & n.

guin·ea (gĭn′ē) n. Former
itish gold coin, orig. of gold from
uinea, and for trade with Guinea,
fluctuating value, but chiefly
rth 1 pound and 1 shilling; ~
wl, **hen**, gallinaceous bird
Numida, esp. N. meleagris) with
ate-colored white-spotted plum-
e, native to Africa but widely
omesticated; ~ **pig**, (origin of
me doubtful) S. Amer. rodent
Cavia porcellus) now domesticated
pet, and also used as subject for
boratory experiments; (also
uman ~ pig) person used in an
xperiment; ~ **worm**, tropical
arasitic nematoid worm (Dracun-
lus medinensis) infesting skin of
an and horse, esp. in legs and
et, and causing sores.

Guin·ea-Bis·sau (gĭn′ē bĭsow′).
epublic on coast of W. Africa,
rmerly Portuguese Guinea;
apital, Bissau.

Guin·e·vere (gwĭn′evĕr).
Arthurian legend) Wife of King
rthur and mistress of Lancelot.

guise (gīz) n. Style of attire, garb
rchaic); external appearance,
mblance, assumed appearance,
etense.

gui·tar (gĭtär′) n. Musical
strument, usu. with six strings,

played with fingers or plectrum.
gui·tar′ist n.

Gui·zhou (gwē′jō′) =
KWEICHOW.

Gu·ja·rat (gōōjaraht′). Region
of W. India; state of W. India.
Gu·ja·ra·ti (gōōjarah′tē) adj. & n.
(Native or inhabitant, language) of
Gujarat.

gulch (gŭlch) n. Small ravine.
gules (gūlz) n. & adj. (her.) Red.
gulf (gŭlf) n. 1. (geog.) Portion
of sea partially enclosed by sweep
of coast, and usu. narrower at
mouth than bay. 2. Deep hollow,
chasm, abyss; (poet.) profound
depth (in river, ocean); impassable
dividing line.

Gulf (gŭlf) **Intracoastal
Waterway.** Inland waterway
composed of rivers, bays and
canals, 1,100 mi. (1,770 km),
extending from NW. Florida to
Brownsville, Texas.

Gulf (gŭlf) **States.** Five south-

ern U.S. states bordering on the
Gulf of Mexico: Florida, Alabama,
Mississippi, Louisiana, and Texas.

Gulf (gŭlf) **Stream.** Great
ocean current of warm water flowing from Gulf of Mexico parallel
with Amer. coast to Newfoundland,
and then E. to the N. Atlantic
Current.

gull¹ (gŭl) n. Any of several
long-winged web-footed sea birds
(family Laridae), usu. white with
mantle varying from pearl-gray to
black, with bright-colored bill and
harsh cry.

gull² (gŭl) n. & v.t. Dupe, fool.
gul′li·ble adj. Easily cheated or
duped. **gul′li·bly** adv. **gul·li-
bil·i·ty** (gŭlɪbil′ɪtē) n.

Gul·lah (gŭl′a) n. 1. One of a
group of descendants of slaves from
W. Africa, inhabiting the Sea
Islands and coastal regions of South
Carolina, Georgia, and N. Florida.
2. English-African patois or dialect

of these people.

gul·let (gŭl´ĭt) *n.* Esophagus; (loosely) throat.

gul·ly (gŭl´ē) *n.* (pl. **-lies**). Deep ditch or channel cut by running water. ~ *v.t.* (**-lied, -ly·ing**). Make gullies in by water action.

gulp (gŭlp) *v.* Swallow (usu. *down*) hastily, greedily, or with effort; perform act of swallowing with difficulty, gasp, choke. ~ *n.* Act of gulping; effort to swallow; large mouthful. **gulp´ing·ly** *adv.*

gum[1] (gŭm) *n.* (usu. pl.) Firm fleshy integument of jaws and bases of teeth; **gum´boil**, abscess on gum. ~ *v.t.* (**gummed, gum·ming**).

gum[2] (gŭm) *n.* 1. Viscous secretion of certain trees and shrubs hardening when dry but usu. soluble in water; chewing gum. 2. (also ~ **tree**) Any tree that exudes gum, esp. eucalyptus, various species of the N. Amer. genus *Nyssa* etc.; hollowed-out log, usu. from gum tree, serving as water trough, etc. 3. ~ **arabic**: see ARABIC; **gum´drop**, small soft candy, of flavored gum arabic or gelatin, with coating of coarse sugar; **gum´shoe**, (1) rubber shoe or overshoe; (2) (slang) detective; hence **gum´shoe** (*v.*) (**-shoeing, -shoed**), (slang) move stealthily, snoop; ~ **tree**: see 2 above. **gum** *v.* (**gummed, gum·ming**). Stiffen, smear, fasten with gum; exude gum; ~ **up**, (colloq.) impede; spoil, ruin. **gum´my** *adj.* (**-mi·er, -mi·est**). Viscid, sticky, abounding in, exuding, gum.

Gum·bo (gŭm´bō) *n.* Creole patois of French W. Indies, Louisiana, etc.

gum·bo (gŭm´bō) *n.* (pl. **-bos**). Okra plant or its pods (*Hibiscus esculentus*); soup thickened with the pods of this plant; (slang) thick mud; goo.

gump·tion (gŭmp´shon) *n.* (colloq.) Resource, enterprising spirit, initiative.

gun (gŭn) *n.* Metal tube for aiming or projecting miss utilizing the explosive force gunpowder or some other pro lant; piece of ordnance, cann musket, fowling piece, rifle, bine; pistol; revolver; (slang) who wears or uses a gun, es gunfighter or professional assas **stick to one's ~s**, maintain o argument; **gun´boat**, small w ship carrying heavy gun(s); arm vessel of light draft, esp. for use rivers; **gun´boat diploma** diplomacy supported by use threat of military force, esp. aga a much weaker nation; **gun´cott** (esp. Brit.) nitrocellulose; **gu fight**, (colloq.) fight with gu **gun´fire**, firing of guns; **gun´m** (pl. **-men**), armed robber; p fessional killer; desperado; **gu metal**, alloy of copper and 1c tin (formerly used for guns); **gun´point**, under threat of inju by a gun; **gun´powder**, explos of saltpeter, sulfur, and charco **Gunpowder Plot**, plot to blow

*The Australian **red gum** (Eucalyptus camaldulensis) grows to 120 ft. high. Its 12-in. leaves clothe the branches spreading from a short, stocky truck.*

Gum *of various kinds is refined from resins and other plant materials. Right: Kauri gum in its dried form. Gum arabic is a common water-soluble gum obtained from plants of the genus Acacia.*

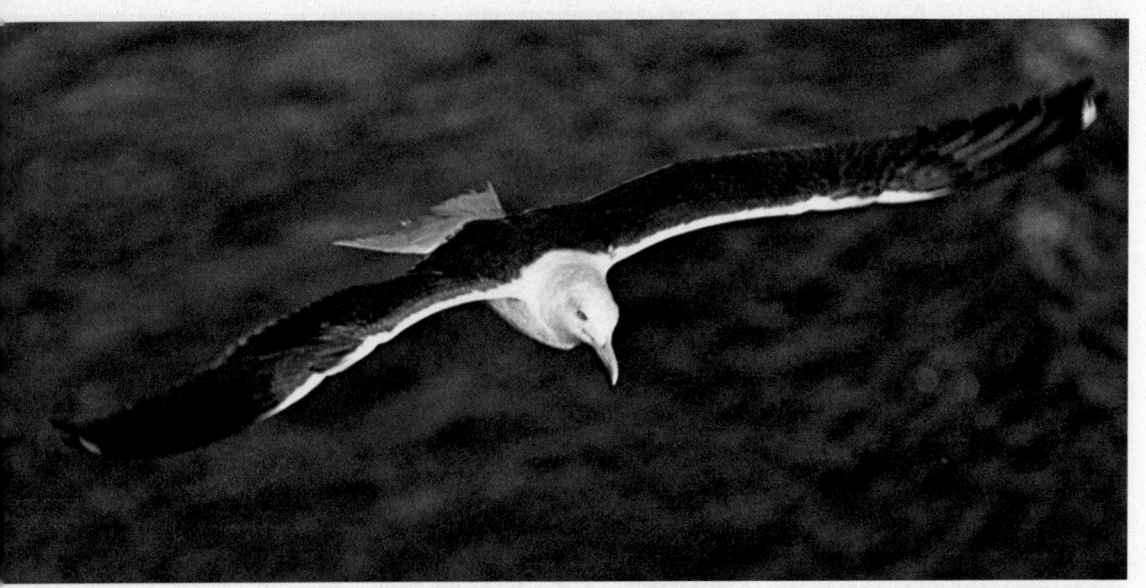

*Above: The **gull** is well adapted to flight. Long narrow wings enable it to soar and glide while its webbed feet enable it to land on and maneuver in water or on land. Most gulls nest on the ground, often on ledges of cliffs or on inaccessible rocks. There are several species including 1: Black-headed. 2: Common and 3: Herring gulls.*

British Houses of Parliament on Nov. 5, 1605, while the king and parliament were assembled there (see FAWKES); **gunpowder tea**, fine kind of green tea with leaves rolled up into pellets; **gun room**, room where guns are kept; compartment on Brit. warship fitted up for junior officers or as lieutenants' mess; **gun′runner, gun′running**, (person engaged in) illegal introduction of firearms into country; **gun′shot**, (1) shot fired from gun; (2) range of gun (*out of, within,* gunshot); **gun-shy**, (esp. of sporting dogs) afraid of the report of gun; **gun′slinger**, (colloq.) gunman; **gun′smith**, maker and repairer of firearms. **gun** *v.* (**gunned, gun′ning**). Shoot with gun; ~ **for**, go in search of with gun (also fig.). [perh. f. *Gunna* pet form of ON. *Gunnhildr* woman's name used as nickname for ballistae and cannon]

gun·nel[1] (gŭn′el) *n.* Eellike fish (*Pholis gunnellus*) of N. Atlantic.

gun·nel[2]: see GUNWALE.

gun·ner (gŭn′er) *n.* One who operates a gun; (naut.) warrant officer in charge of ordnance.

gun·ner·y (gŭn′erē) *n.* Construction and management of guns; firing of guns; hence, ~ **officer**, ~ **sergeant**, etc.

gun·ny (gŭn′ē) *n.* (pl. **-nies**). Coarse sacking, sack, usu. of jute fiber; burlap; **gun′nysack**, sack made of burlap or gunny.

Gun·ther (goon′ter). In the Nibelungenlied, husband of Brunhilde and brother of Kriemhild, by whom he was beheaded in revenge for Siegfried's murder.

gun·wale, gun·nel[2] (gŭn′el) *ns.* Upper edge of ship's or boat's side.

gup·py (gŭp′ē) *n.* (pl. **-pies**). Small W. Indian fish (*Lebistes reticulatus*) freq. kept in aquaria.

gur·gi·ta·tion (gêrjĭtā′shon) *n.* Whirling, surging, bubbling motion or sound.

gur·gle (gêr′gel) *n.* Bubbling sound as of water poured from bottle or running over stones. ~ *v.* (**-gled, -gling**). Make gurgle; utter with gurgle(s).

Gur·kha (gêr′ka, goor′-) *n.* (pl. **-khas**, collect. **-kha**). One of a military people of Hindu descent and Sanskritic speech, who settled in the province of Gurkha, Nepal, in the 18th c.; one of these, or any soldier from Nepal serving in the Brit. or Indian army.

gur·nard (gêr′nerd) *n.* (pl. **-nards**). Marine fish of family Triglidae, esp. of the Old World genus *Trigla* with large spiny head, mailed cheeks, and two or three pairs of finger-shaped processes used as feelers. [OF. *gournart*, lit. = "grunter"]

gu·ru (goo′roo, gooroo′) *n.* Hindu spiritual teacher or head of

religious sect; any wise leader or teacher. [Sansk.]

gush (gŭsh) *n.* Sudden or copious stream (often fig. of speech etc.); effusiveness, sentimental affectation. ~ *v.* Issue in, send forth, gush; emit (water etc.) copiously; speak, behave, with effusiveness. **gush′er** *n.* (esp.) Oil well spouting oil profusely without pumping. **gush′ing·ly** *adv.* **gush′y** *adj.* (**gush·i·er, gush·i·est**). Sentimentally effusive.

gus·set (gŭs′ĭt) *n.* Piece let into garment to strengthen or enlarge some part.

gus·sy (gŭs′ē) *v.* (**-sied, -sy·ing**). (slang) Dress elegantly, decorate, doll up, as in **all gussied up**.

gust[1] (gŭst) *n.* Sudden violent rush of wind; burst of rain, fire, smoke, sound, etc. **gust′y** *adj.* (**gust·i·er, gust·i·est**). **gust′i·ly** *adv.* **gust′less** *adj.*

gust[2] (gŭst) *n.* (archaic and poet.) Sense of taste; keen relish; flavor.

gus·ta·tion (gŭstā′shon) *n.* Tasting. **gus·ta·tive** (gŭs′tatĭv), **gus·ta·to·ry** (gŭs′tatōrē, -tōrē) *adjs.*

gus·to (gŭs′tō) *n.* Zest, enjoyment with which something is done.

gut (gŭt) *n.* 1. (pl.) Bowels or entrails (esp. of animals); (fig. and colloq.) courage, fortitude, pluck; (sing.) particular part of lower alimentary canal, intestine; **blind ~**, cecum. 2. Material for violin strings made from intestines of animals; material for fishing lines made from unspun silk substance in silkworms. 3. Narrow passage or channel. ~ *v.* (**gut·ted, gut·ting**). Take out guts of, clean, (fish); remove or destroy internal fittings of (house etc.). ~ *adj.* (slang) 1. Central, essential, as in ~ **issues**. 2. Strongly emotional, based on emotion rather than intellect, as in ~ **reaction**. 3. (college slang) Easy; ~ **course**, one requiring little or no work.

Gu·ten·berg (goo′tenbêrg), **Johann** (*c*1398–1468). Printer in Mainz, Germany; inventor of

The butterfly **gurnard** (*Paratrig vanessa*) is capable of 'walking' alo sandy bottoms on its three pairs of le like appendages in the course of search for food.

movable printing types.

gut·ta (gŭt′a) *n.* (pl. **gut·tae** gŭt′ē). 1. (archit.) (pl.) Drops in row as ornament esp. in Dor architecture. 2. (med.) Drop.

gut·ta-per·cha (gŭt′a pêr′ch *n.* Grayish rubberlike substan obtained from juice of vario Malayan trees, esp. *Palaquiu gutta*, used in electrical insulatio etc.; any of these trees. [Mal *getāh* gum, *percha* name of tree]

gut·ter (gŭt′er) *n.* Shallo trough below eaves, channel at si of street, carrying off rain wate open conduit for outflow of flui groove; **in, out of, the ~**, in, o of, low, disreputable, or poverty stricken surroundings; **gut′te snipe**, street urchin. **gutter** ~ Furrow, channel; flow in streams.

gut·tur·al (gŭt′eral) *adj.* Of th throat; (of sounds) produced i throat, or by back of tongue an palate. ~ *n.* Guttural sound o letter. **gut′tur·al·ism** *n.* **gut′tur al·ize** *v.t.* (**-ized, -iz·ing** **gut′tur·al·ly** *adv.*

guy[1] (gī) *n.* Rope, chain, etc. guide and steady thing bein hoisted and lowered, or to secure o steady anything liable to shift, or hold tent etc. in place. ~ *v.* (**guyed, guy·ing**). Secure wi guy(s).

guy[2] (gī) *n.* (Brit.) Effigy GUY FAWKES burned on Nov. (Brit.) grotesquely dressed perso fright; man, fellow. ~ *v.t.* (**guyee guy·ing**). Ridicule, make fun of.

Guy·a·na (gēăn′a, -ah′na, gī-Republic on NE. coast of Sout

2

3

Amer. (formerly **British Guiana**); capital, Georgetown. **Guy·a·nese** (gēanēz′, -nēs′, gī-) *adj.* & *n.*

guz·zle (gŭz′el) *v.* (**-zled, -zling**). Drink, eat, greedily; consume in guzzling. **guz′zler** *n.*

Gwyn (gwĭn), **Nell** (1650?-87). (original name, Eleanor Gwynne) English actress and mistress of Charles II.

gym (jĭm) *n.* (colloq.) Gymnasium, gymnastics; **~ shoes**, rubber-soled shoes worn in a gymnasium.

gym·kha·na (jĭmkah′na) *n.* (chiefly Brit.) (Public place with facilities for) athletic or equestrian displays or contests; sporting event, esp. gymnastics. [mixture of *gymnastics* and Hind. *gend-khāna* ball house (racquet court)]

gym·na·si·um (jĭmnā′zēum; for def. 2 also gĭmnah′zēoōm) *n.* (pl. **-si·ums, -si·a** pr. -zēa, -zha). 1. Place, room, or building, with equipment for gymnastics and sports. 2. European, esp. German, academic high school preparing pupils for universities.

gym·nast (jĭm′năst, -nast) *n.* Expert in gymnastics.

gym·nas·tic (jĭmnăs′tĭk) *adj.* Of gymnastics. **gym·nas′ti·cal·ly** *adv.* **gym·nas′tics** *n.pl.* 1. Exercises developing the muscles, esp. such as are performed with special apparatus in gymnasium. 2. (treated as sing.) Art or practice of such exercises.

gym·no·spern (jĭm′nospĕrn) *n.*

(bot.) Plant having its seeds unprotected by seed vessels (opp. ANGIOSPERM). **gym·no·sper′mous** (jĭmnōspĕr′mus) *adj.*

gyn. *abbrev.* Gynecology, gynecological.

gy·nan·dro·morph (gīnăn′dromōrf, jī-, ji-) *n.* (biol.) Individual with characters of both sexes.

gy·nan·drous (gīnăn′drus, jī-, ji-) *adj.* (biol.) Of mixed sex; (bot.) with stamens and pistil united in one column as in orchids.

gyn·e·col·o·gy (gīnekŏl′ojē, jīne-, jĭne-) *n.* Science of diseases of women, esp. of the reproductive system. **gyn·e·co·log′i·cal** *adj.* **gyn·e·col′o·gist** *n.*

gyp, gip (jĭp) *vbs.t.* (colloq.) Cheat, swindle, defraud. **~** *n.* Swindle; cheating; cheater; swindler.

gyp·soph·i·la (jĭpsŏf′ila) *n.* Plant of genus *G~* with small delicate pink or white flowers and including the baby's-breath. [Gk. *gupsos* chalk, *philos* loving]

gyp·sum (jĭp′sum) *n.* Hydrated calcium sulfate, mineral from which plaster of Paris is made by dehydration. **gyp·se·ous** (jĭp′sēus), **gyp·sif·er·ous** (jĭpsĭf′erus) *adjs.*

gyp·sy (jĭp′sē) *n.* (pl. **-sies**). 1. Member of dark-haired tawny-skinned people (called by them-

selves ROMANY), originally fr India, entering Europe in 14th a 15th centuries, now mainly Europe and U.S., still somew maintaining nomadic ways basket makers, horse trade fortunetellers. etc. 2. Their l guage; Romany. 3. One who lo or lives like them. **~** *adj.* **~ c** (colloq.) taxicab operating with proper permission, license, etc.; **moth**, moth (*Porthetria disp*

Sustem Reuther

Chalky soils or ground that contains some mortar rubble are ideal for **gypsophilas**. *They thrive best in a sunny position. The flowers are often dried and used in decorations.*

native to the Old World but introduced to Amer., whose larva is very destructive to trees.

gy·rate (jī′rāt, jīrāt′) *v.i.* (**-rat·ed, -rat·ing**). Go in circle or spiral; revolve, whirl. **gy·ra·tion** (jīrā′shon) *n.* **gy·ra·to·ry** (jī′ratōrē, -tōrē) *adj.*

gyre (jīr) *n.* (lit.) Spiral, vortex; circle; spiral motion.

gyr·fal·con, ger·fal·con (jēr′fawlkon, -faw-) *ns.* Largest of all falcons (*Falco rusticolus*), living in Arctic Amer. and Europe, with plumage in white, gray, and black phases.

gy·ro (jī′rō) *n.* (pl. **-ros**). Gyroscope; **gy′rocompass**, form of gyroscope used as a compass, mounted so that its axis remains parallel to that of the Earth.

gy·ro·plane (jī′roplān) *n.* Flying machine (including the helicopter and autogyro) in which the lift is mainly provided by vanes rotating freely in a more or less horizontal plane.

gy·ro·scope (jī′roskōp) *n.* Instrument to illustrate dynamics of rotating bodies; solid rotating wheel mounted in ring, with axis free to turn in any direction; form of this attached to vessels, aircraft, etc., to maintain equilibrium, measure

*Right: If the flywheel of a **gyroscope** is rotated in the direction of the arrow then a downward force T will result in a motion in the direction P. The gyroscope was used first to demonstrate the Earth's rotation. The device is used in steering and stabilizers. Below: A toy gyroscope.*

angular velocity and accelerat etc. **gy·ro·scop·ic** (jīroskŏp′ĭk) **gy·ro·scop′i·cal·ly** *adv.*

gy·ro·stat (jī′rostăt) *n.* Forr gyroscope in which the whee fixed in a case.

gy·rus (jī′rus) *n.* (pl. **gy·ri** jī′rī). (anat.) Fold, convolut esp. of brain surface.

gyve (jīv, gīv) *n.* (usu. pl. *v.t.* (**gyved, gyv·ing**). (arch Shackle, fetter, esp. for the leg

1. Gi
2. Fly

The letter **H, h** is pronounced as an aspirate in most languages but is variously stressed. The letter and sound derive from a Semitic original which was sounded with a partial coincidence of the back of the tongue and soft palate, giving a guttural sound as used in German today. Italians do not pronounce 'h' but use it to soften attack on vowels that follow and to 'soften' other consonants, such as 'ch'.

Phoenician   Early Greek   Etruscan

Early Latin   Classical Latin   Italian

H, h (āch) (pl. **H's, h's** or **Hs,**). Eighth letter of modern English and ancient Roman alphabet, representing historically Semitic (laryngeal or guttural spirant, rough aspirate), Greek H; in modern English usu. (except in combination with *c, g, s, w*) for simple aspiration or breathing, with just enough narrowing of glottis to be audible before vowel.

H *abbrev.* Hard(ness); henry(s); (song) heroin.

H *symbol.* Hydrogen.

h. *abbrev.* Hecto-; height; high; (baseball) hit(s); hour(s); hundred.

ha[1] (hah) *int.* Exclamation of surprise, joy, suspicion, triumph,

ha[2] *abbrev.* Hectare(s).

ha·be·as cor·pus (hā'bēas kōr'-). Writ requiring a person to be brought before a judge or into court, esp. to investigate whether it has been lawful to hold him in custody. [L., = "you must have the body"]

hab·er·dash·er (hăb'erdăsher) *n.* Dealer in men's furnishings, as shirts, socks, etc.; (Brit.) dealer in sewing notions, as ribbon, tape, etc. **hab'er·dash·er·y** *n.* (pl. **-er·ies**). Shop selling haberdasher's goods.

ha·bil·i·ment (habĭl'iment) *n.* Attire, dress; (pl.) dress suited to particular office or occasion.

hab·it (hăb'ĭt) *n.* 1. Action or behavior so often repeated as to be almost unconscious; settled tendency or practice; mental constitution (~ **of mind**); ~-**forming** (esp. of drugs etc.) addictive. 2. Dress, esp. of religious order; (also **-ing** ~) costume worn by a horseback rider. **habit** *v.t.* 1. Clothe. 2. (archaic) Inhabit. **hab·it·a·ble** (hăb'ĭtabel) *adj.* That can be inhabited. **hab·it·a·bil·i·ty** (hăbĭtabĭl'ĭtē), **hab'it·a·ble·ness** *ns.* **hab'it·a·bly** *adv.*

hab·it·ant (hăb'ĭtant; for def. 2 -tahń') *n.* (pl. **hab·it·ants** pr. -ĭtants; for def. 2 ăbētahń'). 1. Inhabitant. 2. One of the (descendants of) early French settlers in Canada, Louisiana, etc., chiefly farmers.

hab·i·tat (hăb'ĭtăt) *n.* Natural home of plant or animal; habitation. [L., = "(it) inhabits"]

hab·i·ta·tion (hăbĭtā'shon) *n.* Inhabiting; place of abode.

ha·bit·u·al (habĭch'ōōal) *adj.* Customary; constant, continual; given to (specified) habit. **ha·bit'u·al·ly** *adv.* **ha·bit'u·al·ness** *n.*

ha·bit·u·ate (habĭch'ōōāt) *v.t.* (**-at·ed, -at·ing**). Accustom (*to*). **ha·bit·u·a·tion** (habĭchōōā'shon) *n.*

hab·i·tude (hăb'ĭtōōd, -tūd) *n.* Mental or bodily constitution; custom, tendency.

ha·bit·u·é (habĭch'ōōā, -bĭch-ōōā') *n.* Habitual visitor; frequenter of a particular place. [Fr.]

Habs·burg = HAPSBURG.

ha·chure (hăshoor', hăsh'oor) *n.* In map-drawing, one of the short lines of shading indicating differences of slope (close together for steep slopes, wider apart for gradual ones).

ha·ci·en·da (hahsēĕn'da) *n.* (pl. **-das**). In Spanish-speaking

*One of the distinguished members of the **Habsburg** family was Franz Josef, ruler of the Austro-Hungarian Empire from 1848–1916. Two years after his death the empire was dissolved.*

countries, an estate, plantation, or ranch, or the main house on this; ranch house.

hack[1] (hăk) *n.* Mattock; hoe; gash, wound, or blow made by this. ~ *v.* Cut, notch, chop, etc. with a knife, pick, hoe, etc.; strike the arm or kick the shin of (an opponent in sports); deal cutting blows (*at*); emit short dry coughs (so *hacking cough*); **hack'saw**, saw with narrow blade set in a frame, for cutting metal.

hack[2] (hăk) *n.* 1. Horse let out for hire; inferior or worn-out horse; horse for ordinary riding; (hist.) hackney carriage; (colloq.) taxicab. 2. Common (esp. literary) drudge, mere scribbler. ~ *v.* Make common, hackney; ride (horse), ride on horseback, on road at ordinary pace. ~ *adj.* Of or by a hack; routine, banal.

hack·le (hăk'el) *n.* Long feathers on neck of domestic cock and other birds; (also ~ **fly**) angler's artificial fly dressed with hackle; **with ~s up,** (of cock, dog, etc.) angry, ready to fight. **hackle** *v.t.* (**-led, -ling**). Mangle, cut roughly.

hack·ney (hăk'nē) *n.* (pl. **-neys**). Horse of middle size and quality for ordinary riding; (also ~ **carriage,** ~ **coach,** etc.) carriage or coach for hire. ~ *v.t.* (**-neyed, -ney·ing**). Make common or trite by repetition (esp. in past part. **hackneyed**).

had: see HAVE.

had·dock (hăd'ok) *n.* (pl. **-docks,** collect. **-dock**). Fish (*Melanogrammus aeglefinus*) allied to cod but smaller, common in N. Atlantic etc. and much used for food.

Ha·des (hā'dēz). (Gk. myth.) Oldest name of Pluto; his kingdom, abode of departed souls; (often **h** ~) hell.

ha·dith (hahdēth'; *Brit.* hăd'ĭth) *n.* (pl. **-dith, -diths**). Body of traditions relating to Muhammad, now forming supplement to Koran (the *Sunna*).

hadj·i, haj·ji (hăj'ē) *ns.* (pl. **hadj·is, haj·jis** pr. hăj'ēz). Muslim pilgrim who has been to Mecca; **H** ~, title of such.

Ha·dri·an (hā'drēan). Publius

Aelius Hadrianus (76–138 A.D.), Roman emperor 117–38; ~'s Wall, wall from Solway Firth to mouth of the Tyne River, in N. England; built by Hadrian to protect Roman Britain from the tribes of the north.

Built between AD 121–127, **Hadrian's Wall** crosses northern England for 73 miles. The wall is at least 8 ft. thick and it was designed to stop marauders from the north. The section illustrated is in Northumberland.

Hematite occurs as a kidney ore, illustrated, or in crystal, specular oolitic forms. It receives its name from its color of dried blood in the ear state. Crystallized it is steel gray.

Haeck·el (hĕk'el), **Ernst Heinrich** (1834–1919). German biologist and philosopher; 1st German supporter of organic evolution; advocate of MONISM.

hae·mat·ic = HEMATIC.

haem·a·tite = HEMATITE.

hae·ma·tol·o·gy = HEMATOLOGY.

hae·mo·glo·bin = HEMOGLOBIN.

hae·mo·phil·i·a = HEMOPHILIA.

haem·or·rhage = HEMORRHAGE.

haem·or·rhoid = HEMORRHOID.

ha·fiz (hah'fĭz) n. Muslim who knows the Koran by heart; **H~**, title of such. [Arab. *hāfiz*]

haf·ni·um (hăf'nēum) n. (chem.) Rare metallic element, symbol Hf, at. no. 72, at. wt. 178.49, usu. found with zirconium and resembling it in properties. [*Hafnia*, L. name of Copenhagen]

haft (hăft, hahft) n. Handle or hilt (of dagger, knife, etc.). ~ v.t. Furnish with haft.

hag (hăg) n. 1. Ugly old woman; witch; (formerly) evil spirit in female form. 2. (also **hag'fish**) Round-mouthed eellike fish (*Myxine glutinosa*) allied to lamprey and living on dead or dying fish.

Hag·ga·dah (hagah'da; *Heb.* hahgahdah') n. (pl. **-doth** pr. -dōs, -dōt; *Heb.* -dawt', **-dahs**). Legendary part of the Talmud, anecdote, parable, etc., introduced to illustrate a point of the Law; book containing the story of the Exodus and the ritual of the Seder for first

night(s) of Passover.

hag·gard (hăg'erd) adj. Worn-out or wild looking (esp. as result of fatigue, privation, worry, etc.); (of hawk) caught in its adult plumage, untamed. **hag'gard·ly** adv. **hag'gard·ness** n. **haggard** n. Haggard hawk.

hag·gis (hăg'ĭs) n. Scottish dish of the heart, lungs, and liver, of sheep etc., with salt, pepper, onions, suet, etc., and oatmeal, boiled like large sausage in the stomach of the animal.

hag·gle (hăg'el) n. & v.i. (**-gled, -gling**). Dispute, wrangle (esp. *over* or *about* prices or terms).

Hag·i·og·ra·pha (hăgēŏg'rafa, hājē-) n.pl. (considered sing. or pl.) Books of Jewish Scriptures not included under Law and Prophets. **hag·i·og'ra·pher** n. Writer of any of these, or of saints' lives. **hag·i·o·graph·ic** (hăgēŏgrăf'ĭk, hājē-) adj. **hag·i·og'ra·phy** n. Writing of lives of saints.

hag·i·ol·a·try (hăgēŏl'atrē, hājē-) n. Worship of saints.

hag·i·ol·o·gy (hăgēŏl'ojē, hājē-) n. Literature treating of lives and legends of saints.

Hague (hāg), **The.** (Du. 's-Gravenhage) Seat of government of the Netherlands, on the North Sea; seat of the Court of International Justice.

ha-ha[1] (hah hah') int. Representation of sound of laughter.

ha-ha[2] (hah'hah) n. Moat or fence in a ditch bounding park or garden so as not to impair view or scenic appeal.

Hahn (hahn), **Otto** (1879–1968).

German chemist; research atomic fission; co-discoverer w Lise Meitner, of protoactiniu Nobel Prize for chemistry, 1944

Hai·fa (hī'fa). Port of Israel the NW. on Bay of Acre.

hai·ku (hī'kōo) n. (pl. **-k** (English imitation of) Japan poem of three lines of five, sev and five syllables respective [Jap. *hai*, recreation + *ku*, verse

hail[1] (hāl) n. Pellets of co densed and frozen moisture fall in shower, as **hail'storm**; sho of missiles, questions, etc.; **hai stone**, pellet of hail. **hail** v. Precipitate in the form of hail. (fig.) Pour down (words, blov etc.).

hail[2] (hāl) int. of greeti **~-fellow (well met)**, heart congenial man. **hail** v. Salu greet (*as*); call to (ship, person) attract attention; (of ship, pers have come *from* (place). ~ Salutation; **H~ Mary** = A MARIA.

Hai·le Se·las·sie (hī'lē selăs -lah'sē) (1892–1975). Emperor Ethiopia 1930–74; following Ital invasion was forced to leave Ad Ababa, 1936; reinstated in capi 1941; deposed Sept. 1974.

Hai·phong (hī'fŏng'). Port Vietnam near Gulf of Tonkin.

hair (hār) n. One or (colle sing.) all of the fine filame growing from skins of animals, e from human head; (of plants) c growing from epidermis; hairl thing; small amount; **get** (pers **by the short ~s**, (slang) hold that escape is painful; have co

ete control over; **split** ~**s**, make
e or caviling distinctions; be
erly precise; **to a** ~, exactly;
t **turn a** ~, show no sign of
haustion or discomposure; **hair′-**
ll, ball of hair in intestines of
t or other animal that licks its fur,
using distress and often death;
ir′breadth, hairs′breadth,
nute space or distance; narrow
argin; **hair′brush,** brush for
ir; **hair′cut,** act or style of
tting the hair; **hair′do,** way hair
dressed; **hair′dresser,** one who
ts and styles hair; **hair′line,** edge
hair on forehead etc.; very fine
e; **hair′net,** fine or loosely
oven net for keeping hair in place;
ir′piece, toupee, wig; **hair′pin,**
-shaped piece of wire etc. used for
stening up hair; **hairpin curve,**
ry sharp curve where road etc.
ubles back; **hair-raising,**
ough to make hair stand on end
rough fear or excitement; **hair**
irt, ascetic's or penitent's shirt
hair or wiry fabric for mortifying
e flesh; **hair space,** narrowest
ace between words in printing;
ir′splitting, oversubtle(ty);
ir′spray, cosmetic liquid
rayed on hair to hold it in place;
ir′spring, fine spring in watch,

regulating balance wheel; **hair**
trigger, gun trigger responding to
very slight pressure (also fig.
hair-trigger (*adj.*), of temper,
nerves, balance, etc.); **hair′-**
weaving, covering bald spot by
interweaving matched hair with
person's own hair. **hair′i·ness** *n.*
hair′less, hair′like, hair′y *adjs.*
(**hair·i·er, hair·i·est**).

Hai·ti (hā′tē). Republic occupying western part of island of
Hispaniola, W. Indies; capital,
Port-au-Prince. **Hai·tian** (hā′-
shan, -tean) *adj. & n.*

haj·ji = HADJI.

hake (hāk) *n.* (pl. **hakes,** collect.
hake). Any of several codlike food
fishes of the genera *Merluccius* and
Urophycis living in Atlantic waters
from N. Carolina to Newfoundland.

ha·ken·kreuz (hah′kenkroits) *n.*
(pl. **-kreu·ze** pr. -kroitse). Swastika that was used as an emblem of
the Nazi party and the Third Reich.
[Ger., = "hook cross"]

ha·kim, ha·keem (hahkēm′) *ns.*
(esp. in Muslim countries) 1. Wise
and learned man. 2. Muslim
physician. [Arab. *hakīm* wise,
physician]

ha·la·tion (hālā′shon, hă-) *n.*

(phot.) Spreading of light beyond
its proper boundaries on a developed film or plate.

hal·berd (hăl′berd, hawl′-) *n.*
(hist.) Combined spear and battle-
ax. **hal·berd·ier** (hălberdēr′,
hawl-) *n.* Soldier or guard armed
with halberd.

hal·cy·on (hăl′sēon) *n.* 1. Bird
fabled by the ancients to breed in
floating nest on sea at winter
solstice, and to charm wind and
waves into calm for the purpose,
identified with the kingfisher. ~
adj. Calm, peaceful, quiet; prosperous; ~ **days,** 14 days of calm
weather believed by ancients to
occur about winter solstice; period
of peace or prosperity. [Gk. *alkuōn*
kingfisher]

hale[1] (hāl) *adj.* (**hal·er, hal·est**).
Robust, vigorous, in good health, as
in ~ **and hearty.**

hale[2] (hāl) *v.t.* (**haled, hal·ing**).
Drag or draw forcibly (lit. or fig.).

Hale[1] (hāl), **Edward Everett**
(1822–1909). Amer. Unitarian
clergyman and author; best known
for short story, "The Man Without
a Country."

Hale[2] (hāl), **Nathan** (1755–
1776). Amer. Revolutionary War
officer and hero hanged by British
as spy; his last words were: "I only
regret that I have but one life to
lose for my country."

Ha·le·a·ka·la (hahlēahkahlah′).
Dormant volcano on E. Maui
Island, Hawaii; contains largest
crater in the world.

half (hăf, hahf) *n.* (pl. **halves** pr.
hăvz, hahvz). One of two equal or
corresponding parts into which
thing is divided; halfback; one of

*Hair is keratin, a material which in a dif-
ferent form forms fingernails, feathers
and reptile scales. Below: Electron
microscope view of a human hair magnified 200 times. Left: Elaborate
Papuan hair-style.*

The **half-timbered** frames of dome. houses were made of hardwoods, s. as oak. The spaces between the fran were filled with a choice of mater. which lent further range to indivio taste.

The wood frames of **half-timber** houses were cheaply made when raw materials were plentiful up to 1600s. The durability of these str. tures is seen in these houses Stratford-upon-Avon, U.K.

two periods game is divided into; **better** ~: see BETTER; (colloq.) wife; **go halves**, share equally (with person in thing). **half** adj. Forming a half. ~ adv. To the extent of half; (loosely) to a considerable extent; **not** ~ **bad**, (colloq.) not at all bad, quite good. **half** n., adj., or adv. in comb.: ~**-and-**~, (what is) half one thing and half another, esp. mixture of milk and cream; ~**-assed**, (slang, vulgar) incomplete, unprepared, incompetent, unrealistic; **half'back**, (football) one of 2 players usu. flanking quarterback and fullback; (soccer, field hockey) one of 3 players behind forward line; **half-baked**, (fig.) inadequately prepared; half-witted; **half binding**, bookbinding with leather back and corners, cloth or paper sides; **half-breed**, person having parents of different races, esp. the offspring of a Caucasian and an Amer. Indian; **half brother**, brother by one parent only (so **half sister**); **half-caste**, half-breed; esp. offspring of a European and an Asiatic; **half crown**, former British silver or cupronickel coin worth two shillings and sixpence; (usu. **half a crown**) this sum; **half'hearted**, lacking courage or zeal; so **half'heartedly**, **half'-heartedness**; **half hitch**: see HITCH; **half'life**, (phys.) time during which the radioactivity of a substance falls to half its original value; **half-mast, at half-mast**, (of flag) lowered to half height of mast as mark of respect for the dead or on other occasions of mourning; **half measures**, compromise, half-and-half policy etc.; **half-moon**, moon of which only half is illuminated; anything of this shape; **half nelson**: see NELSON; **half pint**, (slang) diminutive person or

animal; **half-seas over**, (slang) drunk; **half sister**: see HALF BROTHER above; **half size**, any fractional size in women's clothing for short women with full figures; **half-slip**, underskirt, petticoat; **half sole**, sole of shoe between shank and toe; **half-timber(ed)**, (archit.) having walls made of timber frame with spaces filled with bricks or plaster; **half time**, (esp.) interval between two halves of play in football, basketball, etc.; **half title**, title of a book printed at head of first page of text, or title of a section of a book printed on the recto of the leaf preceding it; **half tone**, (mus.) = SEMITONE; **half'tone**, (art) tone intermediate between the extreme lights and extreme shades; (photoengraving, printing) illustration printed from a block in which the tones are broken up into small or large dots by the interposition of a glass screen, ruled

The **hallmark** system was established in London in 1300 where it was supervised by the Goldsmith's Hall. Other countries instituted similar systems but many unofficial marks are found on their base metal wares.

22-carat 18-carat 14-carat

9-carat gold sterling silver

standard marks

with fine crosslines, between t camera and the object; this proce **half-track**, (mil.) armored vehi with wheels in front and caterpil treads in back; **half-truth**, sta ment that conveys only part of truth, omitting some relevant fac **half volley** (n.) (tennis, crick etc.) ball hit or returned as soon it touches the ground; **half'wa** equidistant from 2 ends; **halfw house**, (hist.) inn midway betwe 2 towns etc.; home for rehabili tion of former convicts, dr addicts, etc. as they adjust to norn society; **half-witted**, imbecilic.

half·pen·ny (hā'penē, hāp'nē) (pl. **half·pen·nies** for coin, hal **pence** for amount, pr. hā'pen (Brit.) Former bronze coin wor half a penny; this amount.

hal·i·but (hăl'ibut) n. Any several large flat fish (Hippoglos. vulgaris and H. stenolepsis) abu dant in northern seas and mu used for food. [haly holy, butt f fish (because eaten on holy days

Hal·i·car·nas·sus (hălikārnă us). Ancient Greek city in S' Asia Minor; site of tomb Mausolus, the Mausoleum.

hal·ide (hăl'īd, -ĭd, hā'līd)

Birmingham London Sheffield Edinburgh
office marks

maker's marks

lt derived from a halogen.

Hal·i·fax (hăl′ifăks). Capital city
d port of Nova Scotia, Canada.

hal·i·to·sis (hălĭtō′sĭs) *n.* Foul
eath.

hall (hawl) *n.* 1. Large public
om in mansion, palace, etc.;
incipal living room of medieval
use; common dining room in
nglish colleges etc.; large room for
blic business, entrance passage
house; any corridor or passage
building. 2. Building for
udents on college or school
mpus. 3. **hall′way**, entrance hall
corridor in building.

hal·le·lu·jah, hal·le·lu·iah
ălelōō′ya) *interjs. & ns.* Praise ye
e Lord [Heb.] [also **al·le·lu·ia**
elōō′ya)].

Hal·ley (hăl′ē), **Edmund** (1656–
42). English astronomer, mathe-
atician, and inventor; **~'s
met**, comet with a periodicity of
years, the return of which in
58 was predicted by Halley in
82; its last appearance in the 20th
will be in 1986.

hal·liard: see HALYARD.

Hal·li·bur·ton (hăl′ibērton),
ichard (1900–39). Amer. adven-
rer and writer; retraced routes of
ortez, Balboa, Alexander the
reat, Hannibal, etc.; swam
ellespont; lost at sea in typhoon
hile sailing across Pacific.

hall·mark (hawl′märk) *n.* Im-
ession stamped on gold and silver
ticles in England when such
ticles meet established standards
purity; any mark indicating
uality or excellence; any con-
icuous indication of the quality or
aracter of a thing. **~** *v.t.* Mark
ith hallmark. [f. Goldsmiths'
all, London, where gold and
ver articles were orig. appraised
d stamped]

hal·low (hăl′ō) *v.t.* Make holy;
onor as holy.

Hal·low·een, Hal·low·e'en
ălowēn′, hŏl-) *ns.* Eve of All
aints' Day, Oct. 31, on which
ildren go from door to door
gging treats by threatening
icks.

hal·lu·ci·nate (halōō′sināt) *v.t.*
nat·ed, -nat·ing). Produce false
npressions in mind of (person).
al·lu·ci·na·tion (halōōsinā′shon)
Illusion; apparent perception of
xternal object not actually present.
al·lu·ci·na·to·ry (halōō′sinatōrē,
ōrē) *adj.* **hal·lu·ci·no·gen·ic**
aalōōsinojĕn′ĭk) *adj.* (esp., of drug)
iducing hallucination. **hal·lu·-
·no·gen** (halōō′sinojen, hălyu-
n′-) *n.*

ha·lo (hā′lō) *n.* (pl. **-los, -loes**).
ircle of luminous or prismatically
lored light seen around a celestial
ody or light source, esp. that
ound sun or moon caused by
fraction through ice crystals in
in cloud; circle, ring; disk or ring

of light shown around head of a
sacred figure in paintings etc.,
nimbus; (fig.) ideal glory investing
person etc. **~** *v.t.* (**-loed, -lo·ing**).
Surround with halo.

hal·o·gen (hăl′ojen) *n.* (chem.)
Any of the nonmetallic elements,
fluorine, chlorine, bromine, iodine,
and astatine.

hal·o·phyte (hăl′ofīt) *n.* Plant
inhabiting salty soils.

Hals (hahls), **Frans** (*c*1584–
1666). Dutch portrait and genre
painter, most famous work the so-
called "Laughing Cavalier."

halt¹ (hawlt) *n.* Temporary
stoppage on march or journey. **~**
v. Make a halt; (mil.) bring to a
stand.

halt² (hawlt) *adj.* (archaic)
Lame; crippled. **~** *v.i.* Walk
hesitatingly; hesitate (*between*); (of
speech, argument, verse, etc.) be
defective. **halt′ing·ly** *adv.*

hal·ter (hawl′ter) *n.* 1. Rope,
strap, with noose or headstall for
horses or cattle; rope with noose for
hanging person; death by hanging.
2. Woman's garment tied behind
neck and across lower back, leaving
arms, shoulders, and back bare. **~**
v.t. Fasten with halter; hang
(person) with halter.

hal·vah (hahlvah′, hahl′vah) *n.*
Confection, orig. Turkish, of
ground sesame seeds and honey.

halve (hăv, hahv) *v.t.* (**halved,
halv·ing**). Divide into halves;
share equally; reduce to half; (golf)
play (game, hole) in same number
of strokes as opponent.

hal·yard, hal·liard (hăl′yerd)
ns. (naut.) Rope, tackle, for raising
or lowering sail, yard, etc.

Ham (hăm). Second son of Noah
(Gen. 10).

ham (hăm) *n.* Back of thigh;
thigh and buttock; (formerly) the

back of the knee; thigh of hog, esp.
when dried, smoked, salted, or
otherwise cured for food; (colloq.)
licensed amateur radio operator;
(slang) overemphatic actor (also
attrib.).

ham·a·dry·ad (hămadrī′ad,
-ăd) *n.* 1. (Gk. myth.) Nymph
living and dying with the tree she
inhabited. 2. (zool.) KING COBRA.

Ha·man (hā′man). Chief minister of Persian King Ahaseurus;
when his plot against the Jews was
revealed by Esther (Esther 8), he
was hanged on the gallows.

Ham·burg (hăm′bĕrg; *Ger.*
hahm′bōōrχ). City on the Elbe in
northern West Germany.

ham·burg·er (hăm′bĕrger),
ham·burg (hăm′bĕrg) *ns.* Ground
or chopped meat, usu. beef; (also **~
steak**) fried or broiled patty of this
as a meat course; sandwich of this,
usu. on a bun or roll. [f.
Hamburg, Germany, where the
cooked chopped steak was first
popular]

Ham·e·lin (hăm′lin; *Ger.* hah′-
meln). City on the Weser in SW.
West Germany; scene of legend of
"Pied Piper of Hamelin."

Ham·il·ton¹ (hăm′ilton). 1.
City on Lake Ontario, Canada. 2.
Capital of Bermuda, W. Atlantic.
3. River flowing from S. central
Labrador to Lake Melville,
Canada.

Ham·il·ton² (hăm′ilton), **Alexander** (1755–1804). Amer. lawyer
and statesman; secretary and aide-
de-camp to Gen. Washington;
member of Continental Congress;
first U.S. secretary of the Treasury,

*Halifax is the largest of Nova Scotia's
cities and her busiest port. Halifax has
a rich industrial life, including oil refining
nearby, meat packing, sugar refining,
fishing and furniture making.*

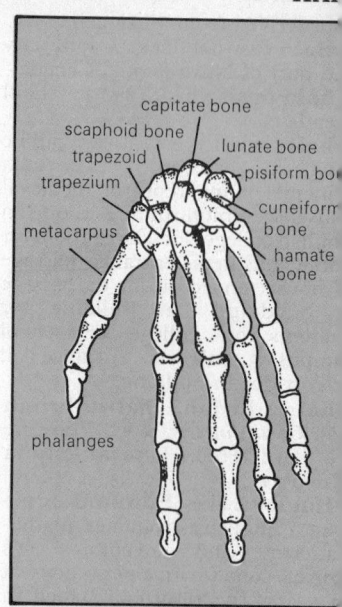

An adult **hamster** grows to 6 ins. long. Above: A few days after birth several golden hamsters fit comfortably into the palm of a hand. Left: Native to temper- ate Europe and west Asia are many species, including this black bellied variety.

The human **hand** has 27 bones and constructed to enable the thumb touch the front of each finger, a gr evolutionary advance on other clumsier primate hands.

1789–95; planned policies establishing national fiscal system; strengthened central government; mortally wounded in duel with Aaron BURR.

Ham·ite (hăm´īt) n. 1. Supposed descendant of HAM. 2. Member of Egyptian, Berber, and other peoples of N. or E. Africa. **Ham·it·ic** (hămĭt´ĭk) adj. Of Hamites; (esp.) of the group of African languages including ancient Egyptian, Berber, Galla, etc.

Ham·let (hăm´lĭt). Legendary prince of Denmark, hero of a tragedy by Shakespeare.

ham·let (hăm´lĭt) n. Small village.

Ham·lin (hăm´lĭn), **Hannibal** (1809–91). Vice president of U.S. under Abraham Lincoln, 1861–5.

ham·mer (hăm´er) n. Instrument for beating, breaking, driving nails, etc., with hard solid (usu. metal) head at right angles to handle; similar contrivance, as for exploding charge in gun, striking string of piano, etc.; auctioneer's mallet used to indicate by rap that article is sold; metal ball weighing 16 pounds (7.257 kg) attached to a wire with a grip handle, used in **throwing the** ~, track-and-field contest in which this is thrown for distance; **come under the** ~, be sold by auction; ~ **and tongs**, with might and main; **ham´merhead**, head of hammer; any of several large sharks of genus *Sphyrna*, with lateral extensions of the head and eyes; **ham´merlock**, (wrestling) position in which a wrestler is held with one arm bent behind his back. **hammer** v. Strike, beat, drive, (as) with hammer; (colloq.) inflict heavy defeat(s) on in war or games; ~ **away**, work hard at; ~ **out**, (fig.) evolve (an agreement) by long and repeated negotiations.

ham·mock (hăm´ok) n. Hanging bed of canvas etc. or netting suspended by cords at ends.

Ham·mond (hăm´ond) **organ.** (trademark) Electronic organ.

Ham·mu·ra·bi (hahmoorah´bē), **Ham·mu·ra·pi** (hahmoorah´pē). (c18th c. B.C.) King and lawgiver of Babylonia; **Code of** ~, famous early civil and criminal legal code attributed to him.

ham·per[1] (hăm´per) n. Large wickerwork basket, usu. with a lid.

ham·per[2] (hăm´per) v.t. Obstruct movement of (person etc.); impede, hinder.

Hamp·ton (hămp´ton) **Roads.** Channel connecting James and Elizabeth Rivers with Chesapeake Bay in SE. Virginia; scene of Civil War naval battle between MERRIMAC and MONITOR, 1862.

ham·shack·le (hăm´shăkel) v (-led, -ling). Hobble (horse et with rope connecting head and foreleg; hinder.

ham·ster (hăm´ster) n. Sm hibernating rodent of gen *Cricetus*, with short tail, and che pouches; **golden** ~, species of th (C. auratus).

ham·string (hăm´strĭng) n. (man) One of the tendons at ba of knee, (in quadrupeds) gre tendon at back of hock, correspon ing to that of heel in man. ~ v (-strung, -stringed, -string ing). Cripple by cutting han string(s); hinder; hold ba (person) by rules, lack of authorit

Han (hahn). Chinese dynast 206 B.C. to 220 A.D., when Chine territory was expanded and unifie literature and art flourished, an Buddhism was introduced.

Han·cock (hăn´kŏk), Joh (1737–93). Amer. statesman; pres dent of Continental Congres 1775–7; first signer of Declaratic of Independence; first governor Massachusetts, 1780–5, and aga 1787–93; **John Hancock**, (colloq signature.

hand (hănd) n. 1. Terminal pa of human being's arm beyond wris similar part in other animals. Possession, charge, authority, di posal (often pl.); agency, instru mentality (often pl.); share in th doing of something; pledge marriage, bestowal in marriage. Side (right or left), quarter. Person, source, from which thin comes; person who does somethin rson in relation to action or in ference to skill in doing something; workman, manual worker; (d.) ship's crew; **all ~s**, whole ew. 5. Skill; style of workmanip; style of writing; (hist.) gnature. 6. Applause. 7. andlike thing, esp. pointer of ock or watch. 8. Linear measure horse's height = 4 inches. 9. rds) Cards dealt to a player; ayer holding these; single round game; game (of cards etc.). 10. **~**, close by; about to happen on; **by ~**, by physical (as opp. to echanical) labor; **(live) from ~ mouth**, improvidently; **in ~**, ld in the hand; at one's disposal; ailable; **on hand**, in one's ssession; in stock; **on (or off) e's hands**, resting on (or passed om) one as a responsibility; **out hand**, without preparation; out control; **to hand**, within reach. . **change hands**, (of property) ss from one person to another; me **to hand**, turn up, be ceived; **keep one's hand in**, be practice; **take in hand**, underke; undertake to teach or train; ith a **heavy hand**, oppressively; ith a **high hand**, boldly, rogantly. 12. **hands down**, sily, without effort; **hands off!**, not touch; **hands up!**, direction persons to hold up their hands be robbed, to preclude resistance, c.; **hand in (or and) glove**, timate (*with*); **hand over hand fist**, with each hand successively ssing over the other, as in imbing rope; rapidly; greedily; **and to hand**, (of conflict etc.) at ose quarters. 13. In comb. = ade, operated, etc., by hand and t by machinery. 14. Special mb.: **hand'bag**, purse carried by oman; **hand'ball**, game played by riking hard rubber ball by hand gainst a wall; **hand'bill**, printed tice circulated by hand; **hand'- ook**, short treatise, manual, uidebook; **hand brake**, brake perated by hand; **hand'car**, small pen railroad car propelled by hand imp, used to transport track orkers; **hand'cart**, cart pushed or awn by hand; **hand'clasp**, asping of hands of two or more ersons to show friendship etc.; **and'craft**, handicraft; **hand'- iffs**, pair of metal rings joined by ort chain, for securing prisoner's ands; **hand'cuff** (v.) secure erson) with these; **hand glass**, nall magnifying glass or mirror ith handle; **hand'gun**, gun that in be held and fired with one hand; istol, etc.; **hand grenade**, small xplosive shell thrown by hand; **and'hold**, something for the ands to grip (in climbing etc.); **and'maid(en)**, (archaic, exc. g.) female servant; **hand-me- own**, (colloq.) article of clothing sed by one person and passed on

to another, usu. member of family; anything secondhand or inferior (also *adj.*); **hand organ**, barrel organ with crank turned by hand; **hand'out**, food, money, etc., handed out to a beggar; publicity or news release handed out to the press; **hand'rail**, railing along edge of stairs etc.; **hand'shake**, shake of person's hand with one's own, as greeting; **hand'spike**, lever for shifting heavy objects, as guns, by hand; spoke of capstan or windlass; **hand'spring**, somersault in which one lands first on one's hands and then on one's feet; **turn hand'- springs**, (esp.) exert special effort (for someone); **hand'work**, handiwork, handicraft; **hand'writing**, writing by hand, esp. of particular person. **hand** *v.t.* Help (person) with the hand (*into*, *out of*, carriage etc.); (naut.) take in, furl (sail); deliver, transfer by hand or otherwise; **~ it to**, acknowledge superiority of.

Han·del (hăn'del; *Ger.* hĕn'del)

*The influence of Buddhism is seen in Chinese art of the **Han dynasty**. Missionary contacts with India developed into broader cultural and trade contacts. This painting is a detail of one found in a Han tomb.*

*Before more advanced implements were developed, the quill was the standard instrument used for **handwriting**.*

(orig. *Haendel*), **George Frederick** (1685–1759). German-born composer of operas and oratorios; settled in England in 1712 and became court composer; famous for his *Messiah*, *Samson*, *Judas Maccabaeus*, etc.

hand·ful (hănd'fool) *n.* (pl. **-fuls**). Quantity that fills the hand; small number (of men etc.); (col-

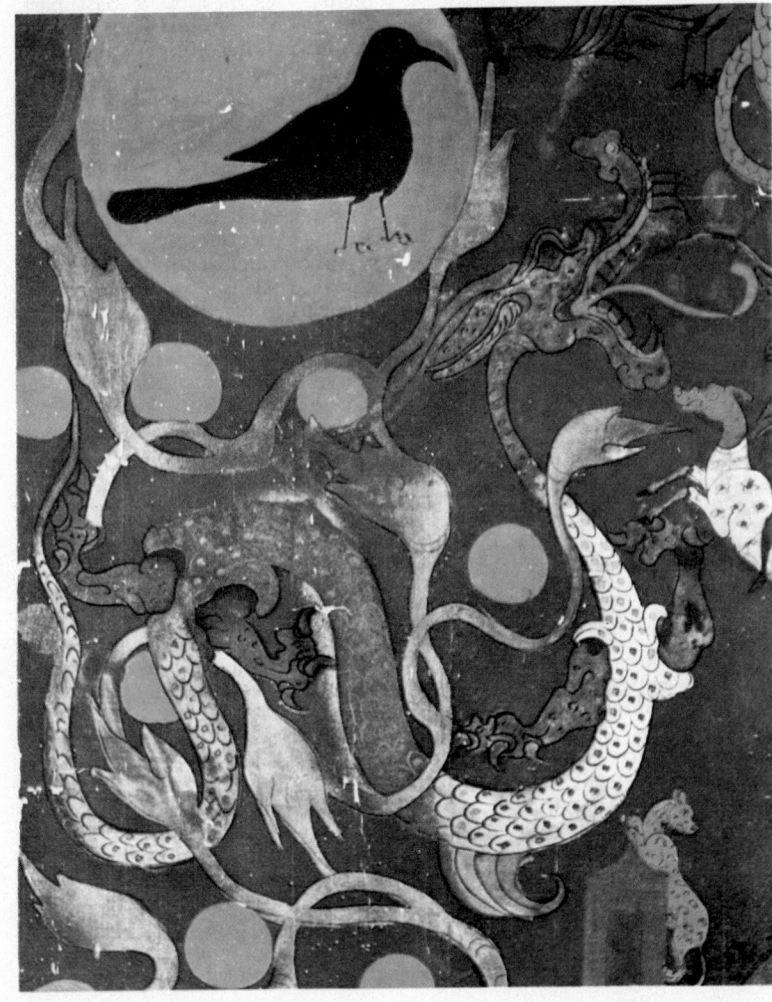

loq.) troublesome person.

hand·i·cap (hăn′dēkăp) *n.* Race or any contest of skill or strength in which to equalize chances of winning, some disadvantage in weight, score, etc. is imposed on a superior competitor, or some advantage is given to an inferior competitor; advantage given or disadvantage imposed; disability of any kind. ~ *v.t.* (**-capped, -cap·ping**). Impose handicap on (competitor); (fig., of circumstances) place (person) at a disadvantage; attempt to predict winner of horse race by comparing past performances, weights carried, etc. **hand′i·capped** *adj.* Suffering from physical or mental disability. **hand′i·cap·per** *n.* (esp.) Racetrack official who assigns weights to be carried by horses in handicap races.

hand·i·craft (hăn′dēkräft, -krahft) *n.* Manual art or trade, as weaving, pottery, etc.; work, articles so produced. **hand′i-crafts·man**, person who practices a handicraft.

hand·i·work (hăn′dēwĕrk) *n.* Work done, thing made, by the hands or by anyone's personal agency.

hand·ker·chief (hăng′kerchĭf, -chēf) *n.* Square of linen, silk, etc., carried in pocket (**pocket-**~) for wiping nose etc.

han·dle[1] (hăn′del) *n.* That part of thing which is made to hold it by; (slang) person's name; (CB jargon) call name. **han′dlebar**, (of bicycle etc.) steering bar with handle at each end.

han·dle[2] (hăn′del) *v.t.* (**-dled, -dling**). Touch, feel with the hands; manipulate; manage (thing, person); treat; treat of; deal in (goods). **han′dler** *n.* (esp.) Person in charge of a trained animal, show dog, etc.

hand·some (hăn′som) *adj.* (**-som·er, -som·est**). Of fine form or figure; (of a man) good-looking; (of conduct etc.) generous; (of price, fortune, etc.) considerable. **hand′some·ly** *adv.* **hand′some·ness** *n.*

hand·y (hăn′dē) *adj.* (**hand·i·er, hand·i·est**). Ready to hand; convenient to handle; clever with the hands; **handyman** *n.* (hăn′dēmăn), person able to do all sorts of odd jobs.

hang (hăng) *v.* (**hung** pr. hŭng, **hanged, hang·ing**). 1. (past t. & past part. **hung**) Suspend, attach loosely (*from, to*); suspend (meat, game) to dry, age, etc.; place (picture) on wall; attach (wallpaper); suspend floating in space; rest (door on hinges) in freeswinging position; let droop; remain, be, suspended; decorate *with* (things suspended); **hanging gardens**: see BABYLON. 2. (past t. & past part. **hanged**) Suspend, be suspended, by the neck

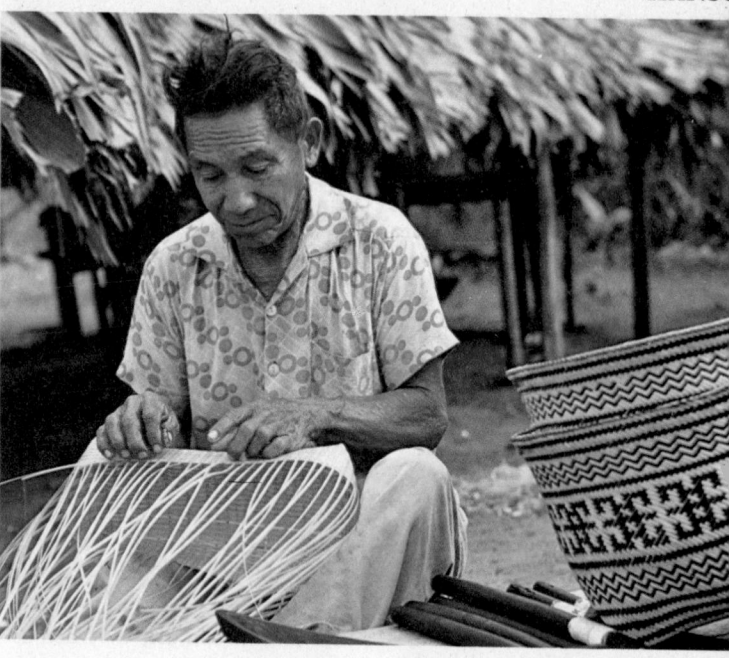

In many communities **handicraft** *is the only form of manufacture. This Guyanese craftsman weaves baskets of characteristic local patterns, using materials from the surrounding country.*

until dead (esp. as capital punishment). 3. (past t. & past part. **hung**) ~ **about** or **around** (colloq.) loiter, linger, about; ~ **back**, show reluctance to act or move; ~ **glider**, kitelike glider controlled by operator suspended in harness beneath; ~ **heavy**, (of time) pass slowly; ~ **in (there)**, persevere in troublesome situation; ~ **on**, attend carefully to (words etc.); stick closely (*to*); keep telephone connection open; persevere; (slang) wait; ~ **out**, suspend from; (slang) frequent (*at* place); ~ **together**, be coherent; ~ **up**, suspend; end telephone conversation by putting receiver back in cradle; **hung over**, (slang) suffering from a hangover. 4. **hang′dog**, base and sneaking; shamed, cringing (expression etc.); **hang′man**, one appointed to hang condemned persons; **hang′nail**, torn skin at root of fingernail; resulting soreness; **hang′out**, (colloq.) place often visited; place where one is usu. found; **hang′-over**, (slang) unpleasant aftereffects of intoxication; **hang′up**, (colloq.) psychological block or fixation. **hang** *n.* Downward droop or bend; way a thing hangs; **get the** ~ **of**, get the knack of, understand.

hang·ar (hăng′ger, hăng′er) *n.* Building for housing aircraft.

hang·er (hăng′er) *n.* (esp.) Loop etc. by which thing is hung; coat hanger; ~**-on**, sycophantic follower.

hang·ing (hăng′ĭng) *n.* (esp., pl.) Drapery with which walls etc. are

hung; **a** ~ **matter**, action (punishable by capital punishme

hank (hăngk) *n.* Circular loop coil, orig. as definite length of ya (naut.) ring of rope, iron, etc., fixing staysails to stays.

hank·er (hăng′ker) *v.i.* Cra long, *after.* **hank′er·ing** *n.*

Hanks (hăngks), **Nancy,** (17 1818). Mother of Abrah Lincoln; married Thomas Linco 1806.

han·ky (hăng′kē) *n.* (pl. **-kie** (colloq.) Handkerchief.

han·ky-pan·ky (hăng′kē păn kē) *n.* (colloq.) Underhand deali mischief, deceit.

Han·ni·bal (hăn′ibal) (3rd B.C.). Carthaginian general; fou against Rome in second Punic W crossed the Alps into Italy a defeated the Romans at La Trasimene (217 B.C.) and Cann (216 B.C.), was eventually forced withdraw from Italy and w defeated by Scipio in N. Africa.

Ha·noi (hănoi′). Capital Vietnam in the NE.

Han·o·ver (hăn′ōver). (G *Hannover*) Town in the north West Germany; once capital of t country of Hanover, which w later a province of Prussia; in 17 the elector of Hanover (Ge Ludwig) became King George I England; **House of** ~, British ro dynasty from 1714 to the death Queen Victoria in 1901.

Hanse (hăns) *n.* Company guild of merchants, esp. politi and commercial league (**Hanseat League**) of Germanic towns, whi flourished in the 14th and 15 centuries. **Han·se·at·ic** (hănsēa ĭk) *adj.* Of the German Hanse.

han·som (hăn′som) *n.* (also **cab**) Cabriolet for two inside, w driver mounted behind and re ing over roof. [J. A. *Hansom* 303–82), Engl. inventor]

Ha·nuk·kah, **Cha·nu·kah** (hah′*nuka*, -nookah; *Heb.* χahnoo-h′) *ns.* Jewish festival commemorating victory of the accabees over the Syrians in 165 c. and the rededication of the emple at Jerusalem (also called ast of Lights, Festival of Lights).

hap·haz·ard (hăphăz′erd) *adj.* asual; unplanned. **hap·haz′ard·** *adv.*

hap·less (hăp′lĭs) *adj.* Unlucky. ap′less·ly *adv.*

hap·loid (hăp′loid) *adj. & n.* iol.) (Organism, cell) with only e set of chromosomes (half the PLOID complement).

hap·pen (hăp′en) *v.i.* 1. (of ent) Occur. 2. Chance, have the rtune, *to* (do); come *upon* by ance. **hap′pen·ing** *n.* 1. Event. Impromptu performance, or one which audience participates.

ap·pen·stance (hăp′enstăns) *n.* oc.) Chance.

hap·py (hăp′ē) *adj.* (**-pi·er,** i·est**). (esp. of circumstance) ucky, fortunate; contented or eased with one's lot; successful, t, felicitous; **~-go-lucky** (*adj.*); eerfully casual. **hap′pi·ly** *adv.* ap′pi·ness *n.*

Haps·burg, Habs·burg (hăps′-rg; *Ger.* hahps′boorχ). German mily (named after the castle of apsburg near Aaran in Switzernd) to which belonged the rulers Austria and many of the Holy oman Emperors from 1273 to 918; branch of the family that led Spain from 1516 to 1700.

ha·ra·ki·ri (hăr′akēr′ē, hăr′-) *n.* uicide by disembowelment, as rmerly practiced by military (or amurai) class in Japan when in sgrace or sentenced to death. ap. *hara* belly, *kiri* cut]

ha·rangue (hărăng′) *n.* Long, ud, or vehement address; tirade. *v.* (**-rangued, -rangu·ing**). lake harangue (to).

har·ass (hăr′as, hărăs′) *v.t.* Vex y repeated attacks; trouble, worry. ar·ass′ment, har′ass·ment *ns.*

Har·bin (härbēn′). (Chinese inkiang) City in central lanchuria; important railroad nction and trade center.

har·bin·ger (här′bĭnjer) *n.* 1. ormerly) One sent to secure dgings for army, royal train, etc. Person or thing that announces nother's approach, forerunner. ~ *t.* Announce approach of.

har·bor, Brit. **har·bour** (här′-er) *ns.* Place of shelter for ships, sp. where they may lie close to and neltered by shore, piers, etc.; nelter. ~ *v.* Give shelter to, ster, cherish (evil thoughts); come anchor in harbor. **har′bor·age,** rit. **har′bour·age** *ns.* (Place of) nelter.

hard (härd) *adj.* 1. Firm, unyielding to touch, solid. 2. Difficult (*to* do); difficult to understand or explain; **~ of hearing,** somewhat deaf. 3. Difficult to bear; unfeeling, harsh; involving undue or unfair suffering; stingy; harsh; (of liquor) distilled or with high alcoholic content; intoxicating; (of drugs) addictive. 4. In phonetics, applied to: (*a*) the letters *c, g* when they have their original guttural sounds, as in *can, get*, as dist. from the palatal and sibilant sounds, as in *center, gin*; (*b*) voiceless as dist. from voiced consonants, as *th* in *think* compared with *th* in *this*. ~ *adv.* Strenuously, severely; with difficulty; **be ~ put to it,** be in difficulties; **~ by,** close by; **~ on,** too severe in criticism or treatment; (of circumstances) bearing with undue severity on. **hard** *adj.* or *adv.* in comb.; **~-and-fast,** (of rules) strict; **hard′ball,** baseball as opp. to softball; (pol.) tough, unscrupulous machinations; **hard-bitten,** tough in fight, stubborn; **hard-boiled,** (of eggs) boiled until white and yolk are solid; hardened, callous; hardheaded; **hard cash,** cash as opp. to credit; **hard cider,** fermented apple juice; **hard coal,** anthracite; **hard core,** (fig.) irreducible nucleus or residue; **hard-core,** inveterate; constituting a difficult social problem; (of pornography) explicit and with no redeeming value; **hard currency,** currency unlikely to depreciate suddenly or fluctuate greatly in value; **hard hat,** light protective helmet worn by construction workers, baseball players, etc.; (colloq.) construction worker; any working-class conservative; **hard′-headed,** practical, not sentimental; **hard′hearted,** unfeeling; **hard-hit,** severely damaged, harmed, or troubled; **hard labor,** compulsory physical labor, as road building, stone breaking, etc., formerly imposed as part of legal punishment on criminals during imprisonment; **hard line,** unyielding adherence to firm policy; **hard-nosed** (colloq.) obdurate, uncompromising; **hard′-pan,** firm subsoil of clay, gravel, or sand; hard unbroken ground; **hard rock,** very loud rock-'n'-roll, with a heavy beat; **hard sauce,** mixture of butter and sugar often with brandy etc. added; **hard sell,** aggressive salesmanship; **hard-shell,** having a hard shell, as **hard-shell crab,** one that has not recently molted; (fig.) rigid and uncompromising in religious orthodoxy; **hard′tack,** hard biscuit made with flour and water only, ship biscuit; **hard up,** in want, esp. of money; at a loss *for*; **hard′ware,** metal goods such as small tools, nails, locks, etc.; (colloq., parts of) machine(s); items of electronic or

mechanical equipment; (esp.) apparatus of a computer; **hard water,** water containing mineral, esp. calcareous, salts that decompose soap, thus making the water unsuitable for washing etc., and causing incrustations in boilers; **hard′wood,** wood of deciduous trees as opp. to pines and firs. **hard′en** *v.* Make or become hard or callous.

Har·ding (här′dĭng), **Warren Gamaliel** (1865–1923). Twenty-ninth president of U.S., 1921–3; senator from Ohio, 1915–21; conservative Republican; opposed League of Nations; died in office.

hard·ly (härd′lē) *adv.* Scarcely; probably or surely not; harshly.

hard·ness (härd′nĭs) *n.* 1. Quality or state of being hard. 2. (min.) Degree of resistance of a mineral to abrasion or scratching, expressed in terms of the following scale, known as MOHS' scale: (i) talc; (ii) gypsum; (iii) calcite; (iv) fluorite; (v) apatite; (vi) orthoclase; (vii) quartz; (viii) topaz; (ix) sapphire (corundum); (x) diamond; thus, in the description of a mineral, "H. 7.5" means that it is harder than quartz but softer than topaz. 3. Quality of water containing dissolved salts of calcium and magnesium, bicarbonates causing temporary hardness, i.e. removable by boiling, and sulfates and chlorides causing permanent hardness, i.e. not removable by boiling.

hard·ship (härd′shĭp) *n.* Hardness of circumstance; severe

The Market Church towering above the Marktplatz in Hanover was completed in 1359. It is a Gothic basilica of brick. After the town's destruction in 1939–45 war, the church became a symbol of Hanover's recovery.

The **hare** is able to run swiftly from predators. It can outdistance most when running uphill, aided by its long back legs. This illustration shows a leveret when surprised.

suffering or privation.

har·dy[1] (här'dē) *adj.* (**-di·er, -di·est**). 1. Bold, audacious. 2. Robust, capable of endurance; (*hort.*, of plants) able to grow in the open air all the year. **har'di·ly** *adv.* **har'di·ness** *n.*

har·dy[2] (här'dē) *n.* (pl. **-dies**). Blacksmith's bar of hard iron for cutting metal on etc.

Har·dy (här'dē), **Thomas** (1840–1928). English novelist and poet; author of many novels of Wessex life, including *Tess of the D'Urbervilles* (1891) and *Jude the Obscure* (1896).

hare (hār) *n.* Quadruped (*Lepus*) resembling a rabbit but larger, with long ears and hind legs, short tail, and divided upper lip, noted for timidity and swiftness; **varying ~**: see SNOWshoe rabbit; **hare'-brained**, silly, rash, wild; **hare'-lip**, fissure of upper lip caused by arrested development of upper lip or jaw.

hare·bell (hār'bĕl) *n.* Perennial plant (*Campanula rotundifolia*) with loose panicle of delicate blue bell-shaped flowers on slender stalk.

ha·rem (hār'em, hăr'-) *n.* Women's part of Muslim dwelling house; its occupants, female members of Muslim family, esp. wives and concubines.

har·i·cot (hăr'ĭkō) *n.* (also ~ **bean**) (chiefly Brit.) Kidney bean; any similar bean of genus *Phaseolus*, eaten as vegetable.

hark (härk) *v.* Listen; **~ back**, (of hounds) retrace course to find scent; recall (hounds); (fig.) revert (*to* subject).

Har·lem (här'lem). Section of New York City at the N. end of Manhattan; founded as a village in 1658; since World War I a major black district.

har·le·quin (här'lekwĭn) *n.* 1. (*usu.* **Harlequin**) Character in Italian comedy; in English pantomime, mute character, invisible to clown and pantaloon, in particolored bespangled tights and visor, and carrying wooden sword or lath as magic wand. 2. (also ~ **duck**) Northern species of duck (*Histrionicus histrionicus*) with distinctively variegated plumage. **har·le·quin·ade** (härlekwĭnād', -kĭ-) *n.* Part of pantomime in which harlequin and clown play principal parts.

Har·ley (här'lē) **Street.** London street associated with eminent or fashionable physicians and surgeons.

har·lot (här'lot) *n.* (archaic) Prostitute. **har'lot·ry** *n.*

harm (härm) *n.* Damage, hurt; mischief, injury; **out of ~'s way**, in safety. **harm** *v.t.* Do harm to; damage, injure. **harm'ful** *adj.* **harm'ful·ly** *adv.* **harm'ful·ness** *n.* **harm'less** *adj.* Doing no harm. **harm'less·ly** *adv.* **harm'less·ness** *n.*

har·mon·ic (härmŏn'ĭk) *adj.* Harmonious, concordant; relating to harmony; (*math.*, of quantities) with reciprocals in arithmetical progression; **~ progression**, (*math.*) series of numbers whose reciprocals are in arithmetical progression, as $\frac{1}{2}, \frac{1}{3}, \frac{1}{4}$, or 12, 15, 20. **har·mon'i·cal·ly** *adv.* **harmonic** *n.* Secondary tone produced by vibration of aliquot parts of sonorous body, usu. accompanying primary or fundamental tone produced by vibration of body as a whole, but sometimes produced independently, as in stringed instrument by light pressure on the string at various points etc.; (*elect.*) one of

The **harebell,** called a bluebel[l] Scotland, grows to between 10 and 1 ft. tall. It thrives in open w[e] lands and grassy places, often in de[?] carpets of color.

the component frequencies [of a] wave or alternating current tha[t is] an integral multiple of the fu[nda]mental frequency.

har·mon·i·ca (härmŏn'ĭka) [n.] Thin rectangular box contain[ing] metal reeds, each tuned to a n[ote,] moved before mouth while a[ir is] blown or sucked through it to [play] tunes.

har·mo·ni·ous (härmō'n[ĭəs]) *adj.* Concordant, forming a c[on]sistent or agreeable whole; [free] from dissent; sweet-sounding; s[?]

Thomas Hardy was born in this b[rick] and thatch cottage in Bockhampto[n,] Dorset hamlet. This author was v[ery] much influenced by 'Wessex', wh[ere] he spent most of his life.

collar
blinkers hames saddle breeching
bit reins
bridle girth

PLOUGH GEAR

crupper

trace
swingle tree

Various types of harness are used in different parts of the world not only for horses but oxen, elephants, camels, dogs and other draught animals. Above: Shire horse in harness. Above right: Harness gear.

The harp was widely used in ancient Mediterranean and near-Eastern civilizations, although it was rare in ancient Greece and Rome. The modern harp has a full chromatic range of notes.

g, playing, tunefully. **har·mo'-·ous·ly** *adv.*

har·mo·ni·um (härmō'nēum) *n.* rganlike musical instrument, in ich the keys operate metal reeds, d a bellows, worked by the ayer's feet, supplies the wind.

har·mo·nize (här'monīz) *v.* **nized, -niz·ing**). Bring into, be harmony (*with*); make, be, agree-le in artistic effect; add notes to elody) to form chords.

har·mo·ny (här'monē) *n.* (pl. ies). 1. Combination or arrange-ent of parts to form consistent d orderly whole, agreement, con-uity; agreeable effect of apt rangement of parts. 2. Combina-on of musical notes to produce easing effect; combination of multaneous) notes to form ords, part of music dealing with rmation and relation of chords. 3. ollation of parallel narratives, ssages on same subject etc., esp. the four Gospels.

har·ness (här'nĭs) *n.* Gear of aft horse or other animal; paratus in loom for shifting warp reads; (hist.) defensive armor; **in** , in the routine of daily work. **ar'ness** *v.t.* Put harness on (horse .); (fig.) utilize (river, waterfall, tural forces) for motive power.

Har·old (här'old). Name of two ngs of England: **Harold I** (d. 40), reigned 1035–40; **Harold II**, ng in 1066; killed in that year at e battle of Hastings.

harp (härp) *n.* Stringed musical strument, roughly triangular, th strings of graduated lengths ayed with fingers, and with pedals r raising tone of strings by one or semitones. ~ *v.i.* Play on harp; ell tediously *on* (subject). arp'ist *n.*

Har·pers (här'perz) **Ferry.** own and tourist resort in NE. st Virginia; site of U.S. arsenal

seized by John Brown's raid in 1859.

har·poon (härpoon') *n.* Barbed spearlike missile with rope attached, for catching whales and large fish; ~ **gun**, gun for firing harpoon. **harpoon** *v.t.* Strike, spear, with harpoon.

harp·si·chord (härp'sĭkôrd) *n.* Keyboard musical instrument resembling in shape and construc-tion the grand piano (which partly superseded it) but producing notes by means of strings plucked with quills or plectra.

Har·py (här'pē) *n.* (pl. **-pies**). 1. (Gk. and Rom. myth.) Rapacious monster with woman's face and body and bird's wings and claws; rapacious person. 2. **h~**, scolding, nagging woman.

har·que·bus (här'kwebus) *n.* (pl. **-bus·es**). (hist.) Early type of portable matchlock gun, supported on tripod by hook or on forked rest.

har·ri·dan (här'ĭdan) *n.* Hag-gard or scolding old woman.

har·ri·er[1] (här'ēer) *n.* One who harries.

har·ri·er[2] (här'ēer) *n.* 1. Hound used for hunting hare. 2. Hawk of genus *Circus*, esp. the marsh hawk (*C. cyaneus hudsonius*).

Har·ris·burg (här'isberg). Capital of Pennsylvania on Susque-hanna in SE. part of state.

Har·ri·son[1] (här'ĭson), **Ben-jamin** (1833–1901). Twenty-third president of U.S., 1889–93; grand-son of William Henry Harrison.

Har·ri·son[2] (här'ĭson), **William Henry** (1773–1841). Ninth president of U.S., 1841; Amer.

general; led Americans during war against Indians, 1811–12; congress-man from Ohio 1816–19; senator, 1825–8; minister to Colombia, 1828–9; died of pneumonia after one month as president.

har·row (här'ō) *n.* Frame with tines or disks that when dragged over soil, stirs it up, breaks clods, covers seed, etc. ~ *v.t.* Draw harrow over (land); distress pain-fully. **har'row·ing** *adj.* Distress-ing.

har·ry (här'ē) *v.t.* (**-ried, -ry·ing**). Ravage, waste, spoil (land); harass.

harsh (härsh) *adj.* Rough to the touch, taste, eye, or ear; cruel, unfeeling. **harsh'ly** *adv.* **harsh'-ness** *n.*

hart (härt) *n.* (pl. **harts,** collect. **hart**). Male of (esp. red) deer, esp. after fifth year; ~**'s-tongue**, fern (*Phyllitis scolopendrium*) with long undivided fronds.

Harte (härt), **(Francis) Bret(t)** (1836–1902). Amer. writer of short stories and humorous verse; best known for his pieces written as a California journalist, including the short stories "The Luck of Roaring Camp" and "The Outcasts of Poker Flat."

har·te·beest (här′tebēst, härt′-bēst) *n.* Common antelope of genus *Alcelephas* of the Sudan and southern Africa, of reddish color with long outward curved horns and long skull.

Hart·ford (härt′ferd). Capital of Connecticut in the central part on the Connecticut River.

har·um-scar·um (här′um skār′um) *adj.* & *n.* Reckless (person,

Harvesting may be a highly mechanized operation, or a simple hand task, as here in Amagon, Arkansas, where this couple are picking cotton.

conduct). ~ *adv.* In reckless manner.

ha·rus·pex (harŭs′pěks, hăr′-uspěks) *n.* (pl. **ha·rus·pi·ces** pr. harŭs′pĭsēz). (Rom. antiq.) Soothsayer of Etruscan origin performing divination by inspection of entrails etc.

Har·vard (här′verd). U.S. university at Cambridge, Massachusetts; named after clergyman John Harvard (1607–38), an English settler who left to the

original college (founded 1636) hi library and half his estate.

har·vest (här′vĭst) *n.* (Seaso for) reaping and gathering in c grain or other products; cro gathered in one season; (fig product of any action; ~ **moon** moon that is full nearest the autum equinox (Sept. 22 or 23). **harves** *v.t.* Reap and collect (crop) a harvest. **har′ves·ter** *n.* 1. Reaper 2. Reaping machine (esp. reape and binder).

Har·vey (här′vē), **Willian** (1578–1657). English physiciar discoverer of circulation of th blood, 1616.

Harz (härts) **Mountains** Mountain range and resort area o

The swift and slender **hartebeest** lives in herds on the open plains and scrublands of Africa. Some species such as Swayne's hartebeest are rare and endangered animals.

orthern West Germany between the Elbe and the Weser.

has·been (hăz'bĭn) *n.* (colloq.) Person no longer useful, successful, or famous.

ha·sen·pfef·fer (hah'senfĕf*er) *n.* Highly seasoned stew of rabbit meat. [Ger. *Hase* = rabbit + *feffer* = pepper]

hash[1] (hăsh) *n.* Dish of hashed meat and potatoes and sometimes vegetables, usually fried or baked, and often made of leftovers; old matter served up in new form; medley; ~ **mark**, (mil. slang) service stripe on sleeve of uniform; **make a ~ of**, spoil in dealing with; **settle a person's ~**, make an end

of, silence, him. **hash** *v.t.* Cut (meat etc.) in small pieces.

hash[2] (hăsh) *n.* (slang) Hashish.

Hash·e·mite (hăsh'emīt) *adj.* & *n.* ~ **Kingdom of the Jordan**: see JORDAN.

Hash·i·mite (hăsh'imīt) *adj.* & *n.* (Member) of an Arab princely family claiming descent from Hashim, great-grandfather of Muhammad.

hash·ish, hash·eesh (hăsh'ēsh, hah'shēsh) *ns.* Top leaves and tender parts of common hemp,

dried for smoking or chewing as narcotic; liquor prepared from this. [Arab., = "herbs"]

Ha·sid (hah'sĭd, hahsĭd'; *Heb.* χahsēd') *n.* (pl. **Ha·sid·im** pr. hahsĭd'ĭm; *Heb.* χahsēdēm'). Member of Jewish sect founded in Poland in 18th c., characterized by mysticism and joyous zeal. **Ha·sid·ic** (hahsĭd'ĭk) *adj.*

hasp (hăsp, hahsp) *n.* Fastening contrivance, esp. clasp passing over staple and secured by padlock or toggle. ~ *v.t.* Fasten with hasp.

has·sock (hăs'ok) *n.* 1. Cushion for kneeling or use as a footstool. 2. Tuft of matted grass etc.

hast (hăst) *v.* (archaic) Second pers. sing. pres. ind. of *have*.

haste (hāst) *n.* Urgency of movement, hurry, precipitancy; **make ~**, be quick. **haste** *v.t.* (poet.) (**hast·ed, hast·ing**). Make haste. **has·ten** (hā'sen) *v.* Cause (person) to make haste; accelerate (work etc.); make haste; come or go in haste.

Has·tings (hās'tĭngz). Town on coast of Sussex, England, on the Strait of Dover, scene of the **Battle of ~**, (1066), in which the Normans, under William of Normandy, defeated the Saxons under HAROLD II.

hast·y (hās'tē) *adj.* (**hast·i·er, hast·i·est**). Hurried; speedy; rash, inconsiderate; quick-tempered; ~ **pudding**, cornmeal mush. **hast'·i·ly** *adv.* **hast'i·ness** *n.*

hat (hăt) *n.* 1. Man's or woman's outdoor head covering, esp. with brim; **opera ~**, collapsible top hat worn in evening; **top ~**, man's tall silk hat. 2. **keep under one's ~**, keep confidential; **pass the ~**, solicit contributions; **talk through one's ~**, exaggerate, make unsupported assertions; **throw one's**

Hats for all occasions — from wide brimmed straw hats, to the ever-popular peaked cotton variety.

*The **hawthorn** is widely cultivated in Europe and North America, particularly in hedges. Its white or pink flowers, which usually grow in clusters, form into small fruit.*

~ **into the ring**, announce one's candidacy for political office. 3. **hat′band**, band of ribbon etc. around hat just above the brim; **hat trick**, (ice hockey, soccer, etc.) scoring of 3 goals by the same player in one game. **hat′ful** *n.* **hat′less** *adj.* **hat′ter** *n.* Person who makes or sells hats; **mad as a hatter**, quite mad (usu. alluding to the Mad Hatter, character in Lewis Carroll's *Alice in Wonderland*, but it may have its origin in the mercury poisoning, causing violent tremors, common among 19th c. hat makers.

hatch[1] (hăch) *n.* Lower half of divided door; aperture in door, wall, floor, or deck; (naut.) (also **hatch′way**) opening in ship's deck for lowering cargo, cover for this; floodgate; (aeron.) opening or door in aircraft or spacecraft; **down the** ~, informal drinking toast.

hatch[2] (hăch) *v.* Bring forth (young birds etc.) from egg; incubate (egg); emerge from egg; (of egg) produce young; contrive and develop (plot etc.). ~ *n.* Hatching; brood hatched. **hatch′-er·y** *n.* (pl. **-er·ies**). Place for hatching eggs, esp. of fish.

hatch[3] (hăch) *v.t.* Mark with (esp. close parallel) lines, as for shading in engraving or drawing. ~ *n.* Shading line in engraving or drawing. **hatch′ing** *n.* Series of engraved or drawn lines producing effect of shading.

hatch·back (hăch′băk) *n.* Automobile with sloping rear door and

window that lift as a unit.

hatch·et (hăch′ĭt) *n.* Light short-handled ax; **bury the** ~, make peace, compose a quarrel; ~ **face**, narrow sharp-featured face; ~ **job**, (colloq.) destructive criticism or gossip intended to damage the recipient; ~ **man**, (colloq.) paid killer; employee whose task it is to carry out unpleasant tasks for his employer.

hate (hāt) *n.* Hatred. ~ *v.t.* (**hat·ed, hat·ing**). Have strong dislike of; bear malice to. **hate′ful** *adj.* Exciting hatred. **hate′ful·ly** *adv.* **hate′ful·ness** *n.*

hath (hăth) *v.* (archaic) Third pers. sing. pres. ind. of *have.*

ha·tred (hā′trĭd) *n.* Active dislike; enmity, ill will.

Hat·ter·as (hăt′erəs), **Cape.** Promontory of Hatteras Island off coast of North Carolina, part of Cape Hatteras National Seashore.

haugh·ty (haw′tē) *adj.* (**-ti·er, -ti·est**). Proud, arrogant; dignified. **haugh′ti·ly** *adv.* **haugh′ti·ness** *n.*

haul (hawl) *v.* Pull, drag, forcibly; transport by cart, wagon, truck, etc.; (naut.) turn ship's course; (of wind) shift; ~ **off**, pull arm back, prepare, to deliver blow. **haul** *n.* Hauling; distance hauled; (fig.) amount gained, acquisition, take; **long** ~, **short** ~, long, short, distance or period of time. **haul·-**

*The **hawk moth**, which is found in most parts of the world, pollinates flowers such as orchids and petunias. The larvae of some North American species are destructive pests to tobacco and potato crops.*

age (haw′lĭj) *n.* Fee charged for hauling.

haunch (hawnch) *n.* 1. Part body (of man and quadrupe between last ribs and thigh; leg a loin of deer etc. as food. 2. S of arch between crown and pier

haunt (hawnt) *v.* 1. Frequ (place); frequent company (person); (of thoughts etc.) v (person) frequently; stay habi ally. 2. (of ghosts etc.) V frequently with manifestations their presence and influence; (p part.) visited, frequented, ghosts. ~ *n.* Place of frequ resort.

Haupt·mann (howpt′mah Gerhart** (1862–1946). Germ dramatist and novelist; Nobel Pr for literature, 1912.

Hau·sa (how′sa, -za) *n.* (pl. **-s** collect. **-sa**). (Member of) wi spread people of the Sudan and Nigeria, of Bantu family with so Hamitic mixture; Hamitic langu of these people, used, esp. commerce, over much of W. Afri

haut·boy (hō′boi, ō′-) *n.* (Cname for) OBOE; oboe player; re stop in organ with tone like obo

haute cou·ture (ōt kōōtü High fashion; (creations of) leadi fashion houses. [Fr.]

haute cui·sine (ōt kwēzēr Elegant style of cooking develop by French chefs. [French]

Ha·van·a (havăn′a). Capital c of Cuba; hence, cigar of Cub tobacco.

have (hăv) *v.* (**had** pr. hăd, **hav ing**). 1. Possess as property or one's disposal; possess as relati

The **hawk** occasionally destroys poultry but usually eats smaller mammals, reptiles and insects. The broad-winged hawk is about the size of a crow; the red-tailed hawk is one of the most common species; the red-shouldered hawk is reddish-brown and about 20 ins. long; and the rough-legged buzzard has fully-feathered legs and is 24 ins. long.

Red-shouldered hawk

Rough-legged buzzard

Red-tailed hawk

Broad-winged hawk

ha·ven (hā′ven) *n.* Harbor, port; refuge.

ha·ver·sack (hăv′ersăk) *n.* (Soldier's, traveler's) stout canvas bag for provisions, carried on back or over shoulder. [Ger. *habersack* (*haber* oats)]

hav·oc (hăv′ok) *n.* Devastation, destruction; **cry ~**, give signal to army to seize spoil (now only fig.); **play ~ with**, destroy.

haw[1] (haw) *n.* (Fruit of) hawthorn; **~finch**, kind of finch with very thick beak (*Coccothraustes coccothraustes*).

haw[2] (haw) *n.* Third eyelid of horse, dog, etc., cartilage within inner corner of eye.

haw[3] (haw) *v.* Hesitate, esp. in speech; stammer; esp. in phrase **hem and ~**.

haw[4] (haw) *int.* Command to animal to turn left (opp. GEE[1]).

Ha·wai·i (hawī′ē, -wī′e). Formerly Sandwich Islands, now state of U.S. comprising a chain of islands in the central Pacific including Hawaii; settled by Polynesians c10th c.; discovered by Europeans under Capt. Cook 1778; annexed by U.S., 1898; admitted to the Union in 1959; capital, Honolulu. **Ha·wai·ian** (hawī′an)

adj. & n. [Polynesian *Hawai'i* or *Havaiki* = Little Sava or Java, legendary home of Polynesians]

hawk[1] (hawk) *n.* Diurnal bird of prey of the order Falconiformes, esp. one of the Accipitridae or true hawks; (pol.) person advocating bellicose policies or nationalism; rapacious or aggressive person; **~-eyed**, keen sighted; **~ moth**, moth of family Sphingidae, noted for its hovering and darting flight; sphinx moth; **hawks' bill, hawks'-bill**, species of turtle (*Eretmochelys imbricata*) with mouth like hawk's beak, inhabiting Indian Ocean and warmer parts of Atlantic, source of tortoise shell; **hawk'weed**, yellow-flowered composite perennial plant of genus *Hieracium*. **hawk** *v.* Attack as hawk does; hunt with trained hawks.

hawk[2] (hawk) *v.t.* Peddle (wares) by crying them in the streets (also fig.). **haw'ker** *n.*

hawk[3] (hawk) *v.* Clear the throat noisily; bring (phlegm etc.) *up* from throat.

hawk[4] (hawk) *n.* Plasterer's or

---

djunct, appendage, attribute, unction, right, etc.; experience, uffer; **~ on**, wear (clothing). 2. ?ossess as duty; be obliged. 3. Retain; entertain in the mind; show, xhibit (sentiment etc.) in action; arry on, engage in (proceeding tc.); **~ in mind**, plan, propose; **~ o do with**, deal with. 4. Express *it*); assert, maintain; **will not ~ it**, efuse to allow or admit. 5. Come nto possession of, obtain, get; slang) deceive, take in; **I ~ it**, I ave found a solution etc. 6. Get nto specified condition, procure or blige (to be done etc.). 7. **~ at**, o at vigorously, attack; **~ it**, win, ave the superiority; **~ had it**, slang) be exhausted, defeated, etc.; **~ it coming**, merit it; **let** (person) **~ it**, give it to him; attack, punish, r reprimand him. **have** *v.aux.* orming (with past part. of verb) ompound tenses, pres. t. of *have* orming perfect, past t. of *have* orming past perfect. **have** *n.* One vho *has*, one belonging to wealthier lasses (usu. in pl., opp. to *have-* ots).

The grasses which produce **hay** are usually cut while still green. They are dried in the field and piled into hay-stacks, like these in Tuscany, Italy.

mason's square board with handle underneath.

hawse (hawz) *n.* Part of ship's bows containing ~ **holes**, openings through which a hawser or cable is passed; space between head of anchored vessel and anchors; situation of cables before ship's stern when moored with two anchors out from forward, one on starboard, other on port bow.

haw·ser (haw′zer) *n.* (naut.) Large rope, small cable, now freq. of steel.

haw·thorn (haw′thŏrn) *n.* Thorny shrub or small tree of genus *Crataegus*, with white, red, or pink blossom and small dark red berry; ~ **china, jar, pattern,** (china, jar, with) decoration of flowering branches of Japanese plum tree in white on dark blue ground.

Haw·thorne (haw′thŏrn), **Nathaniel** (1804–64). Amer. writer of short stories and novels; among his works, *Twice-Told Tales, The Scarlet Letter,* and *The House of Seven Gables.*

hay¹ (hā) *n.* Grass, clover, alfalfa, etc., cut and dried for fodder; **make ~ while the sun shines,** seize opportunities; **hay′-cock,** (chiefly Brit.) hay piled into a conical heap in a field; **hay fever,** allergy with catarrhal and freq. asthmatic symptoms, caused by pollen etc.; **hay′fork,** fork for turning over or loading hay; **hay′-loft,** loft in barn for storing hay; **hay′maker,** one who lifts, tosses, and spreads hay after mowing; instrument for shaking and drying hay; (slang) powerful swinging blow; **hay′mow,** hay stored in

barn; hayloft; **hay′stack,** regular pile of hay with pointed or ridged top for winter storage in the open; **hay′seed,** (slang) rustic, bumpkin; **hay′wire,** wire used to bind a bale of hay, straw, etc.; (*pred. adj.*) in disorder; distracted, crazy. **hay** *v.* Make into hay; make hay; feed hay to (animals).

hay² (hā) *n.* Country dance, or movement in dance, of winding or serpentine kind.

Hay·dn (hī′den), **Franz Josef** (1732–1809). Austrian-born composer of many symphonies, string quartets, masses, oratorios ("The Creation," "The Seasons"), etc.

Hayes (hāz), **Rutherford B(irchard)** (1822–93). Amer. lawyer and soldier; governor of

Ohio 1868–72, 1876–7; 19th predent of U.S., 1877–81, after bei declared the winner over Sam Tilden in a close and disput election.

haz·ard (hăz′erd) *n.* 1. Game dice similar to craps; (somethi causing) danger. 2. (golf) Sand tr or other designed obstacle. ~ *v* Expose to hazard; run the hazard venture on (action, stateme guess).

haz·ard·ous (hăz′erdus) *a* Risky; dangerous; dependent chance. **haz′ard·ous·ly** *adv.*

haze¹ (hāz) *n.* Obscuration atmosphere at or near ground le caused by presence of visible dr lets of water in the air above ground or by a mixing of ascendi hot air and descending colder above hot ground; (fig.) men obscurity or confusion. ~ (**hazed, haz·ing**).

haze² (hāz) *v.t.* (**haze haz·ing**). 1. (naut.) Harass w overwork. 2. Bully, subject to cr horseplay, esp. as part of initiat into college fraternity.

ha·zel (hā′zel) *n.* Bush or sm tree (*Corylus*) bearing nuts; lig brown color of ripe **ha′zeln** (esp. of eyes).

Haz·litt (hăz′lĭt), **Willia** (1778–1830). English critic a essayist.

ha·zy (hā′zē) *adj.* (**-zi -zi·est**). Misty, vague, indistin **ha′zi·ly** *adv.* **ha′zi·ness** *n.*

Hb *abbrev.* Hemoglobin.

H-bomb (āch′bŏm) *n.* Hyd gen bomb.

H.C. *abbrev.* House of Co mons; Holy Communion.

The small trees or hairy-leaved shru of the **hazel** *are found in temper regions. The hazel's hard-shelled nu edible.*

h.d. *abbrev.* Heavy duty.

HE, H.E. *abbrevs.* High explo-
e.

He *symbol.* Helium.

he (hē) *pron.* Third person nom.
g. masc. pronoun, denoting the
le person or animal referred to.
n. Male animal; ∼-**man** (pl.
en), strong virile man.

head (hĕd) *n.* 1. Anterior part of
dy of animal, upper part of
man body, containing mouth,
se organs, and brain; seat of
ellect or imagination; headache
lloq.); image of head, esp. on one
e of coin; person; individual, esp.
cattle. 2. Thing like head in
rm or position, e.g. cutting or
iking part of tool, part of long
ne next to joint, flat end of barrel
cask etc.; rounded or compact
rt of plant, e.g. compact mass of
ves in cabbage or lettuce, flower-
ds in cauliflower, etc.; foam on
p of beer; top (of staircase, page,
.); maturated part of boil etc.;
per end; end of lake at which
er enters it; end of bed etc.
ward which head lies; source of
er or stream; (height of) body of
ter kept at height for supplying
ll etc., force of its fall; pressure
er unit of area) of confined body
steam etc.; front (of procession,
my, etc.); front part of plow,
lding the share; bows of ship;
omontory; underground passage
working coal in mine. 3. Ruler,
ief; headmaster or headmistress
school; position of command;
ain division in discourse;
tegory; culmination, crisis. 4.
lang) Lavatory aboard naval
ssel. 5. **from ∼ to foot**, all
er; **out of one's ∼**, crazy;
lirious; **over one's ∼**, above one;
yond one's comprehension; ∼
d **shoulders** (**above** etc.), (taller
c.) by measure of head and
oulders (freq. fig.); **head'first**,
f plunge etc.) with head foremost;
g.) precipitately; **head of hair**,
ir on head, esp. when long or
ick; **head over heels**, topsy-
rvy, as in a somersault; deeply;
ep one's head, keep calm; **keep**
e's **head above water**, (fig.)
ep out of debt; **lose one's head**,
beheaded; become confused, lose
esence of mind. 6. **head'ache**,
ntinuous pain in head; (colloq.)
oublesome or annoying thing;
ead'band, band worn around
ad; **head'board**, board forming
e head esp. of a bed; **head'dress**,
overing esp. ornamental attire, for
e head; **head'gear**, hat, cap,
address; **head'hunting** (1)
actice of primitive tribes of
eserving enemies' heads as
ophies; (2) similar practice of
vilized hunters with animals; (3)
thless elimination of political or
usiness rivals; (4) (business)
quisition of (esp. executive)

personnel; (5) acquisition of famous
guests by ambitious hostesses;
head'land, promontory; **head'-
light**, (beam from) powerful light
at front of vehicle; **head'line**, line
at top of front page of newspaper
containing title etc. or major news
story; title or subtitle in newspaper;
(pl.) summary of a news broadcast;
head'lock, wrestling hold with arm
around opponent's head; **head'-
master, head'mistress**, director
of a private school; **head-on**, (of
collision etc.) with head or front of
vehicle pointed directly toward or

running full against something, esp.
front of another vehicle; **head'-
phone**, (usu. pl.; radio, telephony)
pair of receivers that can be held
against listener's ears by band passing over head; **head'piece**, hat,
helmet; **head'quarters**, (mil. etc.)
commander in chief's office or place
where commander's orders are
issued; center of operations; **head'-
room**, overhead space; **head'stall**,
part of bridle or halter that fits
around horse's head; **head start**,
early advantage or lead in competition; **head'stone**, gravestone;

right cerebral hemisphere

corpus callosum

septum
pellucidium

hard palate

tongue
pharynx

larynx

oesophagus

pons varolli

tonsil
medulla
oblongata

vertebra

bregma
pterion
sphenoid bone

frontal bone
glabella
nasal
bone

maxilla

mandible

zygomatic bone
parietal bone
temporal bone

lambdoidal
suture

asterion
mastoid
process
tympanic bone

condylus
stylohoid
ligament
hyoid bone

buccinator
masseter

digastric
sterno
mastoid
scalenus
trapezius

*The human **head** contains the brain,
many of whose functions are still
unknown, and the sense-organs. The
anatomy of the head, namely the structure of the skull (above left) and
muscles (right), was known in part by
ancient Greek physicians and medieval
scientists. The mysteries of the brain,
however, still baffle modern scientists.*

The human **heart,** which pumps the blood through the circulatory system, is situated between the two lungs behind the breastbone and slightly to the left of center. In a man the heart weighs about 10–12 ounces and in a woman 8–10 ounces. Above: The structure of the heart showing the direction of blood flow. Above right: The heart's cycle.

A **heart** transplant operation involve the removal of a hopelessly diseas heart and its replacement with a sou heart from a person who has died. Th transplant is being carried out Houston, Texas.

head′wait′er, person who supervises waiters in restaurant, acts as host, etc.; also called maître d'hôtel, (colloq.) maître d.; **head′waters,** stream(s) at upper part of river; **head′way,** progress; rate of progress; (archit.) height of arch etc.; **head′wind,** wind meeting one directly in front; **head′word,** word at head of entry in dictionary etc.; **head′work,** mental work. **head** v. Lop off head of (plant, tree); be, form, the head of; place (name etc.), be placed, at head of (chapter, list, etc.); be, put oneself, at the head of (a company etc.); lead; excel; front (in specified direction); (of ship etc.) make *for* (place, point); (soccer) strike, drive (the ball) with the head; ~ **off,** get ahead of so as to force to turn back or aside. **head′less** adj.

head·er (hĕd′er) n. I. One who puts heads on casks etc. 2. Brick, stone, laid at right angles to face of wall. 3. (colloq.) Headfirst plunge or fall.

head·ing (hĕd′ĭng) n. (esp.) Title etc. at head of page etc., headline; horizontal passage in preparation for tunnel.

head·long (hĕd′lawng, -lŏng) adv. & adj. Head foremost; precipitate(ly); impetuous(ly).

head·most (hĕd′mōst) adj. Foremost.

heads·man (hĕdz′man) n. (pl. -men pr. -men). Executioner who beheads the condemned.

head·strong (hĕd′strawng, -strŏng) adj. Self-willed; obstinate.

head·y (hĕd′ē) adj. (**head·i·er, head·i·est**). Impetuous, violent; (of liquor etc.) apt to intoxicate; (colloq.) tending to make one proud.

heal (hēl) v. Restore to health; cure (*of*); (of wound) become sound or whole. **heal′er** n.

health (hĕlth) n. Soundness of body, mind, etc.; that condition in which functions of body and mind are duly discharged; general condition of body, as **good, bad** ~; toast drunk in person's honor; ~ **food,** food having particularly healthful and unmodified natural qualities, esp. when organically grown.

health·ful (hĕlth′ful) a Health-giving; conducive to mo or spiritual welfare. **health′ful** adv. **health′ful·ness** n.

health·y (hĕl′thē) adj. (**health i·er, health·i·est**). Having go health; conducive to good healt **health′i·ly** adv. **health′i·ness**

heap (hēp) n. Group of thin lying one on another; (colloq., es pl.) large number or amount. ~ v Pile in a heap; load (*with*); accum late (insults etc. *upon*).

hear (hēr) v. (**heard** pr. hē

hear·ing). Perceive (sound etc.), perceive sound(s), with the ear; listen, give audience, to; listen judicially to (case, plaintiff, etc.); grant (prayer); be informed; entertain notion *of*; receive letter or message *from*; ~! ~!, exclamation expressing agreement. **hear′er** *n.*

hear·ing (hēr′ĭng) *n.* 1. Faculty of perception by means of the ear. 2. Opportunity to state one's case; listening to evidence and pleadings in a court of law; trial of a cause, esp. trial before a judge without a jury; ~ **aid**, device worn by person who is hard of hearing.

heark·en (här′ken) *v.i.* (archaic) Listen (*to*).

hear·say (hēr′sā) *n.* What one hears (but does not know to be true), gossip.

hearse (hērs) *n.* Vehicle for conveying coffin at funeral; (formerly) framework supporting coffin at funeral, often adapted for carrying candles.

heart (härt) *n.* 1. Hollow muscular organ that by rhythmic contraction and relaxation drives the blood through the vascular system; consisting in mammals and birds of four chambers. 2. Breast; mind; soul; seat of the emotions, esp. of love; sensibility, tenderness, feeling; courage; enthusiasm, energy. 3. Central part of anything, center, pith, core. 4. Vital part or principle. 5. Heart-shaped thing, esp. conventional symmetrical figure of two similar curves meeting in point at one end and cusp at the other; (playing card with) red heart-shaped figure(s); (pl.) suit of these cards. 6. Phrases: **break** (person's) ~, overwhelm him or her with sorrow; **cry one's** ~ **out**, cry violently; **eat one's** ~ **out**, grieve or yearn inconsolably; **have a** ~!, (colloq.) protesting appeal for sympathy; **have the** ~, be hardhearted or brave enough (*to*); **in one's** ~ **of** ~**s**, in one's inmost feelings; **have one's** ~ **in one's mouth**, be violently alarmed or startled; **set one's** ~ **on**, determine or select; **take** ~, pluck up courage. 7. With prepositions: **at** ~, in one's innermost feelings; **have at** ~, be deeply interested in; **by** ~, in, from, memory; **from (the bottom of) one's** ~, sincerely; **find in one's** ~, prevail on oneself (*to*); **near(est) one's** ~, dear(est) to one; ~-**to**-~, frank, sincere; **take to** ~, be much affected in one's feelings by; **with all one's** ~, sincerely, with the utmost good will. 8. Comb.: **heart′ache**, mental anguish; **heart attack**, heart failure; **heart′beat**, pulsation of heart; **heart′break**, overwhelming distress; **heart′broken**, overwhelmed by grief; **heart′burn**, burning sensation in lower part of chest, due to putrefactive fermenta-

The **heartsease** or wild pansy grows where water is plentiful. It has oval-shaped leaves and the flowers are usually purple, blue and yellow, although there are all-white forms.

tion of food in stomach; **heart failure**, (med.) any derangement of heart's mechanism, not necessarily fatal; (pop.) cessation of heartbeat causing death; **heart′felt**, sincere; **heart′rending**, distressing; **hearts′ease**, pansy, esp. small wild form; **heart′sick**, despondent; **heart′warming**, moving, encouraging; **heart′wood**, dense inner part of tree trunk, containing the hardest timber.

heart·en (här′ten) *v.* Inspirit, cheer; cheer *up*.

hearth (härth) *n.* Floor of fireplace; floor of reverberatory furnace, of smith's forge, etc.; **hearth′stone**, stone forming hearth; soft kind of stone, rubbed with water over hearth, doorstep, etc. to whiten.

heart·i·ly (här′tĭlē) *adv.* With good will, courage, or appetite; very.

heart·less (härt′lĭs) *adj.* Unfeeling, pitiless, cruel. **heart′less·ly** *adv.* **heart′less·ness** *n.*

heart·y (här′tē) *adj.* (**heart·i·er**, **heart·i·est**). Cordial, genial; (of feelings) sincere; vigorous; (of meals) abundant. ~ *n.* Hearty fellow, esp. sailor.

heat (hēt) *n.* 1. Being hot, high temperature; sensation, perception, of this; one of the primary sensations produced by contact with or nearness to fire or any body at a high temperature; (phys.) form of energy arising from the random molecular motion of a substance and capable of transmission by conduction or radiation. 2. Hot weather. 3. Warmth of feeling; anger; violent stage (of debate etc.); (slang) pressure, as in *the* ~ *is on*; (slang) police activity in searching

Heat is an essential ingredient of many operations, especially when it is required to melt a normally solid substance into liquid. Here workers pour gold into 100 ounce ingots.

out felons, as in *put the* ~ *on*. 4. = ESTRUS. 5. Single course in race or other contest. 6. **latent** ~, heat required to convert solid into liquid or vapor, or liquid into vapor (so called because it does not show its presence by an increase in temperature); **prickly** ~: see PRICKLY; **specific** ~, heat required to raise temperature of unit mass of given substance to given extent (usu. 1 degree), calculated relatively to some standard, usu. water; ~ **lightning**, flashes of light without thunder, seen near the horizon on a hot summer evening; ~ **of formation**, thermal change that occurs when substances chemically combine; ~ **shield**, device to protect from excessive heat, esp. on spacecraft during reentry; **heat′-stroke**, prostration from excessive heat; **heat wave**: see WAVE *n.* defs. 3, 4. **heat** *v.* Make hot; inflame (blood etc.); inflame with passion; become hot. **heat′ed·ly** *adv.* Vehemently, angrily.

heat·er (hē′ter) *n.* (esp.) Any contrivance for warming up room etc.; (slang) pistol.

heath (hēth) *n.* (esp. Brit.) Barren flat waste tract of land, esp. if covered with low herbage and dwarf shrubs; plants and shrubs found on heaths, esp. low shrubs of genus *Erica*, heather.

hea·then (hē′dhen) *adj. & n.* (pl. **-thens, -then**). (One who is) neither Christian, Jewish, nor Muslim (in Old Testament, = gentile; hist., used also of Muslims; later restricted to holders of polytheistic religions, esp. when uncivilized); pagan. **hea′then·dom, hea′then·ism** *ns.* **hea′then·ish** *adj.*

heath·er (hĕdh´er) *n.* Species of plant or shrub of genus *Erica*, esp. the common heather, *Calluna vulgaris*, growing on moors and heaths, and bearing purple bell-shaped flowers in autumn; color of heather. **heath´er·y** *adj.*

heave (hĕv) *v.* (**heaved, hove** (naut.) pr. hōv, **heaving**). 1. Lift (heavy thing); utter (groan, sigh) with effort; (naut. and colloq.) throw; (naut.) haul up, haul, by rope; pull (on rope etc.); ~ **to**, bring (vessel) to standstill with head to wind. 2. Rise, swell up; rise with alternate falls, as waves; pant; (colloq.) vomit. ~ *n.* Heaving; (pl.) disease of horses, "broken wind."

heav·en (hĕv´en) *n.* Sky, firmament (in prose now usu. pl.); region of atmosphere in which clouds float, winds blow, and birds fly; (formerly) each of the heavenly spheres; (often cap.) supposed habitation of God and his angels, usu. placed beyond sky; God; providence; place, state, of supreme bliss. **heav·en·ward** (hĕv´enwerd) *adj.* & *adv.* **heav´en·wards** *adv.*

heav·en·ly (hĕv´enlē) *adj.* Of heaven, divine; of the sky; of superhuman excellence. **heav´en·li·ness** *n.*

heav·i·er-than-air (hĕv´ēer dhan ār´) *adj.* (of aircraft) With weight greater than that of air it displaces, as distinct from balloons and dirigibles.

Heav·i·side (hĕv´ēsīd), **Oliver** (1850–1925). English physicist; ~ **layer**, E-layer of the ionosphere.

heav·y (hĕv´ē) *adj.* (**heav·i·er, heav·i·est**). 1. Of great weight; of great specific gravity; weighty because abundant; laden *with*; (of ordnance etc.) large; (mil.) carrying heavy arms or equipment; (of bread etc.) that has not risen properly, compact, dense. 2. Striking or falling with force or violence; (of ground etc.) clinging, difficult to travel over, dig, etc.; (of food)

difficult to digest. 3. Grave, severe; overcast, gloomy; clumsy in appearance or effect; intellectually slow; dull, tedious; oppressive, grievous; sad; despondent; doleful; drowsy; sober, serious. 4. ~ **-duty**, intended to be unusually resistant to stresses in use; ~ **-handed**, clumsy, oppressive; ~ **-hearted**, melancholy, doleful; ~ **hydrogen** = DEUTERIUM; **heav´yset**, having a heavy, stocky build; ~ **water**, deuterium oxide (D_2O), with the same chemical properties as ordinary water, but density about 10% greater; **heav´yweight**, (colloq.) influential person; boxer of heaviest weight. **heav´i·ly** *adv.* **heav´i·ness** *n.* **heavy** *adv.* Heavily. ~ *n.* (colloq.) Villain; gangster; actor who plays a villain or gangster.

The Inner and Outer Hebrides, which are also known as the Western Isles, consist of more than 500 islands, 92 of which are inhabited. The Isle of Lewis, shown here, is the main island of the Outer Hebrides.

Heather is traditionally associated the Scottish Highlands, where it mixed with peat-mud and straw to vide thatching for the Highlanders h Heather is also found throughout A N. America, and Africa.

Heb. *abbrev.* Hebrew; Hebre (New Testament).

He·be (hē´bē). (Gk. my Goddess of youth and spri daughter of Zeus and Hera, a cupbearer of Olympus.

Heb·ei = HOPEI.

He·bra·ic (hĭbrā´ĭk) *adj.* pertaining to, the Hebrews, Hebrew. **He·bra´i·cal·ly** *adv.*

He·bra·ism (hē´brāĭzem, -br *n.* Quality or attribute of Hebrews; Hebrew system thought or religion; Hebrew idi or expression. **He´bra·ist** Hebrew scholar.

He·bra·ize (hē´brāīz) *v.* (-ize -iz·ing). Translate into Hebre make, become, like a Hebrew.

He·brew (hē´broo) *n.* 1. Mer ber of a Semitic people inhabiti ancient Palestine esp. before t Exile, traditionally descended fro Abraham, Isaac, and Jaco (**Epistle to the**) ~ **s**, book of N Testament, traditionally includ among the letters of St. Paul b now usu. held to be nonPaulir 2. Semitic language used by t Hebrews, and in which most of t books of the Old Testament we written; modern form of this, t language of modern Israel. ~ *a* Belonging to the Hebrews; **alphabet**, Semitic alphabet of letters, the vowels being indicat by a system of diacritical marks; **calendar**: see JEWISH. [Aram '*ebrāyā*, Heb. '*ibrī* = "one from t

*The **Heaven Room** in Burghley Hous Lincs., U.K., was painted by Anton Verrio in 1695–6 and depicts t Greek gods on Mt. Olympus. Burgh House, one of the finest Elizabeth houses, also has a Hell Room.*

other side" (of the river)]

Heb·ri·des (hĕb´rĭdēz). Two groups of islands (**Inner** and **Outer** ∼) off the NW. coast of Scotland. **Heb·ri·de·an, He·brid·i·an** (hĕbrĭd´ēan) *adjs.* (Native, inhabitant) of the Hebrides.

Hec·a·te (hĕk´atē). (Gk. myth.) Goddess, said to be of Thracian origin, daughter of Perses and Asteria; in later times identified with Artemis or Persephone, and hence regarded as presiding over witchcraft and magical rites.

heck (hĕk) *int.* (euphem.) Hell.

heck·le (hĕk´el) *v.t.* (**-led, -ling**). 1. Dress (flax etc.) with hackle. 2. Harass (performer or speaker) with gibes, interruptions, awkward questions, etc. **heck'ler** *n.*

hec·tare (hĕk´tār, -tār) *n.* (abbrev. ha) One hundred ares (2.471 acres).

hec·tic (hĕk´tĭk) *adj.* 1. (hist.) ∼ **fever**, that which accompanies consumption and similar diseases, attended with flushed cheeks and hot skin; consumptive; morbidly flushed. 2. Feverishly excited or active. **hec'ti·cal·ly** *adv.*

hecto- *prefix.* One hundred times.

hec·to·gram (hĕk´togrăm) *n.* (abbrev. hg) One hundred grams.

hec·to·li·ter (hĕk´tolēter) *n.* (abbrev. hl) One hundred liters.

hec·to·me·ter (hĕk´tomēter) *n.* (abbrev. hm) One hundred meters.

Hec·tor (hĕk´ter). (Gk. legend) Trojan warrior, son of Priam and Hecuba and husband of Andromache; killed by Achilles, who dragged his body three times around the walls of Troy.

hec·tor (hĕk´ter) *v.t.* Intimidate;

Hebrew or Jewish people claim descent from Abraham and their religion is Judaism. The Wailing Wall in Jerusalem, reputedly on the site of Solomon's Temple, is now a sacred place for prayers and lamentations.

Hedges, like this one outside Mormon Tabernacle in Salt Lake C Utah, have several uses. Some purely decorative; others are prope dividers. In steeplechasing, hedges used as fences to be jumped.

bully. [f. HECTOR]

Hec·u·ba (hĕk´yuba). (Gk. legend) Wife of Priam, king of Troy, and mother of Hector, Paris, and Cassandra, among other children.

hedge (hĕj) *n.* 1. Fence of bushes or low trees. 2. Barrier. 3. Protection against loss in gambling or speculation; **hedge'hop**: see HOP²; **hedge'row**, row of bushes forming hedge. **hedge** *v.* (**hedged, hedg·ing**). 1. Surround with hedge; hem *in*; make, trim, hedges.

2. Secure oneself against loss (bet, speculation, etc.) by con pensating transactions on the oth side; avoid committing onese **hedg'er** *n.*

hedge·hog (hĕj´hŏg, -hawg) Any of several Old World insecti orous mammals of the fam Erinaceidae having a back cover with dense, erectile spines and ab to roll itself into a ball with the bristling in every direction; any various animals armed with spine such as the Amer. porcupine.

he·do·nism (hē′donĭzem) *n.*
:ctrine or ethical theory that
:asure is the chief good, or the
per end of action. **he′do·nist**
he·do·nis·tic (hēdonĭs′tĭk) *adj.*

hee·bie-jee·bies (hē′bē jē′bēz)
l. (slang) State of nervousness
uneasiness.

heed (hēd) *v.t.* Concern oneself
out, take notice of. ~ *n.*
:reful attention; esp. in **take ~,**
y ~, to. heed′ful *adj.* **heed′-**
·ly *adv.* **heed′ful·ness** *n.*
·ed′less *adj.* **heed′less·ly** *adv.*
:ed′less·ness *n.*

hee·haw (hē′haw′) *n.* Donkey's
:ay; loud laugh.

heel[1] (hēl) *n.* 1. Hind part of
:man foot below ankle; corre-
:onding part of hind limb in
:adruped, often raised above
:ound; (pop.) hind part of quad-
:ped's hoof, (pl.) hind feet; **on the**
s of, close behind, in close
:rsuit; **take to one's ~s, show a**
:ean pair of ~s, run away; **turn**
1 one's ~, turn sharply around.
Part of stocking that covers heel;
:rt of boot or shoe that supports or
:ses heel; **down at ~,** (of shoes)
:th heel worn down; (of person)
:earing such shoes, slovenly, desti-
:te. 3. Thing like heel in shape
: position, as lower rear surface of
:lf club, aft end of ship's keel;
:usty end of loaf of bread. 4. Cad,
:shonorable man. **heel** *v.* Touch
:ound with heel, e.g. in dancing;
:rnish (shoe etc.) with heel; chase
: follow closely, esp. of trained
:g. **heeled** *adj.* (esp. slang)
:upplied with money, esp. in **well**

heel[2] (hēl) *v.* (of ship etc.) Lean
:er owing to pressure of wind or
:even load; cause (ship) to do this.
: *n.* (naut.) Inclination of heeling
:ip.

heft (hĕft) *n.* (colloq.) Weight.
: *v.t.* Lift, esp. to judge weight.

heft·y (hĕf′tē) *adj.* (**heft·i·er,**
:eft·i·est). Heavy; sturdy, stal-
:art.

He·gel (hā′gel), **Georg Wil-**
:elm **Friedrich** (1770–1831).
:erman philosopher in whose
:stem of absolute idealism pure
:eing is regarded as pure thought,
:e universe as its development, and
:hilosophy as its dialectical explica-
:on. **He·ge·li·an** (hāgā′lēan, -gē′-)
:dj. & *n.* (Follower) of Hegel or his
:hilosophy. **He·ge′li·an·ism** *n.*

he·gem·o·ny (hĭjĕm′onē, hĕj′-
:nō-) *n.* (pl. **-nies**). Leadership;
:fluence, esp. of one nation over
:thers. **heg·e·mon′ic** *adj.*

He·gi·ra, He·ji·ra (hĭjīr′a,
:ĕj′era) *ns.* Flight of Muhammad
:om Mecca to Medina in 622 A.D.,
:om which the Muslim chrono-
:gical era is reckoned; **h~,** any
:ght or exodus, esp. from danger.
:Arab. *hijra* departure from one's
:untry]

The insect-eating **hedgehog** (above) is
found throughout the whole of Europe
and in Asia and Africa. It hibernates in
winter and, like the African hedgehog
shown here with her young, produces
two litters a year.

Hei·del·berg (hī′delbĕrg; *Ger.*
hī′delbĕrχ). German university city
on the river Neckar in Baden-
Württemberg, West Germany; ~
man, extinct species of man allied
to Neanderthal man, and living in
the Pleistocene period, a fossil jawbone of which was found near
Heidelberg in 1907.

heif·er (hĕf′er) *n.* Young cow
that has not had a calf.

height (hīt) *n.* Measurement
from base to top; elevation above
ground or recognized level, esp.
that of sea; considerable elevation;
high point; top, highest point or
degree; rising ground.

height·en (hī′ten) *v.* Make or
become greater or higher; intensify.

Hei·ne (hī′ne), **Heinrich** (1799–
1856). German lyric poet and
critic.

hei·nous (hā′nus) *adj.* Odious,
atrocious. **hei′nous·ly** *adv.*
hei′nous·ness *n.*

heir (ār) *n.* (fem. **heir·ess** pr.
ār′ĭs). Person receiving or entitled
to receive property or hereditary
rank, title, or office of former
owner, esp. upon death of the latter;
~ **apparent:** see APPARENT; ~
presumptive: see PRESUMPTIVE.

heir·loom (ār′lōōm) *n.* Piece of
personal property that has been in
family for generations.

He·jaz (hĕjăz′). Region on the
Red Sea coast, forming with Nejd
and Asir the Kingdom of Saudi
Arabia.

He·ji·ra: see HEGIRA.

held: see HOLD[2].

Hel·en (hĕl′en) (**of Troy**). (Gk.
legend) Most beautiful woman of
her time, daughter of Zeus and
Leda; wife of Menelaus; her
abduction by PARIS[2] led to the
Trojan War.

Hel·e·na[1] (hĕl′ena). Capital of
Montana in the W. central part.

Hel·e·na[2] (hĕl′ena), **St.** Mother
of the Emperor Constantine; said to

The **helicopter** first came into use in 1942, although the flight principles had been known for centuries. Its designer was the Russian-born American engineer, Igor Sikorsky, whose later design, the Sikorsky Sea King, is shown below. Peaceful uses for the helicopter include the transport of large materials in difficult landscapes (above right), use by police in rescue operations and short-distance taxi services between city centers and airports. During the Vietnam War, helicopters were used extensively both in combat and to recover wounded soldiers.

Above: Four OH6 helicopters fly in formation.

rotor blades

tail plane

tail rotor drive

search radar scanner

rotor brake

rotor head

turbine

overhead panel

pitot head

pilot's seat

instrument panel

tail wheel

navigation light

centre console

control column

crew entry door

main undercarriage

co-pilots seat

access door

he **heliotrope**, *a herbaceous plant und in tropical or temperate regions roughout the world, is cultivated for s fragrant, purple to white clustered wers.*

ve discovered the cross on which hrist was crucified; island in the S. tlantic, the place of Napoleon's ptivity (1815–21).

hel·i·cal (hĕl'ĭkal) *adj.* Of or like helix, as in ~ **gear. hel'i· al·ly** *adv.*

Hel·i·con (hĕl'ĭkŏn, -kon). Mountain in Boeotia, Greece, cred to the Muses.

hel·i·cop·ter (hĕl'ĭkŏpter, hē'li-) Aircraft lifted by rotor blades volving horizontally.

he·li·o·cen·tric (hēlēosĕn'trĭk) *dj.* As viewed from center of sun; king sun as center.

He·li·o·gab·a·lus (hēlēogăb'- lus). Adopted name of Varius vitus Bassianus, Roman emperor 18–22 A.D., famed for folly and rofligacy. [Latinized f. *Elagabal,* yro-Phoenician sun god]

he·li·o·gram (hē'lēogrăm) *n.* lessage transmitted by helio- raph.

he·li·o·graph (hē'lēogrăf, grahf) *n.* Apparatus for signaling ith movable mirror reflecting ashes of sunlight. ~ *v.* Com- unicate by heliograph.

he·li·om·e·ter (hēlēŏm'eter) *n.* stronomical instrument for deter- ining angular distance between elestial bodies (orig. for measuring iameter of sun).

He·li·op·o·lis (hēlēŏp'olĭs). Ruined ancient city in N. Egypt ear Cairo; the Biblical On; ancient ame for BAALBEK.

he·li·o·trope (hē'lēotrōp, hĕl'- o-; *Brit.* also hĕl'ĕotrōp) *n.* 1. lant of genus *Heliotropium* of erbs or shrubs with small clus-

tered purple flowers, esp. *H. arborescens*; color or scent of heliotrope. 2. = BLOODstone.

he·li·o·trop·ic (hēlēotrŏp'ĭk, -trō'pik) *adj.* Phototropic. **he·li- ot·ro·pism** (hēlēŏt'ropĭzem) *n.*

hel·i·pad (hĕl'ĭpăd, hē'li-) *n.* Area used by helicopters to take off or land.

hel·i·port (hĕl'ĭpōrt, -pŏrt, hē'li-) *n.* Airport for helicopter.

he·li·um (hē'lēum) *n.* (chem.) Element, an inert gas occurring in small quantities in the atmosphere and in certain natural gases, and produced during radioactive decay; used, because of its lightness and noninflammability, in balloons and airships; symbol He, at. no. 2, at. wt. 4.00260.

he·lix (hē'lĭks) *n.* (pl. **hel·i·ces** pr. hĕl'ĭsēz, **he·lix·es**). 1. Spiral or coil like corkscrew; (archit. etc.) spiral ornament. 2. (anat.) Curved fold or prominence forming rim of external ear.

hell (hĕl) *n.* Abode of the dead; abode of devils and condemned spirits, figured as place of torment; place, state, of wickedness or misery; **a ~ of a**, an infernal, a very bad, great, loud, etc.; ~

Hell, *as depicted by the 15th century Flemish painter, Hieronymus Bosch, is the product of his bizarre and fantastic imagination. Traditionally, the Hell to which damned souls go is made up of fire and brimstone.*

The **hellebore** *is a genus of some 20 herbaceous perennials from western Asia and southern Europe. The most commonly seen variety is the Helleborus orientalis, known as the Winter or Lenten rose.*

(bent)-for-leather, at breakneck speed; **hell'cat**, (slang) spiteful or furious woman; **hell'fire**, fire of hell; **hell'hole**, any very squalid or disreputable place; **hell'hound**, fiend. **hell'ish** *adj.* **hell'ish·ly** *adv.* **hell'ish·ness** *n.*

Hel·las (hĕl'as). Greece; orig. the name of a district in Thessaly, but applied by the ancient Greeks to the whole of their country.

hel·le·bore (hĕl'ebōr, -bŏr) *n.* Ancient name of various Old World plants supposed to cure madness; (bot.) species of genus *Veratrum* of N. Amer., including false hellebore (*V. viride*) having large leaves and greenish-yellow to green flowers.

Hel·lene (hĕl'ēn) *n.* Greek person. **Hel·len·ic** (helĕn'ĭk) *adj. & n.* (Language) of the Greeks.

Hel·len·ism (hĕl'enĭzem) *n.* Greek idiom or construction; Greek character or culture, esp. that represented by ideals of the classical Greeks; Greek nationality. **Hel'- len·ist** *n.* 1. Greek scholar. 2. One of the Byzantine Greeks who con- tributed to the revival of learning in Europe in the 15th c. 3. One who used the Greek language but was not a Greek, applied esp. to the Jews of the Diaspora. **Hel·len- is·tic** (hĕlenĭs'tĭk) *adj.* 1. Of, pertaining to, the Hellenists. 2. Of, pertaining to, Greek history, language, and culture after Alex- ander the Great.

Hel·len·ize (hĕl'enīz) *v.* (**-ized, -iz·ing**). Make, become, Greek in form or character.

Hel·les·pont (hĕl'espŏnt). Ancient name of the DARDANELLES, named after the legendary Helle, who fell into that part of the sea from the back of a ram with golden fleece and wings, which was carrying her and her brother Phrixus from Thebes to Colchis (see also GOLDEN FLEECE).

Hell (hĕl) **Gate.** Narrow channel in the East River, New York City, between Long Island and Manhattan.

hell·gram·mite (hĕl´gramīt) *n.* Larva (used as fishing bait) of the dobson fly, an aquatic insect of the order Neuroptera (*Corydalus cornutus*).

hel·lion (hĕl´yon) *n.* (colloq.) Mischievous or naughty person, esp. a child or teenager.

hel·lo (hĕlō´, he-, hĕl´ō) *int. & n.* (pl. **-los**). Greeting.

helm (hĕlm) *n.* Tiller, wheel, by which rudder is managed; (fig.) government, guidance, leadership; **helms´man**, person who steers a ship.

hel·met (hĕl´mĭt) *n.* Defensive head cover of soldiers, firemen, football players, etc.; felt or pith hat for hot climates; (bot.) arched upper part of corolla in some flowers, esp. labiates and orchids. **hel´met·ed** *adj.*

Helm·holtz (hĕlm´hōlts), **Hermann Ludwig Ferdinand** (1821–1894). German physicist, physiologist, mathematician, and philosopher.

hel·minth (hĕl´minth) *n.* Worm (esp. intestinal). **hel·min´thic** (hĕlmĭn´thĭk), **hel·min´thoid** *adjs.* **hel·min·thol·o·gy** (hĕlmĭnthŏl´ojē) *n.* Study of worms.

Hé·lo·ïse (ĕl´ōēz, ĕlōēz´) (1101–1163). Learned Frenchwoman, renowned for love affair with ABÉLARD that ended in tragic separation.

Hel·ot (hĕl´ot, hē´lot) *n.* In ancient Sparta, a descendant of the original (chiefly Messenian) inhabitants who were conquered by the Spartans and used by them as serfs.

help (hĕlp) *v.t.* Furnish (person etc.) with what he needs; further the action or purpose of; aid, assist; be of service; make easier; ~ (person) **on with his coat**, help him to put it on; ~ (person) **out**, be of assistance to; ~ (person) **to**, serve him with (food); distribute (food at meal); remedy, prevent, as *it can't be helped, he couldn't ~ being late*; (with neg.) avoid doing, as *I can't ~ hoping that ---*; ~ **oneself to**, (colloq.) take. **help** *n.* 1. Action of helping, assistance; one who or that which helps; domestic servant; employee(s). 2. Remedy. **help´er** *n.*

help·ful (hĕlp´ful) *adj.* (of person or thing) Useful, serviceable. **help´ful·ly** *adv.* **help´ful·ness** *n.*

help·ing (hĕl´pĭng) *n.* (esp.) Portion of food served.

help·less (hĕlp´lĭs) *adj.* Unable to help oneself. **help´less·ly** *adv.* **help´less·ness** *n.*

help·mate (hĕlp´māt) *n.* Helpful companion or partner, usu. husband or wife.

help·meet (hĕlp´mēt) *n.* Helpmate (f. misunderstanding of Gen. 2).

Hel·sin·ki (hĕl´sĭngkē, hĕl-sĭng´-). Capital of Finland in the S. part on the Gulf of Finland.

hel·ter-skel·ter (hĕl´ter skĕl´ter) *adv. & adj.* In disordered haste. ~ *n.* Disordered haste.

Hel·ve·tian (hĕlvē´shan) *adj. & n.* Swiss. [L. *Helvetii*, a people of SE. Gaul]

hem[1] (hĕm) *n.* Border, edge, of cloth etc., esp. border made by turning in edge and sewing it down; **hem´stitch**, (hem *cloth* etc. with) kind of ornamental stitch producing openwork effect by drawing together threads of material. **hem** *v.t.* (**hemmed, hem·ming**). Turn in and sew down edge of (cloth etc.); ~ **in, about, around**, enclose, confine.

hem[2] (hĕm) *int.* Exclamation calling attention or expressing hesitation. ~ *n.* Utterance of "hem." ~ *v.i.* (**hemmed, hem·ming**). Utter "hem"; clear throat; hesitate in speech.

he·mat·ic, hae·mat·ic (hĭmăt´ĭk) *adjs.* Of or containing blood. ~ *n.* Medicine acting on the blood.

hem·a·tite, haem·a·tite (hĕm´atīt, hē´ma-) *ns.* Natural ferric oxide (Fe_2O_3), red, brown, or blackish iron ore.

he·ma·tol·o·gy, hae·ma·tol·o·gy (hēmatŏl´ojē, hĕma-) *ns.* Study of blood and its diseases.

he·ma·to·ma, hae·ma·to·ma (hēmatō´ma, hĕma-) *ns.* (pl. **-mas, -ma·ta** pr. -mata). Localized tumor or swelling filled with blood.

hemi- *prefix.* Half-, affecting one half, etc.

hem·i·he·dral (hĕmĭhē´dral) *adj.* (chem., of crystal) Having half the number of planes required by the highest degree of symmetry belonging to its system.

Hem·ing·way (hĕm´ĭngwā), **Ernest (Miller)** (1899–1961). Amer. novelist, short-story writer, and foreign correspondent; author of *The Sun Also Rises, For Whom the Bell Tolls, The Old Man and the Sea, Death in the Afternoon,* etc.; received Nobel Prize for literature, 1954.

*Eight kings of England were called Henry. 1. **Henry III**, whose inability to rule effectively led to rebellion and to Simon de Montfort's control of government. 2. **Henry IV**, son of John of Gaunt, defeated the rebel barons, Owen Glendower and Sir Henry Percy (1403) and Thomas de Mowbray (1405). 3. **Henry V**, victor of the Battle of Agincourt.*

hem·i·ple·gi·a (hĕmĭplē'jēa, -ja) *n.* Paralysis of one side of body.

he·mip·ter·ous (hĭmĭp'terus) *adj.* Of the Hemiptera, an order of insects with wings leathery at base and membranous at tip, and mouth-parts adapted to piercing and sucking. **he·mip'ter·an** *n.*

hem·i·sphere (hĕm'ĭsfēr) *n.* Half sphere; half the celestial sphere, esp. as divided by equator; (anat.) each half of cerebrum of brain; (geog.) half the Earth, esp. as divided by the equator (into **Northern** and **Southern** ~s), or (loosely) one of those containing Europe, Asia, Australia, and Africa (**Eastern** ~), and America (**Western** ~), respectively. **hem·i·spher·ic** (hĕmĭsfĕr'ĭk), **hem·i·spher'i·cal** *adjs.*

hem·lock (hĕm'lŏk) *n.* 1. Poisonous umbelliferous plant (*Conium maculatum*) with stout-branched, purple-spotted stem, finely divided leaves, and small white flowers, used as powerful sedative; poisonous potion obtained from this (believed to be the poison by which Socrates was put to death). 2. N. Amer. evergreen tree of genus *Tsuga*, esp. *T. canadensis*, from resemblance of branches to hemlock leaves.

hemo- *comb. form.* Blood.

he·mo·glo·bin, hae·mo·glo·bin (hē'moglōbĭn, hĕm'o-) *ns.* Oxygen-carrying pigment contained in the red blood cells of vertebrates.

he·mo·phil·i·a, hae·mo·phil·i·a (hēmofĭl'ēa, -fēl'ya, hĕmo-) *ns.* Constitutional, usu. hereditary, incapacity of blood to clot quickly or at all, involving risk of severe bleeding even from a slight injury. **he·mo·phil'i·ac** *n.* **he·mo·phil'ic** *adj.*

hem·or·rhage, haem·or·rhage (hĕm'erĭj, hĕm'rĭj) *ns.* Escape of blood from blood vessels.

hem·or·rhoid, haem·or·rhoid (hĕm'eroid, hĕm'roid) *ns.* (usu. in pl.) Varicose vein of anus; piles.

he·mo·stat, hae·mo·stat (hē'-mostăt, hĕm'o-) *ns.* Instrument or agent used to stop flow of blood.

hemp (hĕmp) *n.* Annual herbaceous plant, *Cannabis sativa*, native of W. and central Asia, cultivated esp. for its cortical fiber; this fiber used for making cordage and woven into stout fabrics; any of several narcotic drugs, as bhang, hashish, etc., obtained from hemp; any of various other plants yielding useful fiber; ~ **agrimony**, perennial plant (*Eupatorium cannabinum*) of the daisy family, with pale purple flowers and hairy leaves. **hemp'en** *adj.*

hen (hĕn) *n.* Female of common domestic fowl; female of various other birds, or of any bird; **hen'-bane,** (drug extracted from) plant (*Hyoscyamus niger*) of Europe and N. Asia, growing on waste ground, with dull yellow purple-streaked flowers, viscoid stem and leaves, unpleasant smell, and narcotic and poisonous properties; **hen'pecked,** (of husband) dominated by wife.

hence (hĕns) *adv.* 1. (archaic) From here, from this; **hence'-forth', hence'for'ward,** from this time forward. 2. As a result of this; as an inference from this; therefore.

hench·man (hĕnch'man) *n.* (pl. **-men** pr. -men). Squire, page of honor (now only hist.); trusty follower or subordinate; political supporter seeking personal gain.

hendeca- *prefix.* Eleven.

hen·dec·a·syl·lab·ic (hĕndĕka-sĭlăb'ĭk) *adj. & n.* (Verse) of 11 syllables. **hen·dec·a·syl·la·ble** (hĕndĕk'asĭlabel, -dĕkasĭl'-) *n.* Such a verse.

Hen·driks (hĕn'drĭks), **Thomas Andrews** (1819–85). Amer. politician; U.S. vice president under Grover Cleveland, 1885.

hen·na (hĕn'a) *n.* Shrub (*Lawsonia inermis*) of N. Africa and Asia; shoots and leaves of this used as yellowish-red dye for parts of body, hair, etc. ~ *v.t.* Dye or tint with henna.

hen·o·the·ism (hĕn'othēĭzem) *n.* Belief in one god without asserting that he is the only God.

Hen·ri: see HENRY[2].

Hen·ry[1] (hĕn'rē). Name of eight kings of England: **Henry I** (1068–1135), younger son of William I, reigned 1100–35; conquered Normandy; **Henry II** (1133–89), grandson of Henry I, reigned 1154–1189; 1st of Plantagenet line; married Eleanor of Aquitaine; added Anjou and Aquitaine to the English possessions; established his rule in Ireland, and forced the king of Scotland to acknowledge him overlord of that kingdom; **Henry III** (1207–72), son of John, reigned 1216–72; **Henry IV** (1367–1413), grandson of Edward III, deposed Richard II and became first of the Lancastrian kings, 1399–1413; **Henry V** (1387–1422), son of Henry IV, reigned 1413–22; defeated the French at Agincourt, became regent of France and heir to the French throne; **Henry VI** (1421–71, son of Henry V, reigned 1422–61; during his reign the French possessions were lost and the Wars of the Roses, leading to his deposition by the Yorkists, begun; **Henry VII** (1457–1509),

4. Henry VI, the last of the Lancastrians, whose mental instability and the resulting crisis in leadership led to the Wars of the Roses. 5. Henry VII ended the Wars of the Roses, established order at home and diplomacy in foreign affairs. 6. Henry VIII, one of the strongest of English monarchs, was the father of Elizabeth I.

descended from Edward III; 1st of the Tudor line; succeeded Richard III after defeating him at Bosworth Field; reigned 1485–1509; **Henry VIII** (1491–1547), son of Henry VII, reigned 1509–47; his quarrels with the pope resulted in his establishment of the Church of England; married six times; father of Edward VI, Mary I, and Elizabeth I.

Hen·ry[2] (hĕn′rē). (Fr. *Henri*) Name of four kings of France: **Henry I** (d. 1060), reigned 1031–1060; **Henry II** (1519–59), son of Francis I, reigned 1547–59; **Henry III** (1551–89), son of Henry II and Catherine de Médicis, reigned 1574–89; **Henry IV** (1553–1610), king of Navarre, first Bourbon king of France; leader of Huguenots; reigned 1589–1610.

Hen·ry[3] (hĕn′rē), **Joseph** (1797–1878). Amer. physicist; experimented in electromagnetism; unit of induction, HENRY, named for him; first secretary and director of Smithsonian Institution, Washington, D.C., 1846.

Hen·ry[4] (hĕn′rē), **O.** (1862–1910). Pen name of William Sydney Porter, Amer. short-story writer noted for his surprise endings; among his works, "Gift of the Magi," "The Last Leaf."

Hen·ry[5] (hĕn′rē), **Patrick** (1736–99). Amer. lawyer, statesman, and Revolutionary War leader, introduced resolutions in the Virginia legislature opposing the Stamp Act; member of the Continental Congress, 1774–6; remembered for his patriotic demand for freedom from Great Britain, "Give me liberty, or give me death!"

hen·ry (hĕn′rē) *n.* (pl. **-ries, -rys**). (abbrev. H) Electromagnetic unit of inductance, the inductance of a circuit in which the variation of current at the rate of 1 ampere per second induces an electromotive force of 1 volt. [Joseph Henry (1797–1878), Amer. physicist]

hep (hĕp) *adj.* (slang) = HIP[4].

he·pat·ic (hĭpăt′ĭk) *adj.* Of, resembling, the liver; liver-colored, dark brownish-red.

he·pat·i·ca (hĭpăt′ĭkạ) *n.* Any of several small plants of the genus *Hepatica*, having three-lobed leaves and lavender, white, blue, or pink flowers.

hep·a·ti·tis (hĕpătī′tĭs) *n.* Inflammation of the liver.

He·phaes·tus (hĭfĕs′tus). (Gk. myth.) God of fire; identified by the Romans with Vulcan.

Hep·ple·white (hĕp′elhwīt, -wīt), **George** (d. 1786). English cabinetmaker; furniture made by or in the style of Hepplewhite.

hepta- *prefix.* Seven.

hep·tad (hĕp′tăd) *n.* Set, group,

of seven.

hep·ta·gon (hĕp′tagŏn) *n.* Plane figure of seven angles and sides.

hep·tag·o·nal (hĕptăg′onal) *adj.*

hep·ta·he·dron (hĕptahē′dron) *n.* (pl. **-drons, -dra** pr. -drạ). Solid figure of seven faces.

hep·tam·e·ter (hĕptăm′eter) *n.* Verse having seven metrical feet.

hep·tar·chy (hĕp′tärkē) *n.* (pl. **-chies**). Government by seven rulers; **H~**, seven kingdoms supposed to have been established by the Angles and Saxons in Britain.

her (hẽr) *pron.* Objective (accus.) case of SHE. ~ *poss. pron.* Possessive case of SHE used as attrib. adjective and as pred. complement; **hers** (hẽrz), belonging to, affecting, her; used also as subj. or pred. complement.

He·ra (hē′rạ). (Gk. myth.) Daughter of Cronos and Rhea; sister and wife of Zeus; worshipped as queen of the heavens and goddess of power and riches; identified by the Romans with Juno.

Her·a·cli·tus (hĕraklī′tưs). Greek philosopher, of the 6th c.; his melancholy views on the changing character of life led to his being known as the "weeping philosopher."

Her·a·kles, Her·a·cles (hẽr′-aklēz) = HERCULES.

her·ald (hẽr′ald) *n.* 1. Officer who made state proclamations, bore messages between princes, officiated in tournaments, arranged various state ceremonials, regulated use of armorial bearings, etc. 2. Messenger, envoy (freq. as title of newspaper); forerunner. ~ *v.t.* Proclaim the approach of; usher in.

he·ral·dic (hĕrăl′dĭk, he-) *adj.* Of heraldry.

her·ald·ry (hẽr′aldrē) *n.* Science of a herald, esp. art of blazoning armorial bearings and settling right of persons to bear arms or certain bearings; armorial bearings; heraldic pomp.

herb (ẽrb, hẽrb) *n.* Plant whose stem is not woody or persistent but dies down after flowering; plant of which leaves etc. are used for medicine, scent, flavor, etc.; ~ **bennet**, yellow-flowered species of geum; ~ **Robert**, common wild species of plant *Geranium* (*G. robertianum*) with divided leaves and light reddish-purple flowers; ~ **tea**, medicinal brew of herbs.

her·ba·ceous (hẽrbā′shưs, ẽr-) *adj.* Of (the nature of) herb(s).

herb·age (ẽr′bĭj, hẽr′-) *n.* Herbs collectively, esp. grass and other low-growing plants covering large

Heraldic symbols originated as identification devices on shields during the Middle Ages, and developed into hereditary bearings used to distinguish individuals or families. These flags hang in King Henry VIII's chapel at Westminster Abbey, U.K.

extent of ground and used as pa
ture etc.; green succulent parts
herbaceous plants.

her·bal (ẽr′bal, hẽr′-) *adj.* &
(Book with descriptions of herb
herb′al·ist *n.* One skilled in her
or plants (now used of early botan
cal writers).

her·bar·i·um (hẽrbār′ēum, ẽr
n. (pl. **-bar·i·ums, -bar·i·a** p

*The **Hepplewhite** furniture of the la 18th century is characterized by graceful Neo-classical style. This ar chair is of carved mahogany and dated c. 1780 — some years befo the publication of Hepplewhite designs.*

area). (Book, case, room, conning) collection of dried plants.
herb·i·cide (ĕr'bĭsĭd, hĕr'-) *n.*
...y substance, esp. chemical prep-
...tion, used to kill plants.
her·biv·or·ous (hĕrbĭv'erus, ĕr-)
...(of animals) Feeding on plants.
...r·bi·vore (hĕr'bĭvŏr, -vŏr, ĕr'-)

Her·ce·go·vi·na (hĕrtsegovē'na,
...aw'vĭ-): see HERZEGOVINA.
Her·cu·la·ne·um (hĕrkyulā'-
...um). Ancient town in Campania,

*...rbs have been used since ancient
...es to flavor food and also for their
...dicinal value. Popular herbs include
...sley, mint and thyme.*

Italy, buried with Pompeii in
eruption of Vesuvius, 79 A.D.
Her·cu·le·an (hĕrkyulē'an,
-kū'lē-) *adj.* Of Hercules; strong
as Hercules; difficult as his labors.
Her·cu·les (hĕr'kyulēz). 1. (Gk.
and Rom. myth.) Hero of prodigious strength, who performed 12
immense tasks or labors imposed on
him by Eurystheus, and after death
was ranked among the gods;
Pillars of ~, rocks Calpe (Gibraltar) and Abyla (Ceuta) on either
side of Strait of Gibraltar, thought
to have been set up by Hercules
and to be supports of western
boundaries of the world. 2.
(astron.) Northern constellation,

ALENDUL, CAMOMILE, VERVAIN, ELECAMPANE, RUE, CATNIP, LEMON BALM, MALLOW, RED CLOVER, PEPPERMINT, WILD PARSLEY, HOREHOUND, CAYENNE, PENNY ROYAL, YARROW, MULLEIN, COMFREY

figured as a man kneeling on his
right knee.
herd[1] (hĕrd) *n.* Group of animals, esp. cattle, feeding or traveling together; (contempt.) large
number of people; **~ instinct**,
gregariousness and mutual influence as psychological factor;
herds'man (pl. **-men**), keeper of
herds. **herd** *v.* Go, collect, in a
herd (*together, with* others).
herd[2] (hĕrd) *v.t.* Tend (sheep,
cattle). **herd'er** *n.*
here (hēr) *adv.* In this place; in
this country, region, etc.; present to
the sight or mind; in this life, on
earth; at this juncture, at this point
in action, speech, etc.; in the matter
before us or in question; (with verbs
of coming or bringing) to or toward
this place; **~'s to**, formula in drinking toasts; **~ and there**, in various
places; **~, there, and everywhere**, everywhere, all about;
neither ~ nor there, not to the
point, of no importance; **~ goes!**,
(colloq.) exclamation announcing
commencement of bold act; **here'-
abouts**, somewhere near here;
hereaf'ter, in the future, later on;
(in) the world to come; **here'by**,
by this means, as a result; **herein'**,
in this point, book, etc.; **herein-
af'ter**, below (in document etc.);
hereto', (archaic) to this matter;
heretofore', formerly; **hereun'-
der**, below (in book etc.); **here-
upon'**, after this; in consequence
of this; **herewith'**, with this (esp.
of enclosure in letter etc.). **here** *n.*
This place or point.
he·red·i·tar·y (herĕd'ĭtĕrē) *adj.*
Descending by inheritance; transmitted from one generation to
another; like, the same as, that one's
parents had; of, holding position
by, inheritance.
he·red·i·ty (herĕd'ĭtē) *n.* (pl.
-ties). Tendency of like to beget
like, property of organic beings by
which offspring inherit nature and
characteristics of parents or other
ancestors; organic relation between
successive generations; genetic constitution.
Her·e·ford (hĕr'eferd, hēr'ferd).
(One of) a breed of beef cattle
originating in Herefordshire, England (red and white, with white
faces).
he·re·si·arch (herē'zēärk, hĕr'-
esē-) *n.* Leader, founder, of a
heresy.
her·e·sy (hĕr'esē) *n.* (pl. **-sies**).
Opinion or doctrine contrary to the
orthodox doctrine of the Christian
Church, or to the accepted doctrine
on any subject.
her·e·tic (hĕr'etĭk) *n.* Holder of

*Herbaceous gardens, like those sur-
rounding this French cottage in
Périgord, contain flowering plants but
not trees or shrubs. Most herbaceous
gardens are made up of flower beds in
different patterns.*

an unorthodox opinion (orig. in matter of religion). **he·ret·i·cal** (herĕt´ĭkal) *adj.*

her·it·a·ble (hĕr´ĭtabel) *adj.* That passes to heirs (opp. to movable property); transmissible from parent to child; capable of inheriting.

her·it·age (hĕr´ĭtĭj) *n.* What is or may be inherited; inherited lot or portion.

her·i·tor (hĕr´ĭter) *n.* One who inherits.

her·maph·ro·dite (hērmăf´rodīt) *n.* 1. Human being, animal, combining characteristics of both sexes; (zool.) animal having normally both male and female sexual organs; (bot.) plant in which same flower has both stamens and pistils. 2. Person, thing, combining opposite qualities. **her·maph·ro·dit·ic** (hērmăfrodĭt´ĭk) *adj.* Combining both sexes or opposite characteristics. **her·maph´ro·dit·ism** *n.* [Gk. *Hermaphroditos,* son of Hermes and Aphrodite, who became one with the nymph Salmacis]

her·me·neu·tic (hērmenoo´tĭk, -nū´-) *adj.* Of interpretation; interpretive; explanatory. **her·me·neu´tics** *n.pl.* Interpretation, esp. of Scripture. **her·me·neu´ti·cal** *adj.*

Her·mes (hĕr´mēz). 1. (Gk. myth.) Son of Zeus and Maia; represented as messenger of the gods, god of science, commerce, eloquence, etc., identified by the Romans with Mercury, and represented as a youth with winged rod (*caduceus*), brimmed hat (*petasus*), and winged shoes (*talaria*). 2. ~ **Trismegistus** ("thrice-greatest"), name given by Neoplatonists etc. to Egyptian god Thoth, regarded as author of all mysterious doctrines and esp. of secrets of alchemy.

her·met·ic (hērmĕt´ĭk) *adj.* (cap.) Of Hermes Trismegistus; of alchemy, magical, alchemical; completely sealed, airtight. **her·met´i·cal·ly** *adv.*

her·mit (hĕr´mĭt) *n.* One who from religious motives has retired into solitary life, esp. early Christian recluse; person living in solitude; ~ **crab**, crab of family Paguridae, living in mollusk's discarded shell to protect soft abdomen.

her·mit·age (hĕr´mĭtĭj) *n.* 1. Hermit's abode; solitary abode. 2. **H**~, museum of art in Leningrad, containing collections begun by Catherine the Great in 1765 and inheriting its name from the retreat in which she displayed them to her friends.

her·ni·a (hĕr´nēa) *n.* (pl. **-ni·as, -ni·ae** pr. **-nēē**). (path.) Tumor formed by the displacement of part of an organ so that it protrudes through the walls of its containing

Hermit crabs *typically inhabit the discarded shells of mollusks, but some tropical species will move into plant tubes, broken coconut shells and bamboo stems.*

cavity; rupture. **her´ni·al** *adj.*

her·ni·ate (hēr´nēāt) *v.i.* (**-at·ed, -at·ing**). Protrude through an abnormal body opening. **her·ni·a·tion** (hērnēā´shon) *n.*

He·ro (hēr´ō). (Gk. legend) Beautiful priestess of Aphrodite at Sestos on the European shore of the Hellespont, whose lover Leander, a youth of Abydos, swam the strait nightly to visit her; one stormy night he was drowned and Hero in grief threw herself into the sea.

he·ro (hēr´ō) *n.* (pl. **-roes**). 1. (Gk. antiq.) Man of superhuman strength, courage, or ability, favored by the gods; later regarded as intermediate between gods and men, and immortal. 2. Illustrious warrior; man of extraordinary bravery, fortitude, or greatness of soul. 3. Man forming subject of epic; chief male character in poem, play, or story; ~ **sandwich**, large sandwich, usu. a long roll sliced lengthwise and filled with a variety of sliced meats, cheeses, vegetables, pickles, etc.; ~ **worship(er)**, worship(er) of some great man or men or a personal hero.

Her·od (hĕr´od). Name of four rulers in ancient Palestine: **Herod the Great** (d. 4 B.C.), king of the Jews 40–4 B.C., **Herod Antipas**, his son, tetrarch of Galilee and Peraea 4 B.C.–39 A.D., married Herodias and had St. John the Baptist beheaded; **Herod Agrippa I**, (called "Herod" in Acts), grandson of Herod the Great, king of the Jews 41–44 A.D.; put St. James the Apostle to death; **Herod Agrippa II**, his son, king of various territories in N. Palestine 50–c93 A.D.; St. Paul appeared before him (Acts 25).

He·rod·o·tus (hĭrŏd´otus) (5th B.C.). Greek historian; author of history in nine books.

he·ro·ic (hĭrō´ĭk) *adj.* 1. Of, for, a hero; having the qualities a hero; ~ **age**, period of Gree history before the return fro Troy. 2. Describing the deeds heroes, epic; (of meter) used heroic poetry (in Greek and Lati the hexameter; in French, th Alexandrine; in English, Germa and Italian, iambic of 5 feet or syllables); (of language) grand. Bold or daring, attempting gre things. **he·ro´i·cal·ly** *ad* **he·ro´ic** *n.* Grand language sentiments.

her·o·in (hĕr´ōĭn) *n.* Drug, als called diacetylmorphine or diamo phine, prepared from morphin which it resembles in its effect capable of causing addiction.

her·o·ine (hĕr´ōĭn) *n.* Hero woman; chief female character poem, play, or story.

her·o·ism (hĕr´ōĭzem) *n.* Hero conduct or qualities.

her·on (hĕr´on) *n.* (pl. **-on** collect. **-on**). One of the long necked, long-legged wading bir of the family Ardeidae. **her´on·r** *n.* Place where herons breed.

her·pes (hĕr´pēz) *n.* Either of forms of virus affection, ~ **zoste** shingles, an infection of the cuta neous nerves resulting in sever pain and outbreaks of small blister related to the distribution of th nerves, and ~ **simplex**, painles form in which the blisters have n relation to the nerves of the skin.

her·pe·tol·o·gy (hērpetŏl´ojē) Zoology of reptiles. **her·pe·to log·ic** (hērpetolŏj´ĭk), **her·pe·to log´i·cal** *adjs.* **her·pe·tol´o·gist**

Her·rick (hĕr´ĭk), **Rober** (1591–1674). English Cavalie poet; author of *Hesperides* (1648 a collection of some 1,200 mostl idyllic nature poems.

e **heron** is found all over the world
is most common in the tropics. It
ds on frogs, fishes and other aquatic
mals. The great blue heron is a large
d with a wing span of 6 ft.; the grey
common heron is widely distributed
Europe; the boat-billed heron is a
ht bird, feeding in twilight hours and
night and is found in Central and
uth America.

Great white heron

Grey heron

Boat-billed heron

Great blue heron

her·ring (hĕr´ĭng) *n.* Edible fish, *Clupea harengus*, of N. Atlantic, coming near coast in large shoals to spawn; **red** ~ : see RED; **her´ring-bone**, (of masonry, paving) in which stones or tiles are set in zigzag pattern; (of cloth etc.) woven in zigzag pattern; **herring gull**, large gull of N. Atlantic (*Larus argentatus*), with black tips to wings.

hers (hĕrz): see HER.

Her·schel (hĕr´shel), **Sir William** (1738–1822). German-born English astronomer; discoverer of the planet Uranus.

her·self (hersĕlf´) *pron.* Emphatic and reflexive form corresponding to SHE, HER.

Hertz (hĕrts; *Ger.* hĕrts), **Heinrich Rudolph** (1857–94). German physicist; demonstrated electromagnetic radio waves in 1888.

hertz (hĕrts) *n.* (pl. same; abbrev. Hz) Unit of frequency, 1 cycle per second. [f. HERTZ]

Her·ze·go·vi·na (hĕrtsegovĕ´na, -gaw´vĭ-). Region and former province S. of Bosnia, in Yugoslavia.

Her·zl (hĕr´tsel), **Theodor** (1860–1904). Hungarian-born Austrian Jewish writer; founder of Zionism.

He·si·od (hē´sēod, hĕs´ē-) (8th c. B.C.). Greek poet; author of *Works and Days*, descriptive of agricultural life in Boeotia, and probably of the *Theogony*, containing a mythical account of the origin of the world and the genealogy of the gods, and of a *Catalogue of Women* who, being beloved of the gods, became the mothers of heroes. **He·si·od·ic** (hēsēŏd´ĭk, hĕsē-) *adj.*

hes·i·tant (hĕz´ĭtant) *adj.* Hesitating, irresolute. **hes´i·tance** *n.* **hes´i·tan·cy** *n.* (pl. -sies).

hes·i·tate (hĕz´ĭtāt) *v.i.* (**-tat·ed, -tat·ing**). Show, speak with, indecision; be reluctant, *to* (do). **hes´i·tat·ing·ly** *adv.* **hes·i·ta·tion** (hĕzĭtā´shon) *n.* **hes´i·ta·tive** *adj.*

Hes·per·i·des (hĕspĕr´ĭdēz). (Gk. myth.) Three, four, or seven nymphs, daughters of Hesperus; they were guardians, with the aid of a watchful dragon, of the garden in which golden apples grew, in the Islands of the Blessed (see ISLAND).

Hesse[1] (hĕs). (Ger. *Hessen*) Former state of SW. Germany, now a province of West Germany; capital, Wiesbaden.

Hesse[2] (hĕs), **Hermann** (1877–1962). German novelist and poet; author of *Steppenwolf, Das Glasperlenspiel*, etc.; received Nobel Prize for literature, 1946.

Hes·sian (hĕsh´an) *adj.* Of Hesse[1]; ~ **boot**, high boot, with tassels in front at the top, first worn by Hessian troops; ~ **fly**, midge (*Phytophaga destructor*) with larva very destructive to wheat (er-

The **herring gull** *is a common N. Atlantic species, often seen feeding on the wastes of human habitation. It can be recognized by its orange-colored legs, gray mantle and black-and-white wing tips.*

roneously supposed to have been carried to America by Hessian troops). **Hessian** *n.* Native or inhabitant of, soldier from, Hesse; military or political hireling, mercenary (from the Hessian mercenaries used by the British army during the Revolutionary War).

hest (hĕst) *n.* (archaic) Behest.

he·tae·ra (hĭtēr´a) (pl. -tae·ras, -tae·rae pr. -tēr´ē), **he·tai·ra** (hĭtīr´a) (pl. -tai·ras, -tai·rai pr. -tīr´ī) *ns.* Courtesan, esp. in ancient Greece. **he·tae´rism, he·tai´rism** *ns.* Open concubinage; communal marriage in a tribe.

hetero- *prefix.* Other, different.

het·er·o·dox (hĕt´erodŏks) *adj.* Not orthodox. **het´er·o·dox·y** *n.*

het·er·o·dyne (hĕt´erodīn) *n.* Apparatus for, process of, convert-

ing a high-frequency radio wave t one of an audible frequency b superimposing another high frequency wave of nearly the sam period and so producing a pulsa tion. ~ *v.i.* (**-dyned, -dyn·ing**) Produce a heterodyne effect.

het·er·og·a·my (hĕterŏg´amē) *n* (biol.) Alternation of differentl organized generations of animals o plants, as where sexual generatio alternates with parthenogenesis condition of having, or union of gametes of different size and struc ture. **het·er·og´a·mous** *adj.*

het·er·o·ge·ne·ous (hĕteroje´ nēus) *adj.* Diverse in character composed of diverse elements o substances. **het·er·o·ge´ne·ous·ly** *adv.* **het·er·o·ge´ne·ous·ness** *n* **het·er·o·ge·ne´i·ty** *n.* (pl. -ties).

het·er·o·gen·e·sis (hĕterojĕn´ esĭs) *n.* Birth of a living bein otherwise than from parent of sam kind, esp. supposed spontaneou generation from inorganic matter alternation of generation. **het·**

o·ge·net·ic (hĕterōjenĕt´ĭk) *adj.*
scended from different ancestral
ck.

het·er·o·sex·u·al (hĕterosĕk´-
ōoal) *adj.* Relating or belonging
the opposite sex or different
es; sexually attracted to mem-
rs of the opposite sex. ~ *n.*
terosexual person. **het·er·o·-**
x·u·al·i·ty (hĕterōsĕkshooăl´ĭtē)

het·er·o·zy·gote (hĕterozī´gōt) *n.*
Zygote resulting from fusion of
like gametes; Mendelian hybrid
taining dominant and recessive
racters and therefore not breed-
true. **het·er·o·zy´gous** *adj.*
aring two dissimilar alternative
etical factors.

neu·ris·tic (hyurĭs´tĭk) *adj.*
rving to (encourage to) find out
discover.

hew (hū) *v.t.* (**hewed, hewn,**
w·ing). Chop, cut (*down,*
nder, etc.) with ax, sword, etc.;
into shape; fell or cut (wood);
ave. **hew´er** *n.*

hex (hĕks) *v.* Practice witchcraft
); bewitch. ~ *n.* Witch; magic
ll.

hexa-, hex- *prefixes.* Six.

hex·ad (hĕk´săd) *n.* Set, group,
6.

hex·a·gon (hĕk´sagŏn) *n.* Plane
ure of six angles and sides.
x·ag·o·nal (hĕksăg´onal) *adj.*
x·ag´o·nal·ly *adv.*

hex·a·gram (hĕk´sagrăm) *n.*
gure formed by two intersecting
uilateral triangles (the angular
ints coinciding with those of a
xagon); figure of six lines.

hex·a·he·dron (hĕksahē´dron)
(pl. **-drons, -dra** pr. -dra)
lid figure of six faces. **hex·a·-**
´dral *adj.*

hex·am·e·ter (hĕksăm´eter) *n.*

inrich Hertz, the 19th-century Ger-
n physicist, used this oscillator, in-
rporating an induction coil, to demon-
ate the production and reception of
ctromagnetic waves. This formed
basis of radio.

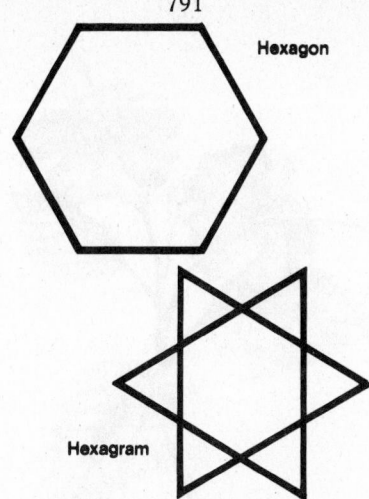

Hexagon

Hexagram

The **hexagon** and **hexagram** are geometrical figures made up of 6 lines. The
Star of David, symbol of the Jewish
religion, which appears on Israel's
national flag, is a hexagram.

Line of six metrical feet, esp. the
dactylic ~ of Latin and Greek epic
poetry, in which the first four feet
may be dactyls or spondees, the
fifth is a dactyl, and the sixth a
spondee or less commonly a trochee.

hey (hā) *int.* Exclamation calling
attention, or of joy, surprise, or
interrogation.

hey·day (hā´dā) *n.* Prime period
(of youth, vigor, prosperity, etc.).

Hey·er·dahl (hā´erdahl), **Thor**
(1914–). Norwegian anthropologist who believed the first Polynesian settlers were from S. Amer.;
to prove this, he sailed a balsa wood
boat from Peru to island near
Tahiti.

Hez·e·ki·ah (hĕzekī´ah). King
of Judah in 8th–7th c. B.C.

HF, H.F., hf, h.f. *abbrevs.* High
FREQUENCY.

Hf *symbol.* Hafnium.

HG, H.G. *abbrevs.* High German.

Hg *symbol.* Mercury.

hg *abbrev.* Hectogram(s).

hgt. *abbrev.* Height.

H.H. *abbrev.* His (*or* Her)
Highness; His Holiness (the Pope).

HI *abbrev.* Hawaii.

H.I. *abbrev.* Hawaiian Islands.

hi (hī) *int.* Exclamation calling
(colloq.) a greeting or (chiefly Brit.)
attention.

hi·a·tus (hīā´tus) *n.* (pl. **-tus·es,**
-tus). Break, gap, esp. in a series,
account, or chain of proof; interruption or loss in time or continuity.

Hi·a·wath·a (hīawŏth´a, -waw´-
tha). Indian hero in long narrative
poem by Henry Wadsworth Long-
fellow, "The Song of Hiawatha."

hi·ba·chi (hībah´chē) *n.* Small
charcoal-fueled grill of Japanese
origin.

hi·ber·nate (hī´bernāt) *v.i.*
(**-nat·ed, -nat·ing**). (of animals)
Spend the winter in torpid state;
(fig.) remain inactive. **hi·ber·na·-**
tion (hībernā´shon) *n.*

Hi·ber·ni·an (hībēr´nēan) *adj.*
& *n.* (Native, inhabitant) of Ireland. [f. L. *Hibernia* Ireland]

hi·bis·cus (hībĭs´kus, hĭ-) *n.*
Malvaceous plant of genus *H*~,
with large bright-colored flowers.

hic·cup, hic·cough (hĭk´ŭp,
-up) *ns.* Involuntary spasm of
respiratory organs, with sudden
closure of glottis and characteristic
sound. ~ *v.* (**-cuped, -cupped,**
-cup·ing, -cup·ping). Make hic-
cup; say, bring out, with hiccup(s).

hick (hĭk) *n.* (colloq.) Provincial,
rustic.

Hick·ok (hĭk´ŏk), **James Butler**
(1837–76). (also known as **Wild**
Bill Hickok) Amer. army scout
and deputy U.S. marshal; toured
with Buffalo Bill Cody, 1872–3.

The former German state, **Hesse,** contained Frankfurt-am-Main as one of its
major cities. Goethe's birth-place,
shown here, is in Frankfurt, today a
thriving industrial city.

Resonator

Spark
gap

To generator

Switch
gear

Induction
coil

Spark
gap

PLAN VIEW OF HERTZ'S OSCILLATOR

Oscillator

hick·o·ry (hĭk´erē) *n.* (pl. **-ries**). N. Amer. tree (*Carya*) closely allied to walnut, with tough heavy wood bearing drupes (usu. with hard woody ring) enclosing edible nuts; wood, stick, of this; hickory nut; **Old H ~**, nickname of President Andrew JACKSON[2].

hid: see HIDE[3].

hi·dal·go (hĭdăl´gō, -dahl´-) *n.* One of the lower nobility in Spain. [Span. *hijo dalgo* son of a "somebody"]

hid·den: see HIDE[3].

hide[1] (hīd) *n.* Animal skin, raw or dressed; (joc.) human skin; **hide´bound**, (of cattle) with skin clinging closely to back and ribs as result of bad feeding; (fig.) narrowminded, rigidly conventional.

hide[2] (hīd) *n.* (hist.) Medieval measure of land, of varying extent; orig., the amount required by one free family and its dependents, or as much as could be tilled with one plow in a year.

hide[3] (hīd) *v.* (**hid** pr. hĭd, **hid·den, hid·ing**). Put, keep, out of sight; keep (fact) secret (*from*); keep from view, obstruct the view of (without implication of intention); conceal oneself; **~-and-(go) seek**, children's game in which one player tries to find others who are hiding (also fig. of dealings with evasive person or thing); **hide´away**, hiding place; refuge; **hide´out**, hiding place.

hid·e·ous (hĭd´ēus) *adj.* Frightful, repulsive, revolting, to senses or mind. **hid´e·ous·ly** *adv.* **hid´e·ous·ness** *n.*

hid·ing[1] (hī´dĭng) *n.* (esp.) **in ~**, hidden; **~ place**, place of concealment.

hid·ing[2] (hī´dĭng) *n.* Thrashing.

hie (hī) *v.i.* (**hied, hie·ing, hy·ing**). (poet.) Go quickly (*to* etc.).

hi·er·arch (hī´erärk) *n.* Chief priest; archbishop.

hi·er·ar·chy (hī´erärkē) *n.* (pl. **-chies**). 1. Each of three divisions of angels (each comprising three orders) in the system of Dionysus the Pseudo-Areopagite; the angels. 2. Priestly government; organized priesthood in successive grades; any graded organization. **hi·er·ar·chic** (hīerär´kĭk), **hi·er·ar´chi·cal** *adjs.*

hi·er·at·ic (hīerăt´ĭk, hīrăt´-) *adj.* Of the priests (esp. of ancient Egyptian cursive writing intermediate between hieroglyphic and demotic); priestly; of traditional styles of art (e.g. Egyptian, Byzantine) in which earlier types and methods are conventionally retained.

hi·er·o·glyph (hī´eroglĭf, hī´ro-) *n.* 1. Figure of an object (pictograph, ideograph, phonogram, or determinative), used to represent a word or sound or syllable in any of the pictorial systems of writing, esp. the ancient Egyptian. 2. Secret

The **hibiscus**, which is found in tropical and semi-tropical regions, is cultivated for its attractive flowers which are large, trumpet-shaped and usually pink, red, yellow or white.

symbol; writing difficult to make out. **hi·er·o·glyph·ic** (hīeroglĭf´ĭk, hīro-) *adj.* Of, written in, hieroglyphs; hard to decipher. **hi·er·o·glyph´ics** *n.pl.* Hieroglyphs.

hi-fi (hī´fī´) *n.* High fidelity; electronic sound reproduction system of high fidelity.

hig·gle (hĭg´el) *v.i.* (**-gled, -gling**). Haggle.

hig·gle·dy-pig·gle·dy (hĭg´eldē pĭg´eldē) *adv., adj., & n.* (In) utter confusion.

*Egyptian **hieroglyphics**, seen here on the temple of Kom-ombo in Upper Egypt, evolved about 3000 B.C. They were deciphered by the French scholar Jean-François Champollion in 1823 from the Rosetta stone.*

high (hī) *adj.* 1. Of great specified upward extent; situate far above ground, sea level, etc upper, inland; (of physical action extending to or from, performed a a height; (of vowel sound) produce with (part of) tongue raised. 2. O exalted rank, position, or qualit important, weighty; (of office etc.) chief. 3. Great, intense, e treme; (of latitude) at great distan from equator; (of time) f advanced; **~ color**, fresh com plexion, flush. 4. (of meat, es game) Slightly tainted. 5. (sounds) Acute in pitch, shrill. Extreme in opinion. 7. (colloq Intoxicated by alcohol or drugs. **with a ~ hand**: see HAND; o **one's ~ horse**: see HORSE; **~ an dry**, (of ship) out of the water; (fig out of the current of events; **~ an low**, (*adv.*) everywhere; **~ an mighty**, arrogant. 9. **~ alta** chief altar of church; **high´bal** whiskey and soda, ginger ale, etc served in tall glass with ice; **high´ boy**, tall chest of drawers on leg **high´brow**, (colloq.) (person) of ir tellectual interests; **high´chair**, in fant's chair for use at meals, wit long legs and usu. tray; **H · Church**, (party, principles of th Anglican Church) giving a hig place to authority of episcopate an priesthood, saving grace of sacra ments, and ritual; hence **H · Churchman; high explosive**, ex plosive detonating very rapidly an with powerful effect; **high´ falutin(g)**, (colloq.) pretentiou bombastic; **high fidelity**, elec tronic reproduction of sound (a recorded, taped, or broadcast musi etc.) with minimum of distortior **high frequency**: see FREQUENCY **High German**: see GERMAN **high´handed**, overbearing, arbi trary; **high jinks**: see JINKS; **high life**, fashionable, luxurious living **high´light(s)**, brightest part(s) esp. of picture etc.; emphasized o most prominent or interesting par **highlight**, (*v.t.*) emphasize, mak prominent; **High Mass**: see MASS **high-minded**, of morally high character; **high noon**, exactl noon; **high-pitched**, (of sound acute in pitch; (of roof etc.) steep **high-pressure**, (of engine machine, etc.) having, driven by high pressure of steam, air, etc (fig.) urgent, intense, as *high pressure salesmanship*; **high pries** chief priest; **high relief**, sculptur in which figures etc. project mor than half their thickness fron background; **high-rise**, (of building) having many stories

*This **hibernating** dormouse spend most of the winter in a state close t death, with its body temperature near t freezing point. It relies on reserve body fat and stored food supplies t keep alive.*

high′road, (chiefly Brit.) main road; (fig.) direct or sure path or way; **high school**, secondary school that includes grades 9–12 or sometimes only 10–12; **high seas**, seas, ocean, outside territorial waters; **high-spirited**, of lofty or courageous spirit; lively; **high spirits**, elated or merry mood; **high-stepper**, horse that steps high; frequenter of fashionable society; one who lives luxuriously; **high-strung**, very sensitive or nervous; **high tea**, (Brit.) substantial early evening meal at which tea is served (usu. a hot supper that is not the main meal of the day); **high-test**, (of gasoline) vaporizing at comparatively low temperature; **high tide**: see TIDE; **high treason**: see TREASON; **high-water mark**, level reached at high tide; highest point of flood. **high** adv. Far up, aloft; in, to, a high degree; at a high price; for high stakes; (of sounds) at, to, a high pitch; **run** ~, (of sea) have strong current with high tide; **high′born**, of noble birth; **high-flown**, extravagant, bombastic; **high′flyer, high′flier**, (fig.) ambitious person; one who has high-flown notions. **high** n. High place; high level; (meteor.) region of high atmospheric pressure; (slang) intoxication by alcohol or euphoria induced by a drug; **on** ~, in a high place, in heaven.

high·lands (hī′landz) n.pl. (freq. **H**~). Mountainous or elevated country; esp. (**H**~) N. part of

Scotland. **high′land** adj. **high′-land·er, High′land·er** ns. Inhabitant of highlands, esp. (**H**~) those of Scotland.

high·ly (hī′lē) adv. In a high degree; at a high price or rate; honorably, favorably (as ~ recommended).

High·ness (hī′nĭs) n. Title of various princes etc., as **His, Her**, (Royal, Serene, Imperial) ~.

high·way (hī′wā) n. Main or principal public road connecting cities or towns; main route by land or water; **high′wayman**, (hist.) man (usu. mounted) who robbed passengers on highway.

hi·jack (hī′jăk) v.t. & n. Seize, seizure of, means of transport or goods etc. in transit. **hi′jack·er** n.

hike (hīk) n. 1. Long walk in the country for pleasure or exercise. 2. (colloq.) Increase (of prices etc.). ~ v. (**hiked, hik·ing**). 1. Walk vigorously or laboriously; go for long walk. 2. Raise or pull up with a jerk. 3. Increase or advance (prices etc.). **hik′er** n.

hi·lar·i·ous (hĭlăr′ēus) adj. Mirthful, joyous, boisterously merry; very funny. **hi·lar′i·ous·ly** adv. **hi·lar′i·ous·ness** n. **hi·lar′i·ty** (hĭlăr′ĭtē, -lār′-) n.

hill (hĭl) n. Natural elevation

*The **Highlands** of Scotland lie north of a line drawn from Dunbarton to Stonehaven and contain Ben Nevis, seen here, the highest mountain in the U.K. at 4,406 ft.*

of earth's surface, small mounta heap, mound, of sand, earth, e **hill′billy**, (colloq., usu. dispar. ing) rustic mountaineer; **hill′bi music, song**, music, song of sim ballad type popular among su people. **hill** v.t. Form into h bank up (plants) with soil. **hi** adj. (**hill·i·er, hill·i·est**). **hill ness** n.

Hill (hĭl), **James Jerome** (18 1916). Amer. railroad promo and financier; formed the Gr Northern Railway, 1890; his sto market battle for control of Northern Pacific Railroad caus the panic of 1901; he became kno as "Empire Builder."

Hil·la·ry (hĭl′erē), **Sir Edmu** (1919–). N.Z. mountaineer; w Sherpa guide Tenzing Norkay, to reach summit of Mount Ever 1953.

hill·ock (hĭl′ok) n. Small hill mound.

Hi·lo (hē′lō). Port and larg city of Hawaii Island, Hawaii, the E. coast.

hilt (hĭlt) n. Handle of sword dagger; handle of other weapon tool; **to the** ~, completely.

hi·lum (hī′lum) n. (bot.) M at point of attachment of seed seed vessel.

him (hĭm) pron. Objective c of HE.

H.I.M. abbrev. His (or H Imperial Majesty.

Hi·ma·la·yas (hĭmalā′az, mahl′yaz). Mountain range in central Asia extending 1,500 (2,414 km), from Jammu Kashmir in the W., to Assam in E.; highest peak, Mt. Ever 29,028 ft. (8,848 m).

him·self (hĭmsĕlf′) pron. E phatic and reflexive form c responding to HE, HIM.

Hi·na·ya·na (hēnayah′na) THERAVADA. [Sansk. hina less yāna vehicle]

hind[1] (hīnd) n. Female of (e red) deer, esp. in and after th year.

hind[2] (hīnd) adj. Situated at t back, posterior; **hind′brain**: s BRAIN; **hind′quarters**, hind l and adjoining parts of quadrupe **hind′sight**, rear sight of a ri perception after the event (op foresight).

Hin·den·burg (hĭn′denbēr **Paul von** (1847–1934). Germ general and statesman; field ma shal then chief of staff during Wo War I; president of Weimar R public, 1925–34; appointed Hit as chancellor, 1933.

hind·er (hĭn′der) v.t. Impe prevent.

Hin·di (hĭn′dē) n. 1. Group Indo-Aryan spoken dialects inclu ing Eastern and Western Hindi. Literary form of Hindustani dra ing literary vocabulary from Sa

...he **Himalayas** *in southern Asia contain*
...0 of the world's highest peaks includ-
...g Everest, Kanchenjunga and Nanga
...arbat; the slopes and foothills provide
...magnificent variety of plant and animal
...e.

...krit and using the Devanagari
...cript.

    hind·most (hīnd′mōst) *adj.*
...arthest behind; most remote.
    hin·drance (hĭn′drɑns) *n.* Ob-
...truction, prevention; obstacle.
    Hin·du, (archaic) **Hin·doo**
...hĭn′dōō) *ns.* One who practices
...linduism. **Hindu,** (archaic) **Hin-**
...loo *adjs.* **Hindu Kush,** moun-
...ain range in S. Asia, extending
...vest from the Himalayas. **Hin′du·**
...**sm** *n.* Religious and social system
...vith adherents, esp. in India, with
...elief in reincarnation, worship of
...everal gods, and caste as basis of
...ociety.
    Hin·du·stan (hĭnd ōōstahn′,
...stăn′). Persian name of India; in
...he stricter sense, India N. of the

The worship of several gods is the basis of **Hindu** religious ceremonies, such as this festival at Katmandu, Nepal. The majority of Indians still adhere to the Hindu caste system, a social as well as religious feature.

Deccan exclusive of Bengal and Bihar. [lit., "place of the Hindus"]
Hin·du·sta·ni (hĭndoōostah´nē, -stăn´ē) *n*. Language based on Western Hindi used widely in northern India and Pakistan; (formerly) = URDU. ~ *adj*. Of Hindustan or its people; of Hindustani.

hinge (hĭnj) *n*. Movable joint, as mechanism like that by which door is hung on side post; natural joint doing similar work, as that of bivalve shell; (fig.) central principle, critical point, on which all turns; small piece of adhesive paper for mounting stamps, photographs, etc. in album. ~ *v*. (**hinged, hing·ing**). Attach (as) with hinge; (of door etc. or fig.) hang and turn *on* (post, principle, etc.). **hinge´less** *adj*.

hin·ny (hĭn´ē) *n*. (pl. **-nies**). Offspring of female donkey by stallion.

hint (hĭnt) *n*. Slight indication; covert or indirect suggestion. ~*v*. Suggest slightly; ~ **at**, give hint of.

hin·ter·land (hĭn´terlănd) *n*. District behind that lying along coast or river bank; remote area.

hip¹ (hĭp) *n*. Projection of pelvis and upper part of thigh bone at each side of body in man and quadrupeds; (archit.) inclined projecting angle of roof from ridge to eaves; ~ **flask**, whiskey flask carried in hip pocket; ~ **pocket**, rear pocket in trousers, just behind hip. **hipped** *adj*.

hip² (hĭp) *n*. Fruit of (esp. wild) rose.

hip³ (hĭp) *n*. Exclamation introducing cheer (~, ~, **hurrah**).

hip⁴ (hĭp), **hep** (hĕp) *adjs*. (slang) Cognizant, wise, esp. to latest attitudes and tastes; in the know.

Hip·par·chus (hĭpär´kus).

Second century B.C. Greek astronomer; originated system of trigonometry and of using latitude and longitude to locate geographical positions.

hip·pie, hip·py (hĭp´ē) *ns*. (pl. **-pies**). Member of a group of young people in the 1960s who rejected customs, career goals, dress styles, etc. of conventional society and turned to communal living, psychedelic drugs, Eastern religions, and sexual freedom.

hip·po (hĭp´ō) *n*. (pl. **-pos**). (colloq.) Hippopotamus.

hippo- *prefix*. Horse.

hip·po·cam·pus (hĭpokăm´pus) *n*. (pl. **-pi** pr. -pī). 1. (myth.) Seahorse, with 2 forefeet, and body ending in fish tail. 2. (anat.) Each of two elongated eminences (~ **major and minor**) on floor of each lateral ventricle of brain.

Hip·poc·ra·tes (hĭpŏk´ratēz) (469–399 B.C.). Most celebrated physician of Greek antiquity. **Hip·po·cra·tic** (hĭpokrăt´ĭk) *adj*. Of Hippocrates or the school of medicine named after him; ~ **oath**, oath embodying the code of medical ethics, preserved in Hippocrates' writings (though prob. of still earlier date), and still taken, in various modified forms, by new physicians.

hip·po·drome (hĭp´odrōm) *n*. (Gk. and Rom. antiq.) Course for chariot races etc.; arena, esp. for horse shows etc.

hip·po·pot·a·mus (hĭpopŏt´a-

mus) *n*. (pl. **-mus·es, -mi** pr. -m Large African quadruped (*amphibius*) with thick heavy almo hairless body, large muzzle a short legs, inhabiting rivers, lak etc. [Gk. *hippos* horse, *potan* river]

hip·py: see HIPPIE.

hip·ster (hĭp´ster) *n*. (slan Person who is well-informed abo newest ideas, styles, etc.

hir·cine (hēr´sĭn, -sĭn) *a* Goatlike.

hire (hīr) *n*. Payment for use thing or for personal service; u or service of for payment; ~ **o** obtain work, esp. as laborer; ~ **ou** exchange or offer one's services f compensation. **hire** *v.t*. (**hire hir·ing**). Employ (person) f wages; procure, grant, tempora use of (thing) for payment.

hire·ling (hīr´lĭng) *n*. (usu. co tempt.) One who serves for hire

Hi·ro·hi·to (hērōhē´tō) (1901– Emperor of Japan 1926– ; aft World War II the Japanese co stitution stripped him of divi rights.

Hi·ro·shi·ma (hēroshē´m hĭrō´shĭ-, hĭrŏsh´ĭ-). Seaport SW. Honshu, Japan, devastated 1st atomic bomb used in warfa Aug. 6, 1945.

hir·sute (hēr´sōot, hērsōot´) *a* Hairy, shaggy; untrimmed. **hir sute·ness** *n*.

his (hĭz) *poss. pron*. Possessi case of, and adjective correspon ing to, HE, belonging to, affectin him.

His·pan·ic (hĭspăn´ĭk) *adj*. C pertaining to, Spain, its people their language. [L. *Hispania* Iberian peninsula]

His·pa·nio·la (hĭspanyō´l Island of the West Indies, E. Cuba, covering about 30,000 sq. m (77,700 sq. km); divided into t Republic of HAITI in the W. pa and the DOMINICAN³ REPUBLIC the E.

hiss (hĭs) *n*. Sharp continuo spirant sound such as is made geese and serpents, and in pr nunciation of "s"; this sou uttered in disapproval or scorn. *v*. Make sound of hiss, esp. expression of disapproval or de sion; express disapproval of thu utter with angry hiss.

hist. *abbrev*. Historian; histo cal; history.

his·ta·mine (hĭs´tamēn, -mĭn) Substance naturally present in t body, responsible for compl physiological phenomena, esp. connection with work of bloc vessels.

his·tol·o·gy (hĭstŏl´ojē) *n*. Stu of the minute structure of organ tissues. **his·to·log´i·cal** *adj*. **his tol´o·gist** *n*.

his·to·ri·an (hĭstōr´ean, -tŏr -tär´-) *n*. Writer of, person learne

, history.

his·tor·ic (hĭstŏr´ĭk, -tär´-) *adj.*
Noted in history. 2. (of tenses of
[ve]rb) Used in narration of past
[eve]nts; ~ **present**, present tense
[us]ed instead of past in vivid nar-
[ra]tion. **his·tor´i·cal** *adj.* Of
[hi]story; belonging to history, not
[le]gend; belonging to the past, not of
[th]e present; (of the study of a sub-
[jec]t) based on analysis of a subject,
[la]nguage, etc., at successive periods
[of] time; (of novel, picture, etc.)
[de]aling with historical events. **his·-**
[to]r´i·cal·ly *adv.*

his·to·ric·i·ty (hĭstŏrĭs´ĭtē) *n.*
Historic quality, character, or
authenticity.

his·to·ri·og·ra·pher (hĭs-
tōrēŏg´rafer, -tor-) *n.* Writer of
history, esp. official historian of a
group, court, etc. **his·to·ri·og´-**

*The **hippopotamus** is found in Africa
from the Upper Nile to South Africa. It is
gregarious and comes ashore at night
to graze. The smaller pygmy hippopotamus lives only on the Ivory Coast,
Liberia and Sierra Leone and is a very
rare and now completely protected
species.*

ra·phy *n.* (pl. **-phies**). Writing of
history.

his·to·ry (hĭs´terē, hĭs´trē) *n.* (pl.
-ries) *n.* 1. Continuous methodical record in order of time, of
important or public events; study of
formation and growth of communities and nations; whole train of
events connected with particular
country, person, thing, etc.; past
events in general, course of human
affairs; **ancient** ~, history usu.
reckoned as ending with fall of
Roman Empire, 476 A.D.; (joc.)
thing that is out of date, or long

Hippopotamus

past. 2. Systematic account of set of natural phenomena (rare exc. in **natural** ~).

his·tri·on·ic (hĭstrēŏn´ĭk) *adj.* Of actors or acting; stagy, overly emotional or dramatic. **his·tri·on'i·cal·ly** *adv.* **his·tri·on'ics** *n.pl.* Theatricals, theatrical act; being dramatic for effect.

hit (hĭt) *v.* (**hit, hit·ting**). 1. Strike with blow or missile; direct blow *at*; (of moving body) strike; strike *against*; deliver (blow, person etc. a blow); (fig.) affect sensibly, wound; (slang) murder; ~**-and-run**, of a motor accident in which driver of vehicle fails to stop; of an attack or raid of short duration by a few attackers or raiders; ~**-or-miss**, ~**-and-miss**, (colloq.) casual, careless; ~**-out**, deal vigorous blows. 2. Fall in with, suit; ~ **it off**, agree; become friends quickly (*with, together*); ~ **on**, come by chance on. **hit** *n.* Blow, stroke; stroke of sarcasm etc. (*at*); stroke of good luck; successful attempt; success; (slang) murder by a paid assassin (~ **man**); (baseball) **base** ~: see BASE². **hit´ter** *n.*

hitch (hĭch) *v.* Move (thing) with jerk; shift; ~ **up**, lift, pull up, with jerk. 2. Fasten with loop, hook, etc.; become so fastened; ~ **up (horses)**, attach them to wagon. 3. (also **hitch'hike**) Travel by soliciting free rides in vehicles. **hitch** *n.* 1. Jerk, abrupt pull or push. 2. (naut.) Noose, knot, of various kinds, by which rope is caught around or temporarily made fast to something, as **half** ~, one formed by passing end of rope around its standing part and then through the bight. 3. Temporary stoppage; impediment.

hith·er (hĭdh´er) *adv.* To, toward, this place; ~ **and thither**, ~ **and yon**, in various directions, here and there; **hith'erto'**, up to this time; **hith'erward**, (archaic) in this direction. **hither** *adj.* Situated on this side; nearer (of two).

Hit·ler (hĭt´ler), **Adolf** (1889–1945). Austrian-born German political leader; founded Nationalist Socialist German Workers' Party (Nazi party) 1919–20; wrote *Mein Kampf*, 1924, describing his aims; President Hindenburg forced to name him chancellor; was granted temporary dictatorial powers by the Reichstag, 1933; combined the offices of chancellor and president upon Hindenburg's death and created the title "Der Führer" as dictator of the Third Reich, 1934–45; was committed to a fanatical policy of establishing

*These **hives** in Spain are made from cork and sacking. Most up-to-date commercial beekeepers, however, use wooden boxes with movable frames in which the bees build their combs.*

Aryan racial supremacy involving elimination of Jews, and to the establishment of Germany as the dominant world power; broke the Treaty of Versailles, withdrew from the League of Nations, 1935, reoccupied the Rhineland, annexed Austria and Sudetenland, 1938, and Czechoslovakia, 1939; his invasion of Poland, Sept., 1939, led to onset of World War II; he committed

suicide in Berlin bunker as A[llies] drew near. **Hit´ler·ism** *n.* **H[it]ler·ite** *adj. & n.*

Hit·tite (hĭt´īt) *n.* 1. Membe[r of] an ancient people who flourishe[d in] Anatolia *c*2000–1200 B.C. and c[on]trolled N. Syria and other part[s of] the Near East. 2. (Old Testame[nt]) People of N. Syria, possibly [de]scended from the Hittites [of] Anatolia or akin to them. [3.] Language of the Hittites [of] Anatolia, known from Babylon[ian] cuneiform inscriptions, related [to] the Indo-European family of l[an]guages. ~ *adj.* Of the Hittites [or] their language.

With a population of 158,000, **Hobart,** State capital of Tasmania, Australia, is built beside the Derwent River. Its deep-water port is the export outlet for zinc, iron, apples and wool from the southern parts of the island.

hobby-horse, associated with the traditional British Morris dance, celebrates rebirth in spring. At Padstow, Cornwall (above), similar dances are staged but they are designed to eliminate evil and death and to encourage human fertility.

hive (hīv) *n.* Habitation for bees; colony of bees living in a hive; (fig.) busy swarming place. ~ *v.* (**-ved, hiv·ing**). Place (bees) in hive; enter hive, live together like bees; store, hoard up (honey etc.) in hive.

hives (hīvz) *n.pl.* (pop.) Any of various physical disorders, as skin eruptions etc.

hl *abbrev.* Hectoliter(s).

hm *abbrev.* Hectometer(s).

H.M. *abbrev.* His (or Her) Majesty.

HMO *abbrev.* Health maintenance organization.

H.M.S. *abbrev.* His (or Her) Majesty's Ship.

Ho *symbol.* Holmium.

ho (hō) *int.* Exclamation expressing surprise, admiration, triumph, derision, calling attention, etc.

hoa·gy, hoa·gie (hō′gē) *ns.* (pl. **-gies**) = HERO SANDWICH.

hoar (hōr, hôr) *adj.* Gray-haired with age; grayish white; (of things)

gray with age; **hoar′frost,** frozen dew forming a white frostlike coating. **hoar** *n.* Hoariness; hoarfrost.

hoard (hōrd, hôrd) *n.* Stock, store (esp. of food, money) laid by; amassed stock of facts etc. ~ *v.t.* Amass (food, money, etc.) and put away, store *up.*

hoar·hound = HOREHOUND.

hoarse (hōrs, hôrs) *adj.* (**hoars′-er, hoars·est**). (of voice) Rough, husky, croaking; (of person) having such a voice. **hoarse′ly** *adv.* **hoarse′ness** *n.* **hoars′en** *v.* Make, become, hoarse.

hoar·y (hōr′ē, hôr′ē) *adj.* (**hoar·i·er, hoar·i·est**). (of hair) Gray, white, with age; having such hair, venerable; ancient, very old; (bot., entom.) covered with short white hairs. **hoar′i·ness** *n.*

hoax (hōks) *v.t.* Deceive, take in (person) by way of joke. ~ *n.* Humorous or mischievous deception.

hob (hŏb) *n.* Part of casing of fireplace having surface level with top of grate, forming stand for kettle, pan, etc.

Ho·bart[1] (hō′bärt). Capital and a port of Tasmania.

Ho·bart[2] (hō′bärt), **Garret Augustus** (1844–99). Amer. lawyer; U.S. vice president under William McKinley, 1897–9.

Hobbes (hŏbz), **Thomas** (1588–1679). English philosopher; expounded his political philosophy, according to which man is a naturally selfish unit, in the *Leviathan* (1651).

hob·ble (hŏb′el) *v.* (**-bled, -bling**). Walk lamely, limp; proceed haltingly; cause to hobble; tie together legs of (horse etc.) to prevent it from straying etc.; tie (legs) thus. ~ *n.* Uneven or infirm gait; rope, clog, etc., for hobbling horse etc.; ~ **skirt,** type of long skirt, popular *c*1910, that was so narrow below the knee it impeded wearer in walking.

hob·ble·de·hoy (hŏb′eldēhoi) *n.* (pl. **-hoys**). Awkward, gawky adolescent boy.

hob·by[1] (hŏb′ē) *n.* (pl. **-bies**). 1. (archaic) Small horse. 2. Subject, activity, or occupation engaged in primarily for pleasure; **hob′by-horse,** stick with horse's head that children bestride as toy horse; rocking horse; favorite theme, obsession.

hob·by[2] (hŏb′ē) *n.* (pl. **-bies**). Small falcon (*Falco subbuteo*).

hob·gob·lin (hŏb′gŏblĭn) *n.* Mischievous, or sometimes evil and ugly, imp; bogey; bugbear.

*The **hockey field**, which measures 100 x 60 yards, is divided into four zones. Two teams of 11 hockey players take up different positions on the field and aim to score hits in their opponent's goal.*

hob·nail (hŏb′nāl) *n.* Heavy-headed nail, for soles of shoes and boots. **hob′nailed** *adj.* Furnished or set with hobnails.

hob·nob (hŏb′nŏb) *v.i.* (**-nobbed, -nob·bing**). Associate familiarly, as drinking companions; hold familiar conversation (*with*).

ho·bo (hō′bō) *n.* (pl. **-boes, -bos**). Migratory worker; tramp.

Hob·son's (hŏb′sonz) **choice.** No choice at all, necessity of taking what one can get. [f. Thomas *Hobson*, 1544?–1631, liveryman of Cambridge, England, who rented out his horses in rotation without allowing his customers to choose among them]

Ho Chi Minh (hō′ chē′ mĭn′) (1890–1969). Vietnamese political leader; president and major leader of North Vietnam, 1954–69, during Vietnam War. ~ **City**, former name of SAIGON.

hock[1] (hŏk) *n.* Joint of quadruped's hind leg between true knee and fetlock.

hock[2] (hŏk) *n.* (esp. Brit.) German white wine, properly that of Hochheim on the river Main.

hock[3] (hŏk) *n.* (colloq.) **in** ~, in pawn; in debt; **hock′shop**, pawnshop. **hock** *v.t.* Pawn.

hock·ey (hŏk′ē) *n.* Field game (also **field hockey**) played with a small hard ball and with sticks hooked or curved at one end between 2 teams of 11 players on each side, the object being to drive the ball through the opponents' goal; **ice** ~, form of hockey played on ice with each side having 6 players on skates and with PUCK instead of ball.

ho·cus (hō′kus) *v.t.* (**-cused, -cus·ing**, Brit. **-cussed, -cus·-sing**). Take in, hoax; stupefy (person) with drugs; drug (food or esp. drink).

ho·cus-po·cus (hō′kus pō′kus) *n.* Sleight of hand, deception; typical conjuring formula. ~ *v.* (**-cused, -cus·ing**, Brit. **-cussed, -cus·sing**). Play tricks on.

hod (hŏd) *n.* 1. Builder's light open trough on staff for carrying mortar etc; ~ **carrier**, worker who carries hod. 2. Coal scuttle.

hodge·podge (hŏj′pŏj), **hotch-potch** (hŏch′pŏch) *ns.* Dish of mixed ingredients; mixture, medley.

Hodg·kin's (hŏj′kĭnz) **disease.** Disease characterized by chronic progressive enlargement and inflammation of the lymph nodes and other lymphoid tissues, esp. of the spleen and often of the kidneys and liver. [T. *Hodgkin* (1798–1866),

Ice hockey is particularly popular in North America. Two teams of 6 players on skates use sticks to hit a hard rubber disc called a puck into the opponent's goal.

English physician]

hoe (hō) *n.* Tool consisting of thin metal blade fixed transversely on long handle, for loosening soil, scraping up weeds, etc.; **hoe′cake**, thin cornmeal cake (perh. orig. baked on broad thin blade of hoe); **hoe′down**, lively dance or party featuring dancing, often square dancing; music for such dancing. **hoe** *v.* (**hoed, hoe·ing**). Weed (crops), loosen (ground), dig *up*, cut *down*, with hoe; use hoe.

Hof·manns·thal (hawf′mahns-tahl), **Hugo von** (1874–1929). Austrian poet and dramatist; a pioneer of the new Romantic movement in German drama.

hog (hawg, hŏg) *n.* Mammal of the family Suidae, including the domesticated pig, the boar, wart

hog, etc.; (esp.) domestic pig weighing over 120 lbs.; (fig.) coa gluttonous, or filthy person; **go whole** ~, do the thing thorough **live (eat) high off (on) the** (colloq.) live luxuriously or extra agantly; **hog′back**, shar crested ridge, steep on each side sloping gradually at each end; **cholera**, often fatal disease swine; **hog′tie**, secure by ty together animal's feet or perso hands and feet; hamper, frustra **hog′wash**, kitchen swill etc. hogs; (colloq.) nonsense; **h weed**, coarse weed of pars family with leaves relished many animals; **hog-wild**, (collo highly enthusiastic; lacking straint. **hog** *v.* (**hogged, hog·gin** Raise (back etc.), rise, archwise center; (slang) appropriate selfish refuse to share. **hog′gish** Piglike, swinish; coarsely s indulgent or gluttonous. **h gish·ly** *adv.* **hog′gish·ness** *n.* **ho·gan** (hō′gahn, -gan) *n.* Na

*The 16th-century German painter and engraver, **Hans Holbein** the Younger, is famous for his accomplished and realistic portraits. This 'Lady with a Squirrel' is the Marchioness Lady Cholmondley.*

ho Indian dwelling built of branches and covered with sod or mud.

Ho·garth (hō´gärth), **William** (1697–1764). English painter and engraver of social and political caricature.

hogs·head (hŏgz´hĕd) *n.* Large cask; liquid measure of 63 gallons, although it can vary as unit of volume or capacity from 62.5 to 140 gallons.

Hoh·en·zol·lern (hō´enzŏlern; *Ger.* hō´entsawlern). German princely family of Swabian origin, from which came the kings of Prussia from 1701 to 1918 and German emperors from 1871 to 1918.

hoicks (hoiks): var. of YOICKS.

hoi pol·loi (hoi´ poloi´). Majority, the masses. [Gk. = "the many"]

hoist[1] (hoist) *v.t.* Raise aloft (esp. flags); raise by means of tackle etc. ~ *n.* Hoisting, shove up; elevator esp. for things; pulley, (eng.) fixed crane.

hoist[2] (hoist) *adj.* ~ **with one's own petard**, ruined by one's own devices against others. [past part. of obs. *hoise* hoist]

hoi·ty-toi·ty (hoi´tē toi´tē) *adj.* Haughty.

hoke (hōk) *v.* (slang) Treat in falsely contrived way (usu. ~ **up**). **hoke** *n.* (slang) = HOKUM. **hok´ey** *adj.*

Hok·kai·do (hawk´kīdō´). Northernmost island of Japan in the Pacific Ocean off the E. coast of Asia covering 30,372 sq. mi. (78,663 sq. km).

ho·kum (hō´kum) *n.* Stage properties, action, etc., designed to have sentimental or melodramatic appeal; fakery; nonsense, bunkum. [perh. blending of *hocus-pocus* and *bunkum*]

Hol·bein (hōl´bīn; *Ger.* hawl´-bīn), **Hans** (1497–1543). German portrait painter; became court painter to Henry VIII of England, 1536; called "the Younger" to distinguish him from his less famous father.

hold[1] (hōld) *n.* Cavity in ship below deck, where cargo is stored.

hold[2] (hōld) *v.* (**held** pr. hĕld, **hold·ing**). 1. Keep fast, grasp; keep (oneself, one's head, etc.) in particular attitude. 2. Possess, be owner or holder or tenant of; have capacity for, contain; keep possession of (place); occupy (place, person's thoughts, etc.); engross (person, his attention); **holding company**, company controlling or holding partial or complete interest in other companies. 3. Keep (person etc.) in specified place, condition, etc.; make (person) adhere *to* (terms, promise). 4. Observe, celebrate, conduct (festival, meeting, conversation). 5. Restrain. 6. Think, believe; (of judge or court) lay down, decide (*that*); entertain specified feelings toward; **hold dear**, regard with affection. 7. Remain unbroken, not give way; keep going; (of laws, rules, etc.) be valid, apply; (archaic) stop, wait; **hold to**, adhere to (choice, purpose, etc.); **hold with**, approve of. 8. **hold one's ground, one's own**, not give way; **hold one's head high**, behave proudly; **hold up one's head**, not be downcast or ashamed; **hold water**, (fig.) be sound, bear examination. 9. **hold oneself aloof**, avoid communication with persons etc.; **hold back**, restrain; hesitate; refrain *from*; **hold down**, continue to occupy (a place or post); retain (a job); **hold forth**, (usu. contempt.) speak publicly; **hold in**, confine, keep in

*e **hogweed** or cow parsnip grows by adsides and in wastes and pastures. is found in northern temperate cli-tes and has small white or pink wers.*

*North and South **Holland** are two provinces of the Netherlands, rich dairying regions also famous for their tulips (above). Haarlem and Amsterdam are in the north and The Hague and Rotterdam in the south. Above right: Typical Dutch windmill. Right: Opening bridge over the River Amstel.*

check; **hold off**, delay; **hold on**, keep one's grasp on something; keep telephone line open; (colloq., imper.) stop; **hold out**, stretch forth; offer (inducement etc.); endure, persist; **hold out for**, refuse to accept anything but (specified terms etc.); **hold over**, postpone; **hold together**, (cause to) cohere; **hold up**, support; exhibit, display (esp. *to* derision etc.); arrest progress of, obstruct, delay; stop and rob; rob; **hold'up**, (*n.*), armed robbery; delay. **hold** *n.* Grasp (esp. in **take, get, keep, ~ of**); opportunity of holding, thing to hold by; means of exerting influence *on, over.*

hold·er (hōl′d*er*) *n.* (esp.) Contrivance for holding something, as a pen, cigarette, etc.

hold·ing (hōl′dĭng) *n.* (esp.) 1. (usu. pl.) Land, stocks, capital, etc. held. 2. (sports) Illegal hampering or blocking of an opponent's movements with the hands or arms.

hole (hōl) *n.* Hollow place in solid body; deep place in stream etc.; animal's burrow; (slang) small mean abode; cavity into which ball etc. must be got in various games, esp. golf; (golf) point scored by player who gets ball from tee to hole

with fewest strokes; perforation; (slang) awkward situation; **in the ~**, (slang) owing money; **make a ~ in**, use a large amount of; **pick ~s in**, find fault with. **hole** *v.* (**holed, hol·ing**). Make holes in; put into hole; hit (golf ball, or abs.) into hole; **~ up**, (slang) hide oneself.

hol·i·day (hŏl′ĭdā) *n.* 1. Day of cessation from work or of recreation; (chiefly Brit.) (usu. pl.) period of this, vacation. 2. Holy day.

ho·li·ness (hō′lēnĭs) *n.* Sanctity; (with possessive) **H~**, title of pope.

Hol·ins·hed (hŏl′ĭnzhĕd, -ĭn-shĕd) or **Hol·lings·head** (hŏl′ĭngz-hĕd), **Raphael** (d. 1580). English historian; wrote *Chronicles of England, Scotland and Ireland*, 1577;

completed a world history begun Reginald Wolfe; his writings w used by Shakespeare and others sources of plots.

ho·lism (hō′lĭzem) *n.* (phil Theory that nature tends to p duce wholes (bodies or organis through ordered grouping of u structures. **ho′list** *n.*

ho·lis·tic (hōlĭs′tĭk) *adj.* 1. or pertaining to holism. 2. Str ing the significance of the wh and the interdependence of units; **~ medicine**, medical tre ment that considers emotior mental, etc., aspects, as well physical symptoms, in treatmen patients. **ho·lis′ti·cal·ly** *adv.*

Hol·land (hŏl′and). Name province of the Northern Neth

nds, now usu. extended by reigners to the kingdom of the ETHERLANDS. **Hol'land·er** n.

hol·lan·daise (hŏl'ăndāz, hŏlan-iz') **sauce.** Sauce for fish, vegebles, etc. of butter, egg yolks, negar, etc. [Fr., = "Dutch"]

hol·ler (hŏl'er) v. & n. (Make, xpress with) loud cry or noise.

hol·low (hŏl'ō) adj. Having a ole, cavity, or depression; not lid, empty inside; empty, incere, false. **hol'low·ly** adv. ol'low·ness n. **hollow** n. Holw place; hole; valley, basin. ~ dv. Completely (esp. in beat ~ c.). ~ v.t. Bend into hollow ape; (also ~ **out**), excavate.

hol·ly (hŏl'ē) n. (pl. **-lies**). vergreen shrub (Ilex, esp. I. aca, Amer. holly, and I. aquilium, English holly) with usu. rk green tough glossy leaves, aving indented edges with sharp iff prickles at the points, and bearg bright red berries, much used r decorating houses etc. at Christas.

hol·ly·hock (hŏl'ēhŏk) n. Tall ant (Althaea rosea) with stout em bearing numerous large owers of many varieties of color a very short stalks. [holy + hock allow]

Hol·ly·wood (hŏl'ēwo͝od). Secon of Los Angeles, California; nter of the U.S. television and otion-picture industry, though ajor studios no longer are conntrated there; (fig.) the motioncture industry, its glamour, etc.

Holmes [1] (hōmz, hōlmz), **Oliver endell** (1809–94). Amer. physian and man of letters; best known r his collected Atlantic Monthly agazine pieces, The Autocrat at e Breakfast Table, and the poems Old Ironsides," "Chambered autilus," and "The Wonderful ne-Hoss Shay"; his son, **Oliver endell** (1841–1935), Amer. rist; associate justice of the U.S. upreme Court, 1902–32; known "the great dissenter," he believed at the law was made for society nd not society for the law, and at law was based on experience, ot logic.

Holmes [2] (hōmz, hōlmz), **Sher-ck.** Private detective, the chief aracter in a number of detective ories by Sir A. Conan Doyle.

hol·mi·um (hōl'mēum) n. hem.) Element of yttrium-rium group found in gadolinite; mbol Ho, at. no. 67, at. wt. 54.9340. [f. Stockholm, near hich yttria-bearing minerals are und]

hol·o·caust (hŏl'okawst, hō'lo-) Whole burned offering; whole-le sacrifice (fig.) or destruction, p. by fire; **the H~**, the murder the Nazis of over 6 million ws.

The **hollyhock** is widely cultivated for its ornamental flowers. The stems grow from 5 to 9 ft. tall and the flowers, usually white, pink, red or yellow are 3 ins. or more across.

ho·lo·gram (hō'logrăm, hŏl'o-) n. (phys.) 1. Pattern produced by interference between coherent light beam and light diffracted etc. from same beam by an object. 2. Photograph of such pattern which, when suitably illuminated, produces an image of the object in two or three dimensions.

hol·o·graph (hŏl'ograf, -grahf, hō'lo-) adj. & n. (Document) written wholly in handwriting of person in whose name it appears (cf. AUTOGRAPH). **hol·o·graph·ic** (hŏlograf'ĭk) adj.

ho·log·ra·phy (hōlŏg'rafē) n. Process or method of producing holograms.

hol·o·thu·ri·an (hŏlothoor'ēan, hōlo-), **hol·o·thu·ri·oid** (hŏlothoor'eoid) adjs. & ns. (Animal) of the Holothurioidea, a class of echinoderms including sea cucumber and characterized by elongated form, tough leathery integument, and a ring of tentacles around the mouth.

Hol·stein (hōl'shtīn). Former Danish duchy; later (after 1866) part of the province of Schleswig-Holstein, Prussia. ~ n. (Any of) a breed of black and white dairy cattle developed in Holstein.

hol·ster (hōl'ster) n. Leather case for pistol, fixed to saddle or worn on belt.

ho·ly (hō'lē) adj. (**-li·er, -li·est**). Consecrated, sacred; morally and spiritually perfect; belonging to, commissioned by, devoted to, God; of high moral excellence; **H~ Alliance**, that formed in 1815, after fall of Napoleon, among Russia, Austria, and Prussia ostensibly to preserve peace and justice in Europe; **H~ Communion**, celebration of the EUCHARIST; ~ **cross**, cross of Christ; **H~ Father**: see FATHER; **H~ Ghost**, third member of the Trinity; ~ **grail**: see GRAIL; ~ **Joe**, (naut. slang) clergyman, pious person; **H~ Land**, western region of PALESTINE, esp. Judea, as scene of life and death of Jesus Christ and of sacred sites, esp. the Holy Sepulcher at Jerusalem; ~ **name**, name of Jesus as object of formal devotion; ~ **orders**: see ORDER; **H~ Roman Empire**: see ROMAN; ~ **Rood**: see ROOD; **H~ Saturday**, Saturday before Easter; ~ **terror**, (slang) formidable person, embarrassing child; **H~ Thursday**, Thursday in Holy Week; (in the Anglican Ch.) Ascension Day; ~ **water**, water dedicated to holy uses and used for ritual purification; water blessed by priest and used in various rites and devotional acts; **H~ Week**, week preceding Easter Sunday; **H~ Writ**: see WRIT [1]. **holy** n. (pl. **-lies**). ~ **of holies**, inner chamber of sanctuary in Jewish temple; innermost shrine.

hom·age (hŏm'ĭj, ŏm'-) n. (in feudal law) Formal and public acknowledgment of allegiance to feudal superior; acknowledgment of superiority; dutiful reverence, respect.

hom·burg (hŏm'berg) n. Man's soft felt hat with slightly curved brim and crown indented lengthwise. [Homburg, town in W. Germany, where first manufactured]

home (hōm) n. 1. Dwelling place, fixed residence of family or household; members of family collectively; private house; ~ **away from** ~, place providing homelike amenities. 2. Native land; place where thing is native or most common. 3. Institution of refuge or rest for destitute or infirm persons. 4. (in games) Goal; (baseball) home plate. 5. **at** ~, in one's own house; at one's ease; familiar with, in (subject etc.); accessible to callers. **home** adj. Of, connected with, home; carried on at home; proceeding from home; in the neighborhood of home; played etc. on team's own ground; carried on, produced, in one's own country; treating of domestic affairs; **home'body**, person who likes to stay at home; **home-brewed**, (beer etc.) brewed at home; **home'-**

Honduras, *a republic in Central America, has an area of 43,227 sq. miles, and a population of 2,930,000. Most of its people are of mixed Indian-European origin. The capital is Tegucigalpa (below right). The principal exports are bananas, coffee, timber and silver.*

coming, arrival at home; **home economics,** science and art of household management, including budgeting, nutrition, child care, cooking, etc.; **home′grown,** grown or produced at home; **home guard,** volunteer armed force of civilians who protect their country while the regular army is fighting in the field; **home′land,** native land; mother country; **home′-made′,** made at home or by oneself; **home′maker,** person who manages household affairs; **home plate,** base at which baseball batter stands, and that must be crossed by runner to score a run; **home′-room,** room in school where a class meets daily to be checked for absences, receive special announcements, etc.; **home rule,** government of country, colony, etc. by its own citizens; **home run,** (baseball) hit that allows batter to circle bases and score a run; **home run ball,** pitch easy to hit for a home run; **home′sick,** depressed by absence from home, longing for home; **home′spun,** (plain coarse woolen cloth) spun at home; (anything) plain, homely; **home′stretch,** straight part of racetrack between final bend and finish line; **home′-work,** office work, piecework, etc. done at home; esp. lessons and exercises to be done by schoolchild at home. **home** *adv.* To one's home or country, as **come, go,** ~ ; arrived at home; to the point aimed at, as **that hits** ~. **home′less, home′like** *adjs.* **home** *v.* (**homed, hom·ing**). 1. Go home (esp. of pigeons); (of aircraft etc.) proceed under guidance of radio signal etc. 2. Bring or send home; bring in (aircraft etc.) under guidance of radio signal etc.

home·ly (hōm′lē) *adj.* (**-li·er, -li·est**). Simple, plain; primitive; unpretending; (of persons or features) uncomely, plain. **home′-li·ness** *n.*

ho·me·op·a·thy (hōmēŏp′athē) *n.* System (founded *c*1796 by Samuel Hahnemann of Leipzig) of treatment of disease by drugs (usu. in minute doses) that in a healthy person would produce symptoms like those of the disease. **ho·me·-o·path** (hō′mēopăth) *n.* **ho·me·o·path·ic** (hōmēopăth′ĭk) *adj.*

ho·me·o·sta·sis (hōmēostā′sĭs) *n.* Tendency toward relatively stable equilibrium between interdependent elements, esp. as maintained by physiological processes. **ho·me·o·stat·ic** (hōmēostăt′ĭk) *adj.*

Ho·mer[1] (hō′mer). Greek epic poet, of uncertain birthplace and date; traditionally believed to be the author of the *Iliad* and the *Odyssey*. **Ho·mer·ic** (hōmĕr′ĭk) *adj.* Of, in the style of, Homer or the poems attributed to him, or the legends and age of which he wrote; heroic, epic.

Ho·mer[2] (hō′mer), **Winslow** (1836–1910). Amer. painter and illustrator noted for realistic portrayals of outdoor life and sea-scapes.

hom·er[1] (hō′mer) *n.* Homi. pigeon.

ho·mer[2] (hō′mer) *n.* Ancie. Hebrew measure of capacity, co. taining 10 ephahs (prob. *c* 10 11 bushels dry measure or 80 100 gallons liquid measure). [He *kōmer* heap]

ho·mer[3] (hō′mer) *n.* HOME ru. **home·stead** (hōm′stĕd) House with outbuildings; far. land claimed by a settler or squatt.

esp. lot of 160 acres granted to
settlers by **Homestead Act** of
Congress, 1862. **homestead** v.
settle and farm a homestead.
home'stead·er n.

home·ward (hōm'wĕrd) adv. &
adj. (Going, leading) toward home;
~ **bound**, (esp. of ship) preparing
to go, on the way, home. **home'-
wards** adv.

home·y, hom·y (hō'mē) adjs.
hom·i·er, hom·i·est). Suggesting home, homelike.

hom·i·cide (hŏm'ĭsīd, hō'mĭ-) n.
1. One who kills a human being.
2. Killing of one human being by
another; MANSLAUGHTER; MURDER;
justifiable ~, killing of a person
where no blame attaches to the
killer. **hom·i·ci·dal** (hŏmĭsī'dal,
hōmĭ-) adj. Having a tendency to
homicide; murderous.

hom·i·let·ics (hŏmĭlĕt'ĭks) n.
Art of preaching. **hom·i·let'ic** adj.
hom·i·ly (hŏm'ĭlē) n. (pl. **-lies**).
Sermon; tedious moralizing discourse.

hom·ing (hō'mĭng) adj. Returning home; ~ **pigeon**: see PIGEON.
hom·i·nid (hŏm'ĭnĭd) n. & adj.
(Member) of the human zoological
family including existing and fossil
man.

hom·i·ny (hŏm'ĭnē) n. (also ~
grits) Hulled and dried kernels
of corn boiled with water or
milk.

Ho·mo (hō'mō) n. Genus of
primates of the family Hominidae,
consisting of mankind now usu.
regarded as a single species, ~
sapiens. [L. homo man, sapiens
wise]

ho·mo (hō'mō) n. (pl. **-mos**).
(slang) Homosexual.

homo- prefix. Same. [Gk.
homos]

ho·mo·cen·tric (hōmōsĕn'trĭk)
adj. Having same center.

ho·mo·ge·ne·ous (hōmōjē'nēus,
-jēn'yus, hŏmō-) adj. Of the same
kind; consisting of parts all of the
same kind, uniform. **ho·mo·ge'-
ne·ous·ly** adv. **ho·mo·ge·ne·i·ty**
(hōmōjenē'ĭtē, hŏmō-), **ho·mo·-
ge'ne·ous·ness** ns.

ho·mo·ge·net·ic (hōmōjenĕt'ĭk,
hŏmō-) adj. Having common
descent or origin.

ho·mog·e·nize (homŏj'enīz) v.t.
(**-nized, -niz·ing**). Treat (milk)
so that fat globules emulsify and
cream does not separate; make
homogeneous.

hom·o·graph (hŏm'ōgrăf,
-grahf) n. Word spelled like
another, but of different meaning
or origin. **hom·o·graph·ic** (hŏmō-
grăf'ĭk) adj.

ho·mol·o·gous (homŏl'ogus)
adj. Having the relation or relative position; corresponding; (biol.,
of limb or organ) similar in position and structure but not necessarily in function (cf. ANALOGOUS).

Homer is the name given to the
author/s of the Greek epic poems, the
'Iliad' and 'Odyssey'. They are believed
to be compilations of earlier oral stories
and were written about 850 B.C.

hom·o·logue, hom·o·log (hŏm'ō-
lawg, -lŏg) ns. Homologous thing.
hom·o·nym (hŏm'ōnĭm) n.
Word of same form as another but
different sense, as *pale* "stake" and
pale "wan"; namesake. **hom·o·-
nym·ic** (hŏmōnĭm'ĭk), **hom·on·y·-
mous** (homŏn'imus) adjs.

Honesty is widely grown for its oval
satin-white seed pods which are used
in many flower arrangements. The best
known species is also known as
moonflower, money or satin flower.

ho·mo·phile (hō'mofīl) n.
Homosexual. ~ adj. Advocating
equal employment opportunities
and other rights of homophiles.
hom·o·phone (hŏm'ofōn) n.
Word having same sound as
another, but of different spelling,
meaning, and origin, as *sew* and *sow*.
hom·o·phon·ic adj. Of same
sound; (mus.) of same pitch, in
unison; having one part or melody
predominating. **hom·o·phon·y** n.
ho·mo·sex·u·al (hōmosĕk'-
shōōal) adj. Sexually attracted only
to members of the same sex; of
those who are so attracted. ~ n.
Homosexual person. **ho·mo·-
sex·u·al·i·ty** (hōmosĕkshōōăl'ĭtē)
n.
ho·mo·zy·gote (hōmozī'gōt) n.
Zygote of like gametes. **ho·mo·-
zy'gous** adj.
ho·mun·cu·lus (hōmŭng'kyu-
lus) n. (pl. **-li** pr. **-lī**). Little
man, manikin.
hom·y: var. HOMEY.
Hon., hon. abbrevs. Honorary;
Honorable.
Ho·nan (hō'năn'). Province of
central China. ~ adj. Of Honan,
esp. its spicy cuisine.
hon·cho (hŏn'chō) n. (pl. **-chos**).
(slang) Leader, boss.
Hon·du·ras (hŏndoor'as,
-dūr'-). Republic of Central Amer.
with a seaboard on the Caribbean,
formerly (until 1821) part of the
Spanish American dominions;
capital, Tegucigalpa; **British** ~,
former name of Belize; **Gulf of** ~,
inlet of the Caribbean bounded by
Belize, Guatemala, and Honduras.
Hon·du'ran adj. & n.
hone (hōn) n. Whetstone, esp.
for razors etc.; any of various stones
as material for this. ~ v.t.
(**honed, hon·ing**). Sharpen on
hone.
hon·est (ŏn'ĭst) adj. Fair and
upright in speech and act, not lying,
cheating, or stealing; sincere; good,
worthy; (of act etc.) showing uprightness; (of gain etc.) earned by
fair means; (of things) unadul-
terated, genuine; (archaic, of
woman) chaste, virtuous; ~
broker, mediator in international,
industrial, etc., disputes; **make an
~ woman of**, marry (seduced
woman); ~ **Injun**: see INJUN.
hon'est·ly adv.
hon·es·ty (ŏn'ĭstē) n. (pl. **-ties**).
1. Uprightness, truthfulness. 2.
Cruciferous plant (*Lunaria annua*)
with large purple (or white) flowers
and flat round semitransparent
fruits.
hon·ey (hŭn'ē) n. (pl. **-eys**).
Sweet viscid yellow fluid, nectar of
flowers collected and worked up for
food by bees and other insects;
(fig.) sweetness; (colloq.) sweet one,
sweetheart, darling; **hon'eybee**,
bee that gathers and stores honey,
esp. the common bee (*Apis melli-*

fera); **hon′eydew**, sweet sticky substance, secreted by aphides, found on leaves and stems; (also **honeydew melon**) melon, variety of *Cucumis melo*, having pale green flesh and a smooth rind; **hon′ey-suckle**, any of various vines or shrubs of the genus *Lonicera*, having fragrant yellowish, white, or pink trumpet-shaped flowers, frequent in woods; other plants of this genus. **hon′eyed** *adj*.

hon·ey·comb (hŭn′ēkōm) *n*. Beeswax structure of hexagonal cells for honey and eggs; any structure, ornament, etc. resembling this. ~ *v.t.* Fill with cavities; mark with honeycomb pattern.

hon·ey·moon (hŭn′ēmōōn) *n*. Holiday or trip taken by newly married couple. ~ *v.i.* Spend honeymoon (*in*, *at*, place). **hon′ey·moon·er** *n*.

Hong Kong (hŏng′ kŏng′). British Crown Colony, consisting of a number of islands and a part of the mainland, situated off the SE. coast of China; first occupied by Gt. Britain 1841 and formally ceded by Treaty of Nanking, 1842; capital, Victoria, is situated on the 32-sq. mi. island of Hong Kong.

honk (hŏngk, hawngk) *n*. Wild goose's cry; sound of automobile etc. horn. ~ *v.i.* Emit or give honk.

*Honey was long used as a sweetener, especially in places where sugar-beet or sugar-cane did not grow. The bees gather nectar from flowers and store it in a **honeycomb**, which is also used to hatch the eggs of the queen-bee.*

hon·ky, hon·key, hon·kie (hŏng′kē, hawng′-) *ns*. (pl. **-kies**). (slang) White person; used derog., esp. by blacks.

honk·y-tonk (hŏng′kē tŏngk, hawng′kē tawngk) *n*. (slang) Cheap, noisy nightclub, barroom, dance hall, etc.

Hon·o·lu·lu (hŏnolōō′lōō). Capital and principal port of HAWAII, on the S. coast of Oahu.

hon·or, Brit. **hon·our** (ŏn′er) *ns*. 1. High respect; glory; reputation, good name. 2. Nobleness of mind; allegiance to what is right or to approved standard of conduct; (of woman) chastity, reputation for this. 3. Exalted position; (with possessive) title for holder of certain offices. 4. Person, thing, that reflects honor on (*to*) another; thing conferred or done as token of respect or distinction; position or title of rank, dignity; (sports, games) right of taking first turn, beginning, etc., as having won previous game, having better record, etc.; (pl.) civilities rendered to guests etc. (**do the** ~**s**);

military ~**s**, marks of respect pa by troops at burial of office statesmen, royalty, etc.; ~**s of wa** privileges granted to capitulati force, as that of marching out wi colors flying etc. 5. (pl., in brid and certain other card games) A king, queen, jack, and sometim 10, of trumps or of all suits. (pl.) Special distinction for pr ficiency beyond that required receive an academic degree; pr gram or course of higher specialized studies for exceptio students. 7. **code of** ~, ru forming conventional or perso standard of conduct; **in** ~ **of**, celebration of; **in** ~ **bound**, bou as a moral duty (*to* do); **be on one** ~, be under moral obligatio **upon my** ~, (colloq.) ~ **brigh** forms of earnest declarati **honor** *v.t.* Respect highly; conf dignity upon; (commerc.) accep pay (bill) when due.

hon·or·a·ble, Brit. **hon·our·a·ble** (ŏn′erabel) *adjs*. 1. Wortl of honor; bringing honor to i possessor; consistent with hono upright. 2. **H**~, (abbrev. Ho title of younger sons of earls ar children of British viscounts ar barons; title of certain officials, ii cluding judges and legislator **Right** ~, title of British pee below rank of marquis, and othe 3. (parl., in conventional use) Tit of members of the British House Commons. **hon·or·a·bly**, Br **hon·our·a·bly** *advs*.

Honeysuckle grows in tempera regions of both hemispheres and also the Himalayas, South Asia and Nor Africa. It has fragrant flowers and is al known as woodbine.

ong Kong has a population of 250,000 people, and most speak the antonese dialect of Chinese. Victoria, e capital (above), has one of the finest tural harbors and is the world's rgest entrepôt port. Right: Map of ng Kong.

hon·o·rar·i·um (ŏnorār'ēum) *n.* l. **-rar·i·ums, -rar·i·a** pr. -ār'ēa). Gift of money in return r voluntary services; payment in eu of fixed fee for professional rvices etc.

hon·or·ar·y (ŏn'orĕrē) *adj.* Con-rred as an honor (without the sual requirements, adjuncts, etc.); olding honorary title or position ithout pay; (of obligations) de-ending on honor, not legally nforceable.

hon·or·if·ic (ŏnorĭf'ĭk) *adj. & n.* Expression) implying respect.

Hon·shu (hŏn'shoo). Island of apan in the Pacific off the E. coast f Asia; largest of Japan's main lands, 88,925 sq. mi. (230,316 sq. m.)

hooch (hooch) *n.* (slang) Alco-olic liquor, esp. inferior or bootleg quor. [abbreviation of Alaskan *Hoochinoo*, a tribe that made a istilled liquor]

hood[1] (hood) *n.* Covering for ead and neck, whether part of loak etc. or separate; leather overing for hawk's head; thing like ood in shape or use, as a carriage

top, the cover for a stove or hearth, etc.; hinged covering over the front of a motor vehicle, covering the engine; ornamental draping of cloth hung from the shoulders of an ecclesiastical, academic, or other robe. ~ *v.t.* Cover with hood. **hood'ed** *adj.*

hood[2] (hood) *n.* (slang) Hoodlum.

Hood (hood), **Mount.** Moun-tain and highest peak, 11,235 ft.

(3,424 m), in NW. Oregon in the Cascade Range.

-hood *suffix.* Having a specified state, condition, or quality (*child-hood, falsehood*).

hood·lum (hood'lum, hood'-) *n.* Hooligan, thug.

hoo·doo (hoo'doo) *n.* Voodoo; bad luck; person or thing bringing bad luck. ~ *v.t.* Bring bad luck to. [Alteration of VOODOO]

hood·wink (hood'wĭngk) *v.t.*

Deceive, humbug; (archaic) blind-fold.

hoo·ey (hoō'ē) *n.* (slang) Non-sense, humbug.

hoof (hoof, hoof) *n.* (pl. **hoofs, hooves**, pr. hoovz, hoovz). Horny casing of foot of ruminants, horses, swine, and allied animals, anatomically a development of the toenail; **cloven ~**: see CLOVEN; **~-and-mouth disease**: see FOOT-and-mouth disease. **hoof** *v.* Strike with hoof; (slang) go on foot; walk; (slang) dance, esp. perform on stage as a dancer. **hoof'er** *n.* (esp.) Dancer, as a professional tap-dancer etc.

hook (hook) *n.* Piece of metal or other material bent back or having sharp angle, for catching hold or for hanging things upon; bent piece of wire, usu. barbed, for catching fish; leftward hooked stroke in golf; (boxing) short swinging blow with elbow bent and rigid; sharp bend, e.g. in river; curved projecting point of land; **~ and eye**, small metal hook and loop as fastening; **by ~ or (by) crook**, by fair means or foul; **off the ~**, no longer in difficulty; (of telephone receiver) not on its rest, thus preventing incoming calls; **on one's own ~**, (colloq.) on one's own account; **~-nose(d)**, (having) aquiline nose; **hook'up**, interconnection of broadcasting stations for special transmissions; **hook'worm**, any of various nematode worms infesting man and some animals, with hook-like mouthparts; disease caused by these. **hook** *v.* Grasp with hook; secure with hook(s); attach with hook (*on, up*, etc.); catch (fish) with hook; (golf) drive (ball) widely to left or (in the case of a left-handed player) to the right; **hook'up (with)**, fasten, connect, etc., (as) with hook. **hooked'** *adj.* Hook-shaped; having, made with, hook(s); **~ on**, (slang) addicted to.

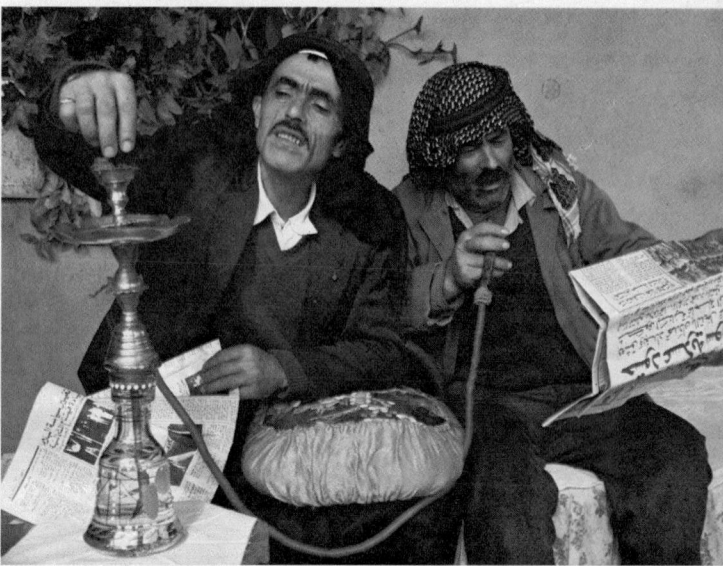

The **hookah** is widely used in the Middle East. The smoke is cooled by being drawn through water, which is often scented. The pipe is passed from person to person.

hook·ah (hook'a) *n.* Oriental smoking pipe with long flexible tube, smoke being drawn through water in vase to which tube and bowl are attached. [Arab. *ḥukka* casket, hookah bottle]

Hooke (hook), **Robert** (1635–1703). English mathematician, physicist, and philosopher.

hook·er[1] (hook'er) *n.* Two-masted Dutch coasting or fishing vessel; one-masted fishing smack.

hook·er[2] (hook'er) *n.* (sla Prostitute.

hook·y (hook'ē) *n.* (colle Truancy from school; **play ~**, p truant.

hoo·li·gan (hoo'ligan) *n.* Yo rowdy; member of street ga **hoo'li·gan·ism** *n.*

hoop[1] (hoop) *n.* Circular banc metal, wood, etc., esp. for bind staves of casks; wooden or i circle trundled along by child; ci of lightweight material expanding woman's hoop sk circle, ring, arc; one of iron arc through which balls must be dri in croquet; **~ skirt**, long full sk flared out into a bell shape b series of connected hoops. **ho** *v.t.* Bind with hoops; surround hoop does.

hoop[2] (hoop) *v.i. & n.* Whoo **hoop·la** (hoop'lah) *n.* (collo 1. Bustling activity or commoti 2. Overblown speech or writi usu. intended to confuse or conceal truth.

hoo·poe (hoo'poo) *n.* Bird, e S. European *Upupa epops*, w conspicuous variegated pluma and large erectile crest.

hoo·ray: see HURRAH.

hoose·gow, hoos·gow (hoo gow) *ns.* (slang) Jail. [Span. Am *juzgao* tribunal, f. L. *judicat* judged]

Hoo·sier (hoo'zher) *n.* (Ni name for) native or inhabitant Indiana.

hoot (hoot) *v.* Make lc sounds, esp. of disapproval (assail (person etc.) with deris shouts; drive (person) *out, off*, e by hooting; (of owl) utter charact istic cry; sound automobile ho train whistle, etc.; (of horn et sound. **~** *n.* Inarticulate sho esp. of derision or disapprobati owl's cry; **don't give, care a** (slang) don't care at all; **not wor a ~**, worthless. **hoot'er** *n.*

The **hoopoe** is so called because of its cry. It is a little larger than a thrush and is found over most of Asia and central and southern Europe. It migrates in winter to Africa and India.

*The **hop** (above), a perennial herbaceous climbing plant used for flavoring beer and ale. **Herbert Hoover** (right): The humanitarian image of him that was widespread during 1914–18 war was tarnished in the Great Depression.*

hoot·en·an·ny (hōō'tenănē, ōot'nănē) *n.* (pl. **-nies**). Gathering of folk singers for public entertainment.

Hoo·ver[1] (hōō'ver), **Herbert Clark** (1874–1964). Amer. mining engineer, businessman, and 31st U.S. president, 1929–33; chairman of the Amer. Relief Committee, 1914–5, and Commission for Relief in Belgium, 1915–9; secretary of commerce, 1921–8; his administration was blamed by many for the Great Depression.

Hoo·ver[2] (hōō'ver) **Dam** (formerly **Boulder Dam**). Dam located on the Colorado River on the border of NW. Arizona and SE. Nevada and forming Lake Mead.

hop[1] (hŏp) *n.* Ripened cones of female hop plant, used for giving bitter flavor to beer etc. (usu. pl.); climbing perennial plant (*Humulus lupulus*) with rough lobed leaves, cultivated for green cones of broad scales borne by female; **hop'head**, (slang) drug addict. **hop** *v.* (**hopped, hop·ping**). Flavor with hops; gather hops; ~ **up**, (slang) stimulate with or as with drugs.

hop[2] (hŏp) *v.* (**hopped, hop·ing**). Spring (of person) on one foot or skip or bound on two feet; (of birds and animals) bound with both or all feet at once; hop over (ditch etc.); (of aircraft) pass low over physical features in a series of movements resembling hops, hence, **hedge-hopping**; jump on to (train etc.); ~**-o'-my-thumb**, dwarf, tiny person; **hop'scotch**, child's game in which players toss a pebble into a section of diagram marked on ground, then hop through all sections of the diagram and retrieve the pebble. **hop** *n.* Hopping; spring; (colloq.) dance, esp. a student dance; distance traversed, esp. in aircraft, at one stretch, one stage of long journey,

esp. by plane; ~ **skip** (or **step**), **and jump**, exercise consisting of these three movements in sequence; (fig.) short distance.

hope (hōp) *n.* Expectation and desire combined (*of, that*); ground of hope, probability; person, thing, that hope centers on; ~ **against** ~, cling to the slightest hope. **hope** *v.* (**hoped, hop·ing**). Look with expectation and desire (*for*); expect and desire.

hope·ful (hōp'ful) *adj.* Feeling hope; inspiring hope, promising. ~ *n.* Promising or aspiring person. **hope'ful·ly** *adv.* With hope; (colloq.) it is to be hoped, let us hope. **hope'ful·ness** *n.*

Hop·ei (haw'pā'), **Heb·ei** (hŏ'bā'). Province of E. China; capital Tientsin.

hope·less (hōp'lĭs) *adj.* Feeling no hope; admitting no hope; impossible; incurable. **hope'less·ly** *adv.* **hope'less·ness** *n.*

Ho·pi (hŏ'pē) *n.* (pl. **-pis**, collect. **-pi**). (Member of) a Pueblo Indian tribe now inhabiting a reservation in NE. Arizona; the Uto-Aztecan language of this tribe.

Hop·kins[1] (hŏp'kĭnz), **Gerard Manley** (1844–89). English poet and Jesuit priest; he is known for his use of internal rhyme and elliptical phrasing, and as the inventor of sprung rhythm.

Hop·kins[2] (hŏp'kĭnz), **Johns** (1795–1873). Amer. financier and philanthropist; founded university and hospital bearing his name, located in Baltimore, Maryland.

hop·per (hŏp'er) *n.* 1. One who hops; hopping insect. 2. Inverted pyramid or cone (orig. with

hopping or shaking motion) through which grain etc. passes in mill; similar contrivance in various machines etc.; barge carrying away mud etc. from dredging machine and discharging it through collapsible bottom; railroad freight car with similar device.

Hop·per (hŏp'er), **Edward** (1882–1967). Amer. painter.

hop·sack·ing (hŏp'săkĭng) *n.* (Coarse material of hemp and jute for making) sack in which hops are packed; woolen fabric of coarse weave with threads in pairs.

ho·ra (hōr'a, hôr'a) *n.* Traditional Israeli folk dance done in a circle; music for this dance.

Hor·ace (hōr'ĭs, hâr'-). Quintus Horatius Flaccus (65–8 B.C.), Roman poet; his work includes the *Satires, Odes, Epodes, Epistles*, and *Ars Poetica*. **Ho·ra·tian** (hōrā'shan) *adj.*

ho·ra·ry (hōr'arē, hôr'-) *adj.* Of the hours; occurring every hour; lasting an hour.

Ho·ra·tius (hōrā'shus). Publius Horatius Cocles, legendary Roman hero famous for defending bridge over Tiber against the Etruscans.

horde (hōrd, hôrd) *n.* Tribe of Tartar or kindred Asiatic nomads, dwelling in tents or wagons and migrating for pasturage or for war or plunder; throng; swarm; gang, troop (usu. contempt.); **Golden H** ~: see GOLDEN. [Turki *ordi, ordu* camp]

hore·hound, hoar·hound (hōr'hownd, hôr'-) *ns.* Labiate herb (*Marrubium vulgare*) with stem and leaves covered with white cottony pubescence, and aromatic bitter juice used as remedy for coughs and as a flavoring; hard candy made of this; allied herb.

ho·ri·zon (horī'zon) *n.* 1. Line at which earth and sky appear to meet; (fig.) limit of mental perception, experience, interest, etc.; **apparent, visible** ~, circle of contact with Earth's surface of a cone whose vertex is the observer's eye; **celestial, true** ~, great circle of celestial sphere, plane of which passes through center of Earth and is parallel to that of sensible horizon of a plane. 2. (geol.) Stratum or set of strata characterized by particular features, as fossils etc.

hor·i·zon·tal (hŏrĭzŏn′tal, hăr-) *adj.* Of, at, the horizon; parallel to the plane of this, at right angles to the vertical; level, flat; (of machinery etc.) having its parts working in horizontal direction; (of manufacturers, corporations, etc.) engaged in a single stage of manufacture or distribution of a product (opp. VERTICAL). **hor·i·zon′tal·ly** *adv.* **horizontal** *n.* Horizontal line, plane, etc.

hor·mone (hŏr′mōn) *n.* (physiol.) Substance secreted by a ductless gland or formed in an organ (as insulin in the pancreas, sex hormone in testis and ovary) and carried by the bloodstream to a specific organ it stimulates; similar substance prepared synthetically. **hor·mo·nal** (hŏrmō′nal) *adj.*

horn (hŏrn) *n.* 1. Hard, permanent outgrowth, freq. one of a pair, often curved and pointed, consisting of epidermal sheath about a bony core, on head of cattle, sheep, goats, and other mammals; projection on head of other animals, e.g. tentacle of snail or slug, crest of feathers on horned owl's head etc.; **pull, draw, in one's** ~s,

restrain one's ardor, draw back; recant. 2. Substance of which horns consist, article made of this, as powder horn, drinking horn, etc.; ~ **of plenty**, cornucopia. 3. Wind instrument orig. made of horn and more or less resembling horn in shape; (esp.) modern brass instrument such as the trumpet and **French** ~, which has an 11-ft. tube coiled in a circle and a system of valves for producing intermediate notes; **basset** ~: see BASSET HORN; **English** ~, large oboe with lower pitch than standard oboe. 4. Funnel- or trumpet-shaped part of early record players etc. for amplifying sound by resonance. 5. Instrument for sounding warning signal. 6. Horn-shaped projection; extremity of moon or other crescent; arm, branch, of bay, river, etc; **on the** ~**s of a dilemma**, forced to choose between two equally distasteful alternatives. 7. **horn′beam**, any of several related trees and shrubs of the family Betulaceae, including Amer. hornbeam (*Carpinus caroliniana*), having smooth, gray bark and very hard, heavy wood, and hop hornbeam (*Ostrya virginiana*) of eastern N. Amer., having fruit that resembles hops; **horn′bill**, bird (of family Bucerotidae) with hornlike excrescence on bill; **horn-rimmed**, (of eyeglasses) rimmed

with horn or tortoise shell. **hor** *v.* Furnish with horns; go with the horns; ~ **in**, (slang intrude (*on*); **horned owl**: se GREAT HORNED OWL; **horned toa** lizard (*Phrynosoma*) of western N Amer. with hornlike projections o its head.

Horn (hŏrn), **Cape.** Headlar on an island of Tierra del Fueg southernmost point of S. Amer discovered by the Dutch navigato Schouten in 1616, and named aft Hoorn, his birthplace.

horn·blende (hŏrn′blĕnd) Dark brown, black, or greenish black mineral, constituent granite and many rocks, compose chiefly of silica, magnesia, and lim and occurring in numerov varieties.

hor·net (hŏr′nĭt) *n.* Large inse of wasp family (esp. Eur. *Vesp crabro* and Amer. *V. maculata* inflicting serious sting.

horn·pipe (hŏrn′pīp) *n.* (hist.) Wind instrument (said t have had bell and mouthpiece o horn). 2. Lively dance, usu. by on person, associated esp. with merry making of sailors; music for this.

horn·y (hŏr′nē) *adj.* (**horn·i·e horn·i·est**). Of, like, horn abounding in horns; hard as horn callous; (slang) sexually aroused **horn′i·ness** *n.*

hor·o·loge (hŏr′olōj, -lŏj, hăr′

*A pair of magnificent **horns** characteristic of the Highland bull (below left) raised on Bodmin moor, Cornwall, U.K. Below right: The trumpet-shaped horn used for amplifying sound in early*

gramophones was also used in som early radios. Facing page: Tibetan mus cal horns are blown to announce th arrival of the new year in Katmandu.

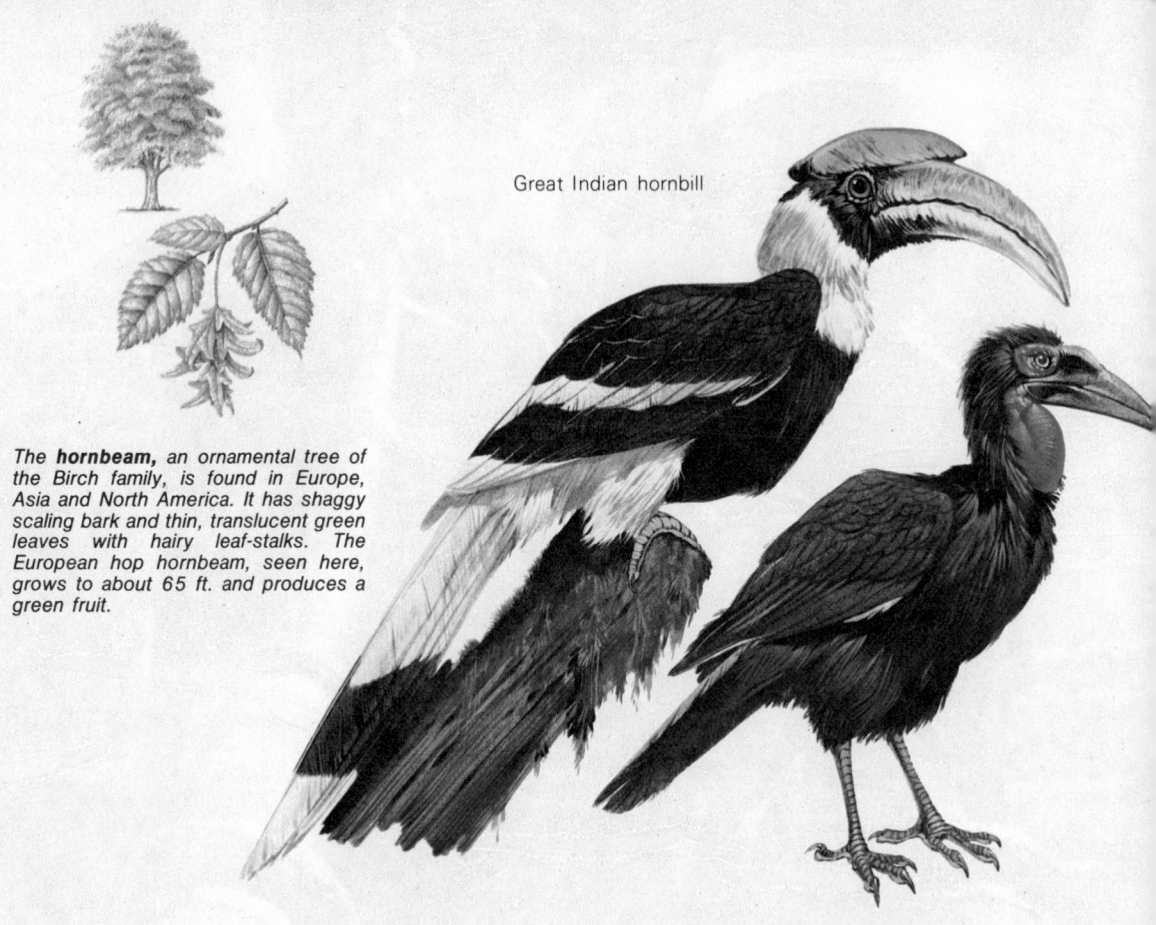

Great Indian hornbill

African Ground hornbill

The **hornbeam,** an ornamental tree of the Birch family, is found in Europe, Asia and North America. It has shaggy scaling bark and thin, translucent green leaves with hairy leaf-stalks. The European hop hornbeam, seen here, grows to about 65 ft. and produces a green fruit.

The **hornbill** is a tropical bird, conspicuous for its fantastic beak. Most species are forest animals living in trees. The great Indian hornbill measures about 5 ft. in length; the African ground species live mainly on open plains.

n. Timepiece, dial, clock. **ho·rol·-o·ger** (horŏl´ojer), **ho·rol´o·gist** *ns.* **ho·rol´o·gy** *n.* Art of measuring time or making clocks. **hor·o·log´-i·cal** *adj.*

hor·o·scope (hŏr´oskōp, hār´-) *n.* 1. (astrol.) Observation of sky and planets at certain moments, esp. at person's birth, supposed to reveal influence on destiny; zodiacal plan showing disposition of heavens at particular moment. 2. Prediction based on such observation or plan. **hor·o·scop·ic** (hŏr´oskŏp´ĭk, -skō´pĭk, hār-) *adj.* **ho·ros·co·py** (horŏs´kopē) *n.*

hor·ri·ble (hŏr´ĭbel, hār´-) *adj.* Exciting, fit to excite, horror; hideous, shocking; unpleasant; offensive. **hor´ri·ble·ness** *n.* **hor´ri·bly** *adv.*

hor·rid (hŏr´ĭd, hār´-) *adj.* Terrible, frightful; (poet., archaic) rough, bristling; unpleasant, very bad, objectionable. **hor´rid·ly** *adv.* **hor´rid·ness** *n.*

hor·ri·fy (hŏr´ĭfī, hār´-) *v.t.* (**-fied, -fy·ing**). Excite horror in; shock; scandalize. **hor·rif·ic** (horĭf´ĭk) *adj.*

hor·ror (hŏr´er, hār´-) *n.* Terrified shuddering; terror, fear; intense dislike (*of*); horrifying thing; **the ~s,** fit of horror or depression, esp. as in delirium tremens; **~-struck, -stricken,**

shocked, horrified.

hors de com·bat (ōr de kawṅbah´). Out of the fight.

hors d'oeu·vre (ōr dērv´; *Fr.* ōr dö´vrɛ) (pl. **hors d'oeu·vres** pr. ōr dērvz´; *Fr.* ōr dö´vrɛ). Canapé or appetizer served with cocktails or before a meal. [*Fr.*]

horse (hōrs) *n.* (pl. **hors·es,** collect. **horse**). 1. Solid-hoofed quadruped (*Equus cabullus*) with flowing mane and tail, used as beast of burden, as draft animal, and for riding on; (esp.) adult male horse; (collect. sing.) cavalry; **hold one's ~s,** (slang) check one's impatience; **~ of a different color,** completely different thing; **on one's high ~,** putting on airs; behaving arrogantly; **on horse´back,** mounted on a horse; **straight from the horse's mouth,** (of information) from authoritative source, esp. from person concerned. 2. Uphol-

stered vaulting block in gym nasium; frame, often with legs, o which something is supported, a **clothes´horse;** (mining) obstruc tion in vein. 3. **horse chestnu** large ornamental tree (*Aescul hippocastanum*), native to Albani Greece, and Iran, with larg digitate leaves, upright conica clusters of showy flowers, and fru consisting of soft thick prickly hu enclosing one or two large har smooth shining brown seeds o bitter taste; nut of this; **horse´ feathers,** (slang) something utterl insignificant; **horse´flesh,** flesh o horse, esp. as food; horses collec tively, esp. racing or riding horses **horse´fly,** any of various large flie of the family Tabanidae, the fema of which sucks the blood of certai mammals; (fig.) any large variety o fly; **horse´hair,** hair from mane o tail of horse, esp. as used i upholstery; **horse´hide,** hide of horse, leather made from thi **horse latitudes,** belt of calms at N and S. edges of trade winds **horse´laugh,** loud coarse laugh **horse´leech,** large European leec (*Haemopsis sanguisuga*); **hors mackerel,** any of various fishe allied to mackerel, esp. the bluefi tuna (*Thunnus thynnus*); **horse´**

an, **horse'woman**, (skilled) ...der on horseback; horse breeder ...trainer; owner of racing stable; ...rse'manship, art of riding, skill ... riding, on horseback; **horse** ...era, (slang) motion picture or ...ay with a western U.S. setting and ...aling with cowboys, Indians, ...nd claim fights, cattle rustling, ...c.; **horse'play**, rough or boister-...s play; **horse'power**, (abbrev. ...p.) unit of power of 33,000 foot-...ounds per minute or 745.7 watts; ...rse race, race between horses ...ith riders); (fig.) contest between ...ually matched opponents; ...orse'radish, cruciferous plant ...(*Armoracia rusticana*) with white

flowers and broad rough leaves, whose pungent root is scraped or grated as condiment; **horse sense**, (colloq.) common sense; **horse'-shoe**, iron shoe for horse, usu. narrow iron plate bent to outline of horse's hoof; thing of this shape; (pl.) game in which horseshoes are tossed at a stake, the player encircling the stake most often with a shoe or coming closest to it being the winner; **horseshoe crab**, any of various horseshoe-shaped marine animals of eastern N. Amer., esp of the genus *Limulus*, having a long, stiff tail; **horse'tail**, tail of horse (formerly used in Turkey as standard, or as ensign

denoting rank of pasha); cryptog-amous plant (*Equisetum*) with hollow jointed stem and whorls of slender branches at joints; **horse'-whip**, whip for horse; (*v.t.*) chastise (person) with this; **horse'woman**: see horseman above. **horse** *v.* (**horsed, hors·ing**). Provide (person, vehicle) with horse(s); mount, ride a horse; (slang) ~ **around**, indulge in horseplay.

hors·y, hors·ey (hōr'sē) *adjs.* (**hors·i·er, hors·i·est**). Concerned with, addicted to, horse, horse-racing, or horseback riding.

hor·ta·tive (hōr'tătĭv), **hor·ta·to·ry** (hōr'tătōrē, -tōrē) *adjs.* Tending, serving, to exhort.

The **horse** has been domesticated since prehistoric times, and has been used as a beast of burden, a draught animal and for riding. Above left: A dapple-grey horse. Above right: The parts of a horse. Below, left to right: Przewalski and Tarpan, earliest surviving forms of horse; and the Shire horse.

hor·ti·cul·ture (hōr´tĭkŭlcher) *n.* Art of plant and garden cultivation. **hor·ti·cul·tur·al** (hōrtĭkŭl´cheral) *adj.* **hor·ti·cul·tur·ist** *n.*

Ho·rus (hōr´us, hôr´-). (Egyptian myth.) God of light, represented with hawk's head.

Hos. *abbrev.* Hosea (Old Testament).

ho·san·na (hōzăn´a) *n.* (pl. **-nas**). Cry of *hosanna*, shout of adoration. [Heb. *hosha‘na*, for *hoshi‘ahnna* save, pray!]

hose (hōz) *n.* 1. (pl. **hose**) Stockings; socks; (obs.) breeches (esp. in **doublet and** ~). 2. (pl. **hos·es**) Flexible tube for conveying liquid for watering plants, putting out fires, etc. **hose** *v.t.* (**hosed, hos·ing**). Drench or water with hose.

Ho·se·a (hōzē´a) (8th c. B.C.). Hebrew minor prophet; book of Old Testament containing his prophecies.

ho·sier (hō´zher) *n.* Dealer in hose and knitted or woven underwear. **ho´sier·y** *n.* (esp.) Stockings and socks.

hos·pice (hŏs´pĭs) *n.* House of rest for travelers, esp. one kept by religious order; home for the destitute or sick, esp. terminally ill.

hos·pi·ta·ble (hŏs´pĭtabel, hŏs-pĭt´a-) *adj.* Giving, disposed to give, welcome and entertainment to strangers or guests. **hos´pi·ta·bly** *adv.*

hos·pi·tal (hŏs´pĭtal) *n.* Institution for care of the sick or wounded; ~ **ship, train**, one equipped for transporting the sick or wounded.

hos·pi·tal·i·ty (hŏspĭtăl´ĭtē) *n.* (pl. **-ties**). Friendly and liberal reception of guests or strangers.

hos·pi·tal·ize (hŏs´pĭtalĭz) *v.t.* (**-ized, -iz·ing**). Put (sick or injured person) into a hospital.

host[1] (hōst) *n.* Large number (*of*); (archaic) army: **Lord (God) of** ~ **s**, frequent title of Jehovah in some Old Testament books.

host[2] (hōst) *n.* One who lodges

and entertains another in his house; landlord of inn; (biol.) animal, plant, sheltering parasite or other organism. ~ *v.t.* Act as host to (person) or at (event).

host[3] (hōst) *n.* (usu. cap.) Bread consecrated in the Eucharist.

hos·tage (hŏs´tĭj) *n.* Person handed over to enemies or allies as pledge for fulfillment of any undertaking or one seized by enemy, terrorist group, etc. to induce compliance with demands.

hos·tel (hŏs´tel) *n.* Inn (archaic); inexpensive lodging for youthful travelers or other special class, YOUTH hostel.

hos·tel·ry (hŏs´telrē) *n.* (pl. **-ries**). (archaic) Inn.

host·ess (hōs´tĭs) *n.* Woman who entertains guests; one who receives or assists clients or visitors.

hos·tile (hŏs´tĭl; *Brit.* hŏs´tīl)

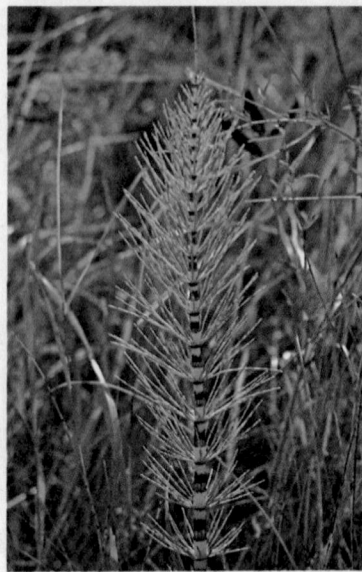

adj. Of an enemy; unfriendl opposed; ~ **witness**, one wh shows that he is hostile to the part calling him and is considered n to give his evidence fairly. **hostil** *n.* Hostile person, esp. N. Ame Indian of late 19th century resistin establishment of tribal reservation **hos´tile·ly** *adv.* **hos·til·i·ty** (hŏs tĭl´ĭtē) *n.* (pl. **-ties**). Enmity state of warfare; opposition; (pl acts of warfare; war.

hos·tler (hŏs´ler, ŏs´-) *n.* Perso who takes care of horses at a inn, stable, etc.; stableman.

hot (hŏt) *adj.* (**hot·ter, hot·test** 1. Of a high temperature; ver warm; communicating or feelin heat; producing the sensation heat; (of pepper etc.) pungen biting. 2. Ardent, passionate angry; (sexually excited) excitin (of dance music) performed wit vigor, virtuosity, and excitemen 3. (hunting, of scent) Strong; (fig of news etc.) fresh, recent; (slang, stolen items) recently stolen easily identifiable and so dangerou to possess. 4. ~ **air,** (slang) excite or boastful talk; **hot´bed,** bed earth heated by fermenting manure (fig.) place very favorable to growth *of* (vice, unpopular ideas, etc.); **hot blooded,** (fig.) ardent, passionate **hot´box,** bearing on an axle or shaf of a railroad car overheated by to much friction; **hot´cake(s),** pan-o griddlecakes, (**sell like hot cakes** be disposed of rapidly); **hot dog** frankfurter or frankfurter sand wich, usu. on a soft roll; (colloq. an exclamation of satisfaction o husiasm; **hot flash**, feeling of a ve of heat passing over the body, en experienced by women ortly before and during meno-use; **hot'foot**, insertion and hting of a match between the sole d upper of an unsuspecting rson's shoe as a practical joke; in t haste; **hot'head**, impetuous rson; **hot'house**, heated building th glass roof and sides for owing plants out of season or in lder climate; **hot line**, direct annel of telephone or teletype mmunication for use by heads of vernment in times of crisis or ergency, specif., the U.S.–.S.S.R. line established in 1963; t **plate**, heated metal plate, rtable heater, for cooking etc.; t **potato**, (colloq.) thing awk-ard to deal with; **hot-press**, press glazed boards and hot metal ates for smoothing paper or cloth; .t.) press (paper etc.) in this; t **rod**, (slang) automobile, often old one, whose engine has been odified to give extra power and eed; hence **hot-rodder**, one who ives such an automobile; **hot at**, (slang) electric chair, (fig.) nbarrassing or difficult situation; t'**shot**, (slang) person who is or

thinks he is very skillful, talented, important, etc.; **hot water**, (fig.) trouble, disgrace, scrape; **hot-water bottle**, bag (usu. rubber) for holding hot water to apply warmth esp. to the body. **hot'ly** *adv.* **hot'-ness** *n.* **hot** *adv.* Hotly, eagerly, angrily. ~ *v.t.* (colloq.) Heat, warm *up*.

hotch·potch: see HODGEPODGE.

ho·tel (hōtĕl') *n.* Commercial establishment providing lodging to the general public, esp. travelers and chiefly for short stays at daily rates.

Hot (hŏt) **Springs.** City and resort in W. central Arkansas, famous for its thermal mineral springs; located within **Hot Springs National Park.**

Hot·ten·tot (hŏt'entŏt) *n.* Member of short stocky people of SW. Africa, related to Bushmen; their language; ~ **fig**, fleshy-leaved South African plant, *Mesembryan-themum edule*, with edible pulpy

Houses in primitive societies make use of local, natural materials and are designed to suit not only the climate but also the community's social structure. These mud and straw-thatched houses are in Mali.

fruit. [Du., perh. = "stammerer"] **hound** (hownd) *n.* Dog for chase, esp. one hunting by scent, of various breeds, as **blood'hound, grey'hound**, etc.; (colloq.) any dog; (slang) enthusiast (in combination, as *photography hound, coffee hound*, etc.); **the hounds**, pack of foxhounds; **hound's-tooth check**, check pattern with reversed diagonal threads giving notched effect. **hound** *v.t.* Chase (as) with hound; urge (person) *on.*

hour (owr) *n.* 1. Twenty-fourth part of day, 60 minutes; appointed or customary time; occasion; time of occupation or duty; time of day; habitual time of getting up or going to bed. 2. Prayer or office to be said at one of seven stated times of day. 3. **hour'glass**, device for measuring intervals of time, consisting of wasp-waisted reversible glass with two bulbs containing sand that takes a definite time in passing from upper to lower bulb, now practically obsolete except for measuring time required to boil an egg; **hour hand**, hand on clock etc. showing hour.

hou·ri (hoor'ē, howr'ē) *n.* (pl. **-ris**). Nymph of Muslim paradise; voluptuously beautiful woman.

[Fr., f. Pers., f. Arab. *hūr* gazelle-like (in the eyes)]

hour·ly (owr′lē) *adj.* & *adv.* (Occurring, done, reckoned) every hour.

Hou·sa·ton·ic (hōōsatŏn′ĭk). River, 148 mi. (238 km), flowing from NW. Massachusetts through Connecticut into Long Island Sound.

house (hows) *n.* (pl. **hous·es** pr. how′zĭz). 1. Building for human habitation or (usu. with defining prefix) occupation; inn, tavern; building for keeping animals or goods; (place of abode of) religious fraternity; (esp. Brit.) college in university; (boys in) boardinghouse forming part of school; (building used by) legislative or deliberative assembly; (audience in) theater etc.; household; family, dynasty; mercantile firm; **the House**, (pol.) House of Representatives; **on the house**, given by the management, free. 2. (transf.) Habitation of any animal; shell of snail, tortoise, etc., in which the animal lives or into which it retires. 3. (astrol.) Twelfth part of heavens as divided by great circles through N. and S. points of horizon; sign of zodiac considered as seat of greatest influence of a particular planet. 4. **keep house**, maintain, manage affairs of, a household; **like a house on fire, afire**, vigorously, fast; **house of cards**, house built of playing cards; (fig.) insecure thing; **house of God**, church, place of worship; **house of ill fame, ill repute**, brothel; **house-to-house**, carried on by means of visits to every house in a neighborhood. 5. attrib. (of animals) Kept in, frequenting, infesting, the house. 6. **house arrest**, detention in one's house, not in prison; **house′boat**, barge-like boat fitted up for living in; **house′boy**, boy or man as servant in house; **house′breaker**, burglar; **house′breaking**, burglary; **house′broken**, (of pets) trained not to excrete indoors; **house′coat**, woman's garment worn indoors as dressing gown or instead of a dress; **house′fly**, common fly, *Musca domestica*, infesting houses; **house′keeper**, woman managing affairs of household; person in charge of house, hotel maids, linens, etc.; **house′keeping**, domestic economy; **house′leek**, succulent herb (*Sempervivum tectorum*) with pink flowers, thick stem, and dense rosette of leaves close to root, growing on walls and roofs; hen and chickens; **house′maid**, female servant serving as maid; **house-maid's knee**, inflammation of the bursa over the kneecap due to kneeling, as from washing floors; **house′-master**, master in charge of school boarding house; **house′mother**, woman in charge of a house, esp. of

The Navajo Indians built **houses** that belied their semi-nomadic existence. They are unusual in that, unlike the homes of most wandering people, they are quite strong and permanent. They are also adapted to the hot, dry climate.

home for orphaned etc. children; **house organ**, periodical or newsletter issued by company for employees or customers; **house party**, party of guests staying overnight or for several days; **house physician**, physician residing in hospital; **house sparrow**, small brown and gray bird (*Passer domesticus*), originally of Europe but introduced into Amer. and other parts of the world, where it readily adapted; English sparrow; **house surgeon**, surgeon residing in hospital; **house′top**, roof (esp. in **shout from the housetops**, give wide publicity to); **house′warm-ing**, party to celebrate moving into new house; **house′work**, domestic work. **house** (howz) *v.* (**housed, hous·ing**). 1. Lodge, shelter (person etc.), store (goods), in house or as house does. 2. Provide houses for (population).

house·hold (hows′hōld) *n.* Those who live under the same roof, as a family etc.; domestic establishment; royal household; ~ **gods**, (Rom. antiq.) lares and penates; ~ **word**, familiar saying or name. **house′holder** *n.* One who occupies house as his own dwelling (esp. formerly, one thus qualified for franchise); head of household.

house·wife (hows′wīf) *n.* (pl.

-wives pr. -wīvz). Mistress o[f] family; married woman who supervises a household. **house′wife·ly** *adv.* **house′wif·er·y** *n.* House-keeping; domestic economy.

hous·ing[1] (how′zĭng) *n.* (esp.) (Provision of) accommodation houses collectively; shelter, covering; socket, casing.

hous·ing[2] (how′zĭng) *n.* Horse'[s] or saddle's cloth covering for protection or ornament.

Hous·man (hows′man, howz′-). **A(lfred) E(dward)** (1859–1936). English classical scholar and lyric poet; author of "A Shropshire Lad" etc.

Hous·ton[1] (hūs′ton). Largest city of Texas, in the SE. part, connected with Gulf of Mexico by Houston Ship Channel; a leading oil and petrochemical center.

Hous·ton[2] (hūs′ton), **Sam(uel)** (1793–1863). Amer. soldier and statesman; commander in chief of Texan army in fight for independence from Mexico; defeated Santa Ana at San Jacinto, 1836; first president of Republic of Texas, 1836–8, and president again 1841–4; became senator and then governor after Texas was admitted to Union, but was deposed when he refused to support the Confederacy.

Hou·yhn·hnm (hōōĭn′ĭm, hwĭn′-, wĭn′-) *n.* One of the civilized talking horses in *Gulliver's Travels*, by Jonathan Swift. [imit. of horse's neigh]

hove: see HEAVE.

hov·el (hŭv′el, hŏv′-) *n.* Open shed, mean dwelling.

hov·er (hŭv′er, hŏv′-) *v.* (of

ird etc.) Hang in the air (over, about, spot); loiter about (person, lace). ~ n. Hovering, state of uspense.

hov·er·craft (hŭv´erkrăft, krahft) n. Vehicle that travels over nd or water on a cushion of com-ressed air provided by a down-vard blast.

how (how) adv. In what way; to vhat extent; (in indirect statement, net. for) that; (in relative clause) in vhatever way, as; ~ **do you do?**, what is your state of ealth? (freq. as form of greeting); ~ **come?**, (colloq.) why?; **here's**

~!, I drink to your good health; ~ **about?**, what about? how come?; ~ **now?**, (archaic) what is the meaning of this?; **that's a fine ~-d'ye'-do**, (colloq.) embarrass-ing situation; ~**'sthat?** what did you say?; can you explain?; **howev'er**, in whatever way; to whatever extent; nevertheless; (archaic) in any case; **howsoev'er**, in whatso-ever manner; to what extent soever; **how-to** (adj.), giving basic instruc-tion in carpentry, electrical wiring, plumbing, etc., and in handicrafts.

how·dah (how´da) n. Seat for two or more, usu. with canopy, on

elephant's back. [Arab. hawdaj litter]

Howe (how), **Elias** (1819–67). Amer. inventor of the sewing machine, etc.

Howe (how), **Julia Ward** (1819–1910). Editor, writer, and social reformer; wrote poem "The Battle Hymn of the Republic," 1862, later set to music; supported women's suffrage, prison reform, and inter-national peace.

How·ells (how´elz), **William Dean** (1837–1920). Amer. writer, editor, and critic; editor of the Atlantic Monthly, 1871–81; author

*This British **Hovercraft** Corporation SR-N4 (bottom) weighs over 160 tons and is in regular use on cross-Channel runs. Below: Four rear-mounted gas-turbine engines each drive one lift fan and one*

propeller which are geared together. Air is drawn in through intakes on the top decking and bleeds into the tubular skirt and fingers to form a stable air-cushion.

forward car ramp
flexible skirt
skirt fingers
forward passenger compartment
12-blade lift fan
air intakes
extension shaft from turbine
main bevel drive gear-box
propeller gear-box
HS Dynamics propeller
air-conditioning packs
main passenger compartment
baggage racks
door to car deck
passenger entrance door
engine intakes
acoustic baffles
Marine Proteus gas-turbine
pylon
fin
car deck
rear car ramp
hatch to auxiliary power unit
crew entry ladder
control deck

of *The Rise of Silas Lapham.*

how·itz·er (how′ĭtser) *n.* Short gun for high-angle firing of shells at low velocities. [Ger. *haubitze,* f. Czech *houfnice* catapult]

howl (howl) *v.* (of animals) Utter long loud doleful cry; (of persons) utter long cry of pain, derision, etc.; utter (words) with howling; (of radio receiver) make howl. ∼ *n.* Long doleful cry of dog, wolf, etc.; loud cry of pain; yell of derision; loud noise like animal's howl in radio receiver, usu. due to low-frequency oscillation.

howl·er (how′ler) *n.* (esp.) 1. (also ∼ **monkey**) S. Amer. monkey of genus *Alouatta.* 2. (colloq.) Ridiculous blunder.

howl·ing (how′lĭng) *adj.* That howls; (bibl., of wilderness) filled with howling, as of wild beasts or wind; (slang) tremendous, very great.

hoy[1] (hoi) *n.* Small vessel, usu. rigged as sloop, carrying passengers and goods esp. for short distances.

hoy[2] (hoi) *int.* Exclamation used to call attention, drive beasts etc., and (naut.) hail or call aloft.

hoy·den (hoi′den) *n.* Boisterous girl.

Hoyle (hoil), **Sir Edmund** (1672–1769). English authority and writer on card games; hence the expression, "according to Hoyle," meaning following the prescribed rules or in a fair manner.

hp, h.p. *abbrevs.* Horsepower.

HQ, hq. *abbrevs.* Headquarters.

hr. *abbrev.* Hour.

H.R.H. *abbrev.* His (or Her) Royal Highness.

hrs. *abbrev.* Hours.

H.S. *abbrev.* High school.

hub (hŭb) *n.* Central part of wheel, rotating on or with axle, and from which spokes radiate; (fig.) center of interest etc.

hub·ble-bub·ble (hŭb′el bŭbel) *n.* Form of hookah; bubbling noise; noisy confusion, hubbub.

hub·bub (hŭb′ŭb) *n.* Confused din; tumult.

hub·by (hŭb′ē) *n.* (pl. **-bies**). (colloq.) Husband.

Hu·bei: see HUPEH.

hu·bris (hū′brĭs, hoo̅′-) *n.* Pride and insolence. **hu·bris·tic** (hū-brĭs′tĭk, hoo̅-) *adj.* [Gk.]

huck·a·back (hŭk′abăk) *n.* Stout linen or cotton fabric with figured weave and rough surface, for towels etc.

huck·le·ber·ry (hŭk′elbĕre̅) *n.* (pl. **-ries**). (Fruit of) common N. Amer. species of genus *Gaylussacia*

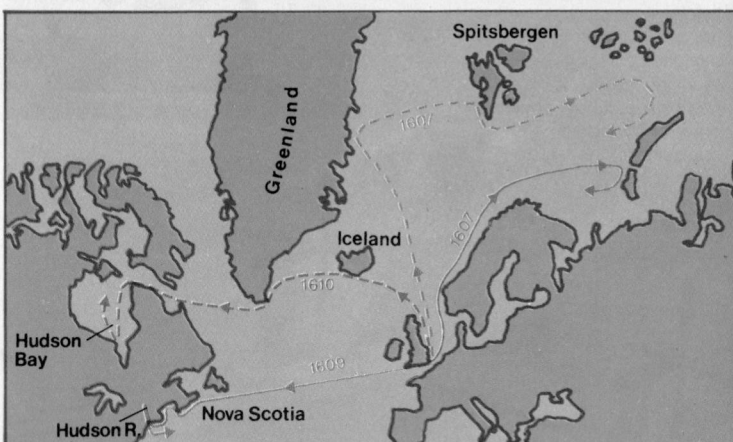

of low berry-bearing shrubs.

huck·ster (huk′ster) *n.* Peddler, hawker; (colloq.) person in advertising business, esp. for television and radio.

hud·dle (hŭd′el) *v.* (**-dled, -dling**). Crowd (things etc.) promiscuously *together, into,* etc.; coil *oneself up;* nestle closely *together;* (football) gather in a huddle; meet to confer or consult. ∼ *n.* Confused array; jumble; densely packed group; (football) brief gathering of team around quarterback to discuss plans, signals, etc.; consultation, discussion; **go into a** ∼, confer.

Hu·di·bras·tic (hū̆dĭbrăs′tĭk) *adj.* In the meter or manner of Samuel Butler's mock-heroic satirical poem "Hudibras" (1663–

1678).

Hud·son (hŭd′son), **Henry** (1611). English navigator ai explorer; hired by Dutch East Inc Company to find a NE. passage the Orient; discovered the Huds River, 1609, sailing his ship t *Half Moon* as far as Albany; la reached **Hudson Bay,** Canac 1610–11; set adrift by his mutino crew to die, 1611; **Hudson Ba** inland sea, covering 480,000 sq. n (1,243,000 sq. km), in E. Northwe Territories, Canada; **Hudsor Bay Company,** joint-stock cor pany, chartered in 1670 by Charl II to deal in fur trading with t Indians of the St. Lawrence Riv region; **Hudson River,** river E. New York, flowing S. 306 n (492 km), from the Adironda

ountains to its mouth at New
ork City on Upper New York Bay,
here it forms the boundary
tween New York and New
rsey; **Hudson Strait**, strait ex-
nding 450 mi. (724 km), in NE.
anada and connecting Hudson
ay to the Atlantic Ocean; navi-
ted by Hudson, 1607–11.

hue[1] (hū) *n.* Color, tint; variety
color caused by mixture with
other; **hued** *adj.*

hue[2] (hū) *n.* ~ **and cry**, clamor
pursuit or assault; outcry
gainst); proclamation for capture
criminal.

huff (hŭf) *v.* (archaic) Bully,
uster; anger; take offense; puff,
ow; inflate. ~ *n.* Fit of
tulance or offended dignity.
ff'ish *adj.* **huff'ish·ly** *adv.*
ff'ish·ness *n.*

hug (hŭg) *v.t.* (**hugged, hug·-
ng**). Squeeze closely in one's
ms, usu. with affection; (of bear)
ueeze between its forelegs; delight
, cling to (prejudices etc.); keep
ose to (shore etc.); ~-**me-tight**,
oman's close-fitting knitted
oolen sleeveless jacket. **hug** *n.*
rong clasp with the arms.

huge (hūj, ūj) *adv.* Very large;
f immaterial things) great.
ge'ness *n.* **huge'ly** *adv.*

Hughes[1] (hūz), **Charles Evans**
862–1948). Amer. jurist and
atesman; governor of New York,
07–10; associate justice of the
S. Supreme Court, 1910–16;
cretary of State, 1921–5; member
the Hague Tribunal, 1926–30;
ief justice of U.S. Supreme
ourt, 1930–41.

Hughes[2] (hūz), **(James) Lang-
on** (1902–67). Amer. poet and
riter about black life in America.

Hu·go (hū'gō; *Fr.* ügō'), **Victor-
arie** (1802–85). French poet,
velist, and dramatist; leader of
e French Romantic movement;
thor of *La Légende des Siècles*, of
e dramas *Ruy Blas, Hernani*, etc.,
d the novels *Notre Dame de Paris*,
s *Misérables*, etc.

Hu·gue·not (hū'genŏt) *n.*
rench Protestant, member of the
alvinistic or Reformed com-
union of France whose liberty of
orship, at first denied, was
fined in the Edict of Nantes
598) and again withdrawn when
e Edict was revoked (1685) by
ouis XIV; to escape persecution
any Huguenots then emigrated to
otestant countries, esp. England
d America. [assimilation of Swiss
er. *eidgenoss* (= confederate) to
me of Geneva burgomaster
ugues]

hu·la (hoō'la) *n.* (also **hula-
la**) Undulating Polynesian
nce pantomiming a story; rhyth-
ic drumbeats, chants, and other
usic for this dance.

hulk (hŭlk) *n.* Body of dis-

mantled, wrecked, or old ship;
(hist.) this used as a warehouse or
prison; unwieldy vessel; (fig.) big or
clumsy person; large, awkward
object. **hulk'ing** *adj.* Bulky;
clumsy.

Hull (hŭl), **Cordell** (1871–
1955). Amer. statesman and
diplomat; U.S. secretary of State
under President F. D. Roosevelt,
1933–44; awarded Nobel Prize for
peace, 1945.

hull[1] (hŭl) *n.* Outer covering of
fruit, esp. pod of peas and beans;
(fig.) covering. ~ *v.t.* Remove hull
of.

hull[2] (hul) *n.* Frame of ship.

hul·la·ba·loo (hŭl'abaloō) *n.* (pl.
-**loos**). Uproar.

Hu·lun Nor (hoō'loōn nōr').
Largest lake in Manchuria, NE.
China; 35 mi. (56 km) long, and 5
mi. (8 km) wide.

hum[1] (hŭm) *v.* (**hummed,
hum·ming**). Make continuous
low-pitched sound, as of bee,
spinning top, machinery, etc.; sing
with closed lips; (colloq.) be in state
of activity or bustle. ~ *n.* Humming sound.

hum[2] (hum) *int.* Exclamation
expressing hesitation, dissent, etc.

hu·man (hū'man, ū'-) *adj.* Of,
belonging to, man (= MAN *n.* def.
1); that is a person or consists of
people; of man as opp. to God;
having, showing, qualities distinctive of man; ~ **rights**, basic rights
of citizens of a nation to express
opinions, hold jobs, move about
freely, etc., within reason, and esp.
freedom to disagree with the
government. **human** *n.* Human
being.

hu·mane (hūmān', ū-) *adj.*
Benevolent, compassionate; of or
promoting human qualities of
mercy, kindness, etc.; civilizing,
refining. **hu·mane'ly** *adv.*
hu·mane'ness *n.*

hu·man·ism (hū'manĭzem, ū'-)
n. 1. Devotion to human interests.
2. (often cap.) Literary culture, esp.
that of the Humanists. 3. Any of
various philosophies concerned
with human (not divine or supernatural) matters, or with the human
race (not the individual), or with

A ship's **hull** *was made of wood until
the 19th century when steel was developed. Repairs to the hull are usually
carried out in dry docks or floating
docks. The giant liner QE2 is seen here
in dry dock.*

man as a responsible and progressive intellectual being. **hu'man·ist** *n.* 1. Student of human nature or human affairs; one versed in the humanities. 2. **H~**, one of the scholars who at the revival of learning in 14th–16th centuries devoted themselves to study of language, literature, and antiquities of Greece and Rome; later disciple of same culture. 3. Adherent of humanism (3). **hu·man·is·tic** (hūmănĭs'tĭk, ū-) *adj.*

hu·man·i·tar·i·an (hūmănĭtār'ēan, ū-) *n.* One who holds that man's duty consists in advancement of welfare of human race; one who devotes himself to welfare of mankind at large, philanthropist. ~ *adj.* Holding, concerned with, views of humanitarians. **hu·man·i·tar'i·an·ism** *n.*

hu·man·i·ty (hūmăn'ĭtē, ū-) *n.* (for def. 4 pl. **-ties**). 1. Human nature; (pl.) human attributes. 2. Human race; human beings collectively. 3. Humaneness, benevolence. 4. (pl.) Learning concerned with human culture, as literature, the arts, philosophy, etc., esp. as opposed to natural and social sciences.

hu·man·ize (hū'manīz, ū'-) *v.* (**-ized, -iz·ing**). 1. Make human, give human character to. 2. Make, become, humane.

hu·man·kind (hū'mankīnd, ū'-) *n.* Mankind.

hu·man·ly (hū'manlē, ū'-) *adv.* In a human manner; by human means; from human point of view; with human feeling.

hum·ble (hŭm'bel) *adj.* (**-bler, -blest**). Having, showing, low estimate of one's own importance; lowly condition; of modest pretensions, dimensions, etc.; **eat ~ pie**, make humble apology, submit to humiliation. **humble** *v.t.* (**-bled, -bling**). Make humble; bring low, abase. **hum'bly** *adv.*

hum'ble·ness *n.*

Hum·boldt (hŭm'bōlt; *Ger.* hoōm'bawlt), **Friedrich Heinrich Alexander von** (1769–1859). German author of the *Kosmos*, a physical description of the universe; naturalist, traveler, and statesman; explored in S. Amer. and Asia; **Humboldt** (hŭm'bōlt) **Current**, cold Pacific Ocean current flowing N. along the coast of Chile and Peru to S. Ecuador.

hum·bug (hŭm'bŭg) *n.* Sham, deception; imposter; nonsense, rubbish. ~ *v.* (**-bugged, -bugging**). Delude, trick (person); be, behave like, a humbug.

hum·drum (hŭm'drŭm) *adj.* & *n.* Commonplace(ness); dull(ness).

Hume (hūm), **David** (1711–76). Scottish philosopher and historian; author of *Treatise of Human Nature* and *Enquiry Concerning Human Understanding*; in his system of philosophical skepticism, human knowledge is restricted to experience of ideas and impressions, and ultimate verification of their truth or falsehood is impossible.

hu·mer·us (hū'merus) *n.* (pl. **-mer·i** pr. -merī'). Bone of upper arm in man; corresponding bone in other vertebrates. **hu'mer·al** *adj.*

hu·mid (hū'mĭd) *adj.* Moist, damp; (of air) containing much water or water vapor. **hu·mid'i·fy** *v.t.* (**-fied, -fy·ing**). **hu·mid'i·ty** *n.* Moisture, dampness; degree of moisture, esp. in atmosphere; **absolute ~**, amount of water vapor in a given volume of air (usu. in grams per cubic meter); **relative ~**, ratio between the amount actually present and the amount

*Many animals have developed ways of storing food for scarce times. In some animals, such as bison and camels, this storage system manifests itself as a characteristic **hump** on the animal's back.*

that would be present if the air were saturated at the same temperature.

hu·mi·dor (hū'mĭdor) *n.* Container for keeping cigars or tobacco moist.

hu·mil·i·ate (hūmĭl'ēat, ū-) *v.* (**-at·ed, -at·ing**). Lower the dignity or self-respect of; mortify. **hu·mil'i·at·ing** *adj.* **hu·mil·i·a·tion** (hūmĭlēā'shŏn, ū-) *n.*

hu·mil·i·ty (hūmĭl'ĭtē, ū-) *n.* Humbleness, meekness.

hum·ming (hŭm'ĭng) *adj.* That hums; **hum'mingbird**, any bird of Amer. (chiefly tropical) family Trochilidae, of very small size, and usu. brilliantly colored, making humming sound by rapid vibration of wings; all species feed while hovering and can fly backward.

hum·mock (hŭm'ok) *n.* Hillock, knoll; rising ground, esp. in marsh; hump or ridge of ice in ice field. **hum'mock·y** *adj.*

hu·mor, Brit. **hu·mour** (hū'mer) *ns.* 1. State of mind, mood, inclination; **out of ~**, displeased. 2. Faculty of perceiving the ludicrous; jocose imagination (less intellectual but more sympathetic than WIT[1]); comicality; facetiousness. 3. (physiol.) Transparent fluid or semifluid substance, esp. **aqueous ~**, between lens of eye and cornea, and **vitreous ~** within eyeball. 4. (hist.) In ancient and medieval physiology, one of four chief fluids of the body (blood, phlegm, choler or bile, and melancholy or black choler) that, by their relative proportions, were supposed to determine a person's physical and mental qualities. **humor** *v.t.* Gratify, indulge (person, taste, temper, etc.); make concessions to. **hu'mor·less** *adj.* Lacking a sense of the ridiculous.

hu·mor·al (hū'meral, ū'-) *adj.* Of the bodily humors (see HUMOR n. 4).

hu·mor·esque (hūmoresk', ū'-) *n.* (mus.) Composition of light capricious character.

hu·mor·ist (hū'merĭst, ū'-) *n.* Facetious person; writer, performer of humorous pieces.

hu·mor·ous (hū'merus, ū'-) *adj.* Full of humor; facetious, funny. **hu'mor·ous·ly** *adv.* **hu'mor·ous·ness** *n.*

hu·mour = HUMOR.

hump (hŭmp) *n.* Protuberance, esp. on back, formed by curved spine or fleshy excrescence, a natural feature in camel, bison, etc.

magnificent rivolis

lodiges racket-tail

ribbon-tailed

sword-billed

sappho comet

erans emerald

ruby and topaz

ruby-throated

frilled coquette

or deformity in man; rounded boss of earth etc.; **hump′back** (person having) back with a hump; **hump-back whale**, whale of genus *Megaptera*, so called because of the low hump on the back; **hump′-backed**, having such a back. **hump** *v.* Make arched or rounded; bend; (vulg.) copulate (*with*). **humped, hump′y** *adjs.* (**hump·i·er, hump·i·est**).

Hum·per·dinck (hōōm′per-dĭngk), **Engelbert** (1854–1921). German composer famous for the fairy tale opera, *Hänsel and Gretel*.

humph (hŭmf) *int.* Exclamation of doubt or mild contempt.

Hum·phrey (hŭm′frē), **Hubert Horatio** (1911–78). Amer. politician; U.S. senator from Minnesota, 1949–64, 1970–8, and vice president under Lyndon Johnson, 1965–1969.

Hump·ty Dump·ty (hŭmp′tē dŭmp′tē). Short dumpy person; (from nursery rhyme in which name is taken to mean an egg) person or thing that once overthrown cannot be restored; (from Lewis Carroll's *Through the Looking-Glass*) person who makes words mean what he chooses.

hu·mus (hū′mus, ū′-) *n.* Decayed vegetable matter, the characteristic organic constituent of the soil formed by the decomposition of plant materials.

Hun (hŭn) *n.* 1. One of the Asiatic race of warlike nomads who invaded Europe *c*375 A.D. and overran much of it under Attila in middle of 5th c. 2. (contempt.) German soldier, German (esp. during World War I). **Hun′nish** *adj.* (fig.) Barbarous, destructive.

Hu·nan (hōō′nahn′). Province of S. China. ~ *adj.* Of Hunan, esp. its spicy cuisine.

hunch (hŭnch) *v.t.* Bend, arch, convexly; thrust *out, up*, to form a hump. ~ *n.* 1. Hump; thick piece, hunk; **hunch′back(ed)**, humpback(ed). 2. Intuition, premonition.

hun·dred (hŭn′drĭd) *n.* (pl. **-dreds**, following a numeral **-dred**). 1. Cardinal number equal to ten times ten (100, c, or C); also as ordinal when followed by other numbers; hundredweight; $100 or a $100 bill; **a ~ percent**, entire(ly); complete(ly); **the ~ s**, between 100 and 999. 2. (chiefly hist.) Subdivision of county or shire in England and Ireland. 3. **hun′-dredweight**, (abbrev. cwt) 100 lb.; (Brit.) 112 lb. avoirdupois. **hun-dred** *adj.* Amounting to 100; **H ~ Days**, period between return of Napoleon I to Paris (Mar. 20, 1815) and his second abdication (June 22); **H ~ Years War**, intermittent war between England and France (1337–1453), arising out of English kings' claim to French crown and

Hunger and malnutrition are perennial problems in the over-populated under-developed countries of the Third World. These children from Nigeria have the pot-bellies and thin limbs characteristic of starvation.

during which England lost all her French lands except Calais. **hun′dred·fold** *adj.* & *adv.* **hun′-dredth** *adj.* & *n.*

hung: see HANG.

Hun·gar·i·an (hŭnggār′ēan) *adj.* Of Hungary or its people or language. ~ *n.* Hungarian person or language; MAGYAR.

Hun·ga·ry (hŭng′gerē). Country of central Europe, forming until the end of World War I the eastern division of Austro-Hungarian Empire; declared an independent republic in 1918; reconstituted as a kingdom, the functions of the monarch being exercised by a regent, in 1920; again declared a republic in 1946; proclaimed a Communist People's Republic, 1949; anti-communist uprisings began in Budapest, 1956, and were quelled by Soviet troops and tanks; capital, Budapest.

hun·ger (hŭng′ger) *n.* Unea sensation, exhausted conditio caused by lack of food; (fig.) stro desire; ~ **strike**, refusal to ta food (esp. by prisoner trying force compliance with h demands). **hunger** *v.i.* Fe hunger; have craving (*for, after*).

hun·gry (hŭng′grē) ac (**-gri·er, -gri·est**). Feeling hunge showing hunger; inducing hunge (fig.) eager, greedy; (of soil) poc barren. **hun′gri·ly** *adv.* **hun′gri ness** *n.*

hunk (hŭngk) *n.* Large piece c off; clumsy piece.

hun·ker (hŭng′ker) *v.i.* Sit squat down on the heels. **hun·ke** *n.pl.* Haunches.

hunk·y (hŭng′kē) *n.* (pl. **hunk ies**). (slang, derog.) Person fro central or eastern Europe.

hunk·y-do·ry (hŭng′kē dōr′

The central European republic **Hungary** has an area of 35,912 s miles and a population of just over million people. The capital is Budape on the river Danube which bisects t country.

*This computer photograph is of **Hurricane Camille** which hit the Mississippi Gulf Coast in August 1969. It caused 157 deaths and the estimated damage from flooding alone was well over a hundred million (U.S.) dollars.*

dŏr′ē) *adj.* (slang) Excellent.

Hun·nish (hŭn′ĭsh): see HUN.

hunt (hŭnt) *v.* 1. Pursue wild nimals or game; chase (these) for ood or sport; pursue with force, iolence, or hostility; shoot (game); eek *after, for, out*; scour (district) n pursuit of game; use (horse, ounds) in hunting; **~-and-peck**, yping method involving search for ach key before striking; **~ down**, ring to bay; **~ out**, track out, find y search; **~ up**, search for. 2. elect. mech.) Be in a state of nstability, oscillate, jump back- vard and forward. **hunt** *n.* Hunt-

ing (lit. and fig.); persons hunting with a pack.

hunt·er (hŭn′ter) *n.* (fem. of def. 1. **hunt·ress** pr. hŭn′trĭs). 1. One who hunts; **hunter's moon**, next full moon after harvest moon. 2. Horse ridden for hunting.

hunt·ing (hŭn′tĭng) *n.* Action of person or animal that hunts;

chase, pursuit; **~ box**, small house used during hunting season; **~ ground**, place where one hunts (freq. fig.); **happy ~ grounds**, those expected by Amer. Indians in world to come (also fig.); **~ leopard** = CHEETAH.

hunts·man (hŭnts′man) *n.* (pl. **-men** pr. -men). Hunter; man in charge of (esp. fox-) hounds.

Hunts·ville (hŭnts′vĭl). City in N. Alabama and site of a NASA space flight center.

Hu·peh (hōō′pä′), **Hu·bei** (hü- böė′). Province of central China.

hur·dle (her′del) *n.* (chiefly Brit.) Portable rectangular frame for temporary fence etc.; wooden frame to be jumped over in **~ race**; (pl.) hurdle race; (hist.) frame on which traitors were dragged to execution. **hurdle** *v.* (**-dled, -dling**). Run in hurdle race; jump as over a hurdle etc. (lit. and fig.). **hur′dler** *n.* One who makes hurdles or runs in hurdle races.

hur·dy-gur·dy (her′dē ger′dē) *n.* (pl. **-gur·dies**). 1. Medieval musical instrument resembling lute, sounded by rosined wheel turned with right hand and keys to "stop" strings played with left hand. 2. Any droning instrument played by turning a handle, as barrel organ.

hurl (herl) *v.t.* Throw violently from some position; throw (missile etc.); (baseball) pitch. **~ n.** Hurling, violent throw. **hurl′er** *n.* (baseball) Pitcher.

hurl·ing (her′lĭng) *n.* Irish game resembling hockey; stick used in this.

hurl·y-burl·y (her′lē ber′lē) *n.* (pl. **-bur·lies**). Commotion, tumult.

Hu·ron[1] (hūr′ŏn, -on) *n.* (Member, language of) confederation of four Iroquoian-speaking Indian tribes formerly occupying the region between Lakes Huron, Erie, and Ontario.

Hur·on[2] (hūr′ŏn), **Lake.** Lake in northern U.S. and southern Canada, covering 23,010 sq. mi. (59,596 sq. km); second largest of the five Great Lakes.

hur·rah (hurah′, -raw′), **hur·ray** (hurā′), **hoo·ray** (hōōrā′) *ints.* Exclamation of exultation or approbation. **~ n. & v.i.** Shout hurrah etc.; **last ~**: see LAST[2] hurrah.

hur·ri·cane (her′ĭkän, hŭr′-; *Brit.* hŭr′ĭkan) *n.* 1. Violent tropical cyclone originating in the Caribbean Sea and tropical regions of the Atlantic Ocean, with heavy rains and winds exceeding 75 m.p.h. around a central calm space or "eye" that follows a N., NW., or NE. path. 2. Any storm in which wind blows with terrific violence; (meteor.) wind of 73 m.p.h. or more (force 12 in BEAUFORT SCALE); ~ **deck**, upper deck on river steamer; ~ **force**, speed of wind 73 m.p.h. or more (Beaufort Scale 12); ~ **lamp**, lamp covered by a glass chimney, orig. so as not to be extinguished by violent wind.

hur·ry (hĕr'ē, hŭr'ē) n. Haste; eagerness to get thing done quickly; eagerness (*to* do thing); (with neg. or interrog.) need for haste; (*not*) **in a** ~, (not) readily; ~-**scurry**, (in) disorderly haste; proceed thus. **hurry** v. (**-ried, -ry·ing**). Carry, drive (person *away, along, into,* etc.) with haste; move, act, with great or undue haste; ~ **up**, make haste. **hur'ried·ly** adv. **hur'ried·ness** n.

hurt (hĕrt) n. Wound, material injury; harm, wrong. — v. (**hurt, hurt·ing**). Cause bodily injury or pain to; damage; inflict injury upon; distress, wound (person, his feelings, etc.); (colloq.) suffer injury or pain. **hurt'ful** adj. **hurt'ful·ly** adv. **hurt'ful·ness** n. **hur·tle** (hĕr'tel) v. (**-tled, -tling**). Strike together, against something else; hurl swiftly; strike *against*; move with clattering sound; come with a crash.

hus·band (hŭz'band) n. Man married to a woman; (archaic) prudent manager. ~ v.t. I. Manage thriftily, economize; (archaic) till (ground), cultivate (plants). 2. (poet.) Provide with husband.

hus·band·ry (hŭz'bandrē) n. Farming; economy; conservation; careful management.

hush (hŭsh) n. Stillness; silence; ~ **money**, money paid to prevent disclosure or hush up something discreditable. **hush** v. Silence, quiet; be silent (esp. as int. **hush!**); ~ **up**, suppress public mention of. **hush'-hush'** adj. (colloq.) Highly confidential, very secret.

husk (hŭsk) n. Dry outer integument of some fruits or seeds; (fig.) worthless outside part of anything. ~ v.t. Remove husk from.

hus·ky¹ (hŭs'kē) adj. (**-ki·er, -ki·est**). I. Of, full of, husks; dry as a husk; (of voice or person) dry, hoarse. 2. (colloq.) Rugged and strong; big, strong, and vigorous. **husk'i·ly** adv. **husk'i·ness** n. **husky** n. (pl. **-kies**). Strong stoutly built vigorous looking person.

hus·ky² (hŭs'kē) n. (pl. **-kies**). Eskimo dog. [app. corrupt. of *Eskimo*]

Huss (hŭs), **John** (1373–1415). Bohemian religious reformer; convicted of heresy by the Council of Constance and burned alive. **Huss'ite** n. Follower of Huss.

hus·sar (hŏozär', -sär') n. One

The **hyacinth** has narrow, untoothed leaves at the base of the plant and fragrant flowers which are usually blue, but may be pink, white or other colors in cultivated species.

of a body of light horsemen organized in Hungary in 15th c.; soldier of light cavalry regiment elsewhere. [O. Serb. *husar*, f. It. *corsaro* corsair]

Hus·sein I (hŏosān'), **King** (1935–). King of Jordan since 1953.

hus·sy (hŭs'ē, hŭz'ē) n. Woman of worthless character; pert girl. [f. *housewife*]

hus·tings (hŭs'tĭngz) n. I. Court formerly held in some British cities by the mayor, recorder, sheriffs or aldermen, etc. for common pleas, probate, appeals against sheriffs' decisions, etc.; platform on which mayor etc. sat for this court (obs.) 2. Platform from which (before 1872) candidates for the Brit. Parliament were nominated; (Brit.) election proceedings. 3. Any platform for political campaigning.

hus·tle (hŭs'el) v. (**-tled, -tling**). Push roughly, jostle; shove (person *into, out of,* etc.); impel unceremoniously; push roughly *against*; push one's way; hurry, bustle; (slang) get money, living etc., by dubious means. ~ n. Hustling. **hus'tler** n. Person who hustles (in good or bad senses), esp. a prostitute.

hut (hŭt) n. Small roughly constructed house or shelter, esp.

for temporary use; (mil.) temporar wooden etc. house for troops. ~ Place (troops etc.) in huts; lodge store in hut.

hutch (hŭch) n. Boxlike pen fc rabbits etc.; hut; storage bir cabinet with some open shelves.

Hutch·in·son (hŭch'ĭnson **Anne** (1591–1643). Religiou leader whose preachings conflicte with beliefs of clergymen i Massachusetts Bay Colony; ex pelled from colony, 1637; settled i Rhode Island; moved to New Yor where she was massacred b Indians.

hut·ment (hŭt'ment) n. Er campment of huts.

hutz·pa, hutz·pah (hŏots'pc *xŏots'-*) = CHUTZPA.

Hux·ley¹ (hŭks'lē), **Aldou Leonard** (1894–1963). Grandsor of Thomas Henry Huxley; Englis novelist and essayist, author c *Brave New World*.

Hux·ley² (hŭks'lē), **Sir Julia Sorell** (1887–1975). Biologist ar writer; brother of Aldous Huxley

Hux·ley³ (hŭks'lē), **Thoma Henry** (1825–95). English phys cian and agnostic philosopher; sup ported Darwinism in his man popular scientific writings.

Huy·gens (hī'genz, hoi'– **Christian** (1629–95). Dutc mathematician and astronome ~'s **principle**, (phys.) principle c wave propagation, according t which every point on an advancin wave front acts as a source c disturbance and sends out smalle waves, the resultant effect of whic constitutes the propagation of th wave as a whole.

huz·za (huzah') int., n., & v. (archaic) Hurrah.

hwy. abbrev. Highway.

hy·a·cinth (hīasĭnth) n. Precious stone (in ancient times blue gem, prob. sapphire); now reddish-orange variety of zirco (occas. also of garnet and topaz 2. Bulbous plant of genus *Hyacir thus* with fragrant bell-shape flowers of various colors, esp purplish blue; deep blue (tradi tional rendering of Homeric epithe applied to hair, perh. meaning dar and glossy). **hy·a·cin'thine** adj.

Hy·a·cin·thus (hīasĭn'thus (Gk. myth.) Beautiful youth beloved by Apollo and Zephyrus accidentally killed by a quoi thrown by Apollo; from his bloo Apollo caused the flower that bear his name to spring up.

Hy·a·des (hī'adēz) n.pl. I. (Gk myth.) Nymphs, daughters o Atlas, placed by Zeus among th Pleiades. 2. (astron.) Cluster o stars in the constellation of Taurus anciently supposed to indicate rain weather when they rose simultane ously with the sun.

hy·ae·na: see HYENA.

hy·brid (hī′brĭd) *n.* Offspring of ⁓o animals or plants of different ⁓ecies or varieties; (fig.) something ⁓ mixed origin or components; ⁓ing, word, composed of incon-⁓uous elements. **⁓** *adj.* Cross-ed, mongrel; heterogeneous. **⁓′brid·ism** *n.* Fact, condition, of ⁓ing hybrid; crossbreeding. **hy⁓-rid·i·ty** (hībrĭd′ĭtē) *n.*

hy·brid·ize (hī′brĭdīz) *v.* (**-ized, ⁓z·ing**). Subject (species etc.) to ⁓ossbreeding; produce hybrids; ⁓terbreed. **hy·brid·i·za·tion** ⁓ībrĭdĭzā′shŏn) *n.*

Hyde (hīd), **Edward**: see ⁓KYLL.

Hyde (hīd) **Park. 1.** Public park ⁓ 361 acres in central London. **2.** ⁓illage in SE. New York on ⁓udson River, home of President ⁓ranklin D. Roosevelt.

Hy·der·a·bad (hīderabahd′, ⁓ăd′, hīdra-). Former state of India, in the Deccan; its capital; now in southern West Pakistan.

Hy·dra (hī′dra). **1.** (Gk. myth.) Many-headed snake of marshes of Lerna, whose heads grew again as they were cut off, killed by Hercules; hence, thing hard to extirpate. **2.** (astron.) Southern constellation represented as water snake or sea serpent.

hy·dra (hī′dra) *n.* (pl. **-dras, -drae** pr. **-drē**). Freshwater polyp of simple structure of genus *H⁓*, with tubular body and mouth surrounded by ring of tentacles with stinging thread cells.

hy·dran·gea (hīdrān′ja, -jēa) *n.*

*The Saronic island of **Hydra** in the Aegean Sea supports sponge-fishing, cotton and silk-weaving, ship-building and tourism. Its chief town, which surrounds this sheltered harbor, is an artists' and writers' colony.*

Shrub of genus *H⁓*, native of temperate regions of Asia and Amer., with white, blue, or pink flowers in large globular clusters.

hy·drant (hī′drant) *n.* Pipe with nozzle to which hose can be attached, for drawing water directly from main, esp. in street, for fire fighting (also **fire ⁓**).

hy·drate (hī′drāt) *n.* (chem.) Compound of water with another compound. **⁓** *v.t.* (**-drat·ed, -drat·ing**). Combine chemically with water. **hy·dra·tion** (hīdrā′-shŏn) *n.*

hy·drau·lic (hīdraw′lĭk, -drŏl′-ĭk) *adj.* Of water (or other liquid) as conveyed through pipes or channels, esp. mechanically; (of machine or other device) operated by resistance offered when water, oil, or other liquid is forced through a pipe or orifice, as **⁓ brake, crane,** etc.; (of cement

*Above: The **hydro-electric** power station, at the foot of the Warragamba Dam in N.S.W., Australia, is operated from Sydney by remote control and is capable of supplying 50 MW to the N.S.W. electricity grid if necessary. The dam was completed in 1960. Below: Section of the dam.*

reservoir

dam

sub-station

stilling basin

power station

spillway

reservoir

dam crest and roadway

dam

spillway

power station

overhead bus-bars

generator transformers

sub-station

circuit breakers

intake

penstock

turbine

generator

stilling basin

etc.) hardening under water. **hy·drau'li·cal·ly** *adv.* **hy·drau'lic** *n.* Science of conveyance of liquid through pipes, etc., esp. as a motiv force.

hydro- *prefix*. 1. Having to d with water. 2. (chem.) Combine with hydrogen.

hy·dro·car·bon (hīdrokär'bor *n.* Chemical compound containin hydrogen and carbon only, a methane and benzene.

hy·dro·ceph·a·lus (hīdrosĕf'a lus) *n.* Disease of brain, esp. i young children, with accumulatio of serous fluid in cavity of craniu and consequent weakness of ment: faculties; water on the brai **hy·dro·ce·phal·ic** (hīdrosefăl'ĭk *adj.* & *n.*

hy·dro·chlo·ric (hīdroklōr'ĭk -klŏr'-) *adj.* ~ **acid**, clea aqueous, acidic, and poisonou solution of hydrogen chlorid (HCl), which fumes in moist ai used in various industrial processe including petroleum productio ore processing, and metal cleanin

hy·dro·cy·an·ic (hīdrosīăn'ĭk *adj.* ~ **acid**, highly poisonou volatile liquid (HCN), hydroge cyanide, with smell like bitte almonds, solution of which i water is PRUSSIC *acid*.

hy·dro·dy·nam·ic (hīdrōdī năm'ĭk), **hy·dro·dy·nam·i·ca** (hīdrōdīnăm'ĭkal) *adjs.* Of th forces acting on or exerted b liquids. **hy·dro·dy·nam'ics** *n.p* Science of the motion, energy, an pressure of moving fluids.

hy·dro·e·lec·tric (hīdroĭlĕk' trĭk) *adj.* Of the utilization of wate power for the production c electricity; of electricity so gener ated.

hy·dro·foil (hī'drofoil) *n.* (Fas motorboat, seaplane, etc., with plate or fin for lifting hull out c water at speed.

hy·dro·gen (hī'drojen) *n* (chem.) Lightest of the elements, colorless odorless gas that burn with pale blue, very hot flame i oxygen (or air) and combines wit oxygen to form water (H₂O symbol H, at. no. 1, at. wt. 1.008c ~ **bomb**, immensely powerfu bomb deriving its energy from th fusion at extremely high temper ature of hydrogen isotopes to forr helium; also called H-bomb, fusio bomb; ~ **fluoride**, colorles: highly corrosive gas (HF), anhy dride of *hydrofluoric acid;* ~ **peroxide**, in its pure anhydrou state, a clear colorless syrupy liqui (H₂O₂), used in aqueous solution a an antiseptic and disinfectan **hy·drog·e·nous** (hīdrŏj'enus) *adj*

hy·dro·gen·ate (hī'drojenā hīdrŏj'e-) *v.t.* (**-at·ed, -at·ing** Charge, cause to combine, wit hydrogen; esp. combine hydroge and unsaturated compound. **hy·**

o·gen·a·tion (hīdrojenā′shon, drŏje-) *n.*

hy·droid (hī′droid) *adj.* & *n.* ol.) (Animal) like, allied to, the dra.

hy·drol·o·gy (hīdrŏl′ojē) *n.* udy of water, esp. its distribution d control. **hy·dro·log·i·cal** (idrolŏj′ĭkal) *adj.*

hy·drol·y·sis (hīdrŏl′isĭs) *n.* litting of compound substance interaction with water. **hy·dro·-t·ic** (hīdrolĭt′ĭk) *adj.*

hy·drom·e·ter (hīdrŏm′eter) *n.* strument for determining specif-gravity of liquids, commonly a aduated stem with a hollow bulb d a weight at lower end, floated right in liquid, of which specific avity is indicated by depth to iich stem is immersed. **hy·dro·-et·ric** (hīdromĕt′rĭk) *adj.* **hy·-om′e·try** *n.*

hy·dro·path·ic (hīdropăth′ĭk) *dj.* Of, concerned with, hydrop-hy. **hy·drop·a·thy** (hīdrŏp′-hē) *n.* Medical treatment by ternal and internal application of iter; water cure.

hy·dro·pho·bi·a (hīdrofō′bēa): e RABIES.

hy·dro·phone (hī′drofōn) *n.* Instrument for the detection or monitoring of sound waves in water.

hy·dro·phyte (hī′drofīt) *n.* Aquatic plant, esp. alga.

hy·dro·plane (hī′droplān) *n.* 1. Light, fast motorboat designed to skim over surface of water. 2. Finlike horizontal device enabling submarine to submerge or rise. 3. Seaplane.

hy·dro·pon·ics (hīdropŏn′ĭks) *n.pl.* Cultivation of plants without soil, in water containing dissolved nutrients.

hy·dro·sphere (hī′drosfēr) *n.* Waters of the Earth's surface.

hy·dro·stat·ic (hīdrostăt′ĭk) *adj.* Of the equilibrium of liquids and the pressure exerted by liquids at rest; (of instruments etc.) involving pressure of liquid as source of power or otherwise, hydraulic. **hy·dro·stat′i·cal** *adj.* **hy·dro·-**

stat′i·cal·ly *adv.* **hy·dro·stat′ics** *n.pl.* Branch of mechanics concerned with the pressure and equilibrium of liquids at rest.

hy·dro·ther·a·peu·tic (hīdrō-thĕrapū′tĭk) *adj.* Hydropathic. **hy·dro·ther′a·py** *n.* Hydropathy.

hy·drous (hī′drus) *adj.* (chem., min.) Containing water.

hy·drox·ide (hīdrŏk′sīd) *n.* (chem.) Compound containing hydroxyl.

hydroxy- *prefix.* Containing hydroxyl.

hy·drox·yl (hīdrŏk′sĭl) *n.* (chem.) Radical OH, which occurs in the structures of many chemical compounds.

hy·dro·zo·an (hīdrozō′an) *adj.* & *n.* (Member) of the Hydrozoa, a class of coelenterate animals, chiefly marine, and simple or compound, including the fresh-water hydra.

hy·en·a, hy·ae·na (hīē′na) *ns.*

surface piercing hydrofoil   fully submerged hydrofoil   ladder hydrofoil

is large **hydrofoil** carries automobiles well as passengers. Hydrofoils skim e surface of the water. They create le disturbance and are less affected wind and turbulence than other sea-aft. The three basic types are the sur-ce piercing foil, the fully submerged e, and a 'ladder' type.

radio and radar antennae

deck seating

bridge

car storage

life boat

davit

engine

surface piercing foil

propeller shaft

passenger seating

ropeller

fully submerged foil

Carnivorous quadruped allied to dog tribe, with powerful jaws, neck, and shoulders, but low and comparatively poorly developed hindquarters; cruel, treacherous, or rapacious person; **laughing** ~, hyena (either **striped** ~, *Hyaena striata*, of Asia and northern Africa, or **spotted** ~, *Crocuta maculata*, of southern Africa) with howl resembling fiendish laughter.

Hy·ge·ia (hījē´a). (Gk. myth.) Goddess of health and daughter of Aesculapius. **Hy·gei´an** *adj*.

hy·giene (hī´jēn, -jēēn) *n*. Science of health and its preservation; practice of measures conducive to this, as cleanliness. **hy·gi·en·ic** (hījēēn´ĭk) *adj*. **hy·gi·en´i·cal·ly** *adv*. **hy·gi·en·ist** (hījē´nĭst, -jĕn´ĭst, hī´jē-, hījēēn´-) *n*.

hygro- *prefix*. Wet, fluid.

hy·grom·e·ter (hīgrŏm´eter) *n*. Instrument for measuring humidity of air or gas. **hy·gro·met·ric** (hīgrŏmĕt´rĭk) *adj*. **hy·grom´e·try** *n*.

hy·gro·scope (hī´grŏskōp) *n*. Instrument indicating approximate humidity of atmosphere. **hy·gro·scop·ic** (hīgrŏskŏp´ĭk) *adj*. Absorbing moisture, esp. from the air.

Hy·men (hī´men). (Gk. and Rom. myth.) God of marriage; represented as a young man carrying torch and veil.

hy·men (hī´men) *n*. Fold of mucous membrane stretched across and partially closing external orifice of vagina of virgin female. **hy·me·ne·al** (hīmenē´al) *adj*. Pertaining to a wedding or marriage. ~ *n*. Marriage song.

hy·me·nop·ter·an (hīmenŏp´teran) *n*. Member of the Hymenop-

tera, a large order of insects, including ants, bees, etc. with two pairs of membranous wings. **hy·me·nop´ter·ous** *adj*.

hymn (hĭm) *n*. Song of praise or prayer to God or other divine being, esp. metrical composition sung in religious service; song of praise. **hymn·book** (hĭm´book) *n*. Book containing collection of hymns for use in religious service. **hymn** *v*. Praise (God etc.) in hymns, express (praise etc.) in hymn; sing hymns. **hym·nal** (hĭm´nal) *adj*. Of hymns. ~ *n*. Hymnbook.

hym·no·dy (hĭm´nodē) *n*. Singing of hymns; composition of hymns; hymns collectively. **hym´no·dist** *n*.

hy·oid (hī´oid) *adj*. ~ **bone**, tongue bone, between chin and thyroid cartilage, in man, horseshoe-shaped and embedded horizontally in root of tongue. ~ *n*. Hyoid bone.

hy·os·cine (hī´osēn, -sĭn) = SCOPOLAMINE.

hy·os·cy·a·mine (hīosī´amēn, -mĭn) *n*. (chem.) Alkaloid, an isomer of atropine, obtained from certain plants (esp. *Hyoscyamus niger* and *Atropa belladonna*) and used as sedative, or, with morphia, to produce partial anesthesia; scopolamine.

hype (hīp) *v.t.* (**hyped**, **hyp·ing**). (slang) 1. Excite, arouse. 2. Publicize by sensational or deceptive means. ~ *n*. (slang) 1.

Sensational or deceptive public to increase interest. 2. Dr addict, esp. user of hypoderm needle.

hyper- *prefix*. Over, abo exceeding, excessive.

hy·per·ac·tive (hīperăk´tĭv) *a* Abnormally or too active. **hy·pe ac·tiv·i·ty** (hīperăktĭv´ītē) *n*.

hy·per·aes·the·sia: see HYP ESTHESIA.

hy·per·bo·la (hīper´bola) (geom.) One of the conic sectio a plane curve consisting of separate, similar, equal, and infin branches, formed by the int section of a cone by a plane maki a larger angle with the base th the side of the cone mak **hy·per·bol·ic** (hīperbŏl´ĭk) *adj*.

hy·per·bo·le (hīper´bolē) (rhet.) Exaggerated statement meant to be taken literally (*big a house*). **hy·per·bol´i·cal** *a* **hy·per·bol´i·cal·ly** *adv*. **hy·pe bo·lism** *n*.

hy·per·bo·loid (hīper´boloid) (geom.) Solid or surface of the 2 degree, some of whose pla sections are hyperbolas, the oth being ellipses or circles.

Hy·per·bo·re·an (hīperbōr´e -bôr´-, -borē´-) *n*. Inhabitant extreme north of Earth; (0 myth.) one of a race living in land of sunshine and plenty beyo the north wind.

hy·per·crit·i·cal (hīperkrĭt´ĭk *adj*. Too critical, esp. of sm faults. **hy·per·crit´i·cal·ly** *a* **hy·per·crit´i·cism** *n*.

hy·per·es·the·sia, hy·per·ae the·sia (hīperĭsthē´zha, -zh -zēa) *ns*. Morbid sensitiveness nerves; excessive sensibility. h **per·es·thet´ic** *adj*.

hy·per·gly·ce·mi·a (hīperglīs mēa) *n*. (path.) Excess of sugar the blood.

Hy·pe·ri·on (hīper´ēon). (0 myth.) One of the Titans, father of Aurora, the Sun, and Moon; in later myth. identif with the Sun itself.

hy·per·me·tro·pi·a (hīperi trō´pēa) *n*. Morbid far-sightedne hyperopia. **hy·per·me·trop** (hīpermĭtrŏp´ĭk) *adj*.

hy·per·o·pi·a (hīperō´pēa) HYPERMETROPIA. **hy·per·op** (hīperŏp´ĭk) *adj*.

hy·per·sen·si·tive (hīpersĕ sĭtĭv) *adj*. Excessively or abn mally sensitive. **hy·per·sen·s tiv´i·ty, hy·per·sen´si·tive·ne** *ns*.

hy·per·son·ic (hīpersŏn´ĭk) *a* (of speed) Greatly in excess of speed of sound, i.e. faster th supersonic.

hy·per·ten·sion (hīpertĕn´sh hī´pertĕn-) *n*. Extreme tensio (path.) raised blood pressure.

hy·per·thy·roid·ism (hīperth roidĭzem) *n*. (path.) Conditi

This spotted or laughing **hyena** *is found in Africa south of the Sahara. It is the most daring of the species and when food is scarce has attacked sleeping people and children.*

sulting from overactivity of
yroid gland.

hy·per·tro·phy (hīpĕr´trofē) n.
l. **-phies**). Excessive develop-
ent, morbid enlargement, of
gan etc. (opp. ATROPHY). **hy-**
er·troph·ic (hīpertrŏf´ĭk) adj.

hy·per·ven·ti·la·tion (hīper-
ĕntĭlā´shon) n. (med.) Abnormally
pid and deep breathing, pro-
ucing carbon dioxide decrease in
ood.

hy·phen (hī´fen) n. Sign (-) used
join two words together, to join
parated syllables of word broken
end of line, or to divide word
to parts. ∼ v.t. Join (words)
ith hyphen. **hy·phen·ate**
i´fenat) v.t. (**-at·ed, -at·ing**).
yphen; **hyphenated**, (colloq.) of
reign birth or mixed national
igin, e.g. Irish-American.

hyp·no·sis (hĭpnō´sĭs) n. (pl.
es pr. -sēz). Artificially produced
eep, esp. that induced by
ypnotism.

hyp·not·ic (hĭpnŏt´ĭk) adj. Of,
roducing, hypnotism; (of drugs)
oporific. ∼ n. Thing that
roduces sleep; person under in-
uence of hypnotism.

hyp·no·tism (hĭp´notĭzem) n.
rtificial production of) state
sembling deep sleep, in which
bject acts only on external
ggestion or direction, to which he
involuntarily and unconsciously
edient. **hyp´no·tist** n. **hyp´no·**
ze v.t. (**-tized, -tiz·ing**).

hy·po (hī´pō) n. (pl. **-pos**).
odium thiosulfate, $Na_2S_2O_3.5H_2O$
ncorrectly called sodium hypo-
ulfite), used in fixing photographic
egatives and prints.

hypo- prefix. Below, under,
ightly.

hy·po·blast (hī´pōblăst) n. Inner
yer of cells in blastoderm.

hy·po·cen·ter (hī´posĕnter) n.
nderground point of origin of an
rthquake (f. EPICENTER).

hy·po·chon·dri·a (hīpokŏn´-
ēa) n. Needless or excessive
xiety about one's health.

hy·po·chon·dri·ac (hīpokŏn´-
rēăk) adj. Of, affected by,
ypochondria. ∼ n. Hypo-
ondriac person. **hy·po·chon-**
ri·a·cal (hīpokondrī´akal) adj.
y·po·chon·dri´a·cal·ly adv.

hy·po·cot·yl (hīpokŏt´ĭl) n. (bot.)
xis of seedling below seed leaves,
rming anatomically a transition
ne between stem and root.

hy·poc·ri·sy (hĭpŏk´risē) n. (pl.
ies). Simulation of virtue or
oodness; dissimulation, pretense.

hyp·o·crite (hĭp´okrĭt) n. Person
uilty of hypocrisy; dissembler,
retender. **hyp·o·crit·i·cal** (hĭpo-
rĭt´ĭkal) adj. **hyp·o·crit´i·cal·ly**
tv.

hy·po·cy·cloid (hīposī´kloid) n.
eom.) Curve traced by a point in
e circumference of a circle which

rolls around the interior circumference of another circle.

hy·po·der·mic (hīpoder´mĭk)
adj. (med., of drugs etc.) Introduced beneath the skin; (anat.)
lying under the skin; ∼ **needle,**
syringe, one used in hypodermic
injection. **hy·po·der´mi·cal·ly**
adv. **hy·po·der´mic** n. Hypodermic injection or syringe.

hy·po·gas·tri·um (hīpogăs´-
trēum) n. Lowest region of
abdomen. **hy·po·gas´tric** adj.

hy·po·gly·ce·mi·a (hīpōglīsē´-
mēa) n. (path.) Deficiency of sugar
(glucose) in the blood.

hy·pog·y·nous (hīpŏj´inus, hĭ-)
adj. (of stamens) Situated below
pistil or ovary; (of flower) having
such stamens.

hy·pos·ta·sis (hīpŏs´tasĭs, hĭ-) n.
(pl. **-ses** pr. -sēz). (metaphys.)
Underlying substance, opp. to
attributes or to what is unsubstantial; (theol.) personality (of
Christ), person (of the Godhead).
hy·po·stat·ic (hīpostăt´ĭk), **hy·po-**
stat´i·cal adjs. **hy·po·stat´i·cal·ly**
adv.

hy·pos·ta·tize (hīpŏs´tatīz) v.t.
(**-tized, -tiz·ing**). Make into or
treat as substance; personify.

hy·pot·e·nuse (hīpŏt´enōos,
-nūs) n. Side of right-angled
triangle opposite the right angle.

hy·poth·e·cate (hīpŏth´ekāt, hĭ-)
v.t. (**-cat·ed, -cat·ing**). Pledge,
mortgage. **hy·poth·e·ca·tion**
(hīpŏthekā´shon, hĭ-) n.

hy·poth·e·sis (hīpŏth´esĭs, hĭ-)
n. (pl. **-ses** pr. -sēz). Supposition
made as basis for reasoning, with-

*The rock **hyrax** lives in groups and is
active by day. It is primarily a vegetarian
and its natural enemies are pythons,
eagles and large cats. It is most prolific
in Africa.*

out reference to its truth, or as
starting point for investigation;
groundless assumption. **hy·po-**
thet·ic (hīpothĕt´ĭk), **hy·po·thet´-**
i·cal adjs. **hy·po·thet´i·cal·ly** adv.

hy·poth·e·size (hīpŏth´esīz, hĭ-)
v. (**-sized, -siz·ing**). Frame a
hypothesis; assume as hypothesis.

hyp·som·e·ter (hĭpsŏm´eter) n.
Instrument for measuring altitudes,
by determining the boiling points of
liquids. **hyp·so·met·ric** (hĭpso-
mĕt´rĭk), **hyp·so·met´ri·cal** adjs.
hyp·som´e·try n.

hy·rax (hī´răks) n. (pl. **hy·rax-**
es, hy·ra·ces pr. hī´rasēz). One of
a small group of mammals of the
order Hyracoida, the coneys, dis-
tantly related to the elephant and
having plantigrade feet with hooves
and including the Syrian rock
rabbit and the South African rock
badger.

hys·sop (hĭs´op) n. Small bushy
aromatic herb of genus Hyssopus,
esp H. officinalis, formerly used
medicinally; (bibl.) plant whose
twigs were used for sprinkling in
Jewish rites, bunch of this used in
purification.

hys·ter·ec·to·my (hĭsterĕk´-
tomē) n. (pl. **-mies**). Surgical
removal of the uterus.

hys·ter·e·sis (hĭsterē´sĭs) n.
(phys.) Lagging or retardation of
an effect when the forces acting on
a body are changed, esp. lagging or
magnetic induction behind the
magnetizing force (**magnetic** ∼).

hys·te·ri·a (hĭstĕr´ēa, -stĕr´-) n.
1. (med., psych.) Functional disturbance of nervous system, of
psychoneurotic origin. 2. Uncontrollable or excessive fear, grief,
etc. **hys·ter·i·cal** (hĭstĕr´ĭkal) adj.
hys·ter´i·cal·ly adv. **hys·ter´ics**
n.pl. Hysterical fits or convulsions;
uncontrollable fit of crying, laughing, etc.

Hz abbrev. Hertz.

Shown here is the evolution from earliest scripts of the letter form **I, i**. In the languages of continental Europe, i is always used phonetically as counterpart of the English e. But in English the letter has two sounds — long (as in 'slide') and short (as in 'bid')

Phoenician   Cretan   Archaic Latin

Cursive Minuscule   Anglo Saxon   Roman

I¹, i (ī) (pl. **I's, i's** or **Is, is**). 1. Ninth letter of modern English and ancient Roman alphabet, in which it was orig. used as symbol both of *i* vowel and of a consonant (orig. *y*, later, in Romanic, developing into "soft g" [j]); differentiation was finally made between these two in English *c*1630–40, the consonant being expressed by the character J, j, orig. merely a variant form of I, i. 2. Roman numeral symbol for I.

I² (ī) *pron.* First person nom. sing. pronoun, denoting the speaker. ~*n.* (pl. **I's**). **the I**, the ego, subject or object of self-consciousness.

I³ *abbrev.* Interstate (highway).

I⁴ *symbol.* Iodine.

I. *abbrev.* Island(s); isle(s).

i. *abbrev.* Interest; intransitive; island(s); isles.

IA, Ia. *abbrevs.* Iowa.

i·amb (ī'ăm, ī'ămb) *n.* Metrical foot of unaccented followed by accented syllable, or of short followed by long syllable.

i·am·bic (ī·ăm'bĭk) *adj.* Of, containing, based on, iambs.

i·am·bus (ī·ăm'bus) *n.* (pl. **-bi** pr. -bī, **-bus·es**) = IAMB.

I·ap·e·tus (ī·ăp'*e*tus). 1. (Gk. myth.) A Titan, father of Atlas, Prometheus, and Epimetheus; hence, regarded as progenitor of mankind. 2. (astron.) Eighth satellite of Saturn.

ib., ibid. *abbrevs.* Ibidem.

I·be·ri·a (ī·bēr'ēa). 1. Ancient name for country comprising Spain and Portugal, and forming peninsula of extreme SW. of Europe. 2. Ancient name of GEORGIA² of the U.S.S.R.

I·be·ri·an (ī·bēr'ēan) *adj.* Of Iberia. ~ *n.* 1. Inhabitant of ancient Iberian peninsula; member of short dark neolithic people, with long heads, who buried their dead and are thought to have built the cairns, dolmens, etc., found in N. Africa, Spain, France, and Gt. Britain. 2. Language of ancient Iberia, supposed to be represented by modern Basque.

i·bex (ī'bĕks) *n.* (pl. **i·bex·es**, **ib·i·ces**, pr. ĭb'ĭsēz, ī'bī-, collect.

i·bex). Species of wild goat (genus *Capra*), with large scimitar-like horns, now rare in Alps but found in Mongolia and Ethiopia.

ib·i·dem (ĭb'ĭdĕm, ĭbī'dem) *adv.* (abbrev. ib., ibid.) In the same book, chapter, passage, etc. [L., = "in same place"]

·i·bis (ī'bĭs) *n.* (pl. **i·bis·es** pr. ī'bĭsĭz, collect. **i·bis**). Any of group of birds, widely distribu in warm climates, of the fam Threskiornithidae, with lo down-curved bills, esp. the wh ibis (*Eudocimus albus*) and glossy ibis (*Plegadis falcinell* **sacred** ~, white ibis, common the Nile basin, venerated by

The European or Alpine **ibex** (right) lives in herds in the mountains of Europe. It has been greatly reduced in numbers and is now protected in the Italian Alps. The Pyrenean or Spanish ibex (below) is one of the critically endangered species.

The **ibis** resembles a stork and occurs in all warm regions except the South Pacific Islands. It usually breeds in vast colonies. This new-born ibis comes from Australia.

cient Egyptians.

-ible *suffix*. Forming adjectives th same meaning as -ABLE (*ter- le, forcible, defensible*).

Ib·sen (ĭb′sen), **Henrik** (1828– o6). Norwegian poet and drama- t, famous for his *A Doll's House, hosts, Hedda Gabler*, etc., examin- g and criticizing social conven- ns.

-ical *suffix*. Forming adjectives rresponding to nouns or adjec- es ending in -*ic* (*classical, histori- l*) or to nouns in -*y* (*pathological*).

Ic·a·rus (ĭk′erus, ī′ker-). (Gk. yth.) Son of DAEDALUS; tried to cape from Crete on wings made his father, but flew so near the n that the wax attaching his ngs was melted and he fell into e Aegean Sea.

ICBM *abbrev*. Intercontinental llistic missile.

ICC *abbrev*. Interstate Com- rce Commission.

ice (īs) *n*. I. Frozen water; ter made solid by exposure to w temperature, a transparent ystalline brittle almost colorless bstance; frozen surface of body water; **break the** ~, (fig.) ake a beginning, break through serve or stiffness; **cut no** ~, have influence or importance, achieve thing; **on** ~, (fig.) held sus- nded, in reserve; absolutely cer- n; **on thin** ~, (fig.) in a risky uation. 2. Frozen dessert made fruit juice, water, and sugar. 3. **Age**, period during the Pleisto- ne, when large parts of Earth were vered by ice; **ice age**, any cold och with extensive glaciation; ~ , ax used by mountain climbers to t footholds in ice slopes; ~ **bag**, all waterproof bag to hold ice for

sacred ibis

scarlet ibis

The sacred **ibis** of South Arabia and Africa south of the Sahara was vener- ated by the ancient Egyptians and is about 30 ins. long. The scarlet ibis is found in tropical America.

cooling head or other part of body; **ice′berg**, floating mass of ice, a detached portion of polar ice sheet or glacier, often traveling great distances in ocean currents before it melts completely; **ice′bound**, hemmed in by ice; **ice′box**, insulated chest in which ice is put to preserve food; (colloq.) refrigerator; **ice′breaker**, boat with reinforced bow for breaking channel through ice of river, harbor, etc.; a means of breaking through reserve or stiffness; **ice′cap**, mass of thick ice covering continent, island, or other region; **ice cream**, food or dessert made from milk, cream, etc., sweetened, flavored, and frozen smooth; **ice cube**, small block of ice made in refrigerator; **ice field**, extensive sheet of floating ice; **ice floe**, flattish free mass of floating ice, smaller than an ice field; **ice hockey**: see HOCKEY; **ice′house**, (hist.) building for storing ice; **ice′man** (pl. **ice′men**), man who sells or delivers ice; **ice milk**, ice cream made from skim milk, or with greatly reduced butterfat; **ice pick**, awl for chipping ice; **ice plant**, plant (*Mesembryanthemum crystallinum*) of S. Africa, Canary Islands, etc., with leaves covered

Ice, in the form of glaciers like this one, is a powerful agent of erosion. Glaciers move slowly, accumulating debris and rocks which scour the landscape, creating smooth troughs.

with pellucid watery vesicles; **ice show**, entertainment by skaters on ice; **ice skate**, metal blade attached to shoe for gliding on ice; **iceskate** (*v.i.*) (**-skated, -skat·ing**), move, glide, over ice on these; **ice water**, iced water. **ice** *v.t.* (**iced, ic·ing**). Freeze; cover (as) with ice; cool (wine) in ice; cover (cake etc.) with icing; (hockey) push (puck) out of one's own territory to far end of ice; (fig.) make secure; put on ice.

Ice·land (īs′land). Large sparsely inhabited island (39,709 sq. mi., 105,240 sq. km), in N. Atlantic between Greenland and Scandinavia; colonized by Scandinavians after 874; united with Norway 1262–4; on union of Norway and Denmark (1831), Iceland was transferred to Denmark, which conceded home rule to Iceland in 1874 and recognized it as a sovereign state, in union with Denmark, in 1918; union dissolved in 1944 when Iceland became an independent republic; capital, Reykjavik; ~ **moss**, species of edible

arctic lichen (*Cetraria islandica* having medicinal properties; **Ice land·er** *n*. Inhabitant, native, Iceland.

Ice·lan·dic (īslăn′dĭk) *adj*. (Iceland. ~ *n*. Language of Ic land, in its oldest form practica identical with Old Norse, which still closely resembles.

I·ce·ni (īsē′nī) *n.pl.* Ancie Celtic tribe inhabiting a district England roughly corresponding modern Norfolk and Suffolk, w were conquered, with their que BOADICEA, by the Romans *c*62 A.

I Ching (ē′jǐng′). The Book Changes, ancient Chinese book divination and mystical speculatic adopted as one of the "Fi Classics" into the Confucian cano

ich·neu·mon (ĭknoo′mon, -nū *n*. 1. N. African mongoo (*Herpestes ichneumon*). 2. ~ fl member of a group of insec related to bees and wasps, who larvae are parasitic on the larv of other insects. [Gk. *ikhneum* tracker]

ichthyo- *Comb. form.* (befo vowel **ichthy-**) Of or like fis [Gk. *ikhthus* fish]

ich·thy·oid (ĭk′thēoid) *a* Fishlike. ~ *n*. Any fishli

This Byzantine **icon** of the Savior was made at the beginning of the 15th century. The subject matter and artistic style were prescribed by the Eastern Church and remained unchanged for centuries.

vertebrate.

ich·thy·ol·o·gy (ĭkthēŏl´ojē) *n.* Study of fishes. **ich·thy·o·log·i·al** (ĭkthēŏlŏj´ĭkal) *adj.* **ich·hy·ol´o·gist** *n.*

ich·thy·oph·a·gous (ĭkthēŏf´a-*us*) *adj.* Fish-eating.

Ich·thy·or·nis (ĭkthēŏr´nĭs) *n.* enus of extinct toothed birds that ad fishlike vertebrae.

ich·thy·o·saur (ĭk´thēosōr), **h·thy·o·saur·us** (ĭkthēosōr´us) s. (pl. **-saurs, -saur·us·es**).

Marine reptile of extinct order Ichthyosauria, with superficial resemblance to the modern dolphin.

-ician *suffix.* (comb. of *-ic* and *-ian*) Forming agent nouns denoting persons skilled in or concerned with arts or sciences having names ending in *-ic(s)* (*politician,*

Iceland is a sparsely populated island republic in the North Atlantic. It contains over 100 volcanoes and earthquakes are frequent. Iceland's map and flag are shown here.

logician).

i·ci·cle (ī´sĭkel) *n.* Tapering ice formation, produced by freezing of successive drops of water trickling from the point of attachment.

ic·ing (ī´sĭng) *n.* 1. Glaze of sugar, water, white of egg, butter, flavoring, etc. for covering or decorating cakes, cookies, etc. 2. Formation of ice on aircraft, roads, etc.

ICJ *abbrev.* International Court of Justice.

ick·y (ĭk´ē) *adj.* (**ick·i·er, ick·i·est**). (slang) Repulsive, sticky; (fig.) cloyingly sentimental.

i·con (ī´kŏn) *n.* Image, picture, statue; (Eastern Churches) painting, mosaic, etc. of sacred personage, itself regarded with reverence.

i·con·ic (īkŏn´ĭk) *adj.* Of (the nature of) an image or portrait; (of statues) following a conventional type.

i·con·o·clasm (īkŏn´oklăzem) *n.* Breaking of images. **i·con´o·clast** *n.* Breaker of images, esp. one who took part in movement in 8th and 9th centuries against use of images in religious worship in Eastern Churches; one who assails cherished beliefs and traditional institutions. **i·con·o·clas·tic** (īkŏnoklăs´tĭk) *adj.*

i·con·og·ra·phy (īkonŏg´rafē) *n.* (pl. **-phies**). 1. Description of a subject by drawings or figures; book containing this. 2. Subject matter of art; study of this. **i·co·nog´ra·pher** *n.* 1. Person who illustrates a subject. 2. Student of iconography. **i·con·o·graph·ic** (īkŏnogrăf´ĭk), **i·con·o·graph´i·cal** *adjs.*

i·co·nol·a·try (īkonŏl´atrē) *n.* Worship of images. **i·co·nol´a·ter** *n.*

i·co·nol·o·gy (īkonŏl´ojē) *n.* 1. Study of icons, images, and symbols. 2. Symbolical representation, symbolism. **i·con·o·log·i·cal** (īkonolŏj´ĭkal) *adj.* **i·co·nol´o·gist** *n.*

i·con·o·scope (īkŏn´oskōp) *n.* (formerly trademark) Television camera tube generating high-velocity electron beam to scan the camera's photoemissive mosaic screen.

i·co·sa·he·dron (īkōsahē´dron, īkŏsa-) *n.* (pl. **-drons, -dra** pr. -dra). (geom.) Solid figure of 20 faces; **regular** ~, one formed by 20 equilateral triangles.

-ics *suffix.* Forming nouns (variously considered pl. or sing.) denoting sciences and systems of practical activity, facts, principles, etc. (*acoustics, ethics, tactics*).

ICU *abbrev.* Intensive care unit (in a hospital).

i·cy (ī'sē) *adj.* (**i·ci·er, i·ci·est**). Abounding in, covered with, ice; very cold. **i·ci·ly** (ī'sĭlē) *adv.* **i·ci·ness** (ī'sēnĭs) *n.*

ID *abbrev.* Idaho; identification.

I.D. *abbrev.* Identification; ~ **card**, identification card; ~ **tag, bracelet**, one showing owner's name etc.

Id., Ida. *abbrevs.* Idaho.

id (ĭd) *n.* (psychol.) Part of the mind that comprises the inherited instinctive impulses of the individual together with memories and fantasies evolved in early infancy (cf. EGO).

id. *abbrev.* Idem.

i.d. *abbrev.* Inside diameter.

I'd (īd) *contr.* I would, I should.

-id[1] *suffix.* Forming nouns denoting belonging to the family of (*Nereid*), and forming names of meteors or comets from their apparent parent constellation or comet (*Andromedid, Geminid*).

-id[2] *suffix.* (zool.) Forming nouns and adjectives indicating members of a zoological family, division, or group (*arachnid, hominid, orchid*).

-id[3] *suffix.* (chem.) Early variant of -IDE (*parotid*).

I·da (ī'da), **Mount.** 1. Mountain range in S. Phrygia, near ancient Troy, from whose summit Zeus was supposed to have watched the progress of the Trojan War; scene of the rape of GANYMEDE and the home of PARIS[2]; highest point 5,810 ft. (1,771 m). 2. Ancient name of chief mountain (Mt. Psiloriti) in Crete, where Zeus is said to have been brought up; 8,195 ft. (2,498 m) high.

-ida *pl. suffix.* (zool.) Forming names of orders and classes (*Arachnida*).

-idae *pl. suffix.* (zool.) Forming taxonomic names of families (*Canidae, Hominidae*).

I·da·ho (ī'dahō). State in northwestern U.S.; admitted to .the Union in 1890; capital, Boise.

-ide *suffix.* (chem.) Forming names of simple compounds by addition to the (usu. abbrev.) name of the more electronegative element of the compound (*carbon sulfide, ferrous oxide*).

i·de·a (ī'dē'a) *n.* 1. Mental conception or impression; thought; motion. 2. Opinion, belief, way of thinking. 3. Intention, plan of action; supposition; fantasy. 4. (philos.) Concept of standard or principle that is desirable or ideal; (in Platonic philos.) eternal archetype or pattern from which natural objects etc. derive their being and of which they are imperfect copies; (in Descartes, Locke, et al.) immediate object of thought or mental perception; (in Kant, et al.) conception of

*This Polynesian **idol**, carved in wood, is a representation of the sea-god Tangaroa. He is creating mankind from the human forms that grow from his body. This sculpture comes from Rurutu in the Austral Islands.*

reason transcending all experience; (in Hegel, et al.) absolute truth of which all phenomenal existence is expression.

i·de·al (ī'dē'al) *adj.* 1. Answering to one's highest conception; perfect or supremely excellent of its kind. 2. Embodying an idea; existing only in idea; visionary. 3. (philos.) Being, relating to, an archetype or Platonic idea. ~ *n.* 1. Conception, standard, or model of perfection. 2. Object or aim of noble character. **i·de·al·ly** *adv.*

i·de·al·ism (ī'dē'alĭzem) *n.* 1. Pursuit or cherishing of noble principles, purposes, etc. 2. Idealizing; representation of things in ideal form. 3. (philos.) Theory that the real is of the nature of thought or that the external object of perception consists of ideas. **i·de·al·ist** *n.* **i·de·al·is·tic** (īdēalĭs'tĭk) *adj.*

i·de·al·ize (ī'dē'alīz) *v.* (**-ized -iz·ing**). Represent in ideal form o character, exalt to ideal perfectio or excellence. **i·de·al·i·za·tior** (īdēalīzā'shon) *n.*

i·de·ate (ī'dēāt, īdē'-) *v.* (**-at·ed -at·ing**). Imagine, conceive; form ideas. **i·de·a·tion** (īdēā'shon) *n* **i·de·a'tion·al** *adj.*

i·dée fixe (ēdā fēks') (*pl.* **i·dées fixes** *pr.* ēdā fēks'). Idea tha dominates the mind, monomania [Fr., = "fixed idea"]

i·dem (ī'děm, ĭd'ĕm) *pron* (abbrev. id.) Same author; sam work. [L., = "the same"]

i·den·ti·cal (īděn'tĭkal) *adj.* (one thing etc. viewed at differen times) Very same; (of differen things) agreeing in every deta (with); (logic, math.) expressing a identity; ~ **twins**, twins resultin from fertilization of single ovun and consequently alike in all re spects, including sex (opp. FRATER NAL). **i·den·ti·cal·ly** *adv.*

i·den·ti·fy (īděn'tĭfī) *v.* (**-fied -fy·ing**). 1. Establish or verify th identity of. 2. Treat (thing) a identical (with); associate onesel (*with*) in feeling, interest, etc **i·den·ti·fi·ca·tion** (īděntĭfīkā' shon) *n.* **identification card**, on serving to identify bearer.

i·den·ti·ty (īděn'tĭtē) *n.* (pl **-ties**). 1. Condition or fact tha person or thing is itself and no something else; individuality, per sonality. 2. Absolute sameness oneness; (alg.) equality of two ex pressions for all values of the litera quantities, equation expressin this; ~ **crisis**, (psych.) distressin emotional conflict or confusion in person concerning his social rol and true self, esp. during adoles cence.

ideo- *comb. form.* Denoting idea character (*ideogram, ideograph*).

id·e·o·gram (ĭd'ēogrăm, ī'dē-) **id·e·o·graph** (ĭd'ēogrăf, -grah ī'dē-) *ns.* Character (e.g., i Chinese pictorial writing, numer als, &, $, etc.) symbolizing an ide or object without expressing th sounds (as in a phonetic system that make up its name.

i·de·o·logue (ī'dēolawg, -lŏg ĭd'ē, īdē'-), **i·de·ol·o·gist** (īdēŏl'o jĭst, ĭdē-) *ns.* Advocate of a ideology; theorist, visionary.

i·de·ol·o·gy (īdēŏl'ojē, ĭdē-) *n.* (pl. **-gies**). 1. Doctrine, set of ideas principles, etc. at basis of som political or economic theory o system. 2. Visionary theorizing 3. (philos.) Study of origin an nature of ideas. **i·de·o·log·i·ca** (īdēolŏj'ĭkal, ĭdē-) *adj.* **i·de·o· log'i·cal·ly** *adv.*

ides (īdz) *n.pl.* (considered sing or pl.) (Rom. antiq.) Eighth da after nones (15th day of Mar. May, July, or Oct.; 13th of othe months); ~ **of March**, day

according to tradition, predicted as
that of the assassination of Julius
Caesar, hence, inauspicious day.

id est (ĭd ĕst´) (abbrev. i.e.) That
is. [L.]

idio- *comb. form.* Individual,
peculiar to one (*idiomatic, idio-
ncrasy*).

id·i·o·cy (ĭd´ēosē) *n.* (pl. **-cies**).
Mental condition of an IDIOT; extreme imbecility, utter foolishness.

id·i·om (ĭd´ēom) *n.* Language of
people, area, or country; specific
character of this; form of expression
peculiar to a language; characteristic mode of expression in art, music,
etc. **id·i·o·mat·ic** (ĭdēomăt´ĭk) *adj.*
characteristic of a particular
language; vernacular, colloquial.
id·i·o·mat'i·cal·ly *adv.*

id·i·o·mor·phic (ĭdēomōr´fĭk)
adj. (min.) Having its own characteristic form, esp. its characteristic
crystallographic faces.

id·i·o·syn·cra·sy (ĭdēosĭng´-
rasē) *n.* (pl. **-sies**). Habit, mannerism, view, mode of expression,
peculiar to a person; (med.) physical
constitution peculiar to a person.
id·i·o·syn·crat·ic (ĭdēōsĭnkrăt´ĭk)
adj.

id·i·ot (ĭd´ēot) *n.* Person so
deficient in mind as to be permanently incapable of rational conduct and having a mental development not exceeding that of an
average normal child of two years
old (the lowest grade of mental
deficiency, next below IMBECILE);
utter fool; ~ **box**, (slang) television
set; ~ **card**, (slang) cue card for
television performer; ~ **light**,
(slang) warning light on automobile
dashboard indicating malfunction
etc. **id·i·ot·ic** (ĭdēot´ĭk) *adj.*
id·i·ot'i·cal·ly *adv.*

i·dle (ī´del) *adj.* (**i·dler, i·dlest**).
1. Unoccupied; lazy, indolent; (of
things) not in use or operation; (of
of money) not in circulation. **2.**
(of words, action, etc.) Worthless,
insignificant, frivolous, groundless; ~ **wheel,** intermediate wheel
transmitting motion between two
geared wheels without changing the
direction of the motion. **i·dle·-
ness** *n.* **i·dly** *adv.* **idle** *v.*
(**i·dled, i·dling**). Be idle; pass
(time etc.) *away* in idleness; saunter, loiter; (of engine etc.) run at
low speed without doing any work.
i·dler *n.*

i·dol (ī´dol) *n.* Image of deity
used as object of worship; false god;
person, thing, that is object of
excessive devotion; (logic) false
mental image or conception.

i·dol·a·ter (īdŏl´ater) *n.* (fem.
i·dol·a·tress pr. īdŏl´atrĭs). Worshipper of idols; devoted admirer
(of). **i·dol'a·try** *n.* (pl. **-tries**).
i·dol'a·trous *adj.* **i·dol'a·trous·ly**
adv.

i·dol·ize (ī´dolīz) *v.* (**-ized, -iz-
ing**). Make an idol of; venerate,

love, to excess; practice idolatry.
i·dol·i·za·tion (īdolīzā´shon) *n.*

Id·u·mae·a, Id·u·me·a (ĭdyu-
mē´a) = EDOM. **Id·u·mae'an** *adj.*
& *n.*

I·dun (ē´dhoon), **I·dun·a** (ē´-
dhoona). (Scand. myth.) Goddess
of spring, wife of Bragi; she kept the
apples that restored the youth of the
gods.

i·dyll (ī´dĭl) *n.* Short description in verse or (**prose ~**) in prose
of pastoral or charmingly simple
scene or incident; episode suitable
for such treatment. **i·dyl·lic**
(īdĭl´ĭk) *adj.* **i·dyl'li·cal·ly** *adv.*

i.e. *abbrev.* *Id est* (L. that is).

-ie *suffix.* Variant of -Y³ (*Charlie,
dearie*).

IF *abbrev.* (radio) Intermediate
frequency.

if (ĭf) *conj.* On the condition or
supposition that; whenever;
whether; even though; **as if,** as the
case would be if, as though. **if** *n.*
Condition, supposition; uncertain
possibility.

if·fy (ĭf´ē) *adj.* (**if·fi·er, if·fi·est**).
(colloq.) Uncertain, doubtful;
chancy.

I·gerne: see IGRAINE.

ig·loo (ĭg´lōō) *n.* (pl. **-loos**).
Eskimo dome-shaped house, esp.
one built of blocks of compact
snow. [Eskimo, = "house"]

Ig·na·tius[1] (ĭgnā´shus), **St.** (Ignatius Theophorus)   Bishop of
Antioch, martyred at Rome early in
2nd c.

Ig·na·tius[2] **Loyola** (ĭgnā´shus)
St. (1491–1556). Spanish soldier
and ecclesiastic, founder of the
Society of Jesus (see JESUIT).

ig·ne·ous (ĭg´nēus) *adj.* Produced by volcanic agency; of fire,
fiery.

ig·nis fat·u·us (ĭg´nĭs făch´ōoĭs)
(pl. **ig·nes fat·u·i** pr. ĭg´nēz
făch´ōoī). Will-o'-the-wisp, phosphorescent light (now rarely) seen
on marshy ground, supposedly due
to the spontaneous combustion of
marsh gas (CH_4), containing traces
of phosphorus compounds; delusive hope, aim, etc. [med. or mod.
L., = foolish fire]

ig·nite (ĭgnīt´) *v.* (**-nit·ed, -nit·-
ing**). Set on fire; take fire; (chem.)
heat to point of combustion or
chemical change. **ig·ni·tion**
(ĭgnĭsh´on) *n.* Igniting; (esp.) process or mechanism that ignites
fuel in cylinder of internal combustion engine.

*The **iguana** is found in tropical America
and Madagascar. It usually lives in trees
but takes readily to water and feeds
mainly on young leaves, flowers and
fruits. Some species are hunted for
their flesh.*

marine iguana

common iguana

The Middle Western State of Illi
contains one of the country's larg
cities, Chicago — the center of
meat-packing industry. The city's
line is shown here.

ig·no·ble (ĭgnō'bel) *adj*. Of low birth, position, or reputation; mean, base, dishonorable. **ig·no'ble·ness** *n*. **ig·no'bly** *adv*.

ig·no·min·y (ĭg'nōmĭnē) *n*. (pl. **-min·ies**). Dishonor, infamy. **ig·no·min·i·ous** (ĭgnōmĭn'ēus) *adj*. Marked by ignominy; humiliating. **ig·no·min·i·ous·ly** *adv*.

ig·no·ra·mus (ĭgnōrā'mus, -răm'us) *n*. (pl. **-mus·es**). Ignorant person. [L., = we do not know]

ig·no·rance (ĭg'norans) *n*. Want of knowledge. **ig'no·rant** *adj*. Lacking knowledge; uninformed (*of*, *in*). **ig'no·rant·ly** *adv*.

ig·nore (ĭgnōr', -nōr') *v.t.* (**-nored, -nor·ing**). Refuse to take notice of or accept.

I·graine (ĭgrān'), **I·gerne**, **Y·gerne** (ĭgĕrn'). (Arthurian legend) Wife of Gorlois of Cornwall and mother (by Uther Pendragon) of Arthur.

i·gua·na (ĭgwah'na) *n*. Any of the large tropical American lizards of the family Iguanidae; most have spiny projections along the back, and some grow to more than 5 ft. (1½ m).

IGY *abbrev*. International Geophysical Year (the 1st being the 18-month period from July 1, 1957, to Dec. 31, 1958, devoted to co-operative international geophysical studies and exploration).

IHS. First three letters of Greek ΙΗΣΟΥΣ (*Iēsous*) Jesus; often taken as initials of *Jesus Hominum Salvator* "Jesus savior of men" or *In Hoc Signo* (vinces) "in this sign (thou shalt conquer)," or *In Hac* (cruce) *Salus* "in this (cross) is salvation."

i·ke·ba·na (ēkĕbah'nah) *n*. Japanese art of flower arranging with strict rules emphasizing form and balance. [Jap., = living flowers]

Ikh·na·ton (ĭknah'ton) = AKHNATON.

IL *abbrev*. Illinois.

il- *prefix*. Form of IN-[1,2] before *l* (*illuminate, illogical*).

ILA *abbrev*. International Longshoremen's Association.

i·lang-i·lang (ē'lahng ē'lahng) = YLANG-YLANG.

Île-de-France (ēl de frahns'). Region and former province of France, with Paris as capital, between rivers Seine, Oise, Marne, and Aisne.

il·e·os·to·my (ĭlēŏs'tōmē) *n*. (pl. **-mies**). (surg.) (Formation of) an opening from the ileum through the abdominal wall.

il·e·um (ĭl'ēum) *n*. (pl. **il·e·a** pr. ĭl'ēa). (anat.) Third and terminal portion of small intestine, opening into large intestine. **il·e·i·tis** (ĭlēī'tĭs) *n*.

i·lex (ī'lĕks) *n*. 1. Holm oak. 2. Tree or shrub of genus *I*~ having small flowers and berrylike fruits; holly.

I.L.G.W.U. *abbrev*. International Ladies' Garment Workers' Union.

il·i·ac (ĭl'ēăk) *adj*. Of the flank or flank bone (ILIUM); but orig. of or affecting the ILEUM.

Il·i·ad (ĭl'ēad). Greek epic poem attributed to Homer, describing incidents in the tenth and last year of the siege of Troy by the Greeks, esp. "the wrath of Achilles."

Il·i·um (ĭl'ēum). Troy. [L. fo of Gk. name *Ilion*]

il·i·um (ĭl'ēum) *n*. (pl. **il·i·a** ĭl'ēa). (anat.) Hipbone, the anter or superior bone of the pelvis.

ilk (ĭlk) *n*. (colloq.) Family, cla or kind.

ill (ĭl) *adj*. 1. Sick; (of physi and mental health) unsound, d ordered. 2. Morally bad; harmf hostile; unkind; wretched, dis trous; ~ **fame**, bad repute; hou **of** ~ **fame**, brothel; ~ w animosity. 3. Unskillful; manners or conduct) improper. *n*. Evil, the opposite of good; har injury; misfortune, calamity, adv sity. ~ *adv*. Badly; unfavorab imperfectly, scarcely; ~ **at ea** embarrassed, uneasy; ~**-advise** imprudent; ~**-advisedly**; **bred**, badly brought up, ru ~**-considered**, unwise, r thoroughly considered; **disposed**, disposed to evil, mal olent; unfavorably disposed, u sympathetic (toward); ~**-fate** destined to, bringing, bad fortu ~**-favored**, uncomely; disple ing, objectionable; ~**-gotte** gained by evil or improper mea ~**-humored**, bad-tempered; **judged**, unwise; ~**-natured**, ba tempered, malevolent; ~**-starre** born under an evil star, unluck ~**-suited**, inappropriate; ~ timed, inopportune; ~**-trea -use**, treat badly.

Ill. *abbrev*. Illinois.

I'll (ĭl). *contr*. I will; I shall.

ill. *abbrev*. Illustrated; illustr tion; illustrator.

il·la·tion (ĭlā'shon) *n*. Dedu tion, conclusion; thing deduce inference.

il·le·gal (ĭlē'gal) *adj*. Not leg contrary to law. **il·le'gal·ly** a **il·le·gal·i·ty** (ĭlēgăl'ĭtē) *n*.

il·leg·i·ble (ĭlĕj'ĭbel) *adj*. N legible. **il·leg·i·bil·i·ty** (ĭlĕ bĭl'ĭtē) *n*. **il·leg'i·bly** *adv*.

il·le·git·i·mate (ĭlĭjĭt'ĭmĭt) *a* Not legitimate; (esp.) born out wedlock. **il·le·git'i·mate·ly** a **il·le·git'i·ma·cy** *n*. illegi **mate** (ĭlĭjĭt'ĭmāt) *v.t.* (**-mat -mating**). Declare illegitimate.

il·lib·er·al (ĭlĭb'eral) a Narrow-minded, bigoted; sting **il·lib'er·al·ly** *adv*. **il·lib·er·al·i** (ĭlĭberăl'ĭtē) *n*. (pl. **-ties**).

il·lic·it (ĭlĭs'ĭt) *adj*. Not p mitted, forbidden; unlawful, u licensed. **il·lic'it·ly** *adv*.

il·lim·it·a·ble (ĭlĭm'ĭtabel) a Boundless. **il·lim·it·a·bil·i** (ĭlĭmĭtabĭl'ĭtē), **il·lim'it·a·ble·ne** *ns*. **il·lim'it·a·bly** *adv*.

Il·li·noi·an (ĭlĭnoi'an) *adj*. pertaining to the third glacial sta

Il·li·nois[1] (ĭlĭnoi′, -noiz′). State
n north-central U.S.; admitted to
he Union in 1818; capital, Spring-
eld.

Il·li·nois[2] (ĭlĭnoi′, -noiz′) *n.*
ndian of confederacy of Algon-
uian tribes formerly living in
llinois and parts of Iowa and Wis-
onsin.

il·lit·er·ate (ĭlĭt′erĭt) *adj.* Un-
ble to read and write; unlearned.
~ *n.* Illiterate person. **il·lit·er·**
·cy (ĭlĭt′erasē), **il·lit·er·ate·ness**
s.

ill·ness (ĭl′nĭs) *n.* Disease,
lment, sickness.

il·log·i·cal (ĭlŏj′ĭkal) *adj.* De-
oid of, contrary to, logic. **il·**
og′i·cal·ly *adv.* **il·log·i·cal·i·ty**
lŏjĭkăl′ĭtē) *n.*

il·lume (ĭlōōm′) *v.t.* (**-lumed,**
lum·ing). (poet.) Light up, make
right.

il·lu·mi·nate (ĭlōō′mĭnāt) *v.t.*
-nat·ed, -nat·ing). Light up,
upply with light; enlighten; throw
ght upon (subject); shed luster
pon; decorate (buildings etc.) pro-
sely with lights; decorate (initial
tter in manuscript etc.) with gold,
lver, and brilliant colors. **il·lu·**
ni·na·tion (ĭlōōmĭnā′shon) *n.* Act
r process of illuminating; supply of
ght; state of being illuminated;
nlightenment; decoration of lights;
olored decorations in a manu-
cript; (optics) surface light density
er unit area on an intercepting
urface (see FOOT candle, LUMEN[1],
UX, PHOT). **il·lu·mi·na·tor** *n.*
·lu·mi·na·tive (ĭlōō′mĭnātĭv,
natĭv) *adj.*

il·lu·mine (ĭlōō′mĭn) *v.t.*
-mined, -min·ing). Light up;
nlighten spiritually; brighten. **il·**
u′min·ism, il·lu′min·ist *ns.*

illus. *abbrev.* Illustrated; il-
stration; illustrator.

il·lu·sion (ĭlōō′zhon) *n.* Decep-
ion, delusion; physical perception
f an external object involving a
alse belief.

il·lu·sion·ist (ĭlōō′zhonĭst) *n.* 1.
onjurer, magician who produces
lusions. 2. One who believes the
naterial world is an illusion.

il·lu·sive (ĭlōō′sĭv) *adj.* Decep-
ve. **il·lu′sive·ly** *adv.* **il·lu′sive·**
ess *n.*

il·lu·so·ry (ĭlōō′serē, -zerē) *adj.*
laving the character of an illusion,
nreal. **il·lu′so·ri·ly** *adv.* **il·lu′-**
o·ri·ness *n.*

il·lus·trate (ĭl′ustrāt, ĭlŭs′-) *v.t.*
-trat·ed, -trat·ing). Make clear,
xplain; make clear by examples;
lucidate (description etc.) by
rawings; ornament (book, news-
aper etc.) with pictures etc. **il′-**
us·tra·tor *n.* **il·lus·tra·tion**
ĭlustrā′shon) *n.* Illustrating; ex-
mple; drawing etc. illustrating
ook or article in paper.

il·lus·tra·tive (ĭlŭs′tratĭv,

ĭl′ustrā-) *adj.* Serving as explanation or example (*of*). **il·lus′tra·**
tive·ly *adv.*

il·lus·tri·ous (ĭlŭs′trēus) *adj.*
Distinguished, renowned. **il·lus′-**
tri·ous·ly *adv.* **il·lus′tri·ous·ness**
n.

Il·lyr·i·a (ĭlēr′ēa). Ancient
region extending along Balkan
coast of Adriatic and including
modern Dalmatia, Bosnia and
Herzegovina, Montenegro, and
part of Albania.

Il·lyr·i·an (ĭlēr′ēan) *adj.* Of
Illyria. ~ *n.* Native, inhabitant,
of Illyria; Indo-European language
(closely related to modern Alba-
nian) of the Illyrians.

I.L.O. *abbrev.* International
Labor Organization.

I·lus (ī′lus). (Gk. legend)
Founder of Troy (Gk. *Ilion*) and
grandfather of Priam.

I'm (īm) *contr.* I am.

im- *prefix.* Form of IN-[1,2] before
b, m, p.

im·age (ĭm′ĭj) *n.* 1. Artificial
imitation of external form of an
object, e.g. statue; form, semblance;
(esp.) figure of saint or divinity as
object of religious veneration. 2.
Optical appearance or counterpart
of object produced by rays of light
reflected from a mirror or refracted
through any transparent medium.
3. Mental picture, idea, conception;
general impression (of person,
party, etc.) given to others. ~ *v.t.*
(**-aged, -ag·ing**). Make an image
of, portray; reflect, mirror; picture,
imagine; describe vividly; typify.

im·age·ry (ĭm′ĭjrē) *n.* (pl. **-ries**).
Images; statuary, carving; figurative illustration.

i·mag·i·na·ble (ĭmăj′inabel) *adj.*
That can be imagined. **i·mag′i·**
na·bly *adv.*

i·mag·i·nar·y (ĭmăj′inĕrē) *adj.*
Existing only in imagination;
(math.) having no real existence,
but assumed to exist for a special
purpose (as an ~ **number**), e.g.
the square root of a negative
quantity.

i·mag·i·na·tion (ĭmăjinā′shon)
n. Imagining; mental faculty form-

ing images of external objects not
present to the senses; fancy; creative
faculty of the mind.

i·mag·i·na·tive (ĭmăj′inatĭv,
-nātĭv) *adj.* Of, given to using,
having or showing in a high degree,
the faculty of imagination. **i·mag′-**
i·na·tive·ly *adv.* **i·mag′i·na·**
tive·ness *n.*

i·mag·ine (ĭmăj′ĭn) *v.* (**-ined,**
-in·ing). Form mental image (*of*);
conceive; guess, suppose, be of
opinion; take into one's head.

im·ag·ism (ĭm′ajĭzem) *n.* Movement in Amer. and Brit. poetry,
originating in 1912 and represented
by Ezra Pound, Amy Lowell, Hilda
Doolittle, and others, in revolt
against romanticism and using free
verse and exact visual images.
im′ag·ist *n.*

i·ma·go (ĭmā′gō) *n.* (pl. **i·ma-**
goes, i·ma·gi·nes pr. ĭmăj′inēz).
1. (entom.) Final and perfect stage
of adult insect after it has undergone all its metamorphoses. 2.
(psychol.) Idealized concept of a
person, esp. a parent, formed in
childhood and retained in the unconscious.

i·mam (ĭmahm′), **i·maum**
(ĭmahm′, ĭmawm′) *ns.* 1. In Muslim communities, name given to the
person who is regarded as taking
Muhammad's place as leader of
Islam, esp. any of 12 successive
heads of Islam, beginning with Ali
and his sons, recognized by the
Shiites, hence, any great spiritual
leader. 2. Official who leads the
prayers in a mosque. 3. Any of the
hereditary rulers of Yemen.
i·mam·ate (ĭmah′māt) *n.* Office,
title, of imam. [Arab. 'imam leader
f. 'amma lead]

im·bal·ance (ĭmbăl′ans) *n.* 1.
Lack of balance; disproportion; esp.
state of having a disproportionately
large number of one racial or
ethnic group (as in a school), or

*Castle at Disneyland, L.A. Many historic
monuments are **illuminated** in this way
so that people can enjoy them by night.
Illumination is also an important safety
measure for motorists and pedestrians
in urban areas.*

disproportion of men or women in a population. 2. (psychol.) Disturbance of mental or bodily equilibrium.

im·be·cile (ĭm´besĭl, -sĭl; *Brit.* ĭm´besēl) *n.* Adult person whose intelligence is equal to that of the average normal child between the ages of 3 and 7 years, or between 25 and 50 per cent of that of the average normal adult (see also IDIOT, MORON); person of weak intellect. ~ *adj.* Mentally weak, stupid, absurd. **im·be·cil·i·ty** (ĭmbesĭl´ĭtē) *n.*

im·bed (ĭmbĕd´) = EMBED.

im·bibe (ĭmbīb´) *v.t.* (**-bibed, -bib·ing**). Drink in, assimilate, (ideas etc.); drink (liquid); inhale (air etc.); absorb (moisture etc.). **im·bi·bi·tion** (ĭmbĭbĭsh´on) *n.*

im·bri·cate (ĭm´brĭkāt) *v.* (**-cat·ed, -cat·ing**). Arrange (leaves, scales of fish, etc.), be arranged, so as to overlap like tiles. ~ (ĭm´brĭkĭt, -kāt) *odj.* So arranged. **im·bri·ca·tion** (ĭmbrĭkā´shon) *n.*

im·bro·glio (ĭmbrōl´yō) *n.* (pl. **-glios**). 1. Confused or complicated state of affairs; difficult predicament; confused heap. 2. Misunderstanding, disagreement.

im·bue (ĭmbū´) *v.t.* (**-bued, -bu·ing**). Saturate (*with*); dye (*with*); permeate, inspire (*with* feelings etc.); imbrue.

I.M.F. *abbrev.* International Monetary Fund.

im·i·ta·ble (ĭm´ĭtabel) *adj.* Capable of being imitated. **im·i·ta·bil·i·ty** (ĭmĭtabĭl´ĭtē) *n.*

im·i·tate (ĭm´ĭtāt) *v.t.* (**-tat·ed, -tat·ing**). Follow example of; mimic, copy; be like. **im·i·ta·tion** (ĭmĭtā´shon) *n.* Imitating; copy; counterfeit (freq. attrib.); **im´i·ta·tor** *n.*

im·i·ta·tive (ĭm´ĭtātĭv) *adj.* Following model or example (*of*); characterized by, consisting in, imitation; fictitious, counterfeit. **im´i·ta·tive·ly** *adv.* **im´i·ta·tive·ness** *n.*

im·mac·u·late (ĭmăk´yulĭt) *adj.* Pure, spotless; faultless; (biol.) not spotted; **I~ Conception**, doctrine that the Virgin Mary was conceived free from taint of original sin (in 1854 declared an article of faith of Roman Catholicism). **im·mac´u·late·ly** *adv.* **im·mac´u·la·cy** *n.*

im·ma·nent (ĭm´anent) *adj.* Indwelling, inherent (*in*); (of God) permanently pervading the universe (opp. TRANSCENDENT). **im´ma·nence, im´ma·nen·cy** *ns.*

Im·man·u·el, Em·man·u·el (ĭmăn´ūel) *n.* Name of the coming Messiah as prophesied by Isaiah (Isa. 7, 8; Matt. 1), represented in Christian exegesis as being Christ. [Heb., = "God with us"]

im·ma·te·ri·al (ĭmatēr´ēal) *adj.* 1. Not relevant, unimportant. 2.

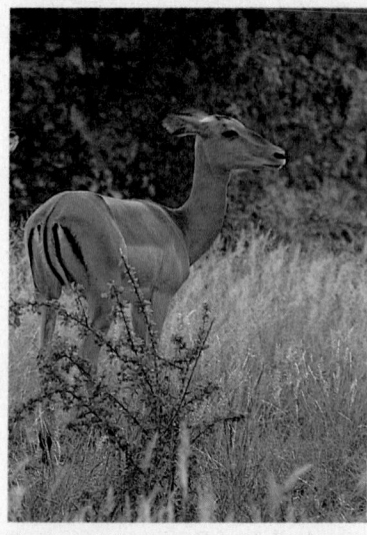

The **Impala** is a species of African antelope which can travel at great speed and can jump up to 30 ft. in length and 10 ft. high when disturbed. Its slight build lends grace to its movements.

Not material, incorporeal. **im·ma·te´ri·al·ism** *n.* Doctrine that there is no material world and all things exist only in the mind or have only spiritual existence. **im·ma·te´ri·al·ist** *n.* **im·ma·te·ri·a·bil·i·ty** (ĭmatērēabĭl´ĭtē) *n.*

im·ma·ture (ĭmatoor´, -tūr´, -choor´) *adj.* Not mature, not developed fully; youthful. **im·ma·tu´ri·ty** *n.*

im·meas·ur·a·ble (ĭmĕzh´erabel) *adj.* Not measurable, immense. **im·meas´ur·a·ble·ness, im·meas·ur·a·bil·i·ty** (ĭmĕzherabĭl´ĭtē) *ns.* **im·meas´ur·a·bly** *adv.*

im·me·di·ate (ĭmē´dēĭt) *adj.* Occurring at once, without delay; of, pertaining to the present time; not separated by or not having any intervening object, agent, or medium, next, nearest; ~ **inference**, (logic) inference from single premise, without intervention of middle term. **im·me´di·ate·ly** *adv.* **im·me´di·ate·ness, im·me·di·a·cy** (ĭmē´dēase) *ns.*

Im·mel·mann (ĭm´elmahn, -man) *turn.* (aviation) Fighter plane or stunt plane maneuver of half loop followed by half roll to gain altitude and reverse direction quickly. [f. Max *Immelmann*, (1890–1916) German aviator]

im·me·mo·ri·al (ĭmemōr´ēal, -mōr´-) *adj.* Ancient beyond memory; very old. **im·me·mo´ri·al·ly** *adv.*

im·mense (ĭmĕns´) *adj.* Vast, huge; **im´mense·ly** *adv.* In an immense degree; (colloq.) very much. **im·men·si·ty** (ĭmĕn´sĭtē) *n.* (pl. **-ties**).

im·merse (ĭmĕrs´) *v.t.* (**-mersed, -mers·ing**). Dip, plunge (*in* liquid); put below surface of water, esp. baptize thus; bury,

embed, (*in*); involve deeply, absor (*in* debt, difficulties, thought, etc.

im·mer·sion (ĭmĕr´zhon, -sho *n.* Immersing; baptism by plungi whole person in water; absorptio (*in* thought etc.); (astron.) di appearance of celestial body in eclipse behind another or in i shadow; ~ **heater**, electrical ele ment, usu. thermostatically con trolled, immersed in water which heats.

im·mi·grate (ĭm´igrāt) (**-grat·ed, -grat·ing**). Come settler (*into* foreign country); im **mi·grant** (ĭm´igrant) *adj.* & **im·mi·gra·tion** (ĭmigrā´shon)

im·mi·nent (ĭm´inent) *adj.* (C events, esp. dangers) impending soon to happen. **im´mi·nent·l** *adv.* **im´mi·nence** *n.*

im·mis·ci·ble (ĭmĭs´ibel) *ad* That cannot be mixed. **im·mis ci·bil·i·ty** (ĭmĭsibĭl´ĭtē) *n.* im **mis´ci·bly** *adv.*

im·mo·bile (ĭmō´bĭl, -bēl) *ad* Immovable; not mobile; motion less. **im·mo·bil·i·ty** (ĭmōbĭl´ĭtē)

im·mo·bi·lize (ĭmō´bĭlīz) *v.* (**-lized, -liz·ing**). Fix immovably render immobile or stationary; kee (limb, patient) restricted in move ment in order to heal; restrict movement of; withdraw (specie from circulation, holding it agains bank notes to create a monetar reserve or a fixed capital. **im·mo bi·li·za·tion** (ĭmōbĭlizā´shon) *n.*

im·mod·er·ate (ĭmŏd´erĭt) *ad* Excessive, wanting in moderation **im·mod´er·ate·ly** *adv.* **im·mod ·er·a·tion** (ĭmŏderā´shon) *n.*

im·mod·est (ĭmŏd´ĭst) *ad* Lacking modesty; shameless; im pudent. **im·mod´est·ly** *adv.* **im mod´es·ty** *n.* (pl. **-ties**).

im·mo·late (ĭm´olāt) *v.t.* (**-lat ed, -lat·ing**). Kill (victim) as sacrifice, as by fire; (fig.) sacrific (thing etc. to another). **im·mo·la tion** (ĭmolā´shon), **im´mo·la·to** *ns.*

im·mo·ral (ĭmŏr´al, -mär´-) *ad* Not conforming to morality morally evil; vicious, dissolute **im·mor´al·ist** *n.* **im·mor´al·ly** *adv.* **im·mo·ral·i·ty** (ĭmorăl´ĭtē) *n.*

im·mor·tal (ĭmôr´tal) *adj.* No mortal, not subject to death; divine remembered or celebrated forever everlasting, perpetual. **im·mor tal·ly** *adv.* **immortal** *n.* Im mortal being, esp. (pl.) gods o classical mythology; person, esp author, of enduring fame; **Th I~s**, 40 members of the Académi Française (so called because eac member's place is filled as soon as he dies); picked body of 10,00 infantry forming ancient Persia royal bodyguard. **im·mor·tal·i·t** (ĭmôrtăl´ĭtē) *n.*

im·mor·tal·ize (ĭmôr´talīz) *v.t* (**-ized, -iz·ing**). Confer enduring fame upon; endow with endless life erpetuate. **im·mor·tal·i·za·tion** (ĭmȯrtălĭzā'shȯn) *n.*

im·mor·telle (ĭmȯrtĕl') *n.* Any several flowers of papery texture taining color and shape after eing dried.

im·mov·a·ble (ĭmoo̅'vabel) *adj.* hat cannot be moved, stationary; otionless; not subject to change; eadfast, unyielding; emotionless; aw, of property) consisting of nd, houses, etc.; = REAL; not anging from one date to another different years, occurring on a xed date of the modern calendar s an ~ **feast** or holiday). **im·- ov'a·ble·ness, im·mov·a·bil·- ty** (ĭmoo̅vabĭl'ĭtē) *ns.* **im·mov'- ·bly** *adv.* **im·mov'a·bles** *n.pl.* nmovable property.

im·mune (ĭmūn') *adj.* Having nmunity, exempt; (esp.) protected om a disease by natural resistance inoculation; ~ **response,** ~ **eaction,** living organism's natural ejection of or reaction to foreign ssues or agents.

im·mu·ni·ty (ĭmū'nĭtē) *n.* (pl. **ties**). 1. Freedom (from); (law) xemption (*from* taxation, jurisdic- on, etc.). 2. (physiol.) That roperty of a living organism by hich infection is resisted and over- ome; **active** ~, increased resist- nce to an invading microbe or its roducts, developed in response to fection (whether a natural infec- on or one introduced artificially), s distinct from **passive** ~, tem- orary resistance acquired pre- atally or by injection of antibody; **cquired** ~, immunity of an rganism that manufactures, or is ijected with, antibodies.

im·mu·nize (ĭm'yunīz) *v.t.* -**nized, -niz·ing**). Render im- une (*against* infection). **im·mu·- i·za·tion** (ĭmyunĭzā'shȯn) *n.*

immuno- *comb. form* (before

vowel **immun-**) = immune, im- munity (*immunology, immunosup- pression*).

im·mu·nol·o·gy (ĭmyunŏl'ojē) *n.* (pl. **-gies**). Study of immunity from disease and the conditions governing it. **im·mu·nol'o·gist** *n.*

im·mu·no·sup·pres·sion (ĭm- yunōsuprĕsh'on) *n.* Medical sup- pression (as by drugs) of natural immune responses. **im·mu·no·- sup·pres'sant** *n.* **im·mu·no·- sup·pres'sive** *adj.*

im·mure (ĭmūr') *v.t.* (**-mured, -mur·ing**). Enclose within walls, imprison, confine; entomb or build into a wall. **im·mure'ment** *n.*

im·mu·ta·ble (ĭmū'tabel) *adj.* Unchangeable; not subject to varia- tion. **im·mu·ta·bil·i·ty** (ĭmūta- bĭl'ĭtē) *n.* **im·mu·ta·bly** *adv.*

Imp. *abbrev.* Emperor; empress; imperial. [L. *imperator, impera- trix*]

imp (ĭmp) *n.* Child of the devil; little devil; mischievous child.

imp. *abbrev.* (gram.) Impera- tive; imperfect; imperfection; im- perial; import; imported; imprima- tur.

im·pact[1] (ĭm'păkt) *n.* 1. Strik- ing, collision. 2. (fig.) Influence, effect.

im·pact[2] (ĭmpăkt') *v.t.* Press, fix, closely or firmly (*into, in*); crowd densely, wedge together. **im·pac·tion** (ĭmpăk'shon) *n.* (esp., surg.) Fracture in which broken parts are driven together so as to become locked; (dentistry) con- dition in which a tooth is so con- fined in its socket as to prevent normal growth through the gum.

*The **Impatiens** genus of plants has widespread distribution particularly in Africa, Asia and North America. The name meaning 'impatient' relates to the speed of seed dispersal.*

im·pair (ĭmpār') *v.t.* Damage, weaken. **im·pair'ment** *n.*

im·pa·la (ĭmpăl'a, -pah'la) *n.* (pl. **-pa·las,** collect. **-pa·la**). African antelope (*Aepyceros melam- pus*) with reddish coat and great leaping ability, the male having lyre-shaped, ringed horns. [f. Zulu]

im·pale (ĭmpāl') *v.t.* (**-paled, -pal·ing**). Transfix (body etc., *with*, sharpened stake, pin, etc., esp. as form of capital punishment). **im·pale'ment** *n.*

im·pal·pa·ble (ĭmpăl'pabel) *adj.* Imperceptible to the touch; not easily grasped by the mind; in- tangible. **im·pal·pa·bil·i·ty** (ĭm- pălpabĭl'ĭtē) *n.* **im·pal'pa·bly** *adv.*

im·pan·el (ĭmpăn'el), **em·- pan·el** (ĕmpăn'el) *vbs.t.* Enter on a panel for jury duty; enroll (a jury). **im·pan'el·ment** *n.*

im·part (ĭmpärt') *v.t.* Com- municate, make known, relate (news, etc. *to*); give share of, bestow.

im·par·tial (ĭmpär'shal) *adj.* Not partial, unprejudiced, fair. **im·par'tial·ly** *adv.* **im·par·ti- al·i·ty** (ĭmpärshēăl'ĭtē) *n.*

im·pass·a·ble (ĭmpăs'abel) *adj.* That cannot be traversed; that cannot be surmounted or overcome. **im·pass'a·ble·ness, im·pass·a·- bil·i·ty** (ĭmpăsabĭl'ĭtē) *ns.*

im·passe (ĭm'păs, ĭmpăs') *n.* Deadlock, unresolvable dilemma; position from which there is no escape; road having no exit, dead end.

im·pas·si·ble (ĭmpăs'ibel) *adj.* Incapable of feeling or emotion; in- capable of suffering injury; not sub- ject to suffering. **im·pas'si·ble·- ness, im·pas·si·bil·i·ty** (ĭmpăsi- bĭl'ĭtē) *ns.* **im·pas'si·bly** *adv.*

im·pas·sion (ĭmpăsh'on) *v.t.* Stir the passions of, excite strongly (chiefly in past part.).

im·pas·sive (ĭmpăs'ĭv) *adj.* De- ficient in feeling or emotion; serene; without sensation; not sub- ject to suffering. **im·pas'sive·ly** *adv.* **im·pas'sive·ness, im·pas·- siv·i·ty** (ĭmpăsĭv'ĭtē) *ns.*

im·pas·to (ĭmpăs'tō, -pah'stō) *n.* (pl. **-tos**). (paint.) Laying on of color thickly; (ceramics) enamel colors on slip standing out in relief from surface of ware.

im·pa·tiens (ĭmpā'shenz, -shens) *n.* Any plant of the genus *I* ~, including the ornamental garden balsam (*I. balsamins*) and the jewelweed. [L. impatient, because seed pods burst and scatter seeds when barely touched]

im·pa·tient (ĭmpā'shent) *adj.* Not patient, not enduring with composure; intolerant *of*; restlessly desirous (*for* thing, *to* do). **im·- pa'tient·ly** *adv.* **im·pa'tience** *n.*

im·peach (ĭmpēch') *v.t.* Call in question, disparage (character, the credibility of, etc.); accuse (person) *of*, charge *with*; find fault with; accuse (a public official) of high crime before competent tribunal. **im·peach′ment** *n.* Calling in question; accusation and prosecution of a public official for high crime or before a competent tribunal, as the presentation of formal charges against a high public official by the lower house of a legislature for possible trial before the upper house. **im·peach′-a·ble** *adj.*

im·pec·ca·ble (ĭmpĕk′abel) *adj.* Faultless, irreproachable; not liable to sin. **im·pec·ca·bil·i·ty** (ĭmpĕkabĭl′ĭtē) *n.* **im·pec′ca·bly** *adv.*

im·pe·cu·ni·ous (ĭmpekū′nēus) *adj.* Having little or no money. **im·pe·cu·ni·os·i·ty** (ĭmpekūnēŏs′-ĭtē) *n.*

im·ped·ance (ĭmpē′dans) *n.* (elect.) Resistance of an electric circuit to the flow of alternating current.

im·pede (ĭmpēd′) *v.t.* (**-ped·ed, -ped·ing**). Retard, hinder.

im·ped·i·ment (ĭmpĕd′ĭment) *n.* Hindrance, obstruction; (also **speech** ~) stammer, stutter.

im·pel (ĭmpĕl′) *v.t.* (**-pelled, -pel·ling**). Drive or urge forward, propel. **im·pel′lent** *n.*

im·pend (ĭmpĕnd′) *v.i.* Be imminent; be a threat or menace; hang, be suspended (*over*). **im·-pend′ence, im·pend′en·cy** *ns.* **im·pend′ent** *adj.*

im·pen·e·tra·ble (ĭmpĕn′etra-bel) *adj.* That cannot be penetrated, pierced, entered, etc.; inscrutable, unfathomable; impervious; (phys.) having that property in virtue of which 2 bodies cannot occupy same place at same time. **im·pen′e·tra·ble·ness, im·pen·e·tra·bil·i·ty** (ĭmpĕnetra-bĭl′ĭtē) *ns.* **im·pen′e·tra·bly** *adv.*

im·pen·i·tent (ĭmpĕn′ĭtent) *adj.* Not penitent. **im·pen′i·tent·ly** *adv.* **im·pen′i·tence** *n.*

imper. *abbrev.* Imperative.

im·per·a·tive (ĭmpĕr′atĭv) *adj.* 1. (gram., of verbal mood, or form belonging to it) Expressing command, request, or exhortation. 2. Commanding, peremptory; urgent; obligatory. **im·per′a·tive·ly** *adv.* **im·per′a·tive·ness** *n.* **im·per′a·tive** *n.* Imperative mood.

im·per·cep·ti·ble (ĭmpersĕp′-tĭbel) *adj.* That cannot be perceived; very slight, gradual, or subtle. **im·per·cep′ti·bly** *adv.* **im·per·cep′ti·ble·ness** *n.*

imperf. *abbrev.* (gram.) Imperfect.

im·per·fect (ĭmpĕr′fĭkt) *adj.* 1. Not fully formed or done, incomplete; faulty. 2. (gram., of tense) Implying action going on but not complete (e.g. *he is, he will be, singing*, but usu. of past time, *as he*

was singing). **im·per′fect·ly** *adv.*

im·per·fec·tion (ĭmperfĕk′shon) *n.* Incompleteness; faultiness; fault, blemish.

im·per·fo·rate (ĭmpĕr′ferĭt, -ferāt), **im·per·fo·rat·ed** (ĭmpĕr′-ferātĭd) *adjs.* Not perforated; (of sheet of postage stamps) without perforations.

im·pe·ri·al (ĭmpēr′ēal) *adj.* Of an empire or sovereign state ranking with an empire; of an emperor or empress; (of weights and measures) appointed by statute for use throughout the United Kingdom; hence, ~ **gallon**, Brit. gallon, equivalent to 1⅕ U.S. gallon. **im·pe′ri·al·ly** *adv.*

Im·pe·ri·al (ĭmpēr′ēal) **Valley.** Agricultural area in SE. California adjacent to Mexico, once part of the Colorado Desert, irrigated by the All-American Canal; land is mostly below sea level and includes the Salton Sink.

im·pe·ri·al·ism (ĭmpēr′ēalĭzem) *n.* Political or economic sway over other nations; (usu. derog.) (belief in desirability of) acquiring colonies and dependencies; principle or spirit of empire, advocacy of what are held to be imperial interests. **im·pe′ri·al·ist** *n.* & *adj.* Adherent of an emperor; advocate of imperial rule; advocate of imperialism. **im·pe·ri·al·is·tic** (ĭm-pērēalĭs′tĭk) *adj.*

im·per·il (ĭmpĕr′ĭl) *v.t.* (**-iled, -il·ing**, esp. Brit. **-illed, -il·ling**). Bring into danger.

im·pe·ri·ous (ĭmpēr′ēus) *adj.* Overbearing, domineering; urgent, imperative. **im·pe′ri·ous·ly** *adv.* **im·pe′ri·ous·ness** *n.*

A young orange grove in **Imperial Valley.** This area, once part of the Colorado Desert, has been extensively irrigated by the All-American Canal and yields a large range of agricultural produce.

im·per·ish·a·ble (ĭmpĕr′ĭs-abel) *adj.* That cannot perish. **im·per·ish·a·bil·i·ty** (ĭmpĕrĭs-abĭl′ĭtē) *n.* **im·per′ish·a·bly** *adv.*

im·per·ma·nent (ĭmpĕr′m-nent) *adj.* Not permanent. **im-per′ma·nence, im·per′ma-nen·cy** *ns.*

im·per·me·a·ble (ĭmpĕr′m-abel) *adj.* That cannot be passed through; that does not permit passage of fluids. **im·per′me-a·bil·i·ty** (ĭmpĕrmēabĭl′ĭtē) *n.* **im·per′me·a·bly** *adv.*

im·per·mis·si·ble (ĭmpermĭs′-ĭbel) *adj.* Not allowable.

im·per·son·al (ĭmpĕr′sona-... *adj.* 1. (gram., of verbs) Used only in 3rd person singular without referring to a person or definite subject; hence, used without a subject or with a merely formal one, as Engl. *it*. 2. Having no personality or personal reference tone. **im·per′son·al·ly** *adv.* **im-per·son·al·i·ty** (ĭmpērsonăl′ĭtē) *n.*

im·per·son·ate (ĭmpĕr′sona-) *v.t.* (**-at·ed, -at·ing**). Represent in bodily form, personify; play the part of, personate; act (character). **im·per·son·a·tion** (ĭmpērsonā′shon), **im·per′son·a·tor** *ns.*

im·per·ti·nent (ĭmpĕr′tĭner-) *adj.* 1. Irrelevant. 2. Presumptuous; insolent, saucy. **im·per′ti·nent·ly** *adv.* **im·per′ti·nen·** *n.*

im·per·turb·a·ble (ĭmpertĕr-babel) *adj.* Not excitable, calm. **im·per·turb′a·ble·ness, im-per·turb·a·bil·i·ty** (ĭmpertĕrb-bĭl′ĭtē) *ns.* **im·per·turb′a·bly** *adv.*

im·per·vi·ous (ĭmpĕr′vēus) *adj.* Not affording passage (*to*); (fig.) impenetrable, not affording entrance *to* (argument, feeling, etc). **im·per′vi·ous·ly** *adv.* **im·per′vi·ous·ness** *n.*

im·pe·ti·go (ĭmpetī′gō) *n.* (pl. **-gos**). Acute inflammatory disease of skin caused by streptococcal and staphylococcal organisms, characterized by pustules chiefly on face and hands.

im·pet·u·ous (ĭmpĕch′ōous) *adj.* Moving violently or rapidly; acting with rash or sudden energy. **im·pet′u·ous·ly** *adv.* **im·pet′u-ous·ness, im·pet·u·os·i·ty** (ĭm-pĕchōōs′ĭtē) *ns.*

im·pe·tus (ĭm′petus) *n.* (pl. **-tus·es**). Force with which a body moves; (fig.) moving force, impulse.

im·pi·e·ty (ĭmpī′etē) *n.* (pl. **-ties**). Ungodliness; want of dutifulness or reverence.

im·pinge (ĭmpĭnj′) *v.* (**-pinged, -ping·ing**). Make impact (*on, upon*); encroach; collide, strike (*against*). **im·pinge′ment** *n.*

im·pi·ous (ĭm′pēus, ĭmpī′-) *adj.* Not pious, profane. **im′pi·ous·ly** *adv.*

imp·ish (ĭm′pĭsh) *adj.* Of, like

imp. **imp'ish·ly** *adv.* **imp'-h·ness** *n.*

im·plac·a·ble (ĭmplăk'abel) *adj.* hat cannot be appeased. **im·-lac·a·bil'i·ty** *n.* **im·plac'a·bly** *dv.*

im·plant (ĭmplănt', -plahnt') ,*t.* Insert, infix (*in*); instill (*in* mind c.); plant. **im·plan·ta'tion** mplăntā'shon) *n.*

im·plau·si·ble (ĭmplaw'zibel) *dj.* Not plausible.

im·ple·ment[1] (ĭm'plement) *n.* Thing serving as equipment or art of outfit. 2. Tool; apparatus, tensil, instrument, etc.

im·ple·ment[2] (ĭm'plemĕnt) *v.t.* ut into effect; provide plan or pro-edure to do so; fulfill. **im·ple·-nen·ta'tion** (ĭmplemĕntā'shon) *n.*

im·pli·cate (ĭm'plĭkāt) *v.t.* -cat·ed, -cat·ing). 1. (archaic) ntwine, entangle. 2. Involve, mply, as inference; involve (*in* harge, crime, etc.). **im·pli·ca-ion** (ĭmplĭkā'shon) *n.*

im·plic·it (ĭmplĭs'ĭt) *adj.* Im-lied though not plainly expressed; irtually contained (*in*). **im·-·lic'it·ly** *adv.* **im·plic'it·ness** *n.*

im·plode (ĭmplōd') *v.* (-plod·-d, -plod·ing). (Cause to) burst nward. **im·plo·sion** (ĭmplō'zhon)

im·plore (ĭmplōr', -plŏr') *v.t.* -plored, -plor·ing). Beg arnestly for; entreat. **im·plor'-ng·ly** *adv.*

im·ply (ĭmplī') *v.t.* (-plied, ply·ing). Involve the truth of thing not expressly asserted); nean; insinuate, hint.

im·po·lite (ĭmpolīt') *adj.* Un-ivil, rude. **im·po·lite'ly** *adv.* **m·po·lite'ness** *n.*

im·pol·i·tic (ĭmpŏl'ĭtĭk) *adj.* Not olitic; inexpedient. **im·pol'i-ic'ly** *adv.*

im·pon·der·a·ble (ĭmpŏn'-lerabel) *adj.* Not capable of being recisely weighed, measured, or valuated. ~ *n.* Imponderable hing.

im·port (ĭmpōrt', -pōrt') *v.t.* 1. Bring, introduce (esp. goods from oreign country *into*). 2. Imply, ndicate, mean; express, make nown. 3. Be of consequence. **m·por·ta'tion** (ĭmpōrtā'shon, -pōr-) *n.* Bringing in, introducing. **m·port'er** *n.* One who imports goods. **import** (ĭm'pōrt, -pōrt) *n.* 1. What is implied, meaning, mportance. 2. (usu. pl.) Com-modity imported.

im·por·tance (ĭmpōr'tans) *n.* Being important; weight, signifi-cance; personal consequence, dig-nity.

im·por·tant (ĭmpōr'tant) *adj.* Carrying with it great consequence (*to*), weighty, momentous; con-sequential. **im·por'tant·ly** *adv.*

im·por·tu·nate (ĭmpōr'chunĭt) *adj.* Persistent, pressing, in solici-tation; (of affairs) urgent. **im·por'-tu·nate·ness** *n.* **im·por'tu-nate·ly** *adv.*

im·por·tune (ĭmpōrtōon', -tūn', -pōr'chun) *v.t.* (-tuned, -tun·ing). Solicit pressingly.

im·pose (ĭmpōz') *v.* (-posed, -pos·ing). 1. Place (thing) *on* (archaic); (print.) lay (pages of type) in proper order and secure them in a chase. 2. Lay (tax, duty, charge, *on*). 3. ~ **on**, take advantage of (person); practice deception upon. **im·po·si·tion** (ĭmpozĭsh'on), **im·-pos'er** *ns.*

im·pos·ing (ĭmpō'zĭng) *adj.* Grand, impressive through size or power, majestic. **im·pos'ing·ly** *adv.*

im·pos·si·ble (ĭmpŏs'ĭbel) *adj.* Not possible; (loosely) not easy, not convenient; (colloq.) outrageous, intolerable. **im·pos·si·bil·i·ty** (ĭmpŏsibĭl'ĭtē) *n.* (pl. -ties). **im·-pos'si·bly** *adv.*

im·post[1] (ĭm'pōst) *n.* Tax, duty, tribute.

im·post[2] (ĭm'pōst) *n.* Upper course of pillar, bearing arch.

im·pos·tor (ĭmpŏs'ter) *n.* One who assumes a false character or passes himself off as someone else.

im·pos·ture (ĭmpŏs'cher) *n.* Fraudulent deception.

im·po·tent (ĭm'potent) *adj.* Powerless; helpless; (of males) in-capable of sexual intercourse; in-capable of fathering a child. **im'po·tent·ly** *adv.* **im'po·tence, im'po·ten·cy** *ns.*

im·pound (impownd') *v.t.* Shut up (cattle) in pound; shut up (person, thing) as in pound; take legal possession of; confiscate. **im·pound'ment** *n.*

im·pov·er·ish (ĭmpŏv'erĭsh) *v.t.* Make poor; exhaust strength of. **im·pov'er·ish·ment** *n.*

im·prac·ti·ca·ble (ĭmprăk'ti-kabel) *adj.* Impossible in practice; impassable (of road etc.); incapable of being done. **im·prac'ti·ca·ble·-ness, im·prac·ti·ca·bil·i·ty** (ĭm-prăktikabĭl'ĭtē) *ns.*

Dog catchers **impound** dogs that are found wandering the streets. After a set waiting period those that have not been claimed are put to sleep.

im·prac·ti·cal (ĭmprăk'tĭkal) *adj.* Not practical or useful. **im·prac·ti·cal·i·ty** (ĭmprăktĭkăl'-ĭtē) *n.*

im·pre·cate (ĭm'prekāt) *v.t.* (-cat·ed, -cat·ing). Invoke, call down, (evil *upon* person etc.). **im·pre·ca'tion** (ĭmprekā'shon) *n.* (esp.) Spoken curse. **im'pre·ca-tor** *n.* **im·pre·ca·to·ry** (ĭm'-prekatōrē, -tōrē) *adj.*

im'preg·na·ble (ĭmprĕg'nabel) *adj.* (of fortress etc.) That cannot be taken by force; (fig.) proof against attack. **im·preg·na·bil·i·ty** (ĭmprĕgnabĭl'ĭtē) *n.* **im·preg'na·bly** *adv.*

im·preg·nate (ĭmprĕg'nāt) *v.t.* (-nat·ed, -nat·ing). 1. Make (female) pregnant; = FERTILIZE def. 2. 2. Fill, saturate, (*with*); imbue, fill. **im·preg·na'tion** *n.*

im·pre·sa·ri·o (ĭmpresär'ēō, -sär'-) *n.* (pl. -sa·ri·os). Organizer of public entertainments, esp. manager of operatic or concert company.

im·press[1] (ĭm'prĕs) *n.* Stamp-ing; mark made by seal, stamp, etc.; (fig.) characteristic mark. ~ (ĭmprĕs') *v.t.* Apply (mark etc.) with pressure, imprint, stamp, (*on*); imprint, enforce, (idea etc. *on* per-son, his mind); mark (thing *with* stamp etc.); affect, influence; affect (person) strongly (*with* idea etc.). **im·press'i·ble** *adj.* **im·press·i·bil·i·ty** (ĭmprĕsibĭl'ĭtē) *n.*

im·press[2] (ĭmprĕs') *v.t.* Force (men) to serve in army or navy; seize (goods etc.) for public service; enlist, make use of, (thing) in argument etc. **im·press'ment** *n.*

im·pres·sion (ĭmprĕsh'on) *n.* 1. Impressing (of mark); mark im-pressed. 2. Individual print taken from type or engraving. 3. Effect produced (esp. on mind or feelings); notion, (vague) belief, impressed on the mind.

im·pres·sion·a·ble (ĭmprĕsh'-onabel) *adj.* Susceptible of impressions, easily influenced.

im·pres·sion·ism (ĭmprĕsh'onĭzem) *n.* (often cap.) Method of painting initiated *c*1870 by a school of French painters (including Manet, Monet, Pissarro, Renoir, and Degas), whose aim was to paint the momentary or transitory appearance of things, and esp. the effects of light and atmosphere, rather than form or structure; method of writing, style of music, resembling this. **im·pres'sion·ist** *n.* & *adj.* **im·pres·sion·is·tic** (ĭmprĕshonĭs'tĭk) *adj.* **im·pres·sion·is·ti·cal·ly** *adv.*

im·pres·sive (ĭmprĕs'ĭv) *adj.* Able to excite deep feeling, making deep impression on mind or senses. **im·pres'sive·ly** *adv.* **im·pres'sive·ness** *n.*

im·pri·ma·tur (ĭmprĭmā'ter, -mah'-) *n.* Official license to print esp. works sanctioned by R.C. Ch.; (fig.) sanction. [mod. L., = "let it be printed"]

im·print (ĭmprĭnt') *v.t.* Stamp (figure etc. *on*); impress (idea etc. *on, in* mind etc.); impress (quality etc. *on, in*); stamp (thing *with* figure). ~ (ĭm'prĭnt) *n.* 1. Impression, stamp. 2. Name of printer or publisher, date and place of printing or publication, at foot or back of title page or at end of book etc.

im·pris·on (ĭmprĭz'on) *v.t.* Put into prison; confine, shut up. **im·pris'on·ment** *n.*

im·prob·a·ble (ĭmprŏb'abel) *adj.* Not likely to be true or to happen. **im·prob·a·bil·i·ty** (ĭmprŏbabĭl'ĭtē) *n.* (pl. **-ties**). **im·prob'a·bly** *adv.*

im·pro·bi·ty (ĭmprō'bĭtē, -prŏb'ĭ-) *n.* Wickedness; dishonesty.

im·promp·tu (ĭmprŏmp'tōō, -tū) *adv.* & *adj.* (Spoken, done) without preparation, extemporaneous. ~ *n.* Improvised or extemporaneous performance or composition. [L. *in promptu* in readiness]

im·prop·er (ĭmprŏp'er) *adj.* Inaccurate, wrong; unseemly, indecent; ~ **fraction**, fraction with numerator greater than denominator. **im·prop'er·ly** *adv.* **im·prop'er·ness** *n.*

im·pro·pri·e·ty (ĭmproprī'etē) *n.* (pl. **-ties**). Incorrectness; unfitness; indecency.

im·prov·a·ble (ĭmprōō'vabel) *adj.* That can be improved. **im·prov'a·ble·ness, im·prov·a·bil·i·ty** (ĭmprōōvabĭl'ĭtē) *ns.*

im·prove (ĭmprōōv') *v.* (**-proved, -prov·ing**). Make, become, better; make good use of; ~ **on**, produce something better than. **im·prove'ment, im·prov'er** *ns.*

im·prov·i·dent (ĭmprŏv'ĭdent) *adj.* Unforeseeing; heedless; thrift-

The fortified **Inca** city of Machu Picchu provided a refuge for priests and nobles after the Spanish capture of Cuzco. It was so well hidden between two mountain peaks that it was not discovered until 1911.

less. **im·prov'i·dent·ly** *adv.* **im·prov'i·dence** *n.*

im·pro·vise (ĭm'provīz) *v.t.* (**-vised, -vis·ing**). Compose, utter, (verse, music, etc.) without preparation; provide, get up, extemporaneously. **im·prov·i·sa·tion** (ĭmprŏvĭzā'shon) *n.* **im·prov·i·sa·to·ri·al** (ĭmprŏvĭzatōr'ēal, -tŏr'-) *adj.* **im·pro·vis·er, im·pro·vi·sor** *ns.*

im·pru·dent (ĭmprōō'dent) *adj.* Rash, indiscreet. **im·pru'dent·ly** *adv.* **im·pru'dence** *n.*

im·pu·dent (ĭm'pyudent) *adj.* Shamelessly forward; unblushing; insolently disrespectful. **im'pu·dent·ly** *adv.* **im'pu·dence** *n.* **im'pu·den·cy** *n.* (pl. **-cies**).

im·pugn (ĭmpūn') *v.t.* Assail by word, call in question (statement, action). **im·pugn'ment, im·pugn'er** *ns.*

im·pulse (ĭm'pŭls) *n.* 1. Impelling, push; (dynamics) force producing momentum; momentum thus produced; product of average value of force multiplied by time during which it acts. 2. Mental incitement; sudden tendency to act

without reflection; impetus.

im·pul·sive (ĭmpŭl'sĭv) *adj.* Tending to impel. 2. (of persons conduct, etc.) Apt to be moved prompted, by sudden impulse **im·pul'sive·ly** *adv.* **im·pul'sive·ness** *n.*

im·pu·ni·ty (ĭmpū'nĭtē) *n.* Exemption from punishment; exemption from injury as consequence o act.

im·pure (ĭmpūr') *adj.* Dirty unchaste; mixed with foreign matter, adulterated; (of color) mixed with another color. **im·pure'ly** *adv.* **im·pur'i·ty** *n.* (pl. **-ties**).

im·pute (ĭmpūt') *v.t.* (**-put·ed -put·ing**). Attribute, ascribe (fault etc. *to*). **im·pu·ta·tion** (ĭmpyōōtā'shon) *n.* **im·put·a·tive** (ĭmpū'tatĭv) *adj.* **im·put'a·tive·ly** *adv.*

IN *abbrev.* Indiana.

In *symbol.* Indium.

in (ĭn) *prep.* Within limits o space, time, circumstance, etc., a ~ *Europe*, ~ *Los Angeles*, ~ *a box* ~ *the day*, ~ *the army*; **nothing little, not much,** ~ **it**, no or little profit or advantage to be gained no or little truth, information, etc contained in (a rumor, message etc.). **in** *adv.* 1. In or at a place, the right or normal state, the fashion, etc.; in season, on the inside, within; at home; in one' fice; at work. **2.** So as to pass ithin. **3.** ~ **for it**, certain to meet ith punishment or something un-easant; ~ **with**, on friendly terms ith. **in** *adj.* That is in; lying c. within. ~ *n.* (pl.) ~**s and uts**, turnings to and fro (usu. fig.), etails (*of procedure etc.*).

in. *abbrev.* Inch(es).

-in *suffix.* Forming names of eutral substances (*gelatin, protein*) nd antibiotics (*penicillin*).

in-[1] *prefix.* In, on, into, ward, against (*insight, influx*).

in-[2] *prefix.* Not (*insane, insepa-*ble).

in·a·bil·i·ty (ĭnabĭl´ĭtē) *n.* Being nable; lack of power or means.

in·ac·ces·si·ble (ĭnaksĕs´ĭbel) dj. That cannot be reached; un-pproachable. **in·ac·ces·si·bil·i·ty** naksĕsĭbĭl´ĭtē) *n.* **in·ac·ces·si·bly** dv.

in·ac·cu·rate (ĭnăk´yerĭt) *adj.* Jot accurate. **in·ac´cu·rate·ly** dv. **in·ac´cu·ra·cy** *n.* (pl. **-cies**).

in·ac·tion (ĭnăk´shon) *n.* Ab-ence of action; sluggishness, inert-ess. **in·ac´tive** *adj.* **in·ac´tive·ly** dv. **in·ac·tiv·i·ty** (ĭnăktĭv´ĭtē) *n.* n·ac·ti·vate (ĭnăk´tĭvāt) *v.t.* -vat·ed, -vat·ing).

in·ad·e·quate (ĭnăd´ekwĭt) *adj.* Jot adequate; insufficient. **in-**d´e·quate·ly *adv.* **in·ad´e-**ua·cy *n.* (pl. **-cies**).

in·ad·mis·si·ble (ĭnadmĭs´ĭbel) dj. That cannot be admitted or llowed. **in·ad·mis·si·bil·i·ty** ĭnadmĭsĭbĭl´ĭtē) *n.* **in·ad·mis´-**i·bly *adv.*

in·ad·ver·tent (ĭnadvĕr´tent) dj. Not properly attentive; negli-ent; (of actions) unintentional. n·ad·ver´ent·ly *adv.* **in·ad-**ert´ence, in·ad·vert´en·cy *ns.* pl. **-cies**).

in·al·ien·a·ble (ĭnāl´yenabel, ā´lēena-) *adj.* Not alienable or ransferable. **in·al·ien·a·bil·i·ty** ĭnālyenabĭl´ĭtē, -ā´lēena-) *n.* **in-**l´ien·a·bly *adv.*

in·am·o·ra·to (ĭnămorah´tō) *n.* pl. **-tos**) (fem. **in·am·o·ra·ta** pr. nămorah´ta; pl. **-tas**). Lover.

in·ane (ĭnān´) *adj.* Empty, void; illy, senseless. **in·ane´ly** *adv.* n·an·i·ty (ĭnăn´ĭtē) *n.* (pl. **-ties**).

in·an·i·mate (ĭnăn´imĭt) *adj.* Jestitute of life; not endowed vith animal life; spiritless, dull. n·an´i·mate·ly *adv.* **in·an´i-**nate·ness *n.*

in·ap·pli·ca·ble (ĭnăp´lĭkabel) idj. Not applicable, unsuitable (*to*). n·ap·pli·ca·bil·i·ty (ĭnăplĭkabĭl´-tē) *n.* **in·ap´pli·ca·bly** *adv.*

in·ap·pre·ci·a·ble (ĭnaprē´shē-ibel, -shabel) *adj.* Imperceptible, iot worth reckoning; negligible, nsignificant. **in·ap·pre´ci·a·bly** idv.

in·ap·pro·pri·ate (ĭnaprō´prēĭt) idj. Not appropriate. **in·ap-**pro´pri·ate·ly *adv.* **in·ap·pro´-**

pri·ate·ness *n.*

in·ar·tic·u·late (ĭnārtĭk´yulĭt) *adj.* **1.** Not jointed. **2.** Not articu-late; unable to speak distinctly; speechless; unable to express one's ideas. **in·ar·tic´u·late·ly** *adv.* **in·ar·tic´u·late·ness** *n.*

in·ar·tis·tic (ĭnārtĭs´tĭk) *adj.* Not following the principles of art; unskilled in art.

in·as·much (ĭnazmŭch´) *adv.* ~ **as**, since, because; in so far as.

in·at·ten·tion (ĭnatĕn´shon) *n.* Want of attention, heedlessness; neglect to show courtesy. **in·at-**ten·tive (ĭnatĕn´tĭv) *adj.* **in·at-**ten´tive·ly *adv.* **in·at·ten´tive-**ness *n.*

in·au·di·ble (ĭnaw´dĭbel) *adj.* That cannot be heard. **in·au·di-**bil·i·ty (ĭnawdĭbĭl´ĭtē) *n.* **in-**au´di·bly *adv.*

in·au·gu·ral (ĭnaw´gyural) *adj.* (of ceremony) Inaugurating; (of speech etc.) given by person who is being inaugurated. ~ *n.* Inaugural speech, esp. by a U.S. president.

in·au·gu·rate (ĭnaw´gyurāt) *v.t.* (**-rat·ed, -rat·ing**). Admit (per-son) to office etc. with ceremony; enter with ceremony upon (under-taking etc.); initiate public use of (building etc.). **in·au·gu·ra·tion** (ĭnawgyurā´shon) *n.*

in·aus·pi·cious (ĭnawspĭsh´us) *adj.* Not of good omen; unlucky. **in·aus·pi´cious·ly** *adv.* **in·aus-**pi´cious·ness *n.*

in·board (ĭn´bōrd, -bōrd) *adv.* & *adj.* (Situated) within sides or toward center of ship or aircraft.

in·born (ĭn´bōrn) *adj.* Im-planted by nature.

in·bound (ĭn´bownd´) *adj.* In-ward bound (of ships, planes, etc.).

in·bred (ĭn´bred´) *adj.* **1.** Innate,

inherent by nature. **2.** Born of closely related parents.

in·breed·ing (ĭn´brēdĭng) *n.* Breeding from animals or persons closely related.

Inc. *abbrev.* Incorporated.

inc. *abbrev.* Incorporated; in-come; increase.

In·ca (ĭng´ka) *n.* Member of Amer. Indian Quechua-speaking people, who at the time of the Spanish expedition, which over-threw them in 1533, had a highly developed civilization and ruled a large region of N.W. South Amer., with center at Cuzco, Peru; member of its ruling class, supposedly descended from the sun; **the** ~, the emperor or chief ruler of the Incas. **In´can** *adj.* & *n.*

in·cal·cu·la·ble (ĭnkăl´kyulabel) *adj.* Too great for calculation; that cannot be reckoned beforehand; uncertain. **in·cal·cu·la·bil·i·ty** (ĭnkălkyulabĭl´ĭtē) *n.* **in·cal´cu-**la·bly *adv.*

in·can·desce (ĭnkandĕs´) *v.* (**-desced, -desc·ing**). (Cause to) glow with heat. **in·can·des·cent** (ĭnkandĕs´ent) *adj.* Glowing with heat; shining brightly; (of gas or electric light etc.) produced by glowing of mantle or filament raised to white heat by flame of burning gas or passage of electricity. **in-**can·des´cence *n.*

in·can·ta·tion (ĭnkăntā´shon) *n.* (Use of) magical formula; spell, charm.

in·ca·ble (ĭnkā´pabel) *adj.*

Incantations are still used by modern witches allegedly to cast spells and charms. In this ceremony the witch holds a sword in one hand and a rope in the other.

Not capable (*of*; freq. = too honest etc. to do); not susceptible (*of* improvement etc.); without ordinary capacity or natural ability. **in·-ca·pa·bil·i·ty** (ĭnkāpabĭl´ĭtē) *n.* **in·ca′pa·bly** *adv.*

in·ca·pac·i·tate (ĭnkapăs´ĭtāt) *v.t.* (**-tat·ed, -tat·ing**). Render incapable or unfit. **in·ca·pac·i·ta·tion** (ĭnkapăsĭtā´shon) *n.*

in·ca·pac·i·ty (ĭnkapăs´ĭtē) *n.* (pl. **-ties**). Inability; disability; legal disqualification.

in·car·cer·ate (ĭnkār´serāt) *v.t.* (**-at·ed, -at·ing**). Imprison. **in·car·cer·a·tion** (ĭnkārserā´shon), **in·car′cer·a·tor** *ns.*

in·car·nate (ĭnkār´nĭt, -nāt) *adj.* Embodied in flesh, esp. in human form. ~ (ĭnkār´nāt, ĭn´kār-) *v.t.* (**-nat·ed, -nat·ing**). Embody in flesh; put (idea etc.) into concrete form, realize; be living embodiment of (quality). **in·car·na·tion** (ĭnkārnā´shon) *n.* Embodiment in (esp. human) flesh, esp. **the I** ~ (of Christ); personification, living type (*of* quality etc.).

in·cau·tious (ĭnkaw´shus) *adj.* Rash. **in·cau′tious·ly** *adv.* **in·cau′tious·ness** *n.*

in·cen·di·ar·y (ĭnsĕn´dēērē) *adj.* Of, guilty of, arson; causing, capable of causing, fire; (mil.) used for setting on fire enemy's property, esp. ~ **bomb**, bomb containing napalm etc. and igniting on impact; (fig.) tending to stir up strife, inflammatory.

in·cense[1] (ĭn´sĕns) *n.* Aromatic gum or other vegetable product, giving sweet smell when burned; smoke of this, esp. in religious ceremonial. ~ *v.t.* (**-censed, -cens·ing**). Fumigate with incense; burn incense to (deity etc.); suffuse with fragrance.

in·cense[2] (ĭnsĕns´) *v.t.* (**-censed, -cens·ing**). Enrage, make angry.

in·cen·tive (ĭnsĕn´tĭv) *adj.* Tending to incite. ~ *n.* Incitement, provocation, motive; (in industry) payment or concession to encourage harder work.

in·cep·tion (ĭnsĕp´shon) *n.* Beginning.

in·cer·ti·tude (ĭnsēr´tĭtōod, -tūd) *n.* Uncertainty.

in·ces·sant (ĭnsĕs´ant) *adj.* Unceasing, continual, repeated. **in·-ces′sant·ly** *adv.*

in·cest (ĭn´sĕst) *n.* Sexual intercourse between person too closely related to be legally married. **in·ces·tu·ous** (ĭnsĕs´chōous) *adj.* **in·ces′tu·ous·ly** *adv.*

inch (ĭnch) *n.* (abbrev. **in.**) Twelfth part of foot in measures of length; (as unit of rainfall) quantity that would cover horizontal surface to depth of 1 in.; (of atmospheric or other pressure) amount that balances weight of column of mercury 1 in. high in mercurial barometer; small amount; (pl.)

stature; **by inches**, bit by bit; **every inch**, entirely; ~ **worm** = MEASURING WORM. **inch** *v.* Move by inches, edge *in*, *forward*, etc.

in·cho·ate (ĭnkō´ĭt) *adj.* Just begun; undeveloped.

in·ci·dence (ĭn´sĭdens) *n.* 1. Falling on, contact with, a thing; range, scope, extent, of influence; (of disease) rate, scale, frequency, of occurrence in a community. 2. (math., phys.) Falling of a line, or a thing moving in a line, upon a surface; **angle of** ~, angle that the incident line, ray, etc., makes with the perpendicular to the surface at the point of contact.

in·ci·dent[1] (ĭn´sĭdent) *adj.* 1. (of light etc.) Falling, striking, (*upon*). 2. Apt to occur, naturally attaching, (*to*).

in·ci·dent[2] (ĭn´sĭdent) *n.* Subordinate or accessory event; event, occurrence; detached event attracting general attention; distinct piece of action in play etc.

in·ci·den·tal (ĭnsĭdĕn´tal) *adj.* Casual, not essential; ~ **music**, music interpolated in spoken play etc. **in·ci·den′tal·ly** *adv.* 1. By chance; casually. 2. Parenthetically; as a subordinate or casual comment.

in·cin·er·ate (ĭnsĭn´erāt) *v.t.* (**-at·ed, -at·ing**). Reduce to ashes; consume by fire. **in·cin·er·a·tion** (ĭnsĭnerā´shon) *n.* **in·cin′er·a·tor** *n.* (esp.) Apparatus for burning rubbish.

in·cip·i·ent (ĭnsĭp´ēent) *adj.* Beginning; in an initial stage. **in·-cip′i·ent·ly** *adv.* **in·cip′i·ence, in·cip′i·en·cy** *ns.*

Incense-burners were widely used [in?] the East. This pottery burner was excavated in 1972 from a 2,100-year-old tomb in China. Inside the pot wer[e] scented herbs.

in·cise (ĭnsīz´) *v.t.* (**-cised, -cis·ing**). Make a cut in; engrave. **in·ci·sion** (ĭnsĭzh´on) *n.* Cutting into a thing; cut.

in·ci·sive (ĭnsī´sĭv) *adj.* Cutting, penetrating; mentally sharp; acute, trenchant. **in·ci′sive·ly** *adv.* **in·ci′sive·ness** *n.*

in·ci·sor (ĭnsī´zer) *n.* Cuttin[g] tooth, any front tooth in either jaw between canine teeth, having shar[p] edge and single fang.

in·cite (ĭnsīt´) *v.t.* (**-cit·ed, -cit·ing**). Urge, stir up (perso[n] etc. *to*). **in·cite′ment** *n.*

in·ci·vil·i·ty (ĭnsivĭl´ĭtē) *n.* (p[l.] **-ties**). Rudeness, discourtesy.

in·clem·ent (ĭnklĕm´ent) *adj.* (o[f] weather etc.) Severe, esp. cold o[r] stormy. **in·clem′en·cy** *n.* (p[l.] **-cies**).

in·cli·na·tion (ĭnklinā´shon) *n[.]* 1. Leaning, slope, slant; difference of direction of 2 lines, esp. a[s] measured by angle between them; (of magnetic needle) = DIP *n.* def 2; (astron.) angle between plane of a planet's orbit and that of th[e] ecliptic. 2. Disposition, propensity (*to, for*); liking, affection (*for*).

in·cline (ĭnklīn´) *v.* (**-clined, -clin·ing**). 1. Bend (head etc.) forward or downward; lean, cause to lean, from vertical etc. 2. Dispose (person, mind, etc., *to*); be disposed; tend (*to*). 3. **inclined plane**, sloping plane (esp. as [a] means of reducing force needed t[o] ise load). **incline** (ĭn'klīn) n. In-ined surface; slope.

in·clude (ĭnklōōd') v.t. (**-clud-l**, **-clud·ing**). Comprise, em-ace, as part of a whole; treat, gard, as so comprised. **in·clu-on** (ĭnklōō'zhon) n.

in·clu·sive (ĭnklōō'sĭv) adj. In-uding, enclosing, comprehend-g; comprising; ~ **of**, embracing, mprising (something specified); uasi- adv.) the term or terms med being included. **in·clu-ve·ly** adv. **in·clu'sive·ness** n.

in·cog·ni·to (ĭnkŏg'nītō, -kŏg-ʹ-) adj. & adv. With one's name, aracter, etc., concealed. ~ n. (pl. os) (fem. **in·cog·ni·ta** pr. ĭnkŏg'-ta, -kŏgnē'-; pl. **-tas**). (Pre-nded identity of) person who is cognito.

in·co·her·ent (ĭnkohēr'ent, -kō-) dj. Not coherent. **in·co·her'-at·ly** adv. **in·co·her'ence** n. ·co·her'en·cy n. (pl. -cies).

in·com·bus·ti·ble (ĭnkombŭs'-ʙel) n. & adj. (Substance, object) at cannot be consumed by fire. ·com·bus·ti·bil·i·ty (ĭnkombŭs-ʙĭl'ĭtē) n.

in·come (ĭn'kŭm) n. Periodical ·ceipts from business, lands, work, vestments, etc.; ~ **tax**, tax levied ·n this; **negative ~ tax**, taxation ·stem by which credits are allowed ·r certain commitments and paid ·s supplementary income to per-·ns for whom they exceed taxable ·come.

in·com·ing (ĭn'kŭmĭng) n. En-·ance, arrival. ~ adj. Entering; ·out to enter, take office, etc.

in·com·men·su·ra·ble (ĭnko-ʙěn'serabel, -shera-) adj. Having ·o common measure integral or ·actional (with another magni-·ade); not capable of being ·easured, compared with, or ·dged. **in·com·men·su·ra-·il'i·ty** n. **in·com·men'su·ra·bly** ·dv.

in·com·men·su·rate (ĭnko-ʙěn'serĭt, -sherĭt) adj. Out of ·roportion, inadequate, (with, to); ·ncommensurable. **in·com·men'-·u·rate·ly** adv. **in·com·men'su-·ate·ness** n.

in·com·mu·ni·ca·ble (ĭnko-ʙū'nĭkabel) adj. That cannot be ·hared; that cannot be told. ·n·com·mu·ni·ca·bil·i·ty (ĭnko-ʙūnĭkabĭl'ĭtē) n. **in·com·mu·ni-·a·bly** adv.

in·com·mu·ni·ca·do (ĭnko-ʙūnĭkah'dō) adj. Without or ·leprived of means of communica-·ion; in solitary confinement.

in·com·mu·ni·ca·tive (ĭnko-ʙū'nĭkātĭv, -katĭv) adj. Not ·ommunicative. **in·com·mu·ni-·a·tive·ly** adv. **in·com·mu·ni-·a·tive·ness** n.

in·com·pa·ra·ble (ĭnkŏm'pera-·ʙel, -prabel) adj. Matchless; that ·annot be compared. **in·com'-**

par·a·ble·ness n. **in·com'par-·a·bly** adv.

in·com·pat·i·ble (ĭnkompăt'-ĭbel) adj. Opposed in character, discordant; (of persons) unable to live, work, etc., together in har-mony; (of drugs) not suitable for taking at the same time; inconsist-ent (with). **in·com·pat·i·bil·i·ty** (ĭnkompătĭbĭl'ĭtē) n. (pl. -ties). **in·com·pat'i·bly** adv.

in·com·pe·tent (ĭnkŏm'petent) adj. Not qualified or able (to do); not legally qualified. **in·com'pe-·tent·ly** adv. **in·com'pe·tence, in·com'pe·ten·cy** ns. (pl. -cies).

in·com·plete (ĭnkomplēt') adj. Not complete. **in·com·plete'ly** adv. **in·com·plete'ness** n.

in·com·pre·hen·si·ble (ĭnkŏm-prĭhĕn'sĭbel) adj. That cannot be understood. **in·com·pre·hen'si-·ble·ness, in·com·pre·hen·si·bil·i·ty** (ĭnkŏmprĭhĕnsĭbĭl'ĭtē) ns. **in·com·pre·hen'si·bly** adv.

in·com·press·i·ble (ĭnkom-prĕs'ĭbel) adj. That cannot be compressed. **in·com·press·i·bil-·i·ty** (ĭnkomprĕsĭbĭl'ĭtē) n.

in·con·ceiv·a·ble (ĭnkonsē'-vabel) adj. That cannot be im-agined. **in·con·ceiv·a·bil·i·ty** (ĭnkonsēvabĭl'ĭtē) n. **in·con·ceiv'-a·bly** adv.

in·con·clu·sive (ĭnkonklōō'sĭv) adj. (of argument etc.) Not deci-sive or convincing. **in·con·clu'-sive·ly** adv. **in·con·clu'sive·ness** n.

in·con·gru·ous (ĭnkŏng'grōōus) adj. Disagreeing, out of keeping, (with); out of place, absurd. **in-**

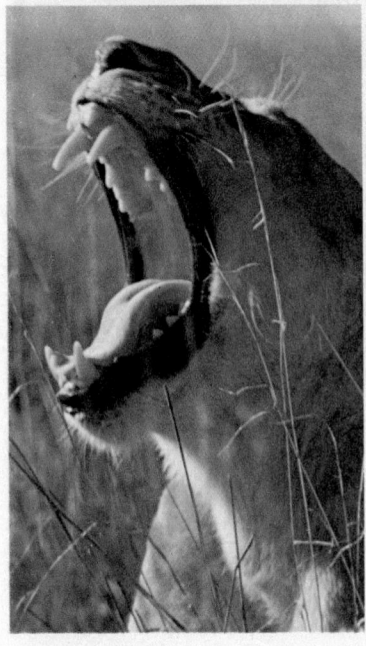
*A lion in the Royal National Park, Nairobi, Kenya, opens its mouth wide, displaying its menacing **incisors**, sharp-edged cutting-teeth that can lacerate and destroy prey.*

con'gru·ous·ly adv. **in·con'-gru·ous·ness** n. **in·con·gru·i·ty** (ĭnkŏnggrōōĭtē) n. (pl. -ties).

in·con·se·quent (ĭnkŏn'se-kwent) adj. Not following natu-rally, irrelevant; wanting in logical sequence; disconnected. **in·con'-se·quent·ly** adv. **in·con'se-quence** n. **in·con·se·quen·tial** (ĭnkŏnsekwĕn'shal) adj. **in·con-se·quen'tial·ly** adv. Unimportant; inconsequent.

in·con·sid·er·ate (ĭnkonsĭd'erĭt) adj. Thoughtless, rash; lacking in regard for feelings etc. of others. **in·con·sid·er·ate·ly** adv. **in·con-sid'er·ate·ness** n.

in·con·sis·tent (ĭnkonsĭs'tent) adj. Not in keeping, discordant, incompatible, (with); acting at variance with one's own principles or former conduct. **in·con·sis'-tent·ly** adv. **in·con·sis'ten·cy** n. (pl. -cies).

in·con·sol·a·ble (ĭnkonsō'label) adj. That cannot be consoled. **in·con·sol'a·bly** adv.

in·con·spic·u·ous (ĭnkonspĭk'-ūus) adj. Not conspicuous; not readily seen or noticed. **in·con-spic'u·ous·ly** adv. **in·con-spic'u·ous·ness** n.

in·con·test·a·ble (ĭnkontĕs'-tabel) adj. That cannot be disputed. **in·con·test'a·bly** adv.

in·con·ti·nent (ĭnkŏn'tinent) adj. Wanting in self-restraint (esp. in regard to sexual appetite); unable to hold in something; unable to control bladder and bowel func-tions. **in·con'ti·nence** n.

in·con·tro·ver·ti·ble (ĭnkŏn-trověr'tibel) adj. Not to be dis-puted. **in·con·tro·vert'i·bly** adv.

in·con·ven·ience (ĭnkonvĕn'-yens) n. Want of adaptation to personal requirement or ease; in-stance of this. ~ v.t. (**-ienced, -ienc·ing**). Put to inconvenience. **in·con·ven'ient** adj. Unfavorable to ease or comfort, troublesome, awkward. **in·con·ven'ient·ly** adv.

in·cor·po·rate (ĭnkōr'perĭt, -prĭt) adj. Formed into a legal corporation; merged; united. ~ (ĭnkōr'porāt) v. (**-rat·ed, -rat·ing**). 1. Unite; combine (ingredients) into one substance. 2. Constitute as, form into, a legal corporation; become incorporated (with). **in-cor·po·ra·tion** (ĭnkōrporā'shon), **in·cor'po·ra·tor** ns.

in·cor·po·re·al (ĭnkōrpor'ēal) adj. Not composed of matter; immaterial; of immaterial beings; spiritual; (law) having no material existence. **in·cor·po're·al·ly** adv.

in·cor·rect (ĭnkorĕkt') adj. Not in conformity with recognized standard, or with fact; improper; erroneous. **in·cor·rect'ly** adv. **in·cor·rect'ness** n.

in·cor·ri·gi·ble (ĭnkōr'ĭjibel, -kâr'-) adj. Incurably bad or de-praved. **in·cor·ri·gi·bil·i·ty** (ĭnkōrĭjĭbĭl´ĭtē, -kär-) *n.* **in·cor´ri-gi·bly** *adv.*

in·cor·rupt·i·ble (ĭnkorŭp´tibel) *adj.* That cannot decay; that cannot be corrupted, esp. that cannot be bribed. **in·cor·rupt·i·bil·i·ty** (ĭnkorŭptibĭl´ĭtē) *n.* **in·cor·rupt´i·bly** *adv.*

in·crease (ĭnkrēs´) *v.* (**-creased, -creas·ing**). Become greater; grow in numbers, esp. by propagation; advance (*in* quality, attainment, etc.); make greater or more numerous; intensify (quality). **in·creas´ing·ly** *adv.* **increase** (ĭn´krēs) *n.* Growth, enlargement; growth in numbers; increased amount; **on the** ~, increasing.

in·cred·i·ble (ĭnkrĕd´ibel) *adj.* That cannot be believed; hard to believe or realize. **in·cred·i·bil·i·ty** (ĭnkrĕdibĭl´ĭtē) *n.* **in·cred´i·bly** *adv.*

in·cred·u·lous (ĭnkrĕj´ulus) *adj.* Unbelieving. **in·cred´u·lous·ly** *adv.* **in·cre·du·li·ty** (ĭnkredoō´lĭtē, -dū´-) *n.*

in·cre·ment (ĭn´krement, ĭng´-) *n.* Increase; amount of this; profit; (math.) small amount by which variable quantity increases.

in·crim·i·nate (ĭnkrĭm´ināt) *v.t.* (**-nat·ed, -nat·ing**). Charge with crime; involve in accusation. **in·crim·i·na·tion** (ĭnkrĭminā´shon) *n.* **in·crim´i·na·to·ry** *adj.*

in·crust (ĭnkrŭst´), **en·crust** (ĕnkrŭst´) *vbs.* Cover with crust; overlay (surface) with ornamental crust of precious material. **in·crus·ta·tion** (ĭnkrŭstā´shon) *n.* Incrusting, being incrusted;

crust, hard coating, esp. of fine or costly material over rough or common substance; calcareous or crystalline concretion or deposit; scab.

in·cu·bate (ĭn´kyubāt, ĭng´-) *v.* (**-bat·ed, -bat·ing**). Sit on eggs, brood; hatch (eggs) thus or by artificial heat; subject (microorganisms) to warmth for a period. **in·cu·ba·tion** (ĭnkyubā´shon, ĭng-) *n.* (esp. path.) Early phase of disease after microorganisms have invaded the host and before symptoms of infection appear. **in´cu·ba·tive** *adj.*

in·cu·ba·tor (ĭn´kyubāter, ĭng´-) *n.* Apparatus maintaining uniform temperature for hatching birds or growing bacterial cultures; apparatus providing controlled temperature, humidity, and oxygen to maintain infants born prematurely.

in·cu·bus (ĭn´kyubus, ĭng´-) *n.* (**pl. -bi** pr. **-bī, -bus·es**). Evil spirit supposed to descend on sleeping persons; nightmare; person, thing, that oppresses like nightmare.

in·cul·cate (ĭnkŭl´kāt, ĭn´kŭl-) *v.t.* (**-cat·ed, -cat·ing**). Urge, impress, persistently (*upon, in,* person, mind). **in·cul·ca·tion** (ĭnkŭlkā´shon), **in·cul´ca·tor** *ns.*

in·cul·pate (ĭnkŭl´pāt, ĭn´kŭl-) *v.t.* (**-pat·ed, -pat·ing**). Accuse,

*The **incubator** is used in hospitals for the care of premature babies and others who need the maintenance of a uniform temperature and humidity. Chickens are also hatched in incubators.*

blame; involve in charge. **in·cul·pa·tion** (ĭnkŭlpā´shon) *n.* **in·cul´pa·to·ry** *adj.*

in·cum·ben·cy (ĭnkŭm´bensē) *n.* (**pl. -cies**). Office, tenure, sphere of an incumbent. **in·cum´bent** *n.* Holder of an office.

in·cum·bent[2] (ĭnkŭm´bent) *adj.* Lying, pressing, (*on*); resting o (person) as duty.

in·cu·nab·u·lum (ĭnkyoōnăb´yulum) *n.* (**pl. -la** pr. **-la**). Early printed book, esp. one produced before 1501. [L. *incunabula* swaddling clothes, infancy]

in·cur (ĭnkēr´) *v.t.* (**-curred -cur·ring**). Fall into, bring on oneself (danger, blame, etc.).

in·cur·a·ble (ĭnkūr´abel) *adj.* & *n.* (Person) that cannot be cured **in·cur´a·ble·ness, in·cur·a·bil·i·ty** (ĭnkūrabĭl´ĭtē) *ns.* **in·cur´a·bly** *adv.*

in·cur·sion (ĭnkēr´zhon, -shon *n.* Hostile invasion; sudder attack.

Ind. *abbrev.* India(n); Indiana Indies.

in·debt·ed (ĭndĕt´ĭd) *adj.* Owing money (*to*); owing gratitude (*to*) **in·debt´ed·ness** *n.*

in·de·cent (ĭndē´sent) *adj.* Immodest; offending against standards of decency. **in·de´cent·ly** *adv.* **in·de´cen·cy** *n.* (**pl. -cies**).

in·de·ci·pher·a·ble (ĭndĭsī´ferabel) *adj.* That cannot be deciphered.

in·de·ci·sion (ĭndĭsĭzh´on) *n.* Want of decision, hesitation.

in·de·ci·sive (ĭndĭsī´sĭv) *adj.* Not decisive; undecided, irresolute. **in·de·ci´sive·ly** *adv.* **in·de·ci´-sive·ness** *n.*

in·de·clin·a·ble (ĭndĭklī´nabel) *adj.* (gram.) Having no inflections.

in·dec·o·rous (ĭndĕk´erus, -dĭkōr´-, -dĭkōr´-) *adj.* Improper; in bad taste. **in·dec´o·rous·ly** *adv.* **in·dec´o·rous·ness** *n.* **in·de·co·rum** (ĭndĭkōr´um, -kōr´-) *n.* Lack of decorum.

in·deed (ĭndēd´) *adv.* In truth, really (freq. placed after a word to emphasize it). ~ *int.* Exclamation of surprise, contempt, etc.

in·de·fat·i·ga·ble (ĭndĭfăt´i-gabel) *adj.* Unremitting, unwearying. **in·de·fat·i·ga·bil·i·ty** (ĭn-dĭfătigabĭl´ĭtē) *n.* **in·de·fat´i-ga·bly** *adv.*

in·de·fen·si·ble (ĭndĭfĕn´sibel) *adj.* Admitting of no defense. **in·de·fen·si·bil·i·ty** (ĭndĭfĕnsi-bĭl´ĭtē) *n.* **in·de·fen´si·bly** *adv.*

in·de·fin·a·ble (ĭndĭfī´nabel) *adj.* That cannot be defined, described, or analyzed. **in·de·fin´-a·bly** *adv.*

in·def·i·nite (ĭndĕf´ĭnĭt) *adj.* 1. Vague, undefined; unlimited. 2. (gram., of adjectives, pronouns, etc.) Not determining the person, thing, time, manner, etc., to which they refer; (of tenses of verbs)

*The American **War of Independence** (1775–83) was the struggle of the 13 Colonies of America for independence from British rule. Washington declared independence on July 4, 1776 although the war continued until 1783.*

denoting an action without specifying whether it is continuous or complete; ~ **article**: see ARTICLE. **in·def′i·nite·ly** *adv.* **in·def′i-nite·ness** *n.*

in·de·his·cent (ĭndĭhĭs′ent) *adj.* (bot.) Not dehiscent; (of fruit) not splitting open when mature, but liberating seed by decay.

in·del·i·ble (ĭndĕl′ibel) *adj.* That cannot be erased, blotted out, etc. **in·del′i·bly** *adv.*

in·del·i·cate (ĭndĕl′ikĭt) *adj.* Coarse, immodest. **in·del′i·cate·ly** *adv.* **in·del′i·ca·cy** *n.* (pl. **-cies**).

in·dem·ni·fy (ĭndĕm′nifĭ) *v.t.* (**-fied, -fy·ing**). Protect, secure (*from*, *against*, harm or loss); secure (person) against legal responsibility (*for* actions); compensate (*for* loss, expenses incurred, etc.). **in·dem·ni·fi·ca·tion** (ĭndĕmnĭfikā′shon) *n.*

in·dem·ni·ty (ĭndĕm′nĭtē) *n.* (pl. **-ties**). Security against damage or loss; legal exemption from penalties etc. incurred; compensation for loss; sum paid for this.

in·de·mon·stra·ble (ĭndemŏn′strabel) *adj.* That cannot be proved.

in·dent (ĭndĕnt′) *v.* 1. Make toothlike notches in; form deep recesses in (coastline etc.). 2. Set in (beginning of printed or written line) from margin, as for new paragraph etc. **in′dent** *n.* Indentation.

in·den·ta·tion (ĭndĕntā′shon) *n.* Indenting; cut, notch; recess in coastline etc.

in·den·tion (ĭndĕn′shon) *n.* Indenting of line in printing or writing; indentation.

in·den·ture (ĭndĕn′cher) *n.* Any binding agreement or contract, esp. that which binds apprentice to master; formal list, certificate, etc.; indentation. ~ *v.t.* (**-tured, -tur·ing**). Bind (person) by indenture, esp. as apprentice.

in·de·pend·ence (ĭndĭpĕn′dens) *n.* Being independent; **Declaration of I** ~, proclamation by which the 2nd Continental Congress, on July 4, 1776, declared the 13 Amer. colonies to be free and independent of Gt. Britain; **I ~ Day**, July 4, an annual holiday celebrating this. **in·de·pend′en·cy** *n.* (pl. **-cies**). Independent state.

in·de·pend·ent (ĭndĭpĕn′dent) *adj.* Not depending on authority of another, autonomous, free; not depending on something else for its validity, efficiency, etc.; unwilling to be under obligation to others; not needing to earn one's livelihood; (of income etc.) sufficient to make one independent. **in·de-pend′ent·ly** *adv.* **independent** *n.* Person who acts (in politics etc.) independently of any party, group, etc.

in·de·scrib·a·ble (ĭndĭskrī-babel) *adj.* Vague, indefinite; too great, beautiful, bad, etc., to be described. **in·de·scrib·a·bil·i·ty** (ĭndĭskrībabĭl′ĭtē) *n.* **in·de·scrib′-a·bly** *adv.*

in·de·struct·i·ble (ĭndĭstrŭk′-tibel) *adj.* That cannot be destroyed. **in·de·struct·i·bil·i·ty** (ĭndĭstrŭktĭbĭl′ĭtē) *n.* **in·de-struct′i·bly** *adv.*

in·de·ter·mi·na·ble (ĭndĭter′-minabel) *adj.* That cannot be definitely fixed or ascertained; that cannot be settled.

in·de·ter·mi·nate (ĭndĭter′minĭt) *adj.* Not fixed in extent, character, etc.; vague; left doubtful; (math., of quantity) not limited to fixed value(s). **in·de·ter′mi-nate·ly** *adv.* **in·de·ter′mi·na·cy, in·de·ter′mi·nate·ness** *ns.* **in·de·ter·mi·na·tion** (ĭndĭtermĭnā′-shon) *n.* Want of determination; being indeterminate.

in·dex (ĭn′dĕks) *n.* (pl. **-dex·es, -di·ces** pr. -dĭsēz). 1. ~ **finger**, forefinger; (on instruments) pointer showing measurement etc.; sign, token, indication (*of* something). 2. Alphabetical list, usu. at end of book, of names, subjects, etc., with references. 3. *I* ~, short for *I* ~ *librorum prohibitorum* (L., = "Index of prohibited books"), list formerly published by authority (abolished 1966), of books

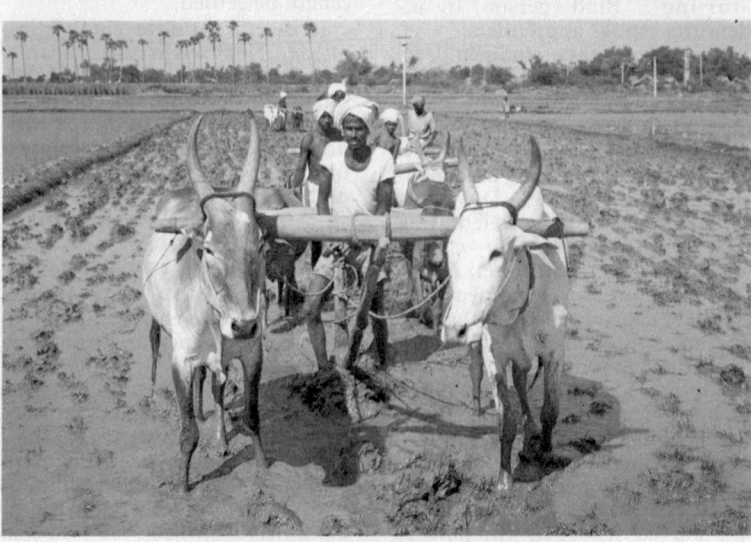

that Roman Catholics were fo
bidden to read, including the *I
expurgatorius* ("Expurgato
Index"), formerly a separate list
passages to be expunged in boo
otherwise permitted. 4. (alg.) E
ponent; ~ **number**, (statistic
number used in comparing wage
prices, etc., at a certain time wi
their value at a standard time; ~
linked, calculated in accordan
with index number; (of wage
pensions, etc.) allowed to rise wi
rise in CONSUMER price inde
index *v.t.* Furnish (book) wi
index; enter (word etc.) in index

In·di·a (ĭn′dēa). 1. Large peni
sula of S. central Asia, bounded o
N. by Himalayas; inhabited b
peoples following Hindu, Muslir
and other religions and speakir
over 200 languages, esp. Hindi ar
Bengali in N. and Tamil ar
Telugu in S.; British interest beg
in early 17th c. with formation
East India Company; in 1858 tl
Brit. government took over th
Company's authority and in 18;
Queen Victoria was proclaime
Empress of India; in 1947 the
provinces (**British** ~) an
numerous native states unde
British protection were divide
between India (see 2 below) an
PAKISTAN. 2. Republic, predom
nantly Hindu, constituted in 195
as a member nation of the Ne
Commonwealth and comprisin
much of the N. and all the S. an
central part of the peninsula
capital, New Delhi. 3. ~ **ink**
ink made from lampblack and
binding agent; ~ **paper**, thin
delicate, uncoated cream or buf
paper esp. used for proofs or firs
impressions of engravings. [Gk
Indos Indus, f. Pers. *hind* = Sansk
sindhu river]

In·di·an (ĭn′dēan) *adj.* 1. O
India or the E. Indies or thei
peoples. 2. Of the original in
habitants of America and the W
Indies. 3. ~ **club**, heavy bottle
shaped wooden club used in gym
nastic exercises; ~ **corn**, (chiefly
Brit.) maize; ~ **file**, single file (s
called because N. Amer. Indian
marched thus); ~ **hemp**, common
HEMP; ~ **meal**, (chiefly Brit.) cor
meal; ~ **Ocean**, ocean to S. o
India, extending from E. coast o
Africa to Malay Archipelago; ~
paintbrush, plant of genus *Castil*
leja, common in W. America, with

*The Republic of **India** occupies an area*
of 1,229,919 sq. miles and has a
population of 586 million people. 1
Coastal craft unload their wares a
Panjim, Goa, which was a Portuguese
possession until 1961. 2. Map and flag
of India. 3. Rice planting in Madras
India is the second-largest producer o
rice. Facing page: A Delhi girl plays the
sitar.

small flowers and bright-colored bracts; ~ **pipe**, leafless saprophytic plant, *Monotropa uniflora*, with a single white flower, resembling a pipe; ~ **summer**, period of calm, dry, mild weather with hazy atmosphere, occurring in late autumn; ~ **Territory**, former U.S. territory covering 31,000 sq. mi. (80,290 sq. km); merged with Oklahoma Territory and became state of Oklahoma, 1907. **Indian** *n.* 1. Native, inhabitant of India. 2. (also called Amer. Indian, (Brit.) Red Indian, or (including Eskimos etc.) Amerind) member of any of the aboriginal N. and S. Amer. peoples who orig. migrated from Asia over the land bridge now called the Bering Strait, and were well established throughout N. and S. America *c*10,000 B.C.; they included a wide variety of cultures from nomadic hunters to builders of vast and complex city-empires (Mayan, Aztec, Inca, etc.). 3. Any or all of the languages of the Amer. Indians.

In·di·an·a (ĭndēăn′a). State in north-central U.S., admitted to the Union in 1816; capital, Indian-

apolis.

In·di·an·ap·o·lis (ĭndēanăp′o-lĭs). Capital and largest city of Indiana in the central part on the White River; site of annual ~ **500** car race.

In·di·a (ĭn′dēa) **rubber** = RUBBER[1] def. 3.

In·dic (ĭn′dĭk) *adj.* & *n.* (Of, pertaining to) language group comprising Sanskrit and its modern descendants.

in·di·cate (ĭn′dĭkāt) *v.t.* (**-cat-ed, -cat·ing**). Point out, make known, show; state briefly; be a sign of, betoken; (med.) suggest, call for, (treatment). **in·di·ca·tion** (ĭndĭkā′shon) *n.*

in·dic·a·tive (ĭndĭk′atĭv) *adj.* 1. Suggestive, giving indications, *of.* 2. (gram., of verbal mood) Stating something as objective fact, not as conception, wish, etc., of speaker. **in·dic′a·tive·ly** *adv.* **indicative** *n.* Indicative mood.

*The **Indianapolis 500** is one of the richest automobile races in the world with prizes worth more than $1 million in the 1970s. It has been held annually since 1911.*

*This woman is a Hopi **Indian**. She weaving a basket, a traditional s amongst women of the Hopi tribe, as the making of pots. The Hopi culture gradually disintegrating in the face modern trends.*

in·di·ca·tor (ĭn′dĭkāter) *n.* Pe son, thing, that points out indicates; mechanical device inc cating condition of apparatus e to which it is attached.

in·dict (ĭndīt′) *v.t.* Accuse (pe son), esp. by legal process. **in dict·a·ble** (ĭndī′tabel) *adj.* Liab rendering one liable, to be indicte **in·dict·ment** (ĭndīt′ment) *n.* Fe mal accusation; (law) legal doc ment charging a party with havi committed a crime, drawn up by prosecuting attorney and found a presented by a grand jury.

In·dies (ĭn′dēz). **the ~**, (fo merly) India and adjacent regio and islands; the East Indies; t West Indies.

in·dif·fer·ence (ĭndĭf′eren -dĭf′rens) *n.* Absence of interest attention (*to, toward*); neutrali unimportance.

in·dif·fer·ent (ĭndĭf′erent, -dĭ rent) *adj.* Impartial, neutral; havi no inclination for or against; neith good nor bad, right nor wror too much nor too little, et mediocre; unimportant. **in·di fer·ent·ly** *adv.*

in·dig·e·nous (ĭndĭj′enus) a Native, belonging naturally; inna intrinsic. **in·dig′e·nous·ly** *adv.*

in·di·gent (ĭn′dĭjent) a Needy, poor. **in′di·gence** *n.*

in·di·gest·i·ble (ĭndĭjĕs′tib -dī-) *adj.* Not digestible; hard digest. **in·di·gest·i·bil·i·ty** (i dĭjĕstɪbĭl′ĭtē, -dī-) *n.* **in·di·ges tion** *n.* Difficulty in digesting foo illness, discomfort from this.

in·dig·nant (ĭndĭg′nant) a Moved by mingled anger and sc or feeling of injured innocenc

·dig′nant·ly *adv.*

in·dig·na·tion (ĭndĭgnā′shon) *n.* nger excited by meanness, in- stice, wickedness, or misconduct. **in·dig·ni·ty** (ĭndĭg′nĭtē) *n.* (pl. ·ies). Unworthy treatment, slight, sult.

in·di·go (ĭn′dĭgō) *n.* (pl. **-gos,** ·goes**).** Blue dye obtained from ·lants of genus *Indigofera*; plant ·om which this is obtained; dark ·ue or bluish-purple color; **~** ·lue,** blue color of indigo; **~ ·unting,** brilliant blue songbird of ·stern U.S., *Passerina cyanea.* ·ik. *indikon* Indian]

in·di·rect′ (ĭndĭrĕkt′, -dī-) *adj.* Not straight; not going straight the point; not directly aimed ; **~ tax,** one paid by consumer form of increased price for the ·xed goods. 2. (gram.) **~ object,** ·rson, thing, affected by action of ·rb but not primarily acted on (e.g. ·m in *give him the book*). **in·- ·rect′ly** *adv.* **in·di·rect′ness** *n.*

in·dis·creet′ (ĭndĭskrēt′) *adj.* In- ·dicious, unwary. **in·dis·creet′ly** ·v.

in·dis·crete (ĭndĭskrēt′, -dĭs′- ·ēt) *adj.* Not divided into distinct ·rts.

in·dis·cre·tion (ĭndĭskrĕsh′on) Injudicious conduct; accidental supposed accidental revelation official secret etc.; imprudence; ·ansgression of social morality.

in·dis·crim·i·nate (ĭndĭskrĭm′i- ·t) *adj.* Confused, haphazard; ·romiscuous; making no distinc- ·ons. **in·dis·crim′i·nate·ly** *adv.* ·dis·crim′i·nate·ness, in·dis- ·rim·i·na·tion** (ĭndĭskrĭminā′- ·on) *ns.*

in·dis·pen·sa·ble (ĭndĭspĕn′- ·bel) *adj.* That cannot be dis- ·nsed with, necessary; (of duty ·c.) that cannot be set aside. ·dis·pen′sa·ble·ness, in·dis- ·n·sa·bil·i·ty** (ĭndĭspĕnsabĭl′ĭtē)

in·dis·pose (ĭndĭspōz′) *v.t.* ·posed, -pos·ing).** Render unfit ·r unable; make averse; (esp. in ·ast part.) put out of health. ·dis·po·si·tion** (ĭndĭspozĭsh′on) Ill health, ailment, (esp. of ·inor kind); disinclination; aver- ·on. **in·dis·posed′** *adj.*

in·dis·pu·ta·ble (ĭndĭspū′tabel, ·dĭs′pyu-) *adj.* That cannot be ·sputed. **in·dis·put′a·ble·ness, ·dis·put·a·bil·i·ty** (ĭndĭspū- ·bĭl′ĭtē) *ns.* **in·dis·pu′ta·bly** *adv.*

in·dis·sol·u·ble (ĭndĭsŏl′yubel) ·dj.** Lasting, stable; that cannot ·e dissolved or decomposed. **in·- ·is·sol·u·bil·i·ty** (ĭndĭsŏlyubĭl′ĭtē) ·dis·sol′u·bly** *adv.*

in·dis·tinct (ĭndĭstĭngkt′) *adj.* ·ot distinct; confused, obscure. ·r·dis·tinct′ly** *adv.* **in·dis·tinct′- ·ess** *n.*

in·dis·tin·guish·a·ble (ĭndĭs- ·ng′gwĭshabel) *adj.* Not distin-

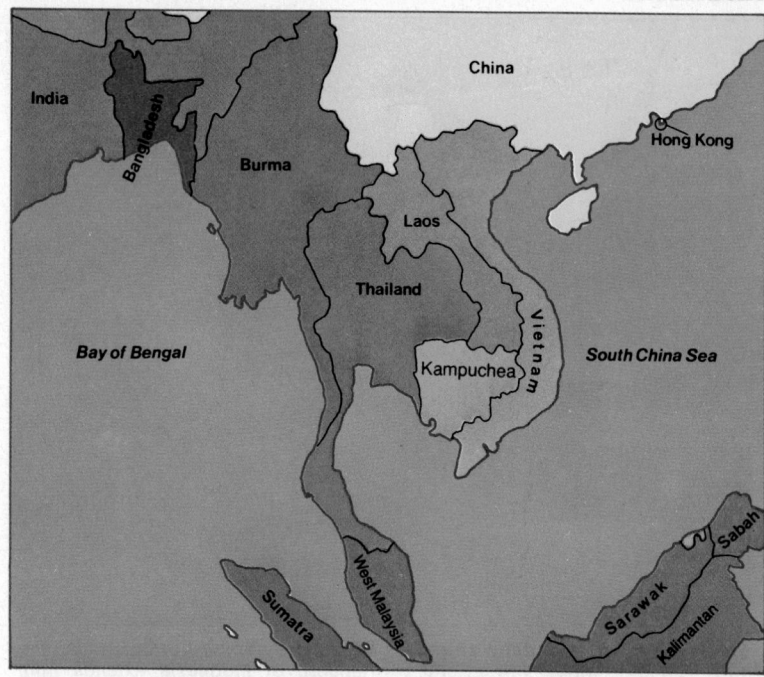

guishable. **in·dis·tin′guish·a·bly** *adv.*

in·di·um (ĭn′dēum) *n.* (chem.) Rare silver-white soft metallic ele- ment, occurring in association with zinc etc.; symbol In, at. no. 49, at. wt. 114.82. [L. *indicum* INDIGO, from two blue lines in the metal's spectrum]

in·di·vid·u·al (ĭndivĭj′ōoal) *adj.* Single; particular, special; having distinct character; of a single per- son or thing, characteristic of an individual. **~** *n.* Single member of a class, group, or number; single human being (opp. to society, the family, etc.); (colloq.) person.

in·di·vid·u·al·ism (ĭndivĭj′ōoa- lĭzem) *n.* 1. Individuality. 2. In- dependence in thought and action. 3. Social theory advocating free and independent action of individual (cf. SOCIALISM). **in·di·vid′u·al·ist** *n.* **in·di·vid·u·al·is·tic** (ĭndivĭjōo- alĭs′tĭk) *adj.*

in·di·vid·u·al·i·ty (ĭndivĭjōoăl′- ĭtē) *n.* (pl. **-ties**). Separate exist- ence; individual character, esp. when strongly marked.

in·di·vid·u·al·ize (ĭndivĭj′ōoa- līz) *v.t.* (**-ized, -iz·ing**). Give individual character to; specify. **in·di·vid·u·al·i·za·tion** (ĭndivĭj- ōoalīzā′shon) *n.*

in·di·vid·u·al·ly (ĭndivĭj′ōoale) *adv.* Personally, in an individual capacity; in a distinctive manner; one by one, not collectively.

in·di·vis·i·ble (ĭndivĭz′ibel) *adj.* Not divisible. **in·di·vis·i·bil·i·ty** (ĭndivĭzabĭl′ĭtē) *n.* **in·di·vis′i·bly** *adv.*

Indo- *prefix.* Indian; Indian and —.

In·do·chi·na (ĭn′dōchī′na). 1.

Indo-China was a French colony from the mid-19th century to 1954. It con- sisted of Laos, Kampuchea (Cambodia) and Vietnam. Today Indo-China may also include Burma, Thailand and West Malaysia.

Peninsula in SE. Asia occupied by Burma, Thailand, Malaya, Laos, Cambodia, and Vietnam. 2. (hist.) Region now occupied by Laos, Kampuchea, and Vietnam, for- merly a French dependency (**French ~**). **In·do·chi·nese** (ĭn′- dōchīnēz′, -nēs′) *adj. & n.* (pl. **-nese**).

in·doc·tri·nate (ĭndŏk′trĭnāt) *v.t.* (**-nat·ed, -nat·ing**). Instruct in a doctrine, ideology, etc.; teach to accept (ideology etc.) uncritically. **in·doc·tri·na·tion** (ĭndŏktrĭnā′- shon) *n.*

In·do-Eu·ro·pe·an (ĭn′dōūro- pē′an) *n. & adj.* (Of) the family of languages spoken over most of Europe and in Asia as far as N. India, including esp. the Indo- Iranian, Balto-Slavonic, Greek, Italic, Celtic, and Germanic groups; (member) of a people speaking one of these languages.

in·do·lent (ĭn′dolent) *adj.* Sloth- ful, lazy; (med., of tumor etc.) causing little or no pain. **in′do- lent·ly** *adv.* **in′do·lence** *n.*

in·dom·i·ta·ble (ĭndŏm′ĭtabel) *adj.* Unyielding; stubbornly per- sistent. **in·dom′i·ta·bly** *adv.*

In·do·ne·sia (ĭndonē′zha, -sha, -zēa, -dō-). Republic of SE. Asia, comprising Sumatra, Java, S. and E. Borneo, Celebes and other islands; formerly belonging to the Netherlands and then known as the Netherlands (or Dutch) East Indies; independent since 1949; capital, Djakarta.

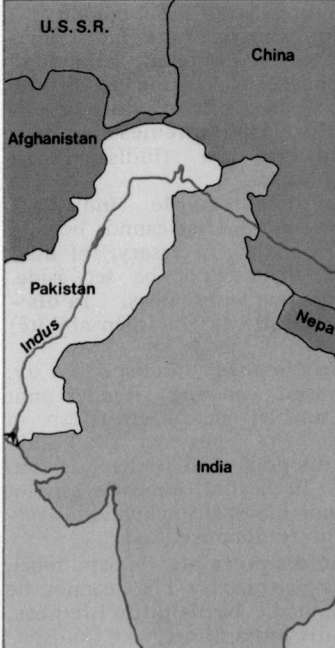

In·do·ne·sian (ĭndonē′zhan, -shan, -zēan, -dō-) *adj.* Of Indonesia or its people, esp. of Sumatra, Java, and Bali; of one of the vast number of SE. Asian languages spoken in Malay Peninsula and Archipelago. ~ *n.* Indonesian person; (esp.) one of a people forming the chief pre-Malay population of Malay Archipelago, and combining Polynesian and Mongoloid characteristics; Indonesian language; ~ **Timor**, (formerly Netherlands Timor) W. section of S. Malay Archipelago island of Timor, the largest and easternmost of the Lesser Sunda Islands; formerly Dutch-ruled, the W. half covers 5,765 sq. mi. (14,931 sq. km) and is now an Indonesian possession; the E. half is a Portuguese province.

in·door (ĭn′dor, -dōr) *adj.* Situated, carried on, within a house or other building. **in·doors′** *adv.* Within a house or other building.

in·dorse (ĭndors′) = ENDORSE.

in·du·bi·ta·ble (ĭndoō′bĭtabel, -dū′-) *adj.* That cannot be doubted. **in·du′bi·ta·bly** *adv.*

in·duce (ĭndoōs′, -dūs′) *v.t.* (**-duced, -duc·ing**). 1. Prevail on, persuade (*to*); bring about, give rise to. 2. (elect.) Produce (current) by induction. **in·duce′ment** *n.* What induces; attraction that leads one on (*to*).

in·duct (ĭndŭkt′) *v.t.* Formally place in an office or benefice; install (*into*); initiate, admit as a member; draft into military service.

in·duct·ance (ĭndŭk′tans) *n.* Setting up of a magnetic field or flux by induction.

in·duc·tion (ĭndŭk′shon) *n.* 1. Inducting. 2. Production (*of* facts) to prove general statement; inferring of general law from particular instances; **mathematical** ~,

With more than 13,000 islands, the Republic of **Indonesia** extends from Sumatra (alongside Western Malaysia) to Irian Jaya — the western half of New

method of proving universal truth of law by showing (i) that if true in a particular case it is true in the next case, and also (ii) that it is true in a particular case. 3. (elect. etc.) Bringing about of electric or magnetic state in a body by proximity (without contact) of electrified or magnetized body; production of electric current in conductor by motion of magnet near it, or by changes in the magnetic field in which it lies due to other causes; (esp.) generation of electric current in a conductor by changes in current in a neighboring conductor; ~ **coil**, apparatus for producing electric currents by induction, consisting normally of a soft iron core, surrounded by a coil of wire (the *primary coil*), which is in turn surrounded by a second and usu. much longer coil (the *secondary coil*): when the current in the primary coil is interrupted, a current of much higher voltage than the original one is induced in the secondary coil; by using very long coils enormous voltages suitable for producing x-rays and conducting many physical and other experiments can be induced.

in·duc·tive (ĭndŭk′tĭv) *adj.* 1. (of reasoning etc.) Of, based on, induction. 2. Of electric or magnetic induction. **in·duc′tive·ly** *adv.*

in·duc·tor (ĭndŭk′ter) *n.* 1. Person who inducts, as into office. 2. Part of electric apparatus that produces induction.

in·dulge (ĭndŭlj′) *v.* (**-dulged, -dulg·ing**). Please by yielding to wishes of; yield to (desire etc.); gratify one's appetite (for); take

Guinea. Above left: Map and flag Indonesia. Above right: Rice paddies Bali. Rice is a major crop in the area

The **Indus** River is 1,800 miles lor and has a drainage basin of 450,00 sq. miles. It is navigable for sm steamers as far as Hyderabad. Its pri cipal dams are the Sukkur and the Kot

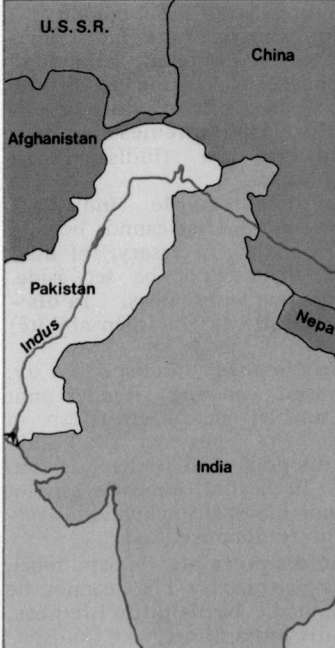

one's pleasure freely *in*. **in·dul′ gent** *adj.* **in·dul′gent·ly** *adv.*

in·dul·gence (ĭndŭl′jens) *n.* 1. Indulging. 2. Privilege granted (R.C. Ch.) remission of tempora punishment still due for sins whos eternal punishment has been re mitted by sacramental absolution.

in·du·rate (ĭn′durāt, -dyu-) *v.* (**-rat·ed, -rat·ing**). Make, be come, hard; make callous or un

The **Industrial Revolution**, which marked the change from domestic industry to the factory system, began in the textile industry. These workers from Wigan's cotton mills in England are shown taking their dinner hour.

eling; become inveterate. **in·du-**·**tion** (ĭndurā´shon) *n.* **in´du·ra**·**ve** *adj.*

In·dus (ĭn´dus). One of the 3 eat rivers of the Indian sub-·ntinent, rising in Himalayas of ´. Tibet, flowing 1900 mi. (3059 n) NW. through Tibet, then SW. rough Pakistan to Arabian Sea.

in·dus·tri·al (ĭndŭs´trēal) *adj.* f industries; engaged in, con-·cted with, industry; having ghly developed industries; **I ~ evolution** (also **i~ r~**), rapid ·velopment of industry through nployment of machinery; this ·velopment in England in late 8th and early 19th c.; **~ union**, ie organized to represent all crafts d trades within an industry; **I~ orkers of the World**, (abbrev. W.W.) international industrial bor organization founded at hicago in 1905 and existing until ie 1920s, advocating syndicalism d international socialism. **in·**·**us´tri·al·ly** *adv.* **in·dus´tri·al**·m, **in·dus´tri·al·ist** *ns.* **in·dus´**·**i·al·ize** *v.t.* (**-ized, -iz·ing**).

in·dus·tri·ous (ĭndŭs´trēus) *adj.* iligent, hardworking. **in·dus´**·**ri·ous·ly** *adv.*

in·dus·try (ĭn´dustrē) *n.* (pl. **·ries**). 1. Diligence; exertion, fort; systematic work; habitual nployment in useful work. 2. ·ranch of trade or manufacture,

esp. one employing much labor and capital; manufacturing in general.

-ine[1] *suffix.* Forming adjectives with sense of "pertaining to," "of the nature of" (*Alpine, equine, marine*).

-ine[2] *suffix.* Forming feminine nouns (*heroine*).

-ine[3] *suffix.* Forming (esp. abstract) nouns (*discipline, medicine*).

in·e·bri·ate (ĭnē´brĕĭt) *adj.* Intoxicated. ~ *n.* Inebriate person, esp. habitual drunkard. ~ (ĭnē´brēāt) *v.t.* (**-at·ed, -at·ing**). Make drunk, intoxicate. **in·e·bri·a·tion** (ĭnēbrēā´shon), **in·e·bri·e·ty** (ĭnĭbrī´etē) *ns.* (Habit of) drunkenness.

in·ed·i·ble (ĭnĕd´ibel) *adj.* Not suitable as food; not edible.

in·ed·u·ca·ble (ĭnĕj´ukabel) *adj.* Incapable of being educated, esp. as a result of mental retardation.

in·ef·fa·ble (ĭnĕf´abel) *adj.* Unutterable. **in·ef´fa·bly** *adj.*

in·ef·fec·tive (ĭnĭfĕk´tĭv) *adj.* Not producing the desired effect; (of person) inefficient. **in·ef·fec´**·**tive·ly** *adv.* **in·ef·fec´tive·ness** *n.*

in·ef·fec·tu·al (ĭnĭfĕk´chōoal) *adj.* Without effect, fruitless.

in·ef·fec´tu·al·ly *adv.* **in·ef·fec´**·**tu·al·ness** *n.*

in·ef·fi·cient (ĭnĭfĭsh´ent) *adj.* Not efficient; wasteful; lacking ability or competence. **in·ef·fi´cient·ly** *adv.* **in·ef·fi´cien·cy** *n.*

in·e·las·tic (ĭnĭlăs´tĭk) *adj.* Not elastic; unadaptable, unyielding. **in·e·las·tic·i·ty** (ĭnĭlăstĭs´ĭtē) *n.*

in·el·i·gi·ble (ĭnĕl´ĭjibel) *adj.* Not eligible. **in·el·i·gi·bil·i·ty** (ĭnĕlĭjibĭl´ĭtē) *n.* **in·el´i·gi·bly** *adv.*

in·e·luc·ta·ble (ĭnĭlŭk´tabel) *adj.* That cannot be avoided or overcome.

in·ept (ĭnĕpt´) *adj.* Out of place; absurd, silly; incompetent; clumsy. **in·ept´ly** *adv.* **in·ept´ness, in·ept´i·tude** *ns.*

in·e·qual·i·ty (ĭnĭkwŏl´ĭtē) *n.* (pl. **-ties**). Want of equality in magnitude, quality, rank, etc.; variableness; (of surface) irregularity.

in·eq·ui·ta·ble (ĭnĕk´wĭtabel) *adj.* Unfair, unjust. **in·eq´ui·ta·bly** *adv.* **in·eq´ui·ty** *n.* (pl. **-ties**).

in·e·rad·i·ca·ble (ĭnĭrăd´ikabel) *adj.* That cannot be erased or rooted out. **in·e·rad´i·ca·bly** *adv.*

in·ert (ĭnĕrt´) *adj.* Without inherent power of action, motion, or resistance; sluggish, slow; (chem., of gases) chemically inactive; esp., belonging to the group of gases comprising helium, neon, argon, krypton, xenon, and radon.

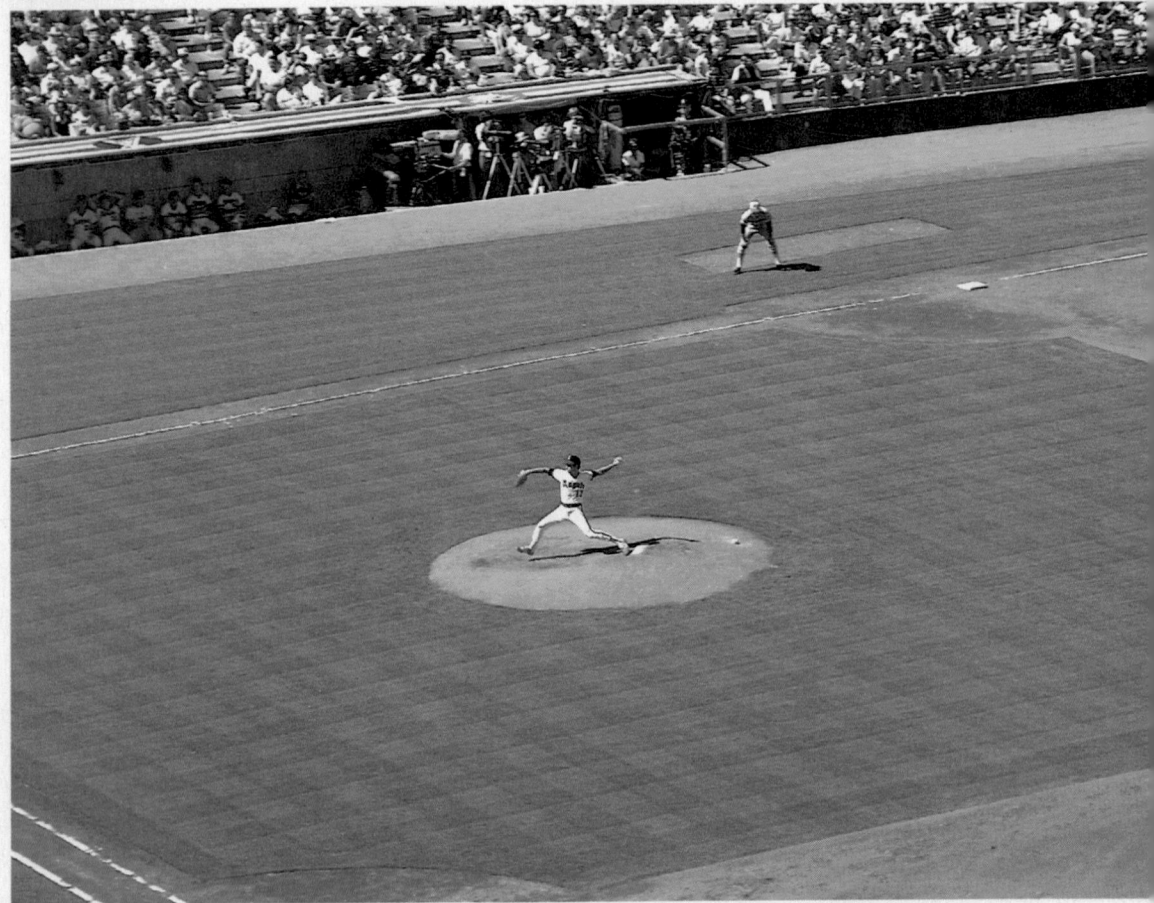

in·ert′ly *adv.* **in·ert′ness** *n.*

in·er·tia (ĭnēr′sha) *n.* 1. (phys.) Property of matter by which it continues in its existing state of rest or uniform motion in a straight line unless that state is changed by an external force. 2. Inertness, sloth. **in·er′tial** *adj.* (esp.) **inertial guidance, navigation**: see GUID-ANCE.

in·es·cap·a·ble (ĭnĕskā′pabel) *adj.* Not to be escaped. **in·es·cap′a·bly** *adv.*

in·es·ti·ma·ble (ĭnĕs′timabel) *adj.* Too great, intense, precious, etc., to be estimated. **in·es′ti·ma·bly** *adv.*

in·ev·i·ta·ble (ĭnĕv′ĭtabel) *adj.* Unavoidable, sure to happen. **in·ev′i·ta·ble·ness, in·ev·i·ta·bil·i·ty** (ĭnĕvĭtabĭl′ĭtē) *ns.* **in·ev′i·ta·bly** *adv.*

in·ex·act (ĭnĭgzăkt′) *adj.* Not exact. **in·ex·act′ly** *adv.* **in·ex·act′ness, in·ex·act′i·tude** *ns.*

in·ex·cus·a·ble (ĭnĭkskū′zabel) *adj.* That cannot be excused or justified. **in·ex·cus′a·bly** *adv.*

in·ex·haust·i·ble (ĭnĭgzaws′ti-bel) *adj.* That cannot be exhausted; limitless. **in·ex·haust·i·bil·i·ty** (ĭnĭgzawstibĭl′ĭtē) *n.* **in·ex·haust′i·bly** *adv.*

in·ex·o·ra·ble (ĭnĕk′serabel) *adj.* Relentless. **in·ex′o·ra·bly** *adv.*

in·ex·pi·a·ble (ĭnĕks′pēabel) *adj.* That cannot be expiated. **in·ex′-**

pi·a·bly *adv.*

in·ex·pli·ca·ble (ĭnĕks′plikabel, -ĭksplĭk′-) *adj.* That cannot be explained or accounted for. **in·ex′pli·ca·bly** *adv.*

in ex·tre·mis (ĭn ĭkstrē′mĭs; *Lat.* ĭn ĕkstrĕ′mēs). At the point of death; also fig. (L., = "in extremity")

in·ex·tri·ca·ble (ĭnĕks′trikabel, -ĕkstrĭk′-) *adj.* That cannot be unraveled, freed, or solved. **in·ex′tri·ca·bly** *adv.*

inf. *abbrev.* Infantry; (gram.) infinitive; information; [L. *infra*] below.

in·fal·li·ble (ĭnfăl′ibel) *adj.* Incapable of erring; unfailing. **in·fal′li·bly** *adv.* **in·fal·li·bil·i·ty** (ĭnfălibĭl′ĭtē) *n.* (esp. as attribute of the pope speaking *ex cathedra*, defined 1870 by Vatican Council).

in·fa·mous (ĭn′famus) *adj.* Of ill fame, notoriously vile; abominable. **in′fa·mous·ly** *adv.* **in′fa·my** *n.* (pl. **-mies**).

in·fan·cy (ĭn′fansē) *n.* (pl. **-cies**). 1. Early childhood, babyhood. 2. (law) = MINORITY def. 1. 3. Early stage of development.

in·fant (ĭn′fant) *n.* Child during earliest period of life; (law) = MINOR *n.* def. 1.

in·fan·ta (ĭnfăn′ta) *n.* (hist.) Daughter of king of Spain or Portugal (usu. eldest daughter), not heir to throne. **in·fan·te** (ĭnfăn′tā, -tē) *n.* (hist.) Son (usu. second son) of king of Spain or Portugal, not heir to throne.

in·fan·ti·cide (ĭnfăn′tĭsīd) *n.* 1. Murder of infant; custom of killing newborn infants. 2. One who kills an infant.

in·fan·tile (ĭn′fantīl) *adj.* Of, as of, infants; in its infancy; childish, silly; ∼ **paralysis**: see POLIOMYE-LITIS.

in·fan·ti·lism (ĭn′fantĭlizem, ĭnfăn′ti-) *n.* Mentally or physically undeveloped state.

in·fan·try (ĭn′fantrē) *n.* (pl. **-tries**). Foot soldiers; **in′fantry-man**, soldier of infantry regiment, trained to fight on foot, usu. equipped with light weapons.

in·farct (ĭnfärkt′, ĭn′färkt) *n.* (path.) Area of dead tissue caused by the blocking of an artery that normally nourishes it. **in·farc′tion** *n.*

in·fat·u·ate (ĭnfăch′ōōāt) *v.t.* (**-at·ed, -at·ing**). Affect (person) with extreme folly; inspire with extravagant passion. **in·fat′u·at·ed·ly** *adv.* **in·fat·u·a·tion** (ĭnfăch-ōōā′shon) *n.*

in·fect (ĭnfĕkt´) *v.t.* Implant disease-forming microorganisms in person, animal, plant, etc.); imbue person *with* opinion etc.). **in·fec´-ive** *adj.* **in·fec´tive·ness** *n.*

in·fec·tion (ĭnfĕk´shŏn) *n.* Communication of disease; diffusive nfluence of example, sympathy, tc.

in·fec·tious (ĭnfĕk´shŭs) *adj.* nfecting with disease, pestilential; of disease) such that the infecting gent can be communicated to the nvironment; (of emotions etc.) apt o spread, catching. **in·fec´tious·ly** *dv.* **in·fec´tious·ness** *n.*

in·fe·lic·i·tous (ĭnfelĭs´ĭtŭs) *adj.* Not felicitous; unfortunate; inppropriate; unhappy. **in·fe·lic´-ty** *n.* Unhappiness; misfortune; naptness of expression etc.

in·fer (ĭnfĕr´) *v.t.* (**-ferred, fer·ring**). Deduce, conclude; erron.) imply.

in·fer·ence (ĭn´ferens) *n.* Infering; (esp., logic) forming of a onclusion from premises either by nduction or deduction; thing inerred. **in·fer·en·tial** (ĭnferĕn´shal) *dj.* **in·fer·en´tial·ly** *adv.*

in·fe·ri·or (ĭnfĕr´ēer) *adj.* 1. ituated below; (bot., of calyx) elow ovary, (of ovary) below alyx; (print., of small letters or gures) placed lower than ordinary etters, e.g. H_2, C_n. 2. Lower in ank, quality, etc. (*to*); of poor uality. **in·fe´ri·or·ly** *adv.* **in-**

ferior *n.* Person inferior to another, esp. in rank. **in·fe·ri·or·-i·ty** (ĭnfereōr´ĭtē, -ār´-) *n.* ~ **complex**, unconscious feeling of inferiority to others, freq. manifested in self-assertive behavior; (pop.) sense of inferiority.

in·fer·nal (ĭnfĕr´nal) *adj.* Of hell; hellish, fiendish; (colloq.) abominable, confounded. **in·fer´-nal·ly** *adv.*

in·fer·no (ĭnfĕr´nō) *n.* (pl. **-nos**). Hell (**The I~**, 1st part of Dante's *Divine Comedy*); scene of horror.

in·fer·tile (ĭnfĕr´tĭl) *adj.* Not fertile. **in·fer·til·i·ty** (ĭnfertĭl´ĭtē) *n.*

in·fest (ĭnfĕst´) *v.t.* Inhabit in large numbers, overrun; swarm in or about, (place). **in·fes·ta·tion** (ĭnfĕstā´shŏn) *n.*

in·fi·del (ĭn´fĭdel) *n.* Person with no religious beliefs; adherent of religion opposed to some particular religion, esp. to Christianity or Islam; unbeliever. ~ *adj.* Unbelieving; of unbelievers.

in·fi·del·i·ty (ĭnfĭdĕl´ĭtē) *n.* (pl.

*Foot-soldiers of the **infantry** have been the backbone of most armies throughout the ages and have a key role even in these days of highly mobile and mechanized warfare. Below Left: Historical re-enactment of Civil War infantry at rest. Below right: Infantrymen ready for deployment during the Vietnam hostilities.*

-ties). 1. Lack of religious beliefs or faith. 2. Disloyalty, esp. to husband or wife; adultery.

in·field (ĭn´fēld) *n.* 1. Farm land around farmhouse. 2. (baseball) Part of field enclosed within baselines; the four infielders: first, second, third basemen and short-stop. **in´field·er** *n.* (baseball) One of the infield.

in·fight·ing (ĭn´fīting) *n.* 1. Boxing at closer quarters than arm's length. 2. (colloq.) Internal strife between (members of) organization(s) etc. **in´fight·er** *n.*

in·fil·trate (ĭnfil´trāt, ĭn´fĭl-) *v.* (**-trated, -trat·ing**). Introduce (fluid) by filtration; permeate by filtration (also fig.). **in·fil·tra´tion** *n.* (esp.) Gradual penetration into territory by small groups of settlers, or into enemy ground by small parties of troops; dissemination of ideas by small group working inside political party etc.; enter an organization as a spy.

in·fi·nite (ĭn´finĭt) *adj.* Boundless, endless; very great; innumerable, very many; (math., of quantity or magnitude) greater than any assignable quantity or magnitude; (of series) that may be continued indefinitely without ever coming to an end. **in´fi·nite·ly** *adv.*

in·fin·i·tes·i·mal (ĭnfĭnĭtĕs´-ĭmal) *adj. & n.* Infinitely or very small (amount). **in·fin·i·tes´i·mal·ly** *adv.*

in·fin·i·tive (ĭnfĭn´ĭtĭv) *adj.* & *n.* (gram.) (Verb form) that expresses the verbal notion without predicating it of any subject (e.g. (*to*) *see*). **in·fin·i·val** (ĭnfĭnĭtĭ´val) *adj.*

in·fin·i·ty (ĭnfĭn´ĭtē) *n.* (pl. **-ties**). Boundlessness; boundless number or extent; (math.) infinite quantity (symbol ∞).

in·firm (ĭnfĕrm´) *adj.* Physically weak, esp. through age; (of person, mind, judgment, etc.) weak, irresolute. **in·firm´ly** *adv.* **in·fir·mi·ty** (ĭnfĕr´mĭtē) *n.* (pl. **-ties**).

in·fir·ma·ry (ĭnfĕr´merē) *n.* (pl. **-ries**). Small hospital or dispensary, esp. in school, factory, etc.

in fla·gran·te de·lic·to (ĭn flagrăn´tē dĭlĭk´tō; *Lat.* ĭn flahgrahn´tĕ dĕlĭk´tō). In the very act of committing an offense. [L., = "in blazing crime"]

in·flame (ĭnflām´) *v.* (**-flamed, -flam·ing**). 1. Set ablaze; catch fire. 2. Excite passionately; become excited; aggravate. 3. Cause inflammation in (body etc.); become affected with inflammation.

in·flam·ma·ble (ĭnflăm´abel) *adj.* Easily set on fire; flammable; easily excited. ~ *n.* (usu. pl.) Inflammable substance. **in·flam·ma·bil·i·ty** (ĭnflămabĭl´ĭtē) *n.*

in·flam·ma·tion (ĭnflamā´shon) *n.* Inflaming; (path.) condition of living tissue marked by heat, swelling, redness, and usu. pain, esp. as reaction to damage or infection.

in·flam·ma·to·ry (ĭnflăm´atōrē, -tōrē) *adj.* Tending to inflame with desire or passion; (path.) of, characterized by, inflammation.

in·flate (ĭnflāt´) *v.t.* (**-flat·ed, -flat·ing**). Distend with air or gas; puff up (*with* pride etc.); resort to inflation of (currency); raise (price) artificially; **inflated**, (of language) bombastic.

in·fla·tion (ĭnflā´shon) *n.* Inflating; (esp.) increase in purchasing power in relation to goods available for purchase, resulting in fall in value of money and general increase in prices. **in·fla·tion·ar·y** (ĭnflā´shonĕrē) *adj.*

in·flect (ĭnflĕkt´) *v.t.* 1. Bend inward, curve. 2. (gram.) Vary termination of (word) to express grammatical relation. 3. Modulate (voice etc.). **in·flec´tion** *n.* 1. Inflecting, bending. 2. Modification of word to express grammatical relationship; inflected form of word; inflectional suffix or element. 3. Modulation of voice; change in pitch or tone. **in·flec´tive** *adj.* Of, characterized by, inflection.

in·flex·i·ble (ĭnflĕk´sĭbel) *adj.* Unbendable; (fig.) unbending, rigid. **in·flex·i·bil´i·ty** *n.* **in·flex´i·bly** *adv.*

in·flict (ĭnflĭkt´) *v.t.* Lay on (blow, etc.); impose (suffering, penalty, etc., *upon*). **in·flic´tion** *n.*

in·flight (ĭn´flīt) *adj.* Served, offered, etc., as food, movies, etc., on plane during flight.

in·flo·res·cence (ĭnflorĕs´ens) *n.* (bot.) Arrangement of flowers of plant in relation to axis and to each other; collective flower of plan flowering.

in·flow (ĭn´flō) *n.* Flowing in.

in·flu·ence (ĭn´flōoens) *n.* Action exercised (*on*); ascendanc moral power (*over, with*); thin person, exercising (usu. no material) power. 2. (astrol.) Su posed flowing from stars of ethere fluid affecting character and destin of man. ~ *v.t.* (**-ence -enc·ing**). Exert influence upo have effect upon.

in·flu·en·tial (ĭnflōoĕn´sha *adj.* Having great influenc **in·flu·en´tial·ly** *adv.*

in·flu·en·za (ĭnflōoĕn´za) Acute infectious febrile disorde caused by a virus, occurring usu. widespread epidemics.

in·flux (ĭn´flŭks) *n.* Flowing i esp. of persons or things (*in* place etc.).

in·fo (ĭn´fō) *n.* (Slang) Inform tion.

in·fold (ĭnfōld´) = ENFOLD.

in·form (ĭnfŏrm´) *v.* 1. Inspir imbue (person, thing, *with* qualit principle, etc.). 2. Tell (person thing, *that, how*, etc.). 3. Brin charge (*against*). **in·form·a** (ĭnfŏr´mant) *n.* (esp.) One who te or gives information.

in·form·al (ĭnfŏr´mal) *adj.* N according to due form; witho formality. **in·for´mal·ly** *ad* **in·for·mal·i·ty** (ĭnfŏrmăl´ĭtē) (pl. **-ties**).

in·for·ma·tion (ĭnfermā´sho *n.* 1. Informing, telling; thing to knowledge, items of knowledg news; ~ **retrieval**, systemat recovery of data from memory ba of computer, files, etc. 2. (la

Simple Raceme　Compound Raceme　Racemose Spike　Racemose Panicle

Cymes

Racemose Corymb

Cymose Corymb
and
Simple Umbel

Compound Umbel

Wild Arum　Androgynous Flower　(Section of Daisy)　(Thistle)

(Guelder Rose)

Composite Flowers

Charge, complaint, lodged with court or magistrate (against).

in·for·ma′tion·al adj.

in·form·a·tive (ĭnfôr′matĭv) adj. Giving information, instructive.

in·formed (ĭnfôrmd′) adj. Instructed, knowing the facts, educated.

in·form·er (ĭnfôr′mer) n. One who informs against another.

in·fra (ĭn′fra) adv. Below, lower down, further on (in book). [L.]

infra- prefix. Below.

in·frac·tion (ĭnfrăk′shon) n. Infringement, violation.

in·fra dig (ĭn′fra dĭg′). (chiefly Brit.) Beneath one's dignity, unbecoming. [abbrev. L. infra dignitatem]

in·fran·gi·ble (ĭnfrăn′jibel) adj. Unbreakable; inviolable.

in·fra·red (ĭnfrarĕd′) adj. (phys.) Lying beyond the red end of the visible spectrum; of, producing, electromagnetic radiations with a wavelength longer than that of red light, perceived as heat and used in heat therapy, cooking devices, etc.

in·fra·struc·ture (ĭn′frastrŭk-cher) n. Fixed installations and facilities necessary to support military operations, as airfields, naval bases, training establishments, supply works, etc.; supporting system of any organization.

in·fre·quent (ĭnfrē′kwent) adj. Not frequent. **in·fre′quent·ly** adv. **in·fre′quen·cy, in·fre′quence** ns.

in·fringe (ĭnfrĭnj′) v.t. (-fringed, -fring·ing). Transgress, violate (law, oath, etc.). **in·fringe′ment** n.

in·fu·ri·ate (ĭnfūr′ēāt) v.t. (-at·ed, -at·ing). Fill with fury, enrage.

in·fuse (ĭnfūz′) v. (-fused, -fus·ing). 1. Pour (into); instill (into). 2. Steep (herb etc.) in liquid to extract its soluble properties; undergo infusion.

in·fu·si·ble (ĭnfū′zibel) adj. That cannot be fused or melted. **in·fus·i·bil·i·ty** (ĭnfūzibĭl′itē) n.

in·fu·sion (ĭnfū′zhon) n. Infusing; liquid extract thus obtained; infused element, admixture.

-ing[1] suffix. Forming nouns f. verbs, denoting action (asking, fighting); product (building); material (clothing).

ing[2] suffix. Forming pres. part. of verbs, often used as adjectives (charming, well-meaning).

in·gen·ious (ĭnjēn′yus) adj. Showing ingenuity. **in·gen′ious·ly** adv. **in·gen′ious·ness** n.

Inflorescence, in its simplest form, is when the stem of a plant bears a series of flower stalks (peduncles) at equal distances apart and with flowers at their tips. The cow parsley (left) is an example. More complex inflorescences occur when there are secondary peduncles (above left).

Gold, silver and steel are cast into **ingots** for further processing, storage or transportation. Steel ingots can weigh more than 100 tons. These steel ingots are ready for forging at the Krupp Works, Essen, W. Germany.

in·gé·nue (ăn'jenōō, -nū, ahn'-zhe-; *Fr.* ahnzhänü') *n.* (pl. **-nues** pr. -nōoz, -nūz; *Fr.* -nü'). Artless girl, esp. as stage type. [Fr.]

in·ge·nu·i·ty (ĭnjenōō'ĭtē) *n.* Cleverness, imagination, inventiveness.

in·gen·u·ous (ĭnjĕn'ūus) *adj.* Open, frank; innocent, artless. **in·gen'u·ous·ly** *adv.* **in·gen'u·ous·ness** *n.*

in·gest (ĭnjĕst') *v.t.* Take in (food etc.) by, or as if by, swallowing. **in·ges·tion** (ĭnjĕs'chon) *n.* **in·ges'tive** *adj.*

in·glo·ri·ous (ĭnglōr'ēus, -glōr'-) *adj.* Shameful, ignominious. **in·glo'ri·ous·ly** *adv.*

in·got (ĭng'got) *n.* Mass (usu. oblong) of cast metal, esp. of gold, silver, or steel.

in·grain (ĭn'grān) *adj.* Inherent, inveterate, thorough.

in·grained (ĭngrānd', ĭn'grānd) *adj.* Deeply rooted, inveterate; thorough.

in·grate (ĭn'grāt) *n.* Ungrateful person.

in·gra·ti·ate (ĭngrā'shēāt) *v.t.* (**-at·ed, -at·ing**). Bring *oneself* into favor *with.* **in·gra·ti·a·tion** (ĭngrāshēā'shon) *n.*

in·grat·i·tude (ĭngrăt'ĭtōod, -tūd) *n.* Lack of gratitude.

in·gre·di·ent (ĭngrē'dēent) *n.* Component part, element, in a mixture.

in·gress (ĭn'grĕs), **in·gres·sion** (ĭngrĕsh'on) *ns.* Going in; right of entrance.

in·grow·ing (ĭngrō'ĭng) *adj.* Growing inward, esp. (of nail) growing into the flesh.

in·gui·nal (ĭng'gwinal) *adj.* Of the groin.

in·hab·it (ĭnhăb'ĭt) *v.t.* Dwell in, occupy (region, town, house, etc.). **in·hab'i·tant** *n.*

in·hal·ant (ĭnhā'lant) *n.* (esp.) Medicinal preparation for inhaling.

The **infra-red** portion of the electromag netic spectrum is invisible to the eye but can be detected as a sensation warmth. This infra-red thermomete used in hospitals, records the tempera ture of an internal section of the body

in·ha·la·tor (ĭn'halāter) *n.* Ap paratus for introducing medicatio or vapor into breathing passages, o for administering anesthetic.

in·hale (ĭnhāl') *v.t.* (**-haled -hal·ing**). Breathe in (air, ga etc.); take (esp. tobacco smoke) int the lungs. **in·ha·la·tion** (ĭn halā'shon) *n.*

This young asthma sufferer has to **inhale** medication to alleviate the breathing difficulties that are an inevitable part of the condition. Prolonged asthmatic attacks can be dangerous if the sufferer is weakened.

that represses a normal physiological process or antagonizes an abnormal one; (chem.) substance that slows down or suppresses a chemical change.

in·hos·pi·ta·ble (ĭnhŏs′pĭtabel, -hŏspĭt′a-) *adj.* Not hospitable; unfriendly; (of region etc.) not affording shelter etc. **in·hos′pi·ta·bly** *adv.* **in·hos′pi·ta·ble·ness**, **in·hos·pi·tal·i·ty** (ĭnhŏspĭtăl′ĭtē) *ns.*

in-house (ĭn′hows′) *adj. & adv.* Within an organization or using its own resources (*an ~ editor, ~ project*).

in·hu·man (ĭnhū′man, ĭnū′-) *adj.* Brutal, unfeeling, barbarous; not of the ordinary human type. **in·hu′man·ly** *adv.* **in·hu·man·i·ty** (ĭnhūmăn′ĭtē) *n.* (pl. **-ties**).

in·im·i·cal (ĭnĭm′ĭkal) *adj.* Hostile; harmful. **in·im′i·cal·ly** *adv.*

in·im·i·ta·ble (ĭnĭm′ĭtabel) *adj.* That defies imitation. **in·im′i·ta·bly** *adv.*

in·iq·ui·ty (ĭnĭk′wĭtē) *n.* (pl. **-ties**). Unrighteousness, wickedness; gross injustice. **in·iq′ui·tous** *adj.* **in·iq′ui·tous·ly** *adv.*

in·i·tial (ĭnĭsh′al) *adj.* Of, existing or occurring at, the beginning; ~ **letter**, letter standing at beginning of word. **in·i′tial·ly** *adv.* **initial** *n.* (esp. pl.) First letter(s) of person's name and surname. ~ *v.t.* (**-tialed, -tialing**, Brit. **-tialled, -tial·ling**). Mark, sign, with initials.

in·i·ti·ate (ĭnĭsh′ēāt) *v.t.* (**-at·ed, -at·ing**). 1. Begin, set going, originate. 2. Admit (person), esp. with introductory rites or forms (*into* society, office, secret, *in* mysteries, science, etc.). **in·i·ti·a·tion** (ĭnĭshēā′shon) *n.* **in·i·ti·a·to·ry** (ĭnĭsh′ēatōrē, -tōrē) *adj.* **initiate** (ĭnĭsh′ēĭt, -āt) *adj. & n.* (Person) who has been initiated.

in·i·ti·a·tive (ĭnĭsh′ēatĭv, ĭnĭsh′-a-) *n.* First step, origination; power, right, or function of originating something; esp., right of citizen(s) outside legislature to initiate legislation; **take the ~**, take the lead. **initiative** *adj.* Beginning, originating.

in·ject (ĭnjĕkt′) *v.t.* Drive, force (fluid, medicine, *into* cavity etc.) by or as by syringe or hypodermic needle; fill (cavity etc.) by injecting.

in·jec·tion (ĭnjĕk′shon) *n.* 1. Injecting; **fuel ~**, direct introduction of fuel under pressure into combustion chamber of internal combustion engine. 2. Liquid or solution injected.

in·ju·di·cious (ĭnjōōdĭsh′us) *adj.*

in·hal·er (ĭnhā′ler) *n.* (esp.) 1. nhalator. 2. RESPIRATOR.

in·here (ĭnhēr′) *v.i.* (**-hered, ·her·ing**). (of qualities etc.) Exist, ·bide, *in*; (of rights etc.) be vested *n.* **in·her·ence** (ĭnhēr′ens, -hěr′-) *n.* **in·her′en·cy** *n.* (pl. **-cies**). **n·her′ent** *adj.* **in·her′ent·ly** *adv.*

in·her·it (ĭnhěr′ĭt) *v.t.* Receive ·y legal descent or succession; ·lerive (quality etc.) from one's ·rogenitors; (abs.) succeed as heir. **·her′i·tance** *n.* Inheriting; what · inherited; **inheritance tax**, tax

on inherited property. **in·her′-it·a·ble** *adj.* Capable of inheriting or of being inherited. **in·her′i·tor** *n.* **in·her·i·trix** (ĭnhěr′ĭtrĭks) *n.fem.* (pl. **in·her·i·tri·ces** pr. ĭnhěr′ĭtri-sēz, -hěrĭtrī′-).

in·hib·it (ĭnhĭb′ĭt) *v.t.* Hinder, restrain (action, process); forbid, prohibit. **in·hi·bi·tion** (ĭnhĭbĭsh′-on) *n.* (esp., psychol.) Blocking of thought or action by emotional resistance.

in·hib·i·tor (ĭnhĭb′ĭter) *n.* Thing that inhibits; (physiol.) substance

Unwise, ill-judged. **in·ju·di´-cious·ly** *adv.* **in·ju·di´cious·ness** *n.*

In·jun (ĭn´jun) *n.* (colloq.) Var. of INDIAN *n.* def 2; **honest ~**, real(ly), true, truly.

in·junc·tion (ĭnjŭnk´shon) *n.* Enjoining; directive, order; (law) court order enjoining or prohibiting a party from a course of action.

in·jure (ĭn´jer) *v.t.* (**-jured, -jur·ing**). Do wrong to; hurt, harm, impair. **in´jured** *adj.* Wronged; hurt; showing sense of wrong, offended.

in·ju·ri·ous (ĭnjoor´ēus) *adj.* Damaging, harmful; (of language) insulting; libelous; slanderous.

in·ju·ry (ĭn´jerē) *n.* (pl. **-ries**). Wrongful action or treatment; harm, damage.

in·jus·tice (ĭnjŭs´tĭs) *n.* Lack of equity, unfairness; unjust act.

ink (ĭngk) *n.* 1. Colored fluid for writing with pen on paper etc. or for printing, consisting of pigment dispersed in water (for writing inks) or in oil, resin, etc., for printing and ballpoint inks; **India ~**: see INDIA. 2. Black inky liquid secreted by cuttlefish etc. and ejected to cloud water and assist escape. 3. **ink blot**, stain of spilled ink on paper, esp. such pattern of such

*The Greenland Fishery **Inn** in King's Lynn, U.K., was built in 1605 as a merchant's house with a cruck-based roof, 17th-century wall paintings and an overhanging upper floor.*

stain used in RORSCHACH test; **ink´well**, (formerly) container for ink fitted into hole in desk. **ink** *v.t.* mark (*in, over*, etc.) with ink; cover (types) with ink. **ink´y** *adj.* (**ink·i·er, ink·i·est**). Of, like ink; black or very dark; covered or stained with ink.

ink·ling (ĭngk´lĭng) *n.* Hint, slight knowledge or suspicion, (*of*).

in·laid (ĭn´lād, ĭnlād´): see INLAY.

in·land (ĭn´lănd, -land) *n.* Interior of country. ~ *adj.* Placed in interior of country, remote from sea or border. **in´land** *adv.* In, toward, the interior.

In·land (ĭn´lănd) **Sea.** Shallow Pacific Ocean inlet extending 240 mi. (386 km), in SW. Japan; bounded on the N. by Honshu, and on the S. by Shikoku and Kyushu.

in-law (ĭn´law) *n.* Relative by marriage.

in-lay (ĭn´lā, ĭnlā´) *v.t.* (**-laid, -lay·ing**). Embed (thing *in* another) so that their surfaces are even; ornament (thing) with another inlaid. **in´lay** *n.* (pl. **-lays**). Inlaid ornament, esp. furniture or woodwork; (dentistry) large filling.

in·let (ĭn´lĕt) *n.* Small arm of sea, creek.

in lo·co pa·ren·tis (ĭn lō´kō parĕn´tĭs). In place of a parent. [L.]

in·mate (ĭn´māt) *n.* Occupant (*of* house, and esp. of a prison, asylum, etc.) esp. along with others.

in me·mo·ri·am (ĭn memôr´ēam, -mōr´-). In memory (of). [L.]

in·most (ĭn´mōst) *adj.* Most inward.

*This 18th-century French games table has **inlays** of ivory and ebony on its tulipwood surface. Its four sides are inset with 26 Sèvres plaques mounted in ormolu.*

inn (ĭn) *n.* House provid[ing] lodging, food, etc., for payme[nt] esp. for travelers; tavern; **in[n] keeper**, one who keeps an inn.

in·nards (ĭn´erdz) *n.pl.* (collo[q.]) Viscera; internal bodily organs.

in·nate (ĭnāt´, ĭn´āt) *adj.* Inbo[rn], natural. **in·nate´ly** *adv.* **in·nat[e]´ ness** *n.*

in·ner (ĭn´er) *adj.* Interi[or], internal; **~ city**, central area [of] city, typically characterized [by] overcrowding, dilapidation, a[nd] poverty; **~ directed**, guided [by] personal standards rather th[an] external social pressure; **~ e[ar]**, internal part of ear compris[ing] vestibule, semicircular canals, a[nd] cochlea; **the ~ man**, man's soul [or] mind; (joc.) stomach; **~ spa[ce]**, space below surface of oce[an]; **in´nerspring (mattress**), hav[ing] enclosed helical springs support[ing] padding; **inner tube**, separ[ate] inflatable rubber tube inside [a] pneumatic tire. **in´ner·most** [adj.] **in´ner** *n.* & *adj.*

in·ning (ĭn´ĭng) *n.* (baseb[all]) Portion of game in which each te[am] is at bat until it has three ou[ts]; **~s**, (usu. considered sin[g.]) (cricket) portion of game in wh[ich] one team is at bat; **~s**, ([any]) opportunity to perform.

In·no·cent (ĭn´osent). Name [of] 13 popes: (esp.) **Innocent III**, po[pe] 1198–1216; champion of suprem[acy] of spiritual over temporal authori[ty], proclaimer of fourth Crusade a[nd] initiator of "crusades" agai[nst] ALBIGENSES; **Innocent IV**, po[pe] 1243–54; canon lawyer, extre[me] supporter of papal claims [to] temporal authority; first bestow[er]

*In the New Guinea highlands a chil[d is] about to take part with a group of oth[ers] in a ceremony of **initiation** into b[oy]-hood. One task will be to kill a pig. [The] cowrie shells have a sacred con[no]-tation*

of red hat on Roman cardinals.

in·no·cent (ĭn′osent) *adj.* Free from moral wrong, sinless; not guilty (*of* crime etc.); simple, guileless; harmless. **in′no·cent·ly** *adv.* **innocent** *n.* Innocent person, esp. young child; simple person. **in′no·cence** *n.*

in·noc·u·ous (ĭnŏk′ūus) *adj.* Not injurious; harmless; banal; not important. **in·noc′u·ous·ly** *adv.* **in·noc′u·ous·ness, in·no·cu·i·ty** (ĭnokū′ĭtē) *ns.*

in·nom·i·nate (ĭnŏm′inĭt) *adj.* Unnamed; (anat.) ∼ **bone**, hip-bone, union of three bones (ilium, ischium, and pubis).

in·no·vate (ĭn′ovāt) *v.i.* (**-vat·ed, -vat·ing**). Bring in novelties; make changes *in.* **in·no·va·tion** (ĭnovā′shon), **in′no·va·tor** *ns.*

in·nu·en·do (ĭnūěn′dō) *n.* (pl. **-dos, -does**). Oblique hint, insinuation, allusive remark (usu. disparaging). [L., = by nodding at, pointing at, meaning (*innuere* nod at, mean)]

In·nu·it (ĭn′ūĭt) *n.* (pl. **-its, -it**). Eskimo of N. America or Greenland as distinct from those of Aleutians or Asia; tribe, language, of these Eskimos. [Eskimo, = people]

in·nu·mer·a·ble (ĭnōō′merabel, -nū′-) *adj.* Countless.

in·oc·u·late (ĭnŏk′yulāt) *v.t.* (**-lat·ed, -lat·ing**). Impregnate (person or animal) *with* agent of disease to induce milder form of it and so safeguard against further attacks. **in·oc·u·la·tion** (ĭnŏkyulā′-shon) *n.*

in·of·fen·sive (ĭnofěn′sĭv) *adj.* Unoffending; not objectionable.

in·of·fen′sive·ly *adv.*

in·op·er·a·ble (ĭnŏp′erabel) *adj.* That cannot be operated; not curable by surgical operation.

in·op·er·a·tive (ĭnŏp′eratĭv) *adj.* Not working or taking effect.

in·op·por·tune (ĭnŏpertoōn′, -tūn′) *adj.* Unseasonable, untimely, tactless. **in·op·por·tune′ly** *adv.* **in·op·por·tune′ness** *n.*

in·or·di·nate (ĭnōr′dinĭt) *adj.* Immoderate, excessive; intemperate; disorderly. **in·or′di·nate·ly** *adv.*

in·or·gan·ic (ĭnōrgăn′ĭk) *adj.* 1. Having no organized physical structure; not existing by natural growth. 2. (chem.) Belonging to any class of substance other than organic compounds; ∼ **chemistry**: see CHEMISTRY. **in·or·gan′i·cal·ly** *adv.*

in·pa·tient (ĭn′pā′shent) *n.* Patient living in a hospital during treatment.

in pet·to (ĭn pět′ō). (of cardinals appointed but not disclosed by the pope) Undisclosed. [It., = in the breast]

in·put (ĭn′pōot) *n.* What is put in, esp. in economic, electrical, or industrial processes; data, programs, etc., supplied to computer; (jargon, colloq.) opinions, facts, etc., offered to decision makers.

in·quest (ĭn′kwěst) *n.* Judicial inquiry to ascertain matter of fact, usu. before a jury; the jury itself; inquiry held by coroner's court to ascertain cause of person's death (also **coroner's** ∼); also fig.

in·quire (ĭnkwīr′) *v.* (**-quired, -quir·ing**). Make search (*into* matter); seek information (*of*

person, *about* thing, etc.); ask abo ask to be told. **in·quir′ing** *adv.*

in·quir·y (ĭnkwīr′ē, ĭn′kwerē) (pl. **-quir·ies**). Asking; questio investigation.

in·qui·si·tion (ĭnkwĭzĭsh′on) 1. Search, investigation; offic inquiry. 2. **I** ∼, (R.C. C ecclesiastical tribunal (the *H Office*) set up in 13th c. und Innocent III for the suppression heresy and punishment of hereti notorious esp. in Spain in 16th for its severities; finally abolish in France 1772, in Spain 18 **in·qui·si′tion·al** *adj.*

in·quis·i·tive (ĭnkwĭz′ĭtĭv) *a* Inquiring, curious; prying. **i quis′i·tive·ly** *adv.* **in·quis′i·tiv ness** *n.*

in·quis·i·tor (ĭnkwĭz′ĭter) *n.* vestigator; questioner; officer of t Inquisition.

in·quis·i·to·ri·al (ĭnkwĭzĭtō′ ēal, -tōr′-) *adj.* Of, like, inquisitor; offensively prying. **i quis·i·to′ri·al·ly** *adv.*

in re (ĭn rē′, rā′) = RE.

I.N.R.I. *abbrev. Iesus Nazarer Rex Iudaeorum* (L., = Jesus Nazareth, King of the Jews).

in·road (ĭn′rōd) *n.* (usu. p Hostile incursion, raid; (fig.) e croachment.

in·rush (ĭn′rŭsh) *n.* Rushing influx.

in·sane (ĭnsān′) *adj.* Not san mad; senseless. **in·sane′ly** *ac* **in·san·i·ty** (ĭnsăn′ĭtē) *n.* (pl. **-tie**

in·sa·tia·ble (ĭnsā′shabel, -sh abel) *adj.* That cannot be satisfie **in·sa·tia·bil·i·ty** (ĭnsāshabĭl′ĭ -shēa-) *n.* **in·sa′tia·bly** *adv.*

in·sa·ti·ate (ĭnsā′shēĭt) *a* Never satisfied.

in·scribe (ĭnskrīb′) *v* (**-scribed, -scrib·ing**). 1. Wr (words etc. *in, on*); enter name (person) on list; dedicate (a copy a book, photograph, etc.) (*to*) writing one's name or a salutati on it. 2. (geom.) Trace (figur within another so that some partic lar points of it lie on the bounda of that other.

in·scrip·tion (ĭnskrĭp′shon) Words inscribed, esp. on mon ment, coin, etc.

in·scru·ta·ble (ĭnskrōō′tab *adj.* That cannot be penetrate wholly mysterious. **in·scru′ta ble·ness, in·scru·ta·bil·i·ty** (i skrōōtabĭl′ĭtē) *ns.* **in·scru′ta·b** *adv.*

in·seam (ĭn′sēm) *n.* Inner sea of trouser leg etc.

in·sect (ĭn′sĕkt) *n.* (pop.) Sm animal with body divided in segments; (zool.) arthropod of t

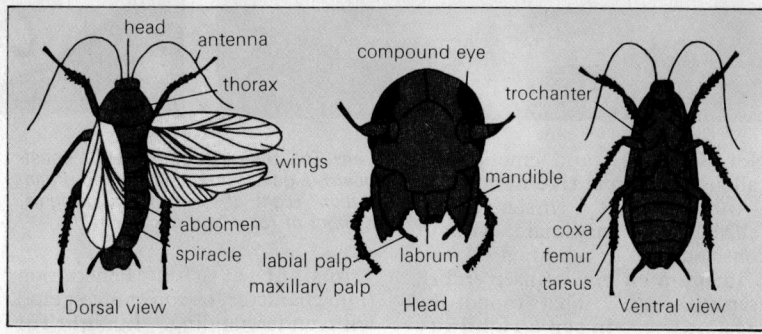

Dorsal view — head, antenna, thorax, wings, abdomen, spiracle, labial palp, maxillary palp

Head — compound eye, labrum

Ventral view — trochanter, mandible, coxa, femur, tarsus

ere are an estimated 2 million cribed species of insects in the rld. 1. The stick insect closely embles the plant on which it feeds. Aphids carry virus diseases from *infected to healthy plants. 3. The cockroach can be a household pest. 4. The Pyrrhocorid plant bug causes discoloration of cotton lint on the plant.*

ss Insecta that breathes through cheae and has a body divided into ee regions (head, thorax, and lomen) and usu., in the adult, ee pairs of legs and two pairs wings.

n·sec·ti·cide (ĭnsĕk′tĭsīd) *n.* eparation used for killing insects. **sec·ti·cid·al** (ĭnsĕktĭsī′dal) *adj.*

n·sec·ti·vore (ĭnsĕk′tĭvōr, -vôr) Insect-eating animal; member the Insectivora, an order of mitive mammals, most members of which (e.g. mole, shrew, hedgehog) usu. feed on insects. **in·sec·-tiv·o·rous** (ĭnsĕktĭv′erus) *adj.* Insect-eating; (of plant) having special structures for trapping and digesting insects.

in·se·cure (ĭnsekūr′) *adj.* 1. Unsafe; not secure; inadequately protected or guarded. 2. Lacking self-confidence; unsure; shaky. **in·se·cure·ly** *adv.* **in·se·cu·ri·ty** *n.* (pl. **-ties**).

in·sem·i·nate (ĭnsĕm′ĭnāt) *v.t.* (**-nat·ed, -nat·ing**). Sow (seed etc.) *in* (lit. and fig.); (biol.) introduce spermatozoa into (female reproductive system, or the eggs of creatures (e.g. frogs) that fertilize externally). **in·sem·i·na′tion** *n.*

in·sen·sate (ĭnsĕn′sāt, -sĭt) *adj.* Without sensibility, unfeeling; without physical sensation; unconscious. **in·sen′sate·ly** *adv.*

in·sen·si·bil·i·ty (ĭnsĕnsibĭl′ĭtē) *n.* (pl. **-ties**). Lack of mental feeling or emotion; indifference (*to*); unconsciousness, swoon.

in·sen·si·ble (ĭnsĕn′sibel) *adj.* Too small or gradual to be perceived; inappreciable; unconscious; unaware. **in·sen′si·bly** *adv.*

in·sen·si·tive (ĭnsĕn′sĭtĭv) *adj.*

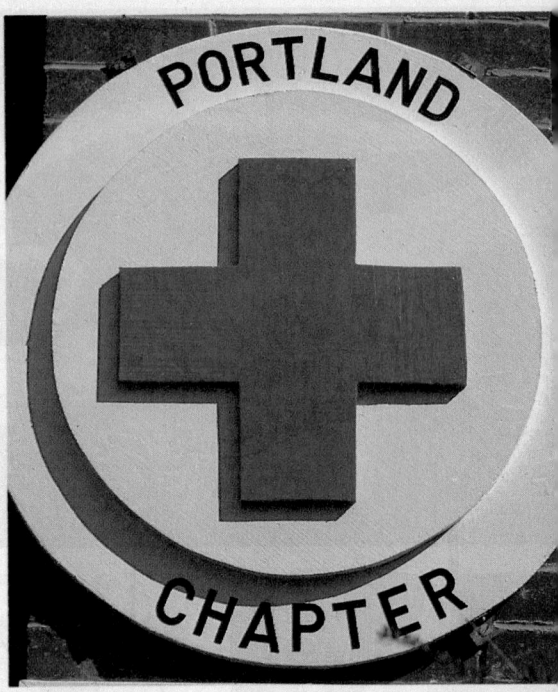

Not sensitive (*to*); emotionless, callous. **in·sen'si·tive·ness** *n.*

in·sen·ti·ent (ĭnsĕn'shēent, -shent) *adj.* Inanimate; without consciousness or sensation.

in·sep·a·ble (ĭnsĕp'erabel, -sĕp'ra-) *adj.* That cannot be separated. **in·sep·a·ra·bil·i·ty** (ĭnsĕperabĭl'ĭtē, -sĕpra-) *n.* **in·sep'a·ra·bly** *adv.*

in·sert (ĭnsērt') *v.t.* Place, fit, thrust, (thing *in, into*, another etc.); introduce (letter, article, etc., *in, into*, written matter, newspaper, etc.). **in'sert** *n.* Thing inserted. **in·ser'tion** *n.* Inserting; thing inserted, esp. in writing or print.

in·set (ĭn'sĕt) *n.* Extra page(s) inserted in sheet or book; small map etc. inserted within border of larger; piece set into dress etc. **in·set'** *v.t.* (-set, -set·ting). Put in as an inset; insert.

in·side (ĭn'sīd, ĭnsīd') *n.* 1. Inner side or surface; (of path) side next to wall or away from road; inner part, interior; ~ **out**, so that inner side becomes outer. 2. **insides** (*n.pl.*), stomach and bowels (colloq.). **in'sides', inside'** *adjs.* Situated on or in, derived from, the inside; ~ **information**, information not accessible to outsiders. **in·side'** *adv.* On or in or to the inside; (slang) in prison; ~ **of**, (colloq.) in less time than. **in'side, inside'** *preps.* On or to the inner side of, within.

in·sid·er (ĭn'sīder) *n.* One who is in some society, organization, etc.; one who has access to secret information.

in·sid·i·ous (ĭnsĭd'ēus) *adj.* Treacherous, crafty; proceeding secretly or subtly. **in·sid'i·ous·ly** *adv.* **in·sid'i·ous·ness** *n.*

in·sight (ĭn'sīt) *n.* Penetration (*into* character, circumstances, etc.) with understanding. **in·sight'ful** *adj.*

in·sig·ni·a (ĭnsĭg'nēa) *n.pl.* (previously pl. of **in·sig·ne** pr. ĭnsĭg'nē, now usu. considered sing., pl. **-ni·as, -ni·a**). Badge(s), distinguishing mark(s) (*of* office, honor, etc.).

in·sig·nif·i·cant (ĭnsĭgnĭf'ĭkant) *adj.* Unimportant, trifling; meaningless. **in·sig·nif'i·cant·ly** *adv.* **in·sig·nif'i·cance** *n.*

in·sin·cere (ĭnsĭnsēr') *adj.* Not sincere. **in·sin·cere'ly** *adv.* **in·sin·cer·i·ty** (ĭnsĭnsĕr'ĭtē) *n.* (pl. **-ties**).

in·sin·u·ate (ĭnsĭn'ūāt) *v.t.* (**-at·ed, -at·ing**). Introduce gradually or subtly; convey indirectly, hint obliquely. **in·sin'u·at·ing·ly** *adv.* **in·sin·u·a·tion** (ĭnsĭnūā'shon), **in·sin'u·a·tor** *ns.* **in·sin·u·a·tive** (ĭnsĭn'ūātĭv, -ūa-) *adj.*

in·sip·id (ĭnsĭp'ĭd) *adj.* Tasteless; wanting in flavor; lifeless, dull, uninteresting. **in·sip'id·ly** *adv.* **in·sip'id·ness, in·si·pid·i·ty** (ĭnsĭpĭd'ĭtē) *ns.*

in·sist (ĭnsĭst') *v.* Dwell long or emphatically (*on*); maintain positively; make a stand *on* as essential. **in·sist'ence, in·sist'en·cy** *ns.* **in·sist'ent** *adj.* **in·sist'ent·ly** *adv.*

in si·tu (ĭn sī'tōo, -tū; *Lat.* ĭn sē'tōo). In its (original) place.

in·so·bri·e·ty (ĭnsobrī'etē) *n.* Lack of sobriety; intemperance.

in·so·far (ĭnsōfär') *adv.* To suc an extent or degree (*as*).

in·sole (ĭn'sōl) *n.* 1. Inner so of the boot or shoe. 2. Flat piec of material worn inside shoe f warmth or comfort.

in·so·lent (ĭn'solent) *adj.* Offe sively contemptuous, insultin, **in'so·lent·ly** *adv.* **in'so·lence** *n*

in·sol·u·ble (ĭnsŏl'yubel) *adj.* That cannot be solved. 2. Th cannot be dissolved. **in·sol'u·ble ness, in·sol·u·bil·i·ty** (ĭnsŏlyubĭl ĭtē) *ns.* **in·sol'u·bly** *adv.*

in·sol·vent (ĭnsŏl'vent) *adj.* & (Debtor) unable to pay debt **in·sol'ven·cy** *n.*

in·som·ni·a (ĭnsŏm'nēa) Chronic inability to sleep. **in som'ni·ac** *n.* & *adj.*

in·sou·ci·ant (ĭnsōō'sēant) *ad* Careless, unconcerned. **in·sou'ci ance** *n.*

in·spect (ĭnspĕkt') *v.t.* Loo closely into; examine officiall **in·spec'tion** *n.*

in·spec·tor (ĭnspĕk'ter) *n.* (esp High-ranking police officer; **general**, (esp.) head of milita department concerned with disc pline, supply, accounts, etc. **in spec·to·ral, in·spec·to·ri·al** (ĭ spĕktōr'ēal, -tōr'-) *adjs.* **in·spec tor·ship** *n.*

in·spi·ra·tion (ĭnspira'shon) 1. Drawing in of breath. Inspiring; divine influence. Thought etc. inspired, promptin sudden happy idea. 4. Inspirin principle. **in·spi·ra'tion·al** *adj.*

in·spire (ĭnspīr') *v.t.* (**-spire -spir·ing**). 1. Breathe in, inha 2. Infuse thought or feeling in (person); animate (person etc. *w* feeling); infuse (feeling *into* perso etc.), create (feeling *in*); suggest rompt expression of a particular pinion etc., prompt writer or peaker to such expression. **·spir·a·to·ry** (ĭnspīr'atōrē, -tōrē) *dj.*

inst. *abbrev.* = INSTANT[1] def. 2.

in·sta·bil·i·ty (ĭnstabĭl'ĭtē) *n.* .ack of stability.

in·stall (ĭnstawl') *v.t.* (**-stalled, stall·ing**). Place (person *in* office r dignity) with ceremonies; estab- sh (*in* place, condition, etc.); place pparatus in position for use. **·stal·la·tion** (ĭnstalā'shon) *n.* Ceremony of) installing; apparatus stalled. **in·stall'er** *n.*

in·stall·ment, in·stal·ment (ĭnstawl'ment) *ns.* Each of several arts, successively falling due, of a m payable; each of several parts pplied etc. at different times; part serial story printed in one issue; **plan**, arrangement for payment installments.

in·stance (ĭn'stans) *n.* Fact llustrating a general truth, xample; particular case; (law) rocess, suit; **for ~**, for example; **t the ~ of**, at the request or aggestion of. **instance** *v.t.* **stanced, -stanc·ing**). (rare) Cite an instance.

in·stant[1] (ĭn'stant) *adj.* 1. rgent, pressing. 2. Immediate; abbrev. inst.) of the current alendar month. 3. (of food) rocessed for quick preparation. 4. **replay**, immediate reshowing of hort section of television broad- ast, esp. of a sports event.

in·stant[2] (ĭn'stant) *n.* Precise :sp. the present) point of time; hort space of time, moment. **·'stant·ly** *adv.*

in·stan·ta·ne·ous (ĭnstantā'- ēus) *adj.* Occurring, done, in an nstant; immediate; existing at a articular instant. **in·stan·ta·ne- us·ly** *adv.* **in·stan·ta·ne·ous- ess** *n.*

in·state (ĭnstāt') *v.t.* (**-stat·ed, stat·ing**). Put in office, install.

in·stead (ĭnstĕd') *adv.* As a ubstitute or alternative; in place *of*.

in·step (ĭn'stĕp) *n.* Upper urface of foot between toe and nkle; part of shoe, etc., fitting ver or under this.

in·sti·gate (ĭn'stĭgāt) *v.t.* (**-gat- d, -gat·ing**). Urge on, incite person *to*); bring about by persua- ion. **in·sti·ga·tion** (ĭnstĭgā'shon), **n'sti·ga·tor** *ns.*

in·still (ĭnstĭl') *v.t.* (**-stilled, stil·ling**). Put in (liquid) by rops; infuse (feeling, idea, etc.) radually. **in·stil·la·tion** (ĭnstĭlā'- non) *n.*

in·stinct (ĭn'stĭngkt) *n.* Innate ropensity to certain seemingly ational acts performed without onscious design; innate impulse; ituition, unconscious skill; (zool.) nborn and usually rigid pattern of ehavior in animals, often in

response to certain simple stimuli. **in·stinc'tive** *adj.* **in·stinc'tive·ly** *adv.*

in·sti·tute (ĭn'stĭtōot, -tūt) *n.* Society, organization, for promo- tion of scientific or other object; building used by this. **~** *v.t.* (**-tut·ed, -tut·ing**). Establish, found; begin (inquiry etc.).

in·sti·tu·tion (ĭnstĭtōo'shon, -tū'-) *n.* 1. Instituting. 2. Estab- lished law, custom, or practice. 3. Organization for promotion of some public object, religious, charitable, educational, etc.; build- ing used by this. 4. Place of confinement, mental hospital, etc. **in·sti·tu·tion·al** *adj.* **in·sti·tu'- tion·al·ly** *adv.* **in·sti·tu'tion·al- ize** *v.t.* (**-ized, -iz·ing**). Make institutional; place, confine (per- son), in institution. **in·sti·tu'tion- al·ism** *n.*

in·struct (ĭnstrŭkt') *v.t.* Teach (person etc. *in* subject); direct, command. **in·struc'tor** *n.*

in·struc·tion (ĭnstrŭk'shon) *n.* 1. Teaching. 2. (pl.) Directions, orders. **in·struc'tion·al** *adj.*

in·struc·tive (ĭnstrŭk'tĭv) *adj.* Tending to instruct, conveying a lesson.

in·stru·ment (ĭn'strument) *n.* 1. Thing used in performing an action; person so made use of; tool, implement, esp. for delicate or

scientific work. 2. Any of several devices, esp. in an airplane or spacecraft, serving to determine position, to measure performance, direction, etc., or to maintain control of operations. 3. (also **musical ~**) Contrivance for pro- ducing musical sounds. 4. Formal, esp. legal, document.

in·stru·men·tal (ĭnstrumĕn'tal) *adj.* 1. Serving as instrument or means (*to, in*). 2. Of, arising from, an instrument. 3. (of music) Performed on or written for instruments. **in·stru·men'tal·ly** *adv.*

in·stru·men·tal·ist (ĭnstru- mĕn'talĭst) *n.* Performer on musical instrument.

in·stru·men·tal·i·ty (ĭnstru- mĕntăl'ĭtē) *n.* (pl. **-ties**). Agency, means.

in·stru·men·ta·tion (ĭnstru- mĕntā'shon) *n.* 1. Composition or arrangement of music for instru- ments; (loosely) orchestration. 2. Use of mechanical instruments in industry etc.

in·sub·or·di·nate (ĭnsubōr'di- nĭt) *adj.* Disobedient, rebellious. **in·sub·or·di·na·tion** (ĭnsubōrdi- nā'shon) *n.*

in·sub·stan·tial (ĭnsubstăn'- shal) *adj.* Not real; lacking solidity or substance. **in·sub- stan·ti·al·i·ty** (ĭnsubstănshĕăl'ĭtē) *n.*

in·suf·fer·a·ble (ĭnsŭf'erabel) *adj.* Unbearably arrogant, con- ceited, etc.; intolerable. **in·suf'- fer·a·bly** *adv.*

Insulation for heat and sound can be carried out easily in modern buildings. A wide variety of materials is used, including porous bricks and quilted 'mattresses' of insulating material.

in·suf·fi·cient (ĭnsu̯fĭsh'ent) *adj.* Not sufficient, inadequate. **in·-suf·fi'cient·ly** *adv.* **in·suf·fi'cien·cy** *n.* (pl. **-cies**).

in·su·lar (ĭn'suler, ĭns'yu-) *adj.* Of (the nature of) an island; of, like, islanders, esp. circumscribed, isolated, narrow-minded. **in'su·lar·ly** *adv.* **in'su·lar·ism, in·su·lar·i·ty** (ĭnsu̯lăr'ĭtē, ĭnsyu-) *ns.*

in·su·late (ĭn'sulāt, ĭns'yu-) *v.t.* (**-lat·ed, -lat·ing**). 1. Detach (person, thing) from surroundings, isolate. 2. Isolate (thing) by interposition of nonconductors, to prevent passage of electricity, heat, or sound. **in·su·la·tion** (ĭnsulā'shon, ĭnsyu-) *n.*

in·su·la·tor (ĭn'sulāter, ĭns'yu-) *n.* That which insulates, esp. a nonconducting substance, as porcelain or glass, for insulating electric wires.

in·su·lin (ĭn'sulĭn, ĭns'yu-) *n.* 1. Hormone secreted by the islets of LANGERHANS in the pancreas of vertebrates, accelerating the passage of glucose from the blood to the tissues and promoting its storage as glycogen in the liver and muscles. 2. Preparation of this substance, used to treat diabetes.

in·sult (ĭnsŭlt') *v.t.* Treat with scornful abuse, offer indignity to; affront. **in·sult'ing·ly** *adv.* **in'sult** *n.* Insulting speech or action, affront.

in·su·per·a·ble (ĭnsōō'perabel, -pra-) *adj.* That cannot be surmounted or overcome. **in·su'per·a·bly** *adv.*

in·sup·port·a·ble (ĭnsupōr'tabel, -pōr'-) *adj.* Unbearable; unjustifiable.

in·sur·ance (ĭnshoor'ăns) *n.* Insuring; sum paid for this, premium.

in·sure (ĭnshoor') *v.t.* (**-sured, -sur·ing**). Secure payment of sum of money in event of loss of or damage to property (esp. by casualty at sea, fire, burglary, etc.), or of the death or disablement of a person, in consideration of the payment of a premium and observance of certain conditions; **the insured**, person to whom such payment is secured. **in·sur'a·ble** *adj.* **in·sur'-er** *n.* One who insures in consideration of premium, underwriter.

in·sur·gent (ĭnser'jent) *adj.* Rising in active revolt. ~ *n.* Rebel. **in·sur'gence, in·sur'gen·cy** *n.*

in·sur·mount·a·ble (ĭnser-mown'tabel) *adj.* Not to be surmounted. **in·sur·mount'a·bly** *adv.*

in·sur·rec·tion (ĭnsurĕk'shon) *n.*

Rising in open resistance to est[ablished] lished authority; incipient reb[el]lion. **in·sur·rec'tion·a·ry** [adj.] **in·sur·rec'tion·ist** *n.*

int. *abbrev.* Interest; inter[jection]; interjection; intransitive; int[ernational] national.

in·tact (ĭntăkt') *adj.* Untouch[ed]; entire; unimpaired.

in·tagl·io (ĭntăl'yō, -tahl'-) [n.] (pl. **-tagl·ios, -tagl·i** pr. -tăl'[..] -tahl'-). Engraved design; inci[sed] carving in hard material; gem w[ith] incised design (opp. CAMEO).

in·take (ĭn'tāk) *n.* Place wh[ere] fluid or gas etc. is taken into chan[nel] or pipe; taking in; thing, amou[nt] taken in.

in·tan·gi·ble (ĭntăn'jibel) [adj.] That cannot be touched; imp[al]pable; that cannot be gras[ped] mentally. **in·tan·gi·bil·i·ty** (ĭntănjibĭl'ĭtē) *n.* **in·tan'gi·bly** ad[v.]

in·te·ger (ĭn'tejer) *n.* Wh[ole] number, undivided quantity; th[ing] complete in itself.

in·te·gral (ĭn'tegral) *adj.* [.] necessary to the completeness o[f a] whole; whole, complete; (math.) [.] denoted by, an integer, involv[ing] only integers; ~ **calculus**, bra[nch] of calculus dealing with integral[s of] functions; used also to incl[ude] solution of differential equatio[ns,] parts of theory of functions, [etc.] **in'te·gral·ly** *adv.* **in·te·gral·i[ty]** (ĭntegrăl'ĭtē) *n.* **integral** *n.* (mat[h.])

quantity of which given function differential or differential coefficient; equation or system of equations from which given equation or system can be derived by differentiation.

in·te·grate (ĭn´tegrāt) v. (**-grat·ed, -grat·ing**). Complete (imperfect thing) by addition of parts; combine (parts) into a whole; combine (religious, ethnic, etc. groups) within a system esp. as equals; cease to segregate (racially); (math.) find the integral of; indicate mean volume or total sum of (area, temperature, etc.); ~**d circuit**, small chip etc. of material designed to replace conventional electric circuit of many components. **in·te·gra·tion** (ĭntegrā´shŏn) n. **in´te·gra·tive** adj.

in·teg·ri·ty (ĭntĕg´rĭtē) n. Completeness; soundness; uprightness, honesty.

in·teg·u·ment (ĭntĕg´yument) n. Skin, husk, rind, or other (usu. natural) covering. **in·teg·u·men·ta·ry** (ĭntĕgyumĕn´terē) adj.

in·tel·lect (ĭn´telĕkt) n. Faculty of knowing and reasoning; person(s) of great intellectual ability.

in·tel·lec·tu·al (ĭntelĕk´chōoal) adj. Of, appealing to, requiring the exercise of, intellect; possessing good understanding, enlightened; given to mental pursuits. **in·tel·lec´tu·al·ly** adv. **in·tel·lec·tu·al´i·ty** n. **in·tel·lec´tu·al·ize** v. (**-ized, -iz·ing**). **intellectual** n. Intellectual person.

in·tel·li·gence (ĭntĕl´ĭjens) n. 1. Intellect, understanding; quickness of understanding, sagacity; rational being; ~ **quotient**, (abbrev. I.Q.) ratio of mental to chronological age; ~ **test**, test designed to ascertain intelligence or mental age, rather than acquired knowledge, of examinee. 2. Information, news; obtaining of (esp. secret) information, persons employed in this; secret service.

in·tel·li·gent (ĭntĕl´ĭjent) adj. Having or showing (usu. a high degree of) understanding. **in·tel´li·gent·ly** adv.

in·tel·li·gent·si·a (ĭntĕlĭjĕnt´sēa, -gĕnt´-) n. collect. (sometimes considered sing.) Class of intellectuals within a society.

in·tel·li·gi·ble (ĭntĕl´ĭjibel) adj. That can be understood; comprehensible to; (philos.) that can be apprehended only by the intellect, not by the senses. **in·tel·li·gi·bil·i·ty** (ĭntĕlĭjibĭl´ĭtē) n. **in·tel´li·gi·bly** adv.

in·tem·per·ate (ĭntĕm´perĭt) adj. Immoderate, unbridled, violent; excessive in indulgence of an appetite; addicted to drinking. **in·tem´per·ate·ly** adv. **in·tem´-**

The commonest example of intaglio is an engraved seal-ring. This beaten metal panel, however, is on a larger scale. Its delicate art nouveau design is by the Scottish artist, Margaret Macdonald, and was executed in 1898–99.

per·ance n.

in·tend (ĭntĕnd´) v.t. Purpose, design; design, destine, for a purpose; mean.

in·tend·ed (ĭntĕn´dĭd) n. (colloq.) Fiancé(e).

in·tense (ĭntĕns´) adj. Existing in a high degree, violent, vehement; having some quality in high degree; eager, ardent; feeling, apt to feel, intense emotion. **in·tense´ly** adv. **in·tense´ness, in·ten´si·ty** ns. (pl. **-ties**).

in·ten·si·fy (ĭntĕn´sĭfī) v. (**-fied, -fy·ing**). Render, become, intense; (phot.) increase opacity of the deposit in a negative by chemical or other means. **in·ten·si·fi·ca·tion** (ĭntĕnsĭfĭkā´shon) n.

in·ten·sion (ĭntĕn´shon) n. (Rare) Intensity; (logic) connotation of a term, sum of the attributes, qualities comprised in a concept.

in·ten·sive (ĭntĕn´sĭv) adj. Of, relating to, intensity as opp. to extent; producing intensity; making intense, esp. (gram.) giving force or emphasis; concentrated, directed to a single point, area, or subject; ~ **care**, constant surveillance, by nurses and electrical etc. devices, of critically ill patients in hospital. **in·ten´sive·ly** adv. **intensive** n. (gram.) Intensive word or prefix.

in·tent[1] (ĭntĕnt´) n. Intention, purpose; **to all ~s and purposes**, practically, virtually.

in·tent[2] (ĭntĕnt´) adj. Resolved, bent (on); sedulously occupied (on); earnest, eager. **in·tent´ly** adv.

*The **interbreeding** of different species of cattle is aimed at producing the best qualities of both breeds in one animal. The Hereford bull (left) crossed with the Friesian (right) produces this large steer (below).*

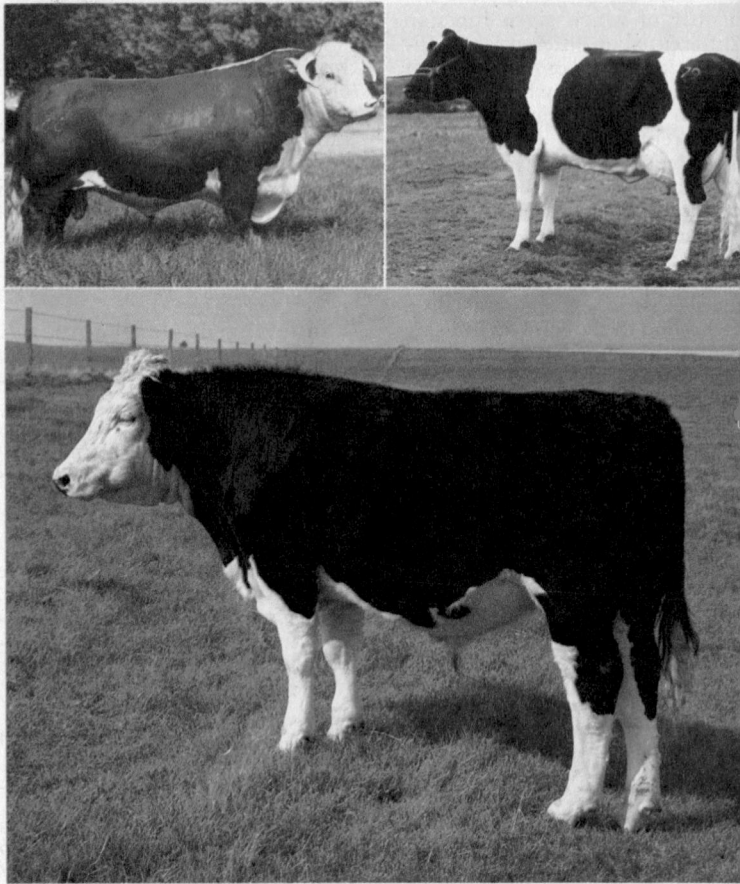

in·ten·tion (ĭntĕn´shon) *n.* Intending; thing intended, purpose; ultimate aim; (pl., colloq.) purposes in regard to proposal of marriage. **in·ten´tion·al** *adj.* Done on purpose. **in·ten´tion·al·ly** *adv.*

in·ter (ĭntēr´) *v.t.* (**-terred, -ter·ring**). Deposit (corpse etc.) in earth, tomb, etc.; bury.

inter- *prefix.* Expressing mutual or reciprocal act or relation, or with sense "among," "between."

in·ter·act (ĭnterăkt´) *v.i.* Act reciprocally, act on each other. **in·ter·ac·tion** (ĭnterăk´shon) *n.* **in·ter·ac´tive** *adj.*

in·ter a·li·a (ĭn´ter ā´lēa; *Lat.* ĭn´tĕr ah´lēah). Among other things. [L.]

in·ter·breed (ĭnterbrēd´) *v.* (**-bred, -breed·ing**). 1. Cross-breed. 2. Breed within a narrow range or population.

in·ter·cede (ĭntersēd´) *v.i.* (**-ced·ed, -ced·ing**). Interpose on behalf of another, plead (*with* one person *for* another).

in·ter·cel·lu·lar (ĭntersĕl´yuler) *adj.* Between or among cells.

in·ter·cept (ĭntersĕpt´) *v.t.* Seize, catch, stop (person, enemy aircraft, etc.) on the way from place to place; pick up (esp. enemy's) radio signal; cut off (light etc. *from*); check, stop; (math.) mark off (space) between two points etc. **in·ter·cep·tion** (ĭntersĕp´shon) *n.* **in·ter·cep´tive** *adj.* **in´tercept** *n.* (math.) Part intercepted.

in·ter·cep·tor, in·ter·cep·ter (ĭntersĕp´ter) *ns.* (esp.) Fighter plane having task of intercepting enemy planes.

in·ter·ces·sion (ĭntersĕsh´on) *n.* Interceding. **in·ter·ces·so·ry** (ĭntersĕs´erē) *adj.*

in·ter·change (ĭnterchānj´) *v.* (**-changed, -chang·ing**). 1. (of 2 persons) Exchange (things) with each other. 2. Put each of (2 things) in the other's place. 3. Alternate. **in·ter·change´a·ble** *adj.* **in·ter·change´a·bly** *adv.* **in·ter·change·a·bil·i·ty** (ĭnterchānjabĭl´ĭtē) *n.* **in´terchange** *n.* Reciprocal exchange; alternation; road junction so arranged that vehicles do not cross any traffic stream.

in·ter·col·le·giate (ĭnterkolē´jĭt) *adj.* (esp. sports) Existing, carried on, between colleges.

in·ter·com (ĭn´terkŏm) *n.* System of internal communication by telephone, radio, etc., between units of an organization, offices in a building, etc.

in·ter·com·mu·ni·cate (ĭnterkomū´nĭkāt) *v.i.* (**-cat·ed, -cat·ing**). Communicate with each other; (of rooms etc.) have free passage to each other. **in·ter·com·mu·ni·ca·tion** (ĭnterkomūnĭkā´shon) *n.*

in·ter·con·ti·nen·tal (ĭnterkŏntĭnen´tal) *adj.* 1. Of, between, or among continents. 2. Capable of traveling between continents, as a guided missile, airplane, etc.

in·ter·cos·tal (ĭnterkŏs´tal) *adj.* Between the ribs.

in·ter·course (ĭn´terkōrs, -kôrs) *n.* 1. Social communication, dealings, between individuals; communion between man and God; communication for purposes of trade etc. between different countries etc. 2. = SEXUAL intercourse.

in·ter·cul·tur·al (ĭnterkŭl´cheral) *adj.* Between or among people of different cultures; **~ education**, education to encourage good relations among people of different races, cultures, religions, etc.

in·ter·de·pend (ĭnterdĭpĕnd´) *v.i.* Depend on each other. **in·ter·de·pend´ence, in·ter·de·pend´en·cy** *ns.* **in·ter·de·pend´ent** *adj.*

in·ter·dict (ĭnterdĭkt´) *v.t.* Prohibit (action); forbid use of; restrain (*from*); forbid (thing *to* person). **in·ter·dic·tion** (ĭnterdĭk´shon) *n.* **in·ter·dic´to·ry** *adj.* **in´terdict** *n.*

Authoritative prohibition; injur tion; (R.C. Ch.) sentence debarri place or person from most ecclesia tical functions and privileges.

in·ter·est (ĭn´terĭst, -trĭst) 1. Legal right, claim, or share something); pecuniary stake commercial undertaking etc.). Advantage, profit; self-interest. Thing in which one is concerne principle in which a party concerned; **~ group**, (usu. po group acting together fr common interest or purpose. Concern, curiosity, or quality e citing them. 5. Money paid for u of money lent or for forbearance debt; **compound ~**, intere reckoned on principal and accumulations of interest; **simp ~**, interest reckoned on princip only. **interest** *v.t.* Cause (perso to take personal interest or sha (*in*); excite curiosity or attention (past part.) having a priva interest, not impartial or d interested. **in´ter·est·ed·ly** *ac* **in´ter·est·ing** *adj.* **in´ter·es ing·ly** *adv.*

in·ter·face (ĭn´terfās) *n.* Surface forming common bounda between 2 regions. 2. Place, piece of equipment, where inte action occurs between 2 systen processes, etc. (also fig.). **in·ter fa·cial** (ĭnterfā´shal) *adj.*

in·ter·fere (ĭnterfēr´) *v*

ered, -fer·ing). Come into llision or opposition (*with*); nder, impede; intrude; meddle; ervene; (sports) illegally obstruct opponent's action; (phys.) oduce interference with another ave; (radio) impede or distort ception.

in·ter·fer·ence (ĭnterfēr'ens) *n.* Interfering. 2. (radio) Intrusion unwanted signals, atmospherics, ., causing poor reception of sired signals. 3. (phys.) Alternate utual neutralization and reinrcement by two beams of sound, ht, electromagnetic waves so as produce alternation of light and rk, silence and sound, etc.

in·ter·fer·om·e·ter (ĭnterfem'eter) *n.* Device for measuring avelengths, astronomical disnces, etc., by means of interrence phenomena.

in·ter·fer·on (ĭnterfēr'ŏn) *n.*

Protein preventing development of virus in cell.

in·ter·fuse (ĭnterfūz') *v.* (**-fused, -fus·ing**). Mix; blend together; blend with each other. **in·ter·fu·sion** (ĭnterfū'zhon) *n.*

in·ter·ga·lac·tic (ĭntergalăk'tĭk) *adj.* Of or in the space between galaxies.

in·ter·gla·cial (ĭnterglā'shal) *adj.* (geol.) Occurring or formed between glacial periods.

in·ter·im (ĭn'terĭm) *n.* Intervening time. ~ *adj.* Intervening; provisional, temporary.

in·te·ri·or (ĭntēr'ēer) *adj.* Situated within; inland, remote from

*This British 'Lightning', jet fighter with strong climbing power, **intercepts** the Soviet long range reconnaissance aircraft 'Bear' during the exercise 'Northern Merger' in September 1974.*

coast or frontier; internal, domestic (opp. *foreign*); existing in mind or soul, inward; ~ **monologue**, form of writing that represents the inner thoughts of a character. **in·te'-ri·or·ly** *adv.* **interior** *n.* Interior part, inside; inland region; inside of building or room; domestic affairs of a country; **Department of the I** ~, government department dealing with these; **interior decoration, design**, art, profession, of designing layout, furnishings, ornament, of the inside of buildings; ~ **decorator**.

in·ter·ject (ĭnterjĕkt') *v.t.* Throw in, interpose (remark etc.) abruptly; remark parenthetically. **in·ter·jec'to·ry** *adj.*

in·ter·jec·tion (ĭnterjĕk'shon) *n.* Exclamation, ejaculation; natural exclamation viewed as part of speech. **in·ter·jec'tion·al** *adj.* **in·ter·jec'tion·al·ly** *adv.*

in·ter·lace (ĭnterlās´) v. (**-laced, -lac·ing**). Bind together intricately, entangle; interweave; mingle; cross each other intricately. **in·ter·lace´ment** n.

in·ter·lard (ĭnterlärd´) v.t. Mix (writing, speech, etc., with).

in·ter·leave (ĭnterlēv´) v.t. (**-leaved, -leav·ing**). Insert leaves between leaves of (book).

in·ter·line[1] (ĭnterlīn´) v.t. (**-lined, -lin·ing**). Insert words between lines of (document etc.); insert (words) thus. **in·ter·lin·e·ar** (ĭnterlĭn´ēer) adj. Written, printed, between the lines. **in·ter·lin·e·a·tion** (ĭnterlĭnēā´shon) n.

in·ter·line[2] (ĭnterlīn´) v.t. (**-lined, -lin·ing**). Put extra lining between ordinary lining and outer material of (garment). **in·ter·lin·ing** n.

in·ter·lock (ĭnterlŏk´) v. Fit together by dovetailing, overlapping etc.; lock, clasp, within each other; connect (switches, apparatus, etc.) so they cannot be operated independently of each other.

in·ter·loc·u·tor (ĭnterlŏk´yuter) n. One who takes part in dialogue or conversation; performer in middle of line of minstrels at minstrel show who acts as announcer and trades jokes with the end men. **in·ter·loc·u·to·ry** (ĭnterlŏk´yutōrē, -tōrē) adj.

in·ter·lop·er (ĭn´terlōper) n. Intruder, one who (esp. for profit) thrusts himself into others' affairs; (hist.) unauthorized trader. **in·ter·lope** (ĭnterlōp´, ĭn´terlōp) v.i. (**-loped, -lop·ing**).

in·ter·lude (ĭn´terlōōd) n. 1. Any intervening period of time, episode, etc. 2. Pause between acts of play; what fills this up; (mus.) instrumental piece played between verses of hymn etc., in intervals of church service etc.

in·ter·lu·nar (ĭnterlōō´ner) adj. Of, pertaining to, the period of the lunar month when the moon is invisible; in the dark of the moon.

in·ter·mar·riage (ĭntermăr´ĭj) n. Marriage between members of different families, tribes, ethnic or religious groups, etc., or (loosely) between near relations.

in·ter·mar·ry (ĭntermăr´ē) v.i. (**-ried, -ry·ing**). Become connected by marriage or intermarriage (with).

in·ter·me·di·ar·y (ĭntermē´dēĕrē) adj. Acting between parties, mediatory; intermediate. ~ n. (pl. **-ar·ies**). Intermediary person or thing, esp. mediator.

in·ter·me·di·ate (ĭntermē´dēĭt) adj. Coming between two things, in time, place, or order. **in·ter·me´di·ate·ly** adv. **intermediate** n. Intermediate thing; (chem.) compound manufactured from a substance obtained directly from raw materials, and used as a basis

These U.S. prisoners of war were **interned** in North Vietnam by Viet Cong forces during the Vietnamese War of 1964–75. They were repatriated after the withdrawal of American troops from the peninsula.

for the synthesis of another product. ~ (ĭntermē´dēāt) v.i. (**-at·ed, -at·ing**). Act between others, mediate (between). **in·ter·me·di·a·tion** (ĭntermēdēā´shon), **in·ter·me´di·a·tor** ns.

in·ter·ment (ĭntĕr´ment) n. Burial.

in·ter·mez·zo (ĭntermĕt´sō, -mĕd´zō) n. (pl. **-mez·zos, -mez·zi** pr. -mĕt´sē, -mĕd´zē). Short light dramatic or musical performance between acts of drama or opera; short movement connecting main divisions of large musical work.

in·ter·mi·na·ble (ĭntĕr´mĭnabel) adj. Endless; tediously long. **in·ter´mi·na·bly** adj.

in·ter·min·gle (ĭntermĭng´gel) v. (**-gled, -gling**). Mix together; mingle (with).

in·ter·mis·sion (ĭntermĭsh´on) n. Pause, cessation; interval; recess; period between acts of a play or

other performance.

in·ter·mit (ĭntermĭt´) v. (**-mit·ted, -mit·ting**). Suspend, d continue; stop for a time (esp. fever, pain, etc., or puls **in·ter·mit´tence** n. **in·ter·mi tent** adj. **in·ter·mit´tent·ly** ad

in·ter·mix (ĭntermĭks´) v. M together.

in·tern[1] (ĭntĕrn´) v.t. Oblige reside within limits of country et confine (esp. enemy aliens a prisoners of war) within prescrib limits. **in·tern·ee** (ĭntĕrnē´) Person interned. **in·tern´ment**

in·tern[2] (ĭn´tĕrn) n. Advanc student or recent graduate und going supervised practical trainir esp. a medical student or gradu acting as assistant doctor in hospital.

in·ter·nal (ĭntĕr´nal) adj. C situated in, the inside of, a thir of the inner nature of a thir intrinsic; of the domestic affairs a country; of the mind or so inward, subjective; ~ **combustic engine**: see COMBUSTION; **evidence**, evidence derived fr what is contained in the thing itse **in·ter´nal·ly** adv.

This criminal portraits file is located in **Interpol's** *Paris headquarters. Interpol provides liaison between member nations in searching for international criminals.*

in·ter·na·tion·al (ĭnternăsh´-nal) *adj.* Existing, carried on, be-ween different nations; **I~ Court f Justice**, judicial court of the nited Nations, established in 945; **~ law**, body of rules egarded by the nations of the world s being binding on them in their :lations with each other, in peace nd war; **I~ Monetary Fund**, .bbrev. I.M.F.) organization aving a monetary pool on which .ember nations can draw, stablished in 1945 to promote iternational trade and stabilization f currencies; **I~ System** (of nits): system based on the meter, ilogram, second, ampere, kelvin, andela, and mole. **in·ter·na´-ion·al·ly** *adv.* **in·ter·na´tion·al** . 1. International firm. 2. Any f various socialist or labor inter-ational organizations, esp. the ollowing: **First I~**, the Inter-ational Working Men's Associa-on; **Second I~**, organization junded at Paris 1889 to celebrate ooth anniversary of French Revo-ition; **Third I~ (Communist ~**, COMINTERN, COMINFORM), junded at Moscow 1919 by

delegates from 12 countries to promote communism and support the Russian Revolution, nominally dissolved 1943; **Fourth I~**, founded 1936 by followers of Trotsky.

In·ter·na·tio·nale (ĭnternăsh-onăl´; *Fr.* ănternăsyawnăl´) *n.* Rev-olutionary hymn composed by Eugène Pottier in 1871 and adopted by various socialist and communist movements.

in·ter·na·tion·al·ist (ĭnter-năsh´onalĭst) *n.* One who advocates community of interests between nations. **in·ter·na´tion·al·ism** *n.*

in·ter·na·tion·al·ize (ĭnter-năsh´onalīz) *v.t.* (**-ized, -iz·ing**). Make international; esp. bring (territory etc.) under combined protection etc. of different nations. **in·ter·na·tion·al·i·za·tion** (ĭnter-năshonalĭzā´shon) *n.*

in·ter·ne·cine (ĭnternē´sēn, -sīn, -něs´ēn, -īn) *adj.* 1. Mutually

destructive; (orig.) deadly. 2. Of a struggle within a nation, organiza-tion, group, etc.

in·ter·plan·e·tar·y (ĭnterplăn´-etĕrē) *adj.* Between planets.

in·ter·play (ĭn´terplā) *n.* Opera-tion of two things on each other; interaction.

In·ter·pol (ĭn´terpōl). Inter-national Criminal Police Commis-sion, with headquarters in Paris.

in·ter·po·late (ĭnter´polāt) *v.t.* (**-lat·ed, -lat·ing**). Make inser-tions in (books etc.), esp. so as to give false impressions as to date etc.; introduce (words) thus; inter-pose (a remark); (math.) insert (intermediate term) in series. **in·ter·po·la·tion** (ĭntĕrpolā´shon), **in·ter´po·la·tor** *ns.*

in·ter·pose (ĭnterpōz´) *v.* (**-posed, -pos·ing**). Insert, make intervene, (*between*); put forth, introduce, (veto, objection, author-ity, etc.) by way of interference; intervene (between disputants etc.); say as an interruption; make an interruption. **in·ter·pos·al** (ĭnter-pō´zal), **in·ter·po·si·tion** (ĭnterpo-zĭsh´on) *ns.*

in·ter·pret (ĭntĕr´prĭt) *v.* Ex-pound the meaning of (abstruse words, writings, etc.); make out the meaning of; translate; bring out the meaning of, render, by artistic rep-resentation or performance; ex-plain, understand, in specified manner; act as interpreter. **in·ter´-pre·ta·tive·ly** *adv.* **in·ter·pre-ta·tion** (ĭntĕrpretā´shon) *n.* **in·ter-pre·ta·tive** (ĭntĕr´pretātĭv), **in·-ter·pre·ta´tion·al** *adjs.*

in·ter·pret·er (ĭntĕr´preter) *n.* One who interprets; one whose office it is to translate orally in their presence the words of persons speaking different languages.

in·ter·reg·num (ĭnterrĕg´num) *n.* (pl. **-reg·nums, -reg·na** pr. -rĕg´na). Period during which government has no normal ruler, esp. between end of king's reign and accession of successor; interval, pause.

in·ter·re·la·tion (ĭnterrĭlā´shon) *n.* Mutual relation. **in·ter·re·la´-tion·ship** *n.*

in·ter·ro·gate (ĭntĕr´ogāt) *v.t.* (**-gat·ed, -gat·ing**). Ask questions of, esp. closely or formally. **in·ter·ro·ga·tion** (ĭntĕrogā´shon) *n.* Asking questions; interview for close questioning; question.

in·ter·rog·a·tive (ĭnterŏg´atĭv) *adj.* Of, having the form or force of, a question; of inquiry; (gram., of words) used in asking question. **in·ter·rog´a·tive·ly** *adv.* **inter-rogative** *n.* Interrogative pro-noun, sentence, etc.

in·ter·rog·a·to·ry (ĭnterŏg´a-tōrē, -tŏre) *adj.* Of inquiry. **~** *n.* (pl. **-ries**). Question, set of questions, esp. (law) one formally put to accused person etc.

in·ter·rupt (ĭnterŭpt´) *v.t.* Break

Interstellar *matter often gathers together in vast clouds of gas and dust to form a nebula like this one in the constellation Serpeus. This was photographed through a 200-inch telescope in California.*

in upon (action, speech, person speaking or working, etc.); break the continuity of. **in·ter·rupt′·ed·ly** *adv.* **in·ter·rupt′er, in·ter·rup′tion** *ns.*

in·ter·sect (ĭntersĕkt′) *v.* Divide (thing) by passing or lying across it; (of lines etc.) cross, cut, each other. **in·ter·sec′tion** *n.* Intersecting; point, line, common to intersecting lines, planes; place where things intersect, esp. 2 or more roads.

in·ter·sperse (ĭnterspers′) *v.t.* (-spersed, -spers·ing). Scatter, place here and there (*between, among*); diversify (thing) *with* (others so scattered). **in·ter·sper·sion** (ĭnterspēr′zhon, -shon) *n.*

in·ter·state (ĭnterstāt′, ĭn′ter-stāt) *adj.* Existing, carried on, between states; **The I~,** U.S. Interstate Highway System; any of the roads of this.

in·ter·stel·lar (ĭnterstĕl′er) *adj.* Between stars.

in·ter·stice (ĭntĕr′stĭs) *n.* Intervening space; crevice. **in·ter·sti-**

tial (ĭnterstĭsh′al) *adj.* Of, forming, occupying interstice(s).

in·ter·twine (ĭntertwīn′) *v.* (-twined, -twin·ing). Entwine; become entwined. **in·ter·twine′-ment** *n.*

in·ter·ur·ban (ĭnterēr′ban) *adj.* Located between or serving to connect cities.

in·ter·val (ĭn′terval) *n.* 1. Intervening time or space; pause; break, gap; **at ~s,** now and then, here and there. 2. (mus.) Difference of pitch between 2 sounds, in melody or harmony. 3. Distance between persons or things. [L. *intervallum* space between ramparts (*vallum* rampart)]

in·ter·vene (ĭntervēn′) *v.i.* (-vened, -ven·ing). Come in, as something extraneous; occur in the meantime; lie, be situated, between;

(of person or thing) come between interfere, so as to prevent modify result etc.; (law) enter int a lawsuit as a 3rd party to protec one's interest. **in·ter·ven′er in·ter·ve′nor, in·ter·ven·tio** (ĭntervĕn′shon) *ns.*

in·ter·view (ĭn′tervū) *n.* Meet ing of persons face to face, esp for purpose of conference; meetin between representative of press an person from whom he seeks t obtain statements for publicatio published report of such meetin meeting between candidate fo employment, college admissio etc., and prospective employe dean, etc. ~ *v.t.* Have interview with (person), esp. with view t publication of statements etc **in′ter·view·er** *n.*

in·ter·weave (ĭnterwēv′) *v.* (-wove, -wo·ven, -weav·ing) Weave together, interlace; blen intimately.

in·tes·tate (ĭntĕs′tāt, -tĭt) *adj* Not having made a legal will; no disposed of by legal will. ~ *n*

Person who dies intestate. **in·tes·-a·cy** (ĭntĕs'tasē) *n.*

in·tes·tine (ĭntĕs'tĭn) *n.* (usu. pl.) Lower part of alimentary canal from pyloric end of stomach to anus; **large ~,** cecum, colon, and rectum; **small ~,** duodenum, jejunum, and ileum. **in·tes'ti·nal** *adj.*

in·ti·mate[1] (ĭn'tĭmĭt) *adj.* Close in acquaintance, familiar; essential, intrinsic; closely personal. **in'ti·mate·ly** *adv.* **in·ti·ma·cy** (ĭn'timasē) *n.* (pl. **-cies**). State of being intimate; intimate act; (euphem.) sexual intercourse. **inti·mate** *n.* Intimate friend.

in·ti·mate[2] (ĭn'timāt) *v.t.* (**-mat·ed, -mat·ing**). Make known; imply, hint. **in·ti·ma·tion** (ĭntimā'shon), **in'ti·mate·ness** *ns.*

in·tim·i·date (ĭntĭm'ĭdāt) *v.t.* (**-dat·ed, -dat·ing**). Inspire with fear, cow, esp. in order to influence conduct. **in·tim·i·da·tion** (ĭntĭmi-dā'shon) *n.*

in·to (ĭn'tŏō, unstressed ĭn'to) *prep.* Expressing (1) motion or direction to a point within a thing, as *come ~ the house, inquire ~ the problem;* (2) change, condition, result, as *water turns ~ ice, collect them ~ heaps.*

in·tol·er·a·ble (ĭntŏl'erabel) *adj.* That cannot be endured. **in·tol'er·a·ble·ness** *n.* **in·tol'er·a·bly** *adv.*

in·tol·er·ant (ĭntŏl'erant) *adj.* Not tolerant (*of*); bigoted, prejudiced (esp. against a racial or religious group, etc.). **in·tol'er·ant·ly** *adv.* **in·tol'er·ance** *n.*

in·to·na·tion (ĭntonā'shon) *n.* (mus.) Opening phrase of a Gregorian chant, sung by priest alone or by one or a few of the choir; intoning, reciting in singing voice; utterance, production, of musical tones; modulation of voice in speaking.

in·tone (ĭntōn') *v.t.* (**-toned, -ton·ing**). Recite, sing, utter in singing voice or with a specific intonation.

in to·to (ĭn tō'tō). Completely; altogether. [L.]

in·tox·i·cant (ĭntŏk'sĭkant) *adj.* & *n.* Intoxicating (liquor).

in·tox·i·cate (ĭntŏk'sĭkāt) *v.t.* (**-cat·ed, -cat·ing**). Make drunk; excite, exhilarate, beyond self-control. **in·tox'i·cat·ing** *adj.* **in·tox·i·ca·tion** (ĭntŏksĭkā'shon) *n.*

intra- *prefix.* On the inside, within.

in·trac·ta·ble (ĭntrăk'tabel) *adj.* Not docile, refractory; (of things) not easily dealt with. **in·trac'ta·ble·ness, in·trac·ta·bil·i·ty** (ĭntrăktabĭl'itē) *ns.* **in·trac'ta·bly** *adv.*

in·tra·mus·cu·lar (ĭntramŭs'kyuler) *adj.* Within or going into a muscle.

intrans. *abbrev.* Intransitive.

in·tran·si·gent (ĭntrăn'sĭjent,

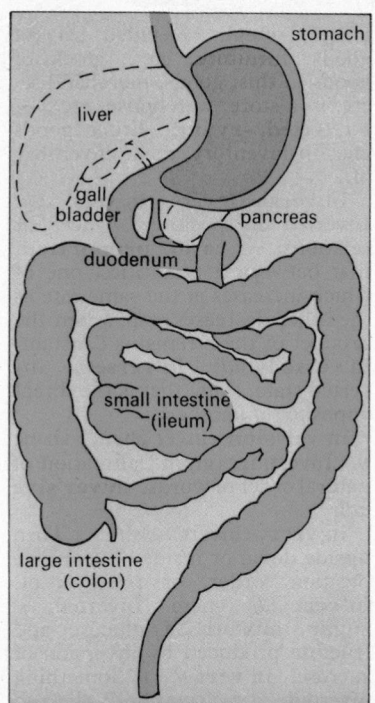

The small **intestine** deals with the digestion of food. In the large intestine water is absorbed from undigested material and anything left passes to the rectum as waste matter.

-zĭ-) *adj.* Uncompromising (person). **in·tran'si·gence, in·tran'si·gen·cy** *ns.* **in·tran'si·gent·ly** *adv.*

in·tran·si·tive (ĭntrăn'sĭtĭv) *adj.* & *n.* (Verb) that does not take a direct object. **in·tran'si·tive·ly** *adv.*

in·tra·state (ĭntrastāt', ĭn'tra-stāt) *adj.* Within a state, esp. one of the states of U.S.

in·tra·u·ter·ine (ĭntraū'terĭn, -rīn) *adj.* Within the uterus; **~ device,** (abbrev. I.U.D.) contraceptive device so placed.

in·tra·ve·nous (ĭntravē'nus) *adj.* Within or going into a vein. **in·tra·ve'nous·ly** *adv.*

in·trep·id (ĭntrĕp'ĭd) *adj.* Fearless, brave. **in·trep'id·ly** *adv.* **in·trep·id·i·ty** (ĭntrepĭd'itē) *n.*

in·tri·cate (ĭn'trĭkĭt) *adj.* Complex; involved. **in'tri·cate·ly** *adv.* **in·tri·ca·cy** (ĭn'trĭkasē) *n.* (pl. **-cies**).

in·trigue (ĭntrēg') *v.* (**-trigued, -trigu·ing**). 1. Carry on underhand plot; employ secret influence (*with*). 2. Excite the interest or curiosity of. **~** (ĭn'trēg, ĭntrēg') *n.* Underhand plotting or plot; secret love affair, liaison.

in·trin·sic (ĭntrĭn'sĭk, -zĭk) *adj.* Belonging naturally, inherent, essential. **in·trin'si·cal·ly** *adv.*

intro- *prefix.* To the inside.

in·tro·duce (ĭntrodōos', -dūs') *v.t.* (**-duced, -duc·ing**). 1. Bring in; place in, insert; bring into use (custom, idea, etc.); usher in, bring

forward, begin. 2. Make known, esp. in formal manner (person *to* another); present formally, as at court or in an assembly; make acquainted with, draw attention of (person) *to;* bring (bill etc.) before legislature. **in·tro·duc'er** *n.* **in·tro·duc·to·ry** (ĭntrodŭk'terē) *adj.*

in·tro·duc·tion (ĭntrodŭk'shon) *n.* Introducing; preliminary matter prefixed to book; introductory treatise; formal presentation.

in·tro·spect (ĭntrospĕkt') *v.i.* Examine one's own thoughts and feelings. **in·tro·spec'tion** *n.* **in·tro·spec'tive** *adj.* **in·tro·spec'tive·ly** *adv.* **in·tro·spec'tive·ness** *n.*

in·tro·vert (ĭntrovert') *v.t.* 1. Turn (mind, thought) inward. 2. (zool.) Withdraw (organ etc.) within its own tube or base, like finger of glove. **in·tro·ver·sion** (ĭntrover'zhon, -shon, ĭn'trover-) *n.* **in'tro·vert** *n.* 1. (psych.) Person given to introversion (opp. EXTRO-VERT); (pop.) unsociable person, one who prefers privacy and lone pursuits. 2. (zool.) Part or organ that is turned inward upon itself.

in·trude (ĭntrōod') *v.* (**-trud·ed, -trud·ing**). Thrust, force, (thing *into*); force (thing *upon* person); come uninvited, thrust oneself in (*into* company, place, etc., *upon* person etc.). **in·trud'er** *n.* One who intrudes; invading enemy; burglar, one who breaks and enters.

in·tru·sion (ĭntrōo'zhon) *n.* Intruding, forcing in; forcing oneself in; (law) illegal appropriation of or entry into property of another.

in·tru·sive (ĭntrōo'sĭv) *adj.* Intruding, tending to intrude. **in·tru'sive·ly** *adv.* **in·tru'sive·ness** *n.*

in·trust (ĭntrŭst') = ENTRUST.

in·tu·it (ĭntōo'ĭt, -tū'-, ĭn'tōo-, -tū-) *v.* Know by intuition.

in·tu·i·tion (ĭntōoĭsh'on, -tū-) *n.* Immediate apprehension by the mind without reasoning; immediate apprehension by sense; immediate insight. **in·tu·i'tion·al** *adj.*

in·tu·i·tive (ĭntōo'ĭtĭv, -tū'-) *adj.* Of, possessing, perceived by, intuition. **in·tu'i·tive·ly** *adv.* **in·tu'i·tive·ness** *n.*

in·tu·mes·cent (ĭntōomĕs'ent, -tyōo-) *adj.* Swelling up. **in·tu·mes'cence** *n.*

in·un·date (ĭn'undāt, ĭnŭn'-) *v.t.* (**-dat·ed, -dat·ing**). Overflow, flood (*with* water etc.; also fig.). **in·un·da·tion** (ĭnŭndā'shon) *n.*

in·ure (ĭnūr', ĭnoor') *v.* (**-ured, -ur·ing**). Accustom, habituate; come into operation, take affect. **in·ure'ment** *n.*

in·vade (ĭnvād') *v.t.* (**-vad·ed, -vad·ing**). Make hostile inroad into; assail; encroach upon. **in·vad'er** *n.*

in·va·lid[1] (ĭn'valĭd) *n.* & *adj.* (Person) enfeebled or disabled by illness or injury. ~ *v.t.* Lay up, disable, (person) by illness. **in′va·lid·ism** *n.*

in·val·id² (ĭnvăl′ĭd) *adj.* Not valid; esp., having no legal force. **in·va·lid·i·ty** (ĭnvəlĭd′ĭtē) *n.* **in·val′id·ly** *adv.*

in·val·i·date (ĭnvăl′ĭdāt) *v.t.* (**-dat·ed, -dat·ing**). Make invalid. **in·val·i·da·tion** (ĭnvălĭdā′shon) *n.*

in·val·u·a·ble (ĭnvăl′ūabel) *adj.* Of value too great to be measured.

in·var·i·a·ble (ĭnvār′ēabel) *adj.* Unchangeable; always the same; (math.) constant, fixed. **in·var′i·a·ble·ness, in·var·i·a·bil·i·ty** (ĭnvāreabĭl′ĭtē) *ns.* **in·var′i·a·bly** *adv.*

in·va·sion (ĭnvā′zhon) *n.* Invading; encroachment.

in·va·sive (ĭnvā′sĭv) *adj.* That invades, esp. (med.) tending to invade healthy tissue.

in·vec·tive (ĭnvĕk′tĭv) *n.* Violent attack in words; abusive oratory.

in·veigh (ĭnvā′) *v.i.* Speak violently, rail, protest loudly, *against.*

in·vei·gle (ĭnvā′gel) *v.t.* (**-gled, -gling**). Entice, seduce (*into*). **in·vei′gle·ment** *n.*

in·vent (ĭnvĕnt′) *v.t.* Devise, originate; produce or construct by original thought etc.; fabricate (false story etc.). **in·ven·tion** (ĭnvĕn′shon) *n.* 1. Inventing; thing invented, contrivance. 2. Inventiveness. 3. Fictitious story. **in·ven′tive** *adj.* **in·ven′tive·ly** *adv.* **in·ven′tive·ness, in·ven′tor** *ns.*

in·ven·to·ry (ĭn′ventōrē, -tōrē)

n. (pl. **-ries**). Detailed list (of goods, furniture, etc.); stock of goods in this; goods, merchandise, etc. in a store, warehouse, etc. ~ *v.t.* (**-ried, -ry·ing**). Enter (goods etc.) in inventory; make inventory of.

in·verse (ĭnvĕrs′, ĭn′vĕrs) *adj.* Inverted in position, order, or relations; ~ **ratio, proportion,** that between 2 quantities, one of which increases at the same rate as the other decreases, esp. when the product of the 2 remains constant. **in·verse′ly** *adv.* **in′verse** *n.* Inverted state; thing that is the direct opposite (*of* another).

in·ver·sion (ĭnvĕr′zhon, -shon) *n.* Inverting; (gram.) alteration of natural order of words. **in·ver′sive** *adj.*

in·vert (ĭnvĕrt′) *v.t.* Turn upside down or inside out; reverse position, order, or relation, of. **in′vert** *adj.* (chem.) Inverted; ~ **sugar,** mixture of glucose and fructose produced by inversion of sucrose. **in′vert** *n.* 1. Something inverted. 2. (psychol.) Person whose sexual instincts are inverted, homosexual.

in·ver·te·brate (ĭnvĕr′tebrĭt, -brāt) *adj.* Not having a spinal column or backbone; (fig.) lacking

The Allied **invasion** *of Normandy on D-Day (June 6, 1944) marked the turning point in the 1939—45 war. This painting by Barnett Freedman shows the Allied forces at Arromanches, 20 days after the landing.*

1. The **invention** of the Mule spinnin frame by Samuel Crompton from 177 to 1779 combined Paul's an Arkwright's method of drawing b rollers and Hargreave's reciprocatin carriage. It was capable of spinning th finest of yarns. 2. A Hammond type writer of 1895. 3. The first practicab photographic process was invented b Louis Daguerre in 1838. Cameras lik these were in wide use by 1900.

firmness of character; (zool.) b longing to the Invertebrata, a class fication of convenience that con prises all animals other than th Vertebrata, and includes princ pally those animals that have n notochord in any state of develop ment. ~ *n.* Invertebrate animal

in·vest (ĭnvĕst′) *v.* 1. (rar Clothe (person etc. *in, with*); cover clothe, endow (person etc. *wi* qualities, insignia of office etc.). (mil.) Besiege, surround. Employ (money in stocks, business etc.); ~ **in,** put money into (stocks (colloq.) lay out money, time effort, on. **in·ves′tor** *n.*

in·ves·ti·gate (ĭnvĕs′tĭgāt) *v.* (**-gat·ed, -gat·ing**). Examine inquire into. **in·ves·ti·ga·tio** (ĭnvĕstĭgā′shon), **in·ves′ti·ga·to** *ns.* **in·ves′ti·ga·to·ry** (ĭnvĕs′tĭga tōrē, -tōrē), **in·ves′ti·ga·tive** *adjs*

in·ves·ti·ture (ĭnvĕs′tĭcher) *n* Formal investing of person (*wit* office), esp. ceremony at whic sovereign or his deputy confer honors; cover, garment.

in·vest·ment (ĭnvĕst′ment) *n.* Investing of money; money in

*The Academy in Athens, an example of the **Ionic** style of architecture developed by the ancient Greeks, but also adopted at a later date by the Romans.*

vested; property, stocks, etc. in which money is invested.   2. Investiture.   3. (mil.) Act of besieging.

in·vet·er·ate (ĭnvĕt′erĭt) *adj.* Long-established; deep-rooted, obstinate. **in·vet′er·ate·ly** *adv.* **in·vet′er·a·cy** *n.*

in·vid·i·ous (ĭnvĭd′ēus) *adj.* (of conduct etc.) Giving offense, esp. by real or seeming injustice, unfair (distinction, discrimination, etc.); (of thing) likely to excite ill feeling against the possessor. **in·vid′i·ous·ly** *adv.* **in·vid′i·ous·ness** *n.*

in·vig·or·ate (ĭnvĭg′orāt) *v.t.* (**-at·ed, -at·ing**). Make vigorous; animate. **in·vig·or·a·tive** (ĭnvĭg′orātĭv) *adj.* **in·vig·or·a·tion** (ĭnvĭgorā′shon) *n.*

in·vin·ci·ble (ĭnvĭn′sĭbel) *adj.* Unconquerable. **in·vin·ci·bil·i·ty** (ĭnvĭnsĭbĭl′ĭtē) *n.* **in·vin′ci·bly** *adv.*

in·vi·o·la·ble (ĭnvī′olabel) *adj.* Safe from assault, trespass, or violation; to be kept sacred from infraction, profanation, etc. **in·vi·o·la·bil·i·ty** (ĭnvīolabĭl′ĭtē) *n.* **in·vi′o·la·bly** *adv.*

in·vi·o·late (ĭnvī′olĭt, -lāt) *adj.* Not violated; unbroken; unprofaned. **in·vi′o·late·ly** *adv.* **in·vi′o·late·ness, in·vi′o·la·cy** *ns.*

in·vis·i·ble (ĭnvĭz′ĭbel) *adj.* That cannot be seen; not to be seen at a particular time; too small to be seen; ∼ **ink**, ink that requires heat, vapor, or the like to make visible what is written in it. **in·vis·i·bil·i·ty** (ĭnvĭzĭbĭl′ĭtē), **in·vis′i·ble·ness** *ns.* **in·vis′i·bly** *adv.* **invisible** *n.*

in·vite (ĭnvīt′) *v.* (**-vit·ed, -vit-** ing). Request courteously to come (*to* dinner, *to* a party, *to* one's house, etc.); request courteously (*to* do); solicit courteously; bring on, tend to bring on (thing) unintentionally; (of thing) present inducements, attract. **in·vit′ing** *adj.* **in·vit′ing·ly** *adv.* **in·vit′ing·ness, in·vi·ta·tion** (ĭnvĭtā′shon) *ns.* **in′-vite** *n.* (slang) Invitation.

in·vo·ca·tion (ĭnvokā′shon) *n.* Invoking, calling upon deity in prayer; appeal to a spirit, one's muse, etc. **in·voc·a·to·ry** (ĭnvŏk′-atōrē, -tōrē) *adj.*

in·voice (ĭn′vois) *n.* List of goods shipped or sent, with prices and charges. ∼ *v.t.* (**-voiced, -voic·ing**). Make an invoice of (goods); bill.

in·voke (ĭnvōk′) *v.t.* (**-voked, -vok·ing**). Call on (deity etc.) in prayer or as witness; appeal to (person's authority etc.); summon (spirit) by charms; ask earnestly for (vengeance, help, etc.); cite in support of one's cause.

in·vo·lu·cre (ĭn′volōoker) *n.* (bot.) Whorl of bracts surrounding inflorescence.

in·vol·un·tar·y (ĭnvŏl′untērē) *adj.* Done without exercise of the will, unintentional. **in·vol·un·tar·i·ly** (ĭnvŏluntĕr′ile, -vŏl′untĕr-) *adv.* **in·vol′un·tar·i·ness** *n.*

in·vo·lute (ĭn′volōot) *adj.* Involved, intricate, curled spirally; (bot.) rolled inward at the edges.

in·vo·lu·tion (ĭnvolōo′shon) Involving; entanglement; intricacy; curling inward; part so curled; (math.) raising of quantity to any power.

in·volve (ĭnvŏlv′) *v.t.* (**-volved, -volv·ing**). Wrap (thing another); entangle (person, thing, etc.) difficulties, mystery, etc.); implicate (*in*); include (*in*); imply; entail. **in·volve′ment** *n.*

in·vul·ner·a·ble (ĭnvŭl′nerabel) *adj.* That cannot be wounded or hurt; immune to attack. **in·vul·ner·a·bil·i·ty** (ĭnvŭlnerabĭl′ĭtē) *n.* **in·vul′ner·a·bly** *adv.*

in·ward (ĭn′werd) *adj.* Situated within; mental, spiritual; directed toward the inside. **in′ward·ly** *adv.* Of the inside; not aloud; in mind or spirit. **in′ward·ness** *n.* Inner nature, essence. **inward, in′wards** *advs.*

i·o·dide (ī′odīd) *n.* Compound of iodine with another element or radical.

i·o·dine (ī′odīn, -dĭn, -dēn) *n.* (chem.) Nonmetallic element widely diffused in nature but never in the free state, used in medicine as an antiseptic; symbol I, at. no. 53, at. wt. 126.9045; tincture or solution of this in alcohol.

i·o·dize (ī′odīz) *v.t.* (**-dized, -diz·ing**). Treat, combine with iodine or an iodide.

i·o (ī′ō) **moth.** Large yellow N. Amer. moth, *Automeris io*, with eyelike spots on hind wings. [f. *Io*, girl in Gk. myth loved by Zeus and tormented by the jealous Hera with a stinging gadfly (the moth's larva stings)]

i·on (ī′on, ī′ŏn) *n.* (phys.)   1. Electrified particle formed when a neutral atom or group of atoms loses or gains one or more electrons, as a *cation*, with positive charge, formed by electron loss, or an *anion*, with negative charge, formed by electron gain.   2. Gaseous particle electrically charged by action of x-rays or other rays. [Gk. *ion* (thing) going]

-ion *suffix.* Forming nouns of action, condition, etc., usu. from verbs (*destruction, infection*).

I·o·ni·a (īō′nēa). Ancient Greek colony on W. coast of Asia Minor; Aegean coast of W. Asia Minor.

I·o·ni·an (īō′nēan) *adj.* Of Ionia or its people; ∼ **Islands**, group of Greek islands in the Ionian Sea; ∼ **Sea**, part of Mediterranean, between Greece and S. Italy. ∼ *n.* Native, inhabitant, of Ionia.

I·on·ic (īŏn′ĭk) *adj.* Of Ionia; of the Ionic dialect, order, or school; ∼ **dialect**, most important of the three main branches of ancient Greek, of which ATTIC was a development; ∼ **order**, (archit.) Greek order characterized by two lateral volutes of the capital.

i·on·ic (īŏn′ĭk) *adj.* Of or

ertaining to ions.

i·on·ize (ī´onīz) *v.* (**-ized, -z·ing**). Convert into, produce ns. **i·on·i·za·tion** (īonīzā´shon) *n.* **i·on·o·sphere** (īŏn´osfēr) *n.* onized region of the upper atmos-here, from altitudes of approxi-ately 30 to 250 mi., able to flect radio waves for transmission ound Earth.

I.O.O.F. *abbrev.* Independent rder of Odd Fellows.

i·o·ta (īō´ta) *n.* Tenth (later nth) letter of Greek alphabet (I, ι) orresponding to *i*; insignificant art, jot, atom.

IOU, I.O.U. (īōū´) *ns.* (pl. **IOUs, O.U.'s**). Signed document bear-g these letters followed by ecified sum, constituting formal knowledgment of debt. [= I owe u]

I·o·wa (ī´owa). State in mid-estern U.S.; admitted to the nion in 1846; capital Des Moines; **River**, flows from N. Iowa to the Mississippi River in the SE.

IPA, I.P.A. *abbrevs.·* Inter-national Phonetic Alphabet.

ip·e·cac (ĭp´ekăk), **ip·e·cac·u-an·ha** (ĭpekăkūăn´a) *ns.* Root of S. Amer. herbaceous or shrubby plant (*Cephaëlis ipecacuanha*) which pos-sesses emetic, diaphoretic, and purgative properties, a common ingredient of cough medicines; the plant itself

Iph·i·ge·ni·a (ĭfĭjenī´a, -nē´a). (Gk. legend) Daughter of Agamem-non and Clytemnestra; she was offered by her father as a sacrifice to Artemis when the Greeks, on their way to the Trojan War, were becalmed at Aulis, but was snatched from the altar by the goddess and borne away to Tauris, where she became a priestess; she was rescued by her brother Orestes.

ip·so fac·to (ĭp´sō făk´tō). By that very fact. [L.]

An unusual perspective of Des Moines, the capital city of the state of Iowa. A large number of German immigrants came to Iowa in the 1850s followed by British, Irish and Scandinavians.

*The dried roots of the **ipecacuanha** produce a drug widely used in medicine as an emetic and as an expectorant. The plant is cultivated commercially in Brazil, Malaysia and Bengal in India.*

IQ, I.Q. *abbrevs.* Intelligence quotient.

ir- *prefix* = IN[1,2] before *r*.

I.R.A. *abbrev.* Irish Republican Army.

I·ran (ĭrăn´, ī-; *Pers.* ērahn´). Formerly Persia; country in SW. Asia S. of Caspian Sea; a monarchy until 1979 when Shah Mohammed Reza Pahlevi left under pressure from a Muslim political group led by Ayatollah Ruhollah Khomeini who returned from exile and took control of government; capital, Teheran. **I·ra·ni·an** (ĭrā´nēan) *adj.* & *n.* (Native, inhabitant) of Iran; (of) a subbranch of the Indo-European family of languages including Persian, Pashto, Avestan, and Kurdish.

I·raq, I·rak (ĭrăk´, ĭrahk´). Republic extending from Kurdistan on N. and NE. to the Persian Gulf on the S. and SE. and from Iran in E. to Syria and the Arabian Desert on W.; formerly known as MESOPOTAMIA; freed from Turkish rule during World War I, then under a British mandate until 1932; a kingdom from 1921 until assassination of Faisal II in 1958, when it became a republic; capital, Baghdad. **I·ra·qi** (ĭrăk´ē, ĭrah´kē) *adj.* & *n.* (pl. **-qis**). (Native, inhabitant) of Iraq; (of) the modern Arabic dialect spoken in Iraq.

i·ras·ci·ble (ĭrăs´ibel) *adj.* Irritable, hot-tempered. **i·ras·ci·bil·i·ty** (ĭrăsibil´itē) *n.*

i·rate (īrāt´, īr´āt) *adj.* Angry. **i·rate'ly** *adv.*

IRBM *abbrev.* Intermediate range ballistic missile.

ire (īr) *n.* Anger. **ire'ful** *adj.*

Ire·land (īr´land). Island in the Atlantic Ocean, to W. of Gt. Britain; made subordinate to the English legislature in 1494; in 1920 the British Parliament divided Ireland into two parts: (1) Southern Ireland, which became an independent country, since 1949 officially called the Republic of Ireland (formerly, 1921–37, the Irish Free State; 1937–49, Eire); capital Dublin; and (2) NORTHERN IRELAND.

ir·i·da·ceous (ĭrĭdā´shus) *adj.* (of plants) Of the iris kind.

ir·i·des·cent (ĭrĭdĕs´ent) *adj.* Showing colors like those of rainbow; changing color with position. **ir·i·des'cence** *n.*

i·rid·i·um (ĭrĭd´ēum, ī-) *n.* (chem.) White metallic brittle

The blue flag **Iris**, native to Eurasia also found in similar habitats in Nor America. There are up to 300 specie of Iris which has become a very popul garden flower and is used widely Japanese floral arrangements.

The republic of Iran has a population of 31,960,000 people, 90% of them Muslim. Below: Map and flag of Iran. Below right: Dome of the Madrasseh Mader-E-Shah at Isfahan, the former captial of Persia and the center of the textile industry. Bottom: Weaving a Persian carpet at Nishapur.

element of platinum group, use esp. to form hard, corrosion-pro alloys with platinum or osmium symbol Ir, at. no. 77, at. w 192.22.

I·ris (īr´ĭs). (Gk. myth.) Goddes who acted as the messenger of th gods, and displayed as her sign th rainbow.

e republic of **Iraq** is bisected by the
ers Tigris and Euphrates which water
fertile center — the site of ancient
esopotamia. Its capital is Baghdad,
d the country produces 80% of the
rld's supply of dates. Above: Aerial
ew of Kadimain mosque. Right: Map
d flag of Iraq.

i·ris (īr´ĭs) *n.* (pl. **i·ris·es,
·i·des** pr. ĭr´ĭdēz, īr´-).   1.
ircular pigmented diaphragm in
terior chamber of eye, with
ntral aperture (the *pupil*) that
mits light to the lens and
ntracts or expands according to
tensity of light; ~ **diaphragm**,
echanical device resembling the
s, used on cameras for controlling
e aperture of the lens by means of
ovable overlapping shutters.   2.
oot.) Plant of genus *I* ~ with tubers
bulbs, sword-shaped leaves, and
owy flowers.

I·rish (īr´ĭsh) *adj.*   1. Of Ireland,
s people, or language; ~ **coffee**,
t coffee and whiskey, with sugar
d whipped cream; ~ **Free State**:
e IRELAND; **I´rishman, I´rish-
oman**, Irish person; **Irish
epublican Army**, (abbrev.

I.R.A.) secret Irish nationalist
organization formed to oppose the
British partition of Ireland and
fight for the unification and independence of all Ireland; has carried
out anti-British terrorist acts since
the 1920s, and is now active chiefly
in Northern Ireland; **Irish Sea**, sea
between Ireland and England;
Irish setter, setter having long,
silky, golden red or reddish-brown

hair; **Irish stew**, stew of meat
(often mutton), potatoes, and
onions; **Irish terrier**, breed of
terrier with rough wiry coat of
reddish-brown color; **Irish
whiskey**: see WHISKEY; **Irish wolfhound**, wolfhound of large tall
Irish breed with rough, shaggy
coat.   2. Of the branch of the
Celtic languages spoken in Ireland.
Irish *n.*   1. (collect.) People of

Ireland. 2. Irish language.

I·rish·ism (īr´ĭshĭzem) *n.* Irish idiom or custom.

irk (ẽrk) *v.t.* Vex; weary, bore.

irk´some *adj.* Tedious, annoying. **irk´some·ly** *adv.* **irk´some·ness** *n.*

IRO, I.R.O. *abbrevs.* International Refugee Organization.

i·ron (īrn, ī´ern) *n.* 1. (chem.) Abundant metallic element, widely distributed in form of ores, silver-white in color, and characterized by great tensile strength, ductility, and magnetic susceptibility; symbol Fe, at. no. 26, at. wt. 55.847; when purified and alloyed with small quantities of other materials, known as STEEL; **cast ~**, iron obtained by smelting from ores, silvery gray when clean, hard, brittle, crystalline in structure, and containing 2–5% of carbon and smaller quantities of sulfur, phosphorus, and silicon; **pig ~**, cast iron as first obtained from the smelting furnace, cast in long blocks (pigs) for convenience; **wrought ~**, highly malleable iron obtained by stirring pig iron when molten (puddling), nearly pure but always containing some slag in the form of filaments and thus showing a fibrous structure. 2. Tool, implement, instrument, made of iron, as **curling ~, grappling ~**; electric appliance with smooth flat undersurface, now usu. heated by

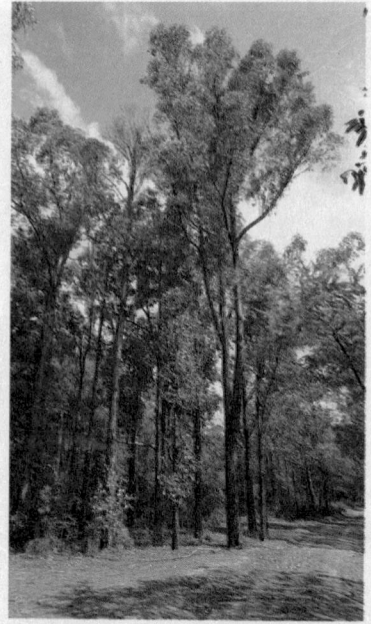

electricity, for smoothing out clothes, linen, etc. (for **flatiron**, see FLAT[2]); golf club with iron or steel head laid back for lofting the ball; (usu. pl.) fetters, shackles. 3. Preparation of iron used in medicine as a tonic. 4. (fig.) Type of hardness, as *man of ~, rod of ~.* 5. Phrases: **strike while the ~ is hot**, act promptly and at a good opportunity; **have many ~s in**

the fire, have many undertakin afoot at the same time. 6. **I ~ Ag** period in the history of a peop following the Bronze Age, chara terized by use of iron implemer and weapons; **i´ronbark,** a species of *Eucalyptus* with har rough bark; **i´ronbound,** boun with iron; (fig.) rigid, inflexib unyielding; (of coast) rugge rocky; **i´ronclad,** covered wit protected by, iron; **Iron Cros** German military decoration; **iro curtain,** (fig.) barrier to passage persons and information at weste boundary of Russian sphere influence in Europe; any simil barrier to spread of ideas etc.; **iro lung,** rigid box enclosing the bo of a patient (leaving the head fre used, in the treatment of paralyzi diseases, for administering pr longed artificial respiration means of mechanical pumps; **iro pyrites**: see PYRITES; **i´ron stone,** name of various hard iro ores; a hard white pottery; **i´ron ware,** generic name for all lig articles made of iron; hardwar **i´ronwood**: see HORNbeam; **i´ron work,** iron parts of a structur casting, moldings, etc., made iron; **i´ronworks,** place where iro

●●●··Symbols indicate importance of production

A bucket wheel reclaimer working on the refined **iron ore** in Port Hedland, Western Australia. The ore is sent down conveyors to a waiting ore carrier.

is smelted or iron goods are made. **iron** *adj.* Made of iron; hard; strong; firm, unyielding. ~ *v.t.* Shackle with irons; smooth (clothes, linen, etc.) with a hot iron; ~ **out**, (fig.) remove (difficulties etc.).

i·ron·ic (īrŏn´ĭk), **i·ron·i·cal** (īrŏn´ĭkal) *adjs.* Of, using, said in, addicted to, irony. **i·ron´i·cal·ly** *adv.*

i·ron·ing (īr´nĭng, ī´er-) *n.* Process of smoothing (clothes etc.) with a heated iron; clothes, linen, etc. to be ironed; ~ **board**, smooth cloth-covered board on which clothes etc. are spread for ironing.

i·ro·ny¹ (ī´ronē, ī´ernē) *n.* (pl. **-nies**). Figure of speech in which the intended meaning is the

*This **iron** bridge over the River Severn was the first of its kind to be built in England. It was constructed between 1775 and 1779 by Abraham Darby and has a single arch.*

opposite of that expressed by the words used, ridicule in which laudatory expressions are used to imply condemnation or contempt; course of events, combination of circumstances, the result of which is the direct opposite of what might be expected as though due to the malice of fate, as in **life's ironie irony of fate**; use of language that has an inner meaning for a privileged audience and an outer meaning for the persons addressed or concerned, as in **tragic iron Socratic irony**, feigned ignorance as means of confuting an opponent in dispute.

i·ron·y² (ī´ernē) *adj.* Of, like, iron.

Ir·o·quoi·an (ĭrokwoi´an) Family of N. Amer. India languages spoken in the eastern U.S. and Canada by the Iroquoi Cherokee, Erie, Wyandotte, and other tribes. ~ *adj.* Of or speaking a language of this family; of the Iroquois.

Ir·o·quois (ĭr´okwoi) *n.* (pl. **-quois** pr. -kwoiz, -kwoi). (Member of) any of several Iroquoian-speaking N. Amer. Indian tribes of a powerful confederacy formerly inhabiting New York State and known as the Five Nations (see FIVE).

ir·ra·di·ate (ĭrā´dēāt) *v.* (-**at·ed, -at·ing**). Subject to radiation, esp. of X-rays, gamma rays, or ultraviolet rays; **ir·ra·di·**

*n X-ray in progress in Japan. The radi-grapher has to **irradiate** the area tended for X-ray which is placed etween an X-ray tube and a film that ontains high levels of silver halide mulsion.*

·tion (ĭrādēāʹshon) *n*. **ir·raʹdi·a-·ive** *adj*.

ir·ra·tion·al (ĭrăshʹonal) *adj*. Unreasonable, illogical, absurd; not ndowed with reason; (math., of oots etc.) not rational, not express-ble by an ordinary (finite) fraction, roper or improper. **ir·ra·tion-·al·i·ty** (ĭrăshonălʹĭtē) *n*. (pl. -ties). ·ra·tion·al·ly *adv*.

ir·re·claim·a·ble (ĭrĭklāʹmabel) *dj*. Not to be reclaimed or eformed. **ir·re·claimʹa·bly** *adv*.

ir·rec·on·cil·a·ble (ĭrĕkonsīʹla-el) *adj*. Implacably hostile; (of deas etc.) incompatible. ~ *n*.

Person who cannot or will not com-promise; idea, belief, or result that cannot be brought into harmony with others. **ir·rec·on·cil·a·bil·i·ty** (ĭrĕkonsīlabĭlʹĭtē), **ir·recʹon-cil·a·ble·ness** *ns*. **ir·recʹon·cil·a-bly** *adv*.

ir·re·cov·er·a·ble (ĭrĭkŭvʹera-bel) *adj*. That cannot be recovered or remedied. **ir·re·covʹer·a·bly** *adv*.

ir·re·cu·sa·ble (ĭrĭkūʹzabel) *adj*. That must be accepted.

Ir·re·den·tist (ĭrĭdĕnʹtĭst) *n*. (It. politics) Advocate of recovery to Italy of all Italian-speaking dis-tricts; **i~**, (of any country) nationalist who advocates recovery of linguistically or historically related area from foreign rule. **ir·re·denʹtism** *n*. [It. (*Italia*) *irredenta* unredeemed Italy]

ir·re·duc·i·ble (ĭrĭdŏōʹsibel,

-dū́-) *adj*. That cannot be brought (*to* desired condition); not capable of being reduced; ~ **minimum**, smallest amount, lowest degree, to which anything can be reduced, or point beyond which further reduc-tion would be useless or unaccept-able. **ir·re·ducʹi·bly** *adv*.

ir·ref·ra·ga·ble (ĭrĕfʹragabel) *adj*. (of statement, argument, person) Indisputable, unanswer-able. **ir·refʹra·ga·bly** *adv*.

ir·re·fran·gi·ble (ĭrĭfrănʹjibel) *adj*. Inviolate; not breakable; (optics) not capable of being refracted.

ir·ref·u·ta·ble (ĭrĕfʹyutabel, ĭrĭ-fūʹta-) *adj*. Not to be refuted. **ir·ref·u·ta·bilʹi·ty** *n*. **ir·refʹu·ta-bly** *adv*.

ir·reg·u·lar (ĭrĕgʹyuler) *adj*. Not regular, contrary to rule, abnormal; not of symmetrical form; (of surface) uneven; uneven in dura-tion, order, etc.; (gram.) not inflected in the usual way; (of troops) not in regular service. ~ *n*. Member of irregular military force. **ir·reg·u·larʹi·ty** (ĭrĕgyu-lărʹĭtē) *n*. (pl. -ties). **ir·regʹu-lar·ly** *adv*.

ir·rel·e·vant (ĭrĕlʹevant) *adj*. Not to the point; not applicable (*to* matter in hand). **ir·relʹe·vance, ir·relʹe·van·cy** *ns*. **ir·relʹe-vant·ly** *adv*.

ir·re·li·gion (ĭrĭlĭjʹon) *n*. Hos-tility to, disregard of, religion. **ir·re·liʹgious·ly** *adv*.

ir·re·me·di·a·ble (ĭrĭmēʹdēabel) *adj*. That cannot be remedied. **ir·re·meʹdi·a·bly** *adv*.

ir·rep·a·ra·ble (ĭrĕpʹerabel) *adj*. (of injury, loss, etc.) That cannot be rectified or made good. **ir·repʹ-a·ra·ble·ness** *n*. **ir·repʹa·ra·bly** *adv*.

ir·re·place·a·ble (ĭrĭplāʹsabel) *adj*. Incapable of being replaced.

ir·re·press·i·ble (ĭrĭprĕsʹabel) *adj*. Not to be repressed or restrained. **ir·re·pressʹi·bly** *adv*.

ir·re·proach·a·ble (ĭrĭprōʹcha-bel) *adj*. Free from blame, faultless. **ir·re·proach·a·bil·i·ty** (ĭrĭprōcha-bĭlʹĭtē) *n*. **ir·re·proachʹa·bly** *adv*.

ir·re·sist·i·ble (ĭrĭzĭsʹtabel) *adj*. Too strong, convincing, charming, etc., to be resisted. **ir·re·sist·i-bil·i·ty** (ĭrĭzĭstabĭlʹĭtē) *n*. **ir·re-sistʹi·bly** *adv*.

ir·re·spec·tive (ĭrĭspĕkʹtĭv) *adj*. ~ **of**, not taking into account, without reference to. **ir·re·specʹ-tive·ly** *adv*.

ir·re·spon·si·ble (ĭrĭspŏnʹsibel) *adj*. Not responsible for conduct; acting, done, without due sense of responsibility. **ir·re·spon·si-bil·i·ty** (ĭrĭspŏnsibĭlʹĭtē) *n*. **ir·re-sponʹsi·bly** *adv*.

ir·re·triev·a·ble (ĭrĭtrēʹvabel) *adj*. That cannot be retrieved. **ir·re·triev·a·bil·i·ty** (ĭrĭtrēvabĭlʹ-ĭtē) *n*. **ir·re·trievʹa·bly** *adv*.

ir·rev·er·ent (ĭrĕv′erent) *adj.* Lacking in reverence. **ir·rev′er·ent·ly** *adv.* **ir·rev′er·ence** *n.*

ir·re·vers·i·ble (ĭrĭvĕr′sĭbel) *adj.* Unalterable; not reversible. **ir·re·vers·i·bil·i·ty** (ĭrĭvĕrsabĭl′ĭtē) *n.* **ir·re·vers′i·bly** *adv.*

ir·rev·o·ca·ble (ĭrĕv′okabel) *adj.* Incapable of being revoked or retracted. **ir·rev·o·ca·bil·i·ty** (ĭrĕvocabĭl′ĭtē) *n.* **ir·rev′o·ca·bly** *adv.*

ir·ri·gate (ĭr′igāt) *v.t.* (**-gat·ed, -gat·ing**). (of streams etc.) Supply land with water; water (land) by system of artificial channels, ditches; (med.) wash, moisten (wound etc.) with flow of liquid. **ir·ri·ga·ble** (ĭr′igabel) *adj.* **ir·ri-**

Irrigation is one of the most ancient techniques in agriculture. 1. Dams like the Burrendong Dam on the Macquarie River, Australia, conserve water for irrigation purposes. 2. A barley field being watered by a portable irrigation system.

ga·tion (ĭrĭgā′shon) *n.*

ir·ri·ta·ble (ĭr′ĭtabel) *adj.* Quick to anger, touchy; (physiol.) (of parts of body, wounds, etc.) excessively sensitive to stimuli; (bot.) capable of responding to external stimulus. **ir·ri·ta·bil·i·ty** (ĭrĭtabĭl′ĭtē) *n.* **ir′ri·ta·bly** *adv.*

ir·ri·tant (ĭr′ĭtant) *adj.* Causing (usu. physical) irritation. ~ *n.* Substance causing irritation (also fig.).

ir·ri·tate (ĭr′ĭtāt) *v.t.* (**-tat·ed,**

3. Cotton is irrigated in Wee Waa, Australia from these artificial troughs. 4. Primitive forms of irrigation, as here in Iran, make use of a well and windlass to draw water.

-tat·ing). Excite to anger, annoy; chafe, inflame, make sore (part of body etc.). **ir′ri·tat·ing** *adj.* **ir′ri·tat·ing·ly** *adv.* **ir·ri·ta·tion** (ĭrĭtā′shon) *n.*

IRS *abbrev.* Internal Revenue Service.

Ir·ving[1] (ēr′vĭng), **Washington** (1783–1859). Amer. writer; best known for his genially satirical *History of New York . . . by Diedrich Knickerbocker*, and the short stories "The Legend of Sleepy Hollow"

Stinging hairs on leaves of the Giant Nettle Tree of Australia, causes an intense **irritation** in the human body.

nd "Rip Van Winkle."

is (ĭz). Third pers. sing. pres. d. of BE.

Is. *abbrev.* Isaiah (Old Testa-ent; also Isa.); Island(s).

I·saac (ī′zak). Hebrew patriarch, n of Abraham and Sarah and ther of Jacob and Esau (Gen. 21 .c.).

Is·a·bel·la I (ĭzabĕl′a) (1451–01). (also known as "The atholic") Queen of Castile, 474–1504, with her husband erdinand of Aragon, joint overeign of Castile and Aragon, 479–1504; gave aid to Columbus

in his expedition to the New World.

I·sa·iah (īzā′a; *Brit.* īzī′a). Hebrew prophet who ministered in Judah in 8th c. B.C. and attacked corruption in the national life; book of Old Testament containing his prophecies.

is·chi·um (ĭs′kēum) *n.* (pl. **-chi·a** pr. -kēa). One of the bones of the pelvis.

I·seult (ĭsōolt′, ĭzōolt′). (Ger. *Isolde*, Fr. *Isoud, Ysoud*) Name of

two characters in medieval legend: (1) ~ **of Ireland**, daughter of the king of Ireland and wife of king Mark of Cornwall, loved by Tristram; (2) ~ **of Brittany**, ~ **of the White Hands**, daughter of the king of Brittany and wife of Tristram.

-ish *suffix.* Of the nature of; somewhat; approximately (*boyish, reddish, fortyish*).

Ish·ma·el (ĭsh′mēal, -māl). Son of Abraham by Sarah's handmaid Hagar, of whom it was predicted, "His hand will be against every man, and every man's hand against

The teachings of **Islam** are preserved in the Koran and the Sunna. Mecca (above) is a holy city and the birthplace of Mohammed. Right: Tunisian prayer-mats. The countries of North Africa are predominantly Muslim.

him" (Gen. 16); hence, an outcast, one at war with society. **Ish'-ma·el·ite** n. (Member of) a desert people believed by ancient Hebrews to be descended from Ishmael; an outcast.

Ish·tar (ĭsh'tär). Assyrian and Babylonian equivalent of ASTARTE.

I·sis (ī'sĭs). (Egyptian myth.) Sister and wife of OSIRIS, and mother of HORUS, regarded as a nature goddess.

Is·lam (ĭs'lam, ĭz'-, ĭslahm'). 1. Religion revealed through the Prophet Muhammad. 2. Muslim world. **Is·lam·ic** (ĭslăm'ĭk, -lah'-mĭk, ĭz-), **Is·lam·it·ic** (ĭslamĭt'ĭk, ĭz-) adjs. **Is·lam·ite** (ĭs'lamīt, ĭz'-) n. [Arab. 'islām resignation to will of God]

Is·lam·a·bad (ĭslah'mabahd, ĭz-). Capital city of Pakistan in NW. Pakistan NE. of Rawalpindi.

is·land (ī'land) n. Piece of land surrounded by water; (fig.) anything detached or isolated; (physiol.) detached portion of tissue or group of cells; ~s of Langerhans: see LANGERHANS; **Islands of the Blest**, (Gk. and Rom. myth.) islands of the Western Ocean, abode of the favorites of the gods after death. **island** v.t. Make into an island; isolate.

is·land·er (ī'lander) n. Native or inhabitant of an island.

isle (īl) n. (esp. poet. or in proper name) Island (usu. small).

is·let (ī'lĭt) n. Little island.

ism (ĭz'em) n. Any distinctive doctrine or practice.

-ism suffix. Forming nouns (1) of action (baptism); (2) of condition or conduct (barbarism, heroism); (3) of system or belief (conservatism); (4) of peculiarity of language (archaism, Gallicism); (5) of pathological condition (alcoholism, Parkinsonism).

Is·ma·il·i (ĭsmāïl'ē, ĭz-) n. Member of a Muslim sect that seceded from the Shiah in 9th c. after the rejection of the claim of Isma'il, a descendant of Muhammad's son-in-law Ali, to be leader (imam) of Islam; the Ismailis now survive mainly in India, Iran, and Afghanistan, and regard the Aga Khan as their imam.

iso- prefix. Equal.

i·so·bar (ī'sobär) n. 1. Line on map connecting places at which atmospheric pressure is the same (at given time or on the average). 2. One of two or more isotopes having the same atomic weight but different chemical properties. **i·so·bar·ic** (ī'sobär'ĭk) adj.

I·soc·ra·tes (īsŏk'ratēz) (436–338 B.C.). Athenian orator and

teacher of rhetoric.

i·so·late (ī'solāt, ĭs'o-) v (-lat·ed, -lat·ing). Place apart alone; (chem.) free substance fro its compounds; subject (person et to quarantine, separate (infectio patient) from others. **i·so·la·tie** (īsolā'shon, ĭso-) n.

i·so·la·tion·ist (īsolā'shonĭ ĭso-) n. One who favors (politic or national) isolation. **i·so·la'tion ism** n.

I·sol·de (ĭsōl'de, ĭzōld') ISEULT.

i·so·mer (ī'sŏmer) *n.* (chem.) One of two or more substances composed of molecules having the same kind of atoms and in the same proportions, but which, by reason of a difference in arrangement of the atoms, have different chemical and physical properties. **i·so·mer·ic** (īsōmĕr'ĭk) *adj.* **i·som'er·ism** *n.*

i·so·met·ric (īsōmĕt'rĭk), **i·so·met·ri·cal** (īsōmĕt'rĭkal) *adjs.* Of equal measure or dimensions; ~ **drawing**, engineer's or architect's drawing in which the three dimensions are represented by three sets of lines 120 apart and all measurements are on same scale (i.e. not in perspective); ~ **exercises, isometrics** (*n.pl.*) system of physical exercises in which muscles are pitted one against another or against a fixed object.

i·so·morph (ī'sōmōrf) *n.* Substance or organism isomorphous with another. **i·so·mor·phic** (īsōmōr'fĭk), **i·so·mor'phous** *adjs.* Having the same form; having the property of crystallizing in the same or closely related geometric forms: *math.,* of groups and other systems) exactly corresponding in form and in the relations between their elements. **i·so·mor'phism** *n.*

i·so·pod (ī'sōpŏd) *n.* Crustacean of large order Isopoda (including, e.g., woodlice) varying greatly in form and often parasitic.

i·sos·ce·les (īsŏs'elēz) *adj.* (of a triangle) Having two equal sides.

i·so·therm (ī'sōthĕrm) *n.* Line on map connecting places having the same temperature. **i·so·ther·mal** (īsōthĕr'mal) *adj. & n.*

i·so·ton·ic (īsōtŏn'ĭk) *adj.* Having equal tension.

i·so·tope (ī'sōtōp) *n.* One or two or more forms of an element having the same atomic number and the same chemical properties and occupying the same place in the periodic table, but differing in atomic weight and in nuclear properties such as radioactivity. **i·so·top·ic** (īsōtŏp'ĭk) *adj.*

Is·ra·el[1] (ĭz'rēel, -rā-). 1. Name given to Jacob after he wrestled with the angel (Gen. 32). 2. Hebrew nation or people traditionally descended from Jacob, whose 12 sons became founders of the 12 tribes; all the Hebrew people, the

*The population of **Israel** doubled in the 10 years after its foundation in 1948, as Jews from the Middle East and Central Europe flooded in. Below: The Church of the Nativity, Bethlehem. Below right: Map and flag of Israel.*

Jews. 3. Northern kingdom of the Hebrews (933–721 B.C.), opp. JUDAH. **Is'ra·el·ite** *adj. & n.* [Heb. = he that strives with God]

Is·ra·el[2] (ĭz'rēel, -rā-). Independent Jewish republic in country formerly called Palestine, bordering on E. of Mediterranean Sea; established in 1948; capital Jerusalem. **Is·rae·li** (ĭzrā'lē) *adj. & n.* (pl. **-lis**, collect. **-li**).

Is·ra·fel (ĭz'rafĕl), **Is·ra·fil** (ĭz'rafēl). In Muslim tradition, angel of music, who will sound the trumpet on the Day of Judgment.

Is·sa·char (ĭs'akär). Hebrew patriarch, son of Jacob and Leah (Gen. 30).

Is·sei (ēs'sā') *n.* (pl. **-sei, -seis**). Japanese immigrant to U.S. or Canada; cf. NISEI and KIBEI. [Jap. = first generation]

is·sue (ĭsh'ōō; *Brit.* ĭs'ū) *n.* 1. Outgoing, outflow; (med.) discharge of blood etc. 2. Place of egress; outlet. 3. Progeny, children. 4. Result, outcome. 5. Point in question; point of discussion, debate, or dispute. 6. Giving out, issuing, (*of* bills of exchange, stamps, etc.); number of coins, notes, copies of newspaper or book etc., issued at one time; ~ *v.* (**-sued, -su·ing**). 1. Go or come

MEDITERRANEAN SEA

Lebanon

Syria

HAIFA

TEL AVIV

JERUSALEM

ISRAEL

Jordan

Egypt

Saudi Arabia

RED SEA

out; be derived, spring, (*from*);
result (*from*); end, result, (*in*). 2.
Come out, be published; send forth;
publish, put into circulation (notes,
newspaper, book, etc.). 3. (mil.)
Supply (soldier) *with* article of
equipment etc. **is'su·a·ble** *adj.*
is'su·ance *n.*

-ist *suffix.* Forming nouns (1) of
agent (*plagiarist, antagonist*); (2) of
adherent of creed etc. (*atheist,*
Methodist); (3) of one concerned
with any subject (*dentist, tobacco-*
nist) esp. as player on musical
instrument (*cellist*).

Is·tan·bul (ĭstănbōōl', -tahn-).
City and port of Turkey on the
European side of the Bosporus
(orig. Byzantium, later CONSTANTI-
NOPLE).

isth·mus (ĭs'mus) *n.* (pl.
-mus·es, -mi pr. -mī). Narrow
portion of land connecting two
larger bodies of land, neck of land;
(anat., bot., zool.) narrow part or
passage connecting two larger ones.

is·tle (ĭst'lē) *n.* Any of several
plants of the genus *Agave*, yielding
a tough fiber. [Mex. Span. *ixtle*]

it (ĭt) *pron.* Third person sing.
pronoun denoting thing or person
in question; as subject of impersonal verb expressing action or
condition of things without reference to agent; as subject of verb,
anticipating deferred virtual subject in apposition; as antecedent to
relative of either number and any
gender, separated by predicate; as
indefinite object with transitive or
intransitive verb; with specific but
unexpressed reference: **with ~**: see
WITH; as quasi-*n.*, (1) in children's
games, player who must catch or
find others; (2) (colloq.) the very
person or thing; perfection.

i.t.a. *abbrev.* Initial teaching
alphabet.

ital. *abbrev.* Italic (type).

I·tal·ian (ĭtăl'yan) *adj.* Of Italy,
its people, or language; (of script)
= ITALIC, 1; **~ sonnet**: see SONNET.

Italian *n.* 1. Italian person.
Language of Italy, one of
modern descendants of La
I·tal·ian·ate (ĭtăl'yanāt, -nĭt) *a*
Of Italian form or character.

I·tal·ic (ĭtăl'ĭk, ī-) *adj.* 1.
ancient Italy or its tribes; of
Greek colonies in southern Ita
~ languages, Indo-Europe
languages of ancient Italy (La
Oscan, Umbrian) as a grou
I·tal·i·cism (ĭtăl'ĭsĭzem, ī-) *n.*

i·tal·ic (ĭtăl'ĭk, ī-) *adj.* 1. Of
kind of handwriting developed
Italy (opp. GOTHIC). 2. Of the ki
of printing type imitating ita
script, introduced by Al
Manutius (1501), in which lett
slope toward the right (now u
employed to emphasize word(s)
distinguish word(s) from others
same context). **~** *n.* (also
Italic type. **i·tal·i·cize** *v.t.* (**-cize**
-ciz·ing). Print in italics;
writing) underline.

It·a·ly (ĭt'alē). Penins
running southward into Medit
ranean from the mass of cent
Europe; formerly divided amo
various mercantile city-states
under foreign domination u
unified in 19th c.; a monarchy fr
1861 until 1946 when a republic v
declared; capital, Rome.

itch (ĭch) *n.* Uneasy sense
irritation in skin; any of vari

contagious skin diseases marked by this sensation, eruptions, etc.; restless desire, hankering; ~ **mite**, mite causing scabies. **itch** *v.i.* Feel irritation in skin; crave uneasily; **itching palm**, avarice. **itch′i·ness** *n.* **itch′y** *adj.* (**itch·i·er, itch·i·est**).

-ite[1] *suffix.* Forming nouns meaning "person or thing belonging to or connected with" (*Trotskyite, Muscovite, anthracite, cordite, vulcanite*). [Gk. *-itēs*].

-ite[2] *suffix.* Forming adjectives (*erudite*), nouns (*appetite*), and verbs (*expedite, unite*). [L. *-itus*]

i·tem (ī′tem) *n.* Article, unit, included in enumeration; entry of this in account etc.; detail of news etc. in newspaper etc. ~ *adv.* Likewise, also, (introducing mention of item). **i′tem·ize** *v.t.* (**-ized, -iz·ing**). Set down by items; specify items of (account etc.). [L. *item* in like manner, also]

it·er·ate (ĭt′erāt) *v.t.* (**-at·ed, -at·ing**). Repeat (quoted words etc.); make (charge, assertion, etc.) repeatedly. **it·er·a·tion** (ĭterā′shon) *n.*

it·er·a·tive (ĭt′erātĭv, -erătĭv) *adj.* Repetitious; (gram., of verb) denoting repetition of action, frequentative.

Ith·a·ca (ĭth′aka). 1. (Gk. *Itháki*) Small island W. of Greece, in the Ionian Sea. 2. Island described by Homer as the kingdom of Odysseus; traditionally identified with modern Ithaca, but thought by some to be the neighboring larger island of Leukas.

i·tin·er·ant (ītĭn′erant, ĭ-) *adj.* Traveling from place to place, esp. to find work or carry out official

task or duty.

i·tin·er·a·ry (ītĭn′erĕrē, ĭ-) *n.* (pl. **-ar·ies**). Route or proposed route, list of stopovers, etc.; record of travel; guidebook. ~ *adj.* Of traveling, of a route.

-itious *suffix.* Forming adjectives corresp. to nouns ending in *-ition* (*ambitious, nutritious*).

-itis *suffix.* Forming nouns indicating inflammatory diseases lit. (*appendicitis, gastritis*) and (colloq.) fig. *baseballitis*.

its (ĭts) *poss. pron.* Possessive

*The **Ivory Coast**, a former French colony, is one of the most stable and prosperous of the West African states. Its main products are cocoa and timber. Below: Pottery market at Adjame. Below right: Map and flag of the country.*

case of IT used as attrib. adjecti belonging to, affecting, it.

it's (ĭts) *contr.* It is.

it·self (ĭtsĕlf′) *pron.* Empha and reflexive form corresponding IT; **by** ~, automatically; apart fr its surroundings; **in** ~, viewed its essential qualities etc.

it·sy-bit·sy (ĭt′sē bĭt′sē), **it·** **bit·ty** (ĭt′ē bĭt′ē) *adjs.* (slang, ba talk) Tiny, insignificant.

IUD, IUCD *abbrevs.* Int uterine (contraceptive) device.

I.V., i.v. *abbrevs.* Intravenou

I·van (ī′van; *Russ.* ēvahn Name of several rulers of Russ **Ivan I** (d. 1341), grand duke Vladimir (1328–41); **Ivan II** 1359), grand duke of Vladim **Ivan III** "the Great" (1440–150 grand duke of Muscovy (140 1505); **Ivan IV** "the Terribl (1530–84), first tsar of Musco (1533–84); a successful ruler, w conquered Kazan and Astrakh and added Siberia to his dominior was subject to fits of rage in c of which he killed his son; **Iv V** (1666–96), associated as tsar fr 1682 with his half-brother Peter t Great; **Ivan VI** (1740–64), empe of Russia (1740–1); imprison from 1742 until his death.

I've (īv) *contr.* I have.

-ive *suffix.* Forming adjectiv meaning "tending to, having t nature of" (*active, evasive*), a nouns (*captive, directive*).

Ives (īvz), **James Merritt**: s CURRIER AND IVES.

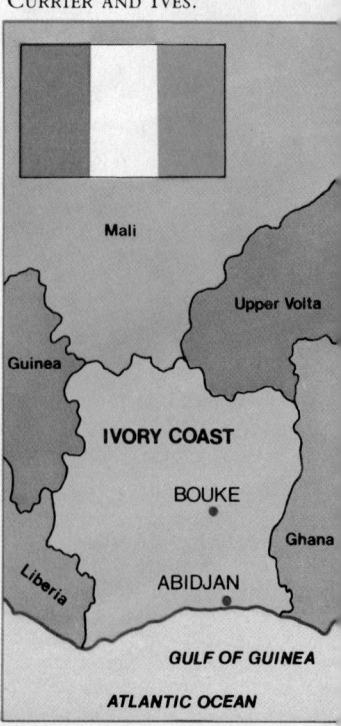

Mali
Upper Volta
Guinea
IVORY COAST
BOUKE
Ghana
Liberia
ABIDJAN
GULF OF GUINEA
ATLANTIC OCEAN

i·vo·ry (ī′verē, īv′rē) *n.* (pl. **-ries**). 1. Hard white fine-grained substance (dentine of exceptional hardness) composing main part of tusks of elephant, hippopotamus, walrus, and narwhal; ~ **tower**, situation or attitude of seclusion from the world or practical affairs (esp. of intellectual seclusion). 2. Color of ivory, ivory-white. 3. (slang, pl.) Teeth; dice, piano keys.

I·vo·ry (ī′verē, īv′rē) **Coast.** Republic of W. Africa, between Liberia and Ghana; formerly a French colony; independent since 1960; capital, Abidjan.

i·vy (ī′vē) *n.* (pl. **i·vies**). Climbing or trailing evergreen shrub (*Hedera helix*) with dark green shining leaves, usu. five-angled;

Ivory is prized for its beauty, durability and suitability for carving. Tusks of African elephants, like this one, average about 6 ft. in length and weigh about 100 lbs. per pair. The tusks of the female Indian elephant are rarely visible.

any of various other climbing or creeping plants, such as POISON ivy; **Ivy League,** association of northeastern U.S. colleges: Brown, Columbia, Cornell, Dartmouth, Harvard, Princeton, University of Pennsylvania, and Yale; (*adj.*) of or like Ivy League traditions.

I·wo Ji·ma (ē′wo jē′ma, ē′wō). Middle and largest of the Japanese Volcano Islands in the Pacific Ocean, S. of Japan; scene of severe fighting during World War II,

when island was completely taken by U.S. forces; returned to Japan, 1968.

I.W.W. *abbrev.* Industrial Workers of the World.

Ix·i·on (ik′sēon). (Gk. myth.) King of Thessaly, father of the Centaurs; tried to seduce Hera, and was condemned to be bound to a fiery wheel revolving unceasingly through the underworld.

-ize *suffix.* Forming verbs meaning (1) treat in a specified way (*patronize, monopolize*); (2) follow specified practice (*gourmandize*); (3) bring or come into specified state (*vaporize, Anglicize*); (4) treat or act according to method (*pasteurize*); (5) provide or affect with (*oxidize, magnetize*).

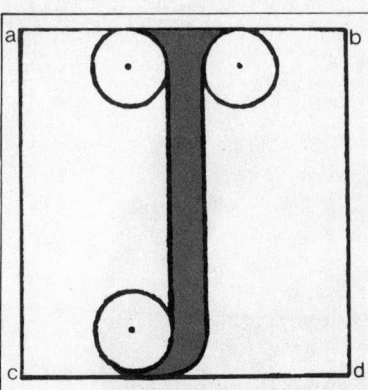

The letter J was unknown as an alphabetic character until the 14th century. The letter J emerged through the ornamental lengthening of I in medieval manuscripts particularly when it appeared as an initial or with another i. It gradually acquired the value of a consonant.

Early Canaanite   Phoenician   Early Greek

Early Etruscan   Early Latin   Classical La

J, j (jā) (pl. **J's, j's** or **Js, js**). Tenth letter of modern English alphabet, a late modification of I; in form, i with a tail (final i was freq. written thus in manuscripts); in modern English representing a voiced composite sound (dzh), corresponding to the voiceless *tsh*.

J *abbrev.* (phys.) Joule(s).

J. *abbrev.* (cards) Jack; judge; justice.

J.A. *abbrev.* Judge Advocate.

jab (jăb) *v.t.* (**jabbed, jab·bing**). Poke roughly; stab; thrust (thing) abruptly (*into*). ~ *n.* Abrupt stabbing blow with pointed thing or fist. **jab'bing·ly** *adv.*

jab·ber (jăb'er) *v.* Speak volubly and with little sense; utter (words) rapidly and indistinctly; chatter, as monkeys etc. ~ *n.* Jabbering talk or sound. **jab'ber·er** *n.*

jab·i·ru (jăb'irōō) *n.* Large white, wading stork, esp. *Jabiru mycteria* of tropical Amer.

jab·o·ran·di (jăborăn'dē) *n.* (pl. **-dis**). Any of several tropical Amer. shrubs of genus *Pilocarpus*; dried leaflets of certain of these, esp. *P. jaborandi*, yielding pilocarpine, a sudorific.

ja·bot (zhăbō'; *Brit.* zhăb'ō) *n.* Ornamental frill on front of woman's bodice; frill on man's shirt front.

ja·ça·na (zhahsanah') *n.* Tropical wading bird of family Jacanidae, including *Jaçana spinosa*, occas. in Florida and Texas, and having very long toes enabling it to walk on floating plants.

jac·a·ran·da (jăkarăn'da) *n.* 1. Any of various tropical Amer. timber trees with heavy dark wood. 2. Tree of genus *J* ~, with trumpet-shaped blue flowers.

jack (jăk) *n.* 1. (usu. **J** ~) Fellow; **every man** ~, (colloq.) every individual man; STEEPLEjack; **J** ~ **Tar,** ~**-tar,** sailor. 2. (cards)

Playing card carrying the pict of a servant or soldier, kna 3. Machine for lifting and suppo ing weights from below; p of various machines; in spin harpsichord, etc., wooden uprig fixed to back of key lever a fitted with quill for plucking stri (elect.) device for connecting o set of wires to a corresponding by the insertion of a single plug. Male of various animals (so JAC ASS); pike, esp. young or small. Ship's flag, smaller than ensi esp. one flown from jackst indicating nationality; **Union J** see UNION. 6. (pl. construed sing.) Game played with set small, six-pointed metal objects. (slang) Money. 8. **jack'boot,** la boot coming above knee; **jack'da** small Eurasian crow (*Cor monedula*), easily tamed and taug to imitate sound of words; **Ja Frost,** frost personified; **jack.**

*The **jacana** is also called the lily-trotter or lotus bird. It has long spidery toes which are equipped with straight claws for walking on vegetation. It is found in tropical regions.*

American jacana

pheasant-tailed jacana

*The **jackal** is a nocturnal animal, which*
ᵉⁿ follows lions and other large cats
order to finish a carcass when the
ᵍᵉʳ animal has eaten its fill. When
ⁿᵗⁱⁿᵍ in packs it can kill antelopes and
ᵉᵉᵖ.

Andrew Jackson, 7th U.S. president,
was elected to the Senate in 1822. His
first run for office failed but he was
elected in 1824 and then again in 1828
for a second term.

ᵃmmer, pneumatic hammer;
ᵃck-in-the-box (pl. **-box·es**), toy
ᵢᵤure that springs out of box when
ᵉned; **jack-in-the-pulpit** (pl.
ᵘˡ·pits), plant (*Arisaema triphyl-*
ᵘⁿ) of eastern N. America, having
ᵃ upright flower spike partly
ᵉclosed by a hoodlike spathe;
ᵃck′knife (pl. **-knives**), large
ᵒcket clasp knife; dive in which
ᵛᵉʳ touches feet or ankles with
ⁿds; **jack′knife** (*v.i.*) (**-knifed,**
ⁿⁱf·ing), double like folding
ⁱfe; **jack′leg** (*adj.*), (slang) not
ᵗᵃined for one's work; incompetent;
ᵃkeshift; without standards; un-
ᵣupulous; **jack-of-all-trades,**
ᵖˡ. jacks-), one who can turn his
ⁿd to anything; **~-o'-lantern**
ᵖˡ.-terns), hollowed-out pumpkin
ⁱⁿtern with a carved face; **jack**
ⁱⁿe, evergreen tree (*Pinus banks-*
ⁿa) of northern N. America,
ᵃⁱⁿg short needles and numerous
ᵒⁿes; **jack′pot,** (in poker) pool
ᵃt cannot be opened until some
ᵃyer has two jacks or better in
ⁱs hand; cumulative stakes or prize
ⁱ lottery etc.; **hit the jackpot,**
ᵃⁱang) have sudden success; **jack**
ᵃbbit, large hare of western N.
ᵐerica with very long ears and
ᵍs; **jack′screw,** machine for
ⁱᵗing heavy loads, operated by
ᵗⁱrning screw; **jack′snipe** (pl.
ⁿⁱpes, collect. **-snipe**), small Old
ᵒʳld species of snipe (*Lymno-*
ᵧptes minima); **jack′straw,** thin
ˡⁱnter of wood, plastic, etc., used
ⁱ game (pl.) in which heap of these
ⁱˢ to be removed one at a time
ⁱᵗhout disturbing the others; **Jack**
ᵃr: see def. 1; **Jack the Ripper,**
ⁱdiscovered murderer of women
ᵢ London (1888–91), who mutilat-
ⁱ his victims. **jack** *v.t.* Hoist
ᵖ) with mechanical jack etc.; usu.

~ up, raise (prices, confidence, in).
[*Jack,* fam. form of name *John*]

jack·al (jăk′al, -awl) *n.* (pl. **-als,**
collect. **-al**). 1. Any of several
members of the dog family found
wild in Asia and Africa, living on
carrion and small animals. 2.
Person who does subordinate
preparatory work or drudgery for
another (because jackals were
formerly believed to hunt up lion's
prey for him). [Turk. *chakāl*]

jack·a·napes (jăk′anāps) *n.* 1.
(archaic) (Tame) ape or monkey. 2.
Impertinent young fellow; coxcomb.

jack·ass (jăk′ăs) *n.* 1. Male ass
or donkey. 2. Stupid person.

*The **Jacob's ladder** or greek valerian*
has loose clusters of drooping flowers,
which are funnel-shaped and usually
blue, violet or white. It grows up to 3 ft.
tall.

jack·et (jăk′ĭt) *n.* 1. Short coat,
coatlike garment for upper part of
body; **life ~:** see LIFE. 2. Any
outer coat or covering, as skin of
potato. 3. Outer covering around
boiler etc. to protect it or cool it
or keep in heat. 4. Wrapper
around book. **jacket** *v.t.* Cover
with jacket. **jack′et·ed, jack′et-**
less *adjs.*

Jack·son¹ (jăk′son). Capital and
largest city of Mississippi, in the
SW. central part, on the Pearl
River.

Jack·son² (jăk′son), **Andrew**
(1767–1845). "Old Hickory," U.S.
soldier and politician; became
national hero as a successful Indian
fighter and defender of New
Orleans against the British in War
of 1812; seventh president of U.S.
1829–37; during his administration
he introduced the spoils system,
paid off the national debt, and
vetoed the charter of the United
States Bank.

Jack·son³ (jăk′son), **Thomas**
Jonathan (1824–63). "Stonewall
Jackson," Amer. general; Lee's
chief assistant in Civil War; commanded Confederate troops at Bull
Run and Shenandoah Valley; was
accidentally killed by the fire of his
own men at Chancellorsville.

Jack·son·ville (jăk′sonvĭl). City
in NE. Florida near the mouth of
the St. Johns River; Confederates
used it as a base for blockade
running during Civil War.

Ja·cob (jā′kob). Hebrew patriarch, son of Isaac and Rebecca,
younger twin brother of Esau, and
traditional founder of Israel (Gen.
25–60); **~'s ladder,** ladder between earth and heaven, with angels
ascending and descending, which
Jacob saw in a dream at Bethel

Jacobean architecture is exemplified in Blickling Hall, Norfolk, built between 1616 and 1624. Its tall chimneys, towers at each corner, decorated stonework and symmetrical plan are typical of the Jacobean style.

(Gen. 28); hence, rope ladder with wooden rungs for ascending ship's rigging; also, blue-flowered perennial plant (*Polemonium caeruleum*) with closely pinnate leaves giving ladderlike appearance.

Jac·o·be·an (jăkobē′an) *adj.* Of the reign of James I of England (1603–25); of the style of building or furniture in England in early 17th c. [L. *Jacobus* James]

Jac·o·bin (jăk′obĭn) *n.* 1. Dominican friar, esp. French member of the order, from their 1st convent near church of St. Jacques in Paris. 2. Member of radical French political club founded 1789 in the old Jacobin convent in Paris, and responsible, under Robespierre, for the Reign of Terror; dissolved 1799. 3. Sympathizer with principles of Jacobins in French Revolution; extreme radical, revolutionary.

Jac·o·bite (jă′kobīt) *n.* Adherent of James II of England after his abdication or supporter of Stuart pretenders after revolution of 1688.

Jac·quard (jăk′ard, jăkärd′; *Fr.* zhäkär′), **Joseph Marie** (1752–1834). French inventor, improver of the loom; ~ **loom**, loom for mechanically weaving fabric of figured patterns (**jacquard**) by means of an endless belt of cards punched with holes arranged to form the required pattern.

jade¹ (jād) *n.* Poor or worn-out horse; (archaic) hussy. **jad′ed** *adj.* Worn out, weary; dulled.

jade² (jād) *n.* 1. Nephrite, a hard translucent light green, bluish, or whitish stone, a silicate of calcium and magnesium, used for ornaments etc. 2. Jadeite, a silicate of sodium and aluminum, closely resembling nephrite in appearance. 3. Carved piece of jadeite or nephrite. 4. (also ~ **green**) Light green. [Span. (*piedra de*) *ijada* (stone of) the colic, f. L. *ilia* flank]

jade·ite (jā′dīt). See JADE², def. 2.

Jaf·fa (jăf′a; *Heb.* yah′fah). City and port of Israel, combined with Tel Aviv into one municipality; (also ~ **orange**) large seedless orange grown near there.

jag¹ (jăg) *n.* Sharp projection. ~ *v.t.* (**jag·ged, jag·ging**). Cut, tear, break, in uneven manner, make indentations in. **jag·ged** (jăg′ĭd) *adj.* **jag·ged·ly** *adv.* **jag·ged·ness** *n.* **jag·gy** *adj.* (**-gi·er, -gi·est**).

jag² (jăg) *n.* (dial.) Small load or portion; (slang) spree, bout.

J.A.G. *abbrev.* Judge Advocate General.

Jag·an·nath (jŭg′anaht, -nawt),

The earliest **jade** carvings in China date from about 2000 B.C. Abrasives such as quartz are used to work the stone into the intricate patterns seen on this jade bowl. In Chinese tradition the stone was 'a mirror of virtues'.

Jag·an·na·tha (jŭganaht′ha), **Jag·-ga·nath** (jŭg′anaht, -nawt). (Hindu myth.) Title of KRISHNA; = JUGGERNAUT.

jag·uar (jăg′war; *Brit.* also jăg′ūer) *n.* (pl. **-uars,** collect. **-uar**). Large carnivorous spotted feline quadruped (*Panthera onca*), of tropical America.

Jah·veh, Jah·ve (yah′vĕ, -vā), **Jah·weh, Jah·we** (yah′wĕ, -wā) = YAHWEH. **Jah·vist** (yah′vĭst), **Jah·wist** (yah′wĭst) = YAHWIST.

Jah·vis·tic (yahvĭs′tĭk), **Jah·wis·tic** (yahwĭs′tĭk) *adjs.*

jai a·lai (hī′lī, hī′alī, hīalī′). Game played in a three-wall cou[rt] and similar to handball, in whi[ch] players strap a long curved bask[et] to the arm to catch a small, ha[rd] ball and throw it against the wal[l].

jail (jāl) *n.* Public prison f[or] detention of persons committe[d] by process of law; **jail′bir[d]** (colloq.) person who is or has be[en] kept in jail; prisoner; **jail′brea[k]** escape from jail; **jail′er,** person [in] charge of jail or prisoners in [it]. **jail** *v.t.* Put in jail, imprison.

Jain (jīn) *n.* Member of asce[tic] non-Brahminical Hindu se[ct] chiefly of India, established in 6th

...e **jaguar** resembles the leopard but larger and more heavily built. It is a solitary predator and stalks animals such as deer, tapirs, fish and birds. It is swift and agile and is found in tropical America.

Strictly speaking a **jalopy** is a dilapidated old car. This Veteran Model T Ford is a shining example of what a renovated jalopy can look like.

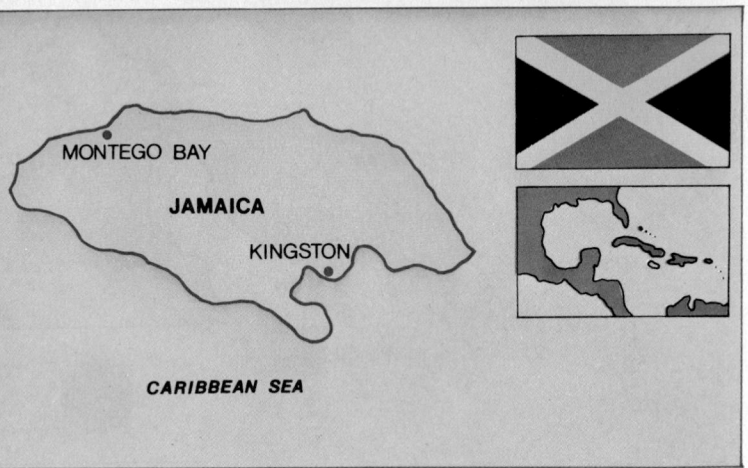

MONTEGO BAY

JAMAICA

KINGSTON

CARIBBEAN SEA

c. B.C., with doctrines closely resembling those of Buddhism. **Jain'ism** *n.* [Sansk. *jina* a Buddha (*ji* conquer, overcome)]

Jai·pur (jī'poor). Commercial city in NW. India noted for its walls and fortifications.

Ja·kar·ta (jakār'ta): = DJAKARTA.

ja·lop·y (jalŏp'ē) *n.* (pl. **-lop·ies**). (colloq.) Old, dilapidated automobile; (transf.) battered old aircraft.

jal·ou·sie (jăl'ose; *Brit.* zhăl'ōozē) *n.* Blind, shutter, with slats sloping upward from without. [Fr., = "jealousy"]

jam¹ (jăm) *v.* (**jammed, jam·ming**). 1. Squeeze between two surfaces or bodies; fill up, block (passage etc.) by crowding into it. 2. Wedge (part of machine) so that it cannot work; become so wedged; ~ **on**, apply (brakes) forcibly. 3. (radio etc.) Cause interference with. **jam** *n.* Crush, squeeze; stoppage (of machine etc.) due to this; crowded mass, esp. accumulation of logs in river or traffic in street etc.; (slang) awkward situation, fix; ~ **packed**, very full; ~ **session**, improvised playing by group of jazz musicians.

jam² (jăm) *n.* Preserves made by boiling whole fruit and sugar to a thick consistency.

Ja·mai·ca (jamā'ka). Island of 4,411 sq. mi. (11,425 sq. km) in the Caribbean Sea S. of Cuba; discovered by Columbus in 1494 and ruled by Spain until captured by England in 1655; independent since 1962; capital, Kingston. **Ja·mai'can** *adj. & n.*

jamb (jăm) *n.* Side post of doorway, window, etc.

jam·bo·ree (jămborē') *n.* Noisy celebration; large rally or assembly, as of Scouts, political party, etc.

James¹ (jāmz). Name of several persons in New Testament: 1. Son of Zebedee and elder brother of St. John the Evangelist (Mark 3); one of the 12 Apostles and the first to be martyred (44 A.D.); called **St. ~ the Great** or **Greater**; commemorated July 25; patron saint of Spain. 2. Person described as brother of Jesus (cf. Mark 6, Gal. 1); traditionally identified with St. James the Less(er); a leader of the church at Jerusalem until put to death by the Sanhedrin in 62 A.D.; **(Epistle of) St. ~**, book of New Testament traditionally ascribed to him. 3. One of the 12 Apostles, son of Alphaeus; called **St. ~ the Less**; commemorated May 1.

James² (jāmz). Name of 7 Stuart

Jamaica has an important tourist trade and is the world's largest producer of bauxite. Coffee grown in the island's Blue Mountains is also highly prized. The country's map and flag are shown here.

kings of Scotland: **James I** (1394–1437); son of Robert III; reigned 1406–37, held captive in England till 1424; **James II** (1430–60), his son, reigned 1437–60; **James III** (1451–88), his son, reigned 1460–1488; **James IV** (1473–1513), his son, reigned 1488–1513; married Margaret Tudor, daughter of Henry VII of England; invaded England, 1513, and was killed at Flodden Field; **James V** (1512–42), son of James IV and father of Mary Queen of Scots; reigned 1513–42; **James VI and VII**: see next entry.

James³ (jāmz). Name of two Stuart kings of England and Scotland: **James I** of England and **VI** of Scotland (1566–1625), son of Lord Darnley and Mary Queen of Scots; on her abdication, became king of Scotland (1567–1625) and, on death of Elizabeth I, king of England (1603–25); patron of the King James Bible; **James II** of England and **VII** of Scotland (1633–1701), son of Charles I and grandson of James I; succeeded his brother, Charles II, 1685; had Catholic sympathies; fled to France, and was succeeded, 1688, by his Protestant son-in-law William of Orange.

James⁴ (jāmz) (1688–1766). James Francis Edward Stuart, son of **James³** II: see Old **PRETENDER.**

James⁵ (jāmz), **Henry** (1843–1916). Amer. novelist living mainly in England; author of *The American, Daisy Miller, The Portrait of a Lady, The Wings of the Dove, The Turn of the Screw,* etc.

James⁶ (jāmz), **Jesse Woodson** (1847–82). Amer. outlaw leader, railroad and bank robber; **James boys**, gang of outlaws led by Jesse and his brother, Frank, 1843–1915.

James⁷ (jāmz), **William** (1842–1910). Amer. philosopher and psychologist; elder brother of Henry **JAMES⁵**; formulator of theory of pragmatism: see **PRAGMATIC**; author of *The Principles of Psychology, The Varieties of Religious Experience,* etc.

James·town (jāmz′town). 1. Village in E. Virginia on the James River; first permanent English settlement in America, 1607. 2. Capital of St. Helena, in the S. Atlantic off Africa.

Jam·mu and Kash·mir (jŭm′-oo, Kăsh′mēr). Former princely State on NW. border of India, divided into two parts, 1949: the NW. controlled by Pakistan, with capital at Muzaffarabad, and the rest made an Indian State with capitals at Srinagar (in summer) and Jammu (in winter), sovereignty disputed by India and Pakistan since 1947.

Jan. *abbrev.* January.

jan·gle (jăng′gel) *v.* (**-gled,**

James I of England was the first of the Stuart kings and the son of Mary Queen of Scots. The Authorized Version of the Bible was published (1611) during his reign.

-gling). Make harsh metallic noise; cause (bell etc.) to do this. ~ *n.* Harsh metallic noise, discordant sound. **jan′gler** *n.* **jan′gly** *adj.*

jan·is·sar·y (jăn′ĭsĕrē) (pl. **-sar·ies**), **jan·i·zar·y** (jăn′ĭzĕrē) (pl. **-zar·ies**) *ns.* (hist.) One of body of Turkish infantry forming sultan's guards and main fighting force of Turkish army from 14th c. to 1826. [Turk. *yeni tsheri* new soldiery]

jan·i·tor (jăn′ĭter) *n.* (fem. **jan·i·tress** pr. jăn′ĭtrĭs). Caretaker of building, office, etc. charged with maintaining and esp. cleaning it. **jan·i·to·ri·al** (jănĭtōr′ēal, -tōr′-) *adj.*

Jan·sen (jăn′sen), **Cornelius** (1585–1638). Dutch R.C. theologian and bishop of Ypres in Flanders.

Jan·sen·ism (jăn′senĭzem) *n.* Theological principles of Cornelius Jansen maintaining that the natural human will is perverse and incapable of good, capacity for the love of God can be attained only by

conversion, and that God conve[rts] whom he pleases; opposed by t[he] Jesuits and condemned as heretic[al] by several popes esp. Clement [XI;] flourished chiefly in France (17th and 18th centuries). **Jan′sen·ist**

Jan·u·ar·y (jăn′ūērē) ([pl.] **-ar·ies**). First month of Gregoria[n] (11th of Julian) calendar, with [31] days. [L. (*mensis*) *Januari*[us] (month) of **JANUS**]

Ja·nus (jā′nus). (Rom. myth[.]) Ancient Italian deity, guardian [of] gates and doorways and of the sta[te] in time of war; represented with tw[o] faces, one at front and one at ba[ck] of his head.

Jap (jăp) *n.* (slang, usu. derog[.]) Japanese.

Jap. *abbrev.* Japan; Japanese.

Ja·pan (japăn′). Country in [W.] Pacific off E. coast of Asia, con[-] sisting of four main islands coveri[ng] 143,750 sq. mi. (372,313 sq. km[.:] Honshu, Hokkaido, Kyushu, an[d] Shikoku; capital, Tokyo; on[ce a] feudalistic society; governed [by] shogun (military dictator) an[d] emperor 12th to 19th c.; 1st conta[ct] with western civilization ar[ound] Christianity, 1542, but trade wi[th] foreign countries restricted to po[rt] of Nagasaki; Commodore Per[ry] entered Tokyo Bay with Ame[r.] fleet, 1854, securing first comme[r-] cial treaty; parliamentary gover[n-] ment retaining empero[r] established, 1889; after short wa[r] with China, acquired Formo[sa] (Taiwan), Pescadores, and part [of] southern Manchuria; defeate[d] Russia and gained additional terr[.]

2

3

4

tory in Manchuria; joined Axis Pact, 1936; invaded China, 1937, attacked Pearl Harbor, 1941, provoking U.S. entry into World War II; surrendered 1945, after destruction of Hiroshima and Nagasaki by U.S. atomic bombs; set up new constitution with bicameral government and elected prime minister, 1947, with emperor as figurehead; large export industry includes cotton textiles, electronic instruments, steel, automobiles, and ships; **Sea of** ~, part of W. Pacific Ocean between Japan on E. and mainland Asia on W.; ~ **Trench**, depression in the Pacific Ocean off the E. coast of Japan, reaching depths over 30,000 ft. (9,144 m).

ja·pan (japăn') *n.* Hard black lacquer or enamel originating in Japan and used to produce a glossy finish; varnish, etc. in imitation of this; object decorated with this. ~ *v.t.* (**-panned, -pan·ning**). Cover with japan; make black and glossy as with japan.

Jap·a·nese (jăpanēz', -nēs') *adj.* Of Japan, its people, or language; ~ **beetle**, bronze and green beetle (*Popillia japonica*), orig. from E. Asia but introduced into N. America, where the larvae and adults are major plant pests; ~ **cherry**, hybrid flowering cherry tree with pink or white, usu. double, flowers; ~ **iris**, tall, beardless iris (*Iris kaempferi*), native of Asia, widely cultivated for its flat, showy flowers; ~ **maple**, small tree (*Acer palmatum*) orig. of E. Asia, prized for its foliage, which is deeply lobed and which turns crimson in the fall. **Japanese** *n.* (pl. **-nese**). 1. Japanese person. 2. Language of Japan, which is agglutinative and written in Chinese ideographs with characters of a syllabary called *kana* for the agglutinative and inflectional endings. [Chinese *Jih-pun* sunrise (*jih* sun, *pun* origin)]

jape (jāp) *n. & v.i.* (**japed, japing**). Jest, quip, joke. **jap'er·y** *n.*

Ja·pheth (jā'fĭth). Third son of Noah (Gen. 10); traditional ancestor of the peoples living around Mediterranean. **Ja·phet·ic** (jafĕt'ĭk) *adj.*

Ja·pu·rá (zhahpōōrah'). River of S. Amer. flowing SE. 1,500 mi. (2,414 km), from the Andes Mountains in SW. Colombia to the Amazon in NW. Brazil.

jar¹ (jär) *n.* Harsh sound; discord; jolt; shock. ~ *v.* (**jarred, jar·ring**). 1. Make discordant sound, make grating impression (*on*, person, his ear, etc.). 2. Be at variance, disagree (*with*). **jar'-ring·ly** *adv.*

jar² (jär) *n.* Cylindrical glass or pottery vessel with a wide mouth and usu. without handles; amount in this.

jar·din·iere (järdinēr', zhärdĭn-yär') *n.* 1. Ornamental pot or stand for display of plants. 2. Dish of mixed vegetables served alone or as garnish with meat. [Fr.]

jar·gon¹ (jär'gon) *n.* Unintelligible or meaningless words; technical or specialized language of a profession, group, etc.; hybrid language or dialect, patois.

jar·gon² (jär'gŏn), **jar·goon** (järgōon') *ns.* Translucent, colorless, or smoky variety of zircon found in Sri Lanka.

jarl (yärl) *n.* (hist.) Scandinavian or Danish chieftain.

Jas. *abbrev.* James.

jas·mine, jas·min (jăz'mĭn, jăs'-), **jes·sa·mine** (jĕs'amĭn) *ns.* Shrub of genus *Jasminum* with white or yellow salver-shaped flowers, esp. **common** or **white** ~ (*J. officinale*), and of genus *Gelsemium*, esp. **yellow** or **Carolina** jessamine (*G. sempervirens*). [Pers. *yāsimīn*]

Ja·son (jā'son). (Gk. legend) Son of Aeson, king of Iolcos; the throne was usurped by Pelias, who promised to surrender it if Jason would bring him the Golden Fleece (see GOLDEN); Jason sailed with the Argonauts and obtained the fleece with the aid of MEDEA, whom he married.

jas·per (jăs'per) *n.* Opaque variety of quartz, usu. red, yellow, or brown.

Jat (jaht, jawt) *n.* Member of a Indo-Aryan people widely dis-tributed in NW. India.

ja·to (jā'tō) *n.* (pl. **-tos**). (aeron Jet-assisted takeoff; auxiliary j engine(s) to provide temporar extra thrust at takeoff.

jaun·dice (jawn'dĭs) *n.* Yello discoloration of skin and normal white part of eyeball due to th presence of pigments in the bloo that are normally excreted in th bile, often caused by an obstructe bile duct; this condition; disordere or discolored vision as character istic of this. **jaun'diced** ad Affected with jaundice; (fig colored by envy, low spirits, etc.

Jasmine is found in warm and temperate climates. It is a climbing shrubby plant with fragrant yellow or whi flowers. It is used in the manufacture perfume.

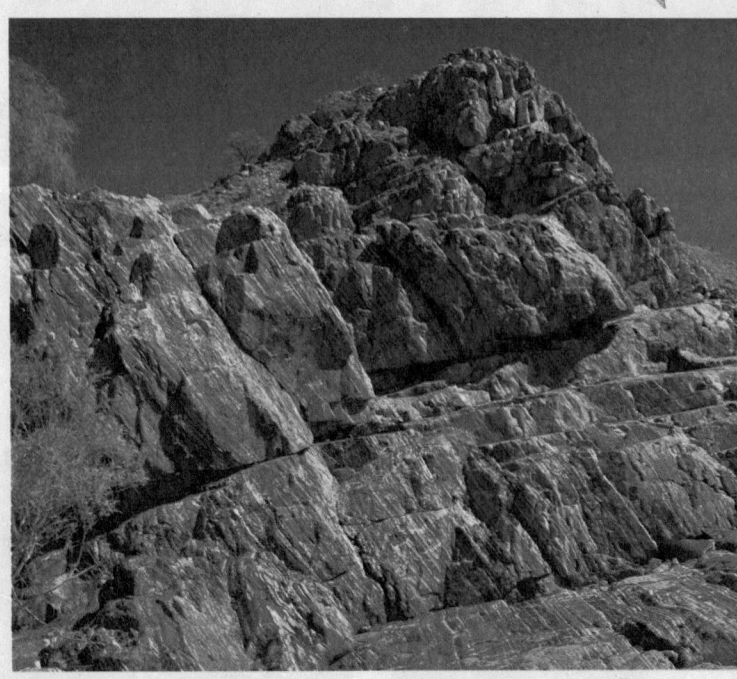

Jasper is usually brick red to brownish red in color. Medicinal values attributed to it include the belief that it strengthened the stomach of the wearer. This jasper rock is in Marble Bar, Western Australia.

*The island of **Java** is the political, economic and cultural center of Indonesia. It is a region of high volcanic mountains like this one (left). Center left: Map of Java.*

jaunt (jawnt) *n.* Excursion, esp. for pleasure. ~ *v.i.* Take a jaunt.

jaun·ty (jawn′tē) *adj.* (**-ti·er, -ti·est**). Having or affecting easy sprightliness, airy self-satisfaction. **jaun′ti·ly** *adv.* **jaun′ti·ness** *n.*

Jav. *abbrev.* Javanese.

Ja·va (jah′va). Large island of Malay archipelago, first settled by Dutch in 17th c. and now part of Indonesia; ~ **man**, fossil hominid *Homo erectus* (formerly *Pithecanthropus erectus*), whose remains were first found in Java in 1891; ~ **Sea**, shallow area of the Pacific Ocean N. of the island of Java and S. of Borneo. **Jav·a·nese** (jăvanēz′, -nēs′) *adj.* & *n.* (Native, inhabitant, Malayan language) of Java.

jav·e·lin (jăv′lĭn, -elĭn) *n.* Light spear thrown with the hand.

jaw (jaw) *n.* 1. One of the bones or sets of bones forming the framework of the mouth and carrying the teeth in vertebrates; in sing. usu. = lower jaw rather than upper; (pl.) bones etc. of mouth including teeth; mouth. 2. (pl.) Structure in invertebrates analogous to vertebrates' jaws. 3. (pl.) Seizing parts of machine, e.g. vise. 4. **jaw′bone**, each of the two bones forming lower jaw in most mammals; these two combined into one in others; **jaw′-breaker**, (colloq.) word hard to pronounce; very hard round candy, often with chewing gum in the center. **jaw** *v.* (colloq.) Speak, esp. at tedious length; scold, lecture *at* (person).

jay (jā) *n.* Any of several birds of the crow family (Corvidae), often having loud, rasping calls, esp. the BLUE JAY and CANADA JAY; **Jay′-hawker**, nickname for Kansan; (sometimes **j**~) Missouri-Kansas border fighter for abolition of slavery before and during Amer. Civil War; **jay′vee**, (colloq.) member of a junior varsity team; **jay′walker**, pedestrian who crosses street without observing regulations; so **jay′walking**.

Jay (jā), **John** (1745–1829). Amer. statesman and diplomat; president, Continental Congress, 1778–9; co-author with Hamilton and Madison of the *Federalist* articles, urging ratification of the Constitution; first chief justice of U.S. Supreme Court, 1789–95; governor of New York, 1795–1801.

Jay·cee (jā′sē′) *n.* Member of a junior chamber of commerce.

jazz (jăz) *n.* Syncopated music, of U.S. black origin, with charac-

***Javelin** throwing was a field event in the ancient Olympics as well as in the modern Games. Ruth Francis is seen here at the 1972 Olympics.*

teristic harmony and ragtime rhythm; (slang) pretentious talk, lies; nonsense; ~ **band**, orchestra playing jazz. **jazz** *v.* Play jazz; ~ **up**, (slang) enliven; make more colorful, interesting, etc. **jazz′i-ness** *n.* **jazz′i·ly** *adv.* **jazz′y** *adj.* (**jazz·i·er, jazz·i·est**).

J.C.S., JCS *abbrevs.* Joint Chiefs of Staff.

jct. *abbrev.* Junction.

JD *abbrev.* Juvenile delinquent.

J.D. *abbrev.* Doctor of Jurisprudence; Doctor of Laws; Department of Justice; juvenile delinquent.

JDL *abbrev.* Jewish Defense League.

Je. *abbrev.* June.

jea·lous (jĕl′*us*) *adj.* 1. Solicitous for preservation *of* (rights etc.); (bibl., of God) intolerant of unfaithfulness; (of inquiry etc.) vigilant. 2. Apprehensive of being displaced in the love or goodwill *of* (wife, lover, friend, etc.; also *of* supposed rival); envious (*of*). **jeal′ous·ly** *adv.* **jeal′ous·y** *n.* (pl. **-ous·ies**). Quality, state, of being jealous.

jean (jēn) *n.* Heavy twilled cotton fabric; (pl.) garment, esp. western-cut pants, of this. [prob. f. Fr. *Gênes* Genoa]

Je·bel Mu·sa (jĕb′el moō′sah). Mountain rising 2,775 ft. (846 m), in NW. Morocco on the Strait of Gibraltar; one of the Pillars of Hercules.

jeep (jēp) *n.* Small, strong, unadorned, all-purpose motor vehicle with four-wheel drive and ¼-ton capacity developed for the armed forces during World War II. **J**~, (trademark) similar vehicle for civil use. [said to have been f. *g p*, initials of *general purposes*]

jeer (jēr) *v.* Scoff derisively (*at*); deride. ~ *n.* Derisive taunt. **jeer′ing·ly** *adv.*

Jef·fers (jĕf′*erz*), **(John) Robinson** (1887–1962). Amer. poet noted for narrative poems based on biblical and classical sources; author of *The Roan Stallion, Tamar and Other Poems*, etc.

Jef·fer·son[1] (jĕf′*erson*), **Thomas** (1743–1826). Amer. statesman and diplomat; champion of states' rights; member of Continental Congress; principal drafter and a signer of the Declaration of Independence; U.S. minister to France, 1785–9, secretary of State, 1790–3, vice president, under John Adams, 1797–1801; as third elected president of U.S., 1801–9, he pushed through the Louisiana Purchase and upheld the Embargo Act.

Jef·fer·son[2] (jĕf′*erson*) **City.** Capital of Missouri, in the central part on the Missouri River.

je·had: see JIHAD.

Je · hosh · a · phat (jehŏsh′*a*făt, -hŏs′-). King of Judah, son of Asa

*The Jefferson Memorial in Washington D.C. commemorates the architect of America's Declaration of Independence, **Thomas Jefferson**, 3rd president of the U.S. Dedicated in 1943 on the 200th anniversary of his birth, it lies in 18 acres of parkland.*

(1 Kings 22; 2 Chron. 20).

Je·ho·vah (jehō′va). 1. Name of God in Old Testament (Exod. 6; cf. YAHWEH). 2. (in Christian use) God; ~'s **Witnesses**, actively evangelical sect founded *c*1879 by Charles Taze Russell (1852–1916) of Pittsburgh, Pa. and believing in the imminent arrival of the millennium. **Je·ho·vist** (jehō′vĭst) = YAHWIST. **Je·ho·vis·tic** (jēhō-vĭs′tĭk) *adj.* [erron. rendering of Heb. JHVH]

Je·hu (jē′hū). King of Israel, son of Jehoshaphat, famous for furious driving of chariot (2 Kings 9).

je·june (jĭjōōn′) *adj.* Meager, not nourishing; insipid; childish; weak. **je·june′ly** *adv.* **je·june′ness** *n.*

je·ju·num (jĭjōō′num) *n.* (anat.) Part of small intestine between duodenum and ileum.

Je·kyll (jĕk′ĭl), **Henry.** Hero of R. L. Stevenson's story "The Strange Case of Dr. Jekyll and Mr. Hyde" (1886); handsome and well-respected, he transformed himself by a potion into the dwarfish and detestable Edward Hyde, in whom was embodied only the evil side of Jekyll; hence, ~ **-and-Hyde character**, dual personality.

jell (jĕl) *v.i.* (colloq.) Set as jelly;

(fig.) take shape.

jel·ly (jĕl′ē) *n.* (pl. **-lies**). Soft stiffish substance, usu. semitransparent, made of gelatin or other gelatinous substance, esp. as food usu. made with meat or with fruit juices; concentrated usu. fruit-flavored preparation of this for dissolving; anything of similar consistency; **jel′lybean**, bean-shaped candy consisting of firm filling and hard sugar coating; **jel′lyfish** (pl. **-fish·es**, collect. **-fish**), any of numerous free-swimming marine coelenterates, having a jellylike body with saucer shape and long tentacles; medusa; (colloq.) spineless person; **jelly roll**, thin flat sponge cake spread with fruit jelly or jam and rolled up. **jelly** *v.* (**-lied, -ly·ing**). Make into jelly; congeal. **jel·lied** (jĕl′ēd) *adj.* Made into, set in, jelly.

je ne sais quoi (zhe ne sā kwŏ′). Indefinable esp. pleasing quality. [Fr., = "I know not what"]

Jen·ghiz Khan (jĕng′gĭz kahn′). = GENGHIS KHAN.

Jen·ner (jĕn′er), **Edward** (1749–1823). English physician and pioneer of vaccination.

jen·net (jĕn′ĭt) *n.* 1. Small Spanish horse. 2. Female donkey or ass.

jen·ny (jĕn′ē) *n.* (pl. **-nies**). 1. The SPINNING JENNY. 2. Female donkey. 3. Female wren; wren. [fam. form of *Jane* or *Janet*]

jeop·ard·ize (jĕp′erdīz) *v.t.* (**-ized, -iz·ing**). Endanger.

jeop·ard·y (jĕp′erdē) *n.* (pl.

ard·ies). Danger, esp. of severe oss or harm. [OF. *ieu parti* ivided (i.e. even) game]

Jeph·thah (jĕf´thǝ). Judge of srael, son of Gilead; sacrificed his aughter in consequence of a vow hat if victorious against the mmonites he would sacrifice the rst living thing that met him on his eturn (Judges 11, 12).

Jer. *abbrev.* Jeremiah (Old estament).

Jer·bo·a (jērbō´a) *n.* Member of amily of rodents including the esert rat (*Dipus*) of N. Africa, with ery long hind legs and tail. [Arab. *arbu'*]

jer·e·mi·ad (jĕremī´ăd) *n.* Lam-ntation, doleful complaint. [f. *eremiah*]

Jer·e·mi·ah (jĕremī´a), **Jer·e-ni·as** (jĕremīas) (*c*650–*c*585 B.C.). Iebrew major prophet, who saw ne fall of Assyria, the vassalage of udah in turn to Egypt and abylon, and the destruction of erusalem; book of Old Testament ontaining his prophecies; hence, oleful person, denouncer of the mes.

Je·rez (hĕrĕth´). (full name ~ **de** a **Frontera**) Town in Andalusia, pain, 15 mi. W. of Cadiz; center f sherry-making industry.

Jer·i·cho (jĕr´ikō). Ancient city ear N. end of the Dead Sea; first anaanite city attacked and taken y Israelites (Joshua 6).

jerk[1] (jĕrk) *n.* 1. Sharp sudden ull, twist, etc. 2. Involuntary pasmodic contraction of muscle. . (slang) Stupid, foolish, or nsignificant person. ~ *v.* Pull, hrust, twist, etc., with a jerk; throw

with suddenly arrested motion; move with a jerk. **jerk'y** *adj.* (**jerk·i·er, jerk·i·est**). **jerk'i·ly** *adv.* **jerk'i·ness** *n.*

jerk[2] (jĕrk) *v.t.* Cure (esp. beef) by cutting in long slices and drying in sun. [Peruv. *echarqui* dried flesh]

jer·kin (jĕr´kǐn) *n.* Man's close-fitting jacket, often of leather (hist.); sleeveless jacket.

jerk·wa·ter (jĕrk´wawtǝr, -wǒt´-er) *adj.* (colloq.) Absurdly unimportant and remote; insignifi-cant.

Jer·o·bo·am (jĕrobō´am). Name of 2 kings in ancient Israel: (1) (10th c. B.C.) first king of northern Israel (I Kings 11–14), "a mighty man of valor," one "who made Israel to sin"; (2) (8th c. B.C.) king of Israel (2 Kings 14).

jer·o·bo·am (jĕrobō´am) *n.* Large wine bottle, holding about $\frac{4}{5}$ of a gallon (3l.). [f. JEROBOAM]

jer·ry-build (jĕr´ēbǐld) *v.* (**-built, -build·ing**). Build with poor and cheap materials. **jer'ry-built** *adj.*

jer·ry (jĕr´ē) **can.** Metal con-tainer esp. for fuel, holding 5 gallons.

jer·sey (jĕr´zē) *n.* (pl. **-seys**). 1. Knitted pullover shirt worn for certain sports. 2. Machine-knitted fabric. 3. **J~**, (one of) a breed of small usu. buff-colored dairy cattle, producing milk of high fat content, orig. raised in Jersey, Channel Islands.

Je·ru·sa·lem (jerōō´salem). Ancient capital of Judea, the holy city of the Jews, sacred also to Christians and Muslims; capital of modern Israel; **the New ~**, the Heavenly City, the abode of God and the saints; **~ artichoke**: see ARTICHOKE.

jes·sa·mine: see JASMINE.

Jesse (jĕs´ē). Father of David (I Sam.).

jest (jĕst) *n.* Joke; witticism; fun; object of derision. ~ *v.i.* Joke, make jests. **jest'ing·ly** *adv.*

desert jerboa

four-toed jerboa

*The **jerboa**, a small nocturnal rodent, looks rather like a miniature kangaroo. It is found in the deserts and dry plains of Asia and North Africa. The desert jer-boa (Jaculus) is found in N. Africa, and the four-toed in Egypt and Asia.*

jest·er (jĕs′ter) *n.* One who jests; (esp., hist.) professional entertainer maintained in court or noble household.

Jes·u·it (jĕzh′ŏŏit, jĕz′ū-, jĕz′ŏŏit) *n.* Member of the Society of Jesus, an order of R.C. priests founded 1534 in Paris by Ignatius Loyola, Francis Xavier, and others, to defend the church and propagate its faith. **Jes·u·it·i·cal** (jĕzhŏŏit′ĭ-kal, jĕzū-, jĕzŏŏ-) *adj.*

Je·sus (jē′zus) (*c*4 B.C.–*c*30 A.D.). (also ~ **Christ**) Source of the Christian religion, accepted by Christians as son of God and as the Messiah; second person of the Trinity; born (traditionally at Bethlehem) of the Virgin Mary; began his public life at about 30; for some three years went about ancient Palestine, chiefly in Galilee, with a band of followers or disciples, teaching and healing; was then arrested in Jerusalem at the time of Passover, handed over to the Roman authorities, and condemned to death by crucifixion; the Christian doctrine is that after three days he rose from the dead; **Society of ~**: see JESUIT.

jet[1] (jĕt) *n.* Hard black coal taking brilliant polish; color of this, deep glossy black. ~ *adj.* (also **~-black**) Deep glossy black.

jet[2] (jĕt) *n.* 1. Stream of water, steam, gas(es), etc., ejected from small opening; spout, nozzle, for

*This painting of **Jesus** carrying the Cross is by El Greco. The artist's spiritual intensity is revealed in his use of strange colors, the elongation of the human figure and the juxtaposition of dark and light.*

emitting water etc. thus. 2. aircraft, stream of gas ejected fr rearward-facing nozzle and p pelling the aircraft forward; aircr propelled thus; hence ~ **pla ~-propelled, ~ propulsion**, e 3. ~ **lag**, delayed bodily effects after long flight by jet aircraft (e owing to difference of local tim **jet′liner**, jet airplane in comm cial passenger service; **jet′po** airport designed for jet aircraft; **set**, wealthy elite making frequ air trips between social or busin engagements; hence **jet setter**; **stream**, narrow current of stro westerly winds in upper tro sphere. **jet** *v.* (**jet·ted, jet·tin** Spout forth in jet(s).

jet·sam (jĕt′sam) *n.* Goo thrown overboard from ship lighten it, and (in mod. use) wash ashore.

jet·ti·son (jĕt′ĭson, -zon) *n* Throwing of goods overboard, e to lighten ship in distress. ~ Throw (goods) overboard th (fig.) abandon.

jet·ty[1] (jĕt′ē) *n.* (pl. **-ties**) Pier or breakwater extending fr shoreline out into the water protect harbor or beach. 2. Lar ing pier; wharf.

jet·ty[2] (jĕt′ē) *adj.* Jet-black.

Jew (jŏŏ) *n.* (fem., now cc sidered offensive, **jew′ess**) Pers of Hebrew descent; one who religion is Judaism; (hist.) Hebr of kingdom of Judah, as opp. those of ten tribes of Isra **Wandering ~**: see WANDERI ~-**baiting**, systematic persecuti of Jews; **jew′fish** (pl. **-fish** collect. **-fish**), any of several lar marine fishes of the family Serra dae, of tropical waters; **jews′ har jew′s-harp**, simple musical instr ment consisting of flexible st tongue affixed at one end to ly shaped metal frame, played holding frame between teeth a striking free end of metal tong with finger.

jew·el (jŏŏ′el) *n.* Ornament precious stone(s), worn for perso adornment; precious stone; hig prized person or thing. ~ *v* (**-eled, -el·ing**, Brit. **-elle -el·ling**). Adorn, furnish, wi jewels; fit (watch) with jewels the pivot holes. **jew′el·er**, B **jew′el·ler, jew′el·ry**, Brit. jew **el·ler·y** *ns.*

jew·el·weed (jŏŏ′elwēd) *n.* A of several plants of the ge *Impatiens*, having yellow flowe sometimes marked with reddi brown spots.

Jew·ish (jŏŏ′ĭsh) *adj.* Of t Jews; ~ **calendar**, lunar calend in use among the Jews, adapted the solar year by various expe ents, having normally 12 mont but 13 months in leap years, whi occur seven times in every cycle

9 years; the years are reckoned
rom the Creation (3761 B.C.). ~
. Yiddish. **Jew·ish·ness** *n.*

Jew·ry (jŏo′rē, joor′ē) *n.* (pl.
·**ries**). 1. (collect.) Jews. 2. (hist.)
ewish ghetto of medieval city.

Jez·e·bel (jĕz′ebĕl, -bel). Ninth
, Phoenician princess, daughter of
ing of Tyre; queen of Israel as
vife of Ahab; denounced by Elijah
or introducing worship of Baal;
illed when Jehu triumphed over
.hab; hence, (often **j**~) shameless
r abandoned woman.

jg, j.g. *abbrevs.* Junior grade.

Jiang·i (jahn′shē′) = KIANGSI.

Jiang·su (jang′sōō′) = KIANGSU.

jib (jĭb) *n.* Triangular staysail
rom outer end of jib boom to
oretop masthead in large ships,
rom bowsprit to masthead in
maller ones; **cut of person's** ~,
is personal appearance; ~ **boom**,
par run out from end of bowsprit;
rojecting arm of crane. **jib** *v.*
ibbed, jib·bing) = JIBE[1].

jibe[1], gybe (jīb) *vbs.* (**jibed,**
ib·ing, gybed, gyb·ing**). 1. Shift
fore-and-aft sail from one side of a
hip to the other. 2. Change course

of a ship so that a fore-and-aft sail
shifts thus.

jibe[2]: see GIBE.

jibe[3](jīb) *v.* (**jibed, jib·ing**).
(colloq.) Fit or agree with.

jif·fy (jĭf′ē) (pl. -**fies**), **jiff** (jĭf)
ns. (colloq.) Very short time,
moment.

jig (jĭg) *n.* 1. Lively dance; music
for this, usu. in $\frac{3}{4}$ or $\frac{6}{8}$ time. 2.
(eng.) Device for holding parts in
appropriate position for drilling or
assembling. 3. Contrivance for
separating ore by agitation. 4.
jig′saw, machine fret saw; (also
jigsaw puzzle) picture pasted on
board etc. and cut in irregular
pieces to be fitted together. **jig** *v.*
(**jigged, jig·ging**). Dance a jig; bob
up and down rapidly and jerkily;
separate coarser and finer portions
of (ore) by shaking it under water
in box with perforated bottom; **in**
~ **time**, quickly; **the** ~ **is up**,
(slang) success is now impossible.

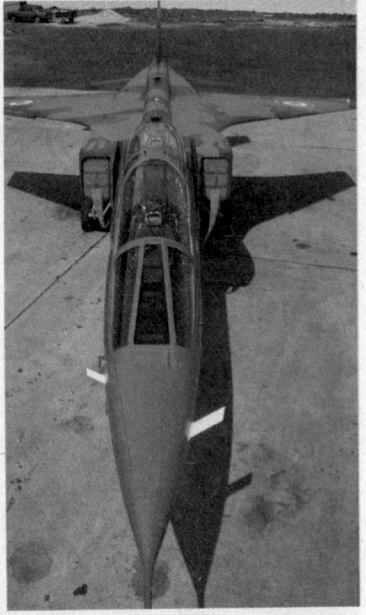

*The construction and testing of **jet
planes** like Concorde and this Anglo-
French Jaguar aircraft, a strike fighter,
is jointly funded by France and Britain.*

heat-resistant tail cone
low-pressure turbine
fan casing
titanium fan (33 blades)
intermediate pressure turbine
high-pressure turbine
guide vanes
annular combustors
bleed air cooling
high-pressure compressor
turbine discs
rear shaft bearings
h-pressure shaft (heat-resistant alloy)
intermediate pressure shaft (steel)
core engine
inlet guide vanes
shaft coupling
low-pressure shaft (steel)

*e jet engine, RB 211-22 built by
olls Royce, is an example of a fan jet
ngine in which a large cowled fan
ows air past the engine, reducing
oise and saving fuel. It is one of the
est known engines in service. There
ere problems with the carbon fiber fan
ades on the original engine, but these
ave been replaced with titanium
ades.*

jig·ger (jĭg′*er*) *n.* 1. (naut.) Small tackle consisting of a double and single block with rope. 2. Small sail rigged out on mast and boom from stern of cutter etc. 3. Any of various mechanical contrivances, used in many trades. 4. Small measure of glass for liquor, usu. holding 1½ ounces.

jig·ger·y-pok·er·y (jĭg′erē pō′-kerē) *n.* (pl. **-er·ies**). (colloq.) Trickery, underhand dealing.

jig·gle (jĭg′*el*) *v.t.* (**-gled, -gling**). Rock or jerk lightly. ~ *n.* Rocking or jerking motion. **jig′gly** *adj.*

ji·had, je·had (jĭhahd′) *ns.* Muslim holy war against unbelievers; (fig.) campaign against a doctrine, policy, etc.; crusade.

Jil·in (chĭl′ēn′) = KIRIN.

jilt (jĭlt) *v.t.* Cast off (lover) after encouragement or promise to marry.

Jim Crow (jĭm′krō′). Segregating of, discrimination against, blacks in U.S.; segregated.

jim-dan·dy (jĭm′dăn′dē) *adj.* (colloq.) Of excellent quality.

jim·my (jĭm′ē) *n.* (pl. **-mies**). Crowbar used by burglars. ~ *v.* (**-mied, -my·ing**). Force or pry open with a jimmy.

jim·son (jĭm′son) **weed.** Highly poisonous tall weed (*Datura stramonium*) having large trumpet-shaped purple or white flowers. [orig. JAMESTOWN-weed]

jin·gle (jĭng′gel) *n.* Mingled noise like that of small bells, links of chain, etc.; repetition of same or similar sounds in words, esp. if designed to catch the attention; words intended to have pleasing or

striking sound without regard to sense; simple repetitious rhyme, esp. as advertising. ~ *v.* (**-gled, -gling**). Make, cause (keys etc.) to make, a jingle; (of writing) be full of alliterations, rhymes, etc. **jin′gler** *n.* **jin′gly** *adv.*

jin·go (jĭng′gō) *n.* (pl. **-goes**). 1. **by ~,** used for emphasis or to express surprise. 2. Blatant patriot, esp. supporter of a belligerent foreign policy (from use of *by jingo* in popular Brit. music hall refrain of 1878, sung by those ready to go to war with Russia). **jin′go·ism** *n.* **jin·go·ist** *n. & adj.* **jin·go·is·tic** (jĭngōĭs′tĭk) *adj.*

jinks (jĭngks) *n.pl.* **high ~,** boisterous sport, frolic.

jinn, djinn (jĭn), **jin·ni** (jĭnē′, jĭn′ē) *ns.* (pl. **jinns, djinns,** collect. **jinn, djinn**). (Islamic myth.) Spirit lower than angels, with supernatural power over men.

jin·rick·sha, jin·rick·shaw, jin·rik·i·sha (jĭnrĭk′shaw, -shah) *ns.* Light two-wheeled hooded vehicle drawn by man or men, first used in Japan c1870. [Jap. *jin-riki-sha* (*jin* man, *riki* strength, power, *sha* vehicle)]

jinx (jĭngks) *n.* (colloq.) Bringer of bad luck, exerciser of evil influence. ~ *v.* Bring bad luck.

jit·ney (jĭt′nē) *n.* (pl. **-neys**). Small bus or taxi carrying passengers at low rates.

jit·ter (jĭt′*er*) *v.t.* Be nervous, nervously; **jit′terbug,** (collo quick-tempo, two-step dance swing music, often with twirls a acrobatic maneuvers, pop. in 1940s; dancer of this. **jit′ters** *n.* (colloq.) Extreme nervousne **jit′ter·y** *adv.*

jiu·jit·su, jiu·jut·su (jōō jĭt′sō see JUJITSU.

jive (jīv) *n.* Swing music, esp. the 1940s; jargon of swing and ja musicians and devotees; (slar deceptive talk, exaggeration. ~ (**jived, jiv·ing**). (slang) Exagg ate, talk deceptively (to).

jnt. *abbrev.* Joint.

Joan of Arc (jōn′ov ārk′), (1412–31). (Fr. *Jeanne d'A* French peasant called "The M of Orleans"; inspired by "voices" St. Catherine and St. Michael, s led the French armies against t English, relieved Orleans, a stood beside Charles VI at l coronation; was tried and co demned for heresy and burned the stake in the marketplace Rouen; canonized 1919; commem orated May 30.

Job (jōb). 1. Book of O Testament, variously dated 5t 2nd c. B.C. 2. Hero of this book wealthy and prosperous ma whose patience and exemplary pie are tried by dire misfortunes, a who, in spite of his bitter lament tions, remains finally confident the goodness and justice of Go hence, a person exhibiting patien under misfortune.

job (jŏb) *n.* 1. Piece of wor esp. small definite one. 2. Pa position of employment. 3. An

hn the Baptist, painted here by
onardo da Vinci, was a cousin of
sus. He preached a mission of
entance in preparation for the immi-
nt coming of the Messiah and
tized his followers.

ng one has to do; (colloq.)
fficult task. 4. **bad, good, ~,**
d, good work, results, state of
airs, etc.; **~ lot,** miscellaneous
ods sold as a single lot; **odd ~s,**
scellaneous tasks; **on the ~,** at
rk, in the course of doing a piece
work; (slang) attentive; alert. 5.
action, organized protest, such
mass absence etc., by employees
rbidden by law to strike; **~ bank,**
mputerized data file to help place
employed workers in suitable
s; **job′holder,** person having a
gular job; **job printer,** printer
o specializes in miscellaneous
ms, such as letterheads, broad-
es, cards, etc.; **job shop,**
ployment agency that places
chnical specialists in short-term
signments under temporary con-
cts. **job** v. (**jobbed, job·bing**).
Do jobs; hire out for definite
ne or job. 2. Act as middleman,
olesaler, or jobber. **job′ber** n.
Person who purchases merchan-
se from manufacturer and sells to
ailers; wholesaler. 2. One who
es odd jobs or works by the job;
eceworker.

job·less (jŏb′lĭs) adj. Out of
rk. **job′less·ness** n.

Jo·cas·ta (jōkăs′ta). (Gk. legend)
aughter of Creon, king of
orinth; mother and wife of
EDIPUS.

jock (jŏk) n. 1. (colloq.) DISC
ckey. 2. (slang) Male athlete. 3.
ck′strap, support or protection
r male genitals, worn esp. by
hletes.

jock·ey (jŏk′ē) n. (pl. **-eys**).
ider in horse races; **~ cap,** cap
ith long peak, worn by jockeys.
ckey v. (**-eyed, -ey·ing**). Ride
horse) as its jockey; cheat, trick
nto, out of, etc.); **~ for position,**
aneuver for advantageous posi-
on (also fig.). [f. Sc. *Jock,* Jack]
jo·cose (jōkōs′) adj. Playful,
aggish. **jo·cos·i·ty** (jōkŏs′ĭtē) n.
joc·u·lar (jŏk′yuler) adj. Mirth-
l; humorous. **joc′u·lar·ly** adv.
c·u·lar·i·ty (jŏkyulăr′ĭtē) n.

joc·und (jŏk′und, jō′kund) adj.
erry, sprightly; pleasant. **joc′-
nd·ly** adv.

jodh·purs (jŏd′perz) n.pl.
iding breeches reaching to the
kle, full above and tight below
e knee. [f. *Jodhpur,* former state
f India]

Joe Mil·ler (jō′mĭl′er). Stale
ke, chestnut. [f. *Joe Miller's
sts,* a jest book (1739) by John
lottley; named after Joseph Miller
684-1738), comedian at Lon-
on's Drury Lane theater]

joe-pie (jō′pī′) **weed.** Any of

*Johannesburg in the Transvaal is the
largest city in South Africa. It is the
industrial center of the world's biggest
gold-mining district (Witwatersrand) and
a livestock and produce market.*

various tall N. Amer. plants
(*Eupatorium*) having whorled,
toothed leaves and flat-topped
clusters of small purplish, pinkish,
or occas. white, flowers.

jog¹ (jŏg) v. (**jogged, jog·ging**).
1. Shake with push or jerk; nudge
(person), esp. to arouse attention;
stimulate (memory). 2. Move up
and down with unsteady motion;

run at a slow steady trot, now esp.
as a regular form of exercise. **~**
n. Shake, push; nudge; slow, steady
trot. **jog′ger** n. (esp.) One who
jogs regularly for exercise.

jog² (jŏg) n. 1. Section of a line
or surface that juts out or recedes.
2. Sudden change of direction. **~**
v. (**jogged, jog·ging**). Turn or
bend abruptly.

jog·gle¹ (jŏg′el) v. (**-gled,
-gling**). Shake, move, (as) by
repeated jerks. **~** n. Slight shake.

jog·gle² (jŏg′el) n. Joint of two
pieces of stone or timber, contrived

to prevent their sliding on one another; notch in one piece, corresponding projection in the other, or small piece let in between both, for this purpose. ~ *v.t.* (**-gled, -gling**). Join by means of a joggle.

Jo·han·nes·burg (jōhăn´ĭsbērg, yōhah´nĭs-). Largest city of the Republic of South Africa.

John[1] (jŏn). Masculine proper name used in various combinations with various meanings, as ~ **Barleycorn**: see BARLEY; ~ **Bull** (from name of character representing English nation in John Arbuthnot's satire *Law is a Bottomless Pit*, 1712), personification of England, typical Englishman, represented as a stoutish red-faced farmerlike man in top hat and high boots; ~ **Doe**, name used in legal proceedings to designate an unidentified or fictitious person or any average man; ~ **Dory**, either of two fishes, *Zenopsis ocellata* or *Zeus faber* of the Atlantic, having a laterally flattened body and long dorsal spines; ~ **Hancock**, (colloq.) person's signature, see HANCOCK.

John[2] (jŏn). Name of 23 popes or antipopes, esp.: **John VIII**, pope 872–82; much involved in imperial politics; **John XXI**, pope 1276–7; identified with Petrus Hispanus, author of medical and philosophical works, and freq. referred to by chroniclers as a magician; **John XXII**, pope at Avignon, 1316–34; accused of heresy; **John XXIII**, antipope, 1410–15; **John XXIIL** (Angelo Giuseppe Roncalli, 1881–1963), pope 1958–63.

John[3] (jŏn) (1167–1216). King of England; called "John Lackland" because as youngest son of Henry II he had no royal lands to maintain him; succeeded his brother Richard Coeur de Lion, 1199; alienated barons and people by bad administration and heavy taxation; was forced by barons to sign MAGNA CARTA.

John[4] (jŏn). Name of six kings of Portugal including: **John I** "the Great," reigned 1385–1433; **John II** "the Perfect," reigned 1481–95; encouraged exploration of sea route to India; **John IV** "the Fortunate," reigned 1541–56; founder of Braganza dynasty; **John VI**, reigned 1816–26.

John[5] (jŏn), **St.** Name of various saints: **St. ~ the Baptist**, son of Elizabeth and Zacharias, a priest (Luke I); preached in the wilderness; forerunner of Jesus Christ; was executed by order of Herod Antipas; **St. ~ Chrysostom**: see CHRYSOSTOM; **St. ~ of the Cross** (1542–91), Spanish mystical poet and Carmelite friar; friend of St. Theresa; canonized 1726; **St. ~ the Evangelist**: see JOHN[6].

John[6] (jŏn), **St.** Apostle, called

Andrew Johnson was vice president when Abraham Lincoln was assassinated during the final months of the American Civil War. He became the 17th president of the U.S.A. His opponents tried to have him impeached.

St. ~ the Evangelist or **St. ~ the Divine**; son of Zebedee, a Galilean fisherman, and brother of James; credited (prob. erron.) with authorship of fourth Gospel and APOCALYPSE, and of three epistles of New Testament; commemorated Dec. 27; fourth Gospel; any of the three epistles attributed to St. John; **St. ~'s wort**, herb or shrub of genus *Hypericum*, with oval leaves and bright yellow flowers.

john (jŏn) *n.* (slang) 1. Lavatory. 2. Man patronizing prostitute.

john·ny (jŏn´ē) *n.* (pl. **-nies**). (slang) Short gown with short sleeves and tied in the back, used by hospital patients; **john'nycake**, corn cake baked on ashes of fire or fried in pan; cornmeal pancake; **johnny-jump-up**, small type of pansy grown esp. in rock gardens; **Johnny Reb**, (colloq.) Confederate soldier in the Civil War. [pet form of *John*]

John Paul (jŏn´pawl´). Name of two popes: **John Paul I** (Albino Luciani, 1912–78) pope Aug. 26–Sept. 28, 1978; **John Paul II** (Karol Wojtyla, 1920–) pope 1978– .

John·son[1] (jŏn´son), **Andrew** (1808–75). U.S. president, 1865–9; member of House of Representatives, 1843–53; Lincoln's vice president; became president after Lincoln's assassination; attempted to carry out Lincoln's Reconstruction policies after Civil War; Congress brought impeachment proceedings against him, 1868, for dismissing Secretary of War Edwin Stanton in defiance of the Tenure of Office Act, but he was acquitted by one vote.

John·son[2] (jŏn´son), **Lyndon Baines** (1908–73). U.S. politician; served in Congress 1937–61; 36th president of U.S., 1963–9; vice president 1961–3; succeeded to presidency on assassination of Kennedy, then elected to a full term; his administration was best known for his social welfare programs and the escalation of the Vietnam War.

John·son[3] (jŏn´son), **Richard Mentor** (1780–1850). U.S. vice president, 1837–41, under Martin Van Buren; only vice president elected by decision of the U.S. Senate, because no candidate received an electoral college majority.

John·son[4] (jŏn´son), (**"Dr."**)

...muel (1709–84). English man of ...ters and lexicographer; famous ...for his landmark *Dictionary of ...English Language*, 1755, and ...versation recorded in his friend ...nes Boswell's *Life of Samuel ...inson*; published a critical edition ...Shakespeare; wrote *Rasselas, ...ves of the Poets*, etc. **John·-ni·an** (jŏnsō′nēan) *adj.* Of ...muel Johnson; esp. of an English ...ose style abounding in words ...rived or made up from Latin, or ...aracterized by weighty and well-...anced sentences.

Jo·hore (johōr′, -hor′). State of ...alaysia at S. end of Malay ...ninsula; capital, Johore Bahru.

joie de viv·re (zhwah de vē′vre). ...refree enjoyment of life. [Fr.]

join (join) *v.* 1. Put together, ...ten, unite; connect (two points) ...a line; unite in marriage, ...endship, alliance, etc.; come ...gether, be united. 2. Take part ...th others (in); come into company ...(person); become member of ...lub etc.); take, resume, one's place ...(regiment, ship, company, etc.); ...**up**, enlist. 3. ~ **battle**, begin ...ghting; ~ **hands**, clasp each ...her's hands; (fig.) combine in ...tion or enterprise. **join** *n.* Joint, ...nction.

join·er (joi′ner) *n.* (esp.) 1. ...hiefly Brit.) Cabinetmaker; furni-...re maker. 2. (colloq.) One who ...ins many clubs, societies, etc.

joint[1] (joint) *n.* 1. Place at which ...vo things are joined together; ...ructure in animal body by which ...vo bones are fitted together; part ...stem from which leaf or branch ...ows; point at which, contrivance ...y which, two parts of artificial ...ructure are joined, rigidly or so as ...allow movement; (geol.) fracture ...rock, esp. one along which there ...as been little or no movement. 2. ...ne of the parts into which butcher ...ivides carcass, esp. large cut of ...eat as served at table. 3. (slang) ...heap or disreputable bar, res-...urant, etc.; (slang) marijuana ...igarette; **out of** ~, out of place or ...ne joint; dislocated; (fig.) dis-...rganized; disordered. **joint** *v.t.* ...Connect by joints. 2. Cut (meat) ...to joints.

joint[2] (joint) *adj.* Held or done ...y, belonging to, two or more ...ersons etc. in conjunction; (of ...ersons) sharing (*with* others in ...ossession, action, state, etc.). ...**oint′ly** *adv.*

joist (joist) *n.* One of parallel ...orizontal beams set from wall to ...vall for ceiling laths or floor-...oards to be nailed to.

joke (jōk) *n.* Thing said or done ...o excite laughter; amusing or ...idiculous thing, person, or circum-...tance; **practical** ~, trick played ...n person in order to have laugh ...t his expense. **joke** *v.i.* (**joked**,

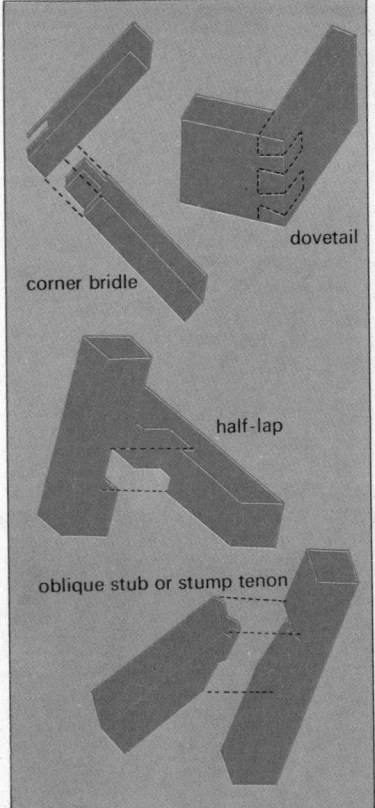

*Wooden **joints** form an essential part of standard furniture, window frames and paneled doors. There are different types of joints but all must have the qualities of strength and rigidity.*

corner bridle
dovetail
half-lap
oblique stub or stump tenon

jok·ing). Make jokes, banter. **jok′ing·ly** *adv.*

jok·er (jō′ker) *n.* 1. One who jokes; (slang) fellow. 2. (cards) Extra card, often with picture of jester, counting in some games (e.g. euchre) as a trump, in others (e.g. certain forms of poker) as any card the holder chooses to make it. 3. Clause unobtrusively inserted in legislation and affecting its opera-tion in some way not immediately apparent; unseen difficulty.

Jo·li·et, Jol·li·et (jō′lēĕt, jōlēĕt′), **Louis** (1645–1700). French-Canadian who, with MARQUETTE, explored Mississippi River as far S. as Arkansas and returned via Illinois River to Lake Michigan; also explored Gulf of St. Lawrence, and the Hudson Bay area.

Jo·liot-Cu·rie (zhawlyō′ küre′), **Frédéric** (orig. name **Joliot**) (1900–58) and **Irene** (1897–1956). French husband and wife physicists who discovered a synthesis of new radioactive elements; jointly awarded Nobel Prize for chemistry, 1935; wife was daughter of Pierre and Marie Curie.

jol·li·ty (jŏl′ĭtē) *n.* (pl. **-ties**). Merrymaking, gaiety.

jol·ly (jŏl′ē) *adj.* (**-li·er, -li·est**). Joyful; festive, jovial; (Brit. colloq.)

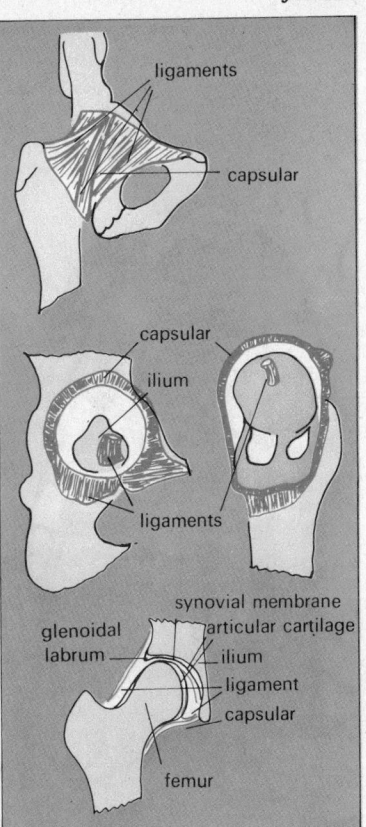

*The **hip-joint** works as a ball-and-socket joint, and has strong muscles and ligaments supporting it. Disorders affecting the joints of the body are mainly various forms of arthritis and dis-location.*

ligaments
capsular
capsular
ilium
ligaments
synovial membrane
glenoidal labrum
articular cartilage
ilium
ligament
capsular
femur

very pleasant, delightful. ~ *adv.* (Brit. colloq.) 1. (with adjective or adverb) Very. 2. ~ **well**: used with verb to give emphasis. **jolly** *v.t.* (**-lied, -ly·ing**). Talk or behave agreeably to (person) in order to put or keep him in good humor. **jol′li·ly** *adv.* **jol′li·ness** *n.*

jolt (jōlt) *v.* Jar, knock, jostle, as with a blow or shove; bump into; (of vehicle) move along in a jerky or bumpy way. ~ *n.* Sudden jerk or jar, as from a blow; surprise, shock. **jolt′y** *adv.*

Jo·nah (jō′na). 1. Hebrew minor prophet; book of Old Testament bearing his name, acc. to which he fled when bidden by God to go to Nineveh and prophesy; God then sent a storm to wreck his ship, and the seamen, holding him respon-sible, threw him overboard; he was swallowed by a great fish and lived in its belly for three days before being cast out on dry land. 2. Person regarded as bringing bad luck to others.

Jon·a·than (jŏn′athan). Eldest son of King Saul and friend of David, killed at battle of Mount Gilboa 1 Sam. 13 etc.).

jon·a·than (jŏn′athan) *n.* Variety of red late-ripening apple.

Jones[1] (jōnz), **Anson** (1798–

1858). President of the Republic of Texas, 1844–6.

Jones² (jōnz), **John Paul** (orig. name, John Paul) (1747–92). Scottish-born Amer. naval commander; when asked to surrender during the Revolutionary War battle between the British warship "Serapis" and the "Bonhomme Richard," Sept., 1779, Jones's famous reply was, "I have not yet begun to fight!"

jon·gleur (zhawṅglör´) *n.* (pl. **-gleurs** pr. -glör´). (hist.) Wandering minstrel in medieval France and England. [Fr.]

jon·quil (jŏng´kwĭl, jŏn´-) *n.* Species of narcissus (*N. jonquilla*) with long linear leaves and clusters of fragrant white and yellow flowers.

Jon·son (jŏn´sŏn), **Ben(jamin)** (1574–1637). English poet and dramatist; author of the plays *Every Man in his Humour*, *Every Man out of his Humour*, *Volpone*, etc., and of

Jordan's stability has been severely tested for 20 years and owes much to the skill and courage of its ruler, King Hussein. Over one third of its Arab population are Palestinian refugees. 1. Arab legionnaires. 2. The ancient forum at Jerash, built in an elliptical shape. 3. Map and flag of Jordan.

song "Drink to Me Only with Thine Eyes." **Jon·so·ni·an** (jŏn-sō´nēan) *adj.*

Jor·dan (jôr´dan). 1. River flowing 200 mi. (322 km) southward from N. Israel through Sea of Galilee and into Dead Sea. 2. Short for **Hashemite Kingdom of the ~**, Arab nation east of the river Jordan, bordered by Israel, Syria, Iraq, and Saudi Arabia; capital, Amman. **Jor·da·ni·an** (jôrdā´nēan) *adj. & n.*

Jo·seph¹ (jō´zef, -sef). Name of several persons in the Bible, esp.: 1. Son of Jacob and Rachel; sold by his brothers into captivity in Egypt, where he attained high office (Gen.

30–50). 2. Carpenter of Nazareth husband of MARY¹. 3. ~ o **Arimathea**, Jew who buried Jesu Christ in a rock-hewn tomb; he wa the subject of many legends, on being that he afterward led mission to England and built th Christian church in England.

Jo·seph² (jō´zef, -sef). Name o two Holy Roman emperors: **Joseph I** (1678–1711), reigned 1705–11 **Joseph II** (1741–90), eldest son o Maria Theresa, reigned 1765–90.

Jo·se·phine (jō´zefēn, -se-) Marie Rose Joséphine Tascher de l Pagerie (1763–1814), a Creole o Martinique; wife of Vicomte Alexander Beauharnais (guillotinec in 1794) and subsequently (1796) o Napoleon Bonaparte; empress o the French from 1804 unti Napoleon divorced her "for reason of state" in 1809.

josh (jŏsh) *v.* (colloq.) Poke fu at in good-natured way. **josh'er** *n* **Josh.** *abbrev.* Joshua (Old Testament).

Josh·u·a (jŏsh'ōōa). Successor of Moses in leadership of Israel; 6th book of Old Testament telling how he conquered the land of Canaan; ~ **tree**, treelike plant (*Yucca brevifolia*) of southwestern U.S., having branches that are like outstretched arms, daggerlike leaves, and pale greenish-white blossoms.

Jo·si·ah (jōsī'a), **Jo·si·as** (jōsī'as) (647–c608 B.C.). King of Judah; carried out complete religious reform based on a book of law (app. Deuteronomy) found in the Temple.

joss (jŏs, jaws) *n.* Chinese idol; ~ **house**, Chinese temple or shrine containing idols; ~ **stick**, stick of incense for burning before a joss. [app. f. Port. *deos* f. L. *deus* god]

jos·tle (jŏs'el) *v.* (**-tled, -tling**). Knock or push (*against* etc.); elbow; vie with for an advantage. ~ *n.* Jostling.

jot[1] (jŏt) *n.* Small amount, whit. [Gk. *iota*, letter i, smallest in alphabet]

jot[2] (jŏt) *v.t.* (**jot·ted, jot·ting**). Write (*down*) briefly or hastily. **jot'ter** *n.*

jot·ting (jŏt'ĭng) *n.* Hastily written note.

joule (jōol) *n.* (phys.) Unit of work or energy in meter-kilogram-second (MKS) system, amount of work done or heat generated by a force of 1 newton acting over a distance of 1 meter (abbrev. J); energy of 1 watt acting for 1 second. [f. JOULE]

Joule (jōol), **James Prescott** (1818–89). English physicist who established the universal constant of proportionality between mechanical work and heat.

jounce (jowns) *v.* (**jounced,**

jounc·ing). Bump, bounce, jolt. ~ *n.* Jouncing motion. **jounc'y** *adj.*

jour·nal (jer'nal) *n.* 1. (in bookkeeping by double entry) Book in which each transaction is entered, with statement of accounts to which it is to be debited and credited. 2. Diary; record of daily transactions of public body or association; (naut.) ship's log; newspaper, other periodical. 3. Part of shaft or axle that rests on bearings; ~ **box**, box enclosing journal or bearings.

jour·nal·ese (jer'nalēz', -lēs') *n.* Slick, superficial style of writing or new word formation characteristic of some newspapers and magazines.

jour·nal·ist (jer'nalĭst) *n.* One who edits or esp. writes for a newspaper or magazine. **jour'nal·ism** *n.* **jour·nal·is·tic** (jernalĭs'tĭk) *adj.* **jour·nal·is'tic·al·ly** *adv.*

jour·ney (jer'nē) *n.* (pl. **-neys**) & *v.i.* (**-neyed, -ney·ing**). Travel from one place to another, esp. by land or air (dist. from *voyage*); (make) expedition to some distance.

jour·ney·man (jer'nēman) *n.* (pl. **-men**). Qualified artisan or workman who works for another (orig. after having completed his apprenticeship in a craft or trade).

joust (jowst, jŭst, jōost), **just**[1] (jŭst, jōost) *vbs.i.* & *ns.* (Engage in) combat between two knights etc. on horseback with lances; (fig.) any combat. **joust'er** *n.*

Jove (jōv). (Rom. myth.) = JUPITER.

jo·vi·al (jō'vēal) *adj.* Merry;

The Joshua Tree National Monument in southern California is noted for its desert plants, amongst which is the Mojave yucca, seen in the foreground of the picture.

convivial. **jo'vi·al·ly** *adv.* **jo·vi·al·i·ty** (jōvĕăl'ĭtē) *n.* [L. *jovialis* of Jupiter]

jowl (jowl) *n.* Flesh under the lower jaw, esp. when prominent; dewlap or wattle. **jowl'y** *adj.*

joy (joi) *n.* Vivid emotion of pleasure, gladness; thing that causes delight; ~ **ride**, (slang) pleasure ride in a car driven carelessly and usu. without permission of the owner (hence ~ **rider**, ~ **rid·ing**); **joy'stick**, (slang) control lever of airplane. **joy'ful** *adj.* **joy'ful·ly** *adv.* **joy'ful·ness** *n.* **joy'less** *adj.* **joy'less·ly** *adv.* **joy'less·ness** *n.* **joy·ous** (joi'us) *adj.* **joy'ous·ly** *adv.* **joy'ous·ness** *n.*

Joyce (jois), **James** (1882–1941). Irish novelist and short-story writer; best known for his novels *Ulysses* (1922) and *Finnegans Wake* (1939), written in a highly allusive style employing the stream-of-consciousness technique.

JP *abbrev.* Jet propulsion.
J.P. *abbrev.* Justice of the Peace.
Jr., jr. *abbrevs.* Junior.

Juan de Fu·ca (jōo'an de fū'ka; *Sp.* hwahn' dĕ fōō'kah) **Strait.** Inlet of the Pacific Ocean extending 100 mi. (161 km), between Vancouver Island, Canada and NW. Washington.

Ju·an Fer·nan·dez (jōo'an fernăn'dĕz; *Sp.* hwahn' fĕrnahn'dĕth). Group of 3 volcanic islands in S. Pacific, 400 mi. (644 km) off coast of Chile, to which they belong; discovered 1563 by a Spanish pilot, Juan Fernandez.

Juá·rez[1] (wär'ĕz; *Sp.* hwah'rĕs). City in N. Mexico opposite El Paso, Texas, on the Rio Grande.

Juá·rez[2] (wär'ĕz; *Sp.* hwah'rĕs), **Benito Pablo** (1806–72). Mexican statesman and reform leader; president of Mexico, 1857–72.

Ju·ba (jōō´bah). River in E. Africa flowing S. 1,000 mi. (1,609 km) from S. central Ethiopia to the Indian Ocean.

ju·bi·late (jōō´bilāt) *v.i.* (**-lat·ed, -lat·ing**). Exult, make demonstrations of joy. **ju·bi·lance** (jōō´bilans), **ju·bi·la·tion** (jōōbilā´shon) *ns.* **ju´bi·lant** *adj.* **ju´bi·lant·ly** *adv.*

ju·bi·lee (jōō´bilē, jōōbilē´) *n.* 1. (Jewish hist.) Year of emancipation and restoration, kept every 50 years, according to Lev. 25; (R.C. Ch.) year during which plenary indulgence may be obtained by performing certain pious acts, granted formerly at various intervals, now at any time. 2. Fiftieth anniversary as occasion for rejoicing (also **golden ~**); **silver ~**, (celebration of) 25th anniversary, **diamond ~**, of 60th. 3. Any season or occasion of celebration or rejoicing. [Heb. *yobel* ram, ram's horn trumpet, jubilee]

Ju·dae·a: see JUDEA.

Ju·dah (jōō´da). 1. Hebrew patriarch, son of Jacob and Leah (Gen. 29); powerful tribe of Israel, traditionally descended from him. 2. Southern kingdom of the Hebrews (opp. ISRAEL[1], def. 3) established by this tribe and the tribe of Benjamin.

Ju·da·ic (jōōdā´ĭk) *adj.* Of Judaism or Jews.

Ju·da·i·ca (jōōdā´ĭka) *n.pl.* Things pertaining to Jews or their religion, esp. books about Jewish history and culture.

Ju·da·ism (jōō´dēĭzem, -dā-) *n.* 1. Monotheistic religion of the Jews, based on Mosaic precepts and rabbinic teaching, with traditions, laws, and moral principles from the Old Testament and the Talmud. 2. (Conformity to) traditional ceremonies, rites, and way of life of the

*The diamond **jubilee** of Queen Victoria's reign in 1897 was celebrated with universal enthusiasm. Her reign had seen rapid industrialization and a vast increase in the wealth of Britain.*

Jews. **Ju·da·ize** (jōō´dēīz, -dā-) *v.* (**-ized, -iz·ing**). Follow Jewish customs or rites; make Jewish.

Ju·das[1] (jōō´das). (also **~ Iscariot**) Apostle who betrayed Jesus Christ for 30 pieces of silver and afterward (acc. to Matt. 27) repented and hanged himself; hence, betrayer, traitor; **~ kiss**, act of betrayal (from kiss which Judas gave to Jesus as a signal to his captors); **~ tree**, (from legend that Judas hanged himself on tree of this kind) leguminous S. European and Asiatic tree (*Cercis siliquastrum*), with abundant purplish-pink flowers appearing in spring before the leaves; any tree of genus *Cercis*, esp. redbud.

Ju·das[2] (jōōdas). St. JUDE.

Ju·das Mac·ca·bae·us (jōō´das măkabē´us): see MACCABEES.

Jude (jōōd), **St.** One of the 12 Apostles, also called Judas (Luke 6, John 14); usu. identified with Jude the brother of James (Jude I); martyred in Persia with St. Simon; commemorated with St. Simon, Oct. 28; **(Epistle of) ~**, last epistle of New Testament, traditionally ascribed to St. Jude.

Ju·de·a, Ju·dae·a (jōōdē´a). Name in Greco-Roman times for S. part of ancient Palestine W. of the Jordan.

Judg. *abbrev.* Judges (Old Testament).

judge (jŭj) *n.* 1. Public official who hears and tries cases in court of justice; person appointed to decide dispute or contest; person who decides a question; person who is qualified to decide on merits of thing or question; **J~ Advocate**

General (pl. **J~ Advocates General, J~ Advocate Generals**) major general serving as senior legal officer in the U.S. Army or Air Force. 2. Officer having temporary authority in Israel in period between Joshua and the kings; **(Book of) Judges**, seventh book of Old Testament, containing history of this period. **judge** *v.* (**judged, judg·ing**). Pronounce sentence on (person) in court of justice; try (cause); decide (question); decide, decree; form a judgment (*of*). **judge´ship** *n.*

judg·ment, judge·ment (jŭj´ment) *ns.* 1. Sentence of court of justice; misfortune viewed as sign of divine displeasure; **Last J~**, final judgment by God of all mankind; **J~ Day**, day of Last Judgment. 2. Criticism; opinion, estimate; critical faculty, discernment; good sense. **judg·men´tal** *adj.*

ju·di·ca·ture (jōō´dikachoor, -kācher) *n.* Administration of justice; function, authority, jurisdiction of a judge or court; body of judges; court of justice.

ju·di·cial (jōōdĭsh´al) *adj.* Of, done by, proper to, a court of law; having the function of judgment; of, proper to, a judge; expressing a judgment; impartial. **ju·di´cial·ly** *adv.*

ju·di·ci·ar·y (jōōdĭsh´ēĕrē, -dĭsh´erē) *n.* (pl. **-ar·ies**). Judges collectively; court system; the judicial branch of government. **~** *adj.* Of or pertaining to the judicial branch, court system, or judges.

ju·di·cious (jōōdĭsh´us) *adj.* Sensible, prudent; sound in discernment. **ju·di´cious·ly** *adv.* **ju·di´cious·ness** *n.*

ju·do (jōō´dō) *n.* Modern form of JUJITSU. **ju·do·ka** (jōōdōkah´) (pl. **-kas, -ka**), **ju´do·ist** *ns.* Judo performer. [Jap. *jiu dō*, f. Chin. *jiu tao* soft way]

Ju·dy (jōō'dē). Wife of PUNCH "Punch and Judy." [dim. of Judith]

jug (jŭg) n. Deep vessel for holding liquids, with handle and su. spout; (slang) prison. ~ v.t. (**ugged, jug·ging**). Stew (hare, rabbit) in jug or jar (usu. in past part.); (slang) imprison. **jug'ful** n. (pl. **-fuls**).

Jug·ger·naut (jŭg'ernawt). (also **Jagannath**) Idol of Krishna at Puri, Orissa, annually dragged in procession in an enormous car under whose wheels devotees are said to have thrown themselves; hence (also **j~**; fig.) institution, notion, to which persons blindly sacrifice themselves or others; large overpowering force, object, etc.

jug·gle (jŭg'el) v. (**-gled, -gling**). Perform feats of dexterity (with objects tossed up); play juggling tricks with; manipulate, change the relative position of; engage in trickery with intent to cheat or deceive. **jug·gler** (jŭg'ler), **jug'gler·y** ns. (pl. **-gler·ies**).

Ju·go·slav (yōō'gōslahv), **Ju·go·sla·vi·a** (yōōgōslah'vēa): see YUGOSLAV(IA).

jug·u·lar (jŭg'yuler, jōō'gyu-) adj. Of the neck or throat; ~ **vein**, any of four great veins at sides of neck, an external pair conveying blood from superficial parts of head and an internal pair from inside of skull. ~ n. Jugular vein.

juice (jōōs) n. Liquid part of vegetable or fruit; fluid part of animal body or substance; (fig.) essence, spirit, of anything; (slang) electricity, electric current.

juic·y (jōō'sē) adj. (**juic·i·er, juic·i·est**). Full of juice, succulent; (colloq.) of rich intellectual quality, interesting. **juic'i·ness** n. **juic'i·ly** adv.

ju·jit·su, ju·jut·su, (jiu·jit·soo, jiu·jut·soo, jōōjit'sōō) ns. Japanese system of self-defense characterized by special holds or maneuvers that turn an opponent's strength and weight against him. [Jap. jūjutsu, f. Chin. jiu shu(t) soft art]

ju·ju (jōō'jōō) n. (W. Afr.) Charm or fetish; supernatural power attributed to this.

ju·jube (jōō'jōōb) n. Edible acid berrylike drupe of certain plants; thorny plant (Zizyphus) of S. Europe and Asia bearing this; fruit-flavored firm candy with such a berrylike shape.

juke·box, juke box (jōōk'bŏks) ns. Machine that automatically plays selected records when a coin is inserted.

Jul. abbrev. July.

ju·lep (jōō'lep) n. (hist.) Sweet syrupy drink, esp. as vehicle for medicine; tall drink (esp. **mint ~**) of liquor, sugar, ice, and flavoring. [Pers. gulāb (gul rose, āb water)]

Ju·lian¹ (jōōl'yan) (332–63).

Flavius Claudius Julianus, Roman emperor 361–3; called Julian the Apostate because, though brought up as a Christian, he reverted to the worship of the old gods and became an opponent of Christianity.

Jul·ian² (jōōl'yan) adj. Of Julius Caesar; ~ **calendar**, reformed calendar introduced by him in 46 B.C. and slightly modified under Augustus, in which ordinary year has 365 days, and every fourth year is a leap year of 366 days (see also GREGORIAN).

ju·li·enne (jōōlēĕn', zhōō-) adj. Cut into long thin strips (esp. vegetables). ~ n. Soup or consomme containing julienne vegetables.

Jul·ius (jōōl'yus). Name of three popes: **Julius I**, St., pope 337–52; **Julius II** (Giuliano della Rovere, 1433–1513), pope 1503–13, statesman and patron of Michelangelo, Raphael, etc.; carried out many reforms; **Julius III** (Giovanni Maria del Monte, 1487–1555), pope 1550–5.

Jul·ius Cae·sar (jōōl'yus sē'zer). Gaius Julius Caesar (prob. 101–44 B.C.), Roman general and statesman; formed 1ST TRIUMVIRATE, 59 B.C.; conducted the Gallic Wars from 58 to 49 B.C. and invaded Britain 55 and 54 B.C.; crossed the RUBICON in defiance of the Senate in 49 B.C., and defeated Pompey in civil war, becoming dictator; was murdered on the Ides of March 44 B.C. by a group of nobles.

Ju·ly (jōōlī', ju-) (pl. **-lies**). Seventh month of Gregorian (fifth of Julian) calendar, with 31 days; ~ **monarchy**, (Fr. hist.) that of Louis Philippe; ~ **revolution**, (Fr. hist.) revolution in July 1830 against Charles X, who fled into exile and was succeeded by Louis Philippe. [f. Julius Caesar]

jum·ble (jŭm'bel) v. (**-bled, -bling**). Move about in disorder; mix up, confuse. ~ n. Confused assemblage; muddle.

jum·bo (jŭm'bō) n. (pl. **-bos**). Big clumsy person, animal, or thing. ~ adj. Larger than average, oversized; ~ **jet**, large jet passenger aircraft wide enough to have two aisles. [after Jumbo, a large elephant exhibited by P. T. Barnum after 1882 and a feature of his circus]

jump (jŭmp) n. Leap, bound, spring from ground; start caused by shock or excitement; abrupt rise in amount, price, value, etc.; sudden transition, gap in series, argument, etc.; **get (have) the ~ on**, (slang) get (have) an advantage at the beginning; ~ **rope**, length of rope with handle at each end, swung over head and under feet during jumping as game or exercise; ~ **suit**, one-piece garment for whole body, orig. worn by paratroops. **jump** v. 1. Spring from ground etc. by flexion and sudden muscular extension of legs or (of fish) tail; move suddenly with leap or bound; start with sudden jerk from excitement, shock, etc.; rise suddenly in price, etc.; come to arrive at (conclusion) hastily; (slang) be very lively; (slang) depart abruptly, esp. without permission; **jump at**, accept (offer, bargain) eagerly; **jump on**, attack (offender etc.) crushingly with word or act. 2. Leap over; (of moving train) leave the rails; pass one piece over another in checkers etc., capturing it. 3. Pounce upon (thing); take summary possession of (claim abandoned or forfeited by former occupant);

Julius Caesar's excessive powers and almost regal honors led to the conspiracy of Brutus and Cassius who assassinated him in the Senate in 44 B.C. He was ancient Rome's outstanding statesman and general.

jump bail, flee while free on bail; **jumping-off place**, starting point; **jump the gun**, make premature start. **jump'a·ble** *adj.* **jump'ing·ly** *adv.* **jump'y** *adj.* (**jump·i·er, jump·i·est**). (esp.) In a state of nervous excitement. **jump'i·ness** *n.*

jump·er¹ (jŭm′per) *n.* 1. Person, animal, or thing that jumps. 2. Person who jumps from airplane with parachute. 3. (elect.) Short wire used to make or break a circuit.

jump·er² (jŭm′per) *n.* Loose outer jacket or protective garment; sleeveless dress worn over a blouse or sweater; child's garment of pants and attached biblike bodice.

Jun., jun. *abbrevs.* June; junior. **junc.** *abbrev.* Junction.

jun·co (jŭng′kō) *n.* (pl. **-cos**). Any of several N. and Central Amer. finches of the genus *Junco*, having black or slate-gray head and white tail feathers.

junc·tion (jŭngk′shon) *n.* Joining; joint, meeting place; esp. place, station, where railroad lines meet and unite. **junc'tion·al** *adj.*

junc·ture (jŭngk′cher) *n.* Joining; place where things join; concurrence of events, state of affairs.

June (jōōn). Sixth month of Gregorian (fourth of Julian) calendar, with 30 days; ~ **beetle**, ~ **bug**, any of various large beetles of genus *Phyllophaga* appearing in late spring; **June'berry**: see SHADbush. [L. prob. orig. f. goddess *Juno*]

Ju·neau (jōō′nō). Port and capital of Alaska in the SE. part near British Columbia, Canada.

Jung (yŏŏng), **Carl Gustav** (1875–1961). Swiss psychologist; orig. a follower of Freud; later founded school of analytical psychology, differing from psychoanalysis in its use of the concepts of unconscious and libido and in its advocacy of a complex classification of types of personality. **Jung'i·an** (yŏŏng′ēan) *adj.*

Jung·frau (yŏŏng′frow). Mountain in Swiss Alps 13,642 ft. (4,158 m). [Ger., = "maiden"]

jun·gle (jŭng′gel) *n.* Land overgrown with tropical vegetation and trees; wild tangled mass; ~ **fever**, severe form of malarial fever. [Hind. *jangal* desert, forest]

jun·ior (jōōn′yer) *adj.* Younger (esp. of son having same name as father); of less standing, of lower position; (in high schools and colleges) belonging to year below senior; ~ **college**, school offering two-year course esp. in preparation for completion at senior college; ~ **high school**, school generally including grades 7, 8, and 9; ~ **miss**: see MISS²; ~ **varsity**, athletic team whose members did not qualify for varsity. **junior** *n.* Junior person; (used as form of

The **junk**, *a classic Chinese sailing vessel of ancient but unknown origin, is still in wide use. Its square sails of linen or matting can be spread or closed like a Venetian blind.*

address to) male child.

ju·ni·per (jōō′niper) *n.* Evergreen shrub of genus *Juniperus*, with prickly leaves and aromatic dark purplish berries of pungent taste.

junk¹ (jŭngk) *n.* 1. (hist.) Old cable cut up for oakum etc. 2. Discarded material, worthless rubbish. 3. (naut.) Hard salt meat. 4. (slang) Narcotic drug, esp. heroin; ~ **food**, food having low nutritive value and usually high caloric count; ~ **mail**, unsolicited advertising matter sent by postal service. **junk** *v.* (colloq.) Discard as rubbish.

junk² (jŭngk) *n.* Flat-bottomed sailing vessel of China seas, with square prow, prominent stem, and lugsails. [app. f. Javanese *djong*]

Jun·ker (yŏŏng′ker) *n.* (hist.) Young German noble; ultrareactionary, overbearing member of Prussian aristocracy.

Jun·kers (yŏŏng′kerz), **Hugo** (1859–1935). German aircraft designer and engineer; built the first all-metal airplane.

jun·ket (jŭng′kĭt) *n.* Dish of sweetened and flavored curds; feast, outing; trip taken by public official on public funds. ~ *v.i.* Feast, go on a junket. **jun·ke·teer** (jŭngketēr′), **jun·ke·ter** *ns.*

junk·ie, junk·y (jŭng′kē) *ns.* (pl junk·ies). (slang) Drug addict.

Ju·no (jōō′nō). 1. (Rom. myth. Chief Roman goddess, wife an sister of Jupiter; worshipped esp by women; identified with HERA 2. (astron.) One of the asteroids **Ju·no·esque** (jōōnōĕsk′) *adj.* Re sembling Juno in stately beauty.

jun·ta (hōōn′ta, hŏŏn′-, jŭn′-hŭn′-), **jun·to** (jŭn′tō) *ns.* (pl. **-tos**) Deliberative or administrative council in Spain or Italy; clique faction, political or other combina tion of persons; group of military officers ruling a country after a coup d'etat.

Ju·pi·ter (jōō′piter). 1. (Rom myth.) Orig. a sky spirit, associated with lightning and thunderbolts later, the chief of the gods, giver of victory, patron of the Roman state, identified with ZEUS. 2 (astron.) Largest planet in solar system, the fifth from the sun revolving in orbit between those of Mars and Saturn, and with four large and several smaller satellites its diameter is approx. 86,000 mi. (138,400 km), its mass over 300 times that of Earth, and its period of revolution around the sun 11.86 years.

Ju·ra (joor′a; *Fr.* zhürä′). System of mountain ranges between rivers Rhine and Rhone forming the frontier between France and Switzerland.

Ju·ras·sic (jōōrăs′ĭk) *adj. & n.* (geol.) (Of) the middle period or

stem of the Mesozoic, between
e Cretaceous and the Triassic
35- to 180-million years ago),
en dinosaurs and the earliest
mmals existed. [f. JURA]

ju·rid·i·cal (jŏŏrĭd´ĭkal), **ju·**
d·ic (jŏŏrĭd´ĭk) *adjs.* Of judicial
oceedings; legal. **ju·rid´i·cal·ly**
v.

ju·ris·dic·tion (jŏŏrĭsdĭk´shon)
Administration of justice; legal
other authority; extent of this,
ritory it extends over. **ju·ris·**
c´tion·al *adj.*

ju·ris·pru·dence (jŏŏrĭsprōō´-
ns) *n.* Science, philosophy, of
v; skill in law. **ju·ris·pru´dent,**
·ris·pru·den·tial (jŏŏrĭs-
ōŏdĕn´shal) *adjs.*

ju·rist (jŏŏr´ĭst) *n.* One versed in
v, esp. an eminent judge or
vyer. **ju·ris·tic** (jŏŏrĭs´tĭk),
·ris´ti·cal *adjs.* Of jurist(s); legal,
ated by law. **ju·ris´ti·cal·ly** *adv.*

ju·ror (jŏŏr´er) *n.* Member of
y.

ju·ry (jŏŏr´ē) *n.* (pl. **-ries**). 1.
dy of persons sworn to render
rdict on question submitted to
em in court of justice; **coroner's**
, jury of persons who pronounce
cision at coroner's inquest;
and ~, jury convened to evalu-
: accusations against person(s)

The Supreme Court building in Washington D.C. The court was formed in 1787 to act in cases involving interpretation of the Constitution and thus represents the apogee of **justice**.

Composed almost entirely of gas **Jupiter** has a mean diameter of 88,700 miles and orbits the sun at a mean distance of 483,310,000 miles. Here, a probe approaches Jupiter's surface.

charged with a crime to determine
whether the evidence warrants an
indictment; ~ **box**, enclosure for
jury in court; **ju′ryman, ju′ry-
woman**, (pl. **-men, -wom·en**)
member of jury; juror. 2. Body of
persons judging competition etc.

just[1]: see JOUST.

just[2] (jŭst) *adj.* Equitable, fair;
deserved; well-grounded; right in
amount etc., proper. **just′ly** *adv.*
just′ness *n.*

just[3] (jŭst) *adv.* Exactly; barely;
merely; exactly at that moment;
(colloq.) positively, quite; ~ **now**,
at this moment; a little time ago.

jus·tice (jŭs′tĭs) *n.* 1. Just
conduct; fairness; exercise of
authority in maintenance of right;
judicial proceedings; **poetic** ~,
ideal justice as shown in poetry or
fiction; **do** ~ **to**, treat fairly; show
due appreciation of; **do oneself** ~,
perform worthily of one's abilities.
2. Judge, esp. of Supreme Court;
Justice of the Peace, (abbrev.
J.P.) local magistrate having
authority in limited area to hear
minor cases, send others to higher
courts, administer oaths, perform
marriages, etc.

jus·ti·ci·a·ble (jŭstĭsh′ēabel)
adj. Subject to trial or court
decision.

jus·ti·ci·ar·y (jŭstĭsh′ēĕrē,

-yerē) *adj.* Of the administration of
justice.

jus·ti·fy (jŭs′tĭfī) *v.t.* (**-fied,
-fy·ing**). 1. Show the justice or
rightness of; vindicate, be such as to

The bark of the **jute** is processed f
fiber which is made into textiles
cordage. The fibers may reach 10
length and are separated by soa
Jute is grown commercially chief
Bengal in India and Bangladesh.

justify; make good (statement e
adduce adequate grounds for.
(theol.) Declare (person) free f
guilt; absolve. 3. (print.) Ad
(line of type) to fill a space ne
jus·ti·fi·a·ble (jŭs′tĭfīabel, jŭ
fī′-), **jus·ti·fi·ca·to·ry** (jŭstĭf′
tōrē, -tōrē, jŭs′tĭfikāterē) *
jus·ti·fi·a·bly *adv.*   **jus·ti·fi·
tion** (jŭstĭfīkā′shon) *n.*

Jus·tin·i·an (jŭstĭn′ēan).
of two Eastern Roman emper
Justinian I (483–565), called "
Great," emperor 527–65; reorg
ized and codified Roman law
Code); built church of St. So
at Constantinople; his gen
Belisarius recovered Africa fr
Vandals, occupied Rome, and o
threw the Gothic kingdom in I
Justinian II (669–711), emp
685–95 and 704–11.

jut (jŭt) *n.* Projection;
truding point. ~ *v.i.* (**jut·
jut′ting**). Stick out; protr
project. **jut′ting·ly** *adv.*

Jute (jōōt) *n.* Member of a
German tribe that invaded Bri
in 5th c. and settled in Kent,
Isle of Wight, etc. [Icel.
people of Jutland]

jute (jōōt) *n.* Fiber from bar
Asian plants (*Corchorus ca
laris* and *C. olitorius*), used
cordage, canvas, etc.; these pla
[Sansk. *juṭa, jaṭa* braid of hair]

Jut·land (jŭt′land). Penin
that forms the continental par
Denmark and Schleswig-Hols
in West Germany.

juv. *abbrev.* Juvenile.

Ju·ve·nal (jōō′venal). Deci
Junius Juvenalis (c60–c130 A
Roman satirist and poet.

ju·ven·ile (jōō′venil, -nīl)
Young, youthful; suited to, cha
teristic of, youth; ~ **delinquer**
criminal or antisocial actions
children or adolescents (~ **de
quents**); ~ **lead**, (theatr.) yout
hero's part in play; actor who t
this. **juvenile** *n.* 1. Young per
2. Book for children. **ju·ve·**
i·ty (jōōvenĭl′ītē) *n.* (pl. **-ties**)

ju·ve·nil·i·a (jōōvenĭl′ēa, -
ya) *n.pl.* Literary or artistic w
produced in youth.

jux·ta·pose (jŭkstapōz′, j
stapōz′) *v.t.* (**-posed, -pos·i**
Place (things) side by side. **jux·**
po·si·tion (jŭkstapozĭsh′on)
Placing, being placed, side by s

JV, J.V. *abbrevs.* Junior var

Map shows the disposition of
opposing British and German
forces during the crucial **Battl**
Jutland in 1916. Despite heavy los
the British Grand Fleet under Ad
Jellicoe remained dominant.

The letter **K, k** an aspirate glottal sound, was adopted by the Greeks from the Syriac 'kaf'. The Greeks called the letter 'kappa', meaning the hollow of the hand and perhaps for this reason placed it after the letter that means 'hand'. In classical Latin, K was used only as an abbreviation because its pronunciation was the same as the letter C.

Phoenician   Cretan   Early Greek

Early Etruscan   Early Latin   Classical Latin

, k (kā) (pl. **K's, k's** or **Ks, ks**). ...venth letter of modern English ...abet, taken from Gk. κ (*kappa*), . **Χ**, from Phoenician and ...eral Semitic **Χ** (*Kaph*); pro- ...nced in modern English as a ...eless stop consonant.

. *abbrev.* Kelvin; kindergarten; ...m.) potassium; (chess) king.

. *abbrev.* Köchel.

. *abbrev.* Karat; kilogram(s); ...ss) king.

.**2.** Peak of the W. Himalayas, ...ı m (28,250 ft.) high, second ...est in the world; also known as ...lwin Austen.

aa·ba, Caa·ba (kah′ba) *ns.* ...red building at Mecca, Muslim ...y of Holies containing sacred ...k stone.

a·bob = KEBAB.

a·bu·ki (kahbōō′kē, -ka-) *n.* ...ditional popular Japanese ...ma with highly stylized song etc. ...d by males only.

a·bul (kah′bōōl). Capital of ...hanistan in the E. central part; **River**, chief river of Afghanistan ...ng W. of Kabul and flowing 360 ...(576 km) to the Indus in ...stan.

ad·dish (kah′dĭsh; *Heb.* kah- ...′) *n.* (pl. **Kad·di·shim** pr. ...dĭsh′ĭm; *Heb.* kahdēshēm′). ...yer in praise of God recited ...ng synagogue service and by ...rners. [Aram. *ḳaddīš* holy]

af·fee klatsch (kah′fā klahch, ...′fē klăch) = COFFEE klatsch.

af·fir, Kaf·ir[1] (kăf′er, kah′fer) ...pl. **-firs, -irs**, collect. **-fir, -ir**). ...tu inhabitant, language, of ...hern Africa (derog. as used by ...bic Muslims), non-Muslim, in- ...l. [Arab. *ḳāfir* infidel]

.af·ir[2] (kah′fēr, kahfēr′) *n.* ...mber of a small group of tribes ...NE. Afghanistan, prob. of ...ian origin, speaking an Indo- ...opean language.

.af·ka (kahf′kah, -ka), **Franz** ...3–1924). Austrian novelist,

born in Prague; author of *The Trial*, *The Castle*, etc. **Kaf·ka·esque** (kahfkahesk′) *adj.* Resembling esp. the nightmare quality of Kafka's writings.

kail: see KALE.

kai·ser (kī′zer) *n.* Emperor; (hist.) German emperor; emperor of Austria; head of Holy Roman Empire; **the K** ~: see WILLIAM[3].

ka·ke·mo·no (kahkamō′nō; *Jap.* kahkĕmaw′naw) *n.* (pl. **-nos**; *Jap.* **-no**). Japanese vertical hanging scroll mounted on rollers, containing either text or painting on silk or paper. [Jap. *kake* hang, *mono* thing]

Ka·la·ha·ri (kahlahhär′ē) **Desert.** Large high barren plateau of

Afghanistan has a mixed population. The Kabul River leads south to the Khyber Pass — the traditional route of invaders. A unifying factor is religion: most of the people are Muslim.

...cs of Mogul rule, as in the Mazar-i- ...rif, are still found in **Kabul** today. ...ar, in the 16th century made Kabul ...tal of the Mogul Empire. Now the ...tal of Afghanistan, the city has a ...ersity and growing industries.

southern Africa, mainly in Botswana.

kale, kail (kāl) *ns.* Variety of
cabbage with wrinkled leaves not
forming compact head (*Brassica
oleracea acephala*).

ka·lei·do·scope (kalī′doskōp) *n.*
Tube through which are seen symmetrical figures, produced by reflections of pieces of colored glass,
and varied by rotation of tube; (fig.)
constantly changing group of bright
objects; series of changing or varied
objects, events, etc. **ka·lei·do·-
scop·ic** (kalīdoskŏp′ĭk), **ka·lei·do·-
scop′i·cal** *adjs.* **ka·lei·do·scop′i·-
cal·ly** *adv.*

kal·ends (kăl′endz): see CALENDS.

Ka·li (kah′lē). (Hindu myth.)
Form of Durga, the bloodthirsty
wife of Siva, represented with black
body, four arms, necklace of human
heads, and protruding bloodstained
tongue.

Kal·muck, Kal·muk (kăl′mŭk)
ns. 1. Member of Buddhist
Mongol people of central Asia
who invaded Russia in 16th and
17th centuries and settled along
lower Volga. 2. Language of the
Kalmucks, one of the Ural-Altaic
family.

ka·long (kah′lŏng) *n.* Malay
flying fox or fruit-eating bat
(*Pteropus vampyrus*), the largest of
the bats, having a wingspread of up
to 5 ft.

Ka·ma (kah′ma). (Hindu myth.)
God of love, represented as a
beautiful youth riding on a sparrow
and armed with bow and arrows.

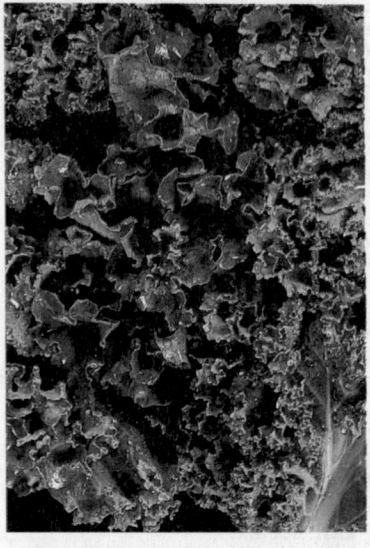

Kam·chat·ka (kahmchaht′kah).
Peninsula of NE. Siberia running
S. between Bering Sea and Sea of
Okhotsk.

Ka·me·ha·me·ha (kamā′hamā′-
ha). Name of five kings of the
Hawaiian Islands who reigned from
1795–1872.

ka·mi·ka·ze (kahmēkah′zē) *n.*
World War II Japanese aircraft
laden with explosives and deliberately crashed by its pilot on its

*The **Kansas State Capitol** in Topeka
which is the capital of Kansas. The
State was named after the Kansa or
Kaw Indians, a hunting and farming
people living in the area.*

target; its pilot. [Jap., = divir
wind]

Kam·pa·la (kahmpah′la). Cap
tal of Uganda, in the E. part, o
Lake Victoria.

Kam·pu·che·a (kahmpōō′chēa
Republic in SE. Asia; once th
powerful kingdom of Khmer;
French protectorate from 1863 a
part of French Indochina; gaine
independence during French
Indochinese war, 1953; now off
cially Democratic Kampuche
capital Phnom Penh.

Ka·nak·a (kanăk′a, -nah′ka)
Native of South Sea Island
[Hawaiian, = "man"]

kan·ga·roo (kănggaroō′) *n.* (p
-roos, collect. **-roo**). Marsupial o
genus *Macropus* with strongl
developed hindquarters and gre
leaping power, native of Australi
Tasmania, etc.; ~ **court**, self
constituted court held by striker
mutineers, etc.; dishonest cour
esp. one determined to pronounc
a person guilty regardless of th
evidence; ~ **rat**, small Austra
marsupial belonging to any
several genera, esp. *Potorous* an
Bettongia; also, Amer. pouche
rodent (*Dipodomys*) of south
western states and Mexico.

kan·ji (kahn′jē) *n.* (pl. **-ji, -jis**
Japanese writing using Chine
characters.

Kans. *abbrev.* Kansas.

Kan·sas (kăn′zas). State
central U.S., admitted to the Uni
in 1861; capital, Topeka; ~ **Cit**
large city in Missouri, on Missou
River; smaller city in Kansa
across river; ~ **River**, river drai
ing N. part of Kansas and flowin
eastward into Missouri Rive
Kan′san *adj.* & *n.*

Kan·su (kahn′sōō′). Extrem
NW. province of China.

Kant (kănt; *Ger.* kahnt), **Im
manuel** (1724–1804). Germa
philosopher, founder of school
transcendental philosophy,
which one of the fundamental pri
ciples is that knowledge of t
external world depends upon sen
impressions coordinated or sy
thesized by the reason, employin
such "categories" or laws
thought as quality, quanti
causation, etc. **Kant′i·an** *adj.* &

ka·o·lin, ka·o·line (kā′olĭn) *n*
Fine white clay formed by the d
composition and weathering
feldspar in granite; used in makir
porcelain, as a filler for paper an
textiles, etc. [Chin. *kao-ling* hi
hill (mountain where orig. o
tained)]

Ka·pell·meis·ter (kahpĕl′n

Above: The **red kangaroo,** a little smaller than the grey kangaroo, is the most widespread of the kangaroo family. It is seen here with a joey climbing out of the female's pouch. Below: A rufous rat kangaroo is about as large as a hare. Left: The black tree kangaroo. Left center: A red kangaroo.

*The seed pod of the **kapok** contains a floss which is dried and cleaned to make an insulating material used to stuff sleeping bags and mattresses. Fats from the seeds are used in the manufacture of soap.*

*The greatest building at **Karnak** in cen tral Egypt is the Temple of Amon. T 134 massive columns of the hypostyl hall, seen here, are arranged in 16 row and cover an area of 388 by 170 The site is 1 mile east of Luxor.*

ster) *n.* (pl. **-ter**). Conductor of orchestra or choir. [Ger.]

ka·pok (kā′pŏk, kăp′ok) *n.* = SILK cotton from tree *Ceiba pentandra.* [Malay *kapoq*]

kap·pa (kăp′a) *n.* Eleventh (later tenth) letter of Greek alphabet (K, k), corresponding to *k*.

ka·put (kahpoot′, -poot′) *adj.* (slang) Finished, done for. [Ger.]

Ka·ra·chi (karah′chē). Seaport and former capital of Pakistan, on an inlet of the Arabian Sea.

kar·a·kul, car·a·cul (kăr′akul) *ns.* Asian sheep whose young have dark curled fleece; fur, wool, made from or resembling this.

Ka·ra Kum, Qa·ra Qum (kărah koom′). Flat desert region of the Turkmen Soviet Socialist Republic in the SW. Soviet Union.

kar·at (kăr′at) *n.* Measure of $\frac{1}{24}$ stating fineness of gold; if e.g. the mass contains 22 parts of gold and two of alloy it is 22 karats fine, or 22-karat gold.

ka·ra·te (karah′tē) *n.* Japanese system of unarmed combat using hands etc. as weapons.

Ka·re·lia (karēl′ya). 1. Area of NW. U.S.S.R. between Finnish border and White Sea. 2. Autonomous republic (properly *Karelian Autonomous Soviet Socialist Republic*) of R.S.F.S.R.; capital, Petrozavodsk. **Ka·re′li·an** *adj. & n.*

Karl-Marx-Stadt (kärl′-

märks′shtaht′). City and textile center of East Germany, SE. of Leipzig; called Chemnitz until 1953.

Karls·bad (kärlz′bahd; *Ger.* kärls′baht). German name of *Karlovy Vary*, town in NW. Czechoslovakia; noted for its mineral springs.

Karls·ru·he (kärlz′rooe). (also **Carlsruhe**) City in SW. West Germany on Rhine River.

kar·ma (kär′ma) *n.* (Buddhism, Hinduism) Sum of person's actions in one of his successive states of existence viewed as deciding his fate in the next; destiny. **kar′mic** *adj.*

Kar·nak (kär′năk). Village of Upper Egypt, on Nile near Luxor, containing magnificent ruins of temple of Ammon on site of ancient Thebes.

karst (kärst) *n.* Barren limestone formation with abrupt ridges, caverns, and underground streams. [*Karst*, limestone plateau in NW. Yugoslavia]

kart (kärt) *n.* Small, low-slung racing car with skeleton body.

ka·sha (kah′sha) *n.* Cracked grain, esp. buckwheat, cooked until mushy; groats.

Kash·mir (kăshmēr′, kăsh′mēr) = JAMMU AND KASHMIR. **Kash·mir′i** *n.* Indo-European language of Kashmir, much influenced by Sanskrit.

ka·ta·ka·na (kahtakah′na) Japanese set of written symbols, syllabary.

Kat·mai (kăt′mī) **Nationa Monument.** Area in S. Alaska the N. end of the Alaska Penin sula covering 4,215 sq. mi. (10,9 sq. km) and including **Mou Katmai**, a volcano rising 6,715 (2,047 m) and the Valley of Te Thousand Smokes.

Kat·man·du (kahtmahndoo′ Capital of Nepal, in a valley of th Himalayas in the E. part.

ka·ty·did (kā′tēdĭd) *n.* Any several large green insects of th genus *Microcentrun* and relate genera, related to the grasshoppe and crickets and producing chara teristic noise by stridulation [imit

Kau·ai (kowī′). Island in th Hawaiian group, NW. of Oah covering 555 sq. mi. (1,437 sq. km

ka·va (kah′va), **ka·va-ka·v** (kah′va kah′va) *ns.* (Intoxicatir beverage prepared from dried roo of) Polynesian shrub, *Piper meth sticum.*

Ka·wa·sa·ki (kahwasah′kē City and industrial center in SI Honshu, Japan, on the W. coast Tokyo Bay.

kay·ak (kī′ăk) *n.* Eskimo one-
n canoe of light wooden frame-
rk covered with sealskins; small
at resembling this.

Ka·zakh, Ka·zak (kazahk′) *ns.*
ember of a Turkic people of S.
eria.

Ka·zakh·stan, Ka·zak·stan
hzahkstahn′). Kazak(h) Soviet
cialist Republic, a constituent
ublic (properly *Kazakh Soviet
cialist Republic*) of U.S.S.R.;
ital, Alma-Ata.

ka·zoo (kazōo′) *n.* Toy musical
trument into which player sings
hums.

kc, kc. *abbrevs.* Kilocycle(s).

K.C. *abbrev.* Knights of Colum-
s.

ke·a (kā′a, kē′a) *n.* Green par-
: (*Nestor notabilis*) of a group
culiar to New Zealand moun-
nous areas, normally living on
it, grubs, and carrion, but re-
ted to kill sheep by pecking at
ir flesh.

Keats (kēts), **John** (1795–1821).
glish lyric poet; author of "The
e of St. Agnes," "Ode on a
ecian Urn," "Ode to a Nightin-
e," "Ode to Autumn," etc.

ke·bab, ka·bob (kebŏb′) *ns.*
iental dish of small pieces of
arinated meat, chicken, seafood,
:., often with onions, green
ppers, cut tomatoes, or other
getables grilled on skewer.

Ke·dah (kā′dah).   State of
alaysia; capital, Alor Star.

Ke·dar (kē′der). Son of ISHMAEL
en. 25), whose descendants were
ribe of nomads identified in later
wish literature with the Arabs.

kedge (kĕj) *v.* (**kedged, kedg·-
g**). (naut.) Change position of
ship by winding in hawser
ached to small anchor at some
tance; (of ship) move thus; move
ip) thus.   ~ *n.* Small anchor
kedging.

ked·ger·ee (kĕj′erē) *n.* Indian
h of rice, lentils, onions, eggs,
:.; European dish of fish, rice,
gs, and condiments.

keel (kēl) *n.* Lowest longitudinal
nber of vessel, on which frame-
rk of whole is built up; similar
uctural member in nonwooden
ssel; (poet.) ship; (in aircraft)
tical fin extending longitudi-
lly underneath; (bot., zool.)
rina; **keel′haul**, haul (person)
der keel of ship as punishment.
el *v.* Turn (ship) keel upward; ~
er, turn, be turned, over, capsize;
nt, drop from exhaustion, shock,
. **keeled, keel′less** *adjs.*

Kee·ling (kē′lĭng) **Islands**: see
cos Islands.

*hn Keats (1795–1821) reading
side a window was painted by his
end Joseph Severn. Severn
rneyed with Keats to Italy in 1820
d cared for him till his death. Keats'
est poems were written between
17 and 1820.*

keen¹ (kēn) *n.* Wailing lamentation for the dead.   ~ *v.* Utter a
keen; bewail (person) thus; utter in
wailing tone.

keen² (kēn) *adj.* Having sharp
edge or point; sharp; (of sound,
light, etc.) penetrating, vivid,
strong, (of cold) intense; (of pain
etc.) acute; (of person, desire,
interest) eager, ardent (colloq. *on*);
(of eyes etc.) sharp, highly sensitive;
intellectually acute. **keen′ly** *adv.*
keen′ness *n.*

*The New Zealand **kea** is a parrot whose
tongue is adapted rather like a brush to
collect nectar from flowers. But the kea
will also eat meat when it needs alternative nourishment.*

keep¹ (kēp) *v.* (**kept, keep·ing**).
1. Pay due regard to, observe, stand
by (law, promise, faith, etc.);
observe, solemnize (feast etc.). 2.
Guard, protect (person, fortress,
etc.); have charge of; maintain in
proper form and order; provide for
sustenance of, maintain, support;
own and manage (animals etc.);
maintain (woman) as mistress,
(man) as lover; have (commodity)
habitually on sale. 3. Retain possession of, not lose; maintain,

*The racing yacht's deep **keel** is seen
clearly as the vessel is lifted out of the
water. The weight of the keel and the
resistance of its surfaces help to
stabilize the boat.*

remain, in proper or specified condition; reserve, admit of being reserved (*for* future time etc.); hide, conceal (secret etc.). 4. Detain (person *in prison* etc.); restrain (*from*); refrain *from*. 5. Continue to follow (way, course); remain in (one's bed, room, house); retain one's place in (the saddle, one's ground, etc.) against opposition; remain (indoors etc.). 6. ~ **house**: see HOUSE. 7. **keep at**, work persistently at; **keep away**, avoid coming; prevent from coming; **keep back**, hold back, retard progress of, conceal; **keep down**, hold in subjection; keep low in amount; **keep in**, confine, restrain (feelings, etc.); keep (fire) burning; **keep one's hand in**: see HAND; **keep off**, ward off, avert; stay at a distance; **keep on**, continue to use, show, etc.; continue (*doing*); **keep out**, not allow to enter; **keep to**, adhere to, confine oneself to; **keep to oneself**, avoid society; refuse to share with others; **keep together**, remain, cause to remain, together; **keep up**, prevent from sinking; maintain; keep in repair; carry on (correspondence etc.); cause (person) to be awake and up at night; bear up, not break down; proceed at equal pace *with*; **keep it up**, not slacken.

keep[2] (kēp) *n.* 1. (hist.) Tower, stronghold. 2. Maintenance, food required for this. 3. **for ~s**, (playing) seriously, intending to keep one's winnings; forever.

keep·er (kē′per) *n.* One who keeps, guards, manages, etc.; custodian; mechanical device for keeping something in place.

keep·ing (kē′pĭng) *n.* (esp.) 1. Custody, charge. 2. Agreement, harmony.

keep·sake (kēp′sāk) *n.* Thing given or kept as a reminder of the giver; memento.

kees·hond (kās′hŏnd) *n.* (pl. **-hon·den** pr. -hŏnden). One of a breed of small Dutch dogs with thick black and gray hair and a tail curled up over the back.

kef·fi·yeh (kĕfē′yĕ), **kaf·fi·yeh** (kahfē′yĕ) *ns.* Bedouin Arab's kerchief worn as headdress.

keg (kĕg) *n.* Small barrel, usu. of less than 10 gallons.

Kel·ler (kĕl′er), **Helen** (**Adams**) (1880–1968). Amer. author, born in Alabama; became blind and deaf in infancy; was taught to speak, read, and use a typewriter; wrote several books, including the story of her life; traveled extensively and did much for the education of those similarly handicapped.

Kel·logg-Bri·and (kĕl′awg brē-ahnd′, -ŏg) **Pact.** Treaty renouncing war as an instrument of national policy; signed in Paris, 1928, by representatives of 15 nations; also called "Kellogg Peace

Kells *in the County of Meath was the seat of a 9th-century bishopric which had earlier associations with Columba. The Book of Kells is probably the finest Irish illuminated work. This page reproduced from it portrays Jesus Christ.*

Pact." [F. B. *Kellogg* (1856–1937), U.S. secretary of state 1924–9]

Kells (kĕlz), **Book of.** Illuminated manuscript of the gospels, now at Trinity College, Dublin; made perh. by Irish monks in 8th or early 9th c. [from *Kells*, town in Co. Meath, Ireland, where it was formerly kept]

kelp (kĕlp) *n.* (Any of the) large seaweeds that are burned for the potash, iodine, etc., they contain; calcined ashes of these.

Kelt (kĕlt): see CELT.

kel·vin (kĕl′vĭn) *n.* Unit of measurement in the Kelvin scale (abbrev. K). [f. KELVIN]

Kel·vin (kĕl′vĭn), **William**

Thomson, 1st Baron (1824–1907). Irish-born physicist who advanced the science of thermodynamics and electricity, improved the system of electrical units, and invented several scientific instruments; **Kelvin scale**, scale of absolute temperature, in which the zero (corresponding roughly to − 273 C) is the temperature at which a perfect gas would occupy zero volume if it could be cooled indefinitely, without liquefaction or solidification.

Ke·mal Pa·sha (kemahl′ pah-shah′): see ATATÜRK.

Kem·ble (kĕm′bel). Name of a family of English actors: **Charles ~** (1775–1854); **Frances Anne ("Fanny") ~** (1809–93), actress, his daughter; **John Philip ~** (1757–1823), his brother; **Roger ~** (1721–1802), actor and manager, father of John and Charles and of Mrs. Siddons.

Kem·pis (kĕm´pĭs), **Thomas à.** Thomas Hämmerken (c1380–1471), named from his birthplace, Kempen, near Düsseldorf; Augusinian monk, author of *De Imitaione Christi*.

ken (kĕn) *n.* Range of sight or knowledge. ~ *v.* (**kenned** or **kent, ken·ning**). (chiefly Sc.) Recognize at sight; know; understand.

Ken·ne·bec (kĕn´ebĕk). River in Maine flowing S. 150 mi. (241 km) from Moosehead Lake to the Atlantic Ocean.

Ken·ne·dy (kĕn´edē). Name of wealthy Amer. family from Massachusetts prominent in politics, including **John Fitzgerald** (1917–1963) 35th president of the U.S. 1961–3); first Roman Catholic to hold this office; member of House of Representatives, 1947–53, and Senate, 1953–60; his term of office is noted for the formation of the Peace Corps, the Alliance for Progress aid program to Latin America, the Cuban missile crisis, in which he forced Soviet withdrawal of offensive atomic missiles, confrontation with Russians concerning the Berlin Wall, and encouragement of full civil rights for blacks; he received Pulitzer Prize, 1957, for collection of essays *Profiles in Courage*; was assassinated Nov. 22, 1963 in Dallas, Texas; 2. **Robert Francis** (1925–1968), brother of John; U.S.

attorney general, 1961–4; U.S. senator from N.Y., 1965–8; assassinated June, 1968, in Los Angeles, Calif., while campaigning for presidency; 3. **Edward Moore ("Ted")** (1932–), brother of John and Robert; U.S. senator from Massachusetts, 1962– ; assistant majority leader, U.S. senate, 1969–1971; 4. **Joseph Patrick** (1888–1969), father of John, Robert, and Edward; Amer. financier and diplo-

*The **keeper** of a zoo is responsible for maintaining the health and general welfare of the animals in his or her care.*

mat; chairman of the Securities and Exchange Commission, 1934–5; U.S. ambassador to the Court of St. James, 1937–41.

ken·nel (kĕn´el) *n.* House, hut, for shelter of dog or dogs; place where dogs are bred or boarded. ~ *v.* (**-neled, -nel·ing**; Brit. **-nelled, -nel·ling**). Live in, go to, kennel; put into, keep in, kennel.

Ken·neth (kĕn´ĭth). Name of two Scottish kings: **Kenneth I MacAlpin** (d. c860), traditional founder of kingdom of Scotland; **Kenneth II** (d. 995).

ken·ning (kĕn´ĭng) *n.* Periphrastic expression used instead of simple name of thing in Old English, Old Norse, etc. poetry e.g. *whale road* = ocean, *ring-giver* = king.

Ken·ny (kĕn´ē), **Elizabeth** (1886–1952). Australian nurse who developed a method of muscle exercise and stimulation in treating paralysis caused by poliomyelitis.

ke·no (kē´nō) *n.* Gambling game resembling bingo.

ke·no·sis (kĭnō´sĭs) *n.* (theol.) Renunciation of divine nature, at least in part, by Christ in incarnation.

Ken·tuck·y (kentŭk′ē). State in southeastern U.S., admitted to the Union in 1792; capital, Frankfort; ~ **Derby**, see DERBY. **Ken·tuck′i·an** *adj. & n.*

Ken·ya (kĕn′ya, kĕn′-). Country of E. Africa between Ethiopia and Tanzania; former British colony, independent since 1963; capital, Nairobi; **Mount** ~, extinct volcano rising 17,040 ft. (5,197 m) in the central part S. of the equator; second highest mountain in Africa. **Ken′yan** *adj. & n.*

Ken·yat·ta (kĕnyah′ta), **Jo·mo** (jō′mō) (1893?–1978). Political leader of Kenya; president, 1963–1978.

kep·i (kā′pē, kĕp′ē) *n.* (pl. **kep·is**). French military cap with visor.

Kep·ler (kĕp′ler), **Johann** (1571–1630). German astronomer, whose three laws of planetary motion provided the basis for much of Newton's work.

Ke·pone (kē′pōn) *n.* (trademark) Pesticide believed to be water pollutant and source of damage to human nervous system.

kept (kĕpt): see KEEP[1]. ~ *adj.* (esp.) Supported financially in exchange for sexual favors.

ker·a·tin (kĕr′atĭn), **cer·a·tin** (sĕr′atĭn) *ns.* Protein or group of proteins found in skin, hair, nails, horns, hoofs, and feathers.

kerb (kĕrb) *n.* (Brit.) Curb.

ker·chief (kĕr′chĭf) *n.* Cloth used to cover head; (poet.) handkerchief.

kerf (kĕrf) *n.* Slit made by cutting, esp. with saw.

Ker·gue·len, Ker·gué·len (kĕr′gelĕn). Desolation Island, uninhabited subantarctic island, belonging to France, in Southern Ocean SE. of Cape of Good Hope and SW. of Australia; discovered (1772) by a Breton navigator, Yves-Joseph de Kerguélen-Trémarec.

ker·mes (kĕr′mēz) *n.* Female of insect *Kermes ilicis*, dried and used in dyeing; red dyestuff prepared from dried bodies of these.

kern[1] (kĕrn) *n.* (print.) Part of a metal type projecting beyond the body or shank, as the curled head of *f* and tail of *j*, etc.

kern[2], **kerne** (kĕrn) *ns.* (hist.) Lightly armed Irish foot soldier; peasant, boor.

Kern (kĕrn), **Jerome David** (1885–1945). Amer. composer famous for musical comedies; his songs include "Ol' Man River," "Smoke Gets in Your Eyes," "The Last Time I Saw Paris," etc.

ker·nel (kĕr′nel) *n.* Softer (usu. edible) part within hard shell of nut or stone fruit; whole seed within husk etc., e.g. grain of wheat; nucleus, center of formation (freq. fig.).

ker·o·sene, ker·o·sine (kĕr′o-sēn, kăr′-, kĕrosēn′, kăr-) *ns.* Fuel oil obtained by distillation of petro-leum, or from coal or shale.

Ker·ry (kĕr′ē). County of th Republic of Ireland, in the SW hence, one of a breed of very sma black dairy cattle orig. produce there; ~ **blue**, Irish breed terrier, with silky blue-gray coat.

kes·trel (kĕs′trel) *n.* Sma falcon, in U.S., the sparrow haw (*Falco sparverius*); in the Old Worl *F. tinnunculus*, with habit of r maining in same place in air wi head to the wind; windhover; s FALCON.

ketch (kĕch) *n.* Small tw masted sailing vessel for coast waters.

ketch·up (kĕch′up, kăch′-**katch·up** (kăch′up, kĕch′-), **cat sup** (kăt′sup, kăch′up, kĕch′-) *n* Sauce of tomatoes (usu.), mus rooms, or walnuts, etc., wi vinegar, raisins, spices, etc., used condiment. [prob. f. Chin. *kôechi* brine of pickled fish]

ke·tone (kē′tōn) *n.* (chem.) O of a group of organic compoun containing carbonyl group (CO doubly united with carbon, us colorless volatile liquids with pu gent ethereal smell, used esp. solvents. [Ger. *keton*, modificatio of *acetone*]

ket·tle (kĕt′el) *n.* 1. Large vess for boiling or stewing, usu. of met with lid; similar but smaller vess with spout and handle, teakettle (geol.) (also ~ **hole**) Sunken area glacial drift, apparent result melting of isolated mass of glac ice. 3. **pretty** ~ **of fish**, awkwa state of affairs; **ket′tledrum**: s

RUM.

key[1] (kē) *n*. (pl. **keys**). I. Metal instrument for moving bolt of lock forward or backward. 2. What gives or precludes opportunity for access to something. 3. (pl., with allusion to Matt. 16) Ecclesiastical authority held to be transmitted to pope as successor of St. Peter. Solution, explanation; translation of book or exercise in foreign language; book of solutions of mathematical problems etc. 5. (mus.) System of tones definitely related to each other and based on **key'note** in which a piece of music is written; (fig.) tone, style, of thought or expression (hence **key-note speech**, address, esp. at political convention, stating basic policies, principles, positions on topical issues, etc., and given by person designated as **key'noter**). Wood or metal pin inserted between parts to secure them. 7. Lever pressed by finger in playing organ, piano, flute, etc.; similar lever in typewriter etc. 8. Small instrument for winding clock etc. **key'board**, set of keys in piano, organ, typewriter, data processing machine, etc.; **key club**, private night club to which each member has personal door key; **key'hole**, hole by which key is put into lock; **key'note**: see sense 5; (fig.) prevailing tone or idea. **key'punch**, machine with which keyboard operator records coded data by punching holes in cards; **key ring**, ring for keeping keys on; **key ignature**, (mus.) one or more flats or sharps written on the staff after the clef to give the key of a composition; **keystone**: see separate entry; **key word**, key to cipher etc. **key'less** *adj*. **key** *v.t.* (**keyed, key·ing**). Fasten (*in, on,* etc.) with pin, wedge, bolt, etc.; **~ up**, (fig.) stimulate.

key[2] (kē) *n*. (pl. **keys**). Low offshore island or reef, of kind common in West Indies or off coast of Florida.

Key[1] (kē), **Francis Scott** (1779–1843). Amer. lawyer; wrote the poem that became lyrics of a popular song, "The Star Spangled Banner," which Congress made national anthem, 1931; Key wrote the poem after seeing the Amer. flag still flying over Fort McHenry in Baltimore following British shelling during War of 1812.

Key[2] (kē) **West.** Resort city on

Key West island, Florida; southernmost U.S. city.

Keynes (kānz), **John Maynard, 1st Baron** (1883–1946). English economist. **Keynes'i·an** *adj.* & *n.*

key·stone (kē'stōn) *n*. I. Stone at summit of arch locking the whole together; (fig.) central principle etc.

on which all depends. 2. **K~ State**, nickname of PENNSYLVANIA. **keystone** *adj*. Of or pertaining to type of slapstick comedy popular in silent films (produced by Keystone Co.) depicting clownlike, inept policemen (**~ cops**).

kg, kg. *abbrevs*. Kilogram(s).

KGB, K.G.B. *abbrevs*. Secret

Top: A map of Kenya with (inset) a location guide to show its position in Africa, and the flag of Kenya. Right: The economy of Kenya is largely based on agriculture. Cattle are raised and coffee, tea, wheat, maize and tobacco grown. Here a worker removes young shoots from tobacco plants.

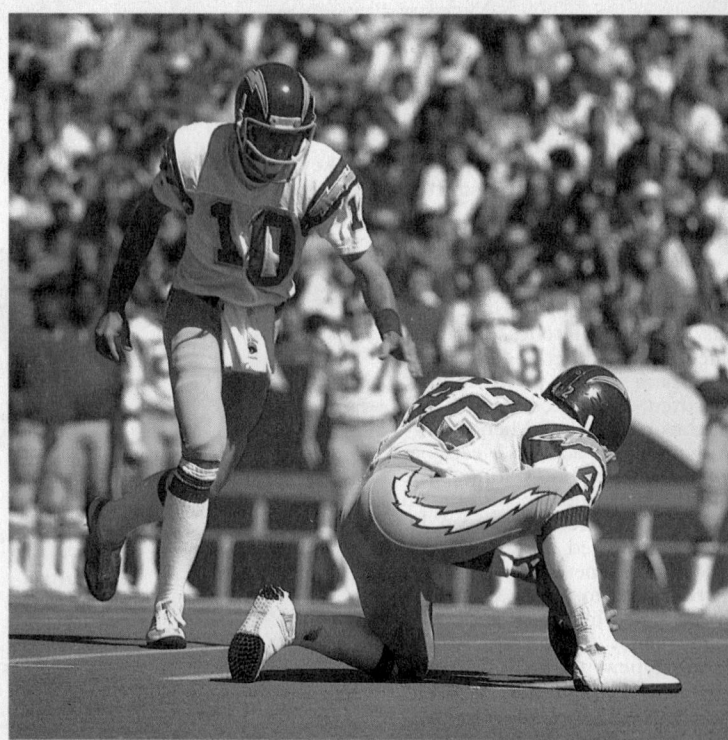

In 1912 when the rules for gridiron football were being changed to make it a less brutal game (in 1905 there had been 18 deaths) the **kickoff,** *previously made from center field, was moved to the kicking side's 40-yard line.*

police of U.S.S.R., which took over functions of M.V.D. in 1960. [initials of Russ. *K*omitét *G*osudár-stvennoĭ *B*ezopásnosti, State security committee]

kha·ki (kăk´ē, kah´kē) *adj.* Dull brownish yellow. ~ *n.* (pl. **-kis**). Khaki fabric used in army for field uniforms. [Hind., = dusty (*khak* dust)]

kha·lif (kahlēf´, kā´lĭf, kăl´ĭf), **kha·li·fa** (kahlē´fah), **khal·i·fate** (kăl´ĭfāt, -fĭt) *ns.* = CALIPH, caliphate.

kham·sin, kam·seen, kam·sin (kăm´sĭn, kămsēn´) *ns.* Oppressive hot S. or SE. wind blowing from the Sahara across Egypt for about 50 days in March, April, and May. [Arab. *ḳamsin* fifty]

khan[1] (kahn, kăn) *n.* (hist.) Title of successors of Genghis Khan, supreme rulers of Turkish, Tartar, and Mongol tribes and emperors of China, in Middle Ages; title of rulers, officials, and men of rank of central Asia, Afghanistan, etc. **khan´ate** *n.* [Turk., perhaps f. *khāgān* king]

khan[2] (kahn, kăn) *n.* Caravansary. [Arab., = "inn"]

Khar·toum (kártoom´). Capital of Sudan, on Blue Nile just above junction with White Nile; besieged 1885 and captured from the British by the Mahdists; recaptured by the British under KITCHENER, 1898.

Khay·yám (kīyahm´, -yăm´), **Omar**: see OMAR KHAYYÁM.

khe·dive (kedēv´) *n.* (hist.) Title of viceroy or governor of Egypt until 1914; orig. accorded to Ismail Pasha by Turkey in 1867.

Khmer[1] (kmĕr, χmār) *n.* 1. Native, inhabitant, of the ancient kingdom of Khmer in SE. Asia, which reached peak of its power in 11th c. and was destroyed by Siamese conquests in 12th and 14th centuries; native, inhabitant, of the Khmer Republic. 2. Monosyllabic language of this people, of Mon-Khmer group of Austro-Asiatic family.

Khmer[2] (kmĕr, χmār) = KAMPUCHEA.

Khru·shchev (kroosh´chĕf, -chawf, kroosh´-; *Russ.* χroosh-chawf´), **Nikita Sergeyevich** (1894–1971). Dictator and premier of U.S.S.R. 1958–64; denounced Stalin at party congresses in 1956 and 1961.

Khy·ber (kī´ber) **Pass.** Chief pass between Afghanistan and Pakistan.

kHz *abbrev.* Kilohertz.

KIA *abbrev.* Killed in action.

ki·ang (kēăng´) *n.* Tibetan ass

(*Equus hemionus*), with thick furry coat, found at altitudes of 15,000 ft. (4,500 m) and upward.

Kiang·si (kyahng´sē). Province of SE. China.

Kiang·su (kyahng´soo´). Coastal province of E. China at outlet of Yangtze Kiang.

kib·ble (kĭb´el) *v.t.* (**-bled, -bling**). Bruise or grind coarsely; crush into small pieces.

kib·butz (kĭboots´) *n.* (pl. **kib·but·zim** pr. kĭbootsēm´). Collective farm or settlement in Israel. [Heb.]

Ki·bei (kē´bā´) *n.* (pl. **-bei, -beis**). Native citizen of U.S., born of immigrant Japanese parents but educated in Japan. Cf. ISSEI; NISEI; SANSEI.

kib·itz·er (kĭb´ĭtser) *n.* (colloq.) Meddlesome person, one who gives advice gratuitously; one who watches game of cards from behind the players; meddlesome onlooker. **kib´itz** *v.*

ki·bosh (kī´bŏsh, kĭbŏsh´) *n.* (slang) **put the** ~ **on**, put an end to.

kick (kĭk) *n.* Act of kicking; (colloq.) power of reaction, resilience; recoil of gun when discharged; (colloq.) complaint, criticism; (slang) sharp stimulant effect, thrill; **kick´back**, (colloq.) strong reaction; (slang) payment for help in making profit, for showing favor, etc.; **kick´off**, (football) kick starting game, second half of game, or play after score is made; (colloq.) start, as of fund drive, political campaign, etc.; **kick´stand**, short metal bar on rear axle of bicycle or motorcycle, used to hold vehicle

The attack that **Khrushchev** *launch on Stalinism released a burst of sep atist activity among the U.S.S.R.'s ellites. He survived this crisis strengthened his position at home a policy of decentralization of indus*

upright when not in u **kick starter**, pedal on motorcy etc. for starting engine by dow ward push with foot. **kick** *v.* Stri out with the foot; (colloq.) sh annoyance, dislike, etc. (*again at*); strike with foot; drive, mov (thing) by kicking; (football) sc (field goal or point after touc down) by a kick; drive forcibly a contemptuously (*out* etc.);

*For centuries the **Khyber Pass** has provided a route to India, either for trade or for invasion. The fort (left) was garrisoned by the British whose regimental badges on plaques record their tours of duty.*

Illinois; its language.

kid[1] (kĭd) *n.* Young of goat; leather from skin of this, used for gloves and boots; (slang) child, young person. ~ *v.i.* (**kid·ded, kid·ding**). Give birth to kid. **kid'dy, kid'die** *ns.* (pl. **-dies**). (slang) Little child.

kid[2] (kĭd) *v.* (**kid·ded, kid·ding**). (colloq.) Tease, josh.

Kidd (kĭd), **William** (c1645–1701). "Captain Kidd," English privateer and pirate; hanged for piracy, 1701.

kid·nap (kĭd'năp) *v.t.* (**-napped, -nap·ping, -naped, -nap·ing**). Abduct (child), carry off (person) by illegal force, esp. to hold for ransom. **kid'nap·per, kid'nap·er** *ns.*

kid·ney (kĭd'nē) *n.* (pl. **-neys**). 1. One of a pair of glandular organs in abdominal cavity of vertebrates, serving mainly to excrete nitrogenous matter from the blood; analogous organ in other animals; kidney of sheep, cattle, or pigs, as food. 2. Kind, disposition, temperament; ~ **bean**, oval-shaped edible seed of common garden bean (*Phaesolus vulgaris*); ~ **stone**, abnormal concretion formed in the kidney.

Kier·ke·gaard (kēr'kegärd; *Dan.* kēr'kegōr), **Sören Aabye** (suh'ren aw'bü) (1813–55). Danish philosopher and theological writer.

Kiev (kē'ĕf, -ĕv). (Russ. **Kiyev**) Capital of Ukrainian S.S.R., U.S.S.R., in the SW. part on the Dnieper River.

Ki·ga·li (kēgah'lē). Capital of Rwanda, in the central part.

Ki·ku·yu (kĭkoo'yoo) *n.* (pl. **-yus,** collect. **-yu**). (Member of) an agricultural Bantu people of Kenya; their language.

Ki·lau·e·a (kēlowā'a). Volcanic crater on the E. side of Mauna Loa, Hawaii; world's largest active volcano, 2 mi. (3 km) wide, 4,090 ft. (1,247 m) high.

Kil·i·man·ja·ro (kĭlimanjär'ō). Mountain in NE. Tanzania, highest mountain in Africa (19,340 ft., 5,895 m).

kill (kĭl) *v.t.* 1. Put to death; cause the death of; perform act of killing, execute; ~ **off**, get rid of (number of animals, persons etc.) by killing; ~ **two birds with one stone**, effect two purposes at once. 2. Destroy vitality of; destroy, put an end to; consume (time) for the sake of doing so; (slang) overwhelm (person) with admiration, amusement, etc.; strike (ball in tennis etc.) so that it cannot be returned; totally defeat (bill in legislature);

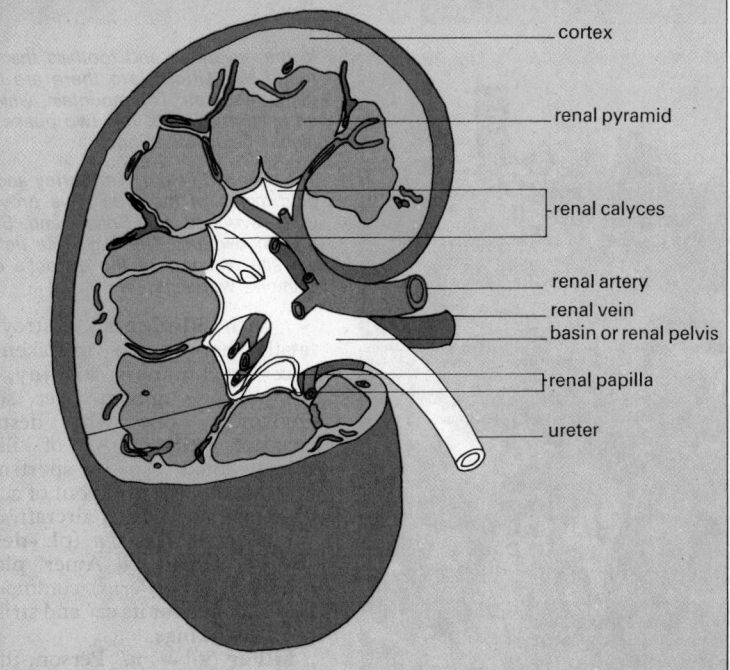

...ammals must have at least one of their ...o kidneys operating effectively. The ...man kidney is about 4 ins. x 2½ ins. ...ood enters the kidney through the ...nal artery, is purified and then passes ...t through the renal vein.

cortex
renal pyramid
renal calyces
renal artery
renal vein
basin or renal pelvis
renal papilla
ureter

·out (**around**), treat person ...ughly or scornfully; discuss (idea) ...systematically; move idly from ...ace to place; be unused or ...wanted; **kick back**, (slang) pay ...ckback; **kick in**, (slang) give ...ne's share), esp. in money; **kick ...f**, (football) put ball in play by

kickoff; (colloq.) start (fund drive etc.); **kick oneself**, be angry with oneself; **kick over**, (colloq.) start, or make start, running, as an internal combustion engine; **kick the bucket**, (slang) die; **kick the habit**, rid oneself of drug addiction, bad habit, etc.; **kick up**, (colloq.) raise (dust); create (fuss, noise). **kick'er** *n.*

Kick·a·poo (kĭk'apoo) *n.* (Member of a) N. Amer. Indian tribe of Algonquin linguistic stock, orig. found in S. Wisconsin and N.

~ **with kindness**, destroy
fatally harm with mistaken
excessive kindness; **kill'joy,** o
who throws gloom over soc
enjoyment, one who destro
pleasure. **kill** *n.* Act of killi
animal killed, esp. by sportsma
destruction or putting out of acti
of enemy submarine, aircraft, et

kill·deer (kĭl'dēr) *n.* (pl. **-dee**
-deer). Large N. Amer. plo
(*Charadrius vociferus*) common
fields, known for its cry and strik
breast markings.

kill·er (kĭl'er) *n.* Person, thi
that kills; murderous ruffian;
whale, a black and white predat
whale (*Orcinus orca*).

kill·ing (kĭl'ĭng) *n.* (es
Murder; kill (of animals, as
hunters); (slang) large, quick pro
~ *adj.* 1. Fatal; exhausting.
(colloq.) Overwhelmingly funny

kiln (kĭl, kĭln) *n.* Furnace, ov
for burning, baking, or drying, e
for calcining lime, baking bricks
drying hops; ~**-dry**, (*v.t.*) dry
kiln.

ki·lo (kē'lō, kĭl'ō) *n.* (pl. **ki·lo**
Kilogram.

kilo- *prefix*. One thousand times (abbrev. k).

kil·o·cy·cle (kĭl´osīkel) *n*. One thousand cycles, as unit in measuring frequency of electromagnetic waves (abbrev. kc).

kil·o·gram (kĭl´ogrăm) *n*. Unit of mass in the metric system (abbrev. kg), equal to the mass of the international prototype of the kilogram at Sèvres (approx. 2.20 lb.).

kil·o·hertz (kĭl´oheͭrts) *n*. (pl. hertz). Unit of vibration frequency = 1,000 cycles per second.

kil·o·joule (kĭl´ojōol) *n*. One thousand joules.

kil·o·li·ter (kĭl´olēter) *n*. One thousand liters (abbrev. kl).

ki·lom·e·ter (kĭl´omēter, lŏm´e-) *n*. One thousand meters (abbrev. km). **kil·o·met´ric** *adj*.

kil·o·ton (kĭl´otŭn) *n*. One thousand tons; unit of explosive power equivalent to 1,000 tons of TNT.

kil·o·watt (kĭl´owŏt) *n*. One thousand watts (abbrev. kw); **-hour**, unit of electrical energy, energy used when a rate of 1 kilowatt is maintained for 1 hour.

kilt (kĭlt) *v.t*. Tuck up (skirts) round body; gather in vertical pleats. ~ *n*. (often **kilts**) Part of highland dress, skirt, usu. of tartan cloth, heavily pleated around back and sides, reaching from waist to knee. **kilt´ed** *adj*.

kil·ter (kĭl´ter) *n*. Good working order (**out of** ~, not working properly).

Kim·ber·ley (kĭm´berlē). Diamond mine, district, and town in N. Cape Province, S. Africa. [1st Earl of *Kimberley*, colonial secretary 1871) when gold mines were taken under protection of Gt. Britain]

ki·mo·no (kĭmō´no, -nō) *n*. (pl. -nos). Long Japanese robe with wide sleeves; one of these, or similar robe, worn as dressing gown etc.

kin (kĭn) *n*. Ancestral stock, family; one's relatives; **kith and** ~: see KITH; **next of** ~: see NEXT. ~ *pred. adj*. Related.

-kin *suffix*. Forming diminutive nouns (*catkin, napkin*).

kind¹ (kīnd) *n*. Class, sort, category, variety; character, quality; (archaic) nature in general; (rare) way, fashion, natural to person, etc.; **in** ~, (of payment) in goods or natural produce, not in money; (of repayment) in something of the same kind as that received; ~ **of**, (colloq.) to some extent; **of a** ~, of the same group, type, etc., similar; **of the** ~, like it.

kind² (kīnd) *adj*. Of gentle or benevolent nature; friendly in one's conduct *to*; (archaic) affectionate. **kind´ness** *n*.

kin·der·gar·ten (kĭn´dergärten,

*The **killer whale** is a member of the dolphin family found in seas all over the world. Unlike other whales that feed off the small shrimp, krill, the killer whale eats sharks, salmon and seals.*

*The **kimono** is actually derived from a Chinese garment and was first worn by the Japanese in about 650 A.D. It is still a popular mode of dress and has changed little.*

For their magnificent plumage or for reasons of size several animals have received the appellation 'king'. Top left: The **kingfisher,** with jewel-like plumage, is a skillful diver in rivers and lakes. Top right: The **king penguin,** largest of penguins, seen here on Macquarie Island, Antarctica. The bird on the left is moulting. Right: The **king snake** is found throughout the U.S., Canada and New Mexico. Strikingly marked, they are non-poisonous.

-den) *n.* School or class in a school for children under six years of age. **kin′der·gart·ner, kin′der·gar·ten·er** *ns.* [Ger., = "children's garden"]

kin·dle (kĭn′del) *v.* (**-dled, -dling**). Set on fire, light; inflame, inspire (passion etc.); stir up (person *to*); catch fire, burst into flame; become animated, glow with passion, etc.; make, become, bright (cause to) glow. **kin′dling** *n.* (esp.) Small wood for starting fires.

kind·ly (kīnd′lē) *adv.* In a kind manner; obligingly; **take ∼**, accept pleasantly; **take ∼ to**, accept tolerantly. **kindly** *adj.* (**-li·er, -li·est**). Kind; pleasant, genial. **kind′li·ness** *n.*

kin·dred (kĭn′drĭd) *n.* Blood relationship; resemblance in character; one's relatives. **∼** *adj.* Related by blood; allied, connected, similar.

kine (kīn). Archaic pl. of COW[1].

kin·e·mat·ic (kĭnemăt′ĭk), **kin·e·mat·i·cal** (kĭnemăt′ĭkal) *adjs.* Of motion considered abstractly without reference to force or mass. **kin·e·mat′ics** *n.* Science of kinematic motion.

kin·e·scope (kĭn′eskōp) *n.* 1. Cathode ray tube used as screen on which televised images are displayed. 2. Motion-picture record of a transmitted television program.

kin·es·the·sia (kĭnĭsthē′zha) *n.* Sense of muscular effort in voluntary movement of body. **kin·es·thet·ic** (kĭnĭsthĕt′ĭk) *adj.*

ki·net·ic (kĭnĕt′ĭk) *adj.* Of, due to, motion; **∼ energy:** see ENERGY; **∼ theory,** theory that heat, gaseous state, is due to motion of particles of matter. **ki·net′ics** *n.* Science of relations between the motions of bodies and the forces acting on them.

king (kĭng) *n.* 1. (Title of) male sovereign (esp. hereditary) ruler of independent state; **K ∼ of Kings,** God; title assumed by many Eastern kings; **the three kings,** wise men who came from the East to worship the newborn Christ; (**1st** and **2nd Book of the Kings**), two historical books of Old Testament, following the two Books of Samuel and covering Jewish history, esp. that of the kingdom of Judah, from the death of David to

the destruction of the Temple (5... B.C.). 2. Great merchant etc.; b... kind (*of* fruits, plants, anima... products, etc.); **king of beas...** lion. 3. (chess) Piece that must ... protected against checkma... (checkers) piece that has be... "crowned"; (cards) one card in ea... suit bearing representation of ki... and usu. ranking next below a... **king's bishop, knight, ro...** chess pieces on king's side of boa... at beginning of game; **king's paw...** pawn in front of king at beginni... of game. 4. **king′bird,** any... several flycatchers, esp. the easte... kingbird (*Tyrannus tyrannus*) ... the western (*T. verticalis*); **kin...** **bolt,** main or large bolt in mecha... cal structure; **King Charl...** **spaniel,** English black-and-tan t... spaniel with long silky coat a... pendulous ears; **king cobra,** larg... extremely venomous snake (*Op...*

*Top left: The **kingcup** is sometimes called a mollyblob. Here kingcups are growing on an alpine pasture, but they are frequently found in marshy ground where they flower in spring. Top right: The **King Charles spaniel** is a sporty rather than a toy breed, and weighs between 8 and 14 lbs.*

ophagus hannah) of tropical Asia, hamadryad; **king crab**, large, edible crab (*Paralithodes camtscha-ica*) of northern Pacific waters; HORSEShoe crab; **king'cup**, (Brit.) marsh marigold; **king'fish** (pl. **-fishes**, collect. **-fish**), name used variously for several large fish of the genus *Menticirrhus* of warm ocean waters; *Genyonemus lineatus*, marine food fish inhabiting Californian coastal waters; **king'fisher**, any of several birds of family Alcedinidae, esp. the belted king-fisher (*Megaceryle alcyon*), feeding on fish it captures by diving; **King James Bible** or **Version** = AUTHORIZED VERSION; **king pen-guin**, large species of penguin (*Aptenodytes petagonica*) of Antarc-tic regions; **king'pin**, (bowling) central or foremost pin; kingbolt; (fig.) most important person in organization etc.; **king post**, up-right post from tie beam to rafter top; **king's** BENCH, ENGLISH, EVI-DENCE: see these words; **king-size (bed)**, usually larger, longer than standard; 6½ by 6½ ft.; (**cigarette**) longer than standard; **king snake**, any of various medium-sized, harm-less snakes (*Lampropeltis*) found from S. Canada through much of the U.S. and feeding on rats, mice, lizards, etc. **king'li·ness** *n.* **king'-less, king'like** *adjs.* **king'ship** *n.* **king** *v.* (checkers) Make into a king.

King¹ (kǐng), **Martin Luther, Jr.** (1929–68). Amer. Baptist minister and civil rights leader; prominent in Montgomery, Ala. bus transportation boycott in fight for desegregation; founder of Southern Christian Leadership Conference; received Nobel Prize for peace, 1964; assassinated April, 1968, in Memphis, Tenn.

King² (kǐng), **William Lyon Mackenzie** (1874–1950). Cana-

dian statesman; prime minister, 1921–6, 1926–30, 1935–48.

King³ (kǐng), **William Rufus DeVane** (1786–1853). Amer. poli-tician; U.S. vice president, 1853, under Franklin Pierce.

king'dom (kǐng'dom) *n.* State with king as its head; monarchical State; territory subject to a king; spiritual reign of God, sphere of this (esp. **K ~ of Heaven**); domain; province of nature (esp. **animal, vegetable, mineral,** ~); ~ **come**, (slang) the next world; **Middle K ~**, imperial state of HONAN under Chan dynasty; **Old, Middle, New K ~**, successive periods of civilization in ancient Egypt.

king·let (kǐng'lǐt) *n.* Either of two small N. Amer. songbirds, the **golden-crowned** ~ (*Regulus sat-rapa*) or the **ruby-crowned** ~ (*R. calendula*), both olive green and having a bright yellow, orange, or red head marking.

king·ly (kǐng'lē) *adj.* (**-li·er, -li·est**). Fit for, appropriate to, a king; kinglike, majestic. **king'li·ness** *n.*

Kings·ton (kǐngz'ton, kǐng'ston). Chief port and capital of JAMAICA, on the SE. coast.

kink (kǐngk) *n.* Back twist in wire, chain, or rope, such as may cause obstruction or a break; tight curl; sharp twist; (fig.) mental twist, eccentricity. ~ *v.* Form a kink; cause (rope) to do this. **kink'y** *adj.* (**kink·i·er, kink·i·est**).

Having kinks; (slang) eccentric, perverted.

kin·ka·jou (kǐng'kajoo) *n.* Car-nivorous arboreal mammal (*Potos flavus*) of Central and S. Amer., allied to raccoon, with prehensile tail.

Kin·sey (kǐn'zē), **Alfred Charles** (1894–1956). Amer. zoologist and sociologist famous for his studies of human sexual be-havior.

kins'folk (kǐnz'fōlk) *n.pl.* Re-lations by blood. **kins'man** (kǐnz'-man) *n.* (pl. **-men** pr. **-men**), fem. **kins'wom·an** (kǐnz'woͦoman) *n.* (pl. **-wom·en** pr. **-wǐmǐn**).

Kin·sha·sa (kǐn'shahsa). (for-merly Léopoldville) Capital of the Republic of Zaire (the former Democratic Republic of the Congo) and major port on the Congo River, on the NW. border.

kin·ship (kǐn'shǐp) *n.* Blood relationship; similarity, alliance, in character.

ki·osk (kēŏsk', kē'ŏsk) *n.* Light open pavilion in Turkey and Iran; structure like this for sale of newspapers etc.

kip¹ (kǐp) *n.* Hide of young or small beast as used for leather.

kip² (kǐp) *n.* (chiefly Brit. slang) Rooming house; bed. ~ *v.i.* (**kipped, kip'ping**). Go to bed; sleep.

Kip·ling (kǐp'lǐng), **Rudyard** (1865–1936). English novelist and poet; born in India; famous for short stories about India, and for children's books; author of *The Jungle Book, Captains Courageous, Just So Stories,* and the poem "Gunga Din."

kip·per (kǐp'er) *n.* Male salmon in spawning season; kippered herring. ~ *v.t.* Cure (salmon, herring, etc.) by splitting open, salting, and smoking.

Kir·ghiz, Kir·giz (kērgēz') *adjs.*

The forked tail of the swallow-tailed **kite** is clearly displayed in flight. The bird is found principally in warm marshy areas. Common kites once scavenged the streets of London.

& ns. (pl. **-ghiz, -ghiz·es**). (Member) of a Turkic, mainly Muslim people of central Asia; (of) their language, one of the Ural-Altaic family; (also **Kir·ghi·zia,** pr. kērgē'zha) constituent republic (properly *Kirghiz Soviet Socialist Republic*) of U.S.S.R., on Chinese frontier; capital, Frunze.

Ki·ri·ba·ti (kǐ'rǐbǎsh). Formerly Gilbert Islands; Brit. dependency, NE. of Solomon Islands; largest island, Tarawa; became independent republic 1979.

During the 1914–18 war **Field Marshal Kitchener** threw the weight of his influence behind a recruiting campaign that increased the British army from 20 divisions to 70 in two years.

Ki·rin (kēr'ǐn). Province of NE. China.

kirk (kērk) *n.* (chiefly Sc.) Church.

kirsch (kērsh), **kirsch-was·ser** (kērsh'vahser) *ns.* Colorless brandy made from cherries.

kish·ke (kǐsh'ke) *n.* Stuffed derma.

kis·met (kǐz'mǐt, kǐs'-) *n.* Destiny. [Arab. *kisma* lot, fate]

kiss (kǐs) *n.* Caress given with lips; light touch, a brushing against; any of various candies; ~ **of peace,** ceremonial kiss of worshippers in eucharistic liturgy as sign of love and union; pax; **kiss-off,** (slang) dismissal. **kiss** *v.t.* Touch with the lips, esp. in sign of affection, greeting, or reverence; touch lightly, brush against; ~ **away,** remove (tears etc.) with kisses; ~ **off,** (slang) get rid of, reject, dismiss.

kiss·er (kǐs'er) *n.* (slang) Face, mouth.

Kis·sin·ger (kǐs'ǐnjer), **Henry** (1923–). German-born Amer. political scientist; special assistant to Pres. Nixon for national security affairs; U.S. secretary of state under Presidents Nixon and Ford, 1973–1977; co-recipient of Nobel Prize for peace, 1973.

kit (kǐt) *n.* (Articles carried in) soldier's knapsack; personal equipment, esp. as packed for traveling; set of tools or other equipment; set of parts or materials to be assembled; ~ **bag,** bag, usu. cylindrical, for carrying soldier's or traveler's kit.

kitch·en (kǐch'en) *n.* Part of house where food is cooked; ~ **garden,** garden for growing fruit and vegetables for table; ~ **police,** (mil.) enlisted men designated to perform menial kitchen tasks.

Kitch·en·er (kǐch'ener), **Horatio Herbert, Earl Kitchener of Khartoum** (1850–1916). British military leader; retook Khartoum with Anglo-Egyptian force 1898; commander in chief in Boer War, 1900–2, and in India; secretary of state for war, 1914–16.

kitch·en·ette, kitch·en·et

(kǐchenĕt') *ns.* Small kitchen alcove used as kitchen.

kite (kīt) *n.* 1. Any large hawk-like bird of family Milvinae or Elaninae with long wings and us. forked tail. 2. Toy consisting of light wooden or plastic frame with paper or other thin material stretched over it, made to fly in strong wind at end of a long string; such a contrivance of box shape (**box-** ~) with open sides; highest or lightest sail of ship, set only in light wind. 3. Bad check or other commercial paper without value, used to get money or credit. **ki** *v.* (**kit·ed, kit·ing**). 1. (Cause to) soar like kite. 2. Get money or credit through use of kites.

kith (kǐth) *n.* ~ **and k** friends and relatives; now fre kinsfolk.

kitsch (kǐch) *n.* Literature, a music, etc., having little cultu merit but produced to appeal popular taste.

kit·ten (kǐt'en) *n.* Young of c **kit'ten·ish** *adj.* **kitten** *v.i.* Gi birth to kittens. **kit'ten·ish·ly** *ac*

kit·ti·wake (kǐt'ēwāk) *n.* Sma est of the strictly marine gu (*Rissa tridactyla*) of Arctic and Atlantic oceans, with black ma ings on usu. white plumage, ve long wings, and very short hind to [imit.]

kit·ty[1] (kǐt'ē) *n.* (pl. **-ties**). name for kitten.

kit·ty[2] (kǐt'ē) *n.* (pl. **-ties**). P or joint fund in games etc.

Kit·ty (kǐt'ē) **Hawk.** Village eastern North Carolina; site of successful airplane flight, Wright Brothers on Dec. 17, 19

Ki·wa·nis (kǐwah'nǐs). Inte national organization (founded Detroit, 1915) of business and pr fessional men, with clubs chiefly U.S. and Canada.

ki·wi (kē'wē) *n.* (pl. **-wis**). New Zealand flightless noctur bird of family Apterygidae, w rudimentary wings and no tail; th as emblem of New Zealand. Fuzzy, brown, edible fruit of a vi (*Actinidia chinensis*) native to su tropical Asia; Chinese gooseberr

K.K.K., KKK *abbrevs.* Ku Kl Klan.

kl, kl. *abbrevs.* Kiloliter(s).

Klam·ath (klǎm'ath) **Mou tains.** Mountain range extendi from NW. California into SW. O gon; **Klamath River,** river flo ing SW. 250 mi. (402 km) fro Oregon through NW. Californ into the Pacific Ocean.

Klan (klǎn) *n.* Ku Klux Klar

Until the early years of the 20th cent the **kitchen** was the center of ho management to a degree no long experienced. Storage and preparat areas had to be large and well planne as at Lanhydrock House, Cornw U.K.

The **kiwi** is a New Zealand flightless bird
of the family Apterygidae. It is so called
because of the male's shrill call. The
kiwi is a shy nocturnal bird about the
size of a chicken.

kla·vier (klavēr´, klăv´ēer, klā´-
vē-): see CLAVIER.

klax·on (klăk´son) *n.* (formerly
trademark) (Electric) horn formerly used on automobiles.

Klee (klā), **Paul** (1879–1940).
Swiss painter of abstract works of
art.

Klein (klīn) **bottle.** (math.)
Closed surface with only one side,
formed by passing neck of bottle
through side of bottle to join hole in
base.

klep·to·ma·ni·a (klĕptomā´nēa)

n. Irresistible impulse to steal in
persons not driven to it by need.
klep·to·ma´ni·ac *n.*

klieg (klēg) **light.** Powerful arc
light used in movie making. [f.
name of inventors, *Kliegl* brothers]

klip·spring·er (klĭp´sprĭnger) *n.*
Small South African mountain
antelope (*Oreotragus oreotragus*)
having large ears.

Klon·dike (klŏn´dīk). Region in
the Yukon Territory, NW. Canada,
where gold was discovered in 1896;
~ **River**, tributary of Yukon River.

km, km. *abbrevs.* Kilometer(s).

kn *abbrev.* Knot(s).

knack (năk) *n.* Acquired faculty
of doing a thing adroitly; ingenious
device, habit, of action, speech,
etc.

knack·wurst, knock·wurst
ŏk´wērst, -woorst, -voorsht) *ns.*
Short, thick, highly seasoned
sausage, similar to frankfurter.

knap·sack (năp´săk) *n.* Soldier's
or traveler's canvas or leather bag,
strapped to back and used for
carrying necessaries. [Low Ger.]

knap·weed (năp´wēd) *n.* Species
of *Centaurea* (esp. *C. nigra*), a
common weed with tough stem and
light purple flowers on dark globular head.

knave (nāv) *n.* 1. Rogue. 2.
(cards) Lowest picture card of each
suit, jack. **knav´er·y** *n.* (pl.
-er·ies). **knav´ish** *adj.* **knav´-
ish·ly** *adv.* **knav´ish·ness** *n.*

knead (nēd) *v.t.* Work up

(dough, clay, etc.) by drawing ou
and pressing or squeezing together
make (bread, pottery) thus; wor
on (muscles etc.) as if kneading
massage. **knead´er** *n.*

knee (nē) *n.* Joint between thigh
and lower leg in man; area abov
this joint considered as place o
which child or object is held; cor
responding joint in animals; part o
garment covering the knee; thin;
like knee in shape or position; o
one's ~s, kneeling, esp. in sup
plication, worship, or submission
bring (person) **to his ~s**, reduc
him to submission; ~ **breeches**
breeches reaching down to or jus
below knee; **knee´cap**, convex bon
in front of knee joint, patella
knee-deep, -high, so deep or high
as to reach the knees; **knee´hole**, (o
writing table etc.) having hole be
tween drawer pedestals to admi
knees. **knee** *v.t.* (**kneed, knee·
ing**). Touch or poke with the knee

kneel (nēl) *v.i.* (**knelt** pr. nĕl
or **kneeled, kneel·ing**). Fall, rest
on the knee(s), esp. in prayer o
reverence (*to*).

knell (nĕl) *n.* Sound of bell
esp. of one rung solemnly afte
death or at funeral; (fig.) anythin
regarded as omen of death or ex

Relics of the gold rush to the Klondyk
remain on the banks of Bonanza Creek
About 18,000 people joined the gol
rush of 1896 and the sudden increas
in the population of the area caused
severe food shortage.

*The **knapsack** has become far more sophisticated in its design and material than the simple rucksack originally used as a convenient carry-all by soldiers.*

*There are several species of **knapweed** of which the commonest is probably the hardhead (Centaurea nigra). The plant grows in heavy soils among grass and it flowers in the summer.*

nction. ~ v. (of bell) Ring, esp.
death or funeral; proclaim as by
knell; (fig.) sound ominously.

Knes·set, Knes·seth (knĕs′ĕt)
s. Israeli parliament.

knew (nōō, nū) v. past t. of
NOW.

Knick·er·bock·er (nĭk′er-
ŏker) n. 1. Descendant of original
Dutch settlers of New York; New
Yorker. 2. (**knickerbockers**)
Loose-fitting breeches gathered in
t knee. [*Knickerbocker*, pretended
uthor of W. Irving's *History of
New York*]

knick·ers (nĭk′erz) n.pl.
Knickerbockers.

knick·knack, nick-nack (nĭk′-
ăk) ns. Small ornamental article,
rinket, gimcrack.

knife (nīf) n. (pl. **knives** pr.
īvz). 1. Blade with sharpened
ongitudinal edge fixed in handle
ither rigidly or with hinge, used
s cutting instrument or as weapon;
harpened cutting blade forming
art of machine, as in paper cutter
tc.; **under the ~,** (colloq.)
undergoing surgical operation. 2.
nife edge, edge of knife; steel
wedge serving as fulcrum on which
alancing beam, lever, etc. works.
nife v.t. (**knifed, knif·ing**). Cut,
tab, with knife; (fig.) betray, seek
o defeat by underhand means.

knight (nīt) n. 1. (hist.) Military
ollower, esp. one devoted to service
f (lady) as attendant or champion
n war or tournament; (hist.) per-
on, usu. one of noble birth who
ad served as page and squire,
aised to honorable military rank
y king or qualified person. 2.
One on whom is conferred rank
orresponding to medieval knight

as reward for personal merit or
services to crown or country. 3.
Piece in game of chess, usu. shaped
like horse's head. 4. **~-errant** (pl.
~s-errant), medieval knight
wandering in search of chivalrous
adventures; (fig.) person of chivalrous or quixotic spirit; **knight-
errantry** (pl. **-tries**), practice,
conduct, of a knight-errant;
Knight of the Round Table, one
of King ARTHUR[1]'S knights;
Knights of Columbus, benevolent society of R.C. men, founded
in the U.S. in 1882; **knight** v.t.
Confer knighthood on. **knight′-
hood** n. Rank, dignity, of a knight.

*The whetting and finishing of a fine edge to a **knife** requires a stone of fine grain and a skillful operator. This knife-grinder in a street in Beirut, Lebanon, works the whetstone by operating a treadle.*

knight′ly adj.

knish (knĭsh) n. Dumpling of
flaky dough filled with cheese,
mashed potatoes, chopped meat,
etc., and baked or fried.

knit (nĭt) v. (**knit·ted, knit·-
ting**). Form (close texture) by
interlooping successive series of
loops of yarn or thread; make
(garments etc.) of this; contract
(brow) in wrinkles; make, become,
close or compact; unite intimately
by means of common interests,
marriage etc.

knit·ting (nĭt′ĭng) n. (esp.) Work
in process of knitting; ~ **needle,**
slender rod of metal, wood, plastic,
etc., two or more of which are used
together in knitting.

knob (nŏb) n. Rounded protuberance, esp. at end or on surface of thing; such handle of door
or drawer. **knobbed** adj. **knob′by**
adj. (**-bi·er, -bi·est**). **knob′bi·-
ness** n.

knock (nŏk) v. 1. Strike with
hard blow; strike door, strike *at,
on the door,* to gain admittances;
drive (thing) *in, out, off,* etc., by
striking; (of internal combustion
engine etc.) make knocking, clang-
ing noise from mechanical defect
or faulty ignition; (colloq.) disparage. 2. ~ **about,** strike repeatedly, treat roughly; wander,
lead irregular life; ~ **against,** collide with; ~ **down,** strike to ground
with blow; take (machinery, furniture) to pieces to save space in
transportation; dispose of (article
to bidder at auction) by knock with
hammer; ~ **off,** strike off with
blow; leave off (work); (colloq.)
dispatch (business) or compose
(verses etc.) rapidly; deduct (sum
from price etc.); ~ **out,** render unconscious with a blow; (boxing)
defeat opponent by knocking him
down for a count of ten (ten
seconds); (colloq.) exhaust completely; (slang) overwhelm with
feeling, emotions, laughter, etc.;
(slang) produce hastily; ~ **together,** put hastily together; ~ **up,**
(slang) impregnate. 3. **knock′-
about,** boisterous, noisy (performance); wandering irregularly; (of
clothes) suitable for rough or casual
use; **knock′down,** (of blow) knocking down the opponent; (of price at
auction) minimum; **knock-kneed,
-knee,** (having) knees turned inward toward each other; **knock′out**
(blow) that knocks boxer out;
(slang) outstandingly beautiful
woman or thing; **knockout drops,**
drops added to drink in order to
make drinker unconscious. **knock**

overhand knot | figure of eight knot | diamond knot | bowline | surgeon's knot | reef knot | granny | sheet bend | double sheet bend variation

sheepshank | slippery hitch | half hitch over a belaying cleat | carrick bend

half hitch | clove hitch | rolling hitch | fishermans bend | timber hitch | round turn and two half hitches

n. Blow; rap, esp. at door; thumping noise in engine etc.

knock·er (nŏk′er) *n.* (esp.) Appendage, usu. of iron or brass, so hinged to door that it can be struck against metal plate to call attention.

knock·wurst: see KNACKWURST.

knoll[1] (nol) *n.* Small hill, mound.

knoll[2] (nōl) *v.* (archaic) Ring (bell); (of bell) sound; knell; toll out (hours); summon by sound of bell.

Knos·sos, Cnos·sus (nŏs′us). Ancient city of Crete; center of the MINOAN civilization, with vast labyrinthine palace (the Palace of MINOS).

knot (nŏt) *n.* 1. Intertwining of parts of one or more ropes, strings, etc., to fasten them together; ribbon etc. so tied as ornament or adjunct to dress; string etc. entangled so it is hard to undo; that which forms or maintains union (esp. marriage); difficulty, problem. 2. (naut.) Unit of speed of 1 nautical mi. per hour (orig. measured by knots on log line; abbrev. kn). 3. Hard lump in animal body; (hard mass formed in trunk at insertion of branch, causing) round cross-grained piece in board, which may fall out, leaving **knot′hole**; node on stem of plant. 4. Group, cluster, of persons or things. 5. **knot′grass**, common weed (*Polygonum aviculare*) with intricately branched creeping stems and small pale pink flowers. **knot** *v.* (**knot·ted, knot·ting**). Tie (string etc.) in knot; entangle. **knot′ty** *adj.* (**-ti·er, ti·est**). Full of knots; (fig.) puzzling, hard to explain or solve.

*There are types of **knots** for various functions: single knots secure the line to itself; double knots join two lines or more; securing knots attach a line to an object, such as a spar, and knots may be used to shorten a line.*

knout (nowt, nōōt) *n. & v.t.* (Flog with) scourge formerly used as instrument of punishment in Russia, often fatal in its effects.

know (nō) *v.* (**knew** pr. nōō, nū, **known** pr. nōn, **know·ing**). 1. Recognize, identify; be able to distinguish; be acquainted with (*by sight, to speak to*, etc.); have personal experience of; be on friendly terms with; be aware of, be aware (*that, how*, etc.); be versed in; ~ **about**, have information about; ~ **better than**, be too well informed of the facts to believe; be too discreet or well behaved (*to* do): ~ **of**, be aware of; ~ **one's own mind**, not vacillate. 2. ~**-it-all**, person claiming or pretending omniscience; ~**-how**, (*n.*) practical knowledge of methods; **know-nothing**, ignorant person; **Know Nothing**, (member of) U.S. political movement in 1850s, hostile to Catholics and immigrants; **you know**, meaningless parenthesis in substandard speech. **know** *n.* **in the** ~, (colloq.) knowing (about) the thing in question or what is not generally known. **know′a·ble** *adj.* **know′er** *n.*

know·ing (nō′ĭng) *adj.* (esp.) Cunning, wide-awake. **know′-ing·ly** *adv.* In a knowing manner; consciously, intentionally.

knowl·edge (nŏl′ĭj) *n.* Knowing, familiarity gained by experience, (*of*); person's range of information;

theoretical or practical understanding (*of*); the sum of what is known; **to my** ~, as far as I know. **knowl′edge·a·ble** *adj.* Well informed, intelligent.

knuck·le (nŭk′el) *n.* Bone at finger joint, esp. at root of finger; projection of carpal or tarsal joint of quadruped; cut of meat consisting of this with parts above and below it; **knuck′lebone**, bone forming knuckle; limb bone with ball-like knob at joint end, this part of animal's leg as cut of meat; metacarpal or metatarsal bone of sheep etc.; **knuckle-duster** (slang) see BRASS knuckles; **knuck′lehead** (*n.*) (colloq.) stupid, bungling person; fool. **knuckle** *v.* (**-led, -ling**). Strike, press, rub, with knuckles; place knuckles on ground when shooting a marble or, esp., shoot (marble) with thumb from knuckle of bent forefinger; ~ **down**, work hard, apply oneself diligently; ~ **under**, give in, submit.

knur (nēr) *n.* Hard excrescence on trunk of tree; hard concretion.

knurl (nērl) *n.* Knot, knob; bead or ridge in metal object, esp. one of a series of ridges to aid in gripping. **knurled** *adj.*

KO, K.O., k.o. (pl. **KO's** *abbrevs.* Knockout; knock out. **KO** *v.t.* (**KO'd, KO'ing**).

ko·a·la (kōah′la) *n.* Tailless arboreal marsupial (*Phascolarctos cinereus*) of the Australian region, feeding almost exclusively on the leaves of the eucalyptus tree.

Ko·be (kō′bā; *Jap.* kaw′bĕ′). City and port in S. Honshu, Japan.

Koch (kawχ), **Robert** (1843–1910). German bacteriologist and hysician, famous for his work on he bacillus of tuberculosis.

Kö·chel (kö′χel) *n.* ~ **number.** Number of a composition by Mozart as listed in complete catalog of his works compiled in 19th c. by Austrian scientist Ludwig von Köchel.

Ko·di·ak (kō′dēăk). Island of Alaska SE. of the Alaska Peninsula in the Gulf of Alaska; noted for salmon fishing industry and as the habitat of the **Kodiak bear,** a large brown bear (*Ursus middendorffi*) inhabiting islands and coasts of Alaska and British Columbia, weighing up to 1500 lbs. and growing up to 9 ft.

K. of C. *abbrev.* Knights of Columbus.

Koh·i·noor, Koh-i-noor (kō′-noor) *ns.* Famous Indian diamond of great size (109 karats), with history going back to 14th c.; one of the British crown jewels since annexation of Punjab, 1849. [Pers. *ōh-i-nūr*, mountain of light]

kohl (kōl) *n.* Preparation, based on powdered sulfide of lead or sulfide of antimony used to darken eyelids etc. [Arab. *kuhl*]

kohl·ra·bi (kōlrah′bē, kōl′rah-) *n.* (pl. **-bies**). Garden vegetable (*Brassica cauloropa*) of cabbage family, bulbous part of steam at ground level being edible.

Koi·ne (koinā′) *n.* Common language of the Greeks from the close of the classical period to the Byzantine era; (**k**~) language shared by various peoples; lingua franca.

Ko·la (kō′la). Peninsula of northwestern U.S.S.R. between Barents Sea and White Sea.

ko·la, co·la (kō′la) *ns.* Either of two trees native to W. Africa and introduced into W. Indies and Brazil, (*Cola nitida* or *C. acuminata*); ~ **nut,** seed of these trees, yielding mildly stimulating extract used in beverages and medicines.

ko·lin·sky (kolĭn′skē) *n.* (pl. **-skies**). Siberian mink; its fur. [Russ., f. Kola]

kol·khoz (kawlkawz′, -χawz′) *n.* Collective farm in U.S.S.R.

Ko·mo·do (komō′dō) **dragon.**

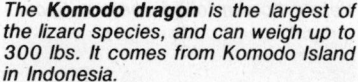

*The **Komodo dragon** is the largest of the lizard species, and can weigh up to 300 lbs. It comes from Komodo Island in Indonesia.*

Very large monitor lizard (*Varanus komodoenis*), of the Indonesian islands of Komodo and Flores, with heavy powerful body, sometimes 15 ft. (4.5 m) long. [*Komodo*, island in Malay Archipelago]

koo·doo: see KUDU.

kook (kook) *n. & adj.* (slang) Crazy or eccentric (person). **kook·y, kook·ie** *adjs.* (**kook·i·er, kook·i·est**).

kook·a·bur·ra (kookabŭr′a, koo′kabēra) *n.* Large kingfisher (*Dacelo novaeguineae*) of S. Australia, having a raucous laughing call, also called "laughing jackass."

Koo·te·nay (koo′tenā). (also **Kootenai**) River flowing 407 mi. (655 km) from SE. British Colum-

*Sometimes called an Australian bear the **koala** is a marsupial. At birth, the ¾ in. long baby crawls to the mother's pouch where it remains for about 8 months. Adults can be 2 ft. 6 in. long.*

bia, Canada, through NW. Montana and N. Idaho, then N. through ~ **Lake** in British Columbia to the Columbia River.

ko·peck, ko·pek, co·peck (kō'pĕk) *ns.* Russian coin = $\frac{1}{100}$ of a ruble.

Ko·ran (kōrahn', -răn, kaw-). Sacred book of Islam, in Arabic, consisting of 114 chapters of revelations orally delivered by Muhammad, collected in writing and put in order after his death by Abu Bakr; the four chief duties that it enjoins are prayer, the giving of alms, fasting, and the pilgrimage to Mecca. [Arab. *kur'ān* the reading]

Ko·re·a (kōrē'a, kaw-). (Chin. *Tai Han*, Jap. *Chōsen*) Country of E. Asia consisting principally of a

Bottom: A map of **Korea,** *a location map and the national flags. The divided country covers about 85,000 sq. miles. People work mostly at agriculture but also exploit mineral deposits. Below: Korean folk dancers in Seoul.*

mountainous peninsula running southward from Manchuria opposite Japan; in Japanese possession 1910–45; at end of World War II occupied by troops of U.S. (for the United Nations) and the U.S.S.R. respectively S. and N. of the 38th parallel; the **Republic of** ~ (capital, Seoul) was proclaimed in S. Korea in July 1948 and the (communist) **Democratic People's Republic of** ~ (capital, Pyongyang) in N. Korea in Sept. 1948; a war between the two lasted 1950–3, with the U.S.-led United Nations forces joining S. Korean forces and with U.S.S.R. pilots and advisors and, eventually, Chinese Communist troops, joining N. Korean forces; **Korea Strait**, channel 120 mi. (193 km) wide between South Korea and SW. Japan connecting the Sea of Japan and the East China Sea. **Ko·re·an** *adj. & n.* (Native, inhabitant) of Korea; (of) the agglutinative language of Korea, which is related to Japanese; ~ **War**, war

between N. and S. Korea, 1950–3

Kos·ci·us·ko (kŏsēŭs'kō, -ōōs'-*Pol.* kawshchōōsh'kō), **Thaddeus** (1746–1817). Polish national hero soldier, and liberal statesman. served in Revolutionary War under Washington; after the second partition of Poland, 1793, he led an uprising against Russia that failed.

ko·sher (kō'sher) *adj.* (of food, or store where food is sold or used. Fulfilling requirements of Jewish dietary law. [Heb. *kāšēr* right, fit]

Kos·suth (kŏs'ōōth, -ōōt; *Hung* kaw'shōōt), **La·jos** (lŭ'yawsh (1802–92). Hungarian national hero and liberal statesman.

Ko·sy·gin (kawsē'gĭn), **Aleksei Nikolayevich** (1904–80). Soviet statesman; premier of U.S.S.R. 1964–80.

ko·to (kō'tō; *Jap.* kaw'taw') *n.* Japanese musical instrument with 13 long silk strings.

Kot·ze·bue (kawt'sebōō), **August Friedrich Ferdinand von** ~ (1761–1819), German dramatist, author of sentimental plays; **Otto von** ~ (1787–1846), his son, navigator and explorer, discoverer of **Kotzebue Sound**, inlet of NW. Alaska.

Kous·se·vitz·ky (kōōsevĭt'skē), **Serge** (1874–1951). Russianborn orchestra conductor; conducted Boston Symphony Orchestra, 1924–49; organized Berkshire Music Center, Tanglewood, Mass.

Kow·loon (kow'lōōn'). City on ~ **Peninsula**, SE. China, opposite Hong Kong Island and part of the crown colony of Hong Kong.

kow·tow (kowtow', kow'tow) *n.* Chinese custom of touching ground with forehead as sign of worship or submission. ~ *v.i.* Make a kowtow; act obsequiously (*to*). [Chin. *k'o t'ou* knock head]

KP, K.P. *abbrevs.* Kitchen police.

K.P.H., k.p.h., kph *abbrevs.* Kilometers per hour.

Kr *symbol.* Krypton.

Kr., kr. *abbrevs.* Krona, krone.

kraal (krahl) *n.* South African village of huts enclosed by stockade; enclosure for cattle or sheep. [Afrikaans, f. Port. *corral*]

Krafft-E·bing (krăft'ĕb'ĭng, krahft'-; *Ger.* krahft'ā'bĭng), **Richard von** (1840–1902). German physician and psychologist; author of *Psychopathia Sexualis*.

kraft (krăft, krahft) *n.* (also ~ **paper**) Strong smooth brown wrapping paper made from unbleached sulfate wood pulp.

Kra·ka·to·a (krăkatō'a), **Kra·ka·tau** (krahkatow'). Small volcanic island of Indonesia in Sunda

*Often called a laughing jackass because of its call, the **kookaburra** is a type of Australian kingfisher with a thick, short beak adapted to killing reptiles and rodents.*

Strait between Java and Sumatra, scene of a great eruption in 1883.

Kra·ków (krah´kow). (English Cracow) City in S. Poland on the Vistula River.

Krem·lin (krĕm´lĭn). Fortified enclosure or citadel within Russian town or city; esp. that of Moscow, containing the old imperial palace and many public buildings, now the political and administrative center of the U.S.S.R.; hence, **the** ~, the Russian Government.

kreut·zer, kreu·zer (kroit´ser) *ns.* Small silver and copper coins formerly current in Germany and Austria. [Ger. *kreuz* cross]

krieg·spiel (krēg´spēl, -shpēl) *n.* War game in which blocks, flags, etc., representing troops etc. are moved about on maps.

Kriem·hild (krēm´hĭlt). In the Nibelungenlied, a Burgundian princess, wife of Siegfried and later of Etzel (Attila), whom she marries in order to be revenged on her brothers for the murder of Siegfried.

krill (krĭl) *n.* Tiny planktonic crustaceans eaten by whales etc.

kris (krĭs, krēs) *n.* Malayan dagger with wavy blade.

Krish·na (krĭsh´na). (Hindu myth.) Great deity or deified hero, worshipped as incarnation of Vishnu.

kró·na, kro·na (krō´na) *ns.* Principal monetary unit of Sweden (pl. **-nor** pr. -nor) = 100 öre; of Iceland (pl. **-nur** pr. -ner).

kro·ne (krō´ne) *n.* (pl. **-ner** pr. -ner). 1. Principal monetary unit of Denmark and Norway = 100 öre. 2. (hist.) Austrian silver coin. 3. (hist.) German ten-mark gold piece. [Ger. and Dan., = "crown"]

Kron·shlot (krawn´shlot). (formerly **Kronstadt, Cronstadt**) Russian fortress and naval base on Kotlin Island in Gulf of Finland, protecting approach to Leningrad.

Kru·ger[1] (krōō´ger; *Du.* krü´χer), **Stephanus Johannes Paulus** (1825–1904). "Oom Paul," Afrikaans soldier and statesman; president of Transvaal republic 1883–1899.

Kru·ger[2] (krōō´ger) **National Park.** Park and wildlife preserve covering 8,000 sq. mi. (20,720 sq. km) in the Republic of South Africa, in the NE. part.

Krupp (krŭp; *Ger.* krōōp), **Alfred** (1812–87). German metallurgist, founder of steel and armament works at Essen.

kryp·ton (krĭp´tŏn) *n.* (chem.) Element, one of the inert rare gases of the atmosphere (1 part in

1,000,000 by volume); symbol Kr, at. no. 36, at. wt. 83.80. [Gk. *krupton* hidden]

KS *abbrev.* Kansas.

Kshat·ri·ya (kshăt´rēa) *n.* Member of second of the four Hindu castes, the military, governing, and professional caste. [Sansk., f. *kshatra* rule]

Kt. *abbrev.* Knight.

kt. *abbrev.* Karat.

Kua·la Lum·pur (kwah´la loompoor´). Capital and commercial center of Malaysia, in the SW. Malay Peninsula.

Ku·blai Khan (kōō´blī kahn´), **Ku·bla Khan** (kōō´bla kahn) (1216–94). Mongol conqueror an emperor, grandson of GENGH KHAN; founder of Mongol dynas (the Yüan) in China.

ku·dos (kōō´dŏz, -dōs, -dŏ kū´-) *n.* Glory, acclaim as a resu of achievement or position; (in correctly misconstrued as *n.pl*

*The **Kremlin** in Moscow covers roughly triangular area of 90 acre Within the walls of its cathedral squar are three cathedrals and the great be tower of Ivan the Terrible.*

*By the 5th century A.D. **Krishna** held an established place in the Hindu pantheon as the 8th incarnation of Vishnu, one of the supreme gods. Here Krishna supports Mt. Govardhana in a painting by Ustad Sahibdin, c. 1690.*

compliments, awards.

ku·du, koo·doo (kōō'dōō) *ns.* Antelope of S. and E. Africa (genus *Strepsiceros*), with vertical white stripes on body and, in the male, twisted horns.

kud·zu (kōōd'zōō) *n.* Rapidly growing perennial vine (*Pueraria lobata*) native to Japan and China and later established in southern U.S.; used for food and forage and as soil stabilizer.

Ku Klux Klan (kōō' klŭks' klăn', kū'-). 1. Secret society formed *c*1865 in southern states by Confederate officers after Civil War; quickly grew into a group aimed at reasserting white su-

premacy by terrorizing blacks and their defenders, the members covering themselves and their horses with white sheets. 2. Similar but more widespread organization that originated in Georgia in 1915; militantly patriotic, anti-Catholic, anti-Jewish, and anti-liberal; influential after World War I; revived 1945. [Gk. *kuklos* circle (*klan* added for effect)]

kuk·ri (kōōk'rē) *n.* Curved knife broadening toward point, used by Gurkhas of India.

ku·lak (kōōlăk', -lahk', kōō'lăk, -lahk) *n.* Well-to-do Russian

Below: The greater kudu survives well even in settled parts of Africa where other antelopes have died out. The lesser kudu is found only in Somaliland and Kenya.

After the 1939–45 war, there was an attempt to revive the Ku Klux Klan in the U.S.A. The attempt failed although the organization still survives despite bans placed on its activities in most States.

peasant, farmer, or trader, esp. (under Soviet) peasant-proprietor tilling land for his own profit; compelled by Stalin to work for the State, 1925–35. [Russ., = "fist"]

Kul·tur (kōōltoor') *n.* Culture and civilization, esp. German, as idealized by exponents and defenders of German imperialism, esp. from 1900 to the end of World War II.

küm·mel (kĭm'el; *Ger.* küm'el) *n.* Sweet colorless liqueur flavored with caraway, anis, or cumin, orig. made in Riga.

kum·quat (kŭm'kwŏt) *n.* Any of several citrus trees (genus *Fortunella*) native of China but cultivated in California, Florida, and the Gulf states for their plum-sized, orange-like fruit.

Kun (kōōn), **Bé·la** (bā'la) (1886–1945). Hungarian communist leader; head of Hungarian communist government that ruled for a few months in 1919.

kung fu (kōōng fōō', gōōng'). Chinese system of self-defense, similar to karate.

Kuo·min·tang (kwō'mĭntăng', -tahng'; *Chin.* gwaw'mĭn'dahng'). Chinese nationalist radical party, founded 1905 by Sun Yat-Sen and led, after his death in 1925, by Chiang Kai-Shek; it led the revolution of 1911; was at first aided by the communists but fought them intermittently from 1927 onward; gained control over most of China and set up a government at Nanking, 1927; in 1949 it was driven out by the communists, and its government withdrew to Taiwan. [Chin., = "national people's party"]

Kurd (kērd, koord) *n.* One of a tall, fair-haired, long-headed nomadic people of Indo-European stock with Turkish admixture, inhabiting Kurdistan.

Kurd·ish (kēr'dĭsh, koor'dĭsh) *adj.* Of the Kurds or their language. ~ *n.* Language of the

Kurds, a dialect of Iranian.

Kur·dis·tan (kĕrdĭstăn′, koor-dĭstahn′). Mountainous region of SE. Turkey, N. Iraq, and NW. Iran, inhabited chiefly by Kurds.

Ku·rile, Ku·ril (koor′ĭl, kōōrēl′) **Islands.** Chain of small islands stretching 700 mi. (1,127 km) northward from Japan to Kamchatka; ceded by Russia to Japan, 1875; regained by Russia at end of World War II.

Ku·wait (kōōwāt′). State on NW. coast of Persian Gulf; former British protectorate, independent since 1961; major oil-producing country; capital, Kuwait.

Kuz·netsk (kōōznĕtsk′) **Basin.** Industrial region in S. central U.S.S.R., important for coal and iron ore deposits.

kvass (kvahs) *n.* Russian fermented beverage similar to beer and made from infusion of rye or barley with malt.

kw *abbrev.* Kilowatt.

Kwa·ja·lein (kwah′jalēn). Island in the W. Pacific in the Marshall Islands; site of Amer. naval base.

There are no national boundaries to **Kurdistan.** *The area inhabited by Kurds is partly in Turkey, Iraq, Iran and Russia. Here, a Kurd leads his herd to pasture beside Lake Van in Turkey.*

Kwang·si-Chuang (kwahng′sē chwahng′; *Chin.* gwahng′sē jwahng′). Autonomous region of China, in the SE.; capital, Nanning.

Kwang·tung (kwahng′tŏong′; *Chin.* gwahng′dŏong′). Coastal province of SE. China.

Kwan·tung (kwahn′tŏong′; *Chin.* gwahn′dŏong′). Territory of S. Manchuria forming S. part of Liaotung peninsula.

Kwan Yin (kwahn′yĭn′). Female divinity worshipped by Chinese Buddhists as incarnation of mercy or compassion. [Chin., = "regard sound," i.e. listen to human cries]

kwash·i·or·kor (kwashēōr′kōr, -ker) *n.* Nutritional disease of infants and children esp. in Africa, caused by protein deficiency.

Kwei·chow (kwā′chow′; *Chin.* gwā′jō′). Province of SW. China.

KY *abbrev.* Kentucky.

ky·mo·graph, cy·mo·graph (kīm*o*grăf, -grahf) *ns.* Instrumen recording variations of pressur (esp. blood pressure), pulsations sound waves, etc. **ky·mo·graph′i** *adj.*

Kyo·to (kyō′tō; *Jap.* kyaw′taw) (also **Kioto**) City and forme capital of Japan, on S. Honsh Island.

Kyr·i·e (kēr′ēā, kĭr′-) *n.* (also ~ **e·le·i·son** pr. ĕlā′ēsawn) Shor petition beginning thus, used in Orthodox and R.C. churches esp at beginning of mass; musica setting of this; response to com mandments in communion service in Episcopal Church. [Gk. *kuri eleēson* Lord have mercy]

Kyu·shu (kū′shōō′). (also **Kiu· shu**) Island of Japan in the Pacific Ocean off the E. coast o Asia; third largest and farthest S. o the four main islands.

The wealth of **Kuwait** *lies solely in its great oil deposits. Below: the port o the same name is the best on the Persian Gulf and serves much of north Arabia. Below left: A map of Kuwait an its flag.*

The letter **L l**, a labio-palatal consonant, is derived from the 12th letter of the ancient Semitic alphabet. The Greek 'lambda' is believed to mean ox-goad, although the letter does not seem to represent the shape of goads discovered in the area. In the Roman cursive form, the horizontal line was used as a link with other letters and was not used when the letter stood alone.

Phoenician   Cretan   Archaic Latin

Early Greek   Early Latin   Classical Latin

L, l (ĕl) (pl. **L's, l's** or **Ls, ls**). Twelfth letter of modern English and 11th of ancient Roman alphabet, representing Greek lambda and Semitic *lamed* (of which earliest known forms are 𐤋 and l), in modern English representing a voiced consonant formed by emission of breath at sides, or one side, of oral passage, with point of tongue in contact with gums or palate. 2. Thing shaped like L; rectangular joint of pipes etc. 3. Roman numeral symbol for 50.

L. *abbrev.* Lake; lambert; Latin; latitude.

l. *abbrev.* Left; length; line; lira; re; liter(s).

£ Symbol for POUND[1], defs. 2 and

La *symbol.* Lanthanum.
La., LA *abbrevs.* Louisiana.
L.A. *abbrev.* Los Angeles.
lab (lăb) *n.* (colloq.) Laboratory.
Lab. *abbrev.* Labrador.
la·bel (lā´bel) *n.* Slip of paper, card, linen, metal, etc., for attaching to object and indicating its nature, owner, name, destination, etc.; (fig.) short classifying phrase or name applied to persons etc. ~ *v.t.* (**-beled, -bel·ing**, Brit. **-belled, -bel·ling**). Attach label to; assign to category.
la·bi·al (lā´bēal) *adj.* 1. Of the lips; (anat., zool.) of, like, serving as, a lip, labial part, or labium; ~ **palp**, sensitive lobe near mouth of certain mollusks; jointed appendage on insect labium. 2. (phon. of sounds) Formed by complete or partial closure of lips, for example, *n, b, f.* **labial** *n.* Labial sound. **la·bi·al·ize** (lā´bēalīz) *v.t.* (**-ized, -iz·ing**).
la·bi·a ma·jo·ra (lā´bēa majōr´a, -jōr´a) (sing. **la·bi·um ma·jus** pr. lā´bēum mā´jus). (anat.) The outer folds of skin of the external female genitalia.
la·bi·a mi·no·ra (lā´bēa mĭnōr´a, -nōr´a) (sing. **la·bi·um mi·nus** pr. lābēum mī´nus). (anat.) The inner folds of skin of the external female genitalia.
la·bi·ate (lā´bēāt, -ĭt) *adj.* (bot.) With corolla or calyx divided into two parts suggesting lips; (bot.,

zool.) like lip or labium. ~ *n.* Labiate plant.
la·bile (lā´bĭl; *Brit.* lā´bīl) *adj.* (phys., chem.) Unstable, liable to displacement or change.
la·bi·um (lā´bēum) *n.* (pl. **-bi·a** pr. -bēa). 1. (anat., usu. in pl.) Lip(s) of female pudendum: see LABIA MAJORA and LABIA MINORA. 2. (zool.) Lower part of insect's mouth, the fused second maxillae. 3. (bot.) Lip, esp. the lower, of labiate corolla.
la·bor, Brit. **la·bour** (lā´ber) *ns.* 1. Bodily or mental toil, exertion, task; (service rendered by) laborers; working classes as a political force; **hard ~**: see HARD; ~ **of love**: see LOVE *n.*, 2; ~ **of Hercules**, task needing enormous strength etc. 2. Uterine contractions in childbirth. 3. **L ~ Day**, day celebrated in honor of workers, in U.S. on first Monday in September; ~ **market**, supply of unemployed labor with reference to demand for it; ~ **pains**, those preceding childbirth; ~ **party**, political party representing in-

*The **labiate** form of the white dead-nettle is clear. Its lower lip has lateral lobes with teeth-like features. The plant flourishes on waste ground and on roadsides, blooming in early summer and in the Fall.*

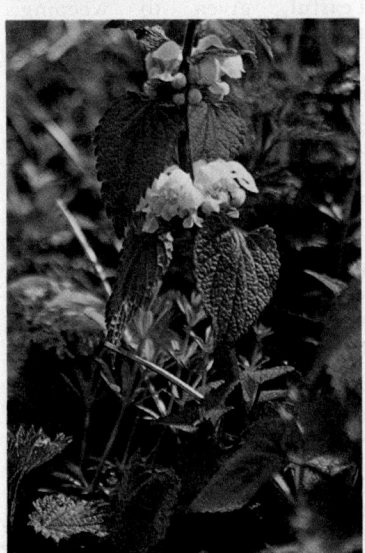

terests of workers; ~ **saving**, tending to reduce amount of work required to accomplish a task; ~ **union**, association of workers organized for mutual benefit and for collective bargaining with company management. **labor** *v.* 1. Exert oneself, work hard; strive (*for, to*). 2. Advance with difficulty; be troubled or impeded; suffer *under* mistake etc. 3. Elaborate, work out in detail, treat at length. **la·bored** *adj.* Showing signs of labor, not spontaneous. **la·bor·er** *n.* (esp.) Unskilled worker doing (esp. heavy) manual work.
lab·o·ra·to·ry (lăb´ratōrē, -tōrē, lăb´era-; *Brit.* labor´aterē, -atrē) *n.* (pl. **-ries**). Room or building used for scientific experiments, tests, etc., or for the preparation of chemical substances etc.; **language ~**, room equipped with tape recorders for study of foreign languages.
la·bo·ri·ous (labōr´ēus, -bōr´-) *adj.* Hard working; showing signs of toil, not facile or fluent. **la·bo´ri·ous·ly** *adv.* **la·bo´ri·ous·ness** *n.*
Lab·ra·dor[1] (lăb´radōr). Eastern coastal part of large peninsula of extreme NE. America, between Hudson Bay and Atlantic; part of the Canadian province of Newfoundland; ~ **Current**, cold ocean current moving southward from Arctic Ocean along part of E. coast of N. America.
Lab·ra·dor[2] (lăb´radōr) *n.* (also ~ **retriever**) Dog of black- or golden-coated breed related to spaniel and setter and used for retrieving game.
la·brum (lā´brum, lăb´rum) *n.* (pl. **la·bra** pr. lā´bra). Ventral lobe of front of insect's head, covering the mouth parts.
la·bur·num (labẽr´num) *n.* Small leguminous tree or shrub of genus *L* ~ with poisonous seeds, of which the commonest species, *L. anagyroides*, has racemes of bright-yellow flowers.
lab·y·rinth (lăb´erĭnth) *n.* Complicated irregular structure with many passages hard to find way through or about without guidance,

The forbidding terrain of **Labrador** delayed its development until well into the 20th century. The potential of the Grand Falls for hydro-electric power and the discovery of huge iron deposits encouraged development.

maze; intricate or tortuous arrangement; (anat.) complex cavity of internal ear. **lab·y·rin·thine** (lăberĭn´thĭn, -thēn) *adj*.

lac (lăk) *n*. Resinous incrustation produced on certain trees in E. Indies by the insect *Tachardia lacca* and used as varnish or as substitute for true lacquer; known, when melted and formed into thin plates, as shellac.

Lac·ca·dive (lăk´adĭv) **Islands.** Group of circular coral reefs in Indian Ocean about 200 miles (322 km) W. of the Malabar Coast of India; administered (with adjacent Minicoy and Amindivi Islands) by India; capital, Kozhikode.

lace (lās) *n*. 1. Cord or leather strip for fastening or tightening opposite edges of boots, shoes, etc., by help of eyelets or hooks. 2. Openwork ornamental patterned fabric of fine, usu. linen, thread, esp. that composed of needlework stitches (**needlepoint** ~), or braided with the aid of bobbins on a pillow (**bobbin** ~). 3. **lace´bark tree**, W. Indian tree (*Lagetta linteria*) with inner bark of lace-like fibers; **lace´wing**, name given to various insects of order Neuroptera. **lac´y** *adj*. (**lac·i·er**, **lac·i·est**). **lace** *v*. (**laced**, **lac·ing**). Fasten, tighten, compress, trim, with lace(s); compress one's waist; embroider (*with* thread etc.); pass (cord etc.) through; diversify *with* streaks of color; flavor, fortify (beverage) *with* whiskey.

lac·er·ate (lăs´erāt) *v.t.* (**-at·ed**, **-at·ing**). Mangle, tear (esp. flesh or tissues); afflict, distress (heart, feelings). **lac·er·a·tion** (lăserā´shon) *n*.

Lach·e·sis (lăk´ĭsĭs). (Gk. myth.) One of the three Fates, who, with her spindle, spun out the course of

human life.

Lach·ry·ma Chris·ti (lăk´rima krĭs´tē). Strong sweet red wine of S. Italy. [L., = "Christ's tear"]

lach·ry·mal, lac·ri·mal (lăk´rimal) *adjs*. Of, for tears; ~ **gland**, (anat.) gland beneath upper eyelid secreting tears, which drain from inner corner of eye through ~ **duct** to nose; ~ **vase**, vase intended to contain tears.

lach·ry·ma·to·ry, lac·ri·ma·to·ry (lăk´rimatōrē, -tŏrē) *adjs*. Of, for tears; causing eyes to water. ~ *n.* (pl. **-ries**). Small vial of kind found in Roman tombs and thought to be bottles meant to contain tears.

lach·ry·mose (lăk´rimōs) *adj*. Tearful, given to weeping. **lach´ry·mose·ly** *adv*.

lac·ing (lā´sĭng) *n.*: see LACE def. I.

lack (lăk) *n*. Deficiency, want, need, *of*; **for** ~ **of**, owing to want or absence of. **lack** *v*. Be without, not have, be deficient in; **lack´-luster**, (of eye etc.) dull. **lack´-ing** *adj*. Not available, inadequate.

lack·a·dai·si·cal (lăkadā´zĭkal) *adj*. Languidly superior, affected; feebly sentimental. **lack·a·dai·si·cal·ly** *adv*. **lack·a·dai·si·cal·ness** *n*. [archaic *lackaday*, -*daisy*, alack]

lack·ey (lăk´ē) *n*. (pl. **-eys**). Footman, manservant (usu. liveried); obsequious person; servant. ~ *v.t.* (**-eyed**, **-ey·ing**). Dance attendance on, behave servilely to.

La·co·ni·a (lakō´nēa). Ancient territory of SW. Greece, now a department, its ancient capital, Sparta, being still the administra-

tive center. **La·co´ni·an** *adj*. & *n*.

la·con·ic (lakŏn´ĭk), **la·con·i·ca** (lakŏn´ĭkal) *adjs*. Brief, concise sententious; given to such speech o: style. **la·con´i·cal·ly** *adv*. [Gk *Lakon* Laconia, from character o. inhabitants]

lac·quer (lăk´er) *n*. 1. (**true** o: **far eastern** ~) Natural sap of ~ **tree** (*Rhus vernicifera*), used since ancient times in China and Japan a: protective and decorative varnish (usu. applied in thin layers t: wooden objects or inlaid on meta wares) or, when solidified, a: medium for sculpture. 2. Varnish imitating this, invented in Europe in 17th c. and prepared from resin lac or shellac (see LAC). **lacquer** *v.t.* Coat with lacquer.

lac·ri·mal (lăk´rimal) = LACH-RYMAL.

la·crosse (lakraws´, -krŏs´) *n*. Game (orig. of N. Amer. Indians) with ten players on each side, in which the ball is flung by and carried in netted rackets, the object being to throw the ball through the opponents' goal. [Fr., so named by Jesuit missionaries f. resemblance of racket to crosier]

lac·tate (lăk´tāt) *n*. Salt of lactic acid. ~ *v.* (**-tat·ed**, **-tat·ing**). Produce or secrete milk. **lac·ta·tion** (lăktā´shon) *n*.

lac·te·al (lăk´tēal) *adj*. Of milk; conveying milky fluid. ~ *n*. One of the minute lymphatic vessels of the mesentery, conveying chyle to the thoracic duct.

lac·tes·cence (lăktĕs´ens) *n*. Milky appearance; milky juice. **lac·tes´cent** *adj*. Milky; yielding milky juice.

lac·tic (lăk´tĭk) *adj*. (chem.) Of milk; ~ **acid**, hygroscopic acid ($CH_3CH(OH)COOH$) formed by the fermentation of sugars etc. and present in sour milk.

lac·to·pro·tein (lăktōprō´tēn, -tēĭn) *n*. Albuminous constituent of milk.

lac·tose (lăk´tōs) *n*. Milk sugar, a substance somewhat similar to cane sugar, present in milk, and manufactured by the evaporation of whey.

la·cu·na (lakū´na) *n*. (pl. **-nae** pr. -nē, **-nas**). Hiatus, blank, missing portion, empty part; cavity in bone, tissue, etc. **la·cu´nal, la·cu´nar, la·cu´nar·y** *adjs*.

la·cus·trine (lakŭs´trĭn) *adj*. Of, dwelling or growing in, lake(s).

lad (lăd) *n*. Boy, youth, young fellow; fellow. **lad·die** (lăd´ē) *n*. (chiefly Scot.).

lad·der (lăd´er) *n*. Set of rungs inserted usu. in two uprights of wood or metal or in two ropes to serve as (usu. portable) means of ascending building etc.; (fig.) means of rising in the world or attaining object; ~**-back chair**, one having back formed of horizontal bars; ~

emales of the order Mammalia **lactate** ⋅ter giving birth to supply their young ⋅ith sustenance. The milk they produce ⋅ries in consistency and content, and ⋅t all have nipples, i.e. monotremes.

⋅titch, crossbar stitch in embroi-⋅ery.

lade (lād) v.t. (**lad·ed, lad·en** or **⋅d·ed, lad·ing**). Put cargo on ⋅oard (ship); ship (goods) as cargo. **⋅d′en** adj. Loaded (with); pain-⋅lly burdened with. **lad′ing** n. **⋅ill of** ~: see BILL[3].

la-di-da, la-de-da, lah-di-⋅ah (lah′dēdah′) adjs. (colloq.) ⋅retentious or affected, esp. in ⋅ronunciation. [imit. of pronunci-⋅tion used, f. comic song of 1880]

La·din (lahdēn′) n. RHAEDO-⋅OMANIC. [Romansh, f. L. latinus ⋅atin]

La·di·no (ladē′nō; Sp. lahdē′-⋅aw) n. Spanish dialect of ⋅ephardic Jews.

Lad·is·laus (lăd′ĭslaws). Name ⋅f several kings of Hungary; ⋅adislaus I, St. (1040–95), king of ⋅Iungary 1077–95; introduced ⋅Catholicism into Croatia, which he ⋅ecured for Hungary; **Ladislaus IV** ⋅262–90), king of Hungary 1272–⋅0; killed after two years of civil ⋅ar; **Ladislaus V (Posthumene)** ⋅1440–57), king of Hungary and ⋅ohemia.

la·dle (lā′del) n. 1. Large spoon, ⋅ith cup-shaped bowl and long ⋅andle, for transferring liquid. 2. ⋅n foundry) Receptacle for molten ⋅etal. ~ v.t. (**-dled, -dling**). ⋅ransfer with ladle.

La·do·ga (lah′dōgah). Largest ⋅uropean lake, 7,100 sq. mi. ⋅8,389 sq. km), in U.S.S.R., near ⋅innish border.

The game of **lacrosse** is played for 4 periods of 20 minutes each. The hard ball is passed from player to player by means of the crosse until a goal is scored by hurling the ball through the 6 ft. by 6 ft. goal.

The **lace** industry was one of the first to be automated but the individuality of handworked lace as produced by this craftswoman working with bobbins on a pillow in Brussels is much sought after by collectors.

end line
side line
59 ft
40 yds
70 yds
wing area
110 yds
goal area
the stick
6 ft
10 ins

la·dy (lā′dē) *n.* (pl. **-dies**). 1. Woman ruling over subjects, or to whom obedience or homage is due (archaic or poet. exc. in ∼ **of the manor, Our L**∼, the Virgin Mary). 2. Woman to whom man is devoted, mistress. 3. Woman of good birth or breeding; ∼ **of the bedchamber**, ∼**-in-waiting**, lady attending a queen or princess. 4. (used courteously) Woman. 5. (Brit.) Prefixed title, part of customary appellation of marchioness, countess, viscountess, baroness; followed by Christian (and family) name of daughter of duke, marquis, or earl; followed by husband's Christian (and family) name of wife of holder of courtesy title *Lord*; followed by surname of wife of baronet or knight; **my** ∼, respectful form of address to holders of title *Lady* and women judges. 6. (poet. or joc.) Wife. 7. **Ladies' Day**, day set aside for women to attend (game, entertainment) at reduced or no cost; **ladies' man**, man fond of female society; **la′dybird** (Brit.) = ladybug; **la′dybug**, coleopterous insect of family Coccinellidae, usu. reddish brown with black spots; **la′dyfinger**, finger-shaped sponge cake; **lady-killer**, man devoting himself to making conquests of women; **la′dylove**, sweetheart; **Lady of the Lake**, (in Arthurian legend) supernatural being (Morgan le Fay, Vivien, Nimue) who gave Arthur the sword Excalibur and was one of the three queens in the ship that bore him to Avalon; **Lady of the Lamp**, Florence NIGHTINGALE, so called in allusion to her visits to hospital wards at night; **lady's maid**, lady's personal maid; **lady's-slipper**, orchidaceous plant of genus *Cypripedium*; **ladies' tresses** (used with sing. or pl. verb), any of various orchids of the genus *Spiranthes*, with a spike of white flowers.

la·dy·like (lā′dēlīk) *adj.* With manners etc. of a lady; befitting a lady.

la·dy·ship (lā′dēshĭp) *n.* (esp.) Respectful form of address to or mention of woman with title of Lady, preceded by *your* or *her.*

la·e·trile (lā′etrĭl) *n.* Drug prepared from apricot pits, used in treatment of cancer.

La·fa·yette (lăfēĕt′, lahfē-, -fā-; *Fr.* lăfăyĕt′), **Marie Joseph Paul Yves Roch Gilbert du Motier, Marquis de** (1757–1834). French general and politician; served as a major general of Amer. troops in Amer. Revolutionary War.

*There are 5,000 species of **ladybird** ranging from red to yellow with black or colored spots. They are important to agriculture because they prey voraciously on harmful aphids. Right: Coccinella semptempunctata.*

Laf·fitte (lahfēt′), **Jean** (1780?–1826). French pirate and smuggler in the Caribbean; aided America during War of 1812 by revealing British plans for attack on New Orleans, then helped Andrew Jackson defend city.

La Fon·taine (lă fawn̈tĕn′), **Jean de** (1621–95). French poet and fabulist.

lag (lăg) *v.* (**lagged, lag·ging**). Go too slow, not keep pace, fall *behind.* ∼ *n.* Delay in time; (amount of) retardation in current or movement, esp. (elect.) of current behind voltage in an alternating current circuit. **lag′gard** (lăg′erd) *n. & adj.* **lag′ging** *adj.*

La·gash (lā′găsh). Ancient Sumerian city in Mesopotamia, excavation of which proved that the Babylonians inherited their culture

Above left: **Lady's finger,** or kidney vetch, grows on sandy or calcareous soils. Above: **Lady's slipper** is rare and found on limestone soil.

and the art of writing from the Sumerians.

la·ger (lah′ger, law′-) *n.* (also ∼ **beer**) Light, orig. German, beer distinguished from other kinds by longer fermentation at lower temperature. [Ger. *lagerbier* beer brewed for keeping]

La·ger·löf (lah′gerlöf), **Selma Ottiliana Louisa** (1858–1940). Swedish novelist; author of *Gösta Berling's Saga*; first woman to receive Nobel Prize for literature (1909).

lag·gard: see LAG.

la·gniappe, la·gnappe (lănyăp′

The city of Venice is surrounded by a **lagoon** whose waters are blocked from the open sea by sand bars and mud banks. This view of the city shows the shallow-draft gondolas well suited to the waters of the area.

ke Cuyamaca in California. Recent *studies* have been attempting to find a *way* of reversing the gradual drying up *process* that occurs in lakes so that the *water* will be available to man.

n'yăp) ns. Unexpected bonus or *gratuity;* something extra.

la·goon (lagoon') *n.* Shallow *stretch* of salt water partly or wholly *separated* from sea by narrow strip *of* land or low sandbank or coral *reef;* enclosed water of atoll.

La·gos (lah'gōs, lā'gŏs). Capital *city* of Nigeria, in the SW., on the *Gulf* of Guinea.

lag (lăg) **screw.** Long, heavy *wood* screw with a square bolt head.

La Guar·di·a (la gwär'dēa), *Fiorello* **H(enry)** (1882–1947). *American* lawyer and congressman; *mayor* of New York City, 1934–45.

La·hore (lahōr'). City in Punjab, W. Pakistan, near Indian frontier; largest in W. Pakistan after Karachi.

la·ic (lā'ĭk) *adj.* Nonclerical, lay; secular, temporal. ~ *n.* Layman. **la·i·cal** (lā'ĭkal) *adj.* **la'i·cal·ly** *adv.*

la·i·cize (lā'ĭsīz) *v.t.* (**-cized, -ciz·ing**). Make lay; commit (school etc.), throw open (office), to laymen. **la·i·ci·za·tion** (lā'ĭsĭzā'shon) *n.*

laid (lād) *adj.:* see LAY[3]; **laid paper,** paper having ribs on surface caused by wires of cylinder on which it was dried.

lain: see LIE[2].

lair (lār) *n.* 1. Wild beast's den. 2. Place of concealment for robbers etc. ~ *v.* Go to, rest or place in, lair.

laird (lārd) *n.* Landed proprietor in Scotland. **laird'ship** *n.*

lais·sez faire (lĕsāfār'; *Fr.* lĕsĕfĕr'). Policy of noninterference; (orig.) freedom from government interference in economic or industrial affairs by tariffs, restrictions on individual enterprise, etc. [Fr.]

la·i·ty (lā'ĭtē) *n.* 1. Body of religious worshippers as distinguished from clergy. 2. People outside a particular profession; those lacking professional knowledge of a subject.

lake[1] (lāk) *n.* Large body of water entirely surrounded by land; **Great Lakes:** see GREAT; **Lake country, district, Lakeland, the Lakes,** region of lakes in NW. England; **lake dweller, dwelling,** (inhabitant of) primitive esp. prehistoric habitation built on piles or other support over a lake; **Lake Ijs·sel:** see IJSSELMEER; **Lake poets,** Coleridge, Southey, and Wordsworth, who lived in Lake district; **Lake Success,** village on Long Island, New York State; early headquarters of the United Nations Security Council, 1946–51.

lake[2] (lāk) *n.* Reddish pigment, orig. made from lac; pigment made from animal, vegetable, or coal tar coloring matter combined with metallic oxide or earth; (dyeing) any insoluble substance resulting from the chemical combination of soluble coloring matter with a mordant.

Laksh·mi (lŭksh′mē). (Hindu myth.) Wife of Vishnu and goddess of fortune or prosperity.

Lal·lan (lăl′an) adj. Of the Lowlands of Scotland. ~ n. (also **Lallans**) Lowland Scots dialect, the vernacular speech of the Lowlands of Scotland, as a literary language.

Lam. abbrev. Lamentations (Old Testament).

lam[1] (lăm) v. (**lammed, lam·ming**). (slang) Thrash, hit hard with cane etc.

lam[2] (lăm) n. (slang) Flight, escape; **on the** ~, fleeing, hiding from the police. **lam** v. (**lammed, lam·ming**). Escape, flee.

la·ma (lah′ma) n. Priest or monk in Lamaism; see DALAI L~, TASHI L~. **La′ma·ism** n. Mahayana form of Buddhism found in Tibet, Mongolia, and nearby regions. **La′ma·ist** n. **la·ma·ser·y** (lah′-masĕrē) n. (pl. **-ser·ies**). Monastery of lamas. [Tibetan blama (silent b)]

La·marck (lamärk′), **Jean-Baptiste Pierre Antoine de Monet, Chevalier de** (1744–1829). French botanist and zoologist, who anticipated Darwin in conceiving the idea of organic evolution, but accounted for it by the theory that acquired characteristics can be inherited by offspring.

La·marck′i·an adj. & n. **La·marck′ism** n. Lamarckian theory.

La·maze (lamahz′) **technique.** System of prenatal training for natural childbirth emphasizing psychological and physical preparation of the expectant mother, including muscle stretching exercises.

lamb (lăm) n. Young of sheep; its flesh as food; young member of church flock; innocent, weak, or dear person; **the L~ (of God)**, Christ; **lamb′skin**, skin of lamb with wool on, used for clothing etc.; leather prepared from skin of lamb; **lamb's quarters** = PIGWEED. **lamb** v. Bring forth lamb; (pass., of lambs) be brought forth. **lamb·kin** (lăm′kĭn) n. Young lamb. **lamb′like** adj.

Lamb (lăm), **Charles** (1775–1834). English essayist and critic; author of Essays of Elia and, with his sister **Mary** (1764–1847), of Tales from Shakespeare.

lam·baste (lămbāst′) v.t. (**-bast·ed, -bast·ing**). (colloq.) Beat, thrash.

lamb·da (lăm′da) n. Twelfth (later 11th) letter of Greek alphabet (Λ, λ), corresponding to l.

lam·bent (lăm′bent) adj. (of

flame etc.) Playing on surfac[e] without burning it, with so[ft] radiance; (of eyes, sky, etc.) soft[,] radiant; (of wit etc.) gentl[y] brilliant. **lam′ben·cy** n. **lam′-bent·ly** adv.

lam·bert (lăm′bert) n. Unit o[f] brightness, equal to that of [a] perfectly diffusing surface radiatin[g] or reflecting light at the rate of on[e] lumen per square centimet[er] (abbrev. L.). [J. H. Lamber[t] (1728–77), German physicist]

lame (lăm) adj. (**lam·e[r,] lam·est**). Disabled by injury o[r] defect in limb, esp. foot or leg[;] limping or unable to walk; (o[f] argument, story, etc.) imperfec[t,] unsatisfactory; (of meter) haltin[g.] **lame′brain**, (slang) stupid perso[n,] half-wit; **lame duck**: see DUCK[.] **lame′ly** adv. **lame′ness** n. **lam[e]** v.t. (**lamed, lam·ing**). Make lam[e,] cripple.

la·mé (lämā′) n. & ad[j.] (Material) with metal thread wove[n] in.

la·mel·la (lamĕl′a) n. (p[l.] **-mel·lae** pr. -mĕl′ē, **-mel·las**[).] Thin plate, scale, layer, or film, es[p.] of bone or tissue. **la·mel·la[r]** (lamĕl′er, lăm′eler), **lam·el·la[te]** (lăm′elāt, -lĭt, lamĕl′āt, -ĭt[),] **lam·el·lat·ed, la·mel·lose** (la[-] mĕl′ōs, lăm′elōs) adjs.

la·ment (lamĕnt′) n. Passionat[e] expression of grief; verse or song o[f] mourning. ~ v. Express or fee[l] grief for or about; be distressed a[t]

*ambing season is usually in the spring, nd the young **lamb** is sold as meat etween 3 and 8 months. The gestation eriod for ewes is 147 days. Some reeds are noted for bearing twins.*

egret; **lamented**, mourned for esp. conventionally of the dead); **he late lamented**, (freq. iron.) he deceased.

lam·en·ta·ble (lăm′entabel, la-něn′-) *adj.* Deplorable, regret-able. **lam′en·ta·bly** *adv.*

lam·en·ta·tion (lămentā′shon) . Lamenting, lament; *Lamen-ations*, poetical book of Old Testament, traditionally ascribed o Jeremiah.

la·mi·a (lā′mēa) *n.* (pl. **-mi·as, mi·ae** pr. -mēē). (Gk. and Rom. nyth.) Monster with head and breasts of a woman and body of a serpent preying on human beings nd sucking children's blood. [L.]

lam·i·na (lăm′ina) *n.* (pl. **-nae** or. -nē, **-nas**). 1. Thin plate, scale, ayer, or flake, or metal, bone, membrane, stratified rock, etc. 2. bot.) Blade of leaf. **lam′i·nar, am·i·nate**[1] (lăm′ināt, -nĭt), **lam-·nose** (lăm′inōs) *adjs.*

lam·i·nate[2] (lăm′ināt) *v.* -nat·ed, -nat·ing). Beat or roll metal) into thin plates; split into ayers or leaves; overlay with metal plates; manufacture by placing

layer on layer. **lam·i·na′tion** *n.*

lam·mer·gei·er, lam·mer-gey·er (lăm′ergīer) *ns.* Bearded vulture (*Gypaetus barbatus*), largest European bird of prey. [Ger. *lämmer* lambs, *geier* vulture]

lamp (lămp) *n.* Vessel with oil and wick for giving light; glass vessel enclosing candle, gas jet, incandescent wire, or other illumi-nant; device that gives radiation; (archaic) sun, moon, star; (fig.) source of spiritual or intellectual light, hope, etc.; **smell of the ~**, betray nocturnal study, be laborious in style, etc.; **lamp′-black**, pigment consisting of finely divided almost pure carbon, made from soot of burning oil or gas; **lamp′lighter**, person who lights

*The Tibetan version of Buddhism is **Lamaism**, which has accretions of the demonolatry of Bon, a primitive atavistic religion of the region. Below: Lamas in Bodhnath, Nepal, dance to drive away evil.*

*Above: The specialized lighting require-
ments of the surgeon are met by having
the **lamp** attached to his head, throwing
a direct light on the subject. Right: The
Spanish 18th-century glass oil-lamp has
spouts for 4 wicks.*

*This old gas **lamp** in Providence, Rhode
Island is typical of the sort used before
electricity became the favored power
source.*

gas street lamps; **lamp′post**, post
usu. of steel or concrete supporting street lamp. **lamp** *v.* (poet.)
Shine, illuminate.

    lam·pi·on (lăm′pēon) *n.* Pot of
usu. colored glass with oil and wick
used in illuminations.

    lam·poon (lămpōon′) *n.* Viru-
lent or scurrilous satire on individual. **~** *v.t.* Write lampoon(s)
against. **lam·poon′er, lam·-
poon′ist** *ns.*

    lam·prey (lăm′prē) *n.* (pl.
-preys). Any of several eel-
shaped aquatic vertebrates (genera
Lampetra and *Petromyzon*) resembling fish but without scales or jaws
and having suckerlike mouth.

    La·na·i (lahnah′ē, lɑnī′). One of
the Hawaiian Islands, 141 sq. mi.

(365 sq. km) in area, W. of Maui.
    la·na·i (lahnah′ē, lɑnī′) *n.* (pl.
-na·is). Veranda. [Hawaiian]

    Lan·cas·ter (lăng′kaster). Name
of English royal house descended
from John of Gaunt, including
Henry IV, Henry V, and Henry VI;
party of the red rose in the Wars
of the Roses. **Lan·cas·tri·an**
(lăngkăs′trēan) *n. & adj.*

    lance (lăns, lahns) *n.* 1. Weapon
with long wooden shaft and pointed
steel head used by horseman in
charging; similar implement for
spearing fish or killing harpooned
whale; **~ corporal**, U.S. Marine
Corps noncommissioned officer of
lowest rank, below corporal;
lance′wood, tough elastic kinds of
W. Indian wood used for fishing
rods etc. 2. Lancet. **lance** *v.t.*
(**lanced, lanc·ing**). 1. (poet.)
Pierce (as) with lance. 2. (surg.)
Prick, cut open, with lancet.

    lance·let (lăns′lĭt, lahns′-) *n.*
Small marine animal of genus
Branchiostoma, one of the lowest
forms of chordate, about 50 mm
long, found in sand of shallow
waters throughout the world.

    Lan·ce·lot (lăn′selot, -lŏt,
lahn′-). (Arthurian legend) Son of
King Ban of Brittany; brought up
by the Lady of the Lake; most

famous of Arthur's knights of th[e]
Round Table; his love affair wi[th]
Queen Guinevere resulted in a wa[r]
with King Arthur.

    lan·ce·o·late (lăn′sēolāt, -lĭ[
adj. Shaped like spearhead, tapere[d]
at ends.

    lan·cer (lăn′ser, lahn′-) *n.*
Soldier of cavalry regiment ori[g]
armed with lances. 2. (pl.) Squar[e]
dance, variant of quadrille, for 8 [or]
16 pairs, derived from cavalr[y]
displays and in vogue in Englan[d]
from *c*1850 to World War I; mus[ic]
for this.

    lan·cet (lăn′sĭt, lahn′-) *n.*
Fine-pointed double-edge[d]
surgical knife. 2. (also **~ arch**
window) High narrow pointe[d]
window or arch in 12th and 13th [
Gothic architecture.

    lan·ci·nat·ing (lăn′sinătĭng
lahn′-) *adj.* (of pain) Acut[e]
shooting.

    land (lănd) *n.* 1. Solid part [of]
Earth's surface; ground, soi[l]
expanse of country; country; lande[d]
property, (pl.) estates. 2. Any of th[e]
divisions between rifling grooves [of]
guns. 3. **~ bank**, bank issuin[g]
notes on security of lande[d]
property; **~ breeze**, breeze blow[-]
ing seaward from land; **~ crab**
any of various crabs that live o[n]

d but breed in sea; **land'fall**, roach to land esp. for first e in voyage or flight; **land nt**, government grant of land, for railroads or colleges; **land'-lder**, proprietor or (usu.) tenant land; **land laws**, law(s) of ded property; **land'locked**, u. of water) almost or quite closed by land; **land'lady**, d'lord**, person who owns land, ldings, etc. for rent to others; d'lubber**, (naut.) person ig-rant of the sea and ships; d'mark**, object marking undary of country, estate, etc.; spicuous object in district etc. ig.) esp. as guide in navigation; .) notable event; **land mine**, losive mine laid in, or dropped parachute on, land; **Land of the dnight Sun**, land N. of the ctic Circle where daylight is tinuous during the short mmer; **Land of the Rising Sun**, an; **land'-office business**, lloq.) a successful, lively siness; **land'owner**, owner of d; **land-poor**, owning much d and little ready money; **Land's d**, rocky promontory in Corn-ll forming westernmost point of gland; **land'slide**, sliding down mass of land, land fallen, from ff or mountain; overwhelming jority of votes in election; **land** x, tax on landed property; **land nd**, land breeze. **land'less** *adj.* d *v.* 1. Set or go ashore; embark (*at*); set down from icle or aircraft. 2. Bring (air-ft) down to ground or surface water; (of aircraft) come down 1s. 3. Bring to, reach, find self in, a certain place, stage, or sition; deal (person blow etc.); ght after jump etc. 4. Bring h) to land; (fig.) win (prize etc.).

Land (lănd), **Edwin Herbert** 909–). American inventor ted for Polaroid Land camera, ich develops film immediately er picture is taken.

an·dau (lăn'daw, -dow) *n.* 1. ur-wheeled carriage with top of ich front and back halves can be dependently raised and lowered. Motor car with collapsible top er rear seat. [*Landau*, town in rmany]

land·ed (lăn'dĭd) *adj.* Possessed land; consisting of land.

land·grave (lănd'grāv) *n.* (hist.) tle of certain German princes; g., count having jurisdiction over ritory, and with inferior counts der him. **land·gra·vine** (lănd'-avēn) *n.* (hist.) Wife of land-ave; woman landgrave.

land·ing (lăn'dĭng) *n.* (esp.) Place for disembarking (also ~ **place**); platform between two flights of stairs; floor, passage at top of staircase on to which rooms open; ~ **craft**, boat, often flat-bottomed and with collapsible side, for carrying troops, armored vehicles, etc., in amphibious operations; ~ **gear**, understruc-ture of an aircraft (wheels etc.) supporting it when landing or taxiing; ~ **net**, net for landing large fish when hooked; ~ **strip**, air-strip.

land·scape (lănd'skāp) *n.* Pic-ture etc. or part of one representing inland scenery; actual piece of such

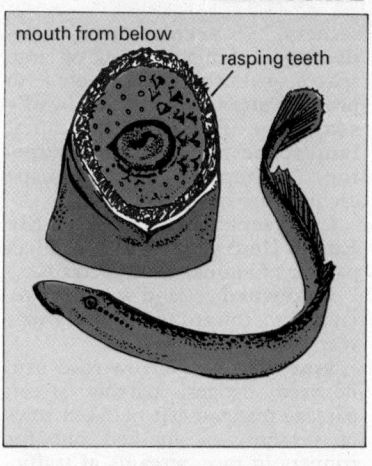

*This Pan-Am airplane carries the stan-dard landing gear for a commercial jet of its size. The principle of retracting **land-ing gear** into the fuselage was intro-duced in the 1930s and improved air-craft performance.*

*The muscular toothed tongue of the **lamprey** rasps pieces of tissue from fish to which the lamprey attaches itself. Its eggs hatch in mud and the larvae stay there for 3 to 4 years before emerging as adults.*

*e story of **Lancelot** first appears in e stories by Chrétien de Troyes in the th century. Right: Lancelot with ncers depicted on a 14th-century minated page. Lancelot was the her of Galahad, purest of knights.*

scenery; ~ **architecture, gardening,** design and layout of large spaces, suburbs, parks, etc., to produce attractive effects. **land'-scap·ist** *n.* Painter of landscapes. **land'scape** *v.t.* (**-scaped, -scap·-ing**). Improve by landscape architecture or gardening.

Land·seer (lănd'sēr, -syer), **Sir Edwin Henry** (1802–73). English painter of animals and portraits.

land·ward (lănd'werd) *adv.* Lying etc. toward the land. **land'-wards** *adj.*

lane (lān) *n.* Narrow road usu. between hedges; narrow street; passage made or left between rows of persons, or marked out for runners in race, streams of traffic, etc.; regular route of ships or aircraft; channel of water in icefield.

lang (lăng) *adj. & n.* (Scot.) Long. ~ *adv.* (Scot.) Long; **(auld)** ~ **syne,** (in) the old days [Scot. pronunc. of old long since]

Lang·er·hans (lăng'erhänz, -hăns; *Ger.* lahng'erhahns), **Paul** (1847–88). German pathologist; **islands (islets) of** ~, groups of small granular cells in the pancreas that secrete INSULIN.

Lang·land (lăng'land), **William** (*c*1330–*c*1400). English poet, author of *Piers Plowman.*

Lan·go·bard (lăng'gobärd) *n.* Lombard.

Lang·try (lăng'trē), **Emily Charlotte** (1853–1929). English actress; known as Lillie Langtry or "the Jersey Lily."

lan·guage (lăng'gwĭj) *n.* Whole body of words and methods of combination of words used by a section or group of people (as a nation, community, etc.); method of expression; words and their use; faculty of speech; person's style of expressing himself; professional or

This **landscape** *is typical of the environment of the beaver who favors lakes, preferably near a forest, so that its source of food and building material is readily available.*

sectional vocabulary; literary style, wording; **bad** ~, oaths and abusive talk; **strong** ~, speech expressing vehement feelings.

langue d'oc (lahngdawk'). Romance dialects of S. provinces of France. [Fr. *langue* language, *oc* Provençal form of *oui* yes]

Langue·doc (lahngdawk'). Old province of S. France stretching from W. bank of Rhône to Pyrenees and including Cévennes and valleys of upper Loire.

langue d'oïl (lahngdawēl'). Romance dialects of France other than those of S. France (cf. LANGUE D'OC). [Fr. *langue* language, OF. *oïl* yes]

lan·guid (lăng'gwĭd) *adj.* Inert, lacking vigor; spiritless, apathetic; sluggish, slow-moving; faint, weak. **lan'guid·ly** *adv.* **lan'guid·ness** *n.*

lan·guish (lăng'gwĭsh) *v.i.* Grow or be feeble, lose or lack vitality; live *under* enfeebling or depressing conditions; droop, pine (*for*); affect languor or sentimental tenderness. **lan'guish·ing·ly** *adv.* **lan'guish·ment** *n.*

lan·guor (lăng'ger) *n.* Faintness, fatigue; inertia, want of alertness; soft or tender mood or effect; slackness, dullness, drooping state. **lan'guor·ous** *adj.* **lan'guor·ous·ly** *adv.*

lan·gur (lŭnggoor') *n.* Long-tailed monkey of southeast Asia, of genus *Presbytis.*

la·nif·er·ous (lanĭf'erus) *adj.* [also **la·nig·er·ous** (lanĭj'erus)]. Wool-bearing.

lank (lăngk) *adj.* Shrunken, spare; tall and lean; long and flaccid; (of hair) straight and limp, not wavy.

lank·y (lăng'kē) *adj.* (**lank·i·er, lank·i·est**). Ungracefully lean and long or tall. **lank'i·ness** *n.*

lan·ner (lăn'er) *n.* Mediterranean species of falcon, *Falco biarmicus;* (in falconry) female of this. **lan'ner·et** (lăn'erĕt) *n.* Male lanner, which is smaller than the female.

Above: The **langur** *(Presbytis entellus can leap through the tree tops for d tances of up to 40 ft. On the jungle flo it moves with the gait typical of a qua ruped.*

lan·o·lin, lan·o·line (lăn'olĭ ns. Fatty matter extracted fro sheep's wool, used as basis ointments and toilet preparations

Lan·sing (lăn'sĭng). Capital Michigan, in the S. central part.

lan·ta·na (lăntā'na, -tah'-) Any of several chiefly tropic plants of the genus *Lantan* cultivated for their aromati brightly colored flowers.

lan·tern (lăn'tern) *n.* 1. (Lam either fixed or portable, ofte burning kerosene, with) tran parent case protecting the flame. (also **magic** ~) Apparatus f projecting image on screen; pr jector. 3. Light chamber lighthouse. 4. ~ **clock,** clo enclosed in metal case like lantern ~ **jaw,** long thin jaw giving hollo look to face, hence ~**-jawed;** **slide,** slide for projection l lantern.

lan·tha·num (lăn'thanum) (chem.) Rare-earth element four in a number of rare minerals and monazite sand; symbol La, at. n 57, at. wt. 138.9055. [Gk. *lanthar* hide]

lan·yard (lăn'yerd) *n.* Sho rope made fast to something (naut. cord attached to knife, whistle, etc to hold it or serve as handle.

La·oc·o·ön (lāŏk'ōŏn). (G legend) Trojan priest; warned t Trojans against the WOODEN hors was crushed to death with his tv sons by two serpents that emerge from the sea.

La·os (lah'ŏs, lā'ŏs). Form kingdom of SE. Asia, incorporate into French Indo-China, 189 gained independence, 1950; no

This **landscape** *(facing page), painte by John Constable in 1802 is Dedham Vale, Essex. Constable, pe haps the greatest English landsca artist of the 19th century, believed th nature was the source of all originali*

Right: A map of Laos with the national flag. Laos has a population of between 3 and 4 million. The administrative capital is Vientiane. Right below: A treasure house in the former royal capital, Luang Prabang.

People's Democratic Republic; capital Vientiane. **La·o·tian** (lāō´shan) *adj. & n.*

Lao-tse, Lao-tzu, Lao-tsze (low´dzoo). (6th c. B.C.) Chinese philosopher and metaphysician; reputed founder of TAOISM and contemporary of Confucius.

lap[1] (lăp) *n.* Hanging part or flap of garment, saddle, etc.; front part of body from waist to knees of seated person, considered with dress as place on which child is nursed or object held; **in one's ~**, in one's charge or control; **in the ~ of luxury**, in luxurious surroundings; **lap´belt**, safety belt across lap of car driver or passenger; **lap´board**, flat board held on lap to use as table; **lap dog**, small pet dog; **lap robe**, rug to cover knees of person seated in vehicle.

lap[2] (lăp) *v.* (**lapped, lap·ping**). 1. Coil, fold, wrap (garment etc. *about, around*); enfold, swathe, *in*; surround, encircle, enfold caressingly. 2. Make overlap; project *over* something; **~ over**, overlap. 3. (racing etc.) Travel over (distance) as lap; pass (competitor) by one or more laps. **lap** *n.* Amount of overlapping, overlapping part; layer or sheet (of cotton etc. being made) wound on roller; single turn of rope, silk, thread, etc., round drum or reel; one circuit of race track.

lap[3] (lăp) *n.* Rotating disk for polishing gems or metal. **~** *v.t.* (**lapped, lap·ping**). Polish with lap.

lap[4] (lăp) *v.* (**lapped, lap·ping**). Drink by scooping with tongue; drink (*up* or *down*) greedily (also fig.); (of wavelets etc.) move, beat, with light slapping sound *against*. **~** *n.* Single act of lapping, amount taken up by it; act or sound of lapping wavelets etc.

lap·a·rot·o·my (lăperŏt´omē) *n.* (pl. **-mies**). Surgical incision through abdominal walls into abdominal cavity.

La Paz (la pahz´; *Port.* lah pahs´). Capital city of Bolivia.

la·pel (lapĕl´) *n.* Part of front of coat etc. folded back toward shoulder. **la·pelled´** *adj.*

lap·i·dar·y (lăp´ĭdĕrē) *adj.* Concerned with stones; engraved on stone; (of style) suitable for inscriptions, monumental. **~** *n.* (pl. **-dar·ies**). Cutter, polisher, or engraver, of stones.

lap·is laz·u·li (lăp´ĭs lăz´ōolē, -lī, lăz´ū-, lăzh´ōo-). (min.) Sodium aluminum silicate containing sulfur, used as bright blue pigment; color of this. [L., = "stone of azure"]

Lap·ith (lăp´ĭth) *n.* (Gk. myth.) Member of a Thessalian people (*Lapithae*) who fought and defeated the Centaurs.

Lap·land (lăp´land, -lănd). Region inhabited by Lapps, most northerly part of Scandinavia (often includes northern area of Finland and NW. U.S.S.R. lying above the Arctic Circle). **Lap´land·er** *n.* Lapp.

Lapp (lăp) *n.* Member of a small-statured Mongoloid people, largely nomadic, inhabiting Lapland. **Lap´pish** *adj. & n.* (Of) the language of the Lapps, one of the Finno-Ugrian family.

lapse (lăps) *n.* Slip of memory etc., slight mistake; weak or careless deviation from what is right, backsliding; decline to lower state; gliding, flow of (water etc.); passage or interval *of* time; (law) termination of right or privilege through disuse; **~ rate**, (meteor.) rate of decrease of temperature as height

increases. **lapse** *v.i.* (**lapsed, laps·ing**). Fail to maintain positi[on] or state for want of effort or vig[or]; fall *back, away*; glide, flow, subsi[de]; pass *away*; (of estate, title, etc.) [fall] in, pass away, become void, rev[ert] *to* someone, by failure of c[on]ditions, heirs, etc.

lap·sus (lăp´sus; *Lat.* lahp´so[o]) *n.* Slip; **~ ca·la·mi** (kăl´amī; *L[at.]* kah´lahmē), slip of the pen; **~ lin·guae** (lĭng´gwē; *Lat.* lĭng´gw[ē]) slip of the tongue. [L.]

La·pu·ta (lapū´ta). In Swif[t's] *Gulliver's Travels*, a flying isla[nd] inhabited by learned men who a[re] absorbed in impractical philosop[hi]cal and scientific speculati[on]. **La·pu´tan** *adj. & n.*

lap·wing (lăp´wĭng) *n.* Bird [of] plover family, *Vanellus vanell[us]* common in temperate parts of [Old] World.

lar (lär) *n.* (pl. **lar·es** [;] lär´ēz, lā´rēz, **lars**). God w[or]shipped, together with the PENAT[ES] households in ancient Rome; **res and penates,** (transf.) easured possessions of a household.

lar·board (lār´bōrd, -bôrd; *aut.* lār´berd) *n.* & *adj.* (naut. s.) Left side of ship looking rward (replaced, to avoid con-sion with *starboard*, by *port*).

lar·ce·ny (lār´senē) *n.* (pl. **-nies**). w) Felonious taking away of other's personal goods with tent to convert them to one's own e; **grand** ~, theft of property of lue above that constituting petit rceny; **petit** ~, **petty** ~, theft of operty of value below a small ked sum. **lar´ce·nous** *adj.* r´ce·nous·ly *adv.*

larch (lärch) *n.* Deciduous niferous tree of genus *Larix*, elding tough timber and bark ed in tanning; tamarack; wood of is.

lard (lärd) *n.* Internal fat of domen of pigs etc., esp. when ndered and clarified for use in oking. ~ *v.t.* Insert strips of con in (meat etc.) before cooking; near (as) with lard; (fig.) garnish lk, writing) *with* particular ords, expressions, etc. **lard´y** *adj.* ard·i·er, lard·i·est).

lard·er (lär´der) *n.* (chiefly Brit.) om or cupboard for storing pro-sions.

La·re·do (larā´dō). City in SW. exas on the Rio Grande on the exican border.

lar·es: see LAR.

large (lärj) *adj.* (**larg·er, larg·-**st). Of considerable or relatively eat magnitude; wide in range or pacity, comprehensive; ~-**scale**, xtensive; made or drawn on a large ale to show detail (of maps, dia-ams, etc.). **large** *n.* **at** ~, at berty, free; (of narration etc.) at ll length, with details; as a body or hole; without particularizing, ithout specific aim; (of representa-

Above: The **larch** *is a swiftly growing softwood tree and, while it is a member of the pine family, it is not evergreen. Male and female cones grow side by side on the same branch.*

tive etc.) representing nation, state, etc. as a whole, not merely a district of it. **large´ness** *n.* **larg´ish** *adj.*

large·ly (lärj´lē) *adv.* (esp.) To a great or preponderating extent.

lar·gess, lar·gesse (lärjĕs´, lär´jĭs) *ns.* Money or gifts freely bestowed, esp. by great person on occasion of rejoicing; generous or plentiful bestowal.

lar·go (lär´gō) *adv.* & *n.* (pl. **-gos**). (mus.) (Passage, piece of music) to be rendered in slow time and with broad, dignified treat-ment. [It.]

lar·i·at (lăr´ēat) *n.* Long rope or leather line for tethering grazing animals; lasso.

lark[1] (lärk) *n.* Any bird of the family Alaudidae, in which the hind claw is usu. greatly elongated; (pop.) SKYLARK; **horned** ~, a N. Amer. lark (*Eremophila alpestris*); also, any of various birds unrelated to these, as **mead´owlark**, N. Amer. songbirds *Sturnella magna* and *S. neglecta.*

lark[2] (lärk) *n.* Frolic, spree; amusing incident. ~ *v.i.* Play tricks, frolic.

lark·spur (lärk´sper) *n.* Plant of genus *Delphinium* with spur-shaped calyx.

La·Roche·fou·cauld (lă rawsh-foōkō´), **François de Marsillac, duc de** (1613–80). French writer of maxims, embodying a cynical philosophy that finds in self-love the prime motive of action.

La·rousse (lăroōs´), **Pierre Athanase** (1817–75). French lexicographer and encyclopedist.

lar·rup (lăr´up) *v.t.* (**-rupped, -rup·ping**). (colloq.) Thrash.

Lars Por·se·na (lärz´ pōr´sena) = PORSENA.

lar·va (lär´va) *n.* (pl. **-vae** pr.

-vē). Insect from time of leaving egg until transformation into pupa; grub; immature form of other animals that undergo metamorpho-sis. **lar´val** *adj.* [L., = "ghost, mask"]

la·ryn·ge·al (larĭn´jēal, lărĭn-jē´al) *adj.* Of the larynx.

lar·yn·gec·to·my (lărĭnjĕk´-tomē) *n.* (pl. **-mies**). Surgical removal of the larynx.

lar·yn·gi·tis (lărĭnjī´tĭs) *n.* In-flammation of lining membrane of larynx.

lar·yn·gol·o·gy (lărĭnggŏl´ojē) *n.* Branch of medicine dealing with diseases of throat. **lar·yn·gol´o·gist** *n.*

la·ryn·go·scope (larĭng´goskōp) *n.* Mirror apparatus for inspecting larynx. **lar·yn·gos·co·py** (lărĭng-gŏs´kopē) *n.* (pl. **-pies**).

lar·yn·go·to·my (lărĭnggŏt´-omē) *n.* Surgical incision into larynx from without, esp. to pro-vide breathing-channel.

lar·ynx (lăr´ĭngks) *n.* (pl. **la·ryn·ges,** pr. larĭn´jēz, **lar·ynx·es**). Cavity in upper part of windpipe with cartilaginous walls which, when moved by muscles, vary the tension of the vocal cords and hence the quality of the sound produced.

la·sa·gna (lazahn´ya) *n.* Dish baked of layers of flat pasta with ground meat, cheese, tomatoes, sauce, etc.

La Salle (la săl´; *Fr.* lă săl´), **René Robert Cavelier, Sieur de** (1640–87). French explorer of the Ohio and Mississippi rivers.

las·car (lăs´ker) *n.* Oriental, esp. E. Indian, sailor, employed on European ships. [Port., f. Hind., f. Arab *al-'askarī* the soldier]

Las·caux (lăskō´). Prehistoric

Below: The **lapwing** *or plover is com-monly seen on the seashore or mudflats where it eats small marine invert-ebrates. The lapwing is also seen on inland pastures.*

elow: The **lark** *nests on the ground here it is well camouflaged. The bird tters its trilling song usually while soar-g and it is often silent while returning earth.*

cave, Dordogne, S. France, containing wall paintings dating from *c*15,000 B.C.

las·civ·i·ous (lasĭv′ēus) *adj.* Lustful, wanton; inciting to lust. **las·civ′i·ous·ly** *adv.* **las·civ′i·ous·ness** *n.*

la·ser (lā′zer) *n.* Device producing an intense narrow beam of light by amplifying radiation that is within or near the frequency range of visible light. [*light* amplification by *s*timulated *e*mission of *r*adiation]

lash (lăsh) *v.* 1. Make sudden movement of limb, tail, etc.; pour, rush, vehemently; strike violently *at*; hit or kick *out*; break *out* into excess, strong language, etc. 2. Beat with lash, flog; (of waves) beat upon; castigate in words, satirize; urge as with whip. 3. Fasten (*down, on, to,* etc.) with cord etc.; ~-**up**, temporary connection of apparatus for experiment or in an emergency. **lash** *n.* 1. Stroke given with thong, whip, etc.; flexible part of whip; thong; goading influence; **the** ~, punishment of flogging. 2. Eyelash. **lash′less** *adj.*

Las Pal·mas (lahs pahl′mahs). Largest city of the Spanish Canary Islands, on the NE. coast of Grand Canary Island.

lass (lăs), **las·sie** (lăs′ē) *ns.* Girl. [chiefly Sc.]

Las·sen (lăs′en) **Peak.** Only active volcano in the continental U.S.; 10,453 feet (3,186 m), in the Cascade Range in N. California.

las·si·tude (lăs′ĭtōod, -tūd) *n.*

Weariness, languor; disinclination to exert or interest oneself.

las·so (lăs·ō′, lăsōō′) *n.* (pl. **-sos, -soes**). Rope, line of untanned hide etc., with running noose esp. for catching cattle. ~ *v.t.* (**-soed, -so·ing**). Catch with lasso.

last[1] (lăst, lahst) *n.* Shoemaker's wooden or metal model on which shoes are shaped.

last[2] (lăst, lahst) *adj.* After all others, coming out or belonging to the end; latest up to now; lowest, of least rank or estimation; only remaining; latest *to be*; least likely or willing or suitable; definitive; utmost, extreme; ~ **day,** Judgment Day; end of the world; ~ **ditch,** (place) of final desperate defense; ~ **hurrah,** (colloq.) a final, futile political campaign; ~-**in, first out,** method of evaluating business inventory on the assumption that the last lot to be received will be the first sold or used; **L**~ **Judgment,** God's final judgment on the world and on each person; ~ **straw,** slight addition that makes something no longer bearable (as with camel's load); limit of tolerance; **L** ~ **Supper,** supper of Jesus Christ and disciples on eve of the Crucifixion; ~ **word:** see WORD; **last** *n.* Last-mentioned person or thing; last day or moments, death; last performance of certain acts; last mention; **at (long)** ~, in the end, after much delay. **last** *adv.* After all others; on the last occasion before the present; in the last place, finally. **last′ly** *adv.*

last[3] (lăst, lahst) *v.* Go on, remain unexhausted or adequate or alive; suffice; ~ **out,** continue (esp. in vigor or use) at least as long as.

Las·tex (lăs′tĕks) *n.* (trademark)

Yarn made of elastic rubber wou with synthetic or natural thread

last·ing (lăs′tĭng, lahs′tĭng) *a* Enduring, permanent; dural **last′ing·ly** *adv.* **last′ing·ness**

Las Ve·gas (lahs vā′gas). C and gambling resort in SE. Neva

Lat. *abbrev.* Latin.

lat. *abbrev.* Latitude.

Lat·a·ki·a (lătakē′a, lahtah Seaport of Syria, the anci Laodicea ad Mare; fine kind Turkish tobacco shipped fr there.

latch (lăch) *n.* Door or g fastening made of small bar fall into catch and lifted by lever, from outside; small springlock outer door catching when door closed and worked by **latch′k** from outside; ~ **onto,** (collo attach oneself to; get; **latch′stri** cord passed through hole in door open latch from outside. **latch** Fasten with latch.

late (lāt) *adj.* (**lat·er, lat·t lat·est, last**). 1. After the due usual time; backward in floweri ripening, etc.; far on in day night, or in time; far on in a peri development, etc. 2. (usu. recent dead; immediately preceding present in office (as *the* ~ *pre dent*); of recent date. **late′ness late** *adv.* After proper time; far in time; (poet.) recently, late ~-**comer,** (of person) rec arrival. **late** *n.* **of** ~, recently.

la·teen (lătēn′) *adj.* ~ **sa** triangular sail on long yard at an of 45 ~ to mast; (of ship etc.) rigged. [Fr. (*voile*) *latine* "La sail," because common in Medit ranean]

late·ly (lāt′lē) *adv.* Not long a in recent times.

La Tène (lă těn′). Archae logical site at E. end of Lake Neufchâtel, Switzerland; ~ **c ture,** that of second Iron Age central and W. Europe, so cal because objects characteristic of were first identified at La Tène.

la·tent (lā′tent) *adj.* Conceal dormant; existing but not deve oped or manifest; ~ **heat:** s HEAT. **la′ten·cy** *n.* **la′tent** *adv.*

lat·er·al (lăt′eral) *adj.* Of, toward, from, the side(s); side-; ~ **branch** (of family), branch scended from brother or sister person in direct line; ~ **pa** (football) pass thrown parallel line of scrimmage or backw (opp. to forward pass). **lat′er·a** *adv.* **lateral** *n.* Side pa member or object, esp. lateral sh or branch; (football) lateral pass

Lat·er·an (lăt′eran). Site Rome containing the basilica of John the Baptist (**St. John** cathedral church of Rome, and ~ **Palace,** now a museum, wh the popes resided until 14th c.;

headstock
chuck cross-slide bed-plate
tool-post saddle tail-stock

lead screw apron
feed-shaft

*Above: The material to be shaped on a **lathe** is secured between the headstock, using a chuck, and the tail-stock. The cutting tool may be attached to or hand-held against the tool-post.*

ouncil, any of the five general clesiastical councils or synods of e Western Church, held in St. hn Lateran (1123, 1139, 1179, 15, 1512–17); ~ **Treaty**, condat between Italy and Holy See, ned 1929 in Lateran Palace, and cognizing as fully sovereign and dependent a new (papal) State led Vatican City.

lat·er·ite (lăt′erīt) n. (geol.) perficial deposit rich in iron and uminum oxides, red or yellow in lor, developed by weathering of cks in some wet tropical climates.

la·tex (lā′tĕks) n. (pl. **lat·i·ces** pr. ′īsēz, **la·tex·es**). Milky fluid of number of plants, exuding from t surfaces and sometimes coaguing rapidly on exposure, used as e raw material of several commercial products, esp. rubber; synthetic oduct resembling this. [L., = iquid'']

lath (lăth, lahth) n. (pl. **laths** pr. dhz, lăths, lahdhz, lahths). Thin rrow strip of wood esp. for use as pport for plaster etc. ~ v.t. ovide (wall, ceiling) with laths.

lathe (lādh) n. Machine for rning wood, metal, etc., by ating the article to be turned inst tools that cut it to the quired shape.

lath·er (lădh′er) n. Froth made agitation of mixture of soap, or her detergent, and water; frothy eat of horse; (fig.) state of citement, as **in a ~. lath′er·y** j. **lather** v. Cover (esp. chin c. for shaving) with lather; (of rse) become covered with lather; f soap etc.) form lather.

lat·i·fun·di·um (lătifŭn′dēum) (pl. **-di·a** pr. -dēa). (Rom. hist.) arge pastoral estate worked by ves or poor tenants.

Lat·in (lăt′īn) n. 1. Indouropean language of ancient tium and of the Romans, orig. at of the people of Latium atini), and spoken by the

Romans, subsequently the language of R.C. Church and used generally in law and the sciences in W. Europe, that of the post-classical period being distinguished chronologically as **Late** ~ (c200–600 A.D.) and **Medieval** ~ (c600–1500 A.D.); **Low** ~, any post-classical Latin; **modern** ~, that of modern times, employed esp. in scientific descriptions and classifications; **pig** ~ : see PIG; **Silver** ~, literary language and style of the century following the death of Augustus (14 A.D.); **Vulgar** ~, popular and provincial forms of Latin, esp. those from which Romance languages developed. 2. Native, inhabitant, of ancient Latium. 3. (hist.) During the Crusades, member of western nations of Europe (as dist. from ''Greeks''). 4. Member of any of the Latin peoples. **Latin** adj. 1. Of Latium or the ancient Latins; of, written in, the Latin language. 2. Of the Latin Church. 3. Of the European peoples speaking languages descended from Latin. 4. ~ **America**, all Western Hemisphere countries S. of U.S. where Spanish or Portuguese is the chief language; ~ **Church**, Roman Catholic Church; ~ **cross**, plain cross with lower member longer than the other three; ~ **League**, (Rom. hist.) confederation of cities of Latium, merged in Roman State 338 B.C.; ~ **Quarter**, district of Paris on left or S. bank of Seine, where students and artists live and principal university buildings are situated.

Lat·in·ism (lăt′inīzem) n. Idiom characteristic of Latin, esp. one used in another language; conformity in style to Latin models.

Lat′in·ist n. Latin scholar.

Lat·in·ize (lăt′inīz) v. (**-ized, -iz·ing**). Give Latin form to (word), put into Latin; make conformable to ideas, customs, etc., of the ancient Romans, Latin peoples, or Latin Church; use Latin forms, idioms, etc.

La·ti·no (lătē′nō) n. Person of Latin-American descent living in U.S.

La·ti·nus (latī′nus). (Rom. legend) Eponymous hero of Latins, son of Faunus and the nymph Marica, king of Latium and father of Lavinia, whom Aeneas married.

la·tis·si·mus dor·si (latĭs′imus dōr′sī) (pl. **la·tis·si·mi dor·si** pr. latĭs′imī dōr′sī). (also ~ **muscle**) Broad flat muscle covering lumbar region.

lat·i·tude (lăt′itood, -tūd) n. 1. Breadth, width (now only joc.); scope, full extent (rare). 2. Freedom from narrowness; liberality of interpretation; tolerated variety of attitude or opinion. 3. (geog.) Angular distance on a meridian, place's angular distance on its meridian, N. or S. of equator, measured from Earth's center; (usu. pl.) regions, climes (esp. with ref. to temperature); (astron.) angular distance of heavenly body from ecliptic. **lat·i·tu′di·nal** adj. **lat·i·tu′di·nal·ly** adv.

lat·i·tu·di·nar·i·an (lătītōodinār′ean, -tū-) n. & adj. (One who is) tolerant; characterized by latitude of opinion, esp. in religious matters. **lat·i·tu·di·nar′i·an·ism** n.

La·ti·um (lā′shēum). Ancient name of district of central Italy lying S. of Apennines and E. of Tiber.

La·to·na (latō′na). (Rom. myth.) = LETO.

la·trine (latrēn′) n. Communal toilet, esp. in military camp etc.

lat·ter (lăt′er) adj. Later, second (archaic); belonging to end of period, world, etc.; secondmentioned (opp. to FORMER); ~-**day**, modern; **L ~ Day Saints**, the MORMONS. **latter** n. Secondmentioned thing or person.

lat·ter·ly (lăt′erlē) adv. Of late; toward the end of some period etc.

lat·tice (lăt′ĭs) n. 1. Framework of wood or other material made of laths crossed diagonally so as to form a netlike structure serving as screen, door, etc.; (also **lat′tice·work**) laths etc. so arranged. 2. Arrangement of points representing the relative position of corresponding atomic or molecular centers in the structure units of a crystal. 3. ~ **window**, one having lattice; one with small panes set in diagonally crossing strips of lead. **lat′ticed** adj.

Lat·vi·a (lăt′vēa). Area on the E. and S. shore of the Gulf of Riga; formerly a Baltic province of the Russian Empire; proclaimed an independent republic in 1918; incorporated in the U.S.S.R. in 1940 as a constituent republic (properly *Latvian Soviet Socialist Republic*); capital, Riga. **Lat′vi·an** *adj. & n.*

laud (lawd) *n.* 1. Praise, hymn of praise (rare). 2. **Lauds**, (R.C. Ch.) canonical HOUR joined to Matins. **laud** *v.t.* Praise, celebrate. **lau·da·tion** (lawdā′shon) *n.* **laud′a·tive, laud·a·to·ry** (law′datōrē, -tōrē) *adjs.*

laud·a·ble (law′dabel) *adj.* Commendable, praiseworthy. **laud·a·bil·i·ty** (lawdabǐl′ǐtē) *n.* **laud′a·bly** *adv.*

lau·da·num (law′danum, lawd′-num) *n.* Tincture of opium. [name given by Paracelsus to a costly medicament, later transferred to preparations containing opium]

laugh (lăf, lahf) *v.* Make the sounds and the movements of face and sides by which lively amusement, sense of the ludicrous, exultation, and scorn, are instinctively expressed; have these emotions; utter laughingly; get (person) *out of* habit, belief, etc., by ridicule; (of objects etc.) be lively with play of movement or light; ridicule; ~ **away**, dismiss (subject) with a laugh; while away (time) with jests; ~ **off**, get rid of (embarrassment etc.) with a jest; ~ **out of court**, deprive of a hearing by ridicule; ~ **out of the other side of one's mouth**, change from pleasure or amusement to sorrow or vexation; ~ **up one's sleeve**, be secretly amused. **laugh** *n.* Sound or act of laughing; **have the last** ~ **(on)**, win after apparent defeat; reverse one's fortunes successfully; trick a trickster. **laugh′a·ble** *adj.* **laugh′a·bly** *adv.* Exciting laughter, amusing.

laugh·ing (lăf′ĭng, lah′fĭng) *n.* (esp.) **no** ~ **matter**, serious thing, not a fit subject for laughter; ~ **gas**, nitrous oxide used as anesthetic, producing exhilarating effects when inhaled; **laugh′ing-stock**, object of general derision; **laughing** *adj.* **laugh′ing·ly** *adv.*

laugh·ter (lăf′ter, lahf′ter) *n.* Act, sound of laughing.

launch¹ (lawnch, lahnch) *v.* 1. Hurl, discharge, send forth (missile, blow, threat, etc.); burst *into* strong language, lengthy speech, etc.; ~, **launching pad**, platform from which rocket or guided missile is launched. 2. Set (vessel) afloat, cause to slide from land or stocks into water; send off,

The fragrance of **lavender** (above: L. officinalis) has earned it a place in gardens of many warm temperate countries. The flowers of L. spica are used in making lavender water.

start, on a course; initiate (an enterprise). **launch** *n.* Process of launching ship.

launch² (lawnch, lahnch) *n.* Large electric or steam or motor-boat for passengers, pleasure trips, etc.; heavy motorboat.

laun·der (lawn′der, lahn′-) *v.* 1. Wash and iron (linen etc.); (of fabric) bear laundering (*well* etc.). 2. (slang) Pass (illicit funds) through (esp. foreign) banks to hide original ownership.

laun·der·ette (lawnderĕt′, lahn-, lawn′derĕt, lahn′-) *n.* Establishment where washing machines may be used for a fee; Laundromat.

laun·dress (lawn′drǐs, lahn′-) *n.* Woman who earns her livelihood by washing clothes etc.

Laun·dro·mat (lawn′dromăt, lahn′-) *n.* (trademark) Self-service establishment equipped with coin-operated washing machines and dryers.

laun·dry (lawn′drē, lahn′-) (pl. **-dries**). Room or establishment for washing linen; batch of clothes etc. sent to or from laundry; ~ **list**, list of items sent to laundry; (colloq.) long ill-assorted list of items.

Lau·ra (lōr′a). Subject of love poems of PETRARCH, by tradition Laura de Noves (c1308–48), wife of Count Hugues de Sade.

lau·re·ate (lōr′ĕĭt) *adj.* Wreathed with, (of wreath) consisting of, laurels; worthy of laurels as poet, orator, etc.; **Nobel** ~, recipient of any of the NOBEL prizes; **poet** ~, (England) poet receiving stipend as officer of British Royal Household, writer of poems for state occasions; (U.S.) outstanding poet receiving comparable honor from state legislature. **laureate** *n.* Poet laureate. **lau′re·ate·ship** *n.*

lau·rel (lōr′el, lăr′-) *n.* 1. Bay tree (*Laurus nobilis*) (also **bay** ~); foliage of this as emblem of victory or poetic merit; **look to one's** ~**s**, beware of losing preeminence; **rest on one's** ~**s**, cease to strive for further glory. 2. Any of various trees and shrubs with leaves resembling those of bay, esp. MOUNTAIN laurel; sweet magnolia, sweet bay, ~ **oak**, N. Amer. species of oak. **laurel** *v.t.* (**-reled**, **-rel·ing**, Brit. **-relled**, **-rel·ling**) Wreathe with laurel.

Lau·rence (lōr′ens, lăr′-), **St** (3rd c.). Roman Christian martyr, usu. represented with a gridiron, the instrument of his martyrdom.

Lau·ren·tian (lawrĕn′shan) **Mountains.** Low mountain range between the St. Lawrence River and Hudson Bay in the province of Quebec, Canada; summer and winter resort area.

lau·rus·ti·nus (lōrustī′nus) *n.* Evergreen flowering shrub, *Virnum tinus.*

la·va (lah′va, lăv′a) *n.* Molten ck which flows down sides of lcano; solid substance this cools to.

la·va·bo (lavā′bō, -vah′-) *n.* tual washing of celebrant's hands offertory in Mass (accompanied y saying of Ps. 26); towel or basin ed for this; washing trough in me medieval monasteries. [L., "I will wash," first wd of Ps. :6]

lav·a·to·ry (lăv′atōrē, -tōrē) *n.* l. -ries). 1. Room or compart-ent with facilities for urination d defecation. 2. Room etc. with cilities for washing face and nds.

lave (lāv) *v.t.* (**laved, lav·ing**). oet.) Wash, bathe; wash against, w along.

lav·en·der (lăv′ender) *n.* Small ac-flowered narrow-leaved shrub genus *Lavandula*, native in S. urope and N. Africa, extensively ltivated for its perfume; flowers d stalks of this laid among linen c.; pale-blue color with trace of d; ~ **water**, perfume made from stilled lavender.

la·ver (lā′ver) *n.* Any of various arine algae, esp. the edible ecies.

La·vin·i·a (lavĭn′ēa). (Rom. gend) Daughter of Latinus, king Latium, and wife of Aeneas.

lav·ish (lăv′ĭsh) *adj.* Giving or roducing without stint, profuse, rodigal; very or too abundant. v′ish·ly *adv.* **lav′ish·ness** *n.* vish *v.t.* Bestow or spread rofusely.

La·voi·sier (lăvwŏzyā′), An-ine Laurent (1743–94). French emist; laid the foundations of odern chemistry by giving a rrect explanation of the part ayed by oxygen in combustion; scovered animal metabolism.

law (law) *n.* 1. Body of enacted customary rules recognized by a community as binding; one of these rules; their controlling influence, law-abiding state of society (freq. ~ **and order**); laws as a system or science, jurisprudence; binding injunction(s); one of the branches of the study of law, laws concerning specified department; statute and common law (opp. EQUITY); legal knowledge; judicial remedy, law courts as providing it, litigation; the ~, the legal profession; (colloq.) the police; **the L~ (of Moses)**: see MOSAIC law; **lay down the ~**, talk authoritatively, hector; **be a ~ unto oneself**, take one's own line, disregard convention; **take the ~ into one's own hands**, redress one's wrong by force. 2. Rule of action or procedure, esp. in an art, department of life, or game; (also ~ **of nature**), correct state-ment of invariable sequence be-tween specified conditions and specified phenomenon; regularity of nature. ~-**abiding**, obedient to law; **law′breaker**, person who violates the law; **law′giver**, one who makes (esp. code of) laws; **law′maker**, one who drafts or enacts laws (often fig.); legislator; **law′man**, esp. sheriff of Old West; **law of nations**, international law, law regulating relations between countries; **law′suit**, prosecution of claim in court of law.

law·ful (law′ful) *adj.* Permitted, appointed, qualified, recognized, by law. **law′ful·ly** *adv.* **law′ful-ness** *n.*

law·less (law′lĭs) *adj.* Without law, not regulated by law; regard-less of, disobedient to, uncontrolled by, law; unbridled, licentious. **law′less·ness** *n.*

lawn[1] (lawn, lahn) *n.* Very fine material of plain weave, made orig. of linen, now usu. of cotton. [prob. f. *Laon* in France]

lawn[2] (lawn, lahn) *n.* Area of closely-cut grass in a garden or park, or used for a game, as *croquet*; ~ **mower**, machine for mowing lawn; ~ **tennis** = TENNIS.

Law·rence[1] (lōr′ens, lār′-), **D(avid) H(erbert)** (1885–1930). English novelist and poet, author of *Sons and Lovers, Lady Chatterly's Lover*, etc.

Law·rence[2] (lōr′ens, lār′-), **Ernest Orlando** (1901–58). Amer-ican physicist; inventor of the cyclotron; received Nobel Prize for physics, 1939.

Law·rence[3] (lōr′ens, lār′-), **T(homas) E(dward)** (1888–1935). Known as "Lawrence of Arabia"; British soldier and scholar; a leader in World War I, of guerrilla warfare against Turks, described by him in *The Seven Pillars of Wisdom*.

law·ren·ci·um (lawrĕn′sēum, lahrĕn′-) *n.* (chem.) Transuranic element; symbol Lw, at. no. 103.

law·yer (law′yer, loi′er) *n.* Member of legal profession, esp. attorney, (Brit.) solicitor; person versed in law.

lax (lăks) *adj.* Loose, not compact; negligent, not strict, vague. **lax′ly** *adv.* **lax′ness, lax′i·ty** *ns.*

lax·a·tive (lăk′satĭv) *adj. & n.* (Medicine) tending to loosen the bowels.

lay[1] (lā) *n.* Short lyric or narrative poem meant to be sung; (loosely) song, poem.

lay[2] (lā) *adj.* Nonclerical, not in orders; of, done by, layman or laity; nonprofessional, not expert; (esp. with ref. to psychoanalysis) not a physician; ~ **brother, sister**, person who has taken habit and vows of religious order but is employed in manual labor and excused from other duties; **lay′-man**, member of the laity; **lay reader**, layman licensed to conduct religious services.

*Below: The layout of a **lawn tennis** court is marked out with white lime. Below left: A men's singles match is played on one of the courts at Wimbledon during the Lawn Tennis Association Championship.*

doubles sideline

base line

21 ft

18 ft

left court

center line

right court

3 ft

singles sideline

service line

78 ft

13 ft 6 ins

27 ft

4 ft 6 ins

lay³ (lā) v. (**laid, layed, lay·-ing**). Place on a surface or in horizontal position; spread, apply (paint etc.); cause to subside (ghost, dust, storm, etc.); impose (obligation etc.); beat down (crops); set (trap) in readiness; aim (cannon); wager (stake); produce (egg); make (rope) by twisting yarn; **~-about** (n.), habitual loafer; **~ by, in**, store; **~ down**, relinquish (office etc.), formulate (principle), store (wine) in cellar; **~ hands on**, attack or seize, (of bishop) confirm or ordain; **~ off** (employee), dismiss temporarily owing to shortage of work; (slang) stop, desist; **lay'off** (n.); **lay on**, provide for supply of (water, electricity, etc.); **lay open**, cut open; expose; **lay out**, prepare (corpse) for burial; dispose, arrange, (site etc.); (slang) kill, knock down, exhaust, (person); **lay'out** (n.), (plan etc. showing) arrangement of site, printed page, etc.; **lay'over** (n.), stopover; **lay papers, bill** (on table), follow procedure for consideration by legislature; **lay table, breakfast**, etc., prepare for meal; **lay to**, impute to; **lay up**, save, store; put (ship or vehicle) temporarily out of active use; confine to bed through illness. **lay** n. Way, position, or direction in which something (esp. country) lies; (of rope) direction or amount of twist given to strands; lie; **~ of the land**, general nature of an area; (fig.) general view or prospects of a matter, the facts of the case.

lay·a·way (lā'awā) **plan.** Reservation of merchandise by payment of deposit.

lay·er (lā'er) n. (esp.) 1. Stratum, thickness of matter (esp. one of several) spread over surface; **~ cake**, one made in layers with filling between. 2. (hort.) Shoot fastened into earth to establish root while attached to parent plant. 3. Oyster bed. **layer** v.t. Propagate in layers; (of plant) form layers.

lay·ette (lāĕt') n. Outfit of clothes, toilet articles, and bedding for newborn child.

lay (lā) **figure.** Jointed usu. wooden figure of human body used by artists, in absence of human model. [Du. led joint]

laz·ar (lăz'er, lā'zer) n. (obs.) Poor and diseased person, esp. leper; **~ house**, lazaretto. [f. LAZARUS¹]

laz·a·ret·to (lăzerĕt'ō), **laz·a·ret, laz·a·rette** (lăzerĕt') ns. (pl. **-tos**). Formerly a hospital for diseased poor, esp. lepers; building or ship for performance of quarantine; after part of ship's hold used for stores.

Laz·a·rus¹ (lăz'erus). 1. Brother of Martha and Mary of Bethany, restored to life by Jesus after four days in the tomb (John 11, 12). 2.

Beggar in the parable of the rich man and the beggar (Luke 16).

Laz·a·rus² (lăz'erus), **Emma** (1849–87). American humanitarian, poet, and philanthropist; champion of Russian Jews during their persecution, 1879–83; best remembered for her sonnet, "The New Colossus," engraved on pedestal of the Statue of Liberty and including the words "Give me your tired, your poor/Your huddled masses, yearning to be free."

laze (lāz) v. (**lazed, laz·ing**). (colloq.) Be lazy; pass (time) away in laziness.

la·zy (lā'zē) adj. (**la·zi·er, la·zi·est**). Averse to labor, slothful; appropriate to, inducing, indolence; (of stream) slow-moving; **la'zybones**, lazy person; **lazy Susan**, revolving tray at center of table that holds serving dishes, condiments, etc.; **lazy tongs**, arrangement of several pairs of levers crossing and pivoted at center like scissors, for picking up objects at a distance. **la'zi·ly** adv. **la'zi·ness** n.

lb. abbrev. Pound, pounds.

lbs. abbrev. Pounds.

L.C. abbrev. Library of Congress.

l.c. abbrev. Loco citato (L., = in the passage already quoted); lower case (of print).

LCD abbrev. Liquid crystal diode.

L.C.D., l.c.d. abbrevs. Lowest common denominator.

LCDR abbrev. Lieutenant commander.

L.C.M. abbrev. Lowest common multiple.

Ld. abbrev. Lord.

L-dopa (ĕl'dō'pa) n. Drug used in treating Parkinson's disease.

lea (lē, lā) n. (poet.) Tract of open ground, esp. grassland.

leach (lēch) v.t. Make (liquid) percolate through some material; subject (bark, ore) to action of percolating fluid; purge (soluble

matter) away etc. by such means

Lea·cock (lē'kŏk), **Stephe (Butler)** (1869–1944). English born Canadian humorist an economist.

lead¹ (lĕd) n. 1. (chem.) Heav soft easily fusible metallic eleme of dull bluish-gray color, us obtained from lead sulfide (th principal ore, PbS) by heating in furnace; symbol Pb, at. no. 82, a wt. 207.2; **red ~**, red oxide of lead used as pigment and in glass making; **white ~**, mixture of lea carbonate and lead hydroxide, use as pigment. 2. Lump of lead use in sounding depth of water. 3. (print.) Metal strip for spacing o (**lead'ing**) lines or letters of typ 4. (pl.) Strips of lead used to cove roof; piece of (esp. horizontal) lead covered roof; lead frames holdin glass of lattices or painted window 5. (also **pencil ~**) Graphite. 6 **~ poisoning**, form of poisonin caused by absorption of lead int the system. **lead** (lĕd) v.t. Cove weight, frame (panes etc.) with lead (print.) separate lines or letters (type) with leads; treat with lead, a in **leaded** or **unleaded** gasoline **lead'ed, lead'less** adjs.

lead² (lēd) v. (**led** pr. lĕd, **lead·ing**). 1. Conduct, guide, esp. b going in front; (of commander direct movements of; **~ the way** act as guide or leader. 2. Conduc (person) by the hand or contact (animal) by halter etc.; guide by per suasion; guide actions or opinion of, induce to do; **~ astray**, (esp. tempt to sin etc. 3. (of road etc. Conduct (usu. abs.) to place; (fig. have as result, as in **~ to happiness** 4. Make (rope, water, etc.) g through pulley, channel, etc. 5 Pass, go through, spend, (life etc.) 6. Have first place in; go first; b

*The resistance of **lead** to corrosio makes it a suitable material for use a cladding on buildings where it protect the structure from the effects of the weather.*

cordate, serrate   ovate, acuminate   lanceolate   sinuate   palmately lobed

reniform, crenate   obtuse   perfoliate   connate

hastate

trifoliate   palmate   alternate   pinnate, opposite, with   bipinnate
                                        mucronate leaflets

pinna

epidermis   cuticle

mesophyll

ligule

stoma   xylem

palisade   phloem

spongy parenchyma

magnified section of leaf

whorled   monocotyledonous leaf

The pattern of veins in a **leaf** is closely related to the shape of the leaf. In a monocotyledonous leaf the veins run parallel along its length. In a dicotyledonous leaf the veins are reticulate and the leaf, such as a maple, may be divided.

expressing editorial opinion; ~ **edge**, forward edge of blade of propeller; foremost edge of aircraft wing, tail, or fin; ~ **lady, man**, actor taking chief part in play etc.; ~ **light**, prominent influential person; ~ **note**, seventh note in ascending scale, leading the ear to expect the tonic; ~ **question**, question that suggests the answer the questioner wishes to receive.

leaf (lēf) *n.* (pl. **leaves** pr. lēvz). 1. Expanded organ (usu. green) of plant springing from side of stem or branch or directly from root; (pop.) petal (esp. **rose** ~); foliage; **in ~**, with leaves out; ~ **miner**, larva of any of numerous insects digging into and feeding on leaves; ~ **mold**, soil composed chiefly of dead leaves. 2. Leaves of plant cultivated for commercial purposes, e.g., tobacco, tea. 3. Single thickness of folded paper, esp. in book; very thin sheet of metal, esp. gold or silver, or horn, marble, etc.; **turn over a new ~**, mend one's ways. 4. Slab inserted in expandable table. **leaf'age** *n.* **leaf'less** *adj.* **leaf'-less·ness** *n.* **leaf'y** *adj.* (**leaf·i·er, leaf·i·est**). **leaf'i·ness** *n.* **leaf** *v.t.* ~ **through**, turn over pages.

leaf·let (lēf'lĭt) *n.* 1. (bot.) One division of compound leaf; young leaf. 2. Small leaf of paper, or sheet folded but not stitched, with printed matter, esp. for distribution.

league[1] (lēg) *n.* Measure of distance, usu. about 3 miles (4.8 km).

league[2] (lēg) *n.* Association for mutual protection and assistance or prosecution of common interests; (sports) group of teams competing chiefly against one another; **in ~ with**, allied with; ~ **standing**, (sports) position of team with respect to championship. **league** *v.* Join in league.

League (lēg) **of Nations.** Association of nations established in 1919 peace treaty "in order to promote international cooperation and to achieve international peace and security"; dissolved in 1946, superseded by the UNITED NATIONS.

lea·guer (lē'ger) *n.* Member of sports league, as *Little Leaguer.*

Le·ah (lē'a, lā'a). Elder daughter of Laban, and wife of Jacob (Gen. 29,30).

leak (lēk) *n.* 1. Perforation through which liquid, steam, or gas makes way into or out of vessel that is immersed in or contains it. 2. Water passing through such a perforation into a ship; liquid etc.

st at some point in race; direct by ample; be official director or ɔkesman of political party, team, .; have chief role in play etc.; :e the offensive (in contest etc.). (cards) Play as first card, be first ɪyer, in trick; play one of (suit) ıen leading; ~ **away from**, lead ːd of suit other than (ace or other ːh card) in one's hand; ~ **up to**, ıy card so as to elicit (specified ːh card, usu. ace) from an ponent's hand. 8. ~ **off**, begin ınce, conversation, etc.); (base-ıl) bat first in inning; **lead'off** ⸴. or *n.*; **lead on**, entice into ıng further than was intended; ⸴d up to, form preparation for, ⁄e to introduce, direct conver-ıon toward (subject). 9. Ply ıtness) with leading questions. ⸴d (lĕd) *n.* 1. Direction given by ıng in front, example; leading ⸴ce, leadership; (theatr.) (player ⸴ chief part; (cards) act or right of

playing first; ~ **time**, interval required between planning and starting or completing a project. 2. (elect.) Connecting wire to or from an electric device (~ **-in**, wire connecting external aerial to radio receiver); channel in ice field. 3. Strap, strip of leather, etc., for leading dog.

lead·en (lĕd'en) *adj.* (As) of LEAD[1]; heavy, slow, burdensome; inert, deadening; lead colored.

lead·er (lē'der) *n.* (esp.) 1. Person or thing that guides or leads; see LOSS ~, MAJORITY ~, MINORITY ~. 2. (mus.) Conductor. 3. Shoot growing at apex of stem or principal branch. 4. (Brit.) LEADING article. 5. (print.) Line of dots or dashes to guide eye. **lead'er·less** *adj.* **lead'er·ship** *n.*

lead·ing (lē'dĭng) *n.* Guidance; direction. ~ *adj.* (esp.) ~ **article**, article in newspaper etc. in prominent position and (Brit.)

escaping through a flaw in a receptacle. 3. Escape of electric charge from an incompletely insulated conductor. 4. (radio) (also **grid** ~) High resistance placed in parallel with a grid condenser to prevent overaccumulation of negative charge on the grid. 5. Divulging of secret information etc.; information etc. divulged; **news** ~. **leak** v. Escape, allow escape of, through leak; divulge (secret information etc.); ~ **out**, become known improperly. **leak'-age** n. **leak'y** adj. (**leak·i·er, leak·i·est**). **leak'i·ness** n.

lean[1] (lēn) adj. Thin, not plump; meager, of poor quality, unnutritious; unremunerative; (of meat) consisting chiefly of muscular tissue, not of fat; ~ **years**, years of scarcity. **lean** n. Lean part of meat.

lean[2] (lēn) v. (**leaned**, Brit. **leant** pr. lĕnt, **lean·ing**). Incline one's body against something for support; be or put in sloping position, against, on; incline body back, forward, etc.; stand obliquely, out of the perpendicular; rely or depend on; have tendency to, be partial to cause, opinion, person, etc.; ~-**to**, (n.) shed etc. with roof leaning against larger building or wall. **lean** n. Inclination, slope.

Le·an·der (lēăn'der). (Gk. legend) Lover of HERO.

leap (lēp) v. (**leaped** or **leapt** pr. lĕpt, lēpt, **leap·ing**). 1. Jump; **leap'frog**, game in which players vault over, by placing hands upon, the bent back or shoulders of others. 2. Act hastily. **leap** n. Jump; thing to be jumped; ~ **in the dark**, hazardous attempt of doubtful issue; **by** ~**s and bounds**, with startlingly rapid progress; ~ **year**, year in which an extra day (Feb. 29) is inserted to make calendar year conform with astronomical YEAR (in Gregorian calendar it occurs every fourth year, i.e., when date is divisible by 4, but not in century years unless divisible by 400); ~ **year proposal**, proposal of marriage made by woman to man, traditionally allowable only in leap year.

Lear[1] (lēr). Legendary British king, a supposed descendant of Aeneas; subject of Shakespeare's tragedy, King Lear.

Lear[2] (lēr), **Edward** (1812–88). English artist and writer of nonsense verse; author and illustrator of The Book of Nonsense (1846), which popularized the LIMERICK, and of "The Owl and the Pussy-cat," (1871).

learn (lĕrn) v. (**learned, learnt, learn·ing**). Get knowledge of or skill in by study, experience, or being taught; commit to memory (esp. ~ **by heart** or **rote**); become aware that, how, etc.; be

The tanning of **leather** is an ancient craft dating back to 400 B.C. The vegetable tannage system, while still in use has been superseded by synthetic methods. The largest producers of hides are the U.S.S.R. and the U.S.A.

informed of, ascertain; receive instruction.

learn·ed (lĕr'nĭd) adj. Deeply read, erudite; showing profound knowledge; (of language, profession, etc.) pursued or studied by, (of words) used by, learned men; ~ **professions**, (chiefly Brit.) divinity, law, and medicine. **learn'ed·ly** adv. **learn'ed·ness** n.

learn·ing (lĕr'nĭng) n. (esp.) (Possession of) knowledge obtained by study, esp. of language or literary or historical science; **the new** ~, studies, esp. of Greek, introduced into England in 16th c.; **book** ~, knowledge gained through reading or formal study rather than through practical experience.

lease (lēs) n. Contract by which landlord (lessor), usu. in consideration of rent, conveys land or tenement to tenant (lessee), either for specified time or for a period terminable at the will of either party; **lease'hold**, (real property) held by lease. **lease** v.t. (**leased, leas·ing**). Grant or take lease of; ~-**lend** = LEND-lease.

leash (lēsh) n. Thong or line by which dogs are held; LEAD[2] (n.). ~ v.t. Connect, hold in, with leash.

least (lēst) adj., superl. of little. Smallest, slightest; **the** ~, (esp. after neg.) any, however small. ~ n. Least amount; **to say the** ~ **of it**, to put the case moderately; **at** ~, at all events, even if a wider statement is disputable; at the lowest computation; **(in) the** ~, in the smallest degree, at all. **least** adv. In the least degree.

least·wise (lēst'wīz), (dial. **least'ways**) adv. (colloq.) Anyway, at least.

leath·er (lĕdh'er) n. Animal skin prepared for use by tanning or similar process; article, or part of one, made of leather, piece of leather for polishing, thong; (slang)

a football; **patent** ~, leather wit fine usu. black varnished surfac **leath'erback**, large soft-shelle sea turtle (Dermochelys coriacea **leath'erjacket**, tough-skinne larva of crane fly, injurious to roo of grass, cereals, etc.; **leath'erneck** (slang) a U.S. Marine. **leathe** adj. Made of leather. **leath'er** adj. **leather** v.t. (colloq.) Bea with strap.

leave[1] (lēv) n. Permission; (als ~ **of absence**) permission to b absent from duty, period for whic this lasts; **on** ~, absent thu **take** ~ **(of)**, bid farewell (to); **tak** ~ **of one's senses**, go mad; **tak French** ~: see FRENCH.

leave[2] (lēv) v.t. (**left** pr. lĕft **leav·ing**). 1. Cause to or le remain, depart without takin bequeath. 2. Abstain from con suming or dealing with, (pass. remain over; let remain in specifie state; commit, refer, to anothe agent etc. than oneself; allow to d something without interference deposit, entrust (thing etc.) to b dealt with, station (person) t discharge function, in one absence. 3. Quit, go away from depart; pass (object) so as to put i in specified relative direction; ceas to reside at, belong to, or serve abandon, forsake; ~ **alone**, no interfere with; ~ **behind**, go awa without; leave as consequence o trace; pass; ~ **off**, discontinue come to, make, an end; ~ **out** omit; ~ **over**, let stand over for time.

leave[3] (lēv) v.i. (**leaved leav·ing**). Put forth leaves.

leav·en (lĕv'en) n. Substanc added to dough to produce fermen tation, esp. fermenting doug reserved from previous batch fo this; (fig.) spreading and transform ing influence (Matt. 13), tinge o admixture of some quality. ~ v.t Ferment (dough) with leaven permeate and transform, modif with tempering element.

leav·ings (lē'vĭngz) n.pl. Wha is left.

Leb·a·non (lĕb′anon). 1. Mountain range extending the ngth of Lebanon, famous in ncient times for its cedars. 2. epublic on E. coast of Mediterranean, between Israel and Syria; ormerly in French-mandated territory with Syria; independent in 944; capital, Beirut. **Leb·a·nese** ĕbanēz′, -nĕs′) *adj. & n.*

Le·bens·raum (lā′bensrowm, benz-) *n.* Area claimed by a ation etc. for its due development lso fig.). [Ger., = "living space"]

lech·er (lĕch′er) *n.* Fornicator, ebauchee. **lech′er·ous** *adj.* Lustl. **lech′er·ous·ly** *adv.* **lech′er·y** (pl. **-er·ies**).

lec·i·thin (lĕs′ithĭn) *n.* (biohem.) Complex fatty substance ontaining phosphorus, occurring plant and animal tissues and egg olk; commercial preparation of is used as an emulsifying agent foods etc.

Le Cor·bu·sier (le kōr′bōozyā′). harles Edouard Jeanneret (1887– 965), French architect of Swiss irth, pioneer in international style f architecture making much use of teel and concrete.

lec·tern (lĕk′tern) *n.* 1. Reading r singing desk in church, esp. aat for the lessons. 2. Similar desk r lecturer etc.

lec·tion·ar·y (lĕk′shonĕrē) *n.* (pl. ar·ies**). Book containing, list of, ortions of Scripture appointed to e read at divine service.

lec·ture (lĕk′cher) *n.* Discourse efore audience or class on given ubject, usu. by way of instruction; ngthy admonition. ~ *v.* (**-tured, tur·ing**). Deliver lecture(s) (*on* ubject); instruct or entertain by ecture; admonish lengthily. **lec′-ur·er** *n.* (esp.) Teacher in a niversity department. **lec′ture·-hip** *n.* Position of lecturer.

Lebanon, was considered the 'middle-man' of the Arab world and tried to protect its commercial strength with political neutrality. In 1975, however, civil war broke out. Left: Dog River, just north of Beirut.

lec·y·thus (lĕs′ithus) *n.* (pl. **-thi** pr. -thī). (Gk. antiq.) Narrow-necked vase or flask.

led *adj.*: see LEAD².

Le·da (lē′da). (Gk. legend) Wife of Tyndareus, king of Sparta; was loved by Zeus, who took the form of a swan; among her children were Castor and Pollux and Helen (all by Zeus), and Clytemnestra.

ledge (lĕj) *n.* Narrow horizontal surface projecting from wall etc.; shelflike projection on side of rock or mountain; ridge of rocks, esp.

below water; (mining) stratum of metal-bearing rock.

ledg·er (lĕj′er) *n.* 1. Principal book of the set used for recording trade transactions, containing debtor and creditor accounts. 2. Horizontal timber in scaffolding, parallel to face of building. 3. Flat gravestone. 4. ~ (*adj.*) (mus.) = LEGER.

lee (lē) *n.* Shelter given by neighboring object; (also ~ **side**) sheltered side, side away from wind (opp. weather side); (attrib.)

Le Corbusier, the French architect, town planner and painter, was one of the best-known exponents of the 'modern' movement in architecture. This church at Ronchamp, France is one of his most famous structures.

The **leg** is the limb which supports the human body. The arteries of the leg are shown in red. The bones of the leg include the femur (the thigh bone), fibula and tibia (the bones below the knee).

labels: deep femoral / femoral / popliteal / peroneal / posterior tibial / anterior tibial / dorsalis pedis / lateral plantar / arcuate / digital

belonging to ship's lee side or to leeward of other object; **lee'board**, plank frame fixed to side of flat-bottomed sailing vessel and let down into water to diminish leeway; **lee shore**, shore to leeward of ship; **lee'way**, lateral drift of ship to leeward of desired course; **make up leeway**, (fig.) make up for loss of time or retardation of progress.

Lee[1] (lē), **Ann** (1736–84). British religious zealot; founder of first Shaker colony in America at Watervliet, N.Y., 1776.

Lee[2] (lē), **Robert E(dward)** (1807–70). American soldier, commander in chief of Confederate armies in Civil War; his father, **Henry** ("Light-Horse Harry") **Lee** (1756–1818), was an American Revolutionary War commander and statesman.

leech[1] (lēch) *n.* (obs.) Physician, healer.

leech[2] (lēch) *n.* Mainly aquatic

bloodsucking worm (*Hirudo medicinalis*) formerly used medicinally for bleeding; person clinging to another, esp. draining his resources.

leek (lēk) *n.* Culinary herb (*Allium porrum*) allied to onion but with cylindrical bulbous part and broad flat leaves; this as Welsh national emblem.

leer (lēr) *v.i.* & *n.* Glance (esp. sideways) with sly, lascivious, or malign expression. **leer'ing·ly** *adv.*

leer·y (lēr'ē) *adj.* (**leer·i·er**, **leer·i·est**). (slang) Knowing, sly; suspicious.

lees (lēz) *n.pl.* Sediment of wine etc.; basest part, refuse.

Lee·u·wen·hoek (lā'venhook; *Du.* lā'üwenhook), **Anton van** (1632–1723). Dutch microscopist and naturalist; using single-lens microscopes of his own making, he was the first to observe bacteria, protozoa, and other minute forms of life.

lee·ward (lē'werd; *naut.* loo'werd) *adj.* & *adv.* On, toward, side sheltered from wind. ~ *n.* Leeward direction or region. **lee'ward·ly** *adv.* (of ship) Apt to fall to leeward.

Lee·ward (lē'werd) **Islands.** Most northerly group of Lesser Antilles, in W. Indies, including Anguilla, Antigua, St. Kitts, Nevis, Montserrat, and the British Virgin Islands (these being the former **British Leeward Islands** colony) and Guadeloupe, Saba, and the U.S. Virgin Islands.

left[1] (lĕft) *adj.* Belonging to side of person's body on which the heart is and of which the hand is normally less used (opp. RIGHT); having corresponding relation to front of any object; (of bank of river etc.) on left hand of person looking

downstream; ~ **hand**, hand on le side; region or direction of this sic of person; ~**-hand**, placed on th left hand; ~**-hand screw**, scre with thread turning to left; ~ **handed**, using left hand more tha right; for use by left-handed pe son; (of blow etc.) struck; mad with left hand; (fig.) awkwar ambiguous, having a contra meaning; ~**-hander**, left-hande person or blow; ~ **turn**, turn the left into a position at rig angles with the original one; ~ **wing**, (esp.) extreme left in politi (see *n.* sense 2). **left** *adv.* On to the left side. ~ *n.* 1. Le hand; (boxing) left-handed blov 2. In many legislatures, membe on left side of chamber, tradition ally the more liberal or radical (c RIGHT); hence, more advanced innovating section of any grou esp. in politics; radicals collectivel **left·ward** (lĕft'werd) *adv.* & *ad* **left'wards** *adv.*

left[2]: see LEAVE[2].

left·ism (lĕf'tĭzem) *n.* Politic views of the left (see LEFT[1] *n.* 2 **left'ist** *n.*

leg (lĕg) *n.* 1. Organ of suppo and locomotion in animal body; (a human) part of this from hip ankle; artificial substitute for thi 2. Leg of animal as food. (archaic) Obeisance made by draw ing back one leg. 4. Support pol prop, of machine etc.; support chair, table, bed, etc. 5. On branch of forked object; side c triangle other than base. Portion of a course, as section c

The **Leeward Islands** in the We Indies include Antigua which was di covered by Columbus (1493) and fir settled by the English in 1632. Primiti* dwellings, like this straw-roofed hut, an still found in remote parts.

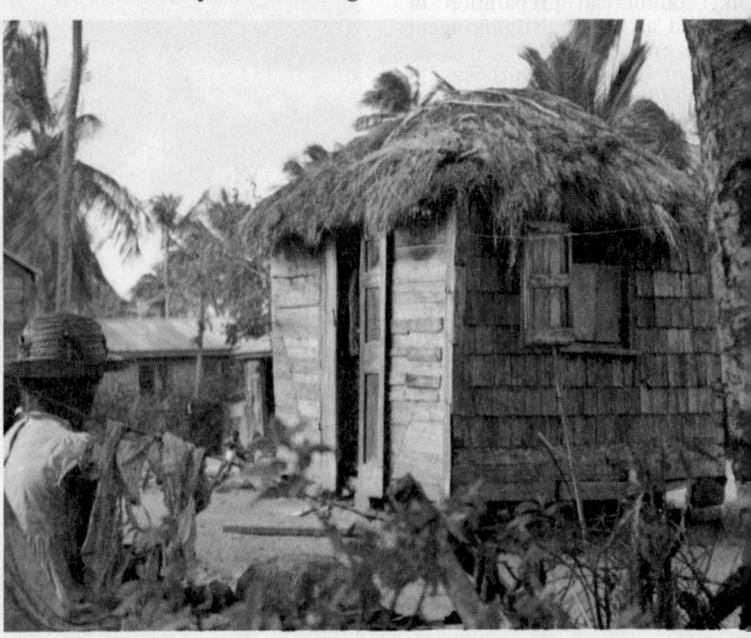

:age of journey; (naut.) run made
n single tack. 7. Part of garment
overing leg. 8. **feel, find, one's
~ s**, get power of standing or walk-
ng (also fig.); **give a ~ up**, help to
mount (horse etc.) or get over
bstacle (also fig.); **on one's last
~ s**, near death or end; **pull
erson's ~**, tease, deceive joking-
v; **shake a ~**, (slang) hurry, dance;
how a ~, get out of bed; **take
o one's ~s**, run away; **walk
erson off his ~s**, tire him out
walking; **without a ~ to stand
n**, unable to support thesis by any
ects or sound reasons. 9. **~-of-
mutton sleeve, sail**, etc., sleeve,
ail, etc., shaped like leg of mutton;
~-pull, (colloq.) piece of teasing;
~ rest**, support for leg of seated
erson. **leg** v.i. (**legged, leg·ging**).
~ it, (slang) walk or run hard; go
way.

leg·a·cy (lĕg′ăsē) n. (pl. **-cies**).
um of money or article be-
ueathed by will; material or
nmaterial thing handed down by
redecessor.

le·gal (lē′gal) adj. Of, based on,
alling within province of, occupied
vith, law; required or appointed by
aw; recognized by law as distinct
rom equity; lawful; (theol.) of the
Mosaic law, of salvation by works
ot faith; ~ **fiction**, statement that
probably fictitious but admitted
s true in order to enable some
seful purpose, as redress of wrong
tc., to be accomplished; ~ **tender**:
ee TENDER². **le′gal·ly** adv.

le·gal·ism (lē′galĭzem) n. Exal-
ation of law or formula, "red tape";
theol.) preference of the law to the
Gospel, doctrine of justification by
vorks. **le′gal·ist** n. **le·gal·is′tic**
dj.

le·gal·i·ty (lēgăl′ĭtē) n. (pl.
ties). Lawfulness; legalism.

leg·ate¹ (lĕg′ĭt) n. 1. Ecclesiastic
eputed to represent pope; ~ **a
atere** (-ah lăt′era), one of highest
lass and full powers. 2. (archaic)
mbassador, delegate. **leg·a·tine**
ĕg′atĭn, -tīn) adj. **leg′ate·ship** n.

le·gate² (lĭgāt′) v.t. (**-gat·ed,
gat·ing**). Bequeath. **le·ga·tor**
ĭgā′ter, lĕgatŏr′) n.

leg·a·tee (lĕgatē′) n. Recipient
f legacy.

le·ga·tion (lĭgā′shon) n. Sending
f legate or deputy; body of
eputies; diplomatic minister and
is staff (esp. when he does not rank
s ambassador), his official resi-
ence; legateship.

le·ga·to (legah′tō; It. lĕgah′taw)
dj. & adv. (mus.) Smooth(ly) and
onnected(ly). [It.]

leg·end (lĕj′end) n. 1. Tradi-
onal story popularly regarded as
istorical, myth; such literature or
adition; (hist.) life of saint,
ollection of such lives or similar
ories; **Golden L ~**: see GOLDEN.
. Inscription or motto, esp. on

Legumes or pod-bearing plants are also known as the pea family. There are more than 12,000 species, including beans, peas, lentils and the carob tree, which has edible fruits, shown here.

coin or medal, below picture, etc.
leg′end·ar·y adj.

leg·er (lĕj′er) adj. ~ **line**, (mus.)
short line added above or below
staff to extend its compass.

Lé·ger (lĕzhĕ′), **Fernand** (1881-
1955). French painter; known for
his cubist paintings.

leg·er·de·main (lĕjerdemān′) n.
Sleight of hand; trickery, sophistry.
[Fr. léger de main light of hand]

leg·ging (lĕg′ĭng) n. (usu. pl.)
Outer covering of leather etc. for
leg up to knee.

leg·gy (lĕg′ē) adj. (**-gi·er,
-gi·est**). Having disproportionately long legs.

Leg·horn (lĕg′hôrn). (Ital.
Livorno) City and seaport of
Tuscany, Italy.

leg·horn (for def. 1 lĕg′hôrn; for
def. 2 lĕg′ern, -hôrn) n. 1. Fine
braided straw for hats etc. imported
from Leghorn, made of stems of a
Mediterranean wheat (Triticum
sativum turgidum) cut green and
bleached; hat of this. 2. One of a
small hardy breed of domestic
poultry.

leg·i·ble (lĕj′ĭbel) adj. Clear,
easily read. **leg·i·bil·i·ty** (lĕji-
bĭl′ĭtē), **leg′i·ble·ness** ns. **leg′i·bly**
adv.

le·gion (lē′jon) n. 1. (Rom. hist.)
Division of 3,000–6,000 men,
including complement of cavalry, in
ancient Roman army. 2. Vast host
or multitude. 3. **American L ~**,
national association of veterans,
founded 1919; **Foreign L ~**, body
of foreign volunteers in modern
(esp. French) army, serving in
colonies or on distant expeditions;
L ~ of Honor, (Fr. légion
d'honneur) French order of dis-

tinction conferred for civil or
military services etc., founded by
Napoleon I in 1802.

le·gion·ar·y (lē′jonĕrē) adj. Of
legion(s). ~ n. (pl. **-ar·ies**). (Rom.
hist.) Soldier of a legion.

le·gion·naire (lējonār′) n. Member of legion, esp. French Foreign
Legion or American Legion.

le·gion·naires' disease (lējonārz′)
Little understood, often
fatal, pneumonia-like infection first
identified after its eruption at an
American Legion convention in
Philadelphia in 1976.

leg·is·late (lĕj′ĭslāt) v.i. (**-lat·ed,
-lat·ing**). Make laws. **leg·is·la·
tion** (lĕjĭslā′shon). (Enacting of)
laws. **leg·is·la·tive** adj. **leg·is·la·
tive·ly** adv.

leg·is·la·tor (lĕj′ĭslāter) n. Lawgiver; member of legislative body.

leg·is·la·ture (lĕj′ĭslācher) n.
Lawmaking body of a government.

le·git·i·mate (lĭjĭt′imĭt) adj.
Born in wedlock; lawful, proper,
regular, conforming to standard
type; logically admissible; (of
sovereign's title) based on strict
hereditary right; (theatr.) of stage
plays not including revues, farces,
etc. **le·git′i·mate·ly** adv. **legit·i·
mate** (lĭjĭt′imāt) v.t. (**-mated,
-mat·ing**). Make legitimate by
decree, enactment, or proof; justify,
serve as justification for. **le·git·i·
ma·tion** (lĭjĭtimā′shon), **le·git′i·
ma·cy** ns. **le·git′i·ma·tize** v.t.
(**-tized, -tiz·ing**). **le·git·i·mize**
(lĭjĭt′imīz) v.t. (**-mized, -miz·ing**).
Make legitimate. **le·git·i·mi·za′-
tion** n.

leg·ume (lĕg′ūm, lĭgūm′) n.
Fruit, edible part, pod, of leguminous plant; such vegetable used for
food.

le·gu·mi·nous (lĭgū′minus) adj.
(bot. etc.) Of the order Leguminosae, including peas, beans, and
other pod-bearing plants.

Le Ha·vre (le hah′vre, -ver; Fr.

le ah′vre). City and port of N. France on English Channel.

le·i (lā′ē, lā) *n.* (pl. **le·is**). Polynesian garland of flowers etc. worn round neck. [Hawaiian]

Leib·niz (līb′nĭts; *Ger.* līp′nĭts), **Gottfried Wilhelm** (1646–1716). German mathematician and philosopher; discoverer of theory of calculus simultaneously with Newton; regarded matter as a multitude of monads, each a microcosm of the universe. **Leib·niz·i·an** (lībnĭt′sēan) *adj.* & *n.*

Leices·ter (lĕs′ter), **Robert Dudley, Earl of** (*c*1532–88). English courtier and general, favorite of Queen Elizabeth.

Lei·den = LEYDEN.

Leif Er·ics·son (lēf ĕr′ĭkson; *Icel.* lāv): see VINLAND.

leis·ter (lēs′ter) *n.* Pronged salmon spear. ~ *v.t.* Spear with this.

lei·sure (lē′zher, lĕzh′er) *n.* (Opportunity *to* do, *for*, afforded by) free time, time at one's own disposal; **at** ~, not occupied; deliberately, without hurry; **at one's** ~, when one has time. **lei′sured** *adj.*

lei·sure·ly (lē′zherlē, lĕzh′er-) *adj.* Having, acting or done at, leisure, deliberate. ~ *adv.* Deliberately, without haste.

leit·mo·tif (līt′mōtēf) *n.* (mus.) Theme associated throughout work with some person, situation, or sentiment. [Ger.]

Le·man (lemahṅ′), **Lake:** see GENEVA.

Le Mans (le mahṅ′). City in W. central France; site of annual 24-hour auto race.

lem·ma (lĕm′a) *n.* (pl. **lem·-mas, lem·ma·ta** pr. lĕm′ata). Assumed or demonstrated proposition used in argument or proof; argument or subject of literary composition; head word of dictionary entry; motto appended to picture etc.

lem·ming (lĕm′ĭng) *n.* (pl. **-mings**, collect. **-ming**). Small rodent of family Muridae inhabiting arctic and subarctic regions, of which one species, the Norway lemming (*Lemmus lemmus*), mi-

Lemmings inhabit the tundra or bordering regions of north Eurasia and North America. The Norway lemming is very prolific and periodically migrates in hordes towards, and often into, the sea, moving chiefly at night.

*Flowers of the **lemon** tree have a distinctive perfume and some of these eventually form into the well-known fruit which is rich in Vitamin C. These trees flourish best in a temperate climate.*

grates in large numbers and has been reported to continue headlong into the sea and drown.

Lem·nos (lĕm′nŏs, -nōs). Large Greek island in N. Aegean. **Lem·ni·an** (lĕm′nēan) *adj.* & *n.*

lem·on[1] (lĕm′on) *n.* Tree (*Citrus limon*), native of Indian Himalayas, now cultivated in U.S. and Mediterranean countries, bearing oval-seeded fruit with pale-yellow skin and acid juice; fruit of this; pale-yellow color; (fig.) defective thing or unpleasant person, esp. a car prone to breakdowns; ~ **drop**, hard lemon-flavored candy; ~ **grass**, tropical grass of genus *Cymbopogon*, yielding fragrant oil.

lem·on[2] (lĕm′on) *n.* ~ **dab, sole**, kind of plaice or flounder resembling sole.

lem·on·ade (lĕmonād′, lĕm′-onād) *n.* Drink of sweetened lemon juice and water; synthetic substitute for this.

le·mur (lē′mer) *n.* Nocturnal mammal of genus *L*~, allied to monkeys but with pointed muzzle, found in Madagascar. **lem·u·roid** (lĕm′yeroid) *adj.* [L. *lemures* spirits of the dead]

Le·na (lē′na; *Rus.* lĕ′nah). River rising W. of Lake Baikal, most

easterly of three great Siberia rivers, it flows 2,650 miles N. the Laptev Sea; famous for th goldfields in its basin.

lend (lĕnd) *v.t.* (**lent** pr. lĕn **lend·ing**). Grant (person) use (thing) on understanding that it its equivalent shall be returned; l out (money) at interest, (books etc for hire; bestow, contribute (som thing of temporary service or effect accommodate *oneself to* some polic or purpose; ~ **(an) ear, one ears**, listen; ~ **a (helping) han** help; **lending library**, library tha lends books, esp. for hire; **lend lease**, arrangement (1941) whereb U.S. supplied equipment etc. countries at war with the Ax powers, orig. as a loan in retur for the use of certain bases. **lend′e** *n.*

L'En·fant (lahṅfahṅ′), **Pierr Charles** (1754–1825). French born Amer. engineer; origina designer of Washington, D.C.

length (lĕngkth, lĕngth) *n.* Thing's measurement from end end, greatest of body's thre dimensions; extent in, of, or wit regard to, time; distance thin extends; long stretch or exten piece of cloth etc. of certain length (pros.) quantity of syllable or vowe **at** ~, in detail or without curtai ment; at last or after a long tim **at full** ~, lying stretched out; full. **length′ways** *adv* & *ad* **length′wise** *adv.* & *adj.*

length·en (lĕngk′then, lĕng then) *v.* Make or become longer (pros.) make (vowel) long.

length·y (lĕngk′thē, lĕng′thē adj. (**length·i·er, length·i·est** Of unusual length, prolix, tediou **length′i·ly** *adv.* **length′i·ness** *n*

le·ni·ent (lē′nēent, lēn′yent) adj Tolerant, gentle, indisposed t severity; (of punishment etc.) mil **le·ni·ent·ly** *adv.* **le·ni·ence** *n* **le·ni·en·cy** *n.* (pl. **-cies**).

Len·in (lĕn′ĭn; *Rus.* lĕnēn′ Assumed name of Vladimir Ilyic Ulyanov (1870–1924), Russia revolutionary, exponent of doc trines of Marx, and founder o Bolshevik party; imprisoned, the exiled from Russia in 190 returned in disguise and took pa in revolution of 1905; escaped 190 and directed revolutionary opera tions from abroad until 1917 whe he returned to Russia and becam first premier of the U.S.S.R., 191 **Lenin Peak**, the highest mountai 23,400 feet (7,133 m), in the Pam Range of the Soviet Unio

*The **lemur**, a slender, large-eyed pr mate, is docile, gregarious and most nocturnal. There are about 15 specie of which the best known is the ringtaile lemur, which is active by day. Othe species include the black lemur (th male only is black), the mouse lemu and the dwarf lemur.*

female

black lemur

male

ruffed lemur

fat-tailed dwarf lemur

ring- tailed lemur

mouse lemur

Verreaux's sifaka lemur

fork-crowned lemur

Len'in·ist, Len'in·ite *adjs.* & *ns.* **Len'in·ism** *n.*

Len·in·grad (lĕn'ĭngrăd; *Rus.* lĕnĭngraht'). Russian city on an inlet of the Gulf of Finland, founded 1703 by Peter the Great and until 1918 capital of Russia; known as St. Petersburg before the Revolution and as Petrograd from 1917 until 1924, when it was renamed after LENIN.

lens (lĕnz) *n.* (pl. **lens·es**). Piece of glass etc. with two curved surfaces, or one plane and one curved, causing regular convergence or divergence of rays of light passing through it, commonly used, either singly or combined, in optical instruments, as a camera, telescope, eyeglass, etc.; (anat.) = CRYSTALline lens; one facet of compound eye; **electron** ~: see ELECTRON.

Lent (lĕnt). Period of fasting before Easter; in western Christian churches, period from Ash Wednesday to Easter eve, of which the 40 weekdays are devoted to fasting and penitence in commemoration of the fasting of Jesus in the wilderness. **Lent'en, lent'en** *adjs.* Of, in, appropriate to, Lent.

lent (lĕnt): see LEND.

len·ti·cel (lĕn'tĭsĕl, -sel) *n.* (bot.) Aeration pore penetrating the young cork of stems and some roots.

len·tic·u·lar (lĕntĭk'yuler) *adj.* Shaped like lentil or lens (esp. ~ **cloud**), double convex; of the lens of the eye.

len·til (lĕn'til) *n.* (Double convex seed of) leguminous plant, *Lens culinaris*, grown for food.

len·to (lĕn'tō) *adj.* & *adv.* (mus.) Slow(ly). [It.]

len·toid (lĕn'toid) *adj.* Lens-shaped.

Le·o¹ (lē'ō). The Lion, a constellation; 5th sign (Ω) of the zodiac which the sun enters about July 21.

Le·o² (lē'ō). Name of 13 popes:

The **lentil** is one of the oldest plants [to] be brought under cultivation. Its edib[le] seed, which contains over 25% pro[]tein, is one of the most nutritious [of] pulses and is important in India, wher[e] it appears as 'dhal'.

Leo I, St., "the Great," pop[e] 440–61, obtained (445) recognitio[n] of the primacy of the popes in th[e] Christian Church; **Leo IV,** pop[e] 847–55, built the LEONINE City[;] **Leo X** (Giovanni de' Medici, 1475[–] 1521), pope 1513–21, excommuni[-] cated Luther and bestowed o[n] Henry VIII of England title o[f] "Defender of the Faith"; **Leo XII[I]** (1810–1903), pope 1878–190[3,] issued encyclical on labor, *Reru[m] Novarum*; "prisoner in Vatican" for refusing to recognize Italia[n] government.

Le·o·nar·do da Vin·ci (lēonär[′] dō d*a* vĭn'chē; *It.* lēawnär'daw d*a* vēn'chē) (1452–1519). Italia[n] painter, sculptor, architect, engi[-] neer, inventor, scientist; among hi[s] paintings are the mural "La[st] Supper" and "La Gioconda" (o[r] "Mona Lisa"); his scientifi[c] accomplishments include origi[-] nating the science of hydraulics, an[d] significant studies in anatomy an[d] mathematics; his notebooks contai[n] visionary sketches for guns an[d]

leopard

snow leopard

The **leopard** (which is also called a pa[n]ther, especially in India), is found [in] Africa and most of Asia. It is a solitar[y] animal of the bush and forest and [is] mainly nocturnal in habit. The sno[w] leopard, a similar feline, inhabits th[e] mountains of central Asia.

Leonardo da Vinci was one of the greatest of the 'universal men' produced by the Renaissance. This painting, 'The Virgin of the Rocks', has a near-duplicate, possibly the work of his pupils, in the Louvre.

annons, airplanes, parachutes, ubmarines, and spiral staircases.

Le·on·ca·val·lo (lĕawnkahvah´-aw), **Ruggiero** (1858–1919). talian composer, famous for his pera *I Pagliacci*.

Le·o·nid (lē´onĭd) *n.* (pl. **Le·o-ids, Le·on·i·des** pr. lēŏn´ĭdēz). One of a shower of meteors adiating from a point in the con-tellation Leo, observable every November but brilliant every 33 ears when Earth passes near the enter of their swarm.

Le·on·i·das (lēŏn´ĭdas). King of parta 491–480 B.C.; hero of efense of pass of Thermopylae gainst invading army of Xerxes, 80 B.C.

Le·o·nine (lē´onīn) *adj.* Of, nade by, a person (esp. a pope) named Leo; ~ **City**, part of Rome n which Vatican stands, walled and fortified by Leo IV; **leonine verse**, medieval form of Latin verse in hexameters or alternate hexam-eters and pentameters, in which final word rhymes with that immediately before the caesura; English verse in which middle and last syllables of two lines rhyme.

le·o·nine (lē´onīn) *adj.* Lionlike, of lions.

leop·ard (lĕp´erd) *n.* 1. Large chiefly nocturnal carnivore (*Felis pardus*) of cat family, with long tail and usu. dark-spotted yellowish-fawn coat, found in Africa and S. Asia, panther; **American** ~, jaguar; **black** ~, Indian species, identical except for black color; **hunting** ~, cheetah; **snow** ~, ounce; ~ **'s bane**, name given to several herbaceous peren-nial plants of family Compositae.

Le·o·pold (lē´opōld). Name of three kings of the Belgians: **Leopold I** (1790–1865), elected king of the Belgians 1831; **Leopold II** (1835–1909), king of the Belgians 1865–1909; **Leopold III** (b. 1901), king of the Belgians from 1934 until his abdication in 1951.

Le·o·pold (lē´opōld), **Lake.** Nine hundred-square-mile (2,331 sq. km) lake in W. central Democratic Republic of the Congo.

Lé·o·pold·ville (lā´opōldvĭl): see KINSHASA.

le·o·tard (lē´otārd) *n.* Close-fitting body garment worn by acrobats, ballet dancers, etc. [f. J.

Lepidoptera, such as butterflies and moths, have four wings covered with minute scales and are often brightly colored. The order comprises more than 100,000 species. These butterflies are common European types.

Léotard, 19th-c. Fr. trapeze performer]

Le·pan·to (lĭpăn′tō; *It.* le′pahntaw), **Strait of.** Entrance to Gulf of Corinth or Lepanto, Greece; scene (1571) of naval battle in which Ottoman sea power was almost completely destroyed by an armada of the Holy League (Pope Pius V, Venice, Spain, Genoa, Savoy, and other Italian States) under Don John of Austria.

lep·er (lĕp′er) *n.* Person suffering from leprosy; (fig.) outcast.

lep·i·dop·ter·ous (lĕpĭdŏp′te-ru̇s) *adj.* Of the Lepidoptera, an order of insects comprising butterflies and moths, with two pairs of membranous wings covered with flattened scales often forming striking color patterns. **lep·i·dop′-ter·ist** *n.* **lep·i·dop′ter·an** *adj.* & *n.* [Gk. *lepis* scale, *pteron* wing]

Lep·i·dus (lĕp′ĭdu̇s), **Marcus Aemilius** (d. 13 B.C.). Roman politician; member of the second TRIUMVIRATE, 43–36 B.C., after death of Julius Caesar.

lep·re·chaun (lĕp′rekawn, -kŏn) *n.* Irish sprite in form of a wizened old man.

lep·ro·sy (lĕp′rosē) *n.* Chronic endemic bacterial disease caused by the organism *Mycobacterium leprae,* characterized by thickening and ulceration of skin with loss of sensation, and, in severe cases, deformity, blindness, and death; once incurable, now readily arrested; now occurring chiefly in tropical and eastern countries but more widely distributed in the Middle Ages; (formerly) any of various diseases causing skin lesions confused with leprosy before recognition of the organism causing it. **lep′rous** *adj.* Having, like, (as) of, leprosy.

lep·ton (lĕp′tŏn) *n.* (pl. **-ta** pr. -ta). (phys.) Any of a family of elementary particles whose mass is equal to or less than that of a muon.

Les·bi·an (lĕz′bēan) *adj.* Of Lesbos; (often **l~**) of homosexuality in women (from the association of the island with Sappho, who was accused of this). **~** *n.* Homosexual woman. **les′bi·an·ism** *n.*

Les·bos (lĕz′bŏs, -bōs). Island in Aegean Sea, off W. coast of Turkey, inhabited from an early date by Aeolians; birthplace of Alcaeus and Sappho.

lese majesty, (lēz) **lèse ma·jes·té** (lāz mahzhĕstā′). Treason; affront to sovereign or ruler; attack on any revered person or institution; (joc.) presumptuous

conduct. [Fr., f. L. *laesa majestas* injured majesty]

le·sion (lē′zhon) *n.* Damage, injury; esp. (path.) morbid change in functioning or texture of organ etc.

Le·so·tho (lĕsō′thō). (formerly *Basutoland*) Kingdom, enclave within the Republic of South Africa; formerly a Brit. protectorate; capital, Maseru.

less (lĕs) *adj.* Smaller; of smaller quantity, not so much, not so much of; of lower rank etc. (rare); (preceding numeral etc.) minus, not including. **~** *n.* Smaller amount, quantity, or number. **~** *adv.* To smaller extent, in lower degree.

les·see (lĕsē′) *n.* Holder of, tenant under, lease. **les·see′ship** *n.*

less·en (lĕs′en) *v.* Make or become less.

less·er (lĕs′er) *attrib. adj.* (superl. **least**). Not so great as the other, or the rest, minor, smaller.

Less·er (lĕs′er) **Antilles.** Chain of islands of the W. Indies stretching from Puerto Rico to S. Amer., including the Virgin Islands, Leeward Islands, Windward Islands,

the islands of the Netherlands W. Indies, Barbados, Trinidad, and Tobago.

Les·sing (lĕs′ĭng), **Gotthold Ephraim** (1729–81). German dramatist and critic, whose influence was of importance in freeing German literature from conventions of French classical school.

les·son (lĕs′on) *n.* 1. Portion of Scripture etc. read at divine service. 2. Thing to be learned by pupil; amount of teaching given at one time, time assigned to it; occurrence, example, rebuke, etc., serving as encouragement or warning; (pl.) systematic instruction in subject.

les·sor (lĕs′ōr, lĕsōr′) *n.* Person who lets on lease.

lest (lĕst) *conj.* In order that ... not, for fear that; (after *fear* etc.) that.

let[1] (lĕt) *v.t.* (**let, let·ting**). Hinder, obstruct. **~** *n.* Stoppage; hindrance (archaic); (tennis) serve that must be repeated, esp. one that hits net and falls into proper part of opponent's court.

let[2] (lĕt) *v.t.* & *auxil.* (**let, let·ting**). 1. Allow (confined fluid,

Leprosy is a disease of the nerves which, if not treated, results in loss of feeling and atrophy of the skin. In advanced cases, hands, feet and face may become deformed. Treatment is with sulphonic drugs.

mands, assumptions, and permissions. **let** *n.* Letting for hire or rent.

le·thal (lē'thal) *adj.* Causing, sufficient or designed to cause, death. **le·thal·i·ty** (līthăl'ītē) *n.*

leth·ar·gy (lĕth'erjē) *n.* (pl. **-gies**). Morbid drowsiness, prolonged and unnatural sleep; torpid, inert, or apathetic state, want of interest and energy. **le·thar·gic** (leth ār'jĭk) *adj.* **le·thar'gi·cal·ly** *adv.*

Le·the (lē'thē). (Gk. myth.) One of the rivers of the underworld, whose water when drunk had the power of making the souls of the dead forget their life on earth. **Le·the·an** (līthē'an, lē'thē-) *adj.* (Gk. *lēthē* oblivion]

Le·to (lē'tō). (Gk. myth.) Daughter of a Titan; mother, by Zeus, of Artemis and Apollo; identified as Roman *Latona*.

Lett (lĕt) *n.* A Latvian.

let·ter (lĕt'er) *n.* 1. Character representing one or more of the elementary sounds used in speech, one of the alphabetic symbols; (print.) type, font of type. 2. Written or printed message addressed to person(s); (freq. pl.) legal or formal statement indicating credentials, authority, etc.; ~**s patent**: see PATENT. 3. Precise terms of statement etc., strict verbal interpretation. 4. (pl.) Literature; acquaintance with books, erudition; **man of** ~**s**, scholar, (now usu.) author; **profession of** ~**s**, authorship. 5. **letter case**, pocketbook for holding letters; **let'terhead**, printed heading on stationery; **let'terpress**, matter printed from letters or types, as distinguished from what is printed from plates

g. blood) to escape. 2. Grant se of for rent or hire; **to** ~, ffered for rent. 3. Allow to, suffer ; cause to (only in ~ **person now**, inform him). 4. ~ **alone**, ot interfere with, not attend to or o; (colloq. use of the imper.) not mention; ~ **be**, let alone; ~ **own** (*v.*), lower; fail (friend) at eed; disappoint; **let'down** (*n.*); t **fall**, drop; (geom.) draw (perendicular) from outside point *on* ne; **let go**, release, set at liberty; se hold of, lose or relinquish old *of*; dismiss from thought; cease restrain; **let in**, admit, open door ; insert into surface of something; t **in for**, involve in (difficulty tc.); **let into**, admit to; insert into urface of; make acquainted with secret etc.); **let loose**, release, unhain; **let off**, discharge (gun etc.); ot punish or compel; punish *with* ght penalty; allow or cause (fluid tc.) to pass away; **let on**, (colloq.) eveal (secret); pretend; **let out**, pen door for exit to; allow to

escape; make (garment) looser; put out to hire, esp. to several tenants; emit; divulge; **let slip**, loose from leash; say inadvertently; miss (opportunity); ~ **up** (*v.*), cease, relax one's efforts; **let'up** (*n.*). 5. *v. auxil.* (followed by inf.) Supplying first and third person of imperative in exhortations, com-

esotho is a small mountainous state — he Maluti Mts are shown here — nclosed by South Africa. Some 25% f its labor force works in the South frican gold mines and on farms.

Levee banks along the Mississippi River are there to control and prevent flooding. Many of the bigger rivers have naturally formed levees as a result of the deposit of silt and sediment.

or blocks. **letter** *v.t.* Impress title etc. on (book cover); inscribe in letters, *with* name etc. **let′tered** *adj.* (esp.) Literate, educated. **let′tering** *n.*

Let′tish (lĕt′ĭsh) *adj. & n.* (Of) the language of the Letts, one of the Baltic group of Indo-European languages, closely related to Lithuanian.

let′tre de ca·chet (*Fr.* lĕtre de kăshĕ′) (pl. *let′tres de ca·chet Fr.* pr. lĕ′tre de kăshĕ′). (Fr. hist.) Letter signed by king of France containing order emanating directly from the king himself, esp. one containing arbitrary order of imprisonment, exile, etc. [Fr., = "sealed letter"]

let·tuce (lĕt′ĭs) *n.* Garden herb of genus *Lactuca* with crisp leaves much used as salad.

Leu·cip·pus (lōōsĭp′us) (5th c. B.C.). Greek philosopher; regarded, with Democritus, as founder of ATOMISM.

leu·co·cyte (lōō′kosīt) *n.* Colorless or white corpuscle in blood, lymph, etc.

leu·cor·rhe·a, leu·cor·rhoe·a (lōōkerē′a) *ns.* (path.) Whitish purulent mucous discharge from vagina and uterine canal.

Leuc·tra (lōōk′tra). Village of Boeotia, scene of a battle (371 B.C.) in which Thebans under Epaminondas defeated Spartans.

leu·ke·mi·a (lōōkē′mēa) *n.* Blood disease affecting the white corpuscles, freq. characterized by excess of these.

Lev. *abbrev.* Leviticus.

Le·vant (levănt′). Eastern part of the Mediterranean with its islands and neighboring countries. **le·vant′er** *n.* Strong Mediterranean easterly wind. [Fr. *levant* sunrise, east]

Le·van·tine (lĕv′antīn, -tēn, lĭvăn′tĭn, -tīn) *n.* Native, inhabitant, of the Levant, esp. one descended from European settlers. ~ *adj.* Of, trading to, the Levant.

lev·ee[1] (lĕv′ē, lĕvē′) *n.* Reception of visitors on rising from bed (hist.); assembly held (in afternoon) by sovereign or his (or her) representative at which men only are received; reception.

lev·ee[2] (lĕv′ē) *n.* Natural embankment of alluvium built up by rivers on either side of their channels; artificial embankment raised to prevent inundations.

lev·el (lĕv′el) *n.* 1. Instrument for testing whether things are horizontal; SPIRIT level; surveyor's instrument for observing levels. 2. Horizontal line or plane; plane or standard in social, moral, or intellectual matters; plane of rank or authority, e.g., *consultation at cabinet level*; **on a ~ with**, in same horizontal plane as; **on the ~**, (colloq.) straightforward(ly), honest(ly). 3. More or less flat surface; flat country. **level** *adj.* 1 Horizontal, perpendicular to the plumb line; on a level or equality (*with*). 2. Even, equable, uniform, well balanced, in quality, style, judgment, etc.; **one's ~ best** (colloq.) one's very best; **~-headed**, mentally well balanced. **lev′el·ly** *adv.* **lev′el·ness** *n.* **level** *v.t.* (**-eled, -el·ing**; Brit. **-elled, -el·ling**). 1. Make level, even, or uniform; place on same level, bring up or *down* to a standard. 2. Raze, lay low; abolish (distinctions). 3. Aim (missile), lay (gun), direct (satire, accusation, etc.) *at, against*.

lev·el·er (lĕv′eler) *n.* (esp.) Person who would abolish social distinctions, advocate of equality, esp. **L ~** (Engl. hist.), one of a party of extreme radical dissenters arising in army of Long Parliament (*c*1647) and advocating leveling of all ranks and completely democratic form of republican government.

lev·er (lĕv′er, lē′ver) *n.* Bar used to pry up heavy or fixed object; (mech.) straight bar or other rigid structure of which one point (*fulcrum*) is fixed, another is connected with the force (*weight*) to be resisted or acted upon, and a third is connected with the force (*power*) applied; **~ escapement**, escapement where connection between balance and escape wheel is made by a pivoted lever bearing the pallets; **~ watch**, watch with lever escapement. **lever** *v.* Use lever, lift, move, act on, with lever.

lev·er·age (lĕv′erĭj, lĕv′rĭj, lē′verĭj, lē′vrĭj) *n.* Action of, way of applying, lever; set or system of levers; power, mechanical advantage gained by use, of lever; means of accomplishing a purpose, power, influence.

Le·vi (lē′vī). Hebrew patriarch, third son of Jacob and Leah (Gen. 29); tribe of Israel, traditionally descended from him.

le·vi·a·than (lĭvī′athan) *n.* Sea monster (bibl.); huge ship; anything very large of its kind.

lev·i·rate (lĕv′erĭt, -āt, lē′verĭt, -āt) *n.* Ancient Jewish custom by which dead man's brother or next of kin had to marry his widow. **lev·i·rat·i·cal** (lĕverăt′ĭkal) *adj.*

lev·i·tate (lĕv′ītāt) *v.* (**-tat·ed, -tat·ing**). (Make) rise and float in air (esp. in spiritualist language). **lev·i·ta′tion** *n.*

Le·vite (lē′vīt) *n.* One of the tribe of Levi, whose members were priests of the sanctuary in ancient Israel (to 586 B.C.) and later (when priesthood was restricted to descendants of Aaron's family) assisted priests in caring for the Temple.

Le·vit·i·cal (lĭvĭt′ĭkal) *adj.* 1. Of the Levites. 2. Of the book of Leviticus.

Le·vit·i·cus (lĭvĭt′ĭkus). Third book of the Pentateuch, containing etails of the law and ritual of the Levites.

lev·i·ty (lĕv´ĭtē) *n.* (pl. **-ties**). Want of thought, frivolity, unreasonable jocularity, inconstancy; light behavior.

lev·u·lose (lĕv´yulōs) *n.* Fructose.

lev·y (lĕv´ē) *n.* (pl. **lev·ies**). Collecting of assessment, tax, etc.; enrolling of men for war etc.; amount or number levied, body of men enrolled; **capital ~**, appropriation by government of fixed proportion of all the wealth in the country. **levy** *v.t.* (**lev·ied, lev·y·ng**). Raise (contribution, taxes), impose (rate, toll); raise (sum) by legal execution or process *on* person's goods; extort; enlist, enroll (soldiers, army); collect men and munitions for, proceed to make war; usu. *on, against*).

lewd (lood) *adj.* Base, worthless bibl.); lascivious, indecent. **ewd´ly** *adv.* **lewd´ness** *n.*

lew·is (loo´ĭs) *n.* Contrivance for gripping heavy blocks of stone for lifting, consisting of a tenon fitting into a shaped hole cut in the stone.

Lewis¹ (lōō´ĭs), **C(live) (taples)** (1898–1963). British religious novelist and essayist, author of *The Screwtape Letters*.

Lewis² (lōō´ĭs), **John L(lewel-yn)** (1880–1969). American labor leader, long president of the United Mine Workers; organizer and president of the C.I.O., 1935–40.

Lew·is³ (lōō´ĭs), **Meriwether** (1774–1809). Explorer; governor of the Louisiana Territory, 1807–9; led **Lewis and Clark Expedition**, 1801–3, with William Clark; they followed the Missouri River to its source, crossed the Great Divide, and descended the Columbia River to the Pacific Ocean, bringing back information on geographical features, flora, fauna, etc.

Lew·is⁴ (lōō´ĭs), **(Harry) Sinclair** (1885–1951). American novelist, author of *Babbitt, Main Street*, etc.; first American to win Nobel Prize for literature, 1930.

Lew·is⁵ (lōō´ĭs) **gun.** Light magazine-fed, gas-operated, air-cooled machine gun. [Col. I. N. *Lewis* (1858–1931) of U.S. Army, inventor]

lew·is·ite (lōō´ĭsīt) *n.* Highly irritant and vesicant persistent poison gas (βchloro-vinyl-dichloro-arsine), a heavy oily liquid. [W. L. *Lewis* (1878–1943), Amer. chemist]

lex·i·cal (lĕk´sĭkal) *adj.* Of the vocabulary of a language; (as) of a lexicon. **lex´i·cal·ly** *adv.*

lex·i·cog·ra·phy (lĕksĭkŏg´rafē) *n.* Dictionary making. **lex·i·cog´-ra·pher** *n.* **lex·i·co·graph·i·cal** (lĕksĭkogrăf´ĭkal) *adj.*

lex·i·con (lĕk´sĭkŏn) *n.* Dictionary, esp. of ancient Greek, Hebrew, Syriac, or Arabic.

Lex·ing·ton (lĕk´sĭngtŏn). Name of several towns and cities of U.S., esp.: (1) in Massachusetts, a town and suburb of Boston; scene of the battle (1775) between British soldiers and Minutemen that began the Amer. Revolution; (2) city in the Bluegrass region of Kentucky; center of thoroughbred horse farms and tobacco growing.

lex ta·li·o·nis (lĕks´tălēō´nĭs). Law of retaliation, an eye for an eye. [L.]

Ley·den, Lei·den (lī´den). City of the SW. Netherlands; university, 1575; **~ jar**, device (invented 1745 at that university) for storing electric charge, consisting of a glass jar coated inside and outside with tinfoil, the electric energy being stored in the glass dielectric between the tinfoil electrodes.

Ley·te (lā´tē). One of the Philippine Islands, 2,785 sq. miles (7,213 sq. km), N. of Mindanao;

*The Battle of **Lexington** and Concord in 1775 marked the beginning of the American War of Independence although it was really more of a skirmish. The colonists were warned by Paul Revere.*

The British Museum library is the second-largest in the world and receives a free copy of every book published in the U.K. Its splendid Reading Room was constructed from designs by Sir Anthony Panizzi and was opened in 1857.

L~ Gulf, inlet between Leyte and Samar Islands; site of a naval battle, 1944, during World War II, in which the Americans defeated the Japanese.

L.F., LF, l.f., l-f *abbrevs*. Low FREQUENCY.

Lha·sa (lah′sa, lăs′a). Capital city of Tibet, in the SE. at an altitude of 12,000 feet (3,658 m).

li·a·bil·i·ty (līabĭl′ĭtē) *n*. (pl. **-ties**). Being liable; what one is liable for; (pl.) debts, pecuniary obligations.

li·a·ble (lī′abel) *adj*. 1. Legally bound; answerable *for*; subject *to* tax or penalty; under obligation *to* do. 2. Exposed or open *to*, apt *to* do or suffer, something undesirable; (colloq.) likely.

li·ai·son (lēāzawn′, lē′azŏn, -zon, lēā′zŏn, -zon; *Fr*. lyĕzawn′) *n*. (pl. **-sons** pr. -zawnz′, -zŏnz, -zonz; *Fr*. -zawn′). 1. Illicit intimacy between a man and a woman. 2. Sounding of ordinarily silent final consonant before vowel or mute *h* in French. 3. (orig. mil.) Connection, communication (*between, with*).

li·a·na (lēah′na, -ăn′a), **li·ane** (lēahn′) *ns*. Woody climbing and twining plant that uses another as support in reaching light, esp. in tropical forest.

Liao·ning (lyow′nĭng′). Province of China, in S. Manchuria.

li·ar (lī′er) *n*. Teller (esp. habitual) of lie(s).

Lib. *abbrev*. Liberal.

li·ba·tion (lībā′shon) *n*. Pouring of wine, wine poured, in honor of a god; (joc.) alcoholic beverage.

Lib·by (lĭb′ē), **Willard Frank** (1908–). American chemist; developed carbon 14 method of dating objects; received Nobel Prize for chemistry, 1960.

li·bel (lī′bel) *n*. 1. (civil and eccles. law) Plaintiff's written declaration. 2. (law) Published statement damaging to person's reputation, act of publishing it; (pop.) false and defamatory statement; (transf.) thing that brings discredit *on*. ~ *v.t*. (**-beled, -bel·ing**, Brit. **-belled, -bel·ling**). Defame by libelous statements, accuse falsely and maliciously; (law) publish libel against; (eccles. etc. law) bring suit against. **li′bel·ous** *adj*. **li′bel·ous·ly** *adv*.

Li·ber (lī′ber). (Rom. myth.) Ancient Roman god of wine and fruitfulness, identified with Dionysus or Bacchus. **Lib·er·a** (lĭb′era). Female counterpart of Liber.

lib·er·al (lĭb′eral, lĭb′ral) *adj*. 1. Fit for a gentleman (now ra... exc. in **education**, educatio... directed to general enlargement ... mind, not professional or techn... cal); ~ **arts**: see ART[1]. 2... Generous, open-handed, n... sparing *of*; abundant. 3. N... rigorous or literal, open-minded... unprejudiced. 4. (Pol.) (Moder... ately) progressive, favoring indivi... ual liberty and democratic reform... **L~ Party**, any political part... favoring liberal principles, esp. on... of the two great parties of Grea... Britain (opp. Tory or Conservativ... Party) in later part of 19th an... early 20th c. **lib′er·al·ly** *ad*... **liberal** *n*. Holder of liberal view... **L~** (member of) Liberal Party... **lib′er·al·ism** *n*.

lib·er·al·i·ty (lĭberăl′ĭtē) *n*. (p... **-ties**). Free giving, munificence... freedom from prejudice, breadth ... mind.

lib·er·ate (lĭb′erāt) *v.t*. (**-at·ed... -at·ing**). Set at liberty; releas... *from*; (chem.) set free from com... bination. **lib·er·a′tion, lib·er·a′... tor** *ns*.

Li·ber·i·a (līber′ēa). Republi... on coast of W. Africa betwee... Ivory Coast and Sierra Leone... founded (1847) and settled by free... U.S. slaves; capital, Monrovia... **Li·ber′i·an** *adj. & n*.

lib·er·tar·i·an (lĭbertār′ēan) *n*... *& adj*. (Person) believing in fre...

ll; (person) advocating extreme
erty, esp. of thought and action.
lib·er·tine (lĭb′ertēn, -tĭn) *n.* 1.
eethinker on religion; anti-
mian; (transf.) one who follows
s own inclinations. 2. Licentious
dissolute person. ~ *adj.* Free-
inking; licentious, dissolute. **lib′-
·tin·age, lib′er·tin·ism** *ns.*

lib·er·ty (lĭb′ertē) *n.* (pl. **-ties**).
Being free from captivity, im-
isonment, slavery, or despotic
ntrol; right or power to do as one
eases or *to* do something; freedom
m despotic rule personified; (pl.)
ivileges, immunities, or rights,
joyed by prescription or grant;
~, free; having the right *to* do;
employed, out of work. 2.
tting aside of rules, license;
ke the ~, presume or venture;
ke liberties, be unduly familiar
th; deal freely *with*. 3. **Liberty
iip**, prefabricated cargo ship
ilt in great numbers by U.S. in
orld War II; **Statue of Liberty**,
lossal bronze figure of a woman
lding up a torch ("Liberty
lightening the World"), gift of
ench people to U.S. to com-
emorate centenary of Amer. in-
pendence, erected on high
anite pedestal on Liberty Island,
ew York harbor, 1885.

li·bid·i·nous (lĭbĭd′inus, -bē′di-)
j. Lustful. **li·bid′i·nous·ly** *adv.*
li·bi·do (lĭbē′dō, -bī′-) *n.*
sychol.) Sexual drive; in
reudian theory the motive force
all human activity. **li·bid′i·nal**
j.

Li·bra (lē′bra, lī′-). The Scales,
constellation; 7th sign (♎) of the
diac, into which the sun enters

at the autumnal equinox.

li·brar·i·an (lībrār′ēan) *n.*
Custodian of library; member of
library staff. **li·brar′i·an·ship** *n.*

li·brar·y (lī′brĕrē, -brerē, -brē)
n. (pl. **-brar·ies**). Room or building containing books for reading or
reference; such a collection of
books, series of books issued by
publisher; **L ~ of Congress**, U.S.
national library, in Washington,
D.C., which receives a copy of
every book copyrighted in the U.S.;
circulating ~, library lending
books for a fee; **free ~**, library
used by public without payment,
esp. one maintained by municipality out of taxes.

li·brate (lī′brāt) *v.i.* (**-brat·ed,
-brat·ing**). Oscillate like beam of
balance. **li·bra·tion** (lībrā′shon) *n.*
Librating; (astron.) real or apparent
motion of oscillating kind; **~ of
moon**, apparent irregularity of
moon's motion making part near
edge of disk alternately visible and
invisible.

li·bret·to (lĭbrĕt′ō) *n.* (pl. **-bret·-
tos, -bret·ti** pr. -brĕt′ē). Text
of opera or other long vocal composition. **li·bret′tist** *n.*

Li·bre·ville (lēbrevēl′). Capital
and a port of Gabon, in the NW.,
on the Gulf of Guinea.

Lib·y·a (lĭb′ēa). 1. Ancient
Greek name for the N. part of
Africa W. of Egypt. 2. Republic
in N. Africa between Egypt and
Tunisia; formerly an Italian colony;
independent 1951; capital, Tripoli.
Lib·y·an (lĭb′ēan) *adj.* Of Libya
or its people; **~ Desert**, E. part
of Sahara, bounded eastward by
River Nile and extending from

Mediterranean to Sudan. **Libyan**
n.

lice: see LOUSE.

li·cense (lī′sens) *n.* 1. Leave,
permission; formal, usu. printed or
written, authority to marry, drive
vehicle, carry on some profession
or trade. 2. Liberty of action, esp.
when excessive; abuse of freedom,
disregard of law or propriety;
licentiousness; writer's or artist's
deviation from conventions of
meter, perspective, etc. (usu.
poetic ~). **license** *v.t.* (**-censed,
-cens·ing**). Grant license to,
authorize by license. **li′censed** *adj.*
(esp.) Allowed complete freedom.
li′cen·sor, li·cen·see (līsensē′) *ns.*

li·cen·ti·ate (līsĕn′shēit, -āt) *n.*
(European practice) Holder of university license or attestation of
competence from collegiate or
examining body.

li·cen·tious (līsĕn′shus) *adj.*
Lascivious, lewd. **li·cen′tious·ly**
adv. **li·cen′tious·ness** *n.*

li·chee, li·chi = LITCHI.

li·chen (lī′ken) *n.* Plant organism of the group Lichenes, composed of fungus and an alga in
association, freq. gray or yellow
and growing on rocks, trees, etc.,
some species of which are edible,
others used in manufacture of dyes,
perfumes and cosmetics.

lic·it (lĭs′ĭt) *adj.* Lawful, not forbidden. **lic′it·ly** *adv.*

*The Arab republic of **Libya** in North
Africa was formerly an Italian colony.
Under its head of state, Muammar
Gaddafi, it became a strict Muslim
country. Below: Map and flag of Libya.
Below left: The **Statue of Liberty**.*

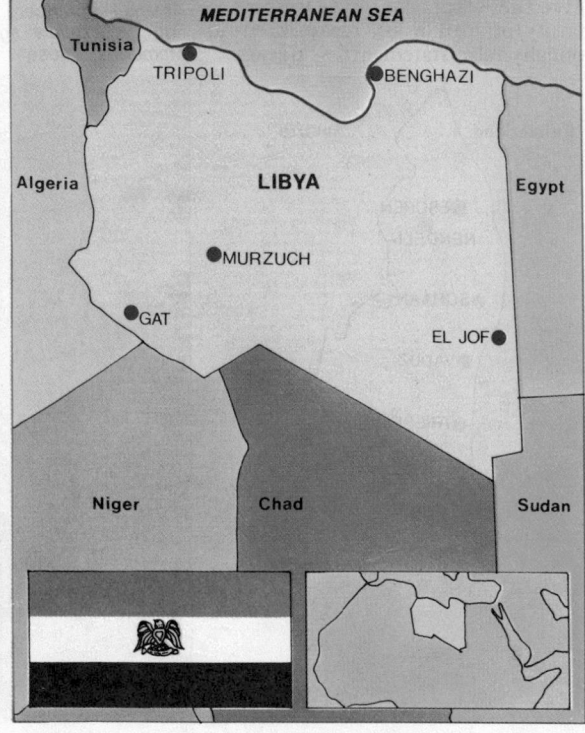

lick (lĭk) *v.* Pass tongue over to taste, moisten, clean, etc.; take *up* or *off*, make *clean*, by licking; (of waves, flame, etc.) play lightly over; (of flame) swallow *up* in passing; (slang) thrash, defeat; ~ **into shape**, mold, make presentable or efficient; ~ **one's wounds**, remain quiet after a defeat; ~ **person's boots** or **shoes**, show servility to him; **lick′spittle**, fawning flatterer, toady. **lick** *n.* Act of licking with tongue; place to which animals resort for salt (also **salt** ~); (slang) rapid pace; a blow; (pl.) (baseball) turn at bat; ~ **and a promise**, hasty performance of a task.

lic·o·rice, li·quo·rice (lĭk′erĭs, -erĭsh, lĭk′rĭsh) *ns.* (Flavoring for medicines, candy, liquor, etc., made from) root of leguminous plant *Glycyrrhiza glabra*.

lic·tor (lĭk′ter) *n.* (Rom. hist.) Officer attending magistrate, bearing fasces as emblem of office and executing sentence on offenders.

lid (lĭd) *n.* Hinged or detached cover for aperture, esp. for opening at top of container; eyelid; (bot., conch.) operculum. **lid′ded, lid′-less** *adjs.*

Li·di·ce (lē′dĕchä, lĭd′ĭsē; *Czech.* lĭ′dyĭtsĕ). Czechoslovakian village completely destroyed by the occupying Nazis, 1942, in reprisal for civilian resistance; rebuilt as a national monument after World War II.

Li·do (lē′dō). Chain of sandy islands separating lagoon of Venice from Adriatic Sea, a fashionable bathing resort.

lie[1] (lī) *n.* Intentional false statement; imposture, false belief; **give the** ~ **to**, belie, serve to show falsity of; **tell a** ~, make intentionally false statement; ~ **detec-**

tor, instrument indicating physiological changes that occur under stress of emotion. **lie** *v.i.* (**lied, ly·ing**). Speak falsely, tell lie(s); take *away*, get *into*, *out of*, by lying; (of things) deceive.

lie[2] (lī) *v.i.* (**lay, lain** pr. lān, **ly·ing**). 1. (of persons or animals) Have one's body in more or less horizontal position along ground or surface; assume lying position (esp. ~ **down**); be kept, remain, in specified state; (archaic) have sexual intercourse *with*; (of the dead) be in the grave *at*, *in*. 2. (of things) Be at rest, usu. more or less horizontally, on surface; be stored up in specified place; remain in specified state; be situated; be spread out to view; exist, be found, reside, be arranged or related, in some position or manner; (of road) lead *through*, *by*, etc.; (of ship) float in berth or at anchor; (law) be admissible or sustainable; ~ **heavy**, be a weight *on* one's stomach or conscience. 3. **lie by**, be unused; keep quiet or retired; **lie down under**, accept without protest; **lie in** (*v.*), be brought to bed in childbirth; **lie off**, (naut.) stand some distance from shore or other ship; **lie over**, be deferred; **lie to**, (naut.) come almost to a stop with head near wind by backing or shortening sail. **lie** *n.* Way, direction, or position in which thing lies; place where beast, bird, or fish, is accustomed to lie; (golf) location of a ball after it has come to a stop.

Lie (lē), **Trygve Halvdan** (1896–1968). Norwegian states-

The miniature alpine principality of **Liechtenstein** *is bordered on the west by the Rhine and on the east by the Austrian Vorarlberg. Below left: Map and flag. Below right: Chapel of St. Mamertus, Triesen.*

man; first secretary-general of t U.N., 1946–53.

Liech·ten·stein (lĭk′tenstī Ger. lĭχ′tenshtīn). Small (6 square-mile, 161 sq. km) indepen ent principality in Rhine vall between Austria and Switzerlan capital, Vaduz.

lied (lēd; *Ger.* lēt) *n.* (**lied·er** pr. lē′der; *Ger.* lē′de German song or poem of ball kind. [Ger.]

lief (lēf) *adv.* (archaic) Glad willingly.

Li·ège (lēäzh′; *Fr.* lyĕzh). Po city in Belgium on the Meu River; first mentioned in histor records in 558 A.D.; noted center learning in the Middle Ages.

liege (lēj, lēzh) *adj.* (of superio Entitled to receive, (of vassa bound to give, feudal service allegiance; ~ **lord**, feudal superio sovereign. **liege** *n.* Liege lor vassal, subject.

lien (lēn, lē′en) *n.* (law) Rig to keep possession of property t debt due in respect of it is di charged.

lieu (lōō) *n.* **in** ~, in plac instead, (*of*).

Lieut. *abbrev.* Lieutenant.

lieu·ten·ant (lōōtĕn′ant, lū *Brit.*, except in the navy, lĕftĕn′an *n.* 1. Deputy, substitute, vicegeren acting for a superior; ~ **governo** deputy governor. 2. (mil.) Office next in rank below captain; (navy junior officer; officer of police forc below captain; ~ **colonel**, arm officer of rank next below colonel′ having actual command of a reg ment; ~ **commander**, officer i navy of rank next below com mander's and above lieutenant's; **general**, officer in army of ran next below general's and abov major general's. **lieu·ten′an·c**

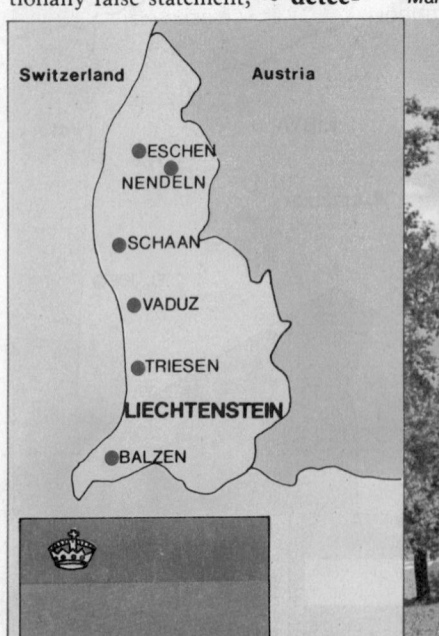

Switzerland | Austria

ESCHEN
NENDELN
SCHAAN
VADUZ
TRIESEN
LIECHTENSTEIN
BALZEN

. (pl. **-cies**).

life (līf) *n.* (pl. **lives** pr. līvz).
. Condition or fact of being living;
hat state of ceaseless change and
unctional activity which con-
titutes the essential difference be-
ween living organisms and dead or
onliving matter; continuance of
nimate existence (opp. death);
nergy, vivacity, animation; vivi-
ying influence; living things; living
orm or model, life-size figure, etc.;
a matter etc.) **of ∼ and death**,
something) on which it depends
vhether a person shall live or die,
f vital importance; **for one's, for
lear ∼**, (as if) to escape death; **as
arge as ∼**, life-size. 2. Period
rom birth to death, birth to present
ime, or present time to death; per-
on considered with respect to ex-
ectation of life; **∼ expectancy**,

*The **life cycle** of the broad bean is
shown here in its successive stages. 1.
Straightening of the plumule. 2.
Closeup of one flower. 3. Ripening
pod. 4. Ripe pod open to show ripe
seed. Bean plants tend to increase soil
reserves of nitrogen and are often used
in a farming rotation system. They are,
like peas, an important vegetable for
human consumption.*

average period that person at specified age may expect to live; **have
the time of one's ∼**, enjoy oneself as never before; **∼ annuity,
sentence**, annuity, sentence, to
continue for the rest of person's life.
3. Individual actions and fortunes,
manner of existence; written story
of these, biography; active part of
existence, business and pleasures of
the world; **eternal, everlasting,
future, the other ∼**, state of

existence after death; **high, low ∼**,
social customs of upper, lower,
classes; **see ∼**, enjoy affairs of the
world, esp. social activities; **this ∼**,
life on earth. 4. Time that an
object etc. may last. 5. **∼ belt**,
belt of buoyant material to support
human body in water; **life′blood**,
blood necessary to life; vitalizing
influence; **life′boat**, boat maintained at **lifeboat station** on shore,
equipped to go to aid of ships in
distress; boat carried by ship for use
in emergency; **life buoy**: see BUOY;
life cycle, (biol.) series of changes
undergone by an organism from the
union of gametes that produced it
until its death (but in some animals
and plants the life cycle includes
the life and death of successive individuals); **life estate**, property
that one holds for life but cannot

dispose of further; **life force**, vit
energy, force conceived as strivin
for survival of individual and rac
life′guard, person guarding safet
of swimmers; **life insurance** (pr
vision for) payment to a beneficiar
on the death of insured person, o
to the person, if he or she lives
a specified age; **life interest**, righ
to life estate; **life jacket**, life pr
server shaped like sleeveless jacke
life line, rope used for life savin
e.g., that attached to life buo
diver's signaling line; **life′lon**
lasting one's life; **life preserve**
buoyant ring, jacket, belt, etc.,
support human body in water; **Li**
Saver, (trademark) hard canc
shaped like a ring life preserve
life-size(d), of same size as obje
represented; **life′time**, duration o
person's life; **life′work**, task pu
sued through one's whole lif
life′less adj. Dead; lacking anim
tion, energy, etc. **life′less·ly** ad
life′less·ness n. **life′like** ad
Resembling life; exactly like re
person or thing.

lif·er (lī′fer) n. (slang) On
sentenced to penal servitude f
life.

Lif·fey (lĭf′ē). River in th
Republic of Ireland flowing 5
miles (81 km) from County Wick
low in Dublin Bay.

LIFO abbrev. Last-in, first-ou

lift (lĭft) v. 1. Raise to highe
position, take up, hoist; rise fro
ground; elevate to higher plane o
thought or feeling; give upwar
direction to; hold or have on hig
hit (golf ball etc.) into air; (of shi
etc. afloat) rise on wave; (of clou
fog, etc.) rise, disperse; **~-of**
vertical take-off of spacecraft o
rocket; **~ one's hand agains**
strike. 2. (slang) Steal (esp.
wallet). 3. **have one's face lifte**
undergo operation to remov
wrinkles etc. on face. **lift** n.
Lifting. 2. Help (esp. given t
walker by taking him some dis
tance in vehicle). 3. One layer o
leather in boot heel. 4. (Brit
Elevator. 5. Lifting power. 6
(slang) Air transport of cargo o
passengers.

lig·a·ment (lĭg′ament) n. (anat
Short band of tough flexible fibrou
tissue binding the two bones at
joint; (loosely) any membranou
fold keeping organ in position
similar part in lower organisms
lig·a·men·tal (lĭgamĕn′tal), **lig·a**
men′ta·ry, lig·a·men′tous adjs.

lig·a·ture (lĭg′acher, -choor) n
1. Thing used in tying, esp. (surg
cord or band used to tie off bloo
vessels to stop hemorrhage o

*Specially designed to negotiate the
surf, the lifeboat (above) is used by
Australian lifeguards. Other equipmen
used by them includes the surf reel and
harness, surfboards and surf skis.*

Aerodynamic **lift** is the upward force acting on the aircraft, equal and opposite to the pull of gravity on the craft and its load. Drag is the resistance the aircraft meets in moving forward through the air. The Bell 205 Helicopter here (RAAF) is lifting a car, increasing the degree of aerodynamic lift needed to fly.

*Above: Beachy Head lighthouse, U.K.
Right: Cross-section of an offshore
lighthouse built of interlocking stone
blocks. The detailed section of the service room and lantern gallery (below)
shows the way the stones are fitted
together. This type of construction can
withstand strong winds and high seas.*

service room and lantern gallery

service room

bedroom

subsidiary
light room

living room

battery room

winch room

oil room

engine
room

obstruct blood flow. 2. Thing that
unites, bond; (mus.) group of two
or more notes sung to one syllable,
slur, tie; (print etc.) two or more
letters joined together in one
character, as æ. ~ v.t. (-**tured,
-tur·ing**). Bind with ligature.

light[1] (līt) *n.* 1. Visible form of
electromagnetic radiation produced
by energy changes within the atoms
of a substance, esp. when excited by
intense heat; that which evokes
functional activity of organ of sight;
natural agent emanating from sun;
medium or condition of space in
which vision is possible; appearance
of brightness; amount of illumination in a place, one's fair or ordinary share of this; daylight; vivacity
in person's eyes; favoring aspect;
come, bring, to ~, be revealed,
reveal; **see the** ~, be born, (also
fig., see below). 2. Object from
which brightness emanates; sun or
other heavenly body; illuminating
agent, as lamp etc., (collect.) lamps
etc. illuminating place; beacon
lamp, esp. of ship or lighthouse;
traffic light; lighthouse; (fig.) eminent person or luminary; **Feast,
Festival, of L**~**s**: see HANUKKAH;
~**s out**, (mil.) last bugle call of the
day, signal for all lights be be put
out. 3. Mental illumination,
illumination of soul by divine truth
or love etc.; elucidation, enlightenment; fact or discovery serving to
explain subject; (pl.) natural or
acquired mental powers; (sing.)
aspect in which thing is viewed; **in
a good or bad** ~, favorably, unfavorably; **see the** ~, become enlightened or convinced. 4. Window
or opening in wall for admission
of light; perpendicular division of
mullioned window; **glazed** compartment of side or roof in green-

house. 5. (paint, etc.) Illuminated
surface, part of picture represented
as lighted up. 6. Flame or spark
serving to ignite; thing used for
igniting, spill, taper, match. 7.
light'house, tower or other structure containing beacon light(s) for
warning or guiding ships at sea;
light'ship, ship, moored or anchored, containing similar lights;
light-year, (astron.) distance that
light travels in one year (approx.
9.46×10^{12} km or 6 trillion miles),
as unit in measuring interstellar
distances. **light'less** *adj.*

light[2] (līt) *adj.* Well provided
with light, not dark; pale-colored,
pale.

light[3] (līt) *v.* (**light·ed, lit,
light·ing**). Set (lamp, fire, etc.)
burning; (of fuel etc.) take fire,
begin to burn; give light to;
brighten with animation; show
(person his) way or surroundings
with a light; ~ **up**, begin to smoke
pipe etc.; kindle or turn on lights
in street, room, etc., at dusk; light

brightly, make conspicuous by light.

light[4] (līt) *adj.* 1. Of little weight, not heavy; deficient in weight; of small specific gravity; having or intended for small load; (of ship, cart, etc.) made lightly for small loads and quick movement; (of building) not looking heavy, graceful, elegant.   2. Acting gently, applied delicately, not violent; not dense, tenacious, or cohesive; easy to digest; not grave or important; trivial; nimble; inconstant; (of wine etc.) not strong; (of syllable) unemphatic.   3. Easily borne or done; aimed or aiming at entertainment merely; (of sleep) easily disturbed, not profound.   4. ~-**fingered**, given to stealing; ~-**footed**, springy, nimble; ~-**handed**, having a light hand, managing tactfully; **light'headed**, slightly disoriented, e.g. from drink or joy; **light heart**, heart free from sorrow; **light'hearted**, gay, untroubled; **light horse**, lightly armed cavalry; **light marching order**, that in which only arms and ammunition are taken; **light-minded**, frivolous, thoughtless; **light'weight**, person etc. of less than average weight; person of no influence; boxer of weight between featherweight and welterweight. **light'ly** *adv.* **light'ness** *n.* **light** *adv.* In light manner.

light[5] (līt) *v.* 1. (naut.) Lift (rope etc.) along, lend a hand in hauling ropes etc.   2. Alight, descend, come down (archaic); chance, come by chance *on.*

light·en[1] (lī'ten) *v.* Shed light upon, make bright; grow bright, shine, flash; emit lightning. **light'-en·er** *n.*

light·en[2] (lī'ten) *v.* Reduce load of (ship etc.), (of ship) have load reduced; relieve (heart etc.), be relieved, of weight; reduce weight of; mitigate; grow lighter.

light·er[1] (lī'ter) *n.* (esp.) Instrument for producing flame or spark for igniting cigarette, gas jet, etc.

light·er[2] (lī'ter) *n.* Boat, usu. flat-bottomed, for unloading and loading ships not brought to wharf and for transporting goods in harbor. **light'er·age** *n.* Transport of goods by lighter. **light'er·man** *n.* **lighter** *v.t.* Remove (goods) in lighter.

light·ning (līt'ning) *n.* Visible electric discharge between clouds or cloud and ground; **forked, chain(ed),** ~, lightning flash in form of zigzag or divided line; **sheet** ~, lightning flash of diffused brightness; **summer, heat** ~, sheet lightning without audible thunder, result of distant storm; **like** ~, with greatest conceivable speed; ~ **bug,** firefly; ~ **conductor, rod,** metal rod or wire fixed to exposed part of building

or to mast to divert lightning into earth or sea. **lightning** *adj.* Very swift; ~ **strike,** sudden strike taking place without warning.

lights (līts) *n.pl.* Lungs of sheep, pigs, etc., used as food esp. for cats and dogs.

light·some (līt'som) *adj.* Gracefully light; merry; agile. **light'-some·ly** *adv.* **light'some·ness** *n.*

light·wood (līt'wŏŏd) *n.* 1. Any of various trees with light wood, in Australia chiefly *Acacia melanoxylon.*   2. Wood used in lighting fire, esp. resinous pinewood.

lign·al·oes (līnăl'ōz, līg-) *n.* (usu. considered sing.). The drug aloes; aloeswood, an aromatic Mexican wood. [L., = "wood of the aloe"]

lig·ne·ous (līg'nēus) *adj.* Woody (esp. of plants).

lig·ni·fy (līg'nifī) *v.* (-**fied, -fy-ing**). Make, become woody. **lig·ni·fi·ca·tion** (līgnĭfĭkā'shon) *n.*

lig·nin (līg'nĭn) *n.* (bot.) Hardening material impregnating cell walls of woody tissues.

lig·nite (līg'nīt) *n.* Brown coal, a deposit formed usu. after the Carboniferous age, showing visible traces of its plant structure and containing much carbon, the oldest approximating to bituminous coal, the newest to peat.

Lightning is a visible discharge of electricity at very high voltage. It usually occurs in cumulonimbus clouds and such discharges may be between two clouds, or between the cloud and the earth.

lig·num vi·tae (līg'num vī'tē). Either of two tropical evergreen Amer. trees, *Guiacum officinale* or *G. sanctum,* with extremely heavy and hard wood. [L., = "wood of life"]

lig·u·late (līg'yulĭt, -lāt) *adj.* Strap-shaped; (bot.) with strap-shaped florets.

lig·ule (līg'ūl) *n.* (bot.) Thin appendage at base of leaf blade, esp. in grasses; ligulate corolla in composites.

Li·gu·ri·a (līgūr'ēa). Region of N. Italy, once forming the republic of Genoa or **Ligurian Republic,** formed 1797 after Napoleon's Italian campaign, annexed to France 1805, and subsequently merged into Italy.

Li·gu·ri·an (līgūr'ēan) *adj.* Of Liguria or its people or language; of an ancient race (**Ligures**) inhabiting NW. Italy, Switzerland, and SE. Gaul and speaking a pre-Italic Indo-European language; ~ **Republic**: see LIGURIA; ~ **Sea,** part of Mediterranean between Corsica and NW. coast of Italy around Genoa. **Ligurian** *n.* Native, inhabitant, language, of Liguria.

like[1] (līk) *adj.* Similar, resembling something, each other, or the original; resembling, such as; characteristic of; in promising state or right mood for *doing*; (archaic) likely (*to*); **what is he** ~?, what sort of person is he?; **look** ~, have the appearance of being; give promise, indicate the presence, of;

~ that, of the kind just seen or referred to; **~-minded**, having same tastes, views, etc. **like** *prep.* In the manner of, to the same degree as; **~ a shot**, without demur, willingly, regardless of consequences; rapidly. **like** *adv.* In the same manner *as* (archaic); (illit.) so to speak. **~** *conj.* (illit. and colloq.) As. **~** *n.* Counterpart, equal, like thing or person; thing(s) of the same kind; **the ~(s) of**, (colloq.) such a person or thing as; **and the ~**, etcetera.

like² (līk) *v.* (**liked, lik·ing**). 1. Be pleasing to (archaic, chiefly impers.). 2. Find agreeable, congenial, or satisfactory; feel attracted by; wish for; **~ to, ~d to**, (slang) almost, came close to. **like** *n.* (usu. pl.) Liking, predilection. **lik'a·ble, like'a·ble** *adjs.* **lik'a·ble·ness, like'a·bil'i·ty** *ns.*

like·li·hood (līk'lēhŏŏd) *n.* Being likely, probability.

like·ly (līk'lē) *adj.* (**-li·er, li·est**). Probably; such as might well happen, or be or prove true, or turn out to be the thing specified; to be expected *to*; promising, apparently suitable *for, to*, capable looking. **~** *adv.* **most** or **very ~**, probably.

lik·en (lī'ken) *v.t.* Find or point out resemblance in (thing) *to*.

like·ness (līk'nĭs) *n.* 1. Being like, resemblance. 2. Representation, copy, portrait; person or thing having exact appearance of another.

like·wise (līk'wīz) *adv. & conj.* Similarly (bibl.); also, moreover.

lik·ing (lī'kĭng) *n.* What one likes, one's taste; regard, taste, *for*.

li·lac (lī'lak) *n.* Oleaceous shrub or small tree of genus *Syringa*, esp. *S. vulgaris* which has fragrant, usu. pale pinkish-violet, blossoms; color of these. **~** *adj.* Of lilac color.

lil·i·a·ceous (lĭlēā'shus) *adj.* Of lilies or the order Liliaceae; lilylike.

Lil·ith (lĭl'ĭth). In the Talmud, the first wife of Adam, dispossessed by Eve; in Jewish folklore, female demon who tries to kill newborn children; in cabalistic literature, symbol of sexual lust.

Li·li·u·o·ka·la·ni (lēlē-ōōōkahlah'nē), **Lydia Kamekeha** (1838–1917). Last native ruler and queen of the Hawaiian Islands, 1891–3; deposed.

Lil·li·put (lĭl'ĭpŭt, -put). In Swift's *Gulliver's Travels*, a country inhabited by people 6 inches high. **Lil·li·pu·tian** (lĭlĭpū'shan) *adj.* Of Lilliput; of diminutive size; petty.

Li·long·we (lēlawng'wā). The designated capital of Malawi, replacing Zomba.

lilt (lĭlt) *v.t.* Sing melodiously or rhythmically. **~** *n.* (Song with) marked rhythmical cadence.

lil·y (lĭl'ē) *n.* (pl. **lil·ies**). 1. Flower of genus *Lilium* of bulbous herbs bearing large showy white, reddish, or purplish flowers, freq. spotted, on tall slender stem, esp. *L. candidum*, the white or madonna lily; any of various plants of allied genera; **tiger ~**: see TIGER; **water ~**: see WATER; **~ of the valley**, spring flower, *Convallaria majalis*, with (usu.) two longish leaves and racemes of fragrant white bell-shaped flowers. 2. Heraldic fleur-de-lis; **the (golden) lilies**, arms of French monarchy, the Bourbon dynasty. 3. (attrib.) Delicately white; pallid; **~-livered**, coward-

ly; **~ pad**, broad flat leaf of wat[er] lily lying on water; **~-white**, wh[ite] as a lily; containing no bla[ck] people; pertaining to groups [or] organizations that discrimina[te] against blacks.

Li·ma (lē'ma). Capital city [of] Peru; **l~** (lī'ma) **bean**, kind of be[an] (*Phaseolus limensis*) native to trop[i]cal America, with flat usu. wh[ite] seeds.

limb¹ (lĭm) *n.* Leg, arm, [or] wing; main branch of tree; bran[ch] of cross; spur of mountain; (colloq[.]) also **~ of the devil, of Sata[n]** mischievous child; **out on a [limb]** (colloq.) in a vulnerable positio[n] isolated. **limb'less** *adj.* **limb** *v[.t.]* Cut off the limbs of.

limb² (lĭm) *n.* Edge of surfac[e] graduated edge of quadrant et[c.] edge of sun, moon, etc.; expand[ed] part of petal, sepal, or leaf.

lim·bate (lĭm'bāt) *adj.* (bio[l.]) Having distinct or different color[ed] border.

lim·ber¹ (lĭm'ber) *n.* Detachab[le] front of gun carriage (two whee[ls,] axle, pole, and ammunition bo[x]) **~** *v.t.* Attach limber to (gu[n)] fasten together two parts of g[un] carriage (usu. *up*).

lim·ber² (lĭm'ber) *adj.* Flexibl[e] lithe, nimble. **~** *v.* Make limb[er] or supple; **~ up**, exercise [in] preparation for athletic etc. exe[r]tion. **lim'ber·ly** *adv.* **lim'ber[·]ness** *n.*

lim·bo¹ (lĭm'bō) *n.* Region [on] border of hell, supposed abode [of] just men who died before Chris[t]

2

3

5

6

*There are about 80 species of **lily** belonging to the genus Lilium, most of which are cultivated as ornamental plants. Shown here are: 1. Tiger lily. 2. Candlestick lily. 3. Spider lily. 4. 'Prosperity lily' (lilium oregon hybrid). 5. African lily. 6. Lily of the Valley, which is not of the genus Lilium but belongs to the lily family. Its scented flowers are distilled for perfume.*

oming and of unbaptized infants; rison; condition of neglect or blivion. [L. *in limbo* at the edge]
lim·bo² (lĭm′bō) *n.* W. Indian ance in which dancer bends back nd passes repeatedly under gradu- lly lowered horizontal bar just bove ground. [Caribbean name]
Lim·burg, Lim·bourg (lĭm′- ‑ĕrg). 1. Ancient duchy of the Low Countries. 2. (**Limbourg**) Prov- nce of NE. Belgium, part of the ld duchy. 3. (**Limburg**) Province f extreme SE. of the Netherlands, ncluding another part of the old uchy. **Lim·burg·er** (lĭm′bĕrger) . (also ~ **cheese**) Soft white ompressed cheese orig. from Lim- ourg, Belgium, with characteristic mell.
lime¹ (līm) *n.* 1. White caustic kaline substance, quicklime (cal- ium oxide, CaO), made by heating chalk or limestone and used for making mortar; (pop., in **car- bonate, chloride**, etc., *of* ~) calcium; (theatr.) limelight. 2. **bird′lime**: see BIRD; ~ **burner**, maker of lime; **lime′kiln**, kiln for burning limestone; **lime′light**, in- tense white light got by heating lime in oxyhydrogen flame, formerly used in theaters to light up important figures etc.; (fig.) glare of publicity; **lime pit**, lime- stone quarry; pit for steeping hides

*The flowers of the **lime** or linden tree are fragrant and rich in nectar. Linden honey, light in color, is highly regarded for its food value. The tree is widely planted for shade.*

to remove hair; **lime'stone**, rock consisting chiefly of calcium carbonate; **lime twig**, twig smeared with birdlime; **lime'water**, solution of calcium hydroxide $(Ca(OH)_2)$ used medicinally as an antacid. **lime** *v.t.* (**limed, lim‑ing**). Smear (twigs), catch (bird), with birdlime; treat with lime.

lime² (līm) *n.* Round fruit of tree *Citrus aurantifolia*, smaller and more acid than lemon; ~ **juice**, juice of this used as beverage and as antiscorbutic.

lime³ (līm) *n.* (also ~ **tree**) Ornamental tree (*Tilia*, esp. *T. glabra*) with heart-shaped leaves and small fragrant yellowish blossom; linden tree.

lime·ade (līmād', lī'mād) *n.* Beverage of sweetened lime juice and water.

li·men (lī'men) *n.* (pl. **li·mens, lim·i·na** pr. lĭm'*i*na). (psych.) = THRESHOLD. **lim·i·nal** (lĭm'*i*nal) *adj.* [L., = "threshold"]

Lim·er·ick (lĭm'erĭk). County in the Republic of Ireland; a town and port at head of estuary of River Shannon.

lim·er·ick (lĭm'erĭk) *n.* Verse, now usu. epigrammatic and freq. indecent, consisting of five lines (two of 3 ft., two of 2 ft., and one of 3 ft.) with rhymes *aabba*; first found c1820, and popularized by Edward LEAR². [said to be f. chorus "Will you come up to Limerick?" sung after extempore verses contributed by each member of party]

lim·ey (lī'mē) *n.* (pl. **-eys**). (slang) English sailor; Englishman.

lim·it (lĭm'ĭt) *n.* Bounding line, terminal point, bound that may not or cannot be passed; **the ~**, (slang) the last straw, the worst, etc., conceivable; **off-~s**, (out of) bounds; **lim'it·less** *adj.* **limit** *v.t.* Confine within limits, set bounds to, restrict *to*; serve as limit to.

lim·i·ta·tion (lĭmĭtā'shŏn) *n.* Limiting; limited condition, disability or inability; limiting rule or circumstance; legally specified period beyond which action cannot be brought, estate or law is not to continue, etc.; **statute of ~s**, statute fixing such period. **lim·i·ta·tive** (lĭm'ĭtātĭv) *adj.*

lim·it·ed (lĭm'ĭtĭd) *adj.* Circumscribed, narrow; scanty; ~ **edition**, edition with limited number of copies; ~ **monarchy**, one in which powers of monarch are restricted by the constitution; ~ **war**, war waged with voluntarily limited ends or means. **limited** *n.* Train or bus making limited number of stops.

limn (lĭm) *v.t.* (archaic) Paint

Limestone *rocks represent 20% of all sedimentary rocks and occur on all continents among strata of every age. This crinoidal limestone is from the Carboniferous period.*

(picture); portray (in words). **limn'er** *n.*

lim·nol·o·gy (lĭmnŏl'ojē) *n.* Study of fresh waters and their inhabitants.

Li·moges (lĭmōzh'). City of W. central France, famous in 16th and 17th centuries for enamel work and later for porcelain.

lim·ou·sine (lĭm'ozēn, lĭmozēn') *n.* Automobile with closed body and partition behind driver; luxurious automobile; large automobile or small bus used to transport passengers to and from airports. [Fr., f. *Limousin*, form province of W. central France]

limp¹ (lĭmp) *v.i.* Walk lame (of verse) halt; (of ship) proce slowly and with difficulty becau of damage. **limp'ing·ly** *ad* **limp** *n.* Lame walk.

limp² (lĭmp) *adj.* Not sti flexible; wanting in energy; (bookbindings) not stiffened wi board. **limp'ly** *adv.* **limp'ness**

lim·pet (lĭm'pĭt) *n.* Gastrop mollusk, as of the famili Acmaeidae or Patellidae, with l conical shell found adhering tight to rocks; (fig.) person who clin persistently.

lim·pid (lĭm'pĭd) *adj.* Pelluci clear, not turbid. **lim'pid·ly** *ad* **lim'pid·ness, lim·pid·i·ty** (lĭ pĭd'ĭtē) *ns.*

Lim·po·po (lĭmpō'pō). River of SE. Africa, rising near Johannesburg and flowing 1,000 miles (1,610 km) to the Indian Ocean.

lin·age (lī'nĭj) *n.* Number of lines in printed matter; payment according to this.

linch·pin (lĭnch'pĭn) *n.* Pin passed through axle end to keep wheel on; (fig.) element or person vital to an organization etc.

Lin·coln[1] (lĭng'kɔn). Capital and commercial center of Nebraska, in the SE.

Lin·coln[2] (lĭng'kɔn), **Abraham** (1809–65). American statesman and 16th president of the U.S., during the Civil War; prominent lawyer, congressman from Illinois, 1847–9; took stand against slavery during famous debates against Stephen A. Douglas; issued Emancipation Proclamation declaring freedom of slaves in all rebellious states; famous for address dedicating national cemetery at Gettysburg, 1863; assassinated in Ford's Theater by John Wilkes Booth, 1865.

Lind (lĭnd), **Johanna Maria ("Jenny")**, afterward Madame Jenny Lind-Goldschmidt (1820–1887). Swedish-born Brit. coloratura soprano.

Lind·bergh (lĭnd'bĕrg, lĭn'-), **Charles A(ugustus)** (1902–74). American aviator; made first non-stop flight of the Atlantic, 1927.

lin·den (lĭn'den) *n.* Any of several trees of the genus *Tilia* with large heart-shaped leaves and fragrant yellowish-white flowers, including *T. americana*, basswood.

Lind·say (lĭn'zē), **(Nicholas) Vachel** (1879–1931). American poet who tried to follow the troubadour tradition; wrote "The Congo" etc.

line[1] (līn) *n.* 1. Piece of rope (esp. naut.); wire or cable for telegraph or telephone, route traversed by this; cord bearing fishhook(s); cord for measuring, leveling, etc.; ~ **of credit**, maximum amount of credit made available by a bank, store, credit card agency, etc., to a customer. 2. Long narrow mark traced on surface; mark limiting games court or ground or special parts of them; thing resembling traced mark, band of color, seam, furrow, wrinkle, fold in palm of hand supposed to indicate fate, character, etc.; equator; straight line; contour, outline; limit, boundary; (as measure) $\frac{1}{12}$ in.; one of the very narrow sections in which televised scenes are photographed and reproduced; (math.) continuous extent (straight or curved) of length without breadth or thickness, curve connecting all points having a common property; (pl.) plan or draft (esp. of ship) in horizontal, vertical, and oblique sections; (pl.) manner of procedure; ~ **drawing**, drawing done with pen or similar instrument; ~ **engraving**, incising of lines on metal plate, print taken from such plate. 3. Row of persons or things; direction indicated by them; row of words in page or newspaper column; short letter; single verse of poetry, (pl.) piece of poetry; (mil.) double row (front and rear ranks) of men ranged side by side; trench, (pl.) connected series of fieldworks; regular fighting force of all arms; (pl.) words of actor's part; **all along the** ~, at every point; **down the** ~; thoroughly, completely; **draw the** ~, restrict, impose a limit; **get a** ~ **on**, gain a clue to; **hold the** ~, remain unyielding; **in** ~ **for**, likely to get; **into** ~, into a straight row or (fig.) agreement; ~ **of battle**: see BATTLE; ~ **of scrimmage**: see SCRIMMAGE; ~-**up**, ~ **up**, (specific order of) persons or things arranged in a line, esp. listing of players in a game and their positions on the team; **on the** ~, (slang) at great risk; with money, as opposed to credit; **out of** ~, (slang) discordant; **read between the** ~s, discover meaning or purpose not expressed or not obvious; **scrimmage** ~: see SCRIMMAGE. 4. Series or regular succession of steamers, buses, aircraft, etc., traveling between certain places; connected series of persons or things following one another in time, esp. several generations of family; family, lineage, stock. 5. Direction, course, track; course followed in riding to hounds; course of procedure, conduct, thought, etc.; department of activity, province, branch of business; (rail.) single track of rails, one branch of system, whole system under one management; (commerc.) class of goods, order for stock of this. **line** *v.* (**lined, lin·ing**). Mark *in, off, out*, with lines on paper etc.; cover with lines; draw *up* in line; come *up*, spread *out*, in lines; post troops etc. along (road etc.), (of troops) form line along; (of things) stand at intervals along (wall etc.).

The Lincoln Memorial in Washington D.C. commemorates the 16th U.S. President Abraham Lincoln, who was assassinated days after the end of the Civil War by John Wilkes Booth.

*The **limpet,** a mollusk with a conical shell, clings mostly to rocks near the shore. This Patella vulgata is a species commonly found in Britain and northern Europe.*

Ling is another name for the common heather. This low evergreen shrub is found in the open woods of western Europe and the British Isles, and in eastern North America.

line² (līn) *v.t.* (**lined, lin·ing**). Apply layer of (usu. different) material to inside of (garment, box, etc.); fill (purse, pocket, stomach, etc.); serve as lining for; ~ **one's pockets**, make money, esp. at the expense of other people. **lin′ing** *n.*

lin·e·age (lĭn′ēĭj) *n.* Lineal descent, ancestry, pedigree.

lin·e·al (lĭn′ēal) *adj.* In the direct line of descent or ancestry; (rare) of, in, line(s), linear. **lin′e·al·ly** *adv.*

lin·e·a·ment (lĭn′ēament) *n.* (usu. pl.) Distinctive feature(s) or characteristic(s), esp. of face.

lin·e·ar (lĭn′ēer) *adj.* 1. Of, in, line(s); (of work of art) conceived or expressed in lines rather than masses. 2. Long, narrow, and of uniform breadth. 3. (math., phys.) Involving measurement in one dimension only. **lin′e·ar·ly** *adv.*

lin·e·a·tion (lĭnēā′shon) *n.* Drawing of, marking with, arrangement of, lines.

line·back·er (līn′băker) *n.* (football) Defensive player, usu. just behind the ends and tackles.

lin·en (lĭn′en) *adj.* Made of flax. ~ *n.* Cloth woven from flax; particular kind of this; (collect.) garments etc. orig. of linen, now of other materials; undergarments, bed linen, table linen.

lin·er¹ (lī′ner) *n.* Ship belonging to line of passenger ships; aircraft belonging to a regular line, esp. for passenger transport.

lin·er² (lī′ner) *n.* Removable metal lining to prevent wear and tear in guns or other machinery; removable substance for lining.

lines·man (līnz′man) *n.* (pl. **-men** pr. -měn). Official assisting umpire or referee by deciding whether or where ball touches or crosses line.

Flax is the plant which produces the fiber to make **linen**. *Here it is seen drying in racks, just one of the processes involved in extracting the fiber. Linen has been used extensively since the time of the pharaohs.*

ling (lĭng) *n.* (collect. **ling**, pl. **lings**). Long slender N. European sea fish (*Molva molva*) used (often salted or split and dried) for food.

lin·ger (lĭng′ger) *v.i.* Put off departure, esp. from reluctance to go; stay about, not depart or arrive at expected or right time; dally *around* place, *over*, *on*, subject; drag *on* a feeble existence; be protracted; be tardy, delay. ~ *v.t.* Throw (time) *away* in delays. **lin′ger·er** *n.* **lin′ger·ing·ly** *adv.*

lin·ge·rie (lahnzherā′, lăn′zheré, -je-) *n.* Women's underclothes.

lin·go (lĭng′gō) *n.* (pl. **-goes**). (slang) Foreign language; language belonging to special subject or class of people. [corrupt. of LINGUA (FRANCA)]

lin·gua fran·ca (lĭng′gwa frăng′ka) (pl. **lin·gua fran·cas, lin·guae fran·cae** pr. lĭng′gwē

frăn′sē). 1. Mixture of Italian, French, Greek, and Spanish, used in Levant. 2. Any language spoken or understood by various peoples over a wide area. [It., = "Frankish tongue"]

lin·gual (lĭng′gwal) *adj.* Of the tongue; of speech or languages. **lin′gual·ly** *adv.*

lin·gui·form (lĭng′gwiform) *adj.* (bot., anat., zool.) Tongue-shaped.

lin·guist (lĭng′gwĭst) *n.* Person skilled in (foreign) languages. **lin·guis·tic** (lĭnggwĭs′tĭk) *adj.* Of the study of languages; of language. **lin·guis′ti·cal·ly** *adv.* **lin·guis′tics** *n.* Study of language.

lin·i·ment (lĭn′iment) *n.* Liquid preparation, usu. made with oil, for application to the skin as treatment for sprains.

link¹ (lĭngk) *n.* One ring or loop of chain; as measure, $\frac{1}{100}$ of surveying chain, 7.92 in.; CUFF¹-link; connecting part, thing or person that unites others, filler of gap, member of series; **missing** ~: see MISSING. **link** *v.* Connect, join *together, to,* or *up*; clasp (hands);

hook (arms, arm *in* or *through* another's); attach oneself *on, in,* to system, company, etc.

link² (lĭngk) *n.* Torch of pitch and tow formerly used for lighting people along streets and carried by **link'man** or **link'boy.**

link·age (lĭng'kĭj) *n.* 1. Act, state, or condition of being linked. 2. (esp. biol.) Relative inseparability of two or more heritable characteristics owing to their factors being in the same chromosome.

links (lĭngks) *n.pl.* Level or undulating sandy ground near seashore, with turf and coarse grass (Sc.); golf course.

Lin·nae·us (lĭnē'us), **Carolus** (1707–78). Latinized name of Carl von Linné, Swedish botanist; originator of system of taxonomy. **Lin·nae'an, Lin·ne'an** *adjs.* Of Linnaeus; (esp.) of his system of botanical binomial classification, dividing all plants into 24 classes, most of which were based on the number or arrangement of stamens.

lin·net (lĭn'ĭt) *n.* Common brown or warm-gray Old World songbird, *Carduelis cannabina.* [Fr. *in* flax, seeds of which are its food]

li·no·le·um (lĭnō'lĕum) *n.* Floor covering of canvas coated with oxidized linseed oil and usu. pigments.

Lin·o·type (lī'nōtīp) *n.* (trademark) Machine that casts a slug or line of type from a line of assembled and justified matrices at a single operation of casting. **lin'o·typ·er** *n.* [= *line o' type*]

lin·sang (lĭn'săng) *n.* 1. Member of an oriental genus (**L~**) of civet cats resembling the true cats in several features. 2. African civet cat of genus *Poiana.*

lin·seed (lĭn'sēd) *n.* Seed of flax; **~ cake,** linseed pressed into cake in process of extracting oil and used as cattle food; **~ oil,** oil obtained by pressure from linseed.

lin·sey-wool·sey (lĭn'zē wŏol'zē) *n.* (pl. **-seys**). Dress material of cotton (orig. linen) warp and wool weft; (fig.) any incongruous mixture.

lin·stock (lĭn'stŏk) *n.* (hist.) Staff with forked end to hold lighted match, used for applying fire to touchhole of a cannon.

lint (lĭnt) *n.* Soft material for dressing wounds, obtained by raveling or scraping linen cloth; fluff of any material; raw cotton fiber. **lint'er** *n.* Machine for stripping off short-staple cotton fiber from cottonseed after ginning; (pl.) these fibers. **lint'y** *adj.* (**lint·i·er, lint·i·est**).

lin·tel (lĭn'tel) *n.* Horizontal timber or stone over door or window.

Li·nus (lī'nus). (Gk. myth.) Hero whose untimely death was celebrated in a dirge sung annually at harvest time; perhaps orig. a corn spirit.

li·on (lī'on) *n.* (pl. **lions,** collect. **lion**). 1. Large member of cat family, a powerful tawny carnivore (*Felis leo*), with tufted tail and (in the male) a mane, now native only in Africa and S. Asia. 2. Courageous person. 3. Person of literary or other celebrity much sought after for social gatherings. 4. Lion as national emblem of Great Britain. 5. **the L~:** see LEO¹. 6. **(American) mountain ~,** puma; **~ and unicorn,** supporters of English royal arms; **li'on-hearted,** courageous; **lion hunter,** person who makes much of celebrities; **Lion of Lucerne,** lion carved in rock at Lucerne, Switzerland, as monument to Swiss Guards who fell defending Louis XVI of France in attack on Tuileries, 1792; **Lion of St. Mark,** winged lion as emblem of St. Mark (from traditional interpretation of Ezek. 1), esp. that in Piazzetta of Venice, of which city he is patron saint; **Lion of the North,** Gustavus Adolphus, king of Sweden; **lion's mouth,** perilous position; **lion's share,** largest or best part. **li·on·ess** (lī'onĭs) *n.* Female lion.

li·on·ize (lī'onīz) *v.t.* (**-ized, -iz·ing**). Treat (person) as celebrity.

*The **linnet** is native to Europe, north Africa and central Asia. It is seed-eating and is brownish-grey and white. About 5 inches long, it is found in hedgerows. Flocks of linnets forage for seed in open country.*

The **lion,** the 'king of beasts', has been, since earliest times, one of the best known of wild animals. It inhabits open country and is found mainly in Africa south of the Sahara, living often in groups or prides. Above: Lion feeding on a wildebeest carcass. Below: Lion family.

lip (lĭp) *n.* 1. One of the fleshy edges of the opening of the mouth; edge of cup, vessel, cavity, wound, etc.; (slang) insolent talk; **bite one's ~**, show vexation; express emotion; **hang on the ~s of**, listen with rapt attention to; **keep a stiff upper ~**, (slang) face adversity courageously; **smack one's ~s**, express relish for food; (fig.) express delight. 2. (attrib., phon.) Formed or produced by lips; **~ reading**, understanding (esp. by deaf person) of what another says by watching movements of lips; **~ salve**, ointment for sore lips; (fig.) flattery; **~ service**, devotion expressed in words only, superficial respect; **lip'stick**, stick of cosmetic for coloring lips; **lip sync, lip synch**, synchronization of filmed or live lip movements with previously recorded sound. **lip** *v.t.* (**lipped, lip'ping**). Touch with lips, apply lips to; (of water) lap.

li·pid (lī'pĭd, lĭp'ĭd) *n.* (chem.) Substance that has the general properties of fats but is not necessarily a glyceride.

Li Po (lē'pō'; *Chin.* lē'baw') = LI TAI PO.

Lip·pi (lĭp'ē; *It.* lē'pē). Name of two Florentine painters of the early Renaissance: **Fra Filippo** or **Lippo ~** (1406–69), and **Filippo**

Fra Filippo Lippi, the 15th-century Florentine painter, was the father of Filippino Lippi. His best known works are brilliant frescoes in the Prato Cathedral, such as the 'Virgin and Child' below.

or **Filippino ~** (1457–1504), his natural son.

li·quate (lī'kwāt) *v.t.* (**-quat·ed, -quat·ing**). Separate or purify (metals) by liquefying. **li·qua·tion** (līkwā'shon) *n.*

liq·ue·fy (lĭk'wefī) *v.* (**-fied, -fy·ing**). Reduce to liquid condition; become liquid. **liq·ue·fa·cient** (lĭkwefā'shent), **liq·ue·fac·tion** (lĭkwefăk'shon) *ns.*

liq·ues·cent (lĭkwĕs'ent) *adj.* Becoming, apt to become, liquid.

li·queur (lĭkēr'; *Brit.* lĭkūr') *n.* Strong sweet drink with base of brandy or other spirit and flavoring of aromatic substances, taken in small quantities usu. after meals; mixture of sugar and certain wines, or sugar and alcohol, used to flavor champagne; **~ glass**, very small glass for liqueurs.

liq·uid (lĭk'wĭd) *adj.* In that condition (the normal condition of water, oil, etc.) in which particles move freely over each other but do not tend to separate like those of gases, fluid; watery; having the transparency, translucence, or brightness, of water or wine; (of sounds) flowing clear, fluent, pure, not grating or discordant, not guttural, vowel-like; not fixed, unstable; (of assets, securities, etc.) easily convertible into cash; **~ air**, air reduced to the liquid state under high pressure and low temperature, used as a refrigerant. **liq'uid·ly** *adv.* **liq'uid·ness, li·quid·i·ty** (lĭkwĭd'ĭtē) *ns.* **liq·uid·ize** (lĭk'wĭdīz) *v.t.* (**-ized, -iz·ing**). **liquid** *n.* 1. Liquid substance. 2. (phon.) Sound of one of the letters *l*, *r* (and sometimes *m*, *n*).

liq·ui·date (lĭk'wĭdāt) *v.* (**-dat·ed, -dat·ing**). Pay, clear off, (debt); wind up, ascertain liabilities and apportion assets of, (company, firm); go into liquidation; put an end to, stamp out, wipe out. **liq·ui·da·tion** (lĭkwĭda'shon) *n.* **go into ~**, (of company) have its affairs wound up, become bankrupt.

liq·uor (defs. 1 and 2 lĭk'er; def. 3 lĭk'wōr) *n.* 1. Liquid part of secretion or product of chemical operation; liquid used as wash etc.; water used in brewing; liquid contained in oysters. 2. Liquid (usu. fermented or distilled) for drinking. 3. (pharm. etc.) Solution of specified drug in water.

liq·uo·rice = LICORICE.

li·ra (lēr'a; *It.* lē'rah) *n.* (pl. **li·re** pr. lēr'a; *It.* lē'rě, **li·ras**). Principal monetary unit of Italy and Turkey.

Lis·bon (lĭz'bon). Capital city and port of Portugal.

The mountain lion or puma is found in the New World from British Columbia to Patagonia in habitats as varied as mountains, deserts and jungles. In some regions, however, it is extinct.

Lisbon is the capital of Portugal and a great port at the mouth of the Tagus. In 1755 an earthquake destroyed half the city which was afterwards rebuilt. Shown here is the National Pantheon.

lisle (līl) *n.* (also ~ **thread**) Fine smooth thread (orig. linen, now cotton) used in manufacture of stockings etc. [former spelling of *Lille* in France]

lisp (lĭsp) *v.* Substitute sound approaching that of English *th* for sibilants in speaking; (of child) speak with imperfect pronunciation. ~ *n.* Lisping pronunciation; (poet.) sound resembling this. **lisp′er** *n.* **lisp′ing·ly** *adv.*

lis·some, **lis·som** (lĭs′om) *adjs.* Lithe, supple, agile. **lis′some·ly**, **lis′som·ly** *advs.* **lis′some·ness**, **lis′som·ness** *ns.*

list[1] (lĭst) *n.* 1. Selvage or edge of cloth, usu. of different material; such edges used for slippers, cushions, etc. 2. (pl.) Palisades enclosing tilting ground (see TILT[2] *n.* def. 2); this ground; (fig.) scene of contest.

list[2] (lĭst) *n.* Roll or catalog of names, of persons or things belonging to a class, of articles with prices, of things to be done etc. ~ *v.* Enter in list.

list[3] (lĭst) *n.* Inclination of ship etc. to one side (owing to leak, shifting cargo, etc.). ~ *v.i.* Lean over to one side.

list[4] (lĭst) *v.* (archaic) Listen, listen to.

lis·ten (lĭs′en) *v.* Make effort to hear something, hear with attention, give ear *to*; yield *to* temptation or request; ~ **in**, tap telephonic communication; listen to radio transmission. **lis′ten·er** *n.*

Lis·ter (lĭs′ter), **Joseph, 1st Baron Lister** (1827–1912). English surgeon; founder of antiseptic surgery.

list·less (lĭst′lĭs) *adj.* Languid; without interest. **list′less·ly** *adv.* **list′less·ness** *n.*

Liszt (lĭst), **Franz** (1811–86). Hungarian pianist and composer, whose best-known compositions are his "Hungarian Rhapsodies."

lit (lĭt): see LIGHT[3].

Li Tai Po (lē′tī′pō′; *Chin.* lē′tī′baw′) (c701–62). One of the greatest Chinese poets.

lit·a·ny (lĭt′anē) *n.* (pl. **-nies**). Series of petitions for use in church services or processions, recited by clergy and responded to usu. in recurring formula(s) by people.

li·tchi, li·chee, li·chi (lē′chē) *ns.* (pl. **-tchis, -chees, -chis**). Sweetish pulpy fruit with shell and single seed; tree bearing this (*Litchi chinensis*) orig. from China, now grown in Bengal and S. Africa.

li·ter, Brit. **li·tre** (lēter) *ns.* Unit of capacity in the metric system, one cubic decimeter (approx. 0.22 gal.).

lit·er·a·cy (lĭt′erasē) *n.* Ability to read and write.

lit·er·al (lĭt′eral) *adj.* Of, in, expressed by, letter(s) of alphabet; following the letter, text, or exact or original words; taking words in their usual or primary sense without mysticism, allegory, or metaphor; so called, so described without exaggeration; (of persons) prosaic, matter-of-fact. **lit′er·al·ly** *adv.* **lit′er·al·ness, lit′er·al·ism, lit·er·al·i·ty** (lĭterăl′ĭtē) *ns.*

lit·er·ar·y (lĭt′erērē) *adj.* Of, constituting, occupied with, literature, polite learning, or books and written records esp. of the kind valued for form; (of word etc.) uncolloquial, affected by writers; ~ **property**, property consisting of written or printed compositions; exclusive right of publication as recognized and limited by law. **lit′er·ar·i·ly** *adv.* **lit′er·ar·i·ness** *n.*

lit·er·ate (lĭt′erĭt) *adj.* Having some acquaintance with literature; (now usu.) able to read and write. ~ *n.* Literate person.

lit·e·ra·ti (lĭterah′tē, -rā′tī) *n.pl.* Men or women of letters; literate or learned class.

lit·er·a·ture (lĭt′eracher, -cho lĭt′ra-) *n.* Literary cultu (archaic); literary production, t literary profession; realm of lette writings of a country or perio writings whose value lies in bea of form or emotional effect; boc etc. treating *of* a subject; (collo printed matter.

lith·arge (lĭth′ärj, lĭthärj′ Lead monoxide (PbO), a ha yellowish-red crystalline substan prepared by prolonged heating lead in air, used in the paint a varnish industry and in the man facture of lead glazes.

lithe (līdh) *adj.* (**lith·er, lith est**). Flexible, supple. **lithe′ne** *n.* **lithe′some** *adj.*

lith·i·a (lĭth′ēa, -ya) *n.* Lithi monoxide (Li$_2$O); ~ **wat** mineral water containing lithiu salts.

lith·ic[1] (lĭth′ĭk) *adj.* Of the sto or calculus; of stone.

lith·ic[2] (lĭth′ĭk) *adj.* (chem.) lithium.

lith·i·um (lĭth′ēum) *n.* (chen Soft, silver-white metallic eleme the lightest of the alkali met occurring in small quantities various minerals; symbol Li, at.

, at. wt. 6.941.

lith·o·graph (lĭth´ogrăf, -grahf) *n.* Print taken from stone block which, after design is traced on it with greasy chalk, is so treated with acid, gum, and water that the un-halked parts reject ink and make no impression; print produced from stone or metal) by variants of this process. **li·thog·ra·phy** (lĭthŏg´rafē) *n.* 1. Art or process of producing a lithograph. 2. Printing process based on this method but using flexible metal plates instead of stones. See also PHOTOLITHOG-RAPHY. **lith·o·graph·ic** (lĭtho-grăf´ĭk) *adj.* **lith´o·graph** *v.i.* Pro-uce, copy, by lithographic process. **li·thol·o·gy** (lĭthŏl´ojē) *n.* science of the nature and composi-on of stones and rocks. **lith·o·og·i·cal** (lĭtholŏj´ĭkal) *adj.*

lith·o·phyte (lĭth´ofīt) *n.* 1. zool.) Polyp whose skeletal sub-tance is calcareous, as some corals. . (bot.) Plant that grows on stone.

lith·o·sphere (lĭth´osfēr) *n.* geol.) Outer crust of Earth, con-isting of soil and rock, dist. from

the BARYSPHERE, which it encloses and the HYDROSPHERE, through which it projects to form the con-tinents.

li·thot·o·my (lĭthŏt´omē) *n.* (pl. **-mies**). Operation of cutting into the bladder and removing stone.

Lith·u·a·ni·a (lĭth ōōā´nēa). Area between Latvia and Poland, on the Baltic Sea; formerly a Baltic province of the Russian Empire; declared an independent republic in 1918; incorporated in 1940 in the U.S.S.R., of which it is a constitu-ent republic (properly *Lithuanian Soviet Socialist Republic*); capital, Vilnius (Vilna). **Lith·u·a´ni·an** *adj. & n.* 1. (native, inhabitant) of

*The main stages of **lithographic** print-ing. Left to right: The drawing is done on the lithographic stone with a stylus. A thin film of nitric acid is spread over the stone. The stone is inked and only the inscribed portions become impreg-nated with ink. The print is taken by placing the sheet of paper on the litho-graphic stone and applying pressure. Below: Lithograph of the Crystal Pal-ace, London, by Vincent Brooks.*

Lithuania. 2. (Of) the language of the Lithuanians, one of the highly inflected Baltic group of Indo-European languages.

lit·i·gate (lĭt´igāt) *v.* (**-gat·ed, -gat·ing**). Go to law, be party to lawsuit; contest (point) at law. **lit´i·gant** *adj. & n.* **lit·i·ga·tion** (lĭtigā´shon) *n.*

li·ti·gious (lĭtĭj´us) *adj.* Given to litigation, fond of going to law; dis-putable at law, offering matter for lawsuit; of lawsuits. **li·ti´gious·ly** *adv.* **li·ti´gious·ness** *n.*

lit·mus (lĭt´mus) *n.* Blue color-ing matter from lichens that is turned red by acids and restored to blue by alkalis; ~ **paper**, unsized paper stained with litmus, as test for acids etc.

lit·o·ral = LITTORAL.

li·to·tes (lī´totēz, -tō-, lĭt´o-, lītō´tēz) *n.* (pl. **-tes**). Ironically moderate form of speech, esp. ex-pression of affirmative by negative of its contrary, as *not bad* for *good*.

li·tre = LITER.

Litt.D. *abbrev. Litterarum doctor* (L., = Doctor of Letters).

Lithuania, *a constituent republic of the U.S.S.R. on the Baltic Sea, is a low-lying region with many lakes. Its chief industries are heavy engineering and shipbuilding.*

lit·ter (lĭt′er) *n.* 1. Vehicle containing bed shut in by curtains and carried on men's shoulders or by beasts; framework with couch for transporting sick and wounded. 2. Straw, rushes, etc., as bedding esp. for animals; straw and dung of farmyard. 3. Odds and ends, leavings; state of untidiness; disorderly accumulation of papers etc. 4. Young (of sow, bitch, etc.) brought forth at one birth. ~ *v.* 1. provide (horse etc.) with litter as bed; spread litter or straw on stable floor etc. 2. Make (place) untidy; scatter and leave lying. 3. (of animals) Bring forth (young).

lit·té·ra·teur, lit·te·ra·teur (lĭterater′; *Fr.* lētĕrahtör′) *ns.* (pl. **-teurs** pr. -tērz′; *Fr.* -tör′). Literary man. [*Fr.*]

lit·ter·bug (lĭt′erbŭg) *n.* One who carelessly litters streets, buildings, etc., with papers and other refuse.

lit·tle (lĭt′el) *adj.* (**less** or **less·er, least** or **lit·tler, lit·tlest**). Small (freq. with emotional implications not present in *small*); not great or big; of smaller or smallest size etc.; young; short in stature, distance, or time; trivial; mean, paltry, contemptible; not much; **in ~**, on a small scale; **L~ America**, American bases for polar exploration in Antarctica on the Ross Ice Shelf; the first base was established by Richard Byrd, 1929; **L~ Bear** or **~ Dipper**, Ursa Minor; **L~ Big Horn**, river in N. Wyoming that joins the Bighorn in S. Montana; along its banks Gen. Custer and his troops were defeated and wiped out by the Indians, 1876; **L~ League**, baseball league for children of ages 8 to 12; **~ magazine**, literary magazine, usu. with experimental writing and in small format; **littleneck**, small young quahog clam suitable for eating raw; **Little Missouri**, river flowing from NE. Wyoming 560 miles (902 km) to the Missouri in North Dakota; **Little Rock**, capital of Arkansas, in the center of the state, on the Arkansas River; **little theater**, small theater, esp. an amateur repertory theater; drama suited to this. **little** *n.* Not much, only a small amount, a mere trifle; a certain but no great amount; (for a) short time or distance; **a ~**, rather, somewhat; **~ by ~**, by degrees; **~ or nothing**, hardly anything; **make ~ of**, look upon or dismiss as unimportant; disparage; **not a ~**, to a great degree; **think ~ of**, consider insignificant or trivial. **little** *adv.* (**less, least**). To a small extent only; not at all.

lit·to·ral, lit·o·ral (lĭt′eral) *adjs.* Of, on, near, the shore. ~ *n.* Region lying along the shore, esp. land lying between high and low tide levels.

lit·ur·gy (lĭt′erjē) *n.* (pl. **-gies**). 1. Communion office of Eastern Church. 2. Form of public worship, set of formularies for this. **li·tur·gi·cal** (lĭtēr′jĭkal) *adj.* **li·tur′gi·cal·ly** *adv.*

live[1] (līv) *adj.* (**liv·er, liv·est**). That is alive, living; full of power, energy, or importance, not obsolete or exhausted; (of combustibles) glowing; (of shell, bomb, etc.) unexploded, unkindled; (of wire) charged with electricity; (of parts of machinery etc.) moving or imparting motion; (of broadcast) heard, viewed, during its occurrence, not recorded; **~ bait**, living fish or worm as fishing bait; **~ oak**, American evergreen oak (*Quercus virginiana*), of southern Atlantic states; **live′stock**, domestic animals kept or dealt in for use or profit; **live wire**, (fig.) person full of energy.

live[2] (līv) *v.* (**lived, liv·ing**). 1.

David Livingstone, the Scott[?] missionary and explorer in Cent[?] Africa, discovered the Victoria Fa[?] (1855) and explored the upper reach[?] of the Congo River.

Be alive, have animal or vegetab[?] life; subsist *on*; depend *on* for su[?] sistence; get livelihood *by* (one[?] wits etc.); (fig.) sustain one's pos[?] tion or repute (*on*). 2. Condu[?] oneself, arrange one's habits, e[?] penditure, feeding, etc., in specifie[?] way; spend, pass, experience (li[?] day, etc.); wear *down* (scandal, pre[?] udice, etc.) by blameless course [?] life; express in one's life; ~ [?] **double life**, sustain two differe[?] characters, act two different part[?] in life; **~ together**, (esp. of u[?] married couples) share livin[?] quarters; **~ up to**, (principle[?] faith, etc.) put (them) into practic[?] **~ with**, tolerate, find congenia[?] share living quarters with. 3. Enj[?] life intensely; **~ it up**, (colloq[?] live gaily and extravagantly. [?] Continue alive, have one's li[?] prolonged; (of things) survive; [?] ship) escape destruction. 5. Dwe[?] spend daytime *in* room; **~ in, ou**[?]

(map labels) BALTIC SEA · KLAIPEDA · SIAULIAI · Latvia · LITHUANIA · R.S.F.S.R. · KAUNAS · VILNIUS · Poland · Byelorussia

parasitic in the liver, esp. (*Fasciola hepatica*) in liver of sheep; **liv·er·wort**, primitive seedless plant allied to mosses. **liv·er·ish** *adj.* Having symptoms of disordered liver; feeling out of sorts, irritable.

liv·er² (lĭv´er) *n.* One who lives in specified way, esp. **high ~**, who lives extravagantly.

liv·er·ied (lĭv´ered, lĭv´red) *adj.* Wearing livery.

Liv·er·pool (lĭv´erpool). City and seaport on the Mersey estuary in SW. Lancashire, England. **Liv·er·pud·li·an** (lĭverpŭd´lēan) *n.* Person who is born in or lives in Liverpool.

liv·er·wurst (lĭv´erwērst, -woorst) *n.* Sausage made with a large amount of chopped pork liver.

liv·er·y (lĭv´erē, lĭv´rē) *n.* (pl. **-er·ies**). 1. Allowance of food or clothing provided esp. for retainers etc. (hist.); allowance of provender for horses; **at ~**, (of horse) kept for owner and fed and groomed for fixed charge. 2. Distinctive clothes worn by a male servant. 3. (law) Legal delivery of property, writ allowing this; **liv´er·y·man**, keeper of or attendant in livery stable; **livery stable**, stable where horses are kept at livery or let out for hire.

Liv·i·a (lĭv´ēa) (58 B.C.–29 A.D.). Roman empress; wife of Tiberius Claudius Nero and mother by him of the Emperor Tiberius; married Octavian (Augustus) after her divorce from her first husband.

liv·id (lĭv´ĭd) *adj.* Of bluish leaden color; discolored as by bruise; (colloq.) furiously angry. **liv´id·ly** *adv.* **li·vid·i·ty** (lĭvĭd´ĭtē), **liv´id·ness** *ns.*

liv·ing (lĭv´ĭng) *n.* (esp.) 1. Livelihood, maintenance; **~ room**, room for general day use; **~ wage**, one on which it is possible to live. 2. (eccles.) Benefice. **living** *adj.* (esp.) 1. Contemporary, now existent; **the ~**, those now alive; **in the land of the ~**, alive; **within ~ memory**, within memory of persons still living. 2. (of likeness) Exact. 3. (of rock) Native, in native condition and site, as part of Earth's crust.

Liv·ing·stone (lĭv´ĭngston), **David** (1813–73). Scottish medical missionary in central Africa; explored the course of the Zambesi and the sources of the Nile; was thought to be missing in Africa and was searched for and found by HENRY STANLEY, 1871, whose first words to him were, "Dr. Livingstone, I presume?"

Liv·ing·stone (lĭv´ĭngston) **Mountains.** Range of high land in Tanzania.

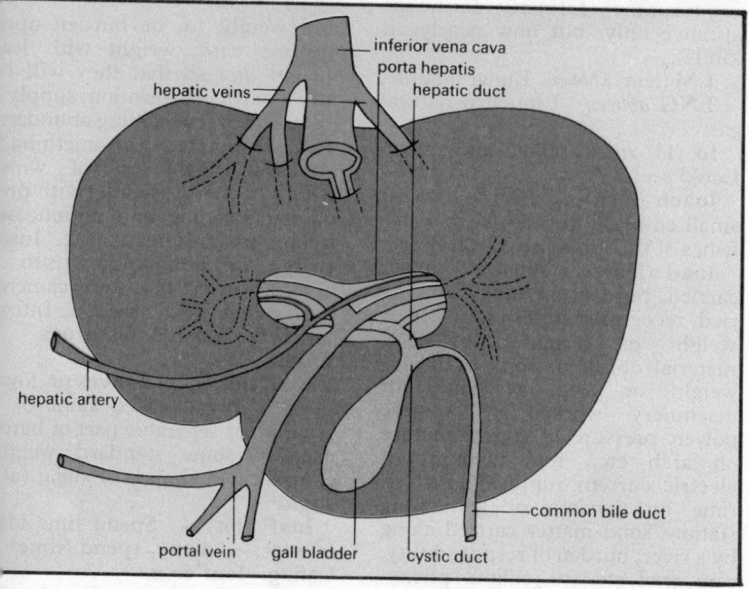

*The functions of the **liver** include: the regulation of blood volume; the manufacture of certain blood-clotting factors; the metabolism of proteins, carbohydrates and fats; and the formation of bile.*

f servant or employee), reside on, f, premises where one works. **v'a·ble, live'a·ble** *adjs.* Fit to e in; that can be lived, bearable; sy to live with, companionable.

live·li·hood (lĭv´lēhŏod) *n.* eans of living, sustenance.

live·long (lĭv´lawng, -lŏng) *adj.* oet., rhet., of time) Whole length (with implication of weariness or light).

live·ly (lĭv´lē) *adj.* (-**li·er, -li·**t). Lifelike, realistic; full of life, ergetic, brisk, interesting; (of lor) bright, gay; (of boat etc.) sing lightly to waves; (joc.) exting, dangerous, difficult. **live'ly** v. **live'li·ness** *n.*

liv·en (lī´ven) *v.* Brighten (up).

liv·er¹ (lĭv´er) *n.* Large dark-red organ in abdomen of vertebrates, the chief site of metabolic reactions, also functioning as a gland, secreting bile; organ of similar function in other animals; flesh of animals' liver used as food; color of liver, dark reddish brown; diseased state of liver; (archaic) liver as set of emotion; **lily ~**, cowardice; **~ fluke**, flatworm

Liv·y (lĭv′ē). **Titus Livius** (59 B.C.–17 A.D.), Roman historian; author of a history of Rome (*Annales*) from the foundation of the city to the death of Drusus (9 B.C.).

lix·iv·i·ate (lĭksĭv′ēāt) *v.t.* (**-at·ed, -at·ing**). Separate (substance) into soluble and insoluble constituents by percolation of water. **lix·iv·i·a·tion** (lĭksĭvēā′shon) *n.*

liz·ard (lĭz′erd) *n.* Reptile of suborder Lacertilia, related to snakes but distinguished by having (usu.) four legs, movable eyelids, eardrums, and fleshy tongue.

ll. *abbrev.* Lines.

lla·ma (lah′ma) *n.* S. Amer. mammal (*Lama glama*) related to the camel but smaller, humpless, and woolly-haired, used as beast of burden; (material made of) its wool; **the ~s**, (zool.) group of camellike S. Amer. mammals including, besides the llama, the alpaca, huanaco, and vicuna.

lla·no (lah′nō; *Sp.* yah′nō) *n.* (pl. **-nos** pr. -nōz; *Sp.* -nōs). Treeless grassland of Orinoco basin and Guiana highlands in S. America.

LL.B., LL.D. *abbrevs. Legum baccalaureus, doctor* (L., = Bachelor, Doctor, of Laws).

Llew·el·lyn (lōoĕl′lĭn). Name of two Welsh princes; **~ ab Iorwerth** (d. 1240) and **~ ab Gruffydd** (d. 1282), his nephew, last Welsh prince of Wales.

Lloyd George (loid jôrj′), **David, 1st Earl Loyd George of Dwyfor** (1863–1945). British Liberal politician; coalition prime minister 1916–22.

Lloyd's (loidz). (also **~ of**

London) London association of underwriters (orig. meeting in coffeehouse opened by Edward Lloyd 1688) and agency for arranging insurance (formerly marine insurance only, but now nearly all kinds).

LM (lĕm) *abbrev.* Lunar module.

LNG *abbrev.* Liquefied natural gas.

lo (lō) *int.* (archaic and poet.) Look! see!

loach (lōch) *n.* Any of several small edible European fresh-water fishes of the subfamily Cobitidinae.

load (lōd) *n.* What is (to be) carried, burden; amount usu. carried, recognized unit in measure or weight of certain substances; material object or force acting as weight or clog, resistance of machinery worked to motive power, pressure of superstructure on arch etc., total amount of electric current supplied at given time by dynamo or generating station; solid matter carried along by a river; burden of responsibility, care, grief, etc.; (pl., colloq.) plenty, superabundance, heaps, lots, *of*; **take a ~ off someone's mind**, relieve him of anxiety; **~-shedding**, cutting off of the electricity supply to an area as a means of avoiding excessive loading of generating plant; **load′star**: see LODE; **load′stone, lode′stone**, variety of magnetite; piece of it used as magnet; thing that attracts. **load** *v.* 1. Put load on or aboard, take load aboard, etc.; place (load, cargo) aboard ship, on vehicle, etc.;

add weight to, be burden upo oppress *with*; weight with lea weight *dice* so that they will fa into a particular position; supply excess or overwhelming abundan *with*; adulterate with something increase weight or (of wine strength; charge (words) with pr udicial meaning or emotion; a weight to (arguments). 2. Ins charge or ammunition into firearm); insert film into (camera **load′ed** *adj.* (esp. slang) 1. Intox cated by alcohol or drugs. Wealthy.

loaf[1] (lōf) *n.* (pl. **loaves** pr. lōv Piece of bread baked alone or separate or separable part of batc usu. of some standard weigh conical molded mass of sugar (al **sugar ~**).

loaf[2] (lōf) *v.* Spend time id saunter; **~ away**, spend (time) loafing. **loaf′er** *n.*

loam (lōm) *n.* 1. Fertile so chiefly of clay and sand with a mixture of decayed vegetab matter; (geog.) deposit of mix sand, silt, and clay. 2. Paste of cl and water; composition moistened clay and sand wi chopped straw etc., used in maki bricks. **loam′y** *adj.* (**loam·i·e loam·i·est**).

There are some 3,000 species of l ard which are grouped in the rept order Lacertilia. Except for legle varieties, all have four legs and dif from snakes by having movable eyeli and openings to the ears. They a found in most parts of the world but a most numerous in warmer regions.

e monitor

plumed basilisk lizard

flying (draco) lizard
ed lizard

blue-tongued skink

common
lizard

horned lizard

slow-worm

loan (lōn) *n.* Thing, esp. sum of money, lent to be returned with or without interest; word, custom, etc., adopted by one people from another; lending or being lent; ~ **shark**, (colloq.) person who lends money at excessive interest rates; usurer; ~ **word**, word adopted from another language. **loan** *v.t.* Lend.

loath, loth (lōth, lōdh) *adjs.* Disinclined, reluctant, unwilling; **nothing** ~, very willing(ly).

loathe (lōdh) *v.t.* (**loathed, loath·ing**). Regard with disgust, abominate, detest. **loath·ing** *n.* **loath·ing·ly** *adv.*

loath·some (lōdh´som, lōth´-) *adj.* Exciting nausea or disgust, offensive to the senses, odious. **loath´some·ly** *adv.* **loath´some·ness** *n.*

lob (lŏb) *v.* (**lobbed, lob·bing**). Walk, run, or move, heavily, clumsily, or slowly; toss, bowl, strike, (ball) slowly or with high arc motion. ~ *n.* Ball sent high in air in tennis or other sport.

lo·bate (lō´bāt) *adj.* (biol.) Having lobe(s). **lo´bate·ly** *adv.* **lo·ba·tion** (lōbā´shon) *n.*

lob·by (lŏb´ē) *n.* (pl. **-bies**). Porch, anteroom, entrance hall, corridor. ~ *v.* (**-bied, -by·ing**). Influence (member of legislature), get (bill etc.) *through* by personal solicitation; frequent a legislature to solicit members' votes. **lob´by·ism, lob´by·ist** *ns.*

lobe (lōb) *n.* Roundish and flattish projecting or pendulous part of an organ, often one of two or more such parts divided by fissure, esp. of cerebrum or lung; lower soft pendulous external part of ear. **lobed** (lōbd) *adj.*

lo·bel·ia (lōbēl´ya) *n.* Herbaceous (rarely shrubby) plant of genus *L*~, with blue, scarlet, purple, or white flowers having deeply cleft corolla without spur. [M. de *Lobel* (1538–1616), Flemish botanist and physician to James I]

lob·lol·ly (lŏb´lŏlē) *n.* (pl. **-lies**). (also ~ **pine**) Tree (*Pinus taeda*) growing in swamps in southern U.S.

lo·bot·o·my (lōbŏt´omē) *n.* (pl. **-mies**). (surg.) Cutting a lobe of the brain, esp. in treatment of mental disorders.

lob·scouse (lŏb´skows) *n.* (naut.) Dish of meat stewed with vegetables and ship's biscuit.

lob·ster (lŏb´ster) *n.* (pl. **-sters**, collect. **-ster**). Large marine crustacean of family Homaridae, a decapod having a pair of heavy pincerlike claws and stalked eyes, which is eaten as a delicacy and turns from bluish black to bright red when boiled; its flesh as food; ~-**eyed**, with protruding eyes; ~ **pot**, basket in which lobsters are trapped.

The 200–300 species of lobelia are native to tropical and sub-tropical areas. Many have been grown for their flowers including the trailing variety (above).

lob·ule (lŏb´ūl) *n.* Small lobe. **lob·u·lar** (lŏb´ūler) *adj.*

lob·worm (lŏb´werm) *n.* Large earthworm used as fishing bait; lugworm.

lo·cal (lō´kal) *adj.* 1. Of, concerned with, place; in regard to place. 2. Belonging to, existing in, or peculiar to, certain place(s); ~ **authority**, body charged with administration of local government; ~ **color**, details characteristic of the scene or time represented in novel or other literary work, inserted to give actuality; the peculiar nature or flavor of a place; ~ **government**, system of administration of local affairs by local authorities; ~ **option**, system by which inhabitants of district may prohibit sale of liquor in it. 3. Affecting, of, a part and not the whole (~ **anesthetic, pain, remedy**); ~ **color**, (in picture) that natural to particular objects as distinct from that seen by painter or chosen for sake of color scheme (see also sense 2 above). 4. (math.) Of a locus. 5. ~ **call**, telephone call to nearby place, charged at local rate. **lo´cal·ly** *adv.* **local** *n.* 1. Person living or working in a particular district. 2. Local train or bus. 3. Local or regional branch of trade union etc.

lo·cale (lōkăl´, -kahl´) *n.* Scene or locality of operations or events.

lo·cal·ism (lō´kalĭzem) *n.* Attachment to a place; limitation of ideas etc., resulting; favoring of what is local; local idiom, custom, etc.

lo·cal·i·ty (lōkăl´ĭtē) *n.* (pl. **-ties**). Position of something, place

where it is, site or scene of something.

lo·cal·ize (lō´kalīz) *v.t.* (**-ized -iz·ing**). Invest with characteristics or particular place; restrict to particular place; attach to districts, decentralize; concentrate (attention) *upon*. **lo´cal·iz·a·ble** *adj* **lo·cal·i·za·tion** (lōkalĭzā´shon) *n.*

Lo·car·no (lōkār´nō). Town at N. end of Lake Maggiore, Switzerland; **Pact (Treaty) of** ~, series of agreements drawn up at Locarno 1925, for peace and arbitration and signed by representatives of Germany, France, Belgium, Great Britain, Italy, Poland, and Czechoslovakia.

lo·cate (lō´kāt, lōkāt´) *v.* (**-cat·ed, -cat·ing**). Establish in a place; (pass.) be situated; state locality of, discover exact place of; take up residence, settle. **lo·ca´tion** *n.* (esp cinemat.) Place, other than studio, chosen for photographing scene of film.

loc. cit. (lŏk´sĭt´) *abbrev.* *Loco citato* (L., = in the passage already quoted).

loch (lŏk, lŏχ) *n.* Scottish lake or narrow or landlocked arm of the sea.

Loch (lŏk, lŏχ) **Ness monster.** Large underwater creature (nicknamed Nessie) alleged to exist in Loch NESS.

lock[1] (lŏk) *n.* Single hair; group of hairs, of head or beard; tuft of wool or cotton; (pl.) hair of head.

lock[2] (lŏk) *n.* 1. Appliance for fastening door, lid, etc., with bolt that requires key of particular shape to work it; appliance to keep wheel from revolving or slewing; mechanism for exploding charge of gun; **under** ~ **and key**, locked up; ~, **stock, and barrel**, whole of thing; completely. 2. Portion of canal or river shut off by folding gates provided with sluices to let the water in and out and thus raise or lower boats from one level to another; (also **air** ~) antechamber to chamber in which engineering work is done in compressed air; similar intermediate chamber. 3. ~ **keeper**, keeper of lock on canal or river; ~ **nut**, extra nut screwed over another to prevent its becoming slack; **lock´smith**, maker and mender of locks; **lock stitch**, sewing or knitting machine stitch by which two threads or stitches are firmly locked together. **lock** *v.* 1. Fasten with lock, shut *up* by fastening doors etc. with lock and key; admit of being so fastened; shut *up, in, into*; (of land, hills, etc.) hem in (usu. pass.); (fig.) store *up, away*, inaccessibly; imprison; keep *out* by locking door (esp. of employer coercing workmen by refusing them work). 2. Come or bring into rigidly fixed position; engage (make) catch, fasten by interlacing

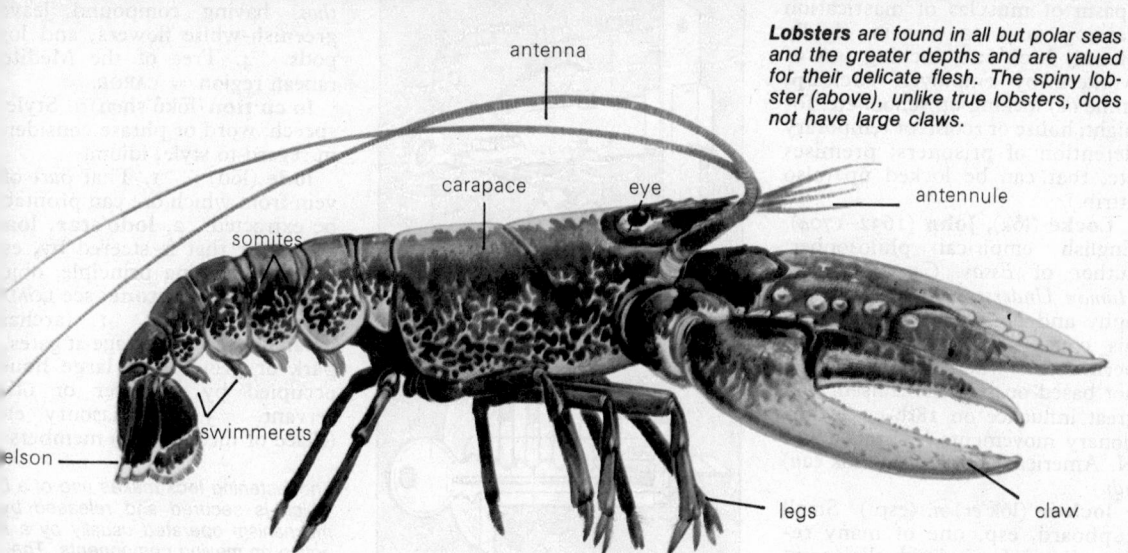

Lobsters are found in all but polar seas and the greater depths and are valued for their delicate flesh. The spiny lobster (above), unlike true lobsters, does not have large claws.

antenna

carapace

eye

antennule

somites

swimmerets

nelson

legs

claw

*This canal **lock,** by controlling the level of the water, provides access from one level reach of navigable water to another. The mitred canal gate, angled into the downward force of the stream, may be Leonardo's invention.*

or fitting of corresponding parts; entangle, (past part.) joined in hostile or other embrace; (mil., of rear rank) march so close to front rank that feet overlap. 3. Provide canal with locks; convey (boat) *up, down,* through lock; go through lock. 4. **lock'jaw** (pop. name for) trismus, a variety of tetanus, tonic spasm of muscles of mastication causing jaws to remain rigidly closed; **lock'out,** locking out of workers by employer; **lock'up,** (time of) locking up school etc. for night; house or room for temporary detention of prisoners; premises etc. that can be locked up (also attrib.).

Locke (lŏk), **John** (1632–1704). English empirical philosopher; author of *Essay Concerning the Human Understanding;* his philosophy and political thinking, esp. his contention that rebellion is permissible when government is not based on popular consent had great influence on 18th-c. revolutionary movements in France and N. America. **Lock·e·an** (lŏk'ēan) *adj.*

lock·er (lŏk'er) *n.* (esp.) Small cupboard, esp. one of many reserved each for individual's use in public room; (naut.) chest or com-

partment for clothes, stores, ammunition, etc.

lock·et (lŏk'ĭt) *n.* Metal plate or band on scabbard; small esp. gold or silver case holding portrait, lock of hair, etc., and usu. hung from neck.

lo·co (lō'kō) *n.* (pl. **-cos**). Locoweed. ~ *adj.* (slang) Insane. [Span., = "insane"]

lo·co·mo·tion (lōkomō'shon) *n.* (Power of) motion from place to place; travel, means (esp. artificial)

RIM LOCK

tumbler spring
bolt
wards on wards bit key
keyhole on key

CYLINDER LOCK

key
cylinder pin spring

of traveling.

lo·co·mo·tive (lōkomō'tĭv) *ac* Of locomotion, (joc.) of trave having power of or given to locomotion, not stationary; effecting loc motion. ~ *n.* Self-propelle vehicle; (esp.) railroad engine.

lo·co·weed (lō'kōwēd) *n.* Leg minous plant of western and south western U.S., causing brai affecting disease in cattle.

loc·ule (lŏk'ūl) = LOCULUS.

loc·u·lus (lŏk'yulus) *n.* (pl. pr. -lī). (anat., bot., zool.) One a number of small separate ca ties.

lo·cum (lō'kum) *n.* (colloc Locum tenens.

lo·cum te·nens (lō'kum tē'něn tĕn'ĭnz) (pl. **lo·cum te·nen·tes** tĕněn'tēz). Deputy acting esp. f clergyman or doctor. **lo·cum-te nen·cy** (lōkum tē'nensē, tĕn'en— [L., "holding place"]

lo·cus (lō'kus) *n.* (pl. **-ci** pr. **-ca** pr. -ka). Locality or exa place of something; (math.) cur etc. made by all points satisfyi particular equation of relation b tween coordinates, or by point, li or surface, moving according mathematically defined conditior ~ **classicus,** best-known or m authoritative passage on a subjec

lo·cust (lō'kust) *n.* 1. Any various kinds of short-horn grasshoppers that migrate swarms and consume vegetation whole areas. 2. **17-year** ~: SEVENTEEN. 3. Any of various tre esp. the eastern N. Amer. **black** (*Robinia pseudoacacia*), havi compound leaves, clusters of wh flowers, and hard, durable woo and **honey** ~ (*Gleditsia triaca thos*) having compound leave greenish-white flowers, and lo pods. 4. Tree of the Medite ranean region = CAROB.

lo·cu·tion (lōkū'shon) *n.* Style speech; word or phrase consider in regard to style, idiom.

lode (lōd) *n.* 1. That part of vein from which ore can profitab be extracted. 2. **lode'star, loa star,** star that is steered by, es polestar; guiding principle, obje of pursuit; **lode'stone:** see LOAD

lodge[1] (lŏj) *n.* 1. (archai Small house. 2. Cottage at gates park or grounds of large hous occupied by gardener or oth servant. 3. (freemasonry et (Place of meeting for) members

*The fastening **lock** makes use of a l which is secured and released by mechanism operated usually by a l acting on moving components. The and cylinder locks are examples.*

Locusts (above and right) are short-horned grasshoppers that often increase greatly in number and migrate long distances in destructive swarms. Once developed, a locust plague is almost impossible to control although destroying egg masses and dusting and spraying are carried out.

branch. 4. Beaver's or otter's lair. 5. N. Amer. Indian's tent or wigwam.

lodge² (lŏj) *v.* (**lodged, lodging**). 1. Provide with sleeping quarters; receive as guest or inmate; establish as resident *in* house or room(s), (pass.) be *well*, *ill*, etc., accommodated in regard to housing. 2. Serve as habitation for, contain, (pass.) be contained *in*. 3. Leave *in* place or *with* person for security. 4. Deposit in court or with official a formal statement of (complaint, information); (pop.) allege (objection etc.). 5. Place (power etc.) *in*, *with*, etc. 6. (Make, let) stick or remain in place without falling or going farther. 7. Reside, be situated; be inmate paying for accommodation, in another's house, hence **lodg'er** *n.*

lodg·ing (lŏj'ĭng) *n.* (esp.) Accommodation in hired rooms; dwelling place, abode, (pl.) room(s) hired elsewhere than in hotel for residing in; ~ **house**, house in which lodgings are let.

lodg·ment (lŏj'ment) *n.* Firm position gained, foothold; accumulation of matter intercepted in fall or transit; (mil.) temporary defensive work on captured part of enemy's works; (law) deposit(ing) of money.

lo·ess (lō'ĕs, lĕs, lŭs) *n.* Light-colored fine-grained deposit formed by windblown dust, very fertile when irrigated, found esp. in Mississippi basin, Rhine valley, an N. China.

loft (lawft, lŏft) *n.* Attic; roo over stable; pigeon house, flock c pigeons; gallery in church or hal upper floor; lofting stroke; back ward slope on face of golf club ~ *v.t.* Hit, throw, etc., (ball) int air over obstacle, etc.; kee (pigeons) in loft.

loft·y (lawf'tē, lŏf'-) *adj.* (**loft· i·er, loft·i·est**). Of imposin height; haughty, exalted, sublime **loft'i·ly** *adv.* **loft'i·ness** *n.*

log¹ (lawg, lŏg) *n.* 1. Unhew piece of felled tree or similar roug mass of wood. 2. Apparatus fo gauging speed of ship; also **log'-book**) book in which all particulars of a ship's or aircraft's voyages are entered. 3. ~ **cabin**, cabin built of logs; **log'jam**, crowded mass of logs in river, (fig.) deadlock; **log'rolling**, (f. phrase **roll my log and I'll roll yours**) mutual help, esp. unprincipled combination in politics; **log'wood**, wood of Amer. tree (*Haemotoxylon campechianum*) used in dyeing. **log** *v.t.* (**logged, log·ging**). Cut into logs; enter in logbook, (of ship or aircraft) make, travel for, (distance or time); enter (seaman's name, with offense committed) in logbook, fine (offender).

log² (lawg, lŏg) *n.* = LOGARITHM (prefixed to number or algebraic symbol).

lo·gan·ber·ry (lō'ganbĕrē) *n.* (pl. **-ries**). Hybrid of raspberry and American blackberry. [raised by Judge *Logan* in California, 1883]

log·a·rithm (law'gerĭdhem, lŏg'e-) *n.* One of a class of arithmetical functions tabulated for simplifying computation; the sum of the logarithms of any numbers is the logarithm of their product; thus, a table of logarithms enables one to substitute addition and subtraction for multiplication and division. **log·a·rith'mic, log·a·rith'mi·cal** *adjs.* **log·a·rith'mi·cal·ly** *adv.*

loge (lōzh) *n.* Box in a theater etc.; front section of balcony in some theaters.

log·ger·head (law'gerhĕd, lŏg'er-) *n.* 1. (archaic) Blockhead. 2. Iron instrument with ball at end heated for melting pitch etc.; post built into boat for catching turn of rope to. 3. Large-headed species of turtle (*Caretta caretta*). 4. **at ~ s** (*with*), disagreeing or disputing (*with*).

log·gia (lŏj'a, law'ja; *It.* lawd'-ah) *n.* (pl. **-gias**; *It.* **-gie** pr. -jĕ). Gallery or arcade having one or more of its sides open to the air; open-sided extension to house etc.

log·ic (lŏj'ĭk) *n.* Science of reasoning; scheme of or treatise on this; chain of reasoning, arguments. **lo·gi·cian** (lōjĭsh'an) *n.*

log·i·cal (lŏj'ĭkal) *adj.* Of logic or formal argument; not contravening the principles of logic, correctly reasoned; following as reasonable inference or natural consequence; capable of correct reasoning; ~ **positivism**, (philos.) form of positivism rejecting transcendental metaphysics and emphasizing the linguistic nature of philosophical problems. **log·i·cal·i·ty** (lŏjĭkăl'-tē), **log·i·cal·ness** *ns.* **log·i·cal·ly** *adv.*

lo·gi·on (lō'gĕŏn, -jē-, lŏg'ē-) *n.* (pl. **lo·gi·a** pr. lō'gēa, -jēa, lŏg'ēa, **lo·gi·ons**). Saying of Christ not recorded in Gospels but preserved

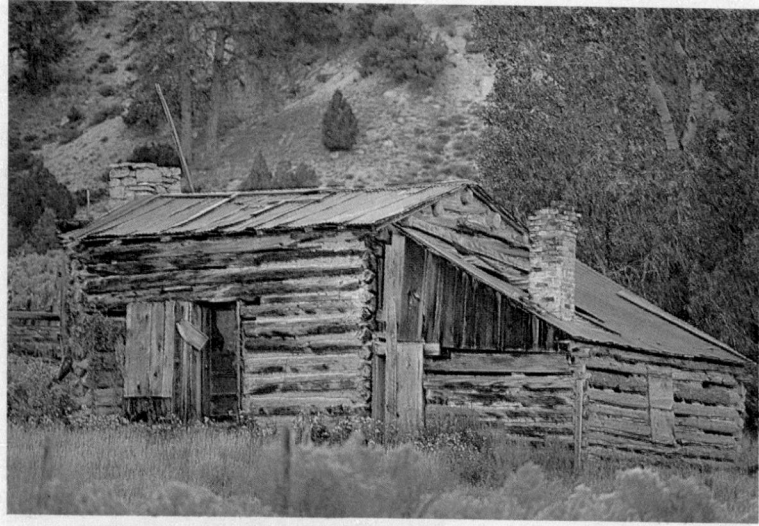

Log cabins have been built and lived in since medieval times. In the U.S.A. they provided shelter for lumberjacks who built them very simply and used local soil and vegetation to seal the joins.

elsewhere.

lo·gis·tics (lōjĭs'tĭks, lo-) *n.* (considered sing. or pl.) Science and practice of moving, lodging, and supplying troops. **lo·gis'tic, lo·gis'ti·cal** *adjs.*

log·jam (lawg'jăm, lŏg') *n.* Immovable mass of floating logs jammed together; (fig.) any similar stoppage, esp. in negotiations or legislation.

log·o·gram (law'gogrăm, lŏg'o-) *n.* Sign or character representing word in shorthand.

lo·gog·ra·pher (lōgŏg'rafer) *n.*

These **logs**, *which have been floated down river to Lake Oyeren in Norway, are sorted for different timber mills. In Norway, where about 25% of the land is forested, pulp and paper are important exports.*

(Gk. antiq.) Writer of traditional history in prose.

log·o·griph (law'gogrĭf, lŏg'o-) *n.* Kind of anagrammatic word puzzle.

lo·gom·a·chy (lōgŏm'akē) *n.* (pl. **-chies**). Dispute about words, controversy turning on merely verbal points.

Lo·gos (lō'gŏs, -gōs, lŏg'ŏs) *n.* (theol.) Word of God, second person of the Trinity.

log·o·type (law'gotīp, lŏg'o-) *n.* (print.) Type containing word, or two or more letters, cast in one piece but not as ligature.

The plain of **Lombardy** in northern Italy is one of Europe's most densely populated areas. Intensive farming (maize, rice and cattle) is carried out on farms like this one.

-logue, -log *suffixes.* Forming nouns denoting talk (*dialogue*) or compilation (*catalog*).

lo·gy (lō'gē) *adj.* (**-gi·er, -gi·est**). Lethargic, sluggish; dull, inert. **lo'gi·ness** *n.*

-logy *suffix.* Forming nouns denoting character of speech or language (*analogy*) or subject of study (*sociology, theology*).

Lo·hen·grin (lō'engrin). (Ger. legend) Son of Parsifal; he was summoned from the temple of the Grail and borne in a swan boat to Antwerp to defend Elsa of Brabant against Frederick of Telramund, who claimed her in marriage; Lohengrin himself married Elsa but was carried away again in the swan boat when she asked his name.

loid (loid) *v.t.* (slang) Open (door) by inserting piece of celluloid, plastic, etc. between the jamb and the edge of the door so as to open a spring lock.

loin (loin) *n.* (pl.) Part of body on both sides of spine between false ribs and hipbones; (sing.) cut of meat including vertebrae of loins; (pl., bibl.) this part of body regarded as part that should be covered by clothing, or as seat of physical strength and generative power; **loin'cloth**, cloth worn about loins.

Loire (lwahr). River rising in S. central France and flowing N. and then W. to the Atlantic.

loi·ter (loi'ter) *v.* Linger on the way, hang about; travel indolently and with frequent pauses; pass (time etc.) *away* in loitering.

loi'ter·er *n.* **loi'ter·ing·ly** *adv.*

loll (lŏl) *v.* Hang (tongue) o (of tongue) hang (*out*); stand, s recline, in lazy attitude; let (hea limbs) rest lazily on something.

Lol·lard (lŏl'erd) *n.* One of t English 14th-c. heretics who we followers of Wycliffe or he opinions similar to his on t necessity for the church to a men to live a life of evangelic poverty and imitate Christ. **Lo lard·ism, Lol'lard·y, Lol'lard** *ns.*

lol·li·pop, lol·ly·pop (lŏl'ēpŏ *ns.* Piece of hard candy on a sm stick.

Lom·bard (lŏm'berd, -bãr lŭm'-) *adj. & n.* (Member) of Germanic people from the low Elbe who invaded Italy in 568 A and founded a kingdom (ove thrown by Charlemagne, 774) the valley of the Po. **Lom·bar'd** *adj.*

Lom·bar·dy (lŏm'berdē, lŭm' Region of N. Italy, lying rough between the Alps and the river F ~ **poplar**, tall columnar variety the black poplar (*Populus nig italica*).

Lo·mé (lōmā'). Capital and port of Togo, on the Gulf Guinea.

lo·ment (lō'měnt) *n.* (bo Legume that is contracted in spac between seeds, breaking up wh mature into one-seeded join **lo·men·ta·ceous** (lōmentā'sh *adj.*

Lo·mond (lō'mond), **Loc** Largest lake in Scotland (about miles long and 5 miles wide), of the Clyde.

Lon·don (lŭn'don). Capital England and of the United Kin dom, a port on the Thames Riv comprising the ancient CITY London, the city of WESTMINST the royal borough of Kensingt and Chelsea, and numerous oth boroughs; ~ **Bridge**, bridge acro Thames about ½ mile above t **Tower of** ~, ancient fortress a prison. **Lon'don·er** *n.* Nati inhabitant, of London.

Lon·don (lŭn'don, Jack (187 1916). American writer a adventurer; wrote *The Call of Wild, The Sea Wolf,* etc.

lone (lōn) *adj.* Solitary, co panionless, single (poet. or rhe ~ **wolf**, person who chooses act or live etc. alone.

lone·ly (lōn'lē) *adj.* (**-li -li·est**). Solitary, companionle isolated; unfrequented. **lone'l ness** *n.*

lone·some (lōn'som) *a* Lonely. **lone'some·ly** *adv.* **lone**

me·ness *n.*

long[1] (lawng, lŏng) *adj.* Measur-
g much from end to end in space
time; (colloq.) tall; far-reaching,
ting at a distance, involving great
terval or difference; in length; of
ongated shape; remarkable for,
stinguished by, concerned with,
ngth or duration; prolix, tedious;
sting, going far back or forward;
honet., pros., of vowel or syllable)
ving the greater of the two
cognized durations; **long'boat**,
ist.) sailing ship's largest boat;
ng'bow, (esp. medieval) bow
awn by hand (as dist. from
ossbow) and discharging long
athered arrow; **long chance**, one
volving much risk; **long dis-
nce**, telephone service between
stant places; **long-distance** (*adj.*
adv.); **long face**, dismal counte-
nce; **long'hair**, (colloq.) (some-
mes **long-haired**) person with
tellectual tastes, esp. in art,
usic, literature; **long'hand**,
dinary writing (opp. SHORThand);
ng-headed, (esp.) sagacious;
ng horn, long-horned ox or cow;
ng-horned grasshopper**, or-
opterous jumping insect with
ry long antennae; **long johns**,
lang) winter underwear covering
tire body except for head, hands,

and feet; **long jump**, jump (as
athletic competition) measured
along ground; **long-lived** (pr.
-līvd), having a long life, durable;
long measure, lineal measure,
measure of length; **long on**,
(colloq.) well supplied with (attribute, money, etc.); **Long Parliament**, English Parliament that sat
from Nov. 1640 to March 1653, was
restored in 1659, and finally dissolved in 1660; **long pig**, sailors'
translation of cannibals' name for
human flesh; **long-playing**, (of
microgroove phonograph record)
playing for about 10 to 30 minutes
a side, esp. one turning at 33⅓
revolutions per minute; **long-
range**, (of gun or projectile) firing
a long distance; (of forecast, plan,
etc.) applying to the more distant
future; **in the long run**, in the end,
ultimately; **long'shore**, found or
employed on the shore; **long'-
shoreman** (pl. **-men**), man employed in loading ships, shore fishing, etc.; **long shot**, bet at long
odds; (cinemat.) shot that includes

*This aerial view of **London** shows the
City, one of the world's leading banking
and financial centers, surrounding the
great dome of St. Paul's Cathedral, built
by Sir Christopher Wren from 1675 to
1710.*

figures or scenery at a distance;
long suit, (cards) suit in which
more than three cards are held;
(fig.) one's strong point; **longterm**, (of plan, policy, etc.)
designed to meet the circumstances
of a long time ahead; **long wave**,
radio wave of more than 800 meters;
long-winded, talking or writing at
tedious length. **long'ish** *adj.* **long'-
ways**, **long'wise** *advs.* **long** *n.*
(usu. colloq.) Long interval or
period; long syllable; **the ~ and
the short of it**, all that need be
said.

long[2] (lawng, lŏng) *adv.* For a
long time; by a long time; throughout specified time; **as** or **so ~ as**,
provided that, if only; (comp.
longer, with **no, any**, etc.) after
implied point of time; **~ ago**,
(belonging to) the distant past;
~-drawn (-out), unduly prolonged; **long'standing**, that has
long existed; **long-suffering**,
(state of) bearing provocation
patiently.

long[3] (lawng, lŏng) *v.i.* Yearn,
wish vehemently (*for, to*). **long'-
ing** *n. & adj.* **long'ing·ly** *adv.*

long. *abbrev.* Longitude.

Long (lawng), **Huey (Pierce)**
(1893–1935). American politician,
called "Kingfish," noted for his

The **loom** is among the most ancient of devices and was in use in 5400 B.C. according to evidence found in tombs. Handlooms are still used for weaving in many countries, and modern high-speed industrial looms work on the same basic principles.

folksy manner while the flamboyant, demagogic, domineering governor of Louisiana, 1928–31, and U.S. senator, 1931–5; known for his "share-the-wealth" public works and public welfare programs and his "every man a king" slogan; assassinated, 1935.

longe: see LUNGE.[1]

lon·ge·ron (lŏn′jeron) n. (usu. in pl.) Longitudinal member of airplane fuselage.

Long·fel·low (lawng′fĕlō, lŏng′-), **Henry Wadsworth** (1807–82). American poet, author of "Hyperion," "Hiawatha," "The Wreck of the Hesperus," "Evangeline," "The Village Blacksmith," "The Children's Hour," etc.

lon·gi·corn (lŏn′jĭkōrn) n. Beetle of the family Cerambycidae with very long antennae.

Lon·gi·nus (lŏnjī′nus). Traditional name of the Roman soldier who pierced with his spear the side of Jesus Christ at the Crucifixion.

Long (lawng, lŏng) **Island.** Island of New York State, adjacent to and including sections of New York City on its W. end; separated from mainland of Connecticut by **Long Island Sound**, an arm of the Atlantic Ocean.

lon·gi·tude (lŏn′jĭtōod, -tūd) n. (geog.) Angular distance along equator E. or W. from standard meridian, as that of Greenwich, to meridian of any place; (astron.) angular distance eastward on ecliptic from vernal equinoctial point to great circle through body or point perpendicular to ecliptic.

lon·gi·tu·di·nal (lŏnjĭtōo′dinal, -tū′-) adj. Of or in length; running lengthwise; of longitude. **lon·gi·tu′di·nal·ly** adv.

loo[1] (lōo) n. (pl. **loos**). (archaic) Round card game, played with three or five cards, with penalties paid to the pool; (having to pay) such penalty.

loo[2] (lōo) n. (Brit. colloq.) Lavatory.

loo·fa, loo·fah (lōo′fa) ns. Fibrous pod of plant (*Luffa aegyptiaca*) used as flesh brush. [Arab. *lufah* (name of the plant)]

look (lŏok) v. 1. Use one's sight; turn eyes in some direction, direct eyes *at*; stare, show surprise; contemplate, examine; express, threaten, show, by one's looks; ascertain or observe by sight; (fig.) make mental search, inquire, aim one's attention *at* and consider; take care or make sure *that*, expect *to* do; **to ~ at**, judging by the looks of; **will not ~ at**, refuses to take,

heddle shafts with heddles
reed
cloth beam
warp beam release
warp beam
cords connecting treadles and lams
treadles
breastbeam
batten

rejects, scorns; **~ here!**, (imper.) formula for demanding attention or expostulating; **~ sharp**, orig., keep strict watch; now, lose no time, bestir oneself. 2. (of things) Face, be turned, have or afford outlook, in some direction; tend, point; have certain appearance, seem; seem to be; **~ alive**, make haste; **~ as if**, suggest by appearance the belief that; **~ like**, seem to be, threaten or promise. 3. (with preps.) **~ about one**, examine one's surroundings, take time to

*The **looper** caterpillar, so called for its movement — arching into loops as it proceeds, is the geometrid moth before its transformation to the chrysalis stage.*

...orm plans; ~ **after**, follow with the eye; seek for; attend to, take care of; ~ **for**, expect, hope or be on the watch for; search for; ~ **into**, examine the inside of; dip into (book); investigate; ~ **on**, regard *as*, regard *with* some feeling; ~ **over**, inspect; ~ **through**, penetrate with a look; glance through (book etc.); ~ **to**, consider, take care of, be careful about; keep watch over; rely on *for*; expect, count upon; aim at. 4. (with advs.) ~ **down on**, consider oneself superior to; ~ **forward to**, anticipate (usu. with pleasure); ~ **in**, make short visit or call; ~ **on**, be (mere) spectator; ~ **out**, direct eyes or put head out of window etc.; be vigilant; keep one's eyes open *for*, be prepared *for*; have or afford outlook *on*, *over*, etc.; ~ **over**, inspect; ~ **through**, survey with searching glance; inspect exhaustively or successively; ~ **up**, search for (esp. word in dictionary, fact in book of reference); call on (person); ~ **up to**, respect, venerate. 5. ~-**alike**, person or thing closely resembling another; **look'ing glass**, mirror made of glass backed with a film of silver etc.; **look'out**, watch, looking out; post of observation; man, party, etc., stationed to look out; view over landscape; prospect of luck; person's own concern; **look-see**, (slang) look. **look** *n.* Act of looking, direction of eyes, glance; appearance (of things etc.); (sing. or pl.) appearance of face, expression, personal aspect.

look·er (look'*er*) *n.* (slang) Good-looking person; ~-**on**, (colloq.) onlooker, one who looks on without taking part.

Look·out (look'owt) **Mountain**. Mountain ridge in SE. Tennessee; site of a victory by Union troops over the Confederates, 1863, during the Civil War.

loom[1] (loom) *n.* 1. Apparatus for weaving threads into fabric by crossing warp with weft, by means of a device that parts the warp threads so that the shuttle carrying the weft can pass between them. 2. (Inboard part of) shaft or oar.

loom[2] (loom) *v.i.* Appear indistinctly, be seen in vague and often magnified or threatening shape. ~ *n.* Indistinct and exaggerated appearance of object first coming into view, esp. at sea.

loon[1] (loon) *n.* (Sc. and archaic) Scamp; fellow.

loon[2] (loon) *n.* Any of several large fish-eating diving birds of the genus *Gavia* of northern waters; the common loon (*G. immer*) is noted for its weird, laugh-like cry.

loon·y (loo'ne) *adj.* (**loon·i·er**, **loon·i·est**) & *n.* (pl. **loon·ies**). (slang) Lunatic; ~ **bin**, (slang) mental hospital.

loop (loop) *n.* Doubling or return into itself of string, thong, etc., so as to leave an aperture between the parts, portion so doubled; stitch in knitting; ring or curved piece of metal as handle etc.; intrauterine contraceptive device; railroad or telegraph line that diverges from main line and joins it again; circuit in roller coaster etc. along top of which passenger travels

Long Island, which is 118 miles long and 12–20 miles wide, serves the city of New York as a dormitory suburb, market garden and beach resort. The boroughs of Brooklyn and Queens are on its western end.

head downward, similar path described by airplane; (skating) curve crossing itself made on single edge; **the L~**, the downtown business district of Chicago. **loop** *v.* Form into loop(s); enclose (as) with loop; fasten (*up*, *back*) or join (*together*) with loops; ~-**the-**~, (of aircraft) describe loop in air.

loop·er (loo'per) *n.* 1. Caterpillar of geometrid moth, progressing by arching itself into loops. 2. Contrivance in sewing machine etc. for making loops.

loop·hole (loop'hol) *n.* Narrow vertical slit in wall for shooting or looking through, or to admit light or air; outlet, means of evading rule, etc.

loose (loos) *adj.* (**loos·er**, **loos·est**). 1. Released from bonds or restraint; detached or detachable from its place; uncombined, as a chemical element; hanging partly free; not rigidly fixed, apt to shift; slack, relaxed, not tense or tight; not compact, dense, or serried; (of bowels) relaxed; **at ~ ends**, without definite occupation; **with a ~ rein**, (fig.) indulgently; **~ change**, money kept or left unsecured for casual use; **~-leaf**, (of ledger etc.) with each leaf separate and detachable; **~ tongue**, one given to blabbing. 2. (of statements, ideas, etc.) Not exact; (of translation) not close or faithful; (of style) ungrammatical. 3. Morally lax; sexually promiscuous. **loose′ly** *adv.* **loose′ness** *n.* **loose** *v.t.* (**loosed, loos·ing**). Release, set free, free from constraint; untie, undo; detach from moorings; relax (hold).

loos·en (lōō′sen) *v.* Make or become less tight or compact or firm; loose (person's tongue); relieve (bowels) from constipation or (cough) from dryness; relax (discipline etc.).

loose·strife (lōō′strīf) *n.* 1. Marsh plant of genus *Lysimachia*, esp. *L. vulgaris*, with golden-yellow flowers. 2. Marsh plant of genus *Lythrum*, esp. *L. salicaria* with purple-red flowers.

loot (lōōt) *n.* Goods taken from enemy, spoil, booty; illicit gains. **~** *v.* Plunder, sack; carry off as booty. **loot′er** *n.*

lop[1] (lŏp) *n.* Small branches and twigs of trees. **~** *v.* (**lopped, lop·ping**). Cut off branches and twigs of (tree); strip tree of (branches etc.); cut off (person's limb or head); make cutting strokes at.

lop[2] (lŏp) *v.* (**lopped, lop·ping**). Hang limply; **~ ear**, kind of rabbit with lop ears; **~ ears**, drooping ears; **lop′sided(ly)**, with one side lower or smaller than the other; unevenly balanced; **lop′sidedness** (*n.*).

lope (lōp) *v.i.* (**loped, lop·ing**) & *n.* (Run with) long bounding stride (esp. of animals).

Lo·pe de Ve·ga (lō′pā de vā′ga; *Sp.* law′pě dhē vě′gah) = VEGA[2].

loq. *abbrev.* *Loquitur* (L., = "speaks," with speaker's name added as stage direction or notice to reader).

lo·qua·cious (lōkwā′shus) *adj.* Talkative; chattering, babbling. **lo·qua′cious·ly** *adv.* **lo·qua′cious·ness** *n.* **lo·quac·i·ty** (lōkwăs′ĭtē) *n.* (pl. **-ties**).

lo·quat (lō′kwŏt, -kwăt) *n.* (Small reddish fruit of) Chinese and Japanese tree, *Eriobotrya japonica*, introduced into S. Europe, California, Australia, etc. [Chin. *luh kwat* rush orange]

lor·an (lōr′an, lôr′-) *n.* Long-range navigational system enabling a navigator to determine his posi-

tion by analyzing time intervals between radio signals from two known positions. [*lo*(ng) *ra*(nge) *n*(avigation)]

Lor·ca (lōr′ka; *Sp.* lôr′kah). **Federico Garcia**: see GARCIA LORCA.

lord (lōrd) *n.* 1. Master, ruler, chief, feudal superior (hist.); magnate in some trade; (poet.) owner; (poet. or joc.) husband; (astrol.) dominant planet; **~s of creation**, mankind. 2. **L~**, God; (usu. **the** or **our L~**) Christ; **in the year of**

The richly decorated chamber of the House of Lords in the Houses of Parliament, U.K. The Palace of Westminster was completely burnt down in 1834 and the new building begun in the Gothic style in 1840.

our L~, Anno Domini; **L~'s Day**, Sunday; **L~'s Prayer** prayer taught by Christ to his disciples (Matt. 6); **L~'s Supper** (Brit.) Holy Communion. 3. Nobleman, peer of the realm or person entitled by courtesy to prefix **Lord** as part of his ordinary style; member (whether peer or not) of board performing duties of high state office put in commission forming part of many official titles as **L~ Chamberlain**, **L~ Chan**

Yellow Loosestrife grows in England and eastern North America and is a member of the Lythraceae family. It is usually found growing on riverbanks.

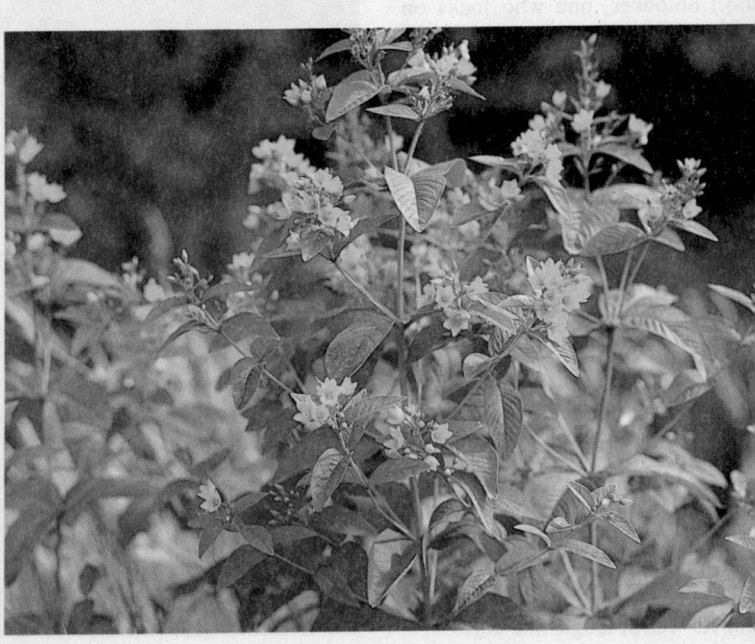

ellor, etc.; **House of Lords**, (also **the Lords**) temporal and spiritual peers of Parliament, forming upper legislative chamber of United Kingdom; building where these meet; committee of specially quali- ied members of this appointed as ultimate judicial court of appeal; **Sea L~**, naval member of Admiralty Board; **~-in-waiting**, ord attending sovereign; **L~ Mayor**, mayor of London, York, and other cities. 4. **L~**, prefixed title, part of customary appellation of marquis, earl, viscount, or baron; followed by Christian (and family) name of younger son of duke or marquis. **lord** v. Play the lord *over*.

lord·ly (lôrd′lē) adj. (**-li·er, -li·est**). Haughty, imperious, lofty, disdainful; grand, magnificent, fit for or belonging to a lord; **lord′- li·ness** n.

lor·do·sis (lôrdō′sĭs) n. (path.) Anterior curvature of spine, pro- ducing convexity in front.

lord·ship (lôrd′shĭp) n. Domin- ion, rule, ownership *of* or *over*, domain, estate, manor; personality of lord.

lore[1] (lōr, lôr) n. Doctrine (archaic); erudition, scholarship (archaic); body of traditions or knowledge relating to some sub- ject.

lore[2] (lōr, lôr) n. (zool.) Space between bird's eye and upper mandible, or between reptile's eye and nostril.

lo·re·al (lôr′ēal, lōr′-) adj. (zool.) Of the LORE[2].

Lor·e·lei (lôr′elī; Ger. lō′relī). Rock or cliff on Rhine River; in German legend, the home of a siren whose song lured sailors to destruc- tion.

lor·gnette (lôrnyĕt′) n. Pair of eyeglasses or opera glasses held in hand, usu. by long handle.

lor·i·cate (lôr′ĭkāt, lār′-, -kĭt)

There are about 60 species of lorikeet. These small, brightly colored parrots are found mostly in south-east Asia and particularly in New Guinea where there are large flocks.

adj. & n. (zool.) (Animal) having defensive armor of bone, plates, scales, etc.

lor·i·keet (lôr′ĭkēt, lār′-, lōrĭkēt′, lār-) n. Any of various small brightly-colored parrots (**rainbow ~, musk ~**, etc.) of Australia etc. [LORY + ending of *parakeet*]

lo·ris (lôr′ĭs, lōr′-) n. (pl. **-ris**). Any of several tailless or stump- tailed nocturnal arboreal primates found in Africa and tropical Asia, related to the lemurs, and including **slender ~** (*Loris tardigradus*), **slow ~** (*Nycticebus coucang*), and potto.

lorn (lôrn) adj. (poet. and joc.) Desolate, forlorn.

Lor·raine (lorān′; *Fr.* lawrĕn′). Medieval kingdom on W. bank of Rhine, extending from North Sea to Italy, and divided into two duchies; Upper Lorraine passed to France in 1766; part of Lorraine was acquired with Alsace by Ger- many in 1871 but was restored to France after World War I; **Cross of ~**, cross having two transoms.

[med. *L. Lotharingia*, f. *Lothair*, name of king]

lor·ry (lŏr′ē, lăr′ē) *n.* (pl. **-ries**). Long low flat sideless wagon; (Brit.) motor truck; truck running on rails.

lo·ry (lōr′ē, lōr′ē) *n.* Any of various bright-plumaged parrots of SE. Asia and New Guinea.

Los Al·a·mos (laws ăl′amōs, lŏs). Town in N. New Mexico; site of the research center that produced the first atomic bomb.

Los An·ge·les (laws ăn′jeles, -lēz, lŏs; sometimes ăng′geles, -lēz). City on coast of S. California with a suburb, Hollywood, which is the center of the American motion-picture industry.

lose (lōoz) *v.* (**lost** pr. lawst, lŏst, **los·ing**). I. Be deprived of, cease, by negligence, misadventure, separation, death, etc., to possess or have; suffer loss or detriment, incur disadvantage, be the worse off in money or otherwise *by* transaction etc.; become unable to find, fail to keep in sight or follow or mentally grasp; spend (time, oppor-

slow loris

tunities, pains) to no purpose, waste; fail to obtain, catch, see, or hear; forfeit (stake), be defeated in (game, battle, lawsuit, etc.); fail to carry (motion); cause person the loss of, cost; ~ **interest**, cease to be interested; cease to interest; ~ **one's life**, be killed; ~ **patience, one's temper**, become impatient, angry; **losing game**, one in which defeat seems inevitable. 2. (pass.) Disappear, perish, die or be dead; (refl. and pass.) go astray; become merged or engrossed (*in*); be obscured in. **los′a·ble** *adj.* **los′er** *n.*

loss (laws, lŏs) *n.* Losing or being lost; person, thing, or amount lost; detriment, disadvantage, resulting from loss; **at a ~**, at less than cost; puzzled; ~ **leader**, (commerc.) article of trade sold at low price to attract customers to buy other things.

lost (lawst, lŏst) *adj.* see LOSE; (esp.) ~ **cause**, one with no hope of success; **L~ Generation**, generation reaching maturity during and after World War I,

lacking cultural and emotion[al] stability; ~ **soul**, damned sou[l]; **L~ Tribes**, ten tribes of Israe[l] taken away c722 B.C. by Sargo[n] II to captivity in Assyria ([2] Kings 17), from which they ar[e] believed never to have returned.

Lot (lŏt). Son of Abraham['s] brother Haran and legendary an[·]cestor of the Ammonites an[d] Moabites; his wife, fleeing with hi[m] from the destruction of Sodom an[d] Gomorrah, looked back, and wa[s] turned into a pillar of salt (Gen. 19[).]

lot (lŏt) *n.* I. One of set o[f] objects used to secure a chanc[e] decision in dividing goods, select[·]ing officials, etc. (now only i[n] **draw, cast, ~s**, and **throw i**[n] **one's ~ with**, share fortunes with[)] this method of deciding, choic[e] resulting from it; what falls to person by lot, share; person['s] destiny, fortune, condition. 2. Plo[t] or portion of land belonging to par[·]ticular owner, piece of land set apar[t] for particular purpose; plot or por[·]tion of land offered for sale. 3[.] Article or set of articles offere[d] separately at sale; item at auction. 4[.] Number or quantity of persons o[r] things of same kind or someho[w] associated; (colloq.) considerabl[e] number or amount, a good or grea[t] deal (also in pl., as ~ **s of money**[)] **the ~**, the whole number o[r] quantity. **lot** *v.t.* (**lot·ted, lot·[·] ting**). Divide (land *out*, or good[s] for sale) into lots.

loth = LOATH.

Lo·thar·i·o (lōthăr′ēō). Name o[f] a seducer in Nicholas Rowe's play *The Fair Penitent*; hence, [a] libertine, deceiver, rake.

Lo·thi·ans (lō′dhēanz, -thē-)[,] **The.** Region of E. Scotland comprising the city of Edinburg[h] and the former counties of Eas[t] Lothian, West Lothian, and most o[f] Midlothian; (hist.) all the E. part o[f] the Scottish Lowlands.

Lo·ti (lawtē′), **Pierre** (1850[-] 1923). Pen name of Louis Mari[e] Julien Viaud, French naval office[r] and romantic novelist.

lo·tion (lō′shon) *n.* Liquid prep[·] aration used externally for healin[g] wounds, beautifying skin, etc.

lot·ter·y (lŏt′erē) *n.* (pl. **-ter·[·] ies**). Arrangement for distributin[g] prizes by chance among holders o[f] tickets; (fig.) thing that defies cal[·]culation.

lot·to (lŏt′ō) *n.* Game of chanc[e] played with boards or cards divide[d] into numbered sections, which ar[e] covered as numbers are drawn, th[e] winning player being the one wh[o]

slender loris

*The **loris**, an Indo-Malay primate, i[s] found in forested regions. The slende[r] loris is found in India and Sri Lanka. Th[e] slow loris is more robust but slower moving. Both feed on insects and sma[ll] animals.*

first covers a row of numbers. Cf. BINGO.

lo·tus, lo·tos (lō'tus) *ns.* (pl. **-tus·es, -tos·es**). 1. Plant represented in ancient Greek legend as inducing luxurious dreaminess and distaste for active life; ∼ **eater**, person given to indolent enjoyment, sybarite. 2. Water lily of Egypt and Asia, species of *Nymphaea* and *Nelumbium*; (archit.) ornament representing Egyptian water lily; ∼ **position**, cross-legged position of meditation.

loud (lowd) *adj.* Strongly audible, sonorous; clamorous, noisy; (of color etc.) obtrusive, flashy; **loud'mouthed**, given to loud, bragging or indiscreet talk; **loud'speaker**, instrument (esp. as part of radio receiving apparatus) for converting electrical impulses into sounds loud enough to be heard at a distance. **loud'ly** *adv.* **loud'ness** *n.* **loud** *adv.*

Lou·is (lōō'ē, lōō'ĭs; *Fr.* lwē). Name of many French kings: **Louis I** (778–840), "the Pious"; third son of Charlemagne; emperor with his father, 813; sole emperor, 814; **Louis II** (846–79), "the Stammerer"; son of Charles the Bald; king of the West Franks 877–9; **Louis III** (*c*863–82), joint king of France with his brother Carloman, 879–82; **Louis IV** (921–54), king of France 936–54; fled to England when his father, Charles III, was imprisoned; **Louis V** (967–87), last Carolingian king of France 986–7; **Louis VI** (1081–1137), "the Fat"; king 1108–37; soldier and popular hero who opposed the English in Normandy; **Louis VII** (*c*1121–1180), king of France 1137–80; proclaimed and led the disastrous second CRUSADE, 1146–9; **Louis VIII** (1187–1226), king of France 1223–6; leader of crusade against the Albigenses; **Louis IX** (1214–1270), St. Louis, king of France 1226–70; went on crusade 1248, was captured 1250 and passed 4 years in Syria; returned to France 1254; sailed for Tunis 1270 on a second crusade, and died there of the plague; canonized 1297; **Louis X** (1287–1316), "the Quarrelsome"; king of France 1314–16; **Louis XI** (1423–83), king of France 1461–1483); ruled as absolute monarch and greatly increased the royal domain; **Louis XII** (1462–1515), king of France 1499–1515; **Louis**

Louis XVI of France, husband of Marie Antoinette, reigned for 18 years. Despite his attempts to accede to the wishes of the Republicans, he and his wife were tried for treason and guillotined in January 1793.

XIII (1601–43), king of France 1610–43; **Louis XIV** (1638–1715), "the Sun King"; king of France 1643–1715; during his minority, power was in the hands of his mother, Anne of Austria, and her minister Mazarin; his own rule was a time of absolute monarchy, wars, and great extravagance at court; **Louis XV** (1710–74), great-grandson and successor of Louis XIV; king of France 1715–74; his reign saw the Seven Years War and the loss to France of India and Canada; **Louis XVI** (1754–93), grandson and successor of Louis XV; king of France from 1774 to 1792, when the Convention of the French Revolution declared royalty abolished; he was guillotined; **Louis XVII** (1785–1795?), titular king of France; second son of Louis XVI; he was reported to have died in prison, but there are many legends of his escape; **Louis XVIII** (1755–1824), younger brother of Louis XVI; fled from France 1791; proclaimed himself king after death of Louis XVII (1795); was restored to the throne after defeat of Napoleon I in 1814.

lou·is d'or (looē dōr´; *Fr.* lwē dōr´) (pl. **lou·is d'or** pr. looēz dōr´; *Fr.* lwē dōr´). French gold coin, first issued by Louis XIII in 1640 and superseded in 1795; gold 20-france piece, napoleon.

Lou·ise (looēz´), **Lake.** Lake in Banff National Park, SW. Alberta, Canada, known for its scenic beauty.

Lou·i·si·an·a (luwēzēăn´a, looīze-looē-). State in southern U.S. with a 397-mile (639 km) coastline on the Gulf of Mexico; capital, Baton Rouge; ~ **Territory**, vast territory extending from the Mississippi River to the Rocky Mountains between the Mexican and Canadian borders; was claimed by France in 1682 and named in honor of Louis XIV, transferred to Spain 1762 and back to France 1800, and finally sold by the French to the U.S. in 1803 for $15,000,000; ~ **Purchase**, territory sold by France to the U.S. in 1803.

Lou·is Phil·ippe (looē; *Fr.* lwē, fēlēp´) (1773–1850). Duke of Orleans, son of Philippe Egalité; spent many years in exile in England and America; was appointed king (called "the Citizen King") of France by the French Chamber after the July revolution of 1830; forced to abdicate in 1848.

Lou·is Qua·torze, Quinze, Seize, (looē; *Fr.* lwē, kătōrz´; kănz; sēz) (of style of furniture,

architecture, etc.) Of the reign of Louis, XIV, XV, XVI, of France.

lounge (lownj) *v.* (**lounged, loung·ing**). Go lazily; loll, recline; idle. ~ *n.* Spell of, place for, lounging; sitting room, esp. in hotel etc.; sofa or deep chair. **loung´er** *n.*

loupe (loop) *n.* Magnifying instrument, esp. for watchmakers, consisting of a system of lenses mounted on a frame.

loup·ing (low´pĭng, lō´-, loo´-) **ill.** Disease of sheep, a form of encephalitis, caused by a virus which occas. attacks other mammals including man.

lour = LOWER².

Lourdes (loord, loordz; *Fr.* loord). Town of SW. France at foot of Pyrenees, site of a shrine and center of pilgrimage where many miraculous cures have been reported (see BERNADETTE).

louse (lows) *n.* (pl. **lice** pr. līs). 1. (zool.) One of various wingless bloodsucking insects of orde Anoplura, parasitic on mammal and Mallophaga, with bitin mouthparts, parasitic on bird esp. the best-known species these (*Pediculus humanus*), whic infests man and is agent in tran mission of many diseases, e.g typhus. 2. (slang, pl. **lous·e** Low contemptible person. **lous** (low´zē) *adj.* (**lous·i·er, lous·i·est** Infested with lice; (slang) disgus ing; (slang) swarming *wit* abundantly supplied *with* mone etc. **lous´i·ness** *n.*

lout (lowt) *n.* Hulking or rough mannered fellow. **lout´ish** *ad* **lout´ish·ly** *adv.* **lout´ish·ness** *n.*

lou·ver (loo´ver) *n.* Dome turretlike erection on mediev hall roof etc., with side openings t let smoke out or air in; (pl arrangement of overlapping board or strips of glass etc. to admit a but exclude light or rain. **lou´ vered** *adj.*

Lou·vre (loo͞ov; *Fr.* loo͞o´vre). Annt palace of the kings of ance, on N. bank of Seine in ris; rebuilt in the reign of Philip I and enlarged by François I and s successors down to Napoleon I; now the principal art museum France.

lov·a·ble, love·a·ble (lŭv´əbel) *js.* Deserving love. **lov´a·ble·ess, love´a·ble·ness** *ns.* **lov´-bly, love´a·bly** *advs.*

lov·age (lŭv´ĭj) *n.* Any of various ants, esp. the S. European mbelliferous herb (*Levisticum ficinale*), grown for use in flavorg etc.

love (lŭv) *n.* 1. Warm affection, tachment, liking, or fondness; ternal benevolence; affectionate votion. 2. Sexual affection, pason, or desire; affection between eethearts, this feeling as literary bject, personified influence, or a d; (**L~**) representation of Cupid of naked winged child symbolizg love; **labor of ~**, task one lights in or does for love of meone; **in ~ (with)**, feeling love or); **fall in ~ (with)**, experience sp. sudden) feelings of love oward); feel strong liking for bject); **make ~**, behave as a ver; engage in sexual intercourse. Beloved one, sweetheart; (colq.) delightful person, pretty oung woman. 4. (tennis) No score, othing, nil; **~ all**, state of game hen neither side has yet scored;

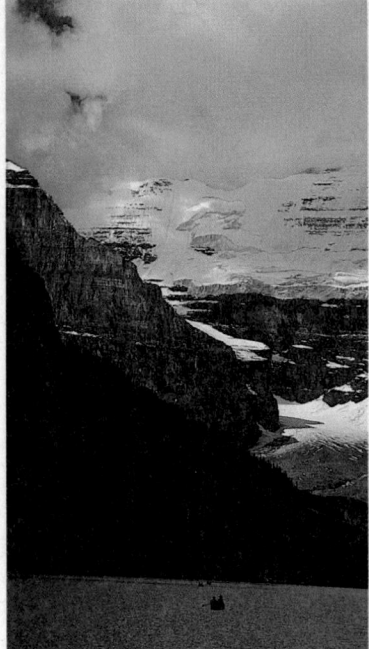

Lake Louise, *situated in the Banff National Park, Alberta, Canada, is renowned for its scenic beauty and draws many visitors each year who also come to explore the mountains.*

~ game, one in which loser has not scored. 5. **~ affair**, temporary relationship between two people who have fallen in love; **~ apple** (old name for) tomato; **love´bird**, one of several species of parakeet,

esp. the W. Afr. *Agapornis pullarius*, remarkable for the affection it shows its mate; **love child**, illegitimate child; **love feast**, meal in token of brotherly love among early Christians; religious service among modern Christian sects; celebration, such as a banquet, held to create good feeling, to honor a special guest, etc.; **love-in-a-mist**, garden plant (*Nigella damascena*), with blue flowers surrounded by green threadlike bracts; S. Amer. passionflower, *Passiflora foetida*, with similar bracts; **love-in-idleness**, wild pansy; **love knot**, intricate knot of ribbon etc. with double bow; **love letter**, letter between sweethearts expressing love; **love-lies-bleeding**, garden plant (*Amaranthus caudatus*), with long drooping spikes of purplish-red bloom; **love´lock**, tress or curl worn on temple or forehead; **love´-lorn**, pining with love, deserted by one's love; **love match**, marriage for the sake of love, not for money or convenience; **love seat**, armchair or sofa for two persons; **love´-sick**, languishing with love; **love song**, song about or expressing love; **love story**, novel etc. of which main theme is love; story of a wooing etc.; **love token**, thing given in sign of love. **love** *v.* (**loved, lov·ing**). Hold dear, bear love for; be in love (with); be fond of; cling to, delight in, enjoy having, be addicted to, admire or be glad

Lovage is cultivated for its stalks and foliage which are used for tea, as a vegetable and to flavor foods, particularly meats. Its flavor is similar to that of celery.

After the Vatican upheld claims that an apparition of the Virgin Mary had been seen, and that a nearby spring had healing powers, the town of Lourdes in the Hautes-Pyrénées has become a shrine for Roman Catholic pilgrims.

Love between people has been celebrated in myth, legend, art and song since the beginning of history. The god of Love (Cupid or Eros) in Greek and Roman mythology was depicted as a winged youth. Left: 'Psyche Crowning Love' a painting by Greuze. Right: 'The Kiss', by Rodin.

of the existence of; be (habitually) inclined *to*; (colloq.) like, be delighted.

Love·lace (lŭv′lās), **Richard** (1618–58). English lyric poet.

love·less (lŭv′lĭs) *adj.* Unloving; unloved. **love′less·ly** *adv.* **love′-less·ness** *n.*

love·ly (lŭv′lē) *adj.* (**-li·er, -li·est**). Attractively or admirably beautiful; (colloq.) delightful, very pleasing, intensely amusing. **love′-li·ness** *n.* **lovely** *n.* (pl. **-lies**). Glamorously beautiful (young) woman.

lov·er (lŭv′er) *n.* 1. Man in love with a woman, (formerly) suitor; man having extramarital sexual relations with a woman; (pl.) two people in love or having a love affair; ∼'s knot, love knot. 2. Admirer, devotee, *of* thing etc. **lov′er·less, lov′er·like** *adjs.*

love·some (lŭv′som) *adj.* (archaic) Lovable; loving.

lov·ing (lŭv′ĭng) *adj.* That loves, affectionate; manifesting or proceeding from love; ∼ cup, large drinking vessel, usu. of silver with two or more handles passed around at banquet; ∼-kindness, tender regard.

low[1] (lō) *v.i.* Utter cry (as) of cow, moo. ∼ *n.* Cow's cry.

low[2] (lō) *adj.* 1. Not reaching far up, not high or tall (not used of persons); not elevated in geographical etc. position. 2. Of small amount as measured by a scale or degrees; (of liquid, receptacle, supply of anything) nearly exhausted or empty; **at low′est**, to mention the least possible amount etc. 3. Of or in humble rank or position; not exalted or sublime,

commonplace, undignified, little civilized, not highly organized; abject, mean, degraded, coarse, vulgar. 4. Weak, dejected; (of diet) not nourishing. 5. (of sound) Not shrill or high, produced by slow vibrations; not loud. 6. (of church etc.) Giving low place to authority of bishops and priests, inherent grace of sacraments, ecclesiastical organization, and ritual; not sacerdotal; approximating to Protestant nonconformity; **L∼ Church, Churchman,** (member of) party in Church of England thus minded. 7. **bring** ∼, depress, reduce, in

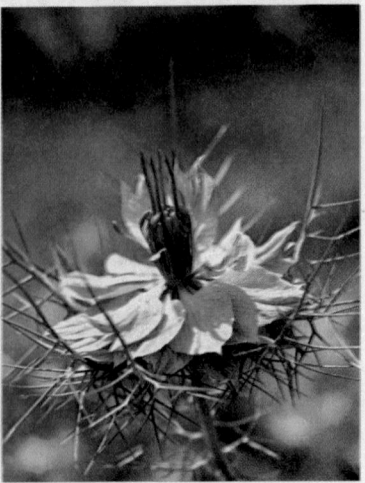

health, wealth, or position; **lay** ∼ overthrow; **lie** ∼, crouch; b prostrate, dead, or abased; (slang keep quiet or out of the way, sa nothing; bide one's time. 8. **low′ boy**, low chest of drawers on leg like the lower part of a highboy **low′brow** (*n.*), **lowbrow** (*adj.* (colloq.) (of person) not highly not pretentiously intellectual; **low browed**, (esp. of rocks) beetling (of building etc.) with low entrance gloomy; **low comedian,** actor low comedy, in which subject an treatment border on farce; **Lo Countries:** see NETHERLAND **low′down,** abject, mean, dishonor able; (slang) facts, correct informa tion; **lower case:** see CASE[2]; lo **frequency** (*n.*), **low-frequenc** (*adj.*): see FREQUENCY; **Low Ger man:** see GERMAN; **low-key,** re strained; **low′land:** see separat entry; **Low Latin:** see LATIN; lo **latitudes,** those near equator; **Lo Mass:** see MASS; **low pitch,** sligh angular elevation of a roof; **lo profile,** deliberately inconspicuou behavior; **low relief,** bas-relie **low-rise,** (of building) having fe stories; **low tide:** see TIDE; **lo water,** (esp.) low tide; **low tide; watermark,** level reached at lo water. **low** *adv.* In or to lo or mean position; on poor diet; fc small stakes; in low tone, on or t low note; **low′born,** of humbl birth; **low′bred,** of vulgar man ners; **low′er·most, low′ish** *adj* **low′ness** *n.* **low** *n.* What

Love-in-a-mist *is a herbaceous plant the buttercup family and is grown gardens in temperate regions of th world. It is 18 to 24 ins. tall and ha blue flowers.*

w; low level or figure; area of low
tmospheric pressure, center of a
epression.

Low·ell[1] (lō'el), **Amy (Law-ence)** (1874–1925). American
oet; leader of the imagist move-
ent in the U.S.; used much free
erse and "polyphonic prose."

Low·ell[2] (lō'el), **James Russell**
1819–91). American poet, essayist,
nd editor; now best remembered
s a distinguished popular poet of
is day and as author of *The
iglow Papers*; he was also a lead-
g linguist, first editor of *The
tlantic Monthly* magazine (1857),
o-editor of *The North American
Review*, and U.S. minister to Spain
nd England.

Low·ell[3] (lō'el), **Percival** (1855–
916). American astronomer;
ounder of the ~ **Observatory** at
lagstaff, Arizona.

Low·ell[4] (lō'el), **Robert**
1917–). American poet; author of
ord Weary's Castle, Imitations,
tc.

low·er[1] (lō'er) v. Let or haul
own; (naut.) let down boat, haul
own sail etc.; diminish height of;
ink, descend, slope downward;
iminish (price etc.); (of price etc.)
ome down; diminish in intensity
r pitch; degrade, disgrace; reduce
odily condition of.

low·er[2], **lour** (low'er) *vbs.i.*
rown, scowl, look sullen; (of
louds etc.) look dark and threaten-
ng. ~ *n.* Scowl; gloominess of sky
tc. **low'er·ing·ly** *adv.* **low'er·y**
dj.

low·land (lō'land) *n.* (usu. pl.)
ess mountainous part of a country,
sp. (Lowlands) that part of Scot-
and S. and E. of Highlands. ~ *adj.*
w'land·er *n.* Inhabitant of low-
ands, esp. (**L**~) those of Scotland.

low·ly (lō'lē) *adj.* (**-li·er, -li·est**).
lumble in feeling, behavior, or
ondition; modest. ~ *adv.* In lowly
nanner. **low'li·ness** *n.*

lox[1] (lŏks) *n.* Smoked salmon.

lox[2] (lŏks) *n.* Liquid oxygen.
(iquid) ox(ygen)]

loy·al (loi'al) *adj.* True, faith-
ul, to duty, love, or obligation
o); faithful in allegiance to
overeign, government, or mother
ountry; enthusiastically devoted to
overeign's person and family;
xhibiting loyalty. **loy'al·ly** *adv.*
oy'al·ism, loy'al·ist *ns.*

loy·al·ty (loi'altē) *n.* (pl. **-ties**).
oyal temper or conduct.

Loy·o·la (loiō'la) = IGNATIUS
OYOLA.

loz·enge (lŏz'inj) *n.* 1. Rhomb,
iamond figure, esp. as bearing in
eraldry; lozenge-shaped shield for
pinster's or widow's arms;
ozenge-shaped facet of cut gem;
ozenge-shaped pane in casement
tc. 2. Small tablet, orig. lozenge-
haped, usu. of flavored or medi-
ated sugar, to be dissolved in

mouth.

LP (pl. **LPs, LP's**). (trademark)
Microgroove phonograph record
making 33⅓ revolutions a minute.

L.P., l.p. *abbrevs.* Low pressure.

LPG *abbrev.* Liquefied petroleum gas.

LPN *abbrev.* Licensed practical
nurse.

L.S., l.s. *abbrevs. Locus sigilli*
(L., = the place of the seal, on
documents).

LSD *abbrev.* Lysergic acid
diethylamide ($C_{20}H_{25}N_3O$), derivative of lysergic acid, powerful
hallucinogenic drug, occas. used in
psychiatric treatment.

£.s.d. *abbrev.* Pounds, shillings,
and pence. [L. *librae, solidi,
denarii*].

Lt. *abbrev.* Lieutenant.

Ltd., ltd. *abbrevs.* (Brit.)
Limited (liability company).

Lu *symbol.* Lutetium.

Lu·an·da (lōoăn'da). Capital
and a seaport of Angola, on the
Atlantic Ocean.

lu·au (lōo'ow) *n.* (pl. **lu·aus**).
Hawaiian-style party.

lub·ber (lŭb'er) *n.* Big clumsy
stupid fellow, lout; clumsy seaman,
unseamanlike fellow; ~'s **line** (or
~ **line**), **mark**, vertical line inside
a compass case, indicating the
direction of the ship's head. **lub'-
ber·ly** *adj.* & *adv.*

*Lubeck, a seaport in Schleswig-
Holstein, West Germany, is linked by
canal with the Elbe. This medieval gate
and adjoining churches survived air
raids in the 1939–45 war.*

Lü·beck (lü'bĕk). City of N.
Germany, a Baltic seaport, formerly
head of the HANSEatic League.

lu·bri·cate (lōo'brĭkāt) *v.t.*
(**-cat·ed, -cat·ing**). Make slippery
or smooth by applying fluid or
lubricant; minimize friction of
(machinery) with grease etc. **lu'-
bri·cant** *adj.* & *n.* **lu·bri·ca·tion**
(lōobrĭka'shon), **lu'bri·ca·tor** *ns.*

lu·bric·i·ty (lōobrĭs'ĭtē) *n.* Slip-
periness, smoothness, oiliness;
lewdness, wantonness.

lu·cent (lōo'sent) *adj.* Shining,
luminous, translucent. **lu'cen·cy**
n. **lu'cent·ly** *adv.*

Lu·cerne (lōosẽrn'). (Ger.
Luzern) Canton and city of central
Switzerland; **Lake of** ~, the principal lake of central Switzerland,
the city is on its NW. shore.

lu·cid (lōo'sĭd) *adj.* Bright
(poet.); clear, pellucid; (entom.,
bot.) with smooth shining surface;
~ **interval**, period of sanity between attacks of madness. **lu'cid·ly**
adv. **lu·cid'i·ty, lu'cid·ness** *ns.*

Lu·ci·fer (lōo'sifer) 1. The
planet Venus when it appears in the
sky before sunrise; the morning
star. 2. By misunderstanding of
Isa. 14 (where the Hebrew epithet
"shining one," translated as *Lucifer*
in the Vulgate, is applied to the
king of Babylon), Satan, the rebel
archangel, before his fall; now
chiefly in phr. **as proud as Lucifer.** [L., = "light bringer"]

Lu·ci·na (lōosī'na). (Rom.
myth.) Goddess who presided over
birth; chiefly as epithet of Juno or
occas. of Diana.

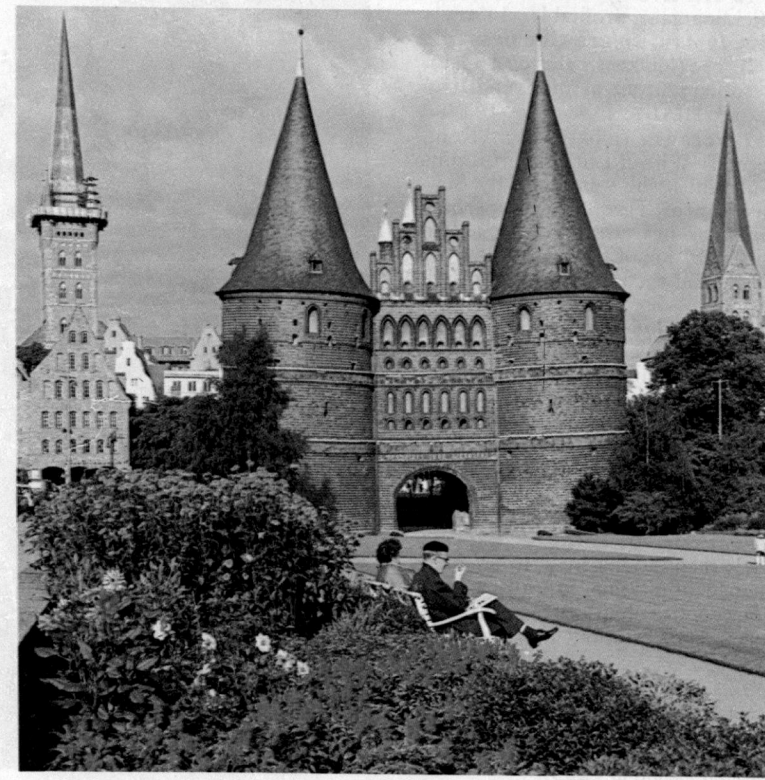

Lucknow, the capital of Uttar Pradesh, India, in the Ganges valley, is a commercial center with textile, chemical and engineering industries. Shown here is the Old Turkish Gateway near the great Inambara Mosque.

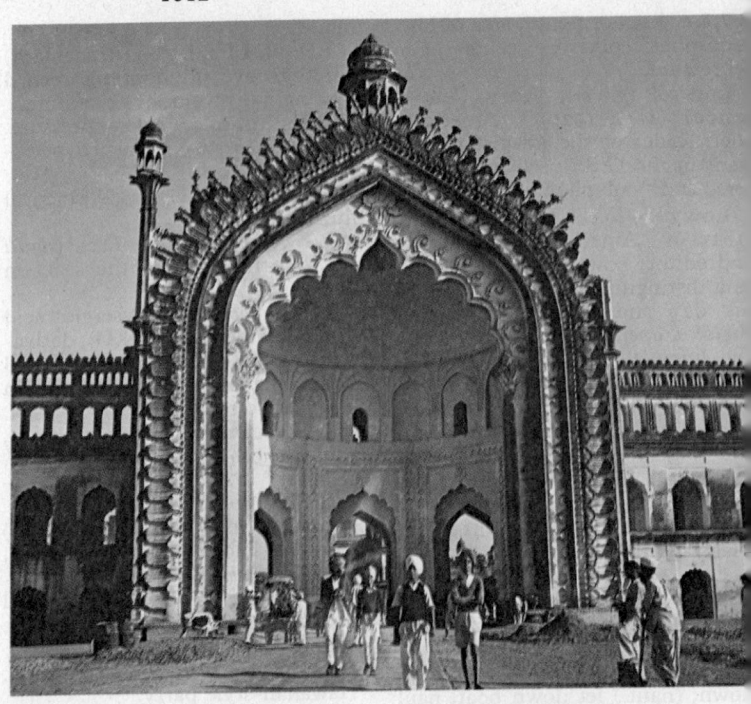

Lu·cite (loo'sīt) *n.* (trademark) Tough unsplinterable transparent acrylic thermoplastic, much lighter than glass, for which it is widely used as a substitute.

luck (lŭk) *n.* (Chance as bestower of) good or ill fortune; fortuitous event affecting one's interests; person's apparent tendency to be (un)fortunate; supposed tendency of chance to bring a succession of (un)favorable events; good fortune, success due to chance; **as ~ would have it**, fortunately or unfortunately; **down on one's ~**, dispirited by misfortune, temporarily unfortunate; **for ~**, to bring good luck; **~ out**, have good luck; **try one's ~**, venture at gambling table etc.; **worse ~**, more's the pity. **luck'less** *adj.* **luck'less·ness** *n.*

luck·i·ly (lŭk'ilē) *adv.* Fortunately.

Luck·now (lŭk'now). Capital city of Uttar Pradesh, India, formerly capital of Oudh.

luck·y (lŭk'ē) *adj.* (**luck·i·er, luck·i·est**). Constantly attended by good luck, enjoying it on a particular occasion; (of guess etc.) right by luck, of the nature of a fluke; occurring by chance and bringing happy results; presaging, bringing, worn, etc. for, good luck, well-omened. **luck'i·ness** *n.*

lu·cra·tive (loo'krativ) *adj.* Yielding gain, profitable. **lu'cra·tive·ly** *adv.* **lu'cra·tive·ness** *n.*

lu·cre (loo'ker) *n.* (derog.) Gain, pecuniary profit as motive; **filthy ~**: see FILTHY.

Lu·cre·tia (lookrē'sha). (Rom. legend) Wife of Lucius Tarquinius Collatinus; she was raped by Sextus, son of Tarquinius Superbus, and took her own life; this led to the expulsion of the Tarquins from Rome and the establishment of the republic.

Lu·cre·tius (lookrē'shus). Titus Lucretius Carus (c94–55 B.C.), Latin poet; author of a philosophical poem "De Rerum Natura," in which he tried to show that the course of the world can be explained without postulating divine intervention.

lu·cu·brate (loo'kyoobrāt) *v.i.* (**-brat·ed, -brat·ing**). Express one's meditations in writing; produce lucubrations. **lu·cu·bra·tion** (lookyoobrā'shon) *n.* Nocturnal study or meditation; literary work

Ludwig II of Bavaria, a patron of Wagner, built this fantastic Gothic castle, Neuschwanstein, in 1869 on a dramatic mountain site. He was declared insane in 1886.

Lake Lugano has an area of 19½ sq. miles, 18 of which are in Ticino canton, Switzerland, and the remainder in Lombardy, Italy. Its wooded shores are mostly precipitous and desolate.

sp. of pedantic or elaborate charac-er. [L. *lucubrare*, work by amplight (*lux*, light)]

Lu·cul·lus (lookŭl'*u*s), **Lucius Licinius** (*c*110–50 B.C.). Roman general; consul 74 B.C.; famous for magnificence and luxury esp. in his banquets. **Lu·cul'lan, Lu·cul·e·an** (lookulē'*a*n), **Lu·cul'li·an** *adjs.*

Lu·cy (loo'sē), **St.** (3rd c. A.D.). Sicilian virgin and martyr, com-memorated Dec. 13; patron saint of the blind.

Lud·dite (lŭdīt') *adj.* & *n.* (Mem-ber) of organized bands of English artisans who in the period 1811–16 destroyed newly introduced machinery in the Midlands and N. of England on the ground that it took away their livelihood. [said to be f. Ned *Ludd*, a feeble-minded person who broke up some machinery in a fit of insane rage]

Lu·den·dorff (loo'dendörf), **Erich von** (1865–1937). German general in World War I; was associated with Hitler in the "Beer-Hall Putsch" at Munich, 1923.

lu·di·crous (loo'dikr*u*s) *adj.* Absurd, ridiculous; exciting or deserving derision. **lu'di·crous·ly** *adv.* **lu'di·crous·ness** *n.*

Lud·wig (lood'vĭg). Name of three kings of Bavaria: **Ludwig I** 1786–1868), king 1825–48; was most popular until he allowed most of the power of government to fall into the hands of his mistress, Lola Montez; abdicated 1848 in favor of his son Maximilian II; **Ludwig II** 1845–86), son of Maximilian II, king 1864–86; patron of the arts, esp. music, and friend of Wagner; built fantastic Gothic castles; was declared insane and committed

suicide 1886; **Ludwig III** (1845–1921), crowned king of Bavaria 1913, abdicated 1918.

Luft·waf·fe (looft'vahfe) *n.* German Air Force. [Ger.]

lug[1] (lŭg) *n.* (also **lug·worm** pr. lŭg'wĕrm). Large marine worm (*Arenicola marina*) burrowing in sand, and used for bait.

lug[2] (lŭg) = LUGSAIL.

lug[3] (lŭg) *v.* (**lugged, lug·ging**). Drag or tug (heavy object) with effort or violence; pull hard *at*; force (person) along. ~ *n.* Hard or rough pull.

lug[4] (lŭg) *n.* Ear (Sc.); projection or handle on vase etc.; projection from a casting etc. by which it may be fixed in place.

Lu·ga·no (loogah'nō), **Lake of.** Lake of N. Italy and S. Switzerland, in foothills of the Alps; center of resort area.

lug·gage (lŭg'ĭj) *n.* Suitcases, bags, etc., (for) containing traveler's belongings

lug·sail (lŭg'sāl; *naut.* lŭg'sal) *n.* Four-cornered sail bent on yard slung at a third or quarter of its length from one end.

lu·gu·bri·ous (loogoo'brē*u*s, -gū'-) *adj.* Doleful, dismal, mourn-ful. **lu·gu'bri·ous·ly** *adv.* **lu·gu'bri·ous·ness** *n.*

lug·worm = LUG.[1]

Luke (look), **St.** Apostle, a physician, possibly the son of a Greek freedman of Rome, closely associated with St. Paul, and author of the third Gospel and the Acts of the Apostles; commemorated Oct. 18; third Gospel.

luke·warm (look'wôrm') *adj.* Moderately warm, tepid; not zealous, indifferent. **luke'warm'-ly** *adv.* **luke'warm'ness** *n.*

lull (lŭl) *v.* Soothe or send to sleep by sounds or caresses; quiet (suspicion etc.); (usu. pass.) quiet (sea, storm); (of storm etc.) lessen, fall quiet. ~ *n.* Intermission in storm, interval of quiet.

lull·a·by (lŭl'*a*bī) *n.* (pl. **-bies**). Soothing refrain or song to put child to sleep. ~ *v.t.* (**-bied, -by·ing**). Sing to sleep.

Lul·ly (loo'lē, *Fr.* lülē), **Jean-Baptiste** (1639–87). Italian-born French violinist, court composer, and composer of operas; founder of French grand opera; wrote the song "Au Clair de la Lune" etc.

lum·ba·go (lŭmbā'gō) *n.* Pain-ful affection, usu. inflammatory, of the muscles of the loins.

lum·bar (lŭm'ber, -bär) *adj.* Of the loin(s).

lum·ber[1] (lŭm'ber) *v.i.* Move in clumsy, blundering, often noisy way. **lum'ber·ing** *adj.* & *n.* **lum'ber·ing·ly** *adv.*

lum·ber[2] (lŭm'ber) *n.* Roughly prepared timber; **lum'ber·jack**, lumberman; **lum'ber·man** (lŭm'-berm*a*n), feller, dresser, or con-veyer of lumber; **lum'ber·mill**, sawmill for cutting up lumber. **lumber** *v.* Cut and prepare forest timber. **lum'ber·er** *n.*

lum·bri·cal (lŭm'brĭkal) *adj.* ~ **muscle**, one of the muscles flexing fingers or toes. **lumbrical** *n.* Lumbrical muscle.

lu·men[1] (loo'men) *n.* (pl. **-mi·na** pr. -min*a*). Unit of light energy or luminous flux, the light energy emitted in a unit solid angle by a uniform point source of one candle; ~ **-hour**, unit of luminous energy, equal to the emission of 1 lumen for 1 hour.

lu·men[2] (loo'men) *n.* (pl. **-mi·na** pr. -min*a*). (physiol.) Canal, duct, or bore of a tubular organ.

Lu·mière (loomyār'; *Fr.* lümyĕr'), **Auguste Marie Louis Nicholas** (1862–1954); his brother, **Louis Jean** (1864–1948). French chemists, inventors, and pioneers in photography and color photog-raphy; invented an early motion-picture camera.

Lu·mi·nal (loo'min*a*l) *n.* (trade-mark) Phenobarbital, a preparation of phenobarbitone ($C_{12}H_{12}O_3N_2$), used medicinally as a sedative.

lu·mi·nance (loo'min*a*ns) *n.* Luminosity; (measure of) bright-ness.

lu·mi·nar·y (loo'minĕrē) *n.* (pl. **-nar·ies**). Natural light-giving body, esp. sun or moon; person of intellectual, moral, or spiritual eminence.

lu·mi·nes·cent (lōōmĭnĕs′ent) *adj.* Emitting light from some cause other than high temperature. **lu·mi·nes′cence** *n.*

lu·mi·nif·er·ous (lōōmĭnĭf′erus) *adj.* Producing or transmitting light.

lu·mi·nous (lōō′mĭnus) *adj.* Emitting or full of light, bright, shining; ~ **paint**, phosphorescent paint making thing conspicuous at night. **lu′mi·nous·ly** *adv.* **lu′mi·nous·ness, lu·mi·nos·i·ty** (lōōmĭnŏs′ĭtē) *ns.*

lump[1] (lŭmp) *n.* Compact shapeless or unshapely mass; great quantity, lot, heap; mass of clay or dough ready for molding or baking; protuberance, excrescence, swelling, bruise; heavy dull person; ~ **in throat**, feeling of pressure caused by emotion; ~ **sugar**, loaf sugar broken or cut into lumps or cubes; ~ **sum**, sum covering or including a number of items; sum paid down at once (opp. INSTALLMENTS). **lump** *v.* Put together in one lump; mass *together*, treat as all alike, disregard differences between or among; rise or collect into lumps; go heavily *along*, sit heavily *down*.

lump[2] (lŭmp) *v.t.* Put up with, endure (unpleasant necessity), as **if you don't like it, ~ it**.

lump·fish (lŭmp′fĭsh) *n.* (pl. **-fish·es**, collect. **-fish**). Sluggish spiny-finned leaden-blue fish (*Cyclopterus lumpus*) of the N. Atlantic with sucking disk on belly.

lump·ish (lŭm′pĭsh) *adj.* Heavy and clumsy; stupid, lethargic. **lump′ish·ly** *adv.* **lump′ish·ness** *n.*

lump·y (lŭm′pē) *adj.* (**lump·i·er, lump·i·est**). Full of or covered with lumps; (of water) cut up by wind into small waves. **lump′i·ly** *adv.* **lump′i·ness** *n.*

lu·na·cy (lōō′nasē) *n.* (pl. **-cies**). Being a lunatic, insanity (formerly of the intermittent kind attributed to moon's changes); great folly.

lu·nar (lōō′ner) *adj.* Of, in, as of, the moon; (of light, glory, etc.) pale, feeble; crescent-shaped; of or containing silver (from alchemists' use of *luna* (L., = moon) for silver); ~ **bone** = LUNATE bone; ~ **caustic**, silver nitrate, esp. in stick form for surgical use; ~ **distance**, distance of moon from sun, planet, or star, used in finding longitude at sea; ~ **module**: see MODULE; ~ **month**: see MONTH; ~ **rainbow**, one made by moon's rays.

lu·nate (lōō′nāt), **lu·nat·ed** (lōō′nātĭd) *adj.* Crescent-shaped; ~ **bone**, crescent-shaped bone in carpal bones. **lunate** *n.* Lunate bone; lunate prehistoric implement, etc.

lu·na·tic (lōō′natĭk) *adj.* Insane; (of action etc.) outrageously foolish. ~ *n.* Insane person; ~ **asylum**, (formerly) mental institution; ~

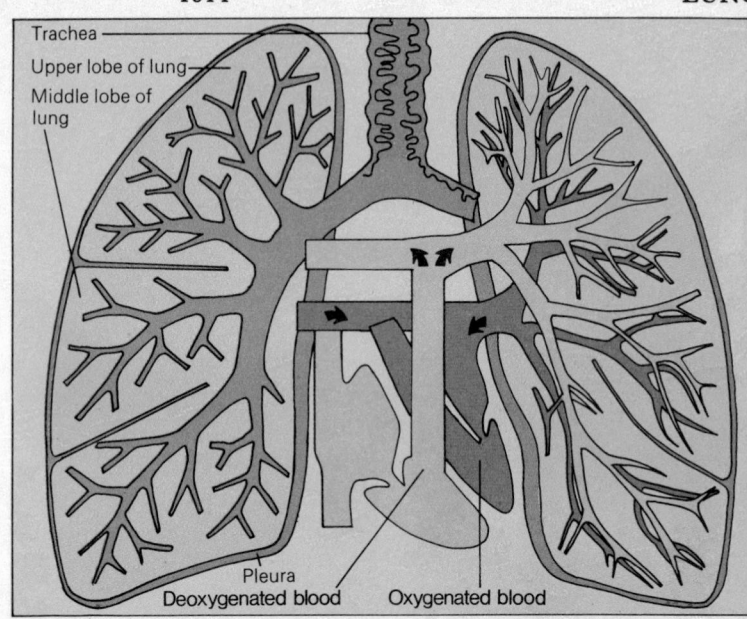

Trachea
Upper lobe of lung
Middle lobe of lung
Pleura
Deoxygenated blood
Oxygenated blood

The human **lungs** (top) are soft, spongy, elastic organs that are responsible for providing the body with air and for discharging certain waste products. Diseases of the lungs can cause serious illness and their incidence has increased. Above: A lung inflamed by exposure to irradiation.

fringe, fanatical or eccentric or visionary minority of political party etc. [L. *luna* moon, because insanity was thought to be caused by the moon's changes]

lu·na·tion (lōōnā′shon) *n.* Time from one new moon to next.

lunch (lŭnch) *n.* (now the more usual word, exc. in formal use, for) Luncheon. ~ *v.* Take lunch; (colloq.) provide lunch for.

lunch·eon (lŭn′chon) *n.* (orig.) Slight repast between two ordinary mealtimes, esp. breakfast and midday dinner; now the midday meal, usu. less substantial and less ceremonious than dinner; ~ **meat**, cooked meat in loaf form ready to cut and eat.

lune (lōōn) *n.* (geom.) Figure formed on sphere or plane by two arcs of circles enclosing a space.

lu·nette (lōōnĕt′) *n.* Arched aperture in concave ceiling to admit light; crescent-shaped or semicircular space in dome or ceiling decorated with painting etc.; watch glass of flattened shape; hole for neck in guillotine.

lung (lŭng) *n.* Either of the pair of saccular respiratory organs in man and other vertebrates, placed within cavity of thorax on either side of heart and communicating with trachea or windpipe; (pl.) open space(s) in or near a city; **lung′fish**, fish having lungs as well as gills; **lung power**, power of voice; **lung′wort**, European plant (*Pulmonaria officinalis*, order Boraginaceae) having leaves with white spots supposed to resemble those of diseased lung; plant of allied Amer. genus *Mertensia*.

lunge[1], **longe** (lŭnj) *ns.* Long rope with which horse trainer holds horse while he makes it canter in circle; circular exercise ground for training horses. ~ *v.t.* (**lunged, lung·ing**). Exercise (horse) with or in lunge.

The **lupin,** of which there are about 0 species, occurs in the western misphere and in the Mediterranean *ion.* The attractive flowers grow in *g* terminal clusters.

lunge² (lŭnj) *n.* Thrust with ord etc., esp. in fencing; sudden ward movement, plunge, rush; ymnastics) forward movement, in ich one foot is advanced, the ee being bent and directly over instep, while the other foot re- ins stationary. ~ *v.* (**lunged,** ng·ing, longed, long·ing). ake lunge in fencing or gym- stics, deliver blow from shoulder boxing; drive (weapon etc.) lently in some direction; rush, ke sudden start in some direc- n.

u·ni·so·lar (loonĭsō´ler) *adj.* Of tual relations or combined ion of sun and moon; ~ **period,** cle of 532 years between agree- nt of solar and lunar cycles hich are of 28 and 19 years); **year,** year with divisions ulated by changes of moon and erage total length made to agree th revolution of sun.

lunk·head (lŭngk´hĕd) *n.* (slang) upid, dull person. **lunk´head·ed** .

Lu·per·cal (loo´perkăl). Cave on latine hill in ancient Rome, red to **Lu·per·cus** (loopēr´kus), Faunus in the guise of a wolf- ity, connected with the story of mulus and Remus. **Lu·per·ca- an** (looperkā´lēan) *adj.*

lu·pine¹, **lu·pin** (loo´pĭn) *ns.* ant of genus *Lupinus,* esp. *L. us,* cultivated in warmer districts Europe for fodder, and the Amer- ecies cultivated in gardens, with g tapering spikes of flowers; su. pl.) seed of any of these.

is Australian **lungfish** is found in ueensland. It uses gills when swim- ing in well oxygenated waters, but hen necessary it can breathe gaseous xygen (air). Similar fish are found in rica and South America.

lu·pine² (loo´pĭn) *adj.* Of wolf or wolves, wolflike.
lu·pus (loo´pus) *n.* Ulcerous disease of skin; ~ **vulgaris,** tuberculosis of the skin.
lurch¹ (lẽrch) *n.* **leave in the** ~, desert (friend, ally) in difficul- ties. [formerly = state of score in some games in which one player was far ahead of the other, f. Fr. *lourche* game like backgammon, also bad defeat in this]
lurch² (lẽrch) *n.* Sudden lean to one side, stagger. ~ *v.i.* Make lurch(es), stagger.
lure (loor) *n.* 1. Falconer's apparatus for recalling hawk, usu. a bunch of feathers (within which hawk finds food during training) attached to cord. 2. Something used to entice; enticing quality *of.* ~ *v.t.* (**lured, lur·ing**). Recall (hawk) with lure; entice (*away, into,* etc.).
lu·rid (loor´ĭd) *adj.* Wan and sallow, ghastly; shining with a red glare or glow amid darkness; ter- rible, ominous, sensational; (bot. etc.) dingy yellowish brown. **lu´- rid·ly** *adv.* **lu´rid·ness** *n.*
lurk (lẽrk) *v.i.* Be hidden *in, under,* etc., prowl; escape notice, exist unobserved, be latent. **lurk´- ing·ly** *adv.*
Lu·sa·ka (loosah´ka). Capital of Gambia in the S. central part.
lus·cious (lŭsh´us) *adj.* Richly sweet in taste or smell; sickly sweet, cloying; (of style etc.) overly rich in sound, imagery, or volup- tuous suggestion. **lus´cious·ly** *adv.* **lus´cious·ness** *n.*
lush¹ (lŭsh) *adj.* 1. (of vegeta- tion, esp. grass) Luxuriant and succulent. 2. Characterized by or having luxuriant vegetation or growth. 3. Opulent; luxurious; abundant. **lush´ness** *n.*
lush² (lŭsh) *n.* (slang) Person who habitually drinks too much whiskey; alcoholic; drunkard.
lust (lŭst) *n.* Sensuous appetite regarded as sinful (esp. bibl., theol.); animal desire for sexual indulgence; passionate enjoyment or desire *of.* ~ *v.i.* Have strong or excessive desire (*after, for*).

The **lungwort,** which is widespread in the open woods and thickets of Europe, is grown as a garden flower. It has drooping pink flowers that turn blue, and white spotted leaves.

lust´ful *adj.* **lust´ful·ly** *adv.* **lust´ful·ness** *n.*
lus·ter, Brit. **lus·tre** (lŭs´ter) *ns.* 1. Quality of shining by reflected light, often with effect of changing color; sheen, gloss; luminous splen- dor, radiant beauty; splendor, glory, distinction. 2. (Prismatic glass pendant of) chandelier. 3. Fabric with lustrous surface. 4. Iridescent glaze applied to pottery and porcelain; ware glazed with this. ~ *v.t.* Put luster on. **lus´ter·less, lus´trous** (lŭs´trus) *adjs.* **lus´trous·ly** *adv.*
lus·tral (lŭs´tral) *adj.* Of, used in, ceremonial purification.
lus·trate (lŭs´trāt) *v.t.* (**-trat- ed, -trat·ing**). Purify by expia- tory sacrifice, ceremonial washing, or other rite. **lus·tra´tion** *n.* [see LUSTRUM]
lus·trum (lŭs´trum) *n.* (pl. **-trums, -tra** pr. -tra). Period of five years. [L. orig. purificatory sacrifice made every five years after census had been taken]
lust·y (lŭs´tē) *adj.* (**lust·i·er, lust·i·est**). Healthy and strong; vigorous, lively. **lust´i·ly** *adv.* **lust´i·ness** *n.*

This **theorbo lute** or bass lute is a modification of the stringed instrument which was so popular in Europe in the Renaissance and Baroque periods. The lute was brought from Arab countries to Europe.

The Grand Duchy of **Luxemburg** in west Europe has an area of 999 sq. miles. Its most important industry is steel, 90% of which is exported. Above: Beaufort Castle in Luxemburg. Above right: Map and flag of Luxemburg.

lu·tan·ist, lu·te·nist (loo'tanĭst) *ns.* Lute player.

lute[1] (loot) *n.* Musical instrument much used in 14th–17th centuries, with pear-shaped body, with strings struck with fingers of right hand and stopped on frets with those of left. [Arab. *al'ud* the lute (*'ud* orig. wood)]

lute[2] (loot) *n.* Tenacious clay or cement used to stop hole, make joint airtight, coat crucible, protect graft, etc. ~ *v.t.* (**lut·ed, lut·ing**). Apply lute to.

lu·te·ous (loo'tēus) *adj.* Greenish or brownish yellow.

lu·te·ti·um (loote'shēum) *n.* (chem.) Metallic element of rare-earth group, resembling ytterbium in properties; symbol Lu, at. no. 71, at. wt. 174.97. [f. *Lutetia*, Latin name of Paris]

Lu·ther (loo'ther), **Martin** (1483–1546). Leader of the Protestant Reformation in Germany; translator (1522–34) of the Bible into German and author of many hymns. **Lu·ther·an** (loo'theran, -thrĭn) *adj.* Of Luther, his opinions and followers, or the Lutheran Church; ~ **Church**, those churches, esp. in Germany and Scandinavia, that accept the doctrines of the Augsburg Confession (1530) and whose cardinal doctrine is that of justification by faith alone.

lux (lŭks) *n.* (pl. **lu·ces** pr. loo'sēz). International unit of illumination, the illumination of a surface at a uniform distance of 1 meter from a symmetrical point source of 1 candle, equal to 1

LUMEN[1] per square meter.

lux·ate (lŭk'sāt) *v.t.* (**-at·ed, -at·ing**). Dislocate (joint etc.). **lux·a'tion** *n.*

Lux·em·bourg[1], **Lux·em·burg** (lŭk'sembērg; *Fr.* lüksahňboor'). Small (999 sq. mile, 2,588 sq. km) constitutional monarchy and grand duchy in W. Europe, S. of Belgium and between France and W. Germany; (also ~ **City**) its capital.

Lux·em·bourg[2] (lŭk'sembērg; *Fr.* lüksahňboor'), **Palais du.** Palace S. of the Seine in Paris, built 1615–20 for Marie de Médicis and now the meeting place of the French Senate, with gardens open to the public.

Lux·or (lŭk'sôr). Town of Upper Egypt on E. bank of the Nile, 415 miles (668 km) S. of Cairo; contains Karnak and the ruins of ancient THEBES.

lux·u·ri·ant (lŭgzhoor'ēant, lŭkshoor'-) *adj.* Prolific, profuse of growth, exuberant, rank; florid, richly ornamented. **lux·u'ri·ant·ly** *adv.* **lux·u'ri·ance** *n.*

lux·u·ri·ate (lŭgzhoor'ēāt, lŭkshoor'-) *v.i.* (**-at·ed, -at·ing**). Revel, enjoy oneself; take one's ease, be luxurious.

lux·u·ri·ous (lŭgzhoor'ēus, lŭkshoor'-) *adj.* Given, contributing, to luxury, self-indulgent, voluptuous, very comfortable. **lux·u'ri·ous·ly** *adv.* **lux·u'ri·ous·ness** *n.*

lux·u·ry (lŭk'shere, lŭg'zhere) *n.* (pl. **-ries**). (Habitual use of) choice or costly food, dress, furniture, etc.; refined and intense enjoyment; thing conducive to comfort or en-

joyment in addition to what are considered necessaries, thing desirable but not essential.

Lu·zon (loozŏn'). Largest island 40,420 square miles (104,688 sq. km), in the N. part of the Republic of the Philippines.

ly·can·thro·py (līkăn'thropē) *n.* 1. Witchcraft consisting in assumption by human beings of form and nature of wolves. 2. Form of insanity in which the sufferer imagines himself a beast and exhibits depraved appetites etc. **ly·can·thrope** (lī'kanthrōp, līkăn'thrōp) *n.* 1. Werewolf. 2. Person afflicted by lycanthropy.

Ly·ca·on (līkā'ŏn, -on). (Gk. legend) King of Arcadia who, at the host of Zeus, offered him human flesh to eat, in order to try his divinity; he was killed by lightning or turned into a wolf.

ly·cée (lēsā') *n.* (pl. **-cées** pr. -sāz'; *Fr.* -sā'). State secondary school in France (dist. from *collège*, municipal secondary school). [Fr. f. LYCEUM]

ly·ce·um (līsē'um) *n.* 1. (**L**~) Grove and gymnasium near Athens, sacred to Apollo Lyceus where Aristotle taught; hence Aristotle's philosophy or followers. 2. Institution providing literary or scientific lectures, concerts, etc.

lych·nis (lĭk'nĭs): see CAMPION.

ly·co·pod (lī'kopŏd) *n.* (bot.) Club moss.

ly·co·po·di·um (līkopō'dēum) *n.* Cryptogamous plant of genus *L~* club moss; highly inflammable powder from spores of species of this, used in fireworks etc.

lydd·ite (lĭd'īt) *n.* High explosive chiefly of picric acid, formerly used in shells. [*Lydd* in Kent where first tested in England]

Lyd·gate (lĭd'gāt, -gĭt), **John** (c1370–c1451). English poet author of devotional, philosophical

nd historical poems and of alle-
ories and moral romances.

Lyd·i·a (lĭd´ea). Ancient king-
om and (7th to 6th c. B.C.)
mpire of W. Asia Minor.

Lyd·i·an (lĭd´ēan) *adj.* 1. Of
ncient Lydia, its people, or their
nguage. 2. ~ **mode**, (mus.)
ncient Greek mode, reputedly
ffeminate in character; fifth of
cclesiastical modes with F as final
nd C as dominant. 3. Soft or
feminate; voluptuous. **Lydian** *n.*
ydian person or language.

lye (lī) *n.* Water made alkaline
y lixiviation of vegetable ashes;
ny strong alkaline solution esp.
r washing, any detergent.

ly·ing[1] (lī´ing) *adj.*: see LIE[1];
sp.) deceitful, false. **ly´ing·ly**
dv.

ly·ing[2] (lī´ing) *adj.*: see LIE[2];
sp.) ~ **down**, (fig.) without prost (of insult etc.). **lying** *n.* (esp.)
-**in**, being confined in childbirth.

Lyl·y (lĭl´ē), **John** (c1554–1606).
nglish author of plays, pamphlets,
nd a prose romance, *Euphues, or
he Anatomy of Wit.*

lymph (lĭmf) *n.* 1. (poet.) Pure
ater. 2. (physiol.) Colorless
ightly alkaline fluid derived from
he blood by permeation through
he walls of the capillaries, and
rains into the lymphatic vessels;
xudation from sore etc.; (also **calf,
accine**, ~) preparation derived
rom cowpox vesicles, used in
accination against smallpox; ~
lands (nodes), small masses of
pecialized tissue at intervals in
mphatic system, filtering off
oreign particles from lymph and
roducting lymphocytes. **lymph·-
id** (lĭm´foid) *adj.*

lym·phat·ic (lĭmfăt´ĭk) *adj.* 1.
Of, secreting, conveying, lymph;
~ **duct, gland**, one in the system
f fine vessels in which lymph cir-
ulates and which communicates
ith the venous system. 2. Flabby-
uscled, pale-skinned, sluggish
qualities formerly attributed to
xcess of lymph). **lymphatic** *n.*
einlike vessel conveying lymph.

lym·pho·cyte (lĭm´fosīt) *n.*
orm of white blood cell.

lyn·ce·an (lĭnsē´an) *adj.* Lynx-
yed, keen-sighted.

lynch (lĭnch) *v.t.* Condemn and
unish by ~ **law**, (1) infliction of
ummary punishment on offender
y self-constituted court with no
egal authority, (2) summary execu-
ion of one charged with some
ffense. **lynch´er, lynch´ing** *ns.*
After Capt. W. *Lynch* (1742–1820)
f Pittsylvania, Virginia]

lynx (lĭngks) *n.* (pl. **lynx·es**,
ollect. **lynx**). Any of various
embers of the cat family found
nly in N. hemisphere, with tufted
ar tips, short tail, spotted fur, esp.
Canada ~ (*L. canadensis*), having
oft gray-brown fur with white

*A street scene in **Luxor**. This city is a centre for tourists wishing to visit the many ruins and monuments of ancient Egypt that are in or near to the city. Its population of about 150 000 is supported by tourism and agriculture.*

*The **lynx** is found in the forests of Europe, Asia and North America. It is nocturnal and climbs and swims well. It feeds on birds and small mammals. Below: Desert or Persian lynx. Bottom: European lynx.*

markings; and **bay** ~ (= BOBCAT); lynx fur; **~-eyed**, sharp-sighted.

Ly·ons (lēawn'). (Fr. **Lyon**) City of E. central France at confluence of Saône and Rhone, famous esp. for manufacture of silk.

Ly·ra (lī'ra). (astron.) The Harp, a northern constellation containing Vega, the 4th brightest star in the heavens.

ly·rate (lī'rāt, -rĭt) adj. (biol.) Lyre-shaped.

lyre (līr) n. (Gk. antiq.) Instrument of harp kind, chiefly used for accompanying voice, with strings supported by two symmetrically curved horns, stopped with the left hand and struck with a plectrum in the right; **lyre'bird**, Australian passerine bird (*Menura superba*), with lyre-shaped tail. **lyr·ist** (līr'ĭst) n. Lyre player.

Ly·san·der (līsăn'der) (d. 395 B.C.). Spartan naval commander in latter part of Peloponnesian War.

ly·ser·gic (līser'jĭk, lī-) adj. ~ **acid**, crystalline solid ($C_{15}H_{15}N_2$ COOH), obtained from ergot or produced synthetically; ~ **acid diethylamide**: see LSD.

Ly·sim·a·chus (līsĭm'akus) (c355–281 B.C.). Macedonian general who served under Alexander the Great and became king of Thrace.

Ly·sip·pus (līsĭp'us) (4th c. B.C.). Greek sculptor of Sicyon who was famous for his statues of Zeus an portraits of Alexander the Great.

ly·sis (lī'sĭs) n. (physiol.) Di integration of bacterial or oth cells.

Ly·sol (lī'sŏl, -sawl, -sŏl) (trademark) Mixture of cresols an soft soap, used as an antiseptic an disinfectant.

Lyt·ton (lĭt'on),   **Edwar George Earle Lytton Bulwer first Baron Lytton** (1803–73 English novelist and politicia author of *Eugene Aram*, *Rienzi*, *T Last Days of Pompeii*, etc.

The **lyre-bird** found only in Australia, so called because of the shape of its t when spread in courtship displa *Menura superba* (left and below) is th most splendid of the two species foun It sings with far-carrying melodio notes and is an excellent mimic.

lyr·ic (lĭr'ĭk) adj. Of or for the lyre, meant to be sung; of the nature of, expressed or fit to be expressed in, song; (of poem) short, usu. divided into stanzas or strophes, and directly expressing poet's own thoughts and sentiments rather than a description of events; (of poet) writing in this manner. ~ n. Lyric poem; (esp. pl., theatr.) words of song.

lyr·i·cal (lĭr'ĭkal) adj. Resembling, couched in, or using language appropriate to, lyric poetry. **lyr'i·cal·ly** adv. **lyr'i·cal·ness** n.

lyr·i·cism (lĭr'ĭsĭzem) n. Lyric character or expression; high-flown sentiments.

M m *is the 13th letter in the English and other west European alphabets. It was the 12th letter in the Greek alphabet and the 14th in early Slavonic alphabets. As a symbol in Roman numeration M stood for 1,000.*

Phoenician   Early Greek   Etruscan

Early Latin   Classical Latin   Italian

The macaw has the brightest plumage of all parrots and the 15 species are found only in Central and South America. The scarlet macaw is about 40 ins. long and is the largest of these birds.

M, m (ĕm) (pl. **M's, m's** or **Ms, ms**). 1. Thirteenth letter of modern English and 12th of ancient Roman alphabet, representing a bilabial nasal (usu. voiced) consonant; the form of the letter is derived from Phoenician ᙍ (early Gk. and L. ᙏ, ᙏ, M). 2. Roman numeral symbol for 1,000. 3. (print.) = EM.

M. *abbrev.* Mega-; monsieur.

m. *abbrev.* Male; mark(s) (coin); married; masculine; meter(s); mile(s); milli-; million(s); minim; minute(s); month; moon; noon.

MA *abbrev.* Massachusetts.

M.A. *abbrev.* Master of Arts.

ma (mah) = MAMA.

ma'am (măm, mahm) *n.* Madam.

Mac (măk) *n.* (slang) Word of address to someone whose name is unknown to speaker.

ma·ca·bre (makahb´re, -kăb´-) *adj.* Grim, gruesome; **danse~**, (Fr.) Dance of Death.

ma·ca·co (makah´kō, -kā´-) *n.* (pl. **-cos** pr. -kōz). Any of several lemurs, esp. the black lemur (*Lemur macaco*).

mac·ad·am (makăd´am) *n.* (Material for) road surface made with successive layers of small broken stones rolled in with some binding material. **mac·ad·am·ize** (makăd´amīz) *v.t.* (**-ized, -iz·ing**). **mac·ad·am·i·za·tion** (makădamīzā´shon) *n.* [John Loudon *McAdam*, Scottish engineer (1756–1836)]

Ma·cao (makow´). Island in the South China Sea 40 mi. (64 km) W. of Hong Kong; **~**, Portuguese colony on the peninsula of this island and name of chief town.

ma·caque (makahk´) *n.* Monkey of genus *Macaca*, of Asia and N. Africa.

mac·a·ro·ni (măkarō´nē) *n.* (pl. **-nis, -nies**). Pasta formed into long tubes; (hist.) 18th-c. dandy affecting continental manners and fashions.

mac·a·ron·ic (măkarŏn´ĭk) *adj.* (of verse) Of burlesque form containing Latin or other foreign words and vernacular words with Latin etc. terminations. **mac·a·ron´ics** *n.pl.* Macaronic verse.

mac·a·roon (măkarōōn´) *n.* Small cookie of ground almonds, white of egg, sugar, etc.

Mac·Ar·thur (makär´ther), **Douglas** (1880–1964). American general; commanded "Rainbow" Division in World War I; superintendent of West Point, 1919–22; department commander in Philippines, 1928–30; Army chief of staff, 1930–5; routed "Bonus Army" from Washington, D.C., 1932; organized Philippine defense forces and appointed field marshal of the Philippines; supreme commander of Allied Forces in the SW. Pacific in World War II; commander of Allied occupation of Japan, 1945–1951; commander of United Nations forces in Korea, 1950–1, until relieved of command by President Harry S. Truman for disagreeing openly with U.S. policy on war aims.

Ma·cas·sar (makăs´er) *n.* Oil said to consist of ingredients obtained from Macassar, a port of Celebes, formerly used as a hairdressing; similar oil or preparation. Also **~ oil.**

Ma·cau·lay (makaw´lē), **Thomas Babington, 1st Baron Macaulay** (1800–59). English historian and essayist.

ma·caw (makaw´) *n.* Any of several large long-tailed brightly colored parrots, mostly native to S. and Central America.

Macc. *abbrev.* Maccabees (Apocr.).

Mac·ca·bees (măk´abēz) *n.pl.* Family of Jews, consisting of Mattathias and his five sons, Jochanan, Simon, Judas, Eleazar, and Jonathan, who led a revolt against the oppression of the Syrian king Antiochus Epiphanes (175–165 B.C.), and established a dynasty of priest-kings that ruled until the time of Herod (40 B.C.); **(Books of) ~**, four books of Jewish history and theology, of which the first two are

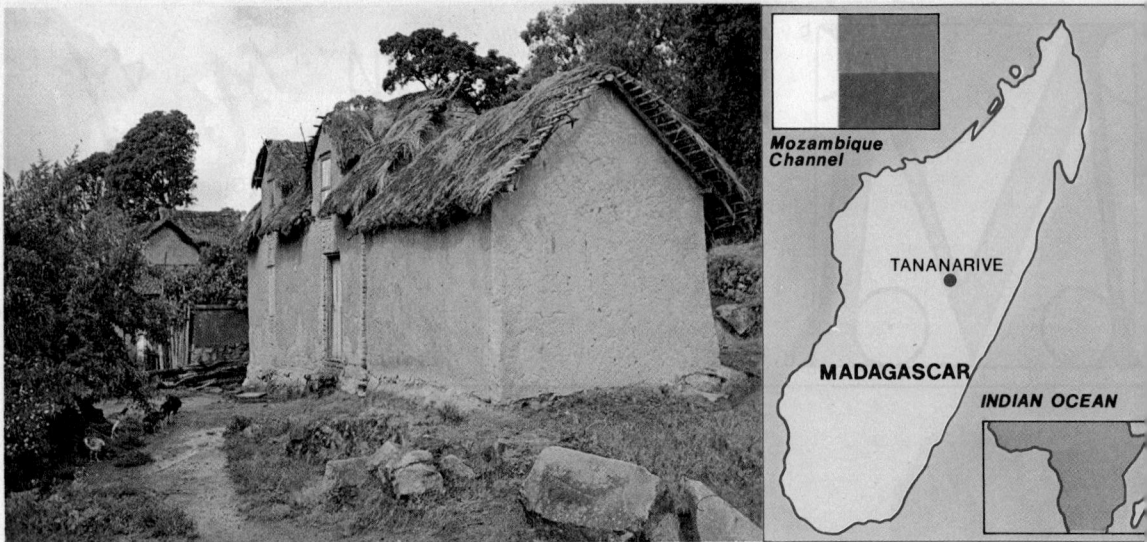

included in the Apocrypha. **Mac·-ca·be·an** (măkabē'an) *adj.*

Mac·Dow·ell (makdow'el), **Edward Alexander** (1861–1908). Amer. composer of piano sonatas, orchestral suites, and symphonic poems.

Mace (mās) *n.* (trademark) Chemical used to incapacitate rioters by causing temporary eye or skin irritation.

mace[1] (mās) *n.* 1. (hist.) Heavy usu. metal-headed and spiked club. 2. Staff of office resembling this; **the M~**, the symbol of the Speaker's authority in the British House of Commons, placed on the table when he is in the chair.

mace[2] (mās) *n.* Dried outer covering of nutmeg, as spice.

mac·é·doine (măsedwahn'; *Fr.* mahsādwahn') *n.* (pl. **-doines** pr. -dwahnz'; *Fr.* -dwahn'). Mixed fruit or vegetables, esp. cut up small. [Fr. *Macedoine* Macedonia]

Mac·e·do·ni·a (măsedō'nēa, -dōn'ya). Mountainous Balkan country, N. of ancient Greece, now divided between Greece and Yugoslavia; under Philip II and his son Alexander III (the Great) it dominated Greece in the 4th c. B.C.:

Madagascar is an island republic about 250 miles off the east coast of Africa, which was known as the Malagasy Republic from 1958 to 1976. Above: Primitive housing on the island. Above right: Map and flag.

in 146 B.C. it became a Roman province, and when the Roman Empire was divided it was assigned to the eastern half; in the 5th c. A.D. Slavs began to invade and colonize it and it became in turn an independent kingdom, a part of the Bulgarian and then of the Serbian Empire; from the end of the 14th c. until the Balkan war of 1912 it was under Turkish rule. **Mac·e·do·ni·an** *adj. & n.*

mac·er·ate (măs'erāt) *v.* (**-at·ed, -at·ing**). Make or become soft by soaking; become emaciated by fasting. **mac·er·a·tion** (măs-erā'shon) *n.*

mach (mahk, măk) *n.* (also ~ **number**) Ratio of the velocity of

Ernst Mach, the Austrian physicist, did much of the pioneer work on projectiles traveling through air at supersonic speeds. Aircraft speeds exceeding that of sound are expressed as 'Mach numbers'.

a body passing through a flu[id] medium to the velocity of sound [in] that medium; ~**meter**. [E. *Ma*[ch] (1838–1916), Austrian physicist]

ma·chet·e (mashĕt'ē, -chĕt'ē) [n.] (pl. **-es**). Broad heavy knife used [in] Central America and W. Indies [as] implement and weapon.

Mach·i·a·vel·li (măkēavĕl'[i], mahkya-), **Niccolo di Bernard**[o] **dei** (1469–1527). Florentin[e] political philosopher, author of [a] famous and influential treatise [on] statecraft, *The Prince* (*Il Princip*[e], 1513), advocating the principle th[at] any political means, howev[er] unscrupulous, are justifiable if the[y] strengthen the power of a govern[-] ment; hence, an unscrupulo[us] schemer, one who practice[s] duplicity in statecraft. **Mach·i·a-vel'li·an** *adj. & n.* **Mach·i·a·vel·li·an·ism, Mach·i·a·vel'lism** *ns*

mach·i·nate (măk'ināt) *v.* (**-nat·ed, -nat·ing**). Lay plot[s], intrigue. **mach·i·na·tion** (măk-inā'shon), **mach'i·na·tor** *ns.*

ma·chine (mashēn') *n.* Ap[-] paratus for applying mechanic[al] power, having several parts eac[h] with definite function (the kin[d] often being specified as **sewin**[g]

MACH less than 1 - Subsonic
Aircraft moving at less than speed of sound, pressure waves in front of aircraft.

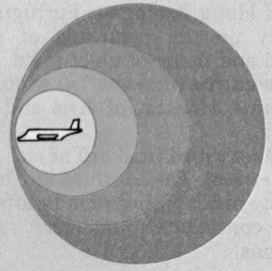

MACH number 1 - Sonic
Pressure waves and aircraft equal in velocity 'Sonic boom' caused by sudden discontinuity of pressure and air temperature in front of aircraft.

Above MACH 1 - Supersonic
Shock waves behind aircraft – Mach cone formed.

rinting ~); bicycle, motorcycle, :c.; aircraft; person who acts nechanically and without intelligence or with unfailing regularity; nstrument directing application of, r transmitting, force; organized ystem for carrying out specific unctions, as the **political, party** ~; ~ **gun**, belt-fed, water-cooled, ingle-barreled gun, firing solid ullets from a fixed mounting, lesigned to utilize part of the nergy of one explosion to extract ne spent cartridge and load and re the next round and capable of ery high rates of continuous firing; ence ~ **gunner;** ~ **tool**, cutting r shaping tool, worked by nachinery, not by hand. **machine** .t. (**-chined, -chin·ing**). Make, perate on, print, sew, etc., with a nachine.

ma·chin·er·y (mashē′nerē) *n.* pl. **-er·ies**). Machines; mechanism; organization.

ma·chin·ist (mashē′nĭst) *n.* Maker of machinery; worker who perates a machine.

ma·chis·mo (machĭz′mō, chēz′-) *n.* Need to prove virility r courage by daring action; also **na·cho** (mah′chō) *n.* Strong, virile nale. **macho** *adj.* Strong, manly. Sp. *macho*, male, f. L. *masculus*]

Ma·chu Pic·chu (mah′chōo bēk′chōo). Site of ruins of an ancient Incan city in the Andes, ltitude about 7,000 ft. (2,100 m), n S. central Peru.

Mac·ken·zie (makĕn′zē), **Sir** Alexander (1764–1820). Scottish xplorer of NW. Canada; **Mac-Kenzie River**, second-longest iver in N. America, flowing 2,500 ni. (4,025 km) from the Canadian Northwest Territories to Mac-kenzie Bay.

mack·er·el (măk′erel, măk′rel) *.* Edible sea fish (*Scomber :combrus*) of N. Atlantic, having a ilvery belly and greenish back with lark blue stripes; ~ **sky**, sky :overed with clouds resembling the patterns on a mackerel's back cirrocumulus).

Mack·i·nac (măk′inaw), **Straits of.** Strait separating Upper and Lower Michigan peninsula connecting lakes Huron and Michigan; **Mackinac Island**, sland and resort in Lake Huron, at the mouth of the strait.

Mac·Leish (maklēsh′), **Archibald** (1892–). Amer. poet and dramatist; librarian of Congress, 1939–44; assistant secretary of state, 1944–5; awarded Pulitzer Prize, 1933, 1953.

Mac·Mil·lan (makmĭl′an), **Harold** (**Maurice**) (1894–). British Conservative statesman; prime minister, 1957–63.

Mâ·con (mahkawń′) *n.* Wine made near Mâcon, a city on the river Saône in central France.

mac·ra·mé (măk′ramā) *n.* Fringe or trimming of knotted thread or cord.

macro- *prefix.* Large (opp. *micro-*).

mac·ro·bi·ot·ic (măkrōbīŏt′ĭk) *adj.* Relating to a diet of grains, vegetables, etc., believed to prolong life. ~ **s**, *n.*

mac·ro·ce·phal·ic (măkrōsefăl′-ĭk) *adj.* Long- or large-headed.

mac·ro·cosm (măk′rokŏzem) *n.* Great world, universe (contrasted with *microcosm*); any great whole.

mac·ro·e·co·nom·ics (măkrō-ēkonŏm′ĭks, ĕko-) *n.* (usu. considered sing.). Study of general economics of large units.

mac·ro·mol·e·cule (măkro-mŏl′ekūl) *n.* Very large molecule like those in proteins, synthetic plastics, etc.

mac·ro·pho·tog·ra·phy (măk-rofotŏg′rafē) *n.* Photography of macroscopic objects.

mac·ro·scop·ic (măkroskŏp′ĭk) *adj.* Visible to the naked eye (opp. *microscopic*). **mac·ro·scop′i·cal·ly** *adv.*

mac·u·la (măk′yula) *n.* (pl. **-lae** pr. **-lē**). Dark spot on sun or moon; spot in mineral due to presence of particles of another mineral; spot, blemish, on the skin; (anat.; also ~ **lu′tea**) region of greatest visual acuity in the retina. **mac′u·lar** *adj.* **mac·u·la·tion** (măkyulā′shon) *n.*

mad (măd) *adj.* Of disordered mind, insane; (of animals) rabid; wildly foolish; (colloq.) annoyed; ~ **about**, (colloq.) infatuated with;

mad′cap, wildly impulsive person; **mad′house**, lunatic asylum; **mad′man** (pl. **-men**), **mad′-woman** (pl. **-women**). **mad′ly** *adv.* **mad′ness** *n.*

Mad·a·gas·car (mădagăs′ker). Fourth largest island in the world, off the SE. coast of Africa; Democratic Republic of **M**~, also Malagasy Republic, co-extensive with Madagascar Island; former French colony; capital, Tananarive.

mad·am (măd′am) *n.* Polite formal address to woman; woman in charge of a brothel. [OF. *ma dame* my lady]

Mad·ame (măd′am, madahm′) *n.* (pl. **Mes·dames**, pr. mādahm′). Title of (corresp. to *Mrs.*) or form of address to French married woman. [Fr.]

mad·den (măd′en) *v.* Make, become, mad; irritate.

mad·der (măd′er) *n.* Herbaceous climbing plant (*Rubia tinctorum*) with yellowish flowers; red dye obtained from its root.

made (mād) *adj.*: see MAKE[1]; ~ **man**, one who has attained success in life; ~**-to-order**, made to particular specifications; custom-made; appropriate.

Ma·dei·ra[1] (madēr′a, -dār′a). Island in Atlantic Ocean, off W.

ATLANTIC OCEAN

MADEIRA

FUNCHAL

The city of **Madras** on the east coast of India is a port and commercial center. Its main industries are textiles, tanning, pottery and dye-making. Shown: the Church of St. Thomas, Madras.

coast of Africa, in Portuguese possession; ~, river in NW. Brazil, 2,000 mi. (3,220 km), flowing from the Bolivian border to the Amazon.

Ma·dei·ra[2] (madēr'a, -dār'a) *n.* 1. Fortified wine produced in Madeira, amber-colored or brownish, varying in sweetness, and resembling sherry. 2. (also ~ **cake**) Kind of rich sweet cake without fruit.

Mad·e·moi·selle (mădemozĕl', mădmwo-) *n.* (pl. **Mes·de·moi·selles** pr. mādmozĕl', mādmwo-). Title of (corresp. to *Miss*) or form of address to French unmarried woman; **m** ~, French governess in U.S. [Fr.]

Ma·di·nat al Shaab (mahdī-naht' ahl shahb'). Administrative capital of the People's Democratic Republic of Yemen, formerly Southern Yemen, in the SE. part.

Mad·i·son[1] (măd'ĭson). Capital of Wisconsin in the S. part.

Mad·i·son[2] (măd'ĭson), **James** (1751–1836). Amer. statesman and fourth president of the U.S., 1809–1817, during War of 1812; co-authored "The Federalist" papers advocating adoption of the Constitution; member of House of Representatives, 1789–97; secretary of state, 1801–9; his wife, **Dolley** (1768–1849), famous as a Washington hostess.

Mad·i·son (măd'ĭson) **Avenue.** Street in Manhattan, New York City, on or near which are located many advertising agencies; hence (fig.) the advertising business.

Ma·don·na (madŏn'a) *n.* (Picture, statue, of) Virgin Mary; ~ **lily,** tall white lily (*Lilium candidum*), as often depicted in pictures of the Annunciation.

Ma·dras (madrăs', -drahs'). Seaport on E. coast of India, capital of Tamil Nadu; **madras,** cotton cloth usu. striped or corded.

mad·re·pore (măd'ropōr) *n.* Perforate coral of genus *Madrepora*; animal producing this. [It. *madre* mother + *poro* corallike but porous substance]

Ma·drid (madrĭd'). Capital city of Spain.

mad·ri·gal (măd'rigal) *n.* Short amatory poem; part song for several voices in elaborate contrapuntal style, usu. without accompaniment.

Mae·an·der (mēăn'der). Ancient name of a river of Phrygia, (now R. *Menderes*) remarkable for its winding course.

Mae·ce·nas (mēse'nas, mī-), **Gaius Cilnius** (c70–8 B.C.). Roman knight; patron of Virgil and Horace and friend and adviser of

Augustus; celebrated for his patronage of learning and letters; hence, generous patron of literature or art.

mael·strom (māl'strom) *n.* Great whirlpool (also fig.). [f. *Maelström*, the whirlpool S. of the Lofoten Is. off W. coast of Norway]

mae·nad (mē'năd) *n.* Bacchante. **mae·nad'ic** *adj.*

maes·tro (mīs'trō) *n.* (pl. **-tros** pr. -trōz, **-tri** pr. -trē). Eminent musical composer, teacher, or conductor.

Mae·ter·linck (mā'terlĭngk), **Maurice** (1862–1949). Belgian poet and dramatist; received Nobel Prize for literature 1911.

Mae West (mā' wĕst'). Inflatable life jacket. [professional name of Amer. film actress (1892–1980)]

Maf·e·king (mah'fekĭng). Town in Cape Province, S. Africa; during the second Boer War a small British force under Baden-Powell with-

Mafeking, a small town in Cape Pr[ov]ince, South Africa, is remembered [for] the siege that took place there dur[ing] the Boer War. The British force, und[er] Baden-Powell, was relieved after sev[eral] months in May 1900.

stood a siege there for sev[eral] months; its relief, in May 190[0], caused riotous rejoicing (**maffic·ing**) in London.

maf·fick·ing (măf'ĭkĭng) *n.:* s[ee] MAFEKING.

ma·fi·a (mah'fēa) *n.* 1. ([In] Sicily) Spirit of hostility to the la[w] and its ministers prevailing amo[ng] a part of the population; also, tho[se] who share in this spirit. 2. (**M** ~) Secret international crimin[al] organization.

ma·fi·o·so (mahfeō'sō) *n.* (pl. -si pr. -sē). Member of the Mafi[a].

Ma·ga·lla·nes (mahgahyah'nĕs). Formerly Punta Arenas, world[s] southernmost city, in Chile o[n] Strait of Magellan.

The **maggot** of the hoverfly feeds on other insects including the black citrus aphid, which it sucks dry. Maggots of other species of insect feed on plants, decaying organic matter, dung and mud.

mag·a·zine (măg′azēn, măg-zēn′) *n.* 1. Store for explosives, arms, or military provisions; receptacle for number of rounds loaded at one time in rifle and various types of automatic gun; reservoir or supply chamber in a machine, store, battery, etc. 2. periodical publication containing articles on various subjects by different writers. [Arab. *makhasin* storehouses]

Mag·da·lene (măg′dalēn), **Mag·da·len** (măg′dalĭn). Appellation of Mary of Magdala (Luke 8), disciple of Christ, commonly identified with the "sinner" of Luke 7 and traditionally represented as a prostitute restored to purity and sanctified by repentance and faith; hence, a reformed prostitute.

Mag·da·le·ni·an (măgdalē′-ĕan) *adj.* Of the paleolithic culture that followed the Aurignacian and Solutrean and is characterized by weapons and tools of horn and bone. [f. rock shelter of La Madeleine, Dordogne, France]

Mag·de·burg (măg′debĕrg). City in E. Germany; ~ **hemispheres**, pair of copper hemispheres joined to form a hollow globe from which the air could be extracted, after which they were practically inseparable, devised by a German physicist, Otto von Guericke (1602–86), to demonstrate the effect of air pressure.

Ma·gel·lan (majĕl′an). **Fernão de Magalhães** (*c*1470–1521), Portuguese navigator; the first European to pass through the strait that bears his name, between Tierra del Fuego and the S. Amer. mainland; he undertook the first

expedition around the world, but perished in the Philippines (only one of his ships completed the voyage).

ma·gen·ta (majĕn′ta) *n.* Brilliant crimson aniline dye (fuchsin), discovered in the year of the battle of Magenta; color of this.

Mag·gio·re (mahjō′rĕ), **Lake.** Alpine lake and resort area between N. Italy and S. Switzerland.

mag·got (măg′ot) *n.* Grub or larva, esp. of bluebottle or cheesefly; (rare) fad, whim. **mag′got·y** *adj.* 1. Full of maggots. 2. (rare) Full of strange whims.

Ma·ghreb, Ma·ghrib (mahgrēb′). Arabic name for the region of NW. Africa usu. including Morocco, Tunisia, Algeria, and sometimes Libya.

Ma·gi (mā′jī): see MAGUS.

mag·ic (măj′ĭk) *n.* Pretended art of influencing events by occult control of nature or of spirits, witchcraft; mysterious agency or power; **black, white, ~,** magic performed by aid of demons, of benevolent spirits. **magic** *adj.* Of, producing, produced by, magic; ~ **latern**: see LANTERN; ~ **square,** square divided into smaller squares each containing a number, so arranged that the sums of the rows, vertical, horizontal, or diagonal, are the same. **mag′i·cal** *adj.* **mag′i·cal·ly** *adv.*

ma·gi·cian (majĭsh′an) *n.* One skilled in magic, wizard.

Ma·gi·not (măzh′inō) **line.** Line of fortifications built in the years preceding World War II along the eastern borders of France from Montmédy to Belfort; crossed by German forces in 1940. [André Maginot (1877–1932), French war minister]

mag·is·te·ri·al (măjĭstēr′ēal) *adj.* Of a magistrate; dictatorial. **mag·is·te′ri·al·ly** *adv.*

mag·is·tra·cy (măj′ĭstrasē) *n.* (pl. **-cies**). Magistrates; magisterial office.

mag·is·trate (măj′ĭstrāt, -strĭt) *n.* Civil officer administering law; person appointed to try minor offenses and small civil cases and conduct preliminary hearing of serious offenses. **mag′is·trate·ship, mag·is·tra·ture** (măj′-ĭstrācher) *ns.*

mag·ma (măg′ma) *n.* (pl. **-mas, -ma·ta** pr. -mata). (geol.) Mixture of molten and crystalline materials that, on cooling, forms igneous rocks.

Mag·na Char·ta, Car·ta (măg′na kär′ta). Great charter of the liberties of England, granted by

King John, under pressure from his barons, at Runnymede in 1215; among its chief provisions was that no freeman should be imprisoned or banished except by the law of the land and that supplies should not be exacted without the consent of the Common Council of the realm. [L. *magna carta* great charter]

mag·na cum lau·de (măg′na kōōm low′de). College or university degree granted with high honors; the winner of such honors. [L., = "with great praise"]

mag·nan·i·mous (măgnăn′-imus) *adj.* Forgiving, free from petty resentment. **mag·nan′-i·mous·ly** *adv.* **mag·na·nim′i·ty** (măgnanĭm′ĭtē) *n.*

mag·nate (măg′nāt, -nĭt) *n.* Man of high position, wealth, authority, power, etc., often with reference to class or occupation, as **financial** ~.

mag·ne·sia (măgnē′zha, -sha, -zēa) *n.* (chem.) Magnesium oxide (MgO); **milk of** ~, suspension of magnesium hydroxide in water, used medicinally. **mag·ne′sian** *adj.*

mag·ne·si·um (măgnē′zēum, -zhum, -shum) *n.* (chem.) Silvery-white metallic element, symbol Mg, at. no. 12, at. wt. 24.305, burning with a bright white light.

mag·net (măg′nĭt) *n.* 1. Piece of iron, steel, cobalt, nickel, or one of their alloys to which has been imparted by contact, induction, or electric current the property of attracting iron and of pointing north. 2. (fig.) Thing that attracts.

mag·net·ic (măgnĕt′ĭk) *adj.* Of or like or acting as magnet; (fig.) very attractive; ~ **declination, deviation**, angular difference between true and magnetic meridians; ~ **dip**, magnetic inclination; ~ **equator**, imaginary line around Earth, at all points along which the magnetic inclination is zero; ~ **field**: see FIELD; ~ **inclination**, vertical angle between the horizontal and the direction of Earth's magnetic field at any point; ~ **mine**, sea mine designed to be detonated by the magnetic field of a steel ship passing near it; ~ **moment**, torque exerted by a magnetic field on any magnetized object within it; ~ **needle**: see NEEDLE def. 2; ~ **north**, magnetic pole some 6 degrees W. of true north; ~ **pole**, either of the poles of a magnet; either of the two

points on Earth's surface toward which the compass needle points and at which it dips vertically; ~ **storm**, erratic disturbance of Earth's magnetism, probably due to solar electric activity; ~ **tape**, strip of usu. plastic material coated with magnetic oxide to make it sensitive to electromagnetism. **mag·net′-i·cal·ly** *adv.* **mag·net′ics** *n.* Branch of physics that deals with magnetic phenomena.

mag·net·ism (măg′netĭzem) *n.* 1. Magnetic phenomena; science of these; **terrestrial** ~, magnetic properties of Earth as a whole. 2. (fig.) Attraction, personal charm.

mag·net·ite (măg′netīt) *n.* Magnetic iron oxide (Fe_3O_4).

mag·net·ize (măg′netīz) *v.t.* (**-ized, -iz·ing**). Make into a magnet; attract as a magnet does. **mag·net·i·za·tion** (măgnetīzā′-shon) *n.*

mag·ne·to (măgnē′tō) *n.* (pl. **-tos**). Magnetoelectric machine, esp. an alternating current generator with permanent magnets used to generate the electric ignition spark in an internal combustion engine.

mag·ne·to·chem·is·try (măg-nētōkĕm′ĭstrē) *n.* That branch of science which treats of the relation of magnetic to chemical phenomena. **mag·ne·to·chem′i·cal** *adj.*

mag·ne·to·e·lec·tric·i·ty (măg-nētōĭlĕktrĭs′ĭtē) *n.* Electricity generated by relative movement of

electric conductors and magne **mag·ne·to·e·lec′tric** *adj.*

mag·ne·tom·e·ter (măgnetŏm′ eter) *n.* Instrument for the mea urement of magnetic forces, es terrestrial magnetism.

mag·ne·to·mo·tive (măgnēt-mō′tĭv) *adj.* ~ **force**, (abbrev. mr or m.m.f.) sum of the magnetizin forces in a magnetic circuit (t) magnetic analogy of electromoti force).

mag·ne·ton (măg′netŏn) *n.* Ur of magnetic moment, used measuring the magnetic moment electrons and protons.

mag·ne·tron (măg′netrŏn) *n.* Kind of thermionic vacuum tube which the motion of the electror is controlled by an external applied magnetic field. 2. Ele tronic device utilizing an axi magnetic field for generating ele tromagnetic radiations of very sho wavelength. [f. *magnet* and *electro*

mag·nif·i·cent (măgnĭf′isen *adj.* Splendid, sumptuou imposing, stately; fine, excellen **mag·nif′i·cent·ly** *adv.* **mag·nif i·cence** *n.*

mag·ni·fy (măg′nĭfī) *v.t.* (**-fie -fy·ing**). Increase apparent size c as with lens, microscope, or conca mirror; exaggerate; (archaic) exto **mag·ni·fi·ca·tion** (măgnĭfĭka shon) *n.* **angular** ~, (optics) rat of the angle subtended by th object.

mag·nil·o·quent (măgnĭl

went) *adj.* Lofty in expression;
astful. **mag·nil'o·quence** *n.*
ag·nil'o·quent·ly *adv.*

mag·ni·tude (măg'nĭtŏod, -tūd)
Largeness; size; importance; one
e classes into which the fixed
rs have been arranged acc. to
ir brilliancy; **of the first ~**,
.) of great importance.

mag·no·lia (măgnōl'ya, -nō'lēa)
(pl. **-lias**, collect. **-lia**). Tree of
nus *M ~*, with conspicuous wax-
e flowers and dark green foliage,
ive in America and Asia. [Pierre
agnol, Fr. botanist (1638–1715)]

mag·num (măg'num) *n.* (Bottle
ntaining) two quarts (of wine
.).

mag·num o·pus (măg'num
us). Chief production of a writer
other artist; great literary under-
.ing. [L., = great work]

Magog: see GOG AND MAGOG.

mag·pie (măg'pī) *n.* Any of
ious birds of the family Corvidae
ch long pointed tail and black and
ite plumage, noted for their
attering; the species *Pica pica* is
mmon in N. Europe and Western
America; (fig.) idle chatterer.

ma·gus (mā'gus) *n.* (pl. **-gi** pr.
). 1. Member of ancient Persian
estly caste; one skilled in
iental magic and astrology. 2.
e Magi, the (traditionally three)
ise men" who came from the
st bearing gifts to the infant Jesus
rist (Matt. 2). **ma·gi·an** (mā'-
n) *adj. & n.* **ma'gi·an·ism** *n.*
octrines, philosophy, of the
rsian magi.

Mag·yar (măg'yär; *Hung.* mŭd'-
r) *n.* Member, language, of a
ongoloid people predominant in
ungary; Hungarian. ~ *adj.* Of
e Magyars.

Ma·ha·bha·ra·ta (mahahbah'-
ta). One of the two great epics

The **magnolia** is native to Asia and North America and has about 80 species. It is valued for its large and fragrant white, yellow, pink or purple flowers which have a waxy quality.

(the other being the Ramayana) of the Hindus, supposed to have been composed *c*500 B.C.

ma·ha·ra·jah ma·ha·ra·ja
(mahharah'ja) *ns.* Title of some Indian princes. **ma·ha·ra·nee, ma·ha·ra·ni** (mahharah'nē) *ns.* Maharajah's wife. [*Hind. mahā* great, *rāja* king, *rānī* queen]

ma·hat·ma (mahaht'ma, -hăt'-) *n.* In Buddhism, one of a class of persons with preternatural powers supposed to exist in India and Tibet; person regarded with reverence. [*Sansk. mahātman* great souled]

Ma·ha·ya·na (mahhayah'na) *n.* One of the two great schools of BUDDHISM, developed in China, Japan, and Tibet. [*Sansk. mahā* great, *yâna* vehicle]

Maidenhair fern, one of 200 species, has delicate and often drooping fronds. It is widely cultivated as an ornamental plant but is susceptible to frost and heat.

mah-jongg, mah-jong (mah'-jŏng', -zhŏng) *ns.* Chinese game for four players played with 144 tiles, in which by discarding and drawing tiles each player attempts to obtain four sets of three tiles each together with one pair.

Mah·ler (mah'ler), **Gustav** (1860–1911). Austrian conductor and composer, esp. of symphonies.

ma·hog·a·ny (mahŏg'anē) *n.* Reddish-brown wood esp. of a tropical Amer. tree (*Swietenia mahogani*), used for furniture etc. and taking high polish; tree producing this; color of this wood.

Ma·hom·et (mahŏm'ĭt). Var. of MUHAMMAD.

ma·hout (mahowt') *n.* Elephant driver.

Ma·ia (mī'a). 1. (Gk. myth.) Daughter of Atlas and mother of Hermes. 2. (Rom. myth.) Goddess associated with Vulcan, and also (by confusion with 1 above) with Mercury. [Gk., = "mother," "nurse"]

maid (mād) *n.* 1. (archaic and poet.) maiden; **the M ~ (of Orleans)**, Joan of Arc; **old ~**, elderly spinster; game of cards; **~ of honor**, unmarried woman attending bride. 2. Female servant.

maid·en (mā'den) *n.* 1. (archaic and poet.) Girl; spinster; virgin. 2. (hist.) One of two supports for bobbin in spinning wheel. 3. (hist.) Kind of guillotine formerly used in Edinburgh. 4. Maiden horse. ~ *adj.* Unmarried (usu. in ~ **aunt, lady**); (obs.) virgin; untried; with blank record; (of horse) that has never won a race; **maidenhair**

The Australian **magpie** has a loud, metallic call and black and white plumage. It is aggressive, especially during the breeding season, and attacks larger birds and even man.

The state of **Maine** is on the extreme north-eastern coast of U.S.A. It was colonized by the English in the 17th and 18th centuries. Agriculture is one of its main industries. Here the blueberry harvest is being sorted.

(**fern**), kind of fern (genus *Adiantum*), with hairlike stalks and delicate fronds; **maidenhair tree**, GINKGO; **maid′enhead**, virginity; hymen; **maiden name**, woman's surname before marriage; **maiden speech**, one made in legislature by a member speaking for the first time. **maid′en·hood** *n.* **maid′-en·ly** *adv.*

mail[1] (māl) *n.* (hist.) Armor of rings or chainwork, or of metal plates; **mailed fist**, (fig.) armed power.

mail[2] (māl) *n.* (Letter etc. conveyed by) post; train or other vehicle carrying post; **mail′box**, public box for depositing outgoing mail; private box for incoming mail; **mail′man**, postman, man who carries and delivers mail; **mail order**, order for goods to be sent by mail; **mail order** (attrib.). **mail** *v.t.* Send by post.

Mail·lol (mahyawl′), **A·ris·tide** (ahrĭstēd′) (1861–1944). French painter and sculptor; known for statues sculpted in the Greek tradition of the 5th c. B.C.

maim (mām) *v.t.* Cripple, mutilate.

Mai·mon·i·des (mīmŏn′idēz). Moses ben Maimon (1135–1204), Spanish-Jewish philosopher and Rabbinic scholar, much influenced by Greek, esp. Aristotelian, philosophy.

Main (mīn). River in West Germany flowing W. from N. Bavaria into the Rhine at Mainz.

main[1] (mān) *adj.* Chief, principal; exerted to the full; ~ **chance**, opportunity for greatest (personal) advantage; **main′land**, country or continent without its adjacent islands; so **main′lander**; **Main Line**, fashionable suburbs W. of Philadelphia along the railroad line; **main line**, principal railroad line or highway; (slang) principal vein esp. as site of drug injection; **main′line** (*v.*) (**-lined, -lin·ing**), (slang) take drugs thus; **main′lin·er** *n.* **main′mast**, principal mast of a ship; **main′sail** (*naut.* pr. mān′sal), (in square-rigged vessel) lowest sail of mainmast; (in fore-and-aft rig) sail set on after part of mainmast; **main′-spring**, chief spring of watch or clock (also fig.); **main′stay**, stay running from top of mainmast to foot of foremast; (fig.) chief support; **main′stream**, (fig.) principal course or trend. **main′ly** *adv.*

main[2] (mān) *n.* Physical force (only in **with might and** ~); (poet.) high sea; principal channel,

Maize (corn) is used as food for both livestock and humans and as a raw material in industry. It is the most important crop in the U.S.A. which produces almost half the world's total supply.

duct, conductor, etc., for water, sewage, electricity, etc.; *Spanish* **M~**: see SPANISH.

Maine (mān). Northeastern state of U.S., on the Atlantic coast; admitted to the Union in 1820; capital, Augusta.

main·tain (māntān′) *v.t.* Carry on, keep up; support; assert as true.

main·te·nance (mān′tenans) Maintaining; (provision of) means of subsistence.

mai·tre d'hô·tel (māter dōtĕ; mātre; *Fr.* mĕtr dōtĕl′) *n.* (**mai·tres d'hô·tel** pr. māte dōtĕl′, mātrez; *Fr.* mĕtr dōtĕ Major-domo; HEADwaiter; (collo **maître d'.** [*Fr.*, = master of hot

maize (māz) *n.* 1. corn. Corncolor, pale yellow.

Maj. *abbrev.* Major.

ma·jes·tic (mạjĕs′tĭk) *a* Characterized by majest imposing, stately. **ma·jes′ti·cal·**

Majorca is the largest of the Balearic Islands in the western Mediterranean. It is a Spanish province and has a mild sunny climate which makes it a popular tourist center. Shown here is La Cartuja Monastery on the island.

maj·es·ty (măj′ĭstē) *n.* (pl. **-s**). 1. Impressive stateliness; ~ereign power; **Your, His, Her, ~**, title used in speaking to or ~overeign. 2. Representation of ~d or Christ (or occas. Virgin ~ry) enthroned within an aureole; **Christ in M~**.

ma·jol·i·ca (majŏl′ĭka, -yŏl′-) *n.* ~ian earthenware coated with an ~que white enamel ornamented ~h metallic colors; modern ~tation of this. [It., f. former ~e of *Majorca*, ships of which brought Spanish wares to Italy]

ma·jor[1] (mā′jer) *n.* Army officer next in rank below lieutenant colonel and above captain.

ma·jor[2] (mā′jer) *adj.* Greater of two things, classes, etc.; senior; (mus.) of intervals, greater by a chromatic semitone than those called minor; normal or perfect; (of keys) in which the scale has a major third; ~ **premise**, (logic) first of a syllogism, containing a statement of the general rule; ~ **suit**, (bridge) spades or hearts; ~ **term**, (logic) predicate of the conclusion of a syllogism. **major** *n.* Person of full legal age; major premise; (in colleges) subject to which special attention is given in a course of study, whence ~ (*v.i.*) take, or qualify *in*, such subject; ~**-do·mo** (-dō′mō), steward or butler; ~ **general**, Army officer ranking next above a brigadier general and below a lieutenant general.

Ma·jor·ca (majōr′ka, -yōr′-). (*Sp.* **Mallorca** pr. mahlyōrkah) Largest of the Balearic Islands.

ma·jor·i·ty (majōr′ĭtē, -jär′-) *n.* (pl. **-ties**). 1. Greater number or part (*of*); **absolute** ~, more than half number of electors or actual voters. 2. Number by which votes cast on one side exceed those on the other. 3. Full legal age. 4. Office of major in military. 5. ~ **leader**, leader of majority party in a legislature, as in U.S. Senate or House.

ma·jus·cule (majŭs′kūl, măj′-us-) *adj.* (paleog.; of a letter) Large (whether capital or uncial); written in majuscule. ~ *n.* Majuscule letter; formal script, orig. based on Roman monumental lettering, used in manuscripts until the development of the MINUSCULE from cursive writing. **ma·jus′cu·lar** *adj.*

Ma·ka·lu (mŭk′alōō). Mountain, 27,790 ft. (8,337 m), in the Himalayas on the Nepal-Tibet border near Mt. Everest.

make[1] (māk) *v.* (**made, mak·ing**). Create, manufacture; cause to exist, bring about; amount to, constitute; bring total up to; represent as being or doing; acquire by effort, earn; win (trick at cards); score (touchdown, goal, etc.); produce by cookery; perform, execute; utter or record (remark etc.); (slang) seduce, persuade to have sexual intercourse; ~ **believe**, pretend; ~**-believe** (*n.*) pretense; ~ **do**, manage *with* what is available or inferior substitute; ~ **for**, take direction of; ~ **good**, fulfill (promise etc.), prove (statement); pay for, repair (damage etc.); succeed in an undertaking; ~ **off**, depart hastily; ~ **off with**, carry away, steal; ~ **out**, draw up or write out (list etc.); prove; represent as; understand; (colloq.) succeed; (slang) neck, pet; **make′shift** (*n. & adj.*) temporary (expedient); **make up**, supply deficiency, complete; arrange; concoct usu. as

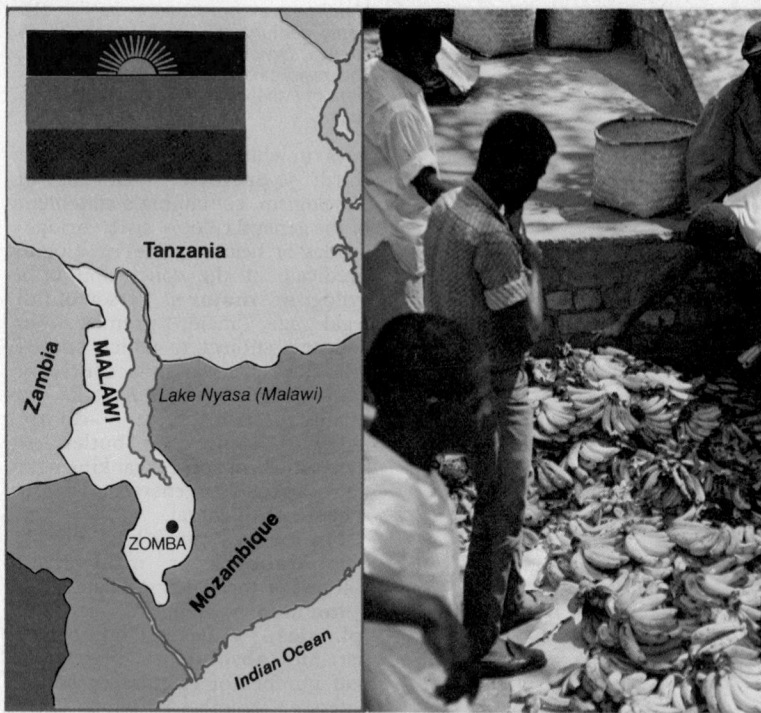

The central African republic of **Malawi** is separated from Mozambique and Tanzania by Lake Nyasa (Malawi), the third largest lake in Africa. Blantyre is one of the main industrial centers, and a market town for crops.

fiction; put an end to (a quarrel); adapt (face etc. of actor) for his part; apply cosmetics (to); **make-up** (*n.*) way actor etc. is made up; way type is made up into pages; fundamental qualities of person's nature; ~ **up to**, curry favor with; **make′-weight**, small quantity added to make up required weight; unimportant argument etc. to supply deficiency.

make[2] (māk) *n.* Way thing is made; figure, shape; brand, sort; **on the** ~, (slang) intent on gain; (slang) or seeking sexual partners.

mak·er (mā′ker) *n.* One who makes; esp. **M** ~, the Creator.

mak·ing (mā′king) *n.* Creating, manufacturing, etc.; (pl.) what one earns; essential qualities, as *he has the* ~*s of a general.*

mal- *prefix.* 1. Bad(ly), as *maltreat.* 2. Un-, as *maladroit.*

Mal·a·bar (măl′abār). Coastal district of SW. India.

Ma·la·bo (mah′lahbō). Formerly Santa Isabel; capital, Equatorial Guinea.

Ma·lac·ca (malăk′a). State of Malaysia, on W. coast Malay Peninsula; its capital; **Strait of** ~, strait *c*500 miles (805 km) long between SW. end of Malay Peninsula and Sumatra; ~ **cane**, rich brown walking cane made of the stem of a palm tree (*Calamus scipionum*).

Mal·a·chi (măl′akī). Prophetic book of the Old Testament, belonging to a period immediately before Ezra and Nehemiah; Malachi is prob. not a personal name. [Heb., = "my messenger"]

mal·a·chite (măl′akīt) *n.* Hydrated copper carbonate, a bright green mineral taking a high polish and used as decorative stone.

mal·ad·just·ment (mălajŭst′-ment) *n.* Faulty adjustment; person's psychological inability to adjust himself, his wishes, etc., to his environment. **mal·ad·just′ed** *adj.*

mal·ad·min·is·tra·tion (măl-admĭnĭstrā′shon) *n.* Faulty administration.

mal·a·droit (măladroit′) *adj.* Bungling; tactless. **mal·a·droit′ly** *adv.* **mal·a·droit′ness** *n.*

mal·a·dy (măl′adē) *n.* (pl. **-dies**). Ailment, disease.

Mal·a·ga[1] (măl′aga; *Sp.* mah′-lahgah). Province of S. Spain, part of the ancient kingdom of Granada;

its capital, a Mediterranean seapo⟨rt⟩

Mal·a·ga[2] (măl′aga) *n.* Da⟨rk⟩ sweet fortified wine produced ne⟨ar⟩ the city of Malaga.

Mal·a·gas·y (mălagăs′ē) *adj.* ⟨&⟩ *n.* (Native, language) ⟨of⟩ Madagascar; ~ **Republic**: s⟨ee⟩ MADAGASCAR.

ma·laise (mălāz′; *Fr.* mălĕz′)⟨.⟩ Feeling of uneasiness or d⟨is⟩comfort.

Mal·a·prop (măl′aprŏp), **M**⟨rs⟩ In Sheridan's play *The Riv*⟨als⟩ (1775), a lady who ludicrous⟨ly⟩ misuses long words, as *illiterate h*⟨im⟩ *from your memory.* **mal′a·prop**⟨-⟩ **ism** *n.* Misapplication of a (lon⟨g⟩) word.

mal·ap·ro·pos (mălăprŏp⟨ō′⟩) *adv.* & *adj.* (Done, said, et⟨c.⟩) inopportunely. ~ *n.* Inopportu⟨ne⟩ remark etc.

ma·lar·i·a (malār′ēa) *n.* Int⟨er⟩mittent and remittent fever, caus⟨ed⟩ by a microorganism (*Plasmodiu*⟨m⟩) which is transmitted by the b⟨ite⟩ of certain mosquitoes of the gen⟨us⟩ *Anopheles.* **ma·lar′i·al, ma·la**⟨r′⟩**i·ous** *adjs.* [It. *mal′aria* bad ⟨air⟩ (because formerly attributed to u⟨n⟩wholesome exhalations of marshe⟨s⟩)]

Ma·la·wi (mahlah′wē). Repub⟨lic⟩ of central Africa; member nati⟨on⟩ of the Brit. Commonweal⟨th⟩; formerly the British protectorate ⟨of⟩ Nyasaland, independent 19⟨64⟩; capital, Lilongwe.

Ma·lay (mā′lā, malā′)⟨.⟩ Member of a light brown peo⟨ple⟩ of mixed Caucasian and Mongoli⟨an⟩ stock, predominating in the Ma⟨lay⟩ Peninsula and Archipelag⟨o⟩; language of this people. ~ *a*⟨dj.⟩ Of Malays or their country ⟨or⟩ language; ~ **Archipelago**, v⟨ery⟩ large group of islands, includ⟨ing⟩ Sumatra, Java, Borneo, the Phi⟨lip⟩pines, and New Guinea, lying S⟨.⟩

The federation of **Malaysia** was est⟨ab⟩lished in 1963. It is the world's lead⟨ing⟩ producer of tin, and palm oil, rub⟨ber⟩ rice and copra are important produ⟨ce⟩. Shown here: Malaysia's map and f⟨lag⟩. Facing page: Women planting rice ⟨in⟩ Sabah.

of Asia and N. and NE. of Australia; **~ Peninsula**, most southerly projection of the mainland of Asia, running southward from Thailand.

Ma·lay·a (malā´a). Known as West Malaysia since 1966; a former federation of 11 Malay States, 1957–63, now part of the Federation of Malaysia.

Ma·lay·sia (malā´zha, -sha). Federation of States within the British Commonwealth, formed in 1963, comprising West Malaysia, Sabah, and Sarawak; capital, Kuala Lumpur. **Ma·lay′sian** *adj. & n.*

mal·con·tent (măl´kontĕnt) *n.* Discontented person, one inclined to rebellion.

măl de mer (măl de mār´). Seasickness. [Fr.]

Mal·dives (măl´dīvz). Formerly called Maldive Islands; a republic consisting of a group of islands in the Indian Ocean SW. of Sri Lanka; formerly a British protectorate, independent since 1965; capital, Malé; **Mal·div·i·an** (măldĭv´ēan) *adj. & n.*

male (māl) *adj.* 1. Of the sex in human beings, other animals, and plants, that begets young by fecundating the female; **~ chauvinist** (*n.*), (derog.) man showing excessive loyalty to other men and prejudice against women; also **~ chauvinist(ic) pig; ~ chauvinism** (*n.*). 2. (of part of machinery etc.) designed to enter or fill the corresponding female (hollow) part; **~ screw**: see SCREW[1]; **~ fern**, fern (*Dryopteris filixmas*), producing an oleoresin used for expelling tapeworms. **male** *n.* Male person, animal, or plant.

Ma·lé (mahlē´). Principal island and capital of the Maldives.

mal·e·dic·tion (măledĭk´shon) *n.* Curse. **mal·e·dic′to·ry** *adj.*

mal·e·fac·tor (măl´efăkter) *n.* Criminal, evildoer. **mal·e·fac·tion** (mălefăk´shon) *n.*

ma·lef·ic (malĕf´ĭk) *adj.* Harmful, baneful. **ma·lef′i·cent** *adj.* Hurtful; criminal. **ma·lef′i·cence** *n.*

ma·lev·o·lent (malĕv´olent) *adj.* Wishing ill to others. **ma·lev′o·lence** *n.* **ma·lev′o·lent·ly** *adv.*

mal·fea·sance (mălfē´zans) *n.* Official misconduct.

mal·for·ma·tion (mălfôrmā´shon) *n.* Faulty formation. **mal·formed** (mălfôrmd´) *adj.*

Ma·li (mah´lē). Republic in W. Africa; formerly the French colony of Sudan; capital, Bamako.

mal·ice (măl´ĭs) *n.* Ill will; desire to do harm. **ma·li·cious** (malĭsh´us) *adj.* **ma·li′cious·ly** *adv.*

ma·lign (malīn´) *adj.* Maleficent; (of disease) malignant. **ma·lign′ly** *adv.* **malign** *v.t.* Speak ill of, slander.

ma·lig·nant (malĭg´nant) *adj.* 1. Feeling or showing intense ill

The republic of **Mali** in West Africa is largely desert and arid grazing land. Timbuktu, the old center of the caravan trade, is located in Mali. These cone-shaped houses are typical village dwellings in Mali.

will. 2. (path., of disease) Of the form that kills, as dist. from milder forms; (of tumor) cancerous, growing into surrounding tissue and destroying it and giving rise to secondary growths in other parts (opp. BENIGN). **ma·lig′nan·cy** *n.* **ma·lig′nant·ly** *adv.*

ma·lig·ni·ty (malĭg´nĭtē) *n.* (pl. **-ties**). Malignant character or feeling.

ma·lin·ger (malĭng´ger) *v.i.* Pretend illness to escape duty. **ma·lin′ger·er** *n.*

mall (mawl, mahl) *n.* Sheltered walk as promenade; shopping area.

mal·lard (măl´erd) *n.* (pl. **-lards**, collect. **-lard**). Wild duck (*Anas platyrhynchos*), from which most domestic ducks are descended, the male being distinguished by a green or dark-blue head and a white ring around the neck.

Mal·lar·mé´ (măl ärmā´), **Stéphane** (1842–98). French symbolist poet; author of "L'Après-midi d'un Faune."

mal·le·a·ble (măl´ēabel) *adj.* (of metal etc.) That can be hammered, beaten, or rolled into a different form without a tendency to return to its original form or to fracture; adaptable, pliable. **mal·le·a·bil′i·ty** *n.*

mal·let (măl´ĭt) *n.* Hammer (usu. wooden); implement for striking croquet or polo ball.

mal·le·us (măl´ēus) *n.* (pl. **-le·i** pr. -lēī). Small bone of middle

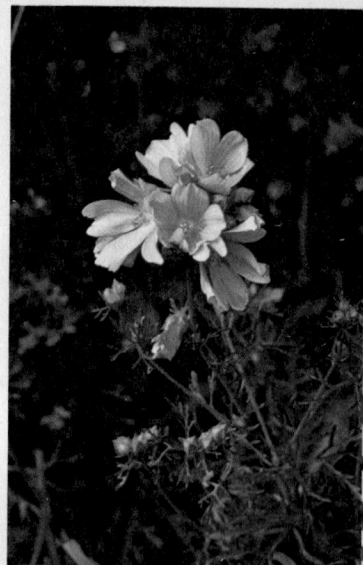

The **mallow** occurs in all except the coldest parts of the world, but is most numerous in the tropics. This musk mallow, which is one of about 1,000 species, is cultivated as a garden plant.

ear transmitting vibrations of tympanum to incus. [L., = "hammer"]

Mal·lor·ca (mahyôr´ka; *Span.* mahlyôr´kah): see MAJORCA.

mal·low (măl´ō) *n.* Plant of genus *Malva*, usu. with purple, pink, or white flowers; any of various related plants, such as **rose ~** or **~ rose** (*Hibiscus moscheutos*).

mal·nu·tri·tion (mălnōōtrĭsh´on, -nū-) *n.* Underfeeding; diet that does not include what is needed for health.

mal·o·dor·ous (mălō´derus) *adj.*

Malta, an independent state in the Mediterranean, comprises the islands of Malta, Gozo and Comino. It was a British naval base during the 1939-45 war. Its capital is Valletta, whose Grand Harbor is shown here.

The **mamba**, a large dangerous and poisonous snake, is found in Africa south of the Sahara where it hunts small animals. This green mamba is about 9ft. long.

Evil-smelling.

Mal·o·ry (măl'erē), **Sir Thomas** (d. 1471). English author; his *Le Morte d'Arthur*, a collection of Arthurian stories, was one of the first books printed by Caxton (1485).

Mal·pi·ghi (mahlpē'gē), **Marcello** (1628–94). Italian physician and anatomist, first to observe the movement of blood through the capillaries. **Mal·pigh·i·an** (mălpĭg'ēan) adj. (anat.) Of certain structures (esp. in the substance of the kidneys)

discovered by Malpighi.

mal·prac·tice (mălprăk'tĭs) n. Wrongdoing; (law) improper treatment of patient by medical attendant; illegal action for one's own benefit while in position of trust.

malt (mawlt) n. Barley or other grain for brewing, steeped in water, allowed to germinate and then dried slowly in a kiln; ~ **liquor**, liquor made from fermented malt (e.g. beer), not by distillation. **malt** v.t. Convert grain into malt.

Mal·ta (mawl'ta). Principal island of a group of three forming a nation in the Mediterranean, south of Sicily; member state of the British Commonwealth, independent 1964; capital, Valletta; occupied successively by Arabs

(870), Sicily (1090), the Order of St. John (1530), France (1788), and Britain (1814).

Mal·tese (mawltēz', -tēs') adj. Of Malta; ~ **cross**, cross of the Knights of Malta, (a military religious order founded in 1099) with four equal limbs broadened at the ends and indented. ~ n. (pl. and collect. **-tese**). Native, inhabitant, of Malta; its language, a dialect of Arabic, written in Roman characters.

Mal·thus (măl'thus), **Thomas Robert** (1766–1835). English clergyman and economist, author of an essay (1798) arguing that population increases faster than the means of subsistence and urging that its increase should be checked, mainly by sexual restraint. **Mal·thu·si·an** (mălthoo'zēan) adj. & n. **Mal·thu·si·an·ism** n.

malt·ose (mawl'tōs) n. (chem.) Sugar obtained by hydrolysis of starch by enzymes present in malt.

mal·treat (măltrēt') v.t. Illtreat. **mal·treat'ment** n.

ma·ma (mah'ma, mamah') n. (Child's name for) mother.

mam·ba (mahm'bah) n. Venomous African snake of genus *Dendraspis*.

mam·bo (mahm´bō) *n*. (pl. **-bos**). Latin-Amer. dance like rumba; music for it. [Amer. Sp. prob. f. Haitian]

mam·ma[1] (mah´ma, mamah´) = MAMA.

mam·ma[2] (măm´a) *n*. (pl. **-mae** pr. -mē). (anat.) Milk-secreting organ of female in mammals; corresponding rudimentary structure in males. **mam·mif·er·ous** (mămĭf´erus) *adj*.

mam·mal (măm´al) *n*. Member of the Mammalia, class of animals having mammae. **mam·ma·li·an** (mamā´lēan, -māl´yan) *adj*. & *n*.

mam·mal·o·gist (mamăl´ojĭst), **mam·mal·o·gy** (mamăl´ojē) *ns*. Student, study, of mammals.

mam·ma·ry (măm´arē) *adj*. Of the mammae.

mammato- *prefix*. (meteor.) Descriptive of clouds resembling rounded festoons, as ~-*cirrus*, ~-*cumulus*.

mam·mil·la (mamĭl´a) *n*. (pl. **-lae** pr. -lē). Nipple of female breast; nipple-shaped organ. **mam·mil·lar·y** (măm´ilĕr´ē), **mam·mil·late** (măm´ilāt) *adjs*.

Mam·mon (măm´on). Aramaic word for "riches" used in Matt. 6 and Luke 16, taken by medieval writers as the proper name of the devil of covetousness; this use was revived by Milton in *Paradise Lost*; hence, as personification, term of opprobrium for wealth regarded as an idol or evil influence. [Aram. *māmôn*]

mam·moth (măm´oth) *n*. Large extinct elephant with long hairy coat and curved tusks whose fossilized remains are found in N. America, northern Europe, and Asia. ~ *adj*. Huge.

Mam·moth (măm´oth) **Cave National Park.** National park in central Kentucky known for its limestone caverns.

mam·my (măm´ē) *n*. (pl. **-mies**). (Child's word for) mother; (chiefly U.S. Southern) black nurse of white children (usu. considered offensive).

man (măn) *n*. (pl. **men** pr. měn). 1. Human being, individual of the genus *Homo*, distinguished from other animals by superior mental development, power of articulate speech, and upright posture, etc.; person; human race. 2. Adult human male; husband; manservant; workman; (pl.) soldiers, the rank and file, as dist. from officers. 3. Piece in chess, checkers, etc. 4. **As one ~**, in unison; **to a ~**, without exception; ~ **about town**, man leading fashionable social life; ~ **and boy** (*adv*.) from boyhood on; ~-**eater**, cannibal; man-eating shark or tiger; ~ **Friday**, male assistant with various duties; **man'han'dle** (*v.t.*) (**-dled, -dling**), handle roughly; **man'-**

hole, opening in floor, pavement, usu. with cover, giving access to a sewer etc.; **man-hour**, one hour's work by one man, as measure of output in industry etc.; **man'hunt**, organized search for person, esp. criminal; **man in the street**, average citizen, ordinary person; **man-of-war**, warship; **man'-power**, amount of men available for military or other service; **The Man**, (black slang) all white men, a white man (derog.). **man** *v.t.* (**manned, man·ning**). Furnish with men for service or defense; place men at (part of ship); fill (post).

Man. *abbrev*. Manitoba.

ma·na (mah´na) *n*. Power, authority; magical or supernatural power. [Polynesian]

man·a·cle (măn´akel) *n*. (usu. pl.) & *v.t.* (**-cled, -cling**). Fetter, handcuff.

man·age (măn´ĭj) *v*. (**-aged, -ag·ing**). Handle, wield (tool etc.); conduct working of (business etc.); have effective control of (household, institution, etc.); subject (animal, person, etc.) to one's

*The **mammoth** was about the same size or slightly smaller than the modern elephant. The woolly mammoth which was found preserved in ice in Siberia was covered in long, reddish-brown hair. Mammoths figure significantly in the art of primitive man.*

control; gain one's ends with (person etc.) by flattery etc.; contrive (*to* do), succeed in one's aim; cope with. **man'age·a·bil·i·ty** (mănĭjabĭl´ĭtē) *n*. **man'age·a·ble** *adj*. **man'age·a·ble·ness** *n*. **man'age·a·bly** *adv*.

man·age·ment (măn´ĭjment) *n*. Act of managing; state of being managed; body of persons managing a business etc.; administration of business concern or public undertaking.

man·ag·er (măn´ĭjer) *n*. Person conducting a business, institution, etc. **man·a·ge·ri·al** (mănĭjēr´ēal) *adj*.

Ma·na·gua (mahnah´gwah) Lake in W. Nicaragua; capital of Nicaragua on the S. shore of the lake.

man·a·kin (măn´akĭn) *n*. One of the small gaily-colored birds of the passerine family Pipridae inhabiting Central and S. America.

Ma·na·ma (mănăm´a). Capital and principal port of Bahrein.

Ma·nas·sas (manăs´as). Town in NE. Virginia where Civil War battles of BULL RUN were fought 1861 and 1862, called Battles of Manassas by Confederates.

man·a·tee (măn´atē, mănatē´) *n*.

Large aquatic herbivorous mammal of genus *Trichechus*, living off W. African and Amer. tropical coasts.

Man·chu (mănchōō′) *adj. & n.* pl. **-chus**, collect. **-chu**). (Member) of a Tartar people who conquered China and founded the Ch'ing dynasty (1644–1912); (of) their language, written in a modified Mongolian script, at one time an official language of China, but now spoken only in parts of N. Manchuria.

Man·chu·kuo (măn′chōō′kwō′): see MANCHURIA.

Man·chu·ri·a (mănchoor′ēa). Region forming the NE. portion of China; in 1932 declared an independent nation by Japan and renamed **Manchukuo**; restored to China in 1945.

*The Toucan has an enormous **mandible** (beak). The reason for its size is not known. There are 37 species of the bird, which live in the tropical forests of America.*

Man·dae·an (măndē′an) *adj. & n.* (Member) of a Gnostic sect, of which a small community survives in Iraq, very hostile to Christianity since Byzantine times.

Man·da·lay (măn′dală, măndalā′). City of central Burma, on the Irrawaddy River.

man·da·mus (măndā′mus) *n.* (pl. **-mus·es**). Judicial writ issued as command to inferior court. [L., = "we command"]

man·da·rin (măn′derĭn) *n.* Former Chinese official in any of the nine grades; (transf.) pedantic official bureaucrat; form of the Chinese language spoken by officials and educated persons and used in official documents. [Sansk. *mantrin* counselor]

man·da·tar·y (măn′datĕrē) *n.* (pl. **-tar·ies**). One to whom a MANDATE is given.

man·date (măn′dāt, -dĭt) *n.* Authoritative command from superior; commission to act for another, esp. one given by League of Nations to a nation (the **mandatary**) to administer certain colonies of the defeated enemy powers in the war of 1914–18 for the benefit of the inhabitants; political instructions inferred from votes of electorate. ~ (măn′dāt) *v.t.* (**-dat·ed, -dat·ing**). Commit (nation etc.) *to* mandatary.

man·da·to·ry (măn′datōrē) *adj.* Of, conveying, a command. ~ *n.* = MANDATARY.

man·di·ble (măn′dĭbel) *n.* Lower jawbone; either part of bird's beak; either half of crushing organ in mouth parts of many arthropods. **man·dib·u·lar** (măndĭb′yuler), **man·dib'u·lar·y** *adjs.*

man·do·lin (măn′dolĭn, măndolĭn′) *n.* Musical instrument of lute kind with paired metal strings stretched on deeply rounded body, played tremolo with a plectrum.

man·drake (măn′drāk, -drĭk), **man·drag·o·ra** (măndrăg′era, -dragōr′a) *ns.* Poisonous plant with emetic and narcotic properties, with root formerly thought to resemble human form and to shriek when plucked up from the ground.

man·drel, man·dril (măn′drel) *ns.* Axis on which material revolves in lathe; rod around which metal etc. is forged or shaped.

man·drill (măn′drĭl) *n.* Large and ferocious baboon (*Mandrillus sphinx*) of W. Africa with highly colored patches and callosities on face and hindquarters.

mane (mān) *n.* Long hair on neck of horse, lion, etc. (also fig. of person's hair).

*The **manatee** is a slow-moving inoffensive creature that feeds on aquatic vegetation. It has no natural enemies but in some areas is hunted for its meat, hide and oil.*

The **mango** is one of the most important and widely cultivated fruits of the tropical world. Its juicy fruit is a rich source of vitamins A, C and D.

These Australian coastal **mangroves** have exposed supporting roots. These project above the mud, and have small openings through which air enters, passing through soft, spongy tissue to the roots beneath the mud.

Ma·nes (mā′nēz) (*c*215–75). (also **Manichaeus**) Founder of MANICHEISM.

ma·nes (mā′nēz; *Lat.* mah′něs) *n.* 1. (usu. considered pl.; Rom. myth.) Deified souls of departed ancestors. 2. (usu. considered sing.) Shade of dead person as object of reverence.

Ma·net (mănā′), **Edouard** (1832–83). French Impressionist painter.

ma·neu·ver (manoo′ver) *n.* Planned movement, (in pl.) large-scale exercise, of troops, warships, etc.; deceptive or elusive movement; skillful plan. ~ *v.* Perform, cause (troops etc.) to perform, maneuvers; employ artifice; force, manipulate, (person, thing *into*, *out*, etc.) by scheming or adroitness. **ma·neu′ver·a·ble** *adj.* **ma·neu·ver·a·bil′i·ty** *n.* (pl. -ties).

man·ful (măn′ful) *adj.* Brave, resolute. **man′ful·ly** *adv.* **man′ful·ness** *n.*

man·ga·bey (măng′gabā) *n.* (pl. -beys). Small long-tailed W. African monkey of genus *Cercocebus.* [name of a region in Madagascar]

man·ga·nese (măng′ganēs, -nēz) *n.* (chem.) Gray brittle metallic element, used in making alloys of steel, symbol Mn, at. no. 25, at. wt. 54.9380; ~ **dioxide**, black mineral (MnO_2) used as an oxidizing agent, esp. in glass-making, electric batteries, etc. [Fr. *manganèse*, corrupt. of MAGNESIA]

mange (mānj) *n.* Skin disease caused by a parasite that destroys hairy coat of animals, occas. communicated to man.

man·ger (mān′jer) *n.* Box or trough in stable etc. for horses or cattle to eat from.

man·gle¹ (măng′gel) *n.* Machine of two or more cylinders between which washed clothes are rolled to press out the water. ~ *v.t.* (-gled, -gling). Press (clothes) in mangle.

man·gle² (măng′gel) *v.t.* (-gled, -gling). Hack, cut about, mutilate; spoil, garble (text, pronunciation, etc.).

man·go (măng′gō) *n.* (pl. -goes, -gos). Fleshy fruit, eaten ripe or used green for pickles etc., of the Indian tree *Mangifera indica*; this tree.

man·grove (măng′grōv, măn′-) *n.* Tropical tree or shrub growing in mud at seashore with aerating roots above ground, esp. the **red** ~ (*Rhizophora mangle*) from coastal Florida to S. America.

man·gy (mān′jē) *adj.* (-gi·er, -gi·est). Having the mange; squalid, shabby. **man′gi·ly** *adv.* **man′gi·ness** *n.*

Man·hat·tan (mănhăt′an, man-). Island and borough of New York City at the mouth of the Hudson River.

man·hat·tan (mănhăt′an, man-. *n.* Cocktail made of sweet vermouth and whiskey with a dash of bitters.

man·hood (măn′hood) *n.* State of being a man; manliness, courage; men of a country etc.

ma·ni·a (mā′nēa) *n.* 1. Mental derangement marked by excitement, hallucination, and violence. 2. Excessive enthusiasm.

ma·ni·ac (mā′nēăk) *n.* Person afflicted with mania. **ma·ni·a·cal** (manī′akal) *adj.* **ma·ni·a·cal·ly** *adv.*

man·ic (măn′ĭk, mā′nĭk) *adj.* Of, affected with, mania; ~ **depressive**, (person) affected with mental disorder characterized by alternating mania and depression.

Man·i·che·ism, Man·i·chae·ism (măn′ikēĭzem) *ns.* Dualistic ascetic religious system, regarding existence as a conflict between the powers of light and the demons of darkness, which was widely accepted from the 3rd to the 5th c., founded by MANES. **Man·i·che′an, Man·i·chae′an** *adjs.* & *ns.*

**Man·i·che'an·ism, Man·i·chae'-
an·ism** *ns.* **Man'i·chee** *n.*
Manichean.

man·i·cure (măn'ĭkūr) *n.*
Cosmetic care and treatment of
hands and (esp.) fingernails. ~
v.t. (-**cured, -cur·ing**). Apply
manicure treatment to. **man'i·
cur·ist** *n.*

man·i·fest[1] (măn'ĭfĕst) *n.* List
of ship's cargo for use of customs
officials.

man·i·fest[2] (măn'ĭfĕst) *adj.*
Clear to sight or mind. **man'i·
fest·ly** *adv.* **manifest** *v.* Show
plainly to eye or mind; be evidence
of, prove; display, evince (quality,
feeling) by one's acts; (of thing)
reveal *itself*; (of ghost) appear.
man·i·fes·ta·tion (măn ifĕstā'-
shon) *n.* **man·i·fes·ta·tive** (măni-
ĕs'tatĭv) *adj.*

man·i·fes·to (măn ifĕs'tō) *n.* (pl.
-**toes**). Public declaration by
sovereign, nation, or body of
individuals, of principles and future
policy.

man·i·fold (măn'ĭfōld) *adj.*
Having various forms, applications,
functions, etc.; many and various.
~ *v.t.* Multiply copies of (letter
etc.). ~ *n.* (mech.) Pipe or
chamber with several openings.
man'i·fold·ly *adv.* **man'i·fold·
ness** *n.*

**man·i·kin, man·a·kin, man·-
ni·kin** (măn'ĭkĭn) *ns.* Little man,
dwarf; artist's lay figure; anatomical
model of the body; mannequin.

Ma·nil·a[1] (manĭl'a). City on
island of Luzon, principal city and
administrative capital of the
Philippine Islands; ~ (or **Manilla**)
hemp, a fibrous material, obtained

Manhattan, *a borough of New York
City consisting of Manhattan Island
(12½ miles long and 2½ miles wide),
is the financial, commercial and cultural
center of the city.*

from the leaves of *Musa textilis*,
a tree native to the Philippines, and
used for ropes, matting, textiles,
etc.; ~ **paper**, brown wrapping
paper orig. made from Manila
hemp.

Ma·nil·a[2], **Ma·nil·la** (manĭl'a)
ns. Manila hemp; Manila paper;
cigar or cheroot made of Philippine
tobacco.

man·i·oc (măn'ĕŏk, mā'nē-)
= CASSAVA. [native Brazilian
mandioca]

man·i·ple (măn'ĭpel) *n.* 1. (Rom.
antiq.) Subdivision of a legion,
containing 120 or 60 men. 2. One
of the Eucharistic vestments, orig.
a napkin, consisting now of a strip
of cloth 2–4 ft. in length, worn
hanging from left arm.

ma·nip·u·late (manĭp'yulāt) *v.t.*
(-**lat·ed, -lat·ing**). Handle; deal
skillfully with; manage craftily.
ma·nip·u·la·tion (manĭpyulā'-
shon), **ma·nip'u·la·tor** *ns.*

Man·i·to·ba (mănĭtō'ba).
Province of central Canada, with
coastline on Hudson Bay; capital,
Winnipeg; **Lake** ~, lake, 1,817 sq.
mi. (2,925 km), in S. part of this
province.

man·i·tou (măn'ĭtōō) *n.* (pl.
-**tous**, collect. -**tou**). (Algonquian
Ind.) Good or evil spirit, thing
having supernatural power.

man·kind (mănkīnd', măn'kīnd)
n. 1. Human species. 2. Male

sex, males.

man·like (măn'līk) *adj.* Like a
man; (of woman) mannish.

man·ly (măn'lē) *adj.* (-**li·er,
-li·est**). Having the qualities or
bearing of a man; befitting a man.
man'li·ness *n.*

Mann[1] (măn), **Horace** (1796–
1859). Amer. educator and lawyer;
revolutionized public school
system; member of U.S. House of
Representatives, 1848–53;
president of Antioch College, 1852–
1859.

Mann[2] (mahn), **Thomas** (1875–
1955). German novelist; U.S.
citizen from 1944; awarded Nobel
Prize for literature, 1929; author
of *Buddenbrooks, Death In Venice,
The Magic Mountain,* etc.

man·na (măn'a) *n.* Substance
miraculously supplied as food to
Israelites in wilderness (Exod. 16).

man·ne·quin, man·i·kin
(măn'ĭkĭn) *ns.* Woman who models
clothing; dummy figure for shop
windows etc.

man·ner (măn'er) *n.* Way a
thing is done or happens; outward
bearing; (pl.) behavior in social
intercourse; habits indicating good
breeding. **man'nered** *adj.* Showing mannerisms, affected; **ill-,
well-** ~, having bad, good,
manners. **man'ner·less** *adj.* Ill-
mannered.

man·ner·ism (măn'erĭzem) *n.* 1.
Trick of speech, gesture, or style;
excessive addiction to a distinctive
manner in art or literature. 2. Style
of art which originated in Italy
c1530 and preceded the Baroque,
characterized by contorted figures,
startling light effects, etc. **man'-**

ner·ist *adj.* & *n.* (Exponent) of mannerism in art, etc.

man·ner·ly (măn′erlē) *adj.* Well-mannered, polite. **man′-ner·li·ness** *n.*

man·nish (măn′ĭsh) *adj.* Characteristic of a man as opp. to a woman; (of woman) masculine. **man′nish·ness** *n.*

Ma·no·le·te (mahnawlĕ′tĕ) (1917–47). Original name, Manuel Laureamo Rodriguez y Sanchez; Spanish matador.

ma·nom·e·ter (manŏm′eter) *n.* Instrument for measuring the pressure of gases and vapors by the difference in level which they produce in a liquid in a U-tube, one side of which may be open to the atmosphere or evacuated and sealed off.

man·or (măn′er) *n.* English territorial unit, orig. feudal, the lord's demesne and lands from whose holders he could exact certain fees etc.; ∼ **house**, house of lord of the manor. **ma·no·ri·al** (manōr′ēal, -nōr′-) *adj.*

man·sard (măn′sard) *n.* Form of roof (usu. ∼ **roof**) in which each face has two slopes, the lower one steeper than the upper, usu. broken by projecting windows. [François *Mansart* (1598–1666), Fr. architect]

manse (măns) *n.* Ecclesiastical residence, esp. that of Scottish Presbyterian minister.

man·sion (măn′shon) *n.* Large residence.

man·slaugh·ter (măn′slawter) *n.* Slaughter of human beings; (law) unlawful killing of a human being without malice aforethought.

man·sue·tude (măn′swetŏod, -tūd) *n.* Gentleness, meekness.

man·ta (măn′ta) *n.* Very large ray of the family Mobubidae, living in tropical seas, with winglike fins; also called ∼ **ray**.

man·tel (măn′tel) *n.* Structure of wood, marble, etc., above and around fireplace; **man′telpiece**, mantel; shelf above fireplace.

man·tel·et, **mant·let** (măn′telĕt, -tlĭt) *ns.* Short mantle or cape; bulletproof screen for gunners.

man·tic (măn′tĭk) *adj.* Of divination.

man·til·la (măntĭl′a, -tē′a) *n.* Lace veil worn by Spanish women over head and shoulders.

man·tis (măn′tĭs) *n.* Orthopterous insect, esp. the **praying** ∼ (*Mantis religiosa*), which holds its forelegs in a position suggesting hands folded in prayer. [Gk., = "prophet"]

man·tis·sa (măntĭs′a) *n.* Decimal part of a logarithm. [L., = "makeweight"]

man·tle (măn′tel) *n.* Loose sleeveless cloak; fragile hood consisting usu. of oxides of thorium and cerium, fixed around gas jet to give incandescent light (also **gas** ∼); (zool.) covering or envelope, as that enclosing body of mollusk; (ornith.) back, scapulars, and wing coverts of bird, esp. when of distinguishing color; (geol.) region lying between

*The **mantis** feeds exclusively on living insects. There are about 1,800 species found mainly in tropical or sub-tropical regions. It may be disguised to resemble foliage, a lichen, a brightly colored flower or an ant.*

*Welding in a steel plant in Chica. Steel **manufacture** is a primary indus. in Chicago, and the volume produce. the highest of any city in the U.S. Allied metal industries are also wi. spread.*

crust and core of Earth; (fi covering. ∼ *v.* (**-tled, -tlin;** Envelop, cover (as) with mant (of liquids) form a scum; (of blocc suffuse cheeks; blush.

man·u·al (măn′ūal) *adj.* Of done with the hands. **man′u·al** *adv.* **manual** *n.* 1. Handbo textbook, primer. 2. Keyboard organ.

man·u·fac·ture (mănyu̇făk cher) *n.* Making of articles physical labor or machinery, e on large scale; branch of such industry; anything manufactur from raw products. ∼ *v.t.* (**-ture -tur·ing**). Produce by labor, e on large scale; invent, fabrica **man·u·fac′tur·er** *n.*

man·u·mit (mănyu̇mĭt′) *v* (**-mit·ted, -mit·ting**). Give fre dom to (slave). **man·u·mis·si** (mănyu̇mĭsh′on) *n.*

ma·nure (manoor′, -nūr′) Substance, esp. dung, used f fertilizing soil. ∼ *v.t.* (**-nure -nur·ing**). Apply manure to.

ma·nus (mā′nus) *n.* (pl. **-nu** (zool.) That part of the forelin of any tetrapod which correspon to the human hand, esp. the bon within it.

man·u·script (măn′yuskrĭp *adj.* & *n.* (Book, documen written by hand, not printed; (c author's written or typed copy f printer (abbrev. MS., pl. MSS.)

The **maple**, of which th
are 200 species, oc
widely in north tempe
regions and is highly va
for its wood. Its leaves
bright yellow, orange or
in the Fall. Maple sugar
by-prod

For long the effective ruler of China and
the chairman of China's Communist
Party, **Mao Tse-Tung,** a poet as well as
a political theorist, was responsible for
China's development as a major power.

Manx (măngks) *adj.* Of the Isle
of Man; of the Celtic language
there; ~ **cat**, cat of tailless breed
originating there. **Manx** *n.*
Manx language.

man·y (měn´ē) *adj.* (**more,
most**) & *n.* (Consisting of) a large
number; **the** ~, the multitude;
~**-sided**, having many sides;
having a variety of interests,
capabilities, etc.; ~**-sidedness** (*n.*).

Ma·o·ri (mahōr´ē, mow´rē) *n.*
(pl. **-ris,** collect. **-ri**). (Member,
language, of) aboriginal people of
New Zealand, of Polynesian stock.

Mao Tse-tung (mow´dze-
dŏong´, tse tŏong´) (1893–1976).
Chinese revolutionary leader;
became head of the Communist
republic in Kiangsi province (SE.
China), 1931; after defeat by
Kuomintang forces, led his
followers on the "long march" of
1934–5 to Shensi province (N.
China) where they established a
new government; chairman of
central committee of Chinese
Communist party from 1936 to
death; chairman of the People's
Republic of China 1949–58.

Mao Ze·dong (mow´dze dŏong´)
= MAO TSE-TUNG.

map¹ (măp) *n.* Representation
on paper etc. of Earth's surface or
part of it, showing physical and
political features etc.; similar
representation of heavens showing
position of stars etc.; **put on the**
~, establish position or vogue of.

map² *v.t.* (**mapped, map·-
ping**). Make map of; ~ **out,** plan
out, arrange in detail.

ma·ple (mā´pel) *n.* Tree or
shrub of genus *Acer* grown for
shade, ornament, wood, or sugar;
~ **leaf,** leaf of maple, emblem of
Canada; ~ **sugar,** sugar from

SUGAR maple.

ma·quis (mahkē´) *n.* (pl. **-quis**
pr. **-kē´**). Dense scrubby forest of
various dwarf trees and shrubs in
Corsica etc.; **M~**, secret army of
patriots in France during the
German occupation (1940–5), so
named as if from hiding in the
undergrowth. **ma·quis·ard**
(mahkēzar´) *n.* Member of the
Maquis. [Fr., f. Corsican It.
macchia thicket]

mar (mar) *v.t.* (**marred, mar·-
ring**). Spoil, impair the perfection
of.

Mar. *abbrev.* March.

mar·a·bou (măr´aboo, măr-
aboo´) *n.* (pl. **-bous,** collect.
-bou). Large W. African stork
(*Leptoptilus crumeniferus*) (also ~
stork); tuft of down from its wings
or tail as trimming for hat etc.

Ma·ra·cai·bo (mărakī´bō),
Lake. Lake in NW. Venezuela,
5,000 sq. mi. (8,050 km), the largest
in South America; seaport of
Venezuela; one of world's leading
oil export centers.

mar·a·schi·no (măraskē´
-shē´-) *n.* Strong sweet lique
made from the *marasca*, a sm
black cherry grown in Dalmatia

ma·ras·mus (mărăz´mus)
(path.) Wasting away of the boc
ma·ras´mic *adj.*

Ma·rat (mără´), **Jean Pa**
(1743–93). French revolutiona
leader, philosopher, and scienti
stabbed to death by Charlo
Corday.

Mar·a·thon (măr´athŏn). Pla
on E. coast of Attica, Greece, whe
the invading Persian army w
defeated by the Athenians a
Plataeans under Miltiades (4
B.C.); the Athenian couri
Pheidippides ran to Sparta to bri
the news of the Persian landing a
ask for help, and is said to ha
completed the distance (150 mile
241.5 km) in two days.

mar·a·thon (măr´athŏn)
Long-distance road race, esp. t
race (26 miles 385 yards 41.86 kr

*The **marabou stork** is a large African bird of the stork family. It is mainly grey and white and has an inflatable throat pouch. It swallows great chunks of carrion whole.*

that is a principal event of the modern Olympic Games (also attrib. of any lengthy feat of great endurance). [f. MARATHON]

ma·raud (mαrawd') *v.i.* Make raid, pillage. **ma·raud'er** *n.*

mar·ble[1] (mar'bel) *n.* Limestone in crystalline or granular state and capable of taking polish, used in sculpture etc.; (pl.) collection of sculptures; small ball of marble, glass, clay, etc., used as toy; **M~ Arch**, arch with three gateways erected (1827) in front of Buckingham Palace, London, and moved (1851) to present site in NE. corner of Hyde Park.

mar·ble[2] (mar'bel) *v.t.* (**-bled, -bling**). Stain, color, to look like variegated marble. Also **mar'ble·ize** (**-ized, -iz·ing**).

mar·ca·site (mar'kasīt) *n.* Crystalline iron pyrites; piece of this used as ornament.

mar·cel (marsĕl') *n.* (also **~ wave**) Kind of deep-grooved artificial wave in hair. **~** *v.t.* (**-celled, -cel·ling**). Wave (hair) in marcel fashion. [f. name of Paris hairdresser]

March (march). Third month of Gregorian (first of Julian) calendar, with 31 days. [L. *Martius* (*mensis*) month of Mars]

march (march) *v.* (Cause to) walk in military manner or with regular paces; progress steadily. **~** *n.* (pl. **march·es**). Marching of troops; progress; distance covered in marching or walking; uniform step of troops etc.; piece of music meant to accompany march, usu. in $\frac{4}{4}$, $\frac{2}{2}$, or $\frac{6}{8}$ time; musical composition, or part of one, of similar character; **steal a ~ on**, gain advantage over, esp. surreptitiously.

mar·chion·ess (mar'shŏnĭs, marshŏnĕs') *n.* (pl. **-ess·es**). Wife, widow, of a marquis; lady holding in her own right rank equal to that of marquis.

march·pane (march'pān) = MARZIPAN.

Mar·co·ni (markō'nē), **Guglielmo** (1874–1937). Italian electrical engineer; inventor of wireless telegraphy; awarded the Nobel Prize for physics in 1909.

Marco Polo: see POLO.

Mar·di gras (mar'dē grah). (Merrymaking on) Shrove Tuesday, the day before Lent; last day of carnival. [F., = "fat Tuesday"]

Marble is capable of taking a high polish and is often veined or mottled. The cutting of these marble blocks at Carrara, Italy, is done by means of a continuous twisted wire driven electrically.

mare (mār) *n.* Female of horse or other equine animal; ~**'s-nest**, illusory discovery; ~**'s-tail**, tall slender plant (*Hippuris vulgaris*) growing in marshy ground; long straight streaks of cirrus cloud.

Mar·ga·ret (mār´gerĭt, -grĭt), **Queen** (d. 1093). Scottish saint and queen of Scotland.

mar·ga·rine (mār´jerĭn, -jerēn, mārj´rĭn) *n.* Edible fat made by the catalytic reduction of unsaturated acids in animal and vegetable oils and fats and freq. colored to resemble butter.

mar·gay (mār´gā) *n.* (pl. -**gays**, collect. -**gay**). Small S. Amer. tiger cat (*Felis tigrina*) related to the ocelot.

mar·gin (mār´jĭn) *n.* Border; strip near edge of anything; plain space around printed page, picture, etc.; extra amount over what is necessary; difference between cost and selling price; sum deposited with stockbroker to cover risk of loss on transaction.

mar·gin·al (mār´jĭnal) *adj.* Of, written in, the margin; of, at, the edge; close to the limit (freq. fig.). **mar´gin·al·ly** *adv.*

mar·gi·na·li·a (mārjinā´lēa, -nāl´ya) *n.pl.* Marginal notes.

mar·grave (mār´grāv) *n.* (hist.) German title, orig. of ruler of a border province; later, hereditary title of some princes of the Holy Roman Empire. **mar·gra·vine** (mār´gravēn) *n.* Margrave's wife.

Mar·gre·the II (mārgrā´te) (1940–). Queen of Denmark since 1972.

mar·gue·rite (mārgerēt´) *n.* Plant (*Chrysanthemum frutescens*), having white or pale yellow flowers resembling those of the daisy. [Gk. *margaritēs* pearl]

ma·ri·a·chi (mārēah´chē) *n.* (pl. -**chi**). 1. (Member of) small band of Mexican strolling musicians dressed in native costume. 2. Music of such bands.

Mar·i·an (mār´ēan) *adj.* Of the Virgin Mary.

Mar·i·a·na (mārēah´na) **Islands, Mar·i·a·nas** (mārēah´naz). Group of islands in the NW. Pacific administered (except for GUAM) by U.S. under trusteeship of U.N.

Ma·rie An·toi·nette (marē´ ăntwŏnĕt´) (1755–93). Daughter of Maria Theresa and queen of Louis XVI of France; guillotined on Oct. 16, 1793.

Ma·rie-Lou·ise (marē´lōōēz´) (1791–1847). Second wife of Napoleon I, 1810, and mother of Napoleon II.

These **Royal Marine Commandos** are on arctic warfare exercises in Norway. Marine troops are specially recruited, trained and organized for service at sea and in land operations related to naval campaigns.

mar·i·gold (mār´igōld) *n.* 1. Any of several plants of genera *Calendula* and *Tagetes*, with bright yellow or golden composite flowers. 2. = MARSH marigold. [f. *Mary* (prob. the Virgin) + *gold*]

ma·ri·jua·na, ma·ri·hua·na (măriwah´na, -hwah´-, măr-) *ns.* Dried leaves of Indian hemp, used to make narcotic cigarettes (reefers); the plant itself.

ma·rim·ba (marĭm´ba) *n.* Primitive African xylophone; modern orchestral instrument evolved from this.

ma·ri·na (marē´na) *n.* Pleasure boat harbor.

mar·i·nade (mărinād´, -nahd´) *n.* Mixture of wine or vinegar with herbs and spices, in which fish or meat is steeped before cooking; ~ (măr´inād) *v.t.* (-**nad·ed, -nad·ing**). Steep in marinade.

mar·i·nate (măr´ināt) *v.* (-**nat·ed, -nat·ing**). Marinade.

ma·rine (marēn´) *adj.* Of, from, beside, the sea; for use at sea; of shipping; ~ **stores**, old ship materials as merchandise; shop selling them. **marine** *n.* Country's fleet of ships, naval or mercantile; member of body of troops trained to fight on land or sea; (pl.) the branch of armed forces (in U.S. Marine Corps).

mar·i·ner (măr´iner) *n.* Sailor; **master** ~, captain of a merchant ship.

mar·i·o·nette (mărēonĕt´) *n.* Puppet worked with strings.

mar·i·tal (măr´ĭtal) *adj.* Of husband; of or between husband

The **marigold,** of which there are about 50 species, is an annual plant grown as garden ornamental. Most species have strongly scented leaves and yellow, orange or red flowers.

The **market,** as a center where sellers display and sell their goods, has existed since earliest times. This pottery market is in Tepotzotlan, Mexico.

and wife. **mar'i·tal·ly** *adv.*

mar·i·time (măr´ĭtĭm) *adj.* Of or connected with the sea or seafaring; situated near the sea; **M ~ Provinces,** common name of three provinces in E. Canada: Nova Scotia, Prince Edward Island, and New Brunswick.

mar·jo·ram (măr´jeram) *n.* Any of several aromatic herbs of genus *Origanum* or esp. O. majorana, used for flavoring.

mark[1] (mărk) *n.* 1. = DEUTSCHE MARK. 2. (abbrev. M.) Monetary unit of the German Democratic Republic.

mark[2] (mărk) *n.* 1. Target, thing aimed at; **beside, wide of, the ~,** not hitting it, (fig.) not to the point; (slang) person easily duped. 2. Trace left by something; stain, scar, spot, dent. 3. Sign, indication, (of quality, character, etc.). 4. Affixed or impressed sign, seal, etc.; written symbol; cross etc. made by person who cannot write his name. 5. Unit in appraising merit of schoolchild's work in class, candidate's in examination, etc. 6. Line serving to indicate position, e.g. starting point in race. 7. **M ~ I, M ~ II,** etc., designation of weapon or piece of equipment indicating first, second, etc., design. **mark ~** *v.* Make a mark on; distinguish with mark; characterize or serve as a mark of; assign marks of merit to; notice, observe, watch; **~ down,** note and remember (place etc.); (also) reduce price of; **~ off,** separate by boundary; **~ out,** trace out (boundary etc.); **~ time,** move feet as in marching, but without advancing (often fig.); **~ up,** raise price of.

Mark (mărk), **St.** Apostle, companion of Peter and Paul; traditional author of the 2nd Gospel

(the earliest in date); commemorated April 25; 2nd Gospel.

marked (mărkt) *adj.* (esp.) Noticeable, conspicuous. **mark·ed·ly** (mär´kĭdlē) *adv.*

mark·er (mär´ker) *n.* 1. Thing used to mark place (in book etc.). 2. Anything used to indicate position on ground to aircraft, course at sea to boats, etc. 3. (slang) I.O.U.

mar·ket (mär´kĭt) *n.* Gathering of people for sale of provisions, livestock, etc.; time of this, space or building used for it; demand *for*; seat of trade; **buyer's ~,** state of purchasing favorable to buyer; so **seller's ~; ~ day,** day on which market is held; **mar'ketplace,** square, open place, where market is held; **market price,** prevailing price in ordinary conditions; **market town,** town where market is held on fixed days; **market value,** salable value. **market** *v.* Buy, offer for sale, in market. **mar'ket·a·ble** *adj.* Fit for sale; sellable.

mark·ing (mär´kĭng) *n.* (esp.) Coloring of feathers, skin, etc.; **~ ink,** indelible ink for marking linen.

marks·man (märks´man) *n.* (pl. -**men** pr. -men). One skilled at aiming at mark, esp. rifleman of certain standard of proficiency. **marks'man·ship** *n.*

mar·lin (mär´lĭn) *n.* (pl. **-lins,** collect. **-lin**). Large sea fish of genus *Makaira*.

mar·line (mär´lĭn) *n.* (naut.) Small line of two strands used for binding shrouds etc.; **mar'line·spike,** pointed tool for separating strands of rope in splicing.

Mar·lowe (mär´lō), **Christopher** (1564–93). English poet and playwright; author of *Tamburlaine, The Jew of Malta,*

Edward II, and *The Tragedy of Dr. Faustus.*

mar·ma·lade (mär´malād) *n.* Preserve of oranges or other citrus fruit, cut up and boiled with the peel and sugar; orange-yellow color, esp. of cats. [Port. *marmelada* f. *marmelo* quince]

Mar·ma·ra (mär´mera), **Sea of.** Small inland sea lying between the Black Sea and the Aegean.

mar·mo·re·al (märmōr´ēal, -mōr´-) *adj.* Of or like marble.

mar·mo·set (mär´mozĕt) *n.* Small tropical Amer. monkey with bushy tail, of several genera in family Callithricidae.

mar·mot (mär´mot) *n.* Any burrowing rodent of the genus *Marmota,* with bushy tail and short legs, found throughout N. hemisphere; WOODCHUCK; WHISTLER.

Marne (märn). River in NE. France; center of battles in World War I, 1914 and 1918, and during World War II, 1944.

Mar·o·nite (măr´onīt) *n.* One of a sect of Syrian Christians living in Lebanon, named after their founder, Maron, who lived probably in the 4th c.

ma·roon[1] (maroon´) *n.* 1. Brownish-crimson color. 2. Explosive device producing loud report. **~** *adj.* Maroon-colored. [Fr. *marron* chestnut]

ma·roon[2] (maroon´) *n.* One of a group of blacks, orig. fugitive slaves, living in mountains of W. Indies; marooned person. **~** *v.t.* Put (person) ashore and leave on desolate island or coast as punishment; leave without means of getting away. [Fr. *marron,* perh. f. Span. *cimarron* wild]

marque (märk) *n.* (hist.) **letters of ~,** license given to private person to fit out armed vessel and employ it in capture of enemy's merchant shipping.

mar·quee (märkē´) *n.* Large tent, esp. one used at fêtes, shows, etc.

*This picture of the surface of **Mars**, taken by Viking 1, shows an orange-red surface covering a darker bedrock. The reddish material is thought to be limonite. The picture was taken at approximately 12 noon Mars time.*

Mar·que·sas (märkä′zaz, -saz, -sas) **Islands.** Group of islands in the Pacific; part of French Polynesia.

mar·que·try, mar·que·te·rie (mär′kĭtrē) *ns.* (pl. **-tries**). Decoration of flat surface, as of furniture, by gluing together shaped pieces of wood, ivory, or other substance(s) so as to cover the whole surface; also, inlay; furniture etc. so decorated.

Mar·quette (märkĕt′), **Jacques (Père)** (1637–75). French Jesuit missionary and explorer in America; accompanied Joliet on voyage down Wisconsin and Mississippi rivers and up Illinois River.

mar·quis (mär′kwĭs, märkē′) *n.* (pl. **-quis·es, -quis** pr. -kwĭsez, -kēz′). (esp. Brit.) **mar·quess** (mär′kwĭs) Noble ranking below duke and above earl or count; **Marquis of Queensbury Rules**, set of rules for boxing in Gt. Britain and the basis for boxing worldwide, based on those drawn up in 1867 under supervision of 8th Marquis of Queensbury, **mar·quis·ate** (mär′kwĭzĭt) *n.*

mar·quise (märkēz′) *n.* (pl. **-quis·es** pr. -kē′zĭz). (also ~ **ring**) Ring with head shaped like ~ **cut,** a boat-shaped brilliant cut.

Mar·ra·kesh (märakĕsh′). City in W. central Morocco, and the former capital; in medieval period, one of the great Islamic cities.

*The **marmot** inhabits open country in mountains or plains and lives in burrows or among boulders. It has strong feet and claws adapted for digging, and feeds on green plants.*

mar·riage (mär′ĭj) *n.* Act, ceremony, or procedure by which a man and a woman are legally united for the purpose of living together; (fig.) intimate union; **communal** ~, (anthrop.) system by which within a small community all the men are regarded as married to all the women; **companionate** ~, probationary union of man and woman; ~ **articles**, agreement concerning rights of property, succession, etc., made before marriage; ~ **license**, official permit for two persons to marry. **mar′riage·a·ble** *adj.*

mar·ron gla·cé (Fr. mărawn′ glăsä′). Chestnut preserved in sugar as sweet.

mar·row (mär′ō) *n.* 1. Soft fatty substance in cavities of bones; essential or best part of anything, essence; **mar′rowbone**, bone containing edible marrow; (pl., facet.) knees; **mar′rowfat (pea)**, kind of large rich pea. 2. (Brit.) (also

vegetable ~) Kind of edible gourd, the fruit of *Cucurbita pepo*. **mar′row·y** *adj.*

mar·ry (măr′ē) *v.* (**-ried, -ry-ing**). Unite, give, or take in marriage; take a wife or husband; (fig.) unite intimately.

Mars (märz). 1. (Rom. myth.) God of war, identified with the Greek ARES. 2. (astron.) Fourth planet in the order of distance from the sun, with an orbit lying between that of Earth and Jupiter. **Mar·tian** (mär′shan) *adj.* & *n.* (Supposed inhabitant) of the planet Mars.

Mar·sa·la (märsah′la) *n.* Fortified wine produced at Marsala, a town on the W. coast of Sicily, orig. as imitation of sherry for English consumption.

Mar·seil·laise (märselāz′, -sāĕz′; Fr. mărsĕyĕz′), **The.** The French national anthem, composed by a young engineer officer, Rouget de Lisle, at Strasbourg in 1792, on the declaration of war against Austria, and first sung in Paris by Marseilles patriots.

Mar·seilles (märsā′). Second-largest city and principal seaport of France in the SE. on the Mediterranean; a military and naval

*The planet **Mars** is the fourth most distant from the sun and has a diameter about half that of earth. In 1976, the American Viking 1 space laboratory landed on this planet.*

station; site of ancient Greek colony of Massilia, settled *c*600 B.C.

marsh (mărsh) *n.* (pl. **marsh·es**). Low-lying land, more or less permanently waterlogged; bog, morass; ~ **gas**, methane; ~ **hawk**, American hawk **Circus cyaneus hudsonius**, nesting in meadows and marshes; ~ **mallow**, shrubby herb with pink flowers (*Althaea officinalis*) growing near salt marshes; **marsh·mal·low** (mărsh′mĕlō, -mălō), soft sweet containing albumen and gum arabic or gelatin; ~ **marigold**, plant (*Caltha palustris*) of family Ranunculus with bright golden flowers, growing in moist meadows, also called cowslip. **marsh′i·ness** *n.* **marsh′y** *adj.* (**marsh·i·er, marsh·i·est**).

mar·shal (mãr′shal) *n.* 1. Official of a royal household or court directing ceremonies, in England the **Earl M** ~. 2. Military officer of highest rank in some foreign armies, in the British Army, a **Field M** ~. 3. Part of title of officers of high rank in the RAF, as **Air (Chief, Vice) M** ~. **marshal** *v.t.* (**-shaled, -shal·ing**). Arrange in due order (soldiers, facts, etc.); lead, conduct, with ceremony; **marshaling yard**, railroad yard in which trains are assembled and distributed.

Mar·shall[1] (mãr′shal), **George C(atlett)** (1880–1959). Amer. general and statesman; with A.E.F. in World War I, 1917–19; aide-decamp to Gen. Pershing, 1919–24; served in China, 1924–7; chief of staff, U.S. Army, 1939–45; U.S. ambassador to China, 1945–7; secretary of state, 1947–9; secretary of defense, 1950–1; awarded Nobel Peace Prize, 1953; **M** ~ **Aid**, financial aid given to certain European countries under the **M** ~ **Plan**, 1948, initiated by Gen. Marshall under the European Recovery Program after World War II.

Mar·shall[2] (mãr′shal), **John** (1755–1835). Amer. jurist and statesman; secretary of state, 1800–1801; chief justice of Supreme Court, 1801–35; established the fundamental principles for interpreting Constitutional law.

Mar·shall[3] (mãr′shal), **Thomas Riley** (1854–1925). Vice president of the U.S. under Woodrow Wilson, 1913–21.

Mars, the ancient Roman god of war, was the most prominent of the military gods worshipped by Roman legions and was second only to Jupiter in prominence. Ares was his Greek equivalent. This painting of Mars is by Velazquez.

Mar·shall[4] (mär´shal), **Thur-good** (1908–). Amer. jurist; first black associate justice of the U.S. Supreme Court, 1967.

Mar·shall (mär´shal) **Islands.** Group of islands in the NW. Pacific administered by U.S. under trusteeship of U.N.

Marsupials are found only in Australia, New Guinea and the Americas. The best-known are the Australian kanga-roos and koalas and the American opossums. The Tasmanian 'wolf' is possibly extinct and was the largest flesh-eating marsupial. Bandicoots eat insects while kangaroos and wallabies feed only on herbage. Some Australian phalangers feed only on plants but others also eat insects.

mar·su·pi·al (märsoo´peal) *adj. & n.* (Animal) of the class of mammals that are born in a very immature condition, as e.g. the kangaroo and opossum, and are carried in a pouch (*marsupium*) until able to fend for themselves; ~ **mole**, small pouched burrowing animal with light-colored fur, native of Australia.

Mar·sy·as (mär´seas). (Gk. myth.) Satyr, who took to flute playing; he challenged Apollo to a musical contest and was flayed alive when he lost.

mart (märt) *n.* Marketplace; auction room; trade center.

mar·ten (mär´ten) *n.* Any of various carnivorous mammals of the genus *Martes*, resembling large weasels, with valuable fur.

Mar·tha (mär´tha). Sister of Lazarus and Mary and friend of Jesus Christ (Luke 10); in Christian allegory she symbolizes the active life and her sister the comtemplative life.

Mar·tha's (mär´thaz) **Vine-yard.** Small island and resort area off the S. coast of Massachusetts.

Flying Phalanger

Ring-tailed Rock Wallaby

Tasmanian Wolf

Brush-tailed Possum

Wombat

Rat Kangaroo

Numbat

Rabbit-eared Bandicoot

Mar·tí (mär·tē′), **José Julian** (1853–95). Cuban lawyer and patriot; inspired Cuban revolution; killed in skirmish with Spanish.

mar·tial (mär′shal) *adj.* Of, suitable for, appropriate to, warfare; militant, ready, eager, to fight; **~ law**, military government, during which ordinary law is suspended. **mar′tial·ly** *adv.* **mar′tial·ize** *v.t.* (**-ized, -iz·ing**). Make suitable, prepare, for war; impart martial spirit to.

mar·tin (mär′tǐn) *n.* Name given to several birds of swallow family, esp. the Amer. purple martin (*Progne subis*), with a glossy blue-black plumage, and the European house martin (*Delichon urbica*).

mar·ti·net (mär·tǐnět′, mär′nět) *n.* Strict (esp. military) disciplinarian. [name of French drillmaster in reign of Louis XIV]

mar·tin·gale (mär′tǐngāl) *n.* 1. strap fastened to bridle and girth of horse to prevent rearing etc. 2. Gambling system of doubling stakes at each venture.

mar·ti·ni (mär·tē′nē) *n.* (pl. **-nis**). Cocktail of gin or vodka and vermouth. [perh. f. name of inventor]

Mar·ti·nique (mär·tǐnēk′). French W. Indian island, one of the Lesser Antilles; capital, Fort de France; the former capital, St. Pierre, was completely destroyed by an eruption of Mont Pelée in 1902.

mart·let (märt′lǐt) *n.* Swift; martin.

mar·tyr (mär′ter) *n.* Person who undergoes death or suffering for any great cause, specif. one who suffers death on account of his adherence to the Christian faith; **~ to**, constant sufferer from (ailment etc.) **martyr** *v.t.* Put to death as martyr; torment. [Gk. *martus* witness]

mar·tyr·dom (mär′terdom) *n.* Sufferings and death of martyr; torment.

mar·tyr·ize (mär′terīz) *v.t.* (**-ized, -iz·ing**). Make martyr of.

mar·vel (mär′vel) *n.* Wonderful thing; wonderful example *of* (quality). **~** *v.i.* (**-veled, -vel·ing**, Brit. **-velled, -vel·ling**). Be surprised (*at, that*); wonder (*how, why*, etc.).

Mar·vell (mär′vel), **Andrew** (1621–78). English poet and political writer of Parliamentarian sympathies.

mar·vel·ous, Brit. **mar·vel·lous** (mär′velus) *adjs.* Astonishing; extravagantly improbable. **mar′vel·ous·ly** *adv.* **mar′vel·ous·ness** *n.*

Marx (märks), **Karl** (1818–83). German revolutionary writer; settled in England after 1849; wrote *Das Kapital* (1867), criticizing the capitalistic system as permitting a diminishing number of capitalists to appropriate the benefits of improved industrial methods, while the laboring class were left in increasing dependency and misery; held the remedy to be total abolition of private property, to be effected by class war; when the community owned all means of production and all property, it would provide every individual with work and the means of subsistence. **Marx′i·an**, **Marx′ist** *adjs. & ns.* **Marx′ism** *n.*

Mar·y¹ (mãr′ē). (**Blessed**) **Virgin ~**, **~ the Virgin**, mother of Jesus Christ; daughter of Joachim and Anne; was betrothed to Joseph of Nazareth at the time of the Annunciation.

Mar·y² (mãr′ē). Name of two reigning queens of England: **Mary I** or Mary Tudor (1516–58), daughter of Henry VIII and Catherine of Aragon; reigned 1553–1558; married Philip II of Spain, 1554; fervently Catholic; known as "Bloody Mary" because of the religious persecutions of her reign; **Mary II** (1662–94), eldest child of James II; married William of Orange, 1677; was invited, with him, to take the throne of England

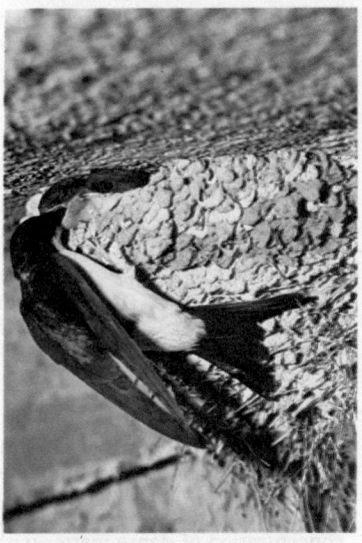

The house **martin** *is a common European swallow which feeds on insects it catches on the wing. It builds a cup-shaped nest of mud which it fastens on the wall of a building under the eaves or in the shelter of a beam.*

Statue of Joan of Arc, saint and visionary, who led the French revolt against the English and Burgundians in the early 15th century. Burned at the stake as a heretic, she became a national heroine and **martyr** *to the French.*

The weasel-like **martens** *are widely distributed in northern lands. They are forest-dwelling and usually solitary. They climb easily and feed rapaciously on animals, fruit and carrion. They are valued for their fur.*

and Scotland after the deposition of her father, and reigned 1689–94.

Mar·y Jane (mār´ē jān´) *n.* (slang) Marijuana.

Mar·y·land (měr´*i*land). State of U.S., on Atlantic coast, one of the original thirteen states of the Union (1788); capital, Annapolis. [named after Henrietta *Maria*, queen of Charles I]

Mar·y (mār´ē) **Magdalene**: see MAGDALENE.

Mar·y (mār´ē), **Queen of Scots** (1542–87). Mary Stuart, daughter of James V of Scotland and great-granddaughter of Henry VII; married the dauphin (François II) of France; claimed English throne on Mary I's death, and returned to Scotland, 1560; married, 1565, her cousin the Earl of Darnley, by whom she had a son (James I); soon after Darnley's mysterious death she married the Earl of Bothwell, 1567; was imprisoned by Elizabeth I, 1567, and was forced to abdicate; was tried for conspiracy, 1586, and beheaded.

mar·zi·pan (mār´zipăn) *n.* Paste of ground almonds, sugar, and white of egg, eaten as sweet and in cakes.

Ma·sac·cio (mahsah´chō), **Tommaso di Giovanni** (1401–1428). Italian painter of the early Renaissance.

Ma·sai (masī´) *n.* (pl. **-sais**, collect. **-sai**). (Member of) pastoral people of mixed Hamitic stock, inhabiting S. Kenya and Tanzania.

Ma·sa·ryk (măs´erĭk), **Thomas Garrigue** (1850–1937). Czech statesman and philosopher; first president of Czechoslovakia, 1918–1935.

mas·car·a (măskăr´a) *n.* Preparation for darkening eyelashes, eyebrows, etc., in make-up. [name of a town in Oran, Algiers]

mas·con (măs´kŏn) *n.* Massive concentration of dense matter with strong gravitational pull beneath surface of moon.

mas·cot (măs´kŏt) *n.* Person, animal, thing, supposed to bring luck; talisman.

mas·cu·line (măs´kyu*l*ĭn) *adj.* 1. (gram.) Of the gender to which appellations of males belong; (of ending) proper to this gender. 2. Of men; manly; mannish. 3. (pros.) ~ **ending**, ending of line of verse with stress on final syllable; ~ **rhyme**, (in French verse) rhyme between words ending in stressed syllables, not *e* mute; hence, rhyme of stressed syllables. **masculine** *n.* (gram.) (Word having) masculine gender. **mas´cu·line·ness, mas·-**

The **Virgin Mary** was the mother of Jesus and according to the Gospel his only human parent. The Virgin Mary is venerated above all the saints in the Roman Catholic Church. This painting of the Nativity is by Piero della Francesca.

cu·lin´i·ty *ns.*

ma·ser (mā´zer) *n.* Device for amplifying microwaves; **optical** ~, laser. [*m*icrowave *a*mplification by *s*timulated *e*mission of *r*adiation]

Mas·er·u (măz´erōō). Capital and largest city of Lesotho in the W. part.

mash[1] (măsh) *n.* Malt mixed with water for brewing; boil grain, bran, etc., given warm horses etc.; soft pulp made crushing, mixing with water, e ~ *v.t.* Make into mash; cru pound, to pulp.

mash[2] (măsh) *v.* (obs. sla Flirt with; force sexual attentic on (a woman). **mash´er** *n.*

mash·ie, mash·y (măsh´ē) (pl. **mash·ies**). Metal-headed g club with lofted face (no. 5 iron

mask (măsk, mahsk) *n.* Covering for concealing the fa 2. Covering of wire, gauze, et worn to protect (part of) face

The **Masai** are nomadic pastoralists of East Africa. They number about 115,000 and inhabit parts of Kenya and Tanzania. Masai is essentially a linguistic term, referring to speakers of this Sudanic language.

2

4

Mary I of England (Mary Tudor), half [sist]er to Elizabeth I, restored [Ca]tholicism to England (1554). Her [reig]n was marked by religious per[se]cution, earning her the title 'Bloody Mary'. 2. **Mary, Queen of Scots** was forced to abdicate (1567) in favor of her son James VI of Scotland. A claimant to the English throne, she was imprisoned by Elizabeth I, and executed after 19 years in prison. 3. **Mary II** married William of Orange and became joint sovereign of England in 1689. 4. **Queen Mary** was the wife of George V and mother of George VI.

Boston, capital of **Massachusetts** and one of the principal cultural centers of the U.S.A., is noted for its contribution to medicine and the sciences.

filter air inhaled or exhaled; respirator. 3. Reproduction of face on cloth etc. worn by actor to symbolize character; grotesque representation of a face worn on festive and other occasions to produce a humorous or terrifying effect; hollow figure of human head esp. as worn by Greek and Roman actors. 4. Likeness of person's face, esp. one made by taking mold from face during life or after death (**life ~, death ~**). 5. (photog.) Screen used to cover or shield part of an image. 6. Face, head, of fox. 7. (fig.) Disguise. ~ *v.t.* Cover with mask; disguise or hide as with mask; **masked ball**, one at which masks are worn. **mask'er** *n.* One who takes part in masque or masquerade.

mas·och·ism (măs'okĭzem, măz'-) *n.* Deriving of pleasure from one's pain or humiliation, esp. as a method of sexual gratification (opp. SADISM). **mas'och·ist** *n.* **mas·och·is'tic** *adj.* [L. von Sacher-*Masoch* (1835-95), Austrian novelist who described it]

ma·son (mā'son) *n.* 1. Worker in stone. 2. Freemason (see FREE). **ma·son·ic** (masŏn'ĭk) *adj.* Of Freemasons. **ma'son·ry** *n.* 1. Stonework. 2. Freemasonry.

Ma·son-Dix·on (mā'son dĭk'son) **line** (also **Mason and Dixon line**). Boundary between Maryland and Pennsylvania, partly surveyed (1763-7) by Charles Mason and Jeremiah Dixon, English astronomers; before the abolition of slavery popularly regarded as demarcation between free and slave states.

masque (măsk, mahsk) *n.* Amateur histrionic and musical performance, orig. in dumb show, later with metrical dialogue etc.; dramatic composition for this. **mas'quer** *n.* Masker.

mas·quer·ade (măskerād') *n.* Masked ball; false show, pretense. ~ *v.i.* (**-ad·ed, -ad·ing**). Appear in disguise; ~ **as**, pretend to be.

Mass (măs) *n.* Celebration (esp. R.C.) of the Eucharist; liturgy, musical setting of liturgy, used in this; **High ~**, with incense, music and assistance of deacon and subdeacon; **Low ~**, without music and with minimum of ceremony. [Low L. *messa*, possibly f. words of dismissal at end of service: *ite, missa est*]

mass (măs) *n.* Coherent body of matter of indefinite shape; dense aggregation, large number, *of*; unbroken expanse *of* (light etc.); majority or main part (*of*); (phys.) quantity of matter a body contains, as determined by comparing the changes in the velocities that result when the body and a standard body impinge; **the masses**, the lower classes of society; **mass-energy**: see ENERGY; **mass hysteria**, uncontrolled panic, enthusiasm, etc., affecting many persons at once; **mass media**, means of communication, as television, radio, newspapers, etc., directed to or reaching the majority of people; **mass meeting**, large assembly of people; **mass production**, production in large quantities of standardized article(s) by standardized mechanical means; hence, **mass-produce(d)**. **mass** *v.* Gather into mass; (mil.) concentrate (troops). **mass'y** *adj.* (**mass·i·er, mass·i·est**). Solid, bulky.

Mass. *abbrev.* Massachusetts.

Mas·sa·chu·setts (măsachōō'sets). New England state, one of the original thirteen states of the Union (1788); capital, Boston; ~ **Bay**, inlet of the Atlantic Ocean along the coast of Massachusetts between Cape Ann and Cape Cod; ~ **Bay Colony**, established 1630, along coast north of Plymouth, under leadership of Governor John Winthrop under auspices of ~ **Bay Company**.

mas·sa·cre (măs'aker) *n.* Indiscriminate killing, esp. of unresisting persons. ~ *v.t.* (**-cred, -cring**). Make a massacre of.

mas·sage (masahzh', -sahj'; *Brit.* măs'ahzh) *n.* Kneading and rubbing of muscles, joints, etc., with hands, to stimulate their action. ~ *v.t.* (**-saged, -sag·ing**). Apply massage to. [Fr., f. L. *massa* lump]

Mas·sa·soit (măs'asoit) (1580?-1661). Wampanoag Indian chief who befriended Mayflower Pilgrims and negotiated peace treaty with them, 1621.

mas·sé (masā'; *Brit.* măs'ē) *n.* (billiards) Stroke made with cue held perpendicularly.

mas·seur (masēr'; *Fr.* măsör') *n.* (pl. **-seurs** pr. -sērz'; *Fr.* -sör') (fem. **mas·seuse** pr. masōos'-sōoz'; pl. **-seus·es** pr. -sōo'sĭz, -sōo'zĭz). One whose profession is providing massage.

mas·sif (măs'ĭf; *Fr.* măsēf') *n.* Mountain heights forming compact group; **M ~ Central**, plateau in central France occupying about a fifth of the country and including the Cévennes, Auvergne, and Limousin mountains.

mas·sive (măs'ĭv) *adj.* Large and heavy or solid; (fig.) solid substantial; (psychol., of sensation etc.) having large volume or magnitude. **mas'sive·ly** *adv* **mas'sive·ness** *n.*

mast[1] (măst, mahst) *n.* Fruit of beech and other forest trees, esp as food for swine.

mast[2] (măst, mahst) *n.* Long pole of timber etc. set upright in ship to support sails etc.; long pole supporting flag, radio aerial, etc. **before the ~**, (hist.) as an ordinary seaman, so described because sailors were quartered in the forecastle; **half-~**: see HALF; **mast'head**, highest part of mast, esp lower mast, as place of observation or punishment.

mas·tec·to·my (măstĕk'tomē) *n* (pl. **-mies**). Excision or amputation of a breast. [f. Gk *mastos* + -ECTOMY]

mas·ter (măs'ter, mah'ster) *n*

Masks have been used throughout the world for social, religious or festive purposes in all periods since the Stone Age. The mask of the African Yaka tribe (above) is worn by boys during initiation ceremonies. The projection under the chin holds the mask in place. Above right: These masked New Guinea 'mudmen' represent evil spirits.

Person having control; captain of merchant vessel; employer; owner of dog etc.; male head of household; one with thorough knowledge of subject or facility in technique; one who has or gets the upper hand. 2. Teacher in private secondary school. 3. Skilled workman or one in business on his own account. 4. Person eminently skilled in an art etc. 5. **M~**, title given to heads of certain colleges at Oxford and Cambridge (as ~ *Balliol*). 6. One holding degree of Master of Arts or Science. 7. (in titles etc.) ~ **at arms**, police officer on warship or liner; **M~** of **Arts** (M.A.), **Science** (M.S.), etc., holder of university degree

ranking above bachelor, and orig. qualifying to teach in university; ~ **of ceremonies**, person presiding over arrangements at entertainment, social gathering, etc. 8. (attrib.) Commanding, superior (as *mas′termind*); principal (as ~ *bedroom*); ~ **key**, one made to open many locks, each also opened by separate key; **mas′terpiece**, consummate piece of workmanship, best work; **mas′tersinger**: see MEISTERSINGER; **master stroke**, masterly action. **master** *v.t.* Overcome; reduce to subjection; acquire complete knowledge of or facility in.

mas·ter·ful (măs′terful, mah′ster-) *adj.* Self-willed, imperious. **mas′ter·ful·ly** *adv.* **mas′ter·ful·ness** *n.*

mas′ter·ly (măs′terlē, mah′ster-) *adj.* Worthy of a master, very

skillful.

Mas·ters (măs′terz, mah′sterz), **Edgar Lee** (1869–1950). Amer. poet and biographer; author of *Spoon River Anthology*, 1915, depicting realistically the life of a fictitious village in the Middle West.

mas·ter·y (măs′terē, mah′sterē) *n.* (pl. **-ter·ies**). Sway; masterly skill, use or knowledge; upper hand.

mas·tic (măs′tĭk) *n.* Gum or resin, exuding from certain trees growing esp. in the Levant, used in making varnish; trees yielding this; mastic color, pale yellow; kind of cement made of mastic.

mas·ti·cate (măs′tĭkāt) *v.t.*

Masonry is the craft of building in stone, with overlapping or bonded stones generally set in mortar but sometimes laid dry. Shown here are the different methods used by masons.

Coping

Pointing

string-course

Long-and-short work

Binder or parpen

Vermiculated rustication

RUSTICATED ASHLAR

ASHLAR

Quoins

COURSED RUBBLE WALLING

DRY WALLING

Plinth

*In bullfighting, the **matador** is the man who works the cape and who must kill the bull with a sword thrust between the animal's shoulder blades. If the thrust is accurately placed the bull dies instantly.*

(-cat·ed, -cat·ing). Grind (food) with teeth, chew. **mas·ti·ca'tion, mas'ti·ca·tor** ns. **mas·ti·ca·to·ry** (măstɪkatōr'ē) adj. ~ n. (pl. **-ries).** Substance chewed to increase saliva.

mas·tiff (măs'tĭf, mah'stĭf) n. Large strong dog with drooping ears and pendulous lips, valuable as a watchdog.

mas·ti·tis (măstī'tĭs) n. Inflammation of the breast.

mas·to·don (măs'todŏn) n. Any of several large extinct mammals esp. of genus *Mammut*, resembling elephants but having nipple-shaped tubercles on crowns of molar teeth.

mas·toid (măs'toid) adj. (anat.) Shaped like female breast; ~ **process,** conical prominence in temporal bone behind ear. **mastoid** n. Mastoid process; (colloq.) mastoiditis. **mas·toid·i'-tis** n. Inflammation of mastoid process.

mas·tur·ba·tion (măsterbā'-shon) n. Sexual stimulation so as to produce orgasm, achieved esp. by manipulation of the genitals, not by coition. **mas'tur·bate** v. **(-bat·ed, -bat·ing).** Practice masturbation (on).

mat¹ (măt) n. Fabric of braided or woven rushes, hemp, etc., or pliant material such as rubber; piece of this as protection or ornament on floor etc.; small rug; small piece of material as protection or

ornament on surface of table etc.; thick pad on floor to cushion falls in gymnastics; sheet of cardboard used to make a border around a picture. ~ v. **(mat·ted, mat·-ting).** Entangle, become entangled, in thick mass.

mat² (măt): see MATTE.

Ma·ta·di (matah'dē). Major port of Zaire, 100 mi. (161 km) from the mouth of the Congo River, in the W.

mat·a·dor (măt'adōr) n. Man appointed to kill bull in bullfight.

Ma·ta Ha·ri (mah'ta hār'ē, măt'a hăr'ē) (1876–1917). Original name, Gertrud Margarete Zelle; French dancer who acted as spy for Germans in World War I and was executed.

match¹ (măch) n. Person equal in some particular, person or thing exactly corresponding, to another; contest in which persons or teams are matched against each other; matrimonial alliance; person viewed in light of eligibility for marriage; **match'board,** board with tongue cut along one edge and groove along another, so as to fit into similar boards; **match'-mak·er,** person fond of trying to arrange marriages; **match play,** (golf) (competition) scored by number of holes won; cf. MEDAL play; **match point,** state of game when one side needs only one point to win the match; the point itself. **match** v. Find or be a match for; place (person etc.) in competition *with,* in conflict *against,* another; be equal, correspond in color, shape, etc.

match² (măch) n. Short strip

of paper or wood (**match'stick**) with tip (**match head**) covered with some combustible substance which ignites when rubbed on rough or (**safety match**) specially prepared surface; fuse for firing cannon etc.; **match'book,** small cardboard folder of cardboard safety matches; **match'box,** box for holding matches; **match'lock** (hist.) (gun with) lock in which match was placed for igniting powder; **match'wood,** wood of suitable size for making matches (wood reduced to) minute splinters.

match·less (măch'lĭs) adj. Without an equal, peerless. **match'less·ly** adv.

mate¹ (māt) n. (chess) = CHECKMATE; **fool's** ~, in which first player is mated at opponent's second move. **mate** v.t. (**mat·ed, mat·ing**). Checkmate.

mate² (māt) n. 1. Companion, fellow worker; (colloq.) friend (also used as form of address among equals).   2. Fitting partner in marriage; one of a pair, esp. of birds.   3. (naut.) Officer on merchant ship who sees to execution of master's commands and deputizes for him. 4. Assistant to some specialist, as *gunner's* ~ **mate** v. (**mat·ed, mat·ing**). Associate as mate; copulate (*with*), cause (animals) to copulate for breeding. **mate'y** adj. (colloq.) Companionable, sociable. **mate'-y·ness, ma'ti·ness** ns.

ma·té (mahtā', mă-) n. Paraguay tea (also **yerba** ~), brew of leaves of S. Amer. shrub *Ilex paraguayensis*; vessel for this.

ma·te·ri·al (matēr'ēal) adj. Concerned with or composed of matter; unspiritual; concerned with bodily comfort, riches, etc; important, essential. **ma·te'ri·al·ly** adv. **material** n. Matter from which thing is made; elements; stuff, fabric; **writing** ~ s requisites for writing.

ma·te·ri·al·ism (matēr'ēalizem) n. Opinion that nothing exists but matter and its movements and modifications and that consciousness and will are wholly due to material agency; (art) tendency to lay stress on material aspect of objects; desire for material rather than spiritual prosperity etc. **ma·te'ri·al·ist** n. & adj. **ma·te·ri·al·is'tic** adj. **ma·te·ri·al·is'ti·cal·ly** adv.

ma·te·ri·al·ize (matēr'ēalīz) v. **(-ized, -iz·ing).** Make, represent as, material; appear, cause (spirit) to appear, in bodily form; make materialistic; become actual fact. **ma·te·ri·al·i·za'tion** n.

ma·te·ri·a med·i·ca (matēr'ē mĕd'ĭka). Remedial substance used in practice of medicine; branch of science dealing with their origin and properties.

ma·té·ri·el, ma·te·ri·el *ns*. Stock of materials, equipment, etc., used in any complex operation (PERSONNEL).

ma·ter·nal (mater'nal) *adj*. Of mothers; motherly; related on mother's side, as ~ **uncle**, mother's brother. **ma·ter'nal·ly** *adv*. **ma·ter'ni·ty** *n*. Motherhood; motherliness; ~ **home, hospital**, institution for care of women during (or immediately after) childbirth.

math (măth) *n*. (colloq.) Mathematics.

math·e·mat·ics (măthemăt'ĭks) *n. pl*. (usu. considered sing.) Abstract science of space and number (also **pure** ~); this applied to branches of physics etc. (also **applied** ~). **math·e·mat'i·cal** *adj*. Of mathematics; (of proof etc.) rigorously precise. **math·e·mat'i·cal·ly** *adv*. **math·e·ma·ti·cian** (măthemătĭsh'an) *n*.

Math·er (mădh'er, măth'-), **Cotton** (1663–1728). Amer. Congregational minister and author of many religious books; leader in educational and charitable fields; father, **Increase Mather**, (1639–1723), Amer. Congregational minister and colonial leader; president of Harvard, 1685–1701; influential in ending witchcraft trials.

mat·i·nee (mătĭnā'; *Brit.* mat'ĭnā) *n*. Afternoon theatrical or musical performance, afternoon cinema show; ~ **idol**, handsome actor.

mat·ins, Mat·ins (măt'ĭnz) *n. pl*. (usu. considered sing.) 1. (R.C. Ch.) Canonical HOUR; service for this, a midnight office, but also recited at daybreak. 2. Morning prayer in Church of England.

Ma·tisse (mătēs'), **Henri** (1869–1954). French Post-Impressionist painter.

ma·tri·arch (mā'trēärk) *n*. Woman corresponding in status to patriarch. **ma·tri·ar'chal** *adj*.

ma·tri·ar·chy (mā'trēärkē) *n*. (pl. **-chies**). Social organization in which the mother is head of the family and descent and relationship are reckoned through mothers.

mat·ri·cide (mat'rĭsīd, mā'trĭ-) *n*. Killing of one's own mother; person guilty of this. **mat·ri·cid'al** *adj*.

ma·tric·u·late (matrĭk'yūlāt) *v*. (**-lat·ed, -lat·ing**). Admit, be admitted, to privileges of university. **ma·tric·u·la'tion** *n*. Matriculating; examination qualifying for this.

mat·ri·mo·ny (măt'rĭmōnē) *n*. (pl. **-nies**). Rite of marriage, state of being married. **mat·ri·mo'ni·al** *adj*. **mat·ri·mo'ni·al·ly** *adv*.

ma·trix (mā'trĭks) *n*. (pl. **-tri·ces** pr. -trĭsēz; **-trix·es**). Womb; place in which thing is developed; mass of rock etc. enclosing gems etc.; mold in which type etc. is cast or shaped; something to be mechanically reproduced; (physiol.) formative part of animal organ; (biol.) substance between cells; (math.) rectangular arrangement of quantities or symbols.

ma·tron (mā'tron) *n*. Married woman; woman managing domestic affairs of schools etc.; woman in charge of nursing in hospital. **ma'tron·age** *n*. **ma'tron·al** *adj*. **ma'tron·hood** *n*. **ma'tron·ly** *adj*. Resembling a married woman in appearance and bearing; staid; portly. **ma'tron·ship** *n*.

Matt. *abbrev*. Matthew (New Testament).

matte, matt (măt) *adjs*. Without luster ~ *v.t*. (**mat·ted, mat·ting**). Make (surface etc.) matte, frost (glass). ~ *n*. Dull gold border around framed picture; lusterless surface or appearance; roughened or frosted groundwork.

mat·ter (măt'er) *n*. 1. Substance(s) of which a physical thing is made; **gray** ~, parts of central nervous system that appear gray owing to presence of massed groups of nerve cells (also, joc., brain, intellectual power), as dist. from **white** ~, parts consisting mainly of nerve fiber tracts. 2. Physical substance in general as dist. from spirit, mind, etc. 3. Content as dist. from form; material for thought or expression; substance of book, speech, etc. 4. Thing(s); material, as *printed* ~. 5. Affair, concern; **no** ~, it is unimportant; ~ **of fact**, what pertains to the sphere of fact (opp. to opinion etc.); **as a** ~ **of fact**, (law) part of a judicial inquiry concerned with truth of alleged facts (opp. to ~ *of law*); **~-of-fact** (*adj*.) unimaginative, prosaic. **matter** *v.i.* Be of importance, signify.

Mat·ter·horn (măt'erhŏrn).

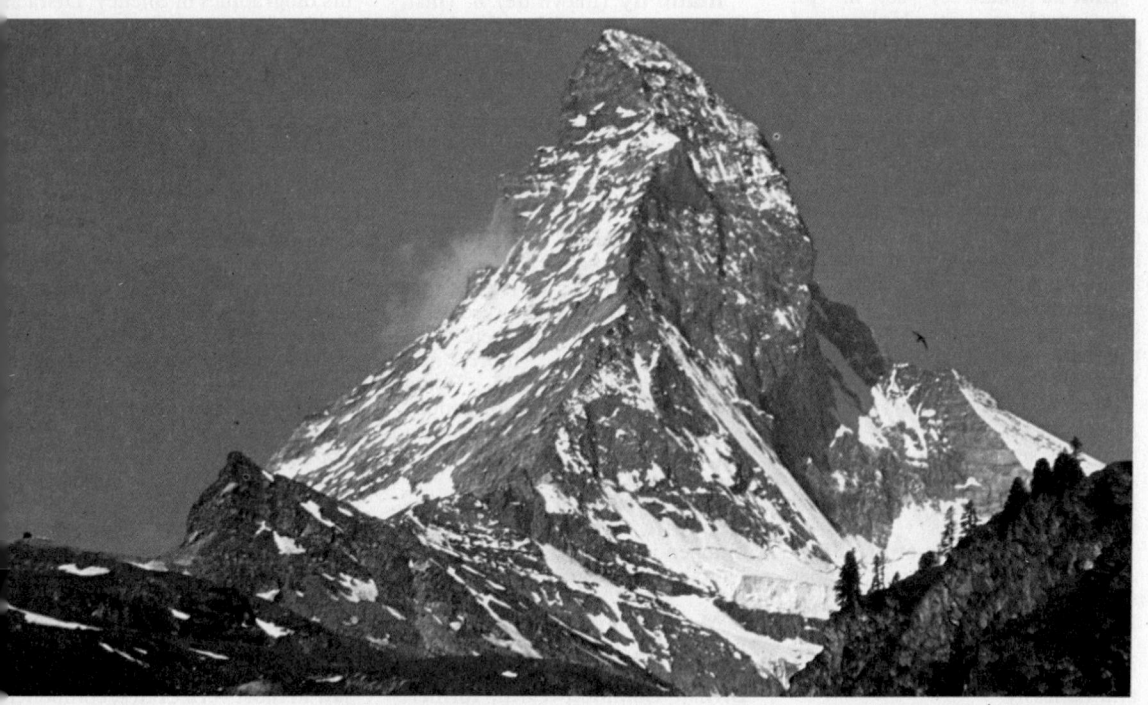

*The **Matterhorn**, the famous mountain in the Pennine Alps, is 14,690 ft. high and is on the Swiss-Italian frontier. It was first climbed by the English mountaineer, Edward Whymper, in 1865.*

Alpine peak (14,701 ft. 4478 m) on Italian-Swiss frontier, first climbed in 1865.

Mat·thew (măth´ū), **St.** Apostle, a tax gatherer from Capernaum; traditionally but erroneously supposed to be the author of the first Gospel, which was written after 70 A.D., and based largely on St. Mark; commemorated Sept. 21; first Gospel.

mat·ting (măt´ĭng) *n.* Material for mats.

mat·tock (măt´ok) *n.* Tool shaped like pick, with adze and chisel edge as ends of head.

mat·tress (măt´rĭs) *n.* Case of canvas or other strong material stuffed with hair, straw, foam rubber, etc., as bed; series of wire springs stretched in frame as support for bed (also **spring** ~); series of wires (**wire** ~) stretched on frame to support mattress of hair etc. [It. *materasso* prob. f. Arab. *almatrah* place, cushion (*taraha* throw)]

mat·u·rate (măch´ŏŏrāt, măt´-yŏŏ-) *v.i.* (**-rat·ed, -rat·ing**). (med.) Attain full development, ripen. **mat·u·ra´tion** *n.* Final series of changes in the growth and formation of germ cells. **ma·tur·a·tive** (măchoor´atĭv, măch´ŏŏrā-, măt´yŏŏrā-) *adj.* Causing maturation.

ma·ture (matoor´, -tūr´, -choor´) *adj.* Fully developed; ripe; adult; (in finance, of bonds etc.) due for payment. **ma·ture´ly** *adv.* **ma·ture´ness, ma·tur´i·ty** *ns.* **mature** *v.* (**-tured, -tur·ing**). Bring to or reach mature state.

ma·tu·ti·nal (matŏŏ´tĭnal, -tū´-) *adj.* Of, in, the morning, early.

mat·zo (maht´so, -sō) *n.* (pl. **-zos, -zoth** pr. -sōt). Unleavened bread for Passover. [Yiddish, f. Heb. *massāh*]

maud·lin (mawd´lĭn) *adj.* Mawkishly sentimental, esp. of tearful and effusively affectionate stage of drunkenness. ~ *n.* Mawkish sentiment. [f. MAGDALEN]

maul (mawl) *n.* Heavy hammer, usu. of wood. ~ *v.t.* Beat and bruise; handle or paw roughly; lacerate; damage by criticism.

maul·stick (mawl´stĭk) *n.* Light stick used by painters to support the hand with the brush. [Du. *maalstok* (*malen* paint, *stok* stick)]

Mau Mau (mow´mow) (pl. **Mau Maus**, collect. **Mau Mau**). (Member of) secret terrorist organization of Kikuyu tribesmen in Kenya rebelling against British rule in the 1950s.

Mau·na Lo·a (mow´na lō´a). Active volcanic mountain, 13,680 ft. (4,104 m), on the island of Hawaii.

maun·der (mawn´der) *v.i.* Talk ramblingly; wander about vaguely and listlessly.

Mauritania is composed mainly of desert. Rich deposits of iron ore and copper have transformed the country's economy, athough social organization is still largely tribal. These nomadic herdsmen tend sheep, goats and camels.

maun·dy (mawn´dē) *n.* (hist.) Ceremony of washing the feet of the poor, performed by royal or other eminent persons on the Thursday before Easter (**M~ Thursday**) in commemoration of Christ's washing of the Apostles' feet, and commonly followed by almsgiving. [L. *mandatum* commandment]

Mau·pas·sant (mōpăsahn´), **Guy de** (1850–93). French novelist, famous as a writer of short stories; author of "The Necklace," "Une Vie," "Bel Ami," etc.

Mau·re·ta·ni·a (mōretă´nēa). Ancient country and Roman province in N. Africa, corresponding roughly to N. Morocco and Algeria. [L., = "country of the Moors" (*Mauri*)]

Mau·ri·ta·ni·a (mōrită´nēa). Republic in NW. Africa; independent since 1960; capital, Nouakchott. **Mau·ri·ta´ni·an** *adj.* & *n.*

Mau·ri·tius (mawrĭsh´us). Island in Indian Ocean E. of Madagascar; member nation of the British Commonwealth; formerly

(1810–1968) a British colony capital, Port Louis. **Mau·ri´tian** *adj.* & *n.*

Mau·rois (mawrwah´), **André** (1885–1967). Pen name of Emil Herzog, French biographer, historian, and novelist; known for his biographies of Shelley, Disraeli, Byron, Proust, and others.

mau·so·le·um (mawsolē´um, -zo-) *n.* (pl. **-le·ums, -le·a** pr. -lē´a). Large, magnificent tomb, orig. that at Halicarnassus in Caria (formerly one of the Seven Wonders of the World) ordered for himself by Mausolus, king of Caria (d. 353 B.C.), and erected by his queen Artemisia (d. 351 B.C.).

mauve (mōv) *n.* Pale purple; delicate purple dye from coal tar aniline. ~ *adj.* [L. *malva* mallow]

mav·er·ick (măv´erĭk, măv´rĭk) *n.* Unbranded calf etc.; unorthodox or undisciplined person.

ma·vin, ma·ven (mā´vĭn) *n.* Expert. [Yiddish f. Heb., = connoisseur]

maw (maw) *n.* Stomach (of animal); abomasum.

mawk·ish (maw´kĭsh) *adj.* Of faint sickly flavor; feebly sentimental. **mawk´ish·ly** *adv.* **mawk´ish·ness** *n.* [obs. *maw* maggot]

max·il·la (măksĭl´a) *n.* (pl. **max·il·lae** pr. măksĭl´ē). Upper jaw in most vertebrates; component

of mouth parts of many arthropods.
max·il·lar·y (măk´sĭlĕrē, măksĭl´-ērē) *adj.* & *n.* (pl. **-lar·ies**).

max·im (măk´sĭm) *n.* General truth drawn from science or experience; principle, rule of conduct.

max·i·mal (măk´simal) *adj.* Greatest possible in size, duration, etc.

Max·i·mil·ian (măksimĭl´yan) (1832–67). Emperor of Mexico; brother of Austrian Emperor Francis Joseph; was offered throne of Mexico 1863; French troops supported him, but after their withdrawal he was defeated by republican forces, captured, and shot.

max·i·mize (măk´simĭz) *v.t.* (**-mized, -miz·ing**). Increase, magnify, to the utmost; interpret (doctrine etc.) vigorously. **max·i·mi·za·tion** (măksimizā´shon) *n.*

max·i·mum (măk´simum) *n.* pl. **-mums, -ma** pr. **-ma**). Highest possible or highest recorded magnitude or quantity (freq. attrib.).

max·well (măks´wel, -wĕl) *n.* Unit of magnetic flux in cgs system, equal to the flux of magnetic induction per square centimeter in a magnetic field whose intensity is one gauss (abbrev. Mx). [f. MAXWELL]

Max·well (măks´wel, -wĕl), **James Clerk** (1831–79). Professor of experimental physics at Cambridge University; contributed to the theory of the conservation of energy and of electricity and

magnetism.

May (mā). Fifth month of Gregorian (third of Julian) calendar, with 31 days; ~ **apple**, plant (*Podophyllum peltatum*) of eastern N. Amer. woodlands, having large leaves, which with roots and seeds are poisonous, one cuplike white flower, and small fruit with edible pulp; ~ **Day**, May 1, traditionally celebrated with dancing around a Maypole, gathering garlands of flowers, and the choice of a May queen; since 1889, the international labor holiday; **may'flower**, flower that blooms in May, used locally for cowslip, lady's smock, etc.; **May-flower**: see separate entry. **may'fly**, insect of the order Ephemeroptera; imitation of this used by anglers; **May'pole**, also **maypole**, gaily colored pole decorated with flowers and ribbons, which is danced around on May Day. [L. *Maius*, perh. f. the Roman goddess *Maia*]

may (mā) *v. auxil.* (past t. **might** pr. mīt). Expressing possibility, permission, request, wish.

Ma·ya (mah´ya) *n.* (pl. **-yas**, collect. **-ya**). Member, language, of an Amer. Indian people, remarkable for their art and knowledge of astronomy, who lived from *c*300 in Guatemala (the "Old Empire")

Mayflower *is any of several plants blooming in May or in early spring. In the U.K. it refers particularly to the hawthorn, shown here, and in America to the trailing arbutus.*

Mauritius is an island nation in the S.W. Indian Ocean. To date its economy has relied only on sugar exports but tea (below) and tobacco are also being grown. Tourism is also expanding.

*The great **Mayan** civilization collapsed in about 900 A.D. Little remains for us to construct a clear picture of the time, although ruins such as these in Guatamala offer some clues.*

in city states, and migrated in 9th c. to Yucatan in E. Mexico ("New Empire"), where their culture partially merged with that of the Toltecs, but disintegrated in mid-15th c. owing to civil wars, and was found in decay by the invading Spaniards in 1511. **Ma'yan** *adj.* & *n.*

may·be (mā′bē) *adv.* Perhaps.

May·day (mā′dā) *n.* International vocal radio-telephonic distress signal from aircraft or ship. [pron. of Fr. *m'aider imp. infin.* "help me!"]

May·flow·er (mā′flowẽr) *n.* Ship that carried Pilgrim Fathers from Southampton, England, to the New World; ~ **compact**, agreement to form government in the New World, entered into on November 11, 1620, aboard the *Mayflower*.

may·hem (mā′hĕm, mā′em) *n.* Crime of causing malicious personal injury; also fig.

May·o (mā′ō), **Charles Horace** (1865–1939). Amer. surgeon; his brother, **William James** (1861–1939), Amer. surgeon; co-founders of the Mayo Clinic, 1889, in Rochester, Minnesota, and of the Mayo Foundation for Medical Education and Research, 1915, affiliated with the Univ. of Minnesota.

may·on·naise (māonāz′, mā′onāz) *n.* Sauce of yolk of eggs, oil, and vinegar used as dressing for salads, fish, etc.

may·or (mā′er, mār) *n.* Head of city, town, village. **may'or·al** *adj.* **may'or·al·ty** *n.* Mayor's (period of) office. **may·or·ess** (mā′erĭs) *n.* (rare) Woman mayor.

Maz·a·rin (măz′erĭn, *Fr.* măzărăn′), **Jules** (1606–61). Italian papal legate in Paris, 1634; became cardinal, 1641, and succeeded Richelieu, 1642, as prime minister of France.

Maz·da·ism (măz′daĭzem) *n.* Zoroastrianism. [Avestan *mazda* good principle in Persian theology (see ORMAZD)]

maze (māz) *n.* Confusing and baffling network of winding and intercommunicating paths with hedges on either side, designed as a puzzle for those who try to find their way in it; labyrinth; (fig.) confusion, bewilderment. ~ *v.t.* (**mazed, maz·ing**). (archaic) Confuse, bewilder. **ma'zy** *adj.* (**-zi·er, -zi·est**). **ma'zi·ly** *adv.* **ma'zi·ness** *n.*

ma·zel tov (mah′zel tawv, tawf, tōv) *int.* Jewish expression of congratulation. [Yiddish f. Heb., = "good luck"]

ma·zur·ka (mazẽr′ka, -zoor′-) *n.* Lively Polish dance; music for this, in triple time. [Polish, = "woman of province of Mazovia"]

M.B.A. *abbrev.* Master of Business Administration.

*A replica of the original ship, **Mayflower** II was built in England, and sailed to Massachusetts in 53 days in 1957.*

Mc·Car·thy (makärthē), **Joseph R(aymond)** (1908–57). U.S. politician; senator from Wisconsin, 1946–57; chairman of Senate Permanent Investigating Subcommittee; conducted controversial investigation of Communists using allegedly irresponsible and sensational methods for which he was formally condemned by Senate; hence **Mc·Car'thy·ism** *n.* unfairness in investigative tactics by any government agency, newspaper, etc.

Mc·Clel·lan (maklĕl′an) **George Brinton** (1826–85). U.S. Army officer; Civil War general; commanded and reorganized the Dept. of the Potomac, 1861; general in chief of Union armies, 1861; commander of Army of the Potomac, 1862; removed from command for not fully pursuing Confederate forces to complete victory; Democratic presidential candidate, 1864, defeated by Lincoln; governor of New Jersey, 1878–81.

Mc·Cor·mick (makōr′mĭk) **Cyrus Hall** (1809–84). Amer. manufacturer; invented reaping machine, 1834.

Mc·Cul·lers (makŭl′erz) **Carson Smith** (1917–67). Amer. novelist and playwright; wrote *The Heart Is a Lonely Hunter, Reflections in a Golden Eye, A Member of the Wedding*, etc.

Mc·Gill (magĭl′), **James** (1744–1813). Scottish-born Canadian philanthropist; founded a college at Montreal which became ~ **University** (1821).

Mc·Guf·fey (magŭf′ē) **William Holmes** (1800–73). Amer. educator and compiler of textbooks; best known as author of *Eclectic Series*, popularly called the McGuffey Readers for children.

Mc·Kin·ley (makĭn′lē) **William** (1843–1901). Twenty-fifth president of U.S., 1897–1901; assassinated by an anarchist; **Mount McKinley**, highest mountain, 20,320 ft. (6,096 m) in N. Amer., in S. central Alaska; also known by its Indian name, Denali.

MD, Md. *abbrevs.* Maryland.

Md *symbol.* Mendelevium.

M.D. *abbrev. Medicinae doctor* (L., = Doctor of Medicine).

ME, Me. *abbrevs.* Maine.

me (mē) *pron.* Objective (accus. dat.) case of I.

mead[1] (mēd) *n.* Alcoholic liquor of fermented honey and water.

mead[2] (mēd) (poet.) = MEADOW

Mead (mēd), **Lake.** Artificial lake formed by Hoover Dam in the Colorado River, in NW. Arizona and SE. Nevada; a resort area.

Mead (mēd), **Margaret** (1901–1978). Amer. anthropologist and psychologist; best known for her books *Coming of Age in Samoa*, and

Growing Up in New Guinea.

Meade (mēd), **George Gordon** (1815–72). General of the U.S. Army of the Potomac during the Civil War; repulsed Confederates under Gen. Lee at Gettysburg, 1863, but was criticized for not following through to obtain total victory.

mead·ow (mĕd'ō) *n.* Piece of grassland, esp. one used for hay; low-lying ground, esp. near river; ~ **beauty**, any plant of genus *Rhexia* of eastern and southeastern U.S., 1 to 3 feet high, with pink, purple, or crimson flowers. ~ **grass**, poa (esp. *Poa pratensis*); **mead'owlark**, Amer. songbird of genus *Sturnella*, related to bobolinks and orioles. **meadow saffron**, autumn crocus; **mead'-owsweet**, rosaceous plant (esp. *Filipendula ulmaria*) common in meadows, growing to a height of about 2 feet, with dense heads of creamy white and very fragrant flowers.

mea·ger (mē'ger) *adj.* Lean, scanty. **mea'ger·ly** *adv.* **mea'-er·ness** *n.*

meal[1] (mēl) *n.* Edible part of any grain or pulse (usu. exc. wheat) rather coarsely ground. **meal'y** *adj.* (**meal·i·er, meal·i·est**). Of,

like, meal; (of boiled potatoes) dry and powdery; **meal'ybug**, any insect of the genus *Pseudococcus*, with body covered with white powder some species of which infest vines, citrus trees, etc.; **mealy-mouthed**, apt to mince matters, soft-spoken. **meal'i·ness** *n.*

meal[2] (mēl) *n.* Customary, or any, occasion of taking food; food so taken; **meal'time**, usual time of eating.

mean[1] (mēn) *n.* 1. Condition, quality, amount, equally removed from two opposite extremes. 2. (pl.) That by which a result is brought about; pecuniary resources; wealth; **by all (manner of)** ~s, certainly, at any cost; **by no (manner of)** ~s, certainly not; **by** ~s **of**, using; (math.) intermediate in value, position, etc., between two other quantities, points, etc.; average. **mean'time, mean'while** *advs.* (also **in** or **for the meantime**) In the intervening time.

mean[2] (mēn) *adj.* Inferior, poor; shabby; ignoble, small-minded; stingy. **mean'ly** *adv.* **mean'ness** (mēn'nĭs) *n.*

mean[3] (mēn) *v.* (**meant** pr. mĕnt, **mean·ing**). Purpose; design, destine; intend to convey or indicate; signify, import. **mean'-**

ing *n.* What is meant. **mean'-ing·ful** *adj.* Significant. **mean'-ing·less** *adj.* **mean'ing·less·ness** *n.* **mean'ing** *adj.* Expressive, significant. **mean'ing·ly** *adv.*

me·an·der (mēăn'der) *v.i.* Wind about; wander at random. ~ *n.* 1. (pl.) Sinuous windings, circuitous journey, winding paths, etc. 2. (geog.) Twisting course of river in its flood plain. 3. Fret pattern (see FRET[1]). [f. MAEANDER]

mea·sles (mē'zelz) *n.* 1. (usu. considered sing. or pl.) Acute infectious disease (*Rubeola*) of man, usu. in childhood caused by a virus, and characterized by fever, skin rash, and inflammation of the conjunctival membranes and air passages; **German** ~: see GERMAN. 2. Disease in swine, caused by tapeworm. **mea'sly** *adj.* (**-sli·er, -sli·est**). Of, affected with, measles; (slang) contemptible, worthless.

meas·ure (mĕzh'er) *n.* 1. Size

Top: **Medals** commemorate an even
or are awarded in recognition of di
tinguished service, or for achievemen
Bottom: **Medicine** has many branche
all of them dedicated to the alleviation
suffering.

movement; carefully weighed.

meat (mēt) n. Animal flesh
food, usu. excluding fish an
poultry; **meat'ball**, chopped me
cooked in shape of a ball; **meat
head**, (slang) stupid or fooli
person. **meat'y** adj. Full of mea
(fig.) full of substance; of or lik
meat.

me·a·tus (mēā′tus) n. (p
-tus·es, -tus). (anat.) Extern
opening of channel, duct, passag
in the body, as **auditory**
channel of the ear.

Mec·ca (mĕk′a). City now
Saudi Arabia, the birthplace
Muhammad and the chief place
Muslim pilgrimage.

me·chan·ic (mekăn′ĭk)
Skilled workman, esp. one wh
makes or uses machiner
me·chan'ics n. Branch of appli
science treating of motio
mechanism, functioning; science
machinery.

me·chan·i·cal (mekăn′ikal) a
Of machines or mechanism; li
machines, automatic; workin
produced, by machines; belongin
to the science of mechanics;
advantage, ratio of load to effo
~ **drawing**, drawing, as
machinery or construction, do
with compasses, rulers, etc.
engineer(ing): see ENGINE
me·chan'i·cal·ly adv. **me·chan
i·cal·ness** n.

mech·an·ism (mĕk′anĭzem)
1. Way a machine works; structur

or quantity found by measuring; vessel of standard capacity for measuring liquids; rod, tape, etc., for measuring; system of measuring; degree, extent, amount; stratum or bed of mineral; (math.) quantity contained in another an exact number of times; **greatest common** ~, largest quantity exactly dividing each of two or more given quantities. 2. Prescribed extent or quantity. 3. Meter; time of piece of music; (archaic) dance. 4. Suitable action; legislative enact-

ment. **measure** v. (**-ured, -ur·- ing**). Ascertain extent or quantity of by comparison with fixed standard or thing of known size; mark off; be of specified length etc.; deal *out*; bring into competition *with*; ~ **up to**, meet the requirements of; **measuring worm**, larva of geometrid moth, which advances approximately one inch at a time (also called *inchworm*); **meas'ur·- a·ble** adj. **meas'ur·a·bly** adv. **meas'ure·ment** n. **meas'ured** adj. Rhythmical, regular in

rts, of a machine; (fig.) frame-
ork, structure, technique;
hysiol.) system of mutually
apted parts working together.
(philos.) Theory that the origin
life can be ascribed to chemical
d physical forces (opp. VITALISM).
ech′a·nist *n.* 1. Expert in
echanics. 2. (philos.) Adherent
mechanism. **mech·a·nis′tic** *adj.*
mech·a·nize (měk′anīz) *v.t.*
nized, -niz·ing). Make
echanical; replace manual labor
th machinery; (mil.) equip with
nks etc. **mech·a·ni·za·tion**
ěkanīza′shon) *n.*

med. *abbrev.* Medical; medicine;
edieval; medium.

med·al (měd′al) *n.* Piece of
etal, usu. in form of coin, struck
cast with inscription and device
commemorate event etc., or
varded as distinction to soldier,
holar, etc., for services rendered;
play, (golf) scored by strokes,
ot by holes as in MATCH¹ play.

med·al·ist (měd′alist) *n.* 1.
inner of medal for golf etc. 2.
ngraver, designer, of medals.

me·dal·lion (medăl′yon) *n.*
arge medal; medal-shaped
cture, panel, etc.

med·dle (měd′el) *v.i.* (**-dled,
lling**). Busy oneself unduly *with*;
terfere *in.* **med′dle·some** *adj.*
iven to meddling. **med′dle·**
ome·ness *n.*

Mede (mēd) *n.* One of the
arliest Iranian inhabitants of
ersia; **the law of the ~s and
ersians**, an immutable law (Dan.
. **Me′di·an, Me′dish** *adjs.*

Me·de·a (medē′a). (Gk. legend)
orceress, daughter of Aeëtes, king
f Colchis; helped JASON to obtain
e Golden Fleece; married him but
as deserted by him in Corinth and
venged herself by killing their two
hildren.

me·di·a¹ (mē′dēa) *n.* (pl. **-di·ae**
r. -dēē). 1. (phonet.) Voiced stop
onsonant (*b, d, g*). 2. (anat.)
liddle membrane of artery or
essel.

me·di·a² (mē′dēa) *n.* Pl. of
EDIUM (esp. sense 2).

me·di·ae·val (mēdēē′val,
ědē-, mĭdē-, mĭdē′-) = MEDIEVAL.

me·di·al (mē′dēal) *adj.* Situated
the middle; of average size.
e′di·al·ly. *adv.*

Me·di·an (mē′dēan): see MEDE.

me·di·an (mē′dēan) *adj.*
ituated in the middle; relating to
a arithmetic median; ~ **strip**,
ividing strip between opposing
nes of automobile traffic.
ledian *n.* 1. (anat.) Median
tery, vein, nerve, etc. 2. (math.)
ach of three lines drawn from the
ngles of a triangle to the middle
oints of the opposite sides and
eeting in a point within it; middle
lue or number in a distribution
series of numbers.

me·di·ate (mē′dēit) *adj.* Involving an intermediary. **me′di·ate·ly**
adv. mediate (mē′dēat) *v.* (**-at·ed,
-at·ing**). Form connecting link;
intervene (between two persons
etc.) for purpose of reconciling
them; be the medium for bringing
about (result). **me·di·a′tion,
me′di·a·tor** *ns.* **me·di·a·tor′i·al,
me′di·a·to·ry** *adjs.*

med·ic (měd′ĭk) *n.* (slang)
Doctor.

med·i·ca·ble (měd′ĭkabel) *adj.*
Admitting of remedial treatment.

Med·i·caid (měd′ĭkād) *n.*
Federal and state insurance for
medical and hospital care for people
of limited means.

med·i·cal (měd′ĭkal) *adj.* Of
medicine; requiring, supplying,
medical not surgical treatment. ~
n. (colloq.) Medical examination for
fitness.

me·dic·a·ment (medĭk′ament,
měd′ĭka-) *n.* Substance used in
curative or palliative treatment.

Med·i·care (měd′ĭkār) *n.*
Federal insurance for medical and
hospital care for the aged.

med·i·cate (měd′ĭkāt) *v.t.*
(**-cat·ed, -cat·ing**). Treat
medically; impregnate with
medicinal substance. **med·i·ca′-
tion** *n.*

Med·i·ci (měd′ĭchē; *It.* mě′-
dēchē). Name of the ruling family
of Florence from 1434; orig.
merchants and bankers; grand
dukes of Tuscany 1569–1737;
patrons of art and letters, esp.
Cosimo dei (or **de′**) ~ (1389–
1464), his son **Piero** (1416–69),
Piero's son **Lorenzo "the
Magnificent"** (1449–92), and
Lorenzo's son **Giovanni** (1475–
1521), who became Pope Leo X;
Giulio (1478–1534) became Pope
Clement VII; **Catarina**
(CATHERINE³ DE MÉDICIS) married
Henri II; **Maria** (Marie de
Médicis) married Henri IV. **Med·-
i·ce·an** (mědīsē′an, -chē-) *adj.*

me·dic·i·nal (medĭs′ĭnal) *adj.*
Of medicine; curative.

med·i·cine (měd′ĭsĭn; *Brit.*
měd′sĭn) *n.* Art of restoring and

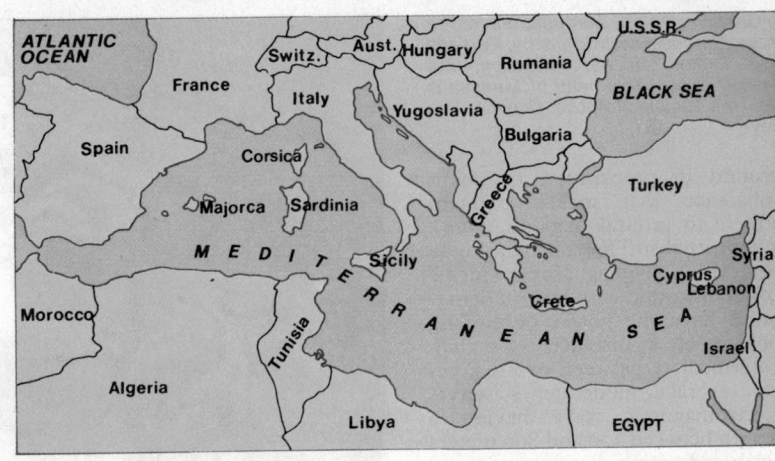

*The **Mediterranean Sea** has been an
important trading area since ancient
times, and was an invaluable trade route
to the East after the opening of the
Suez Canal in 1869.*

preserving health, esp. by means
other than surgery; substance taken
internally for this purpose; ~ **ball**,
large, heavy, stuffed ball to be
thrown and caught for exercise; ~
man, tribal magician of primitive
peoples.

med·i·co (měd′ĭkō) = MEDIC.

me·di·e·val, me·di·ae·val
(mēdēē′val, mědē-, mĭdē-, mĭdē′-
val) *adjs.* Of the Middle Ages.
**me·di·e′val·ism, me·di·ae′val·-
ism, me·di·e′val·ist, me·di·ae′-
val·ist** *ns.*

Me·di·na (medē′na). City now
in Saudi Arabia, to which
Muhammad fled from Mecca and
where he died and was buried.

me·di·o·cre (mēdēō′ker,
mē′dēōker) *adj.* Of middling
quality, indifferent. **me·di·oc′-
ri·ty** (mēdēŏk′rĭtē) *n.* (pl. **-ties**).
Mediocre quality; mediocre person.

med·i·tate (měd′ĭtāt) *v.*
(**-tat·ed, -tat·ing**). Plan mentally;
exercise the mind in contemplation
on. **med·i·ta′tion** *n.* **transcendental** ~: see TRANSCEN-
DENTAL. **med′i·ta·tive** *adj.*
med′i·ta·tive·ly *adv.*

med·i·ter·ran·e·an (mědĭterā′-
nēan) *adj.* (of land) Remote from
coast; (of water surfaces) land-
locked; **M** ~, of the Mediterranean
Sea, the region around it, or the
peoples of this region; **M** ~ **Sea**,
inland sea lying between S.
Europe and N. Africa,
communicating with the Atlantic
by the Strait of Gibraltar and with
the Persian Gulf by the Suez Canal.
M ~ *n.* Mediterranean Sea.

me·di·um (mē′dēum) *n.* (pl.
-di·a pr. -dēa for senses 1–3,
-di·ums for sense 4). 1. Middle
quality, degree, etc. 2. Means,
agency, esp. of communication. 3.
(art) Method by which work of art
is produced, branch of art (e.g.
painting, sculpture); (also) liquid
substance in which pigments are

*In Greek mythology **Medusa,** one of the three Gorgons, was killed by Perseus who looked on her reflection, not directly at her. This head of Medusa is from the Temple of Apollo, Didyma, Turkey.*

ground in preparation of paint; substance that makes pigment adhere to ground (e.g. oil, gum). 4. (spiritualism) Person claiming to be the vehicle for spirits' communication with human beings or to have the power of moving objects at a distance. ~ *adj.* Intermediate between two degrees etc.; average, moderate; ~ **wave,** electromagnetic wave having a length between 100 and 800 meters (in broadcasting, between 200 and 550 meters).

med·lar (mĕd′ler) *n.* (Tree, *Mespilus germanica,* with) fruit like small brown apple, eaten when decayed.

med·ley (mĕd′lē) *n.* (pl. **-leys**). Heterogeneous mixture; ~ **relay,** relay race in which each team member runs a different distance or uses a different swimming stroke.

Mé·doc (mādŏk′; *Fr.* mĕdawk′) *n.* Wine produced in Mĕdoc, a district in the Bordeaux region of France.

me·dul·la (mĕdŭl′a) *n.* (pl. **-dul·las, -dul·lae** pr. -dŭl′ē). 1. Marrow of bones; spinal marrow. 2. Central parts of some organs, esp. kidney. 3. Cellular inner part of animal hair. 4. Soft internal tissue of plants. 5. (also ~ **oblongata**) Brainstem, prolonged hindmost segment of brain. **med·ul·lar·y** (mĕd′ulĕrē, mĕj′u-, medŭl′erē) *adj.*

Me·du·sa (medōō′sa, -za, -dū′-). (Gk. myth.) One of the Gorgons, the only mortal one; slain by Perseus, who cut off her head.

me·du·sa (medōō′sa, -za, -dū′-) *n.* (pl. **-sas, -sae** pr. -sē, -zē). (zool.) Sexually reproductive form of hydrozoan or scyphozoan coelenterates, with jellylike body and stinging tentacles (pop. *jellyfish*).

meek (mēk) *adj.* Piously humble and submissive; tamely submissive. **meek′ly** *adv.* **meek′ness** *n.*

meer·schaum (mēr′shum, -shawm, -showm) *n.* Hydrated magnesium silicate, occurring in soft white masses, used for tobacco pipe bowls; pipe with bowl made of this. [Ger., = "sea foam"]

meet[1] (mēt) *adj.* (archaic) Suitable, fit. **meet′ly** *adv.* **meet′ness** *n.*

meet[2] (mēt) *v.* (**met** pr. mĕt, **meet·ing**). Come into contact or company (with); assemble; become perceptible to; satisfy (demand); experience. ~ *n.* Assembly for hunting, track-and-field, etc.

meet·ing (mē′tĭng) *n.* (esp.)

*The **medlar,** a small tree native to southern Europe and south-west Asia, is cultivated for its brownish fruit which is made into preserves or eaten when partly decayed.*

Assembly of people for entertainment, worship, etc.; duel; race meeting; ~ **house,** Quakers' place of worship.

mega-, meg- *prefixes.* Great; (phys., prefixed to names of units of measurement, force, etc.) one million times (abbrev. M), as in *megacycle, megawatt,* etc.

***Megalith** building spread through the world during the Neolithic Period. Monuments take the forms of tombs, single and multiple stone circles and rows, and single stones.*

meg·a·cy·cle (mĕg′asīkel) *n.* One million cycles, as unit in measuring frequency of electromagnetic waves (abbrev. mc, Mc).

Me·gae·ra (mejēr′a). (Gk. myth.) One of the Furies (see FURY).

meg·a·lith (mĕg′alĭth) *n.* (archaeol.) Large stone used in nstruction or as a monument. **meg·a·lith'ic** *adj.*

meg·a·lo·ma·ni·a (mĕgalomā́- ēa) *n.* 1. (psychiatry) Form of nsanity marked by delusions of randeur. 2. Passion for doing hings on an extravagant scale. **meg·a·lo·ma'ni·ac** *n.*

meg·a·phone (mĕg'afōn) *n.* arge funnel-shaped speaking rumpet, used for making the voice avel to a distance.

meg·a·pod (mĕg'apŏd), **meg·- pode** (mĕg'apōd) *ns.* Member f family of birds, almost all in ustralasian region, whose eggs are ft to hatch without incubation.

meg·a·ton (mĕg'atŭn) *n.* xplosive force equal to 1,000,000 ns of TNT.

meg·a·watt (mĕg'awŏt) *n.* One illion watts (abbrev. mW, W).

Me·gid·do (megĭd'ō). Ancient ty in NW. Palestine from about 500–300 B.C.; probably the rmageddon mentioned in the ible.

me·gil·lah (megĭl'a; *Heb.* ĕgēlah') *n.* (pl. **-gil·lahs** for 1, ǥil·loth** pr. -gēlōt' for 2). 1. lang) Lengthy story or explana- on. 2. Scroll of the Book of Esther, aditionally read in synagogues at e festival of Purim. [Heb., = roll]

me·grim (mē'grĭm) *n.* Mi- raine; whim; (pl.) low spirits. [Fr. igraine (f. Gk. hemi- half, kranion kull)]

mei·o·sis (mīō'sĭs) *n.* (pl. **-ses** r. -sēz). 1. Understatement, freq. onical or jocular. 2. (biol.) plitting of cell or nucleus without ncrease in number of chromo- omes, so that each of the resulting vo cells or nuclei has only half e chromosomes of the original one f. MITOSIS). **mei·ot·ic** (mīŏt'ĭk) dj.

Me·ir (māēr', mī-), **Golda** 898–1978). Russian-born merican woman who became an raeli political leader; premier of rael, 1969–74.

Meis·sen (mī'sen). City on the lbe near Dresden in East ermany where the earliest uropean porcelain factory was unded, 1710, and still exists; ~ hina, porcelain made there (freq. lled *Dresden china*).

meis·ter·sing·er (mī'stersĭnger, ǥing-) *n.pl.* (pl. also **-sing·ers**). erman lyric poets and musicians f 14th–17th centuries, organized guilds and using elaborate chnique; (sing.) member of such uild. [Ger., = "mastersingers"]

Meit·ner (mīt'ner), **Lise** (1878– 1968). Austrian-born Swedish physicist; worked in field of nuclear fission; together with Otto Hahn discovered protoactinium.

Me·kong (mā'kŏng', mē'-, -kawng'). River in SE. Asia flowing 2,600 mi. (4,186 km), from Tibet to the South China Sea; forms the borders between Laos and Burma and Laos and Thailand.

*This **Meissen** clock is decorated with figures of a maiden and cupids, and is surmounted by a cockerel. Its white porcelain case is painted with figures and flowers, and it has an enamel dial with gilt hands.*

mel·an·cho·li·a (mĕlankō'lēa, -kōl'ya) *n.* Mental illness characterized by depression (obsolesc. as psychol. term). [Gk. *melas* black, *khole* bile]

mel·an·chol·ic (mĕlankŏl'ĭk) *adj.* (of person) Melancholy; liable to melancholy.

mel·an·chol·y (mĕl'ankŏlē) *n.* (pl. **-chol·ies**). 1. (Habitual tendency to) sadness and

Megapods or mound-building birds lay eggs in huge mounds built by them from soil and vegetation. The rotting humus provides heat for this incubator. Below: The Mallee Fowl from S.E. Australia.

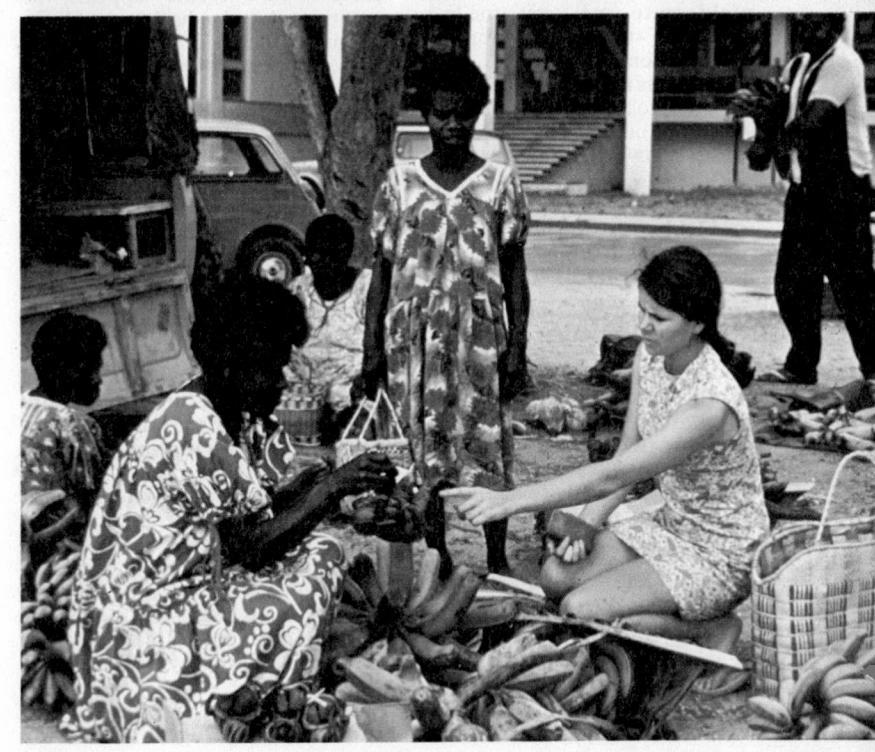

Melanesia, the south-western division f Oceania, includes New Caledonia nd the Bismarck, Solomon, New ebrides, Fiji and smaller archipelagos. his market is in Vila the capital of the ew Hebrides.

depression; pensive sadness. 2. (hist.) One of the four humors. ~ *adj.* Sad, saddening.

Mel·a·ne·sia (mĕlanē'zha,-sha). General term for islands of W. Pacific including New Hebrides, New Caledonia, Fiji, etc. **Mel·a·ne'sian** *adj. & n.* [Gk. *melas* black (from the color of the predominant native race, the Papuans), *nēsos* island]

mé·lange (*Fr.* mĕlahn̄zh') *n.* (pl. **-langes** pr. *Fr.* -lahn̄zh'). Mixture, medley.

mel·a·nin (mĕl'anĭn) *n.* Dark brown or black pigment found in hair, skin, or tissues.

mel·a·nism (mĕl'anĭzem) *n.* Darkness of color resulting from abnormal development of black pigment in epidermis, hair, etc. **mel·a·nis'tic** *adj.*

mel·a·no·ma (mĕlanō'ma) *n.* (pl. **-mas, -ma·ta** pr. -mata). (path.) Dark-colored tumor.

mel·a·no·sis (mĕlanō'sĭs) *n.* Morbid deposit, abnormal development, of black pigment in tissue. **mel·a·not·ic** (mĕlanŏt'ĭk) *adj.*

Mel·ba (mĕl'ba) **toast.** Thin crisp toast. [f. Dame Nellie *Melba,* Australian prima donna d. 1931]

Mel·bourne (mĕl'bern). Capital of Victoria and second largest city in Australia (after Sydney).

Mel·chior (mĕl'kyŏr). Traditional name of one of the Magi, a king of Nubia.

meld (mĕld) *v.* (cards) Declare [card(s)] for score; make meld. ~ *n.* Melding; card(s) melded.

me·lee, mê·lée (mā'lā, mālā', mĕl'ā) *ns.* General fight, brawl, skirmish.

mel·io·rate (mĕl'yerāt, mē'lē-) *v.* (**-rat·ed, -rat·ing**). Improve. **mel·io·ra'tion** *n.*

mel·io·rism (mĕl'yerĭzem, mē'lē-) *n.* Doctrine that the world may be made better by human effort (opp. PESSIMISM). **mel'io·rist** *n.*

mel·lif·er·ous (melĭf'erus) *adj.* Yielding, producing, honey.

mel·lif·lu·ous (melĭf'lŏŏus) *adj.* (of voice, words, music) Sweetsounding. **mel·lif'lu·ence** *n.* **mel·lif'lu·ent** *adj.*

Mel·lon (mĕl'on), **Andrew William** (1855–1937). Amer. financier, industrialist, and philanthropist; secretary of the treasury, 1921–32.

mel·low (mĕl'ō) *adj.* Soft and rich in flavor, color, or sound; softened by age or experience; genial, jovial; partly intoxicated. **mel'low·ly** *adv.* **mel'low·ness** *n.* **mellow** *v.* Make or become mellow; ripen.

me·lod·ic (melŏd'ĭk) *adj.* Of melody; ~ **minor,** (mus.) minor scale with major 6th and 7th when ascending and minor 6th and 7th when descending (so called as more suitable for melody than HARMONIC

minor).

me·lo·di·ous (melō'dēus) *adj.* Of, producing, melody; sweetsounding. **me·lo'di·ous·ly** *adv.* **me·lo'di·ous·ness** *n.* **mel·o·dist** (mĕl'odĭst) *n.* Singer; composer of melodies.

mel·o·dra·ma (mĕl'odrahma, -drāma) *n.* Sensational dramatic piece with violent appeals to emotions and happy ending; language, behavior, suggestive of this; (formerly) play, or passage in play, using spoken voice against musical background. **mel·o·dra·mat·ic** (mĕlodramăt'ĭk) *adj.* **mel·o·dra·mat'i·cal·ly** *adv.* **mel·o·dram·a·tist** (mĕlodrăm'atĭst, -drah'ma-) *n.* **mel·o·dram·a·tize** *v.t.* (**-tized, -tiz·ing**).

mel·o·dy (mĕl'odē) *n.* (pl. **-dies**). Sweet music; arrangement of single notes in musically expressive succession; principal part in harmonized music.

mel·on (mĕl'on) *n.* (Any of several gourds bearing) sweet fruit, esp. the **musk'melon** (*Cucumis melo*) and **wa'termelon** (*Citrullus vulgaris*).

Me·los (mē'lŏs) (also **Mi·los, Mi·lo** pr. mē'lŏs, mē'law). Greek island in the Cyclades; **Venus de Milo,** Hellenistic marble statue of Aphrodite (now in the Louvre) found here in 1820.

Mel·pom·e·ne (mĕlpŏm'enē). (Gk. and Rom. myth.) Muse of tragedy.

melt (mĕlt) *v.* (**melt·ed** or **mol·ten, melt·ing**). (Cause to)

become liquefied by heat; softer be softened; dissolve; pass imperceptibly *into*; ~ **away,** dissolve disappear; ~ **down,** reduce (meta articles etc.) to molten metal fo use as raw material; **melt'down** *n* melting of uranium fuel rods i nuclear reactor, possibly leading t catastrophic accident wit attendant massive radioactive con tamination. ~ *n.* Molten metal.

mel·ton (mĕl'ton) *n.* Kind c cloth with very close-cut nap, use for overcoats etc. [*Melto Mowbray,* town in Leicestershir England]

Mel·ville [1] (mĕl'vĭl), **Herma** (1819–91). Amer. novelist; wrot stories based on his experiences a sea; author of *Omoo, Typee, Moby Dick,* etc.

Jefferson Memorial, viewed from the Washington Monument column, was designed by Pope, Eggers and Higgins and built in the classical style favoured by Jefferson, who is sculptured onto the pediment above the portico.

Mel·ville[2] (mĕl´vĭl) **Island.** Island, 16,500 sq. mi. (26,565 sq. km), in the Canadian Northwest Territories; **Melville Peninsula,** a northward-projecting peninsula, 24,156 sq. mi. (38,891 sq. km), in the E. part of the Canadian Northwest Territories.

mem·ber (mĕm´ber) *n.* 1. Limb or other bodily organ, constituent portion of complex structure. 2. Person belonging to a society etc.; **M ~ of Parliament,** (abbrev. M.P.) person formally elected to the British House of Commons. **mem´ber·ship** *n.*

mem·brane (mĕm´brān) *n.* Fine layer of connective tissue enveloping an organ, lining a cavity, or separating adjacent parts in a living organism; (palaeog.) parchment skin. **mem·bra·nous** (mĕm´branus) *adj.*

me·men·to (memĕn´tō) *n.* (pl. **-tos, -toes**). Object serving as reminder or warning, or kept as memorial; ~ **mori** (mōr´ī, -ē) (L., = remember you must die), warning or reminder of death, e.g. skull.

Mem·non (mĕm´nŏn). (Gk. legend) Ethiopian prince slain at Troy; a colossal statue at Thebes (in reality that of Amenhotep III), which gave forth a musical note when struck by the rays of the rising sun, was supposed to represent him.

mem·o (mĕm´ō) *n.* (pl. **mem·os**). (colloq.) Memorandum.

mem·oir (mĕm´wār, -wōr) *n.* Record, history, written from personal knowledge or special sources of information; (auto)-biography; essay on learned subject by expert.

mem·o·ra·bil·i·a (mĕm-

*The **watermelon** belongs to the gourd family of flowering plants and is now under cultivation on every continent. Its fruit was depicted by early Egyptian artists.*

erabĭl´ēa, -bĭl´ya) *n.pl.* (sing. **-o·rab·i·le** pr. -erăb´ĭlē). Memorable things. [L.]

mem·o·ra·ble (mĕm´erabel) *adj.* Likely or worthy to be remembered. **mem·o·ra·bil´i·ty** *n.* **mem´o·ra·bly** *adv.*

mem·o·ran·dum (mĕmerăn´dum) *n.* (pl. **-dums, -da** pr. -da). Note to help the memory, record for future use; informal letter without signature etc.

me·mo·ri·al (memōr´ēal, -mōr´-) *adj.* Commemorative, of memory. ~ *n.* Memorial object, monument, custom, etc.; **M ~ Day,** formerly May 30, now usu. last Monday in May, a day commemorating dead servicemen of all wars. **me·mo´ri·al·ize** *v.t.* (**-ized, -iz·ing**). Commemorate; address memorial to.

mem·o·rize (mĕm´erīz) *v.t.* (**-rized, -riz·ing**). Commit to memory.

mem·o·ry (mĕm´ere, mĕm´rē) *n.* (pl. **-ries**). 1. Faculty by which things are recalled to or kept in the mind; recollection; posthumous repute; length of time over which memory extends. 2. Part of computer in which information is stored.

mem·sa·hib (mĕm´sahĭb, -ēb, -sahhĭb, -sahhēb): see SAHIB.

men·ace (mĕn´ĭs) *n.* Threat. ~ *v.t.* (**-aced, -ac·ing**). Threaten. **men´ac·ing·ly** *adv.*

mé·nage (mānahzh´, Fr. mĕnahzh´) *n.* (pl. **-nages** pr. -nah´zhĭz, Fr. -nahzh´). Household.

me·nag·er·ie (menăj´ere, -năzh´-) *n.* Collection of wild animals kept in captivity for exhibition etc.

Me·nan·der (menăn´der) (342–291 B.C.). Greek poet and writer of comedies.

Menck·en (mĕng´ken), **H(enry) L(ouis)** (1880–1956). Amer. editor, critic, and satirist; author of books on American language; known especially for *The American Language.*

mend (mĕnd) *v.* Restore to sound condition, repair; improve; rectify; regain health. ~ *n.* Repaired place; **on the ~,** improving.

men·da·cious (mĕndā´shus) *adj.* Lying. **men·da´cious·ly** *adv.* **men·dac·i·ty** (mĕndăs´ĭtē) *n.* (pl. **-ties**).

Men·del (mĕn´del), **Gregor Johann** (1822–84). Abbot of Brünn, Moravia; his experiments in the cross-fertilization of garden peas led to the formulation of ~'s laws of heredity, showing that certain

The study and treatment of **mental** illness has developed into an important science in the 20th century. Mad houses, their inmates treated like animals, like this one depicted by Goya, were once common.

characteristics, as height, color, etc., depend on the presence of hereditary determining factors (later called *genes*), which may be either dominant or recessive. **Men·de·li·an** (měndē′lēan, -dēl′-yan) *adj*. **Men′del·ism** *n*.

Men·de·le·ev (měndelā′ef), **Dmitri Ivanovich** (1834–1907). Russian chemist; discovered the PERIODIC law.

men·de·le·vi·um (měndelē′-vēum) *n*. (chem.) Transuranic element, symbol Md, at. no. 101. [f. MENDELEEV]

Men·dels·sohn (měn′delson; *Ger.* měn′delzawn), **Jacob Ludwig Felix** (1809–47). German musical composer of oratorios, symphonies, overtures, etc.

men·di·cant (měn′dikant) *adj*. Begging; living on alms. ~ *n*. Beggar; mendicant friar. **men′di·can·cy, men·dic·i·ty** (měndĭs′ītē) *ns*.

Men·e·la·us (měnelā′us). (Gk. legend) King of Sparta; brother of Agamemnon, and husband of Helen, who was stolen from him by Paris and restored after the fall of Troy.

men·folk (měn′fōk) *n.pl*. Men collectively, esp. of family or community.

men·ha·den (měnhā′den) *n*. (pl. -den). Kind of large herring (*Brevoortia tyrannus*) found on E. coast of N. America, used for fertilizer and yielding a valuable oil. [Amer. Ind.]

men·hir (měn′hēr) *n*. (archaeol.) Tall upright monumental stone. [Breton, = "long stone"]

me·ni·al (mē′nēal, měn′yal) *adj*. Servile, degrading. ~ *n*. Household servant; servile person. **me′ni·al·ly** *adv*.

me·nin·ges: see MENINX.

men·in·gi·tis (měnĭnjītĭs) *n*. Inflammation of the meninges.

me·ninx (mē′nĭngks) *n*. (pl. **me·nin·ges** pr. menĭn′jēz). Any of three membranes (*dura mater, arachnoid, pia mater*) enveloping brain and spinal cord. **me·nin·ge·al** (menĭn′jēal) *adj*.

me·nis·cus (menĭs′kus) *n*. (pl. **-nis·ci** pr. -nĭs′ī, **-nis·cus·es**). Lens convex on one side and concave on the other; convex or concave upper surface of a column of liquid; (math.) figure of crescent form.

Men·nin·ger (měn′ĭnjer),

Charles F. (1862–1933). Am psychiatrist; with his two so **Karl Augustus,** (1893–) a **William Claire** (1899–196 founded the Menninger Neu psychiatric Clinic in Tope Kansas.

Men·non·ite (měn′onīt) Member of a Christian sect t arose in Friesland in the 16th maintaining principles similar those of the Anabaptists; th baptize only after confession of fa and will not take oaths or und take military or state servi German Mennonites settled Russia under Catherine the Gre but when rendered liable conscription in the 19th c. ma emigrated to U.S. and Brazil; m are farmers. [f. *Menno* Simo (1492–1559), their early leader]

men·o·pause (měn′opawz) Period of life, generally between and 50, in women, at whi menstruation ceases. **men·o·pau sal** *adj*.

me·nor·ah (menōr′a, -nōr′a) Candelabrum used in Jewi worship.

men·or·rha·gi·a (měnerā′jē -ja) *n*. Excessive menstruation.

Me·not·ti (menŏt′ē), **Gia Carlo** (1911–). Italian-bo Amer. operatic composer a

e **merchant** fleet consists of those
ps of a nation used in commerce.
own here are some examples of the
st famous 20th-century funnel mark-
s and colors.

rettist; among his works are the
eras *Amahl and the Night Visitors*
d *The Consul*.

men·ses (mĕn′sēz) *n.pl.* (also
nsidered sing.). Discharge of
ood and tissue debris from uterus
primates, normally at monthly
tervals. [L., = "months"]

Men·she·vik (mĕn′shĕvĭk; *Russ.*
ĕnshĕvĕk′) *n.* (pl. **-viks, -vi·ki**
. -vĭkē, -vēkē; *Russ.* -vēkē′).
ember of the moderate Socialist
rty in Russia, which was in the
inority at the Socialist conference
1903 and was overthrown by
enin and the Bolsheviks at the
evolution of 1917, after being in
wer for a brief period. [Russ.
enshe smaller]

tral) *adj.* 1. Monthly. 2.
hysiol.) Of the menses.

men·stru·ate (mĕn′strōōāt) *v.i.*
at·ed, -at·ing). Discharge the
enses. **men·stru·a′tion** *n.*

men·stru·um (mĕn′strōōum) *n.*
l. **-stru·ums, -stru·a** pr.
trōōa). (pharm.) Solvent.

men·sur·a·ble (mĕn′sherabel)
j. Measurable; (mus.) having
ed time or rhythm.

men·sur·al (mĕn′sheral) *adj.*
f measure; (mus.) measurable.

men·sur·a·tion (mĕnsherā′-
on) *n.* Measuring; (math.) branch
mathematics concerned with
easurement of lengths, areas, and
lumes.

men·tal (mĕn′tal) *adj.* Of,
lating to, the mind; ~ **age**, age
which normal children reach a
rtain stage of mental develop-
ent, used as standard for assessing
telligence (e.g. a boy of 17 who
s the mental development of a
rmal 10-year-old has a mental
e of 10); ~ **arithmetic**, calcula-
ns performed without the use of
ritten figures; ~ **deficiency**,
ngenital feeble-mindedness,
ndition of person who is unequal
the conduct of ordinary affairs;
hospital, institution for care of
rsons suffering from mental
sorder or defect; ~ **patient**, one
der care for disordered mind.
en′tal·ly *adv.*

men·tal·i·ty (mĕntăl′ite) *n.* (pl.
ies). Mental quality; mode of
inking; (degree of) intellectual
wer; (loosely) mind, disposition,
aracter.

men·thol (mĕn′thŏl, -thawl,
hōl) *n.* Crystalline camphorlike
bstance obtained from mint oils.

men·tion (mĕn′shon) *v.t.* Refer
; state incidentally; cite formally
r meritorious achievement; **not**
~, in addition to. **mention**
Mentioning.

Men·tor (mĕn′ter, -tōr). (Gk.

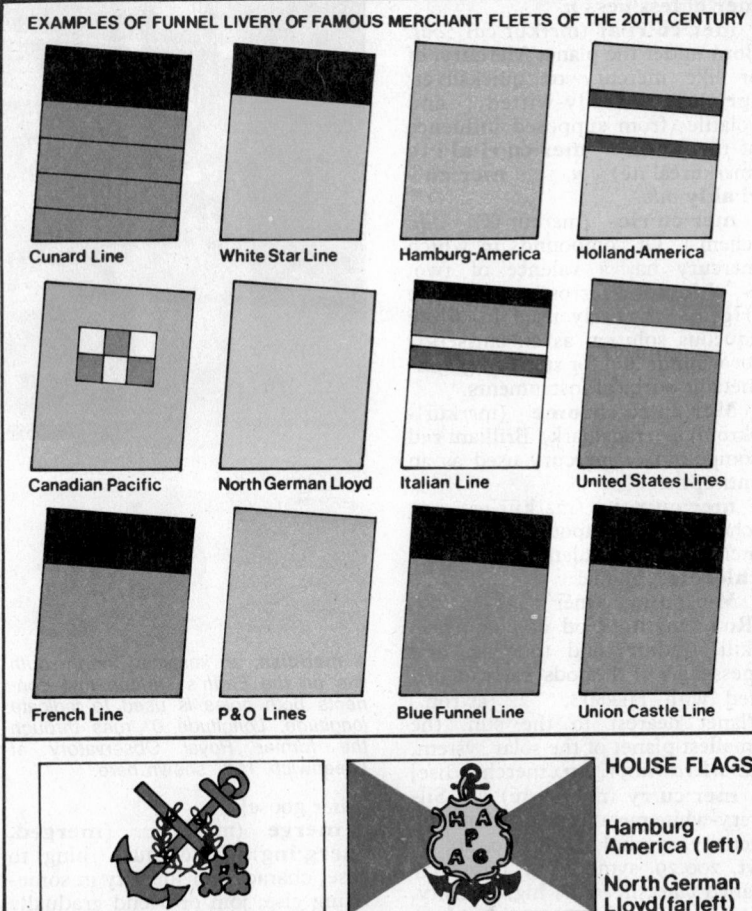

EXAMPLES OF FUNNEL LIVERY OF FAMOUS MERCHANT FLEETS OF THE 20TH CENTURY

Cunard Line — White Star Line — Hamburg-America — Holland-America
Canadian Pacific — North German Lloyd — Italian Line — United States Lines
French Line — P&O Lines — Blue Funnel Line — Union Castle Line

HOUSE FLAGS
Hamburg America (left)
North German Lloyd (far left)

legend) Friend of Odysseus and
guide and adviser of the young
Telemachus.

men·tor (mĕn′ter, -tōr) *n.*
Experienced and trusted counselor.
[f. MENTOR]

men·u (mĕn′ū, mā′nū) *n.* Bill
of fare. [Fr., = "detailed list", f.
adj. = "small"]

me·ow (mēow′) *n. & v.i.* (Make)
cat's cry, mew.

Meph·i·stoph·e·les (mĕfĭstŏf′-
elēz). In the legend of FAUST, the
demon to whom Faust sold his soul.
**Meph·is·to·phe·li·an, Meph·is·-
to·phe·le·an** (mĕfĭstōfē′lēan) *adjs.*

Mer·can·tile (mĕr′kantĕl, -tĭl,
-tĭl) *adj.* Trading; of merchants
or trade; mercenary, fond of
bargaining; ~ **system**, that based
on the old economic theory that
money is the only form of wealth
and that the object of trade is to
export goods at the highest prices.
mer′can·til·ism, mer′can·til·ist
ns.

Mer·ca·tor (merkā′ter),
Gerhard. Latinized name of
Gerhard Kremer (1512–94),
Flemish geographer; inventor of a
system of projecting maps (~
projection) in which the globe is
projected on to a cylinder and the
meridians of longitude are at right
angles to the parallels of latitude.

mer·ce·nar·y (mĕr′senĕrē) *adj.*
Working merely for money or other
reward; having love of money as
motive; hired (now only of soldiers
serving in a foreign army). ~ *n.*
(pl. **-nar·ies**). Hired soldier.
mer′ce·nar·i·ness *n.*

mer·cer·ize (mĕr′serīz) *v.t.*
(**-ized, -iz·ing**). Prepare (cotton)
for dyeing by treating with solution
of caustic potash etc. that produces
a silky luster. [John *Mercer*
(1791–1866), inventor]

mer·chan·dise (mĕr′chandīz,
-dīs) *n.* Mercantile commodities;
goods for sale. ~ (mĕr′chandīz)
v. (**-ised, -is·ing**). Trade (in); buy
and sell; prepare for sale, by display, design, advertising, etc.

mer·chant (mĕr′chant) *n.*
Wholesale trader, esp. one trading
with foreign countries; retail trader;
mer′chantman, merchant ship;
merchant marine, shipping,
commercial shipping; **merchant
ship**, ship of merchant marine.
mer′chant·a·ble *adj.* Salable,
marketable.

mer·ci·ful (mĕr′sĭful) *adj.*
Disposed to mercy; compassionate.
mer′ci·ful·ly *adv.* **mer′ci·ful·-
ness** *n.*

mer·ci·less (mĕr′sĭlĭs) *adj.*
Showing no mercy; pitiless, unrelenting. **mer′ci·less·ly** *adv.*

mer·ci·less·ness *n.*

mer·cu·ri·al (merkūr´ēal) *adj.* Born under the planet Mercury; of or like mercury or quicksilver; sprightly, ready-witted, and volatile (from supposed influence of the planet). **mer·cu·ri·al·i·ty** (merkūrēăl´itē) *n.* **mer·cu´-ri·al·ly** *adv.*

mer·cu·ric (merkūr´ĭk) *adj.* (chem.) Of compounds in which mercury has a valence of two; ~ **chloride**, corrosive sublimate (HgCl$_2$), formerly used in dilute aqueous solution as an antiseptic for wounds and for sterilizing non-metallic surgical instruments.

Mer·cu·ro·chrome (merkūr´-okrōm) *n.* (trademark) Brilliant red compound of mercury used as an antiseptic.

mer·cu·rous (merkūr´us) *adj.* (chem.) Of compounds in which mercury has a valence of one; ~ **chloride**, calomel.

Mer·cu·ry (mer´kyere) 1. (Rom. myth.) God of eloquence, skill, trading, and thieving, and messenger of the gods, early identified with HERMES. 2. (astron.) Planet nearest to the sun, the smallest planet of the solar system. [L. *Mercurius*, f. *merx* merchandise]

mer·cu·ry (mer´kyerē) *n.* Silvery-white metallic element of high density, symbol Hg, at. no. 80, at. wt. 200.29, symbol Hg, popularly called *quicksilver*; its high density, its property of not wetting glass, and the wide range of temperature at which it is liquid make it valuable for scientific instruments, esp. thermometers and barometers; it dissolves many metals, forming amalgams, and its compounds are used in medicine as laxatives and stimulants.

mer·cy (mer´sē) *n.* (pl. **-cies**). Forbearance and compassion toward an offender, enemy, or person in one's power; disposition to forgive; act of mercy, gift of God, blessing; **at the ~ of**, wholly in the power of or subject to; ~ **killing**, killing with the intention of preventing needless suffering; ~ **seat**, golden covering of Ark of Covenant; hence, throne of God.

mere[1] (mēr) *n.* (poet.) Lake.

mere[2] (mēr) *adj.* (*superl.* **mer·est**). Pure, unmixed; barely or only what it is said to be, nothing more than. **mere´ly** *adv.*

mer·e·tri·cious (meretrĭsh´us) *adj.* Showily attractive, flashy. **mer·e·tri´cious·ly** *adv.* **mer·e·tri´cious·ness** *n.* [L. *meretrix* prostitute]

mer·gan·ser (mergăn´ser) *n.* (pl. **-sers**, collect. **-ser**). Any of various fish-eating ducks of great diving powers, with long narrow serrated bill hooked at the tip, inhabiting northern parts of Old World and N. America. [L. *mergus* diver,

*A **meridian**, an imaginary north-south line on the Earth's surface that connects both poles is used to indicate longitude. Longitude 0° runs through the former Royal Observatory at Greenwich, U.K. shown here.*

anser goose]

merge (merj) *v.* (**merged, merg·ing**). Lose, cause (thing) to lose, character or identity in something else; join or blend gradually (*into, with*). **merg´er** *n.* Absorption of estate etc. in another; consolidation of one company or corporation with another.

me·rid·i·an (merĭd´ēan) *n.* Great circle passing through celestial poles and zenith of any place on Earth's surface or passing through the poles and any place on Earth; point at which star or sun attains its highest altitude; prime, full splendor. ~ *adj.* Of noon; (fig.) of the period of greatest splendor, vigor, etc.

me·ringue (merăng´) *n.* Confection made of sugar and beaten white of egg, baked until crisp; shell of meringue filled with whipped cream.

me·ri·no (merē´nō) *n.* (pl. **-nos**). Variety of sheep with fine silky wool, orig. bred in Spain; fine yarn or soft fabric of this wool; fine woolen yarn; (also ~ **sheep**) the chief and best known wool-bearing breed of Australia and N.Z.

mer·i·stem (mer´ĭstĕm) *n.* (bot.) Cell or region where growth is initiated.

mer·it (mer´ĭt) *n.* Quality of deserving well or being entitled to reward or gratitude; goodness; (pl.) good works, deserts; intrinsic rights and wrongs (of case etc., esp. law); **Legion of M~**, U.S. military decoration for outstanding service. **merit** *v.t.* Deserve (reward,

Merino sheep are being inspected f[or] the quality of their fleece at Sydney[´s] Royal Easter Show, Australia. Origina[lly] a Spanish breed, they have bee[n] improved by cross-breeding.

punishment).

mer·i·to·ri·ous (merĭtōr´ĕu[s], -tor´-) *adj.* Deserving prais[e], reward, etc. (often as term [of] limited praise, = well-meant, wel[l-] meaning). **mer·i·to´ri·ous·ly** *ad[v.]* **mer·i·to´ri·ous·ness** *n.*

Mer·lin (mer´lĭn). In Arthuria[n] legend, a magician and bard wh[o] aided and supported King Arth[ur] and made the Round Table.

mer·lin (mer´lĭn) *n.* Sma[ll] European falcon (*Falco columbari[us]* *aesalon*); N. Amer. pigeon hawk (*[F.]* *columbarius columbarius*).

mer·maid (mer´mād) *n.* (mas[c.] **mer·man** pr. mer´măn, pl. **-me[n]** pr. -měn). Fabled being inhabitin[g] the sea, with human head and trun[k] and tail of a fish. [f. *mere*[1]]

mer·o·blast (mer´oblăst) *[n.]* (physiol.) Ovum of two parts, or [one] of which is germinal and the othe[r] nutritive.

Mer·o·vin·gi·an (merovĭn´jēa[n]) *adj. & n.* (Member) of the lin[e] of Frankish kings founded b[y] Clovis (481–511) and reigning i[n] Gaul and Germany until 752.

Mer·ri·mack (mer´ĭmăk[)] Frigate fitted with iron plating use[d] by the Confederates against th[e] Union ship, Monitor, during th[e] Civil War, in an inconclusive batt[le] at Hampton Roads, 1862.

mer·ry (mer´ē) *adj.* (**-ri·e[r],** **-ri·est**). Mirthful, hilarious; fu[ll] of animated enjoyment; slight[ly] tipsy; **make ~**, be festive; ~ **-go-] round**, revolving machine carryin[g] wooden horses, cars, etc., for ridin[g] on or in; busy social lif[e] er'rymaking, festivity. **mer'-ly** *adv.* **mer'ri·ment, mer'ri·ss** *ns.*

me·sa (mā′sa) *n.* High rocky bleland with precipitous sides; ~ **Verde National Park,** area SW. Colorado known for ruins prehistoric cliff dwellings.

Me·sa·bi (mesah′bē) **Range.** ow narrow range of hills in innesota containing vast iron ore d taconite deposits.

mes·cal (měs′kăl, měskăl′) *n.* Strong spirit distilled from rmented sap of wild agave. 2. YOTE.

mes·ca·line (měs′kalēn, -lǐn), es·ca·lin (měs′kalǐn) *ns.* Active gredient in peyote.

mes·en·ter·y (měs′entěrē, ěz′-) *n.* (pl. **-ter·ies**). Fold of ritoneum attaching intestinal nal to posterior wall of abdomen. es·en·ter·ic (měsentěr′ǐk, měz-) j. **mes·en·ter·i·tis** (měsěnterī′-, měz-) *n.* Inflammation of the

mesentery.

mesh (měsh) *n.* One of the spaces between the threads of a net; (pl.) net. ~ *v.* Catch in a net; (of gearwheels etc.) engage, interlock.

Me·shach (mē′shăk). One of three Jewish youths who came unharmed from a furnace into which they were thrown by Nebuchadnezzar (Dan. 3).

mes·mer·ism (měz′merǐzem, měs′-) *n.* (archaic) Hypnotism. **mes·mer·ic** (mězměr′ǐk, měs-) *adj.* **mes′mer·ist** *n.* **mes′mer·ize** *v.t.* (**-ized, -iz·ing**). Hypnotize; fascinate, compel by fascination. [f. F. A. *Mesmer* (1734–1815),

This Stone Age village in the Orkneys is a relic of the **Mesolithic** *Age — in N. W. Europe from about 8,000 B.C. to about 3,400 B.C. — which was technologically intermediate between the cultures using only chipped stone and those using polished stone tools.*

Austrian physician]

mes·o·carp (měz′okārp, měs′-, mē′zo-, -so-) *n.* (physiol.) Middle of three layers of cells formed by embryo at early stage, layer from which skeletal muscles, heart muscle, and blood are developed.

Mes·o·lith·ic (mězolǐth′ǐk, měs-, mē′zo, -so-) *adj.* (archaeol.) Of the Stone Age between Paleolithic and Neolithic.

me·son (mē′zŏn, -sŏn, měz′ŏn, měs′-) *n.* Elementary particle intermediate in mass between proton and electron; **mu** ~ = MUON.

mes·o·phyll (měz′ofǐl, měs′-, mē′zo-, -so-) *n.* (bot.) Inner tissue of leaf.

mes·o·phyte (měz′ofīt, měs′-, mē′zo-, -so-) *n.* Plant needing a moderate amount of moisture.

Mes·o·po·ta·mi·a (měsopotā′mēa). Region of SW. Asia, the larger part of modern Iraq, between the rivers Tigris and Euphrates;

center of the ancient civilizations of SUMER, ASSYRIA, and BABYLON; scene (1915–16) of a disastrous British campaign against the Turks.

Mes·o·po·ta'mi·an *adj.* [Gk., = "(country) between the rivers" (*mesos* middle, *potamos* river)]

mes·o·sphere (měz'osfēr, měs'-, mē'zo-, -so) *n.* Part of atmosphere above stratosphere, in which temperature generally falls with increasing height.

mes·o·tron (měz'otrŏn, měs'-, mē'zo-, -so-) = MESON.

Mes·o·zo·ic (mězozō'ĭk, měs-, mēzo-, -so-) *adj. & n.* (geol.) (Of) the era or group of systems between Caenozoic and Paleozoic, characterized by the appearance of flowering plants and the emergence and extinction of dinosaurs.

mes·quite, mes·quit (měskēt', měs'kēt) *ns.* Any of several deciduous trees or shrubs (genus *Prosopis*) of southwestern U.S. and Mexico, esp. *P. juliflora*, whose seed and pods are used as forage.

mess (měs) *n.* 1. (archaic) Portion of food; concoction, medley. 2. Dirty or untidy state; difficult situation, trouble; **make a ~ of**, bungle. 3. Spilled liquid etc. 4. Company of persons who take meals together, esp. in armed forces; taking of such a meal, place where it is eaten; **~ kit**, soldier's metal utensils, used for cooking. **mess** *v.* 1. Make dirty or untidy; putter *about*. 2. Take meals, esp. as member of a mess. **mess'y** *adj.* Untidy, dirty. **mess'i·ly** *adv.* **mess'i·ness** *n.*

mes·sage (měs'ĭj) *n.* Communication sent from one person to another; inspired utterance of a prophet or sage; teaching or moral of book, play, etc.; mission, errand.

mes·sen·ger (měs'enjer) *n.* Bearer of message.

Mes·si·ah (mesī'a) *n.* In Old Testament prophetic writings, the promised deliverer of the Jews; in Christian doctrine, Jesus Christ, regarded as this deliverer; name of an oratorio by Handel, based on Old Testament prophecies. **Mes·si·an·ic** (měsēăn'ĭk) *adj.* Of or relating to the or a Messiah. [Heb. *māsīah* anointed]

mes·sieurs (měs'erz; *Fr.* mēsyö'): see MONSIEUR.

Mes·si·na (měsē'na). City and harbor of NE. Sicily; **Strait of ~**, that separating Sicily from Italy.

Messrs. (měs'erz) *abbrev.* *Messieurs*; pl. of Mr., prefixed as title to name of firm etc. or introducing list of men.

mes·ti·zo (městē'zō) *n.* (pl. **-zos, -zoes**). Person of Spanish and Amer. Indian ancestry; person of other combinations of ancestry. [Span., f. L. *miscere* mix]

met: see MEET[2].

met·a·bol·ic (mětabŏl'ĭk) *adj.*

Of metabolism.

me·tab·o·lism (metăb'olĭzem) *n.* Process in a cell or organism by which nutritive material is built up into living matter (*anabolism*) or by which protoplasm is broken down to perform special functions (*catabolism*); see BASAL. **me·tab'o·lize** *v.t.* (**-lized, -liz·ing**).

me·tab·o·lite (metăb'olīt) *n.* Substance undergoing change during metabolism.

met·a·car·pus (mětakăr'pus) *n.* (pl. **-pi** pr. **-pī**). (anat.) Set of bones (5 in man) connecting carpus to phalanges; part of hand in which these are situated. **met·a·car'pal** *adj. & n.* (Bone) of the metacarpus.

met·a·gen·e·sis (mětajěn'īsĭs) *n.* (biol.) Reproduction of new generations by processes alternately sexual and asexual. **met·a·ge·net·ic** (mětajenět'ĭk) *adj.*

met·al (mět'al) *n.* 1. One of a class of elements of which gold, silver, copper, iron, lead, and tin are examples; alloy of these. 2. Material for making glass, in molten state. **~** *v.t.* (**-aled, -al·ing**, Brit. **-alled, -al·ling**). Cover or supply with metal.

met·al·ize, met·al·lize (mět'alīz) *vbs.t.* (**-ized, -iz·ing; -lized, -liz·ing**). Render metallic. **met·al·i·za'tion** *n.*

me·tal·lic (metăl'ĭk) *adj.* Of or like metal; yielding metal.

met·al·log·ra·phy (mětalŏg'rafē) *n.* Study, description, of metals and alloys, their structure and properties.

met·al·loid (mět'aloid) *adj.*

*The city of **Messina** in Sicily was almost totally destoyed by an earthquake in 1908. This cathedral of Annunciata dei Catalani, however, survived. Probably of Byzantine origin, it was rebuilt by the Normans in the 12th Century.*

Having form or appearance metal. **~** *n.* Element havin physical properties of a metal ar chemical properties of a nonmeta e.g. tellurium.

met·al·lur·gy (mět'alērjē) Science of the extraction, workin and properties of metals and the alloys. **met·al·lur'gic, met·al lur'gi·cal** *adjs.* **met'al·lur·gist**

met·a·mere (mět'amēr) (zool.) One of a series of mo or less similar segments of an anim body, as of a worm. **met·a·mer** (mětamēr'ĭk) *adj.* (zool.) metameres; (chem.) having sam percentage composition an molecular weight, but differe chemical properties. **me·tam·er ism** (metăm'erĭzem) *n.*

met·a·mor·phic (mětamōr'fĭ *adj.* (geol., of rocks) Altered aft formation by heat or pressure both. **met·a·mor'phism** Metamorphic process.

met·a·mor·pho·sis (mětamōr fosĭs) *n.* (pl. **-ses** pr. **-sēz**). Chang of form, esp. magic transformatio as of person into beast or pla etc.; changed form; change character, circumstance, etc (zool.) change, usually rapi between immature form and adul **met·a·mor·phose** (mětamōr'fō -fōs) *v.t.* (**-phosed, -phos·ing** Change in form, change nature o

met·a·phor (mět'afōr, -fer) Figure of speech in which nam or descriptive term is transferre to an object to which it is n literally applicable (e.g. *a glarin error*); instance of this; **mixed ~** combination of inconsiste metaphors. **met·a·phor** (mětafōr'ĭk, -făr'-), **met·a·phor i·cal** *adjs.* **met·a·phor'i·cal·l** *adv.*

met·a·phys·ics (mětafĭz'ĭks) (considered *sing.*) Branch philosophy dealing with fir principles of things, including suc concepts as being, substance space, time, identity, etc. **met·a phys'i·cal** *adj.* Of metaphysics **~ poets**, term used to designat certain 17th-c. English poet including Donne, Cowley, Herber and Vaughan, addicted to "witt conceits" and far-fetched imagery **met·a·phys'i·cal·ly** *adv.* **met·a phy·si·cian** (mětafĭzĭsh'an) [Gk. *ta meta ta phusika* the work (of Aristotle) placed after th "Physics"]

me·tas·ta·sis (metăs'tasĭs) *n.* (p

2

3

-ses pr. -sēz). (path.) Transference of disease or malignant cells from a primary focus to one in another part of the body by way of natural passages or of blood or lymph vessels. **met·a·stat·ic** (mĕtastăt´ĭk) *adj.* **me·tas´ta·size** *v.i.* (**-sized, -siz·ing**).

met·a·tar·sus (mĕtatär´sus) *n.* (pl. **-si** pr. -sī). Set of bones (5 in man) connecting tarsus to phalanges; part of foot or hind limb in which these are situated. **met·a·tar´sal** *adj. & n.* (Bone) of the metatarsus.

me·tath·e·sis (metăth´esĭs) *n.* (pl. **-ses** pr. -sēz). 1. (gram.) Transposition of letters or sounds. 2. (chem.) Substitution of one radical or atom for another in a molecule. **met·a·thet·i·cal** (mĕtathĕt´ĭkal) *adj.*

met·a·zo·an (mĕtazō´an) *adj. & n.* (zool.) (Member) of the order Metazoa, comprising multicellular animals with differentiated tissues, a nervous system, and coordination between the various cells.

mete (mēt) *v.t.* (**met·ed, met·ing**). (literary) Measure; portion *out*, allot (punishment, reward).

me·tem·psy·cho·sis (metĕm-sīkō´sĭs, mĕtemsī) *n.* (pl. **-sis** pr. -sēz). Supposed migration of soul at death into another body.

me·te·or (mē´tēer, -ör) *n.* One of the small solid bodies in the solar system that become luminous when passing into Earth's atmosphere; (fig.) any bright, dazzling, but transient object. **me·te·or·ic** (mētēör´ĭk, -är´-) *adj.* Of the atmosphere; dependent on atmospheric conditions; of meteors; (fig.) dazzling, rapid.

me·te·or·ite (mē´tēerīt) *n.* Fallen meteor, fragment of rock or nickel iron that has fallen from space on to Earth's surface.

me·te·or·oid (mē´tēeroid) *n.* Body moving through space, of same nature as those which by passing into Earth's atmosphere become visible as meteors. **me·te·or·oid´al** *adj.*

me·te·or·ol·o·gy (mētēerŏl´ojē) *n.* Study of, science treating of, atmospheric phenomena, esp. for forecasting weather. **me·te·or·o·log·i·cal** (mētēerolŏj´ĭkal) *adj.* **me·te·or·o·log´i·cal·ly** *adv.* **me·te·or·ol´o·gist** *n.*

me·ter[1] (mē´ter) *n.* Apparatus for measuring, esp. automatically, and recording quantity of gas, water, electricity, etc., passing through, or time elapsed, etc. **~** *v.t.* Measure with meter.

me·ter[2] (mē´ter) *n.* Any regularly recurring poetic rhythm, determined by character and number of feet; group of metrical feet.

me·ter[3] (mē´ter) *n.* (abbrev. m) Basic unit of length in the metric system (approx. 39.37 in.), orig. representing one ten-millionth (10^{-7}) of a quadrant of the meridian passing through Paris; since 1960 defined as 1,650,763.7 wavelengths in a vacuum of the orange-red radiation of krypton 86 **~-kilogram-second** (*adj.*) (abbrev. mks) applied to a system of units of measurement based on the meter, kilogram, and second as units of length, mass, and time.

meth·ane (mĕth´ān) *n.* (chem.) Colorless inflammable gas (CH_4) formed by decay of vegetable matter in marshy places and coal seams.

meth·a·qua·lone (mĕthăk´walōn) *n.* Sedative drug usu. taken to induce sleep.

meth·od (mĕth´od) *n.* Procedure; way of doing anything esp. according to a regular plan; systematic or orderly arrangement; orderliness and regularity. **me·thod·ic** (methŏd´ĭk) **me·thod´i·cal** *adjs.* **me·thod´i·**

*This vast **meteor** crater in Arizona is 4,000 ft. wide and 600 ft. deep. Its age has been disputed since it was discovered in 1891. Estimates range between 5,000 and 50,000 years.*

The very existence of meteors was questioned by 18th-century rationalists because of the veneration given these stones. A meteor shower in France in 1803 convinced them.

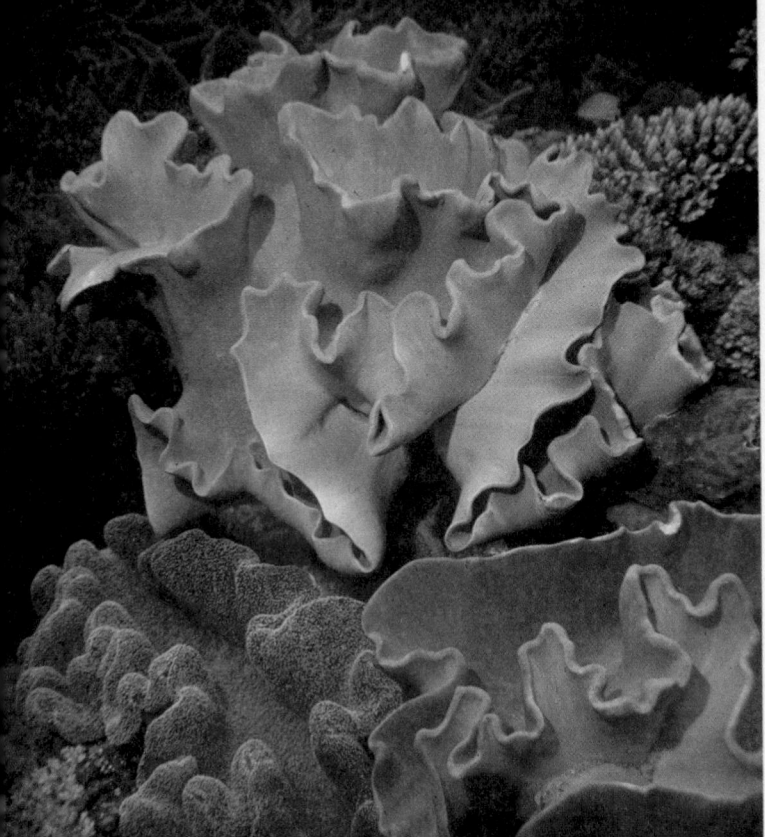

This automatic **parking meter** has to be wound only once a week. It has a weatherproof case and all joints are sealed by neoprene gaskets. The coin slot has a spring-loaded shutter to keep out dust and moisture.

- time scale
- indicator
- signal flag
- coin rotator gear
- coin slot shutter
- hinged cover
- coin window
- neoprene gasket

cal·ly *adv.*

Meth·od·ism (mĕth´odĭzem) *n.* Religious movement, founded by John WESLEY, his brother Charles, and George Whitefield, in reaction against apathy in the Church of England, and developed by missionary tours in U.S. and Gt. Britain; the meetings, often in the open air, were characterized (as now) by lay preaching and hymn singing; the movement later gave rise to various sects, but the principal groups (United Methodist Church, Primitive Methodists, and Wesleyan Methodists) united in 1932. **Meth´od·ist** *adj. & n.* [*Methodists*, applied to associates of the Wesleys at Oxford forming a religious society (nicknamed the "Holy Club"), prob. as following a specified "method" of devotional study]

Me·thu·se·lah (methōō´zela). Patriarch, grandfather of Noah, said (Gen. 5) to have lived 969 years, hence regarded as type of longevity.

meth·yl (mĕth´el) *n.* (chem.) Univalent organic radical (CH_3); ~ **alcohol**, colorless volatile liquid distilled from wood and also made synthetically; wood spirit. **meth·yl·ate** (mĕth´elāt) *v.t.* (-at·ed, -at·ing). Mix (alcohol) with wood spirit, usu. to render it unfit for drinking and therefore exempt from duty, as *methylated spirit.*

me·tic·u·lous (metĭk´yulus) *adj.* Extremely attentive to minute details. **me·tic´u·lous·ly** *adv.*

mé·tier (mā´tyā, mātyā´) *n.* Trade or profession; line.

Me·ton·ic (mĭtŏn´ĭk) **cycle.** Period of 19 solar years, after the lapse of which the new and full moons return to the same day of the year; it was the basis of the Greek calendar and is still used for calculating movable feast days, such as Easter. [f. *Meton*, Athenian astronomer (5th c. B.C.)]

me·ton·y·my (mĭtŏn´imē) *n.* Substitution of name of an attribute or adjunct for that of the thing meant (e.g. *the turf* for *horse racing*). **met·o·nym·i·cal·ly** (mĕtŏnĭm-ĭklē) *adv.*

me·tre (mē´ter) (Brit.) = METER[2], METER[3].

met·ric (mĕt´rĭk) *adj.* Of the meter or metric system; using the metric system; ~ **system**, decimal measuring system based on the meter, orig. devised in 1791 by the French Academy of Sciences, with the meter, liter, and kilogram (orig. the gram) as units of length,

Metazoa includes all animal organisms of more than one cell, except usually sponges. This growing plant-like coral, from Australia's Great Barrier Reef, is a multi-cellular organism.

capacity, and mass; ~ **ton**, 1,000 kilograms. **met·ri·ca·tion** (mĕtrĭkā'shon) *n.* Conversion to the metric system. **met·ri·cate** (mĕt'-rĭkāt) *v.* (**-cat·ed, -cat·ing**).

met·ri·cal (mĕt'rĭkal) *adj.* Of, composed in, meter; of, involving, measurement, as ~ **geometry**. **met'ri·cal·ly** *adv.*

met·ro (mĕt'rō) *n.* (pl. **-ros**). Subway, esp. (**M~**) in Paris.

me·trol·o·gy (mĭtrŏl'ojē) *n.* (pl. **-gies**). Science, system, of weights and measures. **met·ro·log·i·cal** (mĕtrolŏj'ĭkal) *adj.*

met·ro·nome (mĕt'ronōm) *n.* (mus.) Instrument marking time by means of a graduated inverted pendulum with a sliding weight. **met·ro·nom·ic** (mĕtronŏm'ĭk) *adj.*

me·trop·o·lis (metrŏp'olĭs) *n.* Chief city, capital; see of metropolitan bishop. [Gk. *mētropolis* parent state (*mēter* mother, *polis* city)]

met·ro·pol·i·tan (mĕtropŏl'-ĭtan) *adj.* Of a metropolis; of, forming (part of) nation as dist. from its colonies or dependencies; ~ **bishop, archbishop**, one who has authority over the bishops of a province. **metropolitan** *n.* Metropolitan bishop or archbishop; inhabitant of a metropolis. **met·ro·pol·i·tan·ate** (mĕtropŏl'ĭtanĭt) *n.* Office, jurisdiction, of a metropolitan bishop.

Met·ter·nich (mĕt'ernĭk; *Ger.* mĕt'ernĭx). Prince Clemens Wenzel Lothar Metternich-Winneburg (1773–1859), Austrian statesman; led the Congress of VIENNA in devising the settlement of Europe after the Napoleonic Wars.

met·tle (mĕt'el) *n.* Quality of disposition; natural vigor and ardor, spirit, esp. of a horse. **met'tle·some** *adj.* High-spirited.

Meuse (mūz; *Fr.* möz). (*Dutch* **Maas** pr. mahz) River of NE. France, Belgium, and Netherlands.

mew[1] (mū) *n.* Gull, esp. the common gull (*Larus canus*); sea mew.

mew[2] (mū) *v.* (of hawk) Molt; shut up (hawk) in mew; shut *up*, confine. ~ *n.* Cage for hawks.

mew[3] (mū) *n.* & *v.i.* Meow.

mewl (mūl) *v.i.* Cry feebly, whimper; mew like a cat.

mews (mūz) *n.* Series of private stables built around a yard or on both sides of a lane (now freq. converted into dwellings etc.); area containing these. [f. MEW[2], orig. of royal stables on site of hawks' mews]

Mex·i·co (mĕk'sĭkō; *Sp.* mĕ'hēkaw). Federal republic of southern N. Amer.; orig. inhabited by various Amer. Ind. peoples, esp. Maya, Aztecs; was a Spanish colony ("New Spain"), c1519–1821; since then it has been a republic except

for the years 1864–7 when MAXIMILIAN was emperor; the presidency of Diaz (1877–80 and 1884–1911) was followed by a period of revolution; the question of the possession of Texas led to war between the U.S. and Mexico in 1846–8, Texas having applied for admission to the U.S. as early as 1836; capital, Mexico City; **Gulf of** ~, area of Atlantic Ocean, almost surrounded by the southern coast of N. Amer., the coast of Mexico, and Cuba. **Mex'i·can** *adj.* & *n.*

me·ze·re·on (mĭzēr'ēŏn) *n.* Deciduous shrub (*Daphne mezereum*) with fragrant purple flowers.

mez·za·nine (mĕz'anēn, mĕzanēn') 1. *adj.* & *n.* (Low story) between two main stories of a building. 2. Lowest balcony or front part of a theater balcony.

mez·zo (mĕt'sō, mĕd'zō, mĕz'ō) *adv.* (mus.) Moderately; ~ **forte**, moderately loud; ~ **piano**, moderately soft.

mez·zo-so·pran·o (mĕt'sō soprăn'ō, -prah'nō, mĕd'zō, mĕz'ō) *n.* (pl. **-pran·os, -pran·i** pr. -prăn'ē, -prah'nē). (Person with, part for) voice betwee contralto and soprano.

mez·zo·tint (mĕt'sōtĭnt, mĕd zō-, mĕz'ō-) *n.* Method engraving on copper or steel which the plate is roughene uniformly, lights and half-ligh being produced by scraping awa the roughness, deep shadows b leaving it; print produced in th way. ~ *v.t.* Engrave in mezzotin

MF *abbrev.* Medium FREQUENCY

mf *abbrev.* Mezzo forte.

Mg *symbol.* Magnesium.

mg *abbrev.* Milligram(s).

Mgr. *abbrev.* Monseigneur Monsignor (pl. **Mgri.**); manager

mho (mō) *n.* Unit of electrica conductance, the reciprocal of th ohm; thus, a conductor having

Mexico is the largest Spanish speakin nation in the world. Almost half th population are peasants on subsistence economy. Below: The Pa ace of Fine Arts in Mexico City is use for operas, plays and exhibits and i decorated with murals by Rivera Orozco and Tamayo. Bottom: Map an flag of Mexico. Facing page: Harvestin the agave plant from which mescal i made.

resistance of 4 ohms has a conductance of 0.25 mho.

MI *abbrev.* Michigan.

Mi·am·i (mĭăm´ē, -ăm´ĭ). City in SE. Florida; **M ~ Beach**, resort city on an island opposite Miami, across Biscayne Bay.

mi·as·ma (mĭăz´ma, mē-) *n.* (pl. **-ma·ta** pr. -m*a*ta, **-mas**). Noxious exhalation from marshes, putrid matter, etc. **mi·as´mic** *adj.*

Mic. *abbrev.* Micah (Old Testament).

mi·ca (mī´ka) *n.* One of a group of minerals composed of aluminum silicate combined with other silicates, occurring as small glittering scales in granite etc., or as larger crystals separable into thin transparent plates, used as a dielectric and insulator in electrical equipment etc. **mi·ca·ceous** (mīka´shus) *adj.* [L., = "crumb"]

Mi·cah (mī´ka). Hebrew minor prophet, a contemporary of Isaiah; book of Old Testament containing his prophecies.

Mi·caw·ber (mĭkaw´ber), **Mr.** In Dickens' *David Copperfield*, a sanguine idler trusting that some-

thing good will turn up.

mice: see MOUSE.

mi·celle (mĭsĕl´) *n.* (chem.) Minute particle formed by an aggregate of molecules, found in certain colloidal solutions.

Mich. *abbrev.* Michigan.

Mi·chael (mī´kel), **St.** One of the archangels, usu. represented slaying a dragon (Rev. 12); commemorated Sept. 29.

Mi·chael·mas (mĭk´elmas). Feast of St. Michael, Sept. 29; ~ **daisy**, herbaceous perennial of genus *Aster*, native in N. America, flowering at Michaelmas.

Mi·chel·an·ge·lo Buon·ar·ro·ti (mēkĕlahn´jĕlō bwawnahraw´-tē) (1475–1564). Italian sculptor, painter, and poet; one of the greatest artists of the Renaissance; famous esp. for his frescoes in the Sistine Chapel at Rome.

Michelangelo Buonarroti, Italian sculptor, painter, poet and architect of the Renaissance, carved his Pietà (below) in about 1498. He later carved his famous statue of David, painted the frescos on the ceiling of the Sistine Chapel and rebuilt St. Peter's Basilica, Rome.

Mi·chel·son (mī´kelson), **Alber Abraham** (1852–1931). Amer physicist; devised with E. W Morley the **~-Morley experiment**, which attempted to discove the effect of the velocity of Eart on the velocity of light, as a mean of measuring the velocity of Eart through the ether; the failure t discover any such effect was th starting point for the theory c RELATIVITY.

Mich·i·gan (mĭsh´igan). Stat in midwestern U.S., with it northern boundary formed b Lakes Huron and Superior admitted to the Union in 1837 capital, Lansing; **Lake ~**, one c the chain of great lakes in N America.

Mick·ey Finn (mĭk´ē fĭn´ (also **Mickey**) Surreptitiousl drugged alcoholic drink; drink wit knockout drops.

micro- *prefix.* Small, minut (contrasted with MACRO-); also use in names of units, = one millionth of (symbol μ).

mi·crobe (mī´krōb) *n.* (pop. Microorganism, esp. one of th bacteria causing diseases an fermentation. **mi·cro·bi·a** (mīkrō´bēal), **mi·cro´bic** *adjs.*

mi·cro·bi·ol·o·gy (mīkrōbīŏl´ ojē) *n.* Study of microorganisms **mi·cro·bi·ol´o·gist** *n.*

mi·cro·ce·phal·ic (mīkrōsefăl´ ĭk) *adj.* Small-headed.

mi·cro·chip (mī´krōchĭp) *n* Small thin chip of silicon holding a complex electronic circuit.

mi·cro·cosm (mī´krokŏzem) *n* Little world, world in miniature miniature representation *of*; man society, as an epitome of the worl or universe. **mi·cro·cos·mic** (mīkrokŏz´mĭk) *adj.*

mi·cro-dot (mī´krodŏt) *n*

*The **Michaelmas Daisy**, a native o North America but also found in temper ate regions of Europe, flowers from Jul to November. Its roots were often use as a wound-herb.*

otograph reduced to the size of
dot.

mi·cro·e·lec·tron·ics (mīkrō-
ktrŏn´ĭks, -ēlĕk-) *n.* (usu.
nsidered *sing.*). Branch of
ectronics dealing with
niaturized components.

mi·cro·fiche (mī´krofēsh) *n.* (pl.
iche). Sheet of microfilm usu.
× 6 in., usu. showing many 8½ ×
in. pages in reduced size.

mi·cro·film (mī´krofĭlm) *n.*
ry small film; photographic
production on this, projected on
reen for reading etc. ~ *v.t.*
otograph on microfilm.

mi·cro·lith (mī´krolĭth) *n.*
chaeol.) Minute worked flint,
u. for mounting as part of a
mposite tool, found esp. in
esolithic cultures.

mi·crom·e·ter (mīkrŏm´eter) *n.*
ecision instrument, variously
signed, for measuring minute
stances.

mi·cro·min·i·a·tur·i·za·tion
īkrōmĭnēacherīzā´shon) *n.*
aking of electronic devices with
eatly reduced size. **mi·cro-
in·i·a·tur·ize** (mīkrōmĭn´-
cherīz) *v.t.* (**-ized, -iz·ing**).

mi·cron (mī´krŏn) *n.* (pl.
rons, -cra pr. -kra). One
illionth of a meter (symbol μm).

Mi·cro·ne·sia (mīkronē´zha,
ha). Division of Oceania
mprising the small SW. Pacific
ands including the Mariana,
aroline, Marshall, and Gilbert
lands. **Mi·cro·ne´sian** *adj. & n.*

mi·cro·or·gan·ism (mī´-
ōōrganĭzem, mīkrōōr´-) *n.* Any
the organisms not visible to the
naided eye, as bacteria, protozoa,
nicellular algae and fungi, and
ruses.

mi·cro·phone (mī´krofōn) *n.*
strument producing electrical
npulses corresponding to the
brations of sound waves falling
it and thus performing an
sential part in telephonic and
dio transmission. **mi·cro-
hon·ic** (mīkrofŏn´ĭk) *adj.*

mi·cro·pho·to·graph (mī´kro-
tŏgrăf, -grahf, mīkrofō´-) *n.*
otograph reduced to very small
ze.

mi·cro·scope (mī´kroskōp) *n.*
ens or combination of lenses
agnifying near objects so that
tails invisible to the naked eye
e revealed. **mi·cro·scop·ic**
nīkroskŏp´ĭk) *adj.* Of a micro-
ope; with the functions of a
icroscope; so minute as only to
seen clearly with a microscope.
i·cro·scop´i·cal *adj.* Pertaining
a microscope. **mi·cro·scop´i-**

cal·ly *adv.* **mi·cros·co·py**
(mīkrŏs´kopē, mī´kroskōpē), **mi-
cros´co·pist** *ns.*

mi·cro·some (mī´krosōm) *n.*
(*biol.*) Small particle in a cell, not
visible with an ordinary microscope.

mi·cro·struc·ture (mī´-
krōstrŭkcher) *n.* (*metallurgy*)
Arrangement of crystals observable
under a microscope. **mi·cro-
struc·tur·al** (mīkrōstrŭk´cheral)
adj.

mi·cro·tome (mī´krotōm) *n.*
Instrument for cutting very thin
sections of organic tissue for
examination under the microscope.
mi·crot·o·my (mīkrŏt´omē) *n.* (pl.

-mies).

mi·cro·wave (mī´krōwāv) *n.*
Electromagnetic wave having a
wavelength between about 1 mm
and 30 cm.

mi·crur·gy (mī´krērjē) *n.* Art
or science of dissection and
injection under a microscope. **mi-
crur·gi·cal** (mīkrēr´jĭkal) *adj.*

mic·tu·ri·tion (mĭkcherĭsh´on)
n. Urination. **mic·tu·rate** (mĭk´-
cherāt) *v.i.* (**-rat·ed, -rat·ing**).
Urinate.

mid (mĭd) *adj.* Middle of;
intermediate; (*phon.*) pronounced
with the tongue or part of it in
a middle position between high and
low; **mid´brain**: see BRAIN;

reflecting prisms · displacement lens · objective optics · specimen · objective turret · objective barrel · condenser · aperture diaphragm · centring insert · light source prisms · field diaphragm · eyepiece optics · specimen holder · specimen axis controls · focus control · lamp · collector

These **midshipmen** are marching in formation at the U.S. Naval Academy in Annapolis, Maryland. They are the lowest grade of officer in the U.S. Navy.

mid′rib, main vein of a leaf etc.

Mi·das (mī′das). (Gk. legend) King of Phrygia; was given by Dionysus the power of turning everything he touched into gold; unable to eat or drink, he prayed to be relieved of the gift, and was instructed to wash in the river Pactolus, whose sands turned to gold at his touch; another time, when Midas declared Pan a better flute player than Apollo, Apollo turned his ears into the ears of an ass, and Midas tried to hide them, but his barber whispered the secret to some reeds, which repeated it whenever the wind rustled them.

mid·day (mid′dā) *n.* Noon (often attrib.).

mid·dle (mĭd′el) *adj.* Equidistant from extremities; intermediate in rank, quality, etc.; (of languages) in a stage of development between the old and modern forms, as **M ~** ENGLISH; **~ age**, period between youth and old age; **~ -aged** (*adj.*); **M ~ Ages**, period of history intermediate between ancient and modern times, variously calculated, but commonly applied to period from the fall of the Roman Empire in the West (5th c.) to the beginning of the Renaissance (middle of 15th c.); **~ America**, (1) Mexico and Central America; (2) the American middle class; **M ~ Atlantic States**, New York, New Jersey, Pennsylvania, Delaware, and Maryland; **~ class**, class of society between upper and lower, including professional and business classes (often attrib.); **~ distance**, that part of a picture that lies between the foreground and the background; (footracing) races of approximately 1 mile or 1500 meters; **M ~ East**, nations lying between the Near and Far East, including those countries between Egypt and Iran; **M ~ Kingdom**: see KINGDOM; **mid′dleman**, trader intermediate between producer and consumer; **middle-of-the-road**, (of person or course of action) moderate, avoiding extremes; **middle term**, (logic) term in a syllogism common to both premises; **mid′dleweight**, boxer of weight between welterweight and light heavyweight; **Middle West**, that part of the U.S. occupying the N. half of the Mississippi River basin, including the states of Ohio, Indiana, Illinois, Michigan, Wisconsin, Iowa, and Minnesota; **Middle Western(er)**. **middle** *n.* Middle part or point in position or time; middle part of the body, waist. **~** *v.t.* (**-dled, -dling**).

Milan, the second largest city of Italy, is a great communication and industrial center, especially for silks and manmade fibers. Its Gothic cathedral, seen here was begun in 1386.

(naut.) Fold, double, in the middle. **mid·dling** (mĭd′lĭng) *adj. & adv.* Moderately good; second-rate; (colloq.) fairly well (in health). **mid′dlings** *n.pl.* Grades of commodities, such as flour, of second quality or fineness. **mid·dy** (mĭd′ē) *n.* (pl. **-dies**). 1. (colloq.) Midshipman. 2. (also **~ blouse**) Sailor blouse.

Mid·gard (mid′gārd). (Scand. myth.) Region, surrounded by the sea, in which men live; **~ Serpent**, monstrous serpent, the offspring of Loki, thrown by Odin into the sea, where, with its tail in its mouth, it encircled Earth.

midge (mĭj) *n.* Gnat, small insect; (zool.) member of dipterous family Chironomidae.

midg·et (mĭj′ĭt) *n.* Extremely small person; (also attrib.).

Mid·i·an·ite (mĭd′ēanīt) *adj. & n.* (Member) of a nomadic people of N. Arabia often mentioned in the Old Testament, traditionally descended from Midian, son Abraham (Gen. 25), proverbial leading Israel astray.

mid·land (mĭd′land) *n.* Part a country remote from the sea borders; **the Midlands**, counties of England S. of Humber and Mersey Rivers and of the Thames, except Norfo Suffolk, Essex, Hertfordshi Gloucestershire, and the count bordering on Wales. **midland** *a* Of, in, the midland or (**M** Midlands.

Mid·lo·thi·an (mĭdlō′dhē*a* Former Scottish county on S. co of Firth of Forth.

mid·night (mĭd′nīt) *n.* Mid of the night, 12 o'clock at nig (often attrib.).

Mid·rash (mĭd′rahsh; *H* mēdrahsh′) *n.* (pl. **Mid·ra·shi** pr. mĭdrah′shĭm; *He* mēdrahshēm′; **Mid·ra·sho** mĭdrah′shōt; *Heb.* mēdrahshaw′ Ancient Jewish commentary part of the Hebrew scriptures.

mid·riff (mĭd′rĭf) *n.* Diaphra between thorax and abdom region of front of body over th (part of) garment fitted to t region.

foil or yarrow is a common wayside
nt of the daisy family. Its leaves were
oked as tobacco and are still used in
rbal medicine.

mid·ship (mĭd′shĭp) *n.* Middle
rt of ship or boat; **mid′shipman**,
det or student training for
mmission in U.S. Navy or Coast
uard. **mid′ships** *adv.* Amid-
ips.
midst (mĭdst) *n.* Middle. ~ *adv.*
nidst.
mid·sum·mer (mĭd′sŭmer,
′dsŭm′-) *n.* Period of summer
stice, about June 21.
mid·term (mĭd′tērm) *n.*
lloq.) Examination given half-
y through the school term. ~
. Occurring at or near the middle
a term.
Mid·way (mĭd′wā) **Islands.**
nall coral atoll, 1,200 miles
932 km) NW. of Hawaii; scene
decisive battle in which U.S.
val forces repulsed Japanese,
42.
mid·wife (mĭd′wīf) *n.* (pl.

d **mignonette,** which has green
wers, grows wild in Europe and is
mmon on dry wastes, especially in
lk and limestone districts.

Many animals, fish and birds (such as
the ducks shown above) *migrate* from
one place to another either to breed or
to find food or warmth or both.

-**wives** pr. -wīvz). Woman who
assists others in childbirth. **mid·-
wife·ry** (mĭd′wīferē, -wīfrē) *n.*
mien (mēn) *n.* (literary)
Bearing or look.
Mies van der Rohe (mēz′văn
der rō′; *Ger.* mēs′fahn der rō′e),
Ludwig (1886–1969). German-
born American architect.
might[1] (mīt): see MAY; ~-**have-
been,** past possibility.
might[2] (mīt) *n.* Great (bodily
or mental) strength; power to
enforce one's will.
might·y (mī′tē) *adj.* (**might·-
i·er, might·i·est**). Powerful,
strong in body or mind. ~ *adv.*
(colloq.) Very, extremely. **might·-
i·ly** (mī′tĭlē) *adv.* **might′i·ness** *n.*
mi·gnon·ette (mĭnyonĕt′) *n.*
Plant with fragrant grayish-green
blossoms (*Reseda odorata*).
mi·graine (mī′grān) *n.*
Recurrent paroxysmal headache,
often accompanied by nausea,

visual disturbances, and other
severe symptoms. [Fr., f. Gk. *hemi*
half, *kranion* skull]
mi·grant (mī′grant) *adj.* That
migrates. ~ *n.* Migrant bird etc.;
~ **worker,** farm laborer who
moves from one area to another to
do seasonal work.
mi·grate (mī′grāt) *v.i.*
(-**grat·ed, -grat·ing**). Move from
one place of abode, or esp. one
country, to another; (of birds,
fishes, and animals) go from one
habitat to another, esp. come and
go regularly with the seasons.
mi·gra·tion (mīgrā′shon) *n.* **mi-
gra·to·ry** (mī′gratōrē, -tōrē) *adj.*
Mi·ka·do (mĭkah′dō) *n.* (pl.
-**dos**). Popular title, as used by
foreigners, of the Emperor of Japan.
[Jap. *mi* august, *kado* door]
mike (mīk) *n.* (slang) Microphone.
mil (mĭl) *n.* $\frac{1}{1000}$ of an inch,
0.0254 mm.
Mi·lan (mĭlăn′, -lahn′). Second-
largest city of Italy and an
important commercial and
manufacturing center in the N.
central part.

Milkwort, a small European perennial found in meadows, was formerly believed to increase lactation. Herbalists accordingly prescribed it for nursing mothers.

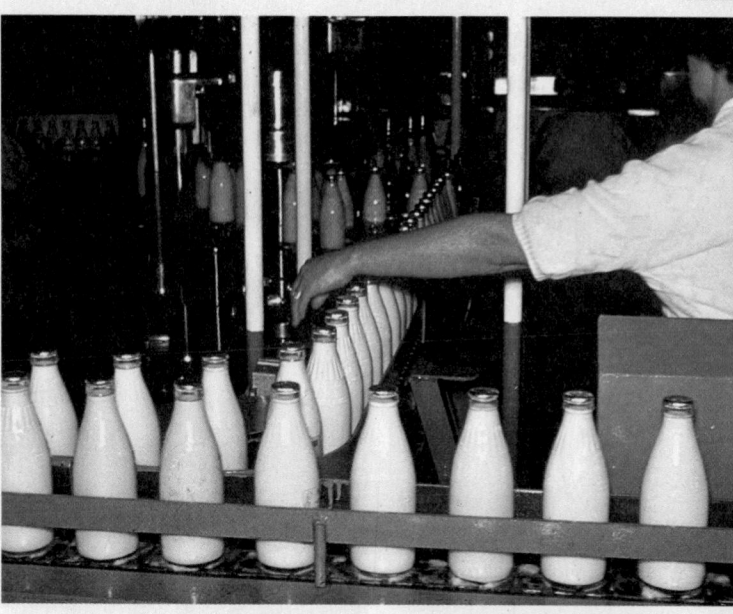

Milk bottling in factories like this one in Australia is carried out under strict hygienic conditions. The milk is processed before bottling to become pasteurized or homogenized.

Mil·an·ese (mĭlanēz′, -nēs′; It. mēlahnĕ′zĕ) adj. Of Milan. ~ n. (pl. **-ese**). Native, inhabitant, of Milan.

milch (mĭlch) adj. Giving, kept for, milk; ~ **cow**, cow kept for milk.

mild (mīld) adj. Gentle; not severe or harsh or drastic; not bitter. **mild′ly** adv. **mild′ness** n. **mild** n. (Brit.) Mild beer.

mil·dew (mĭl′doo, -dū) n. Growth of minute fungi on plants or on leather etc. exposed to damp. **mil′dew·y** adj. **mildew** v. Taint, be tainted, with mildew.

mile (mīl) n. Unit of linear measure of 1,760 yards (1,584 m) (also **statute** ~); race extending over 1 mile; **geographical** ~, 1 minute of longitude (1/60°) measured on the equator, 6,087.2 ft. (1,826.16 m); **nautical, sea,** ~, length of 1 minute of latitude, standardized at 6,080 ft. (1,824 m) but actually varying with latitude (6,046–6,108 ft. 1,813.8– 1,832.4 m); **mile′post, mile′-stone,** post, stone set up on road to indicate the miles to and from a given place; (fig.) stage, event, in life, progress, etc. [L. mille thousand (the Roman mile being 1,000 paces)]

mile·age, milage (mī′lĭj) ns. Distance in miles; traveling allowance at fixed rate per mile; number of miles in which a vehicle uses a given amount of fuel.

mil·er (mī′ler) n. (colloq.) Man, horse, trained specially to run a mile; also in comb. as two-~.

mil·foil (mĭl′foil) n. Common yarrow (Achillea millefolium), which has many finely divided leaves.

mil·i·ar·y (mĭl′ĕĕrē, mĭl′yerē) adj. (path.) Marked by eruption of small red pustules resembling millet seeds; ~ **tuberculosis**, form of tuberculosis, usu. acute, in which small tubercular nodules are distributed throughout the body.

mi·lieu (mĭlyoo′, mēl-; Fr. mēlyö′) n. (pl. **mi·lieus,** Fr. **mi·lieux** pr. mēlyö′). Environment, state of life, social surroundings.

mil·i·tant (mĭl′ĭtant) adj. Engaged in warfare; warlike, combative; **church** ~, Christian church considered at war on earth with the powers of evil, contrasted with the heavenly church triumphant. **mil′i·tan·cy** n. **mil′i·tant·ly** adv. **militant** n. Militant person.

mil·i·ta·rism (mĭl′ĭterĭzem) n. Spirit, tendencies, of the professional soldier; undue reliance on, and exaltation of, military force and methods. **mil′i·ta·rist** n.

mil·i·ta·rize (mĭl′ĭterīz) v.t. (**-rized, -riz·ing**). Make military or warlike; instill principles of militarism into. **mil·i·ta·ri·za·-tion** (mĭlĭterĭzā′shon) n.

mil·i·tary (mĭl′ĭtĕrē) adj. Of, done by, befitting, soldiers, or the army (opp. civil); ~ **age,** age of eligibility for admission to the armed forces; ~ **band,** combination of woodwind, brass, and percussion instruments; ~ **police,** body of soldiers doing police duty in the army. **mil·i·tar·i·ly** (mĭlĭtĕr′ilē, mĭl′ĭtĕr-) adv. **military** n. (pl. **-tar·ies,** collect. **-tar·y**). Soldiery; esp. **the** ~, the defense establishment of a nation.

mil·i·tate (mĭl′ĭtāt) v.i. (**-tat·ed, -tat·ing**). (of facts, evidence, etc.) Have force, tell (against conclusion or result).

mi·li·tia (mĭlĭsh′a) n. Military force, esp. citizen army; all men liable to military service; **mili tiaman,** member of the militia.

milk (mĭlk) n. Opaque white fluid secreted by female mammal for nourishment of their young; cow's milk as article of food; milk-like fluid of certain plants, as the juice of the coconut, the latex of the caoutchouc, etc.; preparation of drugs, herbs, etc., resembling milk in appearance, as ~ **of almonds** ~-**and-water,** feeble, insipid; ~ **bar,** bar selling nonalcoholic drinks, esp. made with milk, and other refreshments; ~ **chocolate,** sweetened chocolate made with milk or other ingredients to impart milky appearance or taste; ~ **fever,** fever to which women are liable after childbirth during

Millipedes of which there are about 8,000 species live among and eat decaying plant matter. Most are slow moving and inoffensive. This giant species is found in Africa.

lactation; ~ **glass**, opaque white glass; ~ **leg**, inflammatory condition of leg, in women after childbirth, accompanied by white swellings; **milk'maid**, woman who milks cows, etc. or is employed in dairy; **milk'man**, man who sells or delivers milk; **milk punch**, drink made of spirits and milk; **milk shake**, glass of milk or milk and egg, flavored and shaken up; ~ **snake**, nonvenomous snake (*Lampropeltis triangulum*) 30 to 50 in. long, having black-rimmed reddish-brown splotches, and feeding on rodents; also known as house snake, milk adder, red king snake; **milk'sop**, effeminate or spiritless fellow; **milk sugar**, lactose; **milk tooth**, one of the first, temporary set of teeth in young mammals; **milk'weed**, any plant of the genus *Asclepias*, esp. the common milkweed (*A. syriaca*), with clusters of purple flowers and pods that release seeds which float through the air on tufts of down or silk; **milk'wort**, any plant of genus *Polygala*, growing in meadows, formerly supposed to increase milk in nursing mothers. **milk** v.t. Draw milk from (cow, ewe, goat, etc.); get money out of, exploit (person); extract juice, venom, etc., from (snake etc.).

milk·y (mĭl'kē) adj. (**milk·i·er**, **milk·i·est**). Of, like, mixed with, milk; (of liquid) cloudy, not clear; effeminate, weakly amiable; **M~ Way**, galaxy as seen from Earth, forming a faintly luminous band of innumerable stars too distant to be seen as separate by the naked eye.

mill¹ (mĭl) n. Building or apparatus for grinding corn; machine for grinding any solid substance to powder; any machine, or building fitted with machinery, for manufacturing processes etc., as **saw'mill, cotton mill; put through, go through, the mill**, subject to, undergo, training or experience; be severely disciplined; **mill'board**, stout pasteboard for bookbinding; **mill'dam**, dam across a stream to make water available for mill; **mill'pond**, pond formed by a milldam; **like a millpond**, said of very calm sea; **mill'race**, current of water that drives mill wheel; **mill'run**, mill-race; output of a sawmill; **mill'-stone**, one of pair of circular stones used in grinding corn; (fig.) heavy burden, crushing weight; **mill'-wright**, one who repairs or constructs mills. **mill** v. Grind or treat in mill; produce grooves etc. in (metal) by rotary cutter; produce regular markings on edge of (coin, esp. in past part.); thicken (cloth) by fulling; beat (chocolate) to a froth; (slang) beat, strike, fight (person) (orig. of cattle etc.) move

A wood pulp factory in Novia Scotia utilizes the offcuts from timber mills, and also timber of a low grade quality which is processed and used to make fiberboard.

around and around in a mass; **milling machine**, rotary cutter for metal.

mill² (mĭl) n. One-thousandth part of a dollar, as a money of account.

Mill (mĭl), **John Stuart** (1806–1873). English political economist; author of *On Liberty* (1859) and *Utilitarianism* (1861).

Mil·lay (mĭlā'), **Edna St. Vincent** (1892–1950). Amer. poet and playwright; awarded Pulitzer Prize, 1923.

mil·le·nar·i·an (mĭlenār'ēan) adj. Of, expecting, the millennium. ~ n. Believer in the millennium.

mil·le·nar·y (mĭl'enĕrē) adj. Consisting of 1,000 (esp. years).

mil·len·ni·um (mĭlĕn'ēum) n. (pl. **-len·ni·ums, -len·ni·a** pr. -lĕn'ēa). Period of 1,000 years; period of 1,000 years foretold in Rev. 20 in which Christ will reign on Earth; period of happiness and prosperity. **mil·len'ni·al** adj.

mil·le·pede = MILLIPEDE.

mill·er (mĭl'er) n. One who works or owns a grain mill; (entom.) popular name for some varieties of white or white-powdered insects; ~'**s-thumb**, pop. name of a small fresh-water fish (*Cottus gobio*), also called the bullhead.

Mil·ler¹ (mĭl'er), **Arthur** (1915–). Amer. playwright; awarded Pulitzer Prize, 1949; author of *All My Sons, Death of a Salesman, A View From the Bridge, The Crucible*.

Mil·ler² (mĭl'er), **Henry** (1891–). Amer. author whose novels include *Tropic of Cancer* (1931) and *Tropic of Capricorn* (1938).

mil·les·i·mal (mĭlĕs'imal) adj. Thousandth.

mil·let (mĭl'ĭt) n. Any of several cereal grasses of the family Gramineae, growing 3 or 4 ft. high and bearing a large crop of minute nutritious seeds, esp. *Panicum miliaceum*; ~ **grass**, tall N. Amer.

woodland grass (*Milium effusum*).

Mil·let (mĭlā'), **Jean François** (1814–75). French landscape and genre painter of the Barbizon school.

milli- prefix. One thousandth of (abbrev. m).

mil·li·bar (mĭl'ibär) n. (meteor.) One thousandth of a BAR² (abbrev. mbar).

mil·li·gram (mĭl'igrăm) n. One thousandth of a gram (abbrev. mg).

Mil·li·kan (mĭl'ikan), **Robert Andrews** (1868–1953). Amer. nuclear physicist; first to isolate electron; awarded Nobel Prize in physics, 1923.

mil·li·li·ter (mĭl'ilēter) n. One thousandth of a liter.

mil·li·me·ter (mĭl'imēter) n. One thousandth of a meter. (abbrev. mm).

mil·li·ner (mĭl'iner) n. Maker or seller of women's hats. **mil·li·ner·y** (mĭl'inĕrē, -nerē) n. [f. MILAN; orig., = vendor of Milan goods]

mil·lion (mĭl'yon) n. (pl. **-lions**, following a numeral **-lion**). Cardinal number equal to one thousand thousand, 1,000,000 (abbrev. m.); also as ordinal when followed by other numbers; one million pounds, dollars, etc.; enormous number. ~ adj. Amounting to one million.

mil·lion·aire (mĭlyonār') n. Person who possesses a million dollars; person of great wealth.

mil·li·pede, mil·le·pede (mĭl'ipēd) ns. Myriapod with numerous legs placed on each of the segments in double pairs.

mil·li·sec·ond (mĭl'isĕkond) n. One thousandth of a second (abbrev. msec.).

Mi·los, Mi·lo: see MELOS.

milt (mĭlt) n. Spleen of mammals; sperm of male fish. **milt·er** n. Male fish in the breeding season.

Mil·ti·a·des (mĭltī'adēz) (d. c488 B.C.). Athenian statesman and general, victor at MARATHON.

Mil·ton (mĭl'ton), **John** (1608–1674). English Puritan poet; author of the epics *Paradise Lost* and *Paradise Regained* and many other poems. **Mil·to·ni·an** (mĭltō'nēan), **Mil·ton·ic** (mĭltŏn'ĭk) adjs.

Mil·wau·kee (mĭlwaw'kē). Largest city and a commercial and industrial center in Wisconsin, in the SE. on Lake Michigan.

mime (mīm) n. 1. (Gk. and Rom. antiq.) Kind of simple farcical drama, characterized by mimicry and dialogue for this. 2. Similar modern performance, play with mimic gestures and action usu. without words. 3. Actor in a mime; buffoon, jester. ~ v. Act in mime.

mim·e·o·graph (mĭm'ēogräf, -grahf) n. Apparatus in which stencils are placed for making copies of written pages. ~ *v.t.* Reproduce by mimeograph.

mi·me·sis (mĭmē′sĭs, mī-) *n.* Representation or imitation of nature in literature and art; (biol.) MIMICRY.

mi·met·ic (mĭmĕt′ĭk, mī-) *adj.* Of, addicted to, imitation, mimicry, or mimesis.

mim·ic (mĭm′ĭk) *adj.* Feigned, esp. to amuse; sham; imitative. ~ *n.* Person who mimics. ~ *v.t.* (-**icked**, -**ick·ing**). Copy speech or gestures of, esp. to amuse others, imitate closely. **mim′ic·ry** *n.* (pl. **-ries**). Mimicking; thing that mimics another; (biol.) protective similarity of one animal species to another, the second being distasteful or poisonous to predators, or to an object in the environment for disguise or concealment.

mi·mo·sa (mĭmō′sa, -za) *n.* (pl. **-sas**, collect. **-sa**). Leguminous plant of genus M~, including the sensitive plant.

mi·na = MYNA.

mi·na·ceous (mĭnā′shus) *adj.* Threatening. **mi·na′ceous·ly** *adv.*

min·a·ret (mĭnerĕt′, mĭn′erĕt) *n.* Tall slender tower or turret of mosque, with projecting balcony, from which muezzin proclaims the hour of prayer. [Arab. *manāra*]

min·a·to·ry (mĭn′atōrē, -tōrē) *adj.* Threatening.

mince (mĭns) *v.* (**minced, minc·ing**). Cut (meat etc.) very small; walk, speak, with affected delicacy; **not ~ words**, be outspoken esp. in condemnation. **mince** *n.* Minced meat; **mince′-meat**, mixture of raisins, currants, apples, suet, spices, etc.; **make mincemeat of**, (fig.) destroy, demolish utterly; **mince pie**, pie

*The **minaret**, the tower from which faithful Muslims are called to prayer, is always connected with a mosque and has one or more balconies or open galleries. Below left: Madresseh minaret, Isfahan, Iran. Below right: The oldest minaret in Baghdad, Iraq.*

*In biology, **mimicry** takes seven forms. Some creatures survive becaus[e] they look like dangerous or unpalatab[le] ones; others have protective shape [or] color like their surroundings, such [as] this stick insect (facing page).*

filled with mincemeat.

mind (mīnd) *n.* Seat [of] consciousness, thought, volitio[n] and emotion; intellectual power[;] memory; opinion; **have a good** [mind] **to**, feel tempted or inclined to (do something). **mind** *v.* Bear in min[d;] heed; take charge of; be vexed; ha[ve] an objection (to).

Min·da·na·o (mĭndanow′[)] Second-largest island, 36,530 s[q.] mi. (58,813 sq. km), in the [S.] part of the Republic of th[e] Philippines; ~ **Deep**, deepe[st] point, 35,400 ft. (10,620 m), of an[y] of the world's oceans, in the W[.] Pacific Ocean off NE. Mindanao[.]

mind·ed (mīn′dĭd) *ad[j.]* Disposed, inclined; (colloq.) ali[ve] to importance of, keenly intereste[d] in, as *air-, politically ~*.

mind·ful (mīnd′ful) *adj.* Takin[g]

thought or care (of). **mind'ful·ly** *adv.* **mind'ful·ness** *n.*

mine¹ (mīn) *poss. pron.* Absolute and predicate form of MY; (archaic and poet., used before initial vowel or silent "h," or following a noun) = MY.

mine² (mīn) *n.* 1. Excavation from which minerals are extracted; (fig.) abundant source (*of* information etc.). 2. (mil.) Subterranean gallery in which explosive is placed to destroy enemy's fortifications etc. 3. (mil., nav.) Case containing charge of high explosive, detonated acoustically, electrically, or on contact; **mine'field**, sea or land area sown with mines; **mine'layer**, vessel for laying sea mines; **mine'-sweeper**, vessel for sweeping and destroying sea mines. **mine** *v.* (**mined, min·ing**). Dig for minerals; burrow or make subterranean passage in; lay, sow, mines under or in.

min·er¹ (mī'ner) *n.* Worker in mine.

min·er² (mī'ner) *n.*: see LEAF-miner.

min·er·al (mĭn'eral, mĭn'ral) *n.* 1. Substance (e.g. metal, coal, salt) obtained by mining. 2. (chem.) Element or compound occurring naturally as a product of inorganic processes. 3. (pop.) Substance that is neither animal nor vegetable. ~ *adj.* Of, belonging to, minerals; belonging to any of the species into which inorganic substances are divided; ~ **water**, water naturally impregnated with mineral(s), esp. those of a medicinal character.

min·er·al·o·gy (mĭnerŏl'ojē, -răl'-) *n.* Scientific study of minerals. **min·er·al·og·i·cal** (mĭneralŏj'ĭkal) *adj.* **min·er·al·og'i·cal·ly** *adv.* **min·er·al·o'gist** *n.*

Mi·ner·va (mĭner'va). (Rom. myth.) Goddess of wisdom, identified with Greek Athene (which led to her being regarded also as the goddess of war).

min·e·stro·ne (mĭnĭstrō'nē; *It.* mĕnĕstraw'nĕ) *n.* Soup containing vegetables and pasta. [It.]

Ming (mĭng). Name of dynasty that ruled in China 1368–1644; hence, porcelain etc. of this period.

min·gle (mĭng'gel) *v.* (**-gled, -gling**). (Cause to) mix; blend; unite *with.*

mini- *prefix.* Miniature, (very) small, as **min'ibus**, small bus, **min'iskirt**, very short skirt.

min·i·a·ture (mĭn'ēacher, mĭn'acher) *n.* 1. Picture in illuminated manuscript. 2. Painted portrait on small scale and with minute finish; reduced image or representation. ~ *adj.* Represented, designed, on a small scale; ~ **camera**, camera producing negatives less than 6 sq. in. in area, (esp.) one using 35-mm film.

min'i·a·tur·ist *n.* Painter of miniatures. **min'i·a·tur·ize** *v.* (**-ized, -iz·ing**). [L. as prec.]

min·i·mal (mĭn'ĭmal) *adj.* Very minute, the least possible.

min·i·mize (mĭn'ĭmīz) *v.t.* (**-mized, -miz·ing**). Reduce to, estimate at, smallest possible amount or degree. **min·i·mi·za·tion** (mĭnĭmĭzā'shon) *n.*

min·i·mum (mĭn'ĭmum) *n.* (pl. **-mums, -ma** pr. -ma). Least amount attainable, usual, etc. (opp. MAXIMUM); ~ **wage**, lowest wage that may legally be offered.

min·ion (mĭn'yon) *n.* Spoiled darling, favorite; (contempt.) servile agent; (print.) size of type (7 point).

overburden tip

surface water

walking dragline

truck

ramps

mechanical shovel

clay

coal seam

limestone

coal seam

shale

sandstone

coal seam

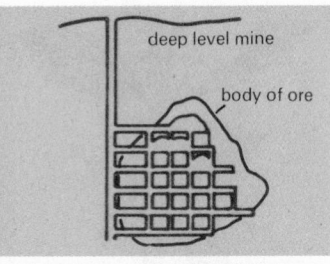

deep level mine

body of ore

Mining *can be broadly classified under two main headings — surface mining and underground mining. Top: Gold mining in South Africa, an example of underground mining. Center: Open-cut mining involves removal of waste material under which ores are situated. Left and below: Different mining systems.*

deep level mine

lode or vein

horizontal mine

opencut mine

drift mine

adit

seam

min·is·ter (mĭn´ĭster) *n.* 1. (Brit.) Executive agent; person in charge of a government department. 2. (Brit.) Diplomatic representative ranking below ambassador. 3. Clergyman. ~ *v.i.* Be serviceable or contributory; officiate as minister of religion.

min·is·te·ri·al (mĭnĭstēr´ēal) *adj.* Of a minister or his office; of the government.

min·is·tra·tion (mĭnĭstrā´shon) *n.* Ministering, esp. in religious matters. **min·is·trant** (mĭn´ĭstrant) *adj. & n.*

min·is·try (mĭn´ĭstrē) *n.* (pl. **-tries**). 1. Priestly office; ministers of a church. 2. (Brit.) Office of minister of state; ministerial department of government, the building belonging to it; ministers forming a government.

mink (mĭngk) *n.* (pl. **minks**, collect. **mink**). Small semiaquatic weasellike animal of the family Mustelidae, esp. *Mustela vison* of N. Amer., valued for its thick brown fur; this fur.

Minn. *abbrev.* Minnesota.

Min·ne·ap·o·lis (mĭnēăp´olĭs). Largest city in Minnesota in the SE. on the Mississippi River.

min·ne·sing·er (mĭn´ĭsĭnger, -zĭng-) *n.* German lyrical poet and songwriter of the 12th to 14th centuries. [OHG. *minna* love]

Min·ne·so·ta (mĭnĭsō´ta). State in north-central U.S. on Canadian border; admitted to the Union in 1858; capital, St. Paul.

min·now (mĭn´ō) *n.* (pl. **-nows**, **-now**). Small fresh-water fish common in streams, ponds, etc.

Mi·no·an (mĭnō´an) *adj. & n.* (Person) of the Bronze Age civilization (lasting from *c*3000 to 1100 B.C.) revealed by excavations made in the Palace of Minos at Knossos in Crete.

mi·nor (mī´ner) *adj.* 1. Lesser (not followed by *than*); comparatively unimportant, as ~ **poet, prophet**; ~ **suit**, (bridge) diamonds or clubs; ~ **term**, (logic) subject of conclusion of categorical syllogism, contained in the ~ **premise**. 2. (mus.) Of intervals less by a semitone than the corresponding major intervals; ~ **key, mode**, one having a scale containing a minor 3rd (and a minor 6th and 7th); **in a ~ key**, (fig.) played down, doleful. **minor** *n.* 1. (law) Person below full age. 2. Minor interval, key, chord, etc. 3. Minor term or premise. 4. MINORITE.

Mi·nor·ca (mĭnôr´ka). Second largest of the Balearic Islands, in W. Mediterranean; hence, (also ~ **fowl**) black domestic fowl introduced from Spain.

Mi·nor·ite (mī´nerĭt) *n.* Franciscan friar, so called because the Franciscans regarded themselves as of humbler rank than members of the other orders.

mi·nor·i·ty (mĭnŏr´ĭtē, -när´-, mī-) *n.* (pl. **-ties**). I. (law) State, period, of being under legal age (see MINOR). 2. Smaller number or part, esp. smaller party voting against majority; number of votes cast for this. 3. Group of persons smaller in number than majority group and differing from the majority in race, religion, language, opinion on an issue, etc. ~ *adj.* Of, relating to or done by a minority, as ~ *rights*; ~ **leader**, head of smaller party in a legislative body.

Mi·nos (mī´nos, -nŏs). Legendary king of Crete; in Attic tradition a cruel tyrant who every year exacted a tribute of Athenian youths and maidens, to be devoured by the Minotaur; **Palace of** ~, name given to the remains of the Bronze Age palace at Knossos.

Min·o·taur (mĭn´otōr). (Gk. myth.) Monster half-man, half-bull, offspring of Pasiphaë and a bull, confined in Crete in a labyrinth made by Daedalus; eventually slain by Theseus.

Minsk (mĭnsk). Important commercial and industrial city in Russia near the Polish border.

min·strel (mĭn´strel) *n.* Medieval singer or musician; poet; one of a band of entertainers with blackened faces, dancing, telling

*One of the original coin-stamping presses used by the **Mint** in Melbourne before 1965. Coins are now made in Australia at the Royal Australian Mint, Canberra.*

jokes, and singing; ~ **show**, stage show with minstrels. **min·strel·sy** (mĭn´strelsē) *n.* Minstrels' art, poetry; body of minstrels.

mint[1] (mĭnt) *n.* Aromatic culinary herb of genus *Mentha*, esp. *M. viridis*, garden mint or spearmint; peppermint; ~ **sauce**, sauce made of finely chopped mint, vinegar, and sugar, used esp. with roast lamb; ~ **julep**: see JULEP.

mint[2] (mĭnt) *n.* Place, usu. under government control, where money is coined; (fig.) source of invention; vast sum *of money*; **in ~ condition**, (as if) newly issued from a mint, perfect. **mint** *v.t.* Coin (money); invent. **mint·age** (mĭn´tĭj) *n.* Coinage, money, esp. that issued from a particular mint at a specified time.

min·u·et (mĭnūĕt´) *n.* Slow stately dance; music for this, in triple time; piece of music in this rhythm and style, often as movement of suite or sonata.

Min·u·it (mĭn´ūĭt), **Peter** (1580–1638). Dutch colonial administrator; purchased Manhattan from the Indians; director-general of New Netherlands (New York), 1626–31.

mi·nus (mī´nus) *prep.* With the deduction of (symbol –); (colloq.) deprived of. ~ *adj.* (indicating subtraction) Less; negative; (after number etc.) less than. ~ *n.* Minus sign or quantity.

mi·nus·cule (mĭn´uskūl, mĭnŭs´kūl) *adj.* Small; (paleog.) written in minuscule. ~ *n.* (paleog.) (Letter in) small cursive script developed in the early Middle

Ages, dist. from MAJUSCULE or uncial; (mod. typ.) lower-case letter.

min·ute[1] (mĭn´ĭt) *n.* I. Sixtieth part of an hour or of a degree (symbol ´); short time. 2. Memorandum, brief summary; (pl.) official record of proceedings at a meeting. 3. ~ **hand**, hand indicating minutes on watch or clock; **min´uteman** (sometimes **M** ~), Revolutionary War militiaman or citizen ready to march at a minute's notice; **minute steak**, thin slice of steak that can be cooked quickly. **minute** *v.t.* (**-ut·ed, -ut·ing**). I. Draft; make minutes of. 2. Time exactly.

mi·nute[2] (mīnōōt´, -nūt´, mī-) *adj.* (**-nut·er, -nut·est**). Very small; precise, going into details. **mi·nute´ly** *adv.* **mi·nute´ness** *n.*

mi·nu·ti·a (mĭnōō´shēa, -sha, -nū´-) *n.* (pl. **-ti·ae** pr. -shēē) Trivial point; small detail.

minx (mĭngks) *n.* Pert or flirtatious girl.

Mi·o·cene (mī´osēn) *adj. &* n. (geol.) (Of) the third epoch or system of the Tertiary period, after the Oligocene and before the Pliocene.

mi·o·sis, my·o·sis (mīō´sĭs) *ns.* (pl. **-ses** pr. -sēz). Constriction of the pupil of the eye.

mir·a·cle (mĭr´akel) *n.* Event due to supernatural agency; remarkable event or object; ~ **play**, mystery play. **mi·rac·u·lous** (mĭrăk´yulus) *adj.* **mi·rac·u·lous·ly** *adv.* **mi·rac·u·lous·ness** *n.*

Mir·a·flo·res (mĭraflōr´es

Mint, an aromatic plant native to Europe, Asia and Australia, is widely cultivated for use as a flavoring. It is used in cooking, and in sweets, drinks, cough medicines etc.

-flŏr'-). Village, artificial lake, and double locks on the W. side of the Panama Canal Zone.

mi·rage (mĭrahzh') *n.* Optical illusion, common in sandy deserts, caused by refraction of nearly horizontal light rays by the hotter and therefore less dense layers of air near the surface, by which a distant object, directly invisible, appears to be near at hand, as though reflected in a sheet of water (also fig.).

mire (mīr) *n.* Swampy ground, boggy place; mud. ~ *v.* (**mired, mir·ing**). Sink in, bespatter with, mud. **mir·y** (mīr'ē) *adj.* (**mir·i·er, mir·i·est**).

mir·ror (mĭr'er) *n.* Polished or very smooth surface that reflects images; looking glass; (fig.) pattern, example; ~ **image**, image etc. with similar parts reversed as if reflected in a mirror. **mirror** *v.t.* Reflect as in a mirror (lit. and fig.).

mirth (mĕrth) *n.* Rejoicing, merriment. **mirth'ful** *adj.* **mirth'ful·ly** *adv.* **mirth'ful·ness** *n.* **mirth'less** *adj.*

MIRV (mĕrv) *n.* Guided missile that carries several warheads, each independently directed. [*m*(ultiple) *i*(ndependently) targeted *r*(eentry) *v*(ehicle)]

mis- *prefix.* Amiss, bad(ly), wrong(ly), unfavorably.

mis·ad·ven·ture (mĭsadvĕn'cher) *n.* Ill luck, bad fortune.

mis·al·li·ance (mĭsalī'ans) *n.* Unsuitable marriage.

mis·an·thrope (mĭs'anthrōp, mĭz'-) *n.* Hater of mankind; one who avoids human society. **mis·an·throp·ic** (mĭsanthrŏp'ĭk, mĭz-), **mis·an·throp'i·cal** *adj.* **mis·an·thro·pist** (mĭsăn'thropĭst, mĭz-), **mis·an'thro·py** *ns.*

mis·ap·ply (mĭsaplī') *v.t.* (**-plied, -ply·ing**). Apply wrongly. **mis·ap·pli·ca·tion** (mĭsăplĭkā'shon) *n.*

mis·ap·pre·hend (mĭsăprehĕnd') *v.t.* Misunderstand. **mis·ap·pre·hen·sion** (mĭsăprehĕn'shon) *n.*

mis·ap·pro·pri·ate (mĭsaprō'preāt) *v.t.* (**-at·ed, -at·ing**). Apply dishonestly to one's own use. **mis·ap·pro·pri·a·tion** (mĭsaprōprēā'shon) *n.*

mis·be·got·ten (mĭsbĭgŏt'en) *adj.* Illegitimate (often as vague term of opprobrium).

mis·be·have (mĭsbĭhāv') *v.* refl. & i. (**-haved, -hav·ing**). Behave improperly. **mis·be·ha·vior** (mĭsbĭhāv'yer) *n.*

misc. *abbrev.* Miscellaneous; miscellany.

mis·cal·cu·late (mĭskăl'kyulāt) *v.* (**-lat·ed, -lat·ing**). Calculate wrongly. **mis·cal·cu·la·tion** (mĭskălkyulā'shon) *n.*

mis·call (mĭskawl') *v.t.* Call by wrong name; (sports) make

Mirrors *using glass with a metallic backing were first produced in Venice in the late 12th century. This mirror with its ornate frame is in the Rococo style and is dated c.1740.*

incorrect call.

mis·car·riage (mĭskăr'ĭj, mĭs'kăr-) *n.* Spontaneous abortion; failure of letter etc. to reach destination; ~ **of justice**, failure of court to do justice. **mis·car·ry** (mĭskăr'ē) *v.i.* (**-ried, -ry·ing**). 1. Fail; go astray. 2. Suffer a miscarriage.

mis·ce·ge·na·tion (mĭsijenā'shon, mĭsĕj-) *n.* Interbreeding between races, esp. sexual union of whites with nonwhites.

mis·cel·la·ne·a (mĭselā'nēa) *n.pl.* Miscellany; odds and ends.

mis·cel·la·ne·ous (mĭselā'nēus) *adj.* Of mixed character, of various kinds.

mis·cel·la·ny (mĭs'elānē; *Brit.* mĭsĕl'anē) *n.* (pl. **-nies**). Medley; miscellaneous writings etc. collected together.

mis·chance (mĭschăns', -chahns') *n.* (Piece of) ill luck, ill success.

mis·chief (mĭs'chĭf) *n.* Harm, evil, wrought by person or particular cause; worker of mischief; vexatious or annoying conduct, esp. of children; playful malice. **mis·chie·vous** (mĭs'chevus) *adj.* **mis·chie·vous·ly** *adv.* **mis'chie·vous·ness** *n.*

mis·ci·ble (mĭs'ĭbel) *adj.* Capable of being mixed, esp. (of liquids) to form a homogeneous substance. **mis·ci·bil·i·ty** (mĭsĭbĭl'ĭtē) *n.*

mis·con·ceive (mĭskonsēv') *v.* (**-ceived, -ceiv·ing**). Have wrong idea of, misunderstand. **mis·con·cep·tion** (mĭskonsĕp'shon) *n.*

mis·con·duct (mĭskŏn'dŭkt) *n.* Bad management; improper

conduct, esp. adultery. ~ (mĭskondŭkt') *v.t.* & refl.

mis·con·strue (mĭskonstrōō') *v.t.* (**-strued, -stru·ing**). Put wrong construction on (word, action). **mis·con·struc·tion** (mĭskonstrŭk'shon) *n.*

mis·count (mĭskownt') *v.t.* Count wrongly. ~ (mĭs'kownt) *n.* Wrong count, esp. of votes.

mis·cre·ant (mĭs'krēant) *n.* Vile wretch, villain.

mis·cue (mĭskū') *v.i.* (**-cued, -cu·ing**). (billiards) Fail to strike the ball properly. ~ *n.* Such a stroke.

mis·date (mĭsdāt') *v.t.* (**-dat·ed, -dat·ing**). Put wrong date on.

mis·deal (mĭsdēl') *v.* (**-dealt** pr. -dĕlt, **-deal·ing**). Make mistake in dealing (cards). ~ *n.* Wrong deal.

mis·deed (mĭsdēd') *n.* Evil deed.

mis·de·mean·ant (mĭsdĭmē'nant) *n.* Person convicted of misdemeanor.

mis·de·mean·or (mĭsdĭmē'ner) *n.* Misdeed; (law) any indictable offense.

mis·di·rect (mĭsdĭrĕkt') *v.t.* Direct wrongly; put wrong name, address, etc., on letter etc.; give wrong instructions to, specif. (of a judge) give wrong instructions to a jury; aim badly or without precision. **mis·di·rec·tion** *n.*

mis·do·ing (mĭsdōō'ĭng) *n.* Misdeed.

mise en scène (mēz ahn sĕn'). Scenery and properties of an acted play; (fig.) setting of an event or action. [Fr.]

mi·ser (mī'zer) *n.* One who lives miserably in order to hoard wealth. **mi'ser·ly** *adj.* **mi'ser·li·ness** *n.*

mis·er·a·ble (mĭz'erabel) *adj.* Wretchedly unhappy, uncomfortable, or poor; causing wretchedness; pitiable, mean. **mis'er·a·bly** *adv.*

mis·er·i·cord (mĭzerĭkŏrd', mĭzĕr'ĭkŏrd) *n.* 1. Room set apart in a monastery, where monks might take special food as an indulgence. 2. Projection on underside of hinged seat in choir stall, serving when seat is turned up to support person standing. 3. (hist.) Thin pointed dagger used in medieval warfare for giving coup de grâce to a fallen knight.

mis·er·y (mĭz'erē) *n.* (pl. **-er·ies**). Wretched state of mind or circumstances.

mis·fea·sance (mĭsfē'zans) *n.* Wrongful exercise of lawful authority, as dist. from MALFEASANCE.

mis·fire (mĭsfīr') *v.i.* (**-fired, -fir·ing**). (of gun) Fail to go off; (of internal combustion engine) fail to ignite (also transf.) ~ *n.* Failure to explode or ignite.

mis·fit (mĭs'fĭt) *n.* Garment etc.

MISFORTUNE 1084 MISSING

*These Russian **missiles** were paraded in Moscow's Red Square in November 1971. A guided missile which is unmanned, may be remotely guided or direct itself to a preselected target.*

that does not fit; (fig.) person badly adjusted to his work or surroundings.

mis·for·tune (mĭsfôr′chun) *n.* Calamity, bad luck.

mis·give (mĭsgĭv′) *v.t.* (**-gave, -giv·en, -giv·ing**). (of heart, mind, etc.) Suggest misgivings to. **mis·giv′ing** *n.* Apprehension, uneasy doubt.

mis·han·dle (mĭshăn′del) *v.t.* (**-dled, -dling**). Handle (person, thing) roughly, rudely, or improperly.

mis·hap (mĭs′hăp, mĭshăp′) *n.* Unlucky accident.

mis·hear (mĭshēr′) *v.t.* (**-heard** pr. -hērd′, **-hear·ing**). Hear amiss or imperfectly.

mish·mash (mĭsh′măsh, -mŏsh) *n.* Confused mixture. [ME., redupl. of MASH[1]]

Mish·nah (mĭsh′na; *Heb.* mĭshnah′) *n.* (pl. **Mish·na·yoth** pr. mĭshnayōt′; *Heb.* mĭshnahyawt′). Collection of precepts forming basis of Talmud and embodying Jewish oral law. **Mish·na·ik** (mĭshnā′ĭk), **Mish′nic, Mish′-ni·cal** *adjs.*

mis·in·ter·pret (mĭsĭntēr′pret) *v.t.* Give wrong interpretation to; make wrong inference from.

mis·lay (mĭslā′) *v.t.* (**-laid, -lay·ing**). Put (thing) by accident where it cannot readily be found; hence, (euphemism for) lose.

mis·lead (mĭslēd′) *v.t.* (**-led** pr. -lĕd′, **-lead·ing**). Lead astray, give wrong impression to.

mis·man·age (mĭsmăn′ĭj) *v.t.* (**-aged, -ag·ing**). Manage badly or wrongly. **mis·man′age·ment** *n.*

mis·name (mĭsnām′) *v.t.* (**-named, -nam·ing**). Call by wrong name.

mis·no·mer (mĭsnō′mer) *n.* Wrongly applied name.

mi·sog·y·ny (mĭsŏj′ĭnē, mī-) *n.* Hatred of women. **mi·sog′y·nist** *n.*

mis·place (mĭsplās′) *v.t.* (**-placed, -plac·ing**). Put in wrong place; bestow (affection etc.) on ill-chosen object. **mis·place′-ment** *n.*

mis·play (mĭs′plā) *n.* (sports) Wrong or faulty play.

mis·print (mĭs′prĭnt) *n.* Error in printing. ~ (mĭsprĭnt′) *v.t.*

mis·pri·sion (mĭsprĭzh′on) *n.* (law) Wrong action or omission, esp. on part of public official; concealment of knowledge of a felony by person not actively involved.

mis·pro·nounce (mĭs-pronowns′) *v.t.* (**-nounced, -nounc·ing**). Pronounce wrongly. **mis·pro·nun·ci·a·tion** (mĭspro-nŭnsēa′shon) *n.*

mis·quote (mĭskwōt′) *v.* (**-quot·ed, -quot·ing**). Quote wrongly. **mis·quo·ta·tion** (mĭ kwōtā′shon) *n.*

mis·read (mĭsrēd′) *v.t.* (**-rea** pr. -rĕd′, **-read·ing**). Read interpret wrongly.

mis·rep·re·sent (mĭsrĕprĭzĕnt *v.t.* Represent wrongly, give fal account of. **mis·rep·re·sen·ta tion** (mĭsrĕprĭzĕntā′shon) *n.*

mis·rule (mĭsrōōl′) *v.t.* (**-rule -rul·ing**). Rule badly. ~ *n.* Ba government.

miss[1] (mĭs) *v.* Fail to hit, reac meet, find, catch, or perceive; pa over; regret absence of; fail. *n.* Failure.

miss[2] (mĭs) *n.* Title of (**M ~** or form of address to girl or u married woman with no superic title; girl (usu. contempt.); **misse** applied to a range of garment siz for women; so **junior mis** (attrib.) for adolescent girls. [a brev. of MISTRESS]

Miss. *abbrev.* Mississippi.

mis·sal (mĭs′al) *n.* (R.C. Ch Book containing the service of th Mass for whole year.

mis·sel (mĭs′el) **thrush** MISTLE THRUSH.

mis·shap·en (mĭs shā′pen) *ac* Deformed.

mis·sile (mĭs′ĭl; *Brit.* mĭs′īl) Object or weapon capable of bei thrown or shot.

miss·ing (mĭs′ĭng) *adj.* N

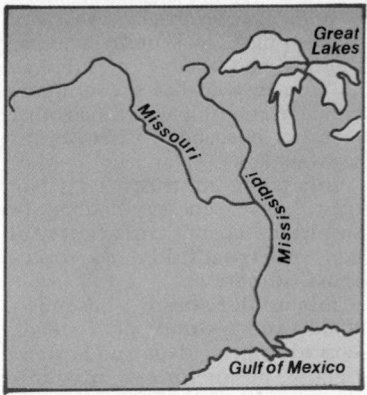

The **Mississippi** (above) together with its main headstream, the Missouri, is the longest river in North America. Its combined length is 3,741 miles and there is a large delta where it enters the Gulf of Mexico.

commonly called **mistletoe**, the *oranthaceae family of semi-parasitic ants is found in all tropical and many mperate zones of the world.*

resent, not found; ~ **link**, pop. ame of hypothetical intermediate pe of animal between anthropoid es and man.

mis·sion (mĭsh´on) *n.* 1. Body persons sent to foreign country conduct negotiations etc. 2. ody sent by religious community convert heathen; field of issionary activity; missionary ost; organization in a district for

conversion of the people; course of religious services etc. for this purpose. 3. Errand of political or other mission. 4. Operational sortie. 5. Person's vocation or divinely appointed work in life.

mis·sion·ar·y (mĭsh´onĕrē) *adj.* Of religious missions. ~ *n.* (pl. **-ar·ies**). Person doing missionary work.

Mis·sis·sip·pi (mĭsĭsĭp´ē). State in southern U.S. on Gulf of Mexico; admitted to Union in 1817; capital, Jackson; ~ **River**, major river in N. Amer., 2,350 mi. (3,783.5 km), flowing from NW. Minnesota to the Gulf of Mexico, and forming borders of several states along its course.

mis·sive (mĭs´ĭv) *n.* Written message, letter.

Mis·sou·ri (mĭzoor´ē, -ĭ). State in central part of the U.S.; admitted to Union, 1821; capital, Jefferson City; ~ **River**, longest river in U.S. flowing from W. Montana, 2,700 mi. (4,347 km), joining Mississippi River 10 mi. (16.1 km) N. of St. Louis, Missouri, and forming borders of several states along its course.

miss·y (mĭs´ē) *n.* (pl. **miss·ies**). Affectionate, playful form of address to girl or young woman, = MISS² (not followed by name).

mist (mĭst) *n.* 1. Water vapor precipitated in droplets smaller and more densely aggregated than those

of rain; (meteor.) state of atmospheric obscurity (less dense than fog) produced by this, in which visibility exceeds 1 km (.621 mi.). 2. Dimness or blurred effect caused by tears in the eyes etc. **mist´y** *adj.* **mist´i·ly** *adv.* **mist´i·ness** *n.* **mist** *v.* Cover, be covered, (as) with a mist.

mis·take (mĭstāk´) *v.* (**-took** pr. -tŏok´, **-tak·en, -tak·ing**). Misunderstand, take in wrong sense; be in error; take (one thing) erroneously *for* another; err in choice of. ~ *n.* Misunderstanding; something incorrectly done through ignorance or inadvertence. **mis·tak´a·ble** *adj.* **mis·tak´en·ly** *adv.* **mis·tak´en·ness** *n.*

mis·ter (mĭs´ter) *n.* 1. (colloq.) Form of address to man, without any name following. 2. (colloq.) = MR.

mis·time (mĭstīm´) *v.t.* (**-timed, -tim·ing**). Time wrongly, do or perform at wrong time.

mis·tle (mĭs´el) **thrush.** Large thrush (*Turdus viscivorous*) that feeds partly on mistletoe berries.

mis·tle·toe (mĭs´eltō) *n.* Any of several evergreen plants of the Loranthaceae family, esp. *Phoradendron flavescens* of eastern N. Amer., parasitic on deciduous or evergreen trees, having thick yellowish-green leaves, small yellowish flowers, and white poisonous berries edible by birds; sprig of the plant often hung as Christmas decoration.

mis·tral (mĭs´tral, mĭstrahl´) *n.* Violent cold northerly or northwesterly wind in Mediterranean provinces of France etc., blowing esp. down Rhône valley. [L. *magistralis* masterful]

mis·tress (mĭs´trĭs) *n.* (pl. **-tress·es**). 1. Woman in authority over servants; female head of household. 2. Woman who has power to control or dispose *of*, as *you are*

~ *of the situation, you are your own*
~ (also fig.). 3. Woman who has thorough knowledge (*of* subject). 4. Woman who has a continuing sexual relationship with a man other than her husband; **wardrobe** ~: see WARDROBE. 5. (archaic) = MRS.

mis·trust (mĭstrŭst´) *v.t.* Not trust; have uneasy doubts or suspicions about. **mis·trust´ful** *adj.* **mis·trust´ful·ly** *adv.* **mis·-trust´ful·ness** *n.*

mis·un·der·stand (mĭsŭnder-stănd´) *v.* (**-stood** pr. -stŏŏd´, **-stand·ing**). Not understand rightly, misinterpret. **mis·un·der·stand´ing** *n.*

mis·use (mĭsūz´) *v.t.* (**-used**, **-us·ing**). Use wrongly, ill-use. ~ (mĭsūs´) *n.*

mite[1] (mīt) *n.* (orig.) Flemish copper coin of small value; hence (pop.) coin of very small value, esp. (also **widow's** ~) small money contribution (Mark 12); small object, esp. a child.

mite[2] (mīt) *n.* Any of several small arachnids of the order Acari, found as parasites.

mi·ter[1], Brit. **mi·tre** (mī´ter) *ns.* Bishop's tall pointed headdress, deeply cleft at the top; episcopal office or dignity. **mi´tered** *adj.* Wearing a miter.

mi·ter[2], Brit. **mi·tre** (mī´ter) *ns.* (carpentry) Joint in which line of junction bisects the angle between the two pieces, as in picture frame; ~ **box**, guide for saw in cutting miter joints. **miter** *v.* (**-tered**, **-ter·ing**). Join in miter; shape to

a miter.

Mith·ras (mĭth´ras). (Pers. myth.) God of light, often identified with the sun. **Mith·ra·ic** (mĭthrā´ĭk) *adj.* **Mith·ra·ism** (mĭth´raĭzem) *n.* Religion involving worship of Mithras, introduced among the Romans under the Empire and spread over most of N. and W. Europe during the first three centuries A.D., becoming the principal rival at that time of Christianity.

Mith·ri·da·tes (mĭthrĭdā´tēz). Name of three kings of Parthia and of several kings of Pontus; **Mithridates VI Eupator** (131–63 B.C.), of Pontus, called "the Great," tried to drive the Romans out of Asia Minor, but was defeated by Sulla, and finally in 66 B.C. by Pompey; he was said to have rendered himself immune to poisons by taking them constantly in small quantities. **Mith·ri·dat·ic** (mĭthrĭdăt´ĭk) *adj.*

mit·i·gate (mĭt´ĭgāt) *v.t.* (**-gat·ed**, **-gat·ing**). Appease; alleviate, reduce severity of. **mit·i·ga·tion** (mĭtĭgā´shon) *n.* **mit·i·ga·to·ry** (mĭt´ĭgatōre, -tōrē) *adj.*

mi·to·chon·dri·on (mītokŏn´-drēon, mĭto-) *n.* (pl. **-dri·a** pr. -drēa). Threadlike or granular

Moats around a town or fortification were usually filled with water and designed to prevent invasion. This moat surrounds the medieval town of Aigues-Mortes in the Camargue, France.

organelle with outer and inner membrane, concerned in release of metabolic energy.

mi·to·sis (mītō´sĭs, mĭ-) *n.* (pl. **-ses** pr. -sēz). (biol.) Splitting of cell or nucleus accompanied by doubling of number of chromosomes, so that both the resulting two cells or nuclei have the same number as the original one (cf. MEIOSIS). **mi·tot·ic** (mītŏt´ĭk, mĭ-) *adj.*

mi·tral (mī´tral) *adj.* (anat.) Of the mitral valve; ~ **valve**, two-cusped valve (so called from fancied resemblance to bishop's miter) between left atrium and ventricle of human heart, preventing reflux of blood into atrium when ventricle contracts.

mi·tre (Brit.) = MITER[1, 2].

mitt (mĭt) *n.* Mitten; (slang, pl.) boxing gloves; baseball glove.

mit·ten (mĭt´en) *n.* Glove leaving fingers and thumb tip bare; glove having no separate partition for fingers, but only for thumb.

mix (mĭks) *v.* (**mixed, mixt, mix·ing**). Mingle, blend, into one mass; compound; ~ **it**, (colloq.) join in fighting; ~ **up**, confuse; ~ **-up** (*n.*), confusion; confused fight, mêlée. **mix** *n.* Mixture of materials (e.g. concrete, plastics) ready for a process.

mixed (mĭkst) *adj.* Of diverse qualities or elements; (of company) not select, containing persons of doubtful status; comprising both sexes; for persons of both sexes; as ~ **bathing**; ~ **farming**, farming involving both crops and livestock; ~ **grill**, dish of various grilled meats and vegetables; ~ **marriage**, marriage between persons of different races or religions; ~ **metaphor**: see METAPHOR; ~ **up**, muddled; (of persons) confused, esp. emotionally.

mix·er (mĭk´ser) *n.* (esp.) 1. In sound films etc., apparatus that controls contributions of various microphones. 2. Apparatus, usu. electrical, for mixing or pulping food in cookery. 3. **good, bad** ~, (colloq.) person who gets on well, badly, in social intercourse with others. 4. Soda or other beverage used in mixed alcoholic drinks. 5. A party designed to help those who attend to meet others.

mix·ture (mĭks´cher) *n.* Mixing; what is mixed, esp. medicinal preparation; mechanical mixing of two or more substances, involving no change in their character, opp. to *chemical combination*; (in internal combustion engine) gas or vaporized fuel mixed with air to form the explosive charges.

miz·zen (mĭz´en) *n.* (naut.) Fore-and-aft sail on after side of **miz´zenmast**, the aftermost mast of a three-masted ship.

mk *abbrev.* Mark (coin).

mks *abbrev.* Meter-kilogram-cond.

ml *abbrev.* Milliliter(s).

M.L.A. *abbrev.* Modern anguage Association.

Mlle. *abbrev.* Mademoiselle (pl. **lles.**).

M.L.S. *abbrev.* Master of ibrary Science.

mm *abbrev.* Millimeter(s).

MM. *abbrev.* Messieurs.

Mme. *abbrev.* Madame (pl. **mes.**).

mmf, m.m.f. *abbrevs.* agnetomotive force.

MN *abbrev.* Minnesota.

Mn *symbol.* Manganese.

mne·mon·ic (nĭmŏn´ĭk) *adj.* Of, tended to aid, the memory. ~ Mnemonic rhyme etc.; (pl.) nemonic art or system.

Mne·mos·y·ne (nĭmŏs´ĭnē, nŏz´-). Mother of the Muses. k., = "memory"].

MO, Mo. *abbrev.* Missouri.

Mo *symbol.* Molybdenum.

M.O. *abbrev.* Money order.

mo·a (mō´a) *n.* Any of various rge extinct flightless birds of New ealand, resembling ostrich (many ecies in family Dinornithidae). aori]

Mo·ab (mō´ăb). Ancient country the Dead Sea.

Mo·ab·ite (mō´ābīt) *n.* (fem. o·a·bit·ess *pr.* mōabī´tĭs). ember of a Semitic people aditionally descended from Lot en. 19), living in Moab. ~ *adj.* f Moab or the Moabites; ~ tone, a monument erected by esha, king of Moab, *c*850 B.C., hich describes the campaign tween Moab and Israel of 2 Kings and furnishes the earliest known scription in the Phoenician phabet; now in the Louvre, Paris.

moan (mōn) *n.* Low inarticulate und expressing pain or grief. ~ Utter moan; lament.

moat (mōt) *n.* Deep, wide, usu. ater-filled, ditch around castle, wn, etc. **moat´ed** *adj.* rrounded by a moat.

mob (mŏb) *n.* Riotous or multuous crowd; rabble; omiscuous gathering. **mob´bish** j. **mob** *v.t.* (**mobbed, mob- ng**). Attack in a mob; crowd ound and molest.

Mo·bile (mōbēl´, mō´bēl). ommercial city and seaport in W. Alabama; ~ **Bay,** inlet of the ulf of Mexico in SW. Alabama; ene of Civil War naval battle, 64, in which the Union under miral Farragut routed the nfederate fleet.

mo·bile (mō´bĭl) *adj.* Movable; aracterized by freedom of move nt; (of troops etc.) that may be sily moved from place to place; changing expression, volatile. o·bil·i·ty (mōbĭl´ĭtē) *n.* **mobile**

(mō´bēl) *n.* Piece of sculpture with parts free to move in currents of air; similar object of cardboard etc.

mo·bi·lize (mō´bĭlīz) *v.* (**-lized, -liz·ing**). Render movable, bring into circulation; call up, assemble, prepare, for war etc. **mo´bi·liz- a·ble** *adj.* **mo·bi·li·za·tion** (mōbĭlīzā´shon) *n.*

Mo·bu·tu (mōbōō´tōō) **Se·se Se·ko** (sĕsĕ sĕ´kō) (1930–). Original name, Joseph Désiré Mobutu; president of Zaire since 1965; Lake **M ~ S ~ S ~**, formerly Lake Albert (see ALBERT).

moc·ca·sin (mŏk´asĭn, -zĭn) *n.* 1. Amer. Inidan soft shoe of deer skin etc. 2. Amer. viper of genus *Ancistrodon.*

mo·cha (mō´ka) *n.* Coffee of fine quality orig. coming from Mocha, seaport of S. Yemen; flavoring of (chocolate and) coffee.

mock (mŏk) *v.* Hold up to ridicule; ridicule by imitation, counterfeit; jeer, scoff; befool, tantalize; **mock´ingbird**, Amer. passerine songbird (*Mimus poly glottos*) that imitates other birds' notes. **mock** *n.* Mockery; object of derision. ~ *adj.* Sham, counterfeit, pretended; **~-heroic,** burlesque imitation of, burlesquely imitating the heroic style; ~ **olive,** Australian olive with succulent fruit and hard wood; ~ **orange,** shrub of genus *Philadelphus* (esp. *P. coronarius*), with creamy-white very fragrant flowers; sometimes called syringa; Australian native laurel (*Pittosporum undulatum*) with citrus-like leaves and heavily scented (usu. white) flowers; ~ **turtle soup,** soup made of calf's

head to imitate real turtle soup; ~ **-up,** scale model.

mock·er·y (mŏk´erē) *n.* (pl. **-er·ies**). Derision; laughingstock; impudent simulation; ludicrously or insultingly futile action.

mod (mŏd) *n.* 1. Style of dress that developed in England in the 1960s, characterized by bright colors, stripes, and designs. 2. British teenager of the 1960s who tried to appear worldly and detached and dressed cleanly and neatly in contrast to ROCKERS. ~ *adj.* 1. Pertaining to or characteristic of the mod style in dress and the people who adopted it. 2. Fashionable, esp. in dress.

mod·al (mō´dal) *adj.* Of mode or form as opp. to substance; (mus.) of mode; (logic) involving affirma tion of possibility, necessity, or contingency; (gram.) of the mood of a verb, (of particle) denoting manner. **mo·dal·i·ty** (mōdăl´ĭtē) *n.* (pl. **-ties**). **mo´dal·ly** *adv.*

mode (mōd) *n.* 1. Way, manner, in which thing is done; prevailing fashion or conventional usage. 2. (mus.) Ancient Greek scale system; any of the scale systems in medieval ecclesiastical music; in more modern music, the two (MAJOR[2] and MINOR) chief scale systems. 3. (statistics) That value of a character or graded quality at which the instances are most numerous.

Model making, as either a hobby or a craft, means producing replicas to scale of various structures such as buildings, automobiles, and human or animal fig ures. This example is of a model railway engine.

mod·el (mŏd′el) *n.* Representation in three dimensions of projected or existing structure or material object; design, pattern; object of imitation; (copy of) garment etc. by recognized designer; person employed to pose for artist etc. or to display clothes by wearing them; dummy for shop windows etc. ~ *adj.* That is a model; exemplary, excellent of its kind. ~ *v.* (-eled, el·ing, Brit. -elled, -el·ling). 1. Mold, fashion; produce in clay, wax, etc. 2. Wear for display; act as artist's model. **mod′el·ing** *n.* Making models, manipulating clay etc.; representation of form in sculpture or of material relief and solidity in painting.

mod·er·ate (mŏd′erĭt) *adj.* Avoiding extremes, temperate; tolerable, mediocre; not excessive. **mod′er·ate·ly** *adv.* **mod′er·ate·ness** *n.* **moderate** *n.* Person, esp. politician, of moderate views. ~ (mŏd′erāt) *v.* (-at·ed, -at·ing). Make or become less violent or excessive; act as moderator.

mod·er·a·tion (mŏderā′shon) *n.* 1. Moderating, moderateness. 2. Retardation of neutrons by MODERATOR.

mod·er·a·tor (mŏd′erāter) *n.* 1. Mediator; Presbyterian minister presiding over presbytery, synod, or general assembly. 2. (nuclear phys.) Material used to dilute fissionable material so as to control nuclear reaction.

mod·ern (mŏd′ern) *adj.* Of the present and recent times; new-fashioned, not antiquated; of school subjects, not concerned with the classics; ~ **face**, style of printing type. **mo·der·ni·ty** (moder′nĭtē, mō-) (pl. **-ties**), **mod′ern·ness** *ns.*

mod·ern·ism (mŏd′ernĭzem) *n.* Modern usage, expression, etc.; modern fashion in art; mode of theological inquiry in which the traditions and doctrines of Christianity are examined in the light of modern thought. **mod′ern·ist** *n.* Person favoring modernism. **mod·ern·is′tic** *adj.* (esp., of style) Following new fashions and innovations, advanced.

mod·ern·ize (mŏd′ernīz) *v.t.* (-ized, -iz·ing). Make modern. **mod·ern·i·za·tion** (mŏdernĭzā′shon) *n.*

mod·est (mŏd′ĭst) *adj.* Not overestimating one's own merits; not excessive; unpretentious; retiring, bashful; decorous, avoiding indecency. **mod′est·ly** *adv.* **mod′es·ty** *n.* (pl. **-ties**).

mod·i·cum (mŏd′ĭkum) *n.* Small quantity or portion.

mod·i·fy (mŏd′ĭfī) *v.t.* (-fied, -fy·ing). Tone down; alter without radical transformation; (gram.)

Modular buildings make use of units which are completely prefabricated before assembly at the site. This method of construction is widely used for low-cost housing, school construction and other purposes.

*The **mole,** of which there are 22 species, is found throughout temperate Eurasia and North America. It is active day and night in rapid cycles of work and rest, and feeds on grubs and worms.*

qualify sense of (word etc.); change vowel by mutation. **mod′i·fi·a·ble** *adj.* **mod·i·fi·ca·tion** (mŏdĭfĭkā′shon) *n.* Act of modifying, state of being modified.

mod·ish (mō′dĭsh) *adj.* Fashionable. **mod′ish·ly** *adv.* **mod′ish·ness** *n.*

mo·diste (mōdēst′; *Fr.* mawdēst′) *n.* (pl. **-distes** pr. -dēsts′; *Fr.* -dēst′). Milliner, dressmaker.

Mo·dred (mō′drĭd) (also **Mordred**). In Arthurian legend, Arthur's nephew, who treacherously seized the kingdom during Arthur's absence and was killed by him in the last battle in Cornwall.

mod·u·lar (mŏj′uler, mŏd′yu-) *adj.* ~ **design**, (archit.) design based on a module or unit that is repeated throughout the building.

mod·u·late (mŏj′ulāt, mŏd′yu-) *v.* (-lat·ed, -lat·ing). 1. Adjust, tone down; attune to a certain pitch or key, vary in tone. 2. (mus.) Pass from one key to another. 3. (radio) Vary the frequency, amplitude, etc., of (a wave) by the effect of another. **mod·u·la·tion** (mŏjulā′shon, mŏdyu-) *n.* Modulating, effect produced by

this; **amplitude** ~, (abbrev. A.M.) transmission of signals modulating the amplitude of t transmitted radio wave but keepi its frequency constant; **frequen** ~, (abbrev. F.M.) transmission signals by modulating t frequency of the radio wave b keeping its amplitude constant.

mod·u·la·tor (mŏj′ulāt mŏd′yu-) *n.* (radio) Apparatus us for modulating a carrier wave.

mod·ule (mŏj′ōol, mŏd′ūl) Unit of standard of measureme as for flow of water; (archit.) u of measurement for determini the proportions of a building, classical architecture usu. half t diameter of a column at the ba independent unit forming secti of spacecraft; **lunar** ~, se contained segment of a spacecra designed to approach and land moon independently.

mod·u·lus (mŏj′ulus, mŏd′y *n.* (math.) 1. Constant multipl or coefficient, esp. for converti

Napierian into common logarithms. 2. Number by which two others are divided.

mo·dus (mō'dus) *n.* Method, manner, mode; ~ **operandi**, method, system, of working; plan of operations; ~ **vivendi**, mode of living, esp. arrangement between disputants pending settlement.

Mo·ga·dish·u (mōgadĭsh'ōō). Capital and port city of Somalia, on the Indian Ocean.

Mo·gul (mō'gul, mōgŭl') *n.* 1. Mongolian, esp. one of the Muslim followers of Babur, who established an empire in India in 1526 that reached its zenith under Akbar and Aurangzeb, but declined after this, the last emperor being deposed by the British in 1857; **Great** ~, Mogul emperor. 2. **m** ~, important or influential person. [Pers. *mugal*, *-ul*, pr. of *Mongol*]

mo·gul (mō'gul) *n.* Small bump on a ski run.

mo·hair (mō'hār) *n.* (Yarn or fabric made from) hair of Angora goat; imitation of this made of a mixture of wool and cotton. [Arab. *mukayyar* cloth of goat's hair (lit. "select, choice," f. *kayyara* choose)]

Mo·ham·med [1] (mōhăm'ĭd, -hah'mĭd) = MUHAMMAD.

Mo·ham·med [2] II (mōhăm'ĭd, -hah'mĭd) (1430–81). Called "The Great" or "The Conqueror"; sultan of Turkey, 1451–81; captured Constantinople, 1453, effectively ending the Byzantine Empire.

Mo·hawk (mō'hawk) *n.* (pl. **-hawks**, collect. **-hawk**). (Member of) a tribe of N. Amer. Indians belonging to the Iroquois; language of this tribe.

Mo·hi·can (mōhē'kan) *n.* (pl. **-cans**, collect. **-can**). (Member of) a warlike tribe of N. Amer. Indians, of Algonquin stock, formerly occupying W. parts of Connecticut and Massachusetts.

mo·ho (mō'hō) *n.* Discontinuity between Earth's crust and mantle; Mohorovicic discontinuity. **mo·hole** (mō'hōl) *n.* Hole drilled through seabed to mantle. [f. *A. Mohorovičić* (1857–1936), Yugoslav seismologist]

Mohs (mōz), **Friedrich** (1773–1839). German mineralogist, inventor of **Mohs' scale**: see HARDNESS def. 2.

moi·e·ty (moi'ĭtē) *n.* (pl. **-ties**). Half, esp. in legal use; (loosely) either of two parts into which thing is divided.

moire (mwār, mōr, mȯr) *n.* Watered silk fabric. [Fr., perh. f. Engl. *mohair*]

moiré (mwahrā', mōrā', mawrā') *adj.* (of silk) Watered; (of metals) having clouded appearance like watered silk. ~ *n.* (Fabric with) appearance like that of watered silk.

[Fr., f. *moirer* water (silk)]

moist (moist) *adj.* Slightly wet, damp; rainy. **moist'ness** *n.*

mois·ten (moi'sen) *v.* Make or become moist.

mois·ture (mois'cher, moish'-) *n.* Liquid diffused through air or solid, or condensed on a surface. **mois'tur·ize** *v.* (-**ized**, -**iz·ing**). Make moist; add moisture to.

Mo·ja·ve (mōhah'vē) **Desert.** Desert region in S. California.

mol *abbrev.* MOLE[4](S).

mo·lar [1] (mō'ler) *adj. & n.* Grinding (tooth), back tooth of mammals. [L. *mola* millstone]

mo·lar [2] (mō'ler) *adj.* (phys.) Of, acting on or by, masses (freq. opp. MOLECULAR); ~ **solution**, (chem.) solution containing one gram molecule of a specified substance per liter.

mo·las·ses (mȯlăs'ĭz) *n.* Thick viscid syrup, drained from raw sugar during manufacture. [Port. *melaço* f. LL. *mellaceus* like honey]

mold, [1] Brit. **mould** (mōld) *ns.* Loose or broken earth, surface soil; earth of the grave; soil rich in organic matter; **mold'board**, curved iron plate at back of plowshare that turns over earth from the furrow.

mold [2] (mōld) *n.* Woolly or furry fungus growth forming on surfaces in moist warm air.

mold [3] (mōld) *n.* Matrix, vessel, in which fluid or plastic material is cast or shaped; pudding etc. shaped in mold; form, shape, distinctive nature. ~ *v.t.* Shape in or as in a mold; shape (bread) into loaves; model. **mold'er** [1] *n.* (esp.) Person employed in making molds for casting.

Mol·da·vi·a (mōldā'vēa, -vya). 1. (hist.) Danubian principality, from which, together with Wallachia, the kingdom of Rumania was formed in 1859. 2. Constituent republic (properly *Moldavian Soviet Socialist Republic*) of the U.S.S.R., formed from territory ceded by Rumania in 1940; capital, Kishinev.

mold·er [2] (mōl'der) *v.i.* Turn to dust by natural decay; crumble away.

mold·ing (mōl'dĭng) *n.* Molded object; ornamental contour given to stone, wood, or metalwork; material, esp. long piece of wood prepared for this.

mold·y (mōl'dē) *adj.* (**mold·i·er, mold·i·est**). Covered with MOLD[2]; moldering; stale, musty.

mole [1] (mōl) *n.* Abnormal pigmented prominence on skin.

mole [2] (mōl) *n.* Any of various small, insect-eating, burrowing mammals of the family Talpidae, having rudimentary eyes and very short strong forelimbs for burrowing; **mole'hill**, mound of earth

thrown up by mole; **mole'skin**, mole's fur; strong, soft, fine-piled cotton twill, used for trousers etc.

mole [3] (mōl) *n.* Massive structure, esp. stone, serving as pier or breakwater.

mole [4] (mōl) *n.* Amount of a particular substance containing as many elementary entities (atoms, molecules, etc.) as there are atoms in 0.012 kg of carbon-12 (abbrev. mol).

mol·e·cule (mŏl'ekūl) *n.* 1. (chem., phys.) One of the minute groups of atoms of which material substances consist; smallest particle to which a compound can be reduced by subdivision without losing its chemical identity. 2. (loosely) Small particle. **mo·lec·u·lar** (mōlĕk'yuler, mo-) *adj.* Of molecules; ~ **weight**, weight of a molecule of a substance relative to weight of hydrogen atom.

mo·lest (mōlĕst') *v.t.* Meddle with injuriously or with hostile intent. **mo·les·ta·tion** (mōlĕstā'shon) *n.*

Mo·lière (mōlyār'; *Fr.* mawlyĕr'). Pen name of Jean Baptiste Poquelin (1622–73), French author of comedies satirizing contemporary manners, including *The Misanthrope* and *The Imaginary Invalid.*

moll (mŏl) *n.* (slang) Gangster's female companion.

mol·li·fy (mŏl'ifī) *v.t.* (-**fied**, -**fy·ing**). Soften, appease. **mol·li·fi·ca·tion** (mŏlifikā'shon) *n.*

mol·lusk, mol·lusc (mŏl'usk) *ns.* Any animal of the phylum Mollusca, which comprises soft-bodied unsegmented invertebrates (usu. having a hard protective shell) and includes limpets, snails, cuttlefish, oysters, etc. **mol·lus·cous** (mȯlŭs'kus) *adj.*

mol·ly·cod·dle (mŏl'ēkŏdel) *n.* Person accustomed to coddling. ~ *v.t.* (-**dled, -dling**). Coddle.

Mo·loch (mō'lŏk, mō'ok). Canaanite god to whose image children were sacrificed as burnt offerings (Lev. 18, 2 Kings 23); hence, power or influence to which everything is sacrificed.

Mo·lo·kai (mō'lokī). One of the Hawaiian Islands, 259 sq. mi. (417 sq. km); originally settled as a leper colony.

Mo·lo·tov (mŏl'otawf, -tŏf, mawl'-; *Russ.* mawl'awtawf), **Vyacheslav Mikhailovich** (1890–). Russian statesman, minister for foreign affairs in U.S.S.R., 1939–49, 1953–6; ~ **cocktail**, crude incendiary hand grenade, consisting of a bottle of inflammable liquid and a wick, orig. used as antitank missile in World War II.

molt, Brit. **moult** (mōlt), *vbs.* (of birds or animals) Shed feathers, fur, skin, etc., which are later replaced by new growth; shed (feathers etc.) thus. ~ *n.* Molting.

mol·ten (mōl'ten) *adj.*: see MELT; (esp.) liquefied by heat.

mol·to (mōl'tō; *It.* mawl'taw) *adv.* (mus.) Very (preceding mus. direction, as ~ *allegro*).

Mo·luc·ca (mŏlŭk'a) **Islands** (formerly Spice Islands). Group of islands forming part of the Republic of Indonesia.

mo·ly (mō'lē) *n.* (pl. **-lies**). (Gk. myth.) Fabulous plant with white flower and black root, given by Hermes to Odysseus as a charm against the sorceries of Circe.

mo·lyb·de·nite (molĭb'denīt, mŏlĭbdē'nĭt) *n.* Molybdenum disulphide (MoS_2), a soft flaky black mineral resembling graphite.

mo·lyb·de·num (molĭb'denum, mŏlĭbdē'num) *n.* (chem.) Grayish-white metallic element resembling tungsten and having a very high melting point, a constituent of special steel alloys; symbol Mo, at. no. 42, at. wt. 95.94. [Gk. *molubdos* lead]

Mom·ba·sa (mŏmbah'sa, -băs'a). Seaport of Kenya in the SE. part on the Indian Ocean.

*These ruins are of the **monastery** of St. Honorat, Iles des Lerins, France. Monastic communities usually separate themselves from general society and are often self-sufficient.*

mo·ment (mō'ment) *n.* Point of time, instant; importance, weight; (mech.) measure of power of a force to cause rotation around an axis.

mo·men·tar·y (mō'mentĕrē) *adj.* Lasting but for a moment. **mo·men·tar·i·ly** (mōmentĕr'ilē, -tār'-, mō'mentĕr-) *adv.* **mo'·men·tar·i·ness** *n.*

mo·men·tous (mōmĕn'tus) *adj.* Important; weighty. **mo·men'·tous·ly** *adv.* **mo·men'tous·ness** *n.*

mo·men·tum (mōmĕn'tum) *n.* (pl. **-ta** pr. -ta, **-tums**). (mech.) Quantity of motion of a moving body, product of mass multiplied by velocity; (pop.) impetus gained by movement.

Mo·mus (mō'mus). (Gk. myth.) God of mockery; expelled from heaven for his criticisms and ridicule of the gods; hence, a fault-finder.

Mon. *abbrev.* Monday.

Mon·a·co (mŏn'akō; *Fr.* mawnăkaw'). Independent principality, under French protection since 1861, on French Riviera, including Monte Carlo within its borders; capital, Monaco.

*This species of **monarch** butterfly (Danaus chrysippus) is found in Africa. It is often called the Plain Tiger butterfly. The best-known of the species is Danaus plexippus.*

mon·ad (mŏn'ăd, mō'năd) *n.* 1. (hist.) Number one, unit. 2. (philos.) Ultimate unit of being (e.g. a soul, an atom, a person, God), esp. in philosophy of LEIBNITZ. 3. (biol.) Primary individual organism assumed as first term in a genealogy. **mo·nad·ic** (monăd'ĭk) *adj.* **mon·ad·ism** (mŏn'adĭzem) *n.* Theory of monadic nature of matter or of substance generally, applied esp. to philosophy of Leibnitz.

Mo·na Li·sa (mō'na lē'za). Portrait, now in the Louvre, of a lady traditionally identified as the wife of Francesco del Gioconda, painted by Leonardo da Vinci and famous for its strange smile.

mon·arch (mŏn'erk) *n.* 1. Sovereign with title of king, queen, emperor, or equivalent; supreme ruler (often fig.) 2. Large orange-and-black butterfly (*Danaus plexippus*). **mo·nar·chal** (monär'kal), **mo·nar'chic, mo·nar'chi·cal** *adjs.*

mon·ar·chism (mŏn'erkĭzem) *n.* Principles of, attachment to, monarchy. **mon'ar·chist** *n.*

mon·ar·chy (mŏn'erkē) *n.* (pl.

*The **Mona Lisa** or 'La Gioconda' is Leonardo da Vinci's most famous painting. It was painted between 1503 and 1506 and portrays the wife of a Florentine official.*

-chies). (Nation under) monarchical government.

mon·as·ter·y (mŏn´astĕrē) *n.* (pl. **-ter·ies**). Residence of community of monks.

mo·nas·tic (monăs´tĭk) *adj.* Of monks or monasteries; secluded, austere. **mo·nas´ti·cal·ly** *adv.* **mo·nas·ti·cism** (monăs´tĭsĭzem) *n.*

mon·a·zite (mŏn´azīt) *n.* Phosphate mineral, containing thorium and rare-earth elements, found in alluvial sands in India and Brazil.

Mon·day (mŭn´dā, -dē) *n.* Second day of the week. [OE. *Monan daeg* (= moon's day), rendering of LL. *lunae dies*]

Mon·dri·an (mŏn´drēahn), **Piet Cornelis** (1872–1944). Dutch painter.

Mo·net (mōnā´; *Fr.* mawnĕ´), **Claude** (1840–1926). French Impressionist painter.

mon·e·tar·y (mŏn´ĭtĕrē, mŭn´-) *adj.* Of coinage or money. **mon´e·ta·rist** *n.* One who advocates control of money as chief method of stabilizing the economy.

mon·ey (mŭn´ē) *n.* (pl. **mon·eys, mon·ies**). 1. Current coin; coin and promissory documents representing it, esp. (**paper** ~) government and bank notes; (econ.) anything generally accepted in

Monet, one of the founders of Impressionism, painted directly from nature. This painting, entitled 'Tempete, Rochers de Belle-Isle', was executed in 1886 when Monet visited this rugged island off Brittany.

settlement of debts. 2. (with pl.) Particular coin. 3. (pl., archaic or legal) Sums of money. 4. ~ **bill**, a bill, originating in the House of Representatives, involving expenditure or raising of money for public purposes; **mon'eychanger**,

one whose business it is to change money at a fixed rate; **mon'ey-grubber**, one bent on accumulating money; avaricious person; **mon'eylender**, one who lends money at interest; **money market**, sphere of operations of dealers in loans, stocks, and shares; **money order**, order for payment of money, issued by a post office or bank; **money supply**, (econ.) amount of currency plus demand or checking account deposits in public hands; **money's worth**, anything recognized as good value for one's money; **mon'eywort**, creeping herb (*Lysimachia nummularia*) with round leaves and single yellow flower; creeping Jenny. **mon'eyed** (mŭn´ēd) *adj.* Wealthy.

mon·ger (mŭng´ger, mŏng-´) *n.* Dealer, trader (chiefly in combination, as **fish'monger, i'ronmonger**, and fig. **scan'dalmonger**).

Mon·gol (mŏng´gol, -gōl, mŏn-´) *adj.* & *n.* 1. (Member, language) of a pastoral people of Mongolia.

Moneywort, a perennial trailing plant of European origin, has round glossy leaves and small yellow flowers in the axils of the leaves. It is also called Creeping Jenny.

2. (Person) with Mongoloid characteristics.

Mon·go·li·a (mŏnggō´lēₐ, mŏngō´-). Region in Asia including **Inner** and **Outer** ~: see MONGOLIAN.

Mon·go·li·an (mŏnggō´lēan, mŏngō´-) *adj.* Of the Mongols or their language; Mongoloid; **Inner ~ Autonomous Region**, autonomous region of China (formerly Inner Mongolia), capital, Huhehot; ~ **People's Republic**, republic N. of China (formerly Outer Mongolia); capital, Ulan Bator. **Mongolian** *n.* Mongolian person.

mon·go·lism (mŏng´golĭzem, mŏn´-) *n.* Type of congenital mental deficiency characterized by a supposedly Mongoloid appearance.

Mon·go·loid (mŏng´goloid, mŏn´-) *adj. & n.* 1. (Person) resembling the Mongolians, esp. (member) of the yellow-skinned division of mankind with high cheekbones, small nose, and broad face, found esp. in Mongolia and adjacent countries and including most of the Asian peoples. 2. **m ~**, (person) suffering from mongolism.

mon·goose (mŏng´gōōs, mŏn´-) *n.* (pl. **-goos·es**). 1. Small carnivorous mammal of Old World tropics esp. of genus *Herpestes*, esp. the Indian gray mongoose (*H. edwardsi*), known for its ability to kill snakes and rodents.

mon·grel (mŏng´grel, mŭng´-) *adj. & n.* (Animal, esp. dog) of no definable breed or type, resulting from various crossings; hybrid. **mon´grel·ism** *n.* **mon´grel·ize** *v.t.* (**-ized, -iz·ing**).

mon·ism (mŏn´ĭzem) *n.* (philos.)

*The **mongoose** is found in Africa, Asia and south Europe. It is an active, bold predator that lives in burrows and feeds on small animals, birds, reptiles and eggs. Shown here are the grey mongoose and the banded species.*

Monkey puzzle, *a tall coniferous tree native to Chile, has stiff, spirally-arranged leaves that discourage animals from attempting to climb the tree. It has edible seeds.*

Any theory denying the duality of matter and mind, as dist. from DUALISM and PLURALISM. **mon´ist** *n.* **mo·nis·tic** (monĭs´tĭk, mō-) *adj.*

mon·i·tor (mŏn´ĭter) *n.* 1. (archaic) One who admonishes. 2. (fem. **mon·i·tress** pr. mŏn´ĭtrĭs) Senior pupil in school with disciplinary functions. 3. One who is appointed to listen to and report on foreign broadcasts, telephone conversations, etc. 4. Receiving apparatus used in monitoring; detector for induced radioactivity, esp. among atomic plant workers. 5. Kind of Old World tropical lizard of genus *Varanus*, supposed to give warning of the vicinity of crocodiles. 6. (hist.) Ironclad vessel with low freeboard and revolving gun turrets, for coast defense, so

called from name of first vessel of this type, designed by Capt Ericsson, in the Civil War, 1862 ~ *v.t.* Act as monitor of (broadcast etc.). **mon·i·to·ry** (mŏn´ĭtōrē -tōrē) *adj.* Admonishing connected with, pertaining to school monitors.

monk (mŭngk) *n.* Member of community of men living apart from the world under religious vows and according to a rule **monks'hood**, aconite. **monk´dom** *n.* **monk´ish** *adj.*

mon·key (mŭng´kē) *n.* (pl **-keys**). 1. One of a group of mammals allied to and resembling man and ranging from anthropoid apes to marmosets; any animal of order Primates except man, the tarsiers, and the lemurs, usu restricted to the small, long-tailed members, as. dist. from the large short-tailed apes. 2. Mischievous playful young person. 3. Machine hammer for pile driving. 4. **have a ~ on one's back**, (slang) be a drug addict; ~ **bread**, fruit of the baobab tree; ~ **business**, (slang) mischief; ~ **engine**, engine that lifts the head of a pile driver; ~ **jacket**, sailor's short close-fitting jacket; ~ **puzzle**, S. Amer coniferous tree (*Araucaria imbricata*) with broad prickly spine growing at intervals down the branches; **mon´keyshines**, (slang) mischief; **monkey wrench**, wrench or spanner with adjustable jaws. **monkey** *v.i.* (**-keyed -key·ing**). Fool *about*, play mischievous tricks (*with*).

mono-, mon- *prefixes.* Alone sole, single.

mon·o·ba·sic (mŏnobā´sĭk) *adj* (chem., of an acid) Having only one acidic hydrogen atom in its molecule.

mon·o·car·pic (mŏnokär´pĭk) **mon·o·car·pous** (mŏnokär´pus *adjs.* (bot.) Bearing fruit once and then dying.

mon·o·chrome (mŏn´okrōm) *n & adj.* (Picture etc.) having only one color, or executed in different shades of one color. **mon·o·chro·mat·ic** (mŏnokrōmăt´ĭk, -ōkro-) *adj.*

mon·o·cle (mŏn´okel) *n.* Single eyeglass.

mon·o·cot·y·le·don (mŏno-kŏtĭlē´don) *n.* Plant having a single cotyledon or seed leaf. **mon·o·cot·y·le´don·ous** *adj.*

mo·noc·u·lar (monŏk´yuler adj. Of, adapted for, one eye, as ~ **microscope**.

Indian grey mongoose

Banded mongoose

*Some common **monkeys** of the Old and New Worlds are shown here. Most monkeys are tree-dwellers and active by day; and many live in groups. They are popular zoo exhibits and are widely used in experimental studies because their physiology is similar to that of man*

oldt s woolly monkey

Geoffreys spider monkey

Red howler monkey

Vervet monkey

colobus monkey

squirrel monkey

mona monkey

sooty mangabey

De Brazza's monkey

Diana monkey

Patas monkey

electric motor

driven wheels

guide wheels

electric motor

ARIEL

box section
with slit

guide rail

supporting rail

*The SAFEGE **monorail** system (above)
was recently constructed in France.
The car is suspended from a box-like
section with a slit on its underside.
Right: Disneyland's main entrance has
this monorail train to carry visitors
around the fair.*

mon·o·dy (mŏn´odē) *n.* (pl.
-dies). 1. (Gk. antiq.) Lyric ode
sung by a single voice. 2. Dirge,
elegy. **mo·nod·ic** (mŏnŏd´ĭk) *adj.*
mon´o·dist *n.*

mo·noe·cious (mŏnē´shus) *adj.*
(bot.) Having reproductive organs
of both sexes on same plant (but,
if a flowering plant, in different
flowers).

mo·nog·a·my (mŏnŏg´amē) *n.*
Condition, rule, or custom of being
married to only one person at a
time, as dist. from *polygamy.*
mo·nog´a·mist *n.* **mo·nog´a·-
mous** *adj.*

mon·o·gram (mŏn´ogrăm) *n.*
Character composed of two or more
interwoven letters. **mon·o·gram·-
mat·ic** (mŏnogramăt´ĭk) *adj.*

mon·o·graph (mŏn´ogrăf,
-grahf) *n.* Treatise on single object
or class of objects. **mo·nog·ra·-
pher** (mŏnŏg´rafer) *n.* **mon·o·-
graph·ic** (mŏnogrăf´ĭk, -grah´fĭk)
adj. **mon·o·graph´i·cal·ly** *adv.*

mon·o·lith (mŏn´olĭth) *n.* 1.
Single block of stone as pillar or
monument. 2. (building) Mass of
concrete, masonry, etc., forming a
solid element in a structure. 3.
Political or social structure
presenting an indivisible or
unbroken unity. **mon·o·lith·ic**
(mŏnolĭth´ĭk) *adj.* Of, like, a
monolith; unified and homogeneous; not exhibiting deviation
or minority interests.

mon·o·logue (mŏn´olŏg, -lawg)
n. Soliloquy; dramatic composition
for a single performer. **mon·o·-
log·i·cal** (mŏnolŏj´ĭkal) *adj.*

mon·o·log·ist (mŏn´olŏgĭst,
-lawg-, monŏl´ojĭst) *n.* **mo·nol·o·-
gize** (monŏl´ojīz) *v.i.* (**-gized,
-giz·ing**).

mon·o·ma·ni·a (mŏnomā´nēa,
-mān´ya) *n.* Form of insanity,
obsession of the mind by a single
idea or interest. **mon·o·ma·ni·ac**
(mŏnomā´nēăk) *n.*

mon·o·mer (mŏn´omer) *n.*
(chem.) 1. One of the units forming
a polymer molecule (see POLYMER).
2. Compound that can undergo
polymerization.

mon·o·met·al·ism (mŏnomĕt´-
alĭzem) *n.* Use of standard currency
based on one metal.

mo·no·mi·al (mŏnō´mēal, mo-)
adj. & n. (alg.) (Expression)
consisting of a single term.

Mo·non·ga·he·la (monŏng-
gahē´la). River flowing from N.
West Virginia joining the
Allegheny to form the Ohio River
at Pittsburgh, Pennsylvania.

mon·o·nu·cle·o·sis (mŏnō-
nōōklēō´sĭs, -nū-, mŏno-) *n.* Acute
infectious disease with symptoms
of sudden fever, benign swelling
of lymph nodes, and presence of

an abnormally large number
leucocytes with single nuclei in t
bloodstream.

mon·o·phon·ic (mŏnofŏn´
adj. (of recording) Sounding
from a single source (opp. STERE
PHONIC).

mon·o·plane (mŏn´oplān)
Airplane with one plane, as distir
from *biplane.*

mo·nop·o·list (monŏp´olĭst)
Holder or supporter of monopol
mo·nop·o·lize (monŏp´olīz) *v*
(**-ized, -iz·ing**). Secure monopo
of. **mo·nop·o·li·za·tion** (monŏ
olīzā´shon) *n.*

mo·nop·o·ly (monŏp´olē) *n.* (
-lies). Exclusive possession
control; exclusive trading privileg
company or group having su
control.

mon·o·rail (mŏn´orāl) *n.* Ra
road in which the track consists
a single rail.

mon·o·so·di·um glu·ta·ma
(mŏnosō´dēum   glōō´tamā
sodium glutamate. Crystallir
water-soluble salt, used to intens
food flavors (abbrev. MSG).

mon·o·syl·la·ble (mŏn´osĭlab
n. Word of one syllable. **mon·**
syl·lab·ic (mŏnosĭlăb´ĭk) *adj.*

mon·o·the·ism (mŏn´othēĭze
n. Doctrine that there is only o
God. **mon´o·the·ist** *n.* **mon·**
the·ist·ic (mŏnothēĭs´tĭk) *adj.*

mon·o·tone (mŏn´otōn) *n.*
Sound continuing or repeated
one note, or without change of tor
mon·o·ton·ic (mŏnotŏn´ĭk) *adj.*
(mus.) In monotone. 2. (mat
With all members of a sequen

ither increasing or decreasing.

mo·not·o·nous (mŏnŏt′onŭs) *adj.* Having no variation in tone or cadence; lacking in variety, always the same. **mo·not′o·nous·ly** *adv.* **mo·not′o·nous·ness, mo·not′o·ny** *ns.*

mon·o·treme (mŏn′otrēm) *n.* (zool.) Mammal of subclass Monotremata, primitive egg-laying forms of Australasia including duck-billed platypus and spiny anteaters.

mon·o·type (mŏn′otīp) *n.* 1. Print taken from a freshly painted card, plate, or block. 2. **M~**, (trademark) printing apparatus that casts and sets up type in single letters by means of a perforated roll that has been previously produced in another part of the apparatus.

mon·o·va·lent (mŏnova′lent) *adj.* (chem.) Having a VALENCE of . **mon·o·va′lence, mon·o·va′len·cy** *ns.*

mon·ox·ide (mŏnŏk′sīd, mŏn-) *n.* (chem.) Oxide with one oxygen atom in the molecule.

Mon·roe (monrō′), **James** (1758–1831). Fifth president of U.S., 1817–25; formulator (1823) of the **Monroe Doctrine** that interference by any European nation in the Spanish-American republics would be regarded as an act unfriendly to the U.S., and that the American continents were no longer open to European colonial settlement.

Mon·ro·vi·a (mŏnrō′vēa). Capital and principal seaport of Liberia in the NW. on the Atlantic.

Mon·sei·gneur (mawn̄sĕnyör′) *n.* (pl. **Mes·sei·gneurs**, pr.

Monsoons, which are periodical winds, change direction between land and sea according to season. When they are reversing direction these winds give rise to disturbances such as tornadoes and hurricanes, but the heavy rains they bring are essential.

Monotremes are egg-laying mammals present today only in Australia and New Guinea. The aquatic platypus (above) lives in burrows at the water's edge. Echidnas are insectivorous and covered with sharp spines.

mĕsĕnyör′). Title or form of address to French dignitaries, esp. princes, cardinals, and bishops (abbrev. Mgr). [Fr.]

mon·sieur (mosyö′) *n.* (pl. **mes·sieurs**, pr. mes′erz; *Fr.* mĕsyör′). Title (corresp. to *Mr.*) or form of address (corresp. to *Sir*) used of or to Frenchman.

Mon·si·gnor (mŏnsē′nyer; *It.* mawnsēnyŏr′) *n.* (pl. **-si·gnors**, *It.* **-si·gno·ri** pr. -sēnyŏr′e). (R.C. Ch.) Ecclesiastical title attached to office or distinction usu. bestowed by pope; in some countries (e.g. France) = MONSEIGNEUR. [It.]

mon·soon (mŏnsōon′) *n.* Seasonal wind prevailing in southern Asia, from southwest (**wet**

Montbretia, although a native of South Africa, has become established in cooler climates as a garden ornamental. It belongs to the iris family and has reddish-orange flowers.

Montreal is the largest city and chief port of Canada. French is spoken by two-thirds of the population, and the old French town (1642) is now the financial district. This view of the city is from Mont Royal Park.

Bernard Law, 1st Viscount Montgomery of Alamein, defeated the German army under Rommel at Alamein in 1942, and was military commander of the Allied invasion of Normandy (1944).

~) in summer and northeast (**dry** ~) in winter; rainy season accompanying SW. monsoon. [prob. f. Arab. *mausim*, lit. season]

mon·ster (mŏn′ster) *n.* 1. Imaginary animal compounded of elements from various creatures. 2. Person or thing of portentous appearance or size. 3. Inhumanly cruel or wicked person. 4. (path.) Grossly malformed product of human conception.

mon·stros·i·ty (mŏnstrŏs′ĭtē) *n.* (pl. **-ties**). Monstrousness; misshapen or outrageous thing.

mon·strous (mŏn′strus) *adj.* Like a monster; huge; outrageous. **mon′strous·ly** *adv.* **mon′strous·ness** *n.*

Mont. *abbrev.* Montana.

mon·tage (mŏntahzh′; *Fr.* mawn̈tahzh′) *n.* 1. (cinemat.) Selection, cutting, and arrangement of shots; presentation of a series of shots as a connected sequence. 2. (Picture etc. produced by) juxtaposition of (parts of) photographs etc.

Mon·taigne (mŏntān′; *Fr.* mawn̈těn′ye), **Michel Eyquem de** (1533–92). French writer; author of *Essais*, which reveal a sagacious and tolerant philosophy of life, stressing the fallibility of the human reason and the relativity of human science.

Mon·tan·a (mŏntăn′a). State on the Canadian border E. of the Rocky Mountains; admitted to the Union in 1889; capital, Helena.

mon·tane (mŏntān′) *adj.* Of, inhabiting, mountainous country.

Mon·tauk (mŏn′tawk) **Point.** Resort area on the E. tip of Long Island, New York State.

Mont Blanc (mawn̈ blahn̈′). Mountain in France on Italian border; highest in Europe (15,782 ft., 4,810 m).

mont·bre·tia (mŏnbrē′sha) *n.* English name of a commonly cultivated and extensively naturalized hybrid plant of two species of the genus *Crocosmia*. [A. F. E. Coquebert de *Montbret* (1780–1801), French botanist]

Mont·calm (mŏntkahm′; *Fr.* mawn̈käm′), **Louis-Joseph de Montcalm-Gozon, Marquis de** (1712–59). French commander of troops in New France; defended Quebec against Wolfe and was mortally wounded in the battle of the Plains of Abraham.

mon·te (mŏn′tē, mŏntā′) *n.* (also **three-card** ~). Spanish-American game of chance, played with 3 cards, in which a player bets that one of the remaining 2 will be matched by the dealer before the last one.

Mon·te Car·lo (mŏn′tĭ kär′lō). One of the three communes of Monaco; famous as a gambling resort.

Mon·te Cas·si·no (mŏn′tĭ kahsē′nō). Hill midway between Rome and Naples, site of the principal monastery of the Benedictine Order, founded by St. Benedict *c*529. The monastery, previously demolished and rebuilt

several times, was almost totally destroyed in a battle between German and Allied forces in 1944 but has since been restored.

Mon·te·go (mŏntē′gō) **Bay.** Resort and seaport on the NW coast of Jamaica, West Indies.

Mon·te·ne·gro (mŏntenē′grō; *It.* mawntĕnĕ′graw). Former monarchy of SE. Europe, on the Adriatic; since 1919 a part of Yugoslavia. **Mon·te·ne·grin** (mŏntenē′grĭn) *adj. & n.*

Mon·tes·quieu (mŏn′teskū; *F.* mawnteskyö′), **Charles Louis de Secondat de** (1689–1755). French political philosopher; author of *L'Esprit des Lois* (1748), in which he analyzed the types of politic

The moon is responsible for the tidal action on the earth. It revolves around the earth in 27 days 7 hours 43 minutes. The first manned landing on the moon (right) was made by U.S. astronauts in Apollo II in 1969.

onstitution and denounced the buses of the French monarchy.

Mon·tes·so·ri (mŏntesōr´ē, sōr´ē), **Maria** (1870–1952). talian educator and physician; riginator of a system of training mall children by the use of pparatus teaching manual exterity, the matching of colors r shapes, etc., under less rigid iscipline than was formerly ommon.

Mon·te·vi·de·o (mŏntevĭdā´ō, vĭd´ēō). Capital and seaport of Uruguay, in the S. part at the mouth of the Rio de la Plata.

Mon·te·zu·ma II (mŏnte-oo´ma) (1466–1520). Aztec mperor of Mexico at the time of he Spanish conquest; was seized nd held as a hostage by Cortez, nd mortally wounded when his eople attempted to rescue him.

Mont·gom·er·y[1] (mŏntgŭm´ere, gŭm´rē). Capital of Alabama in he central part on the Alabama River; first capital of the Confederate States, Feb.–May, 1861.

Mont·gom·er·y[2] (mŏntgŭm´ere, gŭm´rē), **Bernard Law, ´iscount Montgomery of Alamein** (1887–1976). British field marshal; commander of 8th Army from 1942 during the N. African campaign; commander-in-hief of British group of armies in France and Germany, 1944–6.

month (mŭnth) *n.* Period in which moon makes a complete evolution (**lunar ~**); one of 12 portions into which conventional ear is divided (**calendar ~**); loosely) period of four weeks.

month·ly (mŭnth´lē) *adj.* Done, ecurring, payable, etc., once a

month. **~** *adv.* Once a month; every month. **~** *n.* (pl. **-lies**). Magazine etc. published each month; (pl.) menses.

Mon·ti·cel·lo (mŏntĭsĕl´ō). Estate of Thomas Jefferson near Charlottesville, Virginia, including the mansion, which he designed, incorporating many innovations.

Mont·mar·tre (mawn̄mär´tre). District in the N. of Paris; during the 19th c. the artistic quarter and the site of many famous cafés and cabarets.

Mont·par·nasse (mawn̄pär-nahs´). District in the S. of Paris on the left bank of the Seine known for the intellectuals and artists who gather there.

Mont·pe·lier (mŏntpēl´yer). Capital of Vermont in the central part.

Mon·tre·al (mŏntrēawl´, mŭn-). Largest city and a port in Canada, on the St. Lawrence River, in Quebec.

Mont Saint Mi·chel (mawn̄ săn̄ mēshĕl´). Islet off the coast of Normandy, a rocky peak crowned by a medieval Benedictine abbey fortress.

Mont·ser·rat (mŏntserăt´, -raht´, mŏnt´serăt, -raht). Island in the Lesser Antilles and a British dependency; capital, Plymouth.

mon·u·ment (mŏn´yument) *n.* Anything that by its survival commemorates person, action, or event,

esp. erection intended to do this; a natural feature or area of special interest set aside by government as public property; work of enduring value.

mon·u·men·tal (mŏnyumĕn´-tal) *adj.* Like, of, serving as, a monument; colossal, stupendous. **mon·u·men·tal·ly** *adv.* **mon·u·men·tal·i·ty** (mŏnyumĕntăl´ĭtē) *n.*

moo (moō) *v.i.* (**mooed, moo·ing**) & *n.* (pl. **moos**). (Make) lowing sound.

mooch (moōch) *v.i.* (slang) 1. Loaf *about*; slouch *along*. 2. Get food, money, etc. by begging.

mood[1] (moōd) *n.* Frame of mind or state of feelings. **mood´y** *adj.* (**mood·i·er, mood·i·est**). Subject to changes of mood; depressed, sullen. **mood´i·ly** *adv.* **mood´i·ness** *n.*

mood[2] (moōd) *n.* 1. (gram.) Group of forms in conjugation of verb serving to indicate function in which it is used, as INDICATIVE, IMPERATIVE, SUBJUNCTIVE **~** . 2. (logic) Any of the classes into which each of the figures of a valid categorical syllogism is divided.

moon (moōn) *n.* 1. Earth's satellite, a secondary planet reflecting light from sun to Earth during night, and revolving around Earth in one lunar month; first manned landing on moon was made on July 21, 1969, by U.S. astronauts Edwin Aldrin (1930–) and Neil Armstrong (1930–). 2. Aspect of moon at any one time as *full* **~**, *new* **~**, etc. 3. Any planetary satellite. 4. (poet.) Month. 5. **moon´beam**, ray of moonlight; **moon´calf**, born fool; **moon´-light**, light of moon (often attrib.);

*The open **moor**, Exmoor in the U.K., has rich grazing land and its heathland is the home of red deer, grouse, ponies and sheep.*

moon'lighting, working at a second job after one's regular working hours; **moon'lit**, lit up by moon; **moon'scape**, general appearance of the moon's surface or a pictorial representation of it; **moon'shine**, moonlight; (fig.) visionary talk or ideas; illicitly distilled or smuggled spirits, esp. whiskey; hence, **moon'shiner**, illicit distiller, smuggler of spirits; **moon'shot**, (launching of) rocket or spacecraft traveling to moon; **moon'stone**, variety of feldspar having a pearly luster, used as a gem; **moon'struck** (*adj.*), lunatic, distracted or dazed, a condition formerly supposed to be due to the moon's influence; **moon'walk**, astronaut's walk on moon's surface. **moon'y** *adj.* (**moon·i·er, moon·i·est**). Of, like, the moon; listless, stupidly dreamy. **moon** *v.i.* Go *about* dreamily or listlessly.

Moon·ie (mōō'nē) *n.* (pl. **Moon·ies**). (slang) Youthful follower of Rev. Sun Myung Moon (1920?–), Korean anticommunist evangelist proselytizing in the U.S. beginning in the 1970s.

Moor (moor) *n.* One of a Muslim people of mixed Berber and Arab race, inhabiting NW. Africa, who in the 8th c. conquered Spain (see also MOROCCO). **Moor'ish** *adj.*

moor[1] (moor) *n.* (Brit.) Tract of unenclosed, often heather-covered wasteland, or of similar land preserved for shooting (also **moor'land**); **moor'hen**, water hen. **moor'ish, moor'y** (**moor·i·er, moor·i·est**) *adjs.*

moor[2] (moor) *v.t.* Attach (boat etc.) by rope to shore or something fixed. **moor'age** *n.* Place, charge, for mooring. **moor'ings** *n.pl.* Place where vessel can be moored.

Moore[1] (moor), **Henry** (1898–). English semi-abstract sculptor.

Moore[2] (moor), **Marianne Craig** (1887–1972). American poet.

moose (mōōs) *n.* (pl. **moose**). Largest living species of deer (*Alces alces*) of Europe, Asia, and N. Amer.

moot (mōōt) *n.* (hist.) (Legislative or judicial) meeting. ~ *adj.* That can be argued, debatable; hence ~ **court**, in legal training, one in which students try hypothetical cases. **moot** *v.t.* Raise (question etc.) for discussion.

mop (mŏp) *n.* 1. Bundle of yarn etc. fixed to stick for use in cleaning, polishing, etc. 2. (slang) Head of hair, esp. of child. ~ *v.t.* (**mopped, mop'ping**). Clean or wipe with or as with mop; wipe

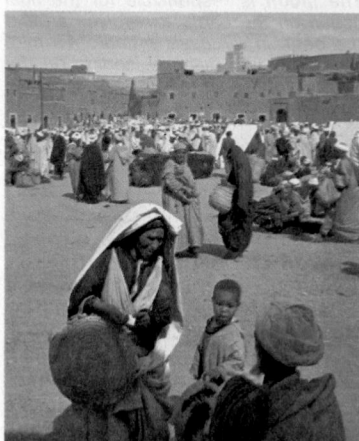

*The **Moors** of north-west Africa were originally called the Mauri and the name was modified when the area was occupied by the Romans. Those (above) are from south of the Atlas Mountains.*

*One of the U.K.'s most eminent sculptors, **Henry Moore,** carves monumental forms of a semi-abstract nature. This photograph shows the sculptor with one of his works.*

tears, sweat, etc., from (brow etc.); ~ **up**, wipe up (as) with mop; (slang) absorb (profits etc.), dispatch, finish off, make an end of; (mil.) complete occupation of (place) by capturing or killing remaining enemy troops; ~ **up the floor with**, (slang) inflict humiliating defeat on.

mope (mōp) *v.i.* (**moped, mop·ing**). Be dull, dejected, and spiritless. ~ *n.* Person who mopes; (chiefly pl.) gloomy state of mind. **mop'ish** *adj.* **mop'ish·ness** *n.*

mo·ped (mō'pĕd) *n.* Motorized bicycle.

mo·raine (morān') *n.* Debris of sand, clay, and boulders deposited by melting glacier.

mor·al (mŏr'al, mär'-) *adj.* Concerned with character or disposition, or with the distinction between right and wrong; morally good, virtuous, righteous; ~ **certainty**, probability so great as to admit of no reasonable doubt; ~ **courage**, courage to encounter odium, contempt, etc., rather than abandon right course; ~ **philosophy**, ethics; **M~ Rearmament**, name of the ideological campaign launched by Dr. Buchman in 1938 as an extension of the Oxford Group founded by him to foster morality in public and private life; ~ **support**, psychological support, encouragement; ~ **victory**, defeat, indecisive result, that eventually produces the moral effects of

Sir Thomas More, *the English states-*
man, humanist scholar and canonized
saint, was a friend of Colet, Erasmus
and other Renaissance figures. His
famous work 'Utopia' (1516) contains
his views of the ideal state.

...ctory. **mor′al·ly** *adv.* **moral** Moral teaching (of fable, story, ...c.); (pl.) habits or conduct from ...int of view of morality.

mo·rale (morăl′) *n.* Mental state ... condition, esp. (of troops) as ...gards discipline and confidence.

mor·al·ist (mor′alĭst, măr′-) *n.* ...ne who practices or teaches ...orality. **mor·al·is·tic** (moralĭs′-...k, măr-) *adj.*

mo·ral·i·ty (morăl′ĭtē, maw-) *n.* ...l. **-ties**). 1. Moral principles or ...les; moral conduct. 2. Kind of ...rama (popular in 16th c.) inculcat-...g moral or spiritual lesson.

mor·al·ize (mor′alīz, măr′-) *v.* ...ized, -iz·ing). Indulge in moral ...flection; interpret morally or ...mbolically. **mor·al·i·za·tion** ...noralĭzā′shon, măr′-) *n.*

mo·rass (morăs′) *n.* Wet ...wampy tract, bog.

mor·a·to·ri·um (morator′ēum, ...ŏr′-, măr-) *n.* (pl. **-to·ri·a** pr. ...ŏr′ēa, -tŏr′ēa, **-to·ri·ums**). Legal ...uthorization to debtor to postpone ...ayment.

Mo·ra·vi·a (morā′vēa, -rah′-). ...istoric region and former ...rovince of Czechoslovakia.

mo·ray (mor′ā, mŏr′ā, mōrā′, ...nawrā′) *n.* (pl. **-rays**). Any of

several dangerous marine eels of the family Muraenidae, found chiefly in tropical coastal waters.

mor·bid (mor′bĭd) *adj.* (of mind, ideas, etc.) Unwholesome, sickly; (med.) of the nature, or indicative, of disease. **mor′bid·ly** *adv.* **mor′-bid·ness** *n.* **mor·bid·i·ty** (mor-bĭd′ĭtē) *n.* Morbidness; prevalence of disease (in a district).

mor·dant (mor′dant) *adj.* (of sarcasm etc.) Caustic, biting; pungent, smarting; (of acids) corrosive. ~ *n.* Substance used for fixing textile dyes; acid used in etching. **mor·da·cious** (mordā′shus) *adj.* **mor·dac·i·ty** (mordăs′ĭtē), **mor·dan·cy** (mor′-dansē) *ns.*

Mor·dred (mor′drĭd) = MODRED.

more (mor, mōr) *adj.* (superl. **most**) & *n.* Greater number, quantity, or degree (of). ~ *adv.* To a greater extent, in a greater degree, additionally.

More (mor, mōr), **Sir Thomas**

(1478–1535). English statesman, author of *Utopia* (1516), a description, in Latin, of an imaginary perfect nation; he succeeded Wolsey as Lord Chancellor, 1529, but resigned in 1532, refusing to take any oath that would impugn the pope's authority or assume the justice of Henry VIII's divorce from Catherine of Aragon; he was therefore indicted of high treason, found guilty, and beheaded; canonized (as **St. Thomas ~**), 1935.

Mo·re·a (morē′a, maw-). Peloponnese.

mo·rel (morĕl′) *n.* Edible mushroom of genus *Morchella*.

more·o·ver (morō′ver, mor-, mor′ō, mor′ō-) *adv.* In addition.

mo·res (mor′āz, -ēz, mor′-) *n.pl.* Customs or conventions regarded as essential to or characteristic of a community. [L. pl. of *mos* custom]

Mor·gan[1] (mor′gan) *n.* (One of) breed of American trotting and saddle horses. [f. Justin *Morgan* (1747–98), who owned the stallion from which the breed descended]

Mor·gan[2] (mor′gan), **J(ohn) P(ierpont)** (1837–1913). Amer. financier, industrialist, and philanthropist; reorganized the railroads and formed U.S. Steel Corp.; art and rare book collector.

mor·ga·nat·ic (morganăt′ĭk) *adj.* (of a marriage) Between man of exalted rank and woman of lower rank in which it is provided that the wife and her children shall not share the rank or inherit the possessions of the husband. [OHG. *morgangeba* gift from husband to wife the morning after consummation of marriage]

Mor·gan le Fay (mor′gan le fā′). "Morgan the Fairy," a magician, sister of King Arthur.

morgue (morg) *n.* Building (esp. one formerly in Paris) in which bodies of persons found dead are held for identification; (journalism) repository of material for obituary notices and other articles.

mor·i·bund (mor′ibŭnd, măr′-) *adj.* In a dying state.

Mor·mon (mor′mon) *n.* Member of the Church of Jesus Christ of Latterday Saints, founded in New York State, 1830, by Joseph Smith of Vermont; he claimed that a parallel volume to the Bible, the "Book of Mormon," had been revealed to him, and that its author, the prophet Mormon, had been one of a race that had colonized America from Palestine in ancient times; the sect grew rapidly but met with hostility esp. for advocating polygamy (which they did until 1890); eventually, led by Brigham YOUNG[1], they migrated to Utah and there founded Salt Lake City in

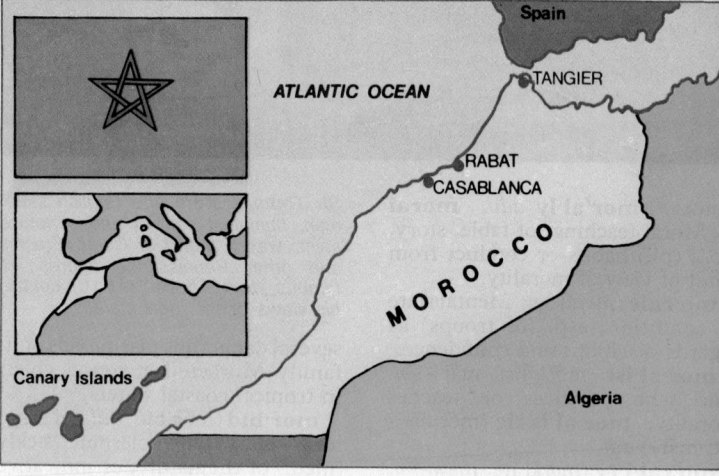

1847. **Mor′mon·ism** *n.*

morn (mōrn) *n.* (poet.) Morning; dawn.

morn·ing (mōr′nĭng) *n.* Early part of daytime, ending at noon or at time of midday meal; **good** ~, form of greeting; ~ **coat**, man's tail coat with front sloped away; ~ **dress**, men's formal daytime wear; ~**-glory**, Amer. plant of genus *Ipomoae*, with showy flowers; ~ **room**, sitting room, other than dining or drawing room; ~ **sickness**, nausea commonly experienced in morning in early months of pregnancy; ~ **star**, Venus (or other planet or bright star) seen to the east before sunrise.

Mo·roc·co (mᴏrŏk′ō). Country of NW. Africa, bounded on N. and

Morocco in North Africa is populated by Arabs and Berbers. Rabat is the capital, although the largest city is Casablanca. Phosphates are the country's major export. Top: Tan-Tan mosque. Above left: Bab Arguenaou, Marrakesh. Above: Map and flag.

W. by the Mediterranean Sea and Atlantic Ocean and on S. and E. by Algeria; inhabited by people descended from Berbers, Arabs, and Moors; formerly a French protectorate, with a Spanish sphere of influence; since 1956 an independent kingdom; capital, Rabat; summer capital, Tangier. **Mo·roc·can** (mᴏrŏk′an) *adj. & n.*

mo·roc·co (mᴏrŏk′ō) *n.* Fine flexible leather made orig. in Morocco, now also elsewhere, from

goatskins tanned with sum imitation of this made from c or sheepskins, grained to resem true morocco; **Levant** ~, hi grade, large-grained morocco, u for bookbinding.

mo·ron (mōr′ŏn, mōr′-) Adult whose mental developm corresponds to that of a norr average child between the ages 8 and 12; (colloq.) very stu person. **mo·ron·ic** (mᴏrŏn′ĭk)

mo·rose (mᴏrōs′) *adj.* S tempered, sullen, and unsoc **mo·rose′ly** *adv.* **mo·rose′ness**

mor·pheme (mōr′fēm) *n.* (philol.) Morphological elem considered in respect of functional relations to a lingui system.

William Morris, the Pre-Raphaelite painter and designer, produced wall-papers, furniture, stained glass and tex-iles. This 'Daffodil Chintz' is an example.

The **Morse code** which was invented by Samuel F. B. Morse of the U.S.A. in 1837 is still used in radio telegraphy. This Morse code operator is from Interpol in Paris.

Morning glory is a widely cultivated twining vine from temperate North America. It has broad, heart-shaped leaves and blue or purplish flowers.

Mor·phe·us (mōr′fēus, -fūs). (Rom. myth.) Son of Somnus, god of sleep, and himself the god of dreams.

mor·phi·a (mōr′fēa) n. Morphine.

mor·phine (mōr′fēn) n. Alkaloid narcotic principle of opium, used to alleviate pain.

mor·phin·ism (mōr′fĭnĭzem) n. Effect of morphine; excessive use of morphine.

mor·phol·o·gy (mōrfŏl′ojē) n. 1. Study of the form of animals and plants. 2. Study of the form of words, branch of philology dealing with inflection and word formation. 3. **social** ~, study of the structure of society, i.e. of social groups and institutions. **mor·pho·log·i·cal** (mōrfolŏj′ĭkal) adj. **mor·pho·log′i·cal·ly** adv. **mor·phol′o·gist** n.

Mor·ris[1] **Jes·up** (mōr′ĭs jĕs′up, măr′ĭs), **Cape.** Northernmost point of land in the world in N. Greenland on the Arctic Ocean.

Mor·ris[2] (mōr′ĭs, măr′-), **William** (1834-96). English designer, printer, poet, and prose writer.

Mor·ris (mōr′ĭs, măr′-) **chair.** Type of plain easy chair with adjustable back. [f. William MORRIS]

mor·ris (mōr′ĭs, măr′-) **dance.** English traditional dance in fancy costume, usu. representing characters from Robin Hood legend. [morys, var. of MOORISH]

mor·row (mōr′ō, măr′ō) n. (literary) Next day.

Morse (mŏrs), **Samuel Finley Breese** (1791-1872). Amer.

inventor of recording telegraph, deviser of the ~ **code**, a telegraphic alphabet in which letters are represented by combinations of short and long electrical contacts, sounds, flashes, etc. ("dots and dashes").

A	·—	S	···
B	—···	T	—
C	—·—·	U	··—
D	—··	V	···—
E	·	W	·——
F	··—·	X	—··—
G	——·	Y	—·——
H	····	Z	——··
I	··	1	·————
J	·———	2	··———
K	—·—	3	···——
L	·—··	4	····—
M	——	5	·····
N	—·	6	—····
O	———	7	——···
P	·——·	8	———··
Q	——·—	9	————·
R	·—·	0	—————

MORSE CODE

mor·sel (mōr′sel) n. Mouthful; small piece, fragment.

mor·tal (mōr′tal) adj. Subject to or causing death, fatal; (of enemy) implacable; (of sin) deadly, entailing spiritual death (opp. VENIAL); accompanying death, as ~ **agony**; ~ **enemy**, implacable enemy; ~ **fear**, dire fear. **mor′tal·ly** adv. **mortal** n. One who is subject to death; person.

mor·tal·i·ty (mōrtăl′ĭtē) n. (pl. -**ties**). Mortal nature; loss of life on large scale; death rate.

mor·tar (mōr′ter) n. 1. Hard vessel in which ingredients are

pounded with a pestle. 2. Short gun with large bore for throwing shells at high angles. 3. Mixture of lime, sand, and water used to make joints between stones and bricks in building; **mor′tarboard**, board for holding builders' mortar; cap with stiff flat square top, resembling this, worn as part of academic dress. **mortar** v.t. Bind, join (bricks or stones) together with mortar; fire upon with mortars.

mort·gage (mōr′gĭj) n. Conveyance of property as security for debt, with provision for re-conveyance on repayment of the sum secured; deed effecting this. ~ v.t. (-**gaged**, -**gag·ing**). Make over by mortgage; pledge in

Moscow, *capital of the U.S.S.R. and the country's chief communications center, has some magnificent examples of Byzantine architecture like the Cathedral of the Assumption pictured.*

For Muslims, the **mosque** is the center of community worship. The early mosques were modelled on the first built at Medina by Muhammad. Seen here is the interior of the Blue Mosque, Istanbul.

advance. **mort·ga·gee** (mōrgajē´) *n.* Holder of mortgage. **mort·ga·gor** (mōr´gajer) *n.* Person who pledges property etc. in mortgage. [OF. *mort gage* dead pledge]

mor·tice = MORTISE.

mor·ti·cian (mōrtĭsh´an) *n.* Undertaker.

mor·ti·fy (mōr´tĭfī) *v.* (**-fied, -fy·ing**). 1. Chasten (the body, passions, etc.) by self-denial. 2. Cause (person) to feel humiliated, wound (feelings). 3. (of flesh) Become gangrenous. **mor·ti·fi·ca·tion** (mōrtĭfĭkā´shon) *n.*

mor·tise, mor·tice (mōr´tĭs) *ns.* Hole or cavity into which end of some other part of framework or structure is fitted; ~ **lock,** lock housed with a mortice. **mortise** *v.t.* (**-tised, -tis·ing**). Cut mortice

in, fasten with mortice.

Mor·ton (mōr´ton), **Levi Parsons** (1824–1920). Vice president of the U.S. under Benjamin Harrison, 1889–93.

mor·tu·ar·y (mōr´chōōĕrē) *adj.* Of or for burial or death. ~ *n.* (pl. **-ar·ies**). Place for temporary reception of corpses.

Mo·sa·ic (mōzā´ĭk) *adj.* Of MOSES; ~ **law,** ancient Hebrew law contained in the Pentateuch.

mo·sa·ic (mōzā´ĭk) *n.* (Production of) picture or pattern of small cubes of colored stone, glass, etc. cemented together (also fig. of any diversified whole); (also ~ **disease**) plant virus disease causing mottled patches on leaves. **mosaic** *adj.* Of or like such work. ~ *v.t.* (**-icked, -ick·ing**). Decorate with mosaics; combine (as) into mosaic. **mo·sa·i·cist** (mōzā´ĭsĭst) *n.* [med. L. *mosaicus,* f. Gk *mousaikos* of the Muses]

mos·cha·tel (mŏskatĕl´, mŏs´katĕl) *n.* Small plant (*Adoxa moschatellina*), having pale green flowers with a musky smell.

Mos·cow (mŏs´kow, -kō) (Russ *Moskva*). Capital city of U.S.S.R. and Russian Soviet Federated Socialist Republic; capital of Russia from 1240 to 1703 (when the capital was transferred to St. Petersburg), and from 1918.

Mo·selle (mōzĕl´) *n.* Dry white wine produced in valley of the Moselle River, which rises in Vosges Mountains and flows into the Rhine at Coblenz.

Mo·ses[1] (mō´zĭz, -zĭs). Hebrew patriarch, the great lawgiver of the Jews; led them from Egypt after the captivity there; was inspired by God on Mount Sinai to write down the Ten Commandments on tablets of stone (Exod. 20); died before the Promised Land was reached (Joshua 1).

Moses,[2] **Anna Mary Robertson**: see GRANDMA MOSES.

mo·sey (mō´zē) *v.i.* (**-seyed, -sey·ing**). (colloq.) Walk (along, in leisurely or aimless manner.

Mos·lem (mŏz´lem, mŏs´-) (pl **-lems,** collect. **-lem**) = MUSLIM.

mosque (mŏsk, mawsk) *n* Muslim place of worship. [Fr *mosquée,* f. Arab. *masjid*]

mos·qui·to (moskē´tō) *n.* (pl **-toes**). Two-winged fly of the family Culicidae, gnat; (esp. species of *Culex, Anopheles,* and *Aëdes,* females of which have a long bloodsucking proboscis; ~ **net** fine-meshed net for keeping mosquitoes from room, bed, etc.

moss (maws, mŏs) *n.* (pl **moss·es**). 1. Any of a variety of small green plants of the class Musci within the division Bryophyta, growing in soft clusters on trees, rocks, or damp ground. 2. Any of a number of similar plants, such as club moss, Spanish moss, algae, and lichens. 3. **moss·back,** old shellfish or turtle with algae growing on its back; (colloq.) very old-fashioned or conservative person; **moss pink,** low-growing plant (*Phlox subulata*) forming mats of brilliant flowers ranging from pink to purple; **moss rose,** cabbage ose (*Rosa centifolia*), with mosslike growth on calyx and stalk. **moss'y** *adj.* (**moss·i·er, moss·i·est**). Of or like moss; overgrown with moss. **moss'i·ness** *n.*

most (mōst) *adj. & n.* Greatest number, quantity, or degree (of). ~ *adv.* In a great or the greatest degree. **most'ly** *adv.* For the most part.

mot (mō) *n.* (pl. **mots** pr. mōz). Witty saying; ~ **juste** (pr. zhüst), expression that conveys a desired shade of meaning with more precision than any other. [Fr.]

mote (mōt) *n.* Particle of dust, esp. speck seen floating in sunbeam.

mo·tel (mōtěl') *n.* Roadside hotel or group of separate small buildings for accommodation of motorists. [blend of *motor* + *hotel*]

mo·tet (mōtet') *n.* (mus.) Sacred musical composition, generally for unaccompanied voices; non-ecclesiastical work on similar lines. [Fr., dim. of *mot* word]

moth (mawth, mŏth) *n.* (pl. **moths** pr. mawdhz, mŏdhz, mawths, mŏths). Popular name for the majority of insects belonging to the order Lepidoptera, those not *butterflies*, distinguished from them by not having clubbed antennae and by being mostly nocturnal in habit; clothes moth or any other insect whose larvae feed on fabrics; (fig.) person hovering around temptation, as a moth flutters about light; **moth'ball**, small ball of naphthalene etc. used to keep moths away from fabrics etc.; (also) air-tight plastic cover sprayed on and enclosing working parts of gun mountings, machinery, etc. of ship; **moth-eaten**, injured by moths; (fig.) antiquated, time-worn. **moth'y** *adj.* (**moth·i·er, moth·i·est**). Infested by moths.

moth·er (mŭdh'er) *n.* Female parent (also transf.); head of female religious community (often ~ **superior**); (familiar) title of or form of address to elderly woman; incubator, artificial apparatus for rearing chickens; ~ **country**, country in relation to its colonies; native land; ~ **earth**, Earth as mother of its inhabitants; **M~ Goose**, legendary author of nursery rhyme collection published in England in 1760; **M~ Hubbard**, person in nursery rhyme; full loose dress, esp. that imposed by missionaries on native women in the Pacific; ~**-in-law**, wife's or husband's mother; ~**-of-pearl**, pearly iridescent lining of certain shells, as of oysters, mussels, etc., used in making buttons etc.; ~ **of**

vinegar, mucilaginous substance produced in vinegar during fermentation by bacteria (usually of the Acetobacter family); **Mother's Day**, day for honoring one's mother, in U.S. a Sunday in May; **mother ship**, ship acting as base for submarines, aircraft, etc.; **mother tongue**, one's native language. **moth'er·hood** *n.* **moth'er·less** *adj.* **mother** *v.* Take care of as a mother; **moth'-ering** *n.*

moth·er·ly (mŭdh'erlē) *adj.* Befitting or resembling a mother. **moth'er·li·ness** *n.*

mo·tif (mōtēf') *n.* Distinctive feature or dominant idea of a design or composition; (mus.) FIGURE.

mo·tile (mō'tǐl) *adj.* (zool., bot.). Capable of motion.

mo·tion (mō'shon) *n.* 1. Moving, movement; gait; gesture. 2. Proposition formally made in deliberative assembly; (law) application to judge or court for some rule or order of court. 3. ~ **picture**, continuous picture showing objects in motion, produced by projecting on to a screen a series of photographs of the scene with successive positions slightly changed. **mo'tion·less** *adj.* **motion** *v.* Make motion to direct or guide (person).

mo·ti·vate (mō'tivāt) *v.t.* (**-vat·ed, -vat·ing**). Supply a motive to, be the motive of. **mo·ti·**

*The **mosquito**, of which there are 2,500 species, is important in public health because of the blood-sucking habits of the females. They are known to transmit such diseases as yellow fever, malaria and dengue.*

*The **club moss** is widely distributed but tropical forms predominate. It is a low, spreading evergreen plant with stems covered with many small leaves. These sometimes resemble normal leaves but can be in clusters.*

***Moths** form with butterflies the insect order Lepidoptera. Generally, moths are active by night, butterflies by day.*

steering wheel
windscreen wipers
windscreen
clutch and brake fluid reservoi

trunk

hood
windscreen washer
cylinder head
carburettor
air cleaner

bumper

rear shock-absorber
rear spring

headlight

differential
propeller shaft
chassis
torsion bar

side-light/
flashing indicator

radiator

parts of a motor-car

wheel nut   brake hose   battery

car bodies   sedan   convertible   coupé   station wagon

The first engine-driven carriage was built by Daimler in 1886. The true automobile was developed between 1881–94. But it was not until the 1900s that **motorcars** were being mass-produced. Their design and production are a major industry throughout the world.

va·tion (mōtivā'shon) *n.*

mo·tive (mō'tĭv) *adj.* Tending to initiate motion; ~ **power**, esp. form of mechanical energy used to drive machinery. **motive** *n.* 1. That which induces a person to act, e.g. desire, fear, circumstance. 2. = MOTIF. **motive** *v.t.* (**-tived, -tiv·ing**). Motivate.

mot·ley (mŏt'lē) *adj.* Multicolored; heterogeneous. ~ *n.* Jester's motley garb.

mo·tor (mō'ter) *n.* Motive agent or force; motor muscle or nerve; apparatus or engine supplying motive power for vehicle or machinery, esp. internal combustion engine; automobile. ~ *adj.* 1. Giving, imparting, or producing motion; ~ **area**, that part of frontal lobe of mammal's brain from which muscular activity of opposite side of body is most easily evoked; ~ **nerve**, any nerve consisting of fibers that carry impulses from spinal cord or brain to induce contractions of muscle. 2. Driven by motor, as **mo'torbike** (colloq.), **mo'torboat, mo'tor-cycle; mo'torcar**, automobile. 3. Of, for, involving, motor vehicles; **mo'torcade**, procession of automobiles; **motor court**, motel; **mo'torman** (pl. **-men**), operator of subway train or streetcar. **motor** *v.* Go, convey, by automobile. **mo'tor·ist** *n.* Driver of automobile.

mo·tor·ize (mō'terīz) *v.t.* (**-ized, -iz·ing**). Supply or equip with motor transport; furnish with motor engine. **mo·tor·i·za·tion** (mōterĭzā'shon) *n.*

mot·tle (mŏt'el) *v.t.* (**-tled, -tling**). Mark or cover with spots or blotches.

mot·to (mŏt'ō) *n.* (pl. **-toes, -tos**). Inscription on some object, expressing appropriate sentiment or aspiration; maxim adopted as rule of conduct; short quotation prefixed to book or chapter,

The **Mountain goat** is a native of the Rockies in the U.S.A. They are closely related to antelopes, living above the timberline, in small bands.

suggestive of the contents.

mou·jik (mōozhĭk', mōo'zhĭk = MUZHIK.

mould (Brit.) = MOLD.

moult (Brit.) = MOLT.

mound (mownd) *n.* Embankment; heap, bank, hillock, of earth etc.; **M~ Builder**, one of prehistoric N. Amer. Ind. people who erected burial mounds and other earthworks chiefly in the Mississippi valley and southeastern U.S. **pitcher's ~**, elevated area from which baseball pitcher delivers ball to batter.

mount[1] (mownt) *n.* Mountain hill (abbrev. Mt. preceding name as **Mt. Everest**).

The image shows a labelled illustration of a glaciated mountain landscape with the following labels: shoulder, col, saddle, peak, cirque, arête, pass, névé, couloir, medial moraine, lateral moraine, chimney, crevasses, séracs, terminal moraine.

mount² (mownt) *v.* Ascend; imb on to; increase in amount; nount *to*; set on horseback, rnish (person) with saddle horse; t in position for use or exhibition; t (picture) in a MOUNT³; fit (gems c.) in gold etc.; fix (object) on icroscope slide; display specimen g. butterfly); put (play) on stage; iil.) organize (an offensive).

mount³ (mownt) *n.* Margin rrounding picture, card on which awing is mounted; ornamental etal parts of thing; horse for rson to ride.

moun·tain (mown´tĭn) *n.* atural elevation of Earth's surface impressive height, esp. over ooo ft. (300 m); large heap or le; ~ **ash**, tree of genus *Sorbus* ith delicate pinnate leaves and arlet berries; ~ **dew**, whiskey, p. illegally distilled; ~ **goat** (also **ocky M~ goat**), long-haired oofed mammal (*Oreamnos ericanus*) of Rocky Mountains ith yellowish-white hair and short rving black horns; ~ **laurel**, N. er. shrub (*Kalmia latifolia*) with

As the plates of the earth's crust shift, ***mountains*** *are formed. Then the forces of erosion — wind, water, heat, cold — attack the upthrust rocks and carve them into widely differing forms. Above: Effects of glacial erosion on a mountainous terrain.*

glossy, evergreen, poisonous leaves and umbels of white or pink flowers; ~ **lion**, tawny long-tailed cat (*Felis concolor*), larger than lynx and smaller than jaguar once common throughout N. and S. America, now rare in U.S. and Canada; also called cougar, catamount, panther, puma, etc.

moun·tain·eer (mowntĭnēr´) *n.* 1. One who lives in the mountains. 2. One who is skilled in climbing mountains.   ~ *v.i.*   Climb mountains.

moun·tain·ous (mown´tĭnŭs) *adj.* Abounding in mountains; huge.

moun·te·bank (mown´tebăngk) *n.* Itinerant quack (archaic); impudent charlatan. [It. *montambanco = monta in banco* mount on bench]

Mountaineering *as a sport was first begun in mid-19th century Switzerland by British tourists and local guides. Today nearly all the world's major peaks have been scaled.*

When a public figure dies, thousands — even tens of thousands — of people unite in their grief and take to the streets in **mourning.**

Moun·tie (mown´tē) *n.* (colloq.) Member of the Royal Canadian Mounted Police.

Mount Rush·more (rŭsh´mōr, -mŏr) **National Monument.** Portraits 60 ft. (18 m) high of presidents Washington, Jefferson, Lincoln, and T. Roosevelt carved in stone by John Gutzon Borglum on side of Mount Rushmore, in the Black Hills of South Dakota.

Mount Ver·non (vēr´nŏn). Estate and burial place of George and Martha Washington on the Potomac River near Washington, D.C.

mourn (mōrn, môrn) *v.* Sorrow, grieve, lament, esp. lament death of; put on mourning. **mourn´er** *n.* One who mourns; person attending funeral.

mourn·ful (mōrn´ful, môrn´-) *adj.* Exhibiting, expressing, or feeling mourning or deep sorrow. **mourn´ful·ly** *adv.* **mourn´ful·ness** *n.*

mourn·ing (mōr´nĭng, môr´-) *n.* (esp.) Feeling or expression of sorrow; (wearing of) black clothes as sign of bereavement; ~ **dove,** wild dove (*Zenaidura macroura*) of N. Amer., grayish brown with delicate pink on breast and having a distinctly sad call; also called turtledove.

mouse (mows) *n.* (pl. **mice** pr. mīs). Small rodent esp. of genus *Mus*; timid or shy person; ~-**ear,** hawkweed; **mouse´trap,** trap for catching mice. **mous·y, mous·ey** (mow´sē, -zē) *adjs.* (**mous·i·er, mous·i·est**). **mouse** (mowz) *v.i.* Hunt for or catch mice; search *about* for something. **mous´er** *n.* Animal that catches mice, esp. cat.

mousse (mōōs) *n.* Dish of whipped cream, or cream and beaten eggs etc., flavored with fruit etc. or containing meat or fish. [Fr., = "froth"]

mous·tache = MUSTACHE.

mouth (mowth) *n.* (pl. **mouths** pr. mowdhz). External orifice in head, with cavity behind it containing apparatus for mastication and organs of vocal utterance; person viewed as consumer of food; opening or entrance of anything; outfall of river; ~ **organ** = HARMONICA; **mouth´piece,** part of some portable wind instruments placed before or between lips; similar part of tobacco pipe; part of telephone spoken into; one who speaks on behalf of others; (slang) lawyer; **mouth-to-mouth,** applied to a method of resuscitation in which a person places his mouth on the patient's and breathes expired air into his lungs; **down in the mouth,** (colloq.) having an unhappy face; depressed, woebegone; **mouth´wash,** liquid antiseptic and breath sweetener for use in cleaning the mouth; **mouth-watering** (*adj.*), highly appetizing; also fig. **mouth** (mowdh) *v.* Utter or speak pompously, declaim; take (food) in, touch with, mouth; train (horse) to answer to bit and reins; grimace. **mouth´ful** *n.* (pl. **-fuls**). Quantity that fills the mouth; small quantity (of food etc.); something difficult to say; (slang) something important said.

mouth·y (mow´dhē, -thē) *adj.* (**mouth·i·er, mouth·i·est**). Ranting, bombastic; prolix.

mou·ton (mōō´tŏn) *n.* (Coat of) sheepskin, sheared and treated to resemble seal or beaver.

mov·a·ble, move·a·ble (mōō´vabel) *adjs.* That can be moved; (of property) that can be removed, personal as opp. to *real*. **mov·a·bil·i·ty** (mōōvabĭl´ĭtē), **mov´a·ble·ness** *ns.*

move (mōōv) *v.* (**moved, mov·ing**). Change position (of); change residence; stir; rouse; cau(bowels) to act; affect with emotio propose as resolution; **movi picture** (see MOTION); **movi staircase,** escalator. **move** Moving of piece at chess etc.; w in which piece is allowed to mo act of moving from rest; chan of abode or premises; device, tric action to some end.

move·ment (mōōv´ment) Moving; moving mechanism watch etc.; principal division (usu. instrumental) musical wor combined action or endeavor body of persons for some spec end, e.g. *the women's rights* ~.

mov·er (mōō´ver) *n.* Individu or company whose business it to move contents of a house, offic etc. from one location to anothe **prime** ~, initial source (natu or mechanical) of motive powe author of fruitful idea.

mov·ie (mōō´vē) *n.* (colloc Moving picture.

mow[1] (mō) *n.* Stack of hay, cor etc.

mow² (mō) v. (**mowed, mown, ow·ing**). Cut down grass, corn, :., with scythe or machine; (fig.) :, sweep down, like grass; **owing machine**, machine for :tting grass etc. **mow'er** n. :rson who mows grass etc.; :wing machine, lawn mower.

Mo·zam·bique (mōzambēk'). :rmer Portuguese colony in E. :rica; independent 1975; capital, :urenço Marques.

Mo·zart (mō'tsärt), **Wolfgang :nadeus** (1756–91). Austrian :nposer of symphonies, chamber :sic, and such operas, as The :arriage of Figaro, Don Giovanni, :e Magic Flute.

moz·za·rel·la (mŏtserĕl'a, mō-) : Soft, white Italian cheese, often :d melted in cooking.

M.P. abbrev. Member of Parlia-:nt; military police.

m.p. abbrev. Melting point.

mpg, m.p.g., mph, m.p.h. :brevs. Miles per gallon, per hour.

Mr. (mĭs'ter) n. (pl. **Messrs.**). :le prefixed to surname of man :h no superior title. [abbrev. :MISTER]

Mrs. (mĭs'ĭz) n. (pl. **Mes·-:mes, Mmes.**) Title prefixed to :me of married woman with no :perior title. [abbrev. of MISTRESS] :MS abbrev. 1. Mississippi. 2. :ultiple sclerosis.

MS. abbrev. (pl. **MSS.**). Manuscript.

Ms., Ms (mĭz) ns. Title prefixed to a woman's name, used to avoid distinguishing between married and unmarried women. [comb. of MRS., MISS²]

ms. abbrev. (pl. **mss.**). Manuscript; milliseconds.

MS. abbrev. 1. Master of Science. 2. Multiple sclerosis.

msec abbrev. Millisecond(s).

MSG abbrev. Monosodium glutamate.

Msgr. abbrev. Monseigneur; Monsignor.

M.Sgt. abbrev. Master Sergeant.

M.S.L. abbrev. Mean sea level.

MST, M.S.T. abbrevs. Mountain Standard Time.

M.S.W. abbrev. Master of Social Work.

MT abbrev. Montana.

Mt. abbrev. Mount.

M.T. abbrev. 1. Metric ton. 2. Mountain Time.

mu (mū, moō) n. Thirteenth (later 12th) letter of Greek alphabet (M, μ), corresponding to m; μ, (phys. etc.) symbol for one millionth; μ, mu, (radio) symbol

*The **Mounties** claim that they always get their man. Founded in 1873, they are today responsible for the enforcement of Federal laws in all Canada except Quebec and Ontario.*

*Almost every part of the world has at least one kind of **mouse**, native or introduced. Mice can be solitary or social, and vary widely in their preferred diets.*

for amplification factor of a valve; ~ **meson**: see MUON.

much (mŭch) adj. & n. Great number, quantity, or degree (of); **make ~ of**, gain much advantage from; give much attention to; attach much importance to. ~ adv. In a great degree; pretty nearly; for a large part of one's time. **much'-ness** n.

mu·ci·lage (mū'sĭlĭj) n. Viscous substance obtained from plants by maceration; adhesive substance. **mu·ci·lag·i·nous** (mūsĭlăj'inus) adj.

muck (mŭk) n. Farmyard manure; (colloq.) dirt, filth. ~ v. Manure; ~ **about**, (Brit. slang) loaf; go about aimlessly; ~ **out**, clean out (stable etc.); ~ **up**, (slang) bungle. **muck'y** adj. (**muck·i·er, muck·i·est**).

muck·a·muck (mŭk'amŭk), **muck·e·ty·muck** (mŭk'etēmŭk) ns. (slang, often derog.) Important person.

muck·rake (mŭk'rāk) v.i. (**-raked, -rak·ing**). Seek out and expose, particularly through the media, corruption in government or business. **muck'rak·er** n.

mu·cous (mū'kus) adj. Secret-ing or covered by mucus; ~ **membrane**, inner surface lining of hollow organs of the body. **mu·cos·i·ty** (mūkŏs'ĭtē) n.

mu·cus (mū'kus) n. Sticky secretion of mucous glands usu. forming a protective covering for mucous membrane.

mud (mŭd) n. Wet soft soil or earthy matter, mire; ~ **bath**, bath in mud impregnated with salts, as a remedy for rheumatism etc.; ~ **flat(s)**: see FLAT² n.; **mud'guard**, guard over wheel of cycle or other vehicle as protection against mud; **mud pie**, mud formed by children in the shape of a pie; **mud'-slinging**, (fig.) personal abuse, invective.

mud·dle (mŭd'el) v. (**-dled, -dling**). Bewilder, confuse; bungle; act in confused, un-methodical, and ineffective manner; ~ **through**, finish successfully despite lack of method. **mud'dleheaded** adj. Mixed up in one's thinking; bungling. **mud-dle** n. Muddled condition.

mud·dy (mŭd'ē) adj. (**-di·er, -di·est**). Like mud; covered with, abounding in, mud; thick, turbid; not clear, mentally confused. **mud'di·ly** adv. **mud'di·ness** n. **muddy** v. (**-died, -dy·ing**). Make or become muddy.

mu·ez·zin (mūĕz'ĭn, moō-) n. Official of Muslim mosque who proclaims hour of prayer from

One of the U.K.'s most spectacular wild plants, common mullein can grow to 7ft. tall with long spikes of yellow flowers rising above large oval leaves clothed with dense, silvery down.

minaret. [Arab. *mu'addin* (*'addana* proclaim)]

muff[1] (mŭf) *n.* Tubular covering esp. of fur into which hands are thrust to keep them warm.

muff[2] (mŭf) *v.t.* Bungle, make muddle of; miss (catch at baseball).

muf·fin (mŭf'ĭn) *n.* Bread made with eggs, usu. baked in cup-shaped mold, often with berries in mix; **English** ~, light, flat, round spongy cake, eaten toasted and buttered.

muf·fle (mŭf'el) *n.* Chamber or covering in furnace or kiln that protects contents from direct contact with fire. ~ *v.t.* (**-fled, -fling**). Wrap, cover *up* for warmth; wrap up (oars, bell, drum, etc.) to deaden sound; wrap up (head of person) to prevent his speaking; repress, deaden, sound of (curse etc., usu. in past part.).

muf·fler (mŭf'ler) *n.* Wrap or scarf worn around neck for warmth; silencer in engine.

muf·ti (mŭf'tē) *n.* (pl. **-tis**). 1. Muslim priest or expounder of law. 2. Plain clothes worn by anyone who has the right to wear a uniform. [Arab. *al-muftī* official expounder of Islamic law]

mug (mŭg) *n.* 1. Drinking vessel, usu. cylindrical and with handle. 2. (slang) Face, mouth. 3. (slang) Stupid person, dupe. 4. (slang) Hoodlum, thug, ruffian. ~ *v.t.* (**mugged, mug·ging**). (slang) 1. Photograph (a person) for police records, official identification, etc. 2. Rob (a person in street), esp. with violence. ~ *v.i.* (slang) Make faces, esp. before an audience, camera, etc. **mug'shot**

n. (slang) Photograph of face for official identification.

mug·ger (mŭg'er) *n.* 1. Broadsnouted Indian crocodile (*Crocodylus palustris*) venerated by many Hindus. 2. (slang) One who assaults others on the street and robs them. 3. (slang) Person who makes faces, esp. before an audience, camera, etc.

mug·gy (mŭg'ē) *adj.* (**-gi·er, -gi·est**). (of weather etc.) Damp, warm, and oppressive. **mug'gi·ness** *n.*

mug·wump (mŭg'wŭmp) *n.* Great man, chief; political independent, (esp.) Republican who refused to support his party's nominee in presidential election of 1884. [N. Amer. Ind.]

Mu·ham·mad (mōōhăm'ad, -hah'mad) (c570–632). Prophet of Islam, whose utterances are preserved in the KORAN; born at Mecca and buried at Medina; declared himself the Prophet, c611, and sought to turn his fellow Arabs from the local gods whom they then worshipped to the ancient religion of Abraham and other Old Testament patriarchs and prophets; meeting opposition in Mecca, he fled to Medina in 622; this flight (the HEGIRA) is regarded as beginning the Muslim era. **Mu·ham'mad·an** *adj.* & *n.* Muslim.

Mu·ham·mad A·li (mōōhăm'ad ah'lē, -hah'mad) (1943–). Name assumed by Cassius Clay, U.S. prizefighter, three times world heavyweight champion.

Muir (mūr), **John** (1838–1914). Scottish-born Amer. naturalist, conservationist, and explorer; influential in establishing national park system and forest reserves; **Muir Woods**, national monument of giant redwood trees in California, N. of San Francisco.

mu·lat·to (mulăt'ō, mū-, -lah'tō) *n.* (pl. **-toes**). Offspring of a white and a black parent. ~ *adj.* Of brownish-yellow color, as mulattoes. [Span. *mulato* young mule]

mul·ber·ry (mŭl'bĕrē, -berē) *n.* (pl. **-ries**). Tree of genus *Morus*, with dark purple or white edible berries, and leaves that are used for feeding silkworms; fruit of this; dark purple color.

mulch (mŭlch) *n.* Half-rotten straw, grass mowings, leaves, etc., spread on the ground to protect roots of plants or trees or conserve moisture etc. ~ *v.t.* Cover or spread with mulch.

mulct (mŭlkt) *v.t.* 1. Punish (person) by a fine; deprive (person *of*). 2. Swindle (person); obtain by swindling. ~ *n.* Fine imposed for offense.

mule[1] (mūl) *n.* 1. Offspring of male ass and mare; hence, stupid

The mulberry is grown all over world both for its red, white, or bla fruit — according to species — and the leaves of the Oriental species which silkworms feed.

or obstinate person. 2. Kind spinning jenny.

mule[2] (mūl) *n.* Kind of u backless slipper.

mu·le·teer (mūletēr') *n.* M driver.

mul·ish (mū'lĭsh) *adj.* Obstina as a mule, intractable. **mul'ish** *adv.* **mul'ish·ness** *n.*

mull[1] (mŭl) *v.t.* Make a m or muddle of; ruminate, pond *over.* ~ *n.* Mess, muddle.

mull[2] (mŭl) *v.t.* Make (win beer) into hot drink with sug spices, yolk of egg, etc.

mul·lah (mŭl'a, mōōl'a, mōō *n.* Muslim learned in theology a sacred law; expounder of t Koran. [Hind. *mulla*, ult. adapt f. Arab. *mawlā*]

mul·lein (mŭl'ĭn) *n.* Herbacec plant of genus *Verbascum*, w woolly leaves and erect woolly sp of yellow flowers.

Mul·ler (mŭl'er), **Johann**: s REGIOMONTANUS.

mul·let (mŭl'ĭt) *n.* (pl. **-le** collect. **-let**). Any of seve spiny-rayed edible fishes of t family Muglidae, distribut worldwide in tropical a temperate waters, esp. the strip ~ (*Mugil cephalus*) of the Am gulf coast and Florida Keys.

mul·li·ga·taw·ny (mŭ gataw'nē) *n.* Highly flavored Indian soup, made with cur powder and hot seasonings; **paste**, curry paste used for th [Tamil *milagutannir* pepper wat

mul·lion (mŭl'yon) *n.* Verti shaft dividing lights in a windo **mul'lioned** *adj.* Furnished w mullions.

multi- *prefix.* Much, many.

mul·ti·far·i·ous (mŭltĭfār´ēus) *adj.* Having great variety. **mul·ti·far´i·ous·ly** *adv.* **mul·ti·far´i·ous·ness** *n.*

mul·ti·form (mŭl´tĭfôrm) *adj.* Having many forms; manifold. **mul·ti·for·mi·ty** (mŭltĭfôr´mĭtē) *n.* Variety, diversity (opp. *uniformity*).

mul·ti·lat·er·al (mŭltĭlăt´eral) *adj.* Having many sides; (of agreement, treaty, etc.) in which more than two sides or nations participate; ~ **trade**, trade carried on among several countries without the necessity of balancing trade or payments between them.

mul·ti·mil·lion·aire (mŭltĭ- nĭlyonār´, mŭltĭ-) *n.* Person with a fortune of several millions (of dollars, pounds, etc.).

mul·tip·a·ra (mŭltĭp´era) *n.* (pl. **·a·rae** pr. -erē) (med.) Pregnant woman who has borne one child or more.

mul·tip·a·rous (mŭltĭp´erus) *adj.* Producing more than one at birth.

mul·ti·par·tite (mŭltĭpär´tīt) *adj.* Divided into many parts.

mul·ti·ple (mŭl´tipel) *adj.* Of many parts, elements or individual components; (math.) repeated, occurring more than once; (elect.) of a circuit with a number of parallel conductors; ~ **choice**, (of question in examination) accompanied by several possible answers from which correct answer is to be selected. ~ **sclerosis**, chronic progressive sclerosis of brain and spinal cord. **multiple** *n.* (math.) Number or quantity containing another an exact number of times; **lowest (least) common** ~, abbrev. L.C.M.) least quantity that contains two or more given quantities exactly, as 12 is the L.C.M. of 3 and 4.

mul·ti·plex (mŭl´tipleks) *adj.* Manifold, of many elements; involving simultaneous transmission of several messages along a channel of communication.

mul·ti·pli·a·ble (mŭl´tiplīabel), **mul·ti·plic·a·ble** (mŭltiplĭk´abel) *adjs.* Capable of being multiplied.

mul·ti·pli·cand (mŭltiplĭkănd´) *n.* (math.) Number that is to be multiplied by another.

mul·ti·pli·ca·tion (mŭltiplĭkā´- shon) *n.* Multiplying; (math.) finding the quantity produced by taking a given quantity (MULTI- PLICAND) as many times as there are units in another given quantity MULTIPLIER); ~ **table**, set of numbers, usu. 1 to 12, with the products of multiplication by the same numbers successively. **mul·ti·pli·ca·tive** (mŭl´tiplĭkātĭv, mŭltiplĭk´a-) *adj.*

mul·ti·plic·i·ty (mŭltiplĭs´ĭtē) *n.*

(pl. **-ties**). Manifold variety; great number *of.*

mul·ti·pli·er (mŭl´tiplīer) *n.* That which multiplies; (math.) number by which another number is multiplied; (elect.) device for multiplying intensity of force, current, etc., to bring it to a desired strength; (econ.) proportion of an increment of a consumer's income to the consequent increment of saving.

mul·ti·ply (mŭl´tiplī) *v.* (**-plied, -ply·ing**). Produce large number of (instances etc.); breed (animals), propagate (plants); (math.) perform process of multiplication (symbol ×).

mul·ti·tude (mŭl´tĭtoōd, -tūd) *n.* Great number; throng; **the** ~, the many, the common people. **mul·ti·tu·di·nous** (mŭltĭtoō´- dinus, -tū´-) *adj.* **mul·ti·tu´di·nous·ly** *adv.* **mul·ti·tu´di·nous·ness** *n.*

mum (mŭm) *adj.* Strictly silent.

mum·ble (mŭm´bel) *v.* (**-bled, -bling**). Speak or utter indistinctly or with lips partly closed. ~ *n.*

mum·bo jum·bo (mŭm´bō jŭm´bō) *n.* (pl. **mum·bo jum·bos**). Meaningless ritual; mystifying or obscure language etc., intended to confuse. [f. name of grotesque idol said to have been worshipped by certain black tribes]

mum·mer (mŭm´er) *n.* Actor

In ancient Egypt the bodies of the nobility were preserved as **mummies***. The soft parts were removed and the rest soaked in various resins, which were later injected into the body, before bandaging.*

in traditional popular performance in dumb show. **mum´mer·y** *n.* (pl. **-mer·ies**). Mummer's performance; buffoonery.

mum·mi·fy (mŭm´ĭfī) *v.t.* (**-fied, -fy·ing**). Make into a mummy. **mum·mi·fi·ca·tion** (mŭmĭfĭkā´shon) *n.*

mum·my[1] (mŭm´ē) *n.* (pl. **-mies**). Dead body preserved from decay by embalming, esp. one so preserved by the ancient Egyptians; dried-up body; rich brown pigment obtained from bitumen; ~ **case**, case of wood, modeled to shape of human body, in which Egyptian mummies were placed for burial. [Arab. *mŭmīyā'*, med. L. *mumia* (Pers. *mŭm* wax)]

mum·my[2] (mŭm´ē) *n.* (pl. **-mies**). (Child's word for) mother.

mumps (mŭmps) *n.* Virus infection that causes acute inflammation of parotid gland and consequent swelling of neck and face.

munch (mŭnch) *v.* Eat with noticeable action of the jaws.

mun·dane (mŭndān´, mŭn´dān) *adj.* Worldly; dull, routine. **mun·dane´ly** *adv.* **mun·dane´- ness** *n.*

Mu·nich (mū´nĭk) (*Ger.* **München**). City of West Germany; ~ **Pact**, agreement among England, France, Germany, and Italy, signed at Munich on Sept. 29, 1938, under which part of Czechoslovakia was ceded to Germany.

mu·nic·i·pal (mūnĭs´ipal) *adj.* Of the local self-government or corporate government of city or town. **mu·nic´i·pal·ly** *adv.*

The beautiful **murex** — related to the whelk — is today valued for its shell. However, 2,000 years ago its flesh was processed to yield a famous, highly prized dye, 'Tyrian purple'.

mu·nic'i·pal·ism, mu·nic'i·pal·ist ns.

mu·nic·i·pal·i·ty (mūnĭsipăl'ĭtē) n. (pl. **-ties**). Town, district, having local self-government; governing body of this.

mu·nif·i·cent (mūnĭf'ĭsent) adj. Splendidly generous. **mu·nif'i·cent·ly** adv. **mu·nif'i·cence** n.

mu·ni·tion (mūnĭsh'on) n. (pl. exc. in comb.). Military weapons, ammunition, equipment, and stores. ~ v. Provide, furnish with munitions.

mu·on (mū'ŏn) n. (phys.) Mu meson, meson having a mass of 206.7 times that of the electron.

mu·ral (mūr'al) adj. Of, on a wall; ~ **crown**, (Rom. antiq.) garland given to soldiers who first scaled walls of a besieged town. **mural** n. A picture painted on a wall.

Mur·chi·son (mēr'chĭson) **Falls**. Waterfall in the Victoria Nile, dropping to Lake Albert in Uganda; **Murchison River**, river in W. Australia flowing into Indian

Ocean.

mur·der (mēr'der) n. Unlawful killing of person with malice aforethought, dist. from (accidental or justifiable) homicide and manslaughter. ~ v.t. Kill unlawfully and with malice aforethought; massacre, butcher; (fig.) spoil by bad execution, representation, etc. **mur'der·er** n. (fem. **mur'der·ess**). **mur'der·ous** adj. **mur'der·ous·ly** adv.

mu·rex (mūr'ĕks) n. (pl. **mu·ri·ces** pr. mūr'isēz, **mu·rex·es**). Mollusc of genus M~, allied to whelks, yielding purple dye.

murk (mērk) n. Darkness, gloom. ~ adj. (archaic, poet.) Dark, gloomy; **murk'y** adj. (**murk·i·er, murk·i·est**). Dark, gloomy; (of darkness) thick.

murk'i·ly adv. **murk'i·ness** n.

mur·mur (mēr'mer) n. Subdued continuous sound; (med.) sound of this kind heard in auscultation; muttered grumbling or repining; subdued or nearly inarticulate speech. **mur'mur·ous** adj. **mur'mur·ous·ly** adv. **mur·mur** v. Produce murmur; speak or say in murmur.

Mur·phy's (mēr'fēz) **Law**. (facetious) Engineers' observation that anything that can go wrong will go wrong.

Mur·ray (mēr'ē, mŭr'ē), **Sir James** (1837–1915). Scottish philologist, editor of A New (later known as The) Oxford English Dictionary.

mur·rhine (mēr'ĭn, -īn) adj. ~ **glass**, Modern delicate glassware from the East, with small particles of colored metal embedded in it. [L. murra substance of which precious vases were made]

mus·ca·dine (mŭs'kadĭn, -dīn) = MUSCAT.

mus·ca·rine (mŭs'kerĭn, -erēn) n. Poisonous alkaloid obtained from fungus Amanita muscaria. **mus·ca·rin·ic** (mŭskerĭn'ĭk) adj.

Mus·cat (mŭskăt'). Capital and a seaport of Oman on the Gulf of Oman.

mus·cat (mŭs'kăt) n. Kind of grape with flavor or odor of musk.

mus·ca·tel (mŭskatĕl', mŭs'katĕl) n. Muscat; strong sweet white wine prepared from muscats; muscat raisin.

mus·cle (mŭs'el) n. Contractile fibrous band or bundle producing motion in animal body, muscular strength; **mus'clebound**, having the muscles stiff and enlarged owing to excessive exercise. **muscle** v.i. (**-cled, -cling**). (slang) Force one's way in. [L. musculus little mouse, f. fancied resemblance to a mouse]

Mus·co·vy (mŭs'kovē). (hist.) Principality of Moscow; Russia in the period (16th and 17th centuries) when that principality was dominant; ~ **duck**, tropical Amer. duck (Cairina moschata) with slightly musky smell. **Mus·co·vite** (mŭs'kovīt) adj. & n. (Native, inhabitant) of Muscovy or of Moscow. [Muscovia, Latinized form of Russ. Moskva Moscow]

mus·cu·lar (mŭs'kyuler) adj. Of, in, the muscles; having well-developed muscles; ~ **atrophy**, ~ **dystrophy**, wasting disorders of the muscles. **mus·cu·lar·i·ty** (mŭskyulăr'ĭtē) n.

mus·cu·la·ture (mŭs'kyulacher)

stored food is converted into energy in muscle tissue: all animal movement, except in unicellular creatures, depends on this process. In higher animals, some muscles directly obey the will while others maintain the body's functions.

n. System, arrangement of muscles.

Muse (mūz) *n.* (Gk. and Rom. myth.) One of the nine goddesses who presided over the arts and sciences (Calliope, epic poetry; Clio, history; Erato, erotic poetry; Euterpe, lyric poetry; Melpomene, tragedy; Polyhymnia, sacred song; Terpsichore, dancing; Thalia,

1. Sternohyoid	18. Gastrocnemius	30. Pectoralis major	48. Peroneus brevis
2. Trapezius	19. Soleus	31. Triceps	49. Splenius capitis
3. Pectoralis minor	20. Flexor digitorum longus	32. Serratus anterior	50. Levator scapulae
4. Triceps	21. Occipitofrontalis frontal	33. External oblique	51. Rhombodeus major
5. Biceps	22. Occipitofrontalis rear	34. Internal oblique	52. Supraspinatus
6. Rectus abdominus	23. Orbicularis oculi	35. Extensor digitorum	53. Infraspinatus
7. Brachioradialis	24. Levator labii superioris alaeque nasi	36. Bicipital aponeurosis	54. Teres minor
8. Pronator teres	25. Levator anguli oris	37. Gluteus medius	55. Teres major
9. Flexor carpi ulnaris	26. Risorius	38. Gluteus maximus	56. Triceps
10. Flexor digitorum superficialis	27. Depressor labii inferioris	39. Sartorius	57. Longissimus thoracis
11. Flexor carpi radialis	28. Sternocleido-mastoid	40. Rectus femoris	58. Serratus posterior
12. Flexor pollicis brevis	29. Deltoid	41. Gracilis	59. Brachioradialis
13. Iliacus		42. Semitendinosus	60. Flexor carpi ulnaris
14. Adductor longus		43. Biceps femoris	61. Gluteus minimus
15. Gracilis		44. Vastus lateralis	62. Piriformis
16. Vastus medialis		45. Gastrocnemius	63. Gemellus
17. Vastus lateralis		46. Tibialis anterior	64. Biceps femoris
		47. Soleus	

comedy; Urania, astronomy); they were daughters of Zeus and Mnemosyne, born at the foot of Mt. Olympus; Mt. Helicon was sacred to them, and Mt. Parnassus was one of their chief seats; hence, **m~**, poet's inspiring goddess, poet's genius.

muse (mūz) *v.i.* (**mused, mus·-ing**). Ponder, reflect (*on*); gaze meditatively (*on* scene etc.).

mu·sette (mūzĕt′) *n.* Small soft-toned French bagpipe; dance for this; pastoral; reed stop on organ; ~ **bag**, small knapsack.

mu·se·um (mūzē′um) *n.* Building or room for storing and exhibiting objects illustrative of antiquities, natural history, the arts, etc.; ~ **piece**, object of quality fit for a museum; person or thing regarded merely as a survival or curiosity. [Gk. *mouseion* seat of the Muses]

mush (mŭsh, *dial.* mŏosh) *n.* Soft pulp; porridge made from corn meal; any soft, thick mass. **mush′y** *adj.* (**mush·i·er, mush·i·est**). Soft, pulpy; (fig.) weakly sentimental, rubbishy. **mush′i·ness** *n.*

mush·room (mŭsh′rŏom) *n.* Popular name of any edible fungus,

These Rwandan **musicians** *bridge the gap between religion and art. In primitive societies song and instrumental music are integrated with the surrounding world in both its material and spiritual aspects.*

esp. *Agaricus campestris*, the common field mushroom, proverbial for its rapid growth; (fig.) upstart; (attrib.) growing suddenly, as ~ *growth, suburb*, etc; ~ **cloud**, mushroom-shaped cloud, esp. resulting from nuclear explosion. **mushroom** *v.i.* Have or assume the shape of a mushroom; spring up rapidly. **mush′room·-ing** *n.* Gathering mushrooms.

mu·sic (mū′zĭk) *n.* Art of combining sounds for reproduction by the voice or various kinds of musical instruments in rhythmic, melodic, and harmonic form so as to express thought or feeling and affect the emotions; sounds so produced; pleasant sound, e.g. song of a bird, murmur of a stream, etc.; written or printed score of musical composition; **face the ~**, face the consequences of actions etc. without shirking; ~ **drama**, Wagnerian form of opera in which music and the other elements are

combined on equal terms and mad subservient to dramatic expression ~ **box**, mechanical music instrument containing a revolvin cylinder furnished with small peg that strike on strips of meta graduated to produce differen notes; ~ **hall**, theater for variet entertainments. [Gk. *mousik (tekhnē)* (art) of the Muses (*Mou* Muse)]

mu·si·cal (mū′zĭkal) *adj.* O resembling, fond of or skilled i music; melodious, harmonious; s to, accompanied by, music; ~ **chairs**, parlor game in which number of players move around row of chairs, less by one in numbe than the players, until music cease when the one who finds no sea is eliminated, and a chair is remove before the next round; ~ **comedy** (also **musical**) light dramat entertainment of songs, dialogu and dancing connected by a plo ~ **glasses**, set of glasses, graduate in tone, struck by small stick similar instrument with glass bow or tubes; ~ **instrument**, any o a variety of instruments with whic music is produced, usu. classifie as *string, wind*, and *percussion*

flintlock musket circa 1800

butt — flintlock — barrel — stock — bayonet stud
trigger — ramrod

blunderbuss circa 1750

pan cover screw and flash-guard support
pan cover — serpent — iron pyrites
lockplate — pan
matchlock circa 1650

dog — dog spring
wheel enclosed in wheel case
wheel-lock circa 1650

upper jaw — flint — steel
cock
pan cover spring
flintlock circa 1740

The musket was the infantryman's long-range weapon for nearly 300 years. The design of the lock changed (match–wheel–flint–percussion) but the basic principle remained.

Many types of mussel are present in both sea and fresh waters throughout the world. Particular species are collected for culinary use, but others may also be eaten.

mu'si·cal·ly *adv.* **mu'si·cal·ness** **musical** *n.* Film or theatrical piece (not opera or operetta) of which music is essential element; musical comedy.

mu·si·cian (mūzĭsh′an) *n.* person skilled in art or practice of music. **mu·si′cian·ship** *n.* Skill, insight, in interpreting and performing music.

mu·si·col·o·gy (mūzĭkŏl′ojē) *n.* all study of music except that directed to proficiency in performance or composition. **mu·si·co·log·i·cal** (mūzĭkolŏj′ĭkal) *adj.* **mu·si·col′o·gist** *n.*

musk (mŭsk) *n.* Odoriferous reddish-brown substance secreted in a gland or sac by male musk deer, used as a basis of perfumes; any of various plants with musky smell; ~ **deer**, small hornless deer (*Moschus*) of Central Asia; ~ **duck**, Muscovy duck; also, an Australian duck (*Biziura lobata*) so called from the musky smell of the male; **musk′melon**, any of several varieties of oblong or round fruits of the melon (*Cucumis melon*), a vine of the gourd family, as the canteloupe; **musk ox**, ruminant (*Ovibos moschatus*) allied to sheep and bovines, with curved horns and shaggy pelt, now found only in Arctic America; **musk′rat**, large aquatic rodent (*Ondatra zibethica*) common throughout N. America; **musk rose**, variety of climbing rose with fragrant white flowers; **musk tree, wood**, any of a variety of trees having a musky smell. **mus′ky** *adj.* (**mus·ki·er, mus·ki·est**).

mus·keg (mŭs′kĕg) *n.* Level swampy or boggy area in some regions of Canada.

mus·kel·lunge (mŭs′kelŭnj) *n.* (pl. **-lunge**). Large N. Amer. pike (*Esox masquinongy*), found esp. in Great Lakes.

mus·ket (mŭs′kĭt) *n.* (hist.) Heavy handgun, esp. unrifled, carried by infantry soldier. [It. *moschetto* sparrow hawk]

mus·ket·eer (mŭskĭtēr′) *n.* (hist.) Soldier armed with musket.

mus·ket·ry (mŭs′kĭtrē) *n.* (mil.) Instruction, practice, in rifle shooting.

Mus·lim (mŭz′lĭm, mōōz′-, mōōs′-) *n.* (pl. **-lims, -lim**). One who professes Islam. ~ *adj.* Of Muslims.

mus·lin (mŭz′lĭn) *n.* Fine delicately woven cotton fabric. [*Mosul*, town in Iraq where muslin was orig. made]

mus·sel (mŭs′el) *n.* Any of several genera of marine or fresh-water bivalve mollusks, esp. *Mytilus*, the common edible sea mussel, and *Unio*, the fresh-water pearl-forming mussel.

Mus·so·li·ni (mōōsolē′nē, mōō-; *It.* mōōsawlē′nē), **Benito** (1883–1945). Italian Fascist politician; dictator 1922–43.

Mus·sul·man (mŭs′ulman) *adj.* & *n.* (pl. **-mans**). Muslim.

must¹ (mŭst) *n.* New wine; unfermented or incompletely fermented grape juice.

must² (mŭst) *aux.v.* (followed by inf. without *to*) Be obliged to; be certain to. ~ *n.* (colloq.) Something that should not be missed.

mus·tache, mous·tache (mŭs′tăsh, mustăsh′) *ns.* Hair growing on upper lip, esp. of a man; similar hair around mouths of some animals, as cats etc.; ~ **cup**, drinking cup with partial cover to prevent the mustache from becoming wet.

Mus·ta·fa Ke·mal (mōōs′tahfah kemahl′) = ATATÜRK.

mus·tang (mŭs′tăng) *n.* 1. Wild or half-wild horse of Mexico, California, etc. 2. Small red Texas grape.

mus·tard (mŭs′terd) *n.* Any of various annual plants (genus *Brassica*), having yellow flowers and slender pods; hot pungent powder made from the crushed

The Lion Gate (right) was the main entrance to the ancient acropolis or fortified section of the city of Mycenae, the principal center of Aegean civilization in about 1,400 B.C.

seeds of this plant, esp. *B. nigra* and *B. alba*, mixed to a paste with water (**English** ~) or with vinegar, spices, etc. (**French** ~) and used as a condiment with meat; ~ **gas**, dichlorodiethyl sulphide, a colorless oily liquid with faint garlic odor, the vapor of which is one of the vesicant gases used in chemical warfare; ~ **plaster**, plaster containing mustard, applied to the skin; ~ **pot**, vessel for holding mustard at table; **cut the** ~, (slang) reach requisite standard.

mus·ter (mŭs′ter) *n.* Assembling of men for inspection, instruction, etc.; **pass** ~, undergo muster without censure; bear examination or inspection; come up to standard; ~ **roll**, official list of officers and men in army or ship's company (also *fig.*). **muster** *v.* Collect or assemble for inspection etc.; collect, bring or come together; summon (courage, strength, etc., *up*).

mus·ty (mŭs′tē) *adj.* (**-ti·er, -ti·est**). Spoiled with damp; moist and fetid; moldy; (*fig.*) stale, antiquated. **mus′ti·ness** *n.*

mu·ta·ble (mū′tabel) *adj.* Liable to change, fickle. **mu·ta·bil·i·ty** (mūtabĭl′ĭtē) *n.*

mu·tant (mū′tant) *adj. & n.* (*biol.*) (Individual) differing from its parents as a result of mutation.

mu·ta·tion (mūtā′shon) *n.* 1. Change, alteration. 2. (*biol.*) Occurrence of a new form differing from its parents as a result of change in the gene structure of a reproductive cell; mutant. 3. (*gram.*) Change in vowel sound through influence of another vowel in following syllable.

mu·ta·tis mu·tan·dis (mūtā′tĭs mūtăn′dĭs; *Lat.* mōōtah′tēs mōōtahn′dēs). With the necessary alterations or changes. [L.]

mute (mūt) *adj.* 1. Silent; not capable of speech, dumb; (of hounds) not giving tongue. 2. Not expressed in speech. 3. (of consonants) Stopped; produced with a closing at some point in throat or mouth, as *b, p, t*, etc.; (of letters) not pronounced, although written, as *e* in *mute*. **mute′ly** *adv.* **mute′ness** *n.* **mute** *n.* 1. Dumb person. 2. (*mus.*) Clip for deadening resonance of strings of violin etc.; pad for deadening sound of wind instrument. 3. Mute consonant. ~ *v.t.* (**mut·ed, mut·ing**). Deaden, soften, sound of a musical instrument with a mute; tone down.

mu·ti·late (mū′tĭlāt) *v.t.* (**-lat·ed, -lat·ing**). Injure, make imperfect, by depriving of part.

mu·ti·la·tion (mūtĭlā′shon) *n.*

mu·ti·neer (mūtinēr′) *n.* One who mutinies.

mu·ti·nous (mū′tinus) *adj.* Guilty of mutiny or rebellion. **mu′ti·nous·ly** *adv.*

mu·ti·ny (mū′tinē) *n.* (pl. **-nies**). Open revolt against constituted authority, esp. refusal of five or more members of armed forces to obey orders of a superior officer. ~ *v.i.* (**-nied, -ny·ing**). Take part in mutiny.

mu·tism (mū′tizem) *n.* Muteness, silence; dumbness.

mut·ter (mŭt′er) *v.* Speak, utter, in low and barely audible tones, with mouth nearly closed. ~ *n.* Muttering.

mut·ton (mŭt′on) *n.* Flesh of sheep as food; **mut′tonchop**, piece of rib or loin of mutton, usu. served fried or grilled; **mut′tonchops**, short bushy whiskers shaped like a muttonchop.

mu·tu·al (mū′chōoal) *adj.* (of feelings, actions, etc.) Felt, done, by each to(ward) the other, as ~ *affection, benefit*; performed by joint action, done in common; (*colloq.*) common to two or more persons, as *our* ~ *friend*; (insurance) of a system by which insured persons are shareholders of a company and share in its profits; ~ **fund**, investment company that invests shareholders' funds in securities (of various types). **mu′tu·al·ly** *adv.* **mu·tu·al·i·ty** (mūchōoăl′ĭtē) *n.* Reciprocity, interdependence.

The familiar millipedes and centipede (above) are both myriapods, althoug very different in their habits. Carnivo ous centipedes are fast-running cre tures — one species can even cat flies — while millipedes are slower mo ing.

muu·muu (mōō′mōō) Woman's loose, brightly colore dress. [Hawaiian]

Mu·zak (mū′zăk) *n.* (trademark Recorded background music trans mitted through telephone or radi to receivers in factories restaurants, offices, etc.

mu·zhik, mou·jik (mōōzhĭk mōō′zhĭk) *ns.* Russian peasant.

muz·zle (mŭz′el) *n.* 1. Project ing part of animal's head includin nose and mouth; snout. 2. Arrange ment of straps or wires ove animal's mouth to prevent it biting, eating, etc. 3. End of firearm from which the projectile is discharged; **muz′zleloader**, firearm loaded at muzzle, dist. f. *breechloader*; **muzzle velocity**, velocity of projectile at its discharge from muzzle of a gun. **muzzle** *v.t.* (-zled, -zling). Put muzzle on (animal, and fig. a person); impose silence on, restrict freedom of speech of.

mV, mv *abbrevs.* Millivolt(s).

MVD *abbrev.* Secret police of U.S.S.R., 1946–60. [initials of Russ. *Ministérstvo Vnútrennikh Del*, ministry of internal affairs]

mW, MW *abbrevs.* Megawatt(s). **Mx** *abbrev.* Maxwell(s).

my (mī) *poss. pron.* Possessive case of *I* used as attrib. adjective, belonging to, affecting, me; prefixed to some terms of address, as ∼ **lord**.

my·ce·li·um (mīsē′lēum) *n.* (pl. -li·a pr. -lēa). (bot.) Vegetative part of a fungus, consisting of microscopic threads.

My·ce·nae (mīsē′nē). City of ancient Greece in the plain of Argos; first inhabited *c*3000 B.C. by peoples akin to the Minoans of Crete; in the Bronze Age (*c*2100–1150 B.C.) occupied by a people whose language was probably an early form of Greek, who built the Lion Gate and beehive tombs, which still survive. **My·ce·nae·an** (mīsīnē′an) *adj. & n.*

my·col·o·gy (mīkŏl′ojē) *n.* Study of fungi. **my·col′o·gist** *n.*

my·cor·rhi·za (mīkorī′za) *n.* (pl. -zae pr. -zē, -zas). (bot.) Association of a fungus with the roots of certain plants, in which the fungus forms a layer around or within the outer tissue of the roots.

my·e·li·tis (mīelī′tĭs) *n.* Inflammation of the spinal cord.

My·lar (mīlär) *n.* (trademark) Tough polyester film used in electrical insulation etc.

my·na, mi·na, my·nah (mī′na) *ns.* One of a number of birds of starling family of India, esp. *Acridotheres tristis*, which has been introduced and has proliferated in other regions (e.g., Hawaii); and *Gracula religiosa*, or hill myna, an excellent mimic that can be trained to talk realistically.

my·o·car·di·um (mīokär′dēum) *n.* Muscular substance of the heart. **my·o·car′di·al** *adj.*

my·ol·o·gy (mīŏl′ojē) *n.* Study of muscles. **my·o·log·i·cal** (mīolŏj′ĭkal) *adj.* **my·ol′o·gist** *n.*

my·op·a·thy (mīŏp′athē) *n.* Any disease of the muscles.

my·ope (mī′ōp) *n.* Near-sighted person.

my·o·pi·a (mīō′pēa) *n.* Near-sightedness, a condition of the eye in which the rays from distant objects are brought to a focus before

The forget-me-not is the member of the genus Myosotis most familiar to gardeners. Its delicate flowers and pale green leaves have made it a popular border perennial.

they reach the retina and so form a blurred image.

my·op·ic (mīŏp′ĭk) *adj.* Near-sighted.

my·o·so·tis (mīosō′tĭs) *n.* (bot.) Small plant of genus *M∼*, of which the forget-me-not is a species, with pink, blue, or white flowers.

myr·i·ad (mĭr′ead) *adj. & n.* Ten thousand; (of) indefinitely great number.

myr·i·a·pod (mĭr′eapŏd) *adj. & n.* (zool.) (Animal) with many legs, of the class of arthropods which includes the centipedes and millipedes.

Myr·mi·don (mer′mĭdŏn, -don) *n.* (pl. -dons, Myr·mid·o·nes pr. mermĭd′onēz). (Gk. legend) One of a warlike people on the S. borders of Thessaly who followed Achilles to the siege of Troy.

myr·mi·don (mer′mĭdŏn, -don) *n.* Faithful follower; unscrupulously faithful attendant.

my·rob·a·lan (mīrŏb′alan, mĭ-) *n.* Dried astringent plumlike fruit of certain E. Indian trees, containing tannin and used in dyeing, tanning, etc.

myrrh (mer) *n.* Gum resin, obtained from certain plants of genus *Commiphora*, used in perfumes and incense, and in medicine as astringent and antiseptic mouthwash.

myr·tle (mer′tel) *n.* (bot.) Shrub of genus *Myrtus*, esp. *M. communis*, the European myrtle with dark glossy evergreen leaves and white fragrant flowers.

my·self (mīsĕlf′) *pron.* (pl. **our′-selves** pr. owrsĕlvz′). Emphatic and reflexive form corresponding to *I*, *me*.

mys·te·ri·ous (mĭstēr′ēus) *adj.* Full of, wrapped in, mystery; (of persons) delighting in, affecting, mystery. **mys·te′ri·ous·ly** *adv.* **mys·te′ri·ous·ness** *n.*

mys·ter·y (mĭs′terē, -trē) *n.* (pl. -ter·ies). 1. Hidden or inexplicable matter; secrecy, obscurity. 2. Religious truth known only by divine revelation; religious rite, esp. (pl.) Eucharist; (pl.) secret religious rites of Greeks, Romans, etc. 3. (also ∼ **play**) Medieval drama based on Bible story or legend of saint.

mys·tic (mĭs′tĭk) *adj.* Spiritually symbolic; occult, esoteric; enigmatical. ∼ *n.* One who seeks by contemplation and self-surrender to attain union with the Deity, or who believes in the spiritual apprehension of truths beyond the understanding. **mys′ti·cal** *adj.* Of mystics or mysticism; spiritually significant, connected with God in some way transcending understanding. **mys′ti·cal·ly** *adv.* **mys′ti·cism** (mĭs′tĭsĭzem) *n.*

mys·ti·fy (mĭs′tĭfī) *v.t.* (-fied, -fy·ing). Bewilder; hoax, humbug. **mys·ti·fi·ca·tion** (mĭstĭfĭkā′shon) *n.*

mys·tique (mĭstēk′) *n.* Atmosphere of mystery and veneration investing some doctrines, arts, professions, etc., or personages; any professional skill or technique that mystifies and impresses the layman.

myth (mĭth) *n.* Fictitious (primitive) tale, usu. involving supernatural persons, embodying some popular idea concerning natural or historical phenomena; fictitious person or thing; fictitious idea or belief etc., esp. one that has been accepted uncritically. **myth′ic, myth′i·cal** *adjs.* **myth′i·cal·ly** *adv.*

myth·i·cize (mĭth′ĭsīz) *v.t.* (-cized, -ciz·ing). Treat (story etc.) as myth, interpret mythically. **myth·i·cism** (mĭth′ĭsĭzem) *n.*

my·thol·o·gy (mĭthŏl′ojē) *n.* (pl. -gies). Body of myths, esp. as relating to particular person or subject or current in a particular country; study of myths; picture etc. illustrating a myth. **my·thol′o·ger, my·thol′o·gist** *ns.* Student of myths. **myth·o·log·i·cal** (mĭtholŏj′ĭkal) *adj.* **myth·o·log′i·cal·ly** *adv.* **my·thol′o·gize** *v.t.* (-gized, -giz·ing). Treat of myths and mythology; invent myths.

myx·e·de·ma (mĭksĭdē′ma) *n.* Disorder due to deficient secretion of the thyroid gland.

myx·o·ma·to·sis (mĭksomatō′-sĭs) *n.* Contagious usu. fatal disease of rabbits, caused by a virus.

'Nun', the Semitic name for **N n**, is thought to have meant 'fish', and the early form of the letter may derive from an ideogram. Over the millennia the letter shape has changed with alterations in writing methods.

Phoenician   Cretan   Early Greek

Etruscan   Roman   Classical Latin

N, n (ĕn) (pl. **N's, n's** or **Ns, ns**). 1. Fourteenth letter of modern English and 13th of ancient Roman alphabet, representing historically Gk. *nu* and Semitic *nun*; earlier Greek forms were N and И, corresponding to Phoenician У; usu. denoting a voiced nasal consonant with front closure (point of tongue touching teeth or teethridge), but sometimes also sonant or vowel, and before *g*, *k*, a nasal with back tongue closure. 2. (print.) = EN. 3. (math.) Indefinite number; **to the nth (power)**, to any required power; (fig.) to any extent, to the utmost.

N *abbrev.* Newton; north(ern).

N *symbol.* Nitrogen.

N. *abbrev.* Navy; new; noon; Norse; north(ern); November.

n. *abbrev.* Name; neuter; new; nominative; noon; north(ern); note; noun; number.

N.A. *abbrev.* North America; not applicable.

NAACP *abbrev.* National Association for the Advancement of Colored People.

nab (năb) *v.t.* (**nabbed, nab‧bing**). (slang) Apprehend, arrest; catch in wrongdoing.

na‧bob (nā′bŏb) *n.* 1. = NAWAB. 2. (hist.) Retired servant of East India Company, esp. between battle of Plassey, 1757, and appointment of Warren Hastings, 1772, returning to England with large fortune and orientalized ways. 3. Any ostentatiously wealthy person. **na′bob‧ish** *adj.* **na′bob‧ism** *n.*

Na‧bo‧kov (nah′bokawf), **Vladímir** (1899–1977). Russian-born author whose novels include *Lolita* (1959).

Na‧both (nā′bŏth). Israelite who was stoned to death because he would not give up his vineyard to Ahab (1 Kings 21); **~'s vineyard**, possession that one will stop at nothing to secure.

na‧celle (nasĕl′) *n.* Outer casing of aircraft's engine.

na‧cre (nā′ker) *n.* (Shellfish yielding) mother-of-pearl. **na‧cre‧ous** (nā′krēus) *adj.*

na‧dir (nā′dēr, -der) *n.* Point of heavens diametrically opposite zenith or directly under observer; (transf.) lowest point, place or time of great depression. [Arab. *nazīr as-samt* opposite to (zenith)]

nag[1] (năg) *n.* Small riding horse or pony; (colloq.) horse.

nag[2] (năg) *v.* (**nagged, nag‧ging**). Find fault or scold persistently (*at* person); annoy thus. **nag′ging** *adj.* (esp. of pain) Gnawing, persistent.

Na‧ga (nah′ga) *n.* 1. (Hindu myth.) One of a race of semihuman serpents, genii of rain, rivers, etc. 2. Member of one of a group of tribes inhabiting parts of Assam and Burma.

na‧ga‧na (nagah′na) *n.* Disease carried by certain species of tsetse fly affecting domestic animals and some wild ones. [Zulu *nakane*]

Na‧ga‧sa‧ki (nahgasah′kē, nāgasăk′ē). Seaport on W. Kyushu Island, Japan; almost half the city was destroyed by U.S. atomic bomb dropped Aug. 9, 1945, during World War II.

Na‧hua‧tl (nah′wahtel) (pl. **-hua‧tls**, collect. **-hua‧tl**) *adj.* & *n.* (Member, language) of a group of peoples of S. Mexico and Central America.

Na‧hum (nā′hum). Hebrew minor prophet; book of Old Testament containing his prophecy against Nineveh (beginning of 7th c. B.C.).

nai‧ad (nī′ăd, nā′-, -ad) *n.* (pl. **-ads, -a‧des** pr. -adēz′). Water nymph (esp. in Gk. myth.).

nail (nāl) *n.* 1. Horny oval-shaped protective covering of modified epidermis on upper surface of tip of finger or toe; claw, talon. 2. Hard excrescence on upper mandible of some softbilled birds. 3. Small metal spike, usu. with point and broadened head, driven in with hammer to hold things together or as peg or ornament; **hit the ~ on the head**, give true explanation, propose or do right thing, hit the mark. 4. **nail′brush**, small brush for cleaning fingernails; **nail′head**, architectural ornament shaped like head of nail; **nail file, nail scissors**, instruments for paring fingernails

nail *v.t.* Fasten with nail(s); fix o keep fixed (person, attention, etc.) secure, catch, engage, succeed i getting hold of; **~ down**, (colloq. establish, settle once and for all **~ to the floor**, (colloq.) follov shady merchant's practice of re fusing to sell (advertised merchan dise). **nail′er** *n.* Nailmaker.

Nai‧ro‧bi (nīrō′bē). Capital o Kenya.

Nai‧smith (nā′smith), **Jame** (1861–1939). Canadian-bor Amer. physical education profes sor; originator of basketball.

na‧ive, na‧ïve (nahēv′), **na‧if na‧ïf** (nahēf′) *adjs.* Artless, inno cent, unsophisticated; amusingl simple. **na‧ive′ly, na‧ïve′ly** *advs* **na‧ive‧té, na‧ïve‧te** (nahēvtā′ **na‧ive‧ty** (nahēv′tē) *ns.*

na‧ked (nā′kĭd) *adj.* 1. Un clothed; not covered by clothing defenseless. 2. Unsheathed; plain undisguised, exposed for examina tion. 3. Devoid *of*; treeless, leafless barren; without ornament; (of rock exposed; (of light, flame, etc.) no placed within case or receptacle (bot., zool.) without pericarp leaves, hairs, scales, etc. 4. Withou addition, comment, support, etc. 5 **~ eye**, eye unassisted by telescope microscope, etc.; **~ truth**, stric truth, without concealment o addition. **na′ked‧ly** *adv.* **na′ked‧ness** *n.*

N.A.M. *abbrev.* Nationa Association of Manufacturers.

nam‧by-pam‧by (năm′bēpăm′ bē) *adj.* & *n.* (pl. **-bies**). Senti mental, pretty, trifling (work o art); (person) lacking in vigor [formed on name of *Ambros Philips* (d. 1749), pastoral poet]

name (nām) *n.* Word by which individual person, animal, place, o thing is spoken of or to; person a known, famed, or spoken of; family clan; reputation; merely nomina existence, practically nonexisten thing; **by the ~ of**, named; **cal names**, described by uncompli mentary names; **in the name of** invoking; acting as deputy for or ir the interest of; **keep one's nam on, take one's name off, the**

...oks, remain, cease to be, member ... organization; **put one's name .wn for**, apply as candidate etc.; .me day, day of saint after whom .rson is named; **name-opping**, familiar mention of ll-known names as form of boast-.; **name of the game**, (colloq.) .tral purpose, essence of action; .me′plate, plate affixed with .ne of occupant etc.; **name′sake**, .rson or thing with same name as .ther. **name** v.t. (**named,** .m′ing). Give name to, call by .ht name, appoint (to office etc.); .cify.

.name·less (nām′lĭs) adj. Ob-.re, left unnamed; unknown; .ring no name or inscription; .efinable; too bad to be named.

.name·ly (nām′lē) adv. That is to .; specifically.

Na·mi·bia (namĭb′ēa). .rmerly South West Africa, now .mandate there under South .rican administration; transfer of .wer to Namibians under negotia-.n; capital, Windhoek.

Na·nak (nah′nak) (1469–1538). .lled "Guru"; Indian religious .der and founder of Sikhism.

Nan·jing (nănzhēng′) = .NKING.

.nan·keen (nănkēn′), **nan·kin** .n′kĭn) ns. Chinese cloth of .tural buff-yellow cotton; cloth of .ed cotton resembling this; pale .ff-yellow color. 2. Chinese .e-and-white porcelain. [f. .NKING]

Although there have been considerable technological advances in China since 1948, many traditional methods survive. Peasants near Nanking (above) use pedal-driven scoops to raise water.

Nan·king (nănkĭng′). City of China, on Yangtze, capital of China early in Ming dynasty, and from 1929 until the Japanese invasion of China in 1937. [Chin., = "southern capital"]

nan·ny (năn′ē) n. (pl. -**nies**). Child's nurse; ~ **goat**, she-goat. [pet form of female name Ann]

nano- prefix. (abbrev. n) One billionth of, as nanosecond.

Nantes (nănts; Fr. nahńt). City of W. France, on Loire River; **Edict of** ~, edict of Henry IV of France (1598) granting toleration to Protestants, revoked by Louis XIV (1685).

Nan·tuck·et (năntŭk′ĭt). Island and resort area of Massachusetts, S. of Cape Cod, in the Atlantic.

Na·o·mi (nāō′mē, -mī). Mother-in-law of RUTH[1] (Ruth I).

nap[1] (năp) v.i. (**napped, nap·ping**). Sleep lightly or briefly;

The town of Aus, situated at the edge of the Namibia Desert. The status of Namibia has been disputed since 1966, when the U.N. declared the South African mandate terminated and assumed responsibility until independence. South Africa has since contested this.

The settlement which gave rise to **Naples** *is very old. Later settlers from Chalcis and Athens built a new 'city' named Neapolis. It is now the third largest Italian city.*

catch napping, find asleep; take unawares or off guard. **nap** *n.* Short sleep, doze, esp. by day.

nap² (năp) *n.* Surface given to cloth by raising the fibers; soft or downy surface. ~ *v.t.* (**napped, nap·ping**). Raise nap on (cloth). **nap′less** *adj.*

na·palm (nā′pahm) *n.* Mixture of aluminum salts of naphthenic acid from crude petroleum with palmitic and stearic acids obtained from coconut oil, for jellying gasoline for incendiary use in war (hence ~ **bomb**). [*na*(phthenic) + *palm*(itic)]

nape (nāp) *n.* Back of neck.

na·per·y (nā′perē) *n.* Household, esp. table, linen.

Naph·ta·li (năf′talī). Son of Jacob and Bilhah (Gen. 30); tribe of Israel traditionally descended from him.

naph·tha (năf′tha, năp′-) *n.* Orig. inflammable volatile liquid (a constituent of asphalt and bitumen) issuing from earth in some places; now, kinds of inflammable oil got by dry distillation of organic substances, esp. coal, shale, and petroleum.

naph·tha·lene (năf′thalēn, năp′-), **naph·tha·line, naph·tha·lin** (năf′thalĭn, năp′-) *ns.* White crystalline aromatic hydrocarbon, $C_{10}H_8$, with peculiar smell and pungent taste, obtained from coal tar etc. and used in the manufacture of dyes and chemicals and for soil fumigation.

naph·thene (năf′thēn, năp′-) *n.* One of a series of hydrocarbons occurring in petroleum, shale tar, etc.

naph·thol (năf′thŏl, -thawl, -thŏl, năp′-) *n.* Either of two white crystalline hydroxyl derivatives of naphthalene, distinguished as α-**naphthol** and β-**naphthol**, used as disinfectants, in manufacture of dyes, etc.

Na·pi·er (nā′pēer, napēr′), **Ne·per** (nā′per), **John** (1550–1617). Scottish mathematician; inventor of logarithms and of the modern notation of decimal numbers. **Na·pier·i·an, Na·per·i·an** (napēr′ēan) *adjs.*

nap·kin (năp′kĭn) *n.* Square of material used for wiping lips or fingers at meals, or in serving certain dishes (**table** ~); ~ **ring**, ring for holding rolled up table napkin.

Na·ples (nā′pelz). (It. **Napoli**) City and seaport of SW. Italy. [L. *Neapolis* f. Gk. *nea polis* new city]

Na·po·le·on (napō′lēon). Name of several French rulers: **Napoleon I**, Napoleon Bonaparte (1769–

1821), French soldier of Corsican family; became first consul of France, 1799, and emperor of the French, 1804; conquered large parts of Europe; after various defeats, abdicated and withdrew to Elba, 1814; returned to Paris, 1815; was defeated at Waterloo three months later and again abdicated; was exiled to St. Helena, where he died; **Napoleon II**, Napoleon Francois Joseph Charles, Duke of Reichstadt (1811–32), son of Napoleon I and Marie Louise; king of Rome; known as Napoleon II (although he never ruled France) because Napoleon I abdicated in his favor in 1814; **Napoleon III**, Charles Louis Napoleon Bonaparte (1808–73), nephew of Napoleon I; elected president of the French Republic 1848; proclaimed emperor 1852; captured by the Germans 1870, and deposed.

na·po·le·on (napō′lēon, -pōl′-yon) *n.* 1. French gold coin of value 20 francs, issued by Napoleon I. 2. Kind of long boot. 3. Rich confection of puff pastry split and filled with cream.

Na·po·le·on·ic (napōlēŏn adj.* Of Napoleon I; ~ **W** series of campaigns (1799–1815 French armies under Napo against Austria, Russia, Gt. Bri Portugal, Prussia, and o powers.

narc, nark (närk) *ns.* (sl. Narcotics agent for the gov ment.

nar·ce·ine (när′sēēn, -ĭn Bitter crystalline narcotic alka present in opium.

nar·cis·sism (när′sĭzĭzem) (psychol.) Excessive or e interest in one's own body personality. **nar·cis·sis·tic** (nä sĭs′tĭk) *adj.* [f. NARCISSUS]

Nar·cis·sus (närsĭs′us). (myth.) Beautiful youth who, fa in love with his reflection

Resistance to **Napoleonic** *imperi encouraged the development of ideas of national identity, springing language and culture, not dynastic tors. After Napoleon's fall these helped to reshape Europe.*

spring, pined away, and was changed into the flower that bears his name.

nar·cis·sus (nārsĭs′us) *n.* Bulbous plant of genus *N~*, including the daffodil, esp. *N. poeticus*, bearing in spring heavily scented single white flower with undivided corona with a red crisped edge.

nar·co·lep·sy (nār′kŏlĕpsē) *n.* Disease characterized by irresistible attacks of true sleep, usually of brief duration. **nar·co·lep·tic** (nārkŏlĕp′tĭk) *adj.*

nar·co·sis (nārkō′sĭs) *n.* Operation or effects of narcotics; state of insensibility.

nar·cot·ic (nārkŏt′ĭk) *adj. & n.* (Substance) inducing drowsiness, sleep, stupor or insensibility (also fig.).

nard (nārd) *n.* (Plant, prob. *Nardostachys jatamansi*, yielding) aromatic balsam of ancients, usu. called *spikenard*.

na·res (nār′ēz) *n.pl.* (sing. **na·ris** pr. nār′ĭs). (anat.) Nostrils.

nar·ghi·le (nār′gĭlē, -lā) *n.* Hookah. [Pers. *nārgīl* coconut]

nark = NARC.

Nar·ra·gan·sett (nărăgăn′sĭt) *n.* (pl. **-setts**, collect. **-sett**). Member, Algonquian language, of an Amer. Indian tribe, formerly inhabiting parts of Rhode Island; ~ **Bay**, inlet of Atlantic in SE. Rhode Island.

nar·rate (nărāt′, nărāt′) *v.t.* (**-rat·ed, -rat·ing**). Relate, recount, give continuous account of. **nar·ra·tion** (nărā′shon), **nar′ra·tor, nar′rat·er** *ns.*

nar·ra·tive (năr′atĭv) *n.* Tale, story, recital of facts; kind of composition or talk that confines itself to these. **~** *adj.* In the form of, concerned with, narration.

nar·row (năr′ō) *adj.* Of small width in proportion to length, confining; restricted; with little margin; illiberal, prejudiced, exclusive, hence **~-minded(ly), ~-mindedness**; searching, precise; (phonet.) tense; **narrow gauge**, (on railroad) gauge of less than 4 ft. 8½ in. **nar′row·ly** *adv.* **nar′row·ness** *n.* **narrow** *n.* (usu. pl.) Narrow part of sound, strait, river, pass, etc. **narrow** *v.* Make or become narrower, diminish, lessen, contract.

nar·thex (nār′thĕks) *n.* Porch or vestibule in early Christian church, extending across width of nave at opposite end from main altar, and used by those not in full communion.

nar·whal, nar·wal (nār′wal),

The original Grand Ole Opry building in **Nashville,** *Tennessee, home of the famous folk music program which began in 1925. Nashville is also the center for country and western music and has a large recording industry.*

nar·whale (nār′hwāl, -wāl) *n.* Arctic cetacean (*Monodon monoceros*), the male having a very long spirally twisted straight tusk developed from one, or sometimes both, of its two teeth.

nar·y (nār′ē) *adj.* (dial.) Not a, no. [var. of *ne'er a*]

NAS *abbrev.* National Academy of Sciences; Naval Air Station.

NASA (năs′a, nah′sa) *n.* U.S. agency responsible for civilian programs of government in aeronautics and space research [N(ational) A(eronautics) and S(pace) A(dministration)]

na·sal (nā′zal) *adj.* Of the nose; (of sounds) produced with nose passages open (as *n*, *m*, *ng*); (of voice etc.) characterized by unusual or disagreeable number of sounds produced by means of nose **na′sal·ly** *adv.* **na·sal·i·ty** (nāzăl′ĭtē) *n.* **na′sal·ize** *v.* (**-ized, -iz·ing**). **na·sal·i·za·tion** (nāzălĭzā′shon) *n.* **nasal** *n.* Nasal letter or sound.

nas·cent (năs′ent, nā′sent) *adj.* In the act of being born; just beginning to be, not yet mature; **~ state**, (chem.) highly active condition of certain elements, esp. hydrogen, at the moment of liberation from a compound. **nas′cen·cy, nas′cence** *ns.*

Nash (năsh), **Ogden** (1902–71) Amer. poet and humorous writer.

The vivid flowers of the **nasturtium** have made it a popular garden plant. Climbing or trailing, its round leaves and orange, red, or yellow blooms provide an attractive splash of color.

A typical **Natchez** antebellum home, for which it is famous. This city in southwest Mississippi takes its name from the Natchez Indians, who were forced to move to Oklahoma after the French-Natchez wars in the 18th century.

nas·ty (năs′tē) *adj.* (**-ti·er, -ti·est**). Unpleasant to taste or smell; disgusting; obscene; spiteful; extremely disagreeable. **nas′ti·ly** *adv.* **nas′ti·ness** *n.*

Na·tal (natăl′, -tahl′). Eastern coastal province of Republic of South Africa; first settled by a few British traders in 1823, then by Boers in 1838, becoming a Boer Republic; annexed by British, 1845; representative government, 1856; responsible government, 1893; province of the Union of South Africa, 1910; capital, Pietermaritzburg. [named *Terra Natalis* by Vasco da Gama because he sighted the entrance to what is now Durban harbor on Christmas Day, 1497].

na·tal (nā′tal) *adj.* Of, from, birth.

na·ta·tion (nātā′shon, nă-) *n.* Swimming.

na·ta·to·ri·al (nātator′eal, -tor′-nāta-), **na·ta·to·ry** (nā′tatōrē, -tōrē) *adjs.* Swimming, of swimming.

Natch·ez (năch′ĭz) *n.* (pl. **-ez**). Member of former Amer. Indian tribe, of lower Mississippi River, conquered and scattered by French in 1730; city and river port in SW. Mississippi.

na·tes (nā′tēz) *n.pl.* (anat.) Buttocks.

Na·than (nā′than). Hebrew prophet of time of David and Solomon (2 Sam.).

na·tion (nā′shon) *n.* Society united under one government in a country; considerable group of

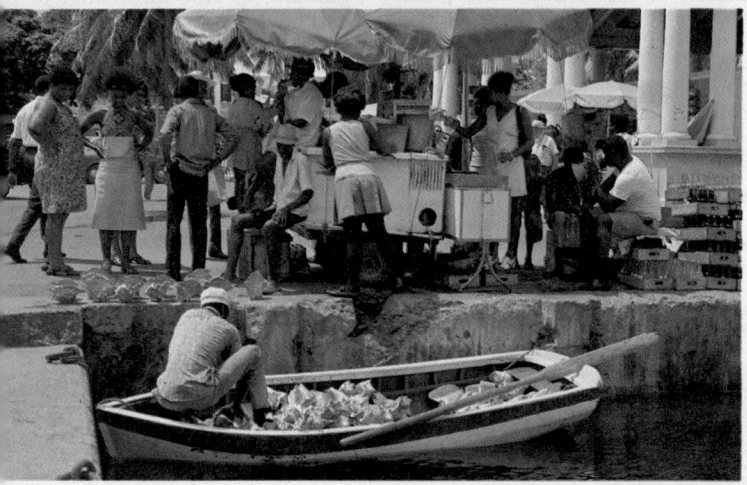

Once the haunt of pirates, the Bahamas are better known today as a resort where scenes such as this on the wharf in **Nassau**, the capital, can be found.

Nash·ville (năsh′vĭl). Capital and commercial city of Tennessee, in the Cumberland River in the N. central part; center of the U.S. country music recording industry.

naso- *prefix.* Of the nose, as in **-frontal**, of nose and forehead.

Nas·sau (năs′aw). Capital city of Bahama Islands, on N. shore of New Providence.

Nas·ser (năs′er, nah′ser), **Gamel Abdel** (1918–70). Egyptian army officer and politician; premier of Egypt 1954–6, president 1956–8; president of United Arab Republic 1958–70; **Lake Nasser**, reservoir formed by the Aswan High Dam on the Nile between S. Egypt and N. Sudan.

Nast (năst), **Thomas** (1840–1902). German-born Amer. political cartoonist; his cartoons were held greatly responsible for reducing political corruption in New York.

na·stur·tium (năster′shum, na-) *n.* Any of various plants of the genus *Tropaeolum* having bright flowers in shades of red, yellow, and orange.

people having common descent or history.

Na·tion (nā′shon), **Carry Amelia Moore** (1846–1911). Amer. leader of temperance movement; notorious for the hatchet she used in wrecking saloons in Kansas.

na·tion·al (năsh′onal) *adj.* Of a (or the) nation; common to the whole nation, concerned with its interests as dist. from those of a faction or region; ~ **anthem**, song adopted by a nation as an expression of patriotism, and played or sung on formal and ceremonial occasions; **N~ Assembly**, (esp., hist.) first revolutionary assembly of France 1789–91; ~ **bank**, any of numerous banks chartered under the federal government; ~ **convention**, convention of major political party to nominate candidate for presidency etc.; ~ **debt**: see DEBT; **N~ Gallery**, gallery for permanent exhibition of pictures belonging to a nation, esp. those in Washington and London; **N~ Guard**, military reserve maintained by each state, subject to call into Federal service; ~ **income**, total money earned within a nation; ~ **park**, extensive area set aside by government for the preservation of historic or prehistoric sites and of flora and fauna, and for the benefit of the public; **N~ Socialist German Workers' Party**, party with extremely nationalistic, anti-Semitic, and totalitarian program, which acquired dictatorial power in Germany under HITLER in 1933; hence **N~ Socialism, N~ Socialist. na′tion·al·ly** *adv.* **national** *n.* Person legally considered a citizen of a specified country.

*Most visitors to London, U.K. include the **National Gallery** in their list of places to visit. Founded in 1824, the gallery contains examples of all older schools of European painting.*

na·tion·al·ism (năsh′onalĭzem) *n.* Patriotic feeling, principle, or efforts; policy of national independence. **na′tion·al·ist** *adj. & n.* **na′tion·al·is·tic** (năshonalĭs′tĭk) *adj.*

Na·tion·al·ist (năsh′onalĭst) **China.** Unofficial name for the Republic of China (TAIWAN).

na·tion·al·i·ty (năshonăl′ĭtē) *n.* (pl. **-ties**). National quality; nation, existence as a nation; ethnic group; fact of belonging to a particular nation or ethnic group; cohesion due to common history etc.; person's status as member of a nation, alterable by legal process.

na·tion·al·ize (năsh′onalīz) *v.t.* (**-ized, -iz·ing**). Make national; make into a nation; transfer (land, mines, railroads, etc.) from private ownership and control to that of the government. **na·tion·al·i·za·tion** (năshonalīzā′shon) *n.*

na·tive (nā′tĭv) *n.* One born in a particular place or country; original or usual inhabitant of country as dist. from strangers or foreigners. ~ *adj.* 1. Belonging to a person or thing by nature, innate, natural *to*; of one's birth; where one was born; belonging to one by right of birth. 2. (of metals etc.) Occurring naturally in pure state; occurring in nature, not produced artificially. 3. Born in a place, indigenous, not exotic; of the natives of a place. **na′tive·ly** *adv.* **na′tive·ness** *n.*

na·tiv·i·ty (natĭv′ĭtē, nā-) *n.* (pl. **-ties**). 1. Birth. 2. (**N~**) Birth of Christ; representation in art, esp. painting, of Christ newborn usu. with Virgin Mary, angels, etc.; festival of birth of Christ (Christmas); (astrol.) horoscope.

NATO (nā′tō) *n.* Alliance for

*In some countries **nationalism** has more or less taken the place of religion. These young Chinese are marching in solemn yet triumphant procession to the Martyrs' Memorial Park, Canton.*

collective defense against aggression established in 1949 by the U.S., Canada, and ten Western European nations. [N(orth) A(tlantic) T(reaty) O(rganization)]

nat·ty (năt′ē) *adj.* (**-ti·er, -ti·est**). Spruce, trim. **nat′ti·ly** *adv.* **nat′ti·ness** *n.*

nat·u·ral (năch′eral, năch′ral) *adj.* 1. Based on the innate moral sense, instinctive, as ~ *law*, ~ *justice*. 2. Constituted by nature; ~ **selection**: see DARWIN[1]. 3. Normal, conformable to the ordinary course of nature, no exceptional or miraculous; ~ **childbirth**, at which mother has been taught to relax so as not to need anesthesia etc.; ~ **death**, death by age or disease, not by violence. 4. Not enlightened, unregenerate, as ~ *man*; not communicated by revelation, as ~ *religion*, ~ *theology*. 5. Physically existing, not spiritual or intellectual or fictitious, as *the ~ world*; ~ **life**, duration of person's life on Earth. 6. Existing in or by nature, not artificial; innate, inherent; self-sown, uncultivated; ~ **gas**, inflammable gas occurring underground, consisting chiefly of methane and other simple paraffins and often found associated with petroleum. 7. Lifelike; unaffected, easy-mannered; not disfigured or disguised. 8. Not surprising; to be expected. 9. Consonant or easy to (person etc.). 10. Destined to be such by nature, as ~ *enemies*. 11. So related by nature only, illegitimate, as ~ *child, son*. 12. Dealing with nature as a study; ~ **classification**, classification of species into natural orders, esp. Jussieu's arrangement of plant species acc. to

*The idea of preserving areas of a country as a **national park** for the whole people originated in 1872, in America, Yosemite, (facing page) was one of the earliest to be established.*

*Revenue for the mountainous province of **Navarre** is from forestry and grazing. Sheep (above) are moved to higher pastures in summer, but feed in the valleys in winter, a procedure established long ago.*

likeness as opp. to Linnaeus's system which was based on the number and characteristics of reproductive organs; ~ **history**, formerly, systematic study of all natural objects, animal, vegetable, and mineral; now usu., study of animal life, freq. implying popular rather than scientific treatment; aggregate of facts about the natural objects or characteristics of a place or class; so ~ **historian**; ~ **order**, (esp.) order resulting from natural classification; ~ **philosophy**, (hist.) natural science; physics; so ~ **philosopher**; ~ **science**: see SCIENCE. 13. (mus.) Not sharp or flat; (of scale or key) having no sharps or flats; ~ **scale**, scale of C major. **nat′u·ral·ness** n. **natural** n. 1. (mus.) Note in natural scale; white key on piano; sign ♮ used to cancel preceding sharp or flat. 2. (colloq.) Person etc. naturally endowed (*for*); easy or obvious choice (*for*). 3. Throw of 7 or 11 at craps.

nat·u·ral·ism (năch′erəlĭzem, năch′ra-) n. 1. Moral or religious system on purely natural basis; philosophy excluding supernatural or spiritual. 2. Faithful representation of nature or reality in literature, art, etc. **nat′u·ral·ist** n. 1. One who believes in or studies naturalism. 2. Student of animals or plants. **nat·u·ral·is·tic** (năcherə-lĭs′tĭk, năchra-) adj. Of, according

to, naturalism in philosophy, literature, etc.; of natural history. **nat·u·ral·is′ti·cal·ly** adv.

nat·u·ral·ize (năch′erəlīz, năch′ra-) v. (**-ized, -iz·ing**). Admit (alien) to citizenship; adopt (foreign word, custom, etc.); introduce (animal, plant) into new environment. **nat·u·ral·i·za·tion** (năch-erəlīzā′shon, năchra-) n.

nat·u·ral·ly (năch′erəlē, năch′-ra-) adv. (esp.) As might be expected, of course.

na·ture (nā′cher) n. 1. Thing's essential qualities, person's innate character; general characteristics and feelings of mankind; specified element of human character; person of specified character; kind, sort, class; **by** ~, innately. 2. Inherent impulses determining character or action; vital force, functions, or needs; **against** ~, unnatural, immoral. 3. Creative and regulative physical power conceived of as immediate cause of phenomena of material world; these phenomena as a whole; these personified; naturalness in art etc.; **in the course of** ~, in the ordinary course; **in** ~, in real fact; **state of** ~, unregenerate condition (opp.

state of grace); condition of ma[n] before society is organized; ur[n]cultivated or undomesticated stat[e] of plants or animals.

naught, nought (nawt) n[.] Nothing, (arith.), cipher, zero; (fig[.]) ruin, failure, thing of no impo[r]tance.

naugh·ty (naw′tē) adj. (**-ti·e[r], -ti·est**). (now used almost e[x]clusively of, to, or by children[.]) Wayward, disobedient, bad[ly] behaved; (archaic) wicked, blam[e]worthy, indecent. **naught′i·ly** ad[v.] **naught′i·ness** n.

nau·se·a (naw′zēa, -zha, -sē[a,] -sha) n. Feeling of sickness; seasic[k]ness; loathing. **nau·se·ate** (naw[′] zēāt, -zhē-, -sē-, -shē-) v.i. & v.[t.] (**-at·ed, -at·ing**). 1. Reject (foo[d,] usu. fig.) with loathing; affect wit[h] nausea, hence ~**ing** adj. 2. Fe[el] sick (*at*), loathe, food, occupatio[n] etc. **nau·se·a·tion** (nawzēā′sho[n,] -zhē-, -sē-, -shē-) n.

nau·seous (naw′shus, -zēus) a[dj.] Causing nausea; offensive to tas[te] or smell, nasty; disgusting, loath[some. **nau′seous·ly** adv. **nau[′]seous·ness** n.

Nau·sic·a·ä (nawsĭk′ēa, -ä[?]) (Gk. legend) Daughter of Alcinou[s;] she found the shipwrecke[d] Odysseus on the shore and took hi[m] to her father's palace.

nau·ti·cal (naw′tĭkal) adj. [Of] sailors or navigation, naval, mar[i]time; ~ **mile**: see MILE. **nau′ti[·]

This early 19th-century patriotic print shows the fierce hand-to-hand fighting common in **naval** battles of the time, with officers and men side by side in attack or defense.

This beautiful **Navajo** silver necklace utilizes the ancient swastika design, which comes from Sanskrit and means 'conducive to well-being'. It is a recurring theme in Navajo art.

·ly *adv.*

nau·ti·lus (naw′ti*lu*s) *n.* (pl. **·es, -li** pr. -lī). 1. (also **paper**) Small two-gilled cephalopod ·llusk of warm seas (genus *gonauta*), related to octopus, the ·nale of which secretes in two of arms a translucent single-·ambered false shell. 2. (also ·ambered or **pearly** ~) Four-·led cephalopod of Indian and ·cific Oceans (genus *N.*), having, ·both sexes, a many-chambered true shell.

Nav·a·ho, Nav·a·jo (năv′ahō, nah′va-) *ns.* (pl. **-hos, -hoes, -jos, -joes,** collect. **-ho, -jo**). (Member of) an Amer. Indian people of N. Arizona and New Mexico; ~ **blanket,** bright-colored woolen blanket with geometrical pattern, made by Navaho women.

na·val (nā′val) *adj.* Of ships, esp. ships of war; of the (or a) navy; ~ **officer,** officer in navy; customs official; ~ **stores,** supplies for war-ships. **na′val·ly** *adv.*

Na·varre (navär′). (Span. **Navarra**) Province of N. Spain; (hist.) medieval kingdom that also included parts of SW. France.

nave (nāv) *n.* Body of church from inner door to chancel or choir, usu. separated by pillars from aisles.

na·vel (nā′vel) *n.* Depression in front of belly left by severance of umbilical cord; central point of anything; ~ **orange,** large orange with navel-like formation at top.

na·vic·u·lar (navĭk′yuler) *adj.* Boat-shaped; ~ **bone,** tarsal bone. **navicular** *n.* also **na·vic·u·lar·e** (navĭkyulār′ē, -lār′ē). Navicular bone.

nav·i·ga·ble (năv′ĭgabel) *adj.* Affording passage for ships; sea-worthy. **nav·i·ga·bil·i·ty** (năvĭga-bĭl′ĭtē), **nav′i·ga·ble·ness** *ns.* **nav′i·ga·bly** *adv.*

nav·i·gate (năv′ĭgāt) *v.* (**-gat·ed, -gat·ing**). Voyage, sail ship; sail over, up, down (sea, river); manage,

1

2

3

4

irect course of (ship, aircraft, etc.)
ith the aid of instruments.

nav·i·ga·tion (năvĭgā′shon) *n.*
Navigating; methods of determining position and course of ship,
airplane, etc., by geometry and
nautical astronomy; voyage; **inland**
~, communication by canals and
rivers. **nav·i·ga′tion·al** *adj.*

nav·i·ga·tor (năv′ĭgāter) *n.* One
charged with or skilled in
navigation; sea explorer.

na·vy (nā′vē) *n.* (pl. **-vies**). 1.
Branch of armed forces using ships;
~ **bean**, any of several varieties of
the kidney bean, grown for their
nutritious white seeds, which are
stored dry and prepared for cooking
and eating by soaking; ~ **blue**, (of)
the dark blue used in naval uniform;
N~ **Cross**, bronze cross
decoration awarded by the U.S.
Navy for great heroism in action
against the enemy; ~ **cut**, cake
tobacco finely sliced; ~ **yard**,
government dockyard. 2. Navy
blue.

na·wab (nawawb′) *n.* 1. Distinguished Muslim in Pakistan. 2.
(hist.) Muslim noble in the Mogul
Empire. [Arab. *nā′ib* deputy]

nay (nā) *n.* Negative vote;
nay′sayer, person who habitually
expresses opposition to proposed
courses of action.

Naz·a·rene (năz′arēn′, năz′arēn)
n. 1. Native, inhabitant, of
Nazareth; **the** ~, Jesus Christ. 2.
(obs., in Muslim and Jewish use)
Christian. 3. Member of an
obscure early Jewish-Christian
sect. ~ *adj.* Of Nazareth or
Nazarenes.

Naz·a·reth (năz′arĭth). Town
of Lower Galilee, now in Israel;
home of Joseph and Mary, parents
of Jesus, who spent his youth there.

Naz·a·rite[1] (năz′arīt) (rare) =
NAZARENE 1.

Naz·a·rite[2] (năz′arīt) *n.* One of
Hebrew sect who abstained from
all products of the vine, from
cutting the hair, etc. (Num. 6).
[Heb. *nāzîr* one consecrated,
devoted]

Na·zi (nah′tsē, năt′sē) *n. & adj.*
(pl. **-zis**). (Member, adherent) of
the NATIONAL Socialist German
Workers' party. **Na·zism** (nah′-
sizem, năt′sĭz-, nah′tseīzem,
năt′sē-) *n.* **na·zi·fy** (nah′tsĭfī,
năt′sĭ-) *v.t.* (**-fied**, **-fy·ing**).
na·zi·fi·ca·tion (nahtsĭfĭkā′shon,
năt-) *n.* [repr. pron. of *Nati-* in Ger.
Nationalsozialist National Social-
ist]

*Naval vessels have become more soph-
isticated with the development of radar
and electronic technology. Most
nations have a **navy** which participates
in exercises designed to test potential
combat situations.
Facing Page: 1. A frigate. 2. A submarine. 3. An aircraft carrier. 4. U.S.S.
John McCain depth charging.*

NB *abbrev.* Nebraska.

Nb *symbol.* Niobium.

N.B. *abbrev.* New Brunswick;
nota bene (L., = note well).

NC, N.C. *abbrevs.* North
Carolina.

N.C.O., NCO *abbrevs.* Noncommissioned officer.

ND, N.D., N.Dak. *abbrevs.*
North Dakota.

Nd *symbol.* Neodymium.

n.d. *abbrev.* No date; not dated.

NE, N.E., n.e. *abbrevs.* North-
east(ern).

Ne *symbol.* Neon.

NEA, N.E.A. *abbrevs.* National
Education Association.

Ne·an·der·thal (nēăn′derthawl,

*For many thousands of years, **navigation** at sea depended on the visibility
of the stars. Only after the 12th century
were inventions such as the sextant (1)
and the compass (2) available.*

-tawl, -tahl). Valley in Rhineland,
Germany; ~ **man**, type of man
widely distributed in paleolithic
Europe in the early stages of the last
glaciation, with long low wide skull,
retreating forehead, and massive
brow ridges (so called because parts
of skeleton were discovered in a
cave in this valley, 1857).

neap (nēp) *adj.* Of those tides
occurring soon after moon's first
and third quarters in which high-
water level is at lowest. ~ *n.* Neap
tide.

Ne·a·pol·i·tan (nēapŏl′ĭtan) *adj.*
Of Naples; ~**ice**, ice cream in
layers of various colors and flavors.
Neapolitan *n.* Native, inhabitant,
of Naples. [see NAPLES]

near (nēr) *adv.* To, at, a short
distance, in(to) proximity in space
or time; nearly; closely; parsi-
moniously; ~ **at hand**, within easy
reach; not far in the future; **near′-**

by, not far off; hence, **nearby** (*adj.*); **come near** (*to do, doing*), nearly do. **near** *prep.* Near in space, time, condition, or resemblance, to. **near** *adj.* 1. Closely related, intimate. 2. (of horse, part of vehicle etc.) Left (i.e. on the side where one mounts; opp. OFF; so ~ **side**). 3. Close at hand, close to, in place or time; (of road or way) direct. 4. (of guess, translation, escape, etc.) Close, narrow. 5. (of persons) Niggardly. 6. ~ **distance**, part of scene between background and foreground; **N ~ East**, SE. parts of Europe; Balkan nations together with Asia Minor; ~ **miss**, (of shell, bomb, etc.) not a hit, but falling close enough to damage the target; something that narrowly misses its objective; ~ **-sighted**, myopic. **near** *v.* Draw near (to), approach. **near'ness** *n.*

near·ly (nēr'lē) *adv.* Closely, almost; **not** ~, nothing like.

neat[1] (nēt) *n.* Any animal of ox kind; (collect.) cattle; **neat'herd**, cowherd; **neat's-foot, -tongue**, foot, tongue, of ox as food; **neat's-foot oil**, light oil obtained from feet and shinbones of cattle, used to dress leather; **neat's leather**, ox hide.

neat[2] (nēt) *adj.* 1. (of liquor, esp. alcoholic) Undiluted. 2. Nicely made or proportioned; pleasantly simple or compact; deft, dextrous, cleverly done; tidy, methodical; (of language, style, etc.) brief, clear, and pointed, cleverly phrased, epigrammatic. **neat'ly** *adv.* **neat'ness** *n.*

'neath, neath (nēth) *preps.* (poet.) Beneath.

Neb., NE *abbrevs.* Nebraska.

neb·bish (nĕb'ĭsh) *n. & adj.* (slang) Submissive, timid (person). [f. Yiddish *nebach* poor thing!]

Ne·bras·ka (nebrăs'ka). State in northwestern U.S., admitted to the Union in 1867; capital, Lincoln.

Neb·u·chad·nez·zar (nĕbukad-nĕz'er, nĕbyu-), **Neb·u·chad·rez·zar** (nĕbukadrĕz'er, nĕbyu-). King of Babylon 605–562 B.C.; built the great walls of the city; after the rebellion of Jehoiakim of Judah he besieged and took Jerusalem 597; when ZEDEKIAH revolted, he took it again and destroyed it, 588.

neb·u·la (nĕb'yula) *n.* (pl. **-las, -lae** pr. -lī, -lē). 1. Clouded speck on cornea causing defective sight. 2. (astron.) Cloud of dust or gas within the galactic system illuminated by neighboring stars. 3. (astron.) Luminous mass believed to consist of an enormous number of stars, usu. not separately dis-

cernible, situated outside the galactic system. **neb'u·lar** *adj.* Of nebula(e); ~ **hypothesis**, theory that solar and stellar systems developed from nebulae.

neb·u·lous (nĕb'yulus) *adj.* 1. Of, like, nebula(e). 2. Cloudlike; hazy, vague, indistinct, formless; clouded, turbid. **neb·u·los·i·ty** (nĕbyulŏs'ĭtē) *n.*

nec·es·sar·i·ly (nĕseser'ĭlē, nĕs-eser-) *adv.* As a necessary result, inevitably.

nec·es·sar·y (nĕs'eserē) *adj.* Indispensable, requisite; requiring to, that must, be done; determined by predestination or natural laws, not by free will; happening or existing by necessity; (of concept etc.) inevitably resulting from nature of things or the mind, inevitably produced by previous state of things; (of agent) having no independent volition. ~ *n.* (pl. **-sar·ies**). Thing without which life cannot be maintained; (loosely) desirable thing not generally regarded as a luxury.

ne·ces·si·tate (nesĕs'ĭtāt) *v.t.* (**-tat·ed, -tat·ing**). Force, compel, *to* do (now rare); render necessary; involve as condition, accompaniment, or result. **ne·ces·si·ta·tion**

(nesĕsĭtā'shon) *n.*

ne·ces·si·tous (necĕs'ĭtus) *adj.* Poor, needy.

ne·ces·si·ty (nesĕs'ĭtē) *n.* (pl. **-ties**). 1. Constraint or compulsion regarded as a law prevailing through the material universe and governing all human action; constraining power of circumstances; state of things compelling to certain courses; **of** ~, unavoidably. 2. Imperative need (*for*); indispensability; indispensable thing necessary. 3. Want, poverty, hardship, pressing need.

neck (nĕk) *n.* 1. Part of body that connects head with shoulders; flesh of animal's neck as food, this as cut of meat; part of garment covering or lying next to neck; **break one's** ~, dislocate cervical vertebrae, be killed so; (colloq.) make great effort; **get it in the** ~, (slang) suffer fatal or severe blow; **save one's** ~, escape being hanged (also transf.); **stick one's** ~ **out**, (colloq.) expose oneself to danger; ~ **and** ~, running even in race. 2. Narrow part *of* vessel, esp. of bottle near mouth, or *of* passage, pass, or channel; pass, narrow channel, isthmus; narrow connecting part between two parts of thing; (archit.

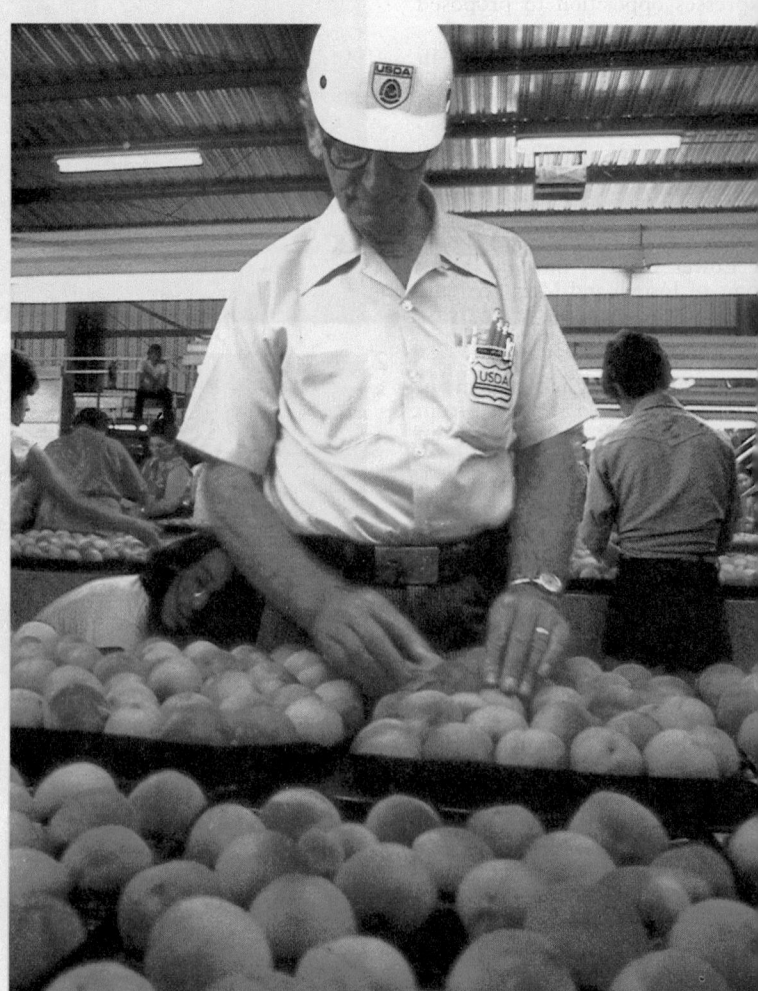

wer part of capital. 3. (geol.) Conical hill consisting of igneous ock that has accumulated in throat f volcano and been exposed later hen the mountain itself weathered way; ~ **of the woods**, (slang) ocality. 4. **neck′band**, part of arment around neck; **neck′cloth**, cravat; **neck′erchief**, kerchief orn around neck; **neck′lace**, rnament of precious stones, beads, tc., worn around neck; **neck′tie**, esp.) narrow band of woven or nitted material placed around neck nd tied in front. **neck** *v.i.* (slang) Iug, exchange kisses and caresses.

nec·ro·man·cy (nĕk′rōmănsē) *n.* Act of predicting by means of ommunication with the dead; nagic, enchantment. **nec′ro·man·cer** *n.* **nec·ro·man·tic** nĕkrōmăn′tĭk) *adj.*

nec·ro·phi·ly (nekrŏf′ĭlē) *n.* Morbid preoccupation with orpses, death, etc.

nec·rop·o·lis (nekrŏp′olĭs) *n.* Cemetery.

nec·rop·sy (nĕkrŏp′sē) (pl. **·sies**), **nec·ros·co·py** (nekrŏs′kopē) *n.* (pl. **-pies**). Postmortem examination, autopsy.

nec·ro·sis (nekrō′sĭs) *n.* (path.) Death of circumscribed piece of tissue, esp. mortification of bones. **ne·crot·ic** (nekrŏt′ĭk) *adj.* **nec′ro·ize** (nĕk′rotīz) *v.i.* (**-tized, -tiz·ing**).

nec·tar (nĕk′ter) *n.* 1. (Gk. myth.) Drink of the gods; any delicious drink. 2. Sweet fluid or oney produced by plants. **nec·tar·e·an** (nĕktār′ēan), **nec·tar′e·ous**, **nec·tar·if·er·ous** nĕkterĭf′erus) *adjs.*

nec·tar·ine (nĕkterēn′, nĕk′terēn) *n.* Kind of peach with thin ownless skin and firm flesh.

nec·ta·ry (nĕk′terē) *n.* (pl. **·ries**). (bot.) Glandular organ or tissue secreting nectar, occurring mainly in flowers, occasionally in eaves and stems.

nee, née (nā) *adjs.* (before married woman's maiden name) Born, as *Mrs. Smith, née Jones.*

need (nēd) *n.* 1. Necessity arising from circumstances of case; imperative demand for presence or possession *of*; **have ~ of**, require, want. 2. Emergency, crisis, time f difficulty; destitution, lack of ecessaries, poverty. 3. Thing wanted, respect in which want is elt, requirement. **need** *v.* (archaic) Be necessary; stand in need of, equire; be needy; be under necessity or obligation to or *to* do. **need′ful** *adj.* Requisite, necessary, ndispensable. **need′ful·ness** *n.*

nee·dle (nē′del) *n.* 1. Instrument

Since prehistoric times, people of all cultures have ornamented themselves with necklaces. Here a Masai woman from Southern Africa shows the local custom of wearing multiple strings of small beads.

Needlework *and embroidery have been used to fulfil a variety of needs. Persian armor in 490 B.C. consisted of embroidered quilting. More recently needlework has become a popular pastime led by an arts and crafts revival.*

used in sewing, usu. small slender piece of polished steel with fine point at one end and hole or eye for thread at other; knitting needle. 2. Piece of magnetized steel used as indicator compass or in magnetic or electrical apparatus (also **magnetic ~**); strip of gold or silver of standard fineness used with touchstone in testing purity of these metals. 3. Pointed etching or engraving instrument; long slender pointed instrument used in surgery; pointed end of hypodermic or other syringe; steel pin exploding cartridge or breechloader; (in

The genus **Nemesia** — part of the fox-glove family — is native to South Africa. Its beautiful, fragrant flowers, however, have made many species popular garden plants.

One of England's distinguished heroe **Nelson** entered the navy at the age 12, and at 20 became a post capta Despite repeated illnesses and seve injuries he was renowned for his bra ery in battle.

phonographs etc.) small pointed instrument transmitting vibrations from record to soundbox; stylus used in recording. 4. Obelisk (**Cleopatra's N** ~); sharp rock, peak; beam of wood, esp. used as temporary support in under-pinning; sharp slender leaf of fir or pine; (chem. etc.) needle-shaped crystal. 5. ~ **bath**, shower bath with fine strong spray; ~ **fish**, any of various fishes with very fine teeth, esp. garfish; ~ **point**, fine sharp point; **nee′dlepoint**: see LACE; **nee′dlewoman**, woman who sews, seamstress; **nee′dlework**, sewing, embroidery, etc. **needle** v. (**-dled, -dling**). Sew, pierce, operate on, with needle; (colloq.) goad, irritate; thread (one's way) between or through things; under-pin with needle beams; form needle-shaped crystals.

need·less (nēd′lĭs) *adj*. Un-necessary, uncalled for. **need′-less·ly** *adv*. **need′less·ness** *n*.

needs (nēdz) *adv*. Of necessity (now only after or before *must*).

need·y (nē′dē) *adj*. (**need·i·er, need·i·est**). Poor, indigent, necessitous. **need′i·ly** *adv*. **need′-i·ness** *n*.

ne'er (nār) *adv*. (poet.) Never; ~ **-do-well**, good-for-nothing (person).

ne·far·i·ous (nefār′ēus, -făr′-) *adj*. Wicked, iniquitous. **ne·far′-i·ous·ly** *adv*. **ne·far′i·ous·ness** *n*.

Nef·er·ti·ti (nĕfertē′tē). Egyptian queen of early 14th c. B.C.; noted for her beauty; wife of AKHNATON.

ne·gate (nĭgāt′, nĕg′āt) *v.t.* (**-gat·ed, -gat·ing**). Nullify; deny existence of, imply or involve non-existence of; be the negation of.

ne·ga·tion (nĭgā′shọn) *n*. 1.

Denying; negative statement or doctrine; refusal, contradiction, denial *of*. 2. (logic) Affirmation of difference or exclusion. 3. Absence or opposite of something actual or positive; negative or unreal thing, nonentity. **neg·a-to·ry** (nĕg′atōrē, -tōrē) *adj*.

neg·a·tive (nĕg′atĭv) *adj*. 1. Expressing or implying denial, prohibition, or refusal; wanting, consisting in the want of, positive attributes; of opposite nature to thing regarded as possible. 2. (math., phys., etc.) Denoting quantities to be subtracted from others; less than zero; in the opposite direction to that which (arbitrarily or by convention) is regarded as positive; (elect.) having a negative charge; ~ **charge**, one of the 2 kinds of electric charge, the charge of an· electron (cf. POSITIVE def. 6); ~ **pole**, region of excess of electrons, cathode; also (magnetism) applied to the south-seeking pole of a magnet and the corresponding (north) pole of Earth; ~ **sign**, minus sign. 3. (phot.) Applied to image in which lights appear dark and shadows light (see *n*. 3 below.) **neg′a·tive·ly** *adv*. **neg′a·tive·ness, neg·a·tiv-i·ty** (nĕgatĭv′ĭtē) *ns*. **negative** *n*. 1. Negative statement, reply, or word; right of veto; **in the** ~,

negative(ly), no. 2. Negati quality, want of something; (math negative or minus· quantity. (phot.) Print in which lights an shadows of nature are reverse made by direct action of light o an emulsion deposited on glass other transparent substance, an used for producing a positive prin **negative** *v.t.* (**-tived, -tiv·ing** Veto, reject, refuse to accept countenance; disprove (inference hypothesis); contradict (statement neutralize (effect).

neg·a·tiv·ism (nĕg′atĭvĭzem) Doctrine characterized by denial accepted beliefs etc. **neg′a·tiv·is** *adj*. & *n*. **neg·a·tiv·is·tic** (nĕg atĭvĭs′tĭk) *adj*.

Ne·gev (nĕ′gĕv), **Ne·ge** (nĕ′gĕb). Semidesert region Israel between Beersheba and th Gulf of Aqaba.

ne·glect (nĕglĕkt′) *v.t.* Dis regard, slight; leave uncared-fo omit *to* do. ~ *n*. Neglecting being neglected; negligence. **ne glect′ful** *adj*. **ne·glect′ful·ly** *adv* **ne·glect′ful·ness** *n*.

neg·li·gee, né·gli·gé (nĕglĭzhā′

ĕg´lĭzhă) *ns.* Free-and-easy or
nceremonious attire, esp.
'oman's loose garment worn on
formal occasions or in dishabille.

neg·li·gence (nĕg´lĭjens) *n.*
Vant of proper care or attention,
piece of) carelessness; **con-**
ibutory ~, negligence on a
erson's part that has helped to
ring about the injury that he has
uffered. **neg´li·gent** *adj.* **neg´li-**
ent·ly *adv.*

neg·li·gi·ble (nĕg´lĭjĭbel) *adj.*
'hat need not be regarded, that
1ay be neglected. **neg·li·gi-**
il·i·ty (nĕglĭjĭbĭl´ĭtē), **neg·li·gi-**
le·ness *ns.* **neg´li·gi·bly** *adv.*

ne·go·ti·ate (nĭgō´shēāt) *v.*
at·ed, -at·ing). 1. Confer (*with*
nother) with view to compromise
r agreement; arrange (affair),
ring about (desired object) by
egotiating. 2. Transfer (bill) to
nother for a consideration; convert
1to cash or notes, get or give value
or (bill, check) in money. 3. Clear,
et over, dispose of (fence, obstacle,
lfficulty). **ne·go·ti·a·ble** (nĭgō´-
nēabel, -sha-) *adj.* **ne·go·ti·ant**
nĭgō´shēant), **ne·go·ti·a·tion**
nĭgōshēā´shon), **ne·go´ti·a·tor** *ns.*

Ne·gress (nē´grĭs) *n.* (now con-
1dered offensive) Black woman.

Ne·gril·lo (nĭgrĭl´ō) *n.* (pl. **-los,**
ollect. **-lo**). Small black person;
ne of dwarf black people of Central
nd S. Africa.

Ne·gri·to (nĭgrē´tō) *n.* (pl. **-tos,**
toes**). One of a small black people
1 Malaya–Polynesian region.

Ne·gro (nē´grō) *n.* (pl. **-groes**).
now considered offensive)
Member, esp. male, of black-
kinned race of mankind. ~ *adj.*
Of black people.

Ne·groid (nē´groid) *adj. & n.*
Member) of the division of
nankind with physical character-
stics of black races.

Ne·gus (nē´gus) *n.* Supreme
uler of Ethiopia.

Ne·he·mi·ah (nēamī´a) (4th c.
3.C.). Jewish governor of Judea
1nder Artaxerxes; rebuilder of
valls of Jerusalem; **Book of** ~,
1istorical book of Old Testament,
;iving account of rebuilding of
valls of Jerusalem and of various
eforms.

Neh·ru (nār´ōō), **Pandit**
awaharlal (1889–1964). Indian
Congress leader; 1st prime minister
f India 1947–64.

neigh (nā) *v.i. & n.* (Utter) cry
as) of horse.

neigh·bor (nā´ber) *n.* Dweller
1ext door, near, in same street,
village, or district, or in adjacent
:ountry, esp. regarded as one who
hould be friendly or as having
:laim on others' friendliness;
verson or thing next to or near
nother; (*attrib.*) neighboring. ~
v. Adjoin, border upon, border
n. **neigh´bor·less** *adj.*

neigh·bor·hood (nā´berhōōd)
n. Neighborly feeling or conduct;
nearness, vicinity *of*; neighbors,
people of a district, district (freq.
attrib., as in ~ *school* etc.).

neigh·bor·ly (nā´berlē) *adj.*
Like a good neighbor, friendly,
helpful. **neigh´bor·li·ness** *n.*

nei·ther (nē´dher, nī´-) *adv.*
(introducing mention of alternatives or different things, about
each of which a negative statement
is made) Not either; not, nor yet;
(strengthening preceding negative)
either. ~ *adj. & pron.* Not the
one or the other.

nek·ton (nĕk´ton, -tŏn) *n.* Group
of forms of free-swimming organic
life found at various depths in the
ocean and in lakes, taken
collectively.

nel·son (nĕl´son) *n.* (wrestling)
Class of holds (**double, full, half,**
quarter ~) in which arm is passed
under opponent's from behind and
the hand applied to his neck.

Nel·son (nĕl´son), **Horatio,**
Viscount Nelson, Duke of
Bronté (1758–1805). British
admiral and naval hero, killed in
battle against French and Spanish
off Trafalgar, 1805.

nem·a·to·cyst (nĕm´atosĭst,
nĭmăt´-) *n.* Cell in jellyfish, sea
anemones, etc., containing coiled
thread that can be projected as
sting.

nem·a·tode (nĕm´atōd) *adj. &*
n. (Worm) of slender unsegmented

cylindrical shape, of the phylum
Nematoda.

Nem·bu·tal (nĕm´byutawl) *n.*
(trademark) Sodium salt of pento-
barbitone, used as sedative and
anticonvulsant.

Nem·e·sis (nĕm´ĭsĭs) *n.* (Gk.
myth.) Goddess of vengeance;
regarded as personification of the
gods' resentment at, and punishment of, insolence toward them;
hence **n** ~, retributive justice.

neo- *prefix.* New; modern, later
or lately found or invented etc.

ne·o·dym·i·um (nēōdĭm´ēum)
n. (chem.) Metallic element of rare-
earth group; symbol Nd, at. no.
60, at. wt. 144.24. [NEO- +
DIDYMIUM]

Ne·o·gene (nē´ojēn) *adj. & n.*
(geol.) (Of) the later period of the
Tertiary era including the Miocene
and Pliocene epochs.

ne·o·lith·ic (nēolĭth´ĭk) *adj.* Of
the later Stone Age (as contrasted
with PALEOLITHIC), characterized
by ground or polished stone implements and by great advances in food
production and simple skills.

ne·ol·o·gism (nēŏl´ojĭzem) (pl.
-gisms), **ne·ol·o·gy** (nēŏl´ojē) (pl.
-gies) *ns.* 1. Coining or using of
new words, newly coined word.

*Peoples such as the pygmies,
Hottentots and Bantu all possess
negroid characteristics. These
Rwandan children show how much variation may occur between the peoples
of a particular country.*

central nervous system

sensory and motor nerves

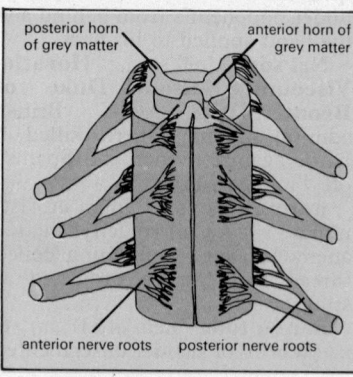

posterior horn of grey matter — anterior horn of grey matter

anterior nerve roots — posterior nerve roots

2. Tendency to, adoption of, novel or rationalistic religious views. **ne·ol·o·gist** *n.* **ne·ol·o·gis·tic** (nēŏlŏjĭs′tĭk), **ne·ol·o·gis′ti·cal** *adjs.*

ne·on (nē′ŏn) *n.* 1. (chem.) Colorless, odorless, inert, gaseous element present in minute quantities in the atmosphere; symbol Ne, at. no. 10, at. wt. 20.179; ~ **light**, bright orange-red light obtained by passing an electrical discharge through a tube or bulb containing neon at low pressure, extensively used for illuminated signs in advertising, etc.; also light of blue, green, etc. obtained by mixing other inert gases with neon; ~ **tetra**, small tropical American freshwater fish.

ne·o·phyte (nē′ofīt) *n.* New convert, esp. among primitive Christians or Roman Catholics; newly ordained R. C. priest, novice of religious order; beginner, novice, tyro.

Ne·o·pla·to·nism (nēōplā′-tonĭzem) *n.* Philosophical and religious system, chiefly consisting of a mixture of Platonic ideas with Oriental mysticism, which originated at Alexandria in the 3rd c. and is represented in the works of Plotinus, Porphyry, and Proclus. **Ne·o·pla·ton′ic** (nēōplatŏn′ĭk) *adj.* **Ne·o·pla′to·nist** *n.*

Ne·op·tol·e·mus (nēŏptŏl′-emus). (Gk. legend) Son of

ACHILLES; in the Trojan War he killed PRIAM, and ANDROMACHE fell to his lot when the TROJAN captives were distributed.

Ne·pal (nāpawl′, -pahl′, -păl′, ne-). Independent kingdom between India and Tibet; capital, Katmandu. **Nep·a·lese** (nĕpalēz′, -lēs′) *adj. & n.*

ne·pen·the (nĭpĕn′thē) *n.* (pl. **-thes** pr. -thēz). Egyptian drug mentioned in the *Odyssey* as banishing grief; (poet.) any drug having this power.

Ne·per (nā′per) = NAPIER.

neph·ew (nĕf′ū; *Brit.* also nĕv′ū) *n.* Brother's or sister's son.

ne·phol·o·gy (nĕfŏl′ojē) *n.* Study of clouds.

neph·rite (nĕf′rīt) *n.* = JADE,[2] def. 1. [Gk. *nephros* kidney, from its supposed value in kidney disease]

ne·phrit·ic (nefrĭt′ĭk) *adj.* Of or in the kidneys, renal.

ne·phri·tis (nefrī′tĭs) *n.* Inflammation of the kidneys.

ne·phro·sis (nefrō′sĭs) *n.* Degenerative disease of kidneys. **ne·phrot·ic** (nefrŏt′ĭk) *adj.*

ne plus ul·tra (nē plŭs ŭl′tra; *Lat.* nĕ plōos ōol′trah). Farthest or highest point attained or attainable. [L., = "not more

Our **nerves** carry information to o brains and orders to our muscles. A elaborate network of specialized ce enables us — with a few tragic exce tions — to perceive, and respor appropriately to our environment.

beyond" (supposed inscription c Pillars of Hercules)]

nep·o·tism (nĕp′otĭzem) Favoritism shown to relatives es in offering employment; (hist practice on the part of som medieval and renaissance popes showing special favor to the natural children, who were know euphemistically as their nephew **nep·o·tist** *n.*

Nep·tune (nĕp′tōon, -tūn). (Rom. myth.) God of the se identified with POSEIDON. (astron.) Third largest of th planets, with two known satellite discovered 1846 as a result mathematical computations of J. C Adams in England and Leverrie in France; symbol Ψ. **Nep·tu ni·an** (nĕptōō′nēan, -tū′-) *adj.*

nep·tu·ni·um (nĕptōō′nēun -tū′-) *n.* (chem.) Transuran element, not found in natur occurring as a temporary stage the formation of plutonium fro uranium 238; symbol Np, at. n 93, at. wt. 237.0482.

Ne·re·id (nēr′eĭd) *n.* 1. (G myth.) One of the sea nymph daughters of Nereus. 2. **n ~**, (zool marine polychaete worm.

Ne·re·us (nēr′ēus, -ōos). (G myth.) Sea deity having the powe like Proteus, of assuming variou forms.

Ne·ro (nēr′ō). Nero Claudiu Caesar Augustus Germanicus (A.[37–68), Roman emperor 54–6 proverbial for tyranny an brutality.

ner·o·li (nĕr′olē, nēr′-) oi Essential oil from flowers of bitt orange, used in perfumery. [f. nam

Both industry and agriculture are being developed in **Nepal** but many of the traditional ways remain unchanged. This ancient fountain still provides water for people living near Katmandu.

of Italian princess supposed to have invented it]

nerv·ate (nēr′vāt) *adj.* (bot.) (of leaves) Having ribs. **ner·va·tion** (nērvā′sh*o*n) *n.*

nerve (nērv) *n.* 1. Sinew, tendon (now only poet. exc. in **strain every** ~, make all possible effort); vigor, energy, well-strung state. 2. (bot.) Rib, esp. midrib, of leaf. 3. (anat.) Fiber or bundle of fibers connecting and conveying impulses of sensation and motion between brain or spinal cord or ganglionic organ and some part of body; nervous fiber; (pl.) bodily state in regard to physical sensitiveness and interaction between brain and other parts, disordered state in these respects, exaggerated sensitiveness, nervousness; **get on one's nerves**, affect one with irritation, impatience, fear, etc.; **nerve center**, ganglion, group of closely connected nerve cells associated in performing some function; **nerve gas**, poison gas that attacks the nervous system, esp. affecting respiration. 4. Coolness in danger; boldness; assurance; (slang) audacity, impertinence; **lose one's nerve**, become timid or irresolute. **nerve** *v.t.* (**nerved, nerv·ing**). Give strength, vigor, or courage to; ~ **oneself**, brace oneself (to face something unpleasant).

nerve·less (nērv′lĭs) *adj.* Inert, wanting in vigor or spirit, listless; undisturbed by danger, cool under attack; (bot., entom.) without nervures; (anat., zool.) without nerves. **nerve′less·ly** *adv.* **nerve′less·ness** *n.*

nerv·ous (nēr′v*u*s) *adj.* 1. Of the nerves; ~ **breakdown**, (colloq.) loss of emotional and mental stability; ~ **system**, system of specialized conducting tissue that enables an organism to coordinate its activity in relation to its environment. 2. Sinewy, muscular. 3. Having disordered or delicate nerves; excitable, highly strung, easily agitated, timid. **nerv′ous·ly** *adv.* **nerv′ous·ness** *n.*

ner·vure (nērv′yer) *n.* 1. One of the tubes strengthening an insect's wing. 2. Principal vein of leaf.

nerv·y (nēr′vē) *adj.* (**nerv·i·er, nerv·i·est**). 1. Nervous; trying to the nerves; irritable, apprehensive. 2. (colloq.) Insolent; courageous.

nes·cience (nĕsh′ens, -ēens) *n.* Not knowing, absence of knowledge *of.* **nes′cient** *adj.* Ignorant (*of*); agnostic.

ness (nĕs) *n.* Promontory, headland, cape.

Ness (nĕs), **Loch.** Lake in

Inverness-shire, Scotland, forming part of Caledonian Canal.

-ness *suffix.* Having a specified state or condition.

Nes·sus (něs′*u*s). (Gk. myth.) Centaur shot by Hercules for trying to carry off his wife Deianira; Nessus' blood-stained tunic, given to Deianira as a charm to reclaim an unfaithful husband, eventually caused Hercules' death.

nest (něst) *n.* Structure or place made or chosen by bird for laying eggs and sheltering young; animal's or insect's abode or spawning or breeding place; snug or secluded retreat, lodging, shelter, bed, receptacle; haunt *of* robbers etc.; fostering place *of* vice etc.; brood, swarm; collection, series of similar objects; set *of boxes, tables,* etc. fitting one inside another; ~ **egg,** real or imitation egg left in nest to induce hen to go on laying there; sum of money kept as reserve or nucleus. **nest** *v.* Make or have nest in specified place; take to nest building; take birds' nests.

nes·tle (něs′*e*l) *v.* (**-tled, -tling**). Make nest (now rare); settle oneself, be settled, comfortably *down, in, among,* etc., leaves, wraps, chair, etc.; press oneself affectionately (*close*) *to* person; lie half-hidden or embedded; push (head, shoulder, etc.) affectionately or snugly *in;* hold embraced (usu. in past. part.). **nes′tler** *n.*

Nes·tor (něs′*ter,* -tōr). (Gk. legend) King of Pylos; in old age led his subjects to the Trojan War, where his wisdom, justice, and eloquence were proverbial; hence, wise old man.

Nes·to·ri·us (něstōr′ē*u*s, -tōr′-)

*The practice of **nest building** is found in all groups of animals, from mammals to insects. Some nests are so ingeniously made as to remind us of human architecture, such as the martin's nest of dried mud (1) and the wasp's elegant paper structure (2).*

(d. *c*451). Syrian ecclesiastic; disciple of St. John Chrysostom and patriarch of Constantinople (428–31); held that Christ had distinct human and divine persons and hence that the Virgin Mary should not be called "Mother of God"; was condemned by the Councils of Ephesus (431) and Chalcedon (451). **Nes′to·ri·an, Nes·to′ri·an·ism** *ns.*

net[1] (nět) *n.* Meshed fabric of twine, cord, hair, etc.; piece of this used for catching fish etc. or for covering, confining, protecting, carrying, etc.; moral or mental snare; reticulation, network; net stroke; ~ **stroke,** stroke in which ball hits this; **net′work,** arrangement with intersecting lines and interstices resembling those of net; complex system *of* railroads, rivers, canals, etc., ramification; broadcasting system of several stations linked together. **net** *v.* (**net·ted, net·ting**). Cover, confine, catch, with net(s); fish (river etc.) with nets, set nets in (river); make netting; make (purse, hammock, etc.) by netting.

net[2] (nět) *adj.* Free from deduc-

tion, remaining after necessar[y] deductions; ~ **price,** real price o[f] which discount is not allowed; ~ **profit,** true profit, actual gain aft[er] working expenses have been paid; ~ **weight,** weight excluding wrap[-] pings. **net** *v.t.* (**net·ted, net·ting**) Gain or yield (sum) as net profit.

neth·er (nědh′*er*) *adj.* (archaic o[r] joc.) Lower. **neth′er·most** *adj.*

Neth·er·lands (nědh′*er*landz) (Du. **Nederland**) 1. Small king[-] dom in N. Europe, in English fre[q.] called Holland; capital, Amsterdam; seat of government, The Hague; principal language, Dutch. 2. (hist.) Low Countries, the whol[e] area of the Rhine, Meuse, an[d] Scheldt deltas, now occupied b[y] Holland, Belgium, Luxembourg, and small parts of France an[d] Germany. During the Middle Age[s] it was divided among numerou[s] countships and dukedoms; by th[e] mid-16th c. these were unite[d] under the Hapsburg empero[r] Charles V, but in the wars o[f] religion the N. (Dutch) par[t] revolted (1555–88) and became a[n] independent Protestant Republi[c] (**United Provinces of the ~,** o[r]

NORTH SEA

AMSTERDAM

THE HAGUE

ROTTERDAM

NETHERLANDS

Germany

Belgium

*Gaining their independence from Spain in the 80 Years' War, the United Provinces of the **Netherlands** have, since the 17th century, grown into a modern industrial State.*

States General); meanwhile the S. part passed to the Spanish Hapsburgs (**Spanish** ~) and later, in 1713, to the Austrian Hapsburgs (**Austrian** ~). In 1815 both N. and S. were united under a monarchy (**Kingdom of the** ~), but the S. revolted in 1830 and became an independent kingdom, BELGIUM. ~ **Antilles**, formerly Dutch West Indies; autonomous territory of the Netherlands in the Caribbean consisting of the islands of Curaçao, Aruba, Bonaire, St. Martin, St. Eustatius, and Saba; capital, Willemstad on Curaçao. **Neth′er·land·er** *n.*

net·su·ke (nĕt′skē, -skā; *Jap.* nĕ′tsōōkĕ′) *n.* Carved or otherwise ornamented piece of ivory etc. once worn by Japanese as bob or button on cord by which articles were suspended from girdle.

net·ting (nĕt′ĭng) *n.* (esp.) Netted string, wire, or thread; piece of this.

net·tle (nĕt′el) *n.* Plant of genus *Urtica*, with two common species (*U. dioica* and *U. urens*) growing profusely on wasteland and noted for stinging properties of leaf hairs; plant resembling this, esp. stinging nettle; ~ **rash**, skin eruption in patches like those produced by nettle stings, URTICARIA. **nettle** *v.t.* (**-tled, -tling**). 1. Beat or sting with nettles; get *oneself* stung with nettles. 2. Irritate, provoke.

neu·ral (noor′al, nūr′-) *adj.* Of the nerves; of the nervous system.

neu·ral·gia (nōōrăl′ja, nyōō-) *n.* Condition of nerves (usu. of head or face) causing intense intermittent pain. **neu·ral′gic** *adj.*

neu·ras·the·ni·a (nōōrasthē′-nēa, nūr-) *n.* Functional nervous weakness, nervous debility. **neu·ras·then·ic** (nōōrasthĕn′ĭk, nūr-) *adj. & n.*

neu·ri·tis (nōōrītĭs, nyōō-) *n.* Inflammation of nerve(s). **neu·rit·ic** (nōōrĭt′ĭk, nyōō-) *adj.*

neuro- *prefix.* Of nerves.

neu·rol·o·gy (nōōrŏl′ojē, nyōō-) *n.* Scientific study of the anatomy, functions, and diseases of the nervous system. **neu·ro·log·i·cal** (nōōrolŏj′ĭkal, nūr-) *adj.* **neu·rol′o·gist** *n.*

*Spinning and weaving with painfully obtained **nettle fibers** was often the lot of the heroine of old European folktales. The plant is, however, the food of many kinds of butterfly larvae.*

*Probably **nets** were among the first of man's inventions, both as an aid to hunting and for carrying provisions. Fishing nets can be fixed, moved by hand (like that of these Portuguese tunny fishers), or towed behind a boat.*

neu·ron (noor´ŏn, nūr´-), **neu·rone** (noor´ŏn, nūr´-) *ns.* Nerve cell with its appendages, the basic structural unit of the nervous system. **neu·ron·ic** (noorŏn´ĭk, nyoo-) *adj.*

neu·rop·ter·ous (noorŏp´terus, nyoo-) *adj.* Of the Neuroptera, an order of insects having four naked membranous transparent wings with netlike vein patterns.

neu·ro·sis (noorō´sĭs, nyoo-) *n.* (pl. **-ses** pr. -sēz). (path., psychol.) Derangement of normal function due to disorders of nervous system, esp. such as are unaccompanied by demonstrable organic change. **neu·rot·ic** (noorŏt´ĭk, nyoo-) *adj. & n.* (Person) affected with neurosis. **neu·rot´i·cal·ly** *adv.*

neu·ter (noo´ter, nū´-) *adj.* 1. (gram.) Neither masculine nor feminine. 2. Neither male nor female; (bot.) having neither pistils nor stamens; (entom.) sexually undeveloped, sterile. ~ *n.* 1. Word of neuter gender. 2. Sexually undeveloped female insect, esp. bee or ant; castrated animal. ~ *v.t.* Castrate.

neu·tral (noo´tral, nū´-) *adj.* 1. Not assisting either of two belligerent nations, belonging to a nation remaining inactive during hostilities, exempted or excluded from warlike operations; taking neither side in dispute or difference of opinion, indifferent, impartial. 2. Not distinctly marked or colored, indefinite, vague, indeterminate; (of color) grayish or brownish; (of sound) indistinct, obscure. 3. (chem.) Neither acid nor alkaline; (elect.) neither positive nor negative. 4. Neuter, asexual. **neu´tral·ly** *adv.* **neu·tral·i·ty** (nootrăl´ĭtē, nū-) *n.* **neutral** *n.* 1. Neutral country or person; citizen of neutral country. 2. (mech.) Position of gear mechanism in which the propelling mechanism can revolve freely without transmitting power to the parts to be driven.

neu·tral·ize (noo´tralīz, nū´-) *v.t.* (**-ized, -iz·ing**). Counterbalance, render ineffective by opposite force or effect; exempt or exclude (place) from sphere of hostilities. **neu·tral·i·za·tion** (nootralīzā´shon, nū-) *n.*

neu·tri·no (nootrē´nō, nū-) *n.* (pl. **-nos**). Neutral elementary particle of negligible mass.

neu·tron (noo´trŏn, nū´-) *n.* Electrically neutral particle of almost the same mass as a proton, present in all atomic nuclei except those of hydrogen.

Nev., NV *abbrevs.* Nevada.

Ne·vad·a (nevădα, -vah´dα). State of western U.S., admitted to the Union in 1864; capital, Carson City. **Ne·vad´an** *adj. & n.* (esp. geol.) Of an episode of mountain formation during the Mesozoic era.

né·vé (nāvā´, nā´vā) *n.* Expanse of granular snow not yet compressed into ice at head of glacier.

nev·er (nĕv´er) *adv.* At no time, on no occasion, not ever; not at all; (colloq., expressing surprise or incredulity) surely not; ~ **a**, not a, no — at all; ~ **a one**, none; ~ **mind, nev´ermind** (*v.*) do not be troubled (about); **nevermore´**, at no future time; **never-never land**, unreal, imaginary place or state of mind; **never so**, (in conditional clauses) to unlimited extent, ever

so; **nevertheless´**, notwithstanding, but for all that.

Ne·vis (nē´vĭs, nĕv´ĭs). Island in the West Indies, part of St. Kitts.

ne·vus (nē´vus) *n.* (pl. **-vi** pr. -vī). (path.) Birthmark, congenital lesion of skin, a network of hypertrophied blood vessels causing sharply defined red patch level with skin surface; (also) pigmented mole.

new (noo, nū) *adj.* Not existing before, now first made, brought into existence, invented, introduced, known or heard of,

*Many people associate **Nevada** with gambling at Las Vegas, but the State also earns large revenue from mining and industry; and there are cattle ranches.*

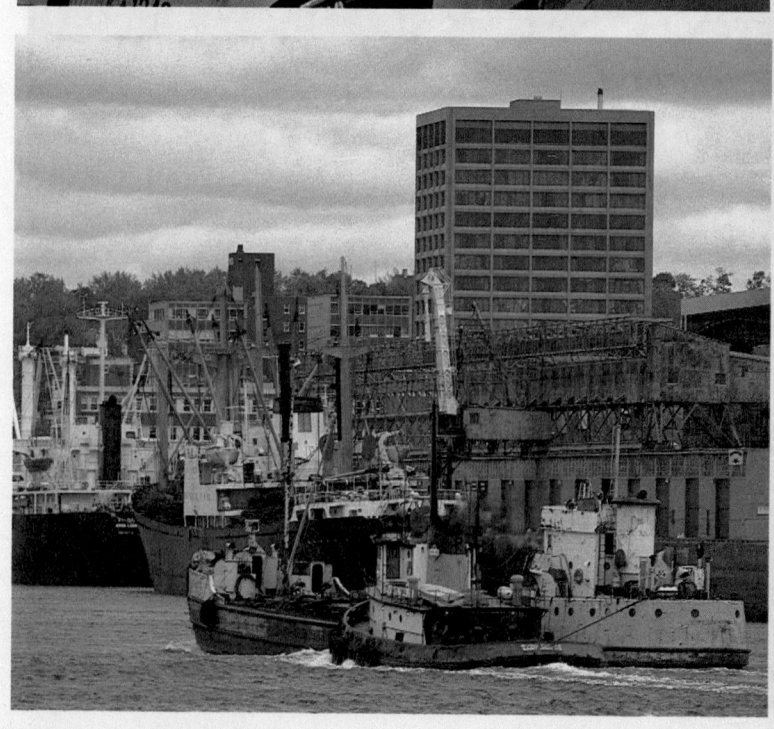

*The Port of St. John in the Bay of Fundy is the principal seaport for the province of **New Brunswick** in Canada. The fishing catch is mainly lobster and sardines.*

experienced, or discovered; un-
miliar *to*; renewed, fresh, further,
dditional; later, modern, new-
ngled; of recent growth, origin,
rival, or manufacture, now first
sed, not worn or exhausted; not yet
ccustomed *to*, fresh *from*; (of
mily or person) lately risen in
osition; **new′comer**, person lately
rrived; **New Deal**: see DEAL³;
ew′fan′gled, different from the
ood old fashion, having no merit
ut novelty; **new-laid**, (of eggs)
ecently laid; **new learning**, study
f the Bible and the Greek classics
their original language at the time
f the Reformation and Renaissance
England; **new moon**, moon
hen first visible as a crescent after
onjunction with sun, time of such
ppearance; **new′speak**, (joc. in
erogatory sense) reformed version
f a language [f. George Orwell's
ovel *1984*]; **New Style**: see STYLE;
ew Testament: see TESTAMENT;
ew World, the Americas, dis-
overed at a comparatively late
eriod; **New Year**, coming or lately
egun year, first few days of year;
ew Year's Day (freq. **New
ear's**), Jan. 1. **new′ish** *adj.*
ew′ness *n.* **new** *adv.* Newly,
ecently, just; anew.

New Britain. Island of Bis-
arck Archipelago.

New Brunswick. SE. maritime
rovince of Canada; capital,
redericton.

New Cal·e·do·ni·a (kălĕdō′nēa,
dōn′ya). Overseas territory of
rance in SW. Pacific 1,000 mi.
,600 km) E. of Australia, consist-
g of this island and several smaller
nes; capital, Nouméa.

*he capitol building in **New Hampshire**,
ew England. The State is one of the
ost industrialized in the U.S.A. With its
eautiful scenery, tourists also contrib-
te a large proportion to the State's
conomy.*

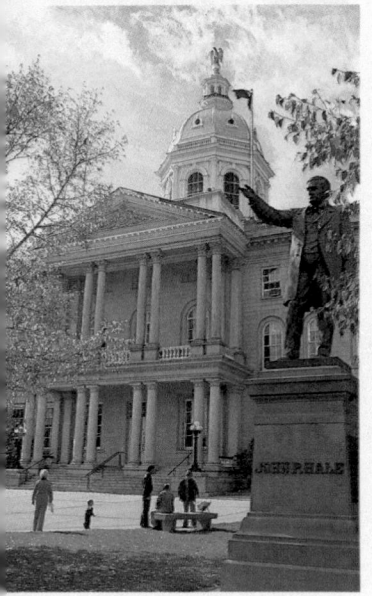

New Del·hi (dĕl′ē). Capital of
India in the N. part on the Jumna
River, S. of Delhi.

new·el (nōō′el, nū′-) *n.* (archit.)
Center pillar or (**open** or **hollow**
~) well of winding stair; post
supporting stair handrail at top or
bottom.

New England. Part of U.S.
comprising NE. states of Maine,
New Hampshire, Vermont, Massa-
chusetts, Rhode Island, and
Connecticut. **New Englander** *n.*
Native, inhabitant, of New
England.

New·found·land (nōō′fund-
lănd, -land, -fun-, nū′-, nōofownd′-
land, nū-). Large island, with
famous fisheries, at mouth of St.
Lawrence River; discovered and
claimed for England 1497 by John
Cabot; formerly a Dominion of the
British Empire; united with Canada
as one of its provinces, 1949;
capital, St. John's; ~ **dog**, large
dog of a breed native to N. Amer.,
with thick coarse coat, noted for
sagacity, good temper, strength,
and swimming powers. **New·-
found·land·er** (nōofownd′land*er*,
nū-) *n.*

*The principal export of **New Britain** is
copra, largely produced in the north of
the island, but native cooperatives grow
considerable amounts of other crops
such as cocoa.*

New Guinea. Pacific island N.
of Australia, divided into (1) the
Indonesian province of West Irian,
and (2) Papua New Guinea.

New Hampshire. NE. state of
U.S., one of the original 13 states
of the Union (1788); capital,
Concord.

New Ha·ven (hā′ven). City and
port in Connecticut on Long Island
Sound; site of Yale University.

New Hebrides. Group of
islands in W. Pacific, under joint
French and British administration;
capital, Vila.

New Jersey. Middle Atlantic
state of U.S., one of the original 13
states of the Union (1787); capital,
Trenton.

new·ly (nōō′lē, nū′-) *adv.* Recently, just; in new manner;

*Newfoundland's economy was at first
based solely on cod fisheries. More
recently, there has been expansion of
mining and forestry.*

1

2

The peoples of **New Guinea** originally had a garden-based economy but Europeans introduced cash cropping of copra, coffee and cocoa. Most of the coffee (1) is grown in the Highlands. The Sepik River is famed for the wood carving (2) of its people.

new′lywed(s) (*adj.* & *n.pl.*), recently married (couple).

New·man (nōō′man, nū′-), **John Henry** (1801–90). English theologian and author; as an Anglican clergyman, was one of the founders of the Oxford or Tractarian movement; was received into R.C. Ch. 1845; published his *Apologia pro Vita sua* 1864; was created cardinal 1879.

New Mexico. State of southwest U.S.; admitted to the Union in 1912; capital, Santa Fe.

New Or·le·ans (ōr′lēenz, -lenz, ōrlēnz′). City and port on Mississippi in Louisiana, 100 mi. (160 km)

N. of Gulf of Mexico; noted for French architecture and Creole cuisine of early settlers; birthplace of jazz music.

New·port (nōō′pōrt, nū′-). Port and summer resort in SE. Rhode Island; site of elaborate mansions; formerly center of fashionable society season.

*Above: As an Anglican and later a Roman Catholic, **John Henry Newman** was a significant leader in the development of religious philosophy in 19th century England.*

*Above left: **New York City,** largest city in the western hemisphere, with five counties in its boundaries. Left: Renovated tenements and housing in the Bronx, one of New York's boroughs.*

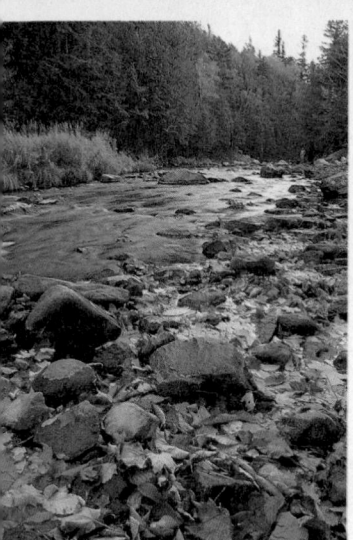

New York State noted for its diverse scenery as well as its industrial and business centres has in the north the beautiful Adirondack Upland, seen here in the Fall.

news (nooz, nūz) *n.* Tidings, new information, fresh event reported; radio or television report of this; **news′cast**, radio or television broadcast of news; **news′caster**, broadcaster of news on radio or television; **news′letter**, (orig.) letter containing news, sent out periodically to country towns etc.; now, periodical sent by mail to subscribers; **news′paper**, printed, now usu. daily or weekly, publication containing news, advertisements, and literary matter; **news′print**, paper for printing newspapers on; **news′reel**, motion picture giving items of recent news;

news′stand, booth for sale of newspapers; **news′vendor**, newspaper seller.

news·y (noo′zē, nū′-) *adj.* (**news·i·er, news·i·est**). (colloq.) Full of (sensational) news.

newt (noot, nūt) *n.* Small-tailed amphibian of the order Urodela.

new·ton (noo′ton, nū′-) *n.* (abbrev. N) Unit of force in meter-kilogram-second system, equal to the force producing an acceleration of 1 meter per second per second on a mass of 1 kilogram.

New·ton (noo′ton, nū′-), **Sir Isaac** (1642–1727). English natural philosopher; formulator of laws of motion and law of gravitation. **New·to·ni·an** (nooto′nēan, nū-) *adj. & n.* (Follower) of Newton or his theory of the universe.

New York. 1. Middle Atlantic state of U.S., one of the original 13 states of the Union (1788); capital, Albany. 2. Largest city of U.S., in New York State at mouth of Hudson River; **New York Bay**, inlet of Atlantic in SE. part of state; divided into Upper and Lower New York Bays, connected by the Narrows; **New York State Barge Canal**, system of waterways including the Erie, Oswego, and Champlain canals, connecting the Hudson River with Lake Erie at Buffalo and with the St. Lawrence through Lake Champlain. **New York′er** *n.* Native, inhabitant, of New York City.

New Zea·land (zē′land). Member nation of the Brit. Commonwealth, occupying 2 large and many

Sir Isaac Newton, *a mathematician and scientist, possessed one of the most original and inquiring minds of his day. His findings in optics, astronomy, and mathematics matched his work on the nature of gravity.*

*Horseshoe Falls, on the Canadian side of **Niagara Falls**. Erosion of the soft top layer of rock is causing the 160 ft. high falls to recede 3 ft. each year upstream.*

smaller islands in S. Pacific *c*1,000 miles (1,610 km) SE. of Australia; the islands were discovered by Tasman, 1642, and visited by Cook, 1769; became an English colony; acquired self-government 1852 and dominion status 1907; capital, Wellington. **New Zea′land·er** *n.* Native, inhabitant, of New Zealand. [f. *Zeeland*]

next (nĕkst) *adj.* Lying, living, being, nearest or nearest *to*; nearest in relationship or kinship; soonest come to, first ensuing, immediately following, coming nearest in order etc., *to*, immediately *before*; ~ **door**, (door of the) nearest or adjoining house (also fig.); **next-door to**, almost. **next** *prep.* In or into the next place, on the next occasion, in the next degree, to. ~ *n.* Next person or thing; ~ **of kin**, person most closely related (*to*).

nex·us (nĕk′sus) *n.* (pl. **nex·us, nex·us·es** pr. nĕk′susĭz). Bond, connection.

Nez Per·cé (nĕz′pĕrs′) (pl. **Nez Per·cés** pr. nĕz′pĕr′sĭz, collect, for def. 1 **Nez Per·cé**). 1. (Member of) a N. Amer. Indian people, formerly in the Pacific Northwest. 2. Sahaptin language of the Nez Percé.

N.F., Nfld., Nfd. *abbrevs.* Newfoundland.

NFL *abbrev.* National Football League.

NH, N.H. *abbrevs.* New Hampshire.

NHL *abbrev.* National Hockey League.

Ni *symbol.* Nickel.

Ni·ag·a·ra (nīăg′ra, -era). N. Amer. river flowing from Lake Erie into Lake Ontario and forming part of boundary between Canada and U.S.; ~ **Falls**, waterfalls in this river comprising Horseshoe or

Canadian Falls, 160 ft. (49 m) high, 2,500 ft. (763 m) wide, and American Falls, 167 ft. (51 m) high, 1,000 ft. (305 m) wide.

Nia·mey (nyahmā′). Capital of Niger in ·SW. part on ~ **River**.

nib (nĭb) *n.* Penpoint; point of tool etc.; (pl.) fragments of crushed cocoa beans.

nib·ble (nĭb′el) *v.* (**-bled, -bling**). Take small bites at; bite gently or cautiously or playfully. ~ *n.* Act of nibbling, esp. of fish at bait.

Ni·be·lungs (nē′belŏongz) *n.f.* (sing. **-lung** pr. lŏong). (German legend) Race of dwarfs in Norwa. **Ni·be·lung·en·lied** (nē′belŏonge lēt) *n.* Thirteenth-c. German poe (embodying a story found in th EDDA) telling of the life and death SIEGFRIED and of KRIEMHILD revenge.

*Rugged mountains, snow covered winter, extend like a backbone throug the South Island of **New Zealand**. Th country also has much thermal activi epitomized by active volcanos ar geysers. Its major exports are agric tural products.*

nib·lick (nĭb´lĭk) *n.* Golf club (no. 9 iron) with heavy lofted head, used esp. for playing out of bunkers.

Ni·cae·a (nīsē´a). (Turk. *Iznik*) Ancient city of Bithynia, scene of two ecumenical councils, the first (325) dealing with the Arian controversy and the second (787) the question of images.

Nic·a·ra·gua (nĭkarah´gwa). Central American republic, between Honduras and Costa Rica; independent since 1821; capital, Managua; **Lake** ∼, largest lake, 3,089 sq. mi. (8,001 sq. km) in Central America in S. Nicaragua. **Nic·a·ra´guan** *adj.* & *n.*

Nice (nēs). Port and resort city of SE. France on the Riviera near Italian border.

nice (nīs) *adj.* (**nic·er, nic·est**). 1. Fastidious; punctilious; requiring precision or discrimination; minute, subtle. 2. (colloq.) Agreeable, delightful; satisfactory; kind, friendly, considerate; generally commendable. **nice´ly** *adv.* **nice´ness** *n.*

Ni·cene (nīsēn´, nī´sēn) *adj.* Of Nicaea; ∼ **Creed**, formal statement of Christian belief based on decisions of first Council of Nicaea, official creed of Orthodox, Roman Catholic, and some Protestant Churches.

nic·e·ty (nī´sĭtē) *n.* (pl. **-ties**). Punctiliousness; precision, accuracy; minute distinction, subtle or unimportant detail, (pl.) minutiae; **to a** ∼, as closely or precisely as possible.

niche (nĭch) *n.* Shallow recess in wall to contain statue, vase, etc.; (fig.) place or position adapted to the character, or suited to the merits, of a person or thing. ∼ *v.t.* (**niched, nich·ing**). Place (as if) in a niche.

Nich·o·las[1] (nĭk´olas). (Russ. *Nikolai*) Name of two emperors of Russia: **Nicholas I** (1796–1855), emperor 1825–55; his accession, after the death of his brother Alexander I and the abdication of his brother Constantine, was marked by the DECEMBRIST revolution, which he subdued and punished mercilessly; **Nicholas II** (1868–1918), emperor of Russia 1894–1917; forced to abdicate, March 1917; killed with his family, 1918.

Nich·o·las[2] (nĭk´olas), **St.** (d. 326). Bishop of Myra in Asia Minor; patron of sailors and of children (cf. SANTA CLAUS), and patron saint of Russia; commemorated Dec. 6.

*Birds and some reptiles have a 'third eyelid' or **nictating membrane**. Usually this semi-transparent tissue is used to clean the eye without total loss of vision.*

Nick (nĭk). **Old** ∼, the Devil.

nick (nĭk) *n.* Notch, groove, serving as catch, guide, mark, etc.; **in the** ∼ **of time**, just at the right moment, only just in time. **nick** *v.* Make nick(s) in, indent; make incision at root of (horse's tail) to make him carry it higher.

nick·el (nĭk´el) *n.* 1. (chem.) Hard silvery-white lustrous malleable ductile metallic element much used esp. in alloys; symbol Ni, at. no. 28, at. wt. 58.71. 2. Five-cent piece. 3. ∼ **silver**, alloy of nickel,

*A wide range of raw materials is exported by **Nicaragua**, including cotton, sugar, and coffee, together with a number of minerals including those used in the manufacture of cement.*

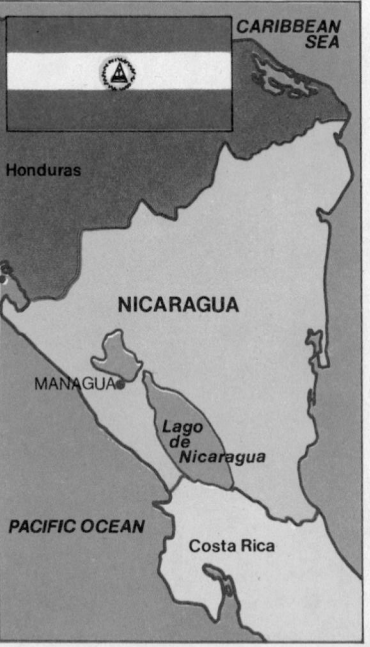

zinc, and copper, formerly used fo cutlery; ∼ **steel**, alloy of iron with nickel. **nickel** *v.t.* (**-eled, -el·ing -elled, -el·ling**). Coat with nickel [abbrev. of Ger. *kupfernicke* copper-colored ore from which nickel was first obtained (*kupfe* copper, *nickel* demon, w. ref. t disappointing nature of ore, which yielded no copper); cf. COBALT]

nick·el·o·de·on (nĭkelō´dēon) *n* 1. In early days of motion pictures theater where admission price wa 5 cents. 2. Early kind of jukebox

Tsar Nicholas I (1796-1855) suc ceeded his brother Alexander in 182 His reign was one in which the corrup Russian administration was given facade of efficiency without any re improvements being made.

nick·nack = KNICK-KNACK.

nick·name (nĭk´nām) *n.* Name added to or substituted for proper name of person, place, or thing. ~ *v.t.* (**-named, -nam·ing**). Call (person etc. by a nickname), give nickname to.

Nic·o·de·mus (nĭkodē´mus). Member of the Sanhedrin who helped Joseph of Arimathea to bury Jesus Christ (John 3, 7, 19).

Nic·o·si·a (nĭkosē´a). Capital of Cyprus in the N. central part.

ni·co·ti·a·na (nĭkōshēā´na,

-ăn´a, -ah´na) *n.* Tobacco plant; any of several plants of genus *N*~, esp. *N. alata*, a garden variety with greenish-white flowers, grown for its sweet scent. [f. Jacques *Nicot*, who introduced tobacco into France in 1560]

nic·o·tine (nĭk´otēn, -tĭn, nĭkotēn´) *n.* Poisonous alkaloid contained in tobacco, from which it is obtained as a pungent oily liquid soluble in water. **nic·o·tin·ic** (nĭkotĭn´ĭk) *adj.* ~ **acid**, crystalline acid ($C_6H_5NO_2$), produced by

oxidation of nicotine, a member of the vitamin B group.

nic·o·tin·ism (nĭk´otēnĭzem, -tĭn-, nĭkotē´nĭzem) *n.* Morbid state produced by excessive use of tobacco.

nic·tate (nĭk´tāt), **nic·ti·tate** (nĭk´tĭtāt) *vbs.i.* (**-tat·ed, -tat·ing**). Close and open the eyes, wink; chiefly in **nict(it)ating membrane**, 3rd or inner eyelid of many animals, vestigial in man. **nic·ta·tion** (nĭktā´shon), **nic·ti·ta·tion** (nĭktĭtā´shon) *ns.*

ni·dus (nī´dus) *n.* (pl. **-di** pr. -dī). Place in which insects etc. deposit eggs; place in which spores or seeds develop; place of origin or development of disease etc.; place in which something is deposited or lodged.

Nie·buhr (nē´boor), **Reinhold** (1892–1971). Amer. Protestant theologian and educator.

niece (nēs) *n.* Brother's or sister's daughter.

ni·el·lo (nēĕl´ō) *n.* (pl. **-el·li** pr. -ĕl´ē). Black metallic amalgam of sulfur added to copper, silver, lead, etc., for filling engraved lines in silver or other metal, as decoration; (specimen of) such ornamental work; ~ **print**, print taken from engraved plate that is to be filled with niello.

Nie·tzsche (nē´che, -chē), **Friedrich Wilhelm** (1844–1900). German philosopher; originator of idea of "superman" and of doctrine of perfectibility of man through forcible self-assertion and superiority to ordinary morality. **Nie´-tzsche·an** *adj. & n.*

nif·ty (nĭf´tē) *adj.* (**-ti·er, -ti·est**). (colloq.) Neat, smart, clever.

Ni·ger (nī´jer). 1. River of W. Africa, flowing in a curve from NE. frontier of Sierra Leone to Gulf of Guinea. 2. Republic in W. central Africa; capital, Niamey.

Ni·ge·ri·a (nījēr´ea). Republic in W. Africa, member of the Brit. Commonwealth, occupying basin of lower Niger, with coastline on Gulf of Guinea; formerly a British protectorate; independent 1960; capital, Lagos.

*The **River Niger** rises in the Loma Mountains of Guinea, flowing north and east through Mali and Niger before reaching the Nigerian coast and forming a delta.*

*The former French colony of **Niger** is now an independent republic. The main exports are cotton and peanuts. Many of the people live by subsistence farming.*

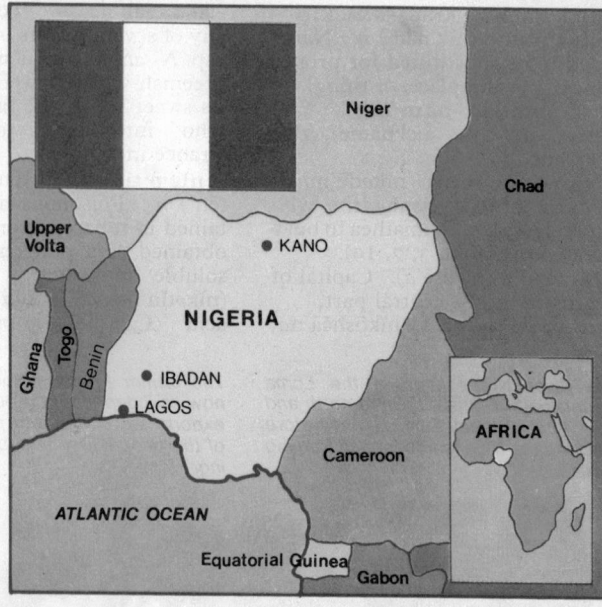

nig·gard (nĭg′erd) *n.* Stingy person, grudging giver *of.* ~ *adj.* (rhet. and poet.) Niggardly.

nig·gard·ly (nĭg′erdlē) *adj.* Parsimonious, stingy, sparing, scanty; giving or given grudgingly or in small amounts. **nig′gard·li·ness** *n.*

nig·gle (nĭg′el) *v.i.* (**-gled, -gling**). Spend time, be overly elaborate, on petty details. **nig′-gling** *adj. & n.* Trifling, petty; lacking in breadth, largeness, or boldness of effect; (of handwriting) cramped.

nigh (nī) *adv., prep., & adj.* (archaic, poet., or dial.) Near.

night (nīt) *n.* Dark period between twilight and dawn, time from sunset to sunrise, darkness then prevailing, the dark; end of daylight; weather, experiences, or occupation of a night; **make a ~ of it,** spend night in festivity; **~ out,** festive evening; evening on which servant is allowed out; **~ blind-ness:** see NYCTALOPIA; **night′cap,** covering for the head, worn in bed; drink taken before going to bed; **night clothes,** clothes worn in bed; **night club,** club open at night for dancing, supper, etc.; **night crawler,** earthworm that comes out of the ground at night; **night′ dress, night′gown,** loose garment worn by women or children in bed; **night′fall,** end of daylight; **night′-hawk,** any of several chiefly nocturnal N. Amer. goatsuckers of the genus *Chordeiles,* related to the whippoorwill; related bird, the European nightjar or goatsucker, *Caprimulgus europaeus*; person who is usu. awake and moving about in the night; **night heron,** any of various nocturnal herons of the genus *Nycticorax*; **night′jar,** any of various nocturnal birds of family Caprimulgidae, with harsh cry; **night′life,** entertainments open at

Above left: Pottery, using local clay, is made by the people of Nigeria, a former British colony. There are up to 250 languages spoken by the many tribes.

night; **night light,** lamp of low wattage for use at night, esp. in bedrooms; **night′mare,** female monster sitting upon and seeming to suffocate sleeper, incubus; oppressive, terrifying, or fantastically horrible dream; haunting fear, thing vaguely dreaded; **night owl,** (colloq.) person who goes about by night; **night′rider,** in the southern U.S., member of a band of mounted men who engaged in acts of terrorism for intimidation or revenge; **night school,** school,

Although tobacco can be grown in gardens, it is usually the related ornamental species of nicotiana which are cultivated in temperate zones.

class, held in evening for those a work during day; **night soil** (archaic) contents of cesspools etc. removed at night; **night stick,** stic carried by police, orig. at night **night watch, night watchman** (person or party keeping) watch b night.

night·in·gale (nī′tin gāl, nī′tĭng gāl) *n.* Small reddish-brow migratory bird of genus *Luscinia* (i Gt. Britain *L. megarhynchos* celebrated for the melodious song o the male, often heard at night durin the breeding season.

Night·in·gale (nī′tin gāl, nī′ tĭnggāl), **Florence** (1820–1910, English reformer; founder o modern nursing profession; organ ized hospital unit for Crimean Wa and established new type of wa hospital in Crimea.

night·ly (nīt′lē) *adj.* Happening done, existing, etc., in the nigh happening every night. ~ *adv* Every night.

night·shade (nīt′shād) *n.* Any o various plants of genus *Solanun* esp. **black ~** (*S. nigrum*), wit white flowers and black poisonou berries, **woody ~** (*S. dulcamara* with purple flowers and bright re berries; **deadly ~,** belladonna **enchanter's ~,** plant of genu *Circaea* with white flowers.

night·y (nī′tē) *n.* (pl. **night·ies** (colloq.) Nightdress.

ni·hil·ism (nī′ilĭzem, nē′-) *n.* Negative doctrines, total rejectio of current beliefs, in religion o morals; (philos.) skepticism tha denies all existence. 2. Doctrine of extreme revolutionary party i 19th- and 20th-c. Russia (orig. use of a small group in the 1860s wh repudiated the established orde and its standards). **ni′hil·ist** *n* **ni·hil·is·tic** (nīilĭs′tĭk, nē-) *adj.* [L *nihil* nothing]

Flying silently and often spending the day resting along instead of across a branch, the **nightjar** is rarely observed even though it may live close to human habitation.

Many plants are given the name of **nightshade**, including the poisonous members of the genus Solanum and other noxious or harmless herbs which resemble them.

Ni·jin·sky (nĭzhĭn´skē, -jĭn´-), **as·lav** (vahtslahf´) (1890–1950). ussian ballet dancer and chore-grapher; most famous and greatest f his time; appeared in "L'Après-Iidi d'un Faun," "Le Spectre de la ose," etc.; in later life he became sane and was confined in an ylum.

-nik suffix. Forming nouns de-oting person associated with pecified thing or quality (beatnik, goodnik). [f. Russ. (as sputnik) nd Yiddish]

Ni·ke (nī´kē). (Gk. myth.) 1. oddess of victory, freq. identified ith Athene; ~ **of Samothrace**: e WINGED Victory. 2. (mil.) One a series of U.S. Army surface-to-r guided missiles for defense gainst enemy aircraft and missiles.

nil (nĭl) n. Nothing.

Nile (nīl). Longest river of Africa, flowing from E. Central Africa 4,000 miles (6,440 km) northward to Mediterranean; **Blue** ~, tributary joining the Nile at Khartoum; **White** ~, part of Nile above Khartoum; ~ **green** = EAU de Nil.

Ni·lot·ic (nīlŏt´ĭk) adj. Of the river Nile, the Nile region, or its inhabitants.

nim·ble (nĭm´bel) adj. (**-bler, -blest**). Quick in movement, agile, swift; (of mind etc.) versatile, clever, quick to apprehend. **nim´-ble·ness** n. **nim´bly** adv.

nim·bo·stra·tus (nĭmbō strā´-tus, -străt´us) n. (meteor.) Type of low cloud, dark gray and sometimes trailing.

nim·bus (nĭm´bus) n. Bright cloud or halo investing deity, person, or thing; bright disk, aureole, around or over head of saint etc. in picture.

Nîmes (nēm). City in S. France; site of famous Roman ruins, including amphitheater.

Nim·rod (nĭm´rŏd). Great-grandson of Noah, traditional founder of the Babylonian dynasty, noted as a great hunter (Gen. 10).

nin·com·poop (nĭn´kompōop, nĭng´-) n. Simpleton.

nine (nīn) adj. Amounting to 9; **the N~**, the Muses; ~ **days' wonder**, novelty that attracts much attention but is soon forgotten; **nine'pin**, pin used in **nine'pins**, game of knocking down nine wooden pins by bowling a ball at them. **nine** n. One more than eight; symbol for this (9, ix, or IX); card with nine pips; nine o'clock; size etc. indicated by 9; set of nine things or persons; baseball team; **to the** ~ **s**, to perfection (esp. in **dressed up to the** ~ **s**). **nine'fold** adj. & n.

nine·teen (nīn´tēn´) adj. & n. One more than 18 (19, xix, or XIX). **nine'teenth'** adj. ~ **hole**, (colloq.) barroom in golf clubhouse.

nine·ty (nīn´tē) adj. Amounting to 90. ~ n. (pl. **-ties**). Cardinal number, 9 times 10 (90, xc, or XC); set of 90 things or persons; **nine-**

Florence Nightingale, during a career lasting from 1851 to 1872, not only radically improved army medical care but raised the standard of general nursing in the U.K. as well.

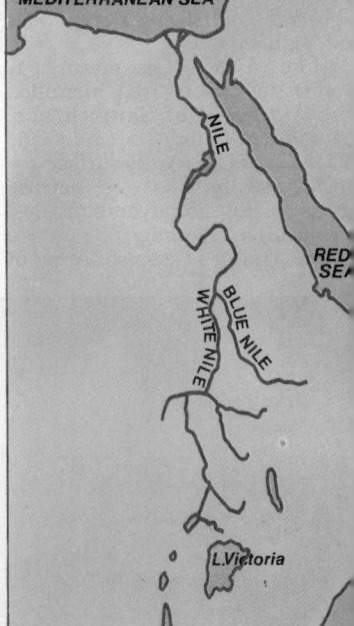

ties, (pl.) numbers etc. from 90 to 99; these years of century or life.

Nin·e·veh (nĭn′eve). Ancient capital of Assyrian Empire, on right bank of Tigris.

nin·ny (nĭn′ē) *n.* (pl. **-nies**). Simpleton.

ninth (nīnth) *adj.* Next after 8th. ~ *n.* Ninth part (see PART[1] def. 1); 9th thing etc.; (mus.) interval of octave and second. **ninth′ly** *adv.*

Ni·o·be (nī′ōbē). (Gk. legend) Daughter of Tantalus; Apollo and Artemis, enraged because she boasted herself superior to their mother Latona, slew her six sons and five of her six daughters; Niobe herself was turned into a rock, and her tears into streams that trickled from it. **Ni·o·bids** (nī′ōbĭdz) *n.pl.* Children of Niobe.

ni·o·bi·um (nīō′bēum) *n.* (chem.) Rare metallic element very similar to tantalum and usu. found associated with it; symbol Nb, at. no. 41, at. wt. 92.9064. [named after NIOBE]

nip[1] (nĭp) *v.* (**nipped, nip·ping**). Pinch, squeeze sharply, bite; pinch *off*; check growth of; (of cold) affect injuriously, pain; (slang) move rapidly or nimbly. ~ *n.* Pinch, sharp squeeze, bite; (check to vegetation caused by) coldness of air; ~ **and tuck**, neck and neck.

nip[2] (nĭp) *n.* Small quantity of liquor etc. ~ *v.* (**nipped, nip·ping**). Take nips (of).

nip·per (nĭp′er) *n.* 1. (Brit. slang) Young boy. 2. (pl.) Implement with jaws for gripping or cutting; forceps, pincers, pliers; (usu. pl.) crustacean's great claw.

nip·ple (nĭp′el) *n.* 1. Small projection in which mammary ducts terminate in mammal of either sex; teat, esp. on woman's breast; teat of nursing bottle. 2. Nipple-like protuberance on skin, glass, metal, etc.; small rounded elevation on mountain; short section of pipe with threading at each end for coupling.

Nip·pon·ese (nĭponēz′, -nēs′) *adj. & n.* Japanese. [f. *Nippon*, Jap. name for Japan, f. *ni-pun* sunrise (*ni* sun, *pon* origin)]

nip·py (nĭp′ē) *adj.* (**-pi·er, -pi·est**). (colloq.) Cold.

nir·va·na (nĭrvah′na, -văn′a, ner-) *n.* In Buddhist theology, extinction of individual existence and absorption into supreme spirit, or extinction of all passions and desires and attainment of perfect beatitude. [Sansk. *nirvāna* blowing out, extinction]

Ni·sei (nē′sā′) *n.* (pl. **-sei**). Person born in U.S. whose parents were immigrants from Japan. [Jap., lit. "2nd generation"]

ni·si (nī′sī) *conj.* (legal) Unless;

*The **Nile** is the longest river in Africa. It is fed by two main tributaries: the White Nile and the Blue Nile. Although used for irrigation since the ancient Egyptian civilizations, recent dams have also allowed its water to produce hydro-electricity.*

decree, order, etc., ~, decree etc valid unless cause is shown fo rescinding it before appointed tim at which it is made absolute.

nit (nĭt) *n.* Egg of louse or othe parasitic insect.

ni·ter, Brit. **ni·tre** (nī′ter) *n.* Saltpeter, potassium nitrat (KNO_3).

nit·pick (nĭt′pĭk) *v.i.* (colloq.

nous (nītrŏj′enus) *adj.* Of, belonging to, containing, nitrogen. **ni·trog·e·nize** (nītrŏj′enīz) *v.t.* (**-ized, -iz·ing**). Combine with nitrogen or nitrogenous compounds.

ni·tro·glyc·er·in (nītroglĭs′e-rĭn), **ni·tro·glyc·er·ine** (nītroglĭs′-erĭn, -erēn) *ns.* Glyceryl trinitrate, a yellowish, oily, violently explosive liquid formed by action of a mixture of nitric and sulfuric acid on glycerine; a constituent of dyna-mite, gelignite, and cordite.

ni·trous (nī′trus) *adj.* Of, like, impregnated with, niter; (chem.) of, containing, nitrogen, esp. of com-pounds in which nitrogen has a lower valence than nitric com-pounds; ~ **acid**, acid (HNO_2) con-taining less oxygen than nitric acid; ~ **oxide**, colorless sweet-smelling gas (N_2O), used as a mild anesthet-ic, laughing gas.

nit·wit (nĭt′wĭt) *n.* (slang) Per-son of little intelligence.

nix[1] (nĭks) *n.* (slang) Nothing.

nix[2] (nĭks) *n.* (pl. **nix·es**). Water elf.

Nix·on (nĭk′son), **Richard Mil-hous** (1913–). Thirty-seventh president of U.S., 1969–74 (re-signed).

NJ, N.J. *abbrevs.* New Jersey.

NKVD, N.K.V.D. *abbrevs.* Secret police of U.S.S.R., 1939–45. [initials of *N*aródnyi *K*omissariát *V*nutrennikh *D*el, people's com-missariat of internal affairs]

NLRB, N.L.R.B. *abbrevs.* National Labor Relations Board.

NM, n.m. *abbrevs.* Nautical mile.

NM, N.M., N.Mex. *abbrevs.* New Mexico.

NNE, N.N.E., n.n.e. *abbrevs.* North-northeast.

NNW, N.N.W., n.n.w. *abbrevs.* North-northwest.

no (nō) *adj.* Not any; not a, quite other than a; hardly any; **no′body** (pl. **-bodies**), no person; person of no importance; **no man**, no person; **no man's land**, piece of waste, unowned or debatable ground, esp. (mil.) the space between opposed lines; **no one**, no person; (as *adj.*) no single; **no-trumps**, (cards), (bid calling for) hand played without trump suit; **no′ways** (archaic), **no′wise**, in no manner, not at all. **no** *adv.* 1. (as alternative after *or*) Not. 2. (with comparatives) By no amount, not at all; ~ **more**, nothing further; not any more; no longer, never again, to no greater extent; just as little, neither. 3. Particle expressing negative reply

Find fault in petty manner. **nit′-pick·er** *n.* **nit′pick·ing** *adj.* & *n.*

ni·trate (nī′trāt) *n.* Salt of nitric acid; potassium or sodium nitrate used as fertilizer. ~ *v.t.* (**-trat·ed, -trat·ing**). Treat, impregnate, or cause to interact, with nitric acid. **ni·tra·tion** (nītrā′shon) *n.*

ni·tric (nī′trĭk) *adj.* Of niter; ~ **acid**, clear, colorless, pungent, highly corrosive liquid (HNO_3); ~ **oxide**, colorless gas (NO), obtained by the action of nitric acid on copper turnings or by the combina-tion of nitrogen and oxygen at high temperatures.

ni·tro·cel·lu·lose (nītrosĕl′yu-lōs) *n.* = CELLULOSE nitrate.

ni·tro·gen (nī′trojen) *n.* Color-less, tasteless, odorless, gaseous element forming about 4/5 of the

atmosphere and occurring also in nature as nitrates, and as proteins in animal and vegetable tissues, used commercially in the large-scale synthesis of ammonia; symbol N, at. no. 7, at. wt. 14.0067; ~ **cycle**, continuous series of processes by which nitrogen and nitrogenous compounds are converted into sub-stances that can be utilized by plants, thence transferred to animals, and finally reconverted by decay of plant and animal tissue; ~ **fixation**, process by which atmos-pheric nitrogen is combined with other elements (1) in the manu-facture of commercially important nitrogen compounds, as nitric acid, fertilizers, etc., (2) in nature by soil bacteria, and thereby made avail-able to plants as food. **ni·trog·e·-**

to request, question, etc. ~ *n.* (pl. **noes, nos**). Word, answer, "no"; (pl.) voters against a motion.

No¹, Noh (nō) *ns.* Traditional Japanese drama evolved from the rites of Shinto worship and practically unchanged since 15th c.

No² (nō), **Lake.** Lake in S. central Sudan; source of White Nile.

No³ *symbol.* Nobelium.

No., no. *abbrevs.* (pl. **Nos.**). Number.

No·a·chi·an (nōā́kēan) *adj.* Of Noah or his times.

No·ah (nṓa). Patriarch, represented as tenth in descent from Adam; at God's command he made the ark that saved his family and specimens of every animal from the flood sent by God to destroy the world; his sons, Shem, Ham, and Japheth were regarded as ancestors of all the races of mankind (Gen. 5–10).

nob (nŏb) *n.* (slang) Head.

No·bel (nōbĕl´), **Alfred Bernhard** (1833–96). Swedish chemist and engineer; inventor of dynamite and other high explosives; founder, by his will, of the five ~ **Prizes**, which are awarded annually to the persons adjudged by Swedish learned societies to have done the most significant work during the year in physics, chemistry, medicine, and literature, and to the person who is adjudged by the Norwegian parliament to have rendered the greatest service to the cause of peace; a ~ **Prize** for economic sciences was added in 1969.

no·bel·i·um (nōbḗlēum) *n.* (chem.) Transuranic element, symbol No, at. no. 102.

no·bil·i·ar·y (nōbĭl´ēērē) *adj.* Of (the) nobility; ~ **particle**, preposition (as French *de*, German *von*) prefixed to title.

no·bil·i·ty (nōbĭl´ĭtē) *n.* (pl. **-ties**). 1. Noble character, mind, birth, or rank. 2. Persons of noble rank as a class; (in England) the peerage.

no·ble (nṓbel) *adj.* (**-bler, -blest**). 1. Illustrious by rank, title, or birth, belonging to the nobility. 2. Of lofty character or ideals; showing greatness of character, magnanimous; splendid, magnificent, stately; impressive in appearance; excellent, admirable; (of metals such as gold, silver, sometimes platinum) resisting chemical action; **no´bleman, no´blewoman**, person of noble rank, peer(ess). **no´ble·ness** *n.* **no´bly** *adv.* **noble** *n.* Nobleman.

no·blesse o·blige (nōblĕś-ōblēzh´). Privilege entails responsibility. [Fr.]

noc·tule (nŏk´chool) *n.* Great bat (*Nyctalus noctula*), largest British species of brown bat.

Alfred Nobel *obtained a large fortune from the development of dynamite and exploitation of oil fields at Baku. He left the money to endow the Nobel Prizes for peace, sciences and the arts.*

noc·tur·nal (nŏktēr´nal) *adj.* Of, in, done by, active in, the night. **noc·tur´nal·ly** *adv.*

noc·turne (nŏk´tērn) *n.* Soft, dreamy musical composition.

nod (nŏd) *v.* (**nod·ded, nod·ding**). Incline head slightly and quickly in salutation, assent, or command; let head fall forward in drowsiness, be drowsy, make mistake from inattention; **nodding acquaintance**, slight acquaintance. **nod** *n.* Nodding of the head; this as sign of absolute power; **land of N~**, (with pun on Gen. 4:16) sleep.

no·dal (nṓdal) *adj.* Of a node.

node (nōd) *n.* 1. (bot.) Point at which leaves spring. 2. (path.) Hard tumor esp. on gouty or rheumatic joint. 3. (astron.) Intersecting point of planet's orbit and ecliptic or of 2 great circles of celestial sphere. 4. (phys.) Point or line of rest in vibrating body. 5. Central point in system. 6. (math.) Point at which curve crosses itself.

nod·ule (nŏj´ool) *n.* Small rounded lump of anything, small node in plant; small knotty tumor, ganglion. **nod·u·lar** (nŏj´uler), **nod·u·lose** (nŏj´ulōs), **nod·u·lous** (nŏj´ulus) *adjs.*

No·el, no·el (nōĕl´) *ns.* Christmas. [OF. f. L. *natalis* natal]

no·et·ic (nōĕt´ĭk) *adj.* Of the intellect; purely intellectual or abstract; given to intellectual speculation. **no·et´ics** *n.* Science of the intellect.

no-fault (nō´fawlt) *adj. & n.* (Of,

pertaining to, requiring) type of automobile insurance that compensates policyholder in case of an accident regardless of liability; divorce granted when neither party is held to blame.

nog¹ (nŏg) *n.* Pin, peg, small block, of wood; wood block built into wall in place of a brick so that interior woodwork can be nailed to it; snag or stump on tree. ~ *v.t.* (**nogged, nog·ging**). Secure with nogs; build in form of nogging. **nog´ging** *n.* Brickwork between wooden quarters of framing.

nog² (nŏg) = EGGnog.

nog·gin (nŏg´ĭn) *n.* Small mug; small measure, usu. 1/4 pint, of liquor. 2. (slang) Head.

Noh (nō) = No¹.

noise (noiz) *n.* Sound, esp. loud or harsh one; din, clamor; ~ **pollution**, contamination of environment by too much loud sound, as of heavy traffic in city streets, airport traffic, etc. **noise´less** *adj.* **noise´less·ly** *adv.* **noise´less·ness** *n.* **noise** *v.t.* (**noised, nois·ing**). Make public, spread *abroad.*

noise·mak·er (noiz´māker) *n.* (esp.) Toy (of paper, metal, etc.) that makes noise.

noi·some (noi´som) *adj.* Harmful, noxious; ill-smelling; objectionable, offensive. **noi´some·ly** *adv.* **noi´some·ness** *n.*

nois·y (noi´zē) *adj.* (**nois·i·er, nois·i·est**). Clamorous, turbulent; full of, making much, noise; loud. **nois´i·ly** *adv.* **nois´i·ness** *n.*

no·lens vo·lens (nṓlĕnz vṓlĕnz) *adv.* Willy-nilly. [L., = "unwilling, willing"]

no·li me tan·ge·re (nṓlī mē tăn´jerē; *Lat.* nṓlē mĕ tahng´gĕrĕ). 1. Warning against interference etc.; person, thing, that must not be touched or interfered with. 2. Painting representing appearance of Jesus Christ to Mary Magdalen at the sepulcher (John 20:17). [L., = "touch me not" (Vulgate, John 20:17)]

nom. *abbrev.* Nominal; nominative.

no·mad (nṓmăd) *n. & adj.* (Member of tribe) roaming from place to place for pasture; wanderer, wandering. **no·mad·ic** (nōmăd´ĭk) *adj.* **no·mad´i·cal·ly** *adv.* **no´mad·ism** *n.*

nom de guerre (nŏm de gār´; *Fr.* nawn de gĕr´) (pl. **noms de guerre** pr. nŏmz de gār´; *Fr.* nawn de gĕr´). Pseudonym, sobriquet, assumed name under which person fights, plays, etc. [Fr., = "war name"]

nom de plume (nŏm de ploom´; *Fr.* nawn de plüm´) (pl. **noms de plume** pr. nŏmz de ploom; *Fr.* nawn de plüm´). Writer's pseudonym, pen name. [Eng. formation on Fr. words *nom* name, *de* of, *plume* pen]

Nome (nōm). Westernmost city of continental U.S., in Alaska on Seward Peninsula; scene of great gold rush after discovery of gold, 1896.

no·men·cla·ture (nō'menklā-her, nōmĕn'kla-) n. System of names for things; terminology of a science etc.; systematic naming. **no·men·cla·tive** (nō'menklātĭv) adj.

nom·i·nal (nŏm'inal) adj. Of, as, like, a noun; of, in, names; existing in name only, (of price etc.) very small, trifling; not real or substantial; consisting of, giving, the names. **nom'i·nal·ly** adv.

nom·i·nal·ism (nŏm'inalĭzem) n. (philos.) Doctrine of the scholastics that universal or abstract concepts are mere names, without any corresponding reality (opp. REALISM). **nom'i·nal·ist** n. **nom·i·nal·is·tic** (nŏminalĭs'tĭk) adj.

nom·i·nate (nŏm'ināt) v.t. -nat·ed, -nat·ing. Name or appoint (date, place); appoint, propose for election, to office. **nom'i·na·tion** (nŏminā'shon) n. (esp.) Right of nominating for appointment. **nom'i·na·tor, nom·i·nee** (nŏminē') ns.

nom·i·na·tive (nŏm'inatĭv, -nā-tĭv) adj. 1. (gram.) Of the case of the subject of a verb. 2. Of, appointed by, nomination. ~ n. (Word in) nominative case; ~ **absolute**, construction like Latin ablative absolute, as in *this being so, I did nothing*.

non- prefix. Not (now freely prefixed to nouns, adjectives, etc.)

non·age (nŏn'ĭj, nō'nĭj) n. Being under age, minority; immaturity, early stage.

non·a·ge·nar·i·an (nŏnajenār'-an, nōna-) adj. & n. (Person) aged 90 years or more but less than 100.

non·a·gon (nŏn'agŏn) n. Plane figure with nine angles and nine sides. **non·ag·o·nal** (nŏnăg'onal) adj.

non·ap·pear·ance (nŏnaper'-ans) n. Failure to appear, esp. in court of law.

no·na·ry (nō'nerē) adj. (arith., of scale of notation) Having nine as basis.

non·bel·lig·er·ent (nŏnbelĭj'e-rent) adj. & n. (Nation) not taking active or open part in war. **non·bel·lig·er·en·cy** n.

nonce (nŏns) n. Time being, present occasion (only in **for the** ~); ~ **word**, word coined for a special occasion and used only for a short time.

non·cha·lant (nŏnshalahnt', nŏn'shalant) adj. Unexcited, unmoved, cool, indifferent. **non·cha·lant'ly** adv. **non·cha·lance'** n.

non·com (nŏn'kŏm) n. (colloq.) Non-commissioned officer.

non·com·bat·ant (nŏnkŏm'ba-tant, nŏnkombăt'ant) adj. Not fighting. ~ n. Civilian in time of war; member of army etc. whose duties do not include fighting.

non·com·mis·sioned (nŏn-komĭsh'ond) adj. Not holding commission (esp. of subordinate army ranks such as *sergeant*, *corporal*).

non·com·mit·tal (nŏnkomĭt'al) adj. Refusing to commit oneself to particular view or course of action.

non com·pos men·tis (nŏn kŏm'pos mĕn'tĭs; *Lat*. nŏn kŏm'pōs mĕn'tĭs). Not in one's right mind. [L.]

non·con·duc·ting (nŏnkondŭk'-tĭng) adj. That does not conduct heat or electricity. **non·con·duc'tor** n.

non·con·form·ist (nŏnkonfōr'-mĭst) n. One who does not conform to established doctrine or discipline, esp. dissenting member of church. **non·con·form'i·ty, non·con·form'ance** ns. Principles, practice, the body, of nonconformists; failure to conform (*to*); want of correspondence between things.

non·co·op·er·a·tion (nŏnkōŏper·ā'shon) n. Refusal or failure to cooperate with authority, esp. as policy of GANDHI and his followers in India from *c*1919.

non·de·script (nŏndĭskrĭpt') adj. & n. (Person, thing) not easily classified, neither one thing nor another, hybrid.

none (nŭn) pron. Not any *of*; no person, no one (now rare); no persons. ~ adj. (usu. ellipt.) No, not any; not to be counted in

These Algerian Berbers following their laden beasts typify the restless life of all **nomads,** *possessions reduced to little beyond necessities.*

specified class. ~ adv. By no amount, not at all. **none'the·less'** adv. Nevertheless.

non·en·ti·ty (nŏnĕn'tĭtē) n. (pl. -ties). Nonexistence, nonexistent thing, figment; person or thing of no importance, cipher.

nones (nōnz) n.pl. (sing. for def. 2 **None** pr. nŏn). 1. (Rom. antiq.) Ninth day (by inclusive reckoning) before IDES; 7th of March, May, July, Oct., and 5th of other months. 2. **N**~, (R.C. Ch.) canonical HOUR, (orig. said at) 9th hour of day (3 p.m.).

non·es·sen·tial (nŏnĭsĕn'shal) adj. & n. (Thing) that is not essential.

none·such, non·such (nŭn'-sŭch') ns. Person or thing that is unrivaled, paragon.

non·ex·is·tent (nŏnĭgzĭs'tent) adj. Not existing. **non·ex·ist'ence** n.

non·fic·tion (nŏnfĭk'shon) adj. & n. (Of) prose writings that are not fiction, poetry, or drama.

non·flam·ma·ble (nŏnflăm'a-bel) adj. Noninflammable.

non·in·flam·ma·ble (nŏnĭn-flăm'abel) adj. That cannot be set on fire.

non·in·ter·ven·tion (nŏnĭnter-vĕn'shon) n. Absence of intervention; esp., in international politics, systematic refusal to interfere in affairs of another nation.

non·pa·reil (nŏnparĕl') adj. Unequaled, peerless. ~ n. 1. Person or thing without equal, something unique. 2. (print.) Size of type (6 point) intermediate between emerald and ruby. 3. Kind of finch. 4. Kind of moth. 5. Chocolate candy lozenge decorated with sugar pellets.

non·plus (nŏnplŭs', nŏn'plŭs) n. State of perplexity, standstill. ~ v.t. (**-plused, -plus·ing**, Brit.

The harbor at Honfleur in **Normandy,** a region of north-western France which has a rich and ancient history. Normandy was the scene of the Allied invasion in the 1939–45 war, which began the liberation of Europe.

-plussed, -plus·sing). Reduce to hopeless perplexity. [L. *non plus* not more]

non·res·i·dent (nŏnrĕz´ĭdent) *adj.* Sojourning in place only for short time or residing elsewhere; not residing at one's place of work. ~ *n.* Nonresident person.

non·re·sis·tance (nŏnrĭzĭs´tans) *n.* (Principle of) not resisting authority even when it is unjustly exercised.

non·sense (nŏn´sĕns, -sens) *n.* Absurd or meaningless words or ideas, foolish or extravagant conduct, worthless things, rubbish (freq. as exclamation of contempt); **no** ~, no foolish or extravagant conduct, no foolery or humbug; ~ **verse(s)**, verse(s) having no sense or an absurd one. **non·sen·si·cal** (nŏnsĕn´sĭkal) *adj.* **non·sen'si·cal·ness** *n.*

non se·qui·tur (nŏn sĕk´wĭter). Illogical inference, paradoxical result. [L., = "it does not follow"]

non·skid (nŏn´skĭd´) *adj.* (of tires or road surface) Designed to prevent or limit skidding.

non·smoker (nŏnsmō´ker) *n.* Person who does not smoke.

non·stop (nŏn´stŏp´) *adj. & adv.* Traveling, performing, etc. without stopping at intermediate points. ~ *n.* Nonstop train etc.

non·such = NONESUCH.

non trop·po (nŏn trŏp´ō; *It.* nawn traw´pō). (mus.) Not too much. [It.]

non·un·ion (nŏnūn´yon) *adj.* Not belonging to a labor union; not made by union labor.

noo·dle[1] (nōo´del) *n.* 1. Simpleton. 2. (slang) Head.

noo·dle[2] (nōo´del) *n.* Strip or ball of pasta, used esp. in soup. [Ger. *Nudel*]

nook (nŏok) *n.* Secluded corner or place; recess.

noon (nōon) *n.* Twelve o'clock in the day; **noon'day,** (poet.) noon. [L. *nona (hora)* 9th hour; orig., 3 p.m.]

noose (nōos) *n.* Loop with running knot, tightening as string is pulled, halter; snare or bond. ~ *v.t.* (**noosed, noos·ing**). Capture with noose, ensnare; make noose on (cord); arrange (cord) in noose *around* neck etc.

no·pal (nō´pal) *n.* Amer. cactus (*Nopalea cochinellifera*) cultivated for breeding cochineal.

nor (nôr) *conj.* Neither (archaic); and not, and no more, neither, and not either.

Nor. *abbrev.* North; Norway; Norwegian.

NOR·AD (nôr´ăd) *n.* North American Air Defense Command.

Nor·dic (nôr´dĭk) *adj. & n.* (Person) of the physical type of the Germanic peoples of N. Europe, esp. the Scandinavians, with tall stature, long narrow head, bony frame, and light coloring of hair, eyes, and skin.

norm (nôrm) *n.* 1. Typical or standard pattern. 2. General level or average.

nor·mal (nôr´mal) *adj.* 1. Rec-

The Cornish font (above, left) and det[a] from the Bayeaux Tapestry (above show clearly many of the feature associated with the art of the **Norma** period.

tangular (rare); standing at rig[h]t angles, perpendicular. 2. Co[n]forming to standard, regular, usua[l] typical; of average intelligenc[e] mentally or emotionally sound; ~ **school,** (formerly) a school f[or] training teachers. **nor'mal·ly** *ad* **nor·mal·i·ty** (nôrmăl´ĭtē), **nor**

*Children in Norwegian national dress. The **Nordic** people are physically tall, and fair. Although Nordic also means people of northern Europe, among whom there are a number of different racial characteristics.*

after Norman Conquest, with characteristic geometrical ornament; ~ **Conquest**, conquest of England by Normans under William of Normandy, 1066; ~ **French**, form of medieval French spoken by Normans; later form of this in English legal use.

Nor·man·dy (nōr'mandē). 1. Region and former province of NW. France with coastline on English Channel; given by Charles the Simple to Rollo, 1st duke of Normandy, 912; united to England intermittently from Norman Conquest until 1204; site of Allied landings in German-occupied France in World War II. 2. Name of English royal house, including William I and II, Henry I, and Stephen.

nor·ma·tive (nōr'matĭv) *adj.* Of, establishing, a norm.

Norse (nōrs) *adj.* Of ancient Scandinavia, esp. Norway; of the language of its inhabitants. ~ *n.* **Old** ~, Germanic language of medieval Scandinavia.

north (nōrth) *adv.* Toward, in, the north. ~ *n.* 1. Point of horizon to the left of an observer who faces the rising sun at the equinox; this direction. 2. Cardinal point of the compass 90 to the left of east and 90 to the right of west. 3. (usu. **the N ~**) That part of a country, district, etc., that lies to the north; in U.S., states lying north of the Mason-Dixon line. 4. **N ~**, bridge player sitting opposite South and to the right of East. **north** *adj.* Lying toward, in, the north; (of wind) blowing from the north; **N ~ Atlantic Treaty Organization**: see NATO; **N ~ Pole**, point on Earth that is farthest north; **N ~ Sea**, part of Atlantic between mainland of

NORSE VOYAGES

al·cy *ns.* **normal** *n.* (geom.) ormal line; usual state, level, mperature, etc.

nor·mal·ize (nōr'malīz) *v.t.* ized, -iz·ing). Make normal. **or·mal·i·za·tion** (nōrmalīzā'- ıon), **nor'mal·iz·er** *ns.*

Nor·man (nōr'man) *n.* Native inhabitant of NORMANDY belong- g to or descended from mixed candinavian and Frankish people habiting that part of France; orig. e of the Northmen or Scan-

dinavians who conquered Normandy in 10th c. ~ *adj.* Of the Normans or Normandy; (archit.) of the style of round-arched Romanesque architecture developed by Normans and employed in England

*Raiders and settlers, the men who voyaged in **Norse** galleys like the Oseberg ship (top) had a lasting impact on the rest of Europe. Voyaging south to Nantes and across to Newfoundland, they played a part in the spread of cultural and other ideas.*

*The linen industry is still among the most important in **Northern Ireland.** However, agricultural products also include large numbers of livestock for dairying and meat (right).*

Europe and E. coast of Gt. Britain; **north star**, polestar. **north'ward** *adv., adj.,* & *n.* **north'ward·ly** *adv.* & *adj.* **north'wards** *adv.*

North America. Northern part of the continent of Amer., including Central Amer., Mexico, U.S., and Canada.

North Cape. Point on island in Arctic Sea off N. Norway; northernmost part of Europe.

North Carolina. South Atlantic state of U.S.; one of the original 13 states of the Union (1789); capital, Raleigh.

North Dakota. State in northwestern U.S.; admitted to the Union in 1889; capital, Bismarck.

north·east (nōrthĕst'; naut. nōrēst') *adv.* & *n.* (Direction or compass point) between north and east. ~ *adj.* Of, in, to, from, the northeast; ~ **passage**, passage for ships along northern coasts of Europe and Asia, formerly thought of as possible route to Far East. **north·east'er** *n.* Northeast wind. **north·east'er·ly** *adj.* & *adv.* **north·east'ern** *adj.* **north·east'-ward** *adv., adj.,* & *n.* **north·east'ward·ly** *adv.* **north·east'wards** *adv.* & *n.*

north·er·ly (nōr'dherlē) *adj.* In the north; (of wind) blowing from the north. ~ *adv.* Toward the north. ~ *n.* North wind.

north·ern (nōr'dhern) *adj.* Of the north; lying or directed toward the north; (poet.) coming from the north; **N ~ hemisphere**: see HEMISPHERE; ~ **lights**, aurora borealis. **north'ern·er** *n.* (also **N ~**) Native, inhabitant, of the north. **north'ern·most** *adj.*

Northern Ireland. Autonomous unit of United Kingdom, constituted in 1920 (see IRELAND); capital, Belfast.

North Korea. Unofficial name of Democratic People's Republic of Korea.

North Platte River. River flowing from Colorado, 680 mi. (1,088 km) to South Platte River in SW. Nebraska; the two form the Platte.

North·um·bri·a (nōrthŭm'-brēa). Ancient Anglo-Saxon kingdom, extending from Humber to Forth. **North·um'bri·an** *adj.* & *n.*

north·west (nōrthwĕst'; naut. nōrwĕst') *adv.* & *n.* (Direction or compass point) between north and west. ~ *adj.* Of, in, to, from, the northwest; ~ **passage**, presumed route along N. coast of Amer. from Atlantic to Pacific; **Northwest Territories**, part of Canada lying

N. of 60th parallel; **Northwest Territory**, region of U.S. N. of the Ohio river. **north·west'er** *n.* Northwest wind. **north·west'er·ly** *adj.* & *adv.* **north·west'ern** *adj.* **north·west'ward** *adv., adj.,*

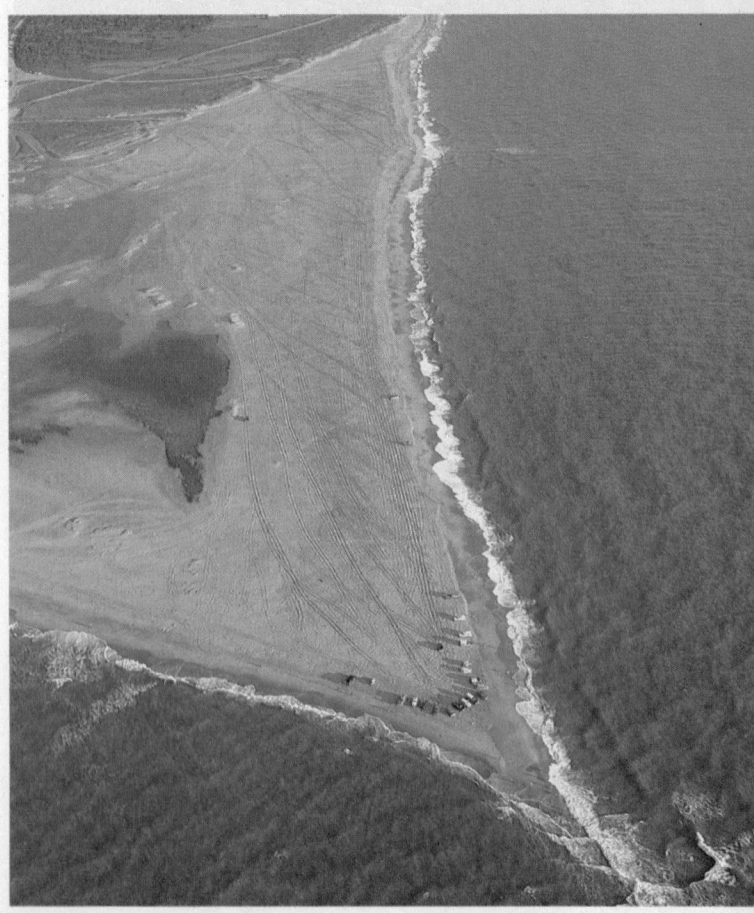

Cape Hatteras, a wild and unspo *beach and dune area of **Nort** **Carolina,** one of the original 13 colo* *ies. Initially an agricultural based eco* *omy it has been industrialized since th 1939—45 war.*

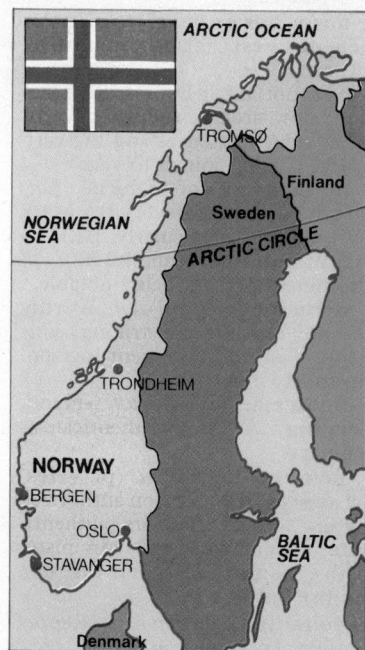

During the summer, the church and houses of Tromso in **Norway** (left) are bathed by the light of the midnight sun. As in all regions very close to the poles the sun does not fully sink below the horizon in midsummer and never rises in midwinter.

north·west′ward·ly *adj.* & *adv.* **north·west′wards** *adv.* & *n.*

Nor·way (nôr′wā). Kingdom of N. Europe occupying W. part of Scandinavian peninsula, founded 872; united with Denmark 1397–1814, and thereafter with Sweden under a personal union of the crowns which was dissolved in 1905; capital, Oslo.

Nor·we·gian (nôrwē′jan) *adj.* Of Norway or its people or language. ∼ *n.* 1. Norwegian person. 2. Language of Norway, in its literary form almost identical with Danish.

nor′west·er (nôrwĕs′ter) = NORTHWESTER.

nose (nōz) *n.* 1. Member of face or head above mouth, containing nostrils and serving as organ of smell; sense of smell; **as plain as the ∼ on your face**, easily seen; **lead by the ∼**, make (person) submissively do one's bidding; **pay through the ∼**, be charged exorbitant price; **poke, thrust, one's ∼**, pry or intrude *into*; **put person's ∼ out of joint**, supplant, disconcert, or frustrate him; **speak through the ∼**, speak with nasal twang; **turn up one's ∼ at**, show disdain for; **under person's ∼**, right in front of him. 2. Open end or nozzle of pipe, tube, bellows, etc.; prow; projecting part. 3. ∼ **bag**, bag of fodder fastened around horse's head; **nose′band**, lower band of bridle passing over nose and attached to cheek straps; **nose cone**, cone-shaped forward section of a rocket or guided missile; **nose dive**, aircraft's downward plunge, with nose first; **nose-dive**, (*v.i.*) perform nose dive; **nose flute**, musical instrument blown with nose, among Siamese, Fijians, etc.; **nose′gay**, bunch of (esp. sweet-scented) flowers; **nose ring**, ring fixed in nose of bull etc. for leading, or worn in person's nose as ornament. **nose** *v.* (**nosed, nos·ing**). Perceive smell of, discover by smell; detect, smell *out* (fig.); rub with the nose, thrust nose against or into; sniff (*at* etc.), pry or search (*after, for*); push one's way, push (one's *way*), with the nose (esp. of ship); ∼ **over**, (of aircraft) fall nose forward.

nos·ey = NOSY.

nosh (nŏsh) *v.* (slang) Eat or drink, esp. between meals. ∼ *n.* (slang) Food or drink, esp. snack. [Yiddish]

no-show (nō′shō′) *n.* Traveler who makes a reservation, esp. on an airplane, but neither uses nor cancels it.

nos·ing (nō′zĭng) *n.* Rounded edge of step, molding, etc., or metal or rubber shield for it.

no·sol·o·gy (nōsŏl′ojē) *n.* (Branch of medical science dealing with) classification of diseases.

nos·tal·gia (nŏstăl′ja, no-) *n.* 1. Severe homesickness. 2. Sorrowful longing *for* conditions of a past age; regretful or wistful memory of earlier time. **nos·tal′gic** *adj.* **nos·tal′gi·cal·ly** *adv.*

nos·toc (nŏs′tŏk) *n.* Unicellular alga of genus N∼ with cells arranged in intertwining rows which form gelatinous mass. [name invented by Paracelsus]

Nos·tra·da·mus (nŏstradā′-mus, -dah′-). Latinized name of Michel de Notredame (1503–66), Provençal astrologer; favorite of Catherine de Médicis and physician to Charles IX of France.

nos·tril (nŏs′trĭl) *n.* Either opening in nose admitting air to lungs and smells to olfactory nerves.

nos·trum (nŏs′trum) *n.* Medicine prepared by person recommending it, quack remedy, patent medicine; pet scheme for political or social reform etc. [L. neut. of *noster* our]

nos·y, nos·ey (nō′zē) *adjs.* (**nos·i·er, nos·i·est**). (slang) Inquisitive, curious.

not (nŏt) *adv.* Expressing negation; now archaic following verbs other than auxiliaries and the verb *be* (freq. as *n't* joined to verb).

no·ta be·ne (nō′ta bē′nē; *Lat.* nō′tah bĕ′nĕ). (abbrev. N.B.) Mark well, observe particularly. [L.]

no·ta·bil·i·ty (nōtabĭl′ĭtē) *n.* Prominent person; being notable.

no·ta·ble (nō′tabel) *adj.* Worthy of note, remarkable, striking, eminent. ~ *n.* Eminent person. **no′ta·bly** *adv.*

no·ta·rize (nō′terīz) *v.t.* (**-rized, -riz·ing**). Attest or authenticate as a notary.

no·ta·ry (nō′terē) *n.* (pl. **-ries**) (also ~ **public**). Person authorized by law to take affidavits, authenticate documents, and administer oaths. **no·tar·i·al** (nōtār′ēal) *adj.* **no·tar′i·al·ly** *adv.*

no·ta·tion (nōtā′shon) *n.* Representing of numbers, quantities, etc., by symbols; any set of symbols used for this, esp. in arithmetic, algebra, and music.

notch (nŏch) *n.* V-shaped indentation or incision on edge or across surface; nick on stick etc., by way of keeping count; deep narrow pass. ~ *v.t.* Make notches in; score, mark, record, by notches. **notched** *adj.*

note (nōt) *n.* 1. Written sign representing pitch and duration of a musical sound; key of piano etc.; single tone of definite pitch made by musical instrument, voice, etc.; (single tone in) bird's song or call. 2. Sign, token, characteristic, distinguishing feature; mark *of exclamation* or *interrogation*; **compare** ~ **s**, exchange ideas or opinions: **strike a false, the right note**, act inappropriately, suitably. 3. Brief record of facts etc. to assist memory or serve as basis for fuller statement or as help in speaking (usu. pl.); annotation appended to passage in book etc. 4. Short or informal letter; formal diplomatic communication; banknote. 5. Distinction, eminence; notice, attention. 6. **note′book**, book for taking notes or containing notes and memoranda; **note′paper**, paper of size or quality used for correspondence. **note** *v.t.* (**not·ed, not·ing**). Observe, notice, give attention to; set down, set *down*, as thing to be remembered or observed; annotate; **not′ed**, celebrated, well-known *for*. **note·wor·thy** (nōt′wērdhē) *adj.* Worthy of note or attention, remarkable.

noth·ing (nŭth′ĭng) *n.* No thing; not anything, naught; trifle, very inferior thing; (arith.) no amount; naught; nonexistence, what does not exist; (with pl.) trifling thing, event, remark, person; **come to**

*Building of the **Notre Dame** cathedral in Paris, the most famous of churches dedicated to the Virgin Mary, began in 1163. It was also the setting for Victor Hugo's novel, 'The Hunchback of Notre Dame'.*

~, turn out useless, fail, not amount to anything; **have ~ on**, (1) possess no advantage over, know of nothing discreditable about; (iron.) be much inferior to; (2) be naked; (3) be free of engagements; **know from ~**, be completely ignorant (of item of information); **make ~ of**, do without hesitation; not understand. **nothing** *adv.* Not at all, in no way.

noth·ing·ness (nŭth′ĭngnĭs) *n.* Nonexistence, the nonexistent; worthlessness, triviality, unimportance.

no·tice (nō′tĭs) *n.* 1. Intimation, warning; placard etc. conveying information or directions; formal intimation of something or instructions *to* do something, announcement by party to agreement that it is to terminate at specified time (esp. between landlord and tenant or employer and employee). 2. Heed, attention, cognizance, observation; **take ~**, give heed. 3. Short comment, review, etc., in newspaper or journal etc. **notice** *v.t.* (**-ticed, -tic·ing**). Remark upon, speak of; perceive, take notice of; treat with attention, favor, or politeness. **no′tice·a·ble** *adj.* **no′tice·a·bly** *adv.*

no·ti·fy (nō′tĭfī) *v.t.* (**-fied, -fy·ing**). Make known, announce, report; inform, give notice to. **no·ti·fi·ca·tion** (nōtĭfĭkā′shon) *n.*

no·tion (nō′shon) *n.* General concept under which particular thing may be classed; idea, conception; view, opinion, theory; in-

clination, disposition, desire; (pl.) haberdashery, small wares, esp cheap useful articles of some ingenuity.

no·tion·al (nō′shonal) *adj.* (o knowledge etc.) Speculative, no based on experiment or demonstration; (of things etc.) existing only in thought, imaginary; (of persons fanciful. **no′tion·al·ly** *adv.*

no·to·chord (nō′tokôrd) *n.* I CHORDATE animals, rudimentary spinal cord, rod of tissue lying along back below nerve cord; in vertebrates, elongated cord of embryonic tissue from which vertebra column develops.

no·to·ri·ous (notôr′ēus, -tôr′ *adj.* Well or commonly known undisguised, talked of, generally known to deserve the name; un favorably known (*for*). **no·to·ri·ous·ly** *adv.* **no·to·ri·e·ty** (nōtorī etē) *n.* (pl. **-ties**).

No·tre Dame (nôtre dām′ dahm′, nōter; *Fr.* nawtre dahm′) Church dedicated to the Virgin Mary, esp. cathedral church o Paris. [Fr., = "Our Lady"]

not·with·stand·ing (nŏtwĭdh stăn′dĭng, -wĭth-) *prep.* In spite of not the less for. ~ *adv.* Never theless, all the same. ~ *conj.* Al though, in spite of the fact *that.*

Nouak·chott (nwahkshŏt′ Capital of Mauritania in SW. par about 3 mi. (4.8 km) from coast.

nou·gat (noō′gat; *Brit.* noō′gah *n.* Confection of sugar, honey almonds or other nuts, and eg white.

nought (nawt) = NAUGHT.

Nou·mé·a (noōmā′a). Capital o New Caledonia on the SW. coast.

noun (nown) *n.* (gram.) Wor used as name of person, place thing, state, or quality.

nour·ish (nĕr´ĭsh, nŭr´-) *v.t.* Sustain with food; foster, cherish, nurse, (feeling, hope, etc.) in one's heart. **nour′ish·ing** *adj.* **nour′-ish·ment** *n.* Sustenance, food; nourishing.

nou·veau riche (noō´vō rēsh´) pl. **nou·veaux riches** pr. noō´vō rēsh´). Newly enriched person, parvenu. [Fr.]

Nov. *abbrev.* November.

no·va (nō´va) *n.* (pl. **-vas, -vae** or. -vē). Star showing sudden great increase in light and energy and then subsiding, formerly mistaken or new star.

No·va Sco·tia (nō´va skō´sha). Province of SE. Canada, comprising peninsula projecting into Atlantic and the adjoining Cape Breton Island; capital, Halifax. **No′va Sco′tian** *adj. & n.*

nov·el[1] (nŏv´el) *n.* Fictitious prose narrative of sufficient length to fill one or more volumes; **the ~**, this type of literature.

nov·el[2] (nŏv´el) *adj.* Of new kind or nature, strange, hitherto unknown.

nov·el·ette (nŏvelĕt´) *n.* Short novel, story of moderate length, romantic novel without literary merit.

nov·el·ist (nŏv´elĭst) *n.* Writer of novels. **nov·el·is·tic** (nŏvelĭs´tĭk) *adj.* **nov·el·is′ti·cal·ly** *adv.*

nov·el·ize (nŏv´elīz) *v.t.* (**-ized, -iz·ing**). Convert into a novel. **nov·el·i·za·tion** (nŏvelĭzā´shon) *n.*

no·vel·la (nŏvĕl´a) *n.* (pl. **-vel·las, -vel·lae** pr. -vĕl´ē). Short novel. [It.]

nov·el·ty (nŏv´eltē) *n.* (pl. **-ties**). New or unusual thing or occurrence; inexpensive trinket; novel character *of* something.

No·vem·ber (nŏvĕm´ber). Eleventh month of Gregorian (ninth of Julian) calendar, with 30 days. [L. *novem* nine.]

no·ve·na (nōvē´na) *n.* (pl. **-nas, -nae** pr. -nē). (R.C. Ch.) Special prayers or services on nine successive days.

nov·ice (nŏv´ĭs) *n.* Person received in religious house on probation before taking the vows; new

Despite the recent growth of industry in **Nova Scotia,** *many of the people still earn their living from fishing. Bottom: A typical port at Peggy's Bay.*

convert; inexperienced person, beginner, tyro.

no·vi·ti·ate, no·vi·ci·ate (nō-vĭsh´ēĭt, -āt) *ns.* Novice's probationary period, initiation, or apprenticeship; novice; quarters assigned to novices.

No·vo·caine, No·vo·cain (nō´-vokān) *ns.* (trademark) Synthetic drug used as a local anesthetic.

now (now) *adv.* 1. At the present time; by this time; immediately; in the immediate past; then, next, by that time; (**every**) ~ **and then, ~ and again,** from time to time, intermittently. 2. In sentences expressing command, request, reproof, etc., with purely temporal sense weakened or effaced. **now** *conj.* Consequently upon or simultaneously with the fact that. ~ *n.* This time, the present (chiefly after prepositions). **now′a·days** *adv.* (At) the present day.

no·where (nō´hwār, -wār) *adv.* In, at, to, no place.

nox·ious (nŏk´shus) *adj.* Harmful, unwholesome. **nox′ious·ly** *adv.* **nox′ious·ness** *n.*

Noyes (noiz), **John Humphrey** (1811–86). Amer. social reformer; founder of Utopian communities, including Oneida, 1848, in New York State.

noz·zle (nŏz´el) *n.* Projecting vent; small spout of hose pipe etc.

Np *symbol.* Neptunium.

N.P., n.p. *abbrevs.* Notary public.

n.p. *abbrev.* No pagination.

nr. *abbrev.* Near.

NRA, N.R.A. *abbrevs.* National Rifle Association of America; National Recovery Administration.

N.S. *abbrev.* New style; Nova Scotia.

n.s. *abbrev.* Not specified.

NSC *abbrev.* National Security Council.

NT, N.T. *abbrevs.* New Testament.

nu (noō, nū) *n.* Fourteenth (later 13th) letter of Greek alphabet (N, ν), corresponding to n.

nu·ance (noō´ahns, nū´-, noō-ahns´, nū-) *n.* Delicate difference in or shade 'of meaning, feeling, opinion, color, etc.

nub (nŭb) *n.* 1. Small knob or lump, esp. of coal. 2. Point or gist (*of* matter or story). **nub′ble** *n.* = NUB def. 1. **nub′bly** *adv.*

Nu·bi·a (noō´bēa, nū´-). Region of NE. Africa in Nile valley between Aswan and Khartoum. **Nu′-bi·an** *adj. & n.* (Native, inhabitant, monosyllabic language) of Nubia.

Nu·bi·an (noō´bēan, nū´-) **Desert.** Desert in NE. Sudan from Nile to Red Sea.

nu·bile (noō´bĭl, -bīl, nū´-) *adj.* Marriageable (esp. of women); of age or physical development appropriate to marriage. **nu·bil·i·ty** (noōbĭl´ĭtē, nū-) *n.*

*Interior (above) and exterior (right) of a prototype fast-breeder **nuclear** reactor at Dounreay, Scotland. This is only one of many similar atomic power stations now contributing to electrical supplies. However, public concern with possible hazards has prevented others from being built.*

nu·cle·ar (nōō′klēer, nū′-) *adj.* 1. Of or constituting a nucleus. 2. Of, using, concerned with, nuclear energy or weapons; ~ **energy**, ATOMIC energy; ~ **fission**, splitting of a heavy nucleus into (usu. 2) parts with resulting release of large amounts of energy; ~ **fuel**, any substance from which atomic energy can be readily obtained; ~ **fusion**, union of atomic nuclei to form heavier nucleus, usu. with release of energy; the utilization of this process as source of energy.

nu·cle·ase (nōō′klēas, nū′-) *n.* (chem.) Enzyme that induces hydrolysis of nucleic acid.

nu·cle·ate (nōō′klēat, nū′-) *v.* (**-at·ed, -at·ing**). Form (into) a nucleus. **nu·cle·a·tion** (nōōklēā′shon, nū-) *n.* **nu·cle·ate** (nōō′klēĭt, -āt, nū′-) *adj.*

nu·cle·ic (nōōklē′ĭk, nū-) **acid.** One of a group of acids found in all living cells, combined with proteins to form nucleoproteins.

nu·cle·o·lus (nōōklē′olus, nū-) *n.* (pl. **-li** pr. -lī). Spherical body observable in nucleus of living rest-ing cells but disappearing during mitosis.

nu·cle·on (nōō′klēŏn, nū′-) *n.* (phys.) Proton or neutron of an atomic nucleus. **nu·cle·on·ics** (nōōklēŏn′ĭks, nū-) *n.* Branch of physics that treats of atomic nuclei esp. in practical applications, as in engineering.

nu·cle·us (nōō′klēus, nū′-) *n.* (pl. **-cle·i** pr. -klēī, **-cle·us·es**). Central part or thing around which others are collected; kernel of aggregate or mass; central part of ovule or seed; body, present in nearly all living cells, containing chromosomes; group of nerve cells in the central nervous system concerned with particular function; (phys., chem. internal core of an atom, su rounded by electrons and contain ing the positive charge of th electrically neutral atom.

nu·clide (nōō′klĭd, nū′-) (phys.) Particular kind of ator defined by composition of i nucleus; hence **nu·clid·ic** (nōōk lĭd′ĭk, nū-) *adj.*

nude (nōōd, nūd) *adj.* Nake unclothed, undraped; ~ **contrac** (law) one lacking a consideratio and therefore void unless und seal. **nude** *n.* Nude figure, i painting, etc.; **the ~**, the undrape human figure; the condition of being naked. **nu·di·ty** (noō'dĭtē, nū'-) *n.*

nudge (nŭj) *v.t.* (**nudged, nudg·ing**). Push slightly with elbow to draw attention privately; draw attention of. ~ *n.* Such a push.

nud·ist (noō'dĭst, nū'-) *n.* One who advocates or practices going unclothed. ~ *adj.* Of nudists. **nud'ism** *n.*

nu·ga·to·ry (noō'gatōrē, -tōrē, nū'-) *adj.* Trifling, worthless, futile; inoperative, not valid.

nug·get (nŭg'ĭt) *n.* Rough lump of native gold or platinum.

nui·sance (noō'sans, nū'-) *n.* Anything injurious or obnoxious to the community or a member of it; obnoxious person, offensive object, annoying action; anything disagreeable.

nuke (noōk, nūk) *n.* (slang) Nuclear or thermonuclear weapon.

Nu·ku·a·lo·fa (noōkoōoalaw'fa). Capital of Tonga on Tongatabu Island.

null (nŭl) *adj.* Not binding, invalid; without character or expression; (rare) nonexistent, amounting to nothing.

nul·li·fy (nŭl'ĭfī) *v.t.* (**-fied, -fy·ing**). Cancel, neutralize. **nul·li·fi·ca·tion** (nŭlifĭkā'shon) *n.*

nul·li·ty (nŭl'ĭtē) *n.* (pl. **-ties**). Being null, invalidity; act, document, etc., that is null; nothingness; a mere nothing.

numb (nŭm) *adj.* Deprived of feeling or power of motion. **numb'ly** *adv.* **numb'ness** *n.* **numb** *v.t.* Make numb; stupefy, paralyze.

num·ber (nŭm'ber) *n.* Count, sum, company, or aggregate, of persons, things, or abstract units; symbol or figure representing such aggregate; person or thing (esp. single issue of periodical) whose place in series is indicated by such figure; numerical reckoning; (sing. or pl.) large (or *large, small,* etc.) collection or company (*of*), (pl.) numerical preponderance; (gram.) property in words of denoting that one, two or more persons or things are spoken of, form of word expressing this; item (as song, dance) esp. on a program; (pl.) groups of musical notes, metrical feet, verses; **Numbers,** fourth book of Old Testament, earlier part of which contains census of Israelites; **his number is up,** he is doomed, his hour is come; **numbers game,** lottery based on occurrence of unpredictable numbers in results of races etc.; (slang) manipulation of statistical data with intention to befuddle (readers); (**times**) **out of number, without number,** innumerable (times); **number one,** oneself, esp. as object of selfish care; **Number 10,** (used for) 10

The cooling tower of a **nuclear** power station, similar to the one which formed a fault at Three Mile Island, threatening the surrounding population.

Downing Street, London, British prime minister's official residence. **num'ber·less** *adj.* **num'ber** *v.t.* Count, ascertain number of; include, regard as, *among, in,* or *with* some class; assign a number to, distinguish with a number; have lived, live (so many years); have, comprise (so many); equal, amount to;

*Throughout the history of art, the **nude** human figure has provided a challenge to artists and sculptors. Velazquez is still renowned for the 'Rokeby Venus' (below).*

(pass.) be restricted or few in number.

nu·mer·a·ble (noō'merabel, nū'-) *adj.* That can be numbered.

nu·mer·al (noō'meral, nū'-) *adj. & n.* (Word, figure, group of figures) denoting a number; of number.

nu·mer·a·tion (noōmerā'shon, nū-) *n.* Method or process of numbering or computing; calculation; assigning of numbers; (arith.) expression in words of number written in figures.

nu·mer·a·tor (noō'merāter, nū'-) *n.* Number above line in common fraction, showing how many of the parts indicated by the denominator are taken; person who numbers.

Nuremberg, possibly best remembered as the location of the trials of War Criminals after the 1939–45 war. A medieval town built around a castle and later walled now forms the town center.

nu·mer·i·cal (nōōměr´ĭkal, nū-) *adj.* Of, in, denoting, etc., number. **nu·mer´i·cal·ly** *adv.*

nu·mer·ol·o·gy (nōōmerŏl´ojē, nū-) *n.* Study of (esp. occult) significance of numbers. **nu·mer·o·log·i·cal** (nōōmerolŏj´ĭkal, nū-) *adj.* **nu·mer·ol´o·gist** *n.*

nu·mer·ous (nōō´merus, nū´-) *adj.* Comprising many units; coming from many individuals. **nu´mer·ous·ly** *adv.*

nu·mi·nous (nōō´minus, nū´-) *adj.* Divine; suggesting or revealing the presence or influence of a god; awe-inspiring, mysterious. [L. *numen* divine will, divinity]

nu·mis·mat·ic (nōōmĭzmăt´ĭk, -mĭs-, nū-) *adj.* Of coins or coinage. **nu·mis·mat´i·cal·ly** *adv.* **nu·mis·mat´ics, nu·mis·ma·tist** (nōōmĭz´matĭst, -mĭs´-, nū-), **nu·mis·ma·tol·o·gy** (nōōmĭzmatŏl´ojē, -mĭs-, nū-) *ns.*

num·skull, numb·skull (nŭm´skŭl) *ns.* Blockhead.

nun (nŭn) *n.* Woman living in convent under religious vow. **nun´like** *adj.*

nun·ci·o (nŭn´shēō, nōōn´-) *n.* (pl. **-ci·os**). Diplomatic representative of the pope at foreign court. **nun·ci·a·ture** (nŭn´shēacher) *n.* (Tenure of) office of nuncio.

nun·ner·y (nŭn´erē) *n.* (pl. **-ner·ies**). House, community, of nuns.

nup·tial (nŭp´shal) *adj.* Of marriage or wedding. ∼ *n.* (usu. pl.) Wedding.

Nu·rem·berg (noor´embẽrg, nūr´-). (Ger. *Nürnberg*) City of Bavaria; ∼ **laws**, series of laws, enacted under the Nazi regime, depriving Jews in Germany of certain civil rights and prohibiting intermarriage between Germans and Jews; ∼ **trials**, trials of war criminals conducted at Nuremberg after World War II.

nurse (nẽrs) *n.* 1. Woman employed to look after young child (so **nurse´maid**, maidservant employed thus); wet nurse. 2. (fig.) Something that nourishes or fosters some quality etc. 3. Person, usu. woman, charged with or trained for care of the sick or infirm; **practical** ∼, one trained in routine nursing but not registered; one with state board certification. 4. (entom.) Sexually imperfect bee, ant, etc., caring for the young brood, worker; (zool.) individual in asexual stage or metagenesis. **nurse** *v.* (**nursed, nurs·ing**). 1. Suckle (child), give suck, act as wet nurse; act as nursemaid to, have charge of; foster,

*The **nyala** is a variety of antelope found only in parts of south-east Africa. The mountain nyala of Ethiopia lives only at altitudes above 4,000 ft. where it grazes on alpine herbs.*

tend, promote development of; manage (plants, estate) with solicitude; cherish (grievance etc.); (pass.) be brought up. 2. Wait upon, attend to, (sick person); try to cure (sickness); **nursing home**, house (freq. under private management) receiving surgical cases, invalids, etc. 3. Clasp or hold carefully or caressingly; conserve (a drink etc.).

nurs·er·y (nẽr´serē) *n.* (pl. **-er·ies**). 1. Room assigned to children and their nurses; **day** ∼, institution taking charge of young children during day. 2. Plot of ground in which young plants are reared for transplantation, esp. one in which trees or plants are reared for sale; fish-rearing pond; place where animal life is developed. 3. **nurs´eryman**, owner of nursery garden; **nursery rhyme**, simple short traditional verse for young children; **nursery school**, school for young children, esp. those under five years of age.

nur·ture (nẽr´cher) *n.* Bringing up, training, fostering care; nourishment. ∼ *v.t.* (**-tured, -tur·ing**). Nourish, rear, foster, train, educate.

nut (nŭt) *n.* 1. Fruit consisting of hard or leathery indehiscent shell enclosing edible kernel; kernel of this; (slang) head; ∼**s about, over**, (slang) devoted to, fond of; **off one's** ∼, (slang) out of one's mind. 2. Small toothed projection on spindle engaging with cogwheel, small spur wheel; small block of metal etc. pierced with female screw for adjusting or tightening bolt; holder for tightening or relaxing horsehair of violin bow. 3. Very small lump of coal etc. 4. (slang) Eccentric or insane person. 5. **nut-brown**, colored like ripe hazelnut; **nut′cracker**, instrument for cracking nuts; corvine bird (*Nucifraga caryocatactes*) of mountain regions in Western U.S., having gray body with white patches on wings and tail; also called Clark's ~; **nut′gall**, gall found on oak; **nut′hatch**, any of several small nut-eating birds (family Sittidae), esp. *Sitta carolinensis* common throughout the U.S. and Canada, predominantly gray but having black on the head and a white throat; **nut′shell**, hard exterior covering of nut; something extremely small; **in a nutshell**, briefest possible way of expressing something; **nut tree**, tree bearing nuts, esp. hazel. **nut′ting** *n.* Gathering nuts.

nu·tant (nōo′tant, nū′-) *adj.* (bot.) Drooping.

nu·ta·tion (nōotā′shon, nū-) *n.* Nodding; (astron.) oscillation of Earth's axis making motion of pole of equator around pole of ecliptic wavy; oscillation of spinning top in its precession around an axis.

nut·meg (nŭt′mĕg) *n.* Hard aromatic spheroidal seed from fruit of evergreen E. Ind. tree (*Myristica fragrans*), used as spice.

nu·tri·a (nōo′trēa, nū′-) *n.* (Fur of the) coypu.

nu·tri·ent (nōo′trēent, nū′-) *adj. & n.* (Substance etc.) serving as or providing nourishment.

nu·tri·ment (nōo′triment, nū′-) *n.* Nourishing food.

nu·tri·tion (nōotrĭsh′on, nū-) *n.* (Supplying or receiving of) nourishment, food. **nu·tri′tion·al** *adj.* Of, relating to, nutrition. **nu·tri′-tion·al·ly** *adv.* **nu·tri′tion·ist** *n.*

nu·tri·tious (nōotrĭsh′us, nū-) *adj.* Nourishing, efficient as food. **nu·tri′tious·ly** *adv.* **nu·tri′-**

*Two species of **nutcrackers**, birds related to crows, are present in northern Europe and America. They collect food in summer which is stored for use in the winter.*

tious·ness *n.*

nu·tri·tive (nōo′trĭtĭv, nū′-) *adj.* Serving as food; concerned in nutrition.

nuts (nŭts) *adj.* (slang) Crazy.

nut·ty (nŭt′ē) *adj.* (**-ti·er, -ti·est**). 1. Abounding in nuts; tasting like nuts, of rich mellow flavor. 2. (slang) Silly.

nux vom·i·ca (nŭks vŏm′ika). Seed of pulpy fruit of E. Ind. tree (*Strychnos nux-vomica*), yielding strychnine.

nuz·zle (nŭz′el) *v.* (**-zled, -zling**). Nose; burrow, press, rub, sniff, with the nose; press nose or press (nose) *into, against*; nestle, lie

*A popular food, these **nuts** are produced by the almond tree, Prunus dulcis, which grows in warm temperate climates. Oil extracted from almonds is used in cosmetics and as a lubricant.*

*The **nuthatch**, a tree-climbing bird found in most parts of the world except the Australian region, may also be aptly described as a tree-runner. The largest is 9 ins. long.*

snug.

NV *abbrev.* Nevada.

NW, N.W., n.w. *abbrevs.* Northwest(ern).

N.W.T. *abbrev.* Northwest Territories (Canada).

NY, N.Y. *abbrevs.* New York.

ny·a·la (nēah′la, nī-) *n.* (pl. **-las**, collect. **-la**). Large S. African antelope (*Tragelaphus angasi*), one of the bush bucks.

N.Y.C. *abbrev.* New York City.

nyc·ta·lo·pi·a (nĭktalō′pēa) *n.* Night blindness, inability to see in a dim light.

ny·lon (nī′lŏn) *n.* Any of a group of long-chain synthetic polymeric amines of which the structural units or molecules can be oriented in one direction, and which are thus capable of being formed into filaments of great tensile strength; textile fiber of this structure and character; (pl.) garments, esp. women's stockings, made of this.

nymph (nĭmf) *n.* 1. (myth.) One of class of semidivine maidens inhabiting sea, rivers, fountains, woods, or trees; (poet.) young and beautiful woman. 2. (zool.) Immature insect that from time of hatching has a general resemblance to the adult. 3. Edible frog.

nym·pho·ma·ni·a (nĭmfomā′nēa) *n.* (path.) Morbid and uncontrollable sexual desire in women. **nym·pho·ma′ni·ac** *adj. & n.*

NYSE *abbrev.* New York Stock Exchange.

nys·tag·mus (nĭstăg′mus) *n.* Rapid involuntary oscillation of eyeball. **nys·tag′mic** *adj.*

N.Z., N. Zeal. *abbrevs.* New Zealand.

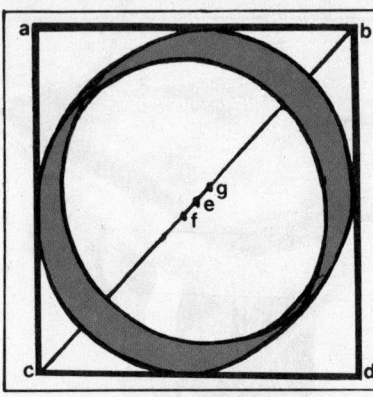

Phoenician Early Greek Etruscan

Early Latin Classical Latin Italian

O¹, o (ō) (pl. **O's, o's** or **Os, os**). 1. Fifteenth letter of modern English and 14th of ancient Roman alphabet, representing a variety of mid-back-round vowels, and corresponding in form to ancient Greek O, derived from Phoenician and ancient Semitic ○, ◇, ▽ (Heb. ע), which represent not a vowel but a glottal stop. 2. O, O-shaped mark, circle; cipher or naught.

O², oh (ō) *ints.* Exclamation expressing various emotions or prefixed to vocative name.

O³ *symbol.* Oxygen.

O. *abbrev.* Ohio.

o' (o, ō) *prep.* Short for *of, on,* in some phrases as (= *of*) *o'clock, will-o'-the-wisp, man-o'-war.*

oaf (ōf) *n.* Awkward lout. **oaf'ish** *adj.* **oaf'ish·ly** *adv.* **oaf'ish·ness** *n.* [ON. *álfr* elf]

O·a·hu (ōah´hoō). One of the Hawaiian Islands, 589 square miles (1,526 sq. km), on which Honolulu, the state capital, is located.

oak (ōk) *n.* 1. Forest tree of genus *Quercus* with hard timber, bearing acorn as fruit; any of various trees or plants resembling this; **~-leaf cluster**, U.S. military decoration granted to the holder of a medal for a second action meriting the same medal; **poison ~**: see POISON. 2. Wood of the oak; this as material for ships. **oak·en** (ō´ken) *adj.* (chiefly poet.) Made of oak.

Oak·land (ōk´land). City in N. California, opposite San Francisco, on San Francisco Bay.

Oak·ley (ōk´lē): see ANNIE OAKLEY.

Oak (ōk) **Ridge.** City in E. Tennessee; site of the original Oak Ridge National Laboratory for development and research of atomic energy and materials.

oa·kum (ō´kum) *n.* Loose fiber gotten by untwisting and picking old hemp ropes and used esp. i caulking.

oar (ōr, ôr) *n.* Long stov wooden shaft widened and flattene at one end into a blade, used t propel (row) a boat by leverag against a rowlock, which serves a fulcrum, esp. pulled by one rowe with both hands, as dist. from scull (one hand) and a sweep (tw rowers); oarsman; **put in one's ~** interfere; **rest on one's ~s,** lea on handles of oars, raising blade out of water; (fig.) suspend one efforts, take things easy; **oar'lock** device, usu. U-shaped, set in swive in gunwale of boat to hold oar **oars'man,** rower; **oars'man ship**.

OAS *abbrev.* Organization American States.

o·a·sis (ōā´sĭs) *n.* (pl. **-ses** p -sēz). Depression in desert wher cultivation is possible owing t presence of water (also fig.).

oat (ōt) *n.* (pl.) (Grain yielde by) hardy cereal (*Avena sativa* grown in cool climates as food fc man and horses; **wild ~s**: see WILI

Oak trees of various types are native to the Americas, Europe, Africa and Asia. English oaks (left) were once essential to shipbuilding. Bark of the American red oak (below) was processed to extract the tannin.

Waikiki Beach on **Oahu,** one of the Hawaiian Islands. Waikiki is a major tourist resort, renowned throughout the world. Honolulu, Hawaii's capital, is on the island. Its name means 'sheltered harbor'.

In desert regions, an **oasis** forms in a depression where underground water accumulates close to the surface. Above: A Tunisian oasis first recorded in Roman times.

Principally a fodder crop, **oats** are also used in breakfast cereals and their stalks used as hay, or processed in silage tanks. Oats are a very hardy plant and can survive in poor soil.

oat′cake, thin unleavened cake of oatmeal; **oat′meal,** meal made from oats; oatmeal porridge; grayish fawn (color).

oath (ōth) *n.* (pl. **oaths** pr. ōdhz, ōths). 1. Solemn appeal to God (or to something scared), in witness of truth of statement or binding character of promise. 2. Name of God, or of something sacred, used as expletive to give emphasis or express anger etc.; piece of profanity in speech.

Ob (ŏb). River of Asiatic U.S.S.R., flowing north into **Gulf of Ob,** an arm of the Arctic Ocean.

ob. *abbrev. Obiit,* obstetrics.

O·ba·di·ah (ōbadī′a). Hebrew minor prophet; shortest book of Old Testament, bearing his name.

ob·bli·ga·to (ŏbligah′tō) *adj.* & *n.* (pl. **-tos,** *It.* **-ti** pr. -tē). (mus.) (Part, accompaniment) forming integral part of composition. [It.]

ob·du·rate (ŏb′dŏorĭt, -dyŏo-) *adj.* Hardened, impenitent, stubborn. **ob′du·rate·ly** *adv.* **ob′du·ra·cy, ob′du·rate·ness** *ns.*

o·be·ah (ō′bēa), **o·bi**[2] (ō′bē) *ns.* Sorcery or witch doctoring associated with the snake god Obi whose worship was introduced by W. African slaves into W. Indies and U.S. **o′be·ah·ism** *n.*

o·be·di·ence (ōbē′dēens) *n.* 1. Obeying as act, practice, or quality; submission to another's rule; compliance with law or command. 2. (eccles., esp. R.C.) (Sphere of) authority; district or body of persons subject to some rule.

o·be·di·ent (ōbē′dēent) *adj.* Submissive to, complying with, superior's will; dutiful. **o·be′di·ent·ly** *adv.*

o·bei·sance (ōbā′sans, ōbē′-) *n.* Gesture, esp. bow or curtsy, expressing submission, respect, or salūtation. **o·bei′sant** *adj.* **o·bei′sant·ly** *adv.*

ob·e·lisk (ŏb′elĭsk) *n.* Tapering shaft of stone, square or rectangular in section, with pyramidal apex; mountain, tree, etc., of similar shape.

O·ber·am·mer·gau (ōberah′mergow). Village in Upper Bavaria; in 1633 the inhabitants vowed that they would perform a Passion Play as an act of thanksgiving for deliverance from the plague; since 1680 the play has been performed every ten years exc. for 1810, 1920, and 1940.

O·ber·on (ō′berŏn). In W. European folklore, king of the fairies.

o·bese (ōbēs′) *adj.* Corpulent. **o·bese′ly** *adv.* **o·bese′ness, o·be·si·ty** (ōbē′sĭtē) *ns.*

o·bey (ōbā′) *v.* Perform bidding of, be obedient (to); execute (command). **o·bey′a·ble** *adj.* **o·bey′er** *n.* **o·bey′ing·ly** *adv.*

ob·fus·cate (ŏb′fŭskāt, ŏbfŭs′-) *v.t.* (**-cat·ed, -cat·ing**). Darken, obscure; stupefy, bewilder. **ob·fus·ca·tion** (ŏbfŭskā′shon) *n.*

o·bi[1] (ō′bē) *n.* Japanese woman's bright-colored sash.

o·bi[2] = OBEAH.

o·bi·it (ō′bēĭt). Died (with date of death). [L.]

o·bit (ō′bĭt, ŏb′ĭt) *n.* Obituary; date of person's death.

ob·i·ter dic·tum (ŏb′ĭter dĭk′tum) (pl. **dic·ta** pr. dĭk′ta). Judge's expression of opinion on matters of law, given in course of argument or judgment but not essential to decision and therefore without binding authority; incidental remark(s). [L.]

o·bit·u·ar·y (ōbĭch′ōoĕrē) *n.* (pl. **-ar·ies**). Notice of death, esp. in newspaper, brief biography of deceased person. ~ *adj.* Recording a death; concerning deceased person.

ob·ject[1] (ŏb′jĭkt, -jĕkt) *n.* 1. Thing placed before eyes or presented to sense; material thing; thing observed with optical instrument or represented in picture. 2. Person or thing of pitiable or ridiculous aspect. 3. Person or thing to which action or feeling is directed, subject *of* or *for*; thing aimed at, end, purpose; **no** ~, not to be taken into account; forming no obstacle. 4. (philos.) Thing thought of or apprehended as correlative to the thinking mind or subject; external thing. 5. (gram.) Substantive word, phrase, or clause governed by active transitive verb or by preposition; **direct, indirect**, ~, that primarily, secondarily, affected by action of verb. 6. ~ **glass, lens**, lens in telescope etc. nearest the object; ~ **lesson**, instruction about material object that is present for inspection; (fig.) striking practical application of some principle.

ob·ject[2] (ŏbjĕkt′) *v.* Bring forward or state in opposition, urge as objection; state objection; express or feel disapproval. **ob·jec′tor** *n.*

ob·jec·ti·fy (objĕk′tifī) *v.t.* (**-fied, -fy·ing**). Present as object of sense; make objective; express in concrete form, embody. **ob·jec·ti·fi·ca·tion** (objĕktifikā′shon) *n.*

ob·jec·tion (objĕk′shon) *n.* Objecting, thing objected; adverse reason or statement; expression or feeling of disapproval or dislike. **ob·jec′tion·a·ble** *adj.* Open to objection; undesirable, unpleasant, offensive. **ob·jec′tion·a·bil·i·ty** (objĕkshonabĭl′ĭtē), **ob·jec′tion·a·ble·ness** *ns.* **ob·jec′tion·a·bly** *adv.*

Obelisks, such as the one from Egypt in the square of Santa Maria Maggiore in Rome, were originally built as central cult objects for worship of the sun.

ob·jec·tive (objĕk′tĭv) *adj.* 1. Belonging to what is presented to consciousness; that is the object of perception or thought, as dist. from perceiving or thinking subject; external to the mind, real. 2. Dealing with outward things and not with thoughts or feelings, exhibiting facts uncolored by exhibitor's feelings or opinions. 3. (gram.) Constructed as, appropriate to, the object. **ob·jec′tive·ly** *adv.* **ob·jec′tive·ness, ob·jec·tiv·i·ty** (ŏbjĕktĭv′ĭtē) *ns.* **ob·jec′tive** *n.* 1. Object glass. 2. (gram.) Objective case. 3. Object or purpose of an action; (mil.) position to the attainment or capture of which an operation is directed, objective point.

ob·jec·tiv·ism (objĕk′tĭvĭzem) *n.* Tendency to lay stress on the objective; doctrine that knowledge of observable phenomena is prior in sequence and importance to that of knowledge of self. **ob·jec′tiv·ist** *n.*

ob·jet d'art (ŏbzhā dār′) (pl. **ob·jets d'art** pr. ŏbzhā dār′). Object (esp. small) of artistic interest, curio. [Fr.]

ob·jur·gate (ŏb′jergāt) *v.t.* (**-gat·ed, -gat·ing**). Chide, scold. **ob·jur·ga′tion, ob′jur·ga·tor** *ns.* **ob·jur·ga·to·ry** (objēr′gatōrē, -tōrē) *adj.*

ob·late[1] (ŏb′lāt) *n.* Person dedicated to monastic or religious life or work. **ob′late·ly** *adv.*

ob·late[2] (ŏb′lāt, ŏblāt′) *adj.* (geom., of spheroid) Flattened at the poles.

ob·la·tion (ŏblā′shon) *n.* (Presenting bread and wine to God in) Eucharist; thing offered to God, sacrifice, victim; donation for pious uses. **ob·la·to·ry** (ŏb′latōrē, -tōrē), **ob·la′tion·al** *adjs.*

ob·li·gate (ŏb′ligāt) *v.t.* (**-gat·ed, -gat·ing**). Bind (person, esp. legally) *to* do; oblige. **ob′li·ga·tor** *n.*

ob·li·ga·tion (ŏbligā′shon) *n.* 1. Binding agreement, esp. one enforceable under legal penalty, written contract, or bond; constraining power of a law, precept, duty, contract, etc.; one's bounden duty, a duty, burdensome task. 2. (Indebtedness for) service or benefit.

ob·lig·a·to·ry (oblĭg′atōrē, -tōrē, ŏb′lĭga-) *adj.* Legally or morally binding; imperative, not merely permissive; constituting an obligation.

o·blige (oblīj′) *v.t.* (**o·bliged, o·blig·ing**). 1. Bind by oath, promise, contract, etc., *to* (archaic, legal); be binding on. 2. Make indebted by conferring favor, gratify *by, with*; (colloq.) make contribution to entertainment (*with*); (pass.) be bound (*to*) by gratitude. 3. Constrain, compel, *to* do.

ob·li·gee (ŏblijē′) *n.* (law) Person to whom another is bound by contract or to whom bond is given.

o·blig·ing (oblī′jing) *adj.* Courteous, accommodating, ready to do kindness, complaisant. **o·blig′ing·ly** *adv.* **o·blig′ing·ness** *n.*

ob·li·gor (ŏbligôr′, ŏb′ligôr) *n.* (law) One who binds himself to another or gives bond.

ob·lique (ōblēk′, oblīk′) *adj.* Slanting; declining from vertical or horizontal; diverging from straight line or course; (geom.) (of line etc.) inclined at other than right angle, (of angle) acute or obtuse, (of cone etc.) with axis not perpendicular to plane of base; (anat.) neither parallel nor perpendicular to body's or limb's long axis; (bot., of leaf) with unequal sides. 2. Not going straight to the point, roundabout, indirect; ~ **speech**, indirect speech. **ob·lique′ly** *adv.* **ob·liq·ui·ty** (oblĭk′wĭtē) *n.*

ob·lit·er·ate (oblĭt′erāt) *v.t.* (**-at·ed, -at·ing**). Blot out, efface, erase, destroy. **ob·lit·er·a·tion** (oblīterā′shon) *n.*

ob·liv·i·on (oblĭv′ēon) *n.* Having or being forgotten; disregard, unregarded state.

ob·liv·i·ous (oblĭv′ēus) *adj.* Forgetful, unmindful, (*of*); (poet.) of, inducing, oblivion. **ob·liv′i·ous·ly** *adv.* **ob·liv′i·ous·ness** *n.*

First recorded in the 13th century, **Oberon** *has been attributed with many forms. To the Germans he was an ugly dwarf. Shakespeare portrayed him as king of the fairies (opposite).*

ob·long (ŏb′lawng) *adj.* Elongated in one direction (usu. as deviation from exact square or circular form); (geom.) rectangular with adjacent sides unequal. ~ *n.* Oblong figure or object.

ob·lo·quy (ŏb′lokwē) *n.* (pl. **-quies**). Abuse, detraction; being generally ill spoken of.

ob·nox·ious (obnŏk′shus) *adj.* Offensive, objectionable, disliked. **ob·nox′ious·ly** *adv.* **ob·nox′ious·ness** *n.*

o·boe (ō′bō) *n.* Musical instrument of woodwind family, played vertically, with a double reed, having a range of nearly three octaves upward from the B flat below middle C, and a plaintive incisive tone; organ reed stop imitating this. **o′bo·ist** *n.*

ob·scene (obsēn′) *adj.* 1. (archaic) Repulsive. 2. Indecent, esp. grossly or repulsively so; lewd; (law, of publications) tending to deprave and corrupt. **ob·scene′ly** *adv.* **ob·scene′ness** *n.* **ob·scen·i·ty** (obsĕn′ītē) *n.* (pl. **-ties**).

ob·scu·rant (obskūr′ant) *n.* Opponent of inquiry, enlightenment, and reform. **ob·scu′rant·ism** *n.* **ob·scu′rant·ist** *n.* & *adj.*

ob·scure (obskūr′) *adj.* (**-scur·er, -scur·est**). 1. Dark, dim; (of color) dingy, dull, indefinite. 2. Indistinct, not clear; (of vowel) not clearly enunciated. 3. Hidden, remote from observation; unnoticed; unknown to fame, humble. 4. Unexplained, doubtful; not perspicuous or clearly expressed. **ob·scure′ly** *adv.* **ob·scure′ness, ob·scu·ri·ty** (obskūr′ītē) *ns.* **ob·scure** *v.t.* (**-scured, -scur·ing**). Make obscure, dark, indistinct, or unintelligible; dim glory of, outshine; conceal from sight. **ob·scu·ra·tion** (ŏbskūrā′shon) *n.*

ob·se·cra·tion (ŏbsekrā′shon) *n.* Earnest entreaty. **ob·se·crate** (ŏb′sekrāt) *v.t.* (**-crat·ed, -crat·ing**).

ob·se·quies (ŏb′sekwēz) *n. pl.* Funeral rites, funeral.

ob·se·qui·ous (obsē′kweus) *adj.* Servile, fawning. **ob·se′qui·ous·ly** *adv.* **ob·se′qui·ous·ness** *n.*

ob·serv·ance (obzēr′vans) *n.* Keeping or performance of law, duty, ritual, etc.; act of religious or ceremonial character, customary rite; rule of a religious order.

ob·serv·ant (obzēr′vant) *adj.* 1. Attentive in observance. 2. Acute or diligent in taking notice. **ob·serv′ant·ly** *adv.*

ob·ser·va·tion (ŏbzērvā′shon) *n.*

*The giant telescope at the **observatory** at Mount Palomar in the U.S.A. This is one of many forms of equipment now used by astronomers to gain better knowledge of the universe.*

1. Noticing or being noticed; peception, faculty of taking notic (mil.) watching of fortress or host position or movements. 2. Obser ing scientifically, accurate watchi and noting of phenomena as th occur in nature; taking of altitu of sun or other heavenly body find latitude or longitude; readi or value of any observed quantit esp. when noted down. 3. Remar statement, esp. one of the natu of comment. **ob·ser′va·tion·** *adj.* **ob·ser′va·tion·al·ly** *adv.*

ob·serv·a·to·ry (obzēr′vātor -tōrē) *n.* (pl. **-ries**). Building e whence natural, esp. astronomic phenomena can be observed.

ob·serve (obzērv′) *v.* (**-serve -serv·ing**). 1. Keep, follow, adhe to, perform duly. 2. Perceiv watch, mark, take notice of, becon conscious of; examine and no (phenomena) without aid of exper ment. 3. Say, esp. by way comment; make remark(s) o **ob·serv′er** *n.* (esp.) Interest spectator; person carried in aircra to note enemy's position et person trained to watch and identi aircraft.

ob·sess (ŏbsēs′) *v.t.* Domina or preoccupy the thoughts of person). **ob·ses·sion** (obsĕsh′o *n.* **ob·ses′sive, ob·ses′sion·al** *ad* **ob·sid·i·an** (obsĭd′ēan) *n.* Da vitreous volcanic rock with appea

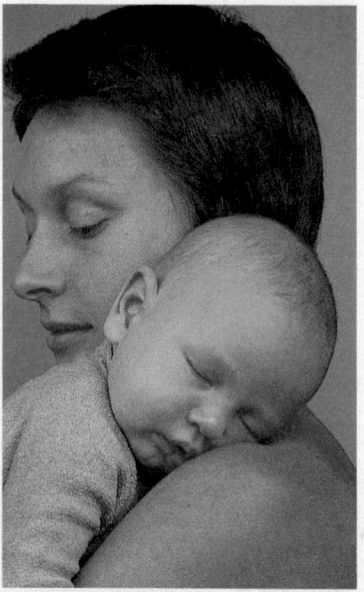

nce like glass, used by primitive ocieties for knives etc. [f. personal name *Obsius*]

ob·so·les·cent (ŏbsoles′ent) *adj.* Becoming obsolete; gradually disappearing. **ob·so·les′cence** *n.*

ob·so·lete (ŏbsolēt′, ŏb′solēt) *adj.* Disused, discarded, antiquated. **ob·so·lete′ly** *adv.* **ob·so·lete′ness** *n.*

ob·sta·cle (ŏb′stakel) *n.* Hindrance, impediment; ~ **race**, one in which artificial or natural obstacles have to be passed.

ob·stet·ric (obstĕt′rĭk), **ob·stet′ri·cal** *adjs.* Of midwifery; of, relating to, obstetrics. **ob·stet′rics** *n.* (usu. considered sing.) Branch of medicine and surgery concerned with the care of women before, during, and immediately after childbirth. **ob·ste·tri·cian** (ŏbstĭtrĭsh′an) *n.*

ob·sti·nate (ŏb′stinĭt) *adj.* Firmly adhering to one's own course, not yielding to argument or persuasion; inflexible, self-willed; (of disease etc.) not yielding readily to treatment. **ob′sti·nate·ly** *adv.* **ob′sti·nate·ness, ob·sti·na·cy** (ŏb′stinasē) *ns.*

ob·strep·er·ous (obstrĕp′erus) *adj.* Noisy, vociferous; turbulent, unruly, noisily resisting control. **ob·strep′er·ous·ly** *adv.* **ob·strep′er·ous·ness** *n.*

ob·struct (obstrŭkt′) *v.* Block up, fill with impediments, make impassable or difficult of passage; prevent or retard progress of, impede; practice obstruction. **ob·struc·tion** (obstrŭk′shon) *n.* Blocking or being blocked, making or becoming more or less impassable; hindering business by talking against time; obstacle. **ob·struc′tion·ist, ob·struc′tion·ism** *ns.*

ob·struc·tive (obstrŭk′tĭv) *adj.* Causing, intended to produce, ob-

struction. **ob·struc′tive·ly** *adv.* **ob·struc′tive·ness** *n.*

ob·tain (obtān′) *v.* 1. Acquire, have granted one, get. 2. Be prevalent, established, or in vogue. **ob·tain′·a·ble** *adj.* **ob·tain′er, ob·tain′ment** *ns.*

ob·trude (obtrōod′) *v.t.* (**-trud·ed, -trud·ing**). Thrust forward (*on, upon*) importunately. **ob·tru·sion** (obtrōo′zhon) *n.* **ob·tru·sive** (obtrōo′sĭv) *adj.* **ob·tru′sive·ly** *adv.* **ob·tru′sive·ness** *n.*

ob·tuse (ŏbtōos′, -tūs′) *adj.* 1. Of blunt form, not sharp or pointed; (geom., of plane angle) greater than right angle. 2. Dull, not acute; stupid, slow of perception. **ob·tuse′ly** *adv.* **ob·tuse′ness** *n.*

ob·verse (ŏbvers′, ŏb′vers) *adj.* 1. Narrower at base or point of attachment than at apex. 2. Answering as counterpart to something else. **obverse** (ŏb′vers) *n.* Side of coin or medal bearing head or principal design (opp. REVERSE); face of anything meant to be presented, front; counterpart of a fact or truth.

ob·vi·ate (ŏb′vēāt) *v.t.* (**-at·ed, -at·ing**). Clear away, get rid of, get around, neutralize (danger, inconvenience, etc.).

ob·vi·ous (ŏb′vēus) *adj.* Open to eye or mind, clearly perceptible, palpable, indubitable. **ob′vi·ous·ly** *adv.* **ob′vi·ous·ness** *n.*

oc·a·ri·na (ŏkarē′na) *n.* Small egg-shaped metal or porcelain musical wind instrument with whistle-like mouthpiece and finger holes, also called "sweet potato." [It. *oca* goose]

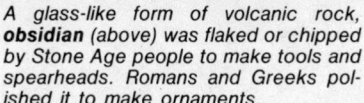

A glass-like form of volcanic rock, **obsidian** *(above) was flaked or chipped by Stone Age people to make tools and spearheads. Romans and Greeks polished it to make ornaments.*

The **obstetric** *branch of medicine deals specifically with the care of women throughout the pregnancy and during and after the birth. This care has dramatically reduced infant mortality.*

O'Ca·sey (ōkā′sē), **Sean** (1884–1964). Irish playwright, author of *Juno and the Paycock, The Plough and the Stars*, etc.

Oc·cam = OCKHAM.

oc·ca·sion (okā′zhon) *n.* Juncture suitable for doing something, opportunity; reason, ground, justification, need; subsidiary, incidental, or immediate cause; (particular time marked by) special occurrence; (pl.) affairs, business. ~ *v.t.* Be the occasion or cause of; bring about, esp. incidentally; cause.

oc·ca·sion·al (okā′zhonal) *adj.* Arising out of, made or meant for, acting on, special occasion(s), as ~ *verse*; happening irregularly as occasion presents itself; coming now and then, not regular or frequent; ~ **table**, small table for use as required. **oc·ca′sion·al·ly** *adv.*

Oc·ci·dent (ŏk′sident) *n.* (chiefly poet.) The West; western Europe; Europe; Europe and America; America; Europe as opp. to Oriental civilization. **oc·ci·den′tal** *adj.* **oc·ci·den′tal·ly** *adv.* **Oc·ci·den′tal·ism** *n.* **Oc·ci·den′tal·ist** *n. & adj.*

oc·ci·put (ŏk′sipŭt) *n.* (pl. **oc·ci·puts, oc·cip·i·ta** pr. ŏksĭp′ĭta). Back of head. **oc·cip′i·tal** *adj.* Of the occiput.

oc·clude (oklōod′) *v.t.* (**-clud·ed, -clud·ing**). Stop up, close, obstruct; (chem.) absorb and retain (gases); **occluded front**, (meteor.) warm front forced upward by cold front when the cold air overtakes the warm and flows in underneath it.

oc·clu·sion (oklōō´zhon) *n*. Act or process of occluding; position of teeth when jaws are brought together, bite; (phonet.) momentary closure of vocal passage as in formation of stop consonants; (chem.) absorption of gases by certain substances.

oc·clu·sive (oklōō´sĭv) *adj*. Tending to occlude; (phonet., of a consonant) produced with occlusion. **oc·clu´sive·ness** *n*.

oc·cult[1] (okŭlt´, ŏk´ŭlt) *adj*. Kept secret, esoteric; recondite, mysterious, beyond the range of ordinary knowledge; involving the supernatural, mystical, magical; **the ~**, the supernatural. **oc·-cult´ly** *adv*. **oc·cult´ness** *n*.

*Originally considered as a river encircling the land of the known world, the name **ocean** was retained when its immensity was later assessed. The name was also applied to certain areas such as the Atlantic (1), Pacific (2) and Antarctic (3) which separate the continents.*

oc·cult[2] (okŭlt´) *v*. Conceal, cut off from view by passing in front (usu. astron.); **occult´ing light**, in lighthouse etc., light that is cut off at regular intervals.

oc·cul·ta·tion (ŏkŭltā´shon) *n*. (astron.) Eclipse of one heavenly body by another, usu. larger, passing between it and the Earth.

oc·cult·ism (okŭl´tĭzem) *n*. Theory of, belief in, occult forces and powers. **oc·cult´ist** *n*. & *adj*

oc·cu·pant (ŏk´yupant) *n*. Pe son holding property, esp. land, actual possession; one wh occupies, resides in, or is in, a plac one who establishes title to owner less thing by taking possession **oc·cu·pan·cy** (ŏk´yupansē) *n*.

oc·cu·pa·tion (ŏkyupā´shon) 1. Occupying or being occupie taking or holding possession, esp of country or district by militar force; tenure, occupancy. 2. Wh occupies one, means of filling one time; temporary or regular employ ment, business, calling, pursui **oc·cu·pa´tion·al** *adj*. (esp. of di ease etc.) Incidental to, caused by one's occupation; **~ therapy**

Ocelot

therapy employing purposeful occupation, as handicrafts, cultural activities, etc.

oc·cu·py (ŏk'yupī) *v.t.* (**-pied, -py·ing**). Take possession of (country etc.) by military force or settlement; hold (office); reside in, tenant; take up or fill (space, time); be in (place, position); keep engaged. **oc'cu·pi·a·ble** *adj.* **oc'cu·pi·er** *n.* Person in (esp. temporary or subordinate) possession, esp. of land or house; holder, occupant.

oc·cur (okēr') *v.i.* (**oc·curred, oc·cur'ring**). Be met with, be found, exist, in some place or conditions; come into one's mind; come into being at a point or period of time.

oc·cur'rence (okēr'ens, okŭr'-) *n.* Happening; incident, event. **oc·cur'rent** *adj.*

o·cean (ō'shan) *n.* Great body of water surrounding the land of the globe; one of the main areas into which this is geographically divided (usu. reckoned as five, the **Atlantic, Pacific, Indian, Arctic** and **Antarctic**); the sea; immense expanse or quantity of anything. **O·ce·an·i·a** (ōshĕăn'ēa, -ah'nēa). Islands of the central, western, and southern Pacific Ocean, usually including Australasia, New Zealand, and Malaysia. **O·ce·an'i·an** *adj.* & *n.*

o·ce·an·ic (ōshĕăn'ĭk) *adj.* Of the ocean; **O ~**, of Oceania. **O·ce·a·nid** (ōsē'anĭd) *n.* (pl. **O·ce·a·ni·des** pr. ōsēăn'ĭdēz). (Gk. myth.) One of the ocean nymphs, daughters of Oceanus and Tethys.

o·cea·nog·ra·phy (ōshanŏg'-rafē) *n.* Branch of science concerned with the study of the ocean, the composition and characteristics of the water, plant, and animal life, and the ocean floor. **o·cea·nog'-ra·pher** *n.*

O·ce·a·nus (ōsē'anus). (Gk. myth.) Son of Uranus and Ge, and father of the Oceanids and river gods; personification of the river encircling the whole world.

o·ce·lot (ŏs'elŏt, ō'se-) *n.* One of the larger cats (*Felis pardalis*) of Central and S. America, with gray body marked with elongated fawn spots edged with black, and white or whitish underparts marked with black.

o·cher, o·chre (ō'ker) *ns.* Mineral or class of minerals consisting of hydrated ferric oxide mixed with varying proportions of clay, used as pigment, ranging in color from light yellow to deep orange or brown. **o'cher·ous, o'chre·ous**

A member of the leopard family the **ocelot** *is found in Central and South America. Its patterned coat is highly distinctive.*

(ō'kerus, ō'krēus) *adjs.*

Ock·ham or **Oc·cam** (ŏk'am), **William of** (c1300–c1349). English scholastic philosopher; founded a speculative sect reviving the doctrines of Nominalism; **Ockham's razor**, principle that assumptions introduced to explain something must not be unnecessarily multiplied.

o'clock (oklŏk') *adv.* (of time) By the clock.

O'Con·nell (ōkŏn'el), **Daniel** (1775–1847). Irish political leader who championed liberation of the Irish catholics and separation of Ireland from Gt. Britain.

OCS *abbrev.* Officer Candidate School.

Oct. *abbrev.* October.

oct. *abbrev.* Octavo.

octa-, oct- *prefixes*. Eight.

oc·tad (ŏk'tăd) *n.* Group of eight. **oc·tad'ic** *adj.*

oc·ta·gon (ŏk'tagŏn) *n.* Plane figure of eight angles and sides; object or building of such section. **oc·tag·o·nal** (ŏktăg'onal) *adj.* **oc·tag'o·nal·ly** *adv.*

oc·ta·he·dron (ŏktahē'dron) *n.* (pl. **-drons, -dra** pr. -dra). Solid figure of eight faces, usu. eight triangles; body, esp. crystal, of regular octahedral form; **regular ~**, figure contained by eight equal and equilateral triangles. **oc·ta·he'dral** *adj.*

oc·tane (ŏk'tān) *n.* (chem.) Hydrocarbon of the paraffin series (C_8H_{18}); **~ number**, measure of the knock prevention properties of gasoline; **high ~**, (of gasoline) having good antiknock properties.

oc·tave (ŏk'tĭv, -tāv) *n.* 1. (eccles.) Eighth day after a festival (both days being counted); period of eight days beginning with a festival. 2. Group or stanza of eight lines, octet. 3. (mus.) Note eight diatonic degrees above or below given note (both notes being counted), and produced by vibrations of twice or half the rate,

Oceania includes many groups of small islands. At left, Pago Pago in American Samoa, Polynesia.

interval between any note and its octave; series of notes etc. extending through this interval; two notes an octave apart played or sung together; organ stop sounding an octave higher than ordinary pitch.

Oc·ta·vi·a (ŏktā'vēa) (d. 11 B.C.). Sister of Augustus and wife of Mark Antony.

oc·ta·vo (ŏktā'vō, -tah'-) n. (pl. **-vos**). (abbrevs. 8vo, oct.). Book or page given by folding sheets three times or into eight leaves; size of this, varying according to size of sheet.

oc·ten·ni·al (ŏktĕn'ēal) adj. Lasting, recurring, every eight years.

oc·tet, oc·tette (ŏktĕt') ns. (Composition for) eight voices or instruments in combination; set of eight; group of eight lines, esp. the first eight of a sonnet.

octo-, oct- prefixes. Eight.

Oc·to·ber (ŏktō'ber). Tenth month of Gregorian (eighth of Julian) calendar, with 31 days; **~ Revolution**: see Russian REVO-LUTION. [L. octo eight]

Oc·to·brist (ŏktō'brĭst) n. Member of Russian moderate liberal political party, whose principles of constitutional government

were proclaimed in the imperial Manifesto of Oct. 1905.

oc·to·dec·i·mo (ŏktodĕs'imō) n. (pl. **-mos**). (abbrev. 18mo) (Size of) book or page given by folding sheets into 18 leaves.

oc·to·ge·nar·i·an (ŏktojenār'-ēan) adj. & n. (Person) aged 80 years or more but less than 90.

oc·to·pod (ŏk'topŏd) n. Cephalopod of the order Octopoda with eight arms.

oc·to·pus (ŏk'topus) n. (pl. **-puses, -pi** pr. pī). Cephalopod mollusk with eight arms, provided with suckers, surrounding mouth.

oc·to·roon (ŏktorōon') n. Person of one-eighth black parentage.

oc·to·syl·lab·ic (ŏktōsĭlăb'ĭk) adj. & n. Eight-syllable (verse). **oc·to·syl·la·ble** (ŏk'tosĭlabel) n. (Verse, word) of eight syllables.

oc·tu·ple (ŏk'tupel) adj. Eightfold. **~** n. Product (of) after multiplication by 8. **~** v.t. (**-pled, -pling**). Multiply by 8.

oc·u·lar (ŏk'yuler) adj. Of, for,

Ranging in size from an inch or two across the longest arms, to a span of several feet, only the blue-ringed octopus of Australia is dangerous to man. Most can adapt their color to their surroundings.

by, with, etc., the eye(s) or sight visual. **~** n. Eyepiece of optica instrument.

oc·u·list (ŏk'yulĭst) n. 1. Medica practitioner who specializes in diseases of the eye; ophthalmologist 2. Optometrist.

OD (ōdē') n. (slang) Overdose esp. of a narcotic. **~** v.i. (**OD'd OD'ing**) (ōdēd', ōdē'ing). Tak an overdose of a narcotic sufficien to cause death.

O.D. abbrev. Doctor of optom etry; officer of the day.

o.d. abbrev. Olive drab; outsid diameter.

o·da·lisque, o·da·lisk (ō'dalĭsk ns. (hist.) Eastern female slave o concubine, esp. in Turkish sultan' seraglio. [Fr., f. Turk. odalik]

odd (ŏd) adj. 1. Remaining ove after division or distribution in pairs; (of number) not exactl divisible by 2; numbered or know by such a number; (appended t number, sum, weight, etc.) wit something over of lower denomina tion etc. by which round number given sum, etc., is exceeded. 2 Additional, casual, beside th reckoning, unconnected, unoccu pied, incalculable; forming part o incomplete pair or set. 3. Extraor dinary, strange, queer, remark able, eccentric. 4. **O ~ Fellow** member of Independent Order o Odd Fellows (founded prob. i early part of 18th c.) with rite imitative of freemasonry; **odd jol** casual disconnected piece of worl **odd'ly** adv. **odd'ness** n. **odd** Anything odd.

odd·i·ty (ŏd'ĭtē) n. (pl. **-ties** Strangeness; peculiar trait; quee person; fantastic object, strang event.

odds (ŏdz) n.pl. Inequalitie difference; variance, strife; balanc of advantage; equalizing allowanc to weaken competitor; rati between amounts staked by parti to bet, advantage conceded by or of the parties in proportion t assumed chances in his favo chances or balance of probabili in favor of some result; **~ an ends**, remnants, stray article **~-on** (adj.), (of chance or prot ability) in favor of some result et

ode (ōd) n. 1. (orig.) Poer meant to be sung; **choral ~**, sor of chorus in Greek play etc. Rhymed (or, rarely, unrhyme lyric, often in form of address, us of exalted style and enthusiast tone, often in varied or irregul meter, and usu. between 50 an 200 lines in length.

O·der (ō'der). River rising N. central Czechoslovakia ar flowing 560 miles (901 km) NV through Poland and E. Germar to the Baltic Sea.

O·din (ō'dĭn). (Scand. myth Supreme god and creator, god

During a war, an **offensive** *is an attempt by one side to gain advantage over the other. In Vietnam in 1968, (left) the civilians suffered more than the armies.*

Economic Cooperation and Development.

O.E.D. *abbrev.* Oxford English Dictionary.

Oed·i·pus (ĕd′ipus, ē′di-). (Gk. legend) Son of Laius king of Thebes, and Jocasta; he unwittingly killed his father and married his mother, and when the facts were discovered, went mad and put out his eyes, while Jocasta hanged herself; ~ **complex**, (psychol.) manifestation of infantile sexuality in relations of (esp. male) child to parents, with attraction towards parent of opposite sex and jealousy of other parent.

oe·no·phile (ē′nofīl) *n.* Connoisseur of wines.

o′er (ōr, ōr) *adv. & prep.* (poet.) = OVER.

oer·sted (ēr′stĕd) *n.* Unit of magnetic intensity in cgs electromagnetic system. [Hans Christian *Oersted* (1777–1851), Danish physicist]

oeu·vre (ö′vre) *n.* (pl. **oeu·vres** pr. ö′vre). (Totality of) works of an author, painter, composer, etc. [F., = work, f. L. *opera*]

of (ŭv, ŏv, ov) *prep.* From; concerning; out of; among; relating to.

off (awf, ŏf) *adv.* Away, at or to a distance; (so as to be) out of position, not on or touching or dependent or attached; loose, separate, gone; so as to break continuity or continuance, discontinued, stopped, not obtainable, abstaining from, averse to; to the end, entirely, so as to be clear; (of food) deteriorated, unfit for consumption; **well, badly, comfortably,** etc., ~, so circumstanced or supplied with money; ~ **and on,** intermittently, waveringly, now and again. **off** *prep.* From; away, down or up from; disengaged or distant from; (so as to be) no longer on; **offcol′or,** offensive, risqué; (of person) slightly unwell; **off′-hand** (*adj.*), extempore, without premeditation, curt, casual, unceremonious; **off′hand′edly** (*adv.*); **off′hand′edness** (*n.*); **off′load:** see own entry; **off-peak,** outside peak hours; **off′print, off′shoot:** see own entries; **off′shore′** (*adv. & adj.*), a short way out to sea; **offshore wind,** one blowing out to sea; **off′side′** (*adj. & adv.*), (soccer, hockey) of a player in a position on the field where he may not kick, handle, or hit the ball or puck; (football) beyond the line of scrimmage before a play begins; **off-the-record** (*adj.*), not for publication or quotation; **off-the-shelf** (*adj.*), readily available, easily adaptable; **off′spring:** see own entry; **off′track′** (*adj.*), pertaining to legalized horse race gambling away from a track; **off** *adj.* 1. Farther, far; (of horse or vehicle) right (opp. NEAR; so **offside**). 2. Subordinate, divergent; disengaged. 3. ~ **chance,** slight or remote chance; ~ **-season,** season when business is less active than usual. **off** *v.* (slang) Kill.

of·fal (aw′fal, ŏf′al) *n.* Refuse, waste stuff, scraps, garbage; parts cut off in dressing carcass of animal killed for food, orig. entrails, now a trade term for edible organs such as liver, kidneys, etc.; carrion, putrid flesh.

of·fend (ofĕnd′) *v.* 1. Commit an offense (*against*). 2. Wound feelings of, anger, cause resentment or disgust in, outrage. **of·fend′-ed·ness, of·fend′er** *ns.*

of·fense (ofĕns′, ŏf′ĕns) *n.* 1. Attacking, aggressive action. 2. Wounding of the feelings; wounded feeling, annoyance, umbrage. 3. Transgression, misdemeanor, illegal act. **of·fense′less** *adj.*

of·fen·sive (ofĕn′sĭv, aw′fĕn-, ŏf′ĕn-) *adj.* 1. Aggressive, intended for or used in attack. 2. Meant to give offense, insulting. 3. Disgusting, repulsive. **of·fen′-sive·ly** *adv.* **of·fen′sive·ness** *n.* **offensive** *n.* Attitude of assailant, aggressive action; attack, offensive campaign or stroke.

of·fer (aw′fer, ŏf′er) *v.* 1. Present to deity, revered person, etc., by way of sacrifice; give in worship or devotion. 2. Hold out in hand, or tender in words or otherwise, for acceptance or refusal; make proposal of marriage; show for sale; give opportunity to enemy for (battle); express readiness *to* to; essay, try to show (violence etc.); show an intention *to* do. 3. Present to sight or notice; present itself, occur. ~ *n.* Expression of readiness to give or do if desired, or to sell on terms; proposal, esp. of marriage; bid. **of′fer·ing** *n.* Thing offered.

of·fer·to·ry (aw′fertōrē, -tōrē, ŏf′er-) *n.* (pl. **-ries**). Part of Mass or Communion service at which offerings are made, offering of these, gifts offered; collection of money at religious service.

of·fice (aw′fĭs, ŏf′ĭs) *n.* 1. Act of kindness, attention, service. 2. Duty attaching to one's position, task, function. 3. Position with duties attached to it; place of authority, trust, or service, esp. of public kind; tenure of official position, esp. that of minister of state. 4. Ceremonial duty; (eccles.) authorized form of worship; (chants at beginning of) Mass or Communion service, any occasional service. 5. Place for transacting business; room etc. in which clerks and others work; consulting room of doctor etc. 6. Quarters, staff,

---

ictory and the dead; represented as an old one-eyed man of great wisdom.

o·di·ous (ō′dēus) *adj.* Hateful, repulsive. **o′di·ous·ly** *adv.* **o′di·ous·ness** *n.*

o·di·um (ō′dēum) *n.* General or widespread dislike or reprobation incurred by person or attaching to action.

o·dom·e·ter (ōdŏm′ĭter) *n.* Instrument for measuring distance traveled.

o·dor, Brit. **o·dour** (ō′der) *ns.* Pleasant or unpleasant smell; fragrance; (fig.) savor, trace; ~ **of sanctity,** sweet or balsamic odor supposed to be exhaled by dying or exhumed saint; reputation for holiness. **o′dor·ful, o′dor·less** *adjs.*

o·dor·if·er·ous (ōderĭf′erus) *adj.* Diffusing scent, fragrant. **o·dor·if′er·ous·ly** *adv.* **o·dor·if′er·ous·ness** *n.*

o·dor·ous (ō′derus) *adj.* Odoriferous. **o′dor·ous·ly** *adv.*

O·dys·se·us (ōdĭs′ēus, ōdĭs′ūs). (Gk. legend) King of Ithaca, called Ulysses by the Romans; renowned for cunning; he was a leader of the Greeks in the Trojan War, and after it Poseidon kept him from home a further ten years while his wife PENELOPE waited in Ithaca.

Od·ys·sey (ŏd′ĭsē) *n.* Greek epic poem attributed to Homer, in 24 books, describing the wanderings and return of Odysseus.

od·ys·sey (ŏd′ĭsē) *n.* (pl. **-seys**). Long adventurous journey.

OECD *abbrev.* Organization for

1

2

3

or collective authority of a business department etc.

of·fic·er (aw'fĭs*er*, ŏf'ĭ-) *n.* I. Holder of public, civil, or ecclesiastical office; appointed or elected functionary; president, treasurer, secretary, etc., of company; policeman. 2. Person holding authority in armed forces or merchant marine, esp. one with a commission in the armed forces.

of·fi·cial (ofĭsh'al) *adj.* Of an office, the discharge of duties, or the tenure of an office; holding office, employed in public capacity; derived from or vouched for by person(s) in office, properly authorized; usual with persons in office. **of·fi'cial·ly** *adv.* **of·fi'cial·dom** (ofĭsh'aldom), **of·fi'cial·ism** *ns.* **of·fi'cial·ize** *v.t.* (**-ized, -iz·ing**). **official** *n.* Person holding public office or engaged in official duties.

of·fi·ci·ate (ofĭsh'ēāt) *v.i.* (**-at·ed, -at·ing**). Discharge priestly office, perform divine service; act in some official capacity, esp. on particular occasion. **of·fi·ci·ant** (ofĭsh'ēant) *n.*

In an attempt to discover fresh reserves of oil, there is increasing exploration for submarine oil-fields. When suitable sites have been located, an oil rig, built ashore, is towed to the site (1). It is

of·fi·cious (ofĭsh'us) *adj.* (Given to) offering service that is not wanted, doing or undertaking more than is required, intrusive, meddlesome. **of·fi'cious·ly** *adv.* **of·fi'-cious·ness** *n.*

off·ing (aw'fĭng, ŏf'ĭng) *n.* Part of visible sea distant from shore or beyond anchoring ground; position at distance from shore; **in the ~**, (fig.) nearby; ready or likely to appear.

off·ish (aw'fĭsh, ŏf'ĭsh) *adj.* (colloq.) Inclined to aloofness. **off'ish·ly** *adv.* **off'ish·ness** *n.*

off·load (awf'lōd', ŏf'-) *v.* (colloq.) Unload (vehicle, airplane, or ship).

off·print (awf'prĭnt, ŏf'-) *n.* Separate copy of article etc. that was originally part of larger publication.

off·set (awf'sĕt, ŏf'-) *n.* I. Short side shoot from stem or root serving

then dropped on to the sea bed (2) a[nd] levelled so that drilling machine[ry] aboard the rig (3) can be used to pe[n]-etrate the sea bed.

for propagation; offshoot, scio[n]. 2. Compensation, setoff, consider[a]-tion or amount diminishing [or] neutralizing effect of contrary on[e]. 3. (surv.) Short distance measure[d] perpendicularly from main line [of] measurement. 4. (archit.) Slopi[ng] ledge in wall etc. where thickne[ss] of part above is diminished. 5. Ben[d] made in pipe to carry it past ob[-] stacle. 6. (printing, engravin[g]) Transfer of ink from a new[ly] printed surface to another surfac[e] so that the final impression is [in] the same sense as the plate or typ[e] (**~ proof**, engraver's trial pro[of] made thus as aid to working[)]. **~ lithography**, method of prin[t]-ing in which ink is transferred fro[m] a lithographic stone or plate t[o] a rubber roller and thence, whil[e] still wet, to paper. **offset** (awfsĕt', ŏf'-) *v.t.* (**-set, -set·ting**). Counter[-] balance, compensate for; print b[y] off·set.

off·shoot (awf′shoot, ŏf′-) *n.* Side shoot or branch; derivative.

off·spring (awf′spring, ŏf′-) *n.* (pl. **-spring, -springs**). Descendant.

oft (awft, ŏft) *adv.* Often (archaic exc. in comb.); **oft′times,** (archaic) often.

of·ten (aw′fen, ŏf′en sometimes awf′ten, ŏf′-) *adv.* Many times, at short intervals; in many instances; **of′tentimes,** (archaic) often.

o·gee (ō·jē′) *n.* S-shaped curve; **~ arch,** arch with two ogee curves meeting at apex.

og·ham, og·am (ŏg′am, aw′-gam) *ns.* Ancient British and Irish alphabet of characters formed by parallel strokes arranged along either side of, or crossing, continuous medial line, e.g. edge of stone; inscription in this; one of the characters.

B	H	M	A
L	D	G	O
V or F	T	NG	U
S	C	ST or Z	E
N	Q	R	I

X as vowel, E; as consonant, C.
OGHAM

To cope with increasing demands for crude oil, tanker sizes have increased and many more **oil-tankers** (1) *have been built. If these ships are wrecked* (2) *there is grave risk of pollution from the spillage.*

o·give (ō′jīv, ōjīv′) *n.* Diagonal groin or rib of vault; pointed or Gothic arch. **o·gi′val** *adj.*

o·gle (ō′gel) *v.* (**o·gled, o·gling**). Cast amorous glances, eye amorously. ~ *n.* Amorous glance.

O·gle·thorpe (ō′gelthōrp), **James Edward** (1696–1785). English army officer, member of Parliament, and humanitarian; founder of the American colony of Georgia, 1733.

OGPU = G.P.U.

o·gre (ō′ger) *n.* (fem. **o·gress** pr. ō′grĭs). (in legend etc.) Man-eating giant; hence, terrifying person. **o′gre·ish** (ō′gerĭsh), **o′grish** *adjs.*

OH *abbrev.* Ohio.

oh (ō) = O².

O'Har·a (ōhăr′a, ōhār′a), **John (Henry)** (1905–70). American novelist and short-story writer; author of "Pal Joey" and the novels *Appointment in Samarra, Butterfield 8*, etc.

O·hi·o (ōhī′ō). State in midwestern U.S. between Ohio River in the S. and Lake Erie in the N.; admitted to the Union in 1803; capital, Columbus; **~ River,** river formed by the Allegheny and Monongahela Rivers at Pittsburgh, Pennsylvania, and flowing 900 miles (1,449 km) SW. to the Mississippi at Cairo, Illinois; chief eastern tributary of the Mississippi.

ohm (ōm) *n.* Unit of electrical resistance, resistance of a circuit in which potential difference of one volt produces current of one ampere. **ohm·ic** (ō′mĭk) *adj.* [f. OHM]

Ohm (ōm), **Georg Simon** (1787–1854). German physicist who determined mathematically the law of the flow of electricity.

oil (oil) *n.* 1. One of a large group of liquid viscid substances with characteristic smooth and sticky feel, lighter than water and insoluble in it, inflammable, and chemically neutral, used as lubricants, in perfumery etc. (**essential** or **volatile ~**), and as fuel etc. (**mineral ~**); **drying ~,** any of those oils which by exposure to air harden into varnishes; **nondrying ~,** one that decomposes by exposure, used as lubricant, in making soap, etc. 2. Oil color (freq. pl.). 3. (pl.) Oilskins. 4. **oil·can,** can for holding oil, esp. with long nozzle for oiling machinery; **oil′cloth,** fabric waterproofed with oil, oilskin; canvas coated with preparation containing drying oil, used to cover tables etc.; **oil color,** paint made by grinding pigment in a drying oil; **oil field,** tract of petroleum-bearing strata; **oil paint,** oil color; **oil painting,** art of painting, picture painted, in oil colors; **oil′paper,** paper made transparent or waterproof by soaking in oil; **oil shale,** rock from which petroleum can be produced by distillation; **oil′skin,** cloth waterproofed with a drying oil; garment or (pl.) coat and trousers of this; **oil′stone,** fine-grained stone used with oil as whetstone; **oil well,** well yielding petroleum. **oil** *v.* 1. Apply oil to, lubricate. 2. Turn into oily liquid. 3. Impregnate or treat with oil. **oiled** (oild) *adj.* (slang) Slightly drunk.

oil·er (oi′ler) *n.* Oilcan for oiling machinery; ship built for carrying oil.

oil·y (oi′lē) *adj.* (**oil·i·er, oil·i·est**). 1. Of, like, covered or soaked with, containing much, oil. 2. (of manner etc.) Fawning, too smooth. **oil′i·ness** *n.*

oint·ment (oint′ment) *n.* Emollient preparation applied to skin to heal or beautify, unguent.

O·jib·wa (ōjĭb´wä, -wa) *n.* (pl. **-was**, collect. **-wa**). (Member of a) tribe of N. Amer. Indians of Algonquian linguistic stock, inhabiting region around the Great Lakes.

O·jib·way (ōjĭb´wä) *n.* (pl. **-ways**, collect. **-way**) = OJIBWA.

OK *abbrev.* Oklahoma.

O.K., o·kay (ō´kā´, ōkā´) *adjs.* (orig. slang) All right. ~ *n.* (pl. **O.K.'s**) & *v.t.* (**O.K.'d, O.K.'ing**). (Mark with) the letters "O.K.," esp. as denoting approval of contents of document etc.; sanction. [possibly initials of *Old Kinderhook* (Kinderhook, near Albany, New York, birthplace of Democratic candidate, Martin van Buren) used *c*1840 as a slogan and passing into a term of approval, being interpreted as abbreviation of *oll korrect*, misspelling of *all correct*]

o·ka·pi (ōkah´pē) *n.* (pl. **-pis**, collect. **-pi**). Rare ungulate mammal, *Okapia johnstoni*, related to giraffes, found in dense forests of W. Africa.

o·kay (ō´kā´, ōkā´) *adj. & v.t.* = O.K.

O·kee·cho·bee (ōkēchō´bē), **Lake.** Lake, over 700 square miles (1,813 sq. km), in S. central Florida, 40 miles (65 km) NW. of Palm Beach; second largest lake wholly within the U.S.; part of cross-Florida waterway.

O' Keeffe (ō kēf´), **Georgia** (1887–). American landscape painter, especially of desert scenes.

O·ki·na·wa (ōkĭnah´wa). Largest of the Ryuku Islands, 794 square miles (2,057 sq. km) S. of Japan; scene of heavy fighting in World War II.

Okla. *abbrev.* Oklahoma.

O·kla·ho·ma (ōklahō´ma). State in southwestern U.S. between Texas on the S. and Kansas on the N.; admitted to the Union in 1907; capital, Oklahoma City.

o·kra (ō´kra) *n.* Tall malvaceous African plant (*Hibiscus esculentus*, called also *gumbo*) cultivated in W. Indies, southern U.S., etc., the young fruits of which are used as a vegetable and for thickening soups, and the stem fibers for ropes.

O·laf (ō´lahf). Name of two kings of Norway; **Olaf I Tryggvason** (*c*969–1000), king 995–1000; raided coast of France and British Isles but ceased when he became a Christian; hero of many legends; **Olaf II** (995–1030), "St. Olaf," patron saint of Norway; king of Norway 1015–28.

old (ōld) *adj.* (**old·er, old·est** or **eld·er, eld·est**). 1. Advanced in age, far on in natural period of existence, not young or near its beginning; having characteristics, experience, feebleness, etc., of age; worn, dilapidated, shabby. 2.

Related to the giraffe ar living only in dens rainforests in central Afric the **okapi** was first four by zoologists in 190 Females are larger tha males and have a should height of 5

(appended to period of time) Of age (as **ten years** ~); (ellipt.) person or animal, esp. race horse, of specified age (as **three-year-** ~). 3. Practiced or inverterate *in* action or quality, or as agent etc. 4. Dating from far back; made long ago; long established, known, familiar, or dear; ancient, not new or recent, primeval; (of language) belonging to the earliest known period or stage; **of** ~ **standing**, long established. 5. Belonging only or chiefly to the past; obsolete, obsolescent, out of date, antiquated, antique; concerned with antiquity; not modern, bygone, former. 6. ~ **age pension(er)**, (person receiving) retirement pension; **O** ~ **Believers**, Russian sect originating in 17th c. in protest against liturgical reforms; ~**-clothes man**, dealer in discarded clothes; **O** ~ **Colony**, part of Massachusetts within original limits of Plymouth colony; ~ **countries**, countries long inhabited or civilized; **the** ~ **country, home**, etc., (used by emigrants etc. of) mother country; **O** ~ **Dominion**, Virginia; ~ **English sheepdog**, medium-sized breed of dog with very long, shaggy whitish coat and short or no tail; **O** ~ **Faithful**, geyser in Yellowstone National Park, Wyoming, erupting regulary at intervals of a little over an hour; ~**-fashioned**,

belonging to a fashion that has gone or is going out; **O** ~ **Fashioned**, cocktail of whiskey, bitters, etc. **O** ~ **Glory**, the Stars and Stripes ~ **gold**, color of tarnished gold ~ **guard**, established influentia conservative group; ~ **hand** practiced workman; person o experience in (*at*) something; **O** ~ **Ironsides**, popular name of Amer frigate, Constitution, active in War of 1812 and subject of poem by Oliver Wendell Holmes; **O** ~ **Hickory**, nickname of Andrew JACKSON[2], from his toughness of character; ~ **lady**, (colloq.) mother or wife; ~ **maid**, (derog.) elderly spinster; person who is overly precise; (cards) game in which object is to avoid holding of unpaired card; ~**-maidish** (*adj.*); ~ **man** (naut. slang) ship's captain: (colloq.) father or husband; ~ **man of the sea**, (from character in Arabian Nights tale of Sindbad the Sailor) person who cannot be shaken off; ~ **master**, (painting by) great painter of former times, esp. 13th–17th centuries in Europe: ~ **school tie**, necktie of characteristic pattern as worn by former members of a particular British school; used symbolically to denote extreme loyalty to a traditional mode of thought or behavior; **O** ~ **Stone Age**, PALEOLITHIC age; **O** ~ **Testament**: see TESTAMENT; ~ -

ime, of former times; **~-timer**, ne whose experience goes back to ld times; one of long standing; old-ashioned person or thing; **O~ Vic** vĭk), theater in London; **~ wives' ale**: see WIFE; **~ woman**, (colloq.) ife; fussy or timid man; **O~ World**, eastern hemisphere; **O~-world**, of the Old World, not American; **~ year**, year just ended r about to end. **old'ish** adj. **old** *a.* Old time (only in **of old** (adj. & adv.) as men of old, of old there were giants). **old'ness** n.

old·en (ōl'den) adj. (archaic and iterary) Old-time, of a former age.

old·ster (ōld'ster) n. Old person.

Ol·du·vai (awl'dŏōvī) **Gorge.** Gorge along line of fault in N. Tanzania, 150 miles (242 km) W. of Mt. Kilimanjaro; archaeological site containing many fossil beds and remains of early man.

o·le·a·ceous (ōlēā'shus) adj. Of the Oleaceae or olive family of plants, including jasmine etc.

o·le·ag·i·nous (ōlēăj'inus) adj. Having properties of or producing oil; oily, fatty, greasy.

o·le·an·der (ō'lēănder, ōlēăn'-) n. Evergreen poisonous Levantine shrub (Nerium oleander) with leathery lanceolate leaves and hand-some red or white flowers.

o·le·fin (ō'lefĭn) n. (chem.) Any member of the ethylene series of hydrocarbons.

o·le·o·mar·ga·rine (ōlēōmär'-arĭn, -rēn) n. Fatty substance extracted from clarified beef fat and made into margarine with addition of butyrin, milk, etc.; margarine.

o·le·o·res·in (ōlēōrĕz'ĭn) n. Natural product containing a volatile oil and a resin, e.g. exuda-tion from coniferous tree.

ol·fac·tion (ōlfăk'shon, ōl-) n. Smelling, sense of smell. **ol·fac'-tive** adj. **ol·fac·to·ry** (ōlfăk'terē, ōl-) adj. Concerned with smelling.

ol·i·garch (ōl'igärk) n. Member of oligarchy.

ol·i·gar·chy (ōl'igärkē) n. (pl. **-chies**). Government, state governed, by a few persons; members of such a government. **ol·i·gar·chic** (ōligär'kĭk), **ol·i·gar'chi·cal** adjs. **ol·i·gar'chi·cal·ly** adv.

Ol·i·go·cene (ōl'igōsēn) adj. & n. (geol.) (Of) the third epoch or system of the Tertiary period.

ol·i·gop·o·ly (ōligŏp'olē) n. State of market allowing limited competition between few producers or sellers.

o·li·o (ō'lēō) n. (pl. **o·li·os**). Mixed dish, hotchpotch, stew of various meats and vegetables; medley, miscellany.

ol·i·va·ceous (ōlivā'shus) adj. Olive-green, of dusky yellowish.

ol·i·va·ry (ōl'ivĕrē) adj. (anat.) Olive-shaped, oval.

ol·ive (ŏl'ĭv) n. 1. Evergreen

*The **Old Faithful** geyser in Yellowstone National Park. Geysers are incorrectly supposed to erupt at regular intervals. Even Old Faithful erupts at varying inter-vals.*

tree (Olea europaea), esp. the cultivated variety, with narrow leaves green above and hoary below and axillary clusters of small whitish flowers, bearing small oval drupes, blackish when ripe, with bitter pulp abounding in oil, and hard stone, cultivated in Mediterranean countries etc. for its fruit and oil; fruit of this tree; any tree of the genus Olea, tree or shrub resembling this. 2. Leaf, branch,

Olives have been eaten and pressed for their oil for centuries. Europe culti-vates more than 75 per cent of the world's olive crop.

or wreath of olive as emblem of peace. 3. Olive-shaped gastropod mollusk (Oliva). 4. Olive color. 5. **~ branch**, branch of olive tree, esp. as emblem of peace (freq. fig.); **~ oil**, clear, pale-yellow, non-drying oil obtained from pulp of olives, used in cooking, salads, as a medicine, as a lubricant, and in the manufacture of toilet soap, etc., **~ drab**, grayish olive color of U.S. Army uniform; hence, (slang) **~ drabs**, such a uniform; **Mount of Olives**, ridge facing Temple mount at Jerusalem on the east, with Garden of Gethsemane on western slope. **olive** adj. Colored like unripe olive, dull yellowish green; (of complexion etc.) brownish yellow; of color of olive foliage, dull ashy green with silvery sheen.

O·liv·i·er (ōlĭv'ēā), **Sir Laurence (Kerr)** (1907–). English actor and director.

Olm·sted (ōm'stĕd), **Frederick Law** (1822–1903). Amer. land-scape architect; cooperated with Calvert Vaux on design of Central Park in New York City, designed Prospect Park in Brooklyn, etc.

O·lym·pi·a (ōlĭm'pēa). 1. Plain on N. bank of river Alpheus about 20 miles from W. coast of Peloponnese; in ancient Greece a great religious center second only to Delphi, and site of OLYMPIC Games. 2. Capital of state of Washington, on Puget Sound.

o·lym·pi·ad (ōlĭm'pēăd) n. (often cap.) 1. Period of four years between celebrations of OLYMPIC Games, used by ancient Greeks in dating events, 776 B.C. being first year of first Olympiad. 2. Meeting of modern Olympic Games.

O·lym·pi·an (ōlĭm'pēan) adj. Of Olympus, celestial; (of manners) magnificent, condescending, superior; aloof. **~ n.** Dweller in Olympus, one of the greater ancient

Greek gods; person of superhuman calm and detachment.

O·lym·pic (ōlĭm′pĭk) *adj.* Of Olympia in Greece; of the Olympic Games; ~ **Games**, (1) athletic contests held by the ancient Greeks every fourth year at Olympia and including foot races, boxing, wrestling, and chariot and horse races; (2) international amateur athletic contests begun in 1896 as revival of ancient Greek games and held every fourth year, organized by an international committee which decides where each festival is to be held, and including athletics, gymnastics, combative sports, swimming, equestrian sports, the pentathlon, and the decathlon. **O·lym′pics** *n.pl.* Olympic Games.

O·lym·pus (ōlĭm′pus), **Mount.** Highest mountain (9,750 feet, 2,972 m) in Greece, about ten miles inland from the Aegean Sea at E. end of range dividing Thessaly from Macedonia; in Greek mythology the court of Zeus and home of the gods.

Om (ŏm). In Hinduism etc., mystic and holy word regarded as summing up all truth.

O·ma·ha (ō′mahah). Industrial city on the Missouri River in E. Nebraska; known for its stockyards and meat-packing plants.

O·ma·ha (ō′mahah) **Beach.** Code name for beach in Normandy, France, as landing place of some units of Amer. troops during invasion of France in World War II, June 6–10, 1944.

O·man (ōmahn′). Sultanate in SE. Arabia; capital, Muscat; **Gulf of** ~, arm of the Arabian Sea, between Oman and Iran, extending toward the Persian Gulf.

O·mar (ō′mär) (c581–644). Second Muslim caliph, 634–44; reputed builder of **Mosque of** ~, on platform of Temple at Jerusalem, a much-altered Byzantine church, containing rock on which, acc. to Jewish legend, Abraham prepared to sacrifice Isaac, and from which, acc. to Muslims, Muhammad ascended to heaven.

O·mar Khay·yám (ō′mär kīyahm′, -yăm). ‘Umar Khayyām (c1100), Persian astronomer, mathematician and poet; author of the *Rubáiyát*.

o·ma·sum (ōmā′sum) *n.* (pl. **-sa** pr. -sa). Ruminant's third stomach.

OMB *abbrev.* Office of Management and Budget.

om·buds·man (ŏm′boodzman) *n.* (pl. **-men** pr. -men). Official who investigates complaints of mal-administration, esp. by government departments. [Swed. = "commissioner"]

o·me·ga (ōmē′ga, ōmā′-, ōmĕg′a) *n.* Last letter of Greek alphabet (Ω, ω), corresponding to

o (pr. ō). [Gk. = "great o"]

om·e·let, om·e·lette (ŏm′lĭt, ŏm′elĭt) *ns.* Dish of eggs lightly beaten and cooked usu. in butter in a frying pan, often with filling; **Western** ~, omelet with filling of diced ham, green pepper, and onion.

o·men (ō′men) *n.* Event or object portending good or evil; prophetic signification.

om·i·cron (ŏm′ikrŏn, ō′mi-) *n.* Sixteenth (later 15th) letter of Greek alphabet (O, o) corresponding to *o* (pr. ŏ). [Gk., = "small o"]

om·i·nous (ŏm′inus) *adj.* Of evil omen, inauspicious, threatening. **om′i·nous·ly** *adv.* **om′i·nous·ness** *n.*

o·mis·sion (ōmĭsh′on) *n.* Omitting, noninclusion; non-performance, neglect, duty not done.

o·mit (ōmĭt′) *v.t.* (**o·mit·ted, o·mit·ting**). Leave out, not insert or include; leave undone, neglect *doing*, fail *to* do.

om·ni·bus (ŏm′nibŭs, -bus) *n.* (pl. **-bus·es**). 1. = BUS. 2. Volume containing a number of stories, plays, etc. ~ *adj.* Serving several objects at once; comprising several items. [L., = "for all," i.e. every-one]

om·ni·di·rec·tion·al (ŏmnĭdirĕk′shonal) *adj.* (of antenna etc.) Receiving or transmitting in all directions.

om·nip·o·tence (ŏmnĭp′otens) *n.* Infinite power; God; great influence. **om·nip′o·tent** *adj.* **om·nip′o·tent·ly** *adv.*

om·ni·pres·ence (ŏmnĭprĕz′ens) *n.* Ubiquity; being widespread or constantly met with. **om·ni·pres′ent** *adj.*

om·nis·cience (ŏmnĭsh′ens) *n.* Infinite knowledge; God; wide information or the affectation of it. **om·nis′cient** *adj.* **om·nis′cient·ly** *adv.*

om·niv·o·rous (ŏmnĭv′erus) *adj.* (of animals) Feeding on both plant and flesh; (fig.) taking in every thing, esp. in choice of reading. **om·niv′o·rous·ly** *adv.* **om·niv′o·rous·ness** *n.* **om·ni·vore** (ŏm′nivŏr, -vōr) *n.*

om·pha·los (ŏm′falos) *n.* 1. (Gk. antiq.) Boss on shield; conical stone at Delphi supposed to be central point of earth. 2. Center, hub. 3. Navel.

on (ŏn, awn) *prep.* 1. (So as to be) supported by, attached to, covering, or enclosing; ~ **one**, about one's person. 2. With axis, pivot, basis, motive, standard, confirmation, or guarantee, consisting in. 3. (So as to be) close to, in the direction of, touching, arrived at, against, just at. 4. (of time) During, exactly at, contemporaneously with, immediately after, as a result of; ~ **time**, punctual(ly). 5. In manner specified by adjective, or state or action specified by noun; concerning, about, while engaged with, so as to affect; taking (a drug) regularly. 6. Added to. 7. Against (a person); (colloq., esp. of treat of any kind) to be paid for by; **have something** ~, have advantage

Since they were instituted in 1896, by Baron Pierre de Coubertin, the modern **Olympic Games** *have been held at four-yearly intervals. However, these games are held in different countries and have far more events than the ones*

in ancient Greece. Ceremonies open with a parade of competitors (below left), the lighting of the Olympic Flame (below) and impressive stadia are often built for athletic and other events (facing).

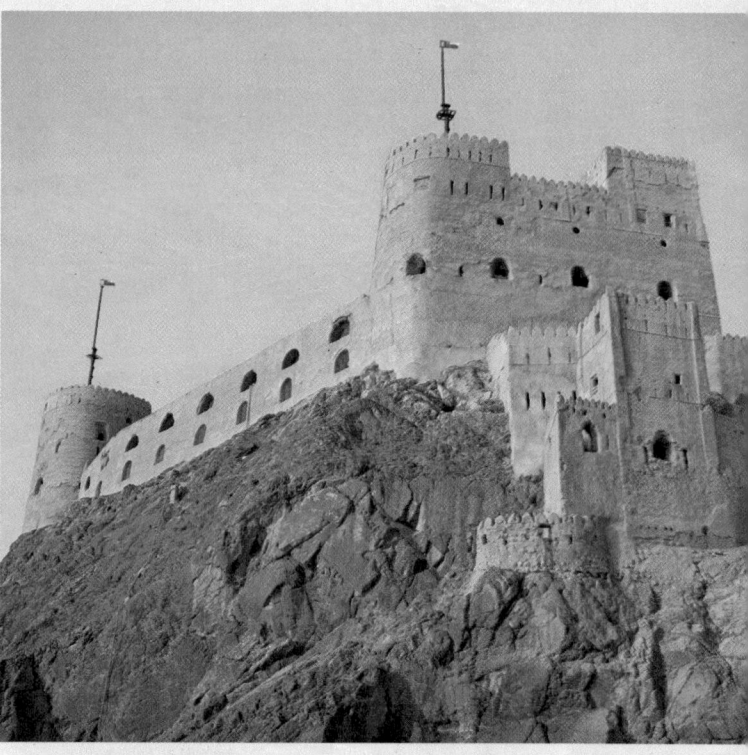

The ancient Muslim Fort Jalali, built on this crag at Muscat, is now the national prison for the Sultanate of **Oman** in the south of the Arabian Peninsula.

over. **on** *adv.* 1. (So as to be) supported by, attached to, covering, enclosing, or touching, something. 2. In some direction, toward something; farther forward, toward point of contact, in advanced position or state; with continued movement or action, in operation or activity; **broadside, end, head,** etc., ~, with that part forward; **line,** (equipment) operating; ~-**line,** (computers) (carried out while) directly connected to the central processing unit, directly controlled by the computer; **send** ~, send in front of oneself, in advance; **gas, water,** etc., **is** ~, gas, water, etc., is turned on, running, or procurable by turning tap; **get, be,** ~, make, have made, bet. 3. ~ **to** (compound prep. corresponding to *on* as *into* to *in*, but often written as two words), to a position on. **on** *adj.*

on·a·ger (ŏn'ajer) *n.* Wild ass, esp. the species *Equus onager* of Central Asia, with broad brown stripe along the back.

o·nan·ism (ō'nanĭzem) *n.* Interrupted coition; masturbation. [f. *Onan* (Gen. 38)]

once (wŭns) *adv.* 1. For one time or on one occasion only; multiplied by one, by one degree; ~ **or twice,** a few times; ~ **(and) for all,** in final manner, definitively; ~ **in a while,** very rarely. 2. (in negative or conditional etc. clause) Ever, at all, even for one or the first time. 3. On a certain but unspecified past occasion; at some period in the past, former(ly). 4. **at** ~, immediately, without

delay; at the same time; **for (this, that)** ~, on one occasion by way of exception; ~-**over,** (colloq.) single and rapid survey or examination. **once** *conj.* As soon as; if once; when once.

on·col·o·gy (ŏngkŏl'ojē) *n.* Science of tumors.

one (wŭn) *adj.* 1. Being, amounting to, the lowest cardinal number, number of a single thing without any more; a; ~ **or two,** a few. 2. Only, without others; forming a unity, united; identical, the same, unchanging; a particular but undefined, to be contrasted with another; **become** ~, coalesce; **made** ~, married. **one** *n.* The lowest cardinal number; its symbol (1, i, or I); one o'clock; size etc. indicated by I; die face or domino with one pip; single thing, person, or example; also, freq. used as substitute for repetition of noun previously expressed or implied; **at** ~, reconciled in agreement; **go** ~ **better,** bid, offer, risk, more by one point; **ten** etc. **to** ~, long odds, high probability; ~ **and all,** all jointly and severally; ~ **another,** formula of reciprocity with *one* orig. subjective and *another* objective or possessive; ~ **too many for,** too hard etc. for ... to deal with; ~ **up (on),** having gained an advantage (over). **one** *pron.* A particular but unspecified person; person of specified kind; any person, esp. the speaker,

spoken of as representing peop in general.

one- (wŭn) in comb.: ~-**arme bandit,** (slang) slot machi operated by pulling down armli handle; ~-**eyed,** having only, blii of, one eye; ~-**horse,** drawn worked by single horse; (fig.) pett poorly equipped; ~-**ma** requiring, consisting of, done managed by, one man; ~-**nigl stand,** (colloq.) single performan of play, concert, etc., in a plac sexual liaison for a single night; ~ **sided,** having, occurring on, o1 side only; larger etc. on one sid partial, unfair, prejudiced; ~ **sidedly** (*adv.*), ~-**sidedness** (*n* ~-**step,** ballroom dance in qui time with steps resembling wal **one'time,** former; ~-**track,** (mind) that is fixed on one line thought or action; ~-**up·man ship** (-ŭp'manshĭp) (*n.*), art practice of demonstratir superiority to gain advantage; ~ **way,** (of thoroughfares) alor which traffic is permitted in o1 direction only.

O·nei·da (ōnī'da) *n.* (pl. **-da** collect. **-da**). Member of a N Amer. Indian tribe of Iroquoia stock, formerly living near Lal Oneida in New York State; **Community,** Christian con munist society founded 1848 a Oneida Creek, New York State, l J. H. Noyes (1811–86), who members held that true sinlessne could be realized through con munion with Christ; dissolve (1881).

O'Neill (ōnēl'), **Eugen**

Toronto, capital of the Canadian Province of **Ontario,** has the largest livestock market in Canada. The city center has been modernized and is elegant, with attractive plazas.

One of the first of the wild horse family to be tamed, the **onager** was used by Sumerians about 2,500 B.C. when the rein-ring (above) was made. These wild asses later drew chariots.

Gladstone) (1888–1953). American playwright, author of *he Emperor Jones, Mourning ecomes Electra, The Iceman ometh, Ah, Wilderness!*, etc.

one·ness (wŭn′nĭs) *n.* Being one, ngleness; singularity, uniqueness; holeness, unity, union, agreement; identity, changelessness.

on·er·ous (ŏn′erus, ō′ner-) *adj.* urdensome, causing or requiring ouble. **on′er·ous·ly** *adv.* **on′er- s·ness** *n.*

one·self, one′s·self (wŭnsĕlf′, ŭnzsĕlf′) *prons.* Emphatic and flexive form corresp. to ONE.

on·ion (ŭn′yon) *n.* (Plant, *llium cepa*, with) edible rounded lb of close concentric leaves, with ngent smell and flavor, used as linary vegetable; **on′ionskin,** termost or any outer coat of ion; very thin smooth translucent nd of paper. **on′ion·y** *adj.*

on·look·er (ŏn′lŏŏker, awn′-) *n.* ne who looks on.

on·ly (ōn′lē) *adj.* That is (or e) the one (or all the) specimen(s) the class, sole. ~ *adv.* Solely, erely, exclusively; and no one or thing more, besides, or else; and at is all. ~ *conj.* Only thing be added being; with this restric- n, drawback, or exception only; t then.

on·o·mat·o·poe·ia (ŏnomăto- ′a, -mahto-) *n.* Formation of mes or words from sounds sembling those associated with e object or action to be named, seemingly naturally suggestive its qualities (e.g. *cuckoo, rustle*); rd so formed. **on·o·mat·o-**

poe′ic, on·o·mat·o·po·et·ic (ŏnomătopoĕt′ĭk, -mahto-) *adjs.* **on·o·mat·o·poe′i·cal·ly, on·o- mat·o·po·et′i·cal·ly** *advs.*

On·on·da·ga (ŏnondaw′ga, -dah′-) *n.* (pl. **-gas,** collect. **-ga**). (Member of) a N. Amer. Indian tribe of Iroquoian stock, formerly living in New York State and Ontario; one of the Six Nations, and guardians of the council fire of the Iroquois.

on·rush (ŏn′rŭsh, awn′-) *n.* Onset.

on·set (ŏn′sĕt, awn′-) *n.* Attack, assault, impetuous beginning.

on·slaught (ŏn′slawt, awn′-) *n.* Onset, fierce attack.

Ont. *abbrev.* Ontario.

On·tar·i·o (ŏntār′ēō). Province of SE. Canada, between Hudson Bay in the N. and the Great Lakes in the S.; capital, Toronto; **Lake ~,** smallest and most easterly of the Great Lakes, lying between the Canadian province and New York State.

on·to (ŏn′tŏŏ, awn′-) *prep.*: see ON def. 3.

on·to·gen·e·sis (ŏntojĕn′ĭsĭs) *n.* = ONTOGENY. **on·to·ge·net·ic** (ŏntōjenĕt′ĭk), **on·to·ge·net′i·cal, on·to·gen′ic** *adjs.* **on·to·ge·net′- i·cal·ly** *adv.*

on·tog·e·ny (ŏntŏj′enē) *n.* (biol.) History of the development of an

individual organism (opp. PHYLOGENY).

on·tol·o·gy (ŏntŏl′oje) *n.* Branch of metaphysics concerned with the essence of things or being in the abstract. **on·to·log·i·cal** (ŏntolŏj′- ĭkal) *adj.* **on·tol′o·gist** *n.*

o·nus (ō′nus) *n.* (pl. **o·nus·es**). Burden, duty, responsibility.

on·ward (ŏn′werd, awn′-) *adv.* & *adj.* (Directed) farther on, toward the front; with advancing motion. **on′wards** *adv.*

on·yx (ŏn′ĭks) *n.* Type of chalcedony with different colors in layers, a form of silica, regarded as semiprecious stone.

oo·dles (ōō′delz) *n.pl.* (colloq.) Superabundance (*of money* etc.).

o·o·gen·e·sis (ōōjĕn′ĭsĭs) *n.* (biol.) Process leading to production of ripe ovum from germ cell.

o·o·lite (ō′olīt) *n.* Rock, freq. a limestone, composed of minute spheres of carbonate, resembling fish roe in appearance, found esp. in the Jurassic strata. **o·o·lit·ic** (oolĭt′ĭk) *adj.*

oo·long (ōō′lawng, -lŏng) *n.* Dark-colored kind of tea grown in China and Taiwan: see TEA. [Chin. *wu* black, *lung* dragon]

oom (ōōm) *n.* (S. Afr.) Uncle; **Oom Paul,** President KRUGER[1].

oo·mi·ak (ōō′mĕăk) *n.* Var. of UMIAK.

ooze (ōōz) *n.* 1. Wet mud, slime,

esp. in riverbed or estuary or on ocean bottom. 2. Tanning liquor, infusion of oak bark etc. 3. Exudation; sluggish flow; something that oozes. **ooz'y** *adj.* **ooz'i·ly** *adv.* **ooz'i·ness** *n.* **ooze** *v.* (**oozed, ooz·ing**). (of moisture) Pass slowly through the pores of a body, exude, percolate; exude moisture; emit (moisture, information, etc.); (fig.) leak *out* or *away*.

Op. *abbrev.* Opus.

O.P. *abbrev.* Observation post.

o.p. *abbrev.* Out of print.

o·pac·i·ty (ōpăs'ĭte) *n.* Being opaque.

o·pal (ō'pal) *n.* Amorphous quartzlike form of hydrated silica, some kinds of which are valued as gems and show changing colors (**common ~**, milk-white or bluish with green, yellow, and red reflections); (commerc.) semitranslucent white glass.

o·pal·es·cence (ōpalĕs'ens) *n.* Changing of color as in an opal. **o·pal·es'cent** *adj.* Showing opalescence, iridescent.

o·pal·ine (ō'palīn, -lēn) *adj.* Opal-like; opalescent. **~** *n.* Opal glass.

o·paque (ōpāk') *adj.* Not transmitting light, not transparent; obscure, not lucid; dull witted. **o·paque'ly** *adv.* **o·paque'ness** *n.*

op (ŏp) **art.** Style of abstract art using contrasting colors, often black and white, to create optical illusions, esp. of movement.

op. cit. *abbrev.* *Opere citato* (L., = in the work quoted).

OPEC (ō'pĕk) *n.* Organization of Petroleum Exporting Countries.

o·pen (ō'pen) *adj.* 1. Not closed or blocked up; allowing of entrance, passage, or access; having gate, door, lid, or part of boundary withdrawn; unenclosed, unconfined, uncovered, bare, exposed, undisguised; public, manifest; not exclusive or limited; (of account) not paid. 2. (of vowel) Produced with wider opening of oral cavity than close vowel; (mus., of organ pipe) not closed at top; (mus., of string) not stopped by finger; (of note) produced by such pipe or string, or without aid of slide, key, or piston. 3. Expanded, unfolded, outspread; spread out, not close, without intervals; porous; communicative, frank. 4. **~ air**, outdoors; **~-and-shut**, (colloq.) immediately obvious; **with ~ arms**, heartily; **~ boat**, undecked boat; **~ country**, country unenclosed or affording wide views; **the ~ door**, principle of free

commerce for all comers; **with ~ eyes**, not unconsciously or under misapprehension; in eager attention or surprise; so **~-eyed** (*adj.*); **~ hand**, freedom in giving, generosity; **o'penhand'ed** (*adj.*) **o'penhand'edly** (*adv.*), **o'penhand'edness** (*n.*); **open-heart surgery**, surgery performed on the exposed heart with the bloodstream diverted around the heart, to a machine and back to the patient's circulatory system; **keep open**

house, entertain all comers; **ope letter**, letter addressing individual but published in new paper etc.; **open mind**, access bility to new ideas; unprejudice or undecided state; **open-minde** (*adj.*), **open-mindedly** (*adv* **open-mindedness** (*n.*); **ope order**, formation with wide spac between men or ships; **ope question**, matter on whi differences of opinion a legitimate; **open syllable**, syllab ending with a vowel; **Ope University**, (Brit.) universi (established 1969) with no form requirement for entry to its fir degree courses, and providi instruction by a combination television, radio, and cor-respondence courses and by audio-visual centers; **o'penwork**, pattern with interstices in material. **o'pen·ness** n. **open** n. the ~, open space or country or air, public view. **open** v. 1. Make or become open or more open; start, establish, set going (business, campaign, etc.); ~ **debate**, be first speaker; ~ **the door to**, give opportunity for; ~ **one's eyes**, show surprise; ~ **the eyes of**, undeceive, enlighten. 2. Commence speaking; make a start; begin to be sold. 3. ~ **out**, unfold, develop, expand; ~ **up**, make accessible; bring to notice, reveal; become communicative; begin firing on. **o'pen·er** n. (esp.) Device for opening bottles, cans, etc.

o·pen·ing (ō'pening) adj. (esp.) Initial, first. ~ n. (esp.) Gap, passage, aperture; commencement, initial part; initial public performance (of a play etc.); opportunity, favorable conjuncture for; (chess) recognized sequence of moves for beginning game.

o·pen·ly (ō'penlē) adv. Without concealment, publicly, frankly.

op·er·a (ŏp'era, ŏp'ra) n. Dramatic performance or composition of which music is an essential part; branch of art concerned with this; **comic** ~, opera of humorous character; **grand** ~, opera, usu. on serious theme, without spoken dialogue; **light** ~, = OPERETTA def. 2; **o·pé·ra bouffe** (Fr. awpérah boof'), **o·pe·ra buf·fa** (It. aw'pĕrah boo'fah) French, Italian, types of comic opera (Ital. buffa comic); **opera glass(es)**, small binoculars for use at opera or theater; **opera hat**: see HAT; **opera**

house, theater for performance of opera.

op·er·a·ble (ŏp'erabel) adj. (med.) That admits of being operated upon. **op·er·a·bil·i·ty** (ŏperabil'ĭtē) n. **op·er·a·bly** adv.

op·er·ate (ŏp'erāt) v. (-at·ed, -at·ing). 1. Be in action, produce an effect, exercise influence; play on, try to act on; have desired effect. 2. Perform surgical or other operation; carry on warlike operations; deal or speculate in stocks and shares. 3. Bring about, accomplish; manage, work, conduct. 4. Conduct, be in charge of (machine, apparatus). **op·er·at·ing** n. (esp.) ~ **table**, table for use in surgery; ~ **theater**, room reserved in hospital etc. for the performance of surgery. **op·er·a·tor** n.

op·er·at·ic (ŏperăt'ĭk) adj. Of, like, opera. **op·er·at·i·cal·ly** adv.

op·er·a·tion (ŏpera'shon) n. 1. Working, action, way thing works; efficacy, validity, scope. 2. Active process, activity, performance; discharge of function; financial transaction. 3. Act or series of acts performed with hand or instrument on some part of body to remedy deformity, injury, disease, pain, etc.; (esp.) piece of surgery. 4. Strategic movement of troops, ships, etc. 5. (math.) Subjection of number or quantity to process affecting its value or form, e.g. multiplication. **op·er·a'tion·al** adj. (esp.) Engaged on, used for,

Ophthalmology is the medical study of the eye and its diseases. A major advance has been the introduction of contact lenses, first conceived by Leonardo da Vinci. Below: an ophthalmologist at work.

warlike operations.

op·er·a·tive (ŏp'erativ, ŏp'erā-) adj. 1. Having effect, in operation, efficacious; practical, not theoretical or contemplative. 2. Of surgical operations. **op·er·a·tive·ly** adv. **op·er·a·tive·ness** n. **operative** n. A secret or trusted agent.

o·per·cu·lum (ōpēr'kyulum) n. (pl. **-la** pr. -la, **-lums**). Gill cover of fish; lid or valve closing aperture of shell when tenant is retracted; similar lidlike structure in plants etc. **o·per·cu·lar, o·per·cu·late** (ōpēr'kyulĭt), **o·per·cu·lat·ed** (ōpēr'kyulātĭd) adjs.

op·er·et·ta (ŏperĕt'a) n. 1. Short opera. 2. Opera in simple popular style. **op·er·et'tist** n.

O·phel·ia (ōfēl'ya). In Shakespeare's *Hamlet*, daughter of Polonius, who went mad and drowned herself because of HAMLET's treatment of her and his killing of her father.

o·phid·i·an (ōfĭd'ēan) adj. & n. (Member) of the Ophidia, a suborder of reptiles including snakes.

oph·thal·mi·a (ŏfthăl'mēa, ŏp-) n. Inflammation of the eye, esp. affecting the conjunctiva.

oph·thal·mic (ŏfthăl'mĭk, ŏp-) adj. Of, relating to, or situated near, the eye.

oph·thal·mol·o·gy (ŏfthăl-mŏl'ojē, -tha-, ŏp-) n. Study of the eye and its diseases. **oph·thal·mol·o·gist** n.

oph·thal·mo·scope (ŏfthăl'-

The Australian Opera presented a magnificent spectacle on stage during its production of 'Turandot', a grand opera composed by Puccini and performed without any spoken words.

moskōp, ŏp-) *n.* Instrument for inspecting the interior of the eye, esp. the retina.

o·pi·ate (ō'pēĭt, -āt) *adj.* Containing opium, narcotic, soporific. ~ *n.* Drug prepared from opium; sleep-inducing drug, narcotic.

o·pine (ōpīn') *v.t.* (**o·pined, o·pin·ing**). Express or hold the opinion (*that*).

o·pin·ion (opĭn'yon) *n.* Judgment or belief based on grounds short of proof; views or sentiment, esp. on moral questions, prevalent among people in general; formal statement by expert consulted; professional advice.

o·pin·ion·at·ed (opĭn'yonātĭd), **o·pin·ion·a·tive** (opĭn'yonātĭv) *adjs.* Obstinate in opinion, dogmatic; self-willed. **o·pin'ion·at·ed·ness** *n.* **o·pin'ion·at·ed·ly** *adv.* **o·pin'ion·at·ive·ly** *adv.* **o·pin'ion·at·ive·ness** *n.*

o·pi·um (ō'pēum) *n.* Dried latex from unripe capsules of a poppy (*Papaver somniferum*), of reddish-brown color, with heavy smell and bitter taste, smoked or eaten as stimulant, intoxicant, or narcotic, and used in medicine as sedative; ~ **den**, haunt of opium smokers.

o·pos·sum (opŏs'um, pŏs'um) *n.* (pl. **-sums**, collect. **-sum**). 1. Any of various small, nocturnal, tree-dwelling Amer. marsupials (family Didelphidae), esp. *Didelphis marsupialis* or *D. virginiana*, of ratlike appearance

Opossums are the only marsupials surviving in America. The North-American variety (above) and the mouse opossum (below) are arboreal but the yapok of South America is aquatic and has webbed feet.

and having the habit of collapsing as if dead when threatened or trapped. 2. Any of several Australian phalangers.

opp. *abbrev.* Opposite.

op·po·nent (opō'nent) *n.* Person opposed or on the opposing side in a contest etc.

op·por·tune (ŏpertoon', -tūn') *adj.* (of time) Suitable, well-selected, favorable; (of action or event) well-timed, done or occurring at favorable conjuncture. **op·por·tune'ly** *adv.* **op·por·tune'ness** *n.*

op·por·tun·ism (ŏpertoo'nĭzem, -tū'-) *n.* Policy of doing what is opportune or at the time expedient, in politics, as opp. to rigid adherence to principles; method or course of action adapted to the circumstances of the moment. **op·por·tun'ist** *n.* **op·por·tun·is'tic** *adj.* **op·por·tun·is'ti·cal·ly** *adv.*

op·por·tu·ni·ty (ŏpertoo'nĭtē, -tū'-) *n.* (pl. **-ties**). Favorable juncture, good chance, opening.

op·pose (opōz') *v.t.* (**-posed, -pos·ing**). 1. Place, produce, or cite as obstacle, antagonist, counterpoise, or contrast to; represent as antithetical. 2. Set

oneself against, withstand, resist, obstruct; propose the rejection of; act as opponent or check. **op·posed'** *adj.* (esp.) Contrary, opposite, contrasted; hostile, adverse. **op·pos'a·ble** *adj.* (of digit, esp. thumb) Capable of being applied so as to meet another.

op·po·site (ŏp'ozĭt, -sĭt) *adj.* 1. Facing, front to front or back to back (with); ~ **number**, person or thing similarly placed in another set etc. to the given one. 2. Of contrary kind, diametrically different *to* or *from*; *the* other of a contrasted pair. **op'po·site·ly** *adv.* **op'po·sit·ness** *n.* **opposite** *n.* Opposite thing or term. ~ *adv.* In opposite place or direction; on opposite sides. ~ *prep.* In an opposite place or direction to; **play** ~, (of lead in play or film) have (specified actor or actress) as one's leading man or lady.

op·po·si·tion (ŏpozĭsh'on) *n.* 1. Placing opposite; diametrically opposite position (esp. astron., of two heavenly bodies when their longitude differs by 180°; opp. CONJUNCTION). 2. Contrast, antithesis; (logic) relation between two propositions with same subject and predicate but differing in quantity or quality or both. 3. Antagonism, resistance, being hostile; any party opposed to some proposal.

op·press (oprĕs') *v.t.* Overwhelm with superior weight or numbers, or irresistible power; lie heavy on, weigh down (spirits etc.); govern tyrannically, keep under by coercion, subject to continual cruelty or injustice. **op·pres'sion** (oprĕsh'on), **op·pres'sor** *ns.* **op·pres'sive** *adj.* **op·pres'sive·ly** *adv.* **op·pres'sive·ness** *n.*

op·pro·bri·ous (oprō'brēus) *adj.* Conveying reproach, abusive vituperative. **op·pro'bri·ous·ly** *adv.* **op·pro'bri·ous·ness** *n.*

op·pro·bri·um (oprō'brēum) *n.* Disgrace attaching to some act or conduct, infamy, crying of shame.

opt (ŏpt) *v.i.* Exercise an option, make a choice; ~ **out (of)** choose not to take part (in).

op·tic (ŏp'tĭk) *adj.* Of the eye or sense of sight; ~ **nerve**, 2nd cranial nerve, from eyeball to forebrain, conducting the impulses responsible for visual sensations. **optic** *n.* Eye (now usu. joc.). **op'tics** *n.* (pl. considered as sing. Science of sight, branch of physics dealing with properties etc. of light.

op·ti·cal (ŏp'tĭkal) *adj.* Visual ocular; of sight or light in relation to each other; belonging to optics constructed to assist sight or on the principles of optics; ~ **activity** (chem.) property possessed by certain transparent solids and liquids of rotating the plane of polarization of polarized light passing through them; ~ **maser**

piates stem from many obscure ources, such as the humble poppy wer. The effects of opiates on West- n nations in the last decades have en devastating, despite the efforts of lice forces.

Garden orache or mountain spinach is a herb native to temperate Europe and Asia which has been grown in England and North America as a substitute for green vegetables. It may also be used in soup.

e MASER. **op'ti·cal·ly** *adv.*

op·ti·cian (ŏptǐsh´an) *n.* Maker seller of optical instruments.

op·ti·mal (ŏp´timal) *adj.* Most tisfactory, best possible under the rcumstances.

op·ti·mism (ŏp´timĭzem) *n.* octrine, esp. as set forth by eibniz, that the actual world is e best of all possible worlds; view

that good must ultimately prevail over evil in the universe; sanguine disposition, inclination to take bright views. **op'ti·mist** *n.* **op·ti-mis'tic, op·tis·mis'ti·cal** *adjs.* **op·ti·mis'ti·cal·ly** *adv.*

op·ti·mum (ŏ´timum) *n.* (pl. **-ma** pr. -ma, **-mums**). (biol.) That degree or amount of heat, light, food, moisture, etc. most

favorable for growth or other vital processes; (also attrib.) best. [L., = "best"]

op·tion (ŏp´shon) *n.* Choice, choosing, thing that is or may be chosen; liberty of choosing, freedom of choice; purchased right to call for or make delivery within specified time of specified stocks etc. at specified rate; **local** ~: see LOCAL. **op'tion·al** *adj.* Not obligatory. **op'tion·al·ly** *adv.*

op·tom·e·try (ŏptŏm´ĭtrē) *n.* Art or profession of measuring certain visual impairments and treating them by corrective lenses or other methods. **op·tom·e·trist** (ŏptŏm´ĭtrĭst) *n.* Practitioner (not usu. a licensed physician) of optometry.

op·u·lent (ŏp´yulent) *adj.* Rich; abounding, abundant, well-stored. **op'u·lent·ly** *adv.* **op'u·lence** *n.*

o·pus (ō´pus) *n.* (pl. **o·pus·es, o·per·a** pr. ō´pera, ŏp´era). Musical composition or set of compositions as numbered among works of composer in order of publication etc. (abbrev. op.); **magnum** ~, great literary undertaking, writer's or other artist's chief production. [L., = "work"]

OR, Or. *abbrevs.* Oregon.

or (ōr, er) *conj.* Introducing alternatives.

or·ach, or·ache (ōr´ach, ār´-) *ns.* Herb or small shrub, often mealy, of various species of genus *Atriplex*, commonest by the seashore.

or·a·cle (ōr´akel, ār´-) *n.* Place at which ancient Greeks etc. were accustomed to consult the gods for advice or prophecy; response, freq. ambiguous or obscure, given at such place; holy of holies or mercy seat in ancient Hebrew temple; (vehicle of) divine inspiration or revelation; infallible guide, test, or indicator; authoritative, profoundly wide, or mysterious judge, judgment, prophet, etc.

o·rac·u·lar (awrăk´yuler) *adj.* Of an oracle; obscure like an oracle. **o·rac'u·lar·ly** *adv.*

o·ral (ōr´al, ōr´-) *adj.* Spoken, verbal, by word of mouth; of the mouth; done or taken by the mouth; ~ **examination**, in which a candidate answers questions put by the examiner in a personal interview (opp. *written*); ~ **stage**, (psychoanalytic theory) the first stage of psychosexual development in which the mouth and the activities associated with it are the source of sexual gratification. **o'ral·ly** *adv.* **oral** *n.* Oral examination.

O·ran (ōrăn´, aw-). Mediterranean port city in NW. Algeria.

Oranges have been grown in Italy since the beginning of the Christian era. They were originally from China or Malaya and their cultivation was propagated by Arab traders.

The glazed and heated structure erected at Heidelberg in 1619 to allow oranges to be grown was known as an **orangery**. The one illustrated is at Uppsala in Sweden.

or·ange (ōr´ĭnj, är´-) *n.* 1. Evergreen tree, *Citrus aurantium* and allied species, native of the East, widely cultivated in S. Europe and other warm, temperate, or subtropical regions, with fragrant white flowers and large globose many-celled berries with subacid juicy pulp and tough outer rind of bright reddish-yellow; fruit of this; **mock ~**: see MOCK; **~ blossom**, flowers of orange or mock orange, freq. worn or carried by bride at wedding; **~ flower water**, fragrant aqueous solution of orange flowers; **~ (wood) stick**, small stick of orangewood used for manicuring nails. 2. Color of orange rind, reddish yellow. **orange** *adj.* Orange-colored. [Arab. *nāranj*]

or·ange·ade (ōrĭnjād´, är-) *n.* Drink of sweetened orange juice and water; synthetic substitute for this.

Or·ange (ōr´ĭnj, är´-) **Free State.** Inland province of the Republic of S. Africa between the Orange and Vaal Rivers; first settled by Boers from Cape Colony (1836–8); annexed by Britain 1848, but restored in 1854 to Boers who established the Orange Free State Republic; annexed again by Britain during the Boer War (1899–1902) and renamed Orange River Colony; province of the Union of South Africa (1910) as Orange Free State; capital, Bloemfontein.

or·ange·ry (ōr´ĭnjrē, är´-) *n.* (pl. **-ries**). Building, hothouse, for protection of orange trees; esp., in 17th c. mansions, (part of) building having solid N. wall and large freq. arched windows on S. side.

o·rang·u·tan, o·rang·ou·tang (ōrăng´ŭtăn, -tăng) *ns.* Large long-armed mainly arboreal anthropoid ape, *Pongo pygmaeus*, of Borneo, Sumatra, and formerly Java. [Malay *orang-uton* man of the woods]

o·rate (ōrāt´, aw- ōr´āt, ōr´-) *v.i.* (**o·rat·ed, o·rat·ing**). (joc.) Make an oration.

o·ra·tion (ōrā´shon aw-) *n.* Formal address, harangue, or discourse, esp. of ceremonial kind.

or·a·tor (ōr´ater, är´-) *n.* Maker of a speech; eloquent public speaker.

or·a·to·ri·o (ōratōr´ēō, -tōr´-, är-) *n.* (pl. **-ri·os**). Semidramatic musical composition usu. on sacred theme performed by soloists, chorus, and orchestra, without action, scenery, or costume. [It., orig. of musical services at Oratory of St. Philip Neri, Rome]

Found only in Indonesia, the **orangutan** is one of the larger apes. The native name meant 'jungle-man' and these primates are considered to be the strongest of all apes, although only 4 ft. 6 ins. tall.

Billy Graham, Christian evange whose **oratory** has captured the imag ation and attention of followers all o the world. Here he is speaking Tampa Stadium in Florida.

or·a·to·ry[1] (ōr´atōrē, -tōrē, är n. (Art of making) speech rhetoric; highly colored preser ment of facts, eloquent exaggerating language. **or·a·to i·cal** (ōratōr´ĭkal, oratär´-) *a* **or·a·tor´i·cal·ly** *adv.*

or·a·to·ry[2] (ōr´atōrē, -tōrē, är n. (pl. **-ries**). Small chapel, pl for private worship.

orb (ōrb) *n.* Circle, disk, ri (now rare); sphere, globe; heaven body; eyeball, eye (poet.); glo surmounted by cross as part regalia, symbolizing domination the world by Christ. **~** *v.* Encl in, gather into, orb.

or·bit (ōr´bĭt) *n.* 1. Eye sock border around eye of bird or inse 2. Curved course esp. of plan comet, satellite, spacecraft, binary star; complete circuit of th (fig.) range, sphere, of action; **~**, traveling in an orbit. **or·** *v.* (Cause to) travel in an orbit.

The orc, or killer whale (Orcinus orca) is usually a very predatory creature. It attacks seals, walruses and, in packs, even large whales. It has a high dorsal fin and rounded flippers. It is found world-wide.

Vehicles launched into space are often placed in an **orbit** which circles the earth or other planets. More recently, orbital laboratories (below) have been launched where experiments can be conducted that are impossible on Earth.

or·bit·al (ōr′bĭtal) *adj.* Of an orbit. ~ *n.* (phys.) That part of the region surrounding an atomic nucleus in which an associated electron is most likely to be found; mathematical equation describing this.

orc (ōrk), **or·ca** (ōr′ka) *ns.* cetacean, esp. the killer whale

CSMJ—2 engine

command-service module

external avionics and telemetry equipment

auxiliary docking port

multiple docking adaptor

water tanks

solar array

airlocks

Apollo telescope mount

solar tracking equipment

ATM solar wings

laboratory body

workshop

sleep compartment

waste compartment

wardroom

missing solar array

or·chard (ōr'cherd) *n.* Enclosure with fruit trees; ~ **grass**, weedy grass (*Dactylis glomerata*), often planted in pastures.

or·ches·tra (ōr'kĭstra) *n.* 1. Semicircular space in front of stage in ancient Greek theater, where chorus danced and sang. 2. Front section of seats in a theater closest to the orchestra pit; entire main floor of theater. 3. Body of instrumental performers, or combination of string, woodwind, brass, and percussion instruments, in theater or concert room; ~ **pit**, pit for orchestra below and in front of stage. **or·ches·tral** (ōrkĕs'tral) *adj.* **or·ches'tral·ly** *adv.*

or·ches·trate (ōr'kĭstrāt) *v.* (**-trat·ed, -trat·ing**). Arrange, or score, (music) for orchestral performance. **or·ches·tra·tion** (ōrkĭstrā'shon), **or'ches·tra·tor, or'ches·trat·er** *ns.*

or·chid (ōr'kĭd) *n.* Plant of the Orchidaceae, a large and widely distributed order of monocotyledons with three sepals and three petals, of which one (the lip or labellum) is usu. much larger than the others and of special color or shape; esp. one of the exotic cultivated species, freq. brilliantly colored or grotesquely shaped.

or·chi·da·ceous (ōrkĭdā'shus) *adj.*

or·chil (ōr'kĭl, -chĭl) *n.* Red or violet dye from certain lichens, esp. *Roccella tinctoria*.

ord. *abbrev.* Ordained; order; ordinance; ordnance.

or·dain (ōrdān') *v.t.* 1. Appoint ceremonially to ministry; confer holy orders (esp. those of priest) on; authorize as a rabbi. 2. Destine, appoint; appoint authoritatively, decree, enact.

or·deal (ōrdēl', -dē'al, ōr'dēl) *n.* Experience that tests character or endurance, severe trial; (hist.) primitive (esp. ancient Teutonic) mode of deciding suspected person's guilt or innocence by subjecting him to physical test such as plunging of hand in boiling water,

In an **orchard**, *it is often necessary to spray at various times to kill insects or their larvae which would damage the fruit, and lower its value when offered for sale.*

safe endurance of which was tak as divine acquittal.

or·der (ōr'der) *n.* 1. Rank community, social division, gra or stratum; definite rank in sta separate and homogeneous set persons. 2. Kind, sort. 3. ~ s **angels**: see ANGEL. 4. Grade Christian ministry; (pl.) status clergyman; **holy** ~ s, orders bishops, priests, and deaco **minor** ~ s, in R.C. Church (ur 1973) orders of acolyte, exorci reader, and doorkeeper; **in** ~ ordained; **take** ~ s, be ordaine 5. (Brit.) Fraternity of monks friars, or formerly of knight bound by common rule of life; o of the companies (**Orders Chivalry**), usu. instituted sovereign, to which distinguish persons are admitted by way honor or reward, insignia worn member of such a company. (archit.) Mode of treatment wi established proportions betwe parts, esp. one of the **five (class cal) orders** of column and entabl ture (Doric, Ionic, Corinthia Tuscan, and Composite, the fi three of Greek origin, the othe Roman). 7. (math.) Degree of coi plexity. 8. (biol.) Classificato group below *class* and above *fami* **natural** ~, (bot.) order of plai allied in general structure, n merely agreeing in single characte istic as in Linnaean system. Sequence, succession, manner following; regular array, conditi in which every part or unit is in right place; tidiness; norm healthy, or efficient state; (mi equipment, uniform, etc., for son purpose; **in (good) order**, fit f use; **out of order**, not syster atically arranged; not workii correctly. 10. Constitution of t world, way things normally happe collective manifestations of natui forces or laws. 11. Stated form divine service; principles of dec um and rules of procedure accept by legislative assembly or pub meeting, or enforced by its pres dent; **rise to (a point of) orde** interrupt debate etc. with inqui whether something being said done is in or out of order, accor ing or not according to rules; **ord of the day**, program, business s down for treatment; prevailing sta of things. 12. Prevalence of coi stituted authority, law-abidi state. 13. Act or instance ordering; authoritative direction instruction (freq. pl.); (bankir etc.) instruction to pay money deliver property signed by own

Only during the 19th century did n instruments enable composers such Berlioz to write music for an **orches** *of more than 100 players. Le Montreal Symphony.*

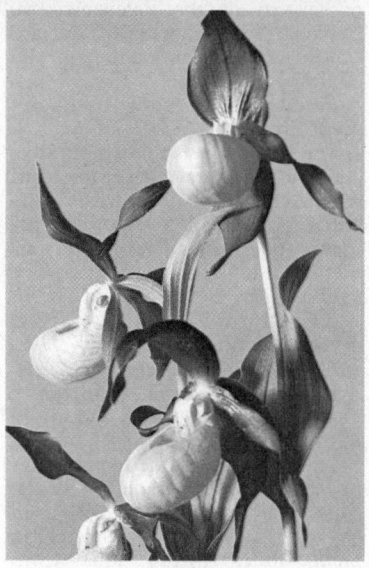

*With 17,000 species described, the variety of **orchid** flowers exceeds the imagination. The Paphiopedilum (top) from the Solomon Islands, the lady's slipper from England (right), and the Australian species (above), are all orchids.*

responsible agent; direction to manufacturer, tradesman, etc., to supply something; **in order**, suitable, fitting, appropriate; **in short order**, without delay, immediately; **large** or **tall order**, (colloq.) difficult undertaking; **made to order**, made according to special directions, to suit individual measurements etc. (opp. *ready-made*); **money**, **postal order**, order issued by post office bank for specific amount of money; **on order**, ordered but not yet supplied. 14. **in order to do**, with a view to, for the purpose of, doing; **in order that**, with the intention or to the end that. 5. **order of magnitude**, class in a system of classification determined by size, usu. by powers 10. **order** *v.t.* 1. Put in order. State with authority that (action must be performed, person must

perform action); prescribe; command or direct to go *to*, *away*, etc.; direct merchant etc. to supply (article).

or·der·ly (ōr′derlē) *adj.* Methodically arranged or inclined, regular, obedient to discipline, not unruly, well-behaved; (mil.) on duty, concerned with carrying out orders; ~ **room**, one set apart in barracks etc. for administrative business. **or′der·li·ness** *n.* **orderly** *n.* (pl. **-lies**). Soldier in attendance on officer to execute orders etc.; attendant in (esp. military) hospital.

or·di·nal (ōr′dinal) *adj.* Of or defining a thing's position in a series (~ **numbers** = *first*, *second*, etc.). **ordinal** *n.* 1. Ordinal number. 2. Prescribed form of ceremony to be observed at consecration of bishops and ordination of priests and deacons; book containing words and directions for this ceremony.

or·di·nance (ōr′dinans) *n.* Authoritative direction, decree; religious rite; statute.

or·di·nar·y (ōr′dinerē) *adj.* 1. Regular, normal, customary, usual; not exceptional, not above the usual, commonplace; ~ **seaman**, (abbrev. O.S.) lower rating than *able seaman*. 2. Having immediate or *ex officio* and not deputed jurisdiction. **ordinary** *n.* (pl. **-nar·ies**). 1. Ordinary authority; **the O** ~, archbishop in province, bishop in diocese. 2. Rule or book laying down order of divine service. 3. Ordinary condition, course, etc.; what is ordinary. **or·di·nar·i·ly** (ōrdi̅na̅r´i̅le̅, -něr´-) *adv.* **or´di·nar·i·ness** *n.*

or·di·nate (ōr´dinĭt, -nāt) *n.* (geom.) Any of series of parallel chords of conic section in relation to bisecting diameter (esp. used of half the chord, from curve to diameter); straight line from any point drawn parallel to one co-ordinate axis and meeting the other (correlative to ABSCISSA).

or·di·na·tion (ōrdina̅´shon) *n.* 1. Arrangement in ranks, classification. 2. Conferring of holy orders, admission to church ministry. 3. Decreeing, ordainment.

ord·nance (ōrd´nans) *n.* Military weapons and ammunition; branch of public service dealing esp. with military stores and materials.

Or·do·vi·cian (ōrdovĭsh´an) *adj. & n.* (geol.) (Of) the second period or system of the Paleozoic era, between Cambrian and Silurian. [*Ordovices*, ancient tribe in N. Wales]

or·dure (ōr´jer, -dūr) *n.* Excrement, dung.

ore (ōr, or) *n.* Solid naturally-occurring mineral aggregate from which one or more valuable constituents may be recovered by treatment; (poet.) metal, esp. precious metal.

Ore. *abbrev.* Oregon.

o·re·ad (ōr´ĕăd, or´-) *n.* (Gk. myth.) Mountain nymph.

Oreg. *abbrev.* Oregon.

Or·e·gon (ōr´egon, -gŏn, ar´-). Pacific NW. state of U.S.; admitted to the Union in 1859; capital, Salem; ~ **pine**, name for Douglas fir, esp. in timber trade; ~ **Trail**, (hist.) major route to the NW. used by settlers, esp. 1942–7, stretching 2,000 miles (3,219 km) from Independence, Missouri, over plains, desert, mountain passes, and rivers to Astoria, Oregon, at the mouth of the Columbia River.

O·res·tes (ōrĕs´tēz, aw-). (Gk. legend) Son of AGAMEMNON and Clytemnestra; killed his mother and her lover Aegisthus in revenge because they had murdered his father; was pursued by the Furies until he was pardoned by Artemis, having rescued her statue (and his sister Iphigenia) from the island of Tauris; became king of Argos, Sparta, and Mycenae, and married Hermione, daughter of Menelaus.

or·gan (ōr´gan) *n.* 1. Part of animal or vegetable body adapted for special vital function, as ~*s of digestion, speech,* etc. 2. Person's voice with ref. to its power or quality. 3. Medium of communication, esp. newspaper or journal representing a party, cause,

Greek Doric

Greek Ionic

Greek Corinthian

Roman Corinthian   Composite   Tuscan

*Architectural **orders** originated in ancient Greece and Rome and were concerned with the proportions and styles of buildings using columns. Eventually later architects analysed these and added variations.*

etc. 4. Musical instrument consisting essentially of pipes arranged in ranks (*stops*) which are supplied with wind by a bellows or electric fan and sounded by means of keys arranged in rows and pedals, each key or pedal controlling the mechanism (usu. a valve) that admits air to a particular pipe. 5. Any of various keyboard instruments producing more or less similar effects by different means, as ELECTRONIC ~. 6. **mouth ~**: see HARMONICA; ~ **grinder**, player on BARREL organ; ~ **loft**, loft or gallery in which organ is placed, freq. above **organ screen**, ornamental screen between nave

and choir in church; ~**-pip cactus**, tall cactus (*Pachycereu marginatus*), of southwest U.S. an Mexico, resembling pipe organ; ~ **stop**, set of pipes of similar ton quality in organ; handle or kno of mechanism that brings such set into action.

or·gan·dy,   or·gan·di (ōr´gandē) *ns.* (pl. **-dies**). Thi stiff translucent cotton or si fabric.

or·gan·elle (ōrganĕl´) *n.* (biol Part of a cell, having a particula function.

or·gan·ic (ōrgăn´ĭk) *adj.* 1. O the bodily organs, vital; (path., o disease) affecting structure of a organ (opp. *functional*). 2. Havin organs or organized physical struc ture; of animals or plants; (chem of compound substances) occurrin naturally as constituent o organized bodies formed from suc

The original musical **organs** *were devised about 250 B.C. but the ancestor of present instruments was made in the 14th century with three keyboards. The organ at St James' Church, Piccadilly, London, was made in the 1600s.*

compounds (all of which contain or are derived from hydrocarbon radicals); ~ **chemistry**: see CHEMISTRY. 3. Constitutional, inherent, fundamental, structural; organized, systematic, coordinated. **or·gan′i·cal·ly** *adv.*

or·gan·ism (ōr′ganĭzem) *n.* Living animal or plant; anything capable of maintaining the processes characteristic of life, esp. reproduction; (material structure of) individual animal or plant; whole with interdependent parts compared to living being. **or·gan·is′mic, or·gan·is′mal** *adjs.*

or·gan·ist (ōr′ganĭst) *n.* Player of organ.

or·gan·i·za·tion (ōr′ganĭzā′-shon) *n.* (esp.) Organized body, system, or society. **or·gan·i·za′tion·al** *adj.* **or·gan·i·za′tion·al·ly** *adv.*

or·gan·ize (ōr′ganīz) *v.* (**-ized, -iz·ing**). 1. Furnish with organs, make organic, make into living being or tissue (usu. in past part.); become organic. 2. Form into an organic whole; give orderly structure to, frame and put into working order; make arrangements for, get up (undertaking involving co-operation). **or′gan·iz·a·ble** *adj.* **or′gan·iz·er** *n.*

or·ga·non (ōr′ganŏn) *n.* (pl. **-nons, -na** pr. -na). Instrument of thought, system of or treatise on logic. [Gk. *organon* tool, work; *Organon* was the title of Aristotle's logical writings, and *Novum* (new) *Organum* that of Bacon's]

or·ga·num (ōr′ganum) *n.* (pl. **-na** pr. -na, **-nums**) = ORGANON.

or·gan·za (ōrgăn′za) *n.* Thin stiff transparent fabric of silk or synthetic fiber.

or·gan·zine (ōr′ganzēn) *n.* Strongest kind of silk thread, in which main twist is in contrary direction to that of strands.

or·gasm (ōr′găzem) *n.* Paroxysm of excitement or rage; climax of sexual excitement esp. in coition. **or·gas′mic, or·gas′tic** *adjs.*

or·gi·as·tic (ōrjĕăs′tĭk) *adj.* Of the nature of an orgy.

or·gy (ōr′jē) *n.* (pl. **-gies**). 1. (Gk. and Rom. antiq., usu. pl.) Secret rites in worship of various gods, esp. festival in honor of Dionysus (Bacchus), celebrated with extravagant dancing, singing,

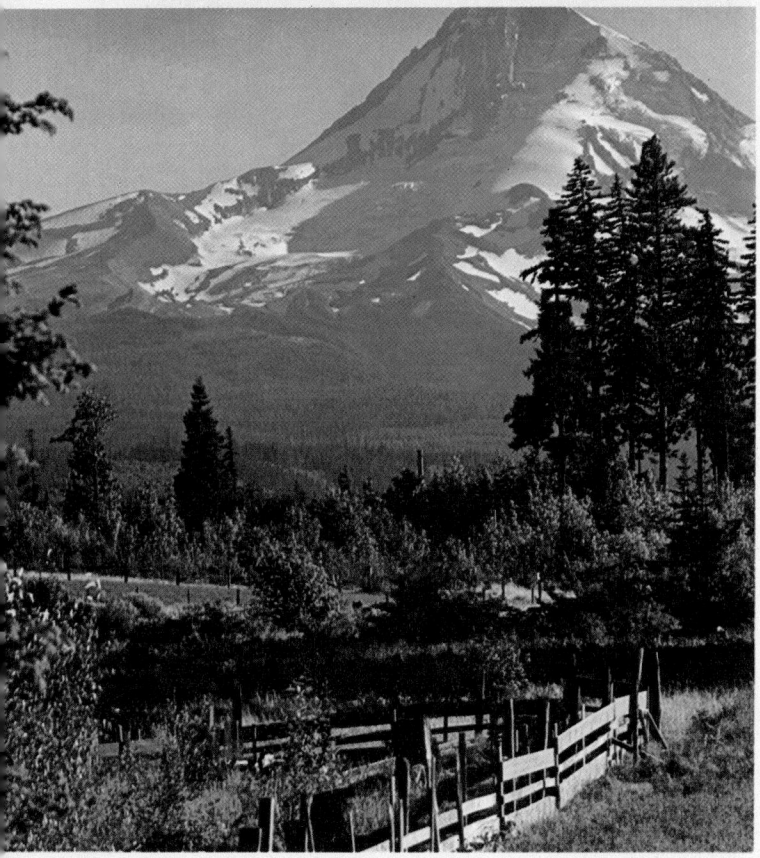

Not all of **Oregon** *is as rugged as Mount Hood (left). The state is the major timber production area for the U.S.A. and irrigation has enabled many other crops to be grown. Fishing also contributes to the economy.*

drinking, etc. 2. Drunken or licentious revel; (pl.) revelry, debauchery.

o·ri·el (ōr´ēel, ŏr´-) *n*. Large windowed polygonal recess projecting usu. from upper story and supported from ground or on corbels; (also ~ **window**) window or oriel, projecting window of upper story.

O·ri·ent (ōr´ēent, ŏr´-, -ĕnt) *n*. 1. The East of Asia, esp. the countries of E. Asia; (poet.) eastward part of sky or earth. 2. (o ~) Orient pearl. **orient**[1] *adj*. 1. (of precious stones, esp. pearls, of finest kinds, as coming anciently from the East) Lustrous, sparkling, precious. 2. (archaic, of sun etc.) Rising, nascent.

o·ri·ent[2] (ōr´ēent, ŏr´-) *v.t.* 1. Place (building etc.) so as to face east; build (church) with chancel end due E.; bury with feet eastward. 2. Place or exactly determine position of with regard to points of compass, settle or find bearings of; (fig.) bring into clearly understood relations; ~ **oneself**, determine how one stands; get one's bearings.

o·ri·en·tal (ōrēĕn´tal, ŏr-) *adj*. Of the Orient, esp. Asiatic; occurring in, coming from, the East, characteristic of its civilization etc.; (of pearls) orient. **o·ri·en´tal·ly** *adv*. **O·ri·en´tal** *n*. Native, inhabitant, of the Orient. **O·ri·en´tal·ism** *n*. **O·ri·en·tal·ize** (ōrēĕn´talīz, ŏr-) *v*. (**-ized, -iz·ing**). Make, become, Oriental.

o·ri·en·tate (ōr´ēĕntāt, ŏr´-) *v.t.* (**-tat·ed, -tat·ing**) = ORIENT. **o·ri·en·ta·tion** (ōrēĕntā´shon, ŏr-) *n*.

O·ri·en·te (ōrēĕn´tā). Province of Cuba where Fidel Castro and his supporters organized the overthrow of Batista, 1959.

or·i·fice (ōr´ifĭs, ăr´-) *n*. Aperture, mouth of cavity, perforation, vent.

or·i·ga·mi (ōrĭgah´mē) *n*. (pl. **-mis**). Japanese art of folding paper into decorative forms; example of this.

or·i·gin (ōr´ĭjĭn, ăr´-) *n*. Derivation, beginning or rising from something; extraction; source, starting point.

o·rig·i·nal (orĭj´inal) *adj*. 1. Existent from the first; primitive, innate, initial, earliest; ~ **sin**, (Christian theol.) innate depravity common to all human beings in consequence of the fall of man. 2. That has served as pattern, of which copy or translation has been made; not derivative or dependent, first-hand, not imitative; novei in

character or style, inventive, creative; thinking or acting for oneself. **o·rig´i·nal·ly** *adv*. **o·rig·i·nal·i·ty** (orĭjinăl´ĭtē) *n*. **original** *n*. Pattern, archetype; thing from which another is copied or imitated; eccentric person.

o·rig·i·nate (orĭj´ināt) *v*. (**-nat·ed, -nat·ing**). Give origin to, initiate, cause to begin; have origin, take rise. **o·rig·i·na·tion** (orĭjinā´shon), **o·rig´i·na·tor** *ns*.

O·ri·no·co (orĭnō´kō). River rising in SE. Venezuela and looping 1,500 miles (2,414 km) W., then N., and finally E. to the Atlantic Ocean.

o·ri·ole (ōr´ēōl, ŏr´-) *n*. 1. Any of a family (Oriolidae) of characteristically bright yellow and black birds of the Old World. 2. Any of a family (Icteridae) of Amer. birds, including the BALTIMORE oriole, the orchard oriole (*Icterus spurius*) and Bullock's oriole (*I. bullockii*), of which the males have bright yellow or orange and black plumage.

O·ri·on (ōrī´on, aw). 1. (Gk. legend) Giant and hunter of Boeotia, changed at his death into a constellation. 2. (astron.) Conspicuous constellation containing many bright stars; ~**'s belt**, three bright stars in short line across Orion.

or·i·son (ōr´ĭzon, ăr´-) (archaic) Prayer.

Ork·ney (ōrk´nē). Group islands off N. coast of Scotland.

Or·lan·do (ōrlăn´dō). City ar resort area in central Florida; si of Disneyworld.

Or·le·ans (ōr´lēanz; *Fr.* c lāahn´). (Fr. *Orléans*) French ci on River Loire; besieged by t English, 1428, and relieved by Jo of Arc.

Or·ly (ōr´lē; *Fr.* ōrlē´). Subu SE. of Paris; site of major inte national airport.

Or·mazd (ōr´mazd). In t Zoroastrian system, the supren deity, principle of goodness ar light, in perpetual conflict wi Ahriman.

or·mo·lu (ōr´molōō) *n*. Gild bronze used for the mounts furniture and other decorati metalwork, esp. in 18th c. Franc imitation of this, esp. gold-colore alloy of copper, zinc, and t articles made of or decorated wi this. [Fr. *or moulu* ground gold (f use in gilding)]

or·na·ment (ōr´nament) *n*. (eccles., usu. pl.) Accessories church or worship (e.g. alta chalice, service books, vestmen organ, bells, etc.). 2. Thing use

With widespread distribution, the golden **oriole** *lives on fruit and insects. Similar birds, grouped into a different genus, are present in the Americas.*

r serving to adorn; quality or
erson whose existence or presence
onfers grace or honor. 3. Adorn-
ng, being adorned, embellishment;
eatures or work added for decora-
ive purposes. 4. (pl. mus.) Grace
otes. **or·na·men'tal** *adj.* **or·na-
men'tal·ly** *adv.* **ornament**
ōr'namĕnt) *v.t.* Adorn, beautify.
r·na·men·ta·tion (ōrnamĕntā-
hon) *n.*

or·nate (ōrnāt') *adj.* Elaborately
dorned; embellished. **or·nate'ly**
dv. **or·nate'ness** *n.*

or·ni·thol·o·gy (ōrnĭthŏl'ojē) *n.*
Branch of zoology dealing with
irds. **or·ni·tho·log·i·cal** (ōrni-
hŏlŏj'ĭkal), **or·ni·tho·log'ic** *adjs.*
r·ni·tho·log'i·cal·ly *adv.* **or·ni-
hol'o·gist** *n.*

o·ro·tund (ōr'otŭnd, ōr'-) *adj.*
Magniloquent, pompous. **o·ro-
un·di·ty** (ōrotŭn'dĭtē, ōr-) *n.* [L.
re rotundo with round mouth]

O·roz·co (awraws'kaw), **José
Clemente** (1883–1949). Mexican
rtist and lithographer associated
vith modernist school; best known
or patriotic murals.

or·phan (ōr'fan) *n.* & *adj.*
Child) bereaved of parent(s). ~
.t.   Bereave   of   parent(s).
r·phan·age (ōr'fanĭj) *n.* (hist.)
nstitution for care of orphans.

Or·phe·us (ōr'fēus, -fūs). (Gk.
egend) Legendary Thracian pre-
Homeric poet; son of Calliope or
nother Muse; played so marvel-
usly on the lyre (given to him by
Apollo) that wild beasts were spell-
ound by his music; visited Hades
nd charmed Pluto into releasing
is wife Eurydice from the dead,
ut lost her because he failed to
bey the condition that he must not
ook back at her until they had
eached the world of the living.

Or·phic (ōr'fĭk) *adj.* Of Orpheus
r Orphism. **Or·phism** (ōr'fĭzem)
. Mystic religion of ancient
Greece, originating in 7th or 6th c.
.c. and based in poems (now lost)
ttributed to Orpheus, emphasizing
he mixture of good (or divine) and
vil in human nature and the
ecessity that the individual should
id himself of the evil part by ritual
nd moral purification throughout
series of reincarnations.

or·pi·ment (ōr'pĭment) *n.*
Bright yellow mineral, arsenic
risulfide (As_2S_3), used as a pig-
nent.

or·pine (ōr'pĭn) *n.* Succulent
erbaceous plant (*Sedum telephium*)
vith smooth fleshy leaves and
orymbs of purple flowers.

or·ris (ōr'ĭs, ăr'-) *n.* (also
r'risroot)   Powdered violet-

1

2

*People of many nations have long used
ornamentation for both body and
elongings. The Indian woman (1) is
avishly adorned with intricate silver-
ork. The beauty of the altar (2)
ymbolizes man's worship of God.*

scented root of three species of iris used in perfumery etc.

ort (ŏrt) *n.* (dial. and archaic; usu. pl.) Refuse, scrap(s), leavings.

Or·te·ga y Gas·set (ŏrtā´gah ē gahsĕt´), **José** (1883–1955). Spanish writer, philosopher, and statesman.

or·tho·chro·mat·ic (ŏrthokrōmăt´ĭk) *adj.* (phot.) Reproducing colors in their correct relative intensities.

or·tho·don·tia (ŏrthodŏn´sha), **or·tho·don·tics** (ŏrthodŏn´tĭks) *ns.* Branch of dentistry concerned with the correction of malformations of the teeth. **or·tho·don´tic** *adj.* **or·tho·don´tist** *n.*

or·tho·dox (ŏr´thodŏks) *adj.* Holding correct or currently accepted opinions esp. on religious doctrine; not heretical, original, or independent in mind; generally accepted as right or true, esp. in theology; in harmony with what is authoritatively established; approved, conventional; **O ~ Church**, (also **Eastern** or **Greek Church**) part of Christian Church separated from Catholic Church in 9th c., recognizing patriarch of Constantinople as head; any of the national Churches of Russia, Bulgaria, Rumania, etc., in communion with this. **or·tho·dox·y** *n.* Being orthodox.

or·tho·e·py (ŏrthō´epē, ŏr´thoĕpē) *n.* Study of correct pronunciation. **or·tho·ep·ic** (ŏrthoĕp´ĭk) *adj.* **or·tho·e·pist** (ŏrthō´epĭst) *n.*

or·tho·gen·e·sis (ŏrthojĕn´ĭsĭs) *n.* View of evolution according to which variations follow a defined direction and are not merely sporadic and fortuitous.

or·thog·ra·phy (ŏrthŏg´rafē) *n.* 1. Correct or conventional spelling; spelling with reference to its correctness. 2. Orthographic projection. **or·tho·graph·ic** (ŏrthogrăf´ĭk) *adj.* (of perspective projection in maps, elevations, etc.) In which point of sight is supposed to be at infinite distance, so that rays are parallel. **or·tho·graph´i·cal** *adj.* Of orthography. **or·tho·graph´i·cal·ly** *adv.*

or·tho·pe·dic (ŏrthopē´dĭk) *adj.* Of, relating to, orthopedics. **or·tho·pe´dics** *n.* Branch of surgery dealing with abnormalities and injuries of the bones and muscles, esp. in children. **or·tho·pe´dist** *n.*

or·thop·ter·ous (ŏrthŏp´terus) *adj.* Of the order Orthoptera of insects, including grasshoppers, crickets, etc., with straight narrow forewings, broad longitudinally folded hind wings, and incomplete metamorphosis.

or·thop·tic (ŏrthŏp´tĭk) *adj.* Of, concerning, the right or normal use of the eyes. **or·thop´tics** *n.* Correction of defective vision by means of exercises of the eye muscles. **or·thop´tist** *n.*

or·tho·rhom·bic (ŏrthorŏm´bĭk) *adj.* (cryst.) Having the three axes mutually at right angles and unequal.

or·tho·scop·ic (ŏrthoskŏp´ĭk)

Osaka, the 2nd-largest city in Japan. No other country in the world has had a more rapid industrial and economic growth since the 1939–45 war. Pictured is the traditional Osaka Castle.

A Greek Orthodox church in Athens, Greece. Declared ecclesiastically independent in 1833, the church has over 8,000,000 followers within Greece.

adj. Having, producing, correct vision; free from, constructed to correct, optical distortion.

or·to·lan (ŏr´tolan) *n.* One of the buntings (*Emberiza hortulana*), a small bird of Europe, N. Africa, and W. Asia, esteemed as table delicacy; the BOBOLINK.

Or·well (ŏr´wĕl), **George** (1903–50). Pseudonym of Eric Arthur Blair, English novelist, essayist, and political satirist; born in India; author of *Animal Farm* (1945), *1984* (1949), etc.

scimitar-horned oryx

fringe-eared oryx

o·ryx (ōr´ĭks, ōr´-, ār´-) *n.* (pl. **o·ryx·es**, collect. **o·ryx**). Large antelope (genus **O ~**) of Africa and Arabia, with long straight pointed horns.

O.S. *abbrev.* Ordinary seaman; out of stock.

O·sage (ō´sāj, ōsāj´) *n.* (pl. **O·sag·es**, collect. **O·sage**). (Member of) N. Amer. Indian tribe of Siouan linguistic stock, formerly occupying territory in Missouri and Arkansas; **~ orange**, N. Amer. thorny tree of mulberry family with large yellow fruit and hard flexible yellow wood; **~ River**, river flowing from E. Kansas to join the Missouri River in central Missouri.

O·sa·ka (ōsah´kah). Industrial city and seaport, second largest city in Japan, on SW. Honshu Island.

Os·can (ŏs´kan) *adj.* & *n.* (Of) the ancient Italic language spoken in Campania and farther S., and surviving only in inscriptions in an alphabet derived from Etruscan.

Os·car (ŏs´ker) *n.* Gold-plated statuette awarded annually by the Academy of Motion Picture Arts and Sciences, of Hollywood, California, for highest achievement in film acting production, etc. (loosely) similar award.

os·cil·late (ŏs´ilāt) *v.* (**-lat·ed, -lat·ing**). 1. Swing like pendulum, move to and fro; vacillate. 2. (of radio receiver) Radiate electromagnetic waves owing to faulty operation or construction. **os·cil·la·tion** (ŏsilā´shon) *n.* **os·cil·la·to·ry** (ŏs´ilatōrē, -tōrē) *adj.*

os·cil·lo·scope (osĭl´oskōp) *n.*

Device in which variations in an electrical quantity produce a temporary trace on the fluorescent screen of a cathode ray tube.

Os·co-Um·bri·an (ŏs´kōŭm´-brēan) *adj.* & *n.* (Of) the group of Italic languages comprising Oscan, Umbrian, and Volscian.

os·cu·lar (ŏs´kyuler) *adj.* Of the mouth; of kissing; (math.) that osculates.

os·cu·late (ŏs´kyulāt) *v.* (**-lat·ed, -lat·ing**). 1. Kiss (usu. joc.). 2. (biol., of species etc.) Have contact through intermediate species etc.; have common characters *with*. 3. (math., of curve or surface) Have contact of higher order with, coincide in three or more points. **os·cu·lant** (ŏs´kyulant), **os·cu·la·to·ry** (ŏs´kyulatōrē, -tōrē) *adjs.* **os·cu·la·tion** (ŏskyulā´shon) *n.*

os·cu·lum (ŏs´kyulum) *n.* (pl. **-la** pr. -la). Mouthlike aperture; mouth of sponge.

Osh·kosh (ŏsh´kŏsh). Resort city on Lake Winnebago in E. Wisconsin.

o·sier (ō´zher) *n.* (Shoot of) species of willow, esp. *Salix viminalis*, with tough pliant branches used in basketwork; attrib., of osiers.

O·si·ris (ōsī´rĭs). (Egyptian myth.) God of the underworld and husband of Isis; sometimes identified with the sun.

Os·ler (ōs´ler, ōz´-) **Sir William** (1849–1919). Canadian physician; founder member of (Brit.) Royal Society of Medicine; was a distinguished teacher and medical historian.

Os·lo (ŏz´lō, ŏs´-). Capital city of Norway, on SE. coast, founded *c*1050; (1624–1925) called Christiania in honor of King Christian IV, who refounded it after its destruction by fire in 1624.

os·mi·um (ŏz´mēum) *n.* (chem.) Metallic element of the platinum group, hard, brittle, bluish-white, and of high density; symbol Os, at no. 76, at. wt. 190.2. [Gk. *osmē* smell]

os·mo·sis (ŏzmō´sĭs, ŏs-) *n.* Tendency of a solvent, when separated from a solution by a suitable membrane (often animal or vegetable), to pass through the membrane so as to dilute the solution. **os·mot·ic** (ŏzmŏt´ĭk, ŏs-) *adj.* **~ pressure**, pressure produced by the solvent in osmosis. **os·mot´i·cal·ly** *adv.*

os·prey (ŏs´prē, -prā) *n.* (pl. **-preys**). 1. Large diurnal bird of prey, *Pandion haliaetus*, found on inland waters and preying on fish; fish hawk. 2. Egret plume formerly worn as ornament on hat etc.

Os·sian (ŏsh´an, ŏs´ēan). Legendary Gaelic 3rd-c. warrior and bard. **Os·si·an·ic** (ŏshēăn´ĭk,

Larger forms of antelope, the **oryx** of Africa and Arabia have had their populations reduced by excessive hunting and by agricultural intrusion on their grazing land. However, some species are now protected.

Jack Lemmon (left) with the **Oscar** he was awarded in 1973 by the Academy of Motion Picture Arts and Sciences. These highly-prized awards have been made since 1927–28.

ŏsē) *adj.* Of Ossian; of the style or character of the rhythmic prose of Macpherson's supposed translation of the poems of Ossian; hence, bombastic, grandiloquent.

os·si·cle (ŏs´ĭkel) *n.* (anat.) Small bone, esp. one of three in the middle ear; small piece of bony, chitinous, or calcareous substance in animal framework. **os·sic·u·lar** (ŏsĭk´yuler), **os·sic·u·late** (ŏsĭk´yulĭt) *adjs.*

os·si·fy (ŏs´ifī) *v.* (**-fied, -fy·ing**). Turn into bone; harden; make or become rigid, callous, or unprogressive. **os´si·fi·er, os·si·fi·ca·tion** (ŏsĭfĭkā´shon) *ns.*

os·su·ar·y (ŏsh´ōŏĕrē, ŏs´-) *n.* (pl. **-ar·ies**). Place or receptacle for bones of the dead.

os·ten·si·ble (ŏstĕn´sĭbel) *adj.* Professed, for show, put forward to conceal the real. **os·ten´si·bly** *adv.*

os·ten·sor·i·um (ŏstĕnsōr´eum, -sōr´-) *n.* (pl. **-sor·i·a** pr. -sōr´ĕa, -sōr´ĕa). Receptacle for displaying the Host to congregation. **os·ten·so·ry** (ŏstĕn´sorē) *n.* (pl. **-ries**).

os·ten·ta·tion (ŏstĕntā´shon) *n.* Pretentious display, esp. of wealth or luxury; showing off; attempt or intention to attract notice. **os·ten·ta·tious** (ŏstĕntā´shus) *adj.* **os·ten·ta´tious·ly** *adv.* **os·ten·ta´tious·ness** *n.*

osteo- *prefix.* Bone.

os·te·o·ar·thri·tis (ŏstēōärthrī´tĭs) *n.* Degenerative arthritis, esp. in elderly persons.

os·te·ol·o·gy (ŏstēŏl´ojē) *n.* Branch of anatomy concerned with the study of the skeleton and the structure of bones. **os·te·o·log·i·cal** (ŏstēolŏj´ĭkal) *adj.* **os·te·o·log´i·cal·ly** *adv.* **os·te·ol´o·gist** *n.*

os·te·o·my·e·li·tis (ŏstēōmīelī´tĭs) *n.* Inflammation of (esp. the marrow) a bone.

os·te·op·a·thy (ŏstēŏp´athē) *n.* Theory of disease and method of cure based on assumption that deformation of part of skeleton, notably the spine, and consequent interference with nerves and blood vessels, are the cause of most diseases. **os·te·o·path·ic** (ŏstēo·păth´ĭk) *adj.* **os·te·o·path´i·cal·ly** *adv.* **os·te·o·path** (ŏs´tēopăth) *n.* Practitioner of osteopathy.

Ost·po·li·tik (awst´pawlĭtēk´) *n.* Policies of a European country toward Communist countries. [Ger. *ost*, east]

os·tra·cize (ŏs´trasīz) *v.t.* (**-cized, -ciz·ing**). 1. (in ancient Athens) Banish (dangerously powerful or unpopular citizen) for 5 or 10 years by voting with potsherds or tiles (*ostraka*) on which name of person to be banished was written. 2. Exclude from society, refuse to associate with. **os·tra·cism** (ŏs´trasĭzem) *n.*

os·trich (aw´strĭch, ŏs´trĭch) *n.* (pl. **-trich·es**, collect. **-trich**). Very large swift-running bird (*Struthio camelus*) of sandy plains of Africa and formerly Arabia, with small wings useless for flight, and habit of swallowing hard substances to assist working of gizzard; proverbial for self-delusion owing to the (unfounded) belief that when pursued the ostrich buries its head in the sand imagining that it cannot then be seen; ~ **plume**, wing or tail feather of ostrich as ornament.

Os·tro·goth (ŏs´trogŏth) *n.*

*The **osprey** or fish-hawk hunts by diving and seizing fish at the surface in its talons. It has wide distribution though populations have been depleted by pesticides which accumulate in fish and sterilize the birds' eggs.*

Member of eastern branch of GOTHS, who toward end of 5th c. conquered Italy, and under their leader THEODORIC established kingdom in Italy, Sicily, and Dalmatia which lasted until 55[?]. **Os·tro·goth´ic** *adj.*

Os·wald (ŏz´wawld), **Lee Harvey** (1939–1963). Alleged assassin of President John F. Kennedy 1963; while being transferred from jail, he was himself shot and killed.

OT, O.T. *abbrevs.* Old Testament.

o·ta·ry (ō´tarē) *n.* Member of the Otariidae, a mainly Antarctic family of seals with small external ear, including fur seals and sea lion; eared seal.

oth·er (ŭdh´er) *adj.* Not the same as one or more or some already mentioned or implied; separate in identity, distinct in kind; alternative, further, or additional; **ever ~**, every alternate; **the ~**, the one remaining; **the ~ day**, a few days ago; **on the ~ hand**, in contrast (with fact or argument just mentioned); ~ **than**, different from; ~ **things being equal**, with conditions alike in everything but the point in question; **the ~ world**, life after death; **oth´er·world´ly** (*adj.*), concerned with or thinking of this or some imagined world to the neglect of the present one. **other** *n.* or *pron.* (orig. elliptic use of *adj.*) Other person, thing, specimen, etc.; **someone or ~**, person unknown. **other** *adv.* Otherwise.

oth·er·wise (ŭdh´erwīz) *adv.* In a different way; if circumstances are or were different, else, or; in other respects; in a different state.

o·tic (ō´tĭk, ŏt´ĭk) *adj.* Of the ear.

o·ti·ose (ō´shēōs, ō´tē-) *adj.* Not required, serving no practical purpose. **o'ti·ose·ly** *adv.* **o'ti·os·-ty** (ōshĕŏs´ĭtē, ōtē-), **o'ti·ose·ness** *ns.*

o·ti·tis (ōtī´tĭs) *n.* Inflammation of the ear.

o·to·lar·yn·gol·o·gy (ōtōlărĭng-gŏl´ojē), **o·to·rhi·no·lar·yn·gol·o·gy** (ōtōrī´nōlărĭnggŏl´ojē) *ns.* Branch of medicine dealing with diseases of ear, nose, and throat. **o·to·lar·yn·gol·o·gist, o·to·rhi´·no·lar·yn·gol·o·gist** *ns.*

ot·ta·va ri·ma (awtah´väh rē´-nah). Italian stanza of eight 11-syllabled lines (ten-syllabled in English), the first six lines rhyming alternately, the last two forming a couplet.

Ot·ta·wa (ŏt´awa). City of Ontario and capital of Canada, situated on the ~ **River**, a tributary of the St. Lawrence.

ot·ter (ŏt´er) *n.* (pl. **-ters**, collect. **-ter**). 1. Aquatic fur-bearing carnivorous mammal of genus *Lutra* and related genera, feeding chiefly on fish, with webbed feet and pointed tail somewhat flattened horizontally; fur of this. 2. (minesweeping) Steel frame shaped like a box kite for holding sweep wires at required depth.

Ot·to·man (ŏt´oman) *adj.* Of the Ottoman Empire; ~ **Empire**, Turkish Empire in SW. Asia, NE. Africa, and SE. Europe, founded *c*1300 and lasting until 1919; capital, Constantinople. **Ottoman** *n.* (pl. **-mans**). Turk.

ot·to·man (ŏt´oman) *n.* (pl. **-mans**). Cushioned seat like sofa or chair without back or arms (freq. a box with cushioned top).

Oua·ga·dou·gou (wahgadoo´-goo). Capital of Upper Volta, in the central region.

ou·bli·ette (ooblēĕt´) *n.* Secret dungeon with entrance only by trapdoor above.

ouch (owch) *int.* Exclamation of pain or annoyance.

ought[1], **aught** (awt) *ns.* (colloq.) Figure denoting nothing, nought.

ought[2] (awt) *v. aux.* Expressing duty, rightness, shortcoming, advisability, or strong probability.

ought[3] (awt) = AUGHT.[1]

Oui·ja (wē´ja, -jē) **board.** (trademark) Board with letters, signs, etc., used with planchette for obtaining messages in spiritualist séances. [Fr. *oui* yes; Ger. *ja* yes]

ounce[1] (owns) *n.* (abbrev. oz.). Unit of weight, $\frac{1}{16}$ lb. in avoirdupois, $\frac{1}{12}$ lb. in troy weight; **fluid** ~, 8 (fluid) drachms, $\frac{1}{16}$ of pint, $\frac{1}{20}$ of imperial pint; (fig.) very small quantity. [L. *uncia* twelfth (of pound or foot)]

ounce[2] (owns) *n.* 1. (poet.) Lynx or other vaguely identified feline beast. 2. (zool.) Snow leopard (*Uncia uncia*) of highlands of central Asia, smaller and lighter in color than leopard but with similar

The largest living bird, the flightless **ostrich,** *was once present in southwest Asia. Today it is confined to east Africa although it is still farmed in South Africa. It can run at 40 m.p.h.*

markings.

our (owr, ow´er, är) *poss. pron.* Possessive case of WE used as attrib. adjective, with absolute and predicate form **ours** (pr. owrz, ow´erz, ärz), belonging to us.

our·self (owrsĕlf´, ower-, är-) *pron.* (pl. **-selves** pr. -sĕlvz). Emphatic and reflexive form corresp. to WE, US.

ou·sel (oo´zel) = OUZEL.

oust (owst) *v.t.* Put out of possession, eject, expel *from*, drive out; force oneself or be put into the place of.

out (owt) *adv.* 1. Away from or not in or at a place, the right or normal state, the fashion, etc.; not at home; (of calculation) inaccurate; (boxing) unable to put up a defense,

giant otter

european otter

*The giant **otter** from Brazil (left) can be up to 8 ft. long and may weigh 75 lb. The European variety (right) is only a third or less of the other's weight. Both are aquatic carnivores.*

e.g. ~ **for the count** (i.e. the counting of seconds from one to ten); not at work, on strike; (of fire etc.) no longer burning. 2. In(to) the open, publicity, hearing, sight, notice, etc.; ~ **for,** ~ **to do,** (colloq.) engaged in seeking; ~ **and about,** able to leave bed or house. 3. To or at an end, completely; (in oral communication by radio etc., as indication) transmission ends; **all** ~, with greatest effort; ~ **and away,** by far; ~ **and** ~, thorough(ly), surpassing(ly). 4. ~ **of,** from within; not within; from among; beyond range of; (so as to be) without; from, owing to, by use of (material); at specified distance from; beyond; transgressing rules of; (of animals) having as dam; ~ **of doors,** in, into the open air; ~ **of it,** not included, forlorn, at a loss; ~-**of-the-way,** remote; uncommon, remarkable; ~ **of this world,** (esp.) superlatively good. **out** *prep.* Out of (now only in **from** ~). **out** *adj.* 1. External, living etc. outside. 2. (baseball) Not successful in reaching base safely. ~ *n.* 1. Way of escape. 2. (baseball) Any play that retires a batter or base runner; player thus retired. 3. (tennis) Return or serve hit out of bounds. 4. (pl.) **ins and** ~s: see IN; **on the** or **at** ~s, at variance or enmity.

out- *prefix.* External; detached; out of; to excess; so as to surpass.

out·back (*adj.* owt'băk'; *n.* owt'-băk) *adj. & n.* (Austral.) (Of the) more remote settlements. **out'-back·er** *n.* Dweller in outback.

out·bid (owtbĭd') *v.t.* (**-bid, -bid·den** or **-bid, -bid·ding**). Outdo in bidding, offer more than.

out·board (owt'bōrd, -bôrd) *adj.* On, toward, nearer to, outside of ship or aircraft; (of motorboat) with engine and propeller attached

outside boat at stern. ~ *adv.* To, toward, outside of ship or aircraft.

out·break (owt'brāk) *n.* Breaking out of emotion (esp. anger), hostilities, disease, fire, volcanic energy, etc.; outcrop; insurrection.

out·build·ing (owt'bĭldĭng) *n.* House, building, shed belonging to and near or built against main house.

out·burst (owt'bẽrst) *n.* Explosion of feeling, esp. expressed by vehement words; volcanic eruption.

out·cast (owt'kăst, -kahst) *adj. & n.* 1. (Person) cast out from home and friends; homeless and friendless (vagabond). 2. (Person) who has lost or been expelled from his caste, or who does not belong to a caste.

out·class (owtklăs', -klahs') *v.t.* Belong to higher class than, completely beat or surpass.

out·come (owt'kŭm) *n.* Issue, result.

out·crop (owt'krŏp) *n.* Emergence of stratum, vein, or rock at surface.

out·cry (owt'krī) *n.* (pl. **-cries**). Clamor, uproar.

out·dis·tance (owtdĭs'tans) *v.t.* (**-tanced, -tanc·ing**). Get far ahead of.

out·do (owtdoō') *v.t.* (**-did, -done, -do·ing**). Surpass, excel.

out·door (owt'dōr, -dôr) *adj.* Done, existing, or used outdoors. **out·doors** (owtdōrz', -dôrz') *adv.* Out of doors.

out·er (ow'ter) *adj.* Farther from center or inside, relatively far out; external, of the outside; objective, physical, not subjective or psy-

chical. **out·er·most** (ow'termōst) *adj.*

out·face (owtfās') *v.t.* (**-faced, -fac·ing**). Look out of countenance, stare down; confront fearlessly or impudently, brave, defy.

out·field (owt'fēld) *n.* Outer part of baseball field, beyond the baseball DIAMOND; hence **out'-field·er** *n.*

out·fit (owt'fĭt) *n.* Complete equipment; party traveling or in charge of herds of cattle etc.; (colloq.) organized group of persons (esp. military unit). ~ *v.t.* (**-fit·ted, -fit·ting**). Provide with outfit; supply *with.* **out'fit·ter** *n.* Supplier of equipment; retailer of men's ready-made clothes.

out·flank (owtflăngk') *v.t.* Get beyond flank of (opposing army), outmaneuver by flanking movement. **out·flank'er** *n.*

out·flow (owt'flō) *n.* What flows out, amount flowing out.

out·fox (owtfŏks') *v.t.* Outwit.

out·gen·er·al (owtjĕn'eral) *v.t.* (**-aled** or **-alled, -al·ing** or **-al·ling**). Defeat by superior generalship.

out·go (owt'gō) *n.* (pl. **-goes**). Expenditure, outlay.

out·go·ing (owt'gōing) *adj.* 1. Friendly. 2. Retiring from a position. 3. (of, ebbing tide) Going out.

out·grow (owtgrō') *v.t.* (**-grew, -grown, -grow·ing**). Grow faster, get taller, than; get too big for (clothes); get rid of (childish habit, ailment, taste) with advancing age.

out·growth (owt'grōth) *n.* Offshoot; consequence.

out·Her·od (owt-hěr'od) *v.t.* Be more violent or hectoring than Herod (represented in old mystery plays as a blustering tyrant); outdo, surpass.

out·house (owt'hows) *n.* (pl.

hous·es pr. -howzĭz). Privy.
out·ing (ow′tĭng) n. Pleasure
rip, holiday away from home.
out·land·er (owt′lănder) n. 1.
esp. poet.) Alien. 2. =
UITLANDER.
out·land·ish (owtlăn′dĭsh) adj.
oreign looking or sounding; un-
miliar, bizarre, uncouth. **out·-
and′ish·ly** adv. **out·land′ish·-
ess** n.
out·last (owtlăst′) v.t. Last
nger than.
out·law (owt′law) n. Person
eprived of protection of the law,
anished or exiled person. ~ v.t.
roscribe, declare outlaw. **out·-
aw′ry** (owt′lawrē) n. Condition of,
ondemnation as, outlaw.
out·lay (owt′lā) n. What one
pends, expenses.
out·let (owt′lĕt, -lĭt) n. Means
f exit or escape, vent, way out;
narket for goods.
out·line (owt′līn) n. Line(s)
nclosing the apparently plane
gure presented by any object to
ght, contour, external boundary;
ketch containing only contour
nes and no shading; rough draft,
erbal description of essential parts
nly, summary; (pl.) main features,
eneral principles. ~ v.t. (**-lined,
lin·ing**). Draw or describe in

outline; mark outline of. **out·-
lin′er** n.
out·live (owtlĭv′) v.t. (**-lived,
-liv·ing**). Live beyond; come
safely through, get over effect of;
live longer than.
out·look (owt′look) n. What one
sees on looking out, view, prospect;
person's general view of life; what
seems likely to happen.
out·ly·ing (owt′līing) adj. Situated far from a center, remote.
out·ma·neu·ver (owtmanoō′-
ver) v.t. Get the better of by
superior strategy.
out·match (owtmăch′) v.t. Be
more than a match for.
out·mod·ed (owtmō′dĭd) adj.
Out of date, old-fashioned.
out·most (owt′mōst) adj.
Outermost.
out·num·ber (owtnŭm′ber) v.t.
Exceed in number.
out·pa·tient (owt′pāshent) n.
One receiving treatment at hospital
etc. without being lodged in it.
out·play (owtplā′) v.t. Surpass
in playing; play better than.
out·point (owtpoint′) v.t. 1.

*In Australia, the **outback** was a term
derived from 'back blocks' — land made
available for grazing after the 1850s
and distant from any centres of population.*

Score more points than. 2. (nautical) Sail closer to the wind than.
3. (boxing) Win through superior
skill rather than through knockout.
out·post (owt′pōst) n. Detachment on guard at some distance
from army to prevent surprise.
out·pour·ing (owt′pōrĭng,
-pōr-) n. Effusion; verbal or literary
expression of emotion.
out·put (owt′poot) n. 1. Amount
produced by manufacture, mining,
labor, etc.; product; current etc.
produced by electrical device. 2.
Information, results, etc. produced
by a computer. ~ v.t. (**-put·ted,
-put·ting**). (of a computer) To
produce such information.
out·rage (owt′rāj) n. Forcible
violation of others' rights, sentiments, etc.; deed of violence, gross
or wanton offense or indignity. ~
v.t. (**-raged, -rag·ing**). Do
violence to, subject to outrage,
injure, insult, violate; infringe (law,
morality, etc.) flagrantly. **out·-
ra·geous** (owtrā′jus) adj.
Immoderate, extravagant, extraordinary; violent, furious; grossly
cruel, immoral, offensive, or
abusive. **out·ra′geous·ly** adv.
out·ra′geous·ness n.
out·rank (owtrăngk′) v.t. Be
superior in rank to.

Outrigger canoes on Sanur beach in Bali. These speedy lightweight canoes have a small sail which adds to their range. The two struts on either side give it an additional stability.

Stone ovens are still used in the open in Bergama, Turkey (above right) and elsewhere. Compared with them, modern kitchen stoves seem to be as advanced mechanically as industrial kilns used by potteries in Northern Ireland (right).

ou·tré (o͞otrā´) *adj.* Outside the bounds of propriety, eccentric. [Fr.]

out·reach (owtrēch´) *v.t.* Reach farther than; surpass; (poet.) stretch out (arm etc.).

out·rid·er (owt´rīd*er*) *n.* Mounted attendant riding before, behind, or with carriage.

out·rig·ger (owt´rĭg*er*) *n.* Beam, spar, framework, rigged out and projecting from or over ship's side for various purposes; bracket supporting rowlock beyond boat's side to enable a long oar to be conveniently used in a narrow boat; boat with such outriggers; ~ **canoe**, canoe having a long float parallel to its side, attached by beams.

out·right (owt´rīt) *adv.* Altogether, entirely, once for all, not by degrees or installments or half-and-half; without reservation, openly. **outright** (owt´rīt) *adj.* Downright, direct, thorough. **out´right·ness** *n.*

out·run (owtrŭn´) *v.t.* (**-ran, -run, -run·ning**). Outstrip in running; pass the limit of.

out·set (owt´sĕt) *n.* Start, commencement.

out·shine (owtshīn´) *v.t.* (**-shone, -shin·ing**). Surpass in brightness, splendor, or excellence.

out·side (owt´sīd´, owt´sīd, out-sīd´) *n.* 1. Outer side or surface; (of path) side away from wall or next to road. 2. Outer part, exterior; outward aspect. 3. Highest computation. **outside** (owtsīd´, owt´sīd) *adj.* Situated on, derived from, the outside; not belonging to some circle or institution; greatest existent or possible; ~ **chance**, remote, very unlikely chance. **outside´** *adv.* On or to the outside, the open air, open sea, etc.; not within. **outside** (owtsīd´, owt´sīd) *prep.* External to; beyond the limits of; at or to the outside of.

out·sid·er (owtsī´d*er*) *n.* Non-member of some circle, party, profession, etc., uninitiated person, layman; person without special knowledge, breeding, etc., or not fit to mix with good society; horse or person not thought to have a chance in race or competition.

out·size (owt´sīz) *n.* Person or thing larger than the normal, esp ready-made article of dress larger than the standard size (also attrib.)

out·skirts (owt´skĕrts) *n.pl* Outer border, fringe, of city, district, etc.

out·smart (owtsmärt´) *v.t.* Outwit, be smarter than.

out·spo·ken (owtspō´ken) *adj* Frank, unreserved. **out·spo´ken·ly** *adv.* **out·spo´ken·ness** *n.*

out·spread (owt´sprĕd´) *adj* Spread out.

out·stand·ing (owtstăn´dĭng) *adj.* Prominent; still unsettled. **out·stand´ing·ly** *adv.* **out·stand´ing·ness** *n.*

out·stay (owtstā´) *v.t.* Stay

*his suburb on the **outskirts** of hoenix, Arizona is a clear indication of at city's encroachment on the agricul- ral surrounds. As the population creases the urban spread continues.*

*When the sky is **overcast,** masses of clouds cover it so that no direct sunlight reaches the earth. Common in temperate zones, this also occurs during the wet season in the tropics.*

eyond limits of, exhaust by staying; stay longer than.

out·strip (owtstrĭp´) *v.t.* **-stripped, -strip·ping**). Pass in unning etc.; surpass in competition or relative progress or ability.

out·vote (owtvōt´) *v.t.* (**-vot·ed, vot·ing**). Outnumber in voting.

out·ward (owt´werd) *adj.* Outer archaic); directed toward the outide; bodily, external, material, isible, apparent, superficial; ~ **orm**, appearance. **outward** *adv.* *also* **out´wards**) In an outward lirection; ~**-bound**, (of ship or passenger) going away from home. **out´ward·ly** *adv.* **out´ward·ness** *n.*

out·weigh (owtwā´) *v.t.* Exceed n weight, value, importance, or nfluence.

out·wit (owtwĭt´) *v.t.* (**-wit·ted, wit·ting**). Prove too clever for, verreach, take in.

out·work (owt´werk) *n.* Part of fortifications lying outside parapet; letached or advanced part of fortiication. **out·work´** *v.t.* (**-worked r -wrought, -work·ing**). Surpass in work.

out·worn (owtwōrn´, -wōrn´) *adj.* Worn out; exhausted, spent.

ou·zel, ou·sel (oo´zel) *ns.* 1. Any of several black European thrushes. 2. see DIPPER.

ou·zo (oo´zō) *n.* (pl. **-zos**). Greek iqueur flavored with anise.

o·val (ō´val) *adj.* Egg-shaped, llipsoidal; having the outline of an egg, elliptical; **the O ~ Office,** White House office of the U.S. President; hence, the Presidency. val *n.* Closed curve with one axis onger than the other, like ellipse r outline of egg; thing with oval utline.

o·va·ry (ō´varē) *n.* (pl. **-ries**).

Organ of female reproductive system, that in which ova or eggs are produced; in plants, lowest part of pistil, ultimately becoming fruit or seed vessel. **o·var·i·an** (ōvār´ēan) *adj.*

o·vate (ō´vāt) *adj.* (biol.) Egg-shaped, oval.

o·va·tion (ōvā´shon) *n.* Enthusiastic reception, spontaneous applause. **o·va´tion·al** *adj.*

ov·en (ŭv´en) *n.* Enclosed chamber or compartment for baking, heating, drying, etc.; **Dutch ~**: see DUTCH; **ov´enware,** dishes that can be used for cooking food in an oven.

o·ver (ō´ver) *adv.* 1. Outward and downward from brink (as *push ~ the edge*) or from erect position (*lean ~*). 2. So as to cover or touch whole surface (*paint it ~*). 3. With motion above something so as to pass across something (*climb ~*). 4. So as to produce fold or reverse position (*bend it ~*; *turn ~*, turn other side of leaf up). 5. Across street or other space or distance; ~ **against**, in opposite situation to, in contrast with. 6. With transference or change from one hand, party, etc., to another; (in radio communication etc., as indication) changing from transmission to reception. 7. Too, in excess; in addition, besides; more; apart, ~ **and above**, moreover, into the bargain. 8. From beginning to end, with repetition, with detailed consideration (*read ~*, *talk (matter) ~*). 9. At an end, done with (*the war is ~*). **over** *prep.* 1. Above, on, at all or various points upon; to and fro upon, all through, round about; concerning, engaged with. 2. With or so as to get or give superiority to; beyond, more

than; ~ **and above**, besides, not to mention. 3. Out and down from, down from edge of; so as to clear; across, on or to the other side of; throughout, through duration of, till end of; **stumble ~**, be tripped up by.

over- *prefix.* Over; upper, outer; superior; excessive.

o·ver·act (ōverăkt´) *v.* Act (part, emotion, etc.), act part, with exaggeration.

o·ver·all (ō´verawl) *n.* Garment worn over others as protection against wet, dirt, etc.; (pl.) trousers with chest piece for dirty work. **o·ver·all´** *adj.* Taking into account all features or aspects; inclusive. ~ *adv.* In all parts; taken as a whole.

o·ver·arm (ō´verārm) *adv. & adj.* = OVERHAND.

o·ver·awe (ōveraw´) *v.t.* (**-awed, -aw·ing**). Restrain, control, or repress by awe.

o·ver·bear (ōverbār´) *v.t.* (**-bore, -borne, -bear·ing**). Bear down or upset by weight or force; put down, repress, by power or authority; surpass in importance etc., outweigh. **o·ver·bear´ing** *adj.* Domineering, masterful **o·ver·bear´ing·ly** *adv.* **o·ver·bear´ing·ness** *n.*

o·ver·blown (ōverblōn´) *adj.* (of flower) Too fully open, past its prime.

o·ver·board (ō´verbōrd, -bord) *adv.* From within ship into water; **throw ~**, (fig.) abandon, discard.

o·ver·bur·den (ōverber´den *v.*; ōv´erber´den *n.*) *v.t.* Burden too much, overload, overcharge. ~ *n.* (geol.) Soil etc. overlying a mineral deposit.

o·ver·call (ōverkawl´) *v.t.* (bridge) Bid more on (hand) than it is worth; bid higher than (opponent, previous bid, one's partner when opponent has not done so). **o´vercall** *n.* Bid made over partner's bid.

o·ver·cap·i·tal·ize (ōverkăp´ĭ-

*An **overpass** in Massachusetts (above) is typical of methods adopted by modern traffic engineers to allow faster traffic flow and to reduce the incidence of accidents by eliminating cross-roads.*

talīz) *v.t.* (**-ized, -iz·ing**). Fix or estimate capital of (company etc.) too high. **o·ver·cap·i·tal·i·za·tion** (ō′verkăpĭtalĭzā′shon) *n.*

o·ver·cast (ōverkăst′, ō′verkăst) *v.t.* (**-cast, -cast·ing**). 1. Cover (sky etc.) with clouds or darkness (usu. in past part. **overcast**). 2. Sew over raw edges of (material, esp. with blanket or buttonhole stitch) to prevent unraveling.

o·ver·charge (ōverchärj′) *v.t.* (**-charged, -charg·ing**). 1. Charge too highly with explosive, electricity, etc. 2. Put exaggerated details or too much detail into (description etc.). 3. Charge too high a price for (thing) or to (person); charge (specified sum) beyond right price. **o′ver·charge** *n.* Excessive charge. **o·ver·charg′er** *n.*

o·ver·coat (ō′verkōt) *n.* Large coat worn over ordinary clothing, esp. in cold weather.

o·ver·come (ōverkŭm′) *v.* (**-came, -come, -com·ing**). Prevail over, master, get the better of; be victorious. ~ *adj.* (esp.) Exhausted, made helpless, deprived

of self-possession.

o·ver·crowd (ōverkrowd′) *v.* Crowd to excess; esp., crowd more people into a space than there is proper accommodation for.

o·ver·do (ōverdoo′) *v.t.* (**-did, -done, -do·ing**). Carry to excess, go too far in; cook too long (esp. in past part.); overtax strength of (esp. in past part.). **o·ver·do′er** *n.*

o·ver·dose (ō′verdōs) *n.* Excessive dose.

o·ver·draft (ō′verdrăft) *n.* Overdrawing of bank account; amount by which check exceeds balance.

o·ver·draw (ōverdraw′) *v.* (**-drew, -drawn, -draw·ing**). 1. Draw check in excess of (one's account). 2. Exaggerate in describing.

o·ver·dress (ōverdrĕs′) *v.* Dress with too much display and ornament.

o·ver·drive (ō′verdrīv) *n.*

(mech.) System by which a speed higher than that maintained by the engine is passed to the propeller shaft.

o·ver·due (ōverdoo′, -dū′) *adj.* More than due; late, in arrear.

o·ver·eat (ōverēt′) *v.* (**-ate, -eat·en, -eat·ing**). Eat to excess.

o·ver·es·ti·mate (ōverĕs′tĭmāt) *v.t.* (**-mat·ed, -mat·ing**). Estimate too highly. ~ (ō′verĕs′-tĭmĭt) *n.* Too high an estimate. **o′ver·es·ti·ma′tion** *n.*

o·ver·flow (ō′verflō) *n.* What overflows or is superfluous; outlet for excess liquid; ~ **meeting**, meeting elsewhere of those who have not found room at demonstration etc. **overflow′** *v.* (**-flowed, -flown, -flow·ing**). Flow over (brim etc.), flood (surface); extend beyond limits of; (of receptacle) be so full that contents overflow; (of kindness, harvest, etc.) be very abundant. **o·ver·flow′ing** *n. & adj.* **o·ver·flow′ing·ly** *adv.*

o·ver·fly (ōverflī′) *v.t.* (**-flew, -flown, -fly·ing**). (of aircraft) Fly over (territory); fly beyond.

o·ver·glaze (ō′verglāz) *n.*

Special mountaineering techniques are needed to negotiate an overhang when a cliff is being scaled. The overhang illustrated above is in the Swiss Alps.

Second glaze applied to pottery over first glaze. ~ *adj*. (of painting etc.) Done on glazed surface.

o·ver·grow (ōvergrō´) *v*. -grew, -grown, -grow·ing). Grow over, cover with growth; grow too large; grow too big etc. for. **o·ver·hand** (ōverhănd) *adv*. & *dj*. (sports) With hand above bject held; with hand above houlder in baseball etc.; with hand r arm out of water in swimming. **´ver·hand·ed** *adv*.

o·ver·hang (ōverhăng´) *v*. -hung, -hang·ing). Jut out over, ut; (fig.) impend (over). **o´ver-ang** *n*. Thing that overhangs; act or amount of overhanging.

o·ver·haul (ōverhawl´) *v.t*. Take part for purpose of examining, xamine condition of and repair; esp. naut.) catch up, come up with. **·ver·haul´er** *n*.

o·ver·head (ōverhĕd´) *adv*. On igh; in the sky; in the story above. **´verhead** *adj*. Placed overhead. ~ *n*. 1. The general expenses of unning a business. 2. A stroke in a acket game made with a downward motion from above head height.

o·ver·hear (ōverhēr´) *v.t*. (-heard, -hear·ing). Hear as eavesdropper or unperceived or unintended listener.

o·ver·joyed (ōverjoid´) *adj*. Transported with joy (*at*).

o·ver·kill (ō´verkĭl) *n*. Amount by which (capacity for) destruction (lit. or fig.) exceeds what is necessary for victory over or annihilation of enemy.

o·ver·lad·en (ōverlā´den) *adj*. Overloaded, overburdened.

o·ver·land (ō´verlănd, -land) *adv*. By land and not sea. ~ *adj*. Entirely or partly by land.

o·ver·lap (ōverlăp´) *v*. (-lapped, -lap·ping). Partly cover; cover and extend beyond; partly coincide. **o´verlap** *n*. Thing that overlaps; fact or amount of overlapping.

o·ver·lay (ōverlā´) *v.t*. (-laid, -lay·ing). Cover surface of *with* coating etc. **o´verlay** *n*. Thing

laid over something, coverlet, small tablecloth, etc.

o·ver·leaf (ō´verlēf) *adv*. On other side of leaf (of book etc.).

o·ver·leap (ōverlēp´) *v.t*. (-leap-ed or -leapt, -leap·ing). Leap over, surmount; omit, ignore.

o·ver·load (ōverlōd´) *v.t*. Load to excess. **o´verload** *n*. Excessive load or charge, as of electric current.

o·ver·look (ōverlook´) *v.t*. 1. Have prospect of or over from above; be higher than. 2. Fail to observe, take no notice of, condone. 3. Superintend, oversee. 4. Bewitch with evil eye.

o·ver·lord (ō´verlōrd) *n*. Supreme lord, suzerain. **o´ver-lord·ship** *n*.

o·ver·ly (ō´verlē) *adv*. Over, excessively.

o·ver·much (ō´vermŭch´) *adj*., *n*., & *adv*. Too much.

o·ver·night (ō´vernīt´) *adv*. On the preceding evening (in relation to following day); through the night (till the following morning). **o´ver·night** *adj*. Done etc. overnight.

o·ver·pass (ō´verpăs) *n*. Road bridge over another road, esp. over a motorway.

o·ver·play (ōverplā´) *v.t*. Play part to excess; give undue importance to; ~ **one's hand** (cards or fig.) be unduly optimistic as to one's capabilities.

o·ver·pow·er (ōverpow´er) *v.t*. Reduce to submission, subdue, master; be too intense or violent for, overwhelm. **o·ver·pow´er·ing** *adj*. **o·ver·pow´er·ing·ly** *adv*. **o·ver·pow´er·ing·ness** *n*.

o·ver·print (ōverprĭnt´) *v.t*. Print (photographic print) darker than intended; print (additional matter or another color) on already printed surface, esp. of postage stamp. **o´ver·print** *n*.

o·ver·rate (ōverrāt´) *v.t*. (-rat·ed, -rat·ing). Have too high an opinion of; assess too high for rating purposes.

o·ver·reach (ōverrēch´) *v*. 1. (refl.) Strain *oneself* by reaching too far; (of horse) injure forefoot by striking it with hind hoof. 2. Circumvent, outwit, get the better of by cunning or artifice.

o·ver·ride (ōverrīd´) *v.t*. (-rode, -rid·den, -rid·ing). 1. Exhaust (horse) by riding. 2. Ride over (enemy's country) with armed force; trample (person) under one's horse's hoofs; (fig.) trample under foot, set aside, refuse to comply with, have or claim superior authority to. **o´verride** *n*. Sales commission paid to executive in addition to that paid to salesperson.

o·ver·rule (ōverrool´) *v.t*. (-ruled, -rul·ing). Set aside (decision, argument, etc.) by superior authority; annul decision

*Making **overstrung** pianos (above) demands painstaking craftsmanship. By placing the bass strings so that they partly overlap the tenor ones, but on a different plane, space is saved and the finished instruments produce greater resonance.*

or reject proposal of (person).

o·ver·run (ōverrŭn´) *v.t.* (**-ran, -run, -run·ning**). Flood, harry and spoil (enemy's country); swarm or spread over; exceed (limit). **o´verrun** *n.* Amount by which (cost, production, etc.) exceeds forecast or estimate, as in *cost ~*.

o·ver·seas (ōversēz´) *adv.* Across or beyond sea. **o´ver·seas´** *adj.*

o·ver·see (ōversē´) *v.t.* (**-saw, -seen, -see·ing**). Superintend, look after (workmen, execution of work, etc.). **o´ver·se·er** *n.*

o·ver·sexed (ōversĕkst´) *adj.* Having unusually great sexual desires.

o·ver·shad·ow (ōvershăd´ō) *v.t.* Cast a shadow over; (fig.) be more conspicuous than, outshine.

o·ver·shoe (ō´vershoō) *n.* Shoe of rubber, felt, etc., worn outside another.

o·ver·shoot (ōvershoōt´) *v.t.* (**-shot, -shoot·ing**). Send missile, go, beyond (mark etc.); ~ **the mark**, go too far, exaggerate, overdo something.

o·ver·shot (ō´vershŏt) *adj.* (of wheel) Turned by water flowing above it.

o·ver·sight (ō´versīt) *n.* 1. Supervision. 2. Omission to notice, mistake of inadvertence.

o·ver·sleep (ōverslēp´) *v.refl.* & *i.* (**-slept, -sleep·ing**). Miss intended hour of rising by sleeping too long.

o·ver·state (ōverstāt´) *v.t.* (**-stat·ed, -stat·ing**). State too strongly, exaggerate. **o´ver·state´-ment** *n.*

o·ver·steer (ōverstēr´) *v.i.* (of vehicle) Have tendency to steer toward the inner side on a curve. **o´versteer** *n.* Oversteering.

o·ver·step (ōverstĕp´) *v.t.* (**-stepped, -step·ping**). Pass over (boundary).

o·ver·strain (ōverstrān´) *v.* Damage by exertion; make to much of (argument etc.).

o·ver·strung (ō´verstrŭng) *ad* 1. (of piano) With strings arrang in sets crossing each oth obliquely. 2. (of person, nerve etc.) Intensely strained.

o·ver·stuff (ōverstŭf´) *v.t.* Stu more than is necessary; ~**ed** (furniture) made soft and con fortable by thick upholster **o´ver·stuffed´** *adj.*

o·ver·sub·scribe (ōversub skrīb´) *v.t.* (**-scribed, -scrib·ing** (usu. in past part.) Subscribe mo than amount of (loan etc.). **o´ver sub·scrib´er, o·ver·sub·scrip tion** *ns.*

o·vert (ōvĕrt´, ō´vĕrt) *ad* Openly done, unconcealed, paten **o·vert´ly** *adv.*

o·ver·take (ōvertāk´) *v.t.* (**-too -tak·en, -tak·ing**). Come up wit catch up; (of storm, misfortun etc.) come suddenly upon; (vehicle) pass (vehicle) traveling same direction.

o·ver·tax (ōvertăks´) *v.t.* Mak excessive demand on (person strength etc.); burden with exce sive taxes.

o·ver·throw (ōverthrō´) *v.* (**-threw, -thrown, -throw·ing** Upset, knock down; cast out fro power; vanquish, subvert; put a end to. **o´verthrow** *n.* Defea subversion.

o·ver·time (ō´vertīm) *ad* Beyond regular hours of work. *n.* Time during which workma etc. works beyond regular hour payment for this.

o·ver·tone (ō´vertōn) *n.* (mus Harmonic; (subtle or elusive secondary quality, color, etc.; im plication.

o·ver·ture (ō´vercher, -choor) *n* 1. Opening of negotiations wit another (usu. pl.); formal proposa or offer. 2. (mus.) Orchestral piec beginning opera, oratorio, etc.

o·ver·turn (ōvertĕrn´) *v.* Upse (cause to) fall down or over; over throw, subvert; abolish. **o´ver turn** *n.*

o·ver·ween·ing (ō´verwē´nĭng *adj.* Arrogant, presumptuous **o·ver·ween´ing·ly** *adv.* **o·ver ween´ing·ness** *n.*

o·ver·weight (ō´verwāt) *n.* Pre ponderance; excessive weight. *adj.* Beyond weight allowed o desirable. **o·ver·weight´** *v.t.* Im pose too great weight or burden on

o·ver·whelm (ōverhwĕlm´ ōverwĕlm´) *v.t.* Bury beneath over lying mass, submerge utterly crush, bring to sudden ruin; over power with emotion etc.; deluge *with.* **o·ver·whelm´ing** *adj.* Ir resistible by reason of numbers amount, etc. **o·ver·whelm´ing·ly** *adv.* **o·ver·whelm´ing·ness** *n.*

o·ver·wind (ōverwīnd´) *v.t*

wound, -wind·ing). Wind too
.r.

o·ver·work (overwērk´) *v.*
worked or **-wrought, -work·-**
ng). (Cause to) work too hard;
eary or exhaust with work. **o´ver-**
ork *n.* Excessive work.

o·ver·wrought (ōverrawt´) *adj.*
Overexcited; suffering reaction
om excitement. 2. Too elaborate.

Ov·id (ŏv´ĭd). Publius Ovidius
`aso (43 B.C.–c18 A.D.), Roman
et; author of *Ars Amatoria,*
Metamorphoses, etc. **O·vid·i·an**
vĭd´ēan) *adj.* **o·vi·duct** (ō´vĭdŭkt)
(anat., zool.) One of pair of ducts
rrying eggs from ovary.

o·vi·form (ō´vĭfōrm) *adj.* Egg-
haped.

o·vine (ō´vīn) *adj.* Of, like,
eep.

o·vip·a·rous (ōvĭp´arus) *adj.*

(zool.) Producing young by means
of eggs expelled from body before
being hatched. **o·vip´ar·ous·ly**
adv.

o·vi·pos·i·tor (ōvĭpŏz´ĭter) *n.*
(zool.) Organ with which female
animal, insect, etc., deposits eggs.

o·void (ō´void) *adj.* Solidly or
superficially egg-shaped, oval with
one end more pointed. ~ *n.*
Ovoid body.

o·vo·tes·tis (ōvōtĕs´tĭs) *n.* (pl.
-tes pr. -tēz). (zool.) Organ in
certain animals that produces both
ova and spermatozoa; hermaphrodite gland.

o·vo·vi·vip·a·rous (ōvōvīvĭp´-
arus) *adj.* (zool.) Producing young
by means of eggs which hatch
before reaching exterior (cf.
OVIPAROUS). **o·vo·vi·vip´ar·ous·ly**
adv.

o·vu·la·tion (ōvyulā´shon, ŏv-
yu-) *n.* Development of ova;
discharge of ova from ovary in
mammals. **o·vu·late** (ō´vyulāt,
ŏv´yu-) *v.i.* (**-lat·ed, -lat·ing).**

o·vule (ō´vūl) *n.* (bot.) Female
germ cell of seed plant. **o·vu·lar**
(ō´vyuler) *adj.*

o·vum (ō´vum) *n.* (pl. **o·va** pr.
ō´va). (biol.) Female germ cell
capable of developing into new
individual when fertilized by male
sperm; egg esp. of mammals, fish,
or insects. [L., = "egg"]

owe (ō) *v.* (**owed, ow·ing).** Be
under obligation to pay, repay, or
render; be in debt (*for*); be indebted
for *to.*

Ow·en (ō´ĭn), **Robert** (1771–
1858). Brit. industrialist and socialist reformer; with his son, **Robert**
Dale (1801–77), he established the

s nocturnal hunters, all owls have
yes about 35 to 100 times more sen-
itive than those of man. Those of the
nowy **owl** are the same size as a man's
nd enable it to hunt at night for the
odents and other small fauna which are
s prey.

Great Grey Owl

Tawny Owl

wy Owl

Long-eared
Owl

A member of the chrysanthemum genus, the **ox-eye daisy** has flowers with a yellow central disk surrounded by long white petals. It is common in England.

Utopian community of New Harmony, Indiana (1825–28).

Ow·ens (ō´ĭnz), **Jesse** (1913–80). Amer. track and field athlete; hero of the Olympic Games in Berlin, 1936.

ow·ing (ō´ĭng) *pred. adj.* Yet to be paid, owed, due; ~ **to** (also used adverbially), attributed to, caused by.

owl (owl) *n.* 1. Bird of prey, esp. nocturnal, of the order Strigiformes, with large head, raptorial beak, large eyes directed forward and soft plumage enabling it to fly noiselessly, feeding on mice, small birds, etc. 2. Solemn person. **owl´ish** *adj.* **owl´ish·ly** *adv.* **owl´ish·ness** *n.*

owl·et (ow´lĭt) *n.* Owl, young owl.

own[1] (ōn) *adj.* (appended to poss. adjective or case) In full ownership, proper, peculiar, individual, and not another's; (abs.) private property, kindred, etc.; **of one's ~**, belonging to one; **hold one's ~**, maintain position, not be defeated; **on one's ~**, (colloq.) independently, on one's own account, responsibility, or resources; **get one's ~ back**, be revenged (*on*).

own[2] (ōn) *v.* 1. Have as property, possess. 2. Acknowledge authorship, paternity, or possession, of; admit as existent, valid, true, etc; ~ **up**, (colloq.) make frank confession. **own´er, own´er·ship** *ns.* **own´er·less** *adj.*

ox (ŏks) *n.* (pl. **ox·en**). Large domestic bovine animal, esp. male castrated and used as draft animal or reared for food; any bovine animal; **ox´eye daisy**, common meadow plant (*Chrysanthemum leucanthemum*) with flowers having a yellow disk and long white rays; **ox´herd**, cowherd; **ox·lip** (ŏks´lĭp), kind of primula; (pop.) hybrid of primrose and cowslip; **ox´tail**, tail of ox, much used for making soup.

ox·al·ic (ŏksăl´ĭk) *adj.* ~ **acid**, highly poisonous and intensely sour acid (COOH)₂ found in wood sorrel etc., used in bleaching etc. [Gk *oxalis* wood sorrel]

Wild cattle were domesticated as early as 4,500 B.C. and **oxen**, males castrated to make them more docile, were used to draw sledges. Below: Modern farmers in Sri Lanka still use oxen.

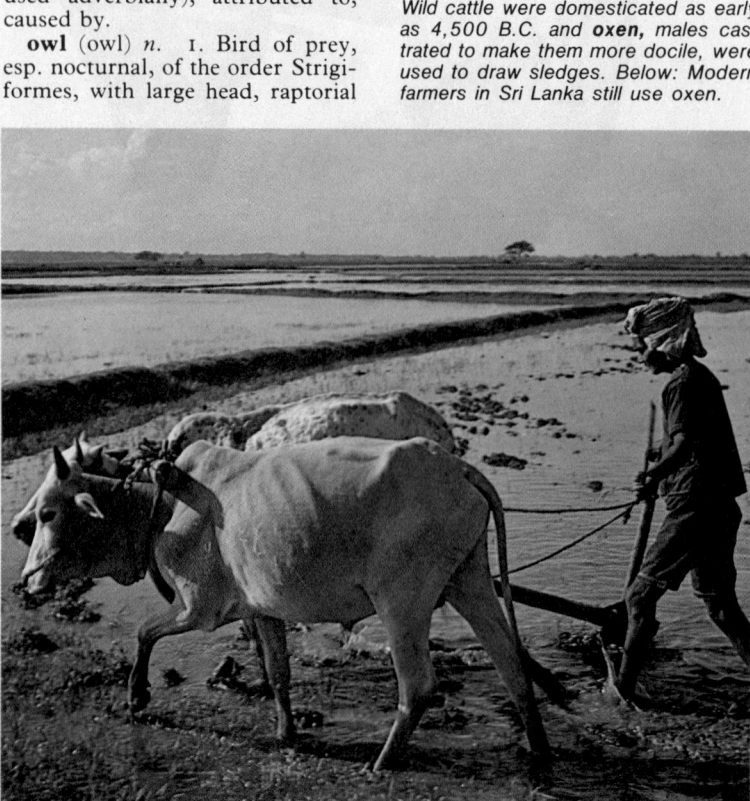

Ox·ford (ŏks´fĕrd). City on Thames River in Oxfordshire, seat of university organized as a *studium generale* soon after 1167, the first of its colleges, University College being founded in 1249; ~ **accent**, style of pronouncing English popularly supposed to be characteristic of members of Oxford University; ~ **blue**, dark blue; ~ **gray**, dark gray; ~ **Group**, religious movement founded by Dr. Frank N.D. Buchman in Oxford in 1921; ~ **movement**: see TRACTARIANISM; ~ **shoe**, kind of low walking shoe laced over instep. **ox´fords** *n.pl.* Oxford shoes. [*ox(en)* + *ford*]

ox·i·dase (ŏk´sĭdās, -dāz) *n.* (physiol., bot.) One of a group of enzymes concerned with the uptake of oxygen by living cells (respiration).

ox·ide (ŏk´sīd) *n.* Compound of oxygen with another element or with a radical.

ox·i·dize (ŏk´sĭdīz) *v.* (**-dized, -diz·ing**). Cause to combine with oxygen; cover (metal) with coating of oxide, make rusty; take up or enter into combination with oxygen, rust; **oxidized silver**, silver with dark coating of silver sulphide. **ox·i·da·tion** (ŏksĭdā´shŏn) *n.* **ox´i·diz·er** *n.*

Oxon. *abbrev. Oxoniensis* (L., = of Oxford); Oxford University.

ox·y·a·cet·y·lene (ŏksēăsĕt´ĭlēn, -ĭlĭn) *adj.* Using mixture of oxygen and acetylene (esp. of flame produced in this way for cutting and welding metals).

ox·y·gen (ŏk´sĭjĕn) *n.* (chem.) Colorless, tasteless, odorless gaseous element, essential to life and to combustion, comprising about one-fifth of the air, and present in combination in water and most minerals and organic substances; symbol O, at no. 8, at. wt 15.9994; ~ **tent**: see TENT[1].

ox·y·gen·ate (ŏk´sĭjenāt) *v.t.* (**-at·ed, -at·ing**). Supply, treat, or mix with oxygen, oxidize; charge (blood) with oxygen by respiration. **ox·y·gen·a·tion** (ŏksĭjenā´shŏn) *n.*

ox·y·gen·ize (ŏk´sĭjenĭz) *v.t.* (**-ized, -iz·ing**). Oxygenate.

ox·y·mo·ron (ŏksĭmôr´ŏn -môr´-) *n.* (pl. **-mo·ra** pr. -môr´a -môr´a). (rhet.) Figure of speech with pointed conjunction of seeming contradictions (e.g. *faithless unfaithful kept him falsely true*).

ox·y·te·tra·cy·cline (ŏksĭtĕtra·sī´klĭn, -klēn, -klīn) *n.* Dull yellow

Oxford is the oldest university in Britain. The town began beside a ford which crossed the Thames and was mentioned about 1,000 years ago. Teaching by monks began in the 12th century. Today, the Bodleian Library has 2 million books.

The **oyster-catcher** (above) has a world-wide distribution and feeds on small mollusks and worms in tidal areas. **Oysters** (right) are the mollusks most valued by man not only as food, but also for pearl-shell and pearls.

crystalline antibiotic powder used in treatment of infections.

oys·ter (oi′ster) *n.* Edible bivalve mollusk of family Ostreidae, usu. eaten alive, esp. the common European *Ostrea edulis* and the Amer. *O. virginica* and *O. lurida* (**Californian** ~); oyster-shaped morsel of meat in fowl's back; ~ **bank, bed**, part of sea bottom where oysters breed or are bred; ~ **bar**, counter where oysters are served; **oys′tercatcher**, maritime wading bird (*Haematopus*) with black-and-white or black plumage and brilliant red feet and beak; **oyster farm**, sea bottom used for breeding oysters; **oyster knife**, knife of shape adapted for opening oysters.

oz. *abbrev.* Ounce(s).

O·zark (ō′zärk) **Mountains.** (also **Ozarks**) Range of low mountains spreading over a 60,000 sq. mile (155,400 sq. km) area between Arkansas and Missouri rivers, mainly in SW. Missouri, NW. Arkansas, and E. Oklahoma.

o·zone (ō′zōn) *n.* 1. Allotropic form of oxygen with three atoms to the molecule (O_3), a pale-blue gas with a peculiarly pungent smell, formed by action of electric discharge or ultraviolet light, used for sterilizing water and purifying air. 2. (pop.) Invigorating, bracing air, esp. that of the seaside. **o·zon·ic** (ōzŏn′ĭk, ōzō′nĭk) *adj.*

Oyster farm at Wallis Lake in N.S.W. Australia. Edible oysters are ready for harvesting within 3 to 5 years. Pearls from edible oysters are valueless.

Phoenician   Early Greek   Etruscan

Early Latin   Classical Latin   Italian

*Shaped like a shepherd's crook, and turning both to right and left during its development, the symbol **P, p** has usually represented the same sound. If combined with 'h' or 's' it results in sounds 'f' and 's' today.*

P, p (pē) (pl. **P's, p's** or **Ps, ps**) xteenth letter of modern English d 15th of ancient Roman phabet, corresponding to Gk. *pi* (ⲡ, π) and Semitic ⲡ, ⲣ, and presenting a voiceless labial stop; **ind one's P's and Q's,** be reful not to do or say the wrong ing.

P *symbol.* Phosphorus.
P. *abbrev.* President.
p. *abbrev.* Page; participle; past; nny, pence, pressure; *piano*[1].
Pa *symbol.* Protactinium.
pa (pah) *n.* (colloq.) Papa.
Pa., PA *abbrevs.* Pennsylvania.
P.A. *abbrev.* Press agent, power attorney, purchasing agent.
p.a. *abbrev.* Per annum.
pab·u·lum (păb´*y*ulum) *n.* 1. od, sustenance. 2. Weak intel-ctual nourishment.
pa·ca (pah´ka, păk´a) *n.* Spotted vy (*Cuniculus paca*), a nocturnal dent of Central and S. Amer.
pace (pās) *n.* 1. Single step in alking or running; space traversed this, as vague measure of distance out 30 in.); space between suc-ssive stationary positions of same ot in walking (about 5 ft.). 2. ode of walking or running, gait; y or various gaits of (esp. trained) rse, etc.; amble; **put (person) rough his ~ s,** test his qualities action, etc. 3. Speed in walking running; rate or progression; **ep ~,** advance at equal rate *with*; **ce´maker,** rider, runner, etc., ho sets pace for another in race c.; electrical device for stimulat-g the heart muscle. **pace** *v.* **aced, pac·ing**). Walk with slow regular pace; traverse thus; easure (distance) by pacing; (of rse) amble; set pace for (rider, nner, etc.). **pac´er** *n.* (esp.) rse that paces.
pa·cha = PASHA.
pa·chin·ko (pachǐng´kō)   *n.* panese form of pinball. [Jap.]
pach·y·derm (păk´ǐdẽrm) *n.* rge thick-skinned mammal esp. ephant or rhinoceros. **pach·y-er´mal, pach·y·der´mous, ach·y·der·ma·tous** (păkǐdẽr´-atus) *adjs.*
pach·y·san·dra (păkǐsăn´dra) *n.*

Any plant of the genus *Pachysandra*, often used as a ground cover.

Pa·cif·ic (pasǐf´ǐk) *adj.* Of, adjoining, the Pacific Ocean; **~ Islands, Trust Territory of the,** approximately 2,000 islands including the Caroline, Marshall, and Mariana Islands under the trusteeship of the U.S., approved by the United Nations in 1947; the 17 islands of the Northern Marianas became a commonwealth under U.S. sovereignty in 1976; **~ Ocean,** largest body of water on Earth's surface, bounded by N. and S. Amer. and Asia and Australia.
Pacific *n.* Pacific Ocean. [so named by Magellan, its first European navigator, because he ex-

*Considered to be the largest expanse of water in the world, the **Pacific Ocean** is broadly bounded by America, Asia and Australia. Large distances separate many of the groups of islands and this isolation has resulted in the development of many diverse cultures.*

perienced calm weather there]
pa·cif·ic (pasǐf´ǐk) *adj.* Tending to peace, of peaceful disposition. **pa·cif´i·cal·ly** *adv.*
pac·i·fi·ca·tion (păsǐfǐkā´shon) *n.* Pacifying; being pacified. **pa·cif·i·ca·to·ry** (pasǐf´ikatōrē, -tōrē) *adj.*
pac·i·fism (păs´ǐfĭzem) *n.* (Support of) policy of avoiding or abolishing war by means of arbitration in settling international disputes. **pac´i·fist** *n.*
pac·i·fy (păs´ǐfī) *v.t.* (**-fied, -fy·ing**). Make calm or quiet; reduce (country etc.) to state of peace. **pac´i·fi·a·ble** *adj.* **pac´i·fi·er** *n.* (esp.) Infant's teething ring or rubber nipple.
pack (păk) *n.* 1. Bundle of things wrapped up or tied together for carrying esp. on shoulders or back; (commerc.) method of packing for the market. 2. Set, lot (usu. derog., as ~ of fools, lies, etc.); large quantity. 3. Number of animals or birds kept together or naturally

The U.S.S. 'Glacier' with its helicopter unloads on **pack-ice** *during the Antarctic winter. This compressed ice forms a stable platform where scientists can make observations of many aspects of the life in such frigid areas.*

congregating; group; set of playing cards. 4. Large area of large pieces of floating ice (~ **ice**) driven or packed together into nearly continuous mass. 5. Quantity of fish, fruit, etc., packed in a season etc. 6. (med.) Swathing of body or part of it in wet sheet, blanket, etc.; sheet etc. so used; wad of gauze etc. for packing an orifice; **ice ~**, compress of crushed ice. 7. Substance (esp. paste) applied to skin or hair as cosmetic treatment; treatment using this. 8. **pack'horse**, horse for carrying packs; **pack rat**, large, hoarding rodent; (fig.) person who saves useless small items; **pack'-saddle**, one adapted for supporting packs; **pack'thread**, strong thread for sewing or typing up packs; **pack train**, line of loaded animals, esp. horses or mules. **pack** *v.* 1. Put (things) together into bundle, box, bag, etc., for transport or storing (freq. ~ **up**, esp. abs.). 2. Prepare and put up (meat, fruit, etc.) in jars, cans, etc. for preservation. 3. Put closely together; crowd together; form into pack. 4. Cover (thing) with something pressed or wedged tightly around; (med.) wrap (body etc.) tightly in wet cloth. 5. Fill (bag, box, etc.) with clothes etc.; cram (space etc. *with*); load (beast) with pack. 6. Take oneself off with one's belongings; **send** (person) **packing**, dismiss him summarily; **pack** (person) **off**, send him away; **pack up**, (slang) retire from fight, contest, etc.; cease to function. 7. **packing case**, case or framework for packing goods; **packing house**, slaughterhouse; establishment for processing and packing foods to be sold to

pack·age (păk'ĭj) *n.* Bundle of things packed, parcel; box etc. in which goods are packed; ~ **deal**, (colloq.) inclusive bargain or transaction; ~ **store**, liquor store; ~ **tour**, planned tour at a fixed inclusive price. **package** *v.t.* (**-aged**, **-ag·ing**). (commerc.) Make up into, enclose in, a unit.

pack·er (păk'er) *n.* (esp.) One who packs meat, fruit, etc., for market.

pack·et (păk'ĭt) *n.* 1. Small package; (colloq.) considerable sum of money (esp. lost or won). 2. Mail or freight boat, usually in coastal waters or rivers.

pact (păkt) *n.* Agreement, covenant.

pad[1] (păd) *v.* (**pad·ded, pad·ding**). Tramp along (road etc.) on foot; travel on foot; walk with dull-sounding steps.

Above: **Paddle-wheel** *boats are still used on lakes at Fairbanks, Alaska, and on other waterways where there is shallow water, or where there can be considerable seasonal variations in the water level.*

pad[2] (păd) *n.* Soft stuffed saddle without frame; part of double harness to which girths are attached; piece of soft stuff used to raise surface, diminsh jarring, absorb fluid, etc.; guard for parts of body in sports; number of sheets of paper fastened together at edge; fleshy cushion forming sole of foot in some quadrupeds; paw of fox, hare, etc.; water lily leaf; flat surface for helicopter takeoff, rocket launching, etc.; (slang) bed, lodging. ~ *v.t.* (**pad·ded, pad·ding**). Furnish with a pad, stuff; fill out (sentence etc.) with superfluous words; **padded cell**, room with padded walls in mental hospital. **pad'ding** *n.* Substance of pad, e.g. felt, hair, kapok, etc.; superfluous words in sentence etc.

pad·dle (păd'el) *n.* 1. Small spade-like implement with a long handle. 2. Short oar with blade at one or both ends used without rowlock; one of the boards fitted around circumference of paddle wheel; paddle-shaped instrument; action or spell of paddling; (zool.)

fin or flipper; ~ **wheel**, wheel f propelling ship, with boards arour and at right angles to the circur ference so as to press backwa against the water. ~ *v.* (**-dle -dling**). Move on water, prop canoe, by means of paddles; r gently; walk with bare feet shallow water; dabble; span thrash.

pad·dock (păd'ok) *n.* Sm field, esp. as part of stud farm; e closure near racecourse, whe horses are assembled before rac ~ *v.t.* Enclose or fence in (a she run etc.); shut up in a paddock.

Pad·dy (păd'ē) (pl. **-die** (Nickname for) Irishman; **pad wagon**, patrol wagon. [pet form *Padraig* Patrick]

pad·dy (păd'ē) *n.* (pl. **-die** Rice in the straw or in the hus rice field. [Malay *padi*]

Pa·de·rew·ski (păderĕf'ski **Ignacy Jan** (1860–1941). Poli pianist, composer and statesma prime minister of Poland 1919–2 and 1940–1.

pad·lock (păd'lŏk) *n.* Detac able lock hanging by hinged pivoted hoop on object fastene ~ *v.t.* Secure with padlock.

pa·dre (pah'drā, -drē) *n.* (m slang). Chaplain. [Port. etc. "father," "priest"]

*Racehorses being led around the **pad-dock** at Newmarket, England. This word also means a small field for grazing horses, or (in Australia) any large field.*

pa·dro·ne (padrō´nē) *n.* Master of Mediterranean trading vessel; Italian employer of street musicians, begging children, etc.; proprietor of Italian inn.

pae·an (pē´an) *n.* Song of praise or thanksgiving; shout or song of triumph, joy, or exultation. [Gk. *paian* hymn to Apollo under name of Paian]

pa·el·la (pah-ĕl´a, -ā´la, -ya; *Sp.* pah-ĕl´yah, -ĕ´yah) *n.* Spanish dish of rice with chicken, vegetables, etc., seasoned with saffron.

pa·gan (pā´gan) *n.* & *adj.* Heathen, esp. in antiquity. **pa´gan·ism** *n.* **pa´gan·ize** *v.* (-ized, -iz·ing).

page[1] (pāj) *n.* Boy employed (esp. in hotels) to attend to door, go on errands, etc. (also ~ **boy**); boy employed as personal attendant of person of rank; small boy attending bride at wedding; (hist.) boy in training for knighthood and attached to knight's service. **page** *v.t.* (**paged, pag·ing**). Communicate with by means of page; call name of (person sought) in public rooms of hotel etc.

page[2] (pāj) *n.* One side of leaf of book etc. ~ *v.t* (**paged, pag·ing**). Put consecutive numbers on pages of (book etc.).

pag·eant (păj´ent) *n.* Brilliant spectacle, esp. procession, arranged for effect; spectacular representation of past history of place etc.; (hist.) tableau, allegorical device, etc., on fixed stage or moving car; (fig.) empty or specious show. **pag·eant·ry** (păj´entrē) *n.* (pl. **-tries**). Slendid display; empty show.

pag·i·nal (păj´inal). Of pages; page for page.

pag·i·nate (păj´ināt) *v.t.* (**-nat·ed, -nat·ing**). Page (book etc.). **pag·i·na·tion** (păjinā´shon) *n.*

pa·go·da (pagō´da) *n.* Temple or sacred building in India, China, etc., esp. tower, usu. of pyramidal form, built over relics of Buddha or a saint; ornamental imitation of this; ~ **tree**, one of several kinds of Chinese, Japanese, and Indian trees, growing in pagoda form.

Pa·go Pa·go (pahn´gō pahn´go). Capital of Amer. Samoa on the S. coast of Tutuila Island.

Pah·la·vi (pah´lavē), **Peh·le·vi** (pā´levē) *ns.* Iranian language, the ancestor of modern Persian, used in Persia from *c*3rd c. onward, distinguished from other dialects of

*Left: The Ban Fu Poh **pagoda** at Penang in Malaysia is one of several forms of temple erected in Asia to exemplify the range and wisdom of the teaching of the founder of Buddhism.*

Middle Persian chiefly by its script, which has some Aramaic characters; **Mohammed Riza** ~ (1919–80), shah of Iran from 1941; forced to leave country, 1979. [Pers. *Pahlav* Parthia]

paid (pād) *adj.*: see PAY[1]; (esp.) **mark** ~, (colloq.) settle the affairs of, finish off; ~**-in capital**, that part of the subscribed capital of an undertaking that has actually been paid.

pail (pāl) *n.* 1. Bucket. 2. (also **dinner** ~) Vessel in which workman's midday meal etc. is carried.

pail·lasse, pal·liasse (păl'yăs, pălyăs') *ns.* Straw mattress.

pain (pān) *n.* 1. Sensation experienced when the body is injured, or afflicted by certain diseases; suffering, distress, of body or mind; (pl.) labor pains of childbirth. 2. (pl.) Trouble taken; **pains'taking**, careful, industrious. 3. Punishment (now only in **on pain of**). **pain** *v.t.* Inflict pain upon. **pain'ful** *adj.* **pain'ful·ly** *adv.* **pain'ful·ness** *n.* **pain'less** *adj.* **pain'-less·ly** *adv.* **pain'less·ness** *n.*

Paine (pān), **Thomas** (1737–1809). Brit.-born pamphleteer and political radical in Amer. and France; in Amer. wrote influential *Common Sense* (1776) urging Amer. Revolution and independence; published the *Crisis* periodical supporting Amer. cause during war of Independence; in Europe, 1787, associated himself with the French Revolution; wrote *The Rights of Man* (1791–2) defending revolutionary France; member of French National Convention 1792–3; wrote *The Age of Reason* (1794, 1796).

paint (pānt) *n.* Solid coloring matter, suspended in a liquid vehicle used to impart color to a surface; something, esp. medicament, put on like paint with brush; cosmetic coloring matter applied to face etc.; ~ **brush**, house painter's or artist's brush. **paint** *v.t.* 1. Portray, represent, in colors; adorn (wall etc.) with painting; (fig.) represent in words vividly as by painting. 2. Cover surface of with paint, apply paint of specified color to; ~ **the town red**, cause commotion by riotous spree etc. 3. Apply liquid or cosmetic to (skin, face, etc.). 4. **painted lady**, orange-red butterfly (*Vanessa cardui*) with black and white spots; **Painted Desert**, plateau area in E. central Arizona known for its colorful eroded rock formations.

paint·er[1] (pān'ter) *n.* 1. One who paints pictures. 2. Workman who coats woodwork etc. with paint. **paint'er·ly** *adj.* (transl. of Ger. *malerisch*) (of work of art) Executed with attention to light and shade, mass, tone, etc., rather than line (opp. LINEAR).

paint·er[2] (pān'ter) *n.* Rope

Thomas Paine, *a revolutionary whose controversial ideas of civic and political freedom were famous, served the revolutionary forces in France and America but died in jail.*

attached to bow of boat for making it fast to ship, stake, etc.

paint·ing (pān'ting) *n.* A painted picture; the art of doing this.

pair (pār) *n.* (pl. **pairs, pair**). 1. Set of two, couple (esp. of things that usu. exist or are used in couples); article consisting of two corresponding parts not used separately; second member of a pair; two playing cards of same denomination. 2. Engaged or married couple; mated couple of animals; two horses harnessed together. 3. Two voters on opposite sides absenting themselves from voting by mutual agreement. ~ *v.* Arrange, be arranged, in couples; unite in love or marriage; mate; unite (*with* one of opposite sex); ~ **off**, put two by two; go off in pairs; make a pair; (colloq.) marry (*with*).

Pais·ley (pāz'lē). Town of Strathclyde near Glasgow; **paisley shawl**, shawl in soft bright colors, orig. made at Paisley; **paisley (pattern)**, characteristic pattern of such shawl.

Pai·ute (pīoot') *n.* (pl. **-utes**, collect. **-ute**). (Member of) either of two distinct Indian tribes of the Shoshonean subfamily, formerly living in southwestern U.S., comprising the **Northern** ~ and **Southern** ~.

pa·ja·mas, py·ja·mas (pajah'-maz, -jăm'az) *ns. pl.* Loose silk or cotton trousers tied around waist, worn by both sexes in the East and adapted esp. for night wear by Europeans; sleeping suit of loose trousers and jacket. [Hind. *pāe jāma, pā jāma* loose drawers]

Pa·ki·stan (pahkĭstahn', păk'ĭ-

stăn). Islamic republic in SE. Asia formed in 1947 from regions wher Muslims predominated; member o the Brit. Commonwealth unt 1972; capital, Islamabad. **Pa·ki·sta·ni** (pahkĭstah'nē, păkĭstăn'ē *adj. & n.* [earlier *Pakstan*, initials of *P*unjab, *A*fghan Frontier *K*ashmir, *S*ind, and last 3 letters o Baluchi*stan*]

pal (păl) *n.* (slang) Comrade friend. ~ *v.i.* (**palled, pal·ling** (usu. ~ **up**) Associate, mak friends (*with*). [Engl. Gypsy *pa* brother, mate]

pal·ace (păl'ĭs) *n.* Officia residence of sovereign, archbishop or bishop; stately mansion; spaciou building for entertainment, re freshment, etc. [L. *Palatiu* PALATINE HILL, Augustus' hous built on it]

pal·a·din (păl'adĭn) *n.* 1. An' of the 12 Peers of Charlemagne' court, of whom the Count Palatin was the chief; knight errant. 2 Heroic champion.

pal·an·quin, pal·an·keen (păl ankēn') *ns.* Covered litter for one in India etc., carried usu. by fou or six men. **pal·an·quin'er, pal an·keen'er** *ns.* [Malya *palangki*]

pal·at·a·ble (păl'atabel) *adj* Pleasant to the taste; (fig.) agree able to the mind. **pal'at·a·bl** *adv.*

pal·a·tal (păl'atal) *adj.* Of th palate; (of sound) produced b placing tongue against or near th palate, usu. hard palate. ~ *n* Palatal sound. **pal'a·tal·ize** *v.t* (**-ized, -iz·ing**). Make palata modify into palatal sound. **pal'a·tal·ly** *adv.*

pal·ate (păl'ĭt) *n.* 1. Roof o the mouth in vertebrates, partl bony and partly fleshy structur separating cavity of mouth from that of nose; **bony or hard** ~ front part of this; **soft** ~, back par of this, pendulous fold of musculo membranous tissue separatin mouth cavity from pharynx. 2 Sense of taste; mental taste, liking

pa·la·tial (palā'shal) *adj.* Like palace; splendid. **pa·la'tial·ly** *adv* **pa·la'tial·ness** *n.*

pa·lat·i·nate (palăt'ĭnāt, -nĭt) *r* Territory under a palatine; **P** ~ (hist., Ger. *Pfalz*), state of th Rhine, constituting with **Upper P** ~ an electorate of the Hol Roman Empire, now part of Wes Germany.

pal·a·tine[1] (păl'atĭn) *adj.* 1. O a palace; palatial. 2. Possessin royal privileges, having jurisdictio (within the territory) such as else where belongs to the sovereig alone. 3. Of or belonging to a coun palatine; **count** ~, orig. in the late Roman Empire a count (*comes* attached to the imperial palace an having supreme judicial authorit in certain causes. **palatine** *n*

Top: Wandering musicians entertaining at a Bugti tribal wedding in **Pakistan**. This Muslim state (see map above) was formed in 1947 but the eastern half seceded to become Bangladesh in 1971 after a very bitter and savage war.

ffice of imperial palace; lord aving sovereign power over prov- ce or dependency of empire or alm; **P ~**, PALATINE HILL.

pal·a·tine² (păl'atīn, -tǐn) *adj.* f the palate. ~ *n.* Either of two ones forming hard palate.

Pal·a·tine (păl'atīn, -tǐn) **Hill.** ne of the seven Hills of Rome, at on which the first Roman ttlement was made; later, site of nperial palaces.

Pa·lau (pahlow'). Group of pproximately 100 small islands in e Caroline Islands.

pa·lav·er (palăv'er. -lah'ver) *n.* onference, discussion, esp. in ibal custom; profuse or idle talk. *v.i.* Engage in palaver.

pale¹ (pāl) *n.* 1. Pointed piece wood for fence etc., stake. 2. oundary; enclosed place; **the P ~**, ist.) part of Ireland under English risdiction.

pale² (pāl) *adj.* (**pal·er, pal·est**). f person or complexion) Of hitish or ashen appearance; (of

colors) faint; faintly colored; of faint luster, dim; **pale'face,** supposed N. Amer. Ind. name for white man. **pale'ly** *adv.* **pale'ness** *n.* **pale** *v.* (**paled, pal·ing**). Grow or make pale; (fig.) become pale in comparison (usu. *before* or *beside*).

Pa·le·o·cene (pā'lēosēn, păl'ē-) *adj. & n.* (geol.) (Of) the earliest epoch of the Tertiary period.

pa·le·og·ra·phy (pālēŏg'rafē, păl'ē-) *n.* Study of ancient writing and inscriptions. **pa·le·og·ra·pher** *n.* **pa·le·o·graph·ic** (pālēogrăf'ĭk, păl'ē-) *adj.*

pa·le·o·lith·ic (pālēolĭth'ĭk, păl'ē-) *adj.* Of the earlier Stone Age (as contrasted with NEOLITHIC), characterized by chipped stone implements and weapons.

pa·le·on·tol·o·gy (pālĕontŏl'ojē,

păle-) *n.* Study of extinct animals and plants. **pa·le·on·tol'o·gist** *n.*

Pa·le·o·zo·ic (pālēozō'ĭk, pălē-) *adj. & n.* (Of) the era or group or systems containing ancient forms of life, including the periods from Cambrian to Permian.

Pal·es·tine (păl'ĭstīn). Former name of country of Asia at E. end of Mediterranean, now divided between ISRAEL and JORDAN; ancient home of the Jews and the Holy Land of Christendom; it was conquered by the Romans, 65 B.C., and by Arabs, 634 A.D.; from then on, except when ruled by Crusaders (1098–1187), it remained under Muslim dominion until the defeat of Turkish and German forces by the British at Megiddo in World War I; under British mandate, 1923–48. **Pal·es·tin·i·an** (pălĭstĭn'ēan) *adj. & n.*

pa·les·tra (palěs'tra) *n.* (pl. **-tras, -trae** pr. -trē). (Gk. antiq.) Wrestling school, gymnasium.

pal·ette (păl'ĭt) *n.* Artist's thin usu. oval or rectangular board or plate, with hole for thumb, for arranging and mixing colors on; range of colors used by particular artist or on particular occasion; ~ **knife**, flexible steel blade with handle for mixing colors, also used for applying them to canvas.

pal·frey (pawl'frē) *n.* (pl. **-freys**). (archaic, poet.) Saddle horse for ordinary riding, esp. for ladies.

Pa·li (pah'lē) *n.* Indo-Aryan language spoken in N. India in the 5th–2nd centuries B.C.; as the language of a large part of the Buddhist scriptures, it was brought to Sri Lanka and Burma, and, though not spoken there, became the vehicle of a large literature of commentaries and chronicles. [fr. Sansk. *pālī-bhāsā* (*pali* canon, *bhāsā* language)]

pal·imp·sest (păl'ĭmpsĕst) *n.* Writing material or manuscript on which the original writing has been effaced to make room for a second writing.

pal·in·drome (păl'ĭndrōm) *n. & adj.* (Word, verse, etc.) that reads the same backward as forward (e.g. *madam*).

pal·ing (pā'lĭng) *n.* (Fence of) pales.

pal·i·sade (pălĭsād') *n.* Fence of pales or of iron railings; (mil.) strong pointed wooden stake, of which a number are fixed deeply in ground in close row as defense; (pl.) line of cliffs. ~ *v.t.* (**-sad·ed, -sad·ing**). Furnish, enclose, with palisade.

pall¹ (pawl) *n.* 1. Cloth, usu. of black, purple, or white velvet, spread over coffin, hearse, or tomb; coffin; **pall'bearer,** one of several persons who carry a coffin, or serve as attendants, at a funeral. 2.

Woolen vestment (now a narrow band passing over shoulders, with short lappets) worn by pope and some metropolitans or archbishops; (fig.) mantle, cloak.

pall² (pawl) *v.* Become insipid (now only fig.); satiate, clog.

Pal·la·di·an (palā′dēan) *adj.* 1. Of Pallas ATHENA. 2. Of PALLADIO or his style (~ **window**). **Pal·la′di·an·ism** *n.* Style, opinions, of the followers of Palladio.

Pal·la·dio (pahlah′dyō). Andrea di Pietro (1508–80), Italian architect of Vicenza, who revived classical Roman styles and had great influence through his *Four Books of Architecture* (1570). [It., = "man of Pallas (Athena)"]

Pal·la·di·um (palā′dēum) *n.* Image of the goddess Pallas in the citadel of Troy, on which the safety of the city was held to depend, reputed to have been brought from there to Rome; (pl. **-di·a** pr. -dēa) (usu. l.c.) safeguard.

pal·la·di·um (palā′dēum) *n.* (chem.) Hard silvery-white metallic element of platinum group; symbol Pd, at. no. 46, wt. 106.4. [f. the asteroid *Pallas*]

Pal·las (păl′as). 1. (Gk. myth.) One of the names (of unknown meaning) of ATHENA. 2. (astron.) Second largest of the asteroids.

pal·let¹ (păl′ĭt) *n.* Straw bed; mattress.

pal·let² (păl′ĭt) *n.* 1. Flat wooden blade with handle, used by potters etc. 2. Projection on part of a machine, engaging with teeth of wheel and converting reciprocating into rotary movement, or vice versa. 3. Portable platform for transporting and storing loads.

pal·liasse = PAILLASSE.

pal·li·ate (păl′ēāt) *v.t.* (**-at·ed, -at·ing**). Alleviate (disease) without curing; extenuate, excuse. **pal·li·a·tion** (pălēā′shon), **pal′li·a·tor** *ns.*

pal·li·a·tive (păl′ēātĭv, -ēatĭv) *adj. & n.* (Thing) serving to palliate.

pal·lid (păl′ĭd) *adj.* Pale, sickly looking. **pal′lid·ly** *adv.* **pal′lid·ness** *n.*

pal·li·um (păl′ēum) *n.* (pl. **-li·a** pr. lēa, **-li·ums**). 1. Man's large rectangular cloak, esp. among Greeks. 2. Archbishop's or pope's PALL¹. 3. Integumental fold or mantle of mollusk.

Pall Mall (pĕl′mel′, păl′măl′). Street in London on site of former pall-mall alley, noted for its clubs.

pall-mall (pĕl′mĕl′, păl′măl′) *n.* Sixteenth- and 17th-c. game in which a boxwood ball was driven

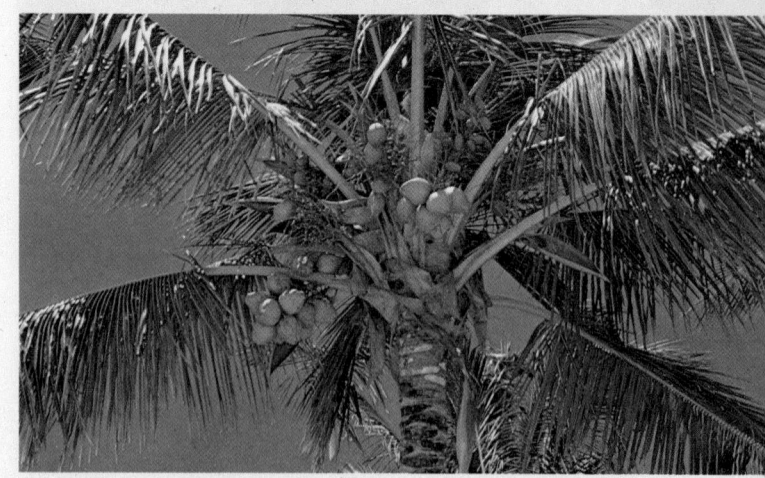

Depending on the species, palm trees can provide food, oil, and timber. Foliage from some varieties has been used for thatching and weaving.

with a mallet through an iron ring suspended at the end of a long alley. [It. *palla* ball, *maglio* mallet]

pal·lor (păl′er) *n.* Paleness.

palm¹ (pahm) *n.* 1. Tree or shrub of an order of monocotyledons widely distributed in warm climates, with stem usu. upright and unbranched, head or crown of very large pinnate or fan-shaped leaves, and fruit of various forms; leaf of palm tree as symbol of excellence; supreme excellence. prize for this. 2. Branch of various trees substituted for palm in northern countries, esp. in celebrating Palm Sunday. 3. ~ **oil**, oil obtained from various palms; **P ~ Sunday**, Sunday before Easter, on which Christ's entry into Jerusalem is celebrated, freq. with processions in which branches

palm are carried. **palm′like** adj.
al·ma·ceous (pălmā′shus, ahmā′-) adj.

palm² (pahm) n. Part of hand etween wrist and fingers, esp. its ner surface; part of glove that vers this; **grease person's ~**, ribe him. **palm** v.t. Impose adulently, pass off (thing on person); conceal (cards, dice, etc.) in and in sleight of hand etc.; bribe.

Pal·ma (pahl′mah). I. (San Miguel de la Palma) Spanish island, art of the Canary Islands in the tlantic off NW. coast of Africa. Capital of the Balearic Islands, n Majorca in the Mediterranean, of Spain.

pal·mate (păl′māt, pah′māt), al·mat·ed (păl′mātĭd, pahmā-) djs. Shaped like open palm or and.

palm·er (pah′mer, pahl′mer) n. Pilgrim who returned from Holy and with palm branch or leaf; nerant monk under vow of overty. 2. (also **palm′erworm**) ne of various kinds of destructive airy caterpillars of migratory or andering habits; hairy artificial y.

pal·met·to (pălmĕt′ō) n. (pl. **-tos, -toes**). Any of various small species of palms, esp. cabbage palmetto (Sabal palmetto) of southeastern U.S.

palm·is·try (pah′mĭstrē) n. Art or practice of telling character or fortunes from the lines etc. in palm of hand. **palm′ist** n.

palm·y (pah′mē) adj. (**palm·i·er, palm·i·est**). Of, like, abounding in, palms; triumphant, flourishing (esp. in ~ days.)

Pal·my·ra (pălmī′ra). (Aram. Tadmor) Ancient city at an oasis in the Syrian Desert on the caravan route from Damascus to the Euphrates.

pal·my·ra (pălmī′ra) n. Species of palm (Borassus flabellifer) grown in India and Sri Lanka with fan-shaped leaves used for matting etc.

pal·o·mi·no (pălomē′nō) n. (pl. **-nos**). Sand-colored horse with white mane and tail.

This non-flying grasshopper, the Horse lubber, is found in parts of Arizona, Texas and Mexico. The **palpus** or feelers enable it to sense food.

palp (pălp) = PALPUS.

pal·pa·ble (păl′pabel) adj. That can be touched or felt; readily perceived by senses or mind. **pal·pa·bil·i·ty** (pălpabĭl′ĭtē), **pal′pa·ble·ness** ns. **pal′pa·bly** adv.

pal·pate (păl′pāt) v.t. (**-pat·ed, -pat·ing**). Examine by touch, handle, esp. in medical examination. **pal·pa·tion** (pălpā′shon) n.

pal·pi·tate (păl′pĭtāt) v.i. (**-tat·ed, -tat·ing**). Pulsate, throb; tremble. **pal·pi·ta·tion** (pălpĭtā′shon) n. Throbbing; increased activity of heart due to exertion, agitation, or disease.

pal·pus (păl′pus) n. (pl. **-pi** pr. -pī). Jointed sense organ in insects etc., feeler.

pal·sy (pawl′zē) n. (pl. **-sies**). Paralysis (also fig.); **cerebral ~**, condition of weakness, imperfect control of movement, and spasticity, following damage to brain at birth. **palsy** v.t. (**-sied, -sy·ing**). Paralyze.

pal·try (pawl′trē) adj. (**-tri·er, -tri·est**). Worthless, petty, contemptible. **pal′tri·ly** adv. **pal′tri·ness** n.

pam·pas (păm′paz, pahm′pas) n.pl. Vast treeless grassy plains of S. Amer. S. of the Amazon, esp. great plain of Argentina stretching from Atlantic coast to Andes, and from Rio Colorado to Gran Chaco; **~ grass**, gigantic grass (Cortaderia selloana) with silvery-colored silky panicles on stalks sometimes 12 or 14 ft. high, introduced into Europe and N. Amer. from S. Amer. [Quechua pampa plain]

pam·per (păm′per) v.t. Overindulge.

pam·phlet (păm′flĭt) n. Small unbound treatise, esp. on subject of current interest. **pam·phlet·eer** (pamflĭtēr′) n. Writer of pamphlets. **~** v.i. Write pamphlets. [prob. f. Pamphilet, Panflet, familiar name of 12th-c. Latin amatory poem or comedy "Pamphilus, seu de Amore"]

Pam·plo·na (pahmplō′na). City in N. Spain, capital of Navarre Province; site of annual "running of the bulls" through streets to bullfight arena.

Pan (păn). (Gk. myth.) God of flocks and shepherds; orig. and chiefly an Arcadian deity, represented with the horns, ears, and legs of a goat; he invented the musical pipe (PANPIPE) and was reputed to cause sudden groundless fear such as that felt by travelers in remote and desolate places.

pan¹ (păn) n. I. Metal or earthenware vessel, usu. shallow

The distinctive colors of a **palomino** can be obtained only by breeding parents of different colors. If palominos are mated, their offspring do not have the colors that breeders want.

and freq. open, for domestic purposes; panlike vessel in which substances are heated etc.; contents of pan, panful. 2. Pan-shaped depression or concavity of any vessel or structure; part of lock that held priming in obsolete types of gun. 3. Hollow in ground, esp. salt pan; **hard** ~, substratum of soil, more or less impervious to moisture. **pan** v. (**panned, pan·ning**). Wash (gold-bearing gravel) in pan; ~ **out**, yield gold, (fig.) succeed, work (*well* etc.).

pan² (pahn) *n.* Betel leaf; combination of this with areca nut etc. for chewing. [Hind. *pān*]

pan³ (păn) *v.* (**panned, pan·ning**). (film) Pivot (camera) to obtain panoramic effect or follow moving object; (of camera) be pivoted thus.

pan- *prefix.* All.

pan·a·ce·a (pănasē'a) *n.* Universal remedy.

pa·nache (panăsh', -nahsh') *n.* Tuft, plume, of feathers, esp. as headdress or on helmet; (fig.) display, swagger.

Pan·a·ma¹ (păn'amah). Republic of Central America, lying between Costa Rica and Colombia; its capital city, at Pacific end of Panama Canal; ~ **Canal**, 50-mile-long ship canal connecting the Atlantic and Pacific through narrow **Isthmus of** ~, completed by the U.S. in 1914. **Panama Canal Zone**, strip of land 50 mi. (80 km) long, and 10 mi. (16 km) wide, across the Isthmus of Panama along the Canal; in a 1903 treaty, the Republic of Panama gave the U.S. perpetual sovereign rights in the Canal Zone in exchange for U.S. building and operating of the canal; in 1978, the U.S. signed a new treaty promising to turn over control of the Canal and the Canal Zone to Panama by the year 2,000. **Pan·a·ma·ni·an** (pănamā'nēan) *adj. & n.*

Pan·a·ma² (păn'amah) *n.* (also ~ **hat**) Fine soft plaited hat made from undeveloped leaves of stemless screw pine (*Carludovica pal-*

mata) of tropical S. Amer., or a imitation of this.

Pan-A·mer·i·can (pănamĕr ĭkan) *adj.* Of all nations of N and S. Amer.; of all Americans.

pan·cake (păn'kāk) *n.* Thin fl cake of batter fried in pan; **flat** a a ~, quite flat; ~ **landing**, (slan landing of aircraft without use undercarriage; ~ **make-up**, mak up in cake form.

pan·chro·mat·ic (pănkrōmăt ĭk) *adj.* (phot.) Equally sensiti to all colors of spectrum, represen ing all colors in proper intensitie **pan·chro·ma·tism** (pănkrō'ma tĭzem) *n.*

pan·cre·as (păn'krēas, păng' *n.* Gland near stomach di charging a digestive secretio (**pancreatic juice**) through duc into duodenum, and also producir INSULIN, which it passes direct into the bloodstream. **pan·cre at·ic** (pănkrēăt'ĭk, păng-) *adj.*

pan·da (păn'da) *n.* Raccoon-lil animal (*Ailurus fulgens*) of S Himalayas, with reddish-brow fur and long bushy ring-marke tail; **giant** ~, large rare bearlil black-and-white mammal (*Ailuro oda melanoleuca*) of E. Tibet ar Szechuan.

Pan·da·rus (păn'darus). (G legend) One of the Trojan leader in the medieval legend of Troilu and Cressida, Cressida's uncle, wl acted as go-between for the lover

pan·dem·ic (pănděm'ĭk) *adj. n.* (Disease, usu. infectious) world-wide distribution.

pan·de·mo·ni·um (păndemō' nēum) *n.* Abode of all demon place of lawless violence or uproa utter confusion. [word coined b Milton]

pan·der (păn'der) *n.* (also **pan der·er**) Go-between in amorou intrigues, procurer; one wl ministers to evil designs. ~ Minister (*to* base passions, ev designs) (also fig.); act as pande to. [f. PANDARUS]

Pan·do·ra (păndōr'a, -dōr'a (Gk. myth.) First woman, made b Hephaestus at the order of Zeus punish the human race becaus PROMETHEUS had stolen fire fro heaven for their use; she becam wife of Epimetheus, brother Prometheus, and from a box (~ **box**) given her by Zeus let loo all the evils that afflict mankin hope alone remaining in the botto of the box.

pan·do·ra (păndōr'a, -dōr'a **pan·dore** (păn'dōr, -dōr) *ns.* Wir stringed musical instrument guitar type.

The 28,575 sq. mile Republic Panama is at the narrowest part of th isthmus linking North and Sou America. The canal (top left) is 40 mile long.

Red (lesser) Panda

Giant Panda

pane (pān) *n.* Single sheet of ass in compartment of window; ctangular division of checkered attern etc. **pane′less** *adj.*

pan·e·gyr·ic (pănĭjēr′ĭk, -jī′rĭk) & *adj.* Laudatory (discourse). **an·e·gyr′i·cal** *adj.* **pan·e·gyr′i-al·ly** *adv.*

pan·e·gy·rize (păn′ĭjirīz) *v.t.* **rized, -riz·ing**). Speak, write, in raise of, eulogize. **pan·e·gyr·ist** ănĭjīr′ĭst, -jī′rĭst) *n.*

pan·el (păn′el) *n.* 1. List of rors, jury. 2. Group of people thered, esp. as experts, to hold scussion, make judgments, etc.; nelists. 3. Distinct section, esp. surface, as of door, etc., often nk below or raised above general vel; strip of material in dress etc. **truck**, small delivery truck aving fully enclosed body. **panel** *t.* (**-eled** or **-elled, -el·ing** or **l·ling**). Saddle (beast) with panel; (wall, door, etc.) with panels; nament (dress etc.) with panels. **an′el·ing, pan′el·ling, pan·el-t** (păn′elĭst) *ns.*

pang (păng) *n.* Shooting pain; dden sharp mental pain.

pan·go·lin (pănggō′lĭn) *n.* Scaly ateater, large mammal of genus *anis* (order Pholidota), of tropical sia and Africa. [Malay *penggoling* ller]

pan·han·dle (păn′hăndel) *n.* andle of pan; narrow prolonga-on of country or territory extend-g between 2 others. ~ *v.* (**-dled,** **lling**). (slang) Beg. **pan′-an·dler** *n.* (slang) Beggar.

Pan·hel·len·ism (pănhĕl′-

Found only in bamboo forests of Yunnan and Szechuan, the giant *panda* can weigh up to 400 lb. The 'fire fox' or lesser panda is cat-sized and is found also in Nepal.

he scale-covered insectivorous angolin is native to Asia and Africa. hen threatened, it rolls itself into a ll, but unlike hedgehogs or spiny ant-aters, some pangolins are arboreal.

enĭzem) *n.* Political union of all Greeks. **Pan·hel·len·ic** (pănhelĕn′ĭk) *adj.*

pan·ic[1] (păn′ĭk) *n.* (also ~ **grass**) Grass of genus *Panicum* including Italian millet, freq. cultivated as cereal grain.

pan·ic[2] (păn′ĭk) *adj.* (of terror) Unreasoning, excessive. ~ *n.* Infectious fright; sudden general alarm leading to hasty measures. ~ *v.* (**-icked, -ick·ing**). Affect, be affected, with panic. **pan′ick·y** *adj.* [Gk. *panikos* of PAN, reputed to cause panic]

pan·i·cle (păn′ĭkel) *n.* (bot.) Compound inflorescence in which some pedicels branch again or repeatedly, forming loose irregu-lar cluster, as in oats. **pan′i·cled** *adj.*

Pan·ja·bi = PUNJABI.

pan·jan·drum (pănjăn′drum) *n.* Mock title of exalted person-age; pompous official or pre-tender. [app. invented by S. Foote, 1720–77, in a piece of non-sense verse]

Pank·hurst (păngk′herst), **Mrs. Emmeline Goulden** (1858–1928). English leader of militant suffragism.

pan·nier, pan·ier (păn′yer, -ēer) *ns.* 1. Basket, esp. one of those carried, usu. in pairs, by beast of burden or on person's shoulders. 2. Frame distending woman's skirt at the hips, part of skirt looped up around hips.

pan·ni·kin (păn′ĭkĭn) *n.* Small metal drinking vessel; its contents.

pan·o·ply (păn′ople) *n.* (pl. **-plies**). Complete suit of armor; (fig.) complete or splendid array. **pan′o·plied** *adj.*

pan·o·ram·a (pănorăm′a, -rah′ma) *n.* Picture of landscape etc. arranged on inside of

waste paper water

cleaning and pulping plant

chemicals

bark stripped

rubbish

water

chemical pulper

water

pulper

mechanical pulper

cylindrical surface or successively rolled out before spectator; continuous passing scene; unbroken view of surrounding region. **pan·o·ram′ic** *adj.* **pan·o·ram′-i·cal·ly** *adv.*

pan·pipe (păn′pīp) *n.* (also **pan′pipes, Pan's′ pipes′**) Musical instrument of graduated series of reeds forming scale, with open ends level. [f. PAN]

pan·sy (păn′zē) *n.* (pl. **-sies**). 1. Wild or cultivated plant (*Viola tricolor*) with variously colored flowers; heartsease. 2. (colloq. offensive) Effeminate man; male homosexual.

pant (pănt) *v.* Gasp for breath; yearn (*for, after, to*); throb violently; utter gaspingly. ~ *n.* Gasp, throb.

Pan·tag·ru·el (păntăg′rŏoĕl, păntagrŏo′el). One of the characters of RABELAIS, giant son of Gargantua, represented as a great eater and drinker and an extravagant and satirical humorist. **Pan·ta·gru·el·i·an** (păntagrŏoĕl′ēan) *adj.*

Pan·ta·loon (păn′talŏon). Venetian character in Italian comedy represented as foolish old man wearing spectacles, pantaloons, and slippers; clown's butt and abettor in harlequinade or pantomime. [It. *Pantalone*, perh. f. San Pantaleone, favorite Venetian saint]

pan·ta·loons (păntalŏonz′) *n.pl.* Garment of breeches and stockings

in one piece; tight-fitting trousers fastened with ribbons or buttons below calf, or strap passing under boots; (archaic) trousers.

pan·the·ism (păn′thēĭzem) *n.* Doctrine that God is everything and everything is God; worship of all the gods. **pan′the·ist** *n.* **pan·the·is′tic, pan·the·is′ti·cal** *adjs.* **pan·the·is′ti·cal·ly** *adv.*

pan·the·on (păn′thēŏn, -on) *n.* 1. Temple dedicated to all the gods, esp. the circular temple still standing in Rome, erected in early 2nd c. A.D. prob. on site of an earlier one built by Agrippa. 2. Building (esp. former church of St. Genevieve in Paris) in which illustrious dead are buried or have memorials. 3. Deities of a people collectively.

pan·ther (păn′ther) *n.* (pl. **-thers**, collect. **-ther**). 1. = LEOPARD, esp. male (now chiefly **black** ~, black form of leopard common in S. India). 2. = MOUNTAIN lion.

pant·ies (păn′tēz) *n.pl.* Underpants worn by women and girls.

pan·to·graph (păn′tograf) *n.* 1. Instrument of four rods jointed together in parallelogram form, with tracing points on one free end and one terminal joint, for copying plans etc. on any scale. 2. (elect.) Device on top of electrically operated vehicle that conveys current from overhead wires. **pan·to·graph′ic** *adj.*

pan·to·mime (păn′tomīm) *n.* 1.

(hist.) Roman actor performing in dumb show. 2. (Brit.) Dramatic entertainment now usu. produced at Christmas time and based on a traditional fairy tale, with singing, dancing, acrobatics, clowning, topical jokes, a transformation scene, and certain stock roles. 3. Dumb show. **pan·to·mim′ic** (păntomĭm′ĭk) *adj.*

pan·try (păn′trē) *n.* (pl. **-tries**). Room in which bread and other

*The **pansy** which now grows wild in some gardens, was bred from a wild flower common in England and the Pyrenees. The multitude of colors has been developed within 170 years.*

size
china clay colour
drying rollers
stock
squeezing roller
wire mesh web
mixer
vacuum
reel of finished paper

provisions, or (**butler's** ~) plates, able linen, etc., are kept.

pants (pănts) *n.pl.* 1. Men's underpants; PANTIES. 2. Trousers.

pan·ty (păn′tē) **hose.** One-piece garment combining PANTIES and stockings.

pan·zer (păn′zer, pahn′tser) *n.* Armor; freq. attrib., as ~ *division.* [Ger.]

pap[1] (păp) *n.* (archaic) Nipple of woman's breast; corresponding part of man.

pap[2] (păp) *n.* Soft or semiliquid food for infants or invalids; mash, pulp.

pa·pa (pah′pa, papah′) *n.* Child's name for) father.

pa·pa·cy (pā′pasē) *n.* (pl. **-cies**). Pope's (tenure of) office; papal system.

pa·pal (pā′pal) *adj.* Of the pope or his office; **P** ~ **States,** district of central Italy until 1870 subject to the Apostolic See. **pa′pal·ly** *adv.* **pa′pal·ism** *n.* **pa′pal·ist** *n. & adj.*

pa·paw (paw′paw, papaw′), **paw·paw** (paw′paw) *ns.* 1. = ᐧPAPAYA. 2. Small N. Amer. tree (*Asimina triloba*) with purple flowers; oblong edible fruit of this, with beanlike seeds embedded in sweet pulp.

pa·pa·ya (papah′ya) *n.* Palmlike tree (*Carica papaya*) of S. Amer.; fruit of this, usu. oblong, of dull orange color, with thick fleshy rind and numerous black seeds embedded in pulp, used as food.

Pa·pe·e·te (pahpēā′tā). Capital of French Polynesia, on the NW. coast of Tahiti Island in the E. Pacific Ocean.

pa·per (pā′per) *n.* 1. Substance composed of fibers interlaced into a compact web, made from linen and cotton rags, straw, wood, certain grasses, etc., which are macerated into a pulp, dried and pressed into a thin flexible sheet, used for writing, printing, drawing, wrapping up parcels, covering the interior of walls, etc.; substance of similar texture, as that made by wasps for their nests; substance made from paper pulp, as papier-mâché etc. 2. Negotiable documents, e.g. bills of exchange; bank notes etc. used as currency (opp. COIN). 3. (slang) (Persons admitted by) free passes to theater etc. 4. (pl.) Documents proving person's or ship's identity, standing, etc.; **send in one's** ~ **s,** resign. 5. Set of questions in examination; essay, dissertation, esp. one read to learned society. 6. Newspaper. 7. Paper used as wrapper or receptacle; small paper parcel; sheet of paper with pins or needles stuck in it. 8. **on** ~, hypothetically, to judge from statistics, etc.; **pa′per-back,** (book) bound in paper, freq. as cheap reprint; **pa′perboy,** boy who sells or delivers newspapers; **pa′perhang·er,** one who hangs wallpaper; **paper knife,** blunt knife for cutting open letters, leaves

of book etc.; **paper mill,** mill in which paper is made; **paper profits,** profits not yet realized; **pa′perweight,** small heavy object laid on loose papers to prevent their being scattered; **paper work,** clerical work involving keeping of records etc. **pa′per·y** *adj.* **paper** *v.t.* Enclose in paper; decorate (wall etc.) with wallpaper; furnish with paper; (slang) fill (theater etc.) by means of free passes. **pa′per·er** *n.*

pa·pier-mâ·ché, pa·per-mâché (pāpermashā′) *ns.* Molded paper pulp used for boxes, trays, etc. [Fr., = "chewed paper"]

pa·pil·la (papĭl′a) *n.* (pl. **-pil·lae** pr. -pĭl′ē). Small nipple-like protuberance in a part or organ of the body; (bot.) small fleshy projection on plant. **pap·il·lar·y** (păp′ĭlĕrē, papĭl′arē), **pap·il·late** (păp′ĭlāt, papĭl′ĭt), **pap·il·lose** (păp′ĭlōs, papĭl′ōs) *adjs.*

pap·il·lon (păp′ĭlŏn) *n.* (Breed of) toy dog with ears suggesting form of butterfly.

pa·pist (pā′pĭst) *n.* Advocate of papal supremacy; (usu. derog.) Roman Catholic. **pa·pis′tic, pa·pis′ti·cal** *adjs.* **pa·pist·ry** (pā′pĭstrē) *n.*

pa·poose, pap·poose (păpōōs′, pa-) *ns.* N. Amer. Ind. young child.

pa·pri·ka (păprē′ka, păp′rĭka) *n.* Ripe fruit of sweet pepper; red condiment made from this. [Hungarian]

*Among the peoples of **Papua New Guinea**, decoration, singing and dancing have always formed an essential part of most aspects of their culture. Today, mass displays are held at the Mount Hagen show.*

Pap (păp) **test, Pap smear.** Method for early detection of cancer, esp. uterine cancer. [f. name of George Papanicolaou, Amer. scientist (1883–1962)]

Pap·u·a (păp´ūa) **New Guinea.** Country in the E. section of the island of New Guinea, covering 178,259 sq. mi. (461,691 sq. km) in the Pacific Ocean N. of Australia; capital, Port Moresby; formerly the Australian territories of Papua and North East New Guinea, which merged in 1945 and became a United Nations trusteeship administered by Australia until independence in 1975.

pap·ule (păp´ūl) *n.* Pimple. **pap·u·lar** (păp´yuler), **pap·u·lose** (păp´yulōs) *adjs.*

pa·py·rus (papī´rus) *n.* (pl. **-rus·es, -ri** pr. **-rī**). Aquatic plant of sedge family (*Cyperus papyrus*), with creeping rootstock sending up long stems that bear spikelets of flowers in large clusters; writing material prepared by ancient Egyptians etc. by soaking, pressing, and drying strips of papyrus stem, laying them side by side, and placing similar layers over these at right angles; manuscript written on this. **pap·y·rol·o·gy** (păpirŏl´ojē) *n.* The scholarly study of papyrus manuscripts. **pap·y·rol´o·gist** *n.*

par (pār) *n.* Equality, equal footing; average or normal amount, degree, or condition; (golf) number of strokes that scratch player should require for hole or course, allowing two putts for each green; **above ~**, at a premium; **at ~**, (of stocks etc.) at face value; **below ~**, at a discount; below the average degree, quality, etc.; not in one's usual health. [L., = "equal(ity)"]

par. *abbrev.* Paragraph; parallel; parenthesis.

para- *prefix.* Beside; beyond; wrong; irregular.

par·a·ble (păr´abel) *n.* Fictitious narrative used to point a moral or illustrate some spiritual relation or condition; short allegory.

pa·rab·o·la (parăb´ola) *n.* Plane curve formed by intersection of cone with plane parallel to its side.

par·a·bol·ic (părabŏl´ĭk), **par·a·bol'i·cal** *adjs.* 1. Of, expressed in, a parable. 2. Of, like, a parabola. **par·a·bol'i·cal·ly** *adv.*

pa·rab·o·loid (parăb´oloid) *n.* Solid some of whose plane sections are parabolas, esp. that generated by revolution of parabola about its axis (**~ of revolution**).

Par·a·cel·sus (părasĕl´sus), **Philippus Aureolus.** Name taken by Theophrastus Bombastus von

*Bundles of **papyrus** near the pyramids. This aquatic reed was the main material used for paper making until the 4th century A.D. Although less is obtained from Egypt today, it is still profuse in east and north Africa.*

Hohenheim (1493–1541), German–Swiss physician, alchemist, and astrologer.

par·a·chute (păr´ashoot) *n.* Umbrella-shaped apparatus of silk or other material attached by ropes to person or heavy object falling or being dropped from a height, esp. from aircraft, and designed to be expanded by the air it is falling through (or other means) and by its resulting drag to reduce the speed of falling to some desired limit, usu. one consistent with safety; **~ troops**, PARATROOPS. **parachute** *v.* (**-chut·ed, -chut·ing**). Convey, descend, by parachute. **par´a·chut·ist** *n.*

pa·rade (parād´) *n.* 1. Display, ostentaion. 2. Muster of troops etc.

for inspection, esp. one he regularly at set hours; ground use for this. 3. Public square promenade. **~** *v.* (**-rad·ed -rad·ing**). 1. Assemble (troop etc.) for review or other purpos march through (streets etc.) wi display; march in procession wi display. 2. Display ostentatiousl **pa·rad´er** *n.*

par·a·digm (păr´adĭm, -dĭm) Example, pattern, esp. of inflectic of noun, verb, etc. **par·a·dig mat·ic** (păradĭgmăt´ĭk) *adj.*

par·a·dise (păr´adĭs) *n.* Garde of Eden (also **earthly ~**); heaver region, state, of supreme bliss; **bir of ~**: see BIRD; **~ duck**, bright colored N.Z. duck (*Tador variegata*), species of sheldrak **par·a·di·sa·i·cal** (păradĭsā´ĭka -zā´-), **par·a·di·sa´ic, par·a·dis· (**păradī´sal, -dī´zal), **par·a·di·si a·cal** (păradĭsī´akal, -zī-´), **par· dis·i·ac** (păradĭs´ēăk, -dĭz´-) ad, [O. Pers, *pairidaeza* park]

A **parade** at Disneyland, California, which was the first of the amusement parks to open in the U.S.A. in 1955. A second park was begun and remained unfinished until 1971, during which time Walt Disney died.

par·a·dox (păr′adŏks) n. Statement contrary to accepted opinion; seemingly absurd though perhaps really well-founded statement; self-contradictory, essentially absurd or false, statement; person, thing, conflicting with preconceived notions of what is reasonable or possible. **par·a·dox′i·cal** adj. **par·a·dox′i·cal·ly** adv. **par·a·dox·i·cal′i·ty** n.

par·af·fin (păr′afĭn) n. 1. (also ~ **wax**) White tasteless odorless waxy substance, chemically a mixture of higher hydrocarbons, solid at ordinary temperatures and obtained by distillation of petroleum etc., used for making candles, rendering paper waterproof (wax paper), etc. 2. (chem.) Any of a series of saturated hydrocarbons of which methane is the simplest member. [L. parum little, affinis having affinity, referring to the relative unreactivity of the paraffins]

par·a·gon (păr′agŏn, -gon) n. 1. Model of excellence, supremely excellent person or thing, model (of virtue etc.). 2. Perfect diamond, 100 carats or more. 3. (print.) Large size of type, between great primer

The bright plumage and long tail feathers of the **bird of paradise** contribute to its spectacular appearance.

Prince Rudolph's Blue Bird of Paradise

...unt Raggis
...d of Paradise

Magnificent Bird of Paradise

Small to medium-sized parrots with long tails have been called **parakeets** *though there is no scientific basis for this discrimination. Many, like the larger ones, have brilliant plumage.*

and double pica (two-line long primer, 20 point).

par·a·graph (păr′agrăf, -grahf) *n.* Distinct passage or section in book etc., usu. marked by indentation of first line; symbol (usu. ¶) formerly used to mark new paragraphs, now as a reference mark; detached short item of news etc. in newspaper. ~ *v.t.* Arrange (article etc.) in paragraphs. **par′a·graph·er** *n.* **par·a·graph′ic** *adj.*

Par·a·guay (păr′agwā, -gwī). Inland republic of S. Amer.; capital, Asunción; ~ **River**, river in S. central S. Amer., flowing 1,584 mi. (2,549 km) from SW. Brazil to the Paraná in SW. Paraguay. **Par·a·guay′an** *adj.* & *n.*

par·a·keet, par·ra·keet (păr′akēt) *ns.* Any of several small esp. long-tailed kinds of parrot; budgerigar. [OF., f. It. *parrochetto* dim. of *parroco* parson, or *parrucchetto* dim. of *parrucca* peruke]

par·al·de·hyde (parăl′dehīd) *n.* Polymer of aldehyde ($C_6H_{12}O_3$), used as a sedative.

par·al·lax (păr′alăks) *n.* Apparent displacement of object, caused by actual change of point of observation; angular amount of this displacement. **par·al·lac′tic** (păralăk′tĭk) *adj.*

par·al·lel (păr′alĕl) *adj.* (of lines) Continuously equidistant (*to*); precisely similar, analogous, or corresponding; ~ **bars**, pair of horizontal parallel bars supported on posts for gymnastic exercises; ~ **circuit**, (elect.) circuit connecting the same two points as are connected by another circuit; ~ **ruler**, two rulers connected by pivoted crosspieces or single ruler fitted with rollers, for drawing parallel lines. **parallel** *n.* 1. (also ~ **of latitude**) Each of the parallel circles marking degrees of latitude on Earth's surface on globe; line on map corresponding to one of these. 2. Person, thing, precisely analogous to another; comparison. 3. Parallel position. 4. Two parallel lines (‖) as reference mark. ~ *v.t.* (**-leled** or **-lelled, -lel·ing** or **-lel·ling**). Represent as similar, compare (*with, to*); find, mention, something parallel or corresponding to; be parallel, correspond, to.

par·al·lel·e·pi·ped (păralĕlepī′pĭd, -pĭp′ĭd) *n.* Solid contained by parallelograms.

par·al·lel·ism (păr′alĕlizem) *n.* Being parallel; comparison or correspondence of successive passages.

par·al·lel·o·gram (păralĕl′ogrăm) *n.* Four-sided rectilineal figure whose opposite sides are parallel.

pa·ral·y·sis (parăl′īsĭs) *n.* (pl. **-ses** pr. -sēz). Impairment or loss of motor or sensory function of nerves; (fig.) state of utter powerlessness.

par·a·lyt·ic (păralĭt′ĭk) *adj.* & *n.* (Person) afflicted with paralysis. **par·a·lyt′i·cal·ly** *adv.*

par·a·lyze (păr′alīz) *v.t.* (**-lyzed, -lyz·ing**). Afflict with paralysis; render powerless, cripple.

Par·a·mar·i·bo (păramăr′ĭbō). Capital and chief seaport of Surinam, on the Surinam River in northeastern S. Amer.

par·a·me·ci·um (păramē′shēum, -sēum) *n.* (pl. **-ci·a** pr. -shēa, -sēa). Ciliated freshwater protozoan of genus **P**~.

pa·ram·e·ter (parăm′īter) *n.* (math.) Quantity constant in case considered, but varying in different cases. **par·a·met·ric** (păramĕt′rĭk), **par·a·met′ri·cal** *adjs.*

par·a·mil·i·tar·y (păramĭl′ĭtĕrē) *adj.* Ancillary to or as substitute for armed forces.

par·a·mo (păr′amō) *n.* (pl. **-mos**). High treeless plateau in tropical S. Amer.

par·a·mount (păr′amownt) *adj.* Supreme; preeminent; superio (*to*). **par′a·mount·cy** *n.* **par′a·mount·ly** *adv.*

par·a·mour (păr′amoor) *n* Illicit lover of married person.

Pa·ra·ná (păranah′). River i central S. Amer. flowing 1,827 mi (2,940 km) from S. Brazil along the S. border of Paraguay to the Rio d la Plata in E. Argentina.

par·a·noi·a (păranoi′a) *n.* Form of mental illness characterized by systematic delusions, esp. o grandeur, persecution, etc. **par·a· noi·ac** (păranoi′ăk, -ĭk) *adj.* & *n.*

par·a·noid (păr′anoid) *adj.* Re sembling, characterized by paranoia.

par·a·pet (păr′apĭt, -pĕt) *n* Low wall at edge of balcony, roof etc., or along sides of bridge etc. (mil.) defense of earth, stone, etc. to conceal and protect troops, esp mound along front of trench **par′a·pet·ed** *adj.* Having parapet.

par·a·pher·nal·ia (părafernāl′ ya, -fenăl′-) *n.pl.* Personal belong ings; accessories, odds and ends o equipment; (formerly) articles o

Female

Male

ersonal property that law allowed
married woman to keep and treat as
er own.

par·a·phrase (păr'afrāz) *n.* Free
rendering or amplification of a
assage, expression of its sense in
ther words. ~ *v.t.* (**-phrased,
-phras·ing**). Express meaning of
passage) in other words. **par·a-
-hras·tic** (părafrăs'tĭk) *adj.* **par-
-phras'ti·cal·ly** *adv.*

par·a·ple·gi·a (păraplē'jēa, -ja)
. Paralysis confined to the lower
mbs. **par·a·ple·gic** (păraplē'jĭk)
dj. & n. (Person) affected with
araplegia.

pa·ra·pro·fes·sion·al (părapro-
ĕsh'onal) *n.* Trained assistant to
eacher, doctor, or other profes-
ional.

par·a·psy·chol·o·gy (păra-
ıköl'ojē) *n.* Study of mental
henomena lying outside the sphere
f ordinary psychology; study of
sychical phenomena. **par·a·psy-
ho·log'i·cal** *adj.*

par·a·se·le·ne (părasĭlē'nē) *n.*
pl. **-nae** pr. -nē). Bright spot on
ınar halo, mock moon; moondog.

par·a·site (păr'asīt) *n.* 1. Inter-
sted hanger-on, toady. 2. Animal,
lant, living in or upon another and
eriving nutriment from it to the
etriment of the host; (loosely)
lant that climbs about another
lant, walls, etc. **par·a·sit·ic** (păra-
ıt'ĭk), **par·a·sit'i·cal** *adjs.* **par·a-
it'i·cal·ly** *adv.* **par'a·sit·ism** *n.*
ar·a·si·tize** (păr'asĭtīz, -sī-) *v.t.*
-tized, -tiz·ing**). Infest as a
arasite.

par·a·sol (păr'asawl, -sŏl) *n.*
.ight umbrella used to give pro-
ection from the sun.

par·a·sym·pa·thet·ic (păra-
ımpathĕt'ĭk) *adj.* Of that part of
he nervous system which consists
f fibers connecting with nerve cells
rouped within or near the viscera,
o called because its peripheral
erves often run alongside those of
he sympathetic system.

par·a·thy·roid (părathī'roid)
dj. (anat.) Situated near the
hyroid; ~ **gland**, one of four small
odies adjacent to thyroid gland,
roducing a secretion that main-
ains the balance between the
alcium in the blood and that in the
ones. **parathyroid** *n.* Para-
hyroid gland.

par·a·troops (păr'atroops) *n.pl.*
ssault troops transported by air-
raft to combat area and then
ropped by parachute. **par'a-
roop·er** *n.*

par·a·ty·phoid (păratī'foid) *n.*
'orm of enteric fever milder than
rue typhoid and bacteriologically
istinguishable from it.

par·a·vane (păr'avān) *n.* Appa-
atus towed from bows of a ship at
depth regulated by its vanes, with
aw-edged jaws for cutting the
oorings of submerged mines.

*Meat and vegetable oils are the main
exports of Paraguay, a land-locked
country in South America. The main
industries are based on the processing
of timber and agricultural products.*

par a·vi·on (păr ăvyawn'). By
air mail. [Fr., by plane]

par·boil (păr'boil) *v.t.* Boil
partially; (fig.) overheat.

par·cel (păr'sel) *n.* 1. Part (esp.
in **part and parcel**); piece of land,
esp. as part of estate. 2. Goods etc.
wrapped up in single package; ~
post, branch of postal service concerned with parcels. **parcel** *v.t.*
(**-celed** or **-celled, -cel·ing** or
-cel·ling). 1. Divide (usu. *out*) into
portions; make (*up*) into parcel(s).
2. (naut.) Cover (caulked seam)
with canvas strips and pitch; wrap
(rope) with canvas strips. **par'cel-
ing, par'cel·ling** *ns.* (esp., naut.)
Strip of canvas, usu. tarred, for
binding around rope.

parch (părch) *v.* Roast slightly;
make or become hot and dry.

parch·ment (părch'ment) *n.*
Skin (strictly, inner part of split
skin of sheep) dressed and prepared
for writing, painting, etc.; parch-
mentlike skin, esp. husk of coffee
bean; ~ **paper**, thick, strong,
specially toughened paper.

par·don (păr'don) *n.* Forgiveness; (law) remission of legal consequences of crime; courteous forbearance (esp. in *I beg your* ~,
formula of apology); (eccles.)
indulgence. **pardon** *v.t.* Forgive;
make allowance for, excuse. **par'-
don·a·ble** *adj.* **par'don·a·bly** *adv.*

par·don·er (păr'doner) *n.* (hist.)
Person licensed to sell pardons or
indulgences.

pare (păr) *v.t.* (**pared, par·ing**).
Trim (thing) by cutting away
irregular parts etc.; cut away skin,
rind, etc., of (fruit etc.); shave, cut
off, away (edges etc.); (fig.)

diminish little by little. **par'er,
par'ing** *ns.*

par·e·gor·ic (părĕgor'ĭk, -găr'-)
n. Camphorated tincture of opium
flavored with aniseed and benzoic
acid, taken for relief of diarrhea and
intestinal pain. ~ *adj.* Soothing.

pa·ren·chy·ma (părĕng'kima)
n. 1. (anat.) Tissue of gland, organ,
etc., as dist. from flesh and
connective tissue. 2. (bot.) Tissue
of cells of about equal length and
breadth placed side by side, usu.
soft and succulent, found esp. in
softer parts of leaves, pulp of fruits,
etc. **pa·ren'chy·mal, par·en-
chym·a·tous** (părĕngkĭm'atus)
adjs.

par·ent (păr'ent, păr'-) *n.* Father
or mother; forefather; animal,
plant, from which others are
derived; (fig.) source, origin.
pa·ren·tal (părĕn'tal) *adj.*
pa·ren'tal·ly *adv.* **par'ent·hood**
n.

par·ent·age (păr'entĭj, păr'-) *n.*
Descent from parents, lineage.

pa·ren·the·sis (părĕn'thĭsĭs) *n.*
(pl. **-ses** pr. -sēz). Word, clause,
sentence, inserted into a passage to
which it is not grammatically
essential, and usu. marked off by
brackets, dashes, or commas; (sing.
or pl.) round brackets ( ) used for
this. **pa·ren·the·size** (părĕn'thĭ-
sīz) *v.t.* (**-sized, -siz·ing**). Insert as
parenthesis; put between marks of
parenthesis; **par·en·thet·ic** (părĕn-
thĕt'ĭk), **par·en·thet'i·cal** *adjs.*
Of, inserted as a, parenthesis;
(fig.) interposed. **par·en·thet'i-
cal·ly** *adv.*

pa·re·sis (părē'sĭs, păr'ĭsĭs) *n.*
Partial paralysis or weakening of
muscular power. **pa·ret·ic**
(parĕt'ĭk, parē'tĭk) *n. & adj.*
pa·ret'i·cal·ly *adv.*

par ex·cel·lence (păr ĕkse-
lahns'). By virtue of special
excellence, above all others that may
be so called. [Fr.]

par·fait (pärfā') *n.* Dessert of layers of ice cream, fruit, etc., served in tall glass.

pa·ri·ah (parī'a, păr'ēa) *n.* Member of very extensive low caste in S. India; member of low or no caste; (fig.) social outcast. [Tamil *paṛaiyar* (hereditary) drummers]

pa·ri·e·tal (parī'ītal) *adj.* 1. Of the wall of the body or of any of its cavities; ~ **bones**, pair forming part of sides and top of skull. 2. (bot.) Of or on the walls of a hollow structure etc. 3. Pertaining to residence within a college, esp. to rules governing visiting hours in dormitories for members of the opposite sex.

par·i·mu·tu·el (păr'īmū'chōōel) *n.* (also ~ **machine**) System of betting, carried on by a mechanical apparatus, in which the winners divide the losers' stakes less a percentage for managerial expenses (see TOTALIZATOR).

Par·is[1] (păr'ĭs). Capital city of France, on Seine River; **plaster of** ~: see PLASTER; ~ **green**, vivid light green pigment prepared from arsenic trioxide and copper acetate. [*Parisii*, L. name of Gallic tribe that settled there]

Par·is[2] (păr'ĭs). (Gk. legend) Son of Priam and Hecuba; as a baby he was left to die because of a prophecy that he would bring destruction upon Troy, but shepherds found him and brought him up; he awarded apple of discord to Aphrodite, who offered him the fairest woman in the world; he chose and abducted HELEN, thus bringing about the Trojan War in which he was killed and Troy sacked.

par·ish (păr'ĭsh) *n.* 1. Subdivision of diocese, having its own church and clergyman; inhabitants of this. 2. County in Louisiana. 3. Members of a parish; all the parishioners of a particular parish.

pa·rish·ion·er (parĭsh'oner) *n.* Member of parish.

Pa·ri·sian (parē'zhan, -rĭzh'an) *adj.* & *n.* (Native, inhabitant) of PARIS[1].

par·i·ty (păr'ĭtē) *n.* 1. Equality; parallelism, analogy; equivalence in another currency, being at par. 2. (med.) Condition of having borne children; number of children borne by one mother.

park (pärk) *n.* 1. Large enclosed piece of ground, usu. with woodland and meadow, in town ornamentally laid out for public recreation; large tract of land kept in natural state for public benefit. 2. (Space occupied by) artillery, stores, etc., in encampment; area where vehicles may be left temporarily. 3. Area or stadium used for sports, as **ball** ~. **park** *v.* Enclose (ground) in or as park; arrange (artillery etc.) compactly in a park; place or leave (vehicle) in park etc. temporarily; (transf.) leave in suitable place until required; **park'ing meter**, coin-operated meter that registers time allowed for a vehicle to be parked.

par·ka (pär'ka) *n.* Long fur jacket with attached hood worn in Arctic regions; garment resembling this.

Park·in·son's (pär'kĭnsonz) **disease.** Chronic progressive disease of the nervous system (*Paralysis agitans*, "shaking palsy") characterized by tremor, muscular rigidity, defective gait, and emaciation. [James *Parkinson*, British physician (1755–1824)]

Park·in·son's (pär'kĭnsonz) **law.** (joc.) Fact that work expands to fill the time available for doing it. [C. N. *Parkinson*, 1909–]

Park·man (pärk'man), **Francis** (1823–93). Amer. historian; famous for his account of his experiences with the Sioux Indians and his trip over the Oregon Trail,

park·way (pärk'wā) *n.* Broa landscaped highway, sometime with landscaped strips.

par·lance (pär'lans) *n.* (Particu lar) way of speaking as regard choice of words (*in common, lega* etc. ~).

par·lay (pär'lā, -lē) *v.t.* Us (money won on bet) as furthe stake; increase in value (as if) b parlaying. ~ *n.* Act of parlaying bet so made.

par·ley (pär'lē) *n.* (pl. **-leys** Conference for debating of poin in dispute, esp. (mil.) discussion c terms. ~ *v.* (**-leyed, -ley·ing** Discuss terms (*with*); speak (es foreign languages).

par·lia·ment (pär'lament) Council forming with the sovereig the supreme legislature of Unite Kingdom, consisting of the Hous of Lords (see LORD) and the Hous of Commons (see COMMONS); co responding legislative assembly other countries; **Long** ~, see LONG

par·lia·men·tar·i·an (pärla mentār'ēan) *n.* Skilled debater i parliament; adherent of parliamer in English civil war of 17th c.

par·lia·men·ta·ry (pärlamēn terē, -trē) *adj.* Of a parliamen enacted, established, by parliamen (of language) admissible in parlia ment; (colloq.) civil; body of rule prescribing procedures to b followed in legislative or organiza tional debate.

par·lor, Brit. **par·lour** (pär'le *ns.* Ordinary sitting room of fami in private house; **beauty** ~, se BEAUTY; ~ **car**, railroad car fitte with individual reserved seats; ~ **game**, game (esp. word game c quiz) played indoors.

par·lous (pär'lus) *adj.* (archai Perilous; hard to deal with.

Par·men·i·des (pärmĕn'ĭdēz (6th c. B.C.) Greek philosopher c Elea (Italy); founder of the ELEAT school, which believed in a sing eternal god not resembling mortal

Par·me·san (pär'mezahn, -zǎ -zan) *adj.* Of Parma; esp. applie to hard, easily grated kind of chees made there and in other parts of N Italy. **par·mi·gia·na** (pärmizhah na), **par·mi·gia·no** (pärmizhah nō) *adjs.* Cooked with Parmesa cheese.

Par·nas·sus (pärnăs'us). Loft mountain of Greece, N. of Delph associated in classical Greece wi worship of Apollo and the Muse

Par·nell (pärnĕl´, pär´nel), **Charles Stewart** (1846–91). Irish nationalist politician; leader of Irish home rule movement.

pa·ro·chi·al (parō´kēal) *adj.* Of a parish; (fig.) confined to narrow area; narrow, provincial. **pa·ro´·chi·al·ism** *n.* **pa·ro´chi·al·ly** *adv.*

par·o·dy (păr´odē) *n.* (pl. **-dies**). Composition in which an author's characteristics are ridiculed by imitation; feeble imitation, travesty. ~ *v.t.* (**-died, -dy·ing**). Imitate (composition etc.) humorously. **par´o·dist** *n.*

pa·role (parōl´) *n.* Word of honor, esp. prisoner's promise that he will not attempt escape, or will return to custody if liberated, or will refrain from taking up arms against captors for stated period; **on** ~, (liberated) on parole. **parole** *v.t.* (**-roled, -rol·ing**). Put (prisoner) on parole.

pa·rot·id (parŏt´ĭd) *adj.* Situated near the ear, esp. ~ **gland**, (in man, largest of three salivary glands) situated in front of ear. ~ *n.* Parotid gland. **par·o·ti·tis** (părotī´tĭs) *n.* (path.) Inflammation of parotid gland, mumps.

par·ox·ysm (păr´oksĭzem) *n.* Fit of disease; fit (*of* rage, laughter, etc.). **par·ox·ys´mal** *adj.* [Gk. *oxunō* goad, render acute]

par·quet (pärkā´, -kĕt´) *n.* Wooden flooring of pieces of wood, freq. of different kinds, arranged in pattern. ~ *v.t.* (**-queted, -quet·ing** pr. -kād´, -kā´ing). Floor (room) thus. **par·quet´ry** (pär´kĭtrē) *n.*

parr (pär) *n.* (pl. **parrs**, collect. **parr**). Young salmon.

Parr (pär), **Catherine** (1512–1548). Sixth wife of Henry VIII, whom she outlived.

par·ra·keet = PARAKEET.

par·ri·cide (păr´ĭsīd) *n.* 1. One who murders his father. 2. Murder of father, parent, near relative, or one whose person is considered sacred. **par·ri·cid´al** *adj.*

par·rot (păr´ot) *n.* Bird of large mainly tropical group (order Psittaciformes) with short hooked bill, and freq. brilliant plumage, many species of which can be taught to repeat words and sentences; person who repeats another's words or imitates his actions unintelligently; ~ **fever**, PSITTACOSIS; ~ **fish**, any of various fishes with brilliant coloring or strong, hard mouth like parrot's bill. **parrot** *v.t.* Repeat (words etc.) mechanically.

par·ry (păr´ē) *v.t.* (**-ried, -ry·ing**). Ward off, avert (weapon, blow, etc.). ~ *n.* (pl. **-ries**). Warding off. [L. *parare* prepare]

parse (pärs) *v.t.* (**parsed, par·sing**). Describe (word) grammatically, stating inflection, relation to sentence, etc.; resolve (sentence) into component parts of speech and describe them grammatically.

par·sec (pär´sĕk) *n.* (astron.) Unit in measuring stellar distances, distance at which a star would have an annual PARALLAX of 1 second of an arc, equivalent to 206,265 astronomical units (3.258 light-years). [*par(allaz)* + *sec(ond)*]

Par·see, Par·si (pär´sē, pärsē´) *adjs.* & *ns.* 1. (One) of the followers of ZOROASTER, descendants of those Persians who fled to India in 7th and 8th centuries to escape Muslim persecution. 2. (Of) the Iranian dialect of the Parsee religious literature.

par·si·mo·ny (pär´simōnē) *n.* Extreme or excessive carefulness in employment of money, etc.; reluctance to give or spend. **par·si·mo´·ni·ous** *adj.* **par·si·mo´ni·ous·ly** *adv.* **par·si·mo´ni·ous·ness** *n.*

pars·ley (pärs´lē) *n.* Biennial umbelliferous plant (*Petroselinum crispum*) with white flowers and aromatic leaves, finely divided and curled in commonly cultivated variety, used for seasoning and garnishing dishes.

pars·nip (pärs´nĭp) *n.* Biennial umbelliferous plant (*Pastinaca sativa*) with pinnate leaves, yellow flowers, and (in cultivated variety) large, pale yellow, sweet, fleshy, and nutritious root used as culinary vegetable; root of this.

par·son (pär´son) *n.* Rector; vicar or any beneficed clergyman; (colloq.) any clergyman; ~**'s nose**, (Brit.) rump of cooked fowl; pope's nose. **par·son·ic** (pärsŏn´ĭk), **par·son´i·cal** *adjs.*

par·son·age (pär´sonĭj) *n.* Parson's official home.

part¹ (pärt) *n.* 1. Some but not all of a thing or number of things; division or section; section of book etc., esp. as much as is issued at one time; each of several equal portions of a whole (as third, fourth, etc. ~, one of three, four, etc. equal parts); individual component of machine etc.; ~ **of**, a part of, some of. 2. Portion allotted; share; interest, concern; person's share in action, his function, business, duty. 3. Character assigned to actor on stage; words spoken by actor on stage; copy of these; (fig.) character sustained by anyone. 4. Melody assigned to particular voice or instrument in harmonic music. 5. (archaic, pl.) Abilities, capacities, (as in *man of* ~s). 6. (pl.) Region. 7. Side in dispute. 8. Dividing line along which something is parted. 9. **for my** ~, as far as I am concerned; **in** ~, partly; **the most** ~, the greatest part, most; **for the most** ~, in most cases, mostly; **take** ~, assist (*in*); **take the** ~ **of**, support, back up; ~ **and parcel**, (emphatic) constituent, element; essential portion; ~ **of speech**, each of the grammatical categories

of words (noun, adjective, pronoun verb, adverb, preposition, con junction, article, interjection); ~ **song**, song for three or more voic parts, usu. without accompanimer and in simple harmony. **part** *adv* In part, partly; ~ **owner** etc owner etc. in common with anothe or others; ~**-time** (*adj.*) employe for, taking up, only part of th working day; ~**-timer** (*n.*).

part² (pärt) *v.* Divide into part suffer division; separate (hair), a with comb, on each side of dividin line or part; separate (combatants friends, etc.); quit one another company; ~ **company**, dissolv companionship (*with*); **part from with**, say good-by to; **part with** give up, surrender (property etc. pay (money). **part·ing** *n.* (esp Leave-taking; ~ **of the way** point at which road divides into or more; (fig.) moment for decisio in choice between alternativ courses.

par·take (pärtāk´) *v.* (**-too -tak·en, -tak·ing**). Take a shar in; take a share (*in, of, with*); tak esp. eat or drink some or (colloq all *of.* **par·tak´er** *n.*

par·terre (pärtār´) *n.* 1. Lev space in garden occupied by flowe beds. 2. Part of ground floor theater under rear balcony.

par·the·no·gen·e·sis (pärthenŏ jĕn´ĭsĭs) *n.* (biol.) Reproductio from gametes without fertilizatio esp. among invertebrates and low plants. **par·the·no·ge·net·ic** (pä thenōjenĕt´ĭk) *adj.* **par·the·no·ge net´i·cal·ly** *adv.*

Par·the·non (pär´thenŏn, -no Temple of Athen Parthenos ("th maiden") on the Acropolis Athens, erected 447–438 B.C. und Pericles' administration and dec rated with sculptures by Phidias his school.

par·tial (pär´shal) *adj.* 1. Biased, unfair; ~ **to**, having a likin for. 2. Forming only a part; nc complete or total. **par´tial·ly** *ad* **par·ti·al·i·ty** (pärshēal´ĭtē, pä shäl´-) *n.* (pl. **-ties**). Bia favoritism; fondness (*for*).

par·ti·ble (pär´tibel) *adj.* Tha can or must be divided (*among*; es of heritable property).

par·tic·i·pate (pärtĭs´ipāt) (**-pat·ed, -pat·ing**). Have shar in; have share (*in*); have somethin *of.* **par·tic·i·pant** (pärtĭs´ipant) & *adj.* **par·tic·i·pa·tion** (pä tĭsipā´shon), **par·tic·i·pa·tor** *ns.*

par·ti·ci·ple (pär´tĭsipel) Verbal adjective ending in *ing* or *e* qualifying noun but retaining som

dian Ring-Necked
arakeet

Princess Alexandra's
Parakeet

Plum-Headed
Parakeet

**African Grey
Parrot**

St. Vincent
Parrot

Red-Winged Parakeet

Bourke's
Parakeet

did
eet

urquoise Grass
arakeet

Crimson Rosella

Blue-Fronted
Parrot

Masked
Lovebirds

Madagascar
Lovebird

properties of verb, e.g., tense and government of object. **par·ti·cip·i·al** (pärtĭsĭp´ēal) *adj.*

par·ti·cle (pär´tĭkel) *n.* Minute portion of matter; smallest possible amount; minor part of speech, esp. short indeclinable one; prefix or suffix having distinct meaning.

par·ti-col·ored (pär´tēkŭlerd) *adj.* Partly of one color, partly of another.

par·tic·u·lar (pertĭk´yuler) *adj.* 1. Relating to one as distinguished from others, special; one considered apart from others, individual. 2. Worth notice, special. 3. Detailed, minute; scrupulously exact; fastidious (*about*). **par·tic·u·lar·i·ty** (pertĭkyulăr´ĭtē) *n.* (pl. **-ties**). **par·tic·u·lar·ly** *adv.* **particular** *n.* Detail, item; (pl.) detailed account; **in** ~, especially.

par·tic·u·lar·ize (pertĭk´yulerīz) *v.t.* (**-ized, -iz·ing**). Name specially or one by one, specify. **par·tic·u·lar·i·za·tion** (pertĭkyulerĭzā´shon) *n.*

par·tic·u·late (pertĭk´yulĭt) *adj.* Of the nature of a particle;

Found in Europe, Asia and Africa, the **partridge** *has long been nurtured in England where hunting it was considered a traditional sport. The grey or common partridge (Perdix perdix, below) is about 12 inches long and has distinctive chestnut breast-markings.*

The purple blooms of the **pasque-flower,** *a wild anemone native to the chalky areas of England, usually flowers in spring and its name is adapted from a French word meaning 'Easter'. Similar spring-flowering anemones grow wild in Europe and North America.*

composed of particles.

par·ti·san (pär´tĭzan) *n.* Ad herent of party, cause, etc., esp unreasoning one; (hist.) member c light irregular troops employed i special enterprises; (in World Wa II) guerrilla (applied orig. Russians resisting in parts of the country occupied by the enemy ~ *adj.* **par´ti·san·ship** *n.*

par·tite (pär´tīt) *adj.* (bot entom.) Divided (nearly) to th base.

par·ti·tion (pärtĭsh´on) Division into parts; such par structure separating 2 such part esp. slight wall. ~ *v.t.* Divide int parts; ~ **off**, separate (part of roo etc.) by a partition.

par·ti·tive (pär´tĭtĭv) *ad* Dividing into parts; (gram denoting part of a collective whol **par´ti·tive·ly** *adv.* **partitive** Partitive word.

part·ly (pärt´lē) *adv.* Wit respect to a part; in some degree.

part·ner (pärt´ner) *n.* Share person associated with others i business of which he shares risl and profits; wife, husband; com panion in dance; player associate with another in bridge, tennis, et ~ *v.t.* Associate as partners; b partner of. **part´ner·ship** *n.*

par·tridge (pär´trĭj) *n.* (p **-tridg·es**, collect. **-tridge**). An f various game birds, esp. British nd central European **common** or ·**ray** ~ (*Perdix perdix*); any of arious birds of grouse or pheasant amily; **partridgeberry**, N. Amer. railing evergreen (*Mitchella repens*) vith white flowers and scarlet ·erries.

par·tu·ri·ent (pärtoor´ēent, ·tūr´-) *adj.* About to bring forth ·oung. **par·tu·ri·tion** (pärturĭsh´- ·n, pärchu-) *n.* Act of bringing orth young.

par·ty (pär´tē) *n.* (pl. **-ties**). 1. Those on one side in a contest etc., ·sp. considered collectively; ·ersons united in maintaining ause, policy, etc., in opposition to ·thers; system of taking sides on ·ublic questions, system of parties. ·. Body of persons traveling or ·ngaged together. 3. Social gather- ·ng, esp. of invited guests at private ·ouse. 4. Each of the two or ·nore persons making the two sides ·n legal action, contract, marriage, ·tc.; **third** ~, person or persons ·ther than these, esp. in insurance ·natters. 5. Participator, accessory *to* action). 6. (now vulg. or joc.) ·erson. 7. ~ **line**, telephone line ·hared by number of subscribers;

(also) set policy of political party.

par·ve·nu (pär´venōō, -nū) *n.* Person of obscure origin who has gained wealth or position, upstart.

pas (pah) *n.* (pl. **pas** pr. pah, pahz). 1. Precedence. 2. Step in dancing (e.g. **pas de deux**, dance for two persons). [Fr.]

Pas·cal (păskăl´), **Blaise** (1623– 1662). French mathematician and religious philosopher; author of *Pensées*.

pas·chal (păs´kal) *adj.* Of the Passover; of Easter; ~ **lamb**, (hist.) lamb slaughtered and eaten at Passover SEDER; **P ~ Lamb**, Christ.

pa·sha, pa·cha (pah´sha, păsh´a, pashah´) *ns.* Title, placed after name, formerly used by senior officers in Turkish dominions. **pa·sha·lik, pa·sha·lic** (pashah´lĭk) *ns.* Jurisdiction of pasha.

Pash·to (pŭsh´tō), **Push·tu** (pŭsh´tōō) *adjs. & ns.* (Of) the language of the Afghans, belonging

to the Eastern Iranıan group of the Indo-European family.

pasque·flow·er (păsk´flower) *n.* Any of several plants of the genus *Anemone*, having large purple, blue, or white cup-shaped flowers; esp. *A. patens* of W. N. Amer. [Fr. *passefleur* surpassing flower, with assim. to *Pasque* Easter]

pass[1] (păs) *v.* 1. Move onward, proceed; circulate, be current; be transported from place to place; change; die; go by; come to an end. 2. Get through, effect a passage; go uncensured, be accepted as adequate; be known as a member of a group other than one's own; (of bill in legislature, proposal, etc.) be sanctioned; (of candidate) satisfy examiner. 3. (law) Adjudicate (*on, upon*); (of judgment) be given (*for* plaintiff etc.). 4. (cards etc.) Decline, declare inability, to play, bid, make trump, etc.; throw up one's hand. 5. Leave on one side or behind as one goes; go across (sea, frontier, mountain range). 6. (of bill) Be examined and approved by legislature; reach standard required by (examiner, examina- tion); ~ **muster**: see MUSTER. 7. Outstrip, surpass; be beyond compass or range of, transcend (any faculty or expression). 8. Transport (usu. with preposition or adverb), move, cause to go; emit from the body as excrement; cause to go by; hand around, transfer; give currency to; (football etc.) transfer (ball) to another player on the same side. 9. Cause, allow, (bill in legislature, candidate for examination, etc.) to proceed after scrutiny. 10. Spend (*time* etc.); utter (criticism, judicial sentence, *upon*). 11. ~ **away**, die, come to an end; ~ **by**, omit, disregard; walk etc. past; ~ **for**, be accepted as; ~ **off**, palm off (thing *for* or *as* what it is not); distract attention from (awkward situation etc.); ~ **out**, (colloq.) distribute (papers, examinations); become unconscious (from drinking etc.); ~ **over**, omit; make no remark upon; ~ **the time**: see TIME; ~ **through**, experience; ~ **up**, (colloq.) reject, as an opportunity. **pass** *n.* 1. Passing, esp. of examination. 2. Critical position, juncture, predicament. 3. Written permission to pass into or out of a place, be absent from quarters etc.; ticket authorizing holder to travel free on railroad etc. 4. Thrust in fencing; juggling trick; passing of hands over anything, esp. in mesmerism; (football etc.) transference of ball to another player on same side; **make a ~ at**, (colloq.) try to attract sexually; try (to do anything). 5. **pass′book**, book

*A **Passion Play** has been performed every ten years by people at Oberammergau in West Germany, since it celebrated the end of a plague in 1634. Once these dramas were performed widely throughout Europe.*

*This ship is on a **passenger** cruise in Alaskan waters. The largest peninsula in the Western Hemisphere, with spectacular coastal scenery, Alaska has been building a successful tourist industry.*

upplied by bank to person having
urrent or deposit account, showing
ll sums deposited and drawn;
pass'key, private key to gate etc.
or special purposes; master key;
pass'word, selected word or
phrase distinguishing friend from
enemy.

pass[2] (păs) *n.* Narrow passage
through mountains; navigable
channel, esp. at river's mouth.

pass·a·ble (păs'abel) *adj.* (esp.)
That can pass muster, fairly good.
pass'a·ble·ness *n.* **pass'a·bly** *adv.*

pas·sa·ca·glia (pahsakahl'ya,
păsa-) *n.* (mus.) Instrumental
composition in ¾ time, based on
an unvarying ground; (orig.)
Spanish or Italian dance tune. [It.,
perh. f. Span. *pasar* pass, *calle*
street, because freq. played in
street]

pas·sage (păs'ij) *n.* 1. Passing,
transit; transition from one state to
another; liberty, right, to pass
through; voyage, crossing from port
to port; right of conveyance as
passenger by sea; **bird of** ~, see
BIRD. 2. Passing of a measure into
law. 3. Way by which person or
thing passes; corridor etc. giving
communication between different
rooms in house. 4. What passes
between two persons mutually,
interchange of confidences, etc. 5.
(also ~ **at arms**) Fight (freq. fig.).
6. Part of speech or literary work
taken for quotation etc.

pas·sé (păsā') *adj.* Past the
prime; behind the times.

passe·men·terie (păsmĕn'trē)
n. Trimming of gold or silver lace,
braid, beads, etc. [Fr.]

pas·sen·ger (păs'enjer) *n.*
Traveler in (public) conveyance by
land, air, or water; traveler in
automobile who is not driving; ~
pigeon, N. Amer. wild pigeon
(*Ectopistes migratorius*) capable of
long sustained flight (now extinct).

passe-par·tout (păspărtoo') *n.*
1. Master key. 2. Adhesive tape
fastening edges of glass to mount of
photograph or small picture as
substitute for frame. [Fr., = "pass
everywhere"]

pass·er (păs'er) *n.* One who
passes; ~ **-by**, one who passes, esp.
casually.

pas·ser·ine (păs'erīn) *adj. & n.*
(Bird) of the order Passeriformes
(perchers).

pas·si·ble (păs'ibel) *adj.* (theol.)
Capable of feeling or suffering.
pas·si·bil'i·ty *n.*

pass·ing (păs'ing) *n.* ~ **bell**, bell
rung at moment of person's death;
in ~, incidentally, by the way; ~
note, (mus.) note not belonging to
harmony, interposed for purpose of
passing smoothly from one to the
other of two notes essential to it.
passing *adj.* (esp.) Transient,
fleeting, cursory, incidental. ~
adv. (archaic) Very.

pas·sion (păsh'on) *n.* 1. Strong
emotion; outburst of anger; sexual
love; strong enthusiasm (*for*). 2.
P ~, sufferings of Christ during
Christ's last days and (esp.) on the
cross; (musical setting of) narrative
of this from Gospels; **pas'sion-
flower**, flower of genus *Passiflora*
of (chiefly climbing) plants with
parts supposed to suggest
instruments of Christ's Passion, the
corona representing the crown of
thorns, etc.; **pas'sionfruit**, grana-
dilla; **Passion Play**, mystery play
representing Christ's Passion;
Passion Sunday, second Sunday
before Easter; **Pas'siontide**,
period of 2 weeks before Easter;
Passion Week, week following
Passion Sunday (but in Anglican
usage freq. = week before Easter,
Holy Week). **passion** *v.i.* (poet.)

*Of about 500 varieties of passion-
flower, those most cultivated produce
passion-fruit or granadillas. The juice
and pulp of the fruits are extracted and
are often canned for export. Below:
Passiflora caerulea.*

Feel or express passion. **pas'sion-
less** *adj.* **pas'sion·less·ly** *adv.*
pas'sion·less·ness *n.*

pas·sion·al (păsh'onal) *adj.* Of,
marked by, passion. ~ *n.* Book of
the sufferings of saints and martyrs.

pas·sion·ate (păsh'onĭt) *adj.*
Easily moved to anger; dominated
by, easily moved to, strong feeling;
due to, showing, passion. **pas'-
sion·ate·ly** *adv.* **pas'sion·ate·-
ness** *n.*

pas·sive (păs'ĭv) *adj.* 1. Suffering action, acted upon; (gram.)
applied to a voice of the verb
comprising those forms in which
action of verb is treated as attribute
of thing toward which action is
directed; (loosely, of verb) in which
the subject is acted on by something or suffers the action. 2.
Offering no opposition, submissive;
~ **resistance**: see RESISTANCE. 3.
Not active, inert. **pas'sive·ly** *adv.*
pas'sive·ness, pas·siv'i·ty *ns.*
passive *n.* Passive voice or form
of verb.

Pass·o·ver (păs'ōver). Jewish
festival beginning with the Seder in

the evening of the 14th of Nisan and lasting eight days (Nisan approx. = April), commemorating the escape of the Jews from Egypt after the "passing over" (i.e. sparing) of their houses whose doorposts were marked with the blood of the lamb, when the Egyptians were smitten with the death of their first-born (Exod. 12).

pass·port (păs′pōrt, -pȯrt) *n.* Document issued by competent authority serving as identification of person and his nationality, esp. when traveling abroad; (fig.) thing that ensures admission.

past¹ (păst, pahst) *adj.* (also rare *past part.* of PASS). (esp.) Gone by in time; just gone by; (gram.) expressing past action or state; ~ **master**, thorough master (*in, of,* subject); ~ **perfect** = PLUPER-FECT. **past** *n.* Past time; what has happened in past time; person's past life or career, esp. one that will not bear inquiry.

past² (păst, pahst) *prep.* Beyond in time or place; beyond the range or compass of. ~ *adv.* So as to pass by, as *hastens* ~.

pas·ta (pah′stɑ) *n.* Dried flour paste used in Italian cooking, in various shapes such as macaroni, spaghetti, vermicelli.

paste (păst) *n.* Flour moistened and kneaded, with lard, butter, suet, etc., as cooking material; any of various sweet doughy confec-

tions; relish of pounded fish, meat, etc.; adhesive; any soft plastic mixture; mixture of clay, water, etc., used in making pottery; hard vitreous composition used in making imitation gems; **paste′-board**, stiff substance made by pasting together sheets of paper; (attrib., fig.) unsubstantial, flimsy. **paste** *v.t.* (**past·ed, past·ing**). Fasten with paste; stick *up* on wall etc. with paste; cover (as) by pasting on or over; (slang) beat, thrash; bomb heavily.

pas·tel (păstĕl′) *n.* Drawing instrument consisting of a stick of powdered pigment bound with gum, usu. covered with paper; drawing made with pastels (usu. in several colors); (attrib., of light color) soft, subdued. **pas·tel′ist, pas·tel′list** *ns.*

Pas·ter·nak (păs′ternăk), **Boris Leonidovich** (1890–1960). Russian translator, novelist, and poet best known for his novel *Doctor Zhivago* (1957); awarded the 1958 Nobel Prize for literature but declined.

Pas·teur (păstȇr′), **Louis** (1822–1895). French chemist and biologist; founder of bacteriology

Trail-riding on horseback is a popular **pastime** *in the U.S.A. The increase in national parks and monuments, plus a growing desire among people to explore their natural environment, has led to a revival of this hobby.*

and inventor of method of inocula-tion for hydrophobia.

pas·teur·ize (păs′cherīz, păs′te-*v.t.* (**-ized, -iz·ing**). Partially sterilize by Pasteur's method prevent or arrest fermentation ir (milk etc.) by keeping for some time at a temperature (55–60 C.) that does not greatly affect chemical composition. **pas·teur·i·za′tion** *n.*

pas·tiche (păstēsh′, pah-) *n.* 1. Medley, esp. musical composition picture, made up from various sources. 2. Literary or other work of art composed in the style of a known author.

pas·tille (păstēl′), **pas·til** (păs′-tĭl) *ns.* 1. Small roll of aromatic paste burned as deodorant etc. 2. Small sweet, freq. medicated, lozenge.

pas·time (păs′tīm) *n.* Recrea-tion; game, sport.

pas·tor (păs′ter) *n.* Minister in charge of church or congregation; person exercising spiritual guid-ance. [Anglo-Fr., f. L. *pastor* shepherd]

pas·to·ral (păs′teral) *adj.* 1. Of shepherds; (of land) used for pasture; (of poems etc.) portraying country life. 2. Of a pastor; **P ~ Epistles**, those of Paul to Timothy and Titus, dealing with pastor's work. **pas′to·ral·ly** *adv.* **pas′-to·ral** *n.* 1. Pastoral play, poem, etc. or picture. 2. (mus.) = PASTORALE. 3. Letter from pastor,

A **pasteurizing** plant in New Zealand. Pasteurizing is a method of preventing the fermentation of various liquids, e.g. milk, by retaining the liquid at a certain temperature.

Left: An early 19th-century **pastil** burner. The scented smoke emerged through the chimney of the porcelain cottage. Today, the oriental types of incense burners are used and aromatic sticks are more popular than pastil.

Cattle grazing in a **pasture**. Where there is low rainfall and no irrigation, stock must feed on natural grasses, but they put on more weight more quickly on specially planted pastures.

esp. bishop, to clergy or people. **pas·to·ral·ism** n. Convention of pastoral poetry etc.

pas·to·rale (păstorahl´, -răl´) n. (pl. **-rales, -ra·li** pr. -rah´lē). 1. Simple opera etc. with rural subject. 2. Slow, quiet instrumental composition.

pas·tor·ate (păs´terĭt) n. Pastor's (tenure of) office; body of pastors.

pas·tra·mi (pastrah´mē) n. Seasoned smoked beef. [Yiddish]

pas·try (pā´strē) n. (pl. **-tries**). Paste of flour, fat, water, etc., rolled and baked; articles of food (pies, tarts, etc.) made wholly or partly of this; ~ **chef**, one who makes pastry, esp. for public sale.

pas·tur·age (păs´cherĭj) n. Pasturing; grass for cattle etc.; pasture land.

pas·ture (păs´cher) n. (Piece of) land covered with grass. ~ v. **(-tured, -tur·ing).** Lead, put, (cattle etc.) to pasture. **pas´tur·a·ble** adj. **pas´tur·er** n.

past·y[1] (păs´tē) n. (pl. **past·ies**). Pie of meat or other food seasoned and enclosed in crust of pastry and baked.

past·y[2] (pā´stē) adj. **(past·i·er, past·i·est).** Of, like, paste; of pale complexion. **past´i·ness** n.

pat[1] (păt) n. Stroke, tap, esp. with hand as caress etc.; small mass (esp. of butter) formed (as) by patting; sound made by striking lightly with something flat, such as hand. ~ v. **(pat·ted, pat·ting).** Strike (thing) gently with flat surface; flatten thus; strike gently with inner surface of fingers, esp. to mark sympathy, approbation, etc.; beat lightly on; ~ **on the back**, express approbation of.

pat[2] (păt) adv. & adj. Apposite(ly), opportune(ly); ready for any occasion; **stand** ~, hold firm to a decision; in poker, make decision not to try to improve one's hand.

Pat·a·go·ni·a (pătagō´nēa, -gōn´ya). Southern region of S. Amer., in Argentina between Andes and Atlantic. **Pat·a·go´ni·an** adj. & n. [f. obs. *Patagon*, one of the S. Amer. Indians inhabiting this region]

patch (păch) n. 1. Piece of cloth, metal, etc., put on to mend hole or rent or strengthen weak place; piece of plaster etc. put over wound; pad worn to protect injured eye. 2. Large or irregular spot on surface; piece of ground; number of plants growing on this: small area, as a ~ **of ice**; ~ **pocket**, pocket sewn on like patch; ~ **test**, test for allergy by applying to the skin patches containing allergenic substances. **patch** v.t. Put patch(es) on; serve as patch to; piece (things) together; appear as patches on (surface); ~ **up**, repair with patches; put to-

Despite the inhospitable appearance of the wind-swept plains of **Patagonia,** the far south of Argentina, very large numbers of Merino, Corriedale and Romney Marsh sheep are bred at altitudes exceeding 2,000 ft.

gether hastily; (fig.) repair; set right (matter, quarrel, etc.); **patch'-work**, work made up of fragments of different colors sewn together (freq. fig.). **patch'y** *adj.* (**patch-i·er, patch·i·est**). **patch'i·ly** *adv.* **patch'i·ness** *n.*

patch·ou·li (păch´ōolē, pachōo´-lē) *n.* Odoriferous plant (*Pogostemon patchouly*) having leaves that yield axomatic oil used in perfume manufacture; penetrating and lasting perfume prepared from this.

pate (pāt) *n.* (colloq.) Head, often as seat of intellect; top of the head.

pa·té (pahtā´) *n.* Paste of meat etc. often baked in pastry; **~ de foie gras** (de fwah grah´), paste of liver of fatted geese. [Fr.]

pa·tel·la (patĕl´a) *n.* (pl. **-tel·lae** pr. -tĕl´ē, **-tel·las**). Kneecap. **pa·tel'lar, pa·tel·late** (patĕl´ĭt) *adjs.*

pat·en (păt´en) *n.* Shallow dish used for bread at Eucharist; thin circular plate of metal.

pat·ent (păt´ent) *adj.* 1. (of rights etc.) Conferred, protected, by **letters ~**, open document under seal of government, granting right, title, etc., esp. sole right for a term to make, use, or sell some invention. 2. Obvious to everyone; plain. 3. **~ leather**: see LEATHER; **~ medicine**, proprietary medicine, esp. one of which formula is not disclosed on container and which is obtainable without a prescription. **pa·ten·cy** (pā´tensē) *n.* **pat'ent·a·ble** *adj.* **pat'ent·ly** *adv.* **patent** *n.* Letters patent;

government grant of exclusive privilege of making or selling new invention; invention, process, so protected. **~** *v.t.* Obtain patent for (invention).

pat·ent·ee (pătentē´) *n.* Holder of a patent, person for the time being entitled to the benefit of a patent.

pa·ter·nal (patēr´nal) *adj.* Of a father; fatherly; related through the father, on the father's side. **pa·ter'nal·ly** *adv.*

pa·ter·ni·ty (patēr´nĭtē) *n.* Fatherhood; one's paternal origin; (fig.) authorship, source.

pa·ter·nos·ter (pā´ternŏs´ter, păt´er-) *n.* (also **Pater Noster**) Lord's Prayer, esp. in Latin; bead in rosary indicating that paternoster is to be said. [L. *pater noster* our father]

path (păth, pahth) *n.* (pl. **paths** pr. pădhz, pahdhz, păths, pahths). Footway, esp. one merely beaten by feet, not specially constructed; track laid for foot or cycle racing; line along which person or thing moves; **path'finder**, person who makes a path for those who follow, esp. in wilderness. **path'less** *adj.*

Pa·than (patahn´) *adj.* & (Member) of a Pashto-speakin people inhabiting E. Afghanistan NW. Pakistan, and other parts o the Indian peninsula.

pa·thet·ic (pathĕt´ĭk) *adj.* Ex citing pity or sadness; of th emotions; **~ fallacy**, ascription o human emotion to inanimat nature. **pa·thet'i·cal·ly** *adv.*

path·o·gen·ic (păthojĕn´ĭk) *ad* Capable of producing disease **path·o·gen** (păth´ojen) *n.*

pa·thol·o·gy (pathŏl´ojē) *n.* (p **-gies**). Systematic study o physical diseases, their causes symptoms, and treatment. **path·o·log·i·cal** (pătholŏj´ĭkal), **path·o·log'ic** *adjs.* **path·o·log'i·cal·ly** *adv.* **pa·thol'o·gist** *n.*

pa·thos (pā´thŏs) *n.* Quality i speech, events, etc., that excites pit or sadness. [Gk., = "suffering"]

pa·tience (pā´shens) *n.* 1. Caln endurance of pain or any provoca tion; forbearance; quiet and self possessed waiting for something perseverance; **have no ~ with** (colloq.) be unable to bear patiently

ut of ~, provoked so as no longer o have patience. **2.** (cards) Game n which object is to arrange cards a some systematic order.

pa·tient (pā′shent) *adj.* Having, howing, patience. **pa′tient·ly** dv. **patient** *n.* Person under nedical treatment, esp. with eference to his doctor.

pat·i·na (păt′ina) *n.* Incrustaon, usu. green, on surface of old ronze, esteemed as ornament; (by xtension) gloss on woodwork etc., roduced by long use.

pa·ti·o (păt′ēō, pah′tēō) *n.* (pl. **ti·os**). Inner court open to sky; aved usu. roofless area adjoining house. [Span.]

pat·ois (păt′wah) *n.* (pl. **pat·ois** r. păt′wahz). Regional dialect of ural people; jargon; mixture of two r more languages.

pa·tri·arch (pā′trēark) *n.* **1.** Father and ruler of family or tribe; ne of the forefathers of Abraham, s ancestors of the human race; Abraham, Isaac, Jacob, or any of acob's 12 sons, as progenitors of he Hebrew peoples. **2.** (in early nd Orthodox Churches) Bishop, sp. of Antioch, Alexandria, Contantinople, Jerusalem, or Rome; in R.C. Ch.) pope, or a bishop anking next above primates and

metropolitans and immediately below the pope. **3.** Founder of an order, science, etc.; venerable old man; oldest living representative (*of*). **pa·tri·ar′chal** *adj.* **pa·tri·ar′chal·ly** *adv.*

pa·tri·ar·chate (pā′trēarkĭt) *n.* Office, see, residence, of ecclesiastical patriarch; rank of tribal patriarch.

pa·tri·ar·chy (pā′trēarkē) *n.* (pl. **-chies**). Government by father or eldest male of tribe or family; community so organized.

pa·tri·cian (patrĭsh′an) *n.* **1.** Ancient Roman noble (contrasted with PLEBEIAN), one belonging to one of the original citizen families from whom, in early years of Republic, senators, consuls and pontifices were exclusively chosen; member of noble order in later Roman Empire; officer representing Roman emperor in provinces of Italy and Africa. **2.** Nobleman, esp. (hist.) in some medieval Italian republics. ~ *adj.* Noble, aristocratic; of the ancient Roman nobility.

*A **patient** has his blood pressure checked. With ever-advancing medical technology, people are living longer, and surviving once-incurable diseases.*

pat·ri·cide (păt′rĭsīd) *n.* Parricide. **pat·ri·cid′al** *adj.*

Pat·rick (păt′rĭk), **St.** (c389–c461). Patron saint and apostle of Ireland; prob. of mixed Roman and British parentage; missionary to Ireland, from which, according to legend, he drove all snakes; commemorated Mar. 17, **St. Patrick's Day**; **St.** ~'**s cross**, red saltire on white ground, the national cross of Ireland.

pat·ri·mo·ny (păt′rimōnē) *n.* (pl. **-nies**). Property inherited from one's father or ancestors, heritage; endowment of church etc. **pat·ri·mo′ni·al** *adj.*

pa·tri·ot (pā′trēot, -ŏt) *n.* One who defends or is zealous for his country's freedom or rights. **pa·tri·ot·ic** (pātrēŏt′ĭk) *adj.* **pa·tri·ot′i·cal·ly** *adv.* **pa·tri·ot·ism** (pā′trēotĭzem) *n.*

pa·tris·tic (patrĭs′tĭk) *adj.* Of (the study of the writings of) the fathers of the church.

Pa·tro·clus (patrō′klus). (Gk. legend) Grecian warrior at siege of Troy, friend of Achilles; slain by Hector.

pa·trol (patrōl′) *n.* Going the rounds of garrison, camp, etc.; tour of town etc. by police; detachment of guard, police officers, assigned to this; ships, aircraft, guarding sea route, etc.; routine operational flight of aircraft; detachment of troops sent out to reconnoiter; unit of Scouts (6 under ~ **leader**); **patrol′man** (pl. **-men**), police officer attached to particular beat or district; **patrol wagon**, police van for prisoners. **patrol** *v.* (**-trolled, -trol·ling**). Act as patrol; go around (camp, town, etc.) as patrol. **pa·trol′ler** *n.* [Fr. *patrouiller*, orig. = "paddle in mud"]

pa·tron (pā′tron) *n.* (fem. **pa·tron·ess** pr. pā′tronĭs). One who countenances, protects, or gives influential support to; customer, esp. regular one, of shop, restaurant, etc.; (usu. ~ **saint**) tutelary saint of person, place, craft, etc.

pa·tron·age (pā′tronĭj) *n.* 1. Support, encouragement, given by patron; customer's support. 2. Right of presentation to benefice or office. 3. Patronizing airs. **pa·tron·ize** (pā′tronīz) *v.t.* (**-ized, -iz·ing**). 1. Act as patron toward, support, encourage. 2. Treat (person, thing) as if with consciousness of one's superiority. **pa′tron·iz·er** *n.* **pa′tron·iz·ing** *adj.* **pa′tron·iz·ing·ly** *adv.*

pat·ro·nym·ic (pătronĭm′ĭk) *adj. & n.* (Name) derived from that of a father or ancestor.

pat·ter[1] (păt′er) *n.* Jargon of any profession or class; oratory, speechifying, of mountebank, conjurer, etc.; rapid speech introduced into (comic) song. ~ *v.* Repeat (prayers etc.) in rapid mechanical way; talk glibly. [f. PATERNOSTER]

pat·ter[2] (păt′er) *v.* Make rapid succession of taps, as rain on windowpane; run with short quick steps; cause (water etc.) to patter. ~ *n.* Succession of taps.

pat·tern (păt′ern) *n.* 1. Excellent example; (attrib.) perfect, ideal, model. 2. Model from which thing is to be made. 3. Sample (of tailor's cloth, etc.). 4. Decorative design as executed on carpet, wallpaper, cloth, etc.; distribution of shots, bombs, etc., on target. 5. (fig.) Arrangement of things or actions, as ~ *of behavior, life,* etc. **pattern** *v.t.* Model (thing *after, upon* design, etc.); decorate with pattern. **pat′ternmaker** *n.*

pat·ty (păt′ē) *n.* (pl. **-ties**). Little pie or pasty; flat, round piece of chopped or ground meat, esp. **hamburger** ~.

pau·ci·ty (paw′sĭtē) *n.* Smallness of number or quantity.

*The name **Paul** has been assumed by various Popes since Paul I was elected in A.D. 757. Paul VI was a controversial Pope in an era of change, during the second Vatican Council in the 1960s.*

Paul[1] (pawl), **St.** (d. *c*67 A.D. (also called Saul, of Tarsus) Jew with the status of a Roman citizen who was converted to Christianit became "Apostle of the Gentiles and the 1st great Christian mis sionary and theologian; h missionary journeys are describe in the Acts of the Apostles, and h letters (*Epistles*) to the Churche form part of the New Testamen he was martyred in Rome; com memorated with St. Peter, June 2

Paul[2] (pawl). Name of six popes including **Paul III** (Alessandr Farnese, 1468–1549), pope 1534 1549, patron of art, established th constitution of the Jesuits (1540 convened the Council of Tren **Paul VI** (Giovanni Battist Montini, 1897–1978), pope 1963 1978.

Paul[3] (pawl). (1754–1801 Emperor of Russia 1796–1801; of Peter III and Catherine th Great; was murdered when h refused to abdicate.

Paul·ine (paw′līn) *adj.* Of S Paul, his writings or his doctrines

Occurring naturally, **patterns** can be seen in rock strata, such as those at Kalbarri, Western Australia (1) or in the forms of a fossilized crinoid in Dorset, England (2), and may have influenced the decorator of the Presbytery ceiling at St. Alban's Cathedral (3).

~ epistles, those in New Testament attributed to St. Paul. **Pauline** n. Member of one of many orders dedicated to St. Paul.

Paul·ing (paw′ling), **Linus Carl** (1901–). Amer. chemist noted for work on molecular structure and on chemical bond; received Nobel Prize for chemistry, 1954, and for peace, 1962.

paunch (pawnch) n. Belly, abdomen; protruding belly. **paunch′y** adj.

pau·per (paw′per) n. Person without means of livelihood, beggar; (hist.) recipient of charity; (law) person allowed to sue or defend *in forma pauperis*. **pau′-per·ism, pau·per·i·za·tion** (paw-perĭzā′shon) ns. **pau′per·ize** v.t. (**-ized, -iz·ing**).

pause (pawz) n. Interval of inaction or silence, esp. from hesitation; break made in speaking or reading; (mus.) mark (⌒ or ⌣)

Pattern-making is a skilled part of a shoemaker's trade. In some traditional companies a model of the customer's foot is taken and kept as a reference for future orders.

*Although constant improvements to welfare services have mostly eliminated the **pauper** from western countries, poverty is still a chronic problem in India and other under-developed countries.*

*The Russian ballerina, **Anna Pavlova**, is best remembered for her creation of the role of 'Le Cygne' choreographed for her by Fokine in 1905. It was one among her large repertoire of ballets.*

*A **pawnbroker** is a money-lender or small-scale banker and the three balls which identify a pawnshop are said to be derived from the arms of the Medici family, who were bankers in Florence.*

placed over or under note or rest as sign that it is to be lengthened; **give** ~ **to**, cause or pause or hesitate. **pause** *v.i.* (**paused, paus·ing**). Make a pause, wait; linger *upon* (word etc.).

pa·vane (pavahn´, -văn´), **pav·an** (păv´an) *ns.* Stately dance of 16th and 17th centuries in which dancers were elaborately dressed; music for this, in slow time.

pave (pāv) *v.t.* (**paved, pav·ing**). Cover (street, floor, etc.) with or as with pavement; (fig.) prepare (*the way for*). **pav·ior** (pāv´yer) *n.*

pave·ment (pāv´ment) *n.* Covering of street, floor, etc., made of stones, tiles, wooden blocks, asphalt, etc.; (zool.) pavementlike formation of close-set teeth etc.

pa·vil·ion (pavĭl´yon) *n.* 1. Tent, esp. large peaked one; light ornamental building, esp. one attached to baseball field etc. for spectators and players; projecting (usu. highly decorated) subdivision of building. 2. Part of brilliant-cut gemstone below girdle. ~ *v.t.* Enclose (as) in, furnish with, pavilion. [L. *papilionem*, butterfly, in LL., tent]

Pav·lov (păv´lŏv; *Russ.* pahv´-lŏf), **Ivan Petrovich** (1849–1916). Russian physiologist; awarded Nobel Prize for medicine, 1904; noted for research on conditioned reflexes.

Pav·lo·va (păvlŏ´va; *Russ.* pahv´-lŏvah), **Anna Matveevna** (1885–1931). Russian ballerina.

paw (paw) *n.* Foot of beast having claws or nails; fur from lower part of animal's leg; (colloq.) hand. ~ *v.* Strike with paw; (of horse) strike (ground), strike ground, with hoofs; (colloq.) handle awkwardly or rudely.

pawl (pawl) *n.* Short pivoted catch engaging with toothed wheel to prevent recoil; (naut.) short bar used to prevent capstan, windlass, etc., from recoiling. ~ *v.t.* Secure (capstan etc.) with pawl.

pawn[1] (pawn) *n.* One of the pieces of smallest size and value in chess; (fig.) unimportant person used by another as a mere tool. [AF. *poun*, f. med. L. *pedonem* foot soldier]

pawn[2] (pawn) *n.* Thing, person, left in another's keeping as security, pledge; state of being pledged; **pawn´broker**, one who lends money at interest on security of personal property pawned; **pawn´-broking**, his occupation; **pawn´-shop**, pawnbroker's place of business; **pawn ticket**, receipt for thing pledged with pawnbroker. **pawn** *v.t.* Deposit (thing) as security for payment of money or performance of action; (fig.) pledge.

Paw·nee (pawnē´) *n.* (pl. **-nees**, collect. **-nee**). Indian of a N. Amer. confederacy, formerly living in Nebraska, now in Oklahoma.

paw·paw = PAPAW.

pax (păks) *n.* 1. Kiss of peace as liturgical form at High Mass. 2. ~ **vo·bis·cum** (vōbĭs´kum), (as

salutation) peace be with you. 3. **Pax Bri·tan·ni·ca** (brĭtăn´ĭka) peace imposed by British rule; **Pax Ro·ma·na** (rōmā´na, rōmah´na), peace between nationalities within Roman Empire. [L., = "peace"]

pay[1] (pā) *v.* (**paid** or for sense 4 **payed, pay·ing**). 1. Give (person) what is due in discharge of debt or *for* services done or goods received; recompense (work); hand over (money owed); hand over amount of (debt, wages, etc.); (fig.) reward, recompense; ~ **for**, hand over the price of, bear the cost of; (fig.) be punished for; ~ **in**, pay to account; ~ **off**, pay in full and discharge or be quit of (ship's crew, creditor, etc.); (colloq.) bring success; ~ (person) **out**, punish or have revenge on him; disburse; ~ **up**, pay full amount of (arrears; or abs.); ~ **one's way**, not get into debt. 2. Render, bestow (attention, court, compliment, etc., *to*). 3. (of business etc.) Yield adequate return to (person); yield adequate return. 4. (naut.) ~ **off**, (of ship) fall off to leeward when helm is put up. ~ **out, away**, let out (rope) by slackening it. 5. ~ **-as-you-go**, policy of managing finances by meeting obligations from current income instead of by borrowing; **pay´off**, time of reckoning, dénouement; (colloq.) bribe. 6. **paying guest**, resident in board-inghouse etc. **pay** *n.* Amount paid; wages, hire, salary; **in the** ~ **of**, employed by; **pay´check**, bank

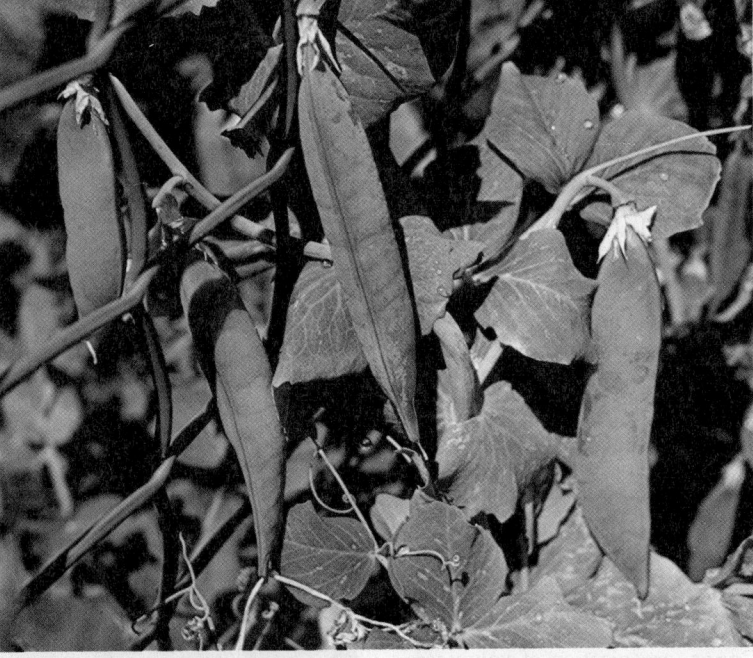

Whether it is used green or dried, the edible **pea** (right), with its valuable protein content, is a staple food in many countries. The family Leguminosae also contains plants such as the everlasting pea (above) whose pods are inedible.

heck given as salary or wages; **ay′day**, day on which payment sp. of wages) is (to be) made; ~ **irt**, (mining) earth or ore containg precious metal or other mineral a sufficient quantity to be profitly worked; (fig.) any source of ealth or income; **pay envelope**, nvelope containing employee's ages; **pay′load**, weight of goods, assengers, etc., carried by aircraft c.; **pay′master**, officer, official, ho pays troops, workmen, etc.; **ay′roll**, list of employees receivg regular pay; **pay phone, pay tation**, public, coin-operated telehone; **pay toilet**, public toilet ith coin-operated door. **paying** dj. Profitable (enterprise, mine, c.).

pay² (pā) v.t. (**payed** or **paid**, ay·ing). (naut.) Smear with tar, itch, etc., to render waterproof.

pay·a·ble (pā′əbel) adj. That ust be paid, due; that may be paid.

pay·ee (pāē′) n. Person to whom ayment is made.

pay·ment (pā′ment) n. Paying; mount paid; (fig.) recompense.

Pb symbol. Lead.

PBB abbrev. Toxic chemical sed in industry, now considered to e contaminating farm products. (oly) b(rominated) b(iphenyl)]

PBS abbrev. Public Broadcasting Service.

PBX abbrev. Private branch exchange (private telephone switchboard).

p.c. abbrev. Percent; petty cash; post card.

PCB abbrev. Toxic chemical used in industry, now considered to be contaminating river fish. [p(oly) c(hlorinated) b(iphenyl)]

Pd symbol. Palladium.

P.D.Q. (pēdēkū′) abbrev. (slang) Pretty damn quick.

P.E. abbrev. Physical education; Professional Engineer; Protestant Episcopal.

pea (pē) n. (pl. **peas**; archaic or Brit. dial. **pease**). Hardy climbing leguminous plant (*Pisum sativum*), with large flowers and long pods each containing a row of round seeds; any of various related leguminous plants; seed of this as food; **green** ~**s**, peas gathered for food while still young and tender; **everlasting** ~, plant (*Lathyrus latifolius*) cultivated for its variously colored flowers; **sweet** ~: see SWEET; **pea′nut**, (fruit of) *Arachis hypogaea*, with pod ripening underground, containing seeds like peas, valued as food and for their oil; **peanut butter**, paste of ground peanuts; **pea′shooter**, toy weapon, tube from which dried peas are shot by blowing; **pea soup**, soup made from (esp. dried) peas; (attrib., esp. of fog) suggestive of this in its dull-yellow color or thick consistency.

orting groundnuts, or **peanuts,** after ne harvest in India, where they are rown extensively. Where the rainfall is nsufficient to sustain the crop irrigation s used. In the U.S.A. half the crop is sed to make peanut-butter.

Related to the almond and nectarine, the sweet, juicy **peach** *(right) has become a popular fruit in warmer regions, far from China where it originated.*

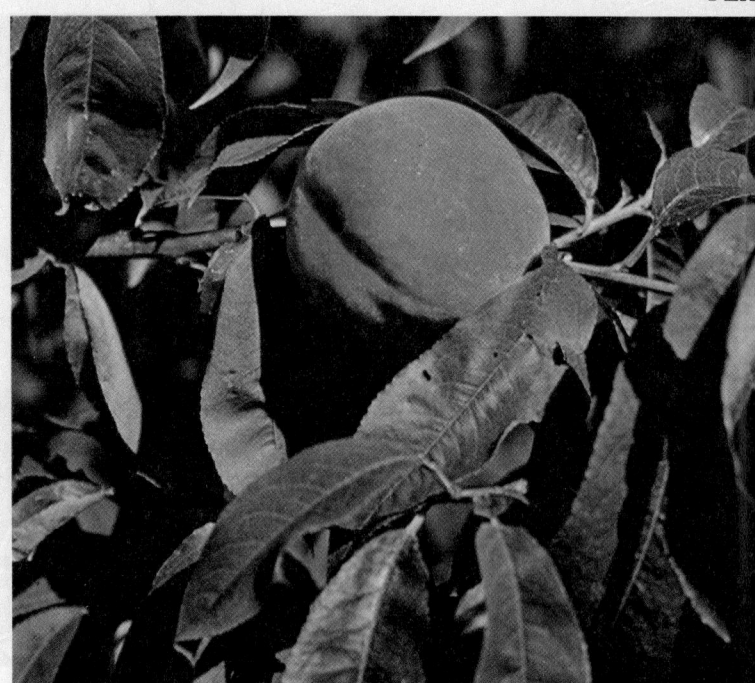

peace (pēs) *n.* 1. Freedom from, cessation of, war; ratification or treaty of peace between powers previously at war. 2. Freedom from civil disorder; general peace of a country as secured by law. 3. Quiet, tranquility; mental calm. 4. **at ~**, in state of friendliness, not at strife (*with*); **hold one's ~**, keep silence; **keep the ~**, prevent, refrain from, strife; **make one's ~** (*with*), become reconciled (*with*); **make ~**, bring hostilities to an end. 5. **peace′keeping**, (committed to) maintaining peace between nations, esp. in *U.N. peacekeeping forces*; **peace′maker**, one who brings about peace; **peace offering**, propitiatory gift; (bibl.) offering presented as thanksgiving to God; **peace officer**, policeman, sheriff; **peace pipe**, calumet; **Peace Corps**, organization of volunteers working in developing countries.

peace·a·ble (pē′sabel) *adj.* Disposed, tending, to peace; free from disturbance, peaceful. **peace′-a·ble·ness** *n.* **peac′a·bly** *adv.*

peace·ful (pēs′ful) *adj.* Characterized by, belonging to a state of, peace; not violating or infringing peace. **peace′ful·ly** *adv.* **peace′-ful·ness** *n.*

peach (pēch) *n.* Large roundish fruit with downy white or yellow skin flushed with red, highly flavored sweet pulp, and rough furrowed stone; tree (*Prunus persica*) bearing this, a native of Asia very early introduced into Europe; peach color; (slang) person or thing of superlative merit, attractive young woman; **~ brandy**, liquor made from peach juice; **peach-color(ed)**, (of) color of ripe peach, soft yellowish pink; **peach Melba**, confection of ice cream and peaches (after Dame Nellie *Melba*, Australian prima donna). **peach′y** *adj.* (**peach·i·er, peach·i·est**). Like a peach, esp. in color and softness. [L. *persicum* (*malum*) Persian (apple)]

pea·cock (pē′kŏk) *n.* (pl. **-cocks**, collect. **-cock**). 1. Male bird of any species of *Pavo*, esp. of *P. cristatus*, native of India, with striking plumage and upper tail coverts marked with iridescent ocelli, able to expand its tail erect like fan (freq. as type of ostentatious display). 2. European butterfly (*Nymphalis io*) with ocellated wings. 3. **peacock blue**, lustrous blue of peacock's neck feathers; **peacock throne**, former throne of kings of Delhi, adorned with representation of fully expanded tail coverts of peacock composed of precious stones. **peacock** *v.i.*

The **peacock** *was a bird native to India and south-east Asia, and related to the pheasant. Peacocks became established in Europe during the Roman era. There they were killed for food until the turkey was brought from America.*

Make display; strut about ostentatiously. **pea′cock·er·y** *n.* **pea′-cock·ish, pea′cock·y** *adjs.*

pea·fowl (pē′fowl) *n.* (pl. **-fowls**, collect. **-fowl**). Peacock or peahen.

pea·hen (pē′hĕn) *n.* Female of the peacock.

pea (pē) **jacket.** Sailor's short double-breasted overcoat of coarse woolen cloth.

peak¹ (pēk) *n.* 1. Projecting part of brim of cap; (naut.) narrow part of ship's hold, esp. (**forepeak**) at bow; upper outer corner of sail extended by gaff. 2. Pointed top, esp. of mountain; point, e.g. of beard; highest point in curve or record of fluctuations (hence **pea load**, greatest frequency maximum of electric power, traffi etc.; **peak hour**, time of day whe this occurs).

peak² (pēk) *v.i.* Waste awa **peak·ed** (pē′kĭd) *adj.* Sharp featured, pinched. **peak′y** *ad* Sickly, puny.

peak³ (pēk) *v.* 1. (naut.) T (yard) vertically; raise (oar blade almost vertically. 2. Reach highe point.

peal (pēl) *n.* Loud ringing bell(s), esp. series of changes on s of bells; set of bells; loud volley sound, esp. of thunder or laughte **~ v.** Sound forth in a peal; rin (bells) in peals; utter sonorously.

pear (pār) *n.* (Fleshy frui tapering toward stalk, of) the tre *Pyrus communis*, or other specie with similar fruit; **alligator ~** AVOCADO. **prickly ~**: see PRICKLY **pear′-shaped** *adj.*

*A **pearl** is formed by an oyster or other bivalve to prevent a grain of sand from irritating it. When the Japanese learnt how to induce this artificially and to keep oysters in enclosures until harvesting, the need for divers was greatly reduced. Left: Sorting pearls at Toba.*

*Mentioned by Homer, the **pear** (above) has been used as a dessert fruit for thousands of years. Today it is grown in many temperate areas and is also canned and dried.*

pearl (pērl) *n.* 1. Concentration, usu. white or bluish-gray, formed around foreign body within shell of certain bivalve mollusks, having beautiful luster and highly prized as gem; precious thing, finest example (*of* its kind); pearllike thing, e.g. dewdrop, tear, tooth; **mother-of-~**: see MOTHER. 2. Small fragment of various substances. 3. **pearl ash**, commercial potassium carbonate; **pearl barley**, barley reduced by attrition to small rounded grains; **pearl button**, button made of mother-of-pearl or imitation of it; **pearl diver**, one who dives for pearl oysters; **pearl fisher**, one who fishes for pearls; **pearl oyster**, oyster of family Pteriidae, which often produce pearls; **pearl shell**, mother-of-pearl as naturally found. **pearl** *v.* Sprinkle with pearly drops; make pearly in color etc.; reduce (barley, etc.) to small pearls;

*Kinder Scout (left) in the **Peak** District of Derbyshire, England, now attracts campers, people on hiking tours, and pot-holers who explore the water-worn caverns in the area.*

Peat (right) is dug by hand in Ireland where it is used as fuel. Its origin is evident from the roots and branches which have not decayed. Archaeologists have also found textiles and other relics in it.

*The **pecan** nut is a member of the walnut family and is an important economic crop in south-eastern U.S.A. It is also grown to a lesser extent in Australia and South Africa.*

form pearllike drops; fish for pearls. **pearl′y** *adj.* (**pearl·i·er, pearl·i·est**). **pearl′i·ness** *n.* **pearl** *adj.* Of the color of pearl.

Pearl (pērl) **Harbor.** Harbor on island of Oahu, near Honolulu, Hawaii, site of U.S. naval base, bombed in surprise attack by Japan, Dec. 7, 1941.

pearl·ite (pēr′līt) *n.* Microstructural constituent of iron, a conglomerate of cementite and ferrite.

Pea·ry (pēr′ē), **Robert Edwin** (1856–1920). Amer. naval officer and Arctic explorer; reached N. Pole on Apr. 6, 1909; **Peary Land**, mountainous peninsula in N. Greenland on the Arctic Ocean.

peas·ant (pĕz′ant) *n.* Countryman, rustic, esp. one working on land as small farmer or laborer. **peas·ant·ry** (pĕz′antrē) *n.* (Body of) peasants.

pease (pēz) *n.* (pl. **pease**). (Brit. or archaic) Peas, esp. in ~ **porridge**.

peat (pēt) *n.* Accumulation of partially decayed vegetable matter found in damp or marshy regions; cut piece of this, used as fuel; ~ **bog**, broken ground from which peats have been cut. **peat′y** *adj.*

peb·ble (pĕb′el) *n.* 1. Small stone worn and rounded by natural action. 2. Colorless transparent rock crystal used for spectacles, lens of this. **peb′bly** *adj.*

pe·can (pĭkahn′, -kăn′, pē′kăn) *n.* Species of hickory (*Carya illinoensis*) common in Ohio and Mississippi valleys; olive-shaped finely flavored nut of this.

pec·ca·ble (pĕk′abel) *adj.* Liable to sin. **pec·ca·bil′i·ty** *n.*

pec·ca·dil·lo (pĕkadĭl′ō) *n.* (pl. **-loes, -los**). Trifling offense.

pec·ca·ry (pĕk′arē) *n.* (pl. **-ries**, collect. **-ry**). Either of two piglike mammals, the collared ~ (*Taxassu tajacu*) or the white-lipped ~, ranging from SW. U.S. to S. Amer. and having a musk gland, sharp tusks, and gray to brown bristles.

pêche mel·ba (pēch′ měl′ba, pěsh′) = PEACH Melba.

peck[1] (pĕk) *n.* Measure of capacity for dry goods, 2 gallons,

*Found only in America from the south west U.S.A. to the Rio Platte in Argentina, the two species of **peccary** travel in groups, usually in isolated areas. They have been tamed and reared like pigs.*

¼ bushel; vessel used as peck measure.

peck[2] (pĕk) *v.* 1. Strike (thing) with beak; pluck *out* thus; make (hole) thus; aim *at* with beak; (colloq.) eat in nibbling fashion. 2. Strike with pick or other pointed tool. 3. **peck′ing order**, hierarchy apparently recognized among domestic birds (also transf.). **peck**

. Stroke with beak; mark made with this; (joc.) kiss like bird's peck; **~ order**, pecking order.

peck·er (pĕk´er) *n.* Bird that ˈecks; (slang) courage, resolution; ˈvulg.) penis.

pec·tin (pĕk´tĭn) *n.* (chem.) ˈhite gelatinous substance soluble ˈn water, closely related to the ˈarbohydrates, formed in the ˈipening of fruits, and constituting ˈhe gelatinizing agent in vegetable ˈuices. **pec´tic** *adj.*

pec·to·ral (pĕk´toral) *adj.* Of the ˈreast or chest; remedying diseases ˈf the chest; worn on the breast; ˈ**~ cross**, cross of precious metal ˈorn on the breast by bishops, ˈardinals, and abbots. **pectoral** *n.* ˈrnamental breastplate, esp. that of ˈewish high priest.

pec·tose (pĕk´tōs) *n.* (chem.) ˈnsoluble substance related to ˈellulose and occurring with it in ˈegetable tissues, esp. in unripe ˈruits and fleshy roots, converted by ˈhe action of acids into PECTIN.

pec·u·late (pĕk´yulāt) *v.* (**-lat**- ˈd, -lat·ing**). Embezzle. **pec·**- ˈ**·la·tion** (pĕkyulā´shon), **pec´u**- ˈa·tor** *ns.*

pe·cu·liar (pĭkūl´yer) *adj.* Be-

longing exclusively *to*; belonging to the individual; particular, special; singular, strange, odd; **~ institution**, (U.S. hist., archaic) institution of slavery peculiar to southern states before the Civil War. **peculiar** *n.* 1. Peculiar property, privilege, etc. 2. (Brit. hist.) Parish, church, exempt from jurisdiction of diocese in which it lies.

pe·cu·li·ar·i·ty (pĭkūlēăr´ĭtē, -kūlyăr´-) *n.* (pl. **-ties**). Being peculiar; characteristic; oddity.

pe·cul·iar·ly (pĭkūl´yerlē) *adv.* As regards oneself alone, individually; especially, more than usually; oddly.

pe·cu·ni·ar·y (pĭkū´nēĕrē) *adj.* (Consisting) of money. **pe·cu·niar·i·ly** (pĭkūnēăr´ĭlē) *adv.*

ped·a·gogue, ped·a·gog (pĕd´agŏg, -gawg) *ns.* Schoolmaster, teacher (usu. contempt.). **ped·agog·ic** (pĕdagŏj´ĭk, -gō´jĭk), **ped·a·gog´i·cal** *adjs.* **ped·a·gog´i·cal·ly** *adv.*

ped·a·go·gy (pĕd´agōjē, -gŏjē), **ped·a·gog·ics** (pĕdagŏj´ĭks, -gō´jĭks) *ns.* Science of teaching.

ped·al[1] (pĕd´al) *n.* 1. Lever worked by the foot to transmit power in machine, e.g. bicycle. 2. Foot lever in various musical instruments; in harp, for altering pitch of strings; in organ, each of keys played upon by feet, (also) foot lever for drawing out several stops at once, opening swell box, etc.; in piano, foot lever for raising dampers from strings, thus sustaining tone and making it fuller (**loud ~**), or for softening tone (**soft ~**) by shifting hammers so as to strike only one or two strings instead of three, by diminishing length of blow, or by interposing strip of cloth between hammers and stings. 3. (mus.) Note sustained or reiterated in one part (usu. bass) through a series of harmonies. 4. **~ board**, row of pedals in an organ or pedal piano; **~ note**, note sounded by the pedals of an organ; (also) in brass instruments, one of the fundamental notes which are below their normal compass; **~ organ**, that part of an organ controlled by the pedals; **~ pushers**, woman's slacks reaching to calf. **ped·al** *v.* (**-aled** or **-alled**, **-al·ing** or **-al·ling**). Work pedals of bicycle etc.; work (bicycle etc.) thus; play on organ pedals.

ped·al[2] (pē´dal) *adj.* (zool.) Of the feet or foot, esp. of mollusk.

ped·ant (pĕd´ant) *n.* One who overrates or parades book learning or technical knowledge, or insists on strict adherence to formal rules. **pe·dan·tic** (pedăn´tĭk) *adj.* **pe·dan´ti·cal·ly** *adv.* **ped·ant·ry** (pĕd´antrē) *n.*

ped·ate (pĕd´āt) *adj.* (zool.) Footed.

ped·dle (pĕd´el) *v.* (**-dled,**

-dling). Follow occupation of peddler; trade or deal in as peddler.

ped·dler, ped·lar, ped·ler (pĕd´ler) *ns.* Traveling vendor of small wares, usu. carried in pack; (fig.) retailer (*of* gossip etc.).

ped·er·as·ty (pĕd´erăstē) *n.* Sodomy with a boy. **ped´er·ast** *n.*

ped·es·tal (pĕd´ĭstal) *n.* Base supporting column in construction; base of statue etc.; each of 2 supports of kneehole writing table; foundation; **~ table**, one with massive central support. **pedestal** *v.t.* (**-taled** or **-talled, -tal·ing** or **-tal·ling**). Set, support, on pedestal.

pe·des·tri·an (pedĕs´trēan) *adj.* Going, performed, on foot; of walking; for those who walk; prosaic, dull, uninspired; **~ crossing**, crossing place for pedestrians over highway. **pedestrian** *n.* One who walks or goes on foot. **pe·des´tri·an·ism** *n.*

pe·di·at·ric (pēdēăt´rĭk) *adj.* Of diseases of children.

pe·di·a·tri·cian (pēdēatrĭsh´an) *n.* Specialist in pediatrics.

pe·di·at·rics (pēdēăt´rĭks) *n.* (usu. considered sing.) Study of children's diseases.

Triangular

Segmental

Broken

Open

The Temple of Manly Fortune in Rome exhibits the classical triangular **pediment**. Originally developed by the Greeks, the Romans took up this feature of Greek architecture and used it widely.

ped·i·cel (pĕd´ĭsel, -sĕl) *n*. (bot zool.) Small, esp. subordinate stalk-like structure in plant or animal. **pe·dic·u·late** (pedĭk´yulĭt, -lāt) *adj*.

pe·dic·u·lar (pedĭk´yuler), **pe·dic·u·lous** (pedĭkyulus) *adjs*. Lousy. **pe·dic·u·lo·sis** (pedĭkyulō´sĭs) *n*. Infestation with lice.

ped·i·cure (pĕd´ĭkūr) *n*. 1. Chiropody. 2. Chiropodist. ~ *v.t.* (**-cured, -cur·ing**). Cure or treat (feet) by removing corns etc. **ped´·i·cur·ist** *n*.

ped·i·gree (pĕd´ĭgrē) *n*. Genealogical table; ancestral line (of man or animal); derivation (of word); ancient descent; (attrib.) having a known line of descent. **ped´i·greed** *adj*. [OF. *pie de grue* crane's foot mark denoting succession in pedigrees]

ped·i·ment (pĕd´iment) *n*. Triangular low-pitched gable crowning front of building in Greek style, esp. over portico; similarly placed member of same or other form in Roman and Renaissance styles; **broken ~**, one without an apex. **ped·i·men·tal** (pĕdimĕn´tal), **ped´i·ment·ed** *adjs*.

ped·lar, ped·ler = PEDDLER.

pe·dol·o·gy (pĭdŏl´ojē) *n*. Science of soils.

pe·dom·e·ter (pĭdŏm´ĭter) *n*. Instrument for estimating distance traveled on foot by recording number of steps taken.

pe·dun·cle (pĭdŭng´kel) *n*. (bot.) Stalk of flower, fruit, or cluster, esp. main stalk bearing solitary flower or subordinate stalks; (zool.) stalk-like process in animal body. **pe·dun·cu·lar** (pĭdŭng´kyuler), **pe·dun·cu·late** (pĭdŭng´kyulĭt, -lāt), **pe·dun´cu·lat·ed** *adjs*.

peek (pēk) *v.i.* Peep, peer; **peek·a·boo** (pēk´abōō), game of hiding and suddenly appearing to child. **peek** *n*. Peep, glance (*take a ~ at*).

peel (pēl) *v*. Strip peel, rind, bark, etc., from (fruit, vegetable, tree, etc.); take *off* (skin, peel, etc.); become bare of bark, skin, etc.; (of bark, surface, etc.) come off like peel; (slang, of person) strip for exercise etc.; (colloq.) **keep one's eyes peeled**, keep a sharp lookout. **peel** *n*. Rind, outer coating, of fruit; **candied ~**, candied rind of various species of citrus fruit, used

The outer coating, called **peel**, of these oranges and mandarins is being cut into strips and is often used in this way in cookery and confectionary.

cookery and confectionery.
peel'a·ble *adj.* **peel'er** *n.* **peel'-
ings** *n.pl.* What is peeled off.

peen (pēn) *n.* Pointed, edged, or
ball-shaped end of hammer opposite face.

peep[1] (pēp) *v.i.* & *n.* (Make)
feeble shrill sound of young birds,
mice, etc.; chirp, squeak.

peep[2] (pēp) *v.i.* Look through
narrow aperture; look furtively;
come cautiously or partly into view,
emerge; (fig.) show itself unconsciously; **peeping Tom**, voyeur (f.
name of tailor in story of Lady
GODIVA). **peep** *n.* Furtive or
peering glance; 1st appearance, esp.
of dawn, of day; **peep'hole**, small
hole to peep through; **peep show**,
small exhibition of pictures etc.
viewed through lens in small
orifice.

peep·er[1] (pē'per) *n.* Any of
various frogs making a shrill call,
esp. the spring peeper (*Hyla
crucifer*).

peep·er[2] (pē'per) *n.* One who
peeps; (slang) eye.

pee·pul = PIPAL.

peer[1] (pēr) *n.* (fem. **peer·ess** pr.
pēr'ĭs). 1. Equal in civil standing
or rank; equal in any respect. 2.
Member of one of the degrees
(duke, marquis, earl, viscount,
baron) of nobility in United Kingdom; noble (of any country); **life
~,** (since 1958) one whose title is
not hereditary; **~ of the realm,**
one of the peers of the United Kingdom, all of whom when of age may
sit in the House of Lords.

peer[2] (pēr) *v.i.* Look narrowly;
appear, peep out; come in sight.

peer·age (pēr'ĭj) *n.* Peers;
nobility, aristocracy; rank of peer;
book containing list of peers with
genealogy etc.

peer·less (pēr'lĭs) *adj.* Having
no equal, unrivaled. **peer'less·ly**
adv. **peer'less·ness** *n.* [f. PEER[1]]

peeved (pēvd) *adj.* (slang) Irritated.

pee·vish (pē'vĭsh) *adj.* Queru-
lous, irritable. **pee'vish·ly** *adv.*
pee'vish·ness *n.*

pee·wit (pē'wĭt, pū'ĭt): see LAP-
WING.

peg (pĕg) *n.* 1. Pin, bolt, of
wood, metal, etc., usu. round and
slightly tapering, for holding together parts of framework etc.,
stopping up vent of cask, hanging
hats etc. on, holding ropes of tent,
tightening or loosening strings of
violin etc., marking cribbage score
etc.; (fig.) occasion, pretext, theme
(*to hang* discourse etc. *on*); **peg'-
board**, board with holes and pegs,
esp. for game, commercial displays,
or home use; **take** (person) **down
a peg or two**, humble him; **peg
leg**, wooden leg; **peg-top
trousers**, trousers wide at hips,
narrow at ankles. 2. (Brit.) Drink,
esp. of whiskey and soda or brandy

*Both an ancient and modern capital of
China,* **Peking** *shows evidence of its
past in (top) the gateway to the old summer palace. Above: Modern city streets
are dominated by huge colored hoard-
ings.*

and soda. **peg** *v.* (**pegged, peg·-
ging**). Fix with peg; (stock exch.)
prevent price of (stock etc.) from
falling or rising by freely buying
or selling at given price; mark score
with pegs on cribbage board; mark
out boundaries of (mining claim
etc.); strike, pierce, aim *at*, with
peg; (slang) throw (stone or baseball), throw stones etc. (*at*); work
(*away*) persistently (*at*); **~ down**,
restrict (*to rules* etc.).

Peg·a·sus (pĕg'asus). 1. (Gk.
myth.) Winged horse, favorite of
the Muses, sprung from blood of
MEDUSA. 2. (astron.) Northern constellation, figured as a winged
horse, containing three stars of the
second magnitude forming with one
star of Andromeda a large square
(**square of ~**).

Peh·le·vi = PAHLAVI.

peign·oir (pānwär', pĕn-) *n.*
Woman's loose dressing gown.

Peirce (pērs), **Charles San-
ders** (1839–1914). Amer. philosopher, mathematician and physicist; founder of pragmatism.

pe·jo·ra·tive (pĭjōr'atĭv, -jär'-,
pĕj'orā-, pē'jo-) *adj.* & *n.* Deprecia-
tory (word).

Pe·kin·ese (pēkinēz', -nēs') =
PEKINGESE def. 2.

Pe·king (pē'kĭng'). Capital city
of China; **~ man**, hominid (*Pithecanthropus pekinensis*) represented
by at least a dozen skulls and other
remains found near Peking from
1929 onward. [Chin., = "northern
capital"]

Pe·king·ese (pēkĭngēz', -ēs',
pēkinēz', -nēs') *adj.* Of Peking. **~**
n. (pl. **-ese**). 1. Native, inhabitant, of
Peking. 2. (Breed of) small dog of
the pug type, with long silky coat,
flat face, and prominent eyes, orig.
brought to Europe from Summer
Palace in Peking in 1860.

male

articular surface of 5th lumbar vertebra
sacrum
ilium
coccyx
pubis
ischium
pubic symphysis
articular surface of head of femur
obturator foramen

female

spine
ureter
spermatic duct
rectum
vas deferens
seminal vesicle
urethra
prostate gland
scrotum enclosing testicles
bladder
penis
erectile tissue
foreskin or prepuce

spine
fallopian tube
ovary
uterus or womb
bladder
urethra
vagina
labium
rectum

pe·koe (pē′kō) *n.* Superior kind of black tea. [Chin. *pek-ho* white down (leaves being picked young with down on them)]

pe·lag·ic (pelăj′ĭk) *adj.* Of, inhabiting, the open sea.

pel·ar·go·ni·um (pĕlärgō′nēum) *n.* Plant of genus *P*~ with showy flowers and fragrant leaves (pop. called *geranium*). [Gk. *pelargos* stork]

pelf (pĕlf) *n.* Money, wealth (usu. contempt.).

pel·i·can (pĕl′ĭkan) *n.* Any of various large aquatic birds (genus *Pelecanus*) of warm regions, including the brown ~ (*P. occidentalis*) of Amer. coastal waters and the white ~ (*P. erythrorhynchos*) ranging from the Pacific Coast to the gulf of Mexico, both being web-footed and having large membranous pouch beneath lower bill.

Pe·li·on (pē′lēon). Wooded mountain near coast of SE. Thessaly, Greece; in Gk. myth., home of centaurs.

pel·la·gra (pelăg′ra, -lā′gra) *n.* Deficiency disease, endemic in countries whose populations live chiefly on cereals with low protein content, characterized by disorders of the skin, digestion, and nervous system. [It., perh. orig. *pelle agra* rough skin]

pel·let (pĕl′ĭt) *n.* Small ball of

*The bones of the **pelvis** act both as a support for the human body and its internal organs, and as pivots for the legs whose uppermost sockets fit into ball-joints on the ends of the pelvis. The shape differs between male and female.*

paper, bread, etc.; pill; small shot. **pel′let·ed** *adj.* Formed into a pellet.

pel·li·cle (pĕl′ĭkel) *n.* Thin skin; membrane; film. **pel·lic·u·lar** (pelĭk′yuler) *adj.*

pel·li·to·ry (pĕl′ĭtōrē, -tōrē) *n.* (pl. **-ries**). (also ~ **of Spain**) Composite plant (*Anacyclus pyrethrum*), native of Barbary, with pungent root used as local irritant etc.

pell-mell, pell·mell (pĕl′mĕl′) *advs.* In disorder, promiscuously; headlong, recklessly. ~ *adj.* Confused; tumultuous. ~ *n.* Confusion, medley, mêlée.

pel·lu·cid (pelōō′sĭd). *adj.* Transparent, clear; clear in style or expression; mentally clear. **pel·lu·cid·i·ty** (pĕlyōosĭd′ĭtē) *n.* **pel·lu′cid·ly** *adv.*

Pel·o·pon·ne·sus (pĕloponē′-sus), **Pel·o·pon·nese** (pĕloponēz′, -nēs′). That part of Greece S. of Isthmus of Corinth. **Pel·o·pon·ne·sian** (pĕloponē′zhan, -shan) *adj.* ~ **War**, war (431–404 B.C.) waged by Sparta and her allies upon Athens and Athenian Empire re-

sulting in the surrender of Athe and transfer, for a brief period, leadership of Greece to Sparta.

pe·lo·ta (pelō′ta) *n.* Jai alai b: used in jai alai. [Span., = "ba (f. L. *pila*)]

pelt[1] (pĕlt) *n.* Skin of sheep goat with short wool on; skin of fu bearing animal, esp. undressed; ra skin of sheep etc. stripped of wc or fur. **pelt·ry** (pĕl′trē) *n.* (p **-ries**). Pelts collectively.

pelt[2] (pĕlt) *v.* Assail wi missiles; (of rain etc.) beat wi violence; strike *at* repeatedly wi missiles; go on throwing (missile ~ *n.* Pelting.

pel·vis (pĕl′vĭs) *n.* (pl. **-vis·e -ves** pr. -vēz). 1. Basin-shape cavity at lower end of trunk in mc vertebrates, formed in man t innominate bones with sacrum a coccyx. 2. Funnel-shaped origin ureter, having a wide end that li within the kidney. **pel·vic** (pĕ vĭk) *adj.*

pem·mi·can, pem·i·can (pĕm ĭkan) *ns.* N. Amer. Ind. food of le: meat dried, pounded, mixed in paste with melted fat and press into cakes; beef similarly treated a1 freq. flavored with currants etc. f Arctic and other travelers.

pen[1] (pĕn) *n.* Small enclosu for cows, sheep, poultry, etc.; e closure resembling this, as su

Very large and highly adapted to swimming and fishing, the **pelican** is famous for the deep pouch beneath its bill, its large webbed feet and its powerful wings.

marine ~; (W. Ind.) farm, plantation. **pen** *v.t.* (**penned** or **pent, pen·ning**). Enclose, shut *up*, shut *in*; shut up (cattle etc.) in pen.

pen² (pĕn) *n.* Quill feather with quill pointed and split into two sections, for writing with ink; small instrument of gold, steel, etc., similarly pointed and split, fitted into rod of wood etc. (**pen′holder**); pen and penholder together; any contrivance for writing with fluid ink; writing, style of this; **ballpoint** ~, **fountain** ~: see BALL[1] and FOUNTAIN; ~**-and-ink**, (attrib., of drawing etc.) done, made, with pen and ink; **pen′knife**, small knife usu. carried in pocket, orig. for making or mending quill pens; **pen′man**, one who writes a (*good, bad*, etc.) hand; author; **pen′manship**, style of handwriting; **pen name**, literary pseudonym; **pen pal**, friend with whom one corresponds without meeting; **pen wiper**, appliance usu. of small pieces of cloth for wiping pen after use. **pen** *v.t.* (**penned, pen·ning**). Write, compose and write (letter etc.).

pen³ (pĕn) *n.* Female mute swan.

pen⁴ (pĕn) *n.* (slang) Prison. [abbrev. of *penitentiary*]

Pen., pen. *abbrevs.* Peninsula.

P.E.N. *abbrev.* (International Association of) Poets, Playwrights, Editors, Essayists, and Novelists.

pe·nal (pē′nal) *adj.* Of punishment, concerned with inflicting this; (of offense) punishable, esp. by law; inflicted as punishment; used as place of punishment, as in ~ *colony.* **pe′nal·ly** *adv.*

pe·nal·ize (pē′nalīz, pĕn′a-) *v.t.* (**-ized, -iz·ing**). Make, declare, penal; subject to handicap or comparative disadvantage (also freq. fig.).

pen·al·ty (pĕn′altē) *n.* (pl. **-ties**). Punishment, esp. (exaction of) sum of money, for breach of law, rule, or contract; money thus paid; (sport etc.) disadvantage imposed on competitor for breaking rule or winning previous contest; (bridge) points added to opponents′ score when declarer fails to make a contract; ~ **box**, (ice hockey) place adjacent to rink for penalized players; ~ **kick**, (soccer) free kick allowed for certain infringements of rules.

pen·ance (pĕn′ans) *n.* (R.C. and Orthodox Churches) Sacrament including contrition, confession, satisfaction, and absolution for sin; act of self-mortification as expression of penitence, esp. one imposed by priest; **do** ~, perform such act.

Pe·nang (pĭnăng′, -nahng′). State of Malaysia consisting of island in SE. Asia off the W. coast of the Malay Peninsula, covering 110 sq. mi. (285 sq. km); and strip of territory on the Malay Peninsula; capital, ~, formerly George Town.

Penang, *an island off the west coast of Malaysia, is about 15 miles long and no more than 8 miles wide. Many of its inhabitants are fishermen (above) and others follow the ancient tradition of making joss sticks, seen drying (right).*

pe·na·tes (penā´tēz, -nah´-) *n.pl.* (Rom. myth.) Gods of the storeroom, worshipped, together with the lares, by households.

pence (pĕns) *n.* (Brit.) Alternative plural of PENNY, esp. in combination, as *sixpence*.

pen·chant (pĕn´chant) *n.* Inclination, liking, (*for*).

pen·cil (pĕn´sil) *n.* 1. (archaic) Artist's paintbrush; (fig.) painter's art or style. 2. Instrument for drawing or writing, esp. (**lead** ~) of graphite enclosed in wooden cylinder or in metal case with tapering end; pencil-shaped object; ~ **case,** case for holding pencils etc. 3. (optics) Set of rays meeting at a point. 4. (geom.) Figure formed by set of straight lines meeting at a point. **pencil** *v.t.* (**-ciled** or **-cilled, -cil·ing** or **-cil·ling**). Tint or mark (as) with lead pencil; jot down with pencil; (esp. in past part.) mark delicately with thin concentric lines of color or shading.

pen·dant (pĕn´dant) *n.* 1. Hanging ornament, esp. one attached to necklace, bracelet, etc. 2. (naut.) Short rope hanging from head of mast etc. with eye at lower end for receiving hooks of tackles; tapering flag, esp. that flown at masthead of vessel in commission. 3. Shank and ring of watch by which it is suspended. 4. Match, parallel, companion, complement (*to*).

pen·dent (pĕn´dent) *adj.* Hanging; overhanging; undecided, pending. **pen´den·cy** *n.* **pen´dent·ly** *adv.*

pend·ing (pĕn´dĭng) *adj.* Undecided, awaiting decision or settlement. ~ *prep.* During; until.

pen·du·late (pĕn´julāt, pĕn´-dyu-) *v.i.* (**-lat·ed, -lat·ing**). Swing like a pendulum.

pen·du·lous (pĕn´julus, pĕn´-dyu-) *adj.* Suspended, hanging down; oscillating. **pen´du·lous·ly** *adv.* **pen´du·lous·ness** *n.*

pen·du·lum (pĕn´julum, -dyu- *n.* Body suspended so as to be free to swing, esp. rod with weighted end regulating movement of clock's works; person, thing, that oscillates.

Pe·nel·o·pe (penĕl´opē). (Gk legend) Wife of Odysseus; when her husband did not return after fall of Troy, she told her importunate suitors that she would marry one of them when she had finished the piece of weaving on which she was engaged, but every night she undid the work that she had done during the day.

pen·e·trate (pĕn´itrāt) *v* (**-trat·ed, -trat·ing**). Find access into or through, pass through; make a way (*with, through, to*); (of sight) pierce through; permeate; imbue (*with*); (fig.) see into, find out, discern (design, the truth, etc.). **pen´e·trat·ing** *adj.* (esp.) Gifted with or suggestive of insight; (of voice etc.) easily heard through or above other sounds. **pen·e·tra·bil·i·ty** (pĕnĭtrabĭl´ĭtē), **pen·e·tra´tion** *ns* **pen·e·tra·ble** (pĕn´ĭtrabel), **pen·e·tra·tive** (pĕn´ĭtrātĭv) *adjs.*

pen·guin (pĕn´gwĭn, pĕng´-) *n* Any bird of the family Spheniscidae, including several genera of seabirds of the southern hemisphere with wings reduced to scaly flippers with which they swim under water

pen·i·cil·late (pĕnĭsĭl´ĭt, -āt) *adj*

Simple Pendulum

suspension

arc of swing   bob

Although Galileo was probably the first man to recognize the properties of the **pendulum**, it was Christian Huyghens in 1657 who first adapted it to regulate a clock, as had been proposed, but not done, by Galileo.

(biol.) Furnished with, forming, small tuft(s); marked with streaks as of pencil or brush.

pen·i·cil·lin (pĕnĭsĭl´ĭn) *n.* Substance obtained from the mold *Penicillium notatum*, effective against many microorganisms of disease (the first ANTIBIOTIC to be used therapeutically, during World War II). [L. *penicillus* painter's brush, f. brushlike sporangia of the mold]

pen·in·su·la (penĭn´sula, -syula) *n.* Piece of land almost surrounded by water, or projecting far into the sea.

pen·in·su·lar (penĭn´suler, -syuler) *adj.* Of (the nature of) a peninsula; **P~ War**, that carried on in Spain and Portugal (1808–1814) between French under Napoleon and English, Spanish and Portuguese under Wellington. **peninsular** *n.* Inhabitant of a peninsula.

pe·nis (pē´nĭs) *n.* (pl. **-nis·es, -nes** pr. -nēz). Organ of urination and copulation in male animals.

pen·i·tent (pĕn´ĭtent) *adj.* That repents, contrite. ~ *n.* Repentant sinner; person doing penance under direction of confessor; (pl.) any of various R.C. congregations or orders associated for mutual discipline, giving religious aid to criminals etc. **pen´i·tent·ly** *adv.* **pen´i·tence** *n.*

pen·i·ten·tial (pĕnĭtĕn´shal) *adj.* Of penitence or penance; ~ **Psalms**, those expressing penitence (Pss. 6, 32, 38, 51, 102, 130, 143). **pen·i·ten´tial·ly** *adv.*

pen·i·ten·tia·ry (pĕnĭtĕn´sharē) *n.* (pl. **-ries**). 1. Office in papal court deciding questions of penance, dispensations, etc.; **grand p~**, cardinal presiding over this. 2. Reformatory prison; state prison. **penitentiary** *adj.* Of penance; of reformatory treatment of criminals.

Penn (pĕn), **William** (1644–1718). English Quaker, founder of Pennsylvania, 1681; framed government to meet popular demands of colonists and granted a liberal charter to the colony.

Penn., Penna. *abbrevs.* Pennsylvania.

pen·nant (pĕn´ant) *n.* = PENNON; flag awarded as distinction, esp. in baseball.

pen·ni·less (pĕn´ēlĭs) *adj.* Having no money; poor, destitute.

*Rock-hopper **penguins** (left), like other species, are unable to fly but use their wings as paddles when swimming. Most live in the cooler latitudes of the southern hemisphere, but one species nests in the Galapagos Islands.*

pen·non (pĕn′on) *n.* Long narrow flag, triangular or swallowtailed; long pointed streamer of ship; flag.

Penn·syl·va·ni·a (pĕnsilvā′nēa, -vān′ya). Middle Atlantic state of U.S.; one of the original 13 states (1787); capital, Harrisburg. [named 1681 in honor of Admiral Sir William *Penn*, father of William PENN, founder of the colony]

pen·ny (pĕn′ē) *n.* (pl. **pen·nies**, collect. **pence**). $\frac{1}{100}$ of a U.S. dollar; $\frac{1}{100}$ of a British POUND[1]; until 1971, $\frac{1}{12}$ of a shilling; (bibl.) denarius; **a bad** ~, someone or something repeatedly present when not desired; ~ **ante**, poker game in which the stakes are a penny or other small amount; **a pretty** ~, a large sum of money; **turn an honest** ~, earn money by an odd job; ~ **candy**, (archaic), candy sold for a penny; ~ **dreadful**: see DREADFUL; **pennies from heaven**,

unexpected benefits; **penny-pinching** (*adj.*) niggardly; (*n.*) niggardliness; **penny stocks**, common stocks, usu. speculative, selling for less than a dollar a share; **pen′nyweight**, (abbrev. dwt) measure of weight, 24 grams, $\frac{1}{20}$ of an ounce troy; **penny-wise**, (overly) careful in small expenditures; **pen′nywort**, name of two plants: (1) **wall penny** (*navelwort*), perennial herb (*Umbilicus rupestris*) with rounded concave leaves, growing in crevices of rocks and walls; (2) **marsh penny** (*white-rot*), small creeping or floating plant (*Hydrocotyle vulgaris*), with rounded

*The 140-mile long **Sinai Peninsula** which extends from the Mediterranean to the head of the Red Sea had settlements as early as 3,400 B.C. One of the oldest biblical texts, the Codex Sinaiticus, was found in a monastery there in 1844.*

leaves, growing in marshy places

pen·ny·roy·al (pĕnēroi′al) Kind of mint (*Mentha pulegium* with small leaves and prostra habit, formerly cultivated for i supposed medicinal virtues.

pe·nol·o·gy (pēnŏl′ojē) *n.* Stud of punishment and of priso management. **pe·no·log·i·c** (pēnolŏj′īkal) *adj.* **pe·nol′o·gist**

pen·sion (pĕn′shon) *n.* Periodical payment made esp. b government or employer in co sideration of past service, old ag widowhood, etc. 2. (pr. pahńsyōn Boardinghouse (in France) whe a fixed rate for board and lodgin is charged. ~ *v.t.* Grant pe sion to; buy over with pension; **off**, dismiss with pension. **pen sion·a·ble** *adj.* Entitled, entitlin person, to pension.

pen·sion·er (pĕn′shoner) Recipient of pension; hirelin creature.

The **Pennsylvania** Canal, built in the mid-1800's to transport freight, is an example of the ingenuity which has characterized the economic development of the state which continues to prosper.

The full-dress uniform of the Chelsea **pensioner**. About 600 invalid soldiers now live at the Royal Hospital, Chelsea, which was founded by Charles II and built by Christopher Wren. Each year Founders Day is celebrated.

pen·sive (pĕn′sĭv) *adj.* Plunged n thought; melancholy. **pen′-ive·ly** *adv.* **pen′sive·ness** *n.*

pen·ste·mon (pĕnstē′mon) = ¡ENTSTEMON.

pent (pĕnt) *adj.* Closely con-ned, shut *in* or *up.* ~ *v.* Past and past part. of PEN[1].

penta-, pent- *prefixes.* Five.

pen·ta·chord (pĕn′takôrd) *n.* Ausical instrument with five ¡rings; system or series of five otes.

pen·ta·cle (pĕn′takel) *n.* Figure sed as symbol, esp. in magic; prop. = pentagram.

pen·tad (pĕn′tăd) *n.* Set, group, f five.

pen·ta·gon (pĕn′tagŏn) *n.* Plane gure of five angles and sides; **P ~,** J.S. Department of Defense head-uarters, Arlington, Va. (from hape of its building). **pen·tag·o-**

nal (pĕntăg′onal) *adj.*

pen·ta·he·dron (pĕntahē′dron) *n.* Solid figure of five faces. **pen·ta·he′dral** *adj.*

pen·tam·e·ter (pĕntăm′ĭter) *n.* (Engl. pros.) Line of verse of 5 ft., e.g. heroic or iambic verse of 10 syllables, thus:

˘/˘˘/˘˘/˘˘/˘/˘/˘/˘/l

pen·tane (pĕn′tān) *n.* Any of a group of paraffin hydrocarbons containing five carbon atoms, including several colorless volatile liquids occurring in petroleum.

Pen·ta·teuch (pĕn′tatook, -tūk) *n.* First five books of Old Testa-ment (Genesis, Exodus, Leviticus,

Numbers, Deuteronomy) tradi-tionally ascribed to Moses. **Pen′-ta·teuch·al** *adj.*

pen·tath·lon (pĕntăth′lon) *n.* 1. In ancient Greece, athletic contest of five events in each of which the same competitors took part (foot race, long jump, javelin-throwing, discus-throwing, wrestling). 2. Similar contest in modern times, comprising five different events.

pen·ta·tom·ic (pĕntatŏm′ĭk) *adj.* (chem.) Containing five atoms in the molecule.

pen·ta·ton·ic (pĕntatŏn′ĭk) *adj.* (mus.) Consisting of five notes or sounds; ~ **scale**, scale without semitones.

pen·ta·va·lent (pĕntavā′lent) *adj.* (chem.) Having a valency of five; quinquivalent.

Pen·te·cost (pĕn′tĭkawst, -kŏst). 1. Christian festival on seventh Sunday after Easter commemorat-ing the descent of the Holy Spirit on the Apostles. 2. Jewish harvest festival (Shabuoth) observed on 50th day after the second day of Passover (Lev. 23). **Pen·te·cos′tal** *adj.* [Gk. *pentēkostē (hēmera)* fiftieth (day)]

Pen·the·si·le·a (pĕnthesĭlē′a). (Gk. legend) Queen of Amazons; came to help of Troy after death of Hector and was slain by Achilles.

pent·house (pĕnt′hows) *n.* Sloping roof, esp. as subsidiary structure attached to wall of main building; awning, canopy, or the like; separate apartment or home atop roof of apartment house.

pen·ti·men·to (pĕntĭmĕn′tō) *n.* (pl. **-ti** pr. **-tē**). Reappearance of earlier underlying painting when layer added later becomes trans-parent, revealing artist's change of mind etc.

pen·to·bar·bi·tal (pĕntōbär′bĭ-tawl) *n.* Narcotic and sedative barbiturate drug.

pen·tode (pĕn′tōd) *n.* Vacuum tube with five main electrodes.

pen·tom·ic (pĕntŏm′ĭk) *adj.* Organized into five battle groups, each with supporting units ready to maneuver in accordance with the needs of atomic warfare.

pen·tose (pĕn′tōs) *n.* (chem.) Sugar with five carbon atoms in the molecule.

Pen·to·thal (pĕn′tothawl) *n.* (trademark) Thiopental.

pent·ste·mon (pĕntstē′mon) *n.* N. Amer. herbaceous plant of genus *P ~,* allied to foxglove with showy flowers, usu. tubular and two-lipped.

pe·nult (pē′nŭlt, pĭnŭlt′), **pe·-nul·ti·mate** (pĭnŭl′tĭmĭt) *ns.* Last

Found throughout the northern hemi-sphere, the **peony** *is now a popular flower in gardens. In ancient times, the strong-smelling roots of the common variety were considered to have med-icinal properties.*

syllable but one. ~ *adjs.* Last but one.

pe·num·bra (pĭnŭm′brɑ) *n.* (pl. **-brae** pr. -brē, **-bras**). Partly shaded region around shadow of opaque body, esp. round total shadow of moon or Earth in eclipse; lighter outer part of sunspot; partial shadow. **pe·num′bral** *adj.*

pe·nu·ri·ous (penoor′ēus, -nūr′-) *adj.* Poor, scanty; stingy, grudging. **pe·nu′ri·ous·ly** *adv.* **pe·nu′ri·ous·ness** *n.*

pen·u·ry (pĕn′yurē) *n.* Destitu-tion, poverty; lack, scarcity, (*of*).

pe·on (pē′on, -ŏn) *n.* 1. In India, office messenger, attendant, orderly. 2. In Spanish Amer., day laborer; in Mexico etc., debtor held in servitude by creditor until debts are worked off. **pe′on·age** *n.* Employment, service, of peons.

pe·o·ny (pē′onē) *n.* (pl. **-nies**). Plant of genus *Paeonia* with large handsome crimson, pink, or white, globular flowers, in cultivation freq. double.

peo·ple (pē′pel) *n.* (pl. **peo·ple**). 1. (pl. **people** or **peoples**) Persons composing community, tribe, race, or nation; persons belonging to a place or forming a company or class etc.; subjects of king etc.; congrega-tion of parish priest etc. 2. Parents or other relatives; commonalty; persons in general. 3. (sing. or pl.) Body of enfranchised or qualified citizens; **People's Charter**: see CHARTIST. **people** *v.t.* (**peo·pled**, **peo·pling**). Fill with people,

populate, fill (place *with*); inhabit, occupy, fill (esp. in past part.).

pep (pĕp) *n.* (colloq.) Vigor, go, spirit; ~ **pill**, pill containing stimulant drug; ~ **rally**, meeting, esp. of students, prior to an athletic contest, to inspire enthusiasm by singing, cheering, speeches, etc.; ~ **talk**, exhortation to exceptional effort etc. **pep** *v.t.* (**pepped, pep·ping**). Fill *up* or inspire with energy and vigor. [abbrev. of *pepper*]

pep·er·o·ni, pep·per·o·ni (pĕp-erō′nē) *ns.* Sausage of highly seasoned beef and pork. [It., = cayenne peppers]

Pep·in (pĕp′ĭn). Name of several members of the Carolingian family: **Pepin I** (of Landen) (d. 639), Frankish mayor of the palace; **Pepin II** (of Héristal) (d. 714), Frankish ruler, father of Charles Martel; **Pepin III** "the Short" (714–68), Frankish king, younger son of Charles Martel and father of Charlemagne.

pep·per (pĕp′er) *n.* 1. Pungent aromatic condiment harvested from dried berries of plants of genus *Piper*, used whole (**peppercorns**) or ground into powder; climbing shrub of East Indies, cultivated also in West Indies, from which this is chiefly obtained; **black** ~, shrub (*P. nigrum*); most usual form of the condiment, prepared from slightly unripe berries; **white** ~, milder form prepared from ripe berries, or from black by removing outer husk.

2. Capsicum; **red** ~, (large red or yellow edible fruit of) plant *Capsi-cum frutescens*; cayenne pepper often eaten when green, **green** ~ also called **sweet** ~. 3. **pepper-and-salt**, (cloth) of dark and ligh threads woven together, showing small dots of dark and ligh intermingled; **pep′perbox**, smal usu. round box with perforated li for sprinkling pepper; **pep′per-corn**, dried berry of black pepper **pepper mill**, utensil for grinding peppercorns by hand; **pepper pot** W. Indian stew of meat with cayenne pepper etc.; **pepper tree** any of various S. Amer. evergreen trees of the genus *Schinus*. **pepper** *v.t.* Sprinkle, treat, with pepper sprinkle as with pepper; pelt with missiles.

pep·per·mint (pĕp′ermĭnt) *n* Kind of mint (*Mentha piperita*) cultivated for its essential oil; thi oil, with characteristic pungen aromatic flavor leaving aftersensa-tion of coolness; candy flavored with this.

pep·per·o·ni = PEPERONI.

pep·per·y (pĕp′erē) *adj.* Of like, abounding in, pepper; (fig. pungent, stinging, hot-tempered.

pep·sin (pĕp′sĭn) *n.* Enzym contained in gastric juice, convert ing proteins into peptones i presence of dilute acid.

pep·tic (pĕp′tĭk) *adj.* Digestive ~ **gland**, gland secreting gastri juice; ~ **ulcer**, any ulcer of th digestive system.

The green pepper is a member of the capsicum family and a native of tropical America. If allowed to ripen properly it becomes a red or yellow color and softens slightly. Usually peppers are eaten crisp and green.

pep·ti·dase (pĕp′tĭdās) *n.* Enzyme that hydrolyzes peptides or peptones and releases amino acids.

pep·tide (pĕp′tīd) *n.* Compound with two or more amino acids linked in linear sequence with elimination of water molecules.

pep·tone (pĕp′tōn) *n.* Any of a class of easily soluble albuminoid substances into which proteins are converted by action of pepsin etc. **pep·to·nize** (pĕp′tonīz) *v.t.* (**-nized**, **-niz·ing**). (esp.) Subject (food) to artificial process of partial digestion, as aid to weak digestion. **pep·ton·ic** (pĕptŏn′ĭk) *adj.*

Pepys (pēps), **Samuel** (1633–1703). English diarist; secretary of Admiralty 1673–9, 1684–8.

per (pēr) *prep.* 1. Through, by means of (esp. in L. phrases, for which see entries); **as ~ usual**, (joc.) as usual. 2. For each; **per annum, per capita:** see own entries; **per cent** (persĕnt′), **per cent′**, (symbol %) in every hundred; **per diem:** see own entry; **per head**, for each person; **per hour**, in each hour (of speed); **per se:** see own entry; **per second per second**, (abbrev. per sec./sec.) per second every second (of rate of acceleration).

per- *prefix.* Completely, very; to destruction, to the bad; (in chem. compounds) denoting maximum of some element in combination.

per·ad·ven·ture (pēradvĕn′cher, pěr-) *adv.* (archaic) Perhaps. **~** *n.* Uncertainty, chance, conjecture; **beyond, without, (all) ~**, without doubt.

per·am·bu·late (perăm′byulāt) *v.t.* (**-lat·ed**, **-lat·ing**). Walk through, over, or about; travel through and inspect (territory). **per·am·bu·la′tion** *n.* **per·am·bu·la·to·ry** (perăm′byulatōre,

-tōrē) *adj.*

per·am·bu·la·tor (perăm′byulāter) *n.* (esp. Brit.) = BABY carriage.

per an·num (pēr ăn′um). (So much) by the year. [L.]

per·cale (perkāl′) *n.* Plain-woven cotton fabric resembling calico, but finer and wider.

per cap·i·ta (pēr kăp′ita). For each person.

per·ceive (persēv′) *v.t.* (**-ceived**, **-ceiv·ing**). Apprehend with the mind, observe, understand; apprehend through one of the senses, esp. sight. **per·ceiv′a·ble** *adj.* **per·ceiv′a·bly** *adv.*

per·cent·age (persĕn′tĭj) *n.* Rate, proportion, percent; (loosely) proportion.

per·cept (pēr′sĕpt) *n.* (philos.) Object of perception; mental product, as opp. to action, of perceiving. **per·cep·tu·al** (persĕp′chōoal) *adj.*

per·cep·ti·ble (persĕp′tibel) *adj.* That can be perceived by senses or intellect. **per·cep·ti·bil′i·ty** *n.* **per·cep′ti·bly** *adv.*

per·cep·tion (persĕp′shon) *n.* Act, faculty, of perceiving; intuitive recognition (*of*); (philos.) action by which the mind refers its sensations to external object as cause. **per·cep′tion·al** *adj.* **per·cep′tive** *adj.* **per·cep′tive·ly** *adv.* **per·cep′tive·ness, per·cep·tiv·i·ty** (pērsĕptĭv′ĭtē) *ns.*

perch¹ (pērch) *n.* (pl. **perch·es**, collect. **perch**). Common N. Amer. spiny-finned freshwater fish

Pepper *is made from the dried seeds of a tree which grows in India and Southeast Asia. White pepper has the skin removed. Cayenne is from the skin of a capsicum, originally from South America.*

(*Perca flavescens*) used as food; related European species (*P. fluviatilis*).

perch² (pērch) *n.* 1. Horizontal bar for bird to rest upon; anything serving for this; (fig.) elevated or secure position; **knock (person) off his ~**, vanquish, destroy, make less confident or condescending. 2. (also POLE¹, ROD) (Brit.) Measure of length, esp. for land, 5½ yds.; measure of area (also **square ~**), 30¼ sq. yds. **perch** *v.* Alight, rest, as bird (*on* bough etc.); settle, alight (*on*); place (as) on perch. **perch′er** *n.* Passerine bird with feet adapted for perching.

per·chance (perchăns′, -chahns) *adv.* (archaic) By chance; possibly, maybe.

Per·che·ron (pēr′cherŏn, -she-) *n.* Strong Swift horse of breed originating in le Perche, district in department of Orne, N. France.

per·chlo·ric (pērklōr′ĭk) *adj.* Containing chlorine in maximum valence.

per·cip·i·ent (persĭp′ēent) *adj.* Perceiving, conscious. **~** *n.* One who perceives, esp. (telepathy etc.) something outside range of senses. **per·cip′i·ence, per·cip′i·en·cy** *ns.*

per·co·late (pēr′kolāt) *v.* (**-lat·ed**, **-lat·ing**). Filter, ooze, through (freq. fig.); permeate;

*This young **peregrine** falcon is tearing at the carcass used to lure it back to its handler. A predator of small and medium-sized birds, the peregrine has been known to nest in cities.*

strain (liquid etc.) through pores etc. **per·co·la'tion** *n.*

per·co·la·tor (pēr'kolātor) *n.* (esp.) Apparatus for making coffee by allowing water to filter repeatedly through ground coffee.

per·cuss (perkŭs') *v.t.* (med.) Tap gently with finger or instrument for purposes of diagnosis etc.

per·cus·sion (perkŭsh'on) *n.* Forcible striking of one (usu. solid) body against another; (med.) percussing; ~ **instrument**, (mus.) instrument played by percussion, esp. struck with a stick or the hand (drum, triangle, tambourine) or struck together in pairs (cymbals); ~ **cap**, small copper cap or cylinder in firearm, containing explosive powder and exploded by percussion of a hammer. **per·cus·sive** (perkŭs'ĭv) *adj.*

per di·em (per dē'em, dīem). (So much) by the day. [L]

per·di·tion (perdĭsh'on) *n.* Eternal death, damnation.

per·dur·a·ble (perdoor'abel, -dūr'-) *adj.* Permanent; eternal; durable. **per·dur·a·bil'i·ty** *n.* **per·dur'a·bly** *adv.*

per·e·gri·nate (pĕr'egrināt) *v.i.* (-nat·ed, -nat·ing). (joc.) Travel, journey. **per·e·gri·na'tion, per'-**

e·gri·na·tor *ns.*

per·e·grine (pĕr'egrĭn, -grēn, -grīn) *n.* (also ~ **falcon**) Species of falcon (*Falco peregrinus*) esteemed for hawking (so called because the young were not taken from the nests but caught on their passages from their breeding places).

per·emp·to·ry (perĕmp'torē) *adj.* 1. Decisive, final; esp. (law) ~ **edict**, one in which the command is absolute; ~ **writ**, enforcing defendant's appearance without option. 2. (of statement or command) Admitting no denial or refusal; absolutely fixed, essential; (of person etc.) dogmatic, imperious, dictatorial. **per·emp'to·ri·ly** *adv.* **per·emp'to·ri·ness** *n.*

per·en·ni·al (perĕn'ēal) *adj.* Lasting through the year; (of stream) flowing through all seasons of the year; lasting long or forever; (of plant) living several years (cf. ANNUAL). **per·en'ni·al·ly** *adv.* **perennial** *n.* Perennial plant.

per·fect (pēr'fĭkt) *adj.* 1.

Complete, not deficient; faultles (of lesson) thoroughly learne thoroughly trained or skilled (in exact, precise; entire, unqualifie 2. (gram., of tense) Denotin completed event or action viewe in relation to the present; **futur** ~, expressing action completed the time indicated. 3. (bot Having all 4 whorls of the flowe (mus., of interval) not augmente or diminished, in normal form; ~ **cadence**, one consisting of dire chord of tonic preceded b dominant or subdominant chor **per'fect·ly** *adv.* **per'fect·ness** **perfect** *n.* Perfect tense. (perfĕkt') *v.t.* Complete, car through; make perfect; improv **per·fect·i·bil·i·ty** (perfĕktibĭl'ĭtē *n.*

per·fec·tion (perfĕk'shon) Completion; making perfect; fu development; faultlessness; perfe person or thing; highest pitc extreme, perfect specimen manifestation (of).

per·fec·tion·ist (perfĕk'shonĭs *n.* One who holds that perfectio may be attained in religion, moral politics, etc.; one who insists upo perfection; **P**~, member of th ONEIDA Community. **per·fec**

tion·ism *n.*

per·fec·to (perfĕk′tō) *n.* (pl. **-tos**). Large thick cigar tapering to point at both ends.

per·fi·dy (per′fĭdē) *n.* (pl. **-dies**). Breach of faith, treachery. **per·fid·i·ous** (perfĭd′ēus) *adj.* **per·fid′i·ous·ly** *adv.* **per·fid′i·ous·ness** *n.*

per·fo·rate (per′forāt) *v.* (**-rat·ed, -rat·ing**). Make hole(s) through, pierce; esp. make rows of holes in (sheet) to separate stamps, coupons, etc.; make an opening into; pass, extend, through; penetrate (*into, through,* etc.). **per·fo·ra′tion** *n.*

per·force (perfors′, -fors′) *adv.* Of necessity.

per·form (perform′) *v.* Carry into effect (command, promise, task, etc.); be agent of; go through, execute (public function, play, piece of music, etc.); act in play, sing, etc.; (of trained animals) execute feats or tricks, esp. at public show. **per·form′er** *n.* **per·form′-ing** *adj.*

per·for·mance (perfor′mans) *n.* Execution (*of* command etc.); carrying out, doing; notable feat; performing of play, public exhibition.

per·fume (per′fūm, perfūm′) *n.* Sweet smell; smell; fluid containing essence of flowers etc., scent. **per′fume·less** *adj.* **perfume** (perfūm′, per′fūm) *v.t.* (**-fumed, -fum·ing**). Impart sweet scent to, impregnate with sweet smell (esp.

in past part.).

per·fum·er (perfū′mer) *n.* Maker, seller, of purfumes. **per·fum′er·y** *n.* (pl. **-er·ies**).

per·func·to·ry (perfŭngk′torē) *adj.* Done merely for sake of getting through a duty, acting thus, superficial, mechanical. **per·func′to·ri·ly** *adv.* **per·func′to·ri·ness** *n.*

per·go·la (per′gola) *n.* Arbor, covered walk, formed of growing plants trained over trellis.

per·haps (perhăps′) *adv.* It may be, possibly.

peri- *prefix.* Around, about.

per·i·anth (pĕr′ēănth) *n.* Outer part or envelope of flower, enclosing stamens and pistils; corolla and calyx, or either of these.

per·i·car·di·um (pĕrĭkär′dēum) *n.* (pl. **-di·a** pr. -dēa). Membranous sac enclosing heart. **per·i·car′di·al, per·i·car′di·ac** *adjs.*

per·i·carp (pĕr′ĭkärp) *n.* Wall of ripened ovary of plant.

per·i·chon·dri·um (pĕrĭkŏn′-drēum) *n.* (pl. **-dri·a** pr. -drēa). Membrane enveloping cartilages (except at joints).

Per·i·cles (pĕr′ĭklēz) (*c*495–429 B.C.). Athenian statesman and military commander, under whose administration (460–429 B.C.) Athens reached the summit of her

Performances of plays, such as this performance of Shakespeare's Othello, have been seen by millions of people over more than 400 years, testimony to the love mankind has for being on the stage and seeing others there.

power. **Per·i·cle′an** *adj.*

per·i·cli·nal (pĕrĭklī′nal) *adj.* (geol.) Domelike.

per·i·cra·ni·um (pĕrĭkrā′nēum) *n.* (pl. **-ni·a** pr. -nēa). Membrane enveloping skull; (joc.) skull, brain; intellect.

per·i·gee (pĕr′ĭjē) *n.* That point in planet's (esp. moon's) orbit at which it is nearest to Earth (opp. *apogee*). **per·i·ge′an, per·i·ge′al** *adjs.*

per·i·he·li·on (pĕrĭhē′lēon, -hēl′yon) *n.* (pl. **-he·li·a** pr. -hē′lēa, -hēl′ya). That point in planet's orbit at which it is nearest sun (opp. *aphelion*).

per·il (pĕr′il) *n.* Danger, risk. **per′il·ous** *adj.* **per′il·ous·ly** *adv.* **per′il·ous·ness** *n.*

pe·rim·e·ter (perĭm′ĭter) *n.* 1. Circumference, outline, of closed figure; length of this. **per·i·met·ric** (pĕrĭmĕt′rĭk), **per·i·met′ri·cal** *adjs.*

per·i·ne·um (pĕrĭnē′um) *n.* (pl. **-ne·a** pr. -nē′a). (anat.) Lower end of trunk with its contents, extending from coccyx or tail bone to pubic symphysis. **per·i·ne′al** *adj.*

pe·ri·od (pēr′ēod) *n.* 1. Length of time marked by recurrence of astronomical coincidences; time of planet's revolution; time during which disease runs its course; menses. 2. Indefinite portion of history, life, etc.; any portion of time; (attrib., esp. of furniture, architecture, etc.) of, characteristic of, a particular (past) period. 3. Full

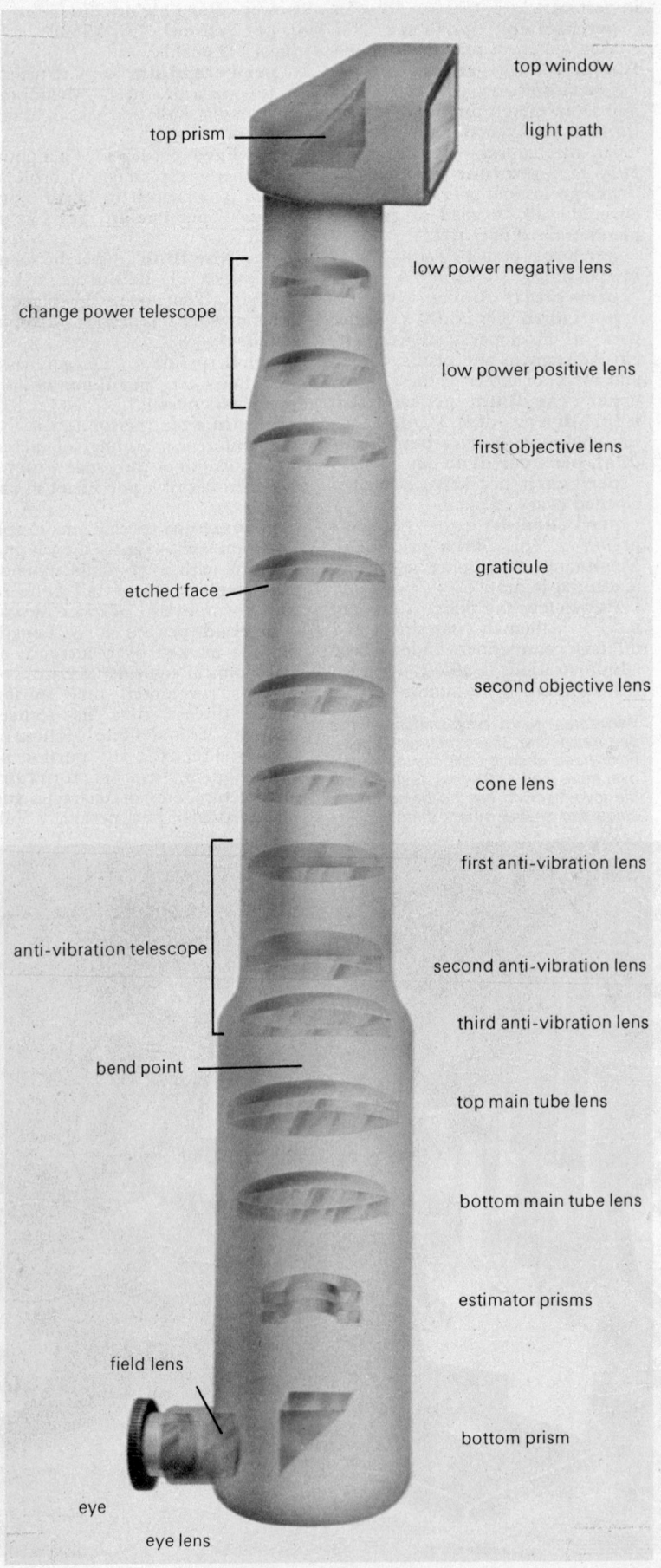

top window

top prism

light path

change power telescope

low power negative lens

low power positive lens

first objective lens

etched face

graticule

second objective lens

cone lens

first anti-vibration lens

anti-vibration telescope

second anti-vibration lens

third anti-vibration lens

bend point

top main tube lens

bottom main tube lens

estimator prisms

field lens

bottom prism

eye

eye lens

pause at end of sentence, point
character (.) marking this; **put a
to**, bring to an end.

pe·ri·od·ic (pērēŏd´ĭk) *adj.*
Of revolution of heavenly body (
motion); recurring at (regula
intervals.   2.   Expressed
(rhetorical) periods. 3. (chem.)
law, statement of fact th
properties of chemical elements a
periodic functions of their atom
weights, i.e. that when they a
arranged in order of those weight
elements having similar chemic
and physical properties occur
regular intervals; ~ **table**, table
chemical elements illustrating th
law. **pe·ri·o·dic·i·ty** (pērēodĭs´ĭt
n.

pe·ri·od·i·cal (pērēŏd´ĭkal) *aa*
= PERIODIC, 1; (of magazin
miscellany, etc.) published
regular intervals, e.g. monthl
pe·ri·od´i·cal·ly *adv.* **periodica**
n. Periodical magazine etc.

per·i·o·don·tal (pĕrēōdŏn´ta
adj. Of the tissues surrounding t
teeth.

per·i·os·te·um (pĕrēŏs´tēum)
(pl. **-te·a** pr. -tēa). Dense fibr
vascular membrane envelopin
bones (except where they a
covered by cartilage), from inn
layer of which bone substance
produced. **per·i·os´te·al** *adj.*

per·i·pa·tet·ic (pĕrĭpatĕt´ĭk) *aa*
1. P ~, of the school of Aristotl
Aristotelian (from Aristotle
custom of teaching while walkir
in the Lyceum at Athens). 2. Wal
ing from place to place on one
business, itinerant. **per·i·pa·tet´i
cal·ly** *adv.* **peripatetic** *n.*

pe·riph·er·y (perĭf´erē) *n.* (p
-er·ies). Bounding line esp.
closed curvilinear figure; extern
boundary or surface. **pe·riph·er·a
(perĭf´eral) *adj.* (esp.)   Of t
periphery, of minor importanc
applied to equipment used in cor
junction with a computer withou
being an integral part of it, and
operations involving such equij
ment.   **pe·riph´er·al·ly   *aa*
peripheral *n.* Peripheral device

pe·riph·ra·sis (perĭf´rasĭs)
(pl. **-ses** pr. -sēz). Roundabout w
of speaking, circumlocutio
roundabout phrase. **per·i·phras
tic** (pĕrĭfrăs´tĭk) *adj.* **per·i·phras
ti·cal·ly** *adv.*

pe·rique (perēk´) *n.* Kind of da
strong-flavored Louisiana tobacc
per·i·scope (pĕr´ĭskōp)
Apparatus of tube and mirro
giving view of things above surfa
to observer in submarine or trenc
or enabling person to see over t
heads of others in a crowd. **per·i

scop·ic (pĕrĭskŏp´ĭk), **per·i·scop´-i·cal** adjs. Enabling one to see distinctly for some distance around axis of vision.

per·ish (pĕr´ĭsh) v. Suffer destruction, lose life, come to untimely end; (of cold or exposure) reduce to distress or inefficiency (usu. in pass.). **per·ish·ing** adj. **per·ish·ing·ly** adv.

per·ish·a·ble (pĕr´ĭshabel) adj. Liable to perish; subject to speedy decay. **per·ish·a·bles** n.pl. Things, esp. foodstuffs in transit, of this nature.

per·i·stal·sis (pĕrĭstawl´sĭs, -stăl´-) n. (pl. **-ses** pr. -sēz). (physiol.) Automatic muscular movement consisting of successive waves of contraction and relaxation, by which contents of alimentary canal etc. are propelled along it. **per·i·stal´tic** adj. **per·i·stal´ti·cal·ly** adv.

per·i·stome (pĕr´ĭstōm) n. 1. (bot.) Fringe of small teeth around mouth of capsule in mosses. 2. (zool.) Part around mouth in various invertebrates.

per·i·style (pĕr´ĭstīl) n. Row of columns surrounding temple, court, cloister, etc.; space so surrounded.

per·i·to·ne·um (pĕrĭtonē´um) n. (pl. **-to·ne·ums, -to·ne·a** pr. -tonē´a). (anat.) Double serous membrane lining cavity of abdomen, of complex form, with numerous folds investing and supporting abdominal viscera. **per·i·to·ne´al** adj. **per·i·to·ni·tis** (pĕrĭtonī´tĭs) n. Inflammation of (part of) peritoneum.

per·i·wig (pĕr´ĭwĭg) n. (archaic) Wig. [Fr. perruque peruke]

per·i·win·kle¹ (pĕr´ĭwĭngkel) n. Plant of genus Vinca, esp. the European **lesser** and **greater** ~ (V. Minor, V. Major), evergreen trailing shrubs with light blue starry flowers; (also ~ **blue**) color of these flowers.

per·i·win·kle² (pĕr´ĭwĭngkel) n. Gastropod mollusk (Littorina), esp. common European and N. Amer. coast species (L. littorea), with dark-colored turbinate shell, much used for food.

per·jure (pĕr´jer) v. refl. (**-jured, -jur·ing**). Give false testimony under oath (~ **oneself**); **perjured**, guilty of perjury; involving perjury. **per´jur·er** n.

per·ju·ry (pĕr´jerē) n. (pl. **-ries**). Swearing to statement known to be false; willful utterance of false evidence while under oath; breach of oath.

perk¹ (pĕrk) n. (Brit. slang) Perquisite.

perk² (pĕrk) v. Lift (up) one's head, carry oneself smartly or briskly; smarten up; hold up (head, tail) self-assertively. **perk´y** adj. (**perk·i·er, perk·i·est**). Self-

*The **periwinkle**, a wild flower native to Europe, North Africa and western Asia, is an evergreen whose pale-blue star-shaped flowers appear in spring. There are five species.*

assertive, saucy, pert. **perk´i·ly** adv. **perk´i·ness** n.

perk³ (pĕrk) v. (colloq.) Percolate (coffee).

per·lite (pĕr´līt) n. Obsidian or other vitreous rock with concentric structure, expansible by heating.

per·ma·frost (pĕr´mafrawst, -frŏst) n. Permanently frozen subsoil etc. in Arctic regions. [f. perma(nent) frost]

perm·al·loy (pĕrmăl´oi, pĕr´-maloi) n. Nickel steel alloy, containing about 78% nickel, characterized by a very high permeability in low magnetic fields. [f. perm-(eable) alloy]

per·ma·nent (pĕr´manent) adj. Lasting, intended to last, indefinitely; ~ **magnet**, one whose

*The **periwinkle** is common in Europe and North America, inhabiting rocky shores and feeding on algae. It has been used as a food source for many centuries.*

property continues after the magnetizing agent has been removed; ~ **press**, (of fabric) requiring little or no ironing after being washed; ~ **wave**, artificial wave in hair that lasts until hair grows out. **per´ma·nent·ly** adv. **per·ma·nence** (pĕr´manens) n. Being permanent. **per´ma·nen·cy** n. Being permanent; permanent thing or arrangement.

per·man·ga·nate (permăng´-ganāt) n. (chem.) Salt of permanganic acid; (also **potassium** ~, ~ **of potash**) crystalline substance (KMnO4), dark purple when dissolved, used as a disinfectant, stain, etc. **per·man·gan·ic** (pĕr-măngăn´ĭk) adj. ~ **acid**, acid (HMnO4) known only in solution and from its salts.

per·me·ate (pĕr´mēat) v. (**-at·ed, -at·ing**). Penetrate, pervade, saturate; diffuse itself through, among, etc. **per·me·a·ble** (pĕr´mēabel) adj. **per·me·a·bil´i·ty** n.

Per·mi·an (pĕr´mēan) adj. & n. (geol.) (Of) the latest period or system of the Paleozoic. [f. Perm, former province of E. Russia]

per·mis·si·ble (permĭs´ibel) adj. Allowable. **per·mis·si·bil´i·ty** n.

per·mis·sion (permĭsh´on) n. Consent or liberty (to do).

per·mis·sive (permĭs´ĭv) adj. Giving permission; tolerant of behavior that some might condemn. **per·mis´sive·ly** adv. **per·mis´sive·ness** n.

per·mit (permĭt´) v. (**-mit·ted, -mit·ting**). Give consent or opportunity; admit of. ~ (pĕr´mĭt, permĭt´) n. Written order giving permission esp. for landing or removal of dutiable goods, entry into a place, etc.

per·mu·ta·tion (pĕrmyutā´-shon) n. (math.) Variation of order of a set of things lineally arranged; each of different arrangement of which such a set is capable. **per·-mu·tate** (pēr'myutāt) *v.t.* (**-tat·ed, -tat·ing**). Arrange in different order or combination.

per·mute (permūt') *v.t.* (**-mut·ed, -mut·ing**). Put in different order, change sequence of (things etc.).

Per·nam·bu·co (pĕrnahmbōō'kō) = RECIFE.

per·ni·cious (pernĭsh'us) *adj.* Destructive, ruinous, fatal; ~ **anemia**, progressive and, unless checked, fatal form of anemia. **per·ni'cious·ly** *adv.* **per·ni'cious·ness** *n.*

per·nick·e·ty (pernĭk'ĭtē), **per·-snick·et·y** (persnĭk'ĭtē) *adjs.* (colloq.) Fastidious; ticklish, requiring careful handling.

Pe·rón (pĕrōn'), **Juan Domingo** (1895–1974). Argentinean general; seized government and became dictator 1943; was elected president 1946, 1951; exiled, after a revolution, 1955; returned to Argentina in 1972; was elected president 1973. **Pe·ro·nis·ta** (pĕronĭs'ta) *n.* Supporter of Perón.

per·o·rate (pĕr'orāt) *v.i.* (**-rat·ed, -rat·ing**). Sum up and conclude speech; speak at length. **per·o·ra'tion** *n.*

per·ox·ide (perŏk'sĭd) *n.* (chem.) Compound of oxygen and another element containing greatest possible proportion of oxygen; (also ~ **of hydrogen**) colorless liquid (H_2O_2) used in aqueous solution as oxidizing and bleaching agent and antiseptic, in pure state a concentrated source of oxygen. ~ *v.t.* (**-id·ed, -id·ing**). Bleach (esp. hair) with peroxide.

per·pen·dic·u·lar (pērpendĭk'yuler) *adj.* 1. At right angles to plane of horizon; (loosely) very steep; erect, upright; (joc.) in standing position. 2. (geom.) At right angles (*to* given line, plane, or surface). 3. **P** ~, (archit.) of the style of English Gothic architecture prevailing from the middle of the 14th c. to the middle of the 16th c., characterized by the vertical lines of its tracery. **per·pen·dic·u·lar·i·ty** (pērpendĭkyulăr'ĭtē) *n.* **per·pen·dic·u·lar·ly** *adv.* **perpendicular** *n.* Plumb rule or other instrument for showing perpendicular line; perpendicular line; **the** ~, perpendicular line or direction.

per·pe·trate (pēr'pĭtrāt) *v.t.* (**-trat·ed, -trat·ing**). Perform, commit (crime, blunder, etc.). **per·pe·tra'tion, per'pe·tra·tor** *ns.*

per·pet·u·al (perpĕch'ōōal) *adj.* Eternal; permanent during life; applicable, valid, forever or for indefinite time; continuous; (colloq.) frequent, repeated; ~ **calendar**, that can be used for any year or over a long period of time; ~ **motion**, motion of hypothetical machine that once set going should continue forever unless stopped by external force or worn out. **per·-pet'u·al·ly** *adv.*

per·pet·u·ate (perpĕch'ōōāt) *v.t.* (**-at·ed, -at·ing**). Make perpetual; preserve from oblivion. **per·-pet·u·a'tion, per·pet'u·a·tor** *ns.*

per·pe·tu·i·ty (pērpĭtōō'ĭtē, -tū'-) *n.* (pl. **-ties**). Quality of being perpetual; perpetual possession or position; perpetual annuity; **in, to, for,** ~, forever.

per·plex (perplĕks') *v.t.* Bewilder, puzzle; complicate, confuse (matter); entangle, intertwine. **per·plexed'** *adj.* **per·plex·ed·ly** (perplĕk'sĭdlē) *adv.* **per·plex'ing** *adj.* **per·plex'ing·ly** *adv.* **per·plex·i·ty** (perplĕk'sĭtē) *n.* (pl. **-ties**). Bewilderment; cause of this; entangled state.

per·qui·site (pēr'kwĭzĭt) *n.* Customary gratuity; incidental income or privilege beyond customary salary.

Per·ry (pĕr'ē), **Matthew Calbraith** (1794–1858). Amer. naval officer; negotiated treaty opening commerce with Japan, 1853–4; his brother, **Oliver Hazard** ~ (1785–1819), an Amer. naval officer, commanded fleet on Lake Erie during the War of 1812, and announced the British defeat in the famous dispatch: "We have met the enemy and they are ours."

per se (per sā', sē'). By or in itself, intrinsically. [L.]

per·se·cute (pēr'sekūt) *v.t.* (**-cut·ed, -cut·ing**). Pursue with enmity and injury (esp. holder of opinion held to be heretical); harass, worry; importune (*with*

Juan Domingo Perón made economic and diplomatic reforms but his rule was marred by graft and civil oppression. His wife, Eva, supported him with her vast popular following.

questions etc.). **per·se·cu'tion** *n.* **delusions of** ~, insane delusions that one is persecuted. **per'se·cu·tive** *adj.* **per'se·cu·tor** *n.*

Per·se·id (pēr'sēĭd) *n.* (astron.) One of a group of shooting stars appearing yearly near beginning of August and radiating from a point near the constellation Perseus.

Per·seph·o·ne (persĕf'onē). (Gk. myth.) Daughter of Zeus and DEMETER; called by the Romans Proserpina; goddess of spring; while gathering flowers she was carried off by Pluto and made queen of Hell; Demeter persuaded Zeus to let her return to earth for some months of each year.

Per·sep·o·lis (persĕp'olĭs). Ancient capital of Persian Empire, now in S. Iran.

Per·se·us (pēr'seus, -sōōs). 1. (Gk. myth.) Hero, son of Zeus and DANAË; cut off the head of the gorgon MEDUSA, and gave it to Athena; saved ANDROMEDA from a sea monster, married her, and founded the city of Mycenae. 2. (astron.) Northern constellation between Cassiopeia and Taurus.

per·se·ver·ance (pērsevēr'ans) *n.* Steadfast pursuit of an aim, constant persistence; (theol.) continuance in state of grace. **per·se·ver'ant** *adj.*

per·se·vere (pērsevēr') *v.i.* (**-vered, -ver·ing**). Continue steadfastly, persist (*in*, *with*). **per·se·ver'ing** *adj.* **per·se·ver'ing·ly** *adv.*

Per·sia (pēr'zha, -sha). Ancient and (now) alternative name of IRAN.

Per·sian (pēr'zhan, -shan) *adj.* Of Persia or its language or people; ~ **blinds**, PERSIENNES; ~ **cat**, cat of domesticated breed, with long silky hair, bushy tail, and round head; ~ **carpet, rug**, carpet or rug made in Persia, usu. oblong, of very fine skillful weave, of silk or wool pile and traditional, freq. geometrical, patterns; ~ **Empire**, empire formed (6th c. B.C.) by conquest of Media, Lydia, and Babylonia under Cyrus, including at its greatest all western Asia, Egypt, and parts of eastern Europe, and overthrown by Alexander the Great, 331 B.C.; ~ **Gulf**, land-locked sea extending in southeasterly direction from confluence of Euphrates and Tigris and communicating with Arabian Sea through Strait of Hormuz and Gulf of Oman; ~ **knot**, kind of knot used in carpet making; ~ **lamb**, caracul; ~ **Wars**, wars in which Darius and Xerxes vainly attempted to conquer Greece (499–449 B.C., but the defeat of Xerxes at SALAMIS, 479, decided the issue). **Persian** *n.* 1. Native, inhabitant, of Persia. 2. Indo-European Iranian language; **Middle** ~, Pahlavi; **Old** ~, ancient W. Iranian language,

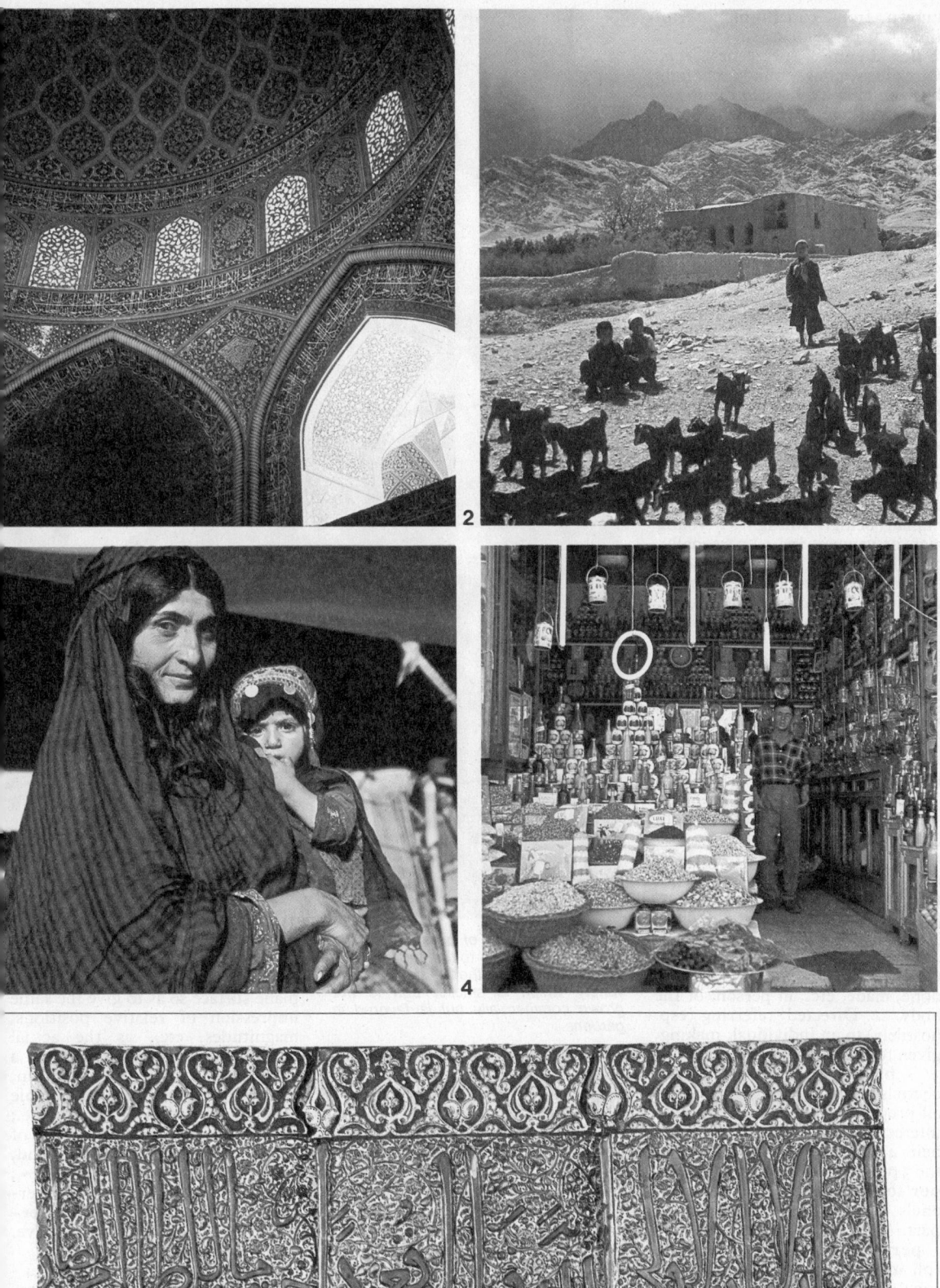

2

4

n Iran, despite the country's recent
noves towards modernization, there is
still a wealth of traditional **Persian** art
nd activities. 1. Intricate mosaics com-
oletely cover the inside of the dome of

Sheikh Lutfullah's mosque built in
1617. 2. In the arid mountains, children
tend flocks of goats. 3. In the same
area women continue to dress in garments similar to those worn for hun-

dreds of years. 4. Even the open-
fronted shops, with their fluorescent
lights, contain a mixture of new and traditional foods. 5. Early 13th-century
wall-tiles from a mosque at Meshhed.

known from cuneiform inscriptions. 3. Persian cat.

per·si·ennes (pērzēěnz´) *n.pl.* Outside window blinds of light horizontal laths; Persian blinds.

per·si·flage (pēr´*si*flahzh) *n.* Light raillery, banter.

per·sim·mon (persĭm´*o*n) *n.* Yellowish-orange plumlike astringent fruit, becoming sweet when softened by frost, of the Amer. tree *Diospyros virginiana*; large red fruit of Chinese and Japanese species (*D. kaki*).

per·sist (persĭst´, -zĭst´) *v.i.* Continue firmly or obstinately (*in* opinion, course, etc.) esp. against remonstrance etc. **per·sist´ence**, **per·sist´en·cy** *ns.* **per·sist´ent** *adj.* (esp., of horns, hair, leaves, etc.) Remaining after such parts normally wither or fall off. **per·sist´ent·ly** *adv.*

per·snick·et·y = PERNICKETY.

per·son (pēr´*so*n) *n.* 1. Individual human being; living body of human being; **young** ~, young man or woman; **in** ~, personally, oneself. 2. (gram.) Each of 3 classes of personal pronouns, and corresponding distinctions in verbs, indicating the person(s) speaking (**first** ~), spoken to (**second** ~), and spoken of (**third** ~).

per·so·na (persō´na) *n.* (pl. **-nae** pr. -nē). (Jungian psychol.) Outer aspect of personality as revealed to other persons.

per·son·a·ble (pēr´*so*nabel) *adj.* Handsome, comely.

per·son·age (pēr´*so*nĭj) *n.* Person of rank or importance; person; character in play etc.

per·so·na (non) gra·ta (persō´na nōn grah´ta, -grăt´a, grā´ta) (pl. **per·so·nae (non) gra·tae** pr. persō´nē nōn grah´tē, grăt´ē, grā´tē). (Un)acceptable person. [L.]

per·son·al (pēr´*so*nal) *adj.* 1. One's own, individual, private; done, made, etc., in person; of the body. 2. Directed, referring (esp. hostilely) to an individual; making, given to making, personal remarks. 3. ~ **property**, **estate**, etc., (law) chattels or chattel interests in land, all property except land and those interests in land that pass to one's heir. 4. (gram.) Of, denoting, one of the 3 persons (esp. in ~ **pronoun**). **per·son·al·ly** *adv.* In person, in one's own person; for one's own part.

per·son·al·i·ty (pērsonal´ĭtē) *n.* (pl. **-ties**). 1. Being a person; personal existence or identity; distinctive personal character; person; ~ **cult**, extreme adulation of an individual person; **multiple** ~, (psych.) apparent existence of two or more distinct and alternating personalities in a single individual. 2. (of remarks) Fact of being personal; (usu. pl.) personal remarks.

per·son·al·ize (pēr´*so*nalīz) *v.t.*

There are 2 types of **persimmon**, the Oriental, introduced to the U.S.A. in the 19th century, and the native American variety which is smaller and is not grown commercially but is favored in gardens.

(**-ized**, **-iz·ing**). Personify; mark with one's name etc. **per·son·al·i·za·tion** (pērsonalīzā´shon) *n.*

per·son·al·ty (pēr´*so*naltē) *n.* (pl. **-ties**). Personal property.

per·son·i·fi·ca·tion (persŏnĭfikā´shon) *n.* Personifying; person, thing, viewed as striking example or embodiment *of.*

per·son·i·fy (persŏn´ĭfĭ) *v.t.* (**-fied**, **-fy·ing**). Attribute personal nature to (abstraction); symbolize (quality) by figure in human form; embody (quality) in one's own person, exemplify typically (esp. in past part.)

per·son·nel (pērsonĕl´) *n.* Body of persons employed in an organization, as distinct from the equipment; ~ **department**, **manager**, those concerned with appointment, advising, training, etc., of employees.

per·spec·tive (perspěk´tĭv) *n.* Art of delineating solid objects on a plane surface so as to give the same impression of relative positions, magnitudes, etc., as the actual objects do when viewed from a particular point; picture so drawn; apparent relation between visible objects as to position, distance, etc.; (fig.) relation in which parts of subject are viewed by the mind; view, prospect (lit. and fig.); **in** ~, drawn according to rules of perspective; foreshortened. **perspective** *adj.* Of, in perspective. **per·spec´tive·ly** *adv.*

per·spi·ca·cious (pērspĭkā´shus) *adj.* Having mental penetration or discernment. **per·spi·ca·cious·ly** *adv.* **per·spi·cac·i·ty** (pērspĭkăs´ĭtē) *n.*

per·spic·u·ous (perspĭk´ūus) *adj.* Easily understood, clearly expressed; (of person) clear in expression. **per·spic´u·ous·ly** *adv.* **per·spi·cu·i·ty** (pērspĭkū´ĭtē) *n.* **per·spic´u·ous·ness** *ns.*

*The Incas of **Peru** were capable of incredible feats of engineering, such as these roads (1) snaking over the mountains to cities like Macchu Picchu (2), near Cuzco.*

per·spi·ra·tion (pĕrspirā'shon) *n.* Sweating; sweat. **per·spir·a·to·ry** (perspī'ratōrē, -tōrē) *adj.*
per·spire (perspīr') *v.* (**-spired, -spir·ing**) Sweat.
per·suade (perswād') *v.t.* (**-suad·ed, -suad·ing**). Cause (person, oneself) to have belief (*of, that*); induce (*to* do, *into* action); **persuaded**, convinced (*of, that*). **per·suad'a·ble**, **per·sua·si·ble** (perswā'sibel) *adjs.* **per·sua·si·bil'i·ty** *n.*
per·sua·sion (perswā'zhon) *n.* Persuading; persuasiveness; conviction; religious belief, sect holding this.
per·sua·sive (perswā'sĭv) *adj.* Able to persuade, winning. **per·sua'sive·ly** *adv.* **per·sua'sive·ness** *n.*
pert (pĕrt) *adj.* Forward, saucy, in speech or conduct; lively, sprightly, cheerful. **pert'ly** *adv.* **pert'ness** *n.*
per·tain (pertān') *v.i.* Belong as part, appendage, or accessory, *to*; be appropriate *to*; have reference, relate, *to*.
per·ti·na·cious (pĕrtinā'shus) *adj.* Stubborn, persistent, obstinate. **per·ti·na'cious·ly** *adv.* **per·ti·nac·i·ty** (pĕrtinăs'ĭtē), **per·ti·na'cious·ness** *ns.*
per·ti·nent (pĕr'tinent) *adj.* Pertaining, relevant, apposite, (*to* matter in hand etc.); to the point. **per'ti·nent·ly** *adv.* **per'ti·nence, per'ti·nen·cy** *ns.*
per·turb (pertĕrb') *v.t.* Upset, disquiet, throw into agitation. **per·tur·ba·tion** (pĕrterbā'shon) *n.*
Pe·ru (peroo'). Republic of Pacific coast of S. Amer.; inhabited during the Middle Ages by the Incas (see INCA); won independence from Spain 1821; capital, Lima; ~ **Current**: see HUMBOLDT CURRENT.
pe·ruke (perook') *n.* Wig, esp. kind worn in 17th–18th c.
pe·ruse (perooz') *v.* (**-rused, -rus·ing**). Read thoroughly or carefully; read; examine carefully. **pe·rus·al** (peroo'zal) *n.*
Pe·ru·vi·an (peroo'vēan) *adj.* Of Peru or its people; ~ **bark**, cinchona bark. **Peruvian** *n.* Native, inhabitant, of Peru. [*Peruvia*, Latinized name of PERU]
per·vade (pervād') *v.t.* (**-vad·ed, -vad·ing**). Spread through, permeate, saturate. **per·va·sion** (pervā'zhon) *n.* **per·va·sive** (pervā'sĭv) *adj.* **per·va'sive·ly** *adv.* **per·va'sive·ness** *n.*
per·verse (pervĕrs') *adj.* Persistent in error; different from what is reasonable or required; wayward; peevish; perverted, wicked; (of ver-

Spraying vineyards in France with pesticide. Excessive use of such chemicals has also killed natural predators of pest species and results in the need for still more spraying.

dict) against weight of evidence or judge's direction. **per·verse′ly** *adv.* **per·verse′ness, per·ver′-si·ty** (perver′sĭtē) *ns.*

per·vert (pervērt′) *v.t.* Turn aside (thing) from its proper use; misconstrue, misapply (words etc.); lead astray (person, mind) from right opinion or conduct, or esp. religious belief. **per·ver′sion** (pervēr′zhon, -shon) *n.* **per·ver′sive** (pervēr′sĭv) *adj.* **pervert** (pēr′vert) *n.* Perverted person; person showing perversion of sexual instincts.

per·vi·ous (pēr′vēus) *adj.* Affording passage (*to*); permeable; (fig.) accessible (*to* reason etc.). **per′vi·ous·ly** *adv.* **per′vi·ous·ness** *n.*

Pe·sach (pā′sahx) = PASSOVER.

Pes·ca·do·res (pĕskadōr′ĭs, -ēz). Group of islands of China in Formosa Strait between China to the W. and Taiwan to the E.

pes·ky (pĕs′kē) *adj.* (**pes·ki·er, pes·ki·est**). (colloq.) Trouble-some, confounded, annoying.

pe·so (pā′sō) *n.* (pl. **-sos**). Principal monetary unit in Argentina, Bolivia, Colombia, Cuba, Dominican Republic, Mexico, Philippines, and Uruguay.

pes·sa·ry (pĕs′arē) *n.* (pl. **-ries**). Instrument, medicated plug, inserted into or worn in vagina to prevent uterine displacements or as contraceptive.

pes·si·mism (pĕs′imĭzem) *n.* Tendency to look at the worst aspect of things; doctrine that this world is the worst possible, or that all things tend to evil. **pes′si·mist** *n.* **pes·si·mis′tic** *adj.* **pes·si·mis′ti·cal·ly** *adv.*

pest (pĕst) *n.* Troublesome or destructive person, animal, or thing; (obs.) pestilence.

Pes·ta·loz·zi (pĕstalŏt′sē), **Johann Heinrich** (1746–1827). Swiss educator; influenced methods of teaching in elementary schools in Amer. and Europe, with an emphasis on primacy of child's sensory experience and use of objects.

pes·ter (pĕs′ter) *v.t.* Trouble, plague. **pes′ter·er** *n.*

pes·ti·cide (pĕs′tĭsīd) *n.* Substance for destroying pests, esp. insects.

pes·tif·er·ous (pĕstĭf′erus) *adj.* Noxious, pestilential; (fig.) having moral contagion, pernicious. **pes′-tif′er·ous·ly** *adv.*

pes·ti·lence (pĕs′tĭlens) *n.* Any fatal epidemic disease, esp. bubonic plague. **pes′ti·lent** *adj.* Destructive to life, deadly; (fig.) injurious to morals etc.; (colloq.) troublesome. **pes′ti·lent·ly** *adv.* **pes·ti·len·tial** (pĕstĭlĕn′shal) *adj.*

pes·tle (pĕs′el, pĕs′tel) *n.* Club-shaped instrument for pounding substances in a mortar; various mechanical appliances for pounding, stamping, etc. ~ *v.* (**-tled, -tling**). Pound (as) with pestle; use pestle.

pet¹ (pĕt) *n.* Animal tamed and kept as favorite or treated with fondness; darling, favorite (often attrib.); ~ **aversion**, what one specially dislikes; ~ **name**, one expressing fondness or familiarity. **pet** *v.* (**pet·ted, pet·ting**). Treat as a pet, fondle, caress; indulge in hugging, kissing, and fondling.

pet² (pĕt) *n.* Offense at being slighted, ill humor.

Pet. *abbrev.* Peter (New Testament).

pet·al (pĕt′al) *n.* Each of the divisions of the corolla of a flower, esp. when separate. **pet·a·loid** (pĕt′aloid) *adj.*

pe·tard (pĭtärd′) *n.* Small engine of war, orig. of metal, later wooden box charged with powder, formerly used to blow in door etc.; kind of firework; **hoist with one's own ~**: see HOIST².

pet·cock (pĕt′kŏk) *n.* (also **pet′cock**) Small valve for draining, letting out steam, etc.

pe·ter (pē′ter) *v.i.* (orig. mining colloq.) ~ **out**, give out, come to an end.

Pe·ter¹ (pē′ter). Name of three tsars of Russia: **Peter I** (1672–1725), "the Great," reigned 1682–1725; founded St. Petersburg (Leningrad); introduced many elements of Western civilization into Russia; **Peter II** (1715–30), grandson of Peter I, reigned 1727–30; **Peter III** (1728–62), maternal grandson of Peter I, reigned 1761–1762; murdered prob. by orders of his wife, CATHERINE¹ the Great.

Pe·ter² (pē′ter), **St.** (d. c67). Apostle, orig. called Simon; most prominent of the disciples during the ministry of Jesus and in the early Church; martyred, probably in Rome; in R.C. tradition, founder and 1st bishop of Church of Rome: in popular belief, keeper of the door of heaven; commemorated with St. Paul, June 29; (**Epistle of St.**) ~, either of the 2 epistles of New Testament ascribed to him; **rob ~ to pay Paul**, take away from one person, cause, etc., to pay, give, etc., to another. [Gk. *petros* rock]

Pe·ter (pē′ter) **Pan.** Hero of J. M. Barrie's play (1904) of the same name, a boy who never grew up.

pet·i·ole (pĕt′ēol) *n.* (bot.) Leaf stalk. **pet·i·o·lar** (pĕt′ēoler), **pet·i·o·late** (pĕt′ēolāt) *adjs.*

pe·tit bour·geois (pĕt′ē boorzhwah′) (pl. **pe·tits bour·geois** pr. same as sing.). Member of lower middle classes.

pe·tite (petēt′) *adj.* (of woman) Of small dainty build.

pe·tit four (pĕt′ē fōr′, fōr′; *Fr.* petē′ foor′) (pl. **pet·its fours** pr.

*Wherever there is salt water, one or more members of the extensive **petrel** family will be found like the Giant Petrel of Antarctica (above).*

Petrified trees in Petrified Fores National Park in Arizona. The wood has gradually been replaced by minerals and become fossilized. In some cases i is still possible to detect the original cel structure which has been preserved in the minerals.

pĕt´ē fŏrz´, fōrz; Fr. petē foor´). Very small fancy cake. [Fr.]

pe·ti·tion (petĭsh´on) *n.* Asking, supplication, request; formal written supplication, request; (law) kind of formal written application to a court. ~ *v.* Make petition to (sovereign etc. *for, to*); ask humbly (*for, to*). **pe·ti´tion·ar·y** *adj.* **pe·ti´tion·er** *n.* (esp.) Plaintiff in divorce suit.

pe·tit lar·ce·ny (pĕ´tē lãr´senē) = PETTY larceny.

pe·tit mal (petē´ măl´, pĕt´ē). Mild form of epilepsy (opp. GRAND MAL). [Fr.]

pe·tit (pĕt´ē) **point.** Embroidery on canvas using small stitches.

Pe·trarch (pē´trärk, pĕt´rärk). Francesco Petrarca (1304–74), Italian poet and humanist; famous for his odes and sonnets to "Laura." **Pe·trar·chan** (pĭtrãr´kan) *adj.* ~ **sonnet**: see SONNET.

pet·rel (pĕt´rel) *n.* Any of various seabirds of the order Procellariiformes (which also includes the shearwaters and albatrosses); **stormy** ~, small bird (*Hydrobates pelagicus*) with black and white plumage.

pe·tri (pē´trē) **dish.** Shallow covered dish used for culture of microorganisms etc. [J. R. Petri (d. 1921), German bacteriologist]

pet·ri·fac·tion (pĕtrĭfăk´shon), **pet·ri·fi·ca·tion** (pĕtrĭfĭkā´shon) *ns.* Petrifying; petrified substance or mass.

Petrified (pĕt´rĭfĭd) **Forest National Park.** Area in E. Arizona covering 93,493 acres

(37,837 hectares) and containing many petrified trees.

pet·ri·fy (pĕt´rĭfī) *v.* (**-fied -fy·ing**). Convert into stone or stony substance, be so converted (esp. of dead organism becoming fossilized); (fig.) paralyze, stupefy, with astonishment, terror, etc.: deprive (mind etc.) of vitality, stiffen.

Pe·trine (pē´trīn) *adj.* Of St. PETER[2].

petro- *prefix.* Rock.

pet·ro·chem·i·cal (pĕtrōkĕm´-ĭkal) *n.* Substance obtained from petroleum or natural gas. ~ *adj.* Of petrochemicals or petro-chemistry.

pe·tro·chem·is·try (pĕtrōkĕm´-ĭstrē) *n.* Chemistry of rocks or of petroleum.

pet·ro·glyph (pĕt´roglĭf) *n.* Rock carving (usu. prehistoric). **pet·ro·glyph´ic** *adj.*

Pet·ro·grad (pĕt´rogrăd). Name of St. Petersburg from 1917 to 1924, when it was renamed LENINGRAD.

pe·trog·ra·phy (pĭtrŏg´rafē) *n.* Scientific description of formation and composition of rocks. **pe·trog´ra·pher** *n.* **pet·ro·graph·ic** (pĕtrogrăf´ĭk), **pe·tro·graph´i·cal** *adjs.*

pe·tro·le·um (petrō´lēum) *n.* Crude oil; inflammable mineral oil, varying from light yellow to dark brown or black, found in many places in the upper strata of Earth, containing large numbers of different hydrocarbons and refined for use as fuel for heating and in internal combustion engines, as illuminant, as dry-cleaning agent, etc.; ~ **jelly**, translucent gelatinous hydrocarbon mixture derived from petroleum and used in ointments etc. [L. and Gk. *petra* rock, L. *oleum* oil]

pe·trol·o·gy (pĭtrŏl´ojē) *n.* Study of origin, structure, etc., of rocks. **pet·ro·log·ic** (pĕtrolŏj´ĭk), **pet·ro·log´i·cal** *adjs.* **pet·ro·log´-i·cal·ly** *adv.* **pe·trol´o·gist** *n.*

Pe·tro·ni·us Ar·bi·ter (pĭtrō´nēus ãr´bĭter), **Gaius** (d. 66 A.D.). Roman satirist, author of the *Satyricon*; arbiter of taste (*elegentiae arbiter*) at Nero's court; committed suicide to avoid being killed by Nero.

pet·rous (pĕt´rus) *adj.* Of, like, rock; esp. (anat.) applied to dense hard part of temporal bone forming protective case for internal ear.

pet·ti·coat (pĕt´ēkōt) *n.*

register

drive to register

meter

vent and flame trap

float

float

filter

tor

on-return valve

check valve

motor

suction elbow

by-pass valve

rotary pump

sight glass

atmosphere

suction

pressure

*Gasoline, refined **petroleum**, fuels much of today's road traffic. Designers have made the pumps which dispense it seem simple, but their sleek outer casing hides intricate machinery to deliver, and register accurately.*

main valve

holding valve

hosecock

from storage tank and check valve

Woman's undergarment hanging from waist or shoulders; ~ **government**, predominance of women in politics or organizational life.

pet·ti·fog (pĕt´ĕfŏg, -fawg) *v.i.* (-**fogged**, -**fog·ging**). Practice legal chicanery; quibble, wrangle, about petty points. **pet´ti·fog·ger**

n. Inferior legal practitioner; rascally attorney; petty practitioner in any department. **pet´ti·fog·ger·y** *n.* **pet´ti·fog·ging** *adj.*

pet·tish (pĕt´ĭsh) *adj.* Peevish, petulant, easily put out. **pet´tish·ly** *adv.* **pet´tish·ness** *n.*

pet·ty (pĕt´ē) *adj.* (-**ti·er**, -**ti·est**). Unimportant, trivial;

small-minded; minor, inferior, on a small scale; ~ **cash**, small cash items of receipt or expenditure; ~ **larceny**, larceny involving goods whose value is below a certain amount (see GRAND larceny); ~ **officer**, officer in navy corresponding in rank to army N.C.O. **pet´ti·ly** *adv.* **pet´ti·ness** *n.*

pet·u·lant (pĕch′ulant) *adj.* Peevishly impatient or irritable. **pet′u·lant·ly** *adv.* **pet′u·lance, pet′u·lan·cy** *ns.*

pe·tu·nia (petoō′nya, -tū′-) *n.* Herbaceous plant of S. Amer. genus *P* ~, with variously colored flowers of funnel shape.

pew (pū) *n.* Place (often enclosed and raised) in church appropriated to a family (**family** ~) or others; fixed bench with back in church. **pew** *v.t.* Furnish with pews, enclose in pew.

pe·wee (pē′wē) *n.* N. Amer. flycatcher of the genus *Contopus.*

pe·wit (pē′wĭt, pū′ĭt): see LAP-WING.

pew·ter (pū′ter) *n.* Gray alloy of tin and lead or other metal, resembling lead in appearance when dull, but capable of receiving a high polish; utensils of this; pewter pot.

pe·yo·te (pāō′tē) *n.* Mexican cactus (*Lophophora williamsii*); hallucinogenic drug produced from tops of this.

Pfc, Pfc., PFC. *abbrevs.* Private first class.

P.G.A. *abbrev.* Professional Golfers' Association.

pH (pēach′) (chem.) Symbol for common logarithm, with sign reversed, of hydrogen ion concentration, expressed in gram equivalents per liter; ~ **scale,** scale on which the acidity or alkalinity of a solution is measured, pH 7.0 representing neutrality, lower values acidity, and higher ones alkalinity.

Phae·dra (fē′dra). (Gr. legend) Daughter of Minos and wife of Theseus; became enamored of Hippolytus, son of Theseus and the Amazon Hippolyta, and engineered his death when he rejected her advances.

Phae·drus (fē′drus) (1st c. A.D.).

The Santa Ines Mission in Solvang, California was built in the early 19th century and its traditional style has been retained with the whitewashed walls and the dark wooden **pews** which have been highly polished.

Macedonian slave; author of fables about animals, based on those of Aesop and others, in Latin verse.

Pha·ë·thon (fā′ethon). (Gk. myth.) Son of the sun god Helios; when he drove his father's chariot too near earth Zeus killed him with a thunderbolt to save earth from destruction.

pha·e·ton (fā′ĭton) *n.* Light four-wheeled open carriage usu. drawn by pair of horses. [f. PHAE-THON]

phage (fāj) *n.* (bacteriology) Destroyer of bacteria.

-phage (*comb. form*) (One) that

eats, destroys.

phag·o·cyte (făg′osīt) *n.* Blood cell, esp. leucocyte, capable of ingesting and destroying dead or foreign material.

-phagous (*comb. form*) Eating.

-phagy (*comb. form*) Eating of.

phal·ange (făl′anj, falănj′) = PHALANX def. 3.

pha·lan·ge·al (falăn′jēal) *adj.* (anat.) Of a phalanx.

pha·lan·ger (falăn′jer) *n.* Any of the Australian opossums, small marsupials (of several genera) of arboreal habits, with thick woolly fur and freq. prehensile tail; **flying** ~, one of those that have a flying membrane, flying opossum. [mod. L. invented by Buffon f. Gk. *phalanggion* spider's web, from webbed toes of hind feet]

pha·lanx (fā′lăngks, făl′ăngks) *n.* (pl. **pha·lanx·es**). 1. (Gk. antiq.) Line of battle, esp. body of Macedonian infantry drawn up in close order. 2. Set of persons banded together for common purpose; community of about 1800 persons, as proposed by Fourier, living together as one family and holding property in common. 3. (pl. **pha·lan·ges** pr. falăn′jēz) (anat.) Any of the bones of the fingers or toes.

phal·a·rope (făl′arōp) *n.* Any of several related species of small wading and swimming bird allied to snipe.

phal·lus (făl′us) *n.* (pl. **phal·li** pr. făl′ī, **phal·lus·es**). Image of penis, venerated in some religious systems as symbolizing generative power in nature. **phal·lic** (făl′ĭk) *adj.* **phal·lism** (făl′īzem), **phal·li·cism** (făl′īsĭzem) *ns.*

phan·tasm (făn′tăzem) *n.* Illusion, phantom; illusive likeness (*of*); supposed vision of absent (living or dead) person. **phan·tas·mal** (făntăz′mal), **phan·tas′·mic** *adjs.*

phan·tas·ma·go·ri·a (făntăz-magōr′ēa, -gōr′-) *n.* Exhibition of optical illusions produced chiefly by means of magic lantern, first shown in London in 1802; shifting scene of real or imagined figures. **phan·tas·ma·gor·ic** (făntăz-magōr′ĭk, -gŏr′-) *adj.*

phan·ta·sy (făn′tasē,-zē) := FANTASY.

phan·tom (făn′tom) *n.* Apparition, specter; image (*of*); vain show, form without substance or reality; mental illusion; (attrib.) apparent, illusive, imaginary.

Phar·aoh (fār′ō). Title of ruler of ancient Egypt. [Hebraized version of Egyptian title meaning "great house"]

The female red-necked **Phalarope** (left) is much brighter than the male. The birds breed in Scandinavia and on the Baltic Coast, then fly south to warmer waters.

phar·ma·cist (fär´masĭst) *n.* Pharmaceutical chemist; qualified person engaged in pharmacy.

phar·ma·col·o·gy (färmakŏl´-ojē) *n.* Science concerned with the nature and action of drugs. **phar·ma·co·log·i·cal** (färmakolŏj´ĭkal) *adj.* **phar·ma·col´o·gist** *n.*

phar·ma·co·poe·ia (färma-kopē´a) *n.* Book (esp. one officially published) containing list of drugs with directions for use; stock of drugs. **phar·ma·co·poe´ial** *adj.*

phar·ma·cy (fär´masē) *n.* (pl. **-cies**). Preparation and (esp. medicinal) dispensing of drugs; pharmacist's shop.

pha·ryn·ge·al (farĭn´jēal, -jal, fărĭnjē´al), **pha·ryn·gal** (farĭng´-gal) *adjs.* Of the pharynx.

phar·yn·gi·tis (fărĭnjī´tis) *n.* Inflammation of the membranes of the pharynx.

pharyngo- *prefix.* Pharyngeal.

pha·ryn·go·scope (farĭng´-goskōp) *n.* Instrument for examining pharynx.

phar·ynx (făr´ĭngks) *n.* (pl. **pha·ryn·ges** pr. farĭn´jēz, **phar·ynx·es**). Cavity, with enclosing muscles and mucous membrane, connecting mouth and nasal passages with esophagus; corresponding part in invertebrates.

phase (fāz) *n.* 1. State of change or development. 2. (astron.) Aspect of moon or planet acc. to amount of illumination (esp. applied to new moon, 1st quarter, full moon, last quarter). 3. (phys.) Particular state or point in a recurring sequence of movements or changes, e.g. a vibration or undulation; time (measured from an arbitrary zero) at which a vibration attains a

Phar·i·see (făr´ĭsē) *n.* Member of Jewish sect of 1st c. B.C. to 1st c. A.D. distinguished by their strict observance of the traditional and written law, represented in New Testament as having pretensions to superior sanctity; hence, self-righteous person; formalist; hypocrite. **Phar·i·sa·ic** (fărĭsā´ĭk), **Phar·i·sa´i·cal** *adjs.* **Phar·i·sa·ism** (făr´ĭsāĭzem), **Phar·i·see·ism** (făr´ĭsēĭzem) *ns.*

phar·ma·ceu·ti·cal (färmasoo´-tĭkal) *adj.* Of, engaged in, pharmacy; of the use or sale of medicinal drugs. **phar·ma·ceu´-ti·cal·ly** *adv.* **phar·ma·ceu´tics** *n.*

*The **pharmaceutical** industry has become a major worldwide commercial enterprise involving highly competitive marketing. Below: Interior of a typical Australian **pharmacy**. The pharmacist is responsible for dispensing prescribed drugs.*

The many members of the **pheasant** family are widely distributed over Europe and Asia, with one — the Congo peafowl — in Africa: this collared pheasant is European.

particular state; **three-** ~ (of alternating currents), supplied in three parts differing in phase by $\frac{1}{3}$ of a period, or 120°; also of electric apparatus, producing or using such currents. 4. (physical chem.) Each of three different physical states, usu. solid, liquid, and gas, in which a substance can exist. **pha′sic** *adj.* **phase** *v.t.* (**phased, phas·ing**). Schedule, order; ~ **in, out**, bring into or out of use gradually.

Ph.D. *abbrev.* *Philosophiae doctor* (L., = Doctor of Philosophy).

pheas·ant (fĕz′ant) *n.* (pl. **-ants,** collect. **-ant**). Long-tailed brightplumaged gallinaceous game bird, esp. *Phasianus colchicus,* long naturalized in Europe; any of various unrelated birds resembling this; ~**-eyed,** (of flowers) with rings of color like pheasant's eye; **pheasant's eye,** any of various flowers with dark center, esp. *Adonis annua* and common narcissus. [Gk. *Phasiános* (bird) of the river Phasis]

Phei·dip·pi·des (fīdĭp′ĭdēz). (Gk. hist.) Athenian runner dispatched to solicit help from Sparta upon the news of the Persian landing at MARATHON, 490 B.C.

phe·nac·e·tin (fenăs′ĭtĭn) *n.* White crystalline substance (ethyl ether of acetanilide), used in medicine as antipyretic.

pheno-, phen- *prefixes.* (chem.) Denoting certain substances derived from coal tar (orig. in manufacture of illuminating gas).

phe·no·bar·bi·tal (fēnōbär′-bĭtawl) *n.* Hypnotic and sedative drug ($C_{12}H_{12}N_2O_3$).

phe·nol (fē′nōl) *n.* 1. Hydroxybenzene (C_6H_5OH), commonly called *carbolic acid,* obtained from coal tar and used esp. as an antiseptic. 2. Any of the hydroxy compounds of benzene and its homologues with the hydroxyl groups attached to the nucleus, e.g. cresol, thymol, pyrogallol.

phe·nom·e·nal (fĭnŏm′enal) *adj.* Of the nature of a phenomenon; cognizable by, evidenced only by, the senses; concerned with phenomena; remarkable, prodigious. **phe·nom′e·nal·ly** *adv.*

phe·nom·e·nal·ism (fĭnŏm′-enalĭzem) *n.* Doctrine that phenomena are the only objects of knowledge. **phe·nom′e·nal·ist** *n.* **phe·nom·e·nal·is′tic** *adj.*

phe·nom·e·non (fĭnŏm′enŏn) (pl. **-na** pr. -na). Thing th appears or is perceived, esp. thir the cause of which is in questio (philos.) that of which a sense the mind directly takes note, in mediate object of perception; (p **-nons**) remarkable person, thin occurence, etc.

phe·no·type (fē′notĭp) *n.* (biol Organism as it appears, as dist. fro its genetic constitution (*genotype* **phe·no·typ·ic** (fēnotĭp′ik), **phe no·typ′i·cal** *adjs.* Appearing in a organism as a result of its genet potentialities in a given environ ment.

phen·yl (fĕn′il, fē′nil) *n.* Mon valent organic radical C_6H_5.

phew (fū, foo, hwū) *int.* E clamation of impatience, disgus exhaustion, relief, etc.

phi (fī) *n.* Letter of Gre alphabet (Φ, ϕ) = ph.

phi·al (fī′al) *n.* Small gla bottle, esp. for medicine.

Phi Be·ta Kap·pa (fī′ bā′ kăp′a, bē′ta). Honor society some U.S. universities and college election for membership is base on high academic qualifications one of three groups: unde graduates studying the liberal art graduates, and distinguishe alumni and faculty member founded in 1776 at the College of William and Mary, Williamsburg, Virginia. [f. the initial letters Φ, β, K, of Gk. *philosophia biou kubernetes* philosophy the guide to life]

Phid·i·as (fĭdˊēas) (5th c. B.C.). Greek sculptor; famous in antiquity for colossal statues of gold and ivory, which have not survived; the sculptures of the Parthenon were prob. made under his supervision.

Phil·a·del·phi·a (fĭladĕlˊfēa). Largest city in Pennsylvania, in the SE. part at the junction of the Delaware and Schuykill rivers; founded by Quaker William Penn, 1681; site of 1st Continental Congress, 1774, which called for colonial boycott of Brit. trade, and Second Continental Congress, 1775–6, which adopted the Declaration of Independence; site of meeting that formulated the Federal Constitution, effective March, 1789. **Phil·a·delˊphi·an** *adj.* & *n.*

phi·lan·der (fĭlănˊder) *v.i.* Make love, esp. insincerely. **phi·lanˊder·er** *n.*

phil·an·throp·ic (fĭlanthrŏpˊĭk) *adj.* Loving one's fellow men, benevolent, humane. **phil·an·thropˊi·cal·ly** *adv.*

phi·lan·thro·pist (fĭlănˊthropĭst) *n.* Lover of mankind; one who exerts himself for the well-being of his fellow men. **phi·lanˊthro·pism** *n.*

phi·lan·thro·py (fĭlănˊthropē) *n.* Love, practical benevolence, toward mankind.

phi·lat·e·ly (fĭlătˊelē) *n.* Study and collection of stamps and other postal material. **phil·a·tel·ic** (fĭlatĕlˊĭk), **phil·a·telˊi·cal** *adjs.* **phi·latˊe·list** *n.* [Gk. *philos* lover of, *ateleia* exemption from payment]

phil·har·mon·ic (fĭlharmŏnˊĭk) *adj.* & *n.* (Person) fond of music (freq. used in names of musical societies, orchestras, etc.).

Phil·ip[1] (fĭlˊĭp). Name of several kings of France: **Philip I** (1052–1108), reigned 1060–1108; **Philip II** (1165–1223), "Philip Augustus," reigned 1180–1223; reconquered Normandy from English; **Philip III** (1245–85), "the Bold," reigned 1270–85; **Philip IV** (1268–1314), "le Bel," reigned 1285–1314; in his reign the papacy was established at Avignon; **Philip V** (c1294–1322), reigned 1316–22; **Philip VI** (1293–1350), reigned 1328–50; his reign saw beginning of Hundred Years War.

Phil·ip[2] (fĭlˊĭp). Name of several kings of Spain: **Philip II** (1527–98), reigned 1556–98; married Mary I of England; launched the Spanish

Armada against England, 1588; **Philip III** (1578–1621), reigned 1598–1621; **Philip IV** (1605–65), reigned 1621–65; **Philip V** (1683–1746), reigned 1700–46; founder of Bourbon dynasty in Spain.

Phil·ip[3] (fĭlˊĭp). (382–336 B.C.) King of Macedonia 359–336; re-organized Macedonian army and conquered Greece; father of Alexander the Great.

Phil·ip[4] (fĭlˊĭp), **King** (d. 1676). Indian name, Metacomet. N. Amer. Ind. chief, son of Massasoit; sachem of Wampanoag tribe, 1662–1676; led Indians against the New England colonists in King Philip's War, 1675–6.

Phi·lip·pi (fĭlĭpˊī). Ancient city of Macedonia, fortified by Philip of Macedon and named after him; scene of battle (42 B.C.) in which Octavian and Mark Antony defeated Brutus and Cassius.

Phi·lip·pi·an (fĭlĭpˊēan) *adj.* Of Philippi. ∼ *n.* Native, inhabitant, of Philippi; (**Epistle to the**) ∼**s**, book of New Testament, epistle of St. Paul to the church at Philippi.

Phi·lip·pic (fĭlĭpˊĭk) *n.* Any of the three speeches of Demosthenes against Philip of Macedon; (also) Cicero's speeches against Antony; hence (**p** ∼) bitter invective.

Phil·ip·pines (fĭlˊĭpēnz, fĭlĭpēnzˊ). Republic in the Pacific Ocean, about 500 mi. (805 km) SE. of Asia, consisting of about 7,000 islands, the largest being Luzon and

*After a long colonial history the **Philippines,** with their varying cultural and linguistic population-groups, are fast becoming a prosperous modern state with many industries as well as the tourism encouraged by landscapes like this.*

Mindanao; capital, Quezon City; discovered by Magellan, 1521, and under Spanish control until 1899 when it was ceded to the U.S. following the Spanish–American War; Commonwealth established, 1935; captured during World War II by Japanese and held until Oct., 1944, when Gen. Douglas MacArthur led U.S. forces into the country; granted independence on July 4, 1946.

Phil·is·tine (fĭl'ĭstēn, -stĭn, fĭlĭs'tĭn, -tēn) *n.* 1. One of the war-like inhabitants of ancient Philistia, a district comprising the fertile Mediterranean coastal plain from Jaffa to Egypt, who in early times constantly harassed the Israelites. 2. Illiberal person, one whose interests are material and commonplace. ~ *adj.* Uncultured, commonplace, materialistic. **Phil·is·tin·ism** (fĭl'ĭstēnĭzem, fĭlĭs'tĭnĭzem) *n.* [Vulgate *Philistīnī*; sense 2 taken f. Ger. *philister*, used by univ. students of townsmen, allegedly since 1693 when a student was killed at Jena in a "town-and-gown" brawl and the sermon at his funeral was based on the text "The Philistines be upon thee!"]

phil·o·den·dron (fĭlodĕn'dron) *n.* (pl. **-drons, -dra** pr. -dra). Tropical Amer. climbing plant (family Araceae) with large shiny leaves, used as house plant.

phi·lol·o·gy (fĭlŏl'ojē) *n.* Science of language. **phi·lol'o·gist** *n.* **phil·o·log·i·cal** (fĭlolŏj'ĭkal) *adj.*

phil·o·log'i·cal·ly *adv.*

Phil·o·me·la (fĭlomē'la). (Gk. myth.) Daughter of Pandion, a legendary king of Athens; was turned into a swallow and her sister Procne into a nightingale (or, in Latin versions, into a nightingale, and Procne into a swallow).

phi·los·o·pher (fĭlŏs'ofer) *n.* Lover of wisdom; student of philosophy; one who shows philosophic calmness in trying circumstances; ~'s **stone**, supreme object of alchemy, substance supposed to change other metals into gold or silver.

phil·o·soph·ic (fĭlosŏf'ĭk), **phil·o·soph·i·cal** (fĭlosŏf'ĭkal) *adjs.* Of, consonant with, philosophy; skilled in, devoted to, philosophy (freq. in titles of societies); wise; calm; temperate. **phil·o·soph·i·cal·ly** *adv.*

phi·los·o·phize (fĭlŏs'ofīz) *v.* (**-phized, -phiz·ing**). Play the philosopher; speculate, theorize; moralize; render philosophic.

phi·los·o·phy (fĭlŏs'ofē) *n.* (pl. **-phies**). 1. Love, study, or pursuit of wisdom or knowledge, esp. that which deals with ultimate reality or with the most general causes and principles of things; philosophical system; system for conduct of life. **moral ~, natural ~:** see these words. 2. Serenity, resignation.

phil·ter (fĭl'ter) *n.* Love potion.

phle·bi·tis (flebĭ'tĭs) *n.* Inflammation of walls of a vein. **phle·bit·ic** (flebĭt'ĭk) *adj.*

phle·bot·o·my (flebŏt'omē) *n.* (pl. **-mies**). Cutting into a vein, bloodletting, an early and now obsolete form of medical treatment.

Phleg·e·thon (flĕg'ethŏn). (Gk. and Rom. myth.) River of fire, one of the 5 rivers of Hades.

phlegm (flĕm) *n.* 1. Thick, slimy substance secreted by mucous membrane of respiratory passages; (hist.) one of the 4 humors. 2. Coolness, sluggishness, apathy (supposed to result from predominance of phlegm in constitu tion). **phleg·mat·ic** (flĕgmăt´ĭk) *adj.* **phleg·mat´i·cal·ly** *adv.*

phlo·em (flō´ĕm) *n.* (bot.) Softer portion of the fibrovascular tissue, as dist. from the xylem or woody portion; soft bast.

phlo·gis·tic (flōjĭs´tĭk) *adj.* Of phlogiston; (med.) inflammatory.

phlo·gis·ton (flōjĭs´ton) *n.* Hypothetical substance formerly supposed to exist in combustible bodies.

phlox (flŏks) *n.* Plant of N. Amer. genus *P* ~ of chiefly herbaceous plants with clusters of usu. showy flowers. [Gk. = "flame"]

Phnom Penh (nŏm´ pĕn´, penawm´ pĕn´). Capital and largest city of Kampuchea (Cambodia), in the S. part on the Mekong River.

pho·bi·a (fō´bēa) *n.* Fear, horror, or aversion, esp. morbid. **pho·bic** (fō´bĭk) *adj.*

phoe·be (fē´bē) *n.* Amer. flycatcher of genus *Sayornis*, with gray or brown back and a short crest.

Phoe·be (fē´bē), **Phoe·bus** (fē´bus). (Gk. myth.) Artemis and Apollo as goddess of moon and god of sun; moon and sun personified. [Gk., = "bright," "radiant"]

Phoe·ni·cia (fĭnĭsh´a, -nē´sha). Ancient country of E. Mediterranean, a narrow strip along the coast of modern Lebanon, including Tyre and Sidon. **Phoe·ni·cian** (fĭnĭsh´an, -nē´shan) *adj.* & *n.* (Member) of the Semitic people who inhabited this area from at least 2000 B.C., famous as pioneers of navigation and trade (Carthage was their colony) and as craftsmen, regarded by the Greeks as inventors of letters, since the Greek alphabet was based on the Phoenician.

Phoe·nix (fē´nĭks). Capital and largest city of Arizona, in the SW. central part.

phoe·nix (fē´niks) *n.* Mythical bird, the only one of its kind, that after living 5 or 6 centuries in the Arabian desert burned itself on a funeral pile and rose from the ashes with renewed youth to live through another cycle; paragon.

phon (fōn) *n.* (phys.) Unit used in measuring sound.

phone[1] (fōn) *n.* Elementary sound of spoken language.

phone[2] (fōn) *n.* & *v.* (**phoned, phon·ing**). (colloq.) Telephone.

pho·neme (fō´nēm) *n.* (phonet). Group of variants regarded as essentially the same vocal sound. **pho·ne·mic** (fonē´mĭk, fō-) *adj.*

pho·net·ic (fonĕt´ĭk) *adj.* Representing vocal sounds, esp. (of systems of spelling) using always same symbol for same sound; of the sounds of spoken language. **pho·net´i·cal·ly** *adv.* **pho·ne·ti·cian** (fōnĭtĭsh´an) *n.* **pho·net´ics** *n.* Study of phonetic phenomena; (as pl.) phonetic phenomena.

pho·ne·tist (fō´nĭtĭst) *n.* One versed in phonetics, advocate of phonetic spelling.

pho·ney = PHONY.

phon·ic (fŏn´ĭk) *adj.* Of sound, acoustic; of vocal sounds.

pho·no·gram (fō´nogrăm) *n.* Symbol representing sound, syllable, or word, without reference to meaning. **pho·no·gram´ic, pho·no·gram´mic** *adjs.*

pho·no·graph (fō´nogrăf) *n.* Machine for reproducing recorded speech, music, etc. **pho·no·graph´ic** *adj.* **pho·no·graph´i·cal·ly** *adv.* **pho·nog·ra·phy** (fōnŏg´rafē) *n.*

pho·nol·o·gy (fōnŏl´ojē) *n.* Science of vocal sounds; system of sounds in a language. **pho·no·log·ic** (fōnolŏj´ĭk), **pho·no·log´i·cal** *adj.* **pho·no·log´i·cal·ly** *adv.* **pho·nol´o·gist** *n.*

pho·ny, pho·ney (fō´nē) *adjs.* (**pho·ni·er, pho·ni·est**). (slang) Sham, false, counterfeit. ~ *n.* (pl. **-nies, -neys**). Phony person or thing.

phos·gene (fŏz´jēn) *n.* Carbonyl chloride ($COCL_2$), a poisonous colorless gas with a characteristic suffocating smell.

phos·phate (fŏs´fāt) *n.* (chem.) Salt or ester of phosphoric acid; substance containing this, used as a fertilizer. **phos·phat·ic** (fŏsfătĭk) *adj.*

phos·phide (fŏs´fīd) *n.* (chem.) Compound of phosphorus with other element or radical.

phos·phor (fŏs´fer) *n.* 1. Phosphorus; esp. in ~ **bronze, copper**, etc., alloys of phosphorus with metals named. 2. Fluorescent material, esp. that used to form screen of cathode ray tube.

phos·pho·res·cence (fŏsferĕs´ens) *n.* Radiation similar to fluorescence but detectable after excitation ceases; emission of light without combustion or perceptible heat. **phos·pho·resce** (fŏsferĕs´) *v.i.* (**-resced, -resc·ing**). Emit phos-phorescence. **phos·pho·res′cent** *adj.*

phos·phor·ic (fŏsfŏr′ĭk, -fär′-) *adj.* Containing phosphorus in its higher valence.

phos·pho·rous (fŏs′ferus, fŏsfŏr′us, fŏr′-) *adj.* Containing phosphorus in its lower (trivalent) valence.

phos·pho·rus (fŏs′ferus) *n.* (pl. **-ri** pr. **-rī**). (chem.) Nonmetallic element found in all animal and vegetable organisms and in some minerals (symbol P, at. no. 15, at. wt. 30.97376) and occurring in several allotropic forms: **yellow ~**, white or cream-colored waxlike highly inflammable solid, not found in free state, oxidizing rapidly in air, appearing luminous, and transformed esp. in sunlight into **red ~**, a stable dark red microcrystalline powder, nonpoisonous and less readily inflammable, used in safety matches. [L. *phosphorus* morning star (Gk. *phōs* light, *phorus* bringing)]

Photosynthesis *is essential to all life on earth, not merely to plants. The complex process, involving light-sensitive pigments, maintains the supply of atmospheric oxygen on which animals and man depend. It also provides a continuous supply of food, directly for herbivores, indirectly for predators.*

phot (fŏt) *n.* (phys.) Unit of illumination equal to 1 LUMEN per sq. cm.

pho·to (fō′tō) *n.* (pl. **-tos**). (colloq.) Photograph; **~ finish**, close finish of race in which winner is identified by photography.

pho·to·chem·is·try (fōtōkĕm′ĭstrē) *n.* Branch of chemistry dealing with the chemical action of light. **pho·to·chem·i·cal** (fōtōkĕm′ĭkal) *adj.*

pho·to·cop·y (fō′tokŏpē) *n.* (pl. **-cop·ies**) & *v.t.* (**-cop·ied, -cop·y·ing**). (Make) photographic copy (of).

pho·to·e·lec·tric (fōtōĭlĕk′trĭk) *adj.* Marked by or utilizing emis-

sion of electrons from solid, liquid, or gaseous bodies when exposed to light of suitable wavelengths; **~ cell**, cell or vacuum tube that uses the photoelectric effect to produce an electric current; also called ELECTRIC EYE. **pho·to·e·lec·tric·i·ty** (fōtōĭlĕktrĭs′ĭtē) *n.*

pho·to·gen·ic (fōtojĕn′ĭk) *adj.* 1. Producing or emitting light. 2. Suitable for photography; photographing well (of person as good subject for photography). **pho·to·gen′i·cal·ly** *adv.*

pho·to·gram·me·try (fōtogrăm′ĭtrē) *n.* Process of making surveys or geodetic measurements by photography.

pho·to·graph (fō′tŏgrăf) *n.* Picture, likeness, taken by means of chemical action of light on sensitive film. **~** *v.* Take photograph of; **~ well, badly**, be a good, bad subject for photography. **pho·tog·ra·pher** (fotŏg′rafer), **pho·tog·ra·phy** (fotŏg′rafē) *ns.* **pho·to·graph·ic** (fōtōgrăf′ĭk), **pho·to·graph′i·cal** *adjs.* **pho·to·graph′i·cal·ly** *adv.*

pho·to·gra·vure (fōtogravūr′) *n.* Printing process in which the subject matter is photographically etched into a polished copper cylinder; this process. **~** *v.t.* (**-vured, -vur·ing**). Reproduce by photogravure.

pho·to·li·thog·ra·phy (fōtōlĭthŏg′rafē) *n.* Lithographic process in which printing plates are made photographically. **pho·to·lith·o·graph** (fōtolĭth′ogrăf) *n.* **pho·to·lith·o·graph′ic** *adj.*

pho·to·me·chan·i·cal (fōtōmekăn′ĭkal) *adj.* Pertaining to the production of pictures by mechanical printing from a photographic plate. **pho·to·me·chan′i·cal·ly** *adv.*

pho·tom·e·ter (fōtŏm′ĭter) *n.* Instrument for measuring intensity of light. **pho·to·met·ric** (fōtomĕt′rĭk), **pho·to·met′ri·cal** *adjs.* **pho·tom·e·try** (fōtŏm′ĭtrē) *n.*

pho·ton (fō′tŏn) *n.* Quantum unit of light or other radiant energy equal to the product of Planck's constant *h* and the frequency *v*.

pho·to-off·set (fōtōawf′sĕt) *n.* Offset printing with plates made photographically.

pho·to·sphere (fō′tosfēr) *n.* Luminous envelope of sun or star from which its light and heat radiate.

Pho·to·stat (fō′tostăt) *n.* (trademark) Apparatus for making photographic copies of documents etc.; (usu. l.c.) copy made by this. **pho·to·stat′ic** *adj.*

pho·to·syn·the·sis (fōtosĭn′thĭsĭs) *n.* (bot.) Process by which carbon dioxide is converted into carbohydrates by chlorophyll under influence of light. **pho·to·syn·thet·ic** (fōtosĭnthĕt′ĭk) *adj.*

pho·to·syn·thet′i·cal·ly *adv.*

pho·to·trop·ic (fōtotrŏp′ĭk) *adj.* (of plant leaves etc.) Bending or turning toward or away from a source of light. **pho·to·trop′i·cal·ly** *adv.* **pho·tot·ro·pism** (fō-tŏt′ropĭzem) *n.*

phrase (frāz) *n.* 1. Mode of expression, diction; idiomatic expression; small group of words, usu. without predicate, esp. preposition with the word(s) it governs, equivalent to adjective, adverb, or noun; short pithy expression; (pl.) mere words. 2. (mus.) Short and more or less independent passage forming part of longer passage or of whole piece. **phras·al** (frā′zal) *adj.* **phrase** *v.t.* (**phrased, phras·ing**). Express in words; divide (music) into phrases; group (notes) in phrase.

phra·se·ol·o·gy (frāzēŏl′ojē) *n.* Choice or arrangement of words; mode of expression. **phra·se·o·log′i·cal** (frāzēolŏj′ĭkal) *adj.* **phra·se·o·log′i·cal·ly** *adv.*

phre·net·ic (frenĕt′ĭk), **phre·-net·i·cal** (frenĕt′ĭkal) = FRENETIC.

phren·ic (frĕn′ĭk) *adj.* (anat.) Of the diaphragm.

phre·nol·o·gy (frĭnŏl′ojē) *n.* Study of external contours of cranium as index to development and position of organs supposedly belonging to the different mental faculties. **phren·o·log·ic** (frĕno-lŏj′ĭk), **phren·o·log′i·cal** *adjs.* **phren·o·log′i·cal·ly** *adv.* **phre·nol′o·gist** *n.*

Phryg·i·a (frĭj′ēa). Ancient region of central and N. Asia Minor.

Phryg·i·an (frĭj′ēan) *adj.* Of Phrygia or its people or language; ~ **mode**, ancient Greek MODE, reputedly warlike in character; 3rd of ecclesiastical modes, with E as final and C as dominant. **Phrygian** *n.* Native, inhabitant, language, of Phrygia.

phthal·ic (thăl′ĭk, fthăl′-) *adj.* ~ **acid**, any of three isomeric acids, $C_6H_4(COOH)_2$.

phthi·sis (thī′sĭs, fthī′-) *n.* Pulmonary tuberculosis; (formerly) any progressive wasting disease. **phthis·ic** (tĭz′ĭk), **phthis′i·cal, phthis′ick·y** *adjs.* Of, having, phthisis.

phy·lac·ter·y (fĭlăk′terē) *n.* (pl. **-ter·ies**). 1. Small leather box containing portions of Hebrew texts (Deut. 6:4–9, 11:13–21; Exod. 13:1–10, 11–16) on vellum, worn by Jews during morning prayer as reminder of obligation to keep the law. 2. Amulet, charm.

phy·le (fī′lē) *n.* (pl. **-lae** pr. -lē). Ancient Greek clan or tribe; in Attica, political, administrative, and military unit, based on geographical division.

phy·let·ic (fīlĕt′ĭk) *adj.* (biol.) Of a phylum or line of descent.

phyl·lox·e·ra (fĭloksēr′a, fīlŏk′-sera) *n.* Any of several plant lice of genus *P~*, esp. species very destructive to grapevine.

phy·lo·gen·e·sis (fīlojĕn′esĭs) = PHYLOGENY.

phy·log·e·ny (fīlŏj′enē) *n.* (biol.) History of the evolution of a kind or type of organism (opp. ON-TOGENY). **phy·lo·ge·net·ic** (fīloje-nĕt′ĭk), **phy·lo·gen·ic** (fīlojĕn′ĭk) *adjs.* **phy·lo·ge·net′i·cal·ly** *adv.*

phy·lum (fī′lum) *n.* (pl. **-la** pr. -la). (biol.) Major division of animals or plants, above CLASS, comprising those of the same general form.

phys·ic (fĭz′ĭk) *n.* (archaic) Art of healing; medical profession; (colloq.) medicine; cathartic. ~ *v.t.* (**-icked, ick·ing**). Treat with physic.

phys·i·cal (fĭz′ĭkal) *adj.* 1. Of matter, material; of the body; of, according to the laws of, natural philosophy; ~ **chemistry**: see CHEMISTRY; ~ **geography**, that dealing with natural features. 2. Of the science of physics. **phys′-i·cal·ly** *adv.*

phy·si·cian (fĭzĭsh′an) *n.* Medical practitioner, esp. one specializing in medical (opp. surgical) diagnosis and treatment; (fig.) healer.

phys·ics (fĭz′ĭks) *n.* Science of the properties and nature of matter in general (excluding chemistry), the various forms of energy, and the mutual interaction of energy and matter. **phys·i·cist** (fĭz′ĭsĭst) *n.*

phys·i·og·no·my (fĭzēŏg′nomē, -ŏn′omē) *n.* (pl. **-mies**). Art of judging character from features of face or form of body; cast of features, type of face; face; external features of country etc.; characteristic (moral or other) aspect. **phys·i·og·nom·ic** (fĭzēŏgnŏm′ĭk, -ēonŏm′-), **phys·i·og·nom′i·cal** *adjs.* **phys·i·og·nom′i·cal·ly** *adv.*

phys·i·og′no·mist *n.*

phys·i·og·ra·phy (fĭzēŏg′rafē) *n.* Description of nature, of natural phenomena, or of a class of objects; physical geography. **phys·i·og′ra·pher** *n.* **phys·i·o·graph·ic** (fĭzēogrăf′ĭk), **phys·i·o·graph′i·cal** *adjs.*

phys·i·ol·o·gy (fĭzēŏl′ojē) *n.* Science dealing with the functions of living organisms or their parts; these functions. **phys·i·o·log·i·cal** (fĭzēolŏj′ĭkal), **phys·i·o·log′ic** *adjs.* **phys·i·o·log′i·cal·ly** *adv.* **phys·i·ol′o·gist** *n.*

phys·i·o·ther·a·py (fĭzēōthĕr′-apē) *n.* Treatment of disease by exercise, massage, heat, light, electricity, or other physical agencies, not by drugs. **phys·i·o·ther′a·pist** *n.*

phy·sique (fĭzēk′) *n.* Bodily structure, organization, and development.

pi[1] (pī) *n.* (pl. **pis**). Seventeenth (later 16th) letter of Greek alphabet (Π, π) corresponding to p; esp. (math.) as symbol of ratio of circumference of circle to diameter (3.14159).

pi[2], **pie**[2] (pī) *ns.* (pl. **pies**). Confused mass of printers' type; (fig.) chaos. ~ *v.t.* (**pied, pi·ing**). Mix (type).

pi·a ma·ter (pī′a mā′ter). (anat.) Delicate fibrous innermost meninx, consisting of a network of blood vessels, covering the brain and spinal cord. [med. L. transl. of Arab. anatomical term, = "tender mother"]

pi·a·nis·si·mo (pēanĭs′imō) *adv., n.* (pl. **-mos**), & *adj.* (mus.) (Passage performed) very soft(ly).

pi·an·ist (pēăn′ĭst, pē′anĭst) *n.* Player of piano.

pi·a·nis·tic (pēanĭs′tĭk) *adj.* Of, adapted for playing on a piano.

pi·a·no[1] (pēah′nō, pyah′nō) *adv., n.* (pl. **-nos**), & *adj.* (mus.) (Passage performed) soft(ly). [It.]

Setting aside a possible medieval precursor, the *piano* as we know it originated in the early 18th century; since then the only major change has been the introduction of the iron frame.

Damper or Sordine — String — Levers lifting hammer — Hammer — Pivot of hammer — Check — Pivot of key — Key

pi·an·o² (pēăn´ō, pyăn´ō) n. (pl. **-an·os**). Large musical instrument played by means of keys that cause hammers to strike on metal strings (the vibrations being stopped by dampers); **baby grand** ~, the smallest size grand piano; **grand** ~, large wing-shaped piano of full tone with strings arranged horizontally; **player** ~, mechanical piano; **spinet** ~, (also **spinet**) small upright piano (see also SPINET); **upright** ~, piano with strings in vertical position; ~ **roll**, in player piano, the paper roll that regulates performance of the instrument. [It., earlier *piano e forte* soft and strong, i.e. loud]

pi·an·o·for·te (pēănofōr´tē, -tā, -fōr´-, -fōrt´, -fōrt´) n. = PIANO².

pi·as·ter, pi·as·tre (pēăs´ter) ns. Small coin of Middle Eastern countries.

pi·az·za (pēăz´a, -ah´za, -ăt´sa, -ah´tsa) n. (pl. **pi·az·zas, pi·az·ze** pr. pēăt´sā, -ah´tsā). Public square or marketplace, esp. in Italian town; verandah of house. [It., ult. f. Gk. *plateia (hodos)* broad (street)]

pi·ca (pī´ka) n. (print.) Size of type (12 point), of about six lines to the inch.

pic·a·dor (pĭk´adōr, pĭkadōr´) n. Mounted man with lance in bullfight.

pic·a·resque (pĭkarĕsk´) adj. (of a style of fiction) Dealing with adventures of rogues.

Pi·cas·so (pĭkah´sō), **Pablo** (1881–1973). Spanish painter in France, a founder of CUBISM., famous esp. for *Guernica* and *The Three Musicians*.

pic·a·yune (pĭkēūn´) n. (formerly) Small coin; (colloq.) small, mean, or insignificant thing. ~ adj. Mean, contemptible, paltry.

pic·ca·lil·li (pĭk´alĭlē) n. (pl. **-lis**). Relish of chopped vegetables, mustard, and hot spices.

pic·co·lo (pĭk´olō) n. (pl. **-los**). Small flute, an octave higher than the ordinary flute. **pic´co·lo·ist** n. [It., = "small"]

*An intrinsic part of the corrida is the skill with which the **picador** does his share of weakening the bull's neck muscles with lance-thrusts.*

pich·i·ci·a·go (pĭchĭsēah´gō -ā´gō) n. (pl. **-gos**). Small pin[k] burrowing armadillo (genu[s] *Chlamyphorus*) of Argentina. [perh[aps] f. native *pichey* little armadillo Span. *ciego* blind]

pick¹ (pĭk) n. Tool consisting o[f] an iron bar, usu. curved with a poin[t] at one end and a point or chise[l] edge at the other, with a woode[n] handle passing through the middl[e] perpendicularly, used for breaking up hard ground etc.; instrument fo[r] picking, toothpick.

pick² (pĭk) v. 1. Break surfac[e] of (ground etc.) with or as wit[h] pick; make (hole etc.) thus. 2. Prob[e] (teeth etc.) with pointed instrumen[t] to remove extraneous matter; clea[r] (bone, carcass) of adherent flesh[.] 3. Detach (flowers, fruit, etc.) fro[m] place of growth. 4. (of birds) Tak[e] up (grains etc.) in bill; (of persons[)] eat in small bits; ~ **at** (food), ea[t] in a fussy way; eat lightly. 5. Sele[ct] carefully; ~ **and choose**, sele[ct] fastidiously. 6. Pull apart; ~ **t[o] pieces**, pull apart; (fig.) criticiz[e] hostilely. 7. ~ **a lock**, open a loc[k] (esp. with intent to rob) wit[h] pointed instrument etc.; ~ [a] **pocket**, steal its contents; ~ [a] **quarrel**, contrive to quarrel *with*[;] ~ **off**, pluck off; shoot deliberatel[y] one by one; (of baseball pitcher[)] throw to first base to put bas[e] runner out; ~ **on**, select; single ou[t] for criticism etc.; ~ **out**, take o[r] choose from a number of others[;] distinguish from surrounding ob[-] jects; relieve (ground color wit[h] another); make out (meaning o[f] passages etc.), play (tune) by ear[;] ~ **up**, break up (ground etc.) wit[h] pick; lay hold of and take up; rais[e] from a fall etc.; gain, acquire (liveli[-] hood, profit, tricks, information)[;] take (person, or thing) along wit[h] one; regain; recover health[;] (colloq.) make acquaintanc[e] casually with (person of opposit[e] sex); succeed in receiving by radio[;] see with searchlight etc.; (games[)] select (sides) by alternate choosing[;] (of motor etc.) recover speed[,] accelerate. 8. ~**-me-up**, stimu[-] lating drink; **pick´pocket**, one wh[o] steals from pockets; **pick´up**, pick[-] ing up (of ball in baseball etc.)[;] game between sides chose[n] casually; (colloq.) casual, esp. un[-] introduced, acquaintance; powe[r] (of motor, etc.) to accelerate[;] mechanism (replacing soundbox o[f] phonograph) that converts im[-] pulses imparted to needle by recor[d] into electrical impulses that ca[n] then be amplified; small moto[r] truck with open body. **pick´er** n[.]

*Reminiscent of Van Gogh, 'Child with [a] Dove' painted by **Picasso** in 190[1] predates his better known Blue Period[.] Later, Picasso experimented in so many ways that he was possibly the leading innovator in 20th-century art.*

Fertile sub-alpine valleys (right) are only part of **Piedmont's** agricultural resources. The wide plain of the Po and the southern hills are highly, and diversely, productive (Italy).

pick *n.* 1. Picking; selection; best part *of.* 2. (weaving) Thread, group of threads, of weft.

pick·a·back (pĭk´a·băk) = PIGGYBACK.

pick·a·nin·ny (pĭk´a·nĭne) *n.* (pl. **-nies**). (offensive) Small black child.

pick·ax, pick·axe (pĭk´ăks) *ns.* (pl. **-ax·es**) = PICK¹. ~ *v.* (**-axed, -ax·ing**). Break (ground etc.) with pickax; work with pickax.

pick·er·el (pĭk´erel) *n.* (pl. **-els**, collect. **-el**). Any of several small N. Amer. freshwater fishes (genus *Esox*), including the Eastern ~ (*E. niger*) and the grass ~ (*E. americanus*).

pick·et (pĭk´ĭt) *n.* 1. Pointed stake or peg driven into ground to form palisade, tether horse, etc.; (hist.) (stake with pointed top on which person stood as) form of military punishment. 2. (mil.) Small body of troops sent out to watch for enemy or held ready in quarters; party of sentinels, outpost; (now, chiefly) camp guard doing police duty in garrison town etc. 3. Person stationed by labor union outside a business that is on strike to dissuade others from work during strike. ~ *v.* Secure (place) with stakes; tether; post (people) as pickets; beset with pickets during strike etc.; act as picket. **pick´et·er, pick´et·ing** *ns.*

pick·ing (pĭk´ĭng) *n.* Act of selecting; (pl.) gleanings, remaining scraps; pilferings.

pick·le (pĭk´el) *n.* Brine, vinegar, or similar liquid in which flesh, vegetables, etc., are preserved; food, esp. (usu. pl.) vegetables preserved in pickle and eaten as relish; acid solution for cleaning purposes etc.; (fig.) plight, predicament. ~ *v.t.* (**-led, -ling**). Preserve in pickle; treat (wood etc.) with acid solution. **pick´led** *adj.* (slang) Drunk.

pick·y (pĭk´ē) *adj.* (**pick·i·er, pick·i·est**). Excessively fastidious.

pic·nic (pĭk´nĭk) *n.* Pleasure party including meal out of doors; ~ **ham, shoulder**, shoulder cut of pork cured like a ham. **picnic** *v.i.* (**-nicked, -nick·ing**). Take part in picnic. **pic´nick·er** *n.*

pic·ric (pĭk´rĭk) *adj.* ~ **acid**, trinitrophenol, intensely bitter yellow crystalline substance used, in aqueous solution, as a treatment for burns etc., and formerly as a high explosive (lyddite).

Pict (pĭkt) *n.* One of an ancient, prob. pre-Celtic, people formerly inhabiting parts of N. Britain and Ireland, later (9th c.) united with

A restored **Pictish** settlement at Jarlshof in the Shetland Islands. These 'painted people' are known from A.D. 297 until their conquest by Kenneth MacAlpine, about A.D. 850.

Scots. **Pict'ish** *adj.* & *n.*

pic·to·graph (pĭk´togrăf, -grahf) *n.* Pictorial symbol that stands for the thing depicted, e.g. representation of an eye standing for "eye"; primitive writing or record consisting of these. **pic·to·graph'ic** *adj.* **pic·to·graph'i·cal·ly** *adv.* **pic·tog·ra·phy** (pĭk·tŏg´rafē) *n.*

pic·to·ri·al (pĭktōr´ēal, -tŏr´-) *adj.* Of, expressed in, pictures; illustrated; picturesque. **pic·to´ri·al·ly** *adv.* **pictorial** *n.* Periodical of which pictures are main feature.

pic·ture (pĭk´cher) *n.* 1. Painting, drawing, of objects esp. as work of art; portrait; beautiful object; (fig.) symbol, type, figure. 2. Scene, total visual impression produced; mental image; **be out of the** ~, not have all the relevant information. 3. Visible reproduction of film; image on television screen; (pl.) exhibition of motion-picture film(s), place where these are exhibited. 4. ~ **card**, one above a 10 in bridge deck; ~ **gallery**, (hall etc. containing) collection of pictures; ~ **hat**, woman's wide-brimmed hat resembling those in pictures by Reynolds and Gainsborough: ~ **postcard**, postcard with picture on back; ~ **tube**, vacuum tube used in television sets etc. to produce visible images; ~ **writing**, mode of recording events etc. by pictures, as in hieroglyphs etc.; ~ **window**, large window

facing attractive view. **picture** *v* (**-tured, -tur·ing**). Represent picture; describe graphicall imagine.

pic·tur·esque (pĭkcheresk´) *ac* Like, fit to be the subject of, striking picture; (of language etc strikingly graphic, vivid. **pic·tur esque'ly** *adv.* **pic·tur·esque'ne** *n.*

pid·dle (pĭd´el) *v.i.* (**-dle -dling**). Work, act, in trifling wa (colloq. or childish) urinate. **pid dling** *adj.* (colloq.) Trivial.

pidg·in (pĭj´in) *n.* Jargon chief of English words used esp. betwee Melanesian or Chinese and Eur pean (also ~ **English**); mixe simplified form of English use elsewhere. [Chin. corrup. of *bus ness*]

pie[1] (pī) *n.* Dish of meat, fruit, c., encased in or covered with or rrounded by crust and baked; any various other baked dishes of eat, fish, etc.; **easy as** ~, very sy; **have a finger in the** ~, be sp. officiously) concerned in the atter; ~ **chart**, one representing lative quantities by areas of ctors of a circle; **pie′crust**, baked ugh of pie; **pie-eyed**, (slang) runk; **pie in the sky**, (slang) rospect of future happiness after resent suffering.

pie[2] (pī) *n.* & *v.* (**pied, pie·ing**) PI[2].

pie·bald (pī′bawld) *adj.* Of 2 lors irregularly arranged, esp. ack and white; (of horse) with ack and white patches on body d legs; (fig.) motley, mongrel.

piece (pēs) *n.* 1. One of the stinct portions of which thing is mposed; **in** ~s, broken; **break** ~s, break into fragments; **pull** **tear to** ~s, (fig.) criticize verely. 2. Enclosed portion *of* nd); detached portion (*of a sub-* ance); definite quantity in which ing is made up; **a** ~ **of one's ind**, one's candid opinion, buke. 3. Example, specimen. Cannon, gun, pistol; man at ess, checkers, etc.; coin; ~ **of ght**, (hist.) Spanish dollar (that s marked with figure 8), of value eight reals; **say one's** ~, (fig.) ve one's opinion; make prepared atement. 5. Picture; literary or usical composition, usu. short; ama. 6. **by the** ~, (bought or

sold) individually; (payment etc.) according to amount done (not time taken); **of a** ~, uniform, consistent, in keeping (*with*); ~ **goods**, textile fabrics (esp. cotton goods) woven in recognized lengths; **piece′work**, work paid for by the piece. **piece** *v.t.* (**pieced, piec·ing**). Put together, form into a whole; join thread in spinning; fit *on* (thing *to* another); eke *out*; make *out* (story, theory, etc.) by combination of parts; join *together*; patch *up*.

pièce de ré·sis·tance (pyĕs de rāzēstahńs′). Principal dish of a meal; most important or remarkable event, picture, etc. [Fr.]

piece·meal (pēs′mēl) *adv.* Piece by piece, part at a time. ~ *adj.* Done etc. piecemeal.

pied (pīd) *adj.* Parti-colored.

Pied·mont (pēd′mŏnt). (It. *Piemonte*) District of NW. Italy, united with Italy 1859. **Pied·mon·tese** (pēdmŏntēz′, -tēs′) *adj.* & *n.* (pl. -tese).

pier (pēr) *n.* Solid structure of stone etc., extending into sea or tidal river, to protect or enclose a harbor; structure of iron or wood, open below, running out into sea, lake, etc. and used as walk and loading area; support of spans of bridge; pillar; solid masonry between windows etc.

Franklin Pierce, 14th president of the U.S.A., unexpectedly won the election in 1852 having resigned from politics some years before. His single term was notable for the opening up of the northwest, railroad development and dissent over slavery.

pierce (pērs) *v.* (**pierced, pierc·ing**). Penetrate; prick (*with* pin etc.); make hole in; force one's way through or into; penetrate *through, into,* etc. **pierc′er** *n.* **pierc′ing** *adj.* **pierc′ing·ly** *adv.*

Pierce (pērs), **Franklin** (1804– 1869). Fourteenth president of U.S., 1853–7.

Pie·ro del·la Fran·ce·sca (pyār′ō dĕla frănchĕs′ka) (1420?– 1492). Italian painter and mathematician; famous for frescoes in the

New Zealand pigeon

Bleeding heart pigeon

Wood pigeon

Victoria crowned pigeon

Crested bronze-wing

White-bellied plumed pigeon

church of St. Francis at Arezzo, *The Legend of the Holy Cross.*

Pierre (pĕr). Capital of South Dakota, in the central part on the Missouri River.

pie·tà (pyätah′) *n.* (often cap.) Picture, sculpture, of Virgin Mary holding dead body of Christ on her lap. [L. *pietas* piety.]

pi·e·tism (pī′etĭzem) *n.* Movement for revival of piety in the Lutheran Church begun by P. J. Spener about 1670; pious sentiment, exaggeration or affectation of this. **pi′e·tist** *n.* **pi·e·tis′tic, pi·e·tis′ti·cal** *adjs.*

pi·e·ty (pī′etē) *n.* Quality of being pious.

pi·e·zo·e·lec·tric·i·ty (pīēzōĭ-lĕktrĭs′ĭtē) *n.* Electricity or electric polarity produced by pressure on

*There is much diversity in size and color among various members of the **pigeon** family, and they are present in most parts of the world. All can produce 'pigeon's milk', a secretion of curd-like material which adults regurgitate from the crop to feed the young. The largest pigeons come from New Guinea.*

a nonconducting crystal. **pi·e·zo-e·lec·tric** (pīēzōĭlĕk′trĭk) *adj.* (also ~ **effect**) Property of certain crystals of generating electricity when subjected to pressure and (conversely) undergoing mechanical stress when subjected to voltage. **pi·e·zo·e·lec′tri·cal·ly** *adv.*

pif·fle (pĭf′el) *v.i.* (**-fled, -fling**). Talk or act feebly, trifle. ~ *n.* Twaddle. **pif′fling** *adj.* Trivial, worthless.

pig (pĭg) *n.* 1. Domesticated h (*Sus scrofa*); flesh of (usu. yo or suckling) pig as meat; (collo greedy, dirty, sulky, obstinate, annoying person; **buy a ~ ir poke,** buy something without s ing it or knowing its value; **ir ~'s eye,** (slang) certainly not. Oblong mass of metal (usu. c iron) cooled in a mold into wh it is run from smelting furna 3. **pig′headed,** obstinate, stup **pig iron;** see def. 2 above, a IRON; **pig Latin,** made-up jarg of schoolchildren; **pig′nut,** bit nut, esp. that of the brown hick (*Carya glabra*) and the tuber *Conopodium denudatum;* **pig′sk** (leather made of) pig's skin, a fo ball; **pig′sticking,** hunting of w boar with spear; **pig′sty,** = st

pig'tail, braid of hair hanging from back of head, esp. as worn by Chinese under the Manchus, by young girls, and formerly by soldiers and sailors; **pig'weed**, herb esp. of genus *Amaranthus* eaten by pigs; wild edible plant (*Chenopodium album*), cooked like spinach, also called *lamb's quarters*. **pig** *v.* (**pigged, pig·ging**). Bring forth (pigs), bring forth pigs; herd together like pigs, live in disorderly or untidy fashion.

pi·geon (pĭj´on) *n.* 1. Bird of the family Columbidae; dove, esp. *Columba livia*, which haunts rocks and large buildings and is also domesticated in many varieties produced by fancy breeding; **carrier** ~, homing pigeon for carrying message attached to its neck or leg; **clay** ~: see CLAY; **homing** ~, pigeon trained to fly home over long distances; **wood** ~, ringdove (*Columba palumbus*), a wild bird eaten as game; ~ **breast**, deformed human breast laterally constricted; **pi'geonhole**, small recess for pigeon to nest in; one of a set of compartments in cabinet etc. for papers, etc.; ~ (*v.t.*) (**-holed, -hol·ing**) deposit (document) in this, put aside (matter) for future consideration; assign (thing) to definite place in memory; **pigeon's**

It is now believed that the domestic pig of Europe originated from two wild species. One was distributed by migrating tribes from the Danube area.

milk, partly digested food with which pigeons feed their young; **pigeon-toed**, (of persons) turning toes or feet inward. 2. (colloq.) Simpleton, person easily swindled.

pig·ger·y (pĭg´erē) *n.* (pl. **-ger·ies**). Pig breeding establishment; pigsty; dirty place; piggishness.

pig·gish (pĭg´ĭsh) *adj.* Like a pig, esp. greedy or dirty. **pig'gish·ly** *adv.* **pig'gish·ness** *n.*

pig·gy (pĭg´ē) *n.* (pl. **-gies**). (nursery, colloq.) Little pig; ~ **bank**, money box, esp. of china, made in the shape of a pig. **piggy** *adj.* Piggish.

pig·gy·back (pĭg´ēbăk) *adv.* On the shoulders or back like a bundle; on the back or top of a larger object.

pig·let (pĭg´lĭt) *n.* Young pig.

pig·ment (pĭg´ment) *n.* Coloring matter in a paint or dye; (biol.) natural coloring matter of a tissue. **pig·men·tal** (pĭgmĕn´tal), **pig·men·tar·y** (pĭg´mentĕrē), **pig'ment·ed** *adjs.* **pig·men·ta·tion** (pĭgmentā´shon) *n.* Coloring (esp. of tissue) by pigment.

Pig·my: see PYGMY.

pi·ka (pē´ka, pī´ka) *n.* Any of several small mammals of family Ochotonidae, akin to rabbit but small-eared.

pike[1] (pīk) *n.* 1. Long wooden shaft with steel or iron head, infantry weapon superseded by bayonet; (dial.) pickax, spike. 2. Peaked top of hill. 3. (pl. **pikes**, collect. **pike**) Large voracious freshwater fish (*Esox · lucuis*) of northern temperate zone, with long slender snout (prob. abbrev. of *pike fish*, from its pointed snout). ~ *v.t.* (**piked, pik·ing**). Thrust through, kill with pike.

pike[2] (pīk) *n.* Turnpike road.

Pike (pīk), **Zeb·u·lon** (zĕb´yulon) **Montgomery** (1779–1813). Amer. Army officer and explorer of the Mississippi, Arkansas, and Red rivers; **Pike's Peak**, mountain in E. central Colorado in the Rocky Mountains, 14,110 ft. (4,300 m) high discovered by him, 1806.

pik·er (pī´ker) *n.* (colloq.) Cautious gambler; petty or very cautious person.

pi·laf, pi·laff (pĭlahf´, pē´lahf) *ns.* Oriental dish of rice usu. with meat, spices, etc.

pi·las·ter (pĭlăs´ter) *n.* Column of rectangular section projecting from a wall.

Pi·late (pī´lat), **Pontuis.** Roman governor of Judea 26–36 A.D.; presided at trial of Jesus Christ.

pil·chard (pĭl´cherd) *n.* Small sea fish (*Sardina pilchardus*) allied to herring but smaller and rounder.

The Berkshire (black), and Gloucester Old Spot are only two of the scores of breeds of pig which have been produced by centuries of breeding for different desired qualities.

When the 'New York Weekly Journal' in the U.S.A. was declared to be libelous in 1734, copies were burned and the printer, John Peter Zenger, was lucky not to be placed in the **pillory**. Instead, he was acquitted.

pile[1] (pīl) *n.* Pointed stake or post; heavy beam or column of wood, concrete, steel, etc., driven or bored into the ground as support for heavy structure; ~ **driver**, machine for driving piles into the ground. **pile** *v.t.* (**piled, pil·ing**). Furnish with piles; drive piles into.

pile[2] (pīl) *n.* 1. Heap of things laid more or less regularly upon one another. 2. (also **voltaic** ~) Series of plates of dissimilar metals, such as copper and zinc, laid one upon another alternately, with cloth or paper moistened with an acid solution placed between each pair, for producing electric current; any similar arrangement for producing electric current. 3. (also **atomic** ~) Nuclear REACTOR. 4. (colloq.) Heap of money, fortune. 5. Heap of combustibles on which corpse is burned. **pile** *v.t.* (**piled, pil·ing**). Heap up (freq. with *up, on*); load (table, etc., *with*); **pile up**, (naut.) run (ship) on rocks or aground; **pile′up**, (colloq.) collision involving several vehicles.

pile[3] (pīl) *n.* 1. Soft hair, down, wool of sheep. 2. Soft surface of some woven fabrics, produced by weaving in extra yarns and cutting them short (as in ~ **velvet**) or by knotting them on to warp threads (as in ~ **carpet**).

pile[4] (pīl) *n.* (Popular name for) hemorrhoid (usu. pl.).

pil·fer (pĭl′fer) *v.* Steal, esp. in small quantities. **pil·fer·age** (pĭl′-ferĭj), **pil′fer·er** *ns.*

pil·grim (pĭl′grĭm, -grĭm) *n.* One who journeys to sacred place as act of religious devotion; person regarded as journeying to a future life; traveler; **P ~ Fathers**, earliest English Puritan settlers of colony of Plymouth, Massachusetts, and esp. those who left Delft Haven and Plymouth, England, in the *Mayflower* in 1620.

pil·grim·age (pĭl′grimĭj) *n.* Pilgrim's journey; (fig.) mortal life viewed as a journey.

pi·lif·er·ous (pīlĭf′erus) *adj.* (chiefly bot.) Having hair.

Pil·i·pi·no (pĭlipē′nō) *n.* Language of Filipinos, based on Tagalog.

pill (pĭl) *n.* 1. Small ball or disk of medicine to be swallowed whole; **the ~**, (colloq.) oral contraceptive. 2. (fig.) Something unpleasant that has to be accepted. 3. (baseball slang) Ball. 4. **pill′box**, shallow cylindrical box for holding pills; hat shaped like this; (mil.) small round concrete emplacement; **pill′wort**, plant of genus *Pilularia*, with small globular involucres.

The **pilot** of a modern military aircraft has to be highly skilled as his cockpit is increasingly filled with technical instruments which he must be able to note and use.

pil·lage (pĭl′ĭj) *n.* Plunder, esp. as practiced in war. ~ *v.t.* (**-laged, -lag·ing**). Sack, plunder. **pil′-lag·er** *n.*

pil·lar (pĭl′er) *n.* Vertical structure of stone, wood, metal, etc slender in proportion to heigh used as support or ornament; pos pedestal; upright mass of air, wate etc.; (mining) solid mass of coal e left to support roof of the workin (fig.) person who is a main su porter (*of*); **from ~ to post**, and fro, from one resource another; **Pil′lars of Hercules**, tw promontories, Calpe (Gibraltar)

Pieces of skull found in 1912 and named **'Piltdown man'** were only exposed as a forgery in 1953–54 when it was shown that the jaw was an orangutan's and the skull had been stained.

Sometimes called the Poor Man's Weatherglass, from its habit of closing when the sky is overcast, the **pimpernel** is a common weed of grassland all over Europe.

Europe and Abyla (Ceuta) in Africa, at E. end of Strait of Gibraltar, anciently supposed to have been parted by the arm of Hercules and regarded as the western limits of the inhabited world. **pillar** v.t. Support (as) with pillars. **pil′lared** adj.

pil·lo·ry (pĭl′orē) n. (pl. **-ries**). Wooden framework with holes for head and hands of offender exposed to public ridicule etc. ~ v.t. (**-ried, ry·ing**). Put in the pillory; (fig.) expose to ridicule.

pil·low (pĭl′ō) n. Cushion as support for head, esp. in bed; (techn.) pillow-shaped block or support; **pil′lowcase, pil′lowslip**, washable cover for pillow; **pillow fight**, mock fight with pillows in bedroom. **pillow** v. Rest, prop up, (as) on pillow.

pi·lose (pī′lōs), **pi·lous** (pī′lus) adjs. Covered with hair. **pi·los·i·ty** (pīlŏs′ĭtē) n.

pi·lot (pī′lot) n. 1. Person qualified to take charge of ships entering or leaving a harbor, or wherever navigation requires local knowledge. 2. One who operates flying controls of an aircraft, one

duly qualified to do so; automatic device for maintaining an airplane in flight. 3. (fig.) Guide, esp. in hunting field; (attrib.) small-scale, experimental. 4. ~ **balloon**, small balloon whose movements are observed as it rises in the air, used to ascertain direction and velocity of currents at various altitudes; ~ **bird**, rare dark brown Australian bird (*Pycnoptilus floccosus*) with loud and distinctive note; ~ **chute**, small parachute serving to bring main one into operation; ~ **engine**, locomotive engine going on ahead of a train to make sure that the way is clear; **pi′lotfish** (pl. **-fish·es**, collect. **-fish**), small silvery-blue dark-barred fish of warm seas (*Naucrates ductor*), said to act for shark as pilot or guide to food; ~ **lamp**, electric indicator light or control light; ~ **light**, small gas burner kept lighted to kindle large burner as required. **pilot** v.t.

Conduct as pilot; act as pilot on. **pi·lot·age** (pī′lotĭj) n. **pi′lot·less** adj. (of aircraft) Without human pilot aboard, guided by remote control.

pi·lous = PILOSE.

Pil·sen (pĭl′zen). German name of Plzen, town of Czechoslovakia, famous for lager beer (**Pil·sen·er** pr. pĭlz′ner, pĭls′-).

Pil·sud·ski (pĭlsoot′skē), **Joseph** (1867–1935). Polish soldier and statesman; 1st marshal of Poland; chief of state 1918–23; prime minister and virtual dictator 1926–1928, 1930–5.

Pilt·down (pĭlt′down). Down near Lewes, England, where prehistoric remains of a human skull and apelike lower jaw, and of worked flints and bone implements, were discovered (1912); they were claimed as belonging to the early Pleistocene period but proved by scientific tests (1953) to have been assembled as a hoax.

pi·men·to (pĭmĕn′tō) n. (pl. **-tos**). 1. (Dried aromatic berry of) West Indian evergreen tree (*Pimenta officinalis*); allspice. 2. (also **pi·mien·to** pr. pĭmyĕn′tō, -mĕn′- pl. **-tos**). Any of various peppers.

pimp (pĭmp) n. Man who solicits clients for a prostitute or brothel. ~ v.i. Act as pimp.

pim·per·nel (pĭm′pernĕl, -nel) n. Small annual (*Anagallis arvensis*) found in cornfields and waste ground, with scarlet (also blue or white) flowers closing in cloudy or rainy weather.

pim·ple (pĭm′pel) n. Small solid round swelling of the skin, usu. inflammatory. **pim′pled, pim′ply** adjs.

pin (pĭn) n. Thin piece of metal with sharp point and round flattened head for fastening together parts of dress, papers, etc.; peg of wood or metal for various purposes; peg on musical instrument; (pl. colloq.), legs; **cotter pin**, metal pin to be passed through hole and held there by gaping of its split end; **pins and needles**, tingling sensation in limb recovering from numbness; **on pins and needles**, in state of mental agitation due to suspense; **pin'cushion**, small cushion for sticking pins in to keep them ready for use; **pin'feather**, ungrown feather; **pin'head**, stupid or silly person; (fig.) minute thing; **pin'hole**, hole made by pin or into which peg fits; **pin money**, (orig.) allowance to women for dress expenses etc.; hence, very small sum; **pin'point**, point of a pin; (attrib. of targets) small and requiring very accurate and precise bombing and shelling; (*v.t.*) locate or bomb (such target) with the accuracy and precision required (also fig.); **pin'prick**, (fig.) trifling irritation; **pin stripe**, very narrow stripe in textile fabric; **pin'tail** (pl. **-tails**, collect. **-tail**), duck or grouse with pointed tail, esp. N. Amer. duck (*Anas acuta*), having long neck, gray, brown, and white plumage, and white underparts; **pin'tuck**, narrow ornamental tuck; **pin'wheel**, small wheel with paper vanes pinned to a stick so as to rotate in the wind; **pin'-worm**, threadworm (*Enterobius vermicularis*) parasitic in human rectum. **pin** *v.t.* (**pinned, pin·ning**). Fasten (*to*, *together*, *up*) with pin(s); transfix with pin, lance, etc.; seize and hold fast; bind (person *down*) *to* (promise, arrangement); ~ **up**, (archit.) underpin; fasten (on wall etc.) by means of a pin; **pin'up** (*n.*) (picture pinned up on wall etc. portraying) sexually attractive woman or man; such a person. **pin'like** *adj.* **pin'ner** *n.*

pin·a·fore (pĭn'afōr, -fŏr) *n.* Washable sleeveless covering worn over dress etc. to protect from dirt.

pince-nez (păns'nā, pĭns') *n.* (pl. **pince-nez** pr. păns'nāz, pĭns'). Pair of eyeglasses with spring to clip on to nose. [Fr., = "pinch-nose"]

pin·cers (pĭn'serz) *n.pl.* (also **pair of** ~) Gripping tool made of two limbs pivoted together forming pair of jaws with manipulating handles; similar organ in crustaceans, etc.; ~ (also **pincer**) **movement**, (mil.) operation involving the convergence of two forces on enemy position like the jaws of a pair of pincers. **pin'cer-like** *adj.*

pinch (pĭnch) *n.* Nip, squeeze; as much as can be taken up with

tips of finger and thumb; (fig.) stress (of poverty etc.); **in a** ~, in a strait or exigency. **pinch** *v.* Nip with finger and thumb, pain or injure by squeezing; (of cold, hunger, etc.) nip, shrivel; stint; be niggardly; sail (vessel) close hauled; (slang) steal; arrest.

Pin·dar (pĭn'der) (518–438 B.C.). Greek lyric poet. **Pin·dar·ic** (pĭndăr'ĭk) *adj.* Of Pindar; resembling the style, diction, etc., of Pindar; ~ **ode**, (English pros.) ode with irregular number of feet in lines and arbitrary disposition of rhymes.

pine[1] (pīn) *n.* Tree of genus *Pinus* with evergreen needle-shaped leaves growing in sheathed clusters of 2 or more, many species of which afford timber, tar, and turpentine; ~ **cone**, characteristic organ of the pine, containing its *e most important use of **pinnacles** in othic architecture was to give strong rtical emphasis, as here: they were :o used to strengthen flying ttresses by adding weight.*

eds; ~ **nut**, edible seed of some ne trees.

pine² (pīn) v.i. (**pined, pin·ing**). anguish, waste away, from grief, sease, etc.; long eagerly (*for, er, to*).

pin·e·al (pĭn´ēal) *adj.* (anat.) aped like a pine cone; ~ **body**, all conical body of unknown nction behind third ventricle of ain.

pine·ap·ple (pīn´ăpel) *n.* Juicy ible collective fruit of *Ananas*, surmounted by crown of small leaves (so called from resemblance to pine cone); (slang) hand grenade, bomb.

ping (pĭng) *n.* Abrupt ringing sound as of rifle bullet flying through air. ~ *v.i.* 1. Produce abrupt ringing sound; fly with this. 2. (of internal combustion engine) Knock, emit dull metallic sound from explosion of (part of) charge, due usu. to poor quality of fuel.

Ping-Pong (pĭng´pŏng) *n.* (trademark) Table tennis.

pin·ion¹ (pĭn´yon) *n.* Terminal segment of bird's wing; any flight feather of wing; (in carving) part of wing corresponding to forearm; (poet.) wing. ~ *v.t.* Cut off pinion

*The garden **pink** and the carnation are both derived from the wild Dianthus which grows in the Mediterranean region. Others grow in Asia and Africa.*

of (wing, bird) to prevent flight; bind the arms of (person), bind (arms); bind (person etc.) fast *to*.

pin·ion² (pĭn´yon) *n.* Small cog-wheel engaging with larger one; cogged spindle engaging with wheel.

pink¹ (pĭngk) *n.* 1. Garden plant, species of *Dianthus* (esp. *D. plumarius*), native to E. Europe, with white, crimson, pink, or variegated sweet smelling flowers; allied or similar plant. 2. Finest example of excellence, flower; **in the ~**, (slang) healthy. 3. Pale red slightly inclining to purple. 4. Fox hunter's red coat; cloth of this; fox hunter. **pink** *adj.* Of pale red color of various kinds, as *rose, salmon, pink*; (joc.) mildly communist; **pink´eye**, contagious ophthalmia in man, marked by red-ness of the eyeball. **pink´ish** *adj.*

pink² (pĭngk) *v.t.* Pierce with sword etc.; ornament (leather etc.) with perforations; cut scalloped or zigzag edge on; adorn, deck (freq. **~ out**); **pink´ing shears**, dress-maker's serrated shears for cutting zigzag edge.

Pink·er·ton (pĭng´kerton), **Allan** (1819–84). Scottish-born Amer. detective; founded (1850) a detective agency; Union intel-ligence agent in Civil War; fore-stalled an attempt on life of Abraham Lincoln, 1861.

pin·nace (pĭn´ĭs) *n.* Man-of-war's double-banked (usu. eight-oared) boat; also applied to other ships' boats, now usu. driven by motor; (hist.) small, usu. two-masted, vessel.

pin·na·cle (pĭn´akel) *n.* Small ornamental turret usu. ending in pyramid or cone, crowning a buttress, roof, etc.; natural peak; (fig.) culmination, climax. ~ *v.t.* (**-cled, -cling**). Set (as) on pinnacle; form the pinnacle of; furnish with pinnacles.

pin·nate (pĭn´āt, -ĭt) *adj.* 1. (bot., of compound leaf) With series of leaflets on each side of common stalk. 2. (zool.) With branches, tentacles, etc., on each side of an axis. **pin´nate·ly** *adv.*

pin·no·there (pĭn´other) *n.* Small crab of genus *Pinnotheres*, inhabiting shells of oysters, mussels, etc., and sharing their food.

pin·nule (pĭn´ūl) *n.* 1. (bot.) Secondary division of pinnate leaf. 2. (zool.) Part, organ, like small wing or fin. 3. Sight at end of index of astrolabe etc. **pin·nu·lar** (pĭn´yuler) *adj.*

pi·noch·le, pi·noc·le (pē´nŭkel, -nŏk-) *ns.* Card game using 48 cards, with two of every card above

*Rock **pipits** are found only on the rocky coasts and offshore islands of western Europe from France to northern Sweden; they nest in crevices on cliffs.*

the 8; occurrence of queen of spades and jack of diamonds together in this game.

pi·ñon (pin′yon, pēn′yōn; *Sp.* pēnyawn′) *n.* (pl. **pi·ñons,** *Sp.* **pi·ño·nes** pr. pēnyaw′něs). Nut pine tree *Pinus edulis monophylla quadrifolia* of western N. Amer.; its edible fruit.

pint (pīnt) *n.* Measure of capacity, liquid or dry, equal to ½ quart.

pin·tle (pĭn′tel) *n.* Bolt or pin, esp. one on which some other part turns.

pin·to (pĭn′tō) *adj.* & *n.* (pl. **-tos**). Piebald (horse); ~ **bean,** mottled kidney bean used for food in Southwest. [Span., = "painted"]

pin·y (pī′nē) *adj.* (**pin·i·er, pin·i·est**). Of, like, abounding in, pines.

pin·yin (pĭn′yĭn′) *n.* System of romanized spelling for Chinese language.

pi·o·neer (pīonēr′) *n.* 1. Member of military unit equipped to prepare road for troops. 2. Initiator of enterprise; original explorer. ~ *v.* Act as pioneer (to); conduct; open up (road etc.) as pioneer.

pi·ous (pī′us) *adj.* Devout, religious; (archaic) dutiful. **pi·ous·ly** *adv.* **pi·ous·ness** *n.*

pip[1] (pĭp) *n.* Disease of poultry, hawks, etc., marked by thick mucus in throat and often by white scale on tip of tongue; **the ~,** (slang) a feeling of disgust, depression, or bad temper.

pip[2] (pĭp) *n.* Each spot on playing cards, dice, or dominoes, or star on army officer's shoulder; single blossom of clustered inflorescence; rhomboidal segment of surface of pineapple; image that an object produces on a radar screen.

pip[3] (pĭp) *n.* Seed of apple, pear, orange, etc.

pi·pal, pee·pul (pē′pal) *ns.* Indian species of fig tree (*Ficus religiosa*) regarded as sacred.

pipe (pīp) *n.* 1. Tube of wood, metal, etc., esp. for conveying water, gas, etc. 2. Musical wind instrument consisting of single tube blown by mouth; each of tubes by which sounds are produced in organ; boatswain's whistle, sounding of this; (pl.) bagpipes. 3. Voice, esp. in singing; song, note, of bird. 4. Tubular organ, vessel, etc., in animal body; cylindrical vein of ore; channel of decoy for wild fowl.

*A re-enactment of a **pioneer** Oregon trail wagon-train in Nebraska. The pioneers suffered the most appalling hardships to reach and open up new territories in the U.S.A.*

Red **piranha** (Rooseveltia natteri) grow up to 12 inches long and, like all other piranhas, are vicious fish. Some piranhas work in packs, devouring quite large animals with their dreadful teeth.

5. Narrow tube of clay, wood, etc., with bowl at one end, for drawing in smoke of tobacco; quantity of tobacco held by this; ~ **of peace, peace** ~, calumet; **put that in your** ~ **and smoke it**, digest that fact etc. if you can. 6. Cask for wine, esp. as measure usu. = about 126 gallons. 7. ~ **clay**, fine white clay used for tobacco pipes and (esp. by soldiers) for cleaning white breeches, belts, etc.; (*v.t.*) whiten with pipe clay; ~ **dream**, (colloq.) kind of extravagant fancy induced by smoking opium; hence, notion unlikely to be realized; ~ **fitter**, mechanic who installs and maintains plumbing pipes, steampipes, etc.; **pipe'line**, line of pipes for conveying petroleum, gas, or water across country; channel of supply, communication, etc.; **pipe rack**, rack for tobacco pipes; **pipe'stone**, hard red clay used by Amer. Indians for tobacco pipes. **pipe** *v.* (**piped, pip·ing**). 1. Play (tune etc.) on pipe; lead, bring, (person etc.) by sound of pipe; summon (crew) by sounding whistle; utter in shrill voice; ~ **down**, (slang) become quiet; ~ **up**, speak up; sing. 2. Trim (garment), ornament (cake etc.) with piping. 3. Furnish with pipes.

pip·er (pī′per) *n.* One who plays on pipe, esp. strolling musician; bagpiper; **pay the** ~, defray cost, bear expense or loss, of proceeding etc.; pay the cost of doing as one pleases.

pi·pette, pi·pet (pīpět′) *ns.*

Slender tube filled usu. by suction, used in laboratories for measuring and transferring small quantities of liquid. ~ *v.* (**-pet·ted, -pet·ting**).

pip·ing (pī′pǐng) *n.* (esp.) Ornamental pipelike fold of cloth, often enclosing cord, for trimming edge of seam of garment, upholstery, etc.; ornamental cordlike line of icing on cake etc. ~ *adj.* Shrill; playing on a pipe. ~ *adv.* ~ **hot**, so hot as to make piping or hissing sound; very hot.

pip·i·strelle (pǐpǐstrěl′, pǐp′-ǐstrěl) *n.* Small bat of genus *Pipistrellus*.

pip·it (pǐp′ǐt) *n.* Bird of a group superficially resembling larks but allied to the wagtails, of *Anthus* and related genera, including **water** ~ (*A. spinoletta*). [prob. imit.]

pip·kin (pǐp′kǐn) *n.* Small earthenware pot or pan.

pip·pin (pǐp′ǐn) *n.* Any of several kinds of apple raised from seed.

pip-squeak (pǐp′skwēk) *n.* (slang) Insignificant person, petty object.

pi·quant (pē′kant, -kahnt, pēkahnt′) *adj.* Agreeably pungent, sharp, appetizing; (fig.) pleasantly stimulating or disturbing to the mind. **pi′quant·ly** *adv.* **pi′-quan·cy, pi′quant·ness** *ns.*

pique (pēk) *v.t.* (**piqued, piqu-ing**). Irritate, wound the pride of; arouse (interest, curiosity); plume (oneself). ~ *n.* Ill feeling, resentment.

pi·qué (pǐkā′, pē-) *n.* Stiff fabric, usu. cotton, with lengthwise ribs.

pi·quet (pǐkět′, -kā′) *n.* Card game for two players with pack of 32 cards, points being scored on various groups or combinations of cards.

pi·ra·cy (pī′rasē) *n.* (pl. **-cies**). Action of a pirate; **air** ~, hijacking of aircraft.

pi·ra·nha (pǐrahn′ya, -răn′-) *n.* Tropical Amer. voracious freshwater fish (*Serrasalmo piraya*) with serrated belly and strong lancet-shaped teeth.

pi·rate (pī′rat) *n.* (Ship used by) sea robber; marauder; one who infringes another's copyright. ~ *v.* (**-rat·ed, -rat·ing**). Plunder; reproduce (book etc.) without authorization of copyright owner; play the pirate; **pi·rat·i·cal** (pǐrăt′ǐkal), **pi·rat′ic** *adjs.* **pi·rat′-i·cal·ly** *adv.*

pir·ou·ette (pǐrooĕt′) *n. & v.i.* (**-et·ted, -et·ting**). (ballet) Spin around on one foot or on point of toe. [Fr., = "top"]

Pi·sa (pē′za). City of Tuscany, N. Italy; **Leaning Tower of** ~, campanile of cathedral, built 1174–1350, about 180 ft. (54.9 m) high and leaning some 16 ft. (4.8 m) from the perpendicular.

pis·ca·to·ry (pǐs′katōrē, -tōrē)

Possibly the most popular form of **pistol**
is the revolver. Its relatively simple
mechanism, developed perhaps 300
years ago, has stood the tests both of
time and of operating conditions such
as sandy deserts. Its greatest practical
advantage, apart from this, is its better
'stopping power' as compared with an
automatic pistol.

adj. Of fishermen or fishing;
addicted to fishing. **pis·ca·to·ri·al**
(pĭskatōr´ēal, -tŏr´-) *adj.*
Pis·ces (pī´sēz, pĭs´ēz). The
Fishes, a constellation; 12th sign
(♓) of the zodiac, which sun enters
about Feb.
Pis·gah (pĭz´ga). Mountain of
Transjordan, NE. of Dead Sea,
from which Moses viewed the
Promised Land (Deut. 3) before his
death.
pis·mire (pĭs´mīr) *n.* Ant. [f.

piss (from smell of ant hill), and
obs. *mire* ant, f. Du. *mier*.]
piss (pĭs) *v.* (**pissed, piss·ing**).
(vulg.) Urinate; discharge with the
urine; wet with urine. ~ *n.* Urine.
pis·ta·chi·o (pĭstăsh´ēō, -stah´-
shēō) *n.* (pl. **-chi·os**). Tree (*Pistacia
vera*) of W. Asia, cultivated in S.
Europe; nut of this, with greenish
edible kernel; color of the kernel.
pis·til (pĭs´tĭl) *n.* Organ of flower
bearing ovules, comprising ovary,
style, and stigma. **pis·til·late**

(pĭs´tĭlĭt, -lāt) *adj.*
pis·tol (pĭs´tol) *n.* Small firearm
usu. with curved butt, held and
fired by one hand; ~ **grip, handle**
handle shaped like butt of pistol
pistol-whip, beat with pistol.
pis·tole (pĭstōl´) *n.* (hist.
Foreign gold coin, esp. Spanish.
pis·ton (pĭs´ton) *n.* Disk or short
cylinder fitting closely within
cylindrical vessel in which it moves
to and fro, used in steam engine
pump, etc., to impart or receive
motion by means of ~ **rod**; sliding
valve in cornet etc.; ~ **ring**
metallic expansible packing ring
fitted on piston.
pit (pĭt) *n.* 1. Natural hole in
ground; hole made in digging for
mineral etc. or for industrial
purposes; (shaft of) coal mine
depression in floor of workshop
enabling persons to reach underside
of motor vehicles for inspection or
repair; covered hole as trap. 2. **the**
~, hell. 3. (hist.) Enclosure for
cockfights etc. 4. Hollow in animal
or plant body or on any surface;
depressed scar, as after smallpox
(bot.) hollow between plant cell
on either side of lamella (~
membrane); ~ **of the stomach**
depression between cartilages of
false ribs. 5. Hard stone of a fruit
6. (Brit.) That part of auditorium
of theater etc. which is on floor
of house; now usu. the part of this
behind stalls; section of theater in
front of stage, used for member
of the orchestra. 7. Part of floor
of commodities exchange appropriated for special branch of business
e.g. *wheat* ~. 8. (usu. pl.) Place
at side of racing track for refueling
etc. 9. **pit´fall**, covered pit as trap
(fig.) unsuspected snare or danger
pit *v.* (**pit·ted, pit·ting**). Put into
a pit; remove pits from (fruit); set
(cocks etc.) to fight in pit (*against*
each other), (fig.) match (*against*)
make pits, esp. scars, in (esp. in
past part.); (of flesh etc.) retain
impression of finger etc. when
touched. **pit´ted** *adj.*
pit·a·pat (pĭt´apăt) *adv.* & *n.*
(With) sound as of light quick steps
Pit·cairn (pĭt´kārn) **Island**
Small island in S. Pacific (British
since 1839) between Tahiti and
Easter Island; settled in 1790 by
mutineers from the BOUNTY and
inhabited by their descendants.
pitch[1] (pĭch) *n.* Black or dark
brown tenacious resinous substance, the residue from distillation
of tar or turpentine, hard when cold
but becoming viscid and semiliquid
when heated, used for caulking
seams of ships, protecting wood
from moisture, road-making, etc

*Buildings like the leaning tower show
the prosperity of medieval **Pisa**. Important even before Roman times, Pisa has
remained a flourishing city to the present day.*

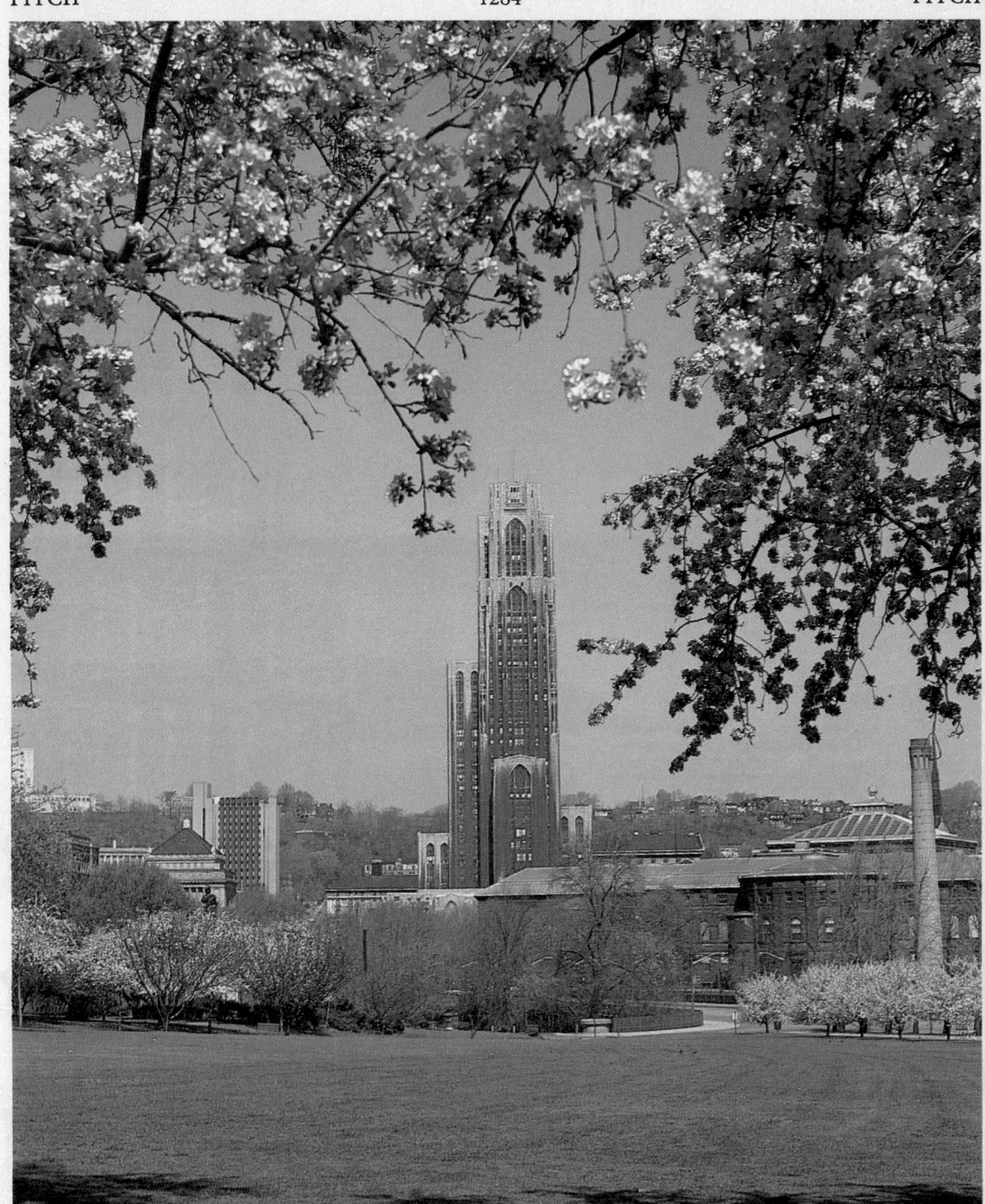

*The Cathedral of Learning at the University of **Pittsburgh, Pennsylvania.** The city of Pittsburgh is one of the U.S.A.'s major steel manufacturers, with a diversity of satellite industries.*

~-**black**, with no light at all; so ~-**dark(ness)**; **pitch'blende**, mineral containing uranium oxide, one of the chief sources of radium and uranium; **pitch pine**, especially resinous kinds of pine. **pitch'y** *adj.* (**pitch·i·er, pitch·i·est**). Of, like, dark as, pitch. **pitch'i·ness** *n*. **pitch** *v.t.* Smear, cover, coat, with pitch.

pitch² (pĭch) *v*. Fix and erect (tent, camp); encamp; fix, plant, (thing) indefinite position; pave (road) with set stones; **pitched' battle**, battle of set kind; battle

with forces intensely committed, not casual. 2. (mus.) Set at particular pitch; (fig.) express in particular style. 3. Throw, fling; (in games) throw (flat object) toward a mark; throw (ball) to batter in baseball etc.; (of ball etc.) land, fall (in specified manner or position); fall heavily. 4. (slang) Tell (tale, yarn); deliver high-

pressure sales talk. 5. (of ship) Plunge in longitudinal direction. 6. Incline, dip (of stratum, roof, etc.). 7. **pitch in**, (colloq.) set to work vigorously; **pitch into**, (colloq..) assail forcibly with blows, words, etc.; make vigorous attack on. **pitch** *n*. 1. Pitching; mode of delivering ball in cricket, baseball, etc. 2. (chiefly Brit.) Place at which street performer is stationed; (cricket) place between and about wickets. 3. Height to which falcon etc. soars before swooping on prey; height, degree, intensity (of quality etc.); (mus.) quality of musical sound depending on comparative rapidity of vibrations producing it, degree of acuteness (international standard pitch is set by fixing the A above middle C at 440 vibrations per second); ~ **pipe**, small pipe blown by mouth to set pitch for singing or tuning. 4. Degree of slope; steepness of roof's slope. 5. (mech.) Distance between successive points or lines, e.g. between successive teeth of cogwheel; ~ **wheel**, toothed wheel engaging with another. 6. (slang) sales talk.

pitch·er[1] (pĭch´er) n. (esp.) Player who delivers ball, esp. in baseball.

pitch·er[2] (pĭch´er) n. Vessel, usu. of earthenware, with handle or two ears and usu. a lip, for holding liquids; (bot.) modified leaf in pitcher form; ~ **plant**, any of various plants with such leaves, freq. containing liquid secretion by which insects are caught and digested. **pitch·er·ful** (pĭch´erfool) n. (pl. **-fuls**).

Pitch·er (pĭch´er), **Molly** (1754–1832). (original name, Mary Ludwig Hays McCauley) Amer. Revolutionary War heroine who carried water to weary and wounded soldiers during the battle of Monmouth, June, 1778, and took her husband's place at his cannon when he was overcome by heat.

pitch·fork (pĭch´fork) n. Long-handled fork with 2 or more sharp prongs for pitching hay etc.; tuning fork. ~ v.t. Cast (as) with pitchfork.

pitch·man (pĭch´man) n. (pl. **-men** pr. -men). 1. Itinerant vendor of small merchandise. 2. (slang) High-pressure salesman.

pit·e·ous (pĭt´ēus) adj. Such as to cause pity, deplorable. **pit´e·ous·ly** adv. **pit´e·ous·ness** n.

pith (pĭth) n. 1. Spongy cellular tissue in stem and branches of dicotyledonous plants; similar tissue lining rind of orange etc.; spinal cord; (fig.) essential part, quintessence. 2. Physical strength, vigor; force, energy. **pith´less** adj. **pith** v.t. Slaughter (animal) by severing spinal cord.

pith·y (pĭth´ē) adj. (**pith·i·er**, **pith·i·est**). Of, like, full of, pith; condensed and forcible, terse. **pith´i·ly** adv. **pith´i·ness** n.

pit·i·a·ble (pĭt´ēabel) adj. Deserving of pity or contempt. **pit´i·a·ble·ness** n. **pit´i·a·bly** adv.

pit·i·ful (pĭt´ĭful) adj. Arousing pity; contemptible. **pit´i·ful·ly** adv. **pit´i·ful·ness** n.

pit·i·less (pĭt´ĭlĭs) adj. Showing no pity. **pit´i·less·ly** adv. **pit´i·less·ness** n.

pi·ton (pē´ton) n. Metal spike or peg used in mountaineering as support or belaying pin.

Pi·tot (pētō´), **Henri** (1695–1771). French physicist; **Pitot tube**, right-angled tube open at both ends, used in anemometers and for determining velocity of fluids; similar device used for measuring velocity of aircraft.

pit·tance (pĭt´ans) n. 1. (hist.) Pious bequest to religious house for extra food etc. 2. Allowance, remuneration, esp. scanty one; small number or amount.

Pitts·burgh (pĭts´bērg). Industrial city and major river port in SW. Pennsylvania, where the confluence of the Allegheny and Monongahela rivers forms the Ohio River.

pi·tu·i·tar·y (pĭtoo´ĭtĕrē, -tū´-) adj. (archaic) Of or secreting phlegm; ~ **gland**, small bilobed ductless gland at base of brain producing hormones that regulate many important bodily functions and coordinate the working of other endocrine organs. **pituitary** n. (pl. **-tar·ies**). Pituitary gland. **pi·tu·i·tous** (pĭtoo´ĭtus, -tū´-) adj. **pi·tu·i·trin** (pĭtoo´ĭtrĭn, -tū´-) n. Hormone produced by pituitary gland; solution of this used medicinally.

pit·y (pĭt´ē) n. (pl. **pit·ies**). 1. Feeling of tenderness aroused by distress or suffering; take ~ **on**, feel or act compassionately toward. 2. Regrettable fact, ground for regret; **more's the ~**, so much the worse. **pity** v.t. (**pit·ied**, **pit·y·ing**). Feel pity for. **pit´y·ing·ly** adv.

Pi·us (pī´us). Name of 12 popes, including **Pius II** (Enea Silvio de Piccolomini, 1405–64); pope 1458–1464; author and patron of letters; **Pius IV** (Giovanni Angelo Medici, 1499–1565); pope 1559–65; re-convened Council of TRENT in 1562; **Pius IX** (Giovanni Maria Mastai-Jenetti, 1792–1878); pope

1846–78; during this pontificate the temporal power of the papacy was lost and the doctrine of papal infallibility proclaimed; **Pius XI** (Achille Ratti, 1857–1939); pope 1922–39; the breach between church and state was healed in this pontificate and the Vatican City State was founded; **Pius XII** (Eugenio Pacelli, 1876–1958); pope 1939–58.

piv·ot (pĭv´ot) n. Short shaft or pin on which something turns or oscillates; (mil.) soldier on whom body of troops on parade wheels; (fig.) cardinal or central point. **piv´ot·al** adj. **pivot** v.i. Turn as on pivot, hinge (on).

pix·ie, pix·y (pĭk´sē) ns. (pl. **pix·ies**). Supernatural being akin to fairy. **pix·i·lat·ed** (pĭk´sĭlātĭd) adj. Enchanted, slightly crazy.

Pi·zar·ro (pĭzär´ō), **Francisco** (c1471–1541). Spanish conquistador; discoverer and conqueror of Peru.

pizz. abbrev. Pizzicato.

piz·za (pēt´sa) n. Italian dish of flat open crust containing cheese etc., therefore, **piz·ze·ri·a** (pētsere´a), place where pizzas are made and sold.

piz·zi·ca·to (pĭtsĭkah´tō) adv., n. (pl. **-tos, -ti** pr. -tē) & adj. (mus.) (Passage, note, played) by plucking string of violin etc. with finger instead of using bow. [It.]

pk. abbrev. (pl. **pks.**). Pack; park; peak; peck.

pkg. abbrev. Package, packages.

pkwy. abbrev. Parkway.

pl. abbrev. Place; plate; plural.

The best-known result of pituitary malfunction is abnormal growth. However the gland is also very important as a controller of other glands, such as the thyroid. Location of the pituitary in the human brain is shown below.

corpus callosum
optic thalamus
choroid plexus
third ventricle
hypothalamus
septum lucidum
cerebral hemisphere
pituitary, anterior lobe
pituitary, posterior lobe
pons
cerebellum
fourth ventricle

plac·a·ble (plăk´*a*bel, plā´k*a*-) *adj.* Easily appeased, mild, forgiving. **plac·a·bil´i·ty** *n.* **plac´a·bly** *adv.*

plac·ard (plăk´ärd, -*e*rd) *n.* Document printed on 1 side of single sheet for posting in a public place, poster. ~ *v.t.* Set up placards on (wall etc.); advertise (wares etc.) by placards; display (poster etc.) as placard.

pla·cate (plā´kāt, plăk´āt) *v.t.* (**-cat·ed, -cat·ing**). Pacify, conciliate. **pla´cat·er, pla·ca´tion** (plākā´sh*o*n) *ns.* **pla·ca´tive, pla·ca·to·ry** (plā´katōrē, -tōrē, plăk´*a*-) *adjs.*

place (plās) *n.* 1. Particular part of space; part of space occupied by person or thing; street. 2. City, town, village, etc.; residence, dwelling; vacation house with surroundings; building, spot, devoted to specified purpose. 3. Particular spot on surface etc.; particular point or passage in book etc. 4. Rank, station; position of figure in series as indicating its value in decimal or similar notation; step in progression of argument, statement, etc.; (racing) second position among those that finish. 5. Proper or natural position; space, seat, accommodation, for person etc. at table, in conveyance, etc.; **in ~ of,** instead of; **~ card,** small card for name of a guest at table; **~ mat,** small mat used at an individual setting at table; **~ setting,** dishes and eating utensils set at a diner's

place at table; **take the ~ of,** substitute for. 6. Office, employment, esp. government appointment; duties of office etc. 7. **give ~ to,** make room for; be succeeded by; **out of, in, ~,** (un)suitable, (in)appropriate; **take ~,** happen. 8. **~ kick,** (football) kick made when ball is held on ground by another player. **place** *v.t.* (**placed, plac·ing**). 1. Put in particular place; arrange in their proper places. 2. Appoint (person) to post; find employment etc. for. 3. Invest (money); dispose of (goods) to customer; put (order for goods etc.) into hands of firm etc. 4. Repose (confidence etc. *in, on*). 5. Assign rank to; locate; state position of (usu. any of first 3 horses or runners) in race; identify fully, determine who (or what) a particular person (or thing) is, assign to a class; **be placed,** be second in race. 6. Get (goal) by place kick.

pla·ce·bo (plasē´bō) *n.* (pl. **-bos, -boes**). 1. Medicine having no intrinsic therapeutic value but given to humor patient (also used in experiments to test the effect of drugs, the drug being given to one group and the placebo to those who act as controls). 2. (eccles.) Vespers

Piux XII, the first Pope to make extensive use of radio as a means of reaching wide audiences, did much to pave the way for the full ecumenical movement.

for the dead, opening chant of t vespers. [L., = "I shall acceptable," 1st word of Ps. 114 in Vulgate]

pla·cen·ta (plasĕnt*a*) *n.* (pl. **-ta -tae** pr. -tē). 1. Spongy vascu structure (in some mammals a some other vertebrates) formed the interlocking of fetal a maternal tissue, through which t fetus is supplied with nutrime and rid of waste products. 2. (bo Part of carpel to which ovules a attached. **pla·cen´tal** *adj.*

plac·er (plăs´*e*r) *n.* Deposit sand, gravel, etc., in bed of strea etc., containing valuable minera in particles.

plac·id (plăs´ĭd) *adj.* Mi peaceful; serene. **plac´id·ly** *aa* **pla·cid·i·ty** (plasĭd´ĭtē), **plac´id ness** *ns.*

pla·gia·rize (plā´j*a*rīz) *v* (**-rized, -riz·ing**). Take and u another person's (thought writings, inventions) as one's ow **pla´gia·rism, pla´gia·rist** *r* **pla´gia·ry** *n.* (pl. **-ries**). Plagiari plagiarism. **pla·gia·ris´tic** *a* **pla·gia·ris´ti·cal·ly** *adv.*

plague (plāg) *n.* 1. Afflictio esp. as divine punishment; (colloc nuisance, trouble. 2. Pestilenc esp. oriental or bubonic plagu

Pizarro conquered the empire of t Incas in 1531 with about 180 men a a few horses. His success was due his capture of Atahualpa which result in a huge ransom being paid.

Freat P ~, bubonic plague that fflicted London in 1665; (fig.) purce or symptom of moral cor- uption. **plague** *v.t.* (**plagued, la·guing**). Afflict with plague; olloq.) annoy, bother.

plaice (plās) *n.* (pl. **plaice, laic·es**). European marine flat- sh, *Pleuronectes platessa*, much sed as food; allied Amer. species f flatfishes and flounders, esp. *Iippoglossoides platessoides.*

plaid (plăd) *n.* Long piece of willed woolen cloth, usu. with heckered or tartan pattern, outer rticle of Highland costume; cloth sed for this, other fabric with artan pattern.

plain (plān) *adj.* 1. Clear, vident; simple, readily under- tood; not elaborate or intricate. . Unembellished, (of drawings tc.) not colored; (of food) not rich r highly seasoned; not luxurious; > ~ **cook**, person able to do ~ ooking, simple cooking. 3. Out- poken, straightforward. 4. Un- ophisticated, ordinary, simple; of omely manners, dress, or appear- nce; not beautiful, ill-favored. . ~ **clothes**, ordinary civil dress, ot uniform or fancy dress, there- ore, **plain·clothes·man** (plăn- lŏz'man) (pl. **-men** pr. -men), oliceman wearing civilian clothing hile on duty; **plain dealing**, can- or, straightforwardness; **plain'- ong**, traditional church music sung n unison in medieval modes and in ree rhythm depending on accen- uation of the words; **plain- poken**, outspoken. **plain** *adv.* learly; plainly. **plain'ly** *adv.* lain'ness *n.* plain *n.* Level tract of ountry. **plains·man** (plānz'man) l. **-men**). Inhabitant of a plain. **Plains** (plānz) **of Abraham.** lateau W. of Quebec, Canada; attle site during the French and ndian War, where the French nder General Montcalm were de- ated by the Brit. under General Volfe, Sept., 1759.

plaint (plānt) *n.* 1. (law) ccusation, charge. 2. (poet.) amentation, complaint.

plain·tiff (plān'tĭf) *n.* Party ho brings suit into court of law, rosecutor.

plain·tive (plān'tĭv) *adj.* Ex- ressive of sorrow; mournful. lain'tive·ly *adv.* **plain'tive- ess** *n.*

plait (plāt, plăt) *n.* 1. Inter- acing of three or more strands of air, ribbon, straw, etc. 2. Fold, rease (now usu. PLEAT). ~ *v.t.* orm (hair, straw, etc.) into plait.

plan (plăn) *n.* Drawing, dia- ram, made by projection on flat urface, esp. one showing relative osition of parts of (floor of) a uilding; large-scale detailed map f town or district; table indicating mes, places, etc., of intended pro-

*Its resistance to most forms of atmos- pheric pollution has made the **plane** a popular tree for city planting.*

ceedings, etc.; scheme of arrange- ment; project, design; way of pro- ceeding; (perspective) any of the imaginary planes, perpendicular to line of vision, passing through objects shown in picture; ~ **posi- tion indicator**, (airborne) radar display used as navigational aid in which position of the detector appears as a spot on a map of the area around the detector. **plan'less** *adj.* **plan** *v.t.* (**planned, plan·- ning**). Make a plan of (ground, existing building); design (building

Jack-plane
Smoothing plane
Trying-plane
Rabbet plane
Router plane
Fillister plane

to be constructed etc.); scheme, arrange beforehand.

planch·et (plăn'chĭt) *n.* Plain disk of metal of which coin is made.

plan·chette (plănshĕt') *n.* Small usu. heart-shaped board (esp. a OUIJA board) supported by two castors and a pencil, which, when one or more persons rest their fingers lightly on the board, is sup- posed to write without conscious direction.

Planck (plahngk), **Max** (1858– 1947). German physicist; received Nobel Prize for physics, 1918; orig- inator of the QUANTUM theory; ~ **'s constant**, (phys.) constant in the expression for the quantum of energy, symbol h, numerical value 6.61×10^{-27}.

plane[1] (plān) *n.* (also ~ **tree**) Tall spreading tree of genus *Plata- nus*, esp. *P. orientalis* and *P. occidentalis* (sycamore or button- wood) with broad angular pal- mately lobed leaves, and bark that scales off in irregular patches.

plane[2] (plān) *n.* Tool for smoothing surface of woodwork by paring shavings from it, consisting of wooden or metal stock from smooth bottom of which projects a steel blade; similar tool for smoothing metal; **molding** ~, one for making moldings; **smoothing** ~, one used to finish surface. **plane** *v.t.* (**planed, plan·ing**). Smooth (wood, metal) with plane; pare *away* or *down* (irregularities) with plane. **plan'er** *n.*

plane[3] (plān) *n.* 1. Surface such that the straight line joining any two points in it lies wholly in it; imaginary surface of this kind in which points or lines in material bodies lie; level surface. 2. Flat thin object, esp. one used in aero- nautical experiments; (one of) the principal supporting surface(s) in an airplane; airplane; each of natural faces of a crystal. 3. (fig.) Level (*of* thought, knowledge, etc.). 4. ~ **sailing**, art of determining ship's place on the theory that the ship is moving on a plane; (fig., now usu. **plain sailing**) simple course. **plane** *v.i.* (**planed, plan·- ing**). Travel, glide (*down* etc.) in airplane; (of speedboat, automobile, etc.) skim over water. ~ *adj.* Per- fectly level, forming a plane; (of angle, figure, etc.) lying in a plane; ~ **chart**, one on which meridians and parallels of latitude are repre- sented by equidistant straight lines, used in plane sailing; ~ **table**, sur- veying instrument used for measur- ing angles in mapping, consisting of a circular drawing table mounted on a tripod and a ruler for pointing

*Although a simple wooden smoothing **plane** has been used by carpenters for many centuries, the metal plane, with its many variations was only invented by Leonard Bailey in the 19th century.*

1

2

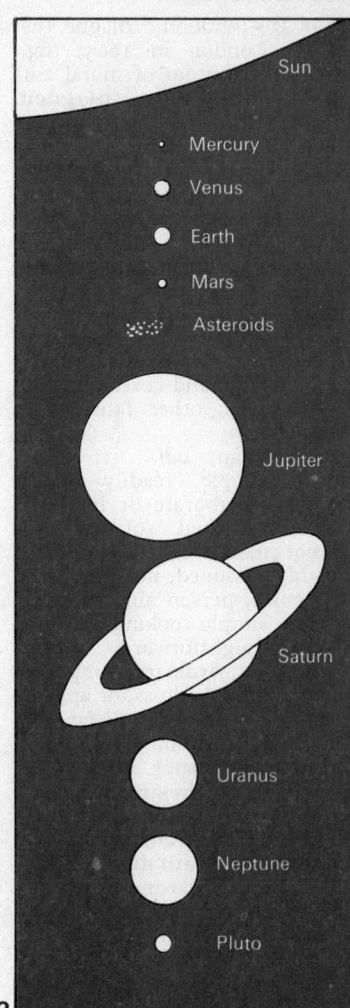

3

The ancient Greeks called the planet 'wandering stars', since they seemed t stray irregularly across the sky. Fiv can be seen with the naked eye advances in telescope design made th discovery of the rest possible. As far a is known there is no life on any of the except the earth. (1. Jupiter; 2. Saturn 3. sizes and positions in relation to th sun.)

at the object observed; **plane-table** (*v.t.*) (**-tabled, -tabling**), survey (area) with this.

plan·et (plăn´ĭt) *n.* 1. (hist.) Heavenly body distinguished from fixed stars by having apparent motion of its own, esp. (astrol.) with reference to its supposed influence on persons and events. 2. Each of the heavenly bodies revolving in approximately circular orbits around sun (**primary** ~**s**), or of those revolving around these (**secondary** ~**s** or *satellites*); **major** ~**s**, (in order of increasing distance from sun) Mercury, Venus, Earth, Mars, Jupiter, Saturn, Uranus, Neptune, Pluto; **minor** ~**s**, asteroids (with orbits between those of Mars and Jupiter); ~ **gear**(**ing**), gearing in which planet wheels are used; ~ **wheel**,

1 of 2 or more gear wheels in mesh with a central sun wheel and an outer annulus that may be free to revolve (giving direct drive) or prevented from revolving (when drive from sun wheel to planet wheels effects a reduction in speed).

plan·e·tar·i·um (plănĭtār´ēum) *n.* (pl. **-tar·i·ums, -tar·i·a** pr. -tār´ēa). Model or structure representing planetary system; apparatus that projects representation of the heavens on inner surface of dome; building housing this.

plan·e·tar·y (plăn´ĭtĕrē) *adj.* Of planets; terrestrial, mundane; wandering.

plan·gent (plăn´jent) *adj.* (of sound) Thrilling, vibrating, moaning, insistent. **plan´gen·cy** *n.*

plank (plăngk) *n.* Long flat piece of smoothed timber thicker

than a board; (fig.) item of politica or other platform or program; **wal the** ~, walk blindfolded into se along plank laid over side of ship esp. as pirates' method of disposing of victims; ~ **bed**, bed of boards without mattress. **plank** *v.t.* Furnish, cover, floor, with planks; cool (fish) by splitting open and fixing to board; (slang) put *down* (esp money on the spot).

plank·ton (plăngk´ton) *n.* (biol. Collective name for all the form of drifting or floating organic lif found at various depths in the ocea or in fresh water.

plano- *prefix.* Flatly, in a flat tened manner; comb. of plane wit another surface.

pla·no-con·cave (plānōkŏn kāv´) *adj.* With one surface plane and the other concave.

pla·no-con·vex (plānōkŏn´věks). *dj.* With one surface plane and ~e the other convex.

plant (plănt) *n.* 1. Living ~rganism generally capable of living ~holly on inorganic substances and ~aving neither power of locomotion ~or special organs of sensation or ~igestion, member of the vegetable ~ingdom (freq. restricted to the ~naller plants, excluding trees and ~nrubs); ~ **louse**, any of various ~sects infesting plants, esp. aphid. . Mode of planting oneself, pose. . Fixtures, implements, machin-~ry, etc., used in industrial process. . (slang) Planned swindle or ~urglary; hoax. **plant** *v.t.* 1. ~lace (tree, shoot, seed, etc.) in ~round that it may take root and ~row; naturalize (animals, fish, ~c.); cause (idea etc.) to take root ~ (mind); ~ **out**, transfer (plant) ~om pot or frame to open ground; ~t out (seedlings) at intervals. 2. ~ix firmly (*in, on,* ground, etc.); ~tation (person), esp. as spy; ~ ~neself, take up a position. 3. ~stablish, found (community, city, ~hurch); settle (person) in place as ~olonist etc. 4. Furnish (land *with* ~lants, district *with* settlers, etc.). . Deliver (blow, thrust) with defi-~ite aim. 6. (slang) Conceal (stolen

goods etc. on innocent person's premises to incriminate him); bury, place (gold dust, ore) in mining claim to encourage prospective buyer; devise (fraudulent scheme).

Plan·tag·e·net (plăntăj´enĭt). Orig., nickname of Geoffrey, Count of Anjou, father of Henry II of England; adopted as surname (*c*1460) by Richard, Duke of York; applied to the whole royal house that occupied English throne 1154–1399 (Henry II to Richard II). [L. *planta* sprig, *genista* broom, with ref. to Geoffrey's habit of wearing on his helmet a sprig of the common broom of Anjou]

plan·tain[1] (plăn´tĭn) *n.* Plant of genus *Plantago,* esp. **greater ~** (*P. major*), low herb with broad flat leaves spread out close to ground and dense cylindrical spikes of seeds.

plan·tain[2] (plăn´tĭn) *n.* Treelike tropical herbaceous plant (*Musa paradisiaca*) allied to banana, with immense undivided oblong leaves, cultivated for its fruit borne in long densely clustered spikes; long pod-shaped somewhat fleshy fruit of this.

plan·tar (plăn´ter) *adj.* (anat.) Of the sole of the foot.

plan·ta·tion (plăntā´shon) *n.* 1.

Assemblage of planted growing plants, esp. trees. 2. Estate on which cotton, tobacco, etc., are cultivated (formerly by servile labor). 3. (hist.) Colonization; colony.

plant·er (plăn´ter) *n.* 1. Cultivator of soil. 2. Occupier of plantation, esp. in tropical and subtropical countries. 3. Machine for planting.

plaque (plăk) *n.* 1. Ornamental tablet of metal, porcelain, etc., plain or decorated; small tablet as badge of rank in honorary order. 2. Film on teeth where bacteria proliferate (also **dental ~**).

plasm (plăz´em) = PLASMA def. 2.

plas·ma (plăz´ma) *n.* 1. Green variety of quartz. 2. (also **plasm**) (physiol.) Coagulable solution of salts and protein in which corpuscles are suspended. 3. (phys.) Ionized gas in which numbers of electrons and positive ions are approximately equal. **plas·mat·ic** (plăzmăt´ĭk), **plas´mic** *adjs.*

plas·mo·di·um (plăzmō´dēum) *n.* (pl. **-di·a** pr. -dēa). 1. (biol.) Mass of naked protoplasm formed by fusion or aggregation of amoeboid bodies. 2. Protozoan of genus *P ~,* causing malaria in man.

plas·mol·y·sis (plăzmŏl´ĭsĭs) *n.* Contraction of protoplasm of vegetable cell due to loss of water to solution with which it is in contact.

plas·ter (plăs´ter) *n.* 1. Curative application consisting of some substance spread upon muslin etc. and capable of adhering at temperature of the body. 2. Soft plastic mixture, esp. of lime, sand, and hair, spread on walls etc. to form smooth surface; **plas'terboard**, board containing plaster core, used for walling, ceilings, etc. 3. Sulfate of lime, gypsum; ~ **of Paris**, fine white plaster of calcined gypsum used to make molds or casts, as cement etc. (orig. prepared from gypsums of Montmartre, Paris). **plas'ter·y** *adj.* **plaster** *v.t.* Cover with or like plaster; apply, stick, etc., like plaster to; coat, bedaub; (slang) bomb or shell heavily; **plas'tered**, (slang) drunk. **plas'-ter·er** *n.*

plas·tic (plăs'tĭk) *adj.* 1. Molding, giving form to clay, wax etc.; produced by molding; capable of being (easily) molded; (fig.) pliant, supple; ~ **arts**, those concerned with modeling, e.g. sculpture, ceramics; ~ **bomb**, bomb of soft pliable explosive substance; ~ **clay**, (geol.) middle group of Eocene beds; ~ **surgery**, repair or replacement of lost, damaged, or deformed tissue etc. 2. Causing growth of natural forms, formative; (biol.) capable of forming living tissue, accompanied by this process. **plas'ti·cal·ly** *adv.* **plastic** *n.* Any of a group of substances, natural or synthetic, chiefly polymers of high molecular weight, that can be molded into any form by heat or pressure or both. **plas'-tic·i·ty** (plăstĭs'ĭtē) *n.*

plas·ti·cize (plăs'tĭsīz) *v.* (**-cized, -ciz·ing**). Make, become, plastic. **plas'ti·ciz·er** *n.*

plat (plăt) *n.* Patch, plot, of ground.

Pla·ta (plah'tah), **Rio de la.** Plate River, long funnel-shaped estuary on E. side of S. Amer., between Argentina and Uruguay; scene (1939) of naval battle between German "pocket battleship" *Admiral Graf Spee*, subsequently scuttled, and three British cruisers, *Ajax, Achilles,* and *Exeter.* [Span., = "river of silver," with ref. to export of silver from the region]

plate[1] (plāt) *n.* 1. Flat thin usu. rigid sheet of metal etc. of even surface and more or less uniform thickness; this as part of mechanism etc., esp. one of the sheets of which a ship's armor and steam boilers are composed; (anat., zool., and bot.) thin flat organic structure or formation. 2. The portion of a denture that fits to the mouth and holds the teeth. 3. Smooth piece of metal etc. for engraving; impression from this, esp. as illustration of book; full-page illustration of book; bookplate. 4. Piece of metal with name or inscription for affixing to something; (baseball) home plate. 5. Stereotype or electrotype

Picking tea on a **plantation** near Hangchow in China. The use of plantations (large organized areas of tree or shrub-borne crops) was essential for economic development in agriculture.

Armor-plating reinforces the hull and deck of the U.S.S. Missouri. Armor **plate** seems to have been used first in the 12th century and gradually became more sophisticated.

*In tropical countries such as Peru (left) the height of a **plateau** above sea level may provide an area where temperate-zone agriculture is possible, despite the latitude.*

cast of page of composed movable types, from which sheets are printed. 6. Thin sheet of metal, glass, etc., coated with sensitive emulsion, for taking photographs. 7. Horizontal timber laid along top of wall to support ends of joists or rafters, or at top or bottom of a framing. 8. (collect. sing.) Table and domestic utensils of silver, gold, or other metals; silver or gold cup as prize for (orig. horse) race, such race. 9. Shallow usu. circular vessel, now usu. of earthenware or china, from which food is eaten; contents of this; similar vessel used for collection in churches etc. 10. ~ **glass**, flat glass of fine quality cast, ground, and polished in a continuous ribbon; ~ **mark** = HALL-MARK; (also) impression left on margin of engraving by edge of plate; imitation of this on mount of photograph; hence ~-**marked** (*adj.*); ~ **rack**, rack in which dining plates are kept or placed to drain after washing. **plate·ful** (plāt´fool) *n.* (pl. **-fuls**). **plate** *v.t.* (**plat·ed, plat·ing**). Cover (esp. ship) with plates of metal for protection, ornament, etc.; cover (other metal) with thin coat of silver, gold, tin, etc.; make a plate of (type) for printing.

pla·teau (plă·tō´) *n.* (pl. **-teaus, -teaux** pr. -tōz´). Elevated tract of comparatively flat or level land, tableland.

plate·let (plāt´lĭt) *n.* (also **blood** ~) Ovoid or circular body suspended in the plasma, important in blood clotting.

plat·en (plăt´en) *n.* Iron plate in printing press by which paper is pressed against inked type; corresponding part in typewriter etc.

plat·er (plā´ter) *n.* One who plates with silver etc.; one who makes or applies plates in shipbuilding; inferior race horse, competing chiefly for plates.

plat·form (plăt´fôrm) *n.* 1. Raised level surface, natural or artificial terrace; raised surface along side of line at railroad station, from which passengers enter the carriages, and upon which they alight on leaving the train. 2. Raised flooring in hall or open air from which speaker addresses audience; (fig.) political basis of party etc. program, esp. declaration of principles, long-range and immediate aims, etc. issued by repre-

*The different artificial substances all called **'plastics'** have between them made possible a whole range of new processes, among them the vacuum-sealing of food for astronauts.*

sentatives of party assembled to nominate candidates for election.

plat·ing (plā'tǐng) *n.* (esp.) Coating of gold, silver, etc.

plat·i·num (plăt'num, plăt'i-num) *n.* (chem.) Somewhat rare metallic element, white, of high density, ductile and malleable, unaffected by simple acids and fusible only at very high temperatures; symbol Pt, at. no. 78, at. wt. 195.09; ~ **black**, platinum in form of finely divided black powder; ~ **blonde**, (woman with) very light, silvery blonde hair.

plat·i·tude (plăt'ĭtōōd, -tūd) *n.* Commonplaceness; commonplace remark, esp. one solemnly delivered. **plat·i·tu·di·nous** (plătĭ-tōō'dǐnus, -tū'-) *adj.* **plat·i·tu'-di·nous·ly** *adv.*

Pla·to (plā'tō) (*c*429–347 B.C.). Greek philosopher, pupil of SOCRATES and author of dialogues (based on his teaching and on the doctrines of Pythagoras), including *Protagoras, Phaedo, Symposium,* and *Republic.*

Pla·ton·ic (platŏn'ĭk, plā-) *adj.* Of Plato or his doctrines; esp. applied to love or affection for one of the opposite sex entirely free from sensual desire (orig. used without reference to women).

Pla·to·nism (plā'tonĭzem) *n.* Philosophical system of Plato, of which central conception is that there exists a world of ideas, divine types, or forms of material objects, and that the ideas alone are real and permanent, while individual material things are but their ephemeral and imperfect imitations. **Pla·to·nist** *adj. & n.* (Follower) of Plato. **Pla·to·nis'tic** *adj.*

pla·toon (platōōn') *n.* 1. (hist.) Small infantry detachment, esp. a unit for volley firing etc.; volley fired by it; (now) subdivision of a company, a tactical unit commanded by a lieutenant and divided into three squads. 2. Group of players within a football team trained as a unit for offense or defense and sent into or taken out of the game as a single unit.

plat·ter (plăt'er) *n.* 1. Flat dish or plate from which food is served. 2. (slang) Phonograph record.

platy- (*comb. form*) Broad, flat.

plat·y·hel·minth (plătĭhĕl'-mĭnth) *n.* One of the phylum Platyhelminthes, including tapeworms and flukes; flatworm.

plat·y·pus (plăt'ĭpus, -pōōs) *n.* (pl. **-pus·es**). (also **duckbill** ~) Primitive aquatic and burrowing mammal (*Ornithorhynchus anatinus*) of Tasmania and SE. Australia, which has a bony ducklike beak and flattened tail, and lays eggs encased in shells. [Gk. *platas* broad, *pous* foot]

plat·yr·rhine (plăt'ĭrīn, -rǐn), **plat·yr·rhin·i·an** (plătĭrǐn'ēan) *adjs.* 1. (anthrop.) Having a broad nose with flat bridge. 2. (zool.) Of the Platyrrhini, a group of New World monkeys with broad flat nose. ~ *n.* Platyrrhine monkey.

plau·dit (plaw'dǐt) *n.* (usu. pl.) Round of applause; emphatic expression of approval. [shortened f. L. *plaudite* applaud, imper. of *plaudere,* customary appeal for applause by Roman actors at end of play]

plau·si·ble (plaw'zǐbel) *adj.* (of arguments etc.) Seeming reasonable or probable; (of persons) fairspoken (usu. implying deceit). **plau·si·bil'i·ty, plau'si·ble·ness** *ns.* **plau'si·bly** *adv.*

Plau·tus (plaw'tus), **Titus Maccius** (d. *c*184 B.C.). Roman comic dramatist.

play (plā) *v.* 1. Move about in lively or capricious manner, frisk, flit, flutter, pass gently; strike lightly; alternate rapidly; (of part of mechanism etc.) have free movement. 2. Allow (fish) to exhaust itself by pulling against line; direct (light *on, over,* etc.); (of light) pass (*over, along,* etc.). 3. Perform, execute (trick, prank, etc.). 4. Amuse oneself, sport, frolic; em-

*When the **platypus** feeds on the bottom of streams, its eyes and ears are closed and it locates the crustacea and insects, which are its food, by means of its sensitive muzzle.*

ploy oneself in the game of; pretend for fun; (of ground etc.) be in good etc. condition for play; contend against (person) in game; employ (person) to play in game, include in team; ~ **at**, engage in (game); (fig.) engage in (work etc.) in trivial or half-hearted way; ~ **ball**, (fig.) cooperate (with); ~ **fair, foul,** play or (fig.) act (un-)fairly; ~ **false,** deceive, betray; ~ **the game,** observe the rules of the game, play fair (freq. fig.); ~ **into the hands of,** act so as to give advantage to (opponent or partner); ~ **the market,** speculate in the stock market; ~ **on words,** pun; ~ **safe,** act with caution; ~ **up,** emphasize; ~ **with,** amuse oneself with, trifle with, treat lightly; **played out,** exhausted of energy, vitality, or usefulness. 5. Move (piece in chess etc.); take (playing card) from one's hand and lay it face upward on table in one's turn; strike (ball) in specified, esp. defensive, manner; **play one's cards well,** (fig.) make good use of opportunities; **play off,** oppose (person *against* another) esp. for one's own advantage; cause (person) to exhibit himself disadvantageously; play extra game or match to decide draw or tie; pass off as something else. 6. Perform on (musical instrument), perform (*on* instrument); perform (music *on* instrument); **play back,** reproduce (newly recorded music etc.); **play** (congregation etc.) **in, out,** play on organ etc., as they come in, go out; **play on,** make use of (person's fears, credulity, etc.). 7. Perform (drama) on stage; act (*in* drama), act (part) in drama; (fig.) act in real life the part of (*the man, truant,* etc.); **play up to,** flatter, toady. **play** *n.* 1. Brisk, light, or fitful movement; activity, operation, freedom of movement, space for this, scope for activity. 2. Amusement; playing of game; manner, style, of this; **at** ~, engaged in playing; **in** ~, not seriously; (of ball) being used in ordinary course of play; **play-off,** extra match or game to decide tie; **play on words**

Pewter platters like these were essential household equipment in the days of massive joints and puddings. Today they find a place, however, which is just decorative.

oun. 3. Dramatic piece, drama.
4. Gaming, gambling. 5. **play'-acting**, playing a part, posing; **play'actor**, actor (usu. contempt.); **play'back**, reproduction of previously recorded sound; **play'bill**, placard, announcing theatrical play; program for this; **play'boy**, man fond of pleasure and gaiety; **play'fellow**, companion in (usu. children's) play; **play'goer**, frequenter of theater; **play'ground**, area used for play, esp. at school; **play group**, group of children below school age, organized for playing etc. under supervision; **play'house**, theater (obs. exc. in title); **play'mate**, playfellow; **play'pen**, portable enclosure for keeping young child out of harm's way; **play'thing**, toy; (fig.) person, etc., treated as mere toy; **play'-wright**, dramatist.

play·er (plā´er) *n.* (esp.) Person engaged at the time, person skillful, in a game; professional baseball player etc.; actor, performer on musical instrument; ~ **piano**: see PIANO[2].

play·ful (plā´ful) *adj.* Frolicsome, sportive; humorous, jocular. **play'ful·ly** *adv.* **play'ful·ness** *n.*

play·ing (plā´ing) *n.* (esp.) ~ **card**: see CARD[2] def. 2.

plea (plē) *n.* Pleading, argument, excuse; (law) formal statement by or on behalf of defendant; (hist.) action at law; **special** ~, defendant's plea alleging new fact; (slang) **cop a** ~,

plead guilty to a lesser offense than the one alleged; hence, ~ **bargain**, seek to settle for such a plea.

plead (plēd) *v.* (**plead·ed** or **pled, plead·ing**). 1. Address court as advocate on behalf of either party; maintain (cause) in court; allege formally as plea; (fig.) allege as excuse etc.; ~ **guilty**, admit liability or guilt, ~ **not guilty**, deny it. 2. Ask earnestly *for* help etc.; ~ **with**, make earnest appeal to (person). **plead'ing** *adj.* **plead'ing·ly** *adv.* **plead'er** *n.*

plead·ing (plē´ding) *n.* (esp.) Formal (now usu. written) statement of cause of action or defense.

pleas·ant (plĕz´ant) *adj.* Agreeable to mind, feelings, or senses. **pleas'ant·ly** *adv.* **pleas'ant·ness** *n.*

pleas·ant·ry (plĕz´antrē) *n.* (pl. **-ries**). Jocularity; humorous speech, jest.

please (plēz) *v.* (**pleased, pleas·ing**). 1. Be agreeable (to); ~ **oneself**, do as one likes, take one's own way; **be pleased with**, derive pleasure from. 2. Be pleased, like; have the will or desire, think proper; (also **if you** ~) if you like (as courteous qualification to request etc.). **pleased, pleas'ing** *adjs.* **pleas'ing·ly** *adv.*

pleas·ur·a·ble (plĕzh´erabel) *adj.* Affording pleasure. **pleas'-ur·a·ble·ness** *n.* **pleas'ur·a·bly** *adv.*

pleas·ure (plĕzh´er) *n.* 1. Feeling of satisfaction; sensuous gratification. 2. Will, desire.

pleat (plēt) *n.* Fold, crease; esp., flattened fold in cloth; **accordion** ~**s**, narrow pleats resembling accordion bellows; **box** ~, double pleat; **inverted** ~, reverse form of box pleat; **knife** ~**s**, narrow overlapping pleats. **pleat** *v.t.* Fold (cloth etc.) in pleats. **pleat'er** *n.*

ple·be·ian (plebē´an) *n.* Commoner in ancient Rome; commoner. ~ *adj.* Of low birth; of the common people; coarse, base, ignoble. **ple·be'ian·ism, ple·be'-ian·ness** *ns.*

pleb·i·scite (plĕb´ĭsĭt, -sĭt) *n.* 1. (Rom. hist.) Law enacted by the commons (plebeians) voting by tribes. 2. Direct vote of all electors of community on important public question; public expression of community's opinion, with or without binding force.

plec·trum (plĕk´trum) *n.* (pl. **-tra** pr. -trᵃ, **-trums**). Small spike of ivory, quill, metal, etc., sometimes attached to a ring fitting on the finger, for plucking strings of guitar, zither, etc.; part of keyboard instrument with same function.

pled (plĕd) *v.* Past t. and past part. of PLEAD.

pledge (plĕj) *n.* 1. Thing handed

*The Seven Sisters, or **Pleiades** — most people can only see six; the seventh is just visible to the keen-sighted — are grouped in fact as well as myth, unlike many constellations.*

over to person as security for ful-fillment of contract, payment of debt, etc., and liable to forfeiture in case of failure; thing put in pawn. 2. Thing given as token of favor etc. or of something to come; drinking of a health, toast. 3. Vow, promise; **the** ∼, solemn engage-ment to abstain from intoxicants. 4. State of being pledged. **pledge** *v.t.* (**pledged, pledg·ing**). I. Deposit as security, pawn.   2. Promise solemnly; bind (oneself) by pledge. 3. Drink to the health of.

Ple·ia·des (plē′*a*dēz, plī′-). I. (Gk. myth.) Seven daughters of Atlas, turned, when they died, into a constellation. 2. (astron.) Con-spicuous constellation or cluster of stars in Taurus.

Pleis·to·cene (plī′stosēn) *adj.* & *n.* (geol.) (Of) the earlier part or system of the Quaternary period, characterized by the formation of glaciers and in which man first appeared. [Gk. *pleistos* most, *kainos* new]

ple·na·ry (plē′*n*ere, plĕn′*a*-) *adj.* Entire, absolute, unqualified; (of assembly) attended by all members. **ple′na·ri·ly** *adv.*

plen·i·po·ten·ti·ar·y (plĕnĭ-potĕn′shēĕrē, -sherē) *adj.* Invested with full power, esp. as ambassador deputed to act at discretion; (of power) absolute.   ∼ *n.*   (pl. **-ar·ies**). Person invested with full power.

plen·i·tude (plĕn′ĭtōōd, -tūd) *n.* Fullness, completeness; abun-dance.

plen·te·ous (plĕn′tē*u*s) *adj.* (chiefly poet.) Plentiful. **plen′te-·ous·ly** *adv.* **plen′te·ous·ness** *n.*

plen·ti·ful (plĕn′tĭf*u*l) *adj.* Abundant, copious. **plen′ti·ful·ly** *adv.* **plen′ti·ful·ness** *n.*

plen·ty (plĕn′tē) *n.* Abundance, as much as one could desire.   ∼ *adv.* (colloq.; with adjective fol-lowed by *enough*) Quite.

ple·num (plē′n*u*m, plĕn′*u*m) *n.* (pl. **ple·nums, ple·na** pr. plē′*n*a, plĕn′*a*). Space filled with matter; full assembly.

ple·o·nasm (plē′onăzem) *n.* (gram.) Redundancy of expression. **ple·o·nas′tic** *adj.* **ple·o·nas′ti-·cal·ly** *adv.*

ple·si·o·sau·rus (plēsēosōr′*u*s) *n.* (pl. **-sau·rus·es, -sau·ri** pr. -sōr′ī).   Member of a genus (*P*∼) of extinct marine reptiles with long neck, small head, short

*Crude versions of **pliers** have been used for many centuries. Remains have been found indicating the use of pliers by Roman carpenters, and blacksmiths who used them to remove old nails from hoofs.*

At the headquarters of Coastal Command of the R.A.F., the modern war officer receives information from many sources. He must **plot** this on huge charts to enable him to make tactical decisions.

tail, and four large paddlelike limbs. [Gk. *plesios* near, *sauros* lizard]

pleth·o·ra (plĕth´era) *n.* Overabundance, glut. **ple·thor·ic** (plethŏr´ĭk, -thăr´-, plĕth´erĭk) *adj.* **ple·thor´i·cal·ly** *adv.*

pleu·ra (ploor´a) *n.* (pl. **pleu·rae** pr. ploor´ē, **pleu·ras**). Either of two serous membranes lining thorax in mammals and enveloping lungs. **pleu´ral** *adj.*

pleu·ri·sy (ploor´ĭsē) *n.* Inflammation of the pleura, marked by pain in chest or side, fever, etc. **pleu·rit·ic** (ploŏrĭt´ĭk) *adj.*

pleu·ron (ploor´ŏn) *n.* (pl. **pleu·ra** pr. ploor´a). Either of the two side plates of the exoskeleton in arthropods.

Plex·i·glas (plĕk´sĭglăs) *n.* (trademark) Transparent acrylic plastic.

plex·us (plĕk´sus) *n.* (pl. **-us·es, -us**). Network of nerve fibers or minute blood vessels in animal body; network, complication.

pli·a·ble (plī´abel), **pli·ant** (plī´ant) *adjs.* Bending, supple; (fig.) yielding, compliant. **pli·a·bil´i·ty, pli´a·ble·ness, pli´an·cy** *ns.* **pli´a·bly, pli´ant·ly** *advs.*

pli·cate (plī´kāt, -kĭt), **pli·cat·ed** (plī´kātĭd) *adjs.* (bot., zool., geol.) folded. **pli·ca·tion** (plīkā´shon), **plic·a·ture** (plĭk´acher) *ns.* Folding; fold; folded condition.

pli·é (plēā´) *n.* (pl. **-és**). (ballet) Bending of knees while holding back straight.

pli·ers (plī´erz) *n.pl.* (also **pair of ~**) Pincers having long jaws, usu. with parallel surfaces, sometimes toothed, for bending wire, holding small objects, etc.

plight[1] (plīt) *v.t.* (literary) Pledge (troth, faith, etc., esp. in past part.); engage *oneself* (*to* person).

plight[2] (plīt) *n.* Condition, state (usu. unhappy).

plinth (plĭnth) *n.* Lower square member of base of column; projecting part of wall (or piece of furniture) immediately above ground.

Plin·y (plĭn´ē). **~ the Elder** (Gaius Plinius Secundus, *c*23–79 A.D.), Roman author of *Natural History*, who perished in the eruption of Vesuvius; **~ the Younger**, his nephew (Gaius Plinius Caecilius Secundus, *c*61–*c*112 A.D.), famous for his published *Letters.*

Pli·o·cene (plī´osēn) *adj.* & *n.* (geol.) (Of) the latest epoch or system of the Tertiary period. [Gk. *pleion* more, *kainos* new]

P.L.O. *abbrev.* Palestine Liberation Organization.

plod (plŏd) *v.* (**plod·ded, plod·ding**). Walk laboriously, trudge; drudge, slave (*at*); make (one's way) laboriously. **~** *n.* Laborious walk or work. **plod´der** *n.* **plod´ding** *adj.* **plod´ding·ly** *adv.*

plo·sive (plō´sĭv) *adj.* & *n.* (phonet.) Explosive (consonant).

plot (plŏt) *n.* 1. Piece of ground, usu. small. 2. Plan, story, of play, poem, novel, etc. 3. Conspiracy; sly plan. **~** *v.t.* (**plot·ted, plot·ting**). Make plan or map of (existing object, place or thing to be laid out, constructed, etc.); mark the position of values of a variable on a graph or the like; plan, contrive (evil object, or abs.). **plot´less** *adj.* **plot´less·ness, plot´ter** *ns.*

Plo·ti·nus (plōtī´nus) (*c*205–69 A.D.). Egyptian-born Roman founder of NEOPLATONISM. His philosophical teachings (*Enneads*, in Greek) were published posthumously.

plov·er (pluv´er, plō´ver) *n.* (pl. **plov·ers**, collect. **plov·er**). Any of several gregarious birds of family Charadriidae, found in open country, esp. by seashores, and nesting on the ground; **green ~**, lapwing.

plow, Brit. **plough** (plow) *ns.* Implement for cutting furrows in soil and turning it up, consisting

*Two types of **plow**, one an antique version drawn by a cable-attachment to a steam-engine (right) and the other by a modern tractor (lower right), demonstrate the progressive mechanization of farming.*

essentially of a vertical blade that cuts the furrow from the unplowed ground, a **plow'share** that cuts the furrow horizontally underneath, and a board that turns it over, drawn by horses etc. (or now, by tractor), and guided by **plow'man**; plowed land; instrument resembling plow, for cutting up blocks of ice, clearing away snow, etc.; **plow'boy**, boy who leads plow horses etc.; **plow'land**, (hist.) as much land as could be plowed by a team of 8 oxen in a year, unit of assessment in N. and E. counties of England after Norman Conquest; arable land; **plowman** and **plowshare**: see above; ~ **tail**, rear of plow. **plow** *v.* 1. Turn up (earth, or abs.) with plow, esp. before sowing; rout *out*, cast *up*, thrust *down* (roots, weeds) with plow; furrow, scratch (surface) as with plow; produce (furrow, line) thus; ~ **back**, plow (grass, clover, etc.) into soil to enrich it; (fig.) reinvest (profits) in business etc. 2. Advance laboriously (*through* snow, book, etc.); (of ship etc.) cleave (surface of water, its way, etc.). **plow'a·ble** *adj.*

ploy (ploi) *n.* Stratagem, maneuver to gain advantage.

pluck (plŭk) *n.* 1. Plucking, twitch. 2. Heart, liver, and lungs, of beast as food. 3. Courage, spirit. ~ *v.* 1. Pull off, pick (flower, feather, hair); pull at, twitch; tug, snatch, *at*; strip (bird) of feathers; (archaic) pull, drag, snatch (*away*, *off*, etc.). 2. (slang) Plunder, swindle. 3. ~ **up spirits**, take courage. **pluck'y** *adj.* (**pluck·i·er**,

pluck·i·est). Brave, spirited. **pluck'i·ly** *adv.* **pluck'i·ness** *n.*

plug (plŭg) *n.* 1. Piece of wood etc. fitting tightly into hole, used to fill gap or act as wedge etc.; freq. in technical use, e.g. pin etc. for making electrical contacts, spark plug (see SPARK[1]); natural or morbid concretion acting thus; kind of stopper for vessel or pipe; fireplug, hydrant. 2. Tobacco pressed into cake or stick; piece of this cut off for chewing. 3. (slang) Worn-out horse. ~ *v.* (**plugged, plug·ging**). Stop (*up*) with plug; (slang) shoot; (slang) strike with fist; (colloq.)

*The golden **plover** mostly breeds near the Arctic circle but migrates to lower latitudes at the end of summer, to spend winter as far south as the Mediterranean or on the shores of the Atlantic.*

plod (*away at* work etc.); (colloq.) popularize (song etc.) by frequent repetition or through publicity.

plum (plŭm) *n.* 1. Any of several small trees (genus *Prunus*) bearing roundish fleshy fruit with sweet pulp and flattish pointed stone. 2. Dried grape or raisin as used for puddings, cakes, etc. 3. (fig.) Good thing; best of a collection; prize in life. 4. ~ **cake**, cake containing raisins, currants, etc.; ~ **pudding**, boiled or steamed pudding containing raisins, currants, eggs, spices, etc., eaten esp. at Christmas.

plum·age (ploō'mĭj) *n.* Bird's feathers.

plumb (plŭm) *n.* Ball of lead, esp. that attached to plumb line; ~ **line**, string with weight attached for testing perpendicularity of wall, etc.; sounding lead, plummet; **out**

*The date when **plums** were introduced to the U.S.A. is uncertain, but it is thought they were introduced by the earliest colonists. There are now myriad varieties grown.*

*Wild species of **plum** are native to Europe, Asia, and North America. Long domestication and selection have resulted in a large range of varieties.*

~, not vertical; ~ **rule,** mason's mb line attached to board. **umb** *adj.* Vertical; level, true; g.) downright, sheer. ~ *adv.* rtically; (fig.) exactly; (colloq.) ite, utterly. ~ *v.* 1. Sound a), measure (depth), with plum-t; make vertical. 2. Work as mber. 3. Examine in order to derstand fully.

plumb·er (plŭm′er) *n.* Mechan-who fits and repairs pipes, terns, tanks, etc.; ~**'s friend** PLUNGER def. 3.

plumb·ing (plŭm′ing) *n.* Sys-n of water and drainage pipes in uilding etc.

plum·bism (plŭm′bizem) *n.* isoning caused by absorption of d into the system.

plume (plōōm) *n.* Feather, esp. ge one used for ornament; athery ornament in hat, hair, etc.; ol.) featherlike part or forma-n. ~ *v.t.* (**plumed, plum·ing**). rnish with plume(s); (of bird) een (feathers). **plume′like** *adj.*

plum·met (plŭm′it) *n.* (Weight ached to) plumb line; sounding d; weight attached to fishing line

to keep float upright. ~ *v.i.* Plunge.

plu·mose (plōō′mōs) *adj.* Feathered; featherlike.

plump¹ (plŭmp) *adj.* (esp. of persons or parts of body) Full, rounded, fleshy, filled out. ~ *v.* Make or become plump, fatten *up,* swell *out.* **plump′ly** *adv.* **plump′-ness** *n.*

plump² (plŭmp) *v.* Drop or plunge with abrupt descent; vote *for* (1 candidate alone, when one might vote for 2); ~ **for,** vote for, choose (something). **plump** *n.* Abrupt plunge, heavy fall. ~ *adv.* With sudden or heavy fall; flatly, bluntly. ~ *adj.* Direct, unquali-fied.

plu·mule (plōōm′ūl) *n.* Rudi-mentary stem of embryo plant; little feather of down. **plu·mu·lar** (plōōm′yuler), **plu·mu·la·ceous** (plōōmyulā′shus) *adjs.*

plun·der (plŭn′der) *v.t.* Rob (place, person) forcibly of goods, esp. as in war; rob systematically; steal, embezzle. ~ *n.* Violent or dishonest acquisition of property; property so acquired; profit, gain. **plun′der·er** *n.*

plun·der·age (plŭn′derij) *n.* Plundering, esp. embezzling of goods on shipboard; spoil thus obtained.

plunge (plŭnj) *v.* (**plunged, plung·ing**). Thrust violently (*into* liquid, cavity, etc.); throw oneself, dive, (*into*); enter impetuously; descend abruptly and steeply; (of horse) throw itself violently for-ward; (of ship) pitch; (slang) gamble deeply, run into debt. ~ *n.* Plunging, dive; place for plunging; (fig.) critical step.

plung·er (plŭn′jer) *n.* (esp.) 1. Part of mechanism that works with plunging motion. 2. (slang) Gambler, speculator. 3. Rubber cup on handle for removal of pipe blockages by suction.

plu·per·fect (plōōper′fikt) *adj.* & *n.* (gram.) (Tense now *past perfect*) expressing action com-pleted prior to some past point of time specified or implied (as *I had seen*). [L. *plus quam perfectum* more than perfect]

plu·ral (ploor′al) *adj.* (gram.) Denoting more than one (or, in languages with dual form, more than two); more than one in number. **plu′ral·ly** *adv.* **plural** *n.* Plural form.

plu·ral·ism (ploor′alizem) *n.* 1. (hist.) Holding of more than one office, esp. benefice, at a time. 2. (philos.) System that recognizes more than one ultimate principle. 3. Form of society in which members of minority groups main-tain independent traditions. **plu′-ral·ist** *n.* **plu·ral·is·tic** *adj.*

plu·ral·i·ty (ploorăl′itē) *n.* (pl. **-ties**). State of being plural; large number, multitude; greater number of votes cast for one candidate than for any other but less than a majority.

plu·ral·ize (ploor'*a*līz) *v.* (**-ized, -iz·ing**). Make plural, express in the plural.

plus (plŭs) *prep.* With the addition of (symbol +); (colloq.) with, and also. ~ *adj.* Extra (indicating addition); positive; (after number etc.) more than; ~ **fours**, long wide knickers, suit with these, freq. associated with golf, so named because, to produce the overhang, the length was orig. increased by 4 in. ~ *n.* Plus sign or quantity; (colloq.) advantage. [L., = "more"]

plush (plŭsh) *n.* Cloth of silk, cotton, etc., resembling velvet but with longer and softer pile. ~ *adj.* Made of plush; luxurious. **plush'ly** *adv.* **plush'ness** *n.* **plush'y** *adj.* (**plush·i·er, plush·i·est**). **plush'·i·ness** *n.*

Plu·tarch (ploo'tärk) (*c*46–120 A.D.). Greek biographer and moral philosopher, author of *The Parallel Lives* of eminent Greeks and Romans.

plu·tar·chy (ploo'tärkē) *n.* Plutocracy.

Plu·to (ploo'tō). 1. (Gk. and Rom. myth.) God of the infernal regions, brother of ZEUS and Poseidon. 2. (astron.) Planet, remoter than Neptune, discovered in 1930.

plu·toc·ra·cy (plootŏk'rasē) *n.* (pl. **-cies**). Rule of the wealthy; ruling class of wealthy persons. **plu·to·crat** (ploo'tokrăt) *n.* **plu·to·crat'ic, plu·to·crat'i·cal** *adjs.*

Plu·to·ni·an (plootō'nēan), **Plu·ton·ic** (plootŏn'ĭk) *adjs.* Of PLUTO or his kingdom; infernal.

plu·to·ni·um (plootō'nēum) *n.* (chem.) Transuranic element, not found in nature, formed from uramium in a nuclear reactor, used as a nuclear explosive; symbol Pu, at. no. 94, principal isotope at. wt. 239. [named after planet PLUTO]

plu·vi·al (ploo'vēal) *adj.* Of rain, rainy; (geol.) caused by rain. ~ *n.* (eccles. hist.) Long cloak as ceremonial vestment.

plu·vi·om·e·ter (ploovēŏm'ĭter) *n.* Rain gauge. **plu·vi·o·met·ric** (ploovēomět'rĭk), **plu·vi·o·met'·ri·cal** *adjs.*

ply[1] (plī) *n.* Fold, thickness, layer, of cloth, etc.; strand of rope, etc.; **two-, three-**, etc. ~, having two etc. thicknesses or strands; **ply'wood**, strong thin board made by gluing or cementing layers of wood together with grains crosswise.

ply[2] (plī) *v.* (**plied, ply·ing**). 1. Use, wield vigorously (tool, weapon); work at (business, task); supply (person etc.) persistently *with* (food etc.); assail vigorously

Plymouth Rock, *traditionally regarded as the landing site of the Pilgrims on the Mayflower. The original rock has been covered by the granite portico. Plymouth's historical past makes it popular with tourists.*

Monument to the Pilgrim Fathers at **Plymouth,** *Massachusetts. The town was founded in 1620 and named by the original settlers after the port of departure in England.*

(*with* questions, arguments). 2. Work to windward (naut.); (of vessel, its master, etc.) go to and fro *betwèen* (places); (of porter, cab driver, etc.) attend regularly for custom (*at* place).

Plym·outh (plĭm'uth). Town in SE. Massachusetts on ~ **Bay**, landing place of Pilgrims from the *Mayflower* (1620); ~ **Colony**, site of settlement in SE. Massachusetts; founded by the Pilgrims, 1620; became part of the Massachusetts Bay Colony, 1691; ~ **Rock**, (1) granite boulder at Plymouth on which Pilgrims are supposed to have stepped from *Mayflower*; (2) domestic fowl of medium size and usu. with gray plumage barred with blackish stripes and yellow beak, legs, and feet.

Pm *symbol.* Promethium.

P.M. *abbrev.* Prime Minister; Provost Marshal; Police Magistrate; *post meridiem.*

p.m. *abbrev. Post meridiem*; (L., = after noon).

pneu·mat·ic (noomăt'ĭk, nyoo-) *adj.* Of, acting by means of, wind or (compressed) air; containing, connected with, air cavities, esp. in bones of birds; ~ **tire**, one inflated with air; ~ **tube**, one for pneumatic delivery (of mail etc.).

pneu·mat'i·cal·ly *adv.* **pneu·mat'ics** *n.* (usu. considered sing. Science of mechanical properties c air or other gases.

pneu·mo·coc·cus (noomokŏk' us, nū-) *n.* (pl. **-coc·ci** pr -kŏk'sī). Infective microorganism (*Diplococcus pneumoniae*) in pneu monia.

pneu·mo·co·ni·o·sis (noomokō nēō'sĭs, nū-) *n.* Any of a group of chronic lung diseases (e.g. sili cosis) caused by inhaling abrasiv dust.

pneu·mo·gas·tric (noomogăs trĭk, nū-) *adj.* Of lungs and stomach; ~ **nerve**, vagus nerve.

pneu·mo·nia (n ōomōn'ya nyoo-) *n.* Acute inflammation o the lungs, converting their nor mally spongy tissue into a soli mass, caused esp. by infection wit pneumococcus. **pneu·mon·i**

*Compressed air has been used in many ways to replace human effort. One of these is the **pneumatic hammer,** by which powerful blows can be delivered in very quick succession, so that the work can be done better and faster than by hand.*

pock·et (pŏk´ĭt) *n.* 1. Small bag inserted in garment for carrying small articles, as money, etc.; (fig.) pecuniary resources; **put one's pride in one's** ~, humble oneself; **in** ~, having money available; having (so much) as profit; **out of** ~, losing money (by some transaction); **out-of-** ~ **expenses**, actual outlay incurred. 2. Pouch at each corner and on each side of billiard table into which balls are driven; pouch-like compartment in bag, suitcase, etc.; cavity in earth filled with gold or other ore; cavity in rock esp. (geol.) filled with foreign matter; AIR pocket; isolated area occupied by the enemy, forces occupying this. 3. (attrib.) Of suitable size or shape for carrying in pocket; small, diminutive; ~ **battleship**, (esp. German) ship armored and equipped like, but smaller than, a battleship; **pock´etbook**, notebook, booklike case for papers, currency, etc., carried in pocket; handbag; **pocket borough**: see BOROUGH; **pocket handkerchief**, one carried in pocket; **pock´etknife**, knife with folding blade(s) to be carried in pocket; **pocket money**, money for occasional expenses, esp. that allowed to children; **pocket veto**, indirect veto of bill by retention in hands of executive without signature until adjournment of legislature. **pock·et·ful** (pŏk´ĭtfŏol) *n.* (pl. **-fuls**). **pocket** *v.t.* Put into one's pocket; confine as in pocket; hem in (competitor) in race; appropriate, usu. dishonestly; (billiards) drive (ball) into pocket. **pock´et·ed** *adj.* Fitted with, enclosed in, pocket(s).

pod¹ (pŏd) *n.* Socket of brace and bit.

pod² (pŏd) *n.* Long seed vessel, esp. of leguminous plants; cocoon of silkworm; case of locust's eggs; narrow-necked eel net. ~ *v.* (**pod·ded, pod·ding**). Form pods; shell (peas etc.). **pod´like** *adj.*

pod³ (pŏd) *n.* Small herd of seals or whales. ~ *v.t.* (**pod·ded, pod·ding**). Drive (seals etc.) into pod or bunch for purpose of clubbing them.

po·di·um (pō´dēum) *n.* (pl. **-di·ums, -di·a** pr. -dēa). Continuous projecting base or pedestal; raised platform around arena of amphitheater; continuous bench around room.

pod·zol (pŏd´zŏl), **pod·sol** (pŏd´sŏl) *ns.* Stratified soil in which various materials have been leached from the upper layers and redeposited in a well-defined lower

compressed air inlet

inlet valve

ontrol lever

outer ompartment

diaphragm valve

exhaust air compartment

piston

inner compartment

piston moving upwards

piston delivering the blow

nitial position

tool

...oomŏn´ĭk, nyoo-) *adj.*

Po *symbol.* Polonium.

P.O. *abbrev.* Petty Officer; ostal (money) order; post office.

poach¹ (pōch) *v.t.* Cook (egg) ithout its shell by boiling in water r steaming; cook (fish, fruit, etc.) y simmering.

poach² (pōch) *v.* 1. Trample, ...t *up* (turf etc.) with hoofs; (of ...nd) become sodden by being ...ampled. 2. Encroach, trespass (*on* ...erson's *preserves* (freq. fig.), lands, ...c.), esp. in order to steal fish or ...ame; trespass on (land etc.); ...apture (game, fish) by illicit or ...nsportsmanlike methods; (in ...arious games) enter on partner's ...ortion of field or court, depriving ...im of some of his share in the ...ame. **poach´er** *n.*

Po·ca·hon·tas (pōkahŏn´tas) ...594–1617). Daughter of Pow-

hatan, an Indian chief in Virginia; acc. to the story of Capt. John Smith, she rescued him from death at the hands of her father, who had imprisoned him; she was seized as a hostage, 1612, and married John Rolfe; was taken to England, 1616, and died there.

po·chard (pō´cherd, -kerd) *n.* (pl. **-chards**, collect. **-chard**). Diving duck, esp. *Aythya ferina*, of Europe, N. Asia, and N. Amer., male of which has bright reddish-brown head and neck.

pock (pŏk) *n.* Eruptive spot esp. in smallpox; pockmark.

stratum. **pod·zol·ize** (pŏd´zolĭz) v. (**-ized, -iz·ing**). Make into, become, podzol. **pod·zol·i·za·tion** (pŏdzolĭzā´shon) n.

POE abbrev. Port of embarkation; port of entry.

Poe (pō), **Edgar Allan** (1809–1849). Amer. short-story writer, poet, and journalist; best known for the poems "The Raven," "Annabel Lee," and "The Bells" and the tales "The Fall of the House of Usher," "The Gold Bug," and "The Murders in the Rue Morgue."

po·em (pō´em) n. Metrical composition, esp. of elevated character; elevated composition in prose or verse; (fig.) something (other than a composition of words) akin or compared to a poem.

po·e·sy (pō´ĭsē, -zē) n. (pl. **-sies**). (archaic) Art, composition, of poetry; poems collectively.

po·et (pō´ĭt) n. (fem. **po·et·ess** pr. pō´ĭtĭs). Writer of poems; writer in verse, esp. one possessing high powers of imagination, expression, etc.; ~ **laureate**: see LAUREATE; **Poets' Corner**, part of south transept of Westminster Abbey, London, containing graves or monuments of several great poets. **po·et·as·ter** (pō´ĭtăster) n. Inferior poet.

po·et·ic (pōĕt´ĭk) adj. Of, proper to, poets or poetry; having the good qualities of poetry; ~ **justice, license**: see JUSTICE, LICENSE. **po·et´i·cal** adj. Of, proper to, poets or poetry; written in verse. **po·et´i·cal·ly** adv. **po·et´ics** n. Part of literary criticism dealing with poetry; treatise on poetry, esp. (**P~**) that of Aristotle.

po·et·ry (pō´ĭtrē) n. Art, work, of the poet; expression of beautiful or elevated thought, imagination, or feeling in appropriate language and usu. in metrical form; poems; quality (in anything) that calls for poetical expression; **prose ~**, prose having all the qualities of poetry except meter.

po·go (pō´gō) **stick.** Toy consisting of a stick with handles and a pair of pedals attached to a spring, used for jumping about.

po·grom (pogrŏm´, -grŭm´, pō-) n. Organized massacre, orig. that of Jews in Russia (1905–6). [Russ. = "destruction" (grom thunder)]

poign·ant (poin´yant, poin´ant) adj. Sharp, pungent, in taste or smell; painfully sharp; pleasantly piquant. **poign´an·cy** n. **poign´ant·ly** adv.

poin·ci·an·a (poinsēā´na) n. Tropical tree (Poinciana pulcher-

rima) with bright red flowers.

poin·set·ti·a (poinsĕt´ēa, -sĕt´a) n. Plant of Mexican species of Euphorbia, E. pulcherrima, with large scarlet bracts surrounding small yellowish flowers. [f. J.R. Poinsett, Amer. minister to Mexico, who discovered it]

point (point) n. 1. Small dot on a surface. 2. Stop or punctuation mark; dot, small stroke, used in Semitic script to indicate vowels or distinguish consonants; dot separating integral from fractional parts in decimals, as two ~ five (2.5). 3. Single item, detail, particular; thing under discussion;

Intensive selection has developed the **pointer** *from its primitive ancestor into a highly specialized hunting dog, bred to indicate the position of the quarry in silence.*

beside the ~, irrelevant(ly); ma[l] a ~, establish proposition, pro[ ] contention; **make a ~ of**, treat essential, insist on; **to the [ ]** relevant(ly). 4. Distinctive tra[ ] characteristic, as **good, bad,** [ ] **strong ~**, thing one is good [ ] 5. Salient feature of story, joke, et[c] pungency, effectiveness. 6. U[ ] in appraising qualities of exhibit show or achievements of competit[ ] in contest; unit (of varying valu[e] in quoting price of stocks etc.; u[ ] of value in rationing; **give ~s t[ ]** allow (opponent) to count so ma[ny] points at starting, (fig.) be superi[ ] to; **win on ~s**, (boxing) win [ ] securing more points in a bout, n[ ] by knockout. 7. (print.) Unit measurement for type bodies, U.S. and Britain 0.0138 in. ($\frac{1}{72}$ i[n] $\frac{1}{12}$ of a pica). 8. (geom.) Th[ ] which has position but not magn[ ]

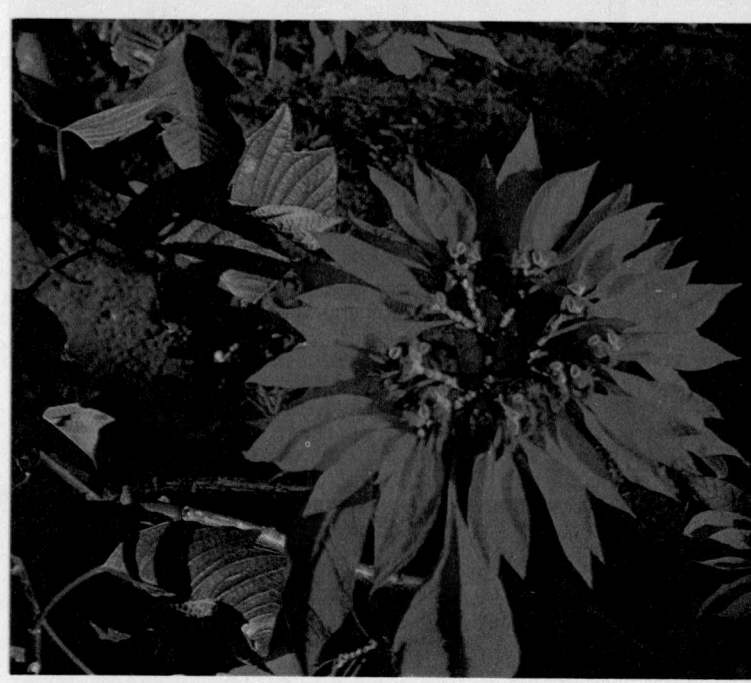

The vivid **poinsettia** *is a tropical and sub-tropical plant which flowers at the end of summer. Although hardy in those regions, it needs particular care when grown in cooler climates.*

ude, as the intersection of two lines. 9. Precise place or spot, as ~ *of contact.* 10. (hunting) Spot to which straight run is made, such run. 11. Stage, degree, in progress or increase, esp. of temperature, as **boiling ~, freezing ~**. 12. Precise moment for action etc.; exact moment (of death etc.). 13. (mus.) Important phrase or subject, esp. in contrapuntal music. 14. Sharp end of tool, weapon, pin, pen, etc.; sharp-pointed tool, e.g. etching needle; (elect.) contact, terminal; socket; (also ~ **lace**) lace made wholly with needle. 15. Tip; promontory, esp. in names, as *Montauk P~*; (pl.) extremities of a horse or dog; (pl., of Siamese cat) colored ears, feet, tail, and face; (ballet, usu. pl.) tips of toes; (mil.) small leading party of advance guard. 16. Tine of deer's horn. 17. Tapering movable rail by which train is directed from one line to another. 18. Tapered division on backgammon board. 19. (hist.) Tagged lace for lacing bodice, attaching hose to doublet, etc. 20. (naut.) Short piece of cord at lower edge of sail for tying up a reef. 21. Horizontal direction on compass; corresponding point of horizon, direction. 22. (of dog) Act of pointing. 23. **at all ~s**, in every part; **in ~ of fact**, as a matter of fact; **on the point of**, on the verge of (action, *doing*); ~ **of honor**, matter regarded as vitally affecting one's honor. **point** *v.* 1. Sharpen (pencil etc.); furnish with point; give point to (words, actions). 2. Insert points in Semitic script; mark ((Psalms etc.) for chanting, by means of points. 3. Fill in joints of (masonry etc.) with mortar etc.; prick *in* (manure), turn *over* (soil), with point of spade. 4. Direct attention *to, at,* by or as by extending finger; (of dog) indicate presence of (game) by standing rigidly, looking toward it; direct (finger, weapon, etc., *at*); direct attention of (person *to*); aim *at*, tend toward; ~ **out**, indicate, show.

point-blank (point'blăngk') *adj.* & *adv.* With aim or weapon level; at short range; (fig.) direct(ly). [prob. f. *blank* white spot in center of target]

point·ed (poin'tĭd) *adj.* Having, sharpened to, a point; (of remark, etc.) having point, penetrating, cutting; emphasized, made evident; (of Semitic script) having the vowels marked. **point'ed·ly** *adv.* **point'-ed·ness** *n.*

point·er (poin'ter) *n.* (esp.) 1. Index hand of clock, balance, etc. 2. Rod used for pointing to words etc. on blackboard, map, etc. 3. Dog that on scenting game stands rigidly, with muzzle stretched toward it and usu. one foot raised. 4. (pl.) Two stars in Great Bear,

straight line through which points nearly to polestar.

poin·til·lé (pwăṅtēyā') *adj.* 1. (of bookbinding) Decorated with gilt dots. 2. (of picture) Painted with numerous small spots of two or more pure colors that at a distance produce the effect of a mixed color, hence **Poin·til·lism** (pwăn'tĭlĭzem) *n.* **poin'til·list** *n.* Painter using technique of Pointillism.

point·ing (poin'tĭng) *n.* (esp.) 1. (Insertion of) points in Semitic script, Psalms, etc. 2. (Insertion of) facing in joints of masonry etc.

point·less (point'lĭs) *adj.* Without a point, blunt; without point, meaningless; not having scored a point. **point'less·ly** *adv.* **point'-less·ness** *n.*

poise (poiz) *v.* (**poised, pois·ing**). Balance; hold suspended or supported; carry (one's head etc.) in specified way; be balanced; hover in air etc. ~ *n.* Balance, equilibrium; state of indecision, suspense; carriage (of head etc.); ease of manner, grace, assurance.

poi·son (poi'zon) *n.* Substance that when introduced into or absorbed by a living organism destroys life or injures health, esp. (pop.) one that rapidly destroys life when taken even in small quantity; (slang) any alcoholic drink; (fig.) baneful principle, doctrine, etc.; ~ **gas**: see GAS; ~ **ivy**, N. Amer. trailing or climbing vine or shrub (*Rhus radicans*), having trifoliate leaves and causing skin rash when touched; ~ **oak**,

The shrub **poison ivy** is native to North America. The normal reaction to contact with poison ivy is the development of a skin rash, or severe dermatitis.

shrub (*Rhus Toxicodendron*) of SE. U.S., similar in appearance and effects to poison ivy; ~ **pen**, anonymous writer of libelous or scurrilous letters; ~ **sumac**, shrub (*Rhus vernix*) of E. U.S. swampy areas, having compound leaves and greenish-white berries and causing severe skin rash on contact. **poi·son·ous** (poi'zonus) *adj.* **poi'son-**

'Sunday Afternoon on the Island of Grande Jatte', a typical work by the **pointillist** *Georges Seurat. He tried to develop impressionism into a scientific art according to color analysis.*

ous·ly *adv.* **poison** *v.t.* Administer poison to; kill, injure, thus; produce morbid effects in (blood etc.); infect (air, water, etc.), smear (weapon) with poison; corrupt, pervert (person, mind); destroy, spoil (pleasure etc.); render (land etc.) foul and unfit for its purpose by noxious applications, etc. **poi'-son·er, poi'son·ing** *ns.*

Poi·tou (pwahtoō'). Former province of W. central France and scene of many battles; Visigoths defeated by Franks, 507; Saracens defeated by Charles Martel, 732; it was occupied by England and France alternately 12th–14th c.; scene of peasant insurrections against French Revolutionary government, 18th c.

poke[1] (pōk) *n.* Bag, sack (now dial. exc. in **buy a pig in a ~**: see PIG).

poke[2] (pōk) *v.* (**poked, pok·ing**). Thrust, push (thing *in*, *up*, *down*, etc.) with hand, arm, point of stick, etc.; stir (fire) with poker; produce (hole etc. *in*) by poking; make thrusts with stick, etc. (*at* etc.); thrust forward, esp. obtrusively; pry (*into*); **~ about**, look here and there; busy oneself in a desultory way; **~ along**, proceed in a desultory manner; **~ fun at**, ridicule. **poke** *n.* 1. Poking; thrust, nudge. 2. Device fastened on cattle etc., to prevent their breaking through fences.

pok·er[1] (pō'ker) *n.* Stiff metal rod with handle, for poking fire.

pok·er[2] (pō'ker) *n.* Card game for two or more players, each of whom receives five or more cards, who bet on the value of their hands, the winner being the one who holds the strongest hand or who succeeds in bluffing the others into throwing in their hands; **~ face**, (person with) face that does not reveal thoughts or feelings.

poke·weed (pōk'wēd) *n.* Tall herb (*Phylotacca americana*) of N. Amer., having purple berries yielding emetic and cathartic.

pok·y, pok·ey (pō'kē) *adjs.* (**pok·i·er, pok·i·est**). 1. (of place, room etc.) Confined, mean, shabby. 2. (of persons) Annoyingly slow.

Po·land (pō'land). Country of NE. Europe, formerly a kingdom, that was divided by partitions of 1772, 1793, and 1795 among Prussia, Russia, and Austria; reconstituted by Napoleon, but repartitioned at the Congress of Vienna (1815); recognized as an independent republic by treaties of Versailles (1919) and Riga (1921);

invaded and overrun by German and later by Russian armies, 1939, and again recognized as an independent republic in 1945; capital, Warsaw.

Po·land Chi·na (pōl'and chī'na). (One of) an American breed of large black-and-white pigs.

po·lar (pō'ler) *adj.* 1. Of, near, either pole of the Earth or of the celestial sphere; **~ bear**, white bear (*Thalarctos maritimus*); **~ circle**, Arctic or Antarctic Circle, at distance of 23° 28' from the poles; **~ distance**, angular distance of point on sphere from nearer pole. 2. Having polarity, having associated positive and negative poles (either electrical or magnetic); (of forces) acting in 2 opposite directions; (of molecules) sym-

metrically arranged in definite directions. 3. (geom.) Relating to a pole. 4. (zool.) Of poles of nerve cell, ovum, etc. 5. (fig.) Analogous to pole of Earth or to polestar; directly opposite in character. **polar** *n.* (geom.) Curve related in particular way to given curve and fixed point called pole; in conic sections, straight line joining points at which tangents from fixed point touch curve.

po·lar·im·e·ter (pōlerĭm'īter) *n.* Instrument for measuring polarized light or degree of polarization. **po·lar·im·e·try** (pōlarĭm'ītrē) *n.* Measurement of polarization.

Po·lar·is (pōlăr'ĭs, -ăr'ĭs) *n.* 1 (astron.) Polestar of North Star; see POLE[2]. 2. A two-stage, solid-propellant intermediate range ballistic missile developed by the

*The intelligent and playful **polecat** is found in varying forms all over Europe and western and northern Asia, living either alone or in temporary family groups of mother and young. Its greatest enemy is man.*

U.S. navy, that can be fired from submerged submarines as well as surface vessels.

po·lar·i·ty (pōlăr′ĭtē, po-) *n.* Tendency of magnetized bar etc. to point with its extremities to magnetic poles of Earth; tendency of a body to place its mathematical axis in particular direction; possession of two poles having contrary qualities; electrical condition of body as positive or negative; (fig.) direction (of thought, feeling, etc.) toward a single point.

po·lar·ize (pō′lerīz) *v.* (**-ized, -iz·ing**). 1. Restrict vibrations of transverse waves, esp. light) so that they have different amplitudes in different directions. 2. Give polarity to. 3. Divide into two groups at opposite extremes of opinion etc. **po·lar·i·za·tion** pōlerĭzā′shon), **po·lar·iz·er** *ns.*

Po·lar·oid (pō′leroid) *n.* (trademark) Thin, transparent, filmlike plastic capable of polarizing light, thereby reducing glare; used in photography, optical devices, etc.

pol·der (pōl′der) *n.* Piece of low-lying land reclaimed from sea or river in Netherlands.

Pole (pōl) *n.* Native or inhabitant of Poland.

pole[1] (pōl) *n.* 1. Long slender rounded piece of wood or metal, esp. as support for tent, telegraph wires, etc., to propel punt etc.; wooden shaft fitted to carriage of vehicle and attached to yokes or collars of horses etc.; ~ **position**, inside track at start of race; ~ **vault**, jump etc. with help of pole held in hands. 2. (as measure) Rod,

perch, 5½ yds.; (also **square** ~) 30¼ sq. yds. **pole** *v.t.* (**poled, pol·ing**). Furnish with poles; push, move, with pole.

pole[2] (pōl) *n.* 1. Either of the 2 points (**north** and **south** ~) in celestial sphere about which the stars appear to revolve; N. and S. extremities of Earth's axis; **pole′-star**, star of Ursa Minor, now about 1¼° distant from north pole of the heavens; Polaris or North Star. 2. (geom.) Each of two points of a circle of the sphere in which axis of that circle cuts surface of sphere; fixed point to which others are referred. 3. Each of two opposite points on surface of magnet at which magnetic forces are manifested; each of two terminal points (POSITIVE and NEGATIVE) of electric cell, battery, etc. 4. (biol.) Extremity of main axis of any spherical or oval organ. 5. (fig.) Each of two opposed principles etc., hence ~s **apart**, as far apart or different as it is possible to be.

pole·ax, pole·axe (pōl′ăks) *ns.* (pl. **-ax·es**). Battle ax; ax formerly used in naval warfare as weapon and for cutting ropes etc.; halbert; butcher's ax with hammer at back. ~ *v.t.* (**-axed, -ax·ing**). Slaughter (beast etc.) with poleax.

pole·cat (pōl′kăt) *n.* (pl. **-cats**, collect. **-cat**). Small dark brown fetid carnivorous European mammal of weasel family, esp.

Mustela putorius; skunk.

po·lem·ic (polĕm′ĭk) *adj.* Controversial, disputatious. ~ *n.* Controversial discussion; (pl.) practice of this, esp. in theology; (sing.) controversialist. **po·lem′i·cal** *adj. & n.* **po·lem′i·cal·ly** *adv.*

po·len·ta (pōlĕn′ta) *n.* Italian dish of milk thickened with corn, barley, etc.

pole·star (pōl′star′): see POLE[2].

po·lice (polēs′) *n.* Civil administration, public order; department of government concerned with this; civil force responsible for maintain-

*The north **pole** lies in a waste of water: it is only possible for its site to be marked because the upper layers of the Arctic Ocean are frozen solid, forming a false 'land'.*

The role of **police** is to maintain law and order and they may be called to help where there has been an accident, even if there are no suspicious factors (1). Some like those in Samoa (2), are armed and have conspicuous uniforms, while men who control traffic in places like Hong Kong (3) must have shelter.

ing public order; (collect.) members of this; any body officially employed to keep order, enforce regulations, etc.; ~ **dog**, dog employed by police to track criminals, etc.; **police'man** (pl. **-men**), **police'woman** (pl. **-women**), member of police force; **police officer**, policeman, policewoman; **police state**, state regulated by means of a national police having secret supervision and control of the citizens' activities; **police station**, office of local police force. **police** *v.t.* (**-liced**, **-lic·ing**). Control (country etc.) by means of police; furnish with police; (fig.) administer, control; ~ (**up**), clean (military barracks, camp, etc.).

pol·i·cy[1] (pŏl'ĭsē) *n.* (pl. **-cies**). Political sagacity; statecraft; prudent conduct, sagacity; craftiness; course of action adopted by government, party, etc.

pol·i·cy[2] (pŏl'ĭsē) *n.* (pl. **-cies**). (also **insurance** ~) Document containing contract of insurance.

po·li·o (pō'lēō) *n.* (colloq.) Poliomyelitis; hence, ~ **vaccine**, one used in immunization against poliomyelitis.

po·li·o·my·e·li·tis (pōlēōmīelī'-tĭs) *n.* (in full **acute anterior** ~) Infectious disease of the central nervous system, with temporary or permanent paralysis. [Gk. *polios* gray, *muelos* marrow]

Po·lish (pō'lĭsh) *adj.* Of Poland or the Poles; ~ **Corridor**: see CORRIDOR. **Polish** *n.* Language of Poland, belonging to Western branch of Slavonic languages.

pol·ish (pŏl'ĭsh) *v.* Make, become, smooth and glossy by friction; (fig.) make elegant or cultured, refine; smarten *up*; ~ **off**, finish off quickly. **pol'ish·er** *n.* **polish** *n.* Smoothness, glossiness, produced by friction; such friction; substance used to produce polished surface; (fig.) refinement.

po·lit·bu·ro (pŏl'ĭtbūr'ō, polĭt'-) *n.* Principal committee of a communist party; (fig.) similar body with controlling power.

po·lite (polīt') *adj.* Of refined manners, courteous; cultivated, cultured; well-bred; (of literature etc.) refined, elegant. **po·lite'ly** *adv.* **po·lite'ness** *n.*

pol·i·tic (pŏl'ĭtĭk) *adj.* 1. (of person) Sagacious, prudent; (of action etc.) judicious, expedient; scheming, crafty. 2. **body** ~: see BODY. **pol'i·tic·ly** *adv.* **pol'i·tics** *n.* Science and art of government;

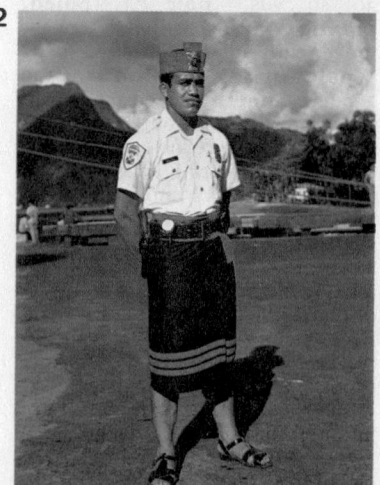

political affairs or life; (as pl.) political principles.

po·lit·i·cal (polĭt'ĭkal) *adj.* 1. Of the state or its government; of public affairs; of politics; (of person) engaged in civil administration. 2. Having an organized polity. 3. Belonging to, taking, a side in politics. 4. ~ **economy**: see ECONOMY; ~ **geography**, that dealing with boundaries, divisions, and possessions of nations; ~ **prisoner**, one imprisoned for a political offense. **po·lit'i·cal·ly** *adv.*

pol·i·ti·cian (pŏlĭtĭsh'an) *n.* One skilled in politics, statesman; one interested or engaged in politics, esp. as profession; one who makes a trade of politics. **pol·i·tick** (pŏl'ĭtĭk) *v.i.* Engage in politics.

po·lit·i·co (polĭt'ĭkō) *n.* (pl. **-cos**). Political agent, officer, or resident.

pol·i·ty (pŏl'ĭtē) *n.* (pl. **-ties**). Condition of civil order; form, process, of civil government; organized society, state.

Polk (pōk), **James Knox** (1795–1849). Eleventh president of U.S.,

Bees transfer **pollen** from male to female flowers but fruit-growers cannot always rely on insects. The earliest records show that date-growers in the Middle East had to pollinate by hand.

Modern industrial advances have given the world the problem of pollution. Both human health (threatened by fumes, above) and wildlife are at risk from poisoning of the environment.

1845–9; under his administration the U.S. obtained the Oregon territory boundary to the 49th parallel, the Texas boundary to the Rio Grande, and California and New Mexico territories from Mexico after the Mexican War.

pol·ka (pŏl´ka, pō´ka) n. Lively dance of Czech origin, with music in double time; music for this; ~ **dot**, one of a pattern of dots of uniform size and arrangement.

poll (pōl) n. 1. Human head (now dial. or joc.); part of head on which hair grows; ~ **tax**, tax levied on every adult, sometimes as a requirement for voting. 2. Counting of voters; voting at election; number of votes recorded. 3. Questioning of a sample of the population in order to estimate trend of public opinion. **poll·ster** (pōl´ster) n. One who takes public-opinion polls. **poll** v. 1. Crop the hair of (archaic), cut off top of (tree, plant), esp. make a pollard of; cut off horns of (cattle, esp. in past part.). 2. Take the votes of; (of candidate) receive (so many votes); give (vote); give one's vote. ~ adj. Polled or cut even at edge.

pol·lack, pol·lock (pŏl´ak) ns. (pl. -lacks, -locks, collect. -lack, -lock). Sea fish (*Pollachius virens*) allied to cod but with lower jaw protruding, used as food.

pol·lard (pŏl´erd) n. 1. Animal that has cast or lost its horns; ox, sheep, goat, of hornless variety. 2. Tree polled so as to produce close rounded head of young branches. 3. Bran sifted from flour; fine bran containing some flour. ~ v.t. Make a pollard of (tree).

pol·len (pŏl´en) n. Fine powdery substance discharged from anther of flower, male element that fertilizes ovules; ~ **count**, index of amount of pollen in air, published as warning to sufferers from respiratory ailments. **pol·lin·ic** (polĭn´ĭk), **pol·li·nif·er·ous** (pŏlinĭf´erus) adjs.

pol·lex (pŏl´ĕks) n. (pl. **pol·li·ces** pr. pŏl´īsēz). Innermost digit of forelimb; in man, thumb.

pol·li·nate (pŏl´ināt) v.t. (-nat·ed, -nat·ing). Sprinkle with pollen, shed pollen upon. **pol·li·na´tion** n.

Pol·lock (pŏl´ok), **Jackson** (1912–56). Amer. abstract expressionist painter famous for his "action paintings" made by dripping paint onto the canvas.

pol·lute (poloōt´) v.t. (-lut·ed, -lut·ing). Destroy the purity or sanctity of; make (water etc.) foul or filthy. **pol·lu´tion** n. (esp.) Contamination or defilement of man's environment.

Pol·lux (pŏl´uks). 1. (Gk. myth.) Twin brother of CASTOR. 2. (astron.) Bright star in the constellation Gemini.

Pol·ly·an·na (pŏlēăn´a). Irrepressibly optimistic person (based on a character in Eleanor

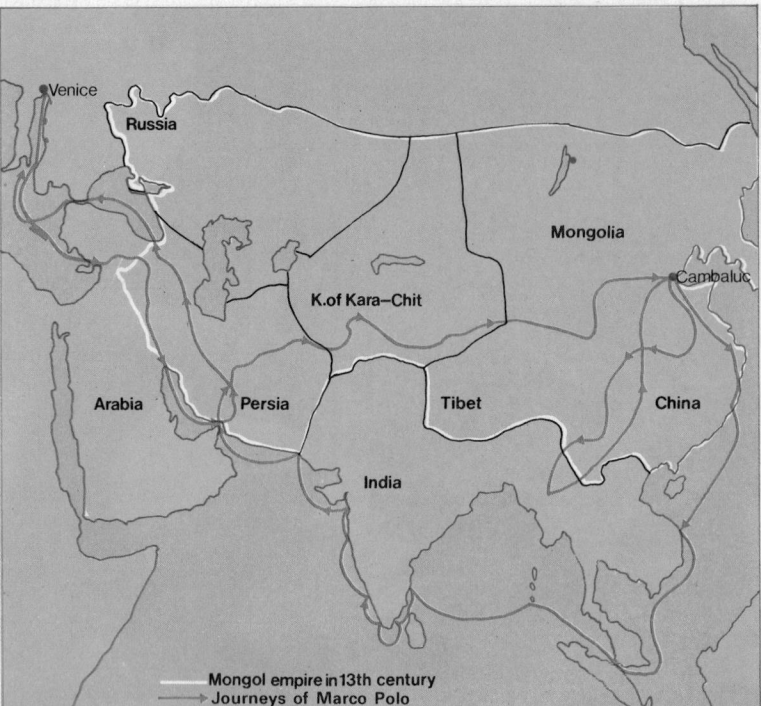

Mongol empire in 13th century
→ Journeys of Marco Polo

Porter's book of the same name, 1913).

po·lo (pō'lō) *n.* Game of Eastern origin resembling hockey, played on horseback by teams of usu. four players, with long-handled mallets (~ **sticks**) and wooden ball; ~ **shirt**, knitted pullover sport shirt; **water** ~, game resembling basketball played by swimmers with ball like soccer ball.

Po·lo (pō'lō), **Marco** (1254–1324). Venetian traveler; reached the court of Kublai Khan in China; spent 17 years in China and wrote an account of his experiences.

pol·o·naise (pŏlonāz', pōlo-) *n.*

Although the word **polo** *is derived from the Tibetan for ball — pulu — the game seems to have started in Persia, at least as far back as the time of Darius the Great.*

1. (hist.) Woman's dress consisting of bodice with skirt open from waist downward. 2. (Music for) slow dance in triple rhythm of Polish origin, with intricate march or procession of dancers in couples. [Fr., fem. of *polonais* Polish]

po·lo·ni·um (polō'nēum) *n.* (chem.) Radioactive metallic element discovered by Pierre and Marie Curie in pitchblende; symbol Po, at. no. 84, principal isotope at.

Taken to the East by his father and uncle, **Marco Polo** remained for 17 years in the service of Kublai Khan. During this time he made notes about everything he saw: some years after their return he had these made into a book.

wt. 210. [med. L. *Polonia* Poland]

pol·ter·geist (pŏl'tergīst) *n.* Noisy spirit manifesting its presence by mischievous behavior such as the overturning of furniture, breaking of crockery, etc. [Ger.]

pol·troon (pŏltroon') *n.* Spiritless coward. **pol·troon'er·y** *n.*

poly- *prefix.* Many.

pol·y·am·ide (pŏlĕăm'ĭd) *n.* (chem.) Polymer containing more than 1 amide group.

pol·y·an·drous (pŏlēăn'drus) *adj.* 1. Of, practicing, polyandry 2. (bot.) With numerous stamens **pol·y·an·dry** (pŏl'ĕăndrē pŏlēăn'-) *n.* Plurality of husbands

pol·y·an·thus (pŏlēăn'thus) *n.* (pl. **-thus·es**). Cultivated primula with flowers of various colors.

pol·y·chaete (pŏl'ĭkēt) *adj. & n.* (Animal) of the Polychaeta, a class of the Annelida comprising worms mostly marine, with many bristles on the foot stumps.

pol·y·chro·mat·ic (pŏlē krōmăt'ĭk), **pol·y·chro·mic** (pŏlēkrō'mĭk), **pol·y·chro'mou** *adjs.* Many-colored.

pol·y·chrome (pŏl'ēkrōm) *adj.* Painted, printed, decorated, in many colors. ~ *n.* Work of art in several colors, esp. colored statue. **pol·y·chro·my** (pŏlē krō'mē) *n.* Art of painting in several colors, esp. as applied to ancient pottery or sculpture.

pol·y·clin·ic (pŏlēklĭn'ĭk) *n.* Clinic or hospital devoted to treatment of various diseases.

pol·y·es·ter (pŏl'ēēster, pŏlēēs'-) *n.* (chem.) Any of several synthetic resins, used esp. in making plastics, fibers, adhesives etc.

pol·y·eth·yl·ene (pŏlēēth'ilēn) *n.* Tough light thermoplastic polymer of ethylene, used for packaging etc.

po·lyg·a·mous (polĭg'amus) *adj.* 1. Having more than one wife or (less usu.) husband at once. 2. (zool.) Having more than one mate at one time. 3. (bot.) Bearing some flowers with stamens only, some with pistils only, some with both on same or different plants. **po·lyg·a·mist** (polĭg'amĭst) **po·lyg·a·my** (polĭg'amē) *ns.*

pol·y·glot (pŏl'ēglŏt) *adj.* Of many languages; speaking or writing several languages; (of book, esp. Bible) written in several languages. ~ *n.* Polyglot person or book.

pol·y·gon (pŏl'ēgŏn) *n.* Figure (usu. plane rectilinear) with many (usu. more than four) angles or sides; ~ **of forces**, polygon

*Generally man is either monogamous or polygamous. Rarely, however, a people develops **polyandry**, living in groups like this: the reason is probably that it keeps family property together.*

illustrating theorem relating to number of forces acting at a point, each represented in magnitude and direction by one side of the figure. **po·lyg·o·nal** (polĭg′onal) *adj.* **po·lyg·o·nal·ly** *adv.*

po·lyg·o·num (polĭg′onum) *n.* Plant of large and widely distributed genus *P~* (including knot grass, etc.) with swollen stem joints sheathed by stipules, and small flowers.

pol·y·graph (pŏl′ēgrăf, -grahf) *n.* 1. Lie detector. 2. Writer of many or various works. **pol·y·graph′ic** *adj.*

po·lyg·y·nous (polĭj′inus) *adj.* 1. Of, practicing, polygyny. 2. (bot.) With many pistils, styles, or stigmas. **po·lyg·y·ny** (polĭj′inē) *n.* Plurality of wives.

pol·y·he·dron (pŏlēhē′dron) *n.* (pl. **-drons, -dra** pr. -dra). Many- (usu. more than six-) sided solid. **pol·y·he′dral** *adj.*

Pol·y·hym·ni·a (pŏlihĭm′nēa). (Gk. and Rom. myth.) Muse of the mimic art.

pol·y·mer (pŏl′imer) *n.* (chem.) Compound formed by the combination of a (usu. very large) number of identical molecules of a simpler substance. **pol·y·mer·ic** (pŏlimĕr′ĭk) *adj.* (of compounds) Composed of the same elements in the same proportions but differing in molecular weight.

po·lym·er·ize (polĭm′erīz, pŏl′imerīz) *v.* (**-ized, -iz·ing**). (chem., of a number of identical molecules) Combine together to form a polymer. **po·lym·er·i·za·tion** (polĭmezā′shon, pŏlimer-) *n.*

pol·y·mor·phism (pŏlēmor′fĭzem) *n.* Diversity occurring within biological populations, determined genetically or by environment.

pol·y·mor·phous (pŏlēmor′fus), **pol·y·mor·phic** (pŏlēmor′fĭk) *adjs.* Multiform; esp. (biol., of a species) of which more than one form exists in a population.

Pol·y·ne·sia (pŏlinē′zha, -sha). One of the three divisions of Oceania; a scattered group of islands in the central and W. Pacific Ocean lying E. of Melanesia and Micronesia, extending from New Zealand N. to the Hawaii Islands and E. to Easter Island. **Pol·y·ne′sian** *adj. & n.*

pol·y·no·mi·al (pŏlēnō′mēal) *adj. & n.* (Expression) of more than two terms, esp. (sum) of terms containing different powers of the same variable(s).

pol·yp (pŏl′ĭp) *n.* 1. (zool.) Single individual of a coelenterate

*The **polychaete** worm, Torrea candida, is well adapted to free-swimming, carnivorous life, with prominent, efficient eyes, bristly paddles along each side, and large jaws which it shoots out at its prey, the smaller creatures of the Mediterranean and similar seas.*

or other colony; similar individual of a noncolonial form, e.g. sea anemone (ill. HYDRA). 2. (path.) Small tumor with a stalk, formed by overgrowth of tissue. **pol·yp·oid** (pŏl′ipoid), **pol′yp·ous** *adjs.*

pol·y·pep·tide (pŏlēpĕp′tīd) *n.* Substance formed by union of three or more amino acids.

Pol·y·phe·mus (pŏlifē′mus). (Gk. legend) CYCLOPS from whom Odysseus and some of his companions escaped by putting out his one eye while he slept.

pol·y·phon·ic (pŏlēfŏn′ĭk), **po·lyph·o·nous** (polĭf′onus) *adjs.* 1. (mus.) Of polyphony, contrapuntal. 2. Producing many sounds.

po·lyph·o·ny (polĭf′onē) *n.* (mus.) Simultaneous combination

*Above: Long clean beaches and lush vegetation have enabled islands in **Polynesia** to develop a tourist industry. This has proved more reliable than the cultivation of the coconut palm as a cash crop (right) to satisfy demands for copra.*

of number of parts, each forming an individual melody; style of composition in which parts are so combined; counterpoint.

pol·y·ploid (pŏl´ēploid) *adj.* & *n.* (biol.) (Organism) having a chromosome number that is a multiple greater than two of the basic group number. **pol·y·ploi·dic** *adj.* **pol´y·ploi·dy** *n.*

pol·y·pod (pŏl´ēpŏd) *adj.* & *n.* (Animal) with many feet.

pol·y·po·dy (pŏl´ēpōdē) *n.* (pl. **-dies**). Fern of large and widely distributed genus *Polypodium*, esp. *P. vulgare*, growing on moist rocks, old walls, and trees.

pol·y·pore (pŏl´ēpōr, -pōr) *n.* Fungus of the family Polyporaceae whose members have large fruiting bodies in which the spores are produced in tubes.

pol·y·pro·pyl·ene (pŏlēprō´pilēn) *n.* (chem.) Plastic polymer of propylene, used esp. for packaging, containers, and electrical insulation.

pol·y·sty·rene (pŏlēstī´rēn) *n.* Transparent thermoplastic material, a polymer of styrene.

pol·y·syl·lab·ic (pŏlēsĭlăb´ĭk) *adj.* (of word) Having many syllables; marked by polysyllables. **pol·y·syl·lab´i·cal·ly** *adv.* **pol´y·syl·la·ble** (pŏl´ēsĭlabel, pŏlēsĭl´-) *n.* Polysyllabic word.

pol·y·tech·nic (pŏlētĕk´nĭk) *adj.* Dealing with, devoted to, various arts. ~ *n.* College of higher education providing courses in various subjects.

pol·y·the·ism (pŏl´ēthēĭzem,

pŏlēthē´-) *n.* Belief in, worship of, many gods or more than one god. **pol´y·the·ist** *n.* **pol·y·the·is´tic** *adj.*

pol·y·un·sat·u·rat·ed (pŏlēŭnsăch´ērātĭd) *adj.* Of fats that have many double bonds in the molecule; in diet they give rise to less cholesterol in blood than other fats.

pol·y·vi·nyl (pŏlēvī´nĭl) *adj.* ~ **chloride**, (abbrev. PVC) vinyl plastic used for insulation, as fabric for clothing and furnishings, etc.

pol·y·zo·an (pŏlēzō´an) = BRYOZOAN.

pom·ace (pŭm´ĭs) *n.* Mass of crushed apples in cider-making before or after juice is pressed out; any pulp; refuse of fish, etc., after oil has been extracted, used as fertilizer.

po·made (pomād´, -mahd´, pō-) *n.* Scented ointment (perh. orig. from apples) for hair and skin of

head. ~ *v.t.* (**-mad·ed, -mad·ing**). Anoint with pomade.

po·ma·tum (pōmā´tum, -mahpo-) *n.* & *v.t.* Pomade.

pome (pōm) *n.* (bot.) Succulen[t] fruit with firm fleshy bo[dy] enclosing carpels forming core, e.[g.] apple, pear, quince; (poet.) appl[e]. **po·mif·er·ous** (pōmĭf´erus) a[dj.] Bearing pomes.

pome·gran·ate (pŏm´grăn[ate,] pŏm´e-, pŭm´-) *n.* Large round[ish] many-celled berry about size [of] orange with tough golden or orang[e] rind and acid reddish pulp envelop[-] ing the many seeds; tree (*Puni[ca] granatum*) bearing this, native [of] N. Africa and W. Asia.

Pom·er·a·ni·a (pŏmerā´nē[a,] -rān´ya). (Ger. *Pommern*) Provin[ce] of Poland with seacoast on Balti[c,] formerly part of Prussia. **Pom·er·a´ni·an** *adj.* & *n.* (Nativ[e or] inhabitant) of Pomerania; (also own also as bracket or shelf fungus, me types of **polypore** grow on the nks of elms and other deciduous es between spring and fall in the rthern hemisphere. Their smell has en likened by some observers to that uncooked tripe.

Polypody, the common name for *Polypodium vulgare* (above), a fern common in Britain, is only one of 75 species at present grouped together by botanists. Another variety is highly specialized and has developed special pouches which collect rain and store it for use in a drought.

The refreshing fruit of the **pomegranate** *has made it popular around the Mediterranean since Biblical times: it was one of the things missed by the Israelites as they wandered in the desert after their departure from Egypt.*

g) dog of small breed with long ick silky hair, usu. black or white, inted muzzle, pricked ears, and ominent eyes.

po·mi·cul·ture (pō´mĭkŭlcher) Fruit-growing.

Pom·mard (pŏmård´, -mär´) *n.* ry red wine produced near mmard in Burgundy.

pom·mel (pŭm´el, pŏm´-) *n.* 1. unded knob esp. at end of sword lt. 2. Upward projecting front rt of saddle. ~ *v.t.* (**-meled** **-melled, -mel·ing** or nel·ling). Pummel.

po·mol·o·gy (pōmŏl´ojē) *n.* ience of fruit-growing. **po·mo·- g·i·cal** (pōmolŏj´ĭkal) *adj.* **po·- ol´o·gist** *n.*

Po·mo·na (pomō´na). (Rom. yth.) Goddess of fruit trees.

pomp (pŏmp) *n.* Splendid splay, splendor.

pom·pa·dour (pŏm´padōr, ōr, -door) *n.* Style of women's irdressing with hair turned back om forehead in high roll. [f. MPADOUR]

Pom·pa·dour (pŏm´padoor, mpadoor´), **Marquise de** (1721– 64). Jeanne Antoinette Poisson Normant d'Étoiles, mistress of uis XV of France.

Pom·peii (pŏmpā´). Ancient wn of Campania, Italy, buried by uption of Mt. Vesuvius in 79 A.D. d since 1755 gradually laid bare excavation.

Pom·pey (pŏm´pē). Gnaeus mpeius Magnus (106–48 B.C.), oman general and consul; ember, with Julius Caesar and

Crassus, of the 1st triumvirate; later he opposed Caesar and was defeated by him at Pharsalia, 48 B.C.

pom-pom (pŏm´pŏm) *n.* 1. Automatic quick-firing gun. 2. Pompon.

pom·pon (pŏm´pŏn) *n.* Ornamental tuft or bunch of silk threads, ribbon, etc., on hat, shoe, dress, etc.; variety of

chrysanthemum or dahlia with small globular flowers.

pomp·ous (pŏm´pus) *n.* Magnificent, splendid; self-important, consequential; (of language) inflated. **pomp´ous·ly** *adv.* **pom·pos·i·ty** (pŏmpŏs´ĭtē), **pomp´ous·ness** *ns.*

Pon·ce de Le·ón (pŏns´ de lē´on; *Sp.* pawn´thĕ dhĕ lĕawn´), **Juan** (c1460–1521). Spanish explorer, conqueror and governor (1510–12) of Puerto Rico, and discoverer of Florida (1513).

pon·cho (pŏn´chō) *n.* (pl. **-chos**). S. Amer. cloak, oblong piece of cloth with slit in middle for head.

pond (pŏnd) *n.* Small body of still water artificially formed by hollowing or embanking; natural pool or small lake; (joc.) sea, esp. Atlantic Ocean; ~ **lily**, water lily; **pond´weed**, aquatic herb (esp. of genus *Potamogeton*) growing in still waters.

pon·der (pŏn´der) *v.* Weigh mentally, think over; think *on*, muse *over.* **pon´der·er** *n.*

pon·der·a·ble (pŏn´derabel) *adj.* Having appreciable weight. **pon·- der·a·bil´i·ty** *n.*

pon·der·ous (pŏn´derus) *adj.* Heavy; unwieldy; laborious; labored. **pon´der·ous·ly** *adv.* **pon´der·ous·ness, pon·der·- os·i·ty** (pŏnderŏs´ĭtē) *ns.*

pone (pōn) *n.* Orig., N. Amer.

The destruction of **Pompeii** *was a tragedy for the citizens, but it has given historians a remarkable insight into everyday Roman life, since so much was preserved under the lava.*

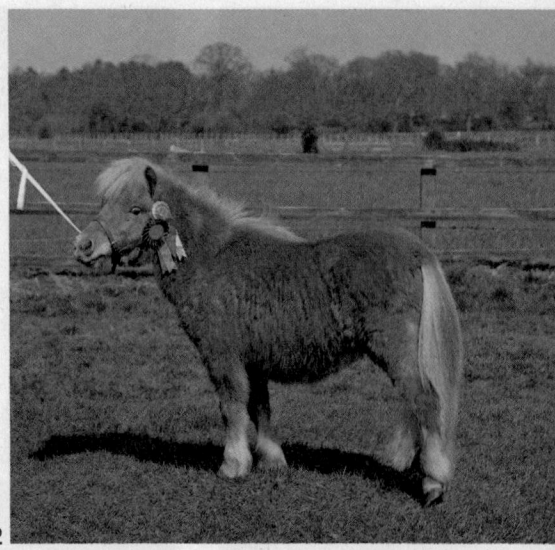

*The Connemara (1) and Shetland (2)
are only two of the many breeds of
pony which exist as a result of natural
and planned selection, from the heavy
types such as the Fell and Dale to yard-
high miniatures. Most have become
popular as children's mounts because
of their intelligence and small size.*

Ind. bread, thin cakes of corn flour cooked in hot ashes; now, in southern U.S., any corn bread; also, very fine light bread made with eggs, milk, etc., and baked in flat cakes.

pon·gee (pŏnjē´, pŏn´jē) *n.* Soft, freq. unbleached fabric of Chinese or Japanese silk, made from cocoons of a wild silkworm feeding on oak leaves; imitation of this in cotton etc. [perh. f. Chin. *pun-chi* own loom]

pon·iard (pŏn´yerd) *n.* Dagger. ~ *v.t.* Stab with poniard.

pons (pŏnz) *n.* (pl. **pon·tes** pr. pŏn´tēz). (anat.) Band of nerve fibers in brain connecting 2 hemispheres of cerebellum, and medulla with cerebrum; also called ~ **Va·ro·li·i** (varō´lēī) ("bridge of Varoli," after an Italian 16th-c. anatomist). [L., = "bridge"]

Pon·ta Del·ga·da (pawn´ta dĕlgah´da). Capital of the Azores, on the SW. coast of São Miguel Island in the N. Atlantic Ocean.

Pont·char·train (pŏn´-chertrān), **Lake**. Lake in SE. Louisiana near New Orleans covering about 600 sq. mi. (1,554 sq. km), and connected with the Gulf of Mexico and the Mississippi River.

Pon·ti·ac (pŏn´tēăk) (d. 1769). Amer. Ind. chief from Ottawa; led Indians in ~**'s War** or **Conspiracy** against British at Detroit, 1763.

pon·ti·fex (pŏn´tĭfĕks) *n.* (pl. **pon·tif·i·ces** pr. pŏntĭf´ĭsēz). (Rom. antiq.) Member of principal college of priests in Rome; ~ **maximus**, head of this; pope.

pon·tiff (pŏn´tĭf) *n.* Pope; bishop; chief priest.

pon·tif·i·cal (pŏntĭf´ĭkal) *adj.* Of, befitting, a pontiff; solemnly dogmatic; **P~ Mass**, Mass celebrated by bishop wearing full vestments. **pon·tif´i·cal·ly** *adv.* **pontifical** *n.* Book of Western

Church containing forms for rites to be performed by bishops; (pl.) vestments and insignia of bishop.

pon·tif·i·cate (pŏntĭf´ĭkĭt, -kāt) *n.* Office of pontifex, bishop, or pope; period of this. ~ (pŏntĭf´-ĭkāt) *v.i.* (**-cat·ed, -cat·ing**). Officiate as bishop, esp. at Mass; assume airs of pontiff, act pompously or dogmatically.

pon·tine (pŏn´tīn, -tēn) *adj.* Of the PONS.

pon·toon (pŏntoon´) *n.* Flat-bottomed boat used as ferryboat etc.; one of several boats, also called ~ **boats**, or hollow metal cylinders, etc., used to support temporary bridge; caisson.

po·ny (pō´nē) *n.* (pl. **-nies**). 1. Horse of any small breed, esp. not more than 13 or (pop.) 14 hands high. 2. (slang) School crib. 3. ~ **express**, formerly in the Amer. West, a rapid postal system using ponies and relays of riders. 4. **po´nytail**, hair worn drawn back, gathered at crown of head, and hanging loose behind.

pooch (pooch) *n.* (colloq.) Dog.

poo·dle (poo´del) *n.* Dog of breed with long curling hair, usu. black or white, often elaborately clipped and shaved. [Ger. *pundel(hund)*, f. *pudeln* splash]

pooh (poo) *int.* Exclamation of impatience or contempt. **pooh´-pooh´** *v.t.* Express contempt for, make light of.

Pooh-Bah (poo´bah´) *n.* Holder of many offices at once. [name of character in Gilbert and Sullivan's *The Mikado*]

pool[1] (pool) *n.* Small body of

still water, usu. of natural form tion; puddle of any liquid; deep st place in river; **swimming** ~: s SWIM.

pool[2] (pool) *n.* 1. (in some ca games) Collective amount players' stakes and fines; recepta for these. 2. Game on billia table with balls numbered from to 15, number of ball pocket being added to player's score. Collective stakes in betting et arrangement between competi. parties by which prices are fix and business is divided to do aw with competition; common fur e.g. of profit of separate firm common supply of commoditi persons, etc. 4. **football** ~, syste of betting on results of footb games. **pool** *v.t.* Place in comm fund; merge (supplies from seve sources); (of competing compan etc.) share (traffic, profits).

poop (poop) *n.* 1. Stern of shi aftermost and highest deck (also **deck**). 2. (slang) Information; new hence ~ **sheet**, fact sheet or pre release distributed to inform. (slang) Feces, esp. of dog; hen **pooper-scooper**, device f picking up dog feces from str for sanitary disposal. **poop** *v.t.* (wave) Break over stern of (shi (of ship) receive (wave) over ste ~ *v.i.* Exhaust; tire out; (sla excrete feces.

poor (poor) *adj.* 1. Lacki means to procure comforts necessities of life; ill supplie deficient (*in* possession or qualit (of soil) unproductive; **the** ~, po people as a class. 2. Scan inadequate, less than is expecte paltry, sorry; spiritless, despicab humble, insignificant. 3. (expr. p or sympathy) Unfortunate, haple 4. ~ **box**, money box esp. church for relief of the poor; **poo house**, (hist.) institution whe paupers were maintained; **po white** (**trash**), (contemp

Pop Art *and* ***Pop Music*** *are often inter-linked: artists may use images of those who have become known as musicians to create dreamlike visions like this of the Beatles (above). Groups like the Rolling Stones (left) have visual elements in their performance.*

Southern white people of no substance; **poor-mouth** (*v.i.*) complain about one's financial status.

poor·ly (poor′lē) *adv.* Scantily, defectively; with no great success.

poor·ness (poor′nĭs) *n.* Defectiveness; lack of some good quality or constituent.

pop¹ (pŏp) *v.* (**popped, pop-ing**). 1. Make small quick explosive sound as of cork when drawn; let off (firearm etc.); fire gun (*at*); **pop′gun**, child's toy gun shooting pellets by compression of air with piston; **pop off**, (slang) die suddenly; speak or write emotionally. 2. Put (*in, out, down,*

Pope's translations made him a wealthy man, but he is best remembered today as the author of such works as 'The Rape of the Lock', a humorous mock-epic.

etc.) quickly or suddenly; move, come, go (*in* etc.) thus; put (question) abruptly; **pop the question**, (colloq.) propose marriage. 3. Parch (corn) till it bursts open; **pop'corn**, corn so parched. **pop** *n*. Abrupt, not very loud, explosive sound; (colloq.) effervescing drink. ~ *adv*. With (the action or sound of) a pop.

pop² (pŏp) = PAPA.

pop³ (pŏp) *adj*. (of music, art, etc.) Popular.

pop. *abbrev.* Population; popular; popularity.

pope¹ (pōp) *n*. 1. Bishop of Rome as head of the R.C. Ch.; **P ~ Joan**, fabulous female pope placed by some chroniclers *c*855, under name of John; **~'s nose**, rump of (cooked) fowl. 2. (fig.) Person assuming or credited with infallibility. **pope'dom** *n*.

pope² (pōp) *n*. Parish priest of Greek Church in U.S.S.R. etc. [Russ. *pop*]

Pope (pōp), **Alexander** (1688–1744). English poet, satirist, and translator of Homer; best known for his mock-heroic poem "The Rape of the Lock" and his "Essay on Man."

pop·er·y (pō'perē) *n*. (in hostile use) Papal system, Roman Catholicism.

pop·in·jay (pŏp'ĭnjā) *n*. 1. (archaic) Parrot; (hist.) figure of parrot on pole as mark to shoot at. 2. Fop, coxcomb, conceited person.

pop·ish (pō'pĭsh) *adj*. Of popery, papistical; **P ~ Plot**, supposed plot to murder Charles II and suppress Protestantism (1678). **pop'ish·ly** *adv*. **pop'ish·ness** *n*.

pop·lar (pŏp'ler) *n*. Large tree of rapid growth (genus *Populus*), freq. with tremulous leaves; soft light loose-textured wood of this.

pop·lin (pŏp'lĭn) *n*. Closely woven fabric with corded surface, orig. of silk warp and worsted woof, now freq. of cotton. [It. *papalina* papal (because made in the papal town of Avignon)]

Po·po·ca·té·petl (pōpokăt'-epĕtel, pawpawkahtĕ'petel). Volcanic mountain, dormant since 1802, in Mexico.

pop·o·ver (pŏp'ōver) *n*. Biscuit made from thin egg-rich batter that expands during baking into a hollow shell.

pop·per (pŏp'er) *n*. Covered basket or other device for popping corn.

pop·py (pŏp'ē) *n*. (pl. -pies). Plant or flower of genus *Papaver* of temperate and subtropical

Despite its name, the Lombardy **poplar** was originally native to the temperate regions of Asia. Its elegant form resulted in its cultivation in Italy, and later in many other parts of the world.

regions, having milky juice with narcotic properties, showy flowers of scarlet or other color, and roundish capsules containing numerous small seeds; artificial poppy (also **Flanders ~**) worn on Veteran's Day; **California ~**, ESCHSCHOLTZIA; **horn(ed) ~**, any plant of genus *Glaucium*, distinguished by its long hornlike

capsules; **opium ~**: see OPIU **prickly ~**, any plant of ger *Argemone*, esp. *A. mexicana*, w yellow or white flowers and pric leaves and capsules; **P ~ D** formerly Armistice Day, n Veteran's Day, on which artific poppies are worn (because popp were very conspicuous on Flanders battlefields); **pop'p head**, capsule of poppy; (arch carved finial crowning end of s in church.

pop·py·cock (pŏp'ēkŏk) (colloq.) Nonsense, rubbish.

pop·u·lace (pŏp′yulas) *n.* Common people.

pop·u·lar (pŏp′yuler) *adj.* 1. Of, carried on by, the people; adapted to the understanding, taste, or means of the people; prevalent among the people; ~ **front**, political group representing leftish elements. 2. Liked, admired, by the people or by people generally or a specified class. **pop′u·lar·ly** *adv.* **pop·u·lar·i·ty** (pŏpyulăr′ĭtē) *n.*

pop·u·lar·ize (pŏp′yulerīz) *v.t.* (-**ized**, -**iz·ing**). Make popular, cause to be generally known or liked; extend to the common people; present in popular form. **pop·u·lar·i·za·tion** (pŏpyulerīzā′shon), **pop′u·lar·iz·er** *ns.*

pop·u·late (pŏp′yulāt) *v.t.* (-**lat·ed**, -**lat·ing**). Inhabit, form the population of (country, town, etc.); supply with inhabitants. **pop·u·la′tion** *n.* Degree in which place is populated; total number of inhabitants; people of a country etc.

Pop·u·list (pŏp′yulĭst) *n.* 1. Adherent of a Russian political movement (*c*1870–80) advocating collectivism. 2. Adherent of a U.S. political party (1892–1904) aiming at public control of railroads, graduated income tax, etc. **pop′u·list** *n.* & *adj.* (Adherent) of political policy claiming to represent the whole of the people.

pop·u·lous (pŏp′yulus) *adj.* Thickly inhabited. **pop′u·lous·ly** *adv.* **pop′u·lous·ness** *n.*

Various species of **porcupine** are native to the Americas, Africa and Asia. All are herbivorous but only the North American porcupine (far right) consistently climbs trees to seek food.

por·ce·lain (pōr′selĭn, pōr′-; pōrs′lĭn, pōrs′-) *n.* Finest and hardest kind of earthenware, consisting largely of kaolin or feldspathic clay, baked at a high temperature and usu. covered with a colored or transparent glaze; article or vessel of this; (attrib.) of porcelain, (fig.) delicate, fragile; ~ **shell**, cowrie. **por·ce·la·ne·ous, por·cel·la·ne·ous** (pōrselā′nēus, pōr-) *adjs.* [It. *porcellana* (*porcella* dim. of *porca* sow, f. resemblance of the shell to hog′s back)]

porch (pōrch, pŏrch) *n.* 1. Covered approach to entrance of

Many kinds of **poppy** *are grown as garden flowers all over the world. One of the best-known is the brilliantly colored oriental poppy shown here.*

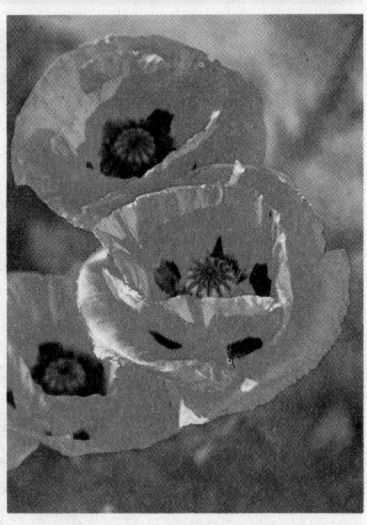

African Crested Porcupine

building. 2. Veranda. 3. **the P** ~, public ambulatory in marketplace of ancient Athens to which Zeno and his disciples resorted; Stoic school or philosophy.

por·cine (pōr′sīn, pōr′-) *adj.* Of or like swine.

por·cu·pine (pōr′kyupīn) *n.* (pl. -**pines**, collect. -**pine**). Rodent, esp. *Erethizon dorsatum*, with body and tail covered with long erectile spines.

pore[1] (pōr, pŏr) *n.* Minute opening in skin of animal body or membrane of plant, for transpiration, absorption, etc.

This charming group was made in biscuit or unglazed **porcelain** *and is typical of the figures made in the late 18th century at the Sèvres factory.*

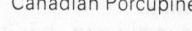
Canadian Porcupine

The porringer has inspired many designers and craftsmen since the form originated. This delicate porcelain one was made at a Derby factory sometime about 1785.

pore² (pōr, por) *v.* (**pored, por·ing**). ~ **over**, be absorbed in studying (book etc.); (fig.) meditate, think intently upon (subject).

por·gy (pōr'gē) *n.* (pl. **-gies, -gy**). Sea fish of family Sparidae related to the bass, of wide distribution.

pork (pōrk, pork) *n.* Flesh of swine as food; ~ **barrel**, (fig.) public treasury viewed as source of grants for local purposes; **pork'-pie**, cylindrical pie of chopped pork; (attrib., of hat) with flat crown and no brim, or brim turned up all around. **pork'like** *adj.*

pork·er (pōr'ker, pōr'-) *n.* Pig raised for food; young fattened hog.

porn (pōrn), **por·no** (pōr'nō) *ns.* (colloq.) Pornography.

por·nog·ra·phy (pōrnŏg'rafē) *n.* Explicit description or exhibition of sexual activity in literature, films, etc., intended to stimulate erotic feelings; literature etc. of this kind. **por·nog'ra·pher** *n.* **por·no·graph·ic** (pōrnogrăf'ĭk) *adj.*

po·rous (pōr'us, pōr'-) *adj.* Full of pores; not watertight. **po'rous·ly** *adv.* **po'rous·ness, po·ros·i·ty** (pōrŏs'ĭtē, paw-, po-) *ns.*

por·phy·rite (pōr'ferīt) *n.* Rock resembling porphyry but with slightly different composition of crystals.

Por·phy·ry (pōr'ferē). Porphyrius (233–c305 A.D.), scholar and philosopher; orig. called Malchus; by birth prob. a Syrian; became a disciple of Plotinus at Rome; author of numerous works in Greek.

por·phy·ry (pōr'ferē) *n.* (pl. **-ries**). Volcanic purplish-red rock composed of large crystals set in a fine-grained ground mass, anciently quarried in Egypt as material for statues etc. **por·phy·rit·ic** (pōrferĭt'ĭk) *adj.*

por·poise (pōr'pos) *n.* (pl. **-poises**, collect. **-poise**). Small whale of genus *Phocaena*, esp. *P. phocaena*, about 6 ft. (1.8 m) long, blackish above and paler beneath, with blunt rounded snout.

por·ridge (pōr'ĭj, păr'-) *n.* Soft food made by stirring oatmeal or other meal or cereal in boiling water or milk.

por·rin·ger (pōr'ĭnjer, păr'-) *n.* Small basin from which soup etc. is eaten.

Porpoises and dolphins are often confused, they are in fact different species of the whale family. Right: Camden Harbour in Maine, an attractive fishing port in an area noted for its wide variety of marine life.

*The **portico** is an architectural feature suited to countries where the midday sun is too hot and bright for comfort. Transferred to northern lands, it can appear incongruous, if elegant, like this one at West Wycombe, U.K.*

portae) formed by union of veins from stomach, intestine, and spleen, conveying blood to the liver.

Port (pōrt, pŏrt) **Arthur.** (now Lüshun) Harbor in S. Manchuria, leased to Russia 1898; besieged and taken by Japanese, 1904, in Russo-Japanese war; restored to U.S.S.R. in 1945.

Port-au-Prince (pōrtōprĭns′, pŏrt-; *Fr.* pŏrtōprăns′). Capital and chief port of Haiti, in the SE. part on the Gulf of Gonave.

port·cul·lis (pōrtkŭl′ĭs, pŏrt-) *n.* Strong heavy grating blocking gateway of fortress, made to slide up and down in vertical grooves.

porte-co·che·re, porte-co·chère (pōrtkōshār′, pŏrt-) *ns.* Gateway and passage for vehicles through house into courtyard. [Fr.]

por·tend (pōrtĕnd′, pŏr-) *v.t.* Foretell, foreshadow, as an omen; give warning of.

por·tent (pōr′tĕnt, pŏr′-) *n.* Omen, significant sign; prodigy, marvelous thing. **por·ten·tous** (pōrtĕn′tŭs, pŏr-) *adj.* **por·ten′tous·ly** *adv.* **por·ten′tous·ness** *n.*

por·ter[1] (pōr′ter, pŏr′-) *n.* Gatekeeper, doorkeeper, esp. of large building, public institution, etc.

por·ter[2] (pōr′ter, pŏr′-) *n.* Person employed to carry burdens, esp. employee of railroad company who handles luggage; attendant in Pullman coaches etc.; ∼'s **knot**, pad resting on shoulders and secured to forehead used by porters in carrying loads. **por·ter·age** (pōr′terĭj, pŏr′-) *n.* Work of porters; charge for this.

por·ter[3] (pōr′ter, pŏr′-) *n.* Dark brown bitter beer, like stout but weaker, brewed from charred or browned malt (now chiefly in Ireland); **por′terhouse,** house at which porter etc., was retailed; place where steaks, chops, etc., were served, chophouse; **por′terhouse steak,** choice cut of beef between sirloin and tenderloin, orig. as served at a porterhouse. [short for *porter's ale* etc., app. because orig. brewed for porters and other laborers]

port·fo·li·o (pōrtfō′lēō, pŏrt-) *n.* (pl. **-li·os**). Case, usu. like large book cover, for keeping loose sheets of paper, drawings, etc.; (fig.) office of high government official; **minister without** ∼., one not in charge of any department of government.

por·ti·co (pōr′tĭkō, pŏr′-) *n.* (pl. **-coes, -cos**). Colonnade, roof supported by columns at regular intervals, usu. attached as porch to

Por·se·na (pōr′sena), **Lars.** (Rom. hist.) King of Clusium in Etruria, who vainly laid siege to Rome (508 B.C.) in an attempt to restore the exiled Tarquinius Superbus (see TARQUIN) or (acc. to another tradition) conquered and ruled Rome.

port[1] (pōrt, pŏrt) *n.* Harbor; town, place, possessing harbor, esp. one where customs officers are stationed; ∼ **of call,** one visited by a ship to take on or discharge cargo or passengers; ∼ **of embarkation,** one from which passengers leave a country, also ∼ **of origin;** ∼ **of entry,** one at which customs officials are stationed to supervise entry of passengers and cargo.

port[2] (pōrt, pŏrt) *n.* 1. (chiefly Sc.) Gate, gateway, esp. of walled town. 2. Opening in side of ship for entrance, loading, etc.; aperture in cylinder for passage of steam, water, etc.; curved mouthpiece of some bridlebits; (also **port′hole**) aperture in ship's or aircraft's side for admission of light and air; aperture in wall etc. for firing through.

port[3] (pōrt, pŏrt) *v.t.* (mil.) carry (rifle, sword) diagonally

across and close to the body, with barrel or blade opposite middle of left shoulder.

port[4] (pōrt, pŏrt) *n.* Left side of ship looking forward (formerly called larboard); corresponding side of aircraft. ∼ *v.* Turn (helm) to left side of ship; (of ship or aircraft) turn to port side.

port[5] (pōrt, pŏrt) *n.* Heavy sweet fortified wine, dark red or (less freq.) white, made in the Douro valley of Portugal; wine of similar type made in other countries. [*Oporto*, seaport where the wine is shipped]

port·a·ble (pōr′tabel, pŏr′-) *adj.* Movable, convenient for carrying. **port·a·bil′i·ty** *n.*

por·tage (pōr′tĭj, pŏr′-) *n.* Carrying, carriage; cost of this; carrying of boats or goods across land between 2 navigable waters, place at which this is necessary. ∼ *v.t.* (**-taged, -tag·ing**). Convey (boat, goods) over a portage.

por·tal[1] (pōr′tal, pŏr′-) *n.* Door(way), gate(way), esp. elaborate one.

por·tal[2] (pōr′tal, pŏr′-) *adj.* Of the *porta* or transverse fissure of the liver; ∼ **vein,** great vein (*vena*

The **Portuguese man-of-war** is not one
animal but a community of three highly
specialized polyps, concerned respectively with feeding, reproduction and killing prey. The stinging tentacles may be
up to 40 ft. long.

a building.

por·tiere, por·tière (pōrtyār´,
pōr-) *ns.* Curtain hung over
doorway.

por·tion (pōr´shon, pōr´-) *n.*
Part, share; dowry; one's destiny,
one's lot; amount of a dish served
to a person in a restaurant etc.;
some (*of*) anything. ~ *v.t.*
Divide (thing) into shares, distribute *out*; assign (*to* person) as
share; give inheritance or dowry to.

Port·land[1] (pōrt´land, pōrt´-).
Seaport city in SW. Maine.

Port·land[2] (pōrt´land, pōrt´-).
City in NW. Oregon, on the Willamette River near its confluence with
the Columbia River.

Port·land[3] (pōrt´land, pōrt´-)
cement. Kind of cement hardening in water and resembling stone
when set.

Port (pōrt, pōrt) **Louis.** Capital
and principal port of Mauritius, in
the Indian Ocean.

port·ly (pōrt´lē, pōrt´-) *adj.*
(**-li·er, -li·est**). Bulky, corpulent;
of stately appearance. **port´li·ness**
n.

port·man·teau (pōrtmăn´tō,
pōrt-, -măntō´) *n.* (pl. **-teaus,
-teaux** pr. -tōz). Oblong case for
carrying clothing etc., opening like
book with hinges in middle of back;
~ **word**, word like those invented
by Lewis Carroll, blending the
sounds and combining the meanings of 2 others (e.g. *slithy* = lithe
and slimy).

Port Mores·by (pōrt mōrz´bē,
pōrt mōrz´-). Capital and administrative center of Papua New Guinea
of SE. coast of New Guinea.

Port-of-Spain (pōrt´ov spān´,
pōrt´-). Capital and chief port of
Trinidad and Tobago, in the NW.
part of Trinidad in the SE. West
Indies.

Por·to·lá (pōrtawlah´), **Gaspar
de** (1723?–84?). Spanish soldier and
explorer; founded San Diego and
Monterey after a 1,000 mi. (1,600
km), march from lower to upper
California; governor of California,
1767–70.

Por·to-No·vo (pōr´tō nō´vo,
pōr´-). Capital and port of the
People's Republic of BENIN, in the
SE. part.

por·trait (pōr´trĭt, -trāt, pōr´-)
n. Likeness of person or animal
made by drawing, painting,
photography, etc.; verbal picture,

Portugal is mainly thought of as a producer of wine, from vineyards like
these. Olive oil, cork, and sardines are
also exported in quantity, together with
fruit, and different kinds of manufactured goods.

PORTUGAL

ATLANTIC
OCEAN

Spain

LISBON

Honey Possum

Pygmy Possum

Leadbeater's Possum

The mouse-sized honey possum has a tongue especially adapted to obtaining nectar but it also eats insects. The rare Leadbeater's variety of south-east Australia is wholly insectivorous. Some pygmy possums store fat in their tails.

graphic description; (fig.) type, similitude. **por′trait·ist** *n.* Maker of portraits.

por·trai·ture (pōr′trĭcher, pōr′-) *n.* Portraying; portrait; graphic description.

por·tray (pōrtrā′, pōr-) *v.t.* Make likeness of; describe graphically. **por·tray′al, por·tray′er** *ns.*

Port Sa·id (pōrt, pōrt sah ēd′). Egyptian seaport at Mediterranean end of Suez Canal.

Por·tu·gal (pōr′chugal, pōr′-). Republic (kingdom until 1910) occupying W. part of Iberian peninsula; capital, Lisbon.

Por·tu·guese (pōrchugēz′, -gēs′, pōr-) *adj.* Of Portugal or its people or language; ~ **man-of-war,** marine hydrozoan of genus *Physalia.* **Portuguese** *n.* (pl.

-guese). Portuguese person; Romance language of Portugal, spoken also in Brazil.

pose[1] (pōz) *n.* Attitude of body or mind, esp. one assumed for effect. ~ *v.* (**posed, pos·ing**). Lay down (assertion, claim, etc.); propound (question); place (artist's model etc.) in certain attitude; assume an attitude, esp. for artistic purposes; set up, give oneself out, as.

pose[2] (pōz) *v.t.* (**posed, pos·-ing**). Puzzle (person) with question or problem. **pos′er** *n.* (esp.)

Puzzling question or problem.

Po·sei·don (pōsī′don, po-). (Gk. myth.) God of the sea, brother of ZEUS and Pluto; identified by the Romans with Neptune.

po·seur (pōzēr′) *n.* Affected person.

posh (pŏsh) *adj.* (slang) Smart, stylish; first-rate, high-class.

pos·it (pŏz′ĭt) *v.t.* Assume as fact, postulate; put in position, place.

po·si·tion (pozĭsh′on) *n.* 1. (chiefly logic and philos.) Proposition; laying down of this. 2. Bodily posture, attitude. 3. Mental attitude, way of looking at question. 4. Place occupied by a thing, site, situation; **in (out of)** ~, in (out of) its proper place; (mil.) place where troops are posted esp. for strategical reasons. 5. Situation in regard to other persons or things; condition. 6. Rank, social status; official employment. **position** *v.t.* Place in position; determine position of. **po·si′tion·al** *adj.*

pos·i·tive (pŏz′ĭtĭv) *adj.* 1. Explicitly laid down; definite; unquestionable. 2. Absolute, not relative; (gram., of degree of adjective or adverb) expressing simple quality, without qualification or comparison; (colloq.) downright, out-and-out. 3. (of person) Confident, assured; opinionated; (also) given to constructive action. 4. (philos.) Dealing only with matters of fact, practical. 5. Marked by presence, not absence, of qualities; tending in the direction regarded as that of increase or progress. 6. (math., phys., etc.) Greater than zero; in the direction which for purposes of calculation is to be regarded as upward from zero; (elect.) having a positive charge; ~ **charge,** one of the 2 kinds of electric charge, that of the atomic nucleus as dist. from the negative charge of the electrons (the terms *positive* and *negative* were applied to electricity before the discovery of electrons, and their meaning is now purely conventional); ~ **pole,** region of deficiency of electrons, anode; also (magnetism) applied to the north-seeking pole of a magnet and the corresponding (south) pole of Earth; ~ **sign,** the sign +, plus sign. 7. (photog.) Showing lights and shadows as seen in nature. **pos′i·tive·ly** *adv.* **pos′i·tive·ness** *n.* **positive** *n.* Positive degree, adjective, quantity, photograph, etc.

pos·i·tiv·ism (pŏz′ĭtĭvĭzem) *n.* Philosophical system of Auguste Comte, recognizing only positive facts and observable phenomena and abandoning all inquiry into causes or ultimate origins; religious system founded upon this. **pos′i·tiv·ist** *n.* & *adj.* **pos·i·tiv·is′tic** *adj.*

*Mail boxes are the starting point of the **post office's** work of delivering mail. From here, mail enters the U.S. Mail's complex system of sorting and transport so that it arrives promptly at destinations all over the world.*

*The **poster** has been used as a form of advertising since ancient times but pictorial versions only became possible with new printing methods in the 19th century (above right). Designs have since reflected changes in art.*

"Oh Mamma don't forget to order BOVRIL"

pos·i·tron (pŏz´ĭtrŏn) *n.* (phys.) Positive particle with mass equal to that of the electron and electrically its counterpart. [*posit(ive elect)ron*]

pos·se (pŏs´ē) *n.* Body of police (also ~ **co·mi·ta·tus** (kŏmĭtah´tus, -tā´-) or of men summoned to aid sheriff in an emergency.

pos·sess (pozĕs´) *v.t.* Hold as property, own; have (faculty, quality, etc.); maintain (*in* patience etc.); (of demon or spirit) occupy, dominate (person etc.); ~ **oneself of**, take, get for one's own; **be possessed of**, own, have. **pos·-ses´sor** *n.*

pos·ses·sion (pozĕsh´on) *n.* 1. Possessing; actual holding or occupancy; (law) visible power of exercising such control as attaches to (but may exist apart from) lawful ownership; **in** ~, (of thing) possessed; (of person) possessing; **in** ~ **of**, having in one's possession; **in the** ~ **of**, possessed or held by; ~ **is nine points (or tenths) of the law**, possession or occupancy gives every advantage short of actual lawful ownership. 2. Thing possessed; subject territory, esp. foreign dominion(s); (pl.) property, wealth.

pos·ses·sive (pozĕs´ĭv) *adj.* Of possession; indicating possession; desirous of keeping as one's own. **pos·ses´sive·ly** *adv.* **pos·ses´-sive·ness** *n.* **possessive** *n.* (Word in) possessive case.

pos·si·bil·i·ty (pŏsĭbĭl´ĭtē) *n.* (pl. **-ties**). State, fact, of being possible; thing that may exist or happen; capability of being used, improved, etc.

pos·si·ble (pŏs´ĭbel) *adj.* That can exist, be done, or happen; that may be or become; tolerable to deal with, reasonable, intelligible. **pos´-si·bly** *adv.* In accordance with possibility; perhaps, maybe, for all one knows to the contrary. **possible** *n.* Highest possible score, esp. in rifle practice; possible candidate, member, etc.

pos·sum (pŏs´um) *n.* (colloq.) Opossum; **play** ~, feign illness, death, etc.

post¹ (pōst) *n.* 1. Stout piece of timber usu. cylindrical or square and of considerable length placed vertically as support in building; stake, stout pole, for various purposes; post marking point in a race; winning post. 2. Vertical mass of coal left as support in mine; thick compact stratum of sandstone etc. 3. ~ **and rail**(s), open fence made of posts and rails. **post** *v.t.* Stick (paper etc., usu. *up*) to post or in prominent place; advertise (fact, thing, person) by placard; enter the name of in a public list; publish name of (ship) as overdue or missing; placard (wall etc.) with bills.

post² (pōst) *n.* 1. (hist.) One of series of men stationed with horses along roads at intervals, the duty of each being to ride forward with letters to next stage; (hist.) courier, letter carrier. 2. (chiefly Brit.) Single dispatch of letters; letters so dispatched; letters taken from post office or mailbox on one occasion; letters delivered at one house on one occasion. 3. (chiefly Brit.) Official conveyance of letters, parcels, etc.; post office or postal letter box; **by return** ~, (hist.) by same courier who brought the dispatch; (now) by next mail in opposite direction. 4. **post´card**, card, usu. with a picture on one side (**picture postcard**), the reverse being left blank for a short

message, address, and postage stamp; **post chaise**, (hist.) traveling carriage hired from stage to stage or drawn by horses so hired; **post haste´**, with great speed; **post horse**, one of those formerly kept at inns etc. for use of posts or travelers; **post´man** (pl. **-men**) one who delivers or collects letters; **post´mark**, official mark stamped on letters etc., formerly giving place, date, and hour of dispatch or arrival, and serving to cancel stamp; **post´mark** (*v.t.*); **post master** (fem. **post´mistress**) official in charge of a post office; **post office**, room or building in which postal business is carried on; **post-office box**, numbered box in post office for receiving letters addressed to particular firm or person; **post´paid´**, on which postage has been paid. **post** *adv.* (archaic) With post horses; express, with haste. ~ *v.* 1. (hist.) Travel with relays of horses; travel with haste, hurry. 2. Put (letter etc.) into post office or mailbox for transmission. 3. (bookkeeping) Carry (entry) from auxiliary book to more formal one, esp. from daybook or journal to ledger; (fig.) supply (person) with full information.

post³ (pōst) *n.* 1. Place where soldier is stationed, (fig.) place of duty; position taken by body of soldiers, force occupying this; (also **trading** ~) place occupied for purposes of trade esp. in undeveloped region. 2. ~ **exchange** (mil.) camp store. 3. Situation, employment. **post** *v.t.* Direct (soldiers etc.) to go to a specific station etc.

post- *prefix.* After, behind.

post·age (pō´stĭj) *n.* Amount charged for carriage of letters etc. by mail, now usu. prepaid by **stamp**, adhesive label to be affixed (or stamp embossed or impressed on envelope etc., having specific value, or by franking.

post·al (pōs´tal) *adj.* Of the

Post-Impressionist painters such as Cézanne (self-portrait right), while continuing to follow many of the trails blazed by the Impressionists, re-emphasized the importance of form as well as color.

POST² n.; ~ **order**: see ORDER def. 3; (**Universal**) **P ~ Union**, union of governments of various countries for regulation of international postage.

post·clas·si·cal (pōstklăs´ĭkal) adj. Occurring later than the classical period of (esp. Greek and Latin) language, literature, or art.

post·date (pōstdāt´) v.t. **-dat·ed, -dat·ing**). Affix, assign, to (document, event, etc.) a date later than the actual one.

post·er (pō´ster) n. 1. One who posts bills. 2. Placard displayed in public place.

pos·te·ri·or (pŏstēr´ēer) adj. 1. Later, coming after in series, order, or time. 2. Hinder; as viewed from behind. ~ n. Buttocks. **pos·te·ri·or·i·ty** (pŏstērēōr´ĭtē, -ār´-) n. **pos·te´ri·or·ly** adv.

pos·ter·i·ty (pŏstĕr´ĭtē) n. Descendants; all succeeding generations.

post·gla·cial (pōstglā´shal) adj. (geol.) Occurring or formed after a glacial period. ~ n. Postglacial period.

post·grad·u·ate (pōstgrăj´ōoĭt, -āt) adj. (of course of study) Carried on after graduation. ~ n. Student taking postgraduate course.

post hoc, er·go prop·ter hoc (pōst hŏk´ ĕr´gō prŏp ter hŏk; Lat. pōst hŏk´ ĕr´gō prŏp´tĕr hŏk). "After this, therefore on account of this," used to ridicule the tendency to confuse sequence with consequence. [L.]

post·hu·mous (pŏs´chumus) adj. Occurring after death; (of child) born after death of its father; (of book etc.) published after author's death.

pos·til·ion, pos·til·lion (pōstĭl´on, pŏ-) ns. One who rides the near horse of the leaders when four or more are used in a carriage, or the near horse when only one pair is used and there is no driver on box.

Post-Im·pres·sion·ism (pōst impresh´onĭzem) n. Comprehensive term for various developments in painting (Neo-Impressionism, Expressionism, Cubism, etc.) which followed IMPRESSIONISM in late 19th and early 20th centuries. **Post-Im·pres´sion·ist** n. One of the painters responsible for Post-Impressionism (as Cézanne, Gauguin, Van Gogh, Picasso). **post-im·pres·sion·is´tic** adj.

post·lude (pōst´lōod) n. (mus.) Concluding piece or movement played at end of oratorio.

post·mas·ter (pōst´măster): see

POST² n.

post me·ri·di·em (pōst merĭd´-ēem). (abbrev. p.m.) Between noon and midnight. **post·me·rid´i·an** adj. [L.]

post·mor·tem (pōstmōr´tem) adj. After death. ~ n. Examination made after death to determine its cause; analysis of event after its occurrence, esp. of game of bridge.

post·na·sal (pōst´nā´zal) **drip.** Trickling of mucus from behind the nose onto the pharynx.

post·na·tal (pōstnā´tal) adj. Occurring after childbirth.

post·nup·tial (pōstnŭp´shal, -chal) adj. Subsequent to marriage.

post·op·er·a·tive (pōstŏp´-eratĭv, -ātĭv) adj. Occurring after surgery.

post·pone (pōstpōn´, pōspōn´) v. (**-poned, -pon·ing**). Cause to take place at later time than the present or the one arranged. **post·pon´-a·ble** adj. **post·pone´ment, post·pon´er** ns.

post·pran·di·al (pōstprăn´dēal) adj. (chiefly joc.). Done etc. after dinner.

post·script (pōst´skrĭpt, pōs´-skrĭpt) n. (abbrev. P.S.) Additional paragraph esp. at end of letter after signature.

pos·tu·lant (pŏs´chulant) *n.* Candidate, esp. for admission into religious order.

pos·tu·late (pŏs´chulĭt, -lāt) *n.* Thing claimed or assumed as basis of reasoning, fundamental condition; prerequisite; (geom.) claim to take for granted possibility of simple operation, e.g. of drawing straight line between any two points; simple problem of a self-evident nature (dist. from AXIOM). ~ (pŏs´chulāt) *v.* (**-lat·ed, -lat·ing**). Demand, require, claim, take for granted; stipulate *for*; (eccles. law) nominate or elect to ecclesiastical dignity, subject to sanction of superior authority. **pos·tu·la′tion, pos′tu·la·tor** *ns.*

pos·ture (pŏs´cher) *n.* Carriage, attitude of body or mind; condition, state (*of* affairs, etc.). ~ *v.* (**-tured, -tur·ing**). Dispose the limbs of (person) in particular way; assume posture.

post·war (pōst´wŏr´) *adj.* Of the period after a war, esp. World War I or II.

po·sy (pō´zē) *n.* (pl. **-sies**). Bunch of flowers; flower; (archaic) short motto, line of verse, etc., inscribed within ring.

pot[1] (pŏt) *n.* 1. Rounded vessel of earthenware, metal, glass etc., for holding liquids or solids; chamber pot; flowerpot, teapot, coffeepot, etc.; such vessel for cooking; drinking vessel of pewter etc.;

contents of pot; **go to** ~, (colloq) be ruined or destroyed. 2. Fis pot, lobster pot; chimney pot. Large sum; (racing slang) large sur staked or betted. 4. **pot′belly** (p -bellies), protuberant belly; **pot′ boiler**, work of literature etc. don merely to make a living; writer c artist who produces this; **po cheese**, cheese of coagulated mil from which water is separated b heating in a pot; **pot′herb**, her grown in kitchen garden; **pot′ hook**, hook over fireplace fo hanging pot etc. on, or for liftin hot pot; curved stroke in hand writing, esp. as made in learnin to write; **pot′luck**, whatever is t be had for a meal; **pot meta** glass melted with stained glass i melting pot so that the colo pervades the whole; cast iron suit able for manufacturing pots; **po roast**, meat cooked slowly i covered dish; **pot′ shot**, shot take at random; an easy shot; casu criticism; **pot still**, kind of still i which heat is applied directly an not by steam jacket. **pot·fu** (pŏt´fool) *n.* (pl. **-fuls**). **pot** *ï* (**pot·ted, pot·ting**). Place (butter fish, meat, etc.) in pot or othe vessel to cook or preserve it; plan (plant) in pot; kill (animal) by po shot; shoot (*at*); seize, secure.

pot[2] (pŏt) *n.* (slang) Marijuana

*The poisonous fruits of the **potato** pres ent no threat to the gardener or farme since the tubers are usually harvestec as here, before the fruits are formed.*

*Making **pots** is one of man's earlie: crafts, and one in which form and dec oration — as in the jars on this Goanes stall — often seem to have come dow unchanged through the millennia.*

*Investigation of a **pot-hole**, while viewed by some people as a new form of adventure, has enabled scientists to discover fossils and other data which give an indication of life in former times in a particular area.*

po·ta·ble (pō′*tabel*) *adj.* Drink-able. **po·ta·bil′i·ty** *n.* **po′ta·-bles** *n.pl.* (usu. joc.) Drinkables. **po·tage** (pōtahzh′) *n.* Thick soup.

pot·ash (pŏt′ăsh) *n.* Alkaline substance, crude potassium carbon-ate; (also **caustic ~**) potassium hydroxide (KOH), white brittle substance, soluble in water and deliquescent in air, with powerful caustic and alkaline properties. [Du. *potasschen*, because orig. gotten by leaching vegetable ashes and evaporating the solution]

po·tas·si·um (potăs′ēum) *n.* (chem.) Light metallic element, one of the alkali metals, which is soft at ordinary temperatures, oxidizes immediately on exposure to air, and instantly decomposes water on contact with it, liberating and igniting hydrogen, which burns with a characteristic violet flame; symbol K (f. *kalium*), at. no. 19, at. wt. 39.102. [Latinized form of POTASH]

po·ta·tion (pōtā′shon) *n.* Drink-ing; (usu. pl.) tippling; draft. **po·ta·to·ry** (pō′tatōrē, -tōrē) *adj.*

po·ta·to (potā′tō) *n.* (pl. **-toes**). Plant (*Solanum tuberosum*), native of Pacific slopes of S. Amer., intro-duced into Europe late in 16th c., with roundish or oval starch-containing tubers used for food; tuber of this; **~ beetle**, **~ bug**, (also called **Colorado beetle**), small beetle native to Rocky Moun-tains but also introduced into Europe, *Leptinotarsa decemlineata*, whose larva is very destructive to potato plants; **potato chip**, thin, crisp slice of fried (and usu. salted) potato [Haitian *batata*]

po·tent (pō′tent) *adj.* Powerful, mighty (chiefly poet. or rhet.); having sexual power; (of reasons etc.) cogent; (of drugs etc.) strong. **po′ten·cy** *n.* **po′tent·ly** *adv.*

po·ten·tate (pō′tentāt) *n.* Monarch, ruler.

po·ten·tial (potĕn′shal) *adj.* Capable of coming into being or action, latent; **~ energy**, (phys.) energy existing in potential form, not as motion. **po·ten′tial·ly** *adv.* **potential** *n.* (Amount of energy or quantity of work denoted by) potential function; possibility, potentiality; resources that can be employed for an undertaking. **po·ten·ti·al·i·ty** (potĕnshēăl′ĭtē) *n.* (pl. **-ties**). Inherent, latent, capacity to exert power; possibility, promise, of development.

po·ten·ti·ate (potĕn′shēāt) *v.t.* (**-at·ed**, **-at·ing**). Endow with power; make possible.

po·ten·ti·om·e·ter (potĕn-shēŏm′ĭter) *n.* Instrument for measuring differences of electrical potential.

poth·er (pŏdh′er) *n.* Choking smoke or cloud of dust; noise, din; verbal commotion or fuss.

pot·hole (pŏt′hōl) *n.* (geol.) Deep hole of more or less cylin-drical shape; esp. one formed by wearing away of rock by rotation of a stone, or gravel, in an eddy of running water, or in glacier bed; depression or hollow in road surface caused by traffic etc. **pot′hol·er**, **pot′hol·ing** *ns.* (Brit.) Explorer, exploring of potholes.

po·tion (pō′shon) *n.* Dose, draft, of liquid medicine or of poison.

Pot·i·phar (pŏt′ifer). Egyptian officer whose wife tried to seduce

*Loading crayfish **pots** at Port Fairy, south-eastern Australia. Closely related to the lobster, they are fished in a simi-lar way with baited pots as a lure, and are a lucrative catch.*

The earliest craftsmen formed ur
from ropes of clay. These **potters**
Singapore (left and below) are using th
potter's wheel, invented
Mesopotamia about 3,500 B.C.
makes more symmetrical earthenwar

Joseph and then falsely accused hi
of an attempt on her virtue (Ge
39).

Po·to·mac (potō'mʌk). Riv
flowing 287 mi. (462 km), from tI
Allegheny Mountains in We
Virginia, along the Virginia ar
Maryland boundary, to Chesapeal
Bay; navigable to Washingto
D.C.

pot·pour·ri (pōpōoorē', pō'po
rē) *n.* (pl. **-ris**). Mixture of dri
petals and spices kept in jar f
its perfume; musical or literaʳ
medley. [Fr., lit. rotten pot]

Pots·dam (pŏts'dăm; *Ge*
pawts'dahm). City in central Ea
Germany, on the Havel River SW
of West Berlin; site of World W
II meeting of Brit., Amer., ar
Soviet leaders to arrange post-wₐ
partition and government
Germany.

pot·sherd (pŏt'shēʳd)
(archaeol.) Broken piece
earthenware.

pot·tage (pŏt'ĭj) *n.* (archaiₙ
Soup, stew (esp. with ref. to Ge
25).

pot·ter (pŏt'er) *n.* Maker
earthenware vessels; ~**'s fiel**
burial place for paupers and uₙ
identified bodies; (after Matt. 27
~**'s wheel**, wheel on which, as
spins rapidly around, the pott
molds the clay. **pot·ter**
(pŏt'erē) *n.* (pl. **-ter·ies**). Earther
ware (sometimes distinguishe
from PORCELAIN); potter's work
workshop.

Pot·ter (pŏt'er), **Helen Beatri**
(1866-1943). English author ar
illustrator of books for children.

pot·to (pŏt'ō) *n.* (pl. **-tos**
Reddish gray loris (*Perodictic*
potto) a slow-moving arbore
mammal of Africa.

pot·ty[1] (pŏt'ē) *adj.* (**-ti·e**
-ti·est). (chiefly Brit. slang)
Insignificant, trivial. 2. Foolisl
crazy.

pot·ty[2] (pŏt'ē) *n.* (pl. **-ties**
Child's chamber pot.

pouch (powch) *n.* Small bag
detachable outside pocket for carry
ing e.g. tobacco; mailbag; baglil
receptacle in which marsupia
carry their undeveloped youn
cheek pouch or other baglil
natural receptacle; (bot.) baglil
cavity in plant, esp. purselike see
vessel. ~ *v.* Put into pouch; ta
possession of, pocket.

poult (pōlt) *n.* Young
domestic fowl, turkey, pheasan
etc.

poul·tice (pōl'tĭs) *n.* Paste
bread, linseed, etc., usu. made wi
boiling water and spread on musl

Bosman's **potto** *lives in the lower
branches of high trees, sometimes
coming down to the ground. It has a
mixed animal and vegetable diet: when
asleep, it rolls up so that the spikes
growing from its spine project.*

etc., applied to sore or inflamed part. ~ *v.t.* (**-ticed, -tic·ing**). Apply poultice to.

poul·try (pōl'trē) *n.* Domestic fowls, ducks, geese, turkeys, etc., reared for food.

pounce[1] (powns) *n.* Claw, talon, of bird of prey; pouncing, sudden swoop. ~ *v.* (**pounced, pounc·ing**). Swoop down upon and seize; make sudden attack *on*, seize eagerly *on*.

pounce[2] (powns) *n.* Fine powder, formerly used to prevent ink from spreading on unsized paper etc.; powdered charcoal etc. dusted over perforated pattern to transfer design to object beneath. ~ *v.t.* (**pounced, pounc·ing**). Smooth (paper etc.) with pumice or pounce; transfer (design) by use of pounce, dust (pattern with pounce).

pound[1] (pownd) *n.* (pl. **pounds**, collect. **pound**). 1. (abbrev. lb.) Measure of weight, 16 oz. avoirdupois, 12 oz. troy. 2. (also ~ **sterling**; written £ before figure) Principal monetary unit of the United Kingdom = 100 pence. 3. Principal monetary unit of various Commonwealth countries and of Egypt (£E), Israel, Lebanon, Sudan (£S), and Syria. 4. ~ **cake**, rich cake containing 1 lb. (or equal weight) of each of chief ingredients; ~ **note**, bank or treasury note for £1; ~ **of flesh**, (fig.) any legal but unconscionable demand (from Shakespeare's *Merchant of Venice*, Shylock's demand for retribution).

pound[2] (pownd) *n.* Enclosure for animals; (fig.) place of confinement.

pound[3] (pownd) *v.* Crush, bruise, as with pestle; thump, pummel, with fists etc.; knock, beat (*to pieces, into a jelly*, etc.); deliver heavy blows, fire heavy shot (*at* etc.); walk, run, ride, make one's way, heavily; ~ **one's ear**, (slang) sleep; ~ **out**, produce (typewritten text, music) with a heavy touch; ~ **the pavement**, (slang) walk the streets, esp. when looking for work. **pound'er** *n.*

Pound (pownd), **Ezra Loomis** (1885–1972). Amer. poet, editor, and critic, esp. of early works of T. S. Eliot, James Joyce, William Carlos Williams, etc.; a founder of IMAGISM; best known for his series of volumes of *Cantos* (1925–40).

pound·al (pown'dal) *n.* (phys.) Unit of force which, when acting on a mass of 1 lb., will impart to it an acceleration of 1 ft. per sec. per sec., corresponding to the DYNE except that pound and foot replace gram and centimeter.

pour (pōr, por) *v.* Cause (liquid, granular substance, light, etc.) to flow, discharge copiously; discharge (missiles etc.) copiously or in rapid succession; send *forth, out* (words, music, etc.); flow (*forth, out, down*) in stream (also fig. of crowd etc.); (of rain) descend heavily; (fig.) come (*in, out*) abundantly. ~ *n.* Heavy fall of rain, downpour; (founding) amount of molten metal etc. poured at a time. **pour'er** *n.* **pour'ing** *adj.*

pout[1] (powt) *v.* Protrude (lips), protrude lips, (of lips) protrude, esp. as sign of displeasure. ~ *n.* Protrusion of the lips. **pout'ing·ly** *adv.* **pout'y** *adj.* (**pout·i·er, pout·i·est**).

pout[2] (powt) *n.* (pl. **pouts** collect. **pout**). Any of several fishes, including the eelpout (family Zoarcidae).

pout·er (pow'ter) *n.* Person, animal, that pouts; (esp.) domestic variety of pigeon with great power of inflating crop.

pov·er·ty (pŏv'ertē) *n.* Indigence, want; deficiency (*in, of*); inferiority, poorness; ~**-stricken**, poor.

POW, P.O.W. *abbrevs.* Prisoner of war.

pow·der (pow'der) *n.* Mass of dry particles or granules, dust; medicine in the form of powder; cosmetic powder applied to face, skin, or hair; gunpowder; (of) pale blue color; ~ **flask**, case for carrying gunpowder; ~ **horn**, powder flask orig. and esp. of horn; ~

magazine, place where gun-powder is stored; ~ **metallurgy**, molding of finely ground (esp. metal) powders into intricate shapes to which solidity is restored afterward by special treatment; ~ **puff**, soft pad for applying powder to skin; ~ **room**, (euphem.) women's lavatory, esp. in restaurant; ~ **snow**, loose dry snow on a ski run, etc.; **take a** ~, (slang) run away, leave without due notice. **powder** *v.t.* Sprinkle powder upon, cover (with powder etc.); apply powder to (hair, face, etc.); decorate (surface) with spots or small figures; reduce to powder; ~ **one's nose**, (slang, of woman) retire to lavatory. **pow'der·y** *adj.* **pow'der·er** *n.*

pow·er (pow'er) *n.* 1. Ability to do or act; vigor, energy; particular faculty of body or mind. 2. Active property, as *heating* ~. 3. Government, influence, authority (*over*); personal ascendancy (*over*); political ascendancy. 4. Authorization, delegated authority; ~ **of**

attorney: see ATTORNEY. 5. Influential person, body, or thing; nation having international influence; **the** ~**s that be**, (w. ref. to Rom. 13) constituted authorities. 6. Deity; (pl.) order of angels (see ANGEL). 7. Mechanical energy as opp. to hand labor (freq. attrib., as ~ *lathe*, ~ *loom*); capacity for exerting mechanical force, esp. horsepower; electrical power distributed to consumer; ~ **factor**, ratio between actual power delivered and apparent power suggested by voltage and current; **pow'erhouse**, power station; (fig.) source of drive or influence. 8. (math., of a number or algebraic quantity) Product of a specified number of factors, each of which is the number or quantity

Pylons and **power-lines** *stride across the countryside in Arizona, bringing electricity to isolated areas which before their installation would have been inaccessible. Appropriately the word pylon comes from the Greek 'gateway'.*

itself, the specified number of factors being the *index*. 9. Magnifying power of lens. 10. **power dive**, (of aircraft), dive made without shutting off the motor power; **power politics**, diplomacy backed by (threat of) force; **power station**, station in which electric power is generated for distribution. **power** *v.t.* Supply with mechanical power. **pow'ered** *adj.*

pow·er·ful (pow'erful) *adj.* Having great power or influence. **pow'er·ful·ly** *adv.* **pow'er·ful·ness** *n.*

pow·er·less (pow'erlĭs) *adj.* Without power; wholly unable (*to* help etc.). **pow'er·less·ly** *adv.* **pow'er·less·ness** *n.*

Pow·ha·tan (powhatăn', -hăt'-en) (1550?–1618). Amer. Algonquian Indian chief of Powhatan confederacy and father of Pocahontas.

pow·wow (pow'wow) *n.* 1. N. Amer. Ind. medicine man or sorcerer. 2. Magic ceremonial, conference, of N. Amer. Indians. 3. (colloq.) Conference or meeting. ~ *v.i.* Hold powwow; (colloq.) confer.

pox (pŏks) *n.* Disease characterized by pocks, esp. syphilis.

pp. *abbrev.* Pages; past participle; *pianissimo*.

P.P., p.p. *abbrevs.* Past participle; parcel post; prepaid; postpaid.

PPI *abbrev.* Plan position indicator.

PPM, ppm, p.p.m. *abbrevs.* Parts per million.

Pr *symbol.* Praseodymium.

pr. *abbrev.* Pair; present; price; pronoun.

P.R. *abbrev.* Proportional representation; Puerto Rico; public relations.

prac·ti·ca·ble (prăk'tĭkabel) *adj.* That can be done, feasible; that can be used, (of road etc.) that can be traversed. **prac·ti·ca·bil'i·ty, prac'ti·ca·ble·ness** *ns.* **prac'ti·ca·bly** *adv.*

prac·ti·cal (prăk'tĭkal) *adj.* 1. Of, concerned with, shown in, practice; available, useful, in practice; engaged in practice, practicing; ~ **joke**: see JOKE. 2. Inclined to action rather than speculation. 3. That is such in effect though not nominally, virtual. **prac'ti·cal·ness, prac·ti·cal·i·ty** (prăktĭkăl'ĭtē) *ns.* **prac'ti·cal·ly** *adv.* In a practical manner; virtually, almost.

prac·tice[1] (prăk'tĭs) *n.* 1. Habitual action or carrying on; method of legal procedure; habit, custom; repeated exercise in an art,

Power comes in many forms, including solar power as seen on this experimental house in Arizona. Solar power has many advantages over conventional fossil-fuel plants, including its cost and minimal disruption to the environment.

Power stations of many types have been developed all over the world since the first steam-driven ones were built in the late 19th century. Fueled by coal, oil, natural gas, or nuclear energy, or driven by the power of tides or falling water, they provide the electrical power required for modern life.

1 visitors' viewing balcony
2 main control room
3 data processing room
4 tank floor and heating plant
5 deaerator
6 visitors' charge face viewing room
7 fuelling machine
8 fuelling machine maintenance crane
9 maintenance area
10 fuelling standpipes
11 pre-stressed concrete reactor vessel
12 boiler
13 gas circulator
14 gas circulator maintenance crane
15 essential supplies room
16 irradiated fuel disposal chute
17 cooling pond
18 flask handling area
19 loading bay
20 turbo generator
21 turbine unit maintenance crane
22 evaporator plant

handicraft, etc.; spell of this. **2.** Professional work, business, or connection, of lawyer or doctor. **3.** (archaic) Scheming, (usu. underhand) contrivance, artifice (esp. pl.); **sharp ~:** see SHARP. **4. in ~,** in the realm of action; actually; skilled through having recently had practice; **put in(to) ~,** carry out. **prac·tice²** (prăk´tĭs) v. (**-ticed, -tic·ing**). Perform habitually, carry out in action; exercise, pursue (profession); exercise oneself in or on (art, instrument, or abs.); exercise (in action or subject); (archaic) scheme, contrive; **~ on,** impose upon, take advantage of. **prac´-ticed** adj. Experienced, expert. **prac·tise (-tised, -tis·ing)** (Brit.). **prac·ti·tion·er** (prăktĭsh´oner) n. Professional or practical worker, esp. in medicine; **general ~:** see GENERAL.

Pra·do (prah´dō). Spanish national museum of painting and sculpture, in Madrid, containing part of the royal collections. [Span., = "meadow," f. the adjoining park]

prae·tor, pre·tor (prē´ter) ns. (Rom. hist.; orig.) Consul as leader of army; (later) annually elected magistrate performing some duties of consul. **prae·to·ri·al** (prētōr´-ēal, -tōr´-) adj.

prae·to·ri·an (prētōr´ēan, -tōr´-) adj. Of a praetor; **P~ Guard,** bodyguard of a Roman general or emperor. **praetorian** n. Man of praetorian rank, soldier of praetorian guard.

prag·mat·ic (prăgmăt´ĭk), **prag·mat·i·cal** (prăgmăt´ĭkal) adjs. **1.** Meddlesome; dogmatic. **2.** Practical, in action or thought, opp. theoretical. **3.** Of philosophical pragmatism. **4. (-ic)** Treating facts of history with reference to their practical lessons. 5. (**-ic**, hist.) Of the affairs of a state. **prag·mat′i·cal·ly** *adv.* **prag·mat′i·cal·ness** *n.* **prag·ma·tism** (prăg′mătĭzem) *n.* 1. Matter-of-fact treatment of things. 2. Philosophical doctrine that evaluates any assertion solely by its practical bearing upon human interests. **prag′ma·tist** *n.*

Prague (prahg). Capital and largest city of Czechoslovakia, in the W. part on the Moldau River.

prai·rie (prār′ē) *n.* Large treeless tract of level or undulating grassland, esp. in N. Amer.; ~ **chicken, hen**, N. Amer. grouse of genus *Tympanuchus*; ~ **dog**, N. Amer. burrowing rodent (*Cynomys*) of squirrel family; ~ **oyster**, raw egg seasoned and swallowed in whiskey; testis of a calf as food; ~ **schooner**, large covered wagon of kind used by pioneers in crossing N. Amer. plains.

praise (prāz) *v.t.* (**praised, prais·ing**). Express warm approbation of, commend the merits of; glorify, extol the attributes of. ~ *n.* Praising, commendation.

prais′er *n.*

praise·wor·thy (prāz′wĕrdhē) *adj.* Worthy of praise, commendable. **praise′wor·thi·ly** *adv.* **praise′wor·thi·ness** *n.*

Pra·krit (prah′krĭt) *n.* Any of the vernacular Indo-European dialects of India, as dist. from Sanskrit; all these collectively.

pra·line (prah′lēn, prā′-) *n.* Candy made by browning nuts in boiling sugar.

pram (prăm) *n.* (Brit.) Perambulator.

prance (prăns) *v.* (**pranced, pranc·ing**). (of horse) Rise by springing from hind legs; cause (horse) to do this; (fig.) walk, behave, in elated or arrogant manner. ~ *n.* Prancing (movement). **pranc′er** *n.* **pranc′ing·ly** *adv.*

pran·di·al (prăn′dēal) *adj.* (joc.) Of dinner.

The site of Prague has been inhabited since the Palaeolithic age, though perhaps not continuously until the 9th century A.D. It became of major European importance in the 14th century as a center of trade and culture.

Prairie dogs are actually rodents belonging to the squirrel family. They live in burrows and are named for the barking sound they make when alarmed.

prank[1] (prăngk) *n.* Mad frolic, practical joke. **prank′ish** *adj* **prank′ish·ly** *adv.* **prank′ish·ness, prank′ster** *ns.*

prank[2] (prăngk) *v.* Dress, deck (*out*); adorn, spangle (*with*); show oneself off.

pra·se·o·dym·i·um (prāzēō- dĭm′ēum) *n.* (chem.) Metallic element of rare-earth group forming leek-green salts; symbol Pr, at. no. 59, at. wt. 140.9077. [Gk. *prasios* leek-green, (DI) DYMIUM]

prate (prāt) *v.* (**prat·ed, prat·ing**). Chatter; discourse foolishly; talk solemn nonsense. **prat′er** *n.* **prat′ing·ly** *adv.*

prat·tle (prăt′el) *v.* (**-tled, -tling**). Talk or say in childish or artless fashion. **prat′tler** *n.* **prattle** *n.* Childish chatter, small talk.

prawn (prawn) *n.* Small lobsterlike marine decapod crustacean of genus *Palaemon, Penaeus*, etc., larger than shrimp. ~ *v.i.* Fish for prawns.

Prax·it·e·les (prăksĭt′elēz) (4th c. B.C.). Greek sculptor, creator of "Apollo Slaying a Lizard" and "Hermes with the Infant Dionysus."

pray (prā) *v.* Make devout supplication to (God, object of worship); beseech earnestly (*for, to, that*); ask earnestly for; engage in prayer, make entreaty; ~ (contr. of *I pray you*), used parenthetically for emphasis, e.g. *what, ~, is the use of that?*

prayer[1] (prār) *n.* Solemn

Prayer is thought by many theologians to be the most important aspect of a religion. Through the ages it has taken many forms, private as in (2), the expression of mass feeling as shown by the packed mosque of (1), or even — strange though it may seem — regulated by devices like the prayer wheels used in Buddhist lands (3).

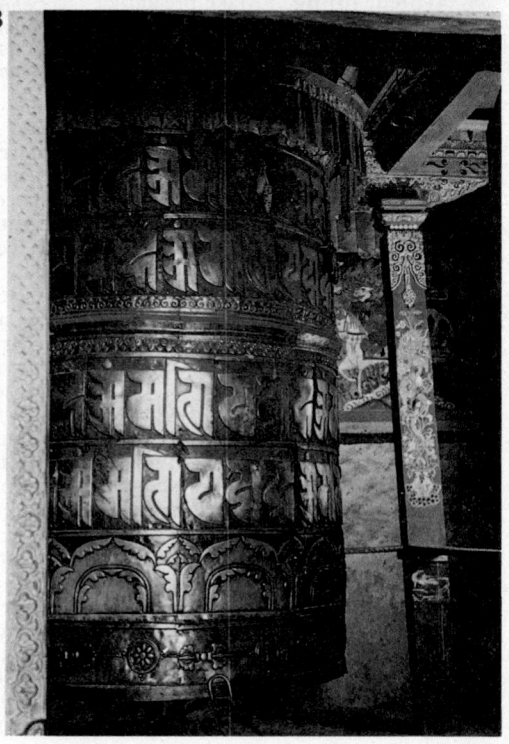

3

request to God or object of worship; formula used in praying; form of divine service consisting largely of prayers; action, practice, of praying; entreaty to a person; thing prayed for; ~ **book**, book of prayers, esp. **Book of Common P**~: see COMMON; ~ **meeting**, religious meeting at which several persons offer prayer; ~ **wheel**, revolving cylindrical box inscribed with or containing prayers, used esp. by Buddhists of Tibet. **prayer·ful** (prār'ful) *adj.* **prayer'ful·ly** *adv.* **prayer'ful·ness** *n.*

pray·er[2] (prā'er) *n.* Person who prays.

pre- *prefix.* Before.

preach (prēch) *v.* Deliver sermon or religious address, deliver (sermon); give moral advice in obtrusive way; proclaim, expound (the Gospel, Christ, etc.) in public discourses; advocate, inculcate (quality, conduct, etc.) thus. **preach'ing** *n.* **preach'ing·ly** *adv.* **preach'er** *n.* **preach'ment** *n.* (usu. contempt.).

preach·i·fy (prē'chĭfī) *v.i.* (**-fied, -fy·ing**). (colloq.) Preach, moralize, hold forth, tediously.

preach·y (prē'chē) *adj.* (**preach·i·er, preach·i·est**). (colloq.) Fond of preaching or holding forth.

pre·ad·am·ite (prēăd'amīt) *adj.* & *n.* (One of supposed race) existing before time of Adam. **pre·a·dam·ic** (prēadăm'ĭk) *adj.*

pre·am·ble (prē'ămbel, prēăm'-) *n.* Preliminary statement in speech or writing; introductory part of statute, deed, etc. ~ *v.i.* (**-bled, -bling**). Make preamble.

pre·ar·range (prēarānj') *v.t.* (**-ranged, -rang·ing**). Arrange beforehand. **pre·ar·range'ment** *n.*

Pre·cam·bri·an (prēkăm'brēan) *adj.* & *n.* (geol.) (Of) the earliest period or system, occurring before the Cambrian.

pre·can·cer·ous (prēkăn'serus) *adj.* Likely to become cancerous.

pre·car·i·ous (prĭkār'ēus) *adj.* Held during the pleasure of another; doubtful, uncertain; dependent on chance; perilous. **pre·car'i·ous·ly** *adv.* **pre·car'i·ous·ness** *n.*

pre·cast (prē'kăst') *adj.* (of concrete) Cast in blocks, slabs, etc. before use in construction.

pre·cau·tion (prĭkaw'shon) *n.* Prudent foresight; measure taken beforehand to ward off evil or ensure good result. **pre·cau·tion·ar·y** (prĭkaw'shonĕrē), **pre·cau·tious** (prĭkaw'shus) *adj.*

pre·cede (prĭsēd') *v.* (**-ced·ed, -ced·ing**). Go before in rank or importance; come before in order; walk or proceed in advance of; come before in time; cause to be preceded

*Many aspects of the various **Pre-Columbian** cultures are still not fully understood, but the skill of their craftsmen, as shown in this Mexican pyramid, needs no interpretation.*

by.

prec·e·dence (prĕs'ĭdens, prĭsē'dens) *n.* Priority in time or succession; superiority, higher position; right of preceding others in ceremonies and social formalities. **prec·e·den·cy** (prĕs'ĭdensē, prĭsē'densē) *n.* (pl. **-cies**). Precedence.

prec·e·dent[1] (prĕs'ĭdent) *n.* Previous case taken as example for subsequent cases or as justification; (law) decision, procedure, etc., serving as rule or pattern. **prec·e·dent·ed** *adj.* Having a precedent; supported by precedent. **prec·e·den·tial** (prĕsĭdĕn'shal) *adj.*

pre·ced·ent[2] (prĭsē'dent, prĕs'ĭdent) *adj.* Preceding in time, order, rank, etc.

pre·cept (prē'sĕpt) *n.* Command, maxim; moral instruction; writ, warrant. **pre·cep·tive** (prĭsĕp'tĭv) *adj.*

pre·cep·tor (prĭsĕp'ter, prē'sĕp-) *n.* (fem. **pre·cep·tress** pr.

prĭsĕp'trĭs). Teacher, instructor. **pre·cep·to·ri·al** (prēsĕptōr'ēal, -tŏr'-), **pre·cep'tor·al** *adjs.* **pre·cep'tor·ship** *n.*

pre·cess (prēsĕs') *v.i.* (of rapidly revolving globe, spinning top, etc.) Sway in such a way that its axis describes a circle.

pre·ces·sion (prēsĕsh'on) *n.* **of the equinoxes**, earlier occurrence of the equinoxes in each successive sidereal year through a slow change in the direction of the Earth's axis, which moves (like the axis of a spinning top) so that the pole of the equator describes an approximate circle around the pole of the ecliptic once in about 25,800 years.

pre-Chris·tian (prēkrĭs'chan) *adj.* Before Christ, before Christianity.

pre·cinct (prē'sĭngkt) *n.* 1. Space enclosed by walls or other boundaries of a place or building, esp. of place of worship; boundary; (pl.) environs. 2. Subdivision of county or city or ward for election and police purposes.

pre·ci·os·i·ty (prĕshēŏs'ĭtē) *n.* (pl. **-ties**). Affectation of refinement or distinction.

pre·cious (prĕsh′us) *adj.* 1. Of great price, costly; of great non-material worth; ~ **metals**, gold, silver, (sometimes) platinum; ~ **stone**, stone of great value, used in ewel. 2. Affectedly refined in anguage, workmanship, etc. 3. Beloved; (abs. as noun) beloved person. ~ *adv.* (colloq.) Extremely, very. **pre′cious·ly** *adv.* **pre′cious·ness** *n.*

prec·i·pice (prĕs′ĭpĭs) *n.* Vertical or steep face of rock, cliff, mountain, etc.

pre·cip·i·tate[1] (prĭsĭp′ĭtāt) *v.t.* -tat·ed, -tat·ing). 1. Throw down headlong, hurl, fling; hurry, urge on; hasten the occurrence of. . (chem.) Cause (a solid substance) o be deposited from a solution by he addition of another solution; ondense (vapor) into drops and so eposit. **pre·cip′i·ta·tor** *n.* **pre-cip·i·ta′tion** *n.* (esp., meteor.) Fall f rain, sleet, snow, or hail. **precipitate** (prĭsĭp′ĭtĭt, -tāt) *n.* chem.) Substance precipitated rom solution; moisture condensed rom vapor by cooling and eposited.

pre·cip·i·tate[2] (prĭsĭp′ĭtĭt -tāt)

*Attractiveness as well as rarity have made gold a **precious** metal: even in a photograph (U.S.A. foreign gold reserves, above) its beauty is apparent. It is not, though, the only precious metal — others are platinum and silver.*

adj. Headlong, violently hurried; hasty, rash, inconsiderate. **pre·cip′i·tate·ly** *adv.* **pre·cip′i·tate·ness, pre·cip′i·tan·cy, pre·cip′i·tance** *ns.*

pre·cip·i·tous (prĭsĭp′ĭtus) *adj.* Of, like, a precipice; steep. **pre·cip′i·tous·ly** *adv.* **pre·cip′i·tous·ness** *n.*

pré·cis (prāsē′, prā′sē) *n.* (pl. -cis pr.- -sēz′, -sēz). Summary, abstract.

pre·cise (prĭsīs′) *adj.* Accurately expressed, definite, exact; punctilious, scrupulous in observance of rules etc. **pre·cise′ly** *adv.* In precise manner; (in emphatic or formal assent) quite so. **pre·cise′ness** *n.*

pre·ci·sion (prĭsĭzh′on) *n.* Accuracy; (attrib., of apparatus) designed for exact or precise work. **pre·ci′sion·ist** *n.*

pre·clas·si·cal (prēklăs′ĭkal) *adj.* Before the classical age (usu.

of Greek and Roman literature or civilization).

pre·clude (prĭklo͞od′) *v.t.* (-clud·ed, -clud·ing). Exclude, prevent, make impracticable. **pre-clu·sive** (prĭklo͞o′sĭv) *adj.* **pre-clu′sive·ly** *adv.* **pre·clu·sion** (prĭklo͞o′zhon) *n.*

pre·co·cious (prĭkō′shus) *adj.* (of plant) Flowering or fruiting early; (of person) prematurely developed in some faculty; (of actions etc.) indicating such development. **pre·co′cious·ly** *adv.* **pre·co′cious·ness, pre·coc·i·ty** (prĭkŏs′ĭtē) *ns.*

pre·cog·ni·tion (prēkŏgnĭsh′on) *n.* 1. Antecedent knowledge. 2. Extrasensory perception of an event before it occurs. **pre·cog·ni·tive** (prēkŏg′nĭtĭv) *adj.*

pre-Co·lum·bi·an (prēkolŭm′-bēan) *adj.* Before the discovery of Amer. by Columbus.

pre·con·ceive (prēkonsēv′) *v.t.* (-ceived, -ceiv·ing). Conceive beforehand, anticipate in thought. **pre·con·cep·tion** (prēkonsĕp′-shon) *n.* (esp.) Prejudice.

pre·con·di·tion (prēkondĭsh′on) *n.* Prior condition, one that must be fulfilled beforehand.

pre·con·scious (prēkŏn'shus) *adj*. Antecedent to consciousness; (psychol.) of the foreconscious.

pre·cur·sor (prĭkēr'ser, prē'-kēr-) *n*. Forerunner, harbinger; one who precedes in office etc. **pre·cur·so·ry** (prĭkēr'serē) *adj*. Preliminary, introductory, serving as harbinger (*of*). **pre·cur·sive** (prĭkēr'sĭv) *adj*.

pre·da·cious, pre·da·ceous (prĭdā'shus) *adjs*. (of animals) Predatory. **pre·dac·i·ty** (prĭdăs'-ĭtē), **pre·da·cious·ness, pre·da'-ceous·ness** *ns*.

pred·a·tor (prĕd'ater) *n*. Animal that preys upon others.

pred·a·to·ry (prĕd'atōrē, -tōrē) *adj*. Of, addicted to, plunder or robbery; (of animals) preying upon others.

pre·de·cease (prēdĭsēs') *v.t*. (-ceased, -ceas·ing). Die before (another).

pred·e·ces·sor (prĕd'ĭsĕser, prē'dĭ-) *n*. Former holder of any office or position; thing to which another thing has succeeded; forefather.

pre·des·ti·nate (prēdĕs'tĭnāt) *v.t*. (-nat·ed, -nat·ing). (of God) Foreordain (person) to salvation or *to* (any fate), *to* (do); determine beforehand. ~ (prēdĕs'tĭnĭt, -nāt) *adj*.

pre·des·ti·na·tion (prēdĕstĭnā'-shon) *n*. God's appointment from eternity of some of mankind to salvation and eternal life; God's foreordaining of all that comes to pass; fate, destiny.

pre·des·tine (prēdĕs'tĭn) *v.t*. (-tined, -tin·ing). Determine beforehand; appoint as if by fate; (theol.) predestinate.

pre·de·ter·mine (prēdĭtēr'mĭn) *v.t*. (-mined, -min·ing). Decree beforehand; predestine; (of motive, etc.) impel (person) beforehand. **pre·de·ter·mi·nate** (prēdĭtēr'-mĭnĭt, -nāt) *adj*. **pre·de·ter·mi·na'tion** *n*.

pred·i·ca·ble (prĕd'ĭkabel) *adj*. That may be predicated or affirmed. **pred·i·ca·bil'i·ty, pred'i·ca·ble·ness** *ns*. **pred'i·ca·bly** *adv*. **predicable** *n*. Predicable thing, esp. (pl.) Aristotle's classes of predicates viewed relatively to their subjects (viz. genus, definition, property, accident).

pre·dic·a·ment (prĭdĭk'ament) *n*. 1. (also pr. prĕd'ĭkament) Thing predicated, esp. (pl.) ten categories of predications formed by Aristotle. 2. Unpleasant, trying, or dangerous situation.

pred·i·cant (prĕd'ĭkant) *adj*. (of religious order, esp. Dominicans) Engaged in preaching.

pred·i·cate (prĕd'ĭkĭt) *n*. (logic) What is predicated; what is affirmed or denied of the subject by means of the copula (e.g. *a fool* in

he is a fool); (gram.) what is said of the subject, including the copula (e.g. *is a fool* in preceding example); quality, attribute. ~ (prĕd'ĭkāt) *v.t*. (-cat·ed, -cat·ing). Assert, affirm, as true or existent; (logic) assert (thing) about subject. **pred·i·ca'tion** *n*.

pred·i·ca·tive (prĕd'ĭkatĭv, -kātĭv) *adj*. Making a predication; (gram., of adjective or noun, opp. attributive) forming part or the whole of the predicate. **pred'i·ca·tive·ly** *adv*.

pre·dict (prĭdĭkt') *v.t*. Forecast, prophesy. **pre·dict'a·ble, pre·dic'tive** *adjs*. **pre·dic'tion** (prĭdĭk'shon), **pre·dic'tor** *ns*.

pre·di·gest (prēdĭjĕst', -dĭ-) *v.t*. Render (food) easily digestible before introduction into stomach. **pre·di·ges'tion** *n*.

pre·di·lec·tion (prēdĭlĕk'shon, prē-) *n*. Special liking, partiality (*for*).

pre·dis·pose (prēdĭspōz') *v.t*. (-posed, -pos·ing). Render liable, subject, or inclined (*to*). **pre·dis·po·si·tion** (prēdĭspozĭsh'on) *n*. State of mind or body favorable *to*.

pre·dom·i·nate (prĭdŏm'ĭnāt) *v.i*. (-nat·ed, -nat·ing). Have or exert control (*over*), be superior; be the stronger or main element, preponderate. **pre·dom·i·nance** (prĭdŏm'ĭnans), **pre·dom'i·nan·cy** *ns*. **pre·dom'i·nant** *adj*. **pre·dom'i·nant·ly** *adv*.

pre·dy·nas·tic (prēdīnăs'tĭk) *adj*. Of the period before the 1st dynasty, esp. in Egypt.

pre·em·i·nent, pre-em·i·nent (prēĕm'ĭnent) *adjs*. Excelling others; distinguished beyond others in some quality. **pre·em'i·nence, pre-em'i·nence** *ns*. **pre·em'i·nent·ly, pre-em'i·nent·ly** *advs*.

pre·empt, pre-empt (prēĕmpt') *vbs.t*. Obtain by preemption; occupy (public land) so as to have right of preemption; appropriate beforehand. **pre·emp'tor, pre-emp'tor** *ns*.

pre·emp·tion, pre-emp·tion (prēĕmp'shon) *ns*. Purchase by on person etc. before opportunity i offered to others; right of actua occupant to purchase public land thus at nominal price, on condition of his improving it. **pre·emp'tive pre-emp'tive** (prēĕmp'tĭv) *adjs* (esp., in bridge, of bid) Highe than necessary, so as to preven opponents from exchanging in formation by bidding. **pre·emp'-tive·ly, pre-emp'tive·ly** *advs*.

preen (prēn) *v.t*. (of bird) Trim (feathers) with beak and oil secreted by gland; trim *oneself*, smooth and adorn *oneself* (also fig., show satisfaction). **preen'er** *n*.

pref. *abbrev*. Preface; preference; preferred; prefix.

pre·fab (prē'făb) *n*. (colloq.) Prefabricated building.

pre·fab·ri·cate (prēfăb'rĭkat) *v.t*. (-cat·ed, -cat·ing). Make (building etc.) in sections for assembly on a site. **pre·fab·ri·ca'tion** *n*.

pref·ace (prĕf'ĭs) *n*. Introduction to book stating subject scope, etc.; preliminary part of a speech; introduction to central par of the Mass. ~ *v*. Furnish (book etc.) with preface, introduce (*with*) lead up to (event etc.); make preliminary remarks. **pref'a·to·ry** (prĕf'atōrē, -tōrē), **pref·a·to'ri·al** *adjs*. **pref'a·to·ri·ly** *adv*.

pre·fect (prē'fĕkt) *n*. 1. (Rom hist.) Any of various civil and military officers e.g. civil governor of province, colony, etc. 2. Chief administrative officer of French department; **P ~ of Police**, head of police administration of Paris and the department of the Seine. 3. (in some Brit. schools) Senior pupil

Mere size is not essential for a pred ator. The tree spider (1) can seize prey larger than itself, although this is no usually the case with birds of prey such as (2): among mammals, a pack may join in bringing down the quarry.

authorized to maintain discipline.
pre·fec·to·ri·al (prĕfĕktōr´ēal, -tōr´-) *adj.*

pre·fec·ture (prē´fĕkcher) *n.* (Period of) office, official residence, district under government, of a prefect. **pre·fec·tur·al** (prĭfĕk´cheral) *adj.*

pre·fer (prĭfĕr´) *v.t.* (**-ferred, -fer·ring**). 1. Promote (person *to* office). 2. Bring forward, submit (statement, information, etc., *to* person in authority etc. *against* offender etc.). 3. Choose, like better, (than someone or something else); **preferred stock**, one on which dividend is paid before any is paid on common stock. **pref·er·a·ble** (prĕf´erabel, prĕf´ra-) *adj.* **pref·er·a·bly** *adv.*

pref·er·ence (prĕf´erens, prĕf´rens) *n.* Liking of one thing better than another; thing one prefers; prior right esp. to payment of debts; favoring of one person or country before others in business relations, esp. favoring of country by admitting its products at lower import duty.

pref·er·en·tial (prĕferĕn´shal) *adj.* Of, giving, receiving, preference; (of duties etc.) favoring particular countries. **pref·er·en´tial·ly** *adv.*

pre·fer·ment (prĭfĕr´ment) *n.* Advancement, promotion; appointment, esp. ecclesiastical, giving social or financial advancement.

pre·fig·ure (prēfĭg´yer) *v.t.* (**-ured, -ur·ing**). Represent beforehand by figure or type; picture to oneself beforehand. **pre·fig·u·ra·tion** (prēfĭgyerā´shon) *n.* **pre·fig·ur·a·tive** (prēfĭg´yerativ) *adj.* **pre·fig´ure·ment** *n.*

pre·fix (prē´fĭks) *n.* Verbal element placed at beginning of word to qualify meaning or (in some languages) as inflectional formative; combining form; word (esp. preposition or adverb) used in combination; title placed before name. ~ (prēfĭks´, prē´fĭks) *v.t.* Add (*to* book etc.) as introduction; join as prefix (*to* word).

pre·form (prēfōrm´) *v.t.* Form beforehand. **pre·for·ma·tion** (prēfōrmā´shon) *n.* Previous formation.

pre·form·a·tive (prēfōr´mativ) *adj.* Forming beforehand; prefixed as formative element, esp. in Semitic languages. ~ *n.* Preformative letter or syllable.

preg·na·ble (prĕg´nabel) *adj.* Capable of being captured.

preg·nant (prĕg´nant) *adj.* 1. (of woman or female animal) With child(ren) or young in the womb. 2. Teeming with ideas, imaginative, inventive; fruitful in results; (of words or acts) having a hidden meaning, significant, suggestive. **preg´nan·cy** *n.* (pl. **-cies**). **preg´-**

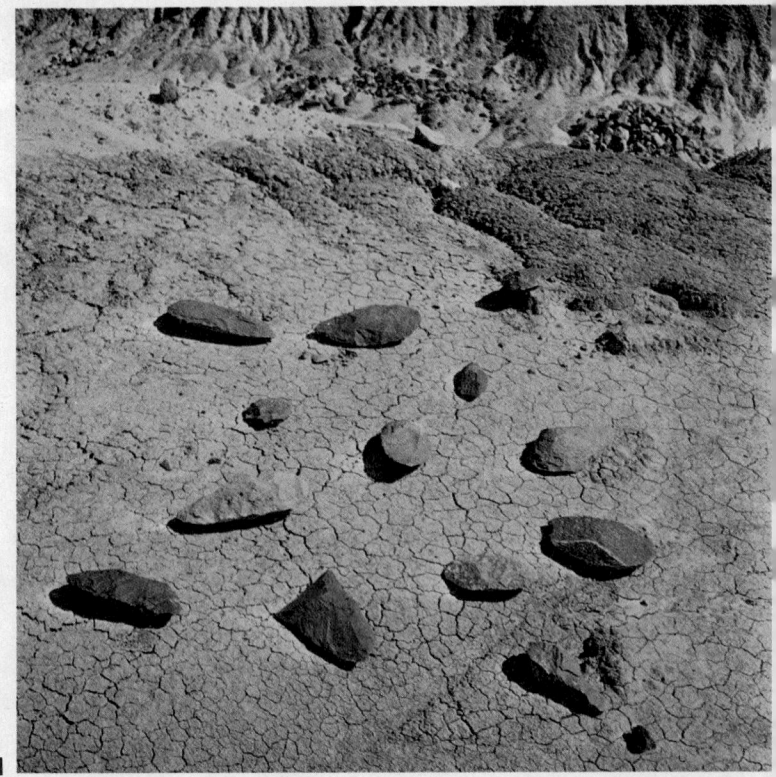

nant·ly *adv.*

pre·hen·sile (prēhĕn´sĭl, -sīl) *adj.* (zool., of tail or limb) Capable of grasping.

pre·his·tor·ic (prēhĭstōr´ĭk, -stär´-), **pre·his·tor´i·cal** *adjs.* Of the period antecedent to history. **pre·his·tor´i·cal·ly** *adv.*

pre·his·to·ry (prēhĭs´terē) *n.* Prehistoric matters or times. **pre·his·to·ri·an** (prēhĭstōr´ēan, -stōr´, -stär´-) *n.*

pre·ig·ni·tion (prēĭgnĭsh´on) *n.* Early ignition in internal combustion engine.

pre·judge (prējŭj´) *v.t.* (**-judged, -judg·ing**). Pass judgment on before trial or proper inquiry; form premature judgment upon. **pre·judg´ment**, esp. Brit. **pre·judge´ment** *ns.*

prej·u·dice (prĕj´udĭs) *n.* Preconceived opinion, bias; injury that results or may result from some action or judgment; **without ~**, without detriment to existing right or claim. **prejudice** *v.t.* (**-diced, -dic·ing**). Impair the validity of (right, claim, etc.); cause (person) to have a prejudice (*against, in favor of*).

prej·u·di·cial (prĕjudĭsh´al) *adj.* Causing prejudice, detrimental (*to*). **prej·u·di´cial·ly** *adv.*

prel·a·cy (prĕl´asē) *n.* (pl. **-cies**). Office, rank, see, of a prelate; prelates collectively; church, government by prelates.

prel·ate (prĕl´ĭt) *n.* High ecclesiastical dignitary, e.g. (arch)bishop, metropolitan, patriarch; (hist.) abbot or prior. **pre·lat·ic**

*All we know of **prehistoric** man comes from the material remains he left. Sometimes, as in the case of these stone tools from Africa (1), their use is clear. but are these Breton monoliths (3) purely ritual or a calendar, these animals from Lascaux (2) magic or art?*

(prĭlăt´ĭk) *adj.*

prel·a·ture (prĕl´acher) *n.* Prelacy.

pre·lim·i·nar·y (prĭlĭm´inĕrē) *adj.* Introductory, preparatory. ~ *n.* (pl. **-nar·ies**). Preliminary arrangement. **pre·lim´i·nar·i·ly** *adv.*

prel·ude (prĕl´ūd, prāl´-, prē´lōōd, prā´-) *n.* Performance, action, event, condition, serving as introduction (*to* another); (mus.) introductory movement or piece of music, esp. one preceding fugue or forming 1st part of suite; short piece of music of similar type and on a theme. ~ *v.* (**-ud·ed, -ud·ing**). Serve as prelude to, introduce, foreshadow; introduce with a prelude; be, give, a prelude *to*; (mus.) play a prelude. **pre·lu·sion** (prĭlōō´zhon) *n.* **pre·lu·sive** (prĭlōō´sĭv) *adj.*

pre·ma·ture (prēmatoor´, -tūr´, -choor´) *adj.* Occurring, done, before the usual or proper time, too early, hasty; ~ **baby**, baby born before expected date or weighing under 5½ lbs. (2,500 g). **pre·ma·ture´ly** *adv.* **pre·ma·ture´ness**, **pre·ma·tu´ri·ty** *ns.*

pre·max·il·la (prēmăksĭl´a) *n.* (pl. **-max·il·lae** pr. -măksĭl´ē) Bone forming front of upper jaw in

*The **Pre-Raphaelite** movement had its roots in a reaction against what its members saw as the falseness of 19th-century art. They drew their inspiration from literature, as in this 'Legend of the Briar Rose'.*

vertebrates, bearing the incisors. **pre·max·il·lar·y** (prĕmăk'sĭlĕrē) *adj.*

pre·med·i·ca·tion (prĕmĕdĭkā'shon) *n.* Administration of sedative or hypnotic drug to patient before giving general anesthetic.

pre·med·i·tate (prĭmĕd'ĭtāt) *v.t.* (**-tat·ed, -tat·ing**). Think out, design, beforehand. **pre·med'i·tat·ed, pre·med'i·ta·tive** *adjs.* **pre·med'i·tat·ed·ly** *adv.* **pre·med'i·ta·tor, pre·med·i·ta'tion** *ns.*

pre·mier (prĭmēr', prēmyēr') *adj.* (now chiefly slang and journalese) First in position, importance, order, or time. ~ *n.* Prime minister. **pre·mier'ship** *n.*

pre·miere, pre·mière (prĭmēr', -myār') *ns.* First performance of play etc.

prem·ise (prĕm'ĭs) *n.* 1. Previous statement from which another is inferred; **major** and **minor** ~ **s**, two propositions from which the conclusion is derived in a SYLLOGISM. 2. (pl.) Aforesaid, foregoing, esp. (law) aforesaid houses, lands, or tenements. 3. (pl.) House, building, with grounds and appurtenances. ~ *v.t.* (**-ised, -is·ing**). Say, write, by way of introduction.

pre·mi·um (prē'mēum) *n.* 1. Reward, prize (now chiefly in **put a ~ on**, provide or act as incentive to). 2. Amount to be paid in consideration of contract of insurance. 3. Sum additional to

interest, wages, etc., a bonus; fee for instruction in profession etc.; charge for changing one currency into another of greater value; **at a ~**, at more than nominal value; (fig.) in high esteem.

pre·mo·lar (prĕmō'ler) *adj. & n.* (Tooth) developed between canines and molars; (in man) bicuspid.

pre·mo·ni·tion (prĕmŏnĭsh'on, prēmo-) *n.* Forewarning; presentiment. **pre·mon·i·to·ry** (prĭmŏn'ĭtōrē, -tōrē) *adj.* **pre·mon'i·to·ri·ly** *adv.*

pre·na·tal (prēnā'tal) *adj.* Existing, occurring, before birth or childbirth. **pre·na'tal·ly** *adv.*

pre·nup·tial (prēnŭp'shal, -chal) *adj.* Before a marriage.

pre·oc·cu·pa·tion (prēŏkyupā'shon) *n.* Prepossession, prejudice; occupation of a place beforehand; occupation, business, that takes precedence over all others; mental absorption.

pre·oc·cu·py (prēŏk'yupī) *v.t.* (**-pied, -py·ing**). Engage beforehand, engross (mind etc.); appropriate beforehand. **pre·oc'cu·pied** *adj.* Distracted, with thoughts elsewhere.

pre·or·dain (prēôrdān') *v.t.* Appoint beforehand; foreordain. **pre·or·di·na'tion** *n.*

prep (prĕp) *adj.* Preparatory (a ~ *school*).

prep. *abbrev.* Preposition.

pre·pack·age (prēpăk'ĭj) *v.t.* (**-aged, -ag·ing**). (also **pre·pack'**) Pack (goods) ready for sale before distributing them.

prep·a·ra·tion (prĕperā'shon) *n.* 1. Preparing; (usu. pl.) thing(s) done to make ready (*for*). 2. Substance, e.g. food or medicine specially prepared.

pre·par·a·to·ry (prĭpăr'atōrē -tōrē, prĕp'era-) *adj.* Serving to prepare, introductory (*to*); ~ **school**, school where pupils are prepared for college. **pre·par'a·to·ri·ly** *adv.*

pre·pare (prĭpār') *v.* (**-pared, -par·ing**). Make ready (*for*); make (food, meal) ready for eating, make mentally ready or fit (*for* news, *to* hear, etc.); get (lesson, speech, etc.) ready by previous study, get (person) ready by teaching (*for* college, examination etc.); make preparations (*for, to do* etc.); make (chemical product etc. by regular process; **be prepared** be ready or willing (*to* do).

pre·pay (prēpā') *v.t.* (**-paid, -pay·ing**). Pay (charge) beforehand; pay (postage), pay postage on (parcel etc.) beforehand, e.g. by affixing stamp. **pre·pay'ment** *n.*

pre·pon·der·ate (prĭpŏn'derāt) *v.i.* (**-at·ed, -at·ing**). Weigh more, be heavier; be of greater moral or intellectual weight; be the chief element, predominate; ~ **over**

*Before the Reformation, church design drew the worshipper's eyes and thoughts to the **presbytery,** and the sacramental part of the service.*

exceed in number, quantity, etc. **pre·pon·der·ance** (prĭpŏn′derəns), **pre·pon′der·an·cy** ns. **pre·pon′der·ant** adj. **pre·pon′der·ant·ly** adv.

prep·o·si′tion (prĕpozĭsh′on) n. Indeclinable word serving to indicate relation between the noun or pronoun it governs and another word (as shown by the italicized prepositions in the following examples: found him *at* home, wait *in* the hall, what did you do it *for?*, the bed he slept *in*, won *by* waiting, came *through* the roof, that is what I was thinking *of*). **prep·o·si′tion·al** adj. **prep·o·si′tion·al·ly** adv.

pre·pos·sess (prĕpozĕs′) v.t. Imbue, inspire (*with*); (of idea etc.) take possession of (person); prejudice, usu. favorably. **pre·pos·sess′ing** adj. (esp.) Making a favorable impression. **pre·pos·sess′ing·ly** adv. **pre·pos·ses′sion** n.

pre·pos·ter·ous (prĭpŏs′terus, -trus) adj. Contrary to nature, reason, or common sense; perverse, foolish; absurd. **pre·pos′ter·ous·ly** adv. **pre·pos′ter·ous·ness** n.

pre·puce (prē′pūs) n. Loose integument covering end of penis. **pre·pu′tial** (prĭpū′shəl) adj.

Pre-Raph·a·el·ite (prērăf′ēelīt, -rā′fē-) adj. & n. (Member, follower) of the ~ **Brotherhood**, a group of young English artists and men of letters including Holman Hunt, Millais, D. G. and W. M. Rossetti, formed c1848 to resist existing con-

ventions in art and literature by a return to standards they supposed to have existed in European art before the time of Raphael. **Pre-Raph′a·el·it·ism** n.

pre·req·ui·site (prĭrĕk′wĭzĭt) adj. & n. (Thing) required as prior condition.

pre·rog·a·tive (prĭrŏg′atĭv) n. 1. royal ~, right of the sovereign, theoretically subject to no restriction. 2. Peculiar right or privilege; natural, or divinely given advantage, privilege, faculty. **pre·rogative** adj. Privileged, enjoyed by privilege; (Rom. hist.) having the right to vote first.

Pres. abbrev. President.

pres·age (prĕs′ĭj) n. Omen, portent; presentiment, foreboding. **pres′age·ful** adj. **pres′age·ful·ly** adv. **presage** (prĕs′ĭj, prĭsāj′) v.t. (-aged, -aging). Portend, foreshadow; give warning of (event etc.) by natural means; (of person) predict; have presentiment of.

pres·by·o·pi·a (prĕzbēō′pēa, prĕs-) n. Form of farsightedness occurring in old age, caused by loss of power of accommodation. **pres·by·op·ic** (prĕzbēŏp′ĭk, prĕs-) adj.

pres·by·ter (prĕz′bĭter, prĕs′-) n. (in early Christian church) One of several officers managing affairs

of local church; (in Episcopal Church) minister of second order, priest; (in Presbyterian Church) elder. **pres·byt·er·al** (prĕzbĭt′eral, prĕs-), **pres·by·te′ri·al** (prĕzbĭtēr′ēal, prĕs-) adjs. **pres·byt·er·ate** (prĕzbĭt′erĭt, -erāt, prĕs-) n.

Pres·by·te·ri·an (prĕzbĭtēr′ēan, prĕs-) adj. Of the ~ **Church**, church recognizing no higher office than that of presbyter or elder and holding doctrines that are Protestant with a strong element of Calvinism; the national Church of Scotland. **Presbyterian** n. Member of the Presbyterian Church. **Pres·by·te′ri·an·ism** n.

pres·by·ter·y (prĕz′bĭtĕrē, prĕs′-) n. (pl. **-ter·ies**). 1. Eastern part of chancel beyond choir, sanctuary. 2. Body of presbyters; district represented by this.

pre·sci·ent (prē′shēent, -shent, prĕsh′ēent, prĕsh′ent) adj. Having foreknowledge or foresight. **pre′sci·ent·ly** adv. **pre′sci·ence** n.

pre·scind (prĭsĭnd′) v. Cut off (part *from* whole), esp. prematurely or abruptly; ~ **from**, leave out of consideration.

Pres·cott (prĕs′kot), **William Hickling** (1796–1859). Amer. historian, author of *History and Conquest of Mexico* and *The Conquest of Peru.*

pre·scribe (prĭskrīb′) v. (-scribed, -scrib·ing). 1. Lay down or impose authoritatively; (med.) advise use of (medicine etc.). 2. Assert prescriptive right or claim (*to, for*).

pre·script (prē′skrĭpt) n. Ordinance, law, command.

pre·scrip·tion (prĭskrĭp′shon) n. 1. Prescribing; physician's (usu. written) direction for composition and use of medicine. 2. (law, also **positive** ~) Uninterrupted use or possession from time immemorial, or for period fixed by law as giving title or right; such title or right; **negative** ~, limitation of the time within which action or claim can be raised; (fig.) ancient custom viewed as authoritative, claim founded on long use.

pre·scrip·tive (prĭskrĭp′tĭv) adj. Prescribing; based on prescription, as ~ **right** (see PRESCRIPTION def. 2); prescribed by custom. **pre·scrip′tive·ly** adv.

pres·ence (prĕz′ens) n. 1. Being present; place where person is; **the** ~, ceremonial attendance on person of high esp. royal rank. 2. Carriage, bearing. 3. ~ **of mind**, calmness and self-command in emergencies.

pres·ent[1] (prĕz′ent) adj. 1. Being in the place in question (chiefly pred.); being dealt with, discussed, etc. 2. (archaic) Ready at hand; ready with assistance. 3. Existing, occurring, being such, now; (gram., of tense) denoting action etc. now going on; true for all time, or future time; ~ **participle**, one used with auxiliary verbs to express continuing or present actions or states of being, e.g. She is *listening*; ~ **perfect**, tense indicating an action or state of being completed at the time of writing or speaking without specifying a past time, e.g. They *have disappeared*. **present** *n.* Present time; present tense; **at** ~, now; **for the** ~, just now, as far as the present is concerned; **by these** ~**s**, by this document (now legal or joc.). **pres·ent²** (prĕz′ent) *n.* Gift. **pre·sent³** (prĭzĕnt′) *v.* 1. Introduce (*to*); introduce (person) to another formally; (of theatr. manager) cause (actor) to take part in play, produce (play); ~ **oneself**, appear esp. as candidate for examination etc. 2. Exhibit (*to*); show (quality etc.); (of idea etc.) offer, suggest *itself*; (physiol., of part of unborn child) be foremost at outlet of womb; (law) bring formally under notice, submit (complaint, offense, *to* authority); (mil. etc.) aim (weapon *at*), hold out (weapon) in position for aiming; hold (firearm) in position for taking aim; (also ~ **arms**) hold firearm etc. in deferential position in saluting. 3. Offer, give, as present; offer (compliments, regards, *to*); deliver (bill, etc.) for acceptance etc.; ~ (person) **with** (thing), present it to him. **pre·sent′er** *n.* **present** (prĕz′ent) *n.* Act of aiming weapon, esp. firearm; position of

weapon when aimed; position of *present arms* in salute.
   pre·sent·a·ble (prĭzĕn′tabel) *adj.* Of decent appearance, fit to be introduced or go into company; suitable for presentation as a gift etc. **pre·sent·a·bil′i·ty, pre·-sent′a·ble·ness** *ns.* **pre·sent′-a·bly** *adv.*
   pres·en·ta·tion (prĕzentā′shon, prēzen-) *n.* Presenting, esp. formal; gift, present; exhibition, theatrical representation, etc.; formal introduction, esp. at court. **pres·en·ta′-tion·al** *adj.*
   pre·sen·tient (prēsĕn′shent, -shēent) *adj.* Having a presentiment (*of*).
   pre·sen·ti·ment (prĭzĕn′timent) *n.* Vague expectation, foreboding.
   pres·ent·ly (prĕz′entlĕ) *adv.* Soon; at present.
   pre·sent·ment (prĭzĕnt′ment) *n.* 1. Theatrical representation. 2. Description (*of*); act, mode, of presenting to the mind. 3. (law) Statement on oath by jury of fact within their knowledge.
   pres·er·va·tion (prĕzervā′shon) *n.* Preserving, being preserved; or keeping from injury or destruction; state of being well or ill preserved.
   pres·erv·a·tive (prĭzĕr′vatĭv)

adj. & n. (Drug, measure, etc tending to preserve; (substance esp. chemical) for preservin perishable foodstuffs etc.
   pre·serve (prĭzĕrv′) *v.* (**-served, -serv·ing**). Keep sa (from harm etc.); keep alive; main tain (state of things); retain (qualit condition); prepare (fruit, mea etc.) by boiling with sugar, pickling etc., to prevent decomposition o fermentation; keep from decompo sition, by chemical treatment etc keep (game, river, etc.) undisturbe for private use; **well-preserved** (of elderly person) showing littl sign of age. **preserve** *n.* 1. (als pl.) Preserved fruit; jam. 2. Groun or water set apart for protection game or fish. **pre·serv′a·ble** *aa* **pre·serv′er** *n.*
   pre·side (prĭzīd′) *v.i.* (**-sid·e -sid·ing**). Occupy chair authority at meeting of society company; sit at head of tabl exercise control, sit or reig supreme; **presiding officer**, pe son in charge of meeting, organiza tion, etc. **pre·sid′er** *n.*
   pres·i·den·cy (prĕz′īdensē) (pl. **-cies**). Office of presiden period of tenure of this.
   pres·i·dent (prĕz′ident) *n.* (ofte **P** ~) Head of temporary permanent body of persons, pr siding over their meetings an proceedings; head of some college person presiding over meetings academy, literary or scientif society, etc.; person presiding ove proceedings of bank or compan

head of advisory council, board, etc.; elected head of government in modern republics. **pres·i·den·tial** (prĕzĭdĕn′shal) *adj.* **pres·i·den′- tial·ly** *adv.*

pre·sid·i·um (prĭsĭd′ēum) *n.* Presiding body or standing com- mittee (esp. in communist organiza- tion).

press[1] (prĕs) *v.* 1. Exert steady force against (thing in contact); move by pressing; exert pressure, bear with weight or force; squeeze (juice etc. *from* etc.); compress, squeeze, (thing) to flatten or shape or smooth it, or to extract juice etc.; iron (clothes etc.). 2. Bear heavily on in attack etc.; weigh down, oppress; produce strong mental or moral impression, esp. weigh heavily *on* (mind, person); **be pressed for**, have barely enough time etc.); **press the button**, set electrical machinery in motion (freq. fig.). 3. Be urgent, demand immediate action; urge, entreat; urge (course etc. *upon* person). 4. Force (offer, gift, etc. *upon*). 5. (sports) Attempt to perform better than can be done with accuracy; (football and basketball) push hard on opposing players. 6. Crowd, throng; hasten, urge one's way, *on*, *forward*, etc. **press** *n.* 1. Crowding; crowd (*of* people etc.); throng, crush, in battle. 2. Pressure, hurry,

of affairs; pressing; (naut.) ~ **of sail, canvas,** as much sail as wind etc. will allow. 3. Instrument for compressing, flattening, or shap- ing, or for extracting juice, etc. 4. Machine for printing; printing house or publisher; art, practice, of printing; newspapers generally; **in the ~,** being printed; **freedom of the ~,** right to print and publish anything without censorship; ~ **agent,** person employed by theater, actor, etc., to attend to advertising and other publicity; ~ **box,** reporters' enclosure, esp. at sports events; ~ **conference,** interview given to journalists by celebrity, official, etc.; ~ **clipping**: see CLIP- PING; ~ **gallery,** gallery for reporters esp. in Congress; **press·- man** (prĕs′man) (pl. **-men**), operator of printing press.

press[2] (prĕs) *v.t.* Force to serve in army or navy, impress[2]. (hist.); ~ **into service,** take for use in an emergency. **press** *n.* (hist.) Com- pulsory enlistment in navy or (less usu.) army; ~ **gang,** (hist.) body of men employed to press men.

*Popular captains who ran their ships well and won prizes in time of war could attract volunteers. Otherwise the Royal Navy depended on the **press-gang** to drag able-bodied men off the streets as in this painting.*

press·ing[1] (prĕs′ĭng) *adj.* (esp.) Urgent; importunate; persistent. **press′ing·ly** *adv.*

press·ing[2] (prĕs′ĭng) *n.* 1. Phonograph record; series of records made at one time from one mold. 2. Act of occupation of ironing clothing.

pres·sure (prĕsh′er) *n.* 1. Exertion of continuous force, force so exerted upon or against a body by another body, or by a liquid or gas, in contact with it; amount of this, expressed by the force upon a unit area; **blood ~**: see BLOOD; **high, low, (atmospheric) ~**: see ATMOSPHERE; **high-~,** (of engines or turbines) used esp. of those in which steam is used at different pressures in different parts of the machine; ~ **casting,** metal casting obtained by injecting fluid metal under pressure into a rigid mold; ~ **cooker,** strong sealed metal vessel for cooking in steam at high pressure; (fig.) place of employment or situation in which people per- form under great pressure; ~ **mine,** mine detonated by pressure. 2. Affliction, oppression; trouble, embarrassment; constraining influ- ence; ~ **group,** body of people exerting pressure upon legislature etc. by concerted agitation. **pres- sure** *v.t.* (**-sured, -sur·ing**). (fig.) Pressurize.

pres·sur·ize (prĕsh'erīz) *v.t.* (**-ized, -iz·ing**). Maintain normal air pressure artificially, esp. in aircraft at high altitudes; (fig.) exert pressure on, force by pressure.

pres·ti·dig·i·ta·tor (prĕstĭdĭj'ĭtāter) *n.* Conjurer. **pres·ti·dig·i·ta'tion** *n.*

pres·tige (prĕstēzh', -stēj') *n.* Influence, reputation, derived from past achievements, associations, etc. **pres·ti·gious** (prĕstĭj'us, -stē'jus) *adj.*

pres·to[1] (prĕs'tō) *adv., n.* (pl. **-tos**) & *adj.* (mus.) (Passage performed) quick(ly). [It.]

pres·to[2] (prĕs'tō) *adv.* (in magician's formula, esp. ~ **change-o!**) Quickly. ~ *adj.* Rapid.

pre·stressed (prēstrĕst') *adj.* (of concrete) Strengthened by compression with steel rods under tension, to counteract stress.

pre·sume (prīzoōm') *v.* (**-sumed, -sum·ing**). Take the liberty, venture (*to* do); assume, take for granted; be presumptuous, take liberties; ~ **upon**, take advantage of, make unscrupulous use of. **pre·sum'a·ble** *adj.* **pre·sum'a·bly, pre·sum'ing·ly** *advs.* **pre·sum'er** *n.*

pre·sump·tion (prīzŭmp'shon) *n.* Arrogance, assurance; taking for granted, thing taken for granted; ground for presuming; (law) ~ **of fact**, inference of fact from known facts; ~ **of law**, assumption of truth of thing until contrary is proved; inference established by law as universally applicable to certain circumstances.

pre·sump·tive (prīzŭmp'tĭv) *adj.* Giving ground for presumption; **heir** ~, one whose right of inheritance is liable to be defeated by birth of nearer heir. **pre·sump'tive·ly** *adv.*

pre·sump·tu·ous (prīzŭmp'chōous) *adj.* Unduly confident, arrogant, forward. **pre·sump'tu·ous·ly** *adv.* **pre·sump'tu·ous·ness** *n.*

pre·sup·pose (prēsupōz') *v.t.* (**-posed, -pos·ing**). Assume beforehand; involve, imply. **pre·sup·po·si·tion** (prēsupozĭsh'on) *n.* Presupposing; thing assumed beforehand as basis of argument etc.

pre·tend (prītĕnd') *v.* 1. Feign, give oneself out (*to* be or do); make believe in play; profess falsely to have; allege falsely. 2. Venture, aspire, presume (*to* do); lay claim *to* (right, title, etc.); ~ **to**, try to win (person, person's hand) in marriage; profess to have (quality etc.). **pre·tend'ed** *adj.* **pre·tend'ing·ly** *adv.*

pre·tend·er (prītĕn'der) *n.* One who makes baseless pretensions (*to* title etc.); **Old P** ~, James Francis Edward Stuart (1688–1766), James II's son, called by Jacobites James III; took part in the unsuccessful Scottish rising of 1715; **Young P** ~, Charles Edward Stuart (1720–1788), son of the Old Pretender; led the rebellion of 1745.

pre·tense, Brit. **pre·tence** (prītĕns', prē'tĕns) *ns.* 1. Claim (*to* merit etc.). 2. Ostentation, display; false profession of purpose, pretext; pretending, make-believe.

pre·ten·sion (prītĕn'shon) *n.* Assertion of a claim; justifiable claim; pretentiousness.

pre·ten·tious (prītĕn'shus) *adj.* Making claim to great merit or importance, esp. when unwar-

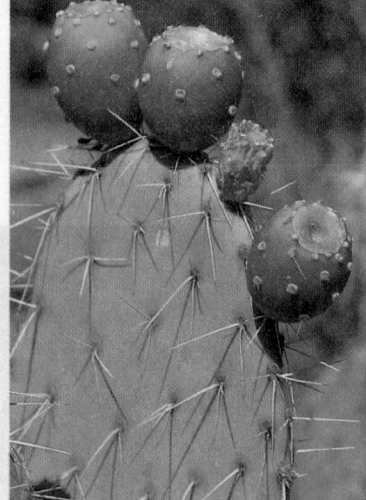

*The **prickly pear** grows throughout southern U.S.A. Introduced to Australia it became a widespread pest until a Mexican insect was found whose larvae killed the plant, controlling its growth.*

ranted; ostentatious. **pre·ten'tious·ly** *adv.* **pre·ten'tious·ness** *n.*

preter- *prefix.* Past, beyond.

pre·ter·hu·man (prēterhū'man) *adj.* Beyond what is human, superhuman.

pret·er·it, pret·er·ite (prĕt'erĭt) *adjs.* (gram.) Expressing past action or state. ~ *n.* Preterit tense or verb.

pret·er·i·tion (prĕterĭsh'on) *n.* Omission, disregard (*of*); (theol.) passing over of the nonelect.

pre·ter·nat·u·ral (prēternăch'eral, -năch'ral) *adj.* Outside the ordinary course of nature; supernatural. **pre·ter·nat'u·ral·ly** *adv.*

pre·text (prē'tĕkst) *n.* Ostensible reason, excuse.

pre·ton·ic (prētŏn'ĭk) *adj.* Coming immediately before stressed syllable.

pre·tor = PRAETOR.

Pre·to·ri·a (prītōr'ēa, -tōr'-). Administrative capital of Republic of South Africa, 35 miles (56 km) NE. of Johannesburg. [Andries Wilhelmus Jacobus *Pretorius* (1799–1853), South African Boer leader, one of founders of Transvaal]

pre·to·ri·an (prītōr'ēan, -tōr'-) = PRAETORIAN.

pret·ti·fy (prĭt'ĭfī) *v.t.* (**-fied, -fy·ing**). Make pretty; represent with finicking prettiness.

pret·ty (prĭt'ē) *adj.* (**-ti·er, -ti·est**). 1. Beautiful in diminutive or trivial way; attractive to eye, ear, or aesthetic sense. 2. Good, fine (also iron.); **a** ~ **penny**, a good deal of money. 3. (abs. as noun) Pretty one, pretty thing. **pret'ti·ly** *adv.* **pret'ti·ness** *n.* **pret'ty·ish** *adj.* **pretty** *adv.* Fairly, moderately, as ~ *good*, ~ *well*.

pret·zel (prĕt'sel) *n.* Crisp salted biscuit, freq. baked in form of a knot.

pre·vail (prĭvāl´) *v.i.* Gain the mastery, be victorious (*against*, *over*); be the more usual or prominent, predominate; exist, occur, in general use or experience, be current; ~ **upon**, persuade. **pre·vail´ing, prev´a·lent** (prĕv´a-lent) *adjs.* **prev´a·lence** *n.* **prev´a·lent·ly** *adv.*

pre·var·i·cate (prĭvăr´ĭkāt) *v.i.* (-cat·ed, -cat·ing). Speak, act, evasively; quibble, equivocate; lie. **pre·var·i·ca´tion, pre·var´i·ca·tor** *ns.*

pre·vent (prĭvĕnt´) *v.t.* 1. Hinder, stop. 2. (archaic) Meet, deal with (wish, question, etc.) before it is expressed; (theol., of God) go before, guide. **pre·vent´a·ble, pre·vent´i·ble** *adjs.* **pre·ven´tion** (prĭvĕn´shon) *n.* **pre·ven·ta·tive** (prĭvĕn´tatĭv) *adj. & n.* Preventive.

pre·ven·tive (prĭvĕn´tĭv) *adj.* Serving to prevent, esp. (med.) to keep off disease; ~ **detention**, (law) incarceration of criminal to prevent crime; (Brit.) imprisonment of habitual criminal for period of corrective training etc. **pre·ven´tive·ly** *adv.* **pre·ven´tive·ness** *n.* **preventive** *n.* Preventive agent, measure, drug, etc.

pre·view (prē´vū) *n.* Viewing of a picture, film, etc., arranged before it is open to public.

pre·vi·ous (prē´vēus) *adj.* Coming before in time or order; prior *to*; (slang) done or acting hastily; ~ **question**, (parl.) question whether vote shall be taken on main question (put to avoid putting of main question). **pre´vi·ous·ly** *adv.* **pre´vi·ous·ness** *n.* **previous** *adv.*

pre·vise (prēvīz´) *v.t.* (-vised, -vis·ing). Foresee, forecast. **pre·vi·sion** (prēvĭzh´on) *n.* **pre·vi´sion·al** *adj.*

pre·war (prē´wôr´) *adj.* Before the war (esp. of World War I or II).

prey (prā) *n.* Animal hunted or killed by carnivorous animal for food; person, thing, that falls a victim (*to* sickness, fear, etc.); **beast of** ~, animal that kills and devours other animals; **bird of** ~: see BIRD. **prey** *v.i.* ~ **on**, seek, take, as prey, plunder; exert baneful or wasteful influence upon.

Pri·am (prī´am). (Gk. legend) Last king of Troy, father of 50 sons and many daughters; slain by Neoptolemus after the fall of Troy.

pri·a·pism (prī´apĭzem) *n.* Licentiousness; (path.) persistent erection of penis. [f. PRIAPUS]

Pri·a·pus (priā´pus). (Gk. myth.) God of fertility whose cult spread from Asia Minor to Greece and Italy; he became the god of gardens and herds and is represented as small, grotesque, and misshapen.

Prib·i·lof (prĭb´ĭlawf) **Islands.** Group of islands belonging to the U.S. in the Bering Sea, SW. of Alaska and N. of the Aleutian Islands; breeding grounds for most of world's fur-bearing seals.

price (prīs) *n.* Money for which thing is bought or sold; (betting)

*Lions eating their **prey** in Uganda. Carnivorous animals can only survive by hunting and killing other animals, which is an essential biological instinct.*

odds; (fig.) what must be given, done, sacrificed, etc., to obtain a thing; **above, beyond, without,** ~, so valuable that no price can be stated; **at any** ~, whatever it may cost; (with neg.) on any terms, for any consideration; **at a** ~, at a relatively high cost; **what** ~ **...?**, (slang) taunting allusion to worthlessness or failure of something; ~ **on person's head**, reward offered for his death or capture. **price** *v.t.* (**priced, pric·ing**). Fix, inquire, the price of (thing for sale); estimate the value of. **priced** *adj.* To which a price is assigned.

price·less (prīs´lĭs) *adj.* Invaluable; (slang) incredibly or extremely amusing, absurd, etc. **price´less·ness** *n.*

prick (prĭk) *n.* Pricking, puncture; mark made by pricking; (archaic) goad for oxen, esp. in **kick against the** ~**s**, (fig.) hurt oneself by useless resistance (Acts 9); ~ **ears**, erect pointed ears of some dogs etc.; conspicuous ears of person. **prick** *v.* Pierce slightly, make minute hole in; cause sharp pain to; feel pricking sensation; make a thrust (*at, into*, etc.); mark off (name etc. in list) with a prick; mark (pattern *off, out*) with dots; (archaic) spur, urge on (horse); advance on horseback; ~ **in, out, off**, plant (seedlings etc.) in small holes pricked in earth; ~ **up**, (of animal) erect (ears) when on the alert; (of animal's ears) rise or stand erect; ~ **up one's ears**, (fig.) become suddenly attentive. **prick´ing** *n.*

prick·er (prĭk´er) *n.* (esp.) Pricking instrument, e.g. awl.

prick·et (prĭk´ĭt) *n.* 1. Male of fallow deer in 2nd year, with straight unbranched horns. 2. Spike to stick candle on.

prick·le (prĭk´el) *n.* Thornlike process developed from epidermis of plant and capable of being peeled off with it; (pop.) small thorn; hardpointed spine of porcupine etc. ~ *v.* (**-led, -ling**). Affect, be affected, with sensation as of prick.

prick·ly (prĭk´lē) *adj.* (**-li·er, -li·est**). Armed with prickles; tingling; ~ **heat**, inflammatory disease of the skin (miliaria) accompanying profuse sweating, caused by blocking of the sweat glands; ~ **pear**, species of cactus of genus *Opuntia*, with pear-shaped fleshy edible fruit; this fruit. **prick´li·ness** *n.*

pride (prīd) *n.* 1. Unduly high opinion of one's own qualities, merits, etc., considered the first of the 7 deadly sins; arrogant bearing or conduct; ~ **of place**, exalted position, consciousness of this, arrogance. 2. (also **proper** ~) Sense of what befits one's position, preventing one from doing unworthy thing; **false** ~, mistaken feeling of this kind. 3. Feeling of elation and pleasure; object of this feeling, e.g., one's child (in *my ~ and joy*); take ~ in, be proud of. 4. Company (of lions). **pride** *v.refl.* (**prid·ed, prid·ing**). ~ **oneself on**, be proud of. **pride'ful** *adj.* **pride'ful·ly** *adv.* **pride'less** *adj.* **pride'ful·ness** *n.*

prie-dieu (prē dyōō′) *n.* (pl. **-dieus, -dieux** pr. -dyōōz′). Kneeling desk; chair with tall sloping back for use in praying.

priest (prēst) *n.* Clergyman, esp. one with authority to administer sacraments and pronounce absolution; Episcopalian minister of the altar; official minister of non-Christian religion (fem. **priest'-ess**); **high** ~: see HIGH; **priest'craft**, ambitious or worldly policy of priests; ~-**ridden**, held in subjection by priest(s). **priest·-hood** (prēst′hōod) *n.* **priest'like** *adj.*

Priest·ley (prēst′lē), **Joseph** (1733–1804). English chemist and clergyman; discoverer of oxygen.

priest·ly (prēst′lē) *adj.* (**-li·er, -li·est**). Of, like, befitting, a priest; **P ~ Code** (Old Testament criticism) one of the constituent elements of the Hexateuch, constituting framework of whole in its existing form.

prig (prĭg) *n.* Person exhibiting excessive precision in speech or manners; conceited or didactic

*Although **Joseph Priestley** is best remembered as one of the discoverers of oxygen, his scientific work was only a hobby. He was a Presbyterian minister and a writer.*

person. **prig·ger·y** (prĭg′erē) *ns.* **prig'gism** *ns.* **prig'gish** *adj.* **prig'gish·ly** *adv.* **prig'gish·ness** *n.*

prim (prĭm) *adj.* (**prim·mer, prim·mest**). Consciously or affectedly precise; formal, demure; ~ *v.* (**primmed, prim·ming**). Assume prim air; form (face, lips etc.) into prim expression. **prim'ly** *adv.* **prim'ness** *n.*

pri·ma·cy (prī′masē) *n.* (pl. **-cies**). Office of a primate; preeminence.

pri·ma don·na (prē′ma dŏn′a, prĭm′a). Principal female singer in opera; (fig.) temperamental person [It., = "first lady"]

pri·ma fa·ci·e (prī′ma fā′shēē, fā′shē, fā′sha) *adv. & adj.* (Arising at first sight, (based) on the first impression. [L.]

pri·mal (prī′mal) *adj.* Primitive, primeval; chief, fundamental. **pri'mal·ly** *adv.*

pri·ma·ry (prī′měrē, -merē) *adj.* Earliest, original; of the first rank in a series, not derived; of the first importance, chief; (geol., **P ~**) of the lowest series of strata, Paleozoic; (biol.) belonging to 1st stage of development; ~ **color**: see COLOR; ~ **coolant system**, system of pipes, pumps, etc., cooling core of nuclear reactor; ~ **education**, that which begins with the rudiments of knowledge, esp. that provided for children under 11 years; ~ **feather**, one of large flight feathers of bird's wing, growing directly from manus; ~ **planets**, those revolving directly around sun as center; ~ **school**, school for primary education. **primary** *n.* (pl. **-ries**). 1. Primary planet, meeting, feather, etc.; **P ~**, (geol.) primary period. 2. Election held among members of a political party.

*The **primates** are an order which at first sight seems to contain animals too different to be grouped together: a gorilla appears to have little in common with a lemur. But anatomy, ancestry, and habits unite them despite dissimilarities.*

PRIMATES

Lemur   Chimpanzee   Gorilla   Man

o choose candidates for elective office. **pri·ma·ri·ly** (prīmĕr´ĭlē, ᵊrī´mĕr-) *adv.*

pri·mate (prī´māt) *n.* 1. (also pr. ᵊrī´mĭt) Archbishop; **P ~ of all England**, archbishop of Canterbury; **P ~ of England**, archbishop of York. 2. (zool.) Member of ᵊrder of mammals including man, ᵃpes, monkeys, tarsiers, and ᵊemurs.

prime[1] (prīm) *n.* 1. State of ʰighest perfection; best part (*of* ʰhing). 2. Beginning, first age, of ᵃnything. 3. Prime number. 4. ᵊmus.) Fundamental note or tone; ᵊower of any 2 notes forming an ᵢnterval. 5. Position in fencing, ᵢirst of the 8 parries or guards in ᵊwordplay, used to protect the head; ʰhrust in such position. ~ *adj.* 1. Chief, most important; ~ **minister**, principal minister of any ᵊovereign or nation (now official ᵗitle of head minister of state in Gt. Britain). 2. First-rate (esp. of beef), ᵊxcellent. 3. Primary, fundamental; ᵃrith.) of number) having no ᵢntegral factors except itself and ᵤnity (e.g. 2, 3, 5, 7, 11). 4. ~ **mover**: see MOVER; ~ **vertical** (**circle**), great circle of the heavens ᵖassing through E. and W. points of ʰorizon and through zenith, where ᵢt cuts meridian at right angles. **prime´ness** *n.*

prime[2] (prīm) *v.* (**primed, prim·ing**). Supply (firearm, or ᵃbs.) with gunpowder for firing ᶜharge (hist.); wet (pump) to make ᵢt start working; equip (person *with* ᵢnformation etc.); inject gasoline ᵢnto (carburetor or cylinder of

*The **primrose** of England, with its pale yellow flowers and delicate perfume, is for many people the epitome of spring. It is in the Primula family.*

internal combustion engine); fill (person *with* liquor); cover (wood, canvas, etc.) with glue, gesso, oil, etc. to prevent paint from being absorbed; (of engine boiler) let water pass with steam into cylinder in form of spray.

prim·er[1] (prī´mer) *n.* 1. Cap, cylinder, etc., used to ignite powder of cartridge etc. 2. Priming coat of paint.

prim·er[2] (prĭm´er) *n.* 1. Elementary schoolbook for teaching

*It is almost unbelievable that these seemingly **primitive** arrangements of lines illustrate complex myths, but the art of Central Australian aborigines is highly stylized.*

children to read; small introductory book; (hist.) prayer book for use of laity esp. before Reformation. 2. **great ~**, (print.) size of type (about 18 points); **long ~**, size of type (about 10 points).

pri·me·val (prīmē´val) *adj.* Of the 1st age of the world; ancient, primitive. **pri·me´val·ly** *adv.*

prim·ing (prī´mĭng) *n.* (esp.) 1. Gunpowder placed in pan of firearm. 2. Train of powder used to ignite charge in blasting etc. 3. Mixture used by painters for preparatory coat. 4. Preparation of sugar added to beer. 5. Hasty imparting of knowledge, cramming.

pri·mip·a·rous (prīmĭp´erus) *adj.* Bearing child for the first time. **pri·mip·a·ra** (prīmĭp´era) *n.* (pl. **-a·ras, -a·rae** pr. -*erē*). Primiparous woman.

prim·i·tive (prĭm´ĭtĭv) *adj.* Ancient; of early, simple, or old-fashioned kind; (anthro.) (of peoples) at an early stage of cultural development; (geol.) Paleozoic; (biol.) appearing in early stage of evolution; only slightly evolved from ancestral types; **P ~ Methodism, Methodist**, principles, member, of **P ~ Methodist Connection**, society of Methodists founded 1810 by Hugh Bourne by secession from main body. **prim´·i·tive·ly** *adv.* **prim´i·tive·ness, prim·i·tiv´i·ty** *ns.* **primitive** *n.* (Picture by) painter of period before Renaissance; (picture by) untutored painter who ignores rules of perspective etc.; primitive word, line, etc.; (**P ~**) Primitive Methodist.

pri·mo·gen·i·tor (prīmojĕn´ĭter) *n.* Earliest ancestor; (loosely) ancestor.

pri·mo·gen·i·ture (prīmojĕn´ĭcher) *n.* Fact of being the first-born of the children of the same parents; (also **right of ~**) right of succession belonging to first-born, esp. feudal rule by which the whole real estate of an intestate passes to the eldest son.

pri·mor·di·al (prīmôr´dēal) *adj.* Existing at or from the beginning, primeval. **pri·mor´di·al·ly** *adv.* **pri·mor·di·al·i·ty** (prīmôrdēăl´ĭtē) *n.*

primp (prĭmp) *v.* Smarten, dress up, esp. in front of a mirror.

prim·rose (prĭm´rōz) *n.* Plant, esp. the **English ~** (*Primula vulgaris*), bearing pale yellowish flowers in early spring, growing wild in woods and hedges and on banks, and with many cultivated varieties; color of flower of this; **evening ~**, plant of genus *Oenothera*, with large pale yellow flowers opening in evening; ~

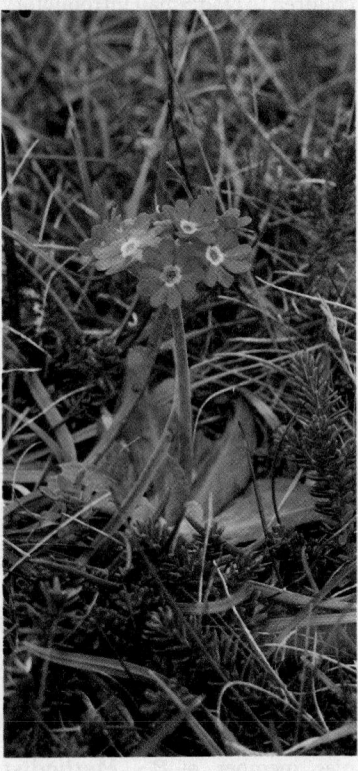

Primula scotica, one plant included in a large genus of herbs which also includes the primrose and the cowslip. More than 500 species are native to the northern hemisphere.

*The **Prince of Wales** derives his title from the formerly independent rulers of Wales who were reduced in status — from kings to princes — after the Anglo-Saxon and Norman wars of the 11th century.*

path, pursuit of pleasure (w. ref. to *Hamlet*, I. iii. 50).

prim·u·la (prǐm′yulɑ) *n.* Herbaceous perennial of genus *P ~*, of low growing habit with yellow, white, pink, or purple flowers mostly borne in umbels. **prim·u·la·ceous** (prǐmyulā′shʊs) *adj.*

pri·mus in·ter pa·res (prī′mʊs ǐn′ter pār′ēz; *Lat.* prē′mōos ǐn′tĕr pah′rĕs). First among equals (in a group). [L., = "first among equals"]

Pri·mus (prī′mʊs) **stove.** (trademark) Portable stove burning vaporized kerosene.

prince (prǐns) *n.* 1. Sovereign ruler (now rhet.); ruler of small state, actually or nominally feudatory to king or emperor; **P ~ of Peace**, Christ; **~ of darkness**, Satan. 2. (Title of) male member of royal family, esp. (in U.K.) son or grandson of king or queen; **P ~ of Wales**, title (since 1301) conferred upon eldest son and heir apparent of British sovereign. 3. (as English rendering of foreign titles) Noble usu. ranking next below duke; (as courtesy title in some connections) duke, marquis, earl; (fig.) chief, greatest (*of*); **~ of the (Holy Roman) Church**, title of cardinal. 4. **~ consort**, husband of reigning female sovereign being himself a prince; esp., Albert, Prince of Saxe-Coburg, as husband

of Queen Victoria; **P ~ Imperial**, Napoléon Eugène Louis Jean Joseph (1856–79), only son of Napoleon III, killed with British forces in Zulu war of 1879; **Princes in the Tower**, Edward V and his brother Richard, Duke of York, sons of Edward IV, alleged to have been lodged in the Tower of London and there murdered in 1483. **prince·dom** (prǐns′dom), **prince·ling** (prǐns′lǐng) *ns.*

Prince (prǐns) **Edward Island.** Smallest province of Canada, a large island in the Gulf of St. Lawrence; capital, Charlottetown.

prince·ly (prǐns′lē) *adj.* (-li·er, -li·est). (Worthy) of a prince; sumptuous, splendid. **prince′li·ness** *n.*

Prince (prǐns) **of Wales Island.** Island in SE. Alaska, largest in the Alexander Archipelago, covering 1,500 sq. miles (3,885 sq. km); island of the Northwest Territories, Canada, in the Arctic Ocean between Victoria and Somerset Islands.

prin·cess (prǐn′sǐs, -sĕs) *n.* 1. (Title of) queen (archaic); wife of prince, daughter or granddaughter of sovereign; **~ royal**, (title conferrable on) sovereign's eldest daughter. 2. (also **prin′cesse**) attrib. (of dress etc.) Made in panels with flared skirt and without a seam at the waist. **prin′cess·ly** *adj.*

Prince·ton (prǐns′ton). City in W. central New Jersey; site of

Princeton University.

prin·ci·pal (prǐn′sipɑl) *adj.* First in rank or importance, chief; main, leading; (of money) constituting the original sum invested or lent; **~ clause** (gram.) one to which another is subordinate; **~ parts**, parts of verb from which the others can be derived. **principal** *n.* 1. Head, ruler, superior; head of some schools. 2. Person for whom another acts as agent etc.; person for whom another is surety; combatant in duel. 3. Capital sum as distinguished from interest, sum lent or invested on which interest is paid. 4. Organ stop of same quality as open diapason, but an octave higher in pitch. **prin′ci·pal·ship** *n.*

prin·ci·pal·i·ty (prǐnsipǎl′ǐtē) *n.* (pl. **-ties**). Government of a prince; state ruled by a prince; (pl.) order of angels (see ANGEL).

prin·ci·pal·ly (prǐn′sipɑlē, -sǐp-lē) *adv.* For the most part, chiefly.

prin·ci·pate (prǐn′sipāt) *n.* 1. (Rom. hist.) Rule of early emperors while some republican forms were retained. 2. State ruled by a prince.

prin·ci·ple (prǐn′sipel) *n.* 1. Fundamental source, primary element; fundamental truth as basis of reasoning etc.; law of nature seen in working of machine etc.; (phys. etc.) general or inclusive law exemplified in numerous cases; general law as guide to action. 2. (pl. and collect. sing.) Personal code of moral conduct; **on ~**, from settled moral motive. 3. (chem.) Constituent of a naturally occurring substance, esp. one giving rise to some quality etc.

print (prǐnt) *n.* 1. Indentation in surface preserving the form left

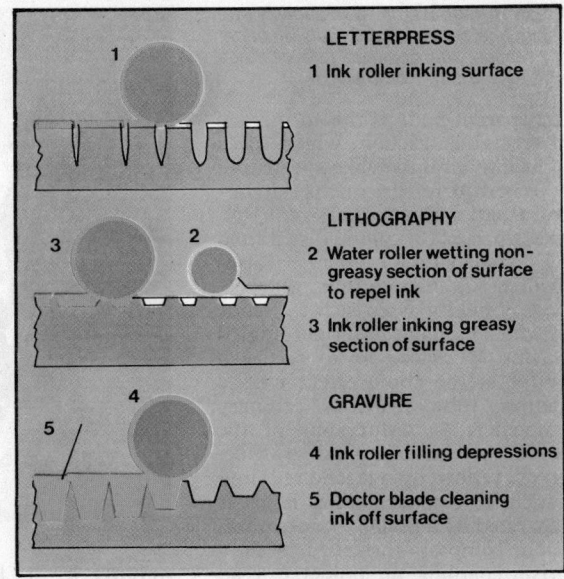

LETTERPRESS

1 Ink roller inking surface

LITHOGRAPHY

2 Water roller wetting non-greasy section of surface to repel ink

3 Ink roller inking greasy section of surface

GRAVURE

4 Ink roller filling depressions

5 Doctor blade cleaning ink off surface

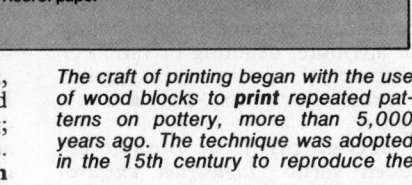

SECOND PRINTING side B

FIRST PRINTING side A

Impression cylinder

Plate cylinder

Inking tray

Reel of paper

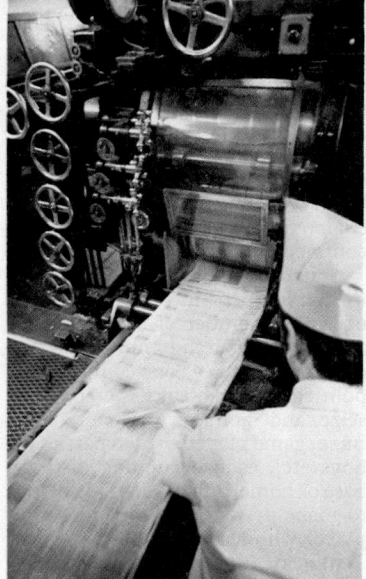

The craft of printing began with the use of wood blocks to print repeated patterns on pottery, more than 5,000 years ago. The technique was adopted in the 15th century to reproduce the

text of manuscripts which were cut on a single slab. Modern printing resulted from Gutenberg's movable type and the development of presses to produce hundreds of newspapers.

pressure of some body; mark, ~ot, stain. 2. Language embodied ~ printed form, printed lettering; ~ndwritten letters imitating this. ~ State of being printed; **book is in** ~, (i) in printed form, (ii) on sale, ~t **out of** ~ (sold out). 4. Printed ~blication, esp. newspaper. 5. ~inted cotton fabric. 6. Picture, ~sign, printed from block or plate; ~hotog.) picture produced from ~gative; **print'out**, computer out-~t in printed form. **print** *v.t.* 1. ~press, stamp, (surface *with* seal, ~e, etc.; mark or figure *on, in,* ~rface); (fig.) impress (*on* mind, ~emory). 2. Produce (book, ~cture, etc., or abs.) by applying ~ked types, blocks, or plates to ~per, vellum, etc.; cause (book, ~S.) to be so printed; express, ~blish, in print; write (words etc.) ~ imitation of typography; ~ **out**, ~oduce computer output in ~inted form. 3. Mark (textile

fabric) with decorative design in colors; transfer (colored design) from paper etc. to unglazed surface of pottery; (photog.) produce (picture) by transmission of light through negative. 4. **print'ed circuit**, (elect.) circuit of conductive strips on a nonconducting material. **print'able** *adj.*

print'er (prĭn'ter) *n.* (esp.) One who prints books; owner of printing business; printing instrument; ~'s **devil**: see DEVIL def. 4.

pri·or[1] (prī'er) *n.* (fem. **pri·or·ess** pr. prī'erĭs). Superior officer of religious house or order; (in abbey) officer next under abbot; (hist.) chief magistrate in some Italian republics. **pri'or·ship** *n.*

pri·or[2] (prī'er) *adj.* Earlier; antecedent in time, order, or importance. ~ *adv.* ~ **to**, before. **pri·or·i·ty** (prīŏr'ĭtē, -ār'-) *n.* (pl. **-ties**). Condition or quality of being earlier in time, or *of* preceding something else; precedence in order, rank, or dignity; interest having prior claim to consideration, often with qualification, as *first, top* ~.

pri·o·ry (prī'erē) *n.* (pl. **-ries**). Monastery, nunnery, governed by prior or prioress.

prise: see PRIZE[3].

prism (prĭz'em) *n.* Solid figure whose two ends are similar, equal, and parallel rectilineal figures and whose sides are parallelograms;

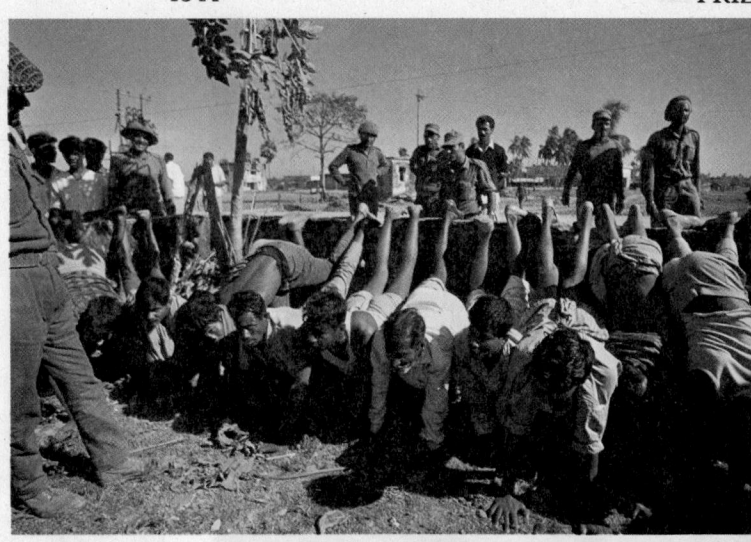

transparent body of this form, usu. of triangular section, which splits light into a rainbowlike spectrum.

pris·mat·ic (prĭzmăt´ĭk), **pris·mat·i·cal** (prĭzmăt´ĭkal) *adjs*. Of, like, a prism; (of colors) distributed by transparent prism, (also) brilliant; ~ **binoculars, glasses**, type of field glasses each telescope of which contains two right-angled prisms so placed as to secure a better stereoscopic effect with a shorter tube than an ordinary binocular; ~ **color**, one of the seven colors (violet, indigo, blue, green, yellow, orange, and red) into which a ray of white light is separated by a prism; ~ **compass**, hand compass furnished with a prism enabling the holder to read the compass while taking a bearing or sight. **pris·mat´i·cal·ly** *adv*.

pris·moid (prĭz´moid) *n*. Body, figure, resembling a prism, with similar but unequal parallel polygonal ends. **pris·moi´dal** *adj*.

pris·on (prĭz´on) *n*. Place in which person is kept in captivity, esp. building to which person is legally committed while awaiting trial or for punishment; custody, confinement.

pris·on·er (prĭz´oner, prĭz´ner) *n*. Person kept in prison; (also ~ **of war**), member of armed forces captured in war and imprisoned; ~ **of state, state** ~, one confined for political reasons; **take** (person) ~, seize and hold as prisoner; ~**s' base**, game played by two parties of boys etc., each occupying distinct base or home, aim of each side being to make prisoner by touching any player who leaves his base.

pris·sy (prĭs´ē) *adj*. (**-si·er, -si·est**). Prim, overly decorous. **pris´si·ly** *adv*. **pris´si·ness** *n*.

pris·tine (prĭs´tēn, prĭsten´) *adj*. Ancient, primitive, unspoiled.

prith·ee (prĭdh´ē) *int*. (archaic) Pray, please. [= (I) pray thee]

pri·va·cy (prī´vasē) *n*. Being withdrawn from society or public interest; avoidance of publicity.

pri·vate (prī´vĭt) *adj*. 1. Not holding public office or official position. 2. Kept, removed, from public knowledge; not open to the public; ~ **detective**, person undertaking special inquiries for pay; ~ **eye**, (slang) private detective; ~ **means**, income not derived from employment; ~ **parts**, genitals; ~ **school**, elementary or secondary school owned and managed by private individual(s). 3. One's own; individual, person, not affecting the community; confidential. 4. (of place) Retired, secluded; (of person, archaic) given to retirement. **pri´vate·ly** *adv*. **pri´vate·ness** *n*.

private *n*. 1. Person enlisted in lowest rank in the U.S. Army or Marine Corps; ~ **first class**, person enlisted in rank above private and below that of corporal in the U.S. Army and of lance corporal in the Marine Corps. 2. Lowest ranking member of Mafia organization. 3. **in** ~, privately; in private life. 4. (pl.) Genitals.

pri·va·teer (prīvater´) *n*. (hist.) Armed vessel owned and officered by private persons holding commission from government (*letters of marque*) and authorized to use it against hostile nation, esp. in capture of merchant shipping; (also **pri·va·teers´man**, pl. **-men**) commander, (pl.) crew, of this.

pri·va·tion (prīvā´shon) *n*. Loss, absence (*of* quality), as *cold is the* ~ *of heat*; want of the comforts or necessaries of life.

priv·a·tive (prĭv´atĭv) *adj*. Consisting in, marked by, the loss, removal, or absence of some quality or attribute; denoting privation or absence of quality etc.; (gram.) expressing privation. **priv´a·tive·ly** *adv*.

priv·et (prĭv´ĭt) *n*. Bushy evergreen shrub (*Ligustrum vulgare*) with smooth dark green leaves, clusters of small white flowers, and small shining black berries, much used for hedges; other species of *Ligustrum* or similar (usu. evergreen) shrub.

priv·i·lege (prĭv´ĭlĭj, prĭv´lĭj) *n*. Right, advantage, immunity, belonging to person, class, or office; special advantage or benefit; special immunity granted to officials and others, esp. members of Congress, to free them from obligations or liabilities. ~ *v.t.* (**-leged, -leg·ing**). Invest with privilege; allow (*to* do) as privilege; exempt (*from* burden etc.). **priv´i·leged** *adj*.

priv·i·ty (prĭv´ĭtē) *n*. (pl. **-ties**). 1. Being privy (*to*). 2. (law) Any relation between 2 parties that is

recognized by law.

priv·y (prĭv´ē) *adj*. Hidden, secluded; secret; ~ **to**, sharing the secret of (person's designs, etc.). **P ~ Council**, sovereign's private counselors; (in Gt. Britain) body of advisers chosen by sovereign (now chiefly as personal dignity), together with princes of the blood, archbishops, etc.; ~ **purse**, allowance from public revenue for monarch's private expenses; keeper of this; ~ **seal**, (hist.) seal affixed to documents that are afterward to pass. **priv´i·ly** (prĭv´ĭlē) *adv*. **privy** *n*. (pl. **priv·ies**). 1. Outhouse. 2. (law) Person having a part or interest in any action, matter, or thing.

prize[1] (prīz) *n*. Reward given as symbol of victory or superiority, to student in school or college who excels in attainments, to competitor in athletic contest, to exhibitor of best specimen of manufactured products, works of art, etc., in exhibition; (fig.) anything striven for or worth striving for; (~) money

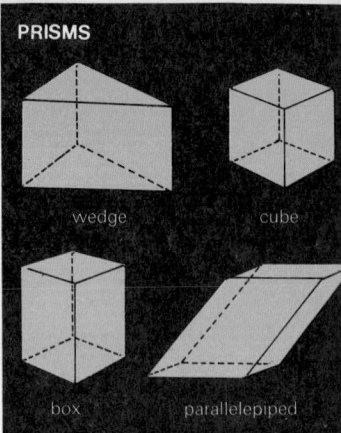

Iso **money** ~) or other reward
fered for competition by chance,
lottery, etc.; **prize′fight**, boxing
atch for money; **prize′fighter**;
rize ring, enclosed area (now usu.
quare), for prizefighting. **prize**
t. (**prized, priz·ing**). Value
ghly.

prize² (prīz) *n.* Ship, property,
ptured at sea in virtue of rights of
ar; (fig.) find or windfall; ~
ourt, one concerned with prizes;
money, money realized by sale
prize. ~ *v.t.* (**prized, priz·ing**).
lake prize of.

prize³, prise (prīz) *v.t.* (**prized,
riz·ing, prised, pris·ing**). (esp.
rit.) Force (lid etc. *up, out*, box
c. *open*) by leverage. ~ *n.* Lever-
e, purchase.

PRO *abbrev.* (mil.) Public
elations Officer.

pro¹ (prō) *n.* (pl. **pros**). (colloq.)
rofessional.

pro² (prō) *adv. & n.* (pl. **pros**).
rgument) in favor of a proposi-
on etc. (usu. pl., in ~**s and cons**,
rguments for and against)). [L.]

pro- *prefix.* 1. In front of, for,
n behalf of, on account of. 2.
avoring or siding with.

prob·a·bi·lism (prŏb′abilĭzem)
Doctrine that where authorities
iffer any course may be followed
r which a recognized doctor of
e church can be cited; theory that
ere is no certain knowledge, but
ere may be grounds of belief
ufficient for practical life. **prob′-**

a·bi·list *n. & adj.*

prob·a·bil·i·ty (prŏbabĭl′ĭtē) *n.*
(pl. **-ties**). Quality of being
probable; (most) probable event;
(math.) likelihood of an event,
measured by the ratio of the
favorable cases to the whole number
of cases possible; **in all** ~, most
likely.

prob·a·ble (prŏb′abel) *adj.*
That may be expected to happen or
prove true, likely. **prob′a·bly** *adv.*

pro·bate (prō′bāt) *n.* Official
proving of will; verified copy of will
with certificate as handed to
executors; ~ **court**, one that
administers wills and estates of dead
persons.

pro·ba·tion (prōbā′shon) *n.*
Testing of conduct or character of
person, esp. of candidate for
membership in religious body, profession, etc.; moral trial or
discipline; (law) method of dealing
with offenders by releasing them
from custody and placing them
under supervision; ~ **officer**,
person appointed to supervise such
offenders. **pro·ba′tion·al, pro-
ba′tion·ar·y** *adjs.* Of, serving for,
done in the way of, probation;
undergoing probation.

pro·ba·tion·er (prōbā′shoner) *n.*
Person on probation, esp. novice in

*Topiary Gardens at Levens Hall in
Cumbria, U.K. **Privet** is one of several
shrubs used for hedges and which can
be trimmed into various shapes.*

religious house, nurse in training,
offender on probation.

pro·ba·tive (prō′batĭv), **pro-
ba·to·ry** (prō′batōrē, -tōrē) *adjs.*
Affording proof, evidential. **pro′-
ba·tive·ly** *adv.*

probe (prōb) *n.* Blunt-ended
surgical instrument for exploring
wound etc.; act of probing; unmanned exploratory spacecraft
transmitting information about its
environment. ~ *v.t.* (**probed,
prob·ing**). Explore (wound, part
of body) with probe; penetrate
(thing) with sharp instrument; (fig.)
examine closely, sound. **prob′er** *n.*
prob′ing *adj. & n.* **prob′ing·ly**
adv.

pro·bi·ty (prō′bĭtē, prŏb′ĭ-) *n.*
Uprightness, honesty.

prob·lem (prŏb′lem) *n.* Doubtful or difficult question; thing hard
to understand; (geom.) proposition
in which something has to be done;
(logic) question (usu. only implied)
involved in a syllogism; (phys.,
math.) inquiry starting from given
conditions to investigate a fact,
result, or law; (chess, bridge, etc.)
arrangement of pieces on board, or
of cards dealt, etc., in which player
is challenged to accomplish specified result, often under prescribed
conditions; (attrib.; of child)
difficult to train; (of literature etc.)
treating subject of social or other
problem.

prob·lem·at·ic (prŏblemăt′ĭk)
adj. Doubtful, questionable; (logic)

enunciating or supporting what is possible but not necessarily true. **prob·lem·at'i·cal** *adj.* **prob·lem·at'i·cal·ly** *adv.*

pro·bos·cis (prŏbŏs´ĭs) *n.* (pl. **-bos·cis·es**, **-bos·ci·des** pr. -bŏs´ĭdēz). Elephant's trunk; long flexible snout of tapir etc.; elongated part of mouth in some insects; sucking organ in some worms; (joc.) human nose; ~ **monkey**, large, long-tailed Bornean ape (*Nasalis larvatus*) the male of which has nose projecting far beyond mouth.

pro·ce·dure (prosē´jer) *n.* Proceeding; mode of conducting business or legal action. **pro·ce'dur·al** *adj.*

pro·ceed (prosēd´) *v.i.* Go on, make one's way, (*to*); go on (*with, in,* action etc., *to* do, *to* another course etc.); adopt course of action; go on to say; come forth, issue, originate; take legal proceedings *against;* (of action) be carried on, take place. **pro·ceed'ing** *n.* (esp.) Action, piece of conduct; (pl.) record of account of doings of a society; **legal** ~**s**, (steps taken in) legal action.

pro·ceeds (prō´sēdz) *n.pl.* Results, profit.

proc·ess (prŏs´ĕs, prō´sĕs) *n.* (pl. **proc·ess·es** pr. prŏs´ĕsĭz, -esēz, prō´sĕsĭz, -sesēz). 1. Progress, course; **in ~ of time**, as time goes on; natural or involuntary operation, series of changes; course of action, proceeding, esp. method of operation in manufacture, printing, photography, etc. 2. (Print from block produced by) method (e.g. chemical or photographic) other than simple engraving by hand; ~ **block**, block for printing from, produced by such method. 3. Action at law; formal commencement of this; summons or writ; ~ **server**, officer of court who serves processes or summonses. 4. (anat., zool., bot.) Outgrowth, protuberance. **process** *v.t.* 1. Institute legal process against (person). 2. Treat (material), preserve (food), reproduce (drawing etc.) by a process. 3. Subject to administrative process, examine, attend to, and dispose of (papers).

pro·ces·sion (prosĕsh´on) *n.* 1. Proceeding of body of persons (or of boats etc.) in orderly succession, esp. as religious ceremony or on festive occasion; body of persons doing this. 2. (theol.) Emanation of the Holy Ghost. ~ *v.* Go in procession; walk along (street) in procession.

pro·ces·sion·al (prosĕsh´onal) *adj.* Of processions; used, carried, sung, in processions. ~ *n.* Processional hymn, (eccles.) office book of processional hymns etc. **pro·ces'sion·al·ly** *adv.*

pro·claim (prōklām´, pro-) *v.t.* Announce publicly and officially; declare (war, peace); announce

Elephants are the only living **proboscideans**, descended through 50,000,000 years of change from a tapir-like creature about 2 ft. tall.

officially the accession of (sovereign); declare (person, thing) officially to be (traitor etc.); declare publicly or openly (thing, *that*); place (district etc.) under legal restrictions, prohibit (meeting etc.), by declaration. **proc·la·ma·tion** (prŏklamā´shon) *n.* **pro·clam·a·to·ry** (prōklăm´atōrē, -tōrē) *adj.*

pro·cliv·i·ty (prōklĭv´ĭtē) *n.* (pl. **-ties**). Tendency (*to, toward,* action or habit, esp. bad one).

Proc·ne (prŏk´nē). (Gk. myth.) Sister of PHILOMELA; for feeding the flesh of her son to her husband, Tereus, she was turned into a swallow.

pro·con·sul (prōkŏn´sul) *n.* 1. (Rom. hist.) Governor of Roman province, in later republic usu. an ex-consul; (under empire) governor of senatorial province. 2. (rhet.) Governor of modern colony etc.; deputy consul. **pro·con'su·lar** *adj.* **pro·con'su·late**, **pro·con'sul·ship** *ns.*

pro·cras·ti·nate (prōkrăs´tĭnāt, pro-) *v.i.* (**-nat·ed**, **-nat·ing**). Defer action, be dilatory. **pro·**

cras·ti·na·tion *n.* **pro·cras'ti·na·tive**, **pro·cras·ti·na·to·ry** (prōkrăs´tinatōre, -tōre, pro-) *adjs.* **pro·cras'ti·na·tor** *n.*

pro·cre·ate (prō´krēāt) *v.t.* (**-at·ed**, **-at·ing**). Generate (offspring). **pro·cre·ant** (prō´krēant) *adj.* **pro·cre·a'tion** *n.* **pro'cre·a·tive** *adj.* **pro'cre·a·tor** *n.*

Pro·crus·tes (prōkrus´tēz). (Gk. legend) Robber who laid travelers on a bed and made them fit it by cutting off their limbs or stretching them; he was killed by Theseus. **Pro·crus'te·an** *adj.* Compelling conformity by violent means.

proc·tor (prŏk´ter) *n.* 1. Person appointed to administer school examinations and guard against cheating. 2. (law) Person managing causes in court (now chiefly eccles. that administers civil or canon law. **proc·to·ri·al** (prŏktōr´ēal, -tōr´ *adj.* **proc'tor·ship** *n.*

proc·to·scope (prŏk´toskōp) *n.* Surgical instrument for inspecting the interior of the rectum.

pro·cum·bent (prōkŭm´bent *adj.* Lying on the face, prostrate (bot.) growing along the ground.

proc·u·ra·tion (prŏkyurā´shon *n.* 1. Procuring, obtaining; bringing about. 2. Function, authorized

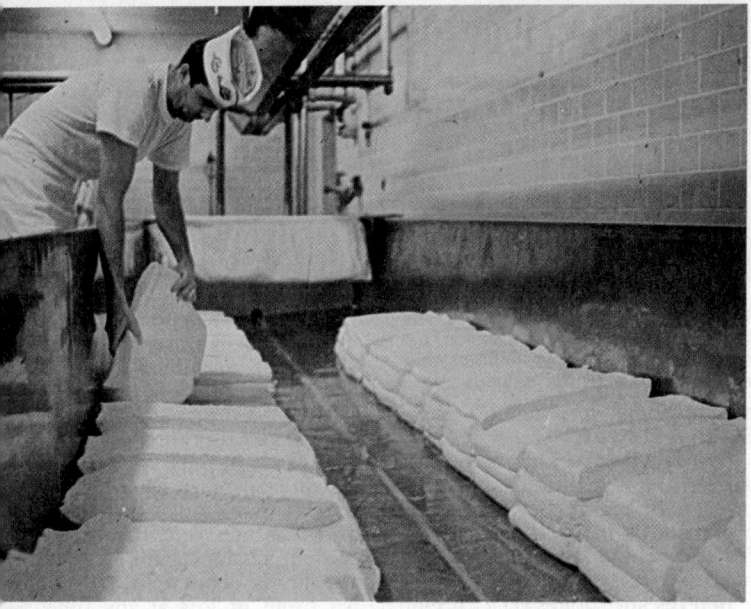

*Food **production** techniques have been mechanized to allow a greater output to be obtained from a smaller workforce. Both beer (1) and cheese (2) were once made by hand but increasing demand is satisfied by use of machinery.*

...ction, of attorney or agent. 3. ...rocurer's trade or offense.

proc·u·ra·tor (prŏk′yurāter) *n.* .. (Rom. hist.) Treasury officer in ...nperial province. 2. Agent, proxy. ...p. one who has power of attorney. .. Magistrate in some Italian cities. **roc·u·ra·to·ri·al** (prŏkyuratōr′-al, -tŏr′-) *adj.* **proc′u·ra·tor·ship**

proc·u·ra·to·ry (prŏk′yuratōrē, ...ōrē) *n.* Authorization to act for ...nother.

pro·cure (prōkūr′) *v.* (**-cured, ...cur·ing**). Obtain by care or effort, ...quire; act as procurer or pro-...uress; (archaic) bring about. **ro·cur′a·ble** *adj.* **pro·cur′ance, ro·cure′ment** *ns.*

pro·cur·er (prōkūr′er) *n.* (fem. **ro·cur·ess** pr. prōkūr′ĭs). Pimp.

prod (prŏd) *v.t.* (**prod·ded, prod·ding**). Poke with pointed instrument, end of stick, etc.; goad, irritate. ~ *n.* Poke, thrust; pointed instrument; **cattle** ~, one equipped with an electrical charger for moving cattle and, sometimes, people in crowd control.

prod·i·gal (prŏd′igal) *adj.* Recklessly wasteful; lavish *of;* **P ~ Son,** repentant wastrel in parable (Luke 15). **prod′i·gal·ly** *adv.* **prod·i·gal·i·ty** (prŏdigăl′ĭtē) *n.* **prodigal** *n.* Prodigal person.

pro·di·gious (prōdĭj′us) *adj.* Marvelous, amazing; enormous; abnormal. **pro·di′gious·ly** ,*adv.* **pro·di′gious·ness** *n.*

prod·i·gy (prŏd′ijē) *n.* (pl. **-gies**). Marvelous thing, esp. one out of the course of nature; wonder-

ful example *of* (some quality); person endowed with surprising qualities or abilities, esp. precocious child.

pro·duce (prodo͞os′, -dūs′) *v.t.* (**-duced, -duc·ing**). 1. Bring forward for inspection or consideration; bring (play, performer, book, etc.) before the public. 2. (geom.) Extend, continue (line *to* a point). 3. Manufacture (goods) from raw materials etc. 4. Bring about, cause (sensation etc.). 5. Yield (produce); bear, yield (offspring, fruit). **pro·duc′i·ble** *adj.* **produce** (prŏd′o͞os, -ūs, prō′do͞os, -dūs) *n.* Amount produced, yield, esp. in assay of ore; agricultural and natural products collectively; result (*of* labor, efforts, etc.).

pro·duc·er (prodo͞o′ser, -dū′-) *n.* 1. (econ.) One who produces articles for consumption (opp. *consumer*); person financing a film, play, etc. and controlling its production. 2. (also **gas ~**) Special form of furnace for making ~ **gas,** an inflammable gas containing carbon monoxide together with nitrogen, made by passing air through red-hot coke.

prod·uct (prŏd′ukt) *n.* Thing produced by natural process or manufacture; result; (math.) quantity obtained by multiplying quantities together; (chem.) compound formed during chemical reaction.

pro·duc·tion (prodŭk′shon) *n.* Producing; thing(s) produced; literary or artistic work.

pro·duc·tive (prodŭk′tĭv) *adj.* Producing, tending to produce; producing abundantly; (econ.) producing salable commodities. **pro·duc′tive·ly** *adv.* **pro·duc′tive·ness** *n.* **pro·duc·tiv·i·ty** (prōdŭktĭv′ĭtē, prŏdŭk-) *n.* (esp.) Efficiency in industrial production.

pro·em (prō′ĕm) *n.* Preface, preamble; beginning, prelude. **pro·e·mi·al** (prōē′mēal) *adj.*

Prof., prof. *abbrevs.* Professor.

pro·fane[1] (prōfān′, pro-) *adj.* Not belonging to what is sacred or biblical; not initiated into religious rites or any esoteric knowledge; (of rites etc.) heathen; irreverent, blasphemous. **pro·fane′ly** *adv.* **pro·fane′ness, pro·fan′er** *ns.* **pro·fan·i·ty** (prōfăn′ĭtē, pro-) *n.* (pl. **-ties**). (esp.) Profane words or acts.

pro·fane[2] (prōfān′, pro-) *v.t.* (**-faned, -fan·ing**). Treat (sacred thing) with irreverence or disregard; violate, pollute (what is entitled to respect). **prof·a·na·-**

Roscoe Tanner, U.S. tennis player. The life of a **professional** player on the international circuit may seem an enviable one, but it can be arduous.

tion (prŏfanā´shon) *n.*

pro·fess (profĕs´, prō-) *v.* 1. Lay claim to (quality, feeling); pretend (*to* be or do); openly declare; take vows of religious order; receive into religious order. 2. Make (law, medicine, etc.) one's profession or business.

pro·fessed (profĕst´, prō-) *adj.* Self-acknowledged; alleged, ostensible; claiming to be duly qualified; that has taken the vows of a religious order. **pro·fess·ed·ly** (profĕs´ĭdlē) *adv.*

pro·fes·sion (profĕsh´on) *n.* 1. Declaration, avowal; declaration of belief in a religion; vow made on entering, fact of being in, a religious order. 2. Vocation, calling, esp. one that involves some branch of higher learning or science; body of persons engaged in this, esp. (theatr. slang) actors.

pro·fes·sion·al (profĕsh´onal) *adj.* Of, belonging to, connected with, a profession; following occupation (esp. one usu. engaged in as pastime or by amateurs) as means of livelihood; making a trade of something usu. or properly pursued from higher motives; maintaining a proper standard, businesslike, not amateurish. ~ *n.* Professional man or woman, esp. (abbrev. pro) athlete playing for money (opp. amateur). **pro·-fes'sion·al·ly** *adv.*

pro·fes·sion·al·ism (profĕsh´-onalĭzem) *n.* Qualities, stamp, of a profession; practice of employing professionals in sport etc. **pro·-fes'sion·al·ize** *v.t.* (-ized, -iz·-ing).

pro·fes·sor (profĕs´er) *n.* 1. One who makes profession (*of* a religion). 2. Teacher or scholar of high rank, sometimes holder of a chair, in a college or university (prefixed as title, abbrev. Prof.). **pro·fes'sor·ate, pro·fes'sor·ship** *ns.* Position, period of activity, of college or university professor. **pro·fes·so·ri·al** (prōfesōr´ēal, -sōr´-, prŏfe-) *adj.* **pro·fes·so'ri·al·ly** *adv.*

prof·fer (prŏf´er) *v.t.* & *n.* (literary) Offer.

pro·fi·cient (profĭsh´ent) *adj.* & *n.* Adept, expert (*in, at*). **pro·-fi'cient·ly** *adv.* **pro·fi'cien·cy** *n.*

pro·file (prō´fīl) *n.* Drawing, silhouette, or other representation, of side view esp. of human face; side outline esp. of human face; flat outline piece of scenery on stage; (fort.) transverse vertical section of fort; comparative thickness of earthwork etc.; (journalism) biographical sketch of a subject, sometimes accompanied by a portrait. ~ *v.t.* (**-filed, -fil·ing**). Represent in profile; give a profile to.

prof·it (prŏf´ĭt) *n.* Advantage, benefit; financial gain, excess of returns over outlay (usu. pl.); ~ **and loss account,** (bookkeeping) account in which gains are credited and losses debited so as to show net profit or loss at any time; ~ **sharing,** sharing of profits esp. between employer and employed. **prof´it·less** *adj.* **prof´it·less·ly** *adv.* **prof´it·less·ness** *n.* **profit** *v.* Be of advantage to; be of advantage; be benefited or assisted.

prof·it·a·ble (prŏf´ĭtabel) *adj.* Beneficial, useful; yielding profit, lucrative. **prof·it·a·bil´i·ty, prof´it·a·ble·ness** *n.* **prof´it·a·bly** *adv.*

prof·it·eer (prŏfĭtēr´) *v.t.* Make inordinate profits on sale of necessary supplies or goods, esp. in time of war or supply shortage. **prof·it·eer´ing** *n.* **profiteer** *n.* Profiteering person.

prof·li·gate (prŏf´lĭgĭt, -gāt) *adj.* & *n.* Licentious, dissolute, or recklessly extravagant (person). **prof´li·gate·ly** *adv.* **prof´li·gate·-ness, prof·li·ga·cy** (prŏf´lĭgasē) *ns.*

Silhouettes, normally of the subject's **profile,** were most popular during the 18th and 19th century. They have also been used in animated cartoons and, as pictured, are continued at Disneyland.

predictive (*of*).

prog·nos·ti·cate (prŏgnŏs´tĭkāt) *v.t.* (**-cat·ed, -cat·ing**). Foretell; presage. **prog·nos·ti·ca'tion** *n.* **prog·nos'ti·ca·tive, prog·nos'ti·ca·to·ry** *adjs.*

pro·gram, Brit. **pro·gramme** (prō´grăm, -gram) *ns.* 1. Descriptive notice of series of events, e.g. of course of study, concert, etc.; definite plan of intended proceedings. 2. Entertainment etc., esp. consisting of several items; a broadcast production. 3. Series of coded instructions for a computer. 4. ~ **music,** music intended to suggest scenes or events. **program** *v.t.* (**-gramed** or **-grammed, -gram·ing** or **-gram·ming**). Express (problem) as a program; instruct (computer) by means of a program. **pro'gram·mer** *n.* **pro·gram·mat·ic** (prōgramăt´ĭk) *adj.*

prog·ress (prŏg´rĕs; *Brit.* prō´grĕs) *n.* Forward or onward movement in space; advance, development. ~ (progrĕs´) *v.i.* Move forward or onward; be carried on; advance, develop.

pro·gres·sion (progrĕsh´on) *n.* 1. Progress. 2. (mus.) Passing from one note or chord to another. 3. (math.) Succession of series of quantities, between every 2 successive terms of which there is some constant relation; **arithmetical** ~, series in which each number increases or decreases by the same quantity, as 2, 4, 6, etc.; **geometrical** ~, series in which the increase or decrease is by a common ratio, as 3, 9, 27. 4. (astron.) Movement of planet in order of signs of zodiac, i.e. from west to east. **pro·gres'sion·al** *adj.*

pro·gres·sive (progrĕs´ĭv) *adj.* 1. Moving forward; proceeding step by step, successive; ~ **bridge** etc., bridge etc. played by several sets of players at different tables, certain players passing after each round to next table; ~ **jazz,** jazz combined with classical elements in dissonant arrangements. 2. Advancing in social conditions, character, efficiency, etc.; favoring progress or reform; (of disease) continuously increasing. **pro·gres'sive·ly** *adv.* **pro·gres'sive·ness** *n.* **progressive** *n.* Advocate of progressive policy.

pro·hib·it (prōhĭb´ĭt) *v.t.* Forbid, debar. **pro·hib'it·ed** *adj.*

pro·hi·bi·tion (prōibĭsh´on, prōhĭ-) *n.* 1. Forbidding; edict, order, that forbids. 2. (also **P** ~) Forbidding by law of sale of intoxicants for common consumption; **P** ~ **Amendment,** 18th Amendment to U.S. Constitution, ratified

pro for·ma (prō fōr´ma). Done for form's sake, as a matter of form. [L.]

pro·found (profownd´) *adj.* 1. Having, showing, great knowledge or insight; demanding deep study or thought. 2. (of state or quality) Deep, intense, unqualified. 3. Having, coming from, extending to, a great depth. **pro·found'ly** *adv.* **pro·found'ness, pro·fun·di·ty** (profŭn´dĭtē) *ns.* **profound** *n.* (poet.) Vast depth.

pro·fuse (profūs´) *adj.* Lavish, extravagant (*in, of*); exuberantly plentiful. **pro·fuse'ly** *adv.* **pro·fuse'ness, pro·fu·sion** (profū´zhon) *ns.*

pro·gen·i·tor (prōjĕn´ĭter) *n.* Ancestor; (fig.) political or intellectual predecessor, original of a copy. **pro·gen·i·to·ri·al** (prōjĕnĭtōr´ēal, -tōr´-) *adj.*

prog·e·ny (prŏj´enē) *n.* (pl. **-nies**). Offspring; descendants; (fig.) issue, outcome.

pro·ges·ter·one (prōjĕs´terōn) *n.* Hormone produced by the ovaries (or prepared synthetically) that prepares the uterus for pregnancy.

prog·na·thous (prŏg´nathus, prŏgnā´-) *adj.* With projecting jaws; (of jaws) projecting. **prog·nath·ic** (prŏgnăth´ĭk) *adj.* **prog·na·thism** (prŏg´nathĭzem) *n.*

prog·no·sis (prŏgnō´sĭs) *n.* (pl. **-ses** pr. -sēz). Prognostication, esp. (med.) forecast of course of disease.

prog·nos·tic (prŏgnŏs´tĭk) *n.* Preindication, omen (*of*); prediction, forecast. ~ *adj.* Foretelling,

1919, which, together with the enabling Volstead Act of Congress, imposed on the nation prohibition of alcoholic drinks in spite of widespread opposition and violation; it was repealed in 1933 by ratification of the 21st Amendment. **pro·hi·bi'tion·ist** *n.* Advocate of prohibition (esp. of sale etc. of intoxicants).

pro·hib·i·tive (prōhĭb'ĭtĭv) *adj.* Prohibiting; (of tax etc.) serving to prevent the use or abuse of something; (of price) so high that it precludes purchase. **pro·hib'i·tive·ly** *adv.* **pro·hib'i·tive·ness** *n.* **pro·hib·i·to·ry** (prōhĭb'ĭtōrē, -tōrē) *adj.*

pro·ject (projĕkt') *v.* 1. Plan, contrive; form a project of. 2. Cast, throw, impel; cause (light, shadow) to fall on surface; (fig.) cause (idea etc.) to take shape. 3. Jut out, protrude. 4. (geom.) Draw straight lines from a center through every point of (given figure) to produce corresponding figure on a surface by intersecting it; draw (such lines), produce (such corresponding figure); make projection of (Earth, sky, etc.). ~ (prŏj'ĕkt) *n.* Plan, scheme; (in schools) scheme of study lasting for a limited period (e.g. 1 term) during which the pupils make their own inquiries and record their findings. **pro·ject'ed, pro·ject'ing** *adjs.*

pro·jec·tile (projĕk'tĭl, -tīl) *adj.*

1. Impelling, as ~ *force.* 2. Capable of being projected by force, esp. from gun. ~ *n.* Projectile missile, shell, bullet.

pro·jec·tion (projĕk'shon) *n.* 1. Throwing, casting. 2. Protruding; protruding thing; thrusting forward. 3. Planning; mental image viewed as objective reality; (psych.) unconscious transfer of one's own impressions or feelings to external objects or persons. 4. (geom.) Projecting of a figure (see PROJECT *v.* def. 4); ~ **of a point**, point in derived figure corresponding to point in original figure. 5. (geog.) Any orderly system of representing the meridians and parallels of Earth (or celestial sphere) by lines on a plane surface, e.g. by first projecting the meridians on to a cone (**conical** ~) or a cylinder (**cylindrical** ~). 6. Display of film in theater by throwing image on screen (and producing corresponding sound). 7. (alchemy) Transmutation of metals by casting **powder of** ~ (powder of philosophers' stone) into crucible containing them.

*One of the map-maker's problems is transferring an accurate image of a curved surface — the earth's — on to a flat one, particularly when the map is of a large area. To solve this, various **projections** have been worked out which limit distortion as much as possible.*

pro·jec·tion·ist (projĕk'shonĭst) *n.* Person who projects slides or film.

pro·jec·tive (projĕk'tĭv) *adj.* Mentally projecting or projected; (geom.) of, derived by, projection; ~ **property** (of a figure), property unchanged after projection. **pro·jec'tive·ly** *adv.*

pro·jec·tor (projĕk'ter) *n.* 1. One who forms a project or scheme. 2. Apparatus for projecting rays of light, as from a lighthouse lantern; apparatus for throwing a picture onto a screen; (**sound** ~, one for sound film, producing corresponding sound at same time).

Pro·kof·iev (prokawf'yef, -yĕf), **Sergei Sergeevich** (1891–1953). Russian composer and pianist, best known for his opera *Love for Three Oranges* and a fairy tale for orchestra and narrator, *Peter and the Wolf.*

pro·lapse (prōlăps') *v.i.* (**-lapsed, -laps·ing**). (path.) Slip forward or down out of place. ~ (prō'lăps, prōlăps'), **pro·lap·sus** (prōlăp'sus) *ns.* (path.) Slipping forward or down of part or organ, esp. of uterus or rectum.

pro·le·gom·e·non (prōlegŏm'enŏn, -non) *n.* (usu. in pl. **-na** pr. -na). Preliminary discourse or matter prefixed to book etc. **pro·le·gom'e·nous** *adj.*

pro·lep·sis (prōlĕp'sĭs) *n.* (pl. **-ses** pr. -sēz). Anticipation; representation of thing as existing

Conical

The meridians are projected on to a cone which touches the earth along a parallel, in this case 40°N.

line of longitude
line of latitude

The surface of projection is a plane tangential to a point on the earth's surface, in this case the North Pole.

Cylindrical or Mercator

The meridians are projected on to a cylinder touching the earth, in this case at the equator.

Zenithal

Epidiascope

projector lens

mirror

reflecting mirror

lamp

s top   manuscript   backing plate

Slide projector

reflector mirror

lamp   heat filter

projection lens

slide

fan   condenser lenses

*development of the projector has
rapid. The projection of a still pic-
ecame possible in the 1850s with
magic lantern, a forerunner of the
projector (above). Moving pic-*

*tures, in 1895, needed advances in
photography and in light transmission
and mechanics. They enabled a much
larger audience to watch performances
and led to a new form of entertainment.*

projector

e-up spool

forward drive clutch

film spool

upper sprocket

upper film loop

shutter

rewind clutch

folding spool
carrier arm

coiled spring
drive belts

projection lens

"gate" and
ssure-plate

former

motor

control knob

cooling fan

sprocket driven by Maltese Cross mechanism

bottom sprocket

bottom film loop

drive chains and sprocket

levelling screw

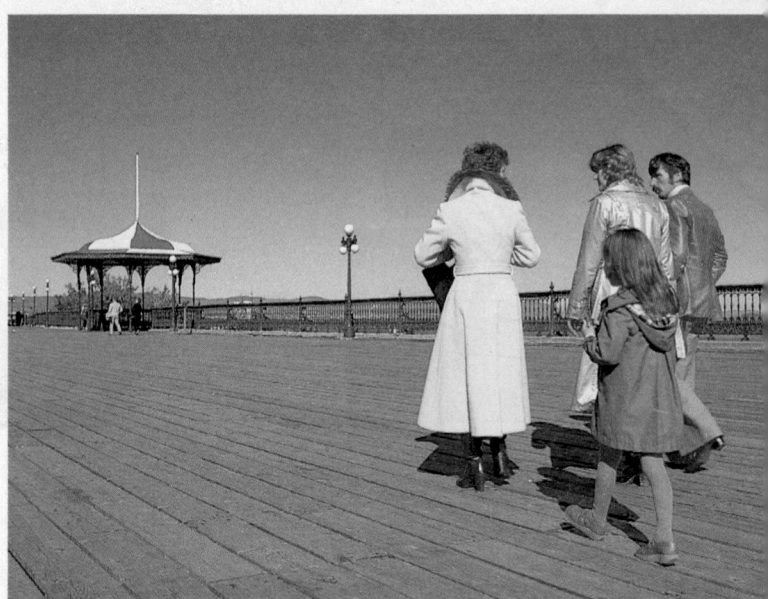

*A **promenade** at Quebec, in Canada. Originally designed to provide a leisure and entertainment location beside the sea, promenades also feature in many cities and towns as an area where people can simply enjoy being out of doors.*

before it actually does or did so; (rhet.) anticipation of possible objections in order to answer them before they are raised. **pro·lep·tic** (prōlĕp´tĭk) *adj.* **pro·lep´ti·cal·ly** *adv.*

pro·le·tar·i·an (prōlĭtār´ēan) *adj. & n.* (Member) of the proletariat. **pro·le·tar´i·an·ism** *n.*

pro·le·tar·i·at (prōlĭtār´ēat) *n.* 1. (Rom. hist.) Lowest class of community in ancient Rome, regarded as contributing nothing to the state but offspring. 2. (freq. contempt.) Lowest class of community; (econ.) class that is dependent on daily labor for subsistence, and has no reserve of capital; sometimes, all wage earners; **dictatorship of the ~**, communist ideal of domination by the proletariat after the suppression of capitalism and the bourgeoisie.

pro·lif·er·ate (prōlĭf´erāt) *v.* (-at·ed, -at·ing). Reproduce itself, grow, by multiplication of elementary parts; produce (cells etc.) thus; (of human beings etc.) multiply. **pro·lif·er·a´tion** *n.* **pro·lif·er·a·tive** *adj.*

pro·lif·ic (prōlĭf´ĭk) *adj.* Producing (much) offspring; abundantly productive (*of*), abounding *in.* **pro·lif´i·cal·ly** *adv.* **pro·lif·i·ca·cy** (prōlĭf´ĭkasē), **pro·lif´ic·ness** *ns.*

pro·lix (prōlĭks´, prō´lĭks) *adj.* Lengthy, wordy, tedious. **pro·lix´ly** *adv.* **pro·lix·i·ty** (prōlĭk´sĭtē) *n.*

pro·logue (prō´lawg, -lŏg) *n.* Preliminary discourse, poem, etc., esp. introducing play; act, event, serving as introduction (*to*). ~ *v.t.* (-logued, -logu·ing). Introduce, furnish, with a prologue.

pro·long (prōlawng´, -lŏng´) *v.t.* Extend in duration; extend in spatial length; lengthen pronunciation of. **pro·lon·ga·tion** (prōlawnggā´shon, -lŏng-) *n.*

prom (prŏm) *n.* (colloq.) Formal dance at school or college.

prom·e·nade (prŏmenād´, -nahd´) *n.* Walk, ride, drive, taken for exercise, amusement, or display, or as social ceremony; place, esp. paved public walk for this; ~ **concert**, one at which (part of) audience is not provided with seats and can move about; ~ **deck**, upper deck on a passenger vessel, where passengers may walk about. **promenade** *v.* (-nad·ed, -nad·ing). Make a promenade through (place); lead (person) about a place esp. for display. **prom·e·nad´er** *n.*

Pro·me·the·us (prōmē´thēus, -thūs). (Gk. myth.) Son of the

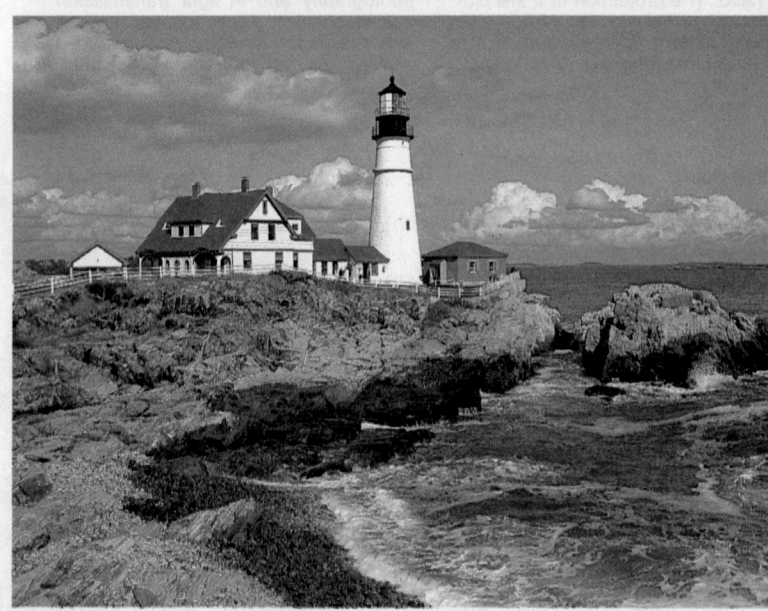

*The **promontory** at Portland Head in Maine. Because of the way the waves are formed on the headland, the surrounding coastline may become selectively eroded.*

Titan Iapetus; he made mankind out of clay, taught them many arts, and stole fire for them from heaven; to punish him, Zeus chained him to a rock in the Caucasus, where a vulture fed each day on his liver, which grew again in the night. **Pro·me·the·an** (prōmē´thēan) *adj.* Of, like, Prometheus in his skill or punishment.

pro·me·thi·um (prōmē´thēum) *n.* (chem.) Radioactive element of the rare-earth group, formed by the fission of uranium; symbol Pm, at. no. 61, principal isotope 145.

prom·i·nent (prŏm´inent) *adj.* Jutting out, projecting; conspicuous; distinguished. **prom´i·nent-**

ly *adv.* **prom´i·nence** *n.* Being prominent; thing that projects; **solar ~**, cloud of incandescent hydrogen projecting from sun.

pro·mis·cu·ous (promĭs´kūus) *adj.* Of mixed and disorderly composition; indiscriminate; (esp.) having sexual intercourse with many persons. **pro·mis´cu·ous·ly** *adv.* **prom·is·cu·i·ty** (prŏmĭskū´-ĭtē, prōmĭ-), **pro·mis´cu·ous·ness** *ns.*

prom·ise (prŏm´ĭs) *n.* Assurance given to a person that one will do or not do something or will give or procure him something; thing promised; (fig.) ground of expectation of future achievements or good results. ~ *v.* (-ised, -is·ing). Make (person) a promise to give or procure him (thing); make (person) a promise (*to, that*); make promise; (fig.) afford expectation of, seem likely (*to*); hold out good etc. prospect; ~ **oneself**, look forward to; **Prom'ised Land**, Canaan, as promised to Abraham and his posterity (Gen. 12, 13, etc.); heaven, any place of expected felicity.

prom·is·ee (prŏmĭsē') n. (law) Person to whom promise is made.

prom·is·ing (prŏm'ĭsĭng) adj. Likely to turn out well, hopeful, full of promise. **prom'is·ing·ly** adv.

prom·is·so·ry (prŏm'ĭsōrē, -sōrē) adj. Conveying or implying a promise; ~ **note**, signed document containing written promise to pay stated sum to specified person or to bearer at specified date or on demand.

prom·on·to·ry (prŏm'ontōrē, -tōrē) n. (pl. **-ries**). Point of high land jutting out into sea etc., headland; (anat.) any of various protuberances in body.

pro·mote (promōt') v.t. (**-mot·ed, -mot·ing**). 1. Advance, prefer (person to position, higher office). 2. Help forward, encourage (process, result); support actively the passing of (law). 3. Advance (child) to next grade (in school). 4. (slang) Obtain by trickery or sharp practice. 5. (slang) Organize (boxing match etc.) **pro·mot'er** n. 1. One who promotes formation of business company (freq. with implication of fraud or sharp practice). 2. One who promotes (sales, boxing matches, etc.). **pro·mo·tion** (promō'shon) n. Promoting; **sales** ~, (commerc.) information or instruction given to dealer by manufacturer or agent to facilitate sale of a product. **pro·mot'a·ble, pro·mo'tive** adjs.

Pro·mo·tor Fi·de·i (promō'ter fĭ'dēī). (R.C. Ch.) Officer of Sacred Congregation of Rites at Rome who advances all possible arguments against candidate for beatification or canonization (pop. called devil's advocate). [L., = "promoter of the faith"]

prompt[1] (prŏmpt) adj. Ready in action, acting with alacrity; made, done, etc., readily or at once. **prompt'ly** adv. **promp·ti·tude** (prŏmp'tĭtood, -tūd), **prompt'ness** ns.

prompt[2] (prŏmpt) v.t. 1. Incite, move (person etc. to); inspire, give rise to (feeling, thought, action). 2. Supply (actor, reciter) with the words that come next; assist (hesitating speaker) with suggestion. ~ n. Thing said to help memory, esp. of actor; **prompt'-book**, copy of play for prompter's use. **prompt'er** n. One who prompts, esp. (theatr.) person stationed out of sight of audience to prompt actors.

prom·ul·gate (prŏm'ulgāt, promŭl'-) v.t. (**-gat·ed, -gat·ing**). Make known to the public, dis-

seminate, proclaim. **prom·ul·ga·tion** (prŏmulgā'shon, prōmul-), **prom'ul·ga·tor** ns.

pro·na·os (prōnā'ŏs) n. (pl. **-na·oi** pr. -nā'oi). (Gk. antiq.) Space in front of body of temple, enclosed by portico and projecting side walls.

pro·nate (prō'nāt) v.t. (**-nat·ed, -nat·ing**). (physiol.) Put (hand, forelimb) into prone position. **pro·na'tion** n.

pro·na·tor (prōnā'ter, prō'nā-) n. (anat.) Muscle that effects or helps pronation.

prone (prōn) adj. 1. Having the front or ventral part downward, lying face downward; (loosely) lying flat, prostrate. 2. (of ground) Having downward aspect or direction; (loosely) steep, headlong. 3. Disposed, liable (to). **prone'ly** adv. **prone'ness** n.

prong (prawng, prŏng) n. Forked instrument, e.g. hayfork; each pointed member of fork; **prong'horn** (antelope), N. Amer. deerlike ruminant (*Antilocapra americana*), both sexes of which have deciduous horns with short prong in front. **prong** v.t. Pierce, stab, turn up (soil etc.) with prong. **prong'like** adj.

pro·nom·i·nal (prōnŏm'inal) adj. Of (the nature of) a pronoun. **pro·nom·i·nal·ly** adv.

pro·noun (prō'nown) n. Word used instead of (proper or other) noun to designate person or thing already mentioned, known from context, or forming subject of inquiry; **demonstrative** ~ s, this, that, these, those; **distributive** ~ s, each, either; **indefinite** ~ s, any, some, etc.; **interrogative** ~ s, who? what? which?; **personal** ~ s, I, we, thou, you, he, she, it, they; **possessive** ~ s; (also *possessive* *adjectives*), representing possessive case of personal pronouns (my, our, etc.) with absolute forms (mine, ours, etc.); **reflexive** ~ s, myself, ourselves, etc.; **relative** ~ s, who, which, that, what.

pro·nounce (pronowns') v. (**-nounced, -nounc·ing**). 1. Utter, deliver (judgment, curse, etc.) formally or solemnly; state, declare, as one's opinion; pass judgment, give one's opinion. 2. Utter, articulate, esp. with reference to different modes of pronunciation; **pronounc'ing dictionary**, one in which pronunciation is indicated. **pro·nounce'a·ble** adj. **pro·nounc'er** n.

pro·nounced (pronownst') adj. (esp.) Strongly marked, decided. **pro·nounc·ed·ly** (pronown'sĭdlē) adv.

pro·nun·ci·a·men·to (pronŭnsēamĕn'tō) n. (pl. **-tos**). Proclamation, manifesto, esp. (in Spanish-speaking countries) one issued by insurrectionists.

pro·nun·ci·a·tion (pronŭnsēā'shon) n. Mode in which a word is pronounced; a person's way of pronouncing words.

proof (proof) n. 1. Evidence sufficing or helping to establish a fact; spoken or written legal evidence; proving, demonstration. 2. Test, trial; (place for) testing of firearms or explosives; ~ **stress**, (eng.) load slightly greater than that which a mechanism etc. will normally have to bear. 3. Standard of strength of distilled alcoholic liquors; ~ **spirit**, standard mixture of pure alcohol and water (containing one-half alcohol by volume) in terms of which the alcoholic strengths of liquors are computed. 4. Trial impression taken from type, in which corrections etc. may be made; each of limited number of careful impressions made before printing; **artist's, engraver's** ~,

*The **prong-horned** antelope became nearly extinct as a result of excessive hunting in the 19th century. Now, however, it is protected and has greatly increased in numbers.*

one taken for examination or alteration by him; **signed** ~, early proof signed by artist; **proof′reader,** person employed in reading and correcting printers' proofs; so **proof′read** (v.) (**-read, -read·-ing**). 5. Rough uncut edges of shorter or narrower leaves of book, left to show it has not been cut down in binding. **proof** adj. (of armor) Of tried strength; impenetrable esp. as second element of compound, as *bomb′proof, wind′-proof.* **proof** v.t. Make (thing) proof; make (fabric etc.) waterproof; submit (mechanism etc.) to proof stress.

prop¹ (prŏp) n. Rigid support, esp. one not forming structural part of thing supported; (fig.) person etc. who upholds institution etc. ~ v.t. (**propped, prop′ping**). Support (as) by prop, hold *up* thus.

prop² (prŏp) n. (colloq.) Stage property; (pl.) property man etc.

prop³ (prŏp) n. (colloq.) Aircraft propeller.

prop. *abbrev.* Proposition; proper; properly.

prop·a·gan·da (prŏpagăn′da) n. 1. (**Congregation, College, of**) **the P** ~, committee of cardinals of R.C. Ch. in charge of foreign missions. 2. Association, organized scheme, for propagation of a doctrine or practice; doctrines, information, etc., thus propagated (freq. with implication of bias or falsity, esp. in politics); efforts, schemes, principles, of propagation. **prop·a·gan·dism** (prŏpagăn′dĭzem) n. **prop·a·gan′dist** n. & adj. **prop·a·gan·dize** (prŏpa-

*The same principle is used to pull a small crop-spraying aircraft (1) and an ocean liner (2). However, the **propeller** of an aircraft rotates at high speed and is narrow, while that of a ship has wider blades and moves more slowly in the denser water.*

găn′dīz) v. (**-dized, -diz·ing**).

prop·a·gate (prŏp′agāt) v (**-gat·ed, -gat·ing**). 1. Multiply specimens of (plant, animal, disease, etc.) by natural process from parent stock; (of plant etc.) reproduce (*itself*). 2. Hand down (quality etc.) from one generation to another. 3. Disseminate (statement, belief, practice). 4. Extend the action or operation of, transmit, convey in some direction or through some medium. **prop·a·ga′tion** n. **prop′a·ga·tive** adj. **prop′a·ga·tor** n.

pro·pane (prō′pān) n. (chem.) Colorless inflammable hydrocarbon gas (C_3H_8), one of the paraffin series, occurring in natural gases.

pro·pel (prọpĕl′) v.t. (**-pelled, -pel·ling**). Drive forward, give onward motion to. **pro·pel′lent** adj. Propelling.

pro·pel·lant (prọpĕl′ant) n

1

2

Single rotation aircraft propeller

Contraprop

Marine propeller or screw

1	blade	5	tail-end shaft
2	back shaft	6	stern tube
3	front shaft	7	shaft
4	boss	8	hull

Construction of the **Propylaea** of the Acropolis at Athens began during the 5th century B.C. But Pericles' concept was never completed, probably because of the costly Peloponnesian War.

propitious. **pro·pi·ti·a·ble** (prō-pĭsh´ēabel, pro-) *adj.* **pro·pi·ti·a´tion** *n.* Appeasement; atonement; (archaic) gift etc. meant to propitiate. **pro·pi´ti·a·tive** *adj.* **pro·pi´ti·a·tor** *n.*

pro·pi·ti·a·to·ry (prōpĭsh´ēatōrē, -tŏrē, pro-) *adj.* Serving, meant, to propitiate.

pro·pi·tious (propĭsh´us) *adj.* Well-disposed, favorable; suitable *for*, favorable *to*. **pro·pi´tious·ly** *adv.* **pro·pi´tious·ness** *n.*

pro·por·tion (propōr´shon, -pōr´-) *n.* Comparative part, share; comparative relation, ratio; due relation of one thing to another or between parts of a thing; (pl.) dimensions; (math.) equality of ratios between two pairs of quantities, set of such quantities; (arith.) method by which, three quantities being given, a fourth is found, having same ratio to third as second has to first. ~ *v.t.* Make proportionate *to.* **pro·por´tioned** *adj.* **pro·por´tion·er, pro·por´tion·ment** *ns.*

pro·por·tion·al (propōr´shonal, -pōr´-) *adj.* In due proportion, corresponding in degree or amount; ~ **representation**, method of legislative representation designed to permit the various political parties to be represented in proportion to their voters and characterized by the use of the transferable vote, i.e. the filling up of seats, where a quota is not secured by 1st choices, by the transference of votes from second choices, and so on. **pro·por·tion·al·i·ty** (propōrshonăl´ītē, -pōr´-) *n.* **pro·por´tion·al·ly** *adv.* **pro·por·tion·ate** (propōr´shonĭt, -pōr´-) *adj.* **pro·por´tion·ate·ly** *adv.*

pro·pos·al (propō´zal) *n.* Act of proposing something; offer of marriage; scheme of action etc. proposed; formal business offer to perform work.

pro·pose (propōz´) *v.* (**-posed, -pos·ing**). Put forward for consideration, propound; set up as an aim; nominate (person) as member of society etc.; offer (person, person's health, etc.) as toast; make offer of marriage (*to*); put forward as a plan; intend, purpose. **pro·pos´a·ble** *adj.* **pro·pos´er** *n.*

prop·o·si·tion (prŏpozĭsh´on) *n.* 1. Statement, assertion, esp. (logic) form of words consisting of predicate and subject connected by copula; (math., abbrev. prop.) formal statement of theorem or problem, freq. including the demonstration. 2. Proposal; task, project, problem for solution. **prop·o·si´tion·al** *adj.* **proposi-**

'ropelling agent; explosive that propels projectile from firearm; fuel or oxidizer for propelling a rocket.

pro·pel·ler (propĕl´er) *n.* (esp.) Revolving shaft with blades usu. set at an angle and twisted like thread of screw, for propelling ship; similar device on an aircraft producing the thrust that drives it forward.

pro·pen·si·ty (propĕn´sĭtē) *n.* pl. **-ties**). Inclination, tendency *to, for*).

prop·er (prŏp´er) *adj.* 1. archaic) Own; (astron.) ~ **mo·ion**, that part of apparent motion of fixed star etc. supposed to be due to its actual movement in space. 2. Belonging, relating, exclusively or distinctively (*to*); ~ **name, noun,** name, part of speech, used to designate an individual person, animal, town, ship, etc. 3. Accurate, correct; (usu. following its noun) strictly so called, real, genuine; thorough, complete colloq.); handsome (archaic); ~ **raction**, one whose value is less than unity. 4. Suitable, right; in conformity with demands of society, decent, respectable. **prop·er·ly** *adv.* Fittingly, suitably; rightly, duly; with good manners; (colloq.) thoroughly. **prop·er·ness** *n.*

prop·er·ty (prŏp´ertē) *n.* (pl. **-ties**). 1. Owning, being owned; thing owned; landed estate; ~ **tax**, one levied directly on property. 2. theatr.) Portable thing, as article of costume, furniture, etc., used on stage; ~ **man**, person in charge of stage properties. 3. Attribute, quality; (logic) quality common to a whole class but not necessary to distinguish it from others.

proph·e·cy (prŏf´ĭsē) *n.* (pl.

-cies). Faculty of a prophet; prophetic utterance; foretelling of future events.

proph·e·sy (prŏf´ĭsī) *v.* (**-sied, -sy·ing**). Speak as a prophet, foretell (future events); (archaic) expound the Scriptures. **proph´e·si·er** *n.*

proph·et (prŏf´ĭt) *n.* (fem. **proph·et·ess**, pr. prŏf´ĭtĭs, tĕs). Inspired teacher, revealer or interpreter of God's will; spokesman, advocate (*of*); one who foretells events; (pl.) prophetic writers of the Old Testament, the first four (Isaiah, Jeremiah, Ezekiel, Daniel) being called the **major** ~s since more of their writings have survived, and the last 12 (from Hosea to Malachi), the **minor** ~s whose extant writings are relatively short; **the P** ~, Muhammad; (also) Joseph Smith, founder of Mormonism.

pro·phet·ic (profĕt´ĭk) *adj.* Of a prophet; predicting, containing a prediction *of.* **pro·phet´i·cal** *adj.* **pro·phet´i·cal·ly** *adv.*

pro·phy·lac·tic (prōfĭlăk´tĭk, prŏfĭ-) *adj. & n.* (Medicine, measure) tending to prevent disease. ~ *n.* CONDOM. **pro·phy·lac´ti·cal·ly** *adv.* **pro·phy·lax·is** (prōfĭlăk´sĭs, prŏfĭ-) *n.* (pl. **-lax·es** pr. -lăk´sēz). Preventive treatment of disease.

pro·pin·qui·ty (prōpĭng´kwĭtē) *n.* Nearness in place; close kinship; similarity.

pro·pi·on·ic (prōpēŏn´ĭk) *adj.* ~ **acid**, colorless liquid with odor resembling that of acetic acid, present in products of the distillation of wood.

pro·pi·ti·ate (prōpĭsh´ēāt, pro-) *v.t.* (**-at·ed, -at·ing**). Appease (offended person etc.); make

1

2

tion *v.t.* Make a proposition to, esp. in regard to illicit sexual relations.

pro·pound (propownd´) *v.t.* Offer for consideration, propose (question, problem, scheme, etc.). **pro·pound´er** *n.*

pro·pri·e·tar·y (proprī´ĭtĕrē) *adj.* Of a proprietor; holding property; held in private ownership (esp. of medicines etc. of which manufacture or sale is restricted by patent or otherwise). ~ *n.* (pl. **-tar·ies**). Proprietorship; body of proprietors.

pro·pri·e·tor (proprī´īter) *n.* (fem. **pro·pri·e·tress**, pr. proprī´ĭtrĭs). Owner. **pro·pri·e·to·ri·al** (proprīītŏr´ēal, -tōr´-) *adj.* **pro·pri·e·to´ri·al·ly** *adv.* **pro·pri´e·tor·ship** *n.*

pro·pri·e·ty (proprī´ĭtē) *n.* (pl. **-ties**). Fitness, rightness; correctness of behavior or morals; (pl.) details of correct conduct.

pro·pul·sion (propŭl´shon) *n.* Driving or pushing forward; means of this; (fig.) impelling influence. **pro·pul·sive** (propŭl´sĭv) *adj.*

pro·pyl (prō´pĭl) *n.* (chem.) Hydrocarbon radical C_3H_7; ~ **alcohol**, colorless liquid (C_3H_7OH), occurring in fusel oil and separated by distillation, used as a solvent. **pro·pyl·ene** (prō´pilēn) *n.* Colorless hydrocarbon gas (C_3H_6), occurring esp. in the gases from the cracking of petroleum.

prop·y·lae·um (prŏpilē´um) *n.* (pl. **-lae·a** pr. -lē´a). Entrance to temple; **Propylaea**, entrance to the Acropolis at Athens.

pro ra·ta (prō rā´ta, rah´ta). Proportional(ly). **pro-ra´ta** *adj.*

pro·sa·ic (prōzā´ĭk) *adj.* Like

prose, lacking poetic beauty; unromantic, commonplace, dull. **pro·sa´i·cal·ly** *adv.* **pro·sa´ic·ness** *n.*

pro·sce·ni·um (prōsē´nēum) *n.* (pl. **-ni·a** pr. -nēa). 1. (Gk. and Rom. antiq.) Stage. 2. (in theater) Space between curtain and orchestra, esp. with the enclosing arch.

pro·scribe (prōskrīb´) *v* (**-scribed, -scrib·ing**). Put (person) out of protection of la banish, exile; reject, denoun (practice etc.) as dangerous et **pro·scrib´er, pro·scrip·tic** (prōskrĭp´shon) *n.* **pro·scrip·tiv** (prōskrĭp´tĭv) *adj.* **pro·scrip´tive ly** *adv.*

prose (prōz) *n.* Ordinary no metrical form of written or spok language; plain matter-of-fa quality; tedious discourse. ~ (**prosed, pros·ing**). Talk prosi **pros·e·cute** (prŏs´ekūt) *v* (**-cut·ed, -cut·ing**). 1. Follow u pursue (inquiry, studies); carry (trade, pursuit). 2. Institute leg proceedings against or with refe ence to. **pros´e·cut·a·ble** *adj.*

pros·e·cu·tion (prŏsekū´shon) Prosecuting; carrying on of leg proceedings against person; pros cuting party; (law) institution ar pursuit of criminal charge befo court.

pros·e·cu·tor (prŏs´ekūter) One who prosecutes, esp. criminal court; **public** ~, la officer conducting criminal pr ceedings in public interest.

pros·e·lyte (prŏs´elīt) *n.* Co vert from one opinion, creed, party, to another; convert another faith. ~ *v.t.* (**-lyt·e -lyt·ing**). Make proselyte **pros·e·lyt·ism** (prŏs´elĭtĭzem, -lī *n.* **pros·e·lyt·ize** (prŏs´elĭtīz, -lī *v.t.* (**-ized, -iz·ing**). **pros´e·lyt iz·er** *n.*

Pro·ser·pi·na (prōsēr´pina **Pro·ser·pi·ne** (prōsēr´pinē, prŏs erpīn) = PERSEPHONE.

pros·o·dy (prŏs´odē) *n.* Scien or study of versification. **pro**

sod·ic (prosŏd´ĭk, -zŏd´-), **pro·-sod'i·cal** *adjs.* **pro·sod'i·cal·ly** *adv.* **pros'o·dist** *n.*

pros·pect (prŏs´pĕkt) *n.* 1. Extensive view of landscape etc.; mental scene. 2. Expectation; what one expects. 3. (colloq.) Possible or likely purchaser, subscriber, etc. 4. (mining) Spot giving prospects of mineral deposit; sample of ore for testing, resulting yield. ~ *v.* Explore region (*for* gold etc.); explore (region) for gold etc., work (mine) experimentally; (of mine) promise (well, ill; specified yield). **pros·pec·tor** (prŏs´pĕkter, pros-pĕk´-) *n.*

pro·spec·tive (prospĕk´tĭv) *adj.* Concerned with, applying to, the future; expected, future, some day to be. **pro·spec'tive·ly** *adv.*

pro·spec·tus (prospĕk´tus) *n.* pl. **-tus·es**). Circular describing chief features of school, commercial enterprise, forthcoming book, etc.

pros·per (prŏs´per) *v.* Succeed, thrive; make successful. **pros'-per·ing** *adj.* **pros·per·i·ty** (prŏs-pĕr´ĭtē) *n.*

pros·per·ous (prŏs´perus) *adj.* Flourishing, successful, thriving; auspicious. **pros'per·ous·ly** *adv.* **pros'per·ous·ness** *n.*

pros·tate (prŏs´tāt) *n.* (also ~ **gland**) Large gland, accessory to male generative organs and sur-rounding neck of bladder and commencement of urethra. **pros'-tat·ic** (prŏstăt´ĭk) *adj.*

pros·the·sis (prŏs´thĭsĭs; also for def. 1 prŏsthē´sĭs) *n.* (pl. **-ses** pr. -sēz). 1. (surg.) Making up of deficiencies (with artificial teeth, limb, etc.); this as branch of surgery. 2. (gram.) Addition of letter or syllable at beginning of word. **pros·thet·ic** (prŏsthĕt´ĭk) *adj.* Of prosthesis; (biochem.) of a group or radical of a different kind added or substituted in a com-pound.

pros·ti·tute (prŏs´tĭtoot, -tūt) *n.* One who engages in indiscriminate sexual intercourse for payment. ~ *v.t.* (**-tut·ed, -tut·ing**). Make a prostitute of; (fig.) sell for base gain, put (abilities etc.) to ignoble use. **pros·ti·tu·tion** (prŏstĭtoo´shon, -tū´-) *n.*

pros·trate (prŏs´trāt) *adj.* Lying with face to ground, esp. as token of submission or humility; lying in horizontal position; overcome, overthrown; physically exhausted; (bot.) lying flat on ground. ~ *v.t.* (**-trat·ed, -trat·ing**). Lay flat on ground; cast *oneself* down prostrate; (fig.) overcome, make submissive; (of fatigue etc.) reduce to extreme physical weakness. **pros·tra·tion** (prŏstrā´shon) *n.*

pro·style (prō´stīl) *adj. & n.*

Proteins are essential parts of animal diet: many of their constituent amino acids cannot be made in the human body and so have to be taken in as food, often in the form of meat, to main-tain tissue growth.

(Portico) with not more than 4 columns.

pros·y (prō´zē) *adj.* (**pros·i·er, pros·i·est**). Commonplace, tedious, dull. **pros'i·ly** *adv.* **pros'i·ness** *n.*

pro·tac·tin·i·um (prōtăktĭn´-ēum) *n.* (chem.) Radioactive element of the actinium series, which by disintegration yields actinium; symbol Pa, at. no. 91, at. wt. 231.0359.

pro·tag·o·nist (prōtăg´onĭst) *n.* Chief person in drama or plot of story; leading person in contest, champion of cause, etc.

Pro·tag·o·ras (prōtăg´eras) (5th c. B.C.). Greek sophist philosopher; portrayed in Plato's dialogue of that name.

pro·ta·mine (prō´tamēn, -mĭn) *n.* (chem.) One of the simple basic proteins, present only in sperm, containing a higher percentage of nitrogen than most proteins.

pro·te·an (prō´tēan, prōtē´-) *adj.* Variable, versatile; of or like Proteus.

pro·tect (protĕkt´) *v.t.* Keep safe, defend, guard (*from, against*); provide (machinery etc.) with appliances to prevent injury from it; (econ.) guard (home, industry) against competition by imposing tariffs on foreign goods. **pro·tect'ing** *adj.* **pro·tect'ing·ly** *adv.*

pro·tec·tion (protĕk´shon) *n.* Protecting, defense; patronage; protecting person or thing; safe conduct; system or policy of pro-tecting home industries by tariffs etc.; security from threatened violence, obtained by payment to racketeers; such payment. **pro·tec'tion·ism, pro·tec'tion·ist** *ns.*

pro·tec·tive (protĕk´tĭv) *adj.* Serving to protect; ~ **custody**, detention of person by government ostensibly for his own protection. **pro·tec'tive·ly** *adv.* **pro·tec'-tive·ness** *n.*

pro·tec·tor (protĕk´ter) *n.* (fem. **pro·tec·tress** pr. protĕk´trĭs). Per-son who protects; thing, device, that protects; regent in charge of kingdom during minority, absence, etc., of sovereign; **Lord P ~ of the Commonwealth**, title of Oliver Cromwell 1653–8 and Richard Cromwell 1658–9. **pro·tec'tor·al** *adj.* **pro·tec'tor·ship** *n.*

pro·tec·tor·ate (protĕk´terĭt) *n.* 1. Office of protector of kingdom or nation; period of this. 2. Authority assumed by a strong nation over a weak or underdeveloped one that it protects and partially controls; period of such authority; state so protected.

pro·té·gé, fem. **pro·té·gée** (prō´-tezhā, prōtezhā´) *ns.* Person under protection or patronage of another.

pro·te·i·form (prōtē´ĭform) *adj.* Multiform, extremely changeable.

pro·tein (prō´tēn, -tēĭn) *n.* Any

Protozoa exist in every conceivable form of habitat including the air and in animal bodies. While some are harmless, others cause malaria, amoebic dysentery and other major diseases.

of a class of organic compounds (of carbon, hydrogen, oxygen, nitrogen, and often sulfur) forming an important part of all living organisms and the essential nitrogenous constituents of the food of animals.

pro·tem·po·re (prō těm´perē). (abbrev. pro tem) For the time, temporary, temporarily. [L.]

pro·test (prō´těst) *n.* Formal statement of dissent or disapproval, remonstrance; (sports) formal objection to (umpire's etc.) decision. ~ *v.* (protěst´, prō-, prō´těst). Affirm solemnly; make (freq. written) protest *against* (action, proposal). **pro·test´er** *n.* **pro·-test´ing·ly** *adv.*

prot·es·tant (prŏt´ĭstant) *n.* 1. **P**~, member, adherent, of any of the Christian churches or bodies that repudiated papal authority and were separated from R.C. communion in the Reformation (16th c.), or of any church or body descended from them; (hist., usu. pl.) those German princes and free cities that dissented from the decision of the Diet of Speyer (1529), which reaffirmed the edict of the Diet of Worms against the Reformation. 2. (also pr. protěs´-tant) One who protests. **Prot´es·-tant·ism** *n.* **Prot´es·tant** *adj.* Of Protestants or Protestantism; ~ **Episcopal Church**: see EPISCO-PAL.

prot·es·ta·tion (prŏtĭstā´shon, prōtĭ-) *n.* Solemn affirmation; protest.

Pro·te·us (prō´tēus, -tūs). (Gk. myth.) Sea god, son of Oceanus and Tethys, with power of assuming different shapes.

pro·tha·la·mi·on (prōthalā´-mēon) *n.* (pl. **-mi·a** pr. -mēa). Song or poem celebrating a marriage.

proth·e·sis (prŏth´ĭsĭs) *n.* (pl. **-ses** pr. -sēz). 1. (eccles.) Placing of the elements etc. in readiness for use in the Mass; table on which elements are placed, part of the church where this stands. 2. (gram.) = PROSTHESIS. **pro·thet·ic** (prōthět´ĭk) *adj.* **pro·thet´i·cal·ly** *adv.*

pro·thon·o·tar·y (prōthŏn´-otěrē, prōthonō´terē) *n.* (pl. **-tar·ies**). Chief clerk in some law courts; **P**~ **Apostolic(al)**, (R.C. Ch.) member of the chief college of prelates in the Curia; ~ **warbler**, brilliant yellow songbird, *Protonotaria citrea*, of eastern U.S.

pro·ti·um (prō´tēum, -shēum) *n.* Common isotope of hydrogen, as dist. from the heavy isotopes deuterium and tritium.

proto- *prefix*. 1. First, primary,

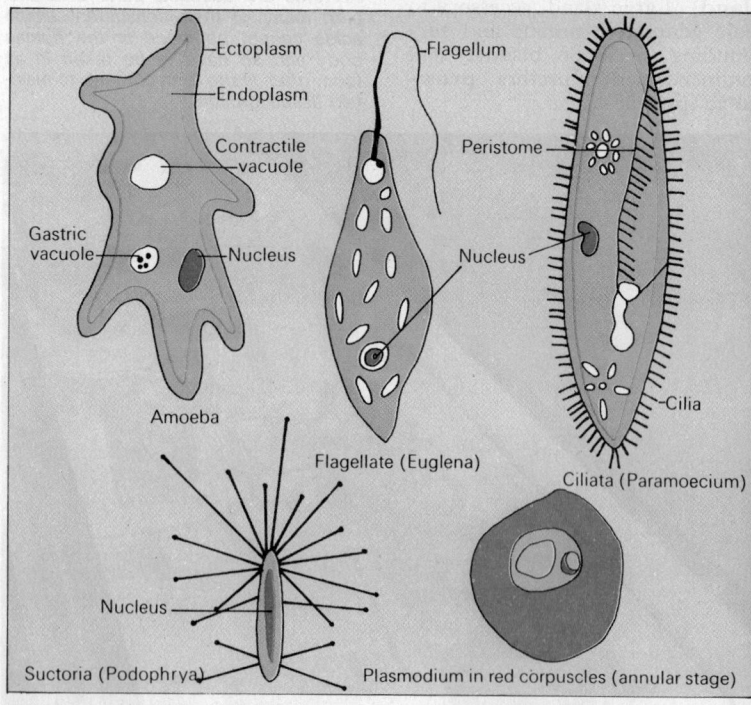

Ectoplasm — Endoplasm — Contractile vacuole — Gastric vacuole — Nucleus — Amoeba
Flagellum — Peristome — Nucleus — Cilia
Nucleus — Flagellate (Euglena) — Ciliata (Paramoecium)
Nucleus — Suctoria (Podophrya) — Plasmodium in red corpuscles (annular stage)

primitive. 2. (chem.) Indicating a substance held to be the parent of the substance to the name of which it is prefixed, as *protoactinium* (= PROTACTINIUM).

pro·to·col (prō´tokawl, -kŏl, -kōl) *n.* Original draft of diplomatic document, esp. of terms of treaty agreed to in conference and signed by the parties; formal statement of transaction; rigid prescription or

observance of precedence an deference to rank as in diplomati and military services; offici formula at beginning and end o such a document. ~ *v.* (**-cole** or **-colled, -col·ing** or **-col·ling** Draw up protocols; record i protocol. [Gk. *protokollon* flylea glued to case of book (*kolla* glue)

pro·to·gy·nous (prōtoji´nu -gī´-) *adj.* Having stigmas ripenin

*The ancient towns of **Provence** such as Les Baux (left), seem almost to have grown out of the rocks, their square, flat-topped houses echoing nature's forms.*

irritated, of moving spontaneously, contracting itself, assimilating other matter, and reproducing itself, differentiated (in most organisms) into the *nucleus*, or reproductive part, and the *cytoplasm*, a viscous fluid forming the general body of the cell. **pro·to·plas·mic** (prṓtoplăz′mĭk) *adj.*

pro·to·plast (prṓtoplăst) *n.* Mass of cytoplasm that is visibly distinct from the rest. **pro·to·plas′tic** *adj.*

pro·to·type (prṓtotīp) *n.* Original thing or person in relation to any copy, imitation, representation, later specimen, improved form, etc. **pro·to·typ·al** (prōtotī′pal), **pro·to·typ·ic** (prōtotĭp′ĭk), **pro·to·typ′i·cal** *adjs.*

pro·to·zo·an (prōtozō′an) *n.* Member of the Protozoa, a division of the animal kingdom comprising animals of the simplest type, each essentially consisting of a simple cell, usu. of microscopic size.

pro·to·zo·ic (prōtozō′ĭk) *adj.* (geol., of strata) Containing earliest traces of living beings.

pro·to·zo·on (prōtozō′ŏn, -on) (pl. **-zo·a** pr. -zō′*a*) = PROTOZOAN.

pro·tract (prōtrăkt′) *v.t.* 1. Prolong, lengthen out; extend. 2. Draw (plan of ground etc.) to scale. **pro·tract′ed** *adj.* **pro·tract′ed·ly** *adv.* **pro·tract′ed·ness** *n.* **pro·tract′i·ble** *adj.* **pro·trac′tive** *adj.*

pro·trac·tile (prōtrăk′tĭl, -tīl) *adj.* (zool.) (of organ etc.) That can be extended.

pro·trac·tion (prōtrăk′shon) *n.* 1. Protracting; action of protractor muscle. 2. Drawing to scale.

pro·trac·tor (prōtrăk′ter) *n.* 1. Instrument for setting off and measuring angles, usu. in form of graduated semicircle. 2. (physiol.) Muscle serving to extend limb etc.

pro·trude (prōtrood′) *v.* (**-trud·ed, -trud·ing**). Thrust forth, cause to project; stick out, project; obtrude. **pro·tru′dent** *adj.* **pro·tru·sion** (prōtroo′zhon) *n.* **pro·tru·si·ble** (prōtroo′sĭbel), **pro·tru′sive** *adjs.*

pro·tu·ber·ant (prōtoo′berant, -tū′-) *adj.* Bulging out, prominent. **pro·tu′ber·ance** *n.* **pro·tu′ber·ant·ly** *adv.*

*The **prow** of a Portuguese fishing boat is similar to that of a Venetian gondola, and may also be a relic of earlier times when prows carried spikes to ram other vessels.*

efore the stamens.

pro·ton (prṓtŏn) *n.* (phys. hem.) Fundamental atomic particle forming part (or in hydrogen he whole) of the nucleus, having a ingle positive electric charge equal nd opposite to that of the electron.

pro·ton·o·tar·y (prōtŏn′otĕrē, ·rōtonō′terē) (pl. **-tar·ies**) = ROTHONOTARY.

pro·to·phyte (prṓtofīt) *n.* Uni-

cellular plant.

pro·to·plasm (prṓtoplăzem) *n.* Viscous translucent substance, the essential matter of living organisms, the substance of which cells principally consist, capable of being

proud (prowd) *adj.* 1. Valuing oneself highly or too highly, esp. on the ground *of* (qualities, rank, etc.); haughty, arrogant; feeling oneself greatly honored; feeling or showing a proper pride; (of actions etc.) showing pride; of which one is or may be justly proud. 2. (of things) Imposing, splendid; slightly projecting; (of flesh) overgrown, around healing wound; (of waters) swollen, in flood. ~ *adv.* **do someone** ~, treat someone generously or lavishly. **proud'ly** *adv.* **proud'ness** *n.*

Proust (proōst), **Marcel** (1871–1922). French novelist; author of the series of volumes grouped under the title *Remembrance of Things Past.*

Prov. *abbrev.* Proverbs (Old Testament); Provence; Provençal; provost; province.

prove (proōv) *v.* (**proved, proved** or **prov·en, prov·ing**). 1. Test qualities of, try (archaic exc. in technical uses); subject (manufactured article etc.) to testing process; (arith.) test correctness of (calculation); take proof impression of (composed type, stereotype plate, etc.). 2. Establish as true, demonstrate truth of by evidence or argument; establish genuineness and validity of, obtain probate of (will). 3. Show itself, turn out, to be (or *to* be or do); ~ **oneself**, prove one's ability, character, etc. **prov·en** (proō'ven) *adj.* **not** ~, not proved (verdict used in certain courts outside the U.S. when evidence is legally insufficient to justify conviction). **prov'a·ble** *adj.* **prov'a·ble·ness** *n.* **prov'a·bly** *adv.* **prov'er** *n.*

prov·e·nance (prŏv'enans) *n.* (Place of) origin.

Pro·ven·çal (prōvensahl', prŏven-; *Fr.* prawvahn̈săl') *adj.* & *n.* Native, inhabitant of Provence; (of) the Romance language spoken in S. France, esp. in the old province of Provence.

Pro·vence (prawvahn̈s'). District, former province, of SE. France; orig. a Roman province, the 1st to be established outside Italy. [L. *provincia (romana)* (the Roman) province]

prov·en·der (prŏv'ender) *n.* Food, provisions, esp. for horses.

prov·erb (prŏv'erb) *n.* Short pithy saying in general use, adage, saw; byword, thing that is proverbial or matter of common talk; (**Book of**) **Proverbs**, didactic poetical book of Old Testament consisting of maxims ascribed to Solomon and others.

pro·ver·bi·al (prover'bēal) *adj.* Of, expressed in, proverbs; that has become a proverb or byword, notorious. **pro·ver'bi·al·ly** *adv.*

pro·vide (prōvīd') *v.* (**-vid·ed, -vid·ing**). 1. Make due preparation (*for, against*); stipulate (*that*); (freq. ~ **with**) give or lend (what is needed); make provision, esp. secure maintenance (*for*). 2. (hist.) Appoint (incumbent *to* benefice); (of pope) appoint (successor *to* benefice not yet vacant). **pro·vid'a·ble** *adj.* **pro·vid'er** *n.*

pro·vid·ed (prōvī'dĭd), **pro·vid·ing** (prōvī'dĭng) *conjs.* On the condition or understanding (*that*).

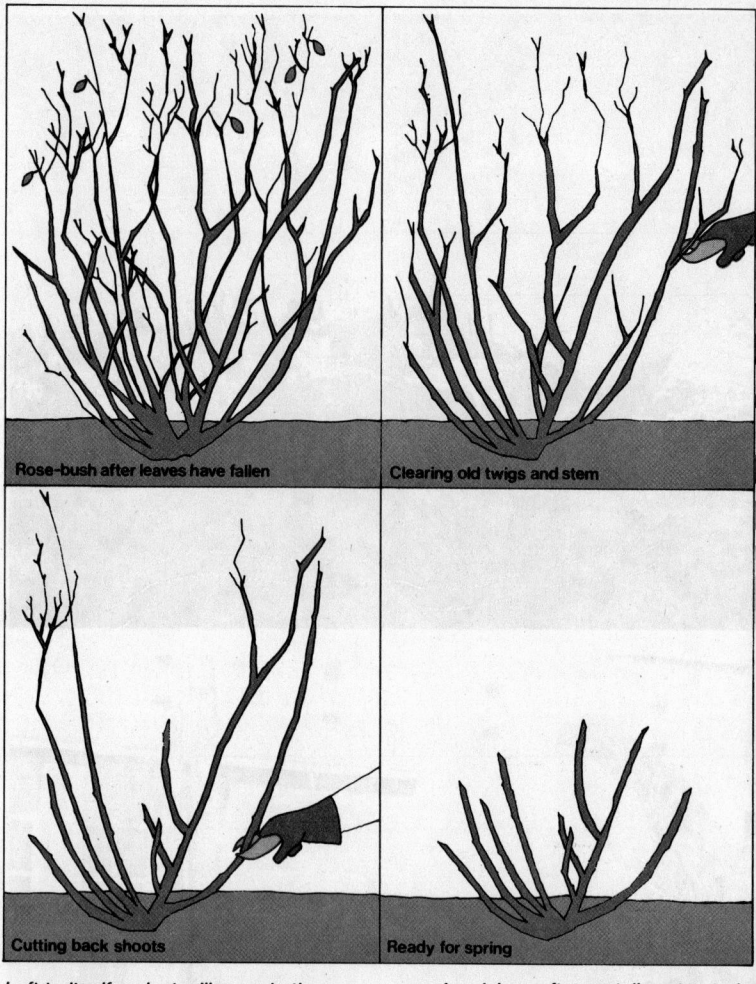

Rose-bush after leaves have fallen

Clearing old twigs and stem

Cutting back shoots

Ready for spring

Left to itself a plant will grow in the way most suited to its needs. A mosaic of leaves will gather all the light available, stem and branches will spread out in accord with the situation. However man's wishes often entail restructuring of the plant by **pruning** *so that it gives more fruit or conforms to a particular shape for decorative purposes.*

Prov·i·dence (prŏv'ĭdens). Capital and largest city of Rhode Island, in the NE. part on Narragansett Bay.

prov·i·dence (prŏv'ĭdens) *n.* 1. Foresight, timely care; thrift. 2. Beneficent care of God or nature; **special** ~, particular instance of this. 3. **P** ~, God.

prov·i·dent (prŏv'ĭdent) *adj.* Having or showing foresight, thrifty. **prov'i·dent·ly** *adv.*

prov·i·den·tial (prŏvĭdĕn'shal) *adj.* Of, by, divine foresight or interposition; opportune, lucky. **prov·i·den'tial·ly** *adv.*

prov·ince (prŏv'ĭns) *n.* 1. (Rom. hist.) Territory outside Italy under Roman governor. 2. Administrative (esp. principal) division of country or government, esp. one that has been historically, linguistically, etc., distinct; (eccles.) district under archbishop or metropolitan; (usu. joc.) **the** ~**s**, all parts of country outside the principal city. 3. Sphere of action, business; branch of learning etc.

pro·vin·cial (prōvĭn'shal) *adj.*

Of a province; of the provinces; having the manners, speech, narrow views or interests, etc., associated with or attributed to inhabitants of provinces. **pro·vin'cial·ly** *adv.* **pro·vin·ci·al·i·ty** (prōvĭnshēăl'ĭtē) *n.* (pl. **-ties**). **pro·vin·cial·ize** (prōvĭn'shalīz) *v.t.* (**-ized, -iz·ing**). **provincial** *n.* 1. Inhabitant of a province or the provinces; countrified person. 2. (eccles.) Head of, chief of religious order in, a province. **pro·vin'cial·ist** *n.*

pro·vin·cial·ism (prōvĭn'shalĭzem) *n.* Provincial manner, mode of thought, etc.; word, phrase, peculiar to province(s); attachment to one's local area, esp. its customs and standards.

pro·vi·sion (prōvĭzh'on) *n.* 1. Providing (*for, against*); provided amount *of* something; (pl.) supply of food and drink. 2. Legal or formal statement providing for something; clause of this; (English hist., pl.) certain statutes or ordinances. ~ *v.t.* Supply with provisions. **pro·vi'sion·er** *n.*

pro·vi·sion·al (prōvĭzh'onal),

pro·vi·sion·ar·y (prŏvĭzh'ŏnĕrĕ) *adjs.* For the time being, temporary, subject to revision. **pro·vi'sion·al·ly** *adv.*

pro·vi·so (prŏvī'zō) *n.* (pl. **-sos, -soes**). Stipulation; clause of stipulation or limitation in document.

prov·o·ca·tion (prŏvŏkā'shŏn) *n.* Incitement, instigation, irritation.

pro·voc·a·tive (prŏvŏk'ătĭv) *adj.* Tending to provocation (of curiosity etc.); intentionally irritating. **pro·voc'a·tive·ly** *adv.* **pro·voc'a·tive·ness** *n.*

pro·voke (prŏvŏk') *v.t.* (**-voked, -vok·ing**). Rouse, incite (*to*); irritate; instigate, tempt, allure; call forth (anger, inquiry, etc.); cause. **pro·vok'er** *n.* **pro·vok'ing** *adj.* **pro·vok'ing·ly** *adv.*

pro·vost (prō'vŏst, prŏv'ost, prō'vost) *n.* 1. Administrative officer in some universities; (hist.) head of chapter or religious community; Protestant clergyman in charge of principal church of town etc. in Germany etc. 2. (mil., usu. prō'vō) Officer of military police in garrison, camp, etc.; ~ **marshal**, head of military police in camp or on active service; naval officer in charge of prisoner to be tried in court martial. **prov'ost·ship** *n.*

prow (prow) *n.* Forepart of boat or ship, bow.

prow·ess (prow'ĭs) *n.* Valor, gallantry; exceptional ability.

prowl (prowl) *v.* Go about in search of plunder or prey; traverse (streets, place) thus. **prowl'er** *n.* **prowl'ing·ly** *adv.* **prowl** *n.* Prowling; **on the** ~, searching stealthily; ~ **car,** (slang) police car.

prox·i·mal (prŏk'sĭmăl) *adj.* (anat.) Situated toward center of body or point of attachment. **prox'i·mal·ly** *adv.*

prox·i·mate (prŏk'sĭmĭt) *adj.* Nearest, next before or after; approximate; nearly accurate.

prox'i·mate·ly *adv.*

prox·im·i·ty (prŏksĭm'ĭtē) *n.* Nearness in space, time, etc.; ~ **of blood,** kinship.

prox·y (prŏk'sē) *n.* (pl. **prox·ies**). Agency of substitute or deputy; person authorized to act for another; writing authorizing person to vote on behalf of another, vote so given; (attrib.) done, given, made, by proxy.

prude (prood) *n.* Person of extreme (esp. affected) propriety in conduct or speech. **prud·er·y** (proo'derē) *n.* **prud'ish** *adj.* **prud'ish·ly** *adv.* **prud'ish·ness** *n.*

pru·dent (proo'dent) *adj.* Sagacious, discreet, worldly wise. **pru'dent·ly** *adv.* **pru'dence** *n.*

pru·den·tial (proodĕn'shăl) *adj.* Of, involving, marked by prudence. **pru·den'tial·ly** *adv.*

prune[1] (proon) *n.* Dried plum; color of its juice, dark reddish purple.

prune[2] (proon) *v.t.* (**pruned, prun·ing**). Trim (tree etc.) by cutting away superfluous branches etc.; lop *off, away* (branches etc.); (fig.) remove (superfluities), clear *of* what is superfluous; **prun'ing hook,** curved knife used for pruning.

pru·ri·ent (proor'ēent) *adj.* Given to the indulgence of lewd ideas. **pru'ri·ence, pru'ri·en·cy** *ns.* **pru'ri·ent·ly** *adv.*

pru·ri·tus (prooʺrī'tus) *n.* (med.) Itching of skin. **pru·rit·ic** (prooʺrĭt'ĭk) *adj.*

Prus·sia (prŭsh'a) (Ger. *Preussen*) Former state of N. Europe; a kingdom 1701–1871; the dominant federal state of Germany 1871–1918; a republic until 1946, when Germany as a political unit was formally dissolved by the Allied Control Council, and the land divided among East and West Germany, Poland, and the U.S.S.R.

Prus·sian (prŭsh'an) *adj.* Of Prussia, its people or language; ~ **blue** (so-called from its discovery in Berlin, 1704), deep greenish-blue pigment of great covering power, formerly regarded as ferric ferrocyanide. ~ *n.* Prussian person or language; **Old** ~, language that became extinct in 17th c., belonging to the Baltic group of languages.

prus·sic (prŭs'ĭk) *adj.* Of, got from, Prussian blue; ~ **acid,** solution in water of hydrocyanic acid.

pry[1] (prī) *v.i.* (**pried, pry·ing**). Look, peer, inquisitively; inquire impertinently *into.* **pry'ing** *adj.* **pry'ing·ly** *adv.*

pry[2] (prī) *v.t.* (**pried, pry·ing**). Raise or move with a lever, crowbar or other tool. ~ *n.* (pl. **pries**). Lever or crowbar for prying.

PS, P.S. *abbrevs.* Postscript; public school.

P.S., Ps., Psa. *abbrevs.* Psalm(s) (Old Testament).

psalm (sahm) *n.* Sacred song, hymn; (**Book of**) **Psalms,** book of Old Testament consisting of psalms (pop. **Psalms of David**). **psalm'ist** *n.* Author of a psalm; **the P** ~, David.

psal·mo·dy (sah'mŏdē, săl'mo-) *n.* (pl. **-dies**). Practice, art, of singing psalms, hymns, anthems, etc., esp. in public worship; arrangement of psalms for singing, psalms so arranged. **psal·mo'dic** (sahmŏd'ĭk, săl-) *adj.* **psal'mo·dist** *n.*

Psal·ter (sawl'ter) *n.* 1. Book of Psalms; version of this. 2. (also **p** ~) Copy of the Psalms esp. for liturgical use.

psal·te·ri·um (sawlter'ēum) *n.* (pl. **-te·ri·a** pr. -ter'ēa). Omasum.

psal·ter·y (sawl'terē) *n.* (pl. **-ter·ies**). Ancient and medieval triangular stringed instrument, like dulcimer, but played by plucking with fingers or plectrum.

pseudo-, pseud- *prefixes.* False(ly), seeming(ly), professed(ly) but not real(ly).

pseu·do·graph (soo'dōgrăf, -grahf) *n.* Literary work purporting to be by a person other than the real author.

pseu·do·morph (soo'dōmôrf) *n.* False form, esp. (min.) crystal etc. consisting of one compound but having the form proper to another. **pseu·do·mor'phic, pseu·do·mor'phous** *adjs.* **pseu·do·mor'phism** *n.*

pseu·do·nym (soo'dŏnĭm) *n.* Fictitious name, esp. one assumed by author. **pseu·don·y·mous** (soodŏn'ĭmus) *adj.* Writing, written, under a false name. **pseu·do·nym'i·ty** *n.*

pseu·do·pod (soo'dŏpŏd) = PSEUDOPODIUM.

Brown University at **Providence,** *Rhode Island, one of the oldest cities in the U.S.A. with a rich history of trading and religious tolerance.*

pseu·do·po·di·um (soōdopō'-dēum) *n.* (pl. **-di·a** pr. -dēa). Temporary protrusion of protoplasm in a protozoan, for movement or feeding.

pshaw (shaw) *int.* & *n.* Exclamation of contempt or impatience. ~ *v.* Say "pshaw!" (*at*).

psi (sī, psē). *n.* (pl. **psis**). Twenty-third letter of Greek alphabet (Ψ, ψ) = ps.

psi, p.s.i. *abbrevs.* Pounds per square inch.

psil·o·cy·bin (sīlosī'bǐn, sīlo-) *n.* Hallucinogen found in Mexican mushrooms of genus *Psilocybe*.

psit·ta·cine (sǐt'asīn) *adj.* Of parrots, parrot-like.

psit·ta·coid (sǐt'akoid) *adj.* Like, akin, to the Psittacidae or parrots.

psit·ta·co·sis (sǐtakō'sǐs) *n.* Contagious disease of birds, esp. parrots, characterized by diarrhea and wasting, and causing bronchial pneumonia when communicated to human beings.

pso·ri·a·sis (sorī'asǐs) *n.* Non-contagious skin disease marked by red scaly patches. **pso·ri·at·ic** (sōrēăt'ǐk, sōr-) *adj.*

Psy·che (sī'kē). (Gk. myth.) Soul personified as beloved of Eros and represented in art with butterfly wings, or as butterfly.

psy·che (sī'kē) *n.* Soul, spirit, mind.

psy·che·del·ic (sīkǐděl'ǐk) *adj.* (of drug) Hallucinatory, giving illusion of freedom from limitations of reality; suggesting experience or effect of such drugs.

psy·chi·a·try (sīkī'atrē, sī-) *n.* Study and treatment of mental illness. **psy·chi·at·ric** (sīkēăt'rǐk), **psy·chi·at·ri·cal** *adjs.* **psy·chi·at'ri·cal·ly** *adv.* **psy·chi·a·trist** (sīkī'atrǐst, sī-) *n.*

psy·chic (sī'kǐk) *adj.* Psychical; susceptible to psychic or occult influences. ~ *n.* Psychic person.

psy·chi·cal (sī'kǐkal) *adj.* 1. Of the soul or mind. 2. Of phenomena and conditions apparently outside domain of physical law and therefore attributed by some to spiritual or hyperphysical agency. **psy'chi·cal·ly** *adv.*

psy·cho·a·nal·y·sis (sīkōanăl'ǐsǐs) *n.* Therapeutic method, devised by FREUD, of dealing with certain mental disorders by bringing to light complexes or repressed affects persisting in the unconscious mind; branch of psychology dealing with unconscious mind. **psy·cho·an·a·lyze** (sīkōăn'alīz) *v.t.* (**-lyzed, -lyz·ing**). **psy·cho·an·a·lyt·ic** (sīkōănalǐt'ǐk), **psy·cho·an·a·lyt'i·cal** *adjs.* **psy·cho·an·a·lyt'i·cal·ly** *adv.* **psy·cho·an·a·lyst** (sīkōăn'alǐst) *n.*

psy·cho·ki·ne·sis (sīkōkīnē'sǐs, -kī-) *n.* Supposed interference with physical causation by mental influence.

psy·cho·log·i·cal (sīkolǒj'ǐkal), **psy·cho·log·ic** (sīkolǒj'ǐk) *adjs.* Of psychology; of, relating to, the mind; ~ **moment**, (f. Fr. mistranslation of Ger. *moment* (neuter) potent element, momentum, as *moment* (masc.) moment of time), psychologically appropriate mo-

*The **ptarmigan** is the smallest member of the grouse family present in the British Isles. It has a mechanism which allows its plumage to change color to give it protective coloration.*

ment; (esp. joc.) nick of time; ~ **warfare,** (achieving aims by) acting on minds of enemy troops or population. **psy·cho·log'i·cal·ly** *adv.*

psy·chol·o·gy (sīkŏl'ojē) *n.* (pl. **-gies**). Science of the nature, functions, and phenomena of human mind and conduct; treatise on, system of, this; mental characteristics; **analytical** ~, introspective analysis of mental processes; (also) method of psychological inquiry akin to psychoanalysis, system elaborated by C. G. JUNG. **psy·chol·o·gist** (sīkŏl'ojǐst) *n.*

psy·chom·e·try (sīkŏm'ǐtrē) *n.* 1. Alleged faculty of divining from physical contact or proximity the qualities of an object or of persons etc. that have been in contact with it. 2. Measurement of mental abilities etc. **psy·cho·met·ric** (sīkōmě'trǐk) *adj.*

psy·cho·mo·tor (sīkōmō'ter) *adj.* Of motion resulting from mental activity.

psy·cho·neu·ro·sis (sīkōnōōrō'sǐs, -nyōō-) *n.* (pl. **-ses** pr. -sēz). Functional disorder of the nervous system characterized by anxiety, depression, or obsessional states, without any ascertainable organic disease. **psy·cho·neu·rot·ic** (sīkōnōōrŏt'ǐk, -nyōō-) *adj.* & *n.*

psy·cho·path (sī'kopăth) *n.* Mentally deranged person; emotionally unstable person. **psy·cho·path'ic** *adj.* **psy·cho·path'i·cal·ly** *adv.*

psy·cho·pa·thol·o·gy (sīkōpathŏl'ojē) *n.* Pathology of the mind.

psy·chop·a·thy (sīkŏp'athē) *n.* Mental disease or disorder, esp. one affecting character or moral sense.

psy·cho·sex·u·al (sīkōsěk'-shōōal) *adj.* Pertaining to the relation between sexual and psychological phenomena.

psy·cho·sis (sīkō'sǐs) *n.* (pl. **-ses** pr. -sēz). Severe form of mental illness involving the entire personality. **psy·chot·ic** (sīkŏt'ǐk) *adj.*

psy·cho·so·mat·ic (sīkōsōmăt'ǐk, -so-) *adj.* (of illness) Involving both mind and body; (esp.) exhibiting physical symptoms but instigated by mental processes. **psy·cho·so·mat'i·cal·ly** *adv.*

psy·cho·ther·a·py (sīkōthěr'apē) *n.* Treatment of disease by action on the mind only, by hypnotism, suggestion, psychoanalysis, etc. **psy·cho·ther·a·peu·tic** (sīkōthěrapū'tǐk) *adj.* **psy·cho·ther·a·pist** (sīkōthěr'apǐst) *n.*

psy·chrom·e·ter (sīkrŏm'ǐter) *n.* Wet-and-dry-bulb thermometer, used for measuring the relative humidity of the atmosphere.

Pt *symbol.* Platinum.

pt. *abbrev.* Part; pint; point.

P.T. *abbrev.* Physical training.

p.t. *abbrev.* Past tense; pro

The John Steinbeck Room at the John Steinbeck Public Library, Salinas, California, a public utility which performs an educational function providing information of interest.

tempore.

P.T.A. *abbrev.* Parent-Teacher Association.

ptar·mi·gan (tär'mĭgan) *n.* (pl. **-gans**, collect. **-gan**). Any of several grouses (genus *Lagopus*) with black, gray, or brown plumage in summer and white in winter, inhabiting high altitudes in Scotland and N. Europe, the Alps and Pyrenees, and western N. Amer.; [Gaelic *tarmachan*] esp. the willow ptarmigan (*L. lagopus*), the rock ptarmigan (*L. mutus*), and the white-tailed ptarmigan (*L. leucurus*).

pter·o·dac·tyl (tĕrodăk'tĭl) *n.* Extinct winged reptile, one of the pterosaurs.

pter·o·pod (tĕr'opŏd) *n.* Mollusk of the group Pteropoda with middle part of foot expanded into winglike lobes for swimming.

pter·o·pus (tĕr'opus) *n.* Member of genus *P*∼ of large tropical and subtropical bats, flying fox.

pter·o·saur (tĕr'osôr) *n.* One of the Pterosauria, an extinct order of mesozoic flying reptiles, with one digit of each forefoot prolonged to great length and supporting flying membrane.

Ptol·e·ma·ic (tŏlemā'ĭk) *adj.* 1. Of the PTOLEMIES. 2. Of the astronomer PTOLEMY; ∼ **system**, astronomical system elaborated by Ptolemy, in which the relative motions of the sun, moon, and planets are explained as taking place around a stationary Earth.

Ptol·e·mies (tŏl'emēz). Dynasty of kings named Ptolemy, of Macedonian origin, that ruled over Egypt from death of Alexander the Great until Roman conquest in the reign of Cleopatra.

Ptol·e·my¹ (tŏl'eme). Claudius Ptolemaeus (2nd c. A.D.), Greek astronomer, mathematician, and geographer of Alexandria.

Ptol·e·my² I (tŏl'eme) (367?–283 B.C.). (also called **Ptolemy Soter**) King of Egypt, 303–285 B.C.; founder of Ptolemaic dynasty.

pto·maine (tō'mān, tomān') *n.* One of a group of organic amine compounds, some of which cause toxic symptoms when injected or taken by mouth; ∼ **poisoning**, (formerly, erron.) food poisoning. [Gk. *ptoma* corpse]

pto·sis (tō'sĭs) *n.* (pl. **-ses** pr. -sēz). (path.) Drooping of one or both upper eyelids; downward displacement of any organ.

Pu *symbol.* Plutonium.

pub (pŭb) *n.* (esp. Brit. colloq.) Public house; ∼ **crawl**, calling at several pubs and drinking at each.

pu·ber·ty (pū'bertē) *n.* Being functionally capable of procreation; **age of** ∼, age at which puberty begins (in common law, 14 in boys, 12 in girls).

pu·bes (pū'bēz) *n.* (pl. **pu·bes**). Hypogastric region, covered with hair in the adult.

pu·bes·cence (pūbĕs'ens) *n.* 1. Arrival at puberty. 2. (bot.) Soft down on leaves and stems of plants; downiness; (zool.) soft down on parts of animals, esp. insects.

pu·bes'cent *adj.*

pu·bic (pū'bĭk) *adj.* Of pubes or pubis.

pu·bis (pū'bĭs) *n.* (pl. **-bes** pr. -bēz). Part of innominate bone forming anterior wall of pelvis.

pub·lic (pŭb'lĭk) *adj.* 1. Of, concerning, the people as a whole. 2. Done by or for, representing, the people. 3. Open to, shared by, the people; provided by, managed or controlled by, the community as a whole; ∼ **accountant**, accountant whose services are available to the general public as opposed to one who is in full-time service with a company; ∼ **address system**, equipment of loudspeakers etc. to enable speaker, musician, etc. to be heard by audience; ∼ **enemy**, criminal whose activities are considered by police to menace the public; ∼ **health**, protection of the public from disease and epidemics by provision of adequate sanitation, standards of hygiene, etc.; ∼ **house**, (Brit.) establishment providing alcoholic liquors to be consumed on the premises; ∼ **law**, law of relations between persons and state; ∼ **nuisance**, (law) illegal act harming community rather than an individual; ∼ **relations**, (esp. good) relations between organization etc. and the general public; ∼ **relations officer**, (abbrev. PRO) person who gives out information to the public in connection with some office of government, corporation, etc.; ∼ **school**, (Brit.) endowed grammar (usu. boarding) school administered by board of governors, and of which the head is a member of the Headmasters' Conference; (U.S.) primary or secondary school provided at public expense and managed by public authority as part of system of public (and usu. free) education; ∼ **servant**, government official, elected or appointed; ∼ **utilities**, services or supplies commonly available in large towns, as buses, drainage, water, gas, electricity, etc. 4. Open to general observation, done or existing in public; of, engaged in, the affairs or service of the people; ∼**-spirited**, animated or prompted by zeal for the common good. **pub'lic·ly** *adv.*

public *n.* 1. (Members of) the community in general; section of the community; **in** ∼, publicly, openly. 2. (Brit. colloq.) Public house, hence **publican**, keeper of the public house.

pub·li·ca·tion (pŭblĭkā'shon) *n.* Making publicly known; issuing of book, engraving, music, etc., to the public; book etc. so issued.

pub·li·cist (pŭb'lĭsĭst) *n.* 1. Writer on, person skilled in, international law. 2. Writer on current public topics, esp. journalist. 3. Publicity agent.

pub·lic·i·ty (pŭblĭs'ĭtē) *n.* Being or making public; esp. (business of) advertising or making events or persons publicly known; ∼ **agent**, person employed for this purpose.

pub·li·cize (pŭb'lĭsīz) *v.t.* (**-cized, -ciz·ing**). Bring to public notice, advertise.

pub·lish (pŭb'lĭsh) *v.t.* Make generally known; announce formally, promulgate (edict etc.);

(Brit.) ask, read (banns of marriage); issue copies of (book etc.) for sale to the public. **pub'lish·a·ble** adj. **pub'lish·er** n. (esp.) One whose business is producing copies of books etc., and distributing them to booksellers etc. or to the public.

Puc·ci·ni (pōochē'nē), **Giaco-mo** (1858–1924). Italian operatic composer, famous for his *La Bohème*, *Tosca*, and *Madame Butterfly*.

puce (pūs) adj. & n. Purplish brown.

Puck (pŭk). Merry mischievous sprite or goblin (as in Shakespeare's *A Midsummer Night's Dream*) believed, esp. in 16th and 17th centuries, to haunt the English countryside; in earlier superstition, an evil demon. **puck'ish** adj. **puck'ish·ly** adv. **puck'ish·ness** n.

puck (pŭk) n. Rubber disk used in ice hockey.

puck·er (pŭk'er) v. Contract, gather (*up*), into wrinkles, folds, or bulges, intentionally or as fault e.g. in sewing; ~ **up**, contract the lips, as before kissing. **pucker** n. Such wrinkle etc.

pud·ding (pood'ing) n. Dish made of a mixture of ingredients, usu. including flour, eggs, and milk as well as seasoning and flavoring.

pud·dle (pŭd'el) n. 1. Small dirty pool, esp. of rain on road etc. 2. Clay (and sand) mixed with water as watertight covering for embankments etc. ~ v. (**-dled, -dling**). 1. Dabble, wallow (*about*) in mud or shallow water; make (water) muddy. 2. Knead (clay and sand) into, make, line (canal etc.) with, puddle. 3. Stir (a mixture of molten cast iron and iron ore) in a furnace so as to expel the carbon and convert it into malleable iron. **pud'dler** n. **pud'dly** adj.

pu·den·dum (pūdĕn'dum) n. (usu. in pl. **-da** pr. -da). External genital organs. **pu·den'dal** adj. [L. *pudere* be ashamed]

pudg·y (pŭj'ē) adj. (**pudg·i·er, pudg·i·est**). Short and fat. **pudg'i·ness** n.

pueb·lo (pwĕb'lō) n. (pl. **-los**). 1. Town or village, esp. communal village or settlement of Indians in Arizona, New Mexico, and adjacent parts of Mexico and Texas. 2. **P~**, member of a group of Indian peoples of several linguistic stocks, dwelling in pueblos in areas in SW. of N. Amer.

pu·er·ile (pūr'īl, -īl pū'erīl, -īl) adj. Boyish, childish; trivial. **pu'er·ile·ly** adv. **pu·er·il·i·ty** (pūerīl'ītē), **pu'er·ile·ness** ns.

pu·er·per·al (pūĕr'peral) adj. Of, due to, childbirth; ~ **fever**, fever following childbirth and caused by uterine infection.

Puer·to Ri·co (pwĕr'to rē'kō, pōr'-, pōr'-). Island of the central

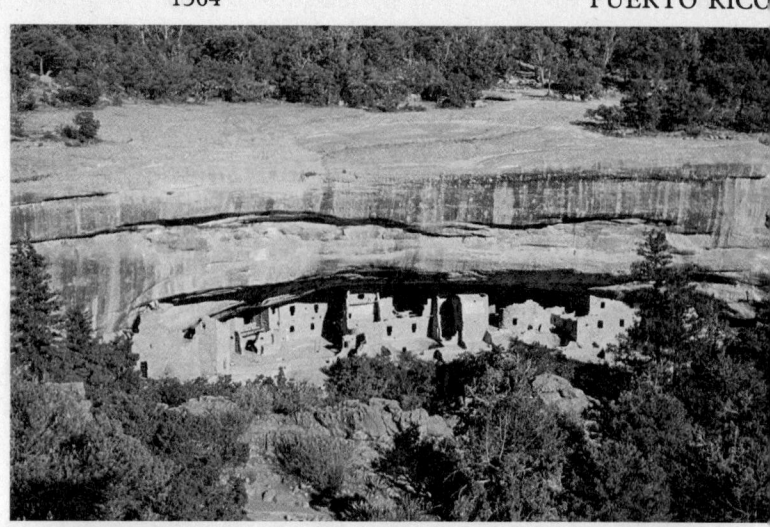

These communal dwellings were built on shelves in the rock walls of the Mesa Verde, Colorado, by the **Pueblo** Indians between 1,200 and 1,500 A.D., as protection against nomadic tribes.

Related to the auk, the **puffin** breeds on oceanic coasts, the nesting female laying only one egg in a burrow of a rabbit or shearwater. Young are fed on fish, caught by either parent.

Puerto Rico is the summit of a long-drowned mountain, one of a range forming the Greater Antilles. Thus while the coastal plains are fertile, much of the island is rugged.

West Indies 100 mi. (160 km) long, 35 mi. (56 km) wide, in the NE. Caribbean Sea; discovered by Columbus, 1493; became U.S. territory after Spanish-American War, 1898; self-governing Commonwealth since 1952; capital, San Juan. **Puer'to Ri'can** *adj.* &

puff (pŭf) *n.* 1. Short quick blast of breath or wind; sound (as) of this; small quantity of vapor, smoke, etc., emitted at one puff. 2. Round soft protuberant mass of material in dress, of hair of head, etc.; POWDER puff. 3. Piece, cake, etc., of light pastry, esp. of ~ **paste, pastry**, light flaky pastry. 4. Unduly or extravagantly laudatory review of book, advertisement of product etc. for sale, esp. in newspaper. 5. ~ **adder**, large venomous African viper (esp. *Bitis arietans*) that inflates upper part of body when excited; **puff'ball**, fungus (*Lycoperdon*) with ballshaped spore case, emitting spores in cloud of fine powder when broken; **puff sleeve**, puffed sleeve. **puff** *v.* 1. Emit puff of air or breath; come *out, up*, in puffs; breathe hard, pant; put out of breath; utter pantingly; emit puffs, move with puffs; blow (dust, smoke, light object, *away, out*, etc.) with puff; smoke (pipe) in puffs. 2. Blow *out, up*, inflate; become inflated, swell *up, out*; ~ **up**, elate, make proud (esp. in past part.); **puffed sleeve**, short very full sleeve gathered at shoulder and lower edge. 3. Advertise (goods etc.) with exaggerated or false praise.

puf·fin (pŭf'ĭn) *n.* Seabird of *Fratercula* and related genera, esp. *F. arctica* of N. Atlantic with very large furrowed particolored bill.

puff·y (pŭf'ē) *adj.* (**puff·i·er, puff·i·est**). Gusty; short-winded; puffed out; corpulent. **puff'i·ness**

pug[1] (pŭg) *n.* Dwarf squat-faced breed of dog like miniature bulldog; ~ **-nose(d)**, (having) short squat or snub nose.

pug[2] (pŭg) *n.* Loam or clay mixed and prepared for brick-making etc. ~ *v.t.* (**pugged, pug·ging**). Prepare (clay) for brickmaking by kneading and working it into soft and plastic condition; pack (space, esp. that under floor, to deaden sound) with pug, cement, etc.

pug[3] (pŭg) *n.* (slang) Pugilist.

Pu·get (pū'jĭt) **Sound.** Pacific Ocean inlet in NW. Washington, extending S. 80 mi. (129 km) from Juan de Fuca Strait to Olympia.

pug·ga·ree, pug·a·ree (pŭg'-arē), **pug·gree** (pŭg'rē) *ns.* Indian's light turban; thin scarf of muslin etc. worn around hat and sometimes hanging down behind to keep off sun.

pu·gil·ist (pū'jĭlĭst) *n.* Boxer, fighter. **pu'gil·ism** *n.* **pu·gil·is'tic** *adj.* **pu·gil·is'ti·cal·ly** *adv.*

pug·na·cious (pŭgnā'shŭs) *adj.* Disposed to fight, quarrelsome. **pug·na'cious·ly** *adv.* **pug·nac·i·ty** (pŭgnăs'ĭtē), **pug·na'cious·ness** *ns.*

puke (pūk) *v.* (**puked, puk·ing**). Vomit.

puk·ka (pŭk'a) *adj.* (Ind.) Real, genuine, true; permanent, solidly built; ~ **sahib**, (freq. derisive) real gentleman. [Hindi *pakkā* cooked, ripe; thorough, permanent]

Pu·las·ki (poolăs'kē), **Casimir** (1748?–79). Polish-born patriot; general in Amer. Revolutionary War.

pul·chri·tude (pŭl'krĭtōod, -tūd) *n.* Beauty. **pul·chri·tu·di·nous** (pŭlkrĭtōo'dĭnus, -tū'-) *adj.*

pule (pūl) *v.i.* (**puled, pul·ing**). Cry querulously or weakly, whine. **pul'er** *n.* **pul'ing** *adj.* **pul'ing·ly** *adv.*

pu·li (poōl'ē, pū'lē) *n.* (pl. **-lis, -lik** pr. poōl'ēk, pū'lēk). One of a breed of Hungarian sheepdogs whose long hair often mats, making the coat appear corded.

Pu·lit·zer (poōl'ĭtser, pū'lĭt-), **Joseph** (1847–1911). Amer. newspaper owner and editor, one of the founders of American sensational journalism; ~ **Prize**, one of a group of money prizes established under his will and offered annually to U.S. citizens for work in music, journalism, American history and biography, poetry, drama, and fiction.

pull (pool) *v.* 1. Exert upon (thing) force tending to draw it to oneself; draw (thing etc.) toward oneself or in direction so regarded; exert pulling force; pluck (plant, freq. *up*) by root; proceed with effort (*up* hill etc.); (of horse) strain against bit; draw or fire (gun etc.); ~ **person's leg**: see LEG. 2. Draw, suck, *at* (pipe, beverage glass, etc.); tear, pluck, *at*. 3. Print upon (sheet), print (copy, proof), orig. in old hand press by pulling bar toward one. 4. Move (boat), move boat, by pulling oar; (of boat) be rowed, be rowed by (so many oars); ~ **one's weight**, row with effect in proportion to one's weight; perform one's due share of work etc. 5. Check (horse), esp. so as to make him lose race. 6. (golf, baseball) Hit (ball) widely to the left, or (of left-handed player) to the right. 7. ~ **down**, demolish (building etc.); lower in health, spirits, price, etc.; ~ **in**, (of train) arrive at station; (of vehicle) move in (nearer) to roadside; (colloq.) arrest (person); ~ **off**, (slang) complete (scheme etc.) successfully; remove (garment); steer (vehicle) to side of road; ~ **out**, row out; draw out of (a position); (colloq.) abandon project etc.; (of train) move out of station; (of vehicle) move out from roadside or line of traffic; **pull'out** (*n.*) page or plate in book that folds out from front edge of leaves to facilitate reference; **pull'over**, garment for upper part of body, pulled on over head; **pull through**, get (person), get oneself, safely through (danger, illness, etc.); **pull together**, work in harmony; **pull oneself together**, rally, recover oneself; **pull up**, cause (person, horse, vehicle) to stop; reprimand; check oneself; advance one's relative position in race etc. **pull** *n.* 1. Act of pulling, wrench, tug; force thus exerted; (fig.) means of exerting influence, interest with the powerful. 2. (print.) Rough proof. 3. Pulling at bridle to check horse; (baseball, golf) pulled stroke; deep drink of liquor; draw at pipe. 4. Handle etc. by which pull is applied. **pull'er** *n.*

pul·let (poōl'ĭt) *n.* Young fowl, esp. hen from time it begins to lay till 1st molt.

*A pre-Reformation 'wine-glass' **pulpit** at Cirencester parish church U.K., is remarkable for its open-tracery stone-work which has been enriched with gilding and paintwork.*

pul·ley (pool′ē) *n.* (pl. **-leys**). One of the simple mechanical powers, consisting of grooved wheel(s) for cord etc. to pass over, mounted in block and used for lifting a weight or changing direction of power; wheel, drum, fixed on shaft and turned by belt, used esp. to increase speed or power. ~ *v.t.* (**-leyed, -ley·ing**). Hoist, furnish, work, with pulley.

Pull·man (pool′man) *n.* (trademark) Type of comfortable railroad car (PARLOR CAR) with fitted tables on which refreshments can be placed; sleeping car. [George M. *Pullman* (1831–97), Amer. designer]

pul·lu·late (pŭl′yulāt) *v.i.* (**-lat·ed, -lat·ing**). (of shoot, bud) Sprout out, bud; (of seed) sprout; (fig.) develop, spring up. **pul·lu·la′tion** *n.*

pul·mo·nar·y (pŭl′monĕrē, pool′-) *adj.* Of, in, connected with, the lungs; having lungs or lunglike organs; affected with, subject to, lung disease. **pul·mo·nate** (pŭl′monāt, -nĭt), **pul·mon·ic** (pŭlmŏn′ĭk) *adjs.*

Pul·mo·tor (pŭl′mōter, pool′-) *n.* (trademark) Apparatus for forcing oxygen into lungs to give artificial respiration.

pulp (pŭlp) *n.* Fleshy part of fruit; any fleshy or soft part of animal body, e.g. nervous substance in interior cavity of tooth; soft formless mass, esp. that of linen, wood, etc., from which paper is made; ore pulverized and mixed with water; ~ **magazine**, trashy magazine; ~ **wood**, timber suitable for making pulp. **pulp** *v.* Reduce to pulp; remove pulp from; become pulpy. **pulp′er, pulp′i·ness** *ns.* **pulp′y** *adj.* (**pulp·i·er, pulp·i·est**).

pul·pit (pool′pĭt, pŭl′-) *n.* Raised enclosed platform from which preacher in church, chapel, or synagogue delivers sermon; profession of preaching, preachers; (in small sailing vessel) guardrail, usu. waist-high, fixed at bow or stern.

pul·que (pool′kē, pool′kā) *n.* Mexican fermented drink from sap of agave etc.

pul·sar (pŭl′sär) *n.* Cosmic source of rapidly pulsating radio signal.

pul·sate (pŭl′sāt) *v.* (**-sat·ed, -sat·ing**). Expand and contract rhythmically, beat, throb; vibrate, quiver, thrill; agitate (diamonds,

*Although only a by-product of a volcanic eruption, **pumice** is of value to man. It can be used as a grinding and polishing medium and replaces gravel in lightweight concrete.*

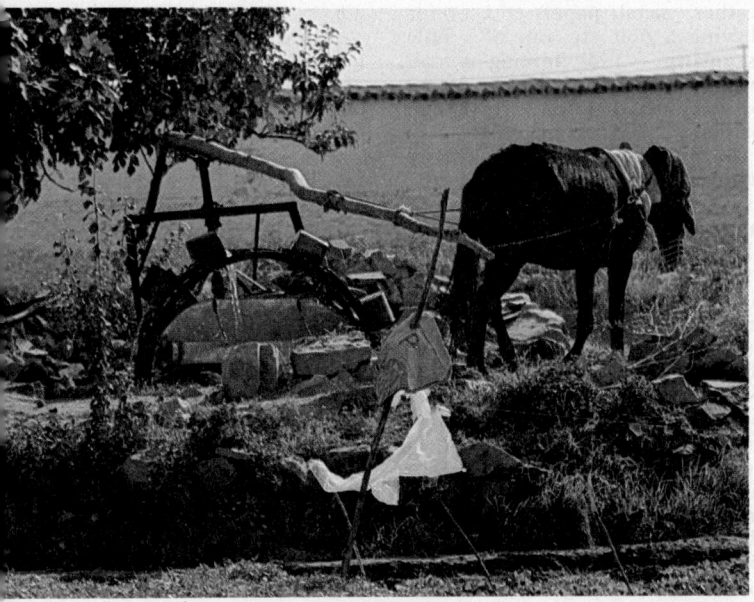

*Despite the many technological advances made by man, not all are adopted in all places. In Spain, animal power is still used to raise water (left) although many types of mechanical **pump** have been designed for continuous operation by wind or engine.*

ROTARY PUMP

liquid in

liquid out

Vanes

Casing

SUCTION PUMP

FORCE PUMP

Air bottle to give even flow

Piston valve

Piston

Flap valve or clack

Delivery valve

stones, etc.) with pulsator. **pul·sa′tion** *n.* **pul·sa·tive** (pŭl′sa̅tĭv), **pul·sa·to·ry** (pŭl′satōrĕ, -tōrĕ) *adjs.* **pul·sa·tor** (pŭl′sāter, pŭlsā′-) *n.* Machine operating with throbbing movement.

pulse[1] (pŭls) *n.* Rhythmical throbbing of arteries as blood is pumped into them from the heart, used, as felt in wrists, temples, etc., to measure the heart rate; each successive beat of arteries or heart; (fig.) throb, thrill, of life or emotion; rhythmical recurrence of strokes, e.g. of oars; single beat or vibration of sound, light, etc.; (mus.) beat. **pulse′less** *adj.* **pulse′less·ly** *adv.* **pulse′less·ness** *n.* **pulse** *v.* (**pulsed, puls·ing**). Pulsate; send *out, in,* etc., by rhythmic beats.

pulse[2] (pŭls) *n.* Edible seeds of leguminous plants, e.g. peas, beans, lentils; (with pl.) any kind of these.

pul·ver·ize (pŭl′verīz) *v.* (**-ized, -iz·ing**). Reduce to powder or dust, crumble into dust; (fig.) demolish, crush, smash. **pul′ver·iz·a·ble, pul′ver·a·ble** *adjs.* **pul·ver·i·za·tion** (pŭlverĭzā′shon), **pul′ver·iz·er** *ns.*

pul·ver·u·lent (pŭlvĕr′yulent) *adj.* Powdery, of dust; covered with powder; (of rock etc.) of slight cohesion, apt to crumble. **pul·ver′u·lence** *n.* **pul·ver′u·lent·ly** *adv.*

pu·ma (pū′ma, poō′-) (pl. **-mas,** collect. **-ma**) = MOUNTAIN lion.

pum·ice (pŭm′ĭs) *n.* (also ∼ **stone**) Very light porous stone formed by the solidified froth on the surface of glassy lava, used, freq. powdered, for polishing and abrading; piece of this for removing stains etc. from the skin.

pum·mel (pŭm′el) *v.t.* (**-meled, -melled, -mel·ing, -mel·ling**). Strike repeatedly, esp. with fist.

pump[1] (pŭmp) *n.* Machine for moving fluid from one place to another, e.g. raising water, for compressing gas, or for similar purpose, e.g. inflating tires, formerly always with rod and piston, now freq. rotary in action; action of working a pump; stroke of pump; ∼ **room,** room where pump is worked. **pump** *v.* I. Work a pump; remove, raise, (water etc.) thus; make *dry* by pumping; inflate (pneumatic tire), inflate tires of (bicycle etc.). 2. Bring out, pour forth (*on*) as by pumping; elicit information from (person) by artful or persistent questions; ∼ **priming,** (fig.) stimulation of national economy, business, etc. by investment, tax cuts, etc. **pump′er** *n.*

pump² (pŭmp) *n.* Light shoe, usu. without fastening, for dancing etc.

pum·per·nick·el (pŭm′per-nĭkel) *n.* German wholemeal rye bread, dark brown, coarse, and sour.

pump·kin (pŭmp′kĭn, pŭm′-) *n.* Trailing plant (*Cucurbita pepo*) with heart-shaped five-lobed leaves; large egg-shaped or globular fruit of this, with edible layer next to rind.

pun (pŭn) *n.* Humorous use of word to suggest different meanings, or of words of same sound with different meanings, play on words. ~ *v.i.* (**punned, pun′ning**). Make puns (**on**). **pun′ning·ly** *adv.*

Punch (pŭnch). Hook-nosed humpbacked buffoon, a stock character derived from Italian popular comedy who appeared in Italy as Pulcinella, in France as Polichinelle, in England and the U.S. as Punchinello or Punch; ~ **and Judy**, open-air puppet show performed at fairs etc. [Neapolitan dial. *policenella*, dim. of *policena* turkey cock, prob. with ref. to its hooked beak]

punch¹ (pŭnch) *n.* Instrument or machine for cutting holes in

*An African monarch butterfly on the point of emerging from its **pupal** casing. Many insects pass through a pupal stage during their metamorphosis from egg to adult.*

leather, metal, paper, etc., or for driving a bolt etc. out of a hole (**starting** ~) or forcing a nail beneath a surface (**driving** ~); tool or machine for impressing design or stamping die on material.

punch² (pŭnch) *v.* 1. Strike, esp. with closed fist; prod with stick etc., esp. drive (cattle) thus; **punch′ing bag**, stuffed or inflated ball held by chain etc., and punched as form of exercise; ~-**up** (*n.*, Brit. slang) fight with fists, brawl. 2. Pierce (metal, leather, railroad ticket, etc.) as or with punch; pierce (hole) thus; drive (nail etc. *in, out*) with punch; ~ (**ed**) **card, tape**, magnetic tape, perforated according to specified code, for conveying instructions to computer etc. **punch** *n.* Blow with fist; **pull one's punches**, refrain from using one's full force; **punch-drunk** (*adj.*) stupefied through being severely and repeatedly punched; (of pugilists), morbid condition marked by muscular failure and mental confusion, resulting from repeated head concussions caused by punches; **punch line**, line giving point of joke etc. **punch′er** *n.*

punch³ (pŭnch) *n.* Drink usu. of wine of whiskey mixed with hot water or milk, sugar, lemons, spice, etc.; similar mixture taken cold; bowl of punch; ~ **bowl**, bowl in which punch is mixed.

pun·cheon¹ (pŭn′chon) *n.* Short post, esp. one supporting roof in coal mine.

pun·cheon² (pŭn′chon) *n.* (hist.) Large cask for liquid etc. holding from 72 to 120 gallons.

Pun·chi·nel·lo (pŭnchinĕl′ō) = PUNCH.

punc·tate (pŭngk′tāt) *adj.* (biol., path.) Marked or studded with points, dots, or holes. **punc·ta′tion** *n.*

punc·til·i·o (pŭngktĭl′ēō) *n.* (pl. -**i·os**). Precise or subtle point of ceremony or honor; petty formality. [It. *puntiglio* little point]

punc·til·i·ous (pŭngktĭl′ēus) *adj.* Attentive to punctilios; very careful about detail. **punc·til′i·ous·ly** *adv.* **punc·til′i·ous·ness** *n.*

punc·tu·al (pŭngk′chōoal) *adj.* Observant of appointed time; in good time, not late. **punc′tu·al·ly** *adv.* **punc·tu·al·i·ty** (pŭngk-chōoăl′ĭtē), **punc′tu·al·ness** *ns.*

punc·tu·ate (pŭngk′chōoāt) *v.t.* (-**at·ed, -at·ing**). Insert periods, commas, etc. in (writing); (fig.) interrupt (speech etc.) with exclamations etc. **punc·tu·a′tion** *n.* Practice, art, of punctuating; marks of punctuation.

punc·ture (pŭngk′cher) *n.* Pricking, prick, esp. accidental pricking of pneumatic tire; hole thus made. ~ *v.* (-**tured, -tur·ing**). Prick, pierce; experience a puncture. **punc′tur·a·ble**

adj.

pun·dit (pŭn′dĭt) *n.* Hindu learned in Sanskrit and in philosophy, religion, and jurisprudence of India; (joc.) learned expert or teacher.

pun·gent (pŭn′jent) *adj.* 1. Sharp-pointed (bot.); (of reproof, etc.) biting, caustic; mentally stimulating, piquant. 2. Affecting organs of smell or taste, or skin etc., with pricking sensation. **pun′gent·ly** *adv.* **pun′gen·cy** *n.*

Pu·nic (pū′nĭk) *adj.* Of Carthage, Carthaginian; of the character attributed by the Romans to the Carthaginians, treacherous, perfidious; ~ **Wars**, three wars between Romans and Carthaginians (264–241, 218–201, 149–146 B.C.); in the first, Rome captured Sicily, her 1st province, from the Carthaginians under Hamilcar; in the second, the Carthaginians under Hannibal invaded Italy and the Romans after long resistance drove them out and destroyed the position of Carthage as a great Mediterranean power; in the third, Carthage itself was besieged and destroyed.

pun·ish (pŭn′ish) *v.t.* Cause (offender) to suffer for offense, chastise, inflict penalty on (offender), inflict penalty for (offense); (colloq.) inflict severe blows on (opponent in boxing), tax severely the powers of (competitor in race etc.); make heavy inroad on (food etc.). **pun·ish·a·bil′i·ty** *n.* **pun′ish·a·ble** *adj.* **pun′ish·er, pun′ish·ment** *ns.*

pu·ni·tive (pū′nĭtĭv) *adj.* Inflicting punishment, retributive. **pu·ni·to·ry** (pū′nĭtōrē, -tôrē) *adj.* **pu′ni·tive·ly** *adv.* **pu′ni·tive·ness** *n.*

Pun·jab (pŭnjahb′, pŭn′jahb). State of India; capital, Chandigarh. **Pun·ja·bi, Pan·ja·bi** (pŭnjah′bē) *ns.* Native, inhabitant, Indo-Aryan language, of Punjab.

punk (pŭngk) *n.* Rotten wood, fungus growing on wood, used as tinder; prepared stick that will smolder, used to light fireworks, drive away night-flying insects; anything worthless; (colloq.) worthless, rotten young hoodlum; ~ **rock**, primitive rock music, usu. with vulgar lyrics.

pun·kah, pun·ka (pŭng′ka) *ns.* (E. Ind.) Portable fan usu. of leaf of palmyra; large swinging cloth fan on frame worked by cord.

pun·ner¹ (pŭn′er) *n.* Maker of puns, punster.

pun·ner² (pŭn′er) *n.* Tool for ramming earth about post etc.

*With a population of 4 million Sikhs including elders of the Nihang (facing), the **Punjab** was subject to partition between India and Pakistan in 1947, the Sikhs staying with India.*

*Village children in India await the start of a **puppet** theatre. This traditional form of entertainment was practiced in ancient Egypt and Greece.*

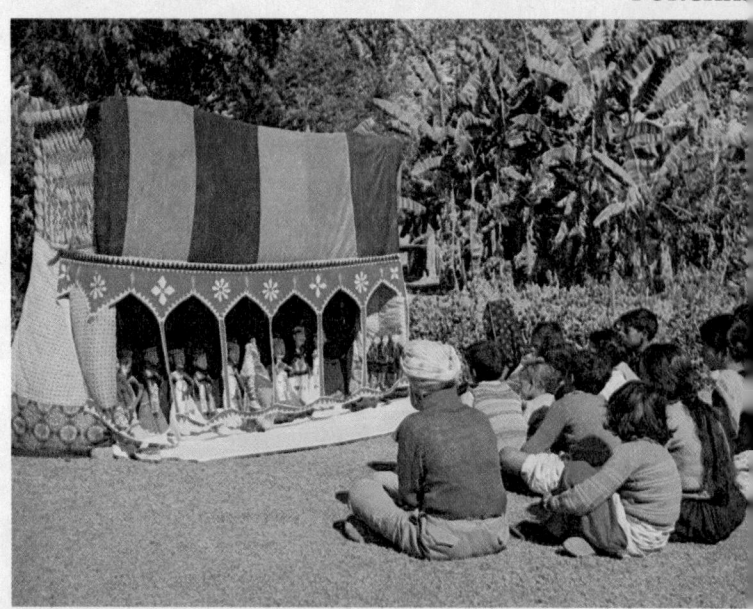

pun·ster (pŭn′stⲉr) *n.* Habitual maker of puns.

punt[1] (pŭnt) *n.* Flat-bottomed shallow boat, broad and square at both ends, propelled by long pole thrust against bottom of river etc. ~ *v.* Propel (punt, boat, or abs.) thus; convey in a punt. **punt′er**[1] *n.*

punt[2] (pŭnt) *v.t.* (football) Kick ball after it has dropped from the hands and before it reaches ground. ~ *n.* Punting kick; player who punts. **punt′er**[2] *n.*

punt[3] (pŭnt) *v.i.* (at faro and other card games) Lay stake against bank; (colloq.) bet on race horse etc. **punt′er**[3] *n.*

pu·ny (pū′nē) *adj.* (**-ni·er, -ni·est**). Undersized; weak, feeble; petty. **pu′ni·ness** *n.*

pup (pŭp) *n.* Puppy; ~ **tent**, small tent of simple design. **pup** *v.i.* (**pupped, pup·ping**). Give birth to puppies.

pu·pa (pū′pa) *n.* (pl. **-pae** pr. **-pē, -pas**). Insect in its inactive preadult form, after larva but before imago, chrysalis of butterfly or moth. **pu′pal** *adj.* **pu·pate** (pū′pāt) *v.i.* (**-pat·ed, -pat·ing**). Become a pupa. **pu·pa′tion** *n.*

pu·pil (pū′pĭl) *n.* 1. One who is taught by another, scholar. 2. Opening (circular, in man) in center of iris of eye regulating passage of light to the retina. **pu·pil·age** (pū′pĭlĭj) *n.* Nonage, minority; being a pupil.

pup·pet (pŭp′ĭt) *n.* Figure, usu. small, representing human being etc., esp. one with jointed limbs moved by strings etc. (MARIONETTE) or one made to fit over the operator's hand so that its head and arms can be manipulated by his fingers; person whose acts are controlled by another; ~ **show**, one with puppets as characters; ~ **state**, one professing to be independent but actually under the control of some greater power. **pup·pet·ry** (pŭp′ĭtrē) *n.* [Fr. *poupette* doll]

pup·py (pŭp′ē) *n.* (pl. **-pies**). Young dog; conceited young man. **pup′py·dom, pup′py·hood** *ns.* **pup′py·ish** *adj.*

pur·blind (pēr′blīnd) *adj.* Partly blind, dim-sighted; (fig.) obtuse, dull. ~ *v.t.* Make purblind. **pur′blind·ly** *adv.* **pur′blind·ness** *n.*

pur·chase (pēr′chas) *n.* 1. Buying; (law) acquisition of

*'The **Purification** of the Temple' by Jacopo da Bassano, a 16th-century Venetian painter, showing people, who had used the temple for commercial purposes, being driven out.*

property by one's personal action, not by inheritance; thing bought; (hist.) practice of buying commissions in army; ~ **money**, price (to be) paid for purchased property etc. 2. Mechanical advantage, leverage, fulcrum; appliance for gaining this, esp. (naut.) rope, windlass, pulley. **purchase** v.t. (**-chased, -chas·ing**). Buy; acquire (with toil, blood, etc.); (naut.) haul up (anchor etc.) by means of pulley, lever, etc. **pur·chas·a·ble** adj. **pur·chas·er** n.

pur·dah (pēr'da) n. (in India, Pakistan, etc.) Curtain, esp. one serving to screen women from sight of strangers; striped material for curtains; (fig.) Indian system of secluding women of rank.

pure (pūr) adj. (**pur·er, pur·est**). Not mixed or adulterated; (of sounds) not discordant, esp. (mus.) perfectly in tune; of unmixed descent, purebred; mere, simple, nothing but, sheer; not corrupt; morally undefiled, guiltless, sincere; sexually chaste; **pure mathematics**, theoretical mathematics, not including practical applications. **pure'bred** adj. Of unmixed descent. **pure'ly** adv. **pure'ness** n.

pu·rée (pyŏŏrā', -rē', pūr'ā, -ē) n. Pulp of cooked vegetables or fruit passed through sieve.

pur·ga·tion (pērgā'shon) n. Purification, purging; purging of bowels; spiritual cleansing, esp. (R.C. Ch.) of soul in purgatory; (hist.) clearing of oneself from accusation or suspicion by oath or ordeal.

pur·ga·tive (pēr'gativ) adj. Cathartic; serving to purify. ~ n. Purgative medicine. **pur'ga·tive·ly** adv. **pur'ga·tive·ness** n.

pur·ga·to·ry (pēr'gatōrē, -tōrē) n. (pl. **-ries**). Condition, place of spiritual purging, esp. (R.C. Ch.) of souls departing this life in grace of God but requiring to be cleansed from venial sins etc.; place of temporary suffering or expiation. ~ adj. Purifying. **pur·ga·to'ri·al** adj.

purge (pērj) v.t. (**purged, purg·ing**). Make physically or spiritually clean; rid (political party, army, etc.) of objectionable, alien, or extraneous elements or members; remove by cleansing process; (of medicine) clear (bowels) by evacuation; clear (of charge, suspicion); (law) atone for, wipe out, (offense, sentence) by expiation and submission. ~ n. 1. Purgative medicine. 2. Purging; ridding of objectionable or hostile elements.

pu·ri·fi·ca·tion (pūrifikā'shon) n. Purifying; ritual cleansing, esp. that of women after childbirth enjoined by Jewish law; **P** ~ (**of the Blessed Virgin Mary**), festival (in Western Church, Feb. 2) of presentation of Christ in the temple on completion of days of Virgin Mary's purification (Luke 2). **pu·ri·fi·ca·to·ry** (pyŏŏrif'ikatōrē, -tōrē) adj.

pu·ri·fi·ca·tor (pūr'ifikāter) n. (eccles.) Cloth used at communion for wiping chalice, and fingers and lips of celebrant.

pu·ri·fy (pūr'ifī) v.t. (**-fied, -fy·ing**). Make pure, cleanse (of, from, impurities, sin, etc.); make ceremonially clean; clear of foreign elements. **pu'ri·fi·er** n.

Pu·rim (poor'im; Heb. pōōrēm'). Jewish festival on 14 and 15 of month Adar (Feb.–March), commemorating defeat of Haman's plot against the Jews (Esther 9).

pur·ist (pūr'ist) n. Stickler for, affecter of, scrupulous purity esp. in language. **pur'ism** n. **pu·ris·tic** (pyŏŏris'tik), **pu·ris'ti·cal** adjs.

Pu·ri·tan (pūr'itan) n. 1. (hist.) Member of that party of English Protestants who regarded the Reformation under Elizabeth I as incomplete and demanded further purification of the church from forms and ceremonies still retained; any of those who later separated from the established church on points of ritual, policy, or doctrine, held by them to be at variance with pure New Testament principles. 2. One who is, or is thought or affects to be, extremely strict, precise, or scrupulous in religion or morals. **pu·ri·tan·ic** (pūrităn'ik), **pu·ri·tan'i·cal** adjs. **pu·ri·tan'i·cal·ly** adv. **pu·ri·tan'i·cal·ness** n. **Pu'ri·tan·ism, pu'ri·tan·ism** ns.

pu·ri·ty (pūr'itē) n. Pureness, cleanness, freedom from physical or moral pollution.

Purslane is the name given to a genus of plants which grow in a wide range of conditions and climates, and whose young shoots are edible.

purl[1] (pērl) n. 1. Cord of twisted gold or silver wire for bordering; chain of minute loops, each loop of this, ornamenting edges of lace, ribbon, etc. 2. (knitting) Stitch in which second needle is inserted through loop on 1st from right to left, and yarn is looped over second needle from the front. ~ v. Border with purl; make purl stitches in knitting.

purl[2] (pērl) v.i. (of brook etc.) Flow with whirling motion and babbling sound. ~ n. Purling motion or sound.

pur·loin (perloin', pēr'loin) v.t. Steal, pilfer. **pur·loin'er** n.

pur·ple (pēr'pel) n. 1. Color mixed of red and blue in varying proportions. 2. (also **Tyrian** ~) Color got from the mollusks Purpura, Thais, and Murex, and associated with the dress and rank or office of emperors, consuls, kings, etc.; crimson; **the** ~, imperial, royal, or consular rank, power, or office; scarlet official dress of cardinal's rank or office. **purple** adj. Of the color purple; **P** ~ **Heart**, U.S. decoration awarded to person wounded in action; ~ **martin**, large N. Amer. swallow (Progne subis) with bluish-black plumage; ~ **passage, prose**, literary passage marked by exaggerated style. **pur·plish** (pēr'plish), **pur·ply** (pēr'plē) adjs. **pur'ple** v. (**-pled, -pling**). Make, become, purple.

pur·port (pēr'pōrt, -pört) n. Meaning, sense, tenor, of document or speech. ~ (perpört', -pört') v.t. (of document or speech) Have as its meaning, convey, state; profess, be intended to seem (to do).

pur·pose (pēr'pos) n. Object, thing intended; fact, faculty, of resolving on something; **on** ~, in order (to, that); designedly, not by accident; **to the** ~, relevant, useful for one's purpose; **to good, little, no**, etc., ~, with good, little, etc., effect or result. **purpose** v.t. (**-posed, -pos·ing**). Design, intend. **pur'pose·ly** adv. **pur'pose·ful** adj. **pur'pose·ful·ly** adv. **pur'pose·ful·ness** n. **pur'pose·less** adj. **pur'pose·less·ly** adv. **pur'pose·less·ness** n.

pur·pos·ive (pēr'posiv) adj. Having, serving, done with, a purpose; having purpose and resolution.

purr (pēr) v. (of cat or other feline animal, fig. of person) Make low continuous vibratory sound expressing pleasure; utter, express (words, contentment) thus. ~ n. Purring sound. [imit.]

purse (pērs) n. Small pouch of leather etc. for carrying money on the person, orig. closed by drawing strings together; (fig.) money, funds; sum collected, subscribed, or given, as present or as prize for

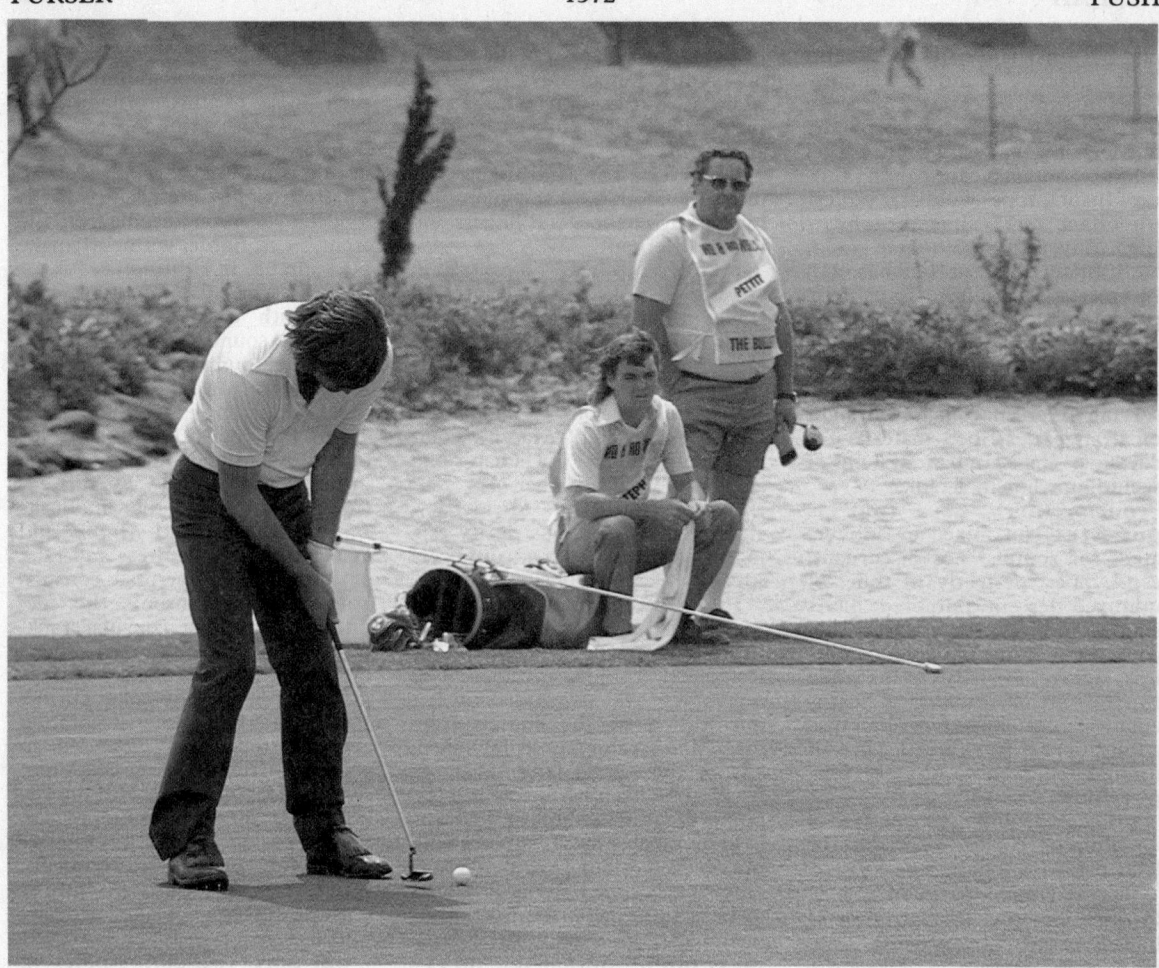

contest; baglike natural or other receptacle, pouch, cyst, etc.; **public ~**, national treasury; **~ strings**, strings for closing mouth of purse; **hold the ~ strings**, have control of expenditure. **purse** v. (**pursed, purs·ing**). Contract (lips etc., freq. up) in wrinkles; become wrinkled.

purs·er (pēr′ser) n. Officer on ship who keeps accounts and usu. has charge of provisions; in passenger ship, head of stewards' department, superintending comfort and requirements of passengers.

purs·lane (pērs′lān, -lĭn) n. Low succulent herb (*Portulaca oleracea* var. *sativa*) formerly used in salads and pickled.

pur·su·ance (persoo′ans) n. Carrying out, pursuing, esp. in **in ~ of** (plan etc.).

pur·su·ant (persoo′ant) adj. Pursuing. **~** adv. Conformably to. **pur·su·ant·ly** adv.

pur·sue (persoo′) v. (**-sued, -su·ing**). Follow with intent to capture or kill; (fig.) persistently attend, stick to; seek after, aim at; proceed in compliance with (plan etc.); proceed along, continue, follow (road, inquiry, studies, etc.); go in pursuit. **pur·su′a·ble** adj. **pur·su′er** n.

pur·suit (persoot′) n. Pursuing;

Putting on the greens at the Australian Golf Club. The game developed in Scotland and was played as early as the 15th century, James I and Mary Stuart were both avid players of the game.

profession, employment, recreation, that one follows.

pu·ru·lent (pūr′ulent, pūr′yu-) adj. Of, full of, discharging, pus. **pu′ru·lent·ly** adv. **pu′ru·lence, pu′ru·len·cy** ns.

pur·vey (pervā′) v. Provide, supply (articles of food) as one's business; make provision, act as purveyor. **pur·vey′a·ble** adj.

pur·vey·or (pervā′er) n. One whose business it is to supply (esp.) articles of food, dinners etc., on large scale.

pur·view (pēr′vū) n. Enacting clauses of statute; scope, intention, range (of act, document, etc.); range of physical or mental vision.

pus (pŭs) n. (path.) Yellowish viscid fluid formed by the liquefaction of dead tissues, usu. containing leucocytes, cell debris, and bacteria.

push (poosh) v. 1. Exert upon (body) force tending to move it away; move thus; exert such pressure; (cause to) project, thrust out, forward, etc.; make one's way forcibly or persistently, force (one's way) thus; **~ off**, (of person in

boat) push against bank etc. with oar to get boat out into stream etc.; (slang) leave, go away. 2. Exert oneself, esp. to surpass others or succeed in one's business etc.; urge, impel; follow up (claim etc.); carry (action, matter, etc.) to further point, or to furthest limit; press the adoption, use, sale, etc., of (goods, etc.) esp. by advertisement; (slang) sell (illicit drugs); press (person) hard, esp. in passive. **push′er** n. (esp., slang) Illegal seller of drugs. **push′ing** adj. **push′ing·ly** adv. **push′y** adj. (**push·i·er, push·i·est**). **push** n. 1. Act of pushing, shove, thrust; thrust of weapon, beast's horn, etc. 2. Vigorous effort, (mil.) attack in force; exertion of influence; pressure of affairs, crisis, pinch. 3. Enterprise, determination to get on, self-assertion. 4. **push′ball**, game in which very large pall is pushed, not kicked, toward opponents' goal; **~ button**, knob or button pressed to operate mechanism; **push-button**, (adj.) operated by pressing a button (also transf.); **push′cart**, handcart; **push′over**, (slang) easy mark, esp. girl or woman easily seduced; **push′up**, (usu. pl.) exercise in which one raises one's prone body by pressing down on hands to straighten arms.

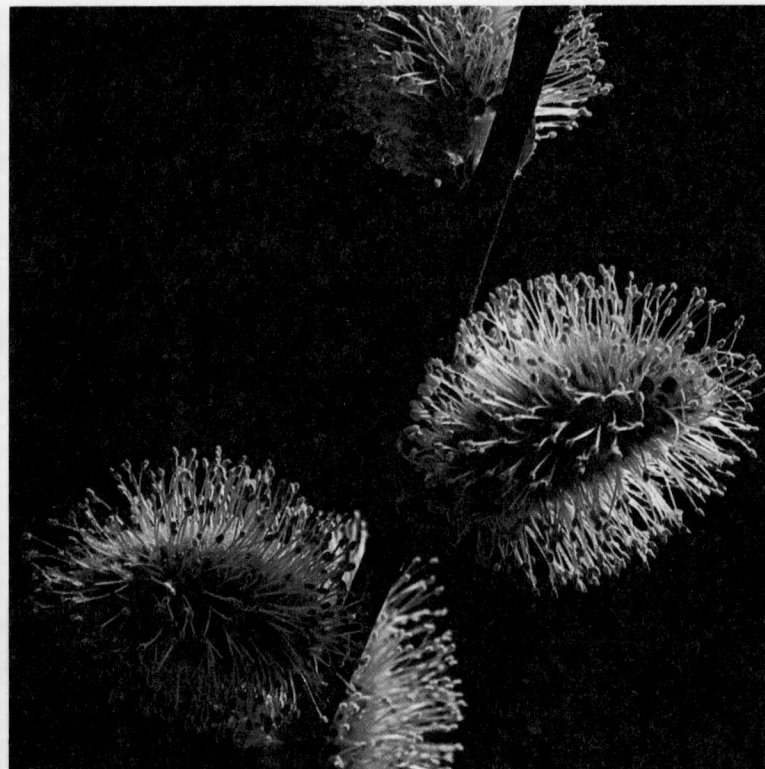

*Open buds of the **pussy willow**, bear little resemblance to the furry or silky catkins which inspired the common name of this tree.*

Push·kin (poosh′kĭn), **Alexander Sergeevich** (1799–1837). Russian poet and prose writer, the first national poet of Russia.

Push·tu = PASHTO.

pu·sil·lan·i·mous (pŭsɪlăn′-imus) *adj.* Faint-hearted, meanspirited. **pu·sil·lan′i·mous·ly** *adv.* **pu·sil·la·nim′i·ty** (pŭsɪlanĭm′ĭtē) *n.*

puss (poos) *n.* Cat (esp. as conventional proper name); (colloq.) girl; ~ **in the corner**, children's game in which player standing in center tries to capture one of the bases as the others change places.

puss·y¹ (poos′ē) *n.* (pl. **puss·ies**). Cat (esp. in nursery use); ~ **willow**, Amer. willow (*Salix discolor*) and allied species, with silky catkins.

pus·sy² (pŭs′ē) *adj.* (**-si·er, -si·est**). Containing or resembling pus.

puss·y·foot (poos′efoot) *v.i.* (colloq.) Tread softly or lightly; proceed warily; avoid committing oneself. [nickname of Amer. prohibition lecturer, W. E. Johnson (1862–1945), given because of his stealthy methods when a magistrate]

pus·tu·late (pŭs′chŭlāt) *v.* (**-lat·ed, -lat·ing**). Form into pustules.

pus·tule (pŭs′chool) *n.* Pimple. **pus·tu·lar** (pŭs′chŭler), **pus·tu·lous** *adjs.*

put (poot) *v.* (**put, put·ting**). 1. Propel, hurl (**the shot**) from hand placed close to shoulder, as athletic exercise; (naut.) proceed, take one's course (*about, back, in, off, out,* etc.). 2. Move (thing etc.) so as to place it in some situation; convey (person) across river etc.; harness (horse etc.) *to* vehicle. 3. Bring into some relation, state, or condition; translate *into* another language, turn (*into* speech or writing, words); apply *to* use or purpose; submit *to* vote etc.; subject *to* (suffering); ~ **an end, stop, to**, bring to an end, stop; ~ **upon**, oppress, victimize; ~ (horse) **at**, urge him toward (obstacle etc.). 4. ~ **about** = TACK¹ *v.* def. 2; ~ **away**, lay by (money etc.) for future use; (slang) consume (food, drink); ~ **back**, check the advance of, retard; move back the hands of (clock); restore to former place; ~ **by**, lay aside esp. for future use; ~ **down**, suppress by force or authority; take down, snub, put to silence; put (animal) to death; cease to maintain (expensive thing); account, reckon; write on paper; ~ **forth**, exert (strength, effort, etc.); (of plant) send out (buds, leaves, etc.); ~ **forward**, thrust into prominence; advance, set forth (theory etc.); ~ **in**, install in office etc.; present formally (evidence, plea, etc.) as in law court; interpose; throw in (additional thing); (colloq.) pass, spend (time); make (an appearance); ~ **off**, postpone; postpone engagement with (person); evade (person, demand, freq. *with* excuse, etc.); hinder, dissuade *from*; foist (thing *upon* person); remove, take off (clothes); (of boat etc.) leave shore; ~ **on**, clothe oneself or another with; assume, take on (character, appearance); develop additional (flesh, weight); add (*to*); stake (*on* horse etc.); bring into action, exert (force, speed, steam, etc.); appoint, arrange for; ~ **out**, (baseball) retire (batter or base runner); extinguish; disconcert, confuse; annoy, irritate; put to inconvenience; exert (strength etc.); lend (money) at interest, invest; give (work) to be done off the premises; ~ **through**, carry out (task); place (person) in telephonic connection with another through exchange(s); ~ **together**, form (whole) by combination of parts; ~ **up**, raise (price); present (petition); propose for election; offer for sale by auction or for competition; place (in jar or can) for preservation; sheathe (knife); lodge and entertain; construct, build; ~ **person's back up**, enrage him; ~ **(person) up to**, incite him; ~ **up with**, submit to, tolerate; ~**-up** (*adj.*) fraudulently concocted (scheme etc.). **put** *n.* Throw, cast, of the shot; **put′down**, (slang) belittling remark; ~**-on**, (slang) trickery (of someone) by taking advantage of his credulity; **put′out**, (baseball) play by which batter or runner is retired.

pu·ta·tive (pū′tatĭv) *adj.* Reputed, supposed. **pu′ta·tive·ly** *adv.*

pu·tre·fy (pū′trefī) *v.i.* (**-fied, -fy·ing**). Become putrid, rot, go bad; fester, suppurate. **pu·tre·fac·tion** (pūtrefăk′shon) *n.* **pu·tre·fac′tive** *adj.*

pu·tres·cent (pūtrĕs′ent) *adj.* In process of rotting; of, accompanying, this process. **pu·tres′cence** *n.*

pu·trid (pū′trĭd) *adj.* Decomposed, rotten; foul, noxious; (fig.) corrupt; (slang) of poor or bad quality, unpleasant. **pu′trid·ly** *adv.* **pu′trid·ness, pu·trid′i·ty** *ns.*

putsch (pooch) *n.* Attempt at revolution, *coup d'état*. [Swiss Ger., = "thrust," "blow"]

putt (pŭt) *v.* Strike golf ball, strike (golf ball) gently and carefully with the putter so as to make it roll along the putting green with the object of getting it into the hole; **putt′ing green**, smooth piece of turf around each hole on golf course on which the ball is putted. **putt** *n.* Putting stroke.

put·tee (pŭt′ē) *n.* Long strip of cloth wound spirally around leg from ankle to knee for protection and support. [Hind. *patti* bandage]

putt·er¹ (pŭt′er) *n.* Straight-faced golf club used in putting.

Pylon *at the temple of Edfu in Egypt. Like similar structures of the period, the walls were decorated with figures and hieroglyphics which usually stated why it was erected and in whose honor, and gave other relevant information.*

put·ter[2] (pŭt'er) *v.* Work in feeble or desultory manner (*at, in*); dawdle, loiter (*about* etc.); trifle *away* (time etc.).

put·ty (pŭt'ē) *n.* (pl **-ties**). 1. (**jewelers'** ~) Powder of calcined tin (and lead) for polishing glass or metal. 2. (**plasterers'** ~) Fine mortar of lime and water without sand. 3. (**glaziers'** ~) Cement of whiting, raw linseed oil, etc., for securing panes of glass, filling up holes in woodwork, etc. **putty** *v.t.* (**-tied, -ty·ing**). Cover, fix, join, fill *up*, with putty.

puz·zle (pŭz'el) *n.* Bewilderment, perplexity; perplexing question, enigma; problem, toy, contrived to exercise ingenuity and patience. ~ *v.* (**-zled, -zling**). Perplex; be perplexed; make *out* by exercising ingenuity and patience. **puz'zle·ment** *n.* **puz'zling·ly** *adv.*

PVC *abbrev.* Polyvinyl chloride.

Pvt. *abbrev.* Private (soldier or marine).

PW *abbrev.* Prisoner of war.

PX *abbrev.* Post Exchange.

py·e·mi·a (pīē'mēa) *n.* Severe infection of the blood by virulent bacteria accompanied by acute fever and formation of abscesses in liver, lungs, kidneys, etc. **py·e·mic** (pīē'mĭk) *adj.*

Pyg·ma·li·on (pĭgmā'lēon, -māl'yon). (Gk. legend) King of Cyprus who made a statue of a woman and fell in love with it; he prayed to Aphrodite for a wife like it, and she endowed the statue with life.

Pyg·my, Pig·my (pĭg'mē) *ns.* (pl. **-mies**). 1. One of a diminutive race of people stated in ancient history and tradition to have inhabited parts of Ethiopia or India. 2. Member of a Negrillo people of very small stature. 3. (**p** ~) Very small person or thing. **p** ~ *adj.* Of pygmies; dwarf; stunted. [Gk. *pugmé* length from elbow to knuckle]

py·ja·mas = PAJAMAS.

py·lon (pī'lŏn) *n.* 1. Gateway, esp. of Egyptian temple, with two truncated pyramidal towers connected by lower architectural member containing the gate. 2. Structure used to mark out airplane course; tall (metal) structure for supporting power cables.

py·lo·rus (pīlōr'us, -lōr'-, pĭ-) *n.* (pl. **-lo·ri** pr. -lōr'ī, -lōr'ī). (anat.)

Pygmies of the Ituri Forest in Zaire. Similar **pygmy** *groups are found in New Guinea and the Andaman Islands, but there is no evidence of any link between these groups.*

Although the **pyramid** is an architectural feature of several early civilizations, here is no known cultural connection. Those at Giza in Egypt (above) were tombs of the pharaohs, while Chichen tza in Mexico and others in Peru and Central America were temples to the Sun and have flat tops.

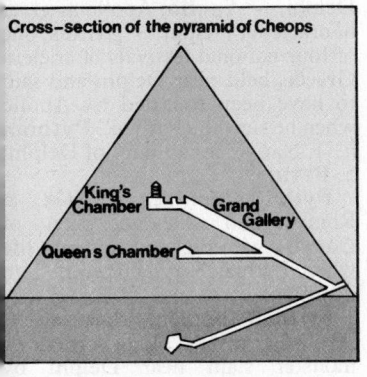

Cross-section of the pyramid of Cheops

King's Chamber
Grand Gallery
Queen's Chamber

Opening from stomach into duodenum; part of stomach where this is. **py·lor·ic** (pīlŏr´ĭk, -lŏr´-, pĭ-) *adj.* [Gk. *pulōros* gatekeeping]

Pyong·yang (pyŭng´yahng´). Capital of Democratic Peoples' Republic of Korea, in the SW. part on the Taedong River.

py·or·rhe·a, py·or·rhoe·a (pīorē´a) *ns.* Disease of the tooth sockets, accompanied by a discharge of pus and slight local hemorrhage. **py·or·rhe´al, py·or·rhoe´al** *adjs.*

pyr·a·can·tha (pĭrakăn´tha, pīra-) *n.* Evergreen thorny shrub of genus *Pyracantha* with white flowers and scarlet berries.

pyr·a·mid (pĭr´amĭd) *n.* Monumental structure of stone etc. with polygonal or (usu.) square base and sloping sides meeting at apex, constructed by ancient Egyptians over a royal burial chamber and by Aztecs and Mayas as stepped platform for a temple; solid of this shape with base of three or more sides; pyramid-shaped thing or pile of things; fruit tree trained in pyramid shape. **py·ram·i·dal** (pĭrăm´ĭdal) *adj.* **py·ram´i·dal·ly** *adv.*

Pyr·a·mus (pĭr´amus). (Rom.

legend) Youth of Babylon, lover of Thisbe; forbidden to marry by their parents, who were neighbors, they conversed through a chink in the wall and agreed to meet at a tomb outside the city; here Thisbe was frightened away by a lioness, and Pyramus, finding her bloodstained cloak and supposing her dead, stabbed himself; Thisbe finding his body, threw herself upon his sword.

pyre (pīr) *n.* Heap of combustible material, esp. funeral pile for burning corpse.

py·rene (pīrēn´) *n.* (chem.) Solid aromatic hydrocarbon obtained from dry distillation of coal etc.

Pyr·e·nees (pĭr´enēz). Range of mountains in SW. Europe separating Spain from France. **Pyr·e·ne´an** adj.

py·re·thrum (pīrē´thrum) n. Any of several chrysanthemums, esp. *Chrysanthemum coccineum* and *C. cinerariaefolium*; insecticide made from powdered heads of this.

Py·rex (pī´rĕks) n. (trademark) Heat-resistant glass used for manufacturing esp. ovenware.

py·rex·i·a (pīrĕk´sēa) n. (med.) Fever.

pyr·i·dine (pĭr´ĭdēn) n. (chem.) Colorless volatile liquid base with offensive odor, present in bone oil and coal tar, from which it is obtained by distillation.

py·ri·tes (pīrī´tēz, pi-, pī´rīts) n. (pl. -tes). (**iron** ~) Iron sulfide (FeS$_2$) occurring as a mineral; (**copper** ~) double sulfide of copper and iron (Cu$_2$S.Fe$_2$S$_3$). **py·ri·tic** (pīrĭt´ĭk, pi-) adj.

pyro- prefix. Fire or heat.

py·ro·gal·lol (pīrogăl´awl, -ōl, -ŏl) n. (also **py·ro·gal·lic** pr. pīrogăl´ĭk **acid**) White crystalline substance, trihydroxybenzene, very soluble in water, used as a developer in photography etc.

py·ro·gen·ic (pīrojĕn´ĭk) adj. Fever-producing.

py·rol·a·try (pīrŏl´atrē) n. Fire worship.

py·ro·man·cy (pī´romănsē) n. Divination by fire. **py´ro·man·cer** n.

py·ro·ma·ni·a (pīromā´nēa) n. Incendiary mania. **py·ro·ma´ni·ac** n.

py·rom·e·ter (pīrŏm´ĭter) n. Instrument for measuring high temperatures. **py·ro·met·ric** (pīromĕt´rĭk), **py·ro·met´ri·cal** adjs. **py·rom´e·try** n.

py·ro·tech·nic (pīrotĕk´nĭk), **py·ro·tech·ni·cal** (pīrotĕk´nĭkal) adjs. Of (the nature of) fireworks; (fig., of wit etc.) brilliant, sensational. **py·ro·tech´ni·cal·ly** adv.

py·ro·tech´nics n. Art of making, display of, fireworks. **py·ro·tech´nist, py´ro·tech·ny** ns.

py·rox·ene (pīrŏk´sēn) n. Black crystalline mineral common in igneous rocks. **py·rox·en·ic** (pīrŏksĕn´ĭk) adj.

py·rox·y·lin (pīrŏk´silĭn), **py·rox·y·line** (pīrŏk´silēn, -lĭn) ns. Any of a class of highly inflammable compounds (nitrates of cellulose), produced by treating vegetable fibers with a mixture of nitric and sulfuric acids.

Pyr·rhic (pĭr´ĭk) adj. Of PYRRHUS; ~ **victory**, victory achieved at too great a cost (from saying attributed to Pyrrhus after battle of Asculum, where he routed

*Unlike the related boas which give birth to live young, the **python** lays eggs. Like all constrictors, this snake lives on small mammals, reptiles and birds which it crushes to death before swallowing whole.*

The Persians are credited with the discovery of the insecticidal properties of **Pyrethrum**. These chrysanthemums were grown in Dalmatia in the 19th century and in Japan, East Africa and, since 1945, Ecuador and Papua New Guinea.

the Romans but lost the flower of his army: "One more such victory and we are lost").

pyr·rhic[1] (pĭr´ĭk) adj. & n. (Of) a war dance of the ancient Greeks, performed in armor, with mimicry of actual warfare.

pyr·rhic[2] (pĭr´ĭk) adj. & n (Metrical foot) of two short or unstressed syllables, ˘˘.

Pyr·rhus (pĭr´us) (319–272 B.C.) King of Epirus, military adventurer who fought a series of campaigns against Rome in Italy and Sicily (280–275); see also PYRRHIC.

Py·thag·o·ras (pĭthăg´eras) (6th c. B.C.). Greek philosopher and mathematician of Samos; his philosophical teaching included the doctrine of the immortality and transmigration of the soul; evolved the idea that the explanation of the universe is to be sought in numbers and their relations. **Py·thag·o·re·an** (pĭthăgerē´an) adj. & n. ~ **theorem**, geometrical proposition, of which Pythagoras is credited with discovering the proof, that the square on the hypotenuse of a right-angled triangle is equal to the sum of the squares on the other two sides.

Pyth·i·a (pĭth´ēa). (Gk. Hist.) Priestess of Apollo at Delphi, who delivered the oracles.

Pyth·i·an (pĭth´ēan) adj. Of Delphi; ~ **Apollo**, Apollo as giver of oracles at Delphi; ~ **games**, one of four national festivals of ancient Greece, held near Delphi and said to have been founded by Apollo when he slew the Python. **Pythian** n. 1. Native, inhabitant, of Delphi 2. PYTHIA.

Pyth·i·as (pĭth´ēas). (Gk. & Rom. legend) Devoted friend of DAMON, who pledged his own life when Pythias was condemned to death.

py·thon (pī´thŏn, -thon) n. 1 (**P** ~, Gk. myth.) Huge serpent or monster slain near Delphi by Apollo. 2. Member of genus P~ of large nonpoisonous snakes inhabiting the tropical regions of the Old World, or of related genera which kill their prey by constriction; other related snakes **py·thon·ic** (pīthŏn´ĭk) adj.

py·tho·ness (pī´thonĭs, pĭth´o- n. Woman soothsayer; see PYTHIA

pyx (pĭks) n. (eccles.) Vessel often of precious metal, in which host is reserved.

*Many religions through the ages have required the dead to be burned on **pyres**. Facing: Balinese mourners near an elaborate structure and decorated coffin, already blazing fiercely.*

The letter **Q, q** derives its form from the Semitic sign koph, probably meaning 'a needle's eye'. It was dropped from the Greek alphabet after the 5th century B.C., only surviving as the sign for 90, but was kept by the Romans.

Phoenician   Early Greek   Early Etruscan

Early Latin   Classical Latin   Italian

Q, q (kū) (pl. **Q's, q's** or **Qs, qs**). Seventeenth letter of modern English and 16th of ancient Roman alphabet, derived from Phoenician φ, φ, ᛞ (representing guttural *k* sound).

q. *abbrev.* Quart, quarto, queen, question, query.

Qa·tar (kah'tār). Independent sheikdom on peninsula on W. coast of Persian Gulf; capital, Doha.

Q.E.D. *abbrev. Quod erat demonstrandum.* [L., = which was to be demonstrated]

Q-fe·ver (kū'fēver). Disease allied to typhus but milder, caused by a different variety of rickettsia. [f. Queensland, Australia, where first observed]

Qi·a·na (kēăn'a, -ah'na) *n.* (trademark) Light nylonlike synthetic fiber.

QM, Q.M. *abbrevs.* Quartermaster.

QMG, Q.M.G. *abbrevs.* Quartermaster General.

qr. *abbrev.* (pl. **qrs.**) Quarter.

qt. *abbrev.* (pl. **qts.**) Quart(s).

q.t. *abbrev.* (slang) Quiet; **on the** ~, silently, stealthily.

qu. *abbrev.* Quart, queen, query, question.

qua (kwā, kwah) *adv.* As, in the capacity of.

Quaa·lude (kwā'lōod, -lūd, kwah-) *n.* (trademark) Methaqualone.

quack[1] (kwăk) *v.i. & n.* (Utter) harsh cry characteristic of duck.

quack[2] (kwăk) *n.* Ignorant pretender to skill esp. in medicine; charlatan. **quack'er·y** *n.* (pl. **-er·ies**). **quack** *adj.* Fraudulent, (esp.) alleged to cure disease.

quad (kwŏd) *n.* (colloq.) Quadrangle; quadraphonic sound system; QUADRAT; quadruplet.

quad·ran·gle (kwŏd'rănggel) *n.* Four-sided figure, esp. square or rectangle; four-sided court (partly) enclosed by parts of large building; such court with buildings around it. **quad·ran·gu·lar** (kwŏdrăng'gyuler) *adj.* **quad·ran'gu·lar·ly** *adv.*

quad·rant (kwŏd'rant) *n.* 1. Quarter of circumference of circle; plane figure enclosed by two radii of circle at right angles and arc cut off by them; quarter of sphere. 2. Object, esp. graduated strip or plate of metal, shaped like quarter circle. 3. Instrument, usu. with calibrated arc of 90°, used for measuring angles and formerly (now superseded by SEXTANT) altitudes. **quad·ran·tal** (kwŏdrăn'tal) *adj.*

quand·ra·phon·ic (kwŏdrafŏn'ĭk) *adj.* Of, pertaining to, or designating method of reproducing recorded sound using four individual transmission channels.

quad·rat (kwŏd'răt, rĭt) *n.* Metal block smaller than metal type, used by printers to create a blank space within printed matter.

quad·rate (kwŏd'rĭt, -rāt) *adj.* Square, rectangular (rare exc. anat. in names of squarish parts of body); ~ **bone**, bone in heads of birds,

*Like many people in the 18th century, Hogarth's Rake (below) visited a **quack**. With his mixture of ancient magic and modern science the quack, then as now, inhabited a medical shadow-world.*

amphibians, reptiles, and fish, b which lower jaw is articulated t skull. **quadrate** *n.* Quadrat bone, muscle, etc.

quad·rat·ic (kwŏdrăt'ĭk) *adj* (math.) Involving the second an no higher power of an unknow quantity or variable (esp. ~ **equation**). **quadratic** *n.* Quad ratic equation. **quad·rat'ics** *n* Branch of algebra dealing wit quadratic equations.

quad·ren·ni·al (kwŏdrĕn'ēa) *adj.* Occurring every, lasting, fou years.

quadri-, quadru-, quadr- (be fore vowel) *prefixes.* Four.

quad·ric (kwŏd'rĭk) *adj.* (math. Of the second degree. ~ *n* Quadric function; surface whos equation is in the second degree.

quad·ri·ceps (kwŏd'rĭsĕps) *n* (pl. **-cep·ses** pr. -sĕpsĭz, **-ceps** Large muscle at front of thigh wit four heads or attachments.

quad·ri·lat·er·al (kwŏdrĭlăt eral) *adj. & n.* (Figure) bounded b four straight lines; (space, area

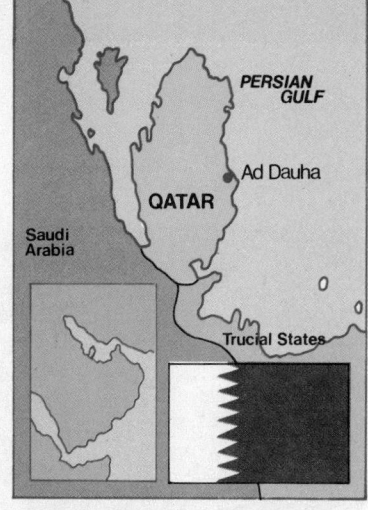

ving four sides.

qua·drille[1] (kwŏdrĭl´) *n.* Card
me fashionable in 18th c., played
four persons with 40 cards (i.e.
ordinary pack without the 8s, 9s,
d 10s).

qua·drille[2] (kwŏdrĭl´) *n.* Square
nce for four couples, containing
e figures; music for this. [Fr. f.
an. *cuadrilla* squadron (*cuadra*
uare)]

quad·ril·lion (kwŏdrĭl´yon) *n.*
fth power of a thousand (1
lowed by 15 zeros). **quad·ril´-**
nth *adj.* & *n.*

quad·ri·par·tite (kwŏdrĭpār´tīt)
j. Consisting of four parts;
ared by or involving four parties.

With a large revenue from oil, **Qatar** *has
introduced television (1) which provides
entertainment for many of its 90,000
people. However, most of the income is
spent on welfare. Old customs continue, including regular attendance at
the huge mosques (2).*

quad·ri·ple·gi·a (kwŏdrĭplē´jēa)
n. Complete paralysis of the body
beginning at the neck. **quad·ri·-
ple´gic** *adj.* & *n.*

quad·ri·va·lent (kwŏdrĭvā´lent,
-drĭv´a-) *adj.* (chem.) Having four
valences.

quad·riv·i·um (kwŏdrĭv´ēum)
n. (pl. **quad·riv·i·a** pr. kwŏdrĭv´-
ēa). In Middle Ages, the higher
division of the seven liberal arts,

comprising arithmetic, geometry,
astronomy, and music.

quad·roon (kwŏdroōn´) *n.* Offspring of white and mulatto, person
having one-quarter black ancestry.

quad·ru·ped (kwŏd´rupĕd) *n.*
Four-footed animal, esp. four-
footed mammal. ~ *adj.* Four-
footed. **quad·ru·pe·dal** (kwŏd-
roō´pedal, kwŏd´rupĕdal) *adj.*

quad·ru·ple (kwŏdroō´pel,
kwŏd´roō-) *adj.* Fourfold, consisting of four parts or involving four
parties; amounting to four times the
number or amount *of*, equivalent to
fourfold the amount of, superior by
four times in amount or number *to*;
~ **rhythm** or **time**, (mus.) with

four beats to a measure. **quad-ru′ple** *n.* Number or amount four times greater than another. ~ *v.* (**-pled, -pling**). Multiply by 4.

quad·ru·plet (kwŏdrŭp′lĭt, -drōo′plĭt, kwŏd′rŭplĭt) *n.* One of four children born at a single birth.

quad·ru·pli·cate (kwŏdrōo′plĭkĭt) *adj.* Fourfold, four times repeated or copied. ~ *n.* **in ~**, in four exactly similar examples or copies; (pl.) four such copies. ~ (kwŏdrōo′plĭkāt) *v.t.* (**-cat·ed, -cat·ing**). Multiply by 4; make in quadruplicate. **quad·ru·pli·ca·tion** (kwŏdrōoplĭkā′shon) *n.*

quaes·tor, ques·tor (kwĕs′ter, kwē′ster) *ns.* (Rom. hist.) Magistrate in charge of public funds, as treasury officer etc. **quaes·to·ri·al** (kwĕstōr′ēal, -stōr′-, kwē-) *adj.* **quaes′tor·ship** *n.*

quaff (kwahf, kwăf, kwawf) *v.* Drink, drain (cup etc.), in long or copious drafts. **quaff′er** *n.*

quag (kwăg, kwŏg) *n.* Quagmire.

quag·ga (kwăg′a) *n.* Species of zebra (*Equus quagga*) of South Africa, now extinct.

quag·mire (kwăg′mīr) *n.* Quaking bog, fen, marsh, slough; (fig.) difficult situation or problem.

qua·hog, qua·haug (kwaw′hŏg, -hawg, kwahawg′, -hŏg′) *ns.* Large,

thick-shelled edible clam species of U.S. Atlantic Coast.

quail[1] (kwāl) *n.* (pl. **quails**, collect. **quail**). Migratory bird of Old World allied to partridge, esp. *Coturnix coturnix*, esteemed as food; any of various Amer. birds (genus *Colinus*) resembling this, esp. the BOBWHITE.

quail[2] (kwāl) *v.* Flinch, be cowed, give way *before*.

quaint (kwānt) *adj.* Attractive or piquant by virtue of unfamiliar, esp. old-fashioned, appearance, ornamentation, manners, etc.; daintily odd. **quaint′ly** *adv.* **quaint′ness** *n.*

quake (kwāk) *v.i.* (**quaked, quak·ing**). Shake, tremble. **quak′y** *adj.* (**quak·i·er, quak·i·est**). **quake** *n.* Act of quaking; earthquake.

Quak·er (kwā′ker) *n.* (fem. **Quak·er·ess** pr. kwā′kerĭs). Member of the religious Society of Friends founded by George Fox in 1648–50, distinguished by peaceful principles and plainness of dre and manners; ~(s′) meeting religious meeting of the Friend silent except when some membe feels stirred to speak; hence, sile meeting, company in which conve sation flags. **Quak′er·ism Quak′er·ly** *adv. & adj.* [nicknam of early members of the societ who were said to "tremble at t Word of the Lord"]

qual·i·fi·ca·tion (kwŏlifĭkā shon) *n.* 1. Modification, restri tion, limitation; restricting limiting circumstance. 2. Qualit accomplishment, etc., fitting pe son or thing (*for* a position etc. 3. Condition that must be fulfille before right can be acquired office held.

qual·i·fy (kwŏl′ifī) *v.* (**-fie -fy·ing**). 1. Attribute quality t describe *as*; (gram., of adjectiv express some quality of noun. Invest or provide with the nece sary qualities, make competent, f or legally entitled (*for, to*); mak oneself competent (*for*) or capab of holding some office, exercisir some function, etc. 3. Modi (statement etc.), make less absolu or sweeping, subject to reservatio or limitation; moderate, mitigat esp. make less violent, severe,

Quagmires are often thought of as useless wasteland, fit only to be drained and reclaimed. But to naturalists they are the homes, feeding areas, or breeding grounds of many fascinating creatures.

*The European **quail** (above) feeds on insects when young, but later eats seeds and shoots too. It is a nocturnal migrant, and spends the summer months in Britain. Gambell's variety (left) is found only in desert areas of the southern States of the U.S.A.*

unpleasant. **qual'i·fied** *adj.* **qual'i·fi·er** *n.*

qual·i·ta·tive (kwŏl'ĭtātĭv) *adj.* Concerned with, depending on, quality.

qual·i·ty (kwŏl'ĭtē) *n.* (pl. **-ties**). 1. Degree of excellence, relative nature or kind or character (opp. QUANTITY); class or grade of thing as determined by this; general excellence. 2. Characteristic trait, mental or moral attribute. 3. (archaic) High rank or social standing; **the** ~, people of high rank or social standing. 4. (logic, of proposition) Being affirmative or negative. 5. (of sound, voice, etc.) Distinctive character apart from pitch or loudness, timbre.

qualm (kwahm, kwawm) *n.* Momentary faint or sick feeling, queasiness; misgiving, sinking of heart; scruple of conscience. **qualm'ish·ly** *adv.* **qualm'ish·ness** *n.*

quan·da·ry (kwŏn'derē) *n.* (pl. **-ries**). State of perplexity, difficult situation, practical dilemma.

quan·ta (kwŏn'ta): see QUANTUM.

quan·ti·fy (kwŏn'tĭfī) *v.t.* (**-fied, -fy·ing**). 1. (logic) Determine application of (term, proposition) by use of *all, some,* etc. 2. Determine quantity of, measure,

express as quantity. **quan'ti·fi·a·ble** *adj.* **quan·ti·fi·ca·tion** (kwŏntĭfĭkā'shon) *n.*

quan·ti·ta·tive (kwŏn'tĭtātĭv) *adj.* Measured or measurable by, concerned with, quantity; of, based on, the quantity of vowels. **quan'·ti·ta·tive·ly** *adv.*

quan·ti·ty (kwŏn'tĭtē) *n.* (pl. **-ties**). 1. Property of things that is regarded as determinable by measurement of some kind; amount, sum; (mus.) length or duration of notes. 2. Specified or considerable portion, number, or amount of something; (pl.) large amounts or numbers, abundance. 3. (math.) Thing having quantity, figure or symbol representing this; **unknown** ~, (fig.) person or thing whose action cannot be foreseen.

quan·tum (kwŏn'tum) *n.* (pl. **-ta** pr. -ta). Sum, amount; share, portion; (phys.) discrete unit quantity of energy, proportional to frequency of radiation, emitted from or absorbed by atom; ~ **electrodynamics, mechanics,** etc., dynamics, etc., taking account of quanta; ~ **number,** one of a set of intergers or half intergers describing the energy level of a particle or system of particles; ~ **jump,** abrupt change in energy level of molecule or atom accom-

panied by absorption or emission of radiant energy equalling the difference between the two levels; (fig.) any abrupt and wide-ranging shift or change; ~ **theory,** theory originated by M. Planck (1910) and extended by N. Bohr, which accounts for certain atomic phenomena by assuming that radiant energy (heat, light, etc.) is emitted from atoms only in discrete amounts or quanta and not continuously.

quar·an·tine (kwŏr'antēn, kwär'-) *n.* (Period, orig. 40 days, of) isolation imposed on infected ship, or on persons (esp. travelers) who might spread contagious or infectious diseases; (period of) isolation for animals (esp. dogs and cats) after landing from abroad. ~ *v.t.* (**-tined, -tin·ing**). Impose such isolation on, put in quarantine. [prob. f. It. *quarantina* 40 days]

quark (kwärk, kwôrk) *n.* (One of three kinds of) hypothetical component of subatomic particles.

quar·rel[1] (kwôr'el, kwär'-) *n.* Short heavy arrow or bolt formerly used in crossbow.

quar·rel[2] (kwôr'el, kwär'-) *n.* Occasion of complaint against person or his actions; violent contention or altercation *between* persons, rupture of friendly relations.

Michelangelo obtained his marble for sculpting from a **quarry** at Carrara (1) which has been worked for 2,000 years, mostly for building materials. In Kent, England (2), chalk is quarried to make lime, used in cement and as a fertilizer.

~ *v.i.* (**-reled, -rel·ing, -relled, -rel·ling**). Take exception, find fault *with*; contend violently (*with* person), fall out, have dispute, break off friendly relations. **quar′rel·some** *adj.* **quar′rel·some·ly** *adv.* **quar′rel·some·ness** *n.*

quar·rel³ (kwŏr′el, kwär′-) *n.* (also **quarry**) Square or diamond shape; object with this shape, as diamond-shaped pane of glass. [f. It. *quadrello*, dim. of *quadro* square]

quar·ry¹ (kwŏr′ē, kwär′ē) *n.* (pl. **-ries**). Object of pursuit by bird of prey, hounds, hunters, etc.; intended victim or prey. [OF. *curée* (*cuir* skin); orig. sense, parts of deer placed on hide and given to hounds]

quar·ry² (kwŏr′ē, kwär′ē) *n.* (pl. **-ries**). Excavation made by taking stone for building etc. from its bed; place from which stone etc., can be extracted. ~ *v.* (**-ried, -ry·ing**). Extract (stone) from quarry; form quarry in (hill etc.); cut or dig (as) in quarry.

quart¹ (kwŏrt) *n.* Measure of capacity, quarter of gallon, two pints; pot or bottle containing this amount.

quart² (kärt) *n.* (in piquet) Sequence of four playing cards in one suit.

quar·ter (kwŏr′ter) *n.* 1. Fourth part; one of four equal or corresponding parts; fourth part of. 2. Quarter of dollar, 25 cents, as amount or coin. 3. One of four parts, each including a limb, into which beast's or bird's carcass is divided; (pl.) similar parts of traitor quartered after execution; (freq. pl.) haunch(es) of living animal or man. 4. Either side of stern of ship to the rear of the beam. 5. Fourth part of cwt., 25 lb. (in Brit. 28 lb.). 6. Quarter-mile race or running distance. 7. Fourth part of year, three months. 8. Fourth part of lunar period, moon's position between first and second or third and fourth of these. 9. Point of time 15 minutes before or after any hour. 10. (Region lying about) point of compass; direction; district, locality; (colloq.) portion or member of community, some thing or things, without reference to actual locality. 11. Division of town, esp. one appropriated to or occupied by special group. 12. (pl.) Lodgings, abode, esp. place where troops are lodged or stationed; assigned or appropriate places, station; **winter ~s**, place occupied, esp. by troops, for winter. 13. Exemption from death offered or

granted to enemy in battle who will surrender. 14. **quar′terback** (*n.* & *v.*), (in football) (player) direct(ing) attacking play (also fig.); **quarter binding**, (of book) with narrow strip of leather at back and none elsewhere; **quar′terdeck**, part of upper deck between stern and after mast, usu. reserved for officers; **quarter horse**, breed of saddle horse in western U.S. (orig. trained for races of ¼ mi.); **quar′termaster**, (naut.) petty officer in charge of steering, signals, hold stowing, etc.; (mil., abbrev. Q.M.) officer with duties of obtaining and looking after food, clothing, equipment, etc.; **quar′termaster general** (pl. **quar′termasters general**) (abbrev. Q.M.G.) (in U.S. Army) major general commanding the **Quartermaster**

Corps, the supply branch of th U.S. Army; **quarter note**, (musi note having ¼ the time value of whole note; **quarter section**, of sq. mi. of land, 160 acre **quar′terstaff**, stout iron-tippe pole 6–8 ft. long formerly used weapon; **quarter tone**, (mus.) ha a semitone. **quarter** *v.t.* 1. Divi into four equal parts; (hist.) divi (traitor's body) into quarters. Put (esp. soldiers) into quarter station or lodge in specified plac 3. (of searchers or search dog Traverse (ground) in order pattern to ensure thorough cove age.

quar·ter·age (kwŏr′terij) Quarterly payment; a quarter wages, allowance, pension, etc.

quar·ter·ly (kwŏr′terlē) *adj.* Occurring every three months.

Divided quarterly or by lines at right angles. ~ n. (pl. **-lies**). Quarterly review or magazine. ~ adv. 1. Once every three months. . In, by quarters.

quar·tet, Brit. **quar·tette** (kwōrtĕt') ns. 1. (mus.) (Composition for) four voices or instruments in combination; players or singers rendering this; **piano** ~, three stringed instruments with piano; **string** ~, two violins, viola, and cello. 2. Set of four persons or things.

quar·tile (kwôr'tĭl, -tīl) n. statistics) One of values of a variable dividing a population into four equal groups having equal frequencies as regards the value of that variable.

quar·to (kwôr'tō) n. (pl. **-tos**). Size given by folding sheet of paper twice (into four leaves); book consisting of sheets so folded.

quartz (kwôrts) n. Any of several varieties of silica occurring in masses or crystals.

quartz·ite (kwôrt'sīt) n. Hard sandstone containing quartz grains.

qua·sar (kwā'zär, -zer, -sär, -ser) n. Any of a number of celestial objects emitting strong radio waves and varying between 4 and 10 billion light-years in distance from Earth. [*quas*(i-stell)*ar* (radio source)]

quash (kwŏsh) v.t. Put an end to; suppress.

qua·si (kwā'zī, -sī, kwah'zē, -sē) adj. & adv. Resembling, seeming to be, as it were, almost, not exactly.

quasi- prefix. Seeming(ly), not real(ly); practical(ly); half-, almost.

quas·sia (kwŏsh'a, -ēa) n. Tropical Amer. tree (*Quassia amara*), found esp. in Surinam; wood, bark, or root of this and other trees (now esp. *Picraena excelsa*, bitter wood tree, of W. Indies etc., yielding bitter medicinal tonic and also much used horticulturally for destroying aphids). [S. Amer. tree named by Linnaeus after *Graman Quassi*, Surinam black slave who discovered its medicinal properties in 1730]

qua·ter·cen·te·na·ry (kwahter-sĕn'tenĕrē, -sĕntĕn'erē; Brit. kwahtersĕntē'nerē) n. Four hundredth anniversary.

qua·ter·na·ry (kwah'ternĕrē, kwahtĕr'nerē) adj. 1. Having four parts; (chem.) compounded of four elements or radicals. 2. **Q** ~, (geol.) of the period or system subsequent to the Tertiary, of recent and present-day formations, yielding fossils of shells, bones, and plants, all of which represent species still living. ~ n. (pl. **-ries**). 1. Set of four things; number 4. 2. **Q** ~, (geol.) Quarternary period or system.

qua·ter·ni·on (kwatĕr'nēon) n. Set of four; (math.) quotient of two vectors or operator that changes one vector into another (so named as depending on four geometrical elements); (pl.) form of calculus of vectors in which this operator is used.

quat·rain (kwŏt'rān; Brit. kwŏt'rĭn) n. Stanza, poem of four lines, usu. with alternate rhymes.

quat·re·foil (kăt'erfoil, kăt're-) n. Four-cusped figure, esp. as opening in architectural tracery, resembling symmetrical four-lobed leaf or flower.

quat·tro·cen·to (kwŏtrōchĕn'-tō) n. Fifteenth century as period of Italian art and literature. [It., = "four hundred," short for *mil quattrocento* 1400]

qua·ver (kwā'ver) v. Vibrate, shake, tremble (esp. of voice or musical sound); use trills in singing; sing with trills; say in trembling tones. ~ n. 1. Trill in singing; tremulousness in speech. 2. (music, chiefly Brit.) Note having ⅛ the time value of a whole note. **qua'ver·ing·ly** adv. **qua'ver·y** adj.

quay (kē, kā, kwā) n. Solid stationary artificial landing place usu. of stone or iron, lying alongside or projecting into water, for (un)loading ships. **quay'age** n.

*Top: A beautifully-crafted **quartz** egg on display at the Smithsonian Institution. Quartz is formed in volcanic rocks, but during geological history may be dissolved by waters passing through the rocks, which then deposit it in cracks.*

*The four-lobed decoration repeated on the frontage of Little Moreton Hall in Cheshire, England, is a **quatrefoil** and was first used in heraldry.*

*The **Quechua** culture, which flourished in the Inca empire in Peru, Ecuador and Bolivia until the Spanish conquest, consequently declined, though the language is still widely spoken.*

Quays collectively; space occupied by quays and their activities; duty levied on ships using quay.

Que. *abbrev.* Quebec.

quea·sy (kwē′zē) *adj.* (**-si·er, -si·est**). (of person, stomach) Easily upset, inclined to sickness or nausea; (of conscience etc.) tender, scrupulous. **quea′si·ly** *adv.* **quea′si·ness** *n.*

Que·bec (kwĭbĕk′, kĭ-). Province of E. Canada; its capital, on the St. Lawrence River, orig. settled by the French, and captured from them by a British force under Wolfe, 1759.

Quech′ua (kĕch′wah, -wa) *n.* (pl. **-uas,** collect. **-ua**). Member of a group of tribes that formed the ruling class of the Incas; language of these tribes, still spoken among Peruvian Indians. **Quech′uan** *adj.* & *n.*

queen (kwēn) *n.* 1. King's wife (also ~ **consort** for distinction from sense 2; ~ **dowager**, wife of late king; ~ **mother**, queen dowager who is mother of sovereign); also prefixed to personal name as title. 2. Female sovereign ruler, usu. hereditary. 3. Adored woman, goddess, etc. (**Q~ of Heaven,** the Virgin Mary; **queen of love,** Venus); majestic woman; belle, mock sovereign, on some occasion (as **Q~ of the May** at May festival); personified best example of anything regarded as feminine. 4. Woman, country, etc. regarded as ruling over some sphere. 5. Fertile female of bee, wasp, ant, or termite. 6. (slang) Male homosexual, esp. one having effeminate traits. 7. (chess) Piece with greatest freedom of movement, placed next to king at beginning of game. 8. One of face cards in each suit of deck of playing cards, bearing figure of a queen. 9. ~ **bee,** fully developed fertile female bee; ~ **post,** one of two upright timbers between tie beam and principal rafters of roof truss; ~**-size** (**bed**), bigger than double bed, but less than king-size, usu. 5 by 6 ft. **queen′like** *adj.* **queen** *v.* 1. Make (woman) queen. 2. (chess) Advance (pawn) to opponent's end of board, where it is replaced by a queen or other piece (of pawn) reach this position.

Queen (kwēn) **Charlotte Islands.** Group of islands in the Pacific off the coast of British Columbia, N. of Vancouver Island.

Queen (kwēn) **Elizabeth Islands.** Group of islands in the Arctic Ocean, N. of the Northwest Territories, N. Canada, and including Ellesmere and Devon Islands, and the Sverdrup and Parry island groups.

queen·ly (kwēn′lē) *adj.* (**-li·er, -li·est**). Fit for, appropriate to, queen; majestic, queenlike. **queen′li·ness** *n.*

Queen (kwēn) **Maud Gulf.** Gulf between SE. Victoria Island and the Northwest Territories in N. Canada; **Queen Maud Land,** section of land in Antarctica bounded by Coats Land in the W. and Enderby Land in the E.; Norwegian dependency since 1949.

Queens·ber·ry (kwenz′bĕrē, -berē) **Rules:** see MARQUIS of Queensberry Rules.

Queens·land (kwenz′lănd, -land). State of NE. Australia; capital, Brisbane.

queer (kwēr) *adj.* Strange, odd, eccentric; of questionable character, shady, suspect; out of sorts, giddy, faint. **queer′ly** *adv.* **queer′ness** *n.* **queer** *n.* (slang) Homosexual. ~ *v.t.* (slang) Spoil, put out of order.

quell (kwěl) *v.t.* Suppress forcibly put an end to; quiet, pacify. **quell′er** *n.*

Que·moy (kĭmoi′). Island in the Formosa Strait off the SE. coast of China, governed by Taiwan.

quench (kwěnch) *v.t.* Extinguish; cool, esp. with water (heat, heated thing); stifle, suppress (desire etc.); slake (thirst). **quench′a·ble** *adj.*

que·nelle (kenĕl′) *n.* (cooking) Seasoned ball of fish or meat pounded to paste and poached.

quern (kwěrn) *n.* Hand mill for grinding grain; small hand mill for pepper etc.

quer·u·lous (kwěr′ulus, -yulus) *adj.* Complaining, peevish. **quer′u·lous·ly** *adv.* **quer′u·lous·ness** *n.*

que·ry (kwēr′ē) *n.* (pl. **-ries**). Question; question mark (?) or word *query* or *qu.,* used to indicate doubt of correctness of statement in writing. ~ *v.* (**-ried, -ry·ing**). Ask, inquire; put a question; call in question, question accuracy of.

quest (kwěst) *n.* Seeking, search thing sought, esp. object of medieval knight's pursuit; **in ~ of** seeking. **quest** *v.* Search for something; go on a quest.

ques·tion (kwěs′chon, kwěsh′on) *n.* 1. Interrogative statement or

*The cores of former volcanoes in the coastal plain of south-east **Queensland**, Australia, the Glasshouse Mountains, can be seen at sea and were named by James Cook.*

some point to be investigated or discussed; problem; subject for discussion in meeting etc.; subject of discussion, debate, or strife; **the ~**, the precise matter receiving or requiring discussion or deliberation; **beg the ~**: see BEG; **in ~**, under consideration; **it is a ~ of**, what is required or involved is; **out of the ~**, not to be considered or thought of; **without ~**, certainly, undoubtedly. 2. Sentence in interrogative form, meant to elicit information, interrogation, inquiry; **~ mark**, punctuation mark (?) placed at end of sentence, phrase, or word to denote a direct question; interrogation mark. 3. Action of questioning. **question** *v.t.* Ask questions of, interrogate, subject (person) to examination; seek information from study of (phenomena, facts); call in question, throw doubt upon, raise objections to. **ques'-tion·er** *n.* **ques'tion·ing·ly** *adv.*

ques·tion·a·ble (kwĕs'chonabel, kwĕsh'-) *adj.* (esp.) Doubtfully true; not clearly consistent with honesty, honor, or wisdom. **ques'tion·a·bly** *adv.* **ques'tion·a·ble·ness, ques·tion·a·bil·i·ty** (kwĕschonabĭl'ĭtē, kwĕsh-) *ns.*

ques·tion·naire (kwĕschonār', kwĕsh-) *n.* Series of printed questions usu. for obtaining information on special points esp. in statistical investigations.

quet·zal (kĕtsahl', -săl; *Brit.* kĕt'sal) *n.* (pl. **quet·zals, quet·za·les** pr. kĕtsah'lās). Beautiful Central Amer. bird (*Pharomachrus mocino*), cock of which has very long golden-green tail feathers. [Aztec *quetzalli* tail feather of this bird]

Quet·zal·co·a·tl (kĕtsahlkōah'-tel). Aztec and Toltec god worshipped as bestower of arts of civilization on mankind, having as symbol a plumed serpent (snake with quetzal feathers instead of scales).

queue (kū) *n.* 1. Pigtail, or long braid of real or artificial hair worn hanging down the back of the neck. 2. Line of persons, vehicles, etc., awaiting their turn to be attended to or proceed. **~** *v.i.* (**queued, queu·ing**). Form *up* in, take one's place in, queue.

Que·zon[1] (kā'zŏn) **City.** Designated capital of the Republic of the Philippines, on S. Luzon Island, NE. of MANILA,[1] which remains the administrative capital.

*The largest park in **Quebec**, the Plains of Abraham, site of the battle that routed the French defenders of Quebec, who had been under seige for two months in 1759, harrassed constantly by British troops.*

Que·zon² (kā′zŏn), **Manuel Luis** (1878–1944). (also called **Quezon y Molina**) Philippine statesman; 1st president of the Commonwealth of the Philippines, 1935–44.

quib·ble (kwĭb′el) *n.* 1. (archaic) Play on words, pun. 2. Equivocation, evasion; unsubstantial or purely verbal argument etc., esp. one depending on ambiguity of word. ~ *v.i.* (**-bled, -bling**). Use quibbles. **quib′bler** *n.* **quib′bling** *adj.*

quiche (kēsh) *n.* Open pastry shell containing baked custardlike dish, often with cheese.

quick (kwĭk) *adj.* 1. (archaic) Living, alive. 2. Vigorous, lively, active; prompt to act, perceive, be affected, etc. 3. Moving rapidly, rapid, swift; done in short time or with little interval. 4. **~-freeze** (*v.t.*), subject (food) to rapid freezing, permitting retention of flavor and juices and indefinite storage at low temperatures; **quick′lime** = LIME¹ def. 1; ~ **one**, (colloq.) quick drink; **quick′sand**, (bed of) loose wet sand readily swallowing up any heavy object resting on it or person or animal walking on it; **quick′silver**, mercury; (*v.t.*) coat back of (mirror glass) with amalgam of tin; **quick′step**, (mus.) march in military quick time; ~ **time**, fast military marching pace of 120 steps per minute; ~ **trick**, (bridge) sure trick that can be taken in 1st or 2nd round of play. **quick′ly** *adv.* **quick** *n.* Tender or sensitive flesh below skin or esp. nails; tender part of wound or sore where healthy tissue begins; seat of feeling or emotion; (also fig.). ~ *adv.* Quickly, at rapid rate, in comparatively short time; ~ *v.* (imper.) make haste.

quick·en (kwĭk′en) *v.* 1. Give or restore natural or spiritual life or vigor to; animate, stimulate, rouse, inspire; receive, come to, life; (of woman) reach stage of pregnancy at which fetus makes clearly perceptible movements. 2. Accelerate; make or become quicker.

quick·ie (kwĭk′ē) *n.* (colloq.) Thing done, made, or consumed hastily; film so produced.

quick·ness (kwĭk′nĭs) *n.* Readiness or acuteness of perception or apprehension; speed, suddenness.

quid¹ (kwĭd) *n.* (pl. **quid**). (Brit.) Sum of £1; one-pound bank note.

quid² (kwĭd) *n.* Lump of tobacco etc. for chewing.

quid·di·ty (kwĭd′ĭtē) *n.* (pl. **-ties**). 1. Essence of a thing, what makes a thing what it is. 2. Quibble, captious subtlety.

quid pro quo (kwĭd prō kwō′) (pl. **quid pro quos**). Compensation, return made, consideration. [L., = "something for something"]

qui·es·cent (kwēĕs′ent, kwī-)

The **quetzal** is found only in the dense mountainous forests of Central America. The 2ft.-long metallic green plumes of the male were worn by native chiefs as a sign of prestige.

adj. Motionless, inert, silent, dormant. **qui·es′cent·ly** *adv.* **qui·es′cence, qui·es′cen·cy** *ns.*

qui·et (kwī′ĭt) *n.* Peaceful condition of affairs in social or political life; silence, stillness; freedom from disturbance, agitation, etc.; rest, repose, peace of mind; unruffled deportment, calm. ~ *adj.* 1. Making no stir, commotion, or noise; not active; free from excess, not going to extremes; avoiding or escaping notice, secret, private. 2. Free from disturbance, interference, or annoyance; calm, unruffled, silent, still. **qui′et·ly** *adv.* **qui′et·ness, qui·e·tude** (kwī′etōod, -tūd) *ns.* **quiet** *v.* Reduce to quietness, soothe, calm; become quiet.

qui·e·tus (kwīē′tus) *n.* (pl. **-tus·es**). Acquittance, receipt, given on payment of account etc. (now rare); release from life, extinction, final riddance; anything that kills or eliminates; finishing blow, final stroke. [med. L. *quietus* (*est*) (he is) quit, used as receipt form]

quill (kwĭl) *n.* Hollow stem of feather; whole large feather of wing or tail; pen, plectrum, or toothpick, made of this; spine of porcupine; bobbin of hollow reed, any bobbin; musical pipe made of hollow stem (archaic); curled up piece of cinnamon or cinchona bark.

quilt (kwĭlt) *n.* Coverlet, esp. made of padding enclosed between 2 layers of fabric and kept in place by lines of stitching. ~ *v.t.* Cover, line, etc., with padded material; make or join together after the manner of a quilt. **quilt′er, quilt′ing** *ns.*

quin·a·crine (kwĭn′akrēn) **hydrochloride.** Antimalarial drug derived from acridine.

quince (kwĭns) *n.* Hard acid fruit like a large yellow apple used as preserve or as flavoring; small tree (*Cydonia oblonga*) bearing this. [ult. f. L. *Cydonium* of Cydonia in Crete]

quin·cen·te·nar·y (kwĭnsĕn′-tenĕrē, -sĕntĕn′erē; *Brit.* kwĭnsĕn-tē′nerē) *n.* Five hundredth anniversary.

quin·cunx (kwĭng′kŭngks, kwĭn′-) *n.* (Arrangement of) five objects set so that four are at corners of square or rectangle and the other at its center, esp. as basis of arrangement in planting trees.

qui·nine (kwī′nīn; *Brit.* kwĭnēn′) *n.* Alkaloid found in cinchona bark and used in treatment of malaria and as febrifuge and tonic; (pop.) quinine sulfate, usual form in which it is taken. [Peruv. *kina* bark]

qui·none (kwĭnōn′, kwĭn′ōn) *n.* 1. Crystalline compound ($C_6H_4O_2$) obtained by oxidizing aniline. 2. General name for a benzene derivative in which two oxygen atoms replace two hydrogen.

quin·qua·ge·nar·i·an (kwĭng-kwajenār′ēan, kwĭnkwa-) *adj. & n.* (Person) aged 50 or more but less than 60.

quinque- *prefix.* Five.

quin·quen·ni·um (kwĭnkwĕn′-ēum, kwĭng-) *n.* (pl. **-quen·ni·ums, -quen·ni·a** pr. -kwĕn′ēa). Five-year period; also **quinquenniad. quin·quen′ni·al** *adj.* Happening every five years; lasting five years.

quin·que·va·lent (kwĭngkwa-vā′lent, kwĭn-, -kwĕv′a-) *adj.* (chem.) Having a valence of 5.

quin·sy (kwĭn′zē) *n.* Abscess forming around the tonsil usu. as a complication of tonsillitis. [Gk. *kunaghkē*(*kuōn* kun- dog, *aghkōm* throttle)]

The Dionne **quintuplets** were born in Callander, Ontario, in 1934. Their survival through childhood was the first case recorded by science. However, one girl died at 20 and another in 1970.

quint (kwĭnt) *n.* (colloq.) Quintuplet.

quin·tal (kwĭn′tal) *n.* Weight of 100 lbs., hundredweight; 100 kilograms. [Arab. *kintār*]

quin·tes·sence (kwĭntĕs′ens) *n.* 1. (ancient and medieval philos.) Fifth substance, apart from the four elements of earth, air, fire, and water, composing the heavenly bodies entirely and latent in all things, extraction of which was one of the aims of alchemy. 2. Most essential part of any substance, refined extract; purest and most perfect form, manifestation, or embodiment, *of* some quality or class. **quin·tes·sen·tial** (kwĭntesĕn′shal) *adj.* [*quinta essentia* fifth essence]

quin·tet, (Brit.) **quin·tette** (kwĭntĕt′) *ns.* 1. (mus.) (Composition for) five voices or instruments in combination; players or singers rendering this; **clarinet, piano,** etc., ∼, four stringed instruments plus instrument named. 2. Set of five persons or things.

Quin·til·ian (kwĭntĭl′yan, -ēan). Marcus Fabius Quintilianus (1st c. A.D.), Roman rhetorician, author of *De Institutione Oratoria*, the tenth book of which contains judgments on Greek and Roman writers.

quin·til·lion (kwĭntĭl′yon) *n.* (pl. **-lions**, following a numeral **-lion**). Cube of a million (1 with 18 zeros).

quin·tu·ple (kwĭntōō′pel, -tū′-, -tŭp′el, kwĭn′tupel, -tyu-) *adj.* Fivefold; consisting of five things or parts. ∼ *v.* (**-pled, -pling**). Multiply, increase, fivefold.

quin·tu·plet (kwĭntŭp′lĭt, -tōō′-plĭt, -tū′-, kwĭn′tuplĭt, -tyu-) *n.* 1. Set of five things. 2. One of five children born at a birth.

quin·tu·pli·cate (kwĭntōō′plĭkĭt, -tū′-) *adj.* Quintuple. ∼ (kwĭntōō′plĭkāt, -tū′-) *v.t.* (**-cat·ed, -cat·ing**).

quip (kwĭp) *n.* Cleverly sarcastic remark, brief offhand witty remark or reply; gibe; quibble. ∼ *v.* (**quipped, quip·ping**).

qui·pu (kē′pōō, kwĭp′ōō) *n.* Ancient Peruvian device for sending messages, keeping accounts, etc., by variously knotting threads of various colors. [Quechua, = "knot"]

quire (kwīr) *n.* Set of four sheets of paper etc. folded to form eight leaves as in medieval manuscripts; any collection of leaves within one another in manuscript or book; 24 sheets (now sometimes 25) of writing paper; **in** ∼**s,** (of book) in folded sheets, unbound.

Quir·i·nal (kwĭr′inal). One of the Hills on which ancient Rome was built; site of Italian royal residence 1870–1947, now of official residence of president of the republic.

quirk (kwĕrk) *n.* 1. Quibble, quip; trick of action or behavior; twist or flourish in drawing or writing. 2. (archit.) Acute hollow between convex part of molding and soffit or fillet. **quirk′y** *adj.* (**quirk·i·er, quirk·i·est**). **quirk′-i·ness** *n.*

quirt (kwĕrt) *n.* Short-handled riding whip with braided leather lash used in western U.S. and Latin America.

quis·ling (kwĭz′lĭng) *n.* Person cooperating with an enemy who has occupied his country. [Major

Quilting exhibition in Texas. Although practiced worldwide, the art of quilting has been perfected in the U.S.A. Many unique designs were created during the 18th and 19th centuries.

Vidkun *Quisling*, a Norwegian who collaborated with the Germans when they invaded Norway 1940]

quit[1] (kwĭt) *pred. adj.* Free, clear, absolved (archaic); rid *of*; **quit'claim**, renunciation of legal right; (*v.t.*) renounce claim to, give up (thing) *to*; **quit'rent**, (usu. small) rent paid by freeholder or copyholder in lieu of service.

quit[2] (kwĭt) *v.* (**quit** or **quit'ted, quit'ting**). 1. (archaic) Rid oneself *of*; behave, acquit, conduct (oneself) *well* etc. 2. Give up, let go, abandon; depart from, leave; (abs., of tenant) leave occupied premises. **quit'ter** *n.* One who abandons project, gives up, etc. easily.

quitch (kwĭch) **grass** = COUCH[2] grass.

quite (kwīt) *adv.* 1. Completely, wholly, entirely, altogether, to the utmost extent, in the fullest sense, positively, absolutely. 2. Rather, to some extent, as ~ *a long time*; ~ *a few*, a fair number.

Qui·to (kē'tō). Capital of Ecuador, on the equator, at an altitude of 9,300 ft. (2,835 m).

quits (kwĭts) *pred. adj.* On even terms by retaliation or repayment.

quit·tance (kwĭt'ens) *n.* Release *from*; acknowledgment of payment, receipt.

quiv·er[1] (kwĭv'er) *n.* Case for holding arrows.

quiv·er[2] (kwĭv'er) *v.* Tremble or vibrate with slight rapid motion; make (something) quiver. ~ *n.* Quivering motion or sound. **quiv'er·er** *n.* **quiv'er·ing·ly** *adv.* **quiv'er·y** *adj.*

qui vive (kē vēv'). **on the** ~, on the alert. [Fr., = "(long) live who?" i.e. "on whose side are you?" as sentinel's challenge]

Qui·xo·te (kēhō'tā), **Don.** Hero of romance (1605–15) by CERVANTES, written to ridicule the books of chivalry; hence, enthusiastic visionary, pursuer of lofty but impracticable ideals.

quix·ot·ic (kwĭksŏt'ĭk) *adj.* Extremely idealistic, chivalrous, and romantic to the point of impracticality. **quix·ot'i·cal·ly** *adv.*

quiz (kwĭz) *n.* (pl. **quiz·zes**). Odd or eccentric person (now rare); informal oral examination of class or pupil; test of knowledge, esp. one organized as an entertainment or competition. ~ *v.t.* (**quizzed, quiz'zing**). Put series of questions to (person). **quiz'zi·cal** *adj.* Questioning; with an air of puzzlement. **quiz'zi·cal·ly** *adv.*

quod e·rat de·mon·stran·dum (kwŏd ĕr'ăt dĕmonstrăn'dum). (abbrev. Q.E.D.) Which was to be proved (formula concluding geometrical demonstration etc.). [L.]

quod vi·de (kwŏd vī'dē). (abbrev. q.v.) Which see (in cross references etc.). [L.]

quoin (kwoin, kwoin) *n.* 1.

External angle of building; stone or brick forming angle, cornerstone. 2. Wedge for locking type in chase, raising level of gun, keeping barrel from rolling, etc. ~ *v.t.* Raise or secure with quoins.

quoit (kwoit, koit) *n.* Heavy, flattish ring of wood, rope, etc., thrown to encircle iron peg or to stick in ground near it; (pl. with sing. verb) game in which quoits are thrown thus.

quon·dam (kwŏn'dam) *adj.* Former. [L., = "formerly"]

Quon·set (kwŏn'sĭt) **hut.** (trademark) Prefabricated, portable, semicylindrical building made of corrugated metal.

quo·rum (kwôr'um, kwōr'-) *n.* Fixed minimum number of members that must be present to make proceedings of assembly, society, board, etc., valid. [L., = "of whom"]

quot. *abbrev.* Quotation.

quo·ta (kwō'ta) *n.* Part or share that is, or ought to be, contributed by one to a total sum or amount; part or share of a total that belongs, is given, or is due, to one; maximum number that is one's share; (colloq.) limit (of number, amount, etc.). [L. *quota* (*pars*) how great (a part), f. *quot* how many]

quo·ta·tion (kwōtā'shon) *n.* Quoting, passage quoted; amount stated as current price of stocks or commodities; ~ **marks**, (' ' or " ") punctuation marks raised above line at beginning and end of quotation.

quote (kwōt) *v.t.* (**quot·ed, quot·ing**). Cite or appeal to (author, book, etc.) in confirmation

*Arrows projecting from the **quiver** of an archer in Australia (right). Although the bow and arrow have been used for centuries, the quiver was not. Even today, hunters in New Guinea carry a variety of arrows in their hands but use no equivalent of the quiver, which allows both hands to remain free.*

Don Quixote, absurd and yet basically good, typified for his creator the Spain which was passing away. The Don attacked imaginary foes, as in this Daumier picture, but for chivalrous if confused reasons.

of some view, repeat or copy out passage(s) from; repeat or copy out (borrowed passage) usu. with indication that it is borrowed; (abs.) make quotations (*from*); adduce or cite *as*; state price of (usu. *at* figure). ~ *n.* (colloq.) Passage quoted; (usu. pl.) quotation mark(s). **quot'a·ble, quo·ta'tion·al** *adjs.* **quo·ta'tion·al·ly** *adv.* **quot'er** *n.*

quo·tid·i·an (kwōtĭd'ēan) *adj.* Daily, of every day; commonplace, trivial.

quo·tient (kwō'shent) *n.* Result given by dividing one quantity by another.

Qu·ran (kōorahn', -răn') = KORAN.

q.v. *abbrev.* Which see. [L. *quod vide*, which see]

Qy., qy. *abbrevs.* Query.

The original symbol which has been transformed into the modern **R, r** was probably a pictograph for a head (the Semitic 'resh'). During its history, its direction was reversed, possibly because of changes in writing.

Phoenician   Early Greek   Early Etruscan

Archaic Latin   Ionic   Classical Latin

R, r (är) (pl. **R's, r's** or **Rs, s**). Eighteenth letter of modern English and 17th of ancient Roman alphabet, derived through early Greek Ρ, Ρ from Phoenician ٩; in modern standard English representing, before a vowel, an open voiced consonant, with almost no trill.

R *abbrev.* (chem.) Radical; (elect.) resistance; restricted (rating of motion picture to which children less than 17 years old are admitted only with an adult); (chess) rook; rupee; **the three ~'s,** reading, (w)riting, and (a)rithmetic, as basis of elementary education.

r *abbrev.* (math.) Radius; (physics) roentgen(s).

R. *abbrev.* Radius; railroad; Réaumur; Regina; Republican; Rex; right; river; road.

r. *abbrev.* (elect.) Resistance; right; rod(s); roentgen(s); (baseball) run(s).

Ra[1] *symbol.* Radium

Ra[2] (rah). (Egyptian myth.) Sun god, freq. represented with head of falcon.

R.A. *abbrev.* Rear admiral; regular army; (astron.) right ascension; Royal Academy.

Ra·bat (rahbaht'). Capital and port of Morocco, on the Atlantic Ocean NE. of Casablanca.

rab·bet (răb'ĭt) *n.* Step-shaped reduction cut along edge, face, or projecting angle of wood, etc., usu. to receive edge or tongue of another piece. **~** *v.t.* (**-bet·ed, -bet·ing**). Join, fix, with rabbet; make rabbet in.

rab·bi (răb'ī) *n.* (pl. **-bis**). 1. Title of Jewish scholar or teacher of civil and religious law from New Testament times on. 2. Ordained spiritual leader of a Jewish congregation. **rab·bin·ate** (răb'ĭnĭt) *n.* 1. Office of rabbi; term of this. 2. Rabbis collectively. **rab'bin·ism** *n.* **rab·bin·i·cal** (rabĭn'ĭkal), **rab·bin'ic** *adjs.* **rab·bin'i·cal·ly** *adv.*

rab·bit (răb'ĭt) *n.* (pl. **-bits**, collect. **-bit**). Burrowing herbivorous gregarious mammal, esp. *Sylvilagus*, the cottontail, allied to the hare but with shorter legs and smaller ears, brownish-gray in the wild, also black, white, or pied in domestication; **~ ears,** (colloq.) television antenna; **~ fever,** TULAREMIA; **~ punch,** (boxing) short (illegal) chop with edge of hand to opponent's nape; **~('s) foot clover,** clover (*Trifolium arvense*) with flowers resembling rabbits' paws. **rabbit** *v.i.* Hunt rabbits.

rab·ble[1] (răb'el) *n.* Disorderly crowd, mob; contemptible or inferior set of people; lowest classes of the populace; **~-rouser,** one who stirs up the rabble in agitation for social or political change.

rab·ble[2] (răb'el) *n.* Iron bar with bent end for stirring molten metal in puddling.

Rabbits are often leading characters in children's books. However, to farmers and gardeners they can be a real pest, causing great damage to crops, and weakening banks by burrowing.

Rab·e·lais (răb'elā; *Fr.* răblě'), **François** (*c*1495–1553). French humanist and satirical writer; author of *Pantagruel* and *Gargantua*. **Rab·e·lai·si·an** (răbelā'zēan, -zhan) *adj. & n.* Of or like Rabelais; having the exuberance and coarse humor characteristic of Rabelais.

rab·id (răb'ĭd) *adj.* Furious, violent, raging, unreasoning; (esp. of dog) affected with rabies; of rabies. **rab'id·ly** *adv.* **rab'id·ness, ra·bid·i·ty** (răbĭd'ĭtē) *ns.*

ra·bies (rā'bēz) *n.* Viral, usu. fatal disease, esp. of dogs, foxes, bats, squirrels, etc., but affecting most warm-blooded animals, including man, and transmitted by the bite of an infected animal; also called hydrophobia, esp. in human beings.

rac·coon, ra·coon (răkoon') *ns.* (pl. **-coons,** collect. **-coon**). Nocturnal N. Amer. carnivore (*Procyon*

lotor), having grayish-brown fur, markings around eyes, sharp snout, and bushy blackringed tail.

race[1](rās) *n.* 1. Onward sweep or movement, esp. strong current in sea or river. 2. Channel of stream; track or channel in which something moves or slides. 3. Contest of speed between runners, ships, horses, etc., or persons doing anything; (pl.) series of these for horses at fixed time on regular course; **race'horse**, horse bred or kept for racing; **race'track**, (usu. oval) track for horse or vehicle races; **race'way**, channel for water; track for trotting or pacing races; track for racing stock cars, hot rods, etc. **race** *v.* (**raced, rac·ing**). Compete in speed *with*; have race with, try to surpass in speed; cause (horse etc.) to race; indulge in horse racing; make (person, thing) move at full speed; go at full speed; (of machinery) move, revolve with uncontrolled speed, when resistance is diminished, as when the propeller of a ship is raised out of the water. **race**[2] (rās) *n.* Group of persons,

animals, or plants connected by common descent; posterity *of* (person); house, family, tribe, or nation regarded as of common stock; (pop.) distinct ethnic stock; any great division of living creatures; descent; kindred; class of persons etc. with some common feature; (biol.) subdivision of a species; variety.

ra·ceme (rāsēm', ra-) *n.* (bot.) Inflorescence opening successively from base to apex, with flowers on short lateral stalks springing from a central stem, as in hyacinth, lily of the valley, etc.

ra·ce·mic (rāsē'mĭk, -sĕm'ĭk, ŕa-) *adj.* (chem.) ~ **acid**, colorless crystalline acid, an optically inactive variety of tartaric acid, found in the juice of grapes.

rac·e·mose (răs'emōs) *adj.* (bot.) Arranged in, having form of, a

*Modern **racing cars** keep to the circuits, which are designed to take them in relative safety: they are now so far removed from ordinary cars that they cannot be driven on the roads.*

raceme; (anat.) arranged in, havin form of, a cluster, as e.g. th pancreas.

rac·er (rā'ser) *n.* (esp. Hors yacht, car, etc., used for racing.

Ra·chel (rā'chel). Second wi of Jacob and mother of Joseph an Benjamin (Gen. 29–35).

ra·chis (rā'kĭs) *n.* (pl. **ra·chi· ses, ra·chi·des** pr. răk'ĭdēz, rā'kĭ- 1. (bot.) Axis of inflorescence wit flower stalks at short intervals, in grasses; axis of pinnately com pound leaf or frond. 2. (anat Vertebral column or cord fro which it develops.

ra·chi·tis (rakī'tĭs) *n.* Ricket **ra·chit·ic** (rakĭt'ĭk) *adj.*

Rach·ma·ni·noff, Rach·ma ni·nov (rahkmah'nĭnawf; *Rus* rahxmah'nĭnawf), **Sergei Vasily evich** (1873–1943). Russian com poser and pianist.

ra·cial (rā'shal) *adj.* Of, belong ing to, characteristic of, rac **ra'cial·ly** *adv.*

Ra·cine (răsēn'), **Jean** (1639 1699). French tragic poet an dramatist; author of *Phèdre, Andr maque*, etc.

rac·ism (rā'sĭzem) *n.* 1. Theor that distinctive characteristic abilities, etc., are determined b race. 2. Belief that one huma race, esp. one's own, is superio social or political system based o this; (encouragement of) antag onism between races. **rac·ist** & *adj.*

rack[1] (răk) *n.* 1. Driving cloud 2. Destruction (only in ~ **an ruin**). **rack** *v.i.* (of clouds) Driv before wind.

rack[2] (răk) *n.* 1. Fixed or mov

aerofoil · air-box · cockpit · extinguisher · roll-over bar · front aerofoil · gearbox · disk caliper · oil-tank · radius arm · spring unit · wishbone · disk air scoop · intake trumpets · front outboard disk · drive shaft · exhaust system · water radiator

First developed as a means of plotting movements of enemy aircraft, radar is now used for various purposes on ships as the different aerials demonstrate (1). In Australia, a form has been developed which will help aircraft to make more accurate instrument landings (2).

...able frame of wooden or metal bars for holding fodder; framework with rails, bars, pegs, or shelves, for keeping articles on or in. 2. Cogged or indented bar or rail gearing with wheel, pinion, or worm, or serving with pegs etc. to adjust position of something; ~ **railway**: see COG railway. **rack** v. Place in or on rack.

rack³ (răk) v.t. Stretch joints of (person) by pulling esp. with instruments of torture made for the purpose; (of disease etc.) inflict tortures on; shake violently, strain, task severely. ~ n. Instrument of torture, frame with roller at each end to which victim's wrists and ankles were tied so that his joints were stretched when rollers were turned; also fig.

rack⁴ (răk) n. Horse's gait between trot and canter, both legs of one side being lifted almost at once, and all four feet being off ground together at moments. ~ v.i. Progress thus.

rack⁵ (răk) v.t. Draw off (wine etc.) from the dregs.

rack·et¹, **rac·quet** (răk´ĭt) ns. 1. Bat used in tennis, badminton, etc.; network of cord, catgut, nylon, etc., stretched across elliptical frame with handle attached. 2. (**racquets**) see RACQUET sense 2. 3. Snowshoe resembling racket.

rack·et² (răk´ĭt) n. 1. Disturbance, uproar. 2. (slang) Line of business; scheme, procedure, for obtaining money etc. by dubious or illegal means, esp. as form of organized crime. **rack´e·ty** adj. Noisy; dissipated.

rack·et·eer (răkĭtēr´) n. Member of criminal gang practicing extortion, intimidation, violence, etc., esp. on large scale. **rack·et·eer´ing** n. Systematic extortion of money by threats, violence, or other illegal methods.

rac·on·teur (răkŏntēr´), fem. **rac·on·teuse** (răkŏntōoz´) ns. Teller of anecdotes.

ra·coon = RACCOON.

rac·quet (răk´ĭt) n. 1. RACKET¹. 2. (pl. with sing. verb) Ball game similar to tennis played by two or four players in a closed four-walled court.

rac·y (rā´sē) adj. (**rac·i·er, rac·i·est**). Of distinctive quality or vigor, not smoothed into sameness or commonness; lively, spirited, piquant; ribald, risqué. **rac´i·ly** adv. **rac´i·ness** n.

rad¹ (răd) n. (phys.) Unit of absorbed dose of ionizing radiation, corresponding to 100 ergs per gram of absorbing material.

rad² abbrev. Radian(s).

ra·dar (rā´dār) n. System for ascertaining direction and range of aircraft, ships, coasts, and other objects by sending out electromagnetic radiations of short wavelength and interpreting the reflections of these produced by certain types of surface; apparatus used for this. [f. radio detection and ranging]

ra·di·al (rā´dēal) adj. 1. Arranged like rays or radii, having position or direction of a radius; having spokes or radiating lines; acting or moving along lines that diverge from a center; ~ **engine**, internal combustion engine, as formerly used in some propeller-driven airplanes, with cylinders arranged like spokes of wheel; ~ **(ply) tire**, motor vehicle tire in which ply cords extend straight across at right angles to travel direction. 2. Of the radius of the forearm. **ra´di·al·ly** adv. **radial** n. Radial part, radius, ray; radial nerve or artery.

ra·di·an (rā´dēan) n. (abbrev. rad) Angle at center of circle (approx. 57.296°) subtending arc whose length is equal to the radius.

ra·di·ant (rā´dēant) adj. Emitting rays of light; beaming with joy, hope, etc.; issuing in rays, bright, shining, splendid; extending or operating radially; ~ **energy**, energy transmitted as electromagnetic waves; ~ **heat**, electromagnetic radiation emitted by hot bodies, having a wavelength greater than that of visible light and capable of crossing a vacuum. **ra´di·ant·ly** adv. **ra´di·ance, ra´di·an·cy** ns. **radiant** n. Point or object from which light or heat radiates; (astron.) apparent origin or focal point of meteoric shower.

ra·di·ate¹ (rā´dēĭt, -āt) adj. Having divergent rays or parts radially arranged. **ra´di·ate·ly** adv.

ra·di·ate² (rā´dēāt) v. (**-at·ed, -at·ing**). Emit rays of light, heat, etc.; issue in rays; diverge or spread from central point; emit (light, heat, etc.) from center.

ra·di·a·tion (rādēā´shon) n. Manner in which the energy of a vibrating body is transmitted in all directions by a surrounding medium; emission and diffusion of heat rays; emission of Roentgen or x-rays, or the rays and particles characteristic of radioactive substances; ~ **sickness**, sickness caused by exposure to ionizing radiation, as from x-rays or radioactive materials, with symptoms ranging from nausea, headache, vomiting, and diarrhea to hemorrhaging, loss of teeth and hair, reduction in blood cell count, sterility, and death.

ra·di·a·tor (rā′dēāter) *n.* (esp.) Metal case containing arrangement of pipes heated with hot air, steam, etc., and radiating warmth into room; that part of the engine cooling system of most motor vehicles etc. in which the circulating fluid is cooled.

rad·i·cal (răd′ĭkal) *adj.* 1. Of the root(s); naturally inherent, essential, fundamental; forming the basis, primary. 2. Affecting the foundation, going to the root; sweeping, extreme, (pol.) desiring or advocating fundamental or revolutionary changes. 3. (philol.) Of the roots of words. 4. (bot.) Of, springing directly from, the root, or the main stem close to it. 5. (math.) Of the root of a number or quantity; ~ **sign**, sign $\sqrt{}$ ($\sqrt[3]{}$ $\sqrt[4]{}$ etc.) used to indicate that the square (cube, fourth, etc.) root of the number to which it is prefixed is to be extracted. **rad′i·cal·ize** *v.t.* (-ized, -iz·ing). **rad′i·cal·ly** *adv.* **radical** *n.* 1. Fundamental thing or principle. 2. (pol.) Person holding radical opinions. 3. (philol.) Root. 4. (math.) Quantity forming or expressed as root of another; radical sign. 5. (chem.) Element or atom, or group of these, forming base of compound and remaining unchanged during ordinary chemical reactions to which this is liable.

rad·i·cle (răd′ĭkel) *n.* 1. Part of plant embryo that develops into primary root; small root. 2. (anat.) Rootlike subdivision of nerve or vein.

ra·di·i: see RADIUS.

ra·di·o (rā′dēō) *n.* (pl. **-os**). 1. Transmission and reception of messages etc. by means of electromagnetic waves of frequency between 10^4 Hz and 3×10^{12} Hz approx. (see FREQUENCY), either as acoustic signals or as Morse code signals; wireless, broadcasting. 2. Radio receiver. 3. (attrib.) Of radio; concerned with phenomena occurring at radio frequency. 4. ~ **astronomy**, branch of astronomy dealing with investigation of celestial bodies by radar, and with electromagnetic radiations from outside Earth's atmosphere; ~ **receiver**, apparatus that detects signals transmitted by radio frequency waves and reproduces

them as audible sounds; ~ **telescope**: see TELESCOPE.

radio- *comb. form.* Connected with: (1) radio (*radiosonde*); (2)

Each year, the versatility of **radio** *increases. At Parkes, Australia (1), huge dish antennae receive radio signals from outer space. To give better reception in long-distance transmissions, log-period aerials (2) have become increasingly complex.*

1

2

radioactivity (*radiocarbon*); (3) rays or radiation (*radioscopy*).

ra·di·o·ac·tive (rādēōăk′tĭv) *adj.* Of, exhibiting, radioactivity. **ra·di·o·ac·tiv·i·ty** (rādēōăktĭv′ĭtē) *n.* (phys.) Property possessed by certain elements of high atomic weight (radium, thorium, uranium, etc.) of spontaneously emitting alpha, beta, or gamma rays (which are capable of penetrating opaque bodies and affecting a photographic plate even when separated from it by thin sheets of metal), by the disintegration of the nuclei of the atoms, or induced in certain non-radioactive elements by exposure to the action of bombarding particles. **ra·di·o·ac′tive·ly** *adv.*

ra·di·o·bi·ol·o·gy (rādēōbīŏl′-ọjē) *n.* Branch of biology concerned with effects of radiation on living organisms and with use of radio-active tracers for biological studies. **ra·di·o·bi·o·log·i·cal** (rādēōbīo-lŏj′ĭkal) *adj.* **ra·di·o·bi·ol·o·gist** *n.*

ra·di·o·car·bon (rādēōkär′bon) *n.* Radioactive isotope of carbon existing in organic matter and having its origin in the radioactive carbon dioxide produced by the interaction of carbon ray neutrons and atmospheric nitrogen at high altitudes; ~ **dating,** method of dating organic materials from ancient deposits, esp. archaeo-logical remains, made possible by the discovery that after the death of plants and animals the radio-carbon content decays at a regular rate (by half in every period of ᴄ5600 years); also called *carbon-14 dating.*

ra·di·o·gram (rā′dēōgrăm) *n.* 1. Image produced on photographic plate by x-rays. 2. Message sent by radiotelegraphy.

ra·di·o·graph (rā′dēōgräf, -grahf) = RADIOGRAM def. 1. **ra·di·o·graph·ic** (rādēōgrăf′ĭk) *adj.*

ra·di·og·ra·phy (rādēŏg′rafē) *n.* Photography by means of x-rays. **ra·di·og′ra·pher** *n.*

ra·di·o·i·so·tope (rādēōī′sotōp) *n.* Radioactive isotope.

ra·di·o·lar·i·an (rādēōlār′ēan) *n.* Protozoan of the order Radio-laria, with siliceous skeleton and radiating pseudopodia.

ra·di·o·lo·ca·tion (rādēōlōkā′-shon) *n.* Determination of the position of course of ships, aircraft, etc., by means of RADAR.

ra·di·ol·o·gy (rādēŏl′ojē) *n.* Scientific study of x-rays, radio-activity, and other radiations, and (esp.) the use of these in medicine. **ra·di·o·log·i·cal** (rādēōlŏj′ĭkal) *adj.* **ra·di·ol′o·gist** *n.*

ra·di·om·e·ter (rādēŏm′eter) *n.* Instrument showing conversion of radiant energy into mechanical force.

ra·di·os·co·py (rādēŏs′kopē) *n.* Examination of the internal structure etc. of opaque bodies by means of x- or other rays.

ra·di·o·sonde (rā′dēōsŏnd) *n.* Miniature radio transmitter, carried aloft in a balloon and descending by parachute, broad-casting to observers on the ground information about atmospheric conditions at various levels.

ra·di·o·tel·e·gra·phy (rādēō-

teleg′rafē) *n.* Transmission and reception of Morse code signals by electromagnetic waves of radio frequency.

ra·di·o·te·leph·o·ny (rādēō-teleēf′onē) *n.* Transmission and reception of acoustic signals by electromagnetic waves of radio frequency. **ra·di·o·tel·e·phone** (rādēōtĕl′efōn), **ra·di·o·phone** (rā′dēōfōn) *ns.* Apparatus used in radiotelephony.

ra·di·o·ther·a·py (rādēōthĕr′-apē) *n.* Treatment of disease by x-rays or other forms of radiation. **ra·di·o·ther′a·pist** *n.*

rad·ish (răd′ĭsh) *n.* Cruciferous plant, *Raphanus sativus*; fleshy slightly pungent root of this, eaten raw.

ra·di·um (rā′dēum) *n.* (chem.) Rare radioactive metallic element isolated from pitchblende in 1898 by P. and M. Curie; symbol Ra, at. no. 88, at. wt. 226.0254; (pop.) any of various salts of this element, used in radiotherapy etc.

ra·di·us (rā′dēus) *n.* (pl. **-di·i** pr. -dēī, **-us·es**). 1. Thicker and shorter bone of forearm in man; corresponding bone in beast's fore-leg or bird's wing. 2. (math.) Straight line from center to circum-ference of circle or sphere; radial line from focus to any point of curve; ~ **vector** (pl. **ra·di·i vec-to·res,** pr. rā′dēī vĕktōr′ēz, -tōr′ēz, ~ **vectors**), variable line drawn to curve from fixed point, esp. (astron.) from sun or planet to path of satellite. 3. Any of set of lines diverging from a point like radii of circle, object of this kind (e.g. spoke). 4. Circular area as measured by its radius.

ra·dix (rā′dĭks) *n.* (pl. **rad·i·ces** pr. răd′ĭsēz, rā′dĭ-, **ra·dix·es**). Number or symbol used as base of a system of numbers; source or origin *of.* [L., = "root"]

ra·dome (rā′dōm) *n.* Dome or covering protecting radar equip-

Radiosondes give essential information about the upper air as the balloons to which they are attached rise through the atmospheric layers. More than 1,000 of these balloons are used each day throughout the world.

*White-water rafting has become a popular sport for those with a taste for adventure. Originally **rafts** were of very simple design and were built to drift with the current, but they can also be navigable and seaworthy.*

ment, esp. on outer surface of aircraft.

ra·don (rā′dŏn) *n.* (chem.) Chemically inert heavy gaseous radioactive element, the first disintegration product of radium; symbol Rn, at. no. 86, principal isotope at. wt. 222. [f. *radium* and the termination of *argon, neon,* etc.]

rad·u·la (răj′ōola) *n.* (pl. **-lae** pr. -lē). File-like structure in mollusks used to scrape off particles of food and draw them into the mouth.

RAF, R.A.F. *abbrevs.* Royal Air Force.

raf·fi·a (răf′ēa) *n.* Palm of genus *Raphia*; soft fiber from leaves of *R. ruffia* and *R. pedunculata*, used for making hats, baskets, mats, etc.

raff·ish (răf′ĭsh) *adj.* Disreputable, dissipated, esp. in appearance. **raff′ish·ly** *adv.* **raff′ish·ness** *n.*

raf·fle[1] (răf′el) *n.* Lottery in which prize is assigned by lot to 1 person of a number who have each bought one or more chances or have paid a certain part of its value. ~ *v.* (**-fled, -fling**). Take part in raffle *for* (thing); sell (thing) by raffle.

raf·fle[2] (răf′el) *n.* Rubbish.

raft (răft, rahft) *n.* Collection of logs, casks, etc., fastened together in the water for transportation; flat floating structure of timber etc., for conveying persons or things, esp. as substitute for boat in emergencies; floating accumulation of trees, ice, etc.; (slang) large collection of things. ~ *v.* Transport (as) on raft; form into a raft; cross (water) on raft(s); work raft.

raft·er (răf′ter, rahf′-) *n.* One of the sloping supporting beams forming framework of pitched roof.

rag[1] (răg) *n.* Torn or frayed piece of woven material; one of the irregular scraps to which cloth etc. is reduced by wear and tear; piece of music in ragtime; (contempt.) flag, handkerchief, newspaper, etc.; (pl.) tattered clothes; (collect.) rags used as material for making paper, stuffing, etc.; **rag′bag**, bag in which scraps of linen etc. are kept for use; **rag doll**, stuffed doll made of cloth; **rag paper**, good quality paper made from rags; **rag′tag (and bobtail)**, riffraff; **rag′time**, elaborately syncopated jazz with steadily accented base accompaniment; **rag′weed**, any of various mainly N. Amer. composite plants (genus *Ambrosia*) having greenish flowers, whose abundant pollen is a major cause of hay fever; **rag′-**

*English Electric's Lightning fighter with its considerable range of weaponry is among the precursors of today's **R.A.F.** aircraft — supersonic, heavily armed and equipped with sophisticated instruments.*

wort, any of several common yellow-flowered ragged-leaved plants, incl. *Senecio aureus*, the golden ragwort of N. Amer.

rag[2] (răg) *n.* Large coarse roofing slate.

rag[3] (răg) *n.* (chiefly Brit.) Act of ragging, noisy disorderly conduct. ~ *v.* (**ragged, rag·ging**).

Annoy, tease, torment; (Brit. university slang) play rough jokes upon, throw into wild disorder (person's room etc.) by way of practical joke; act in this way.

rag·a·muf·fin (răg′amŭfĭn) *n.* Child in ragged dirty clothes.

rage (rāj) *n.* (Fit of) violent anger; violent operation of some natural force or some sentiment; vehement desire or passion (for); object of widespread temporary enthusiasm or fashion. ~ *v.i.* (**raged, rag·ing**). Rave, storm, speak madly or furiously, be full

*The immediately recognizable flowers of **ragged robin** are a common sight during the summer in marshes, fens, and wet woodlands, giving place after fertilization to narrow fruits.*

***Ragweed** is native to North America and is also known by the name American wormwood. It has a very high pollen yield and is a major contributor to the discomfort of hayfever sufferers.*

*Common (left) and marsh **ragworts** have a strong family resemblance. However, the marsh species has glossier leaves and the plants are shorter and more widely branched.*

of anger; (of wind, sea, passion, battle, etc.) be violent, be at the height, operate unchecked, prevail. **rag'ing·ly** *adv.*

rag·ged (răg´ĭd) *adj.* Rough, shaggy, hanging in tufts; of broken jagged outline or surface, full of rough or sharp projections; faulty, wanting finish, smoothness, or uniformity; rent, torn, frayed, in ragged clothes; ~ **robin**, reddish or white wild flower (*Lychnis floscuculi*) with deeply lobed petals. **rag'ged·ly** *adv.* **rag'ged·ness** *n.*

rag·lan (răg´lan) *n.* Coat, jacket, or sweater without shoulder seams, top of sleeve being carried up to neck; ~ **sleeve**, sleeve of this kind. [f. Lord *Raglan*, British commander in Crimean War]

ra·gout (răgōō´) *n.* Meat in small pieces stewed with vegetables and highly seasoned.

rah (rah) *int.* Hurrah.

raid (rād) *n.* Sudden incursion of military force into or upon a country for the purposes of plunder or attack; sudden descent of police etc. upon suspected premises or illicit goods. ~ *v.* Make raid *into* etc.; make raid on. **raid'er** *n.*

rail[1] (rāl) *n.* 1. Horizontal or inclined bar or continuous series of bars of wood or metal used to hang things on, as top of banisters, as part of fence, as protection against contact or falling over, or for similar purpose; any horizontal piece in frame of wooden paneling. 2. Iron bar or continuous line of bars laid on ground as one side or half of railroad track; railroad (esp.

by ~); **rail'head**, farthest point reached by railroad under construction; (mil.) point on railroad where supplies can be unloaded; **rail'road**, (*n.*) track or set

*The first railways were wooden tramways laid down in quarries and collieries, with wagons pulled by horses. With the development of the iron industry, cast-iron **rails** came into use and proved more durable as well as easier to install.*

of tracks of iron or steel rails for passage of trains of cars drawn by locomotive and conveying passengers and freight; tracks of this kind worked by a single company; (hist.) road laid with rails for heavy horsecarts; (*v.*) transport, travel, by rail; (colloq.) accomplish (action) with great speed; (slang) convict unfairly; rush *into*, through, etc.; **rail'way**, railroad esp. in local area service, as street railway;

1

2

3

5

4

*The **rainbow trout** is identified by a spotted body and rainbow-colored band which extends from gills to tail. A native of the U.S., it has been introduced all over the world. Some species migrate to the sea and return to the river of their birth to spawn.*

chiefly Brit.) railroad. **rail** *v.* furnish or enclose with rail (often ~ **in, off**); provide with rail; lay (railroad route) with rails.

rail² (rāl) *n.* (pl. **rails**, collect. **rail**). Any of various small marsh birds of the family Rallidae, characterized by their short wings used only for short flights.

rail³ (rāl) *v.i.* Use abusive language (*at, against*).

rail·ing (rā′lĭng) *n.* (esp.) Fence or barrier of rails etc.

rail·ler·y (rā′lerē) *n.* (pl. **-ler·ies**). (Piece of) good-humored ridicule, banter.

rai·ment (rā′ment) *n.* (poet., rhet.) Clothing, dress.

rain (rān) *n.* Condensed moisture of atmosphere falling visibly in separate drops; fall of such drops; (rain-like descent of) falling liquid or solid particles or bodies; (pl.) showers of rain; **the ~s**, rainy season in tropical countries; ~ **check**, ticket given for later use when baseball game etc. is interrupted by bad weather; (fig.) promise that a postponed offer will still stand; **rain′coat**, (waterproof) coat worn as protection against rain; ~ **day, date**, alternative day on which an outdoor fair, game, etc., is to be held if rain causes it to be canceled on original date; **rain′drop**, single drop of rain; **rain′fall**, shower; quantity of

rain falling within given area in given time; ~ **forest**, forest characteristic of rainy tropical regions; ~ **gauge**, instrument measuring rainfall; **rain′making**, act or process of making or increasing rainfall or trying to do so, esp. by artificial means (**rain′-maker** *n.*); **rain′water**, water that has fallen from clouds as rain (not got from wells, a city water supply, etc.). **rain′less** *adj.* **rain** *v.* 1. **it ~s, it is raining**, rain falls; there is a shower of (something falling etc.); **it ~s cats and dogs**, it rains violently. 2. Send down rain; fall or send down in showers or like rain.

rain·bow (rān′bō) *n.* Arch showing PRISMATIC colors in their order formed in sky (or across waterfall etc.) opposite sun by reflection, double refraction, and dispersion, of sun's rays in falling drops of rain, spray, etc.; (attrib.) many-colored; ~ **trout**, N. Amer. species of trout (*Salmo gairdneri*) with a reddish band on sides and dark spots.

Rai·nier (rānēr′, rā′nēr), **Mount.** Highest peak in Washington, 14,410 ft. (4,392 m), in the Cascade Range in the W. central part.

rain·y (rā′nē) *adj.* (**rain·i·er, rain·i·est**). In or on which rain is falling or much rain usu. falls;

(of clouds, wind, etc.) laden with, bringing, rain; ~ **day**, (fig.) time of need. **rain′i·ness** *n.*

raise (rāz) *v.t.* (**raised, rais·ing**). 1. Set upright, make stand up, restore to or toward vertical position; rouse; ~ **from the dead**, restore to life. 2. Build up, construct; propagate; rear, bring up (a child); utter, make audible; start; give occasion for, elicit; set up, advance; ~ **one's voice**, speak; speak louder. 3. Elevate, put or take into higher position; direct upward; promote to higher rank; make higher or nobler; cause to ascend; make (voice) louder or

Rails can be found almost all over the world, wherever the environment is suitable. Many species, like the American clapper rail (below) are hunted as game birds.

Probably best known as the man who introduced the potato and tobacco to England, **Walter Raleigh** was also renowned as an author and courtier. He fell from favor with James I and was beheaded.

shriller; increase amount of, heighten level of; (naut.) come in sight of (land, ship); ~ **bread** etc., cause it to rise with yeast etc.; ~ **Cain, hell**, etc., (colloq.) make a disturbance; become violently angry; ~ **one's eyebrows**, look supercilious or shocked; also fig. 4. Collect, bring together, procure, manage to get. 5. Relinquish, cause enemy to relinquish (siege, blockade). **raise** *n.* Increase in amount, esp. of stakes at poker, bid at bridge, etc.; rise (in salary etc.).

rai·sin (rā´zĭn) *n.* Partially dried grape.

rai·son d'ê·tre (rā´zōn dĕt´r*e*; *Fr.* rĕzawn´ dĕ´tr*e*) (pl. **rai·sons d'ê·tre** pr. rā´zōnz dĕt´r*e*; *Fr.* rĕzawn´ dĕ´tr*e*). Reason or justification for existing.

raj (rahj) *n.* (Ind.) Sovereignty, rule.

ra·jah, ra·ja (rah´j*a*) *ns.* (hist.) Indian king or prince (also as title of petty dignitary or noble in India, or of Malay or Javanese chief). [Hind. *rājā*]

Raj·put (rahj´pŏŏt). Member of Hindu landowning warrior caste of NW. India.

rake¹ (rāk) *n.* Implement consisting of pole with crossbar toothed like comb at end for drawing together hay etc., or smoothing loose soil or gravel; implement resembling rake used for other purposes, e.g. by croupier drawing in money at gaming table. ~ *v.* (**raked, rak·ing**). Collect, gather *up*, pull *out*, clear *off*, (as) with rake; clean or smooth with rake; search (as) with rake; make *level, clean,* etc., with rake; use rake,

search as with rake; sweep with shot, enfilade, send shot along (ship) from stem to stern; sweep with the eyes; **rake-off**, (slang) profit or commission made, often illegitimately, by one or more persons concerned in a transaction; **rake over, up**, revive memory of (past quarrels, grievances, etc.).

rake² (rāk) *n.* Dissipated or immoral man of fashion.

rake³ (rāk) *v.* (**raked, rak·ing**). (of ship, its bow or stern) Project at upper part of bow or stern beyond keel; (of masts or funnels) incline from perpendicular toward stern; give backward inclination to. ~ *n.* Amount to which thing rakes; raking position or build.

Why **rainbows** occur was first scientifically explained in the 17th century. Before that, various religious or magical reasons were given for their appearance.

rak·ish¹ (rā´kĭsh) *adj.* (As) or like, a RAKE².

rak·ish² (rā´kĭsh) *adj.* (of ship) Smart and fast looking; jaunty [perh. same word as preceding, wit extra association of raking masts]

rale (răl, rahl) *n.* (path.) Soun additional to that of respiratio heard in auscultation of unhealth lungs.

Ra·leigh¹ (raw´lē, rah´-). Capit of North Carolina, in the E. centra part.

Ra·leigh², Ral·egh (raw´lē rah´-), **Sir Walter** (*c*1552–1618) English military and naval com mander, explorer, courtier, an poet; expored the eastern seaboar of Amer. and wrote accounts of h adventures; fell out of favor wit Elizabeth I; was convicted of con spiring against James I, 160 reprieved, but eventually execute

ral·ly¹ (răl´ē) *v.* (**-lied, -ly·ing**) Reassemble, get together agair

Rajput warriors have traditionally provided guards for the palace at Jaipur, and some are still recruited for service despite the modernization of the present Indian army.

Rajah Goman Singh of Kotah, on a 'Lion Hunt' was painted in 1778. It is typical of Mogul painting which was entirely devoted to representations of important people and their activities.

after rout or dispersion, (cause to) renew conflict; bring, come, together as support or for concentrated action; revive (faculty etc.) by effort of will, pull oneself together, assume or rouse to fresh energy. ~ *n*. (pl. **-lies**). 1. Act of rallying, reunion for fresh effort; recovery of energy; mass meeting; competitive automobile race over a fixed course of public roads under specified rules. 2. (tennis etc.) Series of strokes made between service and failure to return the ball.

ral·ly² (răl´ē) *v.t.* (**-lied, -ly·ing**). Banter.

ram (răm) *n*. 1. Uncastrated male sheep. 2. **the R** ~: see ARIES. 3. (hist.) Swinging beam for breaching walls, battering ram; (warship with) projecting beak at bow for charging side of other ships. 4. Falling weight of pile driver; rammer; hydraulic water-raising or lifting machine; piston of hydrostatic press; plunger of force pump; **ram´jet**, jet engine for aircraft in which the motion through the air provides compression. **ram** *v.t.* (**rammed, ram·ming**). 1. Beat down (soil etc.) into solidity with wooden block etc.; make (post, plant, etc.) firm by ramming soil around it; drive (pile etc.) *down, in*, etc., by heavy blows; force (charge) home, pack (gun) tight, with ramrod; squeeze or force into place by pressure; (abs.) use rammer; **ram´rod**, (hist.) rod for ramming home charge of muzzleloader. 2. (of ship) Strike with ram; dash or violently impel *against, at*, etc. **ram´mer** *n*.

Ra·ma (rah´ma). Any of three incarnations of Vishnu: Balarama, Parashurama, or Ramachandra.

Ram·a·dan (răm*a*dahn´, -dăn´). Ninth month of Muslim year, rigidly observed as 30 days of fasting during daylight hours.

Ra·ma·krish·na (rahma-krĭsh´na) (1834–86). Hindu mystic.

Ra·man (rah´man), **Sir Chandrasekhara Venkata** (1888–1970). Indian physicist; awarded Nobel Prize for physics, 1930; ~ **effect**, appearance of additional lines (~ **lines**) in the spectrum of light when scattered by the molecules of a substance; ~ **spectrum**, spectrum so obtained.

Ra·ma·ya·na (rahmah´yana). Ancient Sanskrit epic poem (500–300 B.C.), regarded as sacred text by Hindus, relating the adventures of Ramachandra, the seventh of Vishnu's incarnations.

ram·ble (răm´bel) *v.i.* (**-bled, -bling**). Walk for pleasure and without definite route; wander in discourse, talk or write disconnectedly. ~ *n*. Rambling walk.

ram·bler (răm´bler) *n*. (esp.) Any of several kinds of freely climbing rose.

ram·bling (răm´blĭng) *adj*. Peripatetic, wandering; disconnected, desultory, incoherent; (of plants) straggling, climbing; (of house, street, etc.) irregularly planned. **ram´bling·ly** *adv*.

ram·bunc·tious (rămbŭngk´-sh*u*s) *adj*. Unruly; uncontrollably exuberant. **ram·bunc´tious·ness** *n*.

Ra·meau (rămō´), **Jean Philippe** (1683–1764). French composer of operas and harpsichord music.

ram·e·kin, ram·e·quin (răm´-ekĭn) *ns.* Small quantity of cheese baked with bread crumbs, eggs, etc.; small dish in which this is baked and served.

Ram·e·ses: see RAMSES.

ram·i·fi·ca·tion (rămĭfĭkā´shon) *n.* Ramifying, (arrangement of) tree's branches; subdivision of complex structure comparable to tree's branches.

ram·i·fy (răm´ifī) *v.* (**-fied, -fy·ing**). Form branches, subdivisions, or offshoots; branch out; (usu. pass.) cause to branch out, arrange in branching manner.

ra·mose (rā´mōs, ramōs´) *adj.* Branched, branching.

ramp (rămp) *n.* Slope, inclined plane joining two levels of ground, esp. in fortification, or of wall coping; inclined plane serving instead of steps at entrance of building, connecting different floors or levels etc.; mobile staircase for boarding and leaving airplane; upward bend in stair rail. ~ *v.* (chiefly of lion or other beast) Stand on hind legs with forepaws in air, assume or be in threatening posture.

ram·page (rămpāj´) *v.i.* (**-paged, -pag·ing**). Behave violently, storm, rage, rush about. ~ (răm´pāj) *n.* Violent behavior. **ram·pa´geous** (rămpā´jus) *adj.* **ram·pa´geous·ness, ram·pag´er** *ns.*

ramp·ant (răm´pant) *adj.* Ramping (chiefly of lion in her.); violent or extravagant in action or opinion, arrant, aggressive, unchecked, prevailing; rank, luxuriant; (of arch etc.) having one abutment higher than the other, climbing. **ramp´ant·ly** *adv.* **ramp´an·cy** *n.*

ram·part (răm´pärt) *n.* Broad-topped and usu. stone-parapetted defensive mound of earth; (fig.), defense, protection. ~ *v.t.* Fortify or protect (as) with rampart.

ram·pi·on (răm´pēon) *n.* Flower, esp European campanula (*Campanula rapunculus*), with white tuberous, edible roots; any plant of genus *Phyteuma*, with heads or spikes of blue flowers.

Ram·say (răm´zē), **Sir William** (1852–1916). Brit. chemist; discoverer of helium, argon (with Rayleigh), and neon in the atmosphere; Nobel Prize for chemistry, 1904.

Ram·ses (răm´sēz), **Ram·e·ses** (răm´esēz). Name of several Egyptian kings of 19th and 20th dynasties; **Rameses II** (? 1292–1225 B.C.) is sometimes supposed to have been the Pharaoh who oppressed the Jews.

ram·shack·le (răm´shăkel) *adj.* Tumbledown, rickety.

In many international and some domestic air terminals roll-up ramps have been replaced by permanently installed walkways which protect passengers from any inclement weather and make boarding speedier.

ram·son (răm´son) *n.* Broad-leaved garlic (*Allium ursinum*) bulbous root of this, used in salads and relishes.

ran: see RUN[1].

ranch (rănch, rahnch) *n.* 1 Large farm, esp. in western U.S and Canada, including buildings grazing lands, etc., where cattle sheep, or horses are raised. 2. Any large farm specializing in a crop or particular kind of animal; ~ **house**, suburban house with all rooms on one floor, usu. with attached garage. **ranch** *v.* Operate or work on ranch. **ranch´er** *n.* **ranch´man** *n.* (pl. **-men**). [Span *rancho* mess, persons feeding together]

ran·cid (răn´sĭd) *adj.* Smelling or tasting like rank stale fat. **ran´cid·ness, ran·cid·i·ty** (rănsĭd´ītē) *ns.*

ran·cor (răng´ker) *n.* Inveterate bitterness, malignant hate, spitefulness. **ran´cor·ous** *adj.* **ran´cor·ous·ly** *adv.*

R & D, R. & D. *abbrevs.* Research and development.

Ran·dolph (răn´dŏlf), **Edmund Jennings** (1753–1813). Amer statesman; governor of Virginia 1786–8; delegate to the Constitutional Convention, 1787, where

*Of the twelve Egyptian kings in the 19th Dynasty, Rameses, who used the name **Rameses III** (1198–69 B.C.) is acknowledged to have been one of the greatest. He conquered Ethiopia and fought the Greeks and Philistines.*

The **ramson** or broad-leaved garlic, which was native to western Asia and eastern Europe, has long been considered both a medicinal and a culinary herb. However, ordinary garlic is preferred.

To protect flora and fauna on proclaimed reserves, and other species which may occur outside those areas, governments employ **rangers**. This ranger in N.S.W., Australia is talking to a local property owner.

e presented the Virginia Plan, which provided for two legislative ouses and legislatively selected dicial and executive branches; rst U.S. attorney general, 1789–794; U.S. secretary of State, 1794–795.

ran·dom (răn′dom) *n.* **at** ~, nsystematically; without aim, urpose, or principle. ~ *adj.* Made, done, etc., at random. **ran′-om·ize** *v.t.* (**-ized, -iz·ing**). an′dom·ly *adv.* **ran′dom·ness** [OF. *random* great speed *andir* gallop)]

R & R, R and R *abbrevs.* Rest nd recreation; rest and recupera-on.

ran·dy (răn′dē) *adj.* (**-di·er, -di·est**). Lustful, eager for sexual ratification.

ra·nee: RANI.

rang: see RING².

range (rānj) *n.* 1. Row, line, er, or series, of things, esp. of ountains; horizontal direction, e. 2. Liberty to range; area over hich ranging takes place or is ossible; stretch of grazing or unting ground; piece of ground ith targets for shooting; area over hich plant etc. is distributed, area cluded in or concerned with omething, scope, compass, gister; limits of variation, limited ale or series; distance attainable y gun or projectile, distance tween gun, camera, etc., and

objective; ~ **finder**, instrument for estimating this distance. 3. Large cooking stove, usu. with oven(s), broiler(s), and top plate for boiling, frying, etc. **range** *v.* (**ranged, rang·ing**). 1. Place or arrange in a row or ranks or in specified situation, order, or company; run in a line, reach, lie spread out, extend; be found or occur over specified district; vary between limits; be level (*with*), rank or find right place *with* or *among.* 2. Rove, wander; go all about (place), sail along or about (coast, sea). 3. (of gun) Throw projectile over, (of projectile) traverse, (distance).

rang·er (rān′jer) *n.* (esp.) 1. Warden of forest, national park, etc. 2. Member of commando unit.

Ran·goon (rănggōon′). Capital city and seaport of Burma, on Rangoon River, one of the mouths of the Irrawaddy.

rang·y (rān′jē) *adj.* (**rang·i·er, rang·i·est**). Having long slender form.

ra·ni, ra·nee (rah′nē) *ns.* (pl. **-nis, -nees**). (hist.) Hindu queen or princess. [Hind. *rāṇī, rānī* fem. of RAJAH]

rank¹ (răngk) *n.* 1. Row, line;

(mil.) number of soldiers drawn up in single line abreast; **the** ~**s,** ~ **and file**, common soldiers; (transf.) ordinary people, as dist. from their leaders. 2. Distinct social class, grade of dignity, station; high station; **persons of** ~, members of nobility. 3. Place in a scale. **rank** *v.* Arrange (esp. soldiers) in rank; classify, give certain grade to; have rank or place; have senior position among members of hierarchy etc.

rank² (răngk) *adj.* Too luxuriant, coarse, choked with or apt to produce weeds; foul-smelling, offensive; loathsome, corrupt; flagrant, virulent. **rank′ly** *adv.* **rank′ness** *n.*

Ran·kin (răng′kĭn), Jeanette (1880–1973). Amer. feminist leader and legislator; 1st woman member of U.S. House of Representatives, 1917–19, 1941–3.

ran·kle (răng′kel) *v.i.* (**-kled, -kling**). (of wound etc.) Fester (archaic); (of unpleasant experience, insult, etc.) remain as painful memory, cause continued bitterness or resentment. [OF. (*d*)*rancle* festering sore, f. LL. *dracunculus,* dim. of *draco* serpent]

ran·sack (răn′săk) *v.t.* Thoroughly search; pillage, plunder. **ran′sack·er** *n.*

ran·som (răn′som) *n.* (Liberation of prisoner of war or other captive in consideration of) sum of money or value paid for release; **king's** ~, large sum. **ransom** *v.t.* Buy freedom or restoration of; set free on payment of ransom.

rant (rănt) *v.* Speak, declaim,

*Known both as the lesser celandine and the pilewort, this plant is grouped in the genus **ranunculus**. This contains both annuals and perennials, which are found in temperate and cold areas, and in mountains in the tropics.*

*A martial eagle with a freshly caught rabbit. The eagle is a **raptorial**, or predatory, creature. The term can be used to describe birds or animals which prey on others, such as lions, leopards, hawks and bustards.*

recite in a vehement or loud manner. ~ *n.* Piece of ranting, tirade; empty turgid talk. **rant′er** *n.*

ra·nun·cu·lus (ranŭng′kyul͟us) *n.* (pl. **-lus·es, -li** pr. -lī). Plant of genus *R* ~, including buttercups.

rap[1] (răp) *n.* Smart slight blow; sound made by knocker on door etc.; sound as of striking wooden surface supposed to be produced by spirit at seance; (slang) chat, discussion; (slang) blame, punishment (esp. in **take the** ~); **beat the** ~, (slang) evade punishment. **rap** *v.* (**rapped, rap′ping**). Strike (esp. person's knuckles) smartly; make the sound called a rap; (slang) talk, discuss.

rap[2] (răp) *n.* Counterfeit coin passed for halfpenny in Ireland in 18th c.; the least bit (esp. in *not care a* ~).

ra·pa·cious (rapā′shus) *adj.* Grasping, avaricious; predatory. **ra·pa′cious·ly** *adv.* **ra·pac′i·ty** (rapăs′ĭtē), **ra·pa′cious·ness** *ns.*

rape[1] (răp) *v.t.* (**raped, rap·ing**). Take by force (poet.); violate chastity of, force to submit to sexual intercourse. ~ *n.* Carrying off by force (poet.); ravishing or violation of a person; (law) unlawful sexual intercourse with a woman without her consent. **rap′er, rap′ist** *ns.*

rape[2] (răp) *n.* Plant (*Brassica napus*) grown as fodder and for its seed, **rape′seed**, which yields oil; coleseed.

rape[3] (răp) *n.* Refuse of grapes after wine-making, used in making vinegar.

Raph·a·el[1] (răf′ēel, rā′fē-; *It.* rahfahyĕl′). One of the archangels; commemorated Oct. 24.

Raph·a·el[2] (răf′ēel, rā′fē-; *It.* rahfahyĕl′) (1483–1520). Full name Raffaello Sanzio or Santi; Italian Renaissance painter; famous for "La Belle Jardinière," "Coronation of the Virgin," the Vatican frescoes; chief architect of St. Peter's in Rome. **Raph·a·el·esque** (răf-ēelĕsk′, rahfīlĕsk′) *adj.* In the style of Raphael.

rap·id (răp′ĭd) *adj.* Characterized by, moving or acting with, great speed. **ra·pid·i·ty** (rapĭd′ĭtē), **rap′id·ness** *ns.* **rap′id·ly** *adv.* **rapid** *n.* Steep descent in riverbed, with swift current.

ra·pi·er (rā′pēer) *n.* Light slender sword for thrusting only.

rap·ine (răp′ĭn, -īn) *n.* (rhet.) Plundering, robbery.

Rap·pa·han·nock (răpahăn′ok). River in NE. Virginia, flowing SE. 185 mi., (298 km), from the Blue Ridge Mountains to Chesapeake Bay.

rap·pel (răpĕl′, ra-) *n.* & *v.*

(**-pelled, -pel·ling**). (Make) descent of steep rock face by using doubled rope fixed at higher point

rap·port (răpōr′, -pōr′) *n.* (Esp useful) communication (harmonious) relationship, or connection (*in rapport with*).

rap·proche·ment (rahprawsh-mahn′) *n.* Reestablishment o recommencement of harmoniou relations, esp. between nations [Fr.]

rap·scal·lion (răpskăl′yon) *n* Rogue.

rapt (răpt) *adj.* (orig. past part of RAPE[1]) Carried away in spiri from consciousness or ordinar thoughts and perceptions absorbed, enraptured, intent.

rap·to·ri·al (răptōr′ēal, -tōr′-*adj.* Predatory, (as) of predator birds or animals; (zool.) of th Raptores, an order of birds of prey including eagles, hawks, buzzards etc.

rap·ture (răp′cher) *n.* (Expres sion of) ecstatic delight. **rap·tur ous** *adj.* **rap′tur·ous·ly** *adv.*

ra·ra a·vis (rār′a ā′vĭs; *La* rah′rah ah′wĭs) (pl. **ra·rae a·ve** pr. rār′ē ā′vēz; *Lat.* rah′rī ah′wĕs) Rarity, kind of person or thin rarely encountered. [L., = "rar bird"]

rare[1] (rār) *adj.* (**rar·er, rar·est** 1. (of gases) Not dense; wit constituent particles not closel packed together. 2. Uncommon unusual, seldom found or occur ring; highly valued owing t uncommonness or scarcity; ver amusing. 3. ~ **earth**, (basic oxid of) a ~**-earth** element, any o

Related to the cabbage and similar vegetables, **rape** has long been culti-vated for its seeds which are crushed to produce colza oil. It is used as a lubri-cant, and in soap; and, after process-ing, for cooking in India.

the elements from lanthanum to lutetium inclusive in the PERIODIC table, together with those of scandium and yttrium. **rare′ly** *adv.* **rare′ness** *n.*

rare² (rār) *adj.* (**rar·er, rar·est**). (of meat) Cooked only a short time, still red or pink inside.

rare·bit (rār′bĭt): see WELSH rabbit.

rar·e·fy (rār′efī) *v.* (**-fied, -fy-ing**). Lessen density or solidity of (esp. air); purify, refine.

rar·ing (rār′ĭng) *adj.* (colloq.) Enthusiastic, eager, (*to go* etc.).

rar·i·ty (rār′ĭtē, răr′-) *n.* (pl. **-ties**). Rareness; uncommon thing, thing valued as being rare.

Ra·ro·ton·ga (rărotŏng′ga). Island in the Cook Islands in the S. Pacific Ocean; site of Avarua, capital of the Cook Islands.

ras·cal (răs′kal, rahs′-) *n.* Rogue (freq. used playfully to child etc.). **ras·cal·i·ty** (răskăl′ĭtē, rahs-) *n.* **ras′cal·ly** *adj. & adv.*

rase: RAZE.

rash¹ (răsh) *n.* Eruption of the skin in spots or patches.

rash² (răsh) *adj.* Hasty, im-petuous, overbold, reckless; acting or done without due consideration. **rash′ly** *adv.* **rash′ness** *n.*

rash·er (răsh′er) *n.* Thin slice of bacon; a serving of bacon, usu. three or four slices.

rasp (răsp, rahsp) *n.* Coarse kind of file with separate teeth raised by means of pointed punch; harsh, grating sound. ~ *v.* Scrape with rasp; scrape roughly; grate upon, irritate; make grating sound. **rasp′er** *n.* **rasp′ing·ly** *adv.* **rasp′y** *adj.* (**rasp·i·er, rasp·i·est**).

rasp·ber·ry (răz′bĕrē, -berē, rahz′-) *n.* (pl. **-ries**). 1. (Plant, *Rubus strigosus* of eastern N. Amer. and *R. idaeus* of Europe bearing) usu. red subacid fruit of many small juicy drupelets arranged on conical receptacle. 2. (slang) Sound or gesture expressing derision or dis-like.

Ras·pu·tin (răspū′tĭn; *Russ.* rahspoo′tĭn), **Grigori Efimovich** (1871–1916). Russian monk and mystic who acquired great influence over the household of Nicholas II; he was assassinated as result of a conspiracy among a group of nobles.

Ras·ta·fa·ri·an (rŭstafār′ēan) *adj. & n.* (Member of) Jamaican

This serene painting by **Raphael** of St. Catherine of Alexandria against a placid Italian landscape, is typical of the Renaissance with its expressive pose and subtle coloring.

sect regarding blacks as a chosen people. [f. *Ras Tafari*, title and orig. name of Emperor Haile Selassie of Ethiopia (1891–1975), venerated by sect as a god]

rat (răt) *n.* 1. Rodent of genus *Rattus*, esp. the **black** ~ (*R. rattus*), found esp. on shipboard, and the larger **brown** ~ (*R. norvegicus*) which is now the commoner, both regarded as pests, infesting sewers, warehouses, docks, etc., and acting as carriers of several diseases; any rodent resembling this. 2. (slang) Despicable person; betrayer; informer; sneak. 3. **smell a** ~, have suspicions; ~**s!** (slang) expression of disappointment or disbelief; **rat'catcher**, person whose business is to catch rats; **rat race**, (colloq.) fiercely competitive struggle, struggle to maintain one's position in work or life; **rats'bane**, rat poison; **rat-tail(ed)**, (of file

The Australian black-footed tree **rat** *is one of the true rats found in Australia. Some of these are introduced pest species. The kangaroo rat is more correctly a hopping mouse but in behavior and adaptation it is similar to the jerboa of North Africa.*

etc.) shaped like rat's tail. 4. **rat'trap**, trap for rats. **rat** *v.i.* (**rat·ted, rat·ting**). Hunt or kill rats; betray or inform on one's friends. **rat'ter** *n.*

rat-a-tat (răt'ătăt), **rat-a-tat-tat** (răt'ătăttăt') *ns.* Series of short sharp sounds, as rapid knocks, machine gun fire, etc.

ratch·et (răch'ĭt) *n.* Set of angular or sawlike teeth on edge of bar or wheel, into which a cog, click, or pawl may catch, usu. for the purpose of preventing reverse motion; (also ~ **wheel**) wheel with rim so toothed.

rate[1] (răt) *n.* 1. Estimated value or worth; price, sum paid or asked

African giant rat — stick rat — fat sand rat — wood rat — black rat — brown rat — kangaroo rat

for single thing. 2. Amount or number of one thing corresponding or having some relation to certain amount or number of another thing; value as applicable to each piece or equal quantity of something; basis of exchange; amount (*of* charge or payment), esp. in relation to some other amount or basis of calculation; degree of speed, relative speed; relative amount of variation, increase, etc. 3. Degree of action, feeling, etc. 4. **at any** ~, at all events, at least; **at this (that) rate**, things being so, under these circumstances. **rate** *v.* (**rat·ed, rat·ing**). Estimate worth or value of; assign fixed value to in relation to monetary standard; consider, regard as; rank or be rated *as.*

rate² (rāt) *v.* (**rat·ed, rat·ing**). Scold angrily.

rath·er (rådh´er, rah´dher) *adv.* 1. More truly or correctly, more properly speaking; more readily, all the more. 2. More (so) than not; to some extent, somewhat, slightly. 3. By preference, for choice, sooner (*than*); more properly. 4. (chiefly Brit. colloq., pr. rah´dher´, in answer to question) Most emphatically, yes without doubt.

raths·kel·ler (råt´skěler, raht´-, råth´-) *n.* Restaurant in style of basement of a German town hall (*Rathaus*) where beer is sold.

rat·i·fy (råt´ifī) *v.t.* (**-fied, -fy·ing**). Confirm or make valid (esp. what has been done or arranged for by another) by giving consent, approval, or formal sanction. **rat·i·fi·ca·tion** (rått-ifikā´shon) *n.*

ra·ti·né (råtinā´) *n.* Dress fabric of rough open texture.

rat·ing¹ (rā´tǐng) *n.* (esp.) 1. Classification according to class, grade, or rank. 2. Limit of performance, as of range, operational capability, etc. 3. Estimated standing of person, esp. *credit* rating. 4. Estimated number of audience as index of popularity of a broadcast.

rat·ing² (rā´tǐng) *n.* Angry reprimand.

ra·tio (rā´shō, -shēō) *n.* (pl. **-tios**). Quantitative relation between two similar magnitudes determined by number of times one contains the other integrally or fractionally (*27 and 18 are in the* ~ *of 3 to 2 or 3 : 2; the* ~**s** *1 : 5 and 20 : 100 are the same*).

ra·ti·o·ci·nate (råshēŏs´ǐnāt) *v.i.* (**-nat·ed, -nat·ing**). Reason, carry on process of reasoning. **ra·ti·o-ci·na·tion** (råshēōsǐnā´shon) *n.* **ra·ti·o·ci·na·tive** *adj.* **ra·ti·o´-ci·na·tor** *n.*

ra·tion (råsh´on, rā´shon) *n.* Fixed allowance or individual share of provisions, esp. daily allowance for person in armed forces; (pl.)

Although **rattan** *is now grown widely in Asia, this climbing palm was originally native to Assam and India where its shoots and seeds are eaten, and its vines used for basketwork.*

provisions. ~ *v.t.* Put on fixed allowance of provisions etc.; share (food etc.) in fixed quantities; limit to specific allotment, as during wartime or a time of scarcity.

ra·tion·al (råsh´onal) *adj.* Endowed with reason, reasoning; sensible, sane; based on, derived from, reason or reasoning; not foolish, absurd, or extravagant; (math., of ratio or quantity) expressible without radical signs; ~ **number**, number that can be expressed exactly as an integer or quotient of the integers. **ra·tion·al·ly** *adv.* **ra·tion·al·i·ty** (råshonål´ǐte) *n.* (pl. **-ties**).

ra·tion·ale (råshonål´) *n.* Reasoned exposition of principles; logical or rational basis *of* or *for.*

ra·tion·al·ism (råsh´onalǐzem) *n.* Practice of explaining the supernatural in religion in a way consonant with reason, or of treating reason as the ultimate authority in religion as elsewhere; theory that reason is foundation of certainty in knowledge. **ra·tion·al·ist** *n.* & *adj.* **ra·tion·al·is·tic** (råshonålǐs´tǐk)

adj. **ra·tion·al·is·ti·cal·ly** *adv.*

ra·tion·al·ize (råsh´onalīz) *v.* (**-ized, -iz·ing**). 1. Explain, explain *away*, by rationalism; bring into conformity with reason; be or act as a rationalist. 2. (math.) Clear from irrational quantities. **ra·tion·al·i·za·tion** (råshonalīzā´-shon), **ra·tion·al·iz·er** *ns.*

rat·ite (råt´īt) *adj.* & *n.* (Flightless bird) having a flat unkeeled breastbone, as the ostrich and emu.

rat·line, rat·lin (råt´lǐn) *ns.* (One of) small lines fastened across ship's shrouds like ladder rungs.

ra·toon (råtoon´) *n.* New shoot springing from foot of plant, esp. sugar cane, after cropping ~ *v.* Send up ratoons; cut down (plant) to induce ratooning.

rat·tan (råtån´) *n.* Climbing palm of genus *Calamus* with long thin pliable jointed stems, growing chiefly in E. Indies; piece of rattan stem used as cane or for other purposes; rattans used as material in building etc.

rat·tle (råt´el) *v.* (**-tled, -tling**). 1. Give out rapid succession of short sharp hard sounds, cause such sounds by shaking something; move or fall with rattling noise; make rattle. 2. Say or recite rapidly; talk in lively thoughtless way. 3. (slang) Shake nerves of, fluster, frighten. ~ *n.* 1. Instrument or plaything made to rattle, esp. in order to make music or to amuse babies; end of rattlesnake's tail (see below). 2. Rattling sound; rattling sound in throat caused by partial obstruction; noisy flow of words; empty or trivial talk. 3. **rat´tle-snake**, any of several venomous Amer. snakes of genus *Crotalus* or *Sistrurus*, with horny rings at end of tail making rattling noise when vibrated; **rat´tletrap**, rickety, shaky vehicle.

rat·tler (råt´ler) *n.* (esp.) Rattle-snake.

rat·tling (råt´lǐng) *adj.* (slang) Remarkably good.

rat·ty (råt´ē) *adj.* (**-ti·er, -ti·est**). Ratlike, esp. (slang) shabby, dilapidated.

rau·cous (raw´kus) *adj.* Hoarse, harshsounding. **rau´cous·ly** *adv.* **rau´cous·ness** *n.*

The **rattlesnake's** *rattle is formed, a segment at a time, each time it moults. Part of the old skin is retained at the tip of the tail, forming a kind of bell or cap.*

raun·chy (rawn′chē, rahn′-) *adj.* (**-chi·er, -chi·est**). (slang) 1. Slovenly and dirty. 2. Smutty, obscene. **raun′chi·ness** *adj.*

rau·wol·fi·a (rawōōl′fēa) *n.* Any of several tropical trees and shrubs of the genus $R\sim$ many of which are poisonous and some of which yield medicinal substances, esp. *R. serpentina*, from whose roots the alkaloid reserpine is extracted.

rav·age (răv′ĭj) *v.* (**-aged, -ag·ing**). Devastate, plunder; make havoc. $\sim$ *n.* Devastation, damage, (esp., pl.) destructive effects *of*. **rav′a·ger** *n.*

rave (rāv) *v.* (**raved, rav·ing**). Talk wildly or furiously (as) in delirium; (of sea, wind, etc.) howl, roar; utter with ravings; speak or write with rapturous admiration *about* or *of*, go into raptures. $\sim$ *n.* Act, instance, of raving. $\sim$ *adj.* (of review of play, book, etc.) Extravagantly enthusiastic.

rav·el (răv′el) *v.* (**-eled, -el·ing**, Brit. **-elled, -el·ling**). 1. Entangle or become entangled, confuse, complicate. 2. Disentangle, unravel. $\sim$ *n.* Entanglement, knot, complication; frayed or loose end.

Ra·vel (ravĕl′; *Fr.* rahvĕl′), **Maurice** (1875–1937). French impressionistic musical composer.

ra·ven[1] (rā′ven) *n.* Large black hoarse-voiced bird (*Corvus corax*), both Amer. and European, feeding chiefly on carrion or other flesh; related species. $\sim$ *adj.* Of glossy black.

rav·en[2] (răv′en) *v.* Plunder, go plundering *about*, seek *after* prey or booty; prowl for prey; eat voraciously.

Ra·ven·na (ravĕn′a; *It.* rahvĕn′-nah). City in NE. Italy, founded before Roman era; became the western capital of the Empire after the fall of Rome, and was the seat of Theodoric's court; was added to the Papal States, 1509; passed to Italy, 1860.

rav·e·nous (răv′enus) *adj.* Voracious; very hungry. **rav′e·nous·ly** *adv.* **rav′e·nous·ness** *n.*

ra·vine (ravēn′) *n.* Deep narrow gorge, mountain cleft.

ra·vi·o·li (răvēō′lē) *n.* (considered sing. or pl.) (Italian dish of) small pasta cases containing meat etc., served in sauce. [It.]

rav·ish (răv′ish) *v.t.* 1. Carry off (person, thing) by force (now rare); rape. 2. Enrapture. **rav′ish·ing** *adj.* Entrancing. **rav′ish·ing·ly** *adv.* **rav′ish·ment, rav′ish·er** *ns.*

raw (raw) *adj.* 1. Uncooked; in natural or unwrought state, not yet dressed or manufactured; **raw′hide**, untanned leather; rope or whip of this; **raw material**, that out of which any process of manufacture makes the articles it produces; **raw silk**, silk as reeled from cocoons. 2. Crude, not brought to perfect composition or finish; uncivilized, brutal; **raw deal**, (colloq.) harsh or unfair treatment. 3. Inexperienced, untrained; unskilled. 4. Stripped of skin, excoriated; sensitive to touch from being so exposed; **raw′boned**, with projecting bones hardly covered with flesh, gaunt. 5. (of weather etc.) Damp and chilly, bleak. **raw′ness** *n.*

ray[1] (rā) *n.* 1. Single line or narrow beam of light; straight line in which radiant energy capable of producing sensation of light is propagated to or from given point; analogous propagation line of heat or other nonluminous physical energy; (fig.) remnant or beginning of enlightening or cheering influence; ROENTGEN $\sim$, X-RAY: see these words. 2. Any of the lines forming a set of straight lines pass-

ing through one point; any of a set of radiating lines, parts, or things; (bot.) marginal part of composite flower, as daisy; (zool.) radial division of starfish or other echinoderm. **ray** *v.* Issue, come *forth, off, out*, in rays; radiate (poet.).

ray[2] (rā) *n.* Any of several cartilaginous fishes (order Rajiformes), as the electric ray, stingray, skate, etc., having broad, flat bodies, expanded fins, whiplike tails.

Ray·burn (rā′bĕrn), **Sam(uel Taliaferro)** (1882–1961). Amer. lawyer and politician; member of U.S. House of Representatives, 1913–61, and speaker of the House, 1940–6, 1949–53, 1955–61.

Ray·leigh (rā′lē), **John William Strutt, 3rd Baron** (1842–1919). English mathematician and physicist; discoverer (with Ramsay) of argon; received Nobel Prize for Physics, 1904.

ray·on (rā′ŏn) *n.* Textile fiber made from cellulose; any of various textiles made from such fiber.

raze, Brit. **rase** (rāz) *v.t.* (**razed, raz·ing**, Brit. **rased, ras·ing**). Completely destroy; level with the ground.

ra·zor (rā′zer) *n.* Sharp-edged instrument used in shaving hair from skin; **ra′zorback**, kind of whale, rorqual; $\sim$**-billed auk**, N. Atlantic seabird (*Alca torda*) with black and white plumage; $\sim$ **edge**, keen edge. [f. OF. *rasor*, f. *raser*]

razz (răz) *v.* (slang) Tease, ridicule. $\sim$ *n.* = RASPBERRY sense 2.

raz·zle-daz·zle (răz′eldăz′el) *n.* (slang) Excitement, bustle, stir, etc., often intended to confuse or bewilder.

razz·ma·tazz (răz′matăz) *n.* (slang) 1. Liveliness; excitement. 2. Flashy behavior meant to deceive or mislead.

Rb *symbol.* Rubidium.

r.b.i., rbi *abbrevs.* (baseball) Runs batted in.

R.C. *abbrev.* Red Cross; Roman Catholic.

R.C.A.F., RCAF *abbrevs.* Royal Canadian Air Force.

R.C.M.P. *abbrev.* Royal Canadian Mounted Police.

Rd., rd. *abbrevs.* Road.

R.D. *abbrev.* Rural delivery.

Re *symbol.* Rhenium.

re *prep.* In the matter of, concerning (chiefly in legal and business use as first word of heading stating matter to be dealt with). [L., ablative of *res* thing]

re- *prefix.* 1. Once more; afresh; repeated. 2. Back, with return to previous state.

REA, R.E.A. *abbrevs.* Rural Electrification Administration.

reach (rēch) *v.* Stretch out, extend; stretch out the hand etc.,

The name **raven** is applied to several of the larger members of the genus *Corvus* or crows, which are found in Europe, America, Africa and Australia.

...imilar to sharks in that they have car-...age but no true bones, most of the ...sh called **rays** are adapted to bottom ...welling. Like sharks, most give birth to ...ve young.

make reaching motion or effort (lit. and fig.); succeed in touching or grasping with hand or anything held in it, etc., extend to; come to, arrive at; hand, pass or take with outstretched hand; (naut.) sail with the wind abeam. ~ *n.* 1. Act of reaching out; extent to which hand etc. can be reached out; scope, range, compass. 2. Continuous extent, esp. part of river etc. lying between 2 bends.

re·act (rēăkt′) *v.i.* Act in return (*against* agent or influence); act, display energy, in response to stimulus; act in opposition to some force; move or tend in reverse direction; undergo change (esp. chemical change) under some influence.

re·act·ance (rēăk′tans) *n.* (elect.) That part of the impedance of an alternating current circuit which is due to capacitance or induction or both.

re·ac·tion (rēăk′shon) *n.* 1. Responsive or reciprocal action; return of previous condition after interval of opposite (e.g. depression after excitement); (loosely) opinion, impression; (physiol.) response of organ etc. to external stimulus; (chem.) interaction of 2 or more substances resulting in chemical change. 2. (pol.) (Movement toward) extreme conservatism.

re·ac·tion·ar·y (rēăk′shonĕrē) *adj.* & *n.* (pl. **-ar·ies**). (Person) inclined or favorable to reaction.

re·ac·tive (rēăk′tĭv) *adj.* Tending to react.

re·ac·tor (rēăk′ter) *n.* 1. Person or thing that reacts. 2. (elect.) Element, as a coil, put into a circuit to introduce reactance. 3. Apparatus in which nuclear fission chain reactions are started and controlled for generation of energy and production of medical and experimental materials; atomic pile (reactor), nuclear reactor.

read (rēd) *v.* (**read** pr. rĕd, **read·ing**). 1. Discover or expound significance of (dream, riddle, etc.); foresee, foretell (esp. *the future, one's fortune*). 2. (Be able to) convert into the intended words of meaning (written, printed, or other symbols, or things, expressed by their means); reproduce mentally or vocally, while following their symbols with eyes or fingers, the words of (author, book, letter, etc.); study by reading; find (thing) stated, find statement, in print, etc.; convey when read, run; (of recording instrument) present (figure, etc.) to one reading it; (of computer) copy or transfer (data) from (~ **in**) or to (~ **out**) magnetic

Razorbills spend the bulk of their time in coastal or offshore waters, rather than far out at sea. They are sociable, often associating with guillemots at cliff breeding sites.

tape etc., hence **read'in**, input of data to a computer; **read'out**, retrieval of information from digital computer; such information. 3. Interpret (statement, action) in certain sense; assume as intended in or deducible from writer's words, find implications; (of manuscript, editor, etc.) give as the word(s) probably used or intended by author; **read well, badly**, etc., (of written matter) sound or affect reader thus. 4. Bring into specified state by reading; **read out**, expel (from political party etc.) (as if) by reading form of dismissal. **read** (rĕd) *adj.* (esp., in active sense) **well ~**, versed *in* subject by reading; with good knowledge of literature.

Read (rĕd), **Sir Herbert (Edward)** (1893–1968). English poet and critic; author of *The Philosophy of Modern Art, Poetry and Anarchism*, etc.

read·a·ble (rē'dabel) *adj.* Interestingly written; legible. **read'a·ble·ness, read·a·bil'i·ty** *ns.* **read'a·bly** *adv.*

read·er (rē'der) *n.* (esp.) 1. Person employed by publisher to read and report on proffered manuscripts; proofreader. 2. Person appointed to read aloud, esp. (**lay ~**) parts of service in church. 3. Book containing passages for exercise in reading, instruction in foreign language, etc. **read'er·ship** *n.* Readers of, subscribers to, a publication.

read·i·ly (rĕd'ĭlē) *adv.* Without showing reluctance, willingly; without difficulty.

read·i·ness (rĕd'ĕnĭs) *n.* Prompt compliance, willingness; facility, prompt resourcefulness, quickness in argument or action; ready or prepared state.

read·ing (rē'dĭng) *n.* (esp.) 1. Entertainment at which something is read to audience. 2. Word(s) read or given by an editor etc. or found in manuscript in text of a passage; interpretation, view taken, rendering. 3. Figure etc. shown by graduated instrument. 4. (Specified quality of) matter to be read. 5. **~ desk**, desk for supporting book, etc., lectern; **~ room**, room in library, club, etc., for persons wishing to read.

read·y (rĕd'ē) *adj.* (**read·i·er, read·i·est**). With preparations complete; in fit state; with resolution nerved, willing; apt, inclined; about *to*; prompt, quick, facile; provided beforehand; within reach, easily secured; unreluctant; easy; fit for immediate use; **make ~**, prepare; **~ money**, cash, actual coin; money available for spending. **ready** *adv.* Beforehand, so as not to require doing when the time comes; **~-made**, (of clothes etc.) made in standard shapes and sizes, not custom-made. **ready** *n.* Position in which rifle is ready for use; (slang) ready money. **~** *v.t.* (**read·ied, read·y·ing**). Prepare.

Rea·gan (rā'gan), **Ronald** (1911–). Fortieth president of

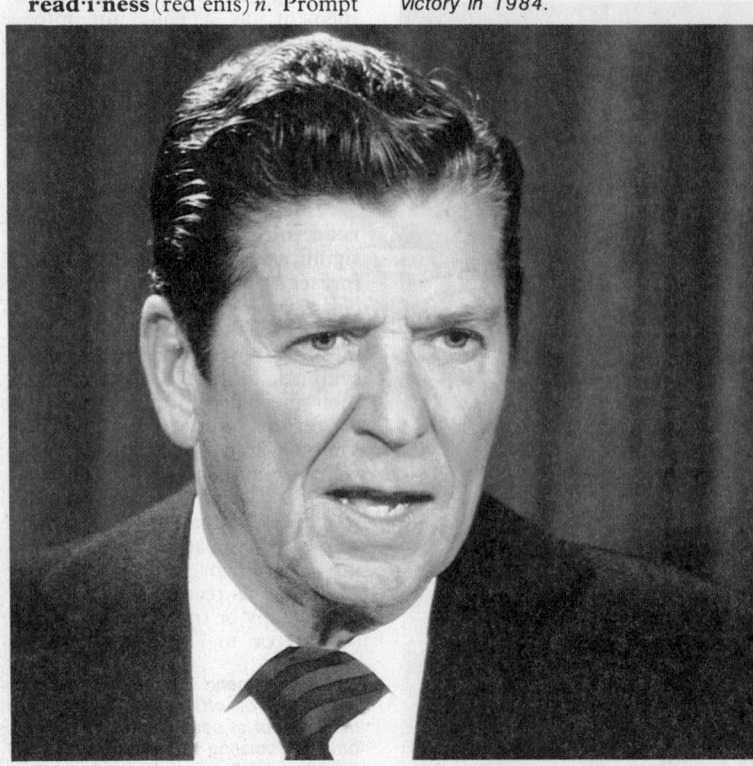

Ronald Reagan, retired Hollywood and T.V. actor and 40th president of the U.S.A. Formerly Governor of California, he defeated Jimmy Carter in the 1980 presidential elections and was re-elected for a 2nd term with a landslide victory in 1984.

the U.S., 1981– ; governor of California, 1966–74. Reagan defeated President Carter in a landslide victory, capturing 43 states and a total of 483 electoral votes, 270 more than needed for election.

re·a·gent (rēā'jent) *n.* Chemical substance used to produce a chemical reaction.

re·al¹ (rē'al, rēl; *Sp.* rěahl') *n.* (pl. **re·als**; *Sp.* **re·a·les** pr. rěah'lěs). Former silver coin and money of account used in Spain and some Spanish-speaking countries. [Spain, f. L. *regalis* regal]

re·al² (rē'al, rēl) *adj.* 1. Actually existing as a thing or occurring in fact, objective; genuine, rightly so called; natural, not artificial or depicted; actually present or involved, not merely apparent; **the ~ thing**, the thing itself, not an imitation or inferior article. 2. (law) Relating to things, esp. stationary or fixed property; **~ estate**: see ESTATE; (philos. etc.) relating to, concerned with, things. **real** *adv.* (colloq. usu. with adjectives) Really; very, extremely. **~** *n.* Real thing; what actually exists, esp. opp. the ideal.

re·al·gar (rēăl'ger) *n.* Arsenic disulfide (As_2S_2), red arsenic occurring as ore, used as pigment and in fireworks. [Arab. *rahj al-gār* dust of the cave]

re·al·ism (rē'alĭzem) *n.* 1. Scholastic doctrine that universal or general ideas have objective existence; belief that matter as object of perception has real existence. 2. Practice of regarding things in their true nature and dealing with them as they are; fidelity of representation, rendering precise details of real thing or scene. **re·al·ist** *n.* **re·al·is·tic** (rēalĭs'tĭk) *adj.* **re·al·is'ti·cal·ly** *adv.*

re·al·i·ty (rēăl'ĭtē) *n.* (pl. **-ties**) Property of being real; resemblance to original; real existence, what is real, what underlies appearances; existent thing; real nature *of*; **~ principle**, (psychoanal.) understanding of and adjustment to environment resulting in satisfaction of needs and achieving of long-range goals.

re·al·ize (rē'alīz) *v.t.* (**-ized, -iz·ing**). 1. Convert (hope, plan, etc.) into fact; give apparent reality to, make realistic, present as reality. 2. Conceive as real; apprehend clearly or in detail. 3. Make a gain or profit of; amass (fortune, specified profit), fetch as price. **re·al·iz·a·ble** *adj.* **re·al·i·za·tion** (rēalĭzā'shon), **re·al·iz·er** *ns.*

re·al·ly (rē'alē, rē'lē) *adv.* In fact, in reality; positively, indeed; (interrog.) is that so?

realm (rělm) *n.* Kingdom sphere, province, domain.

re·al·po·li·tik (rāahlpōlĭtēk') *n*

politics based on realities and material needs, not on ideology or ethics. [Ger., = "real politics"]

Re·al·tor (rē′alter, rēl′-) *n.* (trademark) Real-estate agent who is a member or affiliated member of the National Association of Real Estate Boards.

re·al·ty (rē′altē, rēl′-) *n.* Real estate.

ream¹ (rēm) *n.* Five hundred sheets of paper; (freq. pl.) large quantity; **printers'** ~, 516 sheets. [Arab. *rizmah* bundle]

ream² (rēm) *v.t.* Widen (hole in metal or smoker's pipe) with reamer. **ream′er** *n.* Device, usu. metal, used in reaming.

reap (rēp) *v.* Cut (grain or similar crop), cut grain, etc., with sickle etc. in harvest; gather in thus, or fig. as harvest; harvest crop of field etc.).

reap·er (rē′per) *n.* 1. One who reaps; **grim** ~, death. 2. Mechanical device for reaping crops (and binding sheaves) without manual labor.

rear¹ (rēr) *n.* 1. Hindmost part of army or fleet; back of, space behind, position at back, of, army or camp or person; back part of anything; **bring up the** ~, come last. 2. (attrib.) Hinder, back; ~ **admiral**, officer in navy, next

The 19th-century term **realism** was adopted by writers such as de Maupassant and Flaubert and painters including Courbet, whose 'La Fileuse Endormie' confirms the view that everything should be portrayed objectively.

below vice admiral; ~ **guard**, body of troops detached to protect rear, esp. in retreats. **rear′most** *adj.* Farthest back. **rear′ward, rear′-wards** *adjs. & advs.* **rear′ward** *n.*

rear² (rēr) *v.* 1. Raise, set upright, build. 2. Bring up, raise (children); breed; cultivate. 3. (of horse etc.) Rise on hind feet.

re·arm (rēärm′) *v.* Arm again, esp. with more modern weapons or after disarming. **re·ar′ma-ment** *n.*

rea·son (rē′zon) *n.* 1. (Fact adduced or serving as) argument, motive, cause, or justification; (logic) one of premises of syllogism, esp. minor premise when given after conclusion. 2. Intellectual faculty characteristic esp. of human beings by which conclusions are drawn from premises; intellect personified; (tr. Kant's *Vernunft*) faculty transcending the understanding and providing a priori principles, intuition. 3. Sanity; sense; sensible conduct; what is

right, practical, or practicable; moderation; **listen to** ~, allow oneself to be persuaded; **it stands to** ~, it cannot reasonably be denied. **rea′son·er** *n.* **reason** *v.* 1. Use argument *with* person by way of persuasion; persuade by argument *out of, into.* 2. Form or try to reach conclusions by connected thought; discuss *what, whether,* etc.; conclude, assume as step in argument, say by way of argument, (*that*); express in logical or argumentative form; think *out.* **rea′son·ing** *adj. & n.*

rea·son·a·ble (rē′zonabel) *adj.* 1. Endowed with reason, reasoning (rare). 2. Of sound judgment, sensible, moderate, not expecting too much, ready to listen to reason. 3. Agreeable to reason, not absurd, within the limits of reason; not greatly less or more than might be expected; inexpensive, not extortionate; tolerable, fair. **rea′son-a·ble·ness** *n.* **rea′son·a·bly** *adv.*

re·as·sure (rēashoor′) *v.* (**-sured, -sur·ing**). Restore (person etc.) to confidence; confirm again in opinion or impression; reinsure. **re·as·sur′ance** *n.* **re·as·sur′ing·ly** *adv.*

re·a·ta: RIATA.

Ré·au·mur (rā′umūr; *Fr.* rĕō-mür′), René Antoine Ferchault

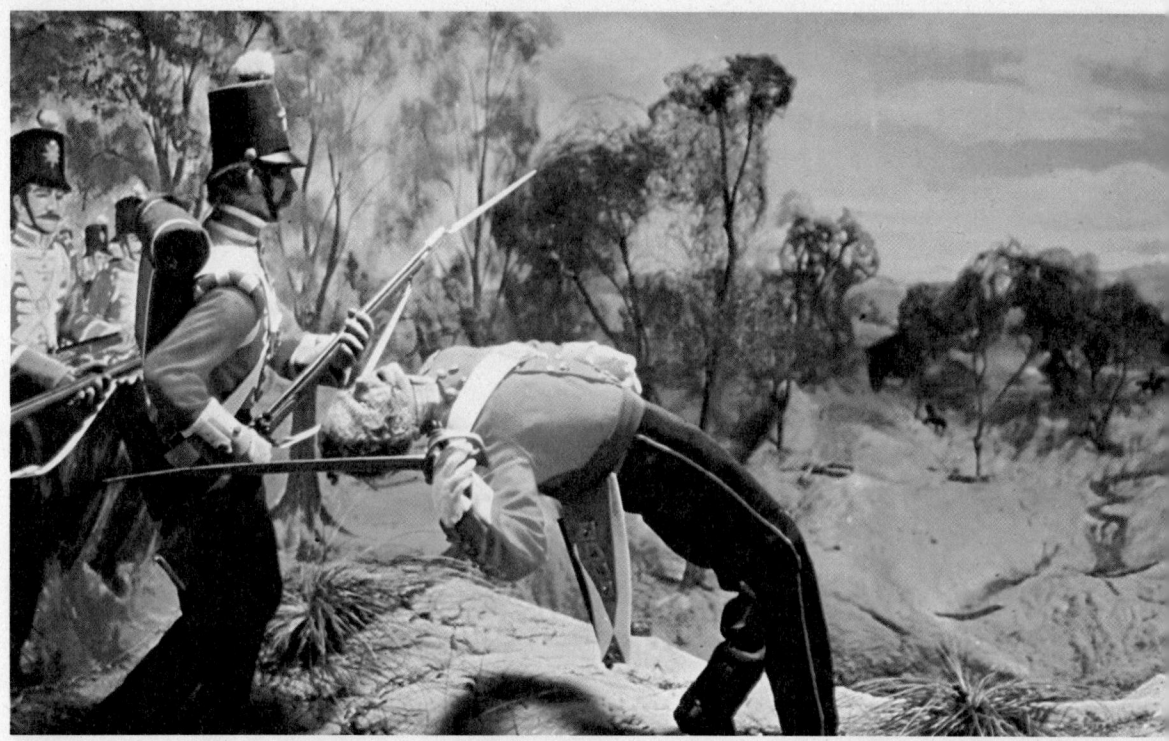

de (1683–1757). French scientist; ~ **scale**, scale in which the freezing point of water is 0° and the boiling point 80°.

reave, reive (rēv) *vbs.* (**reaved** or **reft** pr. rĕft, **reav·ing, reived, reiv·ing**). (archaic, poet.) Commit ravages; forcibly deprive *of* (usu. in past part.); bereave; take by force, carry off. **reiv′er** *n.* Marauder, raider.

re·bate (rē′bāt) *n.* Deduction from sum to be paid, discount, return of part of payment. ~ (rĭbāt′, rē′bāt) *v.t.* (**-bat·ed, -bat·ing**). Deduct or return from payment.

re·bec, re·beck (rē′bĕk) *ns.* Medieval three-stringed instrument, early form of fiddle. [Arab. *rabāb*]

Re·bec·ca (rĭbĕk′a). Wife of Isaac and mother of Jacob and Esau (Gen. 25 ff.).

reb·el (rĕb′el) *n.* Person who rises in arms against, resists, or refuses allegiance to, the established government; person or thing that resists authority or control; (attrib.) rebellious, of rebels, in rebellion. ~ (rĭbĕl′) *v.i.* (**-elled, -el·ling**). Act as rebel (*against*); feel or manifest repugnance to some custom etc. (*against*).

re·bel·lion (rĭbĕl′yon) *n.* Organized armed resistance to established government; open resistance to any authority.

re·bel·lious (rĭbĕl′yus) *adj.* In rebellion; disposed to rebel, insubordinate, defying lawful authority; unmanageable, refractory. **re·bel′·lious·ly** *adv.* **re·bel′lious·ness** *n.*

A law that miners had to pay for licences to prospect at the Ballarat gold rush in Australia in 1854, resulted in a **rebellion** known as the Eureka Stockade. It was the beginning of colonial Australia's move towards self-government.

re·birth (rēbē̆rth′, rē′bē̆rth) *n.* New or second birth (fig.); fresh incarnation; spiritual enlightenment; revival. (John 3).

re·born (rēbōrn′) *adj.* Having undergone rebirth.

re·bound (rĭbownd′) *v.i.* Spring back after impact; have reactive effect, recoil upon agent. ~ (rē′bownd, rĭbownd′) *n.* Act of rebounding, recoil; reaction after emotion.

re·buff (rĭbŭf′) *n.* Check given to one who makes advances, proffers help or sympathy, shows interest or curiosity, makes request, etc.; snub. ~ *v.t.* Give rebuff to.

re·buke (rĭbūk′) *v.t.* (**-buked, -buk·ing**). Convey stern disapproval or censure to (person) *for* fault etc. ~ *n.* Rebuking, being rebuked; reproof. **re·buk′·ing·ly** *adv.*

re·bus (rē′bus) *n.* (pl. **-bus·es**). Enigmatic representation of name, word, etc., by pictures etc. suggesting its syllables.

re·but (rĭbŭt′) *v.t.* (**-but·ted, -but·ting**). Force or turn back, give check to (archaic); refute, disprove (evidence, charge). **re·but′tal, re·but′ter** *ns.*

re·cal·ci·trant (rĭkăl′sĭtrant) *adj. & n.* Obstinately disobedient or refractory (person). **re·cal·ci-**

trance, **re·cal′ci·tran·cy** *ns.*

re·call (rĭkawl′) *v.t.* Summon back from or to a place, from different occupation, inattention, digression, etc.; bring back t memory, cause to remember; recollect, remember; restore; take back withdraw; call back (dangerous o defective manufactured item) fo modification or replacement. ~ (rĭkawl′, rē′kawl) *n.* Summons t return to or from a place; signa to return; possibility of recalling revoking, or annulling; recollection remembrance; act of removing, o right of removal of, an official from public office by popular vote afte petition; process of calling back (esp. automobile) for replacemen or repair. **re·call′a·ble** *adj.*

re·cant (rĭkănt′) *v.* Withdraw and renounce (opinion, statement etc.) as erroneous or heretical disavow former opinion, esp. with public confession of error **re·can·ta·tion** (rēkăntā′shon), **re** **cant′er** *ns.*

re·cap[1] (rē′kăp) *v.* (**-capped -cap·ping**). (colloq.) Recapitulate ~ *n.* Recapitulation.

re·cap[2] (rē′kăp, rēkăp′) *v* (**-capped, -cap·ping**). Put ca back on (bottle etc.); RETREAD.

re·ca·pit·u·late (rēkapĭch′ulāt *v.t.* (**-lat·ed, -lat·ing**). Give gis or substance of (what has already been said); summarize, restat briefly. **re·ca·pit·u·la·tion** (rē kapĭchulā′shon) *n.* **re·ca·pit·u·la·tive** *adj.*

re·cast (rēkăst′, -kahst′) *v.t* (**-cast, -cast·ing**). (esp.) Refashion, remodel, reconstruct; give new form or character to.

recd., rec'd. *abbrevs.* Received.

re·cede (rĭsēd´) *v.i.* (**-ced·ed, -ced·ing**). Go back or farther off; become more distant; slope backward; withdraw (*from* opinion etc.).

re·ceipt (rĭsēt´) *n.* 1. (archaic) Recipe. 2. Amount of money received; fact or action of receiving or being received into person's hands or possession; written acknowledgment of such receipt, esp. of payment of sum due. ~ *v.t.* Write or print receipt on (bill).

re·ceive (rĭsēv´) *v.t.* (**-ceived, -ceiv·ing**). 1. Take into one's hands or possession; accept (something proffered); accept or buy (stolen goods) from thief; take (bread and wine of Eucharist); admit, consent or prove able to hold, provide accommodation for; submit to, endure; admit (impression etc.) by yielding or adaptation of surface. 2. Entertain as guest; greet, welcome; give specified reception to; admit *into* membership of society etc.; (abs.) receive company, hold reception. 3. Acquire, get, come by; be given or provided with; have sent to or conferred or inflicted on one. 4. (radio etc.) Transform incoming electromagnetic waves into the original signal, as sound or as light on screen. **re·ceiv·a·ble** *adj.* (esp.) Awaiting or demanding payment. **re·ceiv´-**

a·bles *n.pl.* Business assets representing amounts due.

re·ceiv·er (rĭsē´ver) *n.* (esp.) 1. Person appointed by court to administer property of bankrupt or property under litigation. 2. Person who receives stolen goods. 3. Receptacle etc. for receiving something in machine or instrument; part of telephone containing ear piece; radio or television receiving set.

re·cen·sion (rĭsen´shon) *n.* Revision of, revised, text.

re·cent (rē´sent) *adj.* Not long past, that happened or existed lately, late; not long established, lately begun, modern; **R ~**, (geol.) of the latter part of the Quaternary period or system, including the present time. **re·cent·ly** *adv.* **re´cent·ness, re´cen·cy** *ns.* **Re´cent** *n.* (geol.) Recent epoch.

re·cep·ta·cle (rĭsep´takel) *n.* 1. Vessel, place, or space that contains. 2. (bot.) Common base of floral organs, axis of cluster.

re·cep·tion (rĭsep´shon) *n.* 1. Receiving, being received; receiving esp. of person, being received, into a place or company; formal or ceremonious welcome; occasion

Spiro Agnew, former Vice-President of the U.S. at a reception in Canberra, Australia, with the then-Australian Prime Minister, Sir John Gorton, who objected to President Johnson's bombing of North Vietnam.

of receiving guests, assembly held for this purpose; ~ **room**, waiting room, room for receiving guests or customers. 2. Receiving of ideas or impressions into the mind. 3. Welcome or greeting of specified kind; demonstration of feeling toward person or project; **warm ~**, enthusiastic welcome; (satirically) vigorous resistance. 4. (radio etc.) Receiving signals, efficiency with which they are received.

re·cep·tion·ist (rĭsep´shonĭst) *n.* Person employed to receive clients, patients, etc.

re·cep·tive (rĭsep´tĭv) *adj.* Able or quick to receive impressions or ideas. **re·cep´tive·ly** *adv.* **re·cep´-tive·ness, re·cep·tiv·i·ty** (rēsep-tĭv´ītē) *ns.*

re·cep·tor (rĭsep´ter) *n.* (physiol.) Minute organ at peripheral end of sensory nerve, capable of specially sensitive response to a particular form of energy, as light or heat.

re·cess (rĭses´, rē´ses) *n.* 1. Temporary cessation from work, short school vacation. 2. Secret or secluded place; niche or alcove of wall; (anat.) fold or indentation in organ. ~ *v.t.* Place in a recess; set back; provide with recess(es).

re·ces·sion (rĭsesh´on) *n.* 1. Receding, withdrawal, from a place or point. 2. Temporary decline or setback in industrial or economic activity or prosperity. **re·ces´sion·ar·y** *adj.*

re·ces·sion·al (rĭsesh´onal) *adj.* Of recession. ~ *n.* Hymn sung while clergy and choir withdraw after church service.

re·ces·sive (rĭses´ĭv) *adj.* 1. Tending to recede. 2. (biol., of an inherited character) Not manifest in the organism that inherits it, though liable to be manifest in the next generation; having its effect obscured by a DOMINANT character.

re·cher·ché (reshār´shā; *Fr.* re-shĕrshā´) *adj.* Devised or got with care or difficulty; choice, farfetched, overrefined.

re·cid·i·vist (rĭsĭd´ĭvĭst) *n.* One who relapses into crime. **re·cid´i·vism** *n.* **re·cid·i·vis·tic** (rĭsĭdĭvĭs´-tĭk), **re·cid´i·vous** *adjs.*

rec·i·pe (res´ĭpē) *n.* 1. Statement of ingredients and procedure for preparing dish etc. 2. (archaic) Medical prescription or remedy prepared from it. 3. Expedient, device, etc., for effecting something. [2nd pers. sing. imp. of L. *recipere* receive (i.e. take) as used in prescriptions]

re·cip·i·ent (rĭsĭp´ēent) *adj.* Receptive. **re·cip´i·ence, re·cip´i·en·cy** *ns.* **recipient** *n.* Person who receives something.

re·cip·ro·cal (rĭsĭp´rokal) *adj.* Given, felt, shown, etc., in return;

felt or shared by both parties, mutual; inversely correspondent, complementary, esp. (math.) based on inverse relationship; (gram.) reflexive, expressing mutual action or relationship (*each other* is a reciprocal pronoun). **re·cip′ro·cal·ly** *adv*. **reciprocal** *n*. Equivalent, counterpart, complement; (math.) function or expression so related to another that their product is unity ($\frac{1}{5}$ is the reciprocal of 5). **re·cip·ro·cate** (rĭsĭp′rokāt) *v*. (**-cat·ed, -cat·ing**). 1. (mech.) Go with alternate backward and forward motion; give such motion to. 2. Give and receive mutually, interchange; return, requite (affection etc.); make a return (*with*). **re·cip·ro·ca·tion** (rĭsĭprokā′shon) *n*. **re·cip′ro·ca·tive, re·cip′ro·ca·to·ry** (rĭsĭp′rokatōrē, -tōrē) *adjs*. **rec·i·proc·i·ty** (rĕsĭprŏs′ĭtē) *n*. (pl. **-ties**). Reciprocal condition, mutual action; principle or practice of give-and-take, esp. interchange of privileges between nations as basis of commercial relations. **re·cit·al** (rĭsī′tal) *n*. 1. Detailed account *of* a number of connected things or facts, relation *of* the facts of an incident etc. 2. Act of reciting; performance of music or dance, esp. by one person or a small group. **re·cit′al·ist** *n*. **rec·i·ta·tion** (rĕsĭtā′shon) *n*. (esp.) Reciting as entertainment, poem or passage recited; oral repetition of prepared lesson or

exercise. **rec·i·ta·tive** (rĕsĭtatēv′) *n*. Musical declamation, between song and ordinary speech, of kind usual in narrative and dialogue parts of opera and oratorio; words, part given in recitative. **re·cite** (rĭsīt′) *v*. (**-cit·ed, -cit·ing**). 1. Repeat aloud or declaim (poem, passage) from memory, esp. before audience; give recitation. 2. Rehearse (facts) in document; mention in order, enumerate. **re·cit′er** *n*. **reck·less** (rĕk′lĭs) *adj*. Devoid of caution, regardless of consequences, rash; heedless *of* danger etc. **reck′less·ly** *adv*. **reck′less·ness** *n*. **reck·on** (rĕk′on) *v*. 1. Ascertain (number, amount), ascertain number or amount of, by counting or usu. by calculation, compute; count, sum up character of; arrive at as total; include *in* computation; make calculations, cast up account or sum; settle accounts *with*. 2. Consider (*to be*); conclude after calculation; be of the confident opinion (*that*); rely, base plans, *on*. **reck′on·er** *n*. **reck·on·ing** (rĕk′onĭng) *n*. (esp.) Statement of amount due, bill;

The problem of **recoil** *has concerned engineers since guns were invented, but the first practical solution was not devised until the early 1900s. At first lead shot was fired in the opposite direction to the main charge.*

day of ∼, time when something must be atoned for or avenged; **dead** ∼: see DEAD. **re·claim** (rĭklām′) *v*. Win back, recall, from wrong course, error etc.; reform, tame, civilize; bring back (land) into cultivation from a waste state or from the sea ∼ *n*. Reclaiming, reclamation. **rec·la·ma·tion** (rĕklamā′shon) *n*. Reclaiming, being reclaimed. **ré·clame** (rāklahm′) *n*. Art or practice by which publicity is secured; public acclaim. [Fr.] **rec·li·nate** (rĕk′lināt, -nĭt) *adj*. (biol.) Bending downward. **re·cline** (rĭklīn′) *v*. (**-clined, -clin·ing**). Lay (esp. one's head, body, limbs) in more or less horizontal or leaning position; assume or be in recumbent position, lie, lean, sit with back or side supported at considerable inclination. **re·clin′er** *n*. (esp.) Easy chair with back and footrest that automatically adjust to reclining position of occupant. **rec·luse** (*adj*. rĭkloos′; rĕk′loos, rĭkloos′) *adj. & n*. (Person) given to or living in seclusion, retirement, or isolation. **re·clu·sive** (rĭkloo′sĭv) *adj*. **rec·og·ni·tion** (rĕkognĭsh′on) *n*. Recognizing, being recognized. **re·cog·ni·zance** (rĭkŏg′nĭzans, -kŏn′ĭ-) *n*. 1. Recorded obligation by which person engages before court or magistrate to observe some condition, e.g. to appear in court

plastic blow-out disk

venturi

priming charge

propellant

detonator

firing pin

rear end cap

cam plate

firing rod

principle of recoilless gun: two shells fired from a single barrel in opposite directions

the Davis system: weight (a charge of lead shot) balances weight of shell

the modern Krupp system: gas from propellant escapes rearwards at high speed through venturi

cutaway of HEAT shell

exploder

distance tube

telescopic sight

propellant

charge

carrying strap

venturi fastening lever

venturi

barrel

tube supporting the firing mechanism

cocking lever

shoulder pad & gun mount

front grip

mainspring

trigger

firing rod

when summoned; sum pledged as urety for such observance. 2. Recognition. **re·cog'ni·zant** *adj.*

rec·og·nize (rĕk'ognīz) *v.t.* -nized, -niz·ing). 1. Acknowledge validity, genuineness, character, claims, or existence of; accord notice or consideration to; discover or realize nature of; treat *as*, acknowledge *for*; realize or admit *that*. 2. Know again, identify as known before. **rec'og·niz·a·ble** *adj.* **rec'og·niz·a·bly** *adv.*

re·coil (rĭkoil') *v.i.* Retreat before enemy etc.; start or spring back, shrink mentally, in fear, horror, or disgust; rebound after impact; spring back to original position or starting point; (of firearms) be driven backward by discharge kick. ~ (rē'koil, rĭkoil') *n.* Act, fact, sensation, of recoiling. **re·coil'less** *adj.* (chiefly of guns).

rec·ol·lect (rĕkolĕkt') *v.t.* Succeed in remembering, recall to mind, remember. **rec·ol·lec·tion** (rĕkolĕk'shon) *n.* Act, power, of recollecting; thing recollected; person's memory, time over which it extends.

rec·om·mend (rĕkoměnd') *v.t.* 1. Give (oneself or another, one's spirit, etc.) in charge *to* God, a person, his care, etc. 2. Speak or write of, suggest, as fit for employment or favor or trial; make acceptable, serve as recommendation of. 3. Counsel, advise. **rec·om·mend'a·ble, rec·om·mend'a·to·ry** (rĕkoměn'datŏrē, -tŏrē) *adjs.* **rec·om·men·da·tion** (rĕkoměn·dā'shon), **rec·om·mend'er** *ns.*

rec·om·pense (rĕk'ompěns) *v.t.* (-pensed, -pens·ing). Requite, reward; make amends to (person) or for (another's loss, injury, etc.). ~ *n.* Reward, requital; atonement or satisfaction for injury; retribution.

rec·on·cile (rĕk'onsīl) *v.t.* (-ciled, -cil·ing). 1. Make friendly after estrangement. 2. Bring into state of acquiescence or submission (*to*). 3. Adjust, settle (quarrel etc.); make (facts, statements, etc.) consistent or accordant; make compatible or consistent, regard or show as consistent (*with*). **rec·on·cil·a·ble** *adj.* **rec·on·cile·ment, rec·on·cil·i·a·tion** (rĕkon·sīlēā'shon) *ns.*

rec·on·dite (rĕk'ondīt, rĭkŏn'-) *adj.* Abstruse, out of the way, little known; dealing in recondite knowledge or allusion, obscure. **rec'·on·dite·ly** *adv.* **rec·on·dite·ness** *n.*

re·con·di·tion (rēkondĭsh'on) *v.t.* Restore to proper, habitable, or usable condition, overhaul, repair.

re·con·nais·sance (rĭkŏn'asans) *n.* Reconnoitering.

rec·on·noi·ter (rēkonoi'ter, rĕko-) *v.* Approach and try to learn

*The first sound **recordings** were made in 1877 by Edison, and developed in the 1880s. The first records were cylinders; in the 1890s Berliner invented the disk, and a way of taking copies from a master negative. From then continual progress was made, and today stereo and quadraphonic reproduction are available.*

position and condition or strategic features of (enemy, area), make reconnaissance.

re·con·struct (rēkonstrŭkt') *v.* Build again; restore (past event) mentally; reorganize.

re·con·struc·tion (rēkonstrŭk'shon) *n.* 1. Process of reconstructing; thing reconstructed. 2. (**R** ~), reincorporation of seceded states into U.S. after Civil War; period during which this occurred (1865-77).

re·cord (rĭkôrd') *v.t.* Register, set down for remembrance or reference, put in writing or other legible shape; represent in some permanent form, esp. on phonograph record, magnetic tape, video disk, film, etc. for reproduction. ~ (rĕk'erd) *n.* 1. State of being recorded or preserved in writing, esp. as authentic legal evidence; official report of proceedings and judgment in cause before a court, copy of pleading etc. constituting case to be decided by a court; piece of recorded evidence or information, account of fact preserved in permanent form, document or monument preserving it; object serving as memorial of something; **matter of** ~, something recorded and thereby established as fact; **off the** ~, unofficial(ly). 2. Track made by marker in groove of revolving disk or cylinder, from which sounds can afterward be reproduced by means of a phonograph or other device; similar track made on tape or wire by mechanical, magnetic, photographic, or other means; grooved

performance — master tape — cutting lathe — black lacquer master disk — heated cutting stylus — grooves on record

master disk is metalized — negative metal master disk — blank disk pressed on both sides — finished record

speakers — amplifier — pick-up

disk, cylinder, etc., bearing such track; **~ player**, apparatus for reproducing sound of phonograph record. 3. Facts known about person's past. 4. Best performance or most remarkable event of its kind on record; (*attrib.*) best hitherto recorded; **break, beat, the ~,** outdo all predecessors.

re·cord·er (rĭkôr′der) *n.* (esp.) 1. One whose official duty is to record. 2. Recording apparatus or instrument. 3. Woodwind flute, played vertically, and varying in range.

re·cord·ing (rĭkôr′dĭng) *n.* (esp.) Process of registering wave form by mechanical, photographic, electrical, or magnetic means for subsequent reproduction by record player, movie projector, radio, television, etc.; disk, film, or tape on which the wave form has been registered; program so reproduced.

re·count[1] (rĭkownt′) *v.t.* Narrate, tell in detail.

re·count[2] (rēkownt′) *v.t.* Count afresh. **re-count, re·count** (rē′kownt) *ns.* Recounting, esp. of election votes.

re·coup (rĭkoop′) *v.* Compensate for (loss), compensate (*for*); (law) deduct, keep back (part of sum due), make such deduction; (refl.) recover what one has expended or lost. **re·coup′ment** *n.*

re·course (rē′kôrs, -kôrs, rĭkôrs′, -kôrs′) *n.* Resorting or betaking of oneself *to* possible source of help; thing resorted to; **have ~ to,** adopt as adviser, helper, or expedient.

re·cov·er (rĭkŭv′er) *v.* 1. Regain possession, use, or control of; acquire or find (out) again; reclaim; (refl.) regain consciousness, calmness, or control of limbs or senses. 2. Secure restitution or compensation, secure (damages) by legal process. 3. Bring or come back to life, consciousness, health, or normal state or position. 4. Retrieve, make up for; get over, cease to feel effects of.

re·cov·er·y (rĭkŭv′erē) *n.* (pl. **-er·ies**). Act or process of recovering or being recovered; restoration to good health; (law) obtaining of a thing, right, damages, etc., by verdict or judgment of a court of law.

rec·re·ant (rĕk′rēant) *adj. & n.* Craven, coward(ly), apostate. **rec′re·ant·ly** *adv.* **rec′re·ance, rec′re·an·cy** *ns.*

rec·re·ate[1] (rĕk′rēāt) *v.* (**-at·ed, -at·ing**). (of pastime, vacation, employment, etc.) Refresh, entertain, agreeably occupy; indulge in recreation. **rec·re·a′tion** (rĕkrēā′shon) *n.* (esp.) Means of recreating oneself, pleasurable exercise or employment. **rec′re·a·tive** *adj.* **rec·re·a′tion·al** *adj.* **recreational vehicle,** camper, trailer, or

*The **recovery** of a spacecraft is an essential part of the entire mission, whether the capsule is manned, as here, or unmanned, especially if the craft has landed on another planet.*

other motor vehicle used for camping.

re·cre·ate[2] (rēkrēāt′) *v.t.* (**-at·ed, -at·ing**). Create anew. **re·cre·a′tion** *n.* **re·cre·a′tive** *adj.*

re·crim·i·nate (rĭkrĭm′ĭnāt) *v.i.* (**-nat·ed, -nat·ing**). Retort accusation, indulge in mutual charges or countercharges. **re·crim·i·na′tion** (rĭkrĭmĭnā′shon) *n.* **re·crim′i·na·tive, re·crim·i·na·to·ry** (rĭkrĭm′ĭnātōrē, -tōrē) *adjs.*

re·cru·desce (rēkroodĕs′) *v.i.* (**-desced, -desc·ing**). (of sore, disease, etc., or fig.) Break out again. **re·cru·des′cence** *n.* **re·cru·des′cent** *adj.*

re·cruit (rĭkroot′) *n.* Newly enlisted and not yet trained member of armed forces; person who joins society etc.; tyro. **~ v.** 1. Enlist recruits for (armed forces, business, etc.); enlist (person) as recruit; get or seek recruits. 2. (rare) Replenish, restore, refresh; (seek to) recover health etc. **re·cruit′er, re·cruit′ment** *ns.*

rec·tal (rĕk′tal) *adj.* Of or by

the rectum. **rec′tal·ly** *adv.*

rec·tan·gle (rĕk′tănggel) *n.* Plane rectilinear four-sided figure with four right angles, esp. one with adjacent sides unequal.

rec·tan·gu·lar (rĕktăng′gyuler) *adj.* Shaped, having base or sides or section shaped, like rectangle; placed, having parts or lines placed, at right angles. **rec·tan′gu·lar·ly** *adv.*

rec·ti·fy (rĕk′tĭfī) *v.t.* (**-fied, -fy·ing**). 1. Put right, correct, amend, reform, adjust (method, calculation, statement, etc.); abolish, get rid of, exchange for what is right (error, abuse, omission, etc.). 2. (chem.) Purify or refine esp. by distillation. 3. (elect.) Change (current) from alternating to direct. **rec′ti·fi·a·ble** *adj.* **rec·ti·fi·ca·tion** (rĕktĭfĭkā′shon), **rec′ti·fi·er** *ns.*

rec·ti·lin·e·ar (rĕktĭlĭn′ēer) *adj.* In or forming a straight line; bounded or characterized by straight lines. **rec·ti·lin′e·ar·ly** *adv.*

rec·ti·tude (rĕk′tĭtood, -tūd) *n.* Moral uprightness, righteousness.

rec·to (rĕk′tō) *n.* (pl. **-tos**). Right-hand page of open book; front of leaf of book or manuscript (opp. VERSO).

rec·tor (rĕk′ter) *n.* 1. (in Ch.

f England) Parish incumbent, hist.) one entitled to receive all thes of parish; (in Protestant and piscopal Ch.) minister in charge f parish; (R.C. Ch.) head parish riest. 2. Head of certain universi- es, colleges, schools, or religious astitutions. **rec·to·rate** (rĕk´- rĭt) *n.* **rec·to·ri·al** (rĕktōr´- al, -tōr´-) *adj.*

rec·to·ry (rĕk´terē) *n.* (pl. **-ries**). ector's benefice; rector's house.

rec·tum (rĕk´tum) *n.* (pl. **-tums,** a pr. -ta). Final section of the arge intestine terminating at the nus. [L. *rectum* (*intestinum*) traight (intestine)]

re·cum·bent (rĭkŭm´bent) *adj.* ying down, reclining. **re·cum´- ent·ly** *adv.* **re·cum´ben·cy** *n.*

re·cu·per·ate (rĭkōō´perāt) *v.* -at·ed, -at·ing). Restore, be estored or recover, from ex- austion, illness, loss, etc. **re·cu- er·a·tion** (rĭkōōperā´shon) *n.* **e·cu·per·a·tive** (rĭkōō´perātĭv, era-) *adj.*

re·cur (rĭk̄er´) *v.i.* (**-curred,** cur·ring). Go back in thought r speech *to*; (of idea etc.) come ack *to* one's mind etc., return to nind; (of problem etc.) come up gain; occur again, be repeated; ecurring decimal, see REPEAT- NG DECIMAL. **re·cur´rence** *n.*

re·cur·rent (rĭk̄er´ent) *adj.* Occurring again, often, or periodi- ally; (of nerve, vein, etc.) turning ack so as to reverse direction. e·cur´rent·ly *adv.*

re·curve (rĭk̄erv´) *v.* (**-curved,** curv·ing). Bend backward. **re- ur·vate** (rĭk̄er´vĭt, -vāt) *adj.*

rec·u·sant (rĕk´yuzant, rĭkū´-) *n.* adj. (Person) who refused to ttend Church of England services hist.); (person) refusing sub- iission to authority or compliance vith regulation. **rec´u·san·cy** *n.*

re·cy·cle (rēsī´kel) *v.* (**-cled,** cling). Return to previous stage f cyclic process, esp. convert waste) to reusable material.

red (rĕd) *adj.* (**red·der, red·- est**). 1. Of or approaching the olor seen at lower or least refracted nd of visible spectrum, of shades arying from crimson to bright rown and orange, esp. those seen n blood, sunset clouds, rubies, lowing coals, and human lips; tained or covered with blood; (of yes) bloodshot, or with lids sore rom weeping; (of persons or nimals) having red or tawny hair; f certain peoples, esp. N. Amer. ndians) having reddish skin. 2. narchistic or communistic; Russian, Soviet. 3. **red'bird**: see ARDINAL *n.* 3 and TANAGER; **red- looded**, full of vigor and zest; irile; **red'breast**: see ROBIN; ed'brick (**university**), applied ttrib. to 19th c. English universi- es built of red brick, to dis-

 1

 2

 3

An English private or **redcoat** *in the uni- form of the mid-18th century (1). This distinctive color was first used in Cromwell's New Model Army and its danger to the wearer was not appreci- ated until the 19th century when less conspicuous uniforms were worn.*

The emblem of the **Red Cross** *(2) as worn by these Australian girls, is adopted from the Swiss flag. Sioux Indians at Wounded Knee when there was trouble between themselves and the authorities (3). Use of the term* **red- skin** *has largely been discontinued.*

tinguish them from Oxford and Cambridge; **red'bud**, any shrub or small tree of genus *Cercis*, esp. *C. canadensis* of Mexico and E. U.S., also called Judas tree, having clusters of pinkish to lavender flowers, and *C. occidentalis* of SW. U.S., having lavender flowers, both species blooming before leaves appear; **red'cap**, railroad station porter; **red carpet**, (fig.) elaborate form of reception for dignitaries

etc.; **red cent**, (colloq.) copper penny (in *not worth, not have a red cent* etc.); **red'coat**, British soldier during the Revolutionary War and the War of 1812, so called from the scarlet uniform coat formerly worn by most regiments of the army; **Red Cross**, emblem of red cross on white ground (Swiss flag with colors reversed) adopted at the Geneva Convention of 1864 for the international societies organized for

direct

*The **redstart** (right) and the **redwing** (below right) are both grouped in the subfamily Turdinae which includes the thrushes and chats. Both are songbirds but the redstart (a chat) is less melodious and breeds in central Africa though it spends the summer in northern Europe. The redwing has a similar range.*

the treatment of sick and wounded in war and borne by ambulances, hospitals, etc., attached to such service; **red deer**, reddish-brown species of deer (*Cervus elaphus*) of Europe, W. Asia, and N. Africa; **red'eye** (pl. **-eyes**, collect. **-eye**), any of various Amer. fishes with red eyes; (slang) whiskey of poor quality; **red'fish** (pl. **-fishes**, collect. **-fish**), any of various Amer. red or reddish fishes; **red flag**, symbol of revolution or socialism; (also) danger signal; **red fox**, any of several foxes of the genus *Vulpes*, typically having reddish fur, including *V. vulpes* of Europe and *V. fulva* of N. Amer.; **red giant**, (astron.) star in intermediate stage of evolution, with reddish hue; **red gum**, (eucalyptus tree yielding) reddish resin; **red-handed**, in the act of crime; **red herring**, herring reddened by being cured in smoke; something introduced to turn attention from the real issue (as *draw a red herring across the track*, with ref. to use of herring in exercising hounds); **red-hot**, heated to redness; highly excited, enthusiastic, furious; **red lead**, red oxide of lead, much used as pigment; **red-letter**, (of day) marked with red letter(s) in calendar as saint's day or festival; memorable as date of joyful occurrence; **red light**, red traffic or danger signal; **red-light district**, district containing many prostitutes, brothels, etc.; **red'lining**, refusal by banks

Redpoll cattle *are found in America, northern Europe and Asia. The distinc-* *tive red crown on their heads has given them their name.*

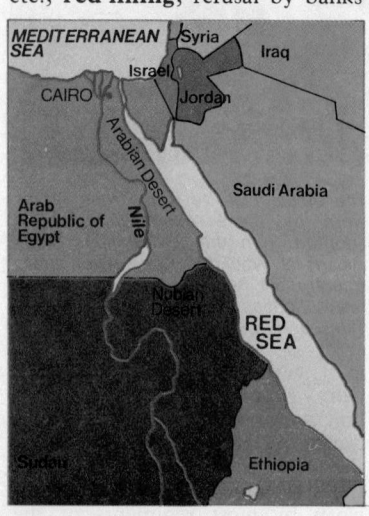

*The **Red Sea** is part of a great system of rifts, stretching south to the great African lakes. Its nearly landlocked nature has made its waters much saltier than those of the oceans.*

to lend mortgage money on property in deteriorating urban areas, designated by red lines on map (**red′line** v.); **red man**, N. Amer. Ind.; **red meat**, beef, venison, etc., as dist. from veal, pork, or chicken; **red′neck**, (derog.) poor, white, uneducated rural farm worker in southern U.S.; **red pepper**: see PEPPER def. 2; **red′poll**, one of two small N. Amer. and Eurasian finches of the genus *Acanthis*, having bright red cap; **Red Poll**, one of a breed of red-haired polled cattle; **Red River**, (1) river in southwestern U.S. flowing 1,018 mi. (1,638 km) from E. New Mexico along the Texas-Oklahoma boundary through Arkansas to the Mississippi River in Louisiana; (2) river in N. central and S. Canada flowing N. 533 mi. (858 km) from the Minnesota-North Dakota boundary to Lake Winnipeg in S. Canada; **Red Sea**, long narrow strip of water between Asia and Africa, connected with Mediterranean by Suez Canal and with Arabian Sea by Gulf of Aden; **red shift**: see SHIFT def. 1; **red′skin**, (offensive) N. Amer. Ind.; **red snapper**, any of several reddish food fishes of the genus *Lutjanus*, esp. *L. blackfordi* found in the Gulf of Mexico; **red′start**, one of two brightly colored N. Amer. warblers of the genus *Setophaga*; any of several Old World thrushes of genus *Phoenicurus*; **red tape**, excessive use of or adherence to formalities esp. in public business (from pink tape used to tie English government and legal documents); **red tide**, brownish-red discoloration of ocean waters, caused by overabundance of one-celled animals, and fatal to fish; **red′wing**, N. Amer. red-winged blackbird (*Agelaius phoeniceus*); **red′wood**: see SEQUOIA. **red′den** v. **red′dish** adj. **red′ly** adv. **red′ness** n. **red** n. Red color; shade of red; red color in roulette etc.; red cloth or clothes; radical, anarchist, or (esp.) communist; **in the ~**, (bookkeeping) showing a deficit; **see ~**, become so angry as to lose self-control.

re·dact (rĭdăkt′) v.t. Put into literary form, edit. **re·dac′tion, re·dac′tor** ns.

redd (rĕd) v.t. (**redd** or **redd·ed, redd·ing**). (regional) Put in order, tidy.

re·deem (rĭdēm′) v.t. 1. Buy back, recover by expenditure of effort or by stipulated payment. 2. Compound for, buy off, (charge or obligation) by payment; perform (promise); purchase the freedom of, save (one's life), by ransom; save, rescue, reclaim; (of God or Christ) deliver from sin and damnation. 3. Make amends for, counter-

The giant **redwood** or sequoia is a type of cypress which grows on the Pacific slopes of the Sierra Nevada at altitudes from 5,000–8,000 ft. The largest trees may be 3,000 years old.

balance (fault, defect); save *from* a defect. **re·deem′a·ble** adj. **re·deem′er** n. (esp., **R~**, of Christ).

re·demp′tion (rĭdĕmp′shon) n. Redeeming or being redeemed, esp. the deliverance from sin and damnation wrought by Christ's atonement; thing that redeems; purchase. **re·demp′tive, re·demp′to·ry** adjs.

red·in·gote (rĕd′ĭnggōt) n. Woman's long double-breasted outer coat with skirt sometimes cut away in front. [Fr., f. English *riding coat*]

red·o·lent (rĕd′olent) adj. Fragrant; having a strong smell; strongly suggestive or reminiscent *of*. **red′o·lence, red′o·len·cy** ns. **red′o·lent·ly** adv.

re·dou·ble[1] (rĭdŭb′el) v. (**-bled, -bling**). Intensify, increase; make or grow greater or more intense or numerous.

re·dou·ble[2] (rĕdŭb′el) v.t. (**-bled, -bling**). (bridge) Double again (bid already doubled by opponent). ~ n. Instance of redoubling.

re·doubt (rĭdowt′) n. (fort.) Outwork or fieldwork, usu. square or polygonal and without flanking defenses.

re·doubt·a·ble (rĭdow′tabel) adj. Formidable.

re·dound (rĭdownd′) v.i. Result in, have effect of, contributing or turning *to* some advantage or disadvantage; turn *to* credit etc.; (of advantage, honor, disgrace, etc.) result, attach, *to* (person), recoil or

come back *upon*.

re·dress (rĭdrĕs′) v.t. Adjust, set straight again; set right, remedy, make up for, rectify (distress, wrong, damage, etc.). ~ (rē′drĕs, rĭdrĕs′) n. Reparation for wrong, redressing of grievances, etc.

re·duce (rĭdoos′, -dūs′) v. (**-duced, -duc·ing**). 1. Bring *to* certain order or arrangement, *to* a certain form or character; convert (*in*)*to* different physical state or form, esp. crush *to* powder etc. 2. Bring by force or necessity *to* some state or action, subdue. 3. Bring down, lower; weaken, impoverish; diminish, contract; degrade (noncommissioned officer) to lower rank; **reduced circumstances**, poverty after prosperity. 4. (surg.) Restore (dislocated, fractured, or ruptured part) to proper position. 5. (chem.) Remove from (a compound) oxygen or other electronegative atom or group; add to (compound) hydrogen or other electropositive atom or group. 6. (arith.) Change (number, quantity) (*in*)*to* another denomination or different form. 7. (logic) Bring syllogism into different form. 8. (intrans.) Lessen one's weight. **re·duc′er** n. **re·duc′i·ble** adj. **re·duc′i·bly** adv.

re·duc·tion (rĭdŭk′shon) n. Reducing or being reduced; reduced copy of picture, map, etc. **re·duc′tive** adj. **re·duc′tion·al** adj.

re·dun·dant (rĭdŭn′dant) adj. Superfluous; repetitive; (of employee or his post) liable to be dispensed with because no longer necessary. **re·dun′dant·ly** adv. **re·dun′dan·cy** n. (pl. **-cies**).

re·du·pli·cate (rĭdoo′plĭkāt, -dū-′) v.t. (**-cat·ed, -cat·ing**). Make double, repeat; (gram.) repeat (letter, syllable); form (tense) by repetition of letter or syllable. **re·du·pli·ca·tion** (rĭdooplĭkā′shon, -dū-′) n.

re·ech·o, re-ech·o, re·ĕch·o (rēĕk′ō) vbs. (**-ech·oed, -ech·o·ing**). Echo; echo again and again, resound.

reed (rēd) n. 1. (Tall straight stalk of) firm-stemmed plant of genus *Phragmites* or *Arundo*; (collect.) reeds, growth or bed of reeds. 2. Musical pipe of reed or straw; one of two vibrating concave wedge-shaped pieces of reed or cane fixed face to face on metal tube as part of mouthpiece of oboe or bassoon; small metal tube with opening closed by vibrating metal tongue in lower end of organ pipe; metal tongue, slip of cane, producing sound by vibration, in organ pipe, clarinet, etc.; (pl.) reed instrument(s). 3. Weaver's instrument of metal wires (formerly thin strips of reed or cane) fixed into parallel bars of wood, for separating threads of warp and beating up weft. 4. (archit.) One of a set of small semicylindrical moldings. 5. **reed′bird**, bobolink; **reed mace**, cattail; **reed pipe**, reeded organ pipe; **reed stop**, organ stop consisting of reed pipes.

Reed (rēd), **Walter** (1851–1902). U.S. Army surgeon; headed commission to study yellow fever in Cuba, 1900, and identified the mosquito that was the source of transmission of the disease.

reed·y (rē′dē) *adj.* (**reed·i·er**, **reed·i·est**). 1. Abounding with reeds; made of reed (chiefly poet.). 2. (of voice) Like reed instrument in tone, scratchy, not round and clear. **reed′i·ness** *n.*

reef[1] (rēf) *n.* One of three or four strips across top of square or bottom of fore-and-aft sail that can be taken in or rolled up to reduce sail's surface; ~ **knot**, square knot. **reef** *v.* Take in reef(s) of sail; shorten (topmast etc.).

reef[2] (rēf) *n.* Ridge of rock, shingle, or sand, at or just above or below surface of water; (gold etc. mining) vein, bedrock.

reef·er[1] (rē′fer) *n.* 1. One who reefs. 2. Close-fitting double-breasted stout jacket.

reef·er[2] (rē′fer) *n.* (slang) Marijuana cigarette.

reek (rēk) *n.* 1. Smoke; vapor. 2. Foul or stale odor; fetid atmosphere. ~ *v.i.* Emit smoke; emit vapor; smell unpleasantly (usu. *of*). **reek′y** *adj.* (**reek·i·er**, **reek·i·est**). **reek′er** *n.*

reel[1] (rēl) *n.* Rotatory apparatus on which thread, silk, yarn, paper, wire, etc., is wound at some stage of manufacture; apparatus capable of easy revolution for winding and unwinding cord, line, etc.; small cylinder, with rim at each end, on which sewing cotton etc. is wound for convenience; cylinder on which length of film, esp. motion-picture film, is wound; quantity wound on a reel. ~ *v.* Wind on reel; take (thread, silk, etc.) *off*, draw (fish etc.) *in* or *up*, by use of reel; rattle (story, list, etc.) *off* without pause or apparent effort.

reel[2] (rēl) *v.i.* Be in a whirl, be dizzy; sway, stagger; stand, walk, or run unsteadily; be shaken physically or mentally; seem to shake.

reel[3] (rē) *n.* Lively Scottish dance; Virginia reel; music for either of these.

re·en·try (rēēn′trē) *n.* (pl. **-tries**). (esp.) 1. (law) Act of reentering upon possession of lands, tenements, etc., previously granted or let to another. 2. Return of rocket etc. into Earth's atmosphere from outer space.

reeve[1] (rēv) *n.* (hist.) Chief magistrate of town or district; (Canada) president of village or town council.

reeve[2] (rēv) *v.t.* (**reeved** or **rove** pr. rōv, **reev·ing**). (naut.) Thread (rope etc.) *through* ring or other aperture; thread (aperture, block, etc.) with rope; fasten (rope, block, etc.) *in*, *on*, *to*, something by reeving.

ref (rĕf) *n.* (colloq.) Referee. ~ *v.* (**reffed**, **ref′fing**).

ref. *abbrev.* Referee; reference; referred; refining; reformation; reformed; refund(ing).

re·fec·tion (rĭfĕk′shon) *n.* Refreshment by food or drink; light meal, repast.

re·fec·to·ry (rĭfĕk′terē) *n.* (pl. **-ries**). Room used for meal in monasteries etc.; ~ **table**, long narrow table.

re·fer (rĭfĕr′) *v.* (**-ferred, -ferring**). 1. Trace or ascribe *to* person or thing as cause or source; assign *to* certain date, place, or class. 2. Send on or direct (person), make appeal or have recourse, *to* some authority or source of information; cite authority or passage. 3. (of statement etc.) Have relation, be directed; make allusion, direct attention, *to*. **ref·er·a·ble** (rĕf′erabel) *adj.* **re·fer′rer** *n.*

ref·er·ee (rĕferē′) *n.* Arbitrator, person to whom dispute is to be or is referred for decision; umpire, esp. in football; ring official supervising boxing match. ~ *v.* (**-eed, -ee·ing**). Act as referee (for), esp. in boxing.

ref·er·ence (rĕf′erens) *n.* 1. Referring of matter for decision, settlement, or consideration, to some authority; scope given to such authority. 2. Relation, respect, correspondence, *to*; **in, with ~ to**, regarding, as regards, about; **without ~ to**, irrespective of. 3. Allusion *to*. 4. Direction *to* book, passage etc. where information may be found; mark used to refer reader of text to note etc.; act of looking up passage etc. or of referring another or applying to person, for information; ~ **book**, book designed for occasional consultation rather than for continuous reading; ~ **library**, library where books may be consulted without being taken away. 5. Person named by one applying for post or offering goods etc. as willing to vouch for him or them; (loosely) testimonial. **ref·er·en·tial** (rĕferĕn′shal) *adj.*

ref·er·en·dum (rĕferĕn′dum) *n.* (pl. **-dums, -da** pr. -da). Referring of question at issue to electorate for direct decision by a general vote; such a vote.

ref·er·ent (rĕf′erent) *n.* What is symbolized by word etc.

re·fill (rēfĭl′) *v.t.* Fill again. ~ (rē′fĭl) *n.* Supply of material to refill container when contents are used up.

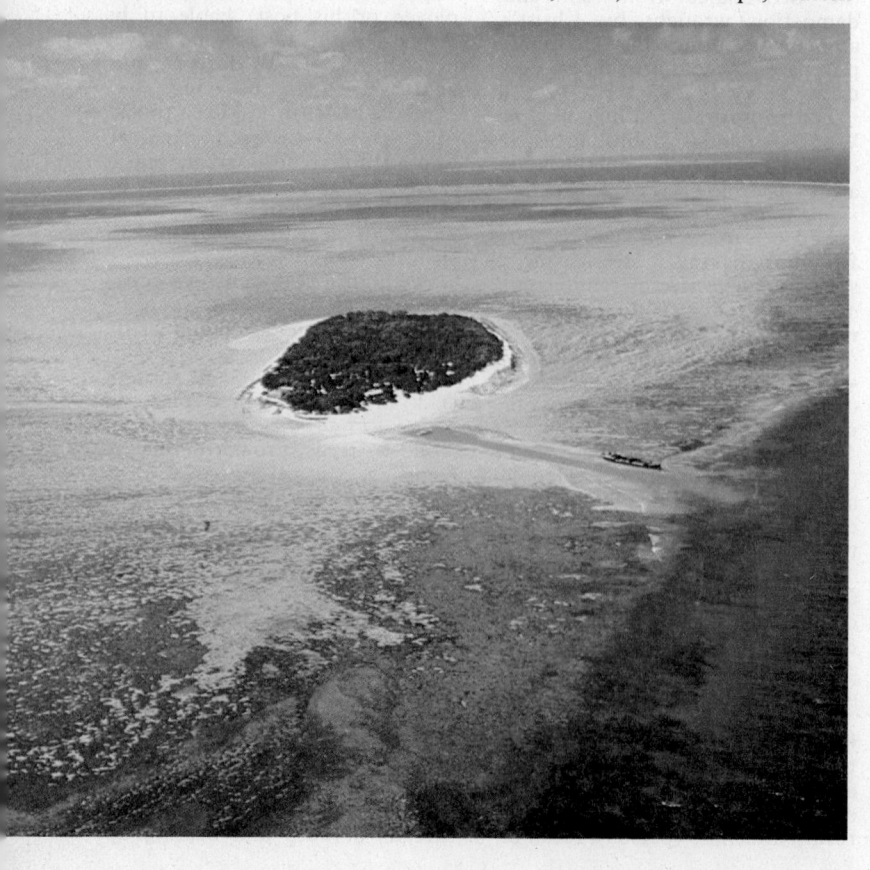

Heron Island on the Great Barrier Reef off eastern Australia is a coral cay. Formation of **reef** *coral is a long and complex process, governed by water temperatures and many other factors.*

re·fine (rĭfīn´) v. (**-fined, -fin·- ing**). 1. Free from dross, im- purities, or defects; purify, clarify; become pure. 2. Polish, improve, make or become more elegant or cultured; use or affect subtlety of thought or language.

re·fine·ment (rĭfīn´ment) n. Re- fining or being refined; fineness of feeling or taste, polished manners, etc.; subtle or ingenious manifesta- tion of (luxury etc.), piece of elaborate arrangement; piece of subtle reasoning, fine distinction.

re·fin·er (rĭfī´ner) n. (esp.) Per- son whose business is to refine metal, sugar, etc. **re·fin´er·y** n. (pl. **-er·ies**). Place where raw material (e.g. sugar, petroleum) is refined.

re·fit (rēfĭt´) v. (**-fit·ted, -fit·- ting**). Restore (ship) to service- able condition; equip and prepare for new or additional use.

re·flect (rĭflĕkt´) v. 1. (of sur- face or body) Throw (heat, light, sound, etc.) back, cause to rebound; (of mirror etc.) show image of, reproduce to eye or mind, exactly correspond in appearance or effect to; (of action etc.) bring back or cause to rebound (credit, discredit, etc.), bring discredit, on person etc. 2. Go back in thought, meditate, or consult with oneself (on).

re·flec·tion, Brit. **re·flex·ion** (rĭflĕk´shon) ns. 1. Reflecting or being reflected; reflected light, heat, color, or image; **angle of ~**, acute angle made by path of a reflected body or reflected light ray with a line at right angles to the surface at the point of reflection. 2. Thing bringing discredit on. 3. Reconsideration, meditation; mental faculty dealing with products of sensation and perception; idea arising in the mind.

re·flec·tive (rĭflĕk´tĭv) adj. 1. Giving back reflection or image. 2. Concerned in reflection or thought; thoughtful, given to meditation. **re·flec´tive·ly** adv.

re·flec·tor (rĭflĕk´ter) n. Body or surface reflecting rays, esp. piece of glass, metal, etc., usu. concave, for reflecting in required direction; (telescope etc. provided with) concave mirror for bringing parallel light to a focus.

re·flex (rē´flĕks) n. 1. Reflected light, color, or glory; reflection, image. 2. Reflex action; **conditioned ~**: see CONDITION v.t. **reflex** adj. Turned backward; reflected; coming by way of return or reflection; **~ action**, in- voluntary action of muscle, nerve, etc., excited as automatic response

to stimulus of sensory nerve (e.g. sneezing); **~ angle**: see ANGLE[1]; **~ camera**, hand camera in which, by means of a pivoted mirror, the reflected image can be seen and focused up to the point of exposure.

*The discovery and exploitation of large deposits of crude oil in Iraq resulted in the construction of this **refinery** at Baghdad. Similar plants have been built in many places.*

reflex (rĭflĕks´) v.t. Bend back, recurve (only in past part.; chiefly bot.).

re·flex·ive (rĭflĕk´sĭv) adj. & n. (gram.) (Word, form) implying agent's action upon himself; (verb) of which subject and object are the same person or thing; (personal pronoun or possessive adjective) referring to subject. **re·flex´ive·ly** adv. **re·flex´ive·ness** n.

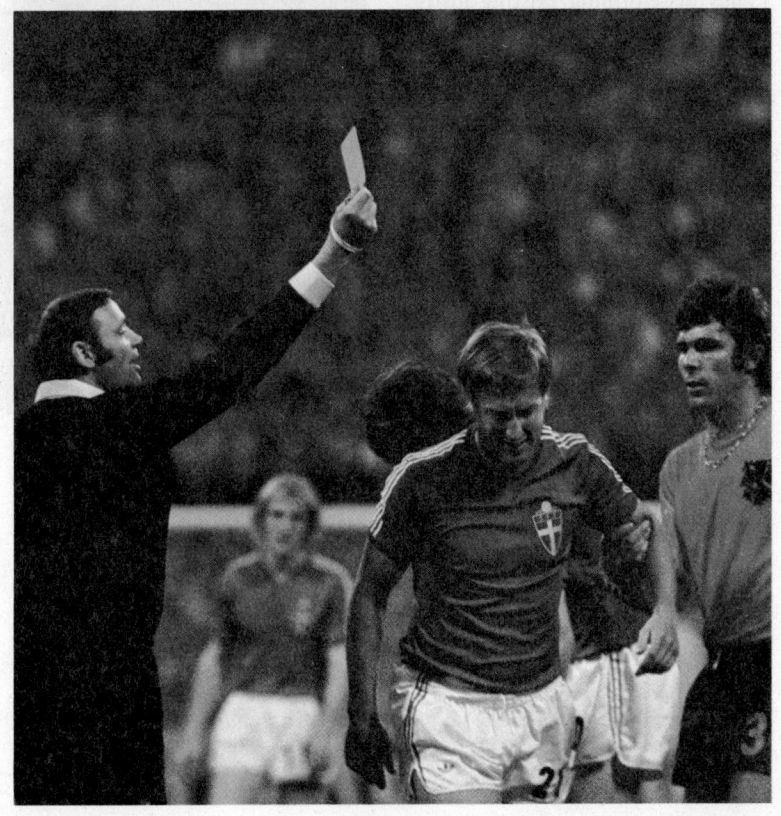

*The **referee** has the crucial role of main- taining fair play by warning players, as in this picture of the 1974 Holland v Sweden World Cup match, or sending them off.*

*The **reflex** camera lets the photographer focus correctly by altering his depth of focus until the reflected image is correct. Reflex reflectors make it easier to see vehicles at night.*

ref·lu·ent (rĕf´loo͞ent) *adj.* Flowing back. **ref´lu·ence** *n.*

re·flux (rē´flŭks) *n.* Flowing back; ebb.

re·form (rĭfôrm´) *v.* Make or become better by removal or abandonment of imperfections, faults, or errors; abolish, cure (abuse, malpractice); **reformed churches**, Protestant denominations that have accepted the principles of the Reformation; esp. **(Reformed)** applied to Calvinist bodies, esp. contrasted with Lutherans. **reform** *n.* Removal of abuse(s) esp. in politics; improvement made or suggested. **re·form´a·ble, re·form´a·tive, re·formed´** *adjs.* **re·form´er** *n.*

ref·or·ma·tion (rĕfermā´shon) *n.* Reforming or being reformed, esp. radical change for the better in political, social, etc. affairs; **R ~**, 16th-c. religious movement to reform doctrines and practices of R.C. Ch., and ending in establishment of reformed or Protestant churches of central and NW. Europe.

re·form·a·to·ry (rĭfôr´matōrē, -tōrē) *adj.* Tending or intended to produce reform. **~** *n.* (pl. **-ries**). Institution to which juvenile offenders are sent for reform purposes.

re·form·ism (rĭfôr´mĭzem) *n.* Policy of reforming existing institutions rather than abolishing or revolutionizing them.

re·fract (rĭfrăkt´) *v.t.* Deflect (ray of light, energy, etc.) at certain angle at point of passage from one medium into another of different density; **refract´ing telescope**: see TELESCOPE. **re·frac´tion, re·frac´tive·ness, re·frac·tiv·i·ty** (rēfrăktĭv´ĭtē) *ns.* **re·frac´tive** *adj.*

re·frac·tor (rĭfrăk´ter) *n.* Refracting medium, lens, or telescope.

re·frac·to·ry (rĭfrăk´terē) *adj.* Stubborn, unmanageable, rebellious; (of wounds etc.) not yielding *to* treatment; (of substances) hard to fuse or work. **re·frac´to·ri·ly** *adv.* **re·frac´to·ri·ness** *n.* **refractory** *n.* (pl. **-ries**). Substance, as graphite, silica, especially resistant to the action of heat and suitable for lining furnaces etc. where high temperatures must be withstood.

re·frain[1] (rĭfrān´) *n.* Recurring phrase or line, esp. at end of stanzas.

re·frain[2] (rĭfrān´) *v.* 1. (archaic) Curb. 2. Abstain (*from*). **re·frain´ment** *n.*

re·fran·gi·ble (rĭfrăn´jĭbel) *adj.* That can be refracted. **re·fran·gi·bil·i·ty** (rĭfrănjĭbĭl´ĭtē), **re·fran´gi·ble·ness** *ns.*

Twin-lens Reflex Camera

Diagrammatic Section through Vehicle Reflector

reflected beam

external surface

reflective surface

deviating mirror

incident beam →

focusing screen

viewing lens

taking lens

film plane

*In times of war, many members of the civilian population may have to leave their homes. They are often accommodated in **refugee** camps like that near Nicosia, Cyprus (above).*

re·fresh (rĭfrĕsh´) *v.* Impart fresh vigor to, by food, rest, etc., reanimate, reinvigorate; freshen up (memory); restore (fire etc.) with fresh supply of fuel etc.; refresh oneself, take refreshment. **re·fresh´ing** *adj.* **re·fresh´ing·ly** *adv.*

re·fresh·er (rĭfrĕsh´er) *n.* 1. That which refreshes. 2. (attrib., of course of instruction etc. Serving to refresh memory or mak up to date.

re·fresh·ment (rĭfrĕsh´ment) *n.* Refreshing or being refreshed i mind or body; thing, esp. (usu. i pl.) food or drink, that refreshes.

re·frig·er·ate (rĭfrĭj´erăt) *v.* (**-at·ed, -at·ing**). Make, become cool or cold; expose (food) to low temperature in order to preserv it. **re·frig´er·ant** *adj. & n.* (Medium etc.) that refrigerates **re·frig·er·a·tion** (rĭfrĭjerā´shon) **re·frig·er·a·tor** (rĭfrĭj´erāter) *n.*

he **regalia** used in the coronation of a ritish monarch all have ancient symbolic significance. The swords denote stice, and mercy; the sceptre — authority; the orb — Christianity.

sp.) Apparatus in which ice can e made and food etc. kept cold y the mechanical production of w temperature.

reft: see REAVE.

re·fu·el (rēfū′el, -fūl) v. (**-eled, el·ing**). Replenish with, take on, esh supply of fuel.

ref·uge (rĕf′ūj) n. (Place of) helter from pursuit, danger, or ouble; person, thing, course, that ives shelter or is resorted to in ifficulties; **city of** ~, in ancient srael, sanctuary for those guilty f manslaughter; **City of R** ~, ational historical part on the island f Hawaii, until 1819 sanctuary for hose vanquished in battle or condemned to death for breaking aboo.

ref·u·gee (rĕfyujē′, rĕf′yujē) n. erson escaped, esp. to foreign ountry, from religious or political ersecution, war, etc.

re·ful·gent (rĭfŭl′jent) adj. hining, gloriously bright. **re·ful′-ent·ly** adv. **re·ful′gence, re·-ul′gen·cy** ns.

re·fund (rĭfŭnd′) v. Pay back money received or taken, expenses ncurred by another); reimburse; make repayment. ~ (rē′fŭnd) n. Repayment. **re·fund′a·ble** adj. e·fund′er n.

re·fus·al (rĭfū′zal) n. 1. Act or nstance of refusing. 2. Right or rivilege of deciding to take or leave thing before it is offered to others.

re·fuse¹ (rĭfūz′) v. (**-fused, fus·ing**). Say or convey by action hat one will not accept, submit to, ive, grant, gratify, consent; deny to person etc.), refuse request of; make refusal; (of horse) stop short at (fence etc.), fail to take jump.

ref·use² (rĕf′ūs) n. & adj. What is) rejected as worthless or eft over after use; rubbish, trash.

re·fute (rĭfūt′) v.t. (**-fut·ed, -fut·ing**). Prove falsity or error of statement, argument, etc.), rebut or repel by argument. **re·fut·a·ble** rĭfū′tabel, rĕf′yu-) adj. **ref·u·ta·tion** (rĕfyutā′shon), **re·fut′er** ns.

reg. abbrev. Regiment; register(ed); region.

re·gain (rĕgān′) v.t. Recover possession of; reach (place) again; recover (feet, footing).

re·gal (rē′gal) adj. Of or by kings; fit for a king, magnificent. **re′gal·ly** adv.

re·gale (rĭgāl′) v. (**-galed, -gal·ing**). Entertain sumptuously with food and drink; give delight to; feast (on). **re·gale′ment** n.

re·ga·li·a (rĭgā′lēa, -gāl′ya) n.pl. Insignia of royalty used at coronations; decorations or insignia of an order.

re·gal·i·ty (rĭgăl′ĭtē) n. (pl. **-ties**). Attribute of kingly power, being king; royal privilege.

re·gard (rĭgärd′) v. 1. Gaze upon; bestow attention or notice on, show interest in. 2. Give heed to; take into account in regulating actions or conduct; show consideration for; pay attention, give heed. 3. Look on as being something; look on with some feeling; consider. 4. Concern, have relation to; **as** ~s, so far as relates to. **re·gard′ing** prep. In or with regard to. **regard** n. 1. Look, gaze; observant attention or heed; consideration; care or concern for. 2. Thing or circumstance looked to or taken into account, respect;

A **refrigerated** road-train travels through the Pilbara in Western Australia taking frozen food and vegetables to remote areas that are not accessible by rail or air. Many isolated communities are dependent on these trucks.

in ~ to, with ~ to, in respect of, with respect or reference to. 3. Esteem, kindly feeling or respectful opinion (*for*); (pl.) as expression of friendliness in letter etc. **re·gard′less** *adj.* Without paying attention; without regard or consideration (*of*). **re·gard′less·ly** *adv.* (colloq.) Anyway; in spite of everything. **re·gard′less·ness** *n.*

re·gat·ta (rĭgăt′a, -gah′ta) *n.* Meeting for boat or yacht races; series of races.

re·gen·cy (rē′jensē) *n.* (pl. **-cies**). (Period of) office of regent or regents; **R ~,** (Engl. hist.) period (1810–20) in which George, Prince of Wales, acted as regent; (attrib.) of the style of architecture, dress, etc., of this period.

re·gen·er·ate (rĭjĕn′erāt) *v.* (**-ated, -at·ing**). 1. Invest with new and higher spiritual nature; improve moral condition of; breathe new, more vigorous, and higher life into. 2. Generate again; bring or come into renewed existence. **re·gen·er·ate** (rĭjĕn′-erĭt), **re·gen′er·a·tive** *adjs.* **re·gen·er·a·tion** (rĭjĕnerā′shon), **re·gen′er·a·cy, re·gen′er·a·tor** *ns.*

re·gent (rē′jent) *n.* 1. Person appointed to administer kingdom during minority, absence, or incapacity of monarch. 2. Member of governing board of some universities etc. **~ adj.** (placed after noun) Acting as, having position of, regent; **Prince R ~,** (Brit. hist.), George, Prince of Wales (later George IV), who was regent 1810–20 during incapacity of George III.

reg·i·cide (rĕj′ĭsīd) *n.* 1. Killer or participator in killing of a king. 2. Killing of a king. **reg·i·cid·al** (rĕjĭsī′dal) *adj.*

re·gime, ré·gime (rezhēm′, rā-) *ns.* Method of government; prevailing system of things; **ancien ~:** see ANCIEN RÉGIME.

reg·i·men (rĕj′imen) *n.* (med.) Prescribed course of exercise, way of life, and esp. diet.

reg·i·ment (rĕj′iment) *n.* Army unit consisting of at least two battalions and usually with a permanent depot and headquarters; large array or number, legion. **~** (rĕj′imĕnt) *v.t.* Form (men) into regiment or regiments; organize (workers etc.) into groups or according to a system; impose uniformity or order upon. **reg·i·men·tal** (rĕjimĕn′tal) *adj.* Of a regiment; military, maintaining or demanding strict discipline. **reg·i·men·tals** *n.pl.* Dress worn by regiment; military uniform. **reg·i·men·ta·tion** (rĕjimĕntā′shon) *n.* Regimenting, organizing.

re·gi·na (rejī′na) *n.* Reigning queen; **R ~,** (abbrev. R.) reigning queen (esp. following name in signature to certain official documents, as *Elizabeth R.*). [L.]

re·gion (rē′jon) *n.* Tract of country, place, space, of more or less definitely marked boundaries or characteristics; separate part of world or universe; sphere or realm of; part of the body around or near some organ etc. **re′gion·al** *adj.* **re′gion·al·ly** *adv.* **re′gion·al·ism** *n.* 1. Quality or trait distinctive in particular region or area. 2. Word, speech, custom, etc. distinctive in certain region.

reg·is·ter (rĕj′ĭster) *n.* 1. Book in which entries are made of details to be recorded for reference; official or authoritative list kept e.g. of births, marriages, and burials or deaths, shipping, medical practitioners, qualified voters in constituency, etc. 2. (Set of pipes controlled by) slides in an organ; compass of voice or instrument (**upper, lower,** etc., **~,** part of this). 3. Adjustable plate for widening or narrowing an opening that admits heated or cooled air into a room. 4. Recording indicator of speed, force, etc. 5. (print.) Exact correspondence or placement of the colors or plates used in printing for clear images. **register** *v.* 1. Set down (name etc.) formally, record in writing; enter or cause to be entered in particular register; write name in register of hotel on arrival; (fig.) make mental note of; send (letter, package, etc.) by registered mail; **registered mail,** mail that is registered at the post office and a receipt given to the sender; **registered nurse,** completely trained nurse who has passed state examination on nursing.

The Venetian painter Canaletto is famous for his pictures of spectacles on the water in and around the city. This glittering **regatta** *scene shows the splendor with which such events were surrounded in the 18th century.*

2

3

The **Regency** period in England was accompanied by extravagance, especially in men's dress as epitomized by 'dandies' (1), in ornate furniture (2) and even in the hair style favored by the future George IV (3) and architecture dominated by ornate curved facades and balconies (4).

services. 2. (of instrument) Record automatically, indicate; (of person) express or show (emotion etc.) in face, or in any manner. 3. (print. etc.) Correspond, make correspond, exactly. **reg·is·tra·tion** (rĕjĭstrā´shon) n.

reg·is·trar (rĕj´ĭsträr, rĕjĭsträr´) n. Official recorder, person charged with keeping register; college or university official who keeps records of the enrollment and academic standing of students; corporate official who keeps records of ownership of corporation's stocks etc.

reg·is·try (rĕj´ĭstrē) n. (pl. **-tries**). 1. Registration. 2. Place, office, where registers are kept. 3. Ship's registered nationality (often for financial or insurance purposes).

reg·nant (rĕg´nant) adj. Reigning; predominant, prevalent.

Reinforced concrete is extensively used in all sorts of building today. This block under construction in Ottawa shows how work proceeds storey by storey, with pre-formed elements swung into place by crane.

re·gorge (rēgōrj′) *v.* (**-gorged, -gorg·ing**). Disgorge.

re·gress (rē′grĕs) *n.* Going back. ~ (rĭgrĕs′) *v.t.* Move backward; return to a previous or less advanced state or condition.

re·gres·sion (rĭgrĕsh′on) *n.* Backward movement, retreat; relapse, reversion. **re·gres′sive** *adj.* **re·gres′sive·ly** *adv.* **re·gres′sive·ness** *n.*

re·gret (rĭgrĕt′) *v.* (**-gret·ted, -gret·ting**). Remember (something lost) with distress or longing, feel sorrow for loss of; grieve at, feel mental distress because of; feel regret. ~ *n.* Sorrow for loss; repentance or sorrow for something done or left undone; (intimation of) sorrow or disappointment at inability to do something, esp. accept invitation. **re·gret′ful** *adj.* **re·gret′ful·ly** *adv.* **re·gret′ta·ble** *adj.* **re·gret′ta·bly** *adv.*

regt. *abbrev.* Regiment.

reg·u·lar (rĕg′yuler) *adj.* 1. (eccles.) Bound by religious rule; belonging to religious or monastic order. 2. Following or exhibiting a principle; harmonious, consistent, systematic; symmetrical; (geom.) having equal sides and angles. 3. Acting, done, recurring, uniformly or calculably in time or manner; habitual, constant, not capricious or casual; orderly; **keep ~ hours**, do same thing at same time daily. 4. Conforming to a standard, in order; properly constituted or qualified, not defective or amateur, devoted exclusively or primarily to its nominal function. 5. (gram., of verbs, nouns, etc.) Following a normal type of inflection. 6. (colloq.) Real; complete, thorough. 7. **R~ Army**, army of professional soldiers as opp. to militia, or temporary soldiers; permanent part of U.S. Army. **reg′u·lar·ly** *adv.* **regular** *n.* One of the regular clergy; regular soldier; (colloq.) regular customer, contributor, etc. **reg·u·lar·i·ty** (rĕgyulăr′ĭtē) *n.* (pl. **-ties**). **reg′u·lar·ize** *v.t.* (**-ized, -iz·ing**). **reg·u·lar·i·za·tion** (rĕgyulerĭzā′shon) *n.*

reg·u·late (rĕg′yulāt) *v.t.* (**-lat·ed, -lat·ing**). Control by rule, subject to restrictions; moderate, adapt to requirements; adjust (machine, clock) to work accurately. **reg·u·la·tive** (rĕg′yulātĭv, -lătĭv), **reg·u·la·to·ry** (rĕg′yulatōrē, -tōrē) *adjs.* **reg·u·la·tion** (rĕgyulā′shon) *n.* 1. Regulating, being regulated. 2. Prescribed rule, authoritative direction; (attrib.) fulfilling what is laid down by regulations, ordinary,

usual, formal.

reg·u·la·tor (rĕg′yulāter) *n.* (esp.) Device for regulating passage of gases, liquids, electric current, etc.; device for regulating speed of watch etc. by adjusting balance.

reg·u·lus (rĕg′yulus) *n.* (pl. **-lus·es, -li** pr. -lī). (chem.) Metallic content of mineral, liberated by reduction and sinking to bottom in crucible; impure metallic product of smelting various ores.

re·gur·gi·tate (rĭgĕr′jĭtāt) *v.* (**-tat·ed, -tat·ing**). Gush back; (of stomach or receptacle) pour or cast out again; vomit. **re·gur·gi·ta·tion** (rĭgĕrjĭtā′shon) *n.*

re·ha·bil·i·tate (rēhabĭl′ĭtāt) *v.t.* (**-tat·ed, -tat·ing**). Restore to

Rehearsal is essential for a successful dramatic performance. These actors in New Zealand have reached the dress rehearsal stage, traditionally the last rehearsal before the opening night.

rights, privileges, reputation, etc. reinstate; restore to previous condition; enable (disabled person, convict, etc.) to earn his living o resume normal life throug therapy, training, etc. **re·ha·bil·i·ta·tion** (rēhabĭlĭtā′shon) *n.* **re·ha·bil·i·ta·tive** (rēhabĭl′ĭtātĭv) *adj.*

re·hash (rēhăsh′) *v.t.* Pu (material) into new form withou real change or improvement repeat, discuss again. ~ (rē′hăsh *n.* Presentation of same materia in new form or words.

re·hears·al (rĭhĕr′sal) *n.* Rehearsing; practicing of play concert, etc. before performing i in public; **in ~**, in process of bein rehearsed.

re·hearse (rĭhĕrs′) *v.t* (**-hearsed, -hears·ing**). Recite say over, repeat from beginning to end; give list of, recount enumerate; have rehearsal of (play part, concert, etc.); practice for late public performance.

Re·ho·bo·am (rēobō´am), **Ro·-bo·am** (rōbō´am). Son of Solomon; succeeded him as king of Israel; the northern tribes broke away from his rule and set up a new kingdom under Jeroboam, after which he continued as 1st king of Judah.

Reich (rīx) *n.* Government or territory of a German empire or republic; **First ~**, the Holy Roman Empire, 962–1806 A.D.; **Second ~**, 1871–1918; **Third ~**, Nazi regime, 1933–45.

Reichs·tag (rīxs´tahx). Supreme legislature of the former German Empire and of the Republic; building in Berlin in which this met, burned down on Nazi accession to power (1933).

reign (rān) *n.* Sovereignty, rule, sway; period during which sovereign reigns; **~ of terror**, time

The common names **reindeer** *and cari-bou are only the European and American terms for the same deer (Rangifer tarandus) which has several subspecies.*

in which community lives in dread of death or outrage, esp. the **R ~ of Terror** (1793–4) during the French Revolution. **reign** *v.i.* Hold royal office, be king or queen; exercise authority, hold sway, rule; be acknowledged as supreme.

re·im·burse (rēĭmbers´) *v.t.* (**-bursed, -burs·ing**). Repay (person who has expended money, out-of-pocket expenses). **re·im·-burs'a·ble** *adj.* **re·im·burse'-ment** *n.*

Reims, Rheims (rēmz; *Fr.* răns). Industrial city and important champagne-producing center in NE. France; site of 13th-c. Gothic cathedral; Germany signed World War II unconditional surrender here, May 7, 1945.

rein (rān) *n.* Long narrow strap with each end attached to bit, used to guide or check horse etc. in riding or driving (freq. pl. in same sense); (fig.) means of control; **give ~ to**, let have free scope. **rein** *v.t.* Check or manage with reins; pull *up* or *back*, hold *in* with reins; guide, control.

re·in·car·nate (rēĭnkär´nāt) *v.t.* (**-nat·ed, -nat·ing**). Incarnate again. ~ (rēĭnkär´nĭt) *adj.*

re·in·car·na·tion (rēĭnkärnā´-shon) *n.* Belief in the return to earth in a new form of the soul after death.

rein·deer (rān´dēr) *n.* (pl. **-deer**). Caribou; subarctic deer of genus *Rangifer* with large branch-ing or palmated antlers in both sexes, used for drawing sleds and kept in herds for its milk, flesh, and hide.

re·in·force (rēĭnfōrs´, -fōrs´) *v.t.* (**-forced, -forc·ing**). Strengthen or support by additional men or material or by increase of numbers, quantity, size, thickness, etc.; **reinforced concrete**, concrete with steel bars or wire netting embedded in it to increase its tensile strength.

re·in·force·ment (rēĭnfōrs´-ment, -fōrs´-) *n.* Reinforcing, being reinforced; anything that re-inforces; (freq. pl.) additional men, ships, aircraft, etc., for military, naval, or air force.

re·in·state (rēĭnstāt´) *v.t.* (**-stat·ed, -stat·ing**). Restore to, replace *in*, lost position, privileges, etc.; restore to health or proper order. **re·in·state'ment** *n.*

re·in·sure (rēĭnshoor´) *v.t.* (**-sured, -sur·ing**). Insure again, esp. (of insurer or underwriter) against risk one has undertaken. **re·in·sur'ance, re·in·sur'er** *ns.*

re·it·er·ate (rēĭt´erāt) *v.t.* (**-at·ed, -at·ing**). Repeat, say over again or several times. **re·it·er·a·tive** (rēĭt´erātĭv, -eratĭv) *adj.*

reive, reiv·er: see REAVE.

re·ject (rĭjĕkt´) *v.t.* 1. Put aside as not to be accepted, practiced, believed, chosen, used, etc. 2. Cast up again, vomit, evacuate. ~ (rē´-jĕkt) *n.* Thing rejected. **re·jec·-tion** (rĭjĕk´shon) *n.* ~ **slip**, formal notice from editor or publisher accompanying rejected manuscript. **re·ject'er** *n.*

re·joice (rĭjois´) *v.* (**-joiced, -joic·ing**). Cause joy to, make glad; feel great joy; be glad (*that, in, at*); make merry, celebrate some event. **re·joic'ing, re·joic'er** *ns.*

re·join (def. 1. rĭjoin´; def. 2 rējoin´) *v.* 1. Reply to charge or pleading, esp. to plaintiff's reply to defendant's plea (law); say in answer, retort. 2. Join again.

re·join·der (rĭjoin´der) *n.* What is rejoined or said in reply, retort.

re·ju·ve·nate (rĭjōō´venāt) *v.*
(**-nat·ed, -nat·ing**). Make or
become young again. **re·ju·ve-
na·tion** (rĭjōōvenā´sh*o*n) *n.*

re·lapse (rĭlăps´) *v.i.* (**-lapsed,
-laps·ing**). Fall back, sink again,
into wrongdoing, error, heresy,
weakness, illness, etc. ~ (rĭlăps´,
rē´lăps) *n.* Act or fact of relapsing,
esp. deterioration in patient's condition after partial recovery.

re·late (rĭlāt´) *v.* (**-lat·ed, -lat-
ing**). 1. Narrate, recount. 2.
Bring into relation, establish
relation between; have reference *to*,
stand in some relation *to*. **re·lat´er**
n. **re·lat´ed** *adj.* (esp.) Connected,
allied, akin by blood or marriage.

re·la·tion (rĭlā´sh*o*n) *n.* 1.
Narration; a narrative; (law)
referring of an act to an earlier date
as the time of its taking effect.
2. Way in which one thing is
thought of in connection with
another; any connection, correspondence, or association between
things or persons; (pl.) dealings or
connections with others, sexual
intercourse. 3. Kinsman, kinswoman, relative. **re·la´tions** *n.*
re·la´tion·ship *n.* Being related;
kinship. **re·la´tion·al** *adj.*

rel·a·tive (rĕl´atĭv) *adj.* 1.
(gram.) Referring, and attaching a
subordinate clause, to an expressed
or implied antecedent; (of clause)
attached to antecedent by relative
word. 2. Comparative; in relation
to something else; proportioned to
something else; involving or implying comparison or relation; having
application or reference *to*, with
reference *to*; ~ **humidity**: see
HUMIDITY. **rel´a·tive·ly** *adv.*
relative *n.* 1. (gram.) Relative
word, esp. pronoun, as *who, which,
that, what.* 2. (philos.) Relative
thing or term. 3. Kinsman,
kinswoman; one related by blood
or marriage. **rel´a·tive·ness** *n.*

rel·a·tiv·ism (rĕl´atĭvĭzem) *n.*
Doctrine that knowledge is of
relations only; theory that ethical
truth is relative to the individual,
time, and place.

rel·a·tiv·i·ty (rĕlatĭv´ĭtē) *n.* 1.
Relativeness. 2. Branch of physics
concerned with correlation of
descriptions of phenomena by
observers using frames of reference
in relative motion with respect to
each other; (**special**) **theory of** ~,
theory, propounded mainly by
Einstein, based on principle of
constant velocity of light and
showing that all motion is relative,
treating space and time as 4 related
dimensions, and invalidating
previous conceptions of geometry;
(**general**) **theory of** ~, that
developed by Einstein in 1915,
extending the special theory to
include cases of acceleration and
the phenomena of gravity.

re·lax (rĭlăks´) *v.* Cause or allow

*These idealized portraits of bygone
writers and thinkers are a section of one
of the **reliefs** on the Albert Memorial,
Queen Victoria's monument commemorating the Prince Consort's support for
the arts.*

to become loose, slack, or limp;
enfeeble, mitigate, abate; grow less
tense, rigid, stern, etc. **re·lax´er,
re·lax´ant** *ns.* **re·lax·a´tion**
(rēlăksā´sh*o*n) *n.* Partial remission
of penalty, duty, etc.; cessation from
work; recreation, amusement;
diminution of tension, severity,
precision, etc.

re·lay (rē´lā; for sense 1 also
rĭlā´) *n.* 1. Set of fresh horses
substituted for tired ones; work
crew, shift, that relieves another.
2. Switch or other device by which
one electric current is made to
control another; instrument used in
long-distance telegraphy to
reinforce weak current with local
battery etc. 3. ~ **race**, one between
teams of which each person does
part of the distance, the 2nd etc.
members starting when the 1st etc.
end. **relay** (rĭlā´) *v.* (**-layed, -lay-
ing**). Arrange in, provide with,
replace by, get, relays; pass on or
rebroadcast (radio signal, program,
etc., originating at, and received
from, another station).

re·lease (rĭlēs´) *v.t.* (**-leased,
-leas·ing**). 1. (law) Remit (debt),
surrender (right), make over
(property) to another. 2. Set free,
liberate, deliver, unfasten (*from*).
3. Exhibit (motion picture etc.) for
1st time, or generally. 4. Make
(information) public. ~ *n.* 1.
Deliverance, liberation, from
trouble, life, duty, confinement,
etc. 2. Written discharge, receipt;

legal conveyance of right or estate
to another, document effecting this.
3. Handle, catch, etc., that releases
part of machine etc. 4. Public
exhibition of motion picture etc.
for 1st time, or generally; film etc.
so shown. 5. Statement etc. containing information, issued for
publication.

rel·e·gate (rĕl´egāt) *v.t.* (**-gat·ed,
-gat·ing**). Banish *to* some place
of exile (rare); consign or dismiss
to some usu. inferior position,
sphere, etc.; transfer (matter) for
decision or execution. **rel·e·ga-
tion** (rĕlegā´sh*o*n) *n.*

re·lent (rĭlĕnt´) *v.i.* Relax
severity, become less stern;
abandon harsh intention, yield to
compassion. **re·lent´less** *adj.* **re·
lent´less·ly** *adv.* **re·lent´less·ness**
n.

rel·e·vant (rĕl´evant) *adj.* Bearing upon, pertinent *to*, the matter
in hand. **rel´e·vant·ly** *adv.* **rel´-
e·vance, rel´e·van·cy** *ns.*

re·li·a·ble (rĭlī´abel) *adj.* That
may be relied upon; of sound and
consistent character or quality.
re·li·a·bil·i·ty (rĭlīabĭl´ĭtē), **re·li´-
a·ble·ness** *ns.* **re·li´a·bly** *adv.*

re·li·ance (rĭlī´ans) *n.* Trust,
confidence; thing depended upon.
re·li´ant *adj.*

rel·ic (rĕl´ĭk) *n.* 1. Part of holy
person's body or belongings kept
after his death as object of
reverence; memento, souvenir; (pl.)
dead body, remains, of person. 2.
(pl.) What has survived destruction
or wasting, remnant, residue,
scraps; (sing.) surviving trace or
memorial *of* custom, period, people,
etc.; object interesting for its age
or associations.

*Each **religion** has its own means of propagating its beliefs. Although dealing with Australian Aboriginals (1) the Roman Catholics adopt a formal approach, far different from the informality of a Salvation Army man in Papua New Guinea (2). Buddhist monks in Bangkok pray in formal splendor (3).*

re·lief[1] (rĭlēf´) *n.* 1. Alleviation of or deliverance from pain, distress, anxiety, etc.; redress of hardship or grievance. 2. Feature etc. that affords a welcome diversion or relaxes tension. 3. Assistance given to the poor or needy; ~ **work**, organized effort to help the poor or victims of earthquake or other calamity. 4. Reinforcement and esp. raising of siege *of* besieged town. 5. (Replacing of person or persons on duty by) persons(s) appointed to take turn of duty; ~ **pitcher**, (baseball) pitcher who replaces another pitcher during game.

re·lief[2] (rĭlēf´) *n.* Method of molding, carving, or stamping in which design stands out from plane or curved surface with projections proportioned and more or less closely approximating to those of objects imitated (HIGH, LOW[2], ~: see the adjectives); piece of sculpture etc. in relief; distinctness of outline, vividness; ~ **map**, map in which the conformation of an area of Earth's surface is shown by (exaggerated) elevations and depressions or by contour lines or colors.

re·lieve (rĭlēv´) *v.t.* (**-lieved, -liev·ing**). 1. Bring, give, be, relief to; ease, free, from pain, discomfort, etc.; make less burdensome, monotonous, etc.; release from watch or other duty by becoming or providing a substitute; raise siege of. 2. Bring into relief, make stand out.

re·li·gion (rĭlĭj´*on*) *n.* 1. Belief in superhuman controlling power and esp. of a personal God or gods entitled to obedience and worship; effect of such recognition on conduct or mental attitude; expression of such belief; particular system of faith and worship, as *Christian, Muslim, Hindu*, ~. 2. **make a ~ of**, make a point of (esp. doing some habitual action).

re·li·gi·ose (rĭlĭj´ēōs, -lĭjēōs´) *adj.* Conspicuously or excessively religious. **re·li·gi·os·i·ty** (rĭlĭjēōs´ĭtē) *n.* Being religious or religiose. **re·li·gious** (rĭlĭj´*us*) *adj.* 1. Imbued with religion, god-fearing, devout. 2. Of, concerned with, religion; scrupulous, conscientious. 3. Of, belonging to, an order of monks or nuns. **re·li´gious·ly** *adv.* **re·li´gious·ness** *n.* **religious** *n.* (pl. **-gious**). Member of a religious order.

re·lin·quish (rĭlĭng´kwĭsh) *v.t.* Give up, abandon, resign, surrender; let go (something held). **re·lin′quish·ment** n.

rel·i·quar·y (rĕl′ĭkwĕrē) n. (pl. **-quar·ies**). Receptacle for religious relic(s).

rel·ish (rĕl′ĭsh) n. 1. Flavor, distinctive taste *of*; appetizing flavor, attractive quality; thing eaten with plainer food to add flavor. 2. Enjoyment of food or other things; zest; liking *for*. ~ v. Give flavor to; make piquant etc.; get pleasure out of, like, be pleased with. **rel′ish·a·ble** adj.

re·luc·tant (rĭlŭk′tant) adj. Unwilling, disinclined (*to*). **re·luc′tant·ly** adv. **re·luc′tance** n.

re·ly (rĭlī′) v.i. (**-lied, -ly·ing**). Put one's trust, depend with confidence, *on*.

REM (rĕm) n. Intermittent, quick, jerky movements of closed eyes during sleep, esp. while dreaming. [*r*(apid) *e*(ye) *m*(ovement)]

rem (rĕm) n. Unit of effective absorbed dose of ionizing radiation in human tissue, equvalent to 1 roentgen of x-rays. [*r*(oentgen) *e*(quivalent) *m*(an)]

re·main (rĭmān′) v.i. 1. Be left over after removal of some part or quantity, or after part has been done

or dealt with in some way. 2. Be in same place or condition during further time; continue to exist, be extant; be left behind; continue to be (something specified). ~ n. (usu. pl.) What remains over, surviving members, parts, or amount; (usu. pl.) relic(s) of obsolete custom or of antiquity; (pl.) dead body.

re·main·der (rĭmān′der) n. 1. (law) Residual interest in estate devised to another simultaneously with creation of estate; right of succession to title or position on holder's decease. 2. Residue, remaining persons or things; (arith.) number left after subtraction; number left over after preliminary division; copies of book etc. left unsold when demand has ceased and often offered at reduced price. ~ v.t. Treat or dispose of (books) as remainders.

re·mand (rĭmănd′, -mahnd′) v.t. Send back (person in custody) to prison, another court, etc., for further proceedings. ~ n. Recommittal to custody. **re·mand′ment** n.

re·mark (rĭmärk′) v. Take notice of, observe; say by way of comment; make comment *on*. ~

n. Observing, commenting; writter or spoken comment, anything said

re·mark·a·ble (rĭmärk′abel) adj Worth notice, exceptional, striking conspicuous. **re·mark′a·ble·nes** n. **re·mark′a·bly** adv.

Rem·brandt (rĕm′brănt -brahnt), (**Harmensz**) **van Rijr** (1606–69). Dutch painter anc etcher; called the "King o Shadows," from his practice o painting pictures illuminated by clear but limited light, emerging in the midst of masses of shadow.

re·me·di·al (rĭmē′dēal) adj Affording a remedy; intended t remedy disease, deficiency, etc. (~ *reading, English*, etc.). **re·me′di·al·ly** adv.

rem·e·dy (rĕm′edē) n. (p **-dies**). Cure for disease, healin, medicine or treatment; means o removing, counteracting, o relieving any evil; redress, legal o other reparation; the small margi within which coins as minted ar allowed to vary from the standarc fineness and weight (also called th *tolerance*). ~ v.t. (**-died, -dy·ing**) Rectify, make good. **re·me·di·a·ble** (rĭmē′dēabel) adj.

re·mem·ber (rĭmĕm′ber) v.t. 1 Retain in, recall to, the memory recollect, not forget (freq. abs.) 2. Fee, reward, tip; convey greetings from (person) *to* another **re·mem′ber·a·ble** adj. **re·mem′ber·er** n.

re·mem·brance (rĭmĕm′brans n. Remembering, being remem bered, memory, recollection; keep sake, souvenir, memorial.

re·mind (rĭmīnd′) v.t. Pu (person) in mind *of, to* do, etc.

re·mind·er (rĭmīn′der) n Thing that reminds or is meant t remind.

Rem·ing·ton[1] (rĕm′ĭngton) **Eliphalet** (1793–1861). Amer firearms manufacturer. After hi death his firm also manufacture typewriters and sewing machines.

Rem·ing·ton[2] (rĕm′ĭngton) **Frederic** (1861–1909). Amer painter and sculptor; noted fo portrayals of the Amer. West.

rem·i·nisce (rĕm*i*nĭs′) v. (**-nisced, -nisc·ing**). Indulge i reminiscence(s).

rem·i·nis·cence (rĕm*i*nĭs′ens) n Remembering; act of recoverin, knowledge by mental effort expression, fact, etc., recallin, something else; remembered fact o incident; (pl.) collection in literar form of person's memories etc.

rem·i·nis·cent (rĕmĭnĭs'ent) *adj.* Recalling past things; given to or concerned with retrospection, mindful or having memories *of*; reminding or suggestive *of.* **rem·i·nis'cent·ly** *adv.*

re·mise (rĭmīz') *v.t.* (**-mised, -mis·ing**). (law) Surrender, make over (right, property).

re·miss (rĭmĭs') *adj.* Careless of duty, lax, negligent; lacking force or energy. **re·miss'ly** *adv.* **re·miss'ness** *n.*

re·mis·si·ble (rĭmĭs'ĭbel) *adj.* That may be remitted or forgiven.

re·mis·sion (rĭmĭsh'on) *n.* Forgiveness *of* sins etc., forgiveness of sins; remittance of debt, penalty, etc.; diminution of force, effect, degree, violence, etc. (esp. of disease or pain). **re·mis'sive** *adj.*

re·mit (rĭmĭt') *v.* (**-mit·ted, -mit·ting**). 1. Pardon (sins etc.); refrain from exacting, inflicting, or executing (debt, punishment, sentence). 2. Abate, slacken, mitigate. 3. Refer (matter for decision etc.) *to* some authority; send back (case) to lower court; send or put back (*in*)*to* previous state; postpone, defer, *to* or *until*. 4. Transmit, get conveyed by post etc. (money etc.).

re·mit·tance (rĭmĭt'ans) *n.* Money sent to person; sending of money; ~ **man**, person living abroad on remittances; person paid to stay away from home.

re·mit·tent (rĭmĭt'ent) *adj.* Abating at intervals.

rem·nant (rĕm'nant) *n.* Small remaining part, quantity, or number; small remaining quantity, part, or piece, esp. end of piece of cloth etc. left over after rest has been used or sold.

re·mon·strance (rĭmŏn'strans) *n.* 1. (hist.) Formal statement of public grievances. 2. Remonstrating, expostulation; protest. **re·mon'strant** *adj. & n.* **re·mon'strant·ly** *adv.*

re·mon·strate (rĭmŏn'strāt, rĕm'on-) *v.* (**-strat·ed, -strat·ing**). Make protest, expostulate; urge in remonstrance. **re·mon·stra·tive** (rĭmŏn'strativ) *adj.* **re·mon·stra·tion** (rĕmŏnstrā'shon, rĭmon-), **re·mon'stra·tor** *ns.*

rem·o·ra (rĕm'era) *n.* Fish (of family Echenaedidae) that attaches itself to sharks, turtles, ships, etc., by means of adhesive organ on top of head.

re·morse (rĭmôrs') *n.* Bitter repentance of wrong committed; compunction, compassionate reluctance to inflict pain or be cruel. **re·morse'ful** *adj.* **re·morse'ful·ly** *adv.* **re·morse'less** *adj.* **re·morse'less·ly** *adv.* **re·morse'less·ness** *n.*

re·mote (rĭmōt') *adj.* (**-mot·er, -mot·est**). Far apart; far away or off in place or time; not closely

*Design of the chateau at Chenonceaux in France was influenced by Diane de Poitiers and Catherine de Medici. It is typical of a new form of architecture used during the **renaissance** in France.*

related; distant, widely different, *from*; out of the way, secluded; (chiefly superl., of idea etc.) slight(est), faint(est); ~ **control**, control of apparatus etc. from a distance by means of electrically operated device, radio, etc. **re·mote'ly** *adv.* **re·mote'ness** *n.*

re·mount (rēmownt') *v.* Mount (horse etc.) again; go up again, get on horseback again; provide (cavalry) with fresh horses. ~ (rē'mownt) *n.* (mil.) Horse to replace another which is worn out or killed.

re·mov·al (rĭmōō'val) *n.* Removing; being removed.

re·move (rĭmōōv') *v.* (**-moved, -mov·ing**). Take off or away from place occupied, convey to another place; change situation of; get rid of, dismiss. **re·moved'** *adj.* (esp.) Distant or remote *from*; (of cousins) **once, twice**, etc., ~, with difference of one, two, etc.,

generations. **re·mov·a·ble** (rĭmōō'vabel) *adj.* **re·mov·a·bil·i·ty** (rĭmōōvabĭl'ĭtē) *n.* **remove** *n.* 1. Act of removing, removal. 2. Distance; stage in gradation, degree, esp. in consanguinity.

re·mu·ner·ate (rĭmū'nerāt) *v.t.* (**-at·ed, -at·ing**). Reward, pay for services rendered; serve as or provide recompense for (toil etc.) or to (person). **re·mu·ner·a·tion** (rĭmūnerā'shon) *n.* **re·mu·ner·a·tive** (rĭmū'nerātĭv, -eratĭv) *adj.* **re·mu'ner·a·tive·ly** *adv.* **re·mu'ner·a·tive·ness, re·mu'ner·a·tor** *ns.*

Re·mus (rē'mus). (Rom. legend) Twin brother of ROMULUS.

Ren·ais·sance (rĕnĭsahns', -zahns', rĕn'ĭsahns, -zahns; *Brit.* rĭnā'sans) *n.* Great revival in 14th–16th centuries of art and letters, under influence of classical models, beginning in Italy; style of art or architecture characteristic of this period (freq. attrib.); **r** ~, any similar revival.

re·nal (rē'nal) *adj.* Of the kidneys.

Re·nan (renahn'), **Ernest**

Now remembered mainly for his sensual nudes, Renoir only began painting them after he was 40. He adopted the colors of the impressionists but retained his own style.

(1823–92). French scholar, philosopher, and historian; author of *Origines du Christianisme*, in which he applied the method of the historian to the biblical narrative.

re·nas·cence (rĭnăs′ens) *n.* (also **R ~**) Rebirth, renewal; RENAISSANCE. **re·nas′cent** *adj.* Springing up anew, being reborn.

rend (rĕnd) *v.* (**rent** pr. rĕnt, **rend·ing**). Tear, wrench (*off*, *away*, *apart*, etc.); split or divide in 2, in pieces, or (usu.) into factions.

ren·der (rĕn′der) *v.t.* 1. Give in return; give back, restore (archaic); hand over, deliver, give up, surrender (chiefly archaic); pay (tribute etc.), show (obedience etc.), do (service etc.); submit produce for inspection or payment. 2. Reproduce, portray; give representation or performance of, execute; translate. 3. Make, cause to be, convert into. 4. Melt (fat) down, extract by melting; cover (stone, brick) with first coat of plaster. **ren′der·ing** *n.* (esp.) Depiction, interpretation of building, dramatic part, musical composition, etc. **ren′der·er** *n.*

ren·dez·vous (rahn′devoo, -dā-; *Fr.* rahṅdĕvoo′) *n.* (pl. **-vous** pr. -vooz; *Fr.* -voo′). Place appointed for assembling of troops, ships, or aircraft; place of common resort; meeting place agreed on, meeting by agreement. **~** *v.i.* (**-voused**, -vood, **-vous·ing**, -vooĭng). Meet at rendezvous.

ren·di·tion (rĕndĭsh′on) *n.* Rendering, performance, of dramatic role, musical piece, etc.; translation.

ren·e·gade (rĕn′egăd) *n.* Apostate; deserter of party or principles, turncoat; outlaw.

re·nege (rĭnĭg′, -nĕg′, -nāg′, -nēg′) *v.* (**-neged, -neg·ing**). 1. Fail to keep one's word. 2. (bridge) Revoke. **re·neg′er** *n.*

re·new (rĭnoo′, -nū′) *v.* 1. Restore to original state, make (as good as) new; regenerate; patch, fill up, reinforce, replace. 2. Get, begin, make, say, or give, anew; grant or be granted continuation of lease, loan, etc. **re·new′a·ble** *adj.* **re·new′al, re·new′er** *ns.*

ren·net (rĕn′ĭt) *n.* Curdled milk found in stomach of unweaned calf, used in curdling milk for making cheese, junket, etc.; preparation of inner membrane of calf's stomach, or of kinds of plant, used for this and other purposes.

Re·no (rē′nō). City in NW. Nevada, N. of Lake Tahoe; tourist center famous for gambling casinos.

Re·noir (rĕn′wär, rĕnwär′), **Pierre Auguste** (1841–1919). French Impressionist painter; his son, **Jean Renoir**, (1894–1979), French motion picture director.

re·nounce (rĭnowns′) *v.* (**-nounced, -nounc·ing**). Resign, surrender, esp. completely and formally; cast off, repudiate; discontinue, give up, esp. openly; (law) refuse or resign right or position, esp. as heir etc. **re·nounce′ment** *n.*

ren·o·vate (rĕn′ovāt) *v.t.* (**-vat·ed, -vat·ing**). Make new again, repair, (house, garment, etc.); restore to good condition. **ren·o·va·tion** (rĕnovā′shon), **ren′-o·va·tor** *ns.*

re·nown (rĭnown′) *n.* Celebrity, fame, high distinction. **re·nowned′** *adj.* Famous, celebrated.

rent[1] (rĕnt) *n.* Tear in garment, etc.; opening in clouds etc. resembling tear; cleft, fissure, gorge.

rent[2] (rĕnt) *n.* Tenant's periodical payment to owner or landlord for use of land or occupancy of building, house, room, etc.; payment for hire of machinery etc.; **~-free**, exempt from rent. **rent** *v.* Take, occupy, use, at a rent; let or hire for rent; be occupied or hired *at* specified rent.

rent[3]: see REND.

rent·al (rĕn′tal) *n.* Income from rents; amount paid or received as rent; property, building, apartment, etc. for renting.

rent·er (rĕn′ter) *n.* One who holds land etc. by payment of rent.

re·nun·ci·a·tion (rĭnŭnsēā′shon, -shē-) *n.* Renouncing, document expressing this; self-denial, giving up of things. **re·nun·ci·a·tive** (rĭnŭn′sēātĭv, -shēa-), **re·nun·ci·a·to·ry** (rĭnŭn′sēātōrē, -tōre, -shēa-) *adjs.*

rep[1], **repp** (rĕp) *ns.* Textile fabric with corded surface, resembling poplin but heavier, used for curtains, upholstery, etc.

rep[2] (rĕp) *n.* (colloq.) Repertory (theater); representative; reputation.

re·pair[1] (rĭpār′) *v.i.* Resort, have recourse, go often or in numbers, *to*.

re·pair[2] (rĭpār′) *v.t.* Restore to good condition, mend, by replacing

or fixing parts or compensating loss or exhaustion; remedy, set right again, make amends for (loss, wrong, error); **repair'man**, person whose work is repairing things.
repair n. Restoring to sound condition; **in good ~**, in good (working) condition. **re·pair'er** n.
rep·a·ra·ble (rĕp'erabel) adj. (of loss etc.) That can be repaired.
rep·a·ra·tion (rĕperā'shon) n. Repairing or being repaired, repair; making of amends, compensation (esp., pl., that paid to victorious country by defeated one for damage done in war). **re·par·a·to·ry** (rĭpăr'atōrē, -tōrē), **re·par'a·tive** adjs.
rep·ar·tee (rĕpărtē', -tā') n. Witty retort; (making of) witty retorts.
re·past (rĭpăst', -pahst') n. (Food supplied for or eaten at) meal.
re·pa·tri·ate (rēpā'trēāt) v.t. (**-at·ed, -at·ing**). Restore or return to native land. **~** n. Person who has been repatriated.
re·pa·tri·a·tion (rēpātrēā'shon) n.
re·pay (rĭpā') v. (**-paid, -pay·ing**). Pay back (money); return, retaliate (blow, service, visit, etc.); give in recompense for; make repayment to (person); make return for, requite (action); make repayment. **re·pay'a·ble** adj. **re·pay'ment** n.
re·peal (rĭpēl') v.t. Revoke, rescind, annul (law etc.). **~** n. Abrogation, repealing; **R ~**, repeal of PROHIBITION. **re·peal'er** n.
re·peat (rĭpēt') v. Say or do over again; recite, report, reproduce; recur, appear again or repeatedly; (of firearm) fire several shots without needing to be reloaded; (refl.) recur in same form, say or do same thing over again; **repeating decimal**, decimal fraction in which same figures are repeated indefinitely. **repeat** n. Repeating; something repeated, shown, or broadcast again; (mus.) passage intended to be repeated, mark indicating this. **re·peat'a·ble** adj. **re·peat'ed·ly** adv.
re·peat·er (rĭpē'ter) n. (esp.) Watch or clock that strikes the hour and will strike it again if required; firearm etc. that repeats.
re·pel (rĭpĕl') v.t. (**-pelled, -pel·ling**). 1. Drive back, repulse, ward off; refuse admission, acceptance, or approach to. 2. Be repulsive or distasteful to. **re·pel'lent** adj.
re·pent[1] (rĭpĕnt') adj. (chiefly bot.) Creeping, esp. growing along or just under surface of ground.
re·pent[2] (rĭpĕnt') v. Feel contrition, compunction, sorrow, or regret for what one has done or left undone; think with contrition or regret of. **re·pent'ance** n. **re·pent'ant** adj. **re·pent'ant·ly** adv.

re·per·cus·sion (rēperkŭsh'on) n. Repulse or recoil after impact; return or reverberation of sound, echo; indirect effect or reaction of event or act. **re·per·cus·sive** (rēperkŭs'ĭv) adj.
rep·er·toire (rĕp'ertwar, -twōr) n. Stock of dramatic or musical pieces etc. that company or player is accustomed or prepared to perform.
rep·er·to·ry (rĕp'ertōrē, -tōrē) n. (pl. **-ries**). 1. Storehouse or repository, where something may be found. 2. Repertoire; **~ company**, theatrical company that keeps a stock of plays ready for performance.
rep·e·ti·tion (rĕpetĭsh'on) n. Repeating or being repeated; recitation of something learned by heart, piece set to be learned and recited; copy, replica. **rep·e·ti·tious** (rĕpetĭsh'us), **re·pet·i·tive** (repĕt'ĭtĭv) adjs. **re·pet'i·tive·ly** adv. **re·pet'i·tive·ness** n.
re·pine (rĭpīn') v.i. (**-pined, -pin·ing**). Fret, be discontented (at).
re·place (rĭplās') v.t. (**-placed, -plac·ing**). Put back in place; take place of, succeed, be substituted for; fill up place of (with, by), find or provide substitute for; (pass.) be succeeded, have one's or its place filled by. **re·place'a·ble** adj. **re·place'ment** n.
re·play (rēplā') v.t. Play (recording, tape) over again. **~** (rē'plā) n. Act of replaying; thing that is replayed; **instant ~**: see INSTANT.[1]
re·plen·ish (rĭplĕn'ĭsh) v.t. Fill up again (with). **re·plen'ish·ment** n.
re·plete (rĭplēt') adj. Filled, stuffed, fully imbued, well stocked, with; gorged, sated (with). **re·ple·tion** (rĭplē'shon) n.
re·plev·in (rĭplĕv'ĭn) n. Restoration or recovery of personal property unlawfully taken; legal action arising out of, replevin. **~** v.t. (**-plev·ined, -plev·in·ing**), **re·plev·y** (rĭplĕv'ē) v.t. (**-plev·ied, -plev·y·ing**). Recover by replevin.
rep·li·ca (rĕp'lĭka) n. Duplicate made by original artist of his picture etc.; facsimile, exact copy.
re·ply (rĭplī') v. (**-plied, -ply·ing**). Make answer, respond, in word or action (to, that). **~** n. (pl. **-plies**). Act of replying; what is replied, response; (law) pleading by plaintiff after delivery of defendant's plea. **re·pli'er** n.
re·port (rĭpōrt', -pōrt') v. Relate, give an account of; convey, repeat (something said or heard); take down (speech etc.) in writing, esp. with view to publication in newspaper etc.; give formal account or statement of; make report; relate or state as result of observation or investigation; name (person) to

superior authority as having offended in some way; (refl. and intrans.) make known to some authority that one has arrived or is present. **~** n. 1. Common talk, rumor; way person or thing is spoken of, repute. 2. Account given or opinion formally expressed after investigation or consideration; account of conduct and progress of a matter, business, etc. (**progress ~**). 3. Sound of explosion; resounding noise. **re·port'a·ble** adj.
re·port·age (rĭpōr'tĭj, -pōr', rĕpōrtahzh', -pōr-) n. (Style of) reporting events for the press.
re·port·er (rĭpōr'ter, -pōr') n. (esp.) One employed to report events for newspaper or radio or television newscast.
re·pose[1] (rĭpōz') v.t. (**-posed, -pos·ing**). Place (trust etc.) in.
re·pose[2] (rĭpōz') v. (**-posed, -pos·ing**). Rest; lay (oneself down) to rest; lie, be lying, esp. in sleep or death. **~** n. Rest, cessation of activity or excitement; sleep; peaceful or quiescent state, stillness, tranquillity; restful effect; composure or ease of manner. **re·pose'ful** adj. **re·pose'ful·ly** adv. **re·pos'er** n.
re·pos·i·to·ry (rĭpŏz'ĭtōrē, -tōrē) n. (pl. **-ries**). Place where things are stored or may be found, museum, warehouse, etc.; burial place; recipient of confidences or secrets.
re·pous·se (rĕpoōsā') adj. & n. (Ornamental metal work) hammered into relief from reverse side.
repp: REP[1].
rep·re·hend (rĕprĭhĕnd') v.t. Rebuke, blame, find fault with.
rep·re·hen·si·ble (rĕprĭhĕn'sĭbel) adj. **rep·re·hen'si·bly** adv. **rep·re·hen·sion** (rĕprĭhĕn'shon) n.
rep·re·sent (rĕprĭzĕnt') v.t. 1. Bring clearly before the mind, esp. by description or imagination; point out explicitly or seriously, freq. in expostulation etc.; describe as having specific character or quality. 2. Display to the eye, make visible; (esp.) exhibit by means of painting, sculpture, etc.; reproduce in action or show, play, perform, act the part of. 3. Symbolize, serve as embodiment of; serve as specimen or example of; stand for or in place of, denote by a substitute; take or fill the place of, be substitute for in some capacity; (esp.) be accredited deputy for (number of persons) in deliberative or legislative assembly. **rep·re·sen·ta·tion** (rĕprĭzĕntā'shon) n. **proportional ~**: see PROPORTIONAL. **rep·re·sent'a·ble** adj.

*This **replica** of the 'Golden Hind' was built in Appledore, U.K., to be sailed approximately along Drake's course to San Francisco where it now is an historical exhibit.*

1

3

rep·re·sen·ta·tive (rĕprĭzĕn′ta-tĭv) *adj.* Serving to represent; esp. typical of a class; holding place of, acting for, larger body of persons (esp. the whole people) in government or legislation; of, based upon, system by which people are thus represented. **rep·re·sent′a·tive·ly** *adv.* **rep·re·sent′a·tive·ness** *n.* **representative** *n.* 1 Sample, specimen; typical embodiment *of.* 2. Agent, delegate, substitute; person appointed to represent sovereign or nation in foreign court or country; one representing section of community as member of legislative body; **R~**, member of the U.S. House of Representatives or of lower house of a state legislature.

re·press (rĭprĕs′) *v.t.* Check, restrain, put down, keep under; reduce to subjection, subdue, suppress, quell; (psychol.) actively exclude (distressing idea or

As the first animals with backbones to become completely adapted to life on land, reptiles are an important source of study for zoologists. Those surviving include the crocodiles (1), tortoises, terrapins and turtles (2), a wide range of lizards including the Australian frilled variety (3), and tree snakes (4). There is also the tuatara of New Zealand.

memory) from the field of conscious awareness. **re·pres·sion** (rĭprĕsh′on) *n.* **re·pres·sive** *adj.* **re·pres′sive·ly** *adv.*

re·prieve (rĭprēv′) *v.t.* (**-prieved, -priev·ing**). Suspend or delay execution of (condemned person); give respite to. ~ *n.* Reprieving, being reprieved; (warrant for) remission, commutation, or postponement of capital sentence; respite.

rep·ri·mand (rĕp′rimănd, -mahnd) *n.* Official rebuke; rebuke, censure. ~ (rĕp′rimănd,

-mahnd, rĕprimănd′, -mahnd′) *v.t.* Rebuke officially; rebuke, censure severely.

re·print (rēprĭnt′) *v.t.* Print again, esp. in new edition. ~ (rē′prĭnt) *n.* Reproduction in print of matter previously printed; new impression.

re·pris·al (rĭprī′zal) *n.* Act of retaliation; (hist.) forcible seizure of foreign subjects' persons or property in retaliation.

re·prise (rĭprēz′) *n.* Repeated passage in music; repeated song etc. in musical program.

re·proach (rĭprōch′) *v.t.* Express, convey, disapproval to (person) for fault etc. ~ *n.* Reproaching; thing that brings disgrace or discredit (*to*); opprobrium, disgraced or discredited state. **re·proach′a·ble, re·proach′ful** *adjs.* **re·proach′ful·ly** *adv.* **re·proach′ful·ness** *n.* **re·proach′ing·ly** *adv.*

re·pro·bate (rĕp′robāt) *v.t.* (-bat·ed, -bat·ing). Express or feel disapproval of, censure; (of God) cast off, exclude from salvation. **rep·ro·ba·tion** (rĕprobā′shon) *n.* **reprobate** *adj.* & *n.* (Person) cast off by God, hardened in sin, of abandoned character, immoral.

re·pro·duce (rēprodoōs′, -dūs′) *v.* (-duced, -duc·ing). (esp.) Produce copy or representation of; multiply by generation. **re·pro·duc·tion** (rēprodŭk′shon) *n.* **re·pro·duc·tive** (rēprodŭk′tĭv) *adj.* **re·pro·duc·tive·ness** *n.* **re·pro·duc·i·ble** *adj.*

re·proof (rĭproōf′) *n.* Blame; rebuke, expression of blame.

re·prove (rĭproōv′) *v.t.* (-proved, -prov·ing). Rebuke. **re·prov·er** *n.* **re·prov·ing·ly** *adv.*

rep·tant (rĕp′tant) *adj.* (biol.) Creeping, crawling.

rep·tile (rĕp′tĭl, -tīl) *n.* Crawling animal; (biol.) member of the Reptilia, a class of cold-blooded, lung-breathing vertebrates, usu. with scales or horny plates, which includes snakes, lizards, crocodiles, turtles, dinosaurs, etc.; also (fig.) a mean, treacherous person. ~ *adj.* Of reptiles; creeping. **rep·til·i·an** (rĕptĭl′yan) *adj.*

re·pub·lic (rĭpŭb′lĭk) *n.* State in which supreme power rests in the people and their elected representatives and officers, as opp. to one governed by king etc.; any community or society with equality between members; **First, Second, Third, Fourth, Fifth R** ~: see FRANCE[1].

re·pub·li·can (rĭpŭb′lĭkan) *adj.* 1. Of, constituted as, characterizing, republic(s); advocating or supporting republican government. 2. **R ~ Party**, the political party that opposes the DEMOCRATIC Party in U.S.; it was formed in 1854 and its 1st leader to achieve the presidency was Abraham Lincoln; (also, hist.) first party that supported Jefferson. **republican** *n.* Person supporting or advocating republican government; **R ~**, member, supporter, of Republican Party. **re·pub′li·can·ism** *n.*

re·pu·di·ate (rĭpū′dēāt) *v.t.* (-at·ed, -at·ing). Cast off, disown (person, thing); refuse to accept or entertain, or to have dealings with; refuse to recognize or obey (authority) or discharge (obligation, debt). **re·pu·di·a·tion** (rĭpūdēā′-shon), **re·pu′di·a·tor** *ns.*

re·pug·nance (rĭpŭg′nans), **re·pug·nan·cy** (rĭpŭg′nansē) *ns.* (logic) Contradiction, incompatibility, of ideas; antipathy, aversion (to).

re·pug·nant (rĭpŭg′nant) *adj.* (logic) Contradictory (to), incompatible (with); distasteful, objectionable, to. **re·pug′nant·ly** *adv.*

re·pulse (rĭpŭls′) *v.t.* (-pulsed, -puls·ing). Drive back (attack, attacking enemy) by force of arms; rebuff (friendly advances etc.); refuse (request, offer, etc.). ~ *n.* Repulsing or being repulsed; rebuff.

re·pul·sion (rĭpŭl′shon) *n.* 1. (phys.) Tendency of bodies to repel each other or increase their mutual distance; **capillary** ~: see CAPILLARY. 2. Aversion, disgust.

re·pul·sive (rĭpŭl′sĭv) *adj.* 1. (phys.) Exercising repulsion. 2. Exciting aversion or loathing, disgusting. **re·pul′sive·ly** *adv.* **re·pul′sive·ness** *n.*

rep·u·ta·ble (rĕp′yutabel) *adj.* Of good repute. **rep′u·ta·bly** *adv.* **rep·u·ta·bil·i·ty** (rĕpyutabĭl′ĭtē) *n.*

rep·u·ta·tion (rĕpyutā′shon) *n.* What is generally said or believed about the character of a person or thing; state of being well reported of, credit, respectability, good fame; *the* credit or distinction *of.*

re·pute (rĭpūt′) *v.t.* (-put·ed, -put·ing). (usu. pass.) Be generally considered, reckoned, spoken or reported of. **re·put′ed** *adj.* (esp.) Supposed, accounted. **re·put′ed·ly** *adv.* **repute** *n.*

re·quest (rĭkwĕst′) *n.* Act of asking for something, petition; thing asked for; **by** ~, in response to expressed wish. ~ *v.t.* Seek permission *to* do; ask to be given, allowed, or favored with; ask (person) *to* do; ask *that.*

Re·qui·em (rĕk′wēem, rē′kwē-) *n.* (also **r** ~) Mass for repose of souls of the dead; musical setting for this; dirge. [L. (accus.), = "rest," first word of Introit in Mass for the Dead]

re·qui·es·cat (rĕkwēĕs′kăt) *n.* Prayer for repose of soul of the dead. [L. *requiescat in pace* "may he rest in peace"]

re·quire (rĭkwīr′) *v.t.* (-quired, -quir·ing). 1. Demand of (person) *to* do; demand or ask in words, esp. as of right; lay down as imperative. 2. Need, call for, depend for success, etc., on. **re·quire′ment** *n.*

*The first **Republican** President was Abraham Lincoln and the sentiments of the Republican Party are embodied in the Lincoln Memorial in Washington.*

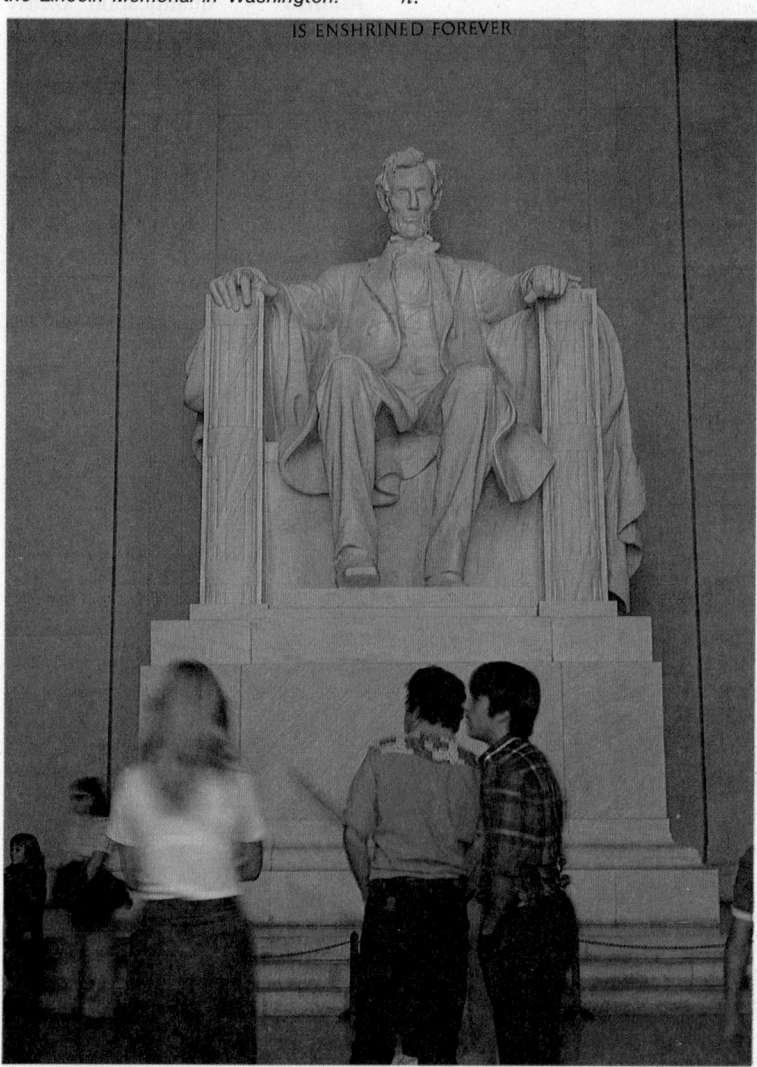

req·ui·site (rĕk′wĭzĭt) *adj.* Required by circumstances, necessary. ~ *n.* Requirement; what is required or necessary. **req′ui·site·ly** *adv.*

req·ui·si·tion (rĕkwĭzĭsh′on) *n.* Requiring, demand made, esp. formal and usu. written demand that some duty be performed, some supplies be furnished, etc. ~ *v.t.* Demand use or supply of for military purposes or public services; demand such supplies etc. from (town, individual, etc.); press into service, call in for some purpose.

re·quite (rĭkwīt′) *v.t.* (**-quit·ed, -quit·ing**). Make return for, reward or revenge (*with*); make return to, repay with good or evil; give in return. **re·quit′al, re·quit′er** *ns.*

re·run (rērŭn′) *v.* (**-ran, -run·ning**). Run (race, film, etc.) again. ~ (rē′rŭn) *n.* Act of rerunning, esp. of film, tape of television program, etc.; film, tape, etc. thus shown.

re·scind (rĭsĭnd′) *v.t.* Abrogate, revoke, annul, cancel. **re·scind′a·ble** *adj.* **re·scis·sion** (rĭsĭzh′on) *n.*

res·cue (rĕs′kū) *v.t.* (**-cued, -cu·ing**). Deliver from or *from* attack, custody, danger, or harm; (law) unlawfully liberate (person), forcibly recover (property). **res′cu·er** *n.* **rescue** *n.* Rescuing, being rescued; deliverance; illegal liberation, forcible recovery.

re·search (rĭsẽrch′, rē′sẽrch) *n.* Careful search or inquiry; (freq. pl.) endeavor to discover facts by scientific study of a subject, course of critical investigation. ~ *v.* Make researches (into). **re·-search′er** *n.*

re·sect (rĭsĕkt′) *v.t.* (surg.) Cut out or pare down (bone, cartilage, nerve, etc.). **re·sec·tion** (rĭsĕk′shon) *n.*

re·se·da (rĭsē′da) *n.* 1. Herbaceous plant of genus **R** ~ that includes mignonette. 2. Pale grayish-green color, as of mignonette.

re·sem·ble (rĭzĕm′bel) *v.t.* (**-bled, -bling**). Be like, have similarity to or some feature or property in common with. **re·sem′blance** *n.*

re·sent (rĭzĕnt′) *v.t.* Show or feel indignation at, feel injured or insulted by. **re·sent′ful** *adj.* **re·sent′ful·ly** *adv.* **re·sent′ment** *n.*

re·ser·pine (resẽr′pĭn, -pēn, rĕs′erpĭn, -pēn) *n.* Alkaloid from plants of genus *Rauwolfia* used as tranquilizer and in treatment of hypertension.

res·er·va·tion (rĕzervā′shon) *n.* (esp.) 1. Tract of land reserved for special purpose, esp. for exclusive occupation by Indian tribe. 2. Express or tacit limitation or exception made about something; **mental** ~, qualification tacitly added in making statement, taking oath, etc. 3. Securing of seat, hotel room, etc., in advance; seat etc. so engaged.

re·serve (rĭzẽrv′) *v.t.* (**-served, -serv·ing**). 1. Keep for future use, enjoyment, or treatment, keep back for later occasion, hold over; keep

The Tennessee Valley Authority reservoir on the Tennessee River. Created in 1933, the authority has been responsible for bringing civilized changes to the lives of many Tennesseans.

oneself in reserve *for*. 2. Retain possession or control of, esp. by legal or formal stipulation; set apart, destine, *for* some use or fate; engage (seat, room, etc.) beforehand; (pass.) be left by fate *for*, fall first or only *to*. **re·served′** *adj.* (esp., of person) Reticent, slow to reveal emotions or opinions, uncommunicative. **re·serv′ed·ly** *adv.* **re·serv′ed·ness** *n.* **reserve** *n.* 1. Something reserved for future use, extra stock or amount; **in** ~, unused but available. 2. (banking) That part of the assets held in the form of cash; (in central banks) that part of the assets held in the form of gold or foreign exchange. 3. (in corporations) That part of the profit not distributed to shareholders but added to capital. 4. Troops withheld from action to reinforce or to cover retreat; forces not in regular service, liable to be called out in emergencies; (in games) extra player chosen in case substitute should be needed. 5. Tract of land reserved for some special purpose = RESERVATION. 6. Limitation, exception, restriction, or qualification, attached to something; **without** ~, fully. 7. Reticence; want of cordiality or friendliness.

re·serv·ist (rĭzẽr′vĭst) *n.* Member of reserve military forces.

res·er·voir (rĕz′ervwār, -vwōr) *n.* Receptacle constructed of earthwork, masonry, etc., in which large quantity of water is stored; any natural or artificial receptacle esp. for or of fluid; place where fluid etc. collects; part of machine, organ of body, holding fluid; reserve supply or collection of knowledge, facts, etc.

re·set (rēsĕt′) *v.t.* (**-set, -set·ting**). Set again (gem, book or its type, etc.).

re·shuf·fle (rēshŭf′el) *v.t.* (**-fled, -fling**). Shuffle again; interchange (appointments, responsibilities, etc.) within a group. ~ *n.*

re·side (rĭzīd′) *v.i.* (**-sided, -sid·ing**). Have one's home, dwell permanently; (of power, rights, etc.) rest or be vested *in* person etc.; (of qualities) be present or inherent *in*. **re·sid′er** *n.*

res·i·dence (rĕz′ĭdens) *n.* Residing; place where one resides, abode *of*; house esp. of considerable pretension, mansion; **in** ~, living or staying regularly at or in some place for the discharge of special duties, or to comply with some regulation.

res·i·den·cy (rĕz′ĭdensē) *n.* (pl. **-cies**). (hist.) Area in a protected state under authority of a resident governor; official residence of such a governor; period of specialized medical training.

res·i·dent (rĕz′ĭdent) *adj.* Residing; (of birds etc.) staying all year.

Resin oozing from a pine trunk damaged by deer, acts in a manner similar to the red corpuscles of the blood. It congeals and forms a protective layer against infection and loss of sap.

A ruler whose authority is no longer accepted has the options, either of clinging to office until removed, or of **resignation:** the Watergate scandal forced Richard Nixon to choose the latter.

not migrating; staying at or in some place in fulfillment of duty or compliance with regulation. ~ *n.* 1. Permanent inhabitant (opp. VISITOR). 2. (hist.) Resident governor or political representative. 3. Physician or other professional person living in, employed in, hospital during specialized medical training, intern.

res·i·den·tial (rězĭděn'shal) *adj.* Suitable for or occupied by private houses; connected with residence. **res·i·den'tial·ly** *adv.*

re·sid·u·al (rĭzĭj'ōōal) *adj.* Remaining, left over, left as residue. ~ *n.* Residual quantity; remainder; residue. **re·sid'u·al·ly** *adv.*

re·sid·u·ar·y (rĭzĭj'ōōĕrē) *adj.* (law) Of the residue of an estate; of a residue.

res·i·due (rĕz'ĭdoo, -dū) *n.* Remainder, rest, what is left over; remains over; what remains of estate after payment of charges, debts, and bequests; (chem. etc.) substance left after combustion or evaporation.

re·sid·u·um (rĭzĭj'ōōum) *n.* (pl. **-sid·u·a** pr. -zĭj'ōōa). What remains, esp. (chem. etc.) residue.

re·sign (rĭzīn') *v.* Relinquish, surrender, give up, hand over (office, right, charge, hope, etc.); reconcile *oneself,* one's *mind,* etc. (*to*); give up office, retire; (chess) discontinue play and admit defeat. **re·signed'** *adj.* Submissive, acquiescent, having resigned oneself to sorrow etc. **re·sign'ed·ly** *adv.*

res·ig·na·tion (rĕzĭgnā'shon) *n.* (esp.) 1. Resigning of an office,

document conveying this. 2. Being resigned, uncomplaining endurance of sorrow, misfortune, etc.

re·sil·ience (rĭzĭl'yens) *n.* Rebound, recoil; elasticity, power of resuming original shape or position after compression, bending, etc. **re·sil'ien·cy** *n.* Resilience; buoyancy, power of recovery. **re·sil'ient** *adj.* **re·sil'ient·ly** *adv.*

res·in (rĕz'ĭn) *n.* Adhesive, highly inflammable substance, hardening on exposure to air, formed by secretion in trees and plants and exuding naturally from many of them (as fir and pine) or obtained by incision, and used in varnishes, medicines, etc. **resin** *v.t.* **res·in·ate** (rĕz'ĭnāt) *v.t.* (**-at·ed, -at·ing**). Rub or treat with resin. **res·in·if·er·ous** (rĕzĭnĭf'erus) *adj.* Yielding, containing, resin.

res·in·ous (rĕz'ĭnus) *adj.* Of, containing, resin.

re·sist (rĭzĭst') *v.* Stop course of, withstand action or effect of; strive against, oppose; offer resistance. **re·sist'ant, re·sist'i·ble, re·sis'tive** *adjs.* **re·sis·tiv·i·ty** (rēzĭstĭv'ĭtē) *n.* **resist** *n.* Composition applied to surfaces for protection. **re·sist'er** *n.*

re·sist·ance (rĭzĭs'tans) *n.* 1. Power of resisting; (also ~ **movement**), any (esp. underground) organization resisting authority, esp. the **R** ~, resisting German authority in occupied countries during World War II; **passive** ~, resistance without resort to violence or active opposition; noncooperation. 2. Hindrance, impeding or

stopping effect, exercised by material thing upon another; (elect., magn., heat) nonconductivity; (elect.) measure of capacity in a conducting body to resist flow of a current (the resistance of a circuit is given by OHM's law as the ratio of the applied voltage (electromotive force) to the current that flows); part of apparatus used to offer definite resistance to current; **line of** ~, direction in which resistance acts; **line of least** ~, (fig.) easiest method or course.

re·sist·less (rĭzĭst'lĭs) *adj.* 1. That cannot be resisted. 2. Unresisting. **re·sist'less·ly** *adv.*

re·sis·tor (rĭzĭs'ter) *n.* Device used to introduce resistance into an electrical circuit.

re·sol·u·ble (rĭsŏl'yubel, -zŏl'-) *adj.* That can be dissolved again.

res·o·lute (rĕz'olōot; *Brit.* rĕz'olūt) *adj.* Determined, decided, bold, not vacillating, unshrinking, firm of purpose. **res'o·lute·ly** *adv.* **res'o·lute·ness** *n.*

res·o·lu·tion (rĕzolōo'shon; *Brit.* rĕzolū'shon) *n.* 1. Separation into components, analysis; (med.) disappearance of inflammation, return of diseased tissue to normal state; (mus.) process by which discord is made to pass into concord; (optics) quality of optical instruments whereby definition of fine detail is obtained. 2. Solving of doubt, problem, question, etc. 3. Formal expression of opinion by legislative body or public meeting; form proposed for this. 4. Resolve, thing resolved on; determined temper or character, boldness and firmness of purpose.

re·solve (rĭzŏlv') *v.* (**-solved, -solv·ing**). 1. Break up into parts, convert or be converted *into;* reduce by mental analysis *into;* (of telescope, microscope) render visible,

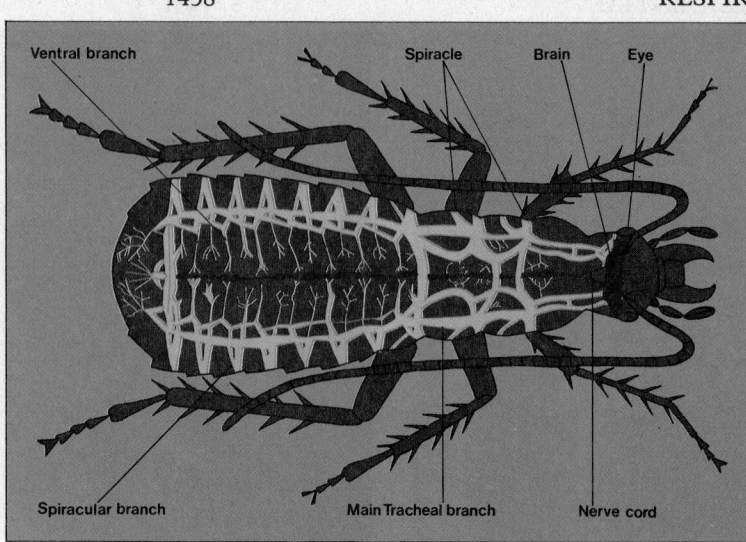

In most insects **respiration** *is not carried out by organs separate from the rest of the body. A network of tubes, the tracheae, carries air through the body, oxygenating the blood.*

distinguish (objects, parts of image); (mus.) convert (discord), be converted, into concord. 2. Solve, explain, clear up, settle. 3. Decide upon, make up one's mind *upon* action or *to* do; form mentally or (of legislative body or public meeting) pass by vote the resolution *that*; (of circumstances etc.) bring (person) to resolution *to* do, *upon* action. **re·solved′** *adj*. **resolve** *n*. Determination or resolution come to in the mind; (poet.) resolution, steadfastness. **re·solv′a·ble** *adj*. **re·solv′er** *n*.

re·sol·vent (rĭzŏl′vent) *adj. & n*. (chiefly med. and chem.) (Drug, application, substance) effecting resolution of tumor etc. or division into component parts.

res·o·nant (rĕz′onant) *adj*. (of sound) Reechoing, resounding; (of body) causing reinforcement or prolongation of sound, esp. by vibration; (of place) echoing, resounding, *with*; (phys.) responding to vibrations of a particular frequency. **res′o·nant·ly** *adv*. **res′o·nance** *n*.

res·o·nate (rĕz′onāt) *v.i*. (**-nat·ed, -nat·ing**). Produce or show resonance. **res′o·na·tor** *n*. (esp.) Appliance for increasing sound by resonance.

res·or·cin·ol (rĭzôr′sĭnōl, -nawl, -nŏl) *n*. Synthetic substance $(C_6H_4(OH)_2)$, used in the production of various dyestuffs and drugs.

re·sort (rĭzôrt′) *v.i*. 1. Turn for aid *to*. 2. Go in numbers or often *to*. ∼ *n*. 1. Thing to which recourse is had, what is turned to for aid, expedient; recourse; **the last** ∼, a last expedient. 2. Place frequented, usu. for specified purpose or quality (as *health, vacation, seaside,* ∼); also attrib., as *resort city*.

re·sound (rĭzownd′) *v*. 1. (of place) Ring or echo (*with*); (of voice, sound, etc.) produce echoes, go on sounding, fill place with sound. 2. Repeat loudly (praises etc.); reecho. **re·sound′ing** *adj*. **re·sound′ing·ly** *adv*.

re·source (rē′sôrs, -sōrs, -zōrs, -zŏrs, rĭsôrs′, -sōrs′, -zōrs′, -zŏrs′) *n*. 1. (usu. pl.) Means of supplying a want, supply that can be drawn on. 2. Expedient, device; skill in devising expedients, ingenuity. **re·source′ful** *adj*. **re·source′ful·ly** *adv*. **re·source′-ful·ness** *n*.

re·spect (rĭspĕkt′) *n*. 1. Reference, relation. 2. Heed or regard *to, of*, attention *to*. 3. Particular detail, point, aspect. 4. Deferential esteem felt or shown toward person or quality; state of being esteemed

Respirators *were first developed during the 1914—18 war, when poison gases such as phosgene were used. Since then developments in the field of chemical warfare have been matched by improvements in respirator design.*

or honored; (pl.) polite messages or attentions. ∼ *v.t*. 1. Refer or relate, to. 2. Treat or regard with deference, esteem, or honor; treat with consideration, spare. **re·spect′er** *n*. **re·spect′ing** *prep*. Having reference to; about, concerning.

re·spect·a·ble (rĭspĕk′tabel) *adj*. 1. Deserving respect. 2. Considerable in number, size, quantity, etc.; fairly good, tolerable. 3. Of good or fair social standing, worthy; befitting respectable persons. **re·spect·a·bil·i·ty** (rĭspĕktabĭl′ĭtē) *n*. **re·spect′a·bly** *adv*.

re·spect·ful (rĭspĕkt′ful) *adj*. Showing deferential esteem. **re·spect′ful·ly** *adv*. **re·spect′ful-**

ness *n*.

re·spec·tive (rĭspĕk′tĭv) *adj*. Pertaining to, connected with, each individual, group, etc., of those in question; separate, several, particular. **re·spec′tive·ly** *adv*.

res·pi·ra·tion (rĕsperā′shon) *n*. Breathing; single inspiration and expiration; (biol.) process by which an organism uses oxygen from its environment and gives out carbon dioxide; **artificial** ∼, any of various methods of restoring the natural function of breathing when this has been suspended.

res·pi·ra·tor (rĕs′perāter) *n*. 1. Apparatus worn over mouth and nose to filter inhaled air or prevent inhalation of noxious materials. 2. Device for maintaining respiration artificially.

re·spire (rĭspīr′) *v*. (**-spired, -spir·ing**). Inhale and exhale air, breathe; breathe again, take breath, recover hope or spirit, get rest or espite. **res·pi·ra·to·ry** (rĕs′pera-ōrē, -tōrē, rĭspīr′a-), **res·pir·a·le** (rĕs′perabel, rĭspīr′a-) *adjs.*

res·pite (rĕs′pĭt) *n.* Delay per-mitted in the discharge of an obli-ation or suffering of a penalty; ıterval of rest or relief. ~ *v.t.* -pit·ed, -pit·ing). Grant respite ; postpone execution or exaction f (sentence, obligation).

re·splend·ent (rĭsplĕn′dent) *adj.* rilliant, dazzlingly or gloriously right. **re·splend′ent·ly** *adv.* **re-**splend′ence, re·splend′en·cy** *ns.*

re·spond (rĭspŏnd′) *v.i.* Make ınswer; act in response (*to*). **re-**pond′er** *n.*

re·spond·ent (rĭspŏn′dent) *adj.* Making answer; responsive *to*; in osition of defendant. ~ *n.* One ho answers; defendant in divorce ase.

re·sponse (rĭspŏns′) *n.* Answer; eccles.) responsory; any part of turgy said or sung by congrega-on in answer to priest; (mus.) epetition by one part of a theme iven by another part.

re·spon·si·bil·i·ty (rĭspŏnsĭbĭl′-ē) *n.* (pl. **-ties**). Being re-onsible; charge for which one is esponsible.

re·spon·si·ble (rĭspŏn′sĭbel) *adj.* iable to be called to account, ınswerable; morally accountable r actions, capable of rational onduct; of good credit and repute, eliable, trustworthy; involving re-onsibility. **re·spon′si·ble·ness re·spon′si·bly** *adv.*

re·spon·sive (rĭspŏn′sĭv) *adj.* ınswering; by way of answer; sponding readily to or *to* some ıfluence, impressionable, sympa-etic; (of liturgy etc.) using esponses. **re·spon′sive·ly** *adv.* e·spon′sive·ness** *n.*

re·spon·so·ry (rĭspŏn′serē) *n.* ol. **-ries**). (eccles.) Anthem said r sung by soloist and choir after sson.

rest[1] (rĕst) *v.* 1. Take repose y lying down, esp. in sleep; lie death or the grave; cease, abstain be relieved from exertion, action, ıovement, or employment; be at ıse or in peace, stay, remain; give est or repose to, lay to rest; allow rest or remain inactive or ıiescent. 2. Have place or posi-on, place, set, lay, (*on*); (of eyes) e directed (*on*); lie or lean, lay, ı for repose or support; rely, epend, be based, base, found, ow to depend *on*. 3. **resting** lace**, place provided or used for sting; **last resting place**, the ave; **rest up**, rest thoroughly. st *n.* 1. Repose or sleep, esp.

in bed at night; intermission of, freedom from, labor, exertion, or activity; freedom from distress, trouble, etc.; quiet or tranquillity of mind; repose of the grave; **at ~**, tranquil, inert; settled; **set at ~**, satisfy, assure; settle; **day of ~**, sabbath; **lay to ~**, bury; dis-pense with. 2. Place of resting or abiding; lodging place or shelter. 3. Prop, support; what something rests on. 4. (mus.) Interval of silence, pause, indicated by various signs according to duration; pause in elocution, caesura in verse. 5. **~ cure**, rest in bed as medical treatment; **~ room**, (euphem.) public lavatory.

*The **restoration** of this house in Williamsburg, Virginia is an example of the care taken by modern-day enthusi-asts who want to keep their heritage.*

hen paintings or other ancient monu-ents need **restoration,** including the mbs in Westminster Abbey, U.K., all forts are devoted to reproducing the iginal impression, often by scientific alysis of the original paint.

rest[2] (rĕst) *v.i.* Remain over (now rare); remain in specified state; **~ with**, be left in the hands or charge of. **rest** *n.* Remainder or remaining parts or individuals (*of*) (with sing. or pl. verb); **for the ~**, as regards anything beyond what has been specially mentioned.

res·tau·rant (rĕs′terant, -te-rahnt, -trant) *n.* Place where meals or refreshments may be had.

res·tau·ra·teur (rĕsteratēr′) *n.* Restaurant owner.

rest·ful (rĕst′ful) *adj.* Favorable to repose, free from disturbing in-fluences, soothing. **rest′ful·ly** *adv.* **rest′ful·ness** *n.*

res·ti·tu·tion (rĕstĭtoō′shon, -tū′-) *n.* Restoring of or *of* thing to proper owner; reparation for in-jury; restoring or return of a pre-vious state or position.

res·tive (rĕs′tĭv) *adj.* (of horse) Refusing to go forward, obstinately moving backward or sideways when being driven or ridden, intractable, resisting control; (of person) un-manageable, rejecting control, fidgety. **res′tive·ly** *adv.* **res′-**tive·ness** *n.*

rest·less (rĕst′lĭs) *adj.* Finding or affording no rest; uneasy, agi-tated, unpausing, fidgeting. **rest′-**less·ly** *adv.* **rest′less·ness** *n.*

res·to·ra·tion (rĕsterā′shon) *n.* (esp.) 1. **R ~**, reestablishment of monarchy in England with return of Charles II to the throne in 1660; period between this and the revolution of 1688. 2. Action or process of restoring to original form or perfect condition.

re·stor·a·tive (rĭstor′ativ, -stōr′-) *adj.* Tending to restore health or strength. ~ *n.* Restora-tive food, medicine, or agency.

re·store (rĭstor′, -stōr′) *v.t.*

(**-stored, -stor·ing**). 1. Give back, make restitution of. 2. Repair, alter, (building, painting, etc.) so as to bring back as nearly as possible to original form, state, etc.; reinstate, bring back *to* dignity or right; bring back *to* health, cure. 3. Reestablish, renew, bring back into use; replace or insert (words etc. in text, missing parts of thing etc.); replace, bring *to* former place or condition. **re·stor′er** *n*.

re·strain (rĭstrān′) *v.t*. Check or hold in *from*, keep in check or under control or within bounds, repress, keep down; confine, imprison. **re·strained′, re·strain′-a·ble** *adjs*. **re·strain′er** *n*.

re·straint (rĭstrānt′) *n*. 1. Restraining, being restrained; check; controlling agency or influence; confinement; **without** ∼, freely, copiously. 2. Constraint, reserve.

re·strict (rĭstrĭkt′) *v.t*. Confine, bound, limit (*to, within*). **re·strict′ed·ly** *adv*. **re·stric′tion** (rĭstrĭk′shon) *n*. **re·stric′tive** *adj*. ∼ **covenant**, real-estate agreement barring free use of property for particular purposes or (usu. clandestine or illegal) for occupancy by or sale to members of specified ethnic group(s). **re·strict′ed** *adj*. **re·stric′tive·ly** *adv*. **re·stric′-tive·ness** *n*.

re·sult (rĭzŭlt′) *v.i*. Arise as consequence, effect, or conclusion *from*; end *in* specified way. ∼ *n*. Consequence, issue, outcome; quantity, formula, etc., obtained by calculation.

re·sult·ant (rĭzŭl′tant) *adj*. Resulting. ∼ *n*. Product, outcome; force that is equivalent of two or more forces acting from different directions at one point; composite or final effect of any two or more forces.

re·sume (rĭzoōm′; *Brit*. rĭzūm′) *v*. (**-sumed, -sum·ing**). 1. Get or take again or back; recover; reoccupy. 2. Begin again; go on (with) after interruption; recommence.

ré·su·mé, re·su·me (rĕz′-oōmā, rā′soō-, rĕzoōma′, rāzoō-) *ns*. Summary, epitome, abstract; (esp.) written summary or list of one's education, qualifications, and previous jobs submitted with job application.

re·sump·tion (rĭzŭmp′shon) *n*. Resuming. **re·sump′tive** *adj*.

re·sur·gent (rĭsẽr′jent) *adj*. That rises or tends to rise again. **re·sur′gence** *n*.

re·sur·rect (rĕzurĕkt′) *v.t*. Raise from the dead; bring back to life; revive practice or memory of.

re·sur·rec·tion (rĕzurĕk′shon) *n*. 1. **R**∼, rising of Christ from the grave; rising again of the dead at the Last Judgment. 2. Revival from disuse, inactivity, or decay; restoration to vogue or memory. **res·ur·rec′tion·al** *adj*.

re·sus·ci·tate (rĭsŭs′ĭtāt) *v*. (**-tat·ed, -tat·ing**). Revive, return or restore to life, consciousness, vogue, vigor, etc. **re·sus·ci·ta·tion** (rĭsŭsĭtā′shon), **re·sus′ci·ta·tor** *ns*. **re·sus′ci·ta·tive** *adj*.

ret (rĕt) *v.t*. (**ret·ted, ret·ting**). Soften (flax, hemp) by soaking in water or exposing to moisture.

ret. *abbrev*. Retired.

re·tail (rē′tāl) *n*. Sale of goods in small quantities to the consumer (freq. attrib. and in adverbial expressions; opp. WHOLESALE). ∼ (rē′tāl for def. 1; rētāl′ for sense 2) *v*. 1. Sell (goods) by retail; (of goods) be retailed. 2. Recount, relate details of. **re′tail·er** *n*.

re·tain (rĭtān′) *v.t*. 1. Keep in

*The **Resurrection** of Jesus Christ is one of the cornerstones of Christianity and has been portrayed frequently in religious art. Below is a 14th-century altar piece from an Italian church, painted in Orcagna's style.*

place, hold fixed; **retaining wall**, one supporting and confining mass of earth or water. 2. Secure services of (esp. lawyer or consultant) by engagement and preliminary payment. 3. Keep possession of, continue to have; continue to practice or recognize, allow to remain or prevail, keep unchanged; bear in mind, remember. **re·tain′ment** *n*.

re·tain·er (rĭtā′ner) *n*. 1. Fee paid to engage the services of a lawyer, consultant, etc.; sum paid to secure special services. 2. One who retains. 3. (hist.) Dependent or follower of person of rank or position; domestic servant. 4. Orthodontic device used to hold teeth in desired position.

re·tal·i·ate (rĭtăl′ēāt) *v*. (**-at·ed, -at·ing**). Repay (esp. injury, insult etc.) in kind; make return or requital (esp. of injury). **re·tal·i·a·tion** (rĭtălēā′shon) *n*. **re·tal·i·a·to·ry** (rĭtăl′ēatōrē, -tōre) *adj*.

re·tard (rĭtärd′) *v*. Make slow

1 pigment layer
2 rods and cones layer
3 limiting membrane
4 outer nuclear layer
5 outer plexiform layer
6 inner nuclear layer
7 inner plexiform layer
8 ganglion cell layer
9 optic nerve fibre layer
10 inner limiting membrane

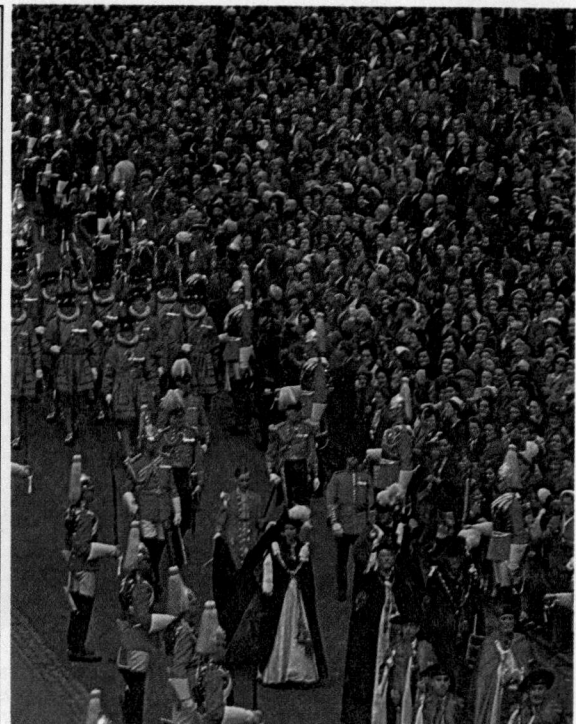

*The **retina** is the area at the back of the eye which is linked by a complicated structure (shown diagrammatically above), which transforms images received through the lens into impulses which are transmitted to the brain.*

*Queen Elizabeth II, on her way to the presentations of the Order of the Garter, is accompanied by a **retinue**, formerly a group of people dependent on the goodwill of the monarch, but whose present-day obligation is to the Crown.*

or late, delay progress, arrival, accomplishment, or happening of. **re·tard·ate** (rĭtār´dāt) *adj.* & *n.* Mentally retarded (person). **re·-tard´ed** *adj.* With mental or physical development behind what is normal. **re·tar·da·tion** (rē-tārdā´shon) *n.* **retard** *n.* Delay; (mus.) slackening of tempo.

re·tard·ant (rĭtār´dant) *n.* (chem.) Substance capable of delaying chemical reaction. ~ *adj.* Able to retard.

retch (rěch) *v.i.* Make motion of vomiting, esp. ineffectually and involuntarily. ~ *n.* Retching motion or sound.

re·ten·tion (rĭtěn´shon) *n.* Retaining; esp. (med.) retaining in body of secretion usually evacuated.

re·ten·tive (rĭtěn´tĭv) *adj.* 1. (of memory) Tenacious, not forgetful. 2. Tending, inclined, apt, to retain. **re·ten´tive·ness, re·ten·tiv·i·ty** (rētěntĭv´ĭtē) *ns.*

ret·i·cence (rět´ĭsens), **ret·i·-cen·cy** (rět´ĭsensē) *ns.* Reserve in speech, avoidance of saying too much or of speaking freely. **ret´i·cent** *adj.* **ret´i·cent·ly** *adv.*

ret·i·cle (rět´ĭkel) *n.* Network of fine threads or lines in object glass of optical instrument to help accurate observation.

re·tic·u·lar (rĭtĭk´yuler) *adj.* Netlike.

re·tic·u·late (rĭtĭk´yulāt) *v.* -lat·ed, -lat·ing). Divide, be divided or marked, into a network; arrange, be arranged, in small squares or with intersecting lines. **·e·tic·u·late** (rĭtĭk´yulĭt, -lāt), **·et´i·cu·lat·ed** *adjs.* **re·tic´u·-**

late·ly *adv.* **re·tic·u·la·tion** (rĭtĭkyulā´shon) *n.*

ret·i·cule (rět´ĭkūl) *n.* 1. Reticle. 2. (archaic) Lady's bag of woven or netlike material carried or worn to serve purpose of pocket.

re·tic·u·lum (rĭtĭk´yulum) *n.* (pl. **-la** pr. -la). 1. Second stomach of ruminant. 2. Netlike structure, reticulated membrane, etc.

ret·i·na (rět´ina) *n.* (pl. **-nas, -nae** pr. -nē). Innermost layer or coating, sensitive to light, at back of eyeball, in which optic nerve terminates. **ret´i·nal** *adj.*

ret·i·nue (rět´inoo, -nū) *n.* Suite or train of persons in attendance upon great personage. **ret´i·nued** *adj.*

re·tire (rĭtīr´) *v.* (-tired, -tir·-ing). 1. Withdraw, go away, seek seclusion or shelter; withdraw *to* usual place or occupation, to bed, etc.; retreat, move back or away, recede. 2. Cease *from* or give up office, profession, employment, or business, esp. to live on savings, income, or pension; compel (officer, employee) to retire; (baseball) cause (batter or side) to conclude an inning. 3. (mil.) Move back. **re·tired´** *adj.* **re·tir´ing** *adj.* (esp.) Shy; fond of seclusion. **re·tir·ee** (rĭtīrē´, -tīr´ē) *n.* One who has retired from a career or occupation.

re·tire·ment (rĭtīr´ment) *n.*

(esp.) Seclusion; secluded place; condition of having retired from work.

re·tort¹ (rĭtôrt´) *v.* 1. Repay (esp. injury) in kind. 2. Reply quickly and sharply; present a counterargument; make, say by way of, repartee. ~ *n.* Incisive reply, repartee; turning of argument or charge against its author; piece of retaliation. **re·tort´er** *n.*

re·tort² (rĭtôrt´) *n.* Vessel usu. of glass with long downward-bent neck used in distilling liquids; clay or iron cylinder in which coal is heated to produce gas; furnace in which iron is heated with carbon to produce steel.

re·touch (rētŭch´) *v.t.* Amend or improve by fresh touches, touch up (esp. photographic negative or print). **re·touch´a·ble** *adj.* **re·touch´er** *n.*

re·trace (rĭtrās´) *v.t.* (-traced, -trac·ing). Trace back to source or beginning; go back over (one's steps, way, etc.). **re·trace´a·ble** *adj.*

re·tract (rĭtrăkt´) *v.* 1. Draw (esp. part of one's body or of machine) back or in; (of such part etc.) shrink back or in, be capable of being retracted; (phonet.) pronounce with tongue retracted. 2. Withdraw, revoke, cancel opinion or statement as erroneous or unjustified. **re·tract´a·ble** *adj.* **re·-**

*The golden labrador is one of the breeds of dogs used as a **retriever** of game and, having a good response to training, is most favored as a guide dog for the blind.*

trac'tion *n.*

re·trac·tile (rĭtrăk'tĭl) *adj.* Capable of being retracted, as cats' claws.

re·tread (rētrĕd') *v.t.* (**-tread·ed, -tread·ing**). Furnish (tire) with fresh tread. ~ (rē'trĕd) *n.* Tire renovated thus.

re·treat (rĭtrēt') *v.* Go back, retire, relinquish a position (esp. of army etc.); recede; (chiefly in chess) move (piece) back from forward or threatened position. ~ *n.* 1. Act of, (mil.) signal for, retreating; (mil.) bugle call signifying lowering of flag at sunset; **beat a ~**, retreat, abandon undertaking. 2. Withdrawing into privacy or security; (place of) seclusion; place of shelter; (place of) temporary retirement for religious exercises.

re·trench (rĭtrĕnch') *v.* 1. Reduce amount of (esp. expenses etc.); economize; remove, delete, omit. 2. (fort.) Furnish with inner line of defense, usu. consisting of trench and parapet. **re·trench'ment** *n.*

re·tri·al (rētrī'al) *n.* Retrying of a case in a court of law.

ret·ri·bu·tion (rĕtrĭbū'shon) *n.* Recompense, usu. for evil, vengeance, requital. **re·trib·u·tive** (rĭtrĭb'yutĭv), **re·trib·u·to·ry** (rĭtrĭb'yutōrē, -tōrē) *adjs.*

re·trieve (rĭtrēv') *v.* (**-trieved, -triev·ing**). 1. (of dogs) Find and bring in (killed or wounded game); find and bring back; get back, regain. 2. Recall to mind, remember. 3. Rescue *from* bad state etc.; restore to flourishing state, revive (esp. fortunes etc.); repair, set right (loss, disaster, error). ~ *n.* (Possibility of) recovery. **re·triev'a·ble** *adj.* **re·triev'al** *n.* Information retrieval: see INFORMATION.

re·triev·er (rĭtrē'ver) *n.* Dog of breed specially adapted for retrieving game.

retro- *prefix.* Backward, back.

ret·ro·act (rĕtrōăkt') *v.i.* React; operate in backward direction; (law) have retrospective effect, be effective as of past date. **ret·ro·ac'tion** *n.* **ret·ro·ac'tive** *adj.* **ret·ro·ac'tive·ly** *adv.*

ret·ro·cede¹ (rĕtrōsēd') *v.i.* (**-ced·ed, -ced·ing**). Move back, recede.

ret·ro·cede² (rĕtrōsēd') *v.t.* (**-ced·ed, -ced·ing**). Cede (territory) back again.

ret·ro·fire (rĕt'rofīr) *v.* (**-fired, -fir·ing**). Ignite (retrorocket).

ret·ro·fit (rĕtrōfĭt') *v.* (**-fit·ted, -fit·ting**). Alter or improve machine, building, etc. already in use by adding more modern features.

ret·ro·gra·da·tion (rĕtrōgrādā'shon) *n.* 1. (astron.) Apparent backward motion of planet in zodiac; apparent motion of heavenly body from east to west among the stars; backward movement of lunar nodes on ecliptic. 2. Retrogression.

ret·ro·grade (rĕt'rogrād) *adj.* 1. (astron.) In or showing retrogradation. 2. Directed backward, retreating; reverting, esp. to inferior state, declining; inverse, reversed. ~ *v.i.* (**-grad·ed, -grad·ing**). Show retrogradation, move backward, recede, retire, decline, revert.

ret·ro·gress (rĕtrōgrĕs', rĕt'rogrĕs) *v.i.* Go back, move backward; deteriorate. **ret·ro·gres'sive** *adj.* **ret·ro·gres'sive·ly** *adv.*

ret·ro·gres·sion (rĕtrōgrĕsh'on) *n.* Backward or reversed movement; return to less advanced state, decline, deterioration.

ret·ro·rock·et, ret·ro·rock·et (rĕt'rōrŏkĭt) *ns.* Auxiliary rocket producing thrust in opposite direction or at oblique angle to course of spacecraft etc., used for decelerating etc.

ret·ro·spect (rĕt'rospĕkt) *n.* Regard or reference *to* precedent, authority, or previous conditions; view or survey of past time or events.

ret·ro·spec·tion (rĕtrospĕk'shon) *n.* Action of looking back, esp. into the past, indulgence or engagement in retrospect. **ret·ro·spec'tive** *adj.* Of, in, proceeding by, retrospection; (of statutes etc.) operative with regard to past time, not restricted to the future, retroactive. **ret·ro·spec'tive·ly** *adv.*

ret·rous·sé (rĕtrōōsā', retrōō'sā) *adj.* (of nose) Turned up at tip.

ret·ro·vert·ed (rĕt'rovērtĭd) *adj.* Turned backward (esp. path., of uterus).

ret·si·na (rĕt'sina, rĕtsē'-) *n.* Resin-flavored Greek wine.

re·turn (rĭtẽrn') *v.* 1. Come or go back; revert. 2. Bring, convey, give, send, put, or pay, back or in return or requital; give, render (thanks). 3. Say in reply, retort. 4. Report in answer to official demand for information, state by way of report or verdict; reelect, reappoint (esp. a legislator, public official) to office. ~ *n.* 1. Coming back; coming around again; return ticket; (**many**) **happy ~s (of the day)**, birthday or festival greeting; **return ticket**, ticket for journey to place and back again to point of departure. 2. Side or part receding, usu. at right angles, from front or direct line of any work or structure. 3. (Coming in of) proceeds or profit of undertaking. 4. Giving, sending, putting, or paying back; thing so given, sent, etc., esp. report in answer to writ or official demand for information, esp. (*income*) *tax return*. **re·turn'a·ble** *adj.* **re·turn'er, re·turn·ee** (rĭtẽrnē', -tẽr'nē) *ns.*

re·tuse (rĭtōōs', -tūs') *adj.* (of leaf, part of insect, etc.) Having a broad or rounded end with depression in center.

Reu·ben (rōō'bĭn). Hebrew patriarch, eldest son of Jacob and Leah (Gen. 29); tribe of Israel traditionally descended from him.

re·un·ion (rēŭn'yon) *n.* Reuniting, being reunited; social gathering of intimates or persons with common interests; esp. of the members of a family once a year (**family ~**) or of a school's graduating class of a particular year (**class ~**).

Ré·un·ion (rēŭn'yon). (formerly

Bourbon) Island and French overseas department, in the Indian Ocean E. of Madagascar, 70 sq. mi. (181 sq. km); capital, Saint-Denis.

re·u·nite (rēūnīt′) v. (**-nit·ed, -nit·ing**). Bring or come together again, join after separation.

rev (rĕv) n. (colloq.) (mech.) Revolution. ~ v. (**revved, rev·ving**). Cause (internal combustion engine) to run quickly, esp. before bringing it into use, speed *up*; (of engine) revolve, be speeded *up*.

Rev. *abbrev.* Revelation (New Testament); Reverend.

re·vamp (rēvămp′) v. Vamp or patch up again; renovate, revise, improve.

re·vanch·ism (rĭvahn′chĭzem) n. (pol.) Policy of seeking to recover lost territory etc.

re·veal (rĭvēl′) v.t. Disclose, make known, divulge; display, show, let appear. **re·veal′ing·ly** adv. **re·veal′ment** n.

re·veil·le (rĭvĕlē) n. Military waking signal sounded in morning on bugle or drums. [Fr. *réveillez*, imper. pl. of *réveiller* awaken, f. L. *vigilare* keep watch]

rev·el (rĕv′el) v.i. (**-eled, -el·ing**, Brit. **-elled, -el·ling**). Make merry, be riotously festive; take keen delight *in*. **rev′el·er**, Brit. **rev′el·ler** ns. **revel** n. Reveling; (occasion of indulgence in) merrymaking (freq. pl.). **rev′el·ry** n. (pl. **-ries**).

rev·e·la·tion (rĕvelā′shon) n. 1. Disclosing of knowledge, knowledge disclosed, esp. to man by divine or supernatural agency; **R ~** (**of St. John the Divine**), (pop. **Revelations**), last book of New Testament, the Apocalypse.

2. Striking disclosure; revealing of some fact. **rev·e·la·to·ry** (rĕvĕl′-atōrē, -tōrē, rĕv′ela-) adj.

re·venge (rĭvĕnj′) v. (**-venged, -veng·ing**). Avenge *oneself* (*on* a person); inflict punishment, exact retribution, for (injury, harm, etc.); avenge (person). ~ n. Revenging, act done in revenging; desire to revenge, vindictive feeling; (in games) opportunity given for re-

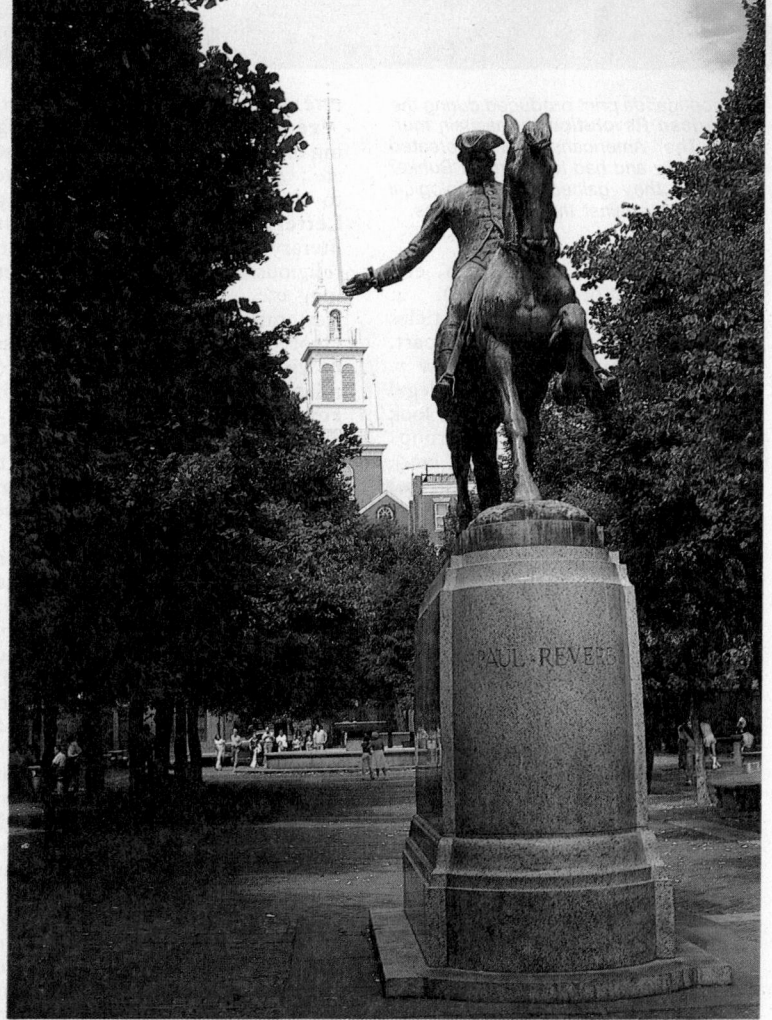

versing former result by return game. **re·venge′ful** adj. **re·venge′ful·ly** adv. **re·venge′ful·ness** n.

rev·e·nue (rĕv′enū, -nōō) n. Income, esp. of large amount, from any source; (pl.) collective items or amounts constituting this; (sing.) annual income of government or state, from which public expenses are met.

re·ver·ber·ate (rĭvĕr′berāt) v. (**-at·ed, -at·ing**). Return, reflect, reecho (sound, light, etc.); be reflected or reechoed; (of flame, heat, etc.) be forced back *into*, *over*, *on* (furnace, substance, etc.); subject to action of reverberatory furnace. **re·ver·ber·a·tion** (rĭvĕrbera′shon) n. **re·ver′ber·ant, re·ver′ber·a·to·ry, re·ver·ber·a·tive** (rĭvĕr′berativ) adjs.

re·vere (rĭvēr′) v.t. (**-vered, -ver·ing**). Regard as sacred or exalted, hold in deep and usu. affectionate or religious respect, venerate.

Re·vere (rĭvēr′), **Paul** (1735–1818). Amer. silversmith, engraver, patriot, famous for his midnight ride from Charlestown to Lexington (1775) to give warning that Brit. troops were advancing from Boston.

rev·er·ence (rĕv′erens) n. Revering; capacity for this; gesture indicating respect; **your, his, R ~**, titles used to, of, clergyman. **rev·er·en·tial** (rĕverĕn′shal) adj. **rev·er·en·tial·ly** adv. **reverence** v.t. (**-enced, -enc·ing**). Regard with reverence, venerate.

rev·er·end (rĕv′erend) adj. Deserving reverence by age, character, or associations; esp. as respectful epithet applied to members of the clergy, freq. (abbrev. Rev.) prefixed to name and designation of clergyman; of, connected with, the clergy, e.g., *Right R ~*, title of Episcopal, Anglican, bishop; *Most Reverend*, of R.C. bishop.

rev·er·ent (rĕv′erent) adj. Feeling or showing reverence. **rev′er·ent·ly** adv.

rev·er·ie (rĕv′erē) n. (Mood of) musing, daydream(ing).

re·verse (rĭvĕrs′) adj. Opposite (*of*) or contrary to in character or order; back or backward, upside down. **re·verse′ly** adv. **reverse** n. 1. Contrary, opposite; gear permitting vehicle to be driven backward; **in ~**, with the position reversed, the other way around; (of vehicle) in reverse gear, moving backward. 2. (Device on) side of coin, medal, etc., that does not bear main device or inscription; verso (of leaf in book etc.); back. 3. Misfortune, disaster, esp. defeat in battle; (pl.) financial setback. **re·verse** v. (**-versed, -vers·ing**). Turn the other way around or up, or inside out; invert; transpose; ~

*A propaganda print produced during the **American Revolution** to maintain morale. The Americans were defeated technically and had to reform at Bunker Hill, but they gained a psychological advantage against the British troops.*

the charges, make recipient of telephone call responsible for payment; convert to opposite character or effect; cause (engine etc.) to work in contrary direction; revoke, annul (decree, act, etc.). **re·vers'er, re·ver'sal** *ns.* **re·vers'i·ble** *adj.* **re·vers·i·bil·i·ty** (rĭvẽrsɪbĭl´ĭtē), **re·vers'i·ble·ness** *ns.*

re·ver·sion (rĭvẽr´zhon, -shon) *n.* 1. (Return to grantor or his estate right of ultimate succession to) estate granted till specified date or event, esp. death of original grantee. 2. Return to a previous state, habit, etc., esp. (biol.) to ancestral type. **re·ver'sion·ar·y** *adj.*

re·ver·sion·er (rĭvẽr´zhoner, -sho-) *n.* One who has the reversion of an estate.

re·vert (rĭvẽrt´) *v.* 1. (of property or money) Return to original owner or his heirs. 2. Return *to* former condition, primitive state, etc.; fall back into wild state. **re·vert'i·ble** *adj.* (of property) Subject to reversion.

re·vet (rĭvĕt´) *v.t.* (**-vet·ted, -vet·ting**). Face (rampart, wall, etc.) with masonry etc., esp. in fortification. **re·vet'ment** *n.* Retaining wall or facing.

re·view (rĭvū´) *n.* 1. Display and formal inspection of troops, fleet, etc.; **pass in ~**, (fig.) examine, be examined. 2. General survey or reconsideration of subject or thing. 3. Published account or criticism of literary work, play, film, etc. (esp. a new or recent one). 4. Periodical publication with articles on current events, new books, art, etc. 5. Second view. **review** *v.* View again; subject to esp. legal revision; survey, glance over, look back on; hold review of (troops etc.); write review of (book etc.), write reviews. **re·view'er** *n.* (esp.) Writer of review(s).

re·vile (rĭvīl´) *v.* (**-viled, -vil·ing**). Call by derogatory names, abuse; talk abusively. **re·vile'ment, re·vil'er** *ns.* **re·vil'ing·ly** *adv.*

re·vise (rĭvīz´) *v.t.* (**-vised, -vis·ing**). Read carefully over, examine, go over again, in order to correct, improve, or amend (literary matter, printer's proofs, law, etc.); **Revised Version**, (abbrev. R.V.) Brit. revision (1870–1884) of 1611 Authorized Version of Bible; **Revised Standard Version**, Amer. revision (1946–57) of the 1901 American Standard Version. **re·vis'al, re·vi·sion** (rĭvĭzh´on) *ns.* **re·vi'sion·ism** *n.* Departure from authoritative (esp. Marxist) doctrine. **re·vi'sion·ist** *n.* **re·vi'sion·al, re·vi·so·ry** (rĭvī´-

zerē) *adjs.* **re·vis'er, re·vi'sor** *ns.*

re·viv·al (rĭvī´val) *n.* 1. Bringing or coming back into vogue, use etc.; restoring of old play etc. to stage etc.; **R ~ of Learning Letters**, the Renaissance in it literary aspect. 2. Reawakening o religious fervor; campaign, meeting, etc., to promote this. 3 Restoration to bodily or menta vigor or to life or consciousness **re·viv'a·lism** *n.* State or kind o religion characterized by revivals **re·viv'al·ist** *n.*

re·vive (rĭvīv´) *v.* (**-vived -viv·ing**). Come or bring back t life, consciousness, existence, vigor notice, activity, validity, or vogue **re·viv'er** *n.*

re·viv·i·fy (rĭvĭv´ĭfī) *v.t.* (**-fied -fy·ing**). Restore to anima tion, activity, vigor, or life. **re· viv·i·fi·ca·tion** (rĭvĭvĭfĭkā´shon) *n*

re·voke (rĭvōk´) *v.* (**-voked -vok·ing**). 1. Repeal, annul, with draw, rescind, cancel (decree, con sent, promise, permission). 2 (bridge etc.) Make a revoke. ~ *n.* (bridge, etc.) Failure to follo suit when able to do so. **rev·o· ca·ble** (rĕv´okabel), **re·vok·a·bl** (rĭvō´kabel), **rev·o·ca·to·ry** (rĕv´ okatōrē, -tōrē) *adjs.* **rev·o·ca· tion** (rĕvokā´shon) *n.*

re·volt (rĭvōlt´) *v.* 1. Cast of allegiance; make, take part in re bellion; fall away *from* or rise *agains* ruler. 2. Feel revulsion or disgus *at*, rise in repugnance against, tur n loathing *from*; affect with strong disgust, nauseate. **re·volt′ing** *adj.* **re·volt′ing·ly** *adv.* **revolt** *n.* 1. Act of revolting, state of having revolted; uprising, insurrection. 2. Sense of loathing; rebellious or protesting mood.

rev·o·lu·tion (rĕvoloō′shon) *n.* 1. Revolving; motion in orbit or circular course, or around axis or center; rotation; single completion of orbit or rotation, time it takes. 2. Complete change, turning upside down, great reversal of conditions, fundamental reconstruction; esp. forcible substitution by subjects of new ruler or polity for the old; **American R~**: see AMERICAN; **English Revolution**, expulsion (1688) of Stuart dynasty under James II and transfer of sovereignty to William and Mary; **French Revolution**: see FRENCH; **Russian Revolution**, series of revolutionary movements in Russia in 1917, beginning with a revolt of workers, peasants, and soldiers in March (February Old Style, hence **February Revolution**) and formation of a provisional government, and culminating in the **Bolshevik Revolution** in November (October Old Style, hence **October Revolu-**

tion), which led to the establishment of the U.S.S.R. **rev·o·lu′-tion·ize** *v.t.* (**-ized, -iz·ing**).

rev·o·lu·tion·ar·y (rĕvoloō′sho-nĕrē) *adj.* Of revolution; involving great and usu. violent changes; **R~**, of or pertaining to the period of the American Revolution. **revolutionary** *n.* (pl. **-ar·ies**). One who instigates or favors political revolution; one who takes part in a revolution.

rev·o·lu·tion·ist (rĕvoloō′sho-nĭst) *n.* Revolutionary.

re·volve (rĭvŏlv′) *v.* (**-volved, -volv·ing**). Turn around (and around); rotate; go in circular orbit; roll along. **re·volv′a·ble** *adj.*

re·volv·er (rĭvŏl′ver) *n.* (esp.) Handgun with mechanism by which set of cartridge chambers is revolved and presented in succession before hammer, so that several shots may be fired without reloading.

re·vue (rĭvū′) *n.* Theatrical entertainment reviewing (often satirically) current fashions, events, etc.; (freq.) entertainment consisting of numerous unrelated scenes or episodes.

re·vul·sion (rĭvŭl′shon) *n.* 1. Sudden violent change of feeling,

esp. to disgust or loathing; sudden reaction in taste, fortune, etc. 2. (rare) Drawing or being drawn away. **re·vul′sive** *adj.*

re·ward (rĭword′) *n.* Return or recompense for service or merit, requital for good or evil; sum offered for detection of criminal, restoration of lost property, etc. ~ *v.t.* Repay, requite, recompense; give a reward; give pleasure or satisfaction.

re·word (rēwerd′) *v.* Change wording of.

re·write (rērīt′) *v.* (**-wrote, -writ·ten**). Write again or differently. ~ (rē′rīt) *n.* Rewriting; thing rewritten; ~ **man**, journalist whose job is to put material submitted by reporter into publishable form.

rex (rĕks) *n.* (also **R~**) (abbrev. R.) Reigning king (cf. REGINA).

Rey·kja·vik (rā′kyavēk). Capital city of Iceland, in the SW. on Faxa Bay.

When the trigger of a double-action ***revolver*** *is squeezed, it performs several functions. It cocks the hammer, rotates and locks the cylinder, and releases the hammer to fire the cartridge. The prototype was invented in 1855: only effective at short range.*

rear sight — bullet in chamber — revolving cylinder — barrel — front sight

hammer (uncocked)

ratchet

hand pivoted trigger lever

main spring

trigger spring

frame

stock

empty chamber

cylinder stop

trigger lever

trigger

hammer

trigger lever

main spring compressed

*The river **Rhine** has been a major north European trade route for many centuries. It still provides vital access for fleets of cargo ships which bring raw materials and leave with export goods.*

*Above right: The nave of the cathedral at **Rheims**, a Gothic building which was begun in A.D. 1211. From the fifth century, French rulers were crowned in this city.*

'The Countess of Pembroke and h son' as portrayed by English painter S Joshua Reynolds (facing). In 1768 h was made President of the newl formed Royal Academy.

Reyn·olds (rĕn´oldz), **Sir Joshua** (1723–92). English portrait painter.

r.f., R.F. *abbrevs.* Radio FREQUENCY.

RFC *abbrev.* Reconstruction Finance Corporation.

RFD *abbrev.* Rural free delivery.

Rh *symbol.* Rhodium.

r.h. *abbrev.* Right hand.

rhab·do·man·cy (răb´dŏmănsē) *n.* Divination by means of a rod, as in dowsing.

Rhad·a·man·thus, Rhad·a·man·thys (rădămăn´thus). (Gk. myth.) Son of Zeus and Europa, and one of the judges in the lower world; hence, stern and incorruptible judge.

Rhae·to-Ro·man·ic (rē´tōrō-măn´ĭk) *adj. & n.* (Of) a group of Romance dialects spoken in some parts of the Alps, esp. in SE. Switzerland and N. Italy; Ladino.

rhap·so·dy (răp´sodē) *n.* (pl. **-dies**). 1. (Gk. antiq.) Epic poem or part of one suitable for recitation at one time. 2. Enthusiastic extravagant high-flown utterance or composition; musical composition of indefinite form and often based on a folk melody. **rhap·sod·ic** (răpsŏd´ĭk), **rhap·sod´i·cal** *adjs.* **rhap·sod´i·cal·ly** *adv.* **rhap·so·dize** *v.* (**-dized, -diz·ing**). Recite epic poetry; talk or write rhapsodies (*about, on,* etc.). **rhap·so·dist** *n.*

Rhe·a (rē´a). (Gk. myth.) One of the Titans, wife of Cronus and mother of Zeus, Demeter, Poseidon, and Hades.

rhe·a (rē´a) *n.* S. Amer. 3-toed ostrichlike bird of genus *R ~*.

Rheims: see REIMS.

Rhen·ish (rĕn´ĭsh) *adj.* Of the Rhine or neighboring regions.

rhe·ni·um (rē´nēum) *n.* (chem.) Rare, very hard, very heavy metallic element resembling manganese in properties, found in ores of tantalum and platinum; symbol Re, at. no. 75, at. wt. 186.2. [L. *Rhenus* Rhine]

rhe·o·stat (rē´ostăt) *n.* Device for varying the resistance to an electric current.

*Related to the ostrich but found only in South America, the **rhea** lives on plants and insects. One male is usually accompanied by 6–8 females, and he helps them make their nests.*

rhe·sus (rē´sus) *n.* Small catar rhine monkey (*Macaca mulatt* common in N. India and widel used in biological and medic research. [arbitrary use of Gl *Rhesus*, mythical king of Thrace]

rhet·o·ric (rĕt´orĭk) *n.* (Treatis on, study of) the art of persuasiv or impressive speaking or writin language designed to persuade impress (freq. with implication insincerity, exaggeration, etc.).

rhe·tor·i·cal (rĭtŏr´ĭkal, -tăr´ *adj.* Expressed with a view persuasive or impressive effec artificial or extravagant in languag of the nature of rhetoric; of th art of rhetoric; given to rhetori oratorical; ~ **question**, questio asked not for information but produce effect. **rhe·tor´i·cal·l** *adv.*

rhet·o·ri·cian (rĕtorĭsh´an) Rhetorical speaker or writer.

rheu·mat·ic (rōomăt´ĭk) *ac* Of, suffering from, rheumatism subject to, producing, produced b this; ~ **fever**, acute febrile diseas mainly in children, with inflam mation and pain of joints, often wit cardiac damage. **rheumatic** Rheumatic patient.

rheu·ma·tism (rōo´matĭzem) Any of several pathologic conditions involving pain and stif ness in joints, tendons, muscle etc.; (pop.) rheumatoid arthritis.

rheu·ma·toid (rōo´matoid) *ac* Having the character rheumatism; ~ **arthritis**, sever chronic progressive disease of ur certain origin, leading to inflam matory changes in the tissues, es joints.

Rh factor. (referring to RHESU

monkey in whose blood the antigen was first discovered) ~ **factor**, inheritable antigen usu. present in human red blood cells, capable of causing a serious reaction in person who lacks them; **Rh positive, Rh negative**, having, not having, the Rh factor; **Rh baby**, infant with hemolytic disorder from its blood being Rh positive and its mother's being Rh negative.

rhi·nal (rī'nal) *adj.* (anat. etc.) Of nostril or nose.

Rhine (rīn). (Ger. *Rhein*) Great European river, rising in Switzerland and flowing northward through West Germany and the Netherlands to North Sea; ~ **wine**, wine produced in valley of Rhine, usu. white, light, and dry. **Rhine·land** (rīn'lănd, -land), valley of

the Rhine.

rhine·stone (rīn'stōn) *n.* Artificial gem of paste or glass cut like diamond. [f. RHINE]

rhi·ni·tis (rīnī'tĭs) *n.* Inflammation of (mucous membrane of) nose.

rhi·no (rī'nō) *n.* (pl. **-nos**, collect. **-no**). (colloq.) Rhinoceros.

rhi·noc·er·os (rīnŏs'eros) *n.* (pl. **-os·es**, collect. **-os**). Large mammal of Africa and S. Asia, usu. with a horn on nose (or, in some species, two) and very thick freq. folded skin.

rhi·nol·o·gy (rīnŏl'ojē) *n.* Branch of medicine dealing with diseases of the nose.

rhi·no·scope (rī'noskōp) *n.* Instrument for inspecting nasal cavity. **rhi·nos·co·py** (rīnŏs'kopē)

n. Examination of nasal cavity with rhinoscope.

rhi·zoid (rī'zoid) *adj.* (bot.) Resembling a root. ~ *n.* Root hair or filament.

rhi·zome (rī'zōm) *n.* Horizontal rootlike stem growing along or under the ground and emitting roots from the lower side and sending up leafy shoots from the upper surface. **rhi·zom·a·tous** (rīzŏm'atus) *adj.*

rho (rō) *n.* (pl. **rhos**). Twentieth (later 17th) letter of Greek alphabet (P, ρ), corresponding to r.

*Although the **black rhinoceros** of Africa is still plentiful, the other species of rhinoceros are all endangered. Estimates of numbers are 25 in Java, 100 in Sumatra and 400 in India.*

white rhino

black rhino

Javan rhino

Indian rhino

Sumatran rhino

*A **rhizome** is an underground stem and serves as food storage to allow leaves to grow to a stage where they can obtain nourishment from the sun. It also has rootlets to obtain food from the soil.*

Rhode (rōd) **Island.** S. New England state, smallest of the U.S., one of the original 13 (1790); capital, Providence; ~ ~ **Red,** (one of) an Amer. breed of domestic fowls with brownish-red plumage.

Rhodes[1] (rōdz). (Gk. *Rhodos*) Most easterly island of Aegean Sea, SW. of Turkey, largest of the Dodecanese, acquired by Italy 1912 and restored to Greece 1946; its principal city and harbor.

Rhodes[2] (rōdz), **Cecil John** (1853–1902). English imperialist, largely instrumental in extending Brit. territory in S. Africa and in development of Rhodesia; **Rhodes scholarship,** one of the scholar-ships endowed at Oxford University under will of Cecil Rhodes, for students from the principal Brit. colonies and dominions and from every state and territory of the U.S.; hence **Rhodes scholar.**

Rho·de·sia (rōdē′zhᴀ, -zēᴀ, -shᴀ). Former name of ZIMBABWE. **Rho·de′sian** *adj. & n.* [named after Cecil RHODES[2]]

rho·di·um (rō′dēᴜm) *n.* (chem.) Hard white metallic element of the platinum group, used as a protective coating for silver articles, and in some special alloys for scientific purposes; symbol Rh, at. no. 45, at. wt. 102.9055. [Gk. *rhodon* rose, from the color of some of its salts]

rho·do·den·dron (rōdodĕn′dron) *n.* Evergreen shrub or low tree with large flowers of genus *R* ~, which includes azaleas. [Gk. *rhodon* rose, *dendron* tree]

rhomb (rŏm, rŏmb) = RHOMBUS.

rhom·bic (rŏm′bĭk) *adj.* Rhombus-shaped.

rhom·bo·he·dron (rŏmbohē′-dron) *n.* (pl. **-drons, -dra** pr. -drᴀ). (Crystal in shape of) solid bounded by 6 equal rhombuses. **rhom·bo·he′dral** *adj.*

rhom·boid (rŏm′boid) *adj.* Of or near the shape of a rhombus. ~ *n.* Quadrilateral figure having its opposite sides and angles equal. **rhom·boi·dal** (rŏmboi′dᴀl) *adj.*

rhom·bus (rŏm′bᴜs) *n.* (pl. **-bus·es, -bi** pr. -bī). Plane equilateral figure with opposite angles equal, two being acute and two obtuse.

Rhône, Rhone (rōn). River rising in Switzerland and flowing 505 mi. (808 km) W. through Lake of Geneva into France and then southward to Mediterranean.

rhu·barb (rōō′bärb) *n.* 1. (Purgative made from) root of Chinese and Tibetan species of the herb *Rheum*, orig. imported into

Cecil Rhodes made a fortune from diamond mining and his ambition was that all of southern Africa should be united as a single British federation. He left money for Rhodes scholarships.

Victoria Falls, on the Zambesi River, probably represents the best-known geographical attraction in Zimbabwe, formerly Rhodesia. The Falls were discovered in 1855 by David Livingstone.

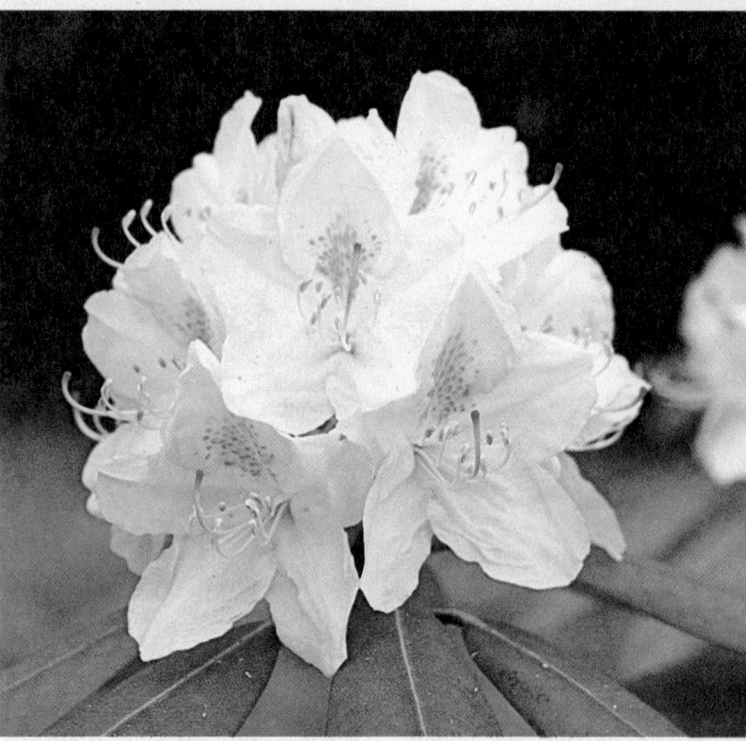

The **rhododendron** probably originated in Asia although the first plants were taken to England in 1629. While some grow into small trees, others remain as shrubs.

Europe through Russia and the Levant, now usu. called **Chinese** ∼. 2. Plant of the genus *Rheum*, esp. any species having heart-shaped smooth deep green leaves, growing on thick fleshy stalks that are cooked and eaten. [L. *rhabarbarum* foreign rha or rhubarb (*rha* Gk. perh. f. ancient name *Rha* of River Volga)]

rhumb (rŭm) *n.* Any of the 32 points of the compass; (also ∼ **line**) line on the surface of a sphere that makes equal oblique angles with all meridians, indicating the course of an object moving always in the same compass direction.

rhyme (rīm) *n.* Agreement in terminal sounds of two or more words or metrical lines, such that (in English prosody) the last stressed vowel and any sounds following it are the same, while the preceding sounds are different (examples: *which*, *rich*; *peace*, *increase*; *decended*, *extended*); verse marked by rhymes; poem with rhymes; employment of rhyme; word providing a rhyme (*with* another); **feminine, masculine** ∼: see FEMININE, MASCULINE; **rhyme royal**, stanzas of seven ten-syllable lines, rhyming *a b a b b c c*; **nursery rhyme**: see NURSERY; **neither rhyme nor reason**, nothing reasonable. **rhyme** *v.* (**rhymed, rhym·ing**). Write rhymes, versify; put or make (story etc.) into rhyme; (of words or lines) terminate in sounds that form a rhyme, form a rhyme *with*; use (words) as rhymes; **rhyming dictionary**, book in which words

are arranged in groups according to the sound of their last syllable or syllables; **rhyming slang**, vocabulary (esp. in Cockney use) dating from early 19th c., of rhyming substitutions for certain words, e.g. *apples and pears* = *stairs*.

rhy·o·lite (rī′olīt) *n.* Fine-grained volcanic rock.

rhythm (rĭdh′em) *n.* Metrical movement determined by relation of long and short, or stressed and unstressed, syllables in foot or line; measured flow of words and phrases in verse or prose; (mus.) systematic grouping of notes, beats, measures, and phrases, giving an effect of forward movement; (art etc.) harmonious correlation of parts, movement with regulated succession of strong and weak elements or of opposite or different conditions; ∼ **method**, method of contraception by avoidance of sexual intercourse as time of ovulation recurs. **rhyth·mic** (rĭdh′mĭk), **rhyth′mi·cal** *adjs.* **rhyth′mi·cal·ly** *adv.*

rhythm-and-blues (rĭdh′em-an-blōōz′) *n.* Form of black music marked by blues themes and strong rhythm.

RI, R.I. *abbrevs.* Rhode Island.

ri·a·ta, re·a·ta (rēah′ta) *ns.* LARIAT.

rib (rĭb) *n.* 1. One of the curved bones articulated in pairs to spine and enclosing and protecting thoracic cavity and its organs; one of these bones from animal carcass, with the meat adhering to it, as food. 2. Denser, firmer, or stronger

part extending along or throug organ or structure; any shaping o supporting part similar to a rib central vein of leaf, shaft or quil of feather; one of ship's curve timbers to which planks are nailed or corresponding ironwork; arc supporting vault, groin, raise molding on groin or across ceilin etc.; hinged rod of umbrella frame combination of plain and pur stitches in knitting, producing riblike fabric with a certai elasticity. ∼ *v.* (**ribbed, rib bing**). Provide with ribs, act a ribs of; mark with ridges; knit i rib stitch; (colloq.) make fun of tease.

rib·ald (rĭb′ald) *adj.* Scurrilous irreverent; vulgar, lewd (esp. o humor). ∼ *n.* Ribald person **rib′ald·ry** *n.*

rib·bon (rĭb′on) *n.* (Piece of length of) silk, satin, or other fin material woven into narrow band esp. for adorning costume; ribbo of special color etc. worn to indicat membership in knightly order possession of medal, order, or othe distinction or membership; lon narrow strip of anything, ribbonlik object or mark; **blue** ∼: see BLUE **rib′bonfish** (pl. **-fishes**, collect **-fish**), any of several marine fishes mainly of the genus *Trachipterus* having long, slender, flattene bodies.

ri·bo·fla·vin (rīboflā′vĭn, rī boflā-) *n.* Factor of vitamin complex required for growth found in milk, egg yolks, fres meat, leafy vegetables, etc., or mad synthetically.

True ribs

Floating ribs

False ribs

*Although its stems are edible, the leaves of **rhubarb** contain oxalic acid which is poisonous. The best stalks for eating are grown by 'forcing' beneath an opaque cover.*

*Bo Sang umbrella village in Thailand. The **ribs** of the umbrellas are covered with durable material. Below: The nave of Exeter Cathedral in Devon, England. Note the **rib-like** fan vaulting.*

*The human **rib cage** consists of 24 rounded bones which form a wall for the thorax. They protect the lungs and are capable of providing substantial resistance to pressure.*

*World **rice** production is slightly less than that of wheat. In the Philippines, it is still winnowed by hand (1); in Malaysia, areas are flooded before seedlings are planted (2). Below: Map of main rice growing areas.*

MAJOR RICE GROWING AREAS OF THE WORLD

ri·bo·nu·cle·ic (rībōnŏōklē´ĭk, -nū-) **acid**: see RNA.

Ri·car·do (rĭkär´dō), **David** (1772–1823). English political economist of the free trade school, author of *Principles of Political Economy and Taxation.* **Ri·car·di·an** (rĭkär´dēan) *adj.*

rice (rīs) *n.* Seeds (usu. pearl white), used as staple food and in puddings etc., of an annual cereal grass (*Oryza sativa*) cultivated in marshy or easily flooded ground in warm climates; this plant; **rice´-bird**, (esp.) bobolink; **rice paper**, thin paper made from rice straw; Chinese painting paper (so named in error) made from pith of tree *Tetrapanax papyriferum*; edible paper used in baking; **rice pudding**, baked pudding of sweetened milk and rice. **rice** *v.* (**riced**, **ric·ing**). Pass (cooked potatoes etc.) through device to form thin strings. **ric´er** *n.*

rich (rĭch) *adj.* 1. Wealthy, having riches; abounding in or *in* natural resources or some valuable possession or production, fertile; abundant, ample. 2. Valuable; splendid, costly, elaborate. 3. (of food) Containing a large proportion of fat; (of cake etc.) containing a large proportion of fat, eggs, fruit, etc. 4. (of colors, sounds, etc.) Mellow, deep, full, not thin. 5. (colloq.) Highly amusing. **rich´-ness** *n.*

Rich·ard (rĭch´erd). Name of three kings of England: **Richard I** (1157–99), "Coeur de Lion" or

"the Lion-Heart," reigned 1189–1199, third son of Henry II; a leader in the third Crusade, on his return from which he was captured and held for ransom by Leopold of Austria; **Richard II** (1367–1400), reigned 1377–99, son of the Black Prince, deposed and imprisoned by Henry IV; **Richard III** (1452–85), reigned 1483–5, last king of House of York; younger brother of Edward IV; defeated and killed at Bosworth Field in the final battle of the Wars of the Roses.

Rich·ard·son (rĭch´erdson), **Samuel** (1689–1761). English novelist, author of *Pamela, Clarissa Harlowe*, etc.

Ri·che·lieu (rĭsh´elōō; *Fr.* rēsh℮lyö´), **Armand Jean du Plessis, Duc de** (1585–1642). French cardinal and statesman; chief minister of Louis XIII, under whom he had virtually dictatorial powers, 1624–42.

rich·es (rĭch´ĭz) *n.pl.* Wealth; valuable possessions.

rich·ly (rĭch´lē) *adv.* In ric manner; amply, fully, thoroughly

Rich·mond (rĭch´mond) Capital and largest city of Virgini on the James River in the central part; capital of th Confederacy during the Civil Wa

Rich·ter (rĭk´ter) **scale** Logarithmic scale, having step graded from 1 to 10, for measurin earthquake intensity.

rick (rĭk) *n.* Stack of ha straw, etc., esp. one regularly bu and thatched or covered f protection from the weather. *v.t.* Form into rick(s).

rick·ets (rĭk´ĭts) *n.* Diseas chiefly of children, marked b softening of the bones and con sequent distortion (bowleg curvature of spine, etc.), resultin from a deficiency of vitamin D lack of exposure to sunlight.

rick·ett·si·a (rĭkĕt´sēa) *n.* (p -si·ae pr. -sēē, **-si·as**). One of group of microorganisms of gen *R ~*, apparently intermedia

Left: **Richard II** *ascended the British throne at the age of 10 and was probably murdered in 1400. In contrast* **Richard III** *(right) only attained the crown after other claimants had been killed.*

between bacteria and viruses, carried as parasites by fleas, lice, and ticks and causing typhus, Rocky Mountain spotted fever, etc. in man. **rick·ett′si·al** *adj.* [Howard T. *Ricketts*, Amer. pathologist]

rick·et·y (rĭk′ĭtē) *adj.* Of (the nature of), suffering from, rickets; shaky, insecure. **rick′et·i·ness** *n.*

rick·ey (rĭk′ē) *n.* Drink of carbonated water, lime juice, and usu. gin.

rick·rack (rĭk′răk) *n.* Zigzag braid trimming for garments.

rick·shaw, rick·sha (rĭk′shaw) = JINRICKSHA.

ric·o·chet (rĭkoshā′, rĭk′oshā) *n.* Rebounding of projectile or other object from an object that it strikes, hit made after this. ~ *v.t.* (**-cheted, -chet·ing**). (of projectile) Glance or skip with rebound(s).

ri·cot·ta (rĭkŏt′a, -kaw′ta) *n.* Italian cottage cheese.

ric·tus (rĭk′tus) *n.* (pl. **-tus, -tus·es**). (anat., zool.) Gape of mouth or beak.

rid (rĭd) *v.t.* (**rid** or **rid·ded, rid·ding**). Make free, disencumber, *of* (often in past part. with *be* or *get*, as *get* ~ *of him*).

rid·dance (rĭd′ans) *n.* (esp. in **good** ~! as exclamation of joy). **rid′der** *n.*

rid·den: see RIDE.

rid·dle[1] (rĭd′el) *n.* Question, statement, etc. designed or serving to test ingenuity of hearers in divining its answer, meaning, or reference; conundrum, enigma; puzzling or mysterious fact, thing, or person. ~ *v.* (**-dled, -dling**). Speak in, propound, riddles; solve (riddle).

rid·dle[2] (rĭd′el) *n.* Coarse sieve for gravel etc. ~ *v.t.* (**-dled, -dling**). 1. Pass (gravel etc.) through riddle, sift. 2. Fill, pierce (ship, person, etc.) with holes esp. of gunshot; (fig.) refute (person, theory) with facts.

ride (rīd) *v.* (**rode** pr. rōd, **rid·den** pr. rĭd′en, **rid·ing**). 1. Sit on and be carried by horse etc.; go on horseback etc. or on bicycle etc. or in automobile, train, or other vehicle; sit, go, be *on* something as on horse; sit on and manage horse; (of boat etc.) lie at anchor; float buoyantly; ~ **for a fall**, ride, (fig.) act, recklessly; ~ **down**, overtake on horseback in automobile, etc., allow one's mount to trample on (person); ~ **high**, (fig.) be

successful; ~ **out the storm**, (of ship, and fig.) come safely through it; ~ **roughshod**: see ROUGH; ~ **to hounds**, go fox hunting; ~ **up**, (of garment) work upward during wear. 2. Traverse on horseback etc., ride over or through. 3. Dominate, tyrannize over; (colloq.) ridicule, annoy. 4. Give ride to, cause to ride. **ride** *n.* Journey in vehicle; spell of riding on horse, bicycle, person's back, etc.; **take for a** ~, (slang) kidnap and murder; make a fool of.

rid·er (rī′der) *n.* (esp.) 1. Additional clause amending or supplementing document. 2. One,

As minister of State to Louis XIII, **Cardinal Richelieu** *became one of the most powerful men in Europe. With almost dictatorial power, he suppressed Spanish influence and made France the dominant nation.*

The mechanism of a Browning automatic **rifle** is operated by gases remaining after a bullet is fired. This system developed from such guns as the Spencer carbine. By depressing the lever, the spent cartridge was ejected and another was thrust into the breech.

rear sight

bolt lock   hammer   firing pin

recess

slide

cartridge

sear

connector

trigger

wooden stock
(sometimes plastic or steel)

piston spring

spring

magazine

barrel   cartridge

hammer

Lever Action (American Spencer carbine)

wooden stock

lever

trigger

breechblock

spring fed magazine tube

who rides. **rid'er·less** *adj.*

ridge (rĭj) *n.* Line of junction of two upward sloping surfaces; any narrow elevation across surface; long narrow hilltop, mountain range, watershed; (agriculture) one of a set of raised strips separated by furrows; (meteor.) elongated region of higher barometric pressure between two of lower; **ridge'pole**, horizontal pole of long tent; horizontal beam at ridge of a roof. **ridge** *v.* (**ridged, ridg·ing**). Mark with, form (into) ridges. **ridg'y** *adj.* (**ridg·i·er, ridg·i·est**).

rid·i·cule (rĭd´ĭkūl) *n.* Holding or being held up as object of contemptuous laughter. ~ *v.t.* (**-culed, -cul·ing**). Treat with ridicule.

ri·dic·u·lous (rĭdĭk´yulus) *adj.* Deserving to be laughed at, absurd, unreasonable. **ri·dic'u·lous·ly** *adv.* **ri·dic'u·lous·ness** *n.*

Rie·mann (rē´man; *Ger.* rē´mahn), **Georg Friedrich Bernhard** (1826–66). German mathematician, originator of a non-Euclidean system of geometry, **Riemann geometry**, based on the postulate that there are no completely parallel lines.

Ri·en·zi (rēĕn´zē), **Ri·en·zo** (rēĕn´zō), **Co·la di** (kaw´lah dē)

(*c*1313–54). Tribune of the people at Rome; led rebellion against nobles and established a republic (1347), but was excommunicated, exiled, and, after returning to Rome, assassinated.

Ries·ling (rēz´lĭng, rēs´-) *n.* (Dry white wine made from) European variety of grape.

Rif[1], **Riff**[1] (rĭf), **Er** (ĕr). Mountain system of Mediterranean coast of Morocco.

rife (rīf) *pred. adj.* Of common occurrence, met with in numbers or quantities, prevailing, current, numerous; well provided *with.* **rife'ness** *n.*

Riff[2], **Rif**[2] (rĭf) *ns.* (pl. **Riffs, Riff·i** pr. rĭf´ē, collect. **Riff**). Member of a Berber people living in Rif area of N. Morocco.

riff (rĭf) *n.* Short repeated phrase in jazz and similar music.

rif·fle (rĭf´el) *n.* 1. Shallow part of stream where water flows brokenly; patch of waves or ripples on water. 2. Process or method of riffling cards. ~ *v.* (**-fled, -fling**). Shuffle (playing cards) rapidly, esp. by flexing and combining 2 halves of pack.

riff'raff (rĭf´răf) *n.* Rabble, disreputable persons.

ri·fle (rī´fel) *v.* (**-fled, -fling**).

1. Search and rob, esp. all that can be found in various pockets or storing places; ransack; pillage. 2. Make spiral grooves in (gun barrel) to produce rotatory motion in projectile; **rifled**, having such grooves. **rifle** *n.* Firearm with rifled bore and designed to be fired from the shoulder; (pl.) troops armed with rifles; **ri'fleman** (pl. **-men**), soldier or other man armed with rifle; shooter of a rifle; **rifle range**, distance coverable by shot from rifle; place for rifle practice. **ri'fling** *n.*

rift (rĭft) *n.* Cleft, fissure, chasm, in earth or rock (freq. fig.); rent, crack, split, in an object, opening in cloud, etc.

rig[1] (rĭg) *v.* (**rigged, rig·ging**). Provide (ship), (of ship) be provided, with necessary spars, ropes, etc.; prepare for sea in this respect; fit (*out, up*) with or *with* clothes or other equipment; set *up* (structure) hastily or as makeshift or by using odd materials. ~ *n.* Way ship's masts, sails, etc., are arranged; special equipment, apparatus, etc. for a particular purpose; wagon or buggy with its horse or horses; (colloq.) outfit, costume.

rig[2] (rĭg) *v.t.* (**rigged, rig·ging**).

bullet   front sight

gas port

gas cylinder

gas piston
(forward end of slide mechanism)

Modern Gas Action

cartridges   firing pin

bolt

bolt mechanism

magazine

trigger

Bolt Action
German WW11 Mauser Kar 98k)

mainspring

*Typical bolt action of a Mauser rifle.
Bullets under spring pressure, are in a
magazine below the bolt. Withdrawing
the bolt ejects the spent cartridge,
another rises and is thrust home by the
bolt.*

Manage or conduct fraudulently.

Ri·ga (rē′ga). Seaport and capital city of the Latvian Republic of the U.S.S.R., on the Baltic Sea; **Gulf of** ~, inlet of Baltic Sea between the Latvian Republic and Estonia.

Ri·gel (rī′jel, -gel). (astron.) Very bright star of first magnitude in foot of constellation Orion.

rig·er (rĭg′er) n. (esp.) Person who assembles parachutes, aircraft parts, etc.

rig·ging (rĭg′ĭng) n. (esp.) Ropes etc. used to support masts and work or set yards, sails, etc.

right (rīt) adj. 1. Straight (archaic; now only in ~ **line, ~-lined**); ~ **angle**: see ANGLE¹; involving right angles, not oblique; **at** ~ **angles**, turning or placed with right angle; ~ **ascension,** (astron.) celestial longitude; ~ **cone, cylinder, prism,** etc., cone, etc., with ends or base perpendicular to axis. 2. Just, morally good, required by equity or duty, proper; (freq. in comb., as ~-**minded,** ~-**principled**). 3. Correct, true; preferable or most suitable; in good or normal condition, sound, sane, satisfactory, well-advised, not mistaken; **get** ~, bring or come into

right state; **put, set,** ~, restore to order, health, etc.; correct mistaken ideas of; **in one's** ~ **mind,** sane, not mad; ~ **side,** side (of fabric etc.) meant for use or show; **on the** ~ **side of,** younger than (specified age); in person's good favor. 4. (archaic) Rightful, real, veritable, properly so called; ~ **whale**: see WHALE¹. 5. (of position) On or toward side of body toward the east when facing north; having corresponding relation to front of any object; (of bank of river etc.) on right hand of person looking downstream; ~-**about,** (turn) so far to right as to face opposite way; ~ **and left,** to or on both sides or all sides; ~ **arm,** (fig.) most reliable helper; ~ **hand,** hand on right side; region or direction on this side of person; chief or indispensable assistant; ~-**hand,** placed on the right hand; ~-**hand man,** chief or indispensable assistant; ~-**handed,** using right hand more than left; ~ **turn,** turn right into a position at right angles with original one; ~ **wing,** (esp.) extreme right in politics (see **right** n., sense 5). **right′ness** n. **right** v. 1. Restore to proper, straight, or vertical position; (refl.) recover one's balance, (of ship) recover vertical position. 2. Make repa-

ration for or to, avenge (wrong, wronged person); correct (mistakes etc.), correct mistakes in, set in order. ~ n. 1. What is just; fair treatment; **the** ~, what is right, the cause of truth or justice; **by right**(s), if right were done; **in the right,** with truth or justice on one's side. 2. Justification; fair claim; being entitled to privilege or immunity; thing one is entitled to; **assert, stand on, one's rights,** refuse to relinquish them; **Declaration** or **Bill of Rights:** see BILL³; **divine right:** see DIVINE²; **right of way,** right of using path etc. over another's ground; path etc. so used; right of one traveling vehicle to take precedence over another. 3. (pl.) Right condition, true state; **set or put to rights,** arrange properly. 4. Right-hand part, region, or direction; (boxing) right-handed blow. 5. (sometimes **Right**) Conservative or reactionary members of legislature, those who sit on right of chamber; hence, conservative political party, group, etc. (**right′ist** adj. & n.). **right** adv. 1. Straight; all the way to etc.; completely off, out, etc.; straight away, immediately. 2. Exactly, quite. 3. Justly, properly, correctly, aright, truly, satisfactorily; **it serves him** ~, it is no worse than he deserves; **R** ~ **Honorable, R** ~ **Reverend**: see these words. 4. To right hand. **right** int. Exclamation of agreement or consent; ~ **on!** (slang) exclamation of approval. **right′er** n.

right·eous (rī′chus) adj. Morally good; acting in a moral way, virtuous; morally justifiable. **right′eous·ly** adv. **right′eous·ness** n.

right·ful (rīt′ful) adj. Equitable, fair; legitimately entitled to position etc.; that one is entitled to. **right′ful·ly** adv. **right′ful·ness** n.

right·ly (rīt′lē) adv. Justly, fairly; properly, correctly, accurately; justifiably.

rig·id (rĭj′ĭd) adj. Not flexible, stiff, unyielding; inflexible, harsh, strict, precise. **rig′id·ly** adv. **ri·gid·i·ty** (rĭjĭd′ĭtē), **rig′id·ness** ns.

rig·ma·role (rĭg′marōl) n. Rambling or meaningless talk or tale; complicated procedure. [app. f. obs. *ragman roll* list, catalog]

rig·or (rĭg′er) n. 1. (path.) Sudden chill with shivering; ~ **mortis,** stiffening of body after death. 2. Severity, strictness, harshness; (pl.) harsh measures; (sing.) strict enforcement of rules etc.; extremity or excess of weather, hardship, famine, etc., great distress; austerity of life, Puritanic strictness of observance or doctrine; logical accuracy, exactitude. **rig′-**

or·ous *adj.* **rig′or·ous·ly** *adv.*

Rig-Ve·da (rĭgvä′da, -vē′-) *n.* Oldest and most important of the Vedas (see VEDA). [Sansk.]

Riks·dag (rĭks′dahg) *n.* Parliament of Sweden.

rile (rīl) *v.t.* (**riled, ril·ing**). Raise anger in, irritate.

Ri·ley (rī′lē), **James Whitcomb** (1849–1916). Amer. poet; noted for simple, dialect poems, as "Little Orphant Annie," "When the Frost is on the Punkin," etc.

Ril·ke (rĭl′kē), **Rainer Maria** (1875–1926). Austrian lyric poet and writer of lyrical prose.

rill, rille (rĭl) *ns.* 1. Small stream, rivulet. 2. (astron.) Long narrow trench or valley on moon's surface.

rim (rĭm) *n.* Outer ring of wheel (not including tire), connected with hub by spokes etc.; edge, margin, border, esp. a raised one, etc., of more or less circular object; **rim′-rock**, outcrop with steep face. **rim** *v.t.* (**rimmed, rim·ming**). Furnish with rim, serve as rim to, edge, border. **rim′less** *adj.*

Rim·baud (rămbō′; *Fr.* răṅbō′), (**Jean Nicolas**) **Arthur** (1854–91). French symbolist poet.

rime¹ = RHYME.

rime² (rīm) *n.* 1. (meteor.) Water droplets from cloud or fog that freeze on hilltops, high branches, etc., esp. in windy weather. 2. (chiefly poet.) Hoar frost. ~ *v.t.* (**rimed, rim·ing**). Cover with rime. **rim′y** *adj.* (**rim·i·er, rim·i·est**).

Rim·i·ni (rĭm′inē). Port and tourist center in NE. Italy, on the

Adriatic Sea.

Rim·sky-Kor·sa·kov, Rim·-ski-Kor·sa·koff (rĭm′skē kōr′-sakawf), **Nikolay Andreevich** (1844–1908). Russian musical composer.

rind (rīnd) *n.* Bark of tree; peel of fruit or vegetable; harder enclosing surface of cheese or other substance; skin of bacon etc.

ring¹ (rĭng) *n.* 1. Circlet, usu. of precious metal and often set with gem(s), worn around finger as ornament or token (esp. of betrothal or marriage) or signet, or (usu. with defining word) hung to or encircling other part of body. 2. Circular object or appliance of any material and any (but esp. of no great) size. 3. Raised, sunk, or otherwise distinguishable line or band around cylindrical or circular object, rim; circular fold, coil, bend, structure, part, or mark; excision of bark around branch or trunk of tree; one of the expanding circular ripples caused by something falling or being thrown into water; (also **annual** ~) one of the concentric circular bands of wood constituting yearly growth of a tree. 4. Persons, trees, etc., disposed in a circle, such disposition; (chem.) number of atoms so united that they can be represented graphically in cyclic form. 5. Combination of traders etc. to monopolize and

*The Swedish **Riksdag** or parliament meets in this late 19th-century building on Helgeandsholmen, in the northern district of old Stockholm, a city containing buildings of many periods.*

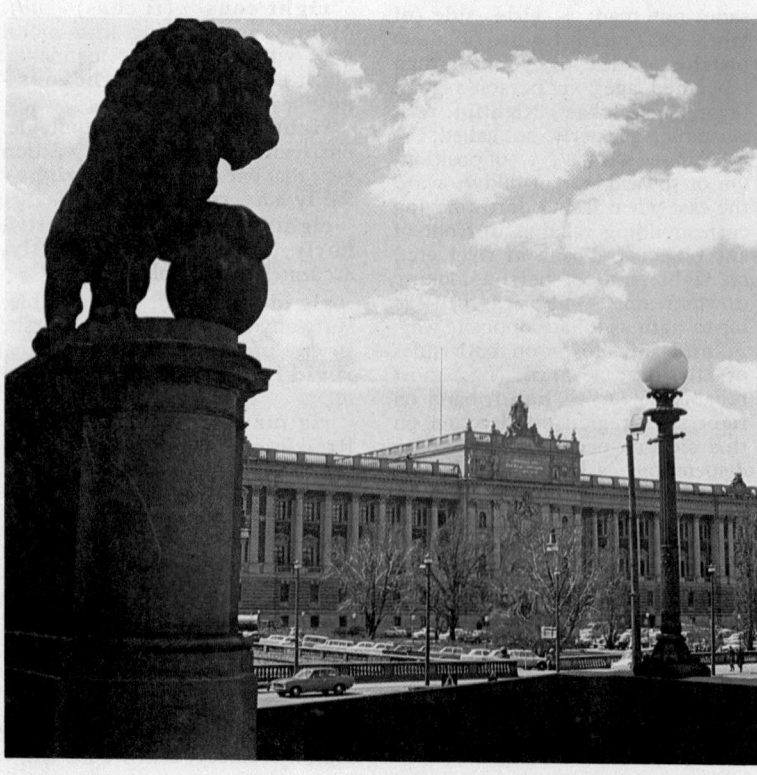

control a particular trade, market, or policy, or to stabilize or keep up price of goods. 6. Circular enclosure for some sport, performance, or exhibition (esp. in circus); space marked off (usu. rectangular) for prize fight or wrestling match, enclosed space for displaying livestock etc. 7. Circular or spiral course; **run rings around**, excel or surpass easily. 8. **ring′bolt**, bolt with ring attached for fastening rope to etc.; **ring′dove**, either of two Old World pigeons, *Columba palumbus* or *Streptopelia risoria*; **ring finger**, third finger, esp. of left hand; **ring′leader**, leader of persons acting in defiance of law or rules etc.; **ring′master**, manager of circus performance; **ring-necked**, with band(s) of color around neck; **ring′side** (**seat**), area, seat close to (boxing or circus etc.) ring; seat providing close view; **ringed snake, ring-necked snake**, common European grass snake; **ring-tailed cat** = CACOMISTLE; **ring′worm**, any of several contagious diseases (*tinea*) of the skin, hair, or nails, caused by fungi and characterized by ring-shaped patches. **ringed, ring′less** *adjs.* **ring** *v.* (**ringed, ring·ing**). 1. (of hawk etc.) Rise in spirals; (of hunted fox) take circular course. 2. Encompass (*around, about, in*); hem in (game, cattle) by riding or beating in circle around them. 3. Put ring upon; put ring in nose of (pig, bull).

ring² (rĭng) *v.* (**rang** pr. răng, **rung** pr. rŭng, **ring·ing**). 1. Give out clear resonant sound (as) of vibrating metal; (of bell) convey summons by ringing; (of place) resound, reecho (*with*); (of utterance or other sound) linger *in* one's ears, memory, etc.; (of ears) be filled with sensation as of bell ringing; ~ **true, false** (of coin tested by throwing on counter, and fig. of sentiments, etc.) sound, genuine, counterfeit. 2. Make (bell) ring; ring bell as summons; sound (peal, knell, etc.) on bell(s); announce (hour etc.) by sound of bell(s); usher *in, out*, with bell ringing; **ring back**, (chiefly Brit.) call back; **ring off**, (chiefly Brit.) terminate telephone call; **ring up**, register sale on cash register; (chiefly Brit.) make telephone call to; **ring the bell**, (colloq.) achieve complete success; strike a sympathetic or responsive note; **ring the changes**: see CHANGE; **ring the curtain up** or **down**, (in theater) direct it by bell to be raised or lowered; (fig.) begin, end. **ring** *n.* Set *of* (church) bells; ringing sound; ringing tone in voice etc.; resonance of coin or vessel; act of ringing bell, sound so produced; (colloq.) call on the telephone.

ring·er (rĭng′er) *n.* 1. Horseshoe

Left: Open air ice-skating **rink** in Central Park, New York. A form of skates was made about 1,500 years ago. Others were used by Dutch soldiers during a battle in 1572.

revel; unrestrained indulgence in or display or enjoyment of something. 2. **run** ~, (orig. of hunting hounds, now usu. fig.) act without restraint or control, disregard all limitations. 3. Disorder, tumult, disturbance of the peace, outbreak of lawlessness, on part of a crowd; **Riot Act**, Brit. act (1715) providing that if 12 or more persons unlawfully or riotously assembled refuse to disperse within an hour after specified law has been read aloud by a competent authority, they shall be considered as felons; hence, (fig.) **read the riot act**, announce that some course of action or conduct must cease; chastise severely. **ri′ot·ous** *adj.* **ri′ot·ous·ly** *adv.* **ri′ot·ous-ness** *n.* **riot** *v.* Make or engage in riot; revel. **ri′ot·er** *n.*

rip[1] (rĭp) *n.* (colloq.) Worthless horse; dissolute person, rake.

rip[2] (rĭp) *v.* (**ripped, rip·ping**). 1. Cut or tear (thing) quickly or forcibly away from something; make long cut or tear in, cut or tear vigorously apart; ~ **off**, (slang) defraud; steal, rob, hence **rip′off** (*n.*); split, saw (wood) with the grain; come violently asunder, split; **rip cord**, cord for releasing parachute, opening balloon gasbag, etc.; **rip-roaring**, (slang) wildly noisy; **rip′saw**, saw for ripping wood; **ripsnort′er**, (slang) person or thing that is very energetic, forceful, wild, etc. 2. Rush along; **let her rip**, (slang) do not check speed or interfere; **rip into**, (colloq.) attack verbally; **rip out**, (colloq.) exclaim violently or suddenly. **rip** *n.* Rent made by ripping. **rip′per** *n.*

rip[3] (rĭp) *n.* Stretch of broken water in river.

R.I.P. *abbrev. Requiesca(n)t in pace* [L., = may he or she, they, rest in peace].

ri·par·i·an (rĭpār′ēan) *adj.* Of, on, riverbank.

ripe (rīp) *adj.* (**rip·er, rip·est**). Ready to be reaped, gathered, eaten, used, or dealt with; fully developed, mellow, mature; prepared or able *to* undergo something, in fit state *for.* **ripe′ly** *adv.* **ripe′ness** *n.* **rip·en** (rī′pen) *v.*

ri·poste, ri·post (rĭpōst′) *ns.* Quick return thrust in fencing; counterstroke; retort. ~ *v.i.* (**-post·ed, -post·ing**). Deliver riposte.

rip·ple[1] (rĭp′el) *n.* Toothed implement used to clear seeds from flax. ~ *v.t.* (**-pled, -pling**). Treat with ripple.

rip·ple[2] (rĭp′el) *n.* Ruffling of water's surface, small wave(s); wavy

Rising in Colorado and flowing south to Mexico, the **Rio Grande** has been dammed in various places to provide water for irrigation. This gorge (above) is near Taos in New Mexico.

quoit thrown so it encircles the g. 2. Bell ringer; device for nging bell. 3. (slang) Substituted cehorse etc.; person's double.

ring·let (rĭng′lĭt) *n.* Curly lock hair, curl; (rare) small ring, fairy ng on grass, ring-shaped mark, c. **ring′let·ed** *adj.*

Ring·ling (rĭng′lĭng). Name of brothers who were Amer. circus wners; bought the Barnum and iley circus, 1907.

rink (rĭngk) *n.* Expanse of ice ed for game of curling; sheet of tural or artificial ice for skating, ilding containing this; floor for ller-skating.

rinse (rĭns) *v.t.* (**rinsed, rins-g**). Wash out or *out* (vessel, outh) by filling with water etc. d shaking and emptying; pour uid over or wash lightly; put othes etc.) through clean water remove soap; clear (soap, purities) *out* or *away* by rinsing.

~ *n.* Rinsing or being rinsed; preparation used for rinsing the hair, esp. for tinting it.

Rio de Ja·nei·ro (rē′ō dā zhanār′ō, ja-, dē, de). Seaport and former capital of Brazil.

Río de la Pla·ta (rē′ō dě lah plah′tah). Atlantic Ocean estuary on the SE. coast of S. Amer., formed by the Paraná and Uruguay rivers; extends inland 171 mi. (275 km) between Argentina and Uruguay.

Rio Grande (rē′ō grănd′, grän′dē, grahn′dā). River rising in S. Colorado and flowing 1,885 mi. (3,034 km) S. and E. to Gulf of Mexico, forming much of the U.S.–Mexican border.

ri·ot (rī′ot) *n.* 1. Loud revelry,

or crinkled appearance in hair, ribbons, etc.; gentle lively sound that rises and falls. **rip′ply** *adj.* (**-pli·er, -pli·est**). **ripple** *v.* Form, flow in, show, agitate or mark with, sound like, ripples.

rip·rap (rĭp′răp) *n.* Loose stone as foundation for structure.

Rip·u·ar·i·an (rĭpūār′ēan) *adj.* Of the ancient Franks living on Rhine between Moselle and Meuse; ~ **law**, code observed by them.

Rip van Win·kle (rĭp′văn wĭng′-kel). Hero of a story (1820) by Washington Irving; he fell asleep in the Catskill Mountains and awoke after 20 years to find the world completely changed.

rise (rīz) *v.* (**rose** pr. rōz, **ris·en** pr. rĭz′en, **ris·ing**). 1. Get up from lying, sitting, or kneeling position; get out of bed; (of meeting etc.) cease to sit for business, adjourn; recover standing or up-right position, become erect; leave ground; come to life again (freq. *from the dead*). 2. Cease to be quiet; abandon submission, revolt; **make one's gorge** ~, disguise, make indignant. 3. Come or go up; grow upward; ascend, soar; project or swell upward; become higher, reach higher position, level, price, pitch, or amount; incline upward; come to surface; (of fish) come to surface of water to take fly, bait, etc.; become or be visible above or *above* surroundings; (of sun, moon, etc.) appear above horizon; develop greater energy or intensity; be progressive; (of dough etc.) swell with yeast or other agent; (of spirits) become more cheerful; **rise in the world**, attain higher social position. 4. Develop powers equal *to* (an *occasion* etc.). 5. Have origin, begin to be, flow, *from, in, at*, etc. **rise** *n.* 1. Ascent, upward slope; knoll; hill. 2. Social advance-ment; upward progress; increase in power, rank, value, price, amount, height, pitch, etc. 3. Movement of fish to surface; **get a** ~ **out of**, (fig. colloq.) draw (person) into display of temper or other foible. 4. Vertical height of step, arch, incline, etc.; riser of staircase. 5. Origin, start; **give rise to**, induce.

ris·er (rī′zer) *n.* (esp.) 1. Vertical piece between treads of staircase. 2. Vertical pipe for flow of liquid or gas.

ris·i·ble (rĭz′ĭbel) *adj.* Inclined to laugh; of laughter; laughable, ludicrous. **ris·i·bil·i·ty** (rĭzĭbĭl′ĭtē) *n.* (pl. **-ties**).

ris·ing (rī′zĭng) *n.* (esp.) Up-rising, insurrection, revolt. ~ *adj.* That rises; advancing toward

maturity (*the* ~ *generation*) or toward a specified age; (of ground) sloping upward.

risk (rĭsk) *n.* Hazard; chance of or *of* bad consequences, loss, etc.; exposure to mischance; **run** ~**s, run a** or **the risk**, expose oneself, be exposed, to loss etc. **risk** *v.t.* Expose to chance of injury or loss; venture on, take the chance of. **risk′y** *adj.* (**risk·i·er, risk·i·est**). **risk′i·ly** *adv.* **risk′i·ness** *n.*

Ri·sor·gi·men·to (rēsōrjē-měn′tō) *n.* Movement of middle 19th c. for union and liberation of Italy associated with names of Cavour, Mazzini, and Garibaldi. [It., = "resurrection"]

ris·qué (rĭskā′) *adj.* Suggestive; bordering on indecency.

ris·sole (rĭsōl′, rĭs′ōl; *Fr.* rēsawl′) *n.* (pl. **ris·soles** pr. rĭsōlz′, rĭs′olz; *Fr.* rēsawl′). Fried ball or cake of minced meat or fish coated with bread crumbs etc.

ris·so·lé (rĭs′olē, rĭsolā′; *Fr.* rēsawlā′) *adj.* Sautéed.

rite (rīt) *n.* Religious or solemn ceremony or observance; form of procedure, action required or usual, in this.

rit·u·al (rĭch′ōoal) *adj.* Of, with, consisting in, involving, religious rites. **rit′u·al·ly** *adv.* **ritual** *n.* Prescribed order of performing religious service; performance of ritual acts.

rit·u·al·ism (rĭch′ōoalĭzem) *n.* (Excessive) practice of ritual. **rit′-u·al·ist** *n.* **rit·u·al·is·tic** (rĭchōo-alĭs′tĭk) *adj.*

ritz·y (rĭt′sē) *adj.* (**ritz·i·er, ritz·i·est**). (colloq.) High-class,

*The **Salt River** in Arizona forms part [of] the Colorado River drainage basin. [An] irrigation project using various dams [...] the area is underway to make fertile t[he] arid region.*

luxurious; ostentatiously sma[rt]. **ritz′i·ness** *n.*

ri·val (rī′val) *n.* Person's co[m-] petitor for some prize (es[p.] woman's or man's love) or in so[me] pursuit or quality (also of thing[s]) ~ *adj.* That is a rival or are riva[ls] ~*v.t.* (**-valed, -val·ing**). Vie wit[h,] be comparable to, seem or clai[m] to be as good etc. as. **ri′val·[ry]** *n.* (pl. **-ries**). [L. *rivalis*, orig. "on same stream," f. *rivus* strea[m]

rive (rīv) *v.* (**rived, riv·en** [pr.] rĭv′en or **rived, riv·ing**). Te[ar]

*Tribesmen in Zaire pay homage in a **rite** to their god of fire. Smoke emitted by their pipes symbolizes the vapor which issues from the vents of a volcano, the god's home.*

*Ruins beside the Appian Way, Italy, (top) testify to the antiquity of what became the prototype of the finest **road** system of ancient times. Above: Modern traffic needs freeways like those in Houston, Texas.*

art, rend, lacerate, tear; split (esp.
ood, stone); rend (heart etc.), be
nt, with painful thoughts or feel-
gs; cleave, split, crack; admit of
litting. **riv·en** (rĭv´en) *adj.*
riv·er¹ (rī´ver) *n.* One who rives
      splits.
riv·er² (rĭv´er) *n.* Copious
eam of water flowing in channel
sea, lake, marsh, or another river;
oious flow or stream *of;* (freq.
rib., prefixed to many names of
imals, plants, and things living
  situated or used on, rivers); ~
ttom, low-lying alluvial land
ng banks of river; **sell down the**
, (colloq.) defraud, betray; **up the**
, (colloq.) into or in prison.
Ri·ve·ra (rĭvār´a; *Sp.* rĕvĕ´rah),
ego (1886–1957). Mexican
inter noted for large, vivid murals
historical subjects.
riv·er·ine (rĭv´erīn, -rĭn) *adj.* Of,

on, river or its banks.
     riv·et (rĭv´ĭt) *n.* Nail or bolt for
holding together metal plates etc.,
its headless end being beaten out
or pressed down after insertion. ~
v.t. (**-et·ed, -et·ing**). Clinch (bolt);
join or fasten with rivets; fix, make
immovable; concentrate, direct intently (eyes etc. *upon*); engross
(attention), engross attention of.
riv´et·er *n.*
     Riv·i·er·a (rĭvēār´a). Strip of
coast and resort area of N. Italy and
S. France, between mountains and
Mediterranean, famous for its
beauty and mild climate.

     riv·u·let (rĭv´yulĭt) *n.* Small
stream.
     Ri·yadh (rēyahd´). Capital of
Saudi Arabia, in the E. central part;
site of royal palace.
     rm. *abbrev.* Room.
     rms *abbrev.* Root mean square.
     Rn *symbol.* Radon.
     R.N. *abbrev.* Registered Nurse;
Royal Navy.
     RNA *abbrev.* Ribonucleic acid,
any of the class of nucleic acids
containing ribose, present in the
nucleoli and cytoplasm of living
cells and concerned in the synthesis
of proteins.
     roach¹ (rōch) *n.* Cockroach;
(slang) butt of marijuana cigarette.
     roach² (rōch) *n.* (pl. **roach·es,**
collect. **roach**). Small freshwater
fish (*Rutilus rutilus*) of the carp
family of N. European rivers; small
fish resembling this, including
some N. Amer. sunfishes.
     road (rōd) *n.* 1. (usu. pl.; also
road´stead) Sheltered area of water
near shore in which ships can ride
at anchor. 2. Open way, course,
or path between places for use of
vehicles, people, and animals; way
of getting *to;* one's way or route;
the ~, the highway; **on the ~,**
traveling; **royal road,** smooth or
easy way (*to* success etc.); **rule of
the ~,** custom regulating side to be
taken by vehicles, riders, or ships
meeting or passing each other; **take
to the ~,** start traveling. 3. Railroad. 4. **road´bed,** foundation that
supports railroad tracks; foundation and traveling surface of highway; **road´block,** obstruction on
road for stopping or slowing traffic;
(fig.) anything that impedes; **road
company,** theatrical group that
visits cities and towns, usu. presenting one play; **road hog,** reckless,
dangerous, or bad-mannered driver
of motor vehicle etc.; **road´house,**
inn, restaurant, bar, or nightclub
on road outside a city; **road´-
runner,** large, crested, terrestrial
bird of SW. Amer. (*Geococcyx
californianus*) feeding on snakes and
lizards; **road´side,** border of road
(esp. attrib.); **road´stead:** see sense
1; **road´way,** road; central part of
road, esp. part used by vehicular
traffic; **road´work,** long-distance
running or jogging as exercise,
conditioning for prizefighters, etc.
     road·a·bil·i·ty (rōdabĭl´ĭtē) *n.*
Qualities that make a vehicle comfortable to travel in and easy to
drive under various road conditions.
     road·ster (rōd´ster) *n.* (archaic)
Horse for use on the road; small
two- or three-seat open automobile.
     roam (rōm) *v.* Ramble, wander;
walk or travel unsystematically
over, through, or about (country,
seas, etc.). **roam´er** *n.* **roam** *n.*
Ramble, rambling walk.
     roan¹ (rōn) *adj.* (of animal) With

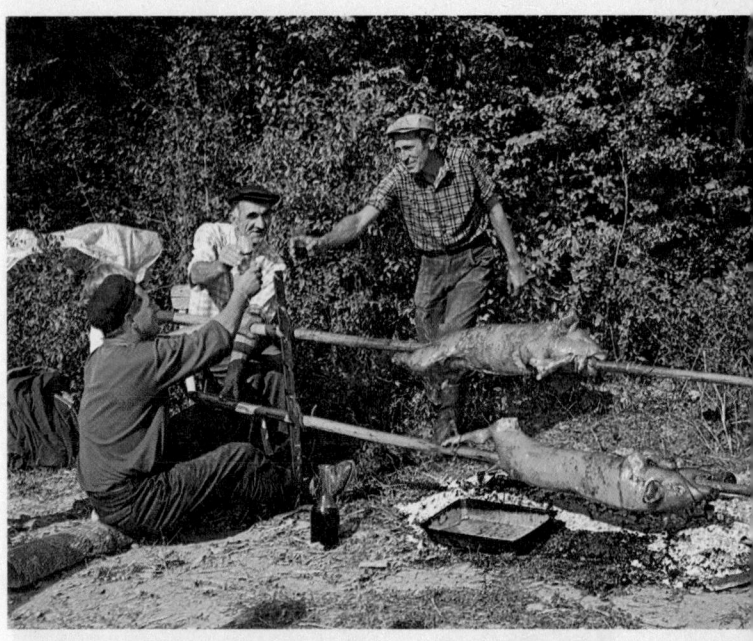

Yugoslavian farmers **roast** pigs on spits over an open fire. This method of spit roasting adds a distinctive flavour to food.

coat in which the prevailing color is thickly interspersed with another, esp. bay, sorrel, or chestnut mixed with white or gray. ~ *n.* Roan horse.

roan² (rōn) *n.* Soft sheepskin leather used in bookbinding as substitute for morocco. [perh. f. *Rouen*]

Ro·a·noke (rō´anōk) **Island.** Island off the coast of North Carolina; site of first attempted English settlement in N. Amer., established by Sir Walter Raleigh, 1585; second attempted colony, called "the lost colony," established 1587; all settlers disappeared.

roar (rōr, rôr) *n.* Loud deep hoarse sound (as) of lion, person or company in pain or rage or loud laughter, the sea, cannon, thunder, furnace, etc. ~ *v.* Utter, send forth, roar; (of place) be full of din, reecho; say, sing, utter (words etc.) in loud tone. **roar´er** *n.*

roar·ing (rōr´ing, rôr´-) *adj.* (esp.) Riotous, noisy, boisterous, brisk.

roast (rōst) *v.* Cook (esp. meat) by exposure to open fire or dry heat in oven; heat or calcine (ore) in furnace; heat (coffee beans) in preparation for grinding; expose to fire or great heat; ridicule, banter, chaff; undergo roasting. ~ *n.* Cut of meat for roasting; roasted meat; operation of roasting.

roast·er (rō´ster) *n.* (esp.) Kind of oven for roasting; large pan for roasting meat in; ore roasting furnace; coffee roasting apparatus; fowl etc. fit for roasting or baking.

roast·ing (rō´sting) *adj.* (esp.) Very hot.

rob (rŏb) *v.t.* (**robbed, rob-bing**). Despoil (person etc.) of or *of* property by violence; feloniously plunder; deprive *of* what is due; (abs.) commit robbery. **rob´ber·y** *n.* (pl. **-ber·ies**). Stealing with (threat of) force.

Rob·bia (rŏb´ēa), **del·la** (dĕl´a). Name of Florentine family of sculptors in glazed terracotta: **Luca** ~ (1400–82); **Andrea** ~, his nephew (1435–1525); **Giovanni** ~, son of Andrea (1469–1529).

robe (rōb) *n.* 1. Long loose outer garment, esp. one worn as indication of wearer's rank, office, profession, etc., gown, vestment; dressing gown, bathrobe. 2. Dressed skin of animal used as garment or rug. ~ *v.* (**robed, rob·ing**). Invest (person) in robe; dress; assume one's robes or vestments.

Rob·ert (rŏb´ert). Name of 3 kings of Scotland: **Robert I**: see BRUCE; **Robert II**, "the Steward" (1316–90), son-in-law of Robert I,

reigned 1371–90; **Robert III** (*c*1340–1406), illegitimate son of Robert II, reigned 1390–1406.

Robe·son (rōb´son), **Paul** (1898–1976). Amer. singer and actor; appeared in the musical, *Showboat*, and the plays *All God's Chillun Got Wings, Emperor Jones, Othello*, etc.

Robes·pierre (rōbz´pēr, -pēar; *Fr.* rawbĕspyĕr´), **Maximilien François Marie Isidore de** (1758–94). French revolutionist; leader of extreme party and chief

*Roman Catholic priests in Lourdes, France. The **robes** worn by the clergy often denote rank. The purple biretta (hat) indicates that the man is a bishop, as do the purple clothes. The man in black is a priest.*

promoter of the Reign of Terr[…] overthrown and guillotined, 179[…]

rob·in (rŏb´in) *n.* Red-breast[…] N. Amer. thrush (*Turdus migr[…] torius*); small brown red-breast[…] European bird (*Erithacus rubecul[…]* any of various birds of Austral[…] New Zealand, India, etc., so[…] having red breasts. [OF. dim. […] *Robert*]

Rob·in (rŏb´in) **Hood.** Legen[…] ary English outlaw, hero of ma[…] ballads and plays, who robbed t[…] rich to aid the poor; said to ha[…] lived in 12th–13th centuries.

Rob·in·son¹ (rŏb´inson), **Edw[…] Arlington** (1869–1935). Ame[…] poet; author of "The Man Wh[…] Died Twice" (1925), a[…] "Tristram" (1927), for which […] won Pulitzer Prizes.

Rob·in·son² (rŏbʹĭnson), **Jack Roosevelt ("Jackie")** (1919–72). Amer. baseball player; first black major league player, signed with the Brooklyn Dodgers, 1947.

Rob·in·son Cru·soe (rŏbʹĭnson kro͞oʹsō). Hero of a novel (1719) by DEFOE, based on adventure of Alexander Selkirk, who lived alone on the uninhabited Pacific island of Juan Fernandez for five years (1704–9).

Ro·bo·am = REHOBOAM.

ro·bot (rōʹbŏt, -bot) *n.* Apparently human automaton; machinelike person, soulless au-

*Fall foliage in **Rochester**, New York. The city was originally laid out in 1811 by Colonel Nathaniel Rochester. Within 20 years it became an industrial and commercial success.*

*A hen **robin** has to feed a cuckoo baby (above) hatched from an egg laid by an interloper. Insects provide the bulk of the diet of both birds. The robin was voted as Britain's national bird in a poll of newspaper readers.*

tomaton. [term for mechanical man in play *R.U.R.* by Karel Čapek; f. Czech *robota* compulsory labor, *robotnik* serf]

Rob Roy (rŏbʹroi′). Robert Macgregor or Campbell (1671–1734), Scottish Highland freebooter, leader of the clan Macgregor, and Jacobite hero.

rob roy (rŏbʹroi′). Cocktail of Scotch, sweet vermouth, and bitters. [f. ROB ROY]

Robt. *abbrev.* Robert.

ro·bust (rōbŭst′, rōʹbŭst) *adj.*

Of strong health and physique; vigorous; (of exercise etc.) tending to or requiring strength, invigorating. **ro·bust′ly** *adv.* **ro·bust′ness** *n.*

roc (rŏk) *n.* Gigantic bird of Eastern legend.

Roch·es·ter (rŏchʹĕstẽr, -ĭs-). 1. Industrial port in W. New York, on the New York State Barge Canal and Genesee River, near Lake Ontario. 2. City in SE. Minnesota, 70 mi. (113 km) SE. of St. Paul; site of Mayo Clinic, established in 1889.

roch·et (rŏchʹĭt) *n.* Surplice-

*Legends telling of **Robin Hood** can be dated to 1377, but no evidence has been found to prove he ever existed. The statue at Nottingham Castle, U.K. (below) is inspired by imagination.*

Rock can be sculpted into remarkable shapes by erosion. Left: Witch Rock in Arizona has been eroded into strange figures. Wave Rock in Western Australia (facing) was smoothed for millions of years by flowing water.

like vestment used chiefly by bishops and abbots.

rock[1] (rŏk) *n.* 1. Large rugged mass of stone forming cliff, crag or prominence; boulder; stone of any size; sure foundation or support, shelter or protection; **on the ~s,** (colloq.) in financial straits; (of drink) served over ice cubes without water or soda. 2. Hard and massive stone; (geol.) any formation of natural origin in the earth's crust, whether composed of a single mineral or an aggregate of many. 3. **~ barnacle**: see BARNACLE; **~ bottom,** (slang, of prices etc.) very lowest; **~-bound,** bordered or enclosed by rocks; **~ candy,** hard candy; large, hard crystals of sugar; **~ crystal,** crystallized quartz; **rock'fish** (pl. **-fishes,** collect. **-fish**), fish (esp. of family Scorpaenidae) frequenting rocks or rocky bottoms; **rock garden,** artificial mound or bank of stones with plants; **rock hound,** (colloq.) person whose hobby is searching for and making collection of rocks; **rock-ribbed,** having rocky out-crop or ridges; (fig.) stern, unyielding, rigid; **rock'rose,** plant of genus *Cistus* or *Helianthemum* with yellow, pink, or salmon flowers; **rock salt**: see SALT *n.* sense 1; **rock wool,** material resembling spun glass, made from molten slag subjected to steam blast and used for building insulation.

rock[2] (rŏk) *v.* Move gently to and fro (as) in cradle; set or keep (cradle etc.), be, in such motion; sway, cause to sway, from side to side; shake, oscillate, reel; **~ the boat,** (colloq.) upset the balance of a situation; **rocking chair,** one mounted on rockers or with seat arranged to rock; **rocking horse,** wooden horse on rockers for child; **rock** *n.* 1. Act of rocking. 2. Rocking motion; **~ and** (or **'n'**) **roll,** (popular dance to) music with heavy beat, simple melody and elements of blues, jazz, and country and western.

Rock·e·fel·ler (rŏk'efĕler) Name of prominent wealthy Amer. family, including **John D(avison ~** (1839–1937), Amer. financier and philanthropist who made a fortune from petroleum and established and endowed four charitable foundations, including the Rockefeller Foundation.

*Various earth movements are responsible for **rock** formation. Above left: The effects of surface folding. Center: Upthrust or collapse. The lower diagram shows the effects of volcanic action and lava penetration.*

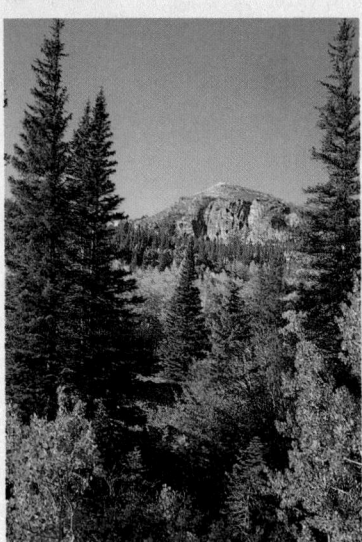

The **Rocky Mountains** extend for more than 3,000 miles, from Alaska to New Mexico. One of the world's youngest mountain ranges, it was formed about 70 million years ago.

established 1913; his son, **John D(avison)** ~ (1874–1960), continued with his father's business and philanthropic interests and planned and built Rockefeller Center in New York City; **Nelson Aldrich** ~ (1908–79), grandson of John D., Sr.; Amer. politician; governor of New York, 1959–73, and U.S. vice president, 1974–7, under Gerald Ford; **Winthrop** ~ (1912–73), grandson of John D., Sr.; Amer. businessman and politician; governor of Arkansas, 1967–70.

rock·er (rŏk′er) n. (esp.) One of the curved bars upon which cradle, chair, etc., rocks; **off one's** ~, (slang) crazy; rocking chair; goldminer's cradle; engraver's cradle for roughening surface of plate; skate with highly curved blade.

rock·er·y (rŏk′erē) n. (pl. **-er·ies**). Artificial heap of rough stones and rock for growing (usu. small) plants adapted to such terrain.

rock·et¹ (rŏk′ĭt) n. Cruciferous plant of genus *Hesperis*, esp. *H. matronalis*, sweet-scented after dark. [It. *ruchetta* f. L. *eruca* because formerly applied to the salad plant *Eruca sativa*]

rock·et² (rŏk′ĭt) n. 1. Cylindrical case that can be projected to a height or distance by the reaction of the gases discharged from the rear when its (highly combustible) contents are ignited, used as fireworks, for signaling, to carry life line, propel military warhead, put spacecraft into orbit, etc. 2. Shell or bomb propelled by rocket. ~ v.t. Bound upward like rocket; fly straight upward, fly fast and high; (of prices) rise rapidly. **rock′et·ry**

n. Science, practice, of rocket propulsion.

Rock·ies (rŏk′ēz) = ROCKY¹ Mountains.

Rock·ne (rŏk′nē), **Knute Kenneth** (1888–1931). Norwegian-born Amer. football player; head coach at the University of Notre Dame, 1918–31.

Rock·well (rŏk′wĕl), **Norman** (1894–1978). Amer. painter; famous for illustrations of typical Amer. family life, many appearing on *Saturday Evening Post* covers.

rock·y¹ (rŏk′ē) adj. (**rock·i·er, rock·i·est**). Of rock, full of or abounding in rocks; like rock in ruggedness, firmness, solidity, etc.; **R~ Mountains**, (also **Rockies**) the major mountain range of western N. Amer., extending 3,000 mi. (4,800 km) from N. Mexico to Alaska; **Rocky Mountain National Park**, area in N. central Colorado NW. of Denver, covering 262,324 acres (106,162 hectares); **Rocky Mountain sheep**: see BIG-horn; **Rocky Mountain (spotted) fever**: see RICKETTSIA. **rock′i·ness** n.

rock·y² (rŏk′ē) adj. (**rock·i·er, rock·i·est**). Unsteady, tottering.

ro·co·co (rokō′kō) adj. Of the style of decoration, originating in France and Italy in the late 17th c. and prevalent in Europe until c1770, characterized esp. by scroll-work, shell motifs, asymmetrical effects, and lightness of coloring; (loosely) frivolous, sophisticated,

Testing a Saturn V **rocket** for the Apollo 16 space mission. These rehearsals are designed to simulate all possible equipment failures which astronauts may have to cope with in space.

Scrolls and shells were used extravagantly in designs for decoration during the **rococo** period. It flourished, especially in France and Italy, for the first 70 years of the 18th century.

overly ornamental. ~ n. Rococo style. [Fr., f. *rocaille* rock work (in ref. to encrusting grottoes with shells)]

rod (rŏd) n. 1. Slender straight round stick growing as shoot on tree or cut from it or made from wood; switch, wand (freq. as symbol of office etc.). 2. Such stick, or bundle of twigs, for use in caning or flogging. 3. Fishing rod. 4. Linear measure equal to 5.5 yards or 5.03 meters. 5. Slender metal bar, connecting bar, shaft; rod-urn 5,F-1(main engine)

oxidizer turbopump

fuel turbopump

gas generator

ignition monitor valve

rocket engine

Two types of engines are used on the Saturn V. Take-off thrust is obtained from five F-1 engines burning kerosene and liquid oxygen. The 5 J-2 second-stage burners use liquid hydrogen and liquid oxygen. A Nerva uses nuclear power to ignite the fuel.

fuel tank (kerosene)

liquid oxygen (lox) transfer pipe

5 F-1 engines

Apollo spacecraft

J-2 engine

lox tank

J-2 engine

fuel tanks(L/hydrogen)

lox tanks

5 J-2 engines

Nerva nuclear engine

liquid hydrogen

pump

turbo exhaust

reactor

nozzle coolant (hydrogen)

rocket nozzle

shaped structure. 6. (slang) Pistol or revolver; **ride the rods**, (slang) steal ride on freight train by hiding beneath car.

ro·dent (rō′dent) *adj*. Of the Rodentia, an order of mammals having only one pair of strong incisors in each jaw and no canine teeth (including rats, squirrels, beavers, mice, etc.). ~ *n*. Rodent mammal.

ro·de·o (rō′dē̄ō, rōdā′ō) *n*. (pl. **-de·os**). Roundup of cattle for branding etc.; public performance, competition of cowboy skills, including bronco riding, calf roping, etc.

Ro·din (rōdăn′; *Fr*. rawdăn′), **(François) Auguste (René)** (1840–1917). French sculptor; noted works include "The Thinker" and "The Kiss."

rod·o·mon·tade (rŏdomŏntād′, -tahd′, rōdo-) *n. & adj*. Boastful, bragging (saying or talk). ~ *v.i*. (**-tad·ed, -tad·ing**). Brag. [It. *Rodomonte*, character in Ariosto's *Orlando Furioso*]

roe[1] (rō) *n*. (pl. **-roe**). (also ~ **deer**) Small European and W. Asiatic species of deer (*Capreolus capreolus*); **roe′buck**, male roe.

roe[2] (rō) *n*. Mass of eggs in fish's ovarian membrane.

Roeb·ling (rō′blĭng), **John Augustus** (1806–69). German-born Amer. civil engineer; designed

*The term **rodent** includes 1,500 species which comprise the largest order of mammals. Its members range in size from the 4-ft. capybara to the tiny wood mouse (above). They are present on all continents except Antarctica.*

and constructed first U.S. suspension bridge, over Niagara Falls; developed plans for Brooklyn Bridge.

roent·gen, rönt·gen (rĕnt′gen, -jen, rŭnt′-) *ns*. Quantity of x or gamma radiation used as a unit of radioactivity.

Roent·gen, Rönt·gen (rĕnt′gen, rŭnt′-; *Ger*. rönt′gen), **Wilhelm Konrad von** (1845–1923). German physicist: received first Nobel Prize for Physics, 1901; discoverer of x-rays, hence freq. called **Roentgen rays; roent·gen·o·ther·a·py** (rĕntgenŏthĕr′apē, -je-; rŭnt-), treatment of disease by x-rays.

Rog·er (rŏj′er). Masculine proper name: **Jolly ~**, pirates' black flag.

rog·er (rŏj′er) *adv*. Response used in oral communication by radio etc. to indicate that a message has been received and understood; (colloq.) all right, O.K.

Rog·ers (rŏj′erz), **Will(iam Penn Adair)** (1879–1935). Amer. humorist, vaudeville and motion-picture actor, and journalist.

Ro·get (rōzhā′), **Peter Mark** (1779–1869). English physician and lexicographer; author of *Thesaurus of English Words and Phrases*.

rogue (rōg) *n*. Idle vagrant (archaic); dishonest, unprincipled person (freq. playfully of mischievous child etc.); ~ **s' gallery** collection of photographs of known criminals etc.; inferior plant among seedlings; wild beast, esp. elephant driven or living apart from the herd and of savage temper. **ro′guer·y** *n*. (pl. **-guer·ies**). **ro′guish** *adj*. **ro′guish·ly** *adv*. **ro′guish·ness** *n*.

roil (roil) *v*. Make (water etc. turbid by stirring; perturb; vex, annoy.

roist·er (roi′ster) *v.i*. Revel noisily, be uproarious (esp. in part. **roistering** as adj.). **roist′er·er** *n*.

Ro·land (rō′land). Hero of medieval (esp. French and Italian) legend, nephew and one of the paladins of Charlemagne; killed in battle against the Saracens at Roncevaux in the Pyrenees.

role, rôle (rōl) *ns*. Actor's part; one's task or function.

Rolfe (rŏlf), **John** (1585–1622). English colonist in Virginia; discovered method of curing tobacco; married Pocahontas, daughter of Indian chief Powhatan.

roll[1] (rōl) *n*. 1. Cylinder formed by turning flexible fabric over and over upon itself without folding; quantity of textile fabric rolled thus (esp. as definite measure of cloth); (slang) quantity of bills rolled together, person's money. 2. Document, esp. official record, in this form. 3. List of names (freq. fig.); ~ **call**, calling over of list (as in school or army) so that each person present answers to his name and absentees are detected; **honor** ~, (esp.) list of those who have died for their country in war; list of outstanding students. 4. More or less (semi-) cylindrical straight or curved mass of anything, however formed; small loaf of bread for one person. 5. Cylinder, roller; in steel mill, grooved cylinder, usu. one of a set revolving simultaneously, beneath which or between which white-hot ingots are passed to shape them. 6. Bookbinder's revolving patterned tool for marking cover.

roll² (rōl) v. 1. Move, send, go, in some direction by turning over and over on axis; (cause to) go, convey, with smooth rolling or sweeping motion (freq. fig.); undulate; make revolve between two surfaces; wrap (*up in*) by rolling motion; (of eyes) change direction (of) with rotatory motion. 2. Wallow, turn about in fluid or loose medium; (of animal) lie on back and kick about; sway or rock, walk with swaying gait as of sailor, reel. 3. (of sound) Utter, be uttered, sound, with vibratory, undulating, or trilling effect. 4. Flatten by passing roller over or by passing between rollers; shape (metal) by passing between

Of all the sculptors in the 19th century, Rodin was one of the most prodigious. His modeling of the human figure was outstanding, as shown by 'The Age of Bronze', Tate Gallery, London, U.K.

The roe or eggs of the Australian lungfish. From these emerge young in a tadpole-like form. Unlike their parents, they need to remain in very shallow water.

or beneath rolls. 5. Turn over and over upon itself into more or less cylindrical shape. 6. Form into cylindrical or spherical shape or accumulate into mass, by rolling. 7. ~ **back**, reduce (wages, prices, etc.) to earlier level, usu. by order of government (**roll'back** n.); **roll bar**, strong metal bar built into automobile roof to protect passenger(s) in case of accidental overturn; **roll on**, (adj.) applying (liquid) by means of a rotating ball in the neck of a container; **roll-top desk**, desk with flexible cover sliding in curved grooves. **roll'ing** adj. & n. (esp.) ~ **mill**, mill that

Originating in the U.S.A., the rodeo is now a familiar form of entertainment in outback towns of Australia. The buckjumping contest (below) is at Katherine in the Northern Territory.

rolls steel into sheets or bars; ~ **pin**, cylindrical roller for rolling out dough; ~ **stock**, railroad's locomotives and cars; ~ **stone**, (fig.) person who has not settled down. **roll** n. 1. Rolling motion; rolling gait; turn of aircraft about its longitudinal axis through 360°. 2. Quick continuous beating of drum; long peal of thunder or shout; rhythmic flow of words.

roll·er (rō'ler) n. (esp.) 1. Cylinder of wood, stone, metal, etc., used alone or as rotating part of machine for lessening friction, pressing, stamping, crushing, flattening, spreading printer's ink, rolling up cloth on, etc.; hollow cylinder of plastic, wire, etc., for rolling hair for setting. 2. ~ **skate**, skate with 4 (occas. 2) small wheels instead of blade, for skating on sidewalks, smooth flooring, etc.; ~ **towel**, towel with ends joined, running on roller.

roll·lick (rŏl'ĭk) v.i. Be jovial, indulge in high spirits, enjoy life boisterously, revel (chiefly in part. **rollicking** as adjective).

ro·ly-po·ly (rō'lēpō'lē) adj. & n. (pl. **-lies**). (Person who is) pudgy, short and plump.

rom, rom. abbrevs. Roman (type).

Rom. abbrev. Romans (New Testament).

Ro·ma·ic (rōmā'ĭk) adj. & n. (Of) the vernacular language of modern Greece.

ro·maine (rōmān') n. Variety of lettuce (*Lactuca sativa longifolia*) having long leaves that form a cylindrical head.

Ro·mains (rawmăṅ'), **Jules.** Pen name of Louis Farigoule (1885–1972), French novelist, poet, and playwright.

Ro·man (rō'man) adj. 1. Of

Legend:

▣ ivory	◆ Au gold	▪ dried fruit
✦ perfumes	◆ Ag silver	△ grain
○ slaves	◆ Cu copper	◇ oil
▽ horses	◆ Pb lead	♥ wine
▼ cattle	◆ Sn tin	▷ fish
▽ hides	◆ Fe iron	▲ timber
● wool	◆ S sulphur	▲ ships
◐ hemp	◆ metalware	◈ marble
◑ silk	▪ coal	▨ glass
◑ linen	▪ salt	◗ ceramics
◔ textiles	▢ dyes	___ trade routes

Map labels: Cu, Au, Pb, Cu, Au, Sn, geese, pigs, pigs, human hair, amber, fur, Cu, Fe, Fe, honey, wax, fur, Au, Sn, Pb, Fe, Ag, Ag, Fe, Au, Au, Ag, Au, Fe, cork, Au, Pb, Sn, nuts, Au, Sn, Cu, Ag, parchment, Cu, Ag, cork, Ag, Cu, Au, Ag, carpets, S, raisins, drugs, drugs, Au, spices, wild animals

ancient or modern Rome or the Roman republic or Empire. 2. Of the R.C. Ch. 3. (of nose) Having prominent upper part or bridge like those seen in portraits of ancient Romans. 4. **r ~**, of the modern kind of lettering or type that most directly represents that used in ancient Roman inscriptions, of the kind now in ordinary use in Amer. and W. Europe; upright, as dist. from *italic*. 5. (of numerals) Expressed in letters of the Roman alphabet, thus: I = 1, V = 5, X = 10, L = 50, C = 100, D = 500, M = 1,000; the letters composing a number are arranged in order of value and the number meant is found by addition, e.g. MDCLXVI = 1,666; if a letter or set of letters is placed before a letter of higher value, it is to be subtracted from it before the addition is done, e.g. XIV = 14; XLIV = 44; MCM = 1,900. 6. **~ candle**, tube discharging colored balls in fireworks; **~ Catholic**, (member) of that part of the Western or Latin Christian Church that owes its allegiance to the Bishop of Rome (the Pope); so **~ Catholicism; ~ Empire**, that established by Augustus 27 B.C. and

divided by Theodosius 395 A.D. into the Western Empire with Rome as its capital and the Eastern Empire with Byzantium as its capital (see BYZANTINE); **Holy ~ Empire**, confederation of Germanic states regarded as the revival of the Western Empire, formed in 962 when Otto I was crowned emperor (or sometimes regarded as originating with Charlemagne in 800); so **Holy ~ Emperor; ~ law**, system of law of ancient Rome, esp. as codified under the Emperor JUSTINIAN; code, modified or derived from the Justinian code, in force in many parts of Europe in modern times; **~ road**, road surviving from the period of Roman rule. **Roman** *n.* 1. Native, inhabitant, of ancient or modern Rome, the Roman republic or Empire; (**Epistle to the**) **~s**, Book of New Testament, an Epistle

written by St Paul to the Christian of Rome. 2. **r ~**, roman letterin or type.

ro·man à clef (rawmahn′ ă klā′ (pl. **ro·mans à clef** pr. rawmahn′z ă klā′). Novel in which real person or events appear in disguise.

Ro·mance (rōmăns′, rō′măns *adj.* & *n.* (Of) the group o languages descended from Latin including French, Spanish, Portu guese, Italian, Rumanian, etc. derived or descended from Latin composed in a Romance language

ro·mance (rōmăns′, rō′măns) *r* 1. Medieval tale, usu. in verse, o some hero of chivalry (orig. becaus written in Romance, i.e. not i Latin). 2. Prose or rarely vers tale (esp. of the class prevalent i 16th and 17th centuries) wit settings and incidents remote fror everyday life; class of literature con sisting of such tales; episode, lov affair, etc., suggesting such tale b its strangeness or moving nature romantic or imaginative characte or quality. **~** (rōmăns′) *v.* (**-manced, -manc·ing**). Inven romances; exaggerate fantastically **ro·manc′er** *n.*

Ro·man·esque (rōmănĕsk′ *adj.* Of the style of art and archi

...cture prevalent in W. Europe ...tween the end of the classical ...riod and the rise of Gothic style, ...p.) of the style prevalent from ...d-11th c. until end of 12th c., ...aracterized by the use of massive ...ne vaulting and the round arch, ...ten with richly carved columns ...d capitals, and sculptured ...ures. ~ n. Romanesque style.

Ro·ma·nia, Ro·mâ·nia: ...MANIA.

Ro·man·ize (rō'manīz) v.t. ...zed, -iz·ing). Render Roman ...character; bring under the in-...ence or rule of Rome; put into ...man alphabet or roman type; ...nvert to Roman Catholicism.

Ro·ma·nov (rō'manawf, -nŏf; ...ss. rawmah'nawf). Surname of ...e imperial dynasty ruling in ...ssia from the accession of ...ichael Romanov (elected tsar ...13) to 1917.

·ro·mansh (rōmănsh', -mahnsh') ...i. & n. (Of) the Rhaeto-Romaic ...alect spoken in the Grisons, E. ...itzerland.

·ro·man·tic (rōmăn'tĭk) adj. ...aracterized by, suggestive of, ...ven to, romance; imaginative, ...mote from experience, visionary; ...f projects etc.) fantastic, im-...actical, quixotic, dreamy; (of ...usic, literary or artistic method, ..., opp. CLASSIC) preferring ...andeur, picturesqueness, ...ssion, or irregular beauty to ...ish and proportion, subordinat-...g whole to parts or form to matter; ...~ **Movement, Revival**, move-...ent of European literature and art ...late 18th and early 19th centuries. ...·man'ti·cal·ly adv. **ro·man'-...cism** (rōmăn'tĭsĭzem), **ro·man'-...cist** ns. **ro·man'ti·cize** v. ...ized, -ciz·ing). **romantic** n. ...mantic person; **R ~**, participant

A rival of Reynolds as a portraitist, **George Romney** was especially able to express character, in subjects as diverse as 'The Parson's Daughter', or those with Lady Hamilton as his model.

in the Romantic Movement.

Rom·a·ny (rŏm'anē, rō'ma-) n. (pl. **-nies**). (Of) the gypsies; (of) the language of the gypsies, an Indo-European language related to Hindi.

Rome (rōm). (It. *Roma*) 1. City on Tiber River, about 20 mi. (32 km) from sea near center of W. coast of Italy, founded 753 B.C.; a republic from *c*500 B.C. until the reign of Augustus (31 B.C.), and conqueror and chief city of most of the known world; in modern times, capital city of Italy. 2. See of the pope and original capital of

Rome, capital of Italy, as seen from the dome of St. Peter's. The basilica is actually located in the Vatican which is a separate State situated within the city of Rome.

Western Christendom; hence, the Roman Catholic Church.

Ro·me·o (rō'mēō). Hero of Shakespeare's romantic tragedy *Romeo and Juliet*; hence, romantic young lover.

Rom·ney (rŏm'nē), **George** (1734–1802). English portrait painter.

romp (rŏmp) v.i. (of children etc.) Play about together, chase each other, wrestle, etc.; (esp. sports slang) get *along*, *past*, etc., without effort, win easily. ~ n. **romp'ers** n.pl. Garment, usu. covering trunk only, for young child to play in.

Rom·u·lus (rŏm'yulus). (Rom. legend) Founder of Rome, son of Mars by the vestal Rhea Silvia; with his twin brother Remus was abandoned at birth and found and suckled by a she-wolf; founded Rome 753 B.C., and became its first king.

Ron·ces·valles (rŏn'sevălz; Sp. rŏnthĕsvahl'yĕs), **Ronce·vaux,** (Fr. rawṅsvō'). Village in Navarre, N. Spain, in W. Pyrenees, site of legendary defeat of rear guard of Charlemagne's army and death of ROLAND.

ron·deau (rŏn'dō) n. (pl. **-deaux**). Poem of 10 or 13 lines having only two rhymes throughout and with opening words used twice as refrain.

ron·del (rŏn'del) n. Poem of 13 or 14 lines, with two rhymes only, and with the first two lines re-curring after the sixth, and the first two or the first only at the end.

The **romantic** movement in literature had its origins in Germany but soon spread to France. One of its exponents was Anne de Stael, portrayed here as 'Corinne', one of her heroines.

*The vault of the cloister at Canterbury Cathedral, U.K. — a form of **roof** no longer built — shows the work of master craftsmen. Below are illustrated various types of roof and their construction.*

ron·do (rŏn′dō) *n.* (pl. **-dos** pr. -dōz). Piece of music (freq. as last movement of sonata) in which principal theme recurs twice or oftener in same key, after introduction of contrasting themes.

Ron·sard (rawn̄sär′), **Pierre de** (1524–85). Chief lyric poet of French renaissance.

Rönt·gen: ROENTGEN.

rönt·gen: ROENTGEN.

rood (rood) *n.* 1. (esp. **holy ~**) Cross of Christ (archaic); crucifix, esp. one raised on middle of **rood screen**, wooden or stone carved screen separating nave and choir. 2. (Brit.) Measure of land, ¼ acre or 40 sq. rods, but varying locally; esp. as loose term for small piece of land.

roof (roof, roof) *n.* (pl. **roofs**). Upper covering of house or building, usu. supported by its walls; top of covered vehicle; **~ of the mouth**, palate; **roof′tree**, ridgepole of roof. **roof′ing, roof′er** *ns.* **roof** *v.t.* Cover with roof; be roof of.

rook[1] (rook) *n.* Common black raucous-voiced European and Asiatic bird (*Corvus frugilegus*) of crow family, nesting in colonies. **~** *v.t.* (slang) Cheat, swindle; charge (customer) extortionately.

rook[2] (rook) *n.* (chess) One of 4 pieces that, at beginning of game, are set in corner squares and have power of moving in a straight line forward, backward, or laterally over any number of unoccupied squares. [f. (ult.) Arab. *rukk*]

rook·er·y (rook′erē) *n.* (pl. **-er·ies**). Breeding and nesting place of colony of rooks; breeding ground of certain other birds and animals, as penguins, seals, etc.

rook·ie (rook′ē) *n.* Untrained recruit; novice or first-year player on baseball team etc.

room (room) *n.* 1. Space that is or might be occupied by something; capaciousness, ability to accommodate contents; **make ~ for**, clear a space for person or thing by removal of others. 2. Opportunity, scope, *to* do or *for.* 3. Part of house or other building enclosed by walls or partitions; (pl.) set of these occupied by person or family, apartments or lodgings; **~ and board**, meals and lodging; **~ clerk**, clerk at motel or hotel in charge of guest registration, room assignments, etc; **~ divider**, piece of furniture used to divide room into separate parts; **room·ette′**, private single compartment in railroad sleeping car; **rooming house**, house where furnished rooms are rented; **room′mate**, person

gable valley
ridge
eaves
hip
Mansard
Gabled   Hipped
principal rafter
common rafter
collar-beam   ridge-pole   king-post
arch-brace   tie-beam   strut
                               wall plate
                                       king-post
purlin   hammer   queen-posts
wind-brace   -beam
arch-braced collar-beam   hammer beam   queen-post

ridge-tile   flashing   tiles
ridge-piece   slates
batten
common rafter   pantiles
wall plate
roof construction   tiles and slate

occupying same room as another; **room service**, (department of hotel responsible for) serving food and drinks to guests in their rooms; **room temperature**, normal temperature of room, about 68° Farenheit (20° Celsius). **room′ful** *n.* (pl. **-fuls**). **room** *v.i.* Have

room(s), share room(s), lodg board. **room′er** *n.* Lodger.

room·y (room′e) *adj.* (**room i·er, room·i·est**). Capacious, larg of ample dimensions.

Roo·se·velt[1] (rō′zevĕlt), **Frank lin Delano** (1882–1945). Ame politician; assistant secretary of th

a   b   c

Annual plants usually have a fibrous **root** *structure (a), but those with a longer life may store food in a tap-root (b). Roots which grow from a stem (c) are known as adventitious.*

Navy 1913–20; governor of New York, 1929–33; 32nd U.S. president, 1933–45, first president to be reelected to a third and fourth term; pledged a "New Deal" to counter the problems of the Depression; established many government programs and agencies; with Winston Churchill drew up the Atlantic Charter formulating Anglo-Amer. international policy, 1941; distant cousin of Theodore Roosevelt.

Roo·se·velt[2] (rō′zevĕlt), **Theodore** (1858–1919). Amer. politician; governor of New York, 1899, 1900; organized and led the "Rough Riders," a volunteer cavalry unit famous for its charge up San Juan Hill during Spanish-Amer. War; U.S. vice president, 1901, becoming 26th U.S. president, 1901–1909, upon William McKinley's death; promised a "Square Deal" to all; his administration was noted for "trust busting," conservation of

national resources, passage of the Pure Food and Drug Act, and the establishment of the Department of Commerce and Labor; received the Nobel Peace Prize, 1906, the first Amer. to receive any Nobel Prize.

roost (rōost) *n.* Bird's perching or resting place, esp. henhouse or part of it in which fowl sleep; **come home to** ~, come back upon originator; **rule the** ~, be the leader or master. **roost** *v.* (of birds etc.) Settle for sleep, be perched or lodged for night. **roos′ter** *n.* Male of the common domestic fowl.

root[1] (rōot, rŏŏt) *n.* 1. Part of plant normally below earth's surface and serving to attach it to earth and convey nourishment to it from soil; (pl.) such part divided into branches or fibers; (sing.) corresponding organ of epiphyte, tendril attaching ivy to its support; permanent underground stock of plant; (hort.) small plant with root

for transplanting; **pull up by the** ~**s**, uproot; **take** ~, begin to draw nourishment from soil; get established; **root′stock**, rootlike stem; source, origin. 2. (Plant, such as turnip, carrot, etc. with) root used for food or in medicine. 3. Imbedded part of some bodily organ or structure, as hair, tooth, nail; part of thing attaching it to greater or more fundamental whole. 4. Source or origin (*of*); basis, dependence, means of continuance, or growth; bottom, essential substance or nature. 5. (math.) Number, quantity, or dimension that, when multiplied by itself a requisite number of times, produces a given expression (symbol $\sqrt{\ }$); value(s) of an unknown quantity that will satisfy a given equation; ~ **mean square**, (abbrev. rms) square root of the arithmetic mean of the squares of a set of numbers. 6. (philol.) Ultimate unanalyzable element of language, forming basis of vocabulary. 7. (mus.) Fundamental note of chord. **root′let** *n.* **root′like**, **root′less** *adjs.* **root** *v.* 1. (Cause to) take root; fix firmly to the spot; establish. 2. Dig up by the roots; ~ **out**, exterminate.

root[2], **rout** (rōot, rŏŏt) *vbs.* 1. (of swine etc.) Turn up ground with snout etc., in search of food; turn *up* (ground) thus. 2. Search *out*, hunt *up*, rummage *in*.

A member of the crow family, the **rook** *is present in Europe and parts of Asia. Some live in large colonies of hundreds of birds, which was the origin of the term 'rookery'.*

Franklin D. Roosevelt, *32nd President of the U.S.A. and arguably one of its greatest. He managed to steer America through 2 of its major crises, the Great Depression and the 1939–45 war, and was elected for 4 terms, although he died a few months into the 4th in 1945.*

Theodore Roosevelt, *the 26th U.S. President and the youngest ever to take office. Then 42, he was regarded by conservatives as a radical and lived up to his reputation in some respects, although his famous 'busting' of business trusts was fairly ineffectual.*

root[3] (root, root) v. Be active *for* another by giving encouraging applause or support. **root'er** n.

Root (root), **Elihu** (1845–1937). Amer. lawyer and statesman; U.S. secretary of War, 1899–1904, secretary of State, 1905–09, senator from New York, 1909–15; received Noble Peace Prize, 1912.

rope (rōp) n. 1. (Length of) stout cord of twisted hemp or other fiber; **the ~**, cord with a noose for hanging person; **the ~ s**, those enclosing boxing ring or other arena; **give one (enough) ~ (to hang himself)**, **plenty of** ~, etc., not check him, trust to his bringing about his own downfall; **know the ~ s**, be familiar with the conditions in some sphere of action; **~ of tobacco** etc., tobacco etc. strung together. 2. Viscid or gelatinous stringy formation in liquid. 3. **~ ladder**, 2 long ropes connected by cross-ropes as ladder. **rop'y** *adj.* (**rop·i·er**, **rop·i·est**). Rope-like;

forming viscid glutinous or slimy threads. **rop'i·ness** n. **rope** v. (**roped**, **rop·ing**). Fasten or secure with rope; catch with rope; lasso; (mountaineering) connect (party) with rope, put on rope; use ropes in towing etc.; enclose, close *in*, shut *off*, (space) with rope; **~ in**, draw into some enterprise.

Roque·fort (rōk'fert, rŏk'-) (**cheese**) n. Blue cheese of a type orig. made at Roquefort, a town in S. France, usu. of ewe's milk and ripened in limestone caves, with strong characteristic flavor.

ror·qual (rōr'kwal) n. Whale of genus *Balaenoptera*, with dorsal fin; also called "finback," "razor-back." [Norw. *raud* red, *hval* whale]

Ror·schach (rōr'shŏk, rōr'-) n. (psych.) **~ test**, in which standard inkblots are successively presented to subject for statement of what they suggest.

ro·sa·ceous (rōzā'shus) *adj.* Of the order Rosaceae, of which the

rose is the type.

ros·an·i·line (rōzăn'ilĭn, -lē -lĭn) n. Magenta dye.

ro·sa·ry (rō'zerē) n. (pl. **-ries**) (R.C. Ch.) (sometimes cap.) For of prayer in which 15 decades Aves ("Hail Mary's") are us repeated, each decade preceded b Paternoster ("Our Father") a followed by Gloria ("Glory be the Father"); book containing thi string of 55 or 165 beads for keepir count in this; similar bead strir used in other religions.

rose[1] (rōz) n. 1. (Prickly bus or shrub of genus *Rosa* bearin beautiful and usu. fragrant flowe usu. of red, yellow, or white colo (with defining word) any of variou other flowering plants; **~ Sharon**, hardy shrub (*Hibisc syriacus*) of mallow family, havir large white, purple, pink, or reddis flowers; (also Brit.) shrublike pla (*Hypericum calycinum*) native Eurasia, having big, yello blossoms and evergreen leaves; **be of** ~, perfect conditions, pleasar easy post or condition. 2. Rep resentation of the flower in herald or decoration; rose-shaped desig rosette worn on shoe or clerical ha rose window; **Wars of the Rose** series of civil wars in Englar during the reigns of Henry V Edward IV, and Richard III (15 c.), between followers of house York (with white rose as badg and of house of Lancaster (re rose), ended by the accession 1485 of the Lancastrian Hen Tudor (Henry VII), who united t 2 houses by marrying Elizabet daughter of Edward IV. 3. Lig crimson color, pink; rosy con

The wild rose (Rosa villosa) (below), one of 250 species from which cu vated varieties like the 'fragrant clo rose' (top left) were bred. The term m also be used for unrelated plants w rose-like blooms. Bottom left: the ro rose (Cistacea).

Hemp being hung to dry in Taiwan is later processed and the fibers drawn and twisted to make yarn, which is formed into various strands which, when combined, become **rope**.

Both as a poet and a painter, **Dante Gabriel Rossetti** was acclaimed in the mid-19th century. 'The Bride' or 'The Beloved' typifies his capability as a colorist.

plexion. 4. **rose′bud**, bud of rose; **rose′bush**, rose plant; **rose chafer**, beetle of genus *Macrodactylus* frequenting roses, very destructive in grub state; **rose-colored**, rosy; (fig.) optimistic, cheerful; **rose fever**, type of hay fever supposedly caused by rose pollen in spring or early summer; **rose water**, perfume distilled from roses; **rose window**, round window, usu. filled with tracery suggesting rose shape or divided by spoke-like mullions; **rose′wood**, any of various kinds of valuable close-grained fragrant cabinet wood. **rose** *adj.* Colored like a pale red rose, of warm pink.

rose²: see RISE.

ro·sé (rōzā′) *n.* Short for *vin rosé*, pink, light table wine, made from red grapes whose skins have been removed during fermentation. [Fr.]

ro·se·ate (rō′zēĭt, -āt) *adj.* Rose-colored, cheerful, optimistic. **ro′se·ate·ly** *adv.*

rose·mar·y (rōz′māre) *n.* (pl. **-mar·ies**). Evergreen fragrant shrub (*Rosmarinus officinalis*), native of S. Europe, with leaves used in perfumery and cooking. [L. *ros* dew, *marinus* marine]

ro·se·o·la (rōzēō′la) *n.* (path.) Any reddish rash; measles, rubeola.

Ro·set·ta (rōzĕt′a) **stone**. Stone found near Rosetta on the W. mouth of the Nile by Napoleon's soldiers in 1799; its inscription, in Egyptian hieroglyphics, demotic characters, and Greek, made it possible to decipher hieroglyphics.

ro·sette (rōzĕt′) *n.* Rose-shaped ornament or badge made of ribbons, silk, etc.; roselike object or arrangement of leaves, parts, etc.; (archit.) carved or molded con-

ventional rose on wall etc.; rose window.

Rosh Ha·sha·nah (rawsh hahshaw′na, -shah′-, rōsh, ha-). Jewish New Year, celebrated in late September or early October.

Ro·si·cru·cian (rōzikrōō′shan, rōzi-) *n.* Member of secret mystical society in 17th and 18th centuries claiming magical knowledge of life, the elements, and elemental spirits; member of the ~ **Order**, or Ancient Mystic Order Rosae Crucis, an international fraternity of religious mysticism. [L. *rosa crux* rose cross, as transl. of Ger. *Rosenkreuz*]

ros·in (rŏz′in) *n.* Resin (esp. of solid residue after distillation of oil of turpentine from crude turpentine). ~ *v.t.* Smear, seal up, rub (e.g. violin bow or string), with rosin.

Ross¹ (raws, rŏs), **Betsy** (**Griscom**) (1752–1836). Amer. patriot formerly credited with making the first U.S. flag; the design of stars and stripes was adopted by the Continental Congress, June 14th, 1777.

Ross² (raws, rŏs), **Sir James Clark** (1800–62). English admiral and explorer of the Arctic and Antarctic; **Ross Sea**, Pacific Ocean inlet in Antarctica, between Edward VII Peninsula and Victoria Land; **Ross Island**, island of Antarctica in the W. part of the Ross Sea, separated from Victoria Land by McMurdo Sound; highest point, Mount Erebus, 12,450 ft. (3,795 m); **Ross Shelf Ice**, also

called **Ross Barrier**, ice wall in Antarctica in the S. part of the Ross Sea, extending 400 mi. (644 km), from Ross Island to Edward VII Peninsula.

Ros·set·ti (rōsĕt′ē, -zĕt′ē). Name of English family of Italian origin: **Dante Gabriel** ~ (1828–1882), poet and painter, and his brother **William Michael** ~ (1829–1919), critic, both members of the PRE-RAPHAELITE Brotherhood; **Christina Georgina** ~ (1830–94), their sister, lyric poet.

Ros·si·ni (rawsē′nē), **Gioacchino Antonio** (1792–1868). Italian composer of *The Barber of Seville*, *William Tell*, and other operas; also composed sacred music, opera bouffe, etc.

Ros·tand (rawstahn′), **Edmond** (1868–1918). French poet and dramatist, author of the play *Cyrano de Bergerac*.

ros·tel·lum (rŏstĕl′um) *n.* (pl. **-tel·la** pr. -tĕl′a). 1. (bot.) Short beak-shaped process on stigma of many violets and orchids. 2. (zool.) Hooked projection on head of tapeworm.

ros·ter (rŏs′ter) *n.* (mil.) List of officers and men enrolled for active duty; list of names. [Du. *rooster* list, orig. gridiron (*rooster* roast) w. ref. to parallel lines]

ros·trum (rŏs′trum) *n.* (pl. **-trums, -tra** pr. -tra). 1. Platform for public speaking (orig. that in Roman forum adorned with beaks of captured galleys); pulpit; office etc. that enables person to gain the public ear. 2. (Rom.

antiq.) Beak of war galley. 3. (zool., entom., bot.) Beak, stiff snout, beaklike part. **ros′tral** *adj.* Of a beak; adorned with beaks. **ros·trate** (rŏs′trāt), **ros′trat·ed** *adjs.* Beaked.

ros·y (rō′zē) *adj.* (**ros·i·er, ros·i·est**). Colored like a red rose (esp. of complexion as indicating health, of blush, sky, etc.); (fig.) rose-colored, promising, hopeful. **ros′i·ly** *adv.* **ros′i·ness** *n.*

rot (rŏt) *n.* I. Decay, putre-faction, rottenness (esp. in timber). 2. (slang; freq. as int. of contempt or ridicule) Nonsense; absurd state-ment, argument, or proposal. ~ *v.* (**rot·ted, rot·ting**). Undergo natural decomposition, decay, putrefy; cause to rot, make rotten; (fig. also ~ **away**) gradually perish from want of vigor or use; **rot′gut,** (slang) cheap liquor.

ro·ta (rō′ta) *n.* I. (chiefly Brit.) List of persons acting, or duties to be done, in rotation; roster. 2. (R.C. Ch.) Supreme ecclesi-astical and secular court. [L., = "wheel"]

Ro·tar·i·an (rōtār′ēan) *adj. & n.* (Member) of a ROTARY Club.

Ro·ta·ry (rō′terē) *adj.* ~ **Club,** local organization of businessmen, founded 1905 by Paul Harris in Chicago; it aims at furthering busi-ness service and social relations and promoting international under-standing and goodwill; **Rotary International,** international organization of Rotary Clubs.

ro·ta·ry (rō′terē) *adj.* Of, acting by, rotation; ~ **engine,** internal combustion engine that supplies power directly without recipro-cating parts. **rotary** *n.* Part, machine, device, etc. that rotates; traffic circle.

ro·tate (rō′tāt, rōtāt′) *v.* (**-tat·ed, -tat·ing**). Move around axis or center, revolve; plant or grow (crops) in fixed order of succession to maintain soil fertility; do, take, schedule in rotation. **ro·tat·a·ble, ro·ta·to·ry** (rō′ta-tōrē, -tōrē), **ro·ta·tive** (rō′tātĭv) *adjs.*

ro·ta·tion (rōtā′shon) *n.* Rotating; recurrence, recurrent series or period, regular succession in office etc. **ro·ta′tion·al** *adj.*

ro·ta·tor (rō′tāter, rōtā′-) *n.* Revolving apparatus or part.

ROTC *abbrev.* Reserve Officers' Training Corps.

rote (rōt) *n.* Mere habituation, knowledge got by repetition, un-intelligent memory (usu. **by** ~).

Roth·schild (rŏth′chĭld, rawth′-). Name of family of financiers, founders in Germany, toward end of 18th c., of famous banking house, with branches at Paris, Vienna, London, and Naples.

ro·ti·fer (rō′tĭfer) *n.* Member of the phylum Rotifera of minute

(usu. microscopic) metazoan animals with (usu.) ring(s) of beat-ing cilia giving the impression of revolving wheels; wheel animalcule.

ro·tis·ser·ie (rōtĭs′erē) *n.* Broiler with motor-driven spit.

ro·to·gra·vure (rōtogravūr′, -grāv′yer) *n.* Intaglio printing pro-cess that transfers images etched on copper cylinders to paper etc. on rotary press; material printed by this process.

ro·tor (rō′ter) *n.* Rotary part of machine; rotating horizontal blades of a helicopter etc.

rot·ten (rŏt′en) *adj.* I. Affected with rot; perishing of decay; falling to pieces, friable, easily breakable or tearable, from age or use. 2. Morally, socially, or politically corrupt. 3. (slang) Disagreeable, regrettable, ill-advised; very bad, wretched. 4. ~ **borough:** see BOROUGH; **rot′tenstone,** de-composed siliceous limestone used as polishing powder. **rot′ten·ly** *adj.* **rot′ten·ness** *n.*

Rot·ter·dam (rŏt′erdăm). City and principal port of the Nether-lands, on the Rhine-Meuse delta.

ro·tund (rōtŭnd′) *adj.* Round, circular (rare); (of speech etc.) as uttered from a rounded mouth,

*The main **rotor** of a helicopter consists of overhead blades. When rotated they produce vertical lift. The tail rotor acts as a rudder and a stabilizer against torque.*

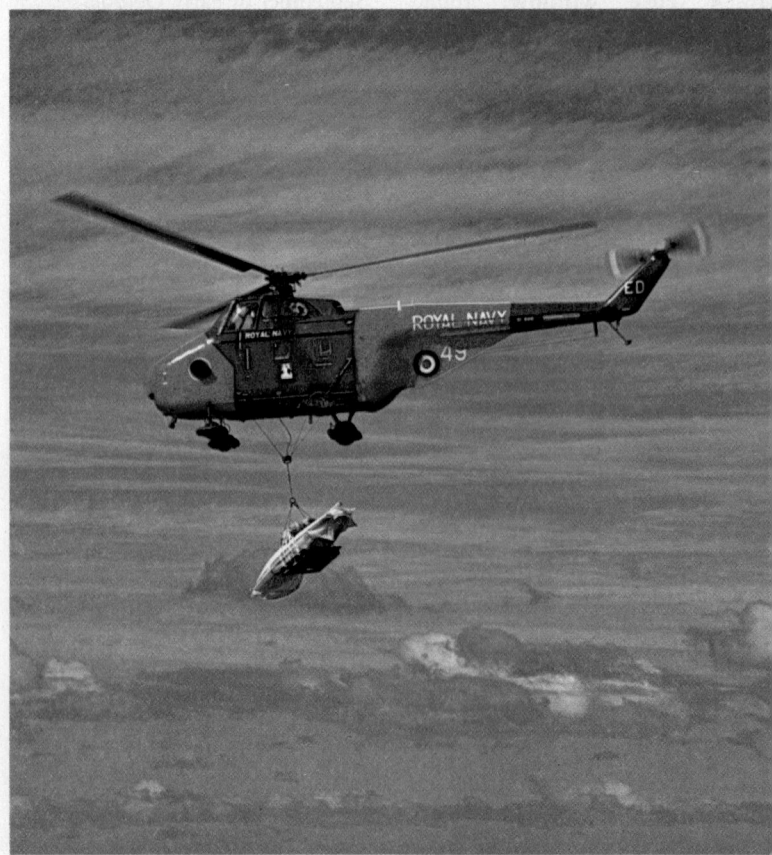

sonorous, sounding, grandiloquent; (of persons) plump, pudgy. **ro·tund′ly** *adv.* **ro·tund′ness** *n.*

ro·tun·da (rōtŭn′da) *n.* Circular building, hall, lobby, etc., esp. one with dome or high ceiling.

Rou·ault (rōō′), **Georges** (1871–1958). French expressionist painter.

rou·ble: see RUBLE.

rou·é (rōōā′) *n.* Debauchee, rake. [Fr., past part. of *rouer* break on wheel, = one deserving this]

Rou·en (rōōahṅ′). City of N. France, on river Seine; ancient capital of Normandy; famous for its cathedral and as Joan of Arc's place of execution.

rouge (rōōzh) *n.* Fine red powder made (orig.) from safflower and used for coloring cheeks and lips; any cosmetic used thus; red powder of ferric oxide, used to polish metal, glass, etc.; red in ~ **et noir,** gambling card game played on table with two red and two black diamond-shaped marks upon which stakes are placed. **rouge** *adj.* Red. ~ *v.* (**rouged, roug·ing**). Color, adorn oneself, with rouge.

rough (rŭf) *adj.* I. Of uneven or irregular surface; not smooth, level, or polished; diversified or broken by prominences; hairy, shaggy, coarse in texture, rugged. 2. Not mild, quiet, or gentle; un-restrained, violent, stormy, boister-ous, disorderly, riotous; harsh, un-feeling; grating, astringent. 3. Deficient in finish, elaboration, or delicacy; incomplete, rudimentary; entirely or partly unwrought; inexact, approximate, preliminary. 4. ~ -and-ready, not overparticular; roughly efficient or effective; ~ -and-tumble, disorderly, regardless of procedural rules; **rough'cast**, (coat, coated, with) plaster of lime and gravel for walls; (v.) (-cast, -cast·ing), coat with roughcast; **rough coat**, 1st coat of plaster laid on; **rough-hew**, (-hewed, -hewed or -hewn, -hew'ing) shape out roughly, give crude form to; (in past part.) uncouth, unrefined; **rough'house**, rowdy play; **rough'neck**, rowdy or pugnacious fellow; **rough on**, bearing, what bears, hard on (person); **rough'rider**, man who can ride unbroken horses; bronco buster; **Rough Riders**, in Spanish-Amer. war, Theodore Roosevelt's volunteer cavalry composed of many cowboys; **rough'shod**, (of horse) having shoes with the nailheads projecting to prevent slipping; **ride roughshod over**, treat arrogantly or inconsiderately. **rough'en** v. **rough'ish** adj. **rough'ly** adv. **rough'ness** n. **rough** adv. In rough manner. ~ n. 1. Rough ground; (golf) rough uncut ground bordering the fairway or between the tee and the green. 2. Rowdy, ruffian. 3. Unfinished or natural state. 4. Rough drawing etc. ~ v.t. 1. Turn *up* (feathers, hair, etc.) by rubbing against the grain. 2. Shape or plan *out*, sketch *in*, roughly; give first shaping to. 3. ~ **it**, do without ordinary conveniences of life.

rough·age (rŭf'ĭj) n. Indigestible fibrous matter or cellulose in foodstuffs.

rou·lade (rōōlahd') n. 1. Florid passage of runs etc. in solo vocal

*The term **roundup** is derived from a method of mustering cattle or sheep whereby they are made to move in a circle to stop any breaking away from the main group.*

music, usu. sung to 1 syllable; drum roll. 2. Slice of meat rolled up around a filling and cooked.

rou·lette (rōōlĕt') n. 1. Gambling game played on table with rotating disk on which small ball is set in motion, and finally drops into one of set of numbered, alternately red and black, slots. 2. Revolving toothed wheel for making dotted lines in engraving, similar wheel for perforating postage stamps.

Rou·ma·nia = RUMANIA.

round[1] (rownd) adj. 1. Spherical, circular, or cylindrical, or approaching these forms; presenting convex outline or surface; done

*Nematodes, which include the **round worm**, are mostly parasites. These worms have no segments and may live in the bodies of humans, horses and many domesticated animals.*

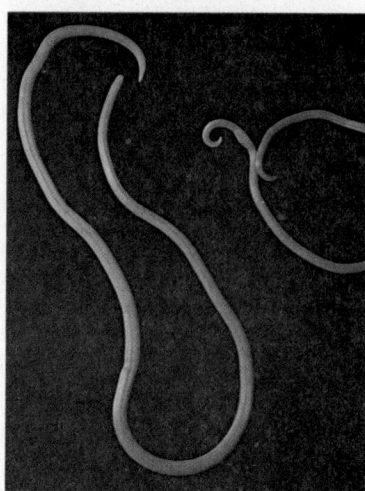

with or involving circular motion; (of cheeks) plump. 2. Entire, continuous, sound, smooth; complete (as ~ dozen); (of tones etc.) full and mellow. 3. ~ **arch**, semicircular arch characteristic of Romanesque architecture; ~ **dance**, one in which dancers form a ring; ~ **figure**(s), round number; figure given as an approximate estimation; **Round'head**, member or supporter of Parliamentary or Puritan party in English Civil War, 1642–9; **round'house**, circular building where locomotives are repaired; (baseball) widely curved pitch; (boxing) blow given with wide swing of arm; **round number**, number (as tens, hundreds, etc.) stated without odd units; **round robin**, tournament in which each competitor plays against every other; petition with signatures in circle to conceal order of signing; letter written by members of a group, each individual contributing short section; **round-shouldered**, having shoulders so bent forward that back is convex; **Round Table**, that around which King Arthur and his knights are supposed to have sat, so that none might have precedence; **round trip**, outward and return journey; **round'worm**, nematode worm, often parasitic, e.g. species infesting human intestines. **round'ish** adj. **round'ness** n.

round[2] (rownd) n. 1. Round object; rung of ladder; large round piece *of* beef, cut from haunch; rounded or convex form. 2. Revolving motion; circular, circuitous, or recurring course; circuit, cycle, series; (often pl.) course of customary places, duties, or actions, as of inspection, deliveries, etc.; (golf) playing of all holes in course once. 3. (mus.) Kind of

Henri Rousseau had a flair for brilliant color and developed an original, if primitive, style. His impressions of tropical flora were gained from hothouse plants and he never left France.

canon for three or more voices singing the same melody, the first voice completing a phrase before the second enters, and so on. 4. Allowance of something distributed or measured out; one of set or series; one bout or spell; one stage in competition; single discharge of shot by firearm; ammunition for this; (archery) fixed number of arrows discharged at fixed distance; **in the ~**, with spectators, congregation, etc. sitting all around central stage, altar, etc.

round[3] (rownd) *adv.* 1. Around. 2. ~ **about**, in a ring (about), all around; on all sides; circuitously; **round′a·bout** (*adj.*) circuitous; circumlocutory; (Brit.) (*n.*) traffic circle. **round** *prep.* Around; throughout; in circumference; ~-**the-clock**, for 24 hours; unceasingly.

round[4] (rownd) *v.* 1. Invest with, assume round shape; round the lips in pronouncing (vowel); bring to complete, symmetrical, or well-ordered state; make round number (freq. ~ **off**). 2. Gather *up* (cattle) by riding around (freq. transf.), hence, **round′up** (*n.*) this action. 3. (naut.) Sail around, double (headland etc.).

roun·del (rown′del) *n.* Small disk, esp. decorative medallion etc.

roun·de·lay (rown′delā) *n.* Short simple song with refrain.

round·ers (rown′derz) *n.* English bat-and-ball game, precursor of baseball.

round·ly (rownd′lē) *adv.* 1. In thoroughgoing manner; bluntly, with plain speech; without qualification, severely. 2. In circular way.

roup (rōōp) *n.* Highly infectious poultry disease characterized by an acute fever generally ending in death.

rouse (rowz) *v.* (**roused, rous·ing**). 1. Startle (game) from lair or cover; bring out of a state of sleep, quiescence, etc.; provoke temper of, inflame with passion; evoke (feelings). 2. Cease to sleep; become active. **rous′ing** *adj.* (esp.) Exciting, stirring; brisk, lively. **rous′er** *n.*

Rous·seau[1] (rōōsō′), **Henri** (1844–1910). French primitive painter; a customs officer, hence called "Le Douanier."

Rous·seau[2] (rōōsō′), **Jean Jacques** (1712–78). French philosopher, advocate of return to natural state, in which man is both good and happy; the *Contrat Social* (1762), expounding the view that society is founded on a contract and that the head of a state is not the

people's master but their man datory, had profound influence o French thought and prepared th way for the Revolution.

roust·a·bout (rows′tabowt) n Deck or dock worker; circu worker who helps put up and tak down tents etc.; any unskilled o migrant worker, as in oil fields, o ranches, etc.

rout[1] (rowt) *n.* 1. Assemblag of company esp. of revelers o rioters; riot, tumult, disturbance clamor, fuss. 2. Disorderly retrea of defeated army or troops; **put t ~**, utterly defeat. **rout** *v.t.* Pu to rout.

rout[2] (rowt, rōōt) *v.* = ROOT (also) force out, eject. **rout′er** *n* (esp.) Kind of plane used in mold ing.

route (rōōt, rowt) *n.* Way take in getting from starting point t destination; customary line o travel; course or territory of a de liveryman, salesman, etc.; highwa (**R ~** when followed by a numbe and used as a highway name). **rout** *v.t.* (**rout·ed, rout·ing**). Pla route of (goods, travelers, etc.) send along a specific route.

rou·tine (rōōtēn′) *n.* Regula course of procedure, unvaryin performance of certain acts; se form, fixed arrangement (e.g. o steps in dancer's performance) (attrib.) performed by rule or habit ually. **rou·tine′ly** *adv.* **rou·tin′-ism, rou·tin′ist** *ns.* **rou·tin·ize** (rōōtē′nīz, rōō′te-) *v.t.* (**-ized, -iz·ing**).

roux (rōō) *n.* (cookery) Flour cooked in melted fat, used to thicken sauces etc. [Fr., = "red," "browned"]

rove[1] (rōv) *v.* (**roved, rov·ing**). Wander without fixed distination, roam, ramble; (of eyes) look in various directions; wander over or through. ~ *n.* Act of roving. **rov′er**[1] *n.* (esp.) Pirate. [orig. term used in archery, = "shoot at casual mark with range not determined"]

rove[2] (rōv) *n.* Sliver of cotton, wool, etc., drawn out and slightly twisted. ~ *v.t.* (**roved, rov·ing**). Form into roves. **rov′er**[2] *n.*

row[1] (rō) *n.* Number of persons or things in a more or less straight line; street with continuous line of buildings on one or each side (freq. in street names); line of seats in theater etc.; row of plants in garden etc.; **a hard ~ to hoe**, difficult task; ~ **house**, one of a line of identical houses, usu. with common walls along sides.

row[2] (rō) *v.* Propel boat, propel (boat), convey (passengers, goods) in boat, with oars or sweeps; pull (oar) as part of racing crew; race *against* by rowing; (of boat) be fitted with (so many *oars*); **row′boat**, boat propelled with oars. **row′er** *n.* **row** *n.* Period of rowing, boat excursion.

row[3] (row) *n.* (colloq.) Disturbance, commotion, noise, dispute; free fight; being reprimanded; **make a ~**, make a fuss or protest.

Roustabouts working on an Indonesian drilling rig. Traditionally, roustabout means an unskilled laborer but rig work requires training for the long hours and hard work.

A *rowing* crew of 4 racing on Lake Torrens in South Australia. Competitive racing began in the early 18th century although the Oxford-Cambridge race did not take place until 1840.

The *rowan*, or mountain ash, grows to a height of 10–30 ft., and is often planted as a garden tree for its foliage, and for the fleshy scarlet berries which cover it in autumn.

row·an (rō´an, row´-): see MOUNTAIN ash.

row·dy (row´dē) *adj*. (**-di·er, -di·est**) & *n*. (pl. **-dies**). Rough, disorderly, and noisy (person). **row´di·ness, row´dy·ism** *ns*.

roy·al (roi´al) *adj*. 1. Of, from, suited to, worthy of, belonging to family of, in service or under patronage of, a king or queen; **R ~ Academy of Arts**, institution, founded 1768 in London under patronage of George III, for annual exhibition of works of contemporary artists and establishment of school of art; **~ blue**, deep vivid blue. 2. Kingly, majestic, stately, (colloq.) splendid, first-rate; on grand scale; of exceptional size etc.; **battle ~**, free fight; heated dispute; **~ fern**, flowering fern (*Osmunda regalis*), with tall upright fronds; **~ flush**, (poker) highest hand in poker, straight flush headed by ace; **~ jelly**, substance secreted by worker bees, fed to all larvae in first few days of life and afterward only to those selected to develop into queens; **~ palm**, any of several fast-growing palm trees (genus *Roystonea*) of W. Indies and Florida, noted for adaptability, having long, bare trunk crowned with large cluster of pinnate leaves. **roy´al·ly** *adv*. **royal** *n*. Size of paper, 19 × 24 in. for writing and 20 × 25 in. for printing.

Roy·al (roi´al) **Gorge**. Canyon in S. central Colorado extending 4.5 mi. (7 km), along the Arkansas River, with walls rising 1,000 ft. (304 m).

roy·al·ist (roi´alĭst) *n*. Monarchist, supporter of monarchy as institution or of the royal side in civil war etc.; esp. (**R ~**), loyal to Britain during Amer. Revolution. **roy´al·ism** *n*. **roy·al·is·tic** (roialĭs´tĭk) *adj*.

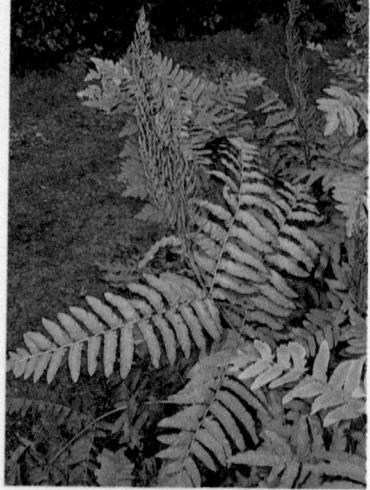

With some ten species growing in temperate and tropical regions, the **royal fern** may attain a height of 6 ft. Its rootstock, similar to that on a tree fern, can be about a foot high.

roy·al·ty (roi´altē) *n*. (pl. **-ties**). 1. Office, dignity, or power of king or queen; sovereignty. 2. Royal persons; member of royal family. 3. Prerogative or privilege of sovereign (usu. pl.). 4. Sum paid to patentee for use of patent or to author, composer, etc., for each copy of book, piece of music, etc., sold, or for each public performance of work.

rpm, r.p.m. *abbrevs*. Revolutions per minute.

Rs., Rs, rs. *abbrevs*. Rupees.

RSFSR, R.S.F.S.R. *abbrevs*. Russian Soviet Federal Socialist Republic.

Rubber sap is 'milked' from a tree once native to Brazil. One tree may yield up to a ton of latex a year. This must then be thickened, pressed into sheets and cured. Annual world output is about 2 million tons.

R.S.V.P., r.s.v.p. *abbrev* Répondez s'il vous plaît (Fr., "answer, if you please").

rte. *abbrev*. Route.

Rt. Hon. *abbrev*. Right Honor able.

Rt. Rev. *abbrev*. Right Reverend

Ru *symbol*. Ruthenium.

rub (rŭb) *v*. (**rubbed, rub bing**). 1. Subject to friction, slid one's hand or an object along, over or up and down the surface of polish, clean, abrade, chafe, mak bare, dry, sore, etc., by rubbing slide (hands, object) *against*, on c *over* something, (objects) *togethe* with friction; bring *away*, *off*, o *out*, force *in*, *into*, *through*, reduc *to* powder, etc., bring size or lev of *down*, spread *over*, groom *dow* freshen or brush *up*, by rubbing (li and fig.); **~ down**, smooth o polish by rubbing; massage; henc **rub´down** *n*. **~ in**, (fig., colloq. emphasize; **~ noses**, rub nos against another's in greeting; **one's hands** (**together**), rub eac with the other, usu. in sign of kee satisfaction; **~ shoulders**, com into close contact *with* (othe people); **~ the wrong way**, strok against the grain, irritate or repe as by stroking cat upward. 2. Pre pare RUBBING. 3. Come into or b in sliding contact, exercise friction *against* or *on*; (of cloth, skin, etc. get frayed, worn, sore, or bare wit friction. **rub** *n*. Spell of rubbing impediment, difficulty (*there's th rub*).

rub-a-dub (rŭb´adŭb) *n*. Roll ing sound of drum. [imit.]

Rub·al Kha·li (rōōb´al kah´lē) (also called Ar Rimal or Grea Sandy Desert) Desert in the S Arabian peninsula covering 250,000 sq. mi. (647,500 sq. km) extending from NE. Yemen t

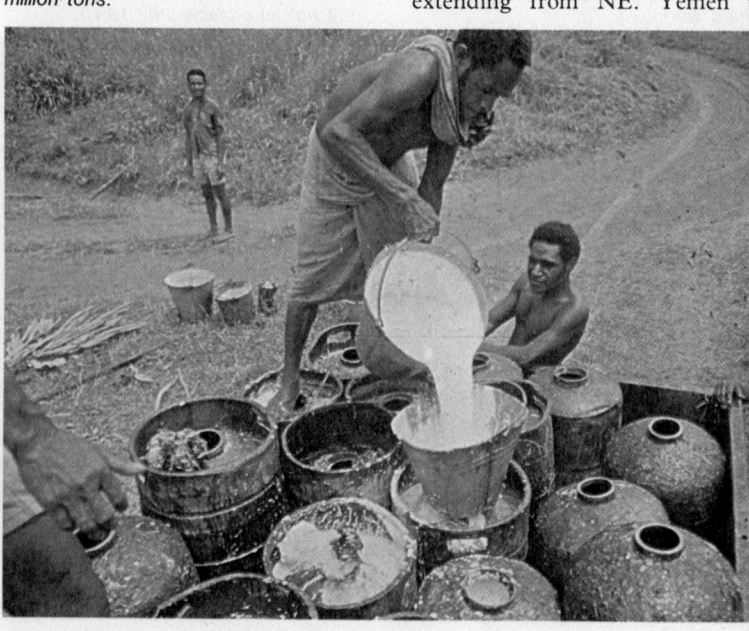

central Oman and including a large section of SE. Saudi Arabia.

rub·ber[1] (rŭb´er) *n.* 1. Person who rubs. 2. Implement used for rubbing. 3. (from its use in erasing pencil marks; also **india rubber**) Elastic solid made from milky juice (latex) of certain plants and trees (esp. *Hevea brasiliensis*) of S. Amer., Africa, the E. Indies, etc., and used for many purposes in industry, e.g. for making tires and waterproofing cloth; (chiefly Brit.) piece of this or other substance for erasing pencil marks; (pl.) galoshes, pair of low rubber overshoes; **rub'berneck**, (slang) sightseeing tourist, inquisitive person; (*v.*) act as rubberneck; **rubber stamp**, stamp for quickly endorsing papers with signature, date, etc., hence **rubber-stamp** (*v.*) give (unconsidered) endorsement to others' decision. **rub'ber·y** *adj.*

rub·ber[2] (rŭb´er) *n.* Three successive games (or two games won by same side) between sides or persons at bridge, whist, cribbage, backgammon, etc.

rub·bing (rŭb´ĭng) *n.* Reproduction of incised or raised surface of sepulchral stone or brass made by rubbing gently with charcoal, colored chalk, etc. on paper placed over surface.

rub·bish (rŭb´ĭsh) *n.* Waste material, debris, refuse, litter; worthless material or articles, trash; absurd ideas or suggestions, nonsense (freq. as excl. of contempt). **rub'bish·y** *adj.*

rub·ble (rŭb´el) *n.* Waste fragments of stone, brick, etc., esp. from old or demolished buildings; pieces of undressed stone used, esp. as filling, for walls; (geol.) loose angular stones etc. forming upper covering of some rocks; waterworn stones. **rub'bly** *adj.*

rube (rōōb) *n.* (slang) Country bumpkin.

ru·be·fa·cient (rōōbefā´shent) *n.* & *adj.* (med.) (Counterirritant etc.) producing redness or slight inflammation. **ru·be·fac·tion** (rōōbefăk´shon) *n.*

ru·bel·la (rōōbĕl´a) = GERMAN measles.

ru·bel·lite (rōōbĕl´ĭt, rōō´belīt) *n.* Red variety of tourmaline.

Ru·bens (rōō´binz), **Sir Peter Paul** (1577–1640). Flemish painter active at Antwerp and in Italy, France, Spain, and England.

ru·be·o·la (rōōbēō´la) = MEASLES.

Ru·bi·con (rōō´bĭkŏn). Ancient name of a small stream flowing into Adriatic, forming part of boundary of Cisalpine Gaul; by taking his army across it, i.e. outside his own province, in 49 B.C., Julius Caesar committed himself to war against the Senate and Pompey; hence, **cross, pass, the** ~, take decisive

The paintings of **Peter Paul Rubens** are renowned for their vivacity and power, well demonstrated in his 'Rape of the Sabine Women', a huge canvas housed in the National Gallery, London, U.K.

The **Royal** family in England are expected to maintain a public profile but to exercise no authority in political matters, although Queen Elizabeth II has weekly meetings with the Prime Minister and may register her opinion.

step, begin undertaking from which one cannot turn back.

ru·bi·cund (rōo´bĭkŭnd) *adj.* (esp. of complexion) Ruddy. **ru·bi·cun´di·ty** *n.*

ru·bid·i·um (rōobĭd´ēum) *n.* (chem.) Rare soft silvery metallic element, one of the alkali metals; symbol Rb, at. no. 37, at. wt. 85.4678. [L. *rubidus* red, from 2 red lines in its spectrum]

Ru·bin·stein[1] (rōo´bĭnstīn), **Anton Grigorevich** (1829–94). Russian pianist and musical composer.

Ru·bin·stein[2] (rōo´bĭnstīn), **Artur** (1886–). Polish-born Amer. concert pianist.

ru·ble, rou·ble (rōo´bel) *ns.* Principal monetary unit of U.S.S.R. = 100 kopecks.

ru·bric (rōo´brĭk) *n.* Heading of chapter, section, etc., also special passage or sentence, written or printed in red or in special lettering; direction for conduct of divine service (prop. in red) inserted in liturgical book; (red-letter entry in) calendar of saints (now rare). **ru´bri·cal** *adj.* **ru´bri·cal·ly** *adv.* **ru·bri·cian** (rōobrĭsh´an) *n.*

ru·bri·cate (rōo´brĭkāt) *v.t.* (-cat·ed, -cat·ing). Mark with, print or write in, red; furnish with rubrics. **ru·bri·ca·tion** (rōobrĭkā´shon) *n.*

ru·by (rōo´bē) *n.* (pl. **-bies**). 1. Rare and valuable precious stone (**true** or **Oriental** ~), a species of corundum, of color varying from deep crimson to pale rose red. 2. Color of ruby, a rich glowing purple-tinged red. **ruby** *adj.* Of ruby color.

ruche (rōosh) *n.* Frill or gathering of lace etc. as trimming, esp. one with both edges sewn to garment; parallel rows of gathering.

ruck[1] (rŭk) *n.* Undistinguished crowd or general run of persons or things.

ruck[2] (rŭk) *n. & v.* Crease, wrinkle.

ruck·sack (rŭk´săk, rōok´-) *n.* Hiker's knapsack slung by straps from both shoulders and resting on back.

ruck·us (rŭk´us) *n.* (colloq.) Ruction.

ruc·tion (rŭk´shon) *n.* (slang, usu. pl.) Disturbance, tumult.

rud·der (rŭd´er) *n.* Broad flat wooden or metal piece hinged to vessel's sternpost for steering with; similar device on an aircraft; (fig.) guiding principle, etc. **rud´der·less** *adj.*

rud·dy (rŭd´ē) *adj.* (-di·er, -di·est). 1. Freshly or healthily red; reddish; ~ **duck**, small Amer. duck (*Oxyura jamaicensis rubida*) having white head, uptilted tail, and (in the male) bright ruddy color. 2. (esp. Brit. slang) = BLOODY sense 3. **rud´di·ly** *adv.* **rud·di-**

Ruin of the temple of Aphaea on Aegina Island, about 17 miles south-west of Athens. In the 12th century the island was a pirates' haven until the Venetians drove them out.

ness *n.*

rude (rōod) *adj.* (rud·er, rud·est). 1. Primitive, simple; in natural state; uncivilized, uneducated; roughly made, contrived, or executed. 2. Violent, not gentle; unrestrained, startling, abrupt. 3. Insolent, impertinent, offensive. **rude´ly** *adv.* **rude´ness** *n.*

ru·di·ment (rōo´diment) *n.* 1. (pl.) Elements or first principles of or *of* knowledge or some subject. 2. (pl.) Imperfect beginning of something that will develop or might have developed. 3. Part or organ incompletely developed, as a vestigial one or one having no function. **ru·di·men·ta·ry** (rōodi-

Common rue is a perennial herb whose leaves are used to flavor meats and sauces. A bitter oil can be distilled from the young shoots and is used in perfumery and for flavorings.

měn´terē) *adj.*

Ru·dolf[1] **I** (rōo´dŏlf). (1218–1291). Founder of Hapsburg dynasty; king of Germany and Holy Roman Emperor, 1273–91.

Ru·dolf[2] (rōo´dŏlf) **of Hapsburg** (1858–1889). Archduke and crown prince of Austria; only son of Emperor Franz Joseph; his death and that of Baroness Marie Vetsera were officially reported as suicides when their bodies were found together at his hunting lodge at Mayerling.

rue[1] (rōo) *v.t.* (**rued, ru·ing**). (pres. part. **rueing**). Repent of, bitterly feel the consequences of, wish undone or unbefallen. **rue** *n.* (archaic) Repentance, dejection at some occurrence. **rue´ful** *adj.* Doleful, dismal. **rue´ful·ly** *adv.* **rue´ful·ness** *n.*

rue[2] (rōo) *n.* Evergreen shrub (*Ruta graveolens*) with bitter strong-scented leaves.

ruff[1] (rŭf) *n.* Deep projecting starched frill of several separately ridged or pleated folds of linen or muslin worn around neck, esp. in 16th c.; projecting or conspicuously colored ring of feathers or hair around bird's or beast's neck. **ruffed** *adj.* ~ **grouse**, Amer. game bird (*Bonasa umbellus*) with strongly marked tail that the male spreads in display while drumming with his wings.

ruff[2] (rŭf) *n.* Small European freshwater fish of perch family (*Acerina cernua*), olive-brown with rough prickly scales and brown and black spots.

ruff[3] (rŭf) *n. & v.* Trump(ing) at bridge, etc.

ruf·fi·an (rŭf´ēan) *n.* Brutal bully, violent lawless person. **ruf´fi·an·ism** *n.* **ruf´fi·an·ly** *adj.*

ruf·fle (rŭf´el) *v.* (-fled, -fling). 1. Disturb smoothness or tranquillity of; (of bird) erect (feathers) in anger etc.; (fig.) irritate, perturb. 2. Suffer ruffling. 3. Gather (lace etc.) into a ruffle. ~ *n.* 1. Perturbation, bustle (rare); rippling effect on water. 2. Ornamental gathered or pleated frill of lace etc. worn at opening of garment, esp. about wrist, breast, or neck; ruff of bird etc.

ru·fous (rōo´fus) *adj.* (Chiefly biol.) Reddish brown.

rug (rŭg) *n.* 1. (chiefly hist.) Large wrap or coverlet of thick wool, animal skin, etc. 2. Piece of shaggy material or thick pile used to cover portion of floor; **pull the** ~ **(out) from under**, (fig.) remove support or concealment of (person).

Rug·by (rŭg´bē). Town in England, site of private school founded 1567; **rugby**, Brit. form of football played with 15 or 13 players on a side, with an elliptical football punted, dribbled, or passed

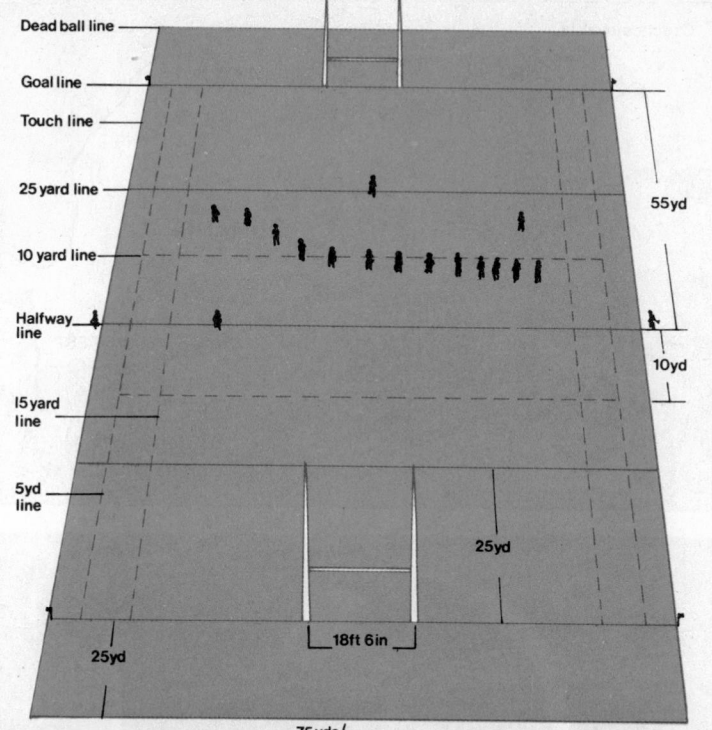

Dead ball line
Goal line
Touch line
25 yard line
10 yard line
Halfway line
15 yard line
5yd line

55yd
10yd
25yd
18ft 6in
25yd
75 yds/

method based on experience or practice, not theory. 2. Sway, government, dominion. 3. (eccles.) Code of discipline observed by religious order; (law) order made by judge or court with reference to particular case only. 4. Graduated, freq. jointed, strip of metal or wood used for measuring, esp. by carpenters etc.; (print.) thin slip of metal for separating headings, columns, etc. **rule** *v.* (**ruled, rul·ing**). 1. Exercise sway or decisive influence over; keep under control, curb; (pass.) consent to follow advice, be guided *by*; **ruling passion**, motive that habitually directs one's actions. 2. Be the ruler(s), have the sovereign control of or *over*, bear rule. 3. Give judicial or authoritative decision; **rule out**, exclude, pronounce irrelevant or ineligible. 4. Make parallel lines across (paper); make (straight line) with ruler or mechanical help.

rul·er (rōō´ler) *n.* 1. Person or thing bearing (esp. sovereign or dictatorial) rule. 2. Straight strip (usu. of wood) used in ruling paper or lines. **rul´er·ship** *n.*

rul·ing (rōō´lĭng) *n.* (esp.) Authoritative pronouncement, judicial decision.

rum (rŭm) *n.* 1. Alcoholic liquor distilled from products of sugar cane, chiefly in W. Indies and Guyana. 2. Any intoxicating liquor; **rum´runner**, (colloq.) smuggler of alcoholic liquor.

Ru·ma·ni·a, Rou·ma·ni·a (rōō-mā´nēa -mān´ya), **Ro·ma·ni·a** (rō-mā´nēa, -mān´ya). Country of SE. Europe, on the Black Sea, formed by union in 1861 of Moldavia and Wallachia; a monarchy from 1881 to 1947, when it was declared a republic; capital, Bucharest. **Ru·ma·ni·an** *adj. & n.* 1. (Native, inhabitant) of Rumania. 2. (Of) the language of Rumania, a Romance language much influenced by Slavonic.

rum·ba (rŭm´ba, rōōm´-) *n.* Cuban dance; ballroom dance imitative of this.

rum·ble (rŭm´bel) *v.* (**-bled, -bling**). Make sound (as) of thunder, earthquake, heavy cart, etc.; go *along, by*, etc., making or in vehicle making such sound; utter, say, give *out, forth*, with such sound. ~ *n.* 1. Rumbling sound; (slang) street fight between teenage gangs. 2. Hind part of carriage; luggage compartment or servant's seat at rear of carriage; ~ **seat**, uncovered folding seat at rear of 2-seater automobile. **rum´bler** *n.* **rum´bling·ly** *adv.* **rum´bly** *adj.*

rom hand to hand, the object being to touch down behind the opponents' line and score a try, and o kick the ball over the crossbar of the H-shaped goal.

rug·ged (rŭg´ĭd) *adj.* Of rough uneven surface; lacking gentleness or refinement; harsh in sound; austere, unbending; involving hardship. **rug´ged·ly** *adv.* **rug´ged·ness** *n.*

ru·gose (rōō´gōs, rōōgōs´) *adj.* (chiefly biol.) Wrinkled, corrugated. **ru´gose·ly** *adv.* **rugos·-ty** (rōōgŏs´ĭtē) *n.*

Ruhr (roor). River of West Germany, flowing into Rhine; coal mining district, with iron and steel and other heavy industries, along his river.

ru·in (rōō´ĭn) *n.* Downfall, fallen or wrecked state (lit. or fig.); (freq. pl.) what remains of building, town, structure, etc., that has suffered ruin; (sing.) what causes ruin, destroying agency, havoc. ~ *v.t.* Reduce (place) to ruins; bring to ruin. **ru·in·a·tion** (rōōĭnā´-shon) *n.*

ru·in·ous (rōō´ĭnus) *adj.* In ruins, dilapidated; bringing ruin, disastrous. **ru´in·ous·ly** *adv.* **ru´in·ous·ness** *n.*

rule (rōōl) *n.* 1. Principle to which action or procedure conforms or is bound or intended to conform; dominant custom, canon, standard, normal state of things; **as a** ~, usually, more often than not; ~ **of thumb**, rough practical

With substantial mineral reserves, including the largest oil fields in eastern Europe, **Rumania** has a thriving manufacturing industry with steelworks, and machinery and chemical plants.

ru·men (rōo′men) *n.* (pl. **-mi·na** pr. -mi*na*). Ruminant's first stomach.

ru·mi·nant (rōo′mi*nant*) *n.* Animal that chews the cud. ~ *adj.* 1. Belonging to the ruminants. 2. Given to, engaged in, rumination.

ru·mi·nate (rōo′mi*nāt*) *v.* (**-nat·ed, -nat·ing**). 1. Chew the cud. 2. Meditate, ponder. **ru·mi·na′tion** *n.* **ru′mi·na·tive** *adj.* **ru′mi·na·tive·ly** *adv.*

rum·mage (rŭm′ĭj) *v.* (**-maged, -mag·ing**). Ransack, make search in or *in*, make search; discover by thorough search; disarrange, throw *about*, in search. ~ *n.* Rummaging; miscellaneous accumulation; ~ **sale**, clearance sale of unclaimed articles at docks etc.; sale of miscellaneous used objects, esp. old clothes, contributed by donors to raise money for charity etc.

rum·my (rŭm′ē) *n.* Card game played by two or more players, the object being to get rid of cards by forming sequences or sets of three or more cards.

ru·mor, Brit. **ru·mour** (rōo′mer) *ns.* General talk, report, or hearsay, of doubtful accuracy; current but unverified statement or assertion. ~ *v.t.* (chiefly pass.) Report by way of rumor.

rump (rŭmp) *n.* 1. Tail end, posterior, buttocks; ~ **roast, steak**, roast, steak cut from steer's rump. 2. Last remaining remnant, esp. of a legislative body considered unrepresentative and having no authority because of expulsion or departure of many original members.

rum·ple (rŭm′pel) *v.t.* (**-pled, -pling**). Crease, ruffle, wrinkle; tousle, disorder.

rum·pus (rŭm′pus) *n.* Disturbance, brawl, row, uproar; ~ **room**, room for games, parties, etc.

run (rŭn) *v.* (**ran** pr. răn, **run, run·ning**). 1. (of persons) Move legs quickly (one foot being lifted before the other is set down) so as to go at faster pace than walking; (of animals) go at quick pace, amble, trot, gallop, etc.; flee, abscond; go or travel hurriedly, precipitately, etc. 2. Compete in or *in* race; seek election etc. (for Congress, president, etc.). 3. Go straight and fast (of fish, ship, etc.); advance (as) by rolling or on wheels, spin around or along, revolve (as) on axle; go with sliding, smooth, continuous, or easy motion; be in action; work freely; be current or operative; (of play) be presented (for specified number of performances etc.) (of train, bus, etc.) go

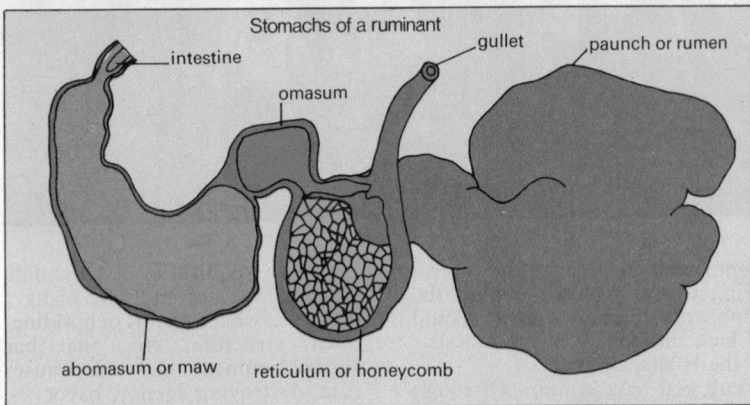

*The multiple stomach of a **ruminant** allows it to digest food at leisure, an advantage to wild animals such as antelopes, but of little value to domesticated cattle and sheep.*

back and forth on route; (of news etc.) spread rapidly from point to point; ~ **in the family**, be found in members of it, as a genetic or other trait. 4. (of color in fabric, ink on paper, etc.) Spread from marked or dyed to other parts. 5. (of thought, eye, etc.) Pass in transitory or cursory way. 6. (of

liquid etc., vessel, faucet, etc. Flow, drip; (of nose, eyes, etc. drop mucus or tears; (of sore suppurate; **make person's bloo** ~ **cold**, horrify, thoroughl frighten; **feeling ~s high**, ex citement, partisanship, etc., i prevalent etc.; ~ **dry**, cease t flow, be exhausted; ~ **low, short** become scanty. 7. Extend, be con tinuous; have a certain course o order, progress, proceed; have tendency, common characteristic or average price or level. 8. (wit cognate object) Pursue, follow, traverse, cover; make way swiftly through or over; perform; ~ **the blockade**: see BLOCKADE; ~ **errands**, perform errands; ~ **the gauntlet**: see GAUNTLET[2]; ~ **rapids**, shoot them; ~ **risk**, see RISK. 9. Chase, hunt; have running race with; ~ **to earth**, chase to its lair; (fig.) discover after long search. 10. Make run or go; smuggle (contraband goods) by evading coast guard etc.; keep (train, bus, ship, business, etc.) going, manage, conduct operations of; ~ **the show**, (slang) dominate in an undertaking etc. 11. **run'-about**, small open car or motorboat; **run'away**, fugitive; unchecked, out of control; **run'way**, track or gangway; specially prepared surface on airfield for taking off and landing; groove in which thing slides; place for fowls to run in. 12. (with preps.) ~ **across**, fall in with; ~ **after**, pursue with attentions; seek society of; ~ **into**, incur difficulties, luck, etc.; be continuous or coalesce with; have collision with; meet unexpectedly; ~ **over**, review, glance over, repeat, recapitulate; (of vehicle) pass over (animal etc.); ~ **through**, examine cursorily; peruse; deal successively with; consume (estate etc.) by reckless or quick spending; pierce, stab; ~ **to**, reach (amount, number, etc.). 13. (with adverbs) ~ **about**, bustle, hurry from one person etc. to another; play or wander without restraint; ~ **away**, flee, abscond, elope; (of horse) bolt; get clear away *from* competitors in race; ~ **away with**, carry off; (slang) win easily; ~ **down**, (of clock etc.) stop for want of winding; (of health etc.) become enfeebled from overwork, lack of proper food, etc.; knock down or collide with; overtake in pursuit; discover after search; disparage; read through hastily; ~ **in**, (football) carry ball over opponents' goal line to score touchdown; (colloq.) arrest and take to prison; ~ **off**, flee; flow away; produce on machine; decide (race) after tie or trial heats; ~ **on**, continue in operation; elapse; speak volubly, talk incessantly; (print.) begin in same line as what precedes; ~ **out**, come to an end; exhaust one's stock of; ~ **out on**, (colloq.) take away support from, desert; ~ **over**, overflow; ~ **through**, pierce with sword etc.; ~ **up**, rise in price; accumulate (sum, debt) quickly; force up (price etc.); raise or construct (building, house, wall, etc.) rapidly; sew (garment) quickly. **run** *n*. 1. Act or period of running; **at a** ~, running; **on the** ~, fleeing or hiding from enemy, police, etc.; retreating; bustling about; **a** ~ **for one's money**, close or strong competition; (a chance for) enjoy-

The great **rune** stone at Jelling near Jutland in Denmark. This early Germanic alphabet seems to have originated in the 2nd or 3rd century A.D. and was used until the Middle Ages.

ment, profit, etc. in return for expenditure or effort. 2. (mus.) Rapid sequence of notes. 3. Continuous stretch, spell, or course; distance traveled by a ship in a specified time; long series or succession; general demand; **in the long** ~; see LONG[1]; **a** ~ **on the bank**, sudden demand from many customers for immediate repayment. 4. Common, general, average, or ordinary type or class; shoal of fish in motion. 5. Regular track of some animals; enclosure for fowls, dogs, etc.; range of pasture; trough for water to run in. 6. Small stream or watercourse. 7. Unraveled tear, ladder in stocking etc. 8. **run'around**, (colloq.) evasion etc. of person's need, request, etc.; **run'back**, (football) run by player after catching kick, pass, etc.; **run'down**, quick summary; **run-in**, (colloq.) quarrel, angry argument; **run-of-the-mill**, (adj.) ordinary, not outstanding; **run'off**, (pol.) election to decide tied vote; deciding race after dead heat; **run-on**, piece of added information or material, as a *run-on in a dictionary definition.*

run·ci·ble (rŭn′sibel) *adj.* (Orig.) nonsense word used by Edward Lear; ~ **spoon**, (now) three-pronged pickle fork, curved like spoon, with one sharp edge.

rune (roon) *n*.   Letter or character of earliest Teutonic

ᚠᚾᚦᚱᚱᚲᚷᚹᚺᚾᛁᛏᛚᛜ

FUThORCGWHNI J̌ I / P
                          A H

ᚤᛏᛗᛒᛗᛦᚻᚠᚫᛩᛨᚱᛄᛦ

[X]ST B E Ng D LM Œ AÆYEa

alphabet (most extensively used by Scandinavians and Anglo-Saxons), dating from at least 2nd or 3rd c. A.D. and based on Roman or Greek letters modified to make them suitable for cutting on wood or stone; similar character of mysterious or magic significance. **ru′nic** *adj.*

rung[1]: see RING[2].

rung[2] (rŭng) *n*. Bar attached at each end as rail, spoke, or crossbar in chair etc., or esp. in ladder.

run·ner (rŭn′er) *n*. (esp.) 1. Messenger; competitor in a race; (baseball) player on base or going toward base. 2. Naked creeping stem thrown out from base of main stem of strawberry or other plant, and itself taking root; any of various kinds of cultivated bean (esp. SCARLET ~) that twine around stakes for support. 3. Ring etc. that slides on rod, strap, etc. 4. Long piece of wood or metal, curved at end(s), supporting body of sled etc.; blade of skate. 5. Groove or rod for thing to slide along; roller for moving heavy article. 6. Long narrow strip of (embroidered) cloth etc., placed along or across table etc., as ornament; long narrow rug or strip of carpet. **runner-up** (pl. **-ners-up**), competitor or team taking 2nd place.

run·ning (rŭn′ing) *n*. (esp.) Condition of ground to be run or raced on; **in, out of, the** ~, with good, no, chance of winning; ~ **board**, narrow footboard extending along either side of older kind of automobile etc. **running** *adj.* That runs; (placed after noun) in

Running the rapids at Lava Falls, Grand Canyon, Arizona — an exhilarating and sometimes dangerous sport which requires great skill and judgement.

Young plant

Parent plant

Runners

*Plants like the strawberry, which are able to propagate by a **runner**, are likely to have a greater chance of survival than those which reproduce by other means.*

succession, following each other without interval; ~ **fight**, continuing fight or disagreement; ~ **head, title**, heading of page, repeated or varying according to content; ~ **jump**, one in which jumper runs to the takeoff; ~ **light**, any of several lights displayed by a ship or airplane at night; ~ **mate**, horse that sets pace for another horse during race; candidate for secondary position in election; ~ **stitch**, one of a line of small straight stitches made by passing needle in and out through material.

run·ny (rŭn´ē) *adj.* (**-ni·er, -ni·est**). Tending to run or flow; excessively fluid.

Run·ny·mede (rŭn´ĭmēd). Meadow at Egham on S. bank of Thames, 19 mi. (31 km) from London, famous for its association with the Magna Carta, which was signed by King John on the meadow or on the island nearby in 1215.

runt (rŭnt) *n.* Smallest animal of a litter; dwarfed or undersized animal or person. **runt´y** *adj.* (**runt·i·er, runt·i·est**). **runt´i·ness** *n.*

ru·pee (rōōpē´, rōō´pē) *n.* Monetary unit of India, Nepal, Pakistan, Sri Lanka, Mauritius, Maldives, and Seychelles. [Hind. *rūpiyah*, f. Sansk. *rūpya* wrought silver]

Ru·pert's (rōō´perts) **Land**. Region in N. and W. Canada owned by Hudson's Bay Company until 1869, then incorporated into the Northwest Territories.

rup·ture (rŭp´cher) *n.* 1. Breach of harmonious relations, disagreement and parting. 2. (path.) Abdominal HERNIA. 3. Breaking, breach. ~ *v.* (**-tured, -tur·ing**). Burst, break (cell, vessel, membrane); sever (connection etc.); affect with hernia; suffer rupture.

ru·ral (rōōr´al) *adj.* In, of, suggesting, the country; pastoral or agricultural; **rural delivery, rural free delivery**, delivery of

mail in rural areas. **ru´ral·ly** *adv.* **ru·ral·i·ty** (rōōrăl´ĭtē) (pl. **-ties**), **ru·ral·i·za·tion** (rōōralīzā´shon) *ns.* **ru´ral·ize** *v.* (**-ized, -iz·ing**).

Ru·rik (rōōr´ĭk), **Ryu·rik** (rūr´ĭk) (d. 879). Reputed founder of Russian empire, Varangian chief who settled in Novgorod in 862; founder of dynasty that ruled Russia until 1598.

ruse (rōōz, rōōs) *n.* Stratagem, feint, trick.

rush[1] (rŭsh) *n.* Marsh plant of order Juncaceae, with naked slender tapering pith-filled or hollow stems, used for making chair bottoms and plaiting baskets etc.;

*Although considered only as marsh plants in England, the stems of **rush** were once used to weave mats and chair seats. The pith was used to make candlewicks and rush lights.*

stem of this; (collect.) rushes as a material; **rush´light, rush candle**, candle made by dipping pith of a rush in tallow.

rush[2] (rŭsh) *v.* 1. Impel, drag, force, carry along, violently and rapidly; (colloq.) be very attentive to, woo intensively; give parties etc. for (prospective members of sorority or fraternity) prior to offering membership; make sudden vehement assault or attack. 2. Run precipitately, violently, or with great speed; go or resort without proper consideration; flow, fall, spread, roll, impetuously or fast; ~ **at**, charge. **rush** *n.* Act of rushing, violent or tumultuous advance, spurt, charge, onslaught; (football) attempt to move the ball by running with it; sudden migration of large numbers, esp. to new goldfield; strong run *on* or *for* some commodity; (pl., motion-picture industry) preliminary showings of film before cutting; (slang) feeling of sudden euphoria after use of narcotic, esp. after injecting narcotic drug into vein; ~ **hour**, time at which traffic is busiest.

Rush (rŭsh), **Benjamin** (1745–1813). Amer. physician and politician; member of the Continental Congress, 1776–7, and signer of the Declaration of Independence.

rusk (rŭsk) *n.* Piece of bread dried and rebaked.

Rus·kin (rŭs´kĭn), **John** (1819–1900). English writer, art critic, and social reformer; author of the 5-volume *Modern Painters, The Seven Lamps of Architecture*, etc.

Rus·sell[1] (rŭs´el), **Bertrand Arthur William, 3rd Earl Russell** (1872–1970). English philosopher and mathematician; author of many works on philosophy, logic, education, economics, and politics; won Nobel Prize for literature, 1950.

Rus·sell[2] (rŭs´el), **George William**: see A.E.

rus·set (rŭs´ĭt) *n.* 1. (hist.) Coarse homespun reddish-brown or gray cloth. 2. Reddish brown. 3. Rough-skinned russet-colored apple. ~ *adj.* 1. Reddish brown. 2. Of russet cloth.

Rus·sia (rŭsh´a). Vast territory of E. Europe and N. Asia, until 1917 an empire under the tzars; since 1917 a federation of socialist republics (see UNION OF SOVIET SOCIALIST REPUBLICS).

Rus·sian (rŭsh´an) *adj.* Of Russia or the U.S.S.R., its people or language; ~ **ballet**, form of ballet developed at the beginning of the 20th c. at the Imperial

*A scene of **rural** tranquility in the Appalachian Mountains. Agricultural production in the U.S.A. increased considerably during the 1950s and 1960s.*

*Located in Red Square, Moscow, the inspirational centre of **Russia**, and near Lenin's tomb, the onion domes of the Cathedral of St. Basil reveal fairytale splendor (below).*

School of Ballet at St. Petersburg from older Italian ballet; ~ **roulette**, firing of revolver held to one's head with one chamber of revolver loaded; ~ **wolfhound** = BORZOI. **Russian** *n.* 1. Russian person. 2. Official language of the U.S.S.R., a Slavic language of the Russian people.

Russian Soviet Federated Socialist Republic. (abbrev. R.S.F.S.R.) Largest and most important of the constituent republics of the U.S.S.R.; occupies more than ¾ of the total area of the U.S.S.R., contains more than half its population, and consists of 12 autonomous republics and numerous provinces; capital, Moscow.

Russo- *prefix.* Russia; of Russia and —; ~**-Japanese War**, war between Russia and Japan, 1904–5, in which Russia was defeated.

rust (rŭst) *n.* 1. Yellowish-brown coating formed on iron or steel by oxidation, esp. as effect of moisture, and gradually corroding the metal; similar coating on other metals; color of this; (fig.) impaired state because of disuse or inactivity, inaction as deteriorating influence. 2. (Plant disease with rust-colored spots caused by) any of various fungi. ~ *v.* Contract rust, undergo oxidation or blight; lose quality or efficiency by disuse or inactivity; effect with rust, corrode.

rus·tic (rŭs′tĭk) *adj.* Rural; having the appearance or manners of country people, characteristic of peasants, unsophisticated, unpolished, clownish; of rude or country workmanship; of untrimmed branches or rough timber; (archit.) with rough-hewn or roughened surface or with chamfered joints. **rus·ti·cal·ly** *adv.* **rus·tic·i·ty** (rŭstĭs′ĭtē) *n.* **rustic** *n.* Countryman, peasant.

rus·ti·cate (rŭs′tĭkāt) *v.* (**-cat·ed, -cat·ing**). Retire to, sojourn in, the country, lead a rural life; countrify. **rus·ti·ca·tion** (rŭstĭkā′-shon) *n.*

rus·tle (rŭs′el) *v.* (**-tled, -tling**). 1. Make sound (as) of dry leaves blown, silk garments, etc. in motion; go with rustle; cause to rustle. 2. (colloq.) Forage, acquire (also ~ **up**); steal (cattle or horses). **rustle** *n.* Sound of rustling. **rus′tler** *n.* Cattle or horse thief. **rus′tling·ly** *adv.*

rust·y (rŭs′tē) *adj.* (**rust·i·er, rust·i·est**). Rusted, affected with rust; out of practice; antiquated, behind the times; impaired by neglect; rust-colored. **rust′i·ly**

adv. **rust′i·ness** *n.*

rut[1] (rŭt) *n.* Track sunk by passage of wheels; established mode of procedure, beaten track, groove. **rut′ty** *adj.* (**-ti·er, -ti·est**). **rut** *v.t.* (**rut·ted, rut·ting**). Mark with ruts (usu. in past part.).

rut[2] (rut) *n.* Periodic sexual excitement of male deer (also of goat, ram, etc.). **rut′tish** *adj.* **rut** *v.i.* (**rut·ted, rut·ting**). Be affected with rut.

ru·ta·ba·ga (rōōtabā′ga) *n.* Turnip (*Brassica napobrassica*) having large, edible, yellow root.

ruth (rōōth) *n.* (archaic) Pity, compassion.

Ruth[1] (rōōth). 1. Moabite woman; her widowed mother-in-law Naomi returned to her own country of Judah, and Ruth being also a widow went with her; in Bethlehem Ruth gleaned corn in the

***Winter rye** growing in Georgia. This grain is grown extensively in Asia, Europe and North America. It is used to make flour for bread, as stock feed and also to produce alcoholic beverages.*

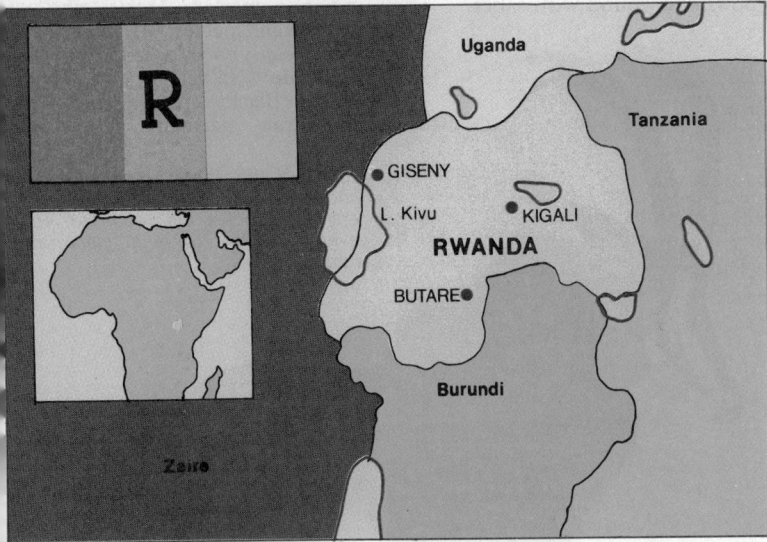

Modern tourist accommodation in **Rwanda** *is designed to simulate the traditional village styles. With much of the country above 5,000 ft., its climate is attractive to visitors and tourists.*

fields of Boaz, who proved to be her husband's kinsman and married her. 2. Book of Old Testament telling story of Ruth.

Ruth² (rooth), **George Herman** ("Babe") (1895–1948). (also called "the Bambino," "The Babe," and "the Sultan of Swat") Amer. baseball player, 1914–35; pitcher for Baltimore and the Boston Red Sox, then outfielder for New York Yankees from 1920; held major league home run records, including hitting 60 home runs in 1927 and 714 in his professional career.

Ru·the·ni·a (rōōthē'nēa). For-

mer province of Czechoslovakia, since 1945 incorporated in the Ukraine. **Ru·the'ni·an** *adj.* & *n.*

ru·the·ni·um (rōōthē'nēum) *n.* (chem.) Rare metallic element of the platinum group, a hard, grayish-white metal; symbol Ru, at. no. 44, at. wt. 101.07. [med. L. *Ruthenia* Russia (from its discovery in the Urals)]

Ruth·er·ford¹ (rŭdh'erferd), **Daniel** (1749–1819). Scottish physician who discovered nitrogen.

Ruth·er·ford² (rŭdh'erferd), **Ernest, 1st Baron Rutherford of Nelson** (1871–1937). New

Zealand-born physicist working in Canada and England; investigated the nature of radioactive transformations and the structure of the atom; received Nobel Prize for chemistry 1908.

ruth·less (rōōth'lĭs) *adj.* Without pity. **ruth'less·ly** *adv.* **ruth'-less·ness** *n.*

RV *abbrev.* Recreational vehicle; Revised Version (of Bible).

R.V. *abbrev.* Revised Version (of Bible).

Rwan·da (rōōwahn'da). Republic of E. central Africa, between Zaire and Tanzania, a former Belgian trust territory; independent since 1962; capital, Kigali.

Rx *abbrev.* (in medical prescriptions) Recipe. [L., = take]

rye (rī) *n.* (Grain of) a cereal, *Secale cereale*, widely grown for use as livestock feed, in making flour, and in making whiskey; (also ~ whiskey) whiskey made from rye; **rye'grass**, fodder grass of genus *Lolium*, esp. *L. perenne*, common rye, and *L. italicum*.

ry·ot (rī'ot) *n.* Indian peasant.

Ryu·kyu (rēōō'kū; *Jap.* rū'kū) **Islands.** Pacific Ocean archipelago extending in a 600 mi. (966 km) arc from Japan S. to Taiwan.

The letter **S, s** is derived from one of 4 sibilants used in Hebrew, Greek and Etruscan. Similar forms were used throughout the Mediterranean but it was not until the 5th century B.C. that rounded forms began to replace jagged ones.

Phoenician   Early Greek   Corinthian

Roman   Ionic   Classical Latin

S, s (ĕs) (pl. **S's, s's** or **Ss, ss**). 1. Nineteenth letter of modern English and 18th of ancient Roman alphabet, derived in form (through early Latin and Greek ⟨, ⟨, ⟩) from Phoenician ⟨ (Hebrew ⟨), representing *s* or *sh* in Semitic languages, in modern English representing chiefly a voiceless sibilant (*s*), the corresponding voiced sound (*z*), and frequently the phonetic combinations (*sy*), (*zy*). 2. Thing shaped like S.

S *symbol*. Sulfur.

S. *abbrev*. (pl. **SS.**). Saint; Signor; South(ern).

s. *abbrev*. Second; shilling; sign; singular; son; south(ern); stere(s); substantive.

-s[1] *suffix*. Denoting pls. of nouns.

-s[2] *suffix*. Denoting third pers. sing. pres. ind. of verbs.

-s[3] *suffix*. Forming adverbs (*besides, afterwards,* etc.).

-'s[1] *suffix*. Denoting possessive case of sing. nouns (*child's, woman's*) and irregularly formed pl. nouns (*children's, women's*).

-'s[2] *suffix*. Used as a contraction of *is* (*she's there*), *has* (*he's walked*), *us* (*let's*), *does* (*what's he say?*).

S.A. *abbrev*. Salvation Army; South Africa; South America.

Saar (zār, sār). River in W. Europe, flowing 150 mi. (241 km), from NE. France to the Moselle River in the west of West Germany.

Sab·ba·tar·i·an (săbatār´ēan) *n.* 1. Person observing Saturday as the Sabbath, as in Judaism etc. 2. Person believing in strict observance of Sunday as the Sabbath. ~ *adj.* Of the Sabbath or Sabbatarian tenets. **Sab·ba·tar′-i·an·ism** *n.*

Sab·bath (săb´ath) *n.* 1. (also ~ **day**) Seventh day of week (Saturday) as day of religious rest enjoined on Israelites; also, the Christian Sunday, esp. as day of obligatory abstinence from work and play. 2. **Witches' Sabbath**: see WITCH[1]. [Heb. *šabbāt*, f. *šābat* to rest]

sab·bat·i·cal (sabăt´ĭkal), **sab·bat·ic** (sabăt´ĭk) *adjs.* Of, appropriate to, the Sabbath; ~ **year,** seventh year in which Israelites were to cease tilling and release debtors and Israelite slaves; year of absence from duty, with pay, for purposes of study and travel, granted to teachers and others in universities etc. at certain intervals, traditionally every seven years. **sab·bat′i·cal·ly** *adv.*

sa·ber, Brit. **sa·bre** (sā´ber) *ns.* Cavalry sword having curved blade; light fencing sword with tapering blade; ~ **rattling**, display of military strength; ~ **saw**, small electric jigsaw; ~ **-toothed tiger**, extinct mammal having long saber-shaped upper canines. **saber** *v.* (**-bered, -ber·ing**, Brit. **-bred, -bring**). Kill, cut down, or wound with saber.

Sa·bin (sā´bĭn), **Albert Bruce** (1906–). Amer. physician and microbiologist; famous for development of **Sabin vaccine**, oral vaccine against polio, made from live virus strains. See SALK.

Sa·bine (sā´bīn) *adj. & n.* (Member) of a tribe in ancient Italy, whose lands were in the neighborhood of Rome, celebrated in legend as having taken up arms against the Romans to avenge the carrying off of their women by the Romans at a spectacle to which they had been invited.

sa·ble[1] (sā´bel) *n.* (pl. **-bles**, collect. **-ble**). Small dark-brown furred arctic and subarctic carnivorous marten (*Martes zibellina*, European species; *M. americana*, American); its skin or fur.

sa·ble[2] (sā´bel) *n.* 1. (poet., rhet.) Black; (poet., rhet.; pl.) mourning garments. 2. ~

Herds of the **sable** *antelope are not uncommon in southern Africa and several sub-species are recorded. However, only 500–700 of the giant variety remain.*

antelope, large stout-horned antelope of S. and E. Africa (*Hippotragus niger*), male of which is dark glossy brown with white belly.

sable *adj.* (poet., rhet.) Black, dusky; somber.

Sa·ble (sā′bel), **Cape.** Cape in SW. Florida, southernmost point in the continental United States.

sab·ot (săb′ō; *Fr.* săbō′) *n.* (pl. **sab·ots** pr. săb′ōz; *Fr.* săbō′). Shoe hollowed out from one piece of wood, worn by French peasants etc.; wooden-soled shoe.

sab·o·tage (săb′otahzh, săbotahzh′) *n.* Deliberate destruction of machinery, damaging of equipment, manufacture of faulty product, etc., by dissatisfied or disaffected workmen, or by hostile agents esp. in wartime. ~ *v.t.* (**-taged, -tag·ing**). Commit sabotage on; (fig.) destroy, render useless. **sab·o·teur** (săbotēr′) *n.* One who commits sabotage.

sa·bra (sah′bra) *n.* Native-born Israeli.

sa·bre: SABER.

SAC *abbrev.* Strategic Air Command.

Sac = SAUK.

sac (săk) *n.* Baglike membrane enclosing cavity in animal or vegetable organism; membranous envelope of hernia, cyst, tumor, etc.

Sac·a·ja·we·a (săkajawē′a) (1788?–1812). Amer. Shoshone Indian woman who acted as guide for Lewis and Clark expedition.

sac·cha·rate (săk′erāt) *n.* Salt of saccharic acid.

sac·char·ic (sakăr′ĭk) *adj.* ~ **acid**, dibasic acid (HOOC(CHOH)₄COOH) formed by oxidation of dextrose.

sac·cha·rin (săk′erĭn) *n.* White intensely sweet crystalline substance prepared from toluene and used as a substitute for sugar.

sac·cha·rine (săk′erĭn, -ĭn) *adj.* Sugary (also fig.); of, containing, like, sugar. **sac′cha·rine·ly** *adv.* **sac·cha·rin·i·ty** (săkerĭn′ītē) *n.*

sac·cha·rose (săk′erōs) = SUCROSE.

sac·cule (săk′ūl) *n.* Small sac or cyst. **sac·cu·late** (săk′yulāt) **sac′cu·lat·ed** *adjs.* **sac·cu·la·tion** (săkyulā′shon) *n.*

sac·er·do·tal (săserdō′tal, săk-) *adj.* Of priest(s) or priesthood, priestly; (of doctrines etc.) ascribing sacrificial functions and supernatural power to ordained priests, claiming excessive authority for the priesthood. **sac·er·do′tal·ly** *adv.* **sac·er·do′tal·ism** *n.*

sa·chem (sā′chem, săch′em) *n.* 1. Supreme chief of some Amer. Ind. tribes. 2. (hist.) One of 12 high officials in Tammany Society.

sa·chet (săshā′; *Brit.* săsh′ā) *n.* Small perfumed bag; (packet of) dry perfume for laying among clothes etc.

For **safety**, laws have been passed in some countries which make it obligatory for motor-cycle riders to wear crash helmets whenever they mount their machines. Frames are also stronger.

sack[1] (săk) *n.* 1. Large, usu. oblong, bag of coarse flax, hemp, etc., usu. open at one end, and used for storing and conveying goods; sack with contents; amount (of wheat, coal, flour, etc.) usu. put in sack as unit of measure or weight. 2. Woman's short loose dress of sacklike shape; (also ~ **dress**). 3. **sack′cloth**, coarse fabric of flax or hemp, sacking; (fig.) mourning or penitential garb (esp. in **sackcloth and ashes**); **sack race**, race between runners with lower part of body in sacks. **sack′ful** *n.* (pl. **-fuls**). **sack** *v.t.* Put into sack(s); (football slang) overwhelm (quarterback) before he can throw the ball. **sack′ing** *n.* Closely woven material of hemp, jute, flax, etc., for sacks etc.

sack[2] (săk) *v.t.* Plunder (captured town etc.). ~ *n.* Act or instance of sacking.

sack[3] (săk) *n.* (hist.) Any of various white wines imported from Spain and the Canary Islands to England in the 16th and 17th centuries. [*Fr. vin sec* dry wine]

sac·ra·ment (săk′rament) *n.* Religious ceremony or act symbolizing or conferring grace (in the Eastern pre-Reformation Western, and R.C. Churches, one of the seven rites of baptism, confirmation, the Eucharist, penance, extreme unction, orders, and matrimony; restricted by many Protestants to baptism and the Eucharist); thing of mysterious and sacred significance, sacred influence, symbol, etc.; oath or solemn engagement taken; (often cap.) (also **blessed** or **holy** ~, ~ **of the altar**) Eucharist; consecrated elements, esp. the bread or Host.

sac·ra·men·tal (săkramen′tal) *adj.* Of (the nature of) a or the sacrament. ~ *n.* Observance analogous to but not reckoned among the sacraments, e.g. use of holy water or sign of the cross. **sac·ra·men′tal·ly** *adv.* **sac·ra·men′tal·ist** *n.*

Sac·ra·men·tar·i·an (săkramĕntār′ēan) *n.* One who holds that the bread and wine of the Sacrament are only symbols of the body and blood of Christ. **s~** *adj.* Pertaining to a sacrament or the sacraments; **S~** pertaining to sacramentarians. **sac·ra·men·tar′i·an·ism** *n.*

Sac·ra·men·to (săkramĕn′tō). Captial of California, in the N. central part, on the **Sacramento River**, longest river in California, flowing 382 mi. (615 km) from NW. California S. to San Francisco Bay.

sa·crar·i·um (sakrār´ēum) *n.* (pl. **-crar·i·a** pr. -krār´ēa). Sanctuary, part of church within altar rails.

sa·cred (sā´krĭd) *adj.* Consecrated, esteemed dear, *to* a deity; dedicated, reserved, appropriated, *to* some person or purpose; made holy by religious association, hallowed; safeguarded or required by religion, reverence, or tradition; indefeasible, inviolable, sacrosanct; ~ **cow**, idea, institution, etc., unreasonably held to be immune from criticism; **S~ Heart**, (R.C. Ch.) heart of Jesus Christ or Mary, as object of devotion. **sa´cred·ly** *adv.* **sa´cred·ness** *n.*

sac·ri·fice (săk´rĭfīs) *n.* 1. Slaughter of animal or person, surrender of possession, as offering to a deity; what is thus slaughtered, surrendered, or done, offering. 2. Give up of thing for the sake of another that is more important, worthy, or urgent; thing thus given up, loss thus entailed; **make the supreme** ~, die for one's country. **sacrifice** *v.* (**-ficed, -fic·ing**). Offer (as) sacrifice (*to*); give up, devote *to*. **sac·ri·fi·cial** (săkrĭfĭsh´al) *adj.* **sac·ri·fi´cial·ly** *adv.* **sac´ri·fic·er** *n.*

sac·ri·lege (săk´rĭlĭj) *n.* Robbery or profanation of sacred building, outrage on consecrated person or thing, violation of what is sacred. **sac·ri·le·gious** (săkrĭlĭj´us, -lē´jus) *adj.* **sac·ri·le´gious·ly** *adv.* **sac·ri·le´gious·ness** *n.* [L. *sacrilegus* one who steals sacred things (*sacer* holy *legere* gather)]

sac·ris·tan (săk´rĭstan), **sa·crist** (săk´rĭst, sā´krĭst) *ns.* Sexton of parish church; official in charge of sacristy.

sa·cris·ty (săk´rĭstē) *n.* (pl. **-ties**). Repository for vestments, vessels, etc., of a church.

sac·ro·il·i·ac (săkrōĭl´ēăk, sā-krō-) *n.* Joint between sacrum and ilium. ~ *adj.* Of, pertaining to, or affecting this joint or its cartilage.

sac·ro·sanct (săk´rōsăngkt) *adj.* Secured by religious sanction against outrage, inviolable. **sac·ro·sanc·ti·ty** (săkrōsăngk´tĭtē) *n.*

sa·crum (sā´krum, săk´rum) *n.* (pl. **sa·cra** pr. sā´kra, săk´ra). Composite triangular bone of ankylosed vertebrae forming back of pelvis. **sa´cral** *adj.* [L. *os sacrum* sacred bone (from sacrificial use)]

sad (săd) *adj.* (**sad·der, sad·dest**). 1. Sorrowful, mournful; showing or causing sorrow. 2. Deplorably bad; sorry. 3. (of color) Dull, neutral-tinted. **sad´den** *v.* **sad´ly** *adv.* **sad´ness** *n.*

Sa·dat (sahdaht´), **Anwar el** (1918–). Egyptian politician; president of Egypt since 1970; co-recipient, with Prime Minister Begin of Israel, of Nobel Peace Prize, 1978.

sad·dle (săd´el) *n.* 1. Rider's seat placed on back of horse etc. (usu.

*Below left: With an Aboriginal guide, visitors go on **safari** in northern Australia. Below: An ancient **sacred** stone from Sarawak whose significance is no longer known.*

concave, of leather, with side flaps and girths and stirrups) or forming part of bicycle etc.; **in the ~** mounted; (fig.) in office or control. 2. Saddle-shaped thing, e.g. ridge between 2 summits; part of back of various animals, as dog; cut *of* meat esp. mutton or venison, consisting of the 2 loins. 3. **~-backed**, with upper outline concave; **sad´dle-bag**, one of pair of bags laid across horse, etc., behind saddle; **sad´dle-bow**, arched front of saddle; **sad´dlecloth**, cloth laid on horse's back under saddle; **saddle horse** horse for riding; **saddle shoe** Oxford shoe with contrasting band across upper part; **sad´dletree** frame of saddle. **saddle** *v.t.* (**-dled, -dling**). Put saddle on (horse etc.), burden (person) *with* task, responsibility, etc.; put (burden) *on* person.

sad·dler (săd´ler) *n.* Maker of or dealer in saddles and other equipment for horses. **sad´dler·y** *n.* (pl. **-dler·ies**).

Sad·du·cee (săj´usē, săd´yu-) *n.* Member of a Jewish sect of 1st c. B.C.-1st c. A.D., opposed to the Pharisees, who repudiated oral tradition and accepted the written Law only, rejecting belief in the resurrection of the body and the existence of angels and spirits. **Sad·du·ce·an** (săjusē´an, sădyu-) *adj.* [Heb. *ṣᵉdûkîy* prob. = descendant of Zadok]

Sade (sahd, săd), **Do·na·tien** (dawnahsyăň´) **Alphonse, Count** (generally known as Marquis) **de**

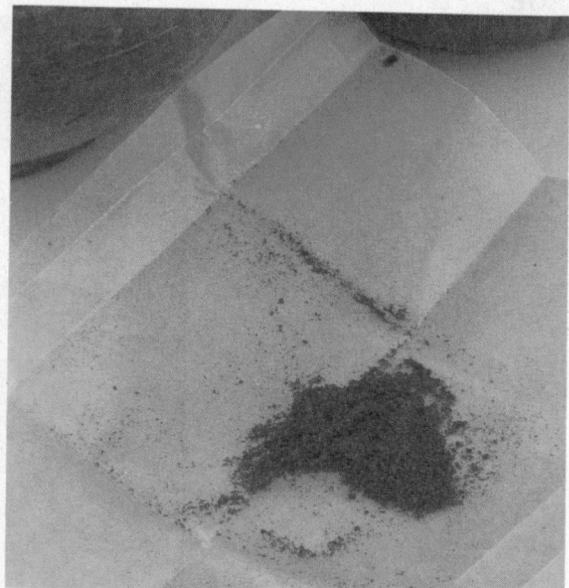

In Kurdistan, ceremonial saddles are covered with ornate embroidery. It is not widely appreciated that the **saddle** was not used until the 3rd or 4th century A.D.

The world's most expensive herb, **saffron,** is made from the dried stigmas of the saffron crocus. It has a strong exotic aroma and a bitter taste.

(1740–1814). French author and libertine, whose accounts of sexual perversions have given his name to SADISM.

sad·ism (săd´ĭzem, sā´dĭz-) *n.* Deriving of pleasure from the infliction of cruelty upon others, esp. as method of sexual gratification. **sad´ist** *n.* **sa·dis·tic** (sadĭs´tĭk) *adj.* [f. Count D. A. de SADE]

sad·o·mas·o·chism (sădōmăs´-okĭzem, sādō-) *n.* Combination of sadism and masochism in one person. **sad·o·mas·o·chist** *n.* **sad·o·mas·o·chis·tic** (sădomăso-kĭs´tĭk, sādō-) *adj.*

SAE, S.A.E. *abbrevs.* Society of Automotive Engineers.

sa·fa·ri (safăr´ē) *n.* (pl. **-ris**). Journey or expedition in E. Africa esp. for hunting or observing wildlife. [Swahili, f. Arab. *safar* journey]

safe[1] (sāf) *n.* Strong locked repository for valuables; **~ deposit,** strongroom or vault, usu. in a bank, containing safe with boxes or drawers for storing papers, jewelry, or other valuables.

safe[2] (sāf) *adj.* (**saf·er, saf·est**). 1. Uninjured (pred. after *bring, keep,* etc.); secure, out of or not exposed to danger. 2. Affording security or not involving danger; **on the ~ side,** with margin of security against risks. 3. Debarred from escaping or doing harm. 4. Cautious and unenterprising; consistently moderate; that can be reckoned on, unfailing, certain *to* do or be; sure to become. 5. **safe-conduct,** (document conveying) privilege granted by sovereign, commander, etc., of being protected from arrest or harm on particular occasion or in district; **safe period,** (colloq.) time during and near menstrual period, when conception is least likely; **safe´-**

keep´ing, custody. **safe´ly** *adv.* **safe´ness** *n.*

safe·guard (sāf´gärd) *n.* Safe-conduct; (usu.) proviso, stipulation, quality, or circumstance that tends to prevent some evil or protect. ~ *v.t.* Guard, protect (esp. rights, etc.) by precaution or stipulation.

safe·ty (sāf´tē) *n.* (pl. **-ties**). 1. Being safe, freedom from danger or risks; safeness, being sure or likely to bring no danger. 2. (football) Play in which offensive team grounds the ball behind its own goal line, scoring two points for opposing team (cf. TOUCHBACK); either of two defensive backs farther behind line of scrimmage; **~ belt** = SEAT belt; **~ (catch),** device for locking gun trigger; **~ glass,** glass so made as to prevent splintering; **~ lamp,** miner's lamp so constructed as to prevent the flame from coming into direct contact with firedamp and causing an explosion; **~ match,** one igniting only on specially prepared surface; **~ pin,** pin bent back on itself so as to form a spring, with guard or sheath to cover point; **~ razor,** razor with blade fitted into holder having guard to prevent it from cutting deeply; **~ valve,** valve in steam boiler etc. opening automatically to relieve excessive pressure; (fig.) means of giving harmless vent to excitement etc.

saf´flow·er (săf´lower) *n.* Thistlelike plant (*Carthamus tinctorius*) with flowers whose dried petals yield red dye, and with seeds that yield oil used in cooking, cosmetics, etc.

saf·fron (săf´ron) *n.* Kind of crocus (*Crocus sativus*) cultivated

for its flowers, the stigmas of which yield an orange-yellow substance used for coloring and flavoring food; this substance; color of this. ~ *adj.* Of saffron color.

sag (săg) *v.* (**sagged, sag·ging**). Sink or subside under weight or pressure; droop; be lopsided; have downward bulge or curve in middle, cause to curve thus; (commerc.) decline in price; (of ship) drift to leeward. ~ *n.* Sagging; amount that rope etc. sags. **sag´gy** *adj.* (**-gi·er, -gi·est**).

sa·ga (sah´ga) *n.* Medieval Icelandic or Norwegian prose narrative, esp. one embodying history of Icelandic family or Norwegian king; story of heroic achievement or adventure; long family chronicle. [ON., = "narrative"]

sa·ga·cious (sagā´shus) *adj.* Mentally penetrating, gifted with discernment, practically wise, acute-minded, shrewd; (of speech etc.) showing wisdom. **sa·ga´cious·ly** *adv.* **sa·gac·i·ty** (sagăs´-ĭtē) *n.* (pl. **-ties**).

sag·a·more (săg´amōr, -môr) *n.* Chief, or subordinate chief, of some Amer. Ind. tribes.

sage[1] (sāj) *n.* Aromatic herb (*Salvia officinalis*) with dull grayish-green leaves; its leaves used in cookery; any plant of the genus *Salvia;* **sage´brush,** any of various N. Amer. hoary-leaved shrubs of genus *Artemisia,* freq. covering large arid tracts in Western states; **sage grouse,** large N. Amer. grouse (*Centrocercus urophasianus*) in sagebrush country, the male's display being spectacular.

Garden **sage,** *an aromatic herb originally from the Mediterranean region, is now grown widely in temperate areas. It is a savory ingredient in meat dishes and soups.*

sage² (sāj) *adj.* (**sag·er, sag·est**). Wise, discreet, judicious, having the wisdom of experience; of or indicating profound wisdom. **sage′ly** *adv.* **sage′ness** *n.* **sage** *n.* Profoundly wise man, esp. any of the ancients traditionally reputed wisest of their time.

Sa·git·ta (sajĭt′a). The Arrow, a northern constellation.

sag·it·tal (săj′ĭtal) *adj.* (anat.) In the same plane as the **sagittal suture** (suture between parietal bones of skull), i.e. longitudinal and from front to back. **sag′it·tal·ly** *adv.*

Sag·it·ta·ri·us (săjĭtār′ēus). The Archer, a southern constellation; 9th sign (♐) of the zodiac, which the sun enters about Nov. 22. **Sag·it·ta′ri·an** *adj. & n.*

sa·go (sā′gō) *n.* (pl. **-gos**). Palm or cycad esp. of genus *Metroxylon*; kind of starch used in cooking, obtained from pith of these plants.

sa·gua·ro (sagwar′ō, sawar′ō) *n.* Giant cactus (*Carnegiea gigantea*) of southwestern U.S. and northern Mexico, growing up to 60 ft. and having thick upward-curving branches, white flowers, and edible fruit.

Sa·hap·tin (sahăp′tĭn) *adj. & n.* (pl. **-tins**, collect. **-tin**). (Member, language) of a N. Amer. Ind. tribe of Washington, Oregon, and Idaho.

Sa·har·a (sahār′a, -här′a). Vast desert in N. Africa, largest in the world, covering 3,500,000 sq. mi. (9,065,000 sq. km), extending from the Atlantic coast E. to the Red Sea and S. to the Sudan. **Sa·ha′ran, Sa·har′i·an** *adjs.*

The largest desert in the world, the **Sahara** *has an area of 3.5 million square miles. Most of it is an elevated plateau and the area covered by sand dunes is relatively small.*

sa·hib (sah′ĭb, -ēb) *n.* (fem. **mem-sa·hib**) Former title or form of address used in colonial India to Europeans.

said (sĕd) *adj.*: see SAY; (esp.) aforesaid.

Sai·gon (sīgŏn′). Capital city and main port of Vietnam, on the ~ **River** in the S. part of the country; now called Ho Chi Minh City.

sail¹ (sāl) *n.* 1. Piece of canvas or other textile material extended on rigging to catch wind and propel vessel; (collect.) some or all of ship's sails; **under** ~, with sails set. 2. (collect.) Ships; ship. 3. Blade of windmill; sailfish's dorsal fin; **sail′cloth,** canvas for sails; kind of coarse linen; **sail′fish** (pl. **-fishes,** collect. **-fish**), any of various tropical, marine game and food fishes of the genus *Istiophorus*, related to swordfish and marlin, 6

The skill needed to handle a **sailing** *vessel is dependent on the captain's ability to assess the strength and direction of the wind and to relate this to the capability of his vessel. The techniques of sailing were evolved long ago, but new designs in boats have resulted in a need for new techniques or variations of earlier ones.*

to 10 ft. long, weighing from 60 to 100 lbs., and having a high, wide, blue dorsal fin and sword-shaped upper jaw.

sail[2] (sāl) v. 1. (of vessel or person on board) Travel on water by use of sails or engine power; start on voyage. 2. Move in stately or smooth manner; travel over or along, navigate, glide through (sea, sky, etc.); (of bird etc.) glide in air. 3. Control navigation of (ship), set (toy boat) afloat. 4. ~ **close to** or **near the wind**, sail nearly against it; come near transgressing a law or moral principle; ~ **into**, (slang) attack physically or verbally. **sail** n. Voyage or excursion in sailing vessel; voyage of specified duration; **sail'boat**, boat or sails propelled by sail; **sail'plane**, soaring glider.

sail·ing (sā'lǐng) n. 1. Act of person or thing that sails. 2. Skill needed to navigate sailing vessel. 3. Sport of riding in or handling sailboat. 4. Departure time of ship or person on it; ~ **ship**, **vessel**,

vessel propelled by sails, not engines.

sail·or (sā'ler) n. One who is employed in navigating a ship; member of ship's crew or company below rank of officer; **good, bad ~**, person not, very, liable to seasickness; **sailor hat**, straw hat with narrow brim and flat top. **sail'or·ly** adj.

sain·foin (sān'foin) n. Low-growing perennial herb (*Onobrychis viciifolia*) with pinnate leaves and pink flowers, cultivated as fodder. [Fr. *sain* wholesome, *foin*, hay]

saint (sānt) adj. Canonized or officially recognized by the R.C. Ch. or certain other Christian churches as having won by exceptional holiness a high place in heaven and veneration on earth, usu. abbrev. St. or S., pl. Sts., SS., as prefix to name(s) of person or

archangel(s) as *St. Paul, St. Michael*; hence, in names of churches and of towns called after their churches, and in Christian and family names, taken from patron saint etc. ~ n. One of the blessed dead or other member of the company of heaven; canonized person; (bibl., archaic, and in some modern sects, esp. Mormon) one of God's chosen people, member of Christian church or of some branch of it (usu. cap.); person of great holiness; **patron ~**, saint selected as heavenly protector of person or place, esp. church, often named after him; **saint's day**, church festival in memory of a saint, freq. observed as holiday. **saint'like** adj. **saint'ly** adj. (**-li·er, -li·est**). **saint'dom, saint'li·ness, saint'-hood** ns. **saint** v.t. Canonize, admit to the calendar of saints; call

1 jigger topsail	13 main topgallant	25 fore skysail	37 flying jib stay
2 spanker	14 main royal	26 upper studding sail	38 flying jib stay
3 mizzen royal	15 main skysail	27 upper topsail studding sail	39 fore royal stay
4 mizzen topgallant	16 main royal staysail	28 lower topsail studding sail	40 fore skysail stay
5 mizzen upper topsail	17 main topgallant staysail	29 lower studding sail	41 fore skysail backstay
6 mizzen lower topsail	18 main topmast staysail	30 fore staysail	42 fore royal backstay
7 mizzen crojack	19 main staysail	31 fore topmast staysail	43 skysail stay
8 mizzen topmast staysail	20 foresail	32 jib	44 foot ropes
9 mizzen topgallant staysail	21 fore lower topsail	33 flying jib	45 skysail braces
10 mainsail	22 fore upper topsail	34 jib martingale	46 royal braces
11 main lower topsail	23 fore topgallant	35 jib stay	
12 main upper topsail	24 fore royal	36 flying jib martingale	

Noted for its vivid red flowers, the **sainfoin** *(Onobrychis viciifolia), is a type of clover which is used both as green fodder and for hay.*

Completed in 1959, the **St. Lawrence Sea·way** *was a joint project between the U.S.A. and Canada, providing large shipping with access to North America.*

or regard as a saint; **saint'ed**, worthy to be so regarded, of saintly life; hallowed, sacred.

Saint (sānt) **Bernard.** Very large dog of breed orig. kept by monks of Hospice on Great St. Bernard Pass in Alps for rescue of travelers.

Sainte-Beuve (sănt böv'), **Charles Augustin** (1804–69). French literary critic, poet, and historian.

Saint-De·nis (săndenē'). 1. Industrial city and suburb of Paris; site of 12th-c. Gothic church containing tombs of many monarchs, including Louis XII and XIII, and Marie Antoinette. 2. Capital of Réunion Island in the Indian Ocean.

Saint-Gau·dens (sāntgaw'denz), **Augustus** (1848–1907). Irish-born Amer. sculptor; noted for his public monuments, including statues of General Sherman, Lincoln, etc.

St. Hel·e·na (sānt helē'na). Island in S. Atlantic, a British possession, the place of Napoleon Bonaparte's exile (1815–21).

St. James's (sānt jāmz'). Old Tudor palace of English monarchs in London, built by Henry VIII; **Court of** ~, official title of British court, to which ambassadors from foreign countries are accredited.

Saint John (sānt jŏn'). Largest city and principal port of New Brunswick, Canada, at the mouth of the St. John River on the Bay of Fundy.

Saint Johns (sānt jŏnz'). Capital of Antigua, one of the Leeward Islands, West Indies.

St. Law·rence (sānt lōr'ens, lär'-) **River.** River in SE. Canada,

flowing NE. 760 mi. (1,223 km), from Lake Ontario, along the New York-Ontario border, to the **Gulf of Saint Lawrence**, gulf of the N. Atlantic between SE. Canada and Newfoundland; **Saint Lawrence Seaway**, water between Montreal, Canada, and Lake Ontario, covering 182 mi. (293 km), along the Saint Lawrence River, enabling deep-draft vessels to travel between the Atlantic Ocean and the Great Lakes; jointly constructed by the U.S. and Canada, 1955–9.

Saint-Saëns (săṅ sahṅ'), **Charles Camille** (1835–1921). French musical composer, noted for his symphonic poems and the

The lives of the saints have provided inspiration for painters throughout history. Adam Elsheimer followed the style of Tintoretto in this study of **Saint John the Baptist.**

opera *Samson and Delilah.*

St. Thom·as (sānt tŏm'as). Second largest island of the U.S. Virgin Islands, covering 28 sq. mi., (73 sq. km), in the Caribbean; capital of the U.S. Virgin Islands, Charlotte Amalie, on S. coast.

St. Wenceslas: see WENCESLAS[1].

Sai·pan (sīpăn'). Largest of the Mariana Islands, covering 70 sq. mi. (181 sq. km), in the W. Pacific Ocean; site of World War II Japanese air base captured by Americans, 1944, and then used as a U.S. air base.

Sa·ïs (sā'ïs). Ancient capital of lower Egypt, in the Nile delta. **Sa·ïte** (sā'īt) *n.* **Sa·it·ic** (sāĭt'ĭk) *adj.*

saith (sĕth) *v.* (archaic) Pres. ind. third pers. sing. of SAY.

sake[1] (sāk) *n.* **for the** ~ **of, for** (someone's or something's) ~, out of consideration for, in the interest of (someone or something); **for goodness', heaven's**, ~, form of entreaty or exclamation; **for old time's** ~, in memory of old days.

sa·ke[2], **sa·ki** (sah'kē) *ns.* Japanese fermented liquor made from rice.

Sa·kha·lin (sahxahlēn'). (formerly *Saghalien*) Island of the U.S.S.R., off the SE. coast N. of Japan in the Sea of Okhotsk; divided in 1905, with the S. part being called Karafuto and belonging to Japan until it was returned to the U.S.S.R. in 1945.

Sa·kya·mu·ni (sahkyamōōn'ē): see BUDDHA.

sal (săl) *n.* Salt. [L.]

sa·laam (salahm') *n.* Muslim salutation "Peace"; obeisance accompanying this, low bow of head and body with right palm on forehead. ~ *v.* Make salaam (to). [Arab. *salām*]

sal·a·ble, sale·a·ble (sā'label) *adjs.* Fit for sale; attractive to purchasers. **sal·a·bil·i·ty** (sālabĭl'-ĭtē) *n.*

There is a noticeable difference in aquatic dependence between different species of **salamander**. The fire variety only enters water to lay eggs, but the mud salamander (behind) spends all its life in water.

Consistent with the upgrading and increase of road systems, vehicle **sales** are also escalating and creating pollution problems in major cities.

sa·la·cious (salā′shus) *adj*. Lustful; (of literature) dealing with or suggestive of lewdness. **sa·la′cious·ly** *adv*. **sa·la′cious·ness**, **sa·lac·i·ty** (salăs′ĭtē) *ns*.

sal·ad (săl′ad) *n*. Cold dish of usu. uncooked vegetables; cold dish of meat, fish, etc., with salad (e.g. *chicken* ~); vegetable (e.g. lettuce, endive) suitable for eating raw in salads; ~ **days**, one's inexperienced youth; ~ **dressing**, mixture of oil and vinegar, or mayonnaise, or other sauce, used on salad; ~ **oil**, olive or other vegetable oil used for dressing salads.

Sal·a·din (săl′adĭn) (1137–93). Sultan of Egypt, who invaded Palestine and captured Jerusalem.

Sal·a·man·ca (sălamăng′ka). Province of W. Spain; capital of this province, scene of a battle (1812) in which the French were defeated by Wellington; the Nationalist capital

during the Spanish Civil War, 1937–38.

sal·a·man·der (săl′amănder) *n*. 1. Lizardlike animal supposed to live in fire. 2. (zool.) Tailed urodele amphibian, related to newts, of family Salamandridae.

sa·la·mi (salah′mē) *n*. Highly seasoned sausage, freq. flavored with garlic.

Sal·a·mis (săl′amĭs; *Gk.* sahlah-mēs′). Island off SW. coast of Attica, near the Piraeus, scene of a naval battle in 480 B.C. in which the Persian fleet under Xerxes was defeated by the Greeks.

sal am·mo·ni·ac (sălamō′nĕăk): see AMMONIAC.

sal·a·ry (săl′erē) *n*. (pl. **-ries**). Fixed periodical payment made to person for services. **sal′a·ried** *adj*. Receiving a salary. [L. *salarium*, orig. soldier's salt money, f. *sal* salt]

sale (sāl) *n*. Exchange of a

commodity for money or other valuable consideration, selling; amount sold; rapid disposal at reduced prices of (part of) store's stock at end of season etc.; **for, on** ~, offered for purchase; **white** ~, sale of household linen etc.; **sales′-man** (pl. **-men**), **sales′woman** (pl. **-women**), **sales′person**, person engaged in selling goods in store etc., or as middleman between producer and retailer; **sales′man-ship**, skill in selling; **sales resistance**, opposition or apathy of the prospective customer regarded as requiring to be overcome by salesmanship; **sales talk**, persuasive reasoning to prospective customer.

sale·a·ble: SALABLE.

Sa·lem[1] (sā′lem). Place mentioned in Gen. 14 as the seat of the kingdom of Melchizedek, doubtfully identified with Jerusalem.

Sa·lem[2] (sā′lem). 1. Massachusetts seaport, in the NE. part, on the Atlantic Ocean; during the 17th c. site of witchcraft trials and executions. 2. Capital of Oregon, in the NW. part, on the Willamette River.

Sa·li·an (sā′lēan, săl′yan) *adj*. & *n*. (Member) of Frankish tribe on the lower Rhine from which the Merovingians were descended.

Sal·ic (săl′ĭk, sā′lĭk), **Sa·lique** (săl′ĭk, săl′ĭk, sā′lĭk) *adjs*. Of the Salian Franks; **Salic Law**, code of law of the Salian Franks that maintains that a woman can have no portion of the inheritance of the

The John Turner House in **Salem**, Massachusetts which was the inspiration for Nathaniel Hawthorne's book, House of the Seven Gables. Today industry and tourism are the city's source of income.

"Salian land"; alleged fundamental law of the French monarchy excluding females from dynastic succession.

sal·i·cin (săl´ĭsĭn) *n.* Bitter crystalline substance gotten from willow bark etc. and formerly used as an analgesic. **sal·i·cyl·ic** (sălĭsĭl´ĭk) *adj.* ~ **acid**, $(C_7H_6O_3)$ orig. obtained from salicin but now made synthetically, used esp. in the form of its acetyl ester, aspirin. **sa·lic·y·late** (sălĭs´ĭlāt, -lĭt, sălĭsĭl´āt, săl´ĭsĭlāt) *n.* Salt of salicylic acid.

sa·li·ent (sā´lēent, sāl´yent) *adj.* 1. Leaping or dancing (pedantic, joc.); (of water etc., poet.) jetting forth. 2. (of angle, esp. in fortification) Pointing outward. 3. Jutting out; prominent, conspicuous, most noticeable. **sa´lient·ly** *adv.* **sa´lience, sa´lien·cy** (pl. **-cies**) *ns.* **salient** *n.* Salient angle or part in fortification; projecting section of line of offense or defense.

sa·li·en·ti·an (sālēĕn´shēan) *adj. & n.* (Member) of the Salientia, an order of amphibians comprising frogs and toads, the adult forms of which have no tails or gills but have strong hind legs for leaping or swimming.

sa·lif·er·ous (sălĭf´erus) *adj.* (geol.) (of stratum) Containing much salt.

sa·line (sā´lēn, -līn) *adj.* (of natural waters, springs, etc.) Impregnated with salt or salts; (of taste) salt; of chemical salts, of the nature of a salt; (of medicines) containing salt(s) of alkaline metals or magnesium. ~ *n.* Saline solution. **sa·lin·i·ty** (sălĭn´ĭtē) *n.*

Sa·lique: SALIC.

Salis·bur·y¹ (sawlz´bĕrē, -berē). Capital city of Zimbabwe, formerly Rhodesia.

*A **salientian**, which can be a frog or toad, is usually a ground dwelling animal. However, tree frogs, such as the one illustrated, are able to gain access to many places.*

Salis·bur·y² (sawlz´bĕrē, -berē) **Plain.** Plateau in S. England; site of Stonehenge.

Salis·bur·y (sawlz´bĕrē, -berē, sălz´-) **steak.** Ground beef, rolled into hamburger patty and fried or broiled.

sa·li·va (sălī´va) *n.* Colorless, normally alkaline liquid, the mixed secretion of salivary glands and mucous glands of the mouth, which mixes with food in mastication; spittle. **sal·i·var·y** (săl´ĭvĕrē) *adj.* Secreting or conveying, of, existing in, saliva.

sal·i·vate (săl´ĭvāt) *v.* (**-vat·ed, -vat·ing**). Produce unusual secretion of saliva in (person), usu. with mercury; secrete or discharge saliva. **sal·i·va·tion** (sălĭvā´shon) *n.*

Salk (sawk, sawlk), **Jonas E(dward)** (1914–). U.S. physician and microbiologist, developed first successful poliomyelitis vaccine (**Salk vaccine**), made from killed virus strains. See SABIN.

sal·low¹ (săl´ō) *n.* European willow, esp. of low-growing or shrubby kinds; shoot or wood of this.

sal·low² (săl´ō) *adj.* (of skin or complexion) Sickly yellow or yellowish-brown color; having skin of this color. ~ *v.* Make, grow, sallow. **sal´low·ness** *n.*

sal·ly (săl´ē) *n.* (pl. **-lies**). 1. Rush (*forth*) from besieged place upon enemy, sortie; excursion; ~ **port**, opening in fortified place for making sallies from. 2. Sudden start into activity, outburst; outburst, flash (esp. *of* wit); witticism, piece of banter, lively remark. **sally** *v.i.* (**-lied, -ly·ing**). Make sally (usu. *forth*); go *forth* on journey, for a walk, etc.

*All **salmon** attempt to return to the stream where they were hatched when the time comes to breed. It has been proved that they locate the correct waterway by its smell.*

Salmon   chum

humpback

sockeye

The **sallow** is a variety of willow tree identified by its handsome catkins which emerge in the spring. Its wood was used for basket making, or burnt to make charcoal for gunpowder.

One of the most vivid flowers in any garden, the **salpiglossis** needs to be grown in sheltered sunny locations in a temperate climate. It thrives in warmer latitudes.

sal·ma·gun·di (sălmagŭn′dē) n. Dish of chopped meat, eggs, anchovies, onions, etc., with oil and condiments; general mixture, miscellaneous collection. [Fr. *salmigondis*]

sal·mi, sal·mis (săl′mē) ns. Ragout, esp. of game birds, partly roasted and then stewed with wine or sauce. [Fr., prob. short for *salmigondis*: see SALMAGUNDI]

salm·on (săm′on) n. (pl. **-ons**, collect. **-on**). Large silver-scaled pink-fleshed fish of genus *Salmo*, esp. *S. salar*, which swims up rivers to spawn, much prized for food and sport; any of various other fishes esp. *Oncorhynchus*) of same family, or resembling salmon; the orange-pink color of salmon flesh. ~ adj. Salmon pink.

sal·mo·nel·la (sălmonĕl′a) n. (pl. **-nel·lae** pr. -nĕl′ē, **-nel·la, -nel·las**). Microorganism of the genus *S*~, members of which are responsible for many forms of enteritis, typhoid fever, etc. [D. E. *Salmon* (1850–1914), Amer. pathologist]

sal·mo·nid (săl′monĭd) adj. & n. (zool.) (Fish) of the family Salmonidae (salmon, trout, etc.).

Sa·lo·me (salō′mē). Stepdaughter of Herod Antipas; she pleased him with her dancing and at the bidding of her mother, Herodias, asked for the head of John the Baptist in a dish as a reward (see Matt. 14).

sa·lon (salŏn′, săl′ŏn) n. Reception room in continental, esp. French, great house; (assembly of prominent people in) reception room of (esp. Parisian) lady of fashion; (exhibition in) gallery etc. for showing works of art, photographs, etc., esp. (**the S**~) annual exhibition of living artists' pictures in Paris; room or establishment where hairdresser, dressmaker, etc., receives clients.

Sa·lo·ni·ka, Sa·lo·ni·ca (salŏn′-ĭka, sălonē′ka). (Gk. *Thessaloniki*, the ancient THESSALONICA) Seaport in NE. Greece, capital of Macedonia.

sa·loon (saloōn′) n. 1. Hall or large room, esp. in hotel or place of public resort, fit for assemblies, exhibitions, etc. 2. Large cabin for first-class or all passengers on ship etc., esp. serving as lounge. 3. Tavern, bar; ~ **keeper**, keeper of saloon or tavern.

sal·pi·glos·sis (sălpĭglŏs′ĭs, -glaw′sĭs) n. Showy-flowered herbaceous garden plant allied to petunia, orig. from Chile. [Gk. *salpigx* trumpet, *glōssa* tongue]

mon Atlantic (European)

chinook

cohoe

sal·si·fy (săl′sĭfē) n. (pl. -fies). Biennial composite plant (*Tragopogon porrifolius*) with long cylindrical fleshy roots eaten as vegetable.

SALT (sawlt) n. & adj. Strategic Arms Limitation Talks.

salt (sawlt) n. 1. (also **common ~**) Sodium chloride, a substance with characteristic taste, very abundant in nature (in the sea, and in crystalline form), used as a condiment, as a preservative of food, and in many industrial processes; **rock ~**, common salt occurring in large solid masses; **table ~**, common salt for table use; **take with a grain of ~**, accept (statement etc.) with reserve; **worth one's ~**, efficient, useful; **the ~ of the earth**, people for whose existence the world is better, moral élite (see Matt. 5). 2. Vessel, usu. open, for table salt, saltcellar (now chiefly in trade use and hist. in **above the ~**, seated with family and their equals, and **below the ~**, among servants and dependents). 3. Sting, piquancy, pungency, wit. 4. (chem.) Substance formed from an acid when all or part of its hydrogen is replaced by a metal or metallic radical. 5. Experienced sailor (esp. **old ~**). 6. **salt′cellar**, vessel holding salt for table use; **salt dome**, mass of salt forced up into sedimentary rocks; **salt grass**, type of grass growing in salt marshes and alkaline regions; **salt lick**, place where animals come to lick earth impregnated with salt; **salt marsh**, marsh frequently overflowed by sea; **salt mine**, mine yielding rock salt; (fig., usu. pl.) place of unremitting toil; **salt′-wort**, any of various maritime and salt marsh plants of the genus *Salsola*. **salt** adj. Impregnated with, containing, tasting of, cured or preserved or seasoned with, salt; (of plants) growing in sea or salt

Church of Guadalupe, in San Salvador, capital of El Salvador. With a population of 3.9 million (1974) and an area of 8,260 sq. miles, this country has the highest population density in Central America.

marshes; **~ water**, water containing a large proportion of salt; sea water; **salt′water**, of, living in, the sea. **salt′ed** adj. **salt′y** adj. (**salt·i·er, salt·i·est**). 1. Containing or tasting of salt. 2. Lively, racy, witty. **salt′i·ness, salt′ness** ns. **salt** v.t. 1. Preserve, season, or treat with salt; **~ away**, (colloq.) put by, store away (money etc.). 2. Render piquant, enliven. 3. Make (mine etc.) appear to be paying one by fraudulently introducing rich ore etc. **salt′er** n.

Salt (sawlt) **Lake City.** Capital

An ornate Vivyan salt cellar made of silver and gilt in 1592–93, has painting on glass panels. Such luxurious salt containers demonstrated the wealth of their owners.

and largest city of Utah, in the N. part on the Jordan River near the Great Salt Lake; founded by Mormons and site of Mormon Temple and Tabernacle and Mormon Church headquarters.

sal·tine (sawltēn′) n. Flat, salted cracker.

salt·pe·ter, Brit. **salt·pe·tre** (sawltpē′ter) ns. Niter, potassium nitrate (KNO_3), white crystalline salty substance used as constituent of gunpowder, in preserving meat etc.; sodium nitrate ($NaNO_3$). [prob. f. L. *sal petrae* salt of stone, because it occurs as an incrustation on stones]

sa·lu·bri·ous (saloo′brēus) adj. Healthy (chiefly of air, climate, etc.). **sa·lu′bri·ous·ly** adv. **sa·lu·bri·ty** (saloo′brĭtē), **sa·lu′bri·ous·ness** ns.

sa·lu·ki (saloo′kē) n. Tall, swift, slender silky-coated dog, developed in Arabia and Egypt.

sal·u·tar·y (săl′yutĕrē) adj. Producing good effect, beneficial.

sal·u·ta·tion (sălyutā′shon) n. (Use of) words spoken or written to convey interest in another's health etc., pleasure at sight of or communication with person, or courteous recognition of person's arrival or departure; greeting.

sa·lute (saloot′) v. (**-lut·ed, -lut·ing**). Make salute or salutation (to). **~** n. Gesture expressing respect, homage, or courteous recognition; (mil., nav., etc.) prescribed movement (esp., of hand to forehead) or position of body or weapons, use of flag(s), discharge of gun(s), in sign of respect; (fencing) formal performance of certain guards, etc., by fencers before engaging. **sa·lut′er** n.

Sal·va·dor (săl′vadōr) EL SALVADOR.

sal·vage (săl′vĭj) n. (Payment made or due for) saving of a ship or its cargo from loss by wreck or

2

Huge deposits of **salt** form naturally from evaporation at Lake Etosha in south-west Africa (1) and at Uyuni, in Bolivia, where it is cut into blocks (2). In the Canary Islands (3) and Australia (4) special areas are deliberately flooded and, when the water evaporates, salt is harvested by machinery.

Salt Lake City is largely influenced by the presence of the Mormon Church, the reason for this city's existence. It was founded in 1847 by Brigham Young and a dedicated group of Mormons escaping religious persecution.

capture; rescue of property from fire etc.; saving and use of waste material of all kinds; property salvaged. ~ v.t. (**-vaged, -vag-ing**). Make salvage of, save from wreck, fire, etc. **sal'vage·a·ble** *adj.*

sal·va·tion (sălvā'shon) *n.* 1. Saving of the soul; deliverance from sin and its consequences, and admission to heaven, brought about by the merits of Christ's death. 2. Preservation from loss, calamity, etc.; thing that preserves from these. **sal·va'tion·al** *adj.*

Sal·va·tion (sălvā'shon) **Army.** Organization founded by the Rev. William Booth in 1878 and established on a quasi-military basis and engaging in evangelical and charitable work among the destitute throughout the world. **Sal·va'tion·ist** *n.* Member of the Salvation Army; (**s~**) person who preaches salvation.

salve[1] (săv, sahv) *n.* Healing ointment for sores or wounds; something that soothes wounded feelings or uneasy conscience. ~ *v.t.* (**salved, salv·ing**). Anoint (wound etc.); soothe (pride, conscience, etc.).

salve[2] (sălv) *v.t.* (**salved, salv·ing**). Save (ship, cargo) from loss at sea or (property) from fire etc.

sal·ver (săl'ver) *n.* Meat tray for handing refreshments or presenting letters etc. [f. Fr. *salve* tray for presenting certain things to king, f. Span. *salva* assaying of food (*salvo*

safe)]

sal·vi·a (săl'vēa) *n.* Plant of genus *S~*, comprising the sages; flower of this cultivated for its bright blue or scarlet color.

sal·vo (săl'vō) *n.* (pl. **-vos, -voes**). Simultaneous discharge of artillery, rockets, etc.; burst of applause, cheers, etc.

sal·vor, sal·ver (săl'ver) *ns.* Person, ship, making or assisting in salvage.

Salz·burg (sawlz'berg; *Ger.* zahlts'boorχ). City and resort in W. central Austria, birthplace of Mozart, where a summer festival of music and drama has been held annually, except in wartime, since 1920.

SAM (săm) *n.* Surface-to-air missile.

Sam. *abbrev.* Samuel (Old Testament).

sam·a·ra (săm'era, samăr'a, -măr'a) *n.* Winged one-seeded indehiscent fruit, single (as in ash) or double (as in sycamore).

Sa·mar·i·a (samār'ēa). Ancient capital of Israel; ancient northern kingdom of Israel (see ISRAEL[1], sense 3); region surrounding this, W. of the Jordan, bounded by Galilee and Judea.

Sa·mar·i·tan (samăr'ĭtan) *n.* 1. Native, inhabitant, language, of Samaria. 2. **good ~**, person always ready to help the unfortunate (with ref. to Luke 10 etc.). **Samaritan** *adj.* Of Samaria or Samaritans.

sa·mar·i·um (samār'ēum) *n.* (chem.) Element of rare-earth group, symbol Sm, at. no. 62, at. wt. 150.4.

Sam·ar·kand (săm'erkănd). City in the SW. Soviet Union, SW. of Tashkent; important stop on the Silk Route from China to Europe during the 7th c.; became capital of Tamburlaine's empire, 1370.

sam·ba (sahm'ba, săm'-) *n.* Brazilian dance of African origin, ballroom dance imitative of this; music for this dance.

Sam Browne (săm' brown') **belt.** Leather belt with a supporting strap passing diagonally over the right shoulder, worn as part of some military and police uniforms [f. name of Brit. Gen. Sir Samuel J. *Browne*, 1824–1901]

same (sām) *adj.* 1. Not different, the very. 2. (pred.) Not changed, not varying; equally acceptable. 3. Aforesaid. 4. (*abs.* and as *pronoun* **the ~**, the same person; the same thing. 5. **the ~** (*adv.*) in the same manner; **all the ~**, nevertheless; **just the ~**, in spite of changed conditions. **same'ness** *n.*

sam·i·sen (săm'ĭsĕn) *n.* Long three-stringed Japanese guitar, played with plectrum.

sam·iz·dat (săm'ĭzdăt) *n.* System of clandestine publication of banned literature in U.S.S.R.

Sam·nite (săm'nīt) *adj. & n.* (Member) of an ancient tribe of S. central Italy, inhabiting the district of Samnium.

Sa·mo·a (samō′a). Group of Polynesian islands, of which the eastern part (**American** ~) is a U.S. territory; **Western** ~, republic, independent since 1962; member nation of the Brit. Commonwealth; capital, Apia. **Sa·mo′an** *adj.* & *n.*

Sa·mos (sā′mŏs, săm′ōs). Greek island in the Aegean off the W. coast of Turkey.

Sam·o·thrace (săm′othrās). Greek island in the NE. Aegean.

sam·o·var (săm′ovär, sămovär′) *n.* Russian tea urn. [Russ., = "self-boiler"]

Sam·o·yed (săm′oyĕd, sămoyĕd′) *n.* 1. (also **Sam·o·yede′**) Member, language, of a Mongolian people of Siberia. 2. Dog of white Arctic breed, used for pulling sleds. **Sam·o·yed·ic** (sămoyĕd′ĭk) *adj.*

sam·pan (săm′păn) *n.* Small boat used in river and coastal traffic of China, Japan, and neighboring islands, rowed with a scull from the stern and usu. having a sail of matting and an awning. [Chin. *san-pan* boat (*san* 3, *pan* board)]

sam·ple (săm′pel, sahm′-) *n.* Small separated part of something illustrating qualities of the mass etc. it is taken from, specimen, pattern. ~ *v.t.* (**-pled, -pling**). Take or give samples, try the qualities, get representative experience, of. **sam′pler**[1] *n.*

sam·pler[2] (săm′pler, sahm′-) *n.* Piece of embroidery worked as specimen of proficiency, usu. containing alphabet and various decorative motifs.

Sam·son (săm′son). Israelite judge famous for his strength (Judges 13–16); he confided to a woman, Delilah, that his strength lay in his hair, and she betrayed him to the Philistines, who cut off his hair while he slept and captured and blinded him; but when his hair grew again, his strength returned and he pulled down the pillars of the house of Gaza, destroying himself and a large concourse of Philistines; hence, man of phenomenal strength.

Sam·u·el (săm′ūel). Hebrew prophet who rallied the Israelites after their defeat by the Philistines and became their ruler; (**First and Second Book of**) ~, two books of Old Testament covering the history of Israel from Samuel's birth to the end of the reign of David.

sam·u·rai (săm′ōōrĭ) *n.* (pl. **-rai**). In Japanese feudal system, military retainer of the chief territorial nobles; any member of military caste.

Sa·n′a (sahnah′). Capital and largest city of Yemen Arab Republic, in the central part of the country, in the SW. Arabian Peninsula.

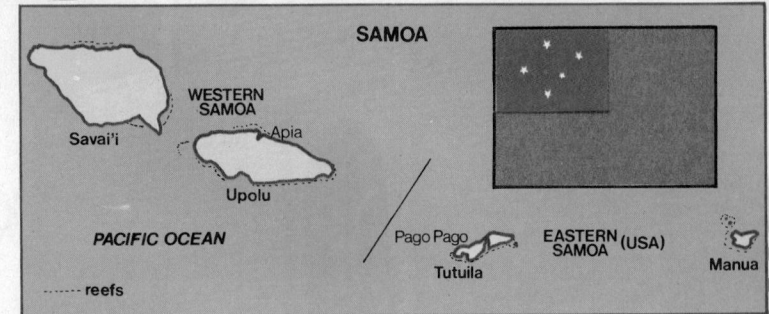

Although **Western Samoa** became the first fully independent Polynesian state in 1962, the eastern islands where Pago Pago (above) is located, are still controlled by the U.S.A.

The **sand dollar** is usually found in warm waters, living and feeding under the sand. It is related to the starfish and sea urchin families. The shell is usually 3 to 4 ins. long.

*Many of the boats which serve as homes to people in Hong Kong are known as a form of **sampan**, although their design may differ from the classical definition.*

*In times when girls stayed at home to learn the arts of housewifery, the **sampler** served as both an achievement and an example of proficiency in needlework. These were made in England in 1832.*

San An·to·ni·o (săn ăntō′nēō). Commercial city in S. central Texas, on the San Antonio River, W. of Austin; site of the Alamo.

san·a·to·ri·um (sănatōr′ēum, -tōr′-) (pl. **-to·ri·ums, -to·ri·a** pr. -tōr′ēa, -tōr′ēa), **san·i·tar·i·um** (sănitār′ēum) (pl. **-tar·i·ums, -tar·i·a** pr. -tār′ēa) ns. 1. Establishment for treatment of chronic diseases (as tuberculosis, mental disorders, etc.) or for convalescents. 2. Health resort.

San·cho Pan·za (săn′chō pän′za, sahn′chō pahn′za). Squire of DON QUIXOTE, who accompanies him on his adventures; he is an ignorant and credulous peasant, but has a store of proverbial wisdom and is thus a foil to his master.

sanc·ti·fy (săngk′tĭfī) v.t. (**-fied, -y·ing**). Consecrate, make holy; purify from sin; give authority to, justify. **sanc·ti·fi·ca·tion** (săngktĭfĭkā′shon), **sanc·ti·fi·er** ns.

sanc·ti·mo·ni·ous (săngktĭmō′nēus) adj. Make a show of sanctity or piety. **sanc·ti·mo′ni·ous·ly** adv. **sanc·ti·mo′ni·ous·ness** n.

sanc·tion (săngk′shon) n. 1. (hist.) Law or decree. 2. Penalty imposed for noncompliance with a law, custom, etc., or with an international agreement. 3. Confirmation or ratification of law etc. by supreme authority; express authoritative permission; countenance or encouragement given to action etc. by custom etc. **sanction** v.t. Authorize; countenance; permit. **sanc′tion·er** n.

sanc·ti·tude (săngk′tĭtōōd, -tūd) n. (now rare) Saintliness.

sanc·ti·ty (săngk′tĭtē) n. (pl. **-ties**). Saintliness; sacredness; inviolability; (pl.) sacred obligations, feelings, etc.

sanc·tu·ar·y (săngk′chōōĕrē) n. (pl. **-ar·ies**). 1. Place recognized as holy part of church within altar rails. 2. Sacred place by retiring to which fugitive from law, or debtor, was secured by medieval church law against arrest or violence; place in which similar immunity was established by custom or law; place of refuge; (right of affording) such immunity. 3. Reserved area where animals, birds, etc. are protected from hunting.

sanc·tum (săngk′tum) n. (pl. **-tums, -ta** pr. -ta). 1. Sacred or holy place; person's private room, study or den. 2. Place in Jewish tabernacle or temple where Ark of the Covenant was located; ~ **sanc·to·rum** (săngktōr′um, -tōr′-), holy of holies.

Sanc·tus (săngk′tus; *Lat.* sahngk′tōōs) n. Hymn (from Isa. 6) beginning *"Sanctus, sanctus, sanctus"* or *"Holy, holy, holy,"* forming conclusion of Eucharistic preface; music for this; ~ **bell**, bell rung at the Sanctus.

sand (sănd) n. Minute fragments resulting from wearing down of esp. siliceous rocks and found covering parts of the seashore, river beds, deserts, etc.; (pl.) expanse or tracts of sand; **sand′bag**, bag filled with sand, used to protect trenches, buildings, etc. against blast and splinters, to protect against floods, as ballast, as weapon leaving no mark on victim, etc.; (v.t.) (**-bagged, -bag·ging**) protect with sandbags; fell with blow from sandbag; **sand′bar**, shoal of sand in sea or river; **sand′blast**, jet of sand impelled by compressed air or steam for giving rough surface to glass, cleaning buildings, etc.; (v.t.) clean, polish, etc. with a sandblast; **sand′box**, large, low box of sand for children to play in; **sand casting**, metal casting obtained from sand mold; process of making such castings; **sand dollar**, round, flat sea urchin; **sand′fly** (pl. **-flies**), any of various biting flies of genus *Phlebotomus;* **sand′hog**, laborer who works under compressed air on underwater or underground construction projects; **sand hopper**, small jumping crustacean of family Talitridae, most species

Sandstone is a sedimentary rock which can be susceptible to erosion. A result of wind-erosion can be seen (above) in grains of sand from the Kalahari Desert. Weathering from wind and rain can cause effects such as those seen in outcrops in Spain (right).

of which burrow in sand of seashore; **sand'lot** (*adj.*), of or pertaining to games, esp. baseball, played by amateurs, orig. in a vacant lot; **sand'man**, (nursery name for) personification of sleep or sleepiness; **sand'paper**, paper with layer of sand or other abrasive stuck on for smoothing or polishing wood etc.; (*v.t.*) polish with sandpaper; **sand'piper**, any of various small wading birds of family Scolopacidae, haunting open wet sandy places; **sand'stone**, sedimentary rock composed of small grains usu. of quartz cemented together; **sand'storm**, desert storm of wind with clouds of sand. **sand** *v.t.* Sprinkle, cover, mix, or polish with sand. **sand'er** *n.*

Sand (sănd; *Fr.* sahṅ), **George.** Pen name of Amandine Lucie Aurore Dupin-Dudevant (1804–1876), French novelist, author of *Indiana, Lélia, Consuelo*, etc.

san·dal (săn'dal) *n.* Sole without upper, attached to foot by thongs passing over instep and around ankle; modification of this, worn by ancient Greeks and Romans, by some Orientals, as modern revival, etc. ~ *v.t.* (**-daled, -dal·ing**). Put sandals on (foot, person; esp. in past part.).

san·dal·wood (săn'dalwŏŏd) *n.* Any of various scented woods, true sandalwood being obtained from species of Asian tree of genus *Santalum.*

san·da·rac (săn'darăk) *n.* Resin exuding from NW. African tree (*Tetraclinis articulata*), used in making varnish.

Sand·burg (sănd'bĕrg, săn'-), **Carl** (1878–1967). Amer. poet and biographer; awarded Pulitzer Prize for history, 1939, for *Abraham Lincoln—The War Years*, and for

poetry, 1951, for *Complete Poems.*

san·der·ling (săn'derlĭng) *n.* Common sandpiper (*Crocethia alba*).

sand·wich (sănd'wĭch, săn'-) *n.* Two or more slices of bread etc. with meat, cheese or other filling between; (also **open-face(d)** ~) slice of bread etc. with meat, cheese, etc. on top; two wafers, cookies, etc. with icing, filling, etc. between; ~ **board**, board carried by sandwich man; ~ **man**, man walking street with two advertising placards hung one before and one behind. **sandwich** *v.t.* Insert (thing, statement, etc.) between two of another character. [perh. f. name of 4th Earl of *Sandwich* (1718–92), said to have eaten slices of cold beef between slices of toast, while gaming for 24 hours]

sand·y (săn'dē) *adj.* (**sand·i·er, sand·i·est**). Covered with sand; sand-colored, (of hair) yellowish red; having such hair. **sand'i·ness** *n.*

sane (sān) *adj.* (**san·er, san·est**). Of sound mind, not mad; sensible, rational. **sane'ly** *adv.* **sane'ness** *n.*

San Fran·cis·co (săn frănsĭs'kō). Port and city in N. California, on the W. side of San Francisco Bay on the Pacific Ocean; severely damaged April 18, 1906 in earthquake caused by movement in the San Andreas Fault, which runs through the ~ peninsula; ~ **Bay**, inlet in N. California, about 60 mi. (97 km) long; connected with the Pacific Ocean by Golden Gate strait.

sang: see SING.

san·ga·ree = SANGRIA.

Sang·er (săng'er) **Margaret** (**Higgins**) (1883–1966). Amer. nurse and social reformer; advocate

of birth control.

sang-froid (sahṅfrwah') *n.* Composure, coolness, in danger or under agitating circumstances [Fr., = "cold blood"]

san·grí·a (sănggrē'a), **san·ga·ree** (sănggerē') *ns.* Cold drink of wine, citrus juices or slices, sugar and spices. [Span., "bleeding," drink of red wine and citrus juices]

san·gui·nar·y (săng'gwĭnĕrē) *adj.* Attended by, delighting in bloodshed or slaughter, bloody, bloodthirsty. **san'gui·nar·i·ly** *adv.* **san'gui·nar·i·ness** *n.*

san·guine (săng'gwĭn) *adj.* Blood-red. 2. (hist.) Belonging to that one of the four HUMORS supposed to be characterized by predominance of blood over other humors, and indicated by ruddy face and courageous, hopeful, and amorous disposition; (mod., of complexion) ruddy, florid. 3. Habitually hopeful, confident; expecting things to go well. **san'guine·ly** *adv.* **san'guine·ness** *n.*

san·guin·e·ous (sănggwĭn'ēus) *adj.* Of blood; blood-colored.

San·he·drin (sănhĕd'rĭn, -hē'drĭn, săn'hĭdrĭn), **San·he·drim** (săn'hĭdrĭm) *ns.* (Jewish hist.) Highest court of justice and supreme council, of 71 members, in ancient Jerusalem, esp. between 5th c. B.C. and 70 A.D. [late Heb., f. Gk. *sunedrion* (*sun* together, *hedra* seat]

san·i·cle (săn'ĭkel) *n.* Umbelliferous plant of genus *Sanicula* having small greenish flowers.

san·i·tar·i·um = SANATORIUM

san·i·tar·y (săn'ĭtĕrē) *adj.* Free from or designed to obviate influences deleterious to health; clean, hygienic; ~ **napkin**, pad used in menstruation. **san'i·tar·i·ly** *adv.*

san·i·ta·tion (sănĭtā'shon)

sank: see SINK[2].

San Ma·ri·no (săn mᴀrē'nō). Small republic occupying 23 sq. mi. (59 sq. km) near Rimini, Italy, on the Adriatic; its capital.

sans (sănz, sahnz) *prep.* (archaic) Without.

San Sal·va·dor (săn săl'vȧdōr). Capital of El Salvador, in the central part of the country.

sans-cu·lotte (sănzkŭlŏt'; *Fr.* sahṅkülawt') *n.* (pl. **sans-cu·lottes** pr. sănzkŭlŏts'; *Fr.* sahṅkülawt'). Republican of Parisian lower classes in French Revolution; any extreme republican or revolutionary. [Fr., lit. "without breeches," the revolutionaries wore pantaloons and men of the upper classes wore knee breeches]

san·sei (sahn'sā') *n.* (pl. **-sei, -seis**). (also **S ~**) U.S.-born grandchild of Japanese who came to Amer. [cf. NISEI]

San·skrit, San·scrit (săn'skrĭt) *adjs. & ns.* (Of) the ancient, classical, and sacred language of the Hindus in India, in which the Vedic hymns were composed, the oldest known member of the Indo-European family of languages. **San·skrit·ic** (sănskrĭt'ĭk) *adj.*

sans ser·if (săn sĕr'ĭf, sahn) *n. & adj.* (Form of type) without serifs.

San·ta Claus (săn'ta klawz). (also *Saint Nicholas, Saint Nick*) Patron saint of children who dispenses gifts to them on Christmas Eve.

San·ta Cruz (săn'ta krōōz') **Islands.** Island group in the SW. Pacific Ocean covering 362 sq. mi. (937 sq. km).

San·ta Fe (săn'ta fā'). Capital of New Mexico, in the N. central part between the Pecos and Rio Grande Rivers; oldest U.S. capital; **~ Trail**, 19th-c. trade route to the West covering 800 mi. (1,287 km) between Independence, Missouri, and Santa Fe, New Mexico.

San·ta·ya·na (săntēăn'a, sahntāah'na), **George** (1863–1952). Spanish-born Amer. poet and philosopher; author of *Persons and Places*, etc., and one novel, *The Last Puritan*.

San·ti·a·go (sahntēah'gō, -tyah'gō). Capital of Chile, in the central part on a plateau W. of the Andes.

San·to Do·min·go (săn'tō dŏmĭng'gō). (formerly Ciudad Trujillo) Capital of the Dominican Republic, on the S. coast, on the Caribbean Sea.

São Mi·guel (sowṅ' mēgĕl'). Largest island of the Azores, covering 288 sq. mi. (746 sq. km).

São Pau·lo (sowṅ' pow'lōō).

San Francisco, financial center of the U.S. west coast, was annexed by America after the Mexican War in 1846. Now a tourist center with a huge population and many industrial and trading interests.

Measures designed to preserve public health, esp. efficient drainage and disposal of sewage, pure water supply, etc.; (specif.) drainage and disposal of sewage.

san·i·tize (săn'ĭtīz) *v.* (**-tized, -tiz·ing**). Make sanitary.

san·i·ty (săn'ĭtē) *n.* Being sane, mental health; tendency to avoid extreme views.

San Jo·sé (sahn hawsě'). Capital and largest city of Costa Rica, in the central part.

San Juan (săn wahn', hwahn'). Capital and seaport of Puerto Rico, on the N. coast; **~ Hill**, hill in SE. Cuba near Santiago de Cuba; site of victory over Spanish by Cuban and Amer. forces, including Theodore Roosevelt and the "Rough Riders," in the Spanish-Amer. War, July, 1898.

Sanicle is a perennial plant whose umbels stand about a foot above the ground during the summer months. It has pink or white flowers which develop into spiny fruits.

Portrait of Nancy, Lady Astor by **J. S. Sargent,** *whose claim to fame relies on his perpetuation of naturalistic techniques when most painters had agreed that modern art needed innovation.*

Largest city in Brazil, in the SE. part of the country.

São Tia·go (sowṅ´ tyah´gōo). Largest of the Cape Verde Islands, covering 383 sq. mi. (991 sq. km); location of the capital of the archipelago, Praia.

· **São To·mé** (sowṅ´ tōomě´). Island in the Gulf of Guinea, off the coast of W. Africa, covering 330 sq. mi. (855 sq. km); became independent from Portugal, 1975.

São To·mé e Prin·ci·pe (sowṅ´ tōomě´ ĕ prĕn´sēpě). Democratic Republic in the Gulf of Guinea off the coast of W. Africa, comprising the islands of São Tomé, Principe, Pedras Tinhosas, and Rolas; Portuguese overseas province until 1975.

sap[1] (săp) *n.* Juice in plants; **sap'wood,** soft layers of wood growing between the bark of trees and the heartwood, alburnum. **sap'py** *adj.* (**-pi·er, -pi·est**). **sap** *v.t.* (**sapped, sap·ping**). (fig.) Exhaust vigor of.

sap[2] (săp) *n.* Making of trenches or tunnels to cover assailant's approach to besieged place or enemy's trenches; covered siege trench. ~ *v.* (**sapped, sap·ping**). Dig sap, approach by sap; undermine, make insecure by removing foundations; (fig.) destroy insidiously.

sap[3] (săp) *n.* (slang) Simpleton, fool. **sap'py** *adj.*

sa·pa·jou (săp´ajōo) *n.* CAPUCHIN monkey.

sa·pi·ent (sā´pēent) *adj.* Wise (now rare); would-be wise, of fancied sagacity, aping wisdom. **sa'pi·ent·ly** *adv.* **sa'pi·ence** *n.*

The ancient citadel of 'La Rocca' in the republic of **San Marino.** *It is located in eastern Italy, about 10 miles southwest of Rimini and was first granted independence in the 13th century.*

sap·ling (săp´lĭng) *n.* Young tree; (fig.) a youth.

sap·o·dil·la (săpodĭl´a) *n.* Large evergreen tropical Amer. tree (*Achras zapota*), with durable wood and edible fruit, and that yields chicle; fruit of this.

sap·o·na·ceous (săponā´shus) *adj.* Of, like, containing, soap; soapy.

sa·pon·i·fy (sapŏn´ĭfĭ) *v.* (**-fied, -fy·ing**). (chem.) Convert (fat or oil) into soap by boiling with alkali; convert (an ester) into its constituent acid and alcohol; be converted thus. **sa·pon·i·fi·ca·tion** (sapŏnĭfĭkā´shon) *n.*

sap·phire (săf´īr) *n.* Transparent blue precious stone, variety of corundum; (min.) any precious transparent crystalline corundum, including sapphire and ruby; bright blue of sapphire, azure. ~ *adj.* Of sapphire blue.

Sap·pho (săf´ō). Greek lyric poetess of Lesbos (flourished 610 B.C.); according to legend, she threw herself into the sea in despair at her unrequited love for Phaon.

sap·ro·phyte (săp´rofĭt) *n.* Vegetable organism living on decayed organic matter. **sap·ro·phyt·ic** (săprofĭt´ĭk) *adj.*

sar·a·band (săr´abănd) *n.* Stately Spanish dance in triple time; music for this or in rhythm of it (often with long note on second

beat of bar).

Sar·a·cen (săr´asen) *n.* (hist.) Member of the nomadic peoples of the Syro-Arabian desert; hence, Arab; by extension, Muslim, esp. with reference to the crusades. **Sar·a·cen·ic** (sărasĕn´ĭk), **Sar·a·cen'i·cal** *adjs.* Of, connected with, the Saracens.

Sar·ah (sār´a, săr´a). Wife of Abraham and mother of Isaac (Gen. 17:ff.).

Sa·ra·je·vo (sărayā´vō). City of Yugoslavia, formerly capital of Bosnia, where the Archduke Francis Ferdinand of Austria was assassinated on June 28, 1914, precipitating World War I.

Sar·a·to·ga (săratō´ga). Scene near the Hudson River, in New York State, of the decisive victory of Amer. army under Gates over the Brit. under Burgoyne in 1777, in the Revolutionary War, and of the surrender of Burgoyne and his army; ~ **trunk,** (19th c.; f. ~ **Springs,** fashionable watering place in New York State) lady's large traveling trunk.

sar·casm (sār´kăzem) *n.* Bitter or wounding irony or ironical remark. **sar·cas·tic** (sārkăs´tĭk) *adj.* **sar·cas'ti·cal·ly** *adv.*

sar·co·ma (sārkō´ma) *n.* (pl. **-mas, -ma·ta** pr. -mata). (path.) Malignant tumor of connective tissue.

sar·coph·a·gus (sārkŏf´agus) *n* (pl. **-gi** pr. -jī, -gī, -gē, **-gus·es**) Stone coffin, esp. one adorned with sculpture or bearing inscription etc [L. f. Gk. *sarkophagos,* orig. = flesh-consuming (stone) (*sar* flesh covering 9,301 sq. mi. (24,090 sq. km); a department of Italy, capital, Cagliari. **Sar·din'i·an** *adj.* & *n.*

Sar·dis (sär'dĭs). Ancient city in W. Asia Minor, once capital of the kingdom of Lydia.

sar·di·us = SARD.

sar·don·ic (särdŏn'ĭk) *adj.* (of laughter etc.) Bitter, scornful, mocking, sneering, cynical. **sar·don'i·cal·ly** *adv.* [Gk. *sardonios* Sardinian, substituted for Homeric *sardanios* (epithet of bitter or scornful laughter) because of belief that convulsive laughter ending in death resulted from eating a Sardinian plant]

sar·don·yx (särdŏn'ĭks, sär'do-nĭks) *n.* Variety of onyx with white layers alternating with brownish-yellow or orange sard.

sar·gas·so (särgăs'ō) *n.* (pl. **-sos**). Seaweed of genus *Sargassum* with berrylike air vessels, found in islandlike masses in Gulf Stream.

Sar·gas·so (särgăs'ō) **Sea.** Region in N. Atlantic, between the West Indies and the Azores, with an abundance of floating sargasso.

sarge (särj) *n.* (colloq.) Sergeant.

Sar·gent (sär'jent), **John Singer** (1856–1925). Amer. portrait and genre painter, chiefly active in England.

sa·ri (sär'ē) *n.* (pl. **-ris**). Length of material wrapped around the body, worn as main garment by Hindu women.

Sark (särk). One of the Channel Islands, 1,274 acres.

sa·rong (sarawng', -rŏng') *n.* Malay and Javanese garment, long piece of cloth worn as skirt, tucked around waist or under armpits.

sar·sa·pa·ril·la (särsparĭl'a, -rĕl'a, săs-) *n.* Any of various tropical Amer. plants of the genus *Smilax*; dried roots of these, or extract of them, used to flavor soft drinks; soft drink with this flavoring.

Sar·to (sär'tō): see ANDREA DEL SARTO.

sar·to·ri·al (särtōr'ēal, -tôr'-) *adj.* Of tailors or tailoring; of men's clothes. **sar·to'ri·al·ly** *adv.*

sar·to·ri·us (särtōr'ēus, -tôr'-) *n.* (pl. **-to·ri·i** pr. -tōr'ēī, -tôr'ēī). Long narrow muscle crossing thigh obliquely in front. [mod. L., so called as being concerned in producing tailor's cross-legged working position]

Sar·tre (sär'tre, särt), **Jean Paul** (1905–1980). French writer and philosopher, leader in existentialist movement; author of *Being and Nothingness*, the play *No Exit*, etc.

sash[1] (săsh) *n.* Ornamental scarf worn over 1 shoulder or around

Sarsaparilla, native to the southern and western coasts of Mexico and Peru, is used as a flavoring for various soft drinks and medical compounds, and used to be drunk as a general tonic.

Sardinia, second-largest island in the Mediterranean, is part of Italy. Sheep and goats are grazed in the hills and agriculture is centered around Cagliari.

-*phagos* eating)]

sard (särd), **sar·di·us** (sär'dēus) *ns.* Yellow or orange chalcedony. [f. *Sardis* in Lydia]

sar·dine (särdēn') *n.* (pl. **-dines**, collect. **-dine**). Young herring or related fishes, freq. cured and tightly canned in oil.

Sar·din·i·a (särdĭn'ēa). Mountainous island in the Mediterranean Sea W. of Italy and S. of Corsica,

Indian woman trying on lengths of material for use as a sari. Despite its apparent simplicity, skill is needed to adjust and wear it effectively.

waist by man, usu. as part of uniform or insignia, or by woman or child around waist. [Arab. *shāsh* muslin, band twisted around head as turban]

sash[2] (săsh) *n.* Frame, usu. of wood, fitted with pane(s) of glass forming (part of) window, esp. sliding frame or one of pair of frames made to slide up and down. [corrupt. of CHASSIS]

sa·shay (săshā′) *v.i.* (colloq.) Walk or move ostentatiously, casually, or diagonally.

sa·shi·mi (sah′shīmē) *n.* Japanese dish of garnished raw fish in thin slices.

Sas·katch·e·wan (săskăch′-ewahn, -wan). 1. River of Canada, flowing from the Rocky Mountains to Lake Winnipeg. 2. Province of central Canada; capital, Regina.

sas·quatch (sahs′kwahch) *n.* (also **S~**) Supposed yeti-like animal of northwestern N. Amer.; also called Bigfoot.

sass (săs) *n.* (colloq.) Impertinence; back talk. **~** *v.t.* (**sassed, sass·ing**) Respond or talk rudely. **sass′y** *adj.* (**sass·i·er, sass·i·est**).

sas·sa·fras (săs′afrăs) *n.* Tree of genus *S~* of laurel family, esp. N. Amer. *S. albidum*, with green apetalous flowers and dimorphous leaves; dried bark of root of this used medicinally and for flavoring.

SAT *abbrev.* Scholastic Aptitude Test.

sat (săt): see SIT.

Sat. *abbrev.* Saturday.

Sa·tan (sā′tan). The devil, Lucifer. **sa·tan·ic** (sătăn′ĭk, sa-), **sa·tan′i·cal** *adjs.* (also **S~**) Of, like, or befitting Satan, diabolical. **sa·tan′i·cal·ly** *adv.* [Heb. *šāṭān* enemy]

Sa·tan·ism (sā′tanĭzem) *n.* Worship of the devil with a travesty of Christian ceremonial and with celebration of the Black Mass; diabolical wickedness. **Sa′tan·ist** *n.*

satch·el (săch′el) *n.* Small bag, esp. for carrying schoolbooks etc., freq. with shoulder strap.

sate (sāt) *v.t.* (**sat·ed, sat·ing**). Gratify (desire, appetite, etc.) to the full; surfeit.

sa·teen (sătēn′) *n.* Cotton fabric, glossy on 1 side, woven like satin.

sat·el·lite (săt′elīt) *n.* 1. Follower, hanger-on; member of great man's retinue, underling. 2. Small or secondary planet revolving around larger one; (also) artificial body launched from Earth and encircling it or other celestial body; **fixed ~**: see FIXED. 3. Nation nominally independent but dominated by powerful neighbor. 4. **~**

town, small town built near larger one to house excess population.

sa·ti·ate (sā′shĕĭt, -āt) *adj.* Sated, satiated. **~** (sā′shēāt) *v.t.* (**-at·ed, -at·ing**). Sate. **sa·ti·a·tion** (sāshēā′shon) *n.*

sa·ti·e·ty (satī′etē) *n.* State of being glutted or satiated; feeling of disgust or surfeit caused by excess.

sat·in (săt′ĭn) *n.* Fabric of silk or similar yarn with glossy surface on one side produced by twill weave in which weft threads are almost concealed by warp, or vice versa; **~ stitch**, in embroidery, long straight stitches laid close together, producing smooth surface; **sat′in·wood**, (hard light-colored wood with satiny surface, of) Indian tree (*Chloroxylon swietenia*) and various W. Indian, Australian, etc., trees. **satin, sat′in·y** *adjs.* Resembling satin; very smooth.

sat·ire (săt′īr) *n.* Poem or prose composition ridiculing vice or folly; lampoon; branch of literature containing such compositions; use of ridicule, sarcasm, or irony to expose folly. **sa·tir·ic** (satĭr′ĭk), **sa·tir′i·cal** *adj.* **sa·tir′i·cal·ly** *adv.* **sat·i·rist** (săt′erĭst) *n.* Writer of satires; satirical person. **sat·i·rize** (săt′erīz) *v.t.* (**-rized, -riz·ing**). Write satires on; describe satirically.

*The **sassafras** of North America is useful to man. Oil for perfumes is obtained from the flowers and roots; dried roots are used by chemists; and beer is made from young leaf shoots.*

sat·is·fac·tion (sătĭsfăk′shon) *n.* 1. Payment of debt, fulfillment of obligation, atonement *for*; thing accepted by way of satisfaction; penance; atonement. 2. Opportunity of satisfying one's honor by

A Syncon communications **satellite**, one of a series now in orbit over the earth, which have had a revolutionary impact on trans-continental telephone, radio and television contacts.

Two schoolchildren are seen here carrying their **satchels**, small bags used especially for carrying schoolbooks.

duel, acceptance of challenge to duel. 3. Satisfying, being satisfied, in regard to desire or want or doubt; thing that satisfies desire or gratifies feeling.

sat·is·fac·to·ry (săt̆ĭsfăk′terē) *adj.* Sufficient, adequate, (of argument) convincing; such as one may be content or pleased with. **sat·is·fac′to·ri·ly** *adv.* **sat·is·fac′to·ri·ness** *n.*

sat·is·fy (săt′ĭsfī) *v.* (**-fied, -fy·ing**). 1. Pay (debt), fulfill (obligation), (now rare except in law); pay (creditor); make atonement or reparation. 2. Meet expectations or desires of, come up to (notion etc.), be accepted by (person etc.) as adequate, content; give satisfaction, leave nothing to be desired; fully supply needs of, put an end to (appetite etc.) by fully supplying it; furnish with adequate proof, convince; adequately meet (objection, doubt, etc.); (math.) be a solution e.g. of an equation; (pass.) be content or pleased (*with*), demand no more than, consider it enough *to* do. **sat′is·fi·er** *n.* **sat′is·fy·ing** *adj.* **sat′is·fy·ing·ly** *adv.*

sa·to·ri (satŏr′ē, -tōr′ē) *n.* (Zen Buddhism) Sudden enlightenment.

sa·trap (sā′trăp, săt′răp) *n.* 1.

Holder of provincial governorship in ancient Persian Empire. 2. Subordinate ruler, colonial governor, etc. (freq. with implication of luxury or tyranny). **sa·trap·y** (sā′trapē, săt′ra-) *n.* (pl. **-trap·ies**). Office, province, of satrap. [Pers. *khsatrapava* province guardian]

Sa·tsu·ma (sah′tsoomah) *n.* (also ~ **ware**) Kind of Japanese glazed pottery with a yellow ground. [former province of Japan]

sat·u·rate (săch′erāt) *v.t.* (**-rat·ed, -rat·ing**). 1. Soak thoroughly, imbue *with*. 2. (phys. etc.) Cause to absorb or hold the maximum quantity of moisture, electrical charge, etc., that can be held under given conditions of temperature etc.; (chem.) cause (a substance) to combine with or dissolve the maximum quantity possible of another substance. 3. Bomb (target) from the air so thoroughly that antiaircraft defenses are powerless. **sat′u·ra·ble** *adj.* **sat′u·rat·ed** *adj.* (esp., of a solution) Containing the maximum quantity possible of the dis-

solved substance at a given temperature (cf. UNSATURATED, able to dissolve more than it contains); (also, of chemical compounds, esp. hydrocarbons) containing no double bonds and hence unable to undergo addition reactions (*unsaturated*, containing one or more double bonds and capable of such reactions). **sat·u·ra·tion** (săchera′-sh*o*n) *n.*

Sat·ur·day (săt′erdē) *n.* Seventh day of the week; ~ **-night special**, (slang) any cheap handgun. [OE., f. L. *Saturni dies* day of Saturn]

Sat·urn (săt′ern). 1. (Rom. myth.) Ancient Italian god of agriculture, ruler of the world in a golden age of innocence and plenty, later identified with the Greek CRONUS. 2. (astron.) Major planet, next in size to Jupiter, distinguished by its 10 satellites or moons and its engirdling system of rings. 3. (alchemy) The metal lead.

Sat·ur·na·li·a (săternā′lēa) *n.* (pl. **-li·a, -li·as**). (also as pl.) (Rom. antiq.) Yearly festival of Saturn, held in December, observed as a time of unrestrained merrymaking with temporary release of slaves; hence, **s~**, scene or time of wild revelry or tumult. **Sa·tur·na′li·an** *adj.*

Sa·tur·ni·an (satẽr′nēan) *adj.* Of the god or the planet Saturn.

sat·ur·nine (săt′ernīn) *adj.* 1. Born under, influenced by, the planet Saturn (astrol.); sluggish, cold and gloomy in temperament, (of looks etc.) suggesting such temperament. 2. Of lead; of, affected by, lead poisoning. **sat·ur·nin·i·ty** (săternĭn′ĭtē), **sat′ur·nine·ness** *ns.*

sa·tyr (sā′ter, săt′er) *n.* (Gk. myth.) One of a class of woodland spirits, usu. represented as being young with ears, tail, and legs of goat, and budding horns; lecher; man afflicted with satyriasis.

sa·tyr·ic (sătĭr´ĭk, sa-) *adj.*

sa·ty·ri·a·sis (sătĭrī´asĭs, sătĭ-) *n.* Excessive sexual desire in males.

sauce (saws) *n.* 1. Preparation, usu. liquid or soft, taken as relish or dressing with some article of food; (fig.) something that adds piquancy; stewed or puréed sweetened fruit as part of meal, as *apple-sauce*; **hard** ~: see HARD; **tartar(e)** ~, sharp-flavored sauce consisting of mayonnaise with chopped pickles, capers, herbs, etc., served with fish. 2. (colloq.) Impudence. 3. **sauce'boat**, vessel in which sauce is served. **sauce** *v.t.* (**sauced, sauc·ing**). 1. Season with sauces or condiments (rare); (fig.) make piquant, add relish to. 2. (colloq.) Be impudent to.

sauce·pan (saws´păn) *n.* Kitchen utensil of metal with handle projecting from side, in which food is boiled, steamed, etc.

sau·cer (saw´ser) *n.* Shallow dish with slight circular depression in center for standing esp. coffee cup or teacup on, to catch liquid that may be spilled from it; any dish or small shallow object resembling this; **flying** ~: see FLYING.

sau·cy (saw´sē) *adj.* (**-ci·er, -ci·est**). Impudent, pert; (slang) smart-looking. **sau´ci·ly** *adv.* **sau´ci·ness** *n.* [orig., = savory, flavored with sauce]

Sau·di (sahoo´dē, sow´dē, saw´-) **Arabia.** Kingdom on the Arabian Peninsula, SW. Asia, with the Red Sea and the Gulf of Aqaba to the W. and the Persian Gulf to the E.; capital, Riyadh. **Sau´di A·ra´bi·an** *adj. & n.*

sau·er·kraut (sow´erkrowt, sowr´-) *n.* Cabbage cut fine and pickled in brine. [Ger.]

Sauk (sawk), **Sac** (sawk, sahk, săk) *ns.* (pl. **Sauks, Sacs**, collect. **Sauk, Sac**). Tribe of Algonquian-speaking N. Amer. Indians, orig. in Michigan, later in Wisconsin, and, after merging with the Fox, in Illinois; now in Iowa and Oklahoma; member of this tribe.

Saul (sawl). 1. First king of Israel (11th c. B.C.). 2. (also ~ **of Tarsus**) Original name of St. PAUL[1].

sau·na (saw´na, sow´-) *n.* Steam bath or bathhouse, of Finnish origin.

saun·ter (sawn´ter, sahn´-) *v.i.* Walk in leisurely way, stroll. ~ *n.* Leisurely ramble or gait. **saun´ter·er** *n.*

sau·ri·an (sôr´ēan) *adj. & n.* (Of or like) a lizard.

sau·sage (saw´sĭj) *n.* Meat minced, seasoned, and stuffed into long cylindrical case made from intestine, bladder, or other animal tissue, or synthetic material; short length of this made by twisting or

Goya's interpretation of '**Saturn** Devouring His Children' shows the power that this painter could demonstrate, especially as works of this type also had an allegorical message.

The National Congress building in Brasilia, capital of the Republic of Brazil, features an unique **saucer**-shaped inverted dome which is the focal point of the building architecturally.

The pampas of Argentina is typical of **savannah** *country, and these vast expanses permit large-scale raising of cattle and sheep, as does similar country in Australia and the U.S.A.*

tying the containing case; ~ **meat**, meat minced and seasoned to be used in sausages or as stuffing etc.

sau·té (sōtā′, saw-) *v.t.* (**-téed** or **-téd**, **-té·ing**). (cooking) Fry lightly in fat. ~ *n.* Sautéed food; sautéed dish.

sau·terne (sōtern′, saw-) *n.* Light sweet white wine from the Bordeaux region of France. [*Sauternes*, name of a district of Gironde, France]

sav·age (săv′ĭj) *adj.* Uncultivated, wild (archaic); uncivilized, in primitive state; fierce, cruel,

furious; (colloq.) angry, out of temper. **sav′age·ly** *adv.* **sav′age·ness** *n.* **sav′age·ry** *n.* (pl. **-ries**). **savage** *n.* Member of savage tribe, esp. one living by hunting or fishing; brutally cruel or barbarous person. ~ *v.t.* (**-aged**, **-ag·ing**). (of animal, esp. horse) Attack and bite (person etc.).

Much of **Saudi Arabia** is overlain with rocks of ancient volcanic origin. However, the oil, which provides the nation's wealth, is in sedimentary rocks.

sa·van·na, sa·van·nah (savăn′a) *ns.* Wide treeless grassland, esp. in tropical Amer.

Sa·van·nah (savăn′a). Seaport and city in Georgia, in the E. part.

sa·vant (săvahnt′, savănt′, săv′ant; *Fr.* săvahn′) *n.* (pl. **sa·vants** pr. săvahnts′, savănts′, săv′ants; *Fr.* săvahn′). Person of learning, scholar.

sa·vate (savăt′, -vaht′) *n.* Kind of French boxing in which blows are given with feet as well as hands. [Fr.]

save[1] (sāv) *v.* (**saved, sav·ing**). 1. Rescue, preserve, deliver from danger, misfortune, harm, or discredit; bring about spiritual salvation of, preserve from damnation; prevent loss of (game etc.), (soccer, hockey, etc.) prevent opponent from scoring; ~ **the day**, find or provide way out of difficulty. 2. Keep for future use, husband, reserve, put by; lay by money; live economically; ~ **up**, accumulate money by economy. 3. Relieve from need of expending (money, trouble, etc.) or from exposure to (annoyance etc.). **save** *n.* Act of preventing other side from scoring in soccer, hockey, etc. **sav′a·ble, save′a·ble** *adjs.* **sav′er** *n.*

save[2] (sāv) *prep.* Except, but. ~ *conj.* (archaic) Useless, but.

sav·in, sa·vine (săv′ĭn) *ns.* European and W. Asiatic small bushy evergreen shrub (*Juniperus sabina*) with dark green leaves and small bluish-purple berries; dried tops of this, used as drug; any of various similar shrubs, esp. red cedar (*J. virginiana* and *J. horizontalis*). [L. (*herba*) *Sabina* Sabine herb]

sav·ing (sā′vĭng) *n.* (esp., usu. pl.) Sum of money saved and put by; ~**s account**, bank deposit receiving interest but allowing withdrawals only with passbook or written authorization, distinct from CHECKING ACCOUNT; ~**s bank**, bank for savings accounts. **saving** *adj.* (esp.) Making a reservation, furnishing a proviso. ~ *prep.* & *conj.* = SAVE[2] *prep.* & *conj.*

sav·ior (sāv′yer) *n.* Deliverer, redeemer; **the, our, S** ~, Christ.

sa·voir-faire (săv′wārfār′). Quickness to see and do the right thing, tact. [Fr.]

Sav·o·na·ro·la (săvonarō′la), **Gi·ro·la·mo** (jǐrŏl′amō) (1452–98). Dominican monk whose sermons at Florence gave expression to the religious reaction against the artistic license and social corruption of the Renaissance; he became the leader of the democratic party in Florence after the expulsion of the

*A large **sawmill** at Kawerau in Auckland, New Zealand. The timber industry in that country is significant as a provider of wood, woodchips for export, and material used in paper-making.*

*Today, a **saw** has been devised for almost every application. However it is little known that saws were used in ancient Rome, though there was little development until the Middle Ages.*

bow-saw

hack-saw

tenon saw

hand-saw

cross-cut saw

circular saw in machine

chain saw

band-saw in machine

Medici, but aroused the hostility of Pope Alexander VI and was excommunicated and burned at the stake as a heretic.

sa·vor (sā′ver) *n.* Characteristic taste, flavor; power of affecting sense of taste; essential virtue or property; tinge, hint, smack, *of.* **sa′vor·i·ness** *adj.*   **savor** *v.* Appreciate flavor of, enjoy; smack or suggest presence *of.*

sa·vor·y[1] (sā′verē) *n.* (pl. **-vor·ies**). Herb of genus *Satureia* of mint family, used in cooking; esp. *S. hortensis* (**summer** ~), and *S. montana* (**winter** ~).

sa·vor·y[2] (sā′verē) *adj.* (**-vor-i·er, -vor·i·est**). With appetizing taste or smell; free from bad smells, fragrant (now only with negative); (of dishes etc.) of stimulating or piquant flavor and not sweet.

Sa·voy (savoi′). Region in SE. France; formerly a duchy and part of the kingdom of Sardinia; ceded to France in 1860.

Sa·voy·ard (savoi′erd, săv′oiärd, săvwahyärd′) *n.*   1. Native of SAVOY. 2. Professional performer or enthusiastic admirer of Gilbert and Sullivan operas, many of which were first presented at London's Savoy Theatre.

sav·vy (săv′ē) *v.* (**-vied, -vy·ing**). (slang) Know. ~ *n.* (slang) Knowingness, wits. [corrupt. of Span. *sabe usted* you know]

saw[1] (saw) *n.* Tool, worked by hand or power, for cutting wood, metal, stone, bone, etc., consisting essentially of plate, band, or tube of steel, one edge of which (except in some stonecutting saws) is formed into continuous series of teeth; **hand′saw**, saw managed by one hand; **saw′buck**, sawhorse, esp. with cross-shaped legs extending above crossbar; (slang) $10 bill; **saw′dust**, tiny fragments of wood produced in sawing, used for stuffing, packing, etc.; **saw′fish** (pl. **-fishes**, collect. **-fish**), sea fish (*Pristis*) with snout ending in long flat projection with teeth on each edge; **saw′fly** (pl. **-flies**), insect of family Tenthredinidae, usu. very destructive to vegetation, with saw-like ovipositor; **saw′horse**, frame or trestle for supporting wood being sawed; **saw′mill**, mill in which wood is sawed into planks or logs by machinery; **saw-whet owl**, (*Aegolius acadicus*), tiny brown and white, tuftless N. Amer. owl, whose note resembles sound of saw being filed. **saw** *v.* (**sawed**, esp. Brit. **sawn, saw·ing**). Cut (wood etc.) with, make (boards etc.) with, use, saw; move backward and forward, divide (the air etc.) with motion as of saw or person sawing; admit of being sawed *easily, badly,* etc.; **saw′bones**, (slang) surgeon; **sawed-off** (*adj.*), (of gun) with part of barrel removed by sawing; (of person, colloq.) undersized.

saw[2] (saw) *n.* Proverbial saying, old maxim.

saw·yer (saw′yer) *n.*   Person employed in sawing timber.

sax (săks) *n.* (colloq.) Saxophone.

sax·a·tile (săk′satĭl) *adj.* Living or growing among rocks.

Saxe-Co·burg-Go·tha (săks′-kō′bĕrggō′tha). Former German duchy; name of the British royal family from the accession of Edward VII in 1901 (dropped during World War I because of its

The wild **saxifrage** (above) and the cultivated varieties (left) are adapted to growing in rock crevices. However, some of these plants are also ideal for planting in borders.

Field **scabious** is one of a group of herbs, which include both annuals and perennial plants. Some have flowers up to 1½ ins. in diameter and are usually blue, though there are pink and white varieties.

German association, and replaced by *Windsor*).

sax·i·frage (săk′sĭfrĭj) *n*. Alpine or rock plant of genus *Saxifraga*, with tufted foliage and panicles of white, yellow, or red flowers. [L. *saxifraga* spleenwort, f. *saxum* rock, *frangere* break (prob. because growing in rock clefts)]

Sax·on (săk′son) *n*. Member, language, of a Germanic people that, in the early centuries of the Christian era, dwelled in a region near the mouth of the Elbe, and of which one portion, distinguished as the Anglo-Saxons, conquered and occupied part of Britain in the 5th and 6th centuries, while the other, the Old Saxons, remained in Germany; native of modern Saxony; Englishman as opp. to Irish and Welsh, Scottish Lowlander as opp. to Highlander; Germanic elements in the English language. ~ *adj*. Connected with, pertaining to, the Saxons, their language or country; (of English words) of Germanic origin.

Sax·on·ism (săk′sonĭzem) *n*. Word, idiom, surviving in English, derived from Anglo-Saxon (opp. LATINISM).

Sax·o·ny (săk′sone). Former duchy of Germany in the E. central part; later became successively an electorate, kingdom, Prussian province, German free state, and republic; absorbed in East Germany, 1952; **Lower** ~, state of West Germany; capital, Hanover.

sax·o·phone (săk′sofōn) *n*. Keyed wind instrument with conical tube, made of brass but regarded as belonging to woodwind group, its mouthpiece being equipped with a reed like that of a clarinet. **sax′o·phon·ist** *n*. [invented c1840 by Adolphe *Sax*, Belgian instrument maker]

say (sā) *v*. (**said** pr. sĕd, **say·ing**). Utter, recite, rehearse, in ordinary speaking voice; put into words, express; adduce or allege in argument or excuse; form and give

opinion or decision; select as example, assume, take as near enough; **that is to** ~, in other words, more explicitly; or at least; **you can** ~ **that** (**again**), (colloq.) I agree emphatically. **say′ing** *n*. (esp.) Sententious remark, maxim. **say** *n*. (Opportunity of saying) what one has to say; share in decision; ~-**so** (pl. ~-**sos**), (colloq.) assertion; authority.

Sb *symbol*. Antimony.

sb. *abbrev*. Substantive.

S.B. *abbrev*. Bachelor of Science. [L. *Scientiae Baccalaureus*]

SBA *abbrev*. Small Business Administration.

SC, S.C. *abbrevs*. South Carolina.

Sc *symbol*. Scandium.

scab (skăb) *n*. 1. Dry rough incrustation formed over sore in healing, cicatrice. 2. Cutaneous disease in animals, resembling scabies. 3. Parasitic disease of plants causing scablike roughness. 4. (slang) Mean low fellow; worker

who refuses to join a union or a strike; strikebreaker. **scab′bi·ly** *adv*. **scab′bi·ness** *n*. **scab′by** *adj*. (-**bi·er, -bi·est**). **scab** *v*. (**scab-bed, scab·bing**). Form scab, heal over.

scab·bard (skăb′erd) *n*. Sheath of sword, bayonet, etc.

sca·bies (skā′bēz) *n.sing*. Contagious skin disease due to a parasite, the mite *Sarcoptes scabiei*. **sca′bi·ous**[1] *adj*.

sca·bi·ous[2] (skā′bēus) *n*. Herbaceous plant of genus *Scabiosa*, with blue, pink, or white pincushion-shaped aggregate flowers. [med. L. *scabiosa* (*herba*); named as specific against itch, f. SCABIES]

scab·rous (skăb′rus, skā′brus) *adj*. 1. (zool., bot., etc.) With rough surface, scurfy. 2. Salacious; indecent. **scab′rous·ness** *n*.

Once a German republic, **Saxony**, with its capital, Hanover, is now part of West Germany. The building (below) is the Neues Rathaus or New Town Hall in Hanover.

scad (skăd) *n.* (pl. **scads**, collect. **scad**). Fish of family Carangidae, including the horse mackerel, with enlarged plates on side of body.

scads (skădz) *n.pl.* (colloq.) Large quantities *of.*

scaf·fold (skăf'old) *n.* 1. Temporary raised platform for execution of criminals. 2. SCAFFOLDING sense 1. ~ *v.t.* Attach scaffolding to.

scaf·fold·ing (skăf'olding) *n.* 1. Temporary structure of wooden poles (or metal tubes) and planks providing platform(s) for workmen to stand on while erecting or repairing building. 2. Materials for making such structure. 3. Temporary framework for other purposes (also fig.).

scal·a·wag, scal·la·wag, scal·-ly·wag (skăl'awăg) *ns.* (colloq.) Rogue or rascal; (hist.) native white of southern state accepting Republican principles after Civil War.

scald (skawld) *v.t.* Injure or pain with hot liquid or vapor; affect like boiling water; cleanse with boiling water; pour hot liquid over; heat (liquid, esp. milk) nearly to boiling point. ~ *n.* Injury to skin by scalding.

scale[1] (skāl) *n.* One of the small thin membranous horny or bony outgrowths or modifications of skin in many fishes, reptiles, etc., freq. overlapping, and forming covering for (part of) the body. 2. Flattened membranous plate of cellular tissue (usu. rudimentary or degenerate leaf) as covering of lead buds of deciduous trees etc. 3. Protective covering of many female insects (~ **insect**) of family Coccidae infesting and injuring various plants. 4. Thin plate, lamina, or film of any kind; (usu. collect.) film of oxide forming on iron or other metal when heated and hammered or rolled; hard deposit in boilers etc. **scaled, scale'less** *adjs.* **scal'y** *adj.* (**scal·i·er,**

*On a Zaire plantation, branches lashed together form **scaffolding**. For the type of building this is just as effective as the steel tubing and planks used by more sophisticated builders.*

scal·i·est). Covered with, having scales. **scale** *v.* (**scaled, scal·ing**) Take away scale(s) from; form come off in, drop, scales; (of scales come *off.*

scale[2] (skāl) *n.* 1. Pan o balance; weighing instrument, esp (also **pair of** ~**s**) one consisting of beam pivoted at middle and with dish, pan, etc., suspended at eithe end; **turn the** ~**s**, exceed weigh in other pan etc. of balance; (fig. outweigh other considerations motives, etc. 2. **the Scales**: se LIBRA. **scale** *v.* (**scaled, scal·ing**) Weigh (specified amount).

scale[3] (skāl) *n.* 1. (mus.) Definit series of sounds ascending or de scending by fixed intervals; any o

DIATONIC

1 2 3 4 5 6 7 8
Major

Harmonic

Melodic   Minor

CHROMATIC

WHOLE TONE

PENTATONIC

SCALES

1. Tonic. 2. Supertonic. 3. Median 4. Subdominant. 5. Dominant. 6. Sut mediant. 7. Leading note. 8. Toni (octave above 1). 1–2, 2–3, 4–5, 5–6–7 are tones; 3–4, 7–8 are semitone

graduated series of sounds int which octave may be divided; an of these series as subject of in struction or practice. 2. Series o degrees, graduated arrangement system, or classification; standarc of measurement, calculation, etc. (arith.) system of numeration o numerical notation, in which the value of a figure depends on it place in the order (the usual is tha in which successive places from right to left represent units, tens hundreds, etc.); relative dimen sions, proportion that representa tion of an object bears to the objec itself. 3. Set of marks at measurec distances on line for use ir

*Each **scale** on a lung-fish (left) is differ ent from that on other fish, and simila only to those found on fossils. Those c a snake (far left) are extensions of th skin and the underneath ones help it t move.*

measuring or making proportional reductions or enlargements; rule determining intervals between these; piece of metal, wood, etc., apparatus, on which they are marked. **scale** v. (**scaled, scal·ing**). 1. Climb with ladder or by clambering; **scaling ladder**, one used for climbing high walls. 2. Represent in dimensions proportional to actual ones; reduce to common scale; **scale up, down**, make larger, smaller, in due proportion. 3. (of quantities etc.) Have common scale, be commensurable.

sca·lene (skā'lēn, skālēn') adj. ~ **cone, cylinder**, one of which axis is not perpendicular to base; ~ **triangle**, triangle with no two sides equal.

scal·la·wag: SCALAWAG.

scal·lion (skăl'yon) n. Onion that fails to bulb but forms long neck and strong blade; young onion before bulb forms; shallot. [OF. *escaloigne*, see SHALLOT]

scal·lop, scol·lop (skŏl'op, kăl'-) ns. 1. Bivalve mollusk of genus *Pecten*, with shell having ridges radiating from middle of hinge and edged with small rounded lobes; edible muscle of this; one valve of this as utensil in which various dishes (of fish, minced meat, etc., with bread crumbs or sauce) are cooked and served. 2. One of series of rounded projections at edge of garment etc. ~ v.t. 1. Bake in scallop shell or similar shallow pan or dish, usu. with milk and bread crumbs. 2. Ornament (edge, material) with scallops. **scal'lop·er** n.

scal·op·pi·ne, scal·op·pi·ni ('skahlopē'nē, skălo-) ns. Very thin slices of meat, esp. veal, cooked slowly in sauce of wine or tomatoes and herbs.

scal·ly·wag: SCALAWAG.

scalp (skălp) n. Skin of upper part of head, with hair covering it; this cut or torn from person's head as battle trophy by Amer. Indians (freq. fig.). ~ v.t. Take scalp of; (fig.) criticize severely; defeat, humiliate; (colloq.) buy (tickets etc.) to resell for quick or high profit; hence **scalp'er** n.

scal·pel (skăl'pel) n. Small straight knife used in surgery and dissection.

scam (skăm) n. (slang) Confidence game; see CONFIDENCE.

scamp[1] (skămp) n. Rascal, knave (freq. joc.).

scamp[2] (skămp) v.t. Do (work etc.) in perfunctory or inadequate way.

scam·per (skăm'per) v.i. Run or caper about nimbly, rush hastily. ~ n. Scampering run.

scam·pi (skăm'pē, skahm'-) n.pl. Large shrimps; dish of these, esp. cooked with garlic. [It.]

The 300 or so species of **scallop** show much difference in markings and size. They move by a form of water-jet propulsion and can attain remarkable acceleration when threatened.

scan (skăn) v. (**scanned, scan·ning**). 1. Analyze, test meter of (verse) by examining number and quantity of feet and syllables; (of verse) be metrically correct. 2. Look intently at all parts successively of. 3. Resolve (a picture) into elements of light and shade in a prearranged number and pattern of lines as a stage in televising. 4. (radar) Traverse (region) with controlled beam. **scan'ner** n.

scan·dal (skăn'dal) n. (Thing that occasions) general feeling of outrage or indignation, esp. as expressed in common talk; malicious gossip. **scan'dal·ous** adj. **scan·dal·ous·ly** adv. **scan·dal·mon·ger** (skăn'dalmŭngger, -mŏng-) n. One who invents or spreads scandals.

scan·dal·ize (skăn'dalīz) v.t. (**-ized, -iz·ing**). Offend moral feelings, sense of propriety, etc.; shock.

Scan·di·na·vi·a (skăndinā'vēa). Geographical term for Sweden, Norway, and Denmark, together with the adjacent islands and sometimes Iceland. **Scan·di·na'vi·an** adj. & n. (Native, inhabitant, family of languages) of Scandinavia.

scan·di·um (skăn'dēum) n. (chem.) Rare metallic element (discovered 1879 in Scandinavian mineral euxenite) usu. included in rare-earth group; symbol Sc, at. no.

21, at. wt. 44.9559. [L. *Scandia* Scandinavia]

scan·ner (skăn'er) n. (esp.) 1. Instrument that scans television pictures. 2. (radar) Apparatus that directs beam in scanning (SCAN sense 4).

scan·sion (skăn'shon) n. Metrical scanning; way verse scans.

scant (skănt) adj. Barely sufficient, deficient, with scanty supply of.

scant·ling (skănt'lĭng) n. 1. Small timber or beam of wood; block or slice of stone of fixed size. 2. Size to which stone or timber is to be cut; set of standard dimensions for parts of structure, esp. in shipbuilding.

scant·y (skăn'tē) adj. (**scant·i·er, scant·i·est**). Of small extent or amount; barely sufficient. **scan'ties** n.pl. (colloq.) Women's short panties. **scant'i·ly** adv. **scant'i·ness** n.

scape (skāp) n. 1. (archit.) Shaft of column. 2. (bot.) Long flower stalk rising directly from root or rhizome of plant having only radical leaves. 3. (entom.) First segment of antenna. 4. (ornith.) Shaft of feather.

scape·goat (skāp'gōt) n. (in Mosaic ritual of Day of Atonement) Goat allowed to escape into wilderness, the sins of the people having been symbolically laid upon it (see Lev. 16); hence, person blamed or punished for sins of others.

scape·grace (skāp'grās) n. Reckless or careless person, esp. young man or boy constantly in scrapes. [= "one who escapes the grace of God"]

scaph·oid (skăf´oid) *adj.* (anat.) Shaped like a boat; ~ **bone**, navicular. **scaphoid** *n.* Scaphoid bone.

scap·u·la (skăp´yula) *n.* (pl. **-lae** pr. **-lē, -las**). Shoulder blade.

scap·u·lar (skăp´yuler) *adj.* Of the scapule; ~ **feather**, feather growing from scapular region. **scapular** *n.* 1. (eccles.) Monk's short cloak covering shoulders; badge of affiliation to religious order consisting of two strips of cloth hanging down breast and back and joined across shoulders, worn under clothing. 2. Scapular feather.

scap·u·lar·y (skăp´yulĕrē) *n.* (pl. **-lar·ies**) = SCAPULAR *n.* def. 1.

scar (skär) *n.* Trace of healed wound, sore, or burn, cicatrice (freq. fig.); mark on plant left by fall of leaf etc.; hilum. ~ *v.* (**scared, scar·ring**). Mark with scar or scars; heal over, form scar.

scar·ab (skăr´ab) *n.* 1. Dung beetle (*Scarabaeus sacer*) revered by ancient Egyptians as symbol of resurrection and immortality. 2. Gem or stone in form of beetle, with intaglio design on flat underside, worn in ring or as pendant around neck, esp. by ancient Egyptians, Etruscans, etc.

scar·a·bae·id (skărabē´ĭd) *adj.* & *n.* (Beetle) of family Scarabaeidae, including June bugs, dung beetles, etc.

scarce (skärs) *adj.* (**scarc·er, scarc·est**). Insufficient, not plentiful, scanty; seldom met with, rare; **make oneself** ~, go away, keep away. **scarce** *adv.* (archaic, poet., rhet.) Scarcely. **scarce′ly** *adv.* Hardly, barely, only just. **scarce′ness, scar′ci·ty** *ns.* (pl. **-ties**).

scare (skär) *v.t.* (**scared, scar·ing**). Strike with sudden terror,

frighten; frighten away, drive off; **scare′crow**, device for frightening birds away from crops, usu. figure of man in ragged clothes; bogy; badly dressed or esp. very thin person. **scare** *n.* Sudden fright or alarm; general public alarm caused by baseless or exaggerated rumors. **scare·mon·ger** (skär´mŭngger, -mŏng-) *n.* Alarmist.

scarf¹ (skärf) *n.* (pl. **scarfs, scarves** pr. skärvz). Long narrow strip of material worn for ornament or warmth around neck over shoulders, from 1 shoulder to opposite hip, or around waist, with ends hanging; square of material worn at neck.

A scarp may be formed naturally when a block of soft rock, capped with a harder substance, is tilted and subjected to erosion. This wears the softer rock more quickly, forming a steeper slope.

A scarab made from blue glass-paste in Egypt about 600 B.C. The dung-beetle on which it was modelled, was thought to symbolize some celestial power which rotated the earth, and also the moon.

scarf² (skärf) *v.t.* Join ends of (pieces of timber, metal, or leather by beveling or notching so that they overlap without increase of thickness and then bolting, brazing, o sewing them together. ~ *n.* (pl **scarfs**). Joint made by scarfing notch, groove.

scar·i·fy (skăr´ĭfī, skär´-) *v.t.* (**-fied, -fy·ing**). Make superficia incisions in (surg.); make sore wound (now fig.); break up ground **scar·i·fi·ca·tion** (skărĭfĭkā´shon skär-) *n.*

Scar·lat·ti (skärlah´tē). Nam of two Italian composers: **Alessandro** ~ (1658–1725), founder o the Neapolitan school of opera (**Giuseppe**) **Domenico** ~ (1685–1757), his son; composer of many sonatas.

scar·let (skär´lĭt) *adj.* O brilliant red color inclining t orange; ~ **fever**, contagious fever

The New Zealand scaup or black teal native to that country but early settler greatly reduced its numbers. Howeve conservation measures have graduall enabled its population to grow.

*Dung-beetles are **scatophagous** creatures, that is, they feed on dung. In doing this they aid in the breakdown of dung and help to reduce it to a form more easily utilised by plants.*

*Vultures in Uganda feed on the carcass of a giraffe. A **scavenger** is part of a natural system which ensures that the bodies of dead animals become a useful part of the ecosystem.*

due to hemolytic streptococcal infection, with scarlet eruptions of skin and mucous membrane of mouth and pharynx; ~ **hat**, cardinal's hat, esp. as symbol of the rank of cardinal; ~ **pimpernel**, red-flowered common pimpernel (*Anagallis arvensis*); ~ **runner**, red-flowered climbing bean (*Phaseolus coccineus*); ~ **tanager**, songbird of eastern U.S. (*Piranga olivacea*), the male in breeding season a brilliant scarlet with black wings and tail; ~ **woman**, prostitute. **scarlet** *n.* Scarlet color; scarlet cloth or clothes. [perh. f. Pers. *sagalat* scarlet cloth]

scarp (skärp) *n.* 1. Line of cliffs caused by geologic faulting or erosion; escarpment. 2. Inner wall or slope of ditch in fortification. ~ *v.t.* Give steep face to, slope steeply.

scar·y (skār'ē) *adj.* (**scar·i·er, scar·i·est**). (colloq.) 1. Causing terror, fright, etc. 2. Easily frightened. **scar'i·ness** *n.*

scat[1] (skăt) *v.i. imper.* (colloq.) Go away quickly: used imperatively.

scat[2] (skăt) *n. & v.* (**scat·ted, scat·ting**). (colloq.) (Sing) wordless jazz song using voice to imitate musical instrument.

scathe (skādh) *v.t.* (**scathed, scath·ing**). Injure, esp. by fire etc. (poet.); wither with fierce invective or satire. **scath'ing** *adj.* **scath'ing·ly** *adv.*

sca·tol·o·gy (skătŏl'ojē, ska-) *n.* 1. (med.) Study of feces. 2. Preoccupation with excrement. 3. Preoccupation with obscenity in literature. **scat·o·log·i·cal** (skăto-lŏj'ĭkal), **scat·o·log'ic** *adjs.*

sca·toph·a·gous (skatŏf'agus) *adj.* Feeding on, eating, dung (as some beetles, flies, etc.).

scat·ter (skăt'er) *v.* 1. Throw here and there, strew, sprinkle; (of gun, cartridge) distribute (shot); (phys.) diffuse by reflection from particles. 2. Separate and disperse in flight etc. 3. **scat'terbrain**, heedless person; **scat'terbrained**, heedless, desultory. **scat'tered** *adj.* (esp.) not situated together, wide apart; sporadic. **scatter** *n.* Act of scattering; extent of distribution, esp. of shot; ~ **rug**, small rug covering part of floor.

scaup (skawp) *n.* (pl. **scaups**, collect. **scaup**). Either of two wild ducks, *Aytha affinis* or *A. marila*, the male of the former having black head glossed with purple, and of the latter a green-glossed head.

scav·eng·er (skăv'ĭnjer) *n.* Person employed to keep streets etc. clean by carrying away refuse; person who collects discarded objects from garbage dumps etc.; animal feeding on carrion, garbage, or any decaying organic matter. **scav'enge** *v.* (**-enged, -eng·ing**). Be, act as, scavenger.

sce·nar·i·o (sĭnär'ēō, -när'-) *n.* (pl. **-nar·i·os**). 1. Skeleton libretto or outline of play, opera, etc. 2. Complete plot of film play, with all necessary directions for actors, details of scenes, etc. **sce·nar·ist** (sĭnär'ĭst, -när'-) *n.* Writer of scenario, sense 2. [It., f. *scena* scene]

scene (sēn) *n.* 1. (hist.) Stage. 2. Place where action of (part of) play, novel, etc., is supposed to take place; locality of event. 3. Portion of a play during which action is

continuous; subdivision (rarely, the whole) of an act; episode, situation, as subject of narrative or description; action, episode, situation, in real life. 4. Stormy encounter or interview; agitated colloquy, esp. with display of temper. 5. Any of the pieces of painted canvas, woodwork, etc., used to represent scene of action on stage; picture presented by these to audience; (transf.) landscape or view spread before spectator like scene in theater; **behind the ~s**, amid actors and stage machinery; (fig.) in private among the principals of a business, group, etc.

sce·ner·y (sē'nerē) *n.* (pl. **-ner·ies**). 1. Accessories used in theater to make stage resemble supposed scene of action. 2. General appearance of natural features etc. of place or district; picturesque features of landscape.

sce·nic (sē'nĭk) *adj.* Of, on, the stage; of the nature of a show; having fine natural scenery, giving landscape views; ~ **railway**, miniature railway running through artificial scenery. **sce'ni·cal·ly** *adv.*

scent (sĕnt) *v.* 1. Discern by smell; perceive as if by smell, detect. 2. Impregnate with odor, perfume. ~ *n.* 1. Distinctive odor, esp. of agreeable kind; odor of man or animal as means of pursuit by hound, trail; **throw off the ~**, deceive by false indications. 2. (of

A lavish **scene** during a performance of the opera 'Aida' at the Royal Opera House, Covent Garden, U.K. Dramatic stage settings are needed to create the correct atmosphere for the production.

animals, esp. dogs) Power of detecting or distinguishing smells.

scep·ter, Brit. **scep·tre** (sĕp´ter) *ns.* Staff borne in hand as symbol of regal or imperial authority; (fig.) royal or imperial dignity, sovereignty.

sch. *abbrev.* School.

sched·ule (skĕj´ool, -ōoul, -ul) *n.* Tabulated statement of details, inventory, list, prices, etc.; timetable; **on ~**, at time provided for in timetable etc. **schedule** *v.t.* (**-uled, -ul·ing**). Make schedule of; enter in schedule.

scheel·ite (shā´līt, shē´-) *n.* (min.) Calcium tungstate, an important ore of tungsten.

Sche·her·a·za·de (shehĕra-zah´de, -zahd´). (Arab. legend) Wife of the sultan of Samarkand who dissuaded him from killing her by narrating *The Arabian Nights' Entertainments.*

sche·ma (skē´ma) *n.* (pl. **-ma·ta** pr. -m*a*ta). Diagram, outline. **sche·mat·ic** (skēmăt´ĭk) *adj.* **sche·mat'i·cal·ly** *adv.* **sche·ma·tize** (skē´m*a*tīz) *v.t.* (**-tized, -tiz·ing**).

scheme (skēm) *n.* 1. Systematic arrangement; table of classification or of appointed times; plan for doing something. 2. Artful or underhand design.   ~ *v.i.* (**schemed, schem·ing**). Make plans, plan esp. in secret or underhand way. **schem'er** *n.* **schem'·ing** *adj.*

scher·zo (skĕr´tsō) *n.* (pl. **-zos, -zi** pr. -tsē). (mus.) Vigorous (properly light and playful) composition, independent or as movement in work of sonata type. [It., f. Teut. (Ger. *Scherz* merriment, prank, jest)]

Schick (shĭk), **Béla** (1877–1967). Hungarian-born Amer. pediatrician; invented **Schick test**, intracutaneous skin test for susceptibility to diphtheria.

Schil·ler (shĭl´er), **Johann Christoph Friedrich von** (1759–1805). German dramatist, lyric poet, and historian; author of the dramas *Wallenstein, William Tell,* etc.

schism (sĭz´em) *n.* Breach of unity of a church, separation into two churches or secession of part of church owing to difference of opinion on doctrine or discipline; offense of promoting schism; splitting of a group into mutually opposing parties.

schis·mat·ic (sĭzmăt´ĭk), **schiz·mat·i·cal** (sĭzmăt´ĭkal) *adjs. & ns.* (Person) tending to, guilty of, schism; (member) of seceded

The **sceptre**, a symbol of authority, is common in the regalia of most nations. Five are held in the British collection and of these, two are used in Coronation ceremonies.

branch of a church. **schis·mat'·i·cal·ly** *adv.*

schist (shĭst) *n.* Fine-grained metamorphic rock with component minerals arranged in more or less parallel layers, splitting in thin irregular plates. **schist·ose** (shĭs´tōs), **schis·tous** (shĭs´t*u*s) *adjs.*

schiz·oid (skĭt´soid, skĭd´zoid) *adj.* Of, resembling, afflicted with, schizophrenia.   ~ *n.* Schizophrenic person.

schiz·o·my·cete (skĭzomīsēt´) *n.* Member of class Schizomycetae of minute, freq. single-celled, lowly organisms between algae and fungi, including bacilli, bacteria, etc. **schiz·o·my·ce'tous, schiz·o·my·ce'tic** *adjs.*

schiz·o·phre·ni·a (skĭtsofrē´nēa, -frēn´ya, skĭdzo-, skĭzo-) *n.* Mental disease characterized by dissociation, delusions, and inability to distinguish reality from imagination. **schiz·o·phren·ic** (skĭtsofrĕn´ĭk, skĭdzo, skĭzo-, -frē´nĭk) *adj. & n.*

schle·miel (shlemēl´) *n.* (slang) Foolish or unlucky person. [Yiddish]

schlep, schlepp (shlĕp) *vbs.* (**schlepped, schlep·ping**). (slang) 1. Haul, drag, carry, etc., with effort or in clumsy manner. 2. Go or move about with difficulty or clumsily.   ~ *n.* 1. Tiresome journey. 2. Stupid, ineffectual person.

Schlie·mann (shlē'mahn), **Heinrich** (1822–90). German archaeologist who excavated Troy, Tiryns, and Mycenae.

schlock (shlŏk) *adj*. & *n*. (slang) Poor quality or secondhand (material). [Yiddish]

schmaltz, schmalz (shmahlts, shmawlts) *ns*. Sickly sentimentality. **schmaltz'y** *adj*. (**schmaltz·i·er, schmaltz·i·est**). [Ger.]

schnapps, schnaps (shnahps)

Schist is found in areas where there have been considerable movements of the earth. The various types are usually named after the dominant mineral but all consist of fine crystalline leaves.

ns. (pl. **schnapps, schnaps**). Strong Holland gin. [Ger. *Schnaps* mouthful, dram of liquor]

schnau·zer (shnow'zer) *n*. Wire-coated black, black-and-brown, or pepper-and-salt terrier of German breed.

schnit·zel (shnĭt'sel) *n*. Veal

cutlet, esp. (**Wiener** ~) one fried in bread crumbs in the Viennese style and garnished with lemon, anchovies, etc.

schnook (shno͞ok) *n*. (slang) Person easily cheated or victimized; dupe. [Yiddish]

schnor·kel = SNORKEL.

schnoz·zle (shnŏz'el) *n*. (slang) Nose. [Yiddish]

schol·ar (skŏl'er) *n*. 1. (archaic) Pupil. 2. Holder of scholarship. 3. Learned person, person versed in literature. **schol'ar·li·ness** *n*. **schol'ar·ly** *adv*.

schol·ar·ship (skŏl'ershĭp) *n*. 1. Attainments of a scholar; learning, erudition. 2. (Right to) emoluments paid, during a fixed period, from funds of charity, school, college, university, etc., or government, for defraying cost of education or studies, usu. granted after competitive examination.

scho·las·tic (skolăs'tĭk), **scho·las·ti·cal** (skolăs'tĭkal) *adjs*. 1. Of schools or other educational establishments; educational, academic; pedantic, formal. 2. (As) of the schoolmen (see SCHOOL¹) dealing in logical subtleties. **scho·las'ti·cal·ly** *adv*. **scho·las·ti·cism** (skolăs'tĭsĭzem) *n*. **scholastic** *n*. 1. Schoolman; modern theologian of scholastic tendencies. 2. Jesuit between novitiate and priesthood.

school¹ (sko͞ol) *n*. 1. Institution for educating children or giving instruction, usu. of more elementary or more technical kind than that given at universities; time given to teaching; being educated in a school; (fig.) circumstances or occupation serving to discipline or instruct. 2. Organized body of teachers and scholars in any of higher branches of study in Middle Ages, esp. as constituent part of medieval university; special division (freq. graduate) of a university; buildings, pupils, of this. 3. Disciples, imitators, followers, of philosopher, artist, etc.; band or succession of persons devoted to some cause, principle, etc. 4. ~ **board**, body of persons appointed or elected by taxpayers of a district etc. to provide and maintain public schools; board of education; **school'boy**, boy at school; **school days**, time of being at school; **school'girl**, girl at school; **school'ma'am, school'marm**, (colloq.) schoolmistress; **school'-man** (pl. **-men**), teacher in medieval university; writer (9th–14th centuries) treating of logic, metaphysics, and theology as taught

*The **Schnauzer**, first bred in 16th century Germany was a work dog before becoming a show dog. Careful breeding produced three varieties, the standard, miniature and great.*

1

2

3

4

in medieval schools or universities of Europe; **school′master, school′mistress,** teacher in school; **school′room,** room used for lessons in school or private house; **school′teacher,** teacher esp. in elementary school. **school** *v.* Send to school, provide for education of (rare); discipline, bring under control, train or accustom *to.* **school′-ing** *n.*

school² (skool) *n.* Great number of fish, whales, etc. swimming in company.

schoon·er¹ (skoo′ner) *n.* Small seagoing fore-and-aft rigged sailing vessel, orig. with only two masts, later with three or four and usu. carrying one or more topsails.

schoon·er² (skoo′ner) *n.* (colloq.) Large, tall beer glass.

Scho·pen·hau·er (shō′pen-hower), **Arthur** (1788–1860). German pessimistic philosopher who taught that the absolute reality is a blind and restless will, that all existence is essentially evil, and that release can be attained only by over-

Whether housed in an old building in England (1) or a modern one in Norway (2), a **school** *serves the same purpose. In New Zealand (3), lessons may sometimes be held in the open air. Lessons may be made more pertinent, like this one in Peking (4), given near the Memorial to the Revolution.*

coming the will to live.

schot·tische (shŏt′ish, shŏtēsh′) *n.* Kind of dance like polka but slower; music for this. [Ger. = "Scottish"]

Schu·bert (shoo′bert), **Franz Peter** (1797–1828). Austrian composer, esp. famous for his songs.

Schu·mann (shoo′mahn), **Robert Alexander** (1810–56). German Romantic composer, author of many songs and much piano and chamber music etc.

schuss (shoos) *n. & v.* (Make) straight downhill run on skis.

Schuy·ler (skī′ler), **Philip John** (1733–1804). Amer. statesman and general in Revolutionary War; delegate to Continental Congress, 1775; U.S. senator, 1789–91, 1797–8.

schwa (shwah) *n.* (phonet.) Indistinct vowel sound, as in second syllable of *common* or *comma,* represented as ə.

Schwei·tzer (shwīt′ser, shvīt′-), **Albert** (1875–1965). French theologian, missionary, doctor, musicologist; founded Lambaréné Hospital in French Equatorial Africa, now called Gabon, 1913; edited organ music of J. S. Bach; received Nobel Peace Prize, 1952.

sci·at·ic (sīăt′ĭk) *adj.* Of the hip; of, affecting, the sciatic nerve; suffering from, liable to, sciatica; ~ **nerve,** each of two divisions of the sacral plexus.

sci·at·i·ca (sīăt′ĭka) *n.* Neuritis or neuralgia of sciatic nerve, with paroxysms of pain along course of nerve and its branches.

sci·ence (sī′ens) *n.* 1. Systematic and formulated knowledge, pursuit of this, principles regulating such pursuit. 2. Branch of knowledge, organized body of the knowledge that has been accumulated on a subject; **abstract** ~

theoretical, not applied, science; **applied** ~, one studied for practical purposes (opp. *pure* ~); **exact** ~, one admitting of quantitative treatment; **natural** ~, science(s) concerned with the physical world (as chemistry, biology) (opp. *abstract* ~); **pure** ~, science studied without its applications to practical use (opp. *applied* ~); ~ **fiction**, form of fiction that assumes an imaginary technological advance or change in environment etc., freq. dealing with space travel and life on other planets.   3. Natural sciences collectively, the systematic study of the phenomena of the material universe and their laws.   4. (in sport, esp. boxing) Expert's skill as opp. to strength or natural ability.

sci·en·tif·ic (sīentĭf´ĭk) *adj.* Of science, esp. the natural sciences; devised according to the rules of science for testing soundness of conclusions etc.; systematic, accurate; assisted by expert knowledge. **sci·en·tif´i·cal·ly** *adv.*

sci·en·tist (sī´entĭst) *n.* One who studies or professes the natural sciences.

sci-fi (sī´fī) *adj. & n.* (slang) Science fiction.

scil·la (sĭl´a) *n.* Liliaceous bulbous plant of genus *S* ~, esp. the frequently cultivated blue-flowered *S. sibirica*; squill.

Scil·ly (sĭl´ē), **Isles of.** (also **Scillies**) Group of small islands off W. extremity of Cornwall, England.

scim·i·tar, scim·i·ter (sĭm´ĭter) *ns.* Oriental short curved single-edged sword, usu. broadening toward point.

scin·til·la (sĭntĭl´a) *n.* Spark, atom.

scin·til·late (sĭn´tĭlāt) *v.t.* (**-lat·ed, -lat·ing**). Sparkle, twinkle (freq. fig.); emit sparks. **scin´til·lat·ing·ly** *adv.* **scin´til·lant** *adj.*   **scin·til·la·tion** (sĭntĭlā´shon) *n.*

sci·o·list (sī´olĭst) *n.* Superficial pretender to knowledge, smatterer. **sci´o·lism** *n.* **sci·o·lis·tic** (sĭolĭs´tĭk) *adj.*

sci·on (sī´on) *n.* Shoot of plant, esp. one cut for grafting or planting; descendant, young member of (esp. noble) family.

scir·rhus (skĭr´us, sĭr´-) *n.* (pl. **scir·rhi** pr. skĭr´ī, sĭr´ī, **scir·rhus·es**). (path.) Hard carcinoma; organ that has hardened. **scir´rhoid, scir´rhous** *adjs.*

scis·sion (sĭzh´on, sĭsh´-) *n.* Cutting, being cut; division, split.

scis·sors (sĭz´erz) *n.pl.*   1. (also

Lilies in the genus **Scilla** may bear flowers which are blue, pink, or white. Several species are now grown in gardens in Britain. Once, gum from them was used to fix flights to arrows.

pair of ~) Cutting instrument consisting of pair of handled blades so pivoted that the instrument can be opened to X-shape and then closed with the object to be cut between the edges of the blades.   2. (wrestling) Hold in which opponent's head or body is clasped between legs; ~ **kick**, (swimming) kick used esp. with sidestroke in which legs move like scissors; **scis´sortail flycatcher**, bird (*Muscivora forficata*) of Texas open country, having spectacularly long-forked tail. **scis´sor** *v.t.* Cut with scissors.

scle·ra (sklēr´a) = SCLEROTIC *n.*

scle·ren·chy·ma (sklĭrĕng´kima) *n.* Hard tissue of coral; tissue of higher plants composed of cells with thickened and lignified walls, forming e.g. nutshell or seed coat.

scle·ro·sis (sklĭrō´sĭs) *n.* (pl. **-ses** pr. -sēz). 1. (path.) Replacement of normal tissue, esp. of nervous system or arteries, by overgrowth of fibrous or supporting tissue, resulting in hardening and and loss of function; **multiple** ~, chronic progressive sclerosis of brain and spinal cord.   2. (bot.) Hardening of cell wall by lignification.

scle·rot·ic (sklĭrŏt´ĭk) *adj.* Of, affected with, sclerosis; of the sclerotic. ~ *n.* Hard opaque white outer coat covering eyeball except over cornea and forming white of eye.

scoff (skŏf, skawf) *v.i.* Speak derisively, esp. of something deserving respect, mock, jeer (*at*);

*The training ship 'Winston Churchill' is a three-masted **schooner**, somewhat larger than the original two-masted vessels which carried the name. However, smaller sailing ships with the older sail arrangement are still numerous.*

scoff'law, (colloq.) person who disregards laws, esp. one who fails to pay traffic fines. **scoff'ing·ly** *adv.* **scoff** *n.* Derisive jest; object of derision or scoffing. **scoff'er** *n.*

scold (skōld) *v.* Castigate (person) verbally for fault etc. **scold'ing** *adj. & n.* **scold'ing·ly** *adv.* **scold** *n.* Railing or nagging woman.

sconce[1] (skŏns) *n.* Flat candlestick with handle; bracket candlestick to hang on wall.

sconce[2] (skŏns) *n.* Small fort or earthwork, usu. covering a ford, pass, etc.

Scone (skōon, skōn). Village in Perthshire, Scotland, ancient capital where Scottish kings were crowned; **Stone of** ~, stone on which Scottish kings sat at coronation ceremony, brought to England by Edward I and now preserved in coronation chair at Westminster Abbey.

scone (skōn, skŏn) *n.* Soft flat cake of flour, freq. with currants etc., usu. round or quadrant-shaped, orig. baked on a griddle.

scoop (skōop) *n.* 1. Short-handled deep shovel for dipping up and carrying such materials as flour, grain, coal; long-handled ladle; instrument with spoon- or gouge-shaped blade for cutting out piece from soft material or removing embedded substance, core, etc.; coal scuttle. 2. Motion as of, act of, scooping; slurring of interval by singer or fiddler. 3. (colloq.) Obtaining of news etc. by newspaper before, or to exclusion of, competitors, news so obtained. ~ *v.t.* 1. Lift (*up*), hollow (*out*), (as) with scoop. 2. (colloq.) Get advantage over (rival) by obtaining newspaper scoop.

scoot (skōot) *v.i.* Run, dart, make off.

scoot·er (skōo'ter) *n.* 1. Child's toy vehicle, consisting of a narrow footboard mounted on 2 tandem wheels, the front one attached to a long steering handle, propelled by pushes of 1 foot on the ground, the other foot resting on the footboard; (also **motor** ~) similar heavier vehicle for adults, with seat and motor. 2. Sailboat with runners for use on either ice or water.

scope (skōp) *n.* End aimed at, purpose (now rare); outlook, purview, sweep or reach of observation or action, range; opportunity, outlet; (naut.) length of cable out when ship rides at anchor; (colloq.) telescope or other instrument whose name ends in -SCOPE.

-scope *suffix.* Forming nouns denoting: (1) thing looked at or through (*kaleidoscope, telescope*); (2) instrument for observing or showing (*gyroscope, oscilloscope*).

Scopes (skōps), **John Thomas**

Grouped with the arachnids (spiders) and represented in fossils that are 300 million years old, the largest **scorpion** is an 8-in. long giant in West Africa. Some smaller ones have lethal stings.

(1901–70). Amer. teacher; convicted for breaking a law prohibiting teaching theory of evolution in Tennessee schools, 1925.

sco·pol·a·mine (skōpŏl'amēn, -mĭn) *n.* Syrupy alkaloid obtained from certain plants of nightshade family (Solanaceae), esp. henbane (*Hyoscamus niger*) and belladonna (*Atropa belladonna*); used as sedative, antispasmodic, and, combined with morphine, as an anesthetic.

scor·bu·tic (skŏrbū'tĭk) *adj. & n.* Of, like, (person) affected with, scurvy.

scorch (skŏrch) *v.* Burn surface of with flame or heat so as to discolor, injure, or pain; affect with sensation of burning; become discolored, slightly burned, etc., with heat; **scorched earth**, policy of a country threatened by invasion of destroying all means of sustenance and supply that might be of use to the invading enemy.

score (skōr, skŏr) *n.* 1. Notch cut, line cut, scratched, or drawn. 2. Account showing amount owed; reckoning, esp. for entertainment. 3. Wrong or grievance for which one seeks redress (**pay off old** ~s). 4. Reason, motive; **on that** ~, so far as that matter is concerned. 5. Number of points made by player or team in many games; **score'board**, large board for publicly displaying score; **score'card**, card for keeping score of game, contest, etc., and identifying players by name, number, and position. 6. Grade given on test or examination. 7. (pl. **score** exc. in **scores** = large numbers) Twenty; set of 20. 8. (mus.) Copy of composition showing instrumental and vocal parts; music for theatrical presentation, motion picture, etc. 9. (colloq.) Piece of good luck; situation, facts;

know the score, (fig.) be aware of essential facts. **score** *v.* (**scored, scor'ing**). 1. Mark with notches, incisions, or lines, slash, furrow; make (line, notch, incision). 2. Mark *up* amount owed; (fig.) mentally record (offense *against* offender). 3. Record (score in games), keep score; win and be credited with, make points in game, secure an advantage, have good luck. 4. Criticize (person) severely. 5. (mus.) Orchestrate; arrange *for* an instrument; write out in score. **score'less** *adj.* **scor'er** *n.*

sco·ri·a (skōr'ēa, skŏr'-) *n.* (pl. **sco·ri·ae** pr. skōr'ēē, skŏr'-). Cellular lava, fragments of this; slag. **sco·ri·a·ceous** (skōrēā'shus, skŏr-) *adj.*

sco·ri·fy (skōr'ĭfī, skŏr'-) *v.t.* (**-fied, -fy'ing**). Reduce to scoria or slag, esp. in assaying. **sco·ri·fi·ca·tion** (skōrĭfĭkā'shon, skŏr-) *n.*

scorn (skŏrn) *v.t.* Hold in contempt, despise; abstain from, refuse *to* do, as unworthy. ~ *n.* Contempt, derision; object of this. **scorn'ful** *adj.* **scorn'ful·ly** *adv.* **scorn'ful·ness, scorn'er** *ns.*

Scor·pi·o (skŏr'pēō), **Scor·pi·us** (skŏr'pēus). The Scorpion, a constellation; eighth sign (♏) of the zodiac, which the sun enters about Oct. 23.

scor·pi·on (skŏr'pēon) *n.* 1. Arachnid with lobsterlike claws and segmented tail that can be bent over to inflict poisoned sting on prey held in claws. 2. (Old Testament) Kind of whip, prob. armed with metal points. 3. **the S** ~: see SCORPIO.

Scot (skŏt) *n.* 1. Native of Scotland. 2. (hist.) One of an ancient Gaelic-speaking people who migrated from Ireland to Scotland in 6th c.

scot (skŏt) *n.* (hist.) Payment corresponding to modern tax or other assessed contribution; ~-**free**, unharmed, unpunished, safe, esp. in *get off, go,* ~-*free*.

Scotch (skŏch) *adj.* Of Scotland or its inhabitants (the modern in-

Rugged coastline at Caithness (above) typifies the severity of some of the landscape in **Scotland**. *Traditional activities include hammer-throwing at the Royal Braemar Gathering held annually in the Grampian region.*

often having a smoky flavor of peat, as distilled in Scotland. **Scotch** *n.* 1. Scottish form of English. 2. (colloq.) Scotch whisky.

sco·ter (skō′ter) *n.* (pl. **-ters**, collect. **-ter**). Any of several large sea ducks (genus *Melanitta*) of northern parts of Northern Hemisphere.

sco·tia (skō′sha) *n.* Concave molding esp. in base of column.

Scot·land (skŏt′land). Northern part of Gt. Britain, formerly a separate kingdom; capital, Edinburgh; the crowns of England and Scotland were united by the accession of James VI of Scotland (James I of England) to the English throne in 1603; the two parliaments were united by the Act of Union in 1707, when Scotland became a part of the United Kingdom.

Scot·land (skŏt′land) **Yard.** Headquarters of London metropolitan police, formerly in Great Scotland Yard, a short street off

...abitants of Scotland usu. prefer ...he form **Scottish** except in such ...xpressions as *Scotch whisky*); in ...he dialect(s) of English spoken in ...cotland; ~ **broth**, mutton broth ...hickened with pearl barley and ...egetables; **Scotch′man** (pl. ...**men**), **Scotch′woman** (pl. ...**women**), (Sc. **Scots-**), native of ...cotland; **Scotch mist**, thick wet

mist; **Scotch** (also **Scots**) **pine**, common pine (*Pinus sylvestris*) native to N. Europe and imported into N. Amer. as ornamental and timber tree; **Scotch tape**, (trademark) adhesive, usu. transparent, cellulose tape; **Scotch terrier**, short-legged terrier with a rough, wiry, grayish coat and short erect tail; **Scotch whisky**, whiskey,

Whitehall; in 1890 moved to New Scotland Yard on Thames Embankment and in 1967 to Broadway, Westminster; allusively, the Criminal Investigation Department (C.I.D.) of the Metropolitan Police Force.

Scoto- *prefix.* Scottish.

Scots (skŏts) *adj.* Scottish; **Scots'man** (pl. **-men**), **Scots'woman** (pl. **-women**), native of Scotland. **Scots** *n.* Scottish (esp. Lowlands) form of English.

Scott[1] (skŏt), **Dred** (1795?–1858). Black slave who sued for freedom on grounds of having spent some time in a nonslave state, but failed, U.S. Supreme Court refusing to recognize his status as a citizen.

Scott[2] (skŏt), **Robert Falcon** (1868–1912). British explorer, leader of 2 Antarctic expeditions, in the 2nd of which the S. Pole was reached on Jan. 18, 1912, but Scott and the rest of the party perished in a blizzard on the return journey.

Scott[3] (skŏt), **Sir Walter** (1771–1832). Scottish writer of historical novels and verse romances, author of *The Lady of the Lake* (in verse), and the novels *Waverley, Ivanhoe,* etc.

Scott[4] (skŏt), **Winfield** (1786–1866). Amer. army officer; commander of U.S. forces in Mexican War.

Scot·ti·cism (skŏt´ĭsĭzem) *n.* Scots phrase, idiom, word, pronunciation, etc.

Scot·tie, Scot·ty (skŏt´ē) *ns.* (pl. **-ties**). (colloq.) Scotch terrier.

Scot·tish (skŏt´ĭsh) *adj.* Con-

Above left: **Robert Falcon Scott,** *the British Antarctic explorer who reached the South Pole in 1912, only to perish on his return. Above right:* **Sir Walter Scott,** *prolific writer of historical novels.*

nected with, pertaining to, Scotland, its people, language, etc.

scoun·drel (skown´drel) *n.* Unscrupulous person, villain, rogue. **scoun'drel·ly** *adj.*

scour[1] (skowr, skow´er) *v.t.* Cleanse or brighten by friction; clean out by flushing with water, or (of water) by flowing through or over; purge drastically; clear (rust, stain) *away, off,* by rubbing etc. ~ *n.* Act, action, of scouring; artificial current or flow for clearing channel etc.; kind of diarrhea in cattle.

scour[2] (skowr, skow´er) *v.* Rove, range, go along hastily; hasten over or along, search rapidly.

scourge (skẽrj) *n.* Whip for punishing persons; person or thing regarded as instrument of divine or other vengeance or punishment. **scourg'er** *n.* **scourge** *v.t.* (**scourged, scourg·ing**). Use scourge on; chastise, afflict, oppress. [LL. *excoriare* strip off the hide]

scout[1] (skowt) *n.* 1. Soldier, plane, ship etc., sent out to reconnoiter position and movements of enemy. 2. Person whose job is to obtain information or locate new talent. 3. Member of the Boy Scouts of America, associated with an international scouting movement founded in 1908 in England by Lord Baden-Powell to develop boys' character by open-air activi-

ties; member of the Girl Scouts of the USA. 4. **scout master**, man in charge of group of scouts (sense 3). **scout** *v.i.* Act as scout.

scout[2] (skowt) *v.t.* Reject with scorn or ridicule.

scow (skow) *n.* Kind of large flat-bottomed square-ended boat used esp. as lighter.

scowl (skowl) *v.i.* Wear sullen look, frown ill-temperedly. ~ *n.* Scowling aspect, angry frown. **scowl'er** *n.* **scowl'ing·ly** *adv.*

Scrab·ble (skrăb´el) *n.* (trademark) Game in which players form words by placing lettered tiles on board similar to crossword puzzle diagram.

scrab·ble (skrăb´el) *v.i.* (**-bled, -bling**). Scratch or grope (*about*) to find or collect something. **scrab'bler** *n.*

scrag (skrăg) *n.* Lean skinny person, animal, etc.; bony part of animal's carcass, esp. of neck of mutton, as food; (slang) person's neck. **scrag'gy** *adj.* (**-gi·er, -gi·est**). **scrag'gi·ly** *adv.* **scrag'gi·ness** *n.* **scrag** *v.t.* (**scragged, scrag·ging**). Hang (on gallows), wring neck of, garotte.

scrag·gly (skrăg´lē) *adj.* (**-gli·er, -gli·est**). Scrubby, ragged, uneven, irregular.

scram (skrăm) *v.i.* (**scrammed, scram·ming**). (slang) Go away quickly, get out (usu. as imper.).

scram·ble (skrăm´bel) *v.* (**-bled, -bling**). 1. Make way over steep or rough ground by clambering, crawling, etc.; struggle to secure as much as possible of something from competitors; deal with in a hasty manner. 2. Cook (eggs) by stirring slightly in pan with butter, milk, etc., and heating; mix together indiscriminately or confusedly; alter frequency of the voice in telephoning or radiotelephony by means of automatic mechanical or electrical devices fitted to the transmitter so as to make the message unintelligible except to a person using a receiver fitted with a similar device. 3. (of military aircraft or their pilots) (Hasten to aircraft and) take off in response to alert. ~ n. 1. Eager struggle or competition (for). 2. Climb or walk over rough ground; motorcycle race over rough ground.

scram·bler (skrăm′blĕr) n. (esp.) Telephone or wireless transmitter fitted with a device for scrambling speech.

scrap[1] (skrăp) n. Small detached piece; shred or fragment; short piece of writing etc.; (pl.) odds and ends, fragments of uneaten food; (collect.) waste material, clippings, etc., of metal collected for reworking; metal wasted in production; residuum of melted fat; **scrap′book**, book for collection of newspaper clippings etc.; **scrap iron, metal**, scrap. **scrap′per** n. **scrap′py** adj. (**-pi·er, -pi·est**). Fragmented, disconnected. **scrap** v.t. (**scrapped, scrap·ping**). Consign to scrap heap; condemn as past use; discard.

scrap[2] (skrăp) n. (colloq.) Fight, quarrel. ~ v.i. Engage in a scrap. **scrap′per, scrap′pi·ness** ns. **scrap′py** adj. (**-pi·er, -pi·est**).

scrape (skrāp) v. (**scraped, scrap·ing**). 1. Clean, clear of projections, abrade, smooth, polish, etc., by drawing sharp or angular edge breadthways over, or by causing to pass over such edge; take (projection, stain, etc.) off, out, away, by scraping. 2. Draw along with scraping sound, produce such sound from, emit such sound. 3. Pass along something so as to graze or be grazed by it or just avoid doing so; ~ **through**, get through with a squeeze or narrow shave (freq. fig.). 4. Amass by scraping, with difficulty, by parsimony, etc.; contrive to gain; practice economy. **scrape** n. 1. Act or sound of scraping; scraping of foot in bowing. 2. Awkward predicament, difficult position, esp. as result of escapade etc. **scrap′er** n. (esp.) Scraping instrument in various technical operations; appliance fixed outside door of house, with horizontal blade for scraping mud etc. from shoes; (archaeol.) primitive wedge-shaped flint implement.

Scratch (skrăch). **Old** ~, the devil.

scratch (skrăch) v. 1. Score surface of, make long narrow superficial wounds in, with nail, claw, or something pointed; get (part of

body) scratched; form, excavate, by scratching; scrape without marking, esp. with fingernails to relieve itching; scratch oneself; make scratch; scrape *together* or *up*. 2. Score (something written) *out*, strike *off* with pencil etc.; erase name of, withdraw, from list of competitors etc. ~ n. 1. Mark or sound made by scratching; sound made by friction of needle in sound-recording apparatus and heard in playing of record etc.; spell of scratching oneself; slight wound. 2. Line from which competitors in race, or those receiving no start in handicap, start; zero, par, in games or contests in which handicaps are allowed; **come up to** ~, be ready to start race, match, etc., at the proper time; (fig.) be ready to embark on an enterprise, to fulfill one's obligations; **start from** ~, have no handicap (also fig.); ~ **pad**, pad of paper for jotting or scribbling on. **scratch** adj. Collected by haphazard, scratched together, heterogeneous.

scratch·y (skrăch′ē) adj. (**scratch·i·er, scratch·i·est**). (of drawing etc.) Done in scratches, careless, unskillful; (of pen) making scratching sound or liable to catch in paper; (of action etc.) uneven, ragged. **scratch′i·ly** adv. **scratch′i·ness** n.

scrawl (skrawl) v. Write, draw, in hurried, sprawling, untidy way; cover with scrawls. ~ n. Something scrawled; hasty or illegible writing. **scraw′ly** adj. (**scrawl·i·er, scrawl·i·est**).

scraw·ny (skraw′nē) adj. (**-ni·er, -ni·est**). Scraggy. **scraw′ni·ness** n.

scream (skrēm) v. Utter piercing cry, normally expressive of terror, pain, sudden or uncontrollable mirth, etc.; make noise like this; utter in screaming tone.

scream′ing adj. **scream′ing·ly** adv. **scream** n. Screaming cry or sound; (slang) irresistibly comical affair, person, or object.

scream·er (skrē′mĕr) n. (esp.) Large S. Amer. bird of family Anhimidae, with harsh cry; (slang) something that raises screams of laughter; (slang) exclamation mark.

scree (skrē) n. (freq. pl.) (Mountain slope covered with) loose stones that slide when trodden on.

screech (skrēch) n. Loud shrill harsh cry; ~ **owl**, small Amer. tufted owl (*Otus asio*) having quavering wail; (occas. pop.) barn owl or other small owl. **screech** v. Make, utter with, screech. **screech′y** adj. (**screech·i·er, screech·i·est**).

screed (skrēd) n. 1. Long and tedious harangue, letter, etc. 2. (plastering etc.) Strip of accurately leveled plaster on wall, ceiling, etc., as guide in running cornice, laying coat of plaster, etc.; board, strip of wood, used for leveling concrete etc.

screen (skrēn) n. 1. Partition partly shutting off part of church or room, esp. that between nave and choir of church; ornamental wall masking front of building. 2. Movable piece of furniture designed to shelter from excess of heat, light, draft, etc., or from observation; any object utilized as shelter esp. from observation, measure adopted for concealment, protection afforded by these; SMOKE screen; wind screen; (window) frame holding wire etc. mesh to let in air but keep out insects; (baseball) high barrier to keep ball

A Chinese lacquer **screen,** *now housed in the Victoria and Albert Museum, U.K., gives some indication of the fine degree of craftsmanship achieved in China during the times of the Emperors.*

*The **screw-palm** or pandanus tree is represented throughout the tropics of Asia, Africa and Australia. The leaves were used for plaiting and the 'nuts' (right) were roasted for eating by Australian Aboriginals.*

from striking spectators, going out of play, etc. 3. Upright surface on which images are projected or received, objects displayed, etc.; (also **silver** ~) moving pictures, films; **screen'play**, (script of) film; **screen'writer**, writer of this script. 4. Body, part of optical, electrical, or other instrument, serving to intercept light, heat, electricity, etc.; (photog.) transparent plate ruled with fine crosslines, through which picture etc. is photographed for halftone reproduction. 5. Large sieve to separate coarser from finer parts of sand, grain, coal, etc. 6. **screen printing**, process like stenciling with ink forced through prepared sheet of fine material (orig. silk), serigraphy. **screen** *v.t.* 1. Afford shelter to; hide partly or completely; (mil.) employ a body of men to cover (troop movement); furnish (radio tube) with screen; prevent from causing electrical interference; ~ **off**, shut off by means of, conceal behind, screen. 2. Show (esp. motion picture) on screen. 3. Clean, sift, grade (coal, gravel, etc.) by passing through a screen; scrutinize, subject (person) to tests to establish reliability etc.

screen·ings (skrē'nĭngz) *n.pl.* Material that has been screened; refuse separated by screening.

screw (skrōō) *n.* 1. Cylinder with spiral ridge (*thread*) running around it outside (**male** ~) or inside (**female** ~); metal male screw with slotted head and sharp point for fastening pieces of wood etc. together, or with blunt end to receive nut and bolt things together; wooden or metal etc. screw as part of appliance for exerting pressure; **have a** ~ **loose**, (colloq.) be

slightly mad; **put the** ~**s on, apply the** ~**s to,** (fig.) put moral pressure on, coerce. 2. (also ~ **propeller**) Propeller. 3. **screw'-driver**, tool with thin wedge-shaped end or blade for turning screws by slot in head; **screw eye**, screw having loop for head; **screw pine**, plant of tropical genus *Pandanus*, with slender palmlike stems and branches, with terminal crown of swordlike leaves; **screw'-worm**, parasitic larva of any of certain Amer. flies (genus *Callitroga*), which often infests wounds, nostrils, navel, etc. of animals, causing injuries, illness, or death. **screw** *v.* 1. Fasten, tighten, etc., by use of screw or screws; turn (screw), twist around like screw; make tauter or more efficient; revolve like screw. 2. Press hard on, oppress. 3. Be miserly; squeeze, extort *out* of. 4. Contort, distort, contract. 5. (vulg., of male) Copulate (with); ~ **up**, (slang) make mess of, bungle.

screw·ball (skrōō'bawl) *n. & adj.* (slang) Mad, crazy (person); (baseball) pitch that curves in opposite direction to normal curve.

screw·y (skrōō'ē) *adj.* (**screw·i·er, screw·i·est**). (slang) Mad,

crazy, suspicious.

scrib·ble (skrĭb'el) *v.* (**-bled, -bling**). Write hurriedly or carelessly. **scrib'bler** *n.* **scribble** *n.* Careless writing, thing carelessly written, scrawl.

scribe (skrīb) *n.* 1. Copyist, transcriber of manuscripts, calligrapher; (obs.) clerk, secretary. 2. Ancient Jewish maker and keeper of records etc.; member of class of professional interpreters of the Law after return from Captivity. 3. Tool for marking or scoring (wood, bricks, etc.) to indicate shape to be cut etc. ~ *v.t.* (**scribed, scrib·ing**). Mark with scribe.

scrim (skrĭm) *n.* Open-weave fabric used in bookbinding, upholstery, plastering, etc.

scrim·mage (skrĭm'ĭj) *n.* Tussle, confused struggle, brawl; (football) play in which center places it flat on ground with long axis at right angles to goal line, and puts it in play; **line of** ~, ~ **line**, imaginary line parallel to goal line passing through point of ball closest to defensive goal line when ball is resting on ground before being put in play. **scrimmage** *v.t.* (**-maged, -mag·ing**). Engage in scrimmage.

*Coastal **scrub** in Crete (left). Vegetation of this type is common in regions of poor soil, aridity and exposure to wind.*

in architecture, made to imitate scroll of parchment more or less exactly; volute of Ionic capital or of chair etc., head of violin etc., flourish in writing; any tracery of spiral or flowing lines. 3. ~ **saw**, fret saw, saw stretched in frame, for carving curved lines; **scroll'-work**, ornament of spiral or curving lines, esp. as cut by scroll saw. **scroll** *v.* Curl or roll up like paper; adorn with scrolls.

Scrooge (skrōōj), **Ebenezer.** Miserly curmudgeon in Charles Dickens' *Christmas Carol*; hence **scrooge**, miser.

scro·tum (skrō'tum) *n.* (pl. **-ta** pr. -ta, -tums). (anat.) Pouch or bag enclosing testicles. **scro'tal** *adj.*

scrounge (skrownj) *v.* (**scrounged, scroung·ing**). (colloq.) Appropriate without permission; cadge; search about. **scroung'er** *n.*

scrub[1] (skrŭb) *n.* (Ground covered with) plant community dominated by shrubs; stunted or insignificant person, animal, etc.; ~ **oak, pine**, stunted oak, pine, of several Amer. species; ~ **typhus**, acute febrile disease, caused by bites of certain larval mites, esp. prevalent in Japan; Japanese river fever. **scrub'by** *adj.* (**-bi·er, -bi·est**).

scrub[2] (skrŭb) *v.* (**scrubbed, scrub·bing**). 1. Rub hard to clean or brighten, esp. with soap and water applied with hard-bristled brush (**scrubbing brush**); use such brush; **scrub-up**, (esp., of surgeons etc.) scrub hands and arms thoroughly before performing surgical operation. 2. **scrub** (colloq.) Drop, cancel, postpone, (plan, event, etc.). 3. Pass (gas) through a scrubber to extract certain components. **scrub** *n.* Scrubbing, being scrubbed; (colloq.) second, usu. inferior, team.

scrub·ber (skrŭb'er) *n.* (esp.) Apparatus for removing impurities etc. from gas, smoke, etc., by passing it through a body or stream of water.

scruff (skrŭf) *n.* (also ~ **of the neck**) Back outer part of neck. **scruff'y** (skrŭf'ē) *adj.* (**scruff·i·er, scruff·i·est**). Unkempt.

scrum (skrŭm) *n.* (Rugby footb.) Formation in which two sets of forwards pack themselves together with heads down and try to obtain ball placed on the ground between them by pushing their opponents away from it.

scrump·tious (skrŭmp'shus) *adj.* (slang) Delicious, delightful.

scrunch (skrŭnch) *n. & v.* = CRUNCH.

scrimp (skrĭmp) *v.* Be frugal or sparing; skimp. **scrimp'y** *adj.*

scrim·shaw (skrĭm'shaw) *n.* Shells, pieces of ivory, etc., adorned with carved or colored designs done by sailors for amusement at sea.

scrip (skrĭp) *n.* 1. Provisional document issued to holder of fractional share of stock. 2. (hist.) Paper money in denominations of less than $1, issued in U.S.; temporary document issued in lieu of and resembling paper currency. [abbrev. of (*sub*)*scrip*(*tion receipt*)]

script (skrĭpt) *n.* 1. (law) Original document. 2. Handwriting, written characters; printed cursive characters, imitation of handwriting in type; style of handwriting in which characters resemble those of print and are not joined together. 3. Manuscript, typescript, of play, film, etc.; text of broadcaster's announcement or talk. ~ *v.i.* (colloq.) Compose script of play etc.

*The **scrum** is a particular feature of Rugby football and it is a means of allowing the forwards of each team to work en masse to obtain possession of the ball.*

Script. *abbrev.* Scriptural; Scripture.

scrip·ture (skrĭp'cher) *n.* Sacred book or writings; (usu. **S~** freq. pl.) Bible; (attrib.) taken from or relating to the Bible. **scrip'-tur·al** *adj.* **scrip'tur·al·ly** *adv.*

scriv·ener (skrĭv'ner) *n.* (hist.) Writer, drafter of documents, notary, broker, moneylender.

scrod (skrŏd) *n.* Young codfish.

scrof·u·la (skrŏf'yula) *n.* Name formerly given to a prob. tubercular condition affecting the lymphatic glands and bones. **scrof'u·lous** *adj.*

scroll (skrōl) *n.* 1. Roll of parchment or paper, esp. written on; book or volume of ancient roll form. 2. Ornamental design, esp.

1 Rustic capitals, 4th-5th c.
2 Uncial, mid-5th c.
3 Half-uncial, 6th c.
4 Insular (Anglo-Saxon) majuscule, early 8th c.
5 Carolingian minuscule, early 9th c.
6 Gothic, circa 1250
7 Humanist script, late 15th c.
8 Italic, late 15th c.
9 Secretary hand, 1593
10 Court hand, 1611
11 Copperplate, 1673

scru·ple (skrōō′pel) n. 1. In apothecaries' weight, unit equivalent to 20 grains or ⅓ drachm; symbol Ə. 2. Doubt, uncertainty, or hesitation in regard to right and wrong, duty, etc. ~ v.i. (**-pled, -pling**). Hesitate owing to scruples *to do*.

scru·pu·lous (skrōō′pyu*lus*) *adj*. Conscientious even in small matters, not neglectful of details, punctilious; overattentive to details, esp. to small points of conscience. **scru′pu·lous·ly** *adv*. **scru′pu·lous·ness** n. **scru·pu·los·i·ty** (skrōōpyu*lŏs′ĭtē*) n. (pl. **-ties**).

scru·ti·nize (skrōō′tinīz) *v.t.* (**-nized, -niz·ing**). Look closely at, examine in detail. **scru′ti·niz·er** n.

scru·ti·ny (skrōō′tinē) n. (pl. **-nies**). Critical gaze; close investi-

The various forms of handwriting or script have often been determined by the writing materials, the time available and the need for legibility. Aesthetic factors have also been influential.

gation, examination into details.

scu·ba (skōō′ba) n. & *adj*. Self-contained underwater breathing apparatus.

scud (skŭd) *v.i.* (**scud·ded, scud·ding**). Run, fly, straight and fast, esp. with smooth or easy motion; (naut.) run before the wind. ~ n. Driving shower of rain, gust of wind.

scuff (skŭf) v. Walk with dragging feet, shuffle; shuffle, drag along (feet); wear, rub, esp. with feet. ~ n. Mark of scuffing; backless slipper.

scuf·fle (skŭf′el) *v.i.* (**-fled, -fling**) & n. (Engage in) confused struggle or scrambling fight.

scull (skŭl) n. Each of pair of light oars used by single rower; oar used to propel boat by working it from side to side over stern, reversing blade at each turn; light, narrow boat for sculling, esp. for racing. ~ v. Propel (boat), propel boat, with scull(s). **scull′er** n. User of sculls; boat intended for sculling.

scul·ler·y (skŭl′erē) n. (pl. **-ler·ies**). Back kitchen, small room attached to kitchen for washing dishes etc.

scul·lion (skŭl′yon) n. (archaic and rhet.) Menial servant, washer of dishes and pots.

scul·pin (skŭl′pĭn) n. (pl. **-pins**, collect. **-pin**). Small Amer. sea fish of family Cottidae, with barbels on head.

sculpt (skŭlpt) v. Sculpture.

sculp·tor (skŭlp′ter), fem.

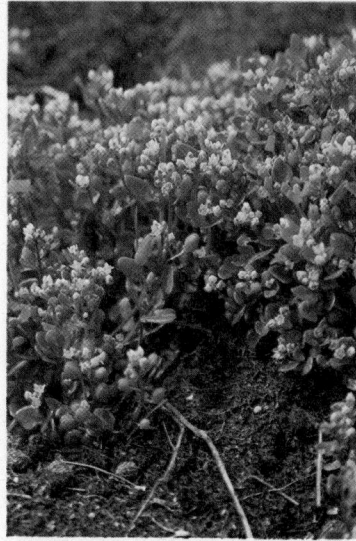

*Despite its name, **scurvy grass** is a form of cress, and not a grass. It grows in Europe and parts of Asia and was once used to prevent scurvy among sailors.*

*Reeds for thatching need to be as long as possible. In marshy areas of Norfolk, U.K., where the mechanical mower cannot be used, a **scythe** will cut them close to the ground.*

sculp·tress (skŭlp′trĭs) *ns*. One who practices sculpture.

sculp·ture (skŭlp′cher) *n*. 1. Art of forming representations of objects etc. or abstract designs in the round or in relief by chiseling stone, carving wood, modeling clay, casting metal, or similar processes; work of sculpture. 2. (zool., bot.) Raised or sunk markings on shell etc. **sculp′tu·ral** *adj*. **sculp′-tu·ral·ly** *adv*. **sculpture** *v*. (**-tured, -tur·ing**). Form by, represent in, sculpture; adorn with sculpture; be sculptor, practice sculpture. **sculp′tured** *adj*. (esp. biol.) With markings etc. like those produced by sculpture; (as though) chiselled.

scum (skŭm) *n*. Impurities that rise to surface of liquid; (fig.) worst part, refuse. **scum′my** *adj*. (**-mi·er, -mi·est**). **scum** *v*. (**scummed, scum·ming**). Take scum from, skim; be, form, scum on; (of liquid) develop scum.

scup·per (skŭp′er) *n*. Opening in ship's side level with deck to drain off water.

scurf (skẽrf) *n*. Flakes on surface of skin cast off as fresh skin develops below, esp. those of head; any scaly matter on a surface. **scurf′y** *adj*. (**scurf·i·er, scurf·i·est**).

scur·ril·ous (skẽr′ilus, skŭr′-) *adj*. Grossly or obscenely abusive; given to, expressed with, low buffoonery. **scur′ril·ous·ly** *adv*. **scur·ril·i·ty** (skurĭl′ĭtē) *n*. (pl. **-ties**).

scur·ry (skẽr′ē, skŭr′ē) *v.i.* (**-ried, -ry·ing**). Run hurriedly, scamper. ~ *n*. Act of scurrying, rush, bustle; flurry.

scur·vy (skẽr′vē) *n*. Disease resulting from deficiency of vitamin C, characterized by swollen gums, hemorrhage, esp. into skin and mucous membrane, and great debility, formerly common among sailors and others who lived for long periods without fresh vegetables; ~ **grass**, any of several cresses used against scurvy, esp. *Cochlearia officinalis*, found in Arctic regions. **scurvy** *adj*. (**-vi·er, -vi·est**). (archaic) Contemptible, low, mean. **scur′vi·ly** *adv*.

scutch (skŭch) *v.t.* Dress (fibrous material, esp. retted flax) by beating. **scutch′er** *n*. Hand tool for scutching flax; machine for scutching; part of threshing machine for striking off the grain. **scutch** *n*. 1. Scutcher. 2. Bricklayer's tool for cutting bricks etc. 3. Refuse of scutched flax.

scutch·eon (skŭch′on) *n*. ESCUTCHEON; pivoted cover of keyhole; plate for name or inscription.

scu·tel·lum (skūtĕl′um) *n*. (pl. **-tel·la** pr. -tĕl′a). Small shield, plate, or scale, in plants; shieldlike part of insect; one of the horny scales on bird's foot. **scu·tel·late** (skūtĕl′ĭt, -āt, skū′telāt), **scu·tel·lat·ed** (skū′telātĭd) *adjs*. **scu·tel·la·tion** (skūtelā′shon) *n*.

scut·tle[1] (skŭt′el) *n*. 1. Shallow open basket for carrying corn, earth, etc. 2. Metal or other recep-

tacle for carrying and holding small supply of coal (**coal** ~) for a fire in a room.

scut·tle[2] (skŭt′el) *n*. Lidded opening smaller than hatchway in ship's deck; similar opening in ship's side for ventilation, lighting, etc.; lidded opening in floor or roof of house; **scut′tlebutt**, ship's cask of drinking water; (colloq.) gossip, rumor. **scuttle** *v.t.* (**-tled, -tling**). Cut hole(s) in (ship, boat, etc.), sink thus; (also fig.).

scut·tle[3] (skŭt′el) *v.i.* (**-tled, -tling**). Scurry, run away, make off. ~ *n*. Hurried gait, precipitate flight or departure.

scu·tum (skū′tum) *n*. (pl. **-ta** pr. -ta). (zool.) Bony, horny, etc., plate, esp. second of three parts forming upper surface of dorsal part of thorax in insects; shieldlike dermal plate in crocodile, turtle, etc.

Scyl·la (sĭl′a). (Gk. myth.) Female sea monster who devoured sailors when they tried to navigate the narrow channel between her cave and the whirlpool CHARYBDIS; later legend substituted a dangerous rock for the monster and located it on the Italian side of the Strait of Messina; hence, ~ **and Charybdis**, dangers such that to avoid the one is to court the other.

scy·pho·zo·an (sīfozō′an) *adj*. & *n*. (Member) of the Scyphozoa, a class of coelenterates comprising the true marine jellyfishes.

scythe (sīdh) *n*. Agricultural implement for mowing and reaping, with long thin slightly curved blade fastened at an angle with handle and wielded with long sweeping stroke. ~ *v.t.* (**scythed, scyth·ing**). Cut with scythe.

SD *abbrev.* South Dakota.

S.D. *abbrev.* South Dakota; special delivery.

S. Dak. *abbrev.* South Dakota.

SE, S.E., s.e. *abbrevs.* Southeast(ern).

Se *symbol.* Selenium.

sea (sē) *n.* 1. Continuous body of salt water covering most of Earth's surface; part of this having certain land limits or washing a particular coast and having a proper name; large lake or landlocked body of water; **at ~**, away from land, aboard ship; (fig.) perplexed, bewildered, at a loss; **the high ~s**: see HIGH; **the seven ~s**, the Arctic, Antarctic, N. and S. Pacific, N. and S. Atlantic, and Indian Oceans. 2. Local motion or state of the sea; swell, rough water. 3. Large quantity or level expanse *of.* 4. **~ anchor**, floating, expanding anchor, usu. of canvas, used to keep a boat's head into the wind in rough weather; drag anchor; **~anemone**, any of numerous usu. large and solitary polyps with bright colors and many petallike tentacles surrounding mouth: **sea′bed**, bottom of ocean; **Sea′bee**, member of

The southern **sea lion** *is one of several varieties of eared-seals. They differ from the fur seals by having blunt snouts, a less luxuriant coat, and different hind-flippers.*

Sea-lions

naval construction battalion; **sea′-bird**, bird frequenting sea; **sea′-board**, coast bordering the sea; **sea′borne**, conveyed by sea; **sea breeze**, cool breeze blowing landward from sea, usu. in daytime; **sea calf**, common seal; **sea chest**, sailor's chest; **sea coal**, (archaic) coal (because formerly brought by sea from Newcastle to London etc.); coal mined from seacoast veins; **sea′coast**, land adjacent to the sea; **sea′cock**, valve by which seawater can be let into ship's interior; **sea′cow**, manatee or other sirenian; **sea cucumber**, one of the holothurians, esp. the bêche-de-mer; **sea dog**, old sailor, privateer or pirate, esp. of Elizabethan days; **sea eagle**, any of the various eagles feeding largely on fish, esp. the white-tailed eagle; **sea ear**, haliotis; **sea elephant**, elephant seal, large seal of S. hemisphere with proboscis; **sea fan**, coral with fanlike skeleton; **sea′farer**, traveler by sea, sailor; **sea′faring** (*adj. & n.*); **sea′food**, sea fish, shellfish, as food; **sea front**, part of town etc. facing sea; **sea′going**, (of ship) designed for open sea, not rivers, etc.; seafaring; **sea green** (*n.*) **sea-green** (*adj.*), (of) bluish green, as of sea; **sea gull**, gull; **sea hog**, porpoise; **sea horse**, hippocampus, small fish covered with rough bony plates, with prehensile tail and forepart of body resembling horse's head and neck; walrus; (Gk. and Rom. myth.) fabulous marine animal with foreparts of horse and tail of fish, drawing sea god's chariot; **sea-island cotton**, fine variety of long-stapled cotton, grown orig. and esp. on islands off coast of Georgia and

South Carolina; **Sealab**, one of several U.S. Navy laboratories for deep-sea research in oceanography etc.; **sea lane**, course prescribed for ocean steamers; **sea lavender**, any maritime herb of genus *Limonium*, of plumbago family; **sea lawyer**, argumentative or captious sailor; **sea legs**, ability to walk on deck of rolling ship; **sea level**, mean level of sea, mean level between high and low tides, used as a standard for measurements of heights and depths; **sea lily**, crinoid; **sea lion**, any of several large-eared seals; **sea′man**, (pl. **-men**), sailor; sailor below rank of officer; navigator; **sea′manship**, skill of good seaman; **sea′mark**, conspicuous object serving to guide or warn sailors in navigation; **sea mew**, common gull; **sea mile**: see MILE; **sea′mount**, underwater mountain; **sea mouse**, pop. name of marine annelid worm, covered with minute iridescent setae, of the genus *Aphrodite*; **sea onion**, squill; **sea otter**, rare (once almost extinct) large otter (*Enhydra lutris*) of the N. Amer. Pacific coast, having lustrous, extremely valuable fur; **sea pink**, see THRIFT def. 2; **sea′plane**, airplane fitted with floats to enable it to alight or take off from water; **sea′port**, (town

Because man has always been a land dweller, it is not surprising that some of the stranger marine organisms were given common names which are based more on their superficial resemblance to land objects, than to their true status. For example, a **sea cucumber** *is not a plant but an animal; a* **sea horse** *is a fish; although a* **sea slug** *is a mollusk.*

male
female
young

1 sea-snail. 2 sea-otter. 3 sea-snake 4 purple starfish. 5 gooseberry sea-squirt. 6 sea-vases. 7 periwinkles. 8 sea-anemones. 9 sea-horses 10 sea-mouse. 11 sea-cucumber 12 sea-urchins. 13 sea-slug.

with) harbor or port on seacoast; **sea power**, naval strength, nation having this; **sea robin**, any of a family (Triglidae) of marine fishes having spiny fins, broad bony heads, and very long pectoral fins; **sea room**, unobstructed space at sea for ship to maneuver in; **sea rover**, pirate; **sea′scape**, picture of a scene at sea; **Sea Scout**, member of organization training SCOUTS (sense 3) in seamanship; **sea serpent**, sea monster of great length and more or less resembling a serpent, freq. alleged to have been seen at sea; **sea′shell**, shell of any saltwater mollusk; **sea′shore**, land close to sea, ground between high- and low-water marks; **sea′sick**, suffering from nausea and vomiting induced by motion of ship at sea; **sea′sickness** (*n.*); **sea′side**, edge of sea, seacoast as health or pleasure resort; **sea slug**, marine gastropod mollusk of which the shell is absent or internal; **sea snake**, any of several poisonous marine snakes

(family Hydrophidae), living chiefly in the Pacific and Indian oceans; **sea squirt**, sessile marine animal of subphylum Urochordata, which squirts water when touched; **sea swallow**, tern; **sea trout**, salmon trout; any of various sea fishes; **sea urchin**, marine animal of order Echinoidea, esp. one of nearly globular form covered with (freq. very sharp) movable spines; **sea′wall**, wall or embankment made to check encroachment of sea or act as breakwater; **sea′ward**, with sea exposure; from the sea; (also **seawards**) in the direction of, or toward, the sea; **sea′weed**, plant growing in sea, esp. marine alga; **sea′worthy**, (of ship) in fit state to put to sea, **sea′worthiness** (*n.*)

Depending on the weather, the **sea** *has many moods. When backed by an ocean and often by storm winds, the effect of waves can have a strong erosive effect on rock.*

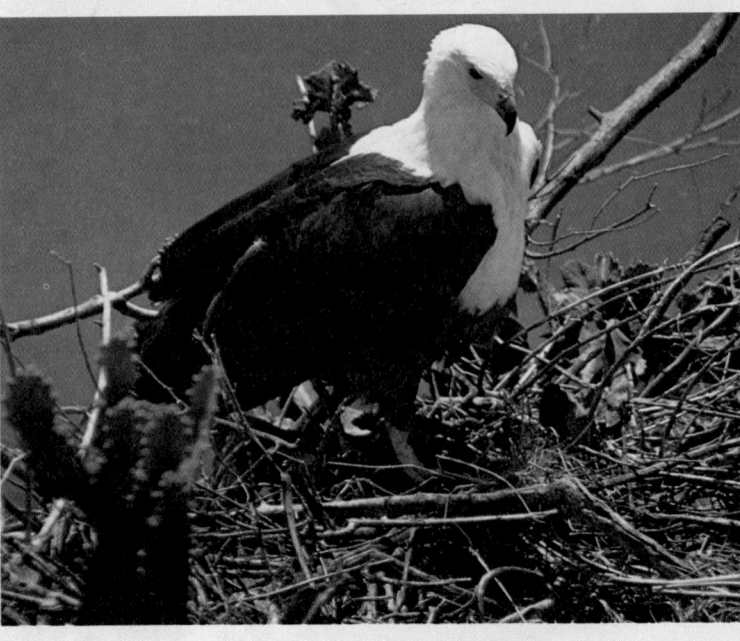

The Madagascar fish or **sea eagle** *is one of the smallest birds in a group of predators which include the bald eagle of the U.S.A. While some birds catch live fish, others eat carrion.*

Sea (sē) **Islands.** Group of islands in the Atlantic Ocean, off the coasts of South Carolina, Georgia, and N. Florida.

seal[1] (sēl) *n.* (pl. **seals**, collect. **seal**). Marine amphibious fish-eating mammal, of family Phocidae, with limbs developed into flippers and adapted for swimming, elongated body covered with thick fur or bristles, and short tail, hunted for its hides and oil; (also **seal′skin**) skin or prepared fur of seals; coat, cape, etc. made of this. **seal** *v.i.* Hunt seals. **seal′er** *n.* (esp.) Ship or man engaged in seal hunting.

seal[2] (sēl) *n.* 1. (Impressed device on) piece of wax etc. attached to document as evidence of authenticity of signature etc., or on folded letter, envelope flap, door, lid of box, etc., so that it cannot be opened without breaking seal; impression stamped on a wafer etc. stuck to document as symbol equivalent to wax seal; decorative adhesive stamp other than postage stamp; (fig.) mark of ownership; obligation to silence or secrecy. 2. Engraved stamp of metal or other hard material used to make impression on wax etc., used as seal; this as mark of office; **Great S ~**, seal used for authentication of important documents issued in name of highest executive authority of nation or state; **~ ring**, finger ring with seal. 3. Substance used to close aperture etc., esp. water standing in drainpipe to prevent ascent of foul air. **seal** *v.t.* Place seal on (document), fasten (letter etc.), esp. with seal or sealing wax; close tightly or hermetically; stop or shut *up*; (fig.) prove authenticity of (devotion etc.) *with* one's life etc.; set significant mark on; set apart, destine, devote; decide irrevocably; **~ off**, cut off (an area) so as to prevent entry or exit. **sealed** *adj.* **seal′ing** *n.* (esp.) **~ wax**, colored mixture of shellac, rosin, and turpentine, which becomes soft when heated and hardens as it cools, thus easily receiving and preserving the impression of a seal, used for sealing letters, documents, etc.

seal·ant (sē′lant) *n.* Sealing substance.

Seal·y·ham (sē′lēhăm, -lēam) *n.* Wiry-haired, long-bodied, short-legged terrier, usu. white with brown or gray markings on head, noted for spirit and gameness. [f. name of estate in Dyfed, Wales]

seam (sēm) *n.* Line of junction between two edges, esp. those of two pieces of cloth etc. sewn together, or of boards fitted edge

1533

Seals are aquatic mammals found in circumpolar waters of both hemispheres of the earth. The largest animal in the group is the elephant seal which may be up to 20 ft. long and an adult male can weigh up to 8,000 lb. In contrast, the ringed seal is only 5 ft. long and rarely exceeds a weight of 200 lb. Other varieties vary between these extremes.

elephant seal

leopard seal

Weddell seal

harp seal

seal and young

ringed seal

banded or ribbon seal

common seal and young

to edge; line, groove, furrow, formed by two abutting edges, mark resembling this; scar; line of purl stitches in knitting resembling sewn seam; thin layer or stratum, esp. of coal, between two wider strata. **~** v. Join *together*, *up*, etc., with seam(s); (knitting) make seam stitch; score or mark with seams, furrow, ridge. **seam'less** *adj.* **seam'er** n.

seam·stress (sēm'strĭs; *Brit.* sĕm'strĭs), **semp·stress** (sĕmp'-strĭs, sĕm'-) ns. Sewing woman.

seam·y (sē'mē) *adj.* (**seam·i·er**, **seam·i·est**). Showing seams; **~ side**, wrong side of garment etc. where rough edges of seams are visible; (usu. fig.) of worst, roughest, or least presentable aspect, esp. of life.

Sean·ad Eir·eann (shăn'adh ār'an). Upper Chamber (Senate) of the Republic of Ireland, with 60 members. [Ir., = "Irish senate"]

sé·ance (sā'ahns) n. Sitting of society or deliberative body; meeting for exhibition or investigation of spiritualistic phenomena.

sear (sēr) *v.t.* Wither up, blast (rare); scorch, esp. with hot iron, cauterize, brand; (fig.) render (conscience etc.) incapable of feeling. **~** *adj.* SERE.

search (sĕrch) v. Examine thoroughly (place, person, etc.) for what may be found or to find something of which presence is known or suspected; make search or investigation (*for*); **~ me!** (slang) exclamation implying that the speaker has no knowledge of some fact or no idea what course to take. **search'ing** *adj.* (of examination etc.) Thoroughgoing, leaving no loopholes. **search'ing·ly** *adv.* **search** n. Act of searching, investigation, quest; **right of ~**, belligerent's right to stop neutral vessel and search it for contraband; **search'light**, lamp designed to throw strong beam of light in any desired direction, used in warfare for discovering hostile aircraft, observing movements of troops, passing ships, etc.; light from this; **search party**, party of persons going out to look for lost or concealed person or thing; **search warrant**, legally issued warrant to enter premises to search for suspected persons, stolen property, or other things kept or concealed in violation of law.

sea·son (sē'zon) n. 1. Each of the periods into which year is divided by Earth's changing position in regard to sun, with particular conditions of weather etc., esp. one of the four equal periods (spring, summer, autumn, winter) marked by passage of sun from equinox to solstice and from solstice to equinox; or each of two periods,

rainy and dry, into which year is divided in tropical climates; time of year when a plant flourishes, blooms, etc., or when an animal pairs, breeds, is hunted, etc., or which is regularly devoted to a particular occupation etc., or when a particular place is most frequented by fashionable society. 2. Proper time, favorable opportunity; period of indefinite or various length; **~ ticket**, ticket issued, usu. at reduced rates, permitting any number of journeys to be taken, performances attended, etc., within specified length of time. **season** v. 1. Bring into efficient or sound condition by habituation, exposure, special preparation, use, or lapse of time; inure, mature; become fit for use by being seasoned. 2. Make palatable or piquant by introduction of salt, condiments, wit, jests, etc.; give zest to, flavor; temper, moderate.

sea·son·a·ble (sē'zonabel) *adj.* Suitable to, of the kind usual at, the season; opportune, meeting the needs of the occasion. **sea'son·a·bly** *adv.* **sea'son·a·ble·ness** n.

sea·son·al (sē'zonal) *adj.* Occur-

A Gipsy **seamstress** *sits on the shafts of a caravan as she sews colorful decorations on to a garment. Some women earn money by sewing at home for clothing manufacturers.*

ring at a particular season; (of trades, workers, etc.) dependent on the seasons, employed only during a particular season. **sea'son·al·ly** *adv.* **sea'son·er** n.

sea·son·ing (sē'zonĭng) n. (esp.) Substance for seasoning food (see SEASON v. sense 2).

seat (sēt) n. 1. Manner of sitting, esp. on horse. 2. Place on which person sits; (right to) use of seat; right to sit as member esp. of legislature, court, etc.; authority or dignity symbolized by sitting on particular seat or throne; something made for sitting upon; part of chair etc. on which occupant sits; sitting part of body, buttocks; part of garment covering this; **~ belt**, strap securing occupant to seat in aircraft, automobile, etc. 3. Site, location; temporary or permanent scene; country mansion, esp. with park or large grounds. **seat** *v.t.* 1. Cause to sit, place *oneself* in sitting posture. 2. Fit or provide with seats; (of room etc.) have seats for (specified number). 3. Mend seat of (chair, trousers, etc.). 4. Establish in position; fix in particular place.

-seater n. (in comb.) **single-~**, **two-~**, etc., automobile, airplane, etc., with seat(s) for one, two, etc.

seat·ing (sē'tĭng) n. (esp.) Seats, arrangement, provision, of seats.

SEATO, S.E.A.T.O. *abbrevs*

*Picking grapes in a South Australian vineyard. In Australia and the U.S.A., there are many **seasonal** workers, who move from district to district, harvesting different crops according to season.*

South East Asia Treaty Organization.

se·ba·ceous (sĭbā′shus) *adj*. Of tallow or fat, fatty; ~ **duct, gland,** etc., organ secreting or conveying fatty matter that lubricates hair and skin.

Se·bas·tian (sĭbăs′chan), **St.** (3rd c.). Roman soldier and Christian martyr, usu. represented as youth pierced by many arrows.

Se·bas·to·pol (sĭbăs′topōl) = SEVASTOPOL.

seb·or·rhe·a (sĕborē′a) *n*. Excessive discharge from the sebaceous glands. **seb·or·rhe′ic, seb·or·rhe′al** *adjs*.

SEC *abbrev*. Securities and Exchange Commission.

sec[1] (sĕk) *n*. (colloq.) SECOND *n*.
sec[2] (sĕk) *adj*. (of wine) Dry.
sec[3] (sĕk) *abbrev*. SECANT *n*. sense 1.

sec. *abbrev*. Secretary.

se·cant (sē′kănt, -kant) *adj*. (math.) Cutting, intersecting. ~ *n.* 1. (trig., function of angle in right-angled triangle) Ratio of side adjacent given acute angle to the hypotenuse (reciprocal of COSINE). 2. (geom.) Line cutting another, esp. straight line cutting curve at two or more points.

se·cede (sĭsēd′) *v.i.* (**-ced·ed, -ced·ing**). Withdraw formally from membership esp. of church or federation of states. **se·ced′er** *n*.

se·ces·sion (sĭsĕsh′on) *n*. Act of seceding, body of seceders; **War of S~,** CIVIL WAR (1861–5), which arose from an attempt by 11 of the southern states to secede from the U.S. **se·ces′sion·al** *adj*. **se·ces′sion·ism, se·ces′sion·ist** *ns*.

se·clude (sĭklood′) *v.t.* (**-clud·ed, -clud·ing**). Keep retired or away from company.

se·clu·sion (sĭkloo′zhon) *n*. Secluding, being secluded; retirement, privacy, avoidance of company; secluded place.

sec·ond (sĕk′ond) *adj*. Next after first in order of time, position, quality, etc.; next in rank, quality, degree, etc., *to*; other, another; (mus., of part) next below highest in concerted music; that performs such a part; ~ **base,** (baseball) base opposite home plate on diamond, touched second by runner; ~ **best,** (what is) next in quality, inferior, to the first; **come off ~ best,** be beaten (in argument etc.); ~ **class,** class next to first; (of postal matter) consisting of periodicals sent from publishing office; ~-**class** (*adj.*) inferior in quality, second-rate; (*adv.*) by the second class; **S~**

Coming, return of Christ in glory, esp. as preliminary to Last Judgment; ~ **cousin**: see COUSIN; **S~ Empire,** (Ger. hist.) see GERMANY; (Fr. hist.) that of Napoleon III (1852–70); ~ **fiddle,** secondary role or person playing such role; ~ **growth,** tree growth in area stripped of virgin forest; ~-**guess** (*v.*), know only by hindsight; predict (event) or correctly guess what another intends; **sec′ondhand,** not new, not original, previously worn, used, etc., by another; **second lieutenant,** U.S. Army, Marine, or Air Force officer of lowest commissioned rank; **second nature,** acquired tendency or habit that has become instinctive; **second person,** (gram.) form of verb or pronoun referring to person(s) addressed; **second-rate,** of inferior quality, value, etc.; **second-rater,** one of inferior quality; **Second Republic,** French Republic of 1848–52; **second sight,** faculty, claimed by, or attributed to, some persons, of seeing, as in a vision, future events; **second-story man,** (colloq.) burglar who enters by climbing to upper story; **second-string,** (colloq.) substitute player for position on football etc. team; lower in rank, significance, etc.; **second thoughts,** reconsideration, decision or opinion after reconsidering matter; **second wind,** breathing with less effort after exhaustion that occurs during initial stages of great effort; renewed energy for continuing any task. **second** *n*. 1. Second thing etc.; second person in race etc.; (person who takes) second class in examination. 2. (mus.) Next to highest part; interval of which the span involves only two alphabetical names of notes; harmonic combination of the two notes thus separated. 3. (pl.) Goods of quality inferior to best. 4. Supporter, helper, esp. person representing and supporting principal in boxing or duel. 5. Sixtieth part of minute of time or angular measurement; vaguely, a short time; ~ **hand,** hand or pointer in some watches and clocks recording seconds. 6. (in motor vehicle) Second gear. **second** *adv*. Second-class. ~ *v.t.* Supplement, support, back up; esp. support (motion, mover) in debate etc. as necessary preliminary to further discussion or adoption of motion. **sec′ond·ly** *adv*. **sec′ond·er** *n*.

sec·ond·ar·y (sĕk′ondĕrē) *adj*. Not in the first class in dignity, importance, etc., of minor importance, subordinate; subsidiary, auxiliary; not original or primary, derivative, belonging to a second stage or period; ~ **accent (stress),** accent weaker than primary accent;

Found only in Africa, south of the Sahara, the **secretary bird** *is conspicuous for its long legs and tail. Its name is derived from its backward sloping crest which was said to resemble a writer in earlier times who had his pens stuck behind his ear. The birds are about 18 ins. tall.*

~ **color**: see COLOR; ~ **education**, education between primary or elementary and higher or university education; ~ **feather**, feather growing from second joint of bird's wing; ~ **school**, school giving secondary education; ~ **sex characteristic**, any physical characteristic distinctive of one sex but not directly related to reproduction. **sec·ond·a·ri·ly** *adv.* **sec'ond·ar·y** *n.* (pl. **-ar·ies**). Secondary feather; **S** ~, (geol.) Secondary period.

sec·ond·ly (sĕk'ondlē) *adv.* In the second place.

se·cre·cy (sē'kresē) *n.* (pl. **-cies**). Being secret.

se·cret (sē'krĭt) *adj.* Hidden, concealed, not (to be) made known; known only to the initiated; not given to revealing secrets; ~ **agent**, spy; ~ **ballot**, ballot in which voters' choices are not made public; ~ **police**, political police of a totalitarian state; ~ **service**, government department that secures information etc. without public disclosure; **S ~ Service**, arm of U.S. Treasury Department responsible for suppression of counterfeiters and guarding the President and his family. **se'cret·ly** *adv.* **secret** *n.* Thing (to be) kept secret; thing known only to

initiated or to a limited number; mystery; **in** ~, secretly.

sec·re·tar·i·at (sĕkrĭtār'ēat) *n.* Office of secretary; members of government administrative office collectively; (premises of) administrative office or department headed by secretary-general.

sec·re·tar·y (sĕk'rĭtĕrē; *Brit.* sĕk'rĭtrē) *n.* (pl. **-tar·ies**). 1. Person employed by another to assist him in correspondence, literary work, and other confidential matters; official appointed by society, company, etc., to keep its records, conduct correspondence, etc. 2. Principal assistant of government minister or ambassador etc.; ~ **-general**, (pl. **-tar·ies-general**), principal administrative officer of organization; ~ **of state**, U.S. Cabinet member who administers State Department and is responsible for conduct of nation's foreign policy. 3. Writing desk, escritoire. 4. ~ **bird**, long-legged long-tailed raptorial African bird (*Sagittarius serpentarius*), with crest of long feathers (thought to resemble pens stuck behind the ear). **sec·re·tar·i·al** (sĕkrĭtĕr'ēal) *adj.* **sec're·tar·y·ship** *n.*

se·crete (sĭkrēt') *v.t.* (**-cret·ed, -cret·ing**). 1. Put into place of concealment. 2. Produce by

secretion. **se·cre·to·ry** *adj.*

se·cre·tion (sĭkrē'shon) *n.* 1. Concealing, concealment. 2. Action of gland etc. in extracting and elaborating certain substances from blood, sap, etc., to fulfill function within body or be excreted; any substance (as saliva, urine, resin) produced by such process.

se·cre·tive (sē'krĭtĭv, sĭkrē'-) *adj.* Given to making secrets, uncommunicative, needlessly reserved. **se'cre·tive·ly** *adv.* **se'cre·tive·ness** *n.*

sect (sĕkt) *n.* Body of persons agreed upon religious doctrines usu. different from those of an established or orthodox church; party or faction in a religious body; religious denomination; school of opinion in philosophy, politics, etc. **sec·tar·i·an** (sĕktār'ēan) *adj. & n.* **sec·tar·i·an·ism** *n.*

sect. *abbrev.* Section.

sec·tion (sĕk'shon) *n.* 1. Cutting (rare exc. in ref. to surgery etc.). 2. Part cut off from something; one of the parts into which something is divided; one of the minor subdivisions of a book etc. (usu. indicated by ~ **mark**, §, as § 15); (mil.) subdivision of platoon; part of community having separate interests or characteristics; thin slice of something cut off for microscopic examination; area of 1 sq. mi., $\frac{1}{36}$ of a township; part of sleeping car containing two berths. 3. Cutting of solid by plane, (area of) figure resulting from this; representation of internal structure of something supposed to be cut thus; **conic** ~ **s**, (math.) study of curves of intersection produced by allowing plane to cut cone at various angles. 4. Section mark (see sense 2) used as mark of reference or to indicate beginning of section. **sec'tion·al** *adj.* **sec'tion·al·ly** *adv.* **section** *v.t.* Arrange in, divide into, sections.

sec·tor (sĕk'ter) *n.* 1. Plane figure contained by two radii and the arc of a circle, ellipse, etc.; anything having this shape; ~ **of a sphere**, solid generated by revolution of plane sector about one of its radii. 2. Mathematical instrument now consisting of two flat rules inscribed with various scales and stiffly hinged together, for mechanical solution of various problems; astronomical instrument, telescope turning about center of graduated arc, for measuring angles. 3. (mil.) Subdivision of defensive position or system under one commander; territory for which one group, e.g. of air-raid wardens, is responsible.

sec·u·lar (sĕk'yuler) *adj.* 1. Occurring once in, lasting for, an age or a century; lasting or going on for ages or an indefinitely long time. 2. Concerned with the affairs of this world, worldly; not sacred not monastic or ecclesiastical, temporal, profane, lay; skeptical of religious truth or opposed to religious education; ~ **clergy**, **priests**, those not belonging to monastic orders (opp. *regular*). **sec'u·lar·ly** *adv*. **sec'u·lar·ism** *n*. **sec'u·lar·ist** *n. & adj*. **sec'u·lar·ize** *v.t*. (**-ized, -iz·ing**). **sec·u·lar·i·za·tion** (sĕkyulerīzā'shon) *n*. **sec·u·lar·i·ty** (sĕkyulăr'īte) *n*. (pl. **-ties**). **secular** *n*. Secular priest. **sec'u·lar·i·zer** *n*.

se·cure (sĭkūr') *adj*. 1. Untroubled by danger or apprehension; safe against attack, impregnable. 2. Reliable, certain not to fail or give way; (usu. pred.) in safe keeping, firmly fastened. 3. Having sure prospect *of*; safe *against, from*. **se·cure'ly** *adv*. **secure** *v.t*. (**-cured, -cur·ing**). 1. Fortify. 2. Confine, enclose, fasten, close, securely. 3. Guarantee, make safe against loss. 4. Succeed in getting, obtain. **se·cure'ness, se·cur'er** *ns*.

se·cu·ri·ty (sĭkūr'īte) *n*. (pl. **-ties**). (esp.) 1. Thing deposited or given as pledge for fulfillment of undertaking or payment of loan; document as evidence of loan; (usu. pl.) certificate of stock, bond, etc. 2. Precautions against theft, espionage, etc. 3. **S~ Council**, council of the General Assembly of the United Nations, consisting of 15 members of which five (People's Republic of China, France, U.K., U.S., U.S.S.R.) are permanent and the remainder elected, charged with the duty of dealing with disputes between nations that threaten the peace of the world.

se·dan (sĭdăn') *n*. 1. (also ~ **chair**) 17th–18th c. portable covered chair for one person, usu. carried on poles by two men. 2. Automobile with enclosed body for four or more persons including driver.

se·date (sĭdāt') *adj*. Tranquil, equable, composed, settled; not impulsive or lively. **se·date'ly** *adv*. **se·date'ness** *n*. **sedate** *v.t*. (**-dat·ed, -dat·ing**). Put (person) under sedation.

se·da·tion (sĭdā'shon) *n*. (med.) Treatment by sedatives.

sed·a·tive (sĕd'atĭv) *adj. & n*. (Drug etc.) tending to soothe.

sed·en·tar·y (sĕd'entĕre) *adj*. Sitting; (of occupation etc.) requiring continuance in sitting posture; (of persons) accustomed or addicted to sitting still, engaged in sedentary occupation; (zool.) permanently attached; (of spiders) lying in wait until prey is in web.

*The spider maintains a **sedentary** position in the web waiting for its prey to become entangled in the sticky substance that prevents escape. When the prey is secured, the spider will advance.*

sed·en·tar·i·ly *adv*. **sed·en·tar·i·ness** *n*.

Se·der (sā'der) *n*. (pl. **Se·ders**, Heb. **Si·dar·im** pr. sĭdăr'ĭm). Ritual for the first night or first two nights of Passover.

sedge (sĕj) *n*. Grasslike plant of genus *Carex*, growing in marshes or by waterside; bed of such plants. **sedg'y** *adj*. (**sedg·i·er, sedg·i·est**).

sed·i·ment (sĕd'ĭment) *n*. Matter that settles to bottom of liquid, lees, dregs; (geol.) waterborne or windborne matter that settles and may become consolidated into rock. **sed·i·men·ta·ry** (sĕdĭmĕn'tere) *adj*. **sed·i·men·ta·tion** (sĕdĭmentā'shon) *n*.

se·di·tion (sĭdĭsh'on) *n*. Conduct or language directed unlawfully against state authority; public commotion, riot, not amounting to insurrection or rebellion and therefore not treason. **se·di·tious** (sĭdĭsh'us) *adj*. **se·di·tious·ly** *adv*. **se·di·tious·ness** *n*.

se·duce (sĭdoos', -dūs') *v.t*. (**-duced, -duc·ing**). Lead astray, tempt into sin or crime; persuade (esp. someone young or innocent) to have sexual intercourse with one. **se·duc'er**, fem. **se·duc'tress** (sĭdŭk'trĭs) *ns*.

se·duc·tion (sĭdŭk'shon) *n*. Seducing, being seduced; thing that seduces.

se·duc·tive (sĭdŭk'tĭv) *adj*. (esp.) Alluring, enticing, winning. **se·duc'tive·ly** *adv*. **se·duc'tive·ness** *n*.

sed·u·lous (sĕj'ulus) *adj*. Diligent, persevering, assiduous, painstaking. **sed'u·lous·ly** *adv*. **sed'u·lous·ness, se·du·li·ty** (sĭdoo'lĭte, -dū'-) *ns*.

se·dum (sē'dum) *n*. Fleshy-leaved plant of genus *S~*, cultivated for its foliage and pink, white, or yellow flowers.

see [1] (sē) *v*. (**saw** pr. saw, **seen**, **see·ing**). Have the faculty of discerning objects with the eyes, exercise this faculty; perceive mentally; learn by reading; look at, visit; admit as visitor; ascertain by inspection, experiment, consideration, etc.; supervise; escort *home, to the door*, etc.; consider, judge; know by observation, experience; imagine; ~ **about**, attend to; take into consideration; ~ **after**, take care of; **Seeing Eye dog**, (named after Seeing Eye, Inc., of N.J.) guide dog; **see red**, (fig.) be enraged; **see stars**, have dancing lights before eyes from blow on head; **see the light**, (fig.) undergo conversion etc.; realize one's errors etc.; **see things**, suffer from hallucinations; **see through**, (esp.,

Despite its grass-like appearance, **sedge** *is a herb, widespread in Asia, Europe and North America. It was often cut for use as straw. Many species have both male and female flowers.*

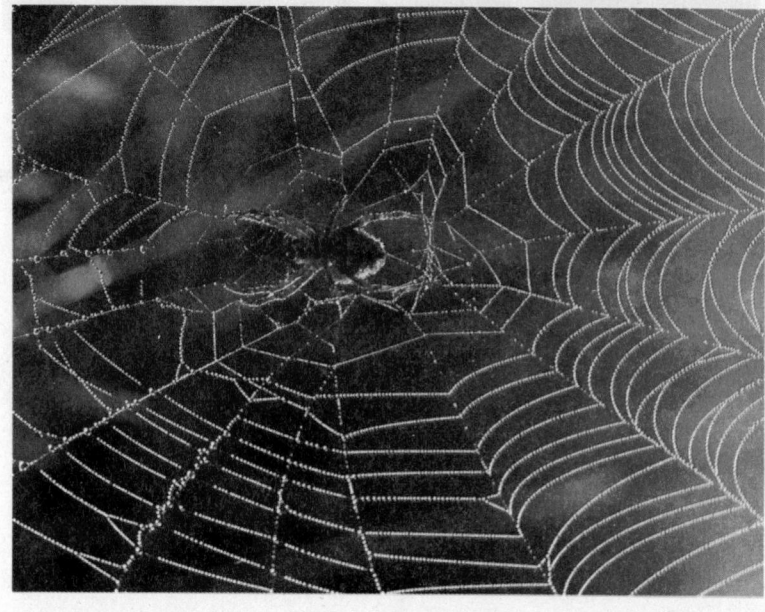

fig.) penetrate, see real character of through disguise or false appearance; continue to watch or take care of until the end, or until difficulties are overcome; **see′through** (*adj.*), (esp. of clothing) transparent; **see to**, attend to; take special care about. **see′a·ble** *adj.*

see² (sē) *n.* Office, position, jurisdiction, of a bishop; **Apostolic, Holy, Papal,** or **Roman S~**, office, jurisdiction, authority, of pope.

seed (sēd) *n.* (pl. **seeds,** collect. **seed**). 1. (One of) grains or ovules of plants, esp. as used for sowing; seedlike fruit, any other part of plant (as bulb) used for propagating new crop; **go, run, to ~**, cease flowering as seed develops; (fig.) become shabby, worn out, etc. 2. (bot.) Fertilized and ripened ovule of flowering plant, containing embryo capable of developing by germination. 3. Sperm, semen, milt; germ or latent beginning *of* (idea etc.). 4. (bibl.) Progeny, descendants. 5. Seeded player. 6. **seed′cake**, cake flavored with caraway seeds; **seed corn**, grain preserved to sow for new crop; **seed money**, money used to launch a project; **seed pearl**, very small pearl; **seeds′man** (pl. **-men**),

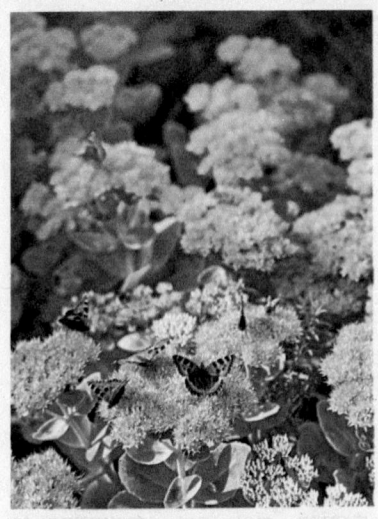

*A succulent plant native to arid areas in various parts of the world, **sedum** from various places has been acclimatized in the U.S.A. and other temperate zones so that its flowers may be grown.*

sower, dealer, in seeds; **seed′time**, sowing season; **seed vessel**, pericarp. **seed′less** *adj.* Having no seeds. **seed** *v.* Go to seed, produce or let fall seed; sprinkle (as) with seed; remove seeds from; disperse chemical material in (cloud) to

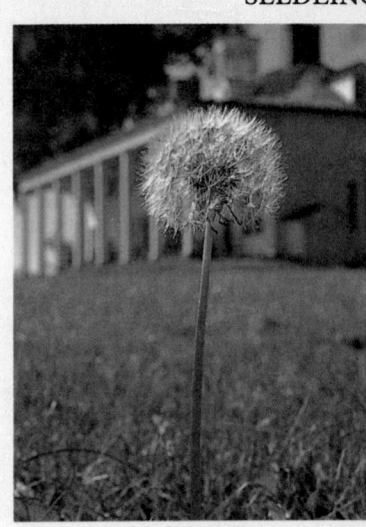

*Dandelion 'clock' on the lawn at Mt Vernon, the estate of George Washington. The clock, which is made up of many **seeds**, is named for the children's game of blowing it to tell the time.*

make rain; (sport, esp. tennis) sor (competitors in tournament) so that the best players do not meet in the early rounds; hence **seeded player**, one so selected.

seed·ling (sēd′lĭng) *n.* Young plant raised from seed.

*Development of a **seed** into a **seedling** is a process which is similar in mos plants, from microscopic spores to giant coconuts. The endosperm serve as a store of food for the embryo but or beans, for example, more food i obtained from the cotyledons.*

longitudinal section of corn grain

- endosperm
- cotyledon
- coleoptile
- epicotyl
- vascular tissue
- hypocotyl
- coleorhiza
- chalaza

micropyle
funiculus
hilum
raphe
vascular bundle
radicle

exterior of broad bean

longitudinal section of pansy seed

plumule
cotyledon

longitudinal section of broad bean

Maize

Kidney Bean

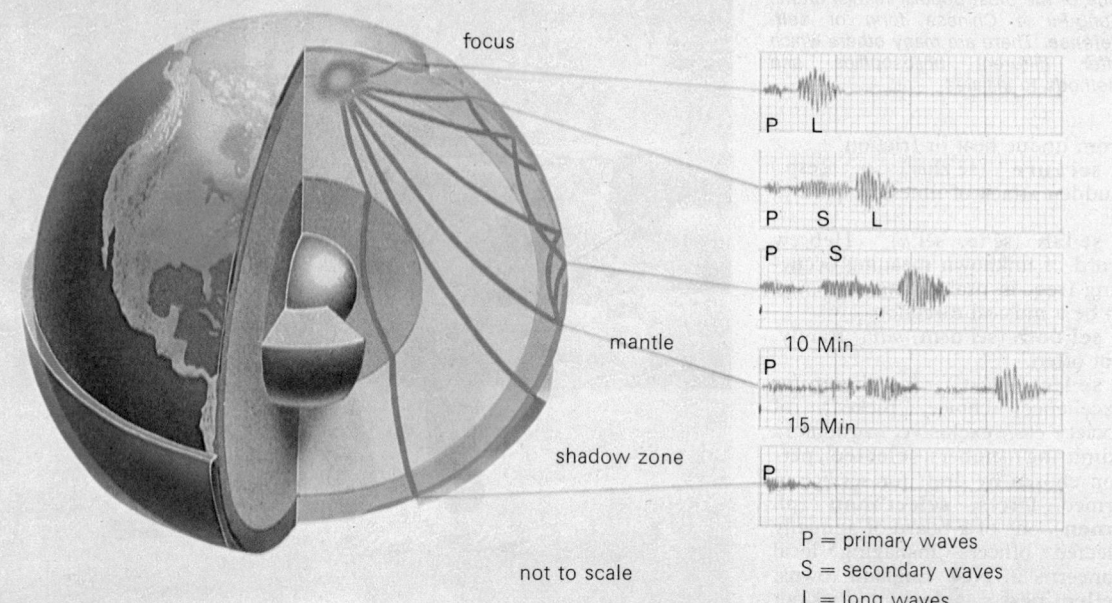

focus

P L

P S L

P S

10 Min

P

15 Min

P

mantle

shadow zone

P = primary waves
S = secondary waves
L = long waves

not to scale

seed·y (sē'dē) adj. (seed·i·er, eed·i·est). I. Full of seed. 2. habby, ill-looking; unwell, out of orts. seed'i·ly adv. seed'i·ness n.

see·ing (sē'ĭng) conj. Considerng the fact that; since, because.

seek (sēk) v. (sought, pr. sawt, eek·ing). Go in search of, look or; try to obtain or bring about, to o; ask for, request; make search. eek'er n.

seem (sēm) v.i. Have the ppearance of, be apparently; ppear to be or do; appear to exist; ppear to be true or the fact. eem'ing adj. Apparent; apparent nly. seem'ing·ly adv. seem'ng·ness n.

seem·ly (sēm'lē) adj. (-li·er, li·est). Decent, decorous, beoming. seem'li·ness n.

seen (sēn): see SEE[1].

seep (sēp) v.i. Ooze, percolate. eep'age n.

seer (sēr, sē'er) n. Visionary, rophet, one gifted with second ight.

seer·suck·er (sēr'sŭker) n. Thin inen, cotton, or other fabric with uckered surface, freq. striped, rig. of Indian manufacture. [Pers. hīr o shakkar milk and sugar]

see·saw (sē'saw) adj. & adv. With backward-and-forward or upnd-down motion. ~ n. Game in which two persons sit at each end of long board balanced on a central upport and move each other up nd down alternately; board thus sed (freq. fig.). ~ v.i. Play at eesaw; move up and down as in ame of seesaw; vacillate.

seethe (sēdh) v. (seethed, eeth·ing). Cook by boiling archaic); (fig.) boil, bubble, be gitated. seeth'ing·ly adv.

seg·ment (sĕg'ment) n. I. geom.) Plane figure contained by

To locate the position and assess the strength of an earthquake, a single seismograph is insufficient. Several are needed, each recording earth movements in horizontal and vertical directions, for triangular plotting.

chord and arc of circle; finite part of line between two points; ~ of a sphere, part cut off by plane; (phys.) each of parts into which length of vibrating string etc. is divided by nodes. 2. Division, section, of something, esp. each of longitudinal divisions of body of some animals. 3. Segmental arch. segment (sĕg'mĕnt') v. Divide into segments; (of cell) undergo cleavage or divide into many cells. seg·men·tal (sĕgmĕn'tal) adj. (esp. of arch, pediment, etc.) Having form of segment of circle. seg·men·tar·y (sĕg'mĕntĕrē) adj. seg·men·ta·tion (sĕgmĕntā'shon) n.

se·go (sē'gō) lily. N. Amer. plant (Calochortus nuttallii) with green and white trumpet-shaped flowers.

seg·re·gate (sĕg'regāt) v. (-gat·ed, -gat·ing). Set apart, isolate; subject (people) to racial segregation; enforce racial segregation in (community, institution, etc.); separate from general mass and collect together, as in crystallization or solidification; (biol., of Mendelian hybrids) separate into dominants, recessives, and hybrids, in conformity with numerical law. seg·re·ga·tion (sĕgregā'shon) n. (esp.) Enforced separation of different racial groups in a country, community, or institution. seg·re·ga'tion·ist n. seg're·gat·ed adj. Isolated, set apart (rare); (zool., bot., etc.) separated from the parent or from one another, not aggregated. ~ (sĕg'regĭt, -gāt) n. (zool.,

bot.) Species separated from aggregate species; (biol.) segregated individual.

sei·gneur (sānyēr'; Fr. sĕnyör') n. (pl. sei·gneurs pr. sānyērz'; Fr. sĕnyör'). Feudal lord, lord of manor (formerly in France and Canada and still in Channel Islands). sei·gneur·i·al (sānyēr'ēal) adj.

Seine (sān; Fr. sĕn). River of N. France flowing 482 mi. (776 km) through Paris NW. to the English Channel near Le Havre.

seine (sān) n. (also ~ net) Fishing net hanging vertically in water, with ends being drawn together to enclose fish. seine v. (seined, sein·ing). Catch, catch fish, with seine; use seine in.

seis·mic (sīz'mĭk, sīs'-), seis·mal (sīz'mal, sīs'-), seis·mi·cal sīz'mĭkal, sīs'-) adjs. Of earthquakes. seis'mi·cal·ly adv. seis·mic·i·ty (sīzmĭs'ĭtē, sīs-) n. (pl. -ties).

seis·mo·graph (sīz'mŏgrăf, -grahf, sīs'-) n. Instrument for recording tremors of earthquakes. seis·mog·ra·phy (sīzmŏg'rafē, sīs-), seis·mol·o·gy (sīzmŏl'ojē, sīs-) ns. Scientific study of earthquakes. seis·mog'ra·pher n. seis·mo·graph·ic (sīzmŏgrăf'ĭk, sīs-), seis·mo·log·i·cal (sīzmolŏj'ĭkal, sīs-) adjs. seis·mol'o·gist n.

seize (sēz) v. (seized, seiz·ing). I. (law) Put in possession of; take possession of, confiscate, by warrant or legal right, impound, attach. 2. Lay hold of forcibly or suddenly, snatch; grasp with hand or mind, comprehend quickly or clearly; lay hold eagerly upon. 3. (naut.) Lash, fasten with several turns of cord. 4. ~ (up), (of bearings or other moving part of machinery) become stuck, jam,

One of the most popular martial arts is Kung-Fu a Chinese form of self-defense. There are many others which offer different philosophies and methods to initiates.

from undue heat or friction.

sei·zure (sē′zher) *n.* (esp.) Sudden attack of illness or paralysis.

se·lah (sē′la, sĕl′a). Hebrew word of unknown meaning occurring freq. in psalms and supposed to be a musical direction.

sel·dom (sĕl′dom) *adv.* Rarely, not often.

se·lect (sĭlĕkt′) *adj.* Chosen for excellence, choice, picked; (of society etc.) exclusive, cautious in admitting members; **selectee′**, person chosen by draft for service in armed forces; **select′man** (pl. **-men**), one of a board of annually elected officers managing local concerns in New England towns. **se·lect′ness** *n.* **select** *v.t.* Pick out as best or most suitable. **se·lec·tion** (sĭlĕk′shon) *n.* Selecting, choice; what is selected; (biol.) sorting out in various ways of the types of animal or plant better fitted to survive, regarded as a factor in evolution. **se·lec′tive** *adj.* Using selection; characterized by selecting; (electr.) able to receive a desired frequency to the exclusion of others; ~ **service**, service in armed forces under conscription. **se·lec′tive·ly** *adv.* **se·lec·tiv·i·ty** (sĭlĕktĭv′ĭtē) *n.*

Se·le·ne (sĭlē′nē). (Gk. myth.) Goddess of the moon, in later myths identified with Artemis.

se·le·nic (sĭlē′nĭk, -lĕn′ĭk) *adj.* ~ **acid**, acid (H_2SeO_4), crystalline when pure, resembling sulfuric acid in many of its characteristics.

se·le·ni·ous (sĭlē′nēus) *adj.* ~ **acid**, colorless crystalline acid (H_2SeO_3).

sel·e·nite (sĕl′enīt) *n.* 1. (min.) Calcium sulfate ($CaSO_4 2H_2O$), gypsum, in crystalline or foliated form; slip of this used to polarize light. 2. (chem.) Salt of selenious acid. **sel·e·nit·ic** (sĕlenĭt′ĭk), **sel·e·nit′i·cal** *adjs.*

se·le·ni·um (sĭlē′nēum) *n.* (chem.) Nonmetallic element, chemically resembling sulfur and tellurium, having the property that its conductivity of electricity increases with intensity of light falling on it and hence used in various photoelectric devices; symbol Se, at. no. 34, at. wt. 78.96; ~ **cell**, piece of selenium to which electrical connections are made, used as a photoelectric device etc. [Gk. *selēnē* moon; named f. its association in nature with *tellurium*]

sel·e·nog·ra·phy (sĕlenŏg′rafē) *n.* Science dealing with the physical geography of the moon, mapping the moon's surface.

*The marine iguana is an example of Darwin's theory of **selection**, which proposed that some species of animal life are better adapted to survival than others. This theory is widely accepted by biologists.*

sel·e·nol·o·gy (sĕlenŏl′ojē) *n.* Science of the moon.

self (sĕlf) *n.* (pl. **selves** pr. sĕlvz). Person's or thing's own individuality or essence, person or thing as object of introspection or reflexive action; one's own interests or pleasure, concentration on these. ~ *adj.* Uniform, the same throughout.

self- *prefix.* Combining form of SELF; ~ **-abuse**, blame or reproach of oneself; masturbation; ~ **-acting**, acting automatically; ~ **-addressed**, addressed for return to sender; ~ **-assertion**, insistence on one's own rights, claims, individu-

*Widespread in Europe, Asia and North America, Prunella vulgaris became known as **self-heal** because of the claims that tea made from its leaves would cure a multitude of sicknesses.*

ality, etc.; self-confidence; ~ **-centered**, centered in oneself, itself, engrossed in self, preoccupied with one's own personality or affairs; ~ **-command**, self-control; ~ **-complacency**, complacency; ~ **-complacent** (*adj.*); ~ **-confidence**, confidence in oneself; ~ **-confident** (*adj.*); ~ **-conscious**, having consciousness of one's identity, actions, sensations, etc.; unduly or morbidly preoccupied with oneself; **~-consciously** (*adv.*), **~-consciousness** (*n.*); **~-contained**, complete in itself; (of person) uncommunicative; **~-control**, control of oneself, one's desires, emotions, etc. **~-defense**, (esp.) in phr. **in ~-defense**, not by way of aggression; (**noble**) **art of ~-defense**, boxing; **~-denial** (*n.*), **~-denying** (*adj.*) sacrificing one's personal desires; **~-determination**, (esp.) a people's decision of its political status, as form of government, independence, etc.; **~-effacing**, keeping oneself inconspicuous; retiring; **~-employed**, running own business etc.; **~-esteem**, favorable opinion of oneself; **~-evident**, not needing demonstration, axiomatic; **~-governing**, (esp., of colony, territory, etc.) governing itself; **~-government** (*n.*); **self′heal**, any of various plants credited with great healing properties, esp. *Prunella vulgaris*, a blue-flowered mint of Europe and Asia; **self-help**, providing for oneself without assistance from others; **self-important**, having an exaggerated idea of one's own importance; **self-importantly** (*adv.*); **self-importance** (*n.*); **self-indulgence**, indulgence of one's own desires for ease, pleasure, etc.; **self-indulgent** (*adj.*), **self-indulgently** (*adv.*); **self-interest**, what one conceives to be for one's own interests; **self-interested** (*adj.*); **self-love**, selfishness, self-centeredness; **self-made**, made by one's own action or efforts; **self-made man**, one who has risen from obscurity or poverty by his own exertions; **self-opinionated**, obstinately adhering to one's own opinion; **self-portrait**, artist's portrait of himself; **self-possessed**, cool, composed, in command of one's faculties or feelings; **self-possession** (*n.*); **self-preservation** (*n.*), (esp.) natural instinct impelling living creatures to go on living and avoid injury; **self-reliance**, reliance on one's own powers etc.; **self-reliant** (*adj.*); **self-respect** (*n.*) proper regard for one's dignity, standard of conduct etc.; **self-righteous**, righteous in one's own esteem, smug; **self-rising**, (*adj.*), (of flour) not needing addition of baking powder etc.; **self-sacrifice**, subordinating private interest and desires to those of others; **self′same** (*adj.*), (the) very same; **self-satisfaction**, conceit; **self-sealing**, having a device for filling up a hole in a structure caused by shot etc.; **self-seeking** (*adj.* & *n.*), seeking one's own advantage only; **self-service**, arrangement of store, restaurant, etc., whereby customers help them-

selves and pay cashier afterward (also attrib. of store etc.); **self-sown**, grown from chance-dropped seed; **self-starter**, device for starting internal combustion engine without use of crank or auxiliary starting engine; person who needs no outside stimulus to work; **self-styled**, having taken name or description on one's own initiative; **self-sufficient**, requiring nothing from outside, independent; sufficient in one's own opinion; **self-sufficiency** (*n.*); **self-will**, obstinate pursuing of one's own desires or opinions; **self-willed** (*adj.*); **self-winding**, (of clock etc.) with automatic winding mechanism. **self′less** *adj.* Oblivious of self, incapable of selfishness. **self′less·ness** *n.*

self·ish (sĕl′fĭsh) *adj.* Deficient in consideration for others, regarding chiefly personal profit or pleasure; actuated by, appealing to,

*In markets all over the world, there can be found people who specialize in **sell·ing**. This vendor of olives and other Mediterranean food is in Sydney, Australia.*

self-interest. **self′ish·ly** *adv.* **self′ish·ness** *n.*

Sel·kirk (sĕl′kẽrk), **Alexander** (1676–1721).- Scottish sailor; at his own request he was put ashore on the uninhabited island of Juan Fernandez, where he remained 1704–9; the original of *Robinson Crusoe*.

sell (sĕl) *v.* (**sold** pr. sōld, **sell·ing**). 1. Make over, dispose of, in exchange for money; keep stock of for sale, deal in; betray for money or other reward; promote sales (of); gain acceptance of, advertise or publish merits of; (of goods) be sold at a specific price; find purchaser(s); **~ off**, sell remainder of (goods), clear out stock, at reduced prices; **~ one's life dear(ly)**, (fig.) do great injury before being killed; **~ out**, (hist.) leave army by selling commission; sell (one's shares in company, whole stock in trade, etc.); (colloq.) turn traitor, betray. 2. (slang) Trick, take in. **sell′er** *n.* One who sells; **~'s market**, market in which supplies are short and prices high. **sell′ing** *n.* **sell** *n.* (slang) Hoax, swindle; disappoint-

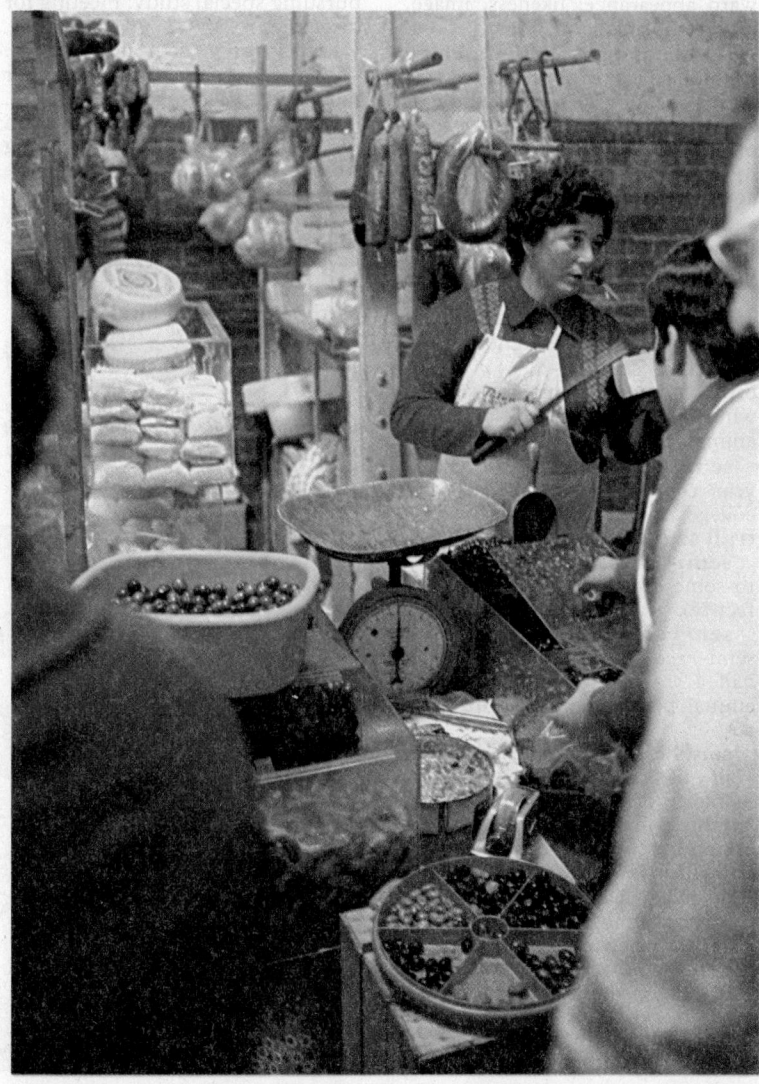

ment; **sell'out**, betrayal; selling of all copies, seats, etc., commercial success.

Selt·zer (sĕlt´ser) n. (also ~ **water**) Effervescent mineral water from Nieder-Selters, near Wiesbaden, Germany; (freq. **s** ~) similar artificial mineral water.

sel·vage, sel·vedge (sĕl´vĭj) ns. Edge of piece of material so woven that weft will not unravel; edge plate of lock with opening for bolt. **sel'vaged** adj.

selves: see SELF.

Sem (sem): SHEM.

se·man·tic (sĭmăn´tĭk) adj. Of meaning. **se·man'tics** n.pl. (usu. w. sing. verb) Branch of philology concerned with meanings. **se·man·ti·cist** (sĭmăn´tĭsĭst) n.

sem·a·phore (sĕm´afōr, -fŏr) n. Signaling apparatus of post with one or more movable arms; signal(ing) by person holding flag in each hand. **sem·a·phor·ic** (sĕmafōr´ĭk, -făr´-) adj. **sem·a·phor'i·cal·ly** adv. **semaphore** v. (**-phored, -phor·ing**). Signal, send, by semaphore.

sem·blance (sĕm´blans) n. Outward appearance; likeness, image, of; resemblance.

se·mei·ol·o·gy, se·mi·ol·o·gy (sēmĭŏl´ojē), **se·mei·ot·ics, se·mi·ot·ics** (sēmĭŏt´ĭks) ns. Study of signs or sign language; (med.) study of symptoms of disease. **se·mei·ot·ic, se·mi·ot·ic, se·mei·ot'i·cal, se·mi·ot'i·cal** adjs.

Sem·e·le (sĕm´elē). (Gk. myth.) Daughter of Cadmus and Harmonia and mother, by Zeus, of Dionysus; she entreated Zeus to come to her in his full majesty and was destroyed by his lightning.

se·men (sē´men, -mĕn) n. Seed, esp. of flowering plants; viscous whitish fluid secreted by male animal, containing spermatozoa.

se·mes·ter (sĭmĕs´ter) n. Half-year course or term in schools, colleges, and universities. **se·mes'tral, se·mes'tri·al** adjs.

semi- prefix. Half-, partly-, to some extent; partial(ly), imperfect(ly).

sem·i·an·nu·al (sĕmēăn´ūal, sĕmī-) adj. Half-yearly; lasting half a year (only). ~ n. Semiannual plant. **sem·i·an'nu·al·ly** adv.

sem·i·cir·cle (sĕm´ĭsērkel) n. Half of circle divided by its diameter, or half its circumference; anything in this shape. **sem·i·cir·cu·lar** (sĕmĭsēr´kyuler) adj. ~ **canal**, any of the three curving fluid-filled channels in ear giving information to the brain to help maintain balance.

sem·i·co·lon (sĕm´ĭkōlon) n. Punctuation mark (;), indicating a more marked separation than the comma, and less than a period.

sem·i·con·duc·tor (sĕmēkon-

dŭk´ter, sĕmī-) n. Electrical conductor with resistance less than that of insulator but greater than that of metal etc.

sem·i·cyl·in·der (sĕmēsĭl´ĭnder, sĕmī-) n. Half of cylinder cut longitudinally. **sem·i·cy·lin·dri·cal** (sĕmēsĭlĭn´drĭkal, sĕmī-), **sem·i·cy·lin'dric** adjs.

sem·i·de·tached (sĕmēdĭtăcht´, sĕmī-) adj. (of house) Joined to another by common wall on one side only.

sem·i·fi·nal (sĕmēfī´nal, sĕmī-) adj. & n. (Match, round) preceding final.

sem·i·flu·id (sĕmēfloō´ĭd, sĕmī-) adj. & n. (Substance) of consistency halfway between fluid and solid.

sem·i·lu·nar (sĕmēloō´ner, sĕmī-) adj. Half-moon-shaped, crescent.

sem·i·nal (sĕm´inal) adj. Of seed, semen, or reproduction; germinal, reproductive, propagative; providing a source of future development; ~ **fluid**, semen. **sem'i·nal·ly** adv.

sem·i·nar (sĕm´inär) n. (Meeting of) group of advanced students pursuing special study; meeting for discussion.

sem·i·nar·y (sĕm´inĕrē) n. (pl. **-nar·ies**). 1. Training college for ministers, priests, rabbis, etc. 2. (archaic) School, esp. institution for higher education of young women. **sem·i·nar·i·an** (sĕminär´ēan) n.

Sem·i·nole (sĕm´inōl) adj. & n. (pl. **-noles**, collect. **-nole**). (Member) of tribe of N. Amer. Indians, allied to Creeks, formerly and still partly resident in Florida.

sem·i·of·fi·cial (sĕmēofĭsh´al, sĕmī-) adj. Having some degree of

Possibly derived from smoke signals **semaphore** *was first put to practical use, in France during the Napoleonic wars, to communicate accurate messages at distances.*

Botanically, the term **semi-annual** *is meaningless, but is usually applied to plants like the pansy which may be either annuals or biennials, depending on the variety, or where they are grown.*

official authority. **sem·i·of·fi·cial·ly** adv.

se·mi·ol·o·gy (sēmĭŏl´ojē), **se·mi·ot·ics** (sēmĭŏt´ĭks): see SEMEIOLOGY.

sem·i·per·me·a·ble (sĕmēpēr´mēabel, sĕmī-) adj. Permeable to small molecules but not large molecules.

sem·i·pre·cious (sĕmēprĕsh´us, sĕmī-) adj. (of gems) Of less value than those called precious (as amethyst, jade, garnet, etc.).

sem·i·pri·vate (sĕmēprī´vĭt, sĕmī-) adj. Partly but not entirely private, as hospital room occupied by several but not many patients.

sem·i·qua·ver (sĕm´ēkwāver) n. (mus. chiefly Brit.) Note having $\frac{1}{16}$ the time value of a whole note (♬).

Semaphore letters and numbers
The thick lines represent the right arm and thin lines the left arm

*Above: Agate and other **semi-precious** stones as they are found. Below center: A finely carved bowl of jade is typical of the objets d'art that these materials may be used for.*

Se·mir·a·mis (sĭmĭr′amĭs). Mythical queen of Assyria, of great beauty and wisdom, wife and successor of Ninus, reputed founder of Nineveh; she built many cities, including Babylon.

sem·i·skilled (sĕmēskĭld′, ĕmĭ-) *adj.* Having or requiring some training but less than skilled work(er).

Sem·ite (sĕm′īt) *n.* Member of any of the peoples supposed to be descended from SHEM (Gen. 10), including Jews, Arabs, Assyrians, Phoenicians, and other peoples of SW. Asia.

Se·mit·ic (sĭmĭt′ĭk) *adj.* 1. Of the group of languages now spoken chiefly in N. Africa and SW. Asia, including Hebrew, Aramaic, Arabic, ancient Assyrian, and Ethiopic. 2. Of the Semites. ~ *n.* 1. Semitic family of languages. 2. Semite.

Sem·i·tism (sĕm′ĭtĭzem; *Brit.* ē′mĭtĭzem) *n.* 1. Semitic characteristics; (esp.) Jewish ideas, influence, etc. 2. Semitic word or idiom.

sem·i·tone (sĕm′ētōn) *n.* (mus.) Interval of (approximately) half a tone.

sem·i·trail·er (sĕm′ētrāler) *n.* Trailer having wheels at back but supported by towing vehicle in front.

sem·o·li·na (sĕmolē′na) *n.* Hard portions of durum wheat that resist action of millstones and are

*Above: Student priests at a **seminary** at Kimmage Manor in Dublin. After ordination, they may serve their church in Ireland, or overseas, either as incumbents of a parish, or as missionaries.*

collected in form of rounded grains and used in puddings and in pasta.

sem·per fi·de·lis (sĕm′per fĭdā′lĭs, -dē′-; *Lat.* sĕm′pĕr fĭdā′lĭs). Always faithful: U.S. Marine Corps motto. [L.]

sem·per pa·ra·tus (sĕm′per parātus; *Lat.* sĕm′pĕr pahrah′tōos). Always prepared: U.S. Coast Guard motto. [L.]

sem·pi·ter·nal (sĕmpĭtēr′nal) *adj.* (rhet.) Everlasting, eternal.

semp·stress: see SEAMSTRESS.

Sen., sen. *abbrevs.* Senate; senator; senior.

sen·ate (sĕn′ĭt) *n.* 1. (Rom. hist.) Roman legislative and administrative body, orig. of representatives elected by patricians, later of appointed members and actual and former holders of various high offices. 2. (cap.) Upper branch of the legislature in U.S. and various other countries. 3. Governing body of some universities; council in some Amer. colleges composed of members of faculty and elected students, and having control of discipline etc.

sen·a·tor (sĕn′ater) *n.* Member of senate. **sen·a·to·ri·al** (sĕnatōr′ēal, -tōr′-) *adj.* **sen·a·tor·ship** *n.*

send (sĕnd) *v.* (**sent** pr. sĕnt, **send·ing**). Cause to go, dispatch, secure conveyance of, to some destination, *to, into, away*, etc.; propel; drive, cause to go, *into* some condition, *to sleep*, etc.; send message or letter; (of deity) grant, bestow, inflict, bring about, cause to be; (slang) excite, put into ecstasy; ~ **down**, (Brit.) suspend, expel, from university; ~ **for**, summon; esp., of head of state, summon politician in order to offer him premiership; ~ **off**, send away; witness departure of (person) as sign of respect, etc.; ~**-off** (*n.*); ~ **up** (**the river**), (slang) send to prison. **send′er** *n.*

Sen·e·ca[1] (sĕn′eka) *n.* (pl. **-cas**, collect. **-ca**). Member, language, of a numerous and warlike tribe of Iroquoian Indians, formerly occupying W. part of New York State.

Sen·e·ca[2] (sĕn′eka), **Lucius Annaeus** (c4 B.C.–65 A.D.). Roman Stoic philosopher and author of tragedies; tutor and adviser to Nero; ordered to take his own life on charge of complicity against Nero conspiracy.

Sen·e·gal (sĕnegawl′). Republic in W. Africa, formerly part of French W. Africa; achieved independence, 1960; capital, Dakar, is westernmost point in Africa. **Sen·e·gal·ese** (sĕnegawlēz′, -lēs′, -ga-) adj. & n. (pl. **-lese**).

se·nes·cent (senĕs′ent) adj. Growing old. **se·nes′cence** n.

se·nile (sē′nīl, sĕn′īl) adj. Belonging, incident, peculiar, to old age; having weakness of old age. **se·nil·i·ty** (sĭnĭl′ĭtē) n.

sen·ior (sēn′yer) adj. More advanced in age, older in standing; superior in age or standing to; of higher or highest degree; senior to another of the same name; belonging to final year in university, school, etc.; ~ **citizen**, elderly person, esp. if retired; ~ **high school**, high school usu. including grades 10, 11, and 12; ~ **partner**, head of firm. **sen·ior·i·ty** (sēnyōr′ĭtē, -yār′-) n. (pl. **-ties**). **senior** n. One superior or worthy of deference etc. by reason of age; person of comparatively long service, standing, etc.; one's elder or superior in length of service, membership, etc.; senior student.

sen·na (sĕn′a) n. (Dried pods or leaflets, used as purgative, of) species of *Cassia*.

se·ñor (sĕnyōr′, -yōr′), **se·ño·ra** (sĕnyōr′a, -yōr′a), **se·ño·ri·ta** (sĕnyorē′ta) ns. (pl. **se·ñors**, Sp.

*Mosque on Gorée, an island opposite Dakar, capital of **Senegal**. This former French colony once relied on peanuts as its main cash crop, but today rice and sorghum are also grown.*

se·ño·res pr. sĕnyōr′ĕs; **se·ño·ras** pr. *Sp.* sĕnyōr′ahs; **se·ño·ri·tas** pr. *Sp.* sĕnyawrē′tahs). (Title of or form of address to) Spanish man, woman, young or unmarried woman.

sen·sa·tion (sĕnsā′shon) n. 1. Consciousness of perceiving or seeming to perceive some state or affection of one's body, its parts or senses, or of one's mind or its emotions; contents of such consciousness. 2. Excited or violent feeling, strong impression, as of horror, surprise, esp. among community; event, person, etc. arousing this. **sen·sa′tion·al** adj. **sen·sa′tion·al·ly** adv.

sen·sa·tion·al·ism (sĕnsā′shonalĭzem) n. 1. (philos.) Theory that sensation is sole source of knowledge. 2. Pursuit of the sensational in literature, journalism, etc. **sen·sa·tion·al·ist** n.

sense (sĕns) n. 1. Any of those faculties, each dependent upon specialized groups of receptors connected with the brain, by which man and other animals are aware of their environment or recognize changes in their own bodily condition such as pain, movement of muscles and joints, or cold and warmth; **the five ~s**, those providing knowledge of the external world (sight, hearing, smell, taste, touch); ~ **datum**, element of experience due to stimulation of a sense

organ; ~ **organ**, part of bod concerned in producing sensatior 2. (pl.) The senses considered a channels for gratifying the desir for pleasure. 3. (pl.) Person's sanit regarded as attested by possessio of the senses. 4. Ability to perceiv or feel; consciousness of; quick c accurate appreciation of; instinc regarding, insight into, specific matter. 5. Practical wisdom, judg ment, common sense, conformity t these. 6. Meaning, way in whic word etc. is to be understooc intelligibility, coherence, pos session of a meaning; **in a ~**, in way, under limitations. 7. Prevail ing sentiment among a number o people. **sense** v.t. (**sensed, sens· ing**). Perceive by sense; (esp.) b vaguely aware of.

sense·less (sĕns′lĭs) adj. 1 Deprived of sensation; uncon scious; unfeeling. 2. Extremel foolish. 3. Meaningless, purpose less. **sense′less·ly** adv. **sense′ less·ness** n.

sen·si·bil·i·ty (sĕnsibĭl′ĭtē) n (pl. **-ties**). 1. Capacity to feel. 2 Susceptibility, sensitiveness (to) delicacy of feeling; oversensitive ness.

sen·si·ble (sĕn′sibel) adj. 1 Perceptible by the senses; grea enough to be perceived, appreci able. 2. Aware, not unmindful, of 3. Of good sense, reasonable judicious; moderate; practical **sen′si·ble·ness** n. **sen′si·bly** adv

sen·si·tive (sĕn′sĭtĭv) adj. Hav ing sensibility to; very open to o acutely affected by external im pressions, esp. those made by th moods or opinions of others ir relation to oneself; (of instrument etc.) readily responding to or recording slight changes of condition; (chem.) readily affected by or responsive *to* appropriate agent; (photog., of paper, etc.) susceptible to influence of light; ~ **plant**, tropical Amer. plant (*Mimosa pudica*) with leaflets that fold together at slightest touch; plant with similar quality. **sen'si·tive·ly** *adv.* **sen'si·tive·ness** *n.* **sen·si·tiv·i·ty** (sĕnsĭtĭv'ĭtē) *n.* ~ **training**, group discussion etc. often involving confrontation, designed to increase learning through feedback from others.

sen·si·tize (sĕn'sĭtīz) *v.t.* (**-tized, -tiz·ing**). Make sensitive; render (photographic paper etc.) sensitive to light; render (organism, tissue) sensitive to substance normally inert, or highly reactive to drug etc. **sen·si·ti·za·tion** (sĕnsĭtīzā'shon) *n.*

sen·sor (sĕn'ser) *n.* Device giving signal for detection or measurement of a physical property to which it responds.

sen·so·ri·al (sĕnsōr'ēal, -sōr'-) *adj.* Of the sensorium, sensation or sensory impressions.

sen·so·ri·um (sĕnsōr'ēum, -sōr'-) *n.* (pl. **-so·ri·ums, -so·ri·a** pr. -sōr'ēa, -sōr'-). Brain as seat of sensation; whole sensory apparatus.

sen·so·ry (sĕn'serē) *adj.* Of sensation or the senses; ~ **nerve**, nerve consisting of fibers conducting impulses from the peripheral sense organs to the central nervous system.

sen·su·al (sĕn'shōoal) *adj.* Of or dependent on the senses only, voluptuous; given to the pursuit of sensual pleasures or gratification of the appetites; licentious. **sen'su·al·ly** *adv.* **sen'su·al·ism, sen'su·al·ist, sen·su·al·i·ty** (sĕnshōoăl'ĭtē) *ns.* **sen·su·al·is·tic**

(sĕnshōoalĭs'tĭk) *adj.*

sen·su·ous (sĕn'shōous) *adj.* Of, derived from, affecting, delighting in pleasures of, the senses. **sen'su·ous·ly** *adv.* **sen'su·ous·ness** *n.*

sent: see SEND.

sen·tence (sĕn'tens) *n.* 1. Judgment or decision of court esp. as to punishment allotted to person condemned in criminal trial (also transf.); the punishment itself. 2. Series of words in connected speech or writing, forming grammatically complete expression of single thought, and usu. containing subject and predicate, and conveying statement, question, command, or request; loosely, part of writing or speech between two periods; SIMPLE, COMPLEX, COMPOUND[1] ~: see these. **sentence** *v.t.* (**-tenced, -tenc·ing**). Pronounce judicial sentence on, condemn *to* a punishment.

sen·ten·tious (sĕntĕn'shus) *adj.* Aphoristic; full of, given to, pointed maxims; pompously moralizing. **sen·ten'tious·ly** *adv.* **sen·ten'tious·ness** *n.*

sen·tient (sĕn'shent) *adj.* Having the power of sense perception, that feels or is capable of feeling. **sen'tience** *n.* **sen'tient·ly** *adv.*

sen·ti·ment (sĕn'timent) *n.* 1. Mental attitude; opinion, view. 2. Mental feeling, emotion, thought, or reflection colored by or proceeding from emotion; emotional thought expressed in literature, art, etc.; feeling or meaning (intended to be) conveyed by passage etc. 3. Refined and tender feeling; emotional weakness, mawkish tenderness, nursing of the emotions. **sen·ti·men·tal** (sĕntimĕn'tal) *adj.*

Best known for their use as a purgative, pods of the **senna** *plant were usually soaked in water, to extract the active ingredients.*

Swayed or dictated by shallow emotion; designed to excite or gratify the softer emotions (~ **value**, value of thing to particular person because of its associations). **sen·ti·men'tal·ly** *adv.* **sen·ti·men'tal·ism, sen·ti·men'tal·ist, sen·ti·men·tal·i·ty** (sĕntimĕntăl'ĭtē) *ns.* **sen·ti·men'tal·ize** *v.* (**-ized, -iz·ing**).

sen·ti·nel (sĕn'tinel) *n.* Sentry (lit. or fig.).

sen·try (sĕn'trē) *n.* (pl. **-tries**). Soldier etc. posted to keep guard; ~ **box**, hut for sentry to stand in.

se·pal (sē'pal, sĕp'al) *n.* (bot.) One of leaves or divisions of calyx.

sep·a·rate (sĕp'erĭt, sĕp'rĭt) *adj.* Divided or withdrawn from others, detached, shut off; forming a unit that is or may be regarded as apart or by itself, distinct, individual, of individuals; ~ **but equal**, of or relating to a policy of segregating the races but providing equal educational etc. opportunities for all. **sep'a·rate·ly** *adv.* **sep'a·rate·ness** *n.* **sep'a·rates** *n.pl.* Separate articles of dress suitable for wearing together in various combinations. **separate** (sĕp'erāt) *v.* (**-rat·ed, -rat·ing**). Make separate, sever, disunite; keep from union or contact; part, secede *from*, go different ways; remove (substance) *from* another with which it is combined or mixed, as cream from milk, esp. by some technical process. **sep·a·ra·ble** (sĕp'erabel, sĕp'ra-), **sep·a·ra·tive** (sĕp'erativ, -erā-) *adjs.*

sep·a·ra·tion (sĕperā'shon) *n.* (esp.) Cessation of conjugal cohabitation without dissolution of marriage tie, either by mutual consent or (**judicial** ~) imposed by judicial decree; ~ **center**, place where members of armed forces are released from military service to return to civilian life.

sep·a·ra·tist (sĕp′erătĭst, sĕp′-ra-, -erā-) *n.* One who favors separation, esp. for political or ecclesiastical independence. **sep′-a·ra·tism** *n.*

sep·a·ra·tor (sĕp′erāter) *n.* (esp.) Machine or appliance for separating, esp. cream from milk by centrifugal force.

Se·phar·di (sefär′dē) *n.* (pl. **Se·phar·dim** pr. sefär′dĭm, sefär-dēm′). Member of one of the two main divisions of Jews, Jews of Spanish or Portuguese descent; cf. ASHKENAZI. **Se·phar′dic** *adj.* [mod. Heb., f. *sᵉpāraḍ*, a country mentioned once in Old Testament and held in late Jewish tradition to be Spain]

se·pi·a (sē′pēa) *n.* (Rich brown color of) pigment made from inky secretion of cuttlefish; a sepia drawing. ~ *adj.* Of color of sepia; drawn in sepia.

se·poy (sē′poi) *n.* (hist.) Native Indian soldier under European, esp. Brit. discipline; **S ~ Rebellion (Mutiny)**, revolt of sepoy troops in Bengal army of Brit. East India Co. (1857–8), which led to abolition of the company and assumption of direct rule by Brit. crown; also called Indian Mutiny. [Hind., f. Pers. *sipāhī* soldier (*sipāh* army)]

sep·pu·ku (sĕpōō′kōō) *n.* Hara-kiri. [Jap.]

sep·sis (sĕp′sĭs) *n.* (pl. **-ses** pr. -sēz). State of poisoning of the tissues or bloodstream, caused by bacteria.

Sept. *abbrev.* September.

sept-, septi- *prefixes.* Seven.

sep·tal (sĕp′tal) *adj.* Of a septum or septa. **sep·tate** (sĕp′tāt) *adj.* Having a septum or septa.

Sep·tem·ber (sĕptĕm′ber). Ninth month of Gregorian (seventh of Julian) calendar, with 30 days. [L. *septem* seven]

Sep·tem·brist (sĕptĕm′brĭst). (Fr. hist.) Supporter of or participator in massacre of political prisoners in Paris Sept. 2–6, 1792.

sep·ten·ni·al (sĕptĕn′ēal) *adj.* Of, for, (recurring) every, seven years. **sep·ten′ni·al·ly** *adv.*

sep·tet, sep·tette (sĕptĕt′) *ns.* 1. (mus.) (Composition for) seven voices or instruments in combination. 2. Set of seven persons or things.

sep·tic (sĕp′tĭk) *adj.* Putrefying; caused by or in a state of sepsis; ~ **tank**, tank in which organic matter in sewage is rapidly decomposed through agency of anaerobic bacteria. **sep′ti·cal·ly** *adv.*

sep·ti·ce·mi·a, sep·ti·cae·mi·a (sĕptĭsē′mēa) *ns.* Disease caused by pathogenic bacteria in the blood, blood poisoning.

sep·tu·a·ge·nar·i·an (sĕpchōōajenār′ēan) *adj. & n.* (Person) aged 70 or more but less than 80.

Sep·tu·a·ges·i·ma (sĕptōōa-

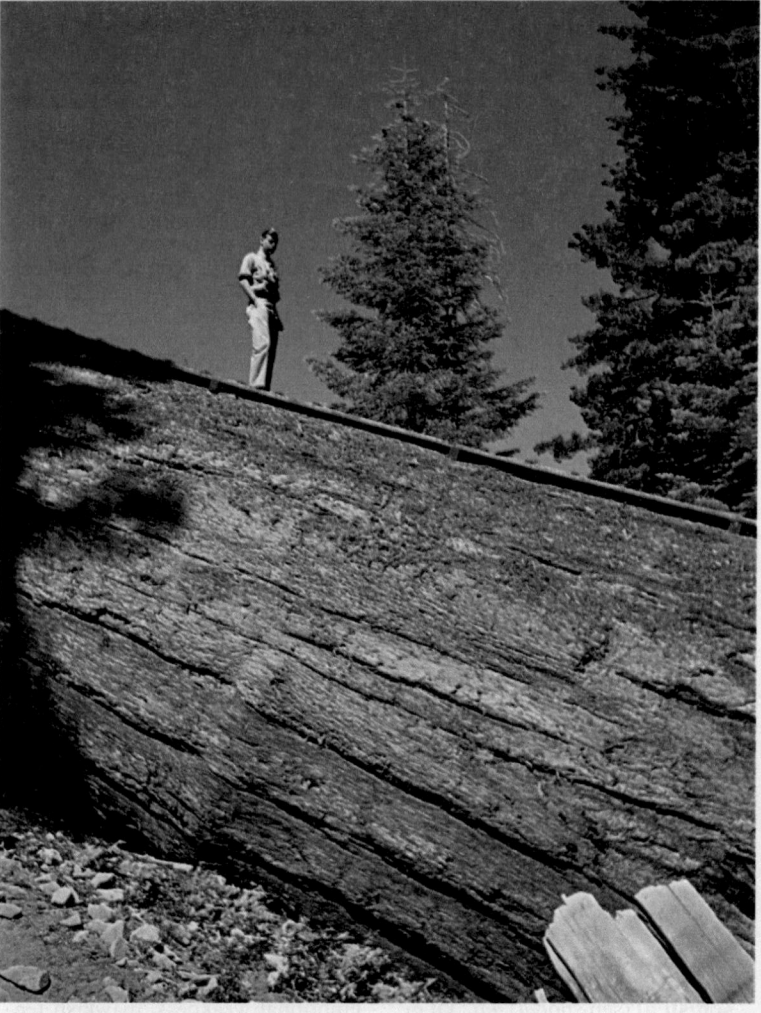

With trunks up to 25 ft. diameter, the **sequoias** of California are claimed to be the largest trees in the world. Some specimens measured had a calculated age of 2,500–3,000 years.

jĕs′ima, -tū-, -chōō-). Third Sunday before Lent. [L., = "70th"]

Sep·tu·a·gint (sĕp′tōōajĭnt, -tū-, -chōō-) *n.* (symbol LXX) Greek version of Old Testament, traditionally said to have been the work of 72 Jewish translators in 3rd c. B.C.; copy of this. **Sep·-tu·a·gint·al** (sĕptōōajĭn′tal, -tū-, -chōō-) *adj.* [L. *septuaginta* 70]

sep·tum (sĕp′tum) *n.* (pl. **-tums, -ta** pr. -ta). (anat., bot., zool.) Partition, dividing wall, membrane, layer, etc., e.g. that between the nostrils.

sep·ul·cher, Brit. sep·ul·chre (sĕp′ulker) *ns.* Tomb, esp. cut in rock or built of stone or brick, burial vault or cave; **Holy S ~**, cave in which Jesus Christ was buried outside walls of Jerusalem; **whited ~**, hypocrite (see Matt. 23).

se·pul·chral (sepŭl′kral) *adj.* Of sepulcher(s) or sepulture; suggestive of the tomb, funereal, gloomy, dismal. **se·pul′chral·ly** *adv.*

seq., seqq. *abbrevs. Sequens, sequentes, -ia.* [L., = "the following"]

se·quel (sē′kwel) *n.* What follows after, continuation or resumption of a story, process, etc., after pause or provisional ending; aftereffects, upshot.

se·que·la (sĭkwē′la) *n.* (pl. **-lae** pr. -lē). (path.) Morbid condition or symptom following upon some disease.

se·quence (sē′kwens) *n.* 1. (Order of) succession. 2. Set of things ranged on some principle of order, series without gaps. 3. (mus.) Phrase or melody repeated at higher or lower pitch. 4. (R.C. Ch.) Hymn occasionally said or sung between gradual and gospel. 5. (cinema) Incident in film story recorded consecutively, corresponding to scene of play. 6. (gram.) ~ **of tenses**, rule or practice according to which tense of verb in subordinate clause depends on that of verb in main clause (e.g. *I think you* are, *thought you* were, *wrong*). **se′quent** *adj.* Following; successive; consecutive. **se·quen·tial** (sĭkwĕn′shal) *adj.* **se·quen′tial·ly** *adv.*

se·ques·ter (sĭkwĕs'ter) *v.t.* 1. Seclude, isolate, set apart. 2. Confiscate, appropriate; seize temporary possession of (debtor's effects).

se·ques·trate (sĭkwĕs'trāt) *v.t.* (**-trat·ed, -trat·ing**) = SEQUESTER (sense 2); divert (income of estate) temporarily from owner until claims are satisfied. **se·ques·tra·tion** (sĕkwĕstrā'shon) *n.*

se·quin (sē'kwĭn) *n.* 1. (hist.) Venetian gold coin. 2. Small circular spangle. **se'quined** *adj.*

se·quoi·a (sĭkwoi'a) *n.* One of 2 California evergreen trees of genus *S~*, the giant sequoia or giant redwood (*S. gigantea*), the largest known tree, or the coast(al) redwood (*S. sempervirens*), the tallest known tree, or a Chinese deciduous conifer, the dawn redwood (*Metasequoia glyptostroboides*) resembling these but much smaller; **S~ National Park**, area in S. central California in the Sierra Nevada Mountains, covering 386,862 acres, (156,590 hectares), noted for its many sequoia trees and mountains. [f. name (*Seqouiah*) of the Cherokee Indian who invented a syllabary for his language]

se·ra: see SERUM.

se·ra·glio (sĭrăl'yō, -rahl'-) (pl. **-glios**), **se·rail** (sĭrīl' -rāl') *ns.* Walled palace, esp. (hist.) that of sultan at Constantinople; harem.

se·ra·i (serah'ē, serī') *n.* (pl. **-ra·is**) = CARAVANSARY. [Pers., = "palace"]

se·ra·pe (serah'pē) *n.* Shawl or blanket worn as cloak in Latin America.

ser·aph (sĕr'af) *n.* (pl. **-aphs, -a·phim** pr. -afĭm). 1. (pl. also **-s**) One of the **seraphim**, in bibl. use, the living creatures with three pairs of wings, seen in Isaiah's vision as hovering above the throne of God. 2. (pl.) Order of angels (see ANGEL). **se·raph·ic** (serăf'ĭk) *adj.* Of or like seraphim; angelic, sublime. **se·raph'i·cal·ly** *adv.*

Se·ra·pis (sĭrā'pĭs). (Egyptian myth.) God combining the Egyptian Osiris with attributes of Zeus, Hades, and Aesculapius invented and introduced into Egypt by Ptolemy I to unite Greeks and Egyptians in common worship.

Serb (sĕrb) *n.* 1. Member, language, of a Slav tribe settled at the invitation of the emperor Heraclius in the Roman province of Moesia, S. of the Danube and N. of Thrace; Serbian. 2. Serbian language.

Ser·bi·a (sĕr'bēa). Former Balkan kingdom, since 1919 part of Yugoslavia. **Ser'bi·an** *adj. & n.* (Native, inhabitant, language) of Serbia.

Ser·bo-Cro·a·tian (sĕrbōkrōā'shan) *adj. & n.* (Of, pertaining to) Slavonic language of Yugoslavia,

Named because of the alleged similarity of its patterns to those on a snakeskin, **serpentine** is a familiar rock in Cornwall, England, especially near the Lizard. It is made into ornaments.

written with Cyrillic letters in Serbia and Roman in Croatia; (of) its speaker(s).

Ser·bo·nis (serbō'nĭs). Boggy lake in the delta of the Nile, in which whole armies were said to have been swallowed up. **Ser·bo·ni·an** *adj.* ~ **bog**, Serbonis; (fig.) difficult position from which escape is impossible.

sere, sear (sēr) *adjs.* (now poet. or rhet.) Dry, withered.

ser·e·nade (serenād') *n.* Performance of music at night in open, esp. by lover under lady's window; piece of music suitable for such performance; instrumental com-

*Chinese women sort cocoons from the moths especially farmed to produce them. **Sericulture** or silk-farming has been practiced in China since prehistoric times.*

position in several movements. ~ *v.* (**-nad·ed, -nad·ing**). Entertain with, perform, a serenade.

Ser·en·dip (sĕrendĭp'), **Ser·en·dib** (sĕrendēb'). Two variants of the ancient name of Sri Lanka.

ser·en·dip·i·ty (sĕrendĭp'ĭtē) *n.* Faculty of making happy discoveries by accident. [coined by Horace Walpole f. title of a tale, "The Three Princes of Serendip"]

se·rene (serēn') *adj.* Clear and calm; unruffled; placid, tranquil, unperturbed. **se·rene'ly** *adv.* **se·ren·i·ty** (serĕn'ĭtē), **se·rene'ness** *ns.*

serf (sĕrf) *n.* Villein, person whose service is attached to the soil and transferred with it (hist.); oppressed person, drudge. **serf'age, serf'dom, serf'hood** *ns.*

Serg., Sergt. *abbrevs.* Sergeant.

serge (sĕrj) *n.* Kind of durable twilled worsted cloth. [L. *serica* silk f. *Seres* the Chinese]

ser·geant (sär'jant) *n.* Non-commissioned officer above corporal; police officer ranking just below inspector or lieutenant; ~**-at-arms** (pl. ~**s-at-arms**), officer who keeps order in legislative chamber, courtroom, etc.; ~ **first class**, enlisted man of seventh grade in U.S. Army, ranking above staff sergeant and below first or master sergeant; ~ **major** (pl. ~**s major**), noncommissioned officer functioning as chief administrative assistant at a U.S. Army, Marine Corps, or Air Force headquarters. **ser'gean·cy** (pl. **-cies**), **ser'geant·ship** *ns.*

se·ri·al (sēr'ēal) *adj.* Of, in, forming, a series; (of story etc.) issued in installments; ~ **number**,

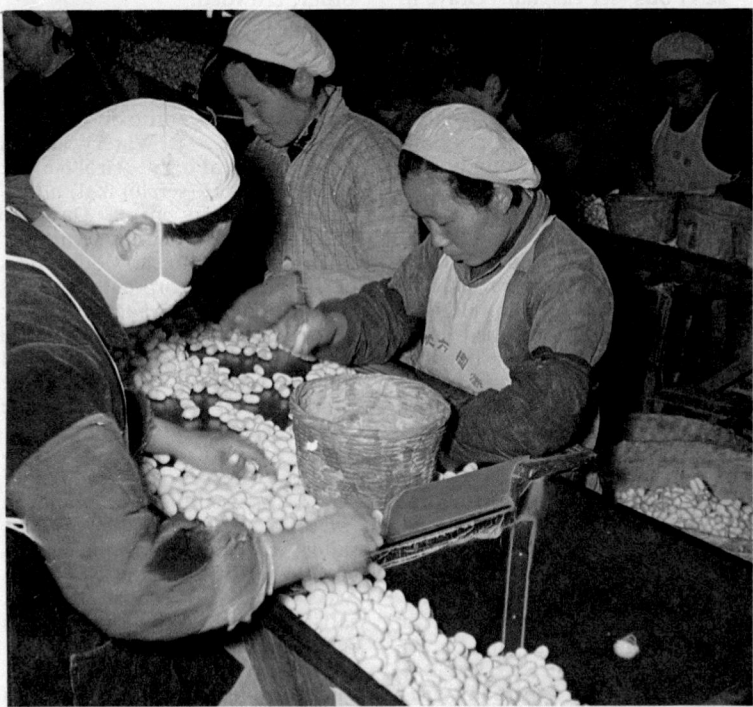

number in series, for identification. **se′ri·al·ly** *adv.* **serial** *n.* Serial story. **se′ri·al·ize** *v.t.* (**-ized, -iz·ing**).

se·ri·a·tim (sērēā′tĭm, sĕr-) *adv.* One after another, one by one in succession.

ser·i·cul·ture (sĕr′ĭkŭlchẽr) *n.* Silkworm breeding, production of raw silk.

se·ries (sēr′ēz) *n.* (pl. **-ries**). Succession, sequence, or set of similar or similarly related things etc.; repertoire of plays presented in successive weeks or on successive nights by same actors, lectures by same speaker, successive games between same teams, esp. (baseball) World Series; set of successive issues of periodical, of literary compositions, of books issued by one publisher in common form and with some similarity of subject or purpose etc.; (geol.) set of strata with common characteristic; (chem.) group of elements with common properties or of compounds related in composition and structure; (math.) set of terms constituting PROGRESSION or having common relation between successive terms; (elect.) set of circuits so arranged (**in ~**) that same current traverses all circuits; (zool.) number of connected genera, families, etc.

ser·if (sĕr′ĭf) *n.* Crossline finishing off a stroke of a letter.

ser·i·graph (sĕr′igrăf, -grahf) *n.* Print made by serigraphy. **se·rig·ra·phy** (sĭrĭg′rafē) *n.* SCREEN printing, esp. by silkscreen. **se·rig′ra·pher** *n.*

se·ri·o·com·ic (sērēōkŏm′ĭk) *adj.* Partly serious and partly comic.

se·ri·ous (sēr′ēus) *adj.* Grave in appearance, manner, intention, purpose, etc., solemn, earnest, not frivolous, trifling, or playful; requiring earnest thought or application; important, not slight; earnest about things of religion, religious-minded. **se′ri·ous·ly** *adv.* **se′ri·ous·ness** *n.*

ser·mon (sĕr′mon) *n.* Discourse delivered from pulpit and usu. based on text of Scripture, by way of religious exhortation or instruction; similar discourse on religious or moral subject delivered elsewhere or published; moral reflection(s), homily. **S~ on the Mount**, discourse of Christ recorded in Matt. 5–7. **ser′mon·ize** *v.* (**-ized, -iz·ing**).

se·rous (sēr′us) *adj.* Of, like, serum; wheylike; **~ membrane**, delicate membrane lining closed cavities of the body.

ser·pent (sĕr′pent) *n.* 1. Snake, esp. large snake; treacherous person. 2. Kind of firework with serpentine motion in air or on ground.

ser·pen·tine (sĕr′pentīn, -tĭn)

Servants, *such as the postillion (above) and the carpenter (right) were employed at one time in the households of wealthy people in Europe and the U.S.A.*

adj. Of or like a serpent, winding; writhing, coiling, tortuous, sinuous; cunning, subtle, treacherous. **~** *n.* 1. (hist.) Kind of cannon. 2. Dull green (or occas. red or brown) soft rock or mineral, chiefly hydrated magnesium silicate, with markings resembling those of snake's skin.

ser·rate (sĕr′ĭt, -āt), **ser·rat·ed** (sĕr′ātĭd, sĭrā′-) *adjs.* Having, forming, row of small projections like teeth of saw; notched like saw. **ser·ra·tion** (sĕrā′shon, sĭ-), **ser·ra·ture** (sĕr′acher) *ns.*

ser·ried (sĕr′ēd) *adj.* (of ranks etc.) Pressed close together, in close order, crowded.

se·rum (sēr′um) *n.* (pl. **se·rums, se·ra** pr. sēr′a). 1. Amber-colored liquid that separates from clot when blood coagulates. 2. Blood serum as antitoxin or therapeutic agent. 3. Watery animal fluid. **se·rol·o·gy** (sĭrŏl′ojē) *n.* **se·ro·log·i·cal** (sĕrolŏj′ĭkal) *adj.*

serv·ant (sĕrv′ant) *n.* One who has undertaken, usu. in return for salary or wages, to carry out orders of individual or corporate employer, esp. one who waits on master or mistress or performs domestic duties in household; devoted follower, person willing to serve another; **civil ~**: see CIVIL; **public ~**, government official.

serve (sĕrv) *v.* (**served, serv·ing**). 1. Be servant (to), render service, be useful (to); be employed (in army, navy, etc.); be soldier, sailor, etc. (in war, against enemy, etc.); **~ at table**, act as waiter. 2. Meet needs (of), avail, suffice, satisfy; punish, requite (serves him right); perform function, be suitable, do what is required for; **~ one's apprenticeship**, go through

training; **~ a (prison) sentence**, undergo it; **~ (one's) time**, undergo imprisonment, serve a sentence; serve apprenticeship. 3. Dish *up*, set (food) on table; set out ready; distribute; supply (person *with*); make legal delivery of (writ etc.), deliver writ etc. to (person); set ball, set (ball) in play; (tennis etc.) start play by striking ball toward opponent, into opposite court etc.; (of male animal) impregnate (the female). **serv′er** *n.* (Usu. lay) attendant on priest at Mass, who brings bread and wine to altar, makes responses, etc., acolyte. **serve** *n.* (tennis etc.) = SERVICE[1] def. 5. **serv′ing** *n.* Single portion of food or drink.

serv·ice[1] (sĕr′vĭs) *n.* 1. Being servant, serving a master; work or duty of a servant; duty that feudal tenant was bound to render to lord; person's disposal or behalf; use, assistance. 2. Department or agency, usually governmental, in which work is done to meet some general need; persons engaged, employment, in this, esp. army, navy, or air force; (attrib.) belonging, issued, etc., to armed force. 3. Liturgical form or office appointed for use on some occasion; single meeting of congregation for worship; musical setting of (parts of) liturgical service. 4. Legal serving of or *of* writ etc. 5. Act of serving ball in tennis etc., way of doing this, ball served. 6. Set of dishes, plates, etc., required for serving meal. 7. Set of trains, steamers, buses, etc., plying at stated times; supply of gas, water, etc., through pipes to private houses etc.; provision of what is necessary, esp. maintenance and repair work carried out by vendor after sale. 8. **~ club**, any of various organizations that benefit their own members and promote community welfare; recreation center for armed forces enlisted personnel; **ser′viceman, service**

woman, person in armed forces; person providing maintenance for appliance etc.; **service module**, module containing main engine and power supplies of spacecraft; **service pipe**, one conveying water or gas from the main to a building; **service station**, place providing maintenance service, gasoline, oil, etc., for motor vehicles; service woman: see SERVICEMAN. **service** *v.t.* (**-iced**, **-ic·ing**). Provide service for, do routine maintenance work on (automobile, washing machine, etc.).

serv·ice² (sẽr'vĭs) *n.* (also ~ **tree**) European tree (*Sorbus domestica*), like mountain ash, with small round or pear-shaped fruit edible when overripe; (also **ser'viceberry** (pl. **-ries**): see SHADBUSH).

serv·ice·a·ble (sẽr'vĭsabel) *adj.* Profitable, useful, capable of rendering service; durable, hard-wearing, for rough or ordinary use rather than ornament. **serv'ice·a·ble·ness**, **serv·ice·a·bil·i·ty** (sẽr-vĭsabĭl'ĭtē) *ns.* **serv'ice·a·bly** *adv.*

ser·vi·ette (sẽrvēĕt') *n.* Table napkin.

ser·vile (sẽr'vĭl) *adj.* Of, being, suitable to, a slave or slaves; slavish; cringing, fawning. **ser'vile·ly** *adv.* **ser·vil·i·ty** (sẽrvĭl'ĭtē) *n.* (pl. **-ties**).

ser·vi·tude (sẽr'vĭtōod, -tūd) *n.* Slavery, subjection, bondage.

ser·vo·mech·a·nism (sẽr'vō-mĕkanĭzem, sẽrvōmĕk'-) *n.* Power-assisted device, usu. for controlling movement (e.g. a brake), freq. deriving its power from the source of energy over which it exercises control.

ses·a·me (sĕs'amē) *n.* (Seeds of)

E. Indian herbaceous plant (*Sesamum indicum*) yielding oil and used as food; **open** ~ , password or charm at which doors or barriers fly open (see ALI BABA).

ses·a·moid (sĕs'amoid) *adj.* Shaped like a sesame seed, nodular (esp. of small independent bones developed in tendons passing over angular structure, as the kneecap or the navicular bone). ~ *n.* Sesamoid bone.

sesqui- *prefix.* One and a half, the ratio 3:2, etc.

ses·qui·cen·ten·ni·al (sĕskwĭ-sĕntĕn'ēal) *adj. & n.* (Of) 150th anniversary. **ses·qui·cen·ten'ni·al·ly** *adv.*

ses·qui·pe·da·li·an (sĕskwĭ-pĭdā'lēan, -dāl'yan), **ses·quip·e·dal** (sĕskwĭp'edal) *adjs.* (of word) Excessively (literally one and one-half feet) long; cumbrous, pedantic.

ses·sile (sĕs'ĭl, -īl) *adj.* (bot., zool.) Immediately attached; without footstalk, peduncle, etc.

ses·sion (sĕsh'on) *n.* Sitting, continuous series of sittings, term of such sittings, of court, legislative or administrative body, etc., for conference or transaction of business; (universities, etc.) part of year during which instruction is given. **ses'sion·al** *adj.*

ses·tet (sĕstĕt', sĕs'tĕt) *n.* Sextet; last six lines of sonnet.

Set (sĕt). (Egyptian myth.) God of evil, brother (or son) of Osiris and his constant enemy; represented with head of beast with long pointed snout.

*A pair of miniature paintings **set** into an elaborate locket which could be closed and worn as a piece of jewellery. The one below was made about 1590.*

set¹ (sĕt) *v.* (**set, set·ting**). 1. Put, lay, stand; apply (thing) *to*; station, place ready; place, turn, in right or specified position or direction; dispose suitably for use, action, or display; plant (seed etc.) in ground; give sharp edge to (razor), bend teeth of (saw) alternately; ~ **sail**, hoist sail; begin voyage; ~ **table**, lay table for meal; ~ **(up) type**, arrange it for printing. 2. Join, attach, fasten; fix; determine, decide, appoint, settle, establish; put parts of (broken bone etc.) into right relative position after fracture or dislocation; insert (precious stone etc.) in gold etc. 3. Bring by placing, arranging, etc., into specified state; make sit down *to* task, cause *to* work, apply oneself *to work*; exhibit or arrange as pattern or as material to be dealt with; draw up (questions, paper) to be answered by examinees; make insertions in (surface) *with*; ~ **to music**, provide (song, words) with music usu. composed for the purpose. 4. Put or come into a settled or rigid position or state; curdle, solidify, harden; take shape, develop into definiteness; fix (hair) when dampened so that it dries in desired style. 5. (of sun, moon, etc.) Appear to descend toward and below horizon. 6. (of tide, current, etc.) Have motion, gather force, sweep along; show or feel tendency. 7. (of sporting dog) Take rigid attitude indicating presence of game; (of dancers) take position facing partners; (of garment) adapt itself to figure, sit *well, badly*, etc. 8. ~ **about**, begin, take steps toward; (colloq.) set on, attack; ~ **against**, contrast or compare, weigh, balance; make hostile or unfriendly toward; ~ **aside**, reserve; reject, disregard; annul; ~ **back**, impede or reverse progress of; (slang) cost (person) specified amount; **set'back** (*n.*), reversal or arrest of progress; (archit.) recession of upper part of building; **set down**, put in writing; attribute *to*, explain or describe oneself *as*; allow (passenger) to alight; **set forth**, make known, declare, expound; begin journey or expedition; **set in**, arise, get vogue, become established; fit (part of garment) into the rest; **set off**, act as adornment or foil to, enhance, make more striking; start (person) laughing, talking, etc.; begin journey; **set'off** (*n.*), thing set off against another, thing of which the amount or effect may be deducted from another by opposite tendency; counterpoise, counterclaim; offset; embellishment, adornment *to* something; (archit.) sloping or horizontal member connecting lower and thicker part of wall etc. with upper receding part; **set on**, urge

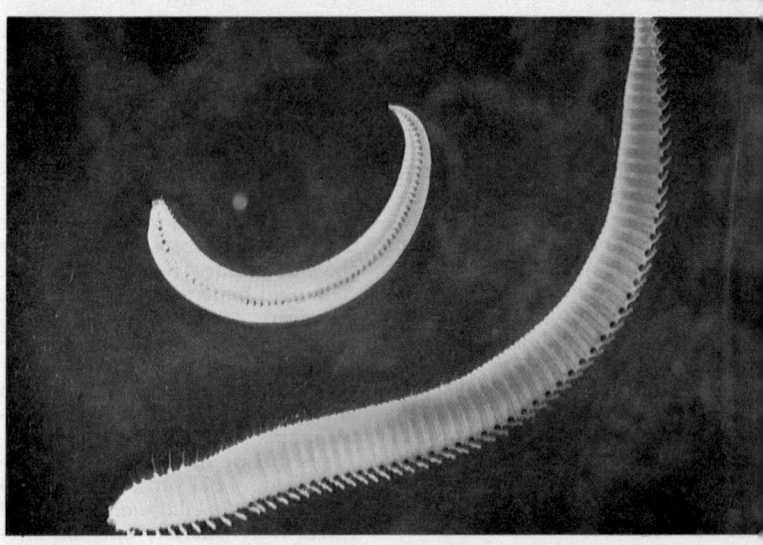

Bristle worms (right) received their name from the rows of setae. They use these to help them move along the ocean bed in search of microscopic organisms which they eat.

(dog etc.) to attack (person etc.); attack; **set out**, demonstrate; exhibit; declare; begin journey; **set to**, begin doing something, esp. fighting or arguing, vigorously; **set-to** (*n.*) (pl. **-tos**), combat, esp. with fists; **set up**, start; occasion, cause; establish (person, oneself) in some capacity; place in view; raise, begin to utter (cry, protest, etc.); propound (theory); prepare (machine) for operation; **set′up** (*n.*), manner or position in which a thing is set up; structure or arrangement of an organization, or the like; (colloq.) faked contest.

set² (sĕt) *adj.* (esp.) Unmoving; fixed; (of persons) determined or resolved *on*; (of speech) composed beforehand; (of phrases) customary; ~ **piece**, fireworks arranged on scaffolding etc.; formal or elaborate arrangement, esp. in art or literature; **of ~ purpose**, intentionally, deliberately; ~ **scene**, stage scene built up of more or less solid material; ~ **screw**, screw to hold 2 parts together or to regulate tension of a spring.

set³ (sĕt) *n.* 1. Number of things or persons belonging together as essentially similar or complementary; group, clique, collection; (tennis etc.) group of games counting as unit of match; radio or television receiving apparatus. 2. Slip or shoot for planting; young fruit just set. 3. (poet.) Setting *of* sun or day. 4. Way current, wind, opinion, etc., sets; drift or tendency *of*; configuration, conformation, habitual posture; warp, bend, displacement, caused by continued pressure or position; (amount of) alternate deflection of sawteeth; fixing of dampened hair. 5. Last coat of plaster on wall; timber frame supporting gallery etc. in coal mine; width of body of type in printing; clutch of eggs; setter's pointing in presence of game; **dead ~**, pointed attack, determined onslaught *at* or *against* (also attrib.). 6. Theatrical or film setting, stage furniture, etc.

se·ta (sē′ta) *n.* (pl. **-tae** pr. -tē). (bot., zool.) Stiff hair, bristle. **se·ta·ceous** (sĭtā′shus), **se·tose** (sē′tōs, sītōs′) *adjs.*

Seth (sĕth). Third son of Adam (Gen. 4).

Se·ton (sē′ton), **Elizabeth Ann** (nee Bayley) (1774–1821). Amer. widow who founded Sisters of Charity of St. Joseph, 1809, and Society for Relief of Poor Widows with Small Children, 1797; canonized on September 14, 1975.

set·tee (sĕtē′) *n.* Long seat with back and usu. arms, for more than one person.

*The distinctive rich golden-chestnut coat of the **Irish setter** has long been admired by dog breeders. The original setters were recognized as a distinct breed as early as 1570.*

set·ter (sĕt′er) *n.* One of several varieties of sporting dogs, with long silky coat, trained to stand rigid on scenting game, as **English ~**, white with brownish and black markings, **Gordon ~**, black with tan markings, **Irish ~**, dark red or chestnut color.

set·ting (sĕt′ĭng) *n.* (esp.) 1. Music composed for particular words. 2. Frame in which jewel is set; surroundings or environment of anything; mounting of play, film, etc., scenery, stage furniture, etc.

set·tle¹ (sĕt′el) *n.* Bench with high back and arms, and freq. with box or chest under seat.

set·tle² (sĕt′el) *v.* (**-tled, -tling**). 1. Establish, become established, in more or less permanent abode, place, or way of life; (cause to) sit down (or *down*) to stay for some time; cease from wandering, motion, change, disturbance, or turbidity; bring to, attain, fixity, composure, certainty, decision etc., determine, decide, appoint. 2 Colonize, establish colonists in, settle as colonists in (country). 3 Subside, sink to bottom of liquid or into lower position. 4. Deal effectually with, dispose or get rid of, do for; pay (bill), pay bill; ~ **up** (**accounts**). 5. Bestow legally for life *on*.

set·tle·ment (sĕt′elment) *n.* (esp.) 1. (law) Conveyance or creation of estate(s) in, property, esp. on marriage. 2. Company of social workers established in poor or crowded district to give educational, medical, recreational, etc., services. 3. Newly settled tract of country, colony. 4. Arrangement, adjustment, of disagreement, strike, etc.; payment of debt etc.

set·tler (sĕt′ler) *n.* (esp.) One who settles in new colony or newly developed country, early colonist.

Se·vas·to·pol (sevăs′topōl). (formerly *Sebastopol*) City and port

*Inspection of underground sewers in London, U.K. Until the 18th century, open drains and cesspools carried refuse. The first underground **sewer** was built in France in the mid-18th century.*

of the Crimea, in U.S.S.R., on the Black Sea; besieged in Crimean War (1854–5) and World War II (1941–2).

sev·en (sĕv′en) *adj.* Amounting to 7; ∼ **deadly sins**: see DEADLY; ∼ **seas**: see SEA; **S∼ Sisters**, the PLEIADES; **S ∼ Weeks' War**, that of 1866 between Austria and Prussia, as result of which Prussia became the predominant German power; **S∼ Wonders of the World**, structures regarded as the most remarkable monuments of antiquity: the Pyramids, the Mausoleum at Harlicarnassus, the Hanging Gardens of Babylon, the temple of Artemis at Ephesus, Phidias's statue of Zeus at Olympia, the Colossus of Rhodes, and the Pharos or lighthouse at Alexandria; **S ∼ Years' War**, that waged 1756–63 by France, Austria, and Russia against Frederick the Great of Prussia and Gt. Britain, in which France lost to Britain her possessions in Amer. and India. **seven** *n.* One more than six; symbol for this (7, vii, or VII);

card with seven pips; seven o'clock; size etc. indicated by 7; set of seven things or persons.

sev·en·teen (sĕv′entēn′) *adj. & n.* One more than 16 (17, xvii, or XVII); ∼-**year locust**, cicada (*Magicicada septendecim*) of eastern U.S. living in soil as larva for 13 to 17 years. **sev′en·teenth′** *adj. & n.*

sev·enth (sĕv′enth) *adj.* Next after sixth; ∼-**day**, Saturday (in Quaker speech and among sects keeping Saturday as sabbath); **S ∼-Day Adventists**, sabbatarian Christian sect; ∼ **heaven**, abode of supreme bliss, highest of seven heavens in Muslim and some Jewish systems. **sev′enth·ly** *adv.* In the seventh place. **seventh** *n.* Seventh part (see PART[1] def. 1); seventh thing etc.; (mus.) interval of which the span involves seven alphabetical names of notes; har-

monic combination of notes thus separated.

sev·en·ty (sĕv′entē) *adj.* Amounting to 70; ∼-**five** (*n.*) 75-mm gun. **seventy** *n.* (pl. **-ties**). Cardinal number, 7 times 10 (70, lxx, or LXX); set of 70 things or persons; **sev′enties**, (pl.) numbers etc. from 70 to 79; these years of century or life. **sev′en·ti·eth** *adj. & n.*

sev·er (sĕv′er) *v.* Separate, divide, part, disunite; cut or break off, take away, (part) from whole. **sev′er·ance** (sĕv′erans, sĕv′rans) *n.* ∼ **pay**, amount paid to dismissed employee in good standing.

sev·er·al (sĕv′eral, sĕv′ral) *adj.* 1. Separate, distinct, individual, respective. 2. A few, more than two or three but not many. ∼ *pron.* Moderate number of persons or things. **sev′er·al·ly** *adv.*

se·vere (sevēr′) *adj.* (**-ver·er, -ver·est**). Austere, strict, harsh; violent, vehement, extreme; trying, making great demands on endurance, energy, skill, etc.; unadorned, without redundance, restrained. **se·vere′ly** *adv.* **se·ver·i·ty** (sevĕr′ĭtē) (pl. **-ties**), **se·vere′ness** *ns.*

Sè·vres (sĕv′re, sĕv). Town near Paris, site of the French national porcelain factory since 1756; porcelain from this factory.

sew (sō) *v.* (**sewed, sewn**, pr. **sōn** or **sewed, sew·ing**). Fasten, join (pieces of material, leather, etc.) by passing thread through series of punctures made by needle carrying the thread or with an awl; make by sewing; fasten together sheets of (book) by passing thread or wire through back fold of each sheet; use needle and thread or sewing machine; ∼ **up**, (colloq.) be sure of; control completely; **sewing machine**, machine for sewing or stitching. **sew′er** *n.*

sew·age (soo′ĭj) *n.* Spent water supply of a community, including wastes from domestic and trade premises etc. and ground water; ∼ **treatment plant**, plant for purifying sewage by artificial methods, rendering it fit for discharge into river, lake, or tidal waters.

Sew·ard (soo′erd), **William Henry** (1801–72). Amer. statesman; senator, 1849–61, secretary of State, 1861–9; remembered for **Seward's Folly**, his purchase of Alaska from Russia in 1867 for $7,200,000; **Seward Peninsula**, peninsula in W. Alaska, extending 180 mi. (290 km) to Cape Prince of Wales on Bering Strait; westernmost point on the N. Amer. continent.

sew·er (soo′er) *n.* Pipe or

*Before the invention of the **sextant** from John Hadley's reflecting quadrant in 1731, navigators on ships had to use a crude cross-staff to measure the angle of sun or stars.*

conduit for conveying sewage. **sew′er·age** *n.*

sewn: see SEW.

sex (sĕks) *n.* Sum of the physiological differences in structure and function that distinguish the male from the female in animals and plants; males or females collectively; (loosely) sexual instincts, desires, etc., or their manifestation; (colloq.) sexual intercourse; (attrib.) arising from sex; ~ **appeal**, qualities attracting members of the opposite sex; ~ **chromosome**, one affecting the determination of sex of an organism; ~**-limited**, (of Mendelian character) expressed only in one sex, although the controlling gene is not on a sex chromosome; ~**-linked**, (of Mendelian character) controlled by a gene that is carried on a sex chromosome. **sex** *v.t.* Examine in order to determine the sex of. **sex′ism** *n.* Discrimination or bias against women. **sex′ist** *n.* One so biased. **sex′less** *adj.* **sex′less·ly** *adv.* **sex′less·ness** *n.* **sex′pot** *n.* (slang) Girl or woman of overly obvious sexual attractiveness.

sex-, sexi- *prefixes.* Six.

sex·a·ges·nar·i·an (sĕksajenār′ĕan) *adj. & n.* (Person) aged 60 years or more but less than 70.

Sex·a·ges·i·ma (sĕksajĕs′ĭma). Second Sunday before Lent. [L., = "60th"]

sex·a·ges·i·mal (sĕksajĕs′ĭmal) *adj.* Proceeding by sixties; of, based on, involving, division into 60 equal parts.

sex·en·ni·al (sĕksĕn′ēal) *adj.* Lasting, (occurring) once in, six years.

sext (sĕkst) *n.* (R.C. Ch.) Canonical HOUR, (orig. said at) sixth hour of day (noon).

sex·tant (sĕks′tant) *n.* Instrument with mirrors and graduated arc of sixth part of circle, used by navigators for finding position by measuring altitudes of heavenly bodies or horizontal angles between terrestrial objects.

sex·tet, sex·tette (sĕkstĕt′, sĕks′tĕt) *ns.* 1. (mus.) (Composition for) six voices or instruments in combination. 2. Set of six persons or things.

sex·ton (sĕks′ton) *n.* Church officer having care of building and contents of church, freq. with duties of bell ringer and gravedigger.

sex·tu·ple (sĕkstōo′pel, -tū′-, -tŭp′el, sĕks′tupel) *adj. & n.* Sixfold (amount). ~ *v.* (**-pled, -pling**). Multiply by six.

sex·u·al (sĕk′shōoᴧl) *adj.* 1. Of

Navigation Sextant

index mirror

horizon mirror

eyepiece of telescope

index arm

graduated arc

decimal micrometer

The dotted lines indicate the direction of light from sun or star and horizon

sex; of, occurring between, members of the two sexes; ~ **inter-course**, copulation, esp. of man and woman. 2. (biol.) Having sex or sexual organs; reproducing by union of male and female gametes (opp. *asexual*). 3. (bot., of classification) Based on distinction of sexes in plants. **sex′u·al·ly** *adv.* **sex·u·al·i·ty** (sĕkshōoăl′ĭtē) *n.*

sex·u·al·ize (sĕk′shōoalīz) *v.t.* (**-ized, -iz·ing**). Make sexual, attribute sex to. **sex·u·al·i·za·tion** (sĕkshōoalĭzā′shon) *n.*

sex·y (sĕk′sē) *adj.* (**sex·i·er, sex·i·est**). (colloq.) Sexually attractive or provocative; engrossed with sex. **sex′i·ly** *adv.* **sex′i·ness** *n.*

Sey·chelles (sāshĕlz′, sāshĕl′). Republic in the Indian Ocean, NE. of Madagascar, consisting of a group of about 90 islands, including Mahé, Praslin, La Digue; capital, Victoria, on Mahé; member of Brit. Commonwealth.

Sey·mour (sē′mōr, -mȯr), **Jane** (c1509–37). Third queen of Henry VIII of England and mother of Edward VI.

sf, SF *abbrevs.* Science fiction.

s.g. *abbrev.* Specific gravity.

*Crude dwellings of corrugated iron and stone on the Black River in Jamaica. Poverty in that country still compels many families to live in **shacks,** although better housing is being built.*

Sgt, Sgt. *abbrevs.* Sergeant.

sh *int.* = HUSH.

Shaan·xi (shĕn´shē´) = SHENSI.

shab·by (shăb´ē) *adj.* (**-bi·er, -bi·est**). Contemptible, paltry, dishonorable; dingy and faded from wear or exposure; worn, dilapidated; shabbily dressed; ∼-**genteel**, attempting to look genteel or keep up appearances in spite of shabbiness. **shab´bi·ly** *adv.* **shab´bi·ness** *n.*

shack (shăk) *n.* Roughly built hut or shanty. ∼ *v.i.* ∼ **up** (**with**), (slang) live (with) as husband or wife without marriage.

shack·le (shăk´el) *n.* Metal loop or staple, bow of padlock, link closed by bolt for connecting chains etc., coupling link; (pl.) fetters, impediments, restraints. ∼ *v.t.* (**-led, -ling**). Fetter, impede trammel. **shack´ler** *n.*

shad (shăd) *n.* (pl. **shads**, collect. **shad**). Any of various deep-bodied herringlike fishes of genus *Alosa*, esp. *A. sapidissima*, much used as food; **shad´bush**, any of several N. Amer. trees and shrubs (genus *Amelanchier*), having creamy white blossoms and small blue-black or purple fruit; also called Juneberry and shadblow.

shad·dock (shăd´ok) *n.* (Tree, *Citrus grandis*, bearing) largest citrus fruit, esp. large coarse pear-shaped varieties of this (the smaller and rounder being called grapefruit). [Captain *Shaddock*, who introduced the plants into Barbados (1696)]

shade (shād) *n.* 1. Comparative or partial darkness, esp. caused by more or less opaque object intercepting rays of sun or other source of light; comparative obscurity; darker part of picture; place sheltered from sun, cool or sequestered retreat; (pl.) darkness *of* night or evening; **the ∼s**, the abode of the dead, Hades. 2. Color, esp. with regard to its depth or as distinguished from one nearly like it; gradation of color; (painting) color darkened by admixture of black; darker tone of a color as dist. from *tint*. 3. Slight difference, small amount; unsubstantial or unreal thing. 4. Soul after death, ghost, disembodied spirit. 5. Screen excluding or moderating light, heat, etc.; eye shield; cover for lamp etc.; **shades**, (slang) sunglasses. **shade´less** *adj.* **shade** *v.* (**shad·ed, shad·ing**). Screen from excessive light; cover, keep off, or moderate power of (luminous object, light) with or as intervening object; make dark or gloomy; darken (parts of drawing etc.), esp. with parallel pencil lines, to give effects of light and shade or gradations of color; (of color, opinion, etc.) pass *off* by degrees into another color or variety, make

The **shackle** on this steam train is an example of those used before the advent of the modern train. Carriages and rolling stock are now secured without the use of retaining chains.

pass thus *into* another. **shad´ed** *adj.* **shad´ing** *n.*

shad·ow (shăd´ō) *n.* 1. Shade; dark part of picture, room, etc.; patch of shade, dark figure projected by body intercepting rays of light, this regarded as appendage of person or thing; (fig.) inseparable attendant or companion. 2. Reflected image; delusive semblance or image; type, foreshadowing, adumbration; slightest trace; phantom, ghost. 3. Protection, shelter. 4. **shad´owboxing**, boxing against imaginary opponent as form of training; **shadow cabinet**, (Brit. politics) members of opposition party who would be cabinet ministers if that party became the government. **shad´ow·less, shad´ow·y** *adjs.* **shadow** *v.t.* 1.

Still a British colony, the **Seychelles** *consists of more than 80 islands and atolls. The people are mostly of African descent and grow coconuts, cinnamon and vanilla as cash crops.*

Cast shadow over. 2. Indicate obscurely, set *forth* dimly or in slight outline, prefigure. 3. Follow closely; follow and watch secretly. **shad´ow·er** *n.*

Shad·rach (shăd´răk). One of three Jewish youths who came unharmed from a furnace into which they were thrown by Nebuchadnezzar (Dan. 3).

shad·y (shā´dē) *adj.* (**shad·i·er, shad·i·est**). 1. Affording shade; shaded; **on the ∼ side of**, older than (specified age). 2. Not able to bear the light, disreputable, of doubtful honesty. **shad´i·ly** *adv.* **shad´i·ness** *n.*

shaft (shăft, shahft) *n.* 1. Long slender rod forming body of spear, lance, or arrow; spear (archaic); arrow; ray *of* light, streak *of* lightning; (fig.) barbed remark, sarcasm. 2. Stem; part of column between base and capital; upright part of cross; part of chimney above roof; rib of feather; more or less long, narrow, and straight part supporting or connecting part(s) of greater thickness etc.; part of golf club between handle and head; handle, haft, of tool, etc. 3. (mech.) Long cylindrical rotating rod upon which

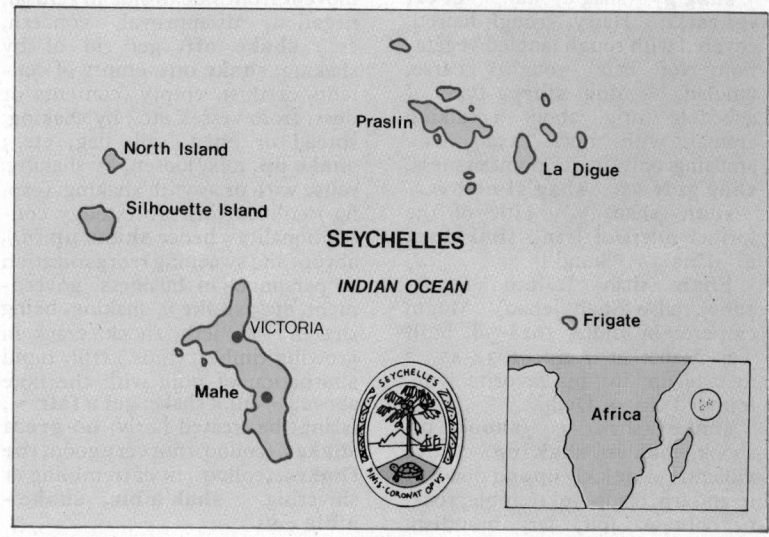

SEYCHELLES

INDIAN OCEAN

North Island
Silhouette Island
Praslin
La Digue
Frigate
VICTORIA
Mahe
Africa

Thomas Hare's impression of workers at the 'Shaft Bottom' of a coal-mine. Coal is no longer hand-winched to the surface in baskets, but brought up by continuous conveyor systems.

are fixed wheels, propeller, gears, etc. for transmission of motive power. **4.** One of long bars between pair of which horse is harnessed to vehicle. **5.** Vertical or inclined well-like excavation giving access to mine, tunnel, etc.; any similar well-like excavation or passage, as that in which elevator runs etc.

shag (shăg) *n.* **1.** Rough growth or mass of hair etc. **2.** (archaic) Long-napped rough cloth. **3.** Strong, coarse kind of cut tobacco. **4.** Cormorant.

shag·bark (shăg′bärk) *n.* (Wood, nut of) hickory tree (*Carya ovata*) having thick, gray, curling bark.

shag·gy (shăg′ē) *adj.* (**-gi·er, -gi·est**). Hairy, rough-haired; covered with rough tangled vegetation; (of hair) rough, coarse, tangled; **~ dog story**, type of anecdote (orig. about a talking animal) with much detail, usu. amusing only in its pointlessness. **shag′gi·ly** *adv.* **shag′gi·ness** *n.*

shah (shah) *n.* Title of the former rulers of Iran. **shah′dom** *n.* [Pers., = "king"]

Shah (shah) **Ja·han** (1592?–1666). (also Shah Jehan) Mogul emperor in India, 1628–58; built Taj Mahal at Agra, 1632–45, a mausoleum for his favorite wife; founded city of Delhi.

shake (shāk) *v.* (**shook** pr. shōŏk, **shak·en, shak·ing**). Move violently or quickly up and down or to and fro; (cause to) tremble, rock, or vibrate; jolt, jar; brandish; weaken, make less firm or stable; agitate, shock, disturb; **~ down**, cause to settle, descend, by shaking; test or try out, as ship or airplane; (slang) extort money from; **shake′-down** (*n.*), improvised bed; (slang) extortion of money by blackmail, violence, etc.; thorough search of person or place; **shake hand(s)**, clasp right hands at meeting or parting, over concluded bargain, in congratulation, etc.; **shake head**, move it from side to side in refusal, negation, disapproval, concern, etc.; **shake off**, get rid of by shaking; **shake out**, empty of contents or dust, empty (contents or dust) from vessel, etc., by shaking; spread or open (sail, flag, etc.); **shake up**, mix, loosen, by shaking; rouse with or as with shaking; (esp. fig.) enliven, disturb (stodgy conventionality); hence **shake′up** (*n.*), abrupt and sweeping reorganization of personnel in business, government, etc.; **shake** *n.* shaking, being shaken; jolt, jerk, shock; crack in growing timber; (mus.) trill, rapid alternation of note with the note above; = MILK shake; **get a fair ~**, (slang) be treated fairly; **no great shakes**, (colloq.) not very good; **the shakes**, (colloq.) fit of trembling or shivering. **shak′a·ble, shake′-a·ble** *adjs.*

shak·er (shā′ker) *n.* (esp.) **1.** Vessel in which ingredients of cocktails are shaken; vessel to sprinkle salt etc. on food. **2.** **S ~**, member of Amer. religious celibate sect living in mixed communities, orig. founded (1747) in Manchester, England, by secession from the Quakers, and named from dancing movements that formed part of their worship.

Shake·speare, Shak·spere (shāks′pēr), **William** (1564–1616). England's greatest dramatist and poet; author of the comedies, *Twelfth Night, A Midsummer Night's Dream, The Tempest, The Merchant of Venice, Much Ado About Nothing,* etc.; the tragedies, *Romeo and Juliet, Julius Caesar, Hamlet, Othello, King Lear, Macbeth,* etc.; the histories, *Henry IV, Henry V, Henry VIII,* etc.; and the poems, "Venus and Adonis," "The Rape of Lucrece," etc., and many sonnets. **Shake·spear′e·an, Shake·spear′i·an, Shak·sper′-i·an** *adjs. & ns.* **~ sonnet**: see SONNET.

shak·o (shăk′ō, shā′kō) *n.* (pl. **shak·os, shak·oes**). Military cap, more or less cylindrical, with peak and upright plume or tuft. [Magyar csákó]

shak·y (shā′kē) *adj.* (**shak·i·er, shak·iest**). Unsteady, trembling, unsound, infirm; unreliable. **shak′i·ly** *adv.* **shak′i·ness** *n.*

shale (shāl) *n.* Very fine-grained laminated sedimentary rock consisting of consolidated mud or clay;

~ **oil**, oil obtained from bituminous shale. **shal′y** *adj.* (**shal·i·er, shal·i·est**).

shall (shăl) *v.aux.* (2nd pers. sing. archaic **shalt** pr. shălt, past and conditional **should** pr. shŏod). Forming compound tenses or moods expressing: (1) (in first pers.) simple future action; (2) (in other person) command; (3) (in all persons) obligation, intention, necessity, etc.

shal·lot (shalŏt′, shăl′ot) *n.* Onionlike plant (*Allium ascalonicum*), native to Syria, with small clustered bulbs, resembling but milder than those of garlic, used for flavoring. [Fr. *eschalotte*, dim. of *eschaloigne* f. L. *ascalonia*, f. *Ascalon* in Palestine]

shal·low (shăl′ō) *adj.* Of little depth (lit. and fig.), superficial, trivial. **shal′low·ly** *adv.* **shal′-low·ness** *n.* **shallow** *n.* Shallow place, shoal. ~ *v.* Become shallower; make shallow.

shalt: see SHALL.

sham (shăm) *n.* Imposture, pretense, humbug; person, thing, pretending or pretended to be something that he or it is not. ~ *adj.* Pretended, counterfeit, imitation. ~ *v.* (**shammed, sham·-ming**). Feign, simulate; pretend to be. **sham′mer** *n.*

sha·man (shah′man, shā′-) *n.* (pl. **-mans**). Priest or witch doctor in shamanism. **sha′man·ism** *n.* Primitive religion of Ural-Altaic peoples of N. Asia in which gods, spirits, and demons influencing all human life are believed to be responsive to shamans; any similar religion, esp. among N. Amer.

This cliff face shows a layer of **shale** compressed between two layers of sandstone, the result of changes in alluvial deposits over long periods of time.

Indians.

sham·ble (shăm′bel) *v.i.* (**-bled, -bling**). Walk, run, in shuffling, awkward, or decrepit way. ~ *n.* Shambling gait.

sham·bles (shăm′belz) *n.pl.* (usu. considered sing.). Butchers' slaughterhouse; scene of carnage or chaotic confusion.

shame (shām) *n.* Feeling of humiliation excited by consciousness of guilt or shortcoming, of appearing ridiculous, or of having offended against propriety etc.; fear of this as restraint on behavior; state of disgrace, ignominy, or discredit; person or thing that brings disgrace; (colloq.) regrettable or unlucky thing. **shame′ful, shame′less** *adjs.* **shame′ful·ly, shame′less·ly** *advs.* **shame′ful·ness, shame′less·ness** *ns.* **shame** *v.t.* (**shamed, sham·ing**). Bring shame on, be a shame to, make ashamed; put to shame by superior

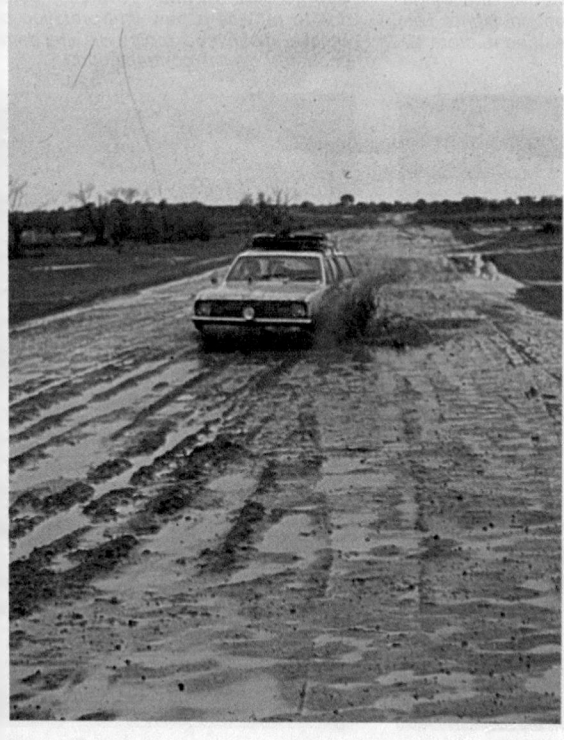

Even when **shallow** water floods an unsurfaced road in the Northern Territory of Australia, cars can get bogged. If they drive too fast, drivers may find that they are in an uncontrollable skid.

If the few proven facts of his life are assessed, it is astonishing that so many books could be written about **William Shakespeare**. The first 'Life' by Nicholas Rowe was published in 1709.

excellence; drive *into, out of,* through shame or fear of shame.

shame·faced (shām´fāst) *adj.* Ashamed; embarrassed. **shame·-fac·ed·ly** (shāmfā´sĭdlē, shām´-fāstlē) *adv.* **shame·fac´ed·ness** *n.*

sham·poo (shămpōo´) *v.t.* (**-pooed, -poo·ing**). Wash (hair) with cleansing preparation; use cleansing preparation on surface of (carpet, upholstery, etc.). ~ *n.* Shampooing (preparation). **sham·poo´er** *n.* [prob. f. Hind. *ćaṅpo,* imper. of *ćaṅpnā* press, knead (dough or limbs)]

sham·rock (shăm´rŏk) *n.* Trifoliate plant, used, according to tradition, by St. Patrick to illustrate doctrine of Trinity, and hence adopted as national emblem of Ireland; (now usu.) lesser yellow trefoil (*Trifolium dubium*). [Ir. *seamróg,* dim. of *seamar* clover]

Shan (shahn, shăn) *n.* (pl. **Shans,** collect. **Shan**). Member, language, of a Thai people of Burma; ~ **State,** state of E. Burma.

Shan·dong (shahn´dawng´) = SHANTUNG.

Shang·hai (shănghī´; *Chin.* shahng·hī´). Principal seaport and commercial center of China, in the E., near the mouth of the Yangtze River.

shang·hai (shănghī´, shăng´hī) *v.t.* (**-haied, -hai·ing**). Drug or otherwise render insensible and ship as sailor while unconscious. [f. SHANGHAI]

Shan·gri·la (shănggrĭlah´, shăng´grĭlah) *n.* Imaginary hidden paradise on Earth. [f. place in James Hilton's novel *Lost Horizon* (1933)]

shank (shăngk) *n.* 1. Leg, lower part of leg from knee to ankle; shinbone, tibia; (part of) leg of bird

(pop.); lower part of foreleg of horse; cut of meat. 2. Stem; straight part of nail, pin, fishhook, etc.; stem of key, spoon, anchor, etc.; shaft of tool between head etc. and handle; narrow part of shoe beneath instep; body of type.

Shan·si (shahn´sē´). Province of N. China.

shan't (shănt, shahnt) *v.* Contr. of *shall not.*

Shan·tung (shăn´tŭng´; *Chin.* shahn·dōong´). Maritime province of NE. China.

shan·tung (shăntŭng´) *n.* Soft undressed Chinese silk, usu. undyed and sometimes mixed with cotton. [f. SHANTUNG]

shan·ty (shăn´tē) *n.* (pl. **-ties**). Hut, cabin; mean roughly constructed dwelling. [Canadian-Fr. *chantier* log hut, f. Fr., = "workshop"]

Shan·xi (shahn´shē´) = SHANSI.

SHAPE (shāp) *n.* Supreme Headquarters Allied Powers Europe.

shape (shāp) *n.* 1. External form, contour, configuration; visible appearance characteristic of person, thing, etc.; guise; concrete presentment, embodiment; phantom (now rare); dimly seen figure. 2. Kind, description, sort. 3. Definite or regular form, orderly arrangement. **shape´less** *adj.* **shape´less·ly** *adv.* **shape´less·ness** *n.* **shape** *v.* (**shaped, shap·ing**). Create, form, construct; model, mold, bring into desired or definite figure or form; frame mentally, imagine; assume form, develop into shape, give

A paussid beetle showing the shiny **shard** *or elytra which cover the wings when the insect is not in flight. The space beneath may be used to store air in aquatic species.*

signs of future shape; ~ **up,** take (specified or favorable) form; behave better; exercise for health.

shape·ly (shāp´lē) *adj.* (**-li·er, -li·est**). Well-formed or proportioned, of pleasing shape. **shape´li·ness** *n.*

shard (shärd), **sherd** (shĕrd) *ns.* 1. = POTSHERD. 2. Hard wing case of beetle, elytron.

share[1] (shār) *n.* Portion detached for individual from common amount; part one is entitled to have or expected to contribute, equitable portion; part one gets or contributes; part proprietorship of property held by joint owners, esp. one of the equal parts into which company's capital is divided; **share´cropper,** tenant farmer paying rent with part of his crop; **share´holder,** owner of shares in corporation. **share** *v.* (**shared, shar·ing**). Apportion, give share of; give away part of; get or have share of; possess, use, endure, jointly with others; have share(s), be sharer(s); (in the language of some religious groups) communicate to others one's spiritual experiences.

share[2] (shār) *n.* PLOWSHARE; blade of cultivator or other agricultural tool for cutting soil.

shark (shärk) *n.* Any of various long-bodied cartilaginous fish, esp. large voracious kinds; rapacious person, swindler; (colloq.) expert in some particular activity; **shark´-skin,** skin of shark used as leather etc.; worsted twill woven fabric, smooth fabric of rayon etc.

As a dramatist, critic or propagandist **George Bernard Shaw** *reveled in paradox to provide a new interpretation of an over-discussed topic. His life demonstrated similar contradictions.*

sharp (shärp) *adj.* 1. Having keen edge or point, not blunt; peaked, pointed, edged; well-defined; abrupt, angular. 2. Keen, pungent, acid, tart; shrill, piercing; biting, harsh, severe, intense, painful. 3. Acute, sensitive, keen-witted, vigilant, clever; quick to take advantage, artful, unscrupulous, dishonest; ~ **practice**, relentless pursuit of advantage; trickery. 4. Vigorous, speedy, impetuous. 5. (mus.) Above true pitch, too high; (following name of note, as *C sharp* etc.) a semitone higher than the note named; (of key) having sharps in the signature. 6. (slang) Very fashionably dressed; ~-**shinned hawk, sharp'shin**, small N. Amer. hawk (*Accipiter striatus*) with long tail and rounded wings. **sharp'ly** *adv.*

sharp'ness *n.* **sharp** *n.* 1. Sewing needle with sharp point. 2. (mus.) Note raised by a semitone above natural pitch; symbol (♯) indicating this raising. 3. (pl.) Finer parts of husk and coarser particles of flour of wheat and other cereals. ~ *adv.* Sharply; abruptly; punctually; (mus.) above true pitch; **sharp'shooter**, skilled marksman; businessman interested in quick profit with no regard for ethical practices. **sharp** *v.i.* Cheat, swindle, esp. at cards. **sharp'er** *n.* Cheat, swindler, esp. at cards. **sharp'en** *v.* Make, become sharp.

shash·lik (shahsh′lĭk, shahsh-lĭk′) *n.* Marinated cubes of meat, esp. lamb, broiled on skewer; shish kebab.

Shas·ta (shăst′a), **Mount.** Extinct volcano in N. California, 14,162 ft. (4,317 m), in the Cascade Mountain Range.

shat·ter (shăt′er) *v.* Break suddenly and violently in pieces;

utterly destroy, wreck; **shat'ter-proof**, able to resist or withstand shattering. **shat'ter·ing·ly** *adv.*

shave (shāv) *v.* (**shaved, shaved** or **shav·en, shav·ing**). 1. Remove (hair), free (chin etc.) of hair, relieve of hair on chin etc., with razor; shave oneself; **shaving brush**, brush for applying lather before shaving. 2. Cut or pare away surface of (wood etc.) with plane or other sharp tool. 3. Pass close to without touching; miss narrowly, nearly graze. **shave** *n.* 1. Shaving, being shaved. 2. Close approach without contact; narrow miss, escape, or failure. 3. Knife blade with handle at each end for shaving wood etc. **shav'a·ble, shave'a·ble** *adjs.*

shav·en (shā′ven) *adj.* Shaved, tonsured; closely clipped.

mako shark

hammer-head shark

Contrary to popular opinion, not all members of the **shark** *order are harmful to man. The largest, the whale shark, eats only microscopic plankton; the smallest is too small to bite a human.*

thresher shark

A **sheaf** of grain could be cut by hand, or by a binder, before being put in stooks to dry. However, today, combine or header harvesters have eliminated the need for early cutting of grain.

Mechanical **shears** have been used for many years. In Australia, scientists are trying to find a substance which, when fed to sheep, will enable the fleece to be shed automatically.

shav·er (shā′ver) *n.* (esp.) 1. (colloq.) Lad, youngster. 2. Electrical appliance for shaving hair from face.

Sha·vi·an (shā′vēan) *adj.* (In the manner) of G. B. SHAW.

shav·ing (shā′vĭng) *n.* (esp.) Thin slice taken from surface with sharp tool; thin slice of wood cut off with plane.

Shaw (shaw), **George Bernard** (1856–1950). Irish playwright and critic; author of the plays *Man and Superman, Back to Methuselah, Pygmalion, Saint Joan*, etc.

shawl (shawl) *n.* Oblong or square piece of fabric, freq. folded into triangle, worn over shoulders or head, around neck, etc., or wrapped around baby. [Pers. *shāl*]

Shaw·nee (shawnē′) *n.* (pl. -nees, collect. -nee). Member of Algonquian-speaking tribe of N. Amer. Indians, formerly of Tennessee Valley area, now in Oklahoma; language of this tribe.

shay (shā) *n.* (dial.) Chaise.

Shays (shāz), **Daniel** (1747?–1825). Amer. officer in Revolutionary War; led unsuccessful **Shays' Rebellion** of farmers in Massachusetts protesting high land taxes and mortgage foreclosures, 1786–7.

she (shē) *pron.* Third person nom. sing. fem. pronoun, denoting the female person, animal, etc. referred to; object, device, country, etc., personified as feminine. ~ *n.* Female animal.

sheaf (shēf) *n.* (pl. **sheaves** pr. shēvz). Large bundle of cereal plants bound together after reaping; cluster or bundle of things laid lengthwise together; bundle or quiverful of 24 arrows. ~ *v.t.*

Bind into sheaf or sheaves.

shear (shēr) *v.* (**sheared, sheared** or **shorn** pr. shōrn, shôrn, **shear·ing**). 1. Cut with sharp instrument (poet. and archaic); clip, cut with scissors or shears; clip wool from (sheep); (fig.) fleece, strip bare. 2. Distort or break, be distorted or broken by, the strain called a shear (see sense 2 of *n.* below). ~ *n.* 1. (pl., with sing. or pl. verb) Cutting instrument with two meeting blades pivoted as in scissors or connected by spring and passing close over each other edge to edge. 2. (mech.) Kind of strain produced by pressure in structure of a substance, its successive layers being shifted laterally over each other. 3. (pl., also

~ **legs**): see SHEERS. **shear′er** *n.*

shear·ling (shēr′lĭng) *n.* (Woo̥ from) sheep shorn once.

shear·wa·ter (shēr′wawte̥ -wŏter) *n.* One of several seabirds ⟨ genus *Puffinus*, with long wing̥ skimming close to water in flight.

sheath (shēth) *n.* (pl. **sheath** pr. shēdhz). Close-fitting cove̥ esp. for blade of weapon or imple̥ ment; (bot., anat., etc.) sheathlik̥ covering, investing membran̥ tissue, skin, horny case, etc.

sheathe (shēdh) *v.t.* (**sheathe̥ sheath·ing**). Put into sheath̥ encase, protect with sheathing̥ **sheath′ing** *n.* Protective layer ⟨ boards, metal plates, etc., on ou̥ side of bottom of wooden ship, o̥ piece of machinery, roof, wall, et̥

The sooty **shearwater**, like oth̥ related birds, feeds in the north̥ oceans during the summer months, b̥ breeds in the southern hemisphe̥ where it nests in burrows.

Classing wool from exhibition class **sheep** *at an Australian show. Although some breeds are raised for wool, others provide meat, and some sheep serve both purposes.*

sheave[1] (shǐv, shēv) *n.* Grooved wheel or pulley of pulley block etc.

sheave[2] (shēv) *v.t.* (**sheaved, sheav·ing**). Gather (corn etc.) into sheaves.

sheaves: see SHEAF.

She·ba (shē′ba), **Queen of.** Balkis, who visited Solomon to test his wisdom (I Kings 10).

she·bang (shebăng′) *n.* (slang) House, hut; matter, business.

shed[1] (shĕd) *n.* Slight structure for shelter, storage, etc., freq. built as lean-to, and sometimes with open front or sides; similar but large and strongly built structure on pier, at airport, etc.

shed[2] (shĕd) *v.t.* (**shed, shed·ding**). Part with, let fall (off), drop; cause (blood) to flow; disperse, diffuse, spread abroad; ∼ **light on**, illuminate, esp. *fig.*

she'd (shĕd). Contr. of *she had, she would.*

sheen (shēn) *n.* Splendor, radiance, luster. **sheen'y** *adj.* (**sheen·i·er, sheen·i·est**).

sheep (shēp) *n.* (pl. **sheep**). Wild or domesticated timid, gregarious, woolly, often horned, ruminant mammal of genus *Ovis*, closely allied to goat, bred for flesh and wool; (usu. pl.) member(s) of minister's flock, parishioners, etc.; person as stupid, poor-spirited, unoriginal, or timid as a sheep; ∼**-dip**, preparation for cleansing sheep of vermin or preserving their wool; place for such cleansing; **sheep'dog**, dog trained to herd sheep; **Old English sheep'dog**, shaggy-coated bobtailed dog used for guarding and herding sheep; **sheep's eyes**, amorous glances; **sheep laurel**, low-growing evergreen (*Kalmia angustifolia*) of eastern N. Amer., having pink flowers and poisonous leaves; **sheep'shank**, knot for temporarily shortening rope, made by doubling rope in three parts and taking hitch over bight at each end; **sheeps'head** (pl. **-head, -heads**), (dish of) head of sheep; large food fish of Atlantic coasts of U.S., with head supposed to resemble sheep's; **sheep'skin**, garment or rug of sheep's skin with wool on; leather of sheep's skin used in bookbinding, etc.; parchment of sheep's skin, diploma engrossed on this; diploma (colloq.).

sheep·ish (shē′pĭsh) *adj.* Embarrassed, shamefaced. **sheep'-ish·ly** *adv* **sheep'ish·ness** *n.*

The ability to train certain breeds of dog into efficient controllers of sheep has resulted in several types of **sheepdog.** *They will round up a flock with as much speed and skill as a horseman.*

sheer[1] (shēr) *adj.* Mere, unqualified, undiluted, absolute; (of textile fabric) thin, diaphanous; (of rock, fall, ascent, etc.) perpendicular, very steep and without a break. ~ *adv.* Plumb, perpendicularly, outright. **sheer'ly** *adv.* **sheer'ness** *n.*

sheer[2] (shēr) *v.i.* (naut.) Deviate from course; ~ **off**, swerve away; make off.

sheer[3] (shēr) *n.* Upward slope of ship's lines toward bow and stern; deviation of ship from course.

sheers, shears (shērz) *ns.* (pl.; also **shear legs** or **sheer legs**) Hoisting apparatus of two or more poles attached at or near top and separated at bottom for masting ships or putting in engines etc., used in dockyards. [var. of SHEAR; named from resemblance to pair of shears]

sheet (shēt) *n.* 1. Rectangular piece of linen, cotton, etc., used as one of a pair of inner bedclothes. 2. Broad, flat piece of some thin material, as paper; complete piece of paper of the size in which it was made; newspaper. 3. Wide expanse of water, snow, ice, flame, color, etc. 4. Rope or chain at lower corner of sail, used to extend it or alter its direction. 5. (pl.) Spaces of open boat forward of (**foresheets**) and abaft (**stern sheets**) thwarts. 6. **in sheets**, (of book) printed but not bound; **three sheets to the wind**, rather or very drunk. 7. **sheet bend**, kind of knot made to join two ropes; **sheet glass**, kind made first as hollow cylinder that is cut open and flattened in furnace; **sheet iron, metal**, etc., spread by rolling, hammering, etc., into thin sheets; **sheet lightning**, sheetlike illumination caused by reflection and diffusion of lightning on clouds; **sheet music**, music published in sheets, not in book form; **Sheet'rock**, (trademark) gypsum plasterboard covered with paper. **sheet** *v.t.* Furnish with sheets; cover with sheet; secure (sail) with sheet.

Shef·field (shĕf'ēld). City in south Yorkshire, England, famous for manufacture of cutlery and steel; ~ **plate**, copperware coated with silver by process now disused.

sheik, sheikh (shēk, shāk) *ns.* Chief, head, of Arab tribe, family, or village; title of eminent Muslim. **sheik'dom, sheikh'dom** *ns.* Office, territory, of sheik.

shek·el (shĕk'el) *n.* Ancient Babylonian, Phoenician, Hebrew, etc., weight; coin of this weight; monetary unit of Israel; (pl., colloq.) money, riches.

shel·drake (shĕl'drāk) *n.* (pl. **-drakes**, collect. **-drake**) (fem. **shel·duck** pr. shĕl'dŭk). Bright-plumaged wild duck of genus *Tadorna*, frequenting sandy coasts

in Europe, N. Africa, and Asia.

shelf (shĕlf) *n.* (pl. **shelves** pr. shĕlvz). Projecting slab of stone or board let into or hung on wall to support things; one of boards in cabinet, bookcase, etc., on which contents stand; ledge, horizontal steplike projection in cliff face etc.; reef or sandbank under water; **on the** ~, (fig.) put aside, done with; ~ **life**, time for which packaged food etc. can be stored and remain usable; ~ **mark**, mark, number, on book indicating its place on library shelf.

shell (shĕl) *n.* 1. Hard outer case enclosing kernel of nut, some

kinds of seed or fruit, egg, some mollusks or crustaceans, etc.; (fig.) reticent attitude concealing emotions. 2. Walls of unfinished or gutted building, ship, etc.; light narrow racing boat; conch-shaped structure for outdoor concerts etc.; domed arena etc. 3. Explosive artillery projectile; cartridge. 4. **shell'back**, (joc.) old sailor; **shell'-bark (hickory)**: see SHAGBARK; **shell'fire**, shooting or firing of explosive shells; **shell'fish** (pl. **-fishes**, collect. **fish**), any aquatic animal with shell, esp. crustacean or mollusk; **shell game**, swindling sleight-of-hand trick with three thimble-shaped cups and pea, and bystanders betting which cup covers pea; any trick or game that takes unfair advantage of customers; **shell jacket**, semi-formal tight-fitting jacket reaching only to waist behind, worn esp. instead of tuxedo by officers; **shell shock**, BATTLE fatigue. **shelled, shell'less, shell'y** *adjs.* (**shell·i·er,**

shell·i·est). **shell** *v.t.* 1. Take out of shell, remove shell or pod from; ~ **out**, (slang) pay up, hand over (money). 2. Bombard, fire at, with shells. **shell'er** *n.*

she'll (shēl). Contr. of *she shall, she will.*

shel·lac, shel·lack (shelăk') *ns.* Purified lac, esp. in thin plates, used in varnishes, insulating materials; (formerly) phonograph records because of its high gloss, adhesiveness, and toughness. ~ *v.t.* (**-lacked, -lack·ing**). Varnish, coat with shellac; (slang) thrash, defeat by wide margin. **shel·lack'ing** *n.* Utter defeat.

Shel·ley (shĕl'ē), **Percy Bysshe** (1792–1822). English Romantic poet, author of "Ode to the West Wind," "To a Skylark," "Ado

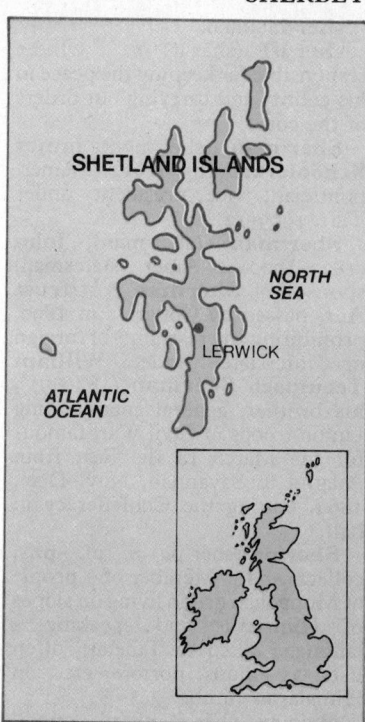

A village built in the Bronze Age at Jarlshof in the **Shetland Islands.** *Today these Scottish offshore islands are known for distinctive woolen garments made by the inhabitants.*

One of the greatest British lyric poets, **Percy Bysshe Shelley** *spent his last years in Italy after offending society by his support of atheism and his rejection of marital fidelity.*

nais," etc. and of the dramas *The Cenci, Prometheus Unbound*, etc.; **Mary Wollstonecraft Shelley** (1797–1851), his second wife, author of *Frankenstein*.

shel·ter (shĕl´ter) *n.* Object serving as shield or barrier against attack, danger, heat, wind, etc.; screen or cabin to keep off wind, rain, etc.; place of safety or immunity; sheltered or protected state (usu. **seek, take** ~); **tax** ~: see TAX. **shelter** *v.* Act or serve as shelter to; protect, conceal, harbor, defend *from* blame, screen, shield; take shelter.

shel·ty, shel·tie (shĕl´tē): see SHETLAND pony, SHETLAND sheepdog.

shelve[1] (shĕlv) *v.t.* (**shelved, shelv·ing**). Put on shelf; provide with shelves, esp. bookshelves; put aside (question etc.) from consideration; remove (person) from office, employment, etc. **shelv´ing** *n.* (esp.) Shelves, material for shelves.

shelve[2] (shĕlv) *v.i.* (**shelved, shelv·ing**). Slope gently.

Shem (shĕm), **Sem** (sĕm). Eldest son of Noah (Gen. 10).

Shen·an·do·ah (shĕnandō´a).

River flowing NE. 55 mi. (88 km), from N. Virginia to Harpers Ferry, West Virginia, emptying into the Potomac River; ~ **National Park**, area in N. Virginia covering 302 sq. mi. (782 sq. km), including part of the Blue Ridge Mountains.

she·nan·i·gan (shenăn´igan) *n.* (usu. pl.) (colloq.) Nonsense; trickery; high-spirited behavior.

Shen·si (shĕn´sē´). Province of N. China.

She·ol (shē´ōl). Hebrew underworld, abode of the dead, represented as subterranean region of thick darkness from which return is impossible.

shep·herd (shĕp´erd), fem. **shep·herd·ess** (shĕp´erdĭs) *ns.* Person who guards, tends, and herds flock of sheep; pastor; ~'**s pie**, pie of chopped or minced meat with crust of mashed potatoes; **shepherd's-purse**, common cruciferous white-flowered weed, *Capsella bursa-pastoris*, with pouchlike pods. **shepherd** *v.t.* Tend as shepherd; marshal, conduct, guide people etc., like sheep.

Sher·a·ton (shĕr´aton), **Thomas** (1751–1806). English furniture designer; light, graceful style of furniture designed by Sheraton.

sher·bet (shẽr´bĭt) *n.* Confection of flavored and frozen water and sugar with added gelatin, egg white, or milk. [f. Turk. Pers. *šerbet* f. Arab. *šarba* drink]

sherd: SHARD.

sher·iff (shĕr´ĭf) *n.* Officer responsible for keeping the peace in his county and carrying out orders of the court.

Sher·man[1] (shĕr´man), **James Schoolcraft** (1855–1912). Amer. politician; vice president under Taft, 1909–12.

Sher·man[2] (shĕr´man), **John** (1823–1900). Amer. statesman; sponsor of **Sherman Antitrust Act**, passed by Congress in 1890, prohibiting any restraints of foreign or interstate trade; **William Tecumseh Sherman** (1820–91), his brother, general commanding Union troops in Civil War; famous for his March to the Sea, from Atlanta to Savannah, Nov.–Dec., 1864, cutting the Confederacy in half.

Sher·pa (shĕr´pa) *n.* (pl. **-pas**, collect. **-pa**). Member of a people of Mongolian origin living on slopes of Himalayas and speaking a language allied to Tibetan, often used as guides, porters, etc., on Himalayan climbs.

sher·ry (shĕr´ē) *n.* (pl. **-ries**). Still wine made near Jerez de la Frontera in Andalusia, Spain, varying in color from pale gold to dark brown and usu. fortified; similar wine made elsewhere. [Span. (*vino de*) *Xeres* (wine of) Jerez]

Shet·land (shĕt´land). **~ Is-lands** (also **Shetlands**), group of islands NNE. of Scottish mainland; **~ pony**, pony of small hardy rough-coated breed orig. from Shetland Islands, also called sheltie; **~ sheepdog**, any of a breed of dogs developed in Shetland Islands and resembling small collie, also called sheltie; **~ wool**, fine thin loosely twisted wool from Shetland sheep. **Shetland** *n.* Shetland pony. **Shet′land·er** *n.*

Shi·ah (shē´a). Muslim sect (chiefly represented by Persians) holding that Muhammad's cousin and son-in-law Ali was the prophet's true successor and that the three first Sunnite caliphs were usurpers. **Shi·ite** (shē´īt) *n. & adj.* [Arab. *al-šī'a* party, sect (of Ali)]

shib·bo·leth (shĭb´olĭth) *n.* Test word, principle, opinion, etc., the use of or inability to use which betrays one's party, nationality, etc. (Judges 12:6) catchword, (esp. outworn or empty) formula, etc., distinguishing a party or sect. [Heb. *šibbōlet*]

shield (shēld) *n.* Article of defensive armor carried in hand or on arm as protection from weapons of enemy; protective plate or screen in machinery etc.; mass of concrete or lead around nuclear reactor to prevent escape of radiation; person or thing serving as protection or defense; shieldlike part in animal or plant; (her.) escutcheon; policeman's shield-shaped badge. **~** *v.t.* Protect, screen, esp. from censure or punishment. **shield′er** *n.*

shift (shĭft) *n.* 1. Change of place or character; substitution of one thing for another; vicissitude; rotation; **red ~**, (astron.) apparent shift in spectra of light from distant galaxies toward the long wave or red end of the spectrum, indicating that the galaxies are receding; **~ key**, key for adjusting typewriter when capitals etc. are to be used. 2. Expedient, device, stratagem, resource; dodge, trick, piece of evasion or equivocation. 3. Chemise. 4. Relay or change of workmen; length of time during which such relay works; **gear′-shift**: see GEAR. **shift** *v.* 1. Change or move from one position to another, change form or character. 2. Use expedients, contrive; manage, get along; **~ for oneself**, depend on one's own efforts.

shift·less (shĭft´lĭs) *adj.* Lacking in resourcefulness; lazy, inefficient. **shift′less·ly** *adv.* **shift′less·ness** *n.*

shift·y (shĭf´tē) *adj.* (**shift·i·er**, **shift·i·est**). Not straightforward, evasive, deceitful. **shift′i·ly** *adv.* **shift′i·ness** *n.*

Shih Tzu (shĭ´dzoo´) (pl. **Shih-Tzus**, collect. **Shih·Tzu**). (Breed of) short-legged toy dog having long, silky hair of various colors. [Chin., "lion dog"]

Shi·ite: see SHIAH.

shik·sa (shĭk´sa) *n.* (disparaging) Non-Jewish girl or woman; Jewish girl or woman with attitudes etc. felt to resemble those of gentiles. [Yiddish]

shill (shĭl) *n.* Person employed to decoy or entice others.

shil·le·lagh, shil·la·lah (shelā´la, -lē) *ns.* Irish cudgel of black-

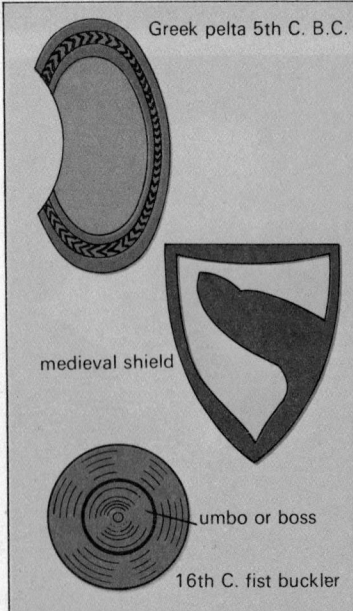

Greek pelta 5th C. B.C.

medieval shield

umbo or boss

16th C. fist buckler

*Left: A steel **shield** made in the 16th century and ornamented with gold. Above: Various designs of shield used at different periods. Shape was determined by the weapons used.*

general cargo ship exterior (port side)

- navigating bridge
- mainmast
- cross-tree
- foremast
- funnel
- derrick
- wheel-house
- crow's-nest
- ensign staff
- jackstaff
- cargo hatch
- winch
- lifeboat
- port-hole
- bilge keel
- cowl ventilators

- boiler casing to funnel
- well-deck
- forecastle
- engine casing to skylight
- bulwark
- well-deck
- poop
- forepeak
- cargo hold
- tween-decks
- watertight bulkhead
- rudder
- engine-room
- boiler-room or stokehold
- propeller or screw
- shaft tunnel

Diagram to show construction (starboard side)

Design of a cargo **ship** is constantly changing as new methods are devised for loading goods. The design shown left is now matched by bulk carriers and container ships.

horn or oak. [*Shillelagh* name of village in County Wicklow]

shil·ling (shĭl´ĭng) *n*. (abbrev. s.) Monetary unit of Kenya, Somalia, Tanzania, and Uganda; until 1971, monetary unit of U.K., = $\frac{1}{20}$ of pound.

shil·ly-shal·ly (shĭl´ē shăl´ē) *n*. Vacillation, irresolution, indecision. ~ *v.i.* (**-lied, -ly·ing**). Vacillate, be irresolute or undecided. **shil·ly-shal·li·er** *n*. [orig. *shill I, shall I*]

shim (shĭm) *n*. Thin slip or wedge used in machinery etc. to make parts fit. ~ *v*. (**shimmed, shim·ming**). Fit or fill up thus.

shim·mer (shĭm´er) *v.i. & n.* (Shine with) tremulous or faint diffused light. **shim´mer·ing·ly** *adv*. **shim´mer·y** *adj*.

shim·my (shĭm´ē) *n*. (pl. **-mies**) *n*. 1. Kind of fox trot of 1920's accompanied by much shaking of body. 2. Abnormal vibration of (front) wheels of automobile. ~ *v*. (**-mied, -my·ing**). 1. Dance a shimmy; move in similar manner. 2. Vibrate abnormally.

shin (shĭn) *n*. Front of human leg below knee; lower part of leg of beef; **shin´bone**, tibia; **shin guard**, guard worn in soccer, hockey, etc. to protect the shins. **shin** *v.i.* (**shinned, shin·ning**). Climb up by using arms and legs, without help of ladder, irons, etc.

shin·dig (shĭn´dĭg) *n*. (colloq.) festive gathering (esp. boisterous one).

shine (shīn) *v*. (**shone** pr. shŏn, **shined, shin·ing**). Emit or reflect light, be bright, glow; be brilliant, excel, in some respect or sphere; (colloq.) make bright, polish (boots etc.); ~ **up to**, (slang) seek to ingratiate oneself with. **shine** *n*. Light, brightness; sunshine; luster, sheen; **take a ~ to**, (slang) take immediate liking to.

shin·er (shī´ner) *n*. (esp.) 1. (slang) Black eye. 2. Any of various small silvery fresh-water fishes of the genus *Notropis*.

shin·gle (shĭng´gel) *n*. 1. Thin rectangular piece of wood etc. thicker at one end, used overlapping for roof or siding; small signboard esp. of doctor, lawyer, etc. 2. Shingled hair. ~ *v.t.* (**-gled, -gling**). 1. Cover, roof, with shingles. 2. Cut (woman's hair) short so that it tapers from back of head to nape of neck. **shin´gler** *n*.

shin·gles (shĭng´gelz) *n*. (pop., considered sing. or pl.) = HERPES zoster. [L. *cingulum* girdle, because eruptions freq. appear around trunk]

shin·ny (shĭn´ē) *v.i.* (**-nied, -ny·ing**). (colloq.) Shin *up* (tree etc.)

shin·splints (shĭn´splĭnts) *n.pl.* (colloq., used with sing. verb) Aching strain in lower leg extensor muscles.

Shin·to (shĭn´tō) *n*. Ancient religion of Japan, based on worship of ancestors and of nature, gradually absorbed and superseded by Buddhism from 6th c. onward, but reestablished as the state religion from 1868 to 1945, with the emperor considered the descendant of the sun; after World War II the emperor disavowed his divinity and governmental support of Shinto was forbidden. **Shin´to·ism** *n*. **Shin´to·ist** *n. & adj.* [Chin. *shin* god, *tao* doctrine, way]

shin·y (shī´nē) *adj.* (**shin·i·er, shin·i·est**). Glistening, shining, polished, rubbed bright. **shin´i-ness** *n*. **shin´i·ly** *adv*.

ship (shĭp) *n*. Any large seagoing vessel, propelled by sails, steam, or other mechanical means; (specif.) sailing vessel with bowsprit and three square-rigged masts, each divided into lower, top, and topgallant mast; aircraft; **~('s) biscuit**, hard coarse kind of biscuit made for keeping, formerly much used on board ship; **ship´board** (*adj.*), used, occurring, done, etc. on ship; **on ship´board**, (adverbial phrase) on board ship; **ship´-builder**, one whose business it is to build ships; **ship´building**; **ship canal**, canal large enough for seagoing vessels; **ship('s) chandler**, dealer supplying ships with stores; **ship´load**, quantity of something forming whole cargo; **ship´mate**, fellow sailor; **ship's company**, crew of a ship, not including the officers; **ship´shape**, in good order, trim and neat; **ship's papers**, documents carried on board ship establishing ownership, nationality, nature of cargo, etc.; **ship´way**, inclined track on which a ship is built and down which it is launched; **ship´worm**, worm-shaped mollusks of the genera *Teredo* and *Barkia* that bore into ship's timbers; **ship´wreck**, (cause, suffer) destruction of ship by storm, foundering, striking rock, etc.; (fig.) ruin; **ship´wright**, shipbuilder, ship's carpenter; **ship´yard**, shipbuilding establishment. **ship** *v*. (**shipped, ship·ping**). 1. Put, take, send away, on board ship; take ship, embark; take service on ship; deliver (goods) to forwarding agent for conveyance by land or water. 2. Fix (mast, rudder, etc.) in its place; remove (oars) from rowlocks and lay them inside boat; (of vessel) take in (water) over the side.

-ship *suffix*. Specified character, office, skill, etc. (*friendship, premiership, seamanship*).

ship·ment (shĭp´ment) *n*. Putting of goods etc. on ship; amount shipped, consignment.

ship·per (shĭp´er) *n*. Merchant etc. who sends or receives goods by ship.

ship·ping (shĭp´ĭng) *n*. (esp.) Ships, esp. the ships of a country, port, etc.; ~ **clerk**, employee who attends to incoming and outgoing shipments of merchandise and keeps records of it.

shirk (shẽrk) *v.t.* Avoid meanly, evade, shrink selfishly from (duty, responsibility, etc.). **shirk′er** *n.*

shirr (shẽr) *v.t.* 1. Gather (material) with several parallel threads. 2. Bake (eggs removed from shells) in shallow dish(es). ~ *n.* Shirring, shirred trimming.

shirt (shẽrt) *n.* Man's loose sleeved garment for upper part of body; **in ~-sleeves**, without coat, or coat and vest; **keep one's ~ on**, (slang) keep one's temper; **lose one's ~**, (slang) lose all one's possessions; ~ **front**, breast of shirt, freq. stiffened or starched; dicky; **shirt′tail**, back part of shirt below waist. **shirt′ing** *n.* Material

for shirts.

shish ke·bab (shĭsh′kebŏb) *n.* Pieces of marinated meat and vegetables cooked on skewers.

shit (shĭt) *v.i.* (**shit, shit·ting**). (vulg.) 1. Evacuate bowels. 2. Speak untruthfully with intent to deceive. ~ *n.* (vulg.) 1. Feces. 2. Act of evacuating bowels. 3. Useless junk. 4. Nonsense. 5. Contemptible person. 6. Narcotic, esp. heroin. ~ *int.* (vulg., used to express anger, contempt, disappointment, etc.).

shiv (shĭv) *n.* (slang) Razor (knife used as weapon.

Shi·va (shē′va), **Si·va** (sē′v shē′va). (Hinduism) One of th supreme gods, third deity of th triad of which Brahma and Vishn are the other members; he repr sents the principle of destructic and the regeneration that follow destruction. **Shi′va·ism, Si′va ism** *ns.* Worship of Shiva.

shiv·er¹ (shĭv′er) *n.* Quiverir or trembling, esp. of body und influence of cold, fear, etc. ~ *v* Tremble, shake, quiver, esp. wit cold or fear. **shiv′er·er** **shiv′er·y** *adj.* **shiv′er·ing·ly** *ad*

shiv·er² (shĭv′er) *n.* One of mar small pieces into which thing shattered by blow or fall. ~ Break into shivers.

shoal¹ (shōl) *adj.* (of wate Shallow. ~ *n.* Shallow place water, sandbank or bar. ~ *v* Grow shallow(er). **shoal′y** *ac* (**shoal·i·er, shoal·i·est**).

shoal² (shōl) *n.* Multitud crowd, great number, esp. of fi swimming in company. ~ *v* Form shoals.

shoat (shōt) *n.* Young (es weanling) pig.

shock¹ (shŏk) *n.* Viole collision, concussion, or impac one of the violent shakes or tremc of part of Earth's surface constitu ing an earthquake; sudden ai disturbing mental or physical in pression; stimulation of nerve(with muscular contraction ar

chamber containing high-pressure air

free piston separating gas and oil

double-acting piston

compartment fitted with special oil

feeling of concussion by passage of electric current through body; (path.) acute state of prostration accompanied by lowering of blood volume and pressure and weakening of pulse and respiration, commonly following accidents, wounds, or burns; ~ **absorber**, device for absorbing vibration in mechanically propelled vehicles; device on aircraft to lessen shock of landing; ~ **tactics**, sudden and violent action; ~ **therapy, treatment**, treatment of mental disorders by application of electric shock to central nervous system; ~ **troops**, picked troops for offensive action; ~ **wave**, disturbance produced when body travels through medium at speed greater than that at which medium transmits sound, or by explosion; (also fig.). **shock**

v.t. Affect with intense aversion, disgust, or strong disapproval, scandalize; outrage sentiments, prejudices, etc., of; cause to suffer shock; administer electric shock to. **shock′proof, shock′ing** *adjs.* **shock′ing·ly** *adv.* **shock′ing·ness** *n.*

shock[2] (shŏk) *n.* Group of sheaves of corn etc. propped upright against each other in field to dry and ripen. ~ *v.t.* Arrange in shocks.

shock[3] (shŏk) *n.* Unkempt or shaggy mass of hair.

shock·er (shŏk′er) *n.* (esp.

At the mouth of many rivers, a shoal may form like that on Mondego in Portugal (below). It may be clearly visible at low tide, but is a navigational hazard in poor light at high water.

colloq.) Sensational novel, film, etc.

shod (shŏd) *adj.*: see SHOE *v.t.;* (esp.) wearing shoes; tipped, edged, or sheathed with metal.

shod·dy (shŏd′ē) *n.* (pl. **shod·-dies**). (Cloth of) woolen yarn made from shreds of knitted or loosely woven woolen fabrics; inferior cloth, anything of worse quality than it claims or seems to have. ~ *adj.* (**-di·er, -di·est**). Of poor material or quality. **shod′-di·ly** *adv.* **shod′di·ness** *n.*

shoe (shoo) *n.* (pl. **shoes**). 1. Outer covering for foot, of leather or other material, with more or less stiff sole and lighter upper part, esp. not reaching above ankle; **fill someone's** ~ **s**, take place of someone; **the** ~ **is on the other foot**, the situation is exactly opposite to what it was; **where the** ~ **pinches**, where one's difficulty or trouble is. 2. Plate of metal, usu. iron, nailed to underside of horse's hoof. 3. Thing like shoe in shape or use, e.g. ferrule or metal sheath for pole etc., wheel drag, socket; part of brake that presses lining against wheel to slow it down; casing of pneumatic tire; (elect.) cast iron block sliding over live rail to collect current therefrom; **shoe′horn**, curved piece of horn, metal, etc., for easing the heel into the back of a shoe; **shoe′lace**, lace for tying up shoe; **shoe′maker**, one who makes, mends shoes; **shoe′-shine**, cleaning and polishing of shoes; one who does this for a fee; (also **shoeshine boy**); **shoe′-string**, shoelace; (*adj.*) cut into long thin strips (**shoestring potatoes**); around the ankles (**shoestring tackle**); **on a shoestring**, (fig.) with minimal expenditure. **shoe** *v.t.* (**shod** pr. shŏd or **shoed** pr. shood, **shoe·ing**). Fit with shoe(s).

sho·far (shō′fer; *Heb.* shōfär′) *n.* (pl. **-fars**; *Heb.* **-froth** pr. -frawt′). Ram's horn trumpet used by Jews in religious ceremonies and as ancient battle signal.

sho·gun (shō′gŭn, -gōōn) *n.* (hist.) Japanese hereditary commander in chief and virtual ruler for some centuries until the office was abolished in 1868. **sho·gun-ate** (shō′gunĭt, -nāt) *n.* [Jap., short for *sei-i-tai shōgun* barbarian-subduing great general]

sho·ji (shō′jē) *n.* (pl. **-ji, -jis**). Translucent rice paper screen used in Japanese houses as sliding door or partition.

shone: see SHINE.

shoo (shoo) *int.* Exclamation used to frighten birds etc. away.

A shoal of yellowtail, a common fish in some Australian waters. Certain species tend to congregate in large numbers when following food in a coastal current.

Although mechanization has been extensively applied to the manufacture of shoes, many details still have to be done by hand.

Although there are far fewer black-smiths than in the past, many horses still need shoeing. When a new shoe is to be fitted, the hoof must be trimmed (1) before the hot shoe is positioned, and nailed to the hoof (2).

~ *v.* (**shooed, shoo·ing**). Utter shoo; drive *away* etc. thus; **shoo'fly pie**, open pie filled with molasses and brown· sugar; **shoo-in**, (colloq.) something easy or certain to succeed.

shoot (shoōt) *v.* (**shot** pr. shŏt, **shoot·ing**). 1. Come or go vigorously or swiftly; pass quickly under (bridge), over (rapids), in boat; ~ **up**, (esp.) grow rapidly. 2. Discharge or propel quickly; discharge (bullet etc.) from gun etc., cause (bow, gun, etc.) to discharge missile, discharge· gun etc.; kill or wound with missile from gun etc.; hunt game etc. with gun; (of gun etc.) go off, send missile; throw (dice); (soccer, basketball) take shot at goal, basket; (slang) inject (drug) intravenously; ~ **down**, bring down (aircraft) by gunfire; ~ **it out**, (slang) engage in decisive gun battle, or **shoot'out** (*n.*); ~ **up**: see sense 1; hit with many shots; (colloq.) terrorize (area) by indiscriminate shooting; (slang) inject (narcotic) into vein. 3. Photograph or (esp.) film. **shoot'er** *n.* **shoot'ing** *n.* (esp.) Right of shooting over particular land; ~ **box**, (Brit.) sportsman's lodge for use in shooting season; ~ **gallery**, place where shooting at targets with rifles is practiced; ~ **iron**, (slang) firearm; ~ **star**, meteor; any of a genus

(*Dodecatheon*) of N. Amer. perennials of the primrose family, having clusters of bright flowers with turned back petals; ~ **war**, one in which there is shooting; ~ **stick**, walking stick that can be adapted to form a seat. **shoot** *n.* 1. Young branch or sucker. 2. Shooting party, expedition, practice, or land.

shop (shŏp) *n.* Building, room, etc., for retail sale of some commodity; small store; workshop of a carpenter, tinsmith, etc.; engineering works or yard; (slang) institution, establishment; one's profession, trade, or business (esp. in **talk** ~); **set up** ~, open or begin business, professional practice, etc.; **close up** ~, cease business for the day or permanently; **shop'keeper**, owner and manager of shop; **shop'-lifter**, pretended customer who steals goods in shop; **shop steward**, union member elected by fellow workers in shop or department of factory etc. to act as their spokesman in dealings with employer; **shop'talk**, specialized vocabulary of an occupation; conversation of people about their work, esp. outside working hours; **shop'worn**, soiled or damaged through being displayed or handled in store; also fig. **shop** *v.* (**shopped, shop·ping**). Go to shop(s) to make purchases. **shop'per** *n.* Person who shops, esp. one who shops carefully. **shop'ping** *n.* ~ **center**, group of stores in one building or several closely related buildings with nearby parking area usu. in suburbs.

shore¹ (shōr, shŏr) *n.* Land that

borders sea or large body of water; (law) land between ordinary high- and low-water marks; **in** ~, on water near(er) to shore; **shore'- bird**, any of various birds that live in seashore areas; **shore leave**, (naut.) permission to go ashore; **shore'line**, line where water and shore meet; **shore patrol**, mem- bers of U.S. Navy, Marine Corps, or Coast Guard assigned to police duties on shore. **shore'less** *adj.* **shore'ward** *adj.* & *adv.*

shore[2] (shōr, shŏr) *n.* Prop, beam, set obliquely against ship, wall, tree, etc., as support. ~ *v.t.* (**shored, shor·ing**). Support, prop *up*, with shores.

shorn: see SHEAR.

short (shŏrt) *adj.* 1. Measuring little from end to end in space or time, soon traversed or finished; of small stature, not tall; not far- reaching, acting near at hand. 2. Deficient, scanty, in want *of*, below the degree *of*; (of weight, change, etc.) less than it should be; concise, brief, curt; (phonet., pros., of vowel or syllable) having the lesser of 2 recognized durations; (of stocks, broker, crops, etc.) sold, selling, etc., when stocks etc. are not in hand, in reliance on getting them in time for delivery. 3. (of pastry, clay, etc.) Friable, crumbling. 4. **short'- bread, short'cake**, crisp dry cake made with flour and butter and sugar without liquid; **short- change'** (*v.t.*), (colloq.) cheat by giving insufficient money as change; **short circuit**, electric circuit through much smaller re- sistance than in the normal circuit, thus allowing a large current to flow through and causing overheating, fusing, etc.; **short-circuit** (*v.t.*) cause short circuit in; shorten (process) by eliminating inter- mediate stages; **short'coming**, failure to come up to a standard, deficiency, defect; **short'cut**, shorter route to reach same loca- tion; (fig.) any means of saving time, work, money, etc.; **short'fall**, output less than expected; shortage; **short'hand**, stenography, system of graphic notation in which speech is recorded at great speed by using contractions, symbols, etc.; **short'- handed**, undermanned, under- staffed; **short'horn**, one of a short-horned breed of cattle; **short-lived**, having a short life; brief, ephemeral; **short order**, food that can be quickly prepared and served, as at diner, lunch counter, etc.; hence **short-order**, *adj.*; **in short order**, immediately; **short-range**, (of gun, missile, etc.) firing or reaching a short distance, (of forecast, plan, etc.) relating to the near future; **short shrift**: see SHRIFT; **short'sighted**, lacking imagination, deficient in foresight; **short'sightedly, short'sighted- ness**; **short'stop**, (baseball) in- fielder between second and third bases; **short story**, story with a fully worked out motif but much shorter than a novel; **short- tempered**, having a temper easily roused; **short-term**, (of plan, policy, etc.) designed to meet the circumstances of a short time ahead; **short'wave**, radio wave- length of 60 meters or less; **short- winded**, short of breath, becoming out of breath after slight exertion; **short-windedly, short-winded- ness. short'ness** *n.* **short** *adv.* Abruptly; before the natural or expected time; in short manner. ~ *n.* Short syllable or vowel, mark indicating that a vowel is short; (colloq.) short circuit; short motion picture film; (pl.) short trousers reaching to any point between crotch and knee; (pl.) men's under- pants. ~ *v.t.* (colloq.) Short- circuit.

short·age (shōr'tĭj) *n.* (Amount of) deficiency.

short·en (shōr'ten) *v.* Become, make, actually or apparently short(er), curtail; reduce amount of (*sail*) spread; make (pastry etc.) flaky or crumbly.

short·en·ing (shōr'tenĭng, shōrt'nĭng) *n.* Fat used for making pastry flaky or crisp.

short·ly (shōrt'lē) *adv.* Before long; a short time *before, after*; in few words, briefly; curtly.

Sho·sta·ko·vich (shŏstakō'- vĭch), **Dmitri** (1906–75). Russian composer of symphonies, operas, piano music, etc.

shot (shŏt) *n.* (pl. **shots**, for def. 1 **shot**). 1. Single missile for cannon or gun, nonexplosive pro- jectile; (pl. same) small lead pellets of which a quantity is used for single charge or cartridge, esp. in

*Clay pigeon shooting allows the partici- pants to enjoy the excitement and expertise of the **shoot** without having to kill. As a recognized sport it is growing in popularity and has been an Olympic event since 1900.*

Above: The Memphis **showboat** anchored on the Mississippi between voyages. These floating theaters were introduced early in the 19th century and ranged from crude rafts to elaborate steamers.

Another obstacle cleared during the Munich Olympics in 1972. **Show jumping** began in Paris in 1886 and equestrian events were introduced to the Olympic Games in 1912.

sporting guns. 2. (colloq.) Injection; (slang) drink of whiskey. 3. Discharge of cannon or gun; attempt to hit with projectile or missile; (fig.) attempt to guess or do something; aim or stroke, esp. in a game, as tennis, golf, billiards; (basketball, soccer, etc.) attempt to score by putting ball into basket, goal, etc. 4. Possessor of specified skill with rifle, gun, pistol, etc. 5. Range, reach, distance to or at which thing will carry or act, as *ear'shot, rifle shot.* 6. Photograph; (portion of) film scene photographed as a unit. 7. **shot'gun**, smoothbore gun for firing small shot; **shot'gun wedding**, forced wedding, esp. one necessitated by pregnancy; **shot put**, athletic event in which heavy metal ball is thrown as far as possible; **shot tower**, tower in which shot is made from molten lead poured through sieves at the top and falling into water at the bottom. **shot** *v.t.* (**shot·ted**, **shot·ting**). Load, weight, etc., with shot.

should: see SHALL.

shoul·der (shōl′dₑr) *n.* Part of body at which arm, foreleg, or wing is attached; either lateral projection below or behind neck; combination of end of upper arm with ends of collarbone and shoulder blade; cut of meat consisting of upper foreleg and adjoining parts; part of mountain, bottle, tool, etc., projecting like human shoulder; (pl.) upper part of back; body regarded as bearing burdens; strip on either side of roadway; **put one's ~ to the wheel**, make effort; **~ blade**, either of the pair of large flat bones of upper back, scapula; **~ patch**, military insigne indicating unit in which wearer serves, sewn onto uniform sleeve just below shoulder; **~ strap**, band over shoulder connecting front and back of (esp. woman's) garment; band at shoulder of uniform keeping shoulder belt in place and bearing name or number of regiment etc.; **straight from the** ~, (of blow or verbal attack) well delivered or frank. **shoulder** v. Push with shoulder, jostle, make one's *way* thus; take (burden) on one's shoulders (also fig.); ~ **arms**, (mil.) hold rifle vertically in front of shoulder with butt resting in palm of hand, the arm being fully extended downward.

shout (showt) n. Loud cry expressing joy, grief, pain, defiance, etc., or to attract attention at a distance. ~ v. Utter shout; speak loudly; say loudly, call out. **shout'er** n.

shove (shŭv) n. (Strong) push. ~ v. (**shoved, shov·ing**). Push, esp. vigorously or roughly; jostle; (colloq.) put; ~ **off**, start from shore in boat; (colloq.) depart.

shov·el (shŭv'el) n. Spadelike implement, freq. with slightly concave blade, for shifting coal, earth, grain, etc. **shovel** v.t. (**-eled, -el·ing**, Brit. **-elled, -el·ling**). Shift with shovel or spade.

shov·el·er, Brit. **shov·el·ler** (shŭv'eler) ns. Brightly colored river duck (*Anas* or *Spatula clypeata*) with large very broad bill.

show (shō) v. (**showed, shown** or **showed, show·ing**). 1. Allow or cause to be seen, expose to view, exhibit, reveal, point out; be visible or noticeable, come into sight; appear in public; have some appearance. 2. Demonstrate, prove, expound; point out. 3. ~ **around**, take (person) to all points of interest; ~ **off**, display to advantage; act or talk for show, make ostentatious display of abilities etc., hence **show'off** (n.), person who shows off; **show up**, make, be, conspicuous or clearly visible; arrive at place; expose (fraud, impostor). 4. **show'down**, final test. **show** n. 1. Showing; display; spectacle, exhibition, entertainment; exhibit; ~ **bill**, advertising sheet or poster; ~ **business**, profession of (esp. theatrical) entertainment (colloq. abbrev. **show-biz**); **show'boat**, passenger boat, esp. on Mississippi, used as theater; **show'case**, (1) glass-enclosed case for exhibiting goods, curiosities, etc.; (2) opportunity for exhibiting (esp. theatrical talent); **show girl**, chorus girl; ~ **of hands**, voting by raising of hands; **show'man** (pl. **-men**), exhibitor or proprietor of show; **show'manship**, (esp.) capacity for exhibiting one's wares, capabilities, etc., to the best advantage; **show'piece**, excellent specimen used for show; **show'place**, place open to public to view its beauty, etc.; **show'room**, room in which goods are exhibited for sale;

The common **shoveller** *is one of the dabbling group of ducks. Before the breeding season, the male has brilliant plumage. It is a surface feeder.*

show-stopper, (colloq.) item in performance receiving prolonged applause; **show window**, (1) window of store where merchandise is on view; (2) outward appearance, semblance; parade, ostentation, pomp, display.

show·er (show'er) n. 1. Brief fall of rain, *of* rain, hail, arrows, dust, etc.; (also ~ **bath**) bath in which water is sprayed from above. 2.

With more than 200 species, the **shrew** *(family Soricidae) forms the largest group in the Insectivora order of mammals. All are aggressive and carnivorous and will attack prey larger than themselves. Some are semi-aquatic.*

elephant shrew

web-footed water shrew

mole shrew

pygmy shrew

piebald shrew

Party for giving presents, esp. to a prospective bride. **show′er·y** *adj.* **show′er·i·ness** *n.* **shower** *v.* 1. Discharge, descend, come, in a shower; bestow (gifts etc.) lavishly (*upon*). 2. Take shower bath.

show·y (shō′ē) *adj.* (**show·i·er, show·i·est**). Striking, making good display; brilliant, gaudy. **show′i·ly** *adv.* **show′i·ness** *n.*

shp *abbrev.* Shaft horsepower.

shrank: see SHRINK.

shrap·nel (shrăp′nel) *n.* Hollow projectile containing bullets scattered in shower by small bursting charge; fragments of any shell, bomb, etc., scattered by explosion. [General H. Shrapnel (1761–1842), inventor of the shell]

shred (shrĕd) *n.* Scrap, fragment; small torn, broken, or cut piece; small remains; least amount. ~ *v.t.* (**shred·ded** or **shred, shred·ding**). Tear or cut into shreds. **shred′der** *n.*

shrew (shrōō) *n.* 1. Small mouselike insectivore of *Sorex* and other genera, with long pointed snout. 2. Scolding woman. **shrew′ish** *adj.* Ill-tempered. **shrew′ish·ly** *adv.* **shrew′ish·ness** *n.*

shrewd (shrōōd) *adj.* Sagacious, sensible, discriminating, astute. **shrewd′ly** *adv.* **shrewd′ness** *n.*

shriek (shrēk) *n. & v.* (Utter) loud shrill cry or sound of terror, pain, mirth, etc.; (make) high-pitched piercing sound.

shrift (shrĭft) *n.* (archaic) Confession (and absolution); now only in **short** ~, little time between condemnation and execution or punishment; scant attention.

shrike (shrīk) *n.* Bird of family Laniidae, with strong hooked beak, preying usu. on insects, but also on mice and small birds, often impaling them on thorns or barbed wire; butcherbird.

shrill (shrĭl) *adj.* (of sound) Piercing and high-pitched; producing such sounds. ~ *v.* (poet. and rhet.) Sound, utter, shrilly. **shril′ly** *adv.* **shrill′ness** *n.*

shrimp (shrĭmp) *n.* (pl. **shrimps**, collect. **shrimp**). Any of the small marine decapod crustaceans of *Crangon* and allied genera, esp. the common shrimp, *C. vulgaris*, inhabiting sandy coasts, a common article of food; (slang) diminutive or puny person. ~ *v.i.* Go catching shrimps.

shrine (shrīn) *n.* Casket, esp. one holding sacred relics; tomb, usu. sculptured or highly ornamented, of saint etc.; place where worship is offered or devotions paid to saint or deity; place hallowed by

*The inverted **shrimp** (Penedi abissal) is caught only in the ocean depths. Most commercial varieties swim closer to the surface and at times many tons may be netted.*

*The great grey **shrike** or butcherbird, like other birds in the Laniidae, impales its prey on a thorn after killing it. This species migrates to Britain in winter and is about 10 ins. long.*

*Boxwood shrubs in a garden at Williamsburg, Virginia. Gardeners find that a **shrub** needs far less maintenance than smaller plants, but can be very effective as decoration.*

memory or associations.

Shrin·er (shrī′ner) *n.* Member of Ancient Arabic Order of Nobles of the Mystic Shrine, established in U.S. in 1872, and open only to Knights Templar and Freemasons of 32nd degree.

shrink (shrĭngk) *v.* (**shrank** pr. shrăngk or **shrunk** pr. shrŭngk, **shrunk** or rarely **shrunk·en**, **shrink·ing**). Become, make, smaller; (of textile fabric) contract when wetted, cause to do this; cower, huddle *together*, recoil, flinch *from*; be averse *from.* **shrink′a·ble** *adj.* **shrink′age** *n.*

shrive (shrīv) *v.t.* (**shrived** or **shrove** pr. shrōv., **shriv·en** pr. shrĭv′en or **shrived, shriv·ing**). (archaic) Hear confession of, assign penance to, and absolve; ~ **oneself**, make one's confession.

shriv·el (shrĭv′el) *v.* (**-eled, -el·ing**, Brit. **-elled, -el·ling**). Contract or wither into wrinkled, folded, contorted, or dried-up state.

shroud (shrowd) *n.* 1. Winding sheet, garment for the dead; (fig.) concealing agency. 2. (pl.) Set of ropes forming part of standing rigging and supporting mast or topmast. ~ *v.t.* Clothe (corpse) for burial; cover or disguise.

Shrove·tide (shrōv′tīd) *n.* Three days before Ash Wednesday, period for confession before Lent; so **Shrove Tuesday**. [f. SHRIVE]

shrub[1] (shrŭb) *n.* Woody plant smaller than tree and usu. divided into separate stems from near the ground. **shrub′by** *adj.* (**-bi·er, -bi·est**).

shrub[2] (shrŭb) *n.* Cordial of juice of acid fruit, sugar, and spirit (usu. rum). [Arab. *sharāb*]

shrub·ber·y (shrŭb′er̄e) *n.* (pl. **-ber·ies**). (Group of) shrubs.

shrug (shrŭg) *n.* Raising and contraction of shoulders to express dislike, disdain, indifference, etc.

~ *v.* (**shrugged, shrug·ging**). Raise (shoulders), raise shoulders, in shrug.

shrunk, shrunk·en: see SHRINK.

shtet·l (shtĕt′el) *n.* (hist.) Jewish village or small community in E. Europe. [Yiddish, f. MHG. diminutive of *stat*, town]

shtick (shtĭk) *n.* (slang) Trait, talent, attribute, etc.; humorous routine or bit of stage business. [Yiddish]

shuck (shŭk) *n.* (colloq.) Husk, pod. **shucks** *int.* Exclamation of contempt or indifference. **shuck** *v.t.* Remove shucks of, shell.

shud·der (shŭd′er) *v.i.* & *n.* (Experience) sudden shivering due to fear, repugnance, or cold. **shud′der·ing·ly** *adv.*

shuf·fle (shŭf′el) *n.* 1. Shuffling movement; shuffling of cards; general change of relative positions. 2. Piece of equivocation or sharp practice. 3. Quick scraping movement of feet in dancing. ~ *v.* (**-fled, -fling**). Move with scraping, sliding, dragging, or difficult motion; manipulate (cards in pack) so that their relative positions are changed; intermingle, confuse, push about or together in disorderly fashion; put *in, off, on,* etc., clumsily or fumblingly; put (responsibility etc.) *off, onto,* another etc., get *out of* shiftily or evasively; keep shifting position, fidget, vacillate; prevaricate, be evasive. **shuf′fler** *n.*

shuf·fle·board (shŭf′elbōrd, -bōrd) *n.* (Shipboard) game in which wooden or iron disks are pushed along decks (or other flat surfaces) with shovel into divisions marked by chalk etc.

shun (shŭn) *v.t.* (**shunned, shun·ning**). Avoid, keep clear of. **shun′ner** *n.* **shun′pike** *v.i.* (**-piked, -pik·ing**). Travel on side roads avoiding turnpikes and expressways. **shun′piker, shun′pik·ing** *ns.*

shunt (shŭnt) *v.* Divert (train, part of an electric current, etc.), diverge, onto a side track. **shunt′er** *n.* Railroad worker shunting trains. **shunt** *n.* Turning, being turned, onto side track; conductor joining 2 points in an electric circuit so as to form a parallel circuit; such a circuit.

shut (shŭt) *v.* (**shut, shut·ting**). Close (door, aperture, window, etc.), close door etc. of (room, box, etc.); become, admit of being, closed; keep *in, out,* etc., by shutting door etc.; ~ **down**, close, terminate operation of (factory, nuclear reactor, etc.); (of factory etc.) cease working, hence **shut′down** (*n.*); **shut′eye** (*n.*), (slang) sleep; **shut one's eyes to,** (fig.) ignore; **shut in,** encircle, prevent free prospect or egress from or access to; **shutin** (*adj.* & *n.*), (invalid) confined to home; **shut off,** stop flow of (water, gas, etc.) by shutting valve; separate *from;* **shut′out** (*n.*), game in which one side fails to score; **shut up,** close doors and windows of (house), close securely, decisively, or permanently, put away in box etc.; imprison; (colloq.) reduce to silence, shut one's mouth, stop talking; **shut up shop,** cease business.

shut·ter (shŭt′er) *n.* (esp.) Movable screen placed outside or inside window to shut off light or ensure privacy or safety; device for opening and closing aperture of photographic lens; **shut′terbug,** (slang) amateur photographer. **shutter** *v.t.* Provide with shutters, put up shutters of.

shut·tle (shŭt′el) *n.* Weft carrier in a loom, a boat-shaped wooden implement with hollowed center to hold the weft thread, thrown from hand to hand by the weaver, or moved by mechanical means backward and forward across and through the warp; thread holder in sewing machine carrying lower thread through the loop of the upper one; (attrib.) denoting an out-and-back course, as in ~ **service, train; shut′tlecock,** small piece of weighted cork or other light material with feathers projecting in a ring from one side, struck to and fro with a racket in badminton.

shy[1] (shī) *adj.* (**shi·er** or **shy·er, shi·est** or **shy·est**). Easily startled, timid, avoiding observation, uneasy in company, bashful; avoiding company *of,* chary *of doing;* elusive; (as second element of compounds) frightened (*of*), averse (to), as gun-, work-~. **shy'ly** *adv.* **shi'er, shy'er, shy'ness** *ns.* **shy** *v.i.* (**shied, shy·ing**). Start suddenly aside in alarm (at object or noise, esp. of horse). ~ *n.* (pl. **shies**). Act of shying.

shy² (shī) *v.* (**shied, shy·ing**). (colloq.) Fling, throw. ~ *n.* (pl. **shies**). Act of shying.

Shy·lock (shī'lŏk). (freq. **s** ~) Hardhearted moneylender. [character in Shakespeare's *Merchant of Venice*]

shy·ster (shīs'ter) *n.* (slang) Tricky, unscrupulous lawyer (or other professional man).

Si *symbol.* Silicon.

si·al (sī'ăl) *n.* (geol.) Lighter outer crust of Earth's surface, composed mainly of solid or molten rocks rich in silica and alumina. [f. *si*lica and *al*umina]

Si·am (sīăm', sī'ăm). Name until 1939 of THAIland.

si·a·mang (sē'amăng) *n.* Largest of the gibbons (*Symphalangus* or *Hylobates syndactylus*), found in Sumatra and the Malay peninsula.

Si·a·mese (sīamēz', -mēs') *adj.* Of Siam or its people or language; ~ **cat**, cat of domesticated breed notable for its raucous cry, having body of grayish or cream color with dark feet, face, and tail; ~ **twins**, two male Chinese born in Siam, Chang and Eng (1814–74), who were congenitally united by a thick fleshy ligament in the region of the waist; any pair of conjoined twins. **Siamese** *n.* (pl. **-mese**). Siamese person; Siamese language, one of the Thai group; Siamese cat.

sib (sĭb) *adj.* (archaic) Related,

Work on the Trans-Siberian Railway, to link the Asian steppes with European Russia, began in 1891. Siberia has an area of more than 6 million sq. miles and has vast mineral deposits.

akin (*to*). ~ *n.* (genetics) Brother or sister (disregarding sex). **sib'-ling** *n.* One of two or more children having one or both parents in common.

Si·be·li·us (sĭbā'lēus, -bāl'yus), **Jean Julius Christian**, (1865–1957). Finnish musical composer of tone poems, symphonies, etc.

Si·be·ri·a (sībēr'ēa). Region of N. Asia between Ural Mountains and Pacific Ocean and from Arctic Ocean to borders of Mongolia and China, forming the larger part of the Russian Soviet Federal Socialist Republic; used under both tsarist and communist regimes as place of exile, concentration camps, etc.;

*With ears too large for its body, this half-grown seal-point **Siamese cat** may be a descendant of the wild golden cat of the Malay peninsula but there is little evidence to prove this.*

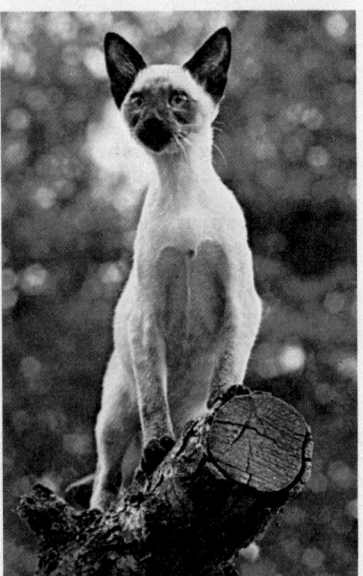

hence (fig.) disgrace, disfavor. **Si·be'ri·an** *adj.* & *n.* Of Siberia; ~ **husky**, dog of breed resembling the Eskimo dog, used for drawing sleds.

sib·i·lant (sĭb'ilant) *adj.* Hissing, sounding like a hiss (of the consonants *s, z, sh*). **sib'i·lance** *n.* **sib'i·lan·cy** *n.* (pl. **-cies**). **sib'i·lant** *n.* (phon.) Sibilant speech sound. **sib'i·lant·ly** *adv.* **sib·i·late** (sĭb'ilāt) *v.* (**-lat·ed, -lat·ing**).

sib·yl (sĭb'ĭl) *n.* Any of the women who in ancient times acted in various places as mouthpiece of a god, uttering prophecies and oracles, the most famous of whom was the sibyl at Cumae in S. Italy

*Unless they share a vital organ, babies connected at birth are now separated surgically. The name **Siamese twins** comes from the Chang brothers, born in Siam (now Thailand) in 1811.*

who (acc. to legend) guided Aeneas through the underworld; prophetess, fortuneteller, witch.

sib·yl·line (sĭb′ĭlīn, -lēn, -lĭn) *adj.* Of a sibyl, oracular, mysteriously prophetic; **S ~ Books**, collection of oracles kept in ancient Rome in temple of Jupiter Capitolinus and freq. consulted by magistrates for guidance; acc. to legend, nine of these books were offered to Tarquin by a sibyl, who burned three of them and then three more when they were refused because of their high price, and finally sold the last three at the same price as she had asked for them all.

sic[1] (sĭk) *v.t.* (**sicked, sick·ing**). Urge (dog) to attack or pursue.

sic[2] (sĭk) *adv.* (freq. parenth.) So, thus (used, spelled, etc.) with implication that this use is incorrect or absurd.

Si·chuan (sī′chwahn′) = SZECHUAN.

Si·cil·ian (sĭsĭl′yan) *adj.* Of Sicily; **~ Vespers**, riot that broke out at a church near Palermo while the vesper bell was ringing on Easter Monday 1282, and developed into a general massacre of the French in Sicily and the expulsion of the Angevins. **Sicilian** *n.* Native, inhabitant, of Sicily.

Sic·i·ly (sĭs′ĭlē). (It. *Sicilia*) Largest island in the Mediterranean Sea, 9,925 sq. mi. (25,706 sq. km); an autonomous Italian region separated from the SW. tip of Italy by the Strait of Messina; capital, Palermo.

sick (sĭk) *adj.* 1. Ill, unwell; disposed to vomit, vomiting. 2. Disordered, perturbed; suffering effects *of*; disgusted; pining *for*; surfeited and tired *of*; (of humor) morbid; suggesting callousness. 3. Of or for sick persons (~ *benefit, leave, pay*). 4. **~ bay**: see BAY[3]; **sick′bed**, invalid's bed; state of being invalid; **sick headache**, headache accompanied by nausea; migraine; **sick list**, list of sick esp. in military unit, aboard ship, etc.; **sick′out**, action against employers by group of employees who stay away from work, alleging illness as their excuse.

sick·en (sĭk′en) *v.* Begin to be ill, show symptoms of illness; feel nausea or disgust (*at* etc.); affect with inclination to vomit, loathing, disgust, weariness, or despair. **sick′en·ing** *adj.* **sick′en·ing·ly** *adv.*

sick·le (sĭk′el) *n.* Reaping hook, short-handled semicircular-bladed implement used for lopping, trimming, etc.; anything sickle-shaped, esp. crescent moon: ~ **cell**, sickle-shaped erythrocyte, esp. as found in ~-**cell anemia**, a severe hereditary anemia occurring chiefly among blacks.

sick·ly (sĭk′lē) *adj.* (**-li·er,** -li·est**). Apt to be ill, chronically ailing; suggesting sickness, as of sick person, languid, pale; causing ill health or nausea; mawkish, weakly sentimental. **sick′li·ness** *n.* **sickly** *v.t.* (**-lied, -ly·ing**).

sick·ness (sĭk′nĭs) *n.* Being ill, disease; a disease; vomiting, inclination to vomit.

side (sīd) *n.* 1. One of the more or less flat surfaces bounding an object, esp. more or less vertical outer or inner surface; such surface as distinguished from top and bottom, front and back, or ends; either surface of thing regarded as

*The dwarf **siamang** is one of the rarest gibbons and is found only in some islands off Indonesia. The common variety is the largest gibbon and is present in both Malaya and Sumatra. It has the typical throat sac of the group.*

having only two; (math.) bounding line of plane rectilinear figure. 2. Either of two lateral surfaces or parts of trunk in persons or animals, esp. extending from armpit to hip or from foreleg to hindleg; part of object in same direction as observer's right or left and not directly toward or away from him, or turned in specified direction; part or region near margin and remote from center, or axis of thing; subordinate, less essential, or more or less detached, part; (attrib.) subordinate; ~ **by** ~, standing close together, esp. for mutual support (also fig.). 3. Region external but contiguous to, specified direction with relation to, person or thing; partial aspect of thing; (cause represented by, position in company with) one of two sets of opponents in war, politics, games, etc.; team; **take ~s**, give support to one side in controversy. 4. Position nearer or farther than, right or left of, dividing line. 5. Line of descent through father or mother. 6. (billiards) Spinning motion given to ball by striking it on side. 7. ~ **arm**, weapon carried at side or in belt, as pistol, sword; **side′arm**

(*adj., adv.*), with sweeping forward motion of extended arm at or below shoulder level; **side′board**, piece of dining room furniture, freq. with drawers and cupboards, for holding dishes, wine, silver, etc.; **side′car**, car for passenger(s) attached to side of motorcycle; cocktail of brandy, orange liqueur, and lemon juice; **side dish**, extra dish, freq. of elaborate kind, at dinner, etc.; **side effect**, secondary, esp. undesirable, effect (as of drug) produced in addition to that intended; **side′kick**, (colloq.) close associate; **side′light**, port or starboard light on ship under way; light coming from the side, (fig.) incidental light *on* subject etc.; **side′line**, (esp.) boundary along side of field of play; subsidiary, secondary, or additional business, pursuit, etc.; **on the sidelines**, (transf.) looking on but not participating; **side road**, minor or subsidiary road; road joining or diverging from main road; **side′saddle**, saddle for rider, usu. woman, with both feet on 1 (usu. left) side of horse; **side′show**, minor show attached to principal one (freq. fig.); **side′slip**, skid; (of aircraft) move, motion, sideways;

side'splitting, causing violent laughter; **side step**, step taken sideways; **side'step** (v.t.) (**-stepped, -step·ping**), avoid, evade, (as) by stepping sideways; **side street**, street lying aside from main streets or roads; **side'stroke**, swimming stroke made lying on the side; **side'track**, siding; (v.t.) turn into siding, shunt, postpone or evade treatment or consideration of; **side view**, view obtained sideways; profile; **side'walk**, paved path for pedestrians at side of road or street; **side'wall**, side of tire between rim of wheel and tread; **side whiskers**, hair left unshaven on cheeks; **side'-winder**, small rattlesnake (*Crotalus cerastes*) of SW. U.S. that moves forward by looping body sideways; (colloq.) powerful sideways blow of fist; (**Sidewinder**) short-range air-to-air missile. **side** v.i. (**sid·ed, sid·ing**). Take part, be on same side, *with*.

side·burns (sīd'bērnz) *n.pl.* Heavy side whiskers worn with mustache and with shaved chin. [f. A. E. *Burnside* (1824–81), Union general in Civil War]

side·long (sīd'lawng, -lŏng) *adv. & adj.* Inclining to one side, oblique(ly).

si·de·re·al (sīdēr'ēal) *adj.* Of the stars; (of time) measured by the stars; ~ **clock**, astronomical clock regulated to sidereal time; ~ **day, year**: see DAY, YEAR.

side·ward (sīd'werd), **sid·-wards** (sīd'werdz) *advs. & adjs.* From, at, to, the side.

side·ways (sīd'wāz), **side·way** (sīd'wā), **side·wise** (sīd'wīz) *advs.*

& *adjs.* Laterally, to or from a side.

sid·ing (sī'dĭng) *n.* 1. Short track by side of railroad line and connected with it by switches, for shunting etc. 2. (Material used for) outer wall of building.

si·dle (sī'del) *v.i.* (**-dled, -dling**). Walk obliquely, esp. in furtive or unobtrusive manner. **si'dling·ly** *adv.*

siege (sēj) *n.* Surrounding or hemming in of a fortified place by a military force to compel its surrender or to take it by direct attack, period during which this lasts; besieging, being besieged.

Sieg·fried (sĭg'frĕd, sēg'-). Hero of first part of Nibelungenlied (see NIBELUNGS), who forged the Nothung sword, slew Fafnir, the dragon guarding the stolen Rhine gold, and helped Gunther to win Brunhild; at the instigation of Brunhild he was treacherously slain by Hagen.

Siegfried (sĭg'frĕd, sēg'-) **Line.** German line of fortifications along the W. border of Germany from Cleves to Basel, constructed prior to World War II.

Sie·na (sēēn'a). City of Tuscany, Italy. **Si·en·ese** (sēenēz', -nēs') *adj. & n.* (pl. **-ese**).

si·en·na (sēēn'a) *n.* Ferruginous earth used as pigment, brownish yellow (**raw** ~) or reddish brown (**burnt** ~). [It. (*terra*) *di Siena* (earth of) SIENA]

si·er·ra (sēēr'a) *n.* Range of mountains with serrated outline. [Span., f. L. *serra* saw]

Si·er·ra Le·one (sēēr'a lēō'nē, lēōn'). Country on W. coast of Africa, between Liberia and Guinea; member nation of the Brit. Commonwealth; independent 1961; capital, Freetown.

Si·er·ra (sēēr'a) **Nevada.** Mountain range in E. California, extending 400 mi. (644 km); highest

peak, Mt. Whitney, 14,495 ft. (4,418 m).

si·es·ta (sĭĕs'ta) *n.* Midday or afternoon rest in hot countries. [Span., f. L. *sexta* (*hora*) 6th (hour)]

sieve (sĭv) *n.* Utensil consisting of usu. circular frame with meshed or perforated bottom, for separating finer from coarser parts of loose material, or for straining liquids or pulping solids; coarsely woven basket for market produce, this as a measure. ~ *v.t.* (**sieved, siev·ing**). Put through, sift with, sieve.

sift (sĭft) *v.* Put through sieve; separate, get *out*, by use of sieve; use sieve; fall as from sieve; sprinkle (sugar etc.) with perforated spoon etc.; closely examine details of, analyze character of. **sift'er** *n.*

Sig. *abbrev.* Signor; signore; signori.

sig. *abbrev.* Signature; signal.

sigh (sī) *n.* Prolonged deep audible respiration expressive of dejection, weariness, longing, relief, etc. ~ *v.* Give sigh or (of wind etc.) sound resembling sigh; utter or express with sighs; yearn, long, *for*. **sigh'er** *n.*

sight (sīt) *n.* 1. Faculty of seeing. 2. Seeing, being seen; way of looking at or considering thing; view, point or position commanding view, of something; range or field of vision; **at, on, ~, at first** ~, as soon as person or thing has been seen; **know by** ~, recognize by appearance alone; ~**-reading, -singing**, reading music, singing, at sight. 3. Thing seen, visible, or worth seeing; display, show, spectacle; ridiculous, shocking, or repulsive sight; (colloq.) great quantity (*of*); **sight'seeing**, act of going to see places or objects of special interest, beauty, etc.; **sight'seer** (*n.*). 4. Device for assisting precise aim with gun,

pinnacle
stop arm
front spectacle
distant arm
'banner' signal
balance weight
gantry
route indicator
stop
proceed
lower quadrant system
stop
proceed
upper quadrant system
route indicator
colour-light signal
identification plate
FJ5

bomb, etc., or observation with optical instrument; **not by a long sight**, (colloq.) not nearly; emphatically not; **out of sight**, not in view; far away; (colloq.) out of or beyond reach; very high, as in quality, cost, etc.; **sight unseen**, without seeing (thing concerned) beforehand. **sight** v.t. Get sight of, esp. by coming near; take observation of (star etc.) with instrument; provide (gun etc.) with sights, adjust sights of; aim (gun etc.) with sights. **sight'ed** adj. Possessing vision; not blind. **sight'ing** n. Instance of seeing something, esp. aircraft etc.

sight·less (sīt'lĭs) adj. Blind.

sight·ly (sīt'lē) adj. (**-li·er, -li·est**). Pleasing to the sight, not unsightly. **sight'li·ness** n.

sig·ma (sĭg'ma) n. Letter of Greek alphabet (Σ, σ, or ς; uncial C) corresponding to s.

sig·moid (sĭg'moid), **sig·moi·dal** (sĭgmoi'dal) adjs. Crescent-shaped, like the uncial sigma C; having double curve like letter s; of the ~ **flexure**, curving portion of intestine between colon and rectum.

sign (sīn) n. 1. Significant gesture; mark or device with special meaning or used to distinguish thing on which it is put; written mark conventionally used for word, phrase, etc., symbol; token, indication, trace (of something); omen, portent; miracle as demonstration of divine power or authority; (path.) objective evidence or indication of disease etc. (cf. SYMPTOM). 2. Board bearing name of business establishment and displayed in front of building housing it. 3. Any of 12 equal divisions of zodiac named

*Despite political upheavals since it attained independence in 1961, **Sierra Leone** is still an exporter of diamonds and iron ore, as well as palm kernels, coffee and cocoa.*

*The magnificent cathedral built between 1288 and 1309 dominates the **Siena** skyline, just as the work of Sienese artists dominated Italian painting from the 13th to the 15th centuries.*

from constellations formerly situated in them. 4. **sign'board**, = sense 2; **sign'post**, post at crossroads etc., with arm(s) indicating direction of place(s); **sign language**, communication by means of hand and finger gestures. **sign** v. 1. Mark *with* sign of the cross; mark with sign; make sign, intimate with sign; use sign language. 2. Attest or confirm by adding one's signature; write (name) as signature; affix one's signature; make *over*, give *away*, etc., by signing; ~ **in, out**, report, indicate, arrival, departure; ~ **off**, end broadcast by announcing one's name; ~ **on**, hire, be hired; ~ **up**, enlist for military duty. **sign'er** n.

sig·nal[1] (sĭg'nal) n. Prearranged or obvious sign conveying information or direction, esp. to person(s) at a distance; message made up of such signs; electrical impulse or radio wave transmitted or received; device, light, sound, gesture to warn, command, direct, as *traffic, railroad* ~; **S ~ Corps**, branch of U.S. Army responsible for radio and other communications, weather studies, etc.; **signal tower**, railroad building with signaling apparatus; **sig'nalman** (pl. **-men**), signaler. **signal** v. (**-naled, -nal·ing**, Brit. **-nalled, -nal·ling**). Make signal(s) to; transmit, announce, by signal, direct (person) *to* do by signal.

sig·nal[2] (sĭg'nal) adj. Remarkable, conspicuous, striking. **sig'nal·ly** adv.

sig·nal·ize (sĭg'nalīz) v.t. (**-ized, -iz·ing**). Distinguish, make conspicuous or remarkable.

sig·na·to·ry (sĭg'natōrē, -tôrē) adj. & n. (pl. **-ries**). (Party, esp. nation) whose signature is attached to document, esp. treaty.

sig·na·ture (sĭg'nacher) n. 1. Name, initials, or mark written with person's own hand as authentication of document or other writing; distinguishing mark; stamp, impression. 2. Letter(s) or figure(s) placed by printer at foot of first page (and freq. other pages) of each sheet of book as guide in making up and binding; a sheet as distinguished by its signature; (mus.) sign(s) placed at beginning of piece of music, movement, etc., to indicate key and time.

sig·net (sĭg'nĭt) n. Small seal, esp. one fixed in finger ring; small seal for official documents etc.

sig·nif·i·cance (sĭgnĭf'ĭkans) n., **sig·nif·i·can·cy** (sĭgnĭf'ĭkansē) n. (pl. **-cies**). Being significant, expressiveness; meaning, import; consequence, importance.

sig·nif·i·cant (sĭgnĭf´ĭkant) *adj.* Having, conveying, a meaning; full of meaning, highly expressive or suggestive; important, notable. **sig·nif´i·cant·ly** *adv.*

sig·ni·fi·ca·tion (sĭgnĭfĭkā´shon) *n.* (esp.) Exact meaning or sense.

sig·nif·i·ca·tive (sĭgnĭf´ĭkătĭv) *adj.* Signifying: having a meaning; serving as sign or indication *of.*

sig·ni·fy (sĭg´nĭfī) *v.* (**-fied, -fy·ing**). Be sign or symbol of; represent, mean, denote; communicate, make known; be of importance, matter.

si·gnor (sēnyōr´, -yōr´), **si·gno·ra** (sēnyōr´a, -yōr´a), **si·gno·ri·na** (sēnyorē´na) *ns.* (pl. **si·gnors**, It. **si·gno·ri** pr. sēnyōr´ē; **si·gno·ras**, It. **si·gno·re** pr. sēnyōr´ē; **si·gno·ri·nas**, It. **si·gno·ri·ne** pr. sēnyorē´nĕ). (Title of or form of address to) Italian man, woman, young or unmarried woman. [It.]

Sikh (sēk) *n.* Member of a monotheistic sect established in India (chiefly in Punjab) since 16th c.; esp., member of a martial community maintained by this sect; ~ **Wars**, wars between Sikhs and British, 1845 and 1848–9, culminating in the British annexation of the Punjab. **Sikh´ism** *n.*

si·lage (sī´lĭj) *n.* Preservation of green fodder in silo or pit without drying; fodder thus preserved.

si·lence (sī´lens) *n.* Abstinence from speech or noise, taciturnity, reticence; absence of sound, stillness, noiselessness; neglect or omission to mention, write, etc. ~ *v.t.* (**-lenced, -lenc·ing**). Make silent, reduce to silence; put down, repress (expression of opinion etc.); compel (gun, ship, etc.) to cease firing.

si·lenc·er (sī´lenser) *n.* (esp.) Device for rendering gun (comparatively) silent.

si·lent (sī´lent) *adj.* Not speaking; not uttering, making, or accompanied by, any sound; (of letter) not pronounced; taciturn, speaking little; not mentioning or referring to, passing over, something; ~ **partner**, partner who invests but does no actual work in business. **si´lent·ness** *n.* **si´lent·ly** *adv.*

Si·le·nus (sīlē´nus). (Gk. myth.) 1. Foster father and teacher of Dionysus, freq. represented as a fat, jolly, drunken old man. 2. (**s~**) Bearded satyr with tail and legs of horse.

Si·le·sia (sīlē´zha, -sha). Ancient duchy and district of E. Europe, partitioned at various times among Prussia, Austria-Hungary, Poland, and Czechoslovakia; now largely under Polish administration.

sil·hou·ette (sĭlooĕt´, sĭl´ooĕt) *n.* Portrait of person in profile showing outline only, this being filled in

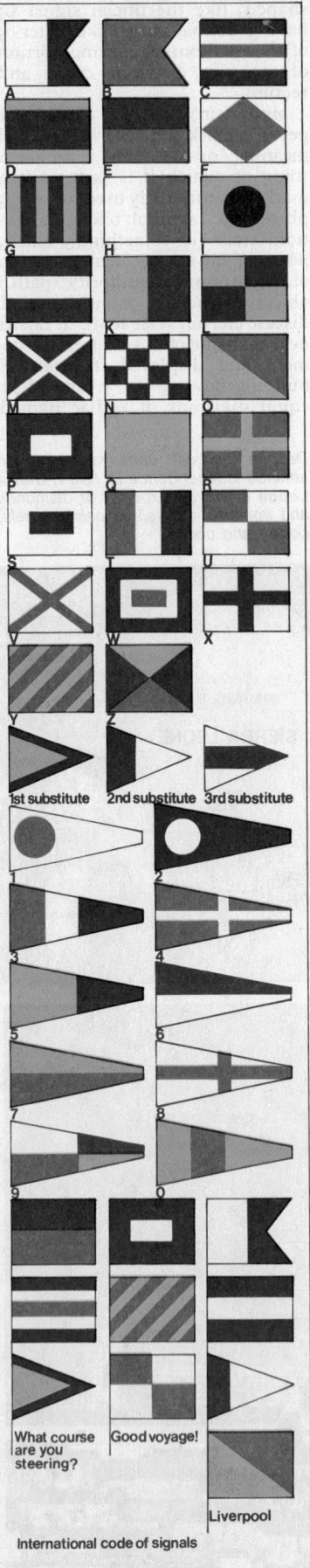

1st substitute   2nd substitute   3rd substitute

What course are you steering?   Good voyage!

Liverpool

International code of signals

with black, cut out in paper, etc.; dark outline, shadow in profile, thrown up against lighter background. ~ *v.t.* (**-et·ted, -et·ting**). Represent, exhibit, in silhouette. [named after Étienne de *Silhouette* (1709–67), French politician]

sil·i·ca (sĭl´ĭka) *n.* Silicon dioxide (SiO_2), a hard, white or colorless, widely distributed mineral present in many precious and other stones, esp. quartz, and sand, used in the manufacture of glass, bricks, etc.

sil·i·cate (sĭl´ĭkĭt, -kāt) *n.* Salt of silicic acid; one of many insoluble compounds of metal(s), silicon, and oxygen, occurring widely in rocks of Earth's crust.

si·li·ceous, si·li·cious (sĭlĭsh´us) *adjs.* Containing or consisting of silica.

sil·i·con (sĭl´ĭkon, -kŏn) *n.* (chem.) Nonmetallic element occurring only in combination, manufactured commercially by reduction of sand and used in the manufacture of certain alloys; symbol Si, at. no. 14, at. wt. 28.086; ~ **carbide**, very hard crystalline compound (SiC), used as an abrasive and as a refractory lining in furnaces etc.

sil·i·cone (sĭl´ĭkōn) *n.* One of many polymeric organic compounds of silicon with high resistance to cold, heat, water, and passage of electricity.

sil·i·co·sis (sĭlĭkō´sĭs) *n.* (pl. **-ses** pr. -sēz). Chronic lung disease caused by inhalation of dust containing silica and freq. affecting coal miners, one of the group of diseases known as pneumoconioses.

silk (sĭlk) *n.* Strong soft lustrous fiber produced, to form their cocoons, webs, etc., by certain insect larvae, spiders, etc., esp. by silkworms (see below); thread or textile fabric made from this; similar lustrous filament or fiber made by chemical processes from cellulose; (in pl.) garments, uniform of such cloth, esp. jockey's cap and jacket in horse owner's colors; (attrib.) made of silk; ~ **cotton**, silky fiber, esp. kapok; ~**-cotton tree**, tree yielding this, esp. *Ceiba pentandra*, kapok tree; ~ **hat**, tall stiff cylindrical hat covered with silk plush; **Silk Route**, overland trade route that went from China through Central Asia and Persia to the Eastern Roman Empire; **silk´screen printing**: see SCREEN printing; **silk-stocking** (*n.* & *adj.*), (fig.) aristocratic, wealthy, luxurious (person); **silk´worm**, mulberry-feeding caterpillar of

The origin of **signal** *flags used by sailors is said to have been the raising of a red cloak in a ship's rigging to tell the Greek fleet to attack the Persians at Salamis in 480 B.C.*

The natural sheen of **silk** enhances dyes and allows material for kimonos (above) to be brilliantly colored. Left: It may take many months to embroider a large wall-hanging by hand.

moth (*Bombyx mori*), which spins cocoon of silk before changing into pupal state; caterpillar of other moths yielding silk cocoons of commerical value; **corn silk**: see CORN.

silk·en (sĭl'ken) *adj.* Made of silk; clad in silk; soft or lustrous as silk.

silk·y (sĭl'kē) *adj.* (**silk·i·er, silk·i·est**). Like silk in smoothness, softness, fineness, or luster; **silky oak** (also **silk oak**), lofty Australian tree (*Grevillea robusta*) with fernlike foliage and attractive mottled wood. **silk'i·ness** *n.*

sill (sĭl) *n.* 1. Horizontal piece or part at base of doorway or esp. window. 2. Horizontal timber, block, etc., serving as foundation for house wall. 3. Sheet of intrusive volcanic rock lying parallel to the bedding of other rocks.

sil·ly (sĭl'ē) *adj.* (**-li·er, -li·est**). Innocent, simple, helpless (archaic); foolish, weakminded, unwise, imbecile. **sil'ly, sil'li·ly** *advs.*

sil'li·ness *n.*

si·lo (sī'lō) *n.* (pl. **-los**). 1. Pit or airtight structure in which fodder is pressed to undergo fermentation for conversion into succulent winter feed. 2. Underground place where guided missile is kept ready for firing. ~ *v.t.* (**-loed, -lo·ing**). Put, store in silo.

silt (sĭlt) *n.* Sediment deposited by water in channel, harbor, etc. ~ *v.* Choke, be choked, (*up*) with silt. **sil·ta·tion** (sĭltā'shon) *n.* **silt'y** *adj.* (**silt·i·er, silt·i·est**).

Sil·u·res (sĭl'yurēz, sĭlūr'-) *n.pl.* Members of a tribe in SE. Wales who resisted the Roman invasion (43 A.D.). **Si·lu·ri·an** (sĭloor'ēan, sī-, -lūr'-) *adj. & n.* 1. (One) of the Silures. 2. (geol.) (Of) the period or system of the Paleozoic between Ordovician and Devonian.

sil·van: SYLVAN.

Sil·va·nus (sĭlvā'nus). (Rom. myth.) Spirit of woods, fields, flocks, etc.

sil·ver (sĭl'ver) *n.* 1. (chem.) White lustrous ductile malleable metallic element, one of the precious metals, used chiefly with alloy of harder metal for coin, jewelry, table utensils, etc., and in form of salts as the light-sensitive materials in photography; symbol Ag, at. no. 47, at. wt. 107.868. 2. Silver coins; cupronickel coins now substituted for these; silverware, silver plate; household cutlery. 3. (attrib.) **sil'versmith**, worker in silver, maker of silverware; **sil'verware**, articles made of silver. **silver** *adj.* Wholly or chiefly of, colored like, silver; having clear ringing sound; eloquent; (of lace etc.) containing silver threads; ~ **age**, (i) (Gk. and Rom. myth.) second age of the world, inferior to golden age; (ii) second phase of classical Latin (see Silver LATIN); ~ **bell** (**tree**), any of various trees or shrubs of the storax family (genus *Halesia*) of southeastern U.S. and China, esp. *H. carolina* having graceful bellshaped white flowers; ~ **birch**, any of several birches (genus *Betula*), from the light color of the bark; **sil'verfish** (pl. **-fishes**, collect. **-fish**), various silvery fishes, esp. white variety of goldfish; small silvery wingless insect (*Lepisma saccharine*) feeding on starch, books, wallpaper, etc.; **silver fox**, color form of Amer. red fox with highly prized black fur that appears silver-tipped because the long hairs are banded with white near tips; **silver gray**, lustrous gray; **silver iodide**, yellow powder that darkens when exposed to light, used in rainmaking, photography, medicine; **Silver Latin**, see LATIN; **silver lining**, sign of hope in gloom; **silver nitrate**, poisonous, colorless, corrosive, crystalline salt, used in photography, as an antiseptic, in silver-plating, mirror manufacturing etc.; **silver-plate** (*v.t.*) (**-plat·ed, -plat·ing**), plate with silver, electroplate; **sil'vertip**: see GRIZZLY; ~ **wedding**, 25th wedding anniversary; **sil'ver-weed**, any of several plants having leaves silvery white underneath esp. *Potentilla argentea* or *P. anserina*. **silver** *v.* Coat or plate with silver; give silvery appearance to; turn (hair etc.), become, white or gray; provide (mirror) with amalgam of tin.

sil·ver·y (sĭl'verē) *adj.* Resembling silver in luster, whiteness, ringing sound, etc. **sil'ver·i·ness** *n.*

si·ma (sī'ma) *n.* (geol.) Part of earth's crust immediately below SIAL. [f. *s*ilicon and *m*agnesium]

Sim·e·on Sty·li·tes (sĭm'ēon stīlī'tēz), **St.** (*c*390–459). First of the stylites; lived for 30 years on top of a pillar near Antioch in Syria.

sim·i·an (sĭm'ēan) *adj. & n.* (Of) one of the apes, esp. the anthropoid apes; ape(like), monkey(like).

sim·i·lar (sĭm'ĭler) *adj.* Like, alike, having mutual resemblance or resemblance *to*, of the same kind; (geom.) having same shape. **sim'i·lar·ly** *adv.* **sim·i·lar·i·ty** (sĭmĭlăr'ĭtē) *n.* (pl. **-ties**).

sim·i·le (sĭm'ĭlē) *n.* Figure of speech in which two unlike things are explicitly compared, usu. with introductory word *like* or *as* ("like a small gray coffeepot sits the squirrel"); passage effecting this.

Silverweed (Potentilla anserina) *which grows wild in many temperate areas of the northern hemisphere. Its roots once served as an emergency food and the leaves were used as a medicine.*

si·mil·i·tude (sĭmĭl'ĭtōōd, -tūd) *n.* Guise, outward appearance; (obs.) simile.

sim·mer (sĭm'er) *v.* Be, keep, on the point of boiling, cook slowly in liquid at temperature just below boiling point (freq. fig.). ~ *n.* Simmering state.

Si·mon (sī'mon). 1. St. PETER[2]. 2. Apostle, member of the Zealot party (~ **Zelotes** or **the Canaanite**); commemorated with St. Jude, Oct. 28. 3. Kinsman of Jesus Christ (Matt. 13, Mark 6). 4. (also ~ **Magus**) Sorcerer of Samaria who was converted by Philip; he offered money to the Apostles if they would confer upon him the power to impart the Holy Ghost, and was rebuked by Peter (Acts 8). 5. ~ **Le·gree** (legrē'), cruel, merciless master, from the character of the slave driver in Harriet Beecher Stowe's novel, *Uncle Tom's Cabin*.

simon-pure (sī'mon pūr') *adj.* Completely pure, genuine, real.

si·mo·ny (sī'monē, sĭm'o-) *n.* Buying or selling of ecclesiastical preferment. [f. SIMON Magus]

sim·pa·ti·co (sĭmpah'tĭkō, -păt'ĭ-) *adj.* Of similar disposition or outlook; congenial.

sim·per (sĭm'per) *n.* Affected and self-conscious smile, smirk. ~ *v.* Smile in silly affected manner, smirk; utter with simper. **sim'per·ing·ly** *adv.* **sim'per·er** *n.*

sim·ple (sĭm'pel) *adj.* (**-pler, -plest**). 1. Not compound, complex, complicated, elaborate, involved, or composite; unmixed,

Except in Peru and Norway, **silver** *is mostly found in combination with other metals, particularly lead and zinc. It is present with gold, in copper deposits at Bougainville, Papua New Guinea.*

consisting of one substance, ingredient, or element; presenting no difficulty; mere, pure, bare; ~ **equation**, one not involving second or any higher power of unknown quantity; ~ **interest**: see INTEREST; ~ **life**, life in more or less primitive conditions, without servants or luxuries; ~ **sentence**, one without subordinate clause. 2. Plain, unsophisticated, natural, artless; inexperienced; weak-minded; of low rank, ordinary; ~**-hearted**, free of guile, sincere, unsophisticated; ~**-minded**, ingenuous, mentally deficient, stupid; **S**~ **Simon**, foolish, silly person, from the nursery rhyme character. **sim'ply** *adv.* In simple manner; without exception, absolutely. **sim'ple·ness, sim·plic·i·ty** (sĭm-plĭs'ĭtē) *ns.* (pl. **-ties**).

sim·ple·ton (sĭm'pelton) *n.* Foolish, gullible, or half-witted person.

sim·pli·fy (sĭm'plĭfī) *v.t.* (**-fied, -fy·ing**). Make simple, make easy to do or understand. **sim·pli·fi·ca·tion** (sĭmplĭfĭkā'shon) *n.*

sim·plism (sĭm'plĭzem) *n.* Affected simplicity; unjustifiable simplification of problem etc. **sim·plis·tic** (sĭmplĭs'tĭk) *adj.*

Sim·plon (sĭm'plŏn; *Fr.* săn-plawn'). Alpine pass in SW. Switzerland; ~ **tunnel**, railroad tunnel, about 12 mi. long, driven through Monte Leone, NE. of the pass.

sim·u·la·crum (sĭmyulā'krum) *n.* (pl. **-cra** pr. **-kra**). Image of something; shadowy likeness, deceptive substitute, mere pretense.

sim·u·late (sĭm'yulāt) *v.t.* (**-lat·ed, -lat·ing**). Feign, counterfeit; pretend to be, wear guise of, mimic. **sim'u·la·tive** *adj.* **sim·u·la·tion** (sĭmyulā'shon)

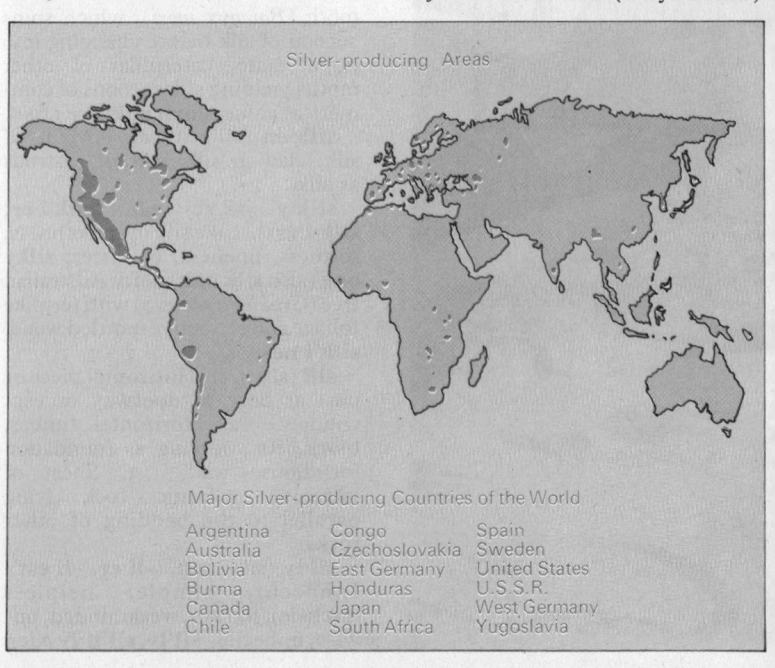

Silver-producing Areas

Major Silver-producing Countries of the World

Argentina	Congo	Spain
Australia	Czechoslovakia	Sweden
Bolivia	East Germany	United States
Burma	Honduras	U.S.S.R.
Canada	Japan	West Germany
Chile	South Africa	Yugoslavia

Silversmith Paul Harrison (below left) adopts the modern design concept of elegant simplicity. Others, anachronistically, attempt to ape the over-ornamentation of the 18th-century wine-cooler by Paul Storr, or the rococo of the Kaendler candelabrum (c. 1750).

n. **sim′u·la·tor** *n.* (esp.) Machine simulating conditions experienced in flying aircraft, driving vehicle, etc., used esp. in training pilots etc.

si·mul·cast (sī′mulkăst, -kahst, sĭm′ul-) *n.* Simultaneous transmission on radio and television.

si·mul·ta·ne·ous (sīmultā′nēus, sĭmul-) *adj.* Existing, occurring, operating, at the same time (*with*); ∼ **equations**, equations involving the same values of the unknown quantity or quantities and solved in conjunction with each other. **si·mul·ta′ne·ous·ly** *adv.* **si·mul·ta′ne·ous·ness, si·mul·ta·ne·i·ty** (sīmultanē′ĭtē, sĭmul-) *ns.*

sin[1] (sĭn) *n.* (A) transgression against divine law or principles of morality; offense *against* good taste, propriety, etc.; DEADLY, MORTAL, ORIGINAL, VENIAL ∼: see these words; **live in** ∼, (esp. colloq.) cohabit without marriage; **seven deadly sins**: see DEADLY. **sin′ful, sin′less** *adjs.* **sin′ful·ly, sin′·less·ly** *advs.* **sin′ful·ness, sin′·less·ness** *ns.* **sin** *v.i.* (**sinned, sin·ning**). Commit sin; offend *against.* **sin′ner** *n.*

sin[2] (sĭn) *abbrev.* Sine.

Si·nai (sī′nī, -nĭī). Peninsula of NE. Egypt, at the N. end of the Red Sea, extending 140 mi. (225 km), between the gulfs of Suez and Aqaba; occupied by Israeli forces June, 1967, during 6-Day War; returned to Egypt by Israeli-Egyptian peace treaty, 1979. **Mount Sinai**, mountain in S. part of this peninsula where the Ten Commandments and the Tables of

the Law were given to Moses.
Si·na·it·ic (sīnāit´ĭk), **Si·na·ic** (sīnā´ĭk, sĭ-) *adjs.*

Sin·bad: SINDBAD.

since (sĭns) *adv.* From that time till now; within the period between then and now, subsequently, later; ago, before now. ~ *prep.* From (specified time) till now; during the period between (specified past time) and now. ~ *conj.* 1. From the time that. 2. Seeing that, because, inasmuch as.

sin·cere (sĭnsēr´) *adj.* (**-cer·er, -cer·est**). Free from pretense or deceit, not assumed or put on, genuine, honest, frank. **sin·cere'ly** *adv.* In a sincere manner; **yours ~**, polite formula used before signature in letter (e.g. to acquaintance) that is neither formal nor intimate. **sin·cer·i·ty** (sĭnsĕr´ĭtē) *n.* (pl. **-ties**).

sin·ci·put (sĭn´sĭpŭt) *n.* (pl. **sin·ci·puts, sin·cip·i·ta** pr. sĭnsĭp´ĭta). Front part of head or skull.

Sind·bad, Sin·bad (sĭn´băd). (also ~ **the Sailor**) Hero of one of the tales in the *Arabian Nights*, who relates his fantastic adventures in a number of voyages.

si·ne (sīn) *n.* (trig., function of angle in right-angled triangle) Ratio of side opposite given acute angle to hypotenuse (abbrev. sin); ~ **curve**, graph in rectangular coordinates showing how this ratio varies with the angle.

si·ne·cure (sī´nekūr, sĭn´e-) *n.* Any office or post that involves little or no work, esp. one that brings profit.

si·ne di·e (sī´nē dī´ē; *Lat.* sī´nĕ dē´ĕ). (Adjourned) without any day for resumption of business etc. being specified; indefinitely. [L., = "without day"]

si·ne qua non (sī´nē kwā nŏn´; *Lat.* sī´nĕ kwah nōn´). Indispensable condition or qualification. [L., = "without which not"]

sin·ew (sĭn´ū) *n.* (Piece of) tough fibrous tissue uniting muscle to bone, tendon; (pl., loosely) muscles, bodily strength, wiriness (freq. fig., esp. in ~**s of war**, money). **sin´ew·y** *adj.*

sing (sĭng) *v.* (**sang** pr. săng or **sung** pr. sŭng, **sung, sing·ing**). Utter words or sounds, utter (words, sounds), in tuneful succession, esp. in accordance with a set tune; produce vocal melody, utter (song, tune); make inarticulate melodious, humming, buzzing, or whistling sounds; compose poetry, celebrate in verse; ~ **out**, (colloq.) call out loudly. **sing´er** *n.*

sing *abbrev.* Singular.

Sin·ga·pore (sĭng´gapōr, -pȯr, sĭng´a-). Republic consisting of the island of Singapore and a number of smaller islands, S. of Malay peninsula; former Brit. colony; member nation of Brit. Common-

wealth, independent 1965.

singe (sĭnj) *n.* Superficial burn. ~ *v.t.* (**singed, singe·ing**). Burn superficially or lightly, burn ends of edges of.

Sin·gha·lese (sĭnggalēz´, -lēs´) *n.* (pl. **-lese**). 1. (Member of) the majority community in Sri Lanka. 2. Indo-European language spoken in Sri Lanka, closely related to Pali, with many Dravidian words. ~ *adj.*

sin·gle (sĭng´gel) *adj.* One only, not double or multiple, undivided, individual, separate; of, for, one person only; solitary, lonely, unaided; unmarried; (of flower) not double, having only one whorl or set of petals; ~**-breasted**, (of garments) having buttons on one edge, not double-breasted; ~ **combat**, combat between two persons; ~ **entry**, simple method of bookkeeping in which transactions are entered in the ledger under one account only (opp. double ENTRY); ~ **file**, line of persons going one behind another, Indian file; ~**-handed**, (done etc.) without help from other persons; ~**-hearted**, sincere, honest; ~**-lens reflex**, type of reflex camera in which image is reflected through same lens onto film and ground glass viewing plate; ~**-minded**, single-hearted; also, keeping one purpose in view; **single-track**, one-track. **sin´gle·-ness** *n.* **sin´gly** *adv.* **single** *n.* One person or thing; theater seat, hotel room, etc. for one person; (pl.) unmarried people collectively; (baseball) one-base hit; (pl., tennis) game for one person only on each side; (colloq.) dollar bill. ~ *v.t.*

(-gled, -gling). Choose *out* as example, to serve some purpose etc.

sin·gle·ton (sĭng´gelton) *n.* 1. (bridge etc.) Card that is the only one of its suit in the hand. 2. Single thing; thing that exists by itself rather than as one of a pair or in a group.

sing·song (sĭng´sawng) *adj.* In, recited with, monotonous rhythm, rising and falling monotonously. ~ *n.* Monotonous rhythm or cadence; impromptu or informal vocal concert.

sin·gu·lar (sĭng´gyuler) *adj.* 1. (gram.) Denoting, expressing, 1 person or thing. 2. Unusual, uncommon, extraordinary, surprising; strange, odd, peculiar. **sin´gu·lar·ly** *adv.* **sin·gu·lar·i·ty** (sĭnggyulăr´ĭtē) *n.* (pl. **-ties**). (esp.) Eccentricity, oddness, strangeness. **singular** *n.* Singular number; word in singular form.

Sin·ha·lese (sĭnhalēz, -lēs´) = SINGHALESE.

sin·is·ter (sĭn´ĭster) *adj.* 1. Of evil omen; unfavorable, harmful; wicked, corrupt, evil; ill-looking, malignant, villainous. 2. (her.) On left side of shield etc. (from bearer's point of view); **bar, bend** ~: see BEND[1].

sin·is·tral (sĭn´ĭstral) *adj.* (of spiral shells) With whorls going to left; (of flat fishes) having left side of body turned uppermost.

sink[1] (sĭngk) *n.* 1. Place in which foul liquid collects (now usu. fig.). 2. Fixed basin with drain and faucets, in bathroom for washing face, hands, etc., in kitchen for washing dishes etc. 3. **heat ~**, device for dissipating heat in electrical circuit or steam engine. 4. Low-lying, poorly drained area.

sink[2] (sĭngk) *v.* (**sank** pr. săngk or **sunk** pr. sŭngk, **sunk** or rarely **sunk·en, sink·ing**). 1. Become wholly or partly submerged in water, quicksand, snow, etc. (freq. fig.); fall slowly downward, subside, descend, pass out of sight; pass, fall gently, lapse, degenerate, *into*; (of sun etc.) appear to move downward toward or pass below horizon; penetrate, make way *in(to)*. 2. Cause or allow to sink; send below surface of liquid or ground; lower level of; excavate, make by excavating; set aside, leave out of consideration; invest (money), lose by investment; (golf, basketball, etc.) get ball into hole, basket, etc.

sink·er (sĭng´ker) *n.* (esp.) Weight used to sink fishing or sounding line; (baseball) curve ball that drops as it crosses home plate.

sink·ing (sĭng′kĭng) n. (esp.) Internal bodily sensation caused by hunger or apprehension; ~ **fund**, fund of money periodically set aside from revenue, usu. to reduce principal of national, municipal, or company's debt.

Sinn Fein (shĭn′ fān′). Irish society, founded 1905 by Arthur Griffith, aiming at political independence and revival of Irish culture and language; policy of this; extreme Irish nationalist party. [Ir., = "we ourselves"]

Sino- *prefix*. Of China and —, as ~ *-Soviet*.

Si·nol·o·gy (sīnŏl′ojē, sĭ-) n. Study of Chinese language, history, customs, etc. **Si·no·logue** (sī′no-lawg, -lŏg), **Si·nol′o·gist** ns. Person versed in this.

Si·no·phile (sī′nofīl), **Si·no·phobe** (sī′nofōb) ns. One who loves, hates, the Chinese.

Si·no-Ti·bet·an (sīnōtĭbĕt′an) adj. & n. (Of) the family of languages, mostly of the isolating type but orig. agglutinative, spoken over an area including N. India, Malay peninsula, China, and most of central and E. Asia (but not Japan).

sin·ter (sĭn′ter) n. Siliceous deposit often found around hot springs; substance produced by sintering. ~ v. (Cause to) coalesce from powder into solid by heating.

sin·u·ous (sĭn′ūus) adj. With many curves, tortuous, serpentine, undulating. **sin′u·ous·ly** adv. **sin′u·ous·ness** n. **sin·u·os·i·ty** (sĭnūŏs′ĭtē) n. (pl. **-ties**). Sinuousness; a curve or bend.

si·nus (sī′nus) n. (pl. **-nus·es**). 1. (anat., zool.) Cavity of bone or tissue, esp. one of the cavities in the bone of the skull that communicate with the nostrils. 2. (path.) Passage communicating with deep-seated abscess, fistula. 3. (bot.) Curve between lobes of leaf.

si·nus·i·tis (sīnusī′tĭs) n. Inflammation of sinus(es).

Sioux (soo) n. (pl. **Sioux** pr. soo, sooz). (Member of) important group of N. Amer. Ind. tribes, orig. of district W. and S. of Lake Superior, later of plains of Minnesota, N. and S. Dakota, and Nebraska. **Siou·an** (soo′an) adj.

sip (sĭp) n. Small mouthful of liquid; act of sipping. ~ v. (**sipped, sip·ping**). Drink in sips, take sip of.

si·phon (sī′fon) n. Pipe or tube bent so that one leg is longer than the other and used for drawing off liquids by atmospheric pressure, which forces liquid up the shorter leg and over the bend in the pipe; (also ~ **bottle**) aerated water bottle from which liquid is forced out by pressure of gas through tube inserted in bottle; (zool.) tubelike organ, esp. in mollusks, serving as canal for passage of fluid etc. **si′phon·al, si·phon·ic** (sīfŏn′ĭk) adj. **siphon** v. Conduct, flow, (as) through siphon.

sir (ser) n. 1. **S~**, title of honor placed before Christian name of knight or baronet. 2. Used (without name) in formal or respectful address to a man; sometimes with scornful, indignant, contemptuous, etc., force; (**Dear**) **Sir**(s), opening of formal letter. **sir** v.t. Address as *sir*.

sire (sīr) n. 1. Father, forefather (poet.); male parent of beast, esp. stallion. 2. (archaic) = "your majesty." ~ v.t. (**sired, sir·ing**). Beget (esp. of stallions).

si·ren (sīr′en) n. 1. (Gk. myth.) Any of several fabulous creatures, women or birds with

women's heads, living on rocky isle to which they lured seafarers by their singing. 2. Sweet singer; dangerously fascinating woman, temptress; (attrib.) irresistibly tempting. 3. Apparatus producing loud sound by revolution of perforated disk over jet of compressed air or steam, used on fire engine, police car, as air raid warning, etc. 4. Eellike tailed amphibian of family Sirenidae, with short forelegs and no hindlegs.

si·re·ni·an (sīrē′nēan) adj. & n. (Member) of order Sirenia of large aquatic herbivorous mammals, including manatee and dugong.

Sir·i·us (sĭr′ēus). (astron.) Dog star, a brilliant white star in the constellation Canis Major, the brightest fixed star.

sir·loin (ser′loin) n. Upper and choicer part of loin of beef.

si·roc·co (sĭrŏk′ō) n. (pl. **-cos**). Hot and blighting oppressive wind blowing from N. coast of Africa over Mediterranean to parts of S. Europe. [It. *s(c)irocco*, f. Arab.

šarŭk east wind]

sir·rah, sir·ra (sĭr′a) *ns.* (archaic) = SIR used in contempt, reproach, reprimand.

sir·up = SYRUP.

si·sal (sī′sal, sĭs′al) *n.* (also ~ **grass, hemp**) Strong durable white fiber of a Mexican agave (*Agave sisalana*) and similar plants, used for cordage etc. [*Sisal*, former seaport of Yucatan]

sis·kin (sĭs′kĭn) *n.* Small sharp-billed finch (*Spinus pinus*) of northern N. Amer., brown with yellow wing and tail patches.

sis·sy (sĭs′ē) *n.* (pl. **-sies**) & *adj.* Effeminate or cowardly boy or man; cowardly or timid person. **sis·si-fied** (sĭs′ĭfīd), **sis′sy·ish** *adjs.*

sis·ter (sĭs′ter) *n.* 1. Daughter of same parents as another person; one considered as or filling the place of a sister. 2. Member of a religious sisterhood, nun; **S~**, title of or form of address to nun; ~-**in-law** (pl. **~s-in-law**), sister of one's husband or wife, wife of one's brother; **sister ship**, vessel built on same design as another.

sis·ter·hood (sĭs′terhood) *n.* 1. Being a sister, relation between sisters. 2. Society of women bound by monastic vows or devoting themselves to religious or charitable work.

Sis·tine (sĭs′tēn, -tīn, -tĭn) *adj.* 1. Of, pertaining to, built by, one of the popes named Sixtus; ~ **Chapel**, chapel in the Vatican, built by Sixtus IV, containing

Michelangelo's painted ceiling and his fresco of the Last Judgment. 2. ~ **Madonna**, painting by Raphael formerly in the Church of San Sisto, Piacenza, and later in Dresden.

Sis·y·phus (sĭs′ifus). (Gk. myth.) Legendary king of Corinth, condemned for his misdeeds to Hades; his eternal task was to roll a large stone to the top of a hill from which it rolled back again to the plain. **Sis·y·phe·an** (sĭsifē′an) *adj.* (As) of Sisyphus, everlastingly laborious.

sit (sĭt) *v.* (**sat** pr. săt, **sit-ting**). 1. Take, be in, position in which weight of body rests on buttocks; occupy seat as judge, with administrative function, as member of council or legislative assembly, etc.; (of assembly) hold a session, transact business; pose (*for* portrait etc. *to* painter etc.); (Brit.) take examination. 2. (of birds and some animals) Rest with legs bent and body close to ground or perch; remain on nest to hatch eggs. 3. (chiefly of inanimate things) Be in more or less permanent position. 4. Seat *oneself* (usu. *down*); cause to sit (usu. *down*); sit on (horse); (of bird) sit on, hatch (eggs). 5. ~ **down**, seat oneself; ~-**down**

(**strike**), one in which strikers refuse to leave the place where they are working; ~-**in**, organized protest in which demonstrators occupy building etc.; ~ **in on**, be present as observer, participant; ~ **on**, hold session concerning; (slang) repress, squash, snub; ~ **out**, remain to end of; outstay; take no part in (dance etc.), sit out dance; ~ **up**, rise from lying to sitting posture; sit erect; (of animal) sit on hind legs with forelegs straight or lifted in begging posture; remain out of bed; (colloq.) be surprised, suddenly interested; **sit′up, sit-up** (*ns.*), exercise in which one raises the body from lying flat on back to sitting position without using arms or bending legs.

si·tar (sĭtär′) *n.* Long-necked seven-stringed Indian musical instrument resembling a lute.

sit·com (sĭt′kŏm) *n.* (colloq.) = SITUATION comedy.

site (sīt) *n.* Ground on which town, building, etc., stood, stands, or is to stand; ground set apart for some purpose. ~ *v.t.* (**sit·ed, sit·ing**). Locate, place, provide with site.

sit·ter (sĭt′er) *n.* (esp.) BABY sitter.

sit·ting (sĭt′ĭng) *n.* (esp.) 1. Time during which one sits or remains seated; single occasion of sitting for artist etc. 2. Clutch of eggs. 3. ~ **room**, space for sitting; room used expressly for sitting in. **sitting** *adj.* (of bird) Not flying;

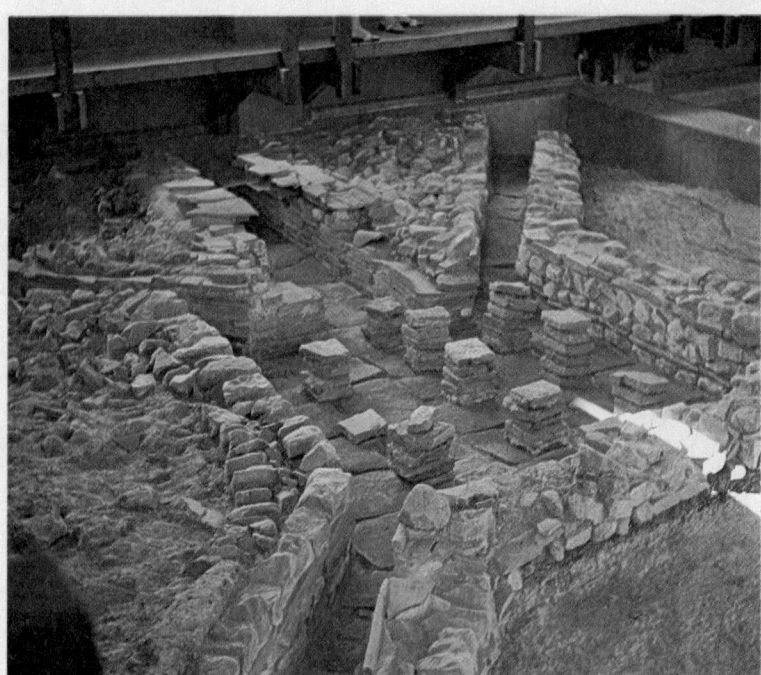

Remains of a hypocaust or Roman form of central heating restored at an archaeological *site* at Fishbourne, in Sussex, England. Such work can indicate what life was like in former times.

(of animal) not running; (of hen) engaged in hatching; ~ **duck,** (colloq.) person or thing easily attacked.

Sit·ting (sĭt´ĭng) **Bull** (1834?–1890). Amer. Indian Sioux chief; leader during Sioux War, 1876–7, and at battle of the Little Big Horn, June 25, 1876, where the Amer. forces under Gen. George S. Custer were massacred.

sit·u·ate (sĭch´ōōāt) *v.t.* **(-at·ed, -at·ing).** Place or put in position, situation, etc. **sit´u·at·ed, situate** (sĭch´ōōĭt, -āt) *adjs.* In specified situation. **sit·u·a·tion** (sĭchōōā´shon) *n.* 1. Place, with its surroundings, occupied by something. 2. Set of circumstances, position in which one finds oneself; critical point or complication, position of affairs, in narrative, drama, etc.; ~ **comedy,** one in which humor derives from characters' misunderstandings and embarrassments. 3. Place or paid office, esp. of domestic servant. **sit·u·a´tion·al** *adj.*

sitz (sĭts, zĭts) **bath.** Hip bath. [Ger. *Sitzbad,* f. *sitzen* sit]

Si·va = SHIVA.

six (sĭks) *adj.* Amounting to 6; ~**-foot,** measuring six feet; **S ~ Nations,** (hist.) confederation of N. Amer. Indians consisting of the FIVE Nations and the Tuscaroras; ~**-pack,** six cans or bottles in one package, esp. when containing beer; **six´pence,** (Brit.) sum of six pence; coin formerly worth this; **six-shooter,** revolver capable of firing six shots without reloading. **six** *n.* One more than 5; symbol for this (6, vi, or VI); card, die face, or domino with six pips; six o'clock; size etc. indicated by 6; set of six things or persons. **six´fold** *adj.* & *adv.*

six·teen (sĭks·tēn´) *adj.* One more than 15. ~ *n.* The number sixteen (16, xvi, or XVI). **six´-teenth´** *adj.* & *n.*

sixth (sĭksth) *adj.* Next after fifth; ~ **sense,** supposed faculty by which a person perceives facts and regulates action without the direct use of any of the five senses. **sixth** *n.* Sixth part (see PART[1] sense 1); sixth thing etc.; **sixth´ly** *adv.* In the sixth place.

Six·tus (sĭks´tus). Name of five popes, esp.: **Sixtus IV,** pope 1471–84, patron of art and letters, builder of the SISTINE Chapel, refounded the Vatican library; **Sixtus V,** pope 1585–90, reorganized the papal finances and issued (1590) an edition of the Vulgate known as the Sistine Vulgate.

six·ty (sĭks´tē) *adj.* Amounting to 60. ~ *n.* (pl. **-ties**). Cardinal number, 6 times 10 (60, lx, or LX); set of 60 things or persons; **six´ties,** numbers etc. from 60 to 69; these years of century or life. **six´ti·eth** *adj.* & *n.*

siz·a·ble, size·a·ble (sī´zabel) *adjs.* Of fairly large size. **siz´a·bly** *adv.*

size[1] (sīz) *n.* Dimensions, magnitude; one of usu. numbered classes into which things, esp. garments, are divided according to size. ~ *v.t.* **(sized, siz·ing).** Group or sort in sizes or according to size; ~ **up,** estimate size of; (colloq.) form judgment of.

size[2] (sīz) *n.* Glutinous substance, preparation of glue, shellac, etc., and water, used for glazing paper, stiffening textiles, mixing with colors, etc. ~ *v.t.* **(sized, siz·ing).** Treat with size.

size·a·ble: SIZABLE.

siz·zle (sĭz´el) *v.i.* **(-zled, -zling).** Make sputtering or hissing sound, esp. in frying, roasting, etc. ~ *n.* Sizzling noise.

S.J. *abbrev.* Society of Jesus.

Skag·er·rak (skăg´erăk). N. part of channel between S. Scandinavia and Denmark connecting North Sea with Baltic.

skate[1] (skāt) *n.* (pl. **skates,** collect. **skate**). Any of various ocean fish (family Rajidae), having a broad flat body and two wing-like dorsal fins.

skate[2] (skāt) *n.* One of a pair of steel blades, each attached beneath shoe sole, enabling wearer to glide over ice; ROLLER skate. ~ *v.i.* **(skat·ed, skat·ing).** Move, glide, (as) on skates. **skat´er** *n.*

As the representative of destruction, *Siva* was always admired by Hindu ascetics. In other forms, he represents dance and free living, and is symbolized by a phallus.

skate·board (skāt´bōrd, -bôrd) *n.* Short, oblong board or length of plastic having pair of roller skate wheels at each end, used for gliding, usu. on inclined surface. ~ *v.* Glide or coast on skateboard. **skate´board·er, skate´board·ing** *ns.*

ske·dad·dle (skĭdăd´el) *v.* **(-dled, -dling).** (colloq.) Run away, retreat hastily. ~ *n.* Precipitate retreat or flight, scurry.

skeet (skēt) *n.* Shooting sport in which clay target is thrown from trap to simulate flight of bird.

skein (skān) *n.* Quantity of yarn or thread coiled and usu. loosely twisted.

The **skeleton** of the dodo (above) and of man (right) show common features which indicate that despite the adaptation of each to different environments, it is probable that all vertebrates originally shared a single ancestor.

1. skull	13. carpal bones
2. mandible	14. metacarpal
3. clavicle	bones
4. sternum	15. trochanter
5. xiphoid	16. femur
process	17. patella
6. ribs	18. tibia
7. spine	19. fibula
8. pelvis	20. tarsal bones
9. scapula	21. metatarsal
10. humerus	bones
11. radius	22. phalanges
12. ulna	

skel·e·ton (skĕl′eton) *n.* 1. Hard internal or external framework of bones, cartilage, shell, woody fiber, etc., supporting or containing animal or vegetable body. 2. Dried bones of human being or other animal fastened together in same relative positions as in life; very thin or emaciated person, etc.; ~ **in the closet**, discreditable or humiliating fact concealed from strangers. 3. Mere outlines, supporting framework, main features or most necessary elements, *of* something; (attrib.) (of staff, company, etc.) of the minimum size, forming a nucleus that can be added to as occasion arises; ~ **key**, key fitting many locks by having large part of bit filed away. **skel′e·tal** *adj.* **kel′e·tal·ly** *adv.* **skel·e·ton·ize** (skĕl′etonīz) *v.t.* (**-ized, -iz·ing**). Reduce to a skeleton.

skep·tic, scep·tic (skĕp′tĭk) *ns.* One who doubts the possibility of real knowledge of any kind; one who doubts the truth of the Christian or of all religious doctrines; person of skeptical attitude, or unconvinced of the truth of a particular fact or theory. **skep′i·cal** *adj.* Inclined to suspense of judgment, given to questioning of facts and soundness of inferences; incredulous, hard to convince. **skep′ti·cal·ly** *adv.* **skep′ti·cism** (skĕp′tĭsĭzem) *n.*

sketch (skĕch) *n.* Preliminary, rough, slight, merely outlined, or unfinished drawing or painting; brief account or narrative without detail, rough draft, general outline; short slight play, freq. of single scene; **sketch′book, sketch book**, book of drawing paper for making sketches on. **sketch** *v.* Make or give sketch of; make sketches. **sketch′er** *n.*

sketch·y (skĕch′ē) *adj.* (**sketch·i·er, sketch·i·est**). Giving only a slight or rough outline; resembling a sketch; light, flimsy, hurried, rough. **sketch′i·ly** *adv.* **sketch′i·ness** *n.*

skew (skū) *v.t.* Make slanting; distort. ~ *v.i.* Move obliquely; twist. ~ *adj.* Oblique, slanting, squint, not symmetrical (now usu.

archit., mech., etc.). ~ *n.* Sloping top of buttress; coping of gable; stone built into bottom of gable to support coping.

skew·er (skū′er) *n.* Pin for holding meat compactly together while cooking. ~ *v.t.* Fasten together, pierce, (as) with skewer.

ski (skē; *Norw.* shē) *n.* (pl. **skis, ski**). One of pair of long slender pieces of wood, plastic, etc., usu. pointed and curved upward at front, fastened to boot and enabling wearer to glide over snow-covered surface; ~ **boots, pants**, etc., garments for wear when skiing; ~ **jump**, steep slope leveling off before sharp drop, allowing skier to leap through air; ~ **lift**, device for transporting skiers up mountain-side, usu. consisting of seats suspended from overhead cable. **ski** *v.i.* (**skied, ski·ing**). Slide, travel on skis.

skid (skĭd) *n.* 1. Piece of frame or timber serving as buffer, support, inclined plane, for logs, etc. 2. Braking device, esp. wooden or metal shoe, fixed under the wheel of a cart etc. and so preventing its turning when descending a steep hill; runner on aircraft to facilitate landing, etc. 3. Act of skidding; ~ **row**, section of city frequented by vagrants, alcoholics, etc. **skid** *v.* (**skid·ded, skid·ding**). 1. Support, move, protect, check, with skid(s). 2. (of wheel etc.) Slide without revolving, fail to grip ground, sideslip; (of vehicle etc.) slide sideways toward outside of curve when turning; slip, slide, esp. with (partial) loss of balance. **skid′dy** *adj.* (**-di·er, -di·est**).

skiff (skĭf) *n.* Any of several types of small open boats having flat bottom, pointed at bow and square at stern, sailed or rowed by one person.

skil·ful: SKILLFUL.

skill (skĭl) *n.* Expertness, practiced ability, dexterity, facility in doing something.

skilled (skĭld) *adj.* (esp., of workman etc.) Properly trained or experienced; (of work) requiring skill and experience.

skil·let (skĭl′ĭt) *n.* Frying pan.

skill·ful, skil·ful (skĭl′fŭl) *adjs.* Having or showing skill (*at, in*); practiced, adept, expert, ingenious. **skill′ful·ly** *adv.* **skill′ful·ness** *n.*

skim (skĭm) *v.* (**skimmed, skim·ming**). Take scum, cream, floating matter, from surface of (liquid), remove (cream etc.) from surface of milk etc.; ~ **the cream off**, (fig.) take best part of; pass over (surface), pass *over, along*, rapidly and lightly with close approach or very slight contact; read superficially, look over cursorily. **skim** *adj.* **skim(med) milk**, milk with the cream removed. **skimming** *n.* (slang) Deliberate failure to report part of income, esp. from gambling, in order to evade tax.

skim·mer (skĭm′er) *n.* (esp.) 1. Ladle, usu. perforated, or other utensil for skimming liquids. 2. Long-winged marine bird of genus *Rynchops*, esp. **black** ~ (*R. nigra*), obtaining food by skimming along surface of water with knifelike lower mandible immersed.

skimp (skĭmp) *v.* Supply meagerly; be parsimonious. **skimp′y** *adv.* (**skimp·i·er, skimp·i·est**). Meager, inadequate. **skimp′i·ly** *adv.* **skimp′i·ness** *n.*

skin (skĭn) *n.* 1. Tough flexible continuous covering of human or other animal body, consisting of

Like most artists, Michelangelo, before he began a full-scale painting or sculpture, made a **sketch** of various features that he wished to incorporate in the final work.

The one class style of yacht racing has become increasingly popular particularly in the smaller classes such as the **skiff**. There is often keen competition for sponsoring rights on successful boats.

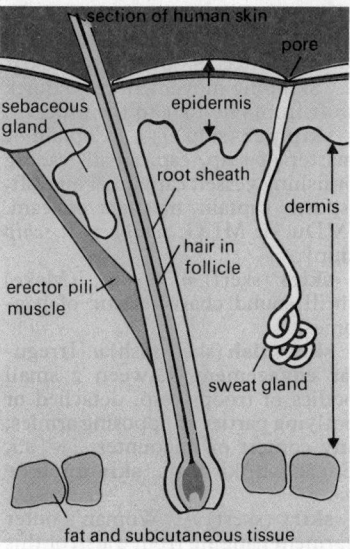

*...etermined skiers no longer need to ...onfine their activities to the winter. ...his Australian competes in a **slalom** ...hich is held on synthetic mats which ...e used to simulate snow.*

*The **ski lift** was designed to encourage people to become skiers, and prevents their wasting much time and energy in ascending those slopes that they wish to descend.*

*The **skin** of a human being consists of two layers and the outer one is constantly being replaced as dead scales are washed or worn away. The pores are remarkable non-return valves.*

...wo layers, the *epidermis* or outer ...yer, and the *dermis* or inner layer, ...ith (in mammals) its sebaceous ...lands, hair follicles, etc.; one of ...e separate layers of which skin ... composed; hide of flayed animal, ...p. of smaller animals, as sheep, ...oat, etc., with or without the hair ...r wool; vessel for wine or water ...ade of animal's whole skin; **...hange one's ~**, undergo impossible change of character etc.; **...et under one's ~**, take a strong ...old on, irritate; **save one's ~**, ...void loss or injury; **thick (thin)**

~, imperviousness (sensitiveness) to affront, reproach, etc. 2. Outer coating, peel, rind, of fruit, vegetable, etc.; thin film or pellicle; outer covering of ribs or frame of ship, boat, or aircraft. 3. **~-deep**, superficial, not deep or lasting; **~-dive** (*v.i.* & *n.*), dive without diving suit (usu. in ref. to deep diving with respirator); so **~ diver**; **~ flick**, (slang) explicitly pornographic motion picture; **skin'flint**, miser; **skin game**, (slang) swindle; **skin graft**, skin cut from another part or person and surgically substituted for damaged part; **skin test**, test for allergy or disease made by observing skin reaction to application of test substance; **skin'tight**, (of garment) very closefitting. **skin** *v*. (**skinned, skin·ning**). 1. Cover

(usu. *over*), as with skin; form, become covered (usu. *over*) with, new skin. 2. Strip skin from, flay; remove skin of. 3. (slang) Swindle, fleece.

skink (skĭngk) *n*. Any lizard of the family Scincidae, with smooth, overlapping scales.

skin·ny (skĭn´ē) *adj*. (**-ni·er, -ni·est**). (esp.) Lean, emaciated; **~-dip** (*v.*), (colloq.) Swim nude; so **~-dipper, -dipping** *ns*.

skip (skĭp) *v*. (**skipped, skip·ping**). Jump about lightly, frisk, gambol, caper, move lightly from one foot to the other; spring or leap lightly and easily, esp. over rope revolved over head and under feet; shift quickly from one subject or occupation to another; omit, make omissions, in reading, dealing with

*...f the 19 families of lizard, none is bet-...r known than the **skink** group. In ...armer regions, the smaller skinks are ...ommon in city gardens, although ...rger species survive in remote areas.*

...e-tongue lizard

blue-tailed skink (young)

stumpy-tail or shingle-back lizard

a series, etc.; cause (bomb) to ricochet from a surface toward a target; hence ~ **bombing. skip** *n.* Skipping movement, esp. quick shift from one foot to the other.

skip·per (skĭp′er) *n.* Captain or master of ship, esp. small trading or fishing vessel; captain of aircraft; (sports) captain, manager of team. [MDu. or MLG. *schipper*, f. *schip* ship]

skirl (skẽrl) *n.* & *v.i.* (Make) shrill sound characteristic of bagpipes.

skir·mish (skẽr′mĭsh) *n.* Irregular engagement between 2 small bodies of troops, esp. detached or outlying parties of opposing armies; any contest or encounter. ~ *v.i.* Engage in skirmish. **skir′mish·er** *n.*

skirt (skẽrt) *n.* Woman's outer garment hanging from waist, or this part of complete garment; underskirt, petticoat (archaic); flap of a saddle; border, rim, outskirts, boundary of anything; diaphragm or midriff of animal (esp. of beef) used for food. **skirt** *v.* Go along, around, or past the edge of; be situated along, go *along*, coast, wall, etc.

skit (skĭt) *n.* Light piece of satire, burlesque; short usu. humorous theatrical sketch.

skit·ter (skĭt′er) *v.i.* Skip or skim along surface, esp., of wildfowl, along water in rising or settling.

skit·tish (skĭt′ĭsh) *adj.* Frivolous, excessively lively; spirited; (of horse etc.) nervous, excitable, fidgety. **skit′tish·ly** *adv.* **skit′-tish·ness** *n.*

skit·tle (skĭt′el) *n.* Pin used in ninepins or tenpins; (pl.) game of ninepins.

skiv·vy (skĭv′ē) *n.* (pl. **-vies**). (slang) 1. (also ~ **shirt**) Man's cotton undershirt; 2. (pl.) Man's undershirt and shorts.

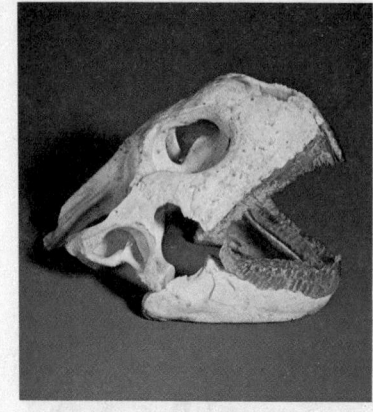

The distinctive bone formation of the marine turtle's **skull** has led palaeontologists to believe that these reptiles separated from others at an early stage of evolution.

sku·a (skū′a) *n.* Large rapacious predatory seabird (*Catharacta skua*), breeding in both Arctic and Antarctic.

skul·dug·ger·y, skull·dug·-ger·y (skŭldŭg′erē) *ns.* Rascally conduct, underhand plotting.

skulk (skŭlk) *v.i.* Lurk, conceal oneself, avoid observation, esp. with sinister motive or in cowardice.

skull (skŭl) *n.* Bony case of the brain, cranium; whole bony framework of head; ~ **and crossbones**, representation of human skull with two thighbones crossed below it, as emblem of death; **skull′cap**, close-fitting brimless cap for top of head; (anat.) cranial portion of skull.

skunk (skŭngk) *n.* (pl. **skunks**, collect. **skunk**). Small N. Amer. mammal of weasel family (genus *Mephitis* and related genera), with black coat striped with white, and bushy tail, able to emit, when attacked, powerful and offensive odor from two anal glands; fur of this; low contemptible person; ~ **bear**, (colloq.) wolverine; ~ **cabbage**, disagreeable-smelling

perennial plant (*Symplocarpu foetidus*) of eastern N. Amer., thriving in swampy, wooded areas and having large leaves, small flowers enclosed in a purplish or greenish hooded spathe, and deep, tough root system; similar plant (*Lysichitum americanum*) growing in western N. Amer. **skunk** *v.t.* (slang) Defeat decisively in game. [Amer. Indian *segongw*]

sky (skī) *n.* (pl. **skies**) Apparent arch or vault of heaven; climate, clime; color of blue sky, sky blue; ~ **blue**, color of clear summer sky; **sky′cap**, porter at air terminal; **sky′diving**, sport of falling freely from aircraft and opening parachute only at last safe moment; **sky-high**, very high(ly); **sky′jack** (*v.t.*), (slang) hijack (aircraft); **Sky′lab**, U.S. space station launched in 1973, to house astronauts engaged in scientific work while they orbited Earth; it fell to Earth (1979); **sky lark**, common European lark, *Alauda arvensis*, which sings continuously while soaring; (*v.i.*) frolic, play tricks or practical jokes, indulge in horseplay; **sky′light**, window in roof; **sky′line**, silhouette of anything against sky; visible horizon; **sky marshal**, armed Federal guard who travels by commercial airlines.

great skua

While resembling a gull, the **skua** is a type of semi-predator, attacking other sea-birds to make them disgorge their catch which the skua then obtains. This bird staunchly defends its territory and will attack man or animal approaching its nest.

pomarine skua

Although spectacular, the land available on Skye offers few opportunities for agriculture. Some people weave plaids at Portree while others work in a factory where diatomite is processed.

o provide security against sky-acking; **sky'rocket**, rocket exploding high in air; (*v.i.*) ascend like skyrocket; **sky'scraper**, very high building; **sky'writing**, legible smoke trails made by aircraft, esp. or advertising purposes. **sky'ey** *adj.* **sky'ward** *adv.* & *adj.* **sky'-wards** *adv.*

Skye (skī). Largest island of Inner Hebrides; ~ **terrier**, small, long-bodied, short-legged, long-haired variety of Scotch terrier, of slate or fawn color.

slab (slăb) *n.* Flat, broad, comparatively thick piece of solid material, as stone, timber, etc.; large flat piece of cake, chocolate, etc.; (logging) rough outside piece cut from log or tree trunk. ~ *v.t.* (**slabbed, slab'bing**). Cut slab(s) from (log, tree); cover, support, protect with slabs.

slack[1] (slăk) *adj.* Sluggish, remiss, relaxed, languid, loose, inactive, negligent; (of heat etc.) gentle, moderate. **slack'ly** *adv.* **slack'ness** *n.* **slack** *n.* Slack part of rope; slack time in business etc.; (pl.) trousers for informal or sports wear. ~ *v.* Slacken, make loose; take rest, be indolent, slow *up*; slake (lime); ~ **off**, abate vigor.

slack[2] (slăk) *n.* Very small or refuse coal, coal dust.

slack·en (slăk'en) *v.* Make, become, loose or slack.

slack·er (slăk'er) *n.* Shirker, lazy person.

slag (slăg) *n.* Dross separated in fused vitreous state in smelting of ores; clinkers; volcanic scoria. **slag** *v.i.* (**slagged, slag·ging**). Form slag, cohere into slaglike mass.

slain: see SLAY.

slake (slāk) *v.t.* (**slaked, slak·ing**). Quench, allay (thirst), cause (lime) to heat and crumble by action of water or moisture.

sla·lom (slah'lom) *n.* 1. Ski race downhill in zigzag course between artificial obstacles, usu. flags. 2. Canoe race in turbulent water through narrow passages (gates) marked by poles.

slam[1] (slăm) *v.* (**slammed, slam·ming**). Shut (door etc.) violently with loud bang; (of door etc.) shut thus; put *down* (object) with similar sound; (colloq.) criticize violently. ~ *n.* Sound (as) of slammed door; ~**-bang** (*adj.* & *adv.*), (colloq.) with noise and violence; recklessly.

slam[2] (slăm) *n.* Winning of all tricks (**grand** ~) or of all tricks but one (**little** ~) in bridge etc.

slan·der (slăn'der) *n.* False re-

port maliciously uttered to person's injury; false oral defamation; defamation, calumny (cf. LIBEL). **slan'der·ous** *adj.* **slan'der·ous·ly** *adv.* **slan'der·er, slan'der·ous·-ness** *ns.* **slander** *v.t.* Utter slander about, defame falsely.

slang (slăng) *n.* Language in common colloquial use but considered to be outside standard educated speech and consisting either of new words or phrases or of current words used in new sense; cant, special language of some class or profession. ~ *adj.* Of, expressed in, slang. ~ *v.t.* Use abusive language to.

slang·y (slăng'ē) *adj.* (**slang·i·er, slang·i·est**). Of the character of, given to the use of, slang. **slang'i·ly** *adv.* **slang'i·ness** *n.*

slant (slănt, slahnt) *n.* Slope, oblique position; point of view, way of regarding something; bias. ~ *adj.* Sloping, inclined, oblique. ~ *v.* Slope, diverge from a line, have or take oblique direction or position; present (news etc.) in biased way. **slant'ing·ly** *adv.* **slant'wise, slant'ways** *advs.* & *adjs.*

*All members of the weasel family have scent glands, but those of the **skunk** are most highly developed. The offensive fluid can be sprayed 10 ft. and will severely irritate a victim's skin.*

slap (slăp) *n.* Smart blow esp. with palm of hand or something flat; sharp rebuke; smack; ~ **in the face**, rebuff, insult. **slap** *v.t.* (**slapped, slap·ping**). Strike with such blow; **slap'dash**, hasty, careless, happy-go-lucky; (*adv.*) in slap-dash manner; **slap'happy**, (colloq.) cheerfully casual; punch-drunk; **slap'stick**, (orig.) flexible lath used by harlequin in pantomime: (of) boisterous knockabout type of comedy. **slap** *adv.* Suddenly, noisily, headlong.

slash (slăsh) *v.* Cut, cut at, with sweep of sharp weapon or instrument; make gashes (in); slit (garment) to show contrasting lining etc.; lash with whip, crack (whip); make drastic economies in (budget etc.). ~ *n.* (Wound or slit made by) slashing cut. **slash'er** *n.*

slat (slăt) *n.* Long narrow strip of wood or metal, lath, esp. one of a series forming a Venetian blind, one of the crosspieces of a bedstead on which the mattress rests. ~ *v.* (**slat·ted, slat·ting**). Flap, strike, with noisy sound, esp. of sails, ropes, etc.

slate (slāt) *n.* 1. Very fine-

*A Lapp family with a **sleigh** drawn by a reindeer. The sleigh, drawn by dogs or horses, is still a commonplace form of winter transport in Canada, the U.S.S.R. and Scandinavia.*

grained gray metamorphic rock that cleaves perfectly in one direction, freq. at an angle to the bedding plane; thin usu. rectangular plate of this or other stone as roofing material; tablet of slate, usu. framed in wood, for writing on. 2. List of candidates supported by a political party. **slat·y** *adj.* (**slat·i·er, slat·i·est**). **slate** *v.t.* (**slat·ed, slat·ing**). 1. Cover, roof, with slates. 2. Designate for candidacy, appointment, etc. **slat·er** *n.*

slath·er (slădh′*er*) *v.t.* (colloq.) Spread thickly; squander.

slat·tern (slăt′*ern*) *n.* Sluttish woman. **slat′tern·ly** *adv.*

slaugh·ter (slaw′*ter*) *n.* Slaying, esp. of many persons or animals at once, carnage, massacre. **slaugh′terhouse**, place for killing cattle or sheep, shambles. **slaughter** *v.t.* Kill in ruthless manner or on great scale; butcher, kill for food. **slaugh′ter·er** *n.* **slaugh′ter·ous** *adj.*

Slav (slahv) *n.* Member of any of the peoples belonging to the Slavonic linguistic group, inhabiting large parts of E. and central Europe, and including Russians, Poles, Czechs, Bulgarians, Serbs, Croats, Slovenes, etc. ~ *adj.* Of the Slavs or their languages.

slave (slāv) *n.* Person who is the legal property of another, servant completely divested of freedom and personal rights; human chattel; helpless victim *to, of,* some influence; submissive or devoted servant; drudge; ~ **bracelet**, wide bracelet freq. worn above ankle; ~ **driver**, superintendent of slaves at work; hard taskmaster; ~ **ship**, ship employed in slave trade; ~ **states**, (hist.) those southern states of U.S. in which slaveholding was legal; ~ **trade**, traffic in slaves, esp. former transportation of African blacks to Amer. **slave** *v.i.* (**slaved, slav·ing**). Work like slave, drudge.

slav·er[1] (slā′*ver*) *n.* Ship or person engaged in slave trade.

slav·er[2] (slăv′*er*, slā′*ver*, slah′-) *n.* Saliva flowing or falling from mouth; nonsense. ~ *v.* Let saliva run from mouth; wet with saliva, slobber.

slav·er·y (slā′*verē*) *n.* Condition of a slave; slaveholding; drudgery.

Slav·ic (slah′vĭk) *adj.* Of, pertaining to, Slavs; ~ **languages**, group of Indo-European languages spoken in E. and central Europe, including Russian, Byelorussian, Ukrainian, Polish, Czech, Bulgarian, Serbo-Croatian, and Slovene.

slav·ish (slā′vĭsh) *adj.* Of, like a slave, servile; showing no originality or independence. **slav′ish·ness** *n.* **slav′ish·ly** *adv.*

Sla·von·ic (slavŏn′ĭk) *adj.* Slavic. ~ *n.* Slavonic languages; **Church** ~, **Old** ~, earliest written Slavonic language, a Bulgarian dialect fixed in writing toward end of 9th c., extinct as a vernacular but remaining the liturgical language of the Orthodox Church in Slav countries.

slaw (slaw) *n.* Coleslaw.

slay (slā) *v.t.* (**slew** pr. slōō, **slain** pr. slān, **slay·ing**). (chiefly poet. and rhet.) Kill.

slea·zy (slē′zē) *adj.* (**-zi·er, -zi·est**). 1. Flimsy, loosely woven. 2. Shoddy, shabby. 3. Squalid. **slea′zi·ly** *adv.* **slea′zi·ness** *n.*

sled (slĕd) *n.* Any of several types of vehicles with attached runners for travel on ice or snow. ~ *v.* (**sled·ded, sled·ding**). Travel, ride, carry, etc. on sled.

sledge[1] (slĕj) *n.* Sled. ~ *v.* (**sledged, sledg·ing**). Travel, go,

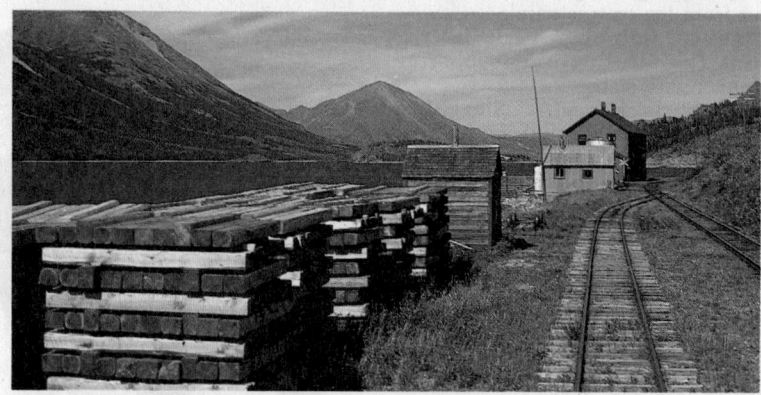

*This railway **sleeper** yard in Alaska will soon be an unusual sight. Wooden sleepers are now being replaced by concrete ones which are more durable and not subject to termite attack.*

convey, on sled.

sledge[2] (slĕj) *n.* (also **sledge′-hammer**) Large heavy hammer usu. wielded with both hands, esp. that used by blacksmith.

sleek (slēk) *adj.* (of hair, fur, surface, etc.) Soft, smooth and glossy; sleek-haired or -skinned; of well-fed comfortable appearance. **sleek′ly** *adv.* **sleek′ness** *n.* **sleek** *v.t.* Make sleek.

sleep (slēp) *n.* Bodily condition regularly and naturally assumed by man and other animals, in which the postural and other muscles are relaxed and consciousness is largely suppressed, though it may be re-established by a sensory disturbance; period or occasion of this; inert condition of some animals in hibernation; (fig.) death; rest, quiet, peace; **sleep′walking**, somnambulism. **sleep** *v.* (**slept** pr. slĕpt, **sleep·ing**). Be in state of sleep; fall, be asleep; rest in death; spend in, affect by, sleeping; stay for the night *at, in,* etc.; **sleep′away** (*adj.*), (slang) (of summer camp) with sleeping accommodations; **sleep-in** (*adj.*), (of domestic servant) living with employer's family; **sleep′ing** *n.* (esp.) ~ **bag**, bag, usu. lined or padded, for sleeping in, esp. out of doors; ~

car, railroad car with berths or beds; ~ **pill**, pill containing drug inducing sleep; ~ **sickness**, (1) freq. fatal disease characterized by extreme lethargy, prevalent in parts of W. and S. Africa and caused by a trypanosome (*Trypanosoma gambiense*) transmitted by the bite of the tsetse fly; (2) ENCEPHA-LITIS lethargica. **sleep′less** *adj*. **sleep′less·ness** *n*.

sleep·er (slē′per) *n*. (esp.) Horizontal wooden member resting on ground, concrete floor, etc., to support flooring; (colloq.) sleeping car; (colloq.) someone or something suddenly and unexpectedly successful; (football) player stationed at distance from teammates in hope he will be un-noticed, play involving this.

sleep·y (slē′pē) *adj*. (**sleep·i·er, sleep·i·est**). Drowsy, ready for sleep; inactive, indolent, without stir or bustle. **sleep′yhead**, sleepy or inattentive person. **sleep′i·ly** *adv*. **sleep′i·ness** *n*.

sleet (slēt) *n*. Hail or snow falling in a half melted state; thin coating of ice formed on road, trees, etc., when rain freezes. **sleet′y** *adj*. (**sleet·i·er, sleet·i·est**).

sleeve (slēv) *n*. Part of garment covering arm; tube or hollow shaft fitting over rod, spindle, etc.; wind sock, drogue; envelope for phonograph record; ~ **valve**, internal combustion engine's valve with sleeve(s) fitting interior of cylinder, sliding with piston, and so designed and controlled that inlet and exhaust ports are uncovered at proper stages in cycle. **sleeved, sleeve′less** *adjs*.

sleigh (slā) *n*. Sled, esp. as passenger vehicle drawn by horse(s); ~ **bells**, small bells attached to sleigh or harness of sleigh horse.

sleight (slīt) *n*. Dexterity, cunning, artifice (archaic exc. in) ~ **of hand**, conjuring, trick(s) displaying great dexterity, esp. performed so quickly as to deceive the eye.

slen·der (slĕn′der) *adj*. Of small girth or breadth; scanty, slight, meager. **slen′der·ly** *adv*. **slen′-der·ness** *n*.

sleuth (slooth) *n*. (colloq.) Detective. **sleuth** *v*. Track, trail; play the detective.

slew[1]: see SLAY.

slew[2], **slue** (sloo) *ns*. (colloq.) Great number; lot.

slew[3]: SLOUGH[1].

slew[4]: SLUE[2].

slice (slīs) *n*. Relatively thin flat broad piece or wedge cut from esp.

Sleeping sickness, transmitted by the tsetse fly, is still prevalent in many parts of Africa, despite W.H.O. and other campaigns to eliminate the disease. In its advanced form, it is fatal.

meat, bread, or cake; share, portion; (tennis, golf, etc.) slicing stroke; kind of implement with thin broad blade used in cookery etc., esp. for lifting or serving fish. **slice′a-ble** *adj*. **slic′er** *n*. **slice** *v*. (**sliced, slic·ing**). Cut into slices, cut (piece) *off*; cut cleanly or easily; (golf etc.) strike (ball) so that it flies or curves to right (in the case of a left-handed player, to the left).

slick (slĭk) *adj*. Sleek; smooth, plausible; adroit, deft, quick, cunning. **slick′ly** *adv*. **slick′ness** *n*. **slick** *n*. (also oil ~) Patch or film of oil on water. **slick** *v.t.* Smooth, sleek.

slick·er (slĭk′er) *n*. Long loose raincoat, usu. oilskin; (colloq.) smooth, tricky person.

slide (slīd) *v*. (**slid** pr. slĭd, **slid·ing**). (Make) progress along smooth surface in continuous contact with that surface; glide over ice without skates in more or less erect posture; glide, go smoothly along, pass easily or gradually; (baseball) throw oneself down and forward, usu. feet first, toward base to avoid being tagged out; **let** ~, let (something) take its own course; ~ **rule**, rule graduated along one edge according to the logarithms of the numbers from 1 to 100 and along the other according to the logarithms of the numbers from 1 to 10 (enabling squares and square roots to be read off directly), and having a similarly graduated sliding piece along its center (enabling numbers to be multiplied or divided by adding or subtracting their logarithms); ~ **valve**, valve with sliding plate for opening and closing orifice, esp. in steam engine. **slide** *n*. Act of sliding; track on ice made by sliding; slope prepared with snow or ice for tobogganing; avalanche; inclined plane down which goods etc. slide to lower level; part(s) of machine on or between which sliding part works; part of machine or instrument that slides. **slid′a·ble** *adj*. **slid′er** *n*. (esp. baseball) Fast pitched ball with slight curve.

slid·ing (slī′dĭng) *adj*. That slides; ~ **door, lid, panel**, etc., door, lid, etc., drawn across aperture by sliding sideways instead of turning on hinges; ~ **scale**, scale (of payments, wages, etc.) rising or falling in established relation to rise or fall of some other standard.

slight (slīt) *adj*. Slender, slim, thin; not good or substantial, rather flimsy or weak; small in amount, degree, etc., unimportant, trifling. **slight′ly** *adv*. **slight′ness** *n*. **slight** *n*. Instance of slighting or being slighted; contemptuous indifference or disregard. ~ *v.t.* Treat with indifference or disrespect, disregard, disdain, ignore.

slim (slĭm) *adj*. (**slim·mer,**

slim·mest). Slender, (gracefully) thin; small, slight, meager. **slim′ly** *adv.* **slim′ness** *n.* **slim** *v.* (**slimmed, slim·ming**). Make, become, slim, esp. by dieting, exercise, etc.

slime (slīm) *n.* Fine oozy mud; any substance of similar consistency. ~ *v.t.* (**slimed, slim·-ing**). Cover with slime.

slim·y (slī′mē) *adj.* (**slim·i·er, slim·i·est**). Of the consistency of slime; covered or smeared with slime; vile, disgusting; repulsively meek or flattering. **slim′i·ly** *adv.* **slim′i·ness** *n.*

sling[1] (slĭng) *n.* 1. (also **sling′-shot**) Weapon, consisting of strap attached to 2 cords or to staff, for hurling stones etc. 2. Belt, rope, etc., formed into loop, with hooks and tackle, for securing bulky or heavy articles while being hoisted or lowered; strap, band, etc., supporting something suspended; bandage etc. formed into loop around neck to support injured arm. ~ *v.* (**slung** pr. slŭng, **sling·ing**). 1. Throw, cast, hurl; hurl (stone etc.) from sling, use sling. 2. Suspend with sling; hoist or transfer with sling; hang up, suspend, esp. between two points. **sling′er** *n.*

sling[2] (slĭng) *n.* Drink of gin and whiskey, sweetened and flavored with lemon.

slink (slĭngk) *v.i.* (**slunk** pr. slŭngk or archaic **slank** pr. slăngk, **slink·ing**). Move, go, in quiet, stealthy, or sneaking manner. **slink′y** *adj.* (**slink·i·er, slink·i·est**). (of woman's garment) Close-fitting and smooth, sinuous.

slip[1] (slĭp) *n.* Finely ground clay, flint, etc., mixed with water to consistency of cream and used for making, cementing, decorating, etc., pottery, tiles, etc.; **slip′ware**, pottery coated with slip.

slip[2] (slĭp) *n.* 1. Act of slipping; blunder, accidental piece of misconduct; slipstream; **give person**

Although some goods which need to be lifted are now built with eyes to which hooks may be attached, the use of a **sling** *for material-handling is still widespread.*

the ~, evade or escape from him. 2. Loose covering or garment, e.g. pillowcase, petticoat. 3. Dog leash. 4. Inclined plane on which ships are built or repaired. 5. Long narrow strip of thin wood, paper, etc. 6. Cutting taken from a plant for grafting or planting; scion, young, esp. slender, person. 7. Dock, pier; space between two piers. **slip** *v.* (**slipped, slip·-ping**). 1. Slide unintentionally for short distance; lose footing, balance, etc., by unintended sliding; go with sliding motion, move easily or unperceived, glide, steal; escape restraint or capture esp. by being slippery or hard to hold; make careless mistake (also, colloq., ~ **up**). 2. Let go (hounds etc.) from restraint of some kind; pull (garment etc.) hastily *on, off*; make pass or move stealthily, casually, or with gliding motion; escape from, (naut.) allow (anchor cable) to run out when leaving anchorage hastily, drop (anchor) thus; (of animals) miscarry with, drop (young) prematurely; **slip′cover**, removable, fitted fabric covering for piece of furniture; **slip′knot**, knot that can be undone by a pull; knot that slips up and down rope etc. and tightens or loosens loop; **slip-on, slip′over**, (shoe, garment, etc.) that can be easily slipped on and off; **slip′page**, act or instance of slipping; amount or extent of slipping; **slipped disk**, rupture of an intervertebral disk of spinal column, causing lumbar pain; **slip′stick**, (slang) slide rule; **slip′stream**, current of air driven astern by propulsion unit of an aircraft producing the thrust that moves the aircraft forward.

slip·per (slĭp′er) *n.* Light loose comfortable indoor shoe; light slip-on shoe for dancing etc.; **slip′per-wort**, any of numerous plants (genus *Calceolaria*) of tropical Amer., having bright slippershaped flowers.

slip·per·y (slĭp′erē) *adj.* (**-per·i·er, -per·i·est**). With smooth, polished, oily, slimy, or greasy surface making foothold insecure, or making object etc. difficult to grasp or hold; (fig.) elusive, unreliable,

shifty, unscrupulous; ~ **elm**, tree (*Ulmus rubra*) of eastern N. Amer., having aromatic, mucilaginous juice once used in medications. **slip′per·i·ness** *n.*

slip·shod (slĭp′shŏd) *adj.* With shoes down at heel; slovenly, careless, unsystematic.

slit (slĭt) *n.* Long incision; long narrow opening comparable to cut. ~ *v.* (**slit, slit·ting**). Cut or tear lengthwise, make slit in, cut into strips; ~ **trench**, narrow trench made to accommodate a soldier.

slith·er (slĭdh′er) *v.i.* Slide unsteadily, go with irregular slipping motion. **slith′er·y** *adj.*

sliv·er (slĭv′er) *n.* Small, thin strip cut or split off; thin strip of wood torn from tree or timber, splinter. ~ *v.* Break off as sliver, break up into slivers.

sliv·o·vitz (slĭv′ovĭts, -wĭts, shlĭv′o-) *n.* Alcoholic spirit distilled from plums esp. in Yugoslavia, plum brandy.

slob (slŏb) *n.* Stupid or careless person.

slob·ber (slŏb′er) *v. & n.* SLAVER[2], drivel. **slob′ber·y** *adj.*

sloe (slō) *n.* (Small bluish-black wild plum, fruit of) blackthorn; ~ **-eyed**, having large eyes of this color; slant-eyed; **sloe gin**, gin flavored with sloes and sweetened.

slog (slŏg) *v.* (**slogged, slog·-ging**). Hit hard and freq. wildly, esp. in boxing; work hard and doggedly, plod. **slog′ger** *n.*

slo·gan (slō′gan) *n.* Party cry, watchword, motto; advertiser's phrase calculated to catch the eye. [Gael. *sluagh* host, *gairm* outcry]

sloop (slōōp) *n.* Small one-masted fore-and-aft-rigged vessel having mainsail and jib.

slop (slŏp) *n.* 1. Soft mud or partly melted snow; slush. 2. Liquid carelessly splashed or

The **sloe** *or blackthorn is a wild plum native to western Europe. The fruit was used to make sloe gin and the timber, which is dark brown, was often made into walking sticks.*

Bale Sling

Butt Sling

three-toed sloth

two-toed sloth

Wholly adapted to an arboreal life, although able to swim, the **sloth** spends its life in the trees which provide the leaves that are its food. It is found only in Central and South America.

spilled. 3. Unappetizing food, esp. when liquid or semiliquid. 4. (usu. pl.) Kitchen waste used for feeding pigs and other animals; swill. ~ *v.* (**slopped, slop·ping**). Spill, (allow to) flow over edge of vessel; spill or splash liquid upon.

slope (slōp) *n.* Stretch of rising or falling ground; inclined surface or way; upward or downward inclination, deviation from horizontal or perpendicular. ~ *v.* (**sloped, slop·ing**). Take, form, move in, be in, place or arrange in, a slope or inclined direction or position.

slop·py (slŏp′ē) *adj.* (**-pi·er, -pi·est**). Wet, splashed, full of puddles; messy with liquid; watery and disagreeable; weak, slovenly, maudlin. **slop′pi·ly** *adv.* **slop′-pi·ness** *n.*

slosh (slŏsh) *v.* Splash about, move with splashing sound; (colloq.) pour (liquid) clumsily, pour liquid on. **sloshed** *adj.*

slot (slŏt) *n.* 1. Groove, channel, slit, long aperture, made in machine, fabric, etc., to admit some other part, esp. slit for coin; ~ **car**, miniature racing car electrically operated by remote control in competition with similar cars on slotted track; ~ **machine**, vending or gambling machine operated by putting coin in slot. 2. (fig.) Place in series etc.; position. **slot** *v.t.* (**slot·ted, slot·ting**). Provide with slot(s).

sloth (slawth, slōth) *n.* 1. Laziness, indolence. 2. Long-haired slow-moving arboreal mammal of tropical Central and S. Amer., with two toes with hooklike claws on each forefoot (genus *Choloepus*) or three toes (*Bradypus*

tridactylus); ~ **bear**, common shaggy black-haired bear (*Melursus ursinus*) of India and Sri Lanka, feeding on fruit, insects, and honey. **sloth′ful** *adj.* **sloth′ful·ly** *adv.* **sloth′ful·ness** *n.*

slouch (slowch) *v.* Droop, hang down negligently; go, stand, etc., with loose ungainly stoop of head and shoulders; pull or bend down brim of hat, esp. over face. ~ *n.* Slouching gait or posture, stoop; downward bend of hat brim; ~ **hat**, soft hat with wide flexible brim. **slouch′y** *adj.* (**slouch·i·er, slouch·i·est**). **slouch′ing·ly** *adv.*

slough[1] (slow, slōō), **slew** (slōō) *ns.* Quagmire, swamp, miry place;

S ~ **of Despond** in Bunyan's *Pilgrim's Progress*, deep miry place between City of Destruction and wicket gate at beginning of Christian's journey; state of hopeless depression. **slough′y** *adj.*

slough[2] (slŭf) *n.* Outer skin periodically cast by snake etc.; any part cast or molted by an animal; dead tissue from surface of wound, ulcer, etc. ~ *v.* Drop off as slough; cast slough.

Slo·vak (slō′vahk, -văk) *adj. & n.* (Member) of a Slavic people inhabiting chiefly Slovakia and S. Moravia; (of) their language. **Slo·va·ki·a** (slōvah′kēa, -văk′ēa). Territory forming the E. part of Czechoslovakia, formerly a part of

Sailing for pleasure is a relatively recent pastime, beginning in the U.S.A. in the late 18th, early 19th centuries. The **sloop** style of yacht was one of the earliest types built to race.

*Very similar to a snail but lacking an external shell, a **slug** is usually nocturnal. Its sensitivity to light and heat prevent movement beyond a certain distance from its underground shelter.*

Hungary.

slov·en (slŭv′en) *n.* Person who is careless, untidy, or dirty in personal appearance or slipshod and negligent in work etc. **slov′·en·ly** *adj.* (**-li·er, -li·est**). **slov′en·li·ness** *n.*

Slo·vene (slōvēn′, slō′vēn) *adj. & n.* (Member, language) of the Slavonic people inhabiting chiefly Slovenia and neighboring parts of Yugoslavia. **Slo·ve·ni·a** (slōvē′nēa, -vēn′ya). Constituent republic of Yugoslavia, bordering on Austria and Italy; capital, Ljubljana. **Slo·ve′ni·an** *adj. & n.* Slovene.

slow (slō) *adj.* 1. Not quick, taking a long time to do a thing or traverse a distance; gradual; tardy, lingering; not hasty; (of clock etc.) behind true time; (of surfaces) tending to cause slowness (*a slow track*, etc.). 2. Dull-witted, stupid; deficient in liveliness or interest, dull, tedious. 3. ~-**motion**, action or speed of a film in which movements appear much slower than in nature, achieved either by exposing the film at high speed or by projecting it at reduced speed; ~ **neutron**, one with low kinetic energy, esp. after moderation; ~ **poison**, poison of which repeated doses are injurious; **slow′poke**, person slow in action, dull of wit, or behind the times in opinions etc.; **slow-witted**, slow to understand; stupid; dull. **slow′ly** *adv.* **slow′ness** *n.* **slow** *adv.* ~ *v.* Reduce one's speed, reduce speed of; **slow′down** (*n.*), action of slowing down.

SLR *abbrev.* Single-lens reflex (camera).

sludge (slŭj) *n.* Thick greasy mud; sewage; muddy or slushy sediment or deposit; accumulation of dirty oil, esp. in sump of internal combustion engine; sea ice newly formed in small pieces. **sludg′y** *adj.* (**sludg·i·er, sludg·i·est**).

slue¹ (slōō): see SLEW².

slue² (slōō) *v.* (**slued, slu·ing**), also **slew** (slōō). Turn or swing around on axis; twist sideways. ~ *n.* Act of sluing.

slug¹ (slŭg) *n.* 1. Gastropod mollusk with rudimentary or no shell, many kinds of which are destructive to small plants. 2. Roughly or irregularly shaped bullet or other piece of metal; (round) bullet; disk of metal used (usu. illegally) instead of coin in slot; (colloq.) drink of straight whiskey; (printing) thick piece of metal used in spacing; line of type in linotype printing. 3. (eng., as

Sluice gates in the power station dam on the Niagara River in Canada. They are needed to reduce water level (and pressure) behind the dam wall in times of heavy rains and floods.

measure in calculating acceleration) That mass to which a force of 1 lb. will impart an acceleration of 1 ft. per second per second.

slug² (slŭg) *n. & v.* (**slugged, slug·ging**). (colloq.) (Strike with) hard heavy blow, esp. with fist or baseball bat; **slug′fest**, boxing match marked by slugging and little attention to defense; baseball game marked by many extra-base hits and runs; **slug′ger** (*n.*), (esp. baseball) strong hitter; player who hits many doubles, triples, and home runs.

slug·a·bed (slŭg′abĕd) *n.* (archaic) One who lies late in bed.

slug·gard (slŭg′erd) *n.* Lazy sluggish person.

slug·gish (slŭg′ĭsh) *adj.* Inert, inactive, slow moving, torpid. **slug′gish·ly** *adv.* **slug′gish·ness** *n.*

sluice (slōōs) *n.* (Gate in) dam or embankment with sliding gate or other contrivance for controlling volume or flow of water; any device

for regulating flow of water; artificial water channel, esp. in gold-washing. ~ *v.* (**sluiced, sluic·ing**). Provide with sluice(s); flood with water from sluice; rinse, pour or throw water freely upon; (of water etc.) rush (as) from sluice.

slum (slŭm) *n.* Dirty squalid overcrowded street, district, etc. inhabited esp. by the very poor; **slum′lord**, landlord of slum housing, esp. one who charges excessive rent and fails to maintain property. **slum′my** *adj.* (**-mi·er, -mi·est**). **slum** *v.i.* (**slummed, slum·ming**). Visit slums.

slum·ber (slŭm′ber) *n. & v.i.* Sleep (chiefly poet. and rhet.). **slum′ber·ous, slum′brous** *adjs.* **slum′ber·ous·ly** *adv.* **slum′ber·er** *n.*

slump (slŭmp) *n.* Sudden decrease (esp. of commercial ventures, prices, etc.; opp. BOOM³); sudden or heavy fall in demand. ~ *v.i.* Undergo slump, fall in price; sit or slop down heavily and slackly.

slung: see SLING¹.

slunk: see SLINK.

slur (slẽr) *v.* (**slurred, slur·ring**). 1. Smudge, blur; pro-

In overcrowded countries where there is widespread poverty, it is surprising how some people survive. This Indian child looks down on the **slum** *shanties which include his home.*

nounce indistinctly, with sounds running into one another; (mus.) sing, play, two or more notes smoothly and connectedly; mark with slur. 2. Pass lightly *over*, conceal, minimize. ~ *n.* 1. Slight, discredit, blame. 2. Slurred sound or utterance; (mus.) curved line (⌢, ⌣) over or under two or more notes to be sung or played without a break or as smoothly as possible.

slurp (slẽrp) *n. & v.t.* Eat(ing) or drink(ing) noisily.

slur·ry (slẽr′ē) *n.* (pl. **-ries**). Thin sloppy cement, mud, etc; suspension of fine material in liquid, esp. water.

slush (slŭsh) *n.* Watery mud or water-saturated snow; soft greasy mixture of oil etc. or other materials, used to lubricate or protect machinery etc.; (fig.) silly sentiment; ~ **fund**, money used for corrupt purposes, esp. bribery of public officials. **slush′y** *adj.* (**slush·i·er, slush·i·est**). **slush′i-ness** *n.*

slut (slŭt) *n.* Slovenly woman; immoral woman. **slut′tish** *adj.* **slut′tish·ly** *adv.* **slut′tish·ness** *n.*

sly (slī) *adj.* (**sli·er, sli·est** or **sly·er, sly·est**). 1. Cunning, wily, deceitful; practicing concealment, working, moving, etc., in stealthy or underhand manner. 2. Knowing, arch, bantering, insinuating. **sly′ly** *adv.* **sly′ness** *n.*

Sm *symbol.* Samarium.

S.M. *abbrev.* Master of Science [L. *Scientiae Magister*]; sergeant major.

smack[1] (smăk) *n.* Flavor, taste; trace, tinge, suggestion, *of* something. ~ *v.i.* Have taste or savor *of*, suggest the presence *of*.

smack[2] (smăk) *n.* Sharp slight sound as of surface struck with palm of hand, lips parted suddenly, etc.; slap, sounding blow; loud kiss. ~ *v.* Strike with palm of hand or with something flat; part (lips) noisily, (of lips) be parted, in eager anticipation or enjoyment of food etc. ~ *adv.* (colloq.) (As) with a smack, slap; outright, exactly.

smack[3] (smăk) *n.* Single-masted sailing vessel, rigged like sloop or cutter, for coasting or fishing; fishing vessel with well for keeping fish alive.

smack[4] (smăk) *n.* (slang) Heroin.

smack·er (smăker) *n.* (slang) Dollar.

At Looe in Cornwall, U.K. (left), the fishermen moor their boats in the local river. The single-masted **smack** *is considered highly suitable for working the inshore waters.*

small (smawl) *adj*. Not large, of comparatively little size, strength, power, or number; consisting of minute units; (of agent) not acting on large scale; poor, mean, humble; ungenerous, not much of; unimportant, trifling; petty, paltry; ~ **arms**, portable firearms, esp. rifle, pistol, light machine gun; ~ **change**, coins as opposed to bills, (fig.) trivial remarks; ~ **fry**, little children; insignificant or unimportant things or persons; **small-scale**, made or occurring on a small scale or in small amounts; **small talk**, ordinary social conversation, chat; **small-time**, (colloq.) of little matter or importance; minor; insignificant; **small-town**, (typical) of small town or village; unsophisticated; countrified. **small** *n*. Small, slender, or narrow part of anything, esp. the back. ~ *adv*. Into small pieces, on small scale, etc. **small'ish** *adj*. **small'ness** *n*.

small·pox (smawl'pŏks) *n*. (hist.) Acute contagious febrile disease (*variola*), often endemic in occurrence, characterized by pustular eruption, usu. leaving scars or pits on skin; worldwide campaign of vaccination apparently resulted by 1978 in total eradication of the disease.

smart¹ (smart) *n*. Sharp pain, stinging sensation. ~ *v.i.* Feel, cause, smart. **smart'ing·ly** *adv*.

smart² (smart) *adj*. 1. Severe, sharp; lively, vigorous, brisk. 2. Clever, quick, ingenious; quick at looking after one's own interests; ~ **al·eck** (ăl'ĭk), would-be clever person (~ **al·eck·y** (ăl'ĭkē) *adj*.); ~ **bomb**, (slang) air-to-surface bomb that reaches target by television or laser beam guidance. 3. Alert, brisk; neat, trim; stylish, fashionable, elegant. **smart'en** *v*. **smart'ly** *adv*. **smart'ness** *n*.

smash (smăsh) *n*. Breaking to pieces; violent fall, collision, or disaster; commercial failure, bankruptcy; violent and heavy blow; very successful thing; (tennis) hard overhand stroke; **smash'up**, complete smash; violent collision of motor vehicles; total ruin or failure. **smash** *v*. Break utterly to pieces, shatter, bash *in*; utterly rout and disorganize; break, come to grief, go bankrupt; (of vehicle etc.) crash; (tennis) hit (ball) in smash. **smash** *adv*. With a smash. **smash'er** *n*.

smat·ter·ing (smăt'ẽrĭng) *n*. Slight superficial knowledge (*of*); small amount.

smaze (smāz) *n*. Mixture of smoke and haze.

smear (smēr) *v*. Daub with greasy or sticky substances or with something that stains, make greasy or sticky marks on; blot, obscure outlines of; blacken character of, discredit publicly; (slang) overpower or defeat. **smear'y** *adj*. (**smear·i·er**, **smear·i·est**). **smear** *n*. Mark, blotch, made by smearing; vilification. **smear'er** *n*.

smell (smĕl) *n*. 1. Faculty of smelling, by which odors are perceived by means of the nose; act of smelling, sniff. 2. Property

A section of the olfactory region of the nasal passage. The nerves are responsible for the sense of smell although the exact mechanism is not fully known.

Olfactory hairs

Supporting cell

Sense cell

Olfactory Nerve

of things affecting sense of smell, odor; bad odor, stench. **smell'y** *adj*. (**smell·i·er**, **smell·i·est**). (colloq.) Smelling strongly, evil smelling. **smell** *v*. (**smelled** or **smelt** *pr.* smĕlt, **smell·ing**). 1. Perceive smell of, detect presence of by smell; use sense of smell, sniff *at*; hunt *out* by smell; (fig.) discover, find *out*, as if by smell; perceive smells, have sense of smell. 2. Emit smell; suggest or recall the smell *of*; stink, be rank. 3. **smelling salts**, preparation of ammonium carbonate and scent, to be sniffed as cure for faintness etc. **smell'i·ness** *n*.

smelt¹ (smĕlt) *n*. (pl. **smelts**, collect. **smelt**). Small edible fish esp. of genus *Osmerus*, allied to salmon, with greenish back, silvery sides and belly, and delicate tender rather oily flesh.

smelt² (smĕlt) *v.t.* Fuse or melt (ore) to extract metal; obtain (metal) thus. **smelt'er** *n*.

smile (smīl) *v*. (**smiled**, **smil·ing**). Express pleasure, amusement, affection, indulgent scorn, incredulity, etc., with slight more or less involuntary movement of features, upward curving of corners of mouth, parting of lips, etc; look *at* with such expression; express by smiling; drive *away*, bring *into* or *out of* (mood), by smiling; be, appear, propitious; look pleasant, have bright aspect; **come up smiling**, (colloq.) recover from adversity and cheerfully face what is to come; **smile on**, show favor to, approve of. **smile** *n*. Act of smiling; smiling expression or aspect. **smil'er** *n*. **smi'ling** *adj*. **smil'ing·ly** *adv*.

smirch (smẽrch) *v.t. & n*. Stain, soil, smear, spot (also fig.).

smirk (smẽrk) *v.i. & n*. (Put on) affected or silly smile; simper.

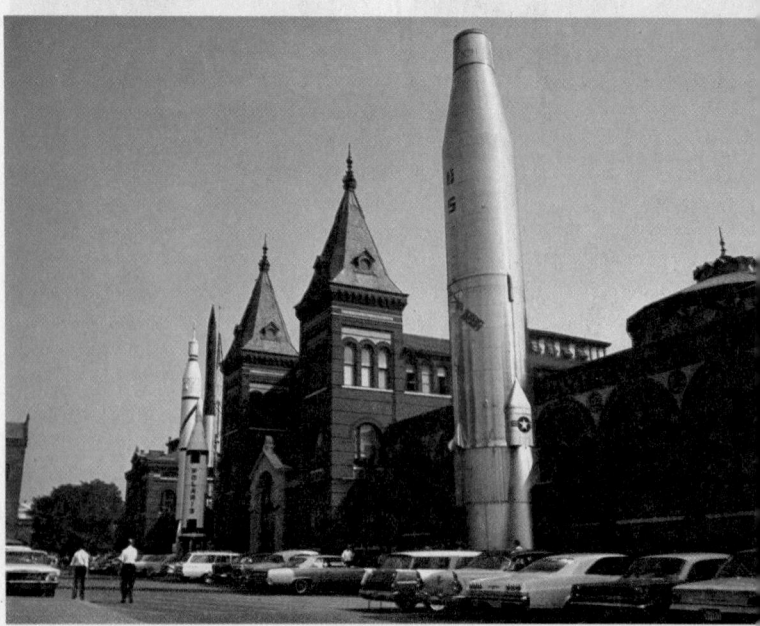

*The outdoor display of missiles and rockets contrasts with the mid-Victorian architecture of the **Smithsonian Institution** in Washington, D.C., the world's largest museum-gallery.*

smirk'er *n.* **smirk'ing·ly** *adv.*

smite (smīt) *v.* (**smote** pr. smōt, **smit·ten** pr. smĭt'en, **smit·ing**). Strike (*upon*), hit, chastise, defeat (chiefly poet. and rhet.); (chiefly in past part. **smitten**) strike, seize, infect, possess, *with* disease, love, etc. **smit'er** *n.*

smith (smĭth) *n.* Worker in metal, esp. iron; blacksmith.

-smith (smĭth) *comb. form.* Worker in (gold, silver, etc.), *goldsmith, silversmith,* etc.

Smith[1] (smĭth), **Adam** (1723–1790). Scottish political economist, author of *The Wealth of Nations* (1776).

Smith[2] (smĭth), **John** (1580–1631). English explorer and colonist; president of Jamestown, Virginia, colony, 1608–09; captured by Indians and saved by Pocahontas, daughter of Chief Powhatan.

Smith[3] (smĭth), **Joseph** (1805–1844). Founder of the MORMON sect.

smith·er·eens (smĭdherēnz') *n.pl.* (colloq.) Small fragments.

Smith·so·ni·an (smĭthsō'nēan) **Institution.** Establishment for increase and diffusion of knowledge, founded 1846 in Washington under will of an English mineralogist and chemist, James Smithson (1765–1829, earlier known as James Lewis Macie); it comprises national museums of natural history, zoology and ethnology, history and technology, air and space, fine arts, and also includes an astrophysical observatory, the John F. Kennedy Center for the Performing Arts, the Radiation Biology Laboratory, the Woodrow Wilson International Center for Scholars, and the Tropical Research Institute.

smith·y (smĭth'ē, smĭdh'ē) *n.* (pl. **smith·ies**). 1. Blacksmith's workshop, forge. 2. Blacksmith.

smock (smŏk) *n.* 1. Chemise (archaic). 2. Loose-fitting outer garment of shirtlike shape, freq. with gathered or smocked yoke. ~ *v.t.* Adorn with smocking. **smock'ing** *n.* Form of needlework with honeycomb ornamentation on basis of very close thick gathers.

smog (smŏg) *n.* Smoky fog. **smog'gy** *adv.* (**-gi·er, -gi·est**).

smoke (smōk) *n.* 1. Visible volatile product given off by burning or smoldering substances; cloud or column of this, esp. used as signal etc.; **go up in** ~, come to nothing. 2. Cigar or cigarette; act of smoking tobacco etc. 3. ~ **bomb**, bomb emitting dense clouds of smoke on bursting, for forming smoke screen; **smoke'house**, building where meat and fish are cured and flavored by smoking; **smoke screen**, dense volume of smoke diffused by funnel of vessel, smoke bomb, etc., to conceal naval or military operations etc.; also fig.; **smoke'stack**, chim-

*This **smog** in Montreal, Canada is one example of the pollution we are exposed to in the modern world. A large proportion of city pollution is caused by exhaust and gasoline fumes.*

ney, chimney pipe. **smoke'less** *adj.* Producing little or no smoke; free from smoke. **smoke** *v.* (**smoked, smok·ing**). 1. Emit smoke or visible vapor, reek, steam; (of chimney, lamp, etc.) emit smoke, be smoky, as result of imperfect draft etc. 2. Color, darken, obscure, with smoke; preserve or cure by exposure to smoke; fumigate, suffocate, stupefy, drive *out*, insects, etc., with smoke; ~ **out**, (fig.) reveal, expose. 3. Inhale and exhale smoke of (tobacco, opium, etc.); **smoking car, compartment**, car etc. for smokers on railroad train; **smoking room**, room set apart for smoking in.

smok·er (smō'ker) *n.* (esp.) Person who habitually smokes tobacco; smoking car on train; men's informal gathering.

smok·y (smō'kē) *adj.* (**smok·i·er, smok·i·est**). Emitting, veiled or filled with, obscure (as) with, smoke; stained with, colored like, smoke; ~ (**bear**), (slang, citizens' band radios) officer of the law. **smok'i·ly** *adv.* **smok'i·ness** *n.*

smol·der, Brit. **smoul·der** (smōl'der) *vbs.i.* Burn and smoke without flame (freq. fig.).

smolt (smōlt) *n.* Young salmon at stage when it migrates to sea for first time.

smooch (smōōch) *v.* (slang) Engage in kissing and caressing.

smooth (smōōdh) *adj.* With surface free from projections, wrinkles, lumps, or undulations; not rough, uneven, or bristly; (of ground etc.) not broken or ob-

structed, easily traversed; not harsh in sound, taste, etc.; pleasant, polite, unruffled; bland, insinuating, flattering; **smooth'bore**, gun with unrifled barrel; **smooth-spoken, -tongued**, smooth, plausible, flattering, in speech; soft-spoken. **smooth'ly** *adv.* **smooth'ness** *n.* **smooth** *v.* Make or become smooth; free from impediments etc.; ~ **over, away**, reduce or get rid of (differences, perplexities, difficulties, faults, etc.) in fact or appearance. **smooth** *n.* Smoothing touch or stroke. **smooth'er** *n.*

smor·gas·bord, smör·gas·bord (shmȯr'gasbȯrd, -bȯrd; *Swed.* smör'gawsboord) *ns.* Buffet meal with a variety of hors d'oeuvres and other dishes. [Swed. *smörgåsbord*]

smote: see SMITE.

smoth·er (smŭdh'er) *v.* Suffocate, stifle, be suffocated or stifled, esp. with smoke; deaden or extinguish (fire) by excluding air with ashes etc.; suppress, conceal, cover (*up*); cover closely or thickly (*in*). ~ *n.* Dense or suffocating smoke, dust, fog, etc. **smoth'er·y** *adj.*

smoul·der (smōl'der): SMOLDER.

smudge[1] (smŭj) *n.* Dirty mark, smear, blur, blot. ~ *v.* (**smudged, smudg·ing**). Soil, stain, smirch, smear. **smudg'y** *adj.*

smudge[2] (smŭj) *n.* Outdoor fire with dense smoke to drive away insects, protect plants etc. against frost.

smug (smŭg) *adj.* (**smug·ger, smug·gest**). Self-satisfied, consciously virtuous. **smug'ly** *adv.* **smug'ness** *n.*

smug·gle (smŭg'el) *v.* (**-gled, -gling**). Convey (goods), convey goods, clandestinely into or out of country to avoid payment of customs duties etc.; convey stealthily or secretly *in*, *out*, put *away* into concealment. **smug′gler** *n*.

smut (smŭt) *n*.   1. Fungous disease of cereals and other plants, with (parts of) grain covered with blackish powdery spores; any fungus causing this. 2. (Black mark, smudge, made by) flake of soot. 3. Indecent or obscene talk or publication. **smut′ty** *adj*. (**-ti·er, -ti·est**). **smut′ti·ly** *adv*.   **smut′ti·ness** *n*.   **smut** *v.t.* (**smut·ted, smut·ting**).

Smuts (smŭts; *Du.* smöts), **Jan Christiaan** (1870–1950). South African general and statesman; founder (1910) and prime minister (1918–24, 1939–48) of the Union of South Africa.

Smyr·na (smêr′na).   Former name of Izmir.

Sn *symbol*.   Tin.

snack (snăk) *n*.   Slight, casual, or hurried meal; ~ **bar**, counter where sandwiches and other snacks may be obtained.

sna·fu (snăfoo′, snăf′oo) *adj.* & *n.* (slang)   (In state of) utter confusion. ~ *v.* (**-fued, -fu·ing**). (slang)   Throw into confusion; jumble. [*S*(ituation) *n*(ormal), *a*(ll) *f*(ouled) *u*(p)]

snag (snăg) *n*.   Jagged projecting point, as stump or branch left on tree after pruning or cutting, trunk or large branch of tree embedded in bottom of river etc., with end pointed upward; (fig.) impediment, obstacle, unexpected drawback. **snag** *v.t.* (**snagged, snag·ging**). Run upon or damage by a snag. **snag′gy** *adj.* (**-gi·er, -gi·est**).

snail (snāl) *n*.   Any aquatic or terrestrial gastropod mollusk with well-developed spiral or whorled shell capable of covering whole body; slow-moving or indolent person.

snake (snāk) *n*.   1. Limbless reptile of suborder Ophidia, serpent; (also, pop.) snakelike limbless lizard or amphibian; treacherous or ungrateful person; long flexible metal band for opening blocked drains; ~ **in the grass**, lurking danger, secret enemy.   2. **S~**, Amer. Ind. of various Shoshone groups of western U.S.   3. **snake′bird**: see ANHINGA; **snake charmer**, person giving exhibition of control of venomous snake with music etc.; **snake dance**, religious ceremony and dance of Hopi Indians, in which rattlesnakes are imitated and handled; informal procession in which participants join hands as they zigzag back and forth in long line; **snake eyes**, (slang) dice throw of 2 ones; **snake fence**, zigzag fence of split rails or poles; **snake′head** = TURTLEHEAD; **snake-hipped** (*adj.*), having slim, supple hips; **snake′mouth**, orchid (*Pogonia ophioglossoides*) of eastern N. Amer., having single rose-

Present on land and in water, **snails**, seem omnipresent and are disliked by gardeners. However, larger varieties in France and Africa have been farmed for food since the Roman era or earlier.

lavender flower with tufted lip; **snake oil**, any liquid misrepresented as curative agent; **snake pit**, overcrowded mental hospital where patients are neglected; **snake plant**, any of various easily cultivated tropical plants (genus *Sansevieria*), having long, stiff, pointed leaves and popular as house plants; **snake′root**, (root of) any of various Amer. plants, esp. *Aristolochia serpentaria* and *Polygala senega*, reputed to be antidotes to snake poison, and used in medicine. **snak′y** *adj.* (**snak·i·er, snak·i·est**). Infested with snakes; snakelike; (chiefly of hair of Gorgons, Furies) composed of snakes.   **snake** *v.i.* (**snaked, snak·ing**).   Make twisting course.

snap (snăp) *n*.   1. (Bite, cut, with) sudden quick closing of jaws or scissors; sudden break or fracture; sound of snapping, quick sharp sound. 2. Small crisp ginger cookie. 3. Spring catch or one closing with snapping sound. 4. (colloq.) Something easy. 5. Sudden, usu. brief, spell of frost or cold. 6. Alertness, vigor, energy; dash. 7. Snapshot. 8. ~ **bean** = STRING bean; **snap′dragon**, any of various perennial plants (genus *Antirrhinum*), esp. a popular horticultural species (*A. majus*) having clusters of white, yellow, pink, crimson, etc., double-lipped closed flowers; **snap fastener**, device for fastening pieces of fabric or clothing by pressing two parts together; **snap lock**, lock shutting automatically with spring when door etc. is

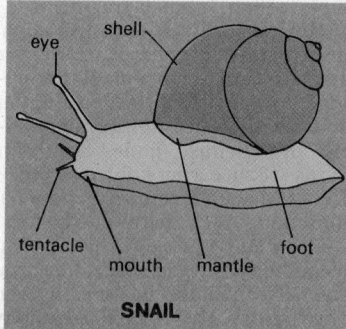

SNAIL

closed; **snap′shot** (*n.*),   taken photograph, esp. with hand camera; **snap′shot** (*v.*) (**-shot·ted, -shot·ting**), take such photograph (of). **snap** *v.* (**snapped, snap·ping**). 1. Make quick or sudden bite; speak irritably; say ill-tempered or spiteful things. 2. Pick *up* (esp. bargain) hastily. 3. Break sharply; produce sudden sharp sound from, emit sharp report or crack; close with snapping sound; ~ **fingers**, make audible fillip (*at*), esp. in contempt. 4. Take snapshot of. 5. **snapping turtle**, any of various large ferocious Amer. freshwater tortoises seizing prey with snap of jaws. **snap** *adj.* (colloq.)   Easy (~ *course*); made on spur of moment (*snap judgment*). **snap′per** *n.* (pl. **-pers**, collect. for *food fish* **-per**). (esp.) Snapping turtle; any of various carnivorous food fishes (family Lutianidae) of warm seas.

snap·pish (snăp′ish) *adj.*   Peevish, testy, malicious, ill-natured. **snap′pish·ly** *adv.* **snap′pish·ness** *n.*

snap·py (snăp′ē) *adj.* (**-pi·er, -pi·est**). 1. Snappish. 2. Quick, vigorous, lively, full of life or spring; **make it ~**, (colloq.) be quick about it.

locomotion

Head of the bushmaster

nose

temperature sensitive pit

poison duct

fangs

poison gland

fang sheath

tongue

tracheal opening

concertina

serpentine

skeleton

side winder

traction

The **snake** is a reptile which has evolved without legs. Some species are terrestrial and others largely aquatic. Methods of progress depend on muscular contractions of the body coupled with use of belly scales as 'anchors'. A speed of 4 m.p.h. can be attained. Contrictors crush their prey, those with venom glands, including the whip snake (right) and Australian bandy-bandy (far right), kill with poison.

snare (snār) *n.* Device for catching birds or animals, esp. with running noose of cord, wire, etc. (freq. fig. of temptation etc.); gut or rawhide string stretched across lower head of drum; ~ **drum**, drum so fitted. **snare** *v.t.* (**snared**, **snar·ing**). Catch with snare.

snarl[1] (snārl) *n.* Tangle, esp. of wool, hair, or the like; tangled condition. ~ *v.* Tangle (*up*), mix together confusedly. **snarl'y** *adj.*

snarl[2] (snārl) *v.* (of dog etc.) Make angry sound with bared teeth;

(of person) grumble viciously, use ill-tempered or surly language; express by snarling. ~ *n.* Act or sound of snarling. **snarl'er** *n.* **snarl'ing·ly** *adv.* **snarl'y** *adj.*

snatch (snăch) *v.* Make sudden snap or catch *at*, seize hurriedly or eagerly; rescue narrowly *from*; carry suddenly *away, from.* ~ *n.* Hasty catch or grasp, grab or snap *at*;

brief period, short spell (*of*); small amount, fragment, short burst (*of* song, talk, etc.); brief view, glimpse. **snatch'y** *adj.* (**snatch·i·er**, **snatch·i·est**). In short spells, disconnected. **snatch'i·ly** *adv.* **snatch'er** *n.*

sneak (snēk) *n.* Mean-spirited or underhanded person; sneaker; ~ **preview**, single public showing of

Both the **snowdrop** *and the* **snowflake** *are European bulbous plants grouped in the Amaryllidaceae. Their common names may be based on the appearance of clumps seen at a distance.*

motion picture in advance of general release; ~ **thief**, one who steals without breaking into buildings, by entering open door or window. **sneak** *v.* (**sneaked, sneak·ing**). 1. Slink, go furtively. 2. (colloq.) Make off with, steal. ~ *adj.* Done without warning (~ *attack*). **sneak'ing** *adj.* (esp.) Furtive, not avowed. **sneak'y** *adj.* (**sneak·i·er, sneak·i·est**). **sneak'ing·ly** *adv.* **sneak'i·ness** *n.*

sneak·er (snē'ker) *n.* Shoe with cloth, usu. canvas, upper and soft sole and heel of one piece of rubber.

sneer (snēr) *v.* Smile derisively (*at*); express or suggest derision or disparagement in speech or writing. ~ *n.* Sneering look or remark. **sneer'er** *n.* **sneer'ful** *adj.* **sneer'ing·ly** *adv.*

sneeze (snēz) *v.i.* (**sneezed, sneez·ing**). Make sudden involuntary convulsive expiration through the nose as a result of irritation of the mucous membrane; ~ **at**, despise, disregard, underrate. **sneeze** *n.* Act of sneezing; sound thus produced. **sneez'er** *n.* **sneez'y** *adj.*

snell (snĕl) *n.* Short length of nylon thread, gut, etc., used to connect hook to fish line.

snick·er (snĭk'er), **snig·ger** (snĭg'er) *ns. & vbs.i.* (Utter) half-suppressed secretive laugh.

snide (snīd) *adj.* (colloq.) Sneering, slyly derogatory. **snide'ness** *n.*

sniff (snĭf) *v.* Draw up air audibly through nose to stop it from running, in smelling *at* something, or as expression of contempt; draw (*up*) (air, liquid, scent), draw up scent of, into nose. ~ *n.* Act or sound of sniffing; amount sniffed up. **sniff'er** *n.* **sniff'ing·ly** *adv.* [imit.]

snif·fle (snĭf'el) *v.* (**-fled, -fling**). Sniff slightly or repeatedly. ~ *n.* Act of sniffling; (pl., usu. **the ~s**) cold in the head.

snif·ter (snĭf'ter) *n.* 1. Brandy glass. 2. (colloq.) Shot of liquor.

snig·ger: SNICKER.

snip (snĭp) *v.* (**snipped, snip·ping**). Cut with scissors etc., esp. in small quick strokes. ~ *n.* Act of snipping; piece snipped off; (colloq.) small, slight, or annoying person; (pl. also **tinsnips**), short strong shears for cutting sheet metal.

snipe (snīp) *n.* (pl. **snipes**, collect. **snipe**). Wading bird (*Capella gallinago*) related to woodcocks, frequenting marshy places and having characteristic long straight bill. ~ *v.* (**sniped, snip·ing**). Shoot snipe; (mil.)

snowdrop   snowflake

shoot at (men) one at a time, usu. from cover and at long range; shoot, shoot *at*, thus; (colloq.) criticize. **snip'er** *n.*

snip·pet (snĭp'ĭt) *n.* Small piece cut off, snipping; (fig.) scrap, fragment, (pl.) odds and ends. **snip'pet·y** *adj.*

snitch (snĭch) *v.* (slang) 1. Act as informer. 2. Steal, purloin.

sniv·el (snĭv'el) *v.i.* (**-eled, -el·ing**). Run at the nose; make sniffling or snuffling sound; be in tearful state, show maudlin emotion. ~ *n.* Running mucus; slight sniff; hypocritical emotion.

snob (snŏb) *n.* Person who meanly or vulgarly admires, imitates, or seeks to associate with, those of superior social position or wealth, and looks down on those he considers inferior; person who despises those whose attainments or tastes he considers inferior to his own. **snob'bish** *adj.* **snob'bish·ly**

A **snow-plough** *at work in Chamrouss in France. The development of suc equipment has made it possible to kee roads open after the worst wint storms.*

adv. **snob'bish·ness** *n.* **snob ber·y** *n.* (pl. **-ber·ies**).

snood (snōōd) *n.* Fillet or ban for woman's hair; net etc. loose confining hair at back.

snook·er (snōōk'er) *n.* (also **pool**) Variety of pool played wi 15 red balls and six balls of oth colors.

snoop (snōōp) *v.i.* (slang) P inquisitively. **snoop'er** *n.* **snoop** *adj.* (**snoop·i·er, snoop·i·est**).

snoot·y (snōō'tē) *adj.* (**snoot·i er, snoot·i·est**). (slang) Contemp tuous, supercilious. **snoot'i·ly** ad **snoot'i·ness** *n.*

snooze (snōōz) *v.i.* (**snooze snooz·ing**) & *n.* (Take) short slee esp. in daytime.

snore (snōr, snôr) *n. & v.* (**snored, snor·ing**). (Make) harsh or noisy respiration through mouth, or mouth and nose, during sleep.

snor·kel (snôr'kel), **schnor·kel** (shnôr'kel) *ns.* Device for supplying air to submerged submarine; breathing tube for underwater swimmer.

snort (snôrt) *n.* 1. Loud or harsh sound made by driving breath violently through nose, or noise resembling this. 2. Expression of contempt, defiance, etc., made by snorting. 3. (slang) Small drink of liquor. **snort** *v.* Make sound of snort; express by snorting, utter with snorts; (colloq.) sniff (cocaine). **snort'er** *n.*

snot (snŏt) *n.* (vulg.) Mucus of the nose; contemptible person. **snot'ty** *adj.* (**-ti·er, -ti·est**). (vulg.) Running or foul with snot; (colloq.) impudent.

snout (snowt) *n.* Projecting part of head of animal, including nose and mouth, (contempt.) person's nose; projecting part, structure, nozzle, etc., resembling snout.

snow (snō) *n.* 1. Atmospheric vapor condensed and frozen into small, usu. hexagonal, crystals, and falling in soft white clusters of these known as flakes; fall of these, layer of them on ground; (usu. pl.) fall or accumulation of snow. 2. Something resembling snow, esp. in whiteness; white hair. 3. (slang) Cocaine. 4. **snow'ball**, snow pressed into ball, esp. as missile; anything growing or increasing rapidly, like snowball rolled along ground; **snow'ball** (*v.*), pelt with, throw, snowballs; increase rapidly; **snow'berry** (pl. **-ries**) (fruit of) any of various plants or shrubs with white berries, esp. *Symphoricarpos albus*; **snow'bird**, any of various small white or partly white birds, esp. junco or snow bunting; **snow-blind**, with vision affected by glare of sun on snow; **snow blower, thrower**, motor-driven, hand-operated machine on wheels, used to remove snow from sidewalks and driveways; **snow'bound**, cut off, isolated, by snow; **snow bunting**, small finch (*Plectrophenax nivalis*) breeding in Arctic regions, migrating to Europe and N. Amer. in winter, with brown and white or black and white plumage; **snow'-drift**, snow piled up in heap by action of wind; **snow'drop**, (flower of) small early-flowering bulbous plant (*Galanthus nivalis*) with white pendent flower; **snow'fall**, (esp.) amount of snow that falls on one occasion or on given area within given time; **snow fence**, temporary fencing of upright laths wired together, used to minimize drifting of snow onto sidewalks, highways, etc.; **snow'flake**, one of flakes or small crystalline masses in which

*The **snorkel**, a simple breathing apparatus, was first used by German submarines in the 1939–45 war so that air could be taken in and exhaust fumes emitted without surfacing. Today it is used widely, particularly by sportsmen.*

snow falls; any (white flower of) plant of bulbous genus *Leucojum*, esp. spring-flowering *L. vernum*, resembling snow drop; **snow goose**, white goose (*Chen hyperborea*) of N. Amer., breeding in Arctic regions; **snow job**, (slang) attempt to deceive by overwhelming with many details; **snow leopard**: see OUNCE[2]; **snow line**, boundary of a region above which snow never completely disappears; **snow'man** (pl. **-men**), mass of snow formed into figure of man; **snow'mobile**, motor vehicle used to travel over snow, esp. one with skis and caterpillar track; **snow'plow**, truck, locomotive, or device equipped with plow for clearing snow from road, railroad track, sidewalk, etc; **snow'shoe**, one of pair of racket-shaped frames of light wood strung with rawhide, enabling wearer to walk on surface of snow; **snowshoe rabbit**, hare (*Lepus americanus*) having large heavily furred feet and coat white in winter and brown in summer (hence called *varying hare*); **snow'storm**, storm with heavy fall of snow; **snow'suit**, heavy clothing for children, in cold-weather, consisting of separate jacket and pants or zippered coverall, usu. with hood, and tightly fitted at ankles, wrists, and neck; **snow tire**, tire having deep tread, and sometimes metal studs, to provide extra for wheel on snow or ice; **snow-white**, white as snow, pure white. **snow'y** *adj.* (**snow·i·er, snow·i·est**). **snow** *v.* 1. **it snows, it is snowing**, snow falls. 2. Let fall as or like snow; strew, cover, (as) with snow; bewilder, overwhelm, with im-

pressive talk, flattery, etc.; **snow in**, block, enclose, with fallen snow; **snow under**, bury in snow, (fig.) submerge, overwhelm.

snub[1] (snŭb) *v.t.* (**snubbed, snub·bing**). 1. Rebuff, reprove, humiliate, in sharp or cutting manner. 2. Check (rope running out) suddenly (by winding it around post). ~ *n.* Snubbing, rebuff. **snub'ber** *n.*

snub[2] (snŭb) *adj.* (of nose) Short and turned up, hence **snub-nosed.**

snuff[1] (snŭf) *n.* Charred part of candle wick, esp. as black excrescence obscuring light. ~ *v.* Trim snuff from (candle, wick) with fingers, scissors, etc.; ~ **out**, extinguish thus; crush, suppress; destroy. **snuf'fers** *n.pl.* Scissors for snuffing candle, with box to catch snuff.

snuff[2] (snŭf) *n.* Powdered tobacco for sniffing up into nostrils; **snuff'box**, small box for holding this; **up to snuff**, (colloq.) reaching acceptable standard. **snuff'y** *adj.* (**snuff·i·er, snuff·i·est**). **snuff** *v.* Sniff (*up, in, at*).

snuf·fle (snŭf'el) *v.* (**-fled, -fling**). Sniff, esp. audibly or noisily; speak or say nasally, whiningly, or like one with a cold. ~ *n.* Sniff; snuffling sound or speech; **the ~s** (colloq.), = the SNIFFLES.

snug (snŭg) *adj.* (**snug·ger, snug·gest**). Sheltered, comfortable, cozy; (of ship etc.) trim, neat, well protected from bad weather. **snug'ly** *adv.* **snug'ness** *n.*

snug·gle (snŭg'el) *v.* (**-gled, -gling**). Move, lie, close *up to* for warmth; hug, cuddle.

so (sō) *adv.* To extent, in manner, with result, described or indicated; of the kind, in the condition, etc., already indicated, by that name or designation; on condition set forth or implied; indeed, as well; **just ~**, (pred.) in precise style etc.; **or ~**, or thereabouts; **so'-and-so** (*n., adj., & adv.*) (pl. **so-and-sos**), used as substitute for name or expression not exactly remembered or not needing to be specified, or (colloq., euphem.) for term of abuse etc.; **so-called** (*adj.*) (epithet calling attention to, or questioning accuracy of description); indifferently, only passably. **so** *conj.* (colloq.) In order that; with the result that; therefore.

So. *abbrev.* South(ern).

s.o. *abbrev.* Strikeout.

soak (sōk) *n.* Soaking; hard drinker. ~ *v.* Place, lie, for some time in liquid, steep; make, be, saturated or wet through; (colloq.) overcharge; take *up*, suck *in*, liquid; (of liquid) make way *in(to), through*, by saturation; drink heavily; ~ **up**, absorb mentally, assimilate readily. **soak'er** *n.*

soap (sōp) *n.* Cleansing agent, essentially sodium salts of fatty acids usu. forming lather when rubbed in water; **soft** ~, kind remaining semifluid, potassium salts of fatty acids; (fig.) flattery; **soap'box**, box or rough platform for open-air orators; (attrib.) of or like open-air oratory; **soap opera**, (colloq.) sentimental radio or television serial; **soap'stone**, steatite; **soap'suds**, water impregnated with dissolved soap; **soap'wort**, herbaceous plant of genus *Saponaria*, yielding detergent substances, esp. *S. officinalis*, or bouncing Bet, with clusters of pink or white flowers. **soap** *v.t.* Rub, smear, lather, treat, with soap; (slang) flatter.

soap·y (sō'pē) *adj.* (**soap·i·er, soap·i·est**). Like, smeared or impregnated with, suggestive of, soap; ingratiating, unctuous, flattering. **soap'i·ly** *adv.* **soap'i·ness** *n.*

soar (sōr, sôr) *v.i.* Fly at, mount to, great height; hover or sail in air without flapping of wings or use of motor power. **soar'er** *n.*

sob (sŏb) *v.* (**sobbed, sob·bing**). Draw breath in convulsive gasps, usu. with weeping; utter with sobs; bring *oneself into* state, *to sleep*, with sobbing. ~ *n.* Convulsive catching of breath, esp. in weeping; ~ **sister**, writer of sentimental stories; ~ **story**, narrative designed mainly to evoke sympathy. **sob'ber** *n.* **sob'bing·ly** *adv.*

so·ber (sō'ber) *adj.* Not drunk; temperate in regard to drink; moderate, well-balanced, sedate, temperate; (of color) quiet, inconspicuous. **so'ber·ly** *adv.* **sober** *v.* Make, become, sober. **so'ber·ness** *n.*

so·bri·e·ty (sobrī'etē, sō-) *n.* Being sober.

so·bri·quet (sō'brikā, -kět, sōbrikā', -kět') *n.* Nickname.

Soc., soc. *abbrevs.* Socialist; society.

soc·cer (sŏk'er) *n.* Type of football in which two teams of 11 players kick round ball up and down rectangular field with goal at either end [abbrev. of Association football].

so·cia·ble (sō'shabel) *adj.* Fitted or inclined for company of others, not averse to society, ready to converse; of, characterized by, friendly or pleasant companionship. **so'cia·bly** *adv.* **so·cia·bil·i·ty** (sōshabǐl'ĭtē) *n.* (pl. **-ties**). **sociable** *n.* Informal social gathering, esp. of church members.

so·cial (sō'shal) *adj.* 1. Of, marked by, friendly intercourse; enjoyed, taken, in company with others; inclined to friendly intercourse, sociable. 2. Living in companies or more or less organized communities, gregarious. 3.

A perennial herb, soapwort received its name because its leaves, when rubbed in water, produce a lather. Saponin is also obtained from the roots and has been used as a soap substitute.

Of, concerned with, interested in, society and its constitution, or the mutual relations of men or classes of men; ~ **contract**, contract assumed by Rousseau (*Contrat Social*, 1762) and other writers by which true freedom was obtained by mutual agreement to substitute a state of law for a state of individualism; **S~ Democrat**, member of socialistic political party esp. (i) that founded in Germany, 1863, by Ferdinand Lassalle, and united with Marxists 1875; (ii) Russian Marxist socialist party; (iii) moderate state socialist party in Germany after 1919; ~ **disease**, venereal disease; ~ **science**, study of human society regarded as a science (freq. taken to include not only sociology but economics, political science, social anthropology, and social psychology); ~ **security**, (governmental provision of) financial and welfare benefits; ~ **services**, welfare services provided by government; ~ **work**, welfare work, work aimed at relieving poverty, improving social conditions, etc.; so ~ **worker**. **so'cial·ly** *adv.* **social** *n.* Social gathering, esp. one organized by club, association, etc.

so·cial·ism (sō'shalǐzem) *n.* Political and economic principle that community as a whole should have ownership and control of all means of production and distribution (opp. CAPITALISM and INDIVIDUALISM); policy aiming at this; state of society in which this principle is accepted. **so'cial·ist** *n.* **so·cial·is·tic** (sōshalǐs'tǐk) *adj.*

so·cial·is·ti·cal·ly *adv.*

so·cial·ite (sō'shalīt) *n.* Person prominent in fashionable society.

so·cial·ize (sō'shalīz) *v.t.* (**-ized, -iz·ing**). Make social or socialistic; **socialized medicine**, provision of medical services for all from public funds. **so·cial·i·za·tion** (sōshalǐzā'shon), **so·cial·iz'er** *ns.*

so·ci·e·ty (sosī'etē) *n.* (pl. **-ties**). 1. State of living in association with other individuals; customs and organization of ordered community; any social community. 2. Leisured, well-to-do, or fashionable persons regarded as distinct part of community. 3. Association with others, companionship, company. 4. Association of persons with common interest, aim, principle, etc.; **S~ of Friends**: see QUAKER; **S~ of Jesus**: see JESUIT; **so·ci'e·tal** *adj.*

So·ci·e·ty (sosī'etē) **Islands.** Group of islands in French Polynesia, including Tahiti.

socio- *comb. form.* Of society or sociology (and), as: **sociocultural**, combining social and cultural factors.

so·ci·ol·o·gy (sōsēŏl'ojē, sōshē-) *n.* Study of human, esp. civilized, society; study of social problems, esp. with a view to solving them. **so·ci·o·log·i·cal** (sōsēolŏj'ĭkal, sōshē-), **so·ci·o·log'ic** *adjs.* **so·ci·o·log'i·cal·ly** *adv.* **so·ci·ol'o·gist** *n.*

sock[1] (sŏk) *n.* (pl. **socks**, also for sense 1 **sox**). 1. Short stocking not reaching knee. 2. Light shoe worn by comic actors on ancient Greek and Roman stage; comedy.

sock[2] (sŏk) *n.* (slang) Hard or violent blow. ~ *v.t.* Hit, strike hard; ~ (person) **one**, give him hard blow.

sock·et (sŏk'ĭt) *n.* Hollow, usu. cylindrical, part or piece for thing to fit into, revolve in, etc.; hollow or cavity in which eye, tooth, bone, etc., is contained; (elect.) device into which electric light bulb or plug fits to make an electrical connection.

sock·eye (sŏk'ī) *n.* Amer. fish, the blueback salmon (*Oncorhynchus nerka*). [Amer. Ind. *sukai*]

Soc·ra·tes (sŏk'ratēz) (469–399 B.C.). Greek philosopher, who was tried at Athens on a charge of corrupting the young by his teaching, and sentenced to death (by drinking hemlock); he left no writings, but his method and doctrines are preserved in the Dialogues of PLATO. **So·crat·ic** (sokrăt'ĭk) *adj. & n.* Of, like, Socrates; ~ **irony**: see IRONY[1]; ~ **method**, method of inquiry and instruction by series of questions. **So·crat'i·cal·ly** *adv.*

sod (sŏd) *n.* Turf, (piece of) upper layer of grassland, with grass growing on it. ~ *v.t.* (**sod·ded,**

od·ding). Cover (ground) with ods.

so·da (sō´da) n. 1. (also **washing ~**) Sodium carbonate (Na_2CO_3) n alkaline substance occurring naturally in mineral state or in solution, used in manufacture of glass, soap, etc., and obtained orig. from ashes of marine plants; **baking ~**, sodium bicarbonate. 2. Soda water (see below). 3. **~ biscuit, cracker**, biscuit, cracker, leavened with sodium bicarbonate; **~ fountain**, apparatus for drawing soda water kept under pressure; counter, shop, apparatus, for making and serving iced drinks, ice cream, sundaes, etc.; **~ jerk(er)**, (slang) attendant at soda fountain; **~ pop**, (colloq.) carbonated, flavored soft drink; **~ water**,

effervescent water charged under pressure with carbon dioxide and used alone or mixed with spirits, syrups, etc., as beverage; club soda.

so·dal·i·ty (sōdăl´ĭtē) n. (pl. **-ties**). Confraternity, association, esp. R.C. religious guild or brotherhood.

sod·den (sŏd´en) adj. Saturated with liquid, soaked; heavy, doughy; stupid or dull with habitual drunkenness. **sod´den·ly** adv. **sod´den·ness** n. [orig. past part. of SEETHE]

so·di·um (sō´dēum) n. (chem.)

*The **sociable** design of an open carriage was very popular for family outings in fine weather. However, an enclosed phaeton or cabriolet was also needed for protection from rain or cold.*

Soft silver-white lustrous metallic element, oxidizing rapidly in air and reacting violently with water, closely resembling potassium in appearance and properties; symbol Na, at. no. 11, at. wt. 22.9898; **~ bicarbonate**, substance ($NaHCO_3$), used in baking (baking soda) and medicinally as an antacid; **~ carbonate**, common washing soda (Na_2CO_3); **~ chloride**, common salt (NaCl); **~ hydroxide**, caustic soda; **~ nitrate**, odorless, crystalline salt ($NaNO_3$), used in explosives and fertilizers; **~ thiosulfate**, white, crystalline salt ($Na_2S_2O_3$), used as bleach and fixative in photography. [named by Sir H. Davy, 1807, f. *soda*]

Sod·om (sŏd´om). Ancient city near the Dead Sea, destroyed, along with Gomorrah, because of its wickedness, by fire from heaven (Gen. 18–19).

sod·om·y (sŏd´omē) n. Unnatural sexual intercourse by a man, esp. with another male or with an animal. **sod·om·ite** (sŏd´omīt) n. Person practicing sodomy. [f. SODOM]

so·ev·er (sōĕv´er) adv. At all, of any kind, in any way (used with generalizing or emphatic force after words or phrases preceded by *how, what, who,* etc.).

-soever suffix. Soever.

so·fa (sō´fa) n. Long seat with raised back and end(s). [Arab. *suffa*]

sof·fit (sŏf´ĭt) n. (archit.) Undersurface of architrave, lintel, arch, etc.

So·fi·a (sō´fēa, sōfē´a). Capital city of Bulgaria.

soft (sawft, sŏft) adj. 1. Not hard; yielding to pressure, malleable, plastic, easily cut. 2. Of smooth surface or fine texture, not rough or coarse. 3. (of water) Not containing calcium or other mineral salts that prevent formation of lather with soap. 4. Not astringent, sour, or bitter; not crude or brilliant; not sharply defined; not strident or loud; (phonet.) voiced; (of the letters *c, g*) pronounced as spirants, not stops. 5. Gentle, quiet, conciliatory; sympathetic, compassionate; maudlin, feeble, flabby, weak; silly; (of drink) nonalcoholic. 6. **soft´ball**, game similar to baseball but played on smaller diamond with larger and softer ball, which is pitched underhand; **soft-boiled**, (of egg) boiled so that yolk remains runny; **soft coal**, bituminous coal; **soft(-core)**, (of pornography) subtle rather than overt; **soft currency**, currency not

*Left: A Tahitian carries pandanus leaves for use in thatching and mat-weaving. The **Society Islands** are mountainous and volcanic, and export coffee, copra and vanilla.*

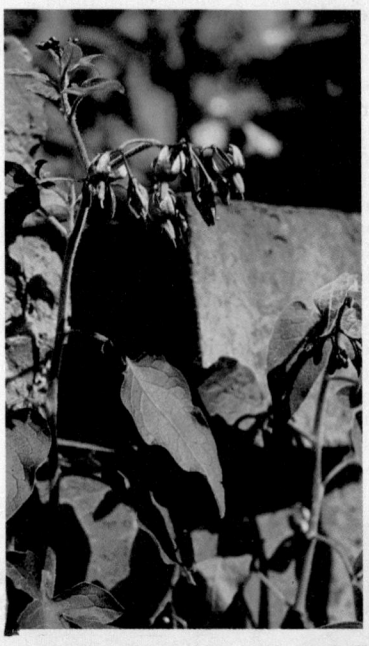

This experimental house in Arizona has **solar** *energy panels installed which enables energy for heating to be generated by the sun. As the world's resources are dwindling, scientists have had to search for alternative methods of producing power. Harnessing the energy of the sun is one of the most feasible possibilities. A solar power station has been built in the Soviet Union.*

Deadly nightshade (above) is one of 1,700 plants in the genus **Solanum.** *Others include the potato (originally from the Andes) and the eggplant of tropical Asia.*

convertible to gold or supported by gold reserves, or not easily exchangeable for other currencies, and therefore likely to depreciate; **soft focus,** (photog.) slight, deliberate blurring of image; **soft goods,** textiles; **soft landing,** landing in which spacecraft etc. reaches ground without being destroyed or damaged; **soft line,** policy of reconciliation and co-operation, esp. in politics, international affairs, etc.; **soft on,** (colloq.) in love with; **soft palate,** rear part of palate; **soft pedal,** (in mus. instr.) foot pedal for making tone softer; **soft-pedal** (*v.*), play with soft pedal down; (fig.) tone down, refrain from emphasizing; **soft sell,** quietly persuasive salesmanship; **soft-shell(ed),** having a soft or flexible shell; having shell not yet hardened owing to recency of molt; **soft-shoe** (*adj.*), of or pertaining to style of tap dancing with no metal taps on shoes; **soft shoulder,** gravel, sand, dirt, etc., strip off paved surface of highway; **soft soap**: see SOAP; **soft spot,** sentimental affection for; **soft'-ware,** (in computer) programs, program material, i.e., tapes, punched cards, etc.; (audio-visual aids) recorded material, such as films, film strips, records, tapes, etc., as opp. to *hardware,* the permanent equipment, such as projectors, record players, etc., in which it is used; **soft'wood,** (wood of) coniferous tree(s). **soft'ly** *adv.* **soft'ness** *n.* **soft** *adv.*

sof·ten (saw'fen, sŏf'en) *v.*

Become, make soft or softer; reduce strength of a defended position by bombing or bombardment (often with *up*); **softening of the brain,** morbid, esp. senile, degeneration of brain. **sof'ten·er** *n.* Person or thing that softens, esp. (i) chemical compound used in water treatment of fabrics to make them soft and light; (ii) WATER softener.

soft·y, soft·ie (sawf'tē, sŏf'-) *n.* (pl. **-ties**). (colloq.) Person who is very sentimental.

sog·gy (sŏg'ē) *adj.* (**-gi·er, -gi·est**). Sodden, saturated, heavy with moisture.

Sog·ne (sawng'ne) **Fjord.** Longest and deepest inlet of Norway, in the Norwegian Sea, on the W. coast; extends 127 mi. (204 km), and reaches depths of 4,081 ft. (1,244 m).

soi·gné, soi·gnée (swahnyā') *adjs.* Carefully or elegantly arranged; well-groomed.

soil[1] (soil) *n.* The ground, upper layer of earth in which plants grow, consisting of disintegrated rock usu. with admixture of organic remains. **soil'less** *adj.*

soil[2] (soil) *v.* Make dirty, smear or stain with dirt; tarnish, defile; admit of being soiled. ~ *n.* Dirty mark, smear, defilement.

soi·ree, soi·rée (swahrā', swār'ā) *ns.* Evening party, social evening.

so·journ (*n.* sō'jẽrn; for *v.* also sōjẽrn') *n. & v.i.* (Make) temporary stay in place. **so'journ·er** *n. & v.i.*

sol (sŏl, sōl) *n.* (phys. chem.) Liquid solution or suspension of colloid. [for *solution*]

sol·ace (sŏl'ĭs) *n.* Comfort, consolation. **sol'ac·er** *n.* **solace** *v.t.* (**-aced, -ac·ing**). Comfort, cheer, console.

sol·a·na·ceous (sŏlanā'shus) *adj.* Belonging to the nightshade family of plants (Solanaceae).

so·lar (sō'ler) *adj.* Of, concerned with, determined by, emanating from, the sun; ~ **battery, cell,** device for converting solar radiation into electrical energy; ~ **day** = DAY sense 2; ~ **month,** exact 12th of the year; ~ **plexus,** (anat.) complex of nerves situated in abdomen behind stomach; ~ **system,** sun with the nine major planets and many minor planets, asteroids, comets, etc., held by its attraction and revolving around it; ~ **wind,** streams of ionized hydrogen and helium particles constantly radiating outward from sun at rate of about a million tons per second.

so·lar·i·um (solār'ēum) *n.* (pl. **-lar·i·a** pr. -lār'ēa). Room, balcony, etc., enclosed in glass or open to air, for sunbathing etc.

sold: see SELL.

sol·der (sŏd'er) *n.* Fusible metal or metallic alloy used for joining metal surfaces or parts. ~ *v.t.* Join with solder. **sol'der·er** *n.*

Practical use of **solar** *energy (facing) includes a French radial house which uses the sun for heating and plant growing; use of solar radiation for air heating; and (top) solar water-heaters devised for roof-installation and now fitted in sunny States such as California and Texas.*

solar water-heater

absorbers

energy transfer loop

electric booster

solar energy in

thermosyphon flow

storage tank

cold water in

hot water out

pipes

solar panels

radial house

thermal storage (hot water)

sleeping area

utter

living area

central fire

er-butt

s and plants

outh

vent

vent

thermal chimney

inner wall with blackened surface

glass

south

French solar house

SOLDIER 1606 SOLUTE

*In geometry, a **solid** is an object of three dimensions: length, breadth and height. Each of these polyhedra is developed from an equilateral polygon or plane figure.*

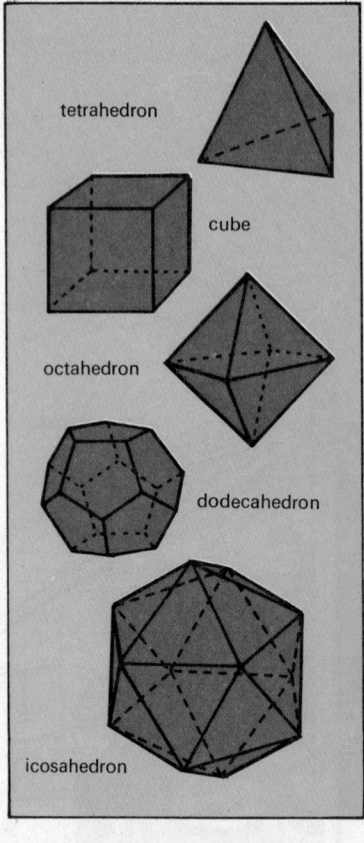

tetrahedron

cube

octahedron

dodecahedron

icosahedron

sol·dier (sōl´jer) *n.* Member of army, esp. private or noncommissioned officer; man of military skill and experience; ~ **of fortune**, one of adventurous character, willing to serve wherever his services are well paid. **sol´dier·ly** *adj.* **soldier** *v.* Serve as soldier; shirk work while on the job. [OF. *soude* pay f. L. *solidus* gold coin]

sol·dier·y (sōl´jerē) *n.* (pl. **-dier·ies**). Soldiers of a nation, in a district, etc.

sole[1] (sōl) *n.* Lower surface of foot, that part of it that rests or is placed on ground in standing or walking; part of boot or shoe on which wearer treads (freq. excluding heel); bottom, foundation, or undersurface, of plow, wagon, golf club head, etc. ~ *v.t.* (**soled, sol·ing**). Provide (boot etc.) with sole.

sole[2] (sōl) *n.* (pl. **soles**, collect. **sole**). Common European flatfish of genus *Solea*, highly esteemed as food; any of various other flatfishes, esp. edible ones.

sole[3] (sōl) *adj.* One and only; exclusive. **sole´ly** *adv.*

sol·e·cism (sŏl´isĭzem) *n.* Offense against grammar or idiom, blunder in speech or writing; violation of good manners or etiquette. **sol´e·cist** *n.* **sol·e·cis·tic** (sŏlĭsĭs´tĭk) *adj.*

sol·emn (sŏl´em) *adj.* Accompanied, performed, with religious rites or with ceremony; formal; ceremonious; impressive, awe-inspiring; serious, grave, earnest. **sol´emn·ly** *adv.* **sol´emn·ness** *n.*

so·lem·ni·ty (sŏlĕm´nĭtē) *n.* (pl. **-ties**). Rite, celebration, festival, ceremony; solemn character, appearance, behavior, etc.

sol·em·nize (sŏl´emnīz) *v.t.* (**-nized, -niz·ing**). Celebrate, honor with ceremonies; duly perform (marriage ceremony); make solemn. **sol·em·ni·za·tion** (sŏl-emnīzā´shon) *n.*

so·le·noid (sō´lenoid) *n.* (elect.) Cylindrical coil of conducting wire that behaves as a bar magnet when a current is passed through it, used for producing magnets. **so·le·noi·dal** (sōlenoi´dal) *adj.*

so·lic·it (solĭs´ĭt) *v.* Make appeals or requests to, importune; ask importunately or earnestly for; (esp. of prostitute) accost and importune for immoral purposes. **so·lic·i·ta·tion** (solĭsĭtā´shon) *n.*

so·lic·i·tor (solĭs´ĭter) *n.* 1. One who solicits or canvasses. 2. (English law) Member of legal profession qualified to advise

clients and instruct barristers, but not to appear as advocate except in certain lower courts. 3. Officer appointed by President to assist attorney general; in some states, chief law officer.

so·lic·i·tous (solĭs´ĭtus) *adj.* Anxious, troubled, concerned; anxious, eager (*to* do); **so·lic´i·tous·ly** *adv.*

so·lic·i·tude (solĭs´ĭtoōd, -tūd) *n.* Being solicitous, anxiety, concern.

sol·id (sŏl´ĭd) *adj.* Of stable shape, not liquid or fluid, rigid, hard and compact; of three dimensions; of solid substance throughout, not hollow, without internal cavities or interstices, uninterrupted; homogeneous, alike all through; firm, substantial, well-grounded, sober, real, genuine; concerned with solids; ~ **state**, (phys.) state of matter in which a body retains its own boundaries without the need of a container; ~**-state**, (elect.) using transistors etc. instead of vacuum tubes etc. **sol´id·ly** *adv.* **sol´id·ness, sol·id·i·ty** (solĭd´ĭtē) *ns.* **so·lid·i·fy** (solĭd´ĭfī) *v.* (**-fied, -fy·ing**). **so·lid·i·fi·ca·tion** (solĭdĭfĭkā´shon) *n.* **solid** *n.* (geom.) Body or magnitude of three dimensions; solid substance or body.

sol·i·dar·i·ty (sŏlĭdăr´ĭtē) *n.* (pl. **-ties**). Community of interests, sympathies, and action.

so·lil·o·quy (solĭl´okwē) *n.* (pl. **-quies**). Talking to oneself or

without addressing any person; instance of this, esp. on part of character in play. **so·lil·o·quize** (solĭl´okwīz) *v.i.* (**-quized, -quiz·ing**). Utter soliloquy.

sol·ip·sism (sŏl´ĭpsĭzem) *n.* (metaphys.) View that the self is the only object of real knowledge or the only really existent thing. **sol·ip·sist** *n.* **sol·ip·sis·tic** (sŏlĭpsĭs´tĭk) *adj.*

sol·i·taire (sŏl´ĭtār) *n.* 1. Precious stone, usu. diamond, set by itself. 2. Card game for one person, patience.

sol·i·tar·y (sŏl´ĭtĕrē) *adj.* Alone, living alone, not gregarious, without companions; single, separate; secluded, lonely. **sol´i·tar·i·ly** *adv.* **sol´i·tar·i·ness** *n.* **solitary** *n.* (pl. **-tar·ies**). Recluse, hermit.

sol·i·tude (sŏl´ĭtoōd, -tūd) *n.* Being solitary; lonely place.

so·lo (sō´lō) *n.* (pl. **-los**, esp. for def. 1 **-li** pr. -lē). 1. Piece of vocal or instrumental music, dance, performed by 1 person or instrument, with or without subordinate accompaniment. 2. Solo flight (see below). ~ *adj.* Alone, without companion or partners; ~ **flight**, unaccompanied flight by pilot in airplane.

so·lo·ist (sō´lōĭst) *n.* Musician etc. who performs alone or takes principal part.

Sol·o·mon (sŏl´omon). King of Israel *c*970–933 B.C., son and successor of David; famed for his wisdom and magnificence; built the Temple at Jerusalem; **Song of ~**: see SONG; **~'s seal**, any of several plants of genus *Polygonatum* with drooping greenish-white flowers on arching stems; also, magic symbol formed by two interlaced triangles forming a six-pointed star. **Sol·o·mon·ic** (sŏlomŏn´ĭk) *adj.*

Sol·o·mon Islands. Island nation in the SW. Pacific Ocean, E. of New Guinea, including Guadalcanal and San Cristobal; scene of severe fighting during World War II; member of the Brit. Commonwealth; capital and largest city, Honiara, on Guadalcanal.

So·lon (sō´lon) (*c*638–558 B.C.). Early Athenian legislator and reformer of the constitution, renowned for his wisdom.

sol·stice (sŏl´stĭs, sōl´-) *n.* Time when sun is farthest from equator and appears to stand still, occurring twice yearly, on June 21 or 22 (**summer ~**) and Dec. 22 or 23 (**winter ~**), and corresponding with the longest and shortest days of the year; point in ecliptic reached by sun at solstice. **sol·sti·tial** (sŏlstĭsh´al, sōl-) *adj.*

sol·u·ble (sŏl´yubel) *adj.* That can be dissolved; that can be solved. **sol·u·bil·i·ty** (sŏlyubĭl´ĭtē) *n.* **sol´u·bly** *adv.*

sol·ute (sŏl´ūt, sōl´-) *n.* & *adj.*

The **Solomon Islands** in the south-west Pacific are partly a British protectorate while Bougainville is included in Papua New Guinea. Above: An islander tribesman in his finery.

As part of his scheme to develop some form of public pride in the country, General Siad Barre, head of **Somalia**, rallied the people of Mogadishu in a mass street-cleaning campaign.

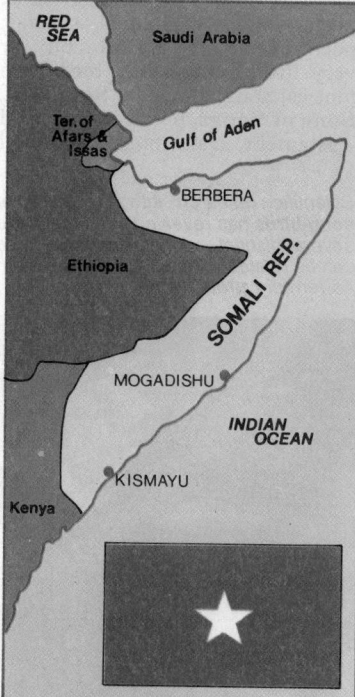

(Of, pertaining to, designating) dissolved substance.

so·lu·tion (soloo'shon) *n.* 1. Solving, being solved; instance or method of solving, explanation, answer. 2. Dissolving, being dissolved, conversion of solid or gas into liquid form by mixture with solvent; dissolved state; fluid substance produced by process of solution. 3. Breaking, breach (chiefly in ~ *of continuity*).

So·lu·tre·an, So·lu·tri·an (soloo'trēan) *adjs.* Of the later paleolithic culture (immediately following the Aurignacian); named from remains found in a rock shelter at La Solutré, central France, with characteristic flint implements; worked by pressure flaking.

solve (sŏlv, sawlv) *v.t.* (**solved, solv·ing**). Explain, resolve, answer; (math.) find answer to (problem etc.). **solv'a·ble** *adj.* **solv·a·bil·i·ty** (sŏlvabĭl'ĭtē, sawl-), **solv'er** *ns.*

sol·ven·cy (sŏl'vensē, sawl'-) *n.* Being financially solvent.

sol·vent (sŏl'vent, sawl'-) *adj.* 1. Able to pay all one's debts or liabilities. 2. That dissolves or can dissolve. ~ *n.* Substance (usu. liquid) capable of dissolving something; dissolving or disintegrating agent.

so·ma (sō'ma) *n.* (biol.) Body of organism in contrast to germ cells.

So·ma·li (somah'lē) *adj. & n.* (pl. **-lis**, collect. **-li**). (Member) of a dark-skinned Muslim Hamitic people inhabiting Somalia; (of) their language, belonging to the Ethiopian group of Hamitic languages.

So·ma·li·a (somah'lēa, -mahl'-ya). Republic on E. coast of Africa, formed (1960) from the former protectorate British Somaliland and the former Italian colony of Somalia; capital, Mogadishu.

So·ma·li·land (somah'lēlănd). Coastal region of E. Africa on the Gulf of Aden and the Indian Ocean, covering 300,000 sq. mi. (777,000 sq. km), and including Djibouti, Somalia, and SE. Ethiopia.

so·mat·ic (sōmăt'ĭk) *adj.* Of the body, corporeal, physical; of the framework of the body as dist. from the internal organs; ~ **cell**, one of the cells forming tissues, organs, etc., of the body (dist. from GERM cell). **so·mat'i·cal·ly** *adv.*

som·ber (sŏm'ber) *adj.* Dark, gloomy, dismal. **som'ber·ly** *adv.* **som'ber·ness** *n.*

som·bre·ro (sŏmbrār'ō) *n.* (pl. **-ros**). Broad-brimmed, usu. felt, hat, of kind common in Spain and Latin Amer.

some (sŭm) *adj.* Particular but unknown or unspecified; certain quantity or number of; appreciable or considerable quantity of; (colloq., emphat.) in the fullest sense, worthy of the name. ~ *pron.* Certain persons or things; certain quantity or number. ~ *adv.* (slang) In some degree; to a great extent.

-some[1] *suffix.* Formerly used to form adjectives with sense "characterized by being" or "apt to" (*bothersome, tiresome*).

-some[2] *suffix.* Forming nouns from numerals to indicate group (*twosome*).

-some[3] *comb. form.* (biol.) Denoting portion of a body, esp. of a cell (*chromosome, ribosome*).

some·bod·y (sŭm'bŏdē, -bodē) *n.* (pl. **-bod·ies**) & *pron.* Person of some note or consequence; some person.

some·how (sŭm´how) *adv.* In some indefinite or unspecified manner, by some means or other.

some·one (sŭm´wŭn) *n.* & *pron.* Somebody.

some·place (sŭm´plās) *adv.* (colloq.) Somewhere.

som·er·sault (sŭm´ersawlt), **som·er·set** (sŭm´ersĕt) *ns.* & *vbs.i.* (Make) acrobatic movement of the body turning head over heels or the reverse, either on the ground or in the air.

some·thing (sŭm´thĭng) *n.* & *pron.* Some thing; some undetermined, unspecified, or unknown thing; important thing or person. ~ *adv.* (archaic, exc. in ~ **like**) In some degree.

some·time (sŭm´tīm) *adv.* At some time; (archaic) formerly. ~ *adj.* Former. **some´times** *adv.* At some times.

some·what (sŭm´hwŭt, -hwŏt, -wŭt, -wŏt) *adv.* In some degree.

some·where (sŭm´hwār, -wār) *adv.* In, at, to, some place.

som·nam·bu·lism (sŏmnăm´-byulĭzem, som-) *n.* Walking or performing other action during sleep; state characterized by this. **som·nam´bu·list** *n.* **som·nam´bu·lis·tic** (sŏmnămbyŭlĭs´tĭk, som-) *adj.*

som·no·lent (sŏm´nolent) *adj.* Sleepy, drowsy; inducing drowsiness. **som´no·lent·ly** *adv.* **som´no·lence, som´no·len·cy** *ns.*

son (sŭn) *n.* 1. Male child in relation to parent; male descendant; offspring, product, native, follower;

~-in-law (pl. **~s-in law**), daughter's husband. 2. **the S~**, second person of the Trinity; **S~ of God, S~ of Man**, Jesus Christ.

so·nant (sō´nant) *adj.* & *n.* Voiced (sound, letter).

so·nar (sō´när) *n.* Device for detecting and locating submerged objects by reflection of sonic and ultrasonic waves.

so·na·ta (sonah´ta) *n.* (orig.) Musical composition for one or two instruments, in several movements contrasted in rhythm and tempo but related in key; **~ form**, musical composition in which two subjects are successively set forth, developed, and restated.

son·a·ti·na (sŏnatē´na) *n.* Shorter or simpler form of sonata.

sonde (sŏnd) = RADIOSONDE.

son et lu·mière (sawn´ā lümyĕr´). Entertainment recounting history connected with a building etc. and using recorded sound together with lighting effects. [Fr., = "sound and light"]

song (sawng, sŏng) *n.* Singing, vocal music; musical utterance of certain birds; short poem set to music or meant to be sung; short poem, esp. in rhymed stanzas; poetry, verse; **buy for a ~**, buy for very little; **song´bird**, bird with musical song; **Song of Solomon, Song of Songs**, poetic book of Old Testament, traditionally ascribed

*Scientific research into the calls of **song-birds** has revealed that most have several distinct 'songs', and that these can be related to specific activities such as territory protection.*

*A well coordinated child learns to do a **somersault** at an early age. Gymnasts however, can turn a simple somersault into a movement of grace and fluidity. Travelling troupes of tumblers were popular entertainers for many centuries.*

to Solomon; **song sparrow**, common sparrow (*Melospiza melodia*) of N. Amer. with streaked brown plumage and sweet song. **song´ful, song´less** *adjs.* **song´ful·ly** *adv.*

song·ster (sawng´ster, sŏng´-), fem. **song·stress** (sawng´strĭs, sŏng´-) *ns.* (poet.) 1. Singer. 2. Songbird.

son·ic (sŏn´ĭk) *adj.* Of, using, sound waves, esp. (of apparatus) determining depth of water by reflection of sound waves; (of a mine) set off by sound vibrations; **~ barrier**, sound barrier; **~ boom**, explosive noise produced by aircraft flying faster than the speed of sound.

son·net (sŏn´ĭt) *n.* Poem of 14 lines arranged according to any of various definite schemes, each line having normally ten syllables in English verse (but in Italian verse 11, in French 12), of which the commonest forms in English are the **Petrarchan** or **Italian ~**, divided into an octave of eight lines rhyming *a b b a a b b a* and a sestet of six lines with three rhymes more freely arranged, and the **Shakespearian** or **English ~**, which consists of three quatrains and a final couplet.

son·ny (sŭn´ē) *n.* (pl. **-nies**). Familiar form of address to boy.

so·no·rous (sonōr´us, -nōr´-, sŏn´erus) *adj.* Resonant, (capable of) giving out esp. loud or rich sound; high-sounding. **so·no´rous·ly** *adv.* **so·no´rous·ness, so·nor·i·ty** (sonōr´ĭtē, -när´-) *ns.* (pl. **-ties**).

soon (sōōn) *adv.* Not long after present time or time in question, in a short time; early; willingly; **as ~**

as, the moment that, not later than, as early as; **sooner or later**, at some time or other. **soon′er** *n*. 1. Person who settled in western U.S. before land was officially open to settlement, thus winning unfair advantage in choosing location. 2. (**S~**), nickname for Oklahoman.

soot (soot) *n*. Black carbonaceous substance or deposit in fine particles formed by combustion of coal, wood, oil, etc. ~ *v.t.* Smear, smudge, cover, choke (*up*). **soot′y** *adj.* (**soot·i·er, soot·i·est**). **soot′i·ly** *adv.* **soot′i·ness** *n*.

soothe (soodh) *v.t.* (**soothed, sooth·ing**). Calm, tranquilize; reduce force or intensity of (passion, pain, etc.). **sooth′er** *n*. **sooth′ing** *adj.* **sooth′ing·ly** *adv.*

sooth·say·er (sooth′sāer) *n*. One who foretells future events, diviner.

SOP, S.O.P. *abbrevs.* (mil.) Standard operating procedure.

sop (sŏp) *n*. Piece of bread etc. dipped or steeped in liquid before eating or cooking. **sop** *v*. (**sopped, sop·ping**). Soak, steep (*in* liquid), take *up* (liquid) by absorption; **sopping** (**wet**), very wet, drenched. **sop′py** *adj.* (**-pi·er, -pi·est**). Soaked, wet; (colloq.) mawkish, foolishly sentimental.

soph·ism (sŏf′ĭzem) *n*. Argument correct in form but fallacious, esp. one intended to deceive or mislead.

soph·ist (sŏf′ĭst) *n*. 1. Paid teacher of rhetoric and philosophy in ancient Greece. 2. Captious or fallacious reasoner, quibbler. **so·phis·tic** (sofĭs′tĭk), **so·phis′ti·cal** *adjs.* **so·phis′ti·cal·ly** *adv.* **soph·is·try** (sŏf′ĭstrē) *n*. (pl. **-tries**).

so·phis·ti·cate (sofĭs′tĭkāt) *v.t.* (**-cat·ed, -cat·ing**). 1. Render somewhat artificial by depriving of natural simplicity, as by education, worldly experience, etc. 2. Falsify by misstatement or alteration. **so·phis′ti·cat·ed** *adj.* (esp.) 1. (of person) Having fashionable tastes or style; (of things) satisfying such persons; (of peoples) of a fully developed culture or stage of civilization. 2. (of machinery etc.) Complex, intricate, and versatile. **so·phis′ti·cat·ed·ly** *adv.* **so·phis·ti·ca·tion** (sofĭstĭkā′shon) *n*. **sophisticate** (sofĭs′tĭkĭt, -kāt) *n*. Sophisticated person.

Soph·o·cles (sŏf′oklēz) (495–406 B.C.). Athenian tragedian; author of *Oedipus Rex, Antigone, Electra*, etc.

soph·o·more (sŏf′omōr, -mor, sŏf′mōr, -mor) *n*. Second-year student in high school or college. **soph·o·mor·ic** (sŏfomor′ĭk, -mär′-) *adj.* Conceited and overly confident of one's knowledge but immature and poorly informed.

sop·o·rif·ic (sŏporĭf′ĭk, sōpo-) *adj. & n.* (Drug) tending to

produce sleep.

so·pra·no (soprah′nō) *n*. (pl. **-nos, -ni** pr. -nē). Highest singing voice in women and boys; singer with such voice; musical part for this.

Sor·bonne (sŏrbŭn′, -bŏn′). Orig. a theological college founded in Paris by Robert de Sorbon, chaplain and confessor to Louis IX, *c*1257; later, faculty of theology in University of Paris, suppressed 1792; now, seat of faculties of science and letters of University of Paris.

sor·cer·er (sŏr′serer), fem. **sor·cer·ess** (sŏr′serĭs) *ns*. User of

magic arts, wizard, magician. **sor·cer·y** (sŏr′serē) *n*. (pl. **-cer·ies**).

sor·did (sŏr′dĭd) *adj.* Dirty, foul, squalid; ignoble, base; avaricious, mercenary. **sor′did·ly** *adv.* **sor′did·ness** *n*.

sore (sōr, sor) *n*. Place where skin or flesh of animal body is diseased or injured so as to be painfully tender or raw. ~ *adj.* (**sor·er, sor·est**). Painful, causing pain, distressing, irritating, grievous; suffering pain; irritable, sensitive; (colloq.) irritated, annoyed; **sore′head**, (colloq.) grumpy person. **sore′ly** *adv.* **sore′ness** *n*.

sor·ghum (sŏr′gum) *n*. Tropical, old-world grass (*Sorghum vulgare*) grown for grain, fodder, and as source of syrup; syrup made from juices of this plant.

so·ror·i·ty (sorōr′ĭtē, -rar′-) *n*. (pl. **-ties**). Society for women in college or university.

sorp·tion (sŏrp′shon) *n*. (phys. chem.) Absorption and adsorption considered jointly.

sor·rel[1] (sŏr′el, sär′-) *n*. Any of various small sour-tasting perennial plants of genera *Rumex* and *Oxalis*, freq. used in salads etc.

sor·rel[2] (sŏr′el, sär′-) *adj. & n.* (Horse) of bright chestnut or reddish-brown color; (having) this color.

mountain sorrel　　common sorrel

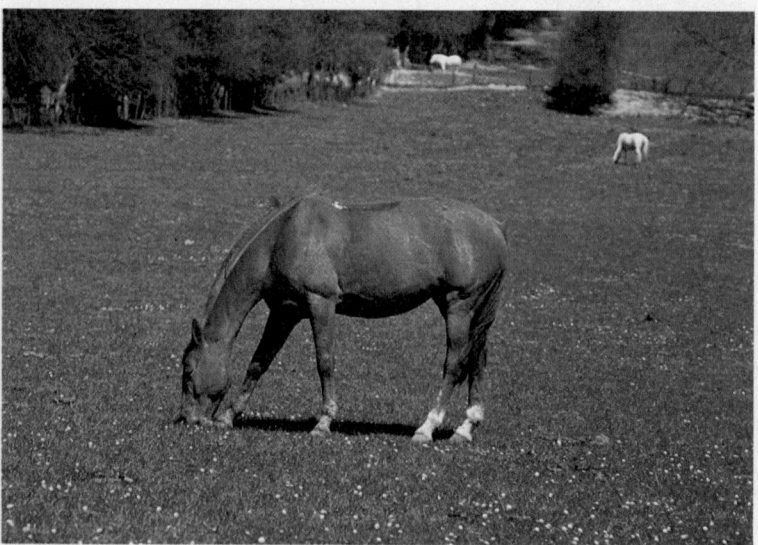

Obviously in the best condition, this **sorrel** *hunter grazes in a Kentish meadow during summer while waiting for the fox-hunting season to begin at the onset of winter in the U.K.*

Each **sorus** *on the underneath of a fern frond contains large numbers of spores. These eventually fall to earth but only a small number germinate and grow to maturity.*

sor·row (săr′ō, sŏr′-) n. Distress of mind caused by loss, suffering, disappointment, etc.; occasion or cause of this, misfortune, trouble. ~ v.i. Grieve, feel sorrow, mourn. **sor′row·ful** adj. **sor′row·ful·ly** adv. **sor′row·ful·ness** n.

sor·ry (săr′ē, sŏr′ē) adj. (-**ri·er**, -**ri·est**). 1. Feeling regret, regretful (freq. in expressions of sympathy or apology). 2. Wretched, paltry, shabby, mean. **sor′ri·ly** adv. **sor′ri·ness** n.

sort (sŏrt) n. Kind, species, variety (of); (print., usu. pl.) any particular letter or character in font of type; **of** ~ **s**, (colloq.) of a not very satisfactory kind; **out of** ~ **s**, out of health, spirits, or temper; slightly unwell; ~ **of**, (slang) in a way. **sort** v. Separate into sorts; take out (certain sorts from others). **sort′er** n. (esp). Letter sorter at a post office.

sor·tie (sŏr′tē) n. Sally, esp. of beleaguered garrison; operational flight by an aircraft.

so·rus (sŏr′us, sŏr′-) n. (pl. **so·ri** pr. sŏr′ī, sŏr′ī). Cluster of spore cases or spores on undersurface of fern leaves, in fungi, lichens, etc.

SOS (ĕs′ō ĕs′) n. International code signal (three dots, three dashes, three dots) of extreme distress, used esp. by ships at sea; (colloq.) urgent appeal for help.

sot (sŏt) n. Person stupefied by habitual drunkenness. **sot′tish** adj. **sot′tish·ly** adv. **sot′tish·ness** n.

sot·to vo·ce (sŏt′ō vō′chē; It. saw′taw vaw′chĕ). In an undertone, aside. [It.]

Sou·bi·rous (soōbēroō′), **Marie Bernarde**: see BERNADETTE.

sou·brette (soōbrĕt′) n. Maidservant or similar character (esp. with implication of pertness, coquetry, intrigue, etc.) in comedy, opera, etc.; actress playing such parts.

souf·flé (soōflā′, soō′flā) n. Light

spongy dish made by mixing a thick sauce or purée with the yolks and stiffly beaten whites of eggs, and baking it.

sough (sow) n. & v.i. (Make) rushing, sighing, or rustling sound, as of wind in trees.

sought (sawt) adj.: see SEEK; (esp.) ~ **-after**, much in demand.

soul (sōl) n. 1. Spiritual or immaterial part of man; moral and emotional part of man; vital principle and mental powers of animals, including man; animating or essential part, person viewed as this; personification or pattern of, embodiment of moral or intellectual qualities. 2. Departed spirit; disembodied spirit. 3. Person. 4. (colloq.) Indigenous culture, racial pride, group solidarity, etc., of black Americans. ~ adj. (colloq.) Of, pertaining to, designating black Americans and their experience in U.S. history: ~ **brother** (**sister**), (colloq.) fellow black; ~ **food**, (colloq.) traditional inexpensive food of Amer. blacks, such as chitterlings, corn bread, turnip greens; ~ **music**, (colloq.) style of music combining elements of rhythm and blues and black gospel singing. **soul′less** adj. **soul′less·ly** adv. **soul′less·ness** n.

soul·ful (sōl′ful) adj. Having, expressing, appealing to, the (esp. higher) emotional or intellectual qualities; (colloq.) excessively emotional. **soul′ful·ly** adv. **soul′ful·ness** n.

sound[1] (sownd) adj. Healthy; not diseased, injured, or rotten; financially solid or safe; correct, logical, well-founded, valid; (of sleep) deep, unbroken; thorough, unqualified. **sound′ly** adv. **sound′-**

ness n. **sound** adv. Deeply, profoundly (asleep).

sound[2] (sownd) n. Sensation produced in organs of hearing when surrounding air etc. vibrates so as to affect these; what is or can be heard; vibrations causing this sensation; utterance, speech, or one of the separate articulations composing this; impression produced by sound, statement, etc.; ~ **barrier**, extremely great resistance of air to object moving at speed near that of sound; **sound(ing) board**, thin resonant board in musical instrument so placed as to reinforce tones; audience whose responses serve as an indication of the effectiveness of the ideas etc. presented; **sound′box**, hollow chamber in musical instrument reinforcing resonance; **sound camera**, motion-picture camera that records sound while taking pictures; **sound effects**, sounds, other than speech or music, broadcast as part of program; **sound engineer**, one who deals with acoustics etc.; **sound film**, film for recording sound; cinema film with soundtrack; **sound′proof**, preventing passage of sound; (v.t.) make soundproof; **sound ranging**, determination of position by measuring time of arrival of sounds from known points; **sound′track**, (area of film carrying) sound record on cinema film; **sound truck**, truck equipped with loudspeakers that broadcast political messages, advertising slogans, etc.; **sound wave**, one of a series of progressive longitudinal vibratory disturbances in air or other medium by which the auditory nerves are stimulated. **sound′less** adj. **sound**

v. Give forth sound (freq. fig., with reference to impression created); cause to sound; utter, pronounce; give notice of by sound, cause to resound, declare, make known; **sound off**, (colloq.) talk loudly, express one's opinions forcefully.

sound[3] (sownd) *v.* Investigate, test depth or quality of bottom of (water), with line and lead or other apparatus; measure (depth) thus; measure temperature etc. of upper atmosphere with **sound'ing balloon** or sonde; (of whale) dive deeply; (usu. **sound out**) inquire, esp. in cautious or indirect manner, into sentiments or inclination of (person); **sounding lead**, lead attached to line (**sounding line**) used in sounding depth of water.

sound[4] (sownd) *n.* Narrow channel, esp. between island and mainland, or connecting two large bodies of water; arm of sea.

sound·ing (sown'ding) *n.* (esp. pl.) Measurement of depth of water at specific places; places where such measurements can be or have been taken.

soup (soop) *n.* 1. Liquid food made by stewing vegetables, meat, etc.; **in the ~**, (slang) in diffi-

culties; **~ kitchen**, public institution where soup etc. is supplied free to the poor or in times of distress. 2. (slang) Nitroglycerine, esp. when used to open safe; **~ up** (*v.t.*), increase power of (engine), supercharge. **soup'y** *adj.* (**soup·i·er, soup·i·est**).

soup·çon (soopsawn', soop'-sawn) *n.* Trace of flavor (*of*); very small amount.

sour (sowr) *adj.* With tart or acid taste, esp. as result of unripeness or of fermentation; rendered acid esp. by fermentation; affected or spoiled thus; (of smell) suggesting fermentation; (of soil) acid; (of person etc.) harsh, peevish, morose; **sour'dough**, prospector, one who lives in the open, esp. in Alaska or Canada (from keeping piece of sour dough for making bread); fermented bread dough; **sour grapes**, scorn or affectation of distaste for something one cannot or does not have; **sour gum**, ornamental tree (*Nyssa sylvatica*) of

*The **sound engineer** in a recording studio is responsible for mixing the various instrument and voice tracks together to produce a final mix for recording purposes. The work requires considerable skill.*

*Johannesburg, capital of **South Africa**. South Africa has come under intense pressure in recent years because of its policy of apartheid.*

moist areas in eastern N. Amer., having shiny, tough leaves that turn brilliant scarlet in fall; also called black gum; pepperidge, tupelo; **sour'puss**, (slang) ill-tempered or gloomy person; **sour'sop**, (large succulent, slightly acid fruit of) tropical Amer. tree (*Anona muricata*). **sour** *n.* Acid solution used in bleaching, tanning, etc.; acid drink, usu. of whiskey or other liquor with lemon or lime juice. **sour'ish** *adj.* **sour'ly** *adv.* **sour'ness** *n.* **sour** *v.* Make, become, sour.

source (sors, sors) *n.* Spring, fountainhead, of stream or river; origin, chief or prime cause, *of*; document, work, etc., giving evidence, esp. original or primary, as to fact, event, etc.; literary work(s) from which later writers have derived inspiration, plots, etc.

souse (sows) *n.* 1. Pickle made with salt; food in pickle, esp. head, feet, and ears of swine. 2. Sousing. 3. Drunkard. **~ v.** (**soused, sous·ing**). Put in pickle; plunge (*into* water etc.), soak (*in* liquid), drench. **soused** *adj.* (slang) Drunk.

sou·tane (sootahn') *n.* Cassock of R.C. priest.

south (sowth) *adv.* Toward, in, the south. **~ n.** 1. Point of horizon directly opposite north; this direction. 2. Cardinal point of the compass opposite north. 3. (usu. **the S~**) That part of a country, district, etc., that lies to the south; (esp.) Southern states of U.S. **south** *adj.* Lying, toward, in, the south; (of wind) blowing from the south; **south'paw**, (colloq.) left-handed (person), esp. in sports;

Typical landscape in the Natal National Park, **South Africa,** *with the Drakensberg Mountains in the background. Elsewhere, much of the country is devoted to agriculture and there are many mines.*

South Pole, point on Earth that is farthest south; **South Seas,** South Pacific. **south'ward** *adv., adj., & n.* **south'wards** *adv.*

South (sowth) **Africa.** Republic in southern Africa; constituted in 1910 (as **Union of ~**) from the self-governing Brit. colonies Cape of Good Hope, Transvaal, Natal, and Orange Free State; member of the Brit. Commonwealth until 1961; administrative capital, Pretoria; seat of legislature, Cape Town. **South African** *adj. & n.*

South (sowth) **America.** Southern part of the continent of Amer., joined to Central Amer. by the isthmus of Panama. **South American** *adj. & n.*

South (sowth) **Carolina.** Southern state of U.S.; one of the original states of the Union (1788); capital, Columbia.

South (sowth) **Dakota.** State in N. central U.S.; admitted to the Union in 1889; capital, Pierre.

south·east (sowthēst') *adv. & n.* (Direction or compass point) between south and east. **~** *adj.* Of, in, to, from, the southeast. **south·east·er** (sowthēs'ter; *naut.* sowē'ster) *n.* Southeast wind. **south'east'er·ly** *adv., adj., & n.* **south'east'ern** *adj.* **south'east'ward** *adv., adj., & n.* **south'east'ward·ly** *adv. & adj.* **south'east'wards** *adv.*

South·east (sowthēst') **Asia.** Region consisting of Cambodia, Indonesia, Laos, Malaysia, Singapore, Thailand, and Vietnam. **South East Asia Treaty Organization,** alliance (1954) of Australia, France, Great Britain, New Zealand, Pakistan, the Philippines, Thailand, and the United States to prevent spread of Communism in the area.

south·er·ly (sŭdh'erlē) *adj.* In the south; (of wind) blowing from the south. **~** *adv.* Toward the south. **~** *n.* South wind.

south·ern (sŭdh'ern) *adj.* Of the south; lying or directed toward the south; (poet.) coming from the south; **S~**, pertaining to the Southern states of the U.S. **S~ Cross:** see CROSS; **S~ hemisphere:** see HEMISPHERE; **~ lights:** see AURORA australis; **S~ states,** esp. those states S. of Mason-Dixon line and E. of New Mexico. **south'ern·er** *n.* (also **S~**) Native, inhabitant, of the south. **south'ern·most** *adj.*

South (sowth) **Korea.** Unofficial name for the Republic of Korea.

south·west (sowthwĕst'; *naut.*

sowwĕst') *adv. & n.* (Direction or compass point) between south and west. **~** *adj.* Of, in, to, from, the southwest. **south'west'er** *n.* 1. Southwest wind. 2. (usu. **sou'wester**) Waterproof hat with broad flap behind to protect the neck. **south'west'er·ly** *adv., adj., & n.* **south'west'ern** *adj.* **south'west'ward** *adv., adj., & n.* **south'west'ward·ly** *adv. & adj.* **south'west'wards** *adv.*

South-West (sowth' wĕst) **Africa:** see NAMIBIA.

sou·ve·nir (soovener', soo'vener) *n.* Thing given, brought, kept, etc., for memento (*of* occasion, place, etc.). [Fr., = remember, f. L. *subvenire* occur to the mind]

sou'west·er (sowwĕs'ter) = SOUTHWESTER.

sov·er·eign (sŏv'rĭn, -erĭn, sŭv'-) *n.* 1. Supreme ruler, esp. monarch. 2. (hist.) English gold coin worth £1. **~** *adj.* Supreme; possessing sovereign power; (of remedies etc.) very good or efficacious. **sov·er-**

eign·ty *n.* (pl. **-ties**).

so·vi·et (sō'vēĕt, -ĭt, sōvēĕt') *n.* Council, esp. elected organ of government of district, republic, etc., or (**Supreme S~**) whole, of U.S.S.R.; **the Soviet,** the U.S.S.R. **so·vi·et·ize** (sō'vēĕtīz) *v.t.* (**-ized, -iz·ing**). Change or convert to a form of government by soviets. **so'vi·et·ism** *n.* [Russ. *sovet* council]

Soviet (sō'vēĕt, -ĭt, sōvēĕt') **Union.** Union of Soviet Socialist Republics (see entry).

sow¹ (sow) *n.* 1. Female of swine, adult female pig, esp. domestic one used for breeding. 2. Trough through which molten iron runs into side channels to form pigs; large block of iron solidified in this. 3. **~ thistle,** plant of genus *Sonchus,* common weed with sharply toothed thistlelike leaves and milky juice.

sow² (sō) *v.t.* (**sowed, sown, sow·ing**). Scatter (seed) on or in the earth; plant (ground *with* seed)

by sowing; (fig.) cover thickly *with*.
sow'er *n*.

sox (sŏks): see SOCK[1].

soy (soi) *n*. (also ~ **sauce, soy-bean sauce**) Sauce for fish etc. made, chiefly in Japan, China, and India, from soybeans pickled in brine; soybean. [Jap. colloq. f. *sho-yu* f. Chin. *shi-yu* (*shi* salted beans, *yu* oil)]

soy·bean (soi'bēn), **soy·a** (soi'*a*) *ns*. (Seed of) a widely cultivated Asiatic bushy leguminous plant (*Soja hispida*), yielding valuable meal (**soy bean flour**), oil, fertilizer, forage, etc. [f. SOY]

Sp. *abbrev*. Spanish.

sp. *abbrev*. Spelling.

S.P. *abbrev*. Shore patrol; shore police.

spa (spah) *n*. Watering place, (place with) mineral spring. [f. *Spa*, watering place in Belgium, fashionable in 18th c.]

space (spās) *n*. 1. Continuous expanse viewed with or without reference to the existence of objects within it; (also **outer** ~) the universe beyond Earth's atmosphere, the immeasurable expanse in which the solar and stellar systems, nebulae, etc., are situated; **space'craft** (pl. **-craft**), **space'-ship**, vehicle designed to travel outside Earth's atmosphere; **space'man**, astronaut or member of spaceship's crew; **space medicine**, medicine dealing with effects of space travel on human body; **space probe**, investigation of conditions in outer space; **space shuttle**, spacecraft for travel be-

South Dakota *is one of the midwestern states of the U.S.A. The badlands are a major tourist attraction famous for their hostile and arid landscapes, and the strange rock formations found there.*

*The yellow flowers of the **sow-thistle** may be seen in Europe from June onwards each summer. In some places its leaves were used as a vegetable and they were also fed to domestic animals.*

*Orbiter I was the first NASA **space shuttle** to be launched, and was thus an uncrewed space flight designed to test the shuttle method, which proved successful.*

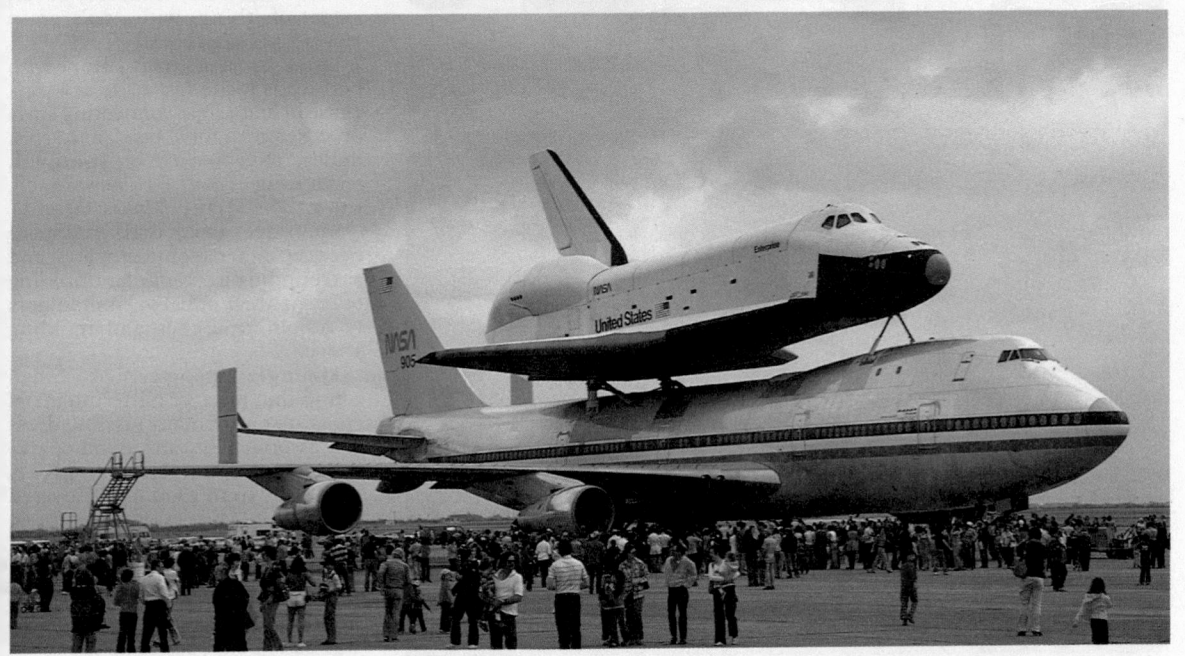

tween Earth and space station in orbit; **space station**, artificial satellite used as base for operations in space; **space′suit**, pressurized suit designed to protect wearer from effects of high acceleration, deceleration, or pull of gravity; **space-time**, (philos.) four-dimensional continuum resulting from fusion of the concepts of space and time; **space′walk**, physical activity by astronaut in space outside spacecraft. 2. Interval between points or objects. 3. Interval of time. 4. (print.) Blank between words etc., piece of type

metal used to separate words etc. 5. **space bar** or **spac′er**, bar on typewriter for making space(s) between words etc.; **space heater**, self-contained unit for heating room etc. **space** *v.* (**spaced, spac·ing**). Set at intervals, put spaces between; make space between words on typewriter etc.; **spaced-out** (*adj.*), (slang) under influence of alcohol, marijuana, etc.

spa·cious (spā′shus) *adj.* Enclosing a large space, having ample space, roomy. **spa′cious·ly** *adv.* **spa′cious·ness** *n.*

spade[1] (spād) *n.* Tool for

digging or cutting ground, turf, etc., usu. with flattish rectangular blade socketed on wooden handle, with grip or crosspiece at upper end, grasped with both hands while blade is pressed into ground with foot; anything resembling this in form or use; **call a ~ a ~**, call things by their names, speak plainly or bluntly; **spade′work**, (fig.) hard, preliminary work. **spade** *v.t.* (**spad·ed, spad·ing**). Dig up with spade.

spade[2] (spād) *n.* (Playing card with) black figure(s) resembling pointed spade; (pl.) suit of these cards. [Span. *espada* sword]

spa·dix (spā′diks) *n.* (pl. **spa·dix·es, spa·di·ces** pr. spādī′sēz, spā′disēz). Inflorescence consisting of thick fleshy spike, usu. enclosed in spathe.

spa·ghet·ti (spagĕt′ē) *n.* Pasta formed into long rods, thinner than macaroni but thicker than vermicelli.

Spain (spān). Country in SW. Europe on the Iberian Peninsula, covering 194,881 sq mi. (504,742 sq. km), and including the Balearic and Canary Islands; capital, Madrid.

spake: see SPEAK.

spall (spawl) *n.* Splinter, chip. **~** *v.* Splinter; (mining) prepare (ore) for sorting by breaking it up.

span[1] (spăn) *n.* Distance from tip of thumb to tip of little finger of fully extended hand; this as measure (9 in.); short distance or time; whole extent of a period of time; full extent or stretch between abutments of arch, piers of bridge, wingtips of aircraft, etc.; arch of bridge. **~** *v.t.* (**spanned, span·ning**). Stretch from side to side of, extend across; bridge (river etc.), form arch across; measure, cover, extent of (thing) with one's grasp etc.

span[2] (spăn) *n.* (naut.) Rope with both ends made fast to afford purchase in loop, rope connecting stays or other uprights; pair of horses, mules, etc. **~** *v.t.* (**spanned, span·ning**). (naut.) Fasten, attach, draw tight. [Du. *spannen* fasten]

span·drel (spăn′drel) *n.* Space between either shoulder of arch and surrounding rectangular molding or framework, or between shoulders of adjoining arches and molding above.

span·gle (spăng′gel) *n.* Small round thin piece of glittering metal etc., esp. one of many sewn to dress etc. as ornament; any small sparkling object. **span′gly** *adj.* (**-gli·er, -gli·est**). **span′gled** *adj.* Covered

*Above left: The Episcopal Palace a[t] Astorga in the north west of **Spain** was built in the twentieth century. However, the city is much older and the cathedra[l] was built in the 15th century.*

oxygen supply pressure gauge

transceiver antenna

emergency oxygen tank

pressurized helmet

back

visor (one of three)

iver

control unit for back pack

er

oxygen supply

cooling tube

ifier

gauge

ump

rock sample pocket

d box

e resisting uit

fabric suit

Saturn 5 launch vehicle
with Apollo spacecraft

command and lunar modules

lunar module

first artificial satellite

sky-lab orbital workshop

lunar orbiter   prospero

1. launch escape system
2. command module
3. service module
4. lunar module housing
5. third stage of Saturn 5 launch vehicle
6. second stage
7. first stage
8. service propulsion engine nozzle
9. S-band antenna
10. heat shield
11. V.H.F. antenna
12. lunar module
13. landing gear
14. rendezvous radar antenna
15. exit platform
16. ladder
17. workshop
18. Solar cell panels
19. radio antenna
20. 36″ parabolic antenna

*Since the launching of the first artificial space satellite, Sputnik 1, by the U.S.S.R. in 1957, **spacecraft** have become increasingly large and more powerful as demands on them increase.*

Although the cabins of spacecraft can now be built so that the crew may live in normal clothing, to emerge onto the surface of the moon, or for any other movement outside the cabin, a space suit must be worn.

(as) with spangles.

Span·iard (spăn´yard) *n*. Native of Spain.

span·iel (spăn´yel) *n*. Dog of various small or medium-sized breeds, usu. with long silky hair, large drooping ears, keen scent, and docile and affectionate disposition, used as sporting dogs esp. for starting and retrieving game, or kept as pets. [OF. *espaignol* Spanish (dog)]

Span·ish (spăn´ĭsh) *adj*. Of Spain or its people or language; ~ **America**, those portions of Amer. settled by Spaniards and now occupied by their descendants, including the greater part of S. Amer. and some of the West Indian islands; ~-**American** (*adj*. & *n*.); ~ **Armada**: see ARMADA; ~ **bayonet**, yucca with stiff sharp-pointed leaves; ~ **fly**, brilliant green beetle (*Lytta vesicatoria*) from which cantharides, used for raising blisters, as aphrodisiac, etc., is obtained; ~ **Inquisition**, inquisition as established in Spain by Ferdinand and Isabella in 1478, and continued thereafter under control of state until formal abolishment in 1834; notorious for harshness, esp. in 16th c., including many executions of those condemned as heretics (cf. INQUISITION); ~ **Main**, mainland of Amer. adjacent to the Caribbean Sea, esp. that portion from the Isthmus of Panama to the mouth of the Orinoco; in later use, the sea contiguous to this; ~ **moss**, epiphytic plant (*Tillandsia usneoides*) of southeastern U.S. and tropical Amer., where long, gray festoons of it grow on trees; ~ **omelet**, omelet with sauce of chopped onions, green peppers, and tomatoes; ~ **rice**, dish made of boiled rice, tomatoes, chopped onions and peppers, and spices.

*A **spare** score is recorded in tenpin bowling if the player has not knocked down all the pins in the first delivery but manages to knock down the remainder with the second.*

Spanish *n*. Language of Spain, one of the Romance group.

spank[1] (spăngk) *v.t.* & *n*. Slap or smack with open hand, esp. on buttocks.

spank[2] (spăngk) *v.t.* Move or travel quickly or dashingly.

spank·ing (spăng´kĭng) *adj*. (esp.) Very large or fine, striking, notable, excellent; (of horse etc.) fast-moving, dashing, showy.

span·ner (spăn´er) *n*. Wrench, usu. with fixed jaws.

Spar, SPAR (spär) *ns*. Member of women's reserve of U.S. Coast Guard. [f. L. *S(emper) Par(atus)* always prepared, motto of Coast Guard]

spar[1] (spär) *n*. Stout pole, esp. such as is used for mast, yard, etc., of ship; either of main lateral members of wing of aircraft, carrying ribs; ~ **varnish**, varnish that provides tough, long-lasting protection against weathering. **spar** *v.t.* (**sparred, spar·ring**). Furnish with spars.

spar[2] (spär) *n*. Any of various more or less lustrous crystalline easily cleavable minerals.

spar[3] (spär) *v.i.* (**sparred, spar·ring**). Make motions of attack and defense with fists, use hands (as) in boxing; (fig.) dispute, bandy words; (of cocks) strike with feet or spurs, fight. ~ *n*. Sparring; boxing match; cockfight.

spare (spär) *adj*. (**spar·er, spar·est**). 1. Scanty, frugal; lean, thin. 2. That can be spared, not required for ordinary use; reserved for future, emergency, or extraordinary use; ~ **part**, duplicate of

*The common **sparrow** has not only adapted itself to life near human habitation, but in some places, has become exceptionally tame. Elsewhere, it has reached plague proportions.*

part of machine, kept in readiness to replace one lost, broken, etc.; ~ **room**, room not ordinarily used, guest room. **spare´ly** *adv*. **spare´ness** *n*. **spare** *n*. 1. Spare part, tire, etc. 2. (bowling) Knocking down all pins with first two balls. ~ *v*. (**spared, spar·ing**). 1. Be frugal or grudging of; be frugal. 2. Dispense with, do without. 3. Refrain from inflicting injury, affliction, or damage or punishment on, deal leniently or gently with; refrain from taking (life). **spar´ing·ly** *adv*. **spar´ing·ness** *n*.

spare·rib (spär´rĭb) *n*. (often pl.) Part of closely trimmed ribs of meat, esp. pork.

spark[1] (spärk) *n*. Fiery particle thrown off from burning substance, or still remaining in one almost extinguished, or produced by impact of one hard body on another; small bright object or point; (elect.) (brilliant flash of light accompanying) sudden disruptive discharge between two conductors separated by air etc.; electric spark for firing explosive mixture in internal combustion engine; **sparks** (colloq.) radio operator on ship; (fig.) flash (of wit etc.); scintilla, particle (of fire, some quality, etc.); **spark plug**, electrical device fitting into the cylinder head of an internal combustion engine, consisting of two electrodes across the space between which the current from the ignition system passes and so produces the spark that fires the explosive mixture in the cylinders; (fig.) person providing impetus in an undertaking. **spark** *v*. Emit

*Left: 'Young **Spartans**' by Degas is a romantic impression of the young people of the Greek civilization which thrived from about 700–370 B.C. Their warrior class believed in austerity.*

hawk: see FALCON, KESTREL.

sparse (spärs) *adj*. (**spars·er, spars·est**). Thinly dispersed or scattered, not crowded or dense, with wide distribution or intervals. **sparse'ly** *adv*. **sparse'ness, spar·si·ty** (spär´sĭtē) *ns*.

Spar·ta (spär´ta). Ancient city of Greece, capital of Laconia, a Dorian city-state of ancient Greece in SE. Peloponnesus, the inhabitants of which were noted for the military organization of their state and for their rigorous discipline, simplicity, and courage.

Spar·ta·cus (spär´takus). Thracian leader of an army of slaves who rebelled against Rome in 73–71 B.C.

Spar·tan (spär´tan) *adj*. Of Sparta (esp. with allusion to the characteristics of the Spartans); hence, austere, hardy. ~ *n*. Native, inhabitant, of Sparta; hardy austere person.

spasm (spăz´em) *n*. Involuntary sudden and violent muscular contraction; sudden convulsive movement, convulsion.

spas·mod·ic (spăzmŏd´ĭk), **spas·mod·i·cal** (spăzmŏd´ĭkal) *adjs*. Of, caused by, subject to, spasm(s); occurring, done, jerkily or by fits and starts. **spas·mod'i·cal·ly** *adv*.

spas·tic (spăs´tĭk) *adj*. Of, characterized by, (esp. tonic) spasm(s). ~ *n*. Person with cerebral PALSY.

spat[1] (spăt) *n*. Spawn of shellfish, esp. oyster. ~ *v*. (**spat·ted, spat·ting**). (of oyster) Spawn.

spat[2] (spăt) *n*. (usu. pl.) Short gaiter covering instep and reaching little above ankle.

spat[3] (spăt) *n*. Tiff, quarrel.

spat[4]: see SPIT[2].

spate (spāt) *n*. River flood, esp. sudden; rush, outburst.

spathe (spādh) *n*. (bot.) Large bract, freq. bright colored, enveloping inflorescence on same axis (spadix), as in arum etc.

spa·tial (spā´shal) *adj*. Of, relating to, occupying, occurring in, space. **spa'tial·ly** *adv*.

spat·ter (spăt´er) *v*. Scatter (liquid, mud, etc.) here and there in small drops, splash (*with* mud, slander, etc.) thus, (of liquid) fall thus or with sound suggesting heavy drops. ~ *n*. Spattering, splash; pattering. **spat'ter·ing·ly** *adv*.

spat·u·la (spăch´ula) *n*. Flat broad-bladed knife-shaped implement used for spreading foods, paints, etc. and for medical examination of certain organs etc. **spat'u·lar, spat·u·late** (spăch´-

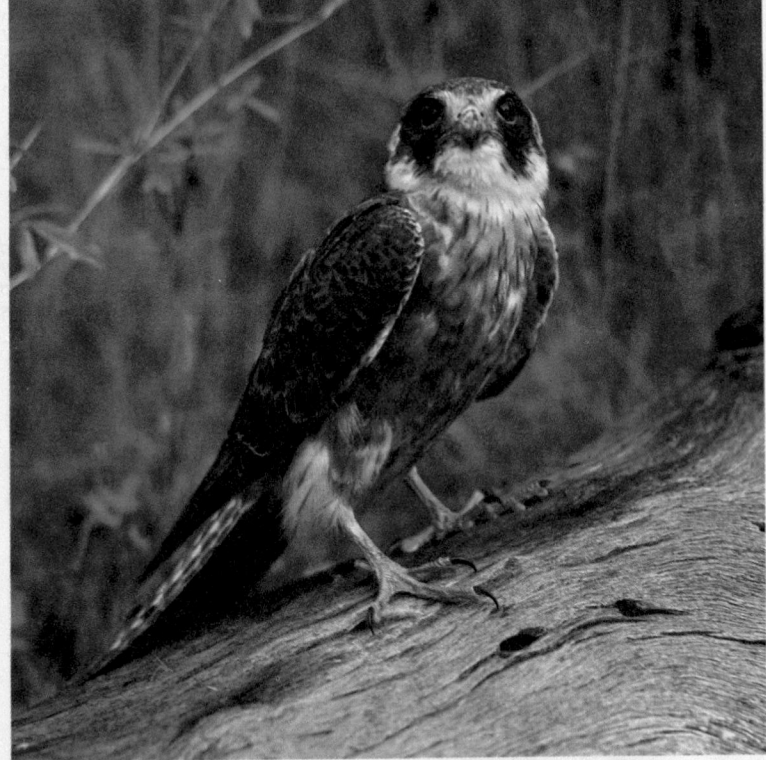

*The collared **sparrow-hawk** is found only in Australia and New Guinea where it preys on smaller birds and mammals. Related birds are found on most continents and have similar behavior.*

spark(s) of fire or electricity; produce sparks at point where electric circuit is broken; (colloq.) begin, animate, set in motion.

spark[2] (spärk) *n*. Outgoing, lively, elegant fellow; gallant. **spark'ish** *adj*. **spark** *v.i.* Play the gallant, woo.

spar·kle (spär´kel) *n*. Sparkling; gleam, spark. ~ *v.i.* (**-kled, -kling**). Emit sparks; glitter, glisten, scintillate. **spar'kler** *n*. (esp., colloq.) Diamond or other sparkling gem. **spar'kling** *adj*. (of wines etc.) Effervescing with small glittering bubbles of carbon dioxide.

spar·row (spăr´ō) *n*. Any of numerous species of small brownish-gray birds of genus *Passer*, commonest being the *house or English* ~ (*P. domesticus*), a native of Europe introduced into N. Amer., abundant in towns and cities; **spar'rowgrass**, (colloq. corrupt. of) asparagus; **sparrow**

spav·in (spăv´ĭn) *n.* Disease of hock in horses, marked by hard bony tumor or excrescence and caused by strain etc. **spav´ined** *adj.*

spawn (spawn) *n.* Minute eggs of frogs, fishes, etc., usu. extruded in large numbers and often forming coherent or gelatinous mass, fertilized by the MILT; (contempt.) brood, (numerous) offspring; mycelium of fungi. ~ *v.* Cast spawn; produce or generate as spawn or in large numbers.

spay (spā) *v.t.* Remove ovaries of (animal).

S.P.C.A. *abbrev.* Society for the Prevention of Cruelty to Animals.

S.P.C.C. *abbrev.* Society for the Prevention of Cruelty to Children.

speak (spēk) *v.* (**spoke** pr. spōk or archaic **spake** pr. spāk, **spo·ken** pr. spō´ken or archaic **spoke**, **speak·ing**). Utter words or articulate sound in ordinary (not singing) voice; hold conversation; make oral address, deliver speech; utter (words); make known (opinion, *the truth*, etc.) thus; use (specified language) in speaking; state in words; be evidence of, indicate; ~ **for**, act as spokesman of or for; ~ **of**, mention; **speak out, up**, speak freely; speak loud(er) or so as to be distinctly heard; **speak´easy** (pl. **-easies**), (slang) place illegally selling liquor, esp. during Prohibition in U.S. **speak´a·ble** *adj.*

speak·er (spē´ker) *n.* 1. One who speaks, esp. one who makes a speech. 2. **S~**, officer of U.S. House of Representatives chosen to preside over debates, preserve order, etc.; similar officer in other legislative bodies. 3. Loudspeaker (see LOUD).

speak·ing (spē´kĭng) *n.* (esp.) Speechmaking; ~ **part**, part in play etc. containing words to be spoken; ~ **terms**, degree of acquaintanceship allowing exchange of conversation (**not on ~ terms**, (usu.) estranged).

spear (spēr) *n.* Thrusting or hurling weapon with long shaft and sharp-pointed head, usu. of iron or steel; sharp-pointed and barbed instrument for catching fish etc.; ~ **grass**, grass with stiff pointed leaves; **spear´head**, (fig.) person(s) leading, anything in forefront of, attack; (*v.t.*) act as spearhead for; **spear´mint**, aromatic herb (*Mentha spicata*) used for flavoring. **spear** *v.t.* Pierce, strike, (as) with spear. **spear´er** *n.*

spec (spĕk) *n.* (colloq.) Speculation; **on ~**, experimentally, as a gamble; specification(s) (usu. pl.).

spe·cial (spĕsh´al) *adj.* Of a particular kind, peculiar, not general; for a particular purpose; exceptional in amount, degree,

kind, etc.; ~ **delivery**, delivery of mail in advance of regular delivery; ~ **handling**, processing as expeditiously as possible of fourth-class or parcel post mail. **spe´cial·ly** *adv.* In special manner, to special degree or extent; of special purpose, expressly. **special** *n.* Special radio or television program, train, edition of magazine, etc.

spe·cial·ist (spĕsh´alĭst) *n.* One who devotes himself to particular branch of profession, science, etc., esp. medicine.

spe·cial·ize (spĕsh´alīz) *v.* (**-ized, -iz·ing**). 1. Make specific or individual; modify, limit (idea, statement). 2. (biol.) Adapt (organ etc.) for particular purpose, differentiate; be differentiated, become individual in character. 3. Be, become, a specialist. **spe·cial·i·za·tion** (spĕshalīza´shon) *n.*

spe·cial·ty (spĕsh´altē) *n.* (pl. **-ties**). Special feature or characteristic; special pursuit, product, operation, etc., thing to which person gives special attention.

spe·cie (spē´shē) *n.* Coin, coined money. [L. *in specie* in kind]

spe·cies (spē´shēz) *n.* (pl. **-cies**). 1. (logic) Group subordinate to genus, containing individuals that

*The **Speaker** presides over debates in the United States House of Representatives. His responsibility is to ensure that rules are obeyed. Here Speaker, Tip O'Neil, sits beside Vice-President Walter Mondale as President Carter addresses Congress.*

have common attribute(s) and are called by a common name. 2. (biol.) Group of organisms that have certain characteristics not shared by other groups, usu. a group that is believed to be reproductively isolated, i.e. whose members will breed among themselves but not normally with members of other groups; subdivision of genus. 3. (loosely) Kind, sort.

spe·cif·ic (spĭsĭf´ĭk) *adj.* 1. Definite; distinctly formulated; precise, particular. 2. Of a species; possessing, concerned with, the properties characterizing a species. 3. (med., of remedies) Specially efficacious for a particular ailment etc.; (path.) characteristic. 4. ~ **gravity**: see GRAVITY; **specific heat**: see HEAT. **spe·cif´i·cal·ly** *adv.* **specific** *n.* Specific remedy. **spec·i·fic·i·ty** (spĕsĭfĭs´ĭtē) *n.*

spec·i·fi·ca·tion (spĕsĭfĭkā´shon) *n.* Specifying; specified detail, esp. detailed description of construction, workmanship, materials, etc., of work undertaken by engineer, architect, etc.; description by applicant for patent of nature, details, and use of invention.

spec·i·fy (spĕs´ĭfī) *v.t.* (**-fied, -fy·ing**). Name expressly, mention definitely; include in specification.

spec·i·men (spĕs´imen) *n.* Indi-

*The **spear** is a standard weapon carried by natives in Uganda and many other places. Broad-bladed spears are used to kill larger animals while the finer tips may be used for birds.*

vidual or part taken as example of class or whole, esp. serving as example of class or thing in question for purposes of investigation or scientific study; (med.) sample; (colloq.) person of a specified sort.

spe·cious (spē'sh*u*s) *adj.* Good in appearance but not in reality; plausible; fair or right only on the surface. **spe'cious·ly** *adv.* **spe'-cious·ness** *n.* **spe·ci·os·i·ty** (spē-shēŏs'ĭtē) *n.* (pl. **-ties**).

speck (spĕk) *n.* Small spot, dot, stain; particle (*of* dirt etc.); spot of rottenness in fruit. **speck'-less** *adj.* **speck** *v.t.* Mark with specks.

speck·le (spĕk'el) *n.* Small speck, mark, or stain. ~ *v.t.* (**-led, -ling**). Mark with speckles.

spec·ta·cle (spĕk'takel) *n.* 1. Public show, specially prepared or arranged display; object of public attention, curiosity, admiration, etc. 2. (**pair of**) ~**s**, eyeglasses. **spec'ta·cled** *adj.* Wearing spectacles; (of animals etc.) marked in way that suggests spectacles.

spec·tac·u·lar (spĕktăk'yuler) *adj.* Of, of the nature of, a spectacle or show; striking; imposing. **spec·tac'u·lar·ly** *adv.*

spec·ta·tor (spĕk'tāter, spĕktā'-) *n.* One who looks on, esp. at show, game, etc. **spec·ta·to·ri·al** (spĕk-tatŏr'ēal, -tŏr'-) *adj.*

spec·ter, Brit. **spec·tre** (spĕk'-ter) *ns.* Ghost, apparition.

spec·tral (spĕk'tral) *adj.* 1. Ghostly, of ghosts. 2. Of spectra or the spectrum.

spec·tre: SPECTER.

spec·tro·gram (spĕk'trogrăm) *n.* Record obtained with spectrograph.

spec·tro·graph (spĕk'trogrăf, -grahf) *n.* Instrument producing representation of a spectrum usu. on a screen or photographic plate. **spec·tro·graph·ic** (spĕktrogrăf'ĭk) *adj.* **spec·tro·graph'i·cal·ly** *adv.*

spec·trom·e·ter (spĕktrŏm'eter) *n.* Spectroscope that can be used for measurement of observed spectra. **spec·tro·met·ric** (spĕtro-mĕt'rĭk) *adj.*

spec·tro·scope (spĕk'troskōp) *n.* Optical instrument for producing and examining spectra. **spec·tro·scop·ic** (spĕktroskŏp'ĭk), **spec·tro·scop'i·cal** *adjs.* **spec·tro·scop'i·cal·ly** *adv.* **spec·tros·co·pist** (spĕktrŏs'kopĭst), **spec·tros'co·py** *ns.*

spec·trum (spĕk'trum) *n.* (pl. **-tra** pr. -tra, **-trums**). 1. Series of images formed when a beam of radiant energy is dispersed and then brought to focus, so that its component waves are arranged in order of wavelength; (esp.) colored band into which beam of light is decomposed by prism etc.; afterimage seen when eyes are turned away from bright-colored object etc.; ~

analysis, analysis, esp. chemical analysis, by means of spectra. 2. Range, series, of interrelated ideas or objects.

spec·u·lar: see SPECULUM.

spec·u·late (spĕk'yulāt) *v.i.* (**-lat·ed, -lat·ing**). 1. Engage in thought or reflection, esp. of confectural or theoretical kind (*on*). 2. Buy or sell commodities etc. in expectation of rise or fall in their market value; engage in commercial operation, make investment, involving risk of loss. **spec·u·la·tive** (spĕk'yulātĭv, -latĭv) *adj.* **spec'u·la·tive·ly** *adv.* **spec'u·la·tive·-ness, spec'u·la·tor** *ns.*

spec·u·la·tion (spĕkyulā'shon) *n.* 1. Meditation on, inquiry into, theory about, a subject. 2. Speculative investment or enterprise, practice of speculating, in business.

spec·u·lum (spĕk'yulum) *n.* (pl. **-la** pr. -la, **-lums**). 1. (surg.) Instrument for dilating cavities of human body for inspection. 2. Mirror, usu. of polished metal, esp.

*People who feel strongly about a topic often give a **speech**. Some do so in formal surroundings; others, like this 'soap-box orator' in Sydney, Australia, attract an audience with their rhetoric.*

in optical instruments; ~ **metal**, alloy of copper and tin taking high polish used as a reflector in telescopes. 3. Lustrous colored patch on wing of some birds. **spec·u·lar** (spĕk'yuler) *adj.*

sped (spĕd): see SPEED.

speech (spēch) *n.* Act, faculty, or manner of speaking; thing said, remark; public address; language, dialect; ~ **therapy**, remedial treatment of defective speech.

speech·i·fy (spē'chĭfī) *v.i.* (**-fied, -fy·ing**). (mildly contempt.) Make speeches, hold forth.

speech·less (spēch'lĭs) *adj.* Dumb; temporarily deprived of speech by emotion etc. **speech'-less·ly** *adv.* **speech'less·ness** *n.*

speed (spēd) *n.* 1. Rate at which something moves, travels, proceeds, or operates; rapidity; transmission gear of motor vehicle; (photog.) sensitivity of film etc. to light; length of exposure; (slang) stimulant drug, as amphetamine. 2. (archaic) Success, prosperity. 3. **speed'ball**, (slang) mixture of cocaine and heroin; **speed'boat**, motorboat etc. capable of very high speed; **speed limit**, maximum speed permitted on road, to vehicle etc.; **speed trap**, stretch of high-

A **speed-boat** designed for competition racing must have special lines and a very powerful motor. Other power boats, for big game fishing, are slower.

Speedwell or veronica is a herb found in northern Europe, Asia and North America whose leaves were used to make a decoction (or tea) said to provide relief from many ailments.

way where police monitor traffic speed to catch drivers who exceed the speed limit; **speed'way**, track for motor racing, road intended only for fast motor vehicles. **speed** v. (**sped** pr. spĕd or **speed·ed, speed·ing**). 1. Go fast; travel at excessive or illegal speed; (archaic) send fast, send on the way. 2. (archaic) Be, make, prosperous; succeed, give success to. 3. Regulate speed of (engine etc.), cause to go at fixed speed; ~ **up**, increase speed of, increase rate of work, production; ~**-up** (n.). **speed'er** n. **speed'ing** adj. & n.

speed·om·e·ter (spēdŏm´ĭter, spī-) n. Instrument for registering speed at which vehicle, esp. car, is moving.

speed·well (spēd´wĕl) n. Plant, flower, of genus Veronica, of small herbaceous plants with leafy stems and small usu. blue flowers.

speed·y (spē´dē) adj. (**speed'·er, speed·i·est**). Rapid, swift; prompt. **speed'i·ly** adv. **speed'·ness** n.

spe·le·ol·o·gy (spēlēŏl´ojē) n. Scientific study of caves. **spe·le·ol'o·gist** n.

spell¹ (spĕl) n. Words, formula, used as charm; incantation; attraction, fascination; **spell'binder**, (colloq.) political speaker who can hold audiences spellbound; **spell'·bound**, bound (as) by spell, fascinated, entranced.

spell² (spĕl) v. (**spelled** or **spelt** or. spĕlt, **spell·ing**). Name or write in order letters of (word etc.); form words etc. thus; (of letters) make

up, form (word); (fig.) signify, imply, involve; ~ **out**, make out (words etc.) laboriously letter by letter; state explicitly, explain in detail. **spell'ing** n. (esp.) ~ **bee**, competition in spelling.

spell³ (spĕl) n. Period of work, or of or at some occupation; short period. ~ v. (**spelled, spell·ing**). (Allow to) rest for short period.

spe·lun·ker (spĭlŭng´ker, spē´lŭng-) n. One who explores caves for sport. **spe·lunk'ing** n.

spend (spĕnd) v.t. (**spent, spend·ing**). Pay out (money) for a purchase etc., pay out money; use, use up, consume, exhaust, wear out; be consumed; live or stay through (period of time); **spend'thrift**, extravagant person, prodigal (freq. attrib. or as adjective). **spend'er** n.

Spen·ser (spĕn´ser), **Edmund** (c1552–99). English poet, author of The Faerie Queene etc. **Spen·se·ri·an** (spĕnsēr´ēan) adj. & n. Of Spenser; s~ **stanza**, stanza invented by Spenser, in which he wrote The Faerie Queene, consisting of eight 5-foot iambic lines, followed by an iambic line of 6 feet, rhyming a b a b b c b c c.

spent (spĕnt) adj.: see SPEND; (esp.) used up; exhausted.

sperm (spĕrm) n. 1. Male generative fluid, semen; (biol.) spermatozoon. 2. ~ **oil**, spermaceti; ~ **whale**, large whale (Physeter catodon) found in warm oceans, with large head cavity containing spermaceti.

sper·ma·ce·ti (spērmasĕt´ē,

-sē´tē) n. White soft scaly solid, a mixture of fatty esters, separating from oil found in head of sperm whale and other cetaceans, and used for ointments, candles, etc. [med. L. f. sperma seed, cetus whale (because it was thought to be whale spawn)]

sper·mat·ic (spērmăt´ĭk) adj. Of sperm or the organ that produces sperm, seminal; ~ **cord**, structure connecting testicles with seminal vesicles.

sper·mat·o·gen·e·sis (spērmăt·ojĕn´esĭs, -mato-) n. Development of spermatozoa. **sper·mat·o·ge·net·ic** (spērmatōjenĕt´ĭk, spērmă·tō-) adj.

sper·mat·o·phore (spērmăt´o·fōr, -fŏr, spēr´mato-) n. (zool.) Capsule formed by some animals containing compact mass of spermatozoa.

sper·mat·o·zo·on (spērmato·zō´on, -măto-) n.(pl. **-zo·a**). Minute active fertilizing cell of male organism.

spew, spue (spū) vbs. Vomit, eject.

sphag·num (sfăg´num) n. Moss of genus S~ growing in boggy and swampy places, used as packing for plants, surgical dressings, etc.

sphe·noid (sfē´noid) adj. Wedge-shaped; ~ **bone**, compound bone at base of skull. **sphenoid** n. (anat.) Sphenoid bone. **sphe·noi·dal** (sfĭnoi´dal) adj.

sphere (sfēr) n. 1. Body or space bounded by surface, every point of which is equidistant from a point within called the center; ball, globe; heavenly body; globe representing Earth or apparent heavens. 2. Any of the (orig. eight, later nine or ten) concentric transparent hollow globes formerly imagined as revolving with harmonious sound (**music of the ~s**) around Earth and carrying with them moon, sun, planets, and fixed stars; sphere occupied by particular planet, star, etc.; field of action, influence, or existence, natural surroundings, place in society. **sphere** v.t. (**sphered, spher·ing**). Enclose (as) in sphere; (poet.) exalt among the spheres, set aloft. **spher·ic** (sfĕr'ĭk) adj. (poet.) Of the heavens, exalted. **sphe·ric·i·ty** (sfĭrĭs'ĭtē) n.

spher·i·cal (sfĕr'ĭkal) adj. 1. Sphere-shaped, globular. 2. Of, concerned with properties of, spheres; (of lines etc.) described in, on surface of, sphere. **spher'i·cal·ly** adv.

spher·ics (sfĕr'ĭks) n. Spherical geometry and trigonometry.

sphe·roid (sfēr'oid) n. Sphere-like but not perfectly spherical body, esp. one generated by revolution of ellipse about one of its axes. **sphe·roi·dal** (sfĭroi'dal) adj.

sphinc·ter (sfĭngk'ter) n. Ring of muscle guarding or closing an orifice in the animal body, e.g. **anal, oral, pupillary,** ~; **cardiac** ~, sphincter guarding upper orifice of stomach.

sphinx (sfĭngks) n. (pl. **sphinx·es, sphin·ges** pr. sfĭn'jēz). 1. (Gk. myth.) Winged monster with woman's head and lion's body, which infested Thebes, killing all who could not answer the riddle it propounded, until the riddle was solved by OEDIPUS; (loosely) enigmatic or mysterious person. 2. Ancient Egyptian figure of a recumbent lion with the head of a man, ram, or hawk, esp. (**the S ~**)

the colossal fourth-Dynasty stone, one near the Pyramids at Giza; any similar figure. 3. (also **sphinx moth**) = HAWK[1] moth.

sphyg·mo·ma·nom·e·ter (sfĭg-mōmanŏm'ĭter), **sphyg·mom·e·ter** (sfĭgmŏm'ĭter) ns. Instrument recording graphically variations in arterial pressure.

Spi·ca (spī'ka) (pl. **-cas**). (astron.) Star of 1st magnitude in constellation Virgo.

spi·ca (spī'ka) n. (pl. **-cae** pr. -sē, **-cas**). (surg.) Form of spiral bandage with reversed turns, suggesting ear of wheat.

spi·cate (spī'kāt) adj. (bot., zool.) Pointed, spiked, spike-shaped.

spice (spīs) n. Any of various strong-flavored or aromatic vegetable substances obtained from tropical plants, as ginger, cinnamon, nutmeg, allspice, used to season or preserve food etc.; spices collectively; slight touch, trace, dash, of some quality etc.; **spice'-bush**, aromatic shrub (Lindera benzoin) of eastern N. Amer. with small yellow flowers and scarlet berries; aromatic shrub (Calycanthus occidentalis) of California, with fragrant light-brown flowers. ~ v.t. (**spiced, spic·ing**). Flavor or season with spice(s).

spick-and-span (spĭk'anspăn') adj. Smart and new; neat, trim. [extended f. ME. span-new (ON. spánn chip)]

spic·u·la (spĭk'yula) n. (pl. **-lae** pr. -lē). Spicule; prickle.

spic·ule (spĭk'ūl) n. Small, slender, pointed or needlelike process or formation; esp. (zool.) small hard calcareous or siliceous body

stiffening tissues of various inverte-brates, as sponges etc. **spic·u·la** (spĭk'yuler), **spic·u·late** (spĭk-yulāt, -lĭt) adjs.

spic·y (spī'sē) adj. (**spic·i·er, spic·i·est**). Of, flavored or fragrant with, spice; (fig.) pungent, sensational, scandalous, somewhat improper. **spic'i·ly** adv. **spic'i·ness** n.

spi·der (spī'der) n. 1. Eight-legged animal of order Araneida of arachnids, many species of which spin webs esp. for capture of insects as food; (loosely) spiderlike arachnid. 2. Frying pan, orig. one with legs or feet. 3. Part of machinery with radiating arms. ~ **crab**, crab of group Oxyrhyncha with long slender legs; **spider monkey**, tropical Amer. monkey of genus Ateles with long slender limbs and prehensile tail; **spi'der·wort**, plant of Amer. genus Tradescantia, with ephemeral white, pink or violet flowers and slender hairy stamens. **spi'der·y** adj. Spider-like, esp. long and slender like spider's legs; like cobweb.

spiel (spēl, shpēl) n. (slang) Talk, sales talk, speech, story (esp. glib or persuasive one). ~ v.i. Talk volubly. [Ger., = "game"]

spif·fy (spĭf'ē) adj. (**-fi·er, -fi·est**). (slang) Smart in dress; stylish; dapper. **spif'fi·ness** n.

spig·ot (spĭg'ot) n. Small peg or plug esp. for insertion into vent hole of cask; plain end of section of pipe fitting into socket of another; faucet.

spike (spīk) n. 1. Sharp point; pointed piece of metal, e.g. forming part of barrier, fixed in shoe sole to prevent slipping, etc.; (pl.) shoe

---

The great **Sphinx** at Giza, Egypt, was built to represent a guardian of the tombs of the ancient pharaohs. It is 239 ft. long and was probably built about 2,550 B.C.

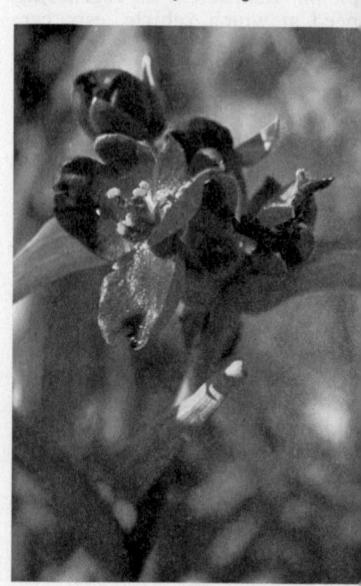

Spiderwort is one of 60 species of a herb native to the Americas. The genus, Tradescantia, was named after a gardener of Charles I who helped to finance the colony of Virginia.

*The pink crab **spider** (above) is usually colored so that it remains inconspicuous among the flowers used by it as a place for an ambush.*

Large, hairy theraphosid spiders are able to attack and kill small vertebrates. However, although their bite may hurt a human, it will not kill.

Originally from south-west Asia, spin-ach has been cultivated in most places where there is a temperate climate. It is sold fresh, canned, or deep-frozen.

1. cervical vertebrae
2. thoracic vertebrae
3. lumbar vertebrae
4. sacrum
5. coccyx
6. atlas
7. axis
8. body of vertebra
9. spine of vertebra
10. intervertebral disc
11. spinal cord
12. posterior root of spinal nerve
13. anterior root
14. foramen for vertebral artery
15. posterior root ganglion
16. grey matter
17. 18. 19. meninges

section of 5th cervical vertebra

SPINAL COLUMN

The spine or vertebral column consists of 26 small bones (vertebrae) in the human adult. This supports the body and also houses the spinal cord which is part of the central nervous system.

The spindle-tree, a member of the genus Euonymus, is native to Europe and northern Asia. Its berries were once used to produce a dye and oi from its seeds was used in soap-making.

fitted with spikes; high, tapering heel on woman's shoe; large stout nail. 2. (bot.) Inflorescence of sessile flowers on elongated simple axis. 3. Young mackerel under 6 in. long. **spik·y** *adj.* (**spik·i·er, spik·i·est**). **spike** *v.t.* (**spiked, spik·ing**). Furnish with spike(s); fix on, pierce, with spike(s); plug up vent of (gun) with spike; (fig.) make useless, put an end to (idea etc.); (colloq.) add alcohol to (drink).

spike·let (spīk′lĭt) *n.* (bot.) Small or secondary spike esp. as part of inflorescence of grasses etc.

spile (spīl) *n.* Wooden peg or plug, spigot; small spout for con-ducting sap from sugar maple etc. ~ *v.t.* (**spiled, spil·ing**). Provide (cask, tree, etc.) with spile.

spill¹ (spĭl) *n.* Thin strip of wood, folded or twisted piece of paper etc., for lighting candle, pipe, etc.

spill² (spĭl) *v.* (**spilled** or **spilt, spill·ing**). Allowing (liquid etc.) to fall or run out from vessel, esp. accidentally or wastefully, run out thus; shed (blood); empty (sail) of wind (naut.); cause to fall from horse or vehicle; **spill′way**, passageway for overflow of surplus water from reservoir etc. **spill** *n.* Throw or fall, esp. from horse or vehicle; tumble. **spill′a·ble** *adj.* **spill′age** *n.*

spin (spĭn) *v.* (**spun** pr. spŭn

or archaic **span** pr. spăn, **spin·-ning**). 1. Draw out and twist (wool, cotton, etc.) into threads, make (yarn) thus; be engaged in, follow, this occupation; (of insects) make (web, cocoon, etc.) by extrusion of fine viscous thread; (fig.) produce, compose (story etc.); ~ **out**, spend, consume (time etc.); prolong, extend. 2. Revolve; (of top etc.) whirl around; (of person or thing) turn *around* quickly, e.g. as result of being struck; (of person's head etc.) be in whirl through dizziness or astonishment; (aviation) make diving descent with continued rotation of aircraft; cause (minnow etc.) to revolve in water as bait for trout etc., fish thus. 3. ~ **off**, produce incidentally, esp. as benefit from industrial or technological development (**spin′off** *n.*). **spin** *n.* Spinning motion, esp. in rifle bullet, in tennis ball, etc., struck aslant, or in airplane in diving descent; brisk or short run, short excursion by automobile etc.; (phys.) intrinsic angular momentum of elementary particle. **spin′ner** *n.* **spin′ning** *n. & adj.*

spin·ach (spĭn′ĭch) *n.* Plant (*Spinacia oleracea*) with succulent leaves used as vegetable.

spi·nal (spī′nal) *adj.* Of the spine; ~ **anesthetic**, anesthetic that anesthetizes lower part of body when injected into spinal cord; ~ **canal**, channel formed by arches

of vertebrae, containing spinal cord; ~ **column**, spine; ~ **cord**, rope-like mass of nerve cells and nerve fibers enclosed within and pro-tected by spinal column, co-ordinating activities of limbs and trunk and transmitting impulse: between the brain and the tissue: of the body. **spi′nal·ly** *adv.*

spin·dle (spĭn′del) *n.* 1. Slende: rounded rod tapering at both ends used to twist fibers of wool, flax etc., into thread in spinning frame steel rod by which thread is twiste and wound on bobbin; varyin: measure of length for yarn. 2. Pin axis, that revolves or on which something revolves. 3. Anythin: spindle-shaped, esp. (biol.) spindle-shaped system of fibers formed during cell division, to which the chromosomes become attached. 4 **spin′dleshanks** (pl. **-shanks**) (person with) long thin legs **spindle tree**, ornamenta European shrub of genus *Euony-mus*, esp. *E. europaeus*, with har fine-grained yellowish woo formerly much used for spindles **spin′dling** *adj.* **spin′dly** *adj* (**-dli·er, -dli·est**). Very thin **spindle** *v.i.* (**-dled, -dling**) Have, grow into, long slender form

spine (spīn) *n.* 1. Invertebrates articulated series of vertebrae ex-tending from skull to the hips (an in some animals continued to form the tail) and forming the supporting axis of the body, backbone. 2. (bot.) Stiff sharp-pointed woody or hardened process, usu. a shoot; (anat.) sharp-pointed slender process of various bones; (zool.) thorn-like process or appendage in certain fishes, insects, etc., prickle of hedgehog, quill of porcupine, etc. 3. Ridge, sharp projection, of rock, ground, etc., resembling backbone. 4. Part of outer cover of book that protects and encloses the back.

spine·less (spīn'lĭs) *adj*. Invertebrate; having no spines; (fig.) limp, weak. **spine'less·ness** *n*.

spin·et (spĭn'ĭt, spĭnĕt') *n*. 1. (hist.) Small keyboard instrument (17th–18th c.) of harpsichord type but smaller, and with only one string to a note. 2. (also ~ **piano**): see PIANO. [prob. f. name of Giovanni *Spinetti* of Venice *c*1550)]

spin·na·ker (spĭn'aker) *n*. Large three-cornered sail carried on mainmast opposite mainsail of racing yacht running before wind. [fanciful formation f. *Sphinx*, name of yacht first using it]

spin·ner (spĭn'er) *n*. (esp.) Spinning machine; manufacturer engaged in (esp. cotton) spinning; kind of (artificial) trout fly, spinning bait.

spin·ner·et (spĭn'erĕt) *n*. 1.

(zool.) Organ or process, esp. nipple-like process on spider's abdomen, tubule on lower lip of silkworm, for producing silk, gossamer, etc. 2. Contrivance of glass or metal with fine holes through which viscous solution is forced, to form filaments or threads of synthetic fiber.

spin·ning (spĭn'ĭng) *n*. (esp.) ~ **jenny**, early spinning machine with several spindles; ~ **wheel**, simple spinning apparatus in which spindle is driven by wheel worked by hand or foot.

spi·nose (spī'nōs, spīnōs'), **spi·nous** (spī'nŭs) *adjs*. Armed or furnished with spines; slender and sharp-pointed like a spine.

Spi·no·za (spĭnō'za), **Baruch** (1632–77). (also known as Benedict de Spinoza) Dutch philosopher; exponent of pantheism; rejected Cartesian dualism and held God to be the immanent cause of the universe with an infinite number of attributes, of which only two, thought and extension, are known to man, all individual things being modes of these. **Spi·no'zism,**

Spi·no'zist *ns*.

spin·ster (spĭn'ster) *n*. Unmarried woman, usu. elderly. **spin'ster·hood** *n*.

spi·nule (spī'nūl, spĭn'ūl) *n*. (bot., zool.) Small spine. **spin·u·lose** (spĭn'yulōs, spī'nyu-) *adj*.

spin·y (spī'nē) *adj*. (**spin·i·er, spin·i·est**). Full of spines, prickly; (fig.) perplexing, troublesome, thorny; ~ **lobster**, any of several edible marine crustaceans (family Palinuridae), similar to true lobster but having spiny shell and lacking large pincers.

spi·ra·cle (spī'akel, spĭr'a-) *n*. (zool.) Orifice or pore that can be opened or closed for respiration in insects etc.; reduced first gill slit in fishes, blowhole of cetacean.

spi·rae·a: SPIREA.

spi·ral (spī'al) *adj*. Coiled in cylindrical or conical manner; curving continuously around fixed point in same plane at a steadily increasing (or diminishing) distance from it. **spi'ral·ly** *adv*. **spiral** *n*. Anything of spiral form; (geom. etc.) continuous curve traced by point moving around fixed point

wheel

maiden

flier

bobbin

mother-of-all

distaff

hackle

footman

spindle

treadle

yarn

in same plane at steadily increasing or diminishing distance; curve traced by point simultaneously moving around and advancing along cylinder or cone; spiral nebula; flight in spiral path; progressive but gradual rise or fall of two or more interdependent quantities alternately, as of wages or prices. ~ *v.i.* (**-raled, -ral·ing**; Brit. **-ralled, -ral·ling**). Wind or move in spiral path, (of aircraft, pilot) descend (or ascend) in spiral path.

spi·rant (spīr′ant) *adj.* & *n.* (phonet.) Fricative.

spire[1] (spīr) *n.* Tapering structure in form of tall cone or pyramid rising above tower, esp. of church; tapering or pointed top of anything. **spir′y** *adj.*

spire[2] (spīr) *n.* Spiral, coil; single fold or convolution of this.

spi·re·a, spi·rae·a (spīrē′a) *ns.* Rosaceous plant or shrub of genus S~, with simple leaves and small pink or white flowers in panicles, racemes, or corymbs.

spir·it (spĭr′ĭt) *n.* 1. Animating or vital principle, intelligent or immaterial part of man, soul; person

A stem of **spiraea** *in full blossom. The profuse blossoms, which range from white to deep red, are a desired feature of plants in this genus. Some may attain a height of ten feet.*

viewed as possessing this, esp. with ref. to particular mental or moral qualities; **the S~, the Holy ~** = HOLY GHOST. 2. Rational or intelligent being not connected with material body; disembodied soul; incorporeal being, ghost, elf, fairy. 3. Person's mental or moral nature or qualities; essential character or qualities, prevailing tone, general meaning, *of* something; mental or moral condition or attribute, mood; mettle, vigor, courage, energy, dash. 4. (chiefly Brit.) Strong alcoholic liquor got by distillation (usu. pl.); distilled extract, alcoholic solution *of* some substance; ~ **gum**, quick-drying gum used in fastening false hair, beard, etc., to actor's skin; ~ **level**, instrument for determining a true horizontal or vertical line or surface, usu. by centering an air bubble in a hermetically sealed glass tube filled with spirit. **spirit** *v.t.* Convey (*away, off,* etc.) rapidly and secretly (as) by agency of spirits.

spir·it·ed (spĭr′ĭtĭd) *adj.* 1. Full of spirit; animated, lively, brisk; courageous. 2. Having specified spirit(s). **spir′it·ed·ly** *adv.* **spir′-**

Below: The **spire** *of Chichester Cathedral and (top right) one at Stockbury in Kent, U.K. Below right: Several variations which show how this architectural device has been applied at different times.*

it·ed·ness *n.*

spir·it·ism (spĭr′ĭtĭzem) = SPIRITUALISM.

spir·it·less (spĭr′ĭtlĭs) *adj.* Wanting in ardor, animation, o courage. **spir′it·less·ly** *adv* **spir′it·less·ness** *n.*

spir·it·u·al (spĭr′ĭchŏoal) *adj.* Of spirit as opp. to matter; of th soul esp. as acted upon by God of, proceeding from, God, holy divine, inspired; concerned with sacred or religious things; ecclesi astical. **spir′it·u·al·ly** *adv.* **spir′it·u·al·ness** *n.* **spiritual** *n.* Reli gious song originating among o characteristic of blacks in southern U.S.

spir·it·u·al·ism (spĭr′ĭchŏoa lĭzem) *n.* Belief that spirits of dea can communicate with the living esp. through a medium; system o doctrines or practices founded on this. **spir′it·u·al·ist** *n.* **spir·it· u·al·is·tic** (spĭrĭchŏoalĭs′tĭk) *adj* **spir·it·u·al·is·ti·cal·ly** *adv.*

spir·it·u·al·i·ty (spĭrĭchŏoăl′ĭte *n.* (pl. **-ties**). 1. Spiritual quality 2. (usu. pl.) What belongs or is du to church or to an ecclesiastic a such.

spir·it·u·al·ize (spĭr′ĭchŏoalīz *v.t.* (**-ized, -iz·ing**). Mak spiritual.

spir·it·u·ous (spĭr′ĭchŏous) *adj* Containing much alcohol; ~ **liquor**, one produced by distilla

1 broach spire
2 lead spire on parapetted tower
3 stone spire of many storeys
4 flèche

tion, not by fermentation alone.

spi·ro·chete, spi·ro·chaete (spīr'ōkēt) *ns.* Any of various slender flexible microorganisms with spiral bodies, many of which cause diseases (esp. syphilis and yaws) in man.

spit[1] (spĭt) *n.* 1. Slender pointed rod thrust into meat for roasting at fire. 2. Small low point of land running into water. ~ *v.t.* (**spit·ted, spit·ting**). Pierce, transfix, (as) with spit.

spit[2] (spĭt) *v.* (**spit** or **spat** pr. spăt, **spit·ting**). Eject saliva; eject (saliva, food, etc., *out*) from mouth; (fig.) utter vehemently; (of cat etc.) make noise as of spitting as sign of anger or hostility; (of rain etc.) fall thinly; (of frying pan etc.) sputter; ~ **and image** (also **spitting image**), exact counterpart of, likeness of; **spit and polish**, neat and cleanness, as for military inspections; **spit'ball**, ball of chewed paper as missile; baseball moistened by pitcher to impart spin; **spit'fire**, fiery-tempered person, esp. woman. **spit** *n.* Spittle; act, instance, of spitting.

spite (spīt) *n.* Ill will, malice; **in ~ of**, notwithstanding. **spite'ful** *adj.* **spite'ful·ly** *adv.* **spite'ful·ness** *n.* **spite** *v.t.* (**spit·ed, spit·ing**). Thwart, mortify, annoy.

Spits·ber·gen (spĭts'bergen). Archipelago in the Arctic Ocean, N. of Norway, under Norwegian sovereignty.

spit·tle (spĭt'el) *n.* Saliva, spit.

spit·toon (spĭtoon') *n.* Receptacle for spittle.

splash (splăsh) *v.* Bespatter (*with* water etc.); dash, spatter (liquid); (of liquid) fly about in drops or scattered portions; cause liquid to do this; step, fall, etc., *into* (water etc.) so as to cause it to splash; mark, mottle, with irregular patches of color etc. **splash'down**, landing of spacecraft in sea. **splash'y** *adj.* (**splash·i·er, splash·i·est**). **splash** *n.* Act, result, or sound of splashing; quantity of fluid splashed; large irregular patch of color etc.; (colloq.) striking or ostentatious display or effect. **splash'er** *n.* **splash'i·ly** *adv.* **splash'i·ness** *n.*

splat·ter (splăt'er) *v.* & *n.* Splash, esp. with continuous and noisy action.

splay (splā) *n.* (archit.) Slope or bevel; embrasure. ~ *adj.* Wide and flat, spread or turned out; **splay'foot** (pl. **-feet**), (having) broad, flat clumsy foot turned outward. **splay** *v.* Bevel; construct (aperture) with divergent sides, be so constructed; spread out (limbs etc.) awkwardly.

spleen (splēn) *n.* Dark red abdominal organ (in mammals situated beneath diaphragm on left side) that is concerned in the

Those ferns given the common name **spleenwort** *are found in many parts of the world, but those in Europe were said to possess medicinal properties, beneficial to the spleen; hence the name.*

formation of antibodies and the destruction of red blood cells; this as the supposed seat of the passions; moroseness, irritability, spite; **spleen'wort**, fern of genus *Asplenium.* **spleen'ful, splen·ic** (splē'nĭk) *adjs.* **spleen'ful·ly** *adv.*

splen·dent (splĕn'dent) *adj.* Shining, bright, brilliant.

splen·did (splĕn'dĭd) *adj.* Mag-nificent, grand, sumptuous, brilliant, gorgeous; excellent, very good or fine. **splen'did·ly** *adv.*

splen·dif·er·ous (splĕndĭf'erus) *adj.* (colloq.) Magnificent, splendid.

splen·dor (splĕn'der) *n.* Great brightness; magnificence; parade, pomp, brilliance. **splen'dor·ous** *adj.*

sple·net·ic (splĭnĕt'ĭk), **sple·-net·i·cal** (splĭnĕt'ĭkal) *adjs.* Ill-tempered, peevish; of the spleen. **sple·net'i·cal·ly** *adv.* **splenetic** *n.* Splenetic person.

splice (splīs) *n.* Joining of two ends of rope etc. by untwisting and interweaving strands at point of junction; overlapping join of two pieces of wood etc. ~ *v.t.* (**spliced, splic·ing**). Join by splice; (colloq.) join in marriage. **splic'er** *n.*

spline (splīn) *n.* Thin strip of material inserted in grooves to join two boards etc.; one of a series of ridges on a shaft fitting into grooves of a hub to transmit torque. ~ *v.* Join by spline.

splint (splĭnt) *n.* Appliance to keep in position or protect injured part, esp. strip of more or less rigid material for holding fractured bone in position. ~ *v.t.* Put into splints, secure with splint(s).

splin·ter (splĭn'ter) *n.* Rough, sharp-edged, or thin piece of wood, bone, stone, etc., broken or split off; ~ **group, party,** (pol.) party (esp. one that is very small in numbers) that has broken away from a larger one. **splin'ter·y** *adj.* Like splinter(s); apt to splinter. **splinter** *v.* Split into splinters.

split (splĭt) *v.* (**split, split·ting**). Break forcibly, be broken, into parts, esp. with the grain or plane of cleavage; divide into parts, thicknesses, shares, etc.; divide into factions, groups, etc; ~ **hairs,** draw very subtle distinctions; ~ **the difference,** take average of two proposed amounts. **split** *adj.* (esp.) ~ **infinitive,** infinitive with adverb etc. inserted between *to* and verb, e.g. *seems to partly correspond*; ~ **-level,** (of building) having some room(s) part of a story higher than the adjacent part; ~ **personality,** alteration or dissociation of personality such as may occur in certain mental illnesses, esp. schizophrenia and hysteria; ~ **second,** very brief moment of time. **split** *n.* Act, result, of splitting; cleft; rupture; anything formed by splitting, as single thickness of split hide; half-bottle of mineral water; (pl.) in acrobatic dancing etc., movement in which body is lowered to floor

- short splice

eye splice -

- thimble eye

becket

The use of a **splice** *is to join two rope ends so that there is no great increase in size, or reduction in strength. It is particularly necessary where a rope has to pass over a pulley.*

between legs widely separated at right angles to trunk.

splotch (splŏch) *n.* Large irregular spot or patch; blot, smear. **splotch'y** *adj.* (**splotch·i·er, splotch·i·est**). **splotch** *v.t.* Cover or splash with splotches.

splurge (splẽrj) *n.* & *v.i.* (**splurged, splurg·ing**). (Make) lavish or showy expenditure. ~ *v.t.* Spend (money) lavishly.

splut·ter (splŭt´er) *v.* Utter, talk, hastily and indistinctly or confusedly; scatter or fly in small splashes or pieces; make sputtering sound. ~ *n.* Spluttering (noise); fuss.

Spode (spōd), **Josiah** (1754–1827). English china manufacturer; hence, china made by him.

spoil (spoil) *v.* (**spoiled** or **spoilt, spoil·ing**). 1. (archaic) Plunder, deprive (*of* thing) by force or stealth. 2. Destroy or impair good, valuable, or effective qualities of; prevent full exercise or enjoyment of; **spoil'sport**, one who spoils sport or enjoyment of others. 3. Injure character of (person) by overindulgence. 4. Deteriorate, decay, go bad. **spoil** *n.* (usu. pl. or collect. sing.) Plunder, booty, taken from enemy in war or acquired by violence; (pl.) public offices etc. distributed among supporters of successful political party; ~**s system**, practice of such distribution. **spoil'age, spoil'er** *ns.*

spoke[1] (spōk) *n.* Each of set of bars or rods radiating from hub to rim of wheel; each radial handle of steering wheel; rung of ladder; **spoke'shave**, tool with blade or plane bit between two handles used for planing curved surface, shaping spokes, etc. **spoke** *v.t.* (**spoked, spok·ing**). Furnish with spokes.

spoke[2] (spōk), **spo·ken**

The 'crumb of bread' **sponge**, commonly found as an encrustation on rocks between high and low tide levels, is small compared with others of the 2500 species.

(spō´ken): see SPEAK.

spokes·man (spōks´man), fem. **spokes·wom·an** (spōks´wŏoman) *ns.* (pl. **-men** pr. -men; fem. **-wom·en** pr. -wĭmĭn). One who speaks for others, representative.

spo·li·a·tion (spōlēā´shon) *n.* 1. Despoiling, plundering, pillaging. 2. (law) Destruction of, tampering with, document to destroy its value as evidence.

spon·da·ic (spŏndā´ĭk), **spon·da·i·cal** (spŏndā´ĭkal) *adjs.* Composed of spondees; (of hexameter) with spondee as fifth foot.

spon·dee (spŏn´dē) *n.* (pros.) Metrical foot of two long or accented syllables, ——.

sponge (spŭnj) *n.* 1. Any of various aquatic (chiefly marine) animals of the group Porifera, with tough elastic skeleton of interlacing fibers. 2. Soft, light, porous, easily compressible, highly absorbent framework remaining after living matter has been removed from various members of this group, used in bathing, cleansing surfaces, etc.; porous rubber etc. used similarly. 3. Thing of spongelike absorbency or consistence; gauze pad to absorb fluid in surgery; soft porous leavened dough in baking. 4. Immoderate drinker, soaker; person who contrives to live at others' expense. 5. Sponging; bath, swill, with sponge. 6. ~ **cake**, very light sweet cake of flour, beaten eggs, and sugar; ~ **cloth**, loose-textured cotton fabric with wrinkled surface; ~ **rubber**, rubber made porous like a sponge. **sponge** *v.* (**sponged, spong·ing**). 1. Wipe, cleanse, with sponge, wet with liquid applied with sponge; wipe out, efface, (as) with sponge; absorb, take *up* (liquid) with sponge. 2. Live on others as parasite, be meanly dependent *on* (esp. ~ **on** person *for* money etc.).

spong·er (spŭn´jer) *n.* (esp.) One who sponges for money etc.

spon·gy (spŭn´jē) *adj.* (**-gi·er, -gi·est**). Spongelike; esp. porous, compressible, absorbent, or soft, as sponge.

spon·son (spŏn´son) *n.* Projection from ship's side, as gun platform; buoyant projection from side of canoe, seaplane, etc.

spon·sor (spŏn´ser) *n.* Person making himself responsible for another; person who present

Josiah Spode introduced bone into the manufacture of porcelain and this gave it added transparency and beauty. The cup and saucer (left) were made by his firm about 1815.

candidate for baptism and makes promises on behalf of infant being baptized, godparent; supporter; advertiser paying cost of broadcast program into which advertisements of his wares are introduced; person subscribing to charity. **spon·so·ri·al** (spŏnsōr´ēal, -sōr´-) *adj*. **spon'sor·ship** *n*. **sponsor** *v.t*. Act as sponsor for; support, advocate.

spon·ta·ne·ous (spŏntā´nēus) *adj*. Acting, done, occurring, without external cause; voluntary; (of movements etc.) involuntary, not due to conscious volition; ~ **combustion**, ignition of mass of material (e.g. straw) from heat generated within itself; ~ **generation**, abiogenesis, development of living organisms from nonliving matter. **spon·ta´ne·ous·ly** *adv*. **spon·ta´ne·ous·ness** *n*. **spon·ta·ne·i·ty** (spŏntanē´ĭtē, -nā´-) *n*. (pl. **-ties**).

spoof (spoof) *n. & v.t*. Swindle, hoax, parody.

spook (spook) *n.* (colloq.) Ghost. **spook'y** *adj*. (**spook·i·er, spook·i·est**).

spool (spool) *n*. Reel for winding thread, wire, photographic film,

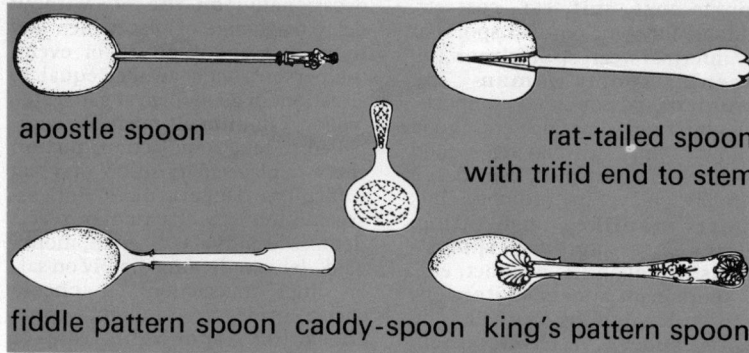

apostle spoon

rat-tailed spoon with trifid end to stem

fiddle pattern spoon   caddy-spoon   king's pattern spoon

fishing line, etc., on. ~ *v.t.* Wind on spool.

spoon (spoon) *n*. Utensil consisting of round or usu. oval bowl and a handle, used for conveying soft or liquid food to mouth, in cooking, etc.; spoon-shaped thing, esp. wooden golf club with slightly concave face; kind of artificial bait used in spinning for fish; **spoon'bill**, any of various wading birds, esp. roseate spoonbill (*Ajaja ajaja*), related to ibises, with long bill expanded and flattened at tip; **spoon'bread**, kind of bread, usu. of corn meal, so soft that it must

be served with spoon; **spoon'fed**, fed with spoon like child; (fig.) pampered, coddled. **spoon** *v.* 1. Take, lift, etc., with spoon. 2. Behave amorously, make love, esp. in sentimental fashion. **spoon'ful** *n*. (pl. **-fuls**).

spoon·er·ism (spoo´nerĭzem) *n*. Accidental transposition of initial or other sounds of two or more words (e.g. *kingquering congs*, for *conquering kings*). [Rev. W. A. *Spooner* (1844–1930), Warden of New College, Oxford]

spoor (spoor, spōr, spôr) *n*. Track, trail, of animal or person. ~ *v.t.* Trace by spoor.

spo·rad·ic (sporăd´ĭk) *adj*. Occurring in isolated instances or very small numbers; scattered, dispersed; occasional. **spo·rad'i·cal·ly** *adv*. **spo·rad'i·cal·ness** *n*.

spo·ran·gi·um (sporăn´jēum) *n*. (pl. **-gi·a** pr. -jēa). (bot.) Receptacle containing spores.

spore (spōr, spôr) *n*. Minute reproductive body produced by plants and some protozoa and capable of development into new individuals independently; ~ **case**, sporangium.

sport (spōrt, spôrt) *n.* 1. Amusement, diversion, fun; jest, mockery (as in *make ~ of*); plaything, toy; pastime(s), game(s), esp. of athletic or open-air character; pastime afforded by taking or killing wild animals, game, or fish; (pl.) (meeting for competition in) athletic pastimes. 2. Animal, plant, etc., exhibiting abnormal variation from parent stock or type. 3. (slang) Good fellow; playboy; sportsman. 4. ~**s car, model**, etc., car of open low-built fast type; **sports'cast**, radio or television broadcast of sports news. **sports'caster** *n*.;

uropean spoonbill

roseate spoonbill

sports-coat, suit, etc., coat etc. suitable for some outdoor sports or for informal wear; **sports'man** (pl. **-men**), **sports'woman** (pl. **-women**), person fond of sports, esp. hunting, shooting, etc.; good fellow; one displaying good qualities of sportsman, esp. desire for fair play, in ordinary life; **sports'manlike**, benefitting, worthy of, a sportsman: **sports'manship**, qualities, conduct, etc., of sportsman; **sports'writer**, one who writes (esp. as journalist) on sports. **sport** v. I. Divert oneself; take part in pastime. 2. (bot. etc.) Become, produce, a sport. 3. Wear, exhibit, produce, esp. ostentatiously.

sport·ing (spor'ting, spor'-) adj. Interested in sport; sportsmanlike; ~ **chance**, one involving risk but offering possibility of success. **sport'ing·ly** adv.

spor·tive (spor'tiv, spor'-) adj. Playful. **spor'tive·ly** adv. **spor'tive·ness** n.

sport·y (spor'te, spor'-) adj. (**sport·i·er, sport·i·est**). (slang) Sporting; characteristic of a sport, showy.

spor·ule (spor'ul, spor'-) n. (Small) spore. **spor·u·lar** (spor'yuler, spar'-) adj.

spot (spot) n. I. Speck, stain, small discoloring or disfiguring mark; eruptive mark on skin, pimple; dark mark on sun etc.; small, usu. roundish mark on surface; moral blemish, stain; (billiards) marked place on table, esp. that on which red ball is placed; **hit the** ~, (colloq.) satisfy a desire or need; **in a** ~ (slang) in difficulties, in an awkward situation; **in** ~**s**, now and then, off and on,

occasionally; **on the** ~, without delay or change of place, then and there, at scene of action or event; (of person) wide awake, equal to situation, in good form at game etc.; (colloq.) in difficult position, compelled to take some action; **put on the** ~, place in position of great difficulty, danger; mark for assassination. 2. Particular place, definite locality. 3. ~ **cash**, money paid, delivered, immediately on sale or other transaction; ~ **check**, check made at random; **spot-check**, (v.t.); **spot'light**, (lamp or projector throwing) concentrated beam of light on one spot, esp. of stage (freq. fig.); (v.t.) illuminate (as) with spotlight, throw into relief, concentrate attention etc. on. **spot'ty** (**-ti·er, -ti·est**), **spot'less** adjs. **spot'less·ly** adv. **spot'ti·ness, spot'less·ness** ns. **spot** v. (**spot·ted, spot·ting**). I. Mark, stain, soil, with spots; (of textile etc.) be (liable to be) marked with spots. 2. (colloq.) Single out, detect, mark out, note; esp. single out (winner in race etc.) beforehand. 3. Act as spotter.

spot·ted (spot'id) adj. (esp.) Marked with spots (freq. in names of animals etc.); **Rocky Mountain** ~ **fever**: see RICKETTSIA.

spot·ter (spot'er) n. (esp.) Watcher on roof, observer in aircraft, etc., noting approach or position of enemy forces, effect of gunfire or bombing, etc.

spous·al (spow'zal) n. (usu. pl.) Nuptials, wedding.

spouse (spows, spowz) n. Husband or wife.

spout (spowt) n. Projecting tube, pipe, or lip, through which rain water is carried off from roof, liquid

is poured from teapot, kettle, etc., or issues from fountain, pump, etc.; jet, column, of liquid, etc.; whale's spiracle; sloping trough down which thing may be shot into receptacle. ~ v. Discharge, issue, forcibly in a jet; utter in declamatory manner, speechify.

S.P.Q.R., SPQR abbrevs. *Senatus Populusque Romanus* (L. = the senate and people of Rome).

sprain (spran) v.t. Wrench (joint of body, esp. ankle or wrist) violently so as to cause pain and swelling. ~ n. Act, result, of spraining.

sprang: see SPRING.

sprat (sprat) n. Small European herring (*clupea sprattus*), common on Atlantic coasts; any similar fish.

sprawl (sprawl) v. Spread oneself, spread (limbs), out in careless or ungainly way; straggle. ~ n. Sprawling movement or attitude; straggling group or mass. **sprawl'er** n.

spray[1] (spra) n. Slender shoot or twig, graceful branch with flowers etc., esp. used for decoration or ornament.

spray[2] (spra) n. Water or other liquid dispersed in small mistlike drops by wind, waves, atomizer, etc.; preparation intended for spraying; instrument or apparatus for applying spray. ~ v. Scatter, diffuse, as spray; sprinkle (as) with spray.

spread (spred) v. (**spread, spread·ing**). Extend surface of, stretch out, cause to cover larger surface, by unrolling, unfolding, smearing, flattening out, etc.; cover surface of; show extended or extensive surface; diffuse, be diffused; prepare (table) for eating. ~ adj. (esp.) ~ **eagle**, representation of eagle with legs and wings extended; something resembling this; ~**- eagle** (v.t.) (**-gled, -gling**), extend, fix, in form of spread eagle; (attrib., in allusion to figure of spread eagle on U.S. emblems etc.) bombastic, noisily patriotic, jingoistic. **spread** n. Spreading; being spread; extent or expanse, breadth, compass, span; cloth cover for bed or table; (colloq.) feast, meal; food to be spread on bread or crackers; printed matter spread across two facing pages or across more than one column. **spread'a·ble** adj. **spread'er** n.

Facing: Children specially garbed for the **Spring** *Festival in Japan. Throughout the world, spring has epitomized the reawakening of life and has been a time for celebration in many ways.*

During the bull games in Minoan Crete, as shown in this fresco from the Palace at Knossos, both boys and girls would grasp the bull's horns as it charged and **spring** *into the air to complete a somersault before landing.*

spree (sprē) *n.* Lively frolic, bout of drinking, etc.

sprig (sprĭg) *n.* 1. Small branch, spray; ornament in form of sprig or spray. 2. (usu. contempt.) Youth, young man. ~ *v.t.* (**sprigged, sprig·ging**). Ornament with sprigs.

spright·ly (sprīt′lē) *adj.* Vivacious, lively, gay. **spright′li·ness** *n.*

spring (sprĭng) *v.* (**sprang** pr. sprăng or **sprung** pr. sprŭng, **sprung, spring·ing**). 1. Leap, jump, move rapidly or suddenly, esp. from constrained position or by action of a spring; arise, take rise; originate; (of wood) warp, split, crack. 2. Rouse (game) from earth or cover; cause to spring, move suddenly, etc.; cause to work by a spring; produce, develop, suddenly or unexpectedly; explode (mine etc.); develop (leak); (slang) contrive the escape of (person from confinement etc.). ~ *n.* 1. Leap; power of springing, elasticity, springiness; place from which vault or arch springs or rises. 2. Elastic contrivance possessing property of returning to normal shape after being compressed, bent, coiled, etc., used for lessening or preventing concussion, as motivating power in clockwork etc.; moving or actuating agency, motive; source, origin. 3. Place where water wells up from underground rocks; flow of water etc. rising from earth. 4. Season between winter and summer, season in which vegetation begins, popularly reckoned in N. hemisphere as comprising March, April, and May, but astronomically as lasting from vernal equinox (March 20 or 21) to summer solstice (June 21 or 22). 5. ~ **balance**, balance measuring weight by elasticity of steel spring; ~ **beauty**, any of a genus (*Claytonia*) of small plants, esp. *C. virginica* of eastern N. Amer. having white or pink flowers; **spring′board**, flexible board, esp. stout projecting board from end of which person jumps or dives; **spring fever**, feeling of laziness affecting many people during first warm days of spring; **spring lock**, lock with bolt closing by means of spring; **spring peeper**: see PEEPER[1]; **spring′tail**, wingless insect of the order Collembola, leaping by means of long elastic caudal appendages; **spring tide**, highest tide, occurring on days shortly after new and full moon; **spring′tide, spring′time**, season of spring; **spring water**, water from spring. **spring′less, spring′like** *adjs.* **spring′y** *adj.* (**spring·i·er, spring·i·est**). **spring′i·ness** *n.*

spring·bok (sprĭng′bŏk) *n.* (pl. **-boks**, collect. **-bok**). S. African species of gazelle (*Antidorcas*

marsupialis), springing lightly and suddenly in air when disturbed. [S. Afr. Du., f. *springen* spring, *bok* antelope]

spring·er (sprĭng′er) *n.* (esp.) 1. (archit.) Support from which arch springs. 2. ~ (**spaniel**), medium-sized hunting dog with black and white or brown and white silky coat.

Spring·field (sprĭng′fēld). Capital of Illinois, in the central part; home and burial place of Abraham Lincoln.

sprin·kle (sprĭng′kel) *v.* (**-kled, -kling**). Scatter in small drops or particles; subject to sprinkling (*with* liquid etc.); (of liquid etc.) fall thus on. **sprin′kler** *n.* Contrivance for sprinkling (water on soil etc.); ~ **system** (system of sprinkling devices for fire protection, actuated by heat on the sprinkler head). **sprinkle** *n.* Slight shower (*of* rain etc.). **sprin′kling** *n.*

sprint (sprĭnt) *v.i.* Run etc. at top speed, esp. for short distance. ~ *n.* Short spell of sprinting; short race run at full speed over whole distance. **sprint′er** *n.*

sprit (sprĭt) *n.* 1. Small spar reaching diagonally from mast to upper outer corner of sail; **sprit-sail** (sprĭt′sāl; *naut.* sprĭt′sal). 1. Sail extended by sprit. 2. = BOWSPRIT.

sprite (sprīt) *n.* Elf, fairy, goblin.

sprock·et (sprŏk′ĭt) *n.* Projec-

The **springbok**, a white-faced gazelle, was once abundant in South Africa; but excessive hunting and use of land for agriculture has driven the remaining flocks into the Kalahari Desert.

tion or tooth on rim of wheel engaging with links of chain; ~ **wheel**, wheel with sprockets.

sprout (sprowt) *v.* Begin to grow, shoot forth, put forth shoots; spring up, grow to a height; produce by sprouting. ~ *n.* Shoot, new growth, from plant; (pl.) young and tender side shoots of plants like cabbage, Brussels sprouts.

spruce[1] (sprōos) *n.* Any of several coniferous evergreen trees (genus *Picea*), having short needle-like leaves and soft wood; any of various similar evergreen trees, or Douglas fir and wood of these; ~ **beer**, fermented drink made from leaves and small branches of spruce.

spruce[2] (sprōos) *adj.* (**spruc·er, spruc·est**). Trim, neat, smart in appearance. **spruce′ly** *adv.* **spruce′ness** *n.* **spruce** *v.t.* (**spruced, spruc·ing**). Smarten (*up*), make spruce.

sprue (sprōo) *n.* Tropical disease with chronic diarrhea and ulceration of mouth. [Du. *spr(o)uw* THRUSH[2]]

sprung (sprŭng) *adj.*: see SPRING; (esp.) 1. Furnished with springs. 2. ~ **rhythm**, verse rhythm invented by G. M. HOPKINS[2] in which each foot consists of a stressed first syllable followed by a varying number of unstressed syllables.

spry (sprī) *adj.* (**spri·er, spri·est** or **spry·er, spry·est**). Active, nimble, lively. **spry′ly** *adv.* **spry′ness** *n.*

spud (spŭd) *n.* 1. Small sharp narrow spade, occas. with prongs instead of blade, for digging up big-rooted weeds etc. 2. (colloq.) Potato. ~ *v.t.* (**spud·ded, spud·ding**). Dig (*up, out*) with spud.

spue: SPEW.

spume (spūm) *n.* & *v.i.* (**spumed, spum·ing**). Froth, foam. **spu′mous** *adj.* **spum′y** *adj.* (**spum·i·er, spum·i·est**).

spu·mes·cence (spūmĕs′ens) *n.* Foaminess.

spu·mo·ne (spumō′nē, -nā), **spu·mo·ni** (spumō′nē) *ns.* Italian frozen dessert of different kinds of ice cream with bits of candied fruit, nuts, etc.

spun (spŭn) *adj.*: see SPIN; (esp.) that has undergone spinning; (of butter, sugar, etc.) drawn out into threads for ornamenting cakes etc.; ~ **glass**, glass drawn into thread while liquid; ~ **silk**, thread or fabric made from floss or waste silk, freq. mixed with cotton; ~ **sugar**, confection of sugar in a fluffy mass, also called cotton candy.

spunk (spŭngk) *n.* Spirit, mettle, pluck. **spunk′y** *adj.* (**spunk·i·er, spunk·i·est**). **spunk′i·ness** *n.* [orig., "spark"]

spur (sper) *n.* 1. Small spike or spiked wheel attached to rider's heel

Despite its name, spurge laurel (above) is not a herb but is a variety of Daphne. This plant is native to Britain and Europe but others are found in China.

Sun spurge (far left) and wood spurge (left) are two English varieties of a widespread group of herbs. Their milky sap has been used for such diverse products as rat poison, and a cosmetic.

for urging horse etc. forward; (fig.) incentive, stimulus; **on the ~ of the moment**, without premeditation; **win one's ~s**, gain knighthood (hist.); gain distinction, make a name. 2. Spur-shaped thing; hard process or projection on cock's leg, steel point fastened to this in cockfight; range, ridge, mountain, etc., projecting from main system or mass; short branch or shoot, esp. one bearing fruit; (bot.) tubular projecting part, usu. nectary, of corolla or calyx; short track connecting with main railroad (**spur track**). **spur** v. (**spurred, spur- -ing**). Prick (horse) with spurs; incite, urge, prompt; provide with spur(s); ride hard, hasten.

spurge (spẽrj) n. Plant of genus Euphorbia, with acrid milky juice with medicinal properties; ~ **laurel**, shrub of European and Asiatic genus Daphne.

spu·ri·ous (spūr'ẽus) adj. Not genuine or authentic; not what it appears, claims, or pretends to be. **spu'ri·ous·ly** adv. **spu'ri·ous- ness** n.

spurn (spẽrn) v. Repel, thrust back, with foot; reject with disdain, treat with contempt.

spurt[1] (spẽrt) v.i. & n. (Make) short sudden violent effort, esp. in racing.

spurt[2] (spẽrt) v. (Cause to) gush out in a jet or stream. ~ n. Sudden gushing out, jet.

sput·nik (spoot'nĭk, spŭt'-) n. Russian earth SATELLITE. [Russ., = 'traveling companion']

sput·ter (spŭt'ẽr) v. Emit with spitting sound; spit, splutter; speak, utter, rapidly or incoherently; speak in rapid or vehement fashion. ~

n. Sputtering; sputtering speech. **sput'ter·er** n.

spu·tum (spū'tum) n. (pl. **-ta** pr. -ta). Expectorated saliva, spittle; thick expectorated matter, mucus, etc.

spy (spī) n. (pl. **spies**). Secret agent, one keeping secret watch on person, place, etc.; person employed by a government, esp. in time of war, to obtain information relating to defenses, military and naval affairs, etc., of other countries. ~ v. (**spied, spy·ing**). 1. Act as spy (on, upon). 2. Discern, make out, esp. by careful observation; ~ **out**, explore secretly, discover thus; **spyglass**, small hand telescope.

sq. abbrev. Square; squadron.

squab (skwŏb) n. Young, esp. unfledged, pigeon; short fat person; thickly stuffed cushion. ~ adj. Short and fat, squat. **squab'by** adj. (**-bi·er, -bi·est**).

squab·ble (skwŏb'el) v.i. (**-bled, -bling**) & n. (Engage in) petty or noisy quarrel.

squad (skwŏd) n. (mil.) Small number of men grouped or assembled for drill etc.; small party of persons; ~ **car**, police car having radio link with headquarters; **flying ~**, detachment of police or other service organized for rapid movement in emergency.

squad·ron (skwŏd'ron) n. 1. Group of naval vessels usu. of same type, esp. naval unit of two or more divisions. 2. Cavalry unit of two to four troops and certain auxiliary units. 3. (Air Force) Unit of two or more flights, usu. part of an air group; at least six aircraft in formation. 4. Any large organized

group.

squal·id (skwŏl'ĭd, skwaw'lĭd) adj. Dirty, foul, wretched, mean in appearance. **squal'id·ly** adv. **squal'id·ness** n.

squall (skwawl) n. 1. Sudden violent gust (of wind, rain, etc.). 2. Discordant cry, scream. **squall'y** adj. (**-li·er, -li·est**). **squall** v. Scream loudly or discordantly; utter in harsh or screaming voice.

squal·or (skwŏl'er, skwaw'ler) n. Squalid condition.

squa·ma (skwā'ma) n. (pl. **-mae** pr. -mē). (zool., anat., bot., etc.) Scale; scalelike portion of bone etc. **squa·mose** (skwā'mōs, skwamōs'), **squa'mous** adjs.

squan·der (skwŏn'der) v.t. Spend wastefully, dissipate.

square (skwãr) n. 1. Plane rectilinear rectangular figure with four equal sides; object (approximately) of this shape; quadrilateral area, open space, esp. enclosed by buildings or houses, buildings surrounding this; block (of buildings), area, surrounded by streets; **on the ~**, at right angles; honest, genuine. 2. Instrument for determining, measuring, or setting out angles. 3. Product of number or quantity multiplied by itself. 4. (slang) Person of conservative or conventional tastes etc., one ignorant of or disliking current trends. **square** adj. (**squar·er, squar·est**). 1. Of the (approximate) shape of a square; rectangular; angular, not round; approximating to square section or outline, solid, sturdy; of stated length on each of four sides forming square; ~ **foot, meter**, etc. (area equal to that of) square whose side is a foot, meter, etc.; ~ **knot**, double knot with free ends paralleling standing parts; ~ **measure**, measure expressed in such units; ~ **root**, number or quantity that, when multiplied by itself, produces given number or quantity. 2. Properly arranged, in good order, on a proper footing; fair, honest; thorough, un-compromising; (of meal) solid, substantial. 3. (slang) Of conservative or conventional tastes etc. 4. ~ **dance**, one in which four couples face inward from four sides; (loosely) country dance; ~ **peg** (**in a round hole**), person unsuited to his job; ~ **-rigged**, having principal sails extended by horizontal yards slung to mast by middle; ~ **sail**, four-sided sail set from yards and slung at right angles to the mast. **square′ly** adv. **square′ness** n. **squar′ish** adj. **square** adv. Squarely. ~ v. (**squared, squar-ing**). I. Make square or rectangular; mark (out) in squares; multiply (number, quantity) by itself; ~ **the circle**, construct square equal in area to given circle (problem incapable of purely geometrical solution); freq. fig., attempt an impossibility. 2. Adjust, make or be consistent (with), reconcile; settle (accounts etc.), also (abs.) ~ **up**; conciliate or satisfy (person) esp. with bribe or compensation. 3. ~ **off**, assume boxing attitude.

squar′rose (skwăr′ōs, skwŏrōs′) adj. (biol.) Rough with scalelike processes.

squash[1] (skwŏsh) v. Crush, squeeze flat or into pulp; be so crushed or squeezed; pack tight, crowd; (fig.) silence (person) with crushing retort. **squash′y** adj. (**squash·i·er, squash·i·est**). **squash′i·ness** n. **squash** n. I. Squashing; something squashed or crushed; crush, crowd; drink made of juice of crushed fruit, freq. in compounds as lemon ~. 2. (also **squash rackets, racquets**): see RACQUET.

squash[2] (skwŏsh) n. (Gourd, used as vegetable etc., of) species of *Cucurbita*, genus of trailing herbaceous annual plants. [Amer. Ind. *askútasquash*]

squat (skwŏt) v. (**squat·ted, squat·ting**). I. Sit with knees drawn up and heels close to or touching hams; crouch; put into this position; (colloq.) sit. 2. Settle on or in uncultivated or unoccupied land, building, etc., without legal title or payment of rent. ~ adj. In squatting posture; short and thick, dumpy. ~ n. Squatting posture. **squat′ness** n.

squat·ter (skwŏt′er) n. Person who settles on land or occupies a building, without right or per-

*Bulbous plants known as **squill**, in the genus Scilla, may be found in Europe, Asia, and South Africa. In pharmacy, the dried bulb of an Indian variety was used as a drug.*

mission.

squaw (skwaw) n. (usu. considered offensive) N. Amer. Ind. woman or wife. [Amer. Ind.]

squawk (skwawk) v.i. & n. (Utter) harsh cry of pain or fear; (make) complaint.

squeak (skwēk) v. I. Emit short, shrill, thin sound; utter in squeaking voice. 2. ~ **by, through**, (colloq.) succeed, win, survive, etc. by slim margin. **squeak** n. Short, thin high-pitched sound; **narrow** ~, narrow escape. **squeak′er** n. I. Person, animal, or thing that squeaks. 2. (colloq.) Game won by narrow margin. **squeak′i·ly** adv. **squeak′y** adj. (**squeak·i·er, squeak·i·est**).

squeal (skwēl) v. I. Utter, emit, more or less prolonged loud shrill noise, esp. of pain or fright; utter with this sound. 2. (slang) Turn informer. ~ n. Sharp shrill sound. **squeal′er** n.

squeam·ish (skwē′mĭsh) adj. Fastidious; easily shocked; of delicate stomach or conscience. **squeam′ish·ly** adv. **squeam′-ish·ness** n.

squee·gee (skwē′jē) n. Implement with rubber blade or roller for scraping, cleaning, squeezing away moisture, etc. ~ v.t. (**-geed, -gee·ing**). Treat with squeegee.

squeeze (skwēz) v. (**squeezed, squeez·ing**). Press, compress hard, esp. so as to crush, drain liquid from, etc.; force by pressure, press out; force one's way; extort money etc. from; bring pressure to bear on, constrain; obtain (money etc.) *from, out of*, by extortion or pressure; take impression of (coin etc.), esp. with sheets of damp

paper. ~ n. Application of pressure; crowd, crush; impression of coin etc.; **put the ~ on**, (colloq.) use forceful methods to secure payment; ~ **bottle**, flexible container whose contents are extracted by squeezing; ~ **play**, (bridge) play in which winning cards are led until opponent is forced to discard important card; (baseball) play in which ball is bunted and runner on third base starts for home as soon as ball is pitched.

squeez·er (skwē′zer) n. (esp.) Device for expressing juice from lemon and other fruits.

squelch (skwělch) v. Fall, stamp on (something soft), with crushing or squashing force; crush; walk heavily in water or wet ground, make sound (as) of this; (colloq.) silence, disconcert, as with sarcasm, stern rebuke, harsh retort, etc. ~ n. (Sound of) squelching; (colloq.) act of silencing with rebuke etc. **squelch′er** n.

squib (skwĭb) n. I. Firework burning with hissing sound and usu. with small explosion at end. 2. Short satirical composition, lampoon.

squid (skwĭd) n. (pl. **squids**, collect. **squid**). Any of various 10-armed cephalopod mollusks, esp. of genus *Loligo* or *Ommastrephes*, some of which are used for food and as fish bait.

squig·gle (skwĭg′el) n. Curly mark. ~ v. (**-gled, -gling**). **squig′gly** adj.

squill (skwĭl) n. Any of several bulbous perennial plants (genus *Scilla*), having stiff, narrow leaves and blue, white, or pink bell-shaped drooping flowers.

squint (skwĭnt) n. Strabismus, abnormality of the eyes in which the visual axes do not coincide at the objective; stealthy or sidelong glance; (colloq.) glance, look. ~ adj. Squinting, looking different ways. ~ v. Have the eyes turned in different directions, have strabismus; look obliquely at; give cast to (eye), cause to look as though squinting. **squint′er** n. **squint′y** adj.

squire (skwīr) n. I. Attendant on knight (hist.); follower; man escorting or attending on lady. 2. Country gentleman, esp. chief landed proprietor in district. ~ v.t. Attend upon, escort (woman).

squirm (skwerm) v.i. Wriggle, writhe (freq. fig.). ~ n. Squirming movement. **squirm′er** n.

*Species of **squirrel** are found in forests of most parts of the world excepting Australia, New Zealand and New Guinea. They range from the pigmy African variety, less than 3 inches long, to the giants of South-East Asia. Most, are diurnal although the 'flying' varieties are active at night.*

giant squirrel

grey squirrel

fox squirrel

flying squirrel

ic ground squirrel

red squirrel

frican
quirrel

Prevost's squirrel

chipmunk

thirteen-lined ground squirrel

Asiatic striped squirrel

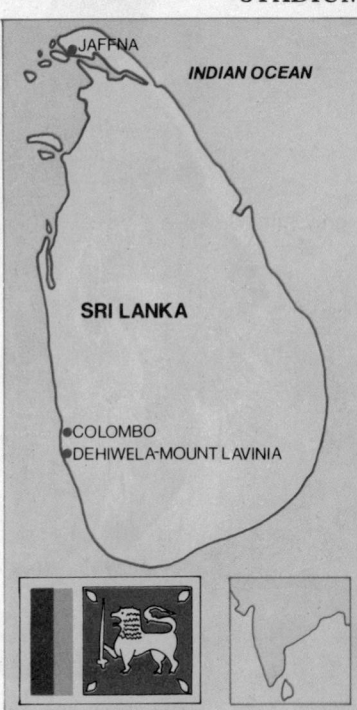

*Interior of a Buddhist temple at Kandy, in **Sri Lanka**. The country is mainly agricultural with tea, rubber and coconuts as the main revenue earners. Graphite and gems are mined and exported; but rice must be imported.*

squirm′y *adj.* (**squirm·i·er, squirm·i·est**).

squir·rel (skwer′el, skwŭr′-) *n.* (pl. **-rels**, collect. **-rel**). Any of various rodents of the family Sciuridae, small and slender with long bushy tail, many being arboreal (**red, gray, flying, ground** ~); ~ **cage**, cage for squirrel etc. with revolving cylinder resembling treadmill; (fig.) repetitiveness, monotony, etc., in job or life; **squir′relfish**, any of several nocturnal fishes (genus *Holocentrus*) of shallow tropical waters; **squirrel monkey**, small soft-haired long-tailed S. Amer. monkey of genus *Saimiri*.

squirt (skwert) *v.* Eject (liquid etc.) in jet as from syringe; be so ejected, spurt. ~ *n.* 1. Syringe; small jet or spray. 2. (colloq.) Insignificant person, whipper-snapper.

Sr *symbol.* Strontium.

sr *abbrev.* Steradian.

Sr. *abbrev.* Senior; señor.

Sra. *abbrev.* Señora.

Sri Lan·ka (srē lăng′ka, shrē lahng′ka). Large island in Indian Ocean near S. point of India, until 1972 called Ceylon; formerly a Brit. colony; independent republic, member of the Brit. Commonwealth, since 1948; capital, Colombo. **Sri Lan′kan** *adj.* [Sanskrit name of the island]

S.R.O. *abbrev.* Standing room only.

SS. *abbrev.* Saints.

ss. *abbrev.* (baseball) Shortstop.

S.S. *abbrev.* (hist.) *Schutz Staffel* (Ger., = protection patrol; Nazi police force); steamship.

SSA *abbrev.* Social Security Act;

Social Security Administration.

SSE, S.S.E., s.s.e. *abbrevs.* South-southeast.

SSR, S.S.R. *abbrevs.* Soviet Socialist Republic.

SSS *abbrev.* Selective Service System.

SST *abbrev.* Supersonic transport.

SSW, S.S.W., s.s.w. *abbrevs.* South-southwest.

St. *abbrev.* Saint; strait; street.

s.t. *abbrev.* Short ton.

sta. *abbrev.* Station; stationary.

stab (stăb) *v.* (**stabbed, stab·bing**). Pierce, wound, with (usu. short) pointed weapon, needle, etc.; aim blow (*at*) with such weapon etc. ~ *n.* Act of stabbing, wound made thus; short stiff stroke with billiard cue, bat, etc.; **have a** ~ **at**, (colloq.) make shot at, try.

sta·bile (stabēl′, stā′bēl; *Brit.* stā′bīl, -bĭl) *n.* Abstract sculpture or structure of wire, wood, metal, etc.

sta·bi·lize (stā′bilīz) *v.t.* (**-lized, -liz·ing**). Make stable, bring into a state of stability. **sta·bi·li·za·tion** (stābĭlĭzā′shon) *n.* (esp.) Maintenance of exchange rate of a country's currency.

sta·bi·liz·er (stā′bilīzer) *n.* (esp.) 1. One of a pair of retractable fins inserted into sides of ship's hull below waterline to prevent rolling. 2. Horizontal tail surface of aircraft.

sta·ble¹ (stā′bel) *n.* Building

with stalls, loose boxes, mangers etc., for keeping horses; establishment for training racehorses, horses belonging to this (also transf.) **sta′bleboy, sta′bleman** (pl -men), one who works in a stable **stable** *v.* (**-bled, -bling**). Put keep, (horse) in stable; be stabled **sta′bling** *n.* (esp.) Accommodation for horses etc.

sta·ble² (stā′bel) *adj.* (**-bler -blest**). Firmly fixed or established, not easily shaken, dislodged decomposed, changed, destroyed etc.; firm, resolute, steadfast **sta·bil·i·ty** (stabĭl′ĭtē) *n.* (pl. **-ties**) **sta′bly** *adv.*

stac·ca·to (stakah′tō) *adv., n.* (pl. **-tos, -ti** pr. -tē) & *adj.* (mus. (Note etc. played) in detached disconnected manner, with break between successive notes.

stack (stăk) *n.* 1. Circular o rectangular pile of hay, straw sheaves of grain, etc., usu. with sloping thatched top; pile, esp. on arranged in an orderly way; (colloq. pl.) large quantity. 2. Group o chimneys etc. standing together chimney of house, factory, ship locomotive, etc.; (pl.) area within library where books are stored aircraft circling airfield at variou altitudes while waiting their turn t land. ~ *v.t.* Pile, arrange, i stack(s); ~ **up**, measure up; kee aircraft circling in air at specifie altitudes until landing space i ready, weather conditions change etc.

sta·di·um (stā′dēum) *n.* (pl **-di·ums, -di·a** pr. -dēa). 1 Ancient Greek and Roman measur (about 600 ft.). 2. Enclosed athletic ground with tiers of seats fo ectators.

staff (stăf, stahf) *n.* (pl. **staffs, aves** pr. stăvz). 1. Stick used as d in walking or climbing (now u. literary); stick, rod, as sign of fice or authority, as **pastoral** ~; aft, pole, as support or handle, **flagstaff**; rod used for measur- g distances, heights, etc., in rveying etc. 2. (mus., pl. **staves**) t of (now five) parallel horizontal es on and between which notes e placed so as to indicate pitch. (pl. **staffs**) Body of officers, not emselves in command, assisting a neral or other commanding ficer; body of people working der central direction, esp. in ctory, educational institution,

o counter the effect of rough seas, odern ships are fitted with some form stabilizer. This may be the use of ed bilge keels; retractable fins; or by ing the hull with tanks which are filled ith water and compensate for the otion of the waves.

etc.; **general** ~, body of officers controlling an army from head- quarters under the commander in chief; ~ **college**, (mil.) establish- ment for instruction and training of officers for staff appointments; **staff sergeant**, (U.S. Army and Marine Corps) noncommissioned officer ranking above sergeant and below (Army) sergeant first class and (USMC) gunnery sergeant; (U.S. Air Force) noncommissioned officer ranking above airman 1st class and below technical sergeant. **staff** *v.t.* Provide with staff of

officers, teachers, servants, etc.

stag (stăg) *n.* Male of deer; (attrib., colloq.) for, of, men only, as ~ *party*; ~ *beetle*, large beetle of family Lucanidae of which males have long denticulated mandibles resembling stag's horns. **stag** *adv.* (of a man) Alone, without female companion (*go* ~).

stage (stāj) *n.* 1. Raised floor or platform, e.g. scaffold for workmen and their tools, platform used as gangway, landing place, etc., surface on which object is placed for inspection through microscope.

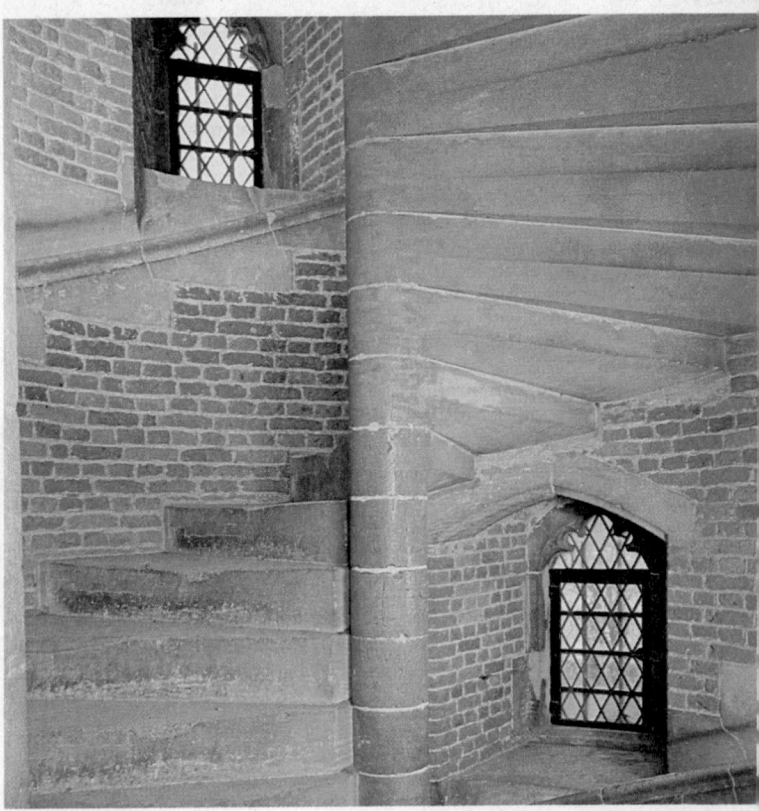

*Spiral **staircase** at Tattershall Castle, in Lincolnshire, England. Built in 1440, the building is said to represent some of the finest examples of the work of East Anglian stonemasons.*

2. Platform on which spectacles, plays, etc., are exhibited, esp. that in theater, with scenery, etc., theater, drama; actor's profession; (fig.) scene of action; **hold the** ~, dominate conversation etc. 3. Division of journey, process, development, etc.; point reached; regular stopping place on stagecoach route where horses were changed; section of bus route for which a particular fare is charged; as much of journey as is performed without stopping for rest etc. 4. Propulsion section of rocket, which can be shed after firing. 5. **stage′coach,** (hist.) coach running regularly between 2 places for conveyance of passengers, parcels, etc.; **stage direction,** instruction in written or printed play for appropriate action etc.; **stage door,** entrance from street for actors etc. to parts of theater behind stage; **stage fright,** nervousness at appearing before audience, esp. for first time; **stage hand,** one of persons handling scenery, lights, etc., during performance on stage; **stage manager,** person in charge of stagehands etc. and having general control of stage during performance, rehearsals, etc.; **stage′struck,** smitten with love for stage, esp. with desire to become actor; **stage whisper,** whisper loud enough to be heard by audience, one meant to be overheard. **stage** v. (**staged, stag·ing**). Put (play) on stage, organize (exhibition, pageant, etc.); organize and carry out; (of play) lend itself to stage production. **stag′y** adj. (**stag·i·er, stag·i·est**).

stag·fla·tion (stăgflā′shon) n. Economic condition combining decline in business activity and growing unemployment with rapid inflation. [*stag*(nation) + (in)*flation*]

stag·ger (stăg′er) v. 1. Walk or stand unsteadily or with swaying movement and irregular devious steps, totter, reel; cause to totter; (cause to) hesitate, waver in purpose, be unsettled or bewildered. 2. Arrange in zigzag, slanting, or overlapping order; time the changing of traffic lights so that steady flow of traffic can be maintained; arrange (hours of work, holidays, etc.) so that they do not coincide with those of others. ~ n. Act, effect, amount, of staggering; (pl. usu. with sing. verb, also **blind** ~**s**) diseased condition in animals resulting in unsteady gait, sudden falling, etc.

stag·ing (stā′jĭng) n. (esp.) 1.

Scaffolding, temporary platform or support. 2. Putting play on stage. 3. Traveling by stages; ~ **point, post,** place marking one stage of journey, esp. place for overnight stay for travelers.

stag·nant (stăg′nant) adj. Not flowing or running, without motion or current (freq. implying unwholesomeness); dull, sluggish, without activity or interest. **stag′nant·ly** adv. **stag′nan·cy** n.

stag·nate (stăg′nāt) v.i. (**-nat·ed, -nat·ing**). Be, become, stagnant. **stag·na·tion** (stăgnā′shon) n.

stag·y (stā′jē) adj. (**stag·i·er, stag·i·est**). Theatrical, dramatically artificial or exaggerated.

staid (stād) adj. Steady, sober, sedate. **staid′ly** adv. **staid′ness** n.

stain (stān) v. 1. Discolor, soil; (fig.) sully, blemish. 2. Color (textile fabrics, paper, wood, etc.) with pigment that penetrates instead of forming coating on surface; color (tissues etc.) with pigment to render structure visible for examination with microscope etc.; color (glass) with translucent colors. ~ n. Discoloration, spot or mark, esp. one caused by contact with foreign matter and not easily removable; dye etc. for staining; (fig.) blot, blemish. **stain′less** adj. (esp. of steel etc.) Alloyed with chromium so as not to be liable to rust or tarnish under ordinary conditions; made of such metal. **stain′er** n.

stair (stār) n. Each of succession

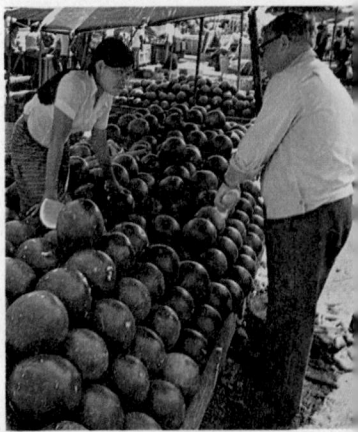

*Throughout the world, street markets provide a shopping area which many customers prefer to enclosed shops. These globular melons are stacked on a **stall** in Vientiane, Laos.*

of steps, esp. indoors; (pl.) set or flight of these; **stair′case, stair′way,** (part of building containing) flight, or series of flights, of stairs; staircase; **stair′well,** open shaft surrounded by staircase.

stake (stāk) n. 1. Stick or post sharpened at one end for driving into ground, used to mark boundary, to support plant, as part of fence, etc.; (hist.) post to which person was tied to be burned alive; **pull up** ~**s,** (colloq.) depart, go to live elsewhere. 2. What is staked or wagered on an event; (pl.) money to be contended for, esp. in horse race; (pl.) such race; (fig.) interes

This old **stallion** has probably been put out to pasture after a long working life. The draft horse is descended from the warhorses of the Middle Ages which had to carry the huge weight of their armored riders.

involved, something to be gained or lost; **at** ~, at issue, in question, risked. 3. (Mormon Ch.) Number of wards administered by a president. **stake** *v.t.* (**staked, stak·ing**). 1. Fasten, secure, support, with stake(s); mark *off, out*, with stakes; ~ **out**, (colloq.) place under surveillance. 2. Wager, risk (*on* event etc.); (fig.) hazard, risk loss of; furnish with money, supplies, etc., esp. in order to share gains.

Sta·kha·nov·ite (stakah′novīt, -χah′-) *adj. & n.* (Member) of Soviet Russian movement aiming at greater output in industry, initiated by Alexei Stakhanov, a Donetz miner, who in 1935 produced a phenomenal quantity of coal by a combination of new method and great energy.

sta·lac·tite (stalăk′tīt, stăl′ak-) *n.* Icicle-like formation of crystalline calcium carbonate formed by dripping of water through overlying limestone and hanging from roof or wall of cavern etc. **stal·ac·tit·ic** (stălaktĭt′ĭk) *adj.*

sta·lag (stăl′ag, stah′lag; *Ger.* shtah′lahk) *n.* German prison camp. [abbrev. of Ger. *Stammlager* (*Stamm* main body, *Lager* camp)]

sta·lag·mite (stalăg′mīt, stăl′-ag-) *n.* Deposit of calcium carbonate or other material on floor of cavern etc. resembling inverted stalactite and similarly formed. **stal·ag·mit·ic** (stălagmĭt′ĭk) *adj.*

stale (stāl) *adj.* (**stal·er, stal·est**). Not fresh; insipid, musty,

*Colored floodlights are used to emphasize the natural beauty of a **stalagmite** and adjoining stalactites at Lake Caves in the Margaret River area of Western Australia.*

or otherwise the worse for age; lacking novelty, trite; (of athlete) overtrained (similarly of other persons whose vigor is impaired by overwork); **stale′mate**, (chess) position in which player can make no move without bringing his king into check, (fig.) deadlock, drawn contest; (*v.t.*) place (player, his king) in position of stalemate. **stale′ly** *adv.* **stale′ness** *n.* **stale** *n.* Urine of horses and cattle. ~ *v.* (**staled, stal·ing**). 1. Make, become, stale or common. 2. (of horse etc.) Urinate.

Sta·lin (stah′lĭn, -lēn). Name adopted by Joseph Vissarionovich Dzhugashvili (1879–1953), Soviet dictator, by birth a Georgian; worked as an underground revolutionary from 1904 until the Bolshevik revolution of 1917; by *c*1927 he was established as undisputed successor to Lenin and leader of the Communist Party and administration, retaining that position until his death; premier of U.S.S.R. 1941–53. **Sta′lin·ism** *n.* **Sta′lin·ist** *adj. & n.* [Russ., = "man of steel"]

Sta·lin·grad (stah′lĭngrăd). See VOLGOGRAD.

stalk¹ (stawk) *n.* Main stem of herbaceous plant, bearing flowers and leaves; attachment or support

of leaf, flower, fruit, animal organ, etc.; stem, shaft, of object. **stalked** *adj.*

stalk² (stawk) *v.* 1. Pursue (game) stealthily; steal up to game under cover; **stalking-horse**, horse, screen, behind which hunter approaches game; (fig.) something used to conceal intentions or efforts; (pol.) candidate put forward to conceal another's candidacy or to draw votes from a rival. 2. Walk with stiff measured steps; stride in stately or imposing manner. ~ *n.* Act of stalking game; stealthy pursuit.

stall¹ (stawl) *n.* 1. (Division for 1 animal in) stable, cattle shed, cow house. 2. Fixed seat enclosed wholly or partly at back and sides, and freq. canopied, in choir or chancel of church or in chapterhouse, for clergyman, dignitary of church, knight, etc.; (fig.) office or dignity of canon etc.; (Brit.) each of set of seats in part of theater nearest stage, usu. between pit and orchestra. 3. Booth, table, stand, in market etc., compartment in building, for exposure and sale of goods. 4. Compartment for occupation by one person in shower baths etc. 5. (Condition or delay resulting from) stalling of engine or aircraft. ~ *v.* 1. Place, keep, (cattle etc.) in stall, esp. for fattening; furnish with stalls. 2. (Cause to) stick fast in mud, snow, etc.; stop (internal combustion engine) accidentally, (of engine) be accidentally stopped; (cause to) lose flying speed to point at which aircraft ceases to respond normally to controls; ~ **speed**, critical speed below which aircraft stalls.

stall² (stawl) *v.* (colloq.) 1. Play for time when being questioned etc. 2. Block, delay, obstruct. ~ *n.* (colloq.) Device, trick, evasion, etc. used in stalling.

stal·lion (stăl′yon) *n.* Uncastrated male horse, esp. one kept for breeding.

stal·wart (stawl′wert) *adj.* (chiefly literary) Stout, strong, sturdy; valiant, courageous, resolute. ~ *n.* Resolute uncompromising partisan, esp. of political party. **stal′wart·ly** *adv.* **stal′wart·ness** *n.*

sta·men (stā′men) *n.* (pl. **stamens, stam·i·na** pr. stăm′ina). (bot.) Male fertilizing organ of flowering plants, with anther containing pollen supported on slender filament.

stam·i·na (stăm′ina) *n.* Staying power, power of endurance.

stam·i·nate (stăm′init, -nāt) *adj.* Having stamens, esp. without pistils.

stam·mer (stăm′er) *v.* Falter or stumble in speech, esp. repeat involuntarily certain sounds in a word etc. several times in rapid succession through inability to complete the articulation; utter with stammer. ~ *n.* Stammering speech, tendency to stammer. **stam′mer·er** *n.* **stam′mer·ing·ly** *adv.*

stamp (stămp) *v.* I. Bring down one's foot, bring down (foot), heavily on ground; ~ **out**, put an end to, crush, destroy; **stamp′ing**

ground, (colloq.) animal's (or colloq., person's) habitual place of resort. 2. Impress pattern, name, mark, upon with die or similar instrument; affix postage or other stamp to (document, envelope, etc.); assign a character to, characterize; impress *on* the memory. 3. Crush, pulverize (ore etc.). **stamp** *n.* I. Act, sound, of stamping, esp. with foot. 2. Instrument for stamping pattern or mark, mark made by this; government's embossed or impressed mark, adhesive label with distinctive device, on deed or other document etc., to certify that duty, tax, etc., has been paid; postage stamp; mark impressed on, label etc. affixed to, commodity as evidence of quality etc.; (fig.) characteristic mark, impress (*of* some quality etc.); character, kind. 3. Heavy pestle operated by machinery for crushing ores, stamp mill. 4. **S~ Act**, act of British Parliament for regulating stamp duties, esp. that of 1765 (repealed

*The **stall** in the private chapel of Petworth House, near Arundel in Sussex, U.K., may have been carved by Grinling Gibbons. The chapel and house were acquired for the nation in 1947.*

1766) levying such duties on Amer. colonies; ~ **mill**, apparatus for crushing ore, usu. with series of stamps.

stam·pede (stămpēd′) *n.* Sudden rush and flight of number of frightened horses, cattle, etc.; sudden unreasoning rush or action of persons in a body or mass. ~ *v.* (**-ped·ed, -ped·ing**). (Cause to) take part in stampede.

stance (stăns) *n.* (golf etc.) Player's position for making stroke; pose, attitude.

stanch, staunch (stawnch, stahnch, stănch) *vbs.t.* Check flow of (esp. blood); check flow from (esp. wound).

stan·chion (stăn′shon) *n.* Upright bar, stay, or support, esp. for confining cattle in stall. ~ *v.t.* Provide, strengthen, support, with stanchion(s).

stand (stănd) *v.* (**stood** pr. sto͞od, **stand·ing**). I. Have, take, assume, erect attitude on one's feet; be set, remain, upright; be of specified height when standing; remain stationary, stop walking or moving on; be set, placed, or situated; remain firm, secure, valid, etc., or in specified condition; present a firm front; (naut.) sail, steer, in specified direction, to sea, etc. 2. Place, set, in upright or specified position. 3. Bear the brunt of, resist; endure, undergo (trial etc.); endure without succumbing or complaining. 4. Provide at one's expense. 5. ~ **by**, uphold, support, side with; adhere to, abide by; stand near, be a bystander, stand and look on; stand ready, be on the alert; **stand′by** (pl. **bys**), thing, person, that can be depended on; **stand a chance**, have a chance or prospect (of success); **stand down**, step down from witness stand; retire, withdraw; go off duty; **stand for**, represent, signify, imply; (colloq.) tolerate, acquiesce in; **stand in**, act as deputy (*for*); be in favor (*with*); **stand-in**, person employed to take place of actor until lights, cameras, etc., are ready; deputy, substitute; **stand off**, move away, keep one's distance; **stand′off**, indecisive contest, tie; **standoff′ish**, distant, reserved, not affable; **standoff′ishly** (*adv.*), **standoff′ishness** (*n.*); **stand on**, insist on, observe scrupulously; **stand out**, hold out, persist in opposition or endurance; be prominent or conspicuous; **stand pat**, (in poker) play hand as dealt; oppose change, maintain one's position; **stand′patter**, (esp. pol.) rigid conservative, opponent of progress; **stand′pipe**, vertical pipe for conveying water, gas, etc., or with spout or nozzle for hose, for attachment to water main; **stand′point**, point of view; **stand′still**, halt, pause, cessation of movement

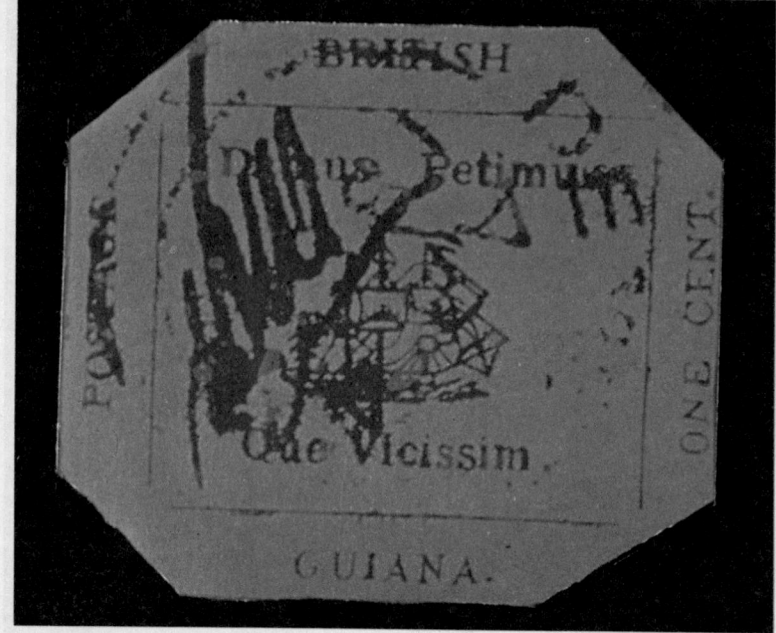

*Claimed to be the most valuable **stamp** in the world, the 1 cent British Guiana of 1856 and the only one of its kind surviving, was insured for £200,000 when exhibited in 1965.*

*Possibly one of the most unusual **stamps** ever issued, a humorous cartoon figure was used in a series to introduce and demonstrate the advantages of metric conversion in Australia.*

or activity; **stand to**, abide by, stick to, not desert; **stand to win, lose**, etc., be reasonably certain to win, lose, etc.; **stand up**, rise to one's feet from sitting position etc.; maintain erect position; (colloq.) fail to keep appointment with; remain durable, convincing; **stand-up**, (of theater, nightclub, etc. entertainer) delivering comic monologue without prop or costume; (of fight) fair and square, in which opponents stand up to one another without flinching or evasion; (of meal etc.) taken standing; **stand up for**, side with, maintain, support. **stand** *n.* 1. Cessation from motion or progress, stoppage; stationary condition, esp. for resistance (*against*); position taken up. 2. Table, set of shelves, rack, etc., on or in which things may be placed; stall in market etc.; standing place for vehicles etc. (as **taxi** ~); raised structure at sports events etc. for persons to sit or stand on (often pl.);

(also **witness** ~) place in courtroom for giving testimony. 3. Standing growth or crop. 4. (of theatrical company, sports team, etc.) Appearance made during tour.   **stand·ard** (stăn′dĕrd) *n.* 1. Distinctive flag, as (*English*) *royal* ~; banner of chief of state; flag of cavalry or armored regiment (opp. to *colors* of infantry); (fig.) rallying principle; (bot.) vexillum, uppermost petal of sweet pea or similar flower. 2. Weight or measure to which others conform or by which the accuracy of others is judged (often attrib. as in *standard pound, yard*, etc.); legal proportion of weight of fine metal and alloy in gold and silver coin (**monetary** ~) or in articles made of these metals;

thing serving as basis of comparison. 3. Degree of excellence etc. required for a particular purpose; thing recognized as model for imitation etc.; (attrib. of book) recognized as possessing merit or authority; (in schools) each of several degrees of proficiency; ~ **of living**, degree of material comfort enjoyed by community, class, or person. 4. Average quality. 5. Upright support; upright water or gas pipe; upright holder for lamp in street or room; tree, shrub, trained on erect stem (not as espalier or dwarfed). 6. ~ **-bearer**, soldier etc. who carries flag; (fig.) prominent leader in cause; ~ **English**, form of English used, with local variations, by the majority of cultured English-speaking people; ~ **time**, time established legally or by custom in country or region, usu. that of a specific time zone.   **stand·ard·ize** (stăn′dĕrdīz) *v.t.* (**-ized, -iz·ing**). Make to conform to standard; make uniform. **stand·ard·i·za·tion** (stănderdīzā′shŏn) *n.*   **stand·ee** (stăndē′) *n.* (colloq.) Person who stands, as at theatrical performance.   **stand·ing** (stan′ding) *n.* (esp.) Estimation in which person is held, repute; duration. ~ *adj.* (esp.)

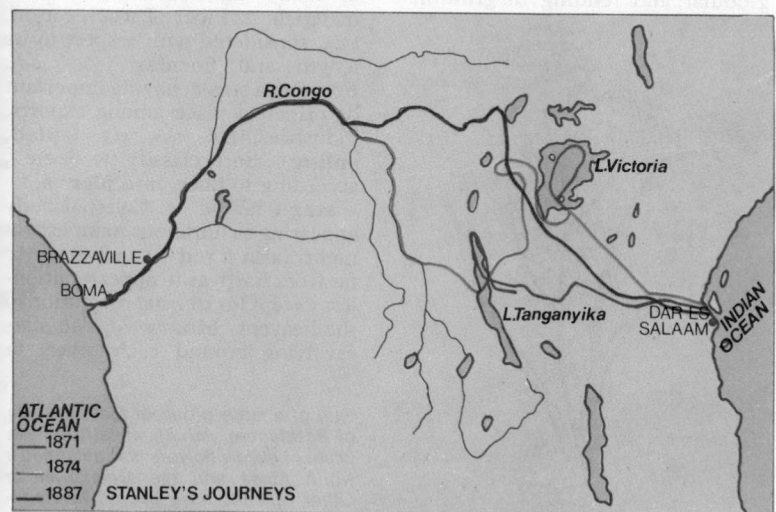

Sir Henry Stanley, the British explorer and journalist, is best known for locating David Livingstone in 1871. However, he also traced the route of the Congo on other expeditions (shown left).

When seen through a 200-inch telescope, the vast number of **stars** shows how little can be seen with the eye. Above: A small section of the Vulpecula constellation.

Established; permanent, not made, formed, etc., for the occasion; stagnant (of water); performed upright (of jump); ~ **orders**, series of instructions remaining in force until countermanded or repealed by a proper authority, esp. (mil.) orders not subject to change by an officer temporarily in command; ~ **room**, area in which to stand, esp. when no seats are available, as at theater.

stank: see STINK.

Stan·ley (stăn′lē), **Sir Henry Morton** (1841–1904). (orig. name John Rowlands) Welsh explorer and journalist; commissioned by the New York *Herald* to search central Africa for David Livingstone; his famous remark on finding him in 1871 was, "Dr. Livingstone, I presume?"; his explorations for Belgium in the Congo region, 1879–1884, helped in establishing the Congo Free State (Belgian Congo); **Stanley Falls**, seven cataracts of the upper Congo River, on the equator in Zaire.

stan·nate (stăn′āt) *n.* (chem.) Salt of stannic acid.

stan·nic (stăn′ĭk) *adj.* Of tin; (chem.) containing tin as quadrivalent element.

stan·nous (stăn′us) *adj.* Containing tin as bivalent element.

Stan·ton (stăn′ton), **Elizabeth Cady** (1815–1902). Amer. feminist leader; organized first women's rights convention, 1848; first president of National Woman Suffrage Association, 1869–90.

stan·za (stăn′za) *n.* Group of (usu. rhymed) lines forming division of song or poem.

sta·pes (stā′pēz) (pl. **sta·pes, sta·pe·des** pr. stapē′dēz) = STIRRUP bone.

staph (stăf) *n.* (colloq.) Staphylococcus.

staph·y·lo·coc·cus (stăfĭlokŏk′-us) *n.* (pl. **-coc·ci** pr. -kŏk′sī). Any of numerous microorganisms, globular and tending to grow in clusters, causing various conditions such as boils, carbuncles, and abscesses. **staph·y·lo·coc′cal** *adj.* [Gk. *staphulē* bunch of grapes, *kokkos* grain]

sta·ple[1] (stā′pel) *n.* U-shaped bar or loop of metal with pointed ends to be driven into post, wall, etc., as hold for hook, bolt, etc.; contrivance of similar shape or function, esp. bent wire used in bookbinding for wire stitching. ~ *v.t.* (**-pled, -pling**). Furnish, fasten, with staple. **sta′pler**[1] *n.* (esp.) Device for stapling.

sta·ple[2] (stā′pel) *n.* 1. Important or principal product or article of commerce; raw material; basic item of food; (fig.) chief element or material. 2. Fiber of wool, cotton, etc., considered with respect to its length and fineness. ~ *adj.* Forming a staple; having important or principal place among exports, industries, etc. ~ *v.t.* (**-pled, -pling**). Sort, classify (wool etc.), according to fiber. **sta′pler**[2] *n.*

star (stär) *n.* 1. Celestial body appearing as luminous point esp. at night; (also **fixed** ~) such body so far from Earth as to appear motionless except for diurnal revolution of the heavens; **binary** ~, two stars revolving around each other, or

One of a large group of lilies, the Star of Bethlehem with its white, greenish white or yellow flowers is widespread in North Africa and the Mediterranean. Other varieties have been cultivated.

around a common center; **double ~**, two fixed stars appearing to naked eye as one, esp. binary star; **multiple ~**, similar group of three to six; **falling, shooting ~**, small meteor looking like rapidly moving star. 2. (astrol.) Heavenly body, esp. planet, considered as influencing human affairs or person's fortunes. 3. Thing suggesting star by its shape, esp. figure or object with radiating points; asterisk; white spot on forehead of horse etc. 4. Actor, singer, athlete, etc., of great celebrity; brilliant or prominent person. 5. **~ chamber**, (judgment, trial) marked by arbitrary, unjust, or clandestine procedure (from **Court of S~ Chamber**, English Privy Council court, abolished 1641); **~ drift**, common proper motion of a number of fixed stars in same region; **star'dust**, multitude of stars looking like dust, (fig.) romantic or dreamlike mood; **star'-fish**, marine echinoderm of the class Asteroidea with usu. five broad arms radiating from a central disk; **star'flower**, any of various small N. Amer. plants (genus *Trientalis*), having pink or white star-shaped flowers; **star'gazer**, esp. impractical idealist; **star'-gazing** (*n.*); **star'light**, light of the stars; (*adj.*, also **star'lit**); **star-nosed mole**, mole (*Condylura cristata*) of eastern N. Amer., having ring of small fleshy tentacles encircling end of snout; **star of Bethlehem**, plant of genus *Ornithogalum*, esp. *O. umbellatum*, with white stellate flowers; any of various other plants; **Star of David**, figure of two interlaced equilateral triangles used as Jewish and Israeli symbol; **star sapphire**, cabochon sapphire giving impression of embedded star; **The Star Spangled Banner**, U.S. national anthem, with ref. to the Stars and Stripes (see below); **star stream**, either of two systematic drifts of stars (one of which comprises the nearer stars and moves toward Orion); **Stars and Stripes**, flag of the U.S. with 13 horizontal stripes, representing the 13 original states, and one star for each of the 50 states in the Union. **star'dom** *n.* Status of star performer (see *n.*, sense 4); realm, sphere, of such stars. **star'let** *n.* Young star (sense 4). **star'less** *adj.* **star'ry** *adj.* (**-ri·er, -ri·est**). **star** *adj.* Brilliant, prominent, preeminent. **~** *v.* (**starred, star·ring**). Set, adorn (as) with stars; mark with asterisk; present (actor etc.), appear, as a star (sense 4).

star·board (stär´berd) *n.* Right-hand side of boat or ship or aircraft looking forward (opp. PORT[4]). **~** *v.t.* Turn, put, (helm) to starboard. [OE. *steor rudder*]

starch (stärch) *n.* White odorless tasteless carbohydrate occurring widely in plants, esp. cereals, potatoes, etc., and forming an important constituent of human food; preparation of this for stiffening linen etc.; (fig.) stiffness of manner or conduct, formality. **starch'y** *adj.* (**starch·i·er, starch·i·est**). **starch'i·ly** *adv.* **starch'i·ness** *n.* **starch** *v.t.* Stiffen with starch.

stare (stär) *v.* (**stared, star·ing**). Gaze fixedly with eyes wide open; open eyes in astonishment, be amazed; reduce (person) to specified condition by staring; be obtrusively conspicuous; **~** (person) **in the face**, (of thing) be glaringly obvious to. **stare** *n.* Staring gaze. **star'er** *n.*

stark (stärk) *adj.* Stiff, rigid; downright, sheer. **~** *adv.* Quite, completely (now chiefly in **~** *mad*, *naked*). **stark'ly** *adv.* **stark'ness** *n.*

star·ling[1] (stär´ling) *n.* Any of various Old World birds of family Sturnidae, esp. *Sturnus vulgaris*, blackbird introduced into N. Amer. and now a gregarious, aggressive, and abundant pest.

star·ling[2] (stär´ling) *n.* Outwork of piles protecting pier of bridge against force of stream, damage by floating objects, etc.

common starling

rose-coloured starling
or rosy pastor

*The common European **starling** is an introduced species in Australia and America where it has reached pest proportions. Other, more vividly colored varieties of this bird, are indigenous to certain tropical countries.*

superb starling

start (stärt) *v.* 1. Make sudden movement from pain, surprise, etc., give start; move suddenly from one's place; rouse (game) from lair etc.; (of timbers etc.) spring from proper position, be displaced by pressure or shrinkage; cause, experience, starting of timbers etc. 2. Set out, begin journey, career, course of action, etc. (*out* or *off*); make a beginning (*on*); begin; originate, set going; cause to begin doing, cause or enable to commence course of action etc.; give signal to (persons) to start in race etc.; (also ~ **up**) cause (engine) to begin to run; (of engine) begin to operate. **start** *n.* 1. Sudden involuntary movement caused by surprise, fright, pain, etc.; (pl.) intermittent and sudden efforts or displays of energy in (esp. *by fits and starts*). 2. Beginning of journey, action, race, career, etc.; starting place of race; opportunity or assistance for starting career, course of action, etc.; advantage gained by starting first in race, journey; position in advance of competitors.

start·er (stär'ter) *n.* (esp.) 1. Person giving signal to start in race. 2. Horse, competitor, starting in race etc. 3. Apparatus for starting engine, esp. **self-~**. 4. **for starters,** (slang) to start with, as a beginning.

start·ing (stär'ting) *n.* (esp.) ~ **block,** shaped block for bracing the feet of runners at start of race; ~ **gate,** movable barrier for securing fair start in horse race.

star·tle (stär'tel) *v.t.* (**-tled, -tling**). Cause to start with surprise or fright; alarm; take by surprise. **star'tling** *adj.*

starve (stärv) *v.* (**starved, starv·ing**). (Cause to) die of hunger; (cause to) suffer from lack of food; (colloq.) feel hungry; force *into* course of action, *out*, etc., by starvation; (fig.) (cause to) suffer mental or spiritual want. **star·va·tion** (stärvā'shon) *n.*

starve·ling (stärv'ling) *n.* Starving or ill-fed person or animal.

sta·sis (stā'sis, stăs'ĭs) *n.* (pl. **sta·ses** pr. stā'sēz, stăs'ēz). Stoppage of circulation of any body fluids, esp. blood.

state[1] (stāt) *n.* 1. Condition; manner or way of existence as determined by circumstances; (colloq.) excited or agitated condition of mind or feeling; ~ **of the art,** stage of development or knowledge of a subject. 2. Rank, dignity; pomp; **in ~,** with all due ceremony; **lie in ~,** (of dead person) be ceremoniously exhibited in public place. 3. Organized political community

under one government, commonwealth, nation; such community forming part of federation with sovereign government; civil government; **the S ~ s,** (colloq.) the United States of America; **States-General,** legislative assembly of clergy, nobles, and commons of whole realm in France before the Revolution, or in Netherlands from 15th c. to 1796. 4. (attrib.) **state capitalism,** system in which capital is owned or controlled by state; **state'craft,** art of conducting affairs of state; **State Department,** department of U.S. government dealing with foreign affairs; **State'house,** building in which legislature of a state holds its sessions; **States rights, States' rights,** rights and powers not delegated to the Federal government but reserved to individual states; **state'room,** passenger's private cabin on ship, train, etc.; **state'side,** (colloq.) of or pertaining to the U.S. (as seen from overseas); **state socialism,** system of state control of industries, railroads, etc. **state'hood** *n.* **state'less** *adj.* Having no legal nationality, esp. because of change

*The invention and use of a **starting-block** has given runners, and especially those in short-distance sprints, the benefit of a non-slip start when the gun is fired.*

*The **starting-gate** was devised for horse racing so that all mounts would have an equal chance to leave the barrier at the same instant, as demonstrated at an Australian race track.*

*In Richmond, Virginia, and other States, the **Statehouse** is where the General Assembly meets. The present building replaced a more modest one which was erected in 1785.*

*'Satyr, nymph and cupid' a **statuette** molded in terracotta by the French 18th-century sculptor Clodion, and much influenced by the styles originally created in Greece and Rome.*

of government or alteration of boundaries of states. **state** *adj*. Of, for, concerned with the state (sense 3); reserved for, employed on, occasions of state or ceremony.

state² (stāt) *v.t.* (**stat·ed, stat·ing**). Express, esp. fully or clearly, in speech or writing; specify (number etc.).

state·ly (stāt′lē) *adj*. (**-li·er, -li·est**). Dignified, imposing, grand. **state′li·ness** *n*.

state·ment (stāt′ment) *n*. Stating, expression in words; presentation of musical theme or subject; thing stated; formal account of facts, as of liabilities and assets; account presented periodically by tradesman to customer.

states·man (stāts′man), fem. **states·wom·an** (stāts′woͦoman) *ns*. (pl. **-men** pr. -men, **-wom·en** pr. -wimĭn). Person skilled or taking leading parts in management of state affairs, esp. sagacious, farsighted politician; **elder s**~: see ELDER².

stat·ic (stăt′ĭk) *adj*. Of forces in equilibrium or bodies at rest (contrasted with *dynamic* or *kinetic*); acting by weight without motion; passive, not active or changing; (elect.) stationary, produced by friction; (of a store of water in a tank) having no pressure of its own and requiring to be pumped. ~ *n*. Static electricity; (slang) opposition, unpleasant remarks, etc. **stat′i·cal** *adj*. Of statics. **stat′ics**

n. Branch of physical science concerned with bodies at rest and forces in equilibrium (contrasted with *dynamics*). **stat′i·cal·ly** *adv*.

sta·tion (stā′shon) *n*. 1. Place in which person or thing stands or is placed, esp. habitually or for definite purpose or duties; building from which radio and television broadcasts are transmitted. 2. Position in life, rank, status. 3. Stopping place on railroad or long-distance bus line with buildings for passengers and freight, or freight only; these buildings. 4. One of a series of holy places, esp. Roman churches, visited in turn for devotions; ~**s of the Cross**, series of 14 pictures or images of Christ's Passion (orig. crosses) in church or occas. in open air, before which devotions are performed. 5. (**station**) **break**, pause between or during television and radio programs for station identification, announcements, or commercials; **station house**, police station; **sta′tionmaster**, official in control of railroad station; **station wagon**, automobile with removable or folding rear seats and wide rear door with tailgate to expedite loading and unloading of luggage etc. **station** *v*. Assign station or post to; post, place, in station.

sta·tion·ar·y (stā′shoněrē) *adj*. Remaining in one place, not moving; fixed, not movable; not changing in condition, quality, or

quantity; ~ **front**, (meteorol.) motionless or nearly motionless boundary between 2 masses of air having different densities; ~ **orbit**, orbit whose period is the same as the period of Earth's rotation on its axis and oriented so that any object in it remains located over one spot on Earth; ~ **satellite**, artificial satellite in such orbit.

sta·tion·er (stā′shoner) *n*. Tradesman selling writing materials etc. **sta·tion·er·y** (stā′shoněrē) *n*. Articles sold by stationer, as paper, pens, ink, etc.

sta·tis·tics (statĭs′tĭks) *n*. Branch of study concerned with collection and classification of (esp.) numerical facts; (as pl.) facts so collected and classified. **sta·tis′ti·cal** *adj*. **sta·tis′ti·cal·ly** *adv*. **stat·is·ti·cian** (stătĭstĭsh′an) *n*.

sta·tor (stā′ter) *n*. Stationary part of machine or device.

stat·u·ar·y (stăch′oͦoěrē) *n*. (pl. **-ar·ies**). (Art of making) statues. ~ *adj*. Of statues; sculptured; suitable for statues.

stat·ue (stăch′oͦo) *n*. Sculptural representation in the round of (esp.) deity, allegorical subject, or human being(s), usu. of life-size proportions.

stat·u·esque (stăchoͦoěsk′) *adj*. Resembling a statue, esp. in beauty or dignity.

stat·u·ette (stăchoͦoět′) *n*. Small statue.

stat·ure (stăch′er) *n*. Height of (esp. human) body; degree of (moral, intellectual, etc.) development attained (by person).

sta·tus (stā′tus, stăt′us) *n*. Social or legal position or condition, rank, standing; superior social etc. position; ~ **symbol**, possession etc. thought of as indicating person's high status; ~ **quo** (**ante**), unchanged position (previous position) of affairs.

stat·ute (stăch′ōōt, -ōōt) *n.* Written law of a legislative body; ordinance of corporation etc. intended to be permanent; ~ **law**, written law as established by legislative enactment; (cf. COMMON law); ~ **mile**, unit of distance (5,280 ft.); ~ **of limitations**, statute setting time limit within which legal action may be taken; **stat′u·ta·ble** *adj.* **stat·u·to·ry** (stăch′ōōtōrē, -tōrē) *adj.* Enacted, required, imposed, by statute; ~ **rape**, sexual intercourse with girl below age of consent.

staunch[1]: STANCH.

staunch[2] (stawnch, stahnch) *adj.* Trustworthy, loyal, firm; (of vessel etc.) watertight, airtight. **staunch′ly** *adv.* **staunch′ness** *n.*

stave (stāv) *n.* 1. Each of the narrow shaped pieces of wood etc. placed together vertically to form sides of cask etc. 2. Stanza, verse, of poem, song, etc. 3. (mus.) = STAFF sense 2. ~ *v.t.* (**staved** or **stove** pr. stōv, **stav·ing**). 1. Break up (cask) into staves, break into, break hole *in* (boat, cask, etc.); crush, bash (*in*). 2. Furnish, fit (cask etc.) with staves. 3. ~ **off**, ward off, defer.

stay[1] (stā) *n.* Rope supporting mast, leading down from masthead; guy or rope supporting flagstaff etc.; tie piece, crosspiece, holding parts together in aircraft etc. **stay**

v.t. (**stayed**, **stay·ing**). Support, steady, with stay(s).

stay[2] (stā) *v.* (**stayed** or archaic **staid**, **stay·ing**). 1. Check, stop (now chiefly literary); postpone (judgment etc.); appease. 2. Support, prop (*up*), as with buttress etc. 3. Remain; dwell temporarily; pause in movement, action, speech; ~ **put**, remain in one's, or its, place. 4. Hold out, show powers of endurance; hold out for (specified distance, *the course*). 5. ~ **-at-home**, (person) remaining habitually at home; **staying power**, endurance. **stay** *n.* 1. Remaining, esp. dwelling temporarily, in a place; duration of this. 2. Suspension of judicial proceedings, esp. ~ **of execution**, of judgment delivered. 3. Prop, support.

S.T.B. *abbrev.* Bachelor of Sacred Theology. [L. *Sanctae Theologiae Baccalaureus*]

St. Croix (sănt kroi′). Largest of the U.S. Virgin Islands, in the N. Lesser Antilles, in the West Indies.

S.T.D. *abbrev.* Doctor of Sacred Theology. [L. *Sanctae Theologiae Doctor*]

stead (stěd) *n.* **stand** (person) **in good** ~, be of advantage or service to; **in person's** ~, instead of him, as his substitute.

*Largely superseded by diesel-electric locomotives, the **steamengine** was a direct development from the first steam locomotives designed by Richard Trevithick and George Stephenson. The fastest exceeded 125 m.p.h. in 1928.*

stead·fast (stěd′făst, -fahst, -fast) *adj.* Constant, firm, unwavering. **stead′fast·ly** *adv.* **stead′fast·ness** *n.*

stead·y (stěd′ē) *adj.* (**stead·i·er**, **stead·i·est**). Firm, not tottering, faltering, rocking, or shaking; stable; unwavering, resolute; settled, unvarying; regular, maintained at even rate of action, change, etc., not erratic. ~ **-state theory**, theory that the universe is in unvarying condition and has not been created by any past event; cf. BIG bang theory. **stead′i·ly** *adv.* **stead′i·ness** *n.* **steady** *adv.* Steadily (chiefly naut.); **go** ~, (colloq.) date regularly only one girl or boy. **steady** *n.* (colloq.) Constant sweetheart. ~ *v.* (**stead·ied**, **stead·y·ing**). Make, become, steady.

steak (stāk) *n.* Thick slice or strip of meat (esp. beef) for grilling, frying, etc., esp. cut from hindquarters of animal; thick slice of fish cut through backbone.

steal (stēl) *v.* (**stole** pr. stōl, **stol·en** pr. stō′len, **steal·ing**). 1. Take away dishonestly, and esp. secretly, what belongs to another; obtain surreptitiously or by surprise; win, get possession of, by insidious arts, attractions, etc.; ~ **the show**, unexpectedly outshine other performers. 2. Move secretly or silently. **steal** *n.* (colloq.) Stealing, theft; thing stolen; bargain.

stealth (stělth) *n.* Secret, secret procedure; **by** ~, surreptitiously, clandestinely. **stealth·y** *adj.* (**stealth·i·er**, **stealth·i·est**).

Steam passes through three different cylinders in a triple-expansion steam engine (bottom). These are connected by side valves (top) which in turn are operated by eccentrics mounted on the crankshaft. Each piston is linked by a piston rod which transmits the drive to the crankshaft, which, in marine engines, provided the driving power to the propeller. The advantage of these engines, used until the late 1940s, was their high torque at low rotation.

steam inlet

slide valve

exhaust port
inlet port

cylinder   piston

steam outlet

steam inlet

slide valve

inlet port
exhaust port

piston   cylinder

steam outlet

slide valve   intermediate pressure cylinder   high pressure cylinder

pressure cylinder

steam inlet

steam exhaust
steam pipe

piston rod

flywheel

connection rod

crank shaft   valve eccentrics

stealth'i·ly *adv.* **stealth'i·ness** *n.*

steam (stēm) *n.* Invisible vapor into which water is converted by heat; this used in specially contrived engines for generation of mechanical power; (pop.) steam mixed with air and with minute particles of water suspended in it, in form of white cloud or mist; (colloq.) energy, go; ~ **bath**, bath in which bather or substance to be heated is immersed in steam; **steam'boat**, boat, esp. large river or coasting boat, driven by steam; **steam engine**, engine in which motive power is steam; freq., steam-driven locomotive; **steam fitter**, person whose occupation is installing and repairing boilers, pipes, and other components of heating, air-cooling, refrigerating, etc., systems; **steam heating**, central heating in which steam is circulated through radiators; **steam jacket**, casing around cylinder etc. with space between to be filled with steam for heating the cylinder etc. **steam'-roller**, steam-driven vehicle with heavy roller for crushing stone, leveling roads, etc.; **steam'ship**, ship driven by steam. **steam'y** *adj.* (**steam·i·er, steam·i·est**). **steam** *v.* 1. Emit, give off, steam or vapor, exhale (steam, vapor), cover, bedew, (surface), (of surface) become covered, with condensed vapor; generate steam. 2. Travel, move, by agency of steam. 3. Treat with steam, expose to action of steam; cook by steam.

steam·er (stē'mer) *n.* (esp.) 1. Boat propelled by steam. 2. Pan in which food is cooked by steam.

ste·a·rate (stē'erāt, stēr'āt) *n.* Salt of stearic acid.

ste·ar·ic (stēăr'ĭk, stēr'ĭk) *adj.* Derived from, containing, stearin; ~ **acid**, white crystalline fatty acid obtained from tallow etc.

ste·a·rin (stē'erĭn, stēr'ĭn) *n.* Any ester of glycerol and stearic acid, esp. white crystalline solid found in tallow and many other animal and vegetable fats; solid portion of any fixed oil or fat; (pop.) stearic acid used for making candles etc.

ste·a·tite (stē'atīt) *n.* (min.) Grayish-green or brown massive variety of talc with soapy feel, soapstone. **ste·a·tit·ic** (stēatĭt'ĭk) *adj.*

steed (stēd) *n.* (poet., rhet., etc.) Horse, esp. warhorse.

steel (stēl) *n.* Various hard, malleable, elastic alloys of purified iron with carbon (up to 1%) and metals such as nickel, manganese, or chromium, used as material for tools, weapons, etc.; this in form of weapons or cutting tools; strip of steel for stiffening corset etc.; ~ **engraving**, engraving on, impression taken from, steel plate; ~ **wool**, very fine steel shavings used as abrasive. **steel** *v.t.* Nerve, harden, fortify (*against*).

Steele (stēl), **Sir Richard** (1672–1729). Irish essayist, playwright, and man of letters; founder of the periodicals *Tatler* and (with ADDISON[1]) *Spectator*.

steel·y (stē'lē) *adj.* (**steel·i·er, steel·i·est**). Of, hard as, steel; inflexible, obdurate.

steen·bok (stēn'bŏk, stän'-) *n.* (pl. **-boks**, collect. **-bok**). Small African antelope (*Raphicerus campestris*).

steep[1] (stēp) *adj.* With precipitous face or slope, sloping sharply; (colloq., of price etc.) exorbitant, unreasonable; (of story etc.) exaggerated, incredible. **steep'ly** *adv.* **steep'ness** *n.* **steep'en** *v.* **steep** *n.* Steep slope, precipice.

steep[2] (stēp) *v.* Soak, be soaked, in liquid; (fig.) permeate, imbue, impregnate. ~ *n.* Process of steeping; liquid in which thing is steeped.

stee·ple (stē'pel) *n.* Lofty structure, esp. tower with spire, rising above roof of church; spire; **stee'plechase**, horse race across country (orig. perh. with steeple as goal) or on made course with hedges, water jumps, and other obstacles; foot race of similar kind; **stee'plejack**, man who climbs steeples, tall chimneys, etc., to do repairs etc.

steer[1] (stēr) *n.* Castrated male ox, bullock usu. raised for beef.

steer[2] (stēr) *v.* Guide (vessel), guide vessel, by rudder, helm, etc.; guide (aircraft, automobile, etc.) by mechanical means; (of vessel etc.) be guided; direct one's course; ~ **clear of**, avoid; **steer'ing wheel**, vertical wheel on ship, hand wheel in car etc. for steering; **steers'man** (pl. **-men**), one who steers ship, hence **steers'manship**. **steer'a·ble** *adj.*

steer·age (stēr'ĭj) *n.* 1. Effect of helm on ship; **steer'ageway**, amount of way or motion sufficient for ship to answer helm. 2. Part of ship allotted to passengers traveling at cheapest rate.

steg·o·saur (stĕg'osōr), **steg·o·sau·rus** (stĕgosōr'us) *ns.* Any of several large (about ten tons), herbivorous dinosaurs (genus *Stegosaurus*) of the Jurassic, having small head and bony plates along the backbone.

stein (stīn) *n.* Large earthenware mug, esp. for beer. [Ger., = "stone"]

Stein (stīn), **Gertrude** (1874–1946). Amer. writer living chiefly in Paris; author of *Three Lives, The Autobiography of Alice B. Toklas, Four Saints in Three Acts*, etc.

Stein·beck (stīn'bĕk), **John Ernst** (1902–68). Amer. writer; author of *Of Mice and Men, The Grapes of Wrath*, etc.; recipient of Nobel Prize for literature, 1962.

ste·le (for def. 1 stē'lē, stēl; for sense 2 stēl, stē'lē) *n.* (pl. **-les, -lae** pr. -lē); also for def. 1 **ste·la** (stē'la) (pl. **-las, -lae** pr. -lē). 1. Upright slab with sculptured design or inscription, esp. as grave-

*Unlike most antelopes, the **steenbock** of east Africa tries to avoid danger by lying in the grass with the neck outstretched, rather than rely on its speed to outpace its enemies.*

suffixes are added. 4. Line of ancestry; branch of family; stock, race. 5. (naut.) Curved upright timber or metal piece at fore end of vessel, to which ship's sides are joined; bows or forepart of vessel. **stem** *v.* (**stemmed, stem·ming**). 1. Remove stem of. 2. Make headway against (tide, current, etc.). 3. ~ **from**, originate in.

stem² (stĕm) *v.t.* (**stemmed, stem·ming**). Check, stop, dam up (stream etc.); (skiing) check (oneself), check progress, by forcing heel of ski(s) outward from line of run; ~ **turn**, turn made by stemming one ski.

stench (stĕnch) *n.* Foul or offensive smell.

sten·cil (stĕn′sil) *n.* Thin sheet of metal, cardboard, etc. with holes cut in such a way that when paintbrush etc. is passed over it, desired design is produced on surface beneath; decoration, lettering, so produced. ~ *v.t.* (**-ciled, -cil·ing**, Brit. **-cilled, -cil·ling**). Produce (pattern) on surface, ornament (surface) with pattern, by means of stencil(s).

Sten·dhal (stĕndahl′). Pen name of Henri Beyle (1783–1842),

stone. 2. (bot.) Axial cylinder in stems and roots of vascular plants.

stel·lar (stĕl′er) *adj.* Of stars; star-shaped.

stel·late (stĕl′ĭt, -āt), **stel·lat·ed** (stĕl′ātĭd) *adjs.* Star-shaped, radiating from center like rays of star.

stem¹ (stĕm) *n.* 1. Main body above ground, ascending axis, of tree, shrub, or other plant; stalk

supporting leaf, flower, or fruit. 2. Stem-shaped part or object, as slender upright support of cup, wineglass, etc., long slender part or tube of key, thermometer, tobacco pipe, etc.; **stem′ware**, glasses with stems; **stem-winder**, watch wound by turning head on end of stem, not by key. 3. Part of word remaining essentially unchanged in inflection, part to which inflectional

*The **stem** of a plant can be distinguished from the root by the bud which is always at its tip. Its function is to provide support for the leaves and to convey food. Young stems are soft but as they age, they become hard and woody. Bulbs and rhizomes are underground stems which store food; runners, on a strawberry, are horizontal stems that produce new plants.*

transverse and longitudinal sections of stems

bundle
loem
xylem
pith
hair
cortex
medulla
phloem
xylem

stele

bres
ermis
vascular bundle
epidermis
cambium
endodermis

maize (monocotyledon)   sunflower (dicotyledon)

heart-wood
sap-wood
bud
thorn
lenticel
leaf-scar
bark
annual ring

transverse section of tree trunk   twigs of horse-chestnut   hawthorn

true leaf   cladode

butcher's broom

*Modern lifting equipment has made the working life of a **stevedore** far less taxing than in the past, when most freight had to be loaded and unloaded by hand.*

French novelist, author of *The Red and the Black* and *The Charterhouse of Parma*.

sten·o (stĕn′ō) *n*. (colloq.) Stenography; stenographer.

ste·nog·ra·phy (stenŏg′rafē) *n*. Art of writing in shorthand. **sten′·o·graph** (stĕn′ogrăf, -grahf) *n*. Writing, machine for writing, in shorthand. ~ *v*. Write in shorthand, act as stenographer. **ste·nog′ra·pher** *n*. **sten·o·graph·ic** (stĕnŏgrăf′ĭk), **sten·o·graph′i·cal** *adjs*. **sten·o·graph′·i·cal·ly** *adv*.

Sten·o·type (stĕn′otīp) *n*. (trademark) Machine like a typewriter that prints letters representing syllables or phonemes.

sten·o·typ·y (stĕn′otīpē) *n*. System of shorthand symbols representing sounds, words, or phrases. **sten·o·typ·ic** (stĕnotĭp′ĭk) *adj*. **sten′o·typ·ist** *n*.

Sten·tor (stĕn′tŏr). In the *Iliad*, a herald with voice as powerful as 50 voices of other men; hence (**s** ~), person with very powerful voice. **sten·to·ri·an** (stĕntōr′ēan, -tŏr′-) *adj*.

step (stĕp) *v*. (**stepped, step′ping**). Lift and set down foot or alternate feet in walking etc.; go short distance, progress in some direction, by stepping; measure (distance) by stepping; (naut.) set up (mast) in step; ~ **down**, retire, resign, take lower position; (elect.) lower voltage of (current) by means of a transformer; ~ **in**, (fig.) intervene to help or hinder; ~**-in** (*n*. & *adj*.), (garment, esp. formerly of woman's underwear) put on by being stepped into without unfastening; ~ **on the gas**: see GAS²; ~ **on it**, (slang) hurry; ~ **out**, walk vigorously, stride;

behave, live, in lively, extravagant, or dissipated manner; ~ **up**, (elect.) increase voltage of (current) by means of a transformer; increase (efficiency, production) in rate, volume, etc., speed up; **stepping stone**, stone set in or projecting above water or muddy place as a help in crossing; (fig.) means of advancement or progress. **step** *n*. 1. Movement of stepping, distance gained by this; progress by stepping, course followed; manner of stepping; sound made by setting foot down; (fig.) action toward result, one of series of measures taken; **in** ~, stepping in time with other person(s) or music, stepping simultaneously and with corresponding legs with other person(s) or animal(s); **out of** ~, not in step. 2. Flat-topped structure, used singly or as one of series, to facilitate person's movement from one level to another; rung of ladder; foot piece for entering, mounting, or alighting from vehicle; notch cut for foot in climbing; (pl.) stepladder; (fig.) degree in an ascending scale, advance from one of these to another. 3. (naut.) Block or socket supporting mast etc.; (mech.) lower bearing on which vertical shaft revolves; step-like part or offset. 4. **step cut**, (of gem) cut in straight facets arranged around center of stone; **step′ladder**, kind of portable short ladder with flat steps and prop hinged to back for steadying.

step- *prefix*. Having a specified relationship resulting from remarriage of a parent, as **step′-brother, step′sister**, child of one's stepfather or stepmother; **step′child** (pl. **-children**), **step′-daughter, step′son**, child by previous marriage of one's wife or husband; **step′father, step′-mother**, husband, wife, of one's mother, father, by subsequent marriage.

steph·a·no·tis (stĕfanō′tĭs) *n*. Tropical woody climbing plant of genus *S* ~ with fragrant white waxy flowers. [Gk., = "fit for a wreath" (*stephanos*)]

Ste·phen¹ (stē′ven), **St.** (d. *c*35 A.D.). First Christian martyr, stoned to death at Jerusalem (Acts 6, 7; commemorated Dec. 26).

Ste·phen² (stē′ven), **St.** (*c*977–1038). First king (997–1038) and patron saint of Hungary; commemorated Sept. 2.

steppe (stĕp) *n*. Vast plain, grassy and largely treeless, esp. in SE. Europe and Siberia. [f. Russ. *step′*]

-ster *suffix*. Used in formation of nouns, sometimes derog., that indicate person who is, does, creates, associates with: *oldster, prankster, teamster, songster, gangster*.

ste·ra·di·an (sterā′dēan) *n*. (abbrev. sr) Solid angle at center of sphere subtending a section on the surface whose area is equal to the square of the radius.

ster·co·ra·ceous (stĕrkerā′-shus), **ster·co·rous** (stĕr′kerus) *adjs*. Of, produced by, dung or feces.

stere (stēr) *n*. One cubic meter.

ster·e·o (stĕr′ēō, stēr′-) *n*. (pl. **-os**). Stereotype; stereoscopic photograph or photography; stereophonic reproduction or equipment. ~ *adj*. Stereotyped; stereoscopic; stereophonic.

stereo- *prefix*. Solid; three dimensional; stereoscopic.

ster·e·o·chem·is·try (stĕrēō-kĕm′ĭstrē, stēr-) *n*. (Branch of chemistry dealing with) spatial arrangement of atoms etc. in molecule. **ster·e·o·chem′i·cal** *adj*.

ster·e·oph·o·ny (stĕrēŏf′onē, stēr-) *n*. System of separate microphones or loudspeakers designed to enhance the realism of broadcast or recorded sounds. **ster·e·o·phon·ic** (stĕrēofŏn′ĭk, stēr-) *adj*. **ster·e·o·phon′i·cal·ly** *adv*.

ster·e·o·scope (stĕr′ēoskōp, stēr-) *n*. Instrument for obtaining single image giving impression of solidity or relief from two pictures (usu. photographs) of object from slightly different points of view. **ster·e·o·scop·ic** (stĕrēoskŏp′ĭk, stēr-) *adj*. Of the stereoscope or stereoscopy. **ster·e·os·co·py** (stĕrēŏs′kopē, stēr-) *n*. Vision of objects as solid or in three dimensions. **ster·e·o·scop′i·cal·ly** *adv*.

ster·e·o·type (stĕr′ēotīp, stēr′-) *n*. Printing plate cast from mold of type in form; method or process of printing from this; conventional image or idea; idea lacking originality. ~ *v.t.* (**-typed, -typ·-ing**). Make stereotype(s) of, print from stereotype(s); (fig.) fix or perpetuate in unchanging form, formalize.

ster·ile (stĕr′il) *adj*. Barren; not producing, incapable of producing, fruit or offspring; free from living microorganisms, as bacteria etc. **ster′ile·ly** *adv*. **ste·ril·i·ty** (sterĭl′ĭtē) *n*.

ster·i·lize (stĕr′ilīz) *v.t.* (**-lized, -liz·ing**). 1. Render (individual) incapable of producing offspring. 2. Render (object) free from contamination by microorganisms by treating with heat, antiseptic, etc. **ster·i·li·za·tion** (stĕrilīza′shon) *n*.

ster·ling (stĕr′lĭng) *n*. 1. British currency. 2. (Articles made of) sterling silver. ~ *adj*. (of coins and precious metals) Genuine, of standard value or purity; (fig.) solidly excellent, genuine, not showy or specious; ~ **silver**, silver of a fineness formerly fixed by law for Brit. silver coinage (92 1/2%

To prevent premature babies risking infection, they are kept in a **sterile** unit which is sufficiently flexible to allow them to be moved about without exposure to the atmosphere.

Of little practical use, although popular during the 19th century to give a three dimensional effect, the **stereoscope** was conceived by Wheatstone but improved by Sir David Brewster.

silver and 7 1/2% copper). [orig. as noun, = the English silver penny]

stern[1] (stern) *n.* After or rear part of aircraft, ship, or boat, specif. that part of the hull abaft the stern-post; buttocks, rump; tail, esp. of oxhound; ~ **chase**, pursuit of ship by another directly in its wake; **stern'post**, central upright timber or iron of stern, attached to keel and usu. bearing rudder; **stern'-wheeler**, (hist.) steamer with 1 large paddle wheel at stern.

stern[2] (stern) *adj.* Severe, strict, not lenient, rigorous in principle, punishment, or condem-nation; hard, grim, harsh, gloomy. **stern'ly** *adv.* **stern'ness** *n.*

ster·nal (stĕr'nal) *adj.* Of the sternum.

Sterne (stern), **Laurence** (1713–68). English novelist, author of *Tristram Shandy* and *A Sentimental Journey.*

ster·num (stĕr'num) *n.* (pl. **-nums, -na** pr. -na). Bone or series of bones running along middle line of front of trunk, usu. articulated with some of ribs; breastbone of bird; ventral plate of body segment of arthropod.

ster·nu·ta·tion (stĕrnyutā'shon) *n.* Sneezing, sneeze. **ster·nu·ta-to·ry** (sternoo'tatōrē, -tōrē, -nū'-) *adj. & n.* (pl. **-ries**). (Substance, e.g. snuff) causing sneezing.

ster·nu·ta·tor (stĕrn'yutātēr) *n.* Chemical agent, esp. poison gas, that acts as a nose irritant.

ster·oid (stĕr'oid, stēr'-) *adj. & n.* (biochem.) (One) of a class of compounds with complex 4-ring molecular structure, found in animal and plant cells or prepared synthetically and including the sterols, bile acids, and certain hormones.

ster·ol (stĕr'awl, -ŏl, -ōl, stēr'-) *n.* (biochem.) One of a class of complex solid alcohols, as cholesterol, ergosterol, widely distributed in animals and plants.

ster·to·rous (stĕr'terus) *adj.* (of breathing etc.) Producing snoring or rasping sound. **ster'to·rous·ly** *adv.* **ster'to·rous·ness** *n.*

stet (stĕt) *n.* Direction to printer, written in margin of manuscript or proof, to cancel a correction made in the text, the letters thus restored being indicated by dots beneath them. ~ *v.t.* (**stet·ted, stet·ting**). [L., = "let it stand"]

steth·o·scope (stĕth'oskōp) *n.* Instrument, consisting of ear tubes and a main tube to be applied to chest etc. for auscultation, esp. of heart or lungs. **steth·o·scop·ic** (stĕthoskŏp'ĭk) *adj.* **steth·o·scop'-i·cal·ly** *adv.* **ste·thos·co·py** (stĕthŏs'kopē) *n.*

Stet·son (stĕt'son) *n.* (trade-mark, colloq.) Man's felt hat with broad brim.

ste·ve·dore (stē'vedōr, -dôr) *n.* Man employed in loading and un-loading ship's cargoes.

Ste·ven·son[1] (stē'venson), **Adlai Ewing** (1835–1914). Amer. statesman; member from Illinois of U.S. House of Representatives, 1875–7, 1879–81; vice president under Grover Cleveland, 1893–7; also his grandson (1900–65) of the same name, U.S. Ambassador to the United Nations from 1961.

Ste·ven·son[2] (stē'venson), **Robert Louis** (1850–94). Scottish essayist, novelist, and poet; author of *Treasure Island, Dr. Jekyll and Mr. Hyde, Kidnapped*, etc.

stew (stoo, stū) *v.* Cook by long simmering in closed vessel with liquid; (fig.) be oppressed by close or moist warm atmosphere; ~ **in one's own juice**, be left to suffer the consequences of one's own actions. **stew** *n.* Dish of stewed meat, usu. with vegetables; (fig.) state of great alarm or excitement; **stew'pan, stew'pot**, pan, covered pot, for stewing.

stew·ard (stoo'erd, stū'-), fem. **stew·ard·ess** (stoo'erdĭs, stū'-) *ns.* 1. Person entrusted with manage-ment of another's property, esp. paid manager of great house or estate. 2. Purveyor of provisions etc. for college, club, ship, etc. 3. Attendant waiting on passengers in ship or aircraft. 4. Official managing meeting, ball, show, etc.

stick (stĭk) *v.* (**stuck** pr. stŭk, **stick·ing**). 1. Thrust point of (pin, weapon, etc.) *in(to), through*; insert pointed thing(s) into, stab; fix *on* pointed thing, be fixed (as) by point *in(to)* or *on*; (colloq.) put in specified position. 2. ~ **out, up**, etc., protrude, (cause to) project; be, make, erect; ~ **up for**, maintain cause or character of, champion; ~ **up**, (slang) rob with violence, hold up; ~ **-up** (*n.*). 3. Fix, become or remain fixed (as) by adhesion of surfaces; (cause to) adhere or cleave; baffle, confuse; (colloq.) endure, bear; ~ **at** or **to it**, persist, not cease trying; ~ **by** or **to**, remain faithful to; ~**-to-it-ive-ness**, (colloq.) perseverance; ~**-to-it-ive** (*adj*.). 4. Lose or deprive of power of motion through friction, jamming, suction, difficulty, etc.; ~**-in-the-mud**, slow, unprogressive (person); **sticking plaster**, adhesive plaster for wounds etc.; **stick'pin**, (ornamental) pin, esp. tie pin, that is merely stuck in, as dist. from safety pin; **stick-up**, (*adj*.) that sticks up or projects. **stick** *n*. 1. Short and relatively slender piece of wood; shoot or branch of tree cut to convenient length for use as walking cane, bludgeon, staff, wand, support for climbing plant, etc.; fiddlestick, drumstick, composing stick, etc.; implement used in hockey or lacrosse; twigs or small pieces of wood as fuel; (fig.) person of no liveliness or intelligence, poor actor; ~ **ball**, baseball played with broom handle and rubber ball; ~ **of furniture**, (esp. in neg. or pl.) piece of furniture; ~ **shift**, manually operated gearshift set in the floor of a car. 2. Slender more or less cylindrical piece *of* any material. 3. Number of aerial bombs released in close succession, or of parachute troops from an

*A **still life** of apples as painted by Gustave Courbet shows the painter's determination to pursue the modes of Velazquez, whom he admired, rather than follow classical trends.*

aircraft. 4. ~ **insect**, insect of family Phasmidae, usu. wingless, with long slender sticklike body resembling twigs of trees in which it lives.

stick·er (stĭk'er) *n*. (esp.) 1. Adhesive label or other paper gummed on back; ~ **price**, retail price for product suggested by manufacturer, esp. as pasted on window of new automobile. 2. Dogged or persistent person.

stick·le·back (stĭk'elbăk) *n*. Any of small spiny-finned fishes (family Gasterosteidae) of N. hemisphere.

stick·ler (stĭk'ler) *n*. 1. (followed by *for*) One who insists on or pertinaciously supports or advocates. 2. Difficult problem.

stick·y (stĭk'ē) *adj*. (**stick·i·er, stick·i·est**). Tending to stick or adhere, glutinous, viscous; (of weather) muggy; covered with wet paint, adhesive, etc.; (slang) highly unpleasant and painful. **stick'i·ly** *adv*. **stick'i·ness** *n*.

stiff (stĭf) *adj*. 1. Rigid, not flexible; unbending, unyielding, uncompromising, obstinate; lacking ease, grace, or freedom; formal, labored, constrained, haughty; ~**-arm** (*v*. & *n*.) (make) motion with extended arm of pushing away or

shoving someone; ~**-necked**, stubborn. 2. Not working freely, sticking, offering resistance; (of joints, limbs, etc.) not supple, unable to move without pain; ~ **neck**, condition in which head cannot be moved without pain. 3. Hard to cope with, trying, difficult. 4. (of moist or semiliquid substance) Thick and viscous, not fluid. **stiff'ly** *adv*. **stiff'ness** *n*. **stiff'en** *v*. **stiff'en·er** *n*. **stiff** *n*. (slang) Corpse.

sti·fle¹ (stī'fel) *v*. (**-fled, -fling**). Smother; (cause to) feel oppressed or unable to breathe. **sti'fling** *adj*. **sti'fling·ly** *adv*.

sti·fle² (stī'fel) *n*. (also ~ **joint**) Joint between femur and tibia in horse and some other quadrupeds, corresponding to knee in man.

stig·ma (stĭg'ma) *n*. (pl. **stig-mas, stig·ma·ta** pr. stĭg'mata, stĭgmah'ta, -măt'a). Mark branded on slave, criminal, etc. (archaic); (fig.) mark of disgrace or infamy, stain on one's good name; (path.) definite characteristic of some disease, morbid red spot on skin, esp. one bleeding spontaneously; (anat., zool.) spot, pore, natural mark, esp. spot on surface of ovary where rupture of Graafian follicle will occur; insect's spiracle; (bot.) receptive surface of the floral pistil to which pollen grains adhere; (pl. **stigmata**) marks resembling wounds on crucified body of Christ, said to have developed on bodies of some saints. **stig·mat·ic** (stĭgmăt´ĭk), **stig·mat´i·cal** adjs.

stig·ma·tize (stĭg´matīz) v.t. (**-tized, -tiz·ing**). Mark with stigmata, produce stigmata upon; (fig.) use opprobrious terms of, describe by disgraceful or reproachful name. **stig·ma·ti·za·tion** (stĭgmatīză´shon) n.

stil·bes·trol (stĭlbĕs´trawl, -trŏl, -trōl) n. Synthetic estrogen, diethylstilbestrol.

stile[1] (stīl) n. Arrangement of steps, rungs, etc., allowing passage to persons over or through fence or wall but excluding cattle etc.

stile[2] (stīl) n. Vertical bar of wainscot, sash, or other wooden framing.

sti·let·to (stĭlĕt´ō) n. (pl. **-tos, -toes**). Short dagger; small pointed implement for making eyelet holes etc.

still[1] (stĭl) adj. Without or almost without motion or sound, silent, quiet, calm; (of wine etc.) not sparkling or effervescing; **still´-birth**, delivery of dead child, so **still´born; still life**, (pl. **still lifes**) representation in painting etc. of inanimate things, as fruit, flowers, etc. **still´ness** n. **still** n. 1. Deep silence. 2. Photograph (other than motion picture), esp. single frame from motion picture film. ~ v. Quiet, calm, appease, make still; (rare) grow still or calm. ~ adv. 1. Without motion or change. 2. Now as formerly; then as before; now, in contrast with future; even then, even now; nevertheless; even, yet; always, even.

still[2] (stĭl) n. Distilling apparatus, consisting essentially of a closed vessel for heating substance to be distilled, and spiral tube or worm for condensing the vapor so produced.

Still·son (stĭl´son) **wrench.** (trademark) Monkey wrench having pivoted, adjustable jaw that tightens its grip on pipes etc. as pressure is applied on handle.

stilt (stĭlt) n. 1. Each of pair of poles, usu. held by hands or under arms, with footrest some way from lower end, for enabling person to walk over marshy ground, stream, etc., with feet raised above ground; one of set of piles or posts supporting building, etc. 2. Marsh bird of the widely distributed genus *Himantopus*, with very long slender legs and sharp slender bill.

stilt·ed (stĭl´tĭd) adj. (As) on stilts; (of style, language, etc.) artificially lofty, formally pompous. **stilt´ed·ly** adv. **stilt´ed·ness** n.

Stil·ton (stĭl´ton) n. (also ~ **cheese**) Rich blue-veined cheese, made principally in England.

stim·u·lant (stĭm´yulant) n. Agent producing temporary increase of activity in part of organism; such a food, beverage, as tea, coffee, etc.; (pop.) alcoholic drink.

stim·u·late (stĭm´yulāt) v.t. (**-lat·ed, -lat·ing**). Apply stimulus to, act as stimulus on; animate, spur on, make more vigorous or active. **stim·u·la·tion** (stĭmyulā´shon) n. **stim´u·la·tive** adj. **stim´-u·lat·ing·ly** adv.

stim·u·lus (stĭm´yulus) n. (pl. **-li** pr. -lī). Something that rouses to activity or energy; rousing effect; thing that rouses organ or tissue to specific activity or function, effect of this. [L., = "goad"]

sting (stĭng) n. 1. Sharp-pointed organ in some insects and other animals, freq. connected with poison gland, and capable of giving painful or dangerous wound; poison fang of snake; (bot.) stiff sharp-pointed hair emitting irritating fluid when touched. 2. Stinging, being stung; wound made, pain or irritation produced, by sting; rankling or acute pain of body or mind; keenness, vigor; stimulus. 3. **sting´ray, stingaree** (stĭng´erē, stĭngerē´), ray esp. of family Dasyatidae, with long tapering tail armed with flattened sharp-pointed serrated spine(s) capable of inflicting severe wounds. **sting** v. (**stung** pr. stŭng, **sting·-ing**). 1. Wound with sting; (of some plants) produce kind of burning or itching rash or inflammation by contact with (skin); feel acute pain; be able to sting, have a sting; **stinging hair**, sting of plant; **stinging nettle**, common NETTLE. 2. (slang, chiefly pass.) Charge heavily, involve in expense, swindle.

stin·gy (stĭn´jē) adj. (**-gi·er, -gi·est**). Meanly parsimonious. **stin´gi·ly** adv. **stin´gi·ness** n.

stink (stĭngk) v. (**stank** pr. stăngk or **stunk** pr. stŭngk, **stunk, stink·ing**). Have, emit, strong offensive smell; drive *out* with stench or suffocating fumes; cause to stink; (slang) be of offensively poor quality. ~ n. Strong offensive smell; **raise a** ~, (colloq.) cause trouble by criticizing or complaining; ~ **bomb**, small bomb giving off offensive smell on bursting; **stink´horn**, any of various ill-smelling fungi, esp. *Phallus impudicus*; **stink´wood**, any of various trees with unpleasant smelling wood.

stink·er (stĭng´ker) n. (colloq.) Person or thing particularly offensive or irritating.

stink·ing (stĭng´kĭng) adj. That stinks (freq. in names of plants etc., e.g. ~ **gum**, eucalyptus with leaves having strong, buglike smell; ~ **Roger**, wild marigold); (slang) objectionable, obnoxious; very drunk.

stint (stĭnt) n. Limitation of supply or effort; fixed or allotted amount (of work etc.). ~ v. Keep on short allowance, supply or give in niggardly amount or grudgingly. **stint´er** n. **stint´ing** adj. **stint´-ing·ly** adv.

stipe (stīp) n. (bot.) Footstalk, esp. stem supporting pileus of fungus, leafstalk of fern etc.; (zool.) stipes.

With legs longer in proportion to its body than any other wading bird, the stilt will feed on shrimps either in salt water estuaries or in grassy areas flooded by freshwater.

The greater **stitchwort** is one of a group of some 80 plants with a wide distribution. Others include common chickweed and the bog variety with large white flowers on foot-high stems.

Reconstructed in the 1950s, the **Stoa of Attalus** still flanks the Agora or ancient civic centre of Athens. A stoa could be a detached portico, or a frontage to a hall as in the example illustrated.

sti·pend (stī′pĕnd) *n.* Salary or pension, esp. of clergyman.

sti·pen·di·ar·y (stīpĕn′dēĕrē) *adj. & n.* (Person) receiving stipend.

sti·pes (stī′pēz) *n.* (pl. **stip·i·tes** pr. stĭp′ītēz). (zool.). Stalklike part or organ, esp. 2nd segment of maxilla of insect, eyestalk, etc.; (bot.) stipe.

stip·ple (stĭp′el) *n.* Method of painting, engraving, etc., by use of dots or small spots to produce gradations of shade or color; layer of paint applied roughly over layer of another color that shows through in places; effect, work, so produced. ~ *v.* Engrave, paint, in stipple.

stip·u·late (stĭp′yulāt) *v.* Require or insist upon as essential condition; make express demand *for* as condition of agreement. **stip·u·la·tion** (stĭpyulā′shon) *n.*

stip·ule (stĭp′ūl) *n.* One of pair of lateral appendages, freq. resembling small leaf or scale, at base of leaf in certain plants.

stir[1] (stẽr) *n.* Commotion, bustle, disturbance, excitement; slight movement; act of stirring. ~ *v.* (**stirred, stir·ring**). Set, keep, (begin to) be, in (esp. slight) motion; agitate (soft or liquid or semiliquid mass) with more or less circular motion, as with spoon, so as to mix ingredients, prevent burning in cooking, etc.; rouse (*up*), excite, animate, inspirit. **stir′ring** *adj.* Exciting, stimulating. **stir′ring·ly** *adv.*

stir[2] (stẽr) *n.* (slang) Prison.

stir·rup (stẽr′up, stĭr′-, stŭr′-) *n.* Support suspended by strap from side of saddle for rider's foot, now usu. iron loop with flattened base; something resembling this, esp. U-shaped clamp or support; (naut.) rope with eye at end supporting footrope; (also ~ **bone**) stirrup-shaped bone of middle ear, stapes; ~ **cup**, (Brit.) parting cup of wine etc. handed to rider on horseback; ~ **jar, vase**, (Gk. antiq.) jar with solid neck joined to body by handle on each side; ~ **leather**, strap suspending stirrup from saddle.

stitch (stĭch) *n.* 1. Sudden sharp pain, esp. in side of the body. 2. Each movement of threaded needle in and out of fabric in sewing, or of awl in shoemaking; loop of thread etc. left in fabric by this movement; single complete movement of needle, hook, etc., in knitting, crochet, embroidery, etc.; part of work produced by this; (surg.) movement of needle in sewing up wound, loop of catgut etc. left in skin or flesh by this; method of making stitch, kind of work produced. 3. **stitch′wort**, chickweed, esp. kind with erect stem and white starry flowers. **stitch** *v.* Sew, make stitches (in); fasten, make, ornament, with stitches.

stitch·er·y (stĭch′erē) *n.* Needlework.

sto·a (stō′a) *n.* (pl. **sto·as, sto·ai** pr. stō′ī, **sto·ae** pr. stō′ē). Portico in ancient Greek architecture.

stoat (stōt) *n.* (pl. **stoats**, collect. **stoat**). ERMINE, esp. in its brown summer coat.

stock (stŏk) *n.* 1. Trunk or stem of tree; stump, butt; plant into which graft is inserted; (bot.) rhizome; (geol.) cylindrical intrusive body of igneous rock (freq. granite) of moderate size. 2. Body piece serving as the base or holder or handle for the working parts of an implement or machine, as whip, lathe, plow, rifle, anchor, etc. 3. (Source of) family or breed; line of descent, ancestry; race, racial strain, or other related group of plants or animals; ethnic group or other major subdivision of human race; group of related (families of) languages. 4. (hist., pl.) Instrument of punishment, wooden framework set up in public place with holes for offender's feet or feet and hands. 5. (pl.) Timbers on which ship rests while building. 6. Cruciferous plant of genus *Mathiola*, with fragrant flowers. 7. Livestock. 8. Liquor or broth made by stewing meat, bones, vegetables, etc., and used as foundation for soup etc. 9. Raw material of manufacture; fund, store ready for drawing on, equipment for trade or pursuit. 10. Specified type or grade of paper; paper for specific job of printing. 11. Outstanding capital of corporation, regarded as transferable property held by subscribers or creditors and subject to fluctuations in market value; see COMMON ~, PREFERRED ~. 12. **take** ~, make inventory of merchandise etc. in hand; (fig.) make careful estimate of one's position, prospects, resources, etc.; **take** ~ **of**, reckon up, evaluate, scrutinize. 13. (attrib. or as *adj.*) Kept regularly in stock for sale or use; commonly used, constantly recurring in discussion etc.; ~ **company**,

Left: Present in the north-temperate forests and tundra of Europe, Asia and North America, the **stoat** *lives on small animals and is a swift hunter. However it in its turn is prey to hawks.*

stock *v.* 1. Fit (gun etc.) with stock. 2. Provide (shop, farm, etc.) with goods, livestock, or requisites. 3. Keep (goods) in stock.

stock·ade (stŏkād') *n.* & *v.t.* (**-ad·ed, -ad·ing**). (Fortify with) enclosure of upright stakes, posts, etc.

Stock·holm (stŏk'hōm, -hōlm; *Swed.* stawk'hawm). Capital city and port of Sweden, on the Baltic Sea.

stock·ing (stŏk'ĭng) *n.* Close-fitting, usu. knitted, covering for foot and leg up to or above knee; ~ **cap**, knitted usu. tapered cap, often having tassel at end.

stock·y (stŏk'ē) *adj.* (**stock·i·er, stock·i·est**). Thickset, short, and strongly built. **stock'i·ly** *adv.* **stock'i·ness** *n.*

stodg·y (stŏj'ē) *adj.* (**stodg·i·er, stodg·i·est**). (of food) Heavy, filling, thick or semisolid; (of person, book, etc.) dull, heavy, solid, uninspired. **stodg'i·ly** *adv.* **stodg'i·ness** *n.*

sto·gie, sto·gy (stō'gē) *ns.* (pl. **-gies**). Kind of long slender cigar or cheroot.

Sto·ic (stō'ĭk) *n.* 1. Philosopher of school founded *c*315 B.C. by ZENO[1], who taught that virtue was the highest good, and inculcated repression of emotion, indifference to pleasure or pain, and patient endurance; later Stoic writers were Seneca, Epictetus, and Marcus Aurelius. 2. (**s~**) Person of great self-control, fortitude, or austerity. **sto'i·cal** *adj.* **sto'i·cal·ly** *adv.* **sto·i·cism** (stō'ĭsĭzem) *n.* [Gk. *stoa* porch, hall in Athens where Zeno taught]

stoke (stōk) *v.* (**stoked, stok·ing**). Feed and tend (furnace), feed furnace of (engine etc.); act as stoker; **stoke'hold**, containing ship's boilers, where furnaces are tended; **stoke'hole**, space in front of furnace where stokers stand, opening through which furnace is tended, stokehold.

stok·er (stō'ker) *n.* One who feeds and tends furnace esp. of ship or steam engine.

STOL *abbrev.* Short takeoff and landing (aircraft).

stole[1] (stōl) *n.* 1. Long loose garment reaching to feet, esp. as outer dress of ancient Roman matron. 2. Ecclesiastical vestment, narrow strip of silk or linen worn over shoulders and reaching to or below knees; woman's fur etc. wrap of similar shape.

stole[2], **stol·en**: see STEAL.

stol·id (stŏl'ĭd) *adj.* Not easily excited or moved, phlegmatic, dull and impassive. **stol'id·ly** *adv.*

company of actors regularly performing together at particular theater; **stock'broker**, broker who buys and sells stocks for clients on commission; **stock'car**, railroad boxcar for carrying livestock; **stock car**, standard passenger automobile modified for use in racing; **stock certificate**, paper given by corporation to stockholder as proof of ownership of specified number of shares of stock; **stock dove**, Old World pigeon (*Columba oenas*) nesting in hollow trees; **stock exchange**, market, building, for buying and selling of stocks esp. *New York Stock Exchange*; association of brokers and jobbers doing business in particular place or market; **stock'fish** (pl. -fishes, collect. -fish), cod, hake, etc., split

Stocks in Williamsburg, Virginia are a reminder of the times when vagabonds and other petty criminals were sentenced to be locked in the wooden bars and exposed to public ridicule.

open and dried in the air without salt; **stock'holder**, holder or owner of stock etc.; shareholder; **stock in trade**, goods kept in stock, all requisites for a particular trade; **stock'man** (pl. **-men**), man employed to look after livestock; man owning and raising livestock; **stock market**, traffic in stocks and shares; **stock'pile**, raw materials purchased and accumulated; **stock'piling**, this practice; **stock-still**, quite motionless; **stock'yard**, enclosure with pens etc. for sorting or temporary keeping of cattle.

sto·lid·i·ty (stolĭd´ĭtē) *n.*

sto·lon (stō´lon) *n.* 1. (bot.) Reclined or prostrate branch that strikes root and develops new plant. 2. (zool.) In hydrozoa etc., extension of body wall that develops buds, giving rise to new zooids.

sto·ma (stō´ma) *n.* (pl. **sto·ma·ta** pr. stō´ma*ta*, stŏm´a-, **sto·mas**). (anat., zool.) Small mouthlike opening, esp. in lower animals; (bot.) minute orifice in epidermis of plants, esp. of leaves, affording communication between outer air and intercellular spaces in interior tissue.

stom·ach (stŭm´ak) *n.* Internal pouch or cavity in human or other animal body in which food is digested; in man, a dilatation of alimentary canal at upper left of abdomen; in some animals, esp. ruminants, one of several digestive cavities; (loosely) abdomen; (archaic) appetite *for* food; (fig.) relish, inclination, desire (*for*) danger, conflict, an undertaking, etc.; **stom´achache**, pain in belly, esp. bowels; **stomach pump**, small pump or syringe for emptying stomach or introducing liquids into it. **stomach** *v.t.* Bear without resistance, endure (insult etc.).

stom·ach·er (stŭm´aker) *n.* (hist.) In women's dress of 15th–17th centuries, ornamental piece, freq. embroidered or set with gems, covering breast and pit of stomach.

stomp (stŏmp) *n.* Lively jazz dance with heavy stamping. ~ *v.* Dance stomp; tread heavily.

stone (stōn) *n.* (pl. **stones, stone** for sense 3). 1. Piece of rock, esp. of small or moderate size; hard compact material of which stones and rocks consist, particular kind

of this; gem; piece of stone of definite form and size, for special purpose, as for building, paving, grinding, as a monument, etc. 2. Hard morbid concretion in body, esp. in kidney, urinary bladder, or gall bladder, calculus; hard wood-like case of kernel in drupe; seed of grape etc. 3. (Brit.) Unit of weight, 14 lbs. 4. **S~ Age**, stage of culture marked by use of implements and weapons of stone, not metal; **stone´crop**, species of sedum, esp *Sedum acre*, with bright yellow flowers and small cylindrical

In the Black Hills of South Dakota is Mt. Rushmore, where the stone has been carved with the faces of 4 U.S. Presidents, Washington, Jefferson, Lincoln and Theodore Roosevelt.

fleshy leaves, growing on rocks, old walls, etc.; **stone´fish** (pl. **-fishes**, collect. **-fish**), (Austral.) tropical fish, (*Synanceja verrucosa*), with erectile dorsal spines containing deadly poison; **stone´fly** (pl. **-flies**), insect of order Plecoptera with larvae often found under stones in streams, used by anglers

Probably the most poisonous of all stinging fish, the stonefish is present in Indo-Pacific waters and off the coasts of northern Australia and South Africa. An antivenin is available.

Stoneware is a particular type of pottery fired at very high temperatures, which makes it vitrified (nonporous and glossy). Because of its nonporous quality it does not require glazing.

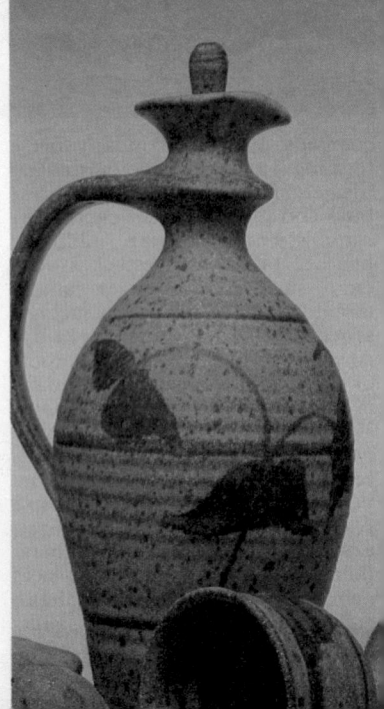

midsummer sunrise

enue
eel stone
ost holes

station stone

trilithons

furthest south
moonrise

oonset

sarsen circle

horseshoe

Aubrey holes

station stone

midwinter sunset

celestial pole

midsummer sunrise

midwinter sunrise

furthest south
moonrise

t north
oonset

mmer sunset

midwinter sunset

Left: Original arrangement and suggested calendar and astronomical functions of Stonehenge. Above: The mammoth uprights and lintels. The outer bank and ditch have been carbon-dated at about 3700 years old and carvings of axheads are between 1600 and 1400 B.C. Beyond its description as 'a prehistoric ritual monument' and its construction and modification in five stages, its true function has not been determined, although it seems likely that it served a religious function.

(freq. fig., esp. police spy, informer). **stool** *v.* Throw up young shoots or stems; act as stool pigeon.

stoop[1] (stōōp) *v.* 1. Bring one's head nearer ground by bending shoulders, trunk, etc., forward; carry head and shoulders bowed forward; incline (head, shoulders, back, etc.) forward and down; (fig.) descend from dignity, rank, etc., *to* action, *to* do. 2. (of falcon or other bird of prey) Swoop, descend steeply and swiftly, on quarry. ~ *n.* 1. Stooping carriage of back or shoulders; act of stooping. 2. Swoop of bird of prey on its quarry. **stoop'ing·ly** *adv.*

stoop[2] (stōōp) *n.* Porch, platform, small verandah, before door of house.

stop (stŏp) *v.* (**stopped, stop·ping**). 1. Close or almost close aperture or cavity by plugging, obstructing, etc.; close (organ pipe) at upper end with plug or cap; prevent or forbid passage through; make impervious or impassable. 2. Put an end to, arrest (motion etc.); check progress, motion or operation of; effectively hinder or prevent; suspend (payment etc.), give instructions to banker not to cash (check etc.). 3. (mus.) Press down (string of violin etc.) with finger to raise pitch of note, produce

---

as bait; **stone fruit**, drupe; **stone lily**, fossil crinoid; **stone'mason**, mason; **Stone of Scone**: see SCONE; **stone's throw**, short or moderate distance; **stone'wall**, obstruct by stonewalling; **stone'-walling**, (pol. slang) parliamentary obstruction; refusal to cooperate; deliberate delay; **stone'ware**, hard dense kind of pottery made from very siliceous clay or mixture of clay with much flint or sand; **stone'work**, masonry. **stone** *v.t.* (**stoned, ston·ing**). Pelt with stones, esp. put to death thus; take stones out of (fruit); face, pave, etc., with stone. ~ - *adv..* (in comb.) Completely, altogether (as ~-*blind*, ~-*broke*, ~-*dead*).

Stone·henge (stōn'hĕnj). Prehistoric stone monument on Salisbury Plain, Wiltshire, England, consisting of concentric circles of huge dressed stones

erected mainly in the Bronze Age; some of the larger stones carry lintels and among the smaller are blue stones that apparently come from SW. Wales.

ston·y (stō'nē) *adj.* (**ston·i·er, ston·i·est**). Full of, covered with, having many, stones; hard, rigid, fixed, as stone, obdurate, unfeeling. **ston'i·ly** *adv.* **ston'i·ness** *n.*

stood: see STAND.

stooge (stōōj) *n.* (slang) Butt, foil, esp. for comedian; person deputed to do routine or undesirable work for another. ~ *v.i.* (**stooged, stoog·ing**). (slang) Act as stooge (*for*); move, travel *about*, *around*, in vehicle or aircraft.

stool (stōōl) *n.* 1. Seat for one person, without arms or back, esp. wooden one on three or four legs; footstool. 2. Feces evacuated. 3. Stump of felled tree etc., esp. with new shoots. 4. ~ **pigeon**, decoy

The development of effective refrigeration was probably the most important development in food preservation. Today, pallets of frozen food can be stacked in cold **storage** until needed.

Elevated grain bunkers in Kansas are a modern and efficient means of **storage**. They are usually built of concrete for economy, speed of construction and durability.

(note, sound) thus. 4. Cease, come to an end, cease from, discontinue; cease from motion, speaking, or action; make halt or pause; (colloq.) remain, stay, sojourn. 5. ~ **by**, **in**, make short visit; ~ **off, over**, interrupt journey. 6. ~ **the clock**, continue discussions past time limit during efforts to negotiate strike settlement, conduct legislative business, etc. 7. ~ **down**, reduce aperture of (lens). **stop′page** n. **stop** n. 1. Stopping, being stopped; pause, check. 2. Punctuation mark, esp. comma, semicolon, colon, or period; **full** ~, period. 3. Batten, peg, block, etc., meant to stop motion of something at fixed point; something stopping aperture, plug. 4. (optics, photog.) Aperture. 5. (mus.) ORGAN stop; closing of hole in tube of wind instrument to alter pitch of note, hole so closed, metal key closing it; pressing with finger on string of violin etc. to raise pitch of note, part of string where this pressure is applied. 6. (phonet.) Consonant in formation of which passage of breath is completely obstructed, mute. 7. **stop-**, in comb.: **stop′cock**, tap or short pipe with externally operated valve to stop or regulate passage of liquid, gas, etc.; key or handle for turning this; **stop′gap**, makeshift, temporary substitute; **stop′light**, red traffic light; light, on rear of motor vehicle, that illuminates when brakes are applied; **stop′-over**, act of stopping over; permission to passenger to break journey; **stop′watch**, watch indicating fractions of a second by a hand that can be instantly stopped at will, used in timing races etc. **stop·per** (stŏp′er) n. (esp.) Plug

for closing bottle etc., usu. of glass or of same material as vessel. ~ v.t. Close or secure with stopper. **stop·ple** (stŏp′el) n. Stopper of bottle or other vessel. ~ v. Close with stopple. **stor·age** (stōr′ĭj, stōr′-) n. Storing of goods, method of doing this; space for storing; cost of warehousing; **cold** ~, storing of provisions under refrigeration; ~ **battery**, electric cell (or group of these connected in series) in which the chemical action that produces the current can be reversed by passing an electric current through it in the opposite direction, and that thus constitutes a means of storing electric energy in the form of chemical energy. **store** (stōr, stōr) n. 1. Abundance, provision, stock of something ready to be drawn upon; **in** ~ **for**, awaiting (person). 2. Building, room, for retail sale of some commodity. 3. (pl.) Articles of particular kind or for special purpose accumulated for use; supply of things needed, stocks, reserves. 4. (attrib.) **store′front**, (rooms etc. at) street front of a store; **store′house**, place where things are stored; store, treasury; **store′-keeper**, person in charge of store(s); **store′room**, room for storing goods or supplies, esp. of ship or household. **store** v.t. (**stored, stor·ing**). Furnish, stock (with something); lay up for future use, form stock of; deposit (goods, furniture, etc.) in warehouse for temporary keeping; have storage accommodation for. **sto·rey**: see STORY[2]. **sto·ried** (stōr′ĕd, stōr′ēd) adj. 1. Adorned with representations of

historical or legendary scenes. 2. Celebrated in history or story. **stork** (stôrk) n. (pl. **storks**, collect. **stork**). Large wading bird of *Ciconia* and allied genera, with long legs and long stout bill, esp. the **common** or **white** ~ (*C. ciconia*), migratory European stork, often nesting on human habitations. **storm** (stôrm) n. Violent disturbance of atmosphere, with high winds and freq. thunder, heavy rain, hail, snow, etc.; wind of particular degree of violence, of force 10 or 11 on BEAUFORT SCALE; heavy discharge or shower (*of* blows etc.); violent disturbance of civil, political, domestic, etc., affairs; tumult, agitation, dispute, etc.; assault on fortified place, capture *of* place by such assault; **take by** ~, take by assault (freq. fig.); ~ **center**, central, comparatively calm, area of cyclonic storm; (fig.) center around which storm of controversy, trouble, etc., rages; ~ **signal**, any device for signaling approach of a storm; ~ **troops**, shock troops, esp. a Nazi semi-military organization; ~ **trooper**, member of this. **storm** v. 1. Take by storm, rush violently, esp. to attack. 2. (of wind etc.) Rage, be violent; bluster, fume; scold. **storm·y** (stôr′mē) adj. (**storm·i·er, storm·i·est**). Characterized, marked, by storm(s); associated or connected with storms; ~ **petrel**: see PETREL. **storm′i·ly** adv. **storm′i·ness** n.

Among the largest wading birds and found in many parts of the world, probably the best-known **stork** is the white species. It winters in Africa but makes its nests on buildings in Europe during the summer. Other species nest in trees or cliffs. Their food consists of freshwater fauna and insects. In flight, they extend the neck and allow the legs to trail behind the body. They have no call but rattle their beaks.

open-billed stork

painted stork

saddle-billed stork

mycteria stork

black stork

white stork

yellow-billed stork

Although this **Stradivarius** violin is among a collection of old instruments in a museum, others made by this master are still used regularly in concert performances by leading violinists.

Stor·thing, Stor·ting (stōr'-tĭng) *ns.* Norwegian parliament. [Norw. *stor* great, *ting* assembly]

sto·ry[1] (stōr'ē, stôr'ē) *n.* (pl. **-ries**). Past course of life of person, institution, etc.; account given of incident or series of events; narrative meant to entertain hearer or reader, tale in prose or verse of actual or fictitious events; legend, myth, anecdote, novel, romance; (amusing) anecdote; plot (of novel, play, etc.); account in newspaper, material for this; (colloq.) lie.

sto·ry[2], Brit. **sto·rey** (stōr'ē, stôr'ē) *ns.* (pl. **-ries, -reys**). Each stage or portion into which house or building is divided horizontally, thing forming horizontal division.

stoup (stoop) *n.* Vessel for holy water, usu. stone basin in wall of church or near church porch; (archaic) flagon, tankard, beaker.

stout (stowt) *adj.* 1. Valiant, undaunted, resolute. 2. Of considerable thickness or strength. 3. Corpulent. **stout'ish** *adj.* **stout'ly** *adv.* **stout'ness** *n.* **stout** *n.* Heavy dark type of beer prepared with well-roasted barley or malt and sometimes caramelized sugar.

stove[1] (stōv) *n.* Portable or fixed closed apparatus to contain burning fuel or consume gas, electricity, etc., for use in warming rooms, cooking, etc.; **stove'pipe**, pipe to carry off smoke and gases from stove; (colloq.) top hat, tall silk hat. **stove** *v.t.* (**stoved, stov·ing**). Dry, heat, in stove.

stove[2]: see STAVE *v.*

stow (stō) *v.* Pack (*away*) in receptacles or convenient places, esp. (naut.) place (cargo) in proper order in hold etc.; fill (receptacle) with articles compactly arranged; (slang) desist, refrain from; ~ **away**, conceal oneself on board ship; **stow'away**, person hiding in ship, aircraft, etc. to avoid paying passage money, to escape by stealth etc. **stow'age** *n.* (Cost of) stowing.

Stowe (stō), **Mrs. Harriet Elizabeth Beecher** (1811–96). Amer. author and abolitionist; famous for novel *Uncle Tom's Cabin.*

S.T.P. *abbrev.* Standard temperature and pressure.

stra·bis·mus (strabĭz'mus) *n.* Disorder of eye muscles in which one eye fails to focus with the other on a given point at the same time. **stra·bis'mal, stra·bis'mic** *adjs.*

strad·dle (străd'el) *v.* (**-dled, -dling**). Spread legs wide apart in walking, standing, or sitting; (of legs) be wide apart; stand or sit across (thing) thus; part (legs) widely; drop shells beyond and short of a target in order to establish its range; drop bombs across (a target) beginning on one side and finishing on the opposite side; (colloq.) be noncommittal, seem to favor both sides of a controversy, vacillate. ~ *n.* 1. Action, position, of straddling. 2. (stock exch.) Contract giving holder right of either calling for or delivering stock at fixed price. **strad'dler** *n.*

Strad·i·var·i·us (strădĭvār'ēus). Latinized name of Antonio Stradivari (*c*1644–1737), most famous of a family of Italian makers of stringed instruments; hence, violin or other stringed instrument made by member of this family.

strafe (strāf, strahf) *v.t.* (**strafed, straf·ing**). Bombard, worry with shells, bombs, sniping, etc.; reprimand sharply, abuse, thrash. ~ *n.* Strafing attack. **straf'er** *n.* [Ger. *strafer* punish]

strag·gle (străg'el) *v.i.* (**-gled, -gling**). Stray from the main body, be dispersed or scattered, grow irregularly or loosely. **strag'gler** *n.* **strag'gling·ly** *adv.* **strag'gly** *adj.* (**-gli·er, -gli·est**). **straggle** *n.*

straight (strāt) *adj.* 1. Not crooked, not curved, bent, or angular; (geom., of line) lying evenly between any two of its points; (of hair) not curly or waving. 2. Direct, undeviating, going direct to the mark. 3. Upright, honest, candid; in proper order or place; (slang) conventional; heterosexual. 4. (of liquor) Unmixed, undiluted; (of playing cards) in sequences, without gap; (of drama) without music. 5. ~ **-arm** (*v.t.*), push away (someone, as tackler in football) by stretching arm out straight; **straight'edge**, strip of wood, steel, etc., with a perfectly straight edge, for testing accuracy of plane surface, drawing straight lines, etc.; **straight face**, intentionally expressionless face, esp. avoiding smile though amused (**straight-faced** *adj.*); ~ **flush**, in poker, a hand with all five cards of the same suit and in sequence; **straight man**, entertainer who acts as foil for a comedian; **straight time**, number of working hours set as standard for specified work period; pay rate for work during such hours. **straight'ness** n. **straight** n. Straight condition; straight part of something, esp. concluding stretch of racetrack; consecutive sequence of cards in poker. **straight** adv. In a straight line, direct, without deviation or circumlocution; in right direction, with good aim; **straight away**, **straight'away**, immediately, at once; **straight off**, without hesitation, deliberation, etc.; **straight out**, frankly, outspokenly.

straight·en (strā'ten) v. Make straight.

straight·forward (strātfōr'-werd) adj. Honest, open, frank; (of task etc.) presenting no complications. **straight·for'ward·ly** adv.

strain[1] (strān) n. Breed, stock; inherited tendency or quality, moral tendency forming part of a character.

strain[2] (strān) n. 1. Straining, being strained, pull, tension, exertion; injury or damage due to excessive exertion, tension, or force; deformation or distortion in any body due to stress, molecular displacement. 2. Melody, tune; passage, snatch, of music, poetry, etc.; tone, mode, etc., adopted in talking or writing; tenor, drift, general tendency or character. ~ v. 1. Stretch tightly, make taut; stretch beyond normal degree, force to extreme effort, exert to utmost; wrest, distort, from true intention or meaning. 2. Overtask; injure, try, imperil, by overuse, by making excessive demands on, etc. 3. Make intense effort; strive intensely after, try at. 4. Clear (liquid) of solid matter by passing through sieve etc.; filter (solids) out from liquid; (of liquid) percolate. **strained** adj. (esp.) Artificial, forced, constrained.

strain·er (strā'ner) n. (esp.) Utensil for straining or filtering.

strait (strāt) adj. Narrow, limited; confined, confining; (archaic exc. in) **strait'jacket**, strong garment for upper part of body, designed to confine the arms, used to restrain violent persons in mental hospital; **strait-jacket** (v.t.) (fig.) restrict severely; **strait-laced**, (now only fig.) severely virtuous, puritanical. **strait** n. 1. Narrow passage of water connecting two seas or large bodies of water. 2. (usu. pl.) Difficult position; need, distress.

strait·en (strā'ten) v.t. (chiefly in past part.) Restrict in amount, scope, or range; reduce to straits;

straitened circumstances, inadequate means of living, poverty.

strake (strāk) n. Section of iron rim of cartwheel; continuous line of planking or plates, of uniform breadth, from stem to stern of ship.

stra·mo·ni·um (stramō'nēum) n. Jimson weed; dried poisonous leaves of this, used in treatment of asthma etc.

strand[1] (strănd) n. Margin of sea, lake, or river, esp. part of shore between tidemarks. ~ v. Run aground. **strand'ed** adj. (esp.) Left in a helpless position or without adequate resources.

strand[2] (strănd) n. Each of strings or wires twisted together to form rope, cord, cable, etc.; thread of woven material, string of beads, pearls, etc.; single hair; group of hairs.

strange (strānj) adj. (**strang·er**, **strang·est**). Foreign, alien, not one's own, not familiar or well known (to); novel, queer, peculiar, surprising, unexpected; fresh or unaccustomed to, unacquainted, bewildered. **strange'ly** adv. **strange'ness** n.

stran·ger (strān'jer) n. Foreigner; person in place, company, etc., to which he does not belong; person unknown to or to one.

stran·gle (străng'gel) v.t. (-gled, -gling). Throttle, kill by

Chatham Strait is a fault-formed passage of the eastern North Pacific in southeast Alaska. It is 150 miles long and was named in 1794 after the 2nd Earl of Chatham.

external compression of throat; hinder growth of (plant) by overcrowding; (fig.) suppress; **stran'-glehold**, deadly grip (usu. fig.). **stran'gler** n.

stran·gles (străng'gelz) n. (usu. considered sing.) Infectious febrile disease, caused by a streptococcus, in equine animals.

stran·gu·late (străng'gyulāt) v.t. (-lat·ed, -lat·ing). Strangle (rare); (med.) constrict (organ, duct, etc.) so as to prevent circulation or passage of fluid; **strangulated hernia**, hernia so constricted as to arrest circulation in protuding part. **stran·gu·la·tion** (stránggyulā'shon) n. Strangling, being strangled; strangulating.

strap (străp) n. Leather band; flat strip of leather etc. of uniform breadth with buckle or other fastening for holding things together etc.; strip of metal used to secure or connect leaf of hinge etc.; **strap'-hanger**, passenger in bus, subway, etc., who must stand and hold on by strap for lack of seat. **strap'-less** adj. Without strap(s); (esp. of dress) without shoulder straps. **strap** v.t. (**strapped, strap·ping**). Furnish, fasten, with strap; beat, flog, with strap; (surg.) close (wound), bind (part) up with adhesive plaster. **strapped** adj. (slang) Lacking money.

strap·ping (străp'ing) adj. (of persons) Strongly and stoutly built.

stra·ta: see STRATUM.

strat·a·gem (străt'ajem) n. Artifice, trick, trickery; device(s)

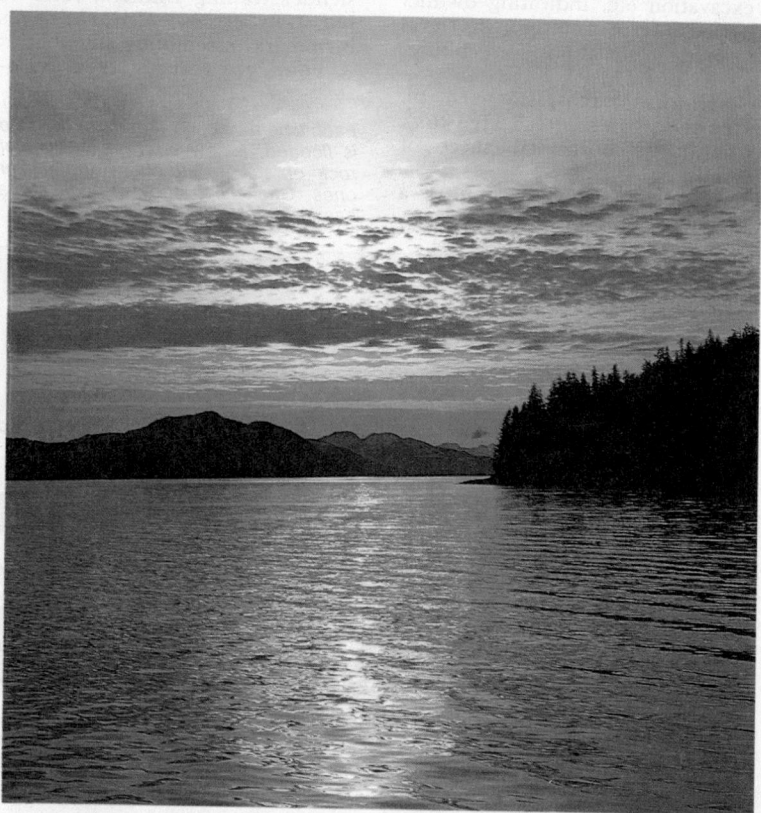

for deceiving enemy.

stra·te·gic (strate´jĭk) *adj.* Of, dictated by, serving the ends of, strategy; **~ bombing**, bombing designed to disrupt the enemy's internal economy, destroy morale, etc. (opp. TACTICAL bombing). **stra·te´gi·cal** *adj.* **stra·te´gi·cal·ly** *adv.*

strat·e·gy (străt´ejē) *n.* (pl. **-gies**). Generalship, art of war; art of planning and directing larger military movements and operations of campaign or war (opp. TACTICS); also fig. **strat´e·gist** *n.*

Strat·ford - up·on - A·von (străt´ferd upŏn ā´vŏn, -vŏn). Town in Warwickshire, England, birthplace and burial place of Shakespeare.

strat·i·fy (străt´ifī) *v.t.* (**-fied, -fy·ing**). Arrange in strata. **strat·i·fi·ca·tion** (strătifĭkā´shŏn) *n.*

stra·to·cu·mu·lus (strătōkū´-myulus, strătō-) *n.* (meteor.) Type of low cloud, a layer of globular masses.

strat·o·sphere (străt´osfēr) *n.* Region of the atmosphere lying above the troposphere, in which the temperature does not decrease with increasing height.

stra·tum (strā´tum, străt´um, strah´tum) *n.* (pl. **stra·ta** pr. strā´ta, străt´a, strah´ta, rarely **stra·tums**). Layer of material, esp. one of several one on top of another; (geol.) layer or bed of sedimentary rock; (biol.) layer of tissue; (archaeol.) layer of deposits in excavation etc. indicating distinct period or form of culture; (fig.) level or grade in social position, culture, etc.

stra·tus (strā´tus, străt´us) *n.* (pl. **stra·ti** pr. strā´tī, străt´ī, **stra·tus**). Continuous horizontal sheet of cloud.

Strauss[1] (strows). Name of a Viennese family of composers, famous esp. for dance music; **Johann ~** (1825–99), composer of the "Blue Danube" waltz and the opera *Die Fledermaus.*

Strauss[2] (strows), **Richard Georg** (1864–1949). German composer of *Der Rosenkavalier* and other operas, and of orchestral music.

straw (straw) *n.* Dry cut stalks of various cereals used for bedding, thatching, litter for animals, plaited or woven as material for hats, beehives, etc.; stem of any cereal plant; single stalk or piece of straw; tube orig. of straw for sucking drink through; insignificant trifle; straw hat; **catch** or **grasp at ~s**, resort to utterly inadequate expedient, like drowning man; **last straw**: see LAST[2]; **straw´board**, coarse yellow cardboard made of straw pulp; **straw boss**, workman who also acts as foreman; assistant foreman; **straw color, straw-colored**, (of) the pale light yellow color of straw; **straw in the wind**, slight hint that suggests much; **straw man**, stuffed effigy; imaginary person, idea, put forward as adversary to divert attention from real issue; **straw vote**, unofficial vote, esp. as sample or indication of public opinion. **straw´y** *adj.* (**straw·i·er, straw·i·est**).

straw·ber·ry (straw´bĕrē, -berē) *n.* (pl. **-ries**). (Juicy edible pulpy, usu. red, fruit, not properly a berry, of) plant of any species of genus *Fragaria*, stemless herbs with trifoliate leaves, white flowers, and slender trailing runners; color of red strawberries; **~ mark**, nevus birthmark, resembling strawberry; **~ roan**, red roan; **~ tree**, Euro-pean evergreen tree (*Arbutus unedo*), with white flowers and strawberry-like fruit; spindle tree.

stray (strā) *v.i.* Wander, go aimlessly; deviate from right way or (fig.) from virtue; lose one's way; get separated from flock, companions, home, or proper place. **~ n.** Lost or strayed domestic animal; homeless, friendless person, esp. child. **~ adj.** Strayed; scattered, sporadic, occasional casually met with. **stray´er** *n.*

streak (strēk) *n.* Thin irregular line of different color or substance from material or surface in which it occurs; flash (of lightning); vein of mineral; trait, strain, element of character, etc. **streak´y** *adj.* (**streak·i·er, streak·i·est**). **streak´i·ly** *adv.* **streak´i·ness** *n.* **streak** *v.* Mark with streak(s); move very rapidly (like streak of lightning); (slang) run nude through public place. **streak´er, streak´ing** *ns.*

stream (strēm) *n.* Body of water flowing in bed, esp. rivulet or brook as dist. from river; current or flow of river, in sea, etc.; flow of any liquid, current of air, gas etc.; continuous flow of persons, traffic, etc. moving in one direction or of words, events, influences, etc. **stream´line**, path of particle of fluid in motion, current of air, etc. form of body (esp. car or aircraft) calculated to offer minimum of resistance to air, water, etc. **stream´line** (*v.t.*), give this shape to (also fig.); **stream of consciousness**, (psychol.) thought and feelings considered as series of states constantly moving forward in time; (attrib.) applied to style of writing presenting individual's thoughts and feelings as continuous monologue. **stream´y** *adj.* (**stream·i·er, stream·i·est**). **stream** *v.* Flow or move as stream; run with liquid; emit stream

Each time a volcano erupts, or the land is flooded, a new **stratum** *or layer of rock or soil is left above the earlier ones. Geological study of such strata can indicate their ages.*

igneous rock
sandstone
limestone
shale
coal seams

anticline

syncline

overthrust

strained effort; (mech.) force exerted between contiguous bodies

STRESSES AND STRAINS

1: Compressive stress. 2. Tensile stress. 3. Shear stress and strain. 4. Torsional stress and strain. α = angle of twist

or parts of a body. 2. Emphasis; greater relative force of utterance given to one syllable of word, one part of a syllable, word in sentence, etc. ~ v.t. Lay the stress on, accent, emphasize; subject to mechanical stress. **stress·or** (strĕs′er, -ōr) n.

stretch (strĕch) v. 1. Make taut; tighten, straighten; place in tightly drawn or outspread state; lay (person) flat; (also ~ **oneself**) extend limbs to tighten muscles after sleeping etc.; ~ **one's legs**, take walking exercise; ~ **out**, extend (hand, foot, etc.) by straightening arm or leg; reach out hand. 2. Strain; exert to utmost or beyond legitimate extent; do violence to; exaggerate. 3. Have specified length or extension; be continuous between points, to or from a point. 4. Draw, be drawn, admit of being drawn, out into greater length, extension, or size. **stretch** n. Stretching, being stretched; continuous expanse, tract, or spell; (slang) term of imprisonment; **stretch′out** (n.), practice in factory operation of having workers do extra work without adequate increase in wages. **stretch′a·ble** adj. **stretch′y** adj. (**stretch·i·er, stretch·i·est**).

stretch·er (strĕch′er) n. (esp.) 1. Brick or stone laid with length in direction of wall, bar or rod used as tie or brace, e.g. between legs of chair; board in boat against which rower presses feet. 2. Frame on which artist's canvas is spread and drawn tight by wedges etc. 3. Oblong frame, with handles at each end, for carrying sick or wounded persons on; ~**-bearer**, one who helps to carry this.

strew (strōō) v.t. (**strewed, strewn, strew·ing**). Scatter (flowers, small objects) over a surface; cover (surface, object) with small objects scattered.

stri·a (strī′a) n. (pl. **stri·ae** pr. strī′ē). (anat., zool., geol., etc.) Linear mark on surface; slight ridge, furrow, or score. **stri·ate** (strī′ĭt, -āt), **stri·at·ed** (strī′ātĭd)

of; float or wave in wind, current of water, etc.

stream·er (strē′mer) n. Pennon; ribbon etc. attached at one end and floating or waving at the other; (pl.) Aurora Borealis.

stream·let (strēm′lĭt) n. Small stream.

street (strēt) n. Road in town or village with houses on one side or both; this with its houses; **the S~**, (esp.) Wall Street; **on the ~**, living by prostitution; **street′car**, public electric passenger car, trolley car; **street theater**, theatrical presentation in street, park, etc., usu. with no admission charge; **street′walker**, prostitute who solicits in street.

strength (strĕngkth, strĕngth) n. 1. Being strong; degree in which person or thing is strong; that which makes strong; number of men in army, regiment, etc., of ships in fleet etc., men enrolled; **on the ~ of**, encouraged by, relying on, arguing from. 2. Significance; effectiveness (of argument).

strength·en (strĕngk′then, strĕng′-) v. Make, become, stronger. **strength′en·er** n.

stren·u·ous (strĕn′ūus) adj. Vigorous, energetic, persistently and ardently laborious (esp. of action or effort). **stren′u·ous·ly** adv. **stren′u·ous·ness** n.

strep (strĕp) n. (colloq.) Streptococcus; ~ **throat**, septic sore throat.

strep·to·coc·cus (strĕptokŏk′us) n. (pl. **-coc·ci** pr. -kŏk′sī). Microorganism of genus S~, of bacteria that form chains, certain species of which produce infections in man, as scarlet fever, endocarditis, strep throat, etc. **strep·to·coc′cal**, **strep·to·coc·cic** (strĕptokŏk′sĭk) adjs.

strep·to·my·cin (strĕptomī′sĭn) n. Antibiotic drug, produced from *Actinomyces griseus*, a moldlike microorganism found in garden soil.

stress (strĕs) n. 1. Pressure of load, weight, some adverse force or influence etc.; condition of things demanding or marked by *adjs.* **striate** (strī'āt) *v.t.* (**-at·ed, -at·ing**). **stri·a·tion** (strīā'shon) *n.*

strick·en (strĭk'en) *adj.*: see STRIKE; (esp., of deer etc.) wounded; (of person, mind, etc.) afflicted with disease, trouble, grief, etc.

strict (strĭkt) *adj.* 1. Exact, precise, accurately determined or defined. 2. Rigorous, allowing no evasion, stringent; (of discipline etc.) admitting no relaxation or indulgence. **strict'ly** *adv.* **strict'ness** *n.*

stric·ture (strĭk'cher) *n.* 1. (usu. pl.) Adverse criticism, critical remark. 2. (path.) Morbid contraction of passage of the body, esp. urethra; contracted part.

stride (strīd) *v.* (**strode** pr. strōd, **strid·den** pr. strĭd'en, **strid·ing**). Walk with long steps; pass over or *over* (obstacle etc.) with one step; bestride. ~ *n.* Striding; long step; distance covered by this; striding gait; **take in one's** ~, (of horse or rider) clear (obstacle) without changing gait; (fig.) deal with incidentally without interrupting course of action etc. **strid'er** *n.*

stri·dent (strī'dent) *adj.* Loud and harsh, grating. **stri'dent·ly** *adv.* **stri'dence, stri'den·cy** *ns.*

strid·u·late (strĭj'ulāt) *v.i.* (**-lat·ed, -lat·ing**). Make harsh grating shrill noise (esp., of grasshoppers etc.) by rubbing together hard parts of body. **strid·u·la·tion** (strĭjulā'shon) *n.*

strife (strīf) *n.* Condition of antagonism or discord; contention, struggle, dispute.

strike (strīk) *v.* (**struck** pr. strŭk, **strick·en** pr. strĭk'en, **strik·**-

ing). 1. Hit, hit upon or *on*, deliver blow(s) or stroke(s); afflict (with infirmity or death); (of disease etc.) attack suddenly; (of lightning) descend upon and blast. 2. Produce or record or bring into specified state by strokes or striking; impress, stamp, print (*with* device etc.); coin (money); touch (string or key of instrument), produce (note) thus; (of clock) sound (hour etc.) with stroke(s) on bell etc.; (of hour) be sounded thus; produce (fire, spark) by percussion of flint and steel, friction of match, etc. 3. Arrest attention of; occur to mind of; produce mental impression on, impress *as*. 4. Lower or take down (sail, flag, tent); signify surrender by striking flag, remove tents of (camp etc.); (theatr.) remove (scene etc.). 5. (of body of employees) Cease work by agreement among themselves or by order of labor union etc. in order to obtain remedy for grievance, better working conditions, etc. 6. (Cause to) penetrate; pierce, stab (as) with sharp weapon. 7. Turn in new direction, go *across*, *down*, *over*, etc.; take specified direction. 8. Assume (attitude) suddenly and dramatically. 9. ~ **from the record** (pp. **stricken**), (law) erase, expunge; **strike home**, (fig.) hit the mark; get blow well in; **strike off**, cancel, erase, (as) by stroke of pen; print; **strike off the register, rolls**, remove (doctor, lawyer) from official list, for misconduct; **strike out**, erase; open up (path, course) *for* oneself; lay about one with fists etc.; begin to swim or skate; (baseball) (be) put out by strikeout

String beans are grown as a commercial crop throughout the U.S.A. and southern Canada. They are also popular with home gardeners, having a high yield and a relatively simple growth cycle.

(see sense 4 of *n.*); **strike up**, begin to play or sing; start (acquaintance, conversation) esp. rapidly or casually; **strike zone**, (baseball) space over plate between batter's knees and armpits. **strike** *n.* 1. Concerted refusal to work by employees till some grievance is remedied; **on** ~, taking part in this; **strike'bound**, immobilized by a strike; **strike'breaker**, one who works for employer whose employees are on strike; **strike pay**, labor union's allowance to workers on strike. 2. Sudden discovery of rich ore, oil, etc.; (fig.) sudden success or piece of good fortune; (bowling) knocking down all the pins on first bowl; score thus made. 3. (geol.) Horizontal course of stratum. 4. (baseball) Pitched ball swung at and missed, or in strike zone and not swung at. **strike'out** (*n.*) (baseball), out made when batter is charged with three strikes.

strik·er (strī'ker) *n.* (esp.) Employee taking part in industrial strike.

strik·ing (strī'kĭng) *adj.* (esp.) Noticeable, arresting, impressive. **strik'ing·ly** *adv.* **strik'ing·ness** *n.*

string (strĭng) *n.* 1. Thin length of twisted fiber; piece of this or of leather, ribbon, or other material, used for tying up, lacing, drawing together, activating puppet, etc.; bowstring; (fig.) condition or limitation imposed; **first, second,**

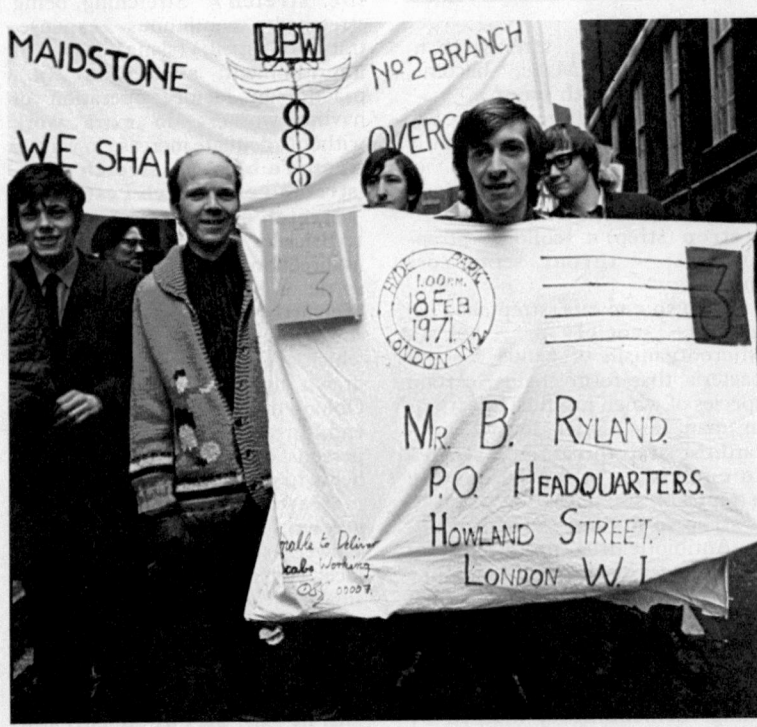

A striker from the British Post Office during industrial unrest in 1971. Such industrial action only became effective after the formation of trade unions during the 19th century.

violin

scroll

peg or pin

neck

back

viola

sound hole or *f*-hole

chin-rest

double-bass

finger-board

violoncello or cello

string

belly

bouts

bridge

tail-piece

stringed instruments of the violin family with bows

The first **stringed** instrument was a type of harp, played at Ur about 4500 years ago. The violin family, like the guitar, probably evolved from the lute, which originated in Persia.

construction of ships (e.g. *deck*, *side* ~) and aircraft; long horizontal timber.

string·y (strĭng′ē) *adj.* (**string·i·er, string·i·est**). Fibrous, like string; (of liquid) ropy. **string′i·ness** *n.*

strip[1] (strĭp) *n.* Long narrow piece or tract (of textile material, land, paper, etc.); narrow flat bar of iron or steel; iron or steel in this form; airstrip; CARTOON, COMIC, strip; ~ **cropping**, practice of planting different crops in alternating strips usu. following contours of terrain, in order to reduce erosion; ~ **lighting**, lighting with usu. tubular lamps arranged in line.

strip[2] (strĭp) *v.* (**stripped, strip·ping**). Denude, lay bare; deprive *of* covering, appurtenance, or property; undress; pull or tear off, *off* or *from* something; tear off (thread from screw, teeth from wheel); extract last milk from udder of (cow); ~ **mine**, mine in open pit formed by removal of earth and rock overlying ore etc.; **strip′tease**, entertainment in which a woman undresses in time to music before an audience. **strip′per** *n.* (esp.) 1. Performer of striptease. 2. Device or solvent for removing paint, varnish, etc.

stripe[1] (strĭp) *n.* (archaic; chiefly pl.) Stroke or lash with whip etc.

stripe[2] (strĭp) *n.* Long narrow portion, usu. of uniform width, on surface, differing in color or texture from adjacent parts; narrow strip of cloth, braid, etc., sewn on garment, esp. chevron indicating rank of noncommissioned officer. **strip′y** *adj.* **stripe** *v.t.* (**striped, strip·ing**). Mark, ornament, with stripe(s). **striped** *adj.* ~ **bass**: see BASS[1]. **strip′er** *n.*

strip·ling (strĭp′lĭng) *n.* Youth approaching manhood.

strive (strīv) *v.i.* (**strove** pr. strōv, **strived, striv·en** pr. strĭv′en, **striv·ing**). Endeavor, try hard, struggle; contend, vie.

strobe (strōb) *n.* 1. Device that emits extremely short, fast flashes of high-intensity light for high-speed photography. 2. (colloq.) Stroboscope.

stro·bile (strō′bĭl, -bīl) *n.* (bot.) Cone of pine etc., inflorescence made up of imbricated scales.

stro·bo·scope (strō′boskōp, strŏb′o-) *n.* Optical instrument employing pulsed illumination to make rapidly moving, rotating, or vibrating objects appear stationary. **stro·bo·scop·ic** (strōboskŏp′ĭk, strŏbo-) *adj.*

strode: see STRIDE.

stroke[1] (strōk) *n.* 1. Blow, shock

etc., ~, person or thing that chief, alternative, etc., reliance is placed on; **have two ~s to one's bow**, have two alternative resources; **pull strings**, control course of affairs; exert (esp. hidden) influence; **without strings**, unconditionally. 2. Tendon, nerve, elongated muscle, etc., in animal body; tough piece connecting two halves of pod in beans etc.; thread of viscid substance. 3. Catgut, wire, etc., yielding musical tone(s) when stretched, in piano, harp, violin, and other instruments; (pl.) stringed instruments played with bow, players of these in orchestra etc. 4. Set of or *of* objects strung together; number of animals etc. in single file; set or stud of horses; number of things in row or line; continuous series or succession. 5. **string bass**, double bass; **string bean**, bush or vine (*Phaseolus vulgaris*) widely grown for its slim, green edible pods; (colloq.) tall, thin person; **string quartet**, quartet of stringed instruments,

esp. two violins, viola, and violoncello; music for this; **string tie**, very narrow necktie. **string** *v.* (**strung** pr. strŭng, **string·ing**). Supply, fit, tie, with string(s); thread (beads etc.) on string; make (bow) ready for use by slipping loop of bowstring into its notch; remove strings of bean pod; brace *up*, bring to specified condition of sensitiveness or tension; connect, put together in continuous series; arrange in row(s) or series; move in string or disconnected line (esp. ~ **out**); ~ **along**, (colloq.) deceive (person); ~ **up**, (colloq.) hang (person).

stringed (strĭngd) *adj.* (esp., of musical instruments) Having strings.

strin·gent (strĭn′jent) *adj.* (of regulations, obligations, etc.) Rigorous, strict, binding, requiring exact performance. **strin′gent·ly** *adv.* **strin′gen·cy** *n.* (pl. -cies).

string·er (strĭng′er) *n.* Longitudinal stiffening member used in given by blow; apoplectic or paralytic seizure; damaging or destructive discharge (of lightning). 2. Single effort put forth, one complete performance of recurrent action or movement; time or way in which such movements are performed; act or method of striking ball etc. in games; (golf) action of hitting (at) ball with club, as unit of scoring; specially successful or skillful effort; ~ **of genius**, original or strikingly successful idea; ~ **of luck**, unforeseen opportune occurrence. 3. Mark made by movement in one direction of pen, pencil, paintbrush, etc.; detail in description etc. 4. Sound made by striking clock; **on the ~ of**, exactly at specified hour. 5. Oarsman rowing nearest stern and setting time of stroke. **stroke** *v.t.* (**stroked, strok·ing**). Act as stroke to (boat, crew).

stroke[2] (strōk) *v.t.* (**stroked, strok·ing**). Pass hand etc. softly and usu. repeatedly in one direction over (hair, skin, etc.), as caress etc. ~ *n.* Act, spell, of stroking.

stroll (strōl) *n.* Leisurely walk or ramble, saunter. ~ *v.i.* Walk in leisurely fashion; **stroll'ing company, players**, etc., actors traveling about and giving performances.

strol·ler (strō'ler) *n.* 1. Person who strolls. 2. Child's light folding

Strip cropping *is a farming method which prevents soil erosion on sloping land. By alternating shallow and deep-rooted crops it is possible to retain moisture that would otherwise be lost through runoff.*

chair on wheels.

strong (strawng, strŏng) *adj.* (**strong·er** pr. strawng'ger, strŏng'-, **strong·est** pr. strawng'gĭst, strŏng'-). 1. Physically powerful, vigorous, or robust; performed with muscular strength; having great muscular, moral, or mental power or strength; powerful in arms, numbers, equipment, authority, etc. 2. Difficult to capture, break into, invade, or escape from, capable of resisting force or strain, resistant, tough. 3. Energetic, effective, vigorous, decided. 4. Convincing, striking; powerfully affecting the senses, passions, mind, etc. 5. (of drink) Having large proportion of flavoring element, solid ingredient, alcohol, etc. 6. (gram., of verbs) Forming inflections by vowel change in root syllable, rather than by addition of suffixes. 7. ~ **-arm**, (colloq.) using force; **strong'box**, strongly made chest or safe for money, documents, etc.; **strong drink**, alcoholic liquors; **strong'hold**, fortified place; secure place of refuge or retreat; center of support for cause etc.; **strong**

language, forcible (esp. profane or abusive) expressions; **strong'man**, (esp.) one who performs feats of strength for entertainment; (colloq.) dictator; **strong-minded**, having strong, vigorous, or determined mind; **strong point**, (esp.) activity or quality in which person or thing excels; **strong'-point**, (mil.) specially fortified position in a defense system. **strong'ly** *adv.* **strong** *adv.* **come on ~**, act aggressively; **be going ~**, be vigorous, thriving, or prosperous.

stron·ti·um (strŏn'shēum, -shum, -tēum) *n.* Soft easily fusible metallic element (silver white when pure); symbol Sr, at. no. 38, at. wt. 87.62; ~ **90**, hazardous radioactive isotope of strontium present in fallout of nuclear fission.

strop (strŏp) *n.* Strip of leather for sharpening razor, implement or machine serving same purpose. ~ *v.t.* (**stropped, strop·ping**). Sharpen on or with strop.

stro·phe (strō'fē) *n.* (Lines recited during) movement made from right to left by chorus in ancient Greek choral dance; series of lines forming division of lyric poem. **stroph·ic** (strō'fĭk, strŏf'ĭk) *adj.*

struc·tur·al (strŭk'cheral) *adj.* Of structure; ~ **linguistics**, study of language as system of interrelated thought and sound elements, the sounds being purely arbitrary; ~ **steel**, strong steel in shapes specially suitable for structural purposes. **struc'tur·al·ly** *adv.*

struc·ture (strŭk´cher) *n.* 1. Manner in which building or other complete whole is constructed; supporting framework or whole of essential parts of something; make, construction. 2. Thing constructed; complex whole; building. ~ *v.t.* (**-tured, -tur·ing**). Arrange, organize, give a structure to.

stru·del (strōō´del, shtrōō´-) *n.* Paper-thin pastry rolled up around a filling and baked.

strug·gle (strŭg´el) *v.i.* (**-gled, -gling**). Throw one's limbs about in violent effort to escape grasp etc.; make violent or determined efforts under difficulties, strive hard; contend *with, against*, make one's way with difficulty *through, along*, etc. ~ *n.* Struggling; resolute contest, continued effort to resist force, free oneself from constraint etc.; determined effort or resistance; ~ **for existence, life**, competition between organic species, esp. as element in natural selection; continued effort to maintain life or obtain means of livelihood. **strug'gler** *n.* **strug'gling** *adj.* (esp.) Experiencing difficulty in making a living, getting recognition, etc. **strug'gling·ly** *adv.*

strum (strŭm) *v.* (**strummed, strum·ming**). Twang strings of stringed instrument; play, esp. unskilfully, *on* (guitar, etc.). ~ *n.* Sound made by strumming.

strum·pet (strŭm´pĭt) *n.*

(archaic) Female prostitute.

strung: see STRING *v.*

strut[1] (strŭt) *n. & v.i.* (**strut·ted, strut·ting**). (Walk with) pompous or affected stiff gait.

strut[2] (strŭt) *n.* Bar, rod, etc., of wood, iron, etc., inserted in framework to resist pressure or thrust in direction of its length; brace. ~ *v.t.* (**strut·ted, strut·ting**).

strych·nine (strĭk´nĭn, -nēn, -nīn) *n.* Highly poisonous vegetable alkaloid obtained from plants of genus *Strychnos*, esp. the nux vomica, used in medicine as stimulant and tonic.

Stu·art[1] (stōō´ert, stū´-). Name of royal house of Scotland from the accession (1371) of Robert II, one of the hereditary stewards of Scotland, and of England from the accession of James VI of Scotland to the English throne as James I (1603) to the death of Queen Anne (1714). (cf. PRETENDER).

Stu·art[2] (stōō´ert, stū´-), **Gilbert Charles** (1755–1828). Amer. portrait painter; famous for portrait of George Washington.

Stu·art[3] (stōō´ert, stū´-), **James Ewell Brown** ("Jeb") (1833–64). Amer. Confederate general and cavalry leader in Civil War.

stub (stŭb) *n.* Stump of tree, tooth, etc., left projecting; short remnant *of* pencil, cigar, etc.; counterfoil of check, ticket, receipt,

etc. **stub** *v.t.* (**stubbed, stub·bing**). Grub up (stubs, roots), clear (land) of stubs; hurt (toe) by striking it against something; extinguish (cigarette) by crushing lighted end against something hard. **stub'by** *adj.* (**-bi·er, -bi·est**). **stub'bi·ness** *n.*

stub·ble (stŭb´el) *n.* Lower ends of grain stalks left in ground after harvest; short stubble-like growth of hair esp. on unshaven face. **stub'bly** *adj.* (**-bli·er, -bli·est**).

stub·born (stŭb´ern) *adj.* Unreasonably obstinate, obdurate, refractory, intractable. **stub'born·ly** *adv.* **stub'born·ness** *n.*

stuc·co (stŭk´ō) *n.* (pl. **-coes, -cos**). Fine plaster used to cover walls, ceilings, etc., and for making cornices, moldings, etc.; coarse plaster or cement for covering exterior surfaces of walls in imitation of stone. ~ *v.t.* (**-coed, -co·ing**). Coat or ornament with stucco.

stuck (stŭk) *adj.*: see STICK; (esp. of animal) that has been stabbed or had throat cut; ~**-up**, (colloq.) conceited, insolently exclusive.

stud[1] (stŭd) *n.* 1. Large-headed nail, boss, or knot, projecting from surface, esp. for ornament; rivet, crosspiece in each link of chain cable; kind of two-headed button passed through one or more eyelets or buttonholes, esp. in shirt front, or to fasten collar to shirt. 2. Upright post in framing for walls, usu. two inches by four inches. ~ *v.t.* (**stud·ded, stud·ding**). Set with studs; be scattered over or about (surface). **stud'ding** *n.* (esp.) Framing woodwork of wall.

stud[2] (stŭd) *n.* Number of

*James I founded the **Stuart** dynasty in England because his mother, Mary Queen of Scots (left) and father, Lord Darnley, shared a Tudor grandmother. Below: The children of Charles I (James' grandchildren).*

horses kept for breeding, hunting, racing, etc.; place where stud, esp. for breeding, is kept; **stud'book, stud book**, book giving pedigree of thoroughbred horses; **stud farm**, place where horses are bred; **stud'horse**, stallion; **stud poker**, kind of poker in which all but first round(s) of cards are dealt with faces up.

stu·dent (stoō'dent, stū'-) *n.* Person engaged in or inclined toward study; person undergoing instruction at university or other place of education or technical training; ~ **teacher**, college student who teaches under supervision as part of requirement for degree in education.

stu·di·o (stoō'dēō, stū'-) *n.* (pl. **-di·os**). Workroom of sculptor, painter, photographer, etc.; room in which movie action is staged; room or premises used for transmission of broadcasts, or for making films or recordings; ~ **apartment**, one-room apartment with kitchenette and bath; ~ **couch**, couch that opens out to form a bed.

stu·di·ous (stoō'dēus, stū'-) *adj.* Given to study, devoted to learning; careful *to* do, anxiously desirous *of*; studied, deliberate, zealous, anxious, painstaking. **stu·di·ous·ly** *adv.* **stu·di·ous·ness** *n.*

stud·y (stŭd'ē) *n.* (pl. **stud·ies**). 1. Devotion of time and thought to acquisition of information esp. from books; (freq. pl.) pursuit of some branch of knowledge; careful examination or observation *of* (subject, question, object, etc.); reverie, deep thought, abstraction. 2. Thing to be secured by pains or attention; thing to be investigated. 3. Literary composition devoted to detailed consideration of a subject or problem or executed as exercise or experiment in style etc. 4. (painting etc.) Careful sketch made for practice in technique or as preliminary experiment for picture etc. or part of it; (mus.) composition designed to develop player's skill. 5. (theatr.) Learning of parts in play; **quick, slow**, ~, person who learns part quickly, slowly. 6. Room used for literary occupation. **study** *v.* (**stud·ied, stud·y·ing**). Make a study of, take pains to investigate or acquire knowledge of (subject) or to ensure (desired result); examine carefully, read attentively, investigate (object); apply oneself to study; take pains *to* do. **stud·ied** *adj.* (esp.) Deliberate, intentional, affected. **stud·i·er** *n.*

stuff (stŭf) *n.* 1. Material of

which thing is made or that is or can be used for some purpose; available supply of something; belongings. 2. Textile material, esp. woolen fabric. 3. Valueless matter; trash, nonsense; **do one's** ~, (colloq.) do what one is expected to do; show one's skill. **stuff** *v.* Pack, cram; stop *up*, fill; distend; fill out (skin of bird, beast, etc.) with material to restore original shape; fill (inside of bird, piece of meat, etc.) with seasoned bread

The term **'studfarm'** *now applies to a place where different types of animals are bred. It includes the Santa Gertrudis cattle stud at Bowral, Australia, where beasts are hand fed.*

crumbs, herbs, etc., before cooking; cram food into, gorge (food); gorge oneself, eat greedily; ram or press into receptacle; place fraudulent votes in (ballot box); ~ **ed shirt**, (colloq.) pompous, incompetent person. **stuff'ing** *n.* (esp.) Ingredients for stuffing fowl etc. in cookery; **knock the** ~ **out of** (person), reduce to state of flabbiness or weakness.

stuff'y (stŭf'ē) *adj.* (**stuff·i·er, stuff·i·est**). Lacking fresh air or ventilation, close; stopped up; without freshness, interest, etc.; easily offended or shocked, strait-laced. **stuff'i·ly** *adv.* **stuff'i·ness** *n.*

stul·ti·fy (stŭl'tifī) *v.t.* (**-fied, -fy·ing**). Reduce to foolishness or

The **studio** *used by Winston Churchill at Chartwell, England. Like many other men who achieved eminence in other spheres, as a hobby, he became skilled as a naturalistic painter.*

The Royal Air Force "Red Arrows" perform highly-skilled aerobatic **stunts** which involve intricate synchronized displays, requiring split-second timing and coordination.

absurdity; render worthless or useless; exhibit in ridiculous light. **stul·ti·fi·ca·tion** (stŭltĭfĭkā′shon) *n.*

stum·ble (stŭm′bel) *v.* (**-bled, -bling**). Lurch forward, have partial fall, from catching or striking foot or making false step; make blunder(s) in doing something; come accidentally *on* or *across*; **stumbling block**, obstacle; circumstance that causes difficulty, hesitation, or scruples; **stum′ble-bum**, (slang) inept, clumsy person, esp. third-rate boxer. **stumble, stum′bler** *ns.* **stum′bling·ly** *adv.*

stump (stŭmp) *n.* Projecting remnant of cut or fallen tree; part remaining of broken branch or tooth, broken-off mast, amputated limb, etc.; stub of cigar, pencil, etc.; stalk of plant (esp. cabbage) with leaves removed; (pl., joc.) legs; stump of tree used by orator to address meeting from; ~ **speech**, open-air speech. **stump** *v.* 1. Walk stiffly, clumsily, and noisily. 2. Nonplus, pose, cause to be at a loss. 3. Make stump speeches; traverse (district) doing this.

stump·y (stŭm′pē) *adj.* (**stump·i·er, stump·i·est**). Thickset, stocky; of small height or length in proportion to girth. **stump′-i·ly** *adv.* **stump′i·ness** *n.*

stun (stŭn) *v.t.* (**stunned, stun·-ning**). (of blow etc.) Knock senseless, reduce to insensibility or stupor; daze, bewilder, with strong emotion, din, etc. **stun′ner** *n.* (esp., slang) Stunning person or thing. **stunning** *adj.* (esp., slang) Splendid, delightful.

stung: see STING *v.*

stunk (stŭngk): see STINK.

stunt¹ (stŭnt) *n.* (colloq.) Special effort, feat; showy performance, skillful trick or maneuver, esp. with aircraft. ~ *v.i.* Perform stunt.

stunt² (stŭnt) *v.t.* Retard growth or development of, dwarf, cramp. **stunt′ed·ness** *n.*

stu·pe·fy (stōo′pefī, stū′-) *v.t.* (**-fied, -fy·ing**). Make stupid or torpid, deprive of sensibility; stun with amazement, fear, etc. **stu·pe·fa·cient** (stōopefā′shent, stū-) *adj.* **stu·pe·fac·tion** (stōopefăk′-shon, stū-) *n.*

stu·pen·dous (stōopĕn′dus, stū-) *adj.* Prodigious, astounding, esp. by size or degree. **stu·pen′-dous·ly** *adv.* **stu·pen′dous·ness** *n.*

stu·pid (stōo′pĭd, stū′-) *adj.* In a state of stupor or lethargy; dull by nature, slow-witted, obtuse, crass, characteristic of persons of this nature; uninteresting, dull. **stu′pid·ly** *adv.* **stu·pid·i·ty** (stōopĭd′ĭtē, stū-) *n.* (pl. **-ties**). **stupid** *n.* Stupid person.

stu·por (stōo′per, stū′per) *n.* Dazed state, torpidity; helpless amazement. **stu′por·ous** *adj.*

stur·dy (stêr′dē) *adj.* (**-di·er, -di·est**). Robust, hardy, vigorous, strongly built. **stur′di·ly** *adv.* **stur′di·ness** *n.*

stur·geon (stêr′jon) *n.* (pl. **-geons**, collect. **-geon**). Any of various large fishes of rivers, lakes, and coastal waters of north temperate zone, with long almost cylindrical body and long tapering snout, esteemed as food and the source of caviar, esp. *Acipenser oxyrhynchus*, of Atlantic coastal regions of Europe and N. Amer.

stut·ter (stŭt′er) *v.* Stammer; speak or say with continued involuntary repetition of parts of words, esp. initial consonants. ~ *n.* Act or habit of stuttering. **stut′ter·er** *n.* **stut′ter·ing·ly** *adv.*

sty¹ (stī) *n.* (pl. **sties**). (also **pigsty**) 1. Pen or enclosure for pigs. 2. Filthy room or dwelling. **sty** *v.* (**stied, sty·ing**). Lodge in sty.

sty² (stī) *n.* (pl. **sties, styes**). Inflamed swelling on edge of eyelid.

Styg·i·an (stĭj′ēan) *adj.* (As) of the Styx or of Hades; murky, gloomy, black as the Styx.

style (stīl) *n.* 1. Ancient writing implement, small rod with pointed end for scratching letters on wax-covered tablets, and flat broad end for erasing and smoothing tablet; (poet.) pen, pencil; stylelike thing, as engraver, blunt-pointed probe; (bot.) narrowed prolongation of ovary supporting stigma; (zool.) small slender pointed process or part; pointed sponge spicule. 2. Manner of writing, speaking, or doing, esp. as opp. to the matter expressed or thing done; manner of execution of work of art etc.; manner characteristic of person, school, period, etc.; (esp. correct or pleasing) way of doing something; kind, sort, pattern, type; mode of behavior, manner of life; fashion, mode, esp. in dress etc.; distinction, noticeably superior quality or manner, esp. with regard to appearance. 3. Descriptive formula, designation of person or thing; full title. 4. Mode of expressing dates; **New S~**, (abbrev. N.S.) according to the reformed or GREGORIAN calendar; **Old Style**, (abbrev. O.S.) according to the JULIAN² calendar, used by all Christian nations until 1582. **styl·ing** *n.* **style** *v.t.* (**styled, styl·ing**). Call by specified name

*Estes Park in northern Colorado is at the eastern entrance of Rocky Mountain National Park and is an example of the **sub-alpine** terrain typified by coniferous vegetation.*

or style; design, arrange, make, etc. in (esp. fashionable) style. **styl′er** *n.*

sty·let (stī′lĭt) *n.* Stiletto; engraving tool, pointed marking instrument; (surg.) slender probe, wire run through catheter for stiffening or cleaning; (zool.) piercing mouthpart of insects etc.

styl·ish (stī′lĭsh) *adj.* Noticeably conforming to fashionable standard of elegance; having good style. **styl′ish·ly** *adv.* **styl′ish·ness** *n.*

styl·ist (stī′lĭst) *n.* Person having or aiming at good style in writing or doing something. **sty·lis·tic** (stīlĭs′tĭk) *adj.* Of literary or artistic style. **sty·lis′ti·cal·ly** *adv.*

sty·lite (stī′līt) *n.* Medieval ascetic living on top of a pillar: see SIMEON STYLITES.

styl·ize (stī′līz) *v.t.* (**-ized, -iz-ing**). Conform (work of art etc., or part of it) to the rules of a conventional style. **styl·i·za·tion** (stīlĭzā′shon) *n.*

sty·lo·bate (stī′lobāt) *n.* Continuous base supporting row(s) of columns.

sty·loid (stī′loid) *adj.* Slender, pointed; ∼ **process**, process projecting from base of temporal bone in man. **styloid** *n.* Styloid process.

sty·lus (stī′lus) *n.* (pl. **-lus·es, -li** pr. -lī). Style, ancient writing implement; tracing point producing indented groove in phonograph record, or following such groove in reproducing sound.

sty·mie, sty·my (stī′mē) *ns.* (pl. **-mies**). (golf) Position on the putting green in which the opponent's ball lies in a direct line between the player's ball and the hole. ∼ *v.t.* (**-mied, mie·ing, -mied, -my·ing**). Put into position of having to negotiate stymie (freq. fig.).

styp·tic (stĭp′tĭk) *adj. & n.* (Substance) that contracts organic tissue and checks bleeding. **styp′sis** *n.*

sty·rene (stīr′ēn) *n.* Liquid hydrocarbon $(C_6H_5CH:CH_2)$, used as basis for many plastics.

Sty·ro·foam (stīr′ofōm) *n.* (trademark) Lightweight polystyrene, used in insulation, as packing, in boatbuilding, etc.

Styx (stĭks). (Gk. myth.) River of Hades over which Charon ferried the souls of the dead. **Styg·i·an** (stĭj′ēan) *adj.*

sua·sion (swā′zhon) *n.* Persuasion, esp. in **moral** ∼.

suave (swahv) *adj.* Bland, soothing, polite. **suave′ly** *adv.* **suav·i·ty** (swah′vĭtē, swăv′ĭ-), **suave′ness** *ns.*

sub (sŭb) *n.* (colloq.) Submarine, substitute. ∼ *v.* (**subbed, sub·bing**). (colloq.) Act as substitute (*for*).

sub- *prefix.* (freq. with letter *b* changed by assimilation) 1. Under, below. 2. More or less, roughly; not quite; on the borders of. 3. Subordinate(ly); secondary; further.

sub·ac·id (sŭbăs′ĭd) *adj.* Moderately acid or tart; somewhat biting.

sub·a·cute (sŭbakūt′) *adj.* (med.) Between acute and chronic.

sub·al·pine (sŭbăl′pīn, -pĭn) *adj.* Of higher slopes of mountains (about 4,000–5,000 ft.), just below the timber line.

sub·al·tern (sŭbawl′tern) *n.* (Brit. mil.) Junior officer below rank of captain.

sub·a·que·ous (sŭbā′kwĕus, -ăk′wē-) *adj.* Existing, formed, performed or taking place, underwater; adapted for use underwater.

sub·arc·tic (sŭbārk′tĭk) *adj.* Of regions somewhat south of Arctic Circle or resembling these in climate etc.

sub·a·tom·ic (sŭbatŏm′ĭk) *adj.* Occurring in, smaller than, an atom.

sub·cla·vi·an (sŭbklā′vēan) *adj.* Lying or extending under clavicle; ∼ **artery**, main trunk of arterial system of upper extremity. **subclavian** *n.* Subclavian artery, vein, or muscle.

sub·clin·i·cal (sŭbklĭn′ĭkal) *adj.* (med.) Not yet presenting definite symptoms.

sub·com·mit·tee (sŭb′komĭtē) *n.* Committee formed from main committee for special purpose.

sub·con·scious (sŭbkŏn'shus) *adj.* Of part of mind or mental field outside range of attention or imperfectly or partially conscious. ~ *n.* Subconscious part of mind. **sub·con'scious·ly** *adv.* **sub·con'scious·ness** *n.*

sub·con·ti·nent (sŭbkŏn'tinent, sŭb'kŏn-) *n.* Land mass of great extent but smaller than those generally called continents. **sub·con·ti·nen·tal** (sŭbkŏntinĕn'tal) *adj.*

sub·con·tract (sŭbkŏn'trăkt, sŭb'kŏn-) *n.* Contract for carrying out (part of) previous contract. ~ (sŭbkontrăkt') *v.* Make subcontract (for). **sub·con·trac·tor** (sŭbkŏn'trăkter, sŭb'kŏn-, sŭbkontrăk'-) *n.*

sub·cor·ti·cal (sŭbkŏr'tikal) *adj.* Situated, formed, etc., below a cortex, esp. the cortex of the brain.

sub·cu·ta·ne·ous (sŭbkūtā'nēus) *adj.* Lying, living, performed, etc., under the skin; hypodermic. **sub·cu·ta'ne·ous·ly** *adv.*

sub·dea·con (sŭbdē'kon, sŭb'dē-) *n.* Minister of order next below deacon; (R.C. Ch.) cleric or lay clerk assisting next below deacon at solemn celebration of Eucharist.

sub·deb (sŭb'dĕb) *n.* (colloq.) Girl who is about to become a debutante.

sub·di·vide (sŭbdivīd', sŭb'divīd) *v.* 1. Divide again after first division. 2. Divide (land) into lots for sale. **sub·di·vi·sion** (sŭb'divĭzhon) *n.* Subdividing; subordinate division; tract of land subdivided into lots.

sub·due (subdoo', -dū') *v.t.* (-dued, -du·ing). Conquer, subjugate, overcome, prevail over; reduce intensity, force, or vividness of (sound, color, light).

su·ber·ic (sōobĕr'ĭk) *adj.* Of cork; (chem.) ~ **acid**, white crystalline dibasic acid obtained by action of nitric acid on cork etc.

su·ber·ose (sōo'berōs), **su·ber·ous** (sōo'berus) *adjs.* (bot.) Of, like, cork, corky.

sub·fam·i·ly (sŭbfăm'ilē, -făm'lē) *n.* (pl. **-lies**). (zool.) Taxonomic category below family and above tribe or genus.

sub·head (sŭb'hĕd), **sub·head·ing** (sŭb'hĕdĭng) *ns.* Subordinate division of subject etc.; subordinate heading or title in chapter, article, etc.

sub·hu·man (sŭbhū'man) *adj.* Less than human; not quite human.

sub·ject (sŭb'jĭkt) *n.* 1. Person owing allegiance to government or ruling power esp. sovereign; any member of a state except the sovereign, any member of a subject state. 2. (logic, gram.) That member of a proposition or sentence about which something is pred-

icated; substantive word, phrase, or clause governing a verb. 3. (philos.) Thinking or feeling entity, the mind, the ego, the conscious self, as opp. to all that is external to the mind; the substance of anything as opp. to its attributes. 4. Theme of or *of* discussion or description or representation; matter (to be) treated of or dealt with; department of study. 5. (chiefly med.) Person to be treated or operated on; person of specified usu. undesirable bodily or mental characteristics, as *hysterical, sensitive*, ~. 6. ~ **catalog, index**, etc., catalog, index, listing books, etc., according to subject; ~ **matter**, matter treated of in book etc. **subject** *adj.* Under government, not independent, owing obedience *to*; liable, exposed, or prone *to*; ~ *to*, conditional(ly) upon, on the assumption of. **subject** (sŭbjĕkt') *v.t.* Subdue, make subject, (*to* one's sway etc.); expose, make liable, treat, *to*. **sub·jec·tion** (sŭbjĕk'shon) *n.*

sub·jec·tive (sŭbjĕk'tĭv) *adj.* 1. Of, proceeding from, taking place within, the thinking subject, having its source in the mind; personal, individual; introspective; imaginary, illusory. 2. (gram.) Of the subject; ~ **case**, nominative. **sub·jec'tive·ly** *adv.* **sub·jec'tive·ness**, **sub·jec·tiv·i·ty** (sŭbjĕktĭv'ĭtē) *ns.*

sub·jec·tiv·ism (sŭbjĕk'tĭvĭzem) *n.* Philosophical theory that all knowledge is merely subjective. **sub·jec'tiv·ist** *n.*

sub·join (sŭbjoin') *v.t.* Add at

*In this photograph of urban development taking over agricultural land the process of **subdivision**, dividing an area of land into plots for sale, is clearly illustrated.*

the end, append.

sub ju·di·ce (sŭb jōo'dĭsē). (law, of case) Under judicial consideration, not yet decided. [L.]

sub·ju·gate (sŭb'jugāt) *v.t.* (-gat·ed, -gat·ing). Bring under the yoke or into subjection, subdue, vanquish. **sub'ju·ga·tor, sub·ju·ga·tion** (sŭbjugā'shon) *ns.*

sub·junc·tive (subjŭngk'tĭv) *adj.* (gram.) Of a verbal mood used in classical language chiefly in subordinate or subjoined clauses; obsolescent in English exc. in certain uses, e.g. to express wish (*I wish it were over*), imprecation (*manners be hanged!*), and contingent or hypothetical events (*if he were here now*). **sub·junc'tive·ly** *adv.* **subjunctive** *n.* Subjunctive mood.

sub·lease (sŭb'lēs) *n.* Lease granted to subtenant. ~ (sŭblēs') *v.t.* (-leased, -leas·ing). Let to subtenant.

sub·let (sŭblĕt') *v.t.* (-let, -let·ting). Sublease.

sub·li·mate (sŭb'limĭt, -māt) *n.* (chem.) Solid produced when a substance is sublimed. ~ (sŭb'limāt) *v.t.* (-mat·ed, -mat·ing). 1. (chem., obs.) = SUBLIME[2]. 2. Transmute into something nobler, more sublime or refined; (psychol.) divert energy of (primitive impulse) into activity more socially useful or regarded as higher in cultural or moral scale. **sub·li·ma·tion** (sŭblimā'shon) *n.* Action, process, of subliming or sublimating.

sub·lime[1] (sublīm') *adj.* Of the most exalted kind, aloof from and raised far above the ordinary; inspiring awe, deep reverence, or lofty emotion by beauty, vastness, grandeur, etc. **sub·lime'ly** *adv.* **sub·lim·i·ty** (sublīm'ĭtē), **sub·lime'ness** *ns.* **sublime** *n.* (usu. **the** ~) What is sublime, sublimity.

sub·lime[2] (sublīm') *v.* (-limed, -lim·ing). 1. (chem.) Subject (substance) to action of heat so as to convert it to vapor that, on cooling, is deposited in solid form; purify (substance) by this means; (of substance) undergo this process; pass from solid to gaseous state without liquefaction. 2. (fig.) Purify or elevate, become pure, as by sublimation; make sublime.

sub·lim·i·nal (sublīm'inal) *adj.* (psychol.) Below threshold of consciousness, too faint or rapid to be recognized; ~ **advertising**, advertising done, e.g. by rapid flashes on motion picture or television screen, which, though not consciously seen by observers, is thought to affect their subsequent behavior. **sub·lim'i·nal·ly** *adv.*

sub·lu·nar·y (sublōo'nerē, sŭb'lōonĕre), **sub·lu·nar** (sublōo'ner) *adjs.* Beneath the moon; between orbits of moon and Earth; subject

*The conventional **submarine** such as the 'Narwhal' (right) is being replaced by nuclear-powered vessels. They have a much longer range and can fire I.C.B.Ms while submerged.*

to moon's influence; of this world, earthly, terrestrial.

sub·ma·chine (sŭbmɑshēn´) **gun.** Lightweight machine gun fired from waist or shoulder.

sub·mar·gin·al (sŭbmär´jinɑl) *adj.* 1. Falling below minimum standards or requirements. 2. Not producing sufficient amount; infertile.

sub·ma·rine (sŭbmɑrēn´, sŭb´-mɑrēn) *adj.* Existing or lying under surface of sea; operating, operated, constructed, laid, intended for use, under surface of sea. ~ *n.* Vessel, esp. warship, that can be submerged and navigated underwater, used esp. for carrying and launching torpedoes and other missiles; ~ **chaser**, small highly maneuverable naval patrol boat equipped for operations against submarines. **sub·ma·rin·er** (sŭbmɑrē´ner, sŭb-mär´i-) *n.* Member of crew of submarine.

sub·max·il·lar·y (sŭbmăk´-silērē) *adj.* Beneath lower jaw.

sub·merge (sŭbmērj´) *v.* (**-merged, -merg·ing**). (Cause to) sink or plunge under water. **sub·mer´gence, sub·mer·sion** (sŭbmēr´zhon, -shon) *ns.* **sub·mer·si·ble** (sŭbmēr´sibil) *adj. & n.* **sub·mer·si·bil·i·ty** (sŭbmērsibil´-itē) *n.*

sub·mi·cro·scop·ic (sŭbmīkro-skŏp´ĭk) *adj.* Too small to be seen by an ordinary microscope.

sub·min·i·a·ture (sŭbmĭn´-ēacher) *adj.* Of greatly reduced size; (of camera) miniature and using 16-mm film. **sub·min´i·a·tur·ize** *v.* (**-ized, -iz·ing**).

sub·mis·sion (sŭbmĭsh´on) *n.* Submissive, yielding, or deferential attitude, condition, conduct, etc.; submitting, being submitted.

sub·mis·sive (sŭbmĭs´ĭv) *adj.* Inclined to submit, yielding to power or authority, humble, obedient. **sub·mis´sive·ly** *adv.* **sub·mis´sive·ness** *n.*

sub·mit (sŭbmĭt´) *v.* (**-mit·ted, -mit·ting**). 1. Surrender oneself, become subject, yield (*to* person, his authority, etc., or *to* judgment, criticism, correction, or condition, etc.). 2. Bring under notice or consideration of person, refer *to* his decision or judgment; urge or represent deferentially (*that*).

sub·nor·mal (sŭbnôr´mɑl) *adj.* Less than normal, below normal. **sub·nor·mal·i·ty** (sŭbnôrmăl´ĭtē) *n.* (pl. **-ties**).

sub·or·bi·tal (sŭbôr´bĭtɑl) *adj.* Of less duration or distance than 1 orbit.

sub·or·der (sŭb´ôrder) *n.* (zool.,

*A bank in Crete showing red earth above limestone **subsoil.** If it is 'double-dug,' or plowed to the surface, and then mixed with topsoil and humus, a greater depth for cultivation can be obtained.*

bot.) Subdivision of order next below order in classification.

sub·or·di·nate (sŭbôr´dinĭt) *adj.* Of inferior importance of rank, secondary, subservient; (gram., of clause) dependent, being syntactically equivalent to noun, adjective, or adverb. ~ *n.* Person under control or orders of superior. **sub·or·di·nate·ly** *adv.* **subordinate** (sŭbôr´dināt) *v.t.* (**-nat·ed, -nat·ing**). Make subordinate, treat or regard as of minor importance, bring or put into subservient relation (*to*). **sub·or·di·na·tion** (sŭbôrdinā´shon) *n.* **sub·or´di·na·tive** *adj.*

sub·orn (sŭbôrn´) *v.t.* Bribe, induce, or procure (person) by underhand or unlawful means to commit perjury or other unlawful act. **sub·or·na·tion** (sŭbôrnā´shon) *n.*

sub·plot (sŭb´plŏt) *n.* Secondary plot in play etc.

sub·poe·na (supē´na) *n.* Writ commanding person's attendance in court of justice. ~ *v.t.* (**-naed, -na·ing**). Serve subpoena on. [L. *sub poena* = "under penalty," first words of writ]

sub·ro·ga·tion (sŭbrogā´shon) *n.* (law) Substitution of one party for another as creditor so that the same rights and duties apply.

sub ro·sa (sŭb rō´za). In confidence, in secret. [L., = "under the rose"]

sub·scribe (subskrīb´) *v.* (**-scribed, -scrib·ing**). 1. Write (one's name) at foot of document, sign one's name to (document etc.), signify assent to by signing one's name; put one's signature *to* in token of assent, approval, etc.;

express one's agreement, acquiescence, etc. 2. Enter one's name in list of contributors; make or promise a contribution, contribute (specified sum) to or *to* common fund, society, party, etc., or *for* common object, raise or guarantee raising of by subscribing thus; ~ **to**, undertake to buy (periodical) regularly. **sub·scrib'er** *n.* **sub·-scrip·tion** (subskrĭp'shon) *n.*

sub·script (sŭb'skrĭpt) *adj.* Written below or underneath (math. etc., of index written below and to right of symbol).

sub·sec·tion (sŭb'sĕkshon) *n.* Subordinate division of section.

sub·se·quent (sŭb'sekwent) *adj.* Following in order, time, or succession, esp. coming immediately after. **sub'se·quent·ly** *adv.* **sub'-se·quence** *n.*

sub·ser·vi·ent (subsēr'vēent) *adj.* 1. Serving as means to further an end or purpose. 2. Subordinate, subject (*to*); cringing, truckling, obsequious. **sub·ser'vi·ent·ly** *adv.* **sub·ser'vi·ence, sub·ser'-vi·en·cy** *ns.*

sub·side (subsīd') *v.i.* (**-sid·ed, -sid·ing**). Sink down, sink to low(er) level (esp. of liquids or soil sinking to normal level); (of swelling etc.) go down; (of person, usu. joc.) sink *into, onto,* chair etc.; (of storm, strong feeling, clamor, etc.) abate, become less agitated, violent, or active; cease from activity or agitation. **sub·sid'ence** (subsī'dens, sŭb'sĭ-) *n.*

sub·sid·i·ar·y (subsĭd'ēērē) *adj.* Serving to assist or supplement, auxiliary, supplementary; subordinate, secondary. ~ *n.* (pl. **-ar·ies**). Subsidiary person or thing.

sub·si·dize (sŭb'sĭdīz) *v.t.* (**-dized, -diz·ing**). Pay subsidy to. **sub·si·di·za·tion** (sŭbsĭdīzā'-shon) *n.*

sub·si·dy (sŭb'sĭdē) *n.* (pl. **-dies**). 1. Money grant from one country to another in return for military or naval aid etc. 2. Financial aid given by government or private organization toward expenses of an undertaking or institution held to be of public utility, or (by government) to producers of commodity etc. to enable goods or services to be provided at low(er) cost to consumer.

sub·sist (subsĭst') *v.* 1. Exist as a reality; continue to exist, remain in being. 2. Maintain, support, keep, provide food or funds for, provision; maintain or support oneself.

sub·sist·ence (subsĭs'tens) *n.*

Subsisting; means of supporting life, livelihood; ~ **allowance**, allowance granted to employee for living expenses while traveling on employer's business; ~ **farming**, farming in which produce is consumed by farm household, with little or no surplus for selling.

sub·soil (sŭb'soil) *n.* Soil lying immediately under surface soil.

sub·son·ic (sŭbsŏn'ĭk) *adj.* (of aircraft etc.) Having speed less than that of sound (opp. SUPERSONIC).

sub·spe·cies (sŭb'spēshēz) *n.* Subdivision of species. **sub·spe·cif·ic** (sŭbspesĭf'ĭk) *adj.* **sub·spe·cif'i·cal·ly** *adv.*

sub·stance (sŭb'stans) *n.* 1. (philos.) What underlies phenomena, permanent substratum of things, that in which accidents or attributes inhere; essential nature; essence or most important part of anything, purport, real meaning. 2. Theme, subject matter, material, esp. as opp. to form; reality, solidity, solid or real thing. 3. (archaic) Possessions, wealth. 4. Particular kind or species of matter.

sub·stand·ard (sŭbstăn'derd) *adj.* Of less than required or normal quality, size, etc.

sub·stan·tial (substăn'shal) *adj.* 1. Having substance, actually existing, not illusory; of real importance or value, of considerable amount. 2. Of solid material or structure, not flimsy, stout; possessed of property, well-to-do, commercially sound. 3. That is such essentially, virtual, practical. **sub·stan'tial·ly** *adv.* **sub·stan·ti·al·i·ty** (substăn-shēăl'ĭtē), **sub·stan'tial·ness** *ns.*

sub·stan·tial·ism (substăn'-shalĭzem) *n.* (philos.) Doctrine that there are substantial realities underlying phenomena.

sub·stan·ti·ate (substăn'shēāt) *v.t.* (**-at·ed, -at·ing**). Give substantial form to; demonstrate or verify by proof or evidence. **sub·-**

stan·ti·a·tion (substănshēā'shon) *n.*

sub·stan·ti·val (sŭbstantī'val) *adj.* Of, consisting of, substantive(s). **sub·stan·ti'val·ly** *adv.*

sub·stan·tive (sŭb'stantĭv) *adj.* 1. Having a separate and independent existence, not merely inferential or implicit or subservient. 2. (gram.) Expressing existence; denoting a noun or its equivalent; ~ **verb**, the verb *be.* 3. (law) Of, consisting of, rules of right administered by court as opp. to forms of procedure. **sub'stan·tive·ly** *adv.* **substantive** *n.* (gram.) Noun.

sub·sti·tute (sŭb'stĭtoot, -tūt) *n.* Person or thing acting or serving in place of another. ~ *v.* (**-tut·ed, -tut·ing**). Put in place of another; (cause to) act as substitute *for.* **sub·sti·tu·tion** (sŭbstĭtoo'shon, -tū'-) *n.* (esp., chem.) Replacement of one atom or radical in molecule by another. **sub·sti·tut·a·bil·i·ty** (sŭbstĭ-tootabĭl'ĭtē, -tū-) *n.* **sub·sti·tu'-tion·al, sub'sti·tu·tive** *adjs.*

sub·strat·o·sphere (sŭbstrăt'-osfēr) *n.* Layer of atmosphere immediately below stratosphere.

sub·stra·tum (sŭbstrā'tum, -străt'um, sŭb'strātum, -strătum) *n.* (pl. **-ta** pr. -ta, **-tums**). What underlies or forms basis of anything.

sub·struc·ture (sŭb'strŭkcher) *n.* Underlying or supporting structure.

sub·sume (subsoom') *v.t.* (**-sumed, -sum·ing**). Bring (one idea, principle, etc.) under another, a rule, or a class. **sub·sump·tion** (subsŭmp'shon) *n.* **sub·sum'a·ble** *adj.*

sub·ten·ant (sŭbtĕn'ant, sŭb'-tĕn-) *n.* One who holds or leases from a tenant. **sub·ten'an·cy** *n.*

sub·tend (sŭbtĕnd') *v.t.* (geom.) (of chord, side of figure, angle) Be opposite to (angle, arc).

This road in Holtville, California has been subjected to an earthquake of 6.7 on the Richter scale, and the ensuing **subsidence** *is a common result of a tremor of that size.*

sub·ter·fuge (sŭb′terfūj) *n.* Evasion, shift; artifice or device adopted to escape or avoid force of argument, condemnation, or censure, or to justify conduct.

sub·ter·ra·ne·an (sŭbterā′nēan) *adj.* Existing, lying, situated, formed, operating, taking place, performed, under surface of the earth; underground. **sub·ter·ra′ne·ous** *adj.* Subterranean. **sub·ter·ra′ne·ous·ly** *adv.*

sub·ti·tle (sŭb′tītel) *n.* Subordinate or additional title of literary work etc.; caption for silent film; television caption; translation printed on screen for foreign-language film. ~ *v.t.* (**-ti·tled, -ti·tling**). Add subtitle(s) to.

sub·tle (sŭt′el) *adj.* (**sub·tler, sub·tlest**). Tenuous, rarefied (archaic); pervasive or elusive by reason of tenuity; fine or delicate, esp. to such an extent as to elude observation or analysis; making fine distinctions, having delicate perceptions, acute; ingenious, elaborate, clever; crafty, cunning. **sub′tly** *adv.* **sub′tle·ty** (pl. **-ties**). **sub′tle·ness** *ns.*

sub·ton·ic (sŭbtŏn′ĭk) *n.* (mus.) Note next below tonic, seventh note of ascending scale.

sub·tract (subtrăkt′) *v.t.* Deduct (part, quantity, number) from or *from* whole or from quantity or number, esp. in arithmetic and algebra. **sub·trac·tion** (subtrăk-

shon) *n.* **sub·trac′tive** *adj.*

sub·tra·hend (sŭb′trahĕnd) *n.* (math.) Quantity or number to be subtracted.

sub·trop·i·cal (sŭbtrŏp′ĭkal) *adj.* (Characteristic of regions) bordering on the tropics.

sub·urb (sŭb′erb) *n.* Residential area lying on or near outskirts of city. **sub·ur·ban** (suber′ban) *adj.* **sub·ur·ban·ite** (suber′banīt) *n.* Person living in a suburb. **sub·ur·bi·a** (suber′bēa) *n.* Suburbs and their inhabitants.

sub·ven·tion (subvĕn′shon) *n.* Grant from government etc., in support of enterprise of public importance, subsidy.

sub·ver·sion (subvēr′zhon, -shon) *n.* Overturning, ruin, overthrow from foundation, esp. overthrowing or undermining of government.

sub·ver·sive (subvēr′sĭv) *adj.* Tending to subvert or overthrow. **sub·ver′sive·ly** *adv.*

sub·vert (subvērt′) *v.t.* Overthrow, overturn, upset, effect destruction or ruin of (religion, government). **sub·vert′er** *n.*

sub·way (sŭb′wā) *n.* Underground electric railroad for rapid

*Dormouse **suckling** her young. Like all mammals the young after birth rely on the mother's milk to provide their total food intake until they are old enough to digest other substances.*

travel in urban area; tunnel for such a railroad.

suc·ceed (suksēd′) *v.* 1. Come next after and take the place of, follow in order, come next (to); be subsequent (to); come by inheritance or in due course to or *to* office, title, or property. 2. Have success, be successful; prosper; accomplish one's purpose; (of plan etc.) be brought to a successful completion or fulfillment. **suc·ceed′er** *n.*

suc·cès d'es·time (sŭksē dĕstēm′). Cordial reception by critics but not by general public. [Fr.]

suc·cess (suksĕs′) *n.* Favorable issue; attainment of object, or of wealth, fame, or position; thing or person that succeeds or is successful. **suc·cess′ful** *adj.* **suc·cess′ful·ly** *adv.*

suc·ces·sion (suksĕsh′on) *n.* 1. Following in order, succeeding; series of things in succession; **in** ~, one after another in regular sequence. 2. (Right of) succeeding to the throne or any office or inheritance; set or order of persons having such right; **apostolic** ~, uninterrupted transmission of spiritual authority through bishops from the apostles downward. **suc·ces′sion·al** *adj.*

suc·ces·sive (suksĕs′ĭv) *adj.* Coming one after another in uninterrupted sequence. **suc·ces′sive·ly** *adv.*

suc·ces·sor (suksĕs′er) *n.* Person or thing succeeding another.

suc·cinct (suksĭngkt′) *adj.* Terse, brief, concise. **suc·cinct′ly** *adv.* **suc·cinct′ness** *n.*

suc·cor (sŭk′er) *v.t.* Come to assistance of, give aid to in need or difficulty. ~ *n.* Aid given in time of need.

suc·co·tash (sŭk′otăsh) *n.* Dish of lima beans and corn kernels cooked together. [Amer. Ind. *msiquatash*]

Suc·coth: SUKKOTH.

suc·cu·ba (sŭk′yuba) (pl. **-bae** pr. -bē), **suc·cu·bus** (sŭk′yubus) (pl. **-bi** pr. -bī, **-bus·es**) *ns.* Female demon supposed to have sexual intercourse with men in their sleep.

suc·cu·lent (sŭk′yulent) *adj.* Juicy; (bot.) having juicy or fleshy tissues, as the cactus. **suc′cu·lent·ly** *adv.* **suc′cu·lence, suc′cu·len·cy** *ns.* **succulent** *n.* Plant with fleshy foliage or stems or both.

suc·cumb (sukŭm′) *v.i.* Sink under pressure, give way to superior force, authority, etc.; (esp.) yield to effects of disease, wounds, etc., die.

such (sŭch) *adj.* 1. Of the character, degree, or extent described, referred to, or implied; previously described or specified; ~ **as**, of the kind or degree that,

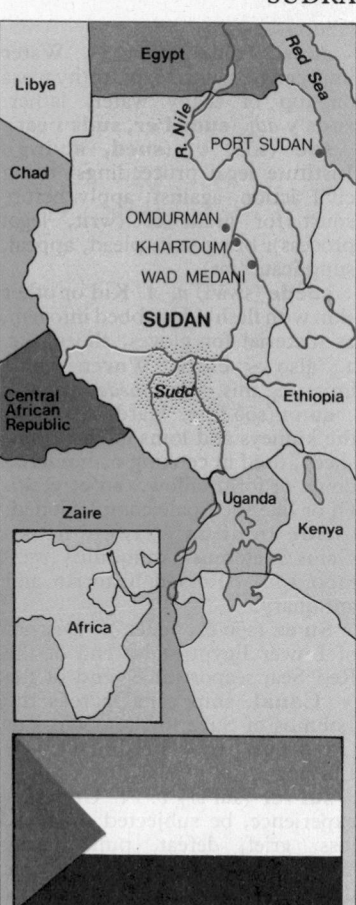

the kind of (person or thing) that; for example, e.g. 2. So great, so eminent, etc. (freq. emphatic and exclamatory); (preceding attrib. adjective, with adverbial force) so. 3. particular, but not specified; ~ **and** ~, a particular but unspecified; **such'like**, (of) such a kind. **such** *pron*. That, the action, etc., referred to; such people *as*, those *who* (chiefly archaic or rhet.); (vulg. or commerc.) the aforesaid thing(s); as ~, as what has been specified.

suck (sŭk) *v*. 1. Draw (liquid, esp. milk from breast) into mouth by contracting muscles of lips, tongue, and cheeks so as to produce partial vacuum; (fig.) imbibe, absorb (knowledge etc.). 2. Apply lips, lips and tongue or analogous organs, to breast, food substance, etc., to absorb nourishment. 3. Perform action of sucking, use sucking action; (of pump etc.) make sucking or gurgling sound, draw in air instead of water. 4. ~ **at**, take pull at (pipe etc.); ~ **down, in**, (of whirlpool, quicksand, etc.) engulf; ~ **dry**, exhaust of contents by sucking; ~ **in**, (slang) cheat, deceive, swindle; ~ **in, up**, (of absorbent substance) absorb; ~ **up to**, (slang) toady to, curry favor with. **suck** *n*. Action, act, spell, of sucking (**give** ~, suckle);

Until the 19th century, the Sudd of **Sudan** *remained isolated from invasion by vast papyrus swamps (above). Today the country is unified and supplies 80 percent of the world's gum arabic.*

drawing action of whirlpool etc.

suck·er (sŭk'er) *n*. 1. Person or thing that sucks, esp. sucking pig or young whale calf; organ adapted for sucking; any of several esp. N. Amer. fish of family Catostomidae with mouths of form that suggests feeding by suction; piston of pump, syringe, etc. 2. Part, organ, or device adapted for adhering to object by suction; fish with suctorial disk by which it adheres to foreign objects. 3. Shoot thrown out by plant, esp. root under ground; axillary shoot to tobacco plant. 4. Lollipop. 5. (slang) Person easily victimized or gulled.

suck·ing (sŭk'ing) *adj*. Not yet weaned; (fig.) budding, unpracticed, immature.

suck·le (sŭk'el) *v.t*. (**-led, -ling**). Give suck to, feed at the breast.

suck'ling *n*. Unweaned child or animal, as ~ *pig*.

su·crose (sōō'krōs) *n*. Sugar ($C_{12}H_{22}O_{11}$) from cane and beet and found widely in many plants.

suc·tion (sŭk'shon) *n*. Action of sucking; production of complete

or partial vacuum so that external atmospheric pressure forces fluid into vacant space or causes adhesion of surfaces; ~ **pump**, pump drawing liquid through pipe into chamber exhausted by piston. **suc'tion·al** *adj*.

suc·to·ri·al (sŭktōr'ēal, -tōr'-) *adj*. (of organ) Adapted for sucking; (of animal) having suctorial organs; of the group Suctoria of protozoa, with tubular suctorial tentacles.

Su·dan (sōōdăn'). 1. Region of Africa, S. of Sahara and Libyan deserts. 2. Republic in NE. Africa, south of Egypt; capital, Khartoum. **Su·da·nese** (sōōdanēs', -nēz') *adj*. & *n*. (pl. **-nese**).

sud·den (sŭd'en) *adj*. Happening, coming, performed, taking place, etc., without warning or unexpectedly, abrupt; ~ **death**, (sports) overtime play to settle tied game, play ending as soon as one side scores the required number of points, goals, etc. **sud'den·ly** *adv*. **sud'den·ness** *n*. **sudden** *n*. (**all**) **of a** ~, suddenly.

su·dor·if·er·ous (sōōderĭf'erus) *adj*. Producing or secreting sweat. **su·dor·if·ic** (sōōderĭf'ĭk) *adj*. & *n*. (Drug) promoting or causing sweating.

Su·dra (sōō'dra) *n*. (Member of) the lowest of the four great Hindu castes, the artisans and laborers.

suds (sŭdz) *n.pl.* Water impregnated with soap; frothy mass on top of soapy water, lather. **suds'y** *adj.* (**suds·i·er, suds·i·est**).

sue (soo) *v.* (**sued, su·ing**). Institute legal proceedings, bring civil action, against; apply before court for grant of (writ, legal process); bring suit; plead, appeal, supplicate (*for*).

suede (swād) *n.* 1. Kid or other skin with flesh side rubbed into nap, as material for gloves, shoes, etc. 2. (also ~ **cloth**) Woven fabric imitating this. [Fr. *Suède* Sweden]

su·et (soo'ĭt) *n.* Hard fat around the kidneys and loins of cattle and sheep, used in cooking or rendered down to form tallow. **su'et·y** *adj.* Of or like suet; pale complexioned.

Sue·to·ni·us (swētō'nēus). Gaius Suetonius Tranquillus (*c*70–*c*100 A.D.). Roman historian and antiquary.

Su·ez (soo'ĕz, sooĕz'). District of Lower Egypt at N. end of the Red Sea; seaport at S. end of the ~ **Canal**, ship canal across the Isthmus of Suez to Port Said, cut (1859–69) by Ferdinand de Lesseps.

suf·fer (sŭf'er) *v.* 1. Undergo, experience, be subjected to (pain, loss, grief, defeat, punishment, etc.); undergo pain, grief, or damage. 2. Permit *to* do; allow, put up with, tolerate. **suf'fer·er, suf'fer·ing** *ns.* **suf'fer·a·ble** *adj.* **suf'fer·ing·ly** *adv.*

suf·fer·ance (sŭf'erans, sŭf'-rans) *n.* 1. (archaic) Long-suffering, forbearance. 2. Sanction, or acquiescence, implied by absence of objection; tacit permission or toleration, esp. in **on** ~, under conditions of bare tolerance or tacit acquiescence.

suf·fice (sufīs') *v.* (**-ficed, -fic·ing**). Be enough, be adequate; satisfy, meet the needs of.

suf·fi·cien·cy (sufĭsh'ensē) *n.* (pl. **-cies**). (esp.) Sufficient supply, adequate provision.

suf·fi·cient (sufĭsh'ent) *adj.* Sufficing; adequate, esp. in amount or number; enough; (archaic) competent, adequate in ability or resources. **suf·fi·cient·ly** *adv.*

suf·fix (sŭf'ĭks) *n.* (gram.) Verbal element attached to end of word as inflectional formative or to form new word. ~ (sŭf'ĭks, sufĭks') *v.t.* Add as suffix. **suf·fix·ion** (sufĭk'shon) *n.*

suf·fo·cate (sŭk'okāt) *v.* (**-cat·ed, -cat·ing**). Kill, stifle, choke, by stopping respiration; produce choking sensation in, smother, overwhelm; feel suffocated. **suf·fo·ca·tion** (sŭfokā'shon) *n.* **suf'fo·cat·ing·ly** *adv.*

suf·fra·gan (sŭf'ragan) *adj.* ~ **bishop**, bishop appointed to assist

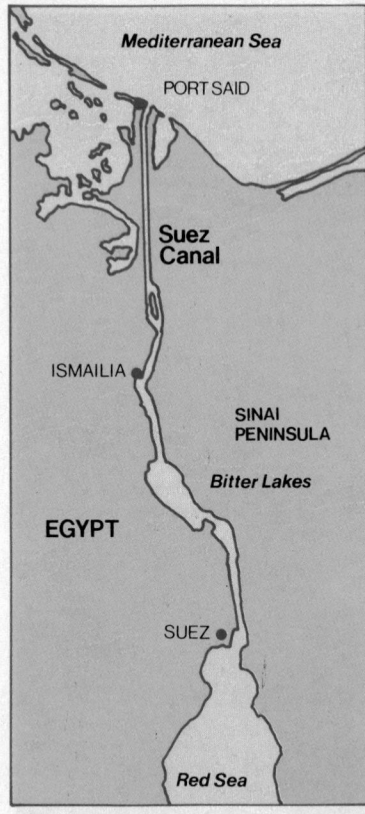

It is believed that the first **Suez Canal,** *while much smaller than the present one, was dug by Seti I of Egypt about 1380 B.C. Another was planned by Napoleon.*

diocesan bishop in particular part of his diocese; bishop in relation to his archbishop. **suffragan** *n.* Suffragan bishop.

suf·frage (sŭf'rĭj) *n.* Vote; approval or consent expressed by voting; right of voting as member of political or other body, franchise; (archaic and eccles.) intercession, prayer. **suf'frag·ism** *n.*

suf·fra·gette (sŭfrajĕt') *n.* (hist.) Woman advocating political enfranchisement of women, esp. militantly or violently.

suf·fra·gist (sŭf'rajĭst) *n.* Advocate of extension of political franchise, esp. to women.

suf·fuse (sufūz') *v.t.* (**-fused, -fus·ing**). Overspread as with a fluid, a color, a gleam of light. **suf·fu·sion** (sufū'zhon) *n.*

sug·ar (shoog'er) *n.* 1. Sweet crystalline substance ($C_{12} H_{22} O_{11}$), white when pure, obtained by evaporation from plant juices, esp. that of sugar cane and sugar beet, and forming important article of human food, saccharose; (pl.) kinds of sugar. 2. (colloq.) Sweet words, flattery, anything serving purpose of sugar put around pill in reconciling person to what is unpalatable. 3. (chem.) Any of a group of carbohydrates, soluble in water and having a sweet taste,

found esp. in plants and including glucose, lactose, saccharose, etc. 4. ~ **beet**, kind of white beet from which sugar is extracted; **sug'-arbush**, grove of sugar maples; **sugar cane**, perennial tropical and subtropical grass (*Saccharum officinarum*), with tall stout jointed stems, cultivated as a source of sugar; **sugar daddy**, (colloq.) elderly man who lavishes gifts on a young woman; **sug'arhouse**, place for refining or processing sugar, esp. shed or other building where maple sugar or syrup is made; **sugar loaf**, conical molded mass of hard refined sugar; anything, esp. hill, in shape of a sugar loaf; **sugar maple**, N. Amer. tree (*Acer saccharum*) yielding fine hardwood for furniture, and sweet sap which is boiled down for maple syrup and sugar; **sug'arplum**, small round or oval candy of boiled sugar; **sugar tongs**, small tongs for picking up lump sugar at table. **sug'ar·less** *adj.* **sugar** *v.t.* Sweeten, coat with sugar; make sweet or agreeable; form sugar, become crystalline or granulated like sugar; spread sugar mixed with gum etc. on (tree) to catch moths; **sug'arcoat**, coat or cover with sugar; make seem more pleasing, less disagreeable; **sugar off**, complete boiling down of maple syrup for sugar.

sug·ar·y (shoog'erē) *adj.* Like sugar; containing (much) sugar; (fig.) cloying, sentimental.

sug·gest (sugjĕst', sujĕst') *v.t.* Cause (idea) to be present to mind, call up idea of; prompt execution of; put forward opinion or proposition (*that*), utter as a suggestion; give hint or inkling of, give impression of existence or presence of.

sug·gest·i·ble (sugjĕs'tĭbel, sujĕs'-) *adj.* (esp.) Capable of being influenced by suggestion. **sug·gest·i·bil·i·ty** (sugjĕstĭbĭl'ĭtē, sujĕs-) *n.*

sug·ges·tion (sugjĕs'chon, sujĕs'-) *n.* Suggesting; idea, plan, or thought suggested, proposal; suggesting of prurient ideas; insinuation of belief or impulse into mind of subject by hypnosis or other means, such belief or impulse.

sug·ges·tive (sugjĕs'tĭv, sujĕs'-) *adj.* (esp.) Suggesting something indecent. **sug·ges'tive·ly** *adv.* **sug·ges'tive·ness** *n.*

su·i·cide (soo'ĭsīd) *n.* 1. Intentional self-slaughter; **commit** ~, kill oneself. 2. (fig.) Action destructive to one's own interests etc. 3. Person who has committed suicide. **suicide** *v.i.* (**-cid·ed, -cid·ing**). (colloq.) Commit suicide. **su·i·ci·dal** (sooĭsī'dal) *adj.* **su·i·ci'dal·ly** *adv.*

su·i ge·ne·ris (soo'ī jĕn'erĭs; *Lat.* soo'ē gĕ'nĕrĭs). Of its own

Sugarcane is grown on the eastern coastal plain of Australia from northern N.S.W. to north Queensland. Miniature locomotives tow canetrolleys from the fields to the crushers.

Cane sugar
Beet sugar

kind, peculiar, unique. [L.]

suit (soot) *n.* 1. Suing in court of law, legal prosecution; process instituted in court of justice, lawsuit. 2. Suing, supplication, petition; courting of a woman, courtship. 3. Set of outer garments, usu. coat (and sometimes vest), and trousers or skirt; set of sails, armor, etc.; **suit'case**, case for carrying clothes, usu. box-shaped with flat hinged lid and one handle. 4. Any of the four sets (spades, clubs, hearts, diamonds) of playing cards in pack, consisting of 13 cards (ten numbered consecutively and three face cards); **follow suit**, play card of suit led; (fig.) follow another's example. **suit** *v.* 1. Accommodate, adapt, make fitting or appropriate, *to.* 2. Be agreeable or convenient to; be fitted or adapted to; be good for, favorable to health of; go well

*Map showing the **sugar** production areas of the world and indicating areas where sugarcane can be grown, and cooler locations where sugarbeet is the alternative.*

with appearance or character of, be becoming to; be fitting or convenient; ~ **up**, put on athletic uniform or special clothing, as for underwater exploration, space travel, etc.; ~ **yourself**, do as you choose; find something that satisfies you. **suit'ing** *n.* (esp.) Material for suits of clothing.

suit·a·ble (soo'tabel) *adj.* Suited *to* or *for*; well fitted for the purpose; appropriate to the occasion. **suit'a·bly** *adv.* **suit·a·bil·i·ty** (sootabǐl'ǐtē), **suit'a·ble·ness** *ns.*

suite (swēt) *n.* 1. Retinue, set of persons in attendance. 2. Set,

series; number of rooms forming unit used by particular person(s) or for particular purpose; set of furniture of same pattern. 3. (mus.) Old form of instrumental composition (*c*1500–*c*1750), later partly superseded by SONATA, and consisting of several (usu. four) movements based on dance tunes, in same or related keys; set of instrumental compositions related in theme etc. and freq. constituting music for ballet, incidental music for play, etc.

suit·or (soo'ter) *n.* 1. Party to lawsuit; petitioner. 2. Wooer, one who seeks woman in marriage.

su·ki·ya·ki (sookēyah'kē, sookē-, skēyah'-) *n.* Japanese dish of sliced meat cooked with vegetables and soy sauce.

Suk·koth, Suc·coth (sook'os; *Heb.* sookawt') *ns.* Feast of Tabernacles or Booths, Jews' autumn festival of thanksgiving for harvest, and commemoration of their wandering in the wilderness when they dwelt in tents. [Heb. *sukkôt* booths]

sul·cus (sŭl'kus) *n.* (pl. **-ci** pr. -sī). Groove, furrow; esp. (anat.) fissure between two convolutions of brain.

sul·fa (sŭl'fa) *adjs.* ~ **drug**, sulfonamide.

sul·fa·nil·a·mide (sŭlfanĭl'-amīd) *n.* Synthetic organic chemical compound ($H_2NC_6H_4SO_2NH_2$), from which most of the sulfa drugs are derived.

sul·fate (sŭl'fāt) *n.* Salt of sulfuric acid. ~ *v.* (**-fat·ed, -fat·ing**). Treat, impregnate, with sulfuric acid or a sulfate; (elect.) form whitish scales of lead sulfate on plates of (storage battery), become sulfated. **sul·fa·tion** (sŭlfā'shon) *n.*

sul·fide (sŭl'fīd) *n.* Compound of sulfur with another element or a radical.

sul·fite (sŭl'fīt) *n.* Salt of sulfurous acid.

sul·fon·a·mide (sŭlfŏn'amīd) *n.* Any of a group of drugs derived from amides of sulfonic acids, capable of killing or preventing the multiplication of bacteria, e.g. streptococci, used in the treatment of many different infections.

sul·fone (sŭl'fōn) *n.* Any of a group of organic compounds containing the radical SO_2 united directly to two carbon atoms. **sul·fon·ic, sul·phon·ic** (sŭlfŏn'ĭk) *adjs.*

sul·fur, sul·phur (sŭl'fer) *ns.* 1. (chem.) Greenish-yellow non-metallic inflammable element,

The fruit of the stag-horn **sumac**, known as the lemonade tree, is used to make lemonade in eastern North America. Other varieties in Europe and Asia provide tannin, resin and wax.

burning with blue flame, widely distributed free and in combination, and used in manufacture of matches, gunpowder, and sulfuric acid, for vulcanizing rubber, as a disinfectant (as sulfur dioxide), and in medicine as a laxative, a sudorific, and an ingredient of ointments; symbol S, at. no. 16, at. wt. 32.06; **flowers of** ~, pure sulfur in form of yellow powder; ~ **dioxide**, poisonous gas formed in burning of sulfur, used in many manufacturing processes and as refrigerant, disinfectant, etc. 2. In popular belief, material of which hellfire and lightning were held to consist; (alchemy) one of the supposed ultimate elements, the principle of combustion. 3. ~ (or ~ **butterfly**), any of various yellow (or orange) butterflies of family Pieridae. 4. ~ **yellow**, (of) the bright pale-yellow color of sulfur.

sul·fu·ric (sŭlfūr'ĭk) *adj.* Of, containing, sulfur; ~ **acid**, dense highly corrosive oily fluid, oil of vitriol (H_2SO_4); ~ **ether**, ether.

sul·fur·ous (sŭl'ferus, sŭlfūr'-) *adj.* 1. Of, like, suggesting, sulfur; with qualities associated with (burning) sulfur; full of sulfur of hell; sulfur yellow. 2. (chem. of compounds) Containing sulfur of lower valence than sulfuric compounds; ~ **acid**, acid (H_2SO_3) present in solutions of sulfur dioxide in water.

sulk (sŭlk) *v.i.* Be sulky. ~ *n.* (usu. pl.) Sulky fit.

sulk·y[1] (sŭl'kē) *adj.* (**sulk·i·er, sulk·i·est**). Sullen, morose; silent, inactive, or unsociable from resentment or ill temper. **sulk'i·ly** *adv.* **sulk'i·ness** *n.*

sulk·y[2] (sŭl'kē) *n.* (pl. **sulk·ies**). Light two-wheeled carriage for one person, esp. one used in trotting races.

Sul·la (sŭl'a), **Lucius Cornelius** (138–78 B.C.). Roman dictator and general; instituted reforms of the constitution designed to increase the power of the senate and reduce that of the people and their tribunes.

sul·len (sŭl'en) *adj.* Gloomy, ill-humored. **sul'len·ly** *adv.* **sul'len·ness** *n.*

Sul·li·van (sŭl'ĭvan), **Sir Arthur Seymour** (1842–1900). English musical composer, in collaboration with W. S. GILBERT[3], of light satiric operas.

sul·ly (sŭl'ē) *v.t.* (**-lied, -ly·ing**). (chiefly poet.) Soil, tarnish; be stain on, discredit.

sul·tan (sŭl'tan) *n.* 1. Sovereign

Although Indonesia has been a unified nation for many years, there are still separate cultural groups. The Menangkabau of south **Sumatra** maintain huge communal houses (above).

of Muslim country, esp. (hist.) of Turkey. 2. Small white domestic fowl with heavily feathered legs and feet, orig. from Turkey. 3. (also **sweet** ~) Either of two sweet-scented annuals, *Centaurea moschata* (purple or white sweet ~) and *C. suaveolens* (yellow ~).

sul·tan·ate (sŭl'tanāt) *n.* Rank, authority, of a sultan; jurisdiction, dominion, of a sultan. [Arab. *sulṭān* ruler, emperor]

sul·tan·a (sŭltăn'a, -tah'na) *n.* 1. Wife or concubine of sultan. 2. Small light-colored seedless raisin grown esp. near Izmir; pale yellow grape from which sultanas are produced.

sul·try (sŭl'trē) *adj.* (**-tri·er, -tri·est**). Oppressively hot, sweltering; (fig.) having strong sexual attraction, passionate,

sensual. **sul'tri·ly** *adv.* **sul'tri·ness** *n.*

sum (sŭm) *n.* 1. Total amount resulting from addition of 2 or more numbers, quantities, magnitudes, etc.; total number or amount *of*; **in** ~, briefly but comprehensively put; ~ **total**, total amount, aggregate (of). 2. Quantity or amount of or *of* money. 3. (Working out of) arithmetical problem. **sum** *v.* (**summed, sum·ming**). 1. Find sum of; reckon, count, or total *up*; collect (*up*) into small compass. 2. ~ **up**, summarize, epitomize; form estimate or judgment of; (of judge in trial, or counsel concluding client's case) recapitulate (evidence or arguments), with any necessary exposition of points of law, before jury considers its verdict; so **summing-up** (*n.*) (pl. **summings-up**).

su·mac, su·mach (soō'măk, shoō'-) *ns.* Shrub or small tree of genus *Rhus*, with feathery leaves and clusters of (usu. red) berries;

one species (*R. vernix*), poison sumac, with white berries, causes acute skin rash like that from poison ivy. [Arab. *summāk*]

Su·ma·tra (soōomah'tra). Large island of Indonesia, separated from the Malay Peninsula by the Strait of Malacca.

Su·mer (soō'mer). Region in ancient Mesopotamia, now part of S. Iraq. **Su·mer·i·an** (soōomēr'ēan, -mĕr'-) *adj.* & *n.* (Native, inhabitant) of Sumer; (of) the agglutinative language of the Sumerian inscriptions written in a cuneiform script.

sum·ma cum lau·de (soōm'a koōm low'dē, -de, sŭm'a kŭm law'dē). With the greatest praise; used of diplomas awarded with highest honors for academic excellence (cf. CUM laude, MAGNA CUM LAUDE). [L.]

sum·ma·rize (sŭm'erīz) *v.t.* (**-rized, -riz·ing**). Make or constitute a summary of, sum up. **sum·ma·ri·za·tion** (sŭmerīzā'-shon) *n.*

sum·ma·ry (sŭm'erē) *adj.* Compendious and (usu.) brief; dispensing with needless detail, performed with dispatch; (law, of proceedings) carried out rapidly by omission of certain formalities required by common law; ∼

In areas where there is geothermal activity, such as the Yellowstone National Park, strong-smelling sulfurous vapors are emitted with steam from hot springs and geysers in the area.

court-martial, court-martial comprising one commissioned officer for judging relatively minor offenses. **sum·mar·i·ly** (sumĕr'īlē, sŭm'er-) *adv.* **summary** *n.* (pl. **-ries**). Summary account or statement, abridgment, epitome.

sum·ma·tion (sŭmā'shon) *n.* Addition, summing (up); finding of total or sum. **sum·ma'tion·al** *adj.*

sum·mer (sŭm'er) *n.* 1. Warmest season of year, popularly reckoned in N. hemisphere as lasting from mid-May to middle or end of August, but astronomically as lasting from summer solstice (June 21 or 22) to autumnal equinox (Sept. 22 or 23); summer weather; (pl.) years of life or age (chiefly poet.); **Indian** ∼: see INDIAN. 2. (*attrib.* or as *adj.*) **sum'merhouse**, (usu. simple and light) building in park or garden providing cool shady place in summer; **summer school**, a program of courses given during summer vacation, esp. at university; **summer solstice**: see SOLSTICE; **sum'mertime**, season of

summer. **summer** *v.* Pass summer (*at* or *in* place); pasture (cattle) *at, in.* **sum'mer·y** *adj.*

sum·mit (sŭm'ĭt) *n.* Highest point, top, apex; highest degree; ∼ **conference**, meeting of heads of nations.

sum·mon (sŭm'on) *v.t.* Call together by authority for action or deliberation, require presence or attendance of, bid approach; call upon *to* do; call *up* (courage, resolution, etc.) to one's aid; cite by authority to appear before court or judge to answer charge or give evidence. **sum'mon·er** *n.*

sum·mons (sŭm'onz) *n.* (pl. **-mons·es**). Authoritative call or urgent invitation to attend on some occasion or to do something; citation to appear before judge or magistrate. ∼ *v.t.* Take out summons against.

su·mo (soō'mō) *n.* (Participant in) Japanese wrestling, in which defeat follows touching of ground except with feet, or failure to keep within marked area.

sump (sŭmp) *n.* Pit or well for collecting water or other fluid, esp. in mine or basement; oil reservoir at bottom of crankcase of internal combustion engine.

sump·tu·ous (sŭmp'choōus) *adj.* Costly, splendid, magnificent

The indescribable beauty of a **sunset** is due to the refraction, reflection and scattering of light. The colors are also affected and intensified by dust particles or smoke.

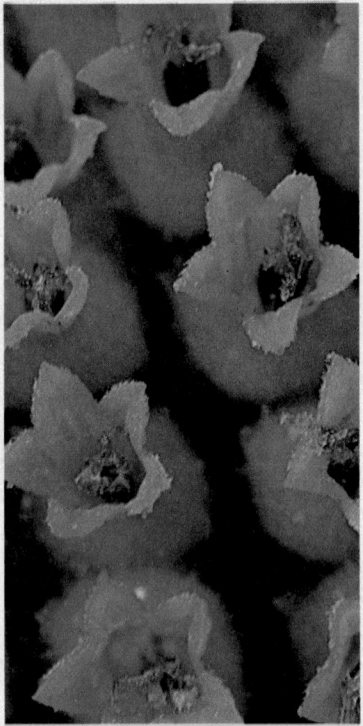

Close-up of the disk florets which occupy the centre of a **sunflower**. These eventually form into large dark seeds which are a rich source of oil, used for culinary and industrial purposes.

Sundew is the common name for a group of about 100 species of insectivorous plants. Prey is trapped in a sticky secretion which forms at the tips of the leaves.

in workmanship, decoration, appearance, etc. **sump′tu·ous·ly** *adv.* **sump′tu·ous·ness** *n.*

sun (sŭn) *n.* Star forming center of system of worlds or planets, esp. the central body of the solar system, around which Earth and other planets revolve, and which supplies them with light and warmth by its radiation; such light or warmth; (poet.) climate, clime; **a place in the** ~, position giving scope for development of individual or national life; **take the** ~, (naut.) make observation of meridian altitude of sun to determine latitude; ~ **bath**, exposure of skin to sun's rays; **sun′bathe** (**-bathed, -bath·ing**), take sunbath; **sun′beam**, beam of sunlight; **Sun′belt**, southern and southwestern area of U.S., having more warm, sunny weather than other regions of nation and, for the past decade, rapid population and economic expansion; **sun′bonnet**, bonnet of cotton etc. shaped so as to shade eyes and neck from sun; **sun′burn**, superficial inflammation of skin caused by exposure to sun; brown color produced thus; **sun′burned, sun′burnt** (*adj.*); **sun′burst**, burst of sunlight; piece of jewelry representing sun surrounded by rays; **sun deck**, flat roof or raised open platform of house etc. for sunbathing etc.; **sun′dew**, plant of genus *Drosera* of small herbs growing in bogs, with leaves covered with glandular hairs secreting viscid drops; **sun′dial**, contrivance for showing time by shadow cast by sun on surface marked with hours; **sun disk**, (archaeol.) winged disk, symbol of sun god; **sun′dog**, parhelion, mock sun; **sun′down**, sunset; **sun′fish** (pl. **-fishes**, collect. **-fish**), large fish of family Molidae of warm seas, with round ungainly body and short fringelike caudal fin; any of various small usu. brilliantly colored Amer. freshwater fishes of family Centrarchidae; **sun′flower**, composite plant of genus *Helianthus*, chiefly native of N. Amer., with conspicuous yellow flower heads whose disk and rays suggest figure of sun; **sun′glasses**, tinted spectacles for protecting eyes from sunlight or glare; **sun′lamp**, large lamp with parabolic mirror reflector used in motion-picture photography; lamp emitting ultraviolet rays; **sun′light, sun′lit**, (illuminated by) light from sun; **sun′lit**, (illuminated by) light from sun; **sun′ray**, sunbeam; (attrib.) emitting, using, ultraviolet rays, esp. therapeutically; **sun′rise**, (time of) sun's apparent ascent above eastern horizon; **sun′roof**, sliding section of automobile roof; **sun′room**, room with walls largely of glass, designed to admit maximum amount of sunshine; **sun′set**, (time of) sun's apparent descent below western horizon at end of day; glow of light or display of color in sky at this time; (fig.) decline, close (esp. of life); **sun′set law**, law requiring periodic evaluation of need for government agencies and programs; **sun′shade**, device providing protection from sun's rays, esp. parasol or awning over window; **sun′shine**, unimpeded sunlight, fair weather; (fig.) cheerfulness, bright influence; **sun′shine law**, law making official meetings and records of most government agencies accessible to public; **sun′spot**, one of the cavities in photosphere appearing as dark spots or patches on sun's surface, lasting from a few hours to several months, recurring in greatest numbers at intervals of a little over 11 years, and freq. accompanied by magnetic disturbances etc. on Earth; **sun′stroke**, prostration or collapse caused by exposure to excessive heat of sun; **sun′tan** (*n.* & *v.*), tan(ning of) skin by exposure to sun; **sun′up**, sunrise; **sun′wise**, in direction of sun's apparent motion, clockwise. **sun′less** *adj.* **sun′less·ness** *n.* **sun** *v.* (**sunned, sun·ning**). Expose to the sun; ~ **oneself**, bask in sun.

Sun. *abbrev.* Sunday.

sun·dae (sŭn′dā) *n.* Confection of ice cream with fruit, nuts, syrup, cream, etc.

Sun·day (sŭn′dā, -dē) *n.* First day of the week, observed by Christians as day of rest and worship; **a month of ∼s**, a very long time; ∼ **best**, best clothes as worn on Sunday; ∼ **punch**, (slang) boxer's most powerful punch; (fig.) anything capable of maximum effectiveness against an opponent; ∼ **school**, school held on Sunday, now only for religious instruction, and usu. attached to parish or church congregation.

sun·der (sŭn′der) *v.* (now poet. or rhet.) Separate, sever, keep apart.

sun·dry (sŭn′drē) *adj.* Diverse, several; **all and ∼**, one and all. **sundry** *n.* (pl. **-dries**). (pl.) Oddments, small items classed together without individual mention.

Sung (soong). Name of dynasty that ruled China 960–1279.

sung: see SING.

sunk (sŭngk), **sunk·en** (sŭng′-ken) *adjs.*: see SINK²; (esp., of eyes, cheeks, etc.) hollow, fallen in.

Sun·na, Sun·nah (soon′a) *ns.* Traditional portion of Muslim law based on Muhammad's words or acts but not written by him, accepted as authoritative by the orthodox but rejected by the Shiites. **Sun·ni** (soon′ē, sŭn′ē), **Sun·nite** (soon′īt, sŭn′-) *adjs.* & *ns.* (Muslim) accepting the Sunna as well as Koran.

sun·ny (sŭn′ē) *adj.* (**-ni·er, -ni·est**). Bright with or as sunlight; exposed to, warm with, the sun; cheery, bright in disposition. **sun′ni·ly** *adv.* **sun′ni·ness** *n.*

Sun Yat-sen (sŭn′yăt′sĕn′, soon′yaht′sĕn′) (1866–1925). Leader of Chinese revolutionary movement, 1911–12; first president of the Chinese Republic, 1921–2.

sup (sŭp) *v.* (**supped, sup·ping**). Take supper.

su·per (soo′per) *n.* (colloq.) Supernumerary actor; building superintendent. ∼ *adj.* (colloq.) Excellent, unusually good.

super- *prefix.* On the top (of); over; beyond, besides, in addition; exceeding, going beyond, more than, transcending; of higher kind; to a degree beyond the usual.

su·per·a·bun·dant (sooperabŭn′dant) *adj.* Very or too abundant. **su·per·a·bun′dance** *n.* **su·per·a·bun′dant·ly** *adv.*

su·per·an·nu·ate (sooperăn′ūat) *v.t.* (**-at·ed, -at·ing**). Dismiss or discharge as too old; discharge with pension. **su·per·an·nu·a′tion** (sooperănūā′shon) *n.* **su·per·an′nu·at·ed** *adj.*

su·perb (soopĕrb′) *adj.* Grand, majestic, splendid, magnificent. **su·perb′ly** *adv.*

su·per·car·go (sooperkăr′gō, soo′perkăr-) *n.* (pl. **-goes, -gos**).

Merchant ship's officer superintending cargo and commercial transactions of voyage.

su·per·charge (soo′percharj) *v.t.* Charge to excess (*with* energy, emotion, etc.); use supercharger on. **su′per·charged** *adj.*

su·per·charg·er (soo′percharjer) *n.* Device supplying internal combustion engine with air or explosive mixture at higher pressure than normal in order to increase its efficiency.

su·per·cil·i·ar·y (soopersĭl′ēĕre) *adj.* Of the eyebrow, over the eye.

su·per·cil·i·ous (soopersĭl′ēus) *adj.* Haughtily contemptuous, disdainful, or superior. **su·per·cil′i·ous·ly** *adv.* **su·per·cil′i·ous·ness** *n.*

su·per·con·duc·tiv·i·ty (sooperkŏndŭktĭv′ĭtē) *n.* Extremely high conductivity shown by certain substances at very low temperatures. **su·per·con·duc·tive** (sooperkondŭk′tĭv) *adj.* **su·per·con·duc′tor** *n.*

su·per·cool (sooperkool′) *v.t.* Cool below freezing point without solidification or crystallization.

su·per·e·go (sooperē′gō, soo′perē-) *n.* (psych.) Part of mind that exerts conscience and responds to social rules.

*The **sundial** was one of the earliest devices used to tell the time but, since they depend on bright sunlight to operate, sundials were replaced by clocks when these became available. Sundials are now purely decorative.*

su·per·er·o·ga·tion (sooperĕrogā′shon) *n.* Performance of more than duty or circumstances require; esp. (R.C. theol.) performance of good works beyond what God requires, which constitute a store of merit that the church may dispense to make up others' deficiencies. **su·per·e·rog·a·to·ry** (soopererŏg′atōrē, -tōre) *adj.*

su·per·fam·i·ly (soo′perfămĭlē, -fămlē) *n.* (pl. **-lies**). (biol.) Set of related families within an order.

su·per·fi·cial (sooperfĭsh′al) *adj.* Of, on, the surface; not going deep, without depth; (of measures) involving two dimensions, of extent of surface, square. **su·per·fi′cial·ly** *adv.* **su·per·fi·ci·al·i·ty** (sooperfĭshēăl′ĭtē), **su·per·fi′cial·ness** *n.*

su·per·flu·id (sooperfloo′ĭd) *n.* (phys.) Fluid, as liquid helium, having frictionless flow at temperatures below 2.18° K and high heat conductivity. **su·per·flu·id·i·ty** (sooperfloo·ĭd′ĭte) *n.*

su·per·flu·i·ty (sooperfloo′ĭte) *n.* (pl. **-ties**). Superfluous amount.

su·per·flu·ous (soopĕr′floous) *adj.* More than enough, excessive, redundant; needless, uncalled-for. **su·per′flu·ous·ly** *adv.* **su·per′flu·ous·ness** *n.*

su·per·heat (sooperhĕt′) *v.t.* Heat to very high temperature; esp. raise temperature of (steam) to increase its pressure. **su·per·heat′er** *n.*

su·per·het·er·o·dyne (sooper-

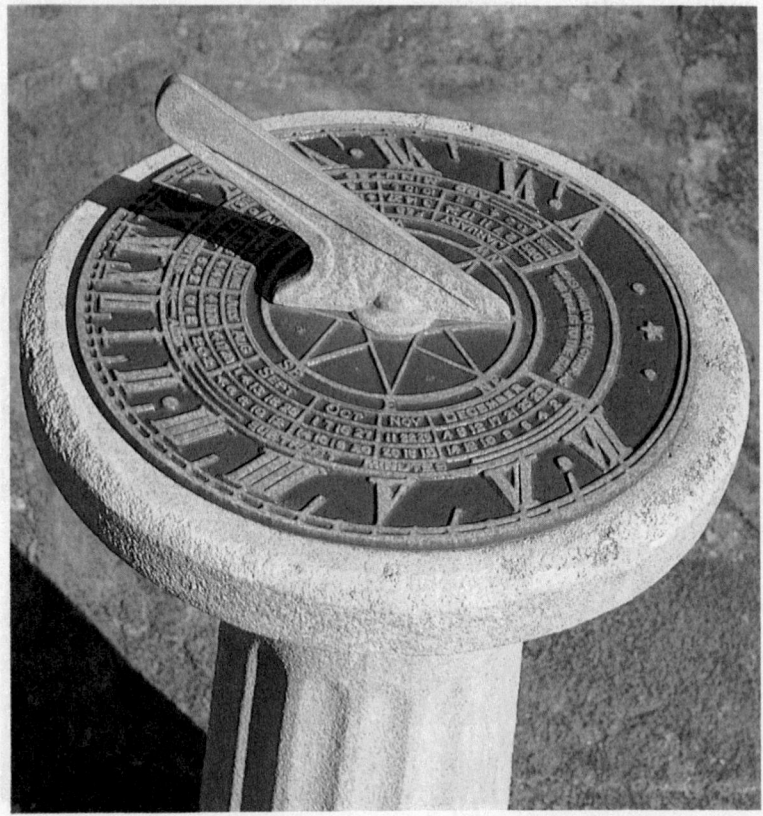

hĕt′erodīn) *adj.* & *n.* (Of) radio reception or receiver in which, by means of a local oscillator, a beat note is set up with the incoming signal and amplified at the resulting intermediate frequency.

su·per·high·way (sōōperhī′wā) *n.* Broad main highway for fast traffic.

su·per·hu·man (sōōperhū′man, -ū′man) *adj.* Beyond (normal) human capacity, strength, etc.; higher than (that of) man.

su·per·im·pose (sōōperĭmpōz′) *v.t.* (**-posed, -pos·ing**). Impose or place *on* or on something else. **su·per·im·po·si·tion** (sōōperĭmpozĭsh′on) *n.*

su·per·in·tend (sōōperĭntĕnd′) *v.* Have or exercise charge or direction (of), oversee, supervise. **su·per·in·tend′ence, su·per·in·tend′en·cy** *ns.* **su·per·in·tend′ent** *n.* Officer or official having control, oversight, or direction of business, institution, etc.; caretaker of building.

su·pe·ri·or (sōōpēr′ēer, su-) *adj.* 1. Upper, higher, situated above or farther up than something else; growing above another part or organ, that is higher than other(s) of the same kind; (printing) above the line or near the top of other figures etc. 2. Higher in rank, dignity, degree, amount, quality, status, etc.; ~ **to**, above the influence or reach of, not affected or mastered by, higher in status or quality than. 3. Conscious, showing consciousness, of superior qualities; lofty, supercilious, dictatorial, etc. **su·pe′ri·or·ly** *adv.* **su·pe·ri·or·i·ty** (sōōpērēor′ĭtē,

-ār′-, su-) *n.* **superior** *n.* 1. Person of higher rank, dignity, or authority, superior officer or official; person or thing of higher quality or value than another. 2. Head of religious community (freq. **Father, Mother,** etc., **S ~**).

Su·pe·ri·or (sōōpēr′ēer, su-), **Lake.** World's largest freshwater lake, covering 31,800 sq. mi. (82,362 sq. km) in N. central U.S. and S. Canada, northernmost and westernmost of the Great Lakes.

su·per·la·tive (sōōpēr′latĭv, su-) *adj.* 1. Raised above or surpassing all others; of the highest degree. 2. (gram., of an inflectional form of an adjective or adverb, as *highest, fastest*) Expressing the highest or very high degree of the quality etc. denoted by the simple word (e.g. *high, fast*). **su·per′la·tive·ly** *adv.* **superlative** *n.* (Word in) the superlative degree. **su·per′la·tive·ness** *n.*

su·per·man (sōō′permăn) *n.* (pl. **-men** pr. -mĕn). Ideal superior man of the future, conceived by NIETZSCHE as evolved from normal human type; man of superhuman powers or achievement. [transl. Ger. *übermensch*]

su·per·mar·ket (sōō′permārkĭt) *n.* Large self-service store selling food and household goods.

su·per·nal (sōōpēr′nal) *adj.* (poet., rhet.) Heavenly, divine; of the sky; lofty.

Crew of the German warship 'Hamburg' lining the decks as it enters port. Originally designed to provide visibility for the helmsman, the **superstructure** *now houses complex equipment.*

su·per·nat·u·ral (sōōpernăch′eral) *adj.* Due to, manifesting, some agency above the forces of nature; outside the ordinary operation of cause and effect. **su·per·nat′u·ral·ly** *adv.* **su·per·nat′u·ral·ness** *n.*

su·per·nat′u·ral·ism (sōōpernăch′eralĭzem) *n.* Belief in supernatural beings, powers, events, etc. **su·per·nat′u·ral·ist** *n.* & *adj.* **su·per·nat·u·ral·is·tic** (sōōpernăcheralĭs′tĭk) *adj.*

su·per·no·va (sōōpernō′va) *n.* (pl. **-vae** pr. -vē, **-vas**). Nova of immense brightness or intensity.

su·per·nu·mer·ar·y (sōōpernōō′merĕrē, -nū′-) *adj.* & *n.* (pl. **-ar·ies**). (Person or thing) in excess of the normal number, esp. (extra person) not belonging to the regular body or staff but associated with it in some need or emergency; (actor) employed in addition to regular company, appearing on stage or in scene but not speaking.

su·per·phos·phate (sōōperfŏs′fāt) *n.* Fertilizer made by treating phosphate containing rock with sulfuric acid.

su·per·pose (sōōperpōz′) *v.t.* (**-posed, -pos·ing**). Place above or on something else; bring into same position so as to coincide. **su·per·pos′a·ble** *adj.* **su·per·po·si·tion** (sōōperpozĭsh′on) *n.*

su·per·pow·er (sōō′perpower) *n.* Extremely powerful nation, esp. one of only a few such.

su·per·sat·u·rate (sōōpersăch′erāt) *v.t.* (**-rat·ed, -rat·ing**). Add to (esp. solution) beyond saturation point. **su·per·sat·u·ra·tion** (sōōpersăcherā′shŏn) *n.*

su·per·scribe (sōō′perskrĭb) *v.t.* (**-scribed, -scrib·ing**). Write upon, put inscription on or over; write (inscription) at top of or outside something. **su·per·scrip·tion** (sōōperskrĭp′shon) *n.* **su·per·script** (sōō′perskrĭpt) *adj.* & *n.*

su·per·sede (sōōpersēd′) *v.* (**-sed·ed, -sed·ing**). Set aside, cease to employ; adopt or appoint another person or thing in place of; take the place of, oust, supplant. **su·per·ses·sion** (sōōpersĕsh′on) *n.*

su·per·son·ic (sōōpersŏn′ĭk) *adj.* With a velocity greater than that of sound. **su·per·son′ics** (*n.pl.* constr. with sing. verb) (Science and application of) supersonic phenomena.

su·per·sti·tion (sōōperstĭsh′on) *n.* Irrational fear of unknown or mysterious, credulity regarding the supernatural; habit or belief based on such tendencies; religious system deemed false or irrational. **su·per·sti′tious** *adj.* **su·per·sti′tious·ly** *adv.* **su·per·sti′tious·ness** *n.*

su·per·struc·ture (sōō′perstrŭkcher) *n.* Building, upper part f building, any material or nmaterial structure, resting upon omething else or with some other art as a foundation; parts of war-nip or 6ther vessel above main eck.

su·per·vene (sooˈpervēnˈ) *v.i.* -**vened, -ven·ing**). Occur as omething additional or ex-raneous, follow closely upon some ther occurrence or condition. **u·per·ven·tion** (sooˈpervenˈshon)

su·per·vise (sooˈpervīz) *v.t.* -**vised, -vis·ing**). Oversee, super-ntend execution or performance of hing), movements or work of erson). **su·per·vi·sion** (sooˈper-ˈizhˈon), **su·per·vi·sor** *ns.* u·per·vi·so·ry (sooˈpervīˈzerē) *adj.*

su·pi·nate (sooˈpināt) *v.t.* -**nat·ed, -nat·ing**). (physiol.) urn (hand or forelimb) so that ack of it is downward or backward pp. PRONATE). **su·pi·na·tion** sooˈpināˈshon) *n.*

su·pine (sooˈpīn) *adj.* 1. Lying ce upward; supinated. 2. Disin-lined to exertion, indolent, thargic, inert. **su·pineˈly** *adv.* u·pineˈness *n.*

sup·per (supˈer) *n.* Meal taken t end of day, esp. evening meal ss formal and substantial than inner; evening meal when dinner s taken at midday; ~ **club**, small nd expensive nightclub having fine ood and drink. **supˈper·less** *adj.*

suppl., supp. *abbrevs.* Supple-ent.

sup·plant (suplăntˈ, -plahntˈ) .t. Dispossess and take the place f, oust, esp. by dishonorable or reacherous means. **sup·plantˈer**

sup·ple (supˈel) *adj.* Easily bent, liant, flexible; (fig.) compliant, ccommodating, artfully or ser-lely obliging or submissive. **sup·**-ly², **sup·ple·ly** (supˈlē) *advs.* upˈple·ness *n.*

sup·ple·ment (supˈlement) *n.* . Something added to supply a eficiency; part added to complete terary work etc., esp. special umber or part of periodical deal-ng with particular item(s). 2. math.) Amount by which arc is ss than semicircle, or angle is less han 180°. ~ (supˈlemĕnt) *v.t.* urnish supplement to.ˈ **sup·ple·-en·tal** (suplemĕnˈtal), **sup·ple·-en·ta·ry** (suplemĕnˈterē) *adjs.* sp.) ~ **angle**, either of 2 angles hat together make 180°. **sup·ple·-en·talˈly** *adv.*

sup·pli·ant (supˈlēant) *n.* Humble petitioner. ~ *adj.* Sup-licating; expressing supplication. upˈpli·ant·ly *adv.*

sup·pli·cate (supˈlikāt) *v.* -cat·ed, -cat·ing**). Make humble etition to or *to* person, for or *for* hing. **supˈpli·cant, sup·pli·ca·-ion** (suplikāˈshon) *ns.* **sup·pli·**-

'Grace Before Meat' by the 17th-century Dutch painter, Jan Steen, is typical of genre painting. He possessed a rare insight which revealed the feel-ings of this family as they prepared for **supper.**

ca·to·ry (supˈlikatōrē, -tôrē) *adj.*

sup·pli·er (suplīˈer) *n.* Person, firm, etc., that supplies.

sup·ply¹ (suplīˈ) *v.t.* (**-plied, -ply·ing**). Furnish, provide (thing needed, or person, receptacle, etc. with or *with* thing needed); make up for (deficiency etc.). ~ *n.* (pl. **-plies**). 1. Provision of what is needed. 2. Stock, store, quantity, of or *of* something provided or available, esp. (econ.) on the market for purchase; (pl.) food and other stores necessary for armed force, expedition, etc.; ~ **and demand**, (econ.) factors regarded as regulat-ing price of commodities.

sup·ply²: see SUPPLE.

sup·port (supôrtˈ, -pôrtˈ) *n.* Supporting, being supported; per-son or thing that supports. ~ *v.t.* 1. Carry (part of) weight of; hold up, keep from falling or sinking; keep from failing or giving way,

give courage, confidence, or power of endurance to. 2. Endure, toler-ate. 3. Supply with necessaries, provide for. 4. Lend assistance or countenance to; back up, second, further; bear out, substantiate; speak in favor of (resolution etc.). **sup·portˈa·ble** *adj.* **sup·portˈ-a·bly** *adv.* **sup·portˈive** *adj.* **sup·portˈer** *n.*

sup·pose (supōzˈ) *v.t.* (**-posed, -pos·ing**). 1. Assume as a hypoth-esis, as ~ *it were true*; in part. or imper. = if, as *supposing white were black you would be right*; also in imper. as formula of proposal, as ~ *we try again*. 2. (of theory, result, etc.) Involve or require as condition, as *design in creation sup-poses a creator*. 3. Assume in default of knowledge, be inclined to think, accept as probably. 4. **be sup-posed**, have as a duty, as *he is supposed to clean the boots*; colloq., with neg., freq. = not be allowed, as *children are not supposed to go in*. **sup·posedˈ** *adj.* Believed to exist or have specified character. **sup·posˈed·ly** *adv.* **sup·posˈa·ble** *adj.*

sup·po·si·tion (supozĭshˈon),

sup·po·sal (supō'zal) *ns.* What is supposed or assumed. **sup·po·si'·tion·al** *adj.*

sup·po·si·tious (sŭpozĭsh'*us*) *adj.* Hypothetical, assumed.

sup·pos·i·ti·tious (supŏzĭ-tĭsh'*us*) *adj.* Substituted for the real; spurious, false. **sup·pos·i·ti'·tious·ly** *adv.* **sup·pos·i·ti'·tious·ness** *n.*

sup·pos·i·to·ry (supŏz'ĭtōrē, -tōrē) *n.* (pl. **-ries**). (med.) Cone or cylinder of medicated easily melted substance introduced into rectum, urethra, etc.

sup·press (suprĕs') *v.t.* Put down, quell, put a stop to activity or existence of; withhold or withdraw from publication; keep secret or unexpressed, refrain from mentioning or showing; (psych.) keep out of one's consciousness; (elect.) partly or wholly eliminate (unwanted frequencies, interference), equip (device) so as to reduce interference due to it. **sup·press'i·ble** *adj.* **sup·pres·sion** (suprĕsh'on) *n.* **sup·pres'sive** *adj.*

sup·pres·sant (suprĕs'ant) *n.* Chemical or drug used for suppressing undesirable behavior or physical condition.

sup·pu·rate (sŭp'yerāt) *v.t.* (**-rat·ed, -rat·ing**). Form or secrete pus, fester. **sup·pu·ra·tion** (sŭpyerā'shon) *n.* **sup'pu·ra·tive** *adj.*

su·pra (sōō'pra) *adv.* Above; previously, before (in a book or writing).

supra- *prefix* = SUPER-, esp. in scientific (esp. anat. and zool.) terms with senses above, higher

than; on.

su·pra·or·bi·tal (sōōpraōr'-bĭtal) *adj. & n.* (Artery, vein, bone, nerve) above the orbit of the eye.

su·pra·re·nal (sōōprarē'nal) *adj. & n.* (Gland) situated above the kidney, adrenal.

su·prem·a·cy (sōōprĕm'asē) *n.* Being supreme, position of supreme authority or power. **su·prem·a·cist** (sōōprĕ'masĭst) *n.* Advocate of supremacy of a group, as *white, black, male* ~.

su·preme (sōōprēm', su-) *adj.* Highest in authority or rank; greatest, of the highest quality, degree, or amount; **the S~ (Being)**, God; **S~ Court**, (esp.) highest judicial body in U.S. Government, consisting of nine members appointed for life by President with Senate's approval; **S~ Soviet**, governing council of U.S.S.R. or one of its constituent republics. **su·preme'ly** *adv.* **su·preme'ness** *n.*

Supt., supt. *abbrevs.* Superintendent.

sur·cease (sērsēs') *n.* (archaic) Cessation, esp. temporary.

sur·charge (sēr'chārj) *n.* Additional or excessive pecuniary charge, or load or burden; additional mark printed on face of stamp, esp. to change its value. ~ (sērchārj') *v.t.* (**-charged,**

-charg·ing**).** Charge (person additional or excessive price o payment; exact (sum) as surcharge overload, fill or saturate to excess print surcharge on (stamp). **sur·charg'er** *n.*

surd (sērd) *adj. & n.* (math.) Irrational (quantity, esp root of integer). 2. Voiceles (speech sound).

sure (shoor) *adj.* (**sur·er, sur·est**). 1. Certain, assured, confident persuaded (*of*); having no doub 2. That may be relied on, trust worthy, unfailing, infallible; cer tainly true or truthful; safe; **sure'-fire**, (colloq.) certain (to succeed) **sure'footed**, treading securely o firmly. 3. Certain *to* do or be **sure of**, certain to get, keep, have etc.; **make sure**, act so as to b certain *of*. **sure'ness** *n.* **sure** *adv* Assuredly, undoubtedly, certainly as certainly as.

sure·ly (shoor'lē) *adv.* 1. Wit certainty or safety (chiefly i **slowly but** ~). 2. Certainly assuredly; (freq., expressing belie without absolute proof, or readines to maintain a statement agains possible denial) as may be con fidently supposed, as must be th case.

sure·ty (shoor'ĭtē, shoor'tē) *n* (pl. **-ties**). 1. Certaint (archaic; chiefly in **of a** ~, cer tainly). 2. Formal engagement

*To ride a **surfboard** along a breaking wave and be carried inshore until all power is spent requires considerable balance, technique and practice as shown by this surfer.*

Independent since November 1975 the former Dutch colony of Surinam has a population of about 410,000 people. Its main revenue comes from bauxite mining and timber felling.

Possibly the most famous work by the Belgian **surrealist** *painter, Paul Delvaux, 'The Call of the Night' uses psychoanalytical symbols in a dream-like setting and reflects Chirico.*

pledge, guarantee, bond, security, for fulfillment of undertaking; person undertaking to be liable for default of another, or for his appearance in court, payment of debt, etc.

surf (sērf) *n.* Swell and white foamy water of sea breaking on rock or (esp. shallow) shore; **surf'bird**, Pacific coast shorebird (*Aphriza virgata*) with gray plumage spotted with black and yellow legs; **surf'board**, long narrow board for riding over heavy surf to shore; (*v.i.*) ride on surfboard; **surf casting**, fishing by casting from water's edge on beach into sea; **surf scoter**, N. Amer. sea duck (*Melanitta perspicillata*) with black plumage and with head and neck marked with white; **surf'riding**, sport of riding on surfboard. **surf'ing** *n.* Surfriding. **surf'er** *n.*

sur·face (sēr'fĭs) *n.* 1. Outermost boundary of any material body, upper boundary on top of soil, water, etc.; superficial area; (fig.) outward aspect or appearance of anything immaterial, what is presented to casual view or consideration. 2. (geom.) Continuous extent with 2 dimensions only (length and breadth, without thickness). 3. ~-active, (of substance) able to affect wetting properties of a liquid; ~ craft, ship navigable on the surface of the sea (opp. SUBMARINE); ~ mail, mail carried by land or sea; (opp. AIR mail); ~ noise, noise in playing phonograph record, due to roughness of groove; ~ tension, (phys.) tension of surface film of liquid, due to attraction between its particles, which tends to bring it into form with smallest superficial area. **surface** *v.* (-faced, -fac·ing).   Put special surface on (paper etc.); raise (submarine etc.), (of submarine etc.) rise, to surface.

sur·feit (sēr'fĭt) *n.* Excess, esp. in eating or drinking; oppression or satiety arising from excessive eating or drinking. ~ *v.* Overfeed; (cause to) take too much of something; cloy, satiate *with*.

surge (sērj) *v.i.* (**surged, surg·ing**). Rise and fall, toss, move to and fro (as) in waves or billows; move suddenly and powerfully (*forward, upward*); increase suddenly; (naut., of rope etc.) slip back or around with jerk. ~ *n.* Waves, a wave; surging motion; (elect.) sudden increase in current; ~ **tank**, standpipe or storage reservoir to neutralize sudden changes of water pressure.

sur·geon (sēr'jon) *n.*   Person skilled in surgery; medical officer in army, navy, or military hospital; **sur'geonfish**, fish of genus *Acanthurus* with sharp movable spine (like lancet) on each side of tail.

sur·ger·y (sēr'jerē) *n.* (pl. for sense 2 -ger·ies). 1. Manual or instrumental treatment of injuries or disorders of the body, esp. (also **operative** ~) involving incision of the skin. 2. Room or department in which surgeon operates.

sur·gi·cal (sēr'jĭkal) *adj.*   Of surgeons or surgery. **sur'gi·cal·ly** *adv.*

Su·ri·name, Su·ri·nam (soorinahm′). Republic on the NE. coast of S. Amer., N. of Brazil and E. of Guyana; formerly Dutch Guiana until Nov., 1975; capital, Paramaribo. **Su·ri·nam′er** *n.*

sur·ly (sẽr′lē) *adj.* (**-li·er, -li·est**). Uncivil, churlishly ill-humored, rude and cross. **sur′li·ly** *adv.* **sur′li·ness** *n.*

sur·mise (sermīz′, sẽr′mīz) *n.* Conjecture, idea formed without certainty and on slight evidence. ~ (sermīz′) *v.* (**-mised, -mis·ing**). Infer doubtfully or conjecturally; conjecture, guess.

sur·mount (sermownt′) *v.t.* 1. Prevail over, overcome, get over (obstacle etc.). 2. Cap, be on the top of. **sur·mount′a·ble** *adj.*

sur·name (sẽr′nām) *n.* Family name, name common to all members of family; (archaic) name or epithet added to person's name(s), esp. one derived from his birthplace or some quality or achievement.

sur·pass (serpăs′, -pahs′) *v.t.* Outdo, excel. **sur·pass′ing** *adj.* That greatly exceeds or excels others, of very high degree. **sur·pass′ing·ly** *adv.*

sur·plice (sẽr′plĭs) *n.* Loose full-sleeved white vestment worn, usu. over cassock, by some clergy.

sur·plus (sẽr′plŭs, -plus) *n.* What remains over, excess; (attrib.) that is in excess of what is taken, used, or needed; ~ **value**, (econ.) difference between value of work done and wages paid. **sur′plus·age** *n.*

sur·prise (serprīz′) *n.* 1. Catch-

*Opened in 1964, the **suspension bridge** over the Forth in Scotland is 1½ miles long and when built, had the greatest single span in Europe and the fourth-longest in the world.*

ing or taking of person(s) unprepared. 2. Emotion excited by the unexpected, astonishment. 3. Thing, event, that excites surprise. ~ *v.t.* (**-prised, -pris·ing**). 1. Assail, capture, by surprise; come upon unexpectedly, take unawares. 2. Affect with surprise; be a surprise to; lead unawares, betray, *into* doing something not intended. **sur·pris′er** *n.* **sur·pris′ing** *adj.* **sur·pris′ing·ly** *adv.*

sur·re·al·ism (surē′alĭzem) *n.* Movement in art and literature, which originated in France (1924), purporting to express the subconscious activities of the mind by representing the phenomena of dreams and similar experiences; art, literature, produced in accordance with this theory. **sur·re′al** *adj.* **sur·re′al·ist** *n.* & *adj.* **sur·re·al·is·tic** (surēalĭs′tĭk) *adj.* **sur·re·al·is′ti·cal·ly** *adv.*

sur·ren·der (surĕn′der) *v.* Yield up, give into another's power or control, relinquish possession of, esp. upon compulsion or demand; abandon claim under (insurance policy) in return for payment of consideration; abandon *oneself*, give *oneself* up *to* some influence, habit, emotion, etc.; (of army, fortress, etc.) yield to enemy or assailant; give oneself up, submit, cease from resistance. ~ *n.* Surrendering, being surrendered; ~ **value**, amount to which insured is entitled if he surrenders insurance policy.

sur·rep·ti·tious (serĕptĭsh′us, sŭrĕp-) *adj.* Underhand, secret, clandestine, done by stealth. **sur·rep·ti′tious·ly** *adv.* **sur·rep·ti′tious·ness** *n.*

sur·rey (sẽr′ē, sŭr′ē) *n.* (pl. **-reys**). (hist.) Light four-wheeled carriage with two seats facing forward.

sur·ro·gate (sẽr′ogāt, -gĭt, sŭr′-) *n.* Deputy, judge with jurisdiction over probate of wills and settlement of estates.

sur·round (surownd′) *v.t.* Come, lie, be, all around or on all sides; invest, enclose, encompass, environ, encircle. **sur·round′ings** *n.pl.* Things (collectively) surrounding person or thing, environs, environment.

sur·tax (sẽr′tăks) *n.* Additional tax; graduated tax on incomes exceeding the amount to which the standard rate applies. ~ (sẽr′tăks, sẽrtăks′) *v.t.* Impose surtax on.

sur·veil·lance (servā′lens) *n.* Supervision; close guard or watch, esp. over person under suspicion of wrongdoing.

sur·vey (servā′) *v.t.* 1. Take general view of, scan. 2. Consider (situation, subject, etc.) as a whole, make or present survey of. 3. Examine condition of (building etc.). 4. Determine form, extent,

*The information gathered by this surveyor will be incorporated into a **survey** which will establish the boundaries and contours of the area to be developed.*

etc., of (tract of ground etc.) by linear and angular measurements so as to settle boundaries or construct map, plan, or detailed description. ~ (sẽr′vā) *n.* (pl. **-veys**). General or comprehensive view of something; inspection, examination in detail, esp. for specific purpose; account given of result of this; department or persons engaged in, operations constituting, act of, surveying of land etc., map or plan setting forth results of such survey. **sur·vey′ing** *n.* (esp.) Science, method of surveying land. **sur·vey′or** *n.*

sur·viv·al (servī′val) *n.* Surviving; person or thing remaining as relic of earlier time.

sur·vive (servīv′) *v.* (**-vived, -viv·ing**). Outlive, continue to live or exist after death or cessation of, or after the occurrence of (disaster, hardship, etc.); continue to live or exist, be still alive or existent. **sur·vi′vor** *n.* **sur·vi′vor·ship** *n.* (esp.) Right of person having some joint interest to take whole estate on death of other(s).

sus·cep·ti·ble (susĕp′tibel) *adj.* 1. (pred.) Admitting *of*; open, liable, accessible, sensitive, *to*. 2. Impressionable; sensitive; readily touched with emotion; touchy. **sus·cep·ti·bil·i·ty** (susĕptĭbĭl′īte) *n.* **sus·cep′ti·bly** *adv.*

sus·pect (suspĕkt′) *v.t.* 1. Imagine something evil, wrong, or undesirable in, have suspicions or doubts about; imagine something, esp. something wrong, about. 2. Imagine to be possible or likely, have faint notion or inkling of; surmise. ~ (sŭs′pĕkt, suspĕkt′) *adj.* Regarded with suspicion or dis-

THEODOLITE

telescope alignment sights

telescope

telescope clamp

scale reading eyepiece

spirit level

vertical angle scale

entry for reading scales

vertical slow motion screw

spirit level

optical plummet

horizontal angle scale

levelling screws

The theodolite is a major tool for a surveyor. It enables a boundary to be located in relation to other landmarks. By measuring the angle to the top of a building and knowing its distance from himself, the surveyor can calculate its height by trigonometry.

account, (bookkeeping) account in which items are temporarily entered until proper place is determined. **sus·pense′ful** *adj.*

sus·pen·sion (suspĕn′shon) *n.* Suspending, being suspended; condition of being diffused in form of particles through fluid medium; (mus.) prolonging note of chord into following chord, dissonance so produced; ~ **bridge**, bridge in which roadway is suspended from ropes, chains, or wire cables extending between steel or masonry towers or other supports.

sus·pen·so·ry (suspĕn′serē) *adj.* That suspends or holds suspended or supported (esp. some part or organ).

sus·pi·cion (suspĭsh′on) *n.* Suspecting; feeling or state of mind of one who suspects; being suspected; slight belief or idea, faint notion, inkling; slight trace, very small amount *of.*

sus·pi·cious (suspĭsh′us) *adj.* Prone to, feeling, indicating, open to, deserving of, exciting, suspicion. **sus·pi′cious·ly** *adv.* **sus·pi′cious·ness** *n.*

sus·tain (sustān′) *v.t.* 1. Uphold or allow validity, rightfulness, truth, correctness, or justice of; be adequate as ground or basis for. 2. Keep from failing or giving way; keep in being, in a certain state or at the proper level or standard; keep up, keep going (sound, effort, etc.); keep up, represent (part, character) adequately. 3. Endure without failing or giving way; withstand; undergo, experience, suffer. 4. Hold up, bear weight of; be support of; bear, support (weight, pressure); **sustain′ing program**, broadcast program without commercial sponsor. **sus·tain′a·ble** *adj.*

sus·te·nance (sŭs′tenans) *n.* Livelihood; means of sustaining life, food.

su·sur·ra·tion (sōosurā′shon) *n.* Whispering, rustling.

su·tra (sōo′tra) *n.* 1. In Sanskrit literature, any of several collections of aphorisms dating from *c*500–200 B.C. and summarizing ritual and law of the Vedic period (*c*1500–200 B.C.). 2. (Buddhism) Any discourse of Buddha. [Sansk. *sūtra* manual of aphoristic rules]

sut·tee (sŭtē′) *n.* (hist.) Hindu widow who immolated herself on husband's funeral pyre; such immolation. **sut·tee′ism** *n.* [Sansk. *satī* virtuous wife]

trust; of suspected character. ~ (sŭs′pĕkt) *n.* Suspected person.

sus·pend (suspĕnd′) *v.t.* 1. Debar from exercise of function or enjoyment of privilege; deprive (temporarily) of office; put a (temporary) stop to, put in abeyance, annul for a time; defer; refrain from forming (judgment, opinion); ~ **payment**, fail to meet financial engagements; become insolvent. 2. (mus.) Prolong (1 note of chord) to following chord. 3. Hang up; hold, cause to be held, in suspension. **sus·pend′ed** *adj.* (esp.) ~ **animation**, temporary cessation of vital physical functions.

sus·pend·er (suspĕn′der) *n.* (esp., pl.) Straps worn over shoulders to support trousers.

sus·pense (suspĕns′) *n.* State of usu. anxious uncertainty, expectation, or waiting for information; doubtfulness, uncertainty; ~

su·ture (soo´cher) *n.* 1. (surg.) Joining of edges of wound etc. by stitch(es), stitch used for this. 2. (anat.) Seamlike line of junction of two bones, esp. of skull; (zool., bot.) line of junction of contiguous parts, as of valves in shell, plant's ovary, etc. **su·tur·al** *adj.* **suture** *v.t.* (**-tured, -tur·ing**). Stitch (wound).

svelte (svĕlt, sfĕlt) *adj.* (**svelt·er, svelt·est**). Slim, willowy.

SW, S.W., s.w. *abbrevs.* Southwest(ern).

Sw. *abbrev.* Sweden, Swedish.

swab (swŏb) *n.* Mop or other absorbent mass used for cleansing or mopping up; pad of cotton wool or other absorbent material for applying medication, cleaning wound, etc.; specimen of morbid secretion etc. taken with swab. ~ *v.t.* (**swabbed, swab·bing**). Clean or wipe (as) with swab, mop *up* (as) with swab.

swad·dle (swŏd´el) *v.t.* (**-dled, -dling**). Swathe in bandages, wrappings, etc.; **swaddling clothes**, narrow bandages wrapped around newborn infant to prevent free movement (now chiefly fig.).

swag (swăg) *n.* 1. Ornamental festoon of flowers, fruit, etc., fastened up at both ends and hanging down in middle; carved or

molded representation of this. 2. (slang) Thief's booty; dishonest gains.

swage (swāj) *n.* Tool for bending cold metal, die or stamp for shaping metal by striking with hammer or sledge; ~ **block**, smith's block of metal with perforations, grooves, etc., for this purpose. ~ *v.t.* (**swaged, swag·ing**). Shape with swage.

swag·ger (swăg´er) *v.i.* Walk, carry oneself, as if among inferiors, with superior, insolent, or blustering manner; talk boastfully or braggingly. ~ *n.* 1. Swaggering gait, talk, or manner. 2. ~ **stick**, short light cane often carried by army officers. **swagger** *adj.* (colloq.) Smart, fashionable. **swag´ger·er** *n.*

Swa·hi·li (swahhē´lē) *n.* (pl. **-lis**, collect. **-li**). (One of) Bantu people of Zanzibar and adjacent coast; (also *Kiswahili*) language of these, used as lingua franca in parts of E. Africa. [lit., "of the coasts," f. Arab. *sawāhil* pl. of *sāhil* coast]

Graceful in its darting flight, the European **swallow** *breeds in northern latitudes but may migrate 7000 miles to South Africa, where it spends several months before returning north.*

swain (swān) *n.* Countryman, young rustic, esp. shepherd (archaic); country gallant or lover; (joc.) suitor, lover.

swal·low[1] (swŏl´ō) *n.* Migratory insect-eating bird of genus *Hirundo* and related genera, with long pointed wings and swift curving flight, esp. the BARN swallow; (loosely) any of various other birds, esp. the unrelated swifts, resembling swallows in some respects; **swal´lowtail**, forked tail like swallow's; butterfly of family Papilionidae, in which border of each hind wing is prolonged into a taillike process; swallow-tailed kite; (freq. pl.) swallow-tailed coat; **swallow-tailed coat**, man's full dress evening coat, with two long tapering tails; **swallow-tailed kite**, white kite (*Elanoides forficatus*) of S. and Central Amer. and Gulf Coast of U.S., with black and white plumage and deeply forked tail; tropical African kite (*Chelictinia riocourii*).

swal·low[2] (swŏl´ō) *v.* Cause or allow (food etc.) to pass down one's throat; engulf, absorb, exhaust (usu. ~ **up**); accept (statement etc.) with ready credulity; put up with, stomach (affront); recant (words); keep down, repress (emotion). ~ *n.* Gullet; act of swallowing; amount swallowed at once; capacity for swallowing.

swam: see SWIM.

swa·mi (swah´mē) *n.* (pl. **-mis**). Hindu religious teacher (esp. as form of address to Brahmin); (transf.) pundit. [Sansk. *svāmin* master, prince]

swamp (swŏmp) *n.* Piece of wet spongy ground, marsh; tract of rich soil with trees etc., too moist for cultivation; (attrib., of many

Despite its bright hindmost colors, this Australian butterfly is described as the **dingy swallowtail** *because many other in the same genus have much more vivid and iridescent markings.*

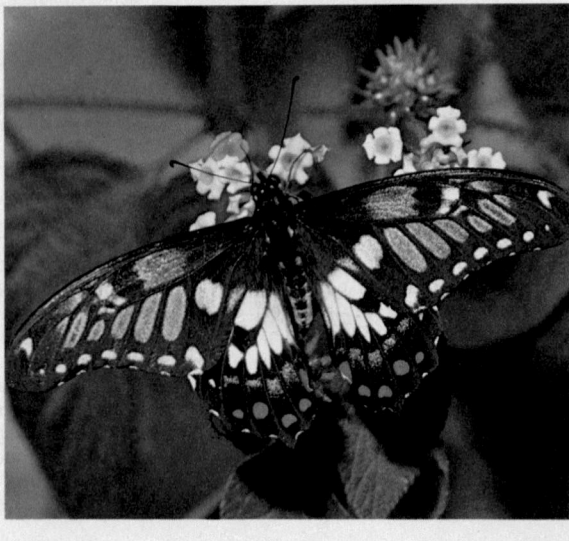

animals, birds, plants, etc.) growing, living, in swamps; ~ **boat** (or **buggy**), automotive vehicle for travel through swamps or muddy areas, usu. amphibious and having extra large tires; flat-bottomed boat driven by propeller rising over stern. **swamp'y** *adj.* (**swamp·i·er, swamp·i·est**). **swamp'i·ness** *n.* **swamp** *v.* Submerge, inundate, soak, with water; (of boat) (cause to) fill with water and sink; overwhelm with numbers or quantity of anything.

swan (swŏn) *n.* (pl. **swans**, collect. **swan**). Large web footed swimming bird usu. of genera *Cygnus* and *Olor*, with long gracefully curved neck, esp. the domestic, mute, or tame swan, *C. olor*, with pure white plumage in adult, black legs and feet and red bill with black knob, occurring wild in NE. Europe and W. Central Asia, and semidomesticated all over Amer. and Europe, formerly supposed to sing melodiously just before its death; (**S** ~, astron.) northern constellation Cygnus; ~ **dive**, forward dive in which spine is curved and arms are outspread, being moved forward and together just before hitting water; **swan's-down, swans'down**, down or fine soft feathers of swan used for powder puffs, trimmings, etc.; soft thick woolen cloth, thick cotton fabric with soft nap; **swan song**, legendary song of dying swan; last (esp. artistic) production of person etc. **swan'like** *adj.*

swank (swăngk) *n.* (colloq.) 1. Fashionable elegance in dress, appearance, etc.; smartness. 2. Ostentatious, swaggering display in speech, behavior, etc. ~ *adj.* (colloq.) Affectedly stylish. **swank·y** (swăng'kē) *adj.* (**swank·i·er, swank·i·est**). (colloq.) Fashionable; ostentatious. **swank'i·ly** *adv.* **swank'i·ness** *n.* **swank** *v.i.* Show off, swagger.

swap, swop (swŏp) *ns. & vbs.* (**swapped, swap·ping, swopped, swop·ping**). (colloq.) Exchange by way of barter. **swap'per** *n.*

swarm[1] (swôrm, swärm) *n.* Cluster of bees leaving hive or main body with queen bee to establish new hive; large or dense body, throng, multitude of persons, insects, etc., esp. moving about. ~ *v.i.* Move in a swarm; (of bees) gather in compact cluster around queen and leave hive in a body; congregate in number, be very numerous; (of places) be overrun or crowded.

swarm[2] (swôrm, swärm) *v.* Climb *up* (rope, pole, tree) by clasping it with arms and legs alternately; climb up or *up* (any steep ascent) by clinging with hands and knees.

swarth·y (swôr'dhē, swär'-) *adj.*

Louisiana's **swamp** *land lies along the coast area of the state on the Gulf of Mexico. Rich in oil and natural gas deposits, this lush subtropical area was not exploited until the 1890s when its economic potential was realized.*

(**swarth·i·er, swarth·i·est**). Dark complexioned, dark in color. **swarth'i·ly** *adv.* **swarth'i·ness** *n.*

swash[1] (swŏsh) *v.* (of water etc.) Wash about, make sound of washing or rising and falling; **swash'-buckler**, swaggering bravo or ruffian, bully. **swash'buckling** *adj. & n.* **swash** *n.* (Sound of) swashing.

swash[2] (swŏsh) *adj.* (turning etc.) Inclined obliquely to axis of

Swahili is the lingua franca of East Africa, and is spoken by 11 million people in Tanzania, Kenya, Zaire, and Uganda. In market places such as this one it is a valuable adjunct to trade.

work; (print., of italic capitals) having flourished strokes at top and bottom, as $\mathcal{J}$, $\mathcal{N}$; ~ **plate**, rotating circular plate set at an oblique angle to its shaft, giving reciprocating motion to rod resting on it and parallel to its shaft.

swas·ti·ka (swŏs'tĭkə) *n.* Primitive and ancient symbol or talisman in form of cross with equal arms, each arm having a limb of same length projecting from its end at right angles, all in same direction

black-necked swan

Representatives of three continents: the black-necked **swan,** *a native of South America; the black variety of Australia; and the mute swan found in Europe. There are four other species.*

black swan

mute swan

*The spires of the old city of Stockholm seen beyond a foreground network of modern freeways and fly-overs. As capital of **Sweden** it reflects both past history and present development.*

(usu. direction of sun's course, i.e. clockwise), found in various parts of the world, esp. Mexico, Peru, and Tibet, used in Germany and Austria from 1918 onward as symbol of anti-Semitism or as emblem of Nazi party. [Sansk. f. *svastika*, f. *svasti* well-being, good fortune, luck]

swat (swŏt) *v.t.* (**swat·ted, swat·ting**). Hit hard, crush (fly etc.) with blow. **swat′ter** *n.*

swatch (swŏch) *n.* Sample of cloth or fabric.

swath (swŏth, swawth), **swathe**[1] (swŏdh, swādh) *ns.* (pl. **swaths** pr. swŏdhz, swawdhz, **swathes** pr. swŏdhz, swawdhz). Row or line of grass, corn, etc., as it falls when mown or reaped; space covered by mower's scythe, width of grass or corn so cut.

swathe[2] (swŏdh, swādh) *v.t.* (**swathed, swath·ing**). Wrap up or around, envelop, like bandage or (as) with wrapping.

sway (swā) *v.* 1. Lean unsteadily to one side or in different directions by turns; have unsteady swinging motion; oscillate irregularly; waver, vacillate; give swaying motion to. 2. Govern the motion of; wield, control direction of; have influence over; govern, rule over. 3. **swayed, sway′back, sway′-backed**, with back abnormally hollowed (esp. of horse). **sway** *n.* 1. Swaying motion or position. 2. Rule, government.

Swa·zi·land (swah′zēländ). Kingdom in SE. Africa between Mozambique, Transvaal, and Natal; member of the Brit. Commonwealth, formerly a Brit. protectorate; independent 1968; capital, Mbabane.

swear (swār) *v.* (**swore** pr. swŏr, **sworn** pr. swŏrn, **swear·ing**). 1. State something, state (thing) on oath, take oath; promise or undertake something by oath; promise to observe or perform (something); confirm by oath; affirm emphatically or confidently; ~ **by**, (colloq.) profess or have great belief in; ~ **off**, forswear. 2. Utter profane oath, use profane language, to express anger or as expletive(s); (of colors) clash unpleasantly (with); **swear′word**, (colloq.) profane oath or word. 3. Cause to take oath, administer oath to; (also **swear in**), admit to office or function by administering oath; **swear out**, obtain (warrant etc.) by making charge on oath. **swear′er** *n.*

sweat (swĕt) *n.* 1. Salty fluid secreted by glands beneath the skin and exuded through the pores, perspiration; something resembling sweat, drops of moisture on a surface; condition or period of sweating; (colloq.) state of impatience or anxiety; **sweat′band**, band of leather etc. as lining of hat or cap; **sweat gland**, minute coiled tubular gland beneath skin secreting sweat; **sweat shirt**, shirt worn esp. by athletes before or after exercise. 2. (chiefly colloq.) Drudgery, toil, laborious task; **sweat′shop**, factory in which workers are made to work hard for very poor wages. **sweat′y** *adj.* (**sweat·i·er, sweat·i·est**). **sweat·i·ly** *adv.* **sweat′i·ness** *n.* **sweat** *v.* (**sweat** or **sweat·ed, sweat·ing**). 1. Exude sweat, perspire; emit or exude, ooze *out*, as or like sweat; cause (horse, athlete, etc.) to sweat by exercise etc.; exude or gather moisture in drops on surface; cause to exude moisture, force moisture out of. 2. Work hard, toil, drudge; employ (workers) at very poor wages for long hours, exploit to the utmost; (of workers) work on such terms. **sweat·er** (swĕt′er) *n.* (esp.) Knitted, crocheted, etc., jacket, jersey, usu. of wool, for informal wear; pullover.

Swed. *abbrev.* Sweden, Swedish.

Swede (swēd) *n.* Native of Sweden.

Swe·den (swē′den). Kingdom of E. Scandinavia; capital, Stockholm.

Swe·den·borg (swē'denborg), **Emanuel** (1688–1772). Swedish religious mystic and philosopher; held that God, as divine man, is infinite love and infinite wisdom, and the end of creation is the approximation of man to God; he taught that there is a symbolic sense to the Scriptures, of which he was the appointed interpreter. **Swe·den·bor·gi·an** (swēdenbor'gēan) *adj.* & *n.* (Follower) of Swedenborg, (member) of the New Jerusalem Church. **Swe·den·bor'gi·an·ism, Swe'den·borg·ism** *ns.*

Swed·ish (swē'dĭsh) *adj.* Of Sweden or its people or language. **Swedish** *n.* Indo-European language of Sweden, one of the Norse group.

sweep (swĕp) *v.* (**swept** pr. swĕpt, **sweep·ing**). 1. Glide swiftly, speed along with impetuous unchecked motion, go majestically; extend in continuous curve, line, or slope. 2. Impart sweeping motion to; carry *along, down, away, off,* in impetuous course; clear *off, away, from,* etc. 3. Traverse or range swiftly, pass lightly across or along; pass eyes or hand quickly along or over; scan, scour, graze; (of artillery etc.) include in line of fire, cover, enfilade, rake. 4. Clear everything from; clear of dust, soot, litter, with broom; win all points, games, etc.; gather *up,* collect, (as) with broom. 5. **sweep'back,** angle at which airplane's wing is set back from position at right angles to body; **sweep (second) hand,** hand on clock or watch moving on same dial as other hands; **sweep'stake(s),** (prize won in) race or contest in which all competitors' stakes are taken by winner(s); form of gambling on horse races etc. in which sum of participators' stakes goes to holder(s) of tickets on winning or placed horse(s); **swept'back** (*adj.*), (of aircraft wing) slanted to the rear from points of connection; **swept'-wing** (*n.* & *adj.*), (aircraft) having sweptback wings. **sweep'er** *n.* **sweep'ing** *adj.* (esp., of statement etc.) General, unqualified, regardless of limitations or exceptions. **sweep'ing** *n.* (esp. pl.) Matter swept up; litter; trash. **sweep** *n.* 1. Sweeping, clearing up or away (now usu. **a clean ~**); moving in continuous curve (of an army, fleet, river, etc.); hostile reconnaissance by group of aircraft; sweeping motion or extension, curve in road, etc.; curved driveway leading to house. 2. Range or compass of something that has curving motion; extent, stretch, expanse, esp. such as can be taken in at one look. 3. Long oar worked by rower(s) standing on barge etc.; long pole mounted as lever for raising bucket from well; gear for clearing submarine mines, usu. consisting of a long wire with a cutting device attached, streamed from a vessel (**minesweeper**) at the required depth. 4. Chimney sweep. 5. Victory in all parts of a contest; winning all games in a series or match. **sweep'ing·ly** *adv.*

sweet (swēt) *adj.* 1. Tasting like sugar, honey, etc., corresponding to one of the primary sensations of taste; (of wine) tasting thus, containing unfermented natural sugar (opp. DRY). 2. Pleasing to the sense of smell, fragrant, perfumed. 3. Fresh and sound, not salt(ed) or sour or bitter or putrid. 4. Agreeable, attractive, gratifying; inspiring affection, dear, amiable, gentle, easy; (colloq.) pretty, charming, delightful; **at one's own ~ will,** as one pleases, arbitrarily; **~ on,** (colloq.) very fond of, (inclined to be) in love with. 5. **~-and-sour,** cooked or prepared with seasoning of both sugar and vinegar or lemon; **~ bay** = BAY[1], 1; (also) N. Amer. magnolia (*Magnolia virginiana*); **sweet'-bread,** pancreas or thymus gland of animal, esp. calf, used for food; **sweet'brier, sweet'briar,** eglantine (*Rosa eglanteria,* and other species), with small hooked prickles, pink flowers, and small aromatic leaves; **sweet corn,** any of several varieties of corn with sweet kernels, eaten when young; also called green corn; **sweet gum,** large tree of N. Amer. (*Liquidambar styraciflua*) having prickly fruit balls and aromatic resin; **sweet'heart,** darling; either of pair of lovers; **sweetheart contract,** (slang) contract with unfavorable terms for union members arranged by secret understanding between officials of union and management; **sweet marjoram,** aromatic cultivated herb (*Marjorana hortensis*); **sweet'meat,** = SWEET *n.* sense 2; **sweet pea,** climbing leguminous annual (*Lathyrus odoratus*) cultivated for its many-colored, sweet-scented flowers; **sweet pepper:** see PEPPER sense 2; **sweet potato,** (large sweet farinaceous tuberous root, eaten as vegetable, of) tropical climbing plant (*Ipomoea batatas*) widely cultivated in warm regions; **sweet-**

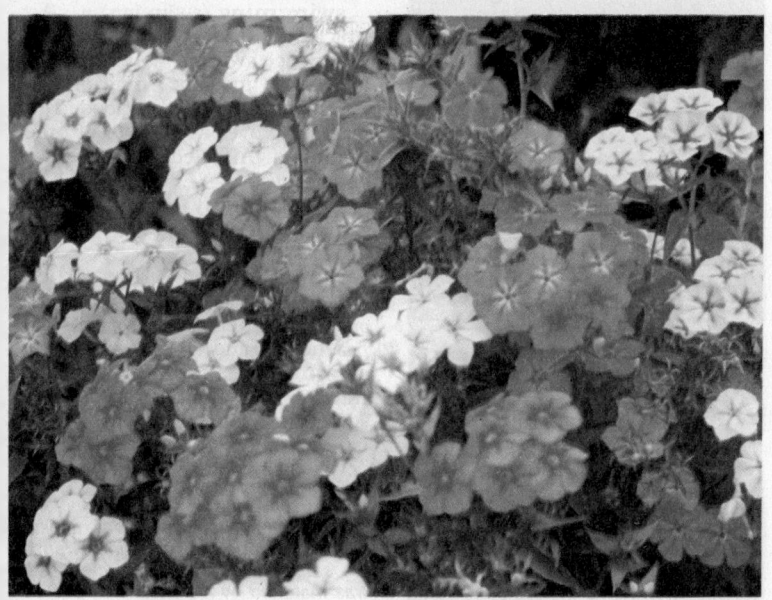

Sweet William, a variety of plants in the genus Dianthus, is a popular garden biennial, especially in borders where the colorful array of blooms provides a vivid foreground to larger plants.

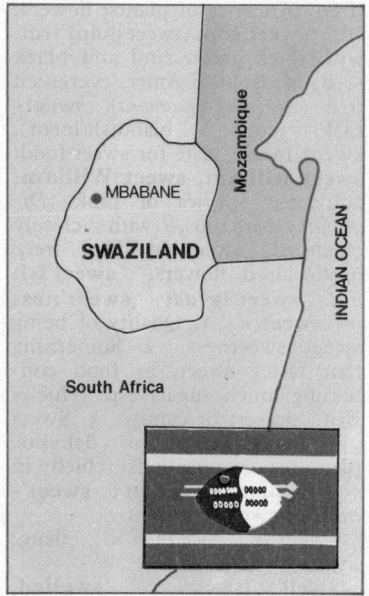

Small and land-locked, the independent Kingdom of Swaziland benefited by being a British protectorate. This forestalled invasion by both the Boers and Zulus.

Despite its apparent similarity to the swallow, the **swift** is considered by ornithologists, to be more closely related to the hummingbird. Nests of an Asian variety are used to make soup.

scented, having a sweet scent (freq. in names of plants, flowers, etc.); **sweet'sop**, (sweet pulpy fruit with thick green rind and black seeds of) tropical Amer. evergreen tree (*Annona squamosa*); **sweet-talk**, (colloq.) blandish(ment); **sweet tooth**, taste for sweet food; **sweet william, sweet William**, cultivated species of pink (*Dianthus barbatus*), with closely clustered sweet-smelling freq. particolored flowers. **sweet'ish** *adj.* **sweet'ly** *adv.* **sweet'ness** *n.* **sweet** *n.* 1. Quality of being sweet; sweetness. 2. Something that tastes sweet, as food containing much sugar, esp. (chiefly Brit.) dessert or candy. 3. Sweet part (chiefly fig.); (pl.) delights, pleasures, gratifications; (chiefly in voc.) darling. **sweet'en** *v.* **sweet'ening, sweet'ener** *ns.*

sweet·ie (swē'tē) *n.* (slang) Sweetheart.

swell (swĕl) *v.* (**swelled,**

swol·len pr. swō'len, **swell·ing**). (Cause to) grow bigger or louder, dilate, expand; rise, raise, *up* from surrounding surface; bulge *out*; increase in volume, force, or intensity; (of emotion) arise and grow in mind with sense as of expansion; (of person, his heart, etc.) be affected with such emotion; **swell'-head**, (colloq.) proud, conceited person; **swelled, swollen head**, (colloq.) conceit. **swell** *n.* 1. Being swollen; swollen part, protuberance, bulge. 2. Heaving of sea etc. with long rolling waves that do not break, as after storm; such waves collectively. 3. Gradual increase in loudness or force of sound. 4. (colloq.) Fashionable or stylish person; person of good social standing. **swell** *adj.* (colloq.) Distinguished, first-rate; stylishly dressed or equipped; of good social position.

swell·ing (swĕl'ĭng) *n.* (esp.) Distention of injured or diseased part of body.

swel·ter (swĕl'ter) *v.i.* Be oppressed or oppressive with heat; sweat profusely, languish, be faint, with excessive heat.

swept: see SWEEP.

swerve (swĕrv) *v.* (**swerved, swerv·ing**). Turn aside, (cause to) deviate from straight or direct course. ~ *n.* Swerving motion;

divergence from course.

swift (swĭft) *adj.* Fleet, rapid, quick; soon coming or passing, not long delayed; prompt, quick *to do*. ~ *adv.* Swiftly (chiefly in comb. as ~-*footed*). **swift'ly** *adv.* **swift'ness, swift** *ns.* Any of various swift-flying insectivorous birds of the family Apodidae, superficially resembling swallows, esp. *Chaetura pelagica*, the chimney swift.

Swift (swĭft), **Jonathan** (1667-1745). Irish satirist and clergyman, dean of St. Patrick's Cathedral, Dublin; author of *A Tale of a Tub*, *Gulliver's Travels*, etc.

swig (swĭg) *v.* (**swigged, swig·ging**). (colloq.) Take drafts (of). ~ *n.* (Act of taking) a draft of liquor.

swill (swĭl) *v.* Wash or rinse (*out*), pour water over or through, flush; drink greedily; feed (usu. pigs) with swill. ~ *n.* 1. Liquid or partly liquid food, chiefly kitchen refuse, given to swine; hogwash; inferior liquor. 2. Rinsing, swilling.

swim (swĭm) *v.* (**swam** pr. swăm, **swum** pr. swŭm, **swim·ming**). 1. Float on or at surface of liquid. 2. Progress at or below surface of water by working legs, arms, tail, webbed feet, fins, etc.; traverse (distance etc.) thus; compete in (race) thus; cause (horse, dog, etc.) to progress thus; (fig.) go with gliding motion. 3. Appear to undulate, reel, or whirl, have dizzy effect or sensation; be flooded or overflow with or *with* or *in* moisture. 4. ~ **bladder**, bladder of many fish. **swim** *n.* Period of swimming; (fig.) main current of affairs (**in, out of, the** ~); **swim'suit**, bathing suit. **swim'mer** *n.*

swim·mer·et (swĭmerĕt', swĭm'erĕt) *n.* Abdominal appendage in some crustaceans.

swim·ming (swĭm'ĭng) *n.* Act, practice, or sport of one who or that which swims. ~ *adj.* 1. Being able to swim; concerning or used in swimming. 2. Flooded or brimming over with water or other liquid. 3. Affected with dizziness or faintness.

swim·ming·ly (swĭm'ĭnglē) *adv.* (esp.) With easy and unobstructed progress.

swin·dle (swĭn'del) *v.* (**-dled, -dling**). Cheat (person, *money out of* person, person *out of* money); practice fraud. **swin'dler** *n.* **swindle** *n.* Piece of swindling; fraudulent scheme, imposition; something represented as what it is not, fraud.

*Best remembered for 'Gulliver's Travels', **Jonathan Swift** was a bitter man whose books all contained trenchant satire. His career as a clergyman was matched by his interest in politics.*

swine (swīn) *n.* (pl. **swine**). Animal of family Tayassuidae of nonruminant hoofed mammals, with stout body, thick skin, longish snout with terminal nostrils, and small tail; hog, pig, domesticated for its flesh and regarded as type of greediness and uncleanness; person of greedy or bestial habits (used esp. as strong term of abuse); ~ **fever**, hog cholera; **swine'herd**, one who tends swine; **swine plague**, infectious bacterial disease of swine resembling swine fever but chiefly affecting lungs. **swin'ish** *adj.* **swin'ish·ly** *adv.* **swin'ish·ness** *n.*

swing (swĭng) *v.* (**swung** pr. swŭng, **swing·ing**). 1. Move with the to-and-fro or curving motion of object having fixed point(s) or side, but otherwise free; sway or so hang as to be free to sway like pendulum, door, etc.; oscillate, revolve, rock, wheel; move back and forth in swing. 2. Go with swinging gait; (slang) be sophisticated, lively, up-to-the-minute, etc., in seeking pleasurable experience; (slang) engage promiscuously in sexual intercourse (colloq.) have decisive influence on (voting, jury, etc.); (colloq.) be executed by hanging. 3. Give (music) the character of swing music. **swing** *n.* 1. Act or process of swinging;

swinging gait or rhythm; movement describing curve; quick trip around country, region, etc.; **in full** ~, at height of activity. 2. Seat slung by ropes or chains for swinging in; period of swinging in either of these. 3. (also **swing music**) Kind of jazz in which the time of the melody (usu. played by single instrument) is freely varied over simple harmonic accompaniment in strict time with strongly marked rhythm. **swing shift**, (colloq.) work shift running from about midafternoon to about midnight. **swing'er** *n.* 1. Person who or thing that swings. 2. (slang) Stylish, up-to-the-minute person who seeks pleasurable experience, esp. sexual freedom.

swing·ing (swĭng'ĭng) *adj.* (superl. **-ing·est**). 1. That swings; **swinging door, gate**, door (esp. in two leaves hung separately and sprung), gate that swings in either direction and closes of itself when released. 2. (of gait, melody, etc.) Vigorously rhythmical. 3. Gay, lively. **swing'ing·ly** *adv.*

swin·gle (swĭng'gel) *n.* Wooden swordlike instrument for beating flax and removing woody parts from it; striking or swinging part of flail; **swin'gletree**, crossbar pivoted in middle, to ends of which traces are fastened in cart, plough,

etc. **swingle** *v.t.* (**-gled, -gling**). Clean (flax) with swingle.

swipe (swīp) *v.* (**swiped, swip'-ing**). 1. (colloq.) Strike with a hard sweeping blow. 2. (slang) Snatch, steal. ~ *n.* Hard sweeping blow.

swirl (swêrl) *n.* Eddy, whirlpool; eddying or whirling motion; twist, convolution, curl. ~ *v.* Eddy, carry (object), be carried, with eddying or whirling motion.

swish (swĭsh) *n.* Sound of switch or similar object moved rapidly through air, of scythe cutting grass, or object moving rapidly through water. ~ *v.* Make, move with, swish; flog with birch or cane.

Swiss (swĭs) *adj.* Of Switzerland or its people; ~ **Guards**, Swiss mercenary troops employed as bodyguards formerly by sovereigns of France etc. and still at Vatican. **Swiss** *n.* Native (collect., people) of Switzerland.

swiss (swĭs) *n.* Fine cotton fabric of plain weave freq. with dots or flecks formed by extra yarns (**dotted** ~).

switch (swĭch) *n.* 1. Slender tapering whip; thin flexible shoot cut from tree, something resembling this. 2. Device for making and breaking contact or altering connections in electric circuit; (on railroad etc.) movable rail or pair of rails pivoted at one end at junction of tracks, used to deflect train etc. from one line to another. 3. Tress of real or false hair, tied at one end, used in hairdressing. 4. **switch'back**, zigzag road, railroad, climbing steep grade; **switch'blade**, pocket knife with blade released by spring; **switch'-board**, board or frame with set of switches for varying connection among a number of electric circuits, as of telephone, telegraph, etc.; **switch hitter**, (baseball) player who can bat with either hand; **switch'man** (pl. **-men**), man who works switch(es), esp. on railroad. **switch** *v.* 1. Strike, whip, (as) with switch; flourish like a switch, whisk, lash, move with sudden jerk. 2.

It is believed by some that a child can easily learn to **swim** *at a very early age, if an adult is nearby to assure safety (left). Swimmers must be a little more advanced to learn the breast stroke and butterfly stroke (below).*

breast-stroke

butterfly

*Highland meadows backed by the snow-covered Alps near Murren in the higher part of **Switzerland**. This small country has diverse and highly productive agricultural regions and its industries are specialized.*

Turn (train etc.) onto another line by means of switch; turn (electric current, light, etc.) *on, off*, by means of switch, change (connection) *over* with switch; (fig.) turn off, divert; **switch'over**, diversion of effort, activity, or production.

Switz·er·land (swĭt′serland). Republic in central Europe, S. of West Germany and N. of Italy, consisting of federation of 22 cantons; capital, Berne.

swiv·el (swĭv′el) *n*. Simple joining or coupling device made so that object fastened can turn freely upon it, or so that each half of the swivel itself can turn independently; ring or staple turning on pin, or the like; ~ **bearing, chain, coupling, gun**, etc., one provided with or mounted on swivel; **swivel chair**, chair with seat turning horizontally on pivot. **swivel** *v*. (**-eled, -el·ing,** *Brit.* **-elled, -el·ling**). Turn (as) on swivel.

swiz·zle (swĭz′el) *n*. Tall mixed drink usu. made with rum, lime, etc.; ~ **stick**, rod for stirring drinks.

swol·len: see SWELL.

swoon (swoōn) *n. & v.i.* (archaic) Faint.

swoop (swoōp) *v*. Come down or *down* with the rush of a bird of prey (often upon prey etc.); attack from a distance; (*up* or *away*) snatch, seize, the whole of. ~ *n*. Act of swooping, esp. sudden pounce of bird of prey; **at one (fell)** ~, at a single blow or stroke.

swop: SWAP.

sword (sōrd, sŏrd) *n*. Offensive weapon for cutting or thrusting, consisting of long straight or curved blade with handle or hilt and cross guard, sharp point, and usu. one or two sharp edges; **at ~s' points**, ready to fight or argue; **cross swords**, fight; dispute violently; **draw, sheathe, the sword**, begin, cease from, war; **sword dance**, dance, esp. folk dance, in which performers go through evolutions with swords, or one which is danced over naked swords laid on ground; **sword'fish** (pl. **-fishes,** collect **-fish**), large sea fish used for food (*Xiphias gladius*), with upper jaw prolonged into swordlike point; **sword grass**, grass with sharp-edged leaves; plant with swordshaped leaves, as the gladiolus; **sword lily**, gladiolus; **sword'play**, fencing; **swords'man** (pl. **-men**), one skilled in use of sword; **swords'-manship. sword'like** *adj*.

sworn (swōrn) *adj.*: see SWEAR;

(esp.) bound by an oath; ~ **brother**, close friend; ~ **enemy, foe**, determined or irreconcilable enemy.

swum: see SWIM.

swung (swŭng) *adj*.: see SWING; (esp.) ~ **dash**, mark (~) used in place of (part of) word previously spelled out.

Syb·a·rite (sĭb′arīt) *n*. Inhabitant of ancient Greek colony of Sybaris in S. Italy noted for

luxury; hence (**s** ~), luxury-loving person. **syb·a·rit·ic** (sĭbarĭt′ĭk) *adj*.

syc·a·more (sĭk′amōr, -mŏr) *n*. 1. Buttonwood or plane tree (*Platanus occidentalis*) of eastern N. Amer., with buttonlike seeds and whitish bark that flakes off in patches. 2. Large Eurasian species of maple (*Acer pseudoplatanus*) grown as shady ornamental tree and for its wood.

*The familiar **sycamore** tree that is grown in streets in England is a hybrid obtained from cross-breeding trees which were originally native to the Near East and North America.*

syc·o·phant (sĭk′ofant) *n.* Flatterer, parasitic person. **syc′o·phan·cy** *n.* (pl. **-cies**). **syc·o·phan·tic** (sĭkofăn′tĭk) *adj.* [Gk. *sukophantes* informer, f. *sukon* fig., *phainō* show (reason for name unknown)]

syl·la·bar·y (sĭl′abĕrē) *n.* (pl. **-bar·ies**). Collection, system, or table of syllables, esp. of written characters each representing a syllable, such as Japanese katakana.

syl·la·bic (sĭlăb′ĭk) *adj.* Of, forming, syllable(s); (of written symbols) denoting a syllable; consisting of such symbols; (pros.) based on number of syllables. **syl·lab′i·cal·ly** *adv.*

syl·lab·i·cate (sĭlăb′ikāt) (**-cat·ed, -cat·ing**), **syl·lab·i·fy** (sĭlăb′ifī) (**-fied, -fy·ing**) *vbs.t.* Divide into syllables. **syl·lab·i·ca·tion** (sĭlăbikā′shon), **syl·lab·i·fi·ca·tion** (sĭlăbifĭkā′shon) *ns.*

syl·la·ble (sĭl′abel) *n.* Vocal sound(s) forming a whole word or part of a word and uttered as an uninterrupted unit; character(s) representing this; least mention, hint, or trace (*of*). ~ *v.t.* (**-bled, -bling**). Pronounce by syllables; articulate distinctly; (poet.) utter, speak. **syl·lab·ic** (sĭlăb′ĭk) *adj.*

syl·la·bus (sĭl′abus) *n.* (pl. **-bus·es, -bi** pr. -bī). 1. Concise

statement of subjects of lectures, course of study, etc. 2. (R.C. Ch.) (also called ~ **of errors**) Catalog of 80 heretical doctrines, practices, or institutions condemned by Pope Pius IX (1864).

syl·lo·gism (sĭl′ojĭzem) *n.* Form of reasoning in which conclusion is deduced from two premises (major and minor) containing a common or middle term that is absent from the conclusion, e.g. (major premise) *All men are mortal*; (minor premise) *Socrates is a man: therefore* (conclusion) *Socrates is mortal*; deductive as opp. to inductive reasoning. **syl·lo·gis·tic** (sĭlojĭs′tĭk) *adj.* **syl·lo·gis′ti·cal·ly** *adv.*

syl·lo·gize (sĭl′ojīz) *v.* (**-gized, -giz·ing**). Use syllogisms; throw (facts, arguments) into syllogistic form.

sylph (sĭlf) *n.* Imaginary, delicate being supposed to inhabit the air; slender graceful woman. **sylph′like** *adj.* Slender and graceful.

syl·van, sil·van (sĭl′van) *adjs.* Of wood(s); consisting of, abounding in, furnished with, woods or trees.

sym- *prefix.* Assim. form of SYN- before *b, m, p.*

sym·bi·o·sis (sĭmbĭō′sĭs, -bē-) *n.* (pl. **-ses** pr. -sēz). (biol.) Association of two different organisms living attached to one another or one as tenant of the other (used esp. of associations advantageous to both organisms, as dist. from *parasitism*). **sym·bi·ot·ic** (sĭm-bĭŏt′ĭk, -bē-) *adj.* **sym·bi·ot′i·cal·ly** *adv.*

sym·bol (sĭm′bol) *n.* Thing standing for or representing something else, esp. material thing taken to represent immaterial or abstract thing, as an idea or quality; written

*First developed in the Bronze Age, and improved and refined as metallurgy developed, the **sword** remained a vital weapon for armed forces, and for dueling, until the development of rifles and revolvers.*

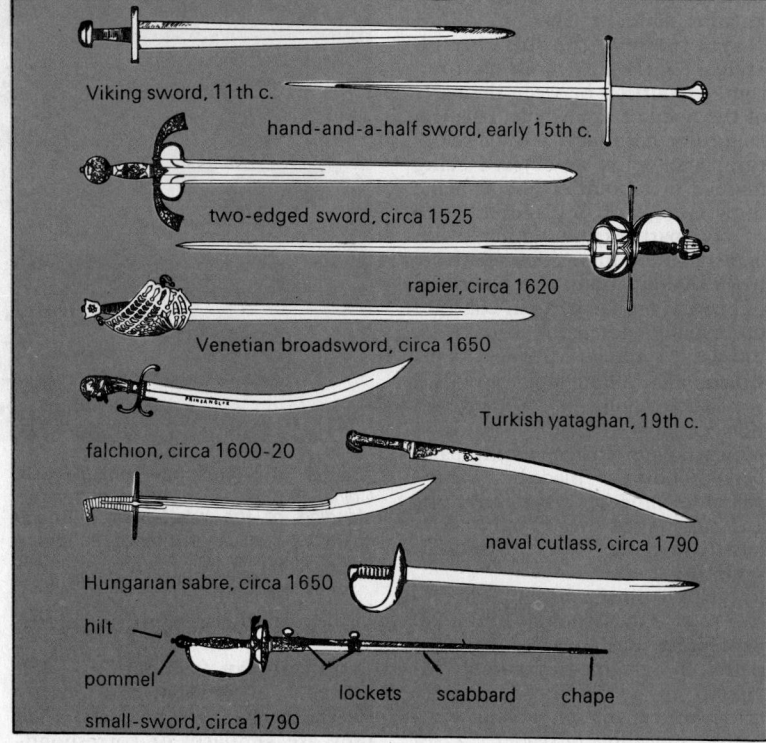

Viking sword, 11th c.

hand-and-a-half sword, early 15th c.

two-edged sword, circa 1525

rapier, circa 1620

Venetian broadsword, circa 1650

Turkish yataghan, 19th c.

falchion, circa 1600-20

naval cutlass, circa 1790

Hungarian sabre, circa 1650

hilt

pommel　　　　lockets　　scabbard　　chape

small-sword, circa 1790

*The true function of the beak of a **swordfish** has yet to be determined. However, one piece of ship's timber now in the British Museum, was penetrated 22 inches by a 'sword'.*

*The **symbiosis** that exists between the sea anemone and the clown fish is illustrated by the ability of the fish to swim and feed among the anemone tentacles which prove fatal to other small fish.*

character conventionally standing for some object, process, etc. **sym·bol·ic** (sĭmbŏl'ĭk), **sym·bol'·i·cal** *adjs.* **sym·bol'i·cal·ly** *adv.*

sym·bol·ism (sĭm'bolĭzem) *n.* System, use, meaning, of symbols; doctrine of the Symbolists. **sym'·bol·ist** *n.* 1. One who uses symbols. 2. **S~**, member of a school of French poets (*c*1880–*c*1900) whose artistic purpose was arousal of emotions by indirect suggestion rather than by direct expression, with particular objects, words, etc. carrying symbolic meaning.

sym·bol·ize (sĭm'bolīz) *v.t.* (**-ized, -iz·ing**). Be symbol of; represent by symbol; treat as symbolic or emblematic. **sym·bol·i·za·tion** (sĭmbolīzā'shon) *n.*

sym·me·try (sĭm'etrē) *n.* (pl. **-tries**). 1. (Beauty resulting from) right proportion between the parts of the body or any whole, balance, congruity, harmony. 2. Such structure as allows of an object's being divided by a point or line or plane or radiating lines or planes into two or more parts exactly similar in size and shape and in position relatively to the dividing point etc.; repetition of exactly similar parts in contrary or equally divergent directions; **axial ~**, symmetry about an axis; **bilateral ~**, about a plane; **radial ~**, about a point. 3. Approximation to such structure; possession by a whole of corresponding parts correspondingly placed. **sym··met·ric** (sĭmĕt'rĭk), **sym·met·ri·cal** *adjs.* **sym·met'ri·cal·ly** *adv.* **sym'me·trize** *v.t.* (**-trized, -triz·ing**).

sym·pa·thet·ic (sĭmpathĕt'ĭk) *adj.* 1. Of sympathy; full of, expressing, due to, effecting sympathy; in agreement; favorably inclined (*to* or *with*); (in literary criticism) capable of evoking sympathy, appealing *to* reader. 2. (of disorder, pain, etc.) Induced in organ or part of body by a similar or corresponding one in another; **~ string**, (mus.) string that vibrates with sympathetic resonance, enriching the tone. 3. (physiol.) Of that part of the nervous system consisting principally of a pair of ganglionated nerve trunks placed alongside the vertebral column and connected with nerve fibers that extend to the blood vessels, viscera, sweat and salivary glands, and pupils. **sym·pa·thet'i·cal·ly** *adv.*

sym·pa·thize (sĭm'pathīz) *v.i.* (**-thized, -thiz·ing**). Feel or express sympathy (*with*); suffer with

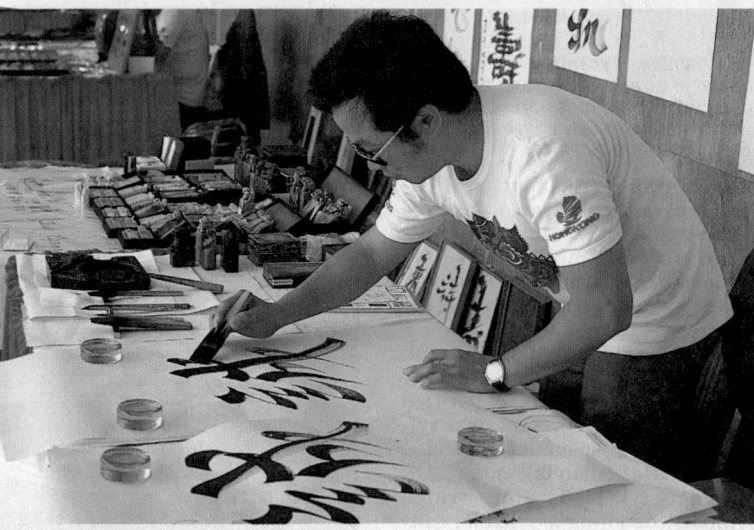

*The art of calligraphy, particularly in China and Japan, requires an understanding of the **symbolism** of each character, which can have an abundance of meanings.*

or like another. **sym'pa·thiz·er** *n.*

sym·pa·thy (sĭm'pathē) *n.* (pl. **-thies**). Affinity or relation between things by virtue of which they are similarly or correspondingly affected by the same influence, or affect or influence each other; tendency to share, state of sharing, emotion, sensation, or condition of another person or thing; mental participation in another's trouble, compassion, commiseration; disposition to agree (*with*) or approve, favorable attitude of mind toward person, cause etc.; **~ strike**, strike of workers not to remedy their own grievances but to support other strikers.

sym·pho·ny (sĭm'fonē) *n.* (pl. **-nies**). Musical composition written in form of SONATA but for full orchestra and usu. comprising four movements; (colloq.) concert by a symphony orchestra; **~ orchestra**, large orchestra including strings, woodwind, brass, and percussion instruments, playing chiefly symphonies or other works of serious artistic quality. **sym·phon·ic** (sĭmfŏn'ĭk) *adj.* **~ poem**, orchestral work, usu. of descriptive or rhapsodic character, freq. resembling first movement of symphony or sonata. **sym·phon'i·cal·ly** *adv.* **sym·pho·nist** *n.*

sym·po·si·um (sĭmpō'zēum) *n.* (pl. **-si·ums, -si·a** pr. -zēa). 1. Ancient Greek drinking party, convivial meeting for drinking, conversation, and intellectual entertainment; **the S~**, title of one of Plato's dialogues recording such conversation. 2. Meeting or conference for discussion of some subject; collection of opinions delivered or articles contributed by number of persons on special topic. **sym·po'si·al** *adj.*

symp·tom (sĭmp'tom) *n.* 1. Perceptible change in the body or its functions indicating presence of disease or injury, esp. (also **subjective ~**) one directly perceptible to the patient only; **objective** ~, one accompanied by signs (see SIGN *n*. sense 1). 2. Evidence or token of the existence of something. **symp·to·mat·ic** (sĭmptŏmăt'ĭk) *adj*. **symp·to·mat·i·cal·ly** *adv*.

    symp·to·ma·tize (sĭmp'-tomatīz) *v.t.* (**-tized, -tiz·ing**). Be a symptom of.

    syn- *prefix*. With, together, alike.

    syn·a·gogue, syn·a·gog (sĭn'-agŏg, -gawg) *ns*. Regular assembly of Jews for religious instruction or worship; building where this is held. **syn·a·gog·al** (sĭnagŏg'al, -gaw'gel), **syn·a·gog·i·cal** (sĭnagŏj'ĭkal) *adjs*.

    syn·apse (sĭn'ăps, sĭnăps') *n*. (anat.). Locus where a nervous impulse passes from the axon of one neuron to the dendrites of another.

    syn·ap·sis (sĭnăp'sĭs) *n*. (pl. **-ses** pr. -sēz). 1. (biol.) Fusion of pairs of chromosomes, the first process in meiotic division of germ cells. 2. (anat.) = SYNAPSE. **syn·ap·tic** (sĭnăp'tĭk) *adj*.

    sync, synch (sĭngk) *ns*. (colloq.) Synchronization. ~ *v*. (colloq.) Synchronize.

    syn·carp (sĭn'kārp) *n*. (bot.)

*Touro **Synagogue** in Newport, Rhode Island is the oldest in the U.S.A., built in 1763 and named a national historic site in 1946.*

Compound fruit, one arising from number of carpels in one flower. **syn·car·pous** (sĭnkār'pus) *adj*.

    syn·chro·mesh (sĭng'krŏmĕsh) *n*. System of gearing, esp. in motor vehicles, in which the sliding gear-wheels are provided with small friction clutches that make contact with the nonsliding wheels before engagement, thus facilitating gear changing by making both wheels revolve at the same speed. [abbrev. f. *synchronized mesh*]

    syn·chro·nize (sĭng'kronīz) *v*. (**-nized, -niz·ing**). Occur at the same time, be contemporary or simultaneous (*with*); keep time (*with*); cause to go at same rate or function simultaneously; cause (clocks etc.) to indicate same time; add dialogue or other sound as synchronous accompaniment to (motion picture). **syn·chro·ni·za·tion** (sĭngkronĭzā'shon), **syn·chro·niz·er** *ns*.

    syn·chro·nous (sĭng'kronus), **syn·chro·nal** (sĭng'kronal) *adjs*. Existing or happening at same time, contemporary, simultaneous, (*with*); keeping time, proceeding at

same pace (*with*), having coincident periods; ~ **orbit**, orbit whose period coincides with period of Earth's rotation on its axis and is so oriented that any body in it holds a position above one point on the surface of Earth. **syn·chro·nous·ly** *adv*.

    syn·chro·tron (sĭng'krotrŏn) *n*. An adaptation of the cyclotron designed for high acceleration of particles combined with a low-frequency magnetic field.

    syn·cline (sĭng'klīn, sĭn'-) *n*. (geol.) Rock bed that forms a trough (opp. ANTICLINE). **syn·cli·nal** (sĭngklī'nal, sĭng'klĭ-) *adj*.

    syn·co·pate (sĭng'kopāt) *v.t.* (**-pat·ed, -pat·ing**). 1. (gram.) Shorten (word) by omitting syllable(s) or letter(s) in the middle. 2. (mus.) Affect, modify, by syncopation. **syn·co·pa·tion** (sĭngkopā'shon) *n*. (esp., mus.) Displacement of accent or beat, by beginning note on normally un-accented part of bar (and freq. prolonging it into normally accented part), putting strong accent on normally weakly accented part of bar etc.

    syn·co·pe (sĭng'kopē, sĭn'-) *n*. 1. (path.) Fainting, sudden temporary loss of consciousness

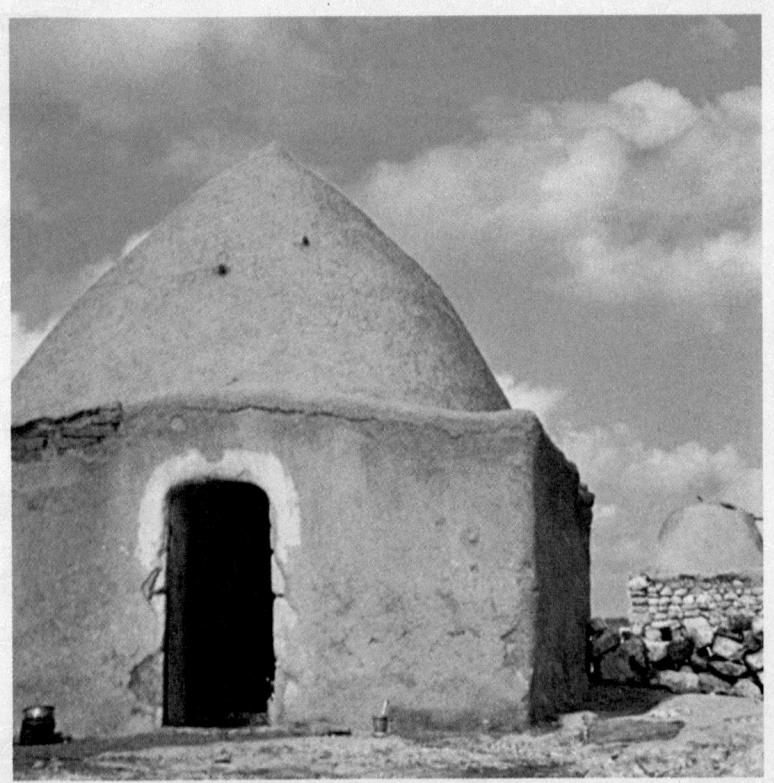

Beehive type huts in a village near Aleppo, **Syria.** Increasing in political power in the Middle East, Syria took a major part in achieving a cease-fire in Lebanon in 1976.

due to cerebral anemia associated with a severe disturbance of the circulation. 2. (gram.) Shortening of word by dropping of syllable(s) or letters in the middle. **syn·co·pal, syn·cop·ic** (sĭnkŏp´ĭk) *adjs.*

syn·cre·tism (sĭng´kretĭzem, sĭn´-) *n.* (Attempted) reconciliation of diverse or opposite tenets or practices, esp. in philosophy or religion. **syn·cret·ic** (sĭnkrĕt´ĭk), **syn·cre·tis·tic** (sĭngkretĭs´tĭk, sĭnkre-) *adjs.*

syn·di·cal·ism (sĭn´dĭkalĭzem) *n.* Movement, orig. and esp. in France, for transfer of control and ownership of means of production and distribution to workers' unions. **syn´di·cal·ist** *adj. & n.* [Fr. *syndicalisme,* f. *syndicat* trade union]

syn·di·cate (sĭn´dĭkĭt) *n.* Combination of financiers etc. for promotion of financial or commercial undertaking; (journalism) agency for syndicating articles etc. in newspapers; (colloq.) organization of gangsters. ~ (sĭn´dĭkāt) *v.* (**-cat·ed, -cat·ing**). Form into syndicate; publish simultaneously in a number of periodicals. **syn·di·ca·tion** (sĭndĭkā´shon), **syn´di·ca·tor** *ns.*

syn·drome (sĭn´drōm) *n.* Concurrence of several symptoms in a disease, set of concurrent symptoms characterizing it.

syn·ec·do·che (sĭnĕk´dokē) *n.* (gram., rhet.). Figure of speech in which the specific is used for the general or vice versa; or the part for the whole or vice versa, e.g. *50 sail* for *50 ships* or *the law* for *a policeman.*

syn·er·gism (sĭn´erjĭzem), **syn·er·gy** (sĭn´erjē) *ns.* (pl. **-gies**). Combined effect of drugs, organs, etc. that exceeds the sum of their individual effects. **syn·er·get·ic** (sĭnerjĕt´ĭk), **syn·er·gic** (sĭnĕr´jĭk), **syn·er·gis·tic** (sĭnerjĭs´tĭk) *adjs.* **syn´er·gist** *n.* **syn·er·gis´ti·cal·ly** *adv.*

syn·od (sĭn´od) *n.* 1. Assembly of clergy of church, diocese, nation, etc., for discussing and deciding ecclesiastical affairs; in Presbyterian churches, assembly of ministers and other elders constituting ecclesiastical court next above presbytery. 2. Any convention or council. **syn´od·al, syn·od·i·cal** (sĭnŏd´ĭkal), **syn·od´ic** *adjs.* **syn·od´i·cal·ly** *adv.*

syn·o·nym (sĭn´onĭm) *n.* Word having same meaning as another in same language; another name (*for*). **syn·on·y·mous** (sĭnŏn´ĭmus) *adj.* **syn·on´y·mous·ly** *adv.*

syn·on·y·my (sĭnŏn´ĭmē) *n.* (pl.

Turkey
Cyprus
● ALEPPO
SYRIA
● HOMS
Iraq
Mediterranean Sea
Lebanon
● DAMASCUS
Israel
Jordan

-mies). Being synonymous; use of synonyms, esp. for amplification or emphasis; subject or study of, a collection of, synonyms.

syn·op·sis (sĭnŏp´sĭs) *n.* (pl. **-ses** pr. -sēz). Brief general survey; summary.

syn·op·tic (sĭnŏp´tĭk) *adj.* Of, forming, furnishing, a synopsis; taking, affording, comprehensive mental view; (meteor.) of, affording, a comprehensive description of atmospheric conditions; **S** ~, of the ~ **Gospels**, those of Matthew, Mark, and Luke, as giving an account of events under same general aspect or from same point of view. **syn·op´ti·cal** *adj.* **syn·op´ti·cal·ly** *adv.* **Syn·op´tist** *n.* Writer of a Synoptic Gospel.

syn·tax (sĭn´tăks) *n.* (gram.) Arrangement of words in sentence showing their connection and relation; rules of grammar dealing with usages of grammatical construction. **syn·tac·tic** (sĭntăk´tĭk), **syn·tac´ti·cal** *adjs.*

syn·the·sis (sĭn´thesĭs) *n.* (pl. **-ses** pr. -sēz). Putting together of parts or elements to make up a complex whole (cf. ANALYSIS); (chem.) formation of a compound by combination of its elements or simpler compounds, esp. artificial production of organic compounds. **syn·the·size** (sĭn´thesīz) *v.t.* (**-sized, -siz·ing**).

syn·thet·ic (sĭnthĕt´ĭk), **syn·thet·i·cal** (sĭnthĕt´ĭkal) *adjs.* Produced by synthesis, artificial. **syn·thet´i·cal·ly** *adv.* Artificially produced fiber etc.

syph·i·lis (sĭf´ĭlĭs) *n.* Venereal disease due to the microorganism

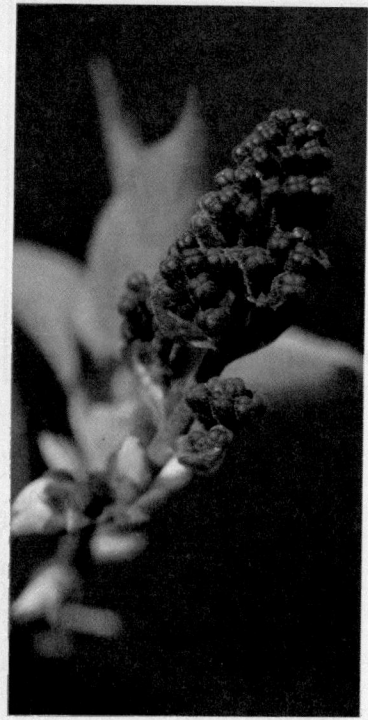

*Better known as lilac, plants in the genus **Syringa** also include others which have flowers with a strong perfume. The plants are believed to have originated in western Asia and southern Europe.*

*Blaise Pascal, French philosopher, physicist and mathematician, was the inventor of the **syringe** in the 17th century. Injection by syringe has become the standard method of introducing fluid drugs into the body.*

Treponema pallidum, communicated by direct contact, usu. sexual intercourse, with an infected person, affecting first some local part (**primary** ∼), secondly skin and mucous membrane (**secondary** ∼), and thirdly bones, muscles, and brain (**tertiary** ∼); **congenital** ∼, condition in which an unborn child is infected through the maternal blood stream. **syph·i·lit·ic** (sĭfĭlĭt′ĭk) *adj. & n.* Of (person) affected with, syphilis. [f. *Syphilus*, character in Latin poem on the subject (1530) by Girolano Fracastoro, Veronese physician]

Syr·i·a (sĭr′ēa, sēr′-). Republic in SW. Asia at E. end of Mediterranean; formed, with nearby regions, part of the Roman Empire from 64 B.C. to 36 A.D.; chiefly under Arab domination until the Ottoman conquest in 1517; French mandated territory 1918–41; capital, Damascus. **Syr·i·an** *adj. & n.* **Syr·i·ac** *adj.* (Of, in) the language of ancient Syria, a branch of Aramaic.

sy·rin·ga (sĭrĭng′ga) *n.* 1. MOCK orange. 2. Shrub of genus *S*∼, esp. *S. vulgaris*, the common lilac. [Gk. *surigx* pipe, with ref. to use of stems cleared of pith as pipestems]

sy·ringe (sĭrĭnj′) *n.* Tube with nozzle and piston or bulb for drawing in quantity of liquid and ejecting it in stream or jet, for making injections, cleansing wounds, spraying plants, etc. ∼ *v.t.* (**-ringed, -ring·ing**). Sluice, spray, with syringe.

syr·up, sir·up (sĭr′up, sēr′-) *ns.* Water (nearly) saturated with sugar, this combined with flavoring as beverage or with drug(s) as medicine; condensed sugar cane juice, part of this remaining uncrystallized at various stages of refining, molasses; **maple** ∼, syrup obtained by boiling down maple sap. **syr′up·y** *adj.* (esp. fig.) Sentimental, excessively sweet in style etc.

sys·tal·tic (sĭstawl′tĭk, -tăl′-) *adj.* Contracting, esp. (physiol.) with alternate contraction (*systole*) and dilatation (*diastole*).

sys·tem (sĭs′tem) *n.* 1. Complex whole, set of connected things or parts, organized body of material or immaterial things; (phys.) group of bodies moving about one another in space under some dynamic law, as that of gravitation, esp. (astron.) group of heavenly bodies moving in orbits about central body; (biol.) set of organs or parts in animal body of same or similar structure or subserving same function, animal body as an organized whole; ∼s **analysis**, technique of analyzing an operation in order to improve efficiency etc.; ∼s **design**, organization of data for electronic processing, or of data processing equipment. 2. Body of knowledge or belief considered as organized whole; comprehensive body of doctrines, beliefs, theories, practices, etc., forming particular philosophy, religion, form of government, etc.; scheme or method of classification, notation, etc.; (cryst.) any of six general methods or types in which substances crystallize. 3. Orderly arrangement or method.

sys·tem·at·ic (sĭstemăt′ĭk), **sys·tem·at·i·cal** (sĭstemăt′ĭkal) *adjs.* Methodical; arranged, conducted, according to system or organized plan; of system(s). **sys·tem·at′i·cal·ly** *adv.* **sys·tem·at·ics** *n.* (with sing. verb) Scientific study of classification of the plant and animal kingdoms, taxonomy. **sys·tem·a·tize** (sĭs′tematīz) *v.t.* (**-tized, -tiz·ing**).

sys·tem·ic (sĭstĕm′ĭk) *adj.* 1. Of, affecting, a system; (esp., physiol.) of the system or body as a whole, or a particular system of bodily organs. 2. Absorbed by a plant so as to be poisonous to insects that feed on it. **sys·tem′i·cal·ly** *adv.*

sys·to·le (sĭs′tolē) *n.* Contraction of heart, alternating with DIASTOLE. **sys·tol·ic** (sĭstŏl′ĭk) *adj.*

syz·y·gy (sĭz′ĭjē) *n.* (pl. **-gies**). (astron.) Point at which the heavenly bodies are in conjunction or opposition, esp. the moon with the sun.

Sze·chwan, Si·chuan (sĕ′chwahn′). Province of China on the Yangtze Kiang.

The earliest forms of the letter 'T, t' were simple crosses which, in Semitic languages, were called 'taw'. It meant a mark or sign. Somewhat surprisingly, its shape has remained relatively constant compared with the changes that have occurred to other letters during their history.

Phoenician   Cretan   Archaic Latin

Etruscan   Corinthian   Latin

T, t (tē) (pl. **T's, t's** or **Ts, ts**). 1. Twentieth letter of modern English and 19th of ancient Roman alphabet, derived in form from Greek *T* (*tau*), from the Phoenician and ancient Semitic † ⨯ ⨯ ⨯, and representing a voiceless dental (or in English, rather alveolar) stop, but in some combinations, as -tion, -tial, it has the sound "sh," in -tual, -tue, -ture freq. the sound represented in this dictionary by "ch"; the combination -th- represents voiced and voiceless dental spirants, simple sounds for which the Roman alphabet has no single symbols; **to a T,** exactly, to a nicety. 2. Object etc. shaped like T; **T-bone steak,** beefsteak from thin end of loin, containing T-shaped bone; **T-shirt,** short-sleeved usu. collarless shirt; **T square,** T-shaped instrument for obtaining or testing right angles and parallel lines.

T *abbrev.* Tesla.

T. *abbrev.* Tablespoon, tablespoonful, tenor, tera-, territory, true, Tuesday.

t. *abbrev.* Teaspoon, teaspoonful, temperature, (grammar) tense, time, ton(s), transitive, troy.

Ta *symbol.* Tantalum.

Taal (tahl) *n.* Cape Dutch, Afrikaans. [Du., = "language"]

tab (tăb) *n.* Short broad strap, flat loop, strip, tag, attached by one end to object, or forming projecting tongue, by which thing can be taken hold of, hung up, fastened, identified, etc.; (colloq.) restaurant or bar bill, check (esp. **keep ~ s on**). **tab** *v.* (**tabbed, tab·bing**).

tab·by (tăb′ē) *n.* (pl. **-bies**). Brownish, tawny, or gray cat with darker stripes (also **tabby cat**); old maid, elderly gossiping woman.

tab·er·nac·le (tăb′ernăkel) *n.* 1. Temporary or slightly built dwelling, hut, booth, tent; **Feast of Tabernacles,** Jewish festival, held in October, commemorating Israelites' sojourn in tents in the wilderness. 2. (Jewish hist.) Curtained tent containing Ark of the Covenant, which served as portable sanctuary of Jews during their wandering in the wilderness. 3.

Place of worship. 4. (eccles.) Canopied niche or recess in wall or pillar; ornamental receptacle for eucharistic elements. **tab·er·nac·u·lar** (tăbernăk′yuler) *adj.* **tabernacle** *v.* (**-led, -ling**). Provide with shelter or tabernacle; dwell temporarily.

ta·bes (tā′bēz) *n.* (path.) Slow progressive emaciation; **~ dor·sa′lis,** locomotor ataxia.

ta·bet·ic (tabĕt′ĭk) *adj.* Of, affected with, tabes, esp. locomotor ataxia. ~ *n.* Tabetic patient.

tab·la·ture (tăb′lacher) *n.* Tabular space or structure.

ta·ble (tā′bel) *n.* 1. Article of furniture consisting of flat top of wood or other solid material supported on legs or central pillar, esp. one on which meals are laid out, articles of use or ornament kept, work done, or games played; each half of folding backgammon board; provision or supply of food for meals, fare; company of persons at a table; **at ~,** at a meal or meals;

*Possibly invented by British officers stationed in India during the 1890s, **table tennis** was adopted in the U.S.A. about 1902. It became internationally accepted in 1926.*

lay on the ~, (in legislative debate) postpone (measure, report). **turn the ~ s,** reverse relation between two persons or parties, cause a complete reversal of state or affairs. 2. Flat, usu. rectangular, horizontal or vertical surface in architecture etc.; flat part of machine tool on which work is put to be operated on; flat upper surface of faceted gem; crystal of flattened or short prismatic form; flat elevated tract of land, plateau, flat mountain top. 3. Slab of wood, stone, etc.; matter written on this; **~ s of the law** (**covenant**), the Ten Commandments, the stones on which they were written; **the Twelve Tables,** laws drawn up by decemviri in Rome, 451 and 450 B.C., embodying most important rules of Roman law. 4. Tabulated statement or arrangement; arrangement of numbers, words, etc., esp. in columns and lines occupying single sheet, so as to exhibit set of facts or relations distinctly and comprehensively for study, reference, or calculation. 5. **ta′ble-cloth,** cloth spread on table, esp. for meals; **table cut,** (of gem) cut with flat upper surface and surrounded by small facets; **ta′ble-**

Left top: A marble-topped and gilt covered **table** *showing the degree of ornamentation used on furniture in the past. Below left: A range of tables showing the variations adopted for different needs.*

console-table

draw-table

Pembroke table

gate-leg table

refectory table

tripod table

trestle table

land, extensive elevated region with level surface, plateau; **table linen**, tablecloths, napkins, etc.; **ta′blespoon**, spoon, used at table for serving vegetables, etc.; tablespoonful; **ta′blespoonful**, amount held by tablespoon, about 4 fluid drams or 3 teaspoonfuls; **table talk**, informal conversation at table; **table tennis**, indoor game resembling lawn tennis, played with small round bats and celluloid ball on table with net stretched across it; **ta′bleware**, utensils and dishes etc. used at table; **table wine**, wine for drinking with meals, containing 8–13 percent alcohol. **table** *v.t.* (**-bled, -bling**). Lay (measure, report, etc.) on table, esp. as way of postponing indefinitely.

tab·leau (tăb′lō, tăblō′) *n.* (pl. **tab·leaux, tab·leaus** pr. tăb′lōz, tăblōz′). Presentation, esp. of group of persons etc., producing picturesque effect; striking or dramatic effect suddenly produced.

ta·bleau vi·vant (tăblō′ vēvahň′) (pl. **ta·bleaux vi·vants** pron. as sing.). Representation of painting, statue, scene, etc., by silent and motionless person or group.

ta·ble d'hôte (tăb′el dōt′, tah′-bel; *Fr.* tăble dōt′) (pl. **ta·bles d'hôte** pr. tăb′elz dōt′, tah′belz; *Fr.* tăble dōt′). (of meal) Served at fixed price for a stated series of courses (opp. *à la carte*). [Fr., = "host's table"]

tab·let (tăb′lit) *n.* Small thin flat piece of ivory, wood, etc., for writing on, esp. each of set fastened together; pad of sheets of notepaper fastened together at top; small slab, esp. with or for inscription; small flat or compressed piece of solid confection, drug, etc., flattened lozenge.

tab·loid (tăb′loid) *n.* 1. Anything in summarized, compressed, or concentrated form. 2. Newspaper of small format, esp. one giving news in concentrated and simplified form. ~ *adj.*

ta·boo, ta·bu (tăbōō′) *adjs.* Set apart as sacred or prohibited. ~ *n.* (pl. **-boos, -bus**). Ban, prohibition. ~ *v.t.* (**-booed, -boo·ing**). Put under taboo. [Polynesian]

tab·u·lar (tăb′yuler) *adj.* 1. Of, arranged in, computed, etc., by means of, tables. 2. Broad, flat, and (usu.) comparatively thin, like a table; formed of, tending to split into, pieces of this form; (of crystal etc.) of short prismatic form with flat base and top. **tab′u·lar·ly** *adv.*

ta·bu·la ra·sa (tăb′yula rā′sa, rah′sa; *Lat.* tah′bŏŏlah rah′sah) (pl.

ta·bu·lae ra·sae pr. tăb′yulē rā′sē, rah′sē; *Lat.* tah′boōlī rah′sī). Erased tablet; (fig.) human mind at birth viewed as having no innate ideas; complete obliteration, a blank. [L., = "scraped tablet," i.e. "clean slate"]

tab·u·late (tăb′yulāt) *v.t.* (**-lat·ed, -lat·ing**). Arrange, summarize, exhibit, in form of a table, scheme, or synopsis. **tab·u·la·tion** (tăbyulā′shon) *n.* **tabulate** (tăb′-yulĭt, -lāt) *adj.* Having flat surface, tabular.

tab·u·la·tor (tăb′yulātᵉr) *n.* (esp.) Typewriter attachment for indenting a selected number of spaces when paragraphing and tabulating.

ta·chis·to·scope (takĭs′toskŏp) *n.* Instrument for very brief measured exposure of objects to eye. **ta·chis·to·scop·ic** (takĭs-toskŏp′ĭk) *adj.*

tach·o·graph (tăk′ogrăf, -grahf) *n.* Device on vehicle, measuring and recording its speed and travel time; tachometer.

ta·chom·e·ter (tăkŏm′etᵉr) *n.* Instrument for measuring the velocity of machines or the rate of flow of liquids. **ta·chom′e·try** *n.*

ta·chy·car·di·a (tăkĭkār′dēa) *n.* (path.) Abnormally rapid action of heart.

tac·it (tăs′ĭt) *adj.* Implied, understood, inferred, but not openly expressed or stated; saying nothing, silent. **tac′it·ly** *adv.* **tac′it·ness** *n.*

tac·i·turn (tăs′ĭtᵉrn) *adj.* Reserved in speech, saying little, uncommunicative. **tac·i·tur·ni·ty** (tăsĭtᵉr′nĭtē) *n.* **tac′i·turn·ly** *adv.*

Tac·i·tus (tăs′ĭtus), **Publius Cornelius** (c56–117 A.D.). Roman historian, son-in-law of Agricola; author of *Agricola* (containing an account of Britain), *Germania*, *Histories*, and *Annals*.

tack[1] (tăk) *n.* 1. Small sharp nail, usu. with large flat head, for fastening thin or light object to more solid one. 2. Fastening together, esp. in slight or temporary way; long slight stitch used in fastening together seams etc. before permanent sewing. 3. Rope used for securing lower corner of some sails; lower windward corner of sail, to which tack is attached. 4. Tacking; ship's course in relation to direction of wind and position of sails; course obliquely opposed to direction of wind, one of consecutive series of such courses with wind alternately on port and starboard side; (fig.) course of action or policy; **on the wrong ~**, with mistaken idea; in error. 5. (of varnish, printing ink, etc.) Viscous condition. 6. Saddles, harness, bridles, etc. and other equipment for riding horse; **~ room**, room in or near stable where this is kept.

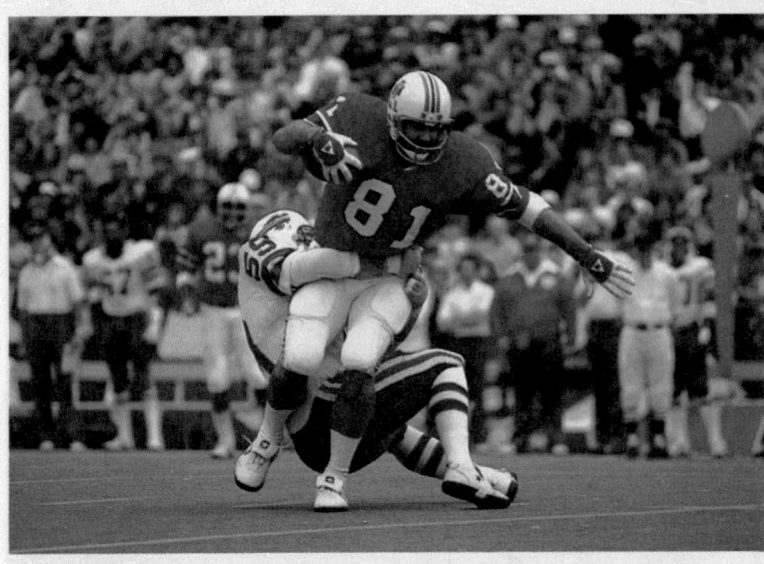

In football, a player receiving the ball expects to be the victim of a **tackle.** *Members of the opposing team either knock him down or hold him so that he cannot advance towards their goal.*

tack *v.* 1. Attach with tacks, or in slight or temporary manner, esp. with long slight stitches; (fig.) annex, append (*to, onto*). 2. Change ship's course by shifting tacks and sails; make run or course obliquely against wind, proceed to windward by series of such courses; (fig.) change one's course, conduct, policy, etc. **tack′er** *n.*

tack[2] (tăk) *n.* Foodstuff (chiefly in **hard′tack**).

tack·le (tăk′el) *n.* 1. Apparatus, utensils, instruments, appliances, esp. for fishing or other sport. 2. (naut.) Rope(s) and pulley block(s) or other mechanism for hoisting weights etc.; windlass with its ropes and hooks; running rigging of ship. 3. (football etc.) Tackling; each of two players (**right ~, left ~**), with positions next to the ends in the line. **tackle** *v.* (**tack·led, tack·ling**). Grapple with, grasp, lay hold of, with endeavor to hold, manage, or overcome; (football etc.) seize and stop, obstruct, intercept (opponent in possession of ball). **tack′ler** *n.*

tack·y (tăk′ē) *adj.* (**tack·i·er, tack·i·est**). (of gum, nearly dry varnish, etc.) Slightly sticky or adhesive; (colloq.) seedy, shabby, or dowdy in appearance. **tack′i·ness** *n.*

ta·co (tah′kō) *n.* (pl. **-cos**). Mexican food of meat etc. in folded or rolled tortilla.

tac·o·nite (tăk′onīt) *n.* Low-grade iron ore obtained from fine-grained, tough, sedimentary rock of quartz, hematite, and magnetite.

tact (tăkt) *n.* Intuitive perception of what is fitting, esp. of the right thing to do or say; adroitness in dealing with persons or circumstances. **tact′ful** *adj.* **tact′ful·ly** *adv.* **tact′ful·ness** *n.* **tact′less** *adj.* **tact′less·ly** *adv.* **tact′less·ness** *n.*

tac·tic (tăk′tĭk) = TACTICS.

tac·ti·cal (tăk′tĭkal) *adj.* Of tactics; adroitly planning or planned; **~ bombing**, aerial bombing carried out in immediate support of military or naval operations. **tac′ti·cal·ly** *adv.*

tac·ti·cian (tăktĭsh′an) *n.* One versed or skilled in tactics.

tac·tics (tăk′tĭks) *n.* (considered sing. or pl.). Art or science of deploying and maneuvering air, military, or naval forces, esp. when in contact with the enemy (contrasted with strategy); (as pl.) procedure, device(s) for gaining some end.

tac·tile (tăk′tĭl, -tīl) *adj.* Of, perceived by, connected with, sense of touch; (painting etc.) appealing to sense of touch, producing effect of solidity. **tac·til·i·ty** (tăktĭl′ĭtē) *n.*

tac·tu·al (tăk′chooal) *adj.* Tactile. **tac′tu·al·ly** *adv.*

tad·pole (tăd′pōl) *n.* Larva of frog or toad, from time it leaves egg until it loses gills and tail, esp. early stage of this when it seems to consist simply of round head with a tail; larva of similar appearance in other animals.

Ta·dzhik·i·stan (tajĭk′ĭstăn; *Russ.* tahjĭkĭstahn′), **Ta·jik·i·stan** (tah′jĭkstahn; *Russ.* tahjĭkstahn′). Constituent republic of U.S.S.R. (properly *Tadzhik Soviet Socialist Republic*), in central Asia; Capital, Dushanbe.

taf·fe·ta (tăf′eta) *n.* Fine plain-woven usu. glossy fabric of silk or

Facing: Known as the Tibet of the U.S.S.R. with one peak exceeding 24,000 ft., **Tadzhikistan** *is on the borders of Afghanistan and China. Many of the people are of Iranian ancestry and raise livestock and grow cotton.*

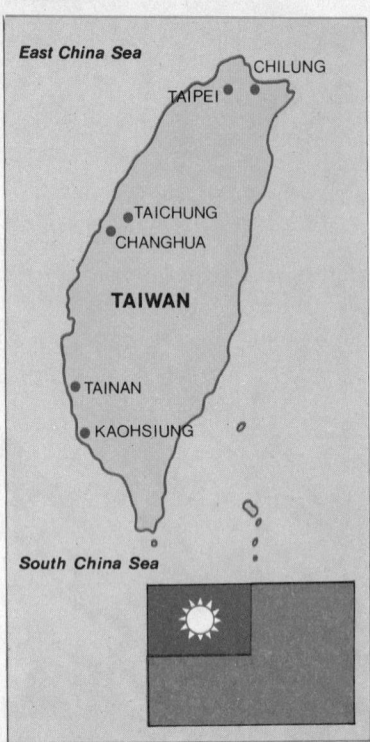

*Helped by massive aid from the U.S.A., the government of Chiang Kai-Shek was established on **Taiwan** (formerly Formosa) in 1949. Since then, it has developed a large export market.*

other material. [Pers. *tāftah* (*tāftan* twist)]

taf·fy (tăf′ē) *n.* Chewy candy of brown sugar or molasses, sometimes containing chopped nuts.

Taft (tăft), **William Howard** (1857–1930). Amer. politician; first civil governor of the Philippines, 1901–04; U.S. secretary of war, 1904–08; 27th U.S. president, 1909–13; chief justice of the U.S. Supreme Court, 1921–30.

tag¹ (tăg) *n.* Metal etc. point at end of shoelace; small hanging piece or part, as loop at back of boot for pulling it on, ragged lock of wool on sheep, address label for tying on, any loose or ragged end; brief and usu. familiar, trite or much-used quotation; refrain or catch of song etc., last words of speech in play etc.; ~ **team**, team of two wrestlers, each of whom competes against either wrestler on similar team, competitors in ring switching with those outside by tagging them. **tag** *v.* (**tagged, tag·ging**). Furnish with a tag; join (*to, onto, together*); find rhymes for (verses), string (rhymes) together; follow closely, trail or drag behind; (in baseball) to touch with the ball or with the ball held in the glove. **tag′ger** *n.*

tag² (tăg) *n.* Children's game in which one pursues the others until he touches one, who in turn becomes pursuer.

Ta·ga·log (tahgah′lŏg, tăg′alŏg)

n. (pl. **-logs**, collect. **-log**). (Member, language) of principal Malayan people of Philippine Islands. [native name, f. *taga* native, *ilog* river]

Ta·gore (tagōr′, -gŏr′, tah′gor), **Sir Ra·bin·dra·nath** (rabēn′-dranaht) (1861–1941). Indian poet and writer; awarded Nobel Prize for literature 1913.

Ta·hi·ti (tahētē, tah-). One of the Society Islands in the S. Pacific, a French protectorate since 1843. **Ta·hi·tian** (tahē′shan) *adj.* & *n.*

Tai = THAI.

tail¹ (tāl) *n.* 1. Hindmost part of animal, esp. when prolonged beyond rest of body; **turn** ~, run away. 2. Thing, part, appendage, resembling this, as luminous train of comet, twisted or braided tress of hair, stem of musical note, pendent posterior part of man's coat, esp. dress coat; appendage of string and paper at lower end of kite; rear end of column, procession, etc.; rear part of aircraft; reverse side of coin; (pl.) full-dress suit. 3. **tail′board**, usu. hinged or removable board at back of cart, truck, etc.; **tail end**, extreme end, concluding part; **tail′gate**, lower gate of canal lock; hinged or removable part of delivery truck, van, station wagon, etc.; (*v.i.*) drive too close behind another vehicle; **tail′-light**, light carried at back of train, cycle, car, etc.; **tail′piece**, piece forming tail; triangular piece of

*In various legal capacities, **W. H. Taft** aroused controversy due to his handling of labor–management disputes, especially secondary boycotts and the right of workers to strike.*

wood to which lower ends of strings are fastened in violin etc.; small decoration at end of book, chapter, etc.; **tail′pipe**, exhaust pipe of motor vehicle; **tail skid**, small skid or runner supporting tail of aircraft in contact with ground; **tail′spin**, (aviation) kind of spinning dive; **tail′stock**, one of two parts (**tail·stock** and **headstock**) that hold work in a lathe; **tail′wind**, wind blowing in same direction as course of aircraft etc. **tail** *v.* Furnish with tail; follow (person) inconspicuously to keep watch on him; cut or pull off what is regarded as tail, esp. of plant or fruit; ~ **away**, **off**, fall away in tail or straggling line; diminish and cease. **tail′less** *adj.* **tail′less·ness** *n.* **tail′like** *adj.*

tail² (tāl) *n.* (law) Limitation of freehold estate or fee to a person and (particular class of) the heirs of his body (freq. in phrase **in** ~). **tail** *adj.* Limited to specified heirs; being in tail.

tai·lor (tā′ler) *n.* Maker of men's outer garments, or of such women's garments as have similar character, e.g. coats, suits, riding clothes; **tailor-made**, made by tailor, usu. with little ornament and with special attention to exact fit. **tailor** *v.* Do tailor's work; make (garments etc.) by tailor's methods; furnish with clothes, dress. **tai′lored** *adj.* (esp., of women's clothes) Made in plain fitted style.

taint (tānt) *n.* Spot, trace, of decay, corruption, or disease; corrupt condition, infection. ~ *v.* Introduce corruption or disease into, infect, be infected. **taint′less** *adj.* **taint′less·ly** *adv.* **taint′less·ness** *n.*

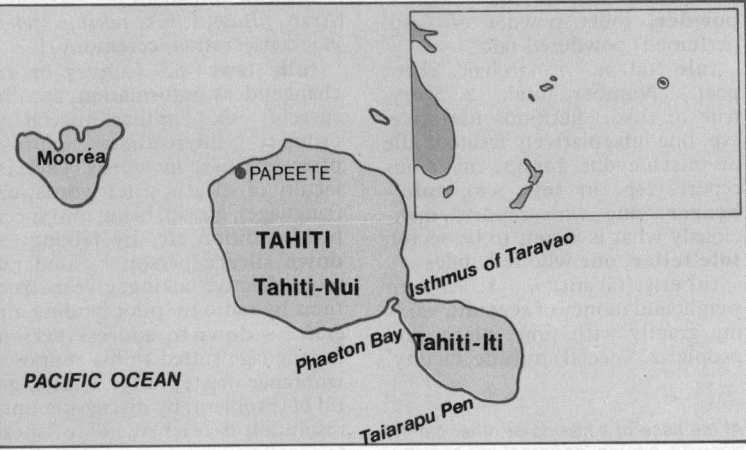

Memorable for the visit of the 'Bounty' and Gauguin's paintings, *Tahiti* is now the base for French nuclear tests. These provoke complaints from N.Z., Australia and other Pacific countries.

some process; write (*down*) (notes, spoken words, etc.); obtain likeness, esp. by photography. 5. Receive, accept, enjoy (pleasure, money, wager, hint, etc.); exact (vengeance etc.); accept as true or correct, or in some specified way; face and attempt to get over, through, etc., negotiate; admit, absorb, contract, be affected by (moisture, infection, dye, a quality, etc.). 6. Grasp with mind, apprehend, understand; suppose, assume; regard, consider (*as*); feel, experience (emotion etc.). 7. Perform, do (action, movement, etc.); raise, make (objection, exception, etc.). 8. Carry, convey, cause to go with one; **take from**, carry away, remove, deprive or rid person or thing of. 9. **take aim**, aim (*at*); **take charge**, make oneself responsible; **take care**, be careful; **take care of**, be careful of; be in charge of; deal with; **take fire**, become kindled or ignited, catch fire; **take hold** (**of**), grasp, seize,

The **tailorbird** is named after its method of stitching together leaves with fibers so that they form a pouch in which a cradle type of nest can be made.

Tai·pei (tī′pā′; *Chin.* tī′bā′). Capital of Taiwan, at N. end of Taiwan Island.

Tai·wan (tī′wahn′). (formerly Formosa) Island in the Pacific Ocean, separated from the SE. coast of mainland China by ∼ **Strait**; in 1949, Chiang Kai-Shek fled mainland Communists, establishing his Nationalist government there; Taiwan lost U.N. recognition as representing China, 1971, to the People's Republic of China; capital, Taipei.

Ta·jik·stan = TADZHIKISTAN.

Taj Ma·hal (tahj″ mahahl′, tazh′). Marble mausoleum of great splendor and beauty at Agra, India, built (1631–45) by the Mogul Emperor Shah-Jahan in memory of his favorite wife. [corrupt. of Pers. *Mumtāz-i-Mahall*, title of wife of Shah-Jahan, f. *mumtāz* distinguished, *mahall* abode]

take (tāk) *v.* (**took** pr. tŏŏk, **tak·en** pr. tā′ken, **tak·ing**). 1.

Seize, grasp; capture; catch; (cards) win (trick); (of plant, seed, etc.) germinate, begin to grow; catch fancy or affection of; (of inoculation etc.) be successful or effective; **be taken ill**, fall ill. 2. Receive into body, as medicine, food, drink, etc.; bring or receive (person) into some relation to oneself; appropriate, enter into possession (of); secure, get, receive, by payment, esp. regularly, as a periodical; assume, charge oneself with, undertake; perform, discharge (function, service, etc.); range oneself on, ally oneself with, (side, in contest etc.); (gram.) have as proper construction; **take it**, (colloq.) endure punishment, affliction, etc., with fortitude. 3. Choose, adopt, take into use or employment; proceed or begin to deal with in some way; proceed to occupy; use (up), consume; need (specified size) *in* shoes, gloves, etc. 4. Obtain, derive, from some source or by take under one's control; **take place**, (esp. of prearranged event) occur; **take possession**, enter into possession (*of*). 10. **take after**, resemble (person, esp. parent) in character, feature, etc.; **take away**, remove, subtract, detract *from*; **take back**, retract (words); **take down**, write down; humiliate, humble; pull down (building), lower, carry or cut down; **take in**, admit, receive (lodgers etc.); undertake (work) to be done in one's own house; conduct into house, room, etc.; include, comprise; reduce (garment etc.) to smaller compass, furl (sail); understand, comprehend; deceive, cheat; believe (false statement); **take off**, remove; conduct away; deduct (part of price); mimic; jump, spring; (of aircraft or pilot) leave ground etc. at beginning of flight; **take'off** (*n.*), caricature; spot from which jump etc. is made; aircraft's leaving of ground etc.; **take on**, undertake (work, responsibility, etc.); play (person) *at* game; (colloq.) show violent emotion, be greatly agitated; **take out**, cause to come out; bring or convey out; remove; accept payment or compensation *in* specified form; procure, get issued (patent, insurance policy, etc.); buy (food etc.) at lunch counter, diner, etc. for eating elsewhere; **take it out of**, exhaust, fatigue; exact satisfaction from; **take over**, succeed to possession or control of; **take'over** (*n.*), assumption of control (esp. of business etc.); **take to**, begin, begin to occupy oneself with; conceive a liking for; **take up**, lift up; shorten (garment); absorb; occupy, engage; enter upon; pursue (occupation, subject, inquiry, etc.); secure, fasten; accept (challenge); subscribe for, subscribe amount of (shares, loan, etc.); **take up with**, begin to consort with. **take** *n.* Amount (of fish, game, etc.) taken or caught; takings; (cinemat.) scene or part of scene photographed at one time without stopping camera, photographing of this.

tak·en: see TAKE.

tak·er (tā′ker) *n.* (esp.) One who takes a bet.

tak·ing (tā′kǐng) *n.* Act of person or thing that takes; thing that is taken; (pl.) business receipts. ~ *adj.* Attractive, captivating, charming. **tak′ing·ly** *adv.*

tal·a·poin (tăl′apoin) *n.* 1. Buddhist priest or monk. 2. Small W. African monkey (*Cercopithecus talapoin*).

talc (tălk) *n.* Soft, translucent, white, green, or gray mineral (a hydrated magnesium silicate) with greasy feel and shining luster, freq. occurring in broad flat plates, and used in making soap, toilet powder, paper, lubricants, etc.; talcum powder.

Native to India, the **tamarisk** is now acclimatized in England where it has proved invaluable for stabilizing sand dunes. Its galls were used for tannin and a dye in Asian countries.

tal·cum (tăl′kum) *n.* Talc; ~ **powder**, toilet powder of (usu. perfumed) powdered talc.

tale (tāl) *n.* 1. (archaic, rhet., poet.) Number, total. 2. Story, true or (usu.) fictitious narrative, esp. one imaginatively treated; idle or mischievous gossip, malicious report (esp. in **tell** ~**s**); **tale′bearer**, one who reports maliciously what is meant to be secret; **tale′teller**, one who tells tales.

tal·ent (tăl′ent) *n.* 1. Ancient weight and money of account, varying greatly with time, place, and people. 2. Special aptitude, faculty,

At the base of a hillside or other natural declivity, a talus (or scree) will accumulate from the eroded material of the hill. The angle at which this material lies is known as the angle of repose.

gift (from the parable of the talents, Matt. 25); high mental ability; ~ **scout**, person engaged in searching for talented people, esp. theatrical etc. performers; ~ **show**, theatrical show in which amateur or unknown performers display abilities as actors, singers, dancers, etc., with hope of winning recognition. **tal′ent·ed** *adj.*

ta·les (tā′lēz) (considered sing. or pl.) *n.* (law) Writ for summoning jurors, list of persons who may be so summoned, to supply deficiency; **tales·man** (tālz′man, tā′lēz-) (pl. **-men** pr. -men), person so summoned. [L. *tales de circumstantibus* such of the bystanders, first words of the writ]

tal·i·pes (tăl′ipēz) *n.* Clubfoot. **tal·i·ped** (tăl′ipĕd) *adj. & n.* Clubfooted (person).

tal·is·man (tăl′ĭsman, -ĭz-) *n.* (pl. **-mans**). Charm, amulet, esp. stone, ring, etc., inscribed with astrological figures or characters and supposed to protect its wearer or bring him good fortune. **tal·is·man·ic** (tălĭsmăn′ĭk, -ĭz-) *adj.* [Arab. *tilsam*, f. Gk. *telesmos* consecration, ceremony)]

talk (tawk) *v.* Convey or exchange ideas, information, etc., by speech, esp. familiar speech of ordinary intercourse; express, utter, discuss, in words; exercise faculty of speech; utter words; use (language); gossip; bring into specified condition etc. by talking; ~ **down**, silence (person) by louder or more effective talking; give instructions by radio to (pilot landing aircraft); ~ **down to**, address (person) in language suited to his supposed ignorance or stupidity; ~ **out**, get rid of (problem) by discussion until resolution is reached; ~ **to**, speak to, (colloq.) reprove; **talk′ing-to** (*n.*, pl. **-tos**), (colloq.) scolding. **talk** *n.* Conversation; short address or lecture in conversational style, esp. one broadcast by radio; theme of gossip.

talk·a·thon (taw′kăthŏn) *n.* Prolonged public discussion.

talk·a·tive (taw′katĭv) *adj.* Fond of talking. **talk′a·tive·ly** *adv.* **talk′a·tive·ness** *n.*

talk·ie (taw′kē) *n.* (archaic slang) Sound motion picture. [abbrev. of talking picture]

talk·ing (taw′kǐng) *n. & adj.* ~ **book**, recording of reading of book, magazine, etc., for use by blind people; ~ **point**, topic for discussion or argument.

tall (tawl) *adj.* 1. (of persons) Of more than average height; (of things) high, lofty, higher than the average or than surrounding objects; of specified height; **tall′boy**, tall chest of drawers, occas. in 2 sections, one standing above the other. 2. (of talk etc.) High-flown; exaggerated, highly colored; **tall**

drink, drink served in tall glass; **tall order**, unreasonable or excessive demand. **tall'ish** *adj.* **tall'ness** *n.*

Tal·la·has·see (tălahăs´ē). Capital of Florida, in the NW. part.

Tal·linn (tahl´lĭn). Seaport and capital of Estonian S.S.R., on the Gulf of Finland opposite Helsinki.

tal·lith (tah´lĭs; *Heb.* tahlēt´) *n.* (pl. **ta·li·thim** pr. tahlē´sĭm; *Heb.* tahlētēm´). Scarf worn by Jews, esp. at prayer.

tal·low (tăl´ō) *n.* Fat of animals, esp. of sheep and cattle, separated by melting and clarifying and used for making candles, soap, etc. **tal'low·y** *adj.*

tal·ly (tăl´ē) *n.* (pl. **-lies**). 1. (obs.) Piece of wood scored across with notches representing amount of debt or payment and split lengthwise across notches, each party keeping half; account so kept. 2. Score, reckoning. 3. Distinguishing mark, ticket, label, attached to thing for identification etc. 4. Corresponding thing, counterpart, duplicate. ~ *v.* (**-lied, -ly·ing**). Record, reckon, by tally; agree, correspond (*with*).

Tal·mud (tahl´mŏŏd, -mŭd, tăl´-) *n.* Body of Jewish civil and ceremonial law, comprising the MISHNAH and the GEMARA. **Tal'mud·ic** (tahlmŏŏd´ĭk, -mŏŏ´dĭk, -mŭ´-, -mŭd´ĭk, tăl-), **Tal'mud'i·cal** *adjs.* **Tal'mud·ist** (tahl´mŭdĭst, tăl´-) *n.*

tal·on (tăl´on) *n.* Claw, esp. of bird of prey; (pinochle etc.) remainder of pack after cards have been dealt; shoulder of bolt against which key presses in turning it; handle end of sword blade.

ta·lus[1] (tā´lus) *n.* (pl. **-lus·es**). Slope, esp. (fort.) sloping side of wall or earthwork; (geol.) mass of rock debris gathering at foot of a cliff.

ta·lus[2] (tā´lus) *n.* (pl. **-li** pr. **-lī**). (anat.) Ankle bone; (path.) form of clubfoot with toes drawn up and heel resting on ground.

tam (tăm) = TAM-O'-SHANTER.

ta·ma·le (tamah´lē) *n.* Mexican dish of cornmeal with pieces of meat or chicken, red pepper, etc., wrapped in corn husks and baked or steamed.

tam·a·rack (tăm´erăk) *n.* (Timber of) any of various Amer. larches, esp. *Larix laricina* of northern N. Amer.

tam·a·rind (tăm´erĭnd) *n.* Large tropical tree (*Tamarindus indica*) with hard heavy timber, dark green pinnate leaves, and racemes of fragrant red-streaked yellow flowers; fruit of this, brown pods with seeds embedded in brown or reddish-black acid pulp, used in medicine, as relish, etc. [Arab. *tamr-hindī* date of India]

tam·a·risk (tăm´erĭsk) *n.* Plant of genus *Tamarix*, esp. *T. gallica*, a graceful evergreen shrub or small tree with slender feathery branches and minute leaves, growing in sandy places.

tam·bour (tăm´boor) *n.* 1. Circular frame consisting of one hoop fitting closely within another, over which material is stretched for embroidering; embroidery worked on it; tambour lace. 2. Drum. 3. (fort.) Small defensive work of palisades, earth, etc., defending entrance or passage. ~ *v.* Decorate, embroider, on tambour.

tam·bou·rin (tam´boorĭn) *n.* (pl. **-rins**). Long narrow drum used in Provence; (music for) dance accompanied by this.

tam·bou·rine (tămberēn´) *n.* Musical instrument consisting of a wooden hoop with a skin stretched over one side and pairs of small cymbals in slots around the circumference, played by shaking, striking with knuckles, or drawing finger(s) across parchment.

Tam·bur·laine (tăm´berlān), **Tam·er·lane** (tăm´erlān). *Timur Lenk* or *Lang* "lame Timur" (c1335–1405), Tartar conqueror of much of Asia and E. Europe; ancestor of the Mogul dynasty in India.

tame (tām) *adj.* (**tam·er, tam·est**). 1. (of animals, birds, etc.) Made tractable, domesticated, not wild; (colloq., of land or plant) cultivated. 2. Submissive, spiritless, insipid. **tame'ly** *adv.* **tame'ness** *n.* **tame** *v.t.* (**tamed, tam·ing**). Make gentle and tractable, break in, domesticate (wild beast, bird, etc.); subdue, curb, humble, reduce to submission. **tam'a·ble, tame'a·ble** *adjs.* **tam'er** *n.*

Tam·il (tăm´ĭl, tŭm´-) *n.* (pl.

*Found only in the Americas and ranging in size from a tit to a finch, the 200 species of **tanager** are better known for the vivid plumage of the males, especially the paradise variety.*

Scarlet Tanager

Western Tanager

Paradise Tanager

Brilliantly conceived and admirably made, this ceramic lion from the **T'ang** dynasty in China demonstrates the degree of art and craftsmanship achieved in the seventh century A.D.

A Victor bomber, converted for use in air-to-air refuelling, acts as a **tanker** or 'mother' for the two Lightnings which carefully maneuver until the fuel supply line is attached.

-ils, collect. **-il**). Member of people of SE. India and part of Sri Lanka; Dravidian language of this people.

Tam·ma·ny (tăm´anē). Fraternal and benevolent society of New York City, founded in 1789, developed out of one of the earlier patriotic societies; political organization of the Democratic Party, identified with this society and notorious in 19th c. for corruption; ~ **Hall**, any of the successive buildings used as headquarters of Tammany; (transf.) members of Tammany. [f. name of Indian chief (late 17th c.) noted for wisdom and friendliness toward whites, and regarded (c1770–90) as "patron saint" of Pennsylvania and other northern colonies]

Tam·muz (tah´mōoz, tah-mōoz´). 1. (myth.) Syrian or Babylonian deity, god of agriculture and flocks, lover of Astarte, who brought him back from the lower world after his death. 2. Tenth month of Jewish calendar.

tam-o'-shan·ter (tăm o shăn´ter) n. Round woolen or cloth cap of Scottish origin, with flat baggy top much wider than headband. [f. hero of Robert Burns's poem "Tam o'Shanter"]

tamp (tămp) v.t. Plug (blast hole etc.) with clay above firing charge; ram down with repeated light strokes.

tamp·er (tăm´per) v.i. ~ **with**, meddle with; alter, corrupt, pervert. **tam´per·er** n.

tam·pi·on (tăm´pēon) n. Plug for top of organ pipe; plug or cover for muzzle of gun.

tam·pon (tăm´pŏn) n. Plug inserted in wound, body cavity, or orifice, to stop hemorrhage or absorb secretions. ~ v.t. Plug with tampon.

tan[1] (tăn) v. (**tanned, tan·ning**). 1. Convert (skin or hide) into leather by soaking in a bath containing oak bark or other substance rich in tannin, or by any other process. 2. Make, become, brown by exposure to sun or weather. 3. (colloq.) Beat, thrash. ~ n. 1. Crushed or bruised bark of oak or other trees, used for tanning (also **tan´bark**); spent bark from tan pits used for covering riding track, circus ring, etc.; track etc. covered with this. 2. Brown color of tan; bronzed color of skin that has been exposed to sun or weather. ~ adj. (**tan·ner, tan·nest**). Of the color of tan or tanned leather, yellowish or reddish brown.

tan[2] abbrev. Tangent.

tan·a·ger (tăn´ajer) n. Amer. bird of family Thraupidae, with numerous species, in which males are usu. brightly colored.

Ta·nan·a·rive (tănănărēv´) (also called Antananarivo). Capital of the Democratic Republic of Madagascar, in the E. central part.

tan·dem (tăn´dem) adv. (of horses in harness) One behind the other; **drive** ~, drive horses so harnessed. **tandem** n. 1. Carriage driven tandem. 2. Bicycle

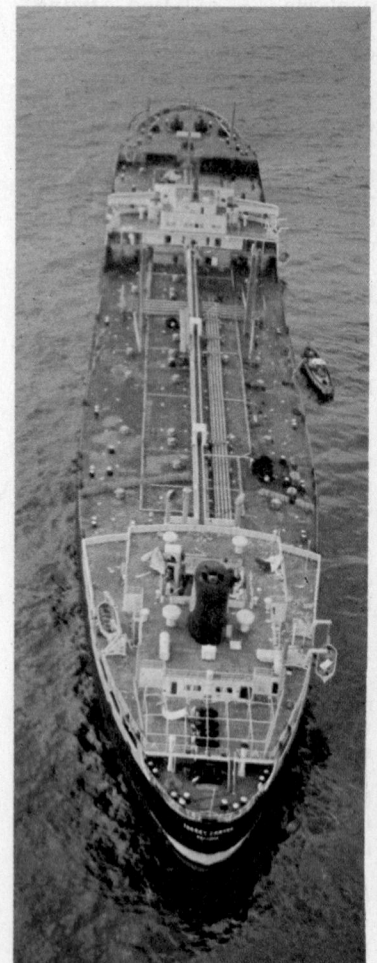

The 'Torrey Canyon' oil **tanker** was one of the first of the larger vessels used in this service to come to grief. Its wreck provided a warning of the pollution hazards that can result.

with 2 or more seats one behind the other, also called ~ **bicycle.** [punning use of L. *tandem* at length (of time)]

Ta·ney (taw′nē), **Roger Brooke** (1777–1864). Amer. jurist; U.S. secretary of the treasury, 1833–34, and chief justice of U.S. Supreme Court, 1836–64.

Tang, T'ang (tahng). Name of dynasty that ruled in China 618–906 A.D., a period noted for territorial conquest and great wealth, and regarded as golden age of Chinese poetry and art; hence, porcelain etc. of this period.

tang (tăng) *n.* 1. Point, projection, esp. extension of knife, chisel, or other metal tool or instrument by which it is secured to its handle. 2. Strong or penetrating taste or smell; characteristic quality; trace, touch, suggestion, *of* something. ~ *v.t.* Furnish with tang. **tang·y** (tăng′ē) *adj.* (**tang·i·er, tang·i·est**).

Tan·gan·yi·ka (tăngɑnyē′kɑ, tănggɑn-). Mainland part of TANZANIA; **Lake** ~, lake in E. central Africa, 420 mi. (676 km) long and 30–45 mi. (48–72 km) wide, covering 12,700 sq. mi.,

(32,893 sq. km) and forming part of the border between Tanzania and Zaire; world's longest freshwater lake. **Tan·gan·yi·kan** *adj.* & *n.*

tan·ge·lo (tăn′jelō) *n.* (pl. **-los**). Hybrid between tangerine and grapefruit.

tan·gent (tăn′jent) *adj.* Of (the nature of) a tangent; (of line or surface) touching a line or surface, but not intersecting it. ~ *n.* 1. Straight line tangent to a curve; **fly, go,** etc., **off at a** ~, diverge suddenly from previous course or direction, or from matter in hand. 2. (trig., function of angle in right-angled triangle) Ratio of side opposite given acute angle to side opposite the other (abbrev. tan). 3. Upright piece that strikes string of clavichord. **tan′gen·cy** *n.* **tan·gen′tial** (tănjĕn′shɑl) *adj.* **tan·gen′tial·ly** *adv.* **tan·gen·ti·al·i·ty** (tănjĕnshĕăl′ĭtē) *n.*

tan·ge·rine (tănjerēn′) *n.* Small flattened deep-colored sweet-scented variety of orange from Tangier; deep orange-yellow color of this. ~ *adj.* Of color of tangerine.

tan·gi·ble (tăn′jɪbel) *adj.* That

can be touched, perceptible by touch; real, objective, definite. **tan′gi·ble·ness, tan·gi·bil·i·ty** (tănjɪbĭl′ĭtē) *ns.* **tan′gi·bly** *adv.*

Tan·gier (tănjēr′). Seaport in N. Morocco, NW. Africa, at the SW. end of the Strait of Gibraltar.

tan·gle (tăng′gel) *v.* (**-gled, -gling**). Intertwine, become twisted or involved, in confused mass; entangle; complicate; (colloq.) quarrel, argue, or fight. ~ *n.* Tangled condition or mass. **tan′gler** *n.*

tan·go (tăng′gō) *n.* (pl. **-gos**). Slow dance of central African origin, brought by Africans to Central Amer. and then to Argentina, where it was influenced by European rhythms, fashionable in ballrooms since *c*1910; music for this, in ⁴⁄₄ time. ~ *v.i.* Dance the tango.

tang·y: see TANG.

tank (tăngk) *n.* 1. Large vessel for liquid, gas, etc.; ~ **car,** railroad car with large tank for carrying liquids; ~ **truck,** truck for transporting large amounts of liquids or gases. 2. (mil.) Armored car carrying guns and mounted on

*Although first conceived in the late 19th century, the **tank** as a weapon of war was never seriously produced until Winston Churchill took the responsibility to order some during the 1914–18 war. The term 'tank' was coined as a code name, for security purposes.*

commander's periscopic rotating binocular

gunner's periscopic sights

fighting compartment

covered spotlight

periscopes

passive night sight

multi-barrel smoke discharger

76mm gun

engine

7.62mm machine gun

ammunition

track with rubber pad

aluminium wheel

driver's hatch

driver's periscope

driver's compartment

headlamp

transmission

Tansy oil is distilled from the flowers and leaves of a plant related to the chrysanthemum. It was considered an effective remedy for intestinal worms but is toxic if over-used.

Raw goatskins and tanned oxhides being dried in the sun outside a Cretan tannery. The drying process is essential if raw hides are not to be attacked by insects, nor tanned ones mildewed.

caterpillar tracks, capable of traversing rough ground; ~ **destroyer**, high-speed armored vehicle on which antitank cannons are mounted. 3. (slang) Prison cell. 4. ~ **farm**, area where petroleum is stored in tanks; ~ **farming**, growing plants in tanks of water without soil; ~ **suit**, simple, one-piece swimsuit for women; ~ **top**, shirt similar to undershirt but having wider shoulder straps; ~ **town**, formerly stopping place on railroad where trains refilled their boilers with water; now small or unimportant town. **tank** *v.t.* Store, put, or process in tank; ~ **up**, (colloq.) fill gasoline tank of vehicle; (slang) drink heavily.

tank·age (tăng′kĭj) *n.* 1. (Charge for) storage in tanks; cubic contents of (tanks). 2. Animal residues remaining after rendering fat from slaughterhouse waste, and used as fertilizer or feed.

tank·ard (tăng′kerd) *n.* Large one-handled drinking vessel, esp. of pewter or silver, freq. with lid.

tanked (tăngkt) *adj.* (slang) Drunk.

tank·er (tăng′ker) *n.* Ship, aircraft, or vehicle for carrying oil or other liquid in bulk.

tank·ful (tăngk′fŭl) *n.* (pl. **-fuls**). As much as a tank will hold.

tan·nate (tăn′āt) *n.* Salt of tannic acid.

tan·ner (tăn′er) *n.* One who tans hides.

tan·ner·y (tăn′erē) *n.* (pl. **-ner·ies**). Place where hides are tanned.

Tann·häu·ser (tahn′hoizer). 1. Legendary 13th-c. German minne-

singer. 2. Opera by Richard Wagner, composed 1843–4.

tan·nic (tăn′ĭk) *adj.* ~ **acid**, complex glucoside found esp. in oak galls, also in tea and many other plants.

tan·nin (tăn′ĭn) *n.* Any of a group of substances extracted from oak galls and various barks and having the property of converting hides into leather; also used in medicine, dyeing, etc.

tan·sy (tăn′zē) *n.* (pl. **-sies**). Erect herbaceous plant of genus *Tanacetum*, esp. the strongly aromatic bitter tasting *T. vulgare*, with deeply divided leaves and corymbs of yellow buttonlike flowers. [Gk. *athanasia* immortality]

tan·ta·lite (tăn′talīt) *n.* Rare heavy black mineral, the principal source of tantalum.

tan·ta·lize (tăn′talīz) *v.t.* (**-lized**, **-liz·ing**). Torment, tease, by sight or promise of something desired that is kept out of reach or withheld. **tan·ta·li·za·tion** (tăn·talīzā′shon), **tan′ta·liz·er** *ns.* **tan′·ta·liz·ing** *adj.* **tan′ta·liz·ing·ly** *adv.* [f. TANTALUS]

tan·ta·lum (tăn′talum) *n.* (chem.) Rare metallic element of vanadium group, a very hard ductile grayish-white metal, used commercially in the manufacture of alloys where hardness and resistance to heat and to the action of acids are of importance, and formerly for electric lamp filaments; symbol Ta, at. no. 73, at. wt. 180.9479. **tan·tal·ic** (tăntăl′ĭk) *adj.*

[f. TANTALUS, with ref. to incapacity of tantalum to absorb acids]

Tan·ta·lus (tăn′talus). (Gk. myth.) King of Phrygia, son of Zeus and the nymph Pluto; he served the flesh of his son Pelops to the gods (or committed some other crime variously described) and after his death was condemned to stand in Tartarus, in water that receded when he tried to drink and under branches of fruit that always eluded his grasp.

tan·ta·mount (tăn′tamownt) *adj.* Equivalent *to*, as *the act was tantamount to a declaration of war*.

tan·ta·ra (tăn′tera, tăntăr′a, -tär′a) *n.* Fanfare, flourish, of trumpets etc.

Tan·tra (tŭn′tra) *n.* 1. One of a class of Hindu writings, in Sanskrit, of a mystical and magical nature. 2. One of a group of Buddhist writings of somewhat similar character. **Tan′tric** *adj.* Of the Tantras; ~ **Buddhism**, form of Buddhism, with emphasis on magic, practiced esp. in Tibet. **Tan′trism** *n.* Tantric Buddhism. [Sansk. *tantra* loom, doctrine, manual]

tan·trum (tăn′trum) *n.* Outburst or display of bad temper or petulance.

Tan·za·ni·a (tănzanē′a, -zăn′ēa, -zā′nēa). Republic in E. central Africa, formed in 1964, consisting of Tanganyika and Zanzibar; member of the Brit. Commonwealth; capital, Dar es Salaam. **Tan·za·ni′an** *adj.* & *n.*

Tao·ism (dow′ĭzem, tow′-) *n.* One of the three religions of China, orig. a system of conduct based on writings attributed to the

Left: A young woman carries a tray of corn or maize meal from the mill at Ngala in **Tanzania.** *Despite a substantial export trade, the majority of the people are subsistence gardeners.*

with tap; pierce (cask, tree, etc.) so as to draw off liquid, draw liquid from (any reservoir); draw off (liquid); (surg.) release (fluid accumulated in body), operate thus on (person); (fig.) broach (subject). 2. Furnish (bolt, hole, etc.) with screw thread. 3. Connect electric circuit to (another circuit), esp. as means of intercepting telegraph or telephone message, stealing current etc. **tap′per** *n.*

tap² (tăp) *v.* (**tapped, tap·ping**). 1. Strike lightly; cause (thing) to strike lightly (*against* etc.); strike gentle blow, rap; do tap dancing. 2. Apply metal to (toe or heel of shoe). ~ *n.* 1. Light blow, rap; sound of this; (pl., mil.) signal sounded on drum or bugle for lights out. 2. Piece of leather or metal put on over toe or heel of shoe in shoe repairing. 3. ~ **dance**, dance in which rhythm, esp. in elaborate syncopation, is tapped out with the feet; ~ **dancer, dancing**; ~ **shoes**, shoes with metal plates attached to toes or heels for dancing.

tape (tāp) *n.* 1. Narrow woven strip of cotton etc. used as string for tying garments etc.; piece of tape stretched across race course at finish line. 2. Strip of tape, flexible metal, etc., used as measuring line etc.; paper strip on which messages are printed in tape machine (see below); strip of magnetic material on which sounds etc. are recorded. 3. ~ **deck**, tape recorder without its own amplifier or speaker; ~ **machine**, receiving instrument of recording telegraph system; ~ **measure**, strip of tape or thin flexible metal marked for use as measure; ~ **recorder**, machine for recording and reproducing sounds on magnetic tape; **tape′worm**, any of numerous cestode worms (*Taenia* and allied genera) parasitic in intestines of man and other vertebrates, and having long flat body of numerous propagative segments. **tape** *v.t.* (**taped, tap·ing**). Furnish, measure, join, with tape(s); record on tape.

ta·per (tā′per) *n.* 1. Slender wax candle; long wick coated with wax for lighting lamp etc. 2. Tapering. ~ *v.* (freq. ~ **off**) Make, become, gradually smaller toward one end; (cause to) grow gradually less. **ta′per·ing·ly** *adv.*

tap·es·try (tăp′ĭstrē) *n.* (pl. **-tries**). Thick handwoven fabric, usu. of wool, with a pictorial or ornamental design formed by the warp threads, these being carried

philosopher LAO-TSE and later invested with magical beliefs and a large pantheon. **Tao′ist** *n.* [f. Chin. *Tao tê king* "the way and its power"]

tap¹ (tăp) *n.* 1. Hollow or tubular plug with device for shutting off or controlling flow, through which liquid or gas can be drawn from pipe, cask, etc.; liquor from a particular tap, particular quality or kind of drink; **on** ~, on draft, ready

for immediate use or consumption. 2. Tool in shape of male screw of hard steel, for cutting female screw thread. 3. **tap′room**, room in hotel etc. where liquors are kept on tap; **tap′root**, straight root growing vertically downward, thick at top and tapering to a point; **tap water**, water from a tap, esp. that supplied through system of pipes and taps to house etc. **tap** *v.t.* (**tapped, tap·ping**). 1. Furnish (cask etc.)

Though the male weighs up to 800 lb., the **tapir** *is defenseless and shy. There are three species present in South America and others in south-east Asian countries.*

back and forth across the parts where their respective colors are needed and not from selvage to selvage; wall-hanging of this; embroidered, painted, or machine-woven fabric imitating or resembling tapestry.

ta·pe·tum (tapē'tum) *n.* (pl. **-ta** pr. -*ta*). 1. (zool.) Irregular sector in eyes of certain animals (e.g. cat), which shines owing to absence of black pigment. 2. (bot.) Layer of nutritive tissue, esp. in reproductive organs.

tap·i·o·ca (tăpēō'ka) *n.* Starchy granular foodstuff prepared from cassava and used in puddings, as a thickener, etc. [Braz. *tipioca* juice of cassava (*tipi* dregs, *og*, *ók* squeeze out)]

ta·pir (tā'per, tāpēr') *n.* (pl. **ta·pirs, ta·pir**). Hoofed piglike mammal of genus *Tapirus* of tropical Amer. and Malaya, with short flexible proboscis, related to rhinoceros.

tap·pet (tăp'ĭt) *n.* Arm, collar, cam, etc., used in machinery to impart intermittent motion.

tar[1] (tär) *n.* Thick viscid inflammable black or dark-colored liquid with heavy resinous or bituminous odor, obtained by distillation of wood, coal, or other organic substance, used for coating and preserving timber, cordage, etc., and as a preservative and antiseptic; source (by distillation) of a number of aromatic hydrocarbons and other substances that are starting materials for the manufacture of numerous chemicals and drugs; substances resembling this; **Tar'-heel**, (colloq.) nickname for inhabitant of North Carolina; **tar'-macadam** (tärmăkăd'am), **Tar'-mac**, (trademark) roadmaking material of crushed stone, slag, etc., mixed or covered with tar or other bituminous binder; **tar paper**, tar-coated thick paper as building material; **tar sands**, (geol.) sandstone deposits or sands from which bituminous oil can be recovered. **tar** *v.t.* (**tarred, tar·ring**). Cover, smear, with tar; **beat (whale) the ~ out of**, (colloq.) defeat utterly, enfeeble, weaken; **~ and feather**, smear (person) with tar and cover him with feathers, as punishment or indignity.

tar[2] (tär) *n.* (colloq.) Sailor. [perh. f. TARPAULIN]

ta·ran·tel·la (tărantĕl'a) *n.* Rapid whirling dance of S. Italian peasants; music for this; instrumental composition in rhythm of tarantella, now always in ⅜ time, increasing in speed toward the end.

ta·ran·tu·la (tarăn'chula) *n.* (pl.

A 16th-century representation of Jezebel made a dramatic subject for this **tapestry**. *Tapestries were originally woven or embroidered as wall-hangings, and their popularity has varied.*

-las, -lae pr. -lē). Large black S. European spider of genus *Lycosa*, with slight poisonous bite; any of various other large venomous spiders, esp. large hairy spiders, family Theraphosidae, of warm parts of America. [f. *Taranto* in S. Italy]

Ta·ra·wa (tahrah'wah). Island

atoll in the N. central Gilbert Islands, in the central Pacific Ocean; site of victory by U.S. Marines over Japanese during World War II, November, 1943.

ta·rax·a·cum (tarăk'sakum) *n.* Plant of genus *T~* of weedy composite herbs, including dandelion, with bitter foliage and usu. yellow flowers; drug prepared from dried roots of dandelion (*T. officinale*) and used as tonic and laxative. [Pers. *talkh chakōk* bitter herb]

tar·boosh (tärbōosh') *n.* Man's

brimless (usu. red) felt etc. cap resembling a fez worn alone or as part of a turban by Muslims in certain countries of E. Mediterranean.

tar·dy (tär´dē) *adj.* (**-di·er, -di·est**). Slow-moving, slow, sluggish; late, coming or done late. **tar´di·ly** *adv.* **tar´di·ness** *n.*

tare[1] (tär) *n.* Any of various vetches; vetch seed; (bibl.) a noxious weed.

tare[2] (tär) *n.* (Allowance made for) weight of wrapping, box, conveyance, etc., in which goods are packed; (chem.) weight of vessel in which substance is weighed. ~ *v.t.* (**tared, tar·ing**). Ascertain, allow for, tare of.

tar·get (tär´gĭt) *n.* Mark, esp. with concentric circles around central ring or spot, for shooting at; anything aimed at; disk-shaped railroad signal indicating position of switch.

tar·iff (tăr´ĭf) *n.* 1. List of duties or customs to be paid on imports or exports; such duties collectively; law imposing these; duty on particular class of goods. 2. List or scale of charges at hotel, on railroad, etc. [Arab. *ta'rīf* notification (*'arrafa* notify)]

Tar·mac (tär´măk): see TAR[1].

tarn (tärn) *n.* Small mountain lake.

tar·na·tion (tärnā´shon) *int.* & *n.* (dial. euphemism) Damnation.

tar·nish (tär´nĭsh) *v.* Dull or dim luster of, discolor by oxidation etc.; lose luster; (fig.) sully, taint, stain. ~ *n.* Tarnishing, being tarnished; stain, blemish, tarnished coating.

ta·ro (tăr´ō, tär´ō) *n.* (pl. **-ros**). Either of two plants of the arum family, *Colocasia esculenta* and *C. antiquorum*, cultivated in Pacific islands and other tropical regions for the starchy edible root; the root of these plants.

tar·ot (tăr´ō, tăr´ō´) *n.* Any of a set of playing cards bearing allegorical representations of vices and virtues and elements of nature, used in fortunetelling.

tar·pau·lin (tärpaw´lĭn, tär´pu-) *n.* Canvas made waterproof by coating or impregnating with tar and used as covering, esp. for ship's hatches, boats, etc.; other waterproof cloth used as covering; sailor's tarpaulin or oilskin hat.

tar·pon (tär´pon) *n.* (pl. **-pons**, collect. **-pon**). Large silvery marine game fish (*Tarpon atlanticus*) found in warmer waters of W. Atlantic.

Tar·quin (tär´kwĭn). Name of two semilegendary, perhaps Etruscan, kings of ancient Rome, Tarquinius Priscus and Tarquinius Superbus (~ **the Proud**); when the latter was expelled (510 B.C.), the Republic was founded.

tar·ra·gon (tăr´agŏn, -gon) *n.* Plant (*Artemisia dracunculus*) allied to wormwood, with aromatic leaves used for flavoring salads etc.; ~ **vinegar**, vinegar flavored with oil or leaves of tarragon. [Arab. *tarkhōn*, perh. f. Gk. *drakōn* dragon]

tar·ry[1] (tär´ē) *adj.* (**-ri·er, -ri·est**). Of, like, smeared or impregnated with, tar. **tar´ri·ness** *n.*

tar·ry[2] (tăr´ē) *v.* (**-ried, -ry·ing**). Remain, stay; wait; delay, be late. **tar´ri·er** *n.*

tar·sal (tär´sal) *adj.* Of the TARSUS.

tar·si·er (tär´sēer) *n.* Small nocturnal tree-climbing animal of E. Indies with soft fur and large prominent eyes (esp. *Tarsius spectrum*), a primate related to the lemurs. [L. *tarsus*, from formation of its foot]

Tar·sus (tär´sus). City in SW. corner of Turkey, home of St. Paul.

tar·sus (tär´sus) *n.* (pl. **-si** pr. -sī). 1. (anat.) Ankle, collection of small bones (seven in man) between metatarsus and leg; third segment of bird's leg; (entom.) terminal segment of limb. 2. Tarsal plate, plate of condensed connective tissue stiffening eyelid.

tart[1] (tärt) *n.* 1. Small pie containing fruit or other sweetened filling; open-faced pie of same type. 2. (chiefly Brit. slang) Girl, woman, esp. of loose morals; female prostitute.

tart[2] (tärt) *adj.* Sharp tasting, sour, acid; cutting, biting. **tart´ly** *adv.* **tart´ness** *n.*

tar·tan (tär´tan) *n.* Woolen cloth with stripes of various colors crossing at right angles, esp. in the distinctive plaid of a Highland clan; such pattern; other fabric with similar pattern. ~ *adj.* Made of, checkered like, tartan.

*Nocturnal in behavior and related to the lemurs, the **tarsier** has abnormally large eyes and a very large angle of neck rotation. It lives on insects in the forests of south-east Asian countries.*

Tar·tar (tär´ter) *n.* 1. (also **Tatar**) Member of any of numerous, mostly Muslim and Turkic, tribes inhabiting various parts of European and Asiatic Russian, esp. parts of Siberia, Crimea, and N. Caucasus, districts along Volga, etc.; one of the mingled horde of Mongols, Turks, Tartars, etc., who overran E. Europe under Genghis Khan. 2. (usu. **t** ~) Violent tempered or intractable or savage person. [Pers. *tātār*; altered to tartar by association with TARTARUS]

tar·tar (tär´ter) *n.* 1. Acid potassium tartrate deposited in form of crust in wine casks etc. during fermentation of grape juice; **cream of** ~, purified tartar in form of white crystals, used in cookery; ~ **emetic**, poisonous white crystalline salt, potassium antimonyl tartrate, used in medicine, and in dyeing as mordant. 2. Hard deposit of calcium phosphate from saliva on teeth. **tar´tar·ous** *adj.*

*The genus **Taraxacum** includes the dandelion (left) whose leaves can be used in salads. Other species include one in south-eastern Europe whose latex can be used to make rubber.*

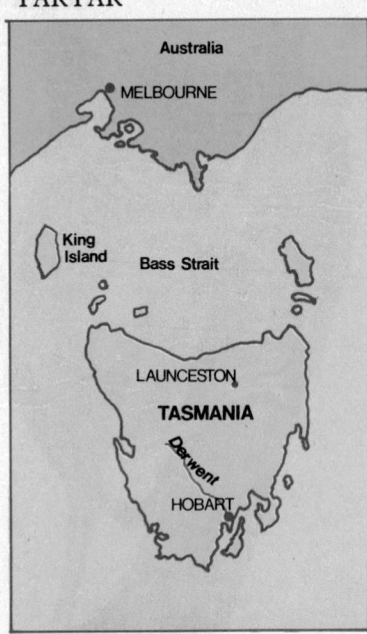

*Separated from the mainland by Bass Strait, **Tasmania** was the second place in Australia to have hydro-electricity. The first aluminum smelter was built on the island, which is also the major producer of orchard fruits.*

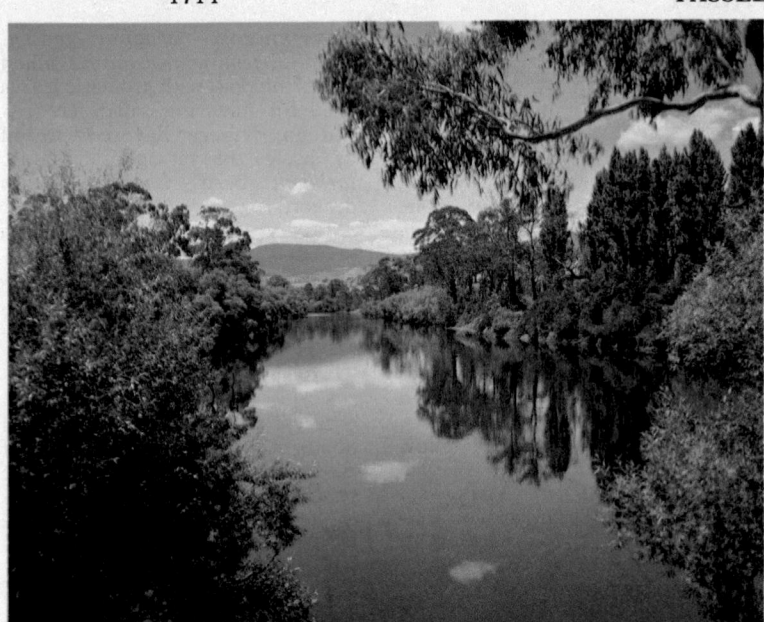

tar·tar, tar·tare (tär´ter) **sauce.** Dressing consisting of mayonnaise with capers, chopped gherkins and herbs, etc., served with fish etc.
tar·tar·ic (tärtăr´ĭk, -tär´-) *adj.* Derived from tartar; ~ **acid**, organic acid present in numerous plants esp. unripe grapes, and used in photography, tanning, manufacture of baking powders and effervescent drinks, etc.
Tar·ta·rus (tär´terus). (Gk. myth.) Infernal regions, or lowest part of them, where the Titans were confined; place of punishment in Hades. **Tar·tar·e·an** (tärtär´ean) *adj.*
tar·trate (tär´trāt) *n.* Salt of tartaric acid.
Ta·shi La·ma (tah´shē lah´ma). Lama second in rank to Dalai Lama; also called Panchen Lama.
task (tăsk, tahsk) *n.* Piece of work imposed or undertaken as a duty etc.; any work that has to be done; **take to** ~, find fault with, rebuke (*for*); ~ **force**, armed force organized for operations under a unified command; similar group organized by government or business to accomplish designated task; **task´master,   task´mistress**, (now usu. fig.) one who sets a task, one who imposes heavy burden or labor. **task** *v.t.* Assign task to; occupy or engage fully, put strain upon.
Tas·ma·ni·a (tăzmā´nēa). State of Australia, consisting of one large and several smaller islands SE. of the continent; discovered 1642 by Abel Janszoon Tasman, Dutch

Tasmanian devil

Tasmanian wolf

*Since Tasmania was cut off from the mainland by rising seas about 10,000 years ago, its fauna evolved in isolation. The thylacine or **Tasmanian 'wolf'** was the largest marsupial carnivore; the 'devil' is smaller but survives.*

navigator; formerly called Van Diemen's Land; capital, Hobart.
Tas·ma·ni·an (tăzmā´nēan) *adj.* Of Tasmania; ~ **devil**, nocturnal carnivorous marsupial (*Sarcophilus harrisii*) of savage appearance, about size of badger, with coarse black hair with white patches; ~ **wolf**, THYLACINE. **Tasmanian** *n.* Native, inhabitant, of Tasmania.
Tass (tăs, tahs). News agency of U.S.S.R. [*T*(elegrafnoye) *A*(gentsvo) *S*(ovyetskovo) *S*(oyuza)]
tas·sel (tăs´el) *n.* Tuft of loosely hanging threads or cords as ornament for cushion, cap, etc.; tassellike head of some plants, esp. staminate inflorescence at top of stalk of corn; ribbon sewn into book to be used as bookmark. ~ *v.*

(**-seled, -sel·ing**). Furnish with tassel; remove tassels of (corn) to strengthen plant; put out tassels. [OF., perh. f. L. *taxillus* small die]

taste (tāst) *v.* (**tast·ed, tast·ing**). Learn flavor of (food etc.) by taking it into the mouth; eat small portion of; experience, have experience *of*; (of food etc.) have specified flavor, have flavor *of*. ~ *n.* 1. Sensation excited in taste buds by contact of some soluble things, flavor; ~ **bud**, one of a number of groups of narrow rod-shaped cells in epithelium of mouth, esp. of tongue. 2. Faculty of perceiving flavor of things by allowing them to touch the tongue. 3. Small portion (*of* food etc.) taken as sample. 4. Liking; predilection *for*; **to one's** ~, in the amount or proportion that gives the desired result. 5. Faculty of discerning and enjoying beauty or other excellence esp. in art and literature; sense of what is harmonious or fitting in art, language, or conduct (**in good** ~, manifesting this faculty; **in bad** ~, showing lack of it).

taste·ful (tāst'ful) *adj.* Having, showing, done in, good taste (TASTE *n.* sense 5). **taste'ful·ly** *adv.* **taste'ful·ness** *n.*

taste·less (tāst'lĭs) *adj.* 1. Flavorless, insipid. 2. Lacking physical sense of taste. 3. Lacking in good taste, or critical discernment and appreciation; not in good taste. **taste'less·ly** *adv.* **taste'less·ness** *n.*

tast·er (tās'ter) *n.* (esp.) 1. Person employed to judge quality of tea, wine, etc., by taste; (hist.) person employed to taste food before it

Tatting is not widely practiced today, but was for hundreds of years a common cottage industry. In France it is known as la frivolite, and in Italy, occhi.

was touched by his employer, esp. to guard against poison. 2. Shallow cup for tasting wines etc.

tast·y (tās'tē) *adj.* (**tast·i·er, tast·i·est**). (colloq.) Savory, appetizing. **tast'i·ly** *adv.* **tast'i·ness** *n.*

TAT *abbrev.* Thematic Apperception Test.

tat (tăt) *v.* (**tat·ted, tat·ting**). Do tatting; make by tatting.

ta·ta·mi (tatah'mē) *n.* (pl. **-mi, -mis**). Japanese standard-sized straw mat, about 3 by 6 ft., used for sitting on; unit of room size in Japan.

Ta·tar (tah'ter) = TARTAR.

tat·ter (tăt'er) *n.* 1. Rag, irregularly torn piece, of cloth, paper, etc. 2. (pl.) Worn, ragged clothing. **tat'tered** *adj.* Reduced to tatters.

tat·ter·de·mal·ion (tăterdĭmāl'yon, -măl'-) *n.* Ragged fellow, ragamuffin.

tat·ter·sall (tăt'ersawl) *n.* Pattern of colored lines forming squares like tartan.

tat·ting (tăt'ĭng) *n.* Kind of notted lace made by hand from thread with small flat shuttle.

tat·tle (tăt'el) *v.i.* (**-tled, -tling**). Gossip idly; inform on wrongdoer; repeat or discuss scandal. ~ *n.* Tattling; gossip. **tat'tler** *n.*

tat·too[1] (tătōo') *n.* (pl. **-toos**). 1. (mil.) Signal by drum or bugle in evening summoning soldiers to quarters; elaboration of this as military entertainment, usu. by torch

*To **tattoo** a man may determine his status in certain societies. This Samoan craftsman has tattooing around his lower torso and more on his legs. Elsewhere, emphasis was on the face.*

or other artificial light, with music, troop exercises, etc. 2. Drumming, rapping; drumbeat. **tattoo** *v.* (**-tooed, -too·ing**). Rap quickly and repeatedly. [Du. *tap-toe*, lit. "close the tap" (of the cask)]

tat·too[2] (tătōo') *v.t.* (**-tooed, -too·ing**). Mark (skin) with permanent pattern or design by puncturing it and inserting pigment; make (design) thus. ~ *n.* Tattooing. **tat·too'er, tat·too'ist** *ns.* [Tahitian *tatau*]

tat·ty (tăt'ē) *adj.* (**-ti·er, -ti·est**). Tattered, shabby; vulgar.

tau (taw, tow) *n.* Letter of Greek alphabet (T, τ), corresponding to *t*; mark or cross (~ **cross**) in shape of this.

taught: see TEACH.

taunt (tawnt, tahnt) *v.t.* Reproach, upbraid, (*with*) insultingly or contemptuously. ~ *n.* Insulting or provoking gibe; scornful reproach. **taunt'er** *n.* **taunt'ing·ly** *adv.*

tau·rine (tōr'īn, -ĭn) *adj.* Of, like, a bull, bovine; of the zodiacal sign Taurus.

tau·rom·a·chy (tawrŏm'akē) *n.* Bullfight(ing).

Tau·rus (tōr'us). The Bull, a constellation; second sign (υ) of the zodiac, which the sun enters about April 21. **Tau·re·an** (tōr'ēan) *adj. & n.*

taut (tawt) *adj.* (of rope etc.) Tightly drawn, not slack; (of ship etc.) trim, neat. **taut'ly** *adv.* **taut'ness** *n.* **taut'en** *v.*

tauto- *prefix.* Same.

tau·tol·o·gy (tawtŏl'ojē) *n.* (pl. **-gies**). 1. Needless repetition of same word or phrase, or of same idea etc., in different words, e.g. *arrived one after the other in succession.* 2. Instance of such repetition. **tau·tol·o·gous** (tawtŏl'ogus), **tau·to·log·i·cal** (tawtolŏj'ĭkal) *adjs.* **tau·to·log'i·cal·ly** *adv.*

tau·tom·er·ism (tawtŏm'erĭzem) *n.* (chem.) Property possessed by some organic compounds of behaving in different reactions as if they possessed two or more different constitutions. **tau·to·mer** (taw'tomer) *n.* Compound having property of tautomerism. **tau·to·mer·ic** (tawtomĕr'ĭk) *adj.*

tav·ern (tăv'ern) *n.* Inn or public house; place where liquor is sold.

taw (taw) *v.t.* Make (hides or skins) into leather by steeping in solution of alum and salt.

taw·dry (taw'drē) *adj.* (**-dri·er, -dri·est**). Showy or gaudy without real value. **taw'dri·ly** *adv.* **taw'dri·ness** *n.* [f. *tawdry lace* sold at *St. Audrey's Fair*, i.e. St. Etheldreda's, in Isle of Ely]

taw·ny (taw'nē) *adj.* (**-ni·er, -ni·est**) & *n.* (Of) brown color with preponderance of yellow or orange. **taw'ni·ness** *n.*

tax (tăks) *n.* Contribution levied

*The art of **taxidermy** is mostly restricted to preparation of fauna for museums. In the past, it was fashionable for big-game hunters to have their trophies mounted and hung at home.*

on person, property, business, or articles of commerce, for the support of the government and for government services; oppressive or burdensome charge etc.; strain, heavy demand *on*; ~ **assessor**, one who assesses taxes or estimates value of property for taxation or insurance purposes; ~ **collector, tax'gatherer**, collector of taxes; **tax-deductible**, (of expenses) that may be paid out of income before deduction of income tax; **tax-exempt**, exempt from taxes, esp. from income taxes; **tax'payer**, one who pays taxes; building meant to pay expenses of a parcel of land until it can be used more profitably; **tax shelter**, any financial investment made for purpose of incurring expenses, depreciation, etc., in order to reduce one's tax obligations. **tax** *v.* 1. Impose tax on, subject to taxation; make demands on, strain, burden. 2. Accuse, charge (*with*); call to account, take to task. **tax'a·ble** *adj.* **tax·a'tion** (tăksā'shon) *n.*

tax·i (tăk'sē) *n.* (pl. **tax·is, tax·ies**). Automobile for hire, esp. one fitted with taximeter; **air** ~, aircraft plying for hire. **taxi** *v.* (**tax·ied, tax·i·ing** or **tax·y·ing**). Go, convey, in taxi; (of aircraft) run along ground or over surface of water before taking off or after alighting.

tax·i·der·my (tăk'sĭdērmē) *n.* Art of preparing and mounting skins of animals with lifelike effect. **tax·i·der·mal** (tăksĭdēr'-mal), **tax·i·der'mic** *adjs.* **tax'i·der·mist** *n.*

tax·i·me·ter (tăk'sēmēter) *n.* Automatic device fitted to taxi indicating fare due.

tax·is (tăk'sĭs) *n.* 1. (biol.) Movement of organism in a particular direction in response to external stimulus (e.g. toward or away from light or heat). 2. (surg.) Manipulative operation to restore displaced part or reduce hernia etc.

tax·on·o·my (tăksŏn'omē) *n.* (biol.) (Laws and principles of) classification. **tax·on'o·mer, tax·on'o·mist** *ns.* **tax·o·nom'ic** (tăksonŏm'ĭk), **tax·o·nom'i·cal** *adjs.* **tax·o·nom'i·cal·ly** *adv.*

Tay·lor (tā'ler), **Zachary** (1784–1850). American soldier; 12th president of U.S., 1849–50.

TB, T.B. *abbrevs.* Tubercle bacillus, hence (colloq.) tuberculosis.

Tb *symbol.* Terbium.

T-bar (tē'bär) **lift.** Ski lift consisting of inverted T-shaped bar against which two skiers may lean as they are pulled uphill.

tbs., tbsp. *abbrevs.* Tablespoon(ful).

Tc *symbol.* Technetium.

Tchai·kov·sky (chīkawf'skē) **Peter Ilyich** (1840–93). Russian composer of ballets including *Swan Lake, Nutcracker*, and symphonies esp. *Fourth Symphony in F Minor, Fifth Symphony in E Minor*, etc.

Tche·khov (chĕk'awf; *Russ.* chĕk'awf): see CHEKHOV.

TD *abbrev.* 1. (also **td, td.**) Touchdown(s). 2. (also **T.D.**) Treasury Department.

Te *symbol.* Tellurium.

tea (tē) *n.* 1. Dried and prepared leaves of the tea plant, classed acc. to their method of manufacture as *green, black,* and *oolong* (the leaves of green tea are rolled and fired immediately, those of black tea are fermented or oxidized before firing, and those of oolong tea are only partially oxidized before firing); drink made by steeping tea leaves in hot water, having slightly

*Nicknamed 'Old Rough and Ready', Zachary **Taylor** (3rd from left) had a distinguished career as a soldier before becoming President, his term was marked by Whig patronage.*

bitter and aromatic flavor and moderately stimulant action, widely used as a beverage; (Brit.) meal at which this is served, esp. light meal in afternoon, or (**high** ~) early evening meal; (slang) marijuana. 2. (also ~ **plant**) Plant from which tea is obtained; shrub (*Thea*) with fragrant white flowers and evergreen lanceolate leaves, cultivated from ancient times in China and Japan and grown also in India, Sri Lanka, etc. 3. Drink made in same way as tea from leaves, blossoms, etc., of other plants, beef extract, fruit preserves,

etc., and freq. used medicinally; (with defining word) plant used for tea, or the beverages prepared from this. 4. ~ **bag**, small permeable bag of tea leaves for steeping; **tea'cup**, cup from which tea is drunk; as measure, about 4 fluid ounces; ~ **dance**, afternoon tea with dancing; **tea gown**, woman's usu. flowing dress worn at tea etc.; **tea'kettle**, kettle with spout and cover for boiling water; **tea leaf** (pl. **leaves**), leaf of tea, esp. (pl. **leaves**), leaf of tea, esp. (pl.) dregs after brewing; **tea plant**: see sense 2; **tea'pot**, vessel with spout in which tea is made; **tea'room**, shop in which tea and other refreshments are served to public; **tea rose**, delicate-scented half-hardy or tender varieties of cultivated rose derived from *Rosa odorata* of

China; **tea set**, set of cups and saucers, plates, etc., for tea; **tea'-spoon**, small spoon used for stirring tea etc.; teaspoonful; **tea'-spoonful**, amount held by tea-spoon, about 1½ fluid drams or ⅓ tablespoonful; **tea'taster**, one whose business is to test quality of tea by tasting samples. [Chin. (Amoy dial.) *t'e*, Mandarin *ch'a*]

teach (tēch) *v.* (**taught** pr. tawt, **teach·ing**). Give (person) instruction or lessons in (a subject); show or make known to person (how to do something); give instruction to, educate; explain, state by way of instruction; be a teacher; ~ **-in** (pl. ~ **-ins**), kind of symposium on subject of topical interest.

teach·a·ble (tē'chabel) *adj.* Apt to learn, docile; (of subject etc.) that can be taught. **teach·a·bil·i·ty** (tēchabĭl'ĭtē), **teach'a·ble·ness** *ns.*

teach·er (tē'cher) *n.* (esp.) One who teaches in a school.

teach·ing (tē'chĭng) *n.* 1. Action or profession of one who teaches. 2. (usu. pl.) What is taught, doctrine; ~ **machine**, mechanical or electronic device that presents the user with educational material in a planned sequence of statements and questions and tells him whether his responses to questions about the material are satisfactory or not.

teak (tēk) *n.* (Yellowish-brown heavy durable oily wood of) large E. Indian tree (*Tectona grandis*) with large egg-shaped leaves and

*A **taximeter** records the distance traveled, the periods spent waiting, and the charges for each function. It is operated by the speedometer cable and a timing device.*

power supply — ratchet and pawl stepping mechanism

read from outside taxi — solenoid switch

tariff selector indicator

electric motor winds clock spring

clock driven wheel

cam

freewheel clutches

solenoid

interchangeable adjustment wheels

read from inside taxi

road driven wheel

swivelling drive

spring driven clock

main fare display — extras (hand set)

speedo cable

trips recorder — tariff selector gearbox — paid mileage recorder — units recorder — extras recorder

cams to change ratios (mechanism not shown)

total mileage recorder

Highlanders picking **tea** near Mount Hagen, Papua New Guinea. Commercial tea-growing began there in the 1960s; within 15 years tea exports exceeded K2 million (about US $1.9 m).

panicles of white flowers; (strong or durable timber of) any of various other trees; also **teak'wood**.

teal (tēl) *n.* 1. Small freshwater duck of *Anas* or other genera, widely distributed in Europe, Asia, and Amer., esp. *A. crecca*. 2. (also **teal blue**) Deep greenish blue.

team (tēm) *n.* 1. Two or more draft animals harnessed together; two or more beasts, or a single beast, with the vehicle they pull. 2. Set of players playing against opposing set in game or sport; set of persons working together; **team'mate**, fellow member of a team; **team spirit**, willingness to act for group rather than individual benefit; **team'work**, combined effort, organized cooperation. **team** *v.* Harness in team; convey, transport, with team; (also ∼ **up**) join, put together in a team (*with*).

team·ster (tēm'ster) *n.* Driver of a team of horses or of a truck used for hauling.

Tea·pot (tē'pŏt) **Dome.** Oil producing region in Wyoming that was designated a naval oil reserve in 1915; associated with scandal, 1922, when Secretary of the Interior Albert B. Fall was found to have leased the lands to private oil concerns from whom he received bribes.

tear[1] (tēr) *n.* 1. Drop of limpid saline fluid secreted by lachrymal gland appearing in or flowing from eye, as result of emotion, esp. grief, or of physical irritation, nervous stimulus, etc.; (pl.) weeping, sorrow, grief. 2. Something resembling a tear, esp. various gums exuding from plants in tear-shaped or globular beads, defect in glass caused by particle of vitrified clay etc. 3. ∼ **gas**, lachrymatory vapor used to disable opponents; ∼-**jerker**, (colloq.) song, story, film, etc., calculated to evoke sadness or sympathy. **tear'ful** *adj.* Shedding tears; mournful, sad. **tear'ful·ly** *adv.* **tear'ful·ness** *n.* **tear'less** *adj.* **tear'less·ly** *adv.* **tear'less·ness** *n.*

tear[2] (tār) *v.* (**tore** pr. tōr, tôr, **torn** pr. tōrn, tôrn, **tear·ing**). 1. Pull apart, away, or asunder, by force; rend, lacerate; make a tear or rent; (of thing) lend itself to tearing. 2. Move violently or impetuously, rush. 3. ∼ **at**, attempt to tear or remove by violent plucking or pulling motions. ∼ **down**, demolish or destroy (house etc.); take apart or dismantle; cause to go to pieces; discredit or disprove (argument etc.) point by point; ∼ **into**, (colloq.) attack violently and,

Japanned enamel metalware **tea urn** made in Pontypool, Wales, U.K., an ironworking center from the 16th century. By the 1700s its craftsmen were decorating sheet iron to resemble lacquerwork.

An ornately decorated **teapot** made in China about 1680 specifically for export to Europe. Each of its six sides is decorated with classical scenes while the spout is imitation bamboo.

often, destructively; attack with words, scold; ~ **off**, (colloq.) do or produce quickly and easily; ~ **up**, tear into small pieces, shred. **tear** *n.* Damage caused by tearing; torn part or place in cloth etc. **tear'-a·ble** *adj.* **tear'er** *n.*

tear·ing (tār'ĭng) *adj.* (esp.) Violent, overwhelming.

tear·y (tēr'ē) *adj.* (**tear·i·er, tear·i·est**). 1. Of or like tears. 2. Tearful; crying. **tear'i·ly** *adv.*

tease (tēz) *v.t.* (**teased, teas·ing**). 1. Pull asunder fibers of, comb, card (wool, flax, etc.); raise surface of (cloth etc.) into nap with teasels etc. 2. Ruffle (hair) by combing toward the scalp. 3. Assail playfully or maliciously, vex, irritate, with jests, questions, or petty annoyances. ~ *n.* Person addicted to teasing.

tea·sel, tea·zel, tea·zle (tē'zel) *ns.* Plant of genus *Dipsacus*, herbs with prickly leaves and flower heads, esp. *D. fullonum*, **fuller's ~**, heads of which have hooked prickles between flowers; dried prickly flower head of fuller's teasel used for teasing cloth etc. so as to raise nap on surface; contrivance used as substitute for this.

teas·er (tē'zer) *n.* (colloq.) Difficult question, problem, or task, thing hard to deal with; a tease.

teat (tēt, tĭt) *n.* Nipple, small protuberance at tip of breast in female mammals, upon which ducts of mammary gland open and from which milk is sucked by young; artificial structure resembling this, esp. contrivance of rubber etc.

Tectonic geology is concerned with the structure of the earth. The theory of plate tectonics, derived from that of continental drift, assumes that the plates of the crust are still moving.

through which milk is sucked from bottle.

teaze (tēz) **tenon.** (carpentry) Steplike tenon on top of a post supporting 2 horizontal pieces of wood that meet each other at right angles.

tea·zle = TEASEL.

tech·ne·ti·um (tĕknē'shēum) *n.* (chem.) Radioactive metallic element not found in nature, the first otherwise unknown element to be produced artificially (1937); symbol Tc, at. no. 43, at. wt. 98.9062. [Gk. *tekhnētos* artificial]

tech·nic (tĕk'nĭk, sometimes tĕknēk') *n.* Technical term or detail, technicality; (pl. rare) technique; (usu. pl.) technology.

tech·ni·cal (tĕk'nĭkal) *adj.* 1. Of or (used) in a particular art, science, profession, handicraft, etc. 2. Of, for, in, the mechanical arts and applied science generally. 3. Regarded in specified way according to a strict interpretation of law or rule(s); ~ **knockout**, referee's termination of prize fight on grounds of boxer's inability to continue, his opponent being declared winner. **tech'ni·cal·ly** *adv.* **tech'ni·cal·ness** *n.* **tech·ni·cal·i·ty** (tĕknĭkăl'ĭtē) *n.* (pl. **-ties**). Technical quality or character; technical point, detail, term, etc.

tech·ni·cal (tĕk'nĭkal) **sergeant.** (U.S. Air Force) Enlisted man of second grade, ranking just below master sergeant and above staff sergeant.

tech·ni·cian (tĕknĭsh'an) *n.* Person skilled in the technique of an art or subject; person expert in the practical application of science.

Tech·ni·col·or (tĕk'nĭkŭler) *n.* (trademark) (cinemat.) Process of color photography in which the colors are separately but simul-

taneously recorded and then transferred to a single positive print.

tech·nique (tĕknēk') *n.* Manner of execution or performance in painting, music, etc.; mechanical part of an art, craft, etc.; (loosely) method of achieving one's purpose.

tech·noc·ra·cy (tĕknŏk'rasē) *n.* (pl. **-cies**). Government or control of society by technical experts. **tech·no·crat** (tĕk'nokrăt) *n.* **tech·no·crat·ic** (tĕknokrăt'ĭk) *adj.*

tech·nol·o·gy (tĕknŏl'ojē) *n.* Scientific study of practical or industrial arts; practical arts collectively; terminology of particular art or subject. **tech·no·log·i·cal** (tĕknolŏj'ĭkal) *adj.* **tech·no·log'i·cal·ly** *adv.* **tech·nol'o·gist** *n.*

tec·ton·ic (tĕktŏn'ĭk) *adj.* Of building or construction; ~ **geology**, that part of geology that deals with deformation of Earth's crust or structural changes caused thereby. **tec·ton'ics** *n.pl.* (usu. considered sing.). 1. Art of producing useful and beautiful buildings, furniture, vessels, etc. 2. (geol.) Structural features as a whole.

tec·trix (tĕk'trĭks) *n.* (pl. **tec·tri·ces** pr. tĕk'trīsēz, tĕktrī'-). (ornith.) = COVERT[1] sense 2.

ted (tĕd) *v.t.* (**ted·ded, ted·ding**). Turn over and spread out (grass, hay) to dry. **ted'der** *n.* Machine for drying hay.

ted·dy (tĕd'ē) **bear.** Child's toy bear. [named after *Theodore* Roosevelt]

Te De·um (tā dā'um; *Brit.* tē dē'um). Ancient Latin hymn of praise beginning *Te Deum laudamus* "We praise thee, O God," sung (usu. in English) at matins in R.C. Ch. and Church of England, and as thanksgiving on special occasions; musical setting of this.

Diverging margins
Converging margins

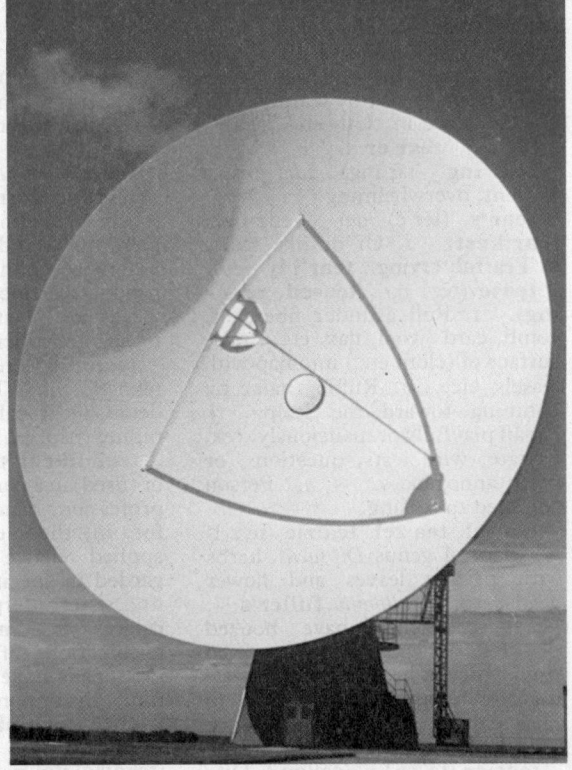

te·di·ous (tē′dēus) *adj.* Tiresomely long, prolix, irksome. **te′di·ous·ly** *adv.* **te′di·ous·ness** *n.*

te·di·um (tē′dēum) *n.* Weariness produced by tediousness, tedious circumstances.

tee¹ (tē) *n.* (pl. **tees**). Letter T; T-shaped thing or part; **~ -shirt, ~ square** = T shirt, T square.

tee² (tē) *n.* (pl. **tees**). (golf) Small mound of sand on which golfer places the ball for driving off at the start and after each hole; small piece of plastic, wood, etc., for the same purpose; (football) similar device for kickoff; place from which the ball is played at the beginning of play for each hole. ~ *v.* (**teed, tee·ing**). Place (ball) on tee; **~ off,** play ball from tee.

teem¹ (tēm) *v.i.* Be prolific, be stocked to overflowing *with,* be abundant.

teem² (tēm) *v.t.* Empty, discharge, pour out (contents of vessel, cart, coal, molten metal, etc.).

teem·ing (tē′mĭng) *adj.* Overflowing or swarming *with.*

teen (tēn) *n.* 1. (pl.) Years of one's age or of century from 13 through 19. 2. Teenager. ~ *adj.* Teenage.

teen·age, teen-age (tēn′āj) *adjs.* In the teens; of or for teenagers. **teen′ag·er** *n.* Person in the teens.

tee·ny (tē′nē) (**-ni·er, -ni·est**), **teen·sy** (tēn′sē) (**-si·er, -si·est**), **tee·ny-wee·ny** (tē′nē wē′nē), **teen·sy-ween·sy** (tēn′sē wēn′sē) *adjs.* (colloq.) Tiny.

Telecommunication techniques have made possible remarkable improvements since the early 1960s. Above left, Papua New Guinea Highlanders can be connected by telephone to anywhere in the world via satellite links such as that at Ceduna, Australia (above right).

tee·ter (tē′ter) *v.* Move like a seesaw; move unsteadily. **tee′ter·board** *n.* Seesaw.

teeth (tēth) *n.* Pl. of TOOTH.

teethe (tēdh) *v.i.* (**teethed, teeth·ing**). Grow or cut teeth. **teeth′ing** *n.* (esp.) ~ **ring,** ring of bone, plastic, etc., for teething infant to bite on.

tee·to·tal (tētō′tal) *adj.* Of, advocating, total abstinence from intoxicants. **tee·to′tal·ism** *n.* **tee·to′tal·ly** *adv.* **tee·to′tal·er** (tētō′taler, tē′tō-) *n.* Total abstainer. [reduplicated form of *total*]

Tef·lon (tĕf′lŏn) *n.* (trademark) Waxlike, tough plastic (polytetrafluorethylene) used for various commercial and industrial purposes.

Te·gu·ci·gal·pa (tĕgōō′sēgahl-pa). Capital of Honduras, in the S. central part, in Central America.

teg·u·ment (tĕg′yument) *n.* Natural covering of (part of) animal body. **teg·u·men·tal** (tĕgyumĕn′tal), **teg·u·men′ta·ry** *adjs.*

Teh·ran, Te·he·ran (tĕrahn′, -răn′, tā-). Capital city of Iran.

tek·non·y·my (tĕknŏn′imē) *n.* Practice of some primitive peoples of naming the parent from the child.

tek·tite (tĕk′tīt) *n.* (geol.) Rounded glassy body of unknown

origin, found in various parts of the world.

tel·aes·the·sia = TELESTHESIA.

tel·a·mon (tĕl′amŏn) *n.* (pl. **tel·a·mo·nes** pr. tĕlamō′nēz). (archit.) Male figure supporting an entablature (cf. CARYATID). [L. f. Gk. *Telamōn* myth. person]

tele- *comb. form.* Far; (esp.) in names of instruments, producing or recording results etc. at a distance; of, for, television.

tel·e·cast (tĕl′ekăst, -kahst) *n.* Program or item broadcast by television. ~ *v.* (**-cast** or **-casted, -cast·ing**). Broadcast by television. **tel′e·cast·er** *n.*

tel·e·com·mu·ni·ca·tion (tĕlekomūnikā′shon) *n.* Communication at a distance by telegraph, telephone, radio, etc.; (freq. pl.) science of this.

tel·e·gen·ic (tĕlejĕn′ĭk) *adj.* (of a person) Suitable by virtue of physical attractiveness for being televised.

tel·e·gram (tĕl′egrăm) *n.* Message sent by telegraph.

tel·e·graph (tĕl′egrăf, -grahf) *n.* Instantaneous conveyance of messages to any distance by means of two instruments so connected by electricity that the working of one excites movements in the other, representing letters etc. acc. to some arranged code; apparatus needed for this; semaphore, signaling apparatus; ~ **key,** device for making and breaking the electric circuit of a telegraph; ~ **line,** telegraphic connection; ~ **plant,** East Indian plant of the bean family whose leaves have spontaneous jerking motion. **telegraph** *v.* Send (message *to* person, or abs.) by telegraph; make signals, convey by signals. **te·leg·ra·pher** (telĕg´ra-fer) *n.*

tel·e·graph·ese (tĕl´egrăfēz, -fēs, tĕlegrăfēz´, -fēs´) *n.* Elliptical style used in telegrams.

tel·e·graph·ic (tĕlegrăf´ĭk) *adj.* Of, by, for, the telegraph; (of style) economically worded, with unessential words omitted. **tel·e·graph´i·cal·ly** *adv.*

te·leg·ra·phy (telĕg´rafē) *n.* Art of constructing, practice of communicating by, telegraph; **wireless** ~, transmission of signals through space by means of electromagnetic waves.

tel·e·ki·ne·sis (tĕlekĭnē´sĭs) *n.* Movement at a distance from the motive cause or agent without material connection, esp. as a spiritualistic phenomenon. **tel·e·ki·net·ic** (tĕlekĭnĕt´ĭk) *adj.*

Te·lem·a·chus (telĕm´akus). In the *Odyssey*, son of Odysseus and Penelope.

tel·e·mark (tĕl´emärk) *n.* Swing turn in skiing used to change direction or to stop short. [f. *Telemark*, district in Norway]

te·lem·e·ter (telĕm´eter, tĕl´emē-) *v.t.* Register (temperature, pressure or other phenomena) at a distant meter, usu. by means of radio devices. ~ *n.* Instrument for this. **te·lem´e·try** *n.*

tel·e·ol·o·gy (tĕlēŏl´ojē, tēlē-) *n.* Doctrine of final causes, view that developments are due to the purpose of design that is served by them. **tel·e·o·log·ic** (tĕlēolŏj´ĭk,

tēlē-), **te·le·o·log´i·cal** *adjs.* **tel·e·o·log´i·cal·ly** *adv.* **tel·e·ol´o·gism, tel·e·ol´o·gist** *ns.*

te·lep·a·thy (telĕp´athē) *n.* Communication of impressions from one mind to another without the aid of the known senses. **tel·e·path·ic** (tĕlepăth´ĭk) *adj.* **tel·e·path´i·cal·ly** *adv.* **te·lep´a·thist** *n.*

tel·e·phone (tĕl´efōn) *n.* Instrument for converting the vibrations caused by sound, esp. those of the voice, into an electric current that passes along a wire and is reconverted into sound at the other end; system of communication by a network of telephones; ~ **exchange**: see EXCHANGE. **tel·e·phon·ic** (tĕlefŏn´ĭk) *adj.* **tel·e·phon´i·cal·ly** *adv.* **telephone** *v.* (-**phoned**, -**phon·ing**). Send (message), speak (*to* person), by telephone.

te·leph·o·ny (telĕf´onē) *n.* Art or science of constructing telephones; the working of a telephone or telephones.

tel·e·pho·to (tĕl´efōtō, tĕlefō´tō) *adj.* Telephotographic; ~ **lens**, lens or combination of lenses for photographing distant objects.

tel·e·pho·tog·ra·phy (tĕlefo-tŏg´rafē) *n.* Photography of objects at a distance by means of a telephoto lens. **tel·e·pho·to·graph·ic** (tĕlefōtogrăf´ĭk) *adj.*

tel·e·print·er (tĕl´eprĭnter) *n.* Telegraphically operated kind of

*The design and construction of a modern **telephoto lens** is complex and calls for extreme accuracy in lens grinding and matching, and in the manufacture of the metal components, so that absolutely accurate focus can be obtained. Results revolutionized photography.*

typewriter.

Tel·e·promp·ter (tĕl´eprŏmp-ter) *n.* (trademark) Electronic device for prompting television speaker by slowly unrolling his text in large letters out of sight of the audience.

tel·e·scope (tĕl´eskōp) *n.* I. Optical instrument for making distant objects appear nearer and larger, consisting of one or more tubes with an arrangement of lenses, or of one or more mirrors and lenses, by which the rays of light are collected and brought to a focus and the resulting image magnified; **reflecting** ~, one in which the image is reproduced by a mirror; **refracting** ~, one in which the image is reproduced by a lens (the object glass). 2. **radio** ~, directional aerial system for collecting radio energy from different parts of the sky as an optical telescope collects light from different stars, either steerable or fixed and directed by Earth's rotation to successive points in the sky. **telescope** *v.* (-**scoped**, -**scoping**). Force or drive one into another like the sliding tubes of a hand telescope; close, slide together, in this manner; be forced one into the other (esp. of colliding railroad trains).

tel·e·scop·ic (tĕleskŏp´ĭk) *adj.* Of, made with, a telescope; visible only through a telescope, as ~ **star**; consisting of sections that telescope. **tel·e·scop´i·cal·ly** *adv.*

te·les·co·pist (telĕs´kopĭst) *n.* User of telescope.

te·les·co·py (telĕs´kopē) *n.* Use and making of telescopes.

tel·es·the·si·a, tel·aes·the·sia (tĕlĭsthē´zha, -zhēa, -zēa) *ns.*

focus distances (metres/feet)   focusing ring

phragm setting ring

of field scale

helical focusing

iris diaphragm

sliding lens hood

light baffles

rear lens group 3 elements/2 groups

front lens group 3 elements/3 groups

astronomical telescopes

object glass

refracting

telescope tube

flat mirror

parabolic concave mirror

declination axis

Newtonian reflecting

Huyghenian eyepiece

polar axis

Ramsden eyepiece

Schmidt photographic

Orthoscopic eyepiece

convex mirror

equatorial
mounting

modified Schmidt giving
flat focal surface

62ft. aerial mast

250ft. reflector
(sheet steel bowl)

railway tracks

radio telescope
(Jodrell Bank)

*The first **telescope** was made by Hans Lippershey in Holland in 1608. In 1668, Newton invented a reflecting telescope (top right) to overcome blurred images. Optical developments are shown (top left) while radio telescopes (lower left and right) are now used to supplement optical work and to locate signals from bodies without light sources.*

(psychol.) Perception of distant occurrences or objects otherwise than by means of the recognized physical senses. **tel·es·thet'ic** *adj.*

tel·e·type·writ·er (tĕletīp′rīter, tĕl′etīp-) *n.* Telegraph instrument for transmitting and receiving messages by typing.

tel·e·view (tĕl′evū) *v.i.* View with a television receiver.

tel·e·vise (tĕl′evīz) *v.t.* (**-vised, -vis·ing**). Transmit by television.

tel·e·vi·sion (tĕl′evĭzhon) *n.* Simultaneous visual reproduction of scenes, objects, performances, etc., at a distance by means of a camera that converts the image into electrical impulses that are transmitted by radio to a receiver, which converts them by means of a CATHODE ray tube into a corresponding image on a screen; apparatus for reception of televised images (also ~ **set**); televised program(s) or matter. **tel·e·vi·sor** *n.* Transmitting apparatus for television. **tel·e·vi·sion·al** (tĕlevĭzh′onal) *adj.* **tel·e·vi·sion·al·ly** *adv.* **tel·e·vi·sion·ar·y** *adj.*

Tel·ex (tĕl′eks) *n.* (trademark) System of telegraphy in which printed messages are exchanged by teleprinters connected to the public telecommunication network; **t~,**
message so sent.

tell[1] (tĕl) *v.* (**told** pr. tōld, **tell·ing**). Relate or narrate; make known, divulge, state, express in words; inform or give information *of, about, how,* etc.; betray secret, inform against (person); ascertain, decide about, distinguish; produce marked effect on; count (votes, esp. in legislature); ~ **one's beads,** use rosary; ~ **person's fortune,** forecast his future by occult means; ~ **off,** number (party etc.), pick out (specified number of persons, person) *for* task or *to* do; (colloq.) scold, reprimand; ~ **on,** inform against; ~ **tales,** reveal another's

*The **telex** system evolved from an invention about 1900 and it allows typed messages to be received and recorded, from all over the world, even when the office is not staffed.*

private affairs, misconduct, etc.; tell falsehoods. **tell′a·ble** *adj.*

tell[2] (tĕl) *n.* Artificial mound found esp. in Near and Middle Eastern countries, consisting of accumulated remains of ancient settlements.

tell·er (tĕl′er) *n.* (esp.) Person appointed to count votes in a legislature; person appointed to receive or pay out money in bank etc.

tell·ing (tĕl′ĭng) *adj.* (esp.) Producing marked effect. **tell′-ing·ly** *adv.*

tell·tale (tĕl′tāl) *n.* 1. Person who tells about another's private affairs; (fig.) thing, circumstance, that reveals person's thoughts, conduct, etc., esp. attrib., as ~ *blush, stain.* 2. Kind of automatic registering device; (naut.) index near wheel to show position of the tiller.

tel·lu·rate (tĕl′yurāt) *n.* Salt of telluric acid.

tel·lu·ri·an (teloor′ēan) *adj. & n.* (Inhabitant) of Earth.

tel·lu·ric[1] (teloor′ĭk) *adj.* Of earth; obtained from earth or soil.

tel·lu·ric[2] (teloor′ĭk) *adj.* Of, derived from, TELLURIUM.

tel·lu·ri·um (teloor′ēum) *n.* (chem.) Rare, brittle, lustrous, silver-colored element, formerly classed among the metals, but chemically belonging to the same family as sulfur and selenium; symbol Te, at. no. 52, at. wt. 127.60.

tel·lu·rous (tĕl′yurus, teloor′-) *adj.* Of, containing, tellurium, esp. of compounds containing a greater proportion of tellurium than those called *telluric.*

Tel·lus (tĕl′us). (Rom. myth.) Goddess of the Earth; Earth personified, the planet Earth.

tel·son (tĕl′son) *n.* Posterior abdominal region of some crustaceans and other arthropods.

Tel·u·gu (tĕl′ugōō) *adj. & n.* (pl. **-gus,** collect. **-gu**). (Language, member) of Dravidian people in Coromandel coast region of India, N. of Madras.

tem·er·ar·i·ous (tĕmerār′ēus) *adj.* (literary) Rash, reckless. **tem·er·ar′i·ous·ly** *adv.*

te·mer·i·ty (temĕr′ĭtē) *n.* Rashness, audacity.

tem·per (tĕm′per) *v.* Bring (clay etc.) to the desired consistency by moistening and kneading; toughen and harden (metal, esp. steel, glass) by heating, sudden cooling, and reheating; (of metal etc.) come to proper hardness and elasticity by this means; modify, mitigate (*justice* etc.) by blending

***Televisions** line the benches of this assembly plant in Singapore; most of the components are designed and built elsewhere and only come together in the final assembly.*

with (*mercy* etc.). ~ *n.* 1. Consistency of clay etc. obtained by tempering; degree of hardness and elasticity in steel etc. produced by tempering. 2. Habitual or temporary disposition of mind; fit of anger; composure under provocation.

tem·per·a (tĕm′pera, -pra) *n.* Painting with colors that have been mixed with a natural emulsion (e.g. egg yolk) or an artificial emulsion (e.g. oil and gum), esp. the method used for movable pictures before the development of oil painting.

tem·per·a·ment (tĕm′pera-ment, -pra-) *n.* Characteristic combination of physical, mental, and moral qualities that together constitute the character of an individual and affect the person's manner of

acting, feeling, and thinking; (also **artistic, musical** ~) emotional character of artist or musician.

tem·per·a·men·tal (tĕmpera-mĕn′tal, -pra-) *adj.* Of, relating to, the temperament; liable to, marked by, variable or unaccountable moods. **tem·per·a·men′tal·ly** *adv.*

tem·per·ance (tĕm′perans, -prans) *n.* Moderation, self-restraint, in speech, conduct, etc., esp. in eating and drinking; moderation in use of, total abstinence from, alcoholic liquors as beverages; (attrib.) nonalcoholic, aimed at the restriction or prohibition of alcoholic drinks, as in ~ **league, movement.**

tem·per·ate (tĕm′perĭt, -prĭt) *adj.* Moderate, self-restrained; abstemious; (of climate) not exhibiting extremes of heat or cold, equable; ~ **zone,** zone between either tropic and the corresponding polar circle. **tem′per·ate·ly** *adv.* **tem′per·ate·ness** *n.*

tem·per·a·ture (těm′peracher, -pra-) *n.* Degree or intensity of sensible heat of a body or of the atmosphere, esp. as shown by the thermometer; (med.) internal heat of the body in man, normally 98.6° F (37° C); (colloq.) body temperature above normal, fever; **take person's** ~, ascertain his internal heat with a clinical thermometer to detect any variation from the normal state of health; ~ **chart**, one showing a temperature curve; ~ **curve**, curve showing variations of temperature, esp. in clinical use.

Temperature (těm′peracher, -pra-) **-Humidity Index.** Quantity giving measure of discomfort due to combined effects of temperature and humidity of air.

tem·pest (těm′pĭst) *n.* Violent storm; (fig.) violent tumult or agitation; ~ **in a teapot**, great excitement over trivial matter.

tem·pes·tu·ous (těmpěs′-cho͞ous) *adj.* (of weather, time, etc., and fig. of person or mood) Stormy, violent. **tem·pes′-tu·ous·ly** *adv.* **tem·pes′tu·ous·ness** *n.*

tem·plate, tem·plet (těm′plĭt) *ns.* Pattern, gauge, usu. thin board or metal plate, used as a guide in cutting or drilling metal, stone, wood, etc.; timber or plate used to distribute weight in a wall or under a beam etc.; wedge for building block under ship's keel.

tem·ple[1] (těm′pel) *n.* Edifice dedicated to service of (esp. ancient Gk., Rom., Egyptian) god; any of the three successive religious edifices of the Jews in Jerusalem; place of Christian public worship, esp. Protestant church in France; (fig.) place in which God resides.

tem·ple[2] (těm′pel) *n.* Flat part of either side of the head between the forehead and the ear.

tem·ple[3] (těm′pel) *n.* Device for keeping cloth taut on a loom.

tem·plet (těm′plĭt) = TEMPLATE.

tem·po (těm′pō) *n.* (pl. **-pos, -pi** pr. -pē). (mus.) Speed at which a passage is (to be) played; (transf.) rate of movement, activity, or progress.

tem·po·ral (těm′peral, -pral) *adj.* 1. Of, in, denoting, time; (gram.) pertaining to time or tense. 2. Of this life only, secular, lay (opp. *spiritual*). 3. (anat.) Of the temples; ~ **bone**, compound bone of the side of the human skull; ~ **lobe**, lobe on each side of cerebral hemisphere. **tem′po·ral·ly** *adv.* **tem′po·ral·ness** *n.* **temporal** *n.* Temporal bone.

tem·po·ral·i·ty (těmperǎl′ĭtē) *n.* (pl. **-ties**). Secular possessions, esp. properties and revenues of a religious body or an ecclesiastic (usu. pl.); (law) temporariness.

tem·po·rar·y (těm′perěrē) *adj.* Lasting only for a time, transient; held, occupied, during a limited

Before the development of oil painting, tempera, having egg yolk as a medium for the pigments, was used by artists such as Domenico Veneziano who painted 'A Miracle of St. Zenobus'.

time only, not permanent; ~ **duty**, duty for limited period with organization to which one is not regularly assigned or attached. **tem·po·rar·i·ly** (těmperār′ĭlē, těm′-perěr-) *adv.* **tem′po·rar·i·ness** *n.* **temporary** *n.* (pl. **-rar·ies**).

tem·po·rize (těm′perīz) *v.i.* (**-rized, -riz·ing**). Pursue indecisive or time-serving policy; avoid committing oneself, act so as to gain time; comply temporarily with requirements of an occasion. **tem·po·ri·za·tion** (těmperĭzā′-shon), **tem′po·riz·er** *ns.*

tempt (těmpt) *v.t.* Entice, incite; attract; (archaic) test or try the resolution of.

temp·ta·tion (těmptā′shon) *n.* Tempting or being tempted; thing that attracts, attractive course.

tempt·er (těmp′ter), fem. **tempt·ress** (těmp′trĭs) *ns.* One who tempts (chiefly in bad sense).

tempt·ing (těmp′tĭng) *adj.* Attractive, inviting. **tempt′ing·ly** *adv.*

ten (těn) *adj.* Amounting to 10; **Ten Commandments**: see COMMANDMENT; **ten-gallon hat**, cowboy's large broad-brimmed hat; **ten′penny**, designating 3-in.-long nail; **ten′pin**, pin used in **ten′pins**, game similar to ninepins, played with ten pins; **ten-spot**, (slang) playing card having ten spots; ten-dollar bill; **ten-strike**, (bowling) = STRIKE *n.* sense 2; (colloq.) wholly successful action. **ten** *n.* One more than 9; symbol for this (10, x, or X); card with ten spots; ten o'clock; size etc. indicated by 10; set of ten things or persons. **ten·fold** (těn′fōld) *adj. & adv.*

ten·a·ble (těn′abel) *adj.* Capable of being maintained or defended against attack or objection; (of office etc.) that can be held *for* a specified time, *by* person, etc. **ten·a·bil·i·ty** (těnabĭl′ĭtē), **ten′-a·ble·ness** *ns.* **ten′a·bly** *adv.*

te·na·cious (tenā′shus) *adj.* Holding fast; keeping firm hold (of property, rights, principles, etc.); (of memory) retentive; adhesive, sticky; strongly cohesive. **te·na′-cious·ly** *adv.* **te·na′cious·ness, te·nac·i·ty** (tenǎs′ĭtē) *ns.*

te·nac·u·lum (tenǎk′yulum) *n.* (pl. **-la** pr. -la). Surgeon's sharp hook used for seizing and holding arteries etc.

ten·an·cy (těn′ansē) *n.* (pl. **-cies**). Act of holding position or property as a tenant; period of such holding; property, land etc., held by a tenant.

ten·ant (těn′ant) *n.* (law) Person holding real property by private ownership; person who occupies land or tenement under a landlord; inhabitant, dweller; ~ **farmer**, one who cultivates farm he does not own. **tenant** *v.t.* Occupy as tenant (esp. in past part.). **ten′-**

Diagram of temples

entablature — pediment — acroterion

antefix
peristyle

reconstruction and plan of the Parthenon

cella or naos

column

portico

inner cella   pronaos

stylobate

distyle in antis

prostyle

amphiprostyle

plans and elevations of temples

tetrastyle   hexastyle   heptastyle

octastyle   decastyle

dipteral   peripteral   pseudo-peripteral

---

ant·less, ten′ant·like *adjs.*

ten·ant·a·ble (těn′antabel) *adj.* Fit to be occupied by a tenant.

tend[1] (těnd) *v.i.* Move, be directed, in a certain direction; be apt or inclined, serve, conduce (*to* action, quality, etc., *to* do).

tend[2] (těnd) *v.* Take care of, look after (flocks, invalid, machine, etc.); wait *upon*; (naut.) watch (ship at anchor) so as to keep turns out of her cable.

tend·en·cy (těn′densē) *n.* (pl. -cies). Bent, leaning, inclination (*toward*, *to*, thing, *to* do).

ten·den·tious, ten·den·cious (těnděn′shus) *adjs.* (of writing etc.) Having an underlying purpose, calculated to advance a cause. ten·den′tious·ly *adv.* ten·den′-tious·ness *n.*

ten·der[1] (těn′der) *n.* (esp.) 1. Small ship in attendance upon a larger one to supply her with stores, convey orders, etc. 2. Car attached to a steam locomotive and carrying fuel, water, etc. [f. TEND[2]]

ten·der[2] (těn′der) *v.* Offer, present, give in (*one's services*, *resignation*, etc.); offer (money etc.) as payment; make a tender (*for* supply of thing or execution of work). ~ *n.* Offer, esp. offer in writing to execute work or supply goods at a fixed price; legal ~, currency recognized by law as acceptable in payment of a debt.

Above: Various designs of temple built by the Greeks. An image of the deity worshipped was housed in the cella (or naos) but the altar was often located outside. The Romans also built temples with a circular plan such as the Tempio Rotondo in Rome (right).

ten′der·a·ble *adj.* ten′der·er *n.*

ten·der[3] (těn′der) *adj.* Soft, not tough or hard; easily touched or wounded, susceptible to pain or grief; delicate, fragile, (lit. and fig., of reputation etc.); loving, affectionate, fond; solicitous, considerate; requiring careful handling, ticklish; ten′derfoot (pl. -foots, -feet), newcomer in camp, settlement, etc., novice, greenhorn; new recruit in Boy Scouts of America; ten′derheart′ed, susceptible to, easily moved by, pity; kindly, compassionate; ten′der-loin, middle part of loin of pork; undercut of sirloin; Tenderloin, former district on W. side of Manhattan, New York City, below 42nd St., center of vice and considered a choice assignment for police accepting bribes; such a district in any U.S. city. ten′-der·ly *adv.* ten′der·ness *n.* ten-der·ize (těn′derīz) *v.t.* (-ized, -iz·ing). Make (more) tender. ten′der·iz·er *n.*

ten·di·nous (těn′dinus) *adj.* Of, connected with, resembling, a ten-

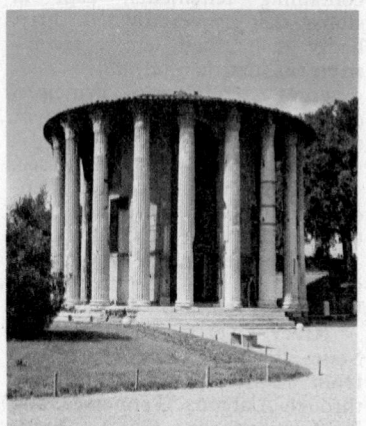

don.

ten·don (těn′don) *n.* Tough, fibrous tissue connecting a muscle to some other part; sinew; Achilles ~: see ACHILLES.

ten·dril (těn′dril) *n.* Slender threadlike organ or appendage of a plant, often spiral in form, which stretches out and attaches itself to some other body so as to support the plant.

Ten·e·brae (těn′ebrā) *n.pl.* or *sing.* (R.C. Ch.) Matins and lauds for the last three days of Holy Week, at which the candles are successively extinguished. [L., = "darkness"]

Although his early works were not appreciated by critics, the poems of **Alfred Lord Tennyson** *became accepted and beloved by most people in England. He was appointed poet laureate in 1850.*

ten·e·ment (tĕn′ement) *n.* (law) Any kind of permanent property, e.g. lands, held from another person; tenement house; dwelling; portion of a house, tenanted as a separate dwelling; ∼ **house**, house containing tenements, esp. in slums, that is overcrowded, dirty, badly maintained, etc. **ten·e·men·tal** (tĕnemĕn′tal) *adj.*

ten·et (tĕn′ĭt) *n.* Principle, dogma, doctrine, of a person or school. [L., = "he holds"]

Tenn., TN *abbrevs.* Tennessee.

ten·ner (tĕn′er) *n.* (colloq.) Ten-dollar bill; (Brit.) ten-pound note, ten pounds.

Ten·nes·see (tĕnĭsē′). State in southeastern U.S., admitted to the Union in 1796; capital, Nashville. ∼ **River**, river in the SE. United States, flowing 652 mi. (1,049 km) from Knoxville, Tennessee, through Alabama, Tennessee, and Kentucky, to the Ohio. **Ten·-nes·see′an** *adj. & n.*

Ten·nes·see (tĕnĭsē′) **Valley Authority.** U.S. Government corporation organized in 1933 to develop cheap hydroelectric power, flood control projects, and irrigation works in the entire Tennessee River basin.

ten·nis (tĕn′ĭs) *n.* Game for two or four persons played by striking ball with racket (formerly with the palm of the hand) over a net stretched across an oblong court, called **lawn tennis** when played on grass court; ∼ **ball**, hollow rubber ball with fuzzy cloth covering; ∼ **court**, court on which tennis is played; ∼ **elbow**, inflammatory

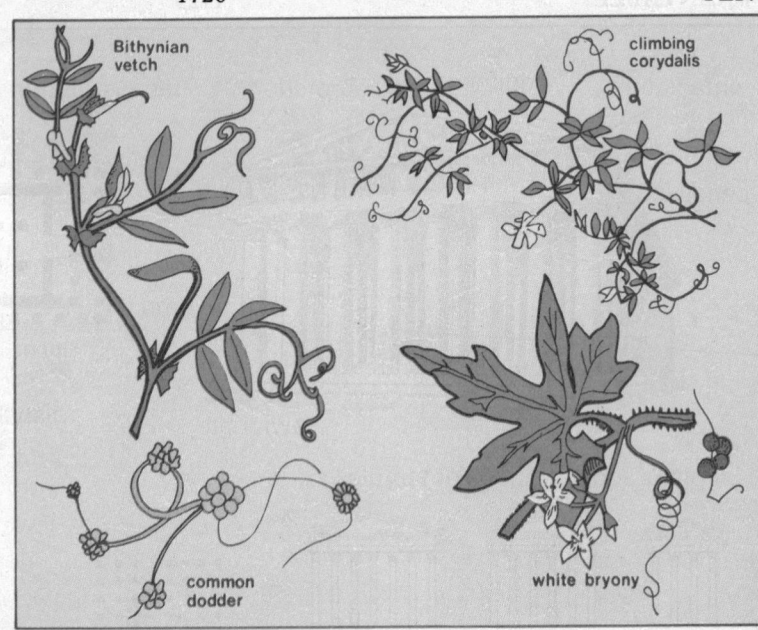

Most **tendrils** *are modified shoots or leaves which climbing plants use to attach themselves to a support. Those of white bryony act as shock absorbers while the whole dodder is a tendril.*

condition of the elbow joint, caused by strain as from playing tennis; ∼ **shoe**, canvas sports shoe with soft rubber sole. [app. f. OF. *tenez* "take," called by server to his opponent]

Ten·ny·son (tĕn′ĭson), **Alfred, 1st Baron** (1809–92). English poet; poet laureate from 1850; author of "In Memoriam," "Maud," "Idylls of the King," etc. **Ten·ny·so·ni·an** (tĕnĭsō′nēan) *adj.*

ten·on (tĕn′on) *n.* Projection fashioned on the end or side of a piece of wood or other material, to fit into a corresponding cavity, or mortise, in another piece; ∼ **saw**, fine saw for making tenons etc., having a thin blade, strong brass or steel back, and small teeth. **tenon** *v.t.* Cut into a tenon; join by means of a tenon.

ten·o·ni·tis (tĕnonī′tĭs) *n.* Painful inflammation of tendon.

ten·or (tĕn′er) *n.* 1. Settled or prevailing course or direction (esp. fig. *of one's life* etc.); general purport, drift (*of* speech, writing, etc.). 2. (mus.) (Music for, singer with) high adult male voice, usually ranging from the octave below middle C to the A above it; viola; (usu. attrib.) applied to an instrument of any kind (∼ **saxophone** etc.) of which the range is approx. that of tenor voice. [L. *tenorem* holding on, (med. L.) chief melody, formerly assigned to adult male voice]

te·not·o·my (tĕnŏt′omē) *n.* (pl. **-mies**). Surgical cutting of a tendon.

tense[1] (tĕns) *n.* Any of the different forms or modifications in the conjugation of a verb that indicate the different times (*past*, *present*, or *future*) at which the action or state denoted by it is viewed as happening or existing, and also (by extension) the different nature of such action or state, as continuing (*indefinite*), (*imperfect*), completed (*perfect*), etc.

tense[2] (tĕns) *adj.* (**tens·er, tens·est**). (of cord, membrane, fig. of nerve, mind, emotion) Stretched tight, strained to stiffness, highly strung. **tense′ly** *adv.* **tense′ness** *n.* **tense** *v.* (**tensed, tens·ing**). Make, become, tense.

ten·si·ble (tĕn′sibel) *adj.* Capable of being stretched out or extended. **ten·si·bil·i·ty** (tĕnsĭbĭl′ĭtē) *n.*

ten·sile (tĕn′sĭl; *Brit.* also tĕn′-sīl) *adj.* Of tension; capable of being drawn out or stretched; ∼ **strength**, maximum of lengthwise stress a material can bear without tearing apart. **ten·sil·i·ty** (tĕnsĭl′-ĭtē) *n.*

ten·sion (tĕn′shon) *n.* Stretching, being stretched; tenseness; mental strain or excitement, strained (political, social, etc.) state; (phys.) effect produced by forces pulling against each other; (elect.) stress along lines of force in a dielectric, formerly used as a synonym for potential, electromotive force, and mechanical force exerted by electricity, still so applied, in industrial and commercial use, in **high** and **low** ∼. **ten′sion·al** *adj.*

ten·sor (tĕn′ser) *n.* (anat.) Muscle that tightens or stretches a part.

tent (tĕnt) *n.* Portable shelter of canvas, cloth, etc., usu. supported by pole(s) and stretched by cords secured to pegs driven into the ground; **oxygen** ∼, tentlike

*French dandies in the late 18th century playing an early form of **tennis**. The game had its origin in England in the 16th century but lawn tennis, as played today did not evolve until the 1870s.*

cover, enclosing head and shoulders or whole body, through which oxygen can be supplied to assist breathing; ~ **bed**, bed with a tent-like canopy; bed for use in a tent; ~ **fly**, piece of canvas pitched outside and over ridge of tent as extra protection from sun, rain, etc.; ~ **stitch**, series of parallel diagonal stitches. **tent** v. Cover (as with a tent; encamp in a tent.

ten·ta·cle (těn′takel) n. Slender flexible process in animals, esp. invertebrates, serving as sensory or attachment organ, (bot.) sensitive hair or filament. **ten′ta·cled, ten·tac·u·lat·ed** (těntăk′yulātĭd) adjs.

tent·age (těn′tĭj) n. Tents collectively; supply or equipment of tents.

ten·ta·tive (těn′tatĭv) adj. Done by way of trial, experimental. **ten′ta·tive·ly** adv. **ten′ta·tive·ness** n.

tent (těnt) **caterpillar**. Any of several caterpillars (genus *Malacosoma*) that live in colonies in tent-like webs constructed among the branches of deciduous trees, which they defoliate.

ten·ter (těn′ter) n. Machine or frame for stretching cloth to set or dry; **ten′terhooks**, hooks to which cloth is fastened on a tenter; **on tenterhooks**, (fig.) in a state of suspense, distracted by uncertainty.

tenth (těnth) adj. Next after ninth. ~ n. Tenth part (see PART¹ sense 1); tenth thing etc. **tenth′ly** adv. In the tenth place.

ten·u·ous (těn′ūus) adj. Thin, slender; (of distinctions etc.) subtle, overrefined. **ten′u·ous·ness** n. **ten′u·ous·ly** adv.

ten·ure (těn′yer) n. Holding *of* a piece of property or office; conditions or period of such holding; permanent appointment after probationary period. **ten′ured** adj.

te·o·cal·li (tēokăl′ē) n. (pl. **-cal·lis**). (archaeol.) Temple of Aztec or other Mexican aborigines, usu. built on a truncated pyramidal mound. [Nahuatl, f. *teotl* god, *calli* house]

Te·o·ti·hua·cán (tāōtēwah-kahn′). Town in Mexico, in the central part, 30 mi. (48 km) NE. of Mexico City; site of many ancient Indian ruins, including the Pyramid of the Sun, Pyramid of the Moon, and the Temples of Tlaloc and Quetzalcoatl.

te·pee (tē′pē) n. Conical tent, hut, or wigwam of the Amer. Indians.

*Nomadic tribes in Afghanistan follow their livestock in the search for grazing. Each family has a low black **tent**, and when groups band together, they form villages of tents.*

tep·id (těp′ĭd) adj. Slightly warm, lukewarm (lit. and fig.). **te·pid·i·ty** (těpĭd′ĭtē), **tep′id·ness** ns. **tep′id·ly** adv.

te·qui·la (tekē′la) n. Mescal or redistilled mescal.

ter·a·tism (těr′atĭzem) n. (biol.) Monstrosity.

ter·a·tol·o·gy (těratŏl′ojē) n. Tale or myth concerning prodigies, marvelous tale, collection of these; (biol.) study of monstrosities or abnormal formations, esp. in man. **ter·a·to·log·i·cal** (těratolŏj′ĭkal) adj.

ter·bi·um (těr′bēum) n. (chem.) Metallic element of rare-earth group found in combination in gadolinite and other minerals; symbol Tb, at. no. 65, at. wt. 158.9254. [f. *Ytterby* in Sweden]

terce (tērs) = TIERCE sense 1.

ter·cel (tēr′sel) n. Male hawk. [L. *tertius* 3rd, from belief that the 3rd egg of a hawk produced a small male bird]

ter·cen·te·nar·y (tērsěn′tenĕrē, tērsěntěn′erē) n. (pl. **-nar·ies**). Three hundredth anniversary. ~ adj. Of 300 (esp. years). **ter·cen·ten·ni·al** (tērsěntěn′ēal) adj. & n. Tercentenary.

Ter·ence (těr′ens). Publius Terentius Afer (*c*190–*c*159 B.C.), Roman playwright, author of comedies, born at Carthage.

Te·resh·ko·va (těrěshkō′va), **Valentina Vladimirovna** (1937–). Soviet cosmonaut; first woman in space, 1963.

ter·gal (tēr′gal) adj. Of the back, dorsal.

ter·gi·ver·sate (tēr′jĭversāt) v.i. (**-sat·ed, -sat·ing**). Turn one's coat, desert one's party or principles, apostatize. **ter·gi·ver·sa·tion** (tērjĭversā′shon) n.

ter·gum (tēr′gum) n. (pl. **-ga** pr. -ga). Dorsal surface of body segment of arthropod.

term (tērm) n. 1. Boundary, limit, esp. of time; limited period; completion of period of pregnancy, (normal) time of childbirth; (law)

*Right: Soldiers of the **termite** genus Psammotermes. Above: Tall **termitary** in S.W. Africa. Despite their destructive ability, termites are highly sensitive to heat and humidity and need the insulation of large nests.*

estate or interest in land, etc., for fixed period; ~ **insurance**, life insurance having specific date of expiration; ~ **paper**, research paper written by student as part of particular course requirements during school term. 2. Figure, post, stone, etc., marking boundary (= TERMINUS sense 3). 3. Each period appointed for sitting of court of law, or for instruction and study in school, university, etc. 4. (math.) Each of two quantities composing a ratio or fraction; each of the quantities forming a series of progression; each of the quantities connected by signs of addition (+) or subtraction (−) in an algebraic expression or equation. 5. (logic) Word(s), notion, that may be subject or predicate of a proposition; hence, any word or group of words expressing a definite conception, esp. in particular branch of study etc.; (pl.) language employed, mode of expression; ~**s of reference**, terms defining scope of inquiry, action, etc. 6. (pl.) Conditions, esp. charge, price; **bring to ~s**, cause to accept conditions; **come to ~s**, yield, give way; **in terms of, in reference to.** 7. (pl.) Relation, footing. **term** *v.t.* Denominate, call.

ter·ma·gant (tẽr´magant) *n.* Brawling turbulent woman. [imaginary deity supposed in medieval times to be worshipped by Muslims]

ter·mi·na·ble (tẽr´minabel) *adj.*

That may be terminated (esp. after stipulated period).

ter·mi·nal (tẽr´minal) *adj.* Of, forming, a limit or terminus; situated at, forming, the end or extremity of something; of, forming, a term; (med.) forming, suffering, the final stage of a fatal disease; ~ **leave**, final leave given to member of armed forces preceding discharge, equal to amount of accumulated unused leave; ~ **moraine**, (geol.) moraine formed at extreme forward edge of glacier; (med.) forming, suffering, the final stage of a fatal disease. **ter´mi·nal·ly** *adv.* **terminal** *n.* Terminating thing, extremity, esp. (structure or device forming) each of free ends of open electrical circuit, by connecting which circuit is closed; end of railroad line, terminus.

ter·mi·nate (tẽr´mināt) *v.* (**-nat·ed, -nat·ing**). Bound, limit; bring, come, to an end, end (*at, in, with*). **ter´mi·na·ble, ter´mi·na·tive** *adjs.* **ter´mi·na·tive·ly** *adv.*

ter·mi·na·tion (tẽrmina´shon) *n.* 1. Act of terminating or state of being terminated. 2. End of something in space or time; boundary; conclusion. 3. Outcome or result of something. 4. Final syllable or letter(s) of word, (inflectional or derivative) ending, suffix.

ter·mi·na·tor (tẽr´mināter) *n.* 1. Person or thing that terminates. 2. Line of separation between dark and light parts of moon or planet.

ter·mi·nol·o·gy (tẽrminŏl´ojē) *n.* (pl. **-gies**). System of terms belonging to a science or subject; technical terms collectively. **ter·min·o·log·i·cal** (tẽrminolŏj´ĭkal) *adj.* **ter·min·o·log´i·cal·ly** *adv.* **ter·mi·nol´o·gist** *n.*

ter·mi·nus (tẽr´minus) *n.* (pl. **-ni** pr. **-nī, -nus·es**). 1. (Brit.) Station at end of line of railroad, bus route, etc. 2. Either end of a railroad line. 3. (Rom. antiq., also **term**) Statue or bust of the god Terminus, who presided over landmarks and boundaries; figure of human bust supported on square pillar.

ter·mite (tẽr´mīt) *n.* Pale-colored soft-bodied social insect of order Isoptera, chiefly tropical, and very destructive to timber; white ant.

tern (tẽrn) *n.* Seabird esp. of genus *Sterna*, resembling gull but usu. smaller and more slender bodied, with long, pointed wing and forked tail; sea swallow.

ter·na·ry (tẽr´nerē) *adj.* Of, in, set(s) of three; composed of three parts or elements.

ter·nate (tẽr´nĭt, -nāt) *adj.* Consisting of, arranged in, threes, esp. (bot.) composed of three leaflets, (of leaves) in whorls of three. **ter´nate·ly** *adv.*

Terp·sich·o·re (tẽrpsĭk´erē) (Gk. and Rom. myth.) Muse of lyric poetry and dance. **Terp·si·cho·re·an** (tẽrpsĭkorē´an, -kōr´ēan, -kōr´-) *adj.* Of Terpsichore; o

There are more than 40 species of **tern** and the Arctic variety actually spends half the year in the northern hemisphere before flying to the Antarctic. Most of these birds live on fish that they catch by diving directly into the water after them.

Caspian tern

Arctic tern

sooty tern

dancing.

terr. *abbrev.* Territorial; territory.

ter·ra al·ba (tĕr′a ăl′ba). Any of various white mineral substances; (esp.) pipe clay. [L.]

ter·race (tĕr′as) *n.* Raised level place, natural or artificial, esp. raised walk in garden or level space in front of building on sloping ground; (geol.) horizontal shelf or beach bordering river, lake, or sea. ~ *v.t.* (**-raced, -rac·ing**). Form into, furnish with, terrace(s).

ter·ra cot·ta (tĕr′a kŏt′a). Hard unglazed pottery of fine quality used for decorative tiles, statuary, architectural decorations, etc.; statuette, figurine of this; brownish-red color of this pottery. ~ *adj.* Of, made of, of the color

of, terra cotta. [It., = "baked earth"]

ter·ra fir·ma (tĕr′a fēr′ma). Dry land, firm ground. [L.]

ter·rain[1] (terān′) *n.* Tract of country considered with regard to its natural features etc., esp. (mil.) its tactical advantages, fitness for maneuvering etc.

ter·rain[2]: see TERRANE.

ter·ra in·cog·ni·ta (tĕr′a ĭn-kŏg′nĭta, ĭnkŏgnē′-; *Lat.* tĕr′ah ĭnkŏg′nĭtah). Unknown or unexplored region. [L.]

Ter·ra·my·cin (tĕramī′sĭn) *n.* (trademark) OXYTETRACYCLINE.

tar·rane, ter·rain (terān′) *ns.* (geol.) Connected series, group, or system of rocks or formations, area over which a group of formations is prevalent.

ter·ra·pin (tĕr′apĭn) *n.* Any of various N. Amer. edible tortoises of family Emydidae, found in fresh or brackish water, esp. the **diamondback** ~, (*Malaclemys*) of salt marshes of coasts of Atlantic and Gulf of Mexico, famous for its delicate flesh.

ter·raz·zo (terăz′ō, -rah′zō) *n.* Flooring material of stone chips set in concrete and given a smooth surface.

ter·rene (tĕrēn′) *adj.* Of Earth, earthy; terrestrial.

ter·res·tri·al (terĕs′trēal) *adj.* Of the Earth, of this world, worldly; of land as opp. to water. **ter·res′tri·al·ly** *adv.*

ter·ri·ble (tĕr′ibel) *adj.* Exciting, fitted to excite, terror; awful, dreadful, formidable; (colloq.) very great, excessive. **ter′ri·bly** *adv.* **ter′ri·ble·ness** *n.*

ter·ri·er (tĕr′ēer) *n.* Any of several kinds of usu. small active hardy dog orig. used to pursue quarry (fox, badger, etc.) into burrow or earth.

ter·rif·ic (terĭf′ĭk) *adj.* Causing terror; (colloq.) of great size, intensity, etc.; very good, admirable, etc. **ter·rif′i·cal·ly** *adv.*

ter·ri·fy (tĕr′ĭfī) *v.t.* (**-fied, -fy·ing**). Fill with terror, frighten. **ter′ri·fy·ing·ly** *adv.* **ter′ri·fi·er** *n.*

ter·rine (terēn′) *n.* Earthenware vessel containing and sold with some table delicacy as pâté de foie gras.

ter·ri·to·ri·al (tĕrĭtōr′ēal, -tōr′-) *adj.* Of territory; of a particular territory or locality, local; **~ waters**, that part of the seas adjacent to its shores over which a nation claims jurisdiction, within a minimum number of (formerly three) miles from low-water mark. **ter·ri·to′ri·al·ly** *adv.*

ter·ri·to·ri·al·ism (tĕrĭtōr′ēal-ĭzem, -tōr′-) *n.* System of church government under which civil rule has religious jurisdiction over the subjects of a nation; principle of predominance of land-owning classes.

ter·ri·to·ri·al·i·ty (tĕrĭtōrēăl′-ĭtē, -tōr′-) *n.* 1. State or quality of being territorial. 2. Behavior pattern of an animal when defending its territory.

ter·ri·to·ry (tĕr′ĭtōrē, -tōr′-) *n.* (pl. **-ries**). 1. Land under jurisdiction of sovereign, nation, city, etc.; (large) tract of land, region; portion of country not yet admitted to full rights of a state or province. 2. District in which salesperson or sales supervisor operates; (zool.) area of habitat that a particular animal or group defends against others of the same species; (in games) half of field regarded as belonging to team whose goal etc. is in it. 3. (fig.) Sphere, province.

ter·ror (tĕr′er) *n.* Extreme fear; person or thing causing this; (colloq.) exasperating or tiresome person, troublesome child.

ter·ror·ist (tĕr′erĭst) *n.* Person attempting to further his views or to rule by coercive intimidation. **ter′ror·ism** *n.* **ter·ror·is·tic** (tĕrerĭs′tĭk) *adj.*

ter·ror·ize (tĕr′erīz) *v.t.* (**-ized, -iz·ing**). Fill with terror; rule or maintain power by terrorism. **ter·ror·i·za·tion** (tĕrerĭzā′shon) *n.*

ter·ry (tĕr′ē) *n.* (pl. **-ries**) & *adj.* (Pile fabric) with loops forming pile left uncut, also called **~ cloth**.

terse (tērs) *adj.* (**ters·er, ters·est**). (of speech, style, writer) Free from cumbrousness and superfluity, smooth and concise; curt. **terse′ly** *adv.* **terse′ness** *n.*

ter·ti·ar·y (tēr′shēērē, -sherē) *adj.* 1. Of the third order, rank, class, stage, etc. 2. **T~**, (geol.) of the period subsequent to the Mesozoic, forming the earlier part of the Cenozoic, characterized by the appearance of mammals other than man. 3. (ornith., of wing feathers) Borne on humerus. 4. **~ color**, (painting) one of the grayish hues obtained by mixing two secondary colors (e.g. purple with green). **tertiary** *n.* 1. Tertiary color; tertiary feather. 2. Member of third order of monastic body. 3. **T~**, (geol.) Tertiary period or system.

ter·va·lent (tērvā′lent) *adj.* (chem.) = TRIVALENT.

ter·za ri·ma (tērt′sa rē′ma). Form of verse in sets of three 10- or 11-syllabled lines rhyming *a b a, b c b*, etc., as in Dante's *Divina Commedia*. [It., = "third rhyme"]

tes·la (tĕs′la) *n.* (abbrev. T) Unit of magnetic induction in M.K.S. system. [f. N. *Tesla* (1856–1943), U.S. electrician]

tes·sel·late, tes·se·late (tĕs′elāt) *vbs.t.* (**-lat·ed, -lat·ing**). Make into mosaic, form (esp. pavement) by combining variously colored blocks into pattern. **tes′sel·lat·ed** *adj.* Composed of, ornamented with, small colored blocks arranged in pattern; (zool., bot.) marked, colored, in regularly arranged squares or patches, reticulated. **tes·sel·la·tion, tes·se·la·tion** (tĕselā′shon) *ns.*

tes·ser·a (tĕs′era) *n.* (pl. **tes·-**

Terrapin is a name applied both to particular varieties of freshwater tortoises in eastern North America, and to freshwater tortoises in general. Tortoises in the genus Terrapene are terrestrial.

ser·ae pr. tĕs′erē). 1. (Gk. and Rom. hist.) Small tablet of wood, bone, ivory, etc., used as token, tally, label, etc. 2. Each of small square pieces of marble, glass, tile, etc., of which mosaic pavement etc. is made up.

test[1] (tĕst) *n.* 1. Critical examination or trial of qualities of person or thing; means of so examining; standard for comparison or trial, cicumstances suitable for this; (chem.) examination of substance under known conditions to determine its identity or that of one of its constituents, reagent used for this. 2. **~ case**, (law) case in which decision is taken as settling a number of other cases involving same question of law; **~ match**, one of series of usu. five cricket games played between sides representing England and Australia or other country, esp. of the Commonwealth, as test of superiority; **~ meal**, meal of specified quantity and composition given to enable gastric secretions etc. to be examined; **~ paper**, school examination paper written by student; **~ pattern**, (television) design transmitted to receivers to test transmission quality; **~ pilot**, one who pilots aircraft on experimental flights; **~ stand**, device that keeps missile or rocket immobilized during test of full engine thrust; **~ tube**, (chem.) tube of thin glass closed at one end, used to hold substance under test etc.; **~-tube baby**, (colloq.) one conceived by artificial insemination, or developing elsewhere than in a mother's body. **test** *v.t.* Put to the test, make trial of; try severely, tax (endurance etc.); subject to chemical test.

test[2] (tĕst) *n.* External covering or shell of tunicates.

tes·ta (tĕs′ta) *n.* (pl. **-tae** pr. -tē). (bot.) Seed coat.

tes·ta·ceous (tĕstā′shus) *adj.* Having a shell, esp. a hard shell; of shells, shelly; (bot., zool.) of color of tile or red brick, brownish red.

tes·ta·cy (tĕs′tasē) *n.* Being testate.

tes·ta·ment (tĕs′tament) *n.* 1. (law) Will, esp. (formerly) disposition of personal as dist. from real property. 2. (colloq.) (Written) statement, affirmation, of (political) beliefs, principles, etc. 3. (bibl.) Covenant between God and man (archaic), hence, **Old, New, T~**, (abbrev. O.T., N.T.) main divisions of Bible consisting respectively of books of old or Mosaic, and new or Christian, dispensation; **T~**, copy of New Testament. **tes·ta·men·ta·ry** (tĕstamĕn′terē) *adj.* Of (nature of), relating to, a will.

tes·tate (tĕs′tāt) *adj. & n.* (Person) who has left a valid will at death.

tes·ta·tor (tĕs′tā̇ter, tĕstā′-) *n.* Person who makes or has died leaving a will. **tes·ta·trix** (tĕstā′-trĭks) *n. fem.* (pl. **-tri·ces** pr. -trisēz).

test·er[1] (tĕs′ter) *n.* Person or thing that tests.

test·er[2] (tĕs′ter) *n.* Canopy, esp. over four-poster bed.

tes·ti·cle (tĕs′tĭkel) *n.* Testis, esp. in man and most other mammals. **tes·tic·u·lar** (tĕstĭk′yuler) *adj.*

tes·tic·u·late (tĕstĭk′yulĭt) *adj.* Having, shaped like, testicles; (bot., of some orchids) having 2 tubers of this shape.

tes·ti·fy (tĕs′tĭfī) *v.* (**-fied, -fy·ing**). Bear witness; (law) give evidence; affirm, declare, be evidence of, evince. **tes′ti·fi·er** *n.*

tes·ti·mo·ni·al (tĕstĭmō′nēal) *n.* Certificate of character, conduct, or qualifications; gift presented, esp. in public at ~ **dinner**, as mark of esteem, in acknowledgement of services, etc. **tes·ti·mo′ni·al·ize** *v.t.* (**-ized, -iz·ing**). Present with testimonial.

tes·ti·mo·ny (tĕs′tĭmōnē) *n.* (pl. **-nies**). Evidence, esp. (law) statement made under oath or affirmation.

tes·tis (tĕs′tĭs) *n.* (pl. **-tes** pr. -tēz). Male organ in which sperms are produced; in man and most other mammals, each of two such organs enclosed in scrotum.

tes·tos·ter·one (tĕstŏs′terōn) *n.* Male sex hormone secreted by testes; synthetic preparation of this.

tes·tu·di·nate (tĕstoo′dinĭt, -nāt, -tū′-) *adj.* Arched, vaulted, like tortoise shell.

tes·ty (tĕs′tē) *adj.* (**-ti·er, -ti·est**). Irritable, touchy. **tes′-**

The Teton Range extends from the southern boundary of Yellowstone to the Teton Pass. The first European to see the mountains was John Colter in 1808 as a member of the Lewis and Clark expedition.

ti·ly *adv.* **tes′ti·ness** *n.*

Tet (tĕt) *n.* Three-day celebration of arrival of lunar new year as observed in SE. Asia.

tet·a·nus (tĕt′anus) *n.* 1. (med.) Painful and often fatal disease caused by microorganism, usu. introduced through wound, and characterized by tonic spasm and rigidity of voluntary muscles. 2. (physiol.) Prolonged contraction of muscle produced by rapidly repeated stimuli. **tet′a·noid** *adj.*

tetch·y, tech·y (tĕch′ē) *adjs.* (**tetch·i·er, tetch·i·est, tech·i·er, tech·i·est**). Peevish, irritable. **tetch′i·ly, tech′i·ly** *advs.* **tetch′i·ness, tech′i·ness** *ns.*

tête-à-tête (tā′tătāt′, tĕt′atĕt′) *n. & adj.* (Of) private conversation or interview between two persons. ~ *adv.* In private, without presence of third person.

*The **tetradactyl** structure of the potto's paws is due to the index finger being reduced to a small knob and the thumb being widely opposed to the remaining digits — an adaptation to life in trees.*

teth·er (tĕdh′er) *n.* Rope, chain, halter, by which grazing animal is confined; **end of one's** ~, extreme limit of one's resources. **tether** *v.t.* Make fast, confine, with tether (freq. fig.).

Te·thys (tē′thĭs). (Gk. myth.) Sea deity, daughter of Uranus and Ge, and wife of Oceanus.

Te·ton (tē′ton) **Range.** Range of the Rocky Mountains, in NW. Wyoming and SE. Idaho; highest peak, Grand Teton, 13,766 ft. (4,196 m) in Grand Teton National Park in Wyoming.

tet·ra (tĕt′ra) *n.* Any of various small freshwater fishes (family Characidae) of the Amer. tropics, kept in home aquariums.

tetra- *prefix.* Four.

tet·ra·cy·cline (tĕtrasī′klĭn, -klēn) *n.* Yellow crystalline compound, $C_{22}H_{24}N_2O_8$, used as a broad spectrum antibiotic.

tet·rad (tĕt′răd) *n.* The number four, set or group of four.

tet·ra·dac·tyl (tĕtradăk′tĭl) *adj. & n.* (Animal) with four fingers or toes. **tet·ra·dac′ty·lous** *adj.*

tet·ra·eth·yl (tĕtraĕth′ĭl) *adj.* (chem.) Containing four ethyl groups; ~ **lead**, heavy colorless liquid used in fuels to prevent knock in internal combustion engines.

tet·ra·flu·o·ro·eth·yl·ene (tĕt-raflooeroĕth′ilēn, -floorō-, -flŏrō-, -flŏrō-) *n.* (chem.) Colorless, water-insoluble inflammable gas, C_2F_4, used to synthesize various polymeric resins.

tet·ra·gram (tĕt′ragrăm) *n.* 1. Word of four letters. 2. Quadrilateral.

Tet·ra·gram·ma·ton (tĕtragrăm′atŏn) *n.* Hebrew word of four consonants (YHWH or JHVH) representing the incommunicable name of God.

tet·ra·he·dron (tĕtrahē′drŏn) *n.* (pl. **-drons, -dra** pr. -dra). Solid figure bounded by four plane triangles; triangular pyramid; crystal of this form. **tet·ra·he′dral** *adj.*

te·tral·o·gy (tĕtrăl′ojē) *n.* (pl. **-gies**). Series of four connected operas, plays, etc., esp. (Gk. antiq.) series of three tragedies and a satyric drama produced at Athens at festival of Dionysus.

te·tram·e·ter (tĕtrăm′ĭter) *n.* 1. (Gk. and L. pros.) Verse consisting of four measures in trochaic, iambic, or anapestic meter. 2. (Engl. pros.) Line of verse of four feet.

tet·ra·pod (tĕt′rapŏd) *adj.* & *n.* (Vertebrate) having two pairs of limbs (zool.; now more usu. than *quadruped* and not necessarily implying walking on four feet).

tet·ra·style (tĕt′rastīl) *adj.* & *n.* (Portico) of four columns.

tet·ra·syl·la·ble (tĕtrasĭl′abel) *n.* Word of four syllables. **tet·ra·syl·la·bic** (tĕtrasĭlăb′ĭk) *adj.*

tet·ra·va·lent (tĕtravā′lent) *adj.* (chem.) Having a VALENCE of four. **tet·ra·va′lence, tet·ra·va′len·cy** *ns.*

tet·rode (tĕt′rōd) *n.* Vacuum tube with four main electrodes.

*After squandering a fortune, **Thackeray** earned his living as a journalist. He was editor of 'Punch' and founded 'Cornhill Magazine'. His novels were written as instalments for magazines.*

Teu·ton (tōō′ton, tū′-) *n.* 1. One of the ancient **Teutones**, or **Teutoni**, a N. European people in ancient Roman times. 2. One of a N. European race of tall stature with long heads, blue eyes, and fair hair and skin, first appearing in Germany, Scandinavia, and the Netherlands. 3. German. **Teu′ton·ize** *v.* (**-ized, -iz·ing**).

Teu·ton·ic (tōōtŏn′ĭk, tū-) *adj.* Of the Teutons or their languages (see GERMANIC).

Tex. *abbrev.* Texas.

Tex·as (tĕk′sas). Second largest state in the United States, in the S. Central part, bordered on the SW. by Mexico and on the SE. by the Gulf of Mexico; discovered and explored by Spanish and by French who claimed it as part of Louisiana; acquired by U.S. with Louisiana Purchase, 1803; relinquished by treaty with Spain, 1819 and became province of Mexico; declared independence after battle of San Jacinto, 1836, and became Republic of Texas; sought annexation and became 28th state admitted to the Union, 1845; capital, Austin. **Tex′an** *adj.* & *n.*

text (tĕkst) *n.* 1. Wording of anything written or printed, esp. the very words and sentences as orig. written, as opp. to translation, commentary, notes, etc. 2. (print.) Type, as opp. to illustrations etc. 3. Passage of Scripture quoted as authority or esp. chosen as subject of sermon etc.; subject, theme. 4. **text′book**, manual of instruction in any branch of science or study,

*The Astrodome at Houston, **Texas**, was built in 1965 and cost $US 31.6m. It was the first air-conditioned, all-purpose stadium and the roof has a diameter of 642 feet.*

work recognized as an authority **text hand**, fine large kind of handwriting esp. used for manuscripts.

tex·tile (tĕks′tĭl, -tīl) *adj.* Of weaving; woven, suitable for weaving. ~ *n.* Textile fabric or material.

tex·tu·al (tĕks′chōōal) *adj.* Of, in, the text. **tex′tu·al·ly** *adv.*

tex·tu·al·ist (tĕks′chōōalĭst) *n.* One who adheres strictly to the letter of the text; one well acquainted with text, esp. of Bible **tex′tu·al·ism** *n.*

tex·ture (tĕks′cher) *n.* Character of textile fabric, resulting from way in which it is woven; arrangement of constituent parts, structure, constitution; representation of surface of objects in work of art (also) character of surface of paint in picture etc. **tex′tur·al** *adj.* **tex′tur·al·ly** *adv.*

Th *symbol.* Thorium.

-th *suffix.* Forming ordinal and fractional numbers with all simple numbers from 4 on (*fourth, fifth twentieth*).

Thack·er·ay (thăk′erē), **William Makepeace** (1811–63). English novelist, author of *Vanity Fair, Henry Esmond, The Virginians*, etc

Thai, Tai (tī, tah′ē) *adjs.* Of Thailand or its people or languages. ~ *ns.* (pl. **Thais, Tais**, collect **Thai, Tai**). 1. Native, inhabitant, of Thailand; (member of) a people of Mongolian stock who migrated southward from S. China (c10th c.) and now inhabit parts of Thailand Burma, Vietnam, and Laos. 2 Language of Thailand. 3. Group of languages spoken over a wide area in SE. Asia. **Thai′land**. Kingdom in SE. Asia, until 1939 called Siam, capital Bangkok. **Thai′land·er** *n.* [Siamese *thai* free]

*Despite the tourist image of golden temples and their dancers, **Thailand** is a major rice producer in South-East Asia. It also exports teak and rubber, and tin and gems are mined.*

Tha·ïs (tā´ĭs, tahēs´). Athenian courtesan who accompanied Alexander the Great on his Asiatic campaign and later became wife of Ptolemy Lagus, king of Egypt; hence, any cultured and intelligent courtesan.

thal·a·mus (thăl´amus) *n.* (pl. **-mi** pr. -mī). 1. (anat.) Interior region of brain where certain important sensory nerves, esp. the optic nerve, originate (hence sometimes called **optic** ~). 2. (bot.) Receptacle of flower. **tha·lam·ic** (thalăm´ĭk) *adj.*

tha·las·sic (thalăs´ĭk) *adj.* Of sea(s), esp. of smaller or inland seas as dist. from oceans.

Tha·les (thā´lēz) (end of 7th c. B.C.). Greek philosopher of Miletus, one of the seven sages, believed to have founded the geometry of lines, discovered several theorems, and advanced the study of astronomy; he regarded water as the principle of all material things.

Tha·li·a (thalī´a, thā´lēa, thāl´ya). (Gk. and Rom. myth.) 1. Muse of comedy. 2. One of the Graces. **Tha·li'an** *adj.*

tha·lid·o·mide (thalĭd´omīd) *n.* Sedative drug, the taking of which by pregnant women was followed *c*1960 by the birth of children with many defects, including malformed limbs; so ~ **child.**

thal·li·um (thăl´ēum) *n.* (chem.) Soft bluish-white leaden-lustered metallic element; symbol Tl, at. no. 81, at. wt. 204.37. **thal'lic, thal'lous** *adjs.* [Gk. *thallos* green shoot, from brilliant green line in its spectrum]

thal·lo·phyte (thăl´ofīt) *n.* Plant whose body is a thallus, e.g. seaweed, liverwort.

thal·lus (thăl´us) *n.* (pl. **thal·li** pr. thăl´ī, **thal·lus·es**). Body of a primitive plant that is not divided into leaves, stem, and roots but consists of more or less uniform tissue. **thal'loid** *adj.*

Thames (tĕmz). Chief river of England, on which London stands, rising in Gloucestershire and flowing 210 mi. (336 km) into North Sea.

Tham·y·ris (thăm´erĭs). (Gk. legend) Thracian poet and musician blinded by the muses for his arrogance.

than (dhăn, unstressed dhan) *conj.* Introducing second member of comparison.

thane (thān) *n.* (Engl. hist.) One holding land of king or other superior by virtue of military service, with rank between ordinary freemen and hereditary nobles; (Sc. hist.) one, ranking with earl's son,

long straw

hazel stick

thatcher's knife

eaves bottles

bottle

side rake

shears

needle

lead apron

subsequent layers of yealms

yealms

leggett

first course laid with spars

liggers and crossrods

Norfolk reed

holding land of the king, chief of a clan.

thank (thăngk) *v.t.* Express gratitude to (person *for* thing); ~ **you**, I thank you (as polite formula of gratitude etc.). **thank** *n.* (now only in pl.) (Expression of) gratitude; ~ **s**, thank you; ~ **s to**, owing to, as the result of; **thanksgiv'ing**, expression of gratitude, esp. to God; form of words for this; **Thanksgiving (Day)**, annual festival and legal holiday, usu. on fourth Thursday of November, first held 1621 by the Plymouth colony in thankfulness for its first harvest. **thank·ful** (thăngk'ful) *adj.* Grateful, expressive of thanks. **thank'ful·ly** *adv.* **thank'ful·ness** *n.*

thank·less (thăngk'lĭs) *adj.* Not feeling or expressing gratitude; (of task etc.) not likely to win thanks, unprofitable. **thank'less·ly** *adv.* **thank'less·ness** *n.*

that (dhăt, unstressed dh*a*t) *pron.* 1. (*demonstr.*) (pl. **those** pr. dhōz) Person or thing referred to, observed, understood, in question,

Cost of labor coupled with fewer men interested in learning the craft of thatching, and a shortage of reed, has resulted in a reduction in the number of buildings roofed with **thatch.** *Many that were formerly thatched have had the old straw replaced with tiles. Reeds used for this purpose had a life of 75 years but straw must be replaced in 20.*

etc.; (coupled or contrasted with *this*) esp., the farther, less immediate or obvious, etc., of two; **and all** ~, and so forth; **at** ~, at that standard, (even) in that capacity; too, besides; ~ **is (to say)**, introducing explanation of preceding word, phrase, etc.; **that's that!** (colloq.) that is taken care of, completed, decided, etc.; **with that**, immediately following; at once. 2. (*rel.*) (introducing defining clause; often omitted) Who, whom, which. **that** *adj.* (pl. **those** pr. dhōz). Designating person or thing referred to etc.; the (used demonstratively not merely definitively); farther or less immediate of the two (opp. this); well known (often implying censure or dislike, but

sometimes admiration). ~ *adv.* (colloq.) To the extent or degree indicated (as ~ **far, much**). **that** *conj.* Introducing dependent clause, esp. expressing result or consequence.

that-a·way (dhăt'awā) *adv.* (colloq.) In the direction or manner indicated.

thatch (thăch) *n.* Roof covering of straw, reeds, etc. ~ *v.t.* Roof or cover with thatch; make (roof) of thatch. **thatch'er** *n.* **thatch'ing** *n.* Thatch.

Thatch·er (thăch'er), **Marga-ret Hilda** (1925–). British Conservative stateswoman, first British woman prime minister, 1979– .

thau·ma·turge (thaw'matērj) *n.* Worker of miracles, wonder-worker. **thau·ma·tur·gic** (thaw-matēr'jĭk), **thau·ma·tur'gi·cal** *adjs.* **thau'ma·tur·gy** *n.*

thaw (thaw) *v.* Reduce (frozen substance) to liquid state by raising its temperature above freezing point; become liquid, flexible, or limp by rise of temperature after being frozen; (fig.) free, be freed, from coldness or stiffness, (cause to) unbend or become genial. ~ *n.* Thawing, melting of ice and snow after frost; warmth of weather that thaws.

the (dh*e* preceding a consonant, dhē preceding a vowel or for emphasis) *definite article*. Denoting, defining, or singling out person(s) or thing(s) already mentioned or under discussion, actually or potentially existent, unique, familiar, or otherwise sufficiently identified; applied to singular nouns as representing species, class, etc.; used with adjectives used abs., *the just, the wicked*; emphatically, applied to person or thing best known or best entitled to the name. ~ *adv.* In that degree, by that amount, on that account; **the ... the**, by how much ... by so much; in what degree ... in that degree.

the·ar·chy (thē´ärkē) *n.* (pl. **-chies**). Theocracy; system or order of gods.

theat. *abbrev.* Theater.

the·a·ter, the·a·tre (thē´ater) *ns.* 1. Building or outdoor area for dramatic performances etc.; (Gk. and Rom. antiq.) open-air structure in form of segment of circle rising gradually; room, hall, for lectures etc., with seats in tiers; ~**-in-the-round**, dramatic performance on stage surrounded by spectators. 2. Scene, field, of action. 3. ~ **of operations**, (mil.) area of military operations and their necessary support in theater of war. 4. Natural formation of land resembling ancient Greek or Roman theater. 5. Dramatic literature or art. ~ **of the absurd**, avant-garde style in drama that emphasizes irrational, incongruous, and aimless elements and omits or distorts traditional ideas of character and plot development in order to raise questions about the nature of reality and to depict the alienation and anxiety of modern man.

the·at·ri·cal (thēăt´rĭkal), **the·at·ric** (thēăt´rĭk) *adjs.* Of or suited to theater; of acting or actors; calculated for effect, showy, artificial. **the·at´ri·cal·ly** *adv.* **the·at´ri·cal·ism, the·at·ri·cal·i·ty** (thēătrĭkăl´ĭtē) *ns.* **the·at´ri·cals** *n.pl.* Theatrical performances, esp. by amateurs.

The·ba·id (thē´bāĭd, -bē-, thēbā´-). 1. Latin epic poem (*c*92 A.D.) by Statius, concerned with legendary expedition against Thebes to recover throne for Polynices from his brother Eteocles. 2. Ancient region in Egypt surrounding Thebes.

Thebes (thēbz). 1. Ancient capital (from time of 12th dynasty) of Upper Egypt, on site of modern Luxor. 2. (Gk. *Thivai*) Ancient city of Greece, subject of many legends, including those of Cadmus, Oedipus, and Antigone; from the late 6th c. B.C., the bitter enemy of Athens, and after the Peloponnesian War the rival of Sparta for the hegemony of Greece; it was razed in 335 B.C. but rebuilt, existed throughout Roman times, and was finally destroyed in 1311. **The´ban** *adj. & n.*

the·ca (thē´ka) *n.* (pl. **-cae** pr. -sē). 1. (bot.) Part of plant serving as receptacle, as pollen sac of anther, spore case, capsule of moss, etc. 2. (zool., anat.) Case or sheath enclosing some organ or part.

thee (dhē) *pron.* Objective (accus., dat.) case of THOU; dial. and among Quakers occas. used for *thou*.

theft (thĕft) *n.* Stealing; (law) act of dishonestly appropriating another's property with intent of permanently depriving him of it.

their (dhār) *poss. pron.* Possessive case of THEY used as attrib. adj. with abs. and pred. form **theirs** (dhārz), belonging to, affecting, them.

the·ism (thē´ĭzem) *n.* Belief in gods or (esp.) a god, as opp. to ATHEISM, PANTHEISM, POLYTHEISM, esp. belief in one God as creator and supreme ruler of universe. **the´ist** *adj. & n.* **the·is·tic** (thēĭs´tĭk), **the·is·ti·cal** *adjs.* **the·is·ti·cal·ly** *adv.*

them (dhĕm) *pron.* Objective (accus., dat.) case of THEY.

the·mat·ic (thĭmăt´ĭk) *adj.* Of, belonging to, constituting, a theme.

The·mat·ic (thĭmăt´ĭk) **Apperception Test.** (psychol.) Projective technique using a series of standard pictures about which person being tested tells stories that presumably reveal psychological components of his or her personality.

theme (thēm) *n.* 1. Subject of discourse, conversation, composition, etc., topic; school essay. 2. (mus.) Subject, tune, or passage developed in musical composition, and recurring as a principal part of its material; tune on which variations are constructed; ~ **song**, recurrent melody in a musical play, film, etc.

The·mis (thē´mĭs, thĕm´ĭs). (Gk.

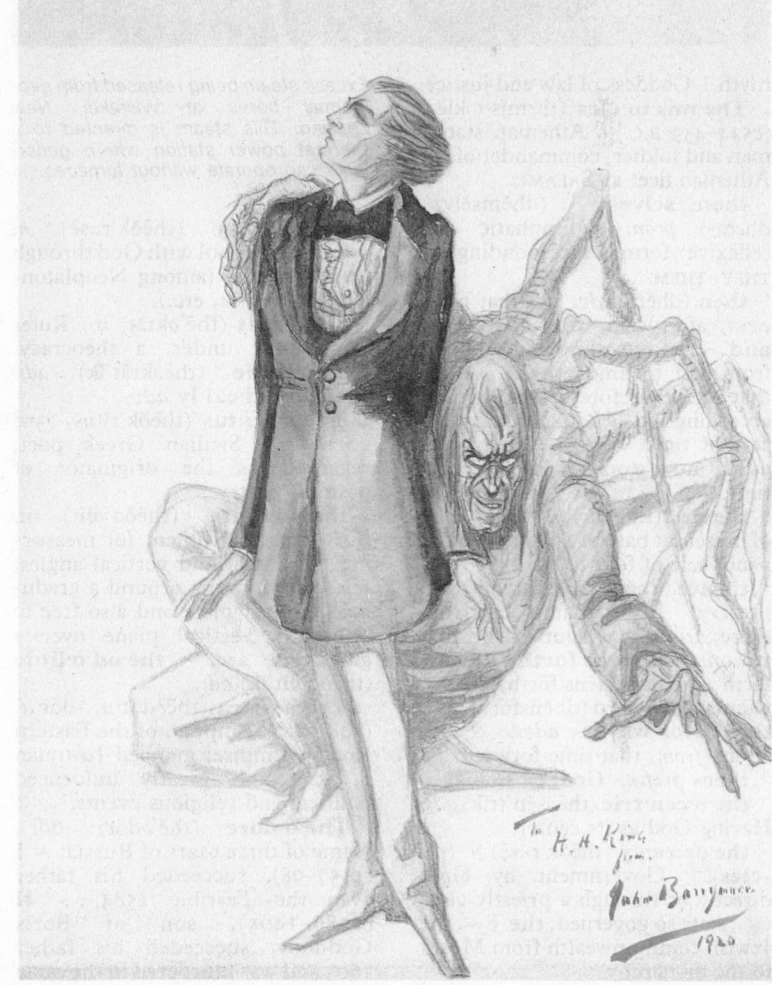

John Barrymore, illustrated here by his self-portrait, was a great romantic actor of the early 1900s up until the 1940s. He had a huge following in **theater,** *screen and radio.*

*Excess steam being released from geo-thermal bores at Wairakei, New Zealand. This steam is directed to a **thermal** power station where generators can operate without furnaces.*

year; ~ **III** (1661–82), succeeded his father Alexey 1679.

The·od·o·ric (thĕŏd´erĭk) (c454–526). King of the Ostrogoths, invader (488–93) and conqueror of Italy, which he ruled from Ravenna; attempted to revive the Western Roman Empire.

The·o·do·si·us (thēodō´shĕus, -shus). Name of three emperors of the Eastern Roman Empire: ~ **I** (c346–95), "the Great," Roman general, born in Spain, became emperor of the East 379; ~ **II** (401–50), succeeded his father Arcadius as emperor 408; ~ **III** (dates uncertain), was proclaimed emperor 715 by the rebellious Byzantine army and deposed 717 by Leo III. **The·o·do´sian** adj. Of Theodosius; (esp.) ~ **Code**, code of all imperial legislation since time of Constantine, promulgated in 438 by Theodosius II.

theol. abbrev. Theologian; theological; theology.

the·o·lo·gian (thēolō´jan, -jēan) n. Person skilled in theology.

the·ol·o·gy (thēŏl´ojē) n. (pl. **-gies**). Science of religion, study of God or gods, esp. of attributes and relations with man etc.; **dogmatic** ~, that based on the authoritative teaching of the Scriptures and the church; **natural** ~, dealing with knowledge of God as gained from evidence by natural human reason without the aid of revelation; **positive, revealed** ~, based on revelation; **speculative** ~, not confined to revelation but giving scope to human speculation; **systematic** ~, methodical arrangement of the truths of religion in their natural connection. **the·o·log´i·cal** (thēolŏj´ĭkal) adj. **the·o·log´i·cal·ly** adv.

the·om·a·chy (thēŏm´akē) n. (pl. **-chies**). Strife among the gods.

the·o·mor·phic (thēomōr´fĭk) adj. Having the form or likeness of a god.

the·o·rem (thē´orem, thēr´em) n. Universal or general proposition, not self-evident but demonstrable by chain of reasoning; algebraic or other rule, esp. expressed by symbols or formulas. **the·o·re·mat·ic** (thēoremăt´ĭk, thēre-) adj.

the·o·ret·i·cal (thēorĕt´ĭkal), **the·o·ret·ic** (thēorĕt´ĭk) adjs. Of, consisting in, relating to, conforming to, theory; existing only in theory, hypothetical; addicted to, constructing, dealing with, theories, speculative. **the·o·ret´ics** n.pl. Theory, theoretical parts of science etc.

the·o·ry (thē´orē, thēr´ē) n. (pl. **-ries**). Scheme or system of ideas or statements held to explain group of facts or phenomena, statement of general laws, principles, or causes of something known or observed; systematic conception or

myth.) Goddess of law and justice.

The·mis·to·cles (themĭs´toklēz) (c524–459 B.C.). Athenian statesman and soldier, commander of the Athenian fleet at SALAMIS.

them·selves (dhĕmsĕlvz´, dhem-) pron. Emphatic and reflexive form corresponding to THEY, THEM.

then (dhĕn) adv. At that time; next, afterward, after that; **now and** ~, at one time and another, from time to time. **then** conj. In that case; therefore; it follows that; accordingly. ~ adj. Existing etc. at that time. ~ n. That time; **every now and** ~, from time to time.

the·nar (thē´när) n. (anat.) Ball of muscle at base of thumb; palm of hand; sole of foot.

thence (dhĕns) adv. (archaic and literary) From that place, from there; from that source, for that reason. **thence·forth** (dhĕnsfōrth´, -fōrth´, dhĕns´fōrth, -fōrth), **thence·for·ward** (dhĕnsfōr´werd), **thence·for´wards** advs. & ns. From (from) that time forward.

theo- prefix. God.

the·o·cen·tric (thēosĕn´trĭk) adj. Having God as its center.

the·oc·ra·cy (thēŏk´rasē) n. (pl. **-cies**). Government by God, directly or through a priestly class etc.; state so governed; **the T** ~, the Jewish commonwealth from Moses to the monarchy.

the·oc·ra·sy (thēŏk´rasē) n. Union of the soul with God through contemplation (among Neoplatonists, Buddhists, etc.).

the·o·crat (thē´okrăt) n. Ruler in, subject under, a theocracy. **the·o·crat·ic** (thēokrăt´ĭk) adj. **the·o·crat´i·cal·ly** adv.

The·oc·ri·tus (thēŏk´rĭtus) (3rd c. B.C.). Sicilian Greek poet; regarded as the originator of pastoral poetry.

the·od·o·lite (thēŏd´olīt) n. Surveying instrument for measuring horizontal and vertical angles; telescope rotating around a graduated circular plate and also free to swivel in vertical plane over a graduated arc. **the·od·o·lit·ic** (thēŏdolĭt´ĭk) adj.

The·o·do·ra (thēodōr´a, -dōr´a) (508?–48). Empress of the Eastern Roman Empire; married Justinian I, 523, and greatly influenced political and religious events.

The·o·dore (thē´odōr, -dōr). Name of three czars of Russia: ~ **I** (1557–98), succeeded his father Ivan the Terrible 1584; ~ **II** (1589–1605), son of Boris Godunov, succeeded his father 1605 and was murdered in the same statement of principles of something, abstract knowledge, formulation of this; branch of art or technical subject concerned with knowledge of its principles or methods, as opp. to practice; systematic statement of general principles of some branch of mathematics; mere hypothesis, conjecture, individual view or notion. **the·o·ti·cian** (thēoretĭsh´an, thēre-), **the´o·rist** *ns*. **the·o·rize** (thē´orīz) *v*. (**-rized, -riz·ing**). **the´o·riz·er** *n*.

the·os·o·phy (thēŏs´ofē) *n*. (pl. **-phies**). Philosophy professing to attain to knowledge of God by spiritual ecstasy, direct intuition, or special individual relations, now usu., doctrines of the Theosophical Society. **the·o·soph·ic** (thēosŏf´ĭk), **the·o·soph´i·cal** *adjs*. (esp.) **T~ Society**, society founded in 1875 in New York, advocating universal brotherhood, and following esp. Brahminic and Buddhistic teachings. **the·o·soph´i·cal·ly** *adv*. **the·os´o·phist** *n*.

ther·a·peu·tic (thĕrapū´tĭk), **ther·a·peu·ti·cal** (thĕrapū´tĭkal) *adjs*. Of the healing of disease, curative; ~ **abortion**, abortion performed when health of mother is endangered by pregnancy. **ther·a·peu´tics** *n.pl*. Branch of medicine concerned with remedial treatment of disease. **ther·a·peu´ti·cal·ly** *adv*.

ther·a·py (thĕr´apē) *n*. (pl. **-pies**). 1. Medical or physical treatment of disease or physical

defects. 2. Healing quality or power. 3. Treatment of patients with psychological, social, or emotional problems, as by PSYCHOTHERAPY. **ther´a·pist** *n*.

Ther·a·va·da (thĕravah´da) *n*. One of the two great schools of Buddhism, surviving esp. in Sri Lanka, Burma, Thailand, and Kampuchea; Hinayanist name for Hinayana.

there (dhār) *adv*. In or at that place; at that point in argument, situation, progress of affairs, etc.; to that place or point; used unemphatically to introduce sentence or clause in which verb comes before its subject (also, with some form of the verb *be*, without inversion); **there´about(s)**, near that place; near that number, quantity, etc.; **thereaf´ter**, (archaic) after that; **thereat´** (archaic) there; thereupon, at that; **thereby´**, (archaic) by or through that; **thereby hangs a tale**, in that connection there is something to be told; **therefor´**, (archaic) for that, for it; for that reason, on that account; **there´fore**, in consequence of that; for that reason, accordingly, consequently; **therein´**, (archaic) in that place; in that respect; **thereinaf´ter**, (archaic) later, in same document etc.; **thereof´**, (archaic) of that, of it;

thereon´, (archaic) to that, to it; in addition; **there´upon**, in consequence of that; soon, immediately, after that; (archaic) upon that; **therewith´**, (archaic) with that; thereupon. **there** *n*. That place or point. ~ *int*. Exclamation expressing confirmation, triumph, dismay, etc.

therm, therme (thẽrm) *ns*. Unit of heat, esp. 100,000 Btu as basis of charge for gas used as fuel. **therm-** = THERMO-. **-therm** *comb. form*. Indicating heat, as in *endotherm, megatherm*.

ther·mal (thẽr´mal) *adj*. Of heat; determined, measured, operated by heat; ~ **capacity**, (of a body) number of heat units required to raise its temperature by 1 degree; ~ **spring**, hot spring; ~ **unit**, unit of heat; **British T~ Unit**, (abbrev. Btu) amount of heat required to raise the temperature of 1 pound of water at its maximum density by 1 degree Fahrenheit. **thermal** *n*. Rising current of warm air. **ther´mic** *adj*. **ther´mal·ly** *adv*.

Ther·mi·dor (thẽr´mĭdor). Eleventh month of French revolutionary calendar, covering parts of July and August. **Ther·mi·do·ri·an** (thẽrmĭdōr´ēan, -dōr´-) *n*. (Fr. hist.) One of those taking part in overthrow of Robespierre on 9

*Development of new equipment has enabled much more accurate data to be obtained. An infra-red **thermometer** can measure radiation from different parts of the body.*

*In the early days of radio, the **thermionic valve** was essential. However, development of transistors and other miniature circuitry has largely eliminated valves.*

Thermidor (July 27, 1794).

therm·i·on (thĕrm´ĭon, thĕr´-mē-) *n.* Electrically charged particle (electron or ion) emitted from a heated body. **therm·i·on·ic** (thĕrmĭŏn´ĭk, thĕrmē-) *adj.* Of, emitting, thermions; ~ **tube,** vacuum tube in which electrons emitted by a heated filament carry electric current in one direction, used as a rectifier of an alternating current and in radio receiving sets for the detection and amplification of radio waves.

therm·is·tor (thĕrmĭs´ter) *n.* Type of semiconductor in which the resistance decreases as the temperature rises.

ther·mite (thĕr´mīt) *n.* Mixture of finely divided aluminum and oxide of iron or oxide of other metal, producing very high temperature (*c*3,000°C) on combustion, used in smelting, welding, and for incendiary bombs.

thermo-, therm- *comb. forms.* Heat (*thermistor, thermodynamics*).

ther·mo·chem·is·try (thĕrmō-kĕm´ĭstrē) *n.* Branch of chemistry dealing with the heat changes accompanying reactions. **ther·mo·chem´i·cal** *adj.* **ther·mo·chem´ist** *n.*

ther·mo·cline (thĕr´moklīn) *n.* Layer of water in ocean or certain lakes between warmer layer near surface and colder, deep-water layer below, with temperature dropping rapidly at greater depths.

ther·mo·cou·ple (thĕr´mo-kŭpel) *n.* Device consisting of two

different metals joined at two places so that when a difference of temperature exists at the junction of the metals, an electromotive force is produced that can be used to measure that difference.

ther·mo·dy·nam·ics (thĕrmo-dīnăm´ĭks) *n.pl.* (usu. considered sing.). Science dealing with the relationship between thermal energy (heat) and all other forms of energy (mechanical, electrical, etc.); **first law of** ~: during transformation of heat into another form of energy there is a constant relation between the amount of heat expended and energy gained; the same is true of the reverse process; **second law of** ~, heat cannot pass of its own accord from a colder to a hotter body. **ther·mo·dy·nam´ic** *adj.* **ther·mo·dy·nam´i·cal·ly** *adv.*

ther·mo·e·lec·tric·i·ty (thĕr-mōĭlĕktrĭs´ĭtē, -ēlĕk-) *n.* Electricity developed by the action of heat at the junction of two different metals. **ther·mo·e·lec·tric** (thĕrmōĭlĕk´trĭk) *adj.*

ther·mol·y·sis (thĕrmŏl´ĭsĭs) *n.* (pl. **-ses** pr. -sēz). (chem.) Dissociation, decomposition, by action of heat.

ther·mom·e·ter (thĕrmŏm´eter) *n.* Instrument for measuring temperature, freq. a graduated glass tube with bulb containing a substance (as mercury, alcohol) whose expansion and contraction under the influence of temperature can be accurately measured. **ther·mo·-**

met·ric (thĕrmomĕt´rĭk), **ther·mo·met´ri·cal** *adjs.* **ther·mo·met´ri·cal·ly** *adv.* **ther·mom´e·try** *n.* Science dealing with the measurement of temperature.

ther·mo·nu·cle·ar (thĕrmō-nōō´klēer, -nū´-) *adj.* Of or concerned with reactions involving the fusion of atomic nuclei at very high temperatures, as in a hydrogen bomb.

ther·mo·pile (thĕr´mopīl) *n.* Set of thermocouples arranged in series, used to detect radiant heat.

ther·mo·plas·tic (thĕrmoplăs´tĭk) *adj.* & *n.* (Substance) that becomes plastic when heated, hardens when cooled, and can do this repeatedly. **ther·mo·plas·tic·i·ty** (thĕrmōplăstĭs´ĭtē) *n.*

Ther·mop·y·lae (thĕrmŏp´ĭlē). Pass in Greece from Locris into Thessaly, orig. narrow but now much widened by recession of sea; scene of the heroic defense (480 B.C.) against the Persian army of Xerxes by 6,000 Greeks, including 300 Spartans under LEONIDAS.

ther·mos (thĕr´mos) *n.* (also ~ **bottle, jug**) Kind of vacuum flask. [orig. trademark]

ther·mo·set·ting (thĕr´mōsĕt-ĭng) *adj.* Becoming permanently hard and rigid when heated.

ther·mo·stat (thĕr´mostăt) *n.* Device that automatically regulates temperature by cutting off and restoring the supply of heat to a piece of equipment or a room etc. **ther·mo·stat·ic** (thĕrmostăt´ĭk) *adj.* **ther·mo·stat´i·cal·ly** *adv.*

ther·mo·tax·is (thĕrmotăk´sĭs) *n.* (physiol.) Regulation of bodily heat.

ther·mo·trop·ic (thĕrmotrŏp´-ĭk) *adj.* (of plants etc.) Bending or turning toward, or away from a source of heat. **ther·mot·ro·pism** (thĕrmŏt´ropĭzem) *n.*

the·saur·us (thĭsōr´us) *n.* (pl. **-saur·i** pr. -sōr´ī, **-saur·us·es**). Storehouse of information; dictionary or encyclopedia, esp. a collection of synonyms and antonyms.

these: see THIS.

The·seus (thē´sēus, -sōos). (Gk. legend) Hero, son of Aegeus, king of Athens (or of Poseidon); slayer of the Cretan Minotaur and hero of other famous exploits.

the·sis (thē´sĭs) *n.* (pl. **-ses** pr. -sēz). Proposition laid down or stated, esp. as theme to be discussed and proved; dissertation to maintain and prove thesis, esp. submitted by candidate for university degree.

Thes·pi·an (thĕs´pēan) *adj.* 1. Of Thespis; of tragedy or the

*The monastery of Aghios Stephanos on a pinnacle in the modern Greek district of **Thessaly**. Subject to invasion by Romans and Turks, such buildings had to be made impregnable.*

dramatic art. 2. Of Thespiae, ancient city of Greece. ~ *n.* 1. Actor or actress. 2. Native, inhabitant, of Thespiae.

Thes·pis (thĕs′pĭs) (6th c. B.C.). Greek dramatic poet, regarded as father of Greek tragedy.

Thess. *abbrev.* Thessalonians (N.T.).

Thes·sa·lo·ni·an (thĕsɑlō′nēɑn) *adj.* Of Thessalonica. ~ *n.* Native, inhabitant, of Thessalonica; **(Epistle to the)** ~ s, either of two books of the New Testament, earliest extant letters of St. Paul, written from Corinth to the new church at Thessalonica.

Thes·sa·lon·i·ca (thĕsɑlŏn′ĭkɑ). Ancient city in Macedonia, founded 316 B.C. by Cassander, a general of Alexander the Great; now SALONIKA.

Thes·sa·ly (thĕs′ɑlē). Region of Greece in the central part of the Greek peninsula bordering the Aegean.

the·ta (thā′tɑ, thē′-) *n.* Ninth (later 8th) letter of Greek alphabet (Θ, θ), = *th.*

The·tis (thē′tĭs). (Gk. myth.) Sea nymph, mother of ACHILLES.

they (dhā) *pron.* Third person nom. pl. pronoun, plural of HE, SHE, IT.

Thi·bet (tĭbĕt′), **Thi·bet·an** (tĭbĕt′ɑn): see TIBET, TIBETAN.

thick (thĭk) *adj.* 1. Of great or specified depth between opposite surfaces; (of line etc.) broad, not fine. 2. Arranged closely, crowded together; numerous; abounding, packed, *with*; of great or considerable density, viscid, stiff; turbid, muddy, cloudy, not clear; (of soup) thickened. 3. Stupid, dull; (of voice) muffled, indistinct; (colloq.) intimate. 4. **thick′head**, blockhead; **thick′headed**, stupid, slow-witted; **thick′set**, set or growing close together; heavily or solidly built; **thick′skinned**, (fig.) not sensitive to criticism, reproach, insult, etc. **thick′ish** *adj.* **thick′ly** *adv.* **thick** *n.* Thick part of anything, esp. fight etc.; **through ~ and thin**, through good times and bad, under all conditions, resolutely. **thick** *adv.* Thickly.

thick·en (thĭk′en) *v.* Make or become thick; make of stiffer consistence. **thick′en·er, thick′en·ing** *ns.*

thick·et (thĭk′ĭt) *n.* Dense growth of small trees, shrubs, undergrowth, etc.

thick·ness (thĭk′nĭs) *n.* Being thick; third dimension, dist. from length and breadth; what is thick; layer.

thief (thēf) *n.* (pl. **thieves** pr. thēvz). One who steals, esp. secretly and without violence.

thieve (thēv) *v.* (**thieved, thiev·ing**). Be a thief, practice stealing; steal (thing). **thiev·er·y** (thē′vere)

As national emblem of Scotland, the **thistle** was taken by migrants to places like Australia. In the warmer climate, growth was prolific and it had to be proclaimed a noxious weed.

n. (pl. **-er·ies**). **thiev′ish** *adj.* **thiev′ish·ly** *adv.* **thiev′ish·ness** *n.*

thigh (thī) *n.* Upper part of human leg, from hip to knee; corresponding part (or part pop. supposed to correspond) in other animals; **thigh′bone**, bone of the thigh, femur.

thim·ble (thĭm′bel) *n.* Bell-shaped sheath of metal etc. worn on end of finger to push needle in sewing; (mech. etc.) ring, tube, sleeve, ferrule, etc.; **thim′bleful** (pl. **-fuls**), small quantity (of whiskey etc.) to drink.

Thim·phu (tĭm′pōō). Capital of Bhutan, in the W. part.

thin (thĭn) *adj.* (**thin·ner, thin·nest**). Having opposite surfaces close together; of small diameter; slender; lean, spare, not plump; not dense; not full or closely packed; of slight density or consistency; wanting body, fullness, volume, or substance; (of lines) narrow, fine; (fig.) shallow, transparent, flimsy; ~ **-skinned**, (fig.) sensitive. **thin′-ly** *adv.* **thin′ness** *n.* **thin′nish** *adj.* **thin** *v.* (**thinned, thin·ning**). Make or become thin; reduce in bulk or number; ~ **out**, reduce number of (esp. seedlings, by pulling up the less promising). **thin** *adv.* Sparsely.

thine: see THY.

thing (thĭng) *n.* 1. What is or may be an object of perception, knowledge, or thought. 2. Entity, being, esp. inanimate object. 3. Piece of property, possession, (pl.) clothes, garments, esp. outdoor garments; (pl.) implements, utensils. 4. (pl.) Affairs, concerns,

matters. 5. What is (to be) done, fact, deed, occurrence; what is said, expression, statement.

thing·um·a·jig (thĭng′umɑjĭg) *n.* (colloq.) Thing indicated vaguely because speaker cannot remember or does not wish to use correct word; what-d'you-call-it; also **thing·um·bob** (thĭng′umbŏb), **thing·a·ma·bob, thing·um·a·bob** (thĭng′amɑbŏb).

think (thĭngk) *v.* (**thought** pr. thawt, **think·ing**). Consider, be of opinion; form conception of; exercise mind in active way, form connected ideas; consider a matter, reflect; conceive notion of doing something, contemplate, intend; ~ **about**, consider; ~ **of**, consider; imagine, intend, contemplate; entertain idea *of*; hit upon; ~ **out**, consider carefully; devise (plan etc.); ~ **over**, reflect upon. **think** *n.* (colloq.) Act of thinking; ~ **piece**, journalistic article dealing with general assessment and interpretation of news etc.; ~ **tank**, (colloq.) organization providing advice and ideas on national, industrial, etc., problems. **think′er** *n.* (esp.) Person of skilled or powerful mind.

think·a·ble (thĭng′kabel) *adj.* Capable of being considered or thought about; conceivable; possible. **think′a·bly** *adv.*

think·ing (thĭng′kĭng) *n.* Act of one who thinks or outcome of such act; thought; opinion; judgment. ~ *adj.* Typified by thoughtfulness; rational; **put on one's ~ cap**, meditate on a problem.

thi·o (thī′ō) *acid.* Acid in which oxygen is partly or wholly replaced by sulfur.

thi·o·cy·an·ic (thīōsīăn′ĭk) *adj.* ~ **acid**, colorless unstable liquid acid (HCNS) with penetrating odor. **thi·o·cy·a·nate** (thīōsī′anāt) *n.* Salt of this.

thi·o·sul·fate (thīōsŭl′fāt) *n.* Salt of thiosulfuric acid ($H_2S_2O_2$), extremely unstable acid; used in photography, formerly called *hyposulphite* (see HYPO).

third (thĕrd) *adj.* Next after second; (baseball) ~ **base**, base between second base and home plate; (baseball) ~ **baseman**, infielder near third base; ~ **-class**, (esp.) poor, inferior; ~ **degree**, severe examination of prisoner to extort confession or information; (freemasonry) degree of master mason; ~ **-degree burn**, severe burn that destroys epidermis and exposes nerve endings; ~ **dimension**, depth in an object as distinguished from length or width, which are the flat surface dimensions; quality of possessing or appearing to possess such depth; quality of appearing real; ~ **gear**, gear next above second gear on motor vehicle or bicycle; **third′-**

Above: **Dylan Thomas** *as painted by Rupert Shepherd. Considered by some critics as an outstanding poet of his generation, he did not attain popular success until 'Under Milk Wood'.*

Right: The **thorax** *of a grasshopper is covered by the large pronotum which, on members of the Acrididae family, has conspicuous crests. Their function is not known.*

hand, (*adj.*) having had two previous owners or users; learned, acquired, etc., through two successive intermediaries; **third mate**, officer on merchant vessel next below second mate; **third party**: see PARTY; **third person**, (gram.) personal pronoun (*he, she, it, they*), verb form denoting person or thing spoken of; **third rail**, (in some electric railroads) rail through which current is conducted, lying alongside those on which train runs; **third-rate**, inferior, decidedly poor, in quality; **Third Reich**: see REICH; **Third World**, underdeveloped countries of Asia, Africa, and Latin Amer., usu. not aligned with either the communist or the Western nations. **third** *n.* Third part (see PART¹ sense 1); third thing, person, place, class, etc.; (in motor vehicle) third gear; (mus.) interval of which the span involves three alphabetical names of notes; harmonic combination of the two notes thus separated. **third'ly** *adv.* In the third place.

thirst (thẽrst) *n.* Uneasy or painful sensation caused by want of drink; desire for drink; (fig.) ardent desire, craving. **thirst'y** *adj.* (**thirst·i·er, thirst·i·est**). Feeling thirst; dry, parched, arid; (colloq.) causing thirst; (fig.) eager, greedy. **thirst'i·ly** *adv.* **thirst'i·ness** *n.* **thirst** *v.i.* Feel thirst.

thir·teen (thẽr'tēn') *adj.* & *n.*

One more than 12 (13, xiii, or XIII). **thir'teenth'** *adj.* & *n.*

thir·ty (thẽr'tē) *adj.* Amounting to 30; **T~-nine Articles**, articles of religion assented to by person taking orders in Church of England; **T~ Years' War**, war (1618–48) originating between Catholics and Protestants of Germany and later involving most of Western Europe. **thirty** *n.* (pl. **-ties**). Cardinal number, 3 times 10 (30, xxx, or XXX); set of 30 things or persons; **thirties**, numbers etc. from 30 to 39; these years of century or life. **thir'ti·eth** *adj.* & *n.*

this (dhĭs) *demonstr. pron.* & *adj.* (pl. **these** pr. dhēz). The (person, thing, event, time) near, present, just mentioned (freq. opp. THAT). ~ *adv.* To the extent or degree indicated (as ~ **far, much**).

This·be (thĭz'bē). (Rom. legend) Lover of PYRAMUS.

this·tle (thĭs'el) *n.* Prickly composite herbaceous, often woody, plant of *Cirsium* and related genera, with stems, leaves, and involucres thickly armed with prickles, usu. globular flower heads and most freq. purple flowers; **this'tledown**, downy appendage of thistle (freq. as type of lightness or flimsiness). **this'tly** *adj.*

thith·er (thĭdh'er, dhĭdh'-) *adv.* (archaic) To that place.

tho, tho' (dhō) = THOUGH.

Thom·as¹ (tŏm'*a*s), **St.** Apostle who refused to believe that Christ had risen again unless he could see and touch his wounds (John 20); commemorated Dec. 21; **doubting** ~, skeptic.

Thom·as² (tŏm'*a*s), **Dylan** (1914–53). Welch poet,; author of *Under Milk Wood*, a play for voices.

Thom·as³ (tŏm'*a*s), **Norman (Mattoon)** (1884–1968). Amer. socialist and politician; U.S. presidential candidate six times between 1928–48.

Thom·as⁴ à Kem·pis (tŏm'*a*s *a* kĕm'pĭs). Thomas Hämmerken (c1380–1471), named for his birthplace, Kempen, near Düsseldorf; Augustinian monk, author of *De Imitatione Christi*.

Thom·as⁵ A·qui·nas (tŏm'*a*s akwī'nas), **St.**: see AQUINAS.

Tho·mism (tō'mĭzem, thō'-). System of theology and philosophy taught by St. Thomas AQUINAS. **Tho'mist** *n.* **Tho·mis·tic** (tōmĭs'tĭk, thō-) *adj.*

Thomp·son¹ (tŏmp'son), **Francis** (1859–1907). English poet; author of "Hound of Heaven," describing the poet's flight from God, the pursuit, and the overtaking.

Thomp·son² (tŏmp'son), **John Taliaferro** (1860–1940). U.S. general; one of the inventors of the **Thompson submachine gun**, a portable automatic weapon.

thong (thŏng) *n.* Narrow strip of hide or leather etc. used as strap etc.

Thor (thōr). (Scand. myth.) God of thunder, war, and agriculture, represented as armed with hammer.

tho·rax (thōr'ăks, thŏr'-) *n.* (pl. **tho·rax·es, tho·ra·ces** pr. thōr'-asēz, thŏr'-). 1. (anat., zool.) Part of body of mammal between neck and abdomen that is enclosed by ribs, breastbone, and vertebrae and contains chief organs of circulation and respiration. 2. (zool.) Middle section of body of insect etc. between head and abdomen. **tho·rac·ic** (thŏrăs'ĭk) *adj.*

Thor·eau (thŏr'ō, thōr'ō, thorō'), **Henry David** (1817–62). Amer. essayist, poet, and naturalist; author of *Walden or Life in the Woods* (1854).

tho·ri·um (thōr'ēum, thŏr'-) *n.* (chem.) Radioactive metallic element that (like uranium) will undergo fission when bombarded with neutrons and is therefore a potential source of atomic energy; symbol Th, at. no. 90, at. wt. 232.0381.

thorn (thôrn) *n.* 1. Stiff sharp-pointed process on stem or other part of plant; thorn-bearing bush or tree, esp. hawthorn, whitethorn, or other species of genus *Crataegus*; ~ **in one's side** or **flesh**, constant source of annoyance (2 Cor. 12:7). 2. Name of Old English and Icelandic runic letter þ (= th). 3. ~ **apple**, poisonous plant of genus *Datura*, esp. *D. stramonium*, Jimson weed. **thorn'y** *adj.* (**thorn·i·er, thorn·i·est**). (esp., fig.) Harassing, vexatious, difficult to handle, delicate, ticklish; ~ **locust**, small tree or spiny shrub (*Robinia neomexicana*) of southwest U.S.

thor·ough (ther'ō, thŭr'ō) *adj.* Complete, unqualified, not superficial, out-and-out; **thor'ough-bred**, (animal, esp. horse) of pure breed; (person) with attractive characteristics associated with a thoroughbred animal; **thor'ough-fare**, any public way open at both ends, esp. main road; **thor'ough-going**, extreme, thorough, out-and-out. **thor'ough·ly** *adv.* **thor'ough·ness** *n.* **thorough** *adv.* & *prep.* (archaic) Through.

those: see THAT.

Thoth (thōth, tōt). (Egyptian myth.) God of wisdom and magic, the scribe of the gods, identified with the Greek Hermes and represented in human form with head of an ibis.

thou (dhow) *pron.* Second person nom. sing. pronoun (now archaic or poet.) denoting person addressed.

though (dhō) *conj.* In spite of the fact that; even if, granting that; **as** ~, as if. **though** *adv.*

(colloq.) And yet, but yet, all the same, none the less.

thought[1] (thawt) *n.* Process, power, capacity, faculty, of thinking; what one thinks, what is or has been thought; idea, notion; consideration, heed; meditation; intention, purpose, design; ~ **transference**, telepathy.

thought[2]: see THINK.

thought·ful (thawt'ful) *adj.* Engaged in, given to, meditation; showing thought or consideration; considerate (*of*), kindly. **thought'-ful·ly** *adv.* **thought'ful·ness** *n.*

thought·less (thawt'lĭs) *adj.* Unthinking, heedless, imprudent; inconsiderate. **thought'less·ly** *adv.* **thought'less·ness** *n.*

thou·sand (thow'zand) *adj.* Amounting to 1,000; (loosely) very many; **T ~ and One Nights**, the "ARABIAN Nights"; **T ~ Island dressing**, salad dressing of mayonnaise and chili sauce with additions of chopped mixed pickles, diced hard-boiled eggs, chopped pimentos, onions, capers, etc.; **T ~ Islands**, group of about 1,000 islands in St. Lawrence River at the outlet of Lake Ontario. **thousand** *n.* (pl. **-sands**, following a numeral **-sand**). Ten hundred; symbol for this (1,000, m, or M). **thou'-sand·fold** *adj.* & *adv.* **thou'-sandth** *adj.* & *n.*

Thrace (thrās). District of eastern Balkan peninsula, in ancient times including Bulgaria and eastern Macedonia. **Thra·cian** (thrā'shan) *adj.* & *n.* (Native, inhabitant) of Thrace; (of) its ancient Indo-European language, closely related to Illyrian, Phrygian, and Armenian.

thrall (thrawl) *n.* Slave; bondage. **thrall'dom, thral'dom** *ns.*

thrash (thrăsh) *v.t.* Beat, esp. with stick or whip; conquer, surpass; thresh; ~ **out**, (fig.) discuss exhaustively, argue thoroughly. **thrash'er**[1] *n.* One who or that which thrashes.

thrash·er[2] (thrăsh'er) *n.* 1. (esp.) Kind of shark (*Alopias vulpinus*), with very long upper division of tail, with which it lashes an enemy. 2. Any of several Amer. songbirds (genus *Toxostoma*) having a long tail and a long curving bill.

thread (thrĕd) *n.* 1. Fine cord of spun-out fibers or filaments of flax, cotton, wool, glass, etc., esp. of two or more twisted together; thread-shaped or threadlike thing, e.g. fine line or streak of color or light; spiral ridge of screw, each complete turn of this. 2. (fig.) Something represented as like thread, esp. course of human life; that which connects successive points in narrative, train of thought, etc., or on which things hang; continuous or persistent feature running through pattern of

anything. 3. **thread'bare**, with nap worn off and threads of warp and woof left bare; wearing such garments, shabby, seedy; (fig.) commonplace, trite, hackneyed; **thread'fish** (pl. **-fishes**, collect. **-fish**), tropical fish of family Polycnemidae, with pectoral fin in long threads; **thread'worm**, any of various threadlike worms, any nematode, esp. the pin worm. **thread'y** *adj.* (**thread·i·er, thread·i·est**). **thread** *v.t.* Pass thread through eye of (needle); string (beads etc.) on thread, make (chain etc.) thus; pick one's way through (street, crowded place, etc.), make one's *way* thus; form screw thread on.

threat (thrĕt) *n.* Declaration of intention to punish or hurt; (law) such menace of bodily hurt or injury to reputation or property as may restrain person's freedom of action; indication of coming evil.

threat·en (thrĕt'en) *v.* Use threats (against); try to influence by threats; announce one's intention (*to* do) as punishment or in revenge etc.; be source of danger to; presage, portend. **threat'en·er** *n.* **threat'-en·ing·ly** *adv.*

three (thrē) *adj.* Amounting to 3; ~ **-color process**, printing process in which colored picture etc. is reproduced by superposition of the three primary colors or their complementary colors; ~ **-cornered**, having three angles or corners; (of contest etc.) between three persons; ~ **-decker**, three-decked ship, esp. (hist.) line-of-battle ship with guns on three decks;

*The drug daturine, which has similar properties to atropine, can be extracted from the **thornapple** and other plants in the genus Datura. Other species contain anesthetic properties.*

Although powered machinery has long been used to **thresh** grain in the U.S.A. and other industrialized countries, hand-operated threshers are still used in the Spanish Pyrenees.

Thrift or sea pink is found in coastal and mountainous areas in north temperate zones. Its leaves once provided a substance used for slimming.

sandwich made with three slices of bread; anything with three layers, tiers, etc.; ~-**dimensional**, (producing effect or illusion of) having depth in space as well as height and width; realistic; ~-**legged**, (of race) run by pairs with one runner's right leg tied to the other's left leg; **T ~ Mile Island**, site of nuclear power plant near Harrisburg, Pa., at which accident occurred in 1979, calling attention of the public to safety problems inherent in conventional reactor designs; ~-**master**, vessel with three masts; ~-**mile limit**, hist. the limit of zone of territorial waters, extending three miles from coast; **threepence** (thrĕp´ens, thrĭp´-, thrŭp´-), (Brit.) sum of three pence; **three-ply**, having, woven with, three strands (of thread, yarn, etc.); (plywood) composed of three layers of wood; **three-point landing**, landing of aircraft so that landing wheels and tail or nose wheel touch down simultaneously; **three-quarter**, (of portraits) showing figure down to hips or knees; **three-quarter time**, (mus.) meter of composition with time signature of $\frac{3}{4}$ and three quarter notes or the equivalent per measure; **the three R's**, reading, (w)riting, (a)rithmetic, regarded as fundamentals of education; basic knowledge in any field; **three´-some**, (game etc., esp. golf) in which three persons take part; **three-wheeler**, vehicle with three wheels, esp. tricycle; **three´fold** *adj.* & *adv.* **three** *n.* One more than 2; symbol for this (3, iii, or III); card, die face, or domino with three pips; three o'clock; size etc. indicated by 3; set of three things or persons; ~ **of a kind**, (poker) three cards of one denomination.

thren·o·dy (thrĕn´odē) (pl. -**dies**), **thre·node** (thrē´nōd, thrĕn´ōd) *ns.* Song of lamentation, esp. for death, dirge. **thre·no·di·al** (thrĭnō´dēal), **thre·nod·ic** (thrĭnŏd´ĭk) *adjs.* **thren´o·dist** *n.*

thresh (thrĕsh) *v.t.* Beat out or separate grain from (wheat etc.) on **thresh´ing floor** (prepared hard level for the purpose) or in **threshing machine**.

thresh·old (thrĕsh´ōld, -hōld) *n.* Piece of stone, timber, etc., lying below bottom of doorway; entrance; (psych.) point at which stimulus begins to produce its effect.

thrice (thrīs) *adv.* (archaic or literary) Three times.

thrift (thrĭft) *n.* 1. Frugality, economical management; ~ **shop**, store that sells discarded clothing, household wares, etc., for bargain prices to raise funds for charity. 2. Plant of genus *Armeria*, esp. *A. maritima* (sea pink), seashore and alpine plant with pink, white, or purple flowers on naked stems rising from tuft of grasslike radical leaves. **thrift´less** *adj.* **thrift´less·ly** *adv.* **thrift´less·ness** *n.* **thrift´y** *adj.* (**thrift·i·er, thrift·i·est**). **thrift´i·ly** *adv.* **thrift´i·ness** *n.*

thrill (thrĭl) *n.* Nervous tremor caused by intense emotion or sensation, wave of feeling or excitement; sensational quality (of story etc.). ~ *v.* Penetrate with wave of emotion or sensation, be thus penetrated or agitated; (of emotion etc.) pass *through*, *over*, etc.; quiver, throb, (as) with emotion. **thrill´er** *n.* (esp.) Sensational play, story, etc. **thrill´ing** *adj.* **thrill´ing·ly** *adv.*

thrips (thrĭps) *n.* (pl. **thrips**). Any minute insect, with four hair-fringed wings, of order Thysanoptera, many of which injure plants by feeding on their juices.

thrive (thrīv) *v.t.* (**thrived** or **throve** pr. thrōv, **thrived** or **thriv·en** pr. thrĭv´en, **thriv·ing**). Grow or develop well and vigorously, flourish; prosper; grow rich. **thriv´er** *n.*

thro, thro' (thrōō) = THROUGH.

throat (thrōt) *n.* 1. Front of neck between chin and collarbone, region containing pharynx and larynx; narrow passage, esp. in or near entrance of something, narrow part in a passage; **sore ~**, inflammation of lining membrane of pharynx etc. **cut one's own ~**, (fig.) bring about one's own defeat; **cut one another's ~s**, compete ruinously; **jump down someone's ~**, (slang) criticize or contradict someone violently and prematurely; **lump in one's ~**, tightness in the throat as emotional reaction; **ram something down someone's ~**, (colloq.) force (thing) on his attention; **stick in one's ~**, be difficult to utter; ~ **microphone**, microphone suspended at neck of speaker etc. and actuated by vibrations of larynx. 2. Forward upper corner of fore-and-aft sail. **throat** *v.t.* Groove, channel.

throat·y (thrō'tē) *adj.* (**throat-i·er, throat·i·est**). Guttural, uttered in the throat, hoarse. **throat'i·ly** *adv.* **throat'i·ness** *n.*

throb (thrŏb) *v.i.* (**throbbed, throb·bing**). (of heart etc.) Beat strongly, palpitate, pulsate, vibrate. ~ *n.* Throbbing, violent beat or pulsation.

throe (thrō) *n.* (usu. pl.) Violent pang(s); desperate · or agonizing struggle, anguish.

throm·bo·sis (thrŏmbō'sĭs) *n.* (pl. **-ses** pr. -sēz). Localized clotting of blood within the heart or blood vessels. **throm·bot·ic** (thrŏmbŏt'ĭk) *adj.*

throm·bus (thrŏm'bus) *n.* (pl. **-bi** pr. -bī). Blood clot formed within vascular system that may impede circulation.

throne (thrōn) *n.* Chair of state for sovereign, bishop, etc., usu. decorated and raised on dais; sovereign power; (pl.) order of angels (see ANGEL); ~ **room**, chamber or hall containing throne where monarch sits in state; (fig.) center of power in government, industrial complex, etc. **throne** *v.t.* (**throned, thron·ing**). Enthrone.

throng (thrŏng) *n.* Crowd, multitude (*of*) esp. in small space. ~ *v.* Come, go, press, in multitudes; fill with crowd or as crowd does.

throt·tle (thrŏt'el) *n.* 1. Throat, gullet (of a horse etc.) 2. Valve controlling flow of steam in steam engine or of fuel in internal combustion engine. ~ *v.t.* (**-tled, -tling**). 1. Choke, strangle. 2. Control, obstruct, flow of (steam, fuel, etc.) in engine, esp. with throttle; (also ~ **down**) slow down (engine) thus.

Throt·tle-bot·tom (thrŏt'el-bŏtom) *n.* (sometimes **t** ~) Inept, unfit public official.

through (thrōō) *prep.* From end to end or side to side of, between the sides, walls, parts, etc., of; from beginning to end of; by reason of, by agency, means, or fault of; up to and including. ~ *adv.* Through something; from end to end; to the end; ~ **and** ~, all the way through, completely, utterly; **be, get,** ~ (**with**), finish (with), come to end (of). **through** *adj.* Going, concerned with going, through; (of railroad etc.) going all the way without change of train, line, etc.; ~ **street**, street where vehicles have right of way over traffic entering from side streets or crossing at intersections; **through'put**, amount of material put through a manufacturing etc. process; work done by a computer in a period of time.

through·out (thrōōowt') *prep.* From end to end of; in every part of. ~ *adv.* In every part or respect.

throw (thrō) *v.* (**threw** pr. thrōō, **thrown, throw·ing**). 1. Shape (pottery) on wheel; prepare and twist (silk etc.) into threads. 2. Project (thing) from hand or arm

Left: The song **thrush,** *is originally from Europe but has been acclimatized in other parts of the world. The ground thrush, below, is an Australian bird related to others in S.E. Asia.*

with jerking motion, esp. with sudden straightening of arm near shoulder level, so that it passes through air or free space; cast, make specified cast, (with) dice; move (esp. part of the body) quickly or suddenly. 3. (of wrestler, horse, etc.) Bring (antagonist, rider) to the ground; (of animals) bring forth (young). 4. Put carelessly or hastily *on, off,* etc. 5. (slang) Give (a party). 6. ~ **away**, (fig.) squander, waste; lose (chance etc.) by neglect; discard (card) when one cannot follow suit; **throw'away** (*n.*), printed paper, advertisement, etc., not intended to be kept; **throw back**, revert to ancestral type or character; **throw'back** (*n.*), such reversion, example of this; **throw in**, add (thing) to bargain without extra charge; interpose (word, remark) in parenthesis or casually; **throw cold water on**, discourage by raising objections, being indifferent, etc.; **throw in one's hand**, give up, withdraw from contest; **throw in one's lot with**, decide to share fortunes of; **throw-in** (*n.*), (soccer or basketball) act of throwing in ball after it has gone out of play; **throw in the sponge** or **the towel**, (slang, esp. boxing) admit defeat; give up; **throw off**, discard; get rid of; abandon (disguise); disturb, distract (person) from train of thought etc.; **throw oneself at**, try hard to gain love or favor of; **throw oneself into**, participate enthusiastically in; **throw oneself on**, place one's reliance on; **throw out**, cast out; suggest, insinuate; reject (bill in legislature); eject; (baseball) put (batter or base runners) out; **throw over**, desert, abandon; **throw the bull**, (slang) talk without point or sequence; boast; **throw up**, vomit; give up; build carelessly. **throw**

n. 1. Throwing, cast; cast of dice; distance missile is or may be thrown; fall in wrestling; (geol., mining) (amount of vertical displacement caused by) fault in stratum. 2. (Extent of) action or motion of slide valve, crank, cam, etc.

throw·er (thrō′er) *n.* One who or that which throws.

thru (throo) *adv. & adj.* (colloq.) Through.

thrum[1] (thrŭm) *n.* Fringe of warp threads remaining on loom when web has been cut off, single thread of this; any loose thread or tuft.

thrum[2] (thrŭm) *v.* (**thrummed, thrum·ming**). Strum; sound monotonously, hum. ~ *n.* (Sound of) thrumming.

thrush[1] (thrŭsh) *n.* Small or medium-sized passerine bird of family Turdidae.

thrush[2] (thrŭsh) *n.* 1. Disease, esp. of infants, characterized by whitish vesicular specks on inside of mouth and throat etc. and caused by fungi of genus *Candida.* 2. Inflammatory pussy disease of foot in animals, esp. the frog of the foot of the horse.

thrust (thrŭst) *v.* (**thrust, thrust·ing**). Push, drive, exert force of impact on or against; pierce *through*; make sudden push *at* with pointed weapon; force oneself *through, past,* etc., make *way* thus. ~ *n.* Thrusting, lunge, stab; (mech. etc.) thrusting force of one part of structure etc. on contiguous part, esp. horizontal or diagonal pressure of part of building against abutment or support, driving force exerted by paddle, propeller shaft,

or jet stream in ship or aircraft, (effect of) compressive strain in Earth's crust; ~ **augmentation**, increase in rocket or jet engine thrust, achieved by afterburning etc. ~ **bearing**, bearing in machinery that absorbs thrusts paralleling axis of revolution; ~ **stage,** (theatr.) stage extending into audience.

thrust·er, thrus·tor (thrŭs′ter) *ns.* (esp.) One who pushes forward in hunting field or rides too close to hounds; pusher.

thru·way (throo′wā) *n.* Highway for high speed traffic, with limited access to it and usu. requiring a toll.

Thu·cyd·i·des (thoosĭd′ĭdēz) (5th c. B.C.). Athenian historian of the Peloponnesian War.

thud (thŭd) *n. & v.i.* (**thud·ded, thud·ding**). (Make, fall with) low dull sound as of blow on soft thing.

thug (thŭg) *n.* Vicious ruffian; **T~,** (hist.) member of an association in India (suppressed 1830–40) of professional robbers and murderers, who strangled their victims. **thug′ger·y** *n.* **Thug·gee** (thŭg′ē) *n.* (hist.) Practice of Thugs.

thu·ja (thoo′ja), **thu·ya** (thoo′ya) *ns.* Tree or shrub of coniferous genus *T~* (the arborvitae) including the N. Amer. (*T. occidentalis*) and Chinese (*T. orientalis*) varieties.

Thu·le[1] (thoo′lē). Ancient Greek and Latin name of country six days' sail N. of Britain, supposed to be most northerly region in world; see ULTIMA THULE.

Thu·le[2] (too′lē) *adj.* Of or pertaining to an Eskimo culture in the Arctic from about 500 to 1400 A.D.

thu·li·um (thoo′lēum) *n.* (chem.) Rare metallic element found in combination in some rare earths; symbol Tm, at. no. 69, at. wt. 168.9342. [f. THULE[1]]

thumb (thŭm) *n.* Short thick inner digit, opposable to fingers, and with only two phalanges, of human hand; any inner digit opposable to and set apart from other digits; part of glove etc. covering thumb; ~ **s-down** (*n.*), act or example of disapproval, dissent; **turn ~ s down; ~ s up!** exhortation to cheerfulness or expression of satisfaction; **rule of ~** : see RULE; **under one's ~** , under influence or domination of; ~ **index**, reference index consisting of grooves cut in, or tabs projecting from, front edges of book, or margins so cut as to show initial letters or titles etc.; **thumb′nail**, nail of thumb; **thumbnail sketch**, small or hasty portrait, brief word picture; **thumb′screw**, screw with flattened or winged head that can be turned with thumb and fingers; instrument of torture for compressing thumb(s); **thumb-sucker**, one, esp. child, with the habit of sucking the thumb; **thumb-sucking** (*n.*); **thumb′tack**, tack with flat head that can be pushed into a soft surface. **thumb′less** *adj.* **thumb** *v.t.* Soil, wear, with thumb; handle with thumb or awkwardly or clumsily; make a request for (a ride in a vehicle) by sticking out a thumb in the direction one wishes to go; ~ **through**, turn over pages of (as if) with thumb.

thump (thŭmp) *n.* Heavy blow, bang; sound of this. ~ *v.* Beat heavily, esp. with fist; deliver heavy blows (*at, on,* etc.). **thump′ing** *adj.* (esp., colloq.) Very large, striking, impressive. **thump′er** *n.*

thun·der (thŭn′der) *n.* Loud noise accompanying lightning (but appearing to follow it because of

---

Lemon-scented thyme, is a cultivated variation of a herb which grows wild in the Mediterranean region. Oil extracted from thyme had culinary and therapeutic uses.

Incorrect functioning of the thyroid may result in an enlargement of the neck known as goiter. Sometimes, minor problems may be avoided by using foods containing iodine.

larynx

thyroid artery and vein

jugular vein

vagus nerve

trachea

difference in speeds of light and sound) and due to sudden violent disturbance of air by the electric discharge; any loud deep rumbling or resounding noise; terrifying, threatening, or impressive utterance(s); **thun′derbird**, in the mythology of some N. Amer. Indians, a great bird that causes thunder, lightning, and rain to come from the heavens; **thun′derbolt**, imaginary bolt or dart formerly supposed to be the destructive agent when thing is struck by lightning, esp. as attribute of Thor, Jupiter, etc.; conventional representation of this; something very startling, terrible, or destructive; **thun′derclap**, loud crash of thunder; **thun′dercloud**, storm cloud charged with electricity and producing thunder and lightning; **thun′derhead**, rounded cumulus cloud near horizon projecting above general body of cloud and portending thunder; **thun′dershower, thun′dersquall**, rain accompanied by thunder and lightning; **thun′derstorm**, storm with thunder and lightning; **thun′derstruck**, (fig.) amazed, terrified, confounded. **thun′der·less, thun′der·ous, thun′der·y** *adjs.* **thunder** *v.* 1. it ~ s, it is thundering, there is thunder. 2. Sound with or like thunder; emit (threats etc.) in loud or impressive manner; fulminate. **thun′der·er** *n.* (esp., **T** ~) Jupiter. **thun′der·ing** *adj. & adv.* (esp., colloq.) Unusual(ly), decided(ly).

thun·der·a·tion (thŭnderā′shon) *int.* Mild oath or exclamation of surprise or irritation.

thu·ri·ble (thoor′ibel) *n.* Censer.

Thu·rin·gi·a (thurin′jēa). (Ger. *Thüringen*) Former state in central Germany; part of East Germany since 1945. **Thu·rin′gi·an** *adj. & n.* (Native, inhabitant) of Thuringia; (member) of an ancient tribe of central Germany conquered by Franks in 6th c.

Thurs., Thur. *abbrevs.* Thursday.

Thurs·day (thērz′dā, -dē) *n.* Fifth day of the week; **Holy** ~ : see HOLY. [OE. *thur(e)sdæg* Thor's day, rendering LL. *dies Jovis* day of Jupiter]

thus (dhŭs) *adv.* In this way, like this, as follows: accordingly, consequently, and so; to this extent, number, or degree.

thwack (thwăk) = WHACK. **thwack′er** *n.*

thwart (thwort) *n.* Seat across boat, on which rower sits. ~ *adv. & adj.* (Lying) athwart. ~ *prep.* Athwart. ~ *v.t.* Frustrate, cross.

thy (dhī) *poss. pron.* Possessive case of THOU used as attrib. adjective with abs. and pred. form (also used before initial vowel and

*A **Tibetan** woman using a portable spinning device as she walks through the mountain meadows with her child on her back. Despite Chinese occupation, many people remain nomadic.*

silent "h") **thine** (dhīn), belonging to, affecting, thee.

Thy·es·tes (thĭĕs′tēz). (Gk. legend) Brother of ATREUS. **Thy·es·te·an** (thĭĕs′tēan) *adj.*

thy·la·cine (thī′lasĭn, -sĭn) *n.* Tasmanian wolf (*Thylacinus cynocephalus*), a carnivorous marsupial resembling a dog in appearance, grayish brown with conspicuous black markings on the hinder half of the back.

thyme (tīm) *n.* Shrubby herb of genus *Thymus* with fragrant aromatic leaves, chiefly of Mediterranean regions, esp. **garden** ~ (*T. vulgaris*), native of Spain and Italy, cultivated as seasoning, and **wild** ~ (*T. serpyllum*), growing on dry banks etc. throughout Europe.

thym·ic (thī′mĭk) *adj.* Of the thymus.

thy·mol (thī′mŏl, -mŏl) *n.* (chem.) White crystalline phenol obtained from oil of thyme, having pleasant aroma and used as antiseptic.

thy·mus (thī′mus) *n.* (pl. **-mus·es, -mi** pr. -mī). (anat.) Ductless glandular body (of uncertain function) situated near base of neck in vertebrates, in man disappearing or diminishing after childhood.

thy·roid (thī′roid) *adj.* (anat.) Of the thyroid gland; ~ **cartilage**, large cartilage of the larynx consisting of two broad plates united in front at an angle, forming the Adam's apple; ~ **gland**, large ductless gland lying near larynx and

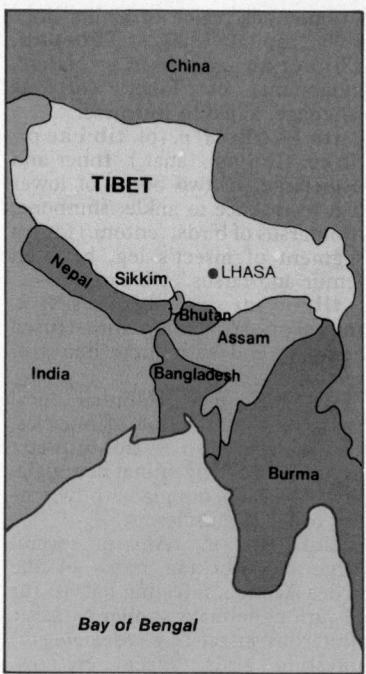

upper trachea in vertebrates and influencing growth and development, so called because of its proximity to the thyroid cartilage. **thyroid** *n.* Thyroid gland; extract prepared from thyroid gland of some animals, used in treating goiter, cretinism, etc.

thy·rox·ine (thīrŏk′sēn, -sĭn), **thy·rox·in** (thīrŏk′sĭn) *ns.* (chem.) Active hormone of thyroid gland.

thyr·sus (ther′sus) *n.* (pl. **-si** pr. -sī). 1. (Gk. antiq.) Staff tipped with ornament like pine cone, attribute of Dionysus. 2. (bot.) Kind of inflorescence in which primary axis is racemose and secondary etc. cymose, as in lilac and horse chestnut.

thy·self (dhīsĕlf′) *pron.* Emphatic and reflexive form corresponding to THOU, THEE.

Ti *symbol.* Titanium.

ti·ar·a (tēăr′a, -är′a, -är′a) *n.* Ancient Persian form of headdress; official headdress of the pope, consisting of a high pointed cap encircled by three crowns, symbolic of the temporal, spiritual, and purgatorial sovereignty claimed by the papacy; papal office; jeweled coronet worn by women.

Ti·ber (tī′ber). River of central Italy flowing from Tuscan Apennines through Rome to Mediterranean Sea at Ostia.

Ti·be·ri·as (tībēr′ēas). 1. Ancient town (built by Herod Antipas *c*21 A.D. and named after Tiberius) on W. shore of Sea of Galilee. 2. **Sea of** ~ : see Sea of GALILEE.

Ti·be·ri·us (tībēr′ēus). Tiberius Claudius Nero (42 B.C.–37 A.D.), Roman emperor 14–37 A.D.

Ti·bet, Thi·bet (tĭbĕt′). Mountainous country of central Asia, an autonomous region of China since 1965; capital, Lhasa. **Ti·bet′an, Thi·bet′an** *adjs.* & *ns.* (Native, inhabitant) of Tibet; (of) its language, allied to Burmese.

tib·i·a (tĭb′ēa) *n.* (pl. **tib·i·ae** pr. tĭb′ēē, **tib·i·as**). (anat.) Inner and usu. larger of two bones of lower leg, from knee to ankle, shinbone; tibiotarsus of birds; (entom.) fourth segment of insect's leg, between femur and tarsus. **tib′i·al** *adj.*

tib·i·o·tar·sus (tĭbēōtär′sus) *n.* (pl. **-si** pr. -sī). Tibia of birds, fused at lower end with some bones of tarsus.

tic (tĭk) *n.* Habitual local spasmodic contraction of muscles, esp. of face; (also ~ **douloureux** pr. dōōlōōrō′) trigeminal neuralgia, severe facial neuralgia with twitching of facial muscles.

tick[1] (tĭk) *n.* Any of several large bloodsucking mites of the order Acarina, infesting hair or fur of various animals; similar parasitic dipterous insect (e.g. *Melophagus*) infesting birds, sheep, etc.; ~ **fever**, fever transmitted by bite of tick.

tick[2] (tĭk) *n.* Case of mattress or pillow. **tick′ing** *n.* Strong cotton or other material for making ticks.

tick[3] (tĭk) *n.* 1. Quick light dry recurring sound, distinct but not loud, esp. of alternate check and release of movement in clock or watch. 2. Mark (dot, check, etc.) used to record review of items in a list. ~ *v.* Mark (*off* item etc.) with tick; make ticking sound; throw *off* (message or passage of time by ticking); **what makes (person)** ~, motivation; ~ **off**, (slang) annoy, exasperate.

tick[4] (tĭk) *n.* (chiefly Brit. colloq.) Credit; **on** ~, on credit. [abbrev. of TICKET]

tick·er (tĭk′er) *n.* (esp., colloq.)

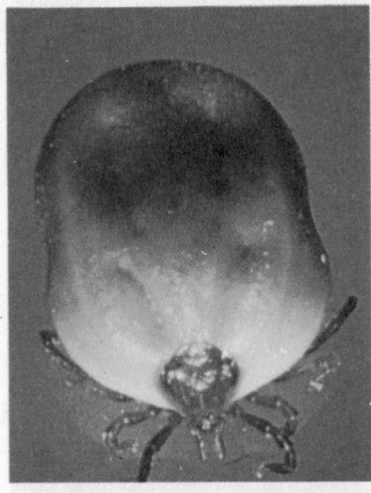

The 700 species of **tick** *can transmit more diseases to man and domestic animals than any arthropod excepting the mosquito. They are more common in tropical and subtropical regions.*

Watch; telegraphic tape machine; (joc.) heart.

ticker (tĭk′er) **tape.** Paper tape from tape machine; this or similar material thrown from windows to greet a celebrity (**ticker-tape parade**).

tick·et (tĭk′ĭt) *n.* Slip, usu. of paper or cardboard, bearing evidence of holder's title to some service or privilege, as railroad journey, seat at entertainment, etc.; certificate of qualifications of pilot, ship's mate, or captain, etc.; list of candidates of one party or group put forward for election; ~ **agency**, agency in the business of selling tickets, esp. for theatrical presenta-

While the gravitational forces in the sun and moon are responsible for **tides** *on earth, the height and frequency may also be affected by ocean currents especially where there is a strait.*

tions and sports events; ~ **agent**, individual selling tickets, as for theatrical and sports events, travel accommodations, etc.; ~ **office**, office where such tickets may be purchased; **parking** ~, notice from police to owner of vehicle parked in violation of regulations that fine must be paid; **the** ~, (slang) what is wanted, expected, etc. **ticket** *v.t.* Put ticket on (article for sale, illegally parked automobile, etc.).

tick·le (tĭk′el) *n.* Act, sensation, of tickling. ~ *v.* (**-led, -ling**). Touch or stroke (person, part of body) lightly with fingertips, feather, etc., so as to excite nerves and usu. produce laughter; cause or feel peculiar uneasy sensation as of being tickled; excite agreeably, amuse, divert; ~**d pink** or **to death**, (colloq.) highly amused or delighted.

tick·lish (tĭk′lĭsh) *adj.* Easily tickled, sensitive to tickling; (of question etc.) difficult, critical, delicate, requiring careful handling. **tick′lish·ly** *adv.* **tick′lish·ness** *n.*

tick-tack-toe, tic-tac-toe (tĭk-tăktō′) *ns.* Game in which nine squares in a block are filled alternately with O's and X's by two players seeking to complete a row of three of either kind.

tick·tock (tĭk′tŏk) *n.* Repetitive sound as of a clock ticking. ~ *v.i.* Make sound of a clock ticking.

Ti·con·der·o·ga (tīkŏnderō′ga). Village and tourist resort in NE. New York State, on Lake Champlain; site of **Fort** ~, captured by the Americans under Ethan Allen, 1775, and then under Burgoyne, 1777, during the Revolutionary War.

tid·al (tī′dal) *adj.* Of tides; ~ **basin**, manmade lake or large pond

▨	twice daily
▨	daily
▨	mixed
▨	more than 6 ft
▨	1 to 6 ft

with access to a river and subject to tidal action; ~ **flat**, muddy or marshy flatland covered with water at full tide and laid bare at low tide; ~ **wave**, wave caused by movement of tide; (pop.) exceptionally large ocean wave or very high water sometimes following earthquake or other local commotion (cf. TSUNAMI); (fig.) widespread manifestation of feeling etc. **tid′al·ly** *adv.*

tid·bit (tĭd′bĭt), Brit. **tit·bit** (tĭt′bĭt) *ns.* Delicate bit, choice morsel.

tid·dly·winks (tĭd′lēwĭngks), **tid·dle·dy-winks** (tĭd′eldēwĭngks) *ns.* Game in which small counters are flipped across table into receptacle.

tide (tīd) *n.* 1. Time, season (archaic exc. in **Eastertide** etc.). 2. Flowing or swelling of sea, or its alternate rising (**flood tide**) and falling (**ebb tide**), twice in each lunar day, due to the attraction of moon (and sun); (fig.) something like a tide in ebbing and flowing, turning, etc.; flood tide; **high, low tide**, completion of the flood, ebb, tide; NEAP, SPRING, **tide**: see these words; **tide gate**, gate through which water passes into dock etc. at flood, and by which it is retained during ebb; **tide lock**, double lock between tidal water and canal, basin, etc., beyond it; **tide′mark**, mark made by tide at high water; **tide′rip**, rough water caused by opposing tides; **tide table**, chart forecasting times and heights of tides for days of month at specific locations; **tide′water**, water affected by ebb and flow of tides; coastal land affected by tide; **tide′-way**, channel in which tidal current runs, tidal part of river; **turn the tide**, reverse a situation. **tide′less** *adj.* **tide** *v.* (**tid·ed, tid·ing**). 1. Drift with tide. 2. ~ **over**, (enable or assist to) get through difficult time, surmount difficulty, etc.

ti·dings (tī′dĭngz) *n.pl.* (now chiefly literary) (Piece of) news.

ti·dy (tī′dē) *adj.* (**-di·er, -di·est**). Neatly arranged, neat, orderly; (colloq.) pretty large, considerable. ~ *v.t.* (**-died, -dy·ing**). Make neat, put in good order. **ti′di·ly** *adv.* **ti′di·ness** *n.*

tie (tī) *v.* (**tied, ty·ing**). 1. Attach, fasten, with cord etc.; secure (shoe etc.) by tightening and knotting lace etc.; form into knot or bow; bind (rafters etc.) by crosspiece etc.; restrict, bind (person etc.); ~ **down**, restrict one's activities, confine; restrain; ~ **in**, make or be consistent; connect; ~ **off**, tie suture around (artery etc.) so as to draw sides together and halt blood circulation within; ~ **one on**, (slang) become drunk; ~ **the knot**, (colloq.) get married; ~ **up**, restrict, esp. annex conditions to (bequest etc.) to prevent its being

sold or diverted from its purpose. 2. Make same score as (competitor) in game etc.; be equal in score *with*. **tie** *n.* 1. Cord, chain, etc., used for fastening. 2. Necktie. 3. Rod, beam, etc., holding parts of structure together; transverse beam on a rail bed supporting railroad tracks. 4. (fig.) Thing that connects or unites in some way, link, bond. 5. Equality of score between competitors or sides in match or contest, drawn match; deciding match played after draw, match between victors in previous matches or heats; match between any pair of several competing players or teams.

6. ~ **beam**, horizontal beam connecting rafters; **tie′clasp, tie′-pin**, ornamental pin worn on necktie; **tie-dye**, (1) Method of producing dyed patterns by tying string etc. to prevent parts of fabric from being dyed; (2) Fabric so decorated or pattern thus made; **tie-in**, of, pertaining to, or designating a sale in which purchaser must buy one or more additional and unwanted items in order to buy the item desired; **tie line**, direct connection between telephone extensions in a switchboard system; **tie-up**, link; obstructed situation, standstill, esp. obstruction of traffic on railroad etc. caused by strike, breakdown, etc.

Tie·po·lo (tēĕp′olō), **Giovanni Battista** (1696–1770). Venetian painter.

tier[1] (tēr) *n.* Row, rank, esp. one of several placed one above another as in theater. ~ *v.t.* Arrange or pile in tiers.

ti·er[2] (tī′er) *n.* One who ties.

tierce (tērs) *n.* 1. **T~**, (R.C. Ch.) canonical hour, (orig. said at) third hour of day (9 a.m.). 2. Position in fencing, third of eight parries or corresponding thrust. 3. (hist.) Measure of capacity, ⅓ of pipe (42 gallons); cask or vessel holding this quantity.

Tier·ra del Fue·go (tyĕr′ah dĕl fwä′gō). (Main island of) archipelago at S. tip of S. Amer., discovered 1520 by Magellan; divided between Chile and Argentina.

tiff (tĭf) *n.* Slight or petty quarrel. ~ *v.i.* Have a tiff.

Tif·fa·ny (tĭf′anē), **Louis Comfort** (1848–1933). Amer. painter, stained-glass decorator, and glass manufacturer, especially of opalescent glass.

tif·fin (tĭf′ĭn) *n. & v.i.* (Brit.) (Take) light meal, lunch. [app. f. obs. *tiff* drink, sip]

ti·ger (tī′ger) *n.* (pl. **-gers**, collect. for senses 1 & 2 **-ger**). 1. Large Asiatic carnivorous feline quadruped (*Panthera tigris*), maneless, of tawny yellow color with blackish transverse stripes and white belly, proverbial for ferocity and cunning. 2. Any of various other feline animals, esp. (in Amer.) the jaguar and puma, and (in S. Africa) the leopard. 3. Fierce, cruel, or rapacious person or animal; formidable opponent in a game; paper tiger, person or thing threatening in appearance but ineffectual. 4. Loud yell at end of burst of cheering. 5. ~ **beetle**, active carnivorous voracious beetle of family Cicindelidae; ~ **cat**, any of various moderate-sized feline beasts resembling tiger in markings etc.; ~ **'s eye, ti′gereye**, yellowish-brown quartz with brilliant luster, used as gem; kind of crystalline pottery glaze resembling this; **tiger lily**, tall garden lily (*Lilium tigrinum*) of Asiatic origin with orange flowers spotted with black; **tiger moth**, moth of family Arctiidae, with striped and spotted wings; **tiger shark**, any of various large voracious spotted or streaked sharks, esp. *Galeocerdo cuvier;* **tiger snake**, venomous and aggressive Australian snake, brown with dark stripes. **ti·gress** (tī′grĭs) *n.* Female tiger.

ti·ger·ish (tī′gerĭsh), **ti·grish** (tī′grĭsh) *adjs.* Like, cruel as, a tiger. **ti′ger·ish·ly** *adv.* **ti′ger·ish·ness** *n.*

tight (tīt) *adj.* 1. Close-textured,

Much of the effect of Muslim architecture was from the use of the painted **tile**. Each was part of a total design. They became used increasingly in Persia from the 13th century onwards.

firmly constructed, so as to be impervious to fluid etc. 2. Closely held, drawn, fastened, fitting, etc.; tense, taut, stretched so as to leave no slack; neat, trim, compact. 3. Produced by, requiring, great exertion or pressure; (colloq., of person) closefisted, (of money) difficult to obtain. 4. (slang)

The Australian **tigermoth,** *Rhodogastria, emits a pungent liquid from the base of its wings as a deterrent against predators.*

Drunk. 5. **tight′fisted**, stingy, closefisted; **tight′rope**, tightly stretched rope, wire, etc., on which acrobats perform; **tight′wad**, (colloq.) tightfisted person. **tight** *adv.* Tightly. **tight′en** *v.* **tight′en·er** *n.* **tight′ly** *adv.* **tight′ness** *n.*

tights (tīts) *n.pl.* 1. (also **pair of** ~) Closely fitting garment covering legs, feet, and lower part of body. 2. Leotard with legs and feet.

Ti·gris (tī′grĭs). River of SW. Asia flowing 1,150 mi. (1,840 km) from Turkey, joining Euphrates to form Shatt al Arab, which flows into Persian Gulf.

ti·grish = TIGERISH.

Ti·jua·na (tēawah′na). City and tourist center of Mexico, in the NW. part on the U.S. border.

Ti·ki (tē′kē). 1. (Polynesian myth.) First man on Earth. 2. (**t~**) (New Zealand) Maori large wooden or small ornamental greenstone image of creator of man or an ancestor.

til·de (tĭl′de) *n.* Diacritical mark (˜) placed in Spanish over *n* to indicate palatalized sound (ny) and in Portuguese over *a* and *o* to indicate nasal sound; swung dash (~).

tile (tīl) *n.* 1. Thin slab of baked clay for covering roof, paving floor, lining wall, fireplace, etc.; material of this; tiles collectively. 2. Decorated piece used in mah-jongg. ~ *v.t.* Cover, line, with tiles.

tile·fish (tīl′fĭsh) *n.* (pl. **-fishes, -fish**). Large deepwater yellow-spotted food fish (*Lopholatilus chamaeleonticeps*), of Atlantic off New England etc.

till[1] (tĭl) *n.* Money drawer etc. in shop etc.

till[2] (tĭl) *n.* Boulder clay, stiff unstratified clay mixed with sand, gravel, and boulders.

till[3] (tĭl) *v.t.* Labor on (land), as by plowing etc. in order to produce crops. **till′age** *n.* 1. Cultivation of land. 2. Tilled land. **till′a·ble** *adj.* **till′er**[1] *n.* One who tills; farmer.

till[4] (tĭl) *prep.* Up to, as late as, until. ~ *conj.* To the time that; up to (the point) when.

till·er[2] (tĭl′er) *n.* Shoot of plant springing from bottom of original stalk; sapling; sucker.

till·er[3] (tĭl′er) *n.* Horizontal bar fixed to rudder head and acting as lever for steering.

till·ite (tĭl′īt) *n.* Rock composed of consolidated TILL[2].

tilt[1] (tĭlt) *n.* Covering or awning of canvas etc. esp. for cart. ~ *v.t.* Furnish with tilt.

tilt[2] (tĭlt) *v.* 1. (Cause to) incline abruptly from vertical or horizontal, (cause to) assume sloping or slanting position, heel over; (fig.) incline toward (one

1749

*Originating in prehistoric times from Siberia, the **tiger** migrated southward to become the major feline in Asia. They are still present in northern regions but populations are low through hunting in India and Sumatra.*

white race of the Indian tiger

Siberian tiger

Sumatran tiger

n tiger

Indian tiger

country, person, etc. or another) in bestowing aid or encouragement; (geol., pass., of strata) be inclined. 2. Engage in tilt; strike, thrust, run, *at*, with weapon; ~ **at windmills**: see WINDMILL. 3. Forge, work, with tilt hammer. **tilt** *n.* 1. Tilting, sloping position. 2. Joust, combat between two armed men on horseback, each trying to throw opponent from saddle with lance; **full** ~, at full speed, with full force or impetus; **tilt′yard**, enclosed place for tilting, tilting ground. 3. (also **tilt hammer**) Heavy forging hammer, fixed on pivot and alternately tilted up and dropped by action of cam or eccentric gear.

tilth (tĭlth) *n.* Tillage, cultivation; depth of soil dug or cultivated.

Tim. *abbrev.* Timothy (New Testament).

tim·bal, tym·bal (tĭm′bal) *ns.* Kettledrum. [Fr. *timbale*, earlier *attabale*, f. Arab. *al tabl* the drum]

tim·bale (tĭm′bal, tĭmbahl′) *n.* Dish of minced meat, fish, etc., cooked in drum-shaped mold of pastry etc. [Fr.]

tim·ber (tĭm′ber) *n.* Wood prepared for building etc.; trees suitable for this; piece of wood, beam, esp. (naut.) any curved piece forming ribs of vessel; **standing** ~, trees, woods; ~ **hitch**, knot used in attaching rope to log or spar; **tim′berland**, land covered with forest yielding timber; **tim′berline**, altitude above which no trees grow, as in mountain or polar regions; **timber wolf**, large gray wolf (*Canis lupus*) of northern N. Amer. **timber** *v.t.* Support (roof of mine or working, sides and roof of tunnel, etc.) with timber. **tim′bered** *adj.* Made of timber or wood, as a ~ **ceiling**; wooded. **tim′ber·ing** *n.*

tim·bre (tĭm′ber, tăm′bre) *n.*

Distinctive quality of musical or vocal sound depending on voice or instrument producing it, tone color. [Fr., = "clock bell," "drum," f. L. *tympanum*]

tim·brel (tĭm′brel) *n.* Tambourine or the like. [f. TIMBRE]

Tim·buk·tu (tĭmbŭktoo′). Town in central Mali near the Niger river; very remote place.

time (tīm) *n.* 1. Indefinite continuous duration regarded as dimension in which sequence of events takes place (freq. personified, **Father T**~, esp. as old man with scythe and hourglass); finite duration as dist. from eternity; more or less definite portion of this associated with particular events or circumstances, historical or other period; (freq. pl.) conditions of life, prevailing circumstances, of a period; allotted or available portion of time, time at one's disposal; moment or definite portion of time destined or suitable for a purpose etc., esp. period of gestation, term of imprisonment, term of apprenticeship, length of round in boxing, part of football or other game, time to begin or end this; point of time; (prison slang) period of imprisonment; season; occasion; (payment for) amount of time worked; (amount of) time as reckoned by conventional standards; STANDARD ~, DAYLIGHT saving ~: see these words; **a good** ~, period of enjoyment. 2. (mus.) Rhythm or measure of musical composition; tempo. 3. (pl.) (Preceded by numeral and followed by number or expression

of quantity etc.) expressing multiplication, comparison, etc. 4. (**work**) **against** ~, with utmost speed so as to reach a goal by a specified time; **ahead of** ~, earlier than expected or promised; **all the** ~, during the whole time referred to; at all times; **at the same** ~, simultaneously; all the same; **at** ~**s**, now and then; **beat (somebody's)** ~, (slang) try to win or win favor of person, esp. woman being wooed by another; triumph over competitor; **behind the** ~**s**, out of style; old-fashioned; **for the** ~ **being**, for the moment; temporarily; **from** ~ **to** ~, occasionally; **in good** ~, at the correct time; before the correct time; **in** ~, not late; early enough; eventually, sooner or later; following the time of music etc.; **in no** ~, rapidly, in a moment; **make** ~, move rapidly, esp. to compensate for lost time; travel at specific, usu. fast, speed; (slang) date, woo, or have affair *with*; **pass the** ~, have short conversation with or greet person; ~ **of day**, hour by clock; current time; now; period of time in a day. 5. ~ **and motion study**, systematic investigation of working methods in order to increase efficiency and establish standards; ~ **bomb**, bomb with fuse or other device so adjusted that it will explode after a predetermined interval, delayed-action bomb; (fig.) precarious, threatening condition; ~ **capsule**, urn or strongbox buried in foundations of new building etc. and containing objects typical of the present time, for discovery in the future; **time′card**, card with record of time worked; **time clock**, clock with device recording times, e.g. of arrival and departure of workmen etc.; **time constant**, mathematical expression giving indication of delay involved in heating, charging, moving, etc., when the process produces an opposing effect proportional to the temperature, charge, speed, etc.; **time-consuming** (*adj.*), taking much time, wasteful of time; **time deposit**, bank deposit not repayable before set date; **time exposure**, (photog.) exposure for regulated length of time, as dist. from instantaneous exposure; **time-honored**, respected because of its antiquity; **time immemorial**, time of long ago and too early to remember; **time'keeper**, watch, clock, esp. in ref. to accuracy; one who records time, esp. of workmen; **time-lag**, interval of time between cause etc. and result or consequence; **time-lapse** (*adj.*), (of motion picture film) containing frames taken at long intervals but shown at normal pace to accelerate view of events, as growth of a plant, construction of a building, etc.; **time limit**, period within which something must be done; **timeout**, time used for rest, leisure, etc.; (football etc.) halt in play, with clock stopped, to permit substitution of players, etc.; **time'piece**, instrument for measuring time, chronometer; **time'server**, opportunist; **time'serving**, opportunism; **time sheet**, sheet of paper recording hours worked by employee(s) etc.; **time signal**, visible or audible signal, esp. radio signal, announcing the time of day; **time'table**, tabular list or schedule of times of classes in school etc., arrival and departure of trains, boats, etc.; **time zone**, one of 24 regions, each bounded by two lines of longitude 15° apart, adopting as standard the mean solar time of the meridian in it distant from Greenwich a complete number of hours. **time** *v.* (**timed, tim·ing**). Choose the time for, do at chosen

Timothy grass, with its long cylindrical spikes, is native in Britain and northern Europe. Being perennial, it has proved useful for cutting and storage as hay.

time; record time of event, duration of action, etc., keep time, harmonize (*with*).

    time·less (tīm′lĭs) *adj.* Unending, eternal; not subject to time. **time′less·ly** *adv.* **time′less·ness** *n.*

    time·ly (tīm′lē) *adj.* (**-li·er, -li·est**). Seasonable, opportune. **time′li·ness** *n.*

    Times (tīmz) **Square.** Area of Manhattan in New York City formed by Broadway crossing Seventh Avenue and extending from 42nd Street to 47th Street, center of New York theatrical district.

    tim·id (tĭm′ĭd) *adj.* Easily alarmed; shy. **tim′id·ly** *adv.* **tim′id·ness, ti·mid·i·ty** (tĭmĭd′ĭtē) *ns.*

    tim·ing (tī′mĭng) *n.* Regulation of speed, control, occurrence, or coordination, as in mechanics, theatrical production, sports, etc., in order to gain best results.

    ti·moc·ra·cy (tīmŏk′rasē) *n.* (pl. **-cies**). 1. In the Aristotelian sense: a state with a property qualification for office. 2. In the Platonic sense: a state (like that of Sparta) in which love of honor is said to be the dominant motive among the rulers. **ti·mo·crat·ic** (tīmokrăt′ĭk), **ti·mo·crat′i·cal** *adjs.*

    Ti·mon (tī′mon) (5th c. B.C.). Athenian who became a misanthrope owing to the ingratitude of his friends.

    Ti·mor (tē′mŏr). Island in the S. Malay Archipelago belonging to Indonesia; largest and easternmost of the Lesser Sunda Islands, covering 13,094 sq. mi. (33,913 sq. km); formerly ruled by the Netherlands in the W. part and Portugal in the E. part; ~ **Sea**, part of Indian Ocean lying between Timor and NW. Australia.

    tim·or·ous (tĭm′erus) *adj.* Timid. **tim′or·ous·ly** *adv.* **tim′or·ous·ness** *n.*

    Tim·o·thy (tĭm′othē). Convert and colleague of St. Paul; either of two Pauline epistles of New Testament addressed to him.

    tim·o·thy (tĭm′othē) *n.* (also ~ **grass**) Meadow grass (*Phleum*

Hauling in the fishing nets on Timor. Formerly divided between Portugal and Indonesia, the country has since been occupied by Indonesia which now claims control of the island.

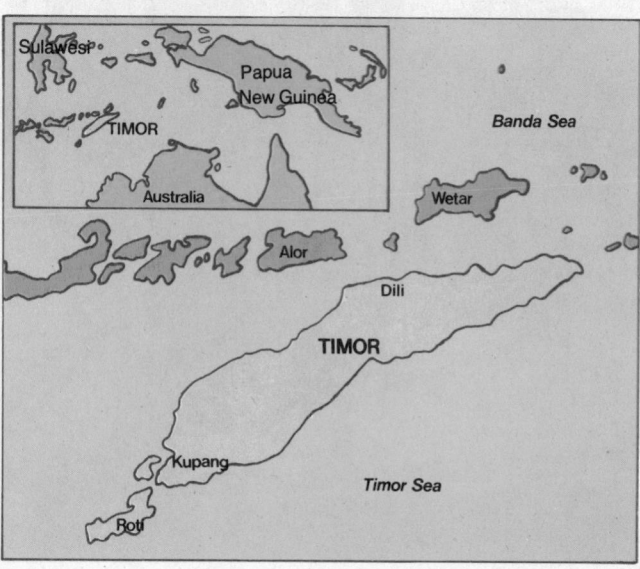

pratense), European grass with long cylindrical spikes, introduced into N. Amer. from England for cultivation for hay. [said to be f. *Timothy Hanson*, who introduced it into N. Amer. c1720]

tim·pa·ni, tym·pa·ni (tǐm′-panē) *ns.pl.* Kettledrums. **tym′-pa·nist** *n.*

tin (tǐn) *n.* 1. (chem.) Metallic element nearly approaching silver in whiteness, highly malleable, and taking a high polish, used in the manufacture of such alloys as bronze and pewter and, because of its resistance to oxidation, for making tinplate and lining culinary and other iron vessels; symbol Sn, at. no. 50, at. wt. 118.69. 2. (chiefly Brit.) Vessel made of tin, or more usu. tinned iron, esp. a vessel in which meat, fish, fruit, etc., is hermetically sealed for preservation; can tinplate, as the material for such vessels. 3. (attrib. or as adj.) **tin′foil,** tin hammered or rolled into a thin sheet; sheet of this rubbed with mercury, formerly used for backing mirrors and precious stones; similar sheet of an alloy of tin and lead used for wrapping and packing; (*v.t.*) cover, coat, with tinfoil; **tin god,** (fig.) base or unworthy object of veneration; **tin hat,** (mil. slang) steel helmet; **tin lizzie,** nickname for a small cheap (orig. Ford) automobile; **Tin Pan Alley,** world of composers, publishers, etc., of popular music; **tin plate, tin′-plate,** sheet iron or sheet steel coated with tin; **tin′smith,** worker in tin, maker of tin utensils; **tin soldier,** miniature toy soldier of metal, esp. lead; **tin′stone,** most commonly occurring form of tin ore, cassiterite (SnO_2). **tin** *adj.* Of tin; (colloq.) of steel or corrugated iron. ~ *v.t.* (**tinned, tin·ning**). Cover, coat, with tin.

tin·a·mou (tǐn′amoo) *n.* S. Amer. bird of the family Tinamidae, resembling grouse but related to rheas.

tin·cal (tǐng′kahl) *n.* Crude borax, found in lake deposits in parts of Asia.

tinc·to·ri·al (tǐngktōr′ēal, -tōr′-) *adj.* Of, used in, dyeing; yielding, using, dye or coloring matter.

tinc·ture (tǐngk′cher) *n.* 1. Solution, usu. in alcohol or alcohol and ether, of medicinal substance, esp. ~ **of iodine.** 2. Slight flavor, spice, smack; smattering; tinge. ~ *v.t.* (**-tured, -tur·ing**). Color slightly; tinge, flavor; affect slightly.

tin·der (tǐn′der) *n.* Any dry inflammable substance readily taking fire from spark, esp. that formerly used in **tin′derbox** to catch spark from flint and steel for kindling fire etc. **tin′der·y** *adj.* Resembling tinder; extremely inflammable.

tine (tīn) *n.* Prong, projecting sharp point of fork etc.

tin·e·a (tǐn′ēa) *n.* (path.) Ringworm.

ting (tǐng) *n.* & *v.i.* (Make) tinkling sound.

tinge (tǐnj) *v.t.* (**tinged, tinge·ing** or **ting·ing**). Color slightly, modify tint or color of; (fig.) qualify, modify, slightly alter tone of. ~ *n.* Tint, slight coloring; flavor, touch.

tin·gle (tǐng′gel) *n.* & *v.* (**-gled, -gling**). (Feel, cause) slight pricking or stinging sensation. **tin′gler** *n.* **tin′gly** *adj.*

tin·ker (tǐng′ker) *n.* Mender (esp. itinerant) of kettles, pans, etc.; (Scotland and N. Ireland) gypsy; jack-of-all-trades; act of tinkering. ~ *v.* Repair, patch (up), roughly; work amateurishly or clumsily *at,* esp. in attempt to repair or improve. **tink′er·er** *n.*

tin·kle (tǐng′kel) *n.* & *v.* (**-kled, -kling**). (Make, cause to make) succession of short light sharp ringing sounds, as of small bell.

tin·ner (tǐn′er) *n.* Tinsmith.

tin·ni·tus (tǐnī′tus) *n.* (med.) Noises heard in the ear not due to external stimulation by sound waves.

tin·ny (tǐn′ē) *adj.* (**-ni·er, -ni·est**). Of or like tin; having a metallic taste; (of sound) thin and metallic.

tin·sel (tǐn′sel) *n.* Shining metallic gold- or silver-colored material used in thin sheets, strips, or threads to give sparkling effect; fabric adorned with tinsel; (fig.) anything having or giving deceptively fine or glittering appearance, gaudy or showy but worthless thing. **tin′sel·ly, tinsel** *adjs.* Showy, gaudy, cheaply splendid. ~ *v.t.* (**-seled, -sel·ing** or **-selled, -sel·ling**). Adorn with tinsel. [L. *scintilla* spark]

tint (tǐnt) *n.* Color, usu. slight or delicate, esp. one of several tones of the same color; (in painting, esp.) lighter tone of a color as dist. from shade, darker one; (engraving) effect produced by fine lines or dots set more or less closely together so as to produce an even tone. ~ *v.t.* Apply tint to, color. **tint′er** *n.*

Tin·tag·el (tǐntǎj′el). Village on coast of N. Cornwall, England, with ruins of castle; traditional birthplace of King Arthur.

Tin·tern (tǐn′tern) **Abbey.**

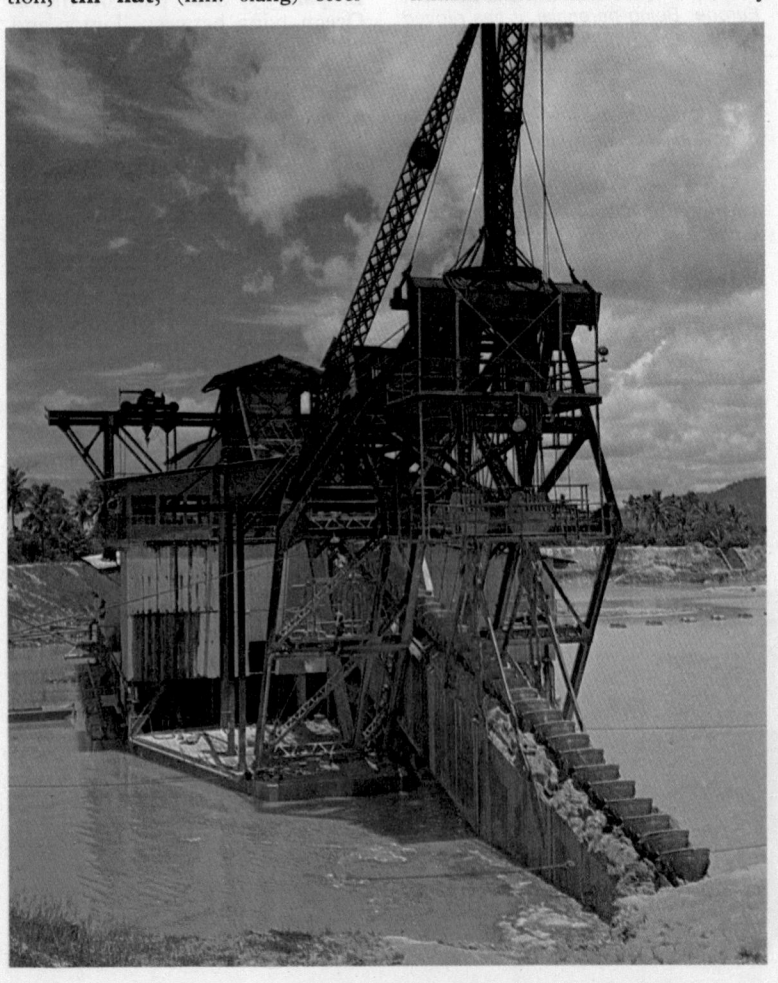

Tin dredge working in Malaysia between Kuala Lumpur and Ipoh. Other major producers include China, Bolivia, the U.S.S.R. and Thailand. World production in 1974 was 232,400 tons.

Tintoretto, a student of Titian, is said to have achieved the peak of his creativity with his paintings of Jesus Christ. Above: 'Christ Washing the Disciples' Feet' at Wilton House, England

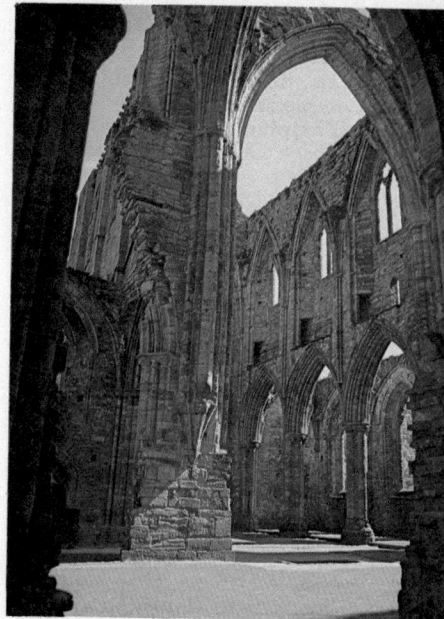

Cistercian monks built **Tintern Abbey** *in 1131 and the church in 1287. The establishment achieved much wealth but was abandoned during the Reformation. The Crown bought the ruins in 1901.*

Ruins, on River Wye, Wales, of a Cistercian abbey, founded 1131 and dissolved by Henry VIII.

tin·tin·nab·u·la·tion (tĭntĭ-năbyulā′shon) *n.* Ringing or tinkling of bell(s).

Tin·to·ret·to (tĭntorĕt′ō). Jacopo Robusti (1518–94), Venetian painter.

ti·ny (tī′nē) *adj.* (**-ni·er, -ni·est**). Very small. **ti′ni·ness** *n.*

tip¹ (tĭp) *n.* Extremity, end, esp. of small or tapering thing; small piece or part attached to thing to form serviceable end; thin flat brush used for gilding; (**on**) **tip′toe** (*n.*), on the tips of the toes, standing or walking with heels raised from ground; **tip′toe** (*v.i.*) (**-toed, -toe·ing**), walk on tiptoe; **tip′top**, highest point of excellence; first-rate. **tip** *v.t.* (**tipped, tip·ping**). Furnish with tip.

tip² (tĭp) *v.* (**tipped, tip·ping**). 1. (Cause to) lean or slant, tilt, topple, esp. with slight effort; overturn, cause to overbalance. 2. Strike or touch lightly; (slang) forecast as winner, esp. informally; ~

off, (colloq.) give private or secret information to; warn of danger etc.; **tip′off** (*n.*) (colloq.) warning, hint; **tip** (**over**), upset, overturn, topple *over*. 3. Give a tip to (see *n.*, sense 4). 4. **tip′cart**, one pivoted so that its contents can readily be tipped out; **tip sheet**, (slang) publication with up-to-the-minute facts and predictions about the stock market, various businesses, racetrack activities, etc. **tip** *n.* 1. Act of tipping or tilting. 2. Light touch or blow. 3. Piece of useful private or special information given by expert, esp. about horse racing, stock market, etc.; useful hint or idea. 4. Small present of money, esp. for service rendered or expected. **tip′per** *n.*

Tip·pe·ca·noe (tĭpekanoō′). River of N. Indiana, flowing SW. 166 mi. (267 km) to the Wabash River near the battlesite of ~,

where Gen. William Henry Harrison defeated Indians led by Tecumseh, 1811; "T~ **and Tyler too**" was Whig party slogan during 1840 presidential campaign, using Harrison's nickname with the last name of his vice presidential running mate.

tip·ple (tĭp′el) *v.* (**-pled, -pling**). Drink intoxicating liquor habitually; take (such) continually in small quantities. **tip′pler** *n.* **tipple** *n.* Intoxicating liquor.

tip·ster (tĭp′ster) *n.* (colloq.) One who gives tips about races etc.

tip·sy (tĭp′sē) *adj.* (**-si·er, -si·est**). (Partly) intoxicated; unsteady, staggering, from effects of drink. **tip′si·ly** *adv.* **tip′si·ness** *n.*

ti·rade (tī′rād, tĭrād′) *n.* Long vehement speech esp. of denunciation or abuse; long declamatory passage. [It. *tirada* volley]

Ti·ra·na (tērah′nah). Capital of Albania, in the central part.

tire¹ (tīr) *v.* (**tired, tir·ing**). Make or grow weary. **tired** *adj.* Weary (*of*); hackneyed; stale. **tired′ly** *adv.* **tired′ness** *n.* **tire′less** *adj.* **tire′less·ly** *adv.* **tire′less·ness** *n.*

tire² (tīr) *n.* 1. Iron or rubber rim or hoop around wheel on vehicle. 2. Air-filled or solid rubber or synthetic elastic tube on wheel of vehicle to reduce shock and supply traction.

tire³ (tīr) *n.* (archaic) Headdress, attire. ~ *v.t.* (**tired, tir·ing**). Adorn, attire.

tire·some (tīr′som) *adj.* Tending to tire, fatiguing, tedious; annoying. **tire′some·ly** *adv.*

tire′some·ness *n.*
  ti·ro = TYRO.
  Tir·ol = TYROL.
  'tis (tĭz). (archaic, poet., or dial.) Contraction of *it is*.
  Ti·siph·o·ne (tĭsĭf′onē). (Gk. myth.) One of the Furies (see FURY).
  tis·sue (tĭsh′oo) *n.* 1. Any (esp. rich or fine) woven stuff. 2. (biol.) Substance of animal or plant body, esp. of a particular part; organized mass of cells of similar kind, as *muscle* ~ etc. 3. (fig.) Interwoven series, set, collection (*of*). 4. (also ~ **paper**) Thin soft gauzelike unsized paper for wrapping delicate articles, toilet use, etc.; piece of tissue paper.
  tit[1] (tĭt): see TITMOUSE.
  tit[2] (tĭt) *n.* ~ **for tat**, equivalent given in return, blow for blow, retaliation.
  tit[3] (tĭt) *n.* Teat; (vulg. slang) breast.
  Tit. *abbrev.* Titus (New Testament).
  Ti·tan (tī′tan) *n.* (Gk. myth.) One of 12 gigantic children of Uranus and Ge (Oceanus, Coeus, Crius, Hyperion, Iapetus, Theia, Rhea, Themis, Mnemosyne, Phoebe, Tethys, Cronus), from two of whom (Cronus and Rhea) Zeus and the Olympians descended; hence, person of superhuman size, strength, etc.
  Ti·ta·ni·a (tĭtä′nēa). In W. European folklore, queen of the fairies, wife of Oberon.
  Ti·tan·ic (tītăn′ĭk). Brit. passenger liner that sank after collision with an iceberg on her maiden voyage, to New York in April 1912.
  ti·tan·ic (tītăn′ĭk) *adj.* 1. **T** ~, of the Titans. 2. Gigantic, colossal.
  ti·ta·ni·um (tītä′nēum) *n.*

(chem.) Gray metallic element widely distributed in combination in many minerals and clays, used esp. in the manufacture of alloy steels, symbol Ti, at. no. 22, at. wt. 47.90. **ti·tan′ous** *adj.*
  tit·bit = TIDBIT.
  ti·ter (tī′ter) *n.* (chem.) Strength of solution as determined by titration.
  tithe (tīdh) *n.* 1. (hist.) Tenth of annual produce of agriculture etc. conceived as due to God and hence payable for support of priesthood, religious establishments, etc. 2. (rhet.) Tenth part. ~ *v.t.*

Left: A blue **titmouse** *collects seeds, which it may store for the winter in its nest in a hollow tree. Below: A great* **titmouse** *in spring looking for insects. In harsh winters these birds may migrate to milder areas.*

Unrecognizable under stereoscan magnification, the **tissue** *of human skin looks more like a view of a tropical swamp. The upright in the foreground is a hair.*

(tithed, tith·ing). Subject to tithes. **tith′ing, tith′er** *ns.*
  Ti·tho·nus (tĭthō′nus). (Gk. myth.) Brother of Priam, loved by the dawn goddess, Eos, who asked Zeus to make him immortal but omitted to ask for eternal youth for him.
  Ti·tian (tĭsh′an, tē′shan). Tiziano Vecellio (1477–1576), Venetian painter; ~ **red**, bright golden auburn, color of the hair favored by Titian in his pictures.
  tit·il·late (tĭt′ĭlāt) *v.t.* (-lat·ed, -lat·ing). Tickle, excite agreeably. **tit′il·lat·ing·ly** *adv.* **tit·il·la·tion** (tĭtĭlā′shon) *n.*

tit·i·vate (tĭt´ivāt) *v.* (**-vat·ed, -vat·ing**). (colloq.) Adorn, smarten; adorn oneself; put finishing or improving touches to appearance (of).

tit·lark (tĭt´lärk) *n.* Any of several larks, esp. PIPIT.

ti·tle (tī´tel) *n.* 1. Name (freq. descriptive) of book, poem, picture, piece of music, etc. 2. Distinctive name or style; personal appellation denoting or relating to rank, function, office, attainment, etc. 3. (law) Legal right to possession of (esp. real) property, title deeds as evidence of this; just or recognized right or claim (*to*). 4. (eccles.) Any of principal or parish churches in Rome, of which incumbents are cardinal priests. 5. Championship in sport. 6. ~ **deed**, document constituting evidence of ownership; **ti´tleholder**, one who holds a title, esp. as champion in some sport; **title insurance**, insurance that

*As an assistant to Giorgione, **Titian** revealed his master's influence in such early works as 'The Three Ages of Man' (above) where the pastoral setting of this allegorical subject reflects the master's treatment.*

protects the owner of or holder of mortgage on real estate from possible legal actions because of a defective title; **title part, role**, part in play etc. from which title is taken; **title page**, page at beginning of book bearing title. **title** *v.t.* (**-tled, -tling**).

ti·tled (tī´teld) *adj.* Having a title of nobility.

tit·mouse (tĭt´mows) *n.* (pl. **-mice** pr. -mis). Any of various small birds, mostly of the common and widely distributed genus *Parus* and including chickadees, having soft, thick plumage, short, pointed bill, and, in some species, a crest on the head. [f. TUFTED TITMOUSE]

Ti·to (tē´tō), **Josip Broz, Marshal** (1892–1980). Prime minister of Yugoslavia 1945–53; president 1953–80.

ti·trate (tī´trāt, tĭt´rāt) *v.t.* (**-trat·ed, -trat·ing**). (chem.) Determine by volume quantity of constituent in (solution) by adding reagent of known strength until a point is reached at which reaction occurs or ceases. **ti·tra·tion** (tītrā´shon, tĭ-) *n.*

tit·ter (tĭt´er) *n. & v.i.* (Produce) laugh of suppressed or covert kind, giggle. **tit´ter·ing·ly** *adv.*

tit·tle-tat·tle (tĭt´el tăt´el) *n. & v.i.* (**-tled, -tling**). (Indulge in) petty gossip, chatter.

tit·u·ba·tion (tĭchoōbā´shon) *n.* Staggering, reeling, unsteadiness in gait or carriage (esp. path.).

tit·u·lar (tĭch´uler, tĭt´yu-) *adj.* Held by virtue of a title; such, existing, only in name; ~ **bishop**, (R.C. Ch.) bishop *in partibus* *infidelium*, one deriving his title from see lost to Roman pontificate; ~ **saint** etc., (R.C. Ch.) sacred person or thing giving name to church. **tit·u·lar·ly** *adv.* **titular** *n.* One who holds title to office, benefice, etc., esp. without performing functions thereof; (esp.) titular bishop.

Ti·tus[1] (tī′tus). Convert and helper of St. Paul; Pauline epistle of New Testament addressed to him.

Ti·tus[2] (tī′tus). Titus Flavius Sabinus Vespasianus (40–81 A.D.), Roman emperor 79–81; took Jerusalem (70 A.D.) after long siege.

tiz·zy (tĭz′ē) *n.* (pl. **-zies**). (colloq.) Dither.

TKO, T.K.O. *abbrevs.* Technical knockout.

Tl *symbol.* Thallium.

Tm *symbol.* Thulium.

tme·sis (temē′sĭs, mē′sĭs) *n.* (gram.) Separation of parts of compound word by intervening word(s), e.g. *to* us *ward*.

TN *abbrev.* Tennessee.

TNT, T.N.T. *abbrevs.* Trinitrotoluene.

to (tŏō) *prep.* 1. In the direction of; as far as, not short of. 2. Used after words expressing comparison, ratio, proportion, relative position, agreement, or adaptation, correspondence, reference, etc. 3. Introducing indirect object, supplying place of dative; indicating person or thing for whose benefit, use, disposal, etc., thing is done etc. 4. Used as sign of infinitive; expressing purpose, consequence, etc. ~ *adv.* To the normal or required position or condition, esp. to a standstill; ~-**and-fro**, backward and forward, up and down, from place to place.

toad (tōd) *n.* Tailless leaping amphibian (*Bufo*), resembling a frog, but terrestrial in habits except at breeding season, more squat in shape, and having a warty skin; **toad′eater**, toady; **toad′fish** (pl. **-fishes**, collect. **-fish**), any of various fishes with large heads or inflated bodies, of family Batrachoididae, of Amer. Atlantic coasts; **toad′flax**, common European and Asiatic herb (*Linaria vulgaris*) with showy spurred orange-spotted yellow flowers; various related plants; **toad′stone**, any of various small stones formerly supposed to be found in head of toad and worn as jewel or amulet; **toad′stool**, fungus with round disklike top and slender stalk, esp. of inedible or poisonous kind.

toad·y (tō′dē) *n.* (pl. **toad·ies**). Sycophant, obsequious parasite. **toad′y·ism** *n.* **toady** *v.i.* (**toad·ied, toad·y·ing**). Fawn upon, behave servilely (*to* person).

toast (tōst) *n.* 1. (Slice of) bread browned by heat. 2. Person or

Widespread in the northern hemisphere, **toadflax** (also known as 'butter and eggs' or 'flaxweed') was once made into a tisane to treat complaints of the bladder and liver.

thing in whose honor a company is requested to drink (hist., reigning belle of season etc.); call to drink, instance of drinking, thus; **toast′-master**, fem. **toast′mistress**, one who proposes or announces toasts at public dinner etc. **toast** *v.t.* 1. Brown, cook (bread, cheese, etc.) by exposure to heat of fire etc.; warm (one's feet etc.) before fire; **toasting fork**, long-handled fork for toasting bread, marshmallows, etc. 2. Drink to health or in honor of. **toast′er** *n.* Electrical etc. device for toasting bread.

to·bac·co (tobăk′ō) *n.* (pl. **-cos, -coes**). Tall annual plant of genus *Nicotiana*, esp. *N. tabacum*, native of tropical Amer., with white or pink tubular flowers and large ovate leaves used for smoking or chewing or as snuff; these dried leaves, or cigars, cigarettes, etc., manufactured from them; plant resembling tobacco or used for same purposes; ~ **heart**, disease of the heart due to excessive tobacco smoking.

to·bac·co·nist (tobăk′onĭst) *n.* Dealer in tobacco.

To·ba·go: see TRINIDAD AND TOBAGO.

to-be (tobē′) *adj.* Future; coming; soon to be what is named, as *bride-to-be*.

to·bog·gan (tobŏg′an) *n.* Long light narrow sled curved up at the

forward end used esp. in sport of coasting down prepared slopes of snow or ice. ~ *v.t.* Ride on toboggan. **to·bog′gan·ist** *n.*

to·by (tō′bē) *n.* (pl. **-bies**). 1. (also T~ **jug**) Mug or small jug for ale etc. in form of stout old man wearing long full-skirted coat and three-cornered hat. 2. **Toby**, name of trained dog in Punch and Judy show, usu. wearing frill round neck. [dim. of name *Tobias*]

toc·ca·ta (tokah′ta) *n.* (mus.) Composition for keyboard instrument, freq. as prelude to fugue etc., designed to exhibit touch and technique of performer.

To·char·i·an, To·khar·i·an (tōkār′ēan, -kār′-) *adj. & n.* (Member) of fairly highly cultured people living in 1st 1,000 years of Christian era in central Asia; (of) Indo-European language of these people, recovered (1904–8) from manuscripts and inscriptions found in ruined temples of northern Chinese Turkestan.

Tocque·ville (tōk′vĭl), Alexis Charles Henri Maurice Clérel de (1805–59). French statesman, historian, and writer; minister of foreign affairs, 1849; author of *Democracy in America* etc.

toc·sin (tŏk′sĭn) *n.* (Bell rung as) alarm or signal. [Provençal *tocarsenh* (*tocar* touch, *senh* signal bell, f. L. *signum* sign)]

to·day, to-day (todā′) *advs. & ns.* (On) this present day; (loosely) nowadays, (in) modern times.

The **holy cross toad**, *shown burrowing into soft mud. Although toads resemble frogs, they prefer land rather than water and have warty, rather than smooth skins.*

Picking **tobacco** leaves in Kenya. They must then be cured in a drying kiln (below left) where heat and humidity are carefully controlled. After 'yellowing', the leaf is then dried and conditioned before grading for quality.

tod·dle (tŏd'el) *n.* Toddling walk. ~ *v.i.* (**-dled, -dling**). (esp. of child) Walk with short unsteady steps; take casual walk. **tod'dler** *n.* (esp.) Child just learning to walk.

tod·dy (tŏd'ē) *n.* (pl. **-dies**). 1. Fresh or fermented sap of various species of palm, used as beverage. 2. Sweetened drink of whiskey and hot water. [Hind. *tārī*, f. *tār* palm tree (Sansk. *tâla* palmyra)]

to-do (todoo') *n.* (pl. **-dos**). Commotion.

to·dy (tō'dē) *n.* (pl. **-dies**). Small insectivorous W. Indian bird of genus *Todus*, allied to the kingfisher.

toe (tō) *n.* One of five terminal members of foot, forepart of foot; part of stocking, shoe, etc., that covers toes; forepart of hoof; something suggesting a toe by its position, shape, etc., esp. outer end of striking surface of golf club; **on one's ~s**, (fig.) alert; **toe'cap**, piece of leather covering toe of boot or shoe; **toe dance**, dance performed on extreme tips of toes; **toe dancer, dancing**; **toe'hold**, minimal foothold (also fig.); **toe-in, -out**, slight forward convergence, divergence, in setting of wheels of vehicle; **toe'nail**, nail of human toe; metal nail driven obliquely through end of board etc.; **toe'shoe**, dance slipper having wooden toe to help dancer dance on toes. **toe** *v.t.* (**toed, toe·ing**). Furnish with toe, put new toe on (stocking etc.); touch or reach with toes; **~ the line, mark**, stand with tips of toes reaching line indicating starting point in race etc.; (fig.) conform strictly to standard or requirement, esp. under pressure.

tof·fee, tof·fy (taw'fē, tŏf'ē) *ns.* (pl. **-fees, -fies**). (chiefly Brit.) Taffy.

tog (tŏg) *v.* (**togged, tog·ging**). (colloq.) Dress (person, oneself, *out* or *up*). ~ *n.pl.* Clothes.

to·ga (tō'ga) *n.* (pl. **-gas, -gae** pr. -jē). Ancient Roman citizen's outer garment, flowing cloak or robe of single piece of cloth covering whole body except right arm, freq. with allusion to civil career or to its assumption at age of manhood; (transf.) gown or other garb associated with some profession. **to'gaed** *adj.*

to·geth·er (togĕdh'er) *adv.* In(to) company or conjunction, so as to unite, in union; simultaneously; uninterruptedly, in unbroken succession.

to·geth·er·ness (togĕdh'ernĭs) *n.* Feeling of belonging together.

tog·gle (tŏg'el) *n.* Short pin put

through eye or loop of rope, link of chain etc. to keep it in place etc.; any similar crosspiece on chain etc.; rod or screw with crosspiece or device enabling it to pass through hole in one position but not in other; movable pivoted crosspiece serving as barb in harpoon; (also ~ **joint**) two plates or rods hinged together endwise, so that force applied at the elbow to straighten the joint is transmitted to the outer end of each plate or rod; ~ **bolt**, anchor bolt having folding wings that open behind wall into which it is driven when screw in center is tightened; ~ **switch**, electric switch with projecting lever to be moved usu. up and down.

To·go (tō´gō). Republic in W. Africa between Ghana and Dahomey; fully independent 1960; capital, Lome.

toil[1] (toil) *v.i.* Work long or laboriously; move painfully or laboriously. **toil'er** *n.* **toil** *n.* Labor, drudgery, hard and continuous work or exertion. **toil'-some** *adj.* **toil'some·ness** *n.*

toil[2] (toil) *n.* (now only in pl.) Net, snare. [OF. *toile* cloth, f. L. *tela* web]

toile (twahl) *n.* Cloth esp. for garments; pattern of garment in muslin etc. for fitting or for use in making copies.

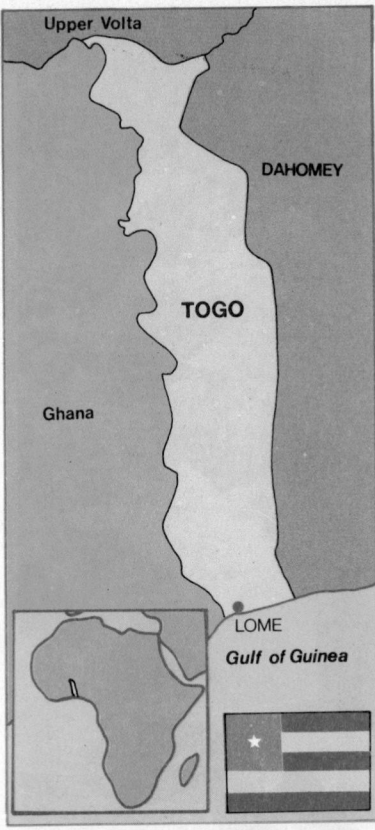

Upper Volta
DAHOMEY
TOGO
Ghana
LOME
Gulf of Guinea

toi·let (toi´lĭt) *n.* Process of dressing, arranging hair, etc.; (style of) dress; dressing room; lavatory; toilet bowl; ~ **bowl**, ceramic bowl in toilet for urination and defecation; ~ **paper**, soft paper for use in lavatories; ~ **powder**, dusting

powder used after bath, shaving, etc.; ~ **seat**, wooden or plastic seat on top of toilet bowl; ~ **set**, set of usu. matching articles used in dressing, as hand mirror, brush, comb, etc.; ~ **water**, scented liquid used after washing. [Fr. *toilette*, orig. = cloth thrown over shoulders in dressing]

toi·let·ry (toi´lĭtrē) *n.* (pl. **-ries**). (also pl.) Articles for use in making one's toilet.

To·kay (tōkā´) *n.* Rich sweet aromatic wine made near Tokay in Hungary; similar wine made elsewhere.

to·ken (tō´ken) *n.* Sign, symbol (*of*); characteristic mark; thing serving to authenticate person, message, etc.; keepsake; small flat piece of stamped metal used in vending machine, toll booth, etc. to receive goods etc.; **by the same** ~, similarly; moreover; in corroboration of what I say; **in ~ of**, in evidence of; ~ **payment**, proportionately small payment made by debtor as indication that debt or obligation is not repudiated.

to·ken·ism (tō´kenĭzem) *n.* Making outward show of meeting requirements of law, principle, etc., by small and merely symbolic gestures.

To·khar·i·an = TOCHARIAN.

To·ky·o (tō´kēō; *Jap.* taw´kyaw).

Above: Tula, capital of the old **Toltec** people. They were noted builders and craftsmen, and gave the cults of the Feathered Serpent, the Coyote, and the Eagle to the Mayan Peoples.

Capital city of Japan, at head of Tokyo Bay on SE. coast of main island; **T ~ Bay**, inlet of the W. Pacific Ocean, extending inland 30 mi. (48 km) into SE. Honshu Island, Japan.

To·le·do (tolē′dō; *Sp.* tawlĕ′-dhaw). City of Spain, Spanish capital 1087–1560 famous for manufacture of finely tempered sword blades.

tol·er·a·ble (tŏl′erabel) *adj.* Endurable; fairly good, not bad. **tol′er·a·ble·ness** *n.* **tol′er·a·bly** *adv.*

tol·er·ance (tŏl′erans) *n.* Willingness to tolerate, forbearance; capacity to tolerate (esp. med.); (eng.) permitted variation in dimension.

tol·er·ate (tŏl′erāt) *v.t.* (**-at·ed, -at·ing**). Endure, permit; allow to exist, be practiced, etc., without interference or molestation; forbear to judge harshly; (med.) sustain use of (drug etc.) without harm. **tol′-er·ant** *adj.* **tol′er·ant·ly** *adv.*

tol·er·a·tion (tŏlerā′shon) *n.* Tolerating; (esp.) recognition of liberty to uphold one's religious opinions and forms of worship or to enjoy all social privileges etc. without regard to religious differences.

toll¹ (tōl) *n.* Tax, duty, charge, paid for passage along public road or over bridge or ferry, for use of telephone, for transport of goods by railroad or canal etc.; **take ~**, (fig.) abstract a portion of; **toll′gate**, bar or gate across road to prevent passage without paying toll; **toll bridge**, bridge at which toll is charged; **toll call**, telephone call for which charge is higher than for local call; **toll′house** (pl.

-houses pr. -howzĭz), house occupied by collector of tolls at tollgate or toll bridge; **tollhouse cookie**, cookie containing bits of chocolate and, sometimes, nuts; **toll road**, road maintained by means of tolls collected on it. **toll** *v.t.* Collect, pay, toll.

toll² (tōl) *v.* Cause (bell) to ring, ring bell, with slow uniform strokes, esp. for death or funeral; (of bell or clock) give out (stroke, knell, hour of day), give out measured sounds. **~** *n.* Tolling, stroke, of bell.

Tol·stoy, Tol·stoi (tŏl′stoi, tōl′-; *Russ.* tŏlstoi′), **Lev (Leo) Nikolaevich, Count** (1828–1910). Russian novelist and social reformer, author of *War and Peace, Anna Karenina*, etc. **Tol′stoy·an, Tol′stoi·an** *adjs. & ns.* (Follower) of doctrines of Tolstoy, who advocated simple living and practice of manual labor and believed that the holding of property is sinful.

Tol·tec (tŏl′tĕk) *n.* (pl. **-tecs**, collect. **-tec**). Member, language, of an Amer. Ind. people, remarkable esp. as architects, who flourished in Mexico from the 9th c. onward, having their capital at Tula, which they abandoned in 1168, when some of them moved to Yucatan and lived in association with the MAYA. **Tol′tec·an** *adj. & n.*

to·lu (tŏlōō′) *n.* (also **balsam of ~, ~ balsam**) Fragrant brown

balsam obtained by incision from tropical S. Amer. tree (*Myroxylon balsamum*) and used to flavor cough syrups and lozenges, as expectorant, and in perfumery. [f. (*Santiago de*) *Tolu* in Colombia]

tol·u·ene (tŏl′ūēn) *n.* Colorless aromatic liquid hydrocarbon (methyl benzene) with smell like benzene and burning taste, orig. obtained from tolu balsam but now esp. from coal tar, used in manufacture of explosives and other compounds. **to·lu·ic** (tolōō′ĭk, tŏl′ūĭk) *adj.* **~ acid**, any of isomeric acids derived from toluene.

tol·u·ol (tŏl′ūōl) *n.* Commercial form of toluene.

Tom (tŏm). Masculine proper name used in various collocations: **Long ~**, large gun with long range; (naut.) long gun formerly carried amidships on swivel carriage; **~ Collins**, drink of gin, sugar, lemon or lime juice, and soda water; **~, Dick, and Harry**, (usu. derog.) persons taken at random, ordinary people; **~ Thumb**, dwarf in nursery tale, no bigger than his father's thumb; any diminutive person; dwarf variety of various plants. **tom** *n.* 1. Male animal, esp. cat (**tom′cat**). 2. **tom′boy**, wild romping girl; **tom′cod** (pl. **-cods**, collect. **-cod**), any of various small Amer. fishes (*Micrograd us*) resembling cod; **tom′fool′**, witless fellow; (*adj.*) stupid, senseless; (*v.i.*) play the fool; **tomfool′ery** (pl. **-er·ies**), foolish trifling, foolish knickknacks, etc.; **tom′tit**, titmouse.

tom·a·hawk (tŏm′ahawk) *n.* Light ax of N. Amer. Indians, used as tool and as weapon of war. **~**

*A Shoshoni Indian with a modern **tomahawk**. Before Europeans arrived, these plateau people used blades of stone or deer horn to butcher buffalo or gut the salmon that were their food.*

v.t. Strike, kill, with tomahawk.

tom·al·ley (tŏm′ălē) *n.* (pl. **-leys**). Fat (often called *liver*) of lobster, green when cooked.

to·ma·to (tomā′tō, -mah′-) *n.* (pl. **-toes**). (Glossy red or yellow fleshy edible fruit of) S. Amer. plant (*Lycopersicon esculentum*) with weak trailing or climbing stem, irregularly pinnate leaves, and yellow flowers, widely cultivated, usu. as annual. [Mex. *tomatl*]

tomb (tōom) *n.* Excavation, chamber, vault, in earth or rock for reception of dead body; sepulchral monument; **tomb′stone**, memorial stone over grave.

tom·bac (tŏm′băk) *n.* Alloy of copper and zinc used as material for cheap jewelry. [Malay]

tome (tōm) *n.* Volume, book, esp. large heavy one.

to·men·tum (tomĕn′tum) *n.* (pl. **-ta** pr. -*ta*). (bot.) Pubescence of matted woolly hairs. **to·men′tose** *adj.*

tom·my (tŏm′ē) *n.* (pl. **-mies**). 1. **T~** (**Atkins**), private in British Army. 2. **T~ gun**, Thompson submachine gun; similar automatic weapon; **tom′myrot**, nonsense. [familiar form of *Tom*]

to·mor·row (tomŏr′ō, -mar′-) *adv. & n.* (On) the day after today; (at) a future time.

Tomp·kins (tŏmp′kĭnz), **Daniel D.** (1774–1825). Amer. politician; governor of New York, 1807–17; U.S. vice president, 1817–25, under James Monroe.

tom-tom (tŏm′tŏm) *n.* Amer. or E. Indian drum, usu. beaten with hands; any barbaric drum; the sound of such a drum. [Hind. *tamtam*, imit.]

ton (tŭn) *n.* 1. (abbrev. t.) Measure of weight; **long ~**, 2,240 lbs. avoirdupois; **metric ~**, unit of mass equal to 1000 kilograms, 2,204.6 lbs. avoirdupois; **short ~**, 2,000 lbs. avoirdupois. 2. Measure of capacity (often varying) for timber (40 cu. ft.), stone (16 cu. ft.), salt (42 bushels), lime (40 bushels), coke (28 bushels), wheat (20 bushels), etc. 3. Unit of internal capacity of ship (for purposes of registered TONNAGE, 100 cu. ft.; for purposes of freight, usu. 40 cu. ft.). 4. (colloq., esp. pl.) Large number or amount. [var. of *tun*]

ton·al (tō′nal) *adj.* Of tone or tones; (of fugue) having **tonal** (opp. real) **answer**, in which intervals are modified rather than repeated exactly.

to·nal·i·ty (tōnăl′ĭtē) *n.* (pl. **-ties**). 1. (mus.) The relation between notes in a composition that constitutes the key; strict observation of key scheme or mode of musical composition. 2. (painting) Coloring in respect of its lightness and darkness, tones of a

*On this experimental farm in California **tomatoes** are tested under various conditions. The end result will, it is hoped, be bigger, tastier tomatoes.*

picture in relation to one another.

tone (tōn) *n.* 1. Sound, esp. with ref. to pitch, quality, and strength. 2. Particular quality, pitch, modulation, etc., of voice; intonation; pitch, inflection, of spoken sound, expressing differences of meaning, esp. (in Chinese and similar languages) any of various inflections or pitches distinguishing words that otherwise have the same sound. 3. (mus.) Sound of definite pitch and character produced by regular vibration of sounding body; musical note; each of the several tones (**fundamental ~** and **overtones**) audible in sound of bell or similar instrument; (also) musical note without overtones. 4. (mus.) Interval of major second, e.g. C-D E-F sharp (freq. **whole tone**, as opp. to **semitone**). 5. (med.) Degree of firmness or tension proper to strong and healthy organs or tissues of body. 6. Prevailing character of morals, sentiments etc., in society or community; state of mind, mood. 7. Degree of lightness or darkness of color(s); general effect of combination of light and shade, esp. in a picture or a scene in nature. 8. **tone arm**, phonograph pickup arm; **tone color** (mus.) timbre; **tone deaf**

part of the soft palate

tonsil

uvula

pharyngeal part of the tongue

vallate papillae

dorsum

fungiform papillae

*Above: The human **tongue** is important for taste, swallowing, and pronunciation.*

*Dancers from **Tonga** in skirts made from tapa or beaten bark. Except for a small export trade of copra and bananas, the Polynesian islanders are self-supporting gardeners.*

deafness, insensitive(ness) to differences in pitch between musical tones; **tone language**, language such as Chinese or Swedish in which similar sounds are distinguished by tones (see sense 2 above); **tone poem**, orchestral composition of indeterminate form and illustrative character, based on poetic or literary rather than purely musical ideas. **tone** *v.* (**toned, ton·ing**). Give tone or quality (of sound or color) to; alter tone or color of (photographic print) in finishing it; harmonize; **tone down**, lower tone, quality, or character of; make, become, less emphatic; become lower or softer in tone or quality; **tone up**, improve tone of, give higher or stronger tone to. **ton'·al·ly** *adv.*

tone·less (tōn'lĭs) *adj.* (esp.) Without distinctive quality of sound or color, dull, lifeless, unexpressive. **tone'less·ly** *adv.* **tone'less·ness** *n.*

tong (tawng, tŏng) *n.* Chinese association, esp. secret society or fraternal association of Chinese in foreign country. [Chin. *t'ang* meeting place]

Ton·ga (tŏng'ga). (also Tongan Islands or Friendly Islands) Group of islands in S. Pacific E. of Fiji;

kingdom, member state of the Brit. Commonwealth, independent since 1970; capital, Nukualofa. **Ton'gan** *adj. & n.*

ton·ga (tŏng'ga) *n.* Light two-wheeled carriage in India.

tongs (tawngz, tŏngz) *n.pl.* (also **pair of** ~) Implement consisting of two limbs connected by hinge, pivot, or spring bringing together lower ends to grasp objects that are inconvenient to lift with hand.

tongue (tŭng) *n.* 1. Organ in floor of mouth, usu. freely movable; in man and many other vertebrates tapering, blunt tipped, muscular, soft and fleshy, used in taking in and swallowing food, as principal organ of taste, and, in people, of articulate speech; animal's tongue as article of food. 2. Action of speaking, faculty of speech, words, talk, language; speech or language of a people; **gift of** ~**s**, power of speaking in unknown languages, esp. as miraculously conferred on early Christians (Acts 2); **lose, find, one's tongue**, be too bashful or surprised to speak, recover power of speech after this; **hold one's tongue**, be silent; **on the tip of one's tongue**, on the point of being said; about to be said, esp. because nearly but not quite remembered; (**speak**) **with one's**

tongue in one's cheek, (speak) insincerely or mockingly. 3. Thing like tongue in shape or function, as pin of buckle, narrow strip of land between two bodies of water, clapper of bell, pole of wagon or other vehicle, strip of leather or cloth closing gap in front of boot or shoe, movable tapered piece of steel in railroad switch, projecting tenon along edge of board, to be inserted into groove or mortise of another board etc. 4. **tongue and groove**, joint in which tongue on edge of one board fits into groove on another; **tongue depressor**, thin piece of wood for holding down patient's tongue during medical examination of mouth and throat; **tongue'fish**, flatfish of family Cynoglossidae; **tongue-lashing**, severe scolding or rebuke; **tongue-tie(d)**, (condition of) having frenum of tongue too short, so that distinct speech is difficult or impossible; speechless, dumb, from embarrassment, shyness, etc.; **tongue twister**, sequence of words difficult to articulate quickly. **tongue** *v.* (**tongued, tongu·ing**). Utter, speak; furnish with tongue; interrupt stream of air with tongue in playing wind instrument. **tongued, tongue'less** *adjs.*

ton·ic (tŏn'ĭk) *adj.* 1. Producing

tension, esp. of muscles; of, maintaining, restoring, tone or normal healthy condition of tissues or organs; **strengthening**, invigorating, bracing; (of spasm) with sustained muscular contraction; ~ **water**, carbonated quinine water esp. for mixing with alcoholic drinks. 2. (mus.) Of, founded upon, tonic or keynote. 3. Of tone or accent in speech. **ton'i·cal·ly** *adv*.

tonic *n*. 1. Tonic medicine or agent; invigorating influence. 2. Tonic water. 3. (mus.) Keynote.

to·nic·i·ty (tōnĭs'ītē) *n*. Tonic quality or condition, tone.

to·night (tonīt') *adv*. & *n*. (On) the present night, (on) the night of today.

ton·ka (tŏng'ka) **bean.** Black fragrant almond-shaped seed of large S. Amer. leguminous tree (*Dipteryx odorata* or *D. oppositifolia*), used for scenting tobacco, as ingredient in perfumes etc.; the tree itself.

Ton·kin (tŏn'kĭn), **Gulf of.** Arm of the China Sea, 300 mi. (483 km) long, between the E. coast of Vietnam and Hainan Island.

ton·nage (tŭn'ĭj) *n*. 1. Carrying capacity of ship expressed in tons of 100 cu. ft.; ships collectively, shipping; charge per ton on cargo or freight; **displacement** ~, weight of water displaced by a ship when loaded up to her load line, used in stating the tonnage of warships; **gross** ~, total cubic capacity of all spaces above and below the tonnage deck; **net** or **register** ~, gross tonnage less space occupied by engines, crew's quarters, etc., tonnage for which vessels are registered and on which the assessment of fees and charges on shipping are based.

to·nom·e·ter (tōnŏm'īter) *n*. Tuning fork or other instrument for measuring the pitch of tones.

ton·sil (tŏn'sĭl) *n*. Either of a pair of small organs on either side of the root of the tongue, composed of lymphatic tissue and instrumental in protecting the throat from infection, but themselves liable to become septic. **ton'sil·lar, ton'sil·ar** *adjs*. Of, affected by, the tonsils.

ton·sil·lec·to·my (tŏnsĭlĕk'tomē) *n*. (pl. **-mies**). Surgical removal of the tonsils.

ton·sil·li·tis (tŏnsĭlī'tĭs) *n*. Inflammation of the tonsils.

ton·so·ri·al (tŏnsōr'ēal, -sōr'-) *adj*. (usu. joc.) Of a barber or his work.

ton·sure (tŏn'sher) *n*. Shaving of head (in Eastern Ch.) or part of it, esp. circular patch on crown (in R.C. Ch., until 1972), as religious practice, esp. as preparation to entering priesthood or monastic order; part of head thus shaved. ~ *v.t.* (**-sured, -sur·ing**).

The **tonsure** of this Benedictine monk is said to represent the 'coronal of St. Peter'. The practice was begun in monasteries in the 5th century, adopted by other clerics, but is now restricted to monks.

Shave head of, give tonsure to.

ton·tine (tŏn'tēn, tŏntēn') *n*. Financial scheme by which subscribers to loan each receive an annuity for life, increasing as their number is diminished by death, until last survivor enjoys whole income; any arrangement, as form of insurance, in which benefits shared among members are increased on death or default of any of them, or in which they are distributed among all remaining members at end of fixed period. [Lorenzo *Tonti*, Neapolitan banker, who instituted scheme in France c1653]

To·ny (tō'nē) *n*. (pl. **-nies**). Any of several awards given each year by the American Theater Wing for outstanding work in the theater as a performer, director, writer, designer, etc.

too (tōō) *adv*. 1. In addition, moreover, besides, also. 2. In excess; more than is right or fitting, more than enough; (colloq.) extremely, very.

tool (tōōl) *n*. Implement for working on something, usu. one held in and operated by hand, but also including simple machines, as lathe; (cutting part of) machine tool; anything used in performing some operation or in any occupation or pursuit; person used as mere instrument by another; (bookbinding etc.) small stamp or roller for impressing design on leather; **tool'box**, box or chest, usu. having compartments, to hold workman's

tools; **tool'house** (pl. **-houses** pr. -howzĭz), **tool'shed**, shed, as in garden, where tools are kept; **tool'maker**, machinist who makes machine tools and parts and maintains and repairs them. **tool** *v*. Work with tool; smooth surface of building stone with large chisel; ornament (leather) with tool; drive, ride, (*along*) esp. in casual or leisurely manner; ~ **up**, equip with tools.

tool·ing (tōō'lĭng) *n*. (esp.) Dressing of stone with broad chisel; impressing of ornamental design with heated tools on leather, such design(s).

toot (tōōt) *n*. Note or short blast of horn, trumpet, or other wind instrument. ~ *v*. Sound (horn or other wind instrument); give out such sound. **toot'er** *n*.

tooth (tōōth) *n*. (pl. **teeth** pr. tēth). 1. Each of the hard processes (in mammals usu. of dentine coated with cement around root and enamel in exposed part) attached, usu. in sockets, in a row to each jaw in most vertebrates except birds, with points, edges, or grinding surfaces, and used for biting, tearing, or chewing food, or as weapons of attack or defense; elephant's tusk; (fig.) sense of taste, taste, liking; **by the skin of one's teeth**, narrowly, barely; **cut one's teeth on**, do at the start of one's career, schooling, etc.; **in the teeth of**, in spite of; in opposition to; in the face of (wind etc.); **long in the tooth**, old; **put teeth in(to)**, make (more) effective, make (law etc.) enforceable; **set one's teeth**, clench teeth firmly from indignation or fixed resolution (freq. fig.); **show one's teeth**, (usu. fig.) show hostility or malice, behave threateningly; (**armed** etc.)

BIRTH

4 YEARS

molars

premolars

canine

incisors

15 YEARS

permanent teeth

milk teeth

Left: Cross sections of the human mouth at various ages showing development of the teeth. Below left: The fossil canine **tooth** of a bear which lived during the Pleistocene, at some time up to 3 million years ago.

on ~, (fig.) supreme, dominant; **on ~ of the world**, (colloq.) exuberant; successful; **the ~s**, (colloq.) (used predicatively) best in ability, popularity, quality, etc.; foremost; **top dog**, victor, master; **top-dog**, of the highest authority; **top′flight**, in highest rank of achievement; **top spin**, spin given to a ball, causing it to rotate forward in direction of its flight. 2. Part of piece forming upper part or covering of something, e.g. platform near head of lower mast of ship, in warship, topsail; upper part of leg of high boot, esp. broad band of material around this; gauntlet part of glove; turned-down part of leg of sock or stocking; stopper of bottle; hood of carriage, automobile, etc. **top** adj. Highest in position or degree, that is at or on top; **top′coat**, overcoat; **top drawer**, uppermost drawer of series; **top-drawer**, of high social position, origin, or quality; **top-dress**, apply material to surface of (land, road, etc.) without working it in; **top dressing**, material, esp. manure, so applied; **topgal′lant**, mast, sail, yard, rigging, immediately above topmast and topsail; **top hat**, tall silk hat; **top-heavy**, overweighted at top, so as to be unstable; **top′knot**, knot, bow of ribbon, tuft, crest, etc., worn or growing on top of head; **topmast** (tŏp′măst, -mahst; naut. tŏp′m*a*st), smaller mast on top of lower mast, esp. second section of mast above deck; **top′notch**, (colloq.) first-rate, excellent; **topsail** (tŏp′sāl; naut. tŏp′s*a*l), in square-rigged vessel, sail next above lower sail, sometimes divided into **upper** and **lower topsails** (**double topsails**); **top-secret**, extremely secret (esp. as security classification); **top sergeant**, (colloq.) first sergeant of company or other military unit; **top′side**, upper part of ship's side, above water line or main deck. **top** v. (**topped, top·ping**). 1. Provide with top or cap; remove top of (plant) to improve growth etc.; reach top of (hill etc.); be at top of, have highest position in; exceed in height; hit (golf ball) above center, make (stroke) thus; ~ **off**, put end or finishing touch to. 2. (naut.) Tip *up*, slant, raise (yard); (of yard) rise, tip up. **top′less** adj. (Seemingly) without a top; (of clothes) having no upper part, (of person) wearing such clothes, bare-breasted.

top² (tŏp) n. Toy, usu. conical, rotating on point when set in

o the teeth, completely, elaborately armed, equipped, etc.; **ooth and nail**, (usu. fig.) vigorously, fiercely. 2. Projecting part or point resembling tooth, as pointed process on margin of leaf; projecting point of rock; prong or line of comb, saw, file, rake, fork, etc.; one of series of projections on edge of wheel, pinion, etc., engaging with corresponding ones on another, cog; (sing. only) rough surface on paper, canvas, etc., to which pencil marks, colors, etc., adhere; roughness made on surfaces to be glued together. 3. **tooth′-ache**, ache in tooth or teeth; **ooth′brush**, small brush used for cleaning teeth; **fine-tooth comb**, comb with closely set teeth; **tooth′-paste, tooth powder**, paste, powder, for cleaning teeth; **tooth′-pick**, small pointed instrument of quill, wood, etc., used for removing matter lodged between teeth; **tooth shell**, (long tubular tusk-shaped

shell of) mollusk of class Schaphopoda or allied genus. **toothed** (tŏōdhd), **tooth′less** adjs. **tooth′less·ly** adv. **tooth′less·ness** n. **tooth** v. Furnish with tooth or teeth; give rough surface to; (of cog wheels etc.) interlock.

tooth·some (tōōth′s*o*m) adj. Pleasant to eat. **tooth′some·ly** adv. **tooth′some·ness** n.

too·tle (tōō′tel) v.i. (**-tled, -tling**). Toot gently or continuously, esp. on flute.

toot·sy (tōōt′sē) n. (pl. **-sies**). (nursery or joc.) [also ~-**wootsy** (-wōōtsē) (pl. **-woot·sies**)] Foot.

top¹ (tŏp) n. 1. Summit, upper part, surface; highest place, rank, degree, etc.; end of anything conventionally regarded as the higher; (usu. pl.) part of plant growing above ground, esp. of vegetable grown for its root; **blow one's ~**, (slang) lose one's temper; lose one's sanity; **from ~ to toe**, from head to foot, in every part;

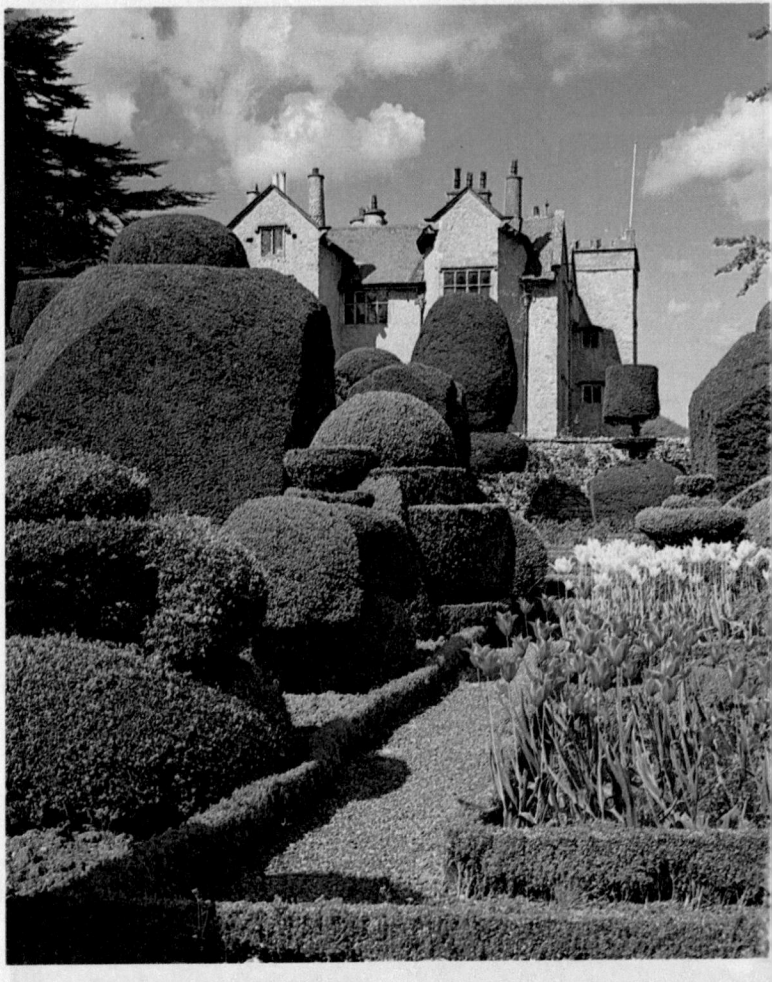

Topiary became fashionable in the gardens of the great English homes during the reign of the Tudors. These shrubs at Leven's Hall in Cumbria are fine examples.

motion by hand, spring, or string; **sleep like a** ~ sleep soundly, (with ref. to apparent stillness of top spinning on vertical axis).

to·paz (tō′păz) *n.* Silicate of aluminum usu. in yellow, white, pale blue, or pale green transparent lustrous prismatic crystals, classed as semiprecious stone; **false** ~, transparent pale yellow variety of quartz; **oriental** ~, precious stone, the yellow sapphire; **pink** ~, rose-colored kind produced by exposing yellow Brazilian topaz to great heat. **to·paz·ine** (tō′pazēn, -zĭn) *adj.*

tope[1] (tōp) *n.* Small European shark, *Galeorhinus galeus*; any of various related sharks.

tope[2] (tōp) *n.* Buddhist monument, usu. a cylindrical tower surmounted by a cupola. [Sansk. *stupa* mound]

tope[3] (tōp) *v.i.* (**toped, top·ing**). (now chiefly literary) Drink to excess, esp. habitually. **top′er** *n.*

to·pee, to·pi (tōpē′, tō′pē) *ns.* Light pith hat or helmet, esp. **sola** ~. [Hind. *topī* hat]

To·pe·ka (topē′ka). Capital of Kansas, in the NE. on the Kansas River.

to·phus (tō′fus) *n.* (pl. **-phi** pᴜ. -fī). (path.) Mineral concretion in the body, esp. on the joints or on a bone, in gout.

to·pi = TOPEE.

to·pi·ar·y (tō′pēĕrē) *adj. & n.* (pl. **-ar·ies**). (Of) the art of clipping and trimming shrubs etc. into ornamental or fantastic shapes. [L. *topia* landscape gardening or painting, f. Gk. *topos* place]

top·ic (tŏp′ĭk) *n.* Subject of discourse, argument, etc., theme; (rhet., logic) class of considerations from which arguments can be drawn.

top·i·cal (tŏp′ĭkal) *adj.* 1. Of topics; of topics of the day, containing local or temporary allusions. 2. (med.) Local. **top′i·cal·ly** *adv.* **top·i·cal·i·ty** (tŏpĭkăl′ĭtē) *n.*

top·most (tŏp′mōst) *adj.* Uppermost.

to·pog·ra·phy (topŏg′rafē) *n.* (pl. **-phies**). Detailed delineation or description, physical features, of place; features of locality collectively; (study of) local distribution; (anat.) regional anatomy. **to·pog′ra·pher** *n.* **top·o·graph·ic** (tŏpŏgrăf′ĭk), **top·o·graph′i·cal** *adjs.* **top·o·graph′i·cal·ly** *adv.*

to·pol·o·gy (topŏl′ojē) *n.* (pl. **-gies**). Branch of mathematics dealing with properties of spaces (sets of points) in respect of their being one connected piece and of

forming a boundary, independently of shape and size. **top·o·log·i·cal** (tŏpolŏj′ĭkal) *adj.* **top·o·log′i·cal·ly** *adv.* **to·pol′o·gist** *n.*

top·per (tŏp′er) *n.* 1. (colloq.) Top hat. 2. One who or thing that tops. 3. (slang) Witticism, joke, etc., better than all that preceded.

top·ple (tŏp′el) *v.* (**-pled, -pling**). (Cause to) tumble or fall headlong, as if top-heavy.

top·sy-tur·vy (tŏp′sētēr′vē) *adv. & adj.* With the top where the bottom should be, upside down; in(to) utter confusion or disorder.

toque (tōk) *n.* Small usu. brimless hat of folded or swathed material.

tor (tōr) *n.* Craggy or rocky hill or peak.

To·rah (tōr′a, tōr′a; *Heb.* tōrah′) *n.* Pentateuch, the Mosaic Law; scroll of this used in synagogue. [Heb. *tôrāh* instruction, direction]

torc = TORQUE.

torch (tōrch) *n.* 1. Light for carrying in hand, consisting of piece of resinous wood or length of twisted hemp or flax soaked in resin, tallow, etc.; (fig.) source of conflagration, illumination, enlightenment, etc.; **carry the** ~ **for**, (slang) have unrequited passion for; **pass on the** ~, pass on tradition.

2. (also **electric** ~) (Brit.) Flashlight. 3. Lamp or other portable device for producing hot flame (also **blow** ~). 4. **torch′bearer**, (esp.) one who guards or hands on light of truth, civilization, etc.; **torch singer**, singer of **torch songs**, popular, esp. jazz, songs about unrequited love.

tore[1]: see TEAR[2].

tore[2] (tōr, tŏr) = TORUS, senses 1 and 3.

tor·e·a·dor (tŏr′ēadōr) *n.* Bullfighter (term still current in English but not in mod. Spanish). [Sp. *toro* bull, f. L. *taurus*]

to·re·ro (torār′ō) *n.* (pl. **-ros**). Bullfighter, esp. a matador. [Sp.]

to·reu·tic (torōō′tĭk) *adj. & n.* (Of) the art of chasing, carving, and embossing, esp. metal. **to·reu′tics** *n.sing.*

tor·ment (tōr′měnt) *n.* Severe bodily or mental suffering; cause of this. ~ (tŏrměnt′) *v.t.* Subject to torment. **tor·men′tor, tor·ment′er** *ns.* **tor·ment′ed·ly, tor·ment′ing·ly** *advs.*

tor·men·til (tōr′měntĭl) *n.* Low-growing yellow-flowered herb (*Potentilla tormentilla*) of Europe and Asia, common on heaths and dry pastures, with strongly astringent roots.

Battery-powered torpedo — gyro — motor — propeller — firing pin — explosive chamber — battery — gear-box

torn: see TEAR[2].

tor·na·do (tŏrnā′dō) *n.* (pl. **-does, -dos**). Violent storm, usu. with heavy rain, in which wind rotates or constantly changes direction, esp., in the midwestern U.S., destructive storm with funnel-shaped (tornado) cloud like waterspout, extending toward the ground and·advancing in narrow path for many miles. **tor·nad·ic** (tŏrnăd′ĭk), **tor·na′do·like** *adjs.*

to·roid (tŏr′oid, tōr′-) *n.* (geom.) Surface generated by the rotation of a plane closed curve about a line lying in its plane. ~ *adj.* Of, resembling, a tore or toroid. **to·roi·dal** (toroi′dal, tŏr′oidal, tōr′-) *adj.*

To·ron·to (torŏn′tō). Capital city of province of Ontario, Canada.

tor·pe·do (tŏrpē′dō) *n.* (pl. **-does**). 1. ELECTRIC ray, esp. *Torpedo nobiliana* found in Atlantic Ocean (also ~ **fish**). 2. Self-propelled submarine missile, usu. equipped with a homing device, cigar-shaped, carrying an explosive that is fired by impact with its objective, used for destroying or disabling ships at sea; similar

The first guided missile was also the ancestor of the **torpedo** *— a small boat filled with explosives and steered on the surface by wires. It was made by Robert Whitehead in 1866.*

missile discharged from aircraft (**aerial** ~); case containing explosive used for various military purposes, explosive cartridge for clearing obstructions etc. in oil well, detonator placed on railroad line as fog signal etc.; small firework consisting of gravel and a percussion cap wrapped in tissue paper, exploding loudly when thrown against a hard surface. 3. (slang) Gangster, thug, etc., who kills for hire; ~ **boat**, small fast lightly armored vessel carrying torpedoes; **~-boat destroyer** (now usu. *destroyer*), larger and more heavily armed torpedo boat, orig. for attacking torpedo boat (see also DESTROYER); ~ **tube**, steel tube through which torpedoes are

A **tor** *is a term peculiar to the west of England and may refer to a small rocky hill, or to a weathered outcrop of rock such as that below, on Bodmin Moor in Cornwall.*

discharged, usu. by compressed air. **torpedo** *v.t.* (**-doed, -do·ing**). Attack, damage, destroy, (as) with a torpedo. [L. name of the fish (*torpere* be numb)]

tor·pid (tŏr′pĭd) *adj.* Benumbed; dormant; sluggish, inactive, dull. **tor′pid·ly** *adv.* **tor·pid·i·ty** (tŏrpĭd′ĭtē), **tor′pid·ness** *ns.*

tor·por (tŏr′per) *n.* Torpidity. **tor·por·if·ic** (tŏrporĭf′ĭk) *adj.* Causing torpor.

torque, torc (tōrk) *ns.* 1. Necklace or collar, usu. of twisted metal, worn esp. by ancient Britons and Gauls. 2. (phys. etc.) Twisting or rotary force in piece of mechanism, moment of system of forces producing rotation; ~ **converter**, device to transmit correct torque from engine to axle in motor vehicle; ~ **wrench**, wrench having dial or other indicator that shows amount of torque exerted.

The roots of **tormentil** *have been found to possess useful qualities. Tannin could be obtained from them; if soaked in brandy, the infusion was used to treat stomach complaints.*

Galapagos tortoise

hinge-backed tortoise (retracted)   radiated tortoise

Land-dwelling **tortoises** *range in size from the giants of Galapagos and the Seychelles up to 4 ft. long, to the tiny spider tortoise of Madagascar which does not exceed 4 ins. Three species are native to Europe but those kept as pets in Britain are all imported from the Mediterranean countries.*

Tor·que·ma·da (tŏrkĕmah'-dhah), **Tomás de** (1420–98). Spanish Dominican monk; first inquisitor general.

torr (tŏr) *n.* Unit of pressure in measuring partial vacuum, equal to $\frac{1}{760}$ of standard atmosphere.

tor·rent (tŏr'ent, tär'-) *n.* Swift violent rushing stream of water etc.; violent downpour of rain; (fig.) violent flow (of words etc.). **tor·ren·tial** (torĕn'shal) *adj.* **tor·ren'·tial·ly** *adv.*

tor·rid (tŏr'ĭd, tär'-) *adj.* Scorched, parched, exposed to great heat; intensely hot, burning; **T~ Zone**, region between the tropics of Cancer and Capricorn. **tor·rid·i·ty** (torĭd'ĭtē), **tor'rid·ness** *ns.*

tor·sion (tŏr'shon) *n.* Twisting, twist; **angle of ~**, (geom.) infinitesimal angle between two consecutive osculating planes of tortuous curve; **~ balance**, apparatus for measuring minute horizontal forces by means of wire or filament that is twisted by the application of the force. **tor'·sion·al** *adj.* **tor'sion·al·ly** *adv.*

tor·so (tŏr'sō) *n.* (pl. **-sos, -si** pr. -sē). Statue lacking head and limbs; trunk of statue, or of human body; mutilated or unfinished work. [It., = "stalk," "stump," "torso," f. L. *thyrsus* (Gk. *thursos*

shaft, wand)]

tort (tŏrt) *n.* (law) Wrongful act (but not breach of contract) that results in injury to person, property, etc., making offender liable to action for damages. [med. L. *tortum* wrong f. L. *torquere* twist]

torte (tŏrt) *n.* Rich cake, often layered, made with many eggs, chopped nuts, spices, and bread or cracker crumbs.

tor·ti·col·lis (tŏrtĭkŏl'ĭs) *n.* (path.) Rheumatic or other condition of muscles causing twisting and stiffness of neck.

tor·til·la (tŏrtē'a) *n.* In Mexican cooking, thin flat cake of corn flour baked on flat plate of iron etc.

tor·tious (tŏr'shus) *adj.* Of, constituting, a tort.

tor·toise (tŏr'tos) *n.* Slow-moving four-footed reptile of land and freshwater species of order Chelonia, with body enclosed in heavy shell, and head and legs retractile.

tortoise (tŏr'tos) **shell.** 1. Carapace of turtle, esp. that of the hawksbill turtle (*Chelone imbricata*), semitransparent, of rich yellowish-brown mottled color, used for ornamental articles, in inlaying, etc. 2. (also ~ **butterfly**) Any of various butterflies with coloring resembling that of tortoise shell, esp. the **small tortoise shell**

(*Aglais urticae*).

tor·to·ni (tŏrtō'nē) *n.* Ice cream made with heavy cream, eggs, and chopped maraschino cherries and usually topped with ground almonds or macaroon crumbs.

tor·tu·ous (tŏr'chōous) *adj.* Full of twists or turns; (geom., of curves of which no two successive portions are in same plane; (fig.) devious, circuitous, crooked, not straightforward. **tor'tu·ous·ly** *adv.* **tor'tu·ous·ness, tor·tu·os·i·ty** (tŏrchōoŏs'ĭtē) *ns.*

tor·ture (tŏr'cher) *n.* Infliction of severe bodily pain, e.g. as punishment or to force confession or extort information; severe physical or mental pain. ~ *v.t.* (**-tured, -tur·ing**). Subject to torture; (fig.) strain, wrench, distort, pervert. **tor'tured·ly** *adv.* **tor'tur·er** *n.*

to·rus (tŏr'us, tŏr'us) *n.* (pl. **to·ri** pr. tŏr'ī, tŏr'ī). (also for sense 1 & 3 **tore**) 1. (archit.) Large convex molding esp. at base of column. 2. (bot.) Receptacle of flower, swollen summit of flower stalk, supporting floral organs; (also) thickening of PIT membrane 3. (Solid enclosed by) surface described by a conic section, esp. circle, rotating about a straight line in its own plane. [L., = "protuberance," "bed"]

To·ry (tŏr´ē, tōr´ē) *adj.* & *n.* (pl. **-ries**). 1. (now chiefly in Brit. colloq. and hostile use) Conservative. 2. (hist.) (Member) of the parliamentary and political party in England that opposed the exclusion of the Duke of York (James II) from the succession, inclined to the Stuarts after 1689, accepted George III and the established order in church and state, opposed the Reform Bill of 1832, and has been known officially (since *c*1830) as "Conservative"; cf. WHIG. 3. In the Amer. Revolution, a colonist loyal to Gt. Britain. **To´ry·ism** *n.* [Ir. *tóraidhe* pursuer, applied orig. to 17th-c. Irish outlaws who robbed and killed English settlers and soldiers]

toss (taws, tŏs) *v.* Throw (*up*, *away*, *to*, etc.), esp. lightly, carelessly, or easily; (of bull etc.) throw (person etc.) up with horns; throw (coin), throw coin (*up*), into air to decide choice etc. by way it falls; settle question or dispute with (person *for* thing) thus; throw back *head*, esp. in contempt or impatience; throw about from side to side, throw oneself about thus in bed etc.; roll about restlessly; roll or swing with fitful to-and-fro motion; throw (pancake) up so that it returns to pan with other side up; ~ **off**, drink off at a draft; dispatch (work etc.) rapidly or without apparent effort; **tossed salad**, salad of mixed greens, tomatoes, sliced onions, cucumbers, etc., with dressing, mixed in large bowl. **toss** *n.* Tossing; sudden jerk, esp. of head; tossing of coin; throw from horseback etc; **toss´up**, tossing of coin; doubtful question; even chance.

tot[1] (tŏt) *n.* Tiny child; (Brit.) small quantity (*of* drink, esp. liquor), dram.

tot[2] (tŏt) *v.* (**tot·ted**, **tot·ting**). Add (*up*), mount *up* (*to*). [abbrev.

of TOTAL or of L. *totum* whole]

to·tal (tō´tal) *adj.* Complete, comprising or involving the whole; absolute, unqualified; ~ **depravity**, Calvinistic belief that man's whole nature, including the rational aspects, has been entirely laid over with sin since the Fall, leaving man totally dependent on Christ for spiritual rebirth before he can do anything pleasing to God; ~ **eclipse**, eclipse in which whole disk of sun or moon is obscured; ~ **recall**, ability to remember every detail of one's experience clearly; ~ **war**, one in which all available resources are employed without reserve. **to´tal·ly** *adv.* **to·tal·i·ty** (tōtăl´ĭtē) *n.* (pl. **-ties**). **total** *n.* Sum of all items, total amount. **total** *v.* (**-taled**, **-tal·ing** or **-talled**, **-tal·ling**) Amount to, mount *up to*; reckon total of.

to·tal·i·tar·i·an (tōtălĭtār´ēan) *adj.* Of, pertaining to, regime that permits no rival loyalties or parties

toco toucan

The largest of the 37 types of **toucan** *has a length of 24 ins. and its beak can be a quarter of that. Despite its size, the beak is light in weight and is an adaptation which allows the bird to obtain soft fruit from stems that are too weak to carry the weight of the bird. These birds are found only in the forests of South America.*

sulphur-breasted or keel-billed toucan

and arrogates to itself all rights, including those normally belonging to individuals. **to·tal·i·tar´i·an·ism** *n.*

to·tal·i·za·tor (tō´talīzāter) *n.* Device for registering or finding total of something; esp. a parimutuel machine for registering and indicating bets on each horse, dog, etc., in a race; tote board. **to´tal·i·sa·tor**, **to´tal·iz·er** *ns.*

to·tal·ize (tō´talīz) *v.* (**-ized**, **-iz·ing**). Collect into a total, find the total of.

tote[1] (tōt) *v.t.* (**tot·ed, tot·ing**). (colloq.) 1. Carry or lug; haul, esp. in one's arms or on one's back. 2. Carry or bear on one's person. 3. Convey, transport, as on truck or boat. ~ *n.* (colloq.) 1. Act of toting. 2. Thing that is toted; burden; ~ **bag**, woman's large bag for carrying parcels etc.

tote[2] (tōt) *v.* (**tot·ed, tot·ing**). (colloq.) Total.

tote (tōt) **board.** (colloq.) Totalizator.

to·tem (tō'tem) *n.* Natural, esp. animal, object assumed as emblem of family or clan; image of this; ~ **pole**, pole or post with carved and painted representation of totem, set up in front of N. Amer. Ind. dwelling. **to'tem·ism** *n.*

toth·er, t'oth·er (tŭdh'ĕr) *prons. & adjs.* (dial.) The other.

tot·ter (tŏt'ĕr) *v.i.* Walk with unsteady steps, go shakily or feebly; rock or shake on its base, as if about to overbalance or collapse. **tot'ter·ing** *adj.* **tot'ter·ing·ly** *adv.* **totter** *n.* Tottering gait. **tot'ter·y** *adj.*

tou·can (tōo'kăn, tōokahn') *n.* Tropical Amer. fruit-eating bird of *Rhamphastos* or allied genera, with huge light thin-walled beak and freq. brilliant coloring.

touch (tŭch) *v.* 1. Put hand or other part of body on or into contact with; bring (thing) into contact *with* another; be in, come into contact (with); (geom.) be tangent (to); (of king or healer) lay hand on (person) as cure for scrofula or other disease (also abs.). 2. Affect in some way by contact; strike (strings, keys) of musical instrument so as to make it sound; mark, draw (*in*), modify, alter, by touching drawing etc. with pencil or brush; add touches to; mark, modify, slightly *with* color, expression, etc.; (of ship etc.) call at (port); reach, (fig.) approach in excellence etc. 3. Affect mentally or morally; affect with tender feeling, soften; rouse painful or angry feeling in; concern. 4. Treat of (subject) lightly or in passing. 5. Affect slightly, produce slightest effect on; have to do with in the slightest degree, esp. hurt or harm in the least degree; (usu. with neg.) eat or drink the smallest quantity of. 6. ~ **at**, (of ship) call at (port); ~ **down**, land on ground from the air; ~ (**someone**) **for**, (slang) beg or borrow (money) from (person); ~ **off**, characterize (someone) precisely; discharge (explosive etc.); ~ **on, upon**, treat (subject) briefly; ~ **up**, give finishing, improving, or heightening touches to; jog (memory). 7. ~ **and go**, ~**-and-go**, delicate state of affairs; of uncertain result, risky; ~**-me-not**, plant of genus *Impatiens*, esp. yellow balsam (*I. noli-me-tangere*) with seed capsules that split open when touched; ~ **wood**, touch (wooden object) to avert bad luck. **touch** *n.* 1. Act or fact of touching, contact; faculty by which material things are perceived by their contact with some part of the body surface; sensation conveyed by touching, feel; light stroke with pencil, brush, etc., detail of any artistic work, slight act or effort in work of any kind; artistic skill, style of artistic work; manner of touching keys or strings of musical, esp. keyboard, instrument, manner or degree in which instrument responds to this. 2. (also ~ **mark**) Manufacturer's identifying mark on article of metal, esp. pewter. 3. Close relation of communication, agreement, sympathy, etc. (esp. **in, out of,** ~ **with; keep in, lose,** ~). 4. **touch'back**, (football) play in which player touches ball to ground behind his own goal line after opponents have caused ball to pass over the line; cf. SAFETY; **touch'down**, (football) scoring by being in possession of ball behind opponents' goal line; landing on ground by airplane; **touch football**, informal style of football played without uniforms or protective equipment and with touching, usu. with both hands, of ball carrier substituted for tackling; **touch'line**, (soccer) boundary line on each side of field of play between goal lines. 5. **touch'hole**, (hist.) small tubular hole in breech of cannon through which fire was applied to powder; **touch needle**, slender rod of gold or silver of known fineness, used with touchstone to test fineness of gold or silver; **touch paper**, paper impregnated with potassium nitrate so as to burn steadily without flame, formerly used for firing gunpowder etc.; **touch'stone**, basanite, used to test fineness of gold and silver alloys by color of streak produced by rubbing them on it; (fig.) standard, criterion; **touch system, typing**, typewriting by touch, i.e. without looking at keys; **touch'-wood**, wood or woody substance in such state as to catch fire readily, used as tinder; esp. soft white long-burning substance into which wood is converted by action of some fungi, punk.

tou·ché (tōoshā') *int.* (fencing) Exclamation acknowledging a touch by opponent's foil; (transf.) acknowledgement of telling thrust in argument. [Fr., = "touched"]

touch·ing (tŭch'ĭng) *prep.* Concerning, about. ~ *adj.* Affecting, pathetic. **touch'ing·ly** *adv.* **touch'ing·ness** *n.*

touch·y (tŭch'ē) *adj.* (**touch·i·er, touch·i·est**). Easily taking offense, oversensitive. **touch'i·ly** *adv.* **touch'i·ness** *n.*

tough (tŭf) *adj.* Of close tenacious substance or texture; hard to break or cut, not brittle; (of food) difficult to chew; (of clay etc.) stiff, tenacious; hardy, able to endure hardship; unyielding, stubborn; difficult; (colloq., of luck etc.) hard, severe, unpleasant; (slang) vicious, rowdy. **tough'ly** *adv.* **tough'ness** *n.* **tough'en** *v.* **tough** *n.* Street ruffian, tough person.

Tou·louse-Lau·trec (tōolōos'-lōtrĕk'; *Fr.* tōolōoz'lôtrĕk'), **Henri de** (1864–1901). French painter and lithographer.

tou·pee (tōopā') *n.* 1. (hist.) Topknot of hair esp. as crowning feature of wig; wig with this. 2. Patch, front, of false hair; man's wig. [OF. *toup* tuft]

tour (toor) *n.* 1. Journey through (part of) a country from place to place; rambling excursion, short journey, walk, esp. for sake of observing what is noteworthy; **grand** ~, (hist.) journey through France, Germany, Switzerland, and Italy, fashionable esp. in 18th c. as finishing course in education of young man of rank; **on** ~, touring. 2. (esp. mil.) Period of duty in service, time to be spent at station; shift. **tour** *v.* Make tour (of); (of actor, theatrical company, etc.) travel from town to town fulfilling engagements, travel about (country) thus, take (entertainment) about thus; so **touring company. touring car** (*n.*), open automobile designed for touring.

tour de force (toor de fôrs', fôrs') (pl. **tours de force** pr. toor de fôrs', fôrs'). Feat of strength or (esp.) skill or artistry. [Fr.]

tour·ism (toor'izem) *n.* Organized touring; accommodation and entertainment of tourists as industry.

tour·ist (toor'ĭst) *n.* Person who makes a tour; person who travels for pleasure; ~ **class**, class of accommodation below first and second class in ships and aircraft; ~ **court**, motel; ~ **home**, private home where travelers may rent rooms; ~ **trap**, place that exploits tourists by overcharging. **tourist** *adv.* In tourist-class accommodation. **tour'ist·y** *adj.* (derog.) Suitable for or visited by tourists.

tour·ma·line (toor'malĭn, -lēn) *n.* Brittle mineral, freq. occurring as crystals, a complex silicate of boron and aluminum with vitreous luster, usu. black or blackish and opaque (*schorl*), also blue (*indicolite*), red (*rubellite*), and other colors, used in optical instruments or as gem. [Sinhalese *tòramalli* (orig. found in Sri Lanka)]

Henri de Toulouse-Lautrec was a caricaturist and a sensitive social commentator. This picture of a man watching a woman adjust her garter (facing) is typical of his style.

tour·na·ment (toor′na*ment,* tēr′-) *n.* 1. (hist.) Medieval martial sport in which mounted combatants in armor fought with blunted weapons for prize of valor; later, meeting for knightly sports and exercises. 2. Any contest in which a number of competitors play a series of games or take part in athletic events.

tour·ne·dos (toor′nedō, toor-nedō′) *n.* (pl. **-dos**). Small slices of fillet of beef served grilled or sauteed.

tour·ney (toor′nē, tēr′-) *n.* (pl. **-neys**) & *v.i.* (hist.) (Take part in) tournament.

tour·ni·quet (tēr′ni*k*ĭt, toor′-) *n.* Bandage for arresting bleeding by compression, tightened by twisting a rigid bar put through it; surgical instrument usu. with pad and screw, for same purpose.

tou·sle (tow′zel) *v.t.* (**-sled, -sling**). Pull about, handle roughly, make (esp. hair) untidy.

Tous·saint L'Ou·ver·ture (*Fr.* tōōsăṅ′ lōōvĕrtür′), **François Dominique** (1743–1803). Black leader of uprising in Haiti in 1791; later became a general in French army, and governor of the island 1796–1802, but was arrested, and died a prisoner in France.

tout (towt) *v.* Solicit business, pester possible customers with calls (*for* orders); give out information on condition of racehorses in training, esp. for a fee; describe flatteringly. ~ *n.* One who touts.

to·va·rich, to·va·rish (tōvär′-ĭsh) *ns.* Comrade. [Russ. *tovarishch*]

tow[1] (tō) *n.* Coarse and broken fibers of flax or hemp, separated by hackling and ready for spinning; **tow′head(ed)**, (having) head of very light-colored straight hair. **tow′y** *adj.*

tow[2] (tō) *v.t.* Pull (boat, barge, etc.) along in water by rope or chain; pull (person, thing) along behind one; **tow′line, tow′rope**, line or rope by which something is towed; **tow′path**, path beside canal or navigable river for use in towing. **tow′age** *n.* **tow** *n.* Towing, being towed; **in ~**, being towed; **take in ~**, (fig.) take under one's guidance or patronage; **~ truck**, truck with special equipment for towing away vehicles that have broken down, are illegally parked, etc.

to·ward (tōrd, tŏrd, towŏrd′), **to·wards** (tōrdz, tŏrdz, towŏrdz′) *preps.* In the direction of; as regards, in relation to; near, approaching (in time); as contribution to.

tow·el (tow′el) *n.* Absorbent cloth, paper, etc., for drying or wiping oneself or thing after washing; ~ **rack**, frame or stand on which towels are hung. **towel** *v.t.* (**-eled, -el·ing** or **-elled, -el·ling**). Wipe or dry with towel. **tow·el·ing** *n.* (esp.) Material for towels.

tow·er (tow′er) *n.* Tall, usu. square or circular structure, freq. forming part of church, castle, or other large building; such structure (or whole fortress or stronghold of which it is part) used as stronghold or prison; (fig.) place of defense, protector (~ **of strength**, (of person) champion, comforter, etc.); **the T~** (**of London**), buildings in London, orig. fortress and palace and later a prison, now used as repository of ancient armor and weapons and other objects of public

a tracked armoured fighting vehicle suspension using transverse torsion bars

idler

track —   — driving sprocket

schematic drawing of the undercarriage of a heavy duty earthmoving dozer tractor

*The idea of a vehicle which moved on its own road was conceived in England in 1770; but it was only in 1906 that the Holt Tractor in the U.S.A. proved that this could be done. A British firm developed the first gasoline-driven caterpillar tractor a year later. Tank designers in the 1914–18 war adapted the **track**.*

track shoe

sprocket

top idler

front idler

final drive

rollers   equalizer bar to hold track roller frames in lateral alignment interest. **tower** *v.i.* Reach high (*above* surroundings); (of eagle etc.) soar, be poised, aloft. **tow′er·ing** *adj.* High, lofty; (fig., of rage, passion) violent. **tow′er·ing·ly** *adv.*

tow·hee (tow′hē, tō′hē) *n.* Any of various small, ground-feeding N. Amer. birds (family Fringillidae), esp. *Pipilo erythrophthalmus*, the male having black, white, and chestnut-brown plumage.

town (town) *n.* Inhabited place usu. larger than a village and smaller than a city; civic community as dist. from members of university (esp. in ~ **and gown**); **go to** ~, work enthusiastically, spend lavishly, etc. (*on*); **man about** ~, sophisticated man seen at many social functions, fashionable night spots, restaurants, theaters, etc.; **on the** ~, (slang) out for an evening of pleasure at restaurants, theaters, nightclubs, bars, etc.; **paint the** ~ **red**, (slang) celebrate boisterously, cause commotion by wild and riotous spree; ~ **clerk**, secretary to town officials, in charge of records, correspondence, etc.; ~ **hall**, building used for transaction of official business of town, often also used for public assembly; **town′-house**, town (as dist. from country) residence; (also) private house (often row house) in town; **town meeting**, meeting of voters of town for transaction of public business, with certain powers of local government; **town planning**, construction of plans for regulating the growth and extension of town(s) etc.; **towns′people, towns′folk**, people of a town; **town talk**, common talk or gossip of people of town.

town·ship (town′shĭp) *n.* Division of county with some corporate powers of local administration, district 6 miles square whether settled or not.

tox·e·mi·a, tox·ae·mi·a (tŏksē′mēa) *ns.* Diseased condition due to presence of toxic substances in blood, usu. of bacterial origin; condition of pregnancy characterized by edema and raised blood pressure. **tox·e′mic** *adj.*

tox·ic (tŏk′sĭk) *adj.* Of, affected or caused by, a poison or toxin; poisonous. **tox′i·cal·ly** *adv.* **tox·ic·i·ty** (tŏksĭs′ĭtē) *n.* [Gk. *toxikon* poison for arrows (*toxa* arrows)]

toxico-, toxic- *comb. forms.* Poison.

tox·i·col·o·gy (tŏksĭkŏl′ojē) *n.* Study of the nature and effects of poisons, their detection and treatment. **tox·i·co·log·i·cal** (tŏk-sĭkolŏj′ikal), **tox·i·co·log′ic** *adjs.* **tox·i·co·log′i·cal·ly** *adv.* **tox·i·col′o·gist** *n.*

tox·in (tŏk′sĭn) *n.* Poisonous substance of animal or vegetable origin; esp. (path.) one of the poisons produced in a human or animal body by microorganisms of disease, provoking the formation of antitoxins.

toy (toi) *n.* Plaything, esp. for child; knicknack, small or trifling thing, thing meant rather for amusement than for serious use; (attrib., of dogs etc.) of diminutive breed or variety. ~ *v.t.* Trifle, amuse oneself (*with*); deal *with* in trifling, fondling, or careless manner.

trace[1] (trās) *v.* (**traced, tracing**). 1. Delineate, mark out, sketch, write esp. laboriously. 2. Copy (drawing etc.) by following and marking its lines, using a transparent sheet placed over it or similar device. 3. Follow the track or path of (person, animal, footsteps, etc.); follow course or line of, decipher; follow course or history of; observe or find vestiges or signs of. **trace′a·ble** *adj.* **trace** *n.* 1. Track left by person or animal walking or running, footprints or other visible signs of course pursued (usu. pl.); path of indicating spot in cathode ray tube, shown as trace on a fluorescent screen. 2. Visible or other sign of what has existed or happened; minute quantity, esp. (chem.) too little to be measured; ~ **element**, substance that is essential, though only in minute amounts, to plant or animal life.

trace[2] (trās) *n.* Each of pair of ropes, chains, or straps connecting collar of draft animal with whiffle-tree etc. of vehicle; **kick over the** ~ **s**, (fig.) become insubordinate, act recklessly.

trac·er (trā′ser) *n.* (esp.) 1. (also ~ **bullet**) Bullet etc. emitting smoke or flame which makes its course visible. 2. (also ~ **element**) Isotope that can be detected in minute quantities because of its radiations, so that the path of a molecule or radical containing it can be traced through a physical, chemical, or biological system to study the system.

trac·er·y (trā′serē) *n.* (pl. **-er·ies**). Decorative stone openwork, esp. in head of Gothic window, in which patterns are formed by placing strips of stone inside a window opening (**bar** ~) or by perforating expanses of flat stone (**plate** ~); interlaced work of vault etc.; anything resembling or suggesting this.

tra·che·a (trā′kēa) *n.* (pl. **tra·che·ae** pr. trā′kēē). 1. Musculo-membranous tube from larynx to bronchial tubes, conveying air to lungs in air-breathing vertebrates. 2. Each of tubes forming respiratory organ in insects etc. 3. (bot.) Duct, vessel. **tra′che·al, tra′che·ate** *adjs.*

tra·che·id (trā′kēĭd) *n.* Water-conducting element in the wood of vascular plants.

tra·che·os·to·my (trākēŏs′tomē) *n.* (pl. **-mies**). Surgical incision to create artificial opening into trachea.

Tracery applied to the windows of The George and Pilgrims, an inn in Glastonbury, Somerset, U.K. This use of stonework decoration was popular in Gothic forms of architecture.

tra·che·ot·o·my (trākēŏt'omē) *n.* (pl. **-mies**). Incision of trachea.

tra·cho·ma (trakō'ma) *n.* Contagious form of conjunctivitis with inflammatory granulation of inner surface of eyelids, scarring of cornea, freq. causing blindness. **tra·cho·ma·tous** (trakŏm'atus, -kō'ma-) *adj.*

trac·ing (trā'sĭng) *n.* (esp.) Copy made by tracing; record of self-registering instrument; ~ **paper**, tough semitransparent paper for copying drawings etc.

track (trăk) *n.* 1. Mark, series of marks, left by passage of anything, as wheel rut, wake of ship, footprints; **in one's ~s**, on the spot, instantly; **on the ~ of**, in pursuit of, having a clue to; **cover (up) ~s**, conceal or screen actions etc. (of); **keep, lose, ~ of**, follow, fail to follow or grasp course, sequence, etc., of; **make ~s (for)**, make off, make for; **off, on, the ~**, (fig.) wandering from, sticking to, the subject; **on the wrong (right) side of the ~s**, in socially inferior (superior) part of town. 2. Path, esp. one beaten by use, rough unmade road; line of travel or motion, course; train, sequence; prepared course for racing etc.; parallel lines of rails with crossties etc.; (mech.) caterpillar track; projection on Earth's surface of route or path of airplane etc.; groove on phonograph record; strip of magnetic tape containing one sequence of signals; ~ **and field**, athletic events performed in competition on running track and adjacent field esp. running, jumping, pole vaulting, shot-putting (~**-and-field** *adj.*); ~ **man**, athlete who participates in track or field events; ~ **meet**, series of athletic contests in track-and-field events; ~ **record**, (esp. fig.) (record of) past achievements; ~ **shoe**, spiked shoe worn by runner. 3. Transverse distance between wheels of vehicle. **track'a·ble**, **track'less** *adjs.* **track'less·ness** *n.* **track** *v.* Follow track of (animal, person, *to* lair etc.; spacecraft etc.); pursue, follow up; (of wheels) run in same track, be in alignment; ~ **down**, find or catch by tracking; **tracking station**, station set up for the purpose of tracking path of and recording data from artificial satellite, spacecraft, etc. by means of radio or radar.

tract[1] (trăkt) *n.* Stretch, extent, region (*of*); region or area of natural structure, esp. bodily organ or system.

tract[2] (trăkt) *n.* Short treatise or discourse, esp. on religious subject.

trac·ta·ble (trăk'tabel) *adj.* (usu. of persons or animals) Easily handled, manageable, pliant, docile. **trac·ta·bil·i·ty** (trăktabĭl'-

Many tractors today offer comforts that pioneer farmers could not have dreamed of — air conditioning, stereo music — and no effort required.

ĭtē), **trac·ta·ble·ness** *ns.* **trac·ta·bly** *adv.*

Trac·tar·i·an (trăktār'ēan) *adj. & n.* (Adherent, promoter) of Tractarianism. **Trac·tar'i·an·ism** *n.* English high church movement of 19th c. (later called the Oxford Movement) intended to restore high church ideals of 17th c. and based on a series of *Tracts for the Times* (1833–41) by Newman and other theologians and clergy in and near Oxford.

trac·tate (trăk'tāt) *n.* Treatise.

trac·tion (trăk'shon) *n.* Drawing, pulling (esp. as dist. from pushing or pressure); drawing of vehicles or loads along road or track, esp. in ref. to form of power used for this; grip of tire on road, wheel or rail, etc.; (med.) sustained pulling on limb etc., esp. by weights and pulleys, to correct dislocation, relieve pressure, etc.; ~ **engine**, steam or diesel engine used for drawing loads on ordinary road, across fields, etc. **trac'tion·al, trac'tive** *adjs.*

trac·tor (trăk'ter) *n.* Motor vehicle for drawing heavy loads etc., esp. one for farm work; such a vehicle for drawing a trailer, ~ **-trailer**.

trade (trād) *n.* 1. Skilled manual or mechanical employment (opp. to PROFESSION), carried on as means of livelihood · or profit; skilled handicraft. 2. Exchange of commodities for money or other commodities. 3. People engaged in a trade. 4. (usu. pl.) Trade wind(s) (see below). 5. ~ **book**, book sold in bookstores and other retail outlets patronized by general public, as dist. from textbook, limited edition, or subscription book; ~ **discount**, deduction from list price allowed by a manufacturer or wholesaler to a retailer or granted reciprocally by firms in the same business; ~ **-in**, used car, appliance, etc., for which credit is allowed on purchase price of new

one; amount so allowed; business deal involving a trade-in; **trade'-mark**, device, word(s), etc., used by manufacturer etc. to distinguish his goods, established by use and legally registered; **trade name**, name of proprietary article; name by which a thing is called by the trade; name under which a person or firm conducts trade; **trade-off**, (also **trade'off**), exchange of one thing for another; esp. surrendering one good thing so as to get another that is thought to be even better; **trade route**, any route generally used by merchant ships, caravans, etc.; **trade secret**, formula, method, or process used by businessman and giving him an advantage over competitors who do not know or use it; **trades'man** (pl. **-men**), person engaged in trade; craftsman, man skilled in one of a number of crafts or trades; **trades'woman** (fem.) (pl. **-women**), woman engaged in trade; **trade union** = LABOR union; **trade unionism, unionist; trade wind**, one of the winds blowing constantly toward the equatorial region of calms from about the 30th parallel north and south, being deflected westward by Earth's rotation so that they blow from the northeast in the N. hemisphere and from the southeast in the S. hemisphere. **trade** *v.* (**trad·ed, trad·ing**). Buy and sell, engage in trade; have commercial transaction (*with*); carry merchandise (*to* place); exchange in commerce, barter (goods); ~ **in**, hand over (e.g. used car) in (part) payment or exchange (*for* thing); **trade on**, take (esp. unscrupulous) advantage of (person's credulity or good nature, one's knowledge of secret etc.); **trade up**, exchange object or property of less value or merit for one of greater value or merit.

trad·ing (trā'dĭng) *n.* (esp.) ~ **post**, station in sparsely populated area for exchanging local products for goods etc.; ~ **stamp**, stamp given by merchant to customer, exchangeable for various articles.

tra·di·tion (tradĭsh'on) *n.* Transmission of statements, beliefs, customs, etc., esp. by word of mouth or by practice without writing; what is thus handed down from generation to generation; long-established and generally accepted custom, practice, etc., an immemorial usage; (theol.) doctrine etc. held to have divine authority but not orig. committed to writing, esp., among Christians, body of teachings transmitted orally from generation to generation from earliest times and by Roman Catholics held to derive from Christ and the apostles or to have divine authority. **tra·di'tion·al** *adj.*

tra·di·tion·al·ly *adv.* **tra·di'-tion·al·ism, tra·di'tion·al·ist** *ns.* **tra·di·tion·al·is'tic** *adj.*

tra·duce (tradoōs', -dūs') *v.t.* (**-duced, -duc·ing**). Calumniate, misrepresent. **tra·duce'ment, tra·duc'er** *ns.*

traf·fic (trăf'ĭk) *n.* 1. Trade (in commodity); now esp. dealing or bargaining in something that should not be the subject of trade, e.g. certain drugs. 2. Transportation of goods, coming and going of persons, goods, or esp. vehicles or vessels, along road, railroad, canal, etc.; amount of this; ∼ **circle**, one-way road around circular island receiving traffic from several streets, designed to expedite traffic flow; ∼ **cop**, (colloq.) policeman regulating road traffic; ∼ **court**, local court that deals with alleged violations of traffic laws; ∼ **jam**, halt or slowdown of highway traffic as result of accident, overcrowding, detour, etc.; ∼ **light, signal**, electrical or mechanical signal for controlling road traffic, esp. at junctions or crossings, by means of colored lights etc; ∼ **manager**, person in charge of transportation of a firm's products; person in transportation company who establishes rates, schedules, etc., for passengers or freight; person in business office in charge of flow of routine business; ∼ **pattern**: see FLIGHT. **traffic** *v.* (**-ficked, -fick·ing**). Trade (*in*), carry on commerce; barter.

trag·a·canth (trăg'akănth) *n.* Gum exuded from various species of *Astragalus*, usu. obtained in dried whitish flakes, and used as vehicle for drugs, in the arts, etc. [Gk. *tragakantha* goat's thorn (*tragos* he-goat, *akantha* thorn)]

tra·ge·di·an (trajē'dēan) *n.* Writer of tragedies; actor in tragedies. **tra·ge·di·enne** (trajē-dēĕn') *n.* Actress in tragedies.

trag·e·dy (trăj'edē) *n.* (pl. **-dies**). Literary composition, esp. play, of serious and usu. elevated character, with fatal or disastrous conclusion; branch of dramatic art dealing with sorrowful or terrible events in serious and dignified style; sad event, calamity, disaster. [Gk. *tragōidia* app. goat song (*tragos* goat, *ōidē* song)]

trag·ic (trăj'ĭk) *adj.* 1. Of, in the style of, tragedy; ∼ **irony**, used in ancient Greek tragedy of words having an inner esp. prophetic meaning for audience unsuspected by speaker. 2. Sad, calamitous, distressing. **trag'i·cal·ly** *adv.*

trag·i·com·e·dy (trăjĭkŏm'edē) *n.* (pl. **-dies**). Drama of mixed tragic and comic elements. **trag'i·com'ic, trag·i·com'i·cal** *adjs.* **trag·i·com'i·cal·ly** *adv.*

trag·o·pan (trăg'opăn) *n.* Asiatic

The **tragopan** from the high mountain forests of Asia, is also known as the horned pheasant because of the two fleshy blue 'horns' on the head of the male. There are five species.

pheasant of genus *T* ∼, with erectile fleshy horns on head of male, horned pheasant. [L. f. Gk. reputed bird in Ethiopia (*tragos* goat + PAN³)]

trail (trāl) *n.* Part drawn behind or in the wake of a thing, long (real or apparent) appendage; hinder end of stock of gun carriage, resting on ground when piece is unlimbered; track left by thing that has moved or been drawn over surface; track, scent; beaten path, esp. through wild region; **at the** ∼, (mil.) (of rifle etc.) being trailed. **trail** *v.* Drawn along behind one, esp. on ground, drag (one's limbs, oneself) along, walk wearily, lag, straggle; hang loosely; (of plant) grow decumbently and stragglingly to some length, esp. so as to touch or rest on the ground; (mil.) carry (rifle etc.) in horizontal or oblique position with arm extended downward; track, follow the track or wake of, shadow.

trail·er (trā'ler) *n.* (esp.) 1. Trailing plant. 2. Vehicle designed to be drawn along behind another, esp. **house** ∼, an automobile-drawn vehicle designed to serve, when parked, as a dwelling, office, etc.; ∼ **camp** (also ∼ **court** or **park**), site for parking house trailers, usu. having piped water, electrical connections, etc. 3. Excerpt(s) of motion picture exhibited in advance as an advertisement.

trail·ing (trā'lĭng) *adj.* That trails; (esp.) ∼ **edge**, rear edge of aircraft wing, tail, or fin.

train (trān) *v.* Bring (person, child, animal) to desired state or standard of efficiency, obedience, etc., by instruction and practice; subject, be subjected to, course of instruction and discipline (*for* profession, art, etc.); teach and accustom (*to* do, *to* action); bring, bring oneself, to physical efficiency by exercise and diet, esp. in preparation for sport or contest; cause (plant) to grow in required shape; point, aim, (firearm, camera, *on* object etc.). ∼ *n.* 1. Trailing thing, esp. elongated part of skirt or robe trailing behind on ground, or sometimes carried on ceremonial occasions by page or attendant; long or conspicuous tail of bird. 2. Body of followers, retinue, suite; succession or series of persons or things; line of gunpowder or other combustible material to convey fire to explosive charge etc.; set of parts in mechanism actuating one another in series, esp. set of wheels and pinions actuating striking part or turning hands of clock or watch. 3. Number of railroad cars, coupled together (usu. including locomotive drawing them); **train'man**, member of railroad train crew or worker in railroad yard; **train sickness**, sickness or nausea caused by rail travel. **train'less** *adj.*

train·ee (trānē') *n.* One who is being trained (for an occupation).

train·er (trā'ner) *n.* (esp.) One who trains persons or animals for athletic performance, as race, boxing match, etc.

train·ing (trā'nĭng) *n.* (esp.) **in** ∼, undergoing physical training, physically fit as a result of this; **out of** ∼, in poor condition from lack or cessation of training; ∼ **pants**, extra-thick cotton shorts, often plastic-coated, for young child out of diapers but not yet ready for regular underclothing; ~ **ship**, ship on which boys are trained for naval service or merchant navy.

train (trān) **oil**. Whale blubber oil [MDu. *traen*, app. = "tear," "drop"]

traipse (trāps) *v.* (**traipsed, traips·ing**). (colloq.) Walk in trailing or untidy way, walk about aimlessly or needlessly, trudge wearily; walk over (thus). ~ *n.*

trait (trāt) *n.* Feature (of face or esp. of mind or character), distinguishing quality.

trai·tor (trā´ter), *fem.* **trai·tress** (trā´trĭs) *ns.* One who is false to his allegiance or acts disloyally (*to* his sovereign or country, his principles, religion, etc.). **trai´-tor·ous** *adj.* **trai´tor·ous·ly** *adv.* **trai´tor·ous·ness** *n.*

tra·jec·to·ry (trajĕk´terē) *n.* (pl. **-ries**). Path of any body moving under action of given forces, esp. that of projectile in its flight through air; (geom.) curve or surface cutting all curves or surfaces of a given system at constant angle.

tram[1] (trăm) *n.* (also ~ **silk**) Silk thread of two or three loosely twisted strands used for woof of some velvets and silks. [L. *trama* woof]

tram[2] (trăm) *n.* 1. Small iron truck running on rails; under-carriage of this. 2. (Brit. also **tram´car**) Passenger car running on rails on public road; **tram´line**, track with rails flush with road surface on which tramcars are run. 3. **tram´way**, cable along which tram runs, esp. system (**aerial tramway**) in which cables are suspended from towers. **tram** *v.* (**trammed, tram´ming**). Convey in tram, perform (journey) in tram; travel by tram. [app. same word as LG. *traam* beam, barrow shaft]

tram·mel (trăm´el) *n.* 1. Fishing net consisting of fine net hung loosely between vertical walls of coarser net, so that fish passing through carry some of the finer net through the coarser and are caught in the pocket thus formed. 2. Shackle, esp. one used in teaching horse to amble; (fig., usu. pl.) impediment to free movement or action. 3. Instrument for drawing ellipses, esp. cross with grooves in which move pins carrying beam and pencil; kind of gauge for adjusting and aligning machine parts; kind of hook for holding kettle etc. at adjustable heights in fireplace. ~ *v.t.* (**-meled, -mel·ing** or **-melled, -mel·ling**). Confine, hamper, with trammels.

tra·mon·tane (tramŏn´tān, trăm´ontān) *adj.* (Situated, living) on other side of mountains, esp. the Alps; (fig., from Italian point

At Kyoto in Japan, athletes in **training** must run up these steep steps to develop strength and stamina. Elsewhere, different techniques are used but all are designed to give the same result.

of view) foreign, barbarous; (of wind) blowing from beyond mountains, esp. the Alps. ~ *n.* Tramontane person, wind.

tramp (trămp) *v.* Walk with firm heavy tread; walk, go, traverse, on foot; be a tramp. ~ *n.* 1. Measured, steady tread of body of persons or animals, sound of heavy footfalls. 2. Tramping, long or tiring walk or march; journey on foot, walking excursion. 3. Person who tramps roads in search of employment or as vagrant. 4. Immoral woman, esp. prostitute. 5. (also ~ **steamer**) Cargo vessel not trading regularly between fixed ports, but taking cargoes wherever obtainable and for any port. **tramp´er** *n.* **tramp´ish** *adj.* **tramp´ish·ly** *adv.* **tramp´ish·-ness** *n.*

tram·ple (trăm´pel) *v.* (**-pled, -pling**). Tread heavily and (esp.) injuriously (upon), crush or destroy thus (freq. fig.); put (fire) *out* by trampling. ~ *n.* Trampling. **tram´pler** *n.*

tram·po·line (trămpolēn´, trăm´polēn) *n.* Canvas sheet attached to horizontal frame by springs, providing resilient platform for acrobatics etc. **tram·-po·lin´er, tram·po·lin´ist** *ns.*

trance (trăns, trahns) *n.* Sleep-like state, with more or less inertness to stimulus and subsequent amnesia; hypnotic or cataleptic condition, similar state of spiritualistic medium; mental abstraction from external things, absorption, ecstasy.

tran·quil (trăng´kwĭl) *adj.* Serene, free from agitation or disturbance. **tran´quil·ly** *adv.* **tran·quil·li·ty, tran·quil·i·ty** (trăngkwĭl´ĭtē) *ns.* **tran´quil·ize** *vbs.t.* (**-ized, -iz·ing; -lized, -liz·ing**). **tran´quil·-iz·er** *n.* (esp.) Sedative drug.

trans- *prefix.* Across, beyond, over, to or on farther side of.

trans·act (trănsăkt´, -zăkt´) *v.t.* Perform, carry on, do (action, business, etc.). **trans·ac´tion** *n.* Transacting, being transacted; what is transacted, piece of business; (pl.) proceedings, dealings; (usu. pl.) learned society's, esp. published, records of its proceedings.

trans·al·pine (trănsăl´pĭn, -pīn, trănz-) *adj.* Situated, living, beyond the Alps (usu. from Italian point of view); passing across or through the Alps; **T~ Gaul**, Roman province including the present France, Switzerland, Belgium, and the Netherlands. **transalpine** *n.* Person born or living beyond the Alps.

trans·at·lan·tic (trănsatlăn´tĭk, trănz-) *adj.* Across the Atlantic; esp., from European point of view,

American; (of boat, aircraft, etc.) crossing the Atlantic.

Trans·cau·ca·sia (trănzkawkā'-zha, -sha). Region of U.S.S.R. lying beyond (i.e. S. of) the Caucasus, including the republics of Armenia, Azerbaijan, and Georgia. **Trans·cau·ca'sian** adj. & n.

trans·ceiv·er (trănsē'ver) n. 1. Combined radio transmitter and receiver. 2. Telephonic device for transmitting and receiving facsimiles of printed material, pictures, etc.

tran·scend (trănsĕnd') v.t. Go beyond, exceed, limits of; rise above, surpass, excel.

tran·scend·ent (trănsĕn'dent) adj. That transcends ordinary limits, preeminent, supreme, extraordinary; (Kantian philos.) transcending, altogether outside, unrealizable in, experience. **tran·scend'ent·ly** adv. **tran·scend'en·cy** n. **transcendent** n. Transcendent thing.

tran·scen·den·tal (trănsĕndĕn'-tal) adj. 1. (Kantian philos.) Not derived from experience, a priori; (of any philosophy) based on recognition of a priori element in experience; (pop., vaguely) abstract, metaphysical, obscure, visionary; **~ meditation**, technique of meditation for purpose of inducing detachment from problems and relief from anxiety etc. 2. (math.) Not capable of being produced by a finite number of

*One **transept** and nave (the second longest in England) of St. Albans Cathedral (formerly the Abbey Church) in Hertfordshire. The original was built with Roman-made bricks and tiles.*

ordinary algebraical operations of multiplication, addition, subtraction, or division.

tran·scen·den·tal·ism (trănsĕndĕn'talĭzem) n. Transcendental philosophy, esp. idealism of Hegel and others (which does not recognize Kantian distinction between *transcendent* and *transcendental*), and religio-philosophical doctrine of Emerson and his followers, emphasizing the spiritual and intuitive rather than the empirical; extravagant, vague, or visionary quality, philosophy, language, etc. **tran·scen·den'tal·ist** adj. & n.

trans·con·ti·nen·tal (trănskŏn-tinĕn'tal) adj. Extending or passing across a continent.

tran·scribe (trănskrīb') v.t. (**-scribed, -scrib·ing**). Copy out (esp. in writing), make copy of; write out (shorthand) in ordinary characters; (mus.) adapt (composition) for voice or instrument other than that for which it was orig. written. **tran·script** (trăn'skrĭpt) n. Written copy; (law) copy of legal record. **tran·scrip·tion** (trănskrĭp'shon) n. **tran·scrip'tive** adj. **tran·scrib'er** n.

trans·duc·er (trănsdoo'ser, -dū'-, trănz-) n. Device that accepts power from one part of a system and emits power in a different form to another part, as between electrical, mechanical, or acoustic parts.

tran·sept (trăn'sĕpt) n. (Either arm of) transverse part of cruciform church. **tran·sep·tal** (trănsĕp'tal) adj. **tran·sep'tal·ly** adv.

trans·fer (trănsfĕr', trăns'fer) v. (**-ferred, -fer·ring**). Convey, transmit, transport, hand over, from one person, place, etc., to another; (law) convey (title, property, etc.) by legal process; convey (design etc.) from one surface to another; change from one station, line, route, etc., to another to continue journey; transfer to another group, job, school, etc. ~ (trăns'fer) n. 1. Transferring, being transferred, esp. (law) conveyance of property, as shares, etc., from one person to another; means or place of transfer, esp. conveyance of passenger and luggage from one station or line to another, place where trains etc. are transferred to ferry for water transport etc.; ticket allowing journey to be continued on another line or route. 2. Transferred thing; design etc. (to be) conveyed from one surface to another, (freq. colored) design or picture on prepared paper from which it can be transferred to another surface, as with water or hot iron. 3. **~ agent**, bank or person empowered to transfer corporation stock between legal owners; **~ company**, company conveying passengers and luggage between stations or from station. **trans·fer·a·bil·i·ty** (trănsfĕrabĭl'-ĭtē, trănsfer-), **trans·fer'al, trans·fer'ral, trans·fer'rer** ns. **trans·fer'a·ble** adj.

trans·fer·ence (trănsfĕr'ens, trăns'ferens) n. (esp., psychol.) Transferring of emotions to new object.

trans·fig·u·ra·tion (trăns-fĭgyerā'shon) n. Transfiguring, being transfigured; esp. change in appearance of Jesus on the mountain (Matt. 17; Mark 9), church festival (Aug. 6) commemorating this, picture representing it.

trans·fig·ure (trănsfĭg'yer) v.t. (**-ured, -ur·ing**). Alter form or appearance of, transform; esp. glorify, change so as to elevate or idealize.

trans·fix (trănsfĭks') v.t. (**-fixed** or **-fixt, -fix·ing**). Pierce with, impale on, sharp-pointed instrument; pierce through, render motionless (with fear, grief, horror, etc.). **trans·fix·ion** (trănsfĭk'-shon) n.

trans·form (trănsfôrm') v.t. Change shape or form of, esp.

considerably; change in character, condition, function, nature, etc.; (phys.) change (one form of energy) into another; (elect.) change (current) in potential (as from high voltage to low) or type (as from alternating to direct).

trans·for·ma·tion (trăns-fĕrmā'shŏn) *n.* Transforming, being transformed; metamorphosis, as of insects; (math.) change of form without alteration of value, as substitution of one geometric figure for another of equal magnitude, or of one algebraic expression for another of same value; change of form of substance, as from solid to liquid, or of potential or type of electric current etc.; wig; (linguistics) production of an equivalent phrase or sentence from one that is grammatically different in structure.

trans·for·ma·tion·al (trăns-fĕrmā'shŏnal) **grammar.** Statement of linguistic transformations to account for construction of a language, as relations between sentence or phrase elements or between word forms.

trans·form·er (trănsfōr'mer) *n.* (esp., elect.) Apparatus for changing potential or type of electric current, usu. consisting of a few turns of comparatively thick wire and a coil of fine wire wound on a laminated iron core.

trans·fuse (trănsfūz') *v.t.* (**-fused, -fus·ing**). Cause (fluid, fig. quality etc.) to flow or pass from one vessel etc. to another; transfer (blood of one person or animal) into veins of another. **trans·fus·er** *n.* **trans·fus'i·ble** *adj.* **trans·fu·sion** (trănsfū'zhŏn) *n.*

trans·gress (trănsgrĕs', trănz-) *v.t.* Violate, infringe (law, command, esp. of God). **trans·gres·sion** (trănsgrĕsh'ŏn, trănz-), **trans·gres'sor** *ns.*

tran·ship = TRANSSHIP.

tran·sient (trăn'shent, -zhent, -zēent) *adj.* Not durable or permanent, brief, momentary, fleeting. ~ *n.* 1. Temporary visitor, worker, etc. 2. Brief oscillation of electrical current in a circuit because of voltage surge etc. **tran'sient·ly** *adv.* **tran'sience, tran'sien·cy** *ns.*

tran·sis·tor (trănzĭs'ter) *n.* Electronic device using the flow of electrons in a solid to perform most of the functions of a vacuum tube; radio set using such device; also attrib., as ~ **radio. tran·sis'tor·ize** *v.t.* (**-ized, -iz·ing**). Design, equip, with transistors instead of vacuum tubes.

trans·it (trăn'sĭt, -zĭt) *n.* 1. Passing, passage, journey, conveyance, from one place to another. 2. (astrol.) Passage of planet across

Invented by three engineers at the Bell Telephone Laboratories and first demonstrated in 1948, the transistor has enabled miniaturization of many electrical circuits.

some region or point of zodiac; (astron.) passage of inferior planet across sun's disk, or of satellite or its shadow across planet's disk; passage of celestial body across meridian. 3. Surveying instrument for measurement of horizontal and occasionally vertical angles. 4. ~ **circle**, astronomical instrument, consisting of transit instrument combined with meridian circle for determining right ascension and declination of star by observation of its transit; ~ **instrument**, astronomical telescope mounted at right angles to horizontal east-and-west axis, for determining time of transit of celestial body over meridian; also same as 3 above. **transit** *v.* 1. (of heavenly body) Make transit (across). 2. Revolve (telescope of a transit) to opposite direction.

tran·si·tion (trănzĭsh'ŏn) *n.* Passage from one condition, action, style, subject, stage of development, etc., to another; period of this; (mus.) modulation, esp. passing or brief, or into remote key. **tran·si·tion·al** *adj.* **tran·si·tion·al·ly** *adv.* **tran·si'tion·ar·y** *adj.*

tran·si·tive (trăn'sĭtĭv, -zĭ-) *adj.* & *n.* (Verb) expressing action that passes over to an object, requiring direct object to complete the sense. **tran'si·tive·ly** *adv.* **tran·si·tiv·i·ty** (trănsĭtĭv'ĭtē, -zĭ-), **tran'si·tive·ness** *ns.*

tran·si·to·ry (trăn'sĭtōrē, -tōrē, -zĭ-) *adj.* Not lasting; fleeting, momentary, brief. **tran'si·to·ri·ly** *adv.* **tran'si·to·ri·ness** *n.*

Trans-Jor·dan (trănsjōr'dan, trănz-). Major part of the Hashemite Kingdom of Jordan, E. of Jordan River.

Trans·kei (trahnz'kā), **The.** Independent enclave in SE. South Africa in E. Cape of Good Hope Province; granted independence by South Africa, 1976; capital, Umtala.

trans·late (trănslāt', trănz-, trăns'lāt, trănz'-) *v.* (**-lat·ed, -lat·ing**). 1. Turn (word, sentence, book, etc.) from one language *into* another, express sense of it in another form of words. 2. Infer or declare the significance of, interpret (signs, movement, conduct, etc.). 3. Convey, introduce (idea, principle, design) *from* one art etc. *into* another. 4. Remove (bishop) to another see. 5. (bibl.) Convey to heaven without death. 6. (teleg.) Retransmit (message). 7. (mech.) Cause (body) to move so that all its parts follow same direction, impart motion without rotation to. **trans·lat'a·ble** *adj.* **trans·la·tor, trans·la·tion** (trănslā'shŏn, trănz-) *ns.* **trans·la'tion·al** *adj.*

trans·lit·er·ate (trănslĭt'erāt, trănz-) *v.t.* (**-at·ed, -at·ing**). Replace (letters of one alphabet or language) with those of another. **trans·lit·er·a·tion** (trănslĭterā'shŏn, trănz-) *n.*

trans·lo·ca·tion (trănslōkā'shŏn, trănz-) *n.* Change of location, esp. (bot.) movement of dissolved substances inside plants.

trans·lu·cent (trănslōō'sent, trănz-) *adj.* Allowing passage of light but so diffusing it as to prevent bodies lying beyond from being clearly distinguished. **trans·lu'cence, trans·lu'cen·cy** *ns.* **trans·lu'cent·ly** *adv.*

trans·lu·nar·y (trăns'lōōnĕrē, trănz'-, trănslōō'nerē, trănz-) *adj.* Lying beyond the moon; (fig.) insubstantial, visionary.

trans·ma·rine (trănsmarēn', trănz-) *adj.* That is beyond the sea; crossing the sea.

trans·mi·grate (trănsmī'grāt, trănz-) *v.t.* (**-grat·ed, -grat·ing**). Migrate; (of soul) pass after death into another body, either human or animal. **trans·mi'grant** *n.* (esp.) Emigrant from one country passing through another in which he does not intend to settle. **trans·mi·gra·tion** (trănsmīgrā'shŏn, trănz-), **trans·mi'gra·tor** *ns.* **trans·mi'gra·to·ry** *adj.*

trans·mis·sion (trănsmĭsh'ŏn, trănz-) *n.* (esp.) 1. Gears by which power is transmitted from engine to axle in automobile etc. 2. Transmitting by radio or television; program etc. so transmitted.

trans·mit (trănsmĭt', trănz-) *v.t.* (**-mit·ted, -mit·ting**). Send, convey, cause to pass or go, to another person, place, or thing;

suffer to pass through, be medium for, serve to communicate (heat, light, sound, electricity, emotion, news). **trans·mis·si·ble** (trăns-mĭs'ĭbel, trănz-), **trans·mis'sive**, **trans·mit'ta·ble** *adjs.* **trans·-mit'tal, trans·mit'tance** *ns.*

trans·mit·ter (trănsmĭt'er, trănz-) *n.* (esp.) Part of telegraphic or telephonic apparatus by means of which message etc. is transmitted; (part of) radio set or station for transmitting radio waves.

trans·mog·ri·fy (trănsmŏg'rĭfī, trănz-) *v.t.* (**-fied, -fy·ing**). (joc.) Transform (esp. utterly, grotesquely, or strangely). **trans·-mog·ri·fi·ca·tion** (trăns-mŏgrĭfĭkā'shon, trănz-) *n.*

trans·mu·ta·tion (trănsmūtā'-shon, trănz-) *n.* Transmuting, being transmuted; (biol.) transformation of one species into another, evolution (esp. in Lamarckian theory).

trans·mute (trănsmūt', trănz-) *v.t.* (**-mut·ed, -mut·ing**). Change form, nature, or substance of; convert (one element, substance, species, etc.) into another; esp. (alchemy) change (baser metal) into gold or silver. **trans·mut'a·ble** *adj.*

trans·o·ce·an·ic (trăns-ōshēăn'ĭk, trănz-) *adj.* Situated, existing, beyond the ocean; crossing the ocean.

tran·som (trăn'som) *n.* Cross-piece, esp. one spanning an opening; horizontal bar across window; crossbar separating door from fanlight above it; window above transom, esp. of door. **tran'somed** *adj.*

tran·son·ic (trănsŏn'ĭk) *adj.* Relating to speeds close to that of sound.

trans·pa·cif·ic (trănspasĭf'ĭk) *adj.* Situated, being, beyond the Pacific Ocean; crossing the Pacific.

trans·par·en·cy (trănspār'ensē, -păr'-) *n.* (pl. **-cies**). Being transparent; transparent object or medium; esp. photograph or picture on transparent substance, to be viewed by transmitted light.

trans·par·ent (trănspār'ent, -păr'-) *adj.* Transmitting light so that bodies lying beyond are completely visible; permeable to specified form of radiant energy, as heat rays, x-rays; easily seen through, manifest, obvious, clear; candid, frank, open. **trans·par'-ent·ly** *adv.*

tran·spire (trănspīr') *v.* (**-spired, -spir·ing**). Emit through excretory organs of skin or lungs, send off in moisture, odor; be emitted thus; (bot., of plant or leaf) exhale moisture; (of gas or liquid) move through capillary tube under pressure; (of secret etc.) come to be known; (misused for) occur,

happen. **tran·spi·ra'tion** *n.*

trans·plant (trănsplănt', -plahnt') *v.* Remove (plant) from one place and plant it in another; remove and establish, esp. cause to live, in another place; (surg.) transfer (living tissue or organ) from one part of body, or one person or animal, to another; bear transplanting. ~ (trăns'plănt, -plahnt) *n.* **trans·plan·ta·tion** (trănsplăntā'shon), **trans·plant'er** *ns.* **trans·plant'a·ble** *adj.*

tran·spon·der (trănspŏn'der) *n.* Radio or radar transceiver for receiving radio signal and automatically transmitting a different signal in response.

trans·port (trănspōrt', -pōrt') *v.t.* 1. Carry, convey, from one place to another. 2. (hist.) Deport, convey (convict) to penal colony. 3. (usu. pass.) Carry away by strong emotion. ~ (trăns'pōrt, -pōrt) *n.* 1. Conveyance, carrying, of goods or passengers, from one place to another; means of conveyance, esp. vessel used in transporting troops or military stores, wagons or other vehicles carrying supplies of army etc. 2. Vehement (usu. pleasurable) emotion; (freq. pl.) fit of joy or rage. **trans·port'er** *n.* **trans·port'-a·ble** *adj.*

trans·por·ta·tion (trănspertā'-shon) *n.* Transporting; deportation transfer to penal settlement;

*Rice is first planted in seed beds. When the seedlings are about 8 inches tall they are **transplanted** to wet paddy fields. In Kiso, Japan, (below) this arduous work is done in July.*

means of transport or conveyance.

trans·pose (trănspōz') *v.t.* (**-posed, -pos·ing**). Alter order of (series of things) or position of (thing in series), interchange; esp. alter order of (letters) in word or (words) in sentence; (algebra) transfer (quantity) from one side of equation to the other; (mus.) put into different key, alter key of. **trans·po·si·tion** (trănspozĭsh'on) *n.*

trans·ship, tran·ship (trănsshĭp') *vbs.* (**-shipped, -ship·ping**). Transfer, change, from one ship, train, etc., to another. **trans·ship'-ment** *n.*

tran·sub·stan·ti·ate (trăn-substăn'shēăt) *v.t.* (**-at·ed, -at·ing**). Change from one substance into another.

tran·sub·stan·ti·a·tion (trăn-substănshēā'shon) *n.* (esp., theol.) Doctrine that in the Eucharist a change is wrought in the elements at consecration, whereby the whole substance of the bread and wine is transmuted into the body and blood of Christ, only the appearances of bread and wine remaining.

trans·u·ran·ic (trănsyoorăn'ĭk, trănz-) *adj.* (chem.) Belonging to a group of radioactive elements having atomic numbers and weights greater than those of uranium, not found in nature but produced artificially, e.g. in atomic pile.

trans·ver·sal (trănsver'sal, trănz-) *adj.* (of line) Cutting two or more lines. ~ *n.* Transversal line.

trans·verse (trănsvērs´, trănz-, trăns´vērs, trănz´-) *adj.* Situated, lying, across or athwart. **trans·- verse´ly** *adv.* **transverse´** *n.* Transverse muscle, piece, etc.

trans·ves·tism (trănsvĕs´tĭzem, trănz-) *n.* Practice of dressing in clothes of opposite sex. **trans·ves- tite** (trănsvĕs´tīt, trănz-) *n.* One who practices transvestism. ~ *adj.*

trap[1] (trăp) *n.* 1. Device, as pitfall, snare, mechanical contrivance, for catching animals; (fig.) something by which one is caught, led astray, etc. 2. Trap door; movable covering of opening, falling when stepped upon; door flush with surface in floor, ceiling, etc. 3. Device for suddenly releasing bird etc. to be shot at; compartment from which greyhound is released at start of race. 4. (chiefly Brit.) Light, esp. two-wheeled horse carriage on springs. 5. Device, usu. U-shaped section of pipe with standing water, for preventing upward escape of air or noxious gases from pipe; contrivance for preventing passage of steam, water, silt, etc. 6. (slang) Mouth. 7. **speed** ~: see SPEED; **trap door**, hinged or sliding door flush with surface of floor, roof, wall, etc.; **trap-door spider**, spider living in burrow closed by one or more hinged lids; **trap´rock** = TRAP[2]; **trap´shooting**, sport of shooting clay pigeons released from spring trap. **trap** *v.* (**trapped, trap·ping**). Catch (as) in trap, snare, ensnare; set traps for game etc.; furnish with trap(s).

trap[2] (trăp) *n.* (also **traprock**) Any of various dark colored fine-grained igneous rocks, freq. columnar in structure, esp. basalt.

trap[3] (trăp) *v.t.* (**trapped, trap·ping**). (chiefly in past part.) Adorn with trappings, caparison. [OF. *drap* cloth, covering]

trap (trăp) **cut** = step cut, see STEP.

tra·peze (trăpēz´) *n.* Horizontal crossbar suspended by ropes as apparatus for acrobatics etc. **tra- pez´ist** *n.* (also **trapeze artist**) Performer on trapeze.

tra·pe·zi·um (trapē´zēum) *n.* (pl. **-zi·ums, -zi·a** pr. **-zēa**). 1. Quadrilateral with two sides (thought of as base and opposite side) parallel. 2. Quadrilateral with no sides parallel. 3. (anat.) Bone of carpus articulating with metacarpal bone of thumb. [Gk. *trapezion*, dim. of *trapeza* table]

tra·pe·zi·us (trapē´zēus) *n.* (pl. **-us·es**). (anat.) Each of pair of large flat triangular muscles of back, extending over back of neck etc.

trap·e·zoid (trăp´ĭzoĭd) *n.* 1. Quadrilateral with two sides parallel and two not parallel. 2. (anat.) Second bone of distal row

of carpus. ~ *adj.* Of, in the form of, a trapezoid. **trap·e·zoi·dal** (trăpĭzoi´dal) *adj.*

trap·per (trăp´er) *n.* (esp.) One engaged in trapping wild animals for their furs.

trap·pings (trăp´ĭngz) *n.pl.* Ornamental housing for horse; ornaments, embellishments, ornamental accessories.

Trap·pist (trăp´ĭst) *adj. & n.* (Monk) of reformed Cistercian order established 1664 at monastery of La Trappe in Normandy, France, and observing extremely austere discipline and perpetual silence except with confessors and in choir.

traps (trăps) *n.pl.* (colloq.) Personal effects, portable belongings, baggage. [app. shortening of *trappings*]

trash (trăsh) *n.* Waste or worthless stuff, refuse, rubbish; stripped-off leaves and tops of sugar cane; worthless or disreputable people; ~ **can**, container for household refuse; **white** ~, (derog.) poor white population of southern U.S. **trash´y** *adj.* (**trash·i·er, trash·i·est**). **trash´- i·ly** *adv.* **trash´i·ness** *n.*

trau·ma (trow´ma, traw´-) *n.*

*The true **trap-door spider** weaves a movable lid over the top of its burrow and lives in a warm climate. In the photograph, the open lid is below the hole.*

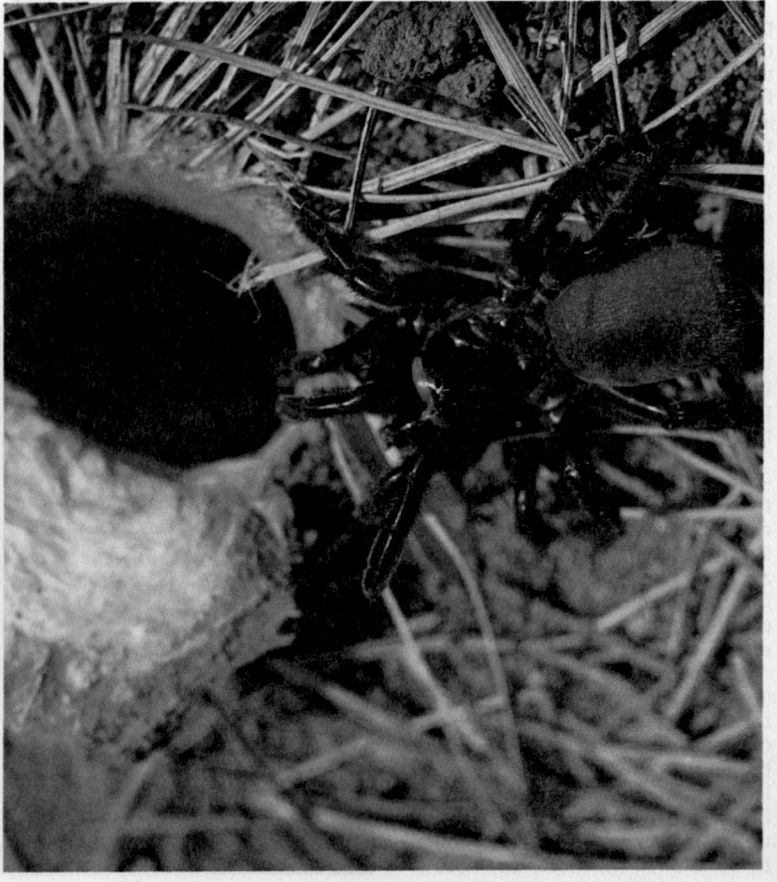

(pl. **-mas, -ma·ta** pr. **-ma**ta). Injury, wound; condition resulting from this; (psychol.) unpleasant or disturbing experience in which neurosis etc. may originate, emotional shock. **trau·mat·ic** (trowmăt´ĭk, traw-, tra-) *adj.* **trau·mat´i·cal·ly** *adv.* **trau´ma- tism** *n.* **trau´ma·tize** *v.t.* (**-tized, -tiz·ing**).

tra·vail (travāl´, trăv´āl) *n. & v.i.* (Suffer) pangs of childbirth; (make) painful or laborious effort. [OF. *travail*, app. f. LL. *trepalium* instrument of torture (L. *tres* three, *palus* stake)]

trav·el (trăv´el) *v.* (**-eled, -el·ing**; Brit. **-elled, -el·ling**). 1. Make journey, esp. of some length or to foreign countries; act as traveling sales representative; pass from one point or place to another, proceed; (of part of mechanism) move, be capable of moving, along fixed course; (colloq.) bear transportation, as in *this wine travels well.* 2. Journey through, pass over, traverse, cover (specified distance); cause (herds etc.) to journey. ~ *n.* 1. Traveling, esp. in foreign countries. 2. Single movement of part of mechanism; range, rate, mode of motion, of this. 3. ~ **agency, agent,** one making arrangements, supplying tickets, etc., for travelers; ~ **time,** time used to travel between home and place of employment or from one place to another as part of one's work.

trav·el·er, Brit. **trav·el·ler** (trăv′eler, trăv′ler) *ns*. One who travels; traveling sales representative; ~**'s check**, check or draft readily redeemable throughout world, sold in sets of various denominations by bank, express agency, etc., to traveler who signs it when receiving it and again when cashing it, check being valid only if signatures match; ~**'s joy**, European shrub (*Clematis alba* and other climbing species of *Clematis*) trailing over wayside hedges.

trav·el·ing, Brit. **trav·el·ling** (trăv′eling, trăv′ling) *ns*. ~ **bag**, small suitcase in which traveler carries most essential items; ~ **crane**, crane that travels along esp. overhead support; ~ **salesman**, business firm's representative who visits stores and other customers to show samples and take orders.

trav·e·logue, trav·e·log (trăv′elawg, -lŏg) *ns*. Illustrated narrative of travel, esp. employing motion pictures.

trav·erse (trăv′ers, travers′) *n*. 1. Movement or part of structure that crosses another; place at which one can cross; crossing; (mountaineering) more or less horizontal motion across face of precipice from one practicable line of ascent or descent to another, place where this is necessary;

(naut.) zigzag course taken owing to contrary winds or currents, each leg of this; (surv.) single line of survey across region, tract of country so surveyed; (mil.) horizontal or lateral movement of gun; (eng.) platform for shifting engine etc. from one line of rails to another; sideways movement of part or machine; (archit.) gallery from side to side of church etc.; (hist.) curtain, partition across room etc., compartment so cut off. 2. (law) Formal denial of matter of fact alleged by other side. ~ (travers′, trăv′ers) *v*. (**-ersed, -ers·ing**). 1. Travel or lie across; make a traverse in climbing; determine position of points, survey (road, river, etc.) by measuring lengths and azimuths of connected series of straight lines; turn (gun); (of needle of compass etc.) turn (as) on pivot; (of horse) walk crosswise; plane (wood) across grain; (of pulley) run over rope etc. that supports it. 2. (fig.) Consider, discuss, whole extent of (subject). 3. Deny, esp. (law) in pleading; thwart, frustrate (plan or opinion). **tra·vers′al** *n*.

trav·er·tine (trăv′ertĭn, -tēn) *n*.

The use of a **trapeze** *as a circus act was only introduced by Leotard in 1859. Other forms of acrobatics had been performed at various locations since ancient Greece and Rome.*

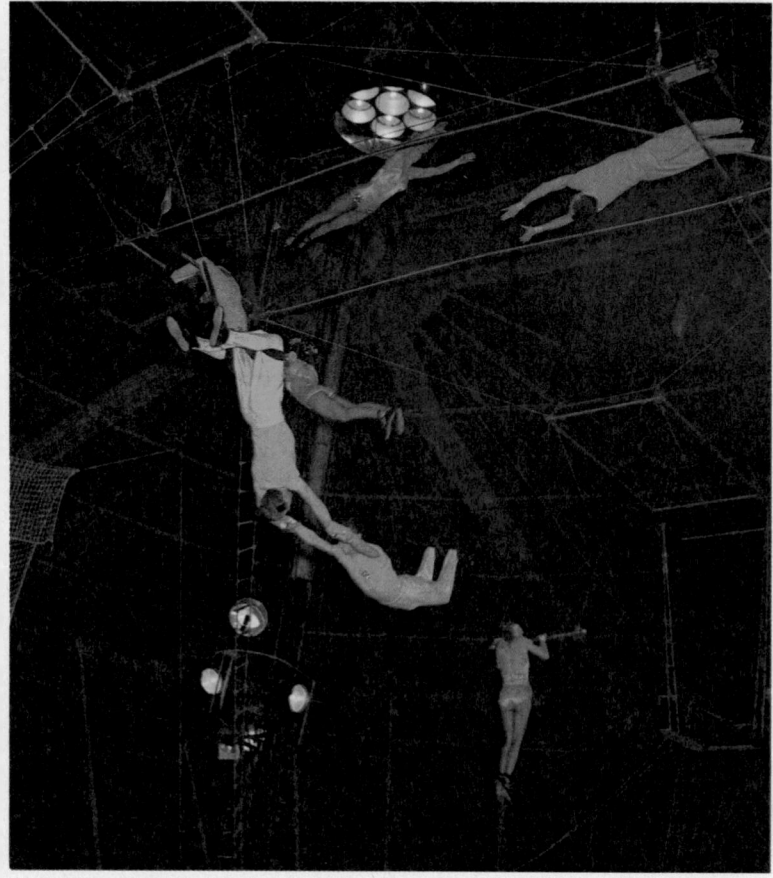

White or light colored crystalline concretionary limestone deposited from springs etc. and used for building. [L. *tiburtinus*, f. *Tibur*, now Tivoli, a town in central Italy]

trav·es·ty (trăv′istē) *v.t.* (**-tied, -ty·ing**). Make ridiculous by gross parody or imitation; be ridiculous imitation of. ~ *n*. (pl. **-ties**). Ridiculing treatment; ridiculous imitation.

trawl (trawl) *n*. Large net (~ **net**) with mouth held open by beam or otherwise, dragged along bottom of sea etc. by boat; ~ **line**, long buoyed line, anchored at ends, and with numerous short baited lines attached, for sea fishing. **trawl** *v*. Fish with trawl or in trawler; catch with trawl.

trawl·er (traw′ler) *n*. One who trawls; vessel used in fishing with trawl net.

tray (trā) *n*. Flat shallow vessel usu. with raised rim for placing or carrying small articles on, steeping specimens in laboratory, holding correspondence on desk, etc.; shallow lidless box forming compartment of trunk.

treach·er·ous (trĕch′erus) *adj*. Violating faith or betraying trust; perfidious; not to be relied on, deceptive. **treach′er·ous·ly** *adv*. **treach′er·ous·ness** *n*. **treach′er·y** *n*. (pl. **-er·ies**).

trea·cle (trē′kel) *n*. 1. (Brit.) Uncrystallized syrup produced in refining sugar; golden syrup. 2. Unrestrained or artificial sentimentality. **trea′cly** *adj*.

tread (trĕd) *v*. (**trod** pr. trŏd, **trod·den, tread·ing**). Set down one's foot, walk, (of foot) be set down; go through (dance) esp. in stately measure; press or crush with feet, trample (*on*); (of male bird) copulate with; ~ **the boards**, be an actor, appear on stage; ~ **down**, press down with feet; trample on, destroy, oppress, crush; ~ **on** someone's **toes** or **corns**, (fig.) offend against his feelings or privileges; ~ **water**, (swimming) keep body erect and head above water while moving feet as in walking upstairs; (fig.) make no progress even though working hard. **tread** *n*. 1. Manner, sound, of walking. 2. Top surface of step or stair; each step of treadmill; rung of ladder. 3. Piece of metal, rubber, or other substance placed on step to lessen wear or sound. 4. Part of wheel that touches ground or rails; part of rails that wheels touch. 5. Part of stilt on which foot rests. 6. Part of sole of shoe etc. that rests on ground. 7. Distance between pedals of bicycle. 8. (of male bird) Copulation. 9. **tread′mill**, appliance for translating motion by the stepping of man or horse etc. on steps fixed to revolving cylinder, esp. kind formerly used in prisons as punishment; (fig.) monotonous routine. **tread'er** *n.*

trea·dle (trĕd'el) *n.* Lever moved by foot and imparting motion to machine, e.g. lathe, sewing machine. ~ *v.* (**-dled, -dling**). Work treadle. **tread'ler** *n.*

treas., Treas. *abbrevs.* Treasurer; treasury.

trea·son (trē'zon) *n.* 1. (also **high** ~) Violation by subject of allegiance to sovereign or chief authority of nation (e.g. plotting or intending sovereign's death, levying war against him, or conspiring with his enemies). 2. Breach of faith, disloyalty (*to cause,* friend, etc.). **trea'son·ous** *adj.*

trea·son·a·ble (trē'zonabel) *adj.* Involving, guilty of, treason. **trea'son·a·ble·ness** *n.* **trea'son·a·bly** *adv.*

treas·ure (trĕzh'er) *n.* Wealth or riches stored, esp. in form of precious metals or gems; accumulated wealth; anything valued or preserved as precious; beloved person, esp. child; (colloq.) very efficient or satisfactory person, esp. servant; ~ **house**, place where treasure is kept, treasury; ~ **trove**, valuable discovery; gold or silver, money, etc., found hidden in ground or other place, owner of which is unknown. **treasure** *v.t.* (**-ured, -ur·ing**). Store as valuable; cherish, prize; (fig.) store (e.g. in memory).

treas·ur·er (trĕzh'erer) *n.* (orig.)

One charged with receipt and disbursement of revenues of king, noble, nation, church, etc.; now, one responsible for funds of public body or any corporation, society, or club; officer of Treasury Department (~ **of the U.S.**) who receives and keeps the federal funds. **treas'ur·er·ship** *n.*

treas·ur·y (trĕzh'erē) *n.* (pl. **-ur·ies**). 1. Room, building, in which precious or valuable objects are preserved (freq. fig.); (esp. in book titles) collection of treasured writings. 2. Funds or revenue of nation, corporation, etc.; **Department of the T** ~, financial agent for the U.S. government, collecting and managing public revenue and advising the president on fiscal policy; ~ **bill**, security given by U.S. government in exchange for a loan of short duration (freq. 91 days); ~ **bond**, any of various series of U.S. government bonds issued by the Treasury, usu. maturing after a long period; ~ **certificate**, bond of U.S. government, usu. maturing in one year and paying interest periodically by redemption of coupons; ~ **note**, demand note issued by the Department of the Treasury and legal tender for all debts except as otherwise provided.

Discovered in 1942-43, the Mildenhall treasure consisted of a host of Roman tableware, mostly made from silver and dated at the 4th century A.D. The great dish (below) is heavily ornamented.

treat (trēt) *v.* 1. Deal, negotiate (*with*), in order to settle terms. 2. Deal with (subject), deal with subject, in speech or writing; deal with in way of art, represent artistically; deal with to obtain particular result, esp. deal with disease etc. in order to relieve or cure. 3. Behave or act toward in specified way. 4. Entertain, esp. with food and drink, regale, feast. ~ *n.* Entertainment, esp. one given gratuitously, pleasure party; treating, invitation to eat or drink; a great pleasure, delight, or gratification. **treat'er** *n.*

trea·tise (trē'tĭs) *n.* Book or writing, longer than essay, treating in formal or methodical manner of particular subject.

treat·ment (trēt'ment) *n.* (Mode of) dealing with or behaving toward person or thing; esp. (method of) treating patient or disease; artistic or literary execution, esp. with regard to style.

trea·ty (trē'tē) *n.* (pl. **-ties**). (Document embodying) formal contract between nations relating to peace, truce, alliance, commerce, etc.

tre·ble (trĕb'el) *adj.* 1. Threefold, triple. 2. Soprano; high-pitched, shrill; of treble pitch; ~ **clef**: see CLEF. **treble** *n.* 1. Treble quantity, stitch, etc. 2. Treble voice, singer, string, etc. ~ *v.* (**-bled, -bling**). Multiply, be multiplied, by 3. **tre'bly** *adv.*

tre·cen·to (trāchĕn'tō) *n.* (also **T** ~) Fourteenth century as period of Italian art and literature. [It., = "three hundred," short for *mil trecento* 1300]

tree (trē) *n.* Perennial plant with self-supporting woody main stem (usu. developing woody branches at some distance from ground); erect bush or shrub with single stem; piece of wood shaped for some purpose (as *shoetree*); genealogical chart like branching tree (**family** ~); **up a** ~, cornered, in difficulty; ~ **creeper**, any of various birds that creep on trunks and branches of trees, esp. *Certhia familiaris*; ~ **fern**, fern usu. of the family Cyatheaceae, with upright woody stem, growing to size of tree, found in tropics, Australia, and New Zealand; ~ **frog**, arboreal amphibian esp. of genus *Hyla*; ~ **of knowledge of good and evil**, tree in Garden of Eden bearing the forbidden fruit, which was tasted by Adam and Eve (Gen. 3); ~ **surgery**, treatment of trees having disease, damaged or decayed branches, etc., by pruning, filling cavities, spraying, feeding, bracing weak parts, etc.; ~ **toad**, tree frog. **tree** *v.t.* (**treed, tree·ing**). Cause to take refuge in tree, drive up a tree; stretch on shoetree. **tree'less** *adj.*

Cedar

Ash

Sycamore

orange   silver birch   acacia   Norway spruce   American elm   weeping willow   desert oak

water moving
upwards to leaves

sap on its downward
journey

outer bark
inner bark or bast

cambium

sap-wood

heart-wood

roots

year of abundant rainfall and rapid growth

thin rings
showing years
of drought

periods of
slow growth

original
sapling

mark of old injury

*Top left to right: Western red cedar, ash
and sycamore are all trees now grown
in northern temperate regions. Left:
Every* **tree** *has the same sort of structure but may have special provisions to
guard against excessive loss of moisture in arid conditions or other special
climatic conditions. By cutting through a
trunk, the history of a tree can be determined with remarkable accuracy, as
shown above.*

tre·foil (trē´foil, trĕf´oil) *n.* 1. Plant of genus *Trifolium* with leaves of three leaflets, clover. 2. Ornamental figure resembling cloverleaf; (archit.) opening divided by cusps suggesting three-lobed leaf.

trek (trĕk) *v.i.* (**trekked, trek-king**). (orig. S. Afr.) Travel, migrate, esp. by ox wagon; make arduous journey or expedition. ~ *n.* (Stage of) journey made by trekking. **trek´ker** *n.*

trel·lis (trĕl´ĭs) *n.* Structure of light bars crossing each other with open square or diamond-shaped spaces between, used as screen, as support for climbing plants, etc.; **trel´liswork**, trellis. **trellis** *v.t.* Furnish, support, (as) with trellis. [L. *trilix* three-ply (f. *licium* warp thread)]

trem·a·tode (trĕm´atōd) *n.* Member of the Trematoda, a class of unsegmented parasitic flatworms having external suckers.

trem·ble (trĕm´bel) *v.i.* (**-bled, -bling**). Shake involuntarily as with fear or other emotion, cold, or weakness; quiver; (fig.) be affected with fear, agitation, suspense, etc. ~ *n.* Trembling, quiver, tremor. **trem´bly, trem´bling** *adjs.* **trem´bling·ly** *adv.*

tre·men·dous (trĭmĕn´dus) *adj.* Awe-inspiring, terrible; (colloq.) extraordinarily great, immense. **tre·men´dous·ly** *adv.* **tre·men´dous·ness** *n.*

trem·o·lo (trĕm´olō) *n.* (pl. **-los**) Tremulous or vibrating effect in certain instruments or human voice; organ stop producing this effect. [It., = "trembling"]

trem·or (trĕm´er, trē´mer) *n.* Tremulous or vibratory movement or sound, vibration, shaking, quaking; (instance, fit, of) involuntary agitation of body or limbs from physical weakness, fear, etc. **trem´or·ous, trem´or·less** *adjs.*

trem·u·lous (trĕm´yulus) *adj.* Trembling, quivering; shaky; timid; tremblingly sensitive or responsive. **trem´u·lous·ly** *adv.* **trem´u·lous·ness** *n.*

trench (trĕnch) *n.* Long narrow usu. deep hollow cut out of ground, esp. with earth thrown up as parapet to protect soldiers under fire or from bombing; ~ **coat**, thick, usu. lined, waterproof overcoat, orig. for wearing in trenches; ~ **foot**, disease of feet resembling chilblains, sometimes with gangrene, due to exposure to extreme cold and wet and prevalent among soldiers serving in trenches; ~ **fever**, low, intermittent, infectious fever carried by lice and common among men serving in trenches; ~ **mortar**, small mortar for throwing bombs etc. into enemy trenches at short range; ~ **mouth**, disease characterized by ulceration of mucous membranes of mouth and pharynx with pain and foul smell; also called Vincent's angina (disease); ~ **warfare**, hostilities carried on from more or less permanent trenches. **trench** *v.* 1. Make trench(es) or ditch(es) in ground; make series of trenches in digging or plowing (ground) so as to bring lower soil to surface; dig

Above: A common European **tree-creeper**. *This bird and related species have remarkably strong feet which enable them to run up and down tree trunks in search of insects.*

A simple latticework **trellis** *is perfect for growing climbing plants. Many species, such as this variegated ivy, are popular for trellis-growing in the U.S.A.*

Common birdsfoot **trefoil** *is only one of some 300 species of plants in the genus Trifolium which is best known for a wide range of clovers. These are widely harvested for fodder.*

*The **trestle** bridge is a very old design, but it is still an extremely effective means of support. Dated examples add immensely to the charm of their surroundings.*

trench(es); cut (groove), cut groove in (wood etc.). 2. Encroach *on*; verge or border closely *on*.

trench·ant (trĕn′chant) *adj.* (archaic and poet.) Keen, sharp; (zool., of tooth etc.) having cutting edge; (fig.) keen, penetrating; vigorous, energetic. **trench′ant·ly** *adv.* **trench′an·cy** *n.*

trench·er (trĕn′cher) *n.* Flat square or usu. circular piece of wood on which meat etc. was formerly cut; any flat round piece of wood; **trench′erman** (pl. **-men**), heavy feeder, eater.

trend (trĕnd) *n.* General direction, course, style, tendency. **trend′y** *adj.* (**trend·i·er, trend·i·est**). (colloq.) Following latest trends of fashion etc. **trend** *v.i.* Have specified direction, course, or general tendency. **trend′i·ness** *n.*

Trent (trĕnt). (It. *Trento*) City of N. Italy; scene of Council of Trent, ecumenical council of R.C. Ch., meeting from time to time, 1545–63, which defined the doctrines of the church in opposition to those of the Reformation, reformed discipline, and strengthened the authority of

the papacy.

tre·pan (trĭpăn′) *n.* 1. Surgeon's cylindrical saw (obs.; superseded by TREPHINE) for cutting holes. 2. (mining etc.) Heavy boring instrument for sinking shafts. ~ *v.t.* (**-panned, -pan·ning**). Operate on with trepan. **trep·a·na·tion** (trĕpană′shon), **tre·pan′ner** *ns.*

tre·phine (trĭfīn′, -fēn′) *n.* Surgeon's cylindrical saw with guiding center pin, for removing part of bone of skull. ~ *v.t.* (**-phined, -phin·ing**). Operate on with trephine. **treph·i·na·tion** (trĕfīnā′shon) *n.*

trep·i·da·tion (trĕpĭdā′shon) *n.* Agitation or alarm, flurry, perturbation.

tres·pass (trĕs′pas) *n.* Transgression, breach of law or duty; (law) actionable wrong committed against person or property of another, esp. wrongful entry upon another's lands with damage (however inconsiderable) to real property. ~ *v.i.* 1. Transgress, sin. 2. (law) Commit trespass, esp. enter unlawfully on land of another or his property or right; (fig.) make unwarrantable claim or undesired

intrusion *on*, encroach *on*, infringe. **tres′pass·er** *n.*

tress (trĕs) *n.* Lock, braid of (esp. woman's long) hair; (pl.) woman's hair.

tres·tle (trĕs′el) *n.* Supporting structure for table etc. consisting of horizontal beam with diverging legs, usu. two at each end, or of two frames hinged together or fixed at an angle; open braced framework of wood or metal for supporting bridge etc.; (naut., pl.) trestletrees; ~ **bridge**, bridge supported on trestles; ~ **table**, table of board(s) laid across trestles or other supports; **tres′tletree**, either of a pair of fore-and-aft horizontal timbers on mast, supporting crosstrees, topmast, etc.

trey (trā) *n.* Three at dice or cards.

tri- *comb. form.* Three, thrice.

tri·ad (trī′ăd) *n.* Group or set of three; (mus.) chord of three notes, esp. note with its third and fifth (e.g. common chord without octave); (chem.) group of three chemical elements having similar properties, as iron, nickel, and cobalt. **tri·ad·ic** (trīăd′ĭk) *adj.* **tri′ad·ism** *n.*

tri·a·del·phous (trīadĕl′fus) *adj.* (bot.) (Having stamens) united by filaments into three bundles.

tri·age (trēahzh′, trē′ahzh) *n.* Assignment of degrees of urgency to decide priority in treatment of wounded etc.

tri·al (trī′al) *n.* 1. Examination and determination of causes at law by judicial tribunal. 2. Testing or putting to proof of qualities of thing; test, probation; experimental treatment, investigation by means of experience; examination of person, esp. for Presbyterian ministry. 3. Being tried by suffering or temptation; painful test of endurance, patience, etc.; affliction, hardship. 4. Attempt, endeavor. 5. Something serving as sample, proof, etc., piece of pottery used to test temperature or progress of firing inside kiln. 6. ~ **and error**, process of attacking a task by trying different methods and eliminating those that fail; ~ **balance**, (in double entry bookkeeping) addition of all entries on each side of ledger to establish that debits balance credits; ~ **balloon**, (fig.) experiment to see how new policy etc. will be received; ~ **marriage**, relationship of man and woman living together without legal marriage, esp. when such marriage is a possibility for the

*Historic photograph of the **trial** of Nazi war criminals at Nuremberg in 1945. Methods and procedures of justice differ between countries but the principal aim remains similar.*

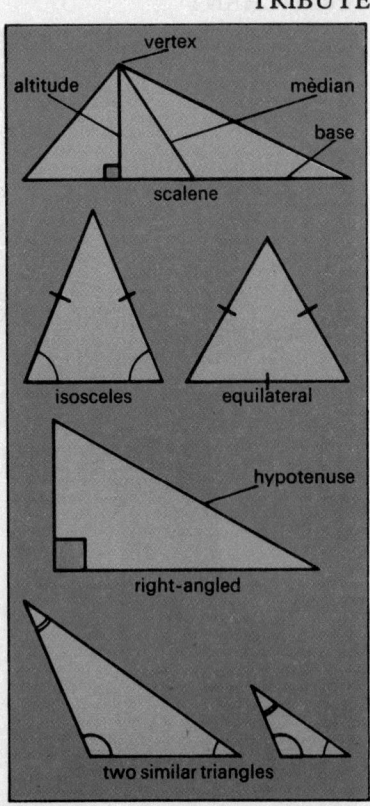

*The relationship between the sides and angles of a **triangle** is the basis of trigonometry. It is invaluable in surveying and other forms of measurement where only some figures are available.*

future; **~ run**, trip to test speed and other qualities of new vessel etc.

tri·an·gle (trī´ănggel) *n.* Geometric figure, esp. plane rectilineal figure, with three angles and three sides; any system of three points not in a straight line, with the three real or imaginary lines joining them; any three-cornered body, object, or space, esp. musical percussion instrument consisting of steel rod bent into a triangle open at one corner and struck with a small steel rod; **eternal ~**: see ETERNAL.

tri·an·gu·lar (trīăng´gyuler) *adj.* Of the shape of a triangle, three-cornered; three-sided; among three persons or parties. **tri·an´gu·lar·ly** *adv.* **tri·an·gu·lar·i·ty** (trīănggyulăr´ĭtē) *n.*

tri·an·gu·late (trīăng´gyulĭt, -lāt) *adj.* Consisting of, marked with, triangles. **tri·an´gu·late·ly** *adv.* **triangulate** (trīăng´gyulāt) *v.t.* (**-lat·ed, -lat·ing**). Divide or convert into triangles; (surveying etc.) measure, map out, by measurement of sides and angles of series of triangles on determined base line(s). **tri·an·gu·la·tion** (trīănggyulā´shon) *n.*

Tri·as (trī´as) = TRIASSIC.

Tri·as·sic (trīăs´ĭk) *adj. & n.* (geol.) (Of) the earliest period or system (also **Trias**) of the Mesozoic. [Gk. *trias* group of three, f. threefold subdivision of Triassic strata]

tri·a·tom·ic (trīatŏm´ĭk) *adj.* Having three atoms in the molecule; having three replaceable atoms or groups.

trib·al (trī´bal) *adj.* Of tribe(s). **trib´al·ly** *adv.*

trib·al·ism (trī´balĭzem) *n.* Tribal system or organization.

tri·ba·sic (trībā´sĭk) *adj.* (chem.) Having three replaceable hydrogen atoms; containing three atoms of a univalent metal or three basic hydroxyl groups.

tribe (trīb) *n.* 1. Group of clans under recognized chiefs. 2. (Rom. hist.) Each of the political divisions of the Romans (orig. three, prob. representing clans, ultimately 35); (Gk. hist.) = PHYLE. 3. Any similar division, whether of natural or political origin; any of the 12 divisions of the people of Israel, each traditionally descended from one of the patriarchs; **Lost T~s**, the ten Israelite tribes (i.e. all but Judah and Benjamin) that revolted from the House of David and were deported by Shalmaneser, after which time their history is lost. 4. (biol.) Group ranking usu. below family and above genus (with name usu. ending in *-ini* for animals and *-eae* for plants). 5. Class, lot, set (usu. contempt.). **tribes´man** *n.* (pl. **-men**). Member of a tribe.

trib·u·la·tion (trĭbyulā´shon) *n.* Great affliction, oppression, or misery. [L. *tribulare* press, oppress, f. *tribulum* threshing sledge]

tri·bu·nal (trībū´nal, trĭbū´-) *n.* 1. Judgment seat; court of justice, judicial assembly; (fig.) place of judgment, judicial authority. 2. Board or committee appointed to adjudicate claims of a particular kind, act as arbiters, etc.

trib·une[1] (trĭb´ūn) *n.* 1. (Rom. hist.) Administrative officer, esp. one of two (later five, then ten) orig. protecting interests and rights of plebeians from patricians; one of six officers of legion, each in command for two months of year. 2. Protector of rights of people, popular leader. **trib·u·nate** (trĭb´yunĭt, -nāt), **trib´une·ship** *ns.*

trib·une[2] (trĭb´ūn) *n.* Raised floor for magistrate's chair in apse of Christian basilica; bishop's throne, apse containing this, in basilica; platform, stage, pulpit; raised and seated area or gallery.

trib·u·tar·y (trĭb´yutĕrē) *adj.* 1. Paying or subject to tribute; furnishing subsidiary supplies or aid, auxiliary, contributory; (of stream) flowing into a larger stream or a lake. **~** *n.* (pl. **-tar·ies**). Tributary person or state; tributary stream.

trib·ute (trĭb´ūt) *n.* Money or equivalent paid by one sovereign or country to another in acknowledgment of submission or for protection or peace; obligation of paying this; (fig.) contribution, offering or gift as mark of respect, affection, etc.

trice[1] (trīs) *n.* **in a ~,** in an instant.

trice[2] (trīs) *v.t.* (**triced, tric-ing**). (naut.) Hoist *up* and secure with rope or lashing, lash *up*.

tri·cen·ten·ni·al (trīsĕntĕn′ēal) *adj. & n.* Tercentenary.

tri·ceps (trī′sĕps) *adj. & n.* (pl. **-ceps·es, -ceps**). (Muscle, esp. great extensor muscle of back of upper arm) with three heads or attachments.

Tri·cer·a·tops (trīsĕr′atŏps) *n.* Gigantic dinosaur of Genus *T~* found in parts of U.S. in the late Cretaceous era, with two large horns above eyes and one on nose.

tri·chi·na (trīkī′na) *n.* (pl. **-nae** pr. -nē). Minute nematode worm (*Trichinella spiralis*) parasitic in muscles and intestines of man, pig, etc. **trich·i·no·sis** (trīkinō′sĭs) *n.* Disease caused by introduction of trichinae from infected pork into alimentary canal. **trich·i·nous** (trīk′inus) *adj.* Of trichinae or trichinosis.

tri·chot·o·my (trīkŏt′omē) *n.* (pl. **-mies**). Division into, classification or arrangement in, three (classes etc.); division of human nature into body, soul, and spirit. **tri·chot′o·mous** *adj.*

tri·chro·ic (trīkrō′ĭk) *adj.* Having or showing three colors; esp. of crystal, presenting three different colors when viewed in three different directions. **tri·chro·ism** (trī′krōĭzem) *n.*

tri·chro·mat·ic (trīkrōmăt′ĭk) *adj.* Trichroic; esp. of or having three fundamental color sensations (red, green, violet) of normal vision; of (printing in) three colors. **tri·chro·ma·tism** (trīkrō′matĭzem) *n.*

trick (trĭk) *n.* 1. Crafty or fraudulent device or stratagem, esp. of mean or base kind; capricious, foolish, or stupid act; clever device or contrivance, stratagem, feat of skill or dexterity; knack (freq. in ~(s) **of the trade**); **do the ~,** achieve the desired result. 2. Peculiar or characteristic practice; habit, mannerism. 3. (cards) Cards played and won in one round; such round, point(s) gained by winning it. 4. (naut.)

Time, usu. two hours, of duty at helm. 5. ~ **knee,** chronic sudden weakening and collapse of knee as result of injury to tendons and ligaments; ~ **or treat,** Hallowe'en children's game of calling at houses with threat of pranks if candy or other treats are not given them. **trick** *v.* 1. Deceive by trick, cheat; cheat *out of,* beguile *into,* by trickery; practice trickery. 2. Dress, deck, decorate (usu. *out, up*). **trick′er·y** *n.* (pl. **-er·ies**).

trick·le (trĭk′el) *v.* (**-led, -ling**). (Cause to) flow in drops or in scanty halting stream; (of baseball) run slowly over surface of ground, cause (baseball) to do this. ~ *n.* Trickling, small fitful stream. **trick′ling·ly** *adv.*

trick·ster (trĭk′ster) *n.* One who tricks; cheat; fraud; deceiver.

trick·y (trĭk′ē) *adj.* (**trick·i·er, trick·i·est**). Crafty, given to tricks, deceitful; skilled in clever tricks or dodges, adroit, resourceful; (colloq.) requiring cautious or adroit action or handling, ticklish. **trick′i·ly** *adv.* **trick′i·ness** *n.*

tri·clin·ic (trīklĭn′ĭk) *adj.* (cryst.) Having the three axes unequal and obliquely inclined.

tri·col·or (trī′kŭler) *n. & adj.* (Flag, esp. that adopted as national flag of France at Revolution) having three colors.

tri·corn, tri·corne (trī′kôrn) *adjs. & ns.* Three-cornered (cocked hat).

tri·cos·tate (trīkŏs′tāt) *adj.* (zool.) Having three ribs, raised lines, or riblike parts.

tri·cot (trē′kō) *n.* Fabric knitted by hand or machine.

tri·cus·pid (trīkŭs′pĭd) *adj.* Having three cusps or points; ~ **valve,** (anat.) valve, consisting of three triangular segments, that guards the opening from the right atrium into the right ventricle of the heart.

tri·cy·cle (trī′sĭkel) *n.* Three-wheeled velocipede or motorcycle. ~ *v.i.* Ride tricycle.

tri·dent (trī′dent) *n.* Three-pronged instrument or weapon, esp. three-pronged fish spear or scepter as attribute of Neptune or of Britannia.

tri·en·ni·al (trīĕn′ēal) *adj.* Existing, lasting, for three years; occurring, done, every three years. **tri·en′ni·al·ly** *adv.* **tri·en′ni·al, tri·en′ni·um** *ns.* Triennial occasion, event, publication, etc.; esp. visitation of diocese by bishop every three years.

tri·fle (trī′fel) *n.* 1. Thing, fact, circumstance, of slight value or importance; small amount, esp. of

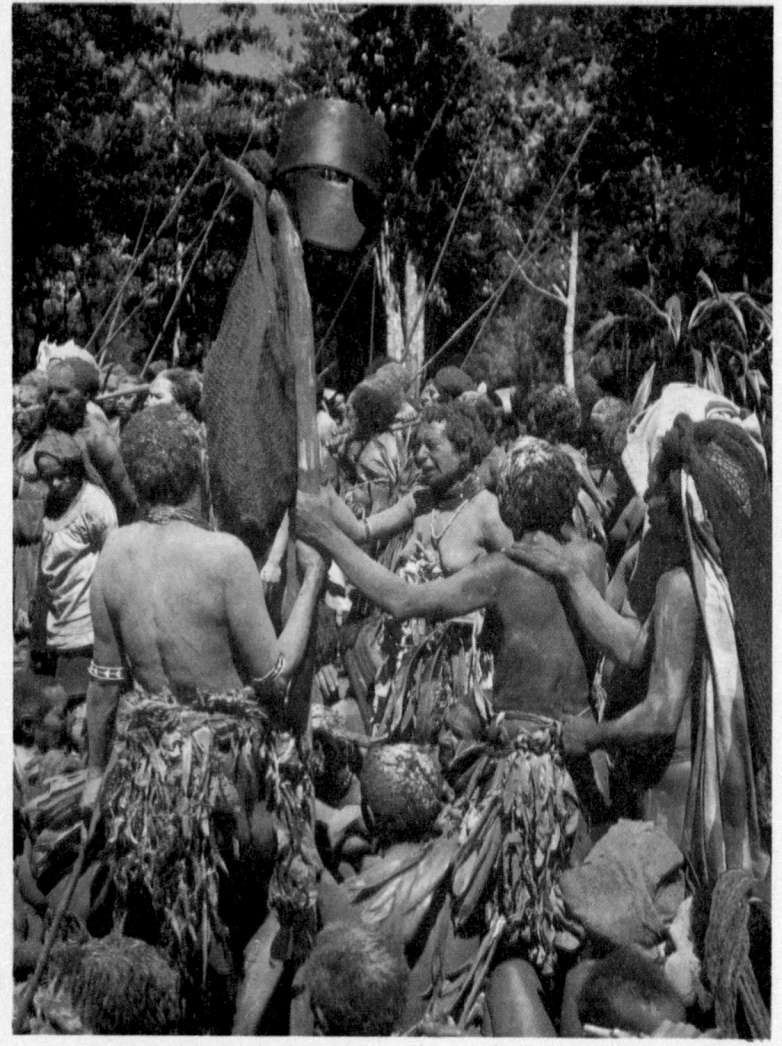

Tribal customs vary from one area to another. While different types of tribalism exist throughout the world it is, perhaps, more easily recognised in some developing countries. Left: a mourning ceremony in Papua New Guinea.

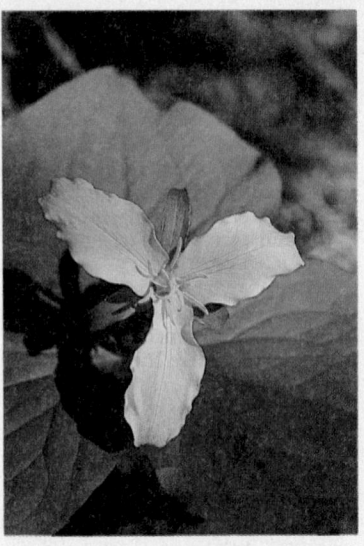

money; small article. 2. (Brit.) Sweet dish of sponge cakes flavored with wine, jam, etc., topped with custard or whipped cream. ~ *v.i.* Toy, play, dally, fidget, *with*; act or speak idly or frivolously. **tri′-fler** *n.* **tri′fling** *adj.* Unimportant, paltry, insignificant; foolish, frivolous, idle. **tri′fling·ly** *adv.*

tri·fo·li·o·late (trīfō′lēolĭt), **tri·-fo·li·ate** (trīfō′lēāt) *adjs.* Three-leaved; consisting of three leaflets; having such leaves.

tri·form (trī′fôrm) *adj.* Having a triple form, existing or appearing in three forms.

trig. *abbrev.* Trigonometry.

tri·gem·i·nal (trījĕm′inal) *adj.* Of the fifth and (in man) largest pair of cranial nerves, dividing into three main branches (ophthalmic, maxillary, and mandibular nerves).

trig·ger (trĭg′er) *n.* Movable catch or lever that is pulled or pressed to release a spring or otherwise set mechanism in motion, esp. small steel catch for releasing hammer of lock in firearm; **quick on the** ~, (fig.) quick to respond; ~ **finger**, forefinger of right hand; **trig′gerfish** (pl. **-fishes**, collect. **-fish**), fish of *Balistes* and related genera, so called because pressure on second spine of anterior dorsal fin depresses first; **trigger-happy**, apt to shoot on slight provocation; **trig′german** (*n.*), (colloq.) gangster specializing in murdering with gun. **trigger** *v.* Initiate, set *off* a reaction etc.

tri·glyc·er·ide (trīglĭs′erīd, -ĭd) *n.* (chem.) Ester derived from glycerol and one to three fatty acids.

tri·glyph (trī′glĭf) *n.* (archit.) Ornament of frieze in Doric order, consisting of block or tablet with two vertical grooves and a half-groove on each side, alternating with metopes.

tri·gon (trī′gŏn) *n.* 1. (archaic) Triangle. 2. (astrol.) Set of three signs of zodiac 120° distant from

each other; each of four such groups (airy, earthy, fiery, watery) into which the 12 signs are divided; triplicity, trine. 3. (zool.) Cutting region of crown of upper molar.

trig·o·nal (trĭg′onal) *adj.* Triangular; having triangular cross section; of a trigon; (geom., cryst., of solid) having triangular faces, having three equal and equally inclined axes. **trig′o·nal·ly** *adv.*

trig·o·nom·e·try (trĭgonŏm′-etrē) *n.* Branch of mathematics dealing with measurement of sides and angles of triangles and with certain functions of their angles or of angles in general. **trig·o·no·met·ric** (trĭgonomĕt′rĭk) *adj.* ~ **function**, any of the basic functions of an angle (as sine, cosine, secant, etc.) expressed as the ratio of two of the sides of a right-angled triangle containing the angle. **trig·o·no·met′ri·cal** *adj.* **trig·o·no·met′ri·cal·ly** *adv.*

tri·graph (trī′grăf, -grahf) *n.* Combination of three letters representing one sound.

tri·he·dron (trīhē′dron, -hĕd′ron) *n.* (pl. **-drons, -dra** pr. -dra). Figure formed by three surfaces meeting in point. **tri·he′dral** *adj. & n.*

tri·ju·gate (trī′jŏogāt, trījŏo′gĭt, -gāt) *adj.* (bot.) With three pairs of pinnate leaves.

tri·lat·er·al (trīlăt′eral) *adj. & n.* (Figure) having three sides; triangle, triangular.

tri·lin·e·ar (trīlĭn′ēer) *adj.* (math.) Of, contained by, having some relation to, three lines.

tri·lin·gual (trīlĭng′gwal) *adj.* Speaking, using, expressed in, three languages.

tri·lith (trī′lĭth), **tri·lith·on** (trīlĭth′ŏn, trī′lithŏn) *ns.* Pre-

historic structure of two upright stones with another resting on them as a lintel.

trill (trĭl) *n.* 1. (mus.) Rapid alternation of two notes a tone or semitone apart, shake. 2. (phon.) Pronunciation of consonant, consonant pronounced, with vibration of tongue or other part of speech organs. 3. Tremulous high-pitched sound or note(s), esp. in singing of birds. ~ *v.* Utter, sing, produce, with trill(s); make trill(s).

tril·lion (trĭl′yon) *n.* Fourth power of a thousand, unit followed by 12 zeros. **tril′lionth** *adj. & n.*

tril·li·um (trĭl′ēum) *n.* Any of several perennial plants of genus *Trillium*, having a single whorl of three leaves borne on an erect stem and one flower of three petals and various colors.

tri·lo·bate (trīlō′bāt, trī′lobāt) *adj.* Having, consisting of, three lobes.

tri·lo·bite (trī′lobīt) *n.* Fossil arthropod with three-lobed body found in Lower Paleozoic rocks.

tril·o·gy (trĭl′ojē) *n.* (pl. **-gies**). (Gk. antiq.) Series of three tragedies performed at Athens at festival of Dionysus; any series or group of three related dramatic or other literary works.

trim (trĭm) *adj.* (**trim·mer, trim·mest**). In good order; well arranged or equipped; neat, spruce. **trim′ly** *adv.* **trim′ness** *n.* **trim** *v.* (**trimmed, trim·ming**). 1. Set in good order, make neat or tidy; remove irregular, superfluous, or unsightly parts from; remove (such parts) by clipping, planing, etc. 2. Ornament (with ribbon, lace, etc.); dress (windows). 3. Adjust

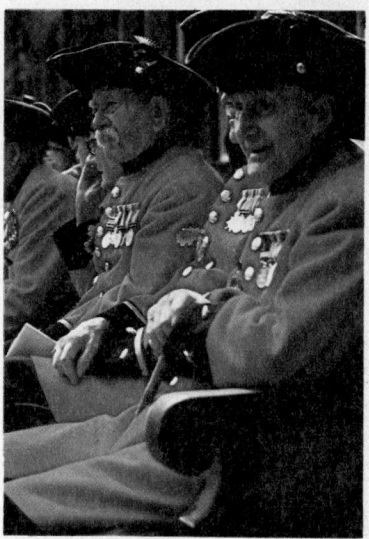

*Chelsea Pensioners U.K. wear a **tricorn** hat with their full-dress uniform. The style evolved in the 17th century from broad-brimmed hats which had their brim pinned to the crown.*

trim·ming (trĭm′ĭng) *n.* (esp.) Ornamental addition to dress, hat, etc.; (pl.) accessories, usual accompaniments, esp. sauces, stuffing, condiments, etc. accompanying main course of a meal; (pl.) pieces cut off in trimming something.

tri·mor·phic (trīmŏr′fĭk), **tri·mor·phous** (trīmŏr′fus) *adjs.* (of species etc.) Having three distinct forms; (bot.) having three distinct forms of organs on individuals of same species; (cryst., of substance) crystallizing in three fundamentally distinct forms. **tri·morph** (trī′-mŏrf), **tri·mor′phism** *ns.*

trine (trīn) *adj. & n.* Threefold, triple (group); (thing) made up of three parts; (astrol.) (aspect) of two heavenly bodies distant from each other by a third part of the zodiac (120°); ~ **immersion**, thrice sprinkling in baptism. **tri′nal, tri′na·ry** *adjs.*

Trin·i·dad (trĭn′ĭdăd) **and To·ba·go** (tōbā′gō). W. Indian islands off coast of Venezuela; member state of the Brit. Commonwealth, independent since 1962; capital, Port of Spain.

Trin·i·tar·i·an (trĭnĭtār′ēan) *adj. & n.* 1. (Member) of religious order of Holy Trinity, founded 1198 to redeem Christian captives from Muslims. 2. (Holder) of doctrine of Trinity. **Trin·i·tar′i·an·ism** *n.*

trin·i·tro·tol·u·ene (trĭnĭtrōtŏl′ūēn), **tri·ni·tro·tol·u·ol** (trīnĭtrōtŏl′ūōl, -awl, -ŏl) *ns.* Derivative of toluene with three nitro (NO_2) groups, high explosive used as shell fillings and as ingredient of various explosives (abbrev. TNT).

balance of (vessel, aircraft) by distribution of cargo, passengers, etc.; arrange (sails etc.) to suit wind; (fig.) hold middle course in politics or opinion, adjust oneself to prevailing opinion, etc. for the sake of expediency; (colloq.) defeat, cheat. ~ *n.* 1. (naut.) State of being trimmed and rigged ready for sailing, battle (**fighting** ~), etc.; state of ship, cargo, etc., in reference to fitness for sailing, esp. proper balance in water on fore-and-aft line; difference between draft forward and draft aft; (aeron.) balance of aircraft in ref. to fore-and-aft in horizontal plane. 2. State, degree, of adjustment, readiness, or fitness; good order. 3. Trimming, being trimmed; interior furnishings of automobile; visible woodwork around openings of house etc.; window dressing. 4. Trimming or cutting off; anything cut off or out, trimmings.

tri·ma·ran (trī′marăn) *n.* Boat

*Although extinct, some 10,000 species of **trilobite** existed in the seas from 450 to 200 million years ago. However, many of the known fossils consist of skins that had been molted.*

resembling catamaran but with three hulls side by side.

tri·mes·ter (trĭmĕs′ter, trī′mĕs-) *n.* Three months; division of academic year into three parts in some colleges and universities.

trim·e·ter (trĭm′īter) *adj. & n.* (Verse) of three measures or feet.

trim·mer (trĭm′er) *n.* 1. One who has no fixed allegiance to a political party or other institution but inclines to each of two opposite sides as interest dictates. 2. One whose business is to stow coal or cargo in loading ship. 3. Short beam framed across an opening (as a stairwell or hearth) to carry the ends of joists that cannot be extended across the opening. 4. Machine or tool for clipping shrubbery, weeds, etc.

*The nation of **Trinidad and Tobago** gained independence in 1962. The islands were discovered by Columbus. Trinidad is now a major producer of oil and asphalt as well as sugar.*

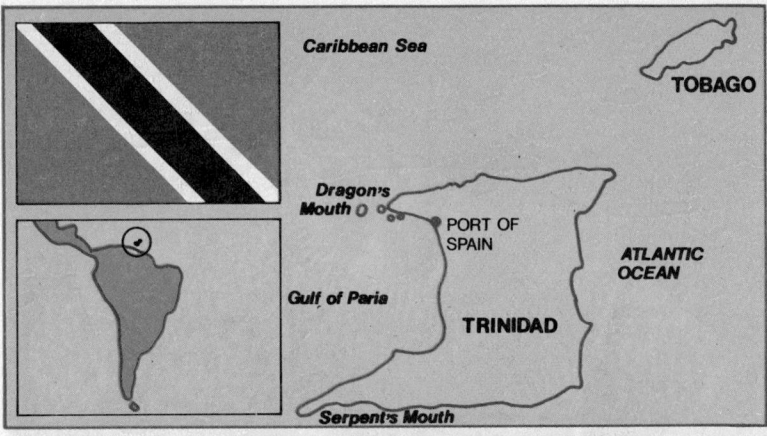

trin·i·ty (trĭn′ĭtē) *n.* (pl. **-ties**). Being three; group of three; **the T ~**, union of three persons or modes of being in the Godhead as conceived in orthodox Christian belief; Father, Son, and Holy Ghost as constituting one God; **T ~ Sunday**, Sunday after Pentecost, observed as festival in honor of the Trinity.

trin·ket (trĭng′kĭt) *n.* Small or trifling ornament or fancy article, esp. piece of jewelry.

tri·nod·al (trīnō′dal) *adj.* (bot.) Having three joints or nodes.

tri·no·mi·al (trīnō′mēal) *adj.* & *n.* (esp., math.) (Algebraical expression) consisting of three terms connected by plus or minus signs.

tri·o (trē′ō) *n.* (pl. **tri·os**). 1. (mus.) (Composition for) three voices or instruments in combination; composition in three parts. 2. Set of three persons or things.

tri·ode (trī′ōd) *n.* Vacuum tube with three main electrodes (anode, cathode, and grid).

tri·oe·cious (trīē′shus) *adj.* Having male, female, and bisexual flowers on different plants.

tri·ox·ide (trīŏk′sīd) *n.* (chem.) Compound of three atoms of oxygen with an element or radical.

trip (trĭp) *v.* (**tripped, trip′-ping**). 1. Walk, dance, (as in ~ **the light fantastic**), skip, etc., with quick light tread, run lightly, move freely and quickly. 2. (freq. with *up*) Make false step, stumble; cause (person) to stumble by entangling or suddenly arresting his feet; make mistake, commit fault, inconsistency, or inaccuracy; detect in stumble, inconsistency, or inaccuracy. 3. Tilt, esp. (naut.) tilt or cant (yard or mast) in lowering it; (naut.) loose (anchor) from its bed and raise it clear of bottom; (mech.) release (catch, lever, etc.) by contact with projection, operate (mechanism) thus. 4. (colloq.) Experience effects of hallucinogenic drug. **trip** *n.* 1. Short voyage or journey, esp. each of series of such journeys over particular route; excursion for pleasure, business, or health; (colloq.) experience induced by hallucinogenic or psychedelic drug. See EGO (sense 2). 2. Stumble; tripping or being tripped up. 3. Contrivance for tripping, projecting part of mechanism coming into contact with another part so as to cause or check movement; **trip′hammer, trip hammer**, massive machine hammer operated by trip.

tri·par·tite (trīpar′tīt) *adj.* Divided into, composed of, three parts or kinds; of, involving, such division; engaged in by, concluded between, three parties.

tripe (trīp) *n.* First or second stomach of ruminant, esp. ox, prepared as food; (slang) worthless or trashy product or thing.

tri·phib·i·ous (trīfĭb′ēus) *adj.* (of military operations) On land, sea, and in the air.

tri·plane (trī′plān) *n.* Aircraft with three sets of wings.

tri·ple (trĭp′el) *adj.* Threefold, three times as much or as many, of three parts; **T ~ Alliance**, (1) alliance of England, Sweden, and Netherlands against France, 1668; (2) that of France, Gt. Britain, and Netherlands against Spain, 1717; (3) that of Germany, Austria, and Italy against Russia and France, 1882–3; **~ crown**, (horse racing) of, pertaining to, victory by same horse in Kentucky Derby, Preakness, and Belmont Stakes; **~-decker**, sandwich having three slices of bread and two layers of filling; **~ play**, (baseball) putting out three runners; **T ~ Entente**: see ENTENTE; **~ threat**, (football) player who excels at running, passing, and kicking; any person having great ability in three fields or three skills in one field; **~ time**, (mus.) rhythm of three beats in the bar. **tri′ply** *adv.* **triple** *n.* Set of three; number or amount three times greater than another; (baseball) hit on which batter gets to third base without a fielding error. **~** *v.* (**tri·pled, tri·pling**). Increase threefold; be three times as great or as many as; (baseball) make a triple.

tri·plet (trĭp′lĭt) *n.* 1. Set of three; esp. three successive lines of verse rhyming together; (mus.) group of three notes performed in the time of two of the same value. 2. Each of three children born at a birth.

tri·plex (trĭp′lĕks) *adj.* Triple, threefold; apartment occupying three floors of a building.

trip·li·cate (trĭp′lĭkĭt, -kāt) *adj.* Threefold, forming three exactly corresponding copies. **~** *n.* Each of set of three exactly corresponding copies or parts; **in ~**, in three exactly corresponding copies. **triplicate** (trĭp′lĭkāt) *v.t.* (**-cat·ed, -cat·ing**). Triple, multiply by three, make or provide in triplicate.

*Using the 'Adoration of the Magi' as a central theme, the Dutch painter of this **triptych** also included the man who commissioned the work, and his wife, as part of the composition.*

trip·li·ca·tion (trĭplᵻkā′shon) *n.*

trip·loid (trĭp′loid) *adj. & n.* (biol.) (Organism or cell) having three times the haploid set of chromosomes.

tri·pod (trī′pŏd) *n.* Three-legged support, table, seat, etc., esp. frame or stand with three diverging legs, usu. hinged at top, for supporting camera, theodolite, etc.; (Gk. antiq.) altar at Delphi on which priestess sat to utter oracles. **tri·pod·al** (trĭp′odal) *adj.*

Trip·o·li (trĭp′olē). Seaport and capital city of Libya.

trip·per (trĭp′er) *n.* (esp.) Excursionist, one who goes on a pleasure trip.

trip·tych (trĭp′tĭk) *n.* Picture or carving, or set of three, in three compartments side by side, with lateral panels usu. hinged so as to fold over central one, used esp. as altarpiece.

tri·reme (trī′rēm) *n.* Ancient Greek or Roman warship with three banks of oars.

tri·sect (trīsĕkt′, trī′sĕkt) *v.t.* Divide into three, esp. (geom.) equal parts. **tri·sec·tion** (trīsĕk′shon) *n.*

tri·sep·al·ous (trīsĕp′alᵤs) *adj.* (bot.) Having three sepals.

tris·mus (trĭz′mᵤs, trĭs′-) *n.* (pl. **-mus·es**). (path.) Lockjaw.

Tris·tram (trĭs′tram). Knight, hero of a medieval legend; lover of ISEULT.

tri·syl·la·ble (trīsĭl′abel) *n.* Word of three syllables. **tri·syl·lab·ic** (trīsĭlăb′ĭk) *adj.* **tri·syl·lab′i·cal·ly** *adv.*

trite (trīt) *adj.* (**trit·er**, **trit·est**). Worn out by constant use or repetition, hackneyed, commonplace. **trite′ly** *adv.* **trite′ness** *n.*

trit·i·um (trĭt′ēum, trĭsh′um) *n.* (chem.) Radioactive isotope of hydrogen (at. wt. 3, half-life 12.5 years).

Tri·ton (trī′ton). (Gk. myth.) Sea god, son of Poseidon and Amphitrite, represented as a merman; one of a number of sea gods in form of mermen, freq. represented with conch shell trumpets.

tri·ton[1] (trī′ton) *n.* (zool.) Marine gastropod of family Tritonidae with large spiral shell.

tri·ton[2] (trī′tŏn) *n.* Tritium nucleus containing one proton and two neutrons.

trit·u·rate (trĭch′erāt) *v.t.* (**-rat·ed, -rat·ing**). Grind, rub, pound, etc., to powder or fine particles, pulverize. **trit·u·ra·tion** (trĭcherā′shon) *n.* **trit·u·ra·ble** *adj.* **trit·u·ra·tor** *n.*

tri·umph (trī′umf) *n.* 1. (Rom. antiq.) Entrance of commander with army and spoils in solemn procession into Rome in celebration of victory. 2. Triumphing; victory, conquest, the glory of this; rejoicing in success, elation, exultation. ~ *v.i.* Celebrate a Roman triumph; be victorious, prevail; rejoice in victory, exult (*over*); rejoice, glory.

tri·um·phal (trīŭm′fal) *adj.* Of, used in, celebrating, commemorating, a triumph or victory; ~ **arch**, arch erected, by Roman emperor or in modern times, in commemoration of victory etc.

tri·um·phant (trīŭm′fant) *adj.* Victorious, successful; triumphing,

exultant. **tri·um′phant·ly** *adv.*

tri·um·vir (trīŭm′ver) *n.* (pl. **-virs, -vi·ri** *pr.* -verī). 1. (Rom. hist.) One of three public officers jointly charged with one department of administration; member of first or second triumvirate (see below). 2. Member of any group of three jointly exercising power.

tri·um·vi·rate (trīŭm′verĭt) *n.* Office or function of triumvir; set of triumvirs; **first** ~, coalition of Pompey, Julius Caesar, and Crassus (60 B.C.); **second** ~, administration of Mark Antony, Octavian (Augustus), and Lepidus (43 B.C.).

tri·va·lent (trīvā′lent) *adj.* (chem.) Having a valence of three. **tri·va′lence, tri·va′len·cy** *ns.*

tri·valve (trī′vălv) *adj. & n.* (Shell) having three valves.

triv·et (trĭv′ĭt) *n.* Stand for pot, kettle, etc., placed over fire, orig. and properly on three feet, now freq. with projection(s) by which it can be secured on top bar of grate; similar stand for hot dishes or pots at table.

triv·i·al (trĭv′ēal) *adj.* Of small value or importance, trifling, slight, inconsiderable. **triv′i·al·ly** *adv.* **triv′i·al·ness, triv′i·al·ism** *ns.* **triv·i·al·i·ty** (trĭvēăl′ĭtē) *n.* (pl. **-ties**). **triv·i·a[1]** (trĭv′ēa) *n.pl.* Matters or information of no importance or usefulness. [L. *trivialis* commonplace f. *trivium* place where three ways ·meet (*via* way)]

triv·i·um (trĭv′ēum) *n.* (pl.

*A **tripod** is essential in photography where a steady hand is required. This is especially so when the camera, such as this movie camera, is heavy.*

*Backed by the ruins of the Coliseum which was completed by Titus, this **triumphal arch** was erected to commemorate his capture of Jerusalem in A.D. 70. He later ruled Rome.*

This woman of the Matmata hills of southern Tunisia is a **troglodyte.** By living in a cave, she enjoys respite from the heat outside. She still grinds corn by primitive means.

With such exact realism that artist Martin Battersby could have been playing a practical joke on his viewers, his **trompe l'oeil** at Mompesson House, Salisbury U.K. is a masterpiece of its type.

triv·i·a² pr. trĭv′ēa). (hist.) Grammar, rhetoric, and logic, forming the lower division (the other being the QUADRIVIUM) of the seven liberal arts in medieval schools. [see TRIVIAL]

tri·week·ly (trīwēk′lē) adj. & adv. (Occurring, appearing, etc.) every three weeks or three times a week.

-trix suffix. Forming fem. agent nouns corresponding to masc. nouns ending in -tor (executrix, testatrix).

tro·cha·ic (trōkā′ĭk) adj. Consisting of trochees, that is a trochee. ~ n. Trochee; (pl.) trochaic verse.

tro·chan·ter (trōkăn′ter) n. (anat., zool.) Prominence or protuberance (usu., as in man, two in number) in upper part of thigh bone, serving for attachment of certain muscles; (entom.) second joint of insect leg.

tro·che (trō′kē) n. Flat, usu. round, medicated tablet or lozenge.

tro·chee (trō′kē) n. (pros.) Metrical foot of two syllables, the first long or accented and the second short or unaccented (— ⌣). [Gk. trokhaios (pous) running (foot) (trekhō, run)]

troch·i·lus (trŏk′ilus) n. (pl. -li pr. -lī). Small Egyptian bird said by ancients to pick teeth of crocodile; small bird, esp. hummingbird.

troch·le·a (trŏk′lēa) n. (pl. -le·ae pr. -lēē). (anat.) Pulley-like structure or arrangement of parts, as surface of inner condyle of humerus at elbow joint, with which ulna articulates, fibrous ring

through which superior oblique muscle of eye passes etc. **troch′-le·ar** adj. Of, connected with, a trochlea; ~ **nerve,** each of fourth pair of cranial nerves, motor nerves for trochlear muscles.

tro·choid (trō′koid) n. (geom.) Curve traced by a point on a circle rolling on a straight line, or by a curve rolling upon another curve; (anat.) pivot joint. ~ adj. (anat., of joint) In which one bone turns upon another with rotary motion. **tro·choi·dal** (trōkoi′dal) adj.

trod·den (trŏd′en) adj.: see TREAD; (esp., of path) formed by treading, beaten.

trog·lo·dyte (trŏg′lodīt) n. Cave dweller, cave man. **trog·lo·dyt·ic** (trŏglodĭt′ĭk) adj.

troi·ka (troi′ka) n. (Russian vehicle drawn by) three horses abreast; group of three persons, nations, etc. acting equally together to exert influence, control, etc. [Russ.]

Troi·lus (troi′lus, trō′i-). (Gk. legend) Son of Priam and Hecuba, killed by Achilles; in medieval legend, forsaken lover of CRESSIDA.

Tro·jan (trō′jan) adj. Of TROY or its inhabitants; ~ **horse,** see below; ~ **War,** (Gk. legend) siege of Troy by Greeks under Agamemnon, undertaken in order to recover his brother's wife, HELEN; it lasted ten years and ended in the destruction of Troy after the

success of the stratagem of the ~ **horse,** a huge wooden figure of a horse concealing soldiers within it which the Greeks caused the Trojans to bring inside the city. **Trojan** n. 1. Native, inhabitant, of Troy. 2. Person of great energy, endurance, or bravery.

troll¹ (trōl) v. 1. Sing out in carefree spirit. 2. Fish for, fish in (water), fish, with rod and line and dead bait or with bait drawn along behind boat. **troll′er** n.

troll² (trōl) n. (Scand. myth.) One of race of supernatural beings formerly conceived as giants, later, in Denmark and Sweden, as dwarfs, inhabiting caves and subterranean dwellings.

trol·ley, trol·ly (trŏl′ē) ns. (pl. -leys, -lies). In streetcar etc., wheel running along overhead electric wire (~ **wire**), the wheel being mounted usu. on a pole (~ **pole**) down which current is conveyed to vehicle; ~ **bus,** bus with motive power derived from trolley; ~ **car,** streetcar.

trol·lop (trŏl′op) n. Slatternly woman, slut.

Trol·lope (trŏl′op), **Anthony** (1815–82). English novelist; author of The Warden, Barchester Towers, etc.

trom·bone (trŏmbōn′, trŏm′-bōn) n. Large brass wind instrument, usu. of tenor or bass range, having a tube that is adjusted in

*Better known for his novels which have enjoyed revivals due to their serialization on television, **Anthony Trollope** was also a writer of travel books. His writing career did not begin until he was in his thirties.*

*Outside the theater of war, **troops** play an important part in ceremonial occasions, such as here at the opening of the new Parliament in Zimbabwe, formerly Rhodesia.*

*The anemone fish is one of many bizarre **tropical fish**. It is protected from predators by living amongst the poisonous anemones, to which it has developed an immunity.*

length for different notes; organ reed stop of similar tone. **trom·-bon'ist** *n.*

trompe l'oeil (trŏmp′ lā′; *Fr.* trawǹp löy′). Painting in which objects represented give the illusion of reality; also attrib. [*Fr.*, = "deceives the eye"]

troop (trōōp) *n.* 1. Body of soldiers, esp. cavalry unit under a captain, artillery unit, or unit of armored vehicles; (pl.) armed forces; ~ **carrier**, aircraft or armored ground vehicle for transporting troops; **troop′ship, troop′train**, vessel, train, for conveyance of troops. 2. Number of persons or things collected together as a group. 3. Unit of Boy Scouts or Girl Scouts. **troop** *v.* Flock, assemble, move along in or as a troop; come or go in great numbers; ~ **the color(s)**, (mil.) perform that part of ceremonial of mounting the guard in which the flag or colors are received.

troop·er (trōō′per) *n.* Cavalryman, horse soldier; **state ~**, in U.S., member of police force operated by, and having authority throughout, a state; **swear like a ~**, swear vigorously and at length.

trope (trōp) *n.* Figurative (e.g. metaphorical, ironical) use of a word; (eccles.) phrase or verse introduced as embellishment into some part of the Mass.

-trope *comb. form.* Turning,

changing in response to specific stimulus (*heliotrope*).

troph·ic (trŏf′ĭk) *adj.* (biol.) Of nutrition; ~ **nerves**, nerves concerned with or regulating nutrition of tissues.

troph·o·blast (trŏf′oblăst) *n.* Layer of cells enclosing embryo, serving to nourish it and (in mammals) to attach it to the wall of the uterus. **troph·o·blas·tic** (trŏfo-blăs′tĭk) *adj.*

tro·phy (trō′fē) *n.* (pl. **-phies**). (Gk. and Rom. antiq.) Arms or other spoils taken from enemy set up as memorial of victory, painted or carved figure of such memorial; (representation of) ornamental or symbolic group of objects; anything taken in war, hunting, etc., esp. if displayed as memorial token or evidence of victory, power, skill, etc.; prize, memento.

-trophy *comb. form.* Nourishment, growth (*hypertrophy, atrophy*).

trop·ic (trŏp′ĭk) *n.* Each of two circles of celestial sphere (northern ~ **of Cancer**, and southern ~ **of Capricorn**) parallel to equator and 23° 28′ north and south of it, where sun reaches its greatest declination north or south; each of two corresponding parallels of latitude on Earth's surface; (pl.) torrid zone, region lying between these parallels. **tropic** *adj.* Tropical; ~ **bird**, seabird of the chiefly tropical genus

Phaethon, resembling terns, with webbed feet, rapid flight, and usu. white plumage marked with black.

trop·i·cal (trŏp′ĭkal) *adj.* Of, occurring in, inhabiting, peculiar to, suggestive of, the tropics; (fig.) very hot, ardent, or luxuriant; ~ **cyclone**, cyclone that originates over tropical oceans and that can develop into severe disturbance known as hurricane, typhoon, or other names used in different regions; ~ **fish**, any of various small usually brightly colored fishes

As its name suggests, the **tropic bird** is found mainly in the warmer parts of the world's oceans. It lives on fish and squid. The conspicuous tail streamers may be twice the body length.

originating in tropical waters and kept in aquariums; ~ **year**: see YEAR, sense I. **trop′i·cal·ly** *adv.*

tro·pism (trō′pĭzem) *n.* (biol.) Turning of organism or part of one in particular direction in response to external stimulus or automatically.

trop·o·pause (trŏp′opawz) *n.* Boundary between the troposphere and the stratosphere.

trop·o·sphere (trŏp′osfēr) *n.* Layer of atmosphere extending from surface of Earth to stratosphere, within which temperature falls with height. **trop·o·spher·ic** (trŏposfĕr′ĭk) *adj.*

trot (trŏt) *n.* Quadruped's gait between walk and gallop, in which legs move in diagonal pairs almost together; similar gait between walking and running of man etc.; (slang) = CRIB sense 7; **the ~s**, (slang) diarrhea. **trot** *v.* (**trot·ted, trot·ting**). (Make) go at a trot; cover (distance) by trotting; bring to specified condition by trotting; ~ **out**, lead out and show off paces of (horse); (fig.) produce, bring forward.

troth (trawth, trōth) *n.* (archaic) Truth; faith, plighted word; **plight one's ~**: see PLIGHT[1].

Trot·sky (trŏt′skē), **Leon.** Lev Davidovich Bronstein (1877–1940), Russian revolutionary leader; advocate of world proletarian revolution; came into conflict with Stalin and was ordered to leave Russia

1929. **Trot′sky·ism, Trot′sky·ist** *ns.*

trot·ter (trŏt′er) *n.* (esp.) Horse specially bred and trained for trotting; animal's foot, esp. used for food.

trot·ting (trŏt′ĭng) **race.** Race at trotting pace between horses, each pulling a sulky on which the driver sits.

trou·ba·dour (trōō′badōr, -dōr, -door) *n.* One of a class of 11th-13th-c. lyric poets living in S. France, E. Spain, and N. Italy and singing in Provençal, chiefly of chivalry and gallantry. [Fr., f. Provençal *trobador*, f. *trobar* find, invent, compose in verse]

trou·ble (trŭb′el) *n.* Affliction, grief, vexation, bother, inconvenience; pains, exertion; thing or person that gives trouble; **get into, be in, ~**, incur censure, punishment, etc.; (euphem., of unmarried

Fauna of the **tropical** regions are often much more vividly colored than their counterparts in cooler areas as exemplified by these sun-birds (above) from Africa.

woman) become, be, pregnant; **troubled waters**, generally disturbed, agitated conditions; **trou′blemaker**, one who stirs up trouble, agitator; **trou′bleshooter**, person employed to trace and remove cause of defective working, discontent, etc. **trouble spot**, place where trouble frequently occurs. **trouble** *v.* (**-bled, -bling**). Disturb, agitate; distress, grieve; be disturbed or worried; subject, be subjected, to inconvenience or exertion.

trou·ble·some (trŭb′elsom) *adj.* Causing trouble, vexatious. **trou′ble·some·ly** *adv.* **trou·ble·some·ness** *n.*

trough (trawf, trŏf) *n.* Long

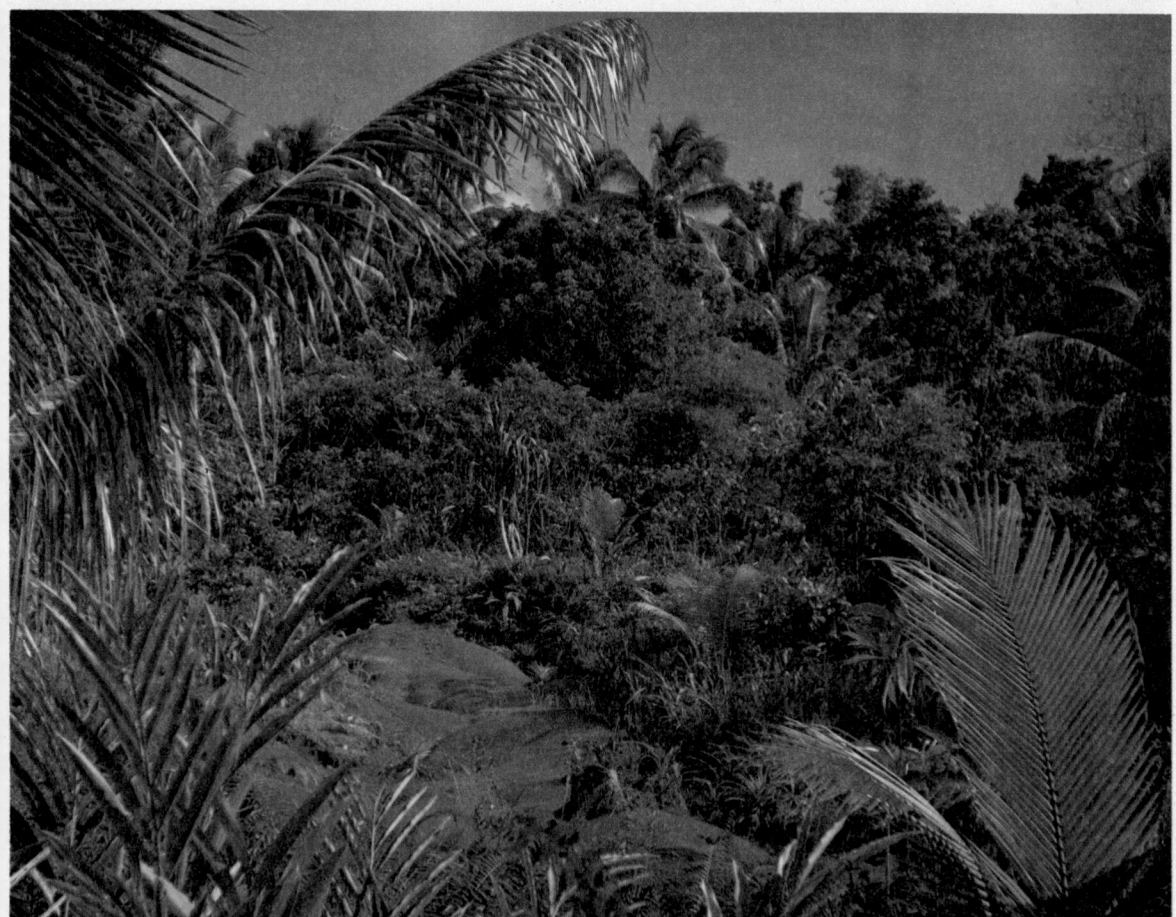

narrow open boxlike wooden or other receptacle for holding water or food for animals, kneading dough, washing ore, etc.; wooden or other channel for conveying liquid; hollow or valley resembling trough; (meteor.) elongated region of lower barometric pressure between two of higher; **feed at the public** ~, gain advantages over and above usual compensation for serving in public office.

trounce (trowns) *v.t.* (**trounced, trounc·ing**). Beat severely, castigate; defeat heavily; scold, abuse.

troupe (trōop) *n.* Company, troop, esp. of actors, acrobats, etc. **troup′er** *n.* 1. (esp.) Actor. 2. (colloq.) Person loyal to a task or enterprise even under adverse conditions.

trou·sers (trow′zerz) *n.* (usu. considered pl.) (also **pair of** ~s)

The popular concept of **tropical** areas being filled with lush vegetation applies only where there is high rainfall. The Sahara and Arabian deserts are also in the tropics; while in West Irian, there is perpetual snow on mountain peaks which are so high that the warmth of the sun has little or no effect.

Loose-fitting two-legged outer garment (sometimes sing.) extending (usu.) from waist to ankles.

trous·seau (trōo′sō, trōosō′) *n.* (pl. **-seaux, -seaus**). Bride's outfit of clothes etc.

trout (trowt) *n.* (pl. **trouts**, collect. **trout**). Any of various small usu. speckled freshwater fish of the salmon family and three genera (*Salmo, Salvelinus, Cristivomer*), inhabiting rivers and lakes of temperate or colder parts of N. hemisphere, fished for sport and esteemed as food.

trove (trōv): see TREASURE trove.

tro·ver (trōver) *n.* (law) Finding and keeping of personal property; (also **action of** ~) action to recover value of personal property illegally converted by another to his own use.

*Left: Map showing the areas of the world encompassed by the **Tropics** of Capricorn and Cancer. In these regions, the sun is directly overhead on one or more days each year.*

trow (trow) *v.t.* (archaic) Think, believe.

trow·el (trow'el) *n.* Flat-bladed tool with short handle used for spreading mortar etc.; gardener's short-handled tool with hollow scooplike blade. ~ *v.t.* (**-eled, -el·ing**; Brit. **-elled, -el·ling**). Spread, smooth, lay on, etc., (as) with trowel.

Troy (troi). Ancient city in NW. Asia Minor, besieged by the Greeks in the TROJAN War; believed to be a figment of Greek legend until its remains were excavated between 1870 and 1890 by Heinrich Schliemann at Hissarlik.

troy (troi) **weight.** System of weights (1 lb. = 12 ounces = 240 pennyweights = 5760 grains) used for precious metals etc. [prob. f. city of *Troyes* in France]

tru·ant (trōō'ant) *n.* One who absents himself from duty or business, esp. child who stays away from school without leave; **play** ~, act thus; ~ **officer**, school official who deals with truants. **truant** *adj.* That plays truant or is a truant; shirking, idle, loitering, wandering. **tru'an·cy** *n.* (pl. **-cies**).

truce (trōōs) *n.* (Agreement for) temporary cessation of hostilities;

respite or intermission from something disagreeable or painful. **truce'less** *adj.*

truck[1] (trŭk) *n.* 1. Barter; (system of) payment of wages otherwise than in money; (fig.) dealings, intercourse. 2. Small miscellaneous articles, sundries; odds and ends, trash, rubbish; vegetables raised for market, hence ~ **crop(s), farming, farm**. **truck** *v.* Exchange, trade, barter; bargain, trade (*in*); pay or deal with on truck system.

truck[2] (trŭk) *n.* 1. Strong usu. four- or six-wheeled vehicle for heavy goods; **truck'driver** = TRUCKER, sense 2; barrowlike frame for moving luggage etc.; hand cart; set of wheels in framework for supporting whole or part of railroad car etc.; **truck'load**, full or nearly full load on truck; minimum weight of particular commodity legally qualified for shipment at rate below that charged for shipments weighing less than the minimum. 2.

*The **truffle** of Europe is esteemed by gourmets. However, as this fungus grows underground, it can only be obtained by specially trained dogs or pigs which locate it by its distinctive smell.*

(naut.) Disk at top of mast with holes for halyards. **truck** *v.t.* Carry, convey, on truck. **truck'age** *n.* (Cost of) conveyance by truck(s).

truck·er (trŭk'er) *n.* 1. Person or company in business of trucking. 2. Person who owns and drives his own truck or serves as driver for trucking company. **truck'ing** *n.* Transportation of goods by truck.

truck·le (trŭk'el) *v.i.* (**-led, -ling**). Submit obsequiously, cringe, (*to*). **truck'ler** *n.* [orig., = to sleep in truckle bed] **truck·le** (trŭk'el) **bed** = TRUNDLE bed.

truc·u·lent (trŭk'yulent) *adj.* Showing ferocity or cruelty; aggressive, savage, harsh. **truc'u·lent·ly** *adv.* **truc'u·lence, truc'u·len·cy** *ns.*

trudge (trŭj) *v.* (**trudged, trudg·ing**). Walk laboriously, wearily, or without spirit, but steadily; perform (distance) thus. ~ *n.* Trudging; laborious or wearisome walk. **trudg'er** *n.*

trudg·en (trŭj'en) *n.* (also ~ **stroke**) Hand over hand or double overarm stroke in swimming with vigorous leg kicks. [f. John *Trudgen* (19th c.), English swimmer]

true (trōō) *adj.* (**tru·er, tru·est**). 1. Consistent with fact or reality, not false or erroneous; **come** ~, be verified in experience, be fulfilled. 2. Agreeing with reason, correct principles, or recognized standard; real, genuine, correct, proper; not spurious, counterfeit, hybrid, or merely apparent; (of voice etc.) in good tune; conformable to the type; accurately placed, fitted, or shaped; (of ground etc.) level, smooth; ~ **bill**, bill of indictment found by grand jury sufficiently well supported to justify hearing of case. 3. Steadfast in adherence (*to*), constant, loyal, faithful, sincere. 4. ~ **-blue**, (fig.) (person) of uncompromising loyalty or orthodoxy; **true'born'**, truly such by birth; **true'bred'**, of true or pure breed, thoroughbred; **true-life**, like what occurs in real life; corresponding to reality; **true** *adv.* Truly. *v.t.* (**trued, tru·ing** or **true·ing**) Make (piece of equipment etc.) true, adjust or shape accurately, make perfectly straight, smooth, level, etc. **true'ness** *n.*

truf·fle (trŭf'el) *n.* Any of various edible fungi of genus *Tuber*, esp. the French *T. melanospora*, usu. shaped like petals, with black warty exterior and rich flavor, esteemed as delicacy. **truf'fled** *adj.*

tru·ism (trōō'izem) *n.* Self-

*Facing: To cater for anglers, especially in areas where the fish have been introduced, **trout** farms have been established. This specimen leaps for its food at a New Zealand hatchery.*

Above: **Harry S. Truman** *took office as President of the U.S.A. when Roosevelt died. He will always be remembered as the man who decided to drop an atom bomb on Japan.*

Metal pieces forming triangular shapes, as in this **truss bridge** *in New Mexico, form a highly stable structure capable of supporting heavy loads over a wide area.*

evident truth, esp. of slight importance; hackneyed truth, platitude.

tru·ly (troō'lē) *adv.* Sincerely, genuinely; faithfully, loyally; accurately, truthfully.

Tru·man (troō'man), **Harry S.** (1884–1972). Thirty-third president of U.S., 1945–53; U.S. senator, 1933–45; U.S. vice president, 1945; formulator (1947) of the ~ **Doctrine**, providing military and economic aid to Greece and Turkey and to any nation "resisting attempted subjugation by armed minorities or outside pressures."

trump (trŭmp) *n.* (also ~s) Playing card of suit ranking temporarily above other three; ~ **card**, card turned up to determine which suit shall be trumps; any card of this suit; (fig.) valuable resource, important means of doing something, gaining one's point, etc. **trump** *v.* Put trump on, take (trick, card) with trump; play trump, take trick with trump; excel, surpass, gain advantage; ~ **up**, fabricate, invent. **trumped-up** *adj.*

trump·er·y (trŭm'perē) *n.* (pl. **-er·ies**). Worthless stuff, trash, rubbish, nonsense. ~ *adj.* Showy but worthless, delusive, shallow. [Fr. *tromper* deceive]

trum·pet (trŭm'pĭt) *n.* Musical wind instrument of bright ringing tone, consisting of narrow cylindrical, usu. metal, straight or curved tube with bell and cup-shaped mouthpiece and now usu. with valves; organ reed stop with power-

ful trumpetlike tone; something shaped like trumpet, tubular corona of daffodil; sound (as) of trumpet, esp. elephant's loud cry; ~ **creeper**, creeper (*Campsis radicans*) of southern U.S., with large scarlet trumpet-shaped flowers; ~ **flower**, any of various plants with trumpet-shaped flowers; ~ **honeysuckle**, vine (*Lonicera sempervirens*) of eastern U.S. having tubular reddish blossoms; ~ **vine**, trumpet creeper; **trum'petweed**, any of several weedlike herbs, esp. of the genus *Eupatorium*. **trumpet** *v.* Proclaim (as) by sound of trumpet; celebrate, extol loudly; (of elephant) make loud sound as of trumpet.

trum·pet·er (trŭm'pĭter) *n.* 1. One who plays on or sounds trumpet, esp. cavalry soldier giving signals with trumpet. 2. Any of various large S. Amer. birds of genus *Psophia*, allied to cranes, with loud, harsh cry; ~ **swan**, large N. Amer. wild swan, *Olor buccinator*, with loud sonorous note.

trun·cate (trŭng'kāt) *adj.* Truncated. ~ *v.t.* (**-cat·ed, -cat·ing**). Cut short, cut off top or end of. **trun'cat·ed** *adj.* (esp.) (of cone or pyramid) With vertex cut off by plane section, esp. parallel to base; (of edge or solid angle) cut off by plane face, esp. one equally inclined to adjacent faces; (of crystal, solid figure, etc.) having such angles; (biol.) looking as if tip or end were cut off. **trun·ca·tion** (trŭngkā'-

shon) *n.*

trun·cheon (trun'chon) *n.* (chiefly Brit.) Short thick staff or club, esp. that carried by policeman. ~ *v.t.* Strike or beat with truncheon.

trun·dle (trŭn'del) *n.* 1. Small wheel; lantern wheel, device of two disks connected by cylinder of parallel staves that engage with teeth of cogwheel; roller with two arms for transmitting motion from stop knob of organ. 2. Trundling; ~ **bed**, low bed on wheels that can be pushed under another. **trundle** *v.* (**-dled, -dling**). (Cause to) roll; draw, be drawn, along on wheel(s) or in wheeled vehicle; walk with a rolling gait. **trun'dler** *n.*

trunk (trŭngk) *n.* 1. Main stem of tree as dist. from roots and branches; shaft of column; human or animal body (apart from head and limbs); main body or line of nerve, artery, etc., or of river, railroad, telegraph, telephone, road, or canal system, as dist. from branches; part of a fish between head and anus. 2. Box or chest with hinged lid for carrying clothes etc. while traveling; compartment in automobile for storing spare tire, luggage, etc. 3. Elephant's long flexible nose. 4. (pl.) Close-fitting shorts worn by swimmers, boxers, etc. 5. ~ **call**, (chiefly Brit.) long-distance telephone call involving use of trunk line; **trunk'fish** (pl. **-fishes**, collect. **-fish**), fish of *Ostracion* and related genera, with body of angular cross section and covered with bony hexagonal plates; **trunk line**, main line of railroad, telephone system, etc. **trunk′ful** *n.* (pl. **-fuls**). **trunk′-less** *adj.*

trun·nion (trŭn′yon) *n.* Supporting cylindrical projection on each side of cannon; hollow structure supporting cylinder in steam engine and giving passage to steam. **trun′nioned** *adj.*

truss (trŭs) *n.* 1. Compact cluster of flowers growing on one stalk. 2. Supporting structure or framework of bridge, roof, etc.; large corbel, projecting from face of wall and freq. supporting cornice etc.; (naut.) tackle for securing yard to mast, metal ring around mast with pivoted attachment to yard at center; ~ **bridge**, bridge supported by trusses. 3. Surgical appliance, now usu. pad with belt or spring, for support in cases of hernia etc. **truss** *v.t.* 1. Tie (*up*), pack, in a bundle or parcel; tie, fasten (*up*) closely or securely; fasten limbs of (fowl etc. for cooking) to body with skewers etc.; (hist.) fasten (*up*) points or laces of (hose), tie up (points), tie up arms of (person). 2. Support or secure with truss(es). **truss′er** *n.*

trust (trŭst) *n.* 1. Confidence in, reliance on, some quality of person or thing, or truth of statement; confident expectation, hope; confidence in future payment for goods etc. supplied, credit; object of trust. 2. Condition of being trusted;

obligation of one in whom confidence is placed or authority vested; (law) confidence reposed in person in whom legal ownership of property is vested to hold or use for benefit of another, property so committed, body of trustees; thing, person, duty entrusted to one or committed to one's care; **in** ~, entrusted to person or body of persons, held as trust; **investment** ~, company whose profits are drawn from investments distributed among a number of other companies and from the sale of these investments; ~ **account**, account of property opened with a trust company by depositor, to be distributed during his lifetime or after death; savings account in a bank with balance going to predesignated beneficiary upon death of depositor; ~ **company**, company formed or authorized to act as trustee or handle trusts; ~ **fund**, money, securities, etc., held in trust; ~ **territory**, one under trusteeship of (country designated by) the United Nations. 3. Illegal combination of producing or trading firms to reduce or defeat competition, control production and distribution, etc., esp. such a combination with central governing body holding majority or whole of stock of combining firms. **trust** *v.* Have faith or confidence (in); place trust in, rely or depend on; hope; believe (statement), rely on truthfulness, etc., of (person); commit care or safety of (thing) *to* or *with* person; place or allow to be *in* place or condition or *to do* something, without fear of the consequences; entrust to care, disposal, etc., of;

give (person) credit *for* (goods). **trust′er** *n.* **trust′a·ble** *adj.*

trus·tee (trŭstē′) *n.* Person to whom property is entrusted for benefit of another; one of number of persons appointed to manage affairs of an institution.

trus·tee·ship (trŭstē′shĭp) *n.* Position of a trustee; status of area for whose government another country is instructed by the United Nations to be responsible.

trust·ful (trŭst′ful) *adj.* Full of trust, confiding. **trust′ful·ly** *adv.* **trust′ful·ness** *n.*

trust·wor·thy (trŭst′wērdhē) *adj.* Worthy of trust, reliable. **trust′wor·thi·ness** *n.*

trust·y (trŭs′tē) *adj.* (**trust·i·er, trust·i·est**). Trustworthy. **trust′i·ly** *adv.* **trust′i·ness** *n.* **trusty** *n.* (pl. **trust·ies**). Trustworthy convict granted special privileges.

truth (trooth) *n.* (pl. **truths** pr. troodhz). Quality, state, of being true; loyalty, honesty, accuracy, integrity, etc.; what is true, true statement or account, true belief or doctrine, reality, fact; ~ **or consequences**, game in which players are asked questions in turn by leader and, failing to reply or give correct answer, must pay penalty or forfeit; ~ **serum** (or **drug**), substance administered in supposition that it will make person tell the truth.

truth·ful (trooth′ful) *adj.* Habitually speaking truth, not deceitful; true. **truth′ful·ly** *adv.* **truth′ful·ness** *n.*

try (trī) *v.* (**tried, try·ing**). 1. Examine and determine (cause, question) judicially, determine

*Found only in tropical forests in South America, the **trumpeter** seldom flies although it roosts in trees. Eggs are laid in holes in a tree trunk and adults are chicken-sized.*

*A Nigerian tribesman plays a traditional form of **trumpet** at a gathering of his people. The earliest known designs of straight trumpets can be traced to the ancient Egyptians.*

Tuba was the Roman name for a military trumpet. The modern **tuba** *(above) which has the lowest notes of any brass wind instrument, only became used, in Germany, sometime after 1820.*

Right: Actually a food storage stem, the **tuber** *of many plants has been used by man for food. These include the potato, yam and Jerusalem artichoke. Inedible ones include the dahlia.*

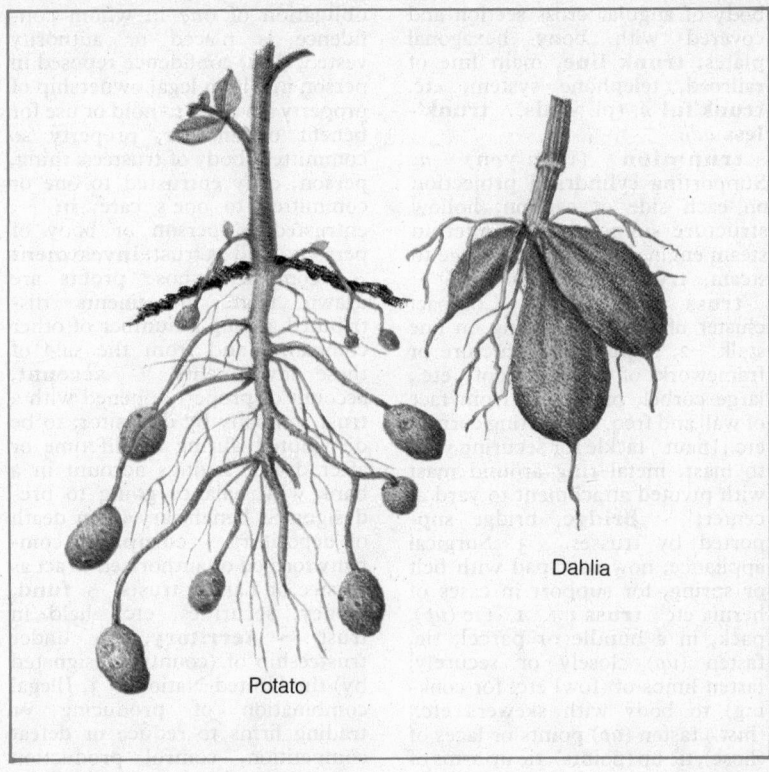

Dahlia

Potato

guilt or innocence of (accused person) by consideration of evidence; test (quality), test qualities of (person, thing) by experiment; test effect or operation of, experiment with; attempt to ascertain by experiment or effort; subject to severe test or strain, strain endurance or patience of; ~ **on**, test fit or style of (garment) by putting it on; ~ **out**, put to the test, test thoroughly. 2. Attempt to do, perform, or accomplish, essay; make an effort, endeavor, attempt; ~ **out for**, attempt to attain (object, position, etc.) or to reach (place); ~ **one's hand**, make attempt *at* for first time. 3. Dress (board etc.) to perfectly flat surface with plane. 4. (also ~ **out**) Extract (oil) from blubber or fat by heat, extract oil from (fat etc.) thus, render. 5. **try'out**, experimental run, esp. of a play or of an actor seeking to gain a role in a play; **try'sail**, small strongly made fore-and-aft sail used as substitute for normal sail in stormy weather; **try square**, carpenter's instrument of two straight edges fixed at right angles, for laying off short perpendiculars. **try** *n.* 1. Act of trying, attempt. 2. (football) (also ~ **for point**) attempt to score additional point(s) after touchdown by place-kicking or other means; **old college ~**, (colloq.) sincere attempt.

try·ing (trī'ĭng) *adj.* That tries; (esp.) exhausting; exasperating; difficult to bear. **try'ing·ly** *adv.*

tryp·a·no·some (trĭp'anosōm, trĭpăn'o-) *n.* Parasite of *Trypano-*

soma or allied genera of flagellate protozoa, infesting blood etc. of man and other animals and often causing disease. [Gk. *trupanon* borer, *soma* body]

tryp·sin (trĭp'sĭn) *n.* Enzyme present in pancreatic juice, converting proteins into peptones.

tryp·tic (trĭp'tĭk) *adj.* Of, produced by, trypsin.

tryst (trĭst) *n.* Appointed meeting, appointment, esp. by lovers. **tryst'ing place**, appointed place for secret meeting of lovers; rendezvous.

tsar, tzar, czar (zär, tsär) *ns.* 1. (hist.) Emperor, title assumed *c*1482 by Ivan Basilovich, Grand Duke of Muscovy, and used by emperors of Russia until 1917. 2. (usu. **czar**) Any person with great power or authority. **tsar'dom** *n.* [Russ. *tsar*, f. L. CAESAR]

tsar·e·vich, tzar·e·vitch, czar·e·vitch (zär'evĭch, tsär'-) *ns.* (hist.) (Title of) son of tsar (in English usage, but erroneously, the eldest son and heir).

tsa·rev·na, tza·rev·na, cza·rev·na (zahrĕv'na, tsah-) *ns.* (hist.) (Title of) daughter of tsar.

tsa·ri·na, tza·ri·na, cza·ri·na (zahrē'na, tsah-) *ns.* (hist.) (Title of) empress of Russia.

tsar·ism, tzar·ism, czar·ism (zär'ĭzem, tsär'-) *ns.* (Devotion to, advocacy of) autocratic rule of tsars. **tsar'ist** *adj. & n.* **tsa·ris·tic** (zahrĭs'tĭk) *adj.*

tsa·rit·za, tza·rit·za, cza·rit·za (zahrĭt'sa, tsah-) *ns.* Tsarina.

tset·se (tsĕt'sē, tsē'tsē) **fly.** Fly

of genus *Glossina*, abundant in parts of central and southern Africa and carrying disease to men and animals, esp. *G. palpalis*, carrier of the trypanosome causing sleeping sickness.

tsp. *abbrev.* Teaspoon(ful).

tsu·na·mi (tsōōnah'mē) *n.* Unusually large wave produced by submarine earthquake. **tsu·na'mic** *adj.*

Tswa·na (tswah'na) *n.* (pl. **-nas**). 1. (Member of) a black people living between the Orange and Zambezi rivers in southern Africa. 2. Bantu language of this people.

Tu. *abbrev.* Tuesday.

tu·a·ta·ra (tōōatah'ra) *n.* Large iguana-like reptile (*Sphaenodon punctatum*) peculiar to N.Z., having a dorsal row of yellow spines. [Maori]

tub (tŭb) *n.* Open cylindrical or slightly concave vessel, usu. of staves and hoops, with flat bottom; measure of capacity for butter or other commodities; (colloq.) bath; (joc.) slow clumsy ship; (mining) box or bucket for conveying coal etc. to surface; (derog.) short fat person. ~ *v.i.* (**tubbed, tub·bing**). (colloq.) Bathe or wash in tub.

tu·ba (tōō'ba, tū'-) *n.* (pl. **-bas, -bae** pr. -bē). (mus.) Brass wind instrument, the bass of the horn family, usu. with wide conical bore and cup-shaped mouthpiece.

tub·by (tŭb'ē) *adj.* (**-bi·er, -bi·est**). Tub-shaped; short and fat, round, corpulent. **tub'bi·ness** *n.*

tube (tōob, tūb) *n.* 1. Long hollow cylinder esp. for conveying or holding liquids, pipe. 2. Main body of wind instrument. 3. Short cylinder of flexible metal with screw cap for holding semi-liquid substance, e.g. toothpaste, artists' paint. 4. Inner tube containing air in pneumatic tire. 5. Hollow cylindrical organ in animal body, as **bronchial** ~; ~ **foot**, one of the tubular projections on body of echinoderm, used for loco-motion and grasping. 6. Cylindrical tunnel in which some railroads or subway trains run; such trains. 7. Vacuum tube. **tube′less** *adj.* (esp., of pneumatic tire) Having no inner tube. **tube** *v.* (**tubed**, **tub·ing**) Furnish with, enclose in, tube(s).

tu·ber (tōo′ber, tū′ber) *n.* 1. Short, thick, more or less rounded, root or stem of plant, freq. bearing eyes or buds from which new plants may grow, as potato etc. 2. (anat.) Rounded swelling or protuberant part.

tu·ber·cle (tōo′berkel, tū′-) *n.* Small rounded projection or pro-tuberance, esp. (path.) small rounded swelling on surface of body or in part or organ, esp. mass of granulation cells charac-teristic of tuberculosis; (bot.) small tuber, or root growth resembling this, small wartlike excrescence; ~ **bacillus**, bacillus *Myobacterium*

tuberculosis causing tuberculosis. **tu·ber′cu·lar** *adj.*

tu·ber·cu·lin (tōober′kyulĭn, tyōo-) *n.* Sterile liquid prepared from cultures of tubercle bacillus and used for diagnosis and treat-ment of tuberculosis, esp. in children and cattle; ~ **test**, injec-tion of tuberculin under skin, causing inflammation in tubercu-lous subjects.

tu·ber·cu·lo·sis (tōoberkyulō′-sĭs, tyōo-) *n.* Infectious disease in men and animals caused by tubercle bacillus and characterized by formation of tubercles in bodily tissues, esp. lungs (**pulmonary** ~). **tu·ber·cu·lous** (tōober′kyu-lus) *adj.* (esp.) Affected with, of the nature of, tuberculosis.

tu·ber·ose (tōo′berōs, tū′-) *adj.* Tuberous. ~ *n.* Tropical liliaceous plant (*Polianthes tuberosa*) with creamy white funnel-shaped fra-grant flowers and tuberous roots. **tu·ber·os·i·ty** (tōoberŏs′ĭtē, tū-) *n.* (pl. **-ties**). Tuberous formation or part; esp. (anat., zool.) large irregular projection of bone, usu. as attachment for muscle. [L. *tuberosus* tuberous]

tu·ber·ous (tōo′berus, tū′-) *adj.* Of the form or nature of a tuber; covered or affected with, bearing, tubers; ~ **root**, (esp.) root thickened so as to resemble tuber but bearing no buds.

tub·ing (tōo′bĭng, tū′-) *n.* (esp.)

Tubes collectively; length or piece of tube; material for tubes.

Tub·man (tŭb′man), **Harriet** (1820?–1913). Black Amer. aboli-tionist leader; best known for guiding many slaves to freedom via the underground railway.

tu·bu·lar (tōo′byuler, tū′-) *adj.* Tube-shaped; cylindrical, hollow, and open at one or both ends; constructed with, consisting of, tubes; ~ **skate**, ice skate having steel blade in aluminum tube. **tu′bu·lous** *adj.*

tu·bule (tōo′būl, tū′-) *n.* Small tube, minute tubular structure in animal or plant.

tuck (tŭk) *n.* 1. Flattened fold in garment etc., secured by stitching, for ornament or to shorten the article. 2. (naut.) Part of vessel where ends of bottom planks meet under stern. 3. Tucking in of ends or edges, anything so tucked in; (*adj.*) (esp., of woman's blouse etc.) designed to be tucked into top of skirt etc. ~ *v.* 1. Put tuck(s) in, shorten or ornament with tuck(s); thrust or put (*away*) object into place where it is snugly held or concealed; thrust or turn (*in*) ends or edges of (anything pendent or loose, now esp. bedcovers) so as to retain or confine them; be so dis-posed of; draw together into small compass. 2. ~ **in, away**, (slang) eat heartily.

tuck·er[1] (tŭk′er) *n.* (esp.) Piece of lace, linen, etc., worn by women inside or around top of bodice in 17th–18th c. (now chiefly in **best bib and** ~, best clothing).

tuck·er[2] (tŭk′er) *v.t.* Tire (*out*), weary; **tuckered out**, exhausted, worn out.

Tu·dor (tōo′der, tū′-). 1. Name of English royal house from Henry VII to Elizabeth I, descended from Owen Tudor, who married Catherine, widowed queen of Henry V. 2. (attrib. or as adjec-tive) Of the architectural style pre-vailing in England during the reigns of Tudors; of, resembling, imitat-ing, the domestic architecture of this period, with much half-timber-ing, brickwork freq. in patterns, elaborate chimneys, many gables, rich oriel windows, much interior paneling and molded plasterwork etc.; ~ **arch**, flattened four-centered arch characteristic of the period.

Tues. *abbrev.* Tuesday.

Tues·day (tōoz′dā, -dē, tūz′-) *n.* Third day of the week. [OE. *Tiwesdæg* (rendering L. *dies Martis*) f. *Tiw*, Germanic deity identified with MARS]

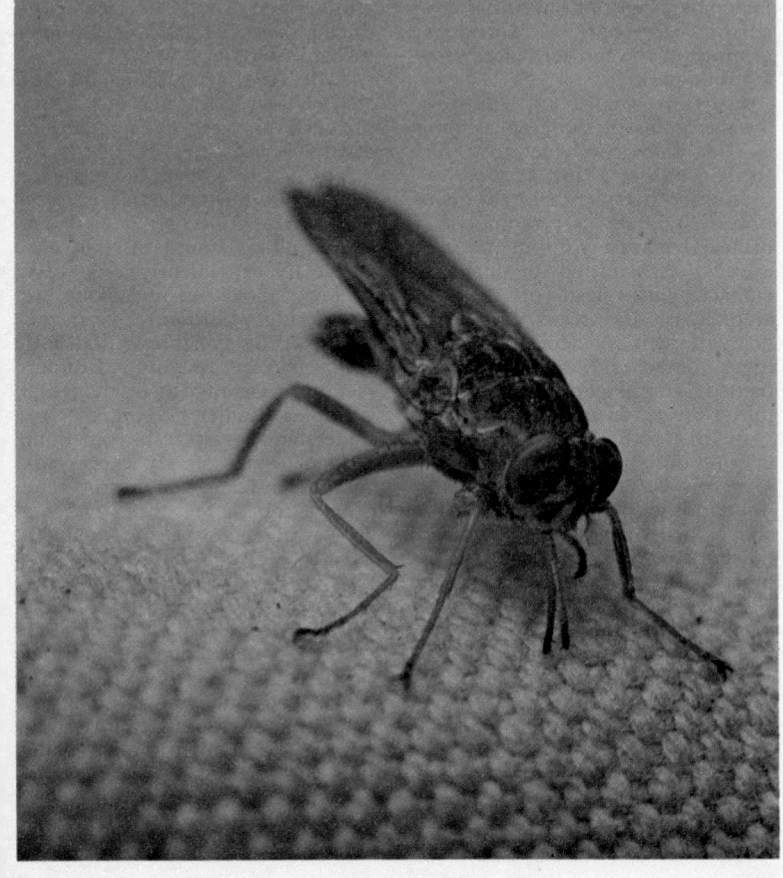

Carrier of the deadly trypanosomes which cause sleeping sickness, the **tsetse fly** *of Africa transfers these organisms to man. Its blood-sucking can also cause disease in cattle.*

tu·fa (tōo´fa, tū´-) *n.* (geol.) Porous deposit of calcium carbonate laid down around mineral springs. **tu·fa·ceous** (tōofā´shus, tū-) *adj.*

tuft (tŭft) *n.* Bunch, collection, of threads, grass, feathers, etc., held or growing together at the base. **tuft´y** *adj.* (**tuft·i·er, tuft·i·est**). **tuft** *v.t.* Furnish with tuft(s); (upholstery) secure padding of (mattress, cushion, etc.) with thread drawn through tightly at regular intervals, producing depressions in surface usu. ornamented with tuft or button. **tuft´ed** *adj.* (esp., of birds) Having tuft of feathers on head, crested; (of plants etc.) growing in tuft(s), clustered, bearing flowers in tufts; ~ **titmouse**, mouse-colored titmouse (*Parus bicolor*) ranging throughout E. and midwestern U.S. and having dull reddish-brown flanks and tufted crest on head.

tug (tŭg) *v.* (**tugged, tug·ging**). Pull with great effort or violently; make vigorous pull *at*; tow (vessel) by means of tugboat. ~ *n.* 1. Tugging, violent pull; ~ **of war**, decisive contest, struggle for supremacy; athletic contest between two teams hauling on rope, each team trying to pull other over line marked between them. 2. Trace, various other parts of harness; any chain, strap, or rope used for pulling. 3. (also **tug´boat**) Small, stoutly built, powerful vessel used to tow other vessels. **tug´ger** *n.*

Tui·ler·ies (twē´lerēz; *Fr.* twēlrē´). Royal palace on N. bank of Seine in Paris, begun 1564 by

Catherine de Médicis and later joined by wings to Louvre; destroyed by fire 1871; ~ **Gardens**, grounds of the former palace, now a public park.

tu·i·tion (tōoǐsh´on, -tū-) *n.* Teaching, instruction, esp. as thing to be paid for; fee for this. **tu·i´tion·al, tu·i´tion·ar·y** *adjs.*

tu·la·re·mi·a, tu·la·rae·mi·a (tōolerē´mēa) *ns.* Severe infectious bacterial disease of rodents, esp. rabbits, transmitted to man by contact with flesh of diseased animals or by insect bites and characterized by aches, irregular fever for several weeks, and inflamed lymph glands; also called rabbit fever. **tu·la·re´mic** *adj.*

tu·lip (tōo´lǐp, tū´-) *n.* (Flower of) bulbous spring-flowering plant of genus *Tulipa*, esp. any of the numerous cultivated varieties, with showy bell-shaped or cup-shaped flowers of various colors and markings; ~ **orchid**, plant (*Cattleya citrina*) that grows in trees of tropical Amer., having single tuliplike yellow flower with white edges; ~ **tree**, large N. Amer. tree (*Liriodendron tulipifera*) with large greenish-yellow tuliplike flowers and soft white wood; any of various other trees with tuliplike flowers, as species of *Magnolia* etc.; **tu´lipwood**, light ornamental wood used for cabinetwork etc., of

tulip tree; any of various colored and striped woods or trees producing these. [Turk. *tülbend-(lale)* turban (tulip)]

tulle (tōol) *n.* Thin soft fine silk, nylon, etc. net, used for dresses, veils, etc. [Fr., name of town]

Tul·ly (tŭl´ē). Familiar name for Marcus Tullius CICERO.

tum·ble (tŭm´bel) *v.* (**-bled, -bling**). 1. (Cause to) fall, esp. helplessly or violently; roll, toss, wallow; move in headlong or blundering fashion; overthrow, demolish; be overthrown, fall into ruin; handle roughly, disorder, rumple, disarrange by tossing; (fig.) stumble, blunder (*on, into*); ~ **to**, understand, grasp (esp. something hidden or not clearly expressed). 2. Perform leaps, somersaults, and other acrobatic feats; (of spaceship etc.) turn end over end in flight. 3. **tum´blebug**, dung beetle that rolls up balls of dung in which to lay its eggs; **tum´bledown**, falling or fallen into ruin, dilapidated; **tum´bleweed**, any of various plants that in late summer are broken off and blown along by wind in light globular rolling mass. **tumble** *n.* Fall; tumbled condition, confused or tangled heap.

tum·bler (tŭm´bler) *n.* (esp.) 1. One who does somersaults, handsprings, etc., acrobat. 2. Variety of domestic pigeon turning over and over backward in flight. 3. Kind of tapering cylindrical or barrel-shaped drinking cup or (now usu.) glass without handle or foot, orig. with rounded or pointed bottom so that it would not stand upright, now with flat usu. heavy bottom. 4. Pivoted plate through which mainspring acts on hammer of gun-lock; pivoted piece in lock that must be moved into proper position by key etc. before lock can be opened; any of various mechanisms or parts, as projecting piece on revolving shaft for operating another piece, movable part of tumbler gear, revolving barrel for washing hides, etc. 5. ~ **gear**, gear with one or more idle wheels on swinging frame for producing reverse motion.

tum·bling (tŭm′blĭng) **barrel.** Rotating drum in which small articles are cleaned and polished by attrition.

tum·brel, tum·bril (tŭm′brel) *ns.* 1. Dump cart, esp. for dung. 2. Cart in which condemned persons were carried to the guillotine during the French Revolution. 3. (archaic) Ammunition cart.

tu·me·fy (tōō′mefī, tū′-) *v.* (-**fied, -fy·ing**). (Cause to) swell; make, become, tumid, turgid, or bombastic. **tu·me·fac·tion** (tōōmefăk′shon, tū-) *n.*

tu·mes·cent (tōōmĕs′ent, tū-) *adj.* Swelling up, becoming tumid. **tu·mes′cence** *n.*

tu·mid (tōō′mĭd, tū′-) *adj.* Swollen, swelling, morbidly affected with swelling; inflated, turgid, bombastic. **tu′mid·ly** *adv.* **tu·mid·i·ty** (tōōmĭd′ĭtē, tū-) *n.*

tum·my (tŭm′ē) *n.* (pl. -**mies**). (esp. nursery) Stomach.

tu·mor (tōō′mer, tū′-) *n.* Abnormal or morbid swelling, overgrowth; BENIGN ~, MALIGNANT ~: see these words. **tu′mor·ous** *adj.*

tu·mult (tōō′mult, tū′-) *n.* Commotion of a multitude, esp. with confused cries and uproar, public disturbance, riot, insurrection; commotion, agitation, disorderly or noisy movement, confused and violent emotion. **tu·mul·tu·ous** (tōōmŭl′chōōus, tū-) *adj.* **tu·mul′tu·ous·ly** *adv.* **tu·mul′tu·ous·ness** *n.*

tun (tŭn) *n.* Large cask or barrel for wine, beer, etc.; measure of capacity, usu. 252 wine gallons.

tu·na (tōō′na) *n.* (pl. -**nas**, collect. -**na**). Any of various large fishes of the family *Scombridae* found in tropical and temperate seas; **yellowfin** ~, an albacore, *Thunnus albacares.*

tun·a·ble (tōō′nabel, tū′-): see TUNE.

tun·dra (tŭn′dra) *n.* Vast level treeless region of N. Europe, Asia, and N. Amer., with arctic climate and vegetation (chiefly mosses and lichens with dwarf shrubs etc.).

tune (tōōn, tūn) *n.* Rhythmical succession of musical tones, air, melody with or without harmony; being in proper pitch, correct intonation in singing or instrumental music; harmony or accordance in respect to vibrations other than those of sound; **call the** ~, have control of events; **change one's** ~, sing another tune, assume a different style of language or manner,

*The **tulip** was first brought to western Europe from Constantinople in 1556. Within 100 years tulip-breeding became an obsession and very large sums were paid for a bulb.*

*Though it may appear desolate, such as here in the Rocky Mountains National Park, **tundra** is home to a wide variety of plant and animal life.*

e.g. change from insolent to respectful tone; **in, out of** ~, in or out of the proper pitch or correct intonation; in or out of order or proper condition; (not) correctly adjusted; in or out of harmony (*with*); **to the** ~ **of**, to the (considerable or exorbitant) amount or sum of; **tune′smith,** (colloq.) composer or arranger of popular music; **tune-up** (*n.*), adjusting of engine to improve operating efficiency. **tune**

*Native to the eastern U.S.A. a **tulip-tree** can attain a height of 200 ft. and a trunk diameter of 12 ft. The timber was used for cabinet-making and was known as whitewood or yellow poplar.*

v. (**tuned, tun·ing**). Adjust tones of (musical instrument) to standard of pitch, put in tune; attune, bring into accord or harmony; bring into proper or desirable condition; adjust (engine etc.) to run smoothly and efficiently, (radio receiver) to desired wavelength etc.; ~ **in**, adjust (radio receiver) to receive transmission; ~ **out**, cut off (radio signal) by tuning receiver; ~ **up**, bring (instrument) up to proper pitch, adjust instruments for playing together; bring (engine etc.) into most efficient working order by esp. fine adjustments. **tun′a·ble**, **tune′a·ble** *adjs.* **tun·a·bil·i·ty** (tōōnabïl′ītē, tū-) *n.* **tun′a·bly** *adv.*

tune·ful (tōōn′ful, tūn′-) *adj.* Melodious, musical. **tune′ful·ly** *adv.* **tune′ful·ness** *n.*

tune·less (tōōn′lïs, tūn′-) *adj.* Untuneful, unmusical; not in tune; songless, silent. **tune′less·ly** *adv.* **tune′less·ness** *n.*

tun·er (tōō′ner, tū′-) *n.* 1. (esp.) One whose occupation is to tune pianos or organs. 2. Electronic circuit or similar device in radio receiver that selects signals of given frequency for amplifying and converting to sound.

tung·sten (tŭng′sten) *n.* (chem.) Heavy steel-gray ductile metallic element, melting only at a very high temperature, occurring in combination in wolfram and other minerals, and used for electric light filaments, electric contacts, spark-plug points, hard steel alloys, etc.; symbol W (*wolfram*), at. no. 74, at. wt. 183.85. **tung·sten·ic** (tŭng-stĕn′ïk), **tung′stic** *adjs.* [Swed.

Above: An oasis in the southern part of **Tunisia** *which borders the Sahara. The main exports are phosphates and crude oil. There is a fertile region in the north bounding the sea.*

tung heavy, *sten* stone]

tung (tŭng) **tree.** Subtropical Asian tree (*Aleurites fordii*) widely cultivated for its seeds, which yield tung oil, used in paints, varnishes, etc.

tu·nic (tōō′nïk, tū′-) *n.* 1. Ancient Greek and Roman short-sleeved body garment reaching almost to knees. 2. Close-fitting short coat of police or military uniform. 3. Woman's loose garment for upper part of body; belted frock worn by women and children at games. 4. (anat., zool.) Membranous sheath or lining of organ or part; (bot.) integument of seed etc.

tu·ni·cate (tōō′nïkït, -kāt, tū′-) *n.* Member of the subphylum Urochordata, having body enclosed in a hard test and, at least in larval stage, a notochord. ~ *adj.* 1. (zool.) Enclosed in a sheath; of the tunicates. 2. (bot.) Consisting of a series of concentric layers, as a bulb.

tun·ing (tōō′nïng, tū′-) **fork.** Small two-pronged steel instrument giving definite musical note of constant pitch when struck.

Tu·nis (tōō′nïs, tū′-). Seaport and capital of Tunisia, in the NE. part on the Mediterranean.

Tu·ni·sia (tōōnē′zha, -sha, -nïzh′a, -nïsh′a). Republic in N. Africa between Algeria and Libya; formerly a French protectorate;

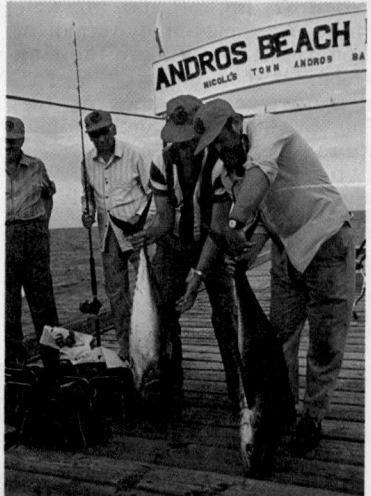

Big game fishermen with their catch of **tunny** *or tuna in the Bahamas. These specimens are small but the larger species may weigh up to 1800 lb. The smaller ones are canned for eating.*

independent 1956; capital, Tunis. **Tu·ni′sian** *adj. & n.*

tun·nel (tŭn′el) *n.* Subterranean passage under hill, river, roadway, etc.; subterranean passage dug by burrowing animal; level or nearly level passage in mine etc.; ~ **of love**, amusement park ride made up of dark, narrow tube through which travel small boats or cars, usu. occupied by couples; ~ **vision**, vision defective in lateral directions. **tunnel** *v.* (**-neled, -nel·ing**). Make tunnel, make tunnel through. **tun′nel·er** *n.*

Turbans *are worn today by several religious groups, including Sikhs and Muslims. In the latter group, however, this has not been an obligation since the early 19th century.*

Below: Cross-section of the **Great St. Bernard Tunnel** *showing how the air within this 7.25 mile road beneath Mont Blanc is kept fresh and how exhaust fumes are extracted.*

fresh-air channels

foul-air channel

lighting and power cables

fresh-air distribution channel

drainage channels

oil pipeline

tun·ny (tŭn´ē) *n.* (pl. **-nies,** collect. **-ny**). (chiefly Brit.) Tuna.

tu·pe·lo (tōō´pelō) *n.* (pl. **-los**). Any of various large N. Amer. trees of genus *Nyssa*, growing in swamps or on river banks in southern U.S.; wood of this.

tur·ban (tẽr´ban) *n.* Oriental men's headdress of Muslim origin consisting of cap with long band or scarf of linen, cotton, or silk wound around it; woman's hat of scarf wound or twisted around. [Turk. *tülbend*]

tur·bid (tẽr´bĭd) *adj.* Muddy, thick, not clear; (fig.) confused, disordered. **tur´bid·ly** *adv.* **tur·bid·i·ty** (tẽrbĭd´ĭtē), **tur´bid·ness** *ns.*

tur·bi·nate (tẽr´bĭnĭt, -nāt), **tur·bi·nat·ed** (tẽr´bĭnātĭd) *adjs.* (of shell) Spiral with whorls decreasing rapidly in size; (bot.) inversely conical; ~ **bone,** (anat.) one of scroll-like bones of the nose.

tur·bine (tẽr´bĭn, -bīn) *n.* Motor in which rotary motion is produced by a fluid (water, steam, gas, etc.) impinging directly upon a series of vanes on the circumference of a revolving cylinder or disk, used to drive a ship, aircraft, generators for electric power, etc.

turbo- *prefix.* Turbine, in compounds forming the name of machines driven by a turbine, or that are themselves turbines, as **tur´bofan; tur´bojet,** power unit of a jet-propelled aircraft; aircraft with turbojet engine; jet produced by a gas turbine.

tur·bot (tẽr´bot) *n.* (pl. **-bots,** collect. **-bot**). Large European flat fish (*Scophthalmus maximus*) much esteemed as food; (loosely) any of various similar fish.

tur·bu·lent (tẽr´byulent) *adj.* Disturbed, in commotion, disorderly, troubled, stormy; tumultuous, unruly, violent. **tur´bu·lent·ly** *adv.* **tur´bu·lence** *n.*

Tur·co·man = TURKOMAN.

turd (tẽrd) *n.* (vulg.) (Lump or piece of) excrement.

tu·reen (tōōrēn´, tyōō-) *n.* Deep covered dish from which soup is served.

turf (tẽrf) *n.* (pl. **turfs, turves**). Covering of grass etc. with matted roots, forming surface of grassland; sod; (slang) area defended by street gang as its own private territory; **the ~,** grassy course used for horse racing; institution, action, or practice of horse racing. **turf´y** *adj.* (**turf·i·er, turf·i·est**). **turf** *v.t.* Cover (ground) with turf.

Tur·ge·nev (tōōrgĕn´yĕf), **Ivan Sergeevich** (1818–83). Russian novelist; author of *Fathers and Sons, Virgin Soil,* etc.

tur·gid (tẽr´jĭd) *adj.* Swollen, distended, puffed out; (fig., of language) pompous, bombastic. **tur´gid·ly** *adv.* **tur·gid·i·ty** (tẽr-

Inhabitants of Iran and the southern U.S.S.R., **Turkoman** horse dealers are renowned, as are the rugs made by their nomadic groups and then sold in the cities.

Right: A coppersmith at Istanbul reflects the traditional crafts of **Turkey.** The nation is mainly agricultural with large exports of tobacco, cotton, nuts and raisins. It is also a major source of chrome and other minerals.

jĭd′ītē), **tur·ges·cence** (tẽrjĕs′ens) ns. **tur·ges′cent** adj.

tur·gor (tẽr′ger) n. (bot.) Rigidity due to uptake of water into living cells or tissues.

Turk (tẽrk) n. 1. Native of Turkey; (hist.) native or inhabitant of the Ottoman Empire. 2. Member of a people speaking a Turkic language.

Tur·key (tẽr′kē). Country of Asia Minor and Europe, formerly part of the Ottoman Empire, declared a republic in 1923; capital (since 1923), Ankara.

tur·key (tẽr′kē) n. (pl. **-keys,** collect. **-key**). Large gallinaceous bird of the Amer. genus *Meleagris,* with handsome plumage and naked wattled head, esp. *M. gallopavo,* found domesticated in Mexico in 16th c. and highly esteemed as table fowl, esp. for Thanksgiving feast; ~ **cock,** male of turkey; ~ **trot,** ragtime ballroom dance in vogue during World War I; ~ **vulture,** Amer. carrion vulture (*Cathartes aura*) with dark plumage and naked reddish head and neck (also ~ **buzzard**). [short for *turkey cock,* orig. guinea fowl, so-called f. being orig. imported through Turkey]

Tur·ki (tẽr′kē, toor′-) adj. & n. (Of, belonging to) a group of Ural-Altaic languages and peoples, including Turkish. **Tur′kic** adj.

Turk·ish (tẽr′kĭsh) adj. Of Turkey or the Turks; Turkic; ~ **bath,** steam bath, inducing perspiration, after which body is washed, massaged, etc.; ~ **delight,** candy made of lumps of jelly flavored with fruit juice and dusted with sugar; ~ **tobacco,** aromatic tobacco grown esp. in Turkey and Greece; ~ **towel,** rough towel with a long nap usu. of uncut loops. **Turkish** n. Language of Turkey.

Turk·man (tẽrk′man) n. (pl. **-men**). Native of Turkmenistan. **Turk·me·ni·an** (tẽrkmē′nean) adj. **Turk·men** (tẽrk′men) n. Turkoman language.

Turk·me·ni·stan (tẽrkmĕnĭstăn´, -stahn´). Constituent republic (properly *Turkmen Soviet Socialist Republic*) of U.S.S.R. lying between the Caspian Sea and Afghanistan; capital, Ashkhabad.

Tur·ko·man, Tur·co·man (tēr´koman) ns. (pl. **-men**). Member of a group of tribes of E. Turkic stock, living chiefly in Turkmenistan and parts of Iran and the Caucasus; Ural-Altaic language of these tribes; ~ **carpet, rug**, soft richly colored carpet made by them. [Pers. *turkumān* Turklike person]

tur·mer·ic (tēr´merĭk) *n.* East Indian herb (*Curcuma longa*) of ginger family; pungent aromatic rhizome of this, used as condiment, esp. as chief ingredient in curry powder and as yellow dye.

tur·moil (tēr´moil) *n.* Agitation, commotion, trouble.

turn (tērn) *v.* I. Move on or as on axis; give rotary motion to, receive such motion; shape (clay on wheel) to form pottery; execute (somersault etc.) with rotary motion; change from one side to another; invert, reverse; (fig.) revolve mentally; ~ **the tables**, (on person, or absolute) reverse relations (between), esp. pass from inferior to superior position; ~ **the tide**, (fig.) reverse trend of events. 2. Give new direction to, take new direction; adapt, be adapted); ~ **one's hand to**, undertake (task of new kind). 3. Move to other side of, go around, flank; pass around (*flank* etc. of army) so as to attack from flank or rear; cause to go, send, put.   4. Change in nature, form, condition, etc.; esp. change for the worse; (cause to) become; (of milk) (cause to) become sour. 5. Shape (object, material) in lathe; (of material) lend itself to treatment in lathe; give (esp. elegant) form to. 6. ~ **about**, turn so as to face in a new direction; ~ **against**, become hostile to; ~ **around**, face about; change to opposite opinion, state of mind, etc.; (of ship) discharge cargo and be ready for new voyage; ~ **down**, fold down; place upside down or face downward; reduce flame of (gas, lamp, etc.) by turning tap etc.; reject (proposal, offer, etc.); ~ **in**, fold inward; incline inward; (colloq.) go to bed; ~ **off**, check flow of (water, electricity, etc.) by turning tap, switch, etc.; (slang) cause to lose interest; ~ **on**, allow passage to (water, electricity, etc.) by turning tap etc.; depend upon; face hostilely, become hostile to; (slang) begin using illegal drugs; (slang) introduce to illegal drugs; (slang) arouse interest of; ~ **out**, expel; (cause to) point or incline outward; produce; put (contents) out of room, pocket, etc.; appear publicly; discharge from employment; extin-

guish (light) by turning switch etc.; (cause to) assemble for duty etc.; get out of bed; be found, prove to be so; ~ **over**, reverse, invert; (cause to) fall over, upset, hand over, make over, transfer; do business to amount of; ~ **to**, apply oneself to, set about; begin work; ~ **up**, turn (playing card) face upward; disinter; appear; happen; fold (cloth, hem, etc.); uncover, find; increase; ~ **upon**, become hostile to (someone). 7. **turn´buckle**, coupling with internal screw thread(s) for connecting metal rods, regulating their length, etc.; **turn button**, small pivoted bar engaging with catch, edge of door, etc.; **turn´coat**, one who changes his principles or party; renegade; **turn´down**, turned-down part of anything; (*adj.*) with upper part turned down; **turn´key**, (pl. **-keys**), jailer; one in charge of keys of prison; **turn´off**, small road branching off from larger one, esp. exit ramp from main highway; **turn´out**, (esp.) assemblage, muster; (style of) equipment, outfit, array; **turn´over**, kind of pie or tart in which filling is laid on half of rolled-out pastry and other half is turned over it; amount of money or merchandise turned over in business; **turn´pike**, (hist.) spiked barrier across road or passage, as defense against attack; (hist.) toll gate; (hist.) road with gates for

collection of tolls; main road, highway; **turn´spit**, spit; (hist., freq. contempt.) man or boy who turned spit upon which meat was cooked; **turn´stile**, post with four radiating arms revolving horizontally as person passes through, in gateway, door, etc., similar device with mechanism for registering number passing through; **turn´table**, revolving platform, table, stand, etc., esp. one for reversing railroad cars or other wheeled vehicles; circular horizontal rotating platform that supports record or phonograph.

turn *n.´* I. Turning; rotation, esp. single revolution of wheel etc.; (single) coil or twist. 2. (mus.) Ornament consisting of note above principal note, note itself, note below and note itself, performed instead of principal note or after it. 3. Change of direction or course, change of position by rotary movement; curved or bent part of anything, bend, angle; turning back (esp. ~ **of the tide**). 4. Change, alteration; change of color, condition, etc.; (colloq.) momentary shock caused by sudden alarm etc. 5. Act of good or ill will, (**good, bad,** ~, service, disservice); attack of illness, faintness, etc. 6. Opportunity, occasion, privilege, obligation, etc., coming successively to each of several persons, etc.; public appearance on stage before or after others; **in** ~, in succession ; ~ **(and** ~**) about,** in turn. 7. Character, tendency, disposition, formation. 8. **at every** ~, con-

*The ocellated **turkey** is found only in Central America and has brighter plumage than the common variety of North America. This bird has minor differences in behavior from the others.*

tinually; **done to a** ~, done (esp. cooked) to just the right degree; **out of** ~, not in correct order; at an unsuitable time or in an unsuitable manner; **take** ~**s**, work etc. alternately.

turn·er[1] (tēr'ner) *n.* (esp.) One who works with a lathe. **turn'er·y** *n.* (pl. **-er·ies**). Use of lathe; objects fashioned on lathe; turner's workshop.

turn·er[2] (tēr'ner) *n.* Gymnast or tumbler, esp. one who belongs to a turnverein.

Tur·ner (tēr'ner), **Nat** (1800–1831). Black Amer. slave leader; leader of slave uprising, Nat Turner's Rebellion, 1831.

turn·ing (tēr'nĭng) *n.* (esp.) 1. Use of, art of using, lathe. 2. Place where road, path, etc., turns or turns off from another; such road; ~ **point**, point at which decisive change takes place.

tur·nip (tēr'nĭp) *n.* Either of two biennial cruciferous plants (*Brassica rapa* and *B. napobrassica*) with fleshy globular and spheroid root, toothed leaves, and yellow flowers; root of these, used as vegetable.

turn·ver·ein (tērn'verīn) *n.* Club of turners or gymnasts.

tur·pen·tine (tēr'pentīn) *n.* Yellowish viscous liquid oleoresins, usu. solidifying on exposure (many varieties acc. to source, most having the same composition, $C_{10}H_{16}$), obtained from various coniferous trees; (also **oil of** ~) colorless or yellowish volatile inflammable oil, of pungent smell and taste, distilled from turpentines and used in mixing paints and varnishes etc.

tur·pi·tude (tēr'pĭtood, -tūd) *n.* Baseness, depravity, wickedness.

turps (tērps) *n.* (colloq.) (Oil of) turpentine.

tur·quoise, tur·quois (tēr'koiz, -kwoiz) *ns.* Opaque or translucent sky blue or blue-green hydrous aluminum phosphate found esp. in Persia and valued as gem; (also ~ **blue**) brilliant greenish-blue color of turquoise. [OF. (*pierre*) *turquoise* Turkish (stone)]

tur·ret (tēr'ĭt, tŭr'-) *n.* Small or subordinate tower, esp. rounded addition to angle of building, freq.

commencing at some height above ground; (mil., nav.) towerlike armored usu. revolving structure in which guns are mounted in fort or tank or (usu.) warship; structure housing guns in aircraft; (mech.) rotating holder for various dies or cutting tools in lathe, drill, etc. **tur'ret·ed** *adj.*

tur·tle (tēr'tel) *n.* (pl. **-tles**, collect. **-tle**). Reptile of any of the marine species (in U.S. also freshwater species) of the order Chelonia resembling tortoise but with limbs compressed into flippers or paddles; flesh of certain turtles as food, much used for soup; **turn** ~, turn over, capsize; **tur'tleback, tur'-tledeck**, arched structure over part of deck of vessel to protect it from heavy sea; **tur'tleneck**, high close-fitting neck of knitted garment.

tur·tle·dove (tēr'teldŭv) *n.* 1. Wild dove of genus *Streptopelia*, esp. the common European *S. turtur* with cinnamon-brown plumage and white-tipped tail feathers, noted for its soft cooing and affection for its mate. 2. = MOURNING DOVE. 3. Sweetheart.

tur·tle·head (tēr'telhĕd) *n.* Any of several plants (genus *Chelone*), esp. *C. glabra* of eastern N. Amer., having tubular white or pink flowers; also called snakehead.

Tus·can (tŭs'kan) *adj.* Of Tuscany; (archit.) of the Tuscan order, simplest of the classical orders. ~ *n.* Native, inhabitant, language, of Tuscany.

Tus·ca·ny (tŭs'kanē). Region of W. central Italy.

Tus·ca·ro·ra (tŭskarōr'a, -rōr'a) *n.* (pl. **-ras**, collect. **-ra**). Indian of tribe orig. of North Carolina, but since admission to Iroquois confederacy living mainly in New York.

tush[1] (tŭsh) *int., n.,* & *v.i.* (archaic) (Make) exclamation of impatient contempt.

tush[2] (tŭsh) *n.* Long pointed tooth, esp. horse's canine tooth; small or stunted tusk in some Indian elephants.

tusk (tŭsk) *n.* Long pointed tooth projecting beyond mouth in certain animals, as elephant, wild

boar, etc.; tusklike thing, as long protruding tooth, kind of tenon, etc. ~ *v.t.* Dig (*up*), tear, wound, with tusk; furnish with tusks. **tusked** *adj.*

tus·sle (tŭs'el) *n.* & *v.i.* (**-sled, -sling**). Struggle, scuffle.

tus·sock (tŭs'ok) *n.* Tuft, clump, small hillock, of grass. ~ **moth**, moth with larva covered with long tufts of hair. **tus'sock·y** *adj.*

Tut·ankh·a·men (tootahnkah'-men) (14th c B.C.). Egyptian king of XVIIIth dynasty who died at age of 18; successor and son-in-law of Akhnaton; his tomb at Karnak, containing remarkable treasures, was excavated in 1922.

tu·te·lage (too'telĭj, tū'-) *n.* Guardianship, being under this; instruction, tuition. **tu'te·lar** *adj.*

tu·te·lar·y (too'telĕrē, tū'-) *adj.* Serving as protector, guardian, or patron, esp. of particular person, place, etc.; of a guardian, protective.

tu·tor (too'ter, tū-) *n.* 1. Private teacher, esp. one having general charge of person's education; (in some Brit. universities) graduate (usu. fellow of a college) directing studies of undergraduates assigned to him; college teacher ranking below instructor. 2. (Rom. law) Guardian of a minor. **tu'tor·age, tu'tor·ship** *ns.* **tu·to·ri·al** (tootōr'ēal, -tōr'-, tū-) *adj.* Of a tutor. ~ *n.* Period of individual instruction given to small group or single student. **tutor** *v.* Act as tutor (to); exercise restraint over, subject to discipline.

tut·ti-frut·ti (too'tēfroo'tē) *n.* & *adj.* (Preserve) made of or flavored with various fruits. [It., = "all fruits"]

tu·tu (too'too) *n.* Dancer's short skirt made of layers of stiffened frills.

tu-whit to-whoo (too hwĭt' too hwoo'). (Make) cry of owl. [imit. of cry of owl]

tux·e·do (tŭksē'dō) *n.* Dinner jacket; man's evening dress including this. [name of fashionable country club at *Tuxedo* Park, N.Y.]

TV (tēvē') *abbrev.* (pl. **TVs, TV's**). Television; terminal velocity.

TVA, T.V.A. *abbrevs.* Tennessee Valley Authority.

twad·dle (twŏd'el) *n.* & *v.i.* (**-dled, -dling**). (Indulge in) senseless, silly, or trifling talk or writing, (talk) nonsense. **twad'-dler** *n.*

Left: The **green turtle,** *Chelonia mydas. Like all marine turtles, the green turtle only comes ashore to lay its eggs.*

The **turret** *of a warship is an armored, revolving structure, often with the purpose of protecting the breech of a large gun.*

DO NOT CLIMB
ON TURRET

twain (twān) *adj.* & *n.* (archaic) Two.

Twain (twān), **Mark.** Pseudonym of Samuel Langhorne Clemens (1835–1910), Amer. humorist, author of *Tom Sawyer* (1876), *Huckleberry Finn* (1884), etc. [call of leadsmen taking soundings on Mississippi where Clemens served as a pilot; = second mark on cable, i.e. 2 fathoms]

twang (twăng) *n.* Sharp ringing sound (as) of taut string of musical instrument or bow when plucked; nasal intonation; distinctive, esp. local, peculiarity of pronunciation. ~ *v.* (Cause to) make twanging sound; play on stringed instrument; utter, speak, with twang. **twang′y** *adj.*

tweak (twēk) *n.* Twist, sharp pull, pinch. ~ *v.t.* Seize and pull sharply with twisting movement, pull at with jerk, twitch.

tweed (twēd) *n.* Twilled woolen (or woolen mixture) cloth of usu. rough surface, dyed, freq. in several colors, before weaving. **tweed′y** *adj.* (**tweed·i·er, tweed·i·est**). [formerly a trademark originating in a misreading of *tweel*, Sc. form of TWILL, influenced by name of river Tweed, Scotland]

twee·dle·dum and twee·dle·-dee (twēdeldŭm′ an twēdeldē′). Two persons or things differing only or chiefly in name, orig. applied to the composers Handel and Bononcini in a satire by John Byrom containing the lines "Strange all this Difference should be Twixt Tweedledum and Tweedledee!"

'tween (twēn) *prep.* Between; ~ **decks,** (space) between decks.

tweet (twēt) *n.* & *v.i.* (Utter) note of small bird.

tweez·ers (twē′zerz) *n.pl.* (also **pair of** ~) Small pincerlike instrument for taking up small objects, plucking out hairs, etc. **tweeze** *v.t.* (**tweezed, tweez·ing**). Use, pull out with, tweezers.

twelfth (twĕlfth) *adj.* Next after 11th; **T ~-day, -night,** 12th day after Christmas, Jan. 6, feast of Epiphany, formerly last day of Christmas festivities and observed as time of merrymaking. **twelfth** *n.* Twelfth part (see PART[1] sense 1); twelfth thing etc.

twelve (twĕlv) *adj.* Amounting to 12. ~ *n.* One more than 11 (12, xii, or XII).

twen·ty (twĕn′tē) *adj.* Amounting to 20. ~ *n.* Cardinal number, twice 10 (20, xx, or XX); set of 20 things or persons; **twenties,** numbers etc. from 20 to 29; these years of century or life. **twen′ti·eth** *adj.* & *n.* **twen′ty·fold** *adj.* & *adv.*

twice (twīs) *adv.* Two times; on two occasions; doubly, in double degree or quantity.

Twilight *creates many dazzling effects, such as here on the St. Lawrence Seaway near Massena, New York State, where the subtly diffused light plays on the water.*

twid·dle (twĭd′el) *n.* Slight twirl, quick twist; twirled mark or sign. ~ *v.* (**-dled, -dling**). Trifle (with); twirl idly, play with idly or absently; ~ **one's fingers, thumbs,** keep turning them idly around each other (for lack of occupation); be idle. **twid′dly** *adj.* **twid′dler** *n.*

twig (twĭg) *n.* Small shoot or branch of tree or plant.

twi·light (twī′līt) *n.* Light diffused by reflection of sun's rays between daybreak and sunrise or (usu.) sunset and dark; period of this; faint light; (fig.) condition of imperfect knowledge, understanding, etc.; **T ~ of the Gods,** (transl. Ger. *Götterdämmerung*; Icel. *ragna rökkr,* orig. *ragna rök* judgment of the gods) in Scand. and Ger. myth., destruction of the gods and the world in conflict with the powers of evil; hence (fig.) complete downfall of a regime etc.; ~ **sleep,** (formerly) partial narcosis for dulling pains of childbirth.

twi·lit (twī′lĭt) *adj.* Dimly illuminated (as) by twilight.

twill (twĭl) *n.* (Textile fabric with) surface of parallel diagonal ribs produced by passing filling threads over 1 and under 2 or more (not 1 as in plain weaving) warp threads. ~ *v.t.* Weave with twill (esp. in past part.). **twilled**

adj. [Sc. and north. variant of obs. *twilly,* OE. *twili,* f. OHG. *zwîlîh,* after L. *bilix* (*licium* thread)]

twin (twĭn) *adj.* Forming, being one of, a closely related pair, esp. of children born together; (bot.) growing in pairs; consisting of 2 closely connected and similar parts; **twin′flower,** species of *Linnaea* (*L. borealis* of northern Europe and Asia and *L. americana* of northern N. Amer.), prostrate plants with fragrant flowers growing in pairs; **twin-screw,** (esp., of steamer) having two screw propellers on separate shafts and revolving in opposite directions. **twin** *n.* One of two children or young carried simultaneously in uterus and born at short interval (FRATERNAL, IDENTICAL, ~ **s**: see these words); each of closely related pair; exact counterpart of person or thing; **T ~ Cities,** Minneapolis and St. Paul, Minnesota, in the SE. part, in the N. central U.S.; **the Twins**: see GEMINI. **twin** *v.* (**twinned, twin·ning**). Bear twins; join intimately together, couple, pair.

twine (twīn) *n.* Strong thread or string of two or more strands of hemp, cotton, etc., twisted together, used for sewing coarse materials, tying packages, making nets, etc.; twining or trailing stem, spray, etc.; coil, twist. ~ *v.* (**twined, twin·ing**). Twist (strands) together to form twine, make (thread) thus; form (garland etc.) by interlacing; wreathe, clasp, twist; coil, wind; (of plant) grow in twisting or spiral manner.

twinge (twĭnj) *n.* Sharp darting pain. ~ *v.* (**twinged, twing·ing**).

twi·night (twī′nīt) *adj.* (baseball) Of, pertaining to, designating, doubleheader that starts late in the afternoon and continues into the evening under lights. **twi′night·er** *n.* A twinight baseball game.

twin·kle (twĭng′kel) *v.* (**-kled, -kling**). Shine with rapidly intermittent light, sparkle, glitter; emit (light etc.) thus; wink, blink, quiver; move to and fro, in and out, etc., rapidly, flit, flicker; **in the twinkling of an eye, in a twinkling,** in an instant. **twinkle** *n.* Wink, blink; twitch, quiver; intermittent or transient gleam. **twin′kler** *n.*

twirl (twerl) *v.* Revolve rapidly, spin, whirl; turn (one's thumbs etc.) around and around idly, twiddle; twist, coil. ~ *n.* Whirling, twirling; anything that twirls, curved line, whorl of shell, etc. **twirl′er** *n.*

twist (twĭst) *v.* Wind (strands etc.) one about another; form (rope etc.) thus; interweave; give spiral form to (rod, column, etc.) as by rotating ends in opposite directions; receive, grow in, spiral form; cause (ball, esp. in baseball) to rotate while following curved path; wrench out of natural shape, distort. ~ *n.* 1. Thread, rope, etc., made by winding two or more strands etc. about one another; kinds of strong silk thread and of cotton yarn; roll of bread, tobacco, etc., in form of twist. 2. Act of twisting, condition of being twisted; manner or degree in which thing is twisted; peculiar tendency of mind, character, etc.; twisting strain, torque; angle through which thing is twisted; dance involving rhythmic gyrations. **twist′a·ble** *adj.*

twit (twĭt) *v.t.* (**twit·ted, twit·ting**). Reproach, upbraid, taunt.

twitch (twĭch) *v.* Pull with light jerk, pull at, jerk at, esp. to call attention; (of features, muscles, etc.) move or contract spasmodically. ~ *n.* Sudden sharp pull or tug, jerk; sudden involuntary, usu. slight, contraction. **twitch′er** *n.*

twitch (twĭch) **grass**: see COUCH².

twit·ter (twĭt′er) *v.* (of bird) Utter succession of light tremulous notes, chirp continuously (freq. fig., of person); utter, express, thus. ~ *n.* Twittering; state of tremulous excitement.

'twixt (twĭkst) *prep.* (poet.) Betwixt.

two (tōō) *adj.* Amounting to 2; ~ **or three**, a few; **two-bagger, -base hit**, (baseball) hit enabling batter to reach second base; double; **two-bit**, costing 25 cents; (fig.) petty; **two-by-four**, 2 (inches,

feet) by 4, hence (colloq.) small, cramped; (*n.*) length of lumber 2 by 4 inches before trimming and, usu., approximately 1⅝ inches by 3⅝ inches trimmed; **two-dimensional,** having height and width; (of literary work) superficial, unconvincing; **two-edged,** having two cutting edges; (fig.) cutting both ways, ambiguous; **two-faced,** having two faces; deceitful, insincere; **two′fer,** (colloq.) card or coupon entitling bearer to buy theater tickets etc. at reduced price; **two-fisted,** (colloq.) vigorous; **two′fold,** double, doubly; **two-handed,** wielded with both hands; worked or wielded by hands of two persons; (of card game etc.) for two persons; **twopence** (tŭp′ens), (Brit.) sum of two pence; **two′penny,** (tŭ′penē) (Brit.) worth, costing, twopence; paltry, trifling; **two-piece,** of a suit of clothes or woman's bathingsuit comprising two separate parts; **two-ply,** of two strands, layers, or thicknesses; **two′some,** two people, couple; **two-step,** ballroom dance with sliding steps in ¾ time; **two-time** (*v.t.*) (**-timed, -tim·ing**), (slang) deceive; **two-way,** (esp.) allowing passage of fluid in either of two directions; **two-way switch,**

*A model of **twins** in the uterus. The ones shown may be known as fraternal and result from two eggs being fertilized at the same time. Identical twins come from a single egg which divides.*

device by which electric current can be switched on or off at either of two points. **two** *n.* One more than 1; symbol for this (2, ii, or II); card, die face, or domino with two pips; two o'clock; size etc. indicated by 2; set of two things or persons; **put ~ and ~ together,** draw inference from facts.

twp *abbrev.* Township.

TWX *abbrev.* Teletypewriter exchange.

TX *abbrev.* Texas.

-ty¹ *suffix.* Forming nouns denoting quality or condition (*cruelty, plenty, safety*).

-ty² *suffix.* Tens (*twenty, sixty, ninety,* etc.).

ty·coon (tīkōōn′) *n.* Business magnate. [Jap. *taikun* great lord, title applied by foreigners to shogun of Japan 1854–68 (Chin. *ta* great, *kuin* prince)]

ty·ing (tī′ing): see TIE.

tyke (tīk) *n.* Dog, cur; child, esp. young boy.

Ty·ler (tī′ler), **John** (1790–1862). Tenth president of U.S., 1841–5.

tym·bal = TIMBAL.

tym·pan (tĭm′pan) *n.* 1. Appliance in printing press interposed between platen etc. and sheet to be printed to equalize pressure, in hand presses usu. double frame covered with sheets of parchment or strong linen, with packing of blanket, rubber, etc., between. 2. (archit.) TYMPANUM.

tym·pa·ni = TIMPANI.

pantograph cutting copy of letter in waxed layer

wax core of letter removed

enlarged copy

wax

glass

original artist's letter

copper deposited on sensitized plate

milling cutter

shell filled with type metal

vertical pantograph

steel punch blank

copper shell

finished punch

pattern (¼ size) of original drawing

relief character

punched out matrices

When **type** is made for printing by mechanical methods, it may be cast from copper shells. These are deposited by electrolysis on wax-coated glass on which the letter was originally inscribed. Other methods are also used.

tym·pan·ic (tǐmpǎn´ĭk) *adj*. Of the or a tympanum; resonant when struck; ~ **bone**, bone supporting tympanic membrane; ~ **membrane**, thin membrane closing middle ear and serving to transmit vibrations from air to inner ear.

tym·pa·num (tǐm´panum) *n*. (pl. **-nums, -na** pr. -na). 1. (anat.) Eardrum, middle ear, cavity in temporal bone filled with air, closed externally by tympanic membrane and containing chain of small bones by which sound vibrations are conveyed to inner ear; tympanic membrane; similar membrane in insects covering organ of hearing in leg etc.; (ornith.) bony labyrinth at base of trachea in some ducks with resonant membranes in walls. 2. (archit.) (also **tympan**) Vertical recessed face (usu. triangular) of pediment; space between lintel and arch of door etc., carving etc. on this.

type (tīp) *n*. 1. Person, thing, event, serving as illustration, symbol, or characteristic specimen, of another thing or of a class. 2. General form, character, etc., distinguishing particular class or group; kind, class, as distinguished by particular character. 3. (biol.) Species or genus regarded as most complete example of essential characteristics of genus, family, etc., and from which family etc. is

named. 4. Biblical event regarded as symbolic or as foreshadowing a later one. 5. Object, conception, work of art, serving as model for later artists. 6. Device on either side of medal or coin. 7. Small block, usu. of metal or wood, with raised letter, figure, etc., on its upper surface for use in printing; (collect.) set, supply, kind, of these. 8. **type´casting**, assignment (of actor) in certain type of role because of predisposing characteristics; **type´face**, (impression made by) inked part of type, set of types in one design; **type metal**, alloy of lead, antimony, and tin from which printing types are cast; **type´script**, (matter) written with typewriter; **type´setter**, compositor; composing machine; **type´write** (*v*.) (**-wrote, -writ·ten, -writ·ing**), write with typewriter; **type´writer**, mechanical or electrical machine for writing in characters similar to those of print, the characters being produced by striking the paper through an inked ribbon by steel types arranged on separate rods or on a wheel or ball and actuated by striking corresponding keys on a keyboard. **type** *v*. (**typed, typ·ing**). 1. Be a type of, typify. 2. Determine type or group of, classify acc. to type. 3. Write with typewriter.

-type *comb. form*. 1. Type, example, model (*prototype*). 2. Printing type, photographic proc-

ess (*monotype, daguerreotype*).

ty·phoid (tī´foid) *n*. (also ~ **fever**) Infectious eruptive febrile disease (formerly supposed to be variety of typhus) caused by ~ **bacillus** (*Bacillus typhosis*) and characterized by inflammation of intestines. **ty·phoi·dal** (tīfoi´dal) *adj*.

ty·phoon (tīfoōn´) *n*. Violent cyclonic storm, esp. one occurring in the China seas and adjacent regions. [f. Chin. *tai fung*, dial. forms of *ta* big, *feng* wind]

ty·phus (tī´fus) *n*. Acute contagious fever transmitted to man by body lice or rat fleas infected by *Rickettsia prowazekii*, and characterized by eruption of rose-colored spots, extreme prostration, and usu. delirium. **ty´phous** *adj*.

typ·i·cal (tǐp´ĭkal) *adj*. Serving as type, symbol, or representative specimen, symbolical, emblematic; distinctive, characteristic. **typ´i·cal·ly** *adv*. **typ´i·cal·ness** *n*.

typ·i·fy (tǐp´ĭfī) *v.t*. (**-fied, -fy·ing**). Represent by type or symbol, foreshadow; serve as type or example of. **typ·i·fi·ca·tion** (tǐpǐfĭkā´shon), **typ´i·fi·er** *ns*.

typ·ist (tī´pǐst) *n*. One who uses a typewriter.

ty·po (tī´pō) *n*. (pl. **-pos**). (colloq.) Mistake in printing or typewriting; typographical error.

ty·pog·ra·phy (tīpŏg´rafē) *n*. Art, practice, of printing from types; style, appearance, of printed matter. **ty·pog´ra·pher** *n*. **ty·po·graph·ic** (tīpŏgrǎf´ĭk), **ty·po·graph´i·cal·ly** *adv*.

ty·pol·o·gy (tīpŏl´ojē) *n*. 1. Classification of archaeological remains etc. according to type. 2. Doctrine, interpretation, of biblical types and antitypes, study of these. **ty·po·log·i·cal** (tīpolŏj´ĭkal) *adj*. **ty·po·log´i·cal·ly** *adv*.

ty·ran·ni·cal (tǐrǎn´ĭkal, tī-) *adj*. Acting like, characteristic of, a tyrant; despotic, arbitrary, oppressive, cruel. **ty·ran´ni·cal·ly** *adv*. **ty·ran´ni·cal·ness** *n*.

ty·ran·ni·cide (tǐrǎn´ĭsīd, tī-) *n*. Killer, killing, of tyrant. **ty·ran·ni·cid·al** (tǐrǎnǐsī´dal, tī-) *adj*.

tyr·an·nize (tĭr´anīz) *v.* (**-nized, -niz·ing**). Play the tyrant; rule despotically or cruelly (*over*).

ty·ran·no·saur (tĭrăn´osōr, tī-) **ty·ran·no·saur·us** (tĭrănosōr´us, tī-) *ns.* Fossil dinosaur (*Tyrannosaurus rex*), largest known carnivore, which walked erect on hind feet, of late Cretaceous period of N. Amer.

tyr·an·nous (tĭr´anŭs) *adj.* Ruling or acting tyrannically; oppressive, unjustly severe or cruel. **tyr·an·nous·ly** *adv.*

tyr·an·ny (tĭr´anē) *n.* (pl. **-nies**). 1. Government of, nation ruled by, tyrant or absolute ruler. 2. Oppressive or despotic government; arbitrary or oppressive exercise of power; tyrannical act or behavior.

ty·rant (tīr´ant) *n.* 1. (Gk. hist.) Absolute ruler who seized sovereign power without legal right; (despotic) usurper. 2. Oppressive, unjust, or cruel ruler, despot; person exercising power or authority arbitrarily or cruelly. 3. ~ **flycatcher**, bird of Amer. passerine family Tyrannidae.

Tyre (tīr). (Arab. *Sur*) Ancient seaport of the Phoenicians on Lebanon coast.

Tyr·i·an (tĭr´ēan) *adj.* Of Tyre or its inhabitants; ~ **purple**, purple dye made from shellfish by the Tyrians and exported by them to ancient Greece and Rome. **Tyrian** *n.* Native, inhabitant, of Tyre.

ty·ro, ti·ro (tīr´ō) *ns.* (pl. **-ros**). Beginner or learner in anything, novice.

Tyr·ol, Tir·ol (tĭr´ol, tĭrōl´). Alpine province of W. Austria, the S. part of which was ceded to Italy after World War I. **Tyr·o·lese, Tir·o·lese** (tĭrolēz´, -lēs´) *adjs. & ns.* (pl. **-lese**).

tzar = TSAR.

tzi·gane (tsĭgahn´) *adj.* Of the Hungarian gypsies or their music. ~ *n.* Hungarian gypsy.

John Tyler *served as President from 1841-1845, gaining office after the death of W. H. Harrison. He tended to follow the philosophies of Thomas Jefferson.*

typeslug typebar keybutton typebar linkage keylever paper bail ribbon spool paper bail holder typeguide card holder platen typebar keyboard carriage keylever carriage return and linespace lever space bar shift key

*Although a **typewriter** was designed in 1714, the first exhibited to the public was the Sholes, a U.S. design, in 1876. Since then, despite refinement in the machinery and electrification, the keyboard has remained unchanged.*

The letter **U, u** is derived from the Semitic 'vau' which in turn came from the hieroglyphic horned asp and a Phoenician symbol. The present sound derived from the Greeks who called it upsilon. The Romans used the shape V to signify the sounds for U and W and they were not separated until the 15th century.

Cretan   Archaic Latin   Corinthian

Ionic   Urban Roman   Classical Latin

U, u (ū) (pl. **U's, u's** or **Us, us**). 1. Twenty-first letter of modern English and 20th of ancient Roman alphabet, where it was identical in form and origin with *v*; now representing a vowel sound except after *g*, where it is freq. silent (*guard*), in final *-que*, where it is always silent (*grotesque*), and after *q* in other positions, where it has the value of *w* (*quick, inquest*), as also in various words after *s* and *g* (*persuade, anguish*). 2. Object etc. shaped like U.

U (o͞o) *n.* Burmese title of respect used before man's name.

U *symbol.* Uranium.

U.A.E. *abbrev.* United Arab Emirates.

UAR, U.A.R. *abbrevs.* United Arab Republic.

UAW, U.A.W. *abbrevs.* United Auto Workers.

U·ban·gi (ūbăng′gē, o͞obahng′-gē). River in Africa flowing about 600 mi. (960 km) to the Zaire River and forming part of boundary between Zaire, Democratic Republic of the Congo, and Central African Empire.

u·biq·ui·ty (ūbĭk′wĭtē) *n.* Omnipresence; being everywhere or in many places at the same time. **u·biq′ui·tous** *adj.* **u·biq′ui·tous·ly** *adv.* **u·biq′ui·tous·ness** *n.*

U-boat (ū′bōt) *n.* German submarine. [Ger. *U-Boot*, abbrev. f. *Unterseeboot* submarine]

U-bolt (ū′bōlt) *n.* Bolt in shape of letter U, with threads and nut at each end.

u.c. *abbrev.* Upper case (of print).

ud·der (ŭd′er) *n.* Pendulous baglike organ, having two or more teats, in which milk is secreted in cows and certain other female animals.

UFO, U.F.O. *abbrevs.* (pl. **UFOs, UFO's**). Unidentified flying object.

U·gan·da (ūgăn′da, o͞ogahn′-dah). Republic in central Africa, N. of Lake Victoria; member of the Brit. Commonwealth, independent since 1962; capital, Kampala. **U·gan′dan** *adj. & n.*

ugh (o͞ox, ŭx, ŭg) *int.* Exclamation expressing disgust etc.

ug·ly (ŭg′lē) *adj.* **(-li·er, -li·est).** Unpleasing or repulsive to sight or hearing; morally repulsive, vile; disquieting, threatening; extremely awkward or unpromising (task, situation); ~ **customer**, unpleasantly formidable person; ~ **duckling**, dull or plain child who becomes brilliant adult (w. ref. to cygnet in a brood of ducklings in Hans Christian Anderson's tale). **ug′li·fy** *v.t.* **(-fied, -fy·ing). ug′li·ly** *adv.* **ug′li·ness** *n.*

U·gri·an (o͞o′grē′an, ū′-), **U·gric** (o͞o′grĭk, ū′-) *adjs. & ns.* (Language, member) of the E. branch of the Finno-Ugrian or Finnic peoples, specif. the Hungarians and Magyars. [*Ugra*, name of the country on both sides of the Ural mountains]

UHF, U.H.F., uhf, u.h.f. *abbrevs.* Ultrahigh FREQUENCY.

uh·lan (o͞o′lahn, ū′lan) *n.* (hist.) Cavalryman armed with lance in some European armies, esp. former German army. [Fr., Ger., f. Polish (*h*)*ulan*, f. Turk. *oğlan* boy, servant]

uit·land·er (oit′länder, ĭt′-, -lahn-) *n.* Outlander, esp. Brit. resident in former S. African republics before Boer War (1899–1902). [(Cape) Du., f. *uit* out, *land* land]

U.K. *abbrev.* United Kingdom.

u·kase (ū′kās, ūkāz′) *n.* 1. (hist.) Decree or edict, with force of law, of former Russian emperor or government. 2. Arbitrary order. [Russ. *ukaz′* command]

U·kraine (ūkrān′, o͞o-). Constituent republic (properly *Ukranian Soviet Socialist Republic*) of U.S.S.R., to the N. of the Black Sea; capital, Kiev. **U·krain′i·an** *adj. & n.*

u·ku·le·le (ūk*u*lā′lē; *Hawaiian* o͞ok*o͞o*lā′lā) *n.* Small four-stringed guitar of Portuguese origin that became popular in Hawaii and subsequently in U.S. and Europe. [Hawaiian, = "jumping flea"]

U·lan Ba·tor (o͞o′lahn bah′tor). Capital of Mongolian People's Republic in the N. Central part.

ul·cer (ŭl′ser) *n.* Open sore on external or internal surface of body, secreting pus; (fig.) corroding or corrupting influence, plague spot. **ul′cer·ous** *adj.* **ul′cer·ous·ly** *adv.*

ul·cer·ate (ŭl′serāt) *v.* **(-at·ed, -at·ing).** Make, become, ulcerous. **ul·cer·a·tion** (ŭlserā′shon) *n.* **ul·cer·a·tive** (ŭl′serātĭv, -atĭv) *adj.*

Ul·fi·las (ŭl′fĭlas), **Wul·fi·la** (wo͞ol′fĭla) (*c*311–83). Gothic bishop who translated the New Testament into Gothic.

u·lig·i·nose (ūlĭj′inōs), **u·lig·i·nous** (ūlĭj′inus) *adjs.* Waterlogged, muddy, swampy; (bot.) growing in muddy places.

ul·lage (ŭl′ĭj) *n.* Amount by which cask or bottle falls short of being quite full; remnant of liquor left in container that has lost part of its contents.

ul·na (ŭl′na) *n.* (pl. **-nae** pr. -nē, **-nas**). Large bone of forearm opposite thumb, extending from elbow to wrist; corresponding bone of foreleg in quadrupeds and of wing in birds. **ul′nar** *adj.*

Ul·ster (ŭl′ster). Former province of Ireland, comprising present Northern Ireland and the counties of Cavan, Donegal, and Monaghan; (loosely) Northern Ireland.

ul·ster (ŭl′ster) *n.* Long loose freq. belted overcoat, orig. of Ulster frieze. [f. ULSTER]

ul·te·ri·or (ŭltēr′ēer) *adj.* Situated beyond; more remote; in the background, beyond what is seen or avowed. **ul·te′ri·or·ly** *adv.*

ul·ti·mate (ŭl′timĭt) *adj.* Last, final; beyond which there is no advance, progress, etc.; fundamental, elemental. **ul′ti·mate·ly** *adv.*

ul·ti·ma Thu·le (ŭl′tima tho͞o′lē; *Lat.* o͞ol′tĭmah to͞o′lĕ). 1. Highest degree (of achievement etc.) attainable; remote goal. 2. Far away region. 3. Point believed by ancient peoples to be farthest north (see THULE).

ul·ti·ma·tum (ŭltimā′tum, -mah′-) *n.* (pl. **-tums, -ta** pr. -ta). Final statement of terms, rejection

Left: The Murchison Falls, **Uganda**. At this point the Nile emerges from Lake Albert and drops 118 ft. through a gorge only 20 ft. wide.

of light at right angles to its optical axis to detect particles beyond the range of an ordinary microscope. **ul·tra·mi·cro·scop·ic** (ŭltra-mīkrŏskŏp′ĭk) *adj.*

ul·tra·mon·tane (ŭltramŏntān′) *adj.* Situated S. of the Alps; Italian; favorable to the absolute authority of the pope in matters of faith and discipline. ~ *n.* One who resides S. of the Alps; person holding ultra-montane views. **ul·tra·mon·tan·ism** (ŭltramŏn′tanĭzem), **ul·tra·mon′tan·ist** *ns.* [L. *ultra* beyond, *mons* mountain]

ul·tra·mun·dane (ŭltramŭn′-dān, -mŭndān′) *adj.* (Of or pertaining to things) lying outside the world or beyond the limits of the solar system.

ul·tra·son·ic (ŭltrasŏn′ĭk) *adj.* (of sound) So high-pitched as to be beyond the range of human hearing; (of sound frequency) above audio frequency range. **ul·tra·son′i·cal·ly** *adv.*

ul·tra·vi·o·let (ŭltravī′olĭt) *adj.* (phys.) Lying immediately beyond the violet end of the visible spectrum; of, producing, electromagnetic radiation with a wavelength shorter than that of visible light rays and having powerful actinic effect.

ul·tra vi·res (ŭltra vīr′ēz). Beyond one's powers; exceeding the powers granted by law. [L.]

ul·tra·vi·rus (ŭltravīr′us) *n.* Ultramicroscopic virus so small that it can pass through pores of finest bacterial filter.

ul·u·late (ūl′yulāt, ŭl′-) *v.i.* (**-lat·ed, -lat·ing**). Howl, wail. **ul·u·la·tion** (ūlyulā′shon, ŭl-) *n.*

Ul·ya·nov (ōolyah′nawf), **Vladimir Ilyich**: see LENIN.

U·lys·ses (ūlĭs′ēz). Roman name for ODYSSEUS.

um·bel (ŭm′bel) *n.* (bot.) Inflorescence with pedicels of nearly equal length springing from common center. **um·bel·late** (ŭm′belĭt, -lāt), **um·bel·lif·er·ous** (ŭmbelĭf′erus) *adjs.* [L. *umbella* sunshade, dim. of *umbra* shadow]

um·ber (ŭm′ber) *n.* Brown earth (iron and manganese) used as pigment. ~ *adj.* Of the color of umber. [Fr. (*terre d'*)*ombre* or It. (*terra di*) *ombra*, either = "shadow" (L. *umbra*) f. fem. of L. *Umber* Umbrian]

um·bil·i·cal (ŭmbĭl′ĭkal) *adj.* Of, affecting, situated near, forming, umbilicus; ~ **cord**, flexible tube attaching fetus to placenta, navel string (also transf.). **um·bil·i·cate** (ŭmbĭl′ĭkĭt, -kāt), **um·bil·i·cat·ed** *adjs.* Resembling a navel.

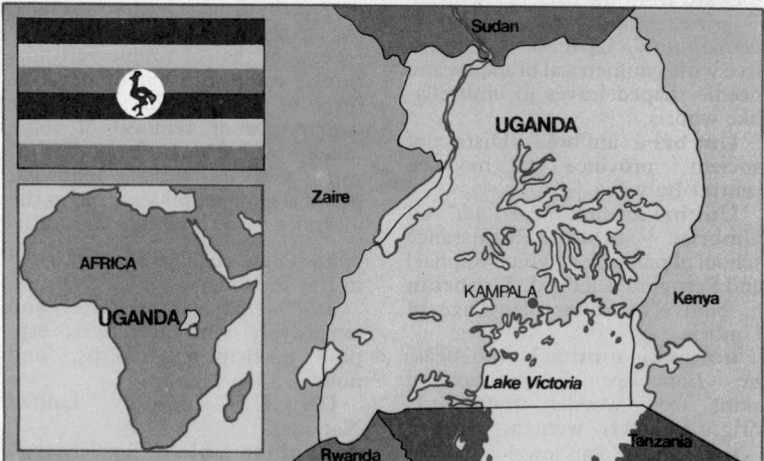

of which by opposite party may lead to rupture, declaration of war, etc.

ul·tra (ŭl′tra) *adj. & n.* (Person) holding extreme views, esp. in religion or politics. [orig. as abbrev. of Fr. *ultra-royaliste*]

ultra- *prefix*. Lying beyond or on the other side of; (with adjectives) going beyond, surpassing; having (the quality etc. expressed by the adjective) in extreme or excessive degree.

ul·tra·con·ser·va·tive (ŭltra-konsẽr′vatĭv) *adj. & n.* (Person who is) conservative to extreme degree,

esp. in political attitudes.

ul·tra·fiche (ŭl′trafēsh) *n.* Microfiche of printed material reduced in size to extreme degree.

ul·tra·high (ŭl′trahī′) **frequency**: see FREQUENCY.

ul·tra·ma·rine (ŭltramarēn′) *adj.* Situated beyond the sea; of the color of ultramarine. ~ *n.* Brilliant deep blue pigment made from lapis lazuli; imitation of this. [L. *ultra* beyond, *mare* sea (w. ref. to foreign origin of lapis lazuli)]

ul·tra·mi·cro·scope (ŭltramī′-kroskōp) *n.* Microscope using beam

The **umbrella bird** is found only in South America, where there are three species. It is named after its distinctive curving crest which opens to cover the head.

Named after the flowers which open like sunshades, **umbelliferous** plants include many that are useful to man. They range from carrots to parsley, chervil (above) and fennel (right).

um·bil·i·cus (ŭmbĭl´ĭkus, -bĭlī´-) n. (pl. **-bil·i·ci** pr. -bĭl´ĭsī, -bĭlī´sī, **-bil·i·cus·es**). Central depression in abdomen, marking point of attachment of umbilical cord, navel; small depression or hollow suggesting this; (geom.) point in surface through which all its lines of curvature pass.

um·bra (ŭm´bra) n. (pl. **-brae** pr. -brē). Earth's or moon's shadow in an eclipse, esp. the complete shadow as dist. from the *penumbra*; dark central part of a sunspot. **um´bral** adj. [L., = "shade"]

um·brage (ŭm´brĭj) n. 1. Sense of slight or injury, offense. 2. (archaic) Shade. **um·bra·geous** (ŭmbrā´jus) adj.

um·brel·la (ŭmbrĕl´a) n. Light portable screen usu. circular and supported on central stick, used in hot countries as protection against sun, and in some Oriental and African countries as symbol of rank or state; portable protection against rain etc., made of silk or similar material fastened on slender ribs that are attached radially to stick and can be readily raised to form an arched circular canopy; structure resembling an umbrella, esp. (zool.) gelatinous disk or bellshaped structure of jellyfish; (conch.) umbrella shell, the part of its shell like an open umbrella; protective screen of fighter aircraft; (fig.) general protection, aegis; ~ **bird**, S. or Central Amer. bird of genus *Cephalopterus*, esp. Brazilian *C. ornatus*, with black plumage and large crest curving forward from the back of the head; ~ **pine**, parasol pine (*Sciadopitys verticillata*), Japanese evergreen tree with symmetrical branches and needle-shaped leaves in umbrella-like whorls.

Um·bri·a (ŭm´brēa). District of ancient, province of modern, central Italy.

Um·bri·an (ŭm´brēan) adj. Of Umbria; ~ **school**, Renaissance school of painting to which Raphael and Perugino belonged. **Umbrian** n. Native, inhabitant, language, of Umbria.

u·mi·ak, u·mi·ack (ōō´mēăk) ns. Long open Eskimo boat of skins over wooden framework, orig. paddled by women.

um·laut (ōōm´lowt) n. (in Germanic languages) Vowel change due to *i*, *j*, etc. (now usu. lost or altered) in following syllable, e.g. Ger. *mann männer, fuss füsse*; diacritical sign (¨) indicating this. [Ger. *um* about, *laut* sound]

um·pire (ŭm´pīr) n. One who decides between disputants or contending parties and whose decision is usu. accepted as final; (law) third person called upon to settle question submitted to arbitrators who cannot agree; person chosen to enforce rules of games or contest and settle disputes or doubtful points. ~ v. (**-pired,** **-pir·ing**). Act as umpire (in). [OF. *nomper* peerless, in sense "odd man" (*non* not, *per* PEER[1])]

ump·teen (ŭmp´tēn´) adj. & n. (slang) Indeterminate but large number (of). **ump´teenth´** adj. [joc. formation, on analogy of *thirteen* etc.]

UMT abbrev. Universal Military Training.

Um·ta·ta (ōōmtah´ta). Capital of The Transkei.

UMW abbrev. United Mine Workers.

un-[1] prefix. Used with verbs and verbal derivatives and in forming new verbs from adjectives, nouns, etc., to signify action contrary to or reverse of that of simple verb (or, rarely, intensification of negative force of verb, as in *unloose*), or deprivation or removal of some quality or property; number of words with this and the following prefix is almost limitless, and as the meaning usu. presents no difficulties, few such words are listed in this dictionary.

un-[2] prefix. Not (used freely and extensively with adjectives, esp. past participles, adverbs, and nouns).

UN, U.N. abbrevs. United Nations.

un·al·ien·a·ble (ŭnā´lēenabel, -āl´ye-) adj. (archaic) Inalienable.

un·al·loyed (ŭnaloid´) adj. Not mixed, pure.

un-A·mer·i·can (ŭnamĕr´ĭkan) adj. Not American; (esp.) not of, not worthy or characteristic of, opposed to, against interests etc. of, the U.S.

u·nan·i·mous (ūnăn´ĭmus) adj. All of one mind, agreeing in opinion; (of opinion, vote, etc.) formed, held, given, etc., with general agreement or consent. **u·nan´i·mous·ly** adv. **u·na·nim·i·ty** (ūnanĭm´ĭtē), **u·nan´i·mous·ness** ns.

un·as·sum·ing (ŭnasōō'mĭng) *adj.* Modest, not pretentious. **un·as·sum'ing·ly** *adv.*

un·a·wares (ŭnawārz') *adv.* Unexpectedly, unconsciously; by surprise.

un·bal·anced (ŭnbăl'anst) *adj.* (esp.) Mentally unstable or deranged.

un·be·known (ŭnbĭnōn'), **un·be·knownst** (ŭnbĭnōnst') *adjs.* & *advs.* Unknown; ~ **to**, without the knowledge of.

un·bend (ŭnbĕnd') *v.* (**-bent** pr. -bĕnt or **-bend·ed, -bend·ing**). Release, relax, from tension; straighten; become unconstrained or genial.

un·bend·ing (ŭnbĕn'dĭng) *adj.* Rigid, uncompromising.

un·bos·om (ŭnbōoz'em, -bōo'-zem) *v.* Disclose, reveal; ~ **oneself**, disclose one's secrets, thoughts, etc.

un·bri·dled (ŭnbrī'deld) *adj.* Unrestrained, uncontrolled. **un·bri'dled·ly** *adv.*

un·called-for (ŭnkawld'fōr') *adj.* Not required or requested; unprovoked, impertinent.

un·can·ny (ŭnkăn'ē) *adj.* Supernatural, mysterious, uncomfortably strange or unfamiliar. **un·can'ni·ly** *adv.* **un·can'ni·ness** *n.*

un·ci·al (ŭn'shēal, -shal) *adj.* Of, written in, a form of majuscule script resembling capitals but with some ascending and descending strokes, used in Greek and Latin manuscripts of the 4th–8th centuries. ~ *n.* Uncial letter; uncial manuscript. [L. *uncialis* in LL. sense "inch-high," "large," f. *uncia* 12th part of foot, inch]

un·cle (ŭng'kel) *adj.* 1. Father's or mother's brother, aunt's husband; (children's colloq.) unrelated man who is a family friend; **cry** (or **say**) ~, (slang) admit defeat, submit; **U~ Sam**, government (or people) of U.S. (perh. facetious expansion of initials *U.S.*); **U~ Tom**, (derog.) black person subservient to whites; **U~ Tomism**, kind of relationship between whites and blacks involving kindness and condescension by the former and meek submissiveness by latter. [after leading character in Harriet Beecher Stowe's novel *Uncle Tom's Cabin* (1852)]

un·com·mon (ŭnkŏm'on) *adj.* Unusual, remarkable. **un·com'mon·ly** *adv.* **un·com'mon·ness** *n.*

un·com·pro·mis·ing (ŭnkŏm'-promīzĭng) *adj.* Refusing compromise; unyielding, stubborn. **un·com'pro·mis·ing·ly** *adv.*

un·con·scion·a·ble (ŭnkŏn'-shonabel) *adj.* 1. Having no conscience, unscrupulous; (of actions) performed against dictates of conscience. 2. Not right or reasonable; excessive, shameless.

un·con·scion·a·bly *adv.*

un·con·scious (ŭnkŏn'shus) *adj.* Not conscious; ~ **mind**, (psychol.) those mental processes whose existence is inferred from their effects. ~ *n.* Unconscious mind; **collective** ~, (Jungian psychol.) unconscious mental processes presumed common to all mankind.

un·con·sti·tu·tion·al (ŭnkŏnstĭtōō'shonal, -tū'-) *adj.* Not in accordance with the political constitution or with procedural rules. **un·con·sti·tu·tion·al·i·ty** (ŭnkŏnstĭtōōshonăl'ĭtē, -tū-) *n.* **un·con·sti·tu'tion·al·ly** *adv.*

un·cork (ŭnkōrk') *v.* 1. Remove cork from. 2. (colloq.) Let loose; let go or propel with force.

un·couth (ŭnkōoth') *adj.* Odd, uncomely, awkward, clumsy, in shape, sound, bearing, etc. **un·couth'ly** *adv.* **un·couth'ness** *n.* [OE. *uncuth* = "unknown," "unfamiliar"]

unc·tion (ŭngk'shon) *n.* 1. Anointing with oil etc. as religious rite or symbol (esp. of investiture with kingship or other office); unguent; **extreme** ~ : SEE EXTREME.

2. (Manner suggesting) deep spiritual or religious feeling; simulation of this, affected enthusiasm, gush.

unc·tu·ous (ŭngk'chōōus) *adj.* 1. Of the nature or quality of an unguent, oily, greasy in feel, appearance, etc. 2. Full of (esp. simulated) unction; complacently agreeable or self-satisfied. **unc'tu·ous·ly** *adv.* **unc'tu·ous·ness, unc·tu·os·i·ty** (ŭngkchōōos'ĭtē) *ns.*

un·der (ŭn'der) *prep.* In or to position lower than, below, at the foot of; within, on the inside, of; inferior to, less than; supporting or sustaining; subjected to, undergoing, liable to, on condition of, subject to; governed, controlled, or bound by; in accordance with; in the form of; in the time of; (**speak** etc.) ~ **one's breath**, in a whisper; ~ **a cloud**: see CLOUD; ~ **the sun**, anywhere on Earth; ~ **way**: see

*The retractable **undercarriage** of modern aircraft takes many forms. Below: The nose wheels of a Lockheed TriStar. The arrows show the directions in which the links move when the undercarriage is withdrawn into the fuselage.*

down lock

bungee springs

retraction actuator

taxi lights

steering actuator

shock strut

torque arms

axle

towing pad

WAY. **under** *adv.* In a lower place or subordinate condition. ~ *adj.* Lower. **un′der·most** *adj.*

under- *prefix.* Below; beneath, lower than; insufficiently, incompletely; situated beneath, subordinate.

un·der·a·chieve (ŭnderachēv′) *v.* Do less or worse than was expected (esp. scholastically). **un′der·a·chiev′er** *n.*

un·der·act (ŭnderakt′) *v.* Underplay.

un·der·arm (ŭn′derärm) *adj. & adv.* (Performed) with arm lower than the shoulder; of the armpit.

un·der·bid (ŭnderbĭd′) *v.* (**-bid, -bid·ding**). Bid less than; bid too little (on); undercut.

un·der·brush (ŭn′derbrŭsh) *n.* Undergrowth in forest.

un·der·car·riage (ŭn′derkărĭj) *n.* Lower framework of a vehicle that supports the superstructure.

un·der·charge (ŭn′derchärj) *v.* Charge too little for (thing) or to (person); give less than proper charge to (gun, electric battery, etc.).

un·der·class·man (ŭn′derklăsman, -klahs-) *n.* (pl. **-men**). Freshman or sophomore in U.S. college.

un·der·clothes (ŭn′derklōz, -klōdhz), **un·der·cloth·ing** (ŭn′derklōdhĭng) *ns.* Clothing worn below outer garments, esp. next to the skin.

un·der·coat (ŭn′derkōt) *n.* Under layer of hair or down in certain long-haired animals; layer of paint used under finishing coat(s). **un′der·coat·ing** *n.* (esp.) Paint for use as undercoat.

un·der·cov·er (ŭnderkŭv′er) *adj.* Acting, done, surreptitiously or secretly.

un·der·cur·rent (ŭn′derkĕrent, -kŭr-) *n.* Current flowing below surface or upper current; (fig.) suppressed or underlying activity, force, etc.

un·der·cut (ŭn′derkŭt, ŭnderkŭt′) *v.t.* (**-cut, -cut·ting**). Cut (away) below or beneath, esp. in carving; supplant by working for lower payment; undersell; (tennis etc.) give backspin to (ball).

un·der·de·vel·oped (ŭnderdĭvĕl′opt, ŭn′derdĭvĕl-) *adj.* Not fully developed; (photog.) not developed enough to give a normal image; (of country etc.) below not (yet) realizing economic potential.

un·der·dog (ŭn′derdawg, -dŏg) *n.* Loser in fight etc.; one in state of subjection or inferiority; person, team, expected to lose game, election, etc.

un·der·done (ŭnderdŭn′) *adj.* Incompletely or insufficiently cooked.

un·der·es·ti·mate (ŭnderĕs′timāt) *v.t.* (**-mat·ed, -mat·ing**). Form or make too low an estimate (of).

un·der·foot (ŭnderfoŏt′): see FOOT.

un·der·gar·ment (ŭn′dergärment) *n.* Article of underwear.

un·der·go (ŭn′dergō, ŭndergō′) *v.t.* (**-went, -gone, -go·ing**). Be subjected to, suffer, endure.

un·der·grad·u·ate (ŭn′dergrăjooĭt, ŭndergrăj′-) *n.* College or university student who has not yet taken a degree.

un·der·ground (ŭn′dergrownd′) *adv.* Below the surface of the ground; in(to) secrecy or concealment. ~ (ŭn′dergrownd) *adj. & n.* (group, movement, etc.) Conducted or existing in secret, esp. in resistance to established order etc.; (Brit.; usu. **the** ~) subway train or system.

un·der·growth (ŭn′dergrōth) *n.* Growth of plants or shrubs under trees etc.

un·der·hand (ŭn′derhănd) *adj. & adv.* 1. Clandestine(ly), secret(ly), not aboveboard. 2. (baseball) Thrown with the arm lower than the shoulder.

un·der·hand·ed (ŭn′derhăn′dĭd) *adj.* UNDERHAND sense 1.

un·der·hung (ŭnderhŭng′) *adj.* (of lower jaw) Projecting beyond upper jaw; (of person, animal) having underhung jaw.

un·der·lay (ŭnderlā′) *v.t.* (**-laid, -lay·ing**). Raise or support or line etc. with something laid under. ~ (ŭn′derlā) *n.* Something laid under esp. carpet or mattress as protection or support.

un·der·lie (ŭnderlī′) *v.t.* (**-lay, -lain, -ly·ing**). Lie, be situated, under; (fig.) be the basis or foundation of, lie under surface aspect of.

un·der·line (ŭn′derlīn, ŭnderlīn′) *v.t.* (**-lined, -lin·ing**). Draw line(s) beneath (words etc.) for emphasis; emphasize.

un·der·ling (ŭn′derlĭng) *n.* (usu. contempt.) Subordinate.

un·der·mine (ŭndermīn′, ŭn′dermīn) *v.t.* (**-mined, -min·ing**). Make mine or excavation under; wear away base or foundation of; injure, wear out, etc., insidiously, secretly, or imperceptibly.

un·der·neath (ŭndernēth′) *adv. & prep.* At or to a lower place (than), below. ~ *adj. & n.* Lower (surface, part).

un·der·pants (ŭn′derpănts) *n.* Short- or long-legged garment worn as underwear on lower part of body.

un·der·pass (ŭn′derpăs, -pahs) *n.* (Crossing with) road etc. passing under another.

un·der·pin (ŭnderpĭn′) *v.t.* (**-pinned, -pin·ning**). Support or strengthen (building etc.) from beneath.

un·der·play (ŭn′derplā) *v.* Act (part) inadequately or with too much restraint.

un·der·priv·i·leged (ŭn′der-priv′ĭlĭjd, -prĭv′lĭjd) *adj.* Not enjoying normal living standard or rights and privileges of member of society.

un·der·rate (ŭnderrāt′, ŭn′derrāt) *v.t.* (**-rat·ed, -rat·ing**). Form too low an estimate of.

un·der·score (ŭn′derskōr, -skŏr, ŭnderskōr′, -skŏr′) *v.* (**-scored, -scor·ing**). Underline.

un·der·sec·re·tar·y (ŭn′dersĕkrĭtĕrē, ŭndersĕk′-) *n.* (pl. **-tar·ies**). Official subordinate to a secretary.

un·der·sell (ŭndersĕl, ŭndersĕl′) *v.* (**-sold** pr. -sōld, **-sel·ling**). 1. (of person) Sell at a lower price than (another person); cut out of competition by selling at a lower rate; (of thing) be sold thus. 2. Sell (thing) at too low a price.

un·der·shoot (ŭn′dershoŏt, ŭndershoŏt′) *v.* (**-shot** pr. -shŏt, **-shoot·ing**). (esp., of aircraft) Land short of (the runway).

un·der·shot (ŭn′dershŏt) *adj.* (of wheel) Turned by water flowing under it.

un·der·signed (ŭn′dersīnd) *adj.* (Whose names are) signed below; **the** ~, undersigned person(s).

un·der·sized (ŭn′dersīzd) *adj.* Of less than normal size.

un·der·slung (ŭn′derslŭng) *adj.* Supported from above; (of vehicle chassis) hanging lower than axles.

un·der·stand (ŭnderstănd′) *v.* (**-stood** pr. -stoŏd, **-stand·ing**). Perceive the meaning of; know how to deal with; infer, esp. from information received; take for granted. **un·der·stand′ing** *n.* (esp.) Intelligence; agreement; convention, thing agreed upon. ~ *adj.* Intelligent, having understanding. **un·der·stand′a·bly**, **un·der·stand′ing·ly** *advs.* **un·der·stand′a·ble** *adj.*

un·der·state·ment (ŭn′derstātment, ŭnderstăt′-) *n.* Statement falling below or coming short of truth or fact; intentionally, ironically, restrained statement. **un·der·state** (ŭn′derstăt, ŭnderstăt′) *v.t.* (**-stat·ed, -stat·ing**).

un·der·steer (ŭn′derstēr, ŭnderstēr′) *v.i.* (of vehicle) Have tendency to steer toward the outer side on a curve. ~ *n.* Understeering.

un·der·stud·y (ŭn′derstŭdē) *n.* (pl. **-stud·ies**). Actor who learns part in order to play it at short notice in absence of usual performer. ~ *v.t.* (**-stud·ied, -stud·y·ing**). Act as understudy to.

un·der·take (ŭn′dertāk, ŭndertāk′) *v.* (**-took** pr. -toŏk, **-tak·en, -tak·ing**). Bind oneself to perform; engage in, enter upon (work, enterprise, etc.); promise (*to* do); guarantee; (colloq.) manage funerals. **un′der·tak·er** *n.* (esp.) One whose business is to carry out arrangements for funerals. **un·-der·tak'ing** *n.* (esp.) Work etc. undertaken, enterprise; business of funeral undertaker.

un·der·tone (ŭn'dertōn) *n.* Low or subdued, underlying or subordinate, tone.

un·der·tow (ŭn'dertō) *n.* Current below sea surface moving in contrary direction to surface current.

un·der·wear (ŭn'derwār) *n.* Underclothes.

un·der·wood (ŭn'derwŏod) *n.* Small trees or shrubs, brushwood, growing beneath trees.

un·der·world (ŭn'derwᵉrld) *n.* (esp. myth.) Abode of souls of the dead; criminal section of society.

un·der·write (ŭn'derrīt, ŭnder-rīt') *v.* (**-wrote** pr. -rōt, -rōt', **-writ·ten** pr. -rīten, -rĭt'en, **-writ·ing**). (esp.) Subscribe (insurance policy), thereby accepting risk of insurance; undertake esp. marine insurance; agree to support (venture financially); agree to buy stock not bought by public in (new company or new issue). **un'der·-writ·er** *n.*

un·dies (ŭn'dēz) *n.pl.* (colloq.) Women's underclothes.

un·dis·trib·ut·ed (ŭndĭstrĭb'yutĭd) *adj.* Not distributed; ~ **middle**, (logic) fallacy resulting from failure of middle term to refer to all members of a class (e.g. *all men are mammals; all apes are mammals; therefore, all men are apes.*).

un·do (ŭndoo', ŭn'doo) *v.t.* (**-did** pr. -dĭd, **-done** pr. -dŭn, -dŭn', **-do·ing**). Annul, cancel; open (parcel etc.); unfasten (laces, buttons, etc.); (poet.) ruin. **un·do'-ing** *n.* (esp.) (Cause of) bringing to ruin. **un·done'** (esp.) Unfastened; (poet.) ruined.

un·dress (ŭndrĕs') *v.* Take off clothes (of). ~ *n.* Ordinary dress; informal dress; negligee.

un·due (ŭndoo', -dū) *adj.* Not owed or suitable; excessive, disproportional.

un·du·lant (ŭn'julant, -du-, -dyu-) *adj.* Undulating, rising and falling like waves; ~ **fever**, persistent remittent fever with profuse perspiration, swollen joints, and enlarged spleen, transmitted through milk esp. of diseased cows.

un·du·late (ŭn'julĭt, -lāt, -dyu-, -du-) *adj.* With wavelike markings; having waved surface or outline, arranged in wavelike curves. ~ (ŭn'julāt, -dyu-, -du-) *v.i.* (**-lat·ed**, **-lat·ing**). Have wavy motion or look. **un'du·lat·ing** *adj.*

un·du·la·tion (ŭnjulā'shon, -dyu-, -du-) *n.* Wavy motion or form, gentle rise and fall, each wave of this; set of wavy lines.

un·du·la·to·ry (ŭn'julatōrē, -tōrē, -dyu-, -du-) *adj.* Undulating,

wavy; of, due to, undulation.

un·du·ly (ŭndoo'lē, -dū'-) *adv.* Unrightfully, improperly; excessively.

un·dy·ing (ŭndī'ĭng) *adj.* Not dying; forever or unceasing. **un·dy'ing·ly** *adv.*

un·earned (ŭnᵉrnd') *adj.* (esp.) ~ **income**, revenue from interest payments etc., dist. from wages etc.

un·earth (ŭnᵉrth') *v.t.* Dig up, disinter; force out of hole or burrow; (fig.) bring to light, disclose, find by searching.

un·earth·ly (ŭnᵉrth'lē) *adj.* Celestial, not of Earth; supernatural, ghostly; (colloq.) not appropriate, absurdly early or inconvenient.

un·eas·y (ŭnē'zē) *adj.* (**-eas·i·er**, **-eas·i·est**). Restless, disturbed, uncomfortable in body or mind. **un·eas'i·ly** *adv.* **un·eas'i·ness** *n.*

un·em·ployed (ŭnĕmploid') *adj.* Not employed or occupied; not in use. **un·em·ploy'ment** *n.*

UNESCO (ūnĕs'kō) *n.* United Nations Educational, Scientific, and Cultural Organization.

un·ex·cep·tion·a·ble (ŭnĭksĕp'-shonabel) *adj.* With which no fault can be found. **un·ex·cep'tion·-a·bly** *adv.*

un·fair (ŭnfār') *adj.* Not equitable or honest or impartial or according to rules. **un·fair'ly** *adv.* **un·fair'ness** *n.*

un·faith·ful (ŭnfāth'ful) *adj.* Failing in loyalty; not true *to*; adulterous. **un·faith'ful·ly** *adv.*

un·fas·ten (ŭnfăs'en, -fah'sen) *v.t.* Make loose; detach; open fastening(s) of.

un·feel·ing (ŭnfē'lĭng) *adj.* Lacking sensibility, without feeling; harsh, cruel. **un·feel'ing·ly** *adv.*

un·fit (ŭnfĭt') *adj.* Not fit, unsuitable; in poor health. ~ *v.t.* (**-fit·ted**, **-fit·ting**). Make unsuitable (for). **un·fit'ly** *adv.* **un·-fit'ness** *n.*

un·flap·pa·ble (ŭnflăp'abel) *adj.* (colloq.) Imperturbable; remaining cool in a crisis. **un·flap·pa·bil'i·ty** *n.* **un·flap'pa·bly** *adv.*

un·fold (ŭnfōld') *v.* Open out; reveal; develop.

un·for·tu·nate (ŭnfōr'chunĭt) *adj.* Unlucky; regrettable; ill-advised. **un·for'tu·nate·ly** *adv.* **un·for'tu·nate·ness** *n.*

un·frock (ŭnfrŏk') *v.t.* Deprive of priestly status.

un·gain·ly (ŭngān'lē) *adj.* Awkward, clumsy, ungraceful. **un·-gain'li·ness** *n.*

un·god·ly (ŭngŏd'lē) *adj.* (**-li·er**, **-li·est**). Impious, wicked; (colloq.) outrageous. **un·god'li·ness** *n.*

un·gov·ern·a·ble (ŭngŭv'erna-bel) *adj.* Uncontrollable.

un·gual (ŭng'gwal) *adj.* Of, like, bearing, a nail, claw, or hoof.

un·guent (ŭng'gwent) *n.* Oint-

ment, salve. **un'guen·tar·y** *adj.*

un·gu·la (ŭng'gyula) *n.* (pl. **-lae** pr. -lē). 1. Hoof, claw, talon. 2. (math.) Cone, cylinder, with top cut off by plane oblique to base.

un·gu·late (ŭng'gyulĭt, -lāt) *adj.* Hoofshaped; (of mammals) having hoofs.

un·hal·lowed (ŭnhăl'ōd) *adj.* Not consecrated; unholy, impious, wicked.

un·hand (ŭnhănd') *v.t.* (archaic) Take one's hands off (person or thing).

un·health·y (ŭnhĕl'thē) *adj.* (**-health·i·er**, **-health·i·est**). Sickly; diseased; prejudicial or hurtful to health; unwholesome; (slang) dangerous. **un·health'i·-ness** *n.*

un·heard (ŭnhᵉrd') *adj.* Not heard; ~ **of**, unknown, unprecedented.

un·hinge (ŭnhĭnj') *v.t.* (**-hinged**, **-hing·ing**). (chiefly in past part.) Derange, disorder (mind).

uni- *prefix.* One; having, composed or consisting of, characterized by, etc., one (thing specified by second element).

u·ni·cam·er·al (ūnikăm'eral) *adj.* Having one (legislative) chamber.

UNICEF (ū'nĭsĕf) *n.* United Nations (International) Children's (Emergency) Fund.

u·ni·cel·lu·lar (ūnisĕl'yuler) *adj.* (esp. of organism) Having, composed of, a single cell.

u·ni·corn (ū'nikōrn) *n.* Fabulous animal represented as having the body of a horse with a single horn projecting from its forehead.

u·ni·cy·cle (ū'nisīkel) *n.* Frame mounted on one wheel with saddle for driver who propels vehicle by pushing pedals.

U·ni·fi·ca·tion (ūnifīkā'shon) **Church.** Anticommunist religious (political?) group led by Rev. Sun Myung Moon (cf. MOONIE).

u·ni·form (ū'nifōrm) *adj.* Being or remaining the same in different places, at different times, etc., unvarying, consistent; plain, unbroken, undiversified; conforming to one standard, rule, or pattern, alike, similar. **u'ni·form·ly** *adv.* **uniform** *n.* Distinctive dress of uniform cut, material, and color worn by all members of particular military or other organization. ~ *v.* Make uniform; dress in uniform. **u'ni·form·ness** *n.*

u·ni·form·i·ty (ūnifōr'mĭtē) *n.* (pl. **-ties**). Being uniform, sameness, consistency, conformity.

u·ni·fy (ū'nifī) *v.t.* (**-fied**, **-fy·ing**). Reduce to unity or uniformity. **u·ni·fi·ca·tion** (ūnifī-kā'shon), **u'ni·fi·er** *ns.*

u·ni·lat·er·al (ūnilăt'eral) *adj.* One-sided; of, affecting, etc., one side (only); made by, binding on,

The combined area of the states of the **Union of Soviet Socialist Republics** is the largest of any nation in the world. Inside its boundaries, the diversity of architecture and activity can range from traditional onion domes on village churches (top left) to huge stores in Moscow which are as large as small towns. However, small village markets still operate in some areas.

affecting, one part only. **u·ni·lat′-er·al·ly** adv.

un·im·peach·a·ble (ŭnĭmpē′-chabel) adj. Giving no opportunity for censure; beyond reproach, question, or doubt. **un·im-peach′a·bly** adv.

un·in·hib·it·ed (ŭnĭnhĭb′ĭtĭd) adj. Not inhibited; free from conventional social customs or restraints. **un·in·hib′it·ed·ly** adv.

un·ion (ūn′yon) n. 1. Uniting, joining, being united, coalition, junction; marriage; concord, agreement. 2. Body formed by combination of parts or members; labor union. 3. Kind of joint or coupling for pipes etc. 4. **the Union**, the UNITED STATES OF AMERICA. 5. ~ **catalog**, library catalog combining catalogs of several libraries or several divisions; **U ~ flag, Jack**, national flag of the United Kingdom; ~ **label**, identification stamped, fastened, etc., on item to show it was made by union labor; ~ **shop**, business or industry, employees of which must belong to union or agree to join within certain time after taking job.

un·ion·ist (ūn′yonĭst) n. 1. Member of a labor union; advocate of labor unions. 2. One who desires or advocates union, esp. particular legislative or political union, supporter of federal union of U.S., esp. (in Civil War) as opp. *secessionist.* ~ adj. Of, supporting, belonging to, union, unionism, or unionists. **un′ion·ism** n.

un·ion·ize (ūn′yonīz) v. (**-ized, -iz·ing**). Bring under labor union organization or rules. **un·ion·i·za-tion** (ūnyonīzā′shon) n.

Un·ion (ūn′yon) **of Soviet Socialist Republics.** (abbrev. U.S.S.R., USSR) Largest country in the world, stretching from E. Europe across Asia, bordered by Pacific on E., Arctic on N., Black and Caspian seas, Iran, Afghanistan, China, and Mongolia on S., and Poland and Rumania on W.; comprising 15 constituent republics (Russian Soviet Federal Socialist Republic, Ukraine, Byelorussia, Uzbekistan, Kazakhstan, Georgia, Azerbaijan, Lithuania, Moldavia, Latvia, Kirghizia, Tadzhikistan, Armenia, Turkmenistan, Estonia) and 20 autonomous republics; capital, Moscow.

u·nique (ūnēk′) adj. Of which there is only one; unmatched, unequaled; having no like, equal, or parallel. **u·nique′ly** adv. **u·nique′ness** n.

u·ni·sex (ū′nĭseks) adj. Of fashions of dress, hairstyle, etc. designed for members of both sexes without distinction.

u·ni·son (ū′nĭson, -zon) n. (mus.) Coincidence in pitch; sound or note of same pitch as another; combination of voices or instruments at same pitch; **in** ~, at same pitch; in concord, agreement, or harmony. **u·nis·o·nal** (ūnĭs′onal), **u·nis′o-nant** adjs.

u·nit (ū′nĭt) n. 1. Single magnitude or number regarded as undivided whole, esp. the numeral "1"; any determinate quantity, magnitude, etc., as basis or standard of measurement for other quantities of same kind. 2. One of the individuals or groups into which a complex whole may be analyzed; that part of collective body or whole regarded as lowest or least to have separate existence; fractional interest in investment trust. 3. Device with specified function forming element in complex mechanism etc.; piece of furniture for fitting with others like it or formed of complementary elements. 4. ~ **pricing**, method of pricing items, esp. food products, that shows price for an ounce, pint, or other standard unit, thus making it easy for shoppers to compare prices of similar items; ~ **rule**, in Democratic Party national convention, rule that all the votes of a state must be given to the candidate chosen by the majority of that state's delegation. **unit** *adj.* Of, being, forming, a unit, individual.

U·ni·tar·i·an (ūnĭtār´ēan) *n.* One who maintains that the Godhead is one person, not a Trinity; member of Christian body that originated in England in 17th c. maintaining this belief; (also) one who advocates individual freedom of belief. ~ *adj.* Of Unitarians or their doctrine. **U·ni·tar´i·an·ism** *n.*

u·nite (ūnīt´) *v.* (**-nit·ed, -nit·ing**). Join together, make or become one, combine, consolidate, amalgamate; agree, combine, cooperate (*in*). **u·nit´ed** *adj.* (esp.) **U~ Brethren**, Moravians; **U~ States**, UNITED STATES OF AMERICA. **u·nit´ed·ly** *adv.*

United Arab Emirates. (abbrev. U.A.E.) Union of seven emirates in the E. part of the Arabian peninsula along Oman and Persian gulfs, comprising Abu Dhabi, Ajman, Dubai, Fujairah, Ras al Khaimah, Sharjah, and Umm al Qaiwain; capital, Abu Dhabi.

United Arab Republic. (abbrev. UAR) Former (1958–71) name of Egypt.

United Church of Christ. U.S. Protestant denomination formed by 1957 merger of Congregational Christian Church and Evangelical and Reformed Church.

United Kingdom. (abbrev. U.K.) Kingdom in W. Europe consisting of Gt. Britain (England, Scotland, and Wales) and Northern Ireland; capital, London.

United Methodist Church. Protestant church formed 1968 in U.S. by union of Methodist Church and Evangelical United Brethren.

United Nations. (orig.) Nations at war with the Axis, 1939–45; hence, international organization of these and other nations established as successor to the League of Nations by the ~ **Charter**, signed at San Francisco on June 26, 1945; its main object is the maintenance of peace and its six principal organs are the General Assembly, Security Council, Secretariat (at New York),

*The **United States of America** consists of the original 48 states together with Alaska (bought in 1867 but only granted statehood in 1959) and Hawaii which also joined the Union in 1959. Each state has certain policies not subject to Federal control.*

International Court (at The Hague), Economic and Social Council, and Trusteeship Council.

United States of America. (abbrev. US, U.S., USA, U.S.A.) Republic of N. Amer. bounded on N. by Canada and on S. by Mexico; federation of 50 states and District of Columbia; capital, Washington, D.C.; colonies were established in N. Amer. beginning in 16th c. by Spanish in S. and W., followed by French in S. and N., Dutch in the E. and English along the Atlantic coast; colonies in E. were ruled by English after defeat of French during French and Indian War, 1754–63; colonies declared independence, 1776, and after defeat of English, during Revolutionary War, 1775–83, the 13 original colonies united under a constitution and chose George Washington as first president; westward expansion of this union resulted from purchase of Louisiana Territory from French, 1803; Florida purchased from Spain, 1819; Texas annexed, 1845; discovery of gold in California further extended westward expansion to Pacific coast; New Mexico and California ceded by Mexico, 1848, after Mexican War; Alaska purchased from Russia, 1867; Hawaiian Islands annexed, 1898.

u·ni·ty (ū´nĭtē) *n.* (pl. **-ties**). State of being one or single or

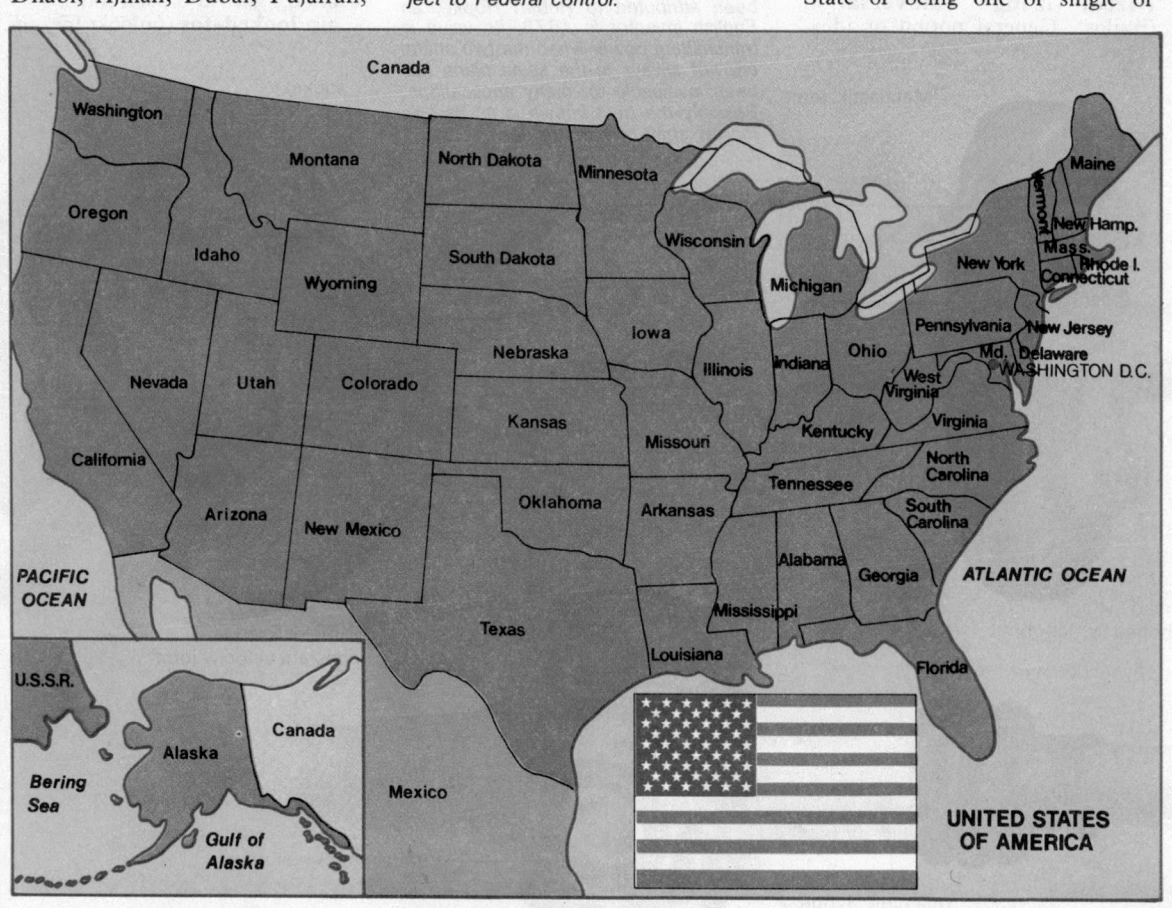

UNITED STATES OF AMERICA

individual; being formed of parts that constitute a whole; due interconnection and coherence of parts; thing showing such unity, thing forming complex whole; (math.) the numeral 1 as basis of number; harmony, concord, between persons etc.; any of the three Aristotelian principles of dramatic composition as adapted by French classical dramatists, by which a play should consist of one main action, represented as occurring at one time and in one place.

Univ. *abbrev.* University.

u·ni·va·lent (ūnivā′lent) = MONOVALENT.

u·ni·valve (ū′nivălv) *adj.* (zool., of shell) Composed of a single valve, (of mollusk) having such shell.

u·ni·ver·sal (ūniver′sal) *adj.* Of, belonging to, done, or used by, etc., all persons or things in the world or in the class concerned; applicable to all cases; covering many or all subjects, very broad (*universal genius*); ~ **joint**, mechanical joint or coupling permitting movement in any direction of the parts joined while transmitting rotary motion; ~ **suffrage**, suffrage extending to all persons over a specified age with the exception of certain minor categories. **u·ni·ver′sal·ly** *adv.* **u·ni·ver·sal·i·ty** (ūniversăl′itē) *n.* (pl. **-ties**). **u·ni·ver′sal·ize** *v.t.* (**-ized, -iz·ing**). **universal** *n.* (philos.) General notion or idea,

thing that by its nature may be predicated of many.

u·ni·ver·sal·ism (ūniver′sa-līzem) *n.* (theol.) Doctrine that all mankind will eventually be saved. **u·ni·ver′sal·ist** *n.* One who holds this doctrine, esp. (**U ~**) member of Protestant denomination holding this doctrine, founded in U.S. in late 18th c., merged with Unitarians in 1961.

u·ni·verse (ū′nivers) *n.* All created or existing things, all creation; = COSMOS[1]; the world or Earth; all mankind.

u·ni·ver·si·ty (ūniver′sitē) *n.* (pl. **-ties**). Whole body of teachers and scholars engaged at particular place in giving and receiving instruction in higher branches of learning; such persons as corporate body with definite organization and powers (esp. of conferring degrees), forming institution for promotion of higher education; colleges, buildings, etc., of such a body.

un·kempt (ŭnkĕmpt′) *adj.* Uncombed, disheveled; untidy, looking neglected.

un·kind (ŭnkīnd′) *adj.* Lacking kindness; unpleasant, harsh. **un·kind′ness** *n.*

un·known (ŭnnōn′) *adj.* Not known; not identified; **U ~ Soldier**, unnamed representative

*Invention of the **universal joint** has been attributed to Robert Hooke, an English inventor in 1676. Its value in transmitting power when the two shafts are not always in the same plane has been invaluable for many applications. Possibly the best known is its use on the tail shaft of a motor car.*

of a country's armed services killed in battle, buried in tomb serving as national memorial, esp. (U.S.) in Arlington National Cemetery.

un·lead·ed (ŭnlĕd′ĭd) *adj.* (of gasoline) Containing no tetraethyl lead; (printing) with no leads for spacing.

un·learn (ŭnlern′) *v.* Cause to be no longer in one's knowledge, memory, or regular behavior.

un·leash (ŭnlēsh′) *v.t.* Free from leash or restraint; set free in order to pursue, attack, etc.

un·less (ŭnlĕs′) *conj.* If . . . not, except when.

un·let·tered (ŭnlĕt′erd) *adj.* Not instructed in learning from books; illiterate.

un·like (ŭnlīk′, ŭn′līk) *adj.* & *prep.* Not like, different (from). **un·like′ness** *n.*

un·like·ly (ŭnlīk′lē) *adj.* Improbable; unpromising. **un·like′li·hood, un·like′li·ness** *ns.*

un·lim·it·ed (ŭnlĭm′ĭtĭd, ŭn′-lĭm-) *adj.* Without limit, unrestricted, very great in number or quantity.

un·list·ed (ŭnlĭs′tĭd, ŭn′lĭs-) *adj.* Not included in list, esp. of stock exchange prices or of telephone numbers.

un·load (ŭnlōd′) *v.* Remove cargo or anything carried or conveyed (from); remove charge from (gun); relieve of burden; (colloq.) get rid of, sell (out).

un·looked-for (ŭnlŏŏkt′for) *adj.*

'Metalastik' joint

rubber 'doughnut'

identical 'spider' on other side

three-armed metal 'spider' bolted to 'doughnut'

socket

caged ball race

outer element

inner element

shaft splined into inner element

Birfield-Rzeppa constant velocity joint

arms of cross

rubber shock absorber

retaining U-bolt

cross type joint

Not expected or foreseen.

un·loose (ŭnlōōs´) v.t. (**-loosed, -loos·ing**). Loose, untie.

un·man (ŭnmăn´) v.t. (**-man- ned, -man·ning**). Deprive of courage, strength, firmness, etc.

un·manned (ŭnmănd´, ŭn´- mănd) adj. (Of) pilotless spacecraft, aircraft without crew and operated by remote or automatic control.

un·mask (ŭnmăsk´, -mahsk´) v. Remove mask from; (fig.) expose true character of.

un·men·tion·a·ble (ŭnmĕn´- shonabel) adj. Unspeakable, that may not (properly) be mentioned.

un·mis·tak·a·ble (ŭnmĭstă´- kabel) adj. That cannot be mistaken or doubted. **un·mis- tak´a·bly** adv.

un·mit·i·gat·ed (ŭnmĭt´ĭgātĭd) adj. Unqualified, absolute. **un- mit´i·gat·ed·ly** adv.

un·nat·u·ral (ŭnnăch´eral) adj. Contrary or not conforming to nature; lacking natural feelings; artificial. **un·nat´u·ral·ly** adv. **un·nat´u·ral·ness** n.

un·nec·es·sar·y (ŭnnĕs´esĕrē) adj. Not necessary; more than necessary. **un·nec·es·sar·i·ly** (ŭnnĕsesār´ĭle, -sĕr´-) adv. **un- nec´es·sar·i·ness** n.

un·nerve (ŭnnērv´) v.t. (**-nerved, -nerv·ing**). Deprive of nerve, courage, self-control, etc.

un·num·bered (ŭnnŭm´berd) adj. Countless; not marked etc. with a number.

un·oc·cu·pied (ŭnŏk´yupīd) adj. 1. Having no occupant. 2. Not busy; idle.

un·or·gan·ized (ŭnôr´ganīzd) adj. 1. Having no system or order. 2. Not acting, talking, etc. in systematic way. 3. Not part of labor union; not unionized.

un·pleas·ant (ŭnplĕz´ant) adj. Disagreeable. **un·pleas´ant·ly** adv. **un·pleas´ant·ness** n.

un·prec·e·dent·ed (ŭnprĕs´- ĭdĕntĭd) adj. For which there is no precedent, novel.

un·prin·ci·pled (ŭnprĭn´sipeld) adj. Not having, not based on, etc., sound or honest principles of conduct.

un·pro·fes·sion·al (ŭnprofĕsh´- onal) adj. Not professional; unworthy of a member of a profession.

un·qual·i·fied (ŭnkwŏl´ifĭd) adj. Not qualified; not modified or limited. **un·qual´i·fied·ly** adv.

un·quote (ŭn´kwōt). Direction used in dictation to indicate the end of a quotation.

un·rav·el (ŭnrăv´el) v. (**-eled, -el·ing**; Brit. **-elled, -el·ling**). Take out of tangled or intertwined condition (freq. fig.); undo, pull out (woven or esp. knitted fabric); come undone, become unknit or disentangled.

un·read (ŭnrĕd´) adj. (Of book

etc.) not read; (of person) uneducated; ignorant.

un·rea·son·a·ble (ŭnrē´zonabel) adj. Not reasonable, esp. having or displaying little intelligence or judgment, irrational; immoderate, excessive. **un·rea´son·a·ble·ness** n. **un·rea´son·a·bly** adv.

un·re·con·struct·ed (ŭnrēkon- strŭk´tĭd) adj. Holding to earlier ideas, beliefs, etc., esp. not accepting the spirit or fact of Reconstruction after the Civil War.

un·re·gen·er·ate (ŭnrĭjĕn´erĭt) adj. Not regenerate; not reborn in spirit; unconverted to a specific belief, attitude, etc.; obstinate, stubborn. **un·re·gen´er·ate·ly** adv.

un·re·mit·ting (ŭnrĭmĭt´ĭng) adj. Incessant.

un·re·served (ŭnrĭzērvd´) adj. Not reserved; without reservations, qualifications, or exceptions; free from reserve, frank, open. **un·re- serv´ed·ly** adv.

un·rest (ŭnrĕst´) n. Disturbance, turmoil, trouble.

UNRRA, U.N.R.R.A. abbrevs. United Nations Relief and Rehabilitation Administration.

un·rul·y (ŭnrōō´lē) adj. (**-rul- i·er, -rul·i·est**). Not amenable to rule or discipline; turbulent. **un·rul´i·ness** n.

un·sat·u·rat·ed (ŭnsăch´erātĭd) adj. (chem.): see SATURATE def. 2. **un·sat·u·rate** (ŭnsăch´erĭt, -răt) n.

un·sa·vor·y (ŭnsā´verē) adj. Not savory; morally offensive. **un·sa´- vor·i·ness** n.

un·scathed (ŭnskādhd´) adj. Not injured or harmed.

un·scram·ble (ŭnskrăm´bel) v. Restore from scrambled state, esp. (electron.) restore (incoming scrambled signals) to understandable form. **un·scram´bler** n.

un·scru·pu·lous (ŭnskrōō´pyu- lus) adj. Not having scruples, shameless, unprincipled. **un- scru´pu·lous·ly** adv. **un·scru´- pu·lous·ness** n.

un·sea·son·a·ble (ŭnsē´zonabel) adj. 1. Not appropriate to the season. 2. Not at the right time, inopportune. **un·sea´son·a·ble- ness** n. **un·sea´son·a·bly** adv.

un·seat (ŭnsēt´) v.t. 1. (of horse) Throw (rider) from saddle. 2. Dislodge, deprive of seat, esp. in legislative body etc.

un·seem·ly (ŭnsēm´lē) adj. Not in accordance with what is customary; improper; unbecoming. **un·seem´li·ness** n.

un·set·tled (ŭnsĕt´eld) adj. Not (yet) settled; liable to or open to change or further discussion; (of bill etc.) unpaid; (of region) unpopulated. **un·set´tled·ness** n.

un·sight·ly (ŭnsīt´lē) adj. Unpleasing to the eye, ugly. **un- sight´li·ness** n.

un·skilled (ŭnskĭld´) adj. Not

having or needing skill or special training.

un·so·lic·it·ed (ŭnsolĭs´ĭtĭd) adj. Not asked for; given or done voluntarily.

un·sound (ŭnsownd´) adj. Not sound; diseased, unhealthy, rotten, ill-founded, fallacious, unreliable. **un·sound´ly** adv. **un·sound´ness** n.

un·spar·ing (ŭnspār´ĭng) adj. Profuse, lavish; merciless. **un- spar´ing·ly** adv.

un·speak·a·ble (ŭnspē´kabel) adj. That may not be spoken; indescribably repulsive or objectionable. **un·speak´a·bly** adv.

un·sta·ble (ŭnstā´bel) adj. Not stable; changeable; showing tendency to sudden mental or emotional changes. **un·sta´ble- ness** n. **un·sta´bly** adv.

un·stead·y (ŭnstĕd´ē) adj. Not steady or firm, changeable, fluctuating; not uniform or regular. **un·stead´i·ly** adv. **un·stead´i- ness** n.

un·stop (ŭnstŏp´) v. Remove stopper from; free from obstruction.

un·strung (ŭnstrŭng´) adj. 1. With strings relaxed or removed. 2. Not threaded on a string. 3. Weakened, unnerved.

un·stuck (ŭnstŭk´) adj. Not stuck, loosened from being stuck; **come ~**, (fig., colloq.) fail, go wrong.

un·sung (ŭnsŭng´) adj. Not sung; not celebrated or honored in verse or song.

un·think·a·ble (ŭnthĭng´kabel) adj. Inconceivable.

un·ti·dy (ŭntī´dē) adj. (**-di·er, -di·est**). Not tidy, slovenly. **un·ti´di·ly** adv. **un·ti´di·ness** n.

un·til (ŭntĭl´) prep & conj. = TILL[4], used esp. when its clause or phrase stands first, and in formal style.

un·time·ly (ŭntīm´lē) adj. Occurring at time not suitable, too soon or too early. **~** adv. Prematurely, unseasonably, inopportunely. **un·time´li·ness** n.

un·to (ŭn´tōō) prep. (archaic) To.

un·told (ŭntōld´) adj. Not told; not counted; beyond count.

un·touch·a·ble (ŭntŭch´abel) n. Noncaste Hindu (whom a caste man may not touch).

un·to·ward (ŭntôrd´, -tôrd´, -tō´werd) adj. Perverse, refractory (archaic); awkward; unlucky; unseemly. **un·to´ward·ly** adv. **un·to´ward·ness** n.

un·truth (ŭntrōōth´) n. Being untrue; falsehood, lie.

un·tu·tored (ŭntōō´terd, -tū´-) adj. 1. Not taught or tutored; uneducated. 2. Unsophisticated, naive.

un·used (for sense 1 ŭnūzd´; for sense 2 ŭnūst´) adj. 1. Not or never having been used. 2. Not

*The African Republic of **Upper Volta** is 600 miles from the sea. Its people are mostly subsistence farmers though some livestock, cotton and peanuts are exported. There is also a textile plant.*

accustomed (*to*).

un·u·su·al (ŭnū′zhōoal) *adj.* Not usual; remarkable. **un·u′su·al·ly** *adv.* **un·u′su·al·ness** *n.*

un·ut·ter·a·ble (ŭnŭt′erabel) *adj.* That cannot be uttered; above or beyond description.

un·var·nished (ŭnvär′nĭsht) *adj.* Not covered (as) with varnish; not embellished, plain.

un·veil (ŭnvāl′) *v.t.* Remove veil from; remove concealing drapery from (statue etc.) as part of ceremony of first public display; (fig.) disclose, reveal, make publicly known. ~ *v.i.* Remove one's veil.

un·voiced (ŭnvoist′) *adj.* Not spoken; (phonet.) not voiced.

un·washed (ŭnwŏsht′, -wawsht′) *adj.* Not washed; not usually washed or clean; **the great ~**, the rabble.

un·well (ŭnwĕl′) *adj.* Not in good health; indisposed.

un·wept (ŭnwĕpt′) *adj.* Not wept for, not lamented.

un·whole·some (ŭnhōl′som) *adj.* Injurious to body or mind; having poor health or appearing to be in bad health; morally corrupt, loathsome. **un·whole′some·ly** *adv.* **un·whole′some·ness** *n.*

un·wield·y (ŭnwēl′dē) *adj.* Slow or clumsy of movement, awkward to handle, wield, or manage, by reason of size, shape, or weight. **un·wield′i·ness** *n.*

un·wind (ŭnwīnd′) *v.* (**-wound** pr. -wownd, **-wind·ing**). (Cause to) become drawn out at length after having been wound; (colloq.) relax.

un·wit·ting (ŭnwĭt′ĭng) *adj.* Not knowing, not aware; not intentional. **un·wit′ting·ly** *adv.*

un·wont·ed (ŭnwŏn′tĭd, -wawn′-, -wŭn′-) *adj.* Not usual, customary, or habitual. **un·wont′-ed·ly** *adv.*

un·wound: see UNWIND.

un·writ·ten (ŭnrĭt′en) *adj.* Not written (down); oral; traditional.

up (ŭp) *adv.* To, in, a high or higher place, position, degree, amount, value, etc.; to or in place farther north or otherwise conventionally regarded as higher; to or in the place in question or where the speaker etc. is; to or in erect or vertical position esp. as favorable to activity, out of bed, out of lying or sitting or kneeling posture, in(to) condition of efficiency or activity; (with verbs, usu.) expressing complete or effectual result etc.; **well ~**, in a high position; **~ against**, in(to) contact or collision with; (colloq.) faced or confronted by; **~ and down**, rising and falling; to and fro along; **~ in**, (colloq.)

expert, well-informed (in subject etc.); **~ to**, as high or far as, up toward, so as to reach or arrive at; until; as many or much as, fit or qualified for, capable of, able to deal with, ready for; on a level with; engaged in, occupying oneself with; (colloq.) obligatory or incumbent on; **~-to-date**, extending to the present time; according to the newest ideas, styles, facts, etc.; keeping abreast of the newest styles, most recent news, etc.; **~-to-the-minute**, (colloq.) with the latest information; in the latest style etc.; **~ with**, so as to overtake; on a level with. **up** *prep.* To a higher point of, on or along in ascending direction; at or in a higher part of; **up′stream**, against the current, farther from mouth of river. **up** *adj.* Moving, sloping, going, toward a higher point; (colloq.) optimistic, cheerful; **~-and-coming**, alert and likely to succeed; **up′beat**, (mus.) unaccented beat, esp. last beat in bar; **up′chuck**, (slang) vomit; **up′coming**, (colloq.) forthcoming, about to appear, anticipated; **up′grade**, upward slope; **on the upgrade**, (fig.) improving; **upgrade** (*v.t.*) (**-grad·ed**, **-grad·ing**), raise in status etc. **up** *n.* **on the ~ and ~**, honest(ly); **~s and downs**, rises and falls; undulating ground; alternately good and bad fortune. **up** *v.* (**upped, up·ping**). 1. Rise or raise abruptly. 2. (colloq.) Begin abruptly or boldly (to do something) (*he ~s and says . . .*).

U·pan·i·shad (ōōpăn′ĭshăd, ōōpah′nĭshahd) *n.* Any of various compositions forming the final part of the Vedic literature, dealing with the nature of the soul and ultimate reality; see VEDA.

up·braid (ŭpbrād′) *v.t.* Chide, reproach.

up·bring·ing (ŭp′brĭngĭng) *n.* Bringing up of young persons, early rearing and training.

up·cast (ŭp′kăst, -kahst) *adj.* Turned upward. ~ *n.* (esp.) 1. (mining and geol.) (Fault caused by) upward dislocation of seam. 2. (mining) ~ **(air-)shaft**, shaft through which air passes out of mine.

up·coun·try (ŭp′kŭntrē) *n., adj., & adv.* (To, in, of) inland part of country.

up·date (ŭp′dāt, ŭpdāt′) *v.t.* (**-dat·ed, -dat·ing**). Advance date of, bring up to date.

up·draft (ŭp′drăft) *n.* Upward flow of air.

up·end (ŭpĕnd′) *v.* Set, rise up, on end.

up·heave (ŭphēv′) *v.* (**-heaved, -hove** pr. -hōv, **-heav·ing**). Lift up, raise; throw up with violence, esp. by volcanic action; raise up. **up·heav′al** *n.*

up·hill (ŭp′hĭl) *adj.* Sloping upward; (fig.) arduous, difficult, laborious. **uphill** *adv.* With upward slope on hill, with slope in upward direction.

up·hold (ŭphōld′) *v.t.* (**-held** pr. -hĕld, **-hold·ing**). Hold up, keep erect, support; give support or countenance to; maintain, confirm (decision etc.). **up·hold′er** *n.*

up·hol·ster (ŭphōl′ster, upōl′) *v.t.* Furnish (room etc.) with hangings, carpets, etc.; provide (chair etc.) with textile covering, padding, etc., cover chair (*with, in*). **up·hol′ster·er** *n.* **up·hol′ster·y** *n.* (pl. **-ster·ies**). [f. obs. *upholster, upholder* one who upholds, i.e. keeps in repair; verb back formation]

UPI *abbrev.* United Press International.

up·keep (ŭp′kēp) *n.* (Cost of) maintenance in good condition or repair.

up·land (ŭp′land, -lănd) *n.* (freq. pl.) Piece of high ground, stretch of hilly or mountainous country. ~ *adj.* Living, growing, situated, etc., on high ground; ~

plover, long-necked, long-tailed brownish bird (*Bartramia longicauda*) of Amer. prairie.

up·lift (ŭplĭft´) *v.t.* Raise up, elevate (esp. fig.). ~ (ŭp´lĭft) *n.* Raising, elevating; (colloq.) moral or intellectual edification. **up·lift´-ment** *n.*

up·on (*u*pŏn´, *u*pawn´) = ON.

up·per (ŭp´er) *adj.* Higher in place, situated above; superior in rank, authority, dignity, etc.; ~ **case**: see CASE²; ~ **class**, class of people holding highest status in society, (~-**class** *adj.*); **upper-class´man**, junior or senior in college, cf. UNDERCLASSMAN; **upper crust**, (colloq.) aristocracy, highest social circles; **up´percut** (-**cut, -cut·ting**), (boxing) upward blow to the chin; **upper deck**, highest continuous deck of ship; **upper hand**, mastery, control, or advantage (*of, over*); **upper house**, higher legislative assembly, esp. U.S. Senate. **upper** *n.* Upper part of boot or shoe; (slang) any stimulant drug, esp. an amphetamine; **on one's ~s**, (colloq.) reduced to penury, having hard luck.

up·per·most (ŭp´ermōst) *adj.* Highest in place or rank. ~ *adv.* On or to the top.

Upper (ŭp´er) **Volta.** Inland republic of W. Africa, formerly part of the French colony of the Ivory Coast; independent since 1960; capital, Ouagadougou.

up·pish (ŭp´ĭsh) *adj.* (colloq.) Self-assertive, pert, putting on airs. **up´pish·ly** *adv.* **up´pish·ness** *n.*

up·pi·ty (ŭp´ĭtē) *adj.* (colloq.) Arrogant, snobbish.

up·raise (ŭprāz´) *v.t.* (-**raised, -rais·ing**). Raise up, elevate, rear.

up·right (ŭp´rīt) *adj.* & *adv.* Erect, vertical; righteous, strictly honorable or honest. **up´right·ly** *adv.* **up´right·ness** *n.* **upright** *n.* Upright PIANO²; post or rod fixed upright esp. as support to some structure.

up·ris·ing (ŭp´rīzĭng) *n.* (esp.) Insurrection, popular rising against authority etc.

up·roar (ŭp´rôr, -rōr) *n.* Tumult, violent disturbance, clamor. **up·roar´i·ous** *adj.* **up·roar´i·ous·ly** *adv.* **up·roar´i·ous·ness** *n.*

up·root (ŭprōōt´, -rŏot´) *v.t.* Tear up by the roots; eradicate, destroy.

up·set¹ (ŭpsĕt´) *v.* (-**set, -set·ting**). Overturn, be overturned; disturb the peace, composure, temper, digestion, etc., of. ~ (ŭp´sĕt, ŭpsĕt´) *n.* Upsetting, being upset.

up·set² (ŭp´sĕt) *adj.* ~ **price**, price fixed as lowest for which property offered at auction will be sold.

up·shot (ŭp´shŏt) *n.* Final issue, conclusion.

up·side down, up·side-down (ŭp´sīd down´) *advs.* & *adjs.* With the upper part under, inverted, in(to) total disorder. [altered from ME. *up so down* up as if down]

up·si·lon (ŭp´sĭlŏn, ūp´-) *n.* Letter of Greek alphabet (Υ, υ), corresponding to *u*.

up·stage (ŭp´stāj) *adv.* Away from front of stage; ~ **of**, farther upstage than. **upstage** *adj.* (slang) Supercilious, haughty. ~ (ŭpstāj´) *v.t.* (-**staged, -stag·ing**). Force (another actor or actress) to face away from audience by getting or keeping upstage; (fig.) outshine; behave superciliously or haughtily toward.

up·stairs (ŭpstārz´) *adv.* Up the stairs. ~ (ŭp´stārz) *adj.* & *n.* (Of, in) upper floor of house etc.

up·stand·ing (ŭpstăn´dĭng) *adj.* Well set up, erect.

up·start (ŭp´stärt) *n.* One who has newly or suddenly risen in position or importance (freq. attrib.).

up·state (ŭp´stāt´) *adj., adv.,* & *n.* (Pertaining to, in) part of state remote from large cities, esp. northern part.

up·stroke (ŭp´strōk) *n.* Upward line made in writing.

up·surge (ŭp´sėrj) *n.* Upward surge, rise.

up·swept (ŭp´swĕpt) *adj.* 1. (of hair) Brushed upward toward top of head. 2. Curved or sloped upward.

up·take (ŭp´tāk) *n.* (colloq.) Understanding, apprehension.

up·thrust (ŭp´thrŭst) *n.* Upward thrust, esp. (geol.) one caused by volcanic or seismic action.

up·tight, up·tight (ŭptīt´) *adjs.* (slang) 1. Tense, worried; annoyed. 2. Stiffly conventional. **up·tight´-ness** *n.*

up·town (ŭp´town´) *adj.* & *n.* (Pertaining to, in) higher or residential part of town or city.

up·turn (ŭp´tėrn) *n.* Upheaval; improvement, upward trend.

up·ward (ŭp´werd) *adj.* & *adv.* (Directed) toward a higher place (lit. & fig.); ~ **mobility**, capacity or tendency to move from lower to higher economic and social position. **up´wards** *adv.* (esp.) ~ **of**, more than. **up´ward·ly** *adv.* **up´ward·ness** *n.*

up·wind (ŭp´wĭnd) *adj.* & *adv.* In the direction opposite to that in which the wind is blowing.

U·ral-Al·ta·ic (ūr´al ăltā´ĭk) *adj.* Of (the people of) the Urals and Altaic mountain ranges of central Asia; of a family of Finnic, Mongolian, Turkic, and other agglutinative languages of N. Europe and Asia.

Ural (ūr´al) **Mountains.** (also **Urals**) Mountain range in U.S.S.R. forming a natural boundary between Europe and Asia.

U·ra·ni·a (yŏōrā´nēa). (Gk. and Rom. myth.) 1. Muse of astronomy. 2. Title of Aphrodite, in her heavenly or pure aspect.

u·ra·ni·um (yŏōrā´nēum) *n.* (chem.) Heavy grayish metallic radioactive element, found in pitchblende and minerals, capable of nuclear fission and hence used in the production of atomic energy and atomic bombs; symbol U, at. no. 92, at. wt. 238.029. **u·ran´ic** (yŏōrăn´ĭk), **u·ran·ous** (ūr´anus, yŏōrăn´-) *adjs.* [f. URANUS]

U·ra·nus (ūr´anus, yŏōrā´-). 1. (Gk. myth.) Personification of the sky, the most ancient of the Greek gods and the first ruler of the universe. 2. (astron.) Seventh of the major planets, farthest from the sun except for Neptune and Pluto. **U·ra´ni·an** *adj.*

Ur·ban (ėr´ban). Name of eight popes: **Urban II**, pope 1088–99, inaugurated the first crusade; **Urban VIII**, pope 1623–44, Florentine scholar and poet.

ur·ban (ėr´ban) *adj.* Of, living or situated in, a city or town; ~ **guerrilla**, terrorist operating in cities; ~ **renewal**, slum clearance and redevelopment with new housing and facilities; ~ **sprawl**, uncontrolled expansion of town or city.

ur·bane (ėrbān´) *adj.* Courteous, civil; bland, suave. **ur·bane´ly** *adv.* **ur·ban·i·ty** (ėrbăn´ĭtē) *n.* (pl. **-ties**). [L. *urbanus* of the city, refined, polished (*urbs* city)]

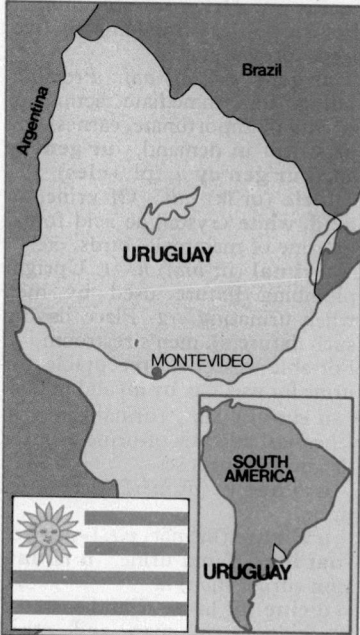

*The smallest country in South America, **Uruguay**, once very prosperous, has suffered from political unrest and inflation. Its exports are mainly wool, meat and hides.*

ur·ban·ize (ĕr'baniz) *v.t.* (**-ized, -iz·ing**). Render urban; remove rural character of (district or population). **ur·ban·i·za·tion** (ĕrbanizā'shon) *n.*

ur·chin (ĕr'chĭn) *n.* 1. Hedgehog (archaic or dial.); **sea ~**: see SEA. 2. Roguish or mischievous boy; little fellow, boy. [ME. *hurcheon* hedgehog, f. L. *ericius*]

Ur·du (ōor'dōō, ōordōō') *n.* Literary form of Hindustani drawing vocabulary from Persian and using Persian-Arabic script; one of the national languages of Pakistan. [Hind., lit. = "camp language"]

-ure *suffix.* Forming nouns with sense (1) (result of) action or process (*composure, enclosure, figure, seizure*); (2) function, state, rank, dignity, office (*judicature, prefecture*); (3) collective body of agents (*legislature*); (4) that by which the action is effected (*closure, ligature*).

u·re·a (yōorē'a, ūr'ēa) *n.* (chem.) Soluble nitrogenous crystalline compound ($CO(NH_2)_2$), present in urine of mammals, birds, and some reptiles, and also in blood, milk, etc.

u·re·mi·a (yōorē'mēa) *n.* (path.) Presence in blood of urinary matter normally excreted by kidneys; condition caused by failure of kidneys to function. **u·re'mic** *adj.*

u·re·ter (yōorē'ter) *n.* Either of two ducts conveying urine from kidney to bladder or cloaca.

u·re·thra (yōorē'thra) *n.* (pl. **-thrae** pr. -thrē, **-thras**). Duct through which urine is discharged from bladder. **u·re'thral** *adj.*

urge (ĕrj) *v.t.* (**urged, urg·ing**). 1. Bring forward (fact etc.) earnestly to someone's attention; state as justification etc.; advocate pressingly. 2. Entreat pertinaciously, incite. 3. Drive forcibly, impel; hasten. **~** *n.* Impelling motive, force, pressure, etc.

ur·gent (ĕr'jent) *adj.* Pressing, calling for immediate action or attention; importunate, earnest and persistent in demand. **ur'gent·ly** *adv.* **ur'gen·cy** *n.* (pl. **-cies**)

u·ric (ūr'ĭk) *adj.* Of urine; **~ acid**, white crystalline acid found in urine of mammals, birds, etc.

u·ri·nal (ūr'ĭnal) *n.* 1. Upright plumbing fixture used by men when urinating. 2. Place having such fixture(s), men's restroom. 3. Portable vessel or receptacle for urine for use, e.g. by invalid in bed.

u·ri·nal·y·sis (ūrĭnăl'ĭsĭs) *n.* Chemical analysis of urine esp. for diagnostic purposes.

u·ri·nar·y (ūr'ĭnĕrē) *adj.* Of urine.

u·ri·nate (ūr'ĭnāt) *v.t.* (**-nat·ed, -nat·ing**). Void urine. **u·ri·na·tion** (ūrĭnā'shon) *n.*

u·rine (ūr'ĭn) *n.* Fluid secreted by kidneys in man and other mammals, stored in bladder and voided at intervals through urethra; similar fluid in other vertebrates. **u'ri·nous** *adj.*

urn (ĕrn) *n.* 1. Vessel or vase with foot and usu. with rounded body, esp. as used for storing ashes of the dead, or as receptacle or measure. 2. Large vessel with spigot, for serving tea or coffee.

u·rol·o·gy (yōorŏl'ojē) *n.* Study of diseases of urinary system. **u·rol'o·gist** *n.*

Ur·sa (ĕr'sa). (astron.) **~ Major**, the Great Bear, a northern constellation, also known as the Big Dipper; **~ Minor**, the Little Bear or Little Dipper, northernmost constellation, containing the polestar. [L., = "she-bear"]

Ur·su·line (ĕr'sulĭn, -lĭn, ĕrs'yu-) *adj.* & *n.* (Nun) of an order founded by St. Angela Merici at Brescia in 1537 for nursing the sick and teaching girls. [named after St. Ursula, patron saint of the foundress]

ur·ti·car·i·a (ĕrtĭkār'ēa) *n.* (path.) Severely itching skin eruptions caused by allergic reaction to external agents (foods etc.) or emotional stimuli; also called hives and nettle rash.

U·ru·guay (ōor'ugwā, -gwī, ūr'-). S. Amer. republic, lying to the E. of the Uruguay river, inaugurated in 1830; capital, Montevideo. **U·ru·guay·an** (ōorugwā'an, -gwī'-, ūr-) *adj.* & *n.*

US, U.S. *abbrevs.* United States (of America).

us (ŭs) *pron.* Objective (accus., dat.) case of WE.

USA, U.S.A. *abbrevs.* United States of America; United States Army.

USAF, U.S.A.F. *abbrevs.* United States Air Force.

us·age (ū'sĭj, ū'zĭj) *n.* Manner of using or treating; treatment; habitual or customary practice, established use (esp. of word); quantity used; (law) habitual but not necessarily immemorial practice.

USCG, U.S.C.G. *abbrevs.* United States Coast Guard.

USDA *abbrev.* United States Department of Agriculture.

use (ūz) *v.* (**used, us·ing**). 1. Employ for a purpose or as instrument or material; exercise; put into operation, avail oneself of; **~ up**, use the whole of, find a use for what remains of; exhaust, wear out. 2. Treat in specified manner. 3. (now only in past t.) Be accustomed, have as constant or frequent practice; (past part.) accustomed; (past part.) (of clothes, vehicles, etc.) secondhand. **us·a·ble** *adj.* **use** (ūs) *n.* 1. Using, employment, application to a purpose; right or power of using; availability, utility, purpose for which thing can be used, occasion for using. 2. Ritual and liturgy of a church, diocese, etc. 3. (law) Benefit or profit of lands etc. held by another solely for the beneficiary. **us·er** (ū'zer) *n.*

use·ful (ūs'ful) *adj.* Of use, serviceable; suitable for use, advantageous, profitable. **use'ful·ly** *adv.* **use'ful·ness** *n.*

use·less (ūs'lĭs) *adj.* Serving no useful purpose, unavailing; of inadequate or insufficient capacity, inefficient. **use'less·ness** *n.*

USES *abbrev.* United States Employment Service.

USGS, U.S.G.S. *abbrevs.* United States Geological Survey.

ush·er (ŭsh'er) *n.* Person who shows people to seats in church, theater, etc. (fem. **ush·er·ette'**); attendant of bridegroom at wedding. **usher** *v.t.* Act as usher to; precede (person) as usher, announce, show *in, out* (freq. fig.). [OF. *uissier* f. L. *ostiarius* doorkeeper (*ostium* door)]

USIA, U.S.I.A. *abbrevs.* United States Information Agency.

USMC, U.S.M.C. *abbrevs.* United States Marine Corps.

USN, U.S.N. *abbrevs.* United States Navy.

USPHS, U.S.P.H.S. *abbrevs.* United States Public Health Service.

U.S.S. *abbrev.* United States Senate; United States Ship (or Steamer, Steamship).

U.S.S.R., USSR *abbrevs.*

US Air Force *Phantoms stationed at Lakenheath, England. There are many strategically positioned bases around the world used by the US Air Force.*

Union of Soviet Socialist Republics.

usu. *abbrev.* Usual(ly).

u·su·al (ū′zhōōal) *adj.* Commonly or ordinarily observed, practiced, used, happening, to be found, etc.; current, ordinary, customary, wonted. **u′su·al·ly** *adv.* **u′su·al·ness** *n.*

u·su·fruct (ū′zufrŭkt, ū′su-, ūz′yu-, ūs′yu-) *n.* (law) Right of enjoying use and advantages of another's property, short of causing damage or prejudice to this; use, enjoyment (*of* something). **u·su·fruc·tu·ar·y** (ūzufrŭk′chōōĕre, ūsu-, ūzyu-, ūsyu-) *adj. & n.* (pl. **-ar·ies**). Of usufruct, (person) enjoying usufruct.

u·su·rer (ū′zherer) *n.* One who lends money at exorbitant or illegal rates of interest.

u·surp (ūserp′, ūzerp′) *v.* Seize, assume, (power, right, etc.) wrongfully. **u·sur·pa·tion** (ūserpā′shon, ūzer-), **u·surp′er** *ns.*

u·su·ry (ū′zhere) *n.* (pl. **-ries**). Practice of lending money at exorbitant interest, esp. at higher interest than is allowed by law; such interest. **u·su·ri·ous** (ūzhoor′eus) *adj.* **u·su′ri·ous·ly** *adv.* **u·su′ri·ous·ness** *n.*

UT, Ut. *abbrevs.* Utah.

U·tah (ū′taw, ū′tah). Western state of U.S., admitted to the Union in 1896; capital, Salt Lake City.

u·ten·sil (ūtĕn′sĭl) *n.* Instrument, implement, vessel, esp. in domestic use.

u·ter·ine (ū′terĭn, -rīn) *adj.* 1. Having the same mother but different fathers. 2. Of, situated in, connected with, the uterus.

u·ter·us (ū′terus) *n.* (pl. **u·ter·i** pr. ū′terī). Womb, organ in which young are conceived, develop, and are protected till birth.

u·til·i·tar·i·an (ūtĭlĭtār′ēan) *adj.* Of, consisting in, based on, utility, esp., regarding the greatest good of the greatest number as the chief consideration of morality; holding utilitarian views or principles. ~ *n.* One who holds or supports utilitarian views; one devoted to mere utility or material interests.

u·til·i·tar·i·an·ism (ūtĭlĭtār′ēanĭzem) *n.* Utilitarian principles, doctrines, etc., esp. as expounded by BENTHAM and J. S. MILL.

u·til·i·ty (ūtĭl′ĭte) *n.* (pl. **-ties**). 1. Usefulness, fitness for some desirable end or useful purpose, profitableness; power to satisfy human wants; useful thing; (**public**) **utilities**, (organizations supplying) gas, water, electricity, transport services, means of communication, etc., provided for some or all members of the community and regarded as so essential to the life of the community that they are subject to various forms of public control. 2. (attrib.) Reared, kept,

made, etc., for useful ends as opp. to display or show purposes; **utility man**, (baseball) reserve player able to play several positions; **utility room**, room containing appliances (e.g. heater, washer, dryer, etc.).

u·ti·lize (ū′tĭlīz) *v.t.* (**-lized, -liz·ing**). Make use of, turn to account, use. **u·ti·li·za·tion** (ūtĭlĭzā′shon) *n.*

ut·most (ŭt′mōst) *adj.* Furthest, extreme; that is such in the highest degree. ~ *n.* Utmost point, degree, limit, extent, etc.; best of one's ability, power, etc.

U·to·pi·a (ūtō′pēa). Name of the imaginary island governed under a perfect political and social system, which forms the title of a book by Sir Thomas More published in 1516; hence, any ideal or perfect social and political system. **U·to·pi·an** *adj. & n.* (Inhabitant) of Utopia; (usu. **u ~**) (characteristic of) an ardent, but unpractical reformer. **u·to′pi·an·ism** *n.* [Gk. *ou* not + *topos* place]

U·tril·lo (ūtrĭl′ō, ōō-), **Maurice** (1883–1955). French painter known especially for scenes of villages and Paris streets.

Awesome. pinnacles tower above the Rec Canyon in the Bryce Canyon Natinal Park, Utah. The result of differential weathering, they will, in time, fall and add to the soil-building process below.

ut·ter[1] (ŭt′er) *adj.* Complete, total, unqualified. **ut′ter·ly** *adv.* **ut′ter·ness** *n.* **ut′ter·most** *adj.*

ut·ter[2] (ŭt′er) *v.t.* 1. Emit audibly; express in spoken or written words. 2. Put (counterfeit money etc.) into circulation. **ut′ter·er** *n.* **ut′ter·ance** *n.* Uttering; power of speech; spoken words.

U-turn (ū′tern) *n.* Turning completely around, esp. of motor vehicle on street to face in opposite direction, without reversing; complete reversal of policy etc.

u·vu·la (ūv′yula) *n.* (pl. **-las, -lae** pr. -lē). Conical fleshy prolongation hanging from middle of pendent margin of soft palate. **u′vu·lar** *adj.*

Ux·mal (ōōshmahl′). Ancient city in Yucatan, Mexico; site of Mayan ruins.

ux·o·ri·ous (ŭksōr′eus, -sōr′-, ŭgzōr′-, -zōr′-) *adj.* Excessively, foolishly fond of one's wife; marked by such fondness. **ux·o′ri·al·ly** *adv.* **ux·o′ri·ous·ness** *n.*

Uz·bek (ōōz′bĕk, ŭz′-), **Uz·beg** (ōōz′bĕg, ŭz′-) *adjs. & ns.* (pl. **-beks, -begs**, collect. **-bek, -beg**). (Member, language) of a Turkic people of Turkestan and Uzbekistan.

Uz·bek·i·stan (ōōzbĕk′ĭstăn, ŭz-, -stahn). Constituent republic (properly *Uzbek Soviet Socialist Republic*) of U.S.S.R., lying S. and SE. of the Aral Sea; capital, Tashkent.

In Latin and in English, use of the letter **V, v** was at first interchangeable with U. This continued in English as late as the 17th century. However, the Latin sound changed earlier (about the end of the Roman Empire) from that of W to its present usage.

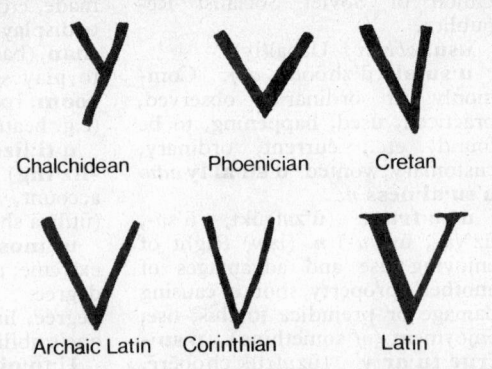

Chalchidean   Phoenician   Cretan

Archaic Latin   Corinthian   Latin

V, v (vē) (pl. **V's, v's** or **Vs, vs**). 1. Twenty-second letter of modern English and 20th of ancient Roman alphabet, adopted in form from early Greek vowel symbol **V**, in English representing a labiodental voiced spirant. 2. Roman numeral symbol for 5. 3. **V**, symbol for allied victory in World War II; **V-E Day**, May 8, 1945, day fixed for the official celebration of the end of hostilities in Europe; **V-J Day**, Aug. 15, 1945, celebrating end of hostilities in Japan. 4. Object etc. shaped like **V**; **V sign**, (orig. in World War II) first two fingers held up in shape of **V**, palm outward, as symbol of victory. Similar sign, palm inward, as vulgar derisory gesture.

V *symbol*. Vanadium.

V, v *abbrevs*. Volt(s).

v. *abbrev*. Verb; verse; versus; *vide*.

VA, V.A. *abbrevs*. Veterans Administration; Virginia.

Va. *abbrev*. Virginia.

V.A. *abbrev*. Vicar Apostolic; Vice Admiral.

va·can·cy (vā′kansē) *n*. (pl. **-cies**). Being vacant; vacant space, breach, gap; lack of intelligence, inanity; unoccupied office, room(s) to let, post, or dignity.

va·cant (vā′kant) *adj*. Empty, not filled or occupied; (of the mind) unoccupied with thought; without intelligence; (of person) with vacant mind. **va′cant·ly** *adv*.

va·cate (vā′kāt) *v.t*. (**-cat·ed, -cat·ing**). Leave (office, position) vacant; give up possession or occupancy of (house etc.); (law) make void, annul, cancel.

va·ca·tion (vākā′shon, va-) *n*. Vacating; part of year constituting fixed period of cessation from work (esp. while still collecting pay) or study; period of recreation, travel, etc.; time during which courts, schools, or universities are closed; cf. HOLIDAY. **va·ca′tion·er, va·ca′tion·ist** *ns*.

vac·ci·nate (văk′sināt) *v.t*. (**-nat·ed, -nat·ing**). Inoculate with a vaccine, esp. against smallpox. **vac·ci·na·tion** (văksinā′shon), **vac′ci·na·tor** *ns*.

vac·cine (văksēn′, văk′sēn) *n*. Preparation of cowpox virus used for inoculation against smallpox; any preparation of microorganisms used as an immunizing agent.

vac·il·late (văs′ilāt) *v.i*. (**-lat·ed, -lat·ing**). Swing or sway unsteadily; hover doubtfully; waver between different opinions, etc.

*Figure labels:*

gas from system

guard ring (cold cap)

top jet

water cooling coils

splash baffle

centre jet

lower jet

to rotary pump

ejector jet

thermal insulating collar

heaters

*To obtain the low pressures needed to achieve a near-perfect **vacuum**, a vapor-diffusion pump is often used. The rotary pump exhausts most of the air and then the heated oil gathers the remaining gas in the system.*

vac·il·la·tor, vac·il·la·tion (văsi-lā′shon) *ns.*

va·cu·i·ty (văkū′ĭtē) *n.* (pl. **-ties**). Empty space; absolute emptiness; vacuousness, vacancy.

vac·u·ole (văk′ūōl) *n.* Space within protoplasm usu. filled with liquid.

vac·u·ous (văk′ūus) *adj.* Empty; void; unintelligent, vacant. **vac′u·ous·ly** *adv.* **vac′u·ous·ness** *n.*

vac·u·um (văk′ūum, -ūm) *n.* (pl. **-u·ms, -u·a** pr. -ūa). Space entirely empty of matter; empty space; vessel, vessel, empty of air, esp. one from which air has been artificially withdrawn; ~ **bottle, jug**, vessel with double wall enclosing vacuum so that liquid in inner receptacle retains its heat or cold; ~ **cleaner**, apparatus for removing dust etc. from carpets, upholstery, etc., by suction; ~-**packed**, sealed after partial removal of air; ~ **pump**, pump for producing a vacuum; ~ **tube**, sealed glass or metal tube or bulb from which almost all the air has been removed, so that electrical current can flow between electrodes inside without disturbance by a gaseous atmosphere; such tube used in radio and electronics. **vacuum** *v.t.* (colloq.) Clean with vacuum cleaner.

va·de me·cum (vā′dē mē′kum, vah′-) *n.* (pl. **va·de me·cums**). Book or other thing carried constantly about the person, esp. handbook or manual. [L., = "go with me"]

Va·duz (vahdōōts′, fah-). Capital of the principality of Liechtenstein.

vag·a·bond (văg′abŏnd) *adj.*

To prevent outbreaks of cholera and other highly-infectious diseases, mass **vaccination** programs have been instituted in India and in other countries where infection is likely to occur.

Wandering, having no settled habitation or home; straying; (as) of a vagabond. ~ *n.* Vagabond person, esp. idle and worthless wanderer, vagrant; (colloq.) scamp, rascal. **vag′a·bond·age, vag′a·bond·ism** *ns.* **vag′a·bond·ish** *adj.*

va·gar·y (vagār′ē, vā′gerē) *n.* (pl. **-gar·ies**). Capricious or extravagant action, notion, etc.; freak, caprice.

va·gi·na (vajī′na) *n.* (pl. **-nas, -nae** pr. -nē). Sheathlike covering, organ, or part; membranous canal leading from vulva to uterus in female mammals; analogous structure in some other animals. **vag·i·nal** (văj′inal) *adj.*

vag·i·ni·tis (văjinī′tĭs) *n.* (pathol.) Inflammation of the vagina.

va·grant (vā′grant) *n.* One without established home or regular work, wandering from place to place, tramp, wanderer; (law) idle and disorderly person liable to arrest and imprisonment. ~ *adj.* That is a vagrant; (as) of a vagrant; roving, itinerant. **va′grant·ly** *adv.*

va·gran·cy (vā′gransē) *n.* (pl. **-cies**).

vague (vāg) *adj.* (**va′guer, va′guest**). Indistinct, not clearly expressed or perceived, of uncertain or ill-defined meaning or character or appearance; forgetful, unbusinesslike. **vague′ly** *adv.* **vague′ness** *n.*

va·gus (vā′gus) *n.* (pl. **va·gi** pr. vā′jī). Either of tenth pair of cranial nerves, with branches to thoracic and abdominal viscera etc.

vain (vān) *adj.* Unsubstantial, empty, of no effect, unavailing; having excessively high opinion (*of* one's own appearance, qualities, possessions, etc.); **in** ~, to no effect or purpose, vainly; **take in** ~, utter, use (name, esp. of God), needlessly, casually, or idly. **vain′ly** *adv.*

vain·glo·ry (vān′glōrē, -glōrē, vānglōr′ē, -glōr′ē) *n.* Boastfulness, extreme vanity. **vain·glo′ri·ous** *adj.* **vain·glo′ri·ous·ly** *adv.* **vain·glo′ri·ous·ness** *n.*

Vais·ya (vīs′ya, vīsh′-). (Member of) the third of the four great Hindu castes, comprising merchants and agriculturalists. [Sansk. *vaiśya* peasant, laborer]

val·ance (văl′ans, vā′lans) *n.* Short curtain around frame or canopy of bedstead, above window or under shelf.

vale[1] (vāl) *n.* Valley (now chiefly poet. or in names); ~ **of tears**, the world as a scene of troubles etc.

va·le[2] (vah′lā, vā′lē; *Lat.* wah′lĕ) *int.* & *n.* Farewell. [L., = "be well!"]

val·e·dic·tion (văledĭk′shon) *n.* (Words used in) bidding farewell.

val·e·dic·to·ri·an (văledĭktōr′-ean, -tōr′-) *n.* Senior student (usu. highest ranking in class) who delivers the valedictory oration on graduation etc.

val·e·dic·to·ry (văledĭk′terē) *adj.* & *n.* (pl. **-ries**). (Speech, oration) bidding farewell.

va·lence (vā′lens), **va·len·cy** (vā′lensē) (pl. **-cies**) *ns.* (chem.) 1. Power that atoms possess of combining with one another to form molecules; ~ **bond**, linkage between two atoms in a molecule, formed either by the transfer of an electron from one atom to the other (*electrovalent bond*) or by the sharing of electrons, two to each link, between the atoms (*covalent bond*). 2. Number indicating the number of atoms of hydrogen with which a single atom of a given element can combine (an element with a valence of 1 is *univalent* or *monovalent*, of 2 *bivalent* or *divalent*, of 3 *tervalent* or *trivalent*, of 4 *quadrivalent* or *tetravalent*, etc.).

Va·len·ci·a (valĕn′shēa, -sēa). Town and province of E. Spain; hence, variety of almond, raisin, orange, and other fruits, produced there.

Va·len·ci·ennes (valĕnsēēnz′; *Fr.* vălahṅsyĕn′). Town in NE. France, formerly Flemish; ~ **lace**, fine bobbin lace made at Valenciennes in 17th and 18th centuries.

va·len·cy = VALENCE.

Val·en·tine[1] (văl′entīn), **St.** Name of several saints of whom the most celebrated are two martyrs whose festivals fall on Feb. 14, both belonging to reign of the emperor

Claudius.

Val·en·tine² (văl'entīn) *n.* 1. St. Valentine's day, Feb. 14, on which birds were believed to mate and sweethearts were chosen. 2. Sweetheart chosen on St. Valentine's day; gift given on this occasion (archaic); (also **v**~) letter or card, of sentimental or comic nature, sent, usu. anonymously, to person of opposite sex on St. Valentine's day.

Va·le·ra (valār'a), **Ea·mon De** (ā'mŏn dě): see DE VALERA.

va·le·ri·an (valēr'ēan) *n.* Any species of widely distributed herbaceous genus *Valeriana*, esp. *V. officinalis*, with small pink or white flowers and strong odor; dried roots etc. of species of valerian used as carminative etc., or in scents etc. **va·ler·ic** (valĕr'ĭk, -lēr'-), **va·le·ri·an·ic** (valērēăn'ĭk) *adjs.* Derived from valerian; ~ **acid**, any of four strong-smelling isomeric fatty acids.

val·et (văl'ĭt, văl'ā, vălā') *n.* (also ~ **de cham·bre** pr. vălǎ *de* shahň'bre) (pl. ~**s de cham·bre** pr. vălǎ *de* shahň'bre). Manservant attending on man's person and having charge of clothes etc.; one who cleans, presses, and mends clothes. **val'et** *v.t.* (**-et·ed**, **-et·ing**). Wait on, act, as valet to.

val·e·tu·di·nar·i·an (văletōōdi-nār'ēan, -tū-) *adj. & n.* (Person) of infirm health, esp. unduly solicitous or anxiously concerned about health. **val·e·tu·di·nar'i·an·ism** *n.* **val·e·tu·di·nar·y** (văletōō'di-nĕrē, -tū'-) *adj. & n.* (pl. **-nar·ies**).

Val·hal·la (vălhăl'a, vahlhah'la). (Scand. myth.) Hall assigned to heroes who have died in battle, in which they feast with Odin.

val·iant (văl'yant) *adj.* Brave, courageous. **val'iant·ly** *adv.* **val'iance, val·ian·cy** (văl'yansē) *ns.*

val·id (văl'ĭd) *adj.* (of reason, argument, etc.) Sound, defensible, well-grounded; (law) sound and sufficient, executed with proper formalities. **val'id·ly** *adv.* **val'id·ness, va·lid·i·ty** (valĭd'ĭtē) *ns.*

val·i·date (văl'ĭdāt) *v.t.* (**-dat·ed**,

In Europe and Asia, **valerian** had many uses. Its roots contained a drug used to treat nervous disorders; perfume was extracted from its leaves which were also used as a condiment.

-dat·ing). Make valid, ratify, confirm. **val·i·da·tion** (vălĭdā'shon) *n.*

va·lise (valēs'; *Brit.* also valēz') *n.* Small piece of hand luggage.

Va·li·um (văl'ēum) *n.* (trademark) Drug used as tranquilizer and muscle relaxant.

Val·kyr·ie (vălkēr'ē, văl'kĭrē) *n.* (Scand. myth.) Each of 12 war maidens supposed to hover over battlefields selecting those to be slain and conducting them to Valhalla.

Val·let·ta (vahllĕt'tah). Capital city and port of Malta.

val·ley (văl'ē) *n.* (pl. **-leys**). Long depression or hollow between hills, freq. with stream or river

The most familiar **valve** used today is the domestic water faucet which is screwed down to stop the passage of water. A rotary valve is used where finer tolerances are needed, as with a gas.

along bottom; stretch of country drained or watered by river system; any depression or hollow resembling valley, esp. trough between waves; angle formed by intersection of two roofs or roof and wall; ~ **of the shadow of death**, experience of being near to death (Ps. 23).

Val·ley (văl'ē) **Forge.** Village in SE. Pennsylvania where George Washington and Amer. Revolutionary army passed winter of 1777–8 in conditions of great hardship.

val·or, *Brit.* **val·our** (văl'er) *ns.* (now chiefly poet. and rhet.) Courage, esp. as shown in war or conflict. **val'or·ous** *adj.* **val'or·ous·ly** *adv.*

Val·pa·rai·so (vălparī'sō, -zō), **Val·pa·ra·i·so** (vahlpahrahē'saw). City and major seaport of Chile on the Pacific.

valse (văls, vahls) *n.* Waltz. [Fr.]

val·u·a·ble (văl'ūabel, -yabel) *adj.* Of great value, price, or worth. ~ *n.* (usu. pl.) Valuable thing or possession esp. small article.

val·u·a·tion (vălyūā'shon) *n.* Estimation (esp. by professional valuer) of thing's worth; worth so estimated, price set on thing.

val·ue (văl'ū) *n.* 1. Amount of commodity, money, etc., considered equivalent for something else; material or monetary worth of thing; worth, desirability, utility, qualities on which these depend; (econ.) amount of commodity, money, etc., for which something else is readily available; FACE, SURPLUS, SURRENDER, ~: see these words; ~ **judgment**, (philos.) subjective estimate of quality etc.; ~ **added tax**, (abbrev. VAT, V.A.T.) tax on amount by which the value of an article is increased by each stage in its production. 2. (math. etc.) Precise number or amount represented by figure, quantity, etc. 3. (mus.) Relative duration of tone signified by note. 4. (painting) Relation of part of picture to others with respect to light and shade, part

stem
(screw spindle)
valve disc
valve seat closed
open
Screw-down Stop valve

Gate or Butterfly valve

Rotary valve or 'gas-tap'

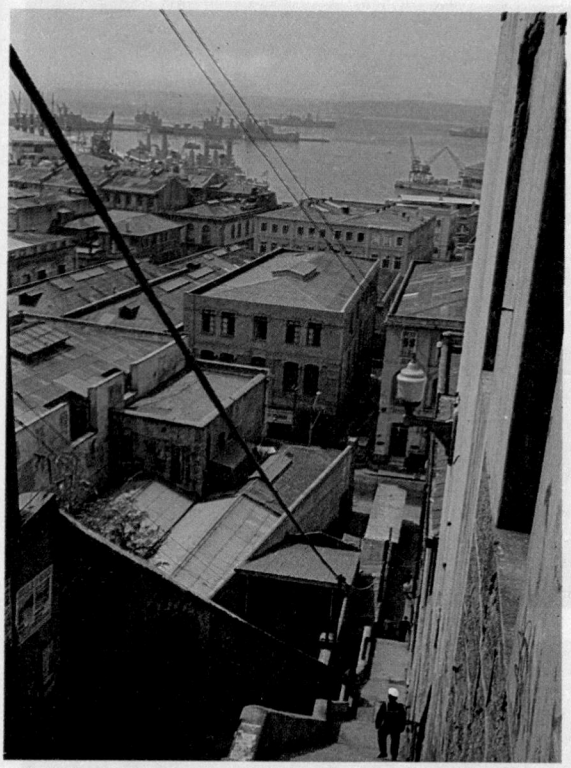

Second-largest city and the major port of Chile, **Valparaiso** *has a population of some 300,000 people. A large percentage of the country's imports is unloaded at this deep-water port.*

The three species of **vampire bat** *live in Central and South America. They feed on the blood of birds and mammals, thus being the only parasitic mammals.*

characterized by particular tone.
value *v.t.* (**-ued, -u·ing**). Estimate value of, appraise, esp. professionally; have high or specified opinion of, prize, esteem, appreciate.
val·ue·less (văl'ūlĭs) *adj.* Worthless. **val'ue·less·ness** *n.*
valve (vălv) *n.* 1. Device for controlling flow of any fluid, usu. acting by yielding to pressure in one direction only. 2. (anat.) Membranous fold or other device in organ or passage of body closing automatically to prevent return flow of blood or other fluid. 3. (Brit.) Vacuum tube. 4. (mus.) Device for varying length of tube in instruments of horn or trumpet kind. 5. (conch.) Each half of hinged shell, single shell of same form; (bot.) each half or section of dehiscent pod, capsule, etc. **valve'-less** *adj.*
val·vu·lar (văl'vyuler) *adj.* Of, like, acting as, furnished with, valve(s).
va·moose (vămoos') *v.i.* (**-moosed, -moos·ing**). (slang) Make off, decamp (from). [Span. *vamos* let us go]
vamp[1] (vamp) *n.* 1. Upper front part of boot or shoe. 2. Something vamped up or patched; (mus.) improvised accompaniment, introductory bars of song etc. ~ *v.* 1. Put new vamp to (boot, shoe); repair, patch *up.* 2. Make *up*, pro-

duce (as) by patching; compose, put together (book etc.) out of old materials; serve up (something old) as new by addition or alteration; (mus.) improvise (esp. accompaniment).
vamp[2] (vămp) *n.* (archaic slang) Adventuress, woman who exploits men. ~ *v.t.* Attract as vamp, allure. [abbrev. of *vampire*]
vam·pire (văm'pīr) *n.* 1. Reanimated corpse supposed in parts of central and E. Europe to leave grave at night and renew its life by sucking blood of sleeping persons; hence, person preying on others. 2. (also ~ **bat**) Any of various small bats of S. Amer. that make an incision with their teeth and lap blood of animals (genera *Desmodus*, *Diaemus*, and *Diphylla*); any of various other bats, chiefly S. American, that do not lap blood, esp. the large **false ~** (*Vampyrus spectrum*). **vam·pir·ic** (vămpĭr'ĭk), **vam'pir·ish** *adj.* **vam'pir·ism** *n.*
van[1] (văn) = VANGUARD.
van[2] (văn) *n.* Closed truck or wagon for carrying goods; (Brit.) baggage car, closed freight car; small closed truck with sleeping, camping facilities, usu. gaudily decorated.
va·na·di·um (vanā'dēum) *n.* (chem.) Extremely hard, steel-white metallic element found in small quantities in combination in

many minerals; symbol V, at. no. 23, at. wt. 50.941; ~ **steel**, steel alloyed with vanadium (and sometimes other elements). **va·nad'ic, van'a·dous** *adjs.*
Van Al·len (văn ăl'en), **James Alfred** (1914–). U.S. physicist; ~ **(radiation) belt**, either of two zones of intense radiation surrounding Earth.
Van Bu·ren (văn būr'en), **Martin** (1782–1862). Eighth president of U.S., 1836–40.
Van·cou·ver (vănkōō'ver). City and seaport of Brit. Columbia, Canada; ~ **Island**, large island off Pacific coast, opposite Vancouver. [George *Vancouver* (1758–98), English navigator and explorer of W. coast of N. Amer.]
Van·dal (văn'dal) *n.* 1. One of an ancient Germanic people who invaded W. Europe, and settled in Gaul, Spain, etc., in 4th and 5th centuries and finally (428–9) migrated to N. Africa; in 455 they sacked Rome in a marauding expedition; their kingdom in N. Africa was overthrown by Belisarius in 533. 2. **v~**, willful or ignorant destroyer of anything beautiful, venerable, or worthy of preservation. **van'dal·ism** *n.* **van·dal·is'-tic** *adj.*
Van de Graaff (văn' de grăf) **generator.** Electrostatic generator producing potentials of over a million volts by using a fast-moving belt inside a hollow spherical conductor, often used as a particle accelerator in nuclear research. [Robert Jemison *Van de Graaf* (1901–67), U.S. physicist]

Van Dyck, Van·dyke (văn dĭk´), **Sir Anthony** (1599–1641). Flemish portrait painter who worked for some years, and died, in England; **Vandyke beard**, neat pointed beard of kind freq. found in his paintings; **Vandyke brown**, deep brown pigment; **Vandyke collar**, broad lace or linen collar with deeply indented edge, seen in portraits by Van Dyck.

vane (vān) *n.* Thin upright plate of metal etc. often in silhouette of cock, ship, arrow, etc., pivoting freely to show direction of wind, often called *weathervane*; windmill sail; blade, wing, or other projection attached to axis etc. so as to be acted on by current of air or liquid; barbs of a feather; sight of surveying instrument.

van Gogh (văn gō´; *Du.* vahn xŏx´), **Vincent** (1853–90). Dutch Post-Impressionist painter, active chiefly in France.

van·guard (văn´gärd) *n.* Front part or foremost division of army, fleet, etc., moving forward or onward; (fig.) leaders of movement etc.

va·nil·la (vanĭl´a) *n.* (Podlike capsule of) tropical climbing orchid of genus *V~*, esp. *V. planifolia*; aromatic extract or synthetic preparation of this, used as flavoring or perfume.

va·nil·lin (văn´ilĭn, vanĭl´-) *n.* (chem.) Fragrant principle of vanilla (C_6H_5CHO).

van·ish (văn´ĭsh) *v.i.* Disappear from sight, esp. suddenly and mysteriously; pass, fade, away; cease to exist; (math.) become zero; **vanishing cream**, face cream that is quickly absorbed by skin; **vanishing point**, in perspective, point at which receding parallel lines appear to meet. **van´ish·er** *n.*

van·i·ty (văn´ĭtē) *n.* (pl. **-ties**). What is vain or worthless; futility, worthlessness, emptiness; empty pride, self-conceit and desire for admiration; woman's dressing table; ~ **bag, case**, woman's small handbag or case containing mirror, face powder, etc.; **V~ Fair**, (from Bunyan's *Pilgrim's Progress*) the world as scene of idle amusement and vain display; fashionable world of society. **van´i·tied** *adj.*

van·quish (văng´kwĭsh, văn´-) *v.t.* (now chiefly rhet.) Conquer, overcome. **van´quish·er** *n.*

van·tage (văn´tĭj, vahn´-) *n.* Advantage (esp. in lawn tennis); ~ **ground**, advantageous position for defense or attack; ~ **point**, position giving wide etc. view.

Portrait of Henry Percy by **Sir Anthony Van Dyck.** *A student of Rubens, he painted in Italy and Holland. He was knighted by Charles I who persuaded him to stay in England.*

vap·id (văp´ĭd) *adj.* Insipid, flat. **vap´id·ly** *adv.* **vap·id·i·ty** (văpĭd´ĭtē) *n.* (pl. **-ties**). **vap´id·ness** *n.*

va·por, Brit. **va·pour** (vā´per) *ns.* Matter diffused or suspended in air, as mist, steam, etc., esp. form into which liquids are converted by action of heat; (phys.) gaseous form of normally liquid or solid substance; vaporized substance; ~ **lock**, blockage of fuel flow in internal combustion engine, caused by pocket of vaporized gasoline as result of excessive heat. **va·por·if·ic** (vāperĭf´ĭk), **va´por·ous**, **va´por·y** *adjs.* **va´por·ous·ly** *adv.* **va´por·ous·ness** *n.* **vapor** *v.i.* Emit vapor; talk fantastically or boastingly.

Variegated plants generally have only two colors in the leaves; this coleus has three. Variegation is rarely found in the wild, for it reduces photosynthesis.

'Cornfield Near Arles' is typical of the expressive brushwork of **Vincent Van Gogh** *in his later years. Despite such originality, few of his paintings sold while he was alive.*

va·por·ize (vā′perĭz) *v.* (**-ized, -iz·ing**). Convert, be converted, into vapor. **va′por·iz·er** *n.* (esp.) Apparatus for vaporizing liquid, fine spray. **va·por·i·za·tion** (vāperĭzā′shon) *n.*

va·pour = VAPOR.

va·que·ro (vahkār′ō) *n.* (pl. **-ros**). (in Latin Amer. and Southwest U.S.) Herdsman, cowboy.

Va·ra·na·si (varah′nasē). (formerly *Benares*) City on the Ganges in India, regarded as sacred by Hindus.

var·i·a·ble (vār′ēabel) *adj.* Apt, liable, to vary or change, capable of variation; modifiable, alterable, changeable, shifting, inconstant; (of star) varying periodically in brightness or magnitude; (math. etc., of quantity etc.) that may assume a succession of values, having different values under different conditions. **var·i·a·bil·i·ty** (vārēabĭl′ĭtē), **var′i·ble·ness** *ns.* **var′i·a·bly** *adv.* **variable** *n.* Variable quantity, star, or other thing; shifting wind, (pl.) parts of sea where steady wind is not expected.

var·i·ance (vār′ēans) *n.* Disagreement, difference of opinion, lack of harmony (esp. in **at** ~); (law) discrepancy between two documents, statements, etc., that should agree; official permission to do something contrary to regulations, esp. authorization to build in contravention of real estate zoning ordinance.

var·i·ant (vār′ēant) *adj.* Differing *from* something or from standard, type, etc. ~ *n.* Variant form, spelling, reading, etc.

var·i·a·tion (vārēā′shon) *n.* 1. Varying, undergoing or making modification or alteration, esp. from normal condition, action, or amount, or from standard or type; extent of this. 2. (astron.) Deviation of heavenly body from mean orbit or motion. 3. (of magnetic needle) Declination. 4. (math.) Change in function(s) of equation due to indefinitely small change of value of constants. 5. (mus.) One of series of repetitions of theme or tune with changes that do not disguise its identity. 6. (ballet) Solo dance.

var·i·co·cele (văr′ĭkōsēl) *n.* Varicose swelling of spermatic veins.

var·i·col·ored (vār′ĭkŭlerd) *adj.* Of various colors, variegated in color.

var·i·cose (văr′ĭkōs, vār′-) *adj.* (of veins) Having permanent abnormal local dilation; affected with, resembling, of, a varix or varices. **var·i·cos·i·ty** (vărĭkōs′ĭtē) *n.*

var·ied (vār′ēd) *adj.* Of differing kinds; changed; ~ **thrush**, songbird of Pacific coast (*Ixoreus naevius*), like robin but having black stripe across breast.

var·i·e·gate (vār′ēegāt, vār′e-, văr′ēe-, văr′e-,) *v.t.* (**-gat·ed, -gat·ing**). Diversify in appearance, esp. in color. **var′i·e·gat·ed** *adj.* **var·i·e·ga·tion** (vārēegā′shon, vāre-, vărēe-, văre-) *n.* Being variegated, esp. (bot.) presence of two or more colors in leaves, petals, etc.; defective or special development leading to such coloring; variegated

marking.

va·ri·e·ty (varī′etē) *n.* (pl. **-ties**). 1. Being varied, diversity, absence of monotony, sameness, or uniformity; collection of different things; ~ **store**, one selling many kinds of small items. 2. Different form *of* some thing, quality, or condition; kind, sort; (biol.) (plant, animal, belonging to) group distinguished by characteristics considered too trivial to permit its classification as distinct species. 3. (also ~ **show**) Entertainment consisting of a number of different independent performances. **va·ri·e·tal·ly** *adv.*

var·i·form (vār′ĭform) *adj.* Of various forms.

var·i·o·rum (vārēōr′um, -ōr′-) *n. & adj.* (Edition, esp. of classical author or text) with notes of various editors or commentators. [L. gen. pl. of *varius* various]

var·i·ous (vār′ēus) *adj.* Different, diverse; separate, several. **var′i·ous·ly** *adv.* **var′i·ous·ness** *n.*

var·ix (vār′ĭks) *n.* (pl. **var·i·ces** pr. vār′ĭsēz). 1. Permanent abnormal dilation of vein or artery, usu. with tortuous development. 2. Prominent longitudinal ridge on surface of shell.

var·let (vär′lĭt) *n.* (hist.) Knight's attendant or page; (archaic) menial, low fellow, scoundrel.

var·mint (vär′mint) *n.* (dial.) Vermin; mischievous or discreditable person or animal.

var·nish (vär′nĭsh) *n.* Resinous matter dissolved in oil or spirit, used for spreading over surface to produce a translucent and usu. glossy protective coating; preparation of certain other substances, e.g. wax, cellulose, for same purpose; surface so formed; gloss; superficial polish of manner; external appearance or display without underlying reality. ~ *v.t.* Coat with varnish; gloss (*over*), disguise.

var·si·ty (vär´sĭtē) *n.* (pl. **-ties**). Principal or first team representing college or school in any sport.

Var·u·na (ver´ōōna). (Hinduism) Supreme cosmic deity, creator, and ruler.

var·y (vār´ē) *v.* (**var·ied, var·y·ing**). Change, make different, modify, diversify; suffer change; be or become different in degree or quality; be of different kinds; ~ **(inversely) as**, change in quantity or value in (inverse) proportion to. **var´y·ing·ly** *adv.*

Vas·co da Ga·ma (vah´skō da gah´ma): see GAMA.

vas·cu·lar (văs´kyuler) *adj.* (biol., anat.) Of tubular vessels; containing, supplied with, these; ~ **system**, system of tubes within an organism for conveying fluid, esp. blood, sap. **vas´cu·lar·ly** *adv.*

vas de·fe·rens (văs dĕf´erĕnz) (pl. **va·sa de·fe·ren·ti·a** pr. vā´sa dĕferĕn´shēa). Spermatic duct. [L. *vas* vessel, *deferens* carrying down]

vase (vās, vāz, vahz) *n.* Vessel, usu. of greater height than width, used as ornament, for holding flowers, etc. or (archaeol.) as container.

vas·ec·to·my (văsĕk´tomē) *n.* (pl. **-mies**). Surgical removal of (part of) the vas deferens, for sterilization.

Vas·e·line (văs´elēn, văselēn´) *n.* (trademark) Kind of petroleum jelly. [f. Ger. *Wasser* water, Gk. *elaion* oil]

vas·o·mo·tor (văsōmō´ter) *adj.* (of nerves) Acting on walls of blood vessels so as to constrict or dilate these and thus regulate flow of blood.

vas·sal (văs´al) *n.* 1. (hist., in feudal system) One holding lands on condition of homage and allegiance to superior. 2. Humble servant or subordinate, slave. **vas´sal·age** *n.* (hist.) Condition, obligations, service, of vassal; servitude, dependence; fief.

vast (văst, vahst) *adj.* Of great extent or area; of great size or amount. **vast´ly** *adv.* **vast´ness** *n.*

VAT, V.A.T. *abbrevs.* Value added tax.

vat (văt) *n.* Large tub, cask, cistern, or other vessel for holding or storing liquids. **vat** *v.* (**vat·ted, vat·ting**). Place, treat, mature, in vat.

Vat·i·can (văt´ĭkan). Pope's palace and official residence on Vatican Hill in Rome; (of or pertaining to) the papal government; ~ **City**, independent papal state in Rome, including Vatican and St. Peter's, established 1929 by Lateran Council; ~ **Council**, ecumenical council of 1869–70, that proclaimed papal infallibility;

similar council held 1962–5; ~ **Hill**, hill in Rome on W. bank of Tiber, opposite ancient Rome.

vaude·ville (vawd´vĭl, vaw´de-) *n.* Variety entertainment. [Fr., prob. f. earlier (*chanson du*) *Vau de Vire* (son of) valley of the Vire, Normandy]

vault[1] (vawlt) *n.* Arched structure of masonry usu. supported by walls or pillars and serving as roof or carrying other parts of building; any arched surface resembling this, esp. apparently concave surface of sky; room or other part of building covered by vault, esp. when subterranean and used as cellar for storing food, wine, etc.; room of this kind without arched roof, underground room, strongroom; (partly) underground burial chamber in cemetery or under church. ~ *v.t.* Construct with, cover (as) with vault; form vault over; make in form of vault. **vault´ed, vault´y** *adjs.*

vault[2] (vawlt) *n.* Leap, spring, performed by vaulting. ~ *v.* Leap, spring, esp. while resting on the hand(s) or with help of pole; spring over thus.

vaunt (vawnt, vahnt) *n.* (archaic or rhet.) Boast. ~ *v.* Boast, brag, (of). **vaunt´ed** *adj.* **vaunt´ing·ly** *adv.*

V.C. *abbrev.* Vice-Chancellor; Vietcong; Victoria Cross.

VD, V.D. *abbrevs.* Venereal disease.

veal (vēl) *n.* Calf's flesh as food.

vec·tor (vĕk´ter) *n.* 1. (math.) Quantity having both magnitude and direction. 2. (path.) Carrier of disease, esp. insect that conveys pathogenic organisms from one host to another. ~ *v.t.* Direct

Wine is kept in a vat for a predetermined period to mature. Once, vats were made from wood, but today stainless steel also is used, especially for white wines.

(aircraft) on a course. **vec·to´ri·al** (vĕktōr´eal, -tŏr-) *adj.*

Ve·da (vā´da, vē-) *n.* Ancient sacred literature of the Hindus; (esp.) the four collections of hymns known as the Rig-Veda, Yarjur-Veda, Sama-Veda, and Atharva-Veda. **Ve´dic** *adj.* [Sansk. *veda* (sacred) knowledge]

Ve·dan·ta (vedahn´ta, -dăn´-) *n.* 1. Final part of the Veda, the Upanishads. 2. Later system of monistic philosophy based on the Upanishads and taught principally by Śandara Ācārya. **Ve·dan´tic** *adj.* [Sansk. VEDA, *anta* end]

vee (vē) *adj.* In the shape of the letter **V**.

veep (vēp) *n.* (colloq.) Vice president, esp. (**V** ~) of the U.S.

veer (vēr) *v.* Change direction, esp. (of wind) in clockwise direction; (of ship) turn with head away from wind, cause to turn thus; (fig.) change from one state, tendency, etc., to another, be variable. **veer´ing·ly** *adv.*

veer·y (vēr´ē) *n.* (pl. **veer·ies**). Amer. thrush (*Hylocichla fuscescens*) noted for its song.

Ve·ga[1] (vē´ga). (astron.) Star in constellation Lyra, fourth brightest in the heavens. [Arab. (*al nasr*) *al wāki* "the falling (vulture)," meaning the constellation Lyra]

Ve·ga[2] (vā´ga; *Sp.* vĕ´gah), **Lo·pe de** (law´pĕ dĕ). Lope Felix de Vega Carpio (1562–1635), prolific Spanish poet and playwright, founder of Spanish drama.

veg·e·ta·ble (vĕj´tabel, vĕj´e-) *n.* Living organism belonging to plant square pins to prevent vertical slipping

boarded formwork

Barrel Vaults

quadrant forms

thick continuous wall

Groin Vaulting

masonry vault

centring frame

longitudinal vault with continuous formwork

windlass supported by tie beams

Erection of a Vault Web

planks

keystone

rib centring

kingdom, plant; (esp.) herbaceous plant cultivated for food. ~ *adj.* Of (the nature of), derived from, concerned with, comprising, plants; ~ **kingdom**, that division of organic nature to which plants belong; ~ **marrow**: see MARROW sense 2.

veg·e·tar·i·an (vĕjetār´ean) *n.* One who eats no animal food, or none that is obtained by destruction of animal life. ~ *adj.* Of vegetarian(s); living on vegetables; consisting of vetetables. **veg·e·tar´i·an·ism** *n.*

veg·e·tate (vĕj´etāt) *v.i.* (**-tat·ed, -tat·ing**). Grow as or like plant(s); (fig.) lead dull monotonous life without intellectual activity or social intercourse. **veg´e·ta·tive** *adj.* 1. Of, concerned with, or typical of vegetation, plants, or plant growth. 2. Of or involved with growth and nutrition, rather than sexual reproduction. 3. Not consciously controlled; passive. **veg´e·ta·tive·ly** *adv.* **veg´e·ta·tive·ness** *n.*

veg·e·ta·tion (vĕjetā´shon) *n.* 1. Vegetating; plants collectively, vegetable growths. 2. (path.) Morbid growth or excrescence on part of body. **veg·e·ta´tion·al** *adj.*

ve·he·ment (vē´ement) *adj.* Intense, violent, acting with great force; exhibiting, caused by, strong feeling or excitement. **ve´he·ment·ly** *adv.* **ve´he·mence, ve´he·men·cy** *ns.*

ve·hi·cle (vē´ĭkel) *n.* 1. Carriage or conveyance for persons or goods, any means of transport, esp. by land. 2. Substance, esp. liquid, used as medium for application, administration, etc., of another substance, as drug; liquid in which pigment is suspended. 3. Thing, person, as means, channel, or in-

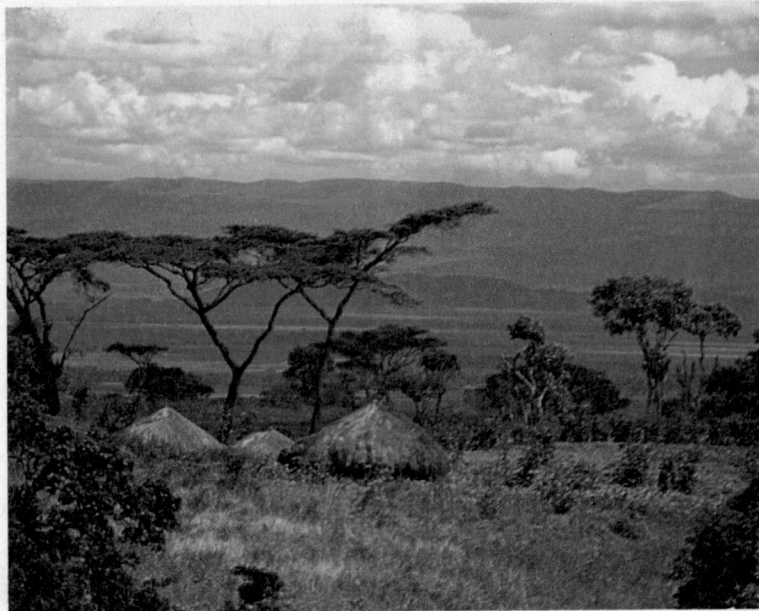

strument of expression, communication, etc. **ve·hic·u·lar** (vēhĭk´yuler) *adj.*

veil (vāl) *n.* 1. Piece of linen or other material as part of nun's headdress, falling over head and shoulders; **take the** ~, become a nun. 2. Piece of thin, usu. more or less transparent, material worn over head or face as part of headdress or to conceal the face or protect it from sun, dust, etc.; curtain; (fig.) disguise, cloak, mask, anything that conceals or covers; **draw a** ~ **over**, conceal, avoid discussing or dealing with. 3. Velum. **veil** *v.t.* Cover

*Observations of nomadic hunter-gatherers have shown that even when man was mainly a meat-eater, he still gathered **vegetables**. Most vegetable varieties have been improved by cultivation.*

*Despite the Dutch application of the world **veld** to South Africa, these grasslands extend much further north to the rift valley in Kenya. Valuable grazing lands are found at the higher altitudes.*

(as) with veil; (fig.) conceal, disguise, mask. **veil´ing** *n.* (esp.) Material for veils, net. **veiled** *adj.*

vein (vān) *n.* 1. Each of the tubular vessels in which blood is conveyed from all parts of body back to heart; (pop.) any blood vessel. 2. (bot.) One of the slender bundles of tissue forming framework of leaf. 3. (entom.) Nervure of insect's wing. 4. Anything suggesting or resembling vein, esp. streak of different color in wood, marble, etc., channel of water in ice etc.; (geol.) crack or fissure in rock, freq. filled with mineral matter; (min.) fissure containing metallic ore. 5. Distinctive character or tendency, cast of mind or disposition, mood. **vein´less, vein´y** (**vein·i·er, vein·i·est**), **veined** *adjs.* **vein** *v.t.* Fill or cover (as) with vein(s). **vein´ing** *n.*

ve·lar (vē´ler) *adj.* Of a velum, esp. velum of palate; (phon., of sound) formed with back of tongue near or touching soft palate. **ve´lar·ize** *v.t.* (**-ized, -iz·ing**). Pronounce with velar articulation.

Ve·láz·quez (velahs´kes; *Sp.* vĕlahth´kĕth), **Diego Rodriguez de Silva y** (1599–1660). Spanish artist, court painter to Philip IV.

veld, veldt (vĕlt, fĕlt) *ns.* (S. Afr.) Fenced or unfenced grassland. [Afrikaans (formerly Du. *veldt* = "field")]

*Although he was court painter to Philip IV of Spain. **Velazquez** did not confine his subject matter to the royal family, as demonstrated (facing) by his realism in 'The Water Seller of Seville', which shows the people, torn clothes and all.*

Street **vendors** offer a wide variety of goods. This one, in San Francisco, has a range of jewelry on sale, probably at below retail cost, but with no guarantees.

Although both skins and papyrus were used for writing in Egypt about 2000 B.C., paper was unknown in Europe before the 11th century A.D. **Vellum** was used for illuminated manuscripts.

vel·lum (věl'um) *n.* Skin (strictly, calfskin) dressed and prepared for writing, painting, etc.; imitations of this, esp. (commerc.) smooth-surfaced writing paper.

ve·loc·i·pede (velŏs'iped) *n.* Any of various light vehicles propelled by riders, esp. early forms of bicycle and tricycle.

ve·loc·i·ty (velŏs'ĭtē) *n.* (pl. **-ties**). Rapidity of motion, operation, or action; (mech.) time rate of change of position of body in a given direction; (loosely) (esp. high) speed; **actual ~**, speed at which a body moving on a curve actually moves as distinct from its **circular ~** (speed at which it is moving around a point) and its **radial ~** (speed at which it is moving away from or toward that point); **terminal ~**, maximum speed of falling object, when resistance of air equals pull of gravity.

ve·lour, ve·lours (veloor') *ns.* (pl. **ve·lours**). Woven fabric with plushlike or velvety pile; felt with similar surface, used for hats; hat of this.

ve·lum (vē'lum) *n.* (pl. **-la** pr. -la). (anat., bot., zool.) Membrane or membranous partition; (esp.) soft PALATE.

vel·vet (věl'vĭt) *n.* Textile fabric having a dense smooth pile on one side formed by loops of additional warp threads, the loops being usu. cut through during the weaving; surface, substance, resembling this in softness or rich appearance, e.g. soft downy skin covering newly grown antlers of deer; (slang) in easy or advantageous position; (slang) gambling winnings, clear profit. **vel'vet·y** *adj.*

vel·vet·een (vělvetēn', věl'vetēn) *n.* Cotton fabric resembling velvet; (pl.) velveteen trousers.

ve·na ca·va (vē'na kā'va) (pl. **ve·nae ca·vae** pr. vē'nē kā'vē). Each of two veins (**inferior ~** and **superior ~**) conveying blood to right atrium of heart.

ve·nal (vē'nal) *adj.* (of person) That may be bribed, willing to lend support, exert influence, or sacrifice principles, from mercenary motive; (of action etc.) characteristic of venal person. **ve'nal·ly** *adv.* **ve·nal·i·ty** (vēnăl'ĭtē, ve-) *n.* (pl. **-ties**).

ve·na·tion (vēnā'shon, ve-) *n.* Arrangement of veins in a leaf or leaflike organ.

vend (věnd) *v.* Sell (now rare exc. law); offer (esp. small articles) for sale, hawk; **vending machine**, coin operated machine for selling small goods. **ven'dor, vend'er** *ns.* **vend'i·ble** *adj.*

ven·det·ta (věndět'a) *n.* Blood feud, esp. one practiced through generations, as in Corsica and parts of Italy; also fig.

ve·neer (venēr') *v.t.* Cover, overlay, (furniture etc.) with thin sheet of finer wood or other more beautiful or valuable material; thin layer used in making plywood; (fig.) give merely specious or superficial appearance of some good quality to, gloss over. **~ n.** Thin outer sheet used in veneering; (fig.) superficial appearance.

ven·er·a·ble (věn'erabel) *adj.* Entitled to veneration because of age, character, etc.; (in Ch. of England) title of archdeacons; (in R.C. Ch.) title of one who has attained lowest of three degrees of

sanctity but is not yet beatified or canonized; **V~ Bede**: see BEDE. **ven·er·a·bil·i·ty** (věnerabĭl'ĭtē), **ven'er·a·ble·ness** *ns.* **ven'er·a·bly** *adv.*

ven·er·ate (věn'erāt) *v.t.* (**-at·ed, -at·ing**). Regard with feelings of respect and reverence; consider as exalted or sacred. **ven·er·a·tion** (věnerā'shon) *n.*

ve·ne·re·al (venēr'ēal) *adj.* Of, connected with, sexual desire or intercourse; infected with venereal disease; **~ disease**, disease, esp. gonorrhea or syphilis, contracted by sexual intercourse with person already infected. [f. VENUS]

Ve·ne·tian (venē'shan) *adj.* Of Venice; **~ blind, v~ blind**, window blind of horizontal slats that can be adjusted so as to admit or exclude light; **Venetian glass**, decorative glassware made at Murano, near Venice, since 15th c., freq. very elaborate and sometimes fusing clear glass with opaque or with glass of various colors; **Venetian lace**, one of several varieties of point lace; **Venetian red**, reddish pigment consisting of ferric oxides; **Venetian School**, school of painting centered in Venice in the 15th and 16th centuries, culminating in the work of Giorgione, Titian, Veronese, and Tintoretto; revival of this in 18th c.; **Venetian window**, PALLADIAN window. **Venetian** *n.* Native, inhabitant, of Venice.

Ven·e·zue·la (věnezwā'la, -zwē'-). S. Amer. republic on Caribbean Sea, formed 1830 after

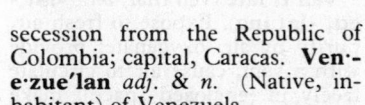

Above left: General view of the sky-scrapers and freeways of Caracas, capital of Venezuela. The prosperity of this country derives from huge reserves of crude oil.

secession from the Republic of Colombia; capital, Caracas. **Ven·-e·zue'lan** *adj.* & *n.* (Native, inhabitant) of Venezuela.

venge·ance (věn´jans) *n.* Avenging oneself on another, retributive or vindictive punishment, hurt or harm inflicted in revenge; **with a ~**, in an extreme degree, with great force or violence.

venge·ful (věnj´ful) *adj.* Seeking vengeance, disposed to revenge, vindictive. **venge'ful·ly** *adv.* **venge'ful·ness** *n.*

ve·ni·al (vē´nēal, vēn´yal) *adj.* (of sin or fault) Pardonable, excusable, not grave or heinous, (theol.) not MORTAL. **ve'ni·al·ly** *adv.* **ve'ni·al·ness, ve·ni·al·i·ty** (věnēăl´ĭtē, věnyăl´-) *ns.*

Ven·ice (věn´ĭs). (Ital. *Venezia*) Seaport of NE. Italy built on numerous islands in a lagoon of the Adriatic; formerly the chief European port for trade with the East, famous esp. for its beauty and (from 15th to 18th c.) as a center of art.

ven·i·punc·ture (věn´ĭpŭngk-ch*er*, vē´ni-) *n.* Puncture of vein, esp. by insertion of hollow needle for medical purposes or for extraction of blood specimen.

ve·ni·re (vĭnī´rē) *n.* (law) Writ directing sheriff to summon jury;

Left: As an oligarchic ruler, the Doge of Venice built the Bridge of Sighs between his palace and the state prison. His enemies were discreetly taken across it after sentencing.

panel thus summoned; **ve·ni′re-man**, member of such a panel.

ven·i·son (vĕn′ĭson, -zon) *n.* Deer's flesh as food.

ven·om (vĕn′om) *n.* Poisonous fluid secreted by certain snakes etc. and injected by biting or stinging; (fig.) bitter or virulent feeling, language, etc. **ven′om·ous** (vĕn′omus) *adj.* **ven′om·ous·ly** *adv.* **ven′om·ous·ness** *n.*

ve·nose (vē′nōs) *adj.* (esp.) Having many or very marked veins. **ve·nos·i·ty** (vĭnŏs′ĭtē) *n.* (esp., med.) Condition in which arteries contain venous blood.

ve·nous (vē′nus) *adj.* Of veins; veined; (of blood) having given up oxygen in capillaries and hence of dark red color, like blood contained in veins (opp. ARTERIAL).

vent[1] (vĕnt) *n.* Opening or slit in garment, esp. slit in back of coat.

vent[2] (vĕnt) *n.* Hole or opening allowing passage out of or into confined space, as flue of chimney, fumarole of volcano, hole in top of barrel to admit air while liquid is drawn out, finger hole in musical instrument, etc.; anus, esp. of lower animals; (fig.) outlet, free passage, free play. ~ *v.t.* Make vent in; give vent or free expression to.

ven·ti·late (vĕn′tĭlāt) *v.t.* (**-lat-ed, -lat·ing**). Expose to fresh air, purify by air, oxygenate; provide with a vent; cause air to circulate freely in (enclosed space); make public, discuss freely. **ven·ti·la·tion** (vĕntĭlā′shon) *n.* **ven′ti·la·tor** *n.* (esp.) Contrivance, e.g. revolving fan, for ventilating building, ship, mine, etc.; opening in wall, freq. with grid, for same purpose. **ven·ti·la·to·ry** (vĕn′tĭlatōrē, -tōrē) *adj.*

ven·tral (vĕn′tral) *adj.* Of the abdomen, abdominal; of the anterior or lower surface (opp. DORSAL). **ven′tral·ly** *adv.*

ven·tri·cle (vĕn′trĭkel) *n.* (anat., zool.) Cavity of body, esp. cavity of heart from which blood is pumped into arteries (in mammals and birds) either of two such cavities; one of series of communicating cavities in brain formed by enlargements of neural canal. **ven·tric·u·lar** (vĕntrĭk′yuler) *adj.*

ven·tril·o·quism (vĕntrĭl′o-kwĭzem), **ven·tril·o·quy** (vĕntrĭl′o-kwē) *ns.* Practice of speaking etc. without visible movement of the lips and in such a manner that the voice appears to come from some other person or object. **ven·tri·lo·qui·al** (vĕntrĭlō′kwēal), **ven·tril·o·quis·tic** (vĕntrĭlokwĭs′tĭk) *adjs.* **ven·tril·o·quist** *n.* **ven·tril·o-**

Of all the operas composed by Verdi, none lends itself more to impressive production than 'Aida'. It was commissioned by an opera house in Cairo to celebrate the opening of the Suez Canal.

Verbena was used as a medicinal herb from the times of ancient Egypt. It was said to alleviate kidney complaints and induce sweating. Aromatic verbena oil is made from another plant.

quize *v.* (**-quized, -quiz·ing**). [L. *venter* belly, *loqui speak*]

ven·ture (vĕn′cher) *n.* Undertaking of a risk, risky undertaking; (archaic) property at stake, thing risked; **at a** ~, at random. **ven′ture·some** *adj.* **ven′ture·some·ly** *adv.* **ven′ture·some·ness** *n.* **venture** *v.* (**-tured, -tur·ing**). Dare; not be afraid, make bold *to* do, hazard (opinion etc.).

ven·tu·ri (vĕntoor′ē) *n.* Short piece of tube between wider sections for measuring flow rate or exerting suction. [G.B. *Venturi* (1740–1822), It. physicist]

ven·ue (vĕn′ū) *n.* (law) County, district, where jury is summoned to come for trial of case; **change of** ~, change location of place of trial to avoid riot, prejudiced jury, etc.; (colloq.) place, rendezvous; position or ground adopted for argument.

Ve·nus (vē′nus). 1. (Rom. myth.) Ancient Italian goddess, identified by the Romans with Aphrodite; ~ **de Milo**: see MELOS; ~**'s flytrap**, N. Amer. insectivorous plant (*Dionaea muscipula*); **Venus's-hair**, delicate maidenhair fern. 2. (astron.) Second planet in order of distance from sun, in orbit between Mercury and Earth; the morning or evening star. **Ve·nu·si·an** (venoō′sēan, -shēan, -shan) *adj.* Of, pertaining to, or characteristic of the planet Venus. ~ *n.* Imagined being living on Venus.

ve·ra·cious (verā′shus) *adj.* Speaking, disposed to speak, the truth; true, accurate. **ve·ra′cious·ly** *adv.* **ve·rac·i·ty** (verăs′-ĭtē) *n.* (pl. **-ties**). **ve·ra′cious·ness** *n.*

ve·ran·da, ve·ran·dah (verăn′da) *ns.* Open roofed portico or gallery along the side of house. [Hindi, f. Port. or Sp. *varanda* railing]

verb (vẽrb) *n.* (gram.) Part of speech that expresses action, occurrence, or being. **verb′less** *adj.*

ver·bal (vẽr′bal) *adj.* 1. Of, concerned with, words; (pop.) oral, not written; verbatim. 2. Of (the nature of) a verb; ~ **noun**, noun derived from verb stem and having some verbal constructions (as English nouns ending in *-ing*). ~ *n.* Verbal noun. **ver′bal·ly** *adv.*

ver·bal·ism (vēr′balĭzem) *n.* Verbal expression; predominance of merely verbal over real significance. **ver′bal·ist** *n.* One concerned with words only, apart from reality or meaning.

ver·bal·ize (vēr′balīz) *v.t.* (-ized, -iz·ing). Make (noun etc.) into verb; express in words; be verbose. **ver·bal·i·za·tion** (vērba-līzā′shon) *n.*

ver·ba·tim (verbā′tĭm) *adv.* & *adj.* Word for word, in the exact words.

ver·be·na (verbē′na) *n.* Plant of genus *V*~, which comprises the vervains, esp. garden variety of this with blue, white, or crimson flowers.

ver·bi·age (vēr′bēĭj) *n.* Needless abundance of words.

ver·bose (verbōs′) *adj.* Using, expressed in, too many words. **ver·bose′ly** *adv.* **ver·bose′ness**, **ver·bos·i·ty** (verbŏs′ĭtē) *ns.*

ver·bo·ten (verbō′ten, fer-) *adj.* Forbidden, esp. by authority. [Ger.]

Ver·cin·get·o·rix (vērsĭnjĕt′-erĭks, -gĕt′-). Gallic chief of the Arverni (occupants of the district now called Auvergne) in 52 B.C. in their war against Julius Caesar.

ver·dant (vēr′dant) *adj.* Green. **ver′dant·ly** *adv.* **ver′dan·cy** *n.*

Ver·di (vār′de; *It.* vĕr′dē), **Gui·sep·pe** (jōōzĕp′pĕ) **Fortunino Francesco** (1813–1901). Italian composer of operas esp. *Aida, Falstaff, Rigoletto*, and church music, esp. *Manzoni Requiem*, etc.

ver·dict (vēr′dĭkt) *n.* Decision of jury in civil or criminal case on issue submitted to them; decision, judgment.

ver·di·gris (vēr′digrēs, -grĭs) *n.* Green or greenish-blue deposit forming on copper or brass as a rust; copper acetate, obtained by action of dilute acetic acid on copper and used as pigment and mordant in dyeing. [OF. *vert de Grece* green of Greece]

ver·dure (vēr′jer) *n.* Fresh green color of flourishing vegetation; green vegetation. **ver·dur·ous** (vēr′jerus) *adj.*

verge[1] (vērj) *n.* 1. Extreme edge, brink, border; grass edging of path, flower bed, etc. 2. Wand, rod, carried before bishop, dean, etc., as emblem of office.

verge[2] (vērj) *v.t.* (**verged, verg·ing**). Incline downward or in specified direction; border *on.*

verg·er (vēr′jer) *n.* (chiefly Brit.) Official carrying rod or other symbol of office before dignitaries of cathedral, church, or university; one who takes care of interior of church and acts as attendant.

ver·i·fy (vĕr′ifĭ) *v.t.* (**-fied, -fy·ing**). Establish the truth or correctness of, examine for this purpose; (pass.) be proved true or correct by result, be borne out. **ver′i·fi·able** *adj.* **ver·i·fi·a·bil·i·ty** (vĕrifīabĭl′ĭtē), **ver·i·fi·ca·tion** (vĕrifĭkā′shon), **ver′i·fi·er** *ns.*

ver·i·ly (vĕr′ĭlē) *adv.* (archaic) Really, in truth.

ver·i·si·mil·i·tude (vĕrĭsĭmĭl′ĭtōōd, -tūd) *n.* Appearance of truth or reality; probability; apparent truth.

ver·i·ta·ble (vĕr′ĭtabel) *adj.* Real, properly or correctly so called. **ver′i·ta·bly** *adv.*

ver·i·ty (vĕr′ĭtē) *n.* (pl. **-ties**). Truth; true statement; reality, fact.

Ver·meer (vermēr′; *Du.* ver-mār′), **Jan** (1632–75). Dutch painter, of Delft.

ver·mi·cel·li (vērmĭsĕl′ē, -chĕl′ē) *n.* Pasta in long slender threads. [It., = "little worms" (L. *vermis* worm)]

ver·mi·cide (vēr′mĭsīd) *n.* Substance used to kill (esp. intestinal) worms.

ver·mic·u·lar (vermĭk′yuler) *adj.* Wormlike in form or movements; of worm-eaten appearance; marked with close wavy lines; (med.) of, caused by, intestinal worms.

ver·mic·u·lat·ed (vermĭk′yulātĭd) *adj.* Covered or ornamented with close wavy markings like those made by gnawing of worms or their sinuous movements. **ver·mic·u·la·tion** (vermĭkyulā′shon) *n.*

ver·mic·u·lite (vermĭk′yulĭt) *n.* Hydrous silicate material, usu. resulting from alteration of mica, and expandable into sponge by heating.

ver·mi·form (vēr′mifôrm) *adj.* Worm-shaped; ~ **appendix**, small wormlike blind tube extending from cecum in man and some other

Trained as a sculptor and a decorative painter, and with canvases monumental in size, **Veronese** *preferred subjects such as 'The Family of Darius before Alexander' (above).*

mammals.

ver·mi·fuge (vēr'mifūj) *n.* Substance that expels worms from intestines.

ver·mil·ion (vermĭl'yon) *n.* Cinnabar; brilliant scarlet color of this. ~ *adj.* Of the color of vermilion. ~ *v.t.* Color (as) with vermilion.

ver·min (vēr'mĭn) *n.* (pl. **-min**). (usu. collect.) Mammals and birds injurious to game crops, etc.; creeping or wingless insects etc. of noxious or offensive kind, esp. those infesting or parasitic on living beings or plants; noxious, vile, or offensive persons. **ver'min·ous** *adj.* (esp.) Infested with, full of, vermin; caused by vermin. **ver'min·ous·ly** *adv.* **ver'min·ous·ness** *n.*

Ver·mont (vermŏnt'). New England state; admitted to Union in 1791; capital, Montpelier. **Ver'mont'er** *n.*

ver·mouth (vermōoth') *n.* White or red wine flavored with wormwood or other aromatic herbs, made esp. in France and Italy. [Fr., f. Ger. *Wermuth* wormwood]

ver·nac·u·lar (vernăk'yuler) *adj.* (of language, idiom, word) Of one's own native country, native, indigenous, not of foreign origin or of learned formation. **ver·nac'u·lar·ly** *adv.* **ver·nac'u·lar·ize** *v.t.* (**-ized, -iz·ing**). **vernacular** *n.* Vernacular language or dialect; homely speech.

ver·nal (vēr'nal) *adj.* Of, appropriate to, coming or happening in, spring; ~ **equinox**: see EQUINOX. **ver'nal·ly** *adv.*

ver·ni·er (vēr'nēer) *n.* Device consisting of graduated scale sliding along fixed scale, for measuring fractional parts of divisions of larger scale. [after Pierre *Vernier* (1580–1637), French mathematician]

Ve·ro·na (verō'na). City of N. Italy.

Ve·ro·nese[1](vĕronēz', -nēs') *adj.* & *n.* (pl. **-nese**). (Native, inhabitant) of Verona.

Ve·ro·ne·se[2] (vĕrawnĕ'zĕ), **Paul Cagliari** (1528–88). Italian painter.

Ve·ron·i·ca (verŏn'ĭka), **St.** 1. Woman who, acc. to legend, wiped the sweat from the face of Christ on the way to Calvary. 2. (often **v** ~) Representation of Christ's face in this scene; the handkerchief or veil used by Veronica to wipe Christ's face.

ve·ron·i·ca (verŏn'ĭka) *n.* 1. Speedwell. 2. Pass in bullfighting in which matador stands motionless while swinging cape away from charging bull. [f. VERONICA]

Ver·ra·za·no (vĕrazah'nō), **Giovanni da** (1485?–1528?). Florentine navigator; explored Atlantic Coast of Amer.; discovered New York Bay.

Ver·sailles (vĕrsī', -sālz'). Town SW. of Paris that contains the royal palace built by Louis XIII and XIV; **Treaty of** ~, treaty that terminated the Amer. War of Independence in 1783; treaty signed on June 28, 1929, that terminated World War I.

ver·sa·tile (vēr'satĭl, -tīl) *adj.* Turning easily or readily from one subject, occupation, etc., to another, showing facility in varied subjects, many-sided, **ver'sa·tile·ly** *adv.* **ver·sa·til·i·ty** (vērsatĭl'ĭtē) *n.*

verse (vērs) *n.* 1. Words arranged according to rules of prosody and forming complete metrical line (now chiefly in ref. to Gk. and Latin poetry). 2. Small number of metrical or rhythmical lines forming either a whole in themselves or a unit in a longer composition; stanza. 3. Metrical composition or structure; poetry esp. with ref. to metrical form as dist. from PROSE. 4. Each of the short sections into which the chapters of the Bible are divided. 5. Short sentence as part of liturgy.

versed[1] (vērst) *adj.* ~ **sine**, quantity obtained by subtracting cosine from unity.

versed[2] (vērst) *adj.* Experienced, practiced, skilled (*in* subject etc.).

ver·si·cle (vēr'sĭkel) *n.* Each of a series of short sentences said or sung in liturgy, esp. sentence said by the minister or priest and followed by another (RESPONSE) from the people; (pl.) versicles and responses collectively.

ver·si·fy (vēr'sĭfī) *v.* (**-fied, -fy·ing**). Make verses; turn into, narrate in, verse. **ver·si·fi·ca·tion** (vērsĭfĭkāshon), **ver'si·fi·er** *ns.*

ver·sion (vēr'zhon, -shon) *n.* Rendering of work, passage, etc., into another language; particular form of statement, account, etc., given by one person or party.

vers li·bre (*Fr.* vĕr lē'bre) FREE verse.

ver·so (vēr'sō) *n.* (pl. **-sos**). Left-hand page of open book; back of leaf of book or manuscript (opp. RECTO); reverse of coin or medal.

verst (vērst, vĕrst) *n.* Russian measure of length, about ⅔ mi.

ver·sus (vēr'sus) *prep.* (abbrev. v., vs.) 1. Against. 2. As compared with.

ver·te·bra (vēr'tebra) *n.* (pl. **-brae** pr. -brā, -brē, **-bras**). Each of the bony segments composing the spinal column (pl., loosely) backbone; **cervical vertebrae**, those of neck; **thoracic**, of ribs; **lumbar**, of loins; **sacral**, of hips;

caudal, of tail. **ver·te·bral** *adj.* **ver·te·bral·ly** *adv.*

ver·te·brate (ver'tebrāt, -brĭt) *adj. & n.* (Animal) belonging to the Vertebrata, the division containing all animals having a cranium and a spinal column or a notochord and including mammals, birds, reptiles, amphibians, and fishes.

ver·te·bra·tion (vĕrtebrā'shon) *n.* Formation of, division into, vertebrae or similar segments.

ver·tex (ver'tĕks) *n.* (pl. **-tex·es**, **-ti·ces** pr. -tĭsēz). Top, highest part or point; top of the head; (math.) point opposite base of (plane or solid) figure, point where axis meets curve or surface, or where lines forming angle meet.

ver·ti·cal (ver'tĭkel) *adj.* Of, at, passing through, vertex or zenith, having position in heavens directly above given place or point; placed, moving, perpendicularly; upright; of, at, affecting, vertex of the head; (econ.) pertaining to all successive processes of manufacture or distribution of a product, as dist. from HORIZONTAL; ~ **takeoff**, (of aircraft) takeoff directly upward (freq. attrib.); **vertical union**: see IN-DUSTRIAL union. **ver·ti·cal·ly** *adv.* **ver·ti·cal·i·ty** (vĕrtĭkăl'ĭtē) *n.* **vertical** *n.* Vertical line, plane, or circle. **ver'ti·cal·ness** *n.*

ver·ti·cil (ver'tĭsĭl) *n.* (bot.) Number of similar organs or parts arranged in circle around axis. **ver·tic·il·late** (vertĭs'ĭlĭt, -lāt, vĕr-tĭsĭl'āt) *adj.*

ver·ti·go (ver'tĭgō) *n.* (pl. **ver·ti·goes**). Dizziness, condition with sensation of whirling and tendency to lose equilibrium. **ver·tig·i·nous** (vertĭj'ĭnus) *adj.* Of vertigo;

causing, tending to cause, giddiness. **ver·tig'i·nous·ly** *adv.* **ver·tig'i·nous·ness** *n.*

ver·vain (ver'vān) *n.* Common herbaceous plant of genus *Verbena*, esp. *V. hastata.*

verve (verv) *n.* Vigor, enthusiasm, energy, esp. in literary work.

ver·y (vĕr'ē) *adj.* (**ver·i·er, ver·i·est**). Real, true, genuine, properly so called or designated; **the ~**, used to emphasize identity, significance, extreme degree, etc. **very** *adv.* (used with adjectives, adverbs, adjectival participles, but not other parts of verbs). In a high degree, to a great extent, extremely; ~ **high frequency**: see FREQUENCY; ~ **well**, formula of consent or approval.

Ve·sa·li·us (vĭsā'lēus), **Andreas** (1514–64). Flemish anatomist and surgeon born in Brussels; considered as father of modern anatomy.

ve·si·ca (vesī'ka) *n.* (pl. **-cae** pr. -sē). 1. (anat.) Bladder. 2. ~ **pis·cis** (pĭs'ĭs, pī'sĭs), pointed oval (◊) used as an aureole in medieval art. **ves·i·cal** (vĕs'ĭkal) *adj.* [L., = "bladder of a fish"]

ves·i·cate (vĕs'ĭkāt) *v.t.* (**-cat·ed, -cat·ing**). Raise blisters on (skin etc.). **ves'i·cant, ves·i·ca·to·ry** (vĕs'ĭkatōrē, -tōrē) *adjs. & ns.* (pl. **-to·ries**). (Substance) causing formation of blisters. **ves·i·ca·tion** (vĕsĭkā'shon) *n.*

ves·i·cle (vĕs'ĭkel) *n.* Small bladderlike vessel, cavity, sac; (path.) small, usu. round, elevation of cuticle containing clear watery fluid. **ve·sic·u·lar** (vesĭk'yuler), **ve·sic·u·late** (vesĭk'yulĭt, -lāt) *adjs.*

Ves·pa·si·an (vĕspā'zhēan, -zhan). Titus Flavius Vespasianus (9–79 A.D.), Roman emperor 69–79 A.D.; began building the Coliseum.

Ves·pers (vĕs'perz) *n.pl.* (R.C. Ch.) Canonical HOUR; office said or sung toward evening, evensong; **Sicilian ~**: see SICILIAN.

ves·per (vĕs'per) **sparrow.** Gray N. Amer. sparrow (*Pooecetes gramineus*), having white outer tail feathers that are conspicuous when bird is in flight, and chestnut wing patch.

Ves·puc·ci (vĕspoo'chē, -spū -), **Amerigo** (1451–1512). Florentine merchant who settled in Spain; he claimed to have made a voyage in 1497 in which he discovered the mainland of S. Amer.; this claim, in virtue of his name was given to the continent of Amer.

ves·sel (vĕs'el) *n.* 1. Hollow receptacle for liquid etc., esp. domestic utensil, usu. round, used for preparing, storing, or serving food or drink; (bibl.) person regarded as containing or receiving some spiritual quality. 2. (anat., zool.) Membranous canal, duct, etc., in which body fluids are contained or circulated, esp. artery or vein (**blood ~**); (bot.) woody duct carrying or containing sap etc., (rare) seed vessel. 3. Any craft or ship, usu. one larger than rowboat.

vest[1] (vĕst) *n.* Short, sleeveless garment for men, buttoning in front and worn under jacket; similar garment worn by woman over dress or blouse; **~-pocket**, (attrib. of

Sold to the U.S. forces, the Hawker Siddeley Harrier is the only aircraft capable of using short runways as well as **vertical takeoff**. *The Russian Yak 36 can only rise vertically. The lift of the Harrier is governed by nozzles which can be swivelled to suit the circumstances.*

articles etc., as cameras) of small size.

vest² (věst) *v.* 1. (chiefly pass.) Invest (person) *with* power, authority, etc.; put in full or legal possession of something, place or secure (something, freq. power or authority) in possession of person(s). 2. Become vested (*in* person), pass into possession of; **vested interests, rights**, etc., interest, rights, etc., possession of which is established in a person by right or by long association and usu. gives rise to expectation of gain; **vesting**, retention by eligible employee of all or some pension benefits, without regard to discontinuation of employment.

Ves·ta (věs′ta). 1. (Rom. myth.) Goddess of hearth and household, daughter of Saturn, with temple in Rome whose sacred fire was tended by vestal virgins. 2. (astron.) One of minor planets or asteroids with orbit between Mars and Jupiter.

ves·tal (věs′tal) *adj.* 1. Of the goodess Vesta or the vestal virgins; ~ **virgin**, (Rom. hist.) one of the (orig. two, later four, then six) virgins consecrated to the service of Vesta and vowed to chastity. 2. Chaste, virgin. **vestal** *n.* Vestal virgin; chaste unmarried woman.

ves·ti·bule (věs′tĭbūl) *n.* 1. Antechamber, hall, lobby, between entrance door and interior of house or other building; porch of church etc. 2. (Gk. and Rom. antiq.) Enclosed or partially enclosed space in front of main entrance of house. 3. Enclosed entrance at end of railroad car giving access to car and usu. communicating with other cars. 4. (anat.) Dilated entrance to a canal or cavity between middle ear and cochlea. **ves·tib·u·lar** (věstĭb′-

*Kidney **vetch** usually has yellow flowers but they may vary and become orange red in a salty atmosphere. Like other plants in the genus Vicia, it has long been used for fodder.*

yuler) *adj.*

ves·tige (věs′tĭj) *n.* Trace, track, evidence (of something no longer existing or present); (biol.) organ or part that is small or degenerate in descendants but in ancestors was fully developed. **ves·tig·i·al** (věs-tĭj′ēal) *adj.* **ves·tig′i·al·ly** *adv.*

vest·ment (věst′ment) *n.* Garment, esp. worn by king or official on ceremonial occasion; any of

*Visitors walk in the crater of the volcano **Vesuvius** during a dormant period. Despite eruptions, the fertility of its slopes has encouraged farming for 2,000 years.*

official garments of priests, assistants, etc., during church service etc., esp. chasuble.

ves·try (věs′trē) *n.* (pl. **-tries**) Room or part of church used for keeping vestments, vessels, records, etc., for robing of clergy and choir, for parish meeting, etc.; (Episcopal Ch.) committee of parishioners that manages business affairs of parish; **ves′tryman** (pl. **-men**), member of parochial vestry.

Ve·su·vi·us (vesoō′vēus). Active volcano in SW. Italy near Naples (3,891 ft., 1,175 m); its eruption destroyed Pompeii and Herculaneum, 79 A.D. **Ve·su′vi·an** (vesoō′vēan) *adj.*

vet¹ (vět) *n.* (colloq.) Veterinary surgeon. ~ *v.t.* (**vet·ted, vet·ting**) Examine, treat (animal, person) medically; work as a veterinarian; submit (scheme, book, etc.) to careful examination.

vet² (vět) *n.* (colloq.) Veteran.

vetch (věch) *n.* Leguminous plant of *Vicia* (esp. *V. sativa*, common tare) or related genera, many or which are valuable for fodder.

vet·er·an (vět′eran, vět′ran) *adj.* Grown old in service; experienced by long practice; (of army) composed of veteran troops; (of service) long continued. ~ *n.* Veteran person, esp. soldier; former serviceman; **Veterans Day**, national holiday honoring all veterans of armed services, orig. Armistice Day and formerly observed on Nov. 11,

*A **veterinarian** giving treatment to a sheep in Australia. Although most people associate these men with domestic pets, the bulk of their work is with farm animals and racehorses.*

now on the fourth Monday of October.

vet·er·i·nar·y (vĕt′erĭnĕrē, vĕt′-ri-) *adj.* Of, for, concerned with (treatment of) diseases and injuries of cattle and other animals. ~ *n.* (pl. **-nar·ies**). **vet·er·i·nar·i·an** (vĕterĭnār′ēan, vĕtri-) *n.* Veterinary surgeon.

ve·to (vē′tō) *n.* (pl. **-toes**). Prohibition of proposed or intended act; (exercise of) constitutional right to prohibit passing or putting in force of an enactment or measure. ~ *v.t.* (**-toed, -to·ing**). Exercise veto against. **ve′to·er** *n.* [L., = "I forbid"]

vex (vĕks) *v.t.* Anger by slight or petty annoyance, irritate.

vex·a·tion (vĕksā′shon) *n.* Being vexed, irritation; vexing thing. **vex·a′tious** *adj.* **vex·a′tious·ly** *adv.* **vex·a′tious·ness** *n.*

vex·il·lum (vĕksĭl′um) *n.* (pl. **vex·il·la** pr. vĕksĭl′a). 1. (Rom. antiq.) Banner of Roman troops; body of troops under this. 2. (eccles.) Small piece of linen or silk wound around upper part of crosier. 3. (bot.) Large upper petal of papilionaceous flower. 4. (ornith.) Vane of feather.

VFD *abbrev.* Volunteer fire department.

VFW, V.F.W. *abbrevs.* Veterans of Foreign Wars.

VHF, V.H.F., vhf, v.h.f. *abbrevs.* Very high FREQUENCY.

VI *abbrev.* Virgin Islands.

v.i. *abbrev.* Verb intransitive.

vi·a (vī′a, vē′a) *prep.* By way of, through (specified place).

vi·a·ble (vī′abel) *adj.* Capable of maintaining separate existence (of child at birth etc.); able to live in particular environment; practi-

Viburnum species are used mainly as decorative shrubs and include the guelder rose, the berries of which are widely used in the U.S.A. as a substitute for cranberries in jelly-making.

cable; (bot., of seeds) having ability to germinate. **vi·a·bil·i·ty** (vĭabĭl′-ĭtē) *n.* **vi′a·bly** *adv.* [Fr., f. *vie* life]

vi·a·duct (vī′adŭkt) *n.* Bridgelike structure carrying railroad or road over valley, river, etc.

vi·al (vī′al, vīl) *n.* Small vessel for liquid medicines, now esp. small glass bottle.

vi·and (vī′and) *n.* (usu. pl.) Article(s) of food, provision(s), victual(s).

vi·at·i·cum (vĭăt′ĭkum) *n.* (pl. **-ca** pr. -ka, **-cums**). 1. Eucharist as administered to one (in danger of) dying. 2. (rare) Sum of money

for traveling expenses, provisions for journey. [L., = "traveling money" f. *via* way]

vibes (vībz) *n.pl.* 1. (colloq.) Vibraphone. 2. (slang) (also **vibrations**) Emotional stimulus one gets from person or place.

vi·brac·u·lum (vībrăk′yulum) *n.* (pl. **-la** pr. -la). Whiplike movable filament in some polyzoan colonies serving e.g. to prevent noxious material from settling.

vi·brant (vī′brant) *adj.* Vibrating, thrilling, resonant. **vi′brant·ly** *adv.* **vi′bran·cy** *n.*

vi·bra·phone (vī′brafōn) *n.* Percussion instrument with lids of resonators kept in constant motion by electric current so as to produce a pulsating effect.

vi·brate (vī′brāt) *v.* (**-brat·ed, -brat·ing**). (Cause to) swing to and fro periodically, oscillate, quiver; set, be, in state of vibration; thrill; (of sound) strike ear with quivering or pulsating effect; (of pendulum) measure (seconds etc.) by vibration. **vi·bra·tile** (vī′bratĭl, -tīl) *adj.*

vi·bra·tion (vībrā′shon) *n.* (esp., phys.) 1. Rapid reciprocating motion to and fro, up and down, etc., of particles of elastic body produced by disturbance of its equilibrium. 2. (pl.) = VIBES sense 2. **vi·bra′tion·al** *adj.*

vi·bra·to (vībrah′tō, vī-) *n.* (pl. **-tos**). (mus.) Tremulous effect in singing or of playing stringed instruments by rapid slight variation of pitch; cf. TREMOLO. [It.]

vi·bra·tor (vī′brāter) *n.* Thing, person, that vibrates. **vi·bra·to·ry** (vī′bratōrē, -tōrē) *adj.* Characterized by, causing, connected with, vibration; capable of vibrating.

vi·bur·num (vībĕr′num) *n.* Shrub of widely distributed genus V~, which includes the cranberry bush.

Vic. *abbrev.* Victoria.

vic·ar (vĭk′er) *n.* 1. Representative; substitute; assistant. 2. (Ch. of England) Parish priest formerly acting in place of rector, now in charge of parish; (Protestant Episcopal) clergyman in charge of a chapel. 3. (R.C. Ch.) Representative of pope or bishop; **V~ of Christ**, the pope as Christ's representative on Earth. **vic′ar·ship** *n.*

vic·ar·age (vĭk′erĭj) *n.* Benefice, residence, of vicar.

vic·ar·i·ous (vīkār′ēus) *adj.* Deputed, delegated; acting, done, endured, for another. **vi·car′i·ous·ly** *adv.* **vi·car′i·ous·ness** *n.*

vice[1] (vīs) *n.* Evil, esp. grossly immoral, habit or conduct; de-

*A granite **viaduct** carrying the railway near St. Austell in Cornwall U.K. Devised by the Romans to carry their aqueducts across river valleys, this device is also used to make roads less steep.*

Ascending the throne at the age of 18, **Queen Victoria** of England had the longest reign of any British monarch and, when she died in 1901, had been queen for 63 years.

Discovered by David Livingstone in 1855, the **Victoria Falls** on the Zambezi River are now used to drive a hydro-electric power station. The canyon beyond the falls is spanned by a bridge.

pravity, serious fault; defect, blemish; fault, bad trick (of horse etc.); ~ **squad**, division of police department enforcing laws against prostitution, gambling, etc.

vice² (vīs) *n.* (chiefly Brit.) Vise.

vi·ce³ (vī′sē) *prep.* In the place of, in succession to.

vice- *prefix.* Acting in place of, assistant, next in rank to.

vice ad·mi·ral (vīs′ăd′merəl). Naval officer ranking next below admiral.

vice·ge·rent (vīsjĕr′ent) *n. & adj.* (Person) exercising delegated power, deputy. **vice·ge′ren·cy** *n.*

vi·cen·ni·al (vīsĕn′ēəl) *adj.* Lasting, happening, every, 20 years.

vice-pres·i·dent (vīs′prĕz′ĭdent) *n.* 1. Officer ranking next to a president. 2. (**V~-P~**) Elected officer second in rank to the President of the U.S. **vice′-pres′i·den·cy** *n.* **vice′-pres·i·den′tial** *adj.*

vice-re·gent (vīs′rē′jent) *n.* One acting in place of regent.

vice·reine (vīs′rān) *n.* Woman viceroy; wife of viceroy.

vice·roy (vīs′roi) *n.* 1. Person acting as governor of country, province, etc., in name and by authority of supreme ruler; (hist.) representative of British Crown in India. 2. Handsome red-and-black Amer. butterfly (*Limenitis archippus*); like monarch but smaller. **vice·re·gal** (vīsrē′gal), **vice·roy·al** (vīsroi′al)

adjs. **vice·roy′al·ty** *n.* (pl. **-ties**).

vi·ce ver·sa (vī′se vēr′sa, vīs′). The other way around, conversely.

Vi·chy (vĭsh′ē; *Fr.* vēshē′). Town in central France noted for mineral waters; ~ **Government**, French government, with headquarters at Vichy, that administered S. part of France (~ **France**) and collaborated with Germans in World War II after French collapse in 1940; ~ **water**, effervescent mineral water from Vichy, freq. bottled; bottled water resembling this.

vi·chy·ssoise (vĭshēswahz′, vĭsh′ēswahz) *n.* Cream soup of potatoes and leeks, usu. served cold.

vi·cin·i·ty (vĭsĭn′ĭtē) *n.* (pl. **-ties**). Surrounding district; nearness in place; close relationship; **in the ~** (**of**), in the neighborhood (of).

vi·cious (vĭsh′us) *adj.* 1. Of the nature of, addicted to, vice; evil; depraved. 2. (of language, reasoning, etc.) Incorrect, faulty, unsound, corrupt; intensifying its own causes; ~ **circle**: see CIRCLE. 3. (esp. of animals) Bad-tempered, spiteful. **vi′cious·ly** *adv.* **vi′cious·ness** *n.*

vi·cis·si·tude (vĭsĭs′ĭtōōd, -tūd) *n.* Change of circumstances, esp. of condition or fortune.

Vicks·burg (vĭks′bĕrg). Town in Mississippi, on the Mississippi River, where, in 1863, the Union

forces under Grant besieged the Confederates, who surrendered on July 4; this victory and Gettysburg marked the turning point in the Civil War.

vic·tim (vĭk′tĭm) *n.* Living creature sacrificed to a deity or in performance of religious rite; person who is killed or made to suffer by cruel or oppressive treatment; (loosely) one who suffers injury, hardship, loss, etc.; **victimless crime**, legal offense, such as prostitution, considered as not having any identifiable victim.

vic·tim·ize (vĭk′timīz) *v.t.* (**-ized, -iz·ing**). Cause to suffer inconvenience, discomfort, annoyance, etc.; cheat, defraud; treat unjustly or with undue harshness, esp. dismiss (employee) for striking, etc. **vic′tim·i·zer, vic·tim·i·za′tion** (vĭktimīzā′shon) *ns.*

vic·tor (vĭk′ter) *n.* Conqueror in battle or contest.

Vic·tor Em·man·u·el (vĭk′ter ĭmăn′ūel). Name of three kings of Sardinia, two of whom became kings of Italy: **Victor Emmanuel I** (1759–1824), king of Sardinia 1802–1821; **Victor Emmanuel II** (1820–78), first king of Italy 1861–1878; **Victor Emmanuel III** (1869–1947), king of Italy 1900–46.

Vic·to·ri·a (vĭktōr′ēa, -tōr-) (1819–1901). Daughter of Edward, Duke of Kent, fourth son of George III; queen of Gt. Britain and Ireland 1837–1901; empress of India 1877–1901; married Prince Albert of Saxe-Coburg-Gotha, 1840; **Lake ~**, largest lake in Africa and chief reservoir of the Nile; ~ **Cross**, (abbrev. V.C.)

decoration awarded for conspicuous bravery to members of Brit. and
Commonwealth armed forces, first
instituted by Queen Victoria in
1856; **~ Falls**, African waterfall on
the Zambezi, discovered by David
Livingstone in 1855.

Vic·to·ri·an (vĭktōr'ēan, -tōr'-)
adj. Of, living in, characteristic of,
the reign of Queen VICTORIA. **~** *n.*
Person living in the reign of Queen
Victoria.

vic·to·ri·ous (vĭktōr'ēus, -tōr'-)
adj. Triumphant, successful in contest or struggle; marked by, producing, victory. **vic·to'ri·ous·ly**
adv. **vic·to'ri·ous·ness** *n.*

vic·to·ry (vĭk'terē) *n.* (pl. **-ries**).
Supremacy achieved by battle or in
war, defeat of enemy; triumph or
ultimate success in any contest or
enterprise.

vict·ual (vĭt'al) *n.* (usu. pl.)
Food, provisions. **~** *v.* (**-ualed,**

Related to the camel and the llama, the
vicuna *of the central Andes lives at*
altitudes up to 16,000 ft. Its wool, the
finest known to man, is rare and
expensive.

Video games *have gained worldwide*
popularity since they first appeared.
Unlike many 'fads', their popularity has
not waned with time.

-ual·ing; *Brit.* **-ualled, -ual·ling**).
Supply with victuals; lay in supply
of victuals; eat.

vi·cu·ña (vĭkoō'na, -ku'-, vĭkoō'-
nya) *n.* (pl. **-ñas**, collect. **-ña**). S.
Amer. mammal (*Vicugna vicugna*)
of N. Andes, related to llama and
alpaca, and with fine silky wool
used for textiles; soft cloth made of
this, imitation of it.

vi·de (vī'dē; *Lat.* wē'dĕ) *v.imp.*
(as direction to reader) Refer to,
consult. [L.]

vi·de·li·cet (vĭdĕl'ĭsĭt; *Lat.*

wēdā'lĭkĕt) *adv.* (abbrev. viz., viz)
That is to say, namely. [L.]

vid·e·o (vĭd'ēō) *n.* Television;
vid'eodisc, vid'eodisk, disk
similar to phonograph record that
can record pictures and sound for
reproducing on television sets;
video game, electronic apparatus
connected to television set,
enabling players in game to control
dots, lines, etc., on screen; **vid'eo-
phone,** telephone transmitting
picture of person speaking; **vid'eo-
tape,** magnetic tape for recording
pictures and sound for reproducing
on television sets.

vie (vī) *v.i.* (**vied, vy'ing**).
Contend or compete for superiority
in some respect (*with*), be rivals.

Vi·en·na (vēĕn'a). (Ger. *Wien*)
Capital of Austria; **Congress of ~**,
conference (1814–15) of European
statesmen that readjusted territories and governments throughout
Europe after the Napoleonic Wars.
Vi·en·nese (vēenēz', -nēs') *adj.* & *n.*

Vien·tiane (vyĕntyahn'). Capital
of Laos in the NW. on the Mekong
River.

Vi·et·cong, Viet Cong (vēĕt-
kŏng', vyĕt-) *n.* (pl. **-cong**).
Communist guerrilla (member of)
force in South Vietnam who, with
aid from North Vietnam, fought
(1954–76) to overthrow the S.
Vietnamese government.

Vi·et·nam (vēĕtnahm', -năm,
vyĕt-). Country in SE. Asia,
formed 1945 from the Tongking,
Annam, and Cochin-China prov-
inces of French Indochina; divided
1954–76 into the **Democratic
Republic of (North) ~** and the
Republic of (South) ~; since
April 1975, united into the
Socialist Republic of ~, capital

Vienna, *capital and largest city of*
Austria, contains many old buildings like
St. Michael's Gate shown above. It is
however, essentially a modern city and
is an important port and major European
railroad center.

A unified country since the civil war ended in 1975, **Vietnam** now has a 'socialist' regime with a single national assembly. Although corruption has been eliminated, work on post-war reconstruction is still behind planned targets.

Hanoi. **Vi·et·nam·ese** (vēĕtna-mēz´, -mēs´, vyĕt-) *adj.* & *n.*

view (vū) *n.* Inspection by eye or mind; power of seeing, range of physical or mental vision; what is seen, scene, prospect; picture etc. representing this; mental survey, mental attitude; **in ~ of**, having regard to, considering; **on ~**, open to inspection; **point of ~**, position from which thing is viewed, way of looking at a matter; **private ~, viewing**, view of exhibition open only to invited guests, usu. on day before public opening; **with a view to**, for the purpose of, as a step toward; with an eye to, in the hope of getting; **view´finder**, attachment to camera showing view in range of camera lens; similar device used by painters; **view´point**, point of view. **view** *v.t.* Survey with eyes or mind, form impression or judgment of.

view·er (vū´er) *n.* (esp.) One who watches television broadcast.

vig·il (vĭj´il) *n.* Keeping awake during usual time for sleep; (pl.) prayers at church service, esp. for the dead; **keep ~**, keep watch.

vig·i·lance (vĭj´ilans) *n.* Watchfulness against danger or action of others, caution, circumspection; **~ committee**, (hist.) in 19th c. U.S. West, self-appointed committee for maintenance of justice and order, esp. for summary punishment of criminals when processes of law were considered inadequate. **vig´i·lant** *adj.* **vig´i·lant·ly** *adv.* **vig´i·lant·ness** *n.*

vig·i·lan·te (vĭjilăn´tē) *n.* Member of vigilance committee.

vi·gnette (vĭnyĕt´, vē-) *n.* Decorative design, usu. small, on blank space in book, having edges shading off into surrounding paper; photograph with edges shading off into background; (fig., literary) character sketch or short description. **~** *v.t.* (**-gnet·ted, -gnet·ting**). Make vignette of esp. by shading off or softening away edges. **vig·nett´ist** *n.* [Fr., = "little vine," ornamental design at end of chapter]

vig·or, Brit. **vig·our** (vĭg´er) *ns.* Active physical strength or energy; flourishing physical condition, vitality; mental or moral strength, force, or energy. **vig·or·ous** (vĭg´erus) *adj.* **vig·or·ous·ly** *adv.* **vig´or·ous·ness** *n.*

Vik·ing (vī´kĭng) *adj.* & *n.* (One) of the Scandinavians during the period (8th–11th centuries) when they became active as traders esp.

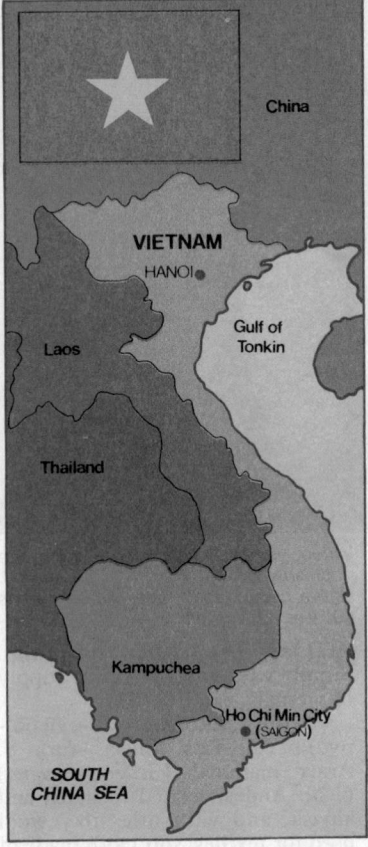

between Russia and W. Europe, and also took to piracy, plundering and temporarily occupying many of the coastal districts and river valleys of N. and W. Europe.

vile (vīl) *adj.* (**vil·er, vil·est**). Despicable on moral grounds, base, depraved; worthless, of poor or bad quality; disgusting, filthy; shameful. **vile´ly** *adv.* **vile´ness** *n.*

vil·i·fy (vĭl´ifī) *v.t.* (**-fied, -fy·ing**). Defame, traduce, speak evil of. **vil·i·fi·ca·tion** (vĭlifĭkā´shon) *n.*

vil·la (vĭl´a) *n.* 1. (hist., esp. Roman) Country estate with house(s), farm(s), etc. 2. Italian country house. 3. Large, usu. luxurious, country house or estate. [L. *villa* farmhouse]

Vil·la (vē´a; *Sp.* vē´yah), **Francisco** (**"Pancho"**) (1877–1923). (orig. name Doroteo Arango) Mexican bandit and revolutionary leader; assassinated.

vil·lage (vĭl´ĭj) *n.* Assemblage of houses etc. in country district, larger than hamlet and smaller than town; small municipality with limited corporate powers. **vil´lag·er** *n.* Inhabitant of village (usu. implying rusticity).

vil·lain (vĭl´an), fem. **vil·lain·ess** (vĭl´anĭs, -nĕs) *ns.* Person guilty or capable of great wickedness, scoundrel; character in play, novel, etc., whose evil motives or actions are important element of plot.

vil´lain·y *n.* (pl. **-lain·ies**).

vil·lain·ous (vĭl´anus) *adj.* Worthy of a villain, wicked, vile; (colloq.) very unpleasant. **vil´lain·ous·ly** *adv.* **vil´lain·ous·ness** *n.*

vil·la·nelle (vĭlanĕl´) *n.* Poem usu. of 19 lines based on two rhymes with some lines repeated.

-ville *suffix.* 1. City or town, used as part of many place names (*Pleasantville, N.Y.*). 2. (colloq.) Forming names of fictitious places with reference to particular quality etc. (*Squaresville, Endsville*).

vil·lein (vĭl´in) *n.* (hist., in feudal system) Peasant cultivator entirely subject to a lord or attached to a manor. **vil´lein·age** *n.* Tenure of villein; being a villein, serfdom.

vil·lose (vĭl´ōs), **vil·lous** (vĭl´us) *adjs.* Covered with (numerous close slender projections resembling) thickset hairs.

vil·lus (vĭl´us) *n.* (pl. **vil·li** pr. vĭl´ī). (bot.) Long slender soft hair; (anat., zool.) slender hairlike projection, esp. of small intestine.

Vil·ni·us (vĭl´nēŏos) *n.* (also Vilna) Capital city of Lithuania.

vim (vĭm) *n.* (colloq.) Vigor, energy.

Vim·i·nal (vĭm´inal). One of the Seven Hills of Rome.

vin·ai·grette (vĭnagrĕt´) *n.* 1. Small ornamental bottle holding aromatic salts etc., smelling bottle. 2. (also **~ sauce**) Sauce of oil,

PLAN OF VIKING ENCAMPMENT AT TRELLEBORG 970-1020

Barracks

Camp Cemetery

Dry moat

Mound Wall

Moat

Barracks

Viking Barrack-house

vinegar, etc., used esp. with salads.

Vin·cent de Paul (vĭn′sent de pawl′), **St.** (1576–1660). French R.C. reformer, founder of Congregation of Priests of the Mission, now usu. known as the Lazarists, and of Sisters of Charity. **Vin·cen·tian** (vĭnsĕn′chan) *adj. & n.* (Member) of society founded by Vincent de Paul.

Vin·ci (vĭn′chē; *It.* vēn′chē): see LEONARDO DA VINCI.

vin·cu·lum (vĭng′kyulum) *n.* (pl. **-la** pr. -la). (math.) Straight line drawn over two or more terms denoting that these are subject to the same operations of multiplication, division, etc., by another term. [L., = "bond"]

vin·di·cate (vĭn′dikāt) *v.t.* (**-cat·ed, -cat·ing**). Maintain the cause of (person, religion, etc.) successfully; establish the existence or merits or justice of (one's veracity, courage, conduct, character, assertion). **vin·di·ca·tion** (vĭndikā′shon), **vin′di·ca·tor** *ns.*

vin·di·ca·to·ry (vĭn′dikatōrē, -tōrē) *adj.* Tending to vindicate; (of laws) punitive.

vin·dic·tive (vĭndĭk′tĭv) *adj.* Revengeful, avenging, given to revenge. **vin·dic′tive·ly** *adv.* **vin·dic′tive·ness** *n.*

vine (vīn) *n.* Trailing or climbing woody plant of genus *Vitis* (esp. *V. vinifera*, from the fruit of which wine is made) bearing grapes; grapevine; any trailing or

climbing plant.

vin·e·gar (vĭn′eger) *n.* Sour liquid (dilute acetic acid) produced by acetous fermentation of wine, cider, etc., and used as condiment, preservative, etc. **vin′e·gar·y** *adj.* Sour like vinegar, acid. [OF. *vin* wine, *aigre* sour]

vin·er·y (vī′nere) *n.* (pl. **-er·ies**). Greenhouse for growing grapes.

vine·yard (vĭn′yerd) *n.* Plantation of grapevines, esp. for wine making.

Vin·land (vĭn′land). Region of N. Amer. explored and briefly settled by Norsemen under Leif Erics(s)on in the 11th c.; remains of a settlement have been discovered at L'Anse au Meadow in Newfoundland.

vin or·di·naire (Fr. văn ōrdēnār′) (pl. *vins or·di·naires* pr. vănz ōrdēnār′). Cheap usu. red wine for ordinary use.

vi·nous (vī′nus) *adj.* Of, like, due to, addicted to, wine. **vi·nos·i·ty** (vīnŏs′ĭtē) *n.*

vin·tage (vĭn′tĭj) *n.* 1. (Season of) grape harvest; wine, esp. of good quality; wine made from grapes of particular district (freq. used with ref. to the age of a wine or the year when it was made). 2. Class of

*Diagram of the large **Viking** stronghold at Trelleborg on the island of West Zealand in Denmark. The size of the settlement, dated between 950 and 1050 A.D. indicates that this may have*

been a staging post for Norse forces. Also it could have been the base for the invasion of England in A.D. 1013 by King Swein of Denmark. Earlier, the Vikings had reached the Mediterranean.

antique objects, automobiles, etc. ~ *adj.* Of high quality, esp. from the past; of a past season.

vint·ner (vĭnt′ner) *n.* Wine merchant.

vi·nyl (vī′nil) *n.* 1. (chem.) Univalent radical (CH_2CH) derived from ethylene, forming the basis of many plastics. 2. Synthetic material made from a vinyl compound; ~ **chloride**, colorless, extremely toxic gas, $CH_2:CHCl$, used in plastics manufacture.

vi·ol (vī′ol) *n.* Late medieval stringed musical instrument (now again in use), similar in shape to violin, but usu. with six strings and held downward on or between the knees; ~ **da gamba, d'amore** = VIOLA[2] da gamba, d'amore.

vi·o·la[1] (vē′ola, vīō′-) *n.* Herbaceous plant of genus *V*~, which includes violets and pansies; hybrid garden plant of this genus, more uniformly and delicately colored than pansy. [L., = "violet"]

vi·o·la[2] (vēō′la) *n.* 1. Member of violin family of musical instruments, slightly larger than violin, of lower pitch (its lowest note being C below middle C) and with less bright, more sonorous tone. 2. ~ **da gam·ba** (da gahm′ba), bass viol; **viola d'a·mo·re** (dah mōr′ā, -mōr′ā), tenor viol with sympathetic strings under fingerboard, having very sweet affecting tone.

vi·o·la·ceous (vīolā′shus) *adj.* (bot.) Of the violet family (Violaceae).

vi·o·late (vī′olāt) *v.t.* (**-lat·ed, -lat·ing**). Break (agreement, law, oath, etc.); treat profanely, break in upon (sanctuary, privacy, etc.); rape. **vi·o·la·tion** (vīolā′shon), **vi·o·la·tor** *ns.* **vi·o·la·ble** (vī′olabel) *adj.*

vi·o·lence (vī′olens) *n.* Violent treatment or conduct, outrage, injury; violent feeling or language, vehemence; intensity (*of*); (law) (intimidation by threat of) unlawful exercise of physical force.

vi·o·lent (vī′olent) *adj.* Involving, caused by, acting with, great physical force or unlawful exercise of force; intense in force, effect, feelings, etc. **vi′o·lent·ly** *adv.*

vi·o·let (vī′olĭt) *n.* 1. Plant of genus *Viola*, esp. (also **sweet ∼**) the sweet-scented *V. odorata*, with purplish-blue, yellow, or white flowers; similar plant of various other genera. 2. Purplish-blue color of the violet, color at opposite end of spectrum to red. **violet** *adj.* Of the color violet.

vi·o·lin (vīolĭn′) *n.* Stringed musical instrument held under chin with left hand and played with bow or occas. by plucking, having a resonant curvilinear soundbox of polished wood over which are stretched four strings tuned in fifths, the lowest note being G below middle C; part for violin in instrumental composition, player of this; **first ∼**, violin player performing FIRST part (see FIRST *adj.*: sense 1); leader of string quartet; **second ∼**, violin player performing

SECOND part; **∼ family**, group of instruments including violin, viola, violoncello, and double bass. **vi·o·lin·ist** *n.* Player of violin. [It. *violino* little VIOLA[2]]

vi·ol·ist (vēō′lĭst) *n.* Player of viol, viola.

vi·o·lon·cel·lo (vēolonchĕl′ō) = CELLO.

VIP, V.I.P. *abbrevs.* (colloq.) Very important person.

vi·per (vī′per) *n.* Venemous snake of family Viperidae, esp. adder; (fig.) malignant or treacherous person. **vi·per·ine** (vī′perĭn, -rīn), **vi′per·ish, vi′per·ous** *adjs.*

vi·ra·go (vĭrā′gō) *n.* (pl. **-goes, -gos**). Turbulent woman, termagant. [L., = "female warrior," f. *vir* man]

vi·ral (vīr′al) *adj.* (of disease) Caused by a VIRUS.

vir·e·o (vĭr′ēō) *n.* (pl. **-os**). Any of several small N. Amer. insectivorous grayish songbirds of genus *Vireo*.

vi·res·cence (vīrĕs′ens) *n.* Greenness, esp. (bot.) in petals etc. normally of some other color. **vi·res′cent** *adj.*

Vir·gil (vēr′jil). Publius Vergilius Maro (70–19 B.C.), Roman poet whose chief works were the *Aeneid*, epic poem on the legendary ancestors of Rome, Aeneas and his Trojans; the *Georgics*, didactic poem on agriculture and rearing of cattle and bees; the *Eclogues* or *Bucolics*, pastoral poems. **Vir·gil·i·an** (verjĭl′ēan) *adj.* Of, in the style of, Virgil.

vir·gin (vēr′jĭn) *n.* 1. Person,

esp. woman, who has had no sexual intercourse; (eccles.) in early Christian times, unmarried or chaste woman distinguished for piety and steadfastness in religion. 2. (**Mary**) **the V ∼**, the (**Blessed**) **V ∼** (**Mary**): see MARY[1]; image or picture representing her. 3. **the V ∼**: see VIRGO. 4. **∼ birth**, (esp.) doctrine that Jesus Christ was born to the Virgin Mary having no human father but conceived by the power of the Holy Spirit; **∼'s-bower**, traveler's joy or other species of plant *Clematis*. **virgin** *adj.* That is a virgin; of, befitting, a virgin; spotless, not yet or not previously touched, handled, or employed; (of metal) made from ore by smelting; **∼ forest**, forest as yet untouched by man; **V∼ Queen**, Elizabeth I of England; **∼ soil**, soil not yet brought into cultivation etc. **vir·gin·i·ty** (verjĭn′ĭtē) *n.* Condition or quality of a virgin.

vir·gin·al (vēr′jinal) *adj.* Being, befitting, belonging to, a virgin. **vir′gin·al·ly** *adv.* **virginal** *n.* (freq. pl.) Keyboard instrument, earliest (16th and 17th centuries) and simplest form of harpsichord, with one string to a note, in box or case, usu. without legs.

Vir·gin·ia (verjĭn′ya). South Atlantic state of U.S., one of the original 13 states of the Union (1788), and site of first English settlement (1607) in Amer.; capital, Richmond; **∼ creeper**, N. Amer. climbing plant (*Parthenocissus quinquefolia*); **∼ reel**, Amer. country dance, in which partners at the start form two lines facing one another and perform a variety of steps together. **Vir·gin′ian** *adj. & n.* [named in honor of Elizabeth I of England (VIRGIN Queen)]

Vir·gin (vēr′jĭn) **Islands.** Group of about 100 small islands in W. Indies, mostly uninhabited; divided between Britain (with capital Road Town) and U.S. (with capital Charlotte Amalie).

Vir·go (vẽr′gō). The Virgin, a constellation; 6th sign (♍) of the zodiac, which the sun enters about Aug. 23.

vir·gule (vẽr′gul) *n*. Slanting line (/) to mark division of words or lines; slash.

vir·i·des·cent (vĭrĭdĕs′ent) *adj*. Greenish, somewhat green. **vir·i·des′cence** *n*.

vi·rid·i·an (vĭrĭd′ēan) *n*. 1. Yellowish-green color. 2. Chromium oxide, an emerald green pigment. ~ *adj*. Of the color viridian.

vi·rid·i·ty (vĭrĭd′ĭtē) *n*. Greenness, esp. of foliage or grass; real or apparent youth, freshness and innocence of mind or body.

vir·ile (vĭr′ĭl; *Brit*. vĭr′īl) *adj*. Of, characteristic of, a man; capable of procreation; having masculine vigor or strength. **vir′i·lism** *n*. (pathol.) Development of secondary male characteristics in female or precociously in male. **vi·ril·i·ty** (vĭrĭl′ĭtē) *n*.

vi·rol·o·gy (vĩrŏl′ojē, vĭ-) *n*.

Study of viruses. **vi·ro·log·i·cal** (vĩrolŏj′ĭkal) *adj*. **vi·rol′o·gist** *n*.

vir·tu·al (vẽr′chōōal) *adj*. That is so in essence or effect, although not formally or actually; ~ **focus** (optics) apparent focus of reflected or refracted rays of light. **vir′tu·al·ly** *adv*. **vir·tu·al·i·ty** (vẽrchōō-ăl′ĭtē) *n*.

vir·tue (vẽr′chōō) *n*. Moral excellence, uprightness, goodness; particular moral excellence, moral quality regarded as of special excellence or importance; chastity, esp. of women; good quality or influence, efficacy; **by, in ~ of**, on the strength or ground of; (pl.) order of angels (see ANGEL). [L. *virtus* worth, valor, f. *vir* man]

vir·tu·o·so (vẽrchōō′sō) *n*. (pl. **-sos, -si** pr. -sē). Person with special interest in or knowledge of works of art; person skilled in technique of an art, esp. of performance on musical instrument. **vir·tu·os·i·ty** (vẽrchōōŏs′ĭtē) *n*. (pl.

Growing to a length of 6 ft. the Gaboon **viper** *is the largest snake in this family. All have venom which is dangerous to man and there is even a European representative, the adder.*

-ties). [It. *virtuoso* learned, skilled, f. L. *virtus* (see VIRTUE)]

vir·tu·ous (vẽr′chōŏus) *adj*. Possessing, showing, moral rectitude; chaste. **vir′tu·ous·ly** *adv*. **vir′tu·ous·ness** *n*.

vir·u·lent (vĭr′yulent, vĭr′u-) *adj*. Poisonous; malignant, bitter; (of disease) extremely violent. **vir′u·lent·ly** *adv*. **vir′u·lence, vir′u·len·cy** *ns*.

vi·rus (vīr′us) *n*. 1. Organic particle, much smaller than bacteria or other classifiable microorganisms, existing only within cells of animal and plant bodies and capable of producing various diseases. 2. Poisonous substance, the product of disease, found in the tissues and body fluids. 3. (fig.) Moral poison, malignity. [L., = "poison"]

vi·sa (vē′za), **vi·sé** (vē′zā, vēzā′) *ns*. Endorsement on passport permitting holder to enter or cross a particular country. ~ *v.t.* (**-saed, -sa·ing; -séed, -sé·ing**). Mark with visa.

vis·age (vĭz′ĭj) *n*. (now chiefly literary) Face.

vis-à-vis (vēzavē′) *n*. Either of two persons or things facing or situated opposite each other. ~ *prep.* & *adv.* Over against, in comparison with; facing, face-to-face (with).

vis·ca·cha, viz·ca·cha (vĭskah′-cha) *ns*. Large burrowing S. Amer. rodent (*Lago stomus maximus*) having long soft fur, gray on back and yellowish-white beneath.

vis·cer·a (vĭs′era) *n.pl.* (sing. **vis·cus** pr. vĭs′kus). Internal organs of principal cavities of animal body, as intestines, heart, liver, etc. **vis′cer·al** *adj*. **vis′cer·al·ly** *adv*.

vis·cid (vĭs′ĭd) *adj*. Glutinous, sticky. **vis·cid·i·ty** (vĭsĭd′ĭtē) *n*. **vis′cid·ly** *adv*.

vis·cose (vĭs′kōs) *n*. Highly viscous solution of cellulose compound obtained by treating wood pulp or cotton fiber with caustic soda and carbon disulfide, used in manufacture of rayon etc.

vis·cos·i·ty (vĭskŏs′ĭtē) *n*. (pl. **-ties**). Quality, degree, of being viscous; (phys.) body's property of resisting alteration in position of its parts relative to each other.

vis·count (vī′kownt) *n*. Member of fourth order of Brit. peerage, between earl and baron; courtesy title of earl's eldest son. **vis′-**

Far left: Plants in the genus Viola include both the colorful **violet** *and the pansy. The violet has long been a source of essence for the perfume industry and is also used in a liqueur.*

Left: **Virginia creeper,** *a native vine of North America, is more closely related to the grape vine than to ivy. The Indians made a dye from its berries.*

Right: Nepalese statue of 'Vishnu float-ing on the waters'. Together with Brahma and Siva, Vishnu forms part of the Hindu trinity. He is considered to act as 'preserver of the universe'.

count·cy (vī′kowntsē), **vis·-count·y** (vī′kowntē) *ns.* **vis·-count·ess** (vī′kowntĭs) *n.* Wife or widow of viscount; peeress of fourth order of nobility.

vis·cous (vĭs′kus) *adj.* Glutinous, gluey, sticky; having viscosity; intermediate between solid and fluid, adhesively soft. **vis′cous·ly** *adv.* **vis′cous·ness** *n.*

vis·cus (vĭs′kus) *n.* (anat.) Internal organ (sing. of VISCERA).

vise, Brit. **vice** (vīs) *ns.* Tool with two jaws worked by screw for gripping firmly and holding thing being worked upon by metal-worker, carpenter, etc.

vi·sé = VISA.

Vish·nu (vĭsh′nōō). (Hinduism) One of the principal deities, identi-fied by his worshippers with the supreme deity and regarded as savior of the world. **Vish′nu·ism** *n.*

vis·i·ble (vĭz′ibel) *adj.* Capable of being seen; that can be seen at particular time, under certain con-ditions, etc.; in sight; that can be perceived or observed, apparent, open, obvious. **vis′i·bly** *adv.* **vis·i·bil·i·ty** (vĭzibĭl′ĭtē) *n.* (pl. **-ties**). (esp.) Conditions of light, atmosphere, etc., with respect to distinguishing of objects by sight; possibility of seeing, range of vision, under such conditions.

Vis·i·goth (vĭz′igŏth) *n.* West Goth, one of that branch of Goths that entered Roman territory toward end of 4th c. and sub-sequently established in Spain a kingdom overthrown by the Moors in 711–12. **Vis·i·goth·ic** (vĭzi-gŏth′ĭk) *adj.*

vi·sion (vĭzh′on) *n.* 1. Act or faculty of seeing, sight; perception of things by means of the light coming from them, which enters the eye. 2. Power of discerning future conditions, sagacity in planning, foresight. 3. Thing, person, seen in dream or trance; supernatural apparition, phantom; thing, esp. of attractive or fantastic character, seen vividly in the imagination; person, sight, of unusual beauty.

vi·sion·ar·y (vĭzh′onĕrē) *adj.* Given to seeing visions or indulging in fanciful theories; seen (only) in a vision, existing only in imagina-tion; unreal, fantastic, unpractical. ∼ *n.* (pl. **-ar·ies**). Visionary person.

vis·it (vĭz′ĭt) *v.t.* Go, come, to see (person, place, etc.) as act of friendship or social ceremony, on business, from curiosity, for official inspection, etc.; (of disease, calamity, etc.) come upon, attack; (bibl.) punish (person, sin), avenge (sins etc.) *upon* person, comfort, bless, (person *with* salvation etc.); **visiting card,** calling card; **visit-ing nurse,** registered or licensed practical nurse who takes care of the sick in their homes; **visiting professor,** college or university professor invited to join faculty at another institution for specified period. **visit** *n.* Call on a person or at a place; temporary residence with a person or at a place; occasion of going *to* doctor, dentist, etc., for examination or treatment, doctor's professional call on patient; formal or official call for purpose of inspection etc. **vis′it·a·ble** *adj.* **vis′i·tor** *n.*

vis·i·tant (vĭz′ĭtant) *n.* 1. Migratory bird, as temporarily frequenting particular locality. 2. (poet., rhet.) Visitor.

vis·it·a·tion (vĭzĭtā′shon) *n.* 1. Official visit of inspection etc., esp. bishop's inspection of churches of his diocese. 2. (colloq.) Unduly protracted visit or social call. 3. Boarding of vessel belonging to another nation to learn her charac-ter and purpose (**right of** ∼, right to do this, not including right of search). 4. Divine dispensation of punishment or reward, notable experience, esp. affliction, com-pared to this. 5. **V** ∼ (**of Our Lady**), visit of Virgin Mary to her cousin Elizabeth (Luke 1); **V** ∼ **day,** July 2, commemorating this; ∼ **rights,** legally decreed right of a divorced or separated parent to visit child in custody of other parent. **vis·it·a′tion·al** *adj.*

vi·sor (vī′zer) *n.* 1. (hist.) Movable front part of helmet, covering face, and with openings for seeing and breathing. 2. (hist.) Mask. 3. Projecting front part of cap. 4. Movable shield fixed inside motor vehicle above windshield to protect eyes from sunlight or glare. **vi′sor·less** *adj.*

VISTA *abbrev.* Volunteers in Service to America. (U.S. govern-ment program established in 1964 under Office of Economic Oppor-tunity to provide volunteers to train and provide other types of assis-tance to residents of economically deprived areas.)

vis·ta (vĭs′ta) *n.* View, prospect, esp. through avenue of trees or other long narrow opening; such an opening; (fig.) mental view of extensive period of time or series of events etc.

vis·u·al (vĭzh′ōoal) *adj.* Of, concerned with, seeing; used in seeing, received through sight; ∼ **aid,** any of a variety of materials, as filmstrips, slides, photographs, picture cards, for students to look at in classrooms, during lectures, etc. as an aid to learning; ∼ **arts,** arts such as painting, etching, sculpture, etc., which are perceived through sense of sight; ∼ **purple,** purple-red pigment present in retinal rods of eyes, abundant in eyes of nocturnal animals. **vis'u-al·ly** *adv.*

vis·u·al·ize (vĭzh'ōōəlīz) *v.t.* (**-ized, -iz·ing**). Make mental vision or image of (something not present or not visible), make visible to imagination. **vis·u·al·i·za·tion** (vĭzhōōəlīzā'shon), **vis'u·al·iz·er** *ns.*

vi·tal (vī'tal) *adj.* Of, concerned with, essential to, organic life; essential to existence or to the matter in hand; affecting life, fatal to life or to success, etc.; ~ **parts**, parts of body essential to life, as lungs, heart, brain, etc.; ~ **signs**, bodily functions, esp. pulse, temperature, and respiration, that are measured to determine organism's efficiency; ~ **statistics**, those relating to births, deaths, health, disease, etc. **vi'tal·ly** *adv.* **vi'tals** *n.pl.* Vital parts of body.

vi·tal·ism (vī'talīzem) *n.* (philos.) Theory that life originates in a vital principle distinct from chemical and physical forces (opp. MECHANISM). **vi'tal·ist** *n.* Adherent of vitalism. **vi·tal·is·tic** (vītalĭs'tĭk) *adj.*

vi·tal·i·ty (vītăl'ĭtē) *n.* (pl. **-ties**). Vital power, ability to sustain life; (fig.) active force or power, activity, animation, liveliness.

vi·tal·ize (vī'talīz) *v.t.* (**-ized, -iz·ing**). Put life or animation into, infuse with vitality or vigor. **vi·tal·i·za·tion** (vītalīzā'shon) *n.*

vi·ta·min (vī'tamĭn) *n.* Any of a number of substances essential for growth and nutrition, occurring in certain foodstuffs or produced synthetically; ~ **A**, present in liver oils, butterfat, green and yellow vegetables, etc.; ~ **B**, any of a group present in yeast products, whole wheat, etc., that comprises a number of separate substances concerned esp. with the formation and functioning of important enzymes in the body; ~ **C**, ASCORBIC acid; ~ **D**, present in fish liver oils and egg yolk and apparently concerned in the deposition of calcium phosphate in bones; ~ **E**, present in wheat germ oil and green leaves, its absence causing sterility; ~ **K**, present in various foodstuffs, esp. green leaves, facilitating clotting of blood. **vi·ta·min·ic** (vītamĭn'ĭk) *adj.* **vi'ta·min·ize** *v.t.* Introduce vitamin(s) into (food). [orig. named *vitamine* f. L. *vita* life and English AMINE, in the belief that an amino acid was present]

vi·tel·lin (vĭtĕl'ĭn, vī-) *n.* (biochem.) Chief protein of egg yolk.

vi·tel·lus (vĭtĕl'us, vī-) *n.* (pl. **-lus·es**). (embryol.) Yolk of an egg. **vi·tel'line** *adj.* Of the vitellus; ~ **membrane**, membrane enclosing vitellus.

vi·ti·ate (vĭsh'ēāt) *v.t.* (**-at·ed,** **-at·ing**). Impair the quality of, corrupt, debase; make invalid or ineffectual. **vi·ti·a·tion** (vĭshēā'shon), **vi'ti·a·tor** *ns.*

vit·i·cul·ture (vĭt'ĭkŭlcher, vī'ti-) *n.* Cultivation of grapes.

vit·re·ous (vĭt'rēus) *adj.* Of (the nature of) glass; resembling glass in composition, brittleness, hardness, luster, transparency, etc.; ~ **humor**: see HUMOR *n.* def 3. **vit're·ous·ly** *adv.* **vit·re·os·i·ty** (vĭtrĕŏs'ĭtē) *n.*

vit·ri·fy (vĭt'rifī) *v.* (**-fied, -fy·ing**). Convert, be converted, into glass or glasslike substance; render, become, vitreous. **vit·ri·fac·tion** (vĭtrifăk'shon), **vit·ri·fi·ca·tion** (vĭtrifikā'shon) *ns.* **vit'ri·fi·a·ble** *adj.*

vit·ri·ol (vĭt'rēol) *n.* 1. Any of various metallic sulfates used in the arts or medicinally, esp. iron sulfate; (also **oil of** ~) concentrated sulfuric acid. 2. (fig.) Causticity, acrimony, of feeling or utterance. **vit·ri·ol·ic** (vĭtrēŏl'ĭk) *adj.* (esp., fig.) Extremely caustic, scathing, bitter, or malignant.

vit·ta (vĭt'a) *n.* (pl. **vit·tae** pr. vĭt'ē). 1. (bot.) Stripe or band of color. 2. (bot.) One of a number of oil tubes in pericarp of fruit of most umbelliferous plants. **vit·tate** (vĭt'āt) *adj.*

vi·tu·per·ate (vītōō'perāt, -tū'-, vĭ-) *v.t.* (**-at·ed, -at·ing**). Revile. **vi·tu·per·a·tion** (vītōōperā'shon, -tū-, vĭ-) *n.* **vi·tu·per·a·tive** (vītōō'perātĭv, -pera-, -tū'-, vĭ-) *adj.* **vi·tu'per·a·tive·ly** *adv.*

Vi·tus (vī'tus), **St.** (*c*300). Child martyr of the DIOCLETIAN persecution; **St. Vitus's dance**, (pop.) = CHOREA.

vi·va (vē'va) *n. & int.* (Salute, greeting, cry, of) "long live ..." [It. third pers. imper. of *vivere* live]

vi·va·ce (vĭvah'chā, -chē) *adv. & n.* (mus.) (Passage performed) in brisk and lively manner. [It.]

vi·va·cious (vĭvā'shus, vī-) *adj.* Lively, animated. **vi·va'cious·ly** *adv.* **vi·vac·i·ty** (vĭvăs'ĭtē, vī-),

vi·va'cious·ness *ns.*

Vi·val·di (vĭvahl'dē), **Antonio** (1680?–1743). Italian violinist and composer.

vi·var·i·um (vĭvār'ēum) *n.* (pl. **-var·i·ums, -var·i·a** pr. -vār'ēa). Place or enclosure for keeping living animals etc. as far as possible under natural conditions, for interest or scientific study.

vi·va vo·ce, vi·va-vo·ce (vī'va vō'sē). Orally; by word of mouth. [L., = "with the living voice"]

vive (vēv) *int.* Cry of "long live," as in ~ **le roi** (rwah), long live the king. [Fr. third pers. sing. imperat. of *vivre* live]

vi·ver·rine (vĭvĕr'ĭn, -īn, vĭ-) *adj.* Of the Viverridae or CIVET family.

viv·id (vĭv'ĭd) *adj.* Strong, intense, glaring (esp. of color, light, etc.); clearly or distinctly perceived or perceptible, intensely or strongly felt or expressed, (capable of) presenting subjects or ideas in clear and striking manner. **viv'id·ly** *adv.* **viv'id·ness** *n.*

viv·i·fy (vĭv'ifī) *v.t.* (**-fied, -fy·ing**). (chiefly fig.) Give life to, animate. **viv·i·fi·ca·tion** (vĭvifikā'shon), **viv'i·fi·er** *ns.*

vi·vip·a·rous (vĭvĭp'erus) *adj.* 1. (zool.) Bringing forth young in developed state, not hatching from egg (cf. OVIPAROUS). 2. (bot.) Germinating while still attached to the parent plant; having such seeds. **vi·vip'a·rous·ly** *adv.* **vi·vip'a·rous·ness, viv·i·par·i·ty** (vĭvipăr'ĭtē) *ns.*

viv·i·sect (vĭv'ĭsĕkt, vĭvĭsĕkt') *v.t.* Perform vivisection upon. **viv·i·sec·tion** (vĭvĭsĕk'shon) *n.* Performance of surgical experiments on living animals in laboratory for the advancement of (esp. medical) knowledge. **viv·i·sec'tion·ist** *n.* One who approves of or advocates this practice.

Related to the chinchilla and the guinea pig, the 2 ft. long **vizcacha** has been hunted in South America for its meat and for its fur. The plains species is in Argentina.

vix·en (vĭk′sen) *n.* 1. Female fox. 2. Ill-tempered quarrelsome woman. **vix′en·ish** *adj.* **vix′en·ish·ly** *adv.*

viz., viz *abbrevs.* (usu. spoken as "namely") = VIDELICET.

viz·ca·cha: see VISCACHA.

vi·zier (vĭzēr′, vĭz′yer), **vi·zir** (vĭzēr′) *ns.* High administrative official in some Muslim countries, esp. (**grand** ~) chief minister of former Turkish Empire. [Arab. *wazīr* caliph's chief minister]

VL, V.L. *abbrevs.* Vulgar Latin.

VLF, V.L.F. *abbrevs.* Very low frequency.

V.M.D. *abbrev.* Doctor of Veterinary Medicine [L. *Veterinariae Medicinae Doctor*].

VOA *abbrev.* Voice of America.

voc. *abbrev.* Vocative.

vo·ca·ble (vō′kabel) *n.* Word, esp. with ref. to form rather than meaning.

vo·cab·u·lar·y (vōkăb′yulĕrē) *n.* (pl. **-lar·ies**). List of words with their meanings, glossary; sum of words used in a language, or in a particular book or branch of science etc., or by a particular person, class, profession, etc.

vo·cal (vō′kal) *adj.* Of, concerned with, uttered by, the voice; (poet.) endowed (as) with a voice; expressive, eloquent; (of music) composed for voice(s) with or without accompaniment; (phonet.) of a vowel, vocalic; ~ **cords**, voice-producing organs, two straplike membranes stretched across the larynx, each having a medial edge that is free to vibrate in the air stream, determining pitch of voice by their length and frequency of vibration, women's being shorter than men's; ~ **score**, musical score showing voice parts in full. **vo′cal·ly** *adv.* **vocal** *n.* 1. Vocal sound. 2. Piece of music for, performance of, singing. 3. (R.C. Ch.) Person entitled to vote in certain elections.

vo·cal·ic (vōkăl′ĭk) *adj.* Of, concerning, vowel(s); of the nature of a vowel; rich in vowels.

vo·cal·ism (vō′kalīzem) *n.* Use of voice in speech or singing; system of vowels in a language. **vo′cal·ist** *n.* Singer.

vo·cal·ize (vō′kalīz) *v.* (**-ized, -iz·ing**). Utter, make vocal; convert into, use as, vowel; furnish with vowels or vowel points; sing without words, but with vowel sound(s). **vo·cal·i·za·tion** (vōkalīzā′shon), **vo′cal·iz·er** *ns.*

vo·ca·tion (vōkā′shon) *n.* Divine call to, sense of fitness for, a career or occupation; occupation, calling. **vo·ca′tion·al** *adj.* **vo·ca′tion·al·ly** *adv.*

voc·a·tive (vŏk′atĭv) *adj.* (gram.) Of the case used in address or invocation. ~ *n.* (Word in) vocative case. **voc′a·tive·ly** *adv.*

*Top: Diagrammatic version of the structure of a **volcano**. Above: Volcanic activity in Tenequia near the Canary Islands in the Atlantic. Above right: A form of volcanic rock sculpted in Egypt about 1800 B.C.*

vo·cif·er·ate (vōsĭf′erāt) *v.* (**-at·ed, -at·ing**). Utter, cry out, noisily; shout, bawl. **vo·cif·er·a·tion** (vōsĭferā′shon) *n.*

vo·cif·er·ous (vōsĭf′erus) *adj.* Clamorous, noisy. **vo·cif′er·ous·ly** *adv.* **vo·cif′er·ous·ness** *n.*

vod·ka (vŏd′ka) *n.* Alcoholic spirit made esp. in Russia by distillation of rye etc. [Russ. dim. of *voda* water]

vogue (vōg) *n.* Popularity, general acceptance or currency; prevailing fashion; **in** ~, in fashion, generally current; ~ **word**, currently popular word. **vogu′ish** *adv.*

voice (vois) *n.* 1. Sound uttered by the mouth, esp. human utterance in speaking, shouting, or singing; use of the voice, esp. in spoken or (fig.) written words; opinion so expressed; right to express opinion; vote; (mus.) singing voice, quality of this; (phonet.) sound uttered with vibration or resonance of vocal cords (dist. from *breath* or *whisper*). **Voice of America**, U.S. radio network broadcasting programs to foreign countries, expressing American point-of-view; **voice-over**, voice heard without speaker in view, as in television commercials; **voice print**, graphic record of speech with respect to frequency, duration, and amplitude; **with one voice**, unanimously. 2. (gram.) Set of forms of a verb showing relation of its subject to the action (ACTIVE, PASSIVE, **voice**). **voice** *v.t.* (**voiced, voic·ing**). Give utterance to, express; (phonet.) utter with voice, change from voiceless to voiced; (mus.) regulate tone quality of organ pipes. **voiced** (voist) *adj.* (esp., phonet.) Uttered with voice, sonant. **voic·ed·ness** (voi′sĭdnĭs) *n.*

voice·less (vois′lĭs) *adj.* Speechless, dumb, mute; (phonet.) not voiced. **voice′less·ly** *adv.* **voice′less·ness** *n.*

void (void) *adj.* Empty, vacant; invalid, not binding; (poet., rhet.) ineffectual, useless; ~ **of**, lacking, free from. **void** *n.* Empty space. ~ *v.t.* Render void or invalid; emit (excrement etc.). **void′a·ble** *adj.* **void′er, void′ance** *ns.*

voi·là (*Fr.* vwălă′) *int.* There it is! There you are! [Fr.]

voile (voil) *n.* Thin semi-transparent cotton, wool, or silk dress material. [Fr., = "veil"]

vol. *abbrev.* (pl. **vols.**). Volume; volunteer.

vo·lar (vō′ler) *adj.* (anat.) Of palm of hand or sole of foot.

vol·a·tile (vŏl′atĭl; *Brit.* vŏl′atīl) *adj.* Readily evaporating at ordinary temperatures; (fig.) changeable, flighty, lively, gay; evanescent, transient; ~ **oil**, essential oil. **vol·a·til·i·ty** (vŏlatĭl′ĭtē) *n.*

vol·a·til·ize (vŏl′atilīz) *v.* (**-ized, -iz·ing**). (Cause to) evaporate; make, become, volatile. **vol·a·til·i·za·tion** (vŏlatĭlĭză′shon) *n.*

vol·can·ic (vŏlkăn′ĭk) *adj.* Of, produced by, a volcano; characterized by volcanoes; ~ **glass**, obsidian. **vol·can′i·cal·ly** *adv.*

vol·ca·no (vŏlkā′nō) *n.* (pl. **-noes, -nos**). Hill or mountain, more or less conical, composed partly or wholly of discharged matter, with crater(s) or other opening(s) in Earth's crust through which steam, gases, ashes, rocks, and freq. streams of molten material are or have been periodically

ejected; (fig.) violent, esp. suppressed, feeling, passion, etc. **vol·-can·ism** (vŏl′kanĭzem) *n.* Volcanic activity. **vol·can·ol·o·gy** (vŏlka-nŏl′ojē) *n.* [It., f. L. *Volcanus* VULCAN]

vole (vōl) *n.* Small rodent with short ears and tail, rounded snout, and herbivorous teeth, of genus *Microtus* and related genera.

Vol·ga (vŏl′ga; *Russ.* vawl′gah). Longest river of Europe, 2,325 mi. (3,743 km), rising in NW. of U.S.S.R. and flowing E., then S. to the Caspian Sea.

Vol·go·grad (vŏl′gogrăd, *Russ.* vawl′gawgraht). City (formerly Stalingrad, 1925–61, previously Tsaritsyn) of U.S.S.R. on the Lower Volga.

vo·li·tion (volĭsh′on) *n.* Act, power, of willing or resolving, exercise of the will. **vo·li′tion·al** *adj.* **vo·li′tion·al·ly** *adv.*

vol·ley (vŏl′ē) *n.* (pl. **-leys**). Salvo, shower, of missiles (or fig. of oaths etc.); (tennis etc.) return stroke at ball before it touches ground; **voll′eyball**, game in which large inflated ball is struck with hands from alternate sides of high net without touching ground. **volley** *v.* (**-leyed, -ley·ing**). Discharge (missiles etc.), return, hit, (ball), in volley; fly in volley; make sound like volleys of artillery.

volt (vōlt) *n.* Unit of electromotive force, the electrical pressure that if steadily applied to a conductor whose resistance is 1 ohm will produce a current of 1 ampere (symb. V, v). [f. VOLTA]

Vol·ta (vōl′ta; *It.* vawl′tah), **A·les·san·dro** (1745–1827). Italian physicist, a pioneer of electrical

science; first devised apparatus for chemically developing electric currents.

volt·age (vōl′tĭj) *n.* Electromotive force expressed in volts.

volt·a·ic (vŏltā′ĭk) *adj.* Producing electricity, (of electricity) generated, by chemical action, after the method discovered by VOLTA; (consisting) of, caused by, connected with, such electricity.

Vol·taire (vōltār′, vŏl-). Pen name of François Marie Arouet (1694–1778), French deist philosopher, historian, dramatist, and writer of historical and satirical poems and tales; famous for anticlericalism, witty skepticism, and influence on the leaders of the French Revolution; author of satirical novels *Candide*, and *Zadig*, and *Philosophical Letters*, etc.

volte-face (vōltfăs′, vŏlt-) *n.* (pl. **volte-face**). Complete change of front in argument, politics, etc. [Fr.]

volt·me·ter (vōlt′mēter) *n.* Any instrument for measuring difference in potential in volts.

vol·u·ble (vŏl′yubel) *adj.* Fluent, glib; speaking, spoken with great readiness or fluency. **vol·u·bil·i·ty** (vŏlyubĭl′ĭtē), **vol′u·ble·ness** *ns.* **vol′u·bly** *adv.*

vol·ume (vŏl′ūm) *n.* 1. Collection of written or esp. printed sheets bound together to form a book; division of work (intended to be) separately bound. 2. Bulk, mass, quantity, esp. large quantity; space occupied by anything, esp. as measured in cubic units; size, dimensions, amount, *of.* 3. (usu. pl.) Plume, coil, rounded mass, of smoke etc. 4. (mus. etc.) Quantity,

Mouse-sized but with a blunter snout and shorter tail, the **vole** *is present in many parts of the northern hemisphere. One species in Russia is rat-sized and has been trapped for its fur.*

Teams from Germany and Japan play **volleyball** *during the 1972 Olympic Games at Munich. This form of 'hand-tennis' was invented in the U.S.A. during the 1890s.*

power, fullness, of tone or sound. **vol·u·met·ric** (vŏlyumĕt´rĭk) *adj*. Of, pertaining to, measurement of volume. **vol·u·met´ri·cal·ly** *adv*.

vo·lu·mi·nous (voloo´minus) *adj*. 1. Containing, consisting of, many coils or convolutions. 2. Consisting of many volumes; (of writer) producing many books etc. 3. Of great volume, bulky, ample. **vo·lu´mi·nous·ly** *adv*. **vo·lu´mi·nous·ness, vo·lu·mi·nos·i·ty** (voloominŏs´ĭtē) *ns*.

vol·un·tar·y (vŏl´untērē) *adj*. Done, acting, able to act, of one's own free will; purposed, intentional, not constrained; (of bodily action etc.) controlled by the will; brought about, produced, maintained, etc., by voluntary action; ~ **hospital**, one maintained by voluntary contributions. **vol·un·tar·i·ly** (vŏl´untĕrile, vŏluntĕr´ile) *adv*. **vol´un·tar·i·ness** *n*. **voluntary** *n*. (pl. **-tar·ies**). (orig.) Extempore performance, esp. as prelude to other music; (now) organ solo played before, during, or after any church service; music composed for this.

vol·un·teer (vŏluntēr´) *n*. Person who voluntarily offers his services or enrolls himself for any enterprise, esp. for service in any of the armed forces. ~ *adj*. Of or pertaining to a volunteer or volunteers; made up of volunteers; serving as volunteer(s). ~ *v*. Undertake, offer, voluntarily; make voluntary offer of one's services; be a volunteer.

vo·lup·tu·ar·y (volŭp´chooĕrē) *n*. (pl. **-ar·ies**) & *adj*. Of, concerned with, (person) given up to, indulgence in luxury and gratification of the senses.

vo·lup·tu·ous (volŭp´choous) *adj*. Of, derived from, marked by, addicted to, promising etc., gratification of the senses. **vo·lup´tu·ous·ly** *adv*. **vo·lup´tu·ous·ness** *n*.

vo·lute (voloot´) *n*. 1. (archit.) Spiral scroll forming chief ornament of Ionic capital and used also in Corinthian and Composite capitals. 2. Spiral conformation; convolution, esp. of spiral shell; marine gastropod of genus *Voluta* and allied genera, chiefly tropical, and freq. with very handsome shell. ~ *adj*. Having the form of a volute, forming spiral curve(s).

vo·lu·tion (voloo´shon) *n*. Convolution, spiral turn, whorl of spiral shell; rolling or revolving movement.

vol·va (vŏl´va) *n*. (bot.) Membranous covering enclosing many fungi in early stages of growth.

vo·mer (vō´mer) *n*. (anat.) Small thin bone separating nostrils in man and most vertebrates.

vom·it (vŏm´ĭt) *v*. Eject contents of stomach through mouth; bring

*Veiled Muslim woman marks the counterfoil of her ballot paper during an election. The power to cast a **vote** is the mark of equality among citizens: one vote, one person.*

up, eject, (as) by vomiting, belch forth, spew out. ~ *n*. Matter ejected from stomach. **vom´it·er** *n*.

voo·doo (voo´doo) *adj*. & *n*. (pl. **-doos**). (Of a) system of religious or magical beliefs and practices of African origin among people of West Indies and Amer.; person skilled in this; voodoo spell; fetish etc. used in voodoo. ~ *v.t*. Bewitch, put voodoo spell on. **voo´doo·ism** *n*.

vo·ra·cious (vōrā´shus, vaw-, vo-) *adj*. Greedy in eating; gluttonous. **vo·ra´cious·ly** *adv*. **vo·ra´cious·ness, vo·rac·i·ty** (vōrăs´ĭtē, vaw-, vo-) *ns*.

-vorous *suffix*. Forming adjectives (usu. with intermediate -i-) with sense "feeding on" (*carnivorous*); so **-vora**, forming names of groups of animals classified by their food (*Insectivora*); **-vore**, forming name of individual of such group (*herbivore*).

vor·tex (vōr´tĕks) *n*. (pl. **-tex·es, -ti·ces** pr. -tĭsēz). 1. Mass of fluid, esp. liquid, with rapid circular movement around axis and tendency to form vacuum or cavity in center toward which bodies are attracted, whirlpool; anything likened to this, esp. by reason of rush or excitement, rapid change, or absorbing effect. 2. Whirling mass of air or vapor; (central part of) whirlwind. **vor·ti·cal** (vōr´tĭkal) *adj*. **vor´ti·cal·ly** *adv*.

vo·ta·ry (vō´terē), fem. **vo·ta·ress** (vō´terĭs, -rĕs) *ns*. One bound by vow(s), esp. to religious life; devotee, devoted or zealous worshipper, ardent follower (*of*).

vote (vōt) *n*. Expression of one's acceptance or rejection signified by ballot, show of hands, voice, or otherwise; right to vote; opinion expressed, resolution or decision carried, by voting; votes collectively. ~ *v*. (**vot´ed, vot·ing**). Give a vote, express choice or preference by ballot, show of hands, etc.; choose, elect, establish, ratify, grant, confer, by vote; pronounce, declare, by general consent; (colloq.) propose, suggest. **vote´less** *adj*. **vot´er** *n*.

vo·tive (vō´tĭv) *adj*. Dedicated, offered, consecrated, etc., in fulfillment of a vow.

vouch (vowch) *v*. Confirm, uphold, (statement) by evidence or assertion; answer, be surety, *for*.

vouch·er (vow´cher) *n*. Document, receipt, etc., to attest correctness of accounts or monetary transactions, authorize or establish payment, etc.; esp. document that can be exchanged for goods or services as token of payment made or promised.

vouch·safe (vowchsāf´) *v.t*. (**-safed, -saf·ing**). Give, grant, bestow, in condescending or gracious manner; deign to give, condescend (*to* do).

vow (vow) *v.t.* Promise, or undertake solemnly, esp. by a vow; make solemn resolve to exact (vengeance), harbor (hatred), etc. ~ *n.* Solemn promise or engagement, esp. to God or to any deity or saint. **vow´er** *n.*

vow·el (vow´el) *n.* Speech sound produced by vibrations of vocal cords, modified or characterized by form of vocal cavities, but without audible friction (opp. to, but not sharply divided from, CONSONANT²); letter or symbol representing such a sound, as a, e, i, o, u; ~ **point**, sign used to indicate vowel in certain alphabets, as Hebrew etc.

vox po·pu·li (vŏks´ pŏp´yulī). (abbrev. **vox pop.**) Voice of the people; public opinion, popular belief, general verdict. [L.]

voy·age (voi´ĭj) *n.* Journey, esp. to distant place or country, by sea or water. ~ *v.* (**-aged, -ag·ing**). Travel by water; traverse, travel over. **voy´ag·er** *n.*

vo·ya·geur (vwahyahzhēr´, voia-) *n.* (in Canada) Man employed in transportation of goods and passengers between trading posts; any guide, woodsman, or boatman of the Canadian wilderness.

vo·yeur (vwahyēr´, voi-) *n.* One who derives gratification from looking at sexual organs or acts of others. **vo·yeur´ism** *n.* **voy·eur·is·tic** (vwahyerĭs´tĭk, voie-) *adj.*

VP, V.P. *abbrevs.* Vice president.

vs. *abbrev.* Verse; versus.

V.S. *abbrev.* Veterinary Surgeon.

V/STOL *abbrev.* Vertical/short takeoff and landing (aircraft).

VT, Vt. *abbrevs.* Vermont.

v.t. *abbrev.* Verb transitive.

VTOL *abbrev.* Vertical takeoff and landing (aircraft).

Vul·can (vŭl´kan). (Rom. myth.) God of fire and patron of workers in metal, identified with Hephaestus.

vul·can·ite (vŭl´kanīt) *n.* Ebonite, black variety of rubber hardened by treatment with sulfur at high temperatures.

vul·can·ize (vŭl´kanīz) *v.t.* (**-ized, -iz·ing**). Harden and make (rubber etc.) more durable by chemical means, esp. by combining it with sulfur, usu. with heat and pressure. **vul·can·i·za·tion** (vŭl·kanīzā´shon), **vul´can·iz·er** *ns.*

Vulg. *abbrev.* Vulgate.

vul·gar (vŭl´ger) *adj.* Of, characteristic of, the common people, plebeian, coarse, low; in common use, generally prevalent; ~ **tongue**, vernacular, popular or native language, esp. opp. Latin; ~ **Latin**, colloq. speech of ancient Rome, opp. of literary or classical Latin. **vul´gar·ly** *adv.* **vul´gar·ism, vul·gar·i·ty** (vŭlgăr´ĭtē) (pl. **-ties**), **vul´gar·ness** *ns.*

vul·gar·i·an (vŭlgār´ēan) *n.* Vulgar (esp. rich) person.

vul·gar·ize (vŭl´gerīz) *v.t.* (**-ized, -iz·ing**). Make vulgar or commonplace; reduce to level of something usual or ordinary. **vul·gar·i·za·tion** (vŭlgerīzā´shon) *n.*

Vul·gate (vŭl´gāt, -gĭt). Latin version of Bible prepared (in the main) by St. Jerome, *c*382–404; recension of this published 1592 by order of Pope Clement VIII, official text of R.C. Ch. [L. *vulgare* make public]

vul·ner·a·ble (vŭl´nerabel) *adj.* That may be wounded, open to attack, injury, or assault, not proof against weapon, criticism, etc.; (in contract bridge) that has won one game toward rubber and therefore is liable to double penalties. **vul·ner·a·bil·i·ty** (vŭlnerabĭl´ĭtē) *n.* **vul´ner·a·bly** *adv.*

vul·pine (vŭl´pīn, -pĭn) *adj.* Of fox(es); characteristic of, like, fox; crafty, cunning.

vul·ture (vŭl´cher) *n.* Any of various large carrion-eating birds of the family Cathartidae in the New World and Accipitridae in the Old World; **turkey** ~: see TURKEY; (fig.) rapacious person. **vul·tur·ine** (vŭl´cherīn, -rĭn), **vul´tur·ous** *adjs.*

vul·va (vŭl´va) *n.* (pl. **-vae** pr. -vē, **-vas**). External female genital organ, esp. external opening of vagina. **vul´val, vul´var** *adjs.*

Below: Red-headed turkey **vulture** and king vulture of America. All have 'bald' heads and most feed on carrion, or the prey of other animals.

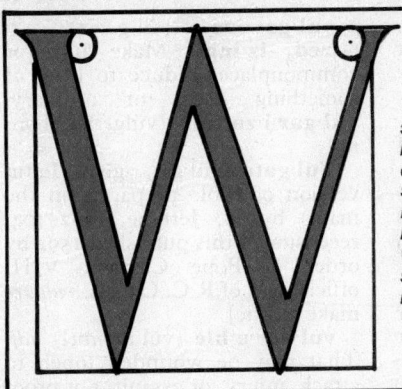

The use of a runic symbol to signify the sound of the present letter **W, w** only seems to have occurred in West Saxon. The sound it represents is not known in German or Slavonic languages. Later two Us or Vs were shown together, side by side, until they were linked into a single letter.

W, w (dŭb′elū) (pl. **W's, w's** or **Ws, ws**). Twenty-third letter of modern English alphabet, originally a ligatured doubling of the Roman letter represented by *u* and *v* of modern alphabets, pronounced as a voiced bilabial spirant and, after vowels, as a *u*-glide, the second element of a diphthong.

W *symbol*. Tungsten. [Ger. *wolfram*]

W. *abbrev*. Watt(s); Wednesday; west(ern).

w. *abbrev*. Watt(s); wide; wife; with.

WA. *abbrev*. Washington.

Wa·bash (waw′băsh). River in Ohio and Illinois flowing 475 mi. (760 km) to the Ohio.

WAC, W.A.C. *abbrevs*. Women's Army Corps. **Wac** (wăk) *n*. Member of WAC.

wack·y (wăk′ē) *adj*. (**wack·i·er, wack·i·est**) & *n*. (slang) Crazy (person).

wad (wŏd) *n*. Small bundle or mass of soft flexible material used as pad etc., esp. plug or disk of felt, cardboard, etc., keeping powder and shot compact in cartridge to prevent gas from passing between shot and barrel when the cartridge is fired; tight roll, esp. of bank notes, (colloq.) wealth, money. ~ *v.t.* (**wad·ded, wad·ding**). Press, compress, roll into wad; line, pad, with wadding; furnish, plug, with wad.

wad·ding (wŏd′ĭng) *n*. (Soft pliable material for making) wads; loose, soft, fibrous material for padding, stuffing, etc.

wad·dle (wŏd′el) *v.i.* (**-dled, -dling**). Walk with short steps and swaying motion natural to stout short-legged person or to bird with short legs set far apart. ~ *n*. Waddling gait. **wad′dler** *n*.

wade (wād) *v*. (**wad·ed, wad·ing**). Walk through water or any soft substance that impedes motion; walk through (stream etc.); ~ **into**, (colloq.) attack (person, task) vigorously; (fig.) progress slowly or with difficulty (*through* book etc.); **wading bird** = WADER sense 1. **wade** *n*. Act of wading.

wad·er (wā′der) *n*. (esp.) 1.

Long-legged bird, as crane, heron, sandpiper, that wades in shallow water. 2. (pl.) High waterproof boots or long waterproof garments covering feet and legs and coming up above waist, worn by fishermen etc.

wa·di, wa·dy (wah′dē) *ns*. (pl. **wa-dis, wa-dies**). In N. Africa etc., rocky ravine or watercourse, dry except in rainy season.

WAF, W.A.F. *abbrevs*. Women in the Air Force. **Waf** (wahf) *n*. Member of WAF.

wa·fer (wā′fer) *n*. Very thin light sweet crisp biscuit or cake; thin disk of unleavened bread used at Eucharist; small disk of gelatine, flour and gum, etc., formerly used for sealing letters; disk of red paper stuck on legal document instead of seal. **wa′fer·y** *adj*. **wafer** *v.t.* Attach or seal with wafer.

waf·fle¹ (wŏf′el) *n*. Small soft crisp batter cake with honeycomb surface; ~ **iron**, utensil, usu. two shallow metal pans hinged together, between which waffle is baked or fried.

waf·fle² (wŏf′el) *v.i.* (**-fled, -fling**) & *n*. (Indulge in) verbose but aimless or ignorant talk or writing.

waft (wăft, wahft) *n*. Act of waving, waving movement; whiff of odor, breath of wind; flag or some substitute, usu. knotted, hoisted as signal, etc. ~ *v.t.* Convey (as) through air or over water, sweep smoothly and lightly along.

wag¹ (wăg) *v*. (**wagged, wag·ging**). Shake or move briskly to and fro, oscillate; **wag′tail**, small Old World bird of genus *Motacilla*, with slender body and long tail that is freq. in wagging motion. **wag** *n*. Single wagging motion.

wag² (wăg) *n*. Facetious person, habitual joker. **wag′ger·y** *n*. (pl. **-ger·ies**). Action(s), humor, of a wag. **wag′gish** *adj*. **wag′gish·ly** *adv*. **wag′gish·ness** *n*.

wage¹ (wāj) *n*. Amount paid periodically, esp. by day or week or month, for work or service of employee (usu. pl); requital, reward (usu. pl.); (pl., econ.) that part of

total production of community that is the reward of all forms of labor (as dist. from remuneration received by capital); **living** ~, pay that permits earner and family to live without fear of privation; ~ **scale**, schedule of rates of wages for related types of jobs in an industry, company, etc.; ~ **slave**, person dependent on income obtained from (esp. unpleasant) labor.

wage² (wāj) *v.t.* (**waged, wag·ing**). Carry on (war etc.).

wa·ger (wā′jer) *n*. Bet, stake; ~ **of battle**, (hist.) trial to decide guilt or innocence by personal combat. **wage** *v.t.* (**waged, wag·ing**). Bet, stake. **wa′ger·er** *n*.

wag·gle (wăg′el) *v*. (**-gled, -gling**). Move (something held or fixed at one end), be moved, to and fro with short quick motions. ~ *n*. Act of waggling. **wag′gly** *adj*.

wag·gon = WAGON.

Wag·ner (vahg′ner), **Richard** (1813–83). German composer of operas, including the Ring Cycle, *Tristan and Isolde, Parsifal*, etc. **Wag·ne·ri·an** (vahgnēr′ēan) *adj*. & *n*.

wag·on, Brit. **wag·gon** (wăg′on) *ns*. Four wheeled vehicle for drawing heavy loads, often with removable semi-cylindrical cover, usu. drawn by two or more horses; (Brit.) open freight car; vehicle for carrying water, hence **on the** ~, (slang) abstaining from alcohol; **tea** ~, small wheeled table for conveying tea etc.

wag·on-lit (văgawn̑lē′) *n*. (pl. **wag·ons·lits** pr. văgawn̑lē′). Sleeping car on continental railroad. [Fr. *wagon* wagon, *lit* bed]

Wah·ha·bi, Wa·ha·bi (wah-hah′bē) *ns*. (pl. **-bis**). Member of Muslim sect, followers of Abd-el-Wahhab (*c*1703–91), who acquired political power in Arabia in early 20th c.

wa·hi·ne (wahhē′nā) *n*. Girl, woman. [Hawaiian and Maori]

wa·hoo (wah′hōō, wahhōō′) *n*. (pl. **-hoos**). Shrub or small tree (*Euonymus atropurpureus*) of eastern N. Amer. having brilliant red leaves in autumn.

waif (wāf) *n*. (law) Any object

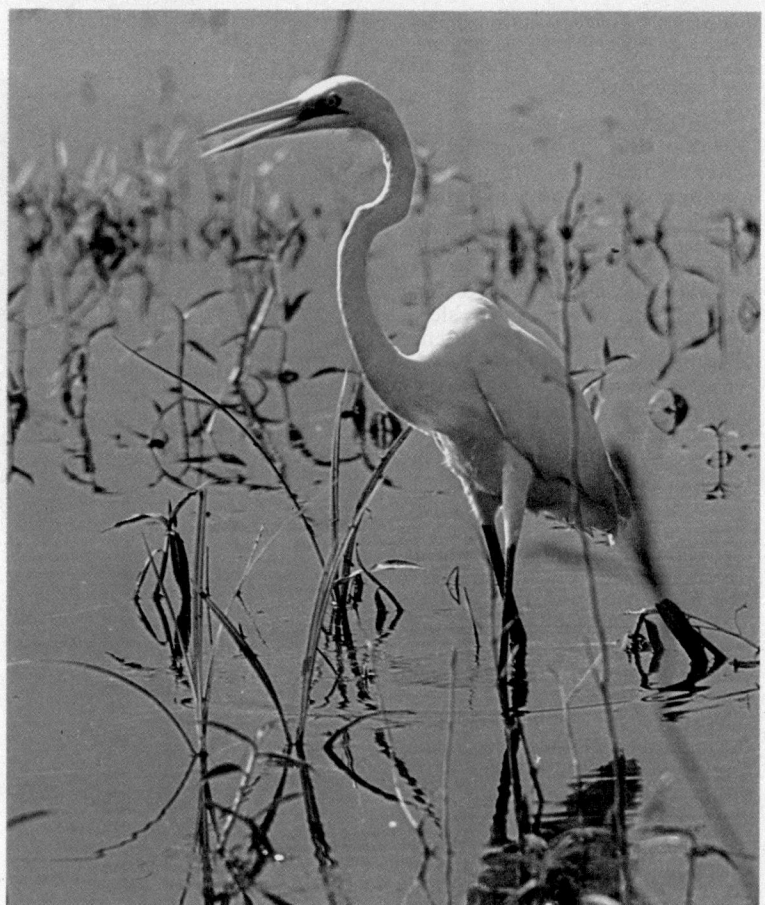

*The great white heron is a **wader** and one of a widespread group of birds mostly conspicuous for long legs and bills. These enable them to walk on mud and feed in shallow water.*

or animal found ownerless; homeless and helpless person, esp. unowned or abandoned child; ~**s and strays**, odds and ends; homeless or neglected children.

Wai·ki·ki (wīkēkē′). Beach and resort area of Honolulu, on SE. Oahu, Hawaii.

wail (wāl) *n.* Prolonged plaintive inarticulate cry of pain, grief, etc.; bitter lamentation; sound resembling cry of pain. ~ *v.i.* Utter wails or persistent and bitter lamentations or complaints; bewail, lament; **Wail′ing Wall**, high wall in Jerusalem, supposed to stand on the site of Solomon's temple, to which Jews go to pray and lament. **wail′er** *n.* **wail′ful** *adj.*

wain·scot (wān′sk*o*t, -sk*o*t) *n.* Wooden paneling or boarding on room wall; (hist.) imported oak of fine quality. ~ *v.t.* (**-scot·ed, -scot·ing** or **-scot·ted, -scot·ting**). Line with wainscot. **wain′-scot·ing, wain′scot·ting** *ns.* Wainscot or material for it.

waist (wāst) *n.* Part of human body between ribs and hip bones, normally slenderer than parts above and below it; middle narrower part of anything; part of garment covering waist, narrowed part of garment corresponding to waist (but sometimes worn higher or lower than position of this); bodice, blouse; **waist′band**, band going around waist, esp. one forming upper part of lower garment; **waist′cloth**, loincloth; **waist′coat**, (also pr. wĕs′k*i*t) (Brit.) vest; **waist′line**, line of waist; measurement of this.

wait (wāt) *v.* 1. Abstain from action or departure until some expected event occurs; pause, tarry; be expectant or on the watch. 2. Await, bide. 3. Act as attendant *on* person; serve food and drink, shift plates at table; ~ **on**, ~ **upon**, serve as attendant to; pay respectful visit to. 4. Defer (meal) till someone arrives. 5. ~**-a-bit**, [f. Afrikaans *wag-'n-bietje*] any of various plants and shrubs, esp. species of *Mimosa*, with hooked and clinging thorns. **wait** *n.* Act or time of waiting; **lie in** ~, lurk in ambush.

wait·er (wā′ter), fem. **wait·ress** (wā′trĭs) *ns.* Person employed at hotel, restaurant, etc., to wait upon guests, take orders for meals, etc.

wait·ing (wā′tĭng) *n.* (esp.) (Period of) official attendance at court; **in** ~, on duty, in attendance; ~ **game**, abstention from attempt to secure advantage in early part of enterprise, game, etc. in order to act more effectively at later

stage; ~ **list**, list of persons waiting for appointment, next chance of obtaining something etc.; ~ **room**, room provided for persons to wait in, esp. at bus or railroad station or for patients waiting to consult doctor etc.

waive (wāv) *v.t.* (**waived, waiv·ing**). Relinquish, refrain

from insisting on, refuse to avail oneself of (advantage, privilege, claim, opportunity, etc.). **waiv′er** *n.* (law) Waiving.

wake[1] (wāk) *v.* (**woke** pr. wōk or **waked, waked** or **wok·en** pr. wō′ken, **wak·ing**). Cease to sleep, rouse from sleep, (freq. ~ **up**); be awake (archaic except in pres. part.); cease, rouse, from sloth, torpidity, inactivity, etc.; rise, raise, from the dead; arouse, excite (feeling, activity, etc.), evoke (sound, echo, etc.); ~**-robin**, liliaceous plant of genus *Trillium*; any of various arums.

wake[2] (wāk) *n.* (chiefly with ref. to Irish custom) Watch by corpse before burial; drinking, lamentation, feasting, etc., associated with this.

*The yellow **wagtail** is one of a widespread group of insectivorous birds. Each has a long tail that is wagged up and down or from side to side.*

*Because of the altitude and topography, agriculture in **Wales** is confined to grazing and stock-breeding. There are also large deposits of coal.*

wake[3] (wāk) *n.* Track left on water's surface by ship or other moving object; **in the ~ of,** following close behind; in imitation of; following as a result or consequence.

wake·ful (wāk´fŭl) *adj.* Keeping awake, esp. while others sleep; unable to sleep; marked by absence or want of sleep. **wake´ful·ly** *adv.* **wake´ful·ness** *n.*

Wake (wāk) **Island.** N. Pacific island under sovereignty of U.S.

wak·en (wā´ken) *v.* Cause to be, become, awake; wake up.

Wal·bur·ga (vahlboor´gah), **St.** (*c*710–79). English missionary to Germany, abbess of Heidenheim; commemorated Feb. 25 and May 1 (see WALPURGIS).

Wal·den (wawl´den) **Pond.** Pond near Concord in NE. Massachusetts; site of Henry David Thoreau's cabin.

Wal·den·ses (wŏldĕn´sēz) *n.pl.* Puritanical religious sect that originated in S. France *c*1170 through preaching of a rich Lyons merchant, Peter Waldo; was banned in 1184 and scattered by persecution into Germany and Bohemia; became a separately organized Church that associated itself with the Protestant Reformation of the 16th c. and still exists, chiefly in N. Italy and in N. and S. Amer., though not officially tolerated until 1848. **Wal·den·si·an** (wŏldĕn´sēan) *adj.* & *n.*

wale (wāl) *n.* 1. WEAL[2]. 2. One of horizontal timbers connecting and bracing piles of trench, dam, etc.; (naut.) one of the broader thicker timbers extending along ship's sides at different heights. 3. One of the parallel ribs in surface of fabric as corduroy. ~ *v.t.* (**waled, wal·ing**). Mark, furnish, with wales.

Wales (wālz). Principality occupying extreme west of central southern portion of Great Britain; orig. independent; conquered by Edward I and united with England by the **Statute of ~** (1284); capital, Cardiff; **Prince of ~**, title usu. conferred (since 1301) on eldest son of reigning sovereign of England.

Wal·hal·la (wahlhah´la, vahl-) = VALHALLA.

walk (wawk) *v.* 1. Travel, go, on foot; perambulate, tread floor or surface of, go over or along on foot; (of bipeds) progress by alternate movements of legs so that one foot is always on the ground, (of quadrupeds) go at gait in which there are always two, and during part of step three, feet on ground (opp. to run, trot, gallop, etc.); (of

*In its wild state, the **wallflower** may have blossoms ranging from yellow to tawny brown. Selective breeding has enabled gardeners to have varieties with flowers from deep red to white.*

ghost etc.) appear. 2. Cause to walk with one; take charge of (dog) on walk; (baseball) give, be given, base on balls. 3. (archaic) Live with specified principle or in specified manner, conduct oneself. 4. ~ **away from,** outdistance easily; ~ **away with,** win (something) easily; ~ **off,** depart, esp. abruptly; ~ **off with,** carry away, steal; win; ~ **on,** play nonspeaking (**walk-on**) part on stage; ~ **out,** (esp., colloq.) strike; hence **walk´out** (*n.*); **walk out on,** abandon, esp. without warning; **walk over,** (of horse) win race in which horse has no competitors going over (course) at walking pace; win a race or other contest with little or no effort; **walk´over** (*n.*), race in which winner walks over; **walk the plank**: see PLANK; **walk the**

*There are 15 species of tree in the genus which includes the **walnut.** The most common commercial variety used in Europe was originally from Asia and Asia Minor.*

streets, (esp.) be a prostitute; **walk-up,** (colloq.) apartment in building without elevator. 5. **walk´ing beam,** overhead oscillating lever, pivoted in the center, for transmitting power, esp. in sidewheel steamers, pumps, etc.; **walking delegate,** (formerly) trade union official who visited sick members, interviewed employers, etc.; **walking stick,** cane; STICK insect. **walk´er** *n.* **walk** *n.* 1. Walking gait, walking pace; manner of walking, spell of walking, esp. short journey on foot for exercise or pleasure; (baseball) base on balls. 2. Place for walking, tree-bordered avenue, broad path in garden or pleasure ground, sidewalk, foot-path; distance to be walked; course or circuit for walking; **cock of the** ~, person whose supremacy in his own circle is undisputed. 3. Sphere of activity, calling, profession, occupation (usu. ~ **of life**).

walk·ie-talk·ie (waw′kē taw′kē) *n.* (pl. **-talk·ies**). Radio transmitting and receiving set carried on the person.

Wal·kyr·ie (wălkēr′ē, wăl′kĭrē, vălkēr′ē, văl′kĭrē) = VALKYRIE.

wall (wawl) *n.* 1. Structure of stone, bricks, earth, etc., of some height, serving as rampart, embankment, defensive enclosure of city, castle, etc., or to enclose or divide off house, room, field, garden, etc.; **drive, send, up the** ~, (slang) drive to distraction. 2. Something resembling wall in appearance or function; outermost part of hollow structure, as tire etc. 3. (anat., zool., bot.) Outermost layer bounding organ, cell, etc. 4. **wall′flower**, plant of genus *Cheiranthus*, esp. *C. cheiri*, with yellow or orange-brown fragrant flowers, growing wild on old walls, rocks, etc., and cultivated in gardens; (colloq.) woman sitting out dances for lack of partners; **wall′paper**, paper for covering interior walls of rooms; **wall pennywort**: see PENNYwort; **wall plate**, timber or other horizontal member laid on or in wall to support rafters, distribute pressure, etc. **wall** *v.t.* Provide or protect with wall; close (*up, in*), block, shut *up*, with wall(s). **walled** *adj.*

Walruses live in large groups, up to 100, frequenting shallow waters in search of clams. These are shoveled out of the shells by the long tusks and whiskers.

wal·la·by (wŏl′əbē) *n.* (pl. **-bies**, collect. **-by**). Any of various smaller species of kangaroo.

Wal·lace[1] (wŏl′ĭs, waw′lĭs), **Henry A(gard)** (1888–1965). Amer. agriculturist and politician; secretary of Agriculture 1933–40; vice president of U.S. under Franklin D. Roosevelt, 1941–5; secretary of Commerce, 1945–6.

Wal·lace[2] (wŏl′ĭs, waw′lĭs), **Sir William** (1270?–1305). National hero of Scotland; resisted the English under Edward I, was captured by treachery and executed in London.

wal·let (wŏl′ĭt) *n.* 1. (archaic) Bag, esp. pilgrim's or beggar's, for holding provisions etc. on journey. 2. Flat folding case for carrying in pocket, closed by flap or opening like book, for holding money, documents, etc.

wall·eye (wawl′ī) *n.* Eye with iris whitish (or occas. streaked, particolored, or different in color from

*The **wallaby** differs from a kangaroo mainly in its smaller size. There are many species but all are confined to Australia and New Guinea. The pretty-faced variety (left) is found in northeastern Australia.*

other eye) or with divergent squint. **wall′eyed** *adj.* Having walleye; (of fishes) with large prominent eyes.

Wal·loon (wŏlōōn′) *adj. & n.* (Member, language) of people, of Gaulish origin and speaking a French dialect, forming chief part of population of SE. Belgium.

wal·lop (wŏl′op) *n.* (colloq.) Heavy resounding blow, whack. ~ *v.t.* Thrash, beat.

wal·lop·ing (wŏl′opĭng) *adj.* (esp., colloq.) Big, strapping, thumping.

wal·low (wŏl′ō) *v.i.* Roll about in mud, sand, water, etc.; (of ship) roll helplessly; (fig.) take delight in gross pleasures etc. ~ *n.* Act of wallowing; place where buffalo, elephants, etc., go to wallow; depression, mudhole, dusthole, formed by this.

Wall (wawl) **Street.** Street in New York City, on or near which are located most of the chief financial institutions of U.S.; Amer. money market.

wal·nut (wawl′nŭt, -nut) *n.* Fruit, consisting of two-lobed seed enclosed in spheroidal shell covered with green fleshy husk, of various trees of genus *Juglans*, esp. *J. regia*; any tree of *Juglans* or some related genera; wood of walnut tree, used in cabinetmaking.

Wal·pur·gis (vahlpoor′gĭs) **Night.** Eve of May 1, on which, acc. to German legend, a witches' Sabbath took place on the Brocken, a peak of the Harz mountains; named after St. WALBURGA, whose feast day on May 1 coincides with an old pagan feast with rites protecting from witchcraft.

wal·rus (wawl′rus, wŏl′-) *n.* (pl. **-rus·es**, collect. **-rus**). Large marine mammal (*Odobenus rosmarus*) of Arctic seas, allied to seals and sea lions, and chiefly distinguished by two long tusks; ~ **mustache**, long thick mustache hanging down on both sides of mouth.

Wal·ton (wawl'ton), **I·zaak** (ī'zak) (1593–1683). English writer, author of *Compleat Angler* (1653) and *Lives* of several contemporary writers.

waltz (wawlts) *n.* Dance performed to music in triple time; music for this, or in its characteristic time and rhythm. ~ *v.* Dance waltz; move lightly, trippingly, etc.; move (person) as in waltz. **waltz′er** *n.*

wam·pun (wŏm′pum, wawm′-) *n.* Cylindrical beads of polished ends of shells threaded to form broad belts; formerly used by N. Amer. Indians of the east coast as currency, as ornaments, or for mnemonic or symbolic purposes, recording treaties, etc.; (slang) money.

wan (wŏn) *adj.* (**wan·ner, wan·nest**). Pale, pallid, colorless, sickly. **wan′ly** *adv.* **wan′ness** *n.*

wand (wŏnd) *n.* Slender rod or staff carried as sign of office by verger, beadle, usher, etc.; staff used in enchantments by fairy or magician.

wan·der (wŏn′der) *v.* Roam, ramble, move idly or restlessly or casually about, stroll, saunter; go from country to country or place to place without settled route or destination; stray, diverge from right way, get lost; wind, meander; be unsettled or incoherent in mind, purpose, talk, etc., be inattentive or delirious, rave; traverse in wandering. **wan′der·er, wan′der·ing** *ns.* **wandering** *adj.* (esp.) **W~ Jew**, (1) person who, according to medieval legend, is condemned to wander the earth without rest until Day of Judgment, as punishment for insulting Christ on way to crucifixion; (2) any of various trailing plants esp. *Tradescantia fluminensis*.

wan·der·lust (wŏn′derlŭst) *n.*

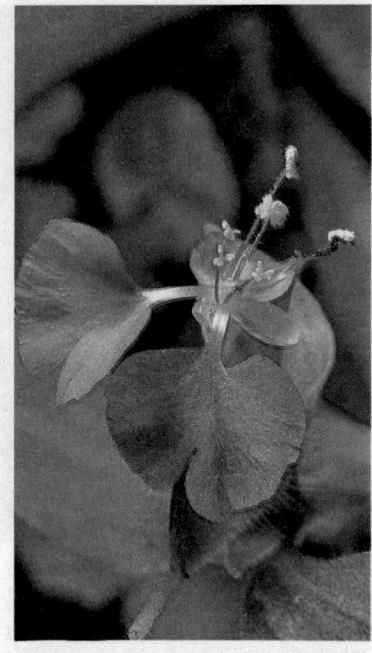

Species of **Wandering Jew**, (Tradescantia) are grown all around the world. They are especially tolerant of low light levels, favoring shady positions.

Strong desire to wander or travel. [Ger.]

wane (wān) *v.t.* (**waned, wan·ing**). Decrease in brilliance, size, or splendor, decline; lose power, vigor, importance, intensity, etc.; (of moon) undergo periodical decrease in extent of visible illuminated portion during second half of lunation. ~ *n.* (Period of) waning, decline.

wan·gle (wăng′gel) *v.t.* (**-gled, -gling**). (slang) Accomplish, obtain, by scheming or contrivance; manipulate, fake, (account, report, etc.). ~ *n.* Act of wangling.

Wan·kel (vahng′kel), **Felix** (1902–). German engineer, inventor of the Wankel rotary internal combustion engine.

want (wŏnt, wawnt) *n.* Lack, absence, deficiency, *of*; penury, destitution; need, condition marked by lack of necessary or desirable thing; (chiefly pl.) something needed or desired; **want ad**, newspaper advertisement by person seeking to obtain employee, buy merchandise, etc. **want** *v.* Be without or have too little of, fall short (by specified amount) *of*; be in want; require; desire, wish for possession or presence of. **want′ed** *adj.* (esp.) Sought by police as suspect. **want′ing** *adj.* (esp.) Lacking *in* quality or quantity; without; not adequate to need or expectation; (colloq.) mentally deficient.

wan·ton (wŏn′ton) *adj.* Sportive, capricious; luxuriant, wild (archaic and poet.); licentious, unchaste; unprovoked, reckless, arbitrary. **wan′ton·ly** *adv.* **wan′ton·ness** *n.* **wanton** *n.* Licentious person. ~ *v.i.* (chiefly archaic and poet.) Gambol, frolic; luxuriate, revel, *in*; sport amorously or lewdly.

wap·i·ti (wŏp′ītē) *n.* (pl. **-tis**, collect. **-ti**). N. Amer. ELK (*Cervus canadensis*).

war (wor) *n.* 1. Strife usu. between nations conducted by force, state of open hostility and suspension of ordinary international law prevalent during such quarrel, attack or series of attacks by armed forces; fighting as profession; (fig.) hostility between persons; **civil ~**, war between parts of one nation for supremacy; **U.S. Civil W~**: see CIVIL War; **cold ~**: see COLD; **holy ~**, war waged in support of some religious cause; **private ~**, feud between persons or families carried on in defiance of laws of murder etc.; (also) armed attack made by members of one nation upon another without government sanction; **W~ Between the States**: see CIVIL War; **W~ of (American) Independence**: see AMERICAN War of Independence; **~ of nerves**, attempt to wear down opponent by gradual destruction of morale; **W~**

Less frequently used today, a 'wanted' poster may still be erected by the authorities in an attempt to obtain information on criminals.

*Facing: the most revolutionary form of internal-combustion engine to be developed since the invention of reciprocating designs, the **Wankel** has a smaller number of moving parts and much smoother operation. It was first used in an NSU car in 1968 and then in the Japanese Mazdas.*

Intake
inlet port

engine housing

rotor

Compression and Ignition
mixture drawn in
space getting larger

crankshaft
(turns at 1½ times rotor speed

mixture compressed

current to spark plug

Power
burning mixture expands

burnt gases forced out

Exhaust

air intake for carburettor

cooling passages in rotor housing

3 phase alternator

combustion chamber

rotor

tip seal

spark plug

chain tensioner

twin drive chains from engine to clutch

electric starter

5 speed gearbox

drive chain to rear wheel

lubricator

kick starter freewheel mechanism

to radiator

thermostatic switch for radiator fan

inlet port

wax thermostat
trochoid pump for metering oil

rotor set

ignition contact breaker

coolant pump rotor

coolant pump volute

oil filter

oil sump inlet strainer

multi-plate clutch

kick starter shaft

of the Secession: see CIVIL War.
2. **be at, make, wage,** ~, carry on hostilities; **declare** ~, announce that hostilities may be expected (also fig.); **go to** ~, begin hostilities. 3. ~ **cloud,** condition in international affairs that threatens war; ~ **correspondent,** newspaper etc. correspondent reporting on war; ~ **cry,** phrase or name shouted in charging or rallying to attack; party catchword; ~ **dance,** dance of primitive people before warlike excursion or after victory; ~ **game,** simulated military operation as part of training for war; ~ **god,** god worshipped as giving victory in war, esp. Ares or Mars; **war'head,** explosive head of torpedo, rocket, etc.; **war'horse,** charger (now chiefly fig. in **old war'horse,** person excited by memories of past combats or controversies); **war'lord,** military commander (transl. of Ger. *Kriegsherr*); **war'monger,** one seeking to bring about war; **war'monger-ing** (*adj.* & *n.*); **war paint,** paint applied to face and body esp. by N. Amer. Indians before battle; (colloq.) one's best clothes, make-up, etc.; **war'path,** (route taken by) warlike expedition of N. Amer. Indians; **on the war'path,** (fig.) engaged in, preparing for, any conflict; **war'plane,** military aircraft; **war'ship,** ship armed and manned for war; **war'time,** time of war; **war whoop,** yell esp. of N. Amer. Indians in charging. **war** *v.* (**warred, war'ring**). (chiefly literary) Make war, be at war. **war'ring** *adj.* (esp.) Contending,

*The launching of a **warship**. The U.S.S. San Diego stands on the slips as guests arrive for the launching ceremony. It was designed as a combat store ship.*

discordant.
war·ble[1] (wŏr'bel) *v.* (**-bled, -bling**). Sing softly and sweetly, sing with trills and quavers. ~ *n.* Warbling sound.
war·ble[2] (wŏr'bel) *n.* Small hard tumor produced by pressure of saddle on horse's back; swelling on back of cattle etc. produced by larva of warble fly; ~ **fly,** any of various dipterous insects whose larvae live under skin of cattle etc.
war·bler (wŏr'bler) *n.* (esp.) Any of various small Amer. insectivorous, migratory birds, many with yellowish markings or plumage, of family Parulidae, also called **wood warblers**; any of various small Old World birds of subfamily Sylviinae.
ward (wŏrd) *n.* 1. Act of guarding or defending (now only in **keep watch and** ~); confinement, custody (archaic); guardianship of minor or other person legally incapable of conducting his affairs. 2. Minor under care of guardian or court. 3. Separate room or division of prison or hospital or (hist.) workhouse. 4. Administrative division of city or town esp. for elections. 5. Each ridge projecting from inside plate of lock, preventing passage of any key not having corresponding incisions; each incision in bit of key corresponding to ward of lock. 6. **ward'room,** messroom or living space of naval commissioned officers below commanding officer. **ward** *v.t.* Have in keeping, protect (chiefly now of God); parry (*off* blow), keep *off* (danger etc.).
-ward *suffix.* Forming adjectives with sense "having specified direction or tendency" (e.g. *backward, downward, homeward, toward*), also used as adverbs (= -WARDS) and nouns (e.g. *to the eastward*).
war·den (wŏr'den) *n.* 1. Chief administrative officer in charge of prison; official in charge of enforcing certain laws, esp. those regulating hunting (*game warden*). 2. Churchwarden. 3. (also **air-raid** ~) Member of civil organization for assistance of civilian population in air raids. **ward'en·-ship** *n.*
ward·er (wŏr'der) *n.* 1. (archaic) Sentinel, watchman on tower. 2. (fem. **ward'ress**) (Brit.) Official in charge of prisoners.
ward·robe (wŏr'drōb) *n.* Place where clothes are kept, esp. large cupboard with hangers, movable trays, drawers, etc.; room where theatrical costumes and properties are kept; in royal or noble household, department charged with care of wearing apparel (chiefly in titles); person's stock of clothes; ~ **mistress,** woman in charge of professional wardrobe of actor, actress, or theatrical company; ~ **trunk,** upright trunk for dresses, suits, etc.
-wards *suffix.* Forming adverbs (and adjectives) with sense "to" or "in the direction of" (e.g. *backwards, towards*).
ware (wār) *n.* Articles made for sale, goods; esp., vessels etc. of baked clay (usu. with defining word, as *Wedgwood* ~); (pl.) things that person has for sale.
ware·house (wār'hows) *n.* (pl. **-hous·es** pr. -howzĭz). (Part of) building used for storage of merchandise, wholesaler's goods for sale, furniture or other property temporarily stored for owner; **bonded** ~: see BOND[1]. **warehouse** (wār'howz, -hows) *v.t.* (**-housed, -hous·ing**). Store in warehouse. **ware·house·man** (wār'howsman) (pl. **-men**), **ware·hous·er** (wār'-howzer, -ser) *ns.*
war·fare (wŏr'fār) *n.* State of war, being engaged in war, conflict.
war·fa·rin (wŏr'ferĭn) *n.* Poisonous, colorless, crystalline powder used for killing rodents and in medicine as an anticoagulant.
war·like (wŏr'līk) *adj.* Martial; skilled in, fond of, war; of, for use in, war; bellicose, threatening war.
war·lock (wŏr'lŏk) *n.* (archaic) Male witch, sorcerer.
warm (wŏrm) *adj.* 1. Of, at, rather high temperature, giving out considerable degree of heat (but less than that indicated by *hot*); (of persons etc.) glowing with exercise, excitement, eating and drinking, etc.; (of clothes etc.) serving to keep one warm. 2. (of feelings etc.) Sympathetic, affectionate, cordial; eager, emotionally excited, indignant; (of conflict) vigorous, harassing; (of scent or trail) fresh, strong; (in children's games) close to the object sought, or to finding or guessing. 3. (of color) Suggesting warmth; esp., of, containing, rich

reds and yellows. 4. **warm'-blood'ed**, (of birds and mammals) having constant body temperature normally higher than that of surrounding medium; (fig.) amorous, emotional; **warm-hearted, warm'heart'ed**, of, showing, proceeding from, generous and affectionate disposition. **warm'ly** *adv.* **warm'ness, warmth** (wŏrmth) *ns.* **warm** *n.* Warming, being warmed; warmth of atmosphere. ~ *v.* Make warm; excite; become warm, animated, or sympathetic; ~ **up**, practice, exercise before game; make, become, warm; reheat (food etc.); (of radio, engine, etc.) come, bring, to efficient working temperature; **warmed up** or **over**, (of food, lit. or fig.) reheated, stale; **warm'up** (*n.*), action of warming up; **warm'ing pan**, long-handled covered metal (usu. brass) pan for holding live coals etc., formerly used for warming beds. **warm'er** *n.*

warn (wŏrn) *v.t.* Give timely notice to (person etc.) of impending danger or misfortune, put on guard, caution *against*; admonish; notify of something requiring attention, give previous notice to; ~ **off**, give notice to person to keep at distance, off private ground, etc.

warn·ing (wŏr'nĭng) *n.* (esp.) Thing that serves to warn; notice of, or caution against possible danger; notice of termination of business relation, esp. between landlord and tenant, employer and employee.

warp (wŏrp) *v.* 1. Make, become, crooked or perverted, bias, change from straight or right or natural state. 2. (naut.) Move (ship) by hauling on rope attached to fixed point; (of ship etc.) progress thus. ~ *n.* 1. Threads stretched lengthwise in loom to be crossed by woof. 2. Rope used in towing or warping. 3. Crooked state produced in lumber etc. by uneven shrinking or expansion; (fig.) perversion or perverse inclination of mind. 4. ~ **and woof**, (fig.) essential structure, base. **warp'er** *n.*

war·rant (wŏr'ant, wär'-) *n.* 1. Act, token, of authorization, sanction; justifying reason or ground for action, belief, etc.; proof, authoritative witness. 2. Document conveying authority or security; esp. written authorization to pay or receive money; executive authority's writ or order empowering officer to make arrest or search, execute judicial sentence, etc.; (mil., naval) official certificate or rank issued to ~ **officer**, officer intermediate in rank between commissioned and noncommissioned officers. **warrant** *v.t.* Serve as warrant for, justify; guarantee. **war'rant·er, war·ran·tor** (wŏr'-antōr, wär'-) *ns.*

war·ran·ty (wŏr'antē, wär'-) *n.* (pl. **-ties**). Authority, justification (*for*); (esp., law) express or implied undertaking by vendor that his title is secure or that thing sold fulfills specified conditions.

war·ren (wŏr'en, wär'-) *n.* Piece of land where rabbits breed or abound; (fig.) densely populated building or district; (hist.) piece of land enclosed and preserved for breeding game.

war·ri·or (wŏr'ēer, wär'-, -yer) *n.* Fighting man, valiant or experienced soldier (now poet. or rhet.); fighting man of tribe etc.

War·saw (wŏr'saw). (Pol. *Warszawa*) Capital city of Poland; ~ **Pact**, treaty of mutual defense and military aid, signed at Warsaw May 14, 1955, by U.S.S.R., Poland, Czechoslovakia, Hungary, Rumania, Bulgaria, Albania, and East Germany.

wart (wŏrt) *n.* Small round dry tough excrescence on skin caused by abnormal growth of papillae and thickening of epidermis over them; rounded excrescence or protuber-

Top to bottom: **Reed warbler** *and its nest; wood warbler; Dartford warbler. Many of these birds have particularly tuneful songs. Some have a restricted range owing to individual needs but others migrate long distances.*

ance on skin of animal, surface of plant, etc.; ~ **hog**, African wild hog (*Phacochoerus aethiopicus*) with large warty excrescences on face and large protruding tusks. **wart′y** *adj.* (**wart·i·er, wart·i·est**).

war·y (wār′ē) *adj.* (**war·i·er, war·i·est**). (Habitually) on one's guard, circumspect, cautious, careful. **war·i·ly** (wār′ĭlē) *adv.* **war·i·ness** (wār′ēnĭs) *n.*

was (wŭz, wŏz): see BE.

wash (wŏsh, wawsh) *v.*   1. Cleanse with liquid; take (stain, dirt, etc.) *out, off, away*, by washing; wash oneself or esp. one's hands (and face); wash clothes; (of textile material, dye, etc.) bear washing without deterioration; (fig.) purify; ~ **down**, clean thoroughly esp. a ship; follow (food) with drink; ~ **one's hands of**, decline responsibility for; ~ **up**, wash (table utensils etc.) after use; sweep (object) on to shore etc.; clean one's face and hands.   2. Moisten; be removed by flow of water; (of sea, river, etc.) flow past, beat upon (shore, walls, etc.), sweep *over*, surge *against*; make (channel etc.) thus.   3. Sift (ore), sift ore, sand, etc. (*for* gold etc.), by action of water; brush thin coating of watery color over (wall, drawing, etc.); coat (inferior metal) thinly with gold etc. **washed** (wŏsht, wawsht) *adj.* (esp.) ~ **out**, (of fabric) faded from being washed; (fig.) enfeebled, limp, exhausted; ~ **up**, (colloq.) having failed completely, defeated. **wash′a·ble** *adj.* **wash** *n.* 1. Washing, being washed; process of being laundered (esp. **in the** ~); quantity of clothes etc. (to be) washed.   2. Lotion; liquid applied to hair esp. to cleanse it.   3. Thin even layer of transparent watercolor or diluted ink.   4. Solution applied to metal to give effect of gold or silver. 5. Visible or audible motion of agitated water, esp. waves caused by passage of vessel; disturbance in air caused by passage of aircraft. 6. Sandbank, tract of land, alternately covered and exposed by sea; low-lying often flooded ground, with shallow pools and marshes; shallow pool, backwater, etc.; dry bed of winter storm. 7. Solid particles carried away or deposited by running water; soil from which gold or diamonds may be washed out. 8. **wash-** *combining form*, **wash-and-wear** = DRIP-dry; **wash′basin**, bowl for washing hands etc.; **wash′board**, corrugated board on which clothes etc. may be scrubbed; **wash′cloth**, small cloth used to wash one's face or body; **wash′day**, day on which clothes are washed; **wash goods**, washable fabrics or clothes; **wash′-out**, (esp.) (site of) removal by flood of part of hillside, road, track, railroad, etc.; (slang) disappointing

failure, fiasco; **wash′room**, room with toilet facilities, lavatory; **wash′tub**, tub for washing clothes etc.

Wash. *abbrev.* Washington.

wash·er[1] (wŏsh′er, waw′sher) *n.* Person, thing, that washes; **wash′erman** (pl. **-men**), **wash′erwoman** (pl. **-women**), person whose occupation is washing clothes.

wash·er[2] (wŏsh′er, waw′sher) *n.* (esp.) Disk or flattened ring of

metal, leather, rubber, fiber, etc., placed between two surfaces, as under nut of bolt or tie rod etc. to relieve rotative friction or prevent lateral motion, under plunger of screw-down water tap etc. to prevent leakage, etc.

wash·ing (wŏsh′ĭng, waw′shĭng) *n.* (esp.) Clothes, linen sent to the wash; ~ **machine**, machine for washing clothes etc.; ~ **soda**, form of sodium carbonate used in washing clothes etc.

Wash·ing·ton[1] (wŏsh′ĭngton, waw′shĭng-). Most northerly of the Pacific states of U.S., admitted to the Union in 1889; capital, Olympia. **Wash·ing·to·ni·an** (wŏshĭngtō′nēan, wawshĭng-) *adj.* & *n.*

Wash·ing·ton[2] (wŏsh′ĭngton, waw′shĭng-), **Booker T(aliaferro**) (1856–1915).   Amer. black educator; established Tuskegee Institute, Alabama.

Wash·ing·ton[3] (wŏsh′ĭngton,

Above left: **George Washington,** *first President of the U.S.A., was a weathy landowner whose commonsense helped to override differences between the States and unify the nation.*

Above: Nest of the **tree wasp** *(Vespula sylvestris). It is made of 'paper' from wood fibers and saliva, by the communal activity of workers.*

waw'shǐng-), **George** (1732–99). Commander in chief of the Continental forces in the Revolutionary War and first president of U.S., 1789–97.

Wash·ing·ton[4] (wǒsh'ǐngton, waw'shǐng-) **D.C.** Administrative capital of U.S., conterminous with the District of Columbia on the NE. bank of the Potomac River; founded during presidency of George Washington and named after him.

wash·y (wǒsh'ē, waw'shē) *adj.* (**wash·i·er, wash·i·est**). (of food etc.) Diluted, weak, thin; (of color) faded looking; (of style, utterance, etc.) feeble, diffuse, lacking vigor. **wash'i·ness** *n.*

WASP, Wasp, wasp[1] (wǒsp) *ns. & adjs.* (usu. derog.) White Anglo-Saxon Protestant.

wasp[2] (wǒsp) *n.* Any of the superfamily Vespoidea of hymenopterous insects, often carnivorous, with slender body, abdomen attached to thorax by narrow stalk, usu. two pairs of fully developed wings, and often formidable sting; ∼ **waist, -waisted,** (having) very slender waist, esp. one produced by tight lacing.

wasp·ish (wǒs'pǐsh) *adj.* Irritable, petulantly spiteful, irascible; caustic. **wasp'ish·ly** *adv.* **wasp'ish·ness** *n.*

wasp·y (wǒs'pē) *adj.* (**wasp·i·er, wasp·i·est**). Wasplike; abounding in wasps.

was·sail (wǒs'al, wǎs'-, wǒsāl') *n.* (archaic) Salutation in presenting cup of wine to guest; festive occasion, drinking bout; liquor in which healths were drunk, esp. spiced ale drunk on Twelfth Night and Christmas Eve. ∼ *v.i.* Make

merry; sit carousing and drinking healths. **was'sail·er** *n.* [ON. *ves heill* "be in good health," form of salutation]

Was·ser·man (wǒs'erman; *Ger.* vah'sermahn), **August von** (1866–1925). German pathologist; ∼ **test,** blood test employed in diagnosis of syphilis.

wast·age (wās'tǐj) *n.* Loss or diminution by use, wear, decay, leakage, etc.; amount wasted.

waste[1] (wāst) *n.* 1. Desert, waste region; dreary scene or expanse. 2. Consumption, loss or diminution from use, wear and tear, etc.; wasting, useless or extravagant expenditure or consumption, squandering (*of*); **run to** ∼, (of liquid) flow away so as to be wasted; (fig.) be expended uselessly. 3. Waste matter; useless remains (esp. of manufacturing process), scraps, shreds; esp. scraps, remnants, from manufacture of cotton, wool, etc., yarn or textiles, used for cleaning machinery, absorbing oil, etc.; ∼ **pipe,** pipe for carrying off used or superfluous water or steam. **waste** *adj.* 1. (of land, region, etc.) Desert, uninhabited, desolate, barren; uncultivated; (fig.) monotonous, without features of interest; not built upon; **lay** ∼, destroy, devastate, ruin; **waste'land,** land not utilized for cultivation or building; (fig.) time, place, society, barren of hope, culture, etc. 2. Superfluous, refuse,

left over; no longer serving a purpose; **waste'paper, waste paper,** paper thrown away as spoiled, superfluous, useless, etc.; **wastepaper basket,** container for this; **waste product,** (usu. useless) byproduct of manufacture or physiological process.

waste[2] (wāst) *v.* (**wast·ed, wast·ing**). 1. Lay waste; (law) bring (estate) into bad condition by damage or neglect. 2. Expend to no purpose or for inadequate result, use extravagantly, squander; run to waste. 3. Wear gradually away, be used up, lose substance or volume by gradual loss, decay, etc.; wither.

waste·ful (wāst'ful) *adj.* Given to, exhibiting, waste; extravagant. **waste'ful·ly** *adv.* **waste'ful·ness** *n.*

wast·rel (wāst'rel) *n.* Wasteful person, spendthrift; idler, good-for-nothing.

watch (wǒch) *v.* (archaic) Remain awake for devotion or other purpose, keep vigil; be on the alert *for,* keep watch, be vigilant; exercise protecting care *over;* keep eyes fixed on, keep under observation, follow observantly. **watch'er** *n.* **watch** *n.* 1. Watching, keeping awake and vigilant at night for guarding, attending, etc.; (hist.) each of (three, four, or five) periods into which night was anciently divided; (naut.) period of time (usu. four hours) during which each division of ship's company remains on duty, sailor's turn of duty; part, usu. half, of officers and crew who together work ship during a watch. 2. Watching, observing, with continuous attention, continued lookout, guard (**keep** ~); one who watches, lookout man; (hist.) man, body of men, charged with patrolling and guarding streets at night, proclaiming the hour, etc. 3. Small timepiece designed to be worn on wrist or carried in pocket etc. 4. **watch′band**, small band of leather, metal, cloth, etc., for securing a watch to the wrist; **watch chain**, chain attaching timepiece to one's person; **watch′dog**, dog kept to guard house, property, etc.; **watch fire**, fire burning at night as signal or for use of sentinel or other person(s) on watch; **watch′man**, (fem.) **watch′woman** (pl. -men; -women), formerly one who patrolled streets at night to safeguard life and property; now esp. person employed to guard building etc., esp. at night; **watch pocket**, small pocket, usu. in vest, for holding a watch; **watch′tower**, tower from which observation is kept of approach of danger; **watch′word**, (hist.) military password; (transf.) word or phrase expressing guiding principle or rule of action of party or individual.

watch·ful (wŏch′ful) adj. Wakeful (archaic); accustomed to, engaged in, watching, vigilant; showing vigilance. **watch′ful·ly** adv. **watch′ful·ness** n.

wa·ter (waw′ter, wŏt′er) n. 1. Transparent, colorless, tasteless, odorless liquid (H_2O) composing seas, lakes, and rivers, falling as rain, issuing from springs, etc., and convertible into steam by heat and into ice by cold; this as supplied for domestic needs, esp. through pipes; liquid resembling (and usu. containing) water, as tears, saliva, urine, etc.; aqueous decoction, infusion, etc., used in medicine or as cosmetic or perfume; (freq. pl.) water of mineral spring(s) used medicinally for bathing or drinking; state of tide (in **high, low,** ~); **heavy** ~: see HEAVY; ~ **on the brain**, hydrocephalus; ~ **on the knee**, accumulation of inflammatory exudate in knee joint. 2. Characteristic transparency and luster of diamond or pearl; **of the first** ~, of the finest quality. 3. ~ `**ballet**, synchronized movements in water by group of swimmers, usu. accompanied by music; ~ **bath**, (esp., chem.) vessel containing water in or over which vessels containing chemical preparations etc. are placed for cooling, evaporating, etc.; ~ **bed**, (bed with) rubber mattress filled with water; ~ **biscuit**, unsweetened biscuit made of flour and

The lower parts of the **water plantain** are poisonous. However, after boiling, the stem and root can be eaten. The leaves were once used to relieve kidney complaints.

water; ~ **boatman**, aquatic insect (*Notonecta*) with boat-shaped body and oarlike legs, which swims upside down over surface of water; **wa′terbuck**, S. African antelope of genus *Kobus*, frequenting riverbanks; **wa′terborne**, (esp. of diseases) communicated by use of contaminated drinking water etc.; (of seaplane) having landed on water; **water buffalo**, common Asiatic buffalo (*Bubalus bubalis*), often domesticated; **Water carrier**: see AQUARIUS; **water chestnut**, Chinese sedge (*Eleocharis dulcis*) growing in thick clumps in water and having buttonlike tubers used as ingredient in Chinese dishes; flating aquatic weed (*Trapa natans*) native to Asia, bearing hard black fruit; **water clock**, water-operated machine for measuring time; **water closet**, (Brit.) (room etc. containing) flush toilet (abbrev. W.C., w.c.); **wa′tercolor**, artists' paint made of pigment mixed usu. with gum and diluted with water; esp., transparent variety of this, aquarelle; picture painted, art or method of painting, with such colors; **water-cooled**, (of internal combustion engine) cooled by means of circulating water; **water cooler**, (esp.) small tank containing cooled drinking water; **wa′tercourse**, (bed or channel of) stream of water, river, brook; **wa′tercress**, hardy perennial cress (*Nasturtium officinale*) often growing in springs and clear running streams, and with pungent leaves used as a salad; **water cure** = HYDROPATHY; **wa′terfall**, more or less perpendicular descent of water from a height, cascade; **wa′terfinder**, DOWSER; **water flag**, yellow iris; **wa′terfowl** (pl. -fowls, collect. -fowl), bird(s) frequenting water,

esp. swimming game bird(s); **wa′terfront**, land or buildings abutting on river, lake, sea, etc.; **water gap**, opening in mountainous or hilly area worn down by stream flow; **water gas**, gas (mixture of hydrogen and carbon monoxide), made by forcing steam over red-hot coke and used as fuel etc.; **water glass, wa′terglass**, tube with glass bottom for observing objects under water; aqueous solution of sodium or potassium silicate, solidifying on exposure to air and used as cement, fireproof paint, for preserving eggs, etc.; **water hammer**, concussion of water made when its flow through pipe is suddenly checked; **water hen**, any of various chickenlike marsh birds, as rail and coot; **water hole**, hole or hollow containing water, esp. in desert or dry bed of stream; **water ice**, frozen dessert of flavored water and sugar; **water jacket**, casing holding water, esp. casing through which water circulates in water-cooled engines, guns, etc.; **water jump**, place where horse must jump over water in steeplechase etc.; **water level**, (height of) surface of water; upward limit of saturation by water; **wa′terlily** (pl. -lil·ies), aquatic plant of *Nymphaea* and related genera, and similar plants with broad floating leaves and showy fragrant flowers; **water line** (1) line on ship's side corresponding to surface of water when ship is afloat, esp. proper line of floating when ship is fully loaded; (2) line left by receding tide or flood indicating greatest height of water; **wa′terlogged**, filled or saturated with water so as to be unbuoyant, heavy and unmanageable; (of ground etc.) made useless by saturation with water; **water main**, chief pipe in system of watersupply; **wa′termark**, distinguishing mark or design in paper visible when paper is held up to light; **wa′termelon**, large fruit (*Citrullus vulgaris*) with smooth hard rind, soft pink or red pulp, and abundant sweet watery juice; plant, native of tropical Africa and widely cultivated, bearing this; **water mill**, mill driven by water; **water moccasin**: see COTTONmouth; **water nymph**, nymph inhabiting or presiding over water, naiad; **water ouzel**: see DIPPER, sense 1; **water plantain**, plant of genus *Alisma*, with plantainlike leaves, growing in ditches etc.; **water polo**, ball game played in water by teams of swimmers; **water power, wa′terpower**, mechanical force derived from weight or motion of water; **wa′terproof** (adj.), impervious to water; (n.), waterproof garment or material; (v.t.), make waterproof; **water rat**, (slang) waterfront vagrant or thief;

*The natural energy from a **waterfall**, such as Russell Fall in Australia (1), enabled man to drive a **water wheel** that turned a millstone, as in Lancashire U.K. (2). The **waterlily** (3) grows wild in warmer areas: and the **watermelon** (4) has been cultivated for 5,000 years.*

water-repellent, not easily penetrated by water; **water-resistant,** resisting but not completely preventing penetration by water; **water right,** legal right, sometimes restricted, to use water of a river etc. for irrigation, navigation, etc.; **wa′tershed,** summit or boundary line separating waters flowing into different rivers or river basins; whole catchment area of river system; **water-ski** (*v.i.*) (**-skied, -ski·ing**), plane over water on water skis, towed by boat; **water ski** (*n.*), ski used on water; **water-ski·er** (*n.*); **water snake,** snake inhabiting or frequenting water, esp. nonpoisonous freshwater snake of *Natrix* and related genera; **water softener,** any of several chemical compounds used to make water soft; **water spaniel,**

large spaniel of variety used for retrieving waterfowl; **wa′terspout,** (esp.) gyrating column of mist, spray, and water produced by action of whirlwind on part of sea

*The **waterbok** is a large African antelope which can weigh up to 475 lb. and have a height of nearly 5 ft. There are five species and only the males carry horns.*

and clouds above it; hole or spout for discharging (esp. rain) water; **water system,** river and all its tributaries; system of reservoirs, filtration plants, pipes, etc., used for storing, treating, and supplying water to a community or region; **water table**, level at which porous rock etc. is saturated by underground water, height to which such water naturally rises in well etc.; **wa'tertight**, so closely constructed or fitted that water cannot leak through; (of argument etc.) unassailable; **watertight compartment**, each of compartments with watertight partitions into which interior of ship is divided for safety; (fig.) division of anything regarded as kept entirely separate from rest; **water tower**, structure supporting elevated tank to secure necessary pressure for water supply; fire-fighting apparatus for delivering water at considerable height; **wa'terway**, navigable channel; (naut.) channel around ship's deck to drain off water; **water wheel**, wheel rotated by action of water and driving machinery; wheel for raising water for irrigation etc. in boxes or buckets fitted on its circumference; **water wings**, inflated floats used as supports by persons learning to swim; **wa'terworks**, assemblage of machinery, buildings, engineering constructions, etc., for supplying town, ornamental fountain, etc., with water through pipes. **wa'ter·less** *adj.* **water** *v.* 1. Give (animal) water to drink, (of animals) go to pool etc. to drink; furnish (ship etc.) with, take in, supply of water; supply water to (plant, crop, etc.), esp. by pouring or sprinkling; add water to (drink etc.), dilute (freq. ~ **down**). 2. (of eyes) Fill and run with moisture; (of mouth) secrete abundant saliva in anticipation of appetizing food etc. 3. (commerc.) Increase nominal amount of (company's stock or capital) by issue of new shares

without corresponding addition to assets. 4. (chiefly in past part.) Produce wavy lustrous finish on (silk or other textiles) by sprinkling with water and passing through calender. 5. **wa'tering can**, portable vessel for watering plants, with long tubular spout; **watering hole**, (slang) bar, cocktail lounge, or nightclub; **watering place**, pool, trough, etc., where animals obtain water; place where supply of water is obtained; (Brit.) spa, seaside holiday or health resort.

Wa·ter·gate (waw'tergāt, wŏt'er-) *n.* Scandal involving abuse of authority and violation of public trust by elected or appointed officials who, to retain power, engage in such acts as deception, perjury, bribery, and burglary. [after *Watergate*, building complex in Washington, D.C., site of Democratic Party offices, burglarized in June 1972, at direction of government officials]

Wa·ter·loo (waw'terlōō, wŏt'er-, wawterlōō', wŏter-). Village S. of Brussels, Belgium, where on June 18, 1815, Napoleon was finally defeated by the British under the Duke of Wellington and the Prussians; hence, **meet one's ~**, suffer final defeat.

wa·ter·y (waw'terē, wŏt'erē) *adj.* Of, consisting of, water (esp. in ~ **grave**, place in which person lies drowned); full of, covered with, containing too much, water; resembling water in color, pale; washed out; (of liquids) too thin, diluted, having little or no taste; (fig.) vapid, insipid, feeble.

WATS (wŏts) *n.* Telephone service that gives customer access to long-distance lines at special monthly rate. [*w*(ide) *a*(rea) *t*(elecommunications) *s*(ervice)]

Wat·son (wŏt'son), **James Dewey** (1928–). Amer. biologist; co-discoverer of DNA molecular structure; received Nobel Prize for medicine, 1962, with CRICK and WILKINS[1].

watt (wŏt) *n.* Unit of power in M.K.S. system, equivalent to 1 joule per second (abbrev. W); **watt'meter**, instrument for measuring electric power in terms of watts. [f. WATT]

Watt (wŏt), **James** (1736–1819). Scottish inventor of the steam engine.

watt·age (wŏt'ij) *n.* Amount of electric power expressed in watts.

wat·tle[1] (wŏt'el) *n.* Interlaced rods and twigs or branches used for fences and walls and roofs of buildings; ~ **and daub**, this plastered with clay or mud as building material for huts etc. **wattle** *v.t.* (-**tled**, -**tling**). Construct of wattle; interlace (twigs etc.) to form wattle; enclose, fill up, with wattle work.

wat·tle[2] (wŏt'el) *n.* Fleshy, usu. bright colored, lobe pendent from head or neck of turkey, domestic fowl, and other birds; barb, fleshy appendage on mouth of some fishes.

Wave (wāv) *n.* Member of the WAVES.

wave (wāv) *n.* 1. Moving ridge or swell of water between two troughs; movement of sea etc. in which such waves are formed. 2. Undulating configuration or line in or on surface, as hair etc. 3. Something resembling or supposed to resemble a wave, esp. temporary heightening of emotion, influence, etc.; **heat, cold, ~**, spell of hot or cold weather. 4. (phys.) Oscillatory condition that is propagated from place to place in such manner that the same type of vibration occurs all along the path with a difference of PHASE (i.e. slightly delayed in time); **heat, light, radio,** ~**s,** electromagnetic waves propagated through space; ~ **band,** (radio and television) range of wavelengths between specified limits; ~ **-form,** shape of wave, graphical or arithmetical specification of this; ~ **front,** surface containing points affected in same way by a wave at given time; **wave′length,** distance between successive points of equal phase in the direction of propagation of a wave; specific electromagnetic wave used by radio transmitting station. 5. Act or gesture of waving. **wave** *v.* (**waved, wav·ing**). 1. Move in waves, undulate; move to and fro, shake, sway; impart waving movement to; wave hand in greeting or as signal; motion (person) *away, back, in,* etc., by movement of hand. 2. Give undulating surface, course, or appearance to, make wavy; (of

hair, lines, etc.) have such appearance, be wavy. **wave′like** *adj.* **wav′er**[1] *n.*

wave·let (wāv′lĭt) *n.* Small wave, ripple.

wa·ver[2] (wā′ver) *v.i.* Change, vary, fluctuate, shake, tremble; be irresolute, show doubt or indecision; falter, show signs of giving way. **wa′ver·er** *n.* **wa′ver·ing·ly** *adv.*

WAVES (wāvz) *n. sing.* or *pl.* Women's branch of U.S. Navy. [*W*(omen) *A*(ppointed for) *V*(oluntary) *E*(mergency) *S*(ervice)]

wav·y (wā′vē) *adj.* (**wav·i·er, wav·i·est**). Undulating; forming undulating line or series of wavelike curves. **wav′i·ly** *adv.* **wav′i·ness** *n.*

wax[1] (wăks) *n.* 1. Beeswax, sticky plastic yellowish substance of low melting point secreted by bees from special abdominal glands, used as

An amazing number of uses have been found for **wax.** *It is applied to surfboards to improve grip and, here, it is being used to make ornamental candles.*

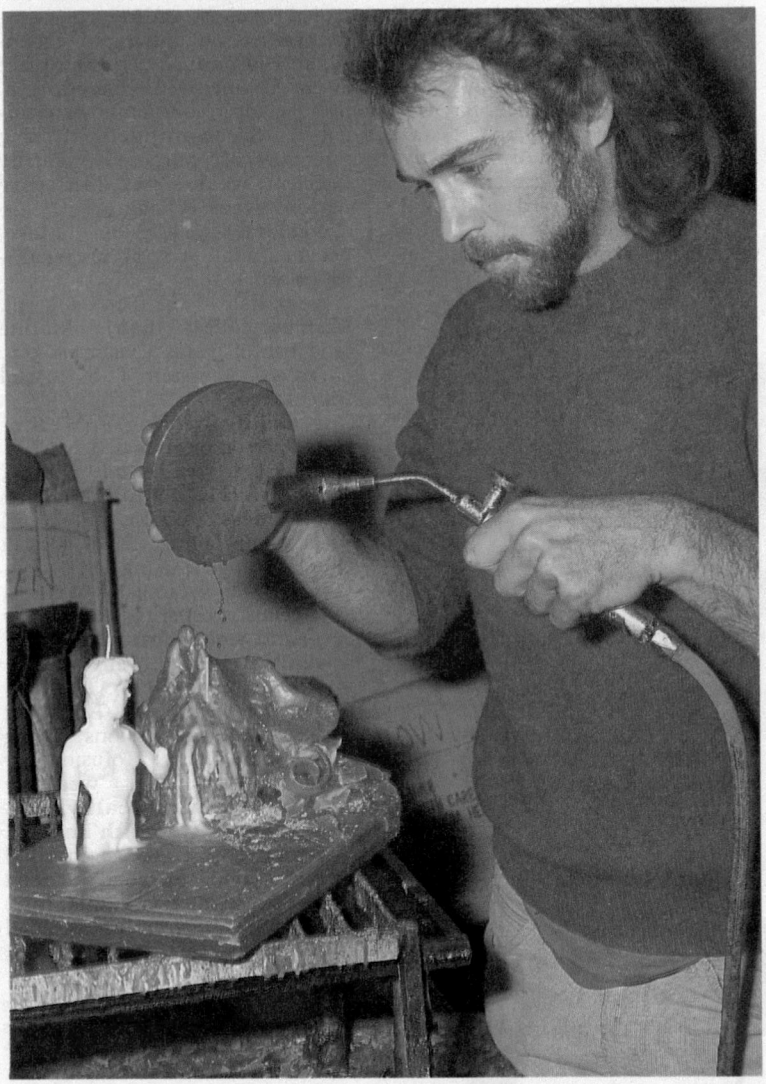

material of honeycomb; white brittle translucent odorless tasteless substance gotten from this by purifying and bleaching, and used for candles, as plastic material for modeling, as basis of polishes, as air-excluding protective coating, etc. 2. Any of class of natural substances of plant or animal origin resembling beeswax in general properties and in being composed of fatty acids and alcohols; any of various hydrocarbons resembling beeswax. 3. Compound, chiefly of lac, used to receive impression of seal, sealing wax. 4. Thick resinous composition used by shoemakers for rubbing thread, cobblers' wax. 5. Cerumen. 6. ~ **bean,** variety of string bean having long, slim yellow pods; edible seed of this plant; **wax′berry** (pl. **-ries**), (fruit of) wax myrtle; **wax candle,** candle of beeswax, paraffin wax, etc.; **wax myrtle,** shrub (*Myrica cerifera*) of southeastern U.S., with aromatic foliage and small hard berries thickly coated with a white wax; **wax, waxed, paper,** paper coated with wax used as waterproof and airtight wrapping etc.; **wax′plant,** tropical Old World vine (*Hoya carnosa*) with pink or white waxy flowers; **wax′wing,** any of various Amer. and Asiatic passerine birds of genus *Bombycilla,* esp. *B. cedrorum,* cedar waxwing, with showy crest and red waxlike tips on wing feathers; **wax′work,** modeling in wax; object modeled in wax, esp. life-size figure of person with wax head, hands, etc., colored and clothed to look lifelike; (pl.) exhibition of such figures. **wax** *v.t.* Smear, coat, polish, treat, with wax. **wax′er** *n.*

wax[2] (wăks) *v.i.* (**waxed, waxed** or **wax·en, wax·ing**). (of moon) Undergo periodical increase in extent of visible illuminated portion in first part of lunation, before full moon (opp. WANE); (archaic and poet.) grow, increase; change by growth or increase, become (*fat* etc.).

wax·en (wăk′sen) *adj.* (archaic) Made of, coated with, wax; resembling wax, esp. in smooth and lustrous surface, pallor, or softness and impressibility.

wax·y (wăk′sē) *adj.* (**wax·i·er, wax·i·est**). Resembling wax, esp. easily molded, or presenting smooth pale translucent surface; (of tissue) affected with amyloid degeneration. **wax′i·ness** *n.*

way (wā) *n.* 1. Road, track, path, street (esp. in phrases **across, over, the** ~, etc.); place of passage through door, crowd, etc.; (pl.) inclined structure, usu. of timber, on which ship is built and down which it is slid at launch; (pl.) parallel sills forming track for carriage or table of lathe or other machine; (pl.) inclined plane of parallel wooden rails or planks for sliding down heavy loads. 2. Route, line or course of travel for reaching place; opportunity for passage or advance, (fig.) freedom of action, scope, opportunity; travel or motion in particular direction, direction of motion, relative position, aspect; distance (to be) traveled, distance between places or to a place; (naut.) progress, rate of progress, through water, impetus gained by vessel in motion; **give ~**, fail to resist; be dislodged or broken under load; make concessions; allow precedence (*to*); abandon oneself (*to* grief etc.); **out of one's** or **the ~**, no longer an obstacle or impediment, disposed of, settled; (of person) imprisoned or killed; **the other ~ around**, conversely, vice versa. 3. Path or course of life or conduct, (pl.) habits of life, esp. with regard to moral conduct; course of action, device, method, means; customary or usual, habitual or characteristic, manner of acting, behaving, speaking, etc., (pl.) habits; condition regarded as hopeful or the contrary; kind, sort (now only in **in the ~ of** and similar phrases), kind *of business*; **on the ~ out**, going out of fashion or use; (slang) near death; **~s and means**, methods, esp. of providing money; **~ out**, method of solving a problem. 4. **make ~**, open a passage (*for*), move to allow person to pass; leave place vacant *for* (successor etc.); **make one's ~**,

proceed in certain direction or to certain place; make progress in career, advance in wealth, reputation, etc.; **pay one's ~**, pay expenses as they arise, without incurring debts; (of business etc.) be carried on at least without loss; **see one's ~**, (esp., fig.) feel justified in deciding *to do* something. 5. **by the ~**, by the roadside; while going along; (fig.) incidentally, in passing; **by ~ of**, via; in capacity or function of, as something equivalent to; in the habit of (*doing*), making a profession of, having a reputation for (*being, doing,* something); **under ~**, (of vessel) having begun to move through water (also freq. fig.). 6. **way'bill**, list of passengers or goods on conveyance; **way'farer**, traveler, esp. on foot; **way'faring**, traveling, itinerant; **way'faring tree**, Old World shrub (*Viburnum lantana*), also grown in U.S., with dense cymes of white flowers, and green berries turning red and then black; **waylay'** (**-laid, -lay·ing**), lie in wait for; wait for and accost or stop (person) to rob or interview him; **way'side**, (land bordering) side of road or path; (*adj.*) situated on, growing at, lying near, etc., wayside. **way** *adv.* Away; (esp.) at or to a great distance, far; **way back**, (colloq.) long ago; distant past; remote or rural district; **way-out**, (slang) exotic, esoteric.

way·ward (wā'werd) *adj.* Childishly or capriciously self-willed or perverse, erratic, freakish, un-

accountable. **way'ward·ly** *adv.* **way'ward·ness** *n.*

Wb *abbrev.* WEBER.

W.C., w.c. *abbrevs.* Water closet.

W.C.T.U. *abbrev.* Women's Christian Temperance Union.

we (wē) *pron.* First person nom. pl. pronoun denoting speaker and other person(s) associated with him as subject of sentence; used by sovereign or ruler, by newspaper writer or editor etc., instead of *I*.

weak (wēk) *adj.* Lacking strength, power or number; fragile, easily broken, bent, or defeated; lacking vigor, feeble, sickly; lacking resolution or power or resisting temptation, easily led; (of action etc.) not effective, showing weakness; (of argument etc.) unconvincing, logically deficient; (of liquid, esp. infusion) watery, thin; (of stress, a speech sound, etc.) having relatively little force etc., (of word or syllable, esp. final syllable or verse) unstressed; (gram., of verbs) forming past tense by addition of suffix, (of nouns or adjectives) belonging to any declension in which Old Teut. stem ended in *-n*; **~ ending**, (in verse) occurrence of unstressed monosyllable in normally stressed place at end of line; **weak-kneed**, (esp. fig.) lacking resolution or determination; **weak-minded**, lacking strength of purpose; mentally deficient; **weak sister**, ineffective person. **weak'ly[1]** *adv.*

weak·en (wē'ken) *v.* Make, become, weak or weaker. **weak'en·er** *n.*

weak·fish (wēk'fĭsh) *n.* (pl. **-fish·es**, collect. **-fish**). Marine food fish of genus *Cynoscion*, esp. *C. regalis* of eastern U.S. coastal waters.

weak·ling (wēk'lĭng) *n.* Weak or feeble person or animal.

weak·ly[2] (wēk'lē) *adj.* (**-li·er, -li·est**). Sickly, not robust, ailing.

weak·ness (wēk'nĭs) *n.* (esp.) Weak point, failing, defect, foolish or self-indulgent liking *for*.

weal[1] (wēl) *n.* (archaic) Welfare, well-being, prosperity (now chiefly in **~ and woe, common ~**).

weal[2] (wēl) *n.* = WELT sense 2. **~** *v.t.* Raise welt(s) on.

wealth (wĕlth) *n.* Abundant means, large possessions, being rich; abundance, profusion or lavish display *of*. **wealth'y** *adj.* (**wealth·i·er, wealth·i·est**). **wealth'i·ly** *adv.* **wealth'i·ness** *n.*

wean (wēn) *v.t.* Accustom (child or other young mammal) to food other than its mother's milk; (fig.) detach, alienate *from* accustomed object of pursuit or enjoyment,

Found in the northern hemisphere, the **waxwing** *is omnivorous. It eats insects in the summer and berries when available.*

cold front

quasi-stationary front

warm front

occluded front

continuous precipitation

showers or squalls

fog or low stratus

isobar

arrow shaft showing direction of wind (from northwest) at a speed of 25 knots

cloud cover represented on an octadic scale by proportional filling

reconcile gradually to privation of something.

wean·ling (wēn′lĭng) *n.* Newly weaned child or other young mammal.

weap·on (wĕp′on) *n.* Instrument used in war or combat as means of attack or defense; any part of body (esp. of bird or beast) used for similar purpose, as claw, horn, etc.; any action or means used against another in conflict.

weap·on·ry (wĕp′onrē) *n.* 1. Weapons collectively. 2. Design and manufacture of weapons.

wear (wār) *v.* (**wore** pr. wōr, **worn, wear·ing**). 1. Be dressed in (habitually or on specific occasion); have on, be covered or decked with; dress (hair, beard, etc.), allow to grow, in specific fashion, or as opposed to shaving or wearing wig; (of ship etc.) fly (flag, colors);

Typical **weather map** *(above left) alongside a legend of some of the more common symbols and their meaning. Coupled with satellite observation, modern weather maps must be accurate to provide data for aircraft.*

(transf. and fig.) bear, carry, exhibit, present (scar, appearance, title, etc.), carry in one's heart, mind, or memory. 2. Waste and impair, damage, deteriorate, gradually by use or attrition; suffer such waste, damage, or deterioration; come or bring into specified state by use, rub *away, down, off, out,* etc.; make (hole, groove, etc.) by attrition; exhaust, tire or be tired

For all man's achievements there is still one thing he cannot control — the **weather.** *The power of an electrical storm or a tornado remains unchallenged.*

out; put *down* by persistence; endure continued use *well, badly,* etc., remain specified time in working order or presentable state, last long; ~ **out,** use, be used, until usable no longer. 3. (of time) Go slowly and tediously *on,* pass (time), be passed, gradually *away.* **wear′-a·ble** *adj.* **wear′er** *n.* **wear** *n.* 1. Wearing or being worn on person, use as clothes; thing to wear, fashionable or suitable apparel. 2. Damage or deterioration due to ordinary use (freq. ~ **and tear**); capacity for resisting wear and tear.

wea·ri·some (wēr′ĕsom) *adj.* Causing weariness, monotonous, fatiguing. **wea′ri·some·ly** *adv.* **wea′ri·some·ness** *n.*

wea·ry (wēr′ē) *adj.* (**-ri·er, -ri·est**). 1. Tired, worn out with exertion, endurance, wakefulness, etc., intensely fatigued; sick or impatient *of;* dispirited, depressed. 2. Tiring, toilsome, tedious, irksome. **wea′ri·ly** *adv.* **wea′ri·ness** *n.* **weary** *v.* (**-ried, -ry·ing**). Make, grow, weary.

wea·sel (wē′zel) *n.* (pl. **-sels,** collect. **-sel**). Small slender-bodied reddish-brown carnivorous mammal (*Mustela frenata*) closely allied to stoats and polecats and remarkable for slyness, ferocity, and bloodthirstiness. **weasel** *v.i.* (colloq.) Equivocate, speak evasively; ~ **words,** (colloq.) equivocal words.

weath·er (wĕdh′er) *n.* Atmospheric conditions prevailing at a specified time or place with respect to heat or cold, quantity of sunshine, presence or absence of rain, snow, fog, etc., strength of wind; adverse, unpleasant, or hurtful

One of the smallest carnivores, the **weasel** *of Europe and Northern America is entirely predatory. Other species are found in the southern hemisphere. All can kill prey as big as themselves.*

condition of atmosphere, rain, frost, wind, etc., as destructive agents; (naut.) direction in which wind is blowing; **make heavy ~ of**, find trying or difficult; **under the ~**, (colloq.) indisposed, not very well; in adversity; **~-beaten**, worn, defaced, damaged, bronzed, hardened, etc., by exposure to weather; **weather-bound**, detained by bad weather; **weath′ercock**, (Brit.) weathervane; (fig.) changeable or inconstant person; **weather eye**, alertness to change in weather; **keep one's weather eye open**, be watchful and alert; **weath′erglass**, barometer; **weath′erman**, (1) meteorologist, esp. one who broadcasts a weather forecast; (2) (**W~**), member of violent revolutionary group in U.S. during late 1960s; **weather map**, chart or map showing state of weather over specific area at particular time; **weath′erproof**, impervious to effects of weather; **weather station**, meteorological observation post; **weath′erstrip**, **weather strip**, strip of material around window to exclude rain etc.; **weather vane**: see VANE sense 1. **weather** *adj.* (naut.) Windward. **~** *v.* 1. Expose to atmospheric changes; wear away, be worn away, disintegrate, discolor, by exposure to weather. 2. Withstand or come safely through (storm etc.); (fig.) come safely through (trouble, adversity, etc.).

weave[1] (wēv) *v.* (**wove** pr. wōv, or **weaved, wo·ven** pr. wō′ven, or **wove, weav·ing**). Form fabric by carrying a continuous thread or threads (the woof) back and forth across a set of lengthwise threads (the warp) so that warp and woof are interlaced; operate loom; make (thread etc.) into fabric, make (fabric) out of thread etc., thus; make (basket, wreath etc.) by interlacing reeds, flowers, etc.; (fig.) intermingle as if by weaving, form or introduce *into* connected whole thus. **~** *n.* Style, method, pattern, of weaving.

weave[2] (wēv) *v.* (Cause to) move from side to side or in devious or intricate course.

weav·er (wē′ver) *n.* (esp.) 1. One who weaves fabrics. 2. (also **weav′erbird**) Any of numerous Asiatic or African tropical birds of family Ploceidae, building elaborately interwoven nests.

web (wĕb) *n.* 1. Woven fabric, esp. whole piece in process of weaving or after coming from loom; (fig.) thing of complicated structure or workmanship, tissue. 2. Spiderweb; (freq. fig.); filmy texture spun by some caterpillars etc. 3. Tissue or membrane in animal body or plant; membrane or fold of skin connecting digits, esp. that between toes of aquatic bird or beast, forming palmate foot; vane of feather; thin flat plate or part connecting more solid parts in machinery; center part of girder between flanges; (papermaking) (large roll of paper made on) endless wire cloth on rollers carrying the pulp. 4. **web′foot** (pl. **-feet**), **web′footed**, (having) foot with webbed toes; **web′worm**, larva of various moths spinning large webs in which to feed or rest. **web** *v.t.* (**webbed, web·bing**). Cover with web or fine network; stretch threads of spider's web across (micrometer etc.); connect (fingers, toes) with web or membrane.

web·bing (wĕb′ĭng) *n.* (esp.) Stout strong closely woven material in form of narrow bands, used in upholstery etc.

Related to the sparrow, the **weaverbird** *is renowned for the complex nest it makes. Some gregarious species in Africa build up to 100 nests so close that they seem to be a single mass.*

we·ber (wĕb′er, vā′ber) *n.* Unit of magnetic flux in M.K.S. system, equal to 10^8 maxwells (abbrev. Wb). [f. WEBER[2]]

We·ber (wĕb′er; Ger. vā′ber), **Wilhelm Eduard** (1804–91). German physicist; devised the centimeter-gram-second system of measurement of electrical quantities.

Web·ster[1] (wĕb′ster), **Daniel** (1782–1852). Amer. lawyer, statesman, and orator.

Web·ster[2] (wĕb′ster), **Noah** (1758–1843). Amer. lexicographer.

wed (wĕd) *v.* (**wed·ded** or **wed, wed·ding**). Marry; unite, join, or couple intimately *with*; **be wedded to**, be obstinately attached to (pursuit etc.).

Wed. *abbrev.* Wednesday.

we'd (wĕd) *contr.* We had; we should; we would.

wed·ding (wĕd′ĭng) *n.* Marriage ceremony with its attendant festivities; specified anniversary of this, as *silver* ~; **~ cake**, highly decorated cake eaten at wedding and sent in small portions to absent friends etc.; ~ **day**, (anniversary of) day of wedding; ~ **march**, march (often Wagner's at beginning, Mendelssohn's at close) for performance at wedding; ~ **ring**, ring placed by bridegroom on bride's finger (usu. third finger of left hand) as part of wedding ceremony and usu. worn there constantly by married woman; one of pair of such rings exchanged by bride and groom at wedding.

wedge (wĕj) *n.* 1. Piece of wood, metal, etc., thick at one end and tapering to thin edge at the other, used as tool operated by percussion or pressure on thick end for splitting wood, stone, etc., forcing things apart, widening opening, rendering separate parts immovable, etc.; (fig.) something that splits or separates. 2. Anything shaped like a wedge. 3. Golf club, a heavy lofted iron used for pitching. **wedge** *v.* (**wedged, wedg·ing**). Tighten, fasten tightly, by driving in wedge(s); split *off*, force *apart*, with wedge; drive, push, squeeze (object) into position where it is held fast; pack or crowd (*together*) in close formation or limited space.

Wedg·wood (wĕj′wǒod), **Josiah** (1730–95). Founder of pottery works near Stoke on Trent, England; hence, ware made at this factory, esp. fine porcelain with small cameo reliefs in white paste on a tinted matte ground; **Wedgwood blue**, shade of blue characteristic of Wedgwood (trademark) ware.

wed·lock (wĕd′lŏk) *n.* Married state; **born in** (or **out of**) ~, having parents married (or not).

Wednes·day (wĕnz′dā, -dē). Fourth day of the week; **Ash** ~: see ASH². [OE. *wódnes daeg* day of WODEN; transl. of LL. *Mercurii dies* day of Mercury]

wee (wē) *adj.* (**we·er, we·est**). Tiny (chiefly Sc. and in nursery use).

weed (wēd) *n.* 1. Plant growing where it is not wanted. 2. (archaic) Tobacco; (colloq.) cigarette; (slang) marijuana. 3. (colloq.) Lanky and weak horse or person. 4. **weed′killer**, substance used to destroy weeds or other plants. **weed′less** *adj.* **weed′y** *adj.* (**weed·i·er, weed·i·est**). **weed** *v.* Clear ground of weeds; free (land, a crop, etc.) from weeds, remove (weeds); eradicate, remove, clear *out* (faults, inferior or superfluous individuals, etc.). **weed′er** *n.*

weeds (wēdz) *n.pl.* Deep mourning worn by widow (usu. **widow's** ~).

week (wēk) *n.* 1. Cycle of seven days usu. understood as beginning with Sunday; period of any seven successive days; work days or hours

of seven-day period, as *five-day* ~. 2. Seven days before or after a specified day. 3. **week′day**, any day other than Saturday and Sunday; **week′end**, holiday period at end of week, usu. from Friday night to Monday; (*v.i.*) make weekend visit, etc.

week·ly (wēk′lē) *adj.* Occurring, done, etc., once a week; of, for, lasting, a week. ~ *adv.* Once a week, every week. ~ *n.* (pl. **-lies**). Weekly newspaper or periodical.

ween (wēn) *v.t.* (archaic and poet.) Think, consider, deem.

wee·nie (wē′nē) *n.* (slang) Wiener, hot dog.

wee·ny (wē′nē) *adj.* (**-ni·er, -ni·est**). (colloq.) Tiny.

weep (wēp) *v.* (**wept**, pr. wĕpt, **weep·ing**). Shed tears; shed tears over, shed (tears), lament, utter, with tears; shed moisture in drops, exude drop of water, exude (water or other liquid); **weeping**, (of trees) having long, slender, drooping branches; esp. **weeping willow**, large Asiatic species of willow (*Salix babylonica*), cultivated as ornamental tree and regarded as symbolic of mourning. **weep′y** *adj.* Inclined to weep, tearful.

wee·vil (wē′vil) *n.* Beetle of the large family Curculionidae, usu. of small size, with head elongated into kind of snout, freq. very destructive to farm crops; any insect damaging stored grain. **wee′viled, wee′-villed, wee′vil·y, wee′vil·ly** *adjs.*

Best known for vases that imitate those of ancient Greece with white cameos on a blue ground, Josiah Wedgwood originally used black as his basic color when he first made this stoneware.

Infested with weevils.

weft (wĕft) *n.* Woof.

Wei (wā). · Name of several dynasties that ruled in China, esp. that of 386–535.

wei·ge·la (wīgē′la, -jē′-, wī′ge-) *n.* Any of various shrubs (genus *Weigela*) of the honeysuckle family, having clusters of tubular flowers, esp. the widely grown *W. florida*, with red, pink, or white flowers.

weigh (wā) *v.* 1. Heave up (ship's anchor) before sailing; ~ **anchor**, sail; ~ **up**, raise (sunk ship etc.) from bottom of water. 2. Find weight of with scales or other machine; balance in hands (as if) to guess weight of; take definite weight of, take specified weight from larger quantity (freq. ~ **out**); be equal to or balance (specified weight) in scales; (fig.) estimate relative value or importance of (*with, against*), consider, ponder, balance in the mind; have specified importance or value, be of account, have influence (*with*); ~ **one's words**, speak deliberately and in calculated terms. 3. ~ **down**, draw, bend, force, down by pressure of weight; depress, oppress, lie heavy on; ~ **in**, (of boxer or wrestler) be weighed before contest; (of jockey) be weighed after race; have one's baggage weighed; hence ~-**in** (*n.*); ~ **in with**, (colloq.) contribute; ~ **on**, be burdensome, heavy, oppressive, on; ~ **out**, (of jockey) be weighed before race; hence ~-**out** (*n.*). 4. **weigh′bridge**, platform scale, flush with road, for weighing vehicles etc. **weigh** *n.* Process or occasion of weighing; **under** ~, corruption (from association with phrase *weigh anchor*) of *under way* (see WAY, *n*. sense 5).

weight (wāt) *n*. 1. Force with which body is attracted to Earth; product of mass of any body and the average force of terrestrial gravitation; mass or relative heaviness as property of material substances; amount that thing etc. weighs, expressed in units of some recognized scale; portion or quantity weighing definite amount; heavy mass, burden, load; (fig.) heavy burden *of* care, responsibility, etc.; importance, influence, authority; persuasive or convincing power (of argument etc.), preponderance (*of* evidence, authority) on one side of question. 2. Any of various systems, with series of units in fixed arithmetical relations, used for stating weight of anything; piece of metal etc. of known weight, used in scales for weighing articles; heavy piece of metal etc. used to pull or press down something, give impulse to machinery (e.g. in clock), act as counterpoise, etc.; ~ **lifting**, athletic sport or exercise of lifting heavy weights; hence ~ **lifter; ~ watcher**, one who takes care not to become unduly fat. **weight'less** *adj*. Having little or no apparent weight as a result of gravitational pull, which has been neutralized by equal and opposing inertial force, as centrifugal force imparted initially to space capsule at launching. **weight'less·ness** *n*. **weight** *v.t*. Attach a weight to, hold down with weight(s); impede or burden with load; add weight to (textiles or other commodities) by addition of adulterant etc.; (statistics) multiply

components of (average) by compensating factors.

weight·y (wā'tē) *adj*. (**weight·i·er, weight·i·est**). Heavy, weighing much; momentous, important; requiring or giving evidence of earnest thought, consideration, or application; influential, authoritative. **weight'i·ly** *adv*. **weight'i·ness** *n*.

Wei·mar (vī'mär). Town in Thuringia, Germany, famous as the residence of Goethe and Schiller and as the seat of the National Assembly of Germany (1919–33); ~ **Republic**, German republic (1919–33), the constitution of which was drawn up at Weimar.

weir (wēr) *n*. Dam or barrier across river etc. to retain water and regulate its flow; fence or enclosure of stakes etc. in river, harbor, etc., to catch or preserve fish.

weird[1] (wērd) *n*. (archaic or Sc.) Fate, destiny.

weird[2] (wērd) *adj*. Connected with fate; uncanny, supernatural; (colloq.) queer, fantastic. **weird'ly** *adv*. **weird'ness** *n*. [f. WEIRD[1], f. phrase ~ *sisters* the Fates, the witches, in Shakespeare's *Macbeth*]

weird·ie, weird·y (wēr'dē) (pl. **weird·ies**), **weird·o** (wēr'dō) (pl. **weird·os**) *ns*. (slang) Unusually odd, eccentric, person or thing.

wel·come (wĕl'kom) *int*. Exclamation of greeting, indicating

pleasure at arrival of person(s) (often in phrases as ~ **home**, ~ **to**). **welcome** *n*. Saying "welcome" to person; kind or glad reception or entertainment of person or acceptance of offer. ~ *v.t*. (**-comed, -com·ing**). Say "welcome" to, receive gladly. ~ *adj*. Gladly received; acceptable as visitor; ungrudgingly permitted *to* do something or given right *to* thing. [OE. *wilcuma* (*wil-*) desire, pleasure, and *cuma* comer, one whose coming is pleasing, later changed to *wel-* (= WELL[2]) after OF. *bien venu*]

weld[1] (wĕld) *n*. Plant *Reseda lutea*; yellow dye yielded by this.

weld[2] (wĕld) *v*. Unite (pieces of metal) into solid mass by hammering or pressure, or by fusion using an electric arc (**arc weld'ing**), usu. when metal is soft but not melted; (of metal) admit of being welded; (fig.) unite intimately or inseparably. **weld'er** *n*. **weld** *n*. Joint made by welding.

wel·fare (wĕl'fār) *n*. Satisfactory state, health and prosperity, well-being (usu. *of* person, society, etc.); maintenance of members of community in such condition, esp. by statutory procedure or social effort; money etc. thus received by those in need; **on** ~, receiving such aid because of poverty, loss of job, etc.; ~ **state**, country having highly

Weir across the Leven River at Newby Bridge, Cumbria, U.K. Adjustable openings (or sluice gates) control floods and allow a navigable depth to be maintained during droughts.

*Rising from ensign to Field Marshal in 27 years, **Wellington** gained honors and cash rewards for his leadership in the Napoleonic campaigns. His political career was conservative.*

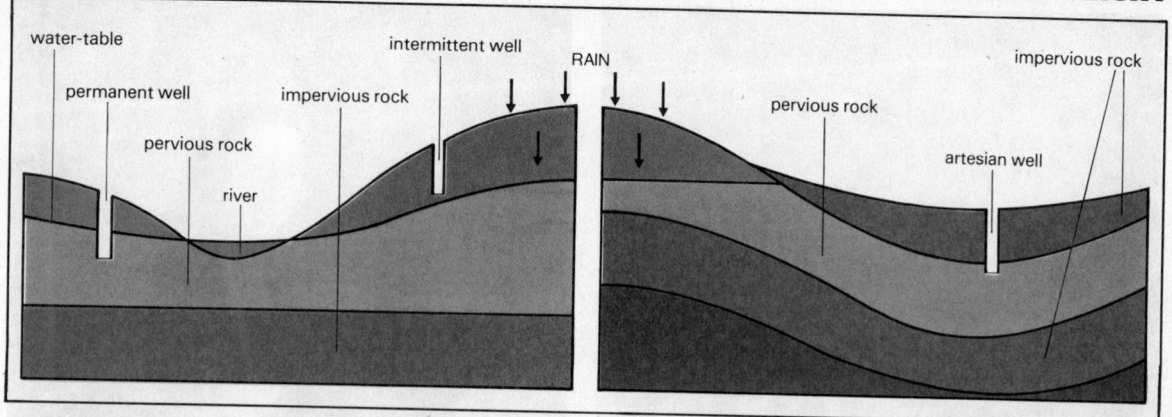

developed social services controlled or financed by the government; ~ **work**, organized effort for welfare of class or group; hence ~ **worker**.

wel·kin (wĕl´kĭn) *n.* (archaic, poet.) Sky, firmament.

well[1] (wĕl) *n.* 1. (archaic and poet.) Spring, fountain; (fig.) source, origin. 2. Pit, esp. circular vertical excavation, usu. lined with masonry, sunk in ground to obtain supply of water; shaft sunk in ground for obtaining oil, gas, brine, etc., for storage of ice, etc. 3. Enclosed space more or less resembling well shaft, esp. central open space of winding or spiral staircase, elevator shaft, deep narrow space between surrounding walls of building(s) for light and ventilation, deep receptacle in piece of furniture, body of vehicle, etc.; receptacle for liquid, esp. for ink. 4. **well´head**, (esp. fig.) chief source, fountainhead; top of a well; **well´spring**, headspring of stream etc.; (fig.) fountainhead, source of perennial emanation or supply. **well** *v.i.* Spring (*up, out, forth*), from or as from fountain.

well[2] (wĕl) *adj.* (**bet·ter, best**). (chiefly predic.) In good health; in satisfactory state or position, satisfactory; advisable, right and proper. ~ *adv.* 1. In good manner or style, satisfactorily, rightly. 2. Thoroughly, carefully, completely, sufficiently; to a considerable degree or extent, quite. 3. Heartily, kindly, approvingly, laudatorily, on good terms. 4. Probably, easily, with reason, wisely, advisably. 5. **as** ~, with equal reason; preferably; in addition; **as** ~ **as**, (esp.) to the same extent, in the same degree, as much ... as; in addition to, both ... and, not only ... but also. 6. In comb., esp. with past and present participles of verbs, and with adjectives ending in *-ed*, as ~-**advised**, (esp.) prudent, wary, wise; ~-**appointed**, properly equipped or fitted out; ~-**balanced**, sensible, sane; equally matched; ~-**being**, happy, healthy, or prosperous condition; **well´born**, of noble or dis-

tinguished family; **well-bred**, having or displaying good manners, courteous; of good breed; **well-conditioned**, of good disposition, morals, or behavior; sound, healthy, in good physical condition; **well-defined**, clearly indicated or determined; **well-disposed**, (esp.) disposed to be friendly or favorable (*toward, to*); **well-done** (*int.*), exclamation of approval; skillfully or rightly done; (of meat etc.) cooked thoroughly; **well-favored**, good-looking; **well-fed**, appearing to be well nourished; **well-founded**, (esp.) having foundation in fact, based on reason; **well-groomed**, (esp. of persons) with hair, skin, etc., carefully tended; **well-grounded**, well-founded; well-trained in rudiments; **well-heeled**, (colloq.) rich; **well-informed**, having mind fully furnished with general or special knowledge; **well-intentioned**, having, showing, based on, good intentions; **well-knit**, (esp., of person, his frame) strongly and compactly built, not loosely made; **well-known**, widely known; fully or thoroughly known; **well-made**, (of thing) skillfully manufactured; **well-meaning**, well-intentioned (freq. with implication of inefficiency or unwisdom); **well-nigh**, very nearly, almost wholly; **well-off**, fortunately situated; sufficiently rich; **well-preserved**, kept in good condition; (of elderly person) of more youthful appearance than age merits; **well-read**, well-informed by reading, learned (*in*), versed or skilled (*in*); **well-rounded**, symmetrical, (of sentence etc.) full and well-turned; (of person) broadly educated; **well-spoken**, (esp.) having good or ready speech, refined in speech; **well-timed**, timely, opportune; **well-to-do**, prosperous, well off; **well-tried**, often tried or tested with good result; **well-turned**,

(esp., of speech) neatly finished, happily expressed; **well-wisher**, one who wishes well to another, a cause, etc.; **well-worn**, (esp.) trite, hackneyed. **well** *int.* Exclamation introducing remark or statement, expressing astonishment, relief, concession, etc., or resumption of talk or subject, qualified recognition of point, expectation, resignation, etc.

we'll (wēl) *contr.* We shall; we will.

Wel·ling·ton[1] (wĕl´ĭngton). Capital of New Zealand, in North Island.

Wel·ling·ton[2] (wĕl´ĭngton), **Arthur Wellesley, 1st Duke of** (1769–1852). British general and statesman; led the British.forces in the Peninsular War, defeated Napoleon at Waterloo (1815); prime minister 1828–30.

Welsh (wĕlsh, wĕlch) *adj.* Of Wales or its people or language; ~ **corgi**: see CORGI; **Welsh´man** (pl. **-men**), **Welsh´woman** (pl. **-women**), native of Wales; **Welsh rabbit**, dish consisting of seasoned melted or toasted cheese on buttered toast, sometimes incorrectly called **Welsh rarebit**. **Welsh** *n.* 1. (collect.) People of Wales. 2. Language of Wales, one of the Celtic group of languages.

welsh (wĕlsh, wĕlch) *v.* (also ~ **on**); swindle by not paying debt; fail to meet obligation; fail to pay gambling debt. **welsh´er** *n.*

welt (wĕlt) *n.* 1. Strip of leather sewn between edge of sole and turned-in edge of upper in soling boot or shoe; ribbed or reinforced border of knitted garment. 2. Ridge on flesh, esp. mark of heavy blow or healed wound, weal. ~ *v.t.* 1. Provide with welt. 2. Raise weals on, beat, flog.

wel·ter (wĕl´ter) *v.i.* Roll, wallow; be tossed or tumbled about; lie prostrate *in* (blood or gore); (fig.) be sunk or deeply involved *in*. ~ *n.* State of turmoil or upheaval; surging or confused mass.

wel·ter·weight (wĕl´terwāt) *n.* Boxer of weight between light-weight and middleweight.

wen (wĕn) *n.* More or less
permanent benign tumor on skin,
esp. of scalp.

Wen·ces·las¹, Wen·ces·laus¹
(wĕn′seslaws) (1361–1419). King
of Bohemia (as Wenceslas IV), king
of Germany and Holy Roman
Emperor (1378–1419).

Wen·ces·las², Wen·ces·laus²
(wĕn′seslaws), **St., Duke of
Bohemia** (early 10th c.). National
saint of Bohemia, commemorated
Sept. 28.

wench (wĕnch) *n.* (now dial. or
joc.) Girl or young woman. ~
v.i. (archaic) Associate with female
prostitutes.

Wend (wĕnd) *n.* Member of a
Slavonic people of eastern
Germany.

wend (wĕnd) *v.* (**wend·ed** or
went, wend·ing). Direct one's
way; (archaic) go.

Wend·ish (wĕn′dĭsh) *adj.* Of the
Wends or their language. ~ *n.*
Western-Slavonic language of the
Wends.

went: see GO¹.
wept: see WEEP.
were (wēr): see BE.
we're (wēr) *contr.* We are.
weren't (wēr′ent) *contr.* Were not.
were·wolf, wer·wolf (wēr′-
wŏolf, wār′-, wēr′-) *ns.* (pl. **-wolves**
pr. -wŏolvz). In folklore, human
being who changes into a wolf.

Wes·ley (wĕs′lē, wĕz′-). **John** ~
(1703–91), Anglican clergyman,
evangelist, and founder of METHOD-
ISM; **Charles** ~ (1707–88), his
brother, author of many hymns.
Wes·ley·an (wĕs′lēan, wĕz′-) *adj.*
& *n.* (Follower) of John Wesley or
his teaching. **Wes′ley·an·ism** *n.*

Wes·sex (wĕs′ĭks). 1. Kingdom
of West Saxons. 2. Those counties

*The **Western Church** has developed
many sects and branches, possibly
more so than in any other religion. This
splintering has at times, led to bloody
conflict.*

of SW. England, principally
Dorset, that are the scene of
Thomas Hardy's novels.

west (wĕst) *adv.* Toward, in, the
west; **go** ~, (esp.) go to the western
states; (fig.) die, perish, be
destroyed. **west** *n.* 1. Point on
horizon where sun sets at equinox;
this direction. 2. Cardinal point of
the compass lying opposite east. 3.
(usu. the **W**~) That part of a
country, district, etc., that lies to
the west; Europe and America as
dist. from Asia; (esp.) western
Europe and America as dist. from
communist states of Asia and
eastern Europe; states of U.S. west
of Mississippi River. **west** *adj.*
Lying toward, in, the west; coming
from the west (~ **wind**); **W**~
Germany: see GERMANY; **W**~
Point, town in SE. New York
State, on west bank of Hudson
River, site of the U.S. Military
Academy. **west′ward** *adv., adj.,* &
n. **west′ward·ly** *adv.* & *adj.*
west′wards *adv.*

west·er·ly (wĕs′terlē) *adj.* In the
west; (of wind) blowing from the
west. ~ *adv.* Toward the west.
~ *n.* (pl. **-lies**). West wind.

west·ern (wĕs′tern) *adj.* Of the
west; occidental; lying or directed
toward the west; (poet.) in, coming
from, the west; **W**~, of the West as
dist. from communist countries;
W~ **Church**, Latin or R.C. Ch.
(occas. including Anglican Church
or all Churches of western
Christendom) as dist. from Orthodox Church; **W**~ **Empire**: see

*John Wesley founded a new movement
in the church. He preached in the open
and is said to have given 40,000 sermons. He founded Methodism in 1784
and had 100,000 followers.*

ROMAN Empire; **W**~ **Hemisphere**, half of Earth that includes
N. and S. Amer. and the surrounding islands and oceans. **western** *n.*
(esp.) Film or novel about adventures of cowboys, rustlers, etc., in
western parts of N. Amer. **west′-
ern·er** *n.* (also **W**~) Native,
inhabitant, of the west, esp. of
western U.S. **west′ern·most** *adj.*

West (wĕst) **Indies.** Chain of
islands extending from coast of
Florida to Venezuela and enclosing
Caribbean Sea; **West Indies
Associated States**, group of
former British colonies; in 1967
became self-governing territories in
association with the United King-
dom, including Antigua, Dominica,
St. Lucia, St. Christopher–Nevis–
Anguilla, and St. Vincent. **West
Indian** *adj.* & *n.*

West (wĕst) **Malaysia.** Federa-
tion of 11 states forming part of
Malaysia; formerly Malaya, in the
Malay Peninsula.

West·min·ster (wĕst′mĭnster).
City and inner London borough
containing the Houses of Parliament (**Palace of** ~) and many
government offices etc.; hence,
British parliamentary life or
politics; ~ **Abbey**, collegiate
church of St. Peter in the city of
Westminster, several times reconstructed from a church orig. built
by Edward the Confessor in the
11th c., scene of the coronation of
English monarchs and burial place
of kings, statesmen, soldiers, poets,
etc.

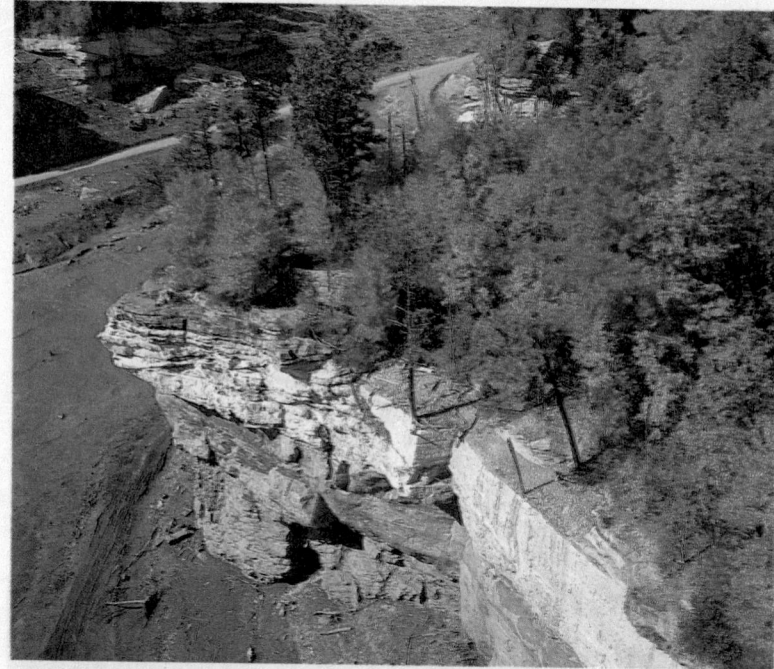

West Virginia became the 35th State of the U.S.A. in 1863. In the fall, deciduous trees of West Virginia turn on a magnificent display as the leaves change color.

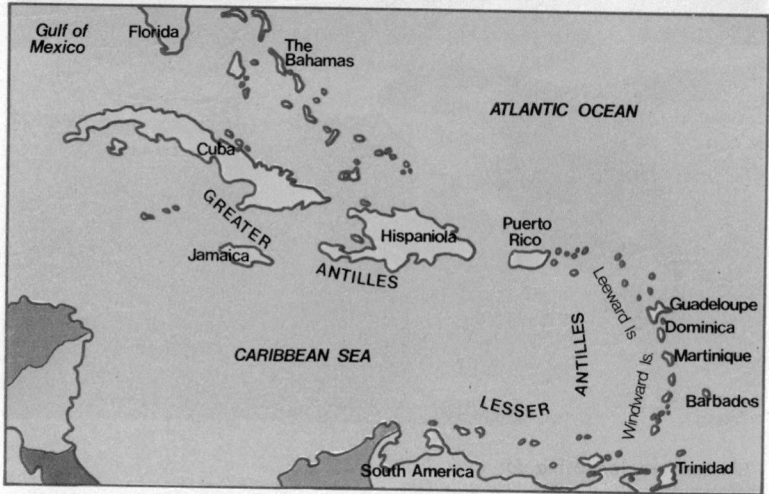

Named because Columbus believed he had reached India, the **West Indies** is an archipelago whose islands have an area of 100,000 square miles. The Bahamas lies beyond this region.

Formerly controlled by the British, the **West Indies** are fast becoming a popular tourist destination. The islands have few natural resources, and arable land is minimal.

West (wĕst) **Virginia.** South Atlantic state of U.S., admitted to the Union in 1863; capital, Charleston. **West Virginian** *adj.* & *n.*

wet (wĕt) *adj.* (**wet·ter, wet·-test**). 1. Soaked, covered, supplied with, etc., water or other liquid; rainy; employing, done by means of, water or other liquid. 2. (colloq.) Permitting or favoring sale of alcoholic liquors. 3. **all ~,** (slang) completely mistaken; **wet'back,** (derog.) illegal immigrant from Mexico to U.S.; **wet blanket**: see BLANKET; **wet bulb thermometer,** one having its bulb covered with wet muslin so that the difference between its reading and that of a dry bulb thermometer indicates the amount of water vapor in the air; **wet cell,** battery cell having electrolyte in liquid form; **wet fly,** (angling) artificial fly used under water; **wet'lands,** swamps and other damp areas of land; **wet nurse,** woman employed to suckle another's child; **wet-nurse** (*v.t.*) (**-nursed, -nurs·ing**), act as wet nurse to; foster, coddle; **wet pack,** (med.) form of bath, in which patient is wrapped in wet sheets, esp. to reduce fever. **wet'ly** *adv.* **wet'ness** *n.* **wet'tish** *adj.* **wet** *v.t.* (**wet** or **wet·ted, wet·ting**). Make wet; **wet'ting agent,** substance that helps water to spread or penetrate. **wet** *n.* Moisture, liquid that wets something, rainy weather; (colloq.) person in favor of allowing sale of alcoholic drinks. **wet'ter** *n.*

weth·er (wĕdh'*er*) *n.* Castrated male sheep.

we've (wēv) *contr.* We have.

wf., w.f. *abbrevs.* (print.) Wrong font.

WFTU, W.F.T.U. *abbrevs.* World Federation of Trade Unions.

whack (hwăk, wăk) *n.* Heavy resounding blow, esp. with stick; **have, take, a ~ at,** (colloq.) attempt; **out of ~,** (colloq.) out of order. **whack** *v.t.* Beat or strike vigorously.

whale[1] (hwāl, wāl) *n.* (pl. **whales,** collect. **whale**). Any marine mammal of order Cetacea, with short forelimbs and tail with horizontal flukes, esp. one of the larger of these, hunted for oil, whalebone, etc.; (colloq.) something impressive in size or amount, or superlative in quality (**~ of a ...**); **blue ~,** large bluish-gray whale, hunted for its oil; **Greenland ~,** whalebone whale, with very large head; **right ~,** whalebone whale, esp. of genus *Balaena*; **whale'back,** anything shaped like back of whale, esp. arched structure over deck of ship, kind of steamboat, much used on the Great Lakes in early 20th c., with spoon bow and main decks covered in and rounded over; **whale′boat**, long narrow rowboat, pointed at both ends, used in whale fishing or carried as lifeboat; **whale′bone**, elastic horny substance growing in series of thin parallel plates in upper jaw of some whales and used in feeding, baleen; strip of this, used as stiffening in clothes etc.; **whale-bone whale**, whale of suborder Mysiceti having whalebone plates in upper jaw; **whale oil**, oil obtained from blubber of whales. **whale** *v.i.* (**whaled, whal·ing**). Fish for whales. **whal′er** *n.* Ship, man, engaged in whale fishing.

whale² (hwāl, wāl) *v.* (**whaled, whal·ing**). Beat, thrash; perform action vigorously or vehemently.

wham (hwăm, wăm) *int.* Expressing sound of forcible impact. ~ *n. & v.* (**whammed, wham·ming**). (Make, strike with) such sound.

wham·my (hwăm′ē, wăm′ē) *n.* (slang) (Thing with) supernatural power, esp. one bringing bad luck.

whang (hwăng, wăng) *v.* (colloq.) Strike heavily and loudly; (of drum etc.) sound (as) under heavy blow. ~ *n.* Whanging sound or blow.

wharf (hwôrf, wôrf) *n.* (pl. **wharves** pr. hwôrvz, wôrvz, **wharfs**). Substantial structure of stone, timber, etc., at water's edge for loading or unloading of ships lying alongside. ~ *v.t.* Discharge (cargo), accommodate (ships), at wharf. **wharf′age** *n.* Provision of accommodation at wharf; charge

made for this; wharves collectively.

Whar·ton (hwôr′ten, wôr′-), **Edith** (1862–1937). American novelist, author of *The House of Mirth, The Age of Innocence, Ethan Frome*, etc.

what (hwŭt, hwŏt, wŭt, wŏt) *pron.* 1. (interrog.) What thing(s)?; what did you say?; ~ **about?**, what is the news concerning?; how do you dispose of the question of?; what do you think of?; ~ **for?**, for what reason or purpose?; ~ (would result) **if?**; ~ **of it?**, the fact has no immediate relevance or interest. 2. **know ~'s what**, have good judgment; know the matter in hand, know what is fitting or profitable; **what′not**, other things of the same kind, anything; some indefinite or trivial thing; (19th c.) piece of furniture with shelves for knick-knacks; **what's-his** (or **-her)-name, what d'you-call-it**, person, thing, whose name the speaker cannot recall. 3. (exclam.) What thing(s)!; how much! 4. (rel.) That or those which; the thing(s) that; anything that; a thing that. **what** *adj.* 1. (interrog.) Asking for selection from indefinite number or for specification of amount, number, kind, etc. 2. (exclam.) How great, how strange, how remarkable in some way; (before adjectives) how. 3. The ... that, any ... that, as much or many ... as. ~ *adv.* 1. (interrog.) To what extent or degree?; how much? 2. ~ **with**, because of, considering. **what** *int.* Exclamation of surprise.

what·ev·er (hwŭtĕv′er, hwŏt-, wŭt-, wŏt-) *pron.* Anything that; any quantity etc. that; no matter what; something of the same kind; (colloq.) as emphatic extension of

Whales are renowned for their high intelligence, and are used for entertainment at places such as Sea World, San Diego, where this killer whale has been taught to perform.

Right from top to bottom: Blue, humpback and sperm **whales**. *Populations of these huge marine mammals have been greatly reduced by modern methods of hunting. After killing, they are taken to shore bases where flensers (above) strip the blubber for making* **whale oil**.

blue whale

hump-backed whale
sperm whale

felloe   spoke

hub or nave

linchpin

axle or arbor   axle-tree

strake

wooden cart-wheel

copper clasps

Mesopotamian circa 2050 B.C.   locomotive driving wheel

*Above left: The **wheatear** migrates to Britain each summer from tropical Africa and India. It is about 6 ins. long and is mainly insectivorous. Once they were killed for food.*

*The earliest representation of a **wheel** on a vehicle is from Uruk, Mesopotamia about 3200 B.C. It is believed that the spoked wheel may have been developed later in Syria.*

"what" implying perplexity or surprise. ~ *adj.* All; any quantity etc. of; (with negatives) at all.

what·so·ev·er (hwŭtsōĕv′er, hwŏt-, wŭt-, wŏt-) *pron. & adj.* (emphat.) Whatever.

wheat (hwēt, wēt) *n.* Cereal plant of genus *Triticum*, esp. *T. aestivum*, closely related to barley and rye; its grain, furnishing meal or flour, the chief ingredient of bread in temperate countries; ~ **germ**, embryo of wheat kernel, added to breads, cereals, etc. for additional vitamins. **wheat′en** *adj.* Of wheat, of grain or flour of wheat.

wheat·ear (hwēt′er, wēt′-) *n.* Small passerine bird (*Oenanthe oenanthe*) of N. parts of Europe, Asia, and Amer., with black wings and distinctive white rump and upper tail feathers. [prob. *whit eeres* white arse]

Wheat·stone (hwēt′stōn, wēt′-), **Sir Charles** (1802–75). English physicist and inventor; ~ **bridge**, device utilizing galvanometer for comparison of electrical resistances.

whee·dle (hwē′del, wē′-) *v.* (**-dled, -dling**). Entice or persuade by soft words or flattery; obtain by such action; use soft words or flattery. **whee′dler** *n.*

wheel (hwēl, wēl) *n.* 1. Circular frame or disk arranged to revolve on axis and used to facilitate motion of vehicle or for various mechanical purposes; wheellike structure or thing; instrument or appliance with wheel as essential part, e.g. bicycle; revolving firework in form of spiral; ancient instrument of torture. 2. Motion as of wheel, circular motion, motion of line as on pivoted end, esp. as military maneuver; **left, right,** ~, words of command to troops in line to swing around on left, right, flank as pivot. 3. **on** ~**s,** (fig.) with rapid easy motion; ~**s within** ~**s,** intricate machinery; indirect or secret agencies. 4. **wheel′barrow,** shallow open box with shafts and one wheel for carrying small loads on; **wheel′base,** distance between points of contact with ground or rail of front and back wheels of vehicle; **wheel′chair,** invalid's chair on wheels; **wheel′horse,** horse harnessed next to wheels and behind another; (fig.) steady, reliable worker; **wheel′house,** structure enclosing large wheel, esp. (naut.) superstructure containing steering wheel; **wheel lock,** (gun with) lock in which powder was fired by friction of small wheel against flint; **wheel′wright,** one who makes or mends wooden wheels of farm vehicles. **wheel** *v.* 1. Turn on axis or pivot, (cause to) move in circle or spiral; change direction, face another way, turn *around* or *about*. 2. Push or pull (wheelchair, bicycle, etc.); ~ **and deal,** engage in political or commercial scheming. **wheeled** *adj.* (esp.) Having wheels. **wheel′less** *adj.*

wheel·er (hwē′ler, wē′-) *n.* (esp.) Wheel horse; (in comb.) vehicle etc. having specified no. of wheels, e.g. *three-*~; ~**-dealer,** (colloq.) schemer.

Wheel·er (hwē′ler, wē′-), **William Almon** (1819–87). Vice president of the U.S. under Rutherford B. Hayes, 1877–81.

wheeze (hwēz, wēz) *v.* (**wheezed, wheez·ing**). Breathe hard with audible whistling or piping sound from dryness or obstruction in throat; utter with wheezing. ~ *n.* 1. Sound of wheezing. 2. (orig., theatr. slang) Joke, esp. one frequently repeated; (slang) catch phrase, trick or dodge. **wheez′y** *adj.* (**wheez·i·er, wheez·i·est**). **wheez′i·ly** *adv.* **wheez′i·ness** *n.*

whelk[1] (hwĕlk, wĕlk) *n.* Marine gastropod mollusk of *Buccinum* and allied genera, with spiral shell, esp. *B. undatum*, common in Europe and N. Amer. and much used for food.

whelk[2] (hwĕlk, wĕlk) *n.* Pimple.

whelp (hwĕlp, wĕlp) *n.* Young dog, puppy; (archaic) young of lion, tiger, bear, and wolf; (derog.) youth. ~ *v.* Bring forth (whelp(s)).

when (hwĕn, wĕn) *adv.* (interrog.) At what time, on what occasion, in what case or circumstances?; **say** ~, (in pouring drink etc.) tell me when to stop. **when** *conj.* At the time that, on the occasion etc., that; at which time etc., and (just) then; seeing that, considering that, since; whereas. ~ *pron.* What or which time.

whence (hwĕns, wĕns) *adv. & conj.* (literary) From where, from what or which place, source, circumstance, etc.; (with *place* etc.) from which.

when·ev·er (hwĕnĕv′er, wĕn-) *adv. & conj.* At whatever time, on whatever occasion; every time that.

when·so·ev·er (hwĕnsōĕv′er, wĕn-) *adv. & conj.* (emphat.) Whenever.

where (hwār, wār) *adv.* (interrog.) At or in what place, position,

The term **'whipsnake'** is a common name applied on the basis of appearance. Above: A southern European Coluber viridiflavus which is a constrictor. Others are venomous.

A species of curlew, the **whimbrel** is more oriented to a terrestrial existence and spends less time than the larger curlew in marshy and coastal locations.

or circumstances?; in what respect, in what, from what source, etc.?; to what place?; in comb. with prepositions, with the general meaning of the preposition followed by *what* or *which* (chiefly archaic or formal), as **whereat′, whereby′, where′fore, wherein′, whereof′, whereon′, whereto′, whereupon′, where′-upon, wherewith′. where** *conj.* In, at, to, etc., place in or at which; and there. ~ *pron.* What place, the place in which.

where·a·bouts (hwār′abowts, wār′-) *adv.* About where, in or near what place or position? ~ *n.pl.* (Approximate) position or situation (of), place in or near which person or thing is.

where·as (hwārǎz′, wār-) *conj.* In view or consideration of the fact that, inasmuch as (chiefly in preamble of legal or other formal document); while on the contrary, but on the other hand.

where·fore (hwār′fōr, -fŏr, wār′-) *adv.* For what?; for what purpose, reason, cause, or end, why?; on which account, for which reason, and therefore; (archaic) because of which, in consequence or as a result of which.

where·so·ev·er (hwārsŏĕv′er, wār-) *adv.* (emphat.) Wherever.

wher·ev·er (hwārĕv′er, wār-) *adv.* At or to whatever place etc.

where·with·al (hwār′wĭdhawl, wār′-) *adv.* (archaic) Wherewith. ~ *n.* (colloq.) Means (esp. pecuniary).

whet (hwĕt, wĕt) *n.* Sharpening; something that whets the appetite, esp. small drink of liquor as appetizer. ~ *v.t.* (**whet′ted, whet′ting**). Sharpen; make (interest, wits, appetite, etc.) (more) acute, keen, or eager; **whet′stone**,

shaped stone, natural or artificial, for giving sharp edge to cutting tools; any hard fine-grained rock from which whetstones are made. **whet′ter** *n.*

wheth·er (hwĕdh′er, wĕdh′-) *conj.* Introducing dependent question or its equivalent expressing doubt, choice, etc., between alternations, or, freq. as ordinary sign of indirect interrogation (*if*). ~ *pron.* & *adj.* (archaic) Which of the two.

whew (hwū) *int.* Exclamation of astonishment, consternation, etc.

whey (hwā, wā) *n.* Serum or watery part remaining after separation of curd from milk, esp. in cheese-making. **whey′ey** (hwā′ē, wā-) *adj.*

which (hwĭch, wĭch) *adj.* & *pron.* 1. (interrog.) What one(s) of a stated or implied set of persons, things, or alternatives. 2. (rel.) Relative adjective and pronoun, introducing additional statement about the antecedent. = "and that (it, they, etc.)," "that."

which·ev·er (hwĭchĕv′er, wĭch-) *adj.* & *pron.* Any or either (of definite set of persons or things) that . . .; no matter which.

which·so·ev·er (hwĭchsŏĕv′er, wĭch-) *adj.* & *pron.* (emphat.) Whichever.

whiff (hwĭf, wĭf) *n.* 1. Puff, waft, of air, smoke, odor, etc. 2. Slight smell (also fig.). 3. ~ **of grapeshot**, (fig.) violent suppression of riot, protest, etc. **whiff** *v.* Blow or puff lightly; (baseball slang) strike out.

whif·fle (hwĭf′el, wĭf′-) *v.* (**-fled, -fling**). 1. Puff lightly; move as if blown by puff of air. 2. Make light whistling sound. ~ *n.* Slight movement of air.

whif·fle·tree (hwĭf′eltrē, wĭf′-) *n.* Crossbar pivoted in middle, to ends of which traces are fastened in cart, plow, etc.

Whig (hwĭg, wĭg) *adj.* & *n.* 1. (Member) of political party in Great Britain that, after the Revolution of 1688, aimed at subordinating the power of the Crown to that of Parliament and the upper classes, passed the 1832 Reform Bill, and in the 19th c. was succeeded by the Liberal party. 2. (Amer. hist.) Supporter of the Revolution. 3. (Member) of political party formed c1834 in opp. to Democratic Party and remaining one of the two chief U.S. parties until its collapse in 1852. **Whig′-ger·y, Whig′gism** *ns.* **Whig′gish** *adj.* **Whig′gish·ly** *adv.* **Whig′gish·ness** *n.* [used earlier of Scotch Covenanters, prob. short for *whiggamer, -more,* of uncertain origin]

while (hwīl, wīl) *n.* Space of time, esp. time spent in doing something (now only in **worth (one′s)** ~, worth doing, advantageous); **a** ~, (colloq.) a considerable time, some time; **all the, this,** ~, during the whole time (that). **while** *conj.* During the time that, for as long as, at the same time as; when on the contrary, whereas, although; and at the same time, besides that. ~ *v.t.* (**whiled,** **whil·ing**). Pass (time etc.) *away* in leisurely manner or without weariness.

whi·lom (hwī′lom, wī′-) *adv.* & *adj.* (archaic) (That existed, or was such) at some past time; former(ly).

whilst (hwīlst, wīlst) *adv.* & *conj.* (Brit.) = WHILE.

whim (hwĭm, wĭm) *n.* Sudden fancy, caprice, freakish notion.

whim·brel (hwĭm′brel, wĭm′-) *n.* Small curlew (*Numenius phaeopus*) of both Amer. and European coasts.

whim·per (hwĭm′per, wĭm′-) *v.i.* Cry querulously, whine softly. ~ *n.* Feeble whining broken cry. **whim′per·ing·ly** *adv.*

whim·si·cal (hwĭm′zĭkal, wĭm′-) *adj.* Capricious, fanciful, characterized by whims. **whim′-si·cal·ly** *adv.* **whim·si·cal′i·ty** *n.* (pl. **-ties**).

whim·sy (hwĭm′zē, wĭm-) *n.* (pl. **-sies**). Crotchet, whim.

whine (hwīn, wīn) *n.* Long-drawn complaining cry (as) of dog; suppressed nasal tone; feeble, mean, or undignified complaint. ~ *v.* (**whined, whin·ing**). Utter whine(s); utter, complain, whiningly. **whin′y** *adj.* (**whin·i·er, whin·i·est**) **whin′er** *n.* **whin′-ing·ly** *adv.*

whin·ny (hwĭn′ē, wĭn′-) *v.i.* (**-nied, -ny·ing**). Neigh gently or joyfully. ~ *n.* Whinnying sound.

whip (hwĭp, wĭp) *n.* 1. Instrument for flogging or beating, or for urging on horse etc., consisting usu. of lash attached to short or long stick. 2. Official, in legislative body, appointed to maintain discipline among members of his party, give them necessary information, and secure their attendance esp. when a bill is up for voting. 3. Whipping or lashing motion, esp. slight bending movement produced by sudden strain. 4. Dessert made with whipped cream or egg whites. 5. **whip′cord**, thin tough kind of hempen cord for whiplashes etc.; close-woven worsted fabric with fine close diagonal ribs, used for riding breeches etc.; **whip hand**, hand in which whip is held; (fig.) upper hand, control (*of*), advantage; **whip′lash**, lash of whip; object resembling this; **whiplash injury**, injury to neck caused by sudden jerk of head in collision of vehicle etc.; **whip′saw**, saw with very long narrow tapering blade; two-man crosscut saw; (fig.) swindle or defeat (opponent) by collusion of two poker players, political allies, etc.; **whip scorpion**, arachnid resembling scorpion but without sting and usu. with lashlike organ at end of body; **whip′snake, whip snake**, any of various slender snakes; **whip stitch**, (sew with) whipping stitch (*v.* sense 3). **whip**

v. (**whipped, whip·ping**). 1. Move suddenly or briskly, snatch, dart; make *up* quickly or hastily. 2. Beat, drive or urge on, (as) with whip; lash, flog; beat up (eggs, cream, etc.) into froth; (angling) throw line or bait on water with movement like stroke of whip; (colloq.) overcome, defeat. 3. Bind around (rope, stick, etc.) with close covering of twine, thread, etc.; sew over and over, overcast, esp. hem, or gather (fabric) by overcasting rolled edge with fine stitches. 4. ~ **graft**, (make) graft with slit in end of both scion and stock, tongue of each being inserted in slit of the other.

whip·per·snap·per (hwĭp′er-snăper, wĭp′-) *n.* (colloq.) Small child; young and insignificant but impertinent person.

whip·pet (hwĭp′ĭt, wĭp′-) *n.* Small dog like greyhound used for racing, and orig. bred (19th c.) in N. of England from cross between greyhound and terrier or spaniel.

whip·ping (hwĭp′ĭng, wĭp′-) *n.* (esp.) Overcasting of hem; ~ **boy**, (hist.) boy educated with young prince and chastised in his stead (also fig.); ~ **post**, post to which offenders were tied to be whipped.

whip·poor·will (hwĭp′erwĭl, wĭp′-, hwĭperwĭl′, wĭp′-) *n.* (pl. **-wills**, collect. **-will**). Nocturnal insectivorous bird (*Caprimulgus vociferus*) of eastern N. Amer.; an unusually skillful flier. [f. its cry]

whir (hwer, wer) *n.* & *v.i.* (**whirred, whir·ring**). (Make) continuous buzzing or vibratory sound, as of bird's rapidly fluttering wings, swiftly turning wheel, etc.

whirl (hwerl, werl) *v.* Swing

Known by various names around the world — tornado, twister willy-willy — whirlwinds can be devastating in settled districts. This one in Kenya caused minimal damage.

around and around, revolve rapidly; send, travel, swiftly in orbit or curve; convey, go, rapidly in wheeled conveyance; (of brain, senses, etc.) be giddy, seem to spin around; **whirl′pool**, part of river, sea, etc., where water is in constant and usu. rapid circular motion; **whirlpool bath**, therapeutic bath in which current of hot water is swirled by agitating device around immersed body or parts of body; **whirl′wind**, mass of air whirling rapidly around and around and moving progressively over surface of land or water (also fig. of violent motion); tornado; (also attrib.) hurried, intense and hasty; **whirl′ybird**, (slang) helicopter. **whirl** *n.* Whirling, swift, or violent movement; disturbance, commotion; distracted or dizzy state. **whirl′er** *n.*

whirl·i·gig (hwer′lĭgĭg, wer′-) *n.* Spinning toy like sails of windmill revolving on stick; merry-go-round; revolving motion.

whisk (hwĭsk, wĭsk) *n.* 1. Bunch of twigs, grass, hair, bristles, etc., for brushing or dusting; instrument for beating up eggs, cream, etc., into a froth; slender hairlike part or appendage, as on tails of certain insects etc.; panicle of certain plants, esp. common millet. 2. Quick sweeping movement (as) of whisk, animal's tail, etc. ~ *v.* Convey, go, move with light rapid sweeping motion; brush or sweep lightly and rapidly from surface; beat up (eggs, cream, etc.), esp. with whisk.

whisk·er (hwĭs′ker, wĭs′-) *n.* 1. (usu. pl.) Hair on cheeks or sides of face of man. 2. Each of set of projecting hairs or bristles on upper lip or about mouth of cat or other animals, birds, etc. **whisk′ered, whisk′er·y** *adjs.*

whis·key, Brit. and Canadian **whis·ky** (hwĭs′kē, wĭs′-) *ns.* (pl.

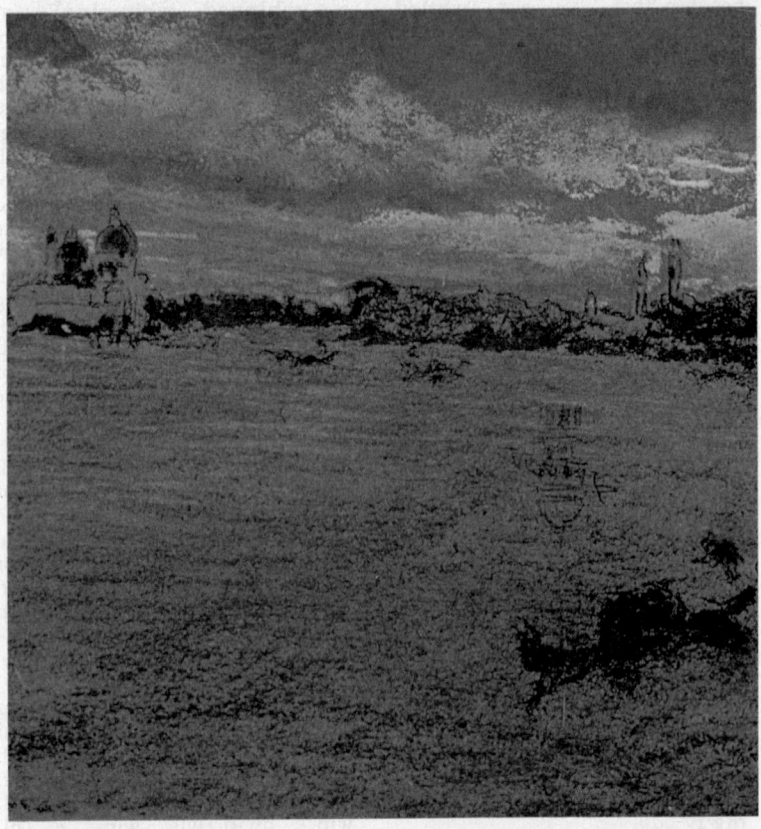

Influenced by Courbet and prints of Japanese painters, **Whistler** was concerned with color as displayed in 'Stormy Sunset' (above). However, his work was noted for its individuality and was not linked to any movement.

-keys, -kies). Alcoholic liquor distilled, orig. in Scotland and Ireland, from malted barley, rye, corn, or other grains; drink of whiskey; ~ **jack** = CANADA jay; ~ **sour**, cocktail of whiskey, lemon juice, and sugar.

whis·per (hwĭs′per, wĭs′-) *n.* Speech or vocal sound without vibration of vocal cords; remark uttered thus; soft rustling sound; insinuation, rumor, hint. ~ *v.* Utter in whisper, esp. for sake of secrecy; communicate etc. quietly or confidentially; (of leaves etc.) make soft rustling sound;

whist (hwĭst, wĭst) *n.* Game of cards, played (usu.) by two pairs of opponents with pack of 52 cards, in which one suit is trumps and tricks are taken by highest card of suit led or highest trump.

whis·tle (hwĭs′el, wĭs′-) *n.* 1. Tubular wind instrument of wood, metal, etc., producing shrill tone by forcing air or steam against a sharp edge or into a bell and causing it to vibrate, used for giving signal or alarm; also as musical toy, usu. of tin and pierced with six holes; (joc., colloq.) mouth or throat (esp. in **wet one's** ~, take a drink); ~ **stop**, (colloq.) small unimportant town on railroad; pause of train at such a station for politician to make speech [from practice of announcing stop at country place by sounding train whistle]. 2. Whistling, clear shrill sound produced by forcing breath through lips contracted to narrow opening; similar sound made by whistle or pipe; clear shrill note of bird; any similar sound, as of wind blowing through trees or missile flying through air. **whistle** *v.* (**-tled, -tling**). Make sound of whistle with mouth, esp. as call or signal, expression of derision, contempt, astonishment, enthusiasm, etc.; utter, produce, clear shrill sound or note; blow whistle; produce, utter, by whistling; call, send, (*away, off, up*) by whistling; ~ **for**, (colloq.) seek or expect in vain, go without.

whis·tler (hwĭs′ler, wĭs′-) *n.* One who whistles; (local) any of various whistling birds; (also **whistling marmot**) marmot (*Marmota caligata*) common in mountains of northwestern N. Amer.

Whis·tler (hwĭs′ler, wĭs′-), **James Abbott McNeill** (1834–1903). American-born painter, etcher, and wit, active chiefly in England.

whit (hwĭt, wĭt) *n.* (chiefly with neg.) Particle, least possible amount.

white (hwīt, wīt) *adj.* (**whit·er, whit·est**). Of the color of snow or milk, of color produced by reflection or transmission of all kinds of light in proportions in which they exist in complete visible spectrum, without apparent absorption; of some color approaching this, pale, less dark than other things of the same kind; (fig.) innocent, unstained, harmless; of a light-skinned race or people; Caucasian; (pol., usu. Russian) of royalist, counterrevolutionary, or reactionary tendency (opp. RED); ~ **ant**, termite; **white′bait** (pl. -**bait**), any of various small silvery-white fish cooked and eaten whole; **white bear**, polar bear; **white′cap**, white-crested wave; **white-collar**, engaged in, being, nonmanual work; **white corpuscle**, (also **white blood cell, white blood corpuscle**) leucocyte; **white dwarf**, one of class of small stars of great density radiating white light; **white-eye** (pl. -**eyes**), Old World passerine bird (family Zosteropidae) with white ring around eye; **white elephant**, Indian elephant with pale-colored skin, venerated as rarity in Siam etc.; (fig.) burdensome or useless possession (from story that kings of Siam made presents of these animals to those whom they wished to ruin by cost of their maintenance); **white feather**, symbol or emblem of cowardice (from white feather in gamecock's tail, held to show that he is not purebred); **white′fish** (pl. -**fish, -fish·es**), any light-colored or silvery fish, as cod, haddock, whiting, etc.; lake fish of *Coregonus* and allied genera, resembling salmon and valued as food; **White Friar**, Carmelite; **white gold**, white-colored alloy of gold, esp. alloy with nickel and zinc, resembling platinum; **white-haired** (or -**headed**) **boy**, favorite; **white heat**, degree of temperature (higher than red heat) at which body radiates white light (freq. fig. of passions etc.); **white-hot**, at white heat; **White House**, official residence of U.S. president, Washington, D.C.; **white lead**, basic lead carbonate, a heavy white powder, used as white pigment; **white lie**, innocent, harmless, or trivial lie, fib; **white man's burden**, (hist.) supposed task of leading subject colonial people of dark races; **white meat**, light-colored meat of poultry; **white metal**, white or silver-colored alloy, esp. one that is easily fusible and so suitable for lining high-speed bearings; **White Nile**: see NILE; **white noise**, almost inaudible sound containing many frequencies with approximately equal energies; **white′out**, atmospheric condition, esp. in polar regions, marked by dense snow cloud and total obscuration of physical features; **white paper**,

The **White House**, a 100-room mansion, was completed in 1800 after a design by James Hoban. He supervised reconstruction after it was burnt during the British invasion of 1814.

white part of eyeball surrounding colored iris; member of a light-skinned race or people, Caucasian; white butterfly, pigeon, pig, etc.; member of political party called "white," reactionary, legitimist, extreme conservative; player having white (or light-colored) pieces in chess etc.

White·field (hwīt′fēld, wīt′-), **George** (1714–70). English religious reformer, one of the founders of METHODISM, who engaged in evangelical preaching in N. Amer., adopted Calvinistic views, and formed a party of Calvinistic Methodists.

whit·en (hwī′ten, wī′-) v. Make, become, white or whiter. **whit′en·er, whit′en·ing** ns.

White (hwīt, wīt) **Sands National Monument.** Area 219 sq. mi. (567 sq. km) in south central New Mexico containing world's largest surface deposit of gypsum; **White Sands Proving Grounds**, area SW. of White Sands National Monument used as test range for missiles; site of explosion of first atom bomb, 1945.

whit·ey (hwī′tē, wī′-) n. 1. (slang) Very blond man or boy. 2. (slang, derog.) White person or white people as group.

whith·er (hwĭdh′er, wĭdh′-) adv. (archaic) To where.

whit·ing[1] (hwī′tĭng, wī′-) n. Preparation of finely powdered chalk used for paints, putty, etc.

whit·ing[2] (hwī′tĭng, wī′-) n. (pl. **-ings**, collect. **-ing**). Common

governmental report disclosing and explaining official position; **white race**, (loosely or pop.) Caucasian people; **White Russia**, Byelorussia; **White Russian**, (native, language) of White Russia; **white sale**: see SALE; **white sapphire**, colorless variety of sapphire; **white sauce**, sauce of flour or cornstarch, milk, and butter, variously flavored; **White Sea**, gulf of Arctic Ocean in U.S.S.R.; **white slave**, woman held unwillingly for purpose of prostitution, esp. one transported from one state or country to another; **white slaver, slavery** (ns.); **white-tailed deer**, N. Amer. deer (*Odocoileus virginianus*) having a tail white on the underside; **white′thorn**, hawthorn; **white′-**

throat, **white-throated sparrow**, N. Amer. sparrow (*Zorotrichia albicollis*) with sweet plaintive song and white patch on throat; **white′wall**, rubber automobile tire with white band on outer wall; **white′wash**, liquid composition of lime and water or whiting, size, and water, for whitening walls, ceilings, etc.; (fig.) glossing over person's or institution's faults; **white′wash** (v.), apply whitewash to (lit. and fig.). **white′ly** adv. **white′ness** n. **whit′ish** adj. **white** n. White or light-colored part of anything; white or nearly white color; white pigment; white clothes or material; translucent viscid fluid surrounding yolk of egg, becoming white when coagulated; sclerotic coat,

The **golden whistler** (*Pachycephala pectoralis*) is found only in coastal regions of eastern, south-eastern and south-western Australia where it inhabits fairly dense woodland.

The large copper stills at Cardew Distillery in Scotland. Malted barley liquor is heated by furnaces beneath the stills and the **whiskey** produced is colorless. The color is added before bottling.

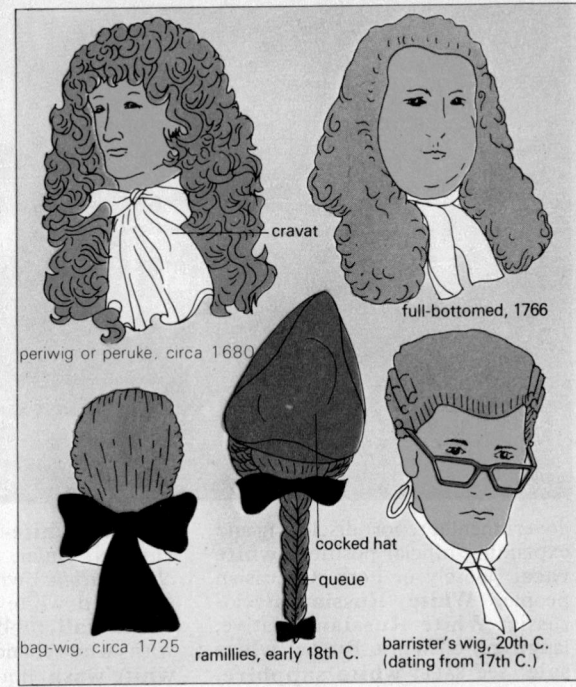

cravat

full-bottomed, 1766

periwig or peruke, circa 1680

cocked hat

queue

bag-wig, circa 1725

ramillies, early 18th C.

barrister's wig, 20th C. (dating from 17th C.)

small codlike fish (genus *Menticirrhus*) with pearly white flesh, used as food; fish resembling this.

Whit·man (hwĭt′man, wĭt′-), **Walt(er)** (1819–92). Amer. poet; author of *Leaves of Grass, Drum Taps*, etc.

Whit·ney[1] (hwĭt′nē, wĭt′-), **Eli** (1765–1825). Amer. inventor of cotton gin, 1793.

Whit·ney[2] (hwĭt′nē, wĭt′-), **Mount.** Highest mountain, 14,495 ft. (4,421 m), in U.S., excluding Alaska, in Sierra Nevada range in E. central California.

Whit·ti·er (hwĭt′ēer, wĭt′-), **John Greenleaf** (1807–92). Amer. poet; author of *The Barefoot Boy, Snow-Bound, Barbara Frietchie*, etc.

whit·tle (hwĭt′el, wĭt′-) *v.* (**-tled, -tling**). Dress, pare, with knife; cut thin slices or shavings from surface of, make or shape thus; (fig.) reduce amount or effect of by successive abstractions, pare *down*, take *away* by degrees.

whiz, whizz (hwĭz, wĭz) *vbs.* (**whizzed, whiz·zing**). (Cause to) make sound as of body rushing through air; move swiftly (as) with such sound. **whiz** *n.* Act, sound, of whizzing; (slang) person of outstanding skill, wizard.

WHO *abbrev.* World Health Organization.

who (hōō) *pron.* (obj. **whom** pr. hōōm, poss. **whose** pr. hōōz). 1. (interrog.) What or which person(s); what sort of person(s) in regard to origin, position, authority, etc.; *Who's Who*, title of reference book of contemporary biography (first issued 1849) and of similar works. 2. (rel.) (Person or persons) that; and, but, he (she,

they); (archaic) the or any person(s) that.

whoa (hwō, wō) *int.* Word of command to horse etc. to stop or stand still.

who·dun·it (hōōdŭn′ĭt) *n.* (slang) Detective or mystery story.

who·ev·er (hōōĕv′er) *pron.* Whatever person(s), any(one) who; no matter who.

whole (hōl) *adj.* In sound condition, uninjured, not broken or divided, intact; integral, without fractions; undiminished, without subtraction; all, all of; **with one's ~ heart**, heartily, with concentrated effort, etc., hence **whole′heart′ed, whole′heart′-edly, whole′heart′edness; go the whole hog**, go to the utmost limit; act etc. without reservation; **whole milk**, milk as given by the cow, containing all its butterfat and other elements; **whole note**, note having duration of four beats; **whole number**, number that can be got from zero by adding or subtracting units; **whole-wheat**, made from the entire wheat kernel. **whole** *n.* Full, complete, or total amount (*of*); complete thing; organic unity, complex system, total made up of parts. **whole′ness** *n.*

whole·sale (hōl′sāl) *n.* Selling of articles in large quantities to be retailed by others. **~** *adj.* Selling by wholesale; pertaining to sale in bulk; unlimited, indiscriminate; doing, done, largely or profusely. **~** *adv.* In large quantities, in bulk;

in abundance, extensively, indiscriminately. **whole′sal·er** *n.* One who sells wholesale. **whole·sale** *v.* (**-saled, -sal·ing**).

whole·some (hōl′som) *adj.* Promoting, conducive to, health or well-being; beneficial, salutary, salubrious; not morbid, healthy. **whole′some·ly** *adv.* **whole′some·ness** *n.*

who′ll (hōōl) *contr.* Who shall; who will.

whol·ly (hō′lē, hōl′lē) *adv.* Entirely, completely, to the full extent, altogether; exclusively.

whom (hōōm) *pron.* Objective (accus., dat.) case of WHO.

whom·ev·er (hōōmĕv′er) *pron.* Objective case of WHOEVER.

whom·so·ev·er (hōōmsōĕv′er) *pron.* Objective case of WHOSOEVER.

whoop (hōōp, hwōōp, wōōp) *int.* Cry expressing excitement, exultation, etc. (used esp. by N. Amer. Indians as signal or war cry). **~** *n.* Cry of "whoop"; characteristic drawing-in of breath after coughing in whooping cough. **~** *v.i.* Utter whoop; **whoop·ing** (hōō′ping, hōōp′ing) **cough**, infectious disease, esp. of children, with violent convulsive cough followed by whoop, caused by a bacillus, *Haemophilus pertussis*; **whoop′ing crane**, very large white wading bird (*Grus americana*), nearly extinct. **whoop′er** *n.*

whoop·ee (hwōōp′ē′, wōōp′ē′, hwōō′pē′, wōō′-) *int.* (slang) Exclamation of exuberant joy.

(hwo͞o´e͝, wo͝o´e͝, hwo͞o´pe͞, wo͞o´-)
n. (slang) Cry of "whoopee"; **make ~**, (slang) rejoice noisily or hilariously, have a good time.

whoosh (hwo͞osh, wo͝osh, hwo͝osh, wo͞osh) *int.* Expressing sound of rushing air or water. **~** *n. & v.* (Make or cause) such sound.

whop (hwŏp, wŏp) *v.t.* (**whopped, whop·ping**). (slang) Thrash, defeat, overcome. **whop´-ping** *adj.* Very large or great. **whop´per** *n.* Very large thing; monstrous falsehood.

whore (hōr, hôr, hoor) *n.* Female prostitute. **whore´dom** *n.* Fornication. **whore´mong·er** *n.* Fornicator; pimp. **whore** *v.i.* (**whored, whor·ing**). Have to do with whore(s), fornicate; (fig., archaic, after Deut. 31) **go a-whoring after strange gods** etc., practice idolatry or iniquity. **whor´ish** *adj.*

whorl (hwẽrl, wẽrl, hwôrl, wôrl) *n.* Small flywheel or pulley on spindle to steady its motion; convolution, coil, something suggesting whirling movement, esp. (of fingerprint) complete circle formed by central papillary ridges; each turn of spiral shell or any spiral structure; (bot.) ring of leaves, flowers, etc., springing from stem or axis at same level. **whorled** *adj.*

who's (ho͞oz) *contr.* Who has; who is.

whose (ho͞oz) *pron.* Possessive case of WHO.

who·so·ev·er (ho͞oso͝ev´er) *pron.* (emphat.) Whoever.

why (hwī, wī) *adv.* 1. (interrog.) On what ground, for what reason, with what purpose. 2. (rel.) On account of which. **~** *n.* (pl. **whys**). Reason, cause, explanation, esp. in **~(s) and wherefore(s)**. **why** *int.* Exclamation expressing (esp. mild or slight) surprise, slight protest, etc., or emphasizing or calling attention to following statement, in opposition to possible doubt or objection.

WI *abbrev.* Wisconsin.

W.I. *abbrev.* West Indies.

wick (wĭk) *n.* Bundle of fiber, now usu. loosely twisted or woven cotton, immersed at one end in oil or grease of lamp, candle, etc., and drawing it up to maintain flame at other end.

wick·ed (wĭk´ĭd) *adj.* Sinful, iniquitous, vicious, morally depraved; (colloq., usu. joc.) very or excessively bad, malicious, mischievous, roguish; **W ~ Bible**, English edition of 1632 with "not" omitted in 7th commandment. **wick´ed·ly** *adv.* **wick´ed·ness** *n.*

wick·er (wĭk´er) *n.* Plaited pliant twigs or reeds as material of baskets, chairs, mats, etc.; **wick´erwork**, things made of wicker; craft of making them.

Wickerwork abounds in Asian countries such as here in Sri Lanka. The elephants make interesting decorations while the baskets serve a practical purpose.

wick·et (wĭk´ĭt) *n.* 1. (also **~ gate**) Small gate or door, esp. one made in or placed beside large one. 2. (cricket) Either of two sets of stumps at which bowler aims ball and which batsman defends; **wick´-etkeeper**, fielder stationed behind wicket; **sticky wicket**, difficult or unpleasant situation. 3. (croquet) Small wire arch through which player tries to drive ball.

wide (wīd) *adj.* (**wid·er, wid·est**). 1. Measuring much from side to side; broad, not narrow; in width (as *20 ft.* **~**). 2. Extending far, embracing much, of great extent; not tight, close, or restricted; loose, free, liberal, unprejudiced, general. 3. Open to full extent. 4. At considerable distance from point or mark, not within reasonable distance of. 5. **~-angle**, (of lens) having short focus and field extending through wide angle; **wide-eyed**, with eyes wide open, gazing intently; (fig.) wondering, naïve; **wide´mouthed**, with a wide mouth; with mouth opened wide in astonishment etc. **wide´ly** *adv.* **wide** *adv.* Over or through large space or region, far abroad (now only in **far and ~**); at wide interval(s), far apart; with wide opening, to full extent, at a distance to one side, so as to miss mark or way, astray; **wide-awake**, fully awake; (colloq.) on the alert, fully aware of what is going on, sharp-witted, knowing; **wide´-spread´**, widely disseminated or

diffused.

wid·en (wīden) *v.* Make, become, wide or wider. **wid´en·er** *n.*

widg·eon, wi·geon (wĭj´on) *ns.* (pl. **-eons**, collect. **-eon**). Either of two surface-feeding ducks, *Mareca americana* of N. Amer., having white head, or *M. penelope* of the Old World, having rusty head.

wid·ow (wĭd´ō) *n.* Woman who has lost her husband by death and has not married again; **widow's mite**: see MITE[1]; **widow's peak**, V-shaped growth of hair in center of forehead. **wid´ow·hood** *n.* **widow** *v.t.* Make widow or widower of (usu. in past part.); bereave, deprive *of.*

wid·ow·er (wĭd´ōer) *n.* Man who has lost his wife by death and has not married again.

width (wĭdth) *n.* Distance or measurement from side to side; large extent; piece of material of same width as when woven, esp. one of such pieces sewn together to make garment etc.

wield (wēld) *v.t.* Control, sway, hold and use, manage. **wield´er** *n.*

wie·ner (wē´ner) *n.* Frankfurter.

wife (wīf) *n.* (pl. **wives** pr. wīvz). 1. Married woman esp. in relation to her husband. 2. Woman, esp. one who is old and rustic or uneducated (now rare exc. in **old wives' tale**, foolish or superstitious tradition). **wife´hood** *n.* **wife´less** *adj.* **wife´ly** *adj.* (**-li·er, -li·est**).

wig (wĭg) *n.* Artificial head of hair worn esp. to conceal baldness, or as part of professional, ceremonial, or fashionable costume.

wi·geon = WIDGEON.

wig·gle (wĭg´el) v.t. (**-gled, -gling**). (colloq.) (Cause to) move from side to side.

wig·wag (wĭg´wăg) v. (**-wagged, -wag·ging**). (colloq.) Wag; esp. wave flag, light, etc., to and fro in signaling.

wig·wam (wĭg´wŏm, -wawm) n. Tent or cabin of N. Amer. Indian tribes of region of Great Lakes and eastward, formed of bark, matting, or hides stretched over frame of converging poles.

wild (wīld) adj. 1. Living or growing in state of nature, not domesticated, tame, or cultivated. 2. Uncivilized, barbarous. 3. Rebellious, lawless; not under control or restraint; tempestuous; rash, random. 4. Violently excited or agitated; passionately desirous (to do); elated, enthusiastic; haphazard, reckless, extravagant. 5. **wild´cat** (pl. **-cats**, collect. **-cat**), N. Amer. wild species of cat of genus Lynx, larger and stronger than domestic cat and similar in color and marking to tabby; any of various small undomesticated cats, as lynx, serval, ocelot, etc.; (colloq.) unsound or risky enterprise (freq. attrib.); **wildcat** (v.t.) (**-catted, -catting**), prospect esp. for oil in unexplored or unpromising area; **wildcat strike**, unofficial strike; **wild-eyed**, (1) having angry, distraught, or demented look in the eyes; (2) extremely foolish, irrational, or impractical; **wild´fire**, highly inflammable composition very difficult to extinguish, formerly used in warfare etc. (now chiefly in **spread like wildfire**, spread with immense rapidity); phos-

phorescent light; vast conflagration; **wild´fowl** (pl. **-fowls**, collect. **-fowl**), wild birds, esp. wild game; **wild goose**, any undomesticated goose, in England usu. graylag, in N. Amer. the Canada goose; **wild-goose chase**, foolish, fruitless, or hopeless quest; **wild indigo**, any of a genus (Baptisia) of N. Amer. leguminous plants, esp. B. tinctoria, having trifoliate leaves and yellow flowers; **wild man**, savage; **wild oat**, wild grass of genus Avena, resembling oats; **sow one's wild oats**, indulge in youthful indiscretions and escapades; **wild pitch**, (baseball) pitch that catcher cannot be expected to stop and that allows a runner to advance; **wild rice**, tall aquatic grass (Zizania aquatica) of eastern N. Amer. yielding edible grains; **Wild West, wild West**, western states of U.S. during period in which they were lawless frontier districts; **wild´-wood**, (chiefly poet.) uncultivated or unfrequented wood. **wild´ly** adv. **wild´ness** n. **wild** n. (usu. pl.) Desert, wild tract.

Wilde (wīld), **Oscar Fingal O'Flahertie Wills** (1854–1900). Irish-born author of comedies, novels, and verse; wrote The Picture of Dorian Gray, The Importance of Being Ernest, Lady Windermere's Fan, etc.

wil·de·beest (wĭl´debēst) n. (pl. **-beests**, collect. **-beest**). Gnu. [S. Afr. Du., = "wild beast"]

wil·der·ness (wĭl´dernĭs) n.

Desert, uncultivated and un-inhabited land or tract; mingled, confused, or vast assemblage of; **in the ~**, (of political party, with ref. to Num. 14) out of office.

wild´ing (wīl´dĭng) n. Wild plant, esp. wild crab apple; fruit of such plant.

wile (wīl) n. Trick, cunning procedure, artifice. ~ v.t. (**wiled, wil·ing**). Lure.

wil·ful = WILLFUL.

Wil·kins[1] (wĭl´kĭnz), **Maurice Hugh Frederick** (1916–). British physicist; co-discoverer of DNA molecular structure; received Nobel Prize for medicine, 1962, with WATSON and CRICK.

Wil·kins[2] (wĭl´kĭnz), **Roy** (1901–). Amer. Civil rights leader; executive secretary and director of NAACP, 1955–77.

will[1] (wĭl) n. 1. Faculty or function that is directed to conscious and intentional action; act, action, of willing; intention or determination that something shall be done or happen; desire, wish, inclination (to do); (archaic or poet.) what one desires; **against one's ~**, unwillingly; **at ~**, according to one's volition or choice, as one will; at the command or disposal (of); **with a ~**, resolutely, determinedly, energetically; **will´-power**, (strength of) will, esp. power to control one's own actions etc. 2. Person's formal declaration, usu. in writing, of his intention as to disposal of his property etc. after

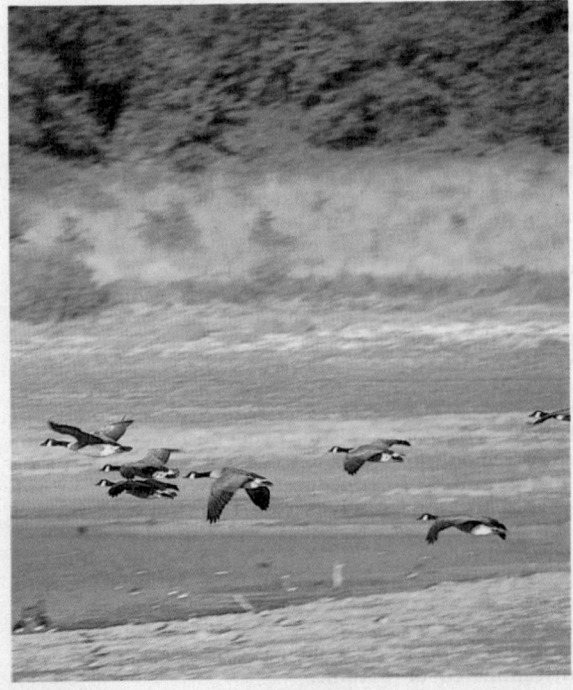

*All species of non-domesticated ducks and geese can be termed **wildfowl**. These Canadian geese take off from a pond in North America.*

*Despite a superficial resemblance to cattle, the **wildebeest** is the largest antelope. Although fierce in the wild, youngsters raised in captivity have been domesticated.*

his death; document in which this is expressed. **will** *v.* (**willed, will·ing**). 1. Determine by the will, choose or decide to do something or that something shall be done; exercise the will; bring, get, (*into* etc.) by exercise of will; control (person), induce (another) *to do*, by exercise of one's will. 2. Direct by will or testament; dispose of by will, bequeath. **willed** *adj.*

will[2] (wǐl) *v.t.* (past **would** pr. wo͞od). Desire (thing; archaic); want, desire, choose, to; wish that; consent, be prevailed on, to; intend unconditionally; be accustomed, be observed from time to time, to; be likely to. ～ *v.aux.* Forming compound tenses or moods expressing (in second and third pers.) plain future or conditional statement or question, (in first pers.) future or conditional statement expressing speaker's will or intention.

Wil·lem·stad (wǐl'emstaht). Capital of Netherlands Antilles on S. coast of Curaçao.

wil·let (wǐl'ǐt) *n.* (pl. **-lets**, collect. **-let**). Large N. Amer. shorebird of sandpiper family (*Catotrophorus semipalmatus*), with warbling call and striking wing pattern in flight.

will·ful, wil·ful (wǐl'fŭl) *adjs.* Asserting or disposed to assert one's own will against instruction, persuasion, etc.; obstinately self-willed; deliberate, intentional, showing perversity or self-will. **will'ful·ly** *adv.* **will'ful·ness** *n.*

Wil·liam[1] (wǐl'yam). Name of four kings of England: ～ **I** (*c*1027–1087), "the Conqueror," Duke of Normandy, claimed the English throne, invaded England and

defeated Harold at the Battle of Hastings (1066); reigned 1066–87; ～ **II** (1056–1100), "Rufus," son of William I; reigned 1087–1100; ～ **III** (1650–1702), Prince of Orange, married Mary, daughter of James II, and reigned jointly with her 1689–94, and alone (after her death) until 1702; ～ **IV** (1765–1837), third son of George III, succeeded his brother, George IV in 1830.

Wil·liam[2] (wǐl'yam). Name of three princes of Orange: ～ **I** (1533–84), "the Silent," led the insurrection of the Netherlands

William III of Great Britain was born in the Netherlands. He accepted joint rule of England with Mary to obtain forces to save Holland from France.

Oscar Wilde as portrayed by Toulouse-Lautrec in 1895, not long before he was sentenced to two years jail for homosexuality. Wilde's finest plays were written between 1891 and 1895.

against Spain and became (1580) the first chief magistrate of the United Provinces of the Netherlands; ～ **II** (1626–50); ～ **III** = William III of England (see WILLIAM[1]).

Wil·liam[3] (wǐl'yam). Anglicized form of name (*Wilhelm*) of two German emperors and kings of Prussia: ～ **I** (1797–1888), king of Prussia 1861–88, first German emperor 1871–88; ～ **II** (1859–1941), "the Kaiser," grandson of William I, succeeded his father, Frederick III, 1888, abdicated 1918 after the defeat of Germany, and fled to Holland.

Wil·liams[1] (wǐl'yamz), **Roger** (1603?–83). English clergyman in Amer.; founded Providence, earliest settlement in Rhode Island.

Wil·liams[2] (wǐl'yamz), **Tennessee** (1914–). (orig. name Thomas Lanier Williams) Amer. playwright; author of *A Streetcar Named Desire, Summer and Smoke*, etc.

wil·lies (wǐl'ēz) *n.pl.* (slang) Nervous feeling of discomfort or fear.

will·ing (wǐl'ǐng) *adj.* Consenting, disposed (*to* do); ready to be of use or service; given, rendered, performed, etc., will-

Better known as the 'sailor king' of England, William IV reigned only for 7 years. However during the first two years of his reign, he had considerable influence on British politics.

ingly. **will'ing·ly** *adv.* **will'ing·- ness** *n.*

wil·li·waw (wĭl'iwaw) *n.* Sudden blast of chill wind gusting down from mountains near the sea, as in Alaska and the Strait of Magellan.

will-o'-the-wisp (wĭl'odhe wĭsp') *n.* = IGNIS FATUUS; (fig.) person or thing that deludes or misleads by fugitive appearances. [orig. *Will with the wisp* (= handful of lighted flax etc.)]

wil·low (wĭl'ō) *n.* Tree or shrub of genus *Salix*, widely distributed in temperate and cold regions, usu. growing by water and with pliant branches and long narrow drooping leaves; ~ **herb**: see FIREWEED; **wil'lowware**, white china with blue pattern including willow tree etc., of Chinese origin, introduced into England in late 18th c. by Thomas Turner. **wil'low·y** *adj.* 1. Abounding in willows, bordered or shaded with willows. 2. Lithe and slender. .

wil·ly-nil·ly (wĭl'ē nĭl'ē) *adv.* & *adj.* With or against the will of the persons concerned, whether one will or not, willing(ly) or un-willing(ly).

Wil·son¹ (wĭl'son), **Henry** (1812–75). (orig. name Jeremiah Jones Colbath) Vice president of U.S. under Ulysses S. Grant, 1873–5.

Wil·son² (wĭl'son), **(Thomas) Wood·row** (1856–1924). Twenty-eighth president of U.S., 1913–21; U.S. representative at the peace treaty negotiations after World War I and sponsor of the covenant of the League of Nations.

wilt¹ (wĭlt) *v.* (Cause to) fade,

droop, become limp.

wilt² (wĭlt) *v.* (archaic) Second person sing., pres. ind. of WILL².

. **wil·y** (wī'lē) *adj.* (**wil·i·er, wil·i·est**). Full of wiles, crafty, cunning. **wil'i·ly** *adv.* **wil'i·- ness** *n.*

wim·ple (wĭm'pel) *n.* Cloth of linen or silk so folded as to cover head, chin, sides of face, and neck, formerly worn by women and retained in dress of nuns. ~ *v.* (**-pled, -pling**). Envelop in wimple, veil; fall in folds.

win (wĭn) *v.* (**won** pr. wŭn, **win·ning**). Be victorious in (game, battle, race, etc.); gain victory; get, gain, secure, esp. by effort or competition, as price or reward, by merit, or in gambling or betting; gain affection or allegiance of, bring *over* to one's party or cause; make one's way to, make one's way *to, through,* etc.; ~ **out** (colloq.), **through**, gain one's end, be successful. **win'ner** *n.* **win** *n.* (colloq.) Victory in game or contest.

wince (wĭns) *v.i.* (**winced, winc·ing**). Make involuntary shrinking movement, start, with pain, in alarm, etc., flinch. ~ *n.* Such movement. **winc'er** *n.*

winch (wĭnch) *n.* Crank of wheel or axle; hoisting or hauling apparatus consisting essentially of revolving horizontal drum worked by a crank.

wind¹ (wĭnd) *n.* 1. Air in motion, current of air of any degree of force perceptible to senses occurring naturally in atmosphere; this in reference to direction from which it blows or (naut.) its direction or position in relation to

*The direction and regularity of a **wind** depends on topography and climatic conditions. Trade winds are due to semi-permanent anticyclones over sub-tropical oceans.*

ship; air artificially put in motion by passage of missile, action of bellows, etc.; scent, esp. of person or animal in hunting etc., conveyed on wind; **get ~ of**, (fig.) begin to suspect, hear rumor of; **in the ~**, happening or ready to happen, astir, afoot; **like the ~**, swiftly; **sail** etc. **close to the ~**, (fig.) come very near indecency or dishonesty; **take ~ out of person's sails**, (fig.) put him at a disadvantage, esp. by anticipating his arguments etc. 2. Gas in stomach or intestines. 3. Breath as needed in exertion, power of drawing breath without difficulty while running etc.; **second ~**, regular breathing regained after breathlessness during continued exertion (also fig.). 4. Breath as used in speaking, esp. (fig.) empty talk. 5. Breath or air as used for sounding musical instrument, as horn, flute, organ pipe; (players of) wind instruments of orchestra collectively. 6. **wind'- age**, effect of the wind in deflection of a missile; degree of such deflection; **wind'bag**, wordy talker; **wind'break**, something, esp. row of trees, used to break force of wind or as protection against it; **wind chill factor**, (meteorol.) temperature of still air having same perceived effect on exposed human flesh as a specified combination of air temperature and wind velocity; **wind'fall**, something blown down by wind, esp. fruit; (fig.) piece of unexpected good fortune, esp. legacy; **wind'flower**, anemone; **wind instrument**, musical instru-ment in which sound is produced by current of air, esp. by breath; **wind'jammer**, (colloq.) sailing ship; **wind'pipe**, air passage between throat and bronchi or lungs, trachea; **wind'proof**, affording protection from wind; **wind'row**, row of mown grass or

*Once confined to classical music, **wind instruments** are finding their way into diverse forms of music including jazz, rock and even country and western.*

Tornado region in U.S.A.

Tropical cyclones:
- ⇐ less than 2 a year
- ⇐ 2 to 4
- ⇐ 5 to 10
- ← more than 10

Prevailing westerlies

Equatorial belt of variable winds and calms

→ Warm winds from hot deserts

→ Cold winds bringing polar air

◄ Warm descending winds (Föhn type)

◄ Cold descending winds (Bora type)

windshaft
brake-wheel
brake
wallower
fantail
stock
whip
shutters
curb
sack hoist
toothed ring
grain bin
main vertical shaft
stone cases
stone nuts
spur wheel
centrifugal governor for
controlling gap between
stones
gallery

*Numerous small sails are used to drive this **windmill** in the Cyclades, Greece (above). Sprung shutters, similar to those on a Venetian blind, were invented by Meikle in 1772 and used in western Europe. Modern windmills (below) have much lighter machinery.*

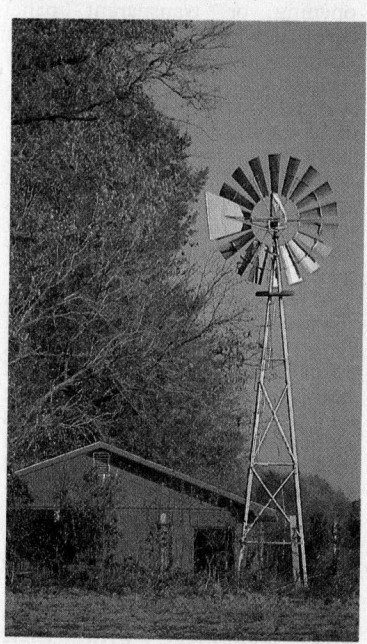

hay raked up to dry before being bundled; **wind′shield**, screen to keep off wind, esp. sheet of glass etc., in front of driver of motor vehicle etc.; **wind sleeve, wind′-sock**, piece of cloth shaped like truncated cone, held open at larger end by ring of wire and used to indicate direction of wind, drogue; **wind′swept**, swept by winds, exposed; **wind′tight**, constructed so as to keep out wind; **wind tunnel**, enclosed chamber through which wind may be blown at known velocities, for testing (models of) aircraft etc.; **wind′ward**, (region) lying in direction from which wind blows, facing the wind. **wind′less**

adj. **wind** *v.* (**wind·ed** or for sense 1. **wound** pr. wownd, **wind·ing**). 1. Sound (horn or bugle) by blowing; blow (note, call, etc.) on horn etc. 2. Detect presence of by scent. 3. Deprive of breath, make out of breath; hence **wind′ed** (*adj.*), out of breath.

wind² (wīnd) *v.* (**wound** pr. wownd, **wind·ing**). Move, traverse, in curved or sinuous course; coil, wrap closely, around something or upon itself, encircle or enclose thus; haul or hoist by turning windlass etc.; tighten (*up*) coiled spring of (clock etc.), or (fig.) tension, intensity, or efficiency of; ∼ **up**, bring or come

to conclusion, conclude; arrange and adjust affairs of (company) on its dissolution; **wind′up**, finish, conclusion; (baseball) preparatory motions of pitcher before throwing ball to batter; **winding sheet**, shroud. **wind′er** *n.* Person, thing, that winds; winding step in staircase.

Wind·hoek (vĭnt′hook). Capital city of Namibia.

wind·lass (wĭnd′las) *n.* Mechanical contrivance for hauling or hoisting, consisting essentially of horizontal roller or beam on supports, with rope or chain wound around. ∼ *v.t.* Hoist or haul with windlass.

wind·mill (wĭnd′mĭl) *n.* Mill worked by action of wind on sails; toy consisting of stick with shaped card or other light substance fixed to its end and revolving when moved through air; **fight, tilt at, ~ s,** expend energy contending against imaginary opponents or difficulties (in allusion to story of Don Quixote's tilting at windmills under the delusion that they were giants).

win·dow (wĭn′dō) *n.* Opening, usu. filled with glass, in wall or roof of building, ship, car, train, etc., to admit light or air and afford view of what is outside or inside; window space or opening, esp. used for display of goods, advertisements, etc., in shop etc.; any opening resembling window in shape or function; **~ box,** box on outside window sill in which flowers and plants are grown; **~ dresser,** one who arranges display in store window etc.; **~ dressing,** art of arranging such display; (fig.) adroit presentation of facts etc. to give falsely favorable impression; **~ envelope,** envelope with opening or transparent panel through which address inside is visible; **windowpane,** pane of glass set in window frame; **window seat,** seat below window, usu. in recess or bay; **window shade,** curtain or shade for window, usu. consisting of heavy cloth, paper, or plastic on spring roller; **window-shopping,** looking at store displays without buying; **window sill,** sill of window.

Wind·sor (wĭn′zer). English town on bank of Thames, site of royal residence, **~ Castle;** surname assumed by English royal house in 1917; **Duke of ~,** title conferred on Edward VIII on his abdication in 1936; **~ chair,** kind of wooden chair with back formed of upright spokes surmounted by curved crosspiece.

Wind·ward (wĭnd′werd) **Islands.** 1. Group of islands in the West Indies consisting of Grenada, St. Vincent, St. Lucia, and Dominica, with their dependencies. 2. Group of islands in southern part of Lesser Antilles, including British and French territories.

wind·y (wĭn′dē) *adj.* (**wind·i·er, wind·i·est**). Windswept; exposed to, blown upon or through, by wind; in which wind is frequent or prevalent, accompanied by (much) wind; verbose, empty. **wind′i·ly** *adv.* **wind′i·ness** *n.*

wine (wīn) *n.* 1. Fermented grape juice for drinking, varying in color from *red* (usu. a purplish crimson) to *white* (pale gold);

*The glazed **window** was used by the Greeks and Romans but its use declined in the Middle Ages so that churches seem to have been the only buildings with glazing. Its use in private dwellings increased only with the availability of glass.*

dessert ~, wine for drinking with dessert or after meal; **fortified** ~, wine (esp. port and sherry) to which brandy is added during manufacture; **table** ~, wine for drinking at meal. 2. Fermented drink more or less resembling wine, made from juice of other fruits or flowers or root vegetables. 3. Color of red wine. 4. **wine cellar,** cellar used for storing wine; contents of this; **wine-cooler,**

vessel in which bottles of wine are cooled with ice; **wine′glass,** small drinking glass, usu. with stem and foot, for wine; **wine press,** press in which grape juice is extracted for making wine; **Wine′sap,** large red Amer. winter apple; **wine′skin,** skin of goat etc. sewn together to make primitive wine vessel. **win′y** *adj.* (**win·i·er, win·i·est**). **wine** *v.* (**wined, win·ing**). Drink wine; entertain with wine; **~ and dine,**

lancet, early 13th C. (interior)

plate tracery, early 13th C.

geometric bar tracery, late 13th C.

curvilinear tracery with ogee arch, 14th C.

embrasure, rear-arch, rear-vault, dripstone, iron stanchion, quatrefoil, cusp, foil

perpendicular tracery, 15th C.

rose window, 14th C.

oriel window, 15th C.

bay window, 15th C.

mullion window, 16th C.

mullion, transom, light

casement window with leaded lights

dormer window

Venetian window, 18th C.

sash window, 18th C.

sash window, 18th C. (interior)

French window, early 19th C.

lintel, architrave, glazing bar, pane, sill

pelmet, curtain, window seat

shutter in reveal, balcony

entertain generously.

wing (wĭng) n. 1. Organ of flight of any flying animal, in birds a specially modified forelimb; in bats, extension of skin attached to modified parts of forelimb; in insects, membranous expansions attached to thorax in addition to limbs; **on the ~,** flying; **take ~,** fly away; **take under one's ~,** treat as protégé. 2. Anything resembling wing in form or function, esp. one of the main supporting surfaces (planes) of aircraft. 3. Lateral part or appendage. 4. Either of two divisions on each side of main body of army or fleet in battle. 5. (soccer etc.) Position, player, on outside of forward line. 6. Section of political party etc. holding views deviating from center: see RIGHT wing, LEFT[1] wing. 7. Subordinate part of building on one side of main or central part. 8. (usu. pl.) Space at side of stage where actors stand before going on stage; **waiting in the ~s,** (fig.) holding oneself in readiness. 9. (anat., bot.) Lateral part or projection of some organ or structure, as lateral cartilage of nose, thin membranous appendage of seed or fruit serving for its dispersal by wind etc. 10. Division of air force, usu. comprising three groups. 11. (pl.) Representation of pair of bird's wings worn as badge by those who have passed flying tests. 12. **wing′back,** (football) back positioned on offense, flanking the end of the line; position played by this back; **wing case,** horny covering of functional wings in certain insects; **wing chair,** chair with sidepieces projecting forward at top of high back, for protection from drafts; **wing collar,** man's stiff collar with upper corners turned down; **wing covert:** see COVERT[1] sense 2; **wing load-(ing),** total weight of loaded aircraft divided by area of supporting surfaces; **wing nut,** nut with projections for thumb and fingers to turn it by; **wing′span, wing′-spread,** extreme measurement between tips of wings of bird or aircraft; **wing tip,** outer end or tip of wing of bird or aircraft. **wing** v. Equip with wings; enable to fly or mount; send in flight, lend speed to; travel, traverse, on wings; wound (esp. game bird) in the wing.

wing·ding (wĭng′dĭng) n. (slang) Lively, noisy party or celebration.

winged (wĭngd; occas. wĭng′ĭd) adj. Having wings; swift, rapid, flying; (of speech) conveying its message swiftly and effectively; ~ **god,** Mercury; ~ **horse,** Pegasus; **W~ Victory,** statue of Nike, Greek goddess of victory, with wings, esp. Hellenistic statue found in Samothrace, preserved in Louvre.

wing·less (wĭng′lĭs) adj. Having no wings; (of birds) having rudimentary wings not used for flight.

wink (wĭngk) v. Blink; close one eye momentarily in flippant or frivolous manner; close (an eye, eyes) for a moment; move swiftly, (cause to) flicker like an eyelid, twinkle; give (signal, message, etc.) by flashing lights; ~ **at,** shut one's eyes to, connive at. **wink** n. Act of winking, esp. as signal; **not a ~ (of sleep),** no sleep at all. **wink′er** n.

win·ning (wĭn′ĭng) adj. That wins; charming, attractive. ~ n. 1. Act of winning. 2. (pl.) Money won by gambling or betting. **win′ning·ly** adv.

win·now (wĭn′ō) v.t. Fan (grain) free of chaff etc., fan (chaff) away, out, from; sift, separate, clear of worthless or inferior element, extract, select (out) thus.

win·o (wī′nō) n. (pl. **win·os**). (slang) Alcoholic.

win·some (wĭn′som) adj. Attractive, charming. **win′-some·ly** adv. **win′some·ness** n.

win·ter (wĭn′ter) n. 1. Coldest season of year, popularly reckoned in N. hemisphere as comprising December, January, and February, but astronomically as lasting from winter solstice (Dec. 21 or 22) to vernal equinox (Mar. 20 or 21); (opp. SUMMER[1]) colder half of year. 2. (attrib. or adj.) Of, characteristic of, winter; occurring, used, etc., in, lasting for, winter; (of fruit) ripening late or keeping well until or during winter; ~ **aconite,** small perennial herb (*Eranthis hyemalis*) producing bright-yellow starry flowers in winter; **win′tergreen,** any of various creeping or low shrubby plants with leaves remaining green in winter, esp. N. Amer. *Gaultheria procumbens,* with drooping white flowers, edible scarlet berries, and aromatic leaves yielding oil used in medicine and for flavoring; **win′terkill,** kill or be killed by exposure to cold temperatures, ice, snow, etc.; **winter solstice:** see SOLSTICE; **win′tertide** (poet.), **win′tertime,** season of winter; **winter wheat (oats** etc.), wheat (oats etc.) sown in autumn and remaining in ground all winter. **winter** v. Spend winter (at, in); keep, feed, during winter.

win·ter·ize (wĭn′terīz) v.t. (**-ized, -iz·ing**). Adapt for operation or for use in cold weather.

win·try (wĭn′trē) (**-tri·er, -tri·est**), **win·ter·y** (wĭn′terē) (**-ter·i·er, -ter·i·est**) adj. Characteristic of winter, having the temperature, storminess, etc., appropriate to winter, cold, windy, cheerless; (of smile, greeting, etc.) devoid of warmth. **win′tri·ness** n.

wipe (wīp) v. (**wiped, wip·ing**). Clean or dry surface of by rubbing with cloth etc.; clear away (moisture, dust, etc.) thus; apply soft or liquid substance over surface by rubbing it on, esp., (plumbing) apply solder to (joint) thus; ~ **out,** (colloq.) destroy, annihilate, exterminate; ~ **the floor with,** (slang) humiliate (person) by defeat

*During the middle of **winter** in the high altitudes of the Canadian Rocky Mountains, nearly everything is covered with snow. Nevertheless, some animals are able to survive in such conditions without hibernating.*

*Just as a Christian may utter a prayer, followers of Shinto in Japan may express a **wish** by writing it on paper or cloth and attaching it to the fence in front of a shrine.*

or correction. **wipe** *n.* Act of wiping.

wip·er (wī′per) *n.* (esp., also **windshield** ~) Mechanical device that wipes windshield of motor vehicle.

wire (wīr) *n.* (Piece of) metal drawn into slender flexible rod or thread; length or line of this used for various purposes, esp. for fencing, as conductor of electric current, etc.; wire netting, framework of wire; snare of wire etc.; (colloq.) telegram; (horse racing) the finish line; (pl.) lines by which puppets are worked (chiefly fig., in **pull** (**the**) ~ **s**); **under the wire**, barely meeting the deadline; **wire cloth**, fabric (for strainers etc.) woven from wire; **wire cutter**, tool for cutting wire; **wire entanglement**, entanglement of barbed wire stretched over ground to impede enemy's advance; **wire gauge**, gauge for measuring diameter of wire etc.; standard series of sizes to which wire etc. is made; **wirehaired**, (of dogs, esp. terriers) having rough hard wiry coat; **wire′puller**, (colloq.) politician etc. who privately influences others; **wire′pulling** (*adj. & n.*); **wire service**, business organization that collects news and photographs for distribution to subscribing newspapers and broadcasting stations; **wire′tap** (*v.*) (**-tapped, -tapping**), make secret connection with (telephone or telegraph wire) in order to eavesdrop on telephone conversations; **wire′worm**, slender yellow larva of any click beetle destructive to plants; (also) millipede that destroys plant roots. **wire** *v.* (**wired, wir·ing**). Furnish, support, stiffen, secure, with wire; snare with wire; (colloq.) telegraph. **wir′ing** *n.* (esp.) Electrical system of building.

wire·less (wīr′lĭs) *adj.* Without wire(s), esp. (of telegraphy, telephony) with no connecting wire between transmitting and receiving stations; (archaic) radio. ~ *n.* (archaic) Radio receiver or transmitter; telegraphy or telephony. ~ *v.* Send (message etc.), inform, by wireless.

wir·y (wīr′ē) *adj.* (**wir·i·er, wir·i·est**). Made of wire; tough and flexible like wire; (of persons) tough, sinewy, untiring. **wir′i·ly** *adv.* **wir′i·ness** *n.*

Wis., Wisc. *abbrevs.* Wisconsin. **Wis·con·sin** (wĭskŏn′sĭn). State in N. central U.S., admitted to Union in 1848; capital, Madison.

wis·dom (wĭz′dom) *n.* Being wise; soundness of judgment in matters relating to life and conduct;

*Although the status of a **witch doctor** (above) has declined in Africa, in some places, including Zambia, they retain an important role in tribal life and wield considerable influence.*

knowledge, enlightenment, learning; **W** ~ **of Solomon**, book of the Apocrypha; ~ **of Jesus the son of Sirach**, Ecclesiasticus; **W** ~ **literature**, biblical books of Job, Proverbs, Ecclesiastes, Wisdom of Solomon, Ecclesiasticus, and Epistle of James; ~ **tooth**, hindmost molar tooth on each side of upper and lower jaws in humans, usu. appearing about age of 20.

wise[1] (wīz) *n.* (archaic) Way, manner, guise.

wise[2] (wīz) *adj.* (**wis·er, wis·est**). Having, exercising, proceeding from, indicating, sound judgment resulting from experience and knowledge; sagacious, prudent, sensible; having knowledge (*of*); (archaic) skilled in magic or occult arts; (slang) offensively knowledgeable; insolent; **be, get,** ~ **to**, (colloq.) be, become, aware of; **put** ~ (**to**), inform (of); **wise′crack**, smart remark, witticism; (*v.i.*) make wisecracks; **wise guy**, (slang) cocksure person; **wise man**, man of good judgment or discernment; (archaic) one skilled in magic, wizard, esp. one of the Magi; **wise woman**, witch, female soothsayer, esp. harmless or beneficent one. **wise′ly** *adv.*

-wise *suffix.* In (specified) manner, way, or respect. [f. WISE[1]]

wise·a·cre (wīz′ā′ker) *n.* One who pretends to, or affects an air of, wisdom. [MDu. *wijsseggher* soothsayer]

wish (wĭsh) *n.* (Expression of)

desire or aspiration; request; (pl.) expression of desire for another's welfare, success, etc.; **wish'bone**, forked bone between neck and breast of cooked bird (because when two persons have pulled it apart the holder of the larger piece is entitled to the magical fulfillment of a wish); **wish fulfillment**, (psychoanal.) gratification of unconscious wishes, esp. symbolically in dreams, fantasy, etc. **wish** v. Have, feel, express, a wish for; express desire or aspiration *for*; want (*to* do, person *to* do); request; (esp. in expressions of goodwill, greeting, etc.) desire (something, esp. something good) for a person etc. **wish'er** n.

wish·ful (wĭsh'fŭl) *adj*. Wishing, desirous; ~ **thinking**, believing a thing to be so because it is desired or desirable. **wish'-ful·ly** *adv*. **wish'ful·ness** *n*.

wish·y-wash·y (wĭsh'ē wŏshē, -wawshē) *adj*. Thin, sloppy; feeble or poor in quality or character. **wish'y-wash·i·ness** n.

wisp (wĭsp) n. Small bundle or twist of straw, hay, etc.; thin, narrow, filmy, or slight piece or scrap (of). **wisp'y** *adj*. (**wisp·i·er, wisp·i·est**).

wis·ter·i·a (wĭstēr'ēa), **wis·tar·i·a** (wĭstār'ēa) *ns*. Leguminous plant of genus *Wisteria* of N. Amer., Japan, and China, forming hardy climbing deciduous shrubs with pendulous racemes of blue, purple, or white

papilionaceous flowers. [Caspar *Wistar* or *Wister*, Amer. anatomist (1761–1818)]

wist·ful (wĭst'fŭl) *adj*. Yearningly or mournfully expectant or eager. **wist'ful·ly** *adv*. **wist'ful·ness** *n*.

wit[1] (wĭt) n. 1. (sing. or pl.) Intelligence, understanding; **at one's ~'s end**, utterly perplexed; **have one's wits about one**, be mentally alert; **live by one's wits**, get one's living by clever or crafty devices, without any settled occupation; **out of one's wits**, mad, distracted. 2. Unexpected combining or contrasting of previously unconnected ideas or expressions; power of causing surprise and delight by this; capacity for making brilliant observations in an amusing way. 3. Person with this capacity; (archaic) person of great mental ability, man of talent.

wit[2] (wĭt) v. (**wist, wit·ting**). (archaic) Know; **to ~**, this is to say, namely.

witch[1] (wĭch) n. Sorceress, woman supposed to have dealings with devil or evil spirits; (fig.) fascinating or bewitching woman; **old ~**, (colloq.) malevolent or ugly old woman; **witch'craft**, sorcery; **witch doctor**, tribal magician of primitive people; **witches' Sabbath**, midnight meeting of demons, sorcerers, and witches, presided over by the Devil, supposed in medieval times to have been held annually as orgy or festival; **witch hunt, hunting**, searching out and persecution of (formerly) supposed witches, or (now) persons suspected of un-

popular or unorthodox political views, etc. **witch** v.t. Bewitch; (fig.) fascinate, charm; **witch'ing time** (**of night**), (*Hamlet*, III. ii) time when witches are active, midnight. **witch'er·y** n. (pl. -er·ies).

witch[2]: see WYCH.

with (wĭdh, wĭth) *prep*. 1. (of conflict, rivalry, etc.) Against, in opposition to. 2. In or into company of or relation to, among, beside. 3. Agreeably or in harmonious relation to. 4. Having, carrying, possessed of, characterized by; ~ **child, young**, pregnant. 5. In the care, charge, or possession of. 6. By use of as instrument or means, by addition or supply of, by operation of, owing to. 7. In same way, direction, degree, at same time, as. 8. In regard to, concerning, in the mind or view of. 9. Despite, notwithstanding, the presence of. 10. **with it**, (colloq.) up-to-the-minute, (capable of) understanding new ideas etc.

with·al (wĭdhawl', wĭth-) *adv*. & *prep*. (archaic) With (it); in addition, moreover, as well, at the same time.

with·draw (wĭdhdraw', wĭth-) v. (-**drew** pr. -drōō', -**drawn**, -**draw·ing**). 1. Pull aside or back; take away, remove; retract. 2. Retire from presence or place, go aside or apart. **with·draw'al** n. **with·drawn'** *past part*. as *adj*. Shy, unresponsive.

A possible ancestor of the dog, the **wolf** *lives as one of a pack within which there is a complex social structure. It inhabits the cooler isolated regions of the northern hemisphere.*

Posthumously awarded the status of hero, and romanticized in paintings (above) **James Wolfe** *led his men to capture Quebec. It has been suggested that the plan came from his brigadiers.*

with·er (wĭdh´*er*) *v.* Make, become, dry or shriveled (*up*); deprive of or lose vigor, vitality, freshness, importance; decline, languish, decay; blight, paralyze (*with* look of scorn etc.). **with´-er·ing** *adj.* **with´er·ing·ly** *adv.*

with·ers (wĭdh´*erz*) *n.pl.* Ridge between shoulder blades of horse and some other animals. [part that takes strain of collar, f. OE. *wither* against]

with·hold (wĭthhōld´, wĭdh-) *v.t.* (**-held, -hold·ing**). Hold back, restrain; refuse to give, grant, or allow; **withholding tax**, tax deducted from wages or salary.

with·in (wĭdhĭn´, wĭth-) *adv.* Inside, internally, inwardly; indoors. ∼ *prep.* To, on, in, the inside of; enclosed by; in the limits of; not beyond, above, outside, or farther than the extent of; in the scope or sphere of action of.

with·out (wĭdhowt´, wĭth-) *adv.* (literary or archaic) Outside, externally. ∼ *prep.* 1. (archaic) Outside of. 2. Not having, not with; devoid of; lacking; free from.

with·stand (wĭthstănd´, wĭdh-) *v.t.* (**-stood** pr. -stŏŏd´, **-stand·-ing**). Resist, oppose.

wit·less (wĭt´lĭs) *adj.* (archaic and literary) Lacking in wits, senseless; lacking wit. **wit´less·ly** *adv.* **wit´less·ness** *n.*

wit·ness (wĭt´nĭs) *n.* 1. Testimony, evidence; confirmation. 2. Person giving sworn testimony in court or for legal purpose; person attesting execution of document by adding his signature; thing or person whose existence, position, etc., is testimony *to* or proof *of*; person present as spectator or auditor; ∼ **stand**, stand from which witness gives evidence. **witness** *v.* State in evidence (archaic); give evidence, serve as evidence; indicate, serve as evidence of; see, be spectator of; sign (document) as witness.

wit·ted (wĭt´ĭd) *adj.* Having wit; usu. in comb., as *quick-* ∼ , *slow-* ∼ , etc.

wit·ti·cism (wĭt´ĭsĭzem) *n.* Witty saying, piece of wit; esp. jeer, witty sarcasm. [coined by Dryden from WITTY, after *criticism*]

wit·ting (wĭt´ĭng) *adj.* Knowing or intending, conscious. **wit´ting·ly** *adv.* [f. WIT²]

wit·ty (wĭt´ē) *adj.* (**-ti·er, -ti·est**). Capable of, given to, saying or writing brilliantly or sparklingly amusing things; full of wit. **wit´ti·ly** *adv.* **wit´ti·ness** *n.*

wive (wīv) *v.* (**wived, wiv·ing**). (archaic) Provide with, take, wife.

wives: see WIFE.

wiz·ard (wĭz´erd) *n.* Magician, sorcerer, male witch; extremely skillful person; person who effects seeming impossibilities. **wiz´-ard·ry** *n.*

wiz·en (wĭz´en), **wiz·ened** (wĭz´end) *adjs.* Of shriveled or dried-up appearance.

wk. *abbrev.* Week.

wkly. *abbrev.* Weekly.

WL, w.l. *abbrevs.* Wavelength.

WNW, W.N.W., w.n.w. *abbrevs.* West-northwest.

WO, W.O. *abbrevs.* Warrant Officer.

w/o *abbrev.* Without.

woad (wōd) *n.* European biennial plant (*Isatis tinctoria*); blue dye formerly obtained from this.

wob·ble (wŏb´el) *v.i.* (**-bled, -bling**). Move unsteadily or with uncertain direction from side to side or backward and forward; shake, rock, quiver; (fig.) vacillate, hesitate, waver. ∼ *n.* Wobbling motion. **wob´bly** *adj.* (**-bli·er, -bli·est**). **wob´bli·ness** *n.*

Wob·bly (wŏb´lē) *n.* (pl. **-blies**). (slang) Member of the Industrial Workers of the World (I.W.W.).

[prob. f. mispronunciation of letter *W*]

Wo·den (wō´den) = ODIN.

woe (wō) *n.* (chiefly poet. or joc.) Affliction, bitter grief, distress; (pl.) calamities, troubles; ∼ **is me!**, alas!; **woe´begone**, dismal looking. **woe´ful** *adj.* **woe´ful·ly** *adv.* **woe´ful·ness** *n.*

wok (wŏk) *n.* Large bowllike metal pan used in Chinese cooking. **woke**: see WAKE¹.

wolf (wŏŏlf) *n.* (pl. **wolves** pr. wŏŏlvz). 1. Any of various large mammals of dog tribe (*Canis*, esp. *C. lupus*) of Europe, Asia, and N. Amer., with gray or brownish-gray fur, erect pointed ears, and bushy tail, noted for fierceness and rapacity; rapacious or greedy person; (slang) man who pursues women; **cry** ∼ , raise false alarm; **keep** ∼ **from the door**, ward off hunger or starvation; ∼ **in sheep's clothing**, person concealing malicious intentions under guise of friendliness etc. 2. ∼ **dog, wolf´-hound**, any of various large varieties of dog kept for hunting wolves; **wolfs´bane**, *Aconitum lycoctonum*, with yellow flowers; dried root of this, used as poison; **wolf whistle**, expressive whistle uttered by man as indication of sexual attraction to woman. **wolf´-ish** *adj.* **wolf´ish·ly** *adv.* **wolf´-ish·ness** *n.* **wolf** *v.t.* Devour ravenously.

Wolfe (wŏŏlf), **James** (1727–1759). English general; commanded the British forces at the siege of Quebec, in which he was killed.

wolf·ram (wŏŏlf´ram) *n.* Ore

(FeWO₄) yielding tungsten.

wol·ver·ine (wŏŏlverēn´) *n.* Very large voracious weasel (*Gulo gulo*) of N. Amer. and N. Europe, with shaggy black fur, white markings, and bushy tail; also called "glutton."

wom·an (wŏŏm´an) *n.* (pl. **wom·en** pr. wĭm´ĭn). Adult human female; female servant or attendant; (without article) the average or typical woman, the female sex; (attrib.) female, as ~ **doctor**, ~ **friend; wom'ankind**, women in general; **women's lib** (sometimes derog.), movement urging liberation of women from domestic duties and subservient status; **women's rights**, rights claimed for women of privileges and opportunities equal with those of men; **woman suffrage**, right of women to vote. **wom'an·hood** *n.* State of being a woman; womanliness; womankind.

wom·an·ish (wŏŏm´anĭsh) *adj.* Characteristic of woman as opp. to man; (of man) effeminate. **wom'an·ish·ly** *adv.* **wom'an·ish·ness** *n.*

wom·an·ize (wŏŏm´anīz) *v.* (**-ized, -iz·ing**). Make womanish; (of men) philander. **wom'an·iz·er** *n.*

wom·an·like (wŏŏm´anlīk) *adj.* Like a woman.

wom·an·ly (wŏŏm´anlē) *adj.* Having the qualities or bearing of a woman; befitting a woman. **wom'an·li·ness** *n.*

womb (wŏŏm) *n.* Uterus, (fig.) place where anything is generated or produced.

wom·bat (wŏm´băt) *n.* Burrowing herbivorous marsupial, esp. of genus *Phascolomis*, native to S. Australia and Tasmania, with thick heavy body, short legs, rudimentary tail, and general resemblance to small bear.

*The common **wombat** is found in eastern and south-eastern Australia from southern Queensland to the islands of Bass Strait and Tasmania. The three other species have limited distribution.*

*A **witness** is required for almost all legal proceedings, including this naturalization ceremony.*

*The **withers** of a horse form a prominent ridge between the shoulder blades; they are quite sensitive to pressure.*

wom·en·folk (wĭm´ĭnfōk), **wom·en·folks** (wĭm´ĭnfōks) *n.pl.* Women collectively, esp. of family or community.

won: see WIN.

won·der (wŭn´der) *n.* 1 Marvel, miracle, prodigy; astonishing thing, deed, event, occurrence, etc.; **no ∼**, (it is) not surprising; **Seven W∼s of the World**: see SEVEN. 2. Emotion excited by something novel and unexpected, or inexplicable; astonishment mixed with perplexity, bewildered curiosity, or admiration. 3. **wonder drug**, any drug supposed to have remarkable power to relieve symptoms of or cure illness; **won´derland**, imaginary realm of wonders, fairyland; **won´derworker**, one who performs wonders or miracles. **wonder** *v.* 1. Be affected with wonder, marvel; **I shouldn't ∼**, (colloq.) I should not be surprised. 2. Feel some doubt or curiosity, be desirous to know or learn. **won·der·er, won·der·ment** (wŭn´derment) *ns.*

won·der·ful (wŭn´derful) *adj.* Marvelous, surprising; surprisingly large, fine, excellent, etc. **won´der·ful·ly** *adv.* **won´der·ful·ness** *n.*

won·drous (wŭn´drus) *adj.* & *adv.* (poet., rhet.) Wonderful(ly). **won´drous·ly** *adv.* **won´drous·ness** *n.*

wont (wōnt, wawnt, wŭnt) *adj.* (archaic) Accustomed, used (*to* do). **∼** *n.* Custom; habit. **wont´ed** *adj.* Habitual.

won't (wōnt, wŭnt) *contr.* Will not.

woo (woō) *v.* COURT[2]. **woo´er** *n.*

wood (woōd) *n.* 1. Collection of trees growing more or less thickly together, of considerable extent; piece of ground covered with trees; (now rare) wooded country, woodland; **out of the ∼s**, clear of a difficulty, danger, etc. 2. Hard compact fibrous substance making up trunks and branches of trees and shrubs between bark and pith, whether growing or cut down for use in construction or cabinetwork, for fuel, etc.; particular kind of wood. 3. Something made of wood, esp. cask in which wine etc. is stored; (mus.) wooden wind instrument, woodwind; golf club used for driving. 4. **wood alcohol**, methyl alcohol; **wood anemone**, any of various common wild anemones, abundant in woods and flowering in early spring; **wood´bine**, VIRGINIA creeper; any of various climbing plants, esp. honeysuckle of genus *Lonicera*; **wood´block**, block of wood, e.g. for paving or esp. with design for printing from; **wood´cock** (pl. **-cocks**, collect **-cock**), common European migratory bird (*Scolopax rusticola*), allied to snipe,

great spotted woodpecker

Arizona woodpecker

Above: A common British species, the spotted woodpecker. Left: The Arizona woodpecker. Both may eat seeds as well as insects. Below: Autumnal leaves cast a golden glow over an English wood. Because land was needed for farming and houses, wooded areas in that country have been reduced.

*The **woodcock** is unusual because the female carries the young in flight. The usual position is between the feet and body, but occasionally, they have also been seen on her back.*

with long bill, large eyes, and mottled plumage, esteemed as food; similar but smaller N. Amer. *Philohela minor*; **wood'craft**, knowledge of and skill in forest conditions applied to hunting, maintaining oneself, making one's way, etc.; **wood'cut**, print obtained from design cut in relief on block of wood (usu. sawn along the grain); this art; **wood'cutter**, one who fells or lops trees for timber or fuel; **wood engraving**, print obtained from design engraved on block of wood (usu. sawn across grain); this art; **wood ibis**, large wading bird of southern swampland (*Mycteria americana*), the only Amer. stork; **wood'land**, wooded country, woods; (attrib.) of, in, growing or dwelling in, consisting of, etc., woodland; **wood louse**, small terrestrial isopod crustacean of *Oniscus* or related genera, found in old wood, under stones, etc.; **wood'man** (pl. -men), forester, woodcutter; **wood nymph**, nymph of the woods, dryad; **wood'pecker**, any bird of numerous genera and species of family Picidae, found in most parts of world, with plumage usu. bright colored and variegated, characterized by habit of pecking holes in trunks and branches of trees to find insects for food or make cavities for laying eggs; **wood pigeon**: see PIGEON; **wood pulp**, pulp made by mechanical or chemi-

cal disintegration of wood fiber, used for making paper etc.; **wood'ruff**, low-growing European woodland herb (*Asperula odorata*) with clusters of small white flowers and whorls of strongly sweet-scented leaves; **woods'man** (pl. -men), man living in or frequenting woods, one skilled in woodcraft; **wood sorrel**, low-growing spring-flowering woodland plant (*Oxalis acetosella*) with delicate trifoliate leaves and small white flowers streaked with purple; other species of *Oxalis*; **wood tar**, tar obtained in dry distillation of wood; **wood warbler**: see WARBLER; **wood'wind**, wooden wind instruments of orchestra; **wood'work**, work done in wood, wooden part *of* anything, esp. wooden interior parts of building; **wood'worm**, wood-boring larva of a furniture beetle *Anobium punctatum*. **wood'ed** *adj.* Covered with growing trees; abounding in woods.

wood·chuck (wŏod'chŭk) *n.* Thick-bodied reddish-brown marmot (*Marmota monax*) of northeastern U.S. and Canada. [f. Amer. Ind. name, cf. Cree *wuchak*, *otchock*]

*Modern automatic machinery at a mill in Galashiels, Scotland. Current demand for **wool** has resulted in most early methods of spinning and weaving being superseded.*

wood·en (wŏod'en) *adj.* Made, consisting, of wood; resembling wood; dull and inert, stiff and lifeless, inexpressive; **wood'en-head**, blockhead; **woodenheaded** (*adj.*); **wooden horse**, wooden figure of a horse made by Greeks in TROJAN War; **wood'enware**, kitchen utensils made of wood. **wood'en·ly** *adv.* **wood'en·ness** *n.*

wood·y (wŏod'ē) *adj.* (**wood·i·er, wood·i·est**). Covered with trees, abounding in woods, well wooded; of the nature of, consisting of, wood; resembling (that of) wood; (of plant) forming wood, having woody stems and branches; ~ **nightshade**: see NIGHTSHADE. **wood'i·ness** *n.*

woof (wŏof, wŏof) *n.* Threads crossing from side to side of web and interwoven with warp; yarn for woof threads.

wool (wŏol) *n.* Fine soft curly hair forming fleecy coat of domesticated sheep and similar animals, characterized by overlapping of the filaments, to which is due its property of felting, and used chiefly in prepared state for making cloth; twisted woolen yarn used for knitting etc.; woolen garment or cloth; short soft underhair or down of some animals; something resembling wool, esp. downy substance found on some plants: any fine fibrous substance naturally or artificially produced; **dyed in the ~**, dyed before spinning; (fig.) thoroughgoing, out-and-out; **pull the ~ over person's eyes**, hoodwink; **wool'gathering**, gathering fragments of wool torn from sheep by bushes etc.; absent-minded-(ness), indulging or indulgence in idle imagining. **wool** *adj.* (commerc.) Made of wool throughout. (cf. WOOLEN).

wool·en, Brit. **wool·len** (wŏol'en) *adjs.* Made, consisting, of wool or of yarns containing wool fibers, esp. when coarse or loosely woven. ~ *n.* (usu. pl.) Woolen clothing or fabric.

Woolf (wŏolf), **Virginia** (1882–1941). English novelist and critic.

wool·len = WOOLEN.

wool·ly (-li·er, -li·est), **wool·y** (**wool·i·er, wool·i·est**) (wŏol'ē) *adjs.* Bearing, naturally covered with, wool or woollike hair; resembling or suggesting wool in softness, texture, etc.; confused, blurred, hazy; (of thought) lacking clarity; (of plants) pubescent, downy; **wild and ~**, vigorous, rough, lawless (orig. applied to West of U.S. in frontier days);

woolly bear, (colloq.) large hairy caterpillar, esp. larva of tigermoth. **wool·ly** (pl. **-lies**), **wool·y** (pl. **wool·ies**) *ns*. Woolen, esp. knitted, garment. **wool'li·ness, wool'i·ness** *ns*.

word (wērd) *n*. 1. Vocal sound or combination of sounds, or written or printed symbols of these, constituting minimal element of speech having a meaning as such and capable of independent grammatical use; ~ **for** ~, verbatim, exact(ly); **last** ~, final utterance in conversation or esp. dispute; (pl.) last utterance before death; final or conclusive statement, latest thing. 2. Thing(s) said, speech, utterance (usu. pl.); (pl.) text of song, actor's part, etc.; verbal expression contrasted with action or thought; (pl.) contentious or violent talk, altercation; (with negative etc.) anything at all (said or written); watchword, password; report, tidings, information; command, order; promise, undertaking; declaration, assurance; **the W** ~ (**of God**), the Bible or some part of it; second person of Trinity; **man of his** ~, one who keeps his promises. 3. ~**-blind**, (path.) unable as result of brain injury or disease to understand written or printed words; **word'book**, book with list(s) of words, vocabulary; **word-deaf**, (path.) unable to understand speech though capable of hearing the sounds; **word painting**, vivid descriptive writing; **word'play**, joke using features of words, pun, etc.; **word square**, series of words so arranged as to read the same vertically and horizontally, puzzle of which solution is such a series.

word'less *adj*. **word'less·ly** *adv*. **word** *v.t*. Put into words, phrase, select words to express. **word'ing** *n*. (esp.) Form of words used, phrasing.

word·age (wēr'dĭj) *n*. 1. Words collectively, esp. number of words in story, book, etc. 2. Use of too many words; verbiage. 3. Wording.

Words·worth (wērdz'wērth), **William** (1770–1850). English Romantic lyric poet, one of the Lake poets (see LAKE[1]); poet laureate from 1843.

word·y (wēr'dē) *adj*. (**word·i·er, word·i·est**). Verbose; in, consisting of, words. **word'i·ly** *adv*. **word'i·ness** *n*.

wore: see WEAR[2].

work (wērk) *n*. 1. Action involving effort or exertion, esp. as means of gaining livelihood; labor done in making something, as dist. from materials used; (phys. etc.) operation of a force in producing movement or other physical change, esp. as measurable quantity; something to do or to be done, employment, business, function; act, deed, proceeding, (pl.) doings; (theol., pl.) moral action considered in relation to justification; **at** ~, engaged in work, working, operating; **out of** ~, without work to do, unemployed; **set to** ~, set (person), apply oneself, to a task, or to do something; **the** ~ **of** ..., a proceeding occupying (a stated time).

*Some modern critics tend to dismiss the poetry of **William Wordsworth** yet his recommendation that the language of ordinary speech be used was a strong influence on his contemporaries.*

2. Product of labor, thing(s) made; result of action; (pl.) architectural or engineering operations; (mil.) fortified building, defensive structure, fortification; literary or musical composition, product of any fine art, as statue, picture, etc., (pl. or collect. sing.) person's writings, compositions, paintings, etc., as a whole; sewing, embroidery, knitting, etc. 3. (pl.) Establishment, building with machinery, etc., where industrial process, esp. manufacture, is carried on; (pl.) internal mechanism, moving parts of piece of machinery, etc., esp. clock or watch. 4. **workahol'ic**, (colloq.) person having obsessive need to work; **work'bag, work'basket, work'box**, bag etc. holding materials and implements for needlework; **work'bench**, bench for mechanical work, esp. carpentry; **work'book**, book containing instructions and suggestions for study work in the form of questions, exercises, etc.; book for recording work done or planned; handbook containing directions for workman; **work'day**, day on which work is ordinarily performed, weekday; **work'horse**, horse (or fig. person or machine etc.) that performs arduous labor; **work'house**, (hist.) public institution for maintenance of paupers, in which able-bodied were set to work; **work'load**, amount of work that can be performed by a person, machine, etc. in a specified time; **work'man** (pl. **-men**), man hired to do work or (usu.) manual labor, esp. skilled labor; craftsman; one who works in specified manner; **work'manlike, work'manly**, characteristic of a good workman, efficient; **work'manship**, skill as a workman, craftsmanship exhibited in piece of work; **work'room**, room in which work is done; **work sheet**, sheet of paper for recording work schedules, working time, instructions, etc.; sheet of paper having questions, problems, etc., to be solved by pupils; sheet of paper setting forth in preliminary form ideas, plans for action; **work'shop**, room or building in which manual work is carried on; seminar or group of meetings for sharing ideas, group study, demonstrating methods, etc.; **work'table**, table for holding working implements; **work'week**, total number of days or hours worked in a week for base pay. **work'less** *adj*. & *n*. **work** *v*. (**worked** or **wrought** pr. rawt,

1

2

3

work·ing). 1. Engage, be engaged, in work; carry on operations; make efforts; be craftsman (*in* some material); (of machine, plan, etc.) operate, act, (of person) put or keep (machine etc.) in operation; keep (person, machine, etc.) at work or going, exact toil from; purchase (*passage* etc.) with labor instead of money. 2. Carry on, manage, control; have influence or effect, exercise influence on; bring about, effect, accomplish, produce as result. 3. Be in motion, be agitated; cause agitation; ferment. 4. (Cause to) make way, make (way etc.), slowly or with difficulty or by shifting motions; gradually become (tight, free, etc.) by motion. 5. Knead, hammer, fashion, into shape or desired consistency; artificially and gradually excite (person) *into* (a rage etc.). 6. Do, make by, needlework or the like. 7. Solve (sum) by mathematical processes. 8. **~ off**, get rid of, free oneself from; finish working at; pass off, palm off; **~ out**, find (amount etc.), solve (sum) by calculation, (of amount etc.) be calculated (*at*); exhaust (mine etc.) by working; accomplish, attain, with difficulty; develop, elaborate, plan or provide for details of; discharge (debt, obligation), pay for, by labor instead of money; (of athlete, team, etc.) box, play, etc., for practice and exercise not in contest; **work'-out**, exercise; practice game, bout, run, etc.; **work up**, bring gradually to efficient state; elaborate in description; advance gradually *to* (climax); excite, incite, stir up, arouse (*to*); stir up, make up (materials), compose, produce, construct; study (subject) carefully

and in detail.

work·a·ble (wēr′kabel) *adj.* That can be worked, fashioned, manipulated, managed, conducted, etc. **work·a·bil·i·ty** (wērkabĭl′ĭtē), **work'a·ble·ness** *ns.*

work·a·day (wēr′kadā) *adj.* Of, characteristic of, workday or its occupations; of ordinary humdrum everyday life.

work·er (wēr′ker) *n.* (esp.) 1. One employed for a wage, esp. in manual or industrial work; one who works either with hand or brain (opp. capitalist; see CAPITAL[2]). 2. Neuter or undeveloped female of certain social hymenopterous and other insects, as ants and bees, which supplies food and performs other services for community.

work·ing (wēr′kĭng) *n.* (esp.) Way thing works, result of its working; action, operation; **~ capital**, capital used in actual conduct of business, not invested in buildings, machinery, etc.; **~ day**, workday, number of hours of work entitling workman to day's pay, portion of day devoted to work; **~ drawing(s)**, scale drawing(s) from which workmen carry out construction; **~ order**, (of a machine, system, etc.) working efficiently. **working** *adj.* (esp.) Engaged in manual or industrial work; **~ class(es)**, grade(s) of society comprising those employed for wages, esp. in manual or industrial occupations; **~-class**, of, for, the working class; **work'ingman, work'ing-**

woman, (pl. **-men; -women**), person of working class; **working model**, model of machine etc. capable of doing work on small scale, or of being operated.

world (wērld) *n.* 1. Human existence, (also **this ~**) present life; pursuits and interests, affairs and conditions of life; secular or lay life and interests; **next, other, ~**, life after death; **~ without end**, endlessly, eternally. 2. Earth considered as a planet; Earth and all created things upon it; planet or other heavenly body, esp. one viewed as inhabited; material universe as ordered system, system of created things; everything, all phenomena; countries of Earth and their inhabitants, all people; human society; particular section of this, esp. high or fashionable society; sphere of interest, action, or thought; (freq. pl.) great quantity, vast or infinite amount or extent; **for all the ~**, in every respect (like); **man, woman, of the ~**, one knowing the ways of society; **not for (all) the ~**, not on any account. 3. **New World**, Western Hemisphere, containing the nations of the Americas; **Old World**, Eastern Hemisphere, comprising the continents of Europe, Asia, Africa, and Australia; **World Bank**, (colloq.) International Bank for Reconstruction and Development, established in 1945 as an agency of the United Nations; **world history**, history embracing

When scientists first began to classify animals, the term **worm** *was even used to describe snakes. However, today, marine bristle worms (below) are in the same phylum as the earthworm.*

Plants named **woundwort** *include Stachys palustris whose leaves were used as a poultice; and resin from the root of Laserpitium prutenicum was used to make 'Thaspia plasters'.*

events of whole world; **world language**, artificial language intended for universal use; **world politics**, international politics, politics based upon considerations affecting whole world; **world power**, state or nation dominating world politics; **world series** (often **W ~ S ~**), annual series of baseball games between the two U.S. major league pennant winners to decide championship; **world war**, war affecting (most of) the world; **World War I, First World War**, that of 1914–18, fought mainly in Europe and the Middle East between the Allied Powers (Great Britain, U.S., France, etc.) and the Central Powers (Germany, Austria-Hungary, etc.); **World War II, Second World War**, that of 1939–45, fought between the Allies (Great Britain, U.S., France, Soviet Union) and the Axis (Germany, Italy and Japan); **world-weary**, weary of (the life of) the world; **world'wide**, spread over the world, known or found everywhere, universal.

world·ling (wērld'ling) *n.* Worldly person.

world·ly (wērld'lē) *adj.* (**-li·er, -li·est**). Temporal, earthly; exclusively or predominantly concerned with or devoted to affairs of this life, esp. to pursuit of wealth or pleasure; ~ **goods**, property; ~**-minded**, intent on worldly things; ~ **wisdom**, esp. prudence in advancing one's own interests; ~ **-wise**, having worldly wisdom, sophisticated. **world'li·ness** *n.*

worm (wērm) *n.* Slender burrowing invertebrate animal esp. of genus *Lumbricus*, usu. brown or reddish with soft body divided into segments, earthworm; any annelid (**ringed** or **segmented** ~), nematode (**round'worm**), or platyhelminth (**flat'worm**); platyhelminth or nematode living as parasite in intestine of man or other animal; (pl.) disorder characterized by presence of these; larva of insect, maggot, grub, esp. one feeding on or destructive to fruit, leaves, timber, paper, flesh, etc.; maggot supposed to eat dead bodies in the grave; SHIPworm. 2. Abject, miserable, or contemptible person. 3. (fig.) Grief or passion that preys stealthily on the heart or torments the conscience. 4. Natural or artificial object resembling earthworm; small worm-shaped ligament in dog's tongue; any of various spiral implements, esp. spiral of screw (also **worm gear**) endless or tangent screw whose thread gears with teeth of toothed wheel etc.; long spiral or coiled tube connected to head of still, in which vapor is condensed. 5. **worm-eaten**, eaten into by worm(s), full of wormholes; decayed, decrepit, antiquated; **worm**

In Scotland, some types of seaweed have long been used as a vegetable. **Bladder-wrack** (above) is used as mulch and as winter feed for livestock. It was also used to combat scurvy and goiter.

gear, see sense 4; worm wheel; **worm'hole**, hole in wood, fruit, book, etc., made by burrowing insect larva; **worm wheel**, toothed wheel gearing with worm. **worm'y** *adj.* (**worm·i·er, worm·i·est**). **worm** *v.* 1. Hunt for worms; rid (plants etc.) of worms or grubs; cure (puppies etc.) of worms; extract worm from tongue of (dog) as supposed safeguard against madness. 2. Progress or move sinuously; make one's way insidiously, insinuate *oneself, into* (person's confidence, secrets, etc.); ~ **out**, extract (secret etc.) by insidious questioning.

worm·wood (wērm'wŏŏd) *n.* European woody herb (*Artemisia absinthium*) with bitter aromatic taste, yielding dark green oil, and formerly used as tonic and vermifuge and now for making vermouth and absinthe; (fig.) bitter humiliation or its cause.

Worms (wērmz; *Ger.* vōrmz), **Diet of**: see DIET[1].

worn (wŏrn; wōrn) *adj.*: see WEAR; (esp.) impaired by use, exposure, or wear; enfeebled, exhausted, by toil, age, anxiety, etc.; ~**-out**, no longer of use or service; utterly wasted in strength or vitality; stale, trite.

wor·ry (wē'ĕ; wŭr'ĕ) *n.* (pl. **-ries**). Harassing anxiety or solicitude; cause of this, matter for anxiety, (pl.) cares, troubles; **wor'rywart**, (colloq.) person who habitually worries unduly. **worry** *v.* (**-ried, -ry·ing**). 1. (of dog etc.) Seize by throat with teeth and tear or lacerate, kill or injure by biting

and shaking; (fig.) harass, work at, get *along* or *through* with persistent aggression or dogged effort or struggle; vex or distress by inconsiderate or importunate behavior, pester with repeated demands, requests, etc. 2. Make anxious and ill at ease; give way to anxiety or mental disquietude. **wor'ri·er** *n.*

worse (wērs) *adj. & adv.* Used as comparative of *bad, evil, badly, ill*, or as opposite of *better*. ~ *n.* Worse thing(s); worse condition. **wors'en** *v.* Make or become worse, deteriorate.

wor·ship (wēr'shĭp) *n.* 1. Reverence paid to being or power regarded as divine; acts, rites, or ceremonies displaying this; adoration or devotion comparable to this felt or shown to person or principle; **public** ~, church service. 2. (Brit.) Respectful form of address to or mention of certain magistrates in court, also (formerly) persons of high rank etc. **worship** *v.* (**-shiped, -ship·ing**, Brit. **-shipped, -ship·ping**). Adore as divine, pay religious homage to; idolize, regard with adoration; attend public worship; be full of adoration. **wor'ship·er**, Brit. **wor'ship·per** *ns.*

wor·ship·ful (wēr'shĭpfŭl) *adj.* 1. Reverent, filled with spirit of veneration. 2. (archaic) Entitled to honor and respect. **wor'ship·ful·ly** *adv.* **wor'ship·ful·ness** *n.*

worst (wērst) *adj. & adv.* Used as superlative of *bad, evil, badly, ill*; least good or well. ~ *n.* Worst part, feature, state, event, possible issue, action, etc.; **at (the)** ~, in the most evil or undesirable possible state; even on the most unfavorable view or surmise; **do one's** ~, do the utmost evil or harm possible; **get** (etc.) **the ~ of**, be

Sir Christopher Wren attained eminence as an astronomer before he became an architect at the age of 30. His plan for the redesign of London was never completed, but his churches still stand.

worsted in; **if (the) ~ come(s) to (the) ~**, if things turn out as badly as possible or conceivable. **worst** *v.t.* Get the better of, defeat, outdo.

wor·sted (woos'tĭd, wer'stĭd) *n.* Fine smooth-surfaced yarn spun from long staple wool that has been combed so that fibers lie parallel; fabric woven from this. ~ *adj.* Made of worsted. [f. *Worste(a)d* in Norfolk, England]

wort (wert) *n.* Plant or herb used for food or medicine (archaic exc. as second element of plant names).

worth (werth) *predic. adj.* Of the value of (a specified amount or sum); of specified or certain value in other than material respects; sufficiently valuable or important to be equivalent or good return for (something); possessed of, owning; deserving or worthy of (something); **worth'while'**, that is worth time or effort expended. **worth'less** *adj.* **worth'less·ly** *adv.* **worth'less·ness** *n.* **worth** *n.* What a thing is worth, value; equivalent *of* specified sum or amount.

wor·thy (wer'dhē) *adj.* (**-thi·er, -thi·est**). Estimable; having high moral standard; of sufficient worth, value, desert, or merit (*to*), deserving (*of*). ~ *n.* (pl. **-thies**). Distinguished, eminent, or famous person, esp. hero of antiquity.

would (wood): see WILL[2]; **~-be** (*adj.*) desiring or professing to be, posing as.

wound[1] (woond) *n.* Injury done by cutting, stabbing, lacerating, etc., animal or vegetable tissues with hard or sharp instrument, bullet, etc. (freq. fig.); **wound'-wort**, plant used for healing or dressing wounds, esp. species of kidney vetch, goldenrod, etc. **wound** *v.* Inflict wound (on); inflict pain or hurt on, pain, grieve deeply.

wound[2]: see WIND[2].

wove (wōv) *adj.*: see WEAVE; (esp. of paper) made on mold of closely woven wire.

wo·ven: see WEAVE.

wow[1] (wow) *n.* (slang) Striking success.

wow[2] (wow) *n.* Waver, tremolo, in reproduced sound, due to fluctuations in record speed.

w.p. *abbrev.* (baseball) Wild pitch(es).

WPA *abbrev.* Works Progress Administration.

wpm, w.p.m. *abbrevs.* Words per minute.

wrack (răk) *n.* Seaweed or other marine vegetation cast up or growing on tidal seashore; (archaic) wreck; destruction (= RACK[1]); vestige.

wraith (rāth) *n.* Apparition, ghost, of dead person; spectral appearance of living person supposed to portend his death.

wran·gle (răng'gel) *v.* (**-gled, -gling**). 1. Brawl; engage in noisy, vehement, or contentious argument or quarrel; gain or bring about by wrangling. 2. Herd, round up, horses etc. ~ *n.* Noisy, vehement dispute. **wran'gler** *n.*

wrap (răp) *v.* (**wrapped** or **wrapt, wrap·ping**). Enfold, enclose, pack, swathe, (freq. *up*) in garment or folded or soft encircling material; form wrap or covering for; involve, enfold, *in* something obscuring or disguising; fold, wind, draw (covering, garment, etc.) *about, around,* etc.; ~ *up*, put on wraps; (colloq.) finish, settle, summarize; **wrapped up**, (esp.) engrossed, centered, absorbed, *in*; bound up with, involved *in.* **wrap** *n.* Wrapper, covering; blanket, rug, etc., (usu. pl.) additional outer garment worn as defense against wind and weather; woman's shawl, scarf, or the like; **wrap'around**, (designating) garment, skirt, robe, etc., that wraps around body and overlaps its full length; **wrap'up**, (colloq.) brief summary.

wrap·per (răp'er) *n.* (esp.) Protective covering for parcel etc.; paper enclosing newspaper etc. for posting; paper cover of pamphlet or periodical; book jacket; loose enveloping robe or gown; tobacco leaf of superior grade used for outer cover of cigar.

wrap·ping (răp'ĭng) *n.* (esp. pl.) Wraps, enveloping garments; ~ **paper**, paper for packing or wrapping parcels, packages, etc.

wrath (răth) *n.* (chiefly poet. or rhet.) Anger, indignation. **wrath'ful** *adj.* **wrath'ful·ly** *adv.* **wrath'ful·ness** *n.*

wreak (rēk) *v.t.* Gratify (anger etc.), inflict (vengeance etc.), *on.*

wreath (rēth) *n.* (pl. **wreaths** pr. rēdhz). Flowers or leaves strung or woven or wound together into ring for wearing on head, for Christmas ornament, or for decorating statue, building, coffin, etc.; carved imitation of this; similar ring of soft twisted material, as silk; curl *of* smoke, circular or curved band of cloud, light drift-in mass of sand, snow, etc.

wreathe (rēdh) *v.* (**wreathed, wreath·ing**). Encircle as (or with, or as with) a wreath; form into wreath; entwine; wind, turn (flexible object) around or over something; (of smoke etc.) move in wreathlike shape.

wreck (rĕk) *n.* Disabling, destruction, ruin, overthrow, esp. of ship; ship that has suffered wreck; what remains *of* thing or person that has suffered ruin, waste, disablement, dilapidation, etc., anything broken down or ruined, person of undermined or shattered constitution; (law) goods etc. cast up by sea, piece of wreckage. ~ *v.* Cause wreck of (ship, train, person's constitution, undertaking, etc.); suffer wreck.

wreck·age (rĕk´ĭj) *n.* Fragments or remains of wrecked or shattered vessel, structure, etc.; (fig.) act or process of wrecking.

wreck·er (rĕk´er) *n.* (esp.) One who tries from shore to bring about shipwreck in order to plunder or profit by wreckage; one who steals wreckage; person employed in recovering wrecked ship or its contents; vehicle to tow wrecked car; one who obstructs undertaking etc.

wren (rĕn) *n.* Any of numerous species of genus *Troglodytes* and related genera of small songbirds, esp. the *T. aedon*, the house wren, a very small dark brown mottled bird with short erect tail.

Wren (rĕn), **Sir Christopher** (1632–1723). English architect; designer of St. Paul's Cathedral and many other London churches and buildings after the fire of 1666.

wrench (rĕnch) *n.* 1. Violent twist, turn, or pull; (fig.) pain or anguish caused by parting. 2. Instrument or tool of various forms for gripping or turning bolthead, nut, etc., consisting essentially of metal bars with (freq. adjustable) jaws. ~ *v.* Twist, turn; pull around or sideways, violently or with effort; pull *away*, *off*, *out*, thus; injure, pain, by straining or stretching.

wrest (rĕst) *v.* Twist, deflect, distort, pervert; force or wrench away from person's grasp. ~ *n.* Tuning key of wire-stringed instrument, as harp, piano; ~ **pins**, pegs to which piano strings are attached.

wres·tle (rĕs´el) *n.* (**-tled, -tling**). Wrestling match; hard struggle. ~ *v.* Strive to overpower and throw another to the ground, esp. in contest governed by fixed rules, by grappling with him and tripping or overbalancing

him; have wrestling match with; contend, grapple, struggle, *with* thing, difficulties, feelings, forces, etc.; throw (cattle) for branding. **wres'tler, wres'tling** *ns.*

wretch (rĕch) *n.* Miserable, unhappy, or unfortunate person; contemptible or vile person, one without conscience or shame (freq. as term of playful abuse).

wretch·ed (rĕch´ĭd) *adj.* Miserable, unhappy, afflicted; inferior, of poor quality, of no merit; contemptible; unsatisfactory; causing discontent, discomfort, or nuisance. **wretch'ed·ly** *adv.* **wretch'ed·ness** *n.*

wrig·gle (rĭg´el) *n.* (**-gled, -gling**). Wriggling movement. ~ *v.* Twist or turn body about with short writhing movements; (fig.) be slippery, practice evasion; move (oneself, part of body, etc.) with wriggling motion, make (*way*) by wriggling. **wrig'gly** *adj.* (**-gli·er, -gli·est**). **wrig'gler** *n.* (esp.) Larva of a mosquito.

Wright[1] (rīt), **Frank Lloyd** (1869–1959). Amer. architect known for his exceptionally original and innovative designs.

Wright[2] (rīt), **Orville** (1871–1948) and **Wilbur** (1867–1912). Two brothers, Amer. technicians, who built and flew (1903) the first heavier-than-air motor-driven flying machine.

wring (rĭng) *v.t.* (**wrung** pr. rŭng, **wring·ing**). Press, squeeze, or twist, with hands or machine, esp. so as to drain or make dry, strain (moisture etc.) by squeezing or torsion from moist or wet thing; twist forcibly, break by twisting, torture, distress, rack; extort, get (money, concession, etc.) *out of* or *from* by exaction or importunity; press or clasp (person's *hand*) forcibly or with emotion; ~ **one's hands**, clasp and twist them to-

gether in distress or pain. **wring** *n.* Squeeze, act of wringing.

wring·er (rĭng´er) *n.* (esp.) Device for wringing water from laundered clothes etc., usu. consisting essentially of two rollers between which article is squeezed.

wrin·kle (rĭng´kel) *n.* 1. Furrowlike crease, depression, or ridge in skin (esp. of kind produced by age, care, etc.) or in other flexible surface. 2. (colloq.) Useful hint; clever expedient. **wrin'kly** *adj.* (**-kli·er, -kli·est**). **wrinkle** *v.* (**-kled, -kling**). Acquire or assume wrinkles; produce wrinkles in.

wrist (rĭst) *n.* Joint in man connecting hand with forearm, carpus; analogous joint in other animals; part of garment covering wrist; **wrist'band**, band of sleeve covering or fastening about wrist; wristlet; **wrist pin**, (mech.) pin, stud, joining connecting rod to piston; **wrist'watch**, small watch worn on strap or bracelet around wrist.

wrist·let (rĭst´lĭt) *n.* Band, bracelet, strap, worn on wrist to strengthen or guard it, as ornament, to hold watch, etc.

writ[1] (rīt) *n.* 1. **Holy, Sacred, W~**, sacred writings collectively, esp. the Bible. 2. Formal written order issued by court in name of government, state, etc., directing person(s) to whom it is addressed to do or refrain from doing specified act.

writ[2] (rīt) *v.* (archaic and poet.) Wrote, written.

write (rīt) *v.* (**wrote** pr. rōt, **writ·ten** pr. rĭt´en, **writ·ing**). Form symbols representing letter(s) or word(s) esp. on paper, parchment, etc., with pen, pencil, brush, etc., form (such symbols), set (words etc.) down in writing, express in writing; chronicle, make record or account of; convey (message, information, etc.) by letter; engage in writing or authorship; produce writing; ~ **down**, set down in writing; write in disparagement or depreciation of; reduce (total, assets, etc.) to lower amount; ~ **in**, add (extra name) on list of candidates when voting (so **write-in** *n.*); **write off**, record canceling of (bad debt, depreciated stock, etc.); reckon as lost or worthless; **write-off** (*n.*), something that must be regarded as total loss or wreck, failure; **write out**, make written copy of; transcribe in full or detail; **write up**, write full account

common wren

cactus wren

blue wren

*As with many animals in the colonies the name **wren** was given to small birds which are unrelated to the true varieties. Most of these birds are insectivorous and the common wren of Europe is only 4 ins. long. In contrast, the cactus wren in the south-west U.S.A. grows to 8½ inches long.*

or record of; give full or elaborate description of; commend by appreciative writing, praise in writing; **write-up** (*n.*), review or report.

writ·er (rī´ter) *n.* One who writes; person writing books, articles, etc., esp. as profession; ~**'s cramp**, painful spasmodic cramp affecting muscles of hand and fingers used in writing, and resulting from excessive writing.

writhe (rīdh) *v.* (**writhed, writh·ing**). Twist or roll oneself about (as) in acute pain, squirm; twist (*body* etc.) about, contort. ~ *n.* Act of writhing. **writh´ing·ly** *adv.*

writ·ing (rī´tĭng) *n.* (esp.) Written document; (piece of) literary work; personal script, handwriting; **put in** ~, write down; **the W ~s** = HAGIOGRAPHA; **writing desk**, desk; **writing paper**, paper for writing on with ink, esp. notepaper; **writing table**, desk.

writ·ten (rĭt´en) *adj.*: see WRITE; (esp.) that is in writing, esp. opp. *oral* or *printed*.

wrong (rawng, rŏng) *adj.* 1. Not morally right or equitable, unjust; doing or prone to do evil; not correct or proper; not true, mistaken; judging, acting, etc., contrary to facts, in error; ~**-headed, wrong´head´ed**, perversely or obstinately wrong, characterized by perversity of judgment; **wrong-headedness, wrong´headed´ness** (*ns.*). 2. Not in good order or condition, amiss; not what is required or intended, unsuitable, inappropriate; (of way etc.) leading in, tending to, direction other than

what is intended, desired, or expected; **wrong end**, end or limit less adapted or suitable for particular purpose; **get hold of the wrong end of the stick**, (fig.) be mistaken in judgment etc.; **wrong side**, side (of fabric etc.) not meant for use or show; **on the wrong side of**, older than (specified age); under a person's disapproval or disfavor; **get up, get out of bed, on the wrong side**, be in irritable mood; (**the**) **wrong way**, in contrary or opposite way to proper or usual one. **wrong´ly** *adv.* **wrong´ness, wrong´er** *ns.* **wrong** *adv.* Amiss, in wrong course or direction; mistakenly, erroneously; in improper or unfitting manner; **get person** ~, misunderstand him; **get in** ~ **with person**, (colloq.) incur his dislike; **get person in** ~, bring him into disfavor; **go** ~, go astray; happen amiss or unfortunately; get out of gear or working order; take to bad ways. **wrong** *n.* What is morally wrong; wrong action; unjust action or treatment; being wrong in attitude, procedure, or belief (freq. **in the** ~); **wrong´doing**, transgression against moral or established law. **wrong** *v.t.* Treat unjustly, do wrong to; do injustice to by statement, opinion, etc.; dishonor by word or thought.

wrong·ful (rawng´ful, rŏng´-)

Empty hay cart in the rodeo parade at Cheyenne, Wyoming. This mountain State is a major center of cattle breeding although the greatest income is derived from mining, and oil and gas.

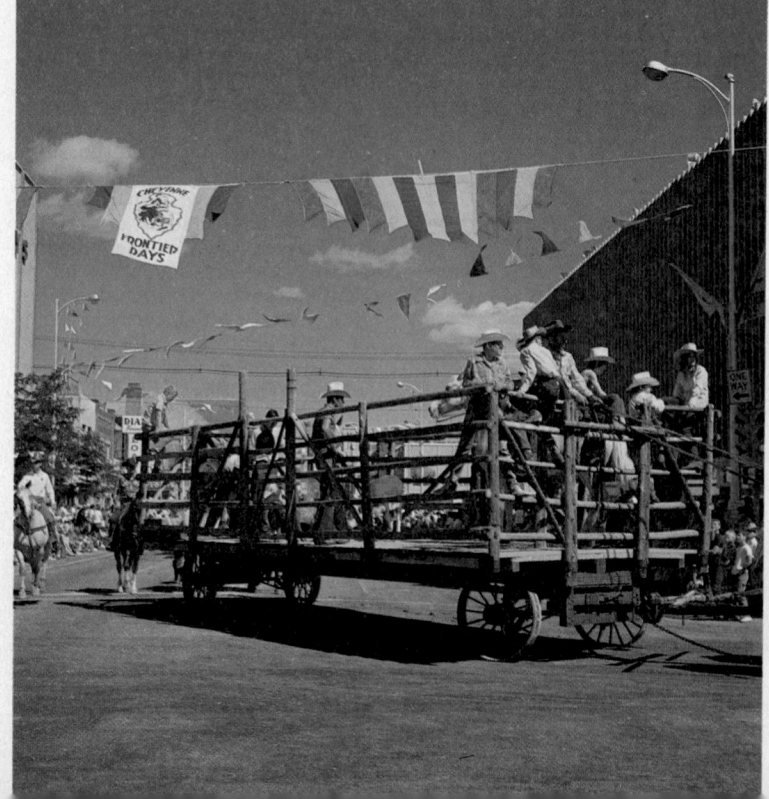

adj. Marked by wrong, unfairness, injustice, etc.; contrary to law, etc., unlawful, illegal; (of persons) holding office, possession, etc., unlawfully or without legitimacy or right. **wrong´ful·ly** *adv.* **wrong´ful·ness** *n.*

wrote: see WRITE.

wroth (rawth, rŏth; *Brit.* also rōth) *pred. adj.* (poet. and rhet.) Angry, stirred to wrath.

wrought (rawt) *adj.* Worked, processed, manufactured, worked into shape; (literary) put together, worked, made; (of metals) beaten out or shaped with hammer etc.; ~ **iron**: see IRON; **wrought-up**, stirred up, excited or agitated.

wrung: see WRING.

wry (rī) *adj.* (**wri·er, wri·est**). Distorted, turned to one side; temporarily twisted or contorted in disgust, disrelish, etc.; **wry mouth** (pr. rī´mowth) (pl. **-mouth**, collect. **-mouths** pr. -mowdhz), any of numerous large fish of family Stichaeidae, of blenny kind, the ghostfish of northern Atlantic coasts of N. Amer.; **wry´neck**, deformity with contortion of neck and face and lateral inclination of head, torticollis; species of genus *Jynx* of small migratory birds allied to woodpeckers, esp. *J. torquilla* of Europe and Asia, with peculiar manner of writhing neck and head. **wry´ly** *adv.* **wry´ness** *n.*

WSW, W.S.W., w.s.w. *abbrevs.* West-southwest.

wt. *abbrev.* Weight.

Wul·fi·la (wŏŏl´fila): see ULFILAS.

WV, W.Va. *abbrevs.* West Virginia.

WY *abbrev.* Wyoming.

Wy·an·dotte (wī´andŏt) *n.* (pl. **-dottes**, collect. for def. 1 **-dotte**). 1. Member of tribe of N. Amer. Indians. 2. Domestic fowl of medium-sized breed, orig. white laced with black but now bred in various colors.

wych, witch² (wĭch) *ns.* In names of various trees with pliant branches: ~**-elm**, species of elm (*Ulmus glabra*) with broader leaves and more spreading branches than common elm; ~ **hazel**, N. Amer. shrub (*Hamamelis virginiana*) with yellow flowers blooming in late autumn or winter.

Wyc·liffe, Wyc·lif (wĭk´lĭf), **John** (*c*1320–84). English religious reformer; attacked the papacy and asserted the right of every man to examine the Bible for himself; instituted the first translation into English of the whole Bible, himself translating the Gospels and probably other parts; his doctrines were taken up by the Lollards.

Wyo. *abbrev.* Wyoming.

Wy·o·ming (wīō´mĭng). State of northwestern U.S., admitted to the Union in 1890; capital, Cheyenne.

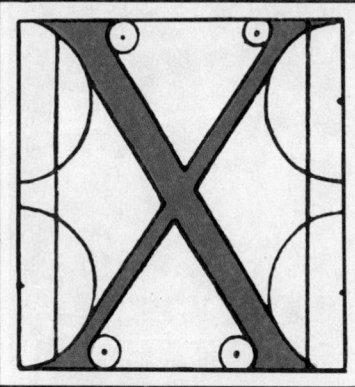

Although the letter **X, x** appeared in the Greek alphabet, about 600 B.C., it was derived from a symbol used in Egyptian hieroglyphics and a later Phoenician character. The sound attributed to it in Greek was as in 'fix' but if used at the beginning of a word, then sounded as in 'xylophone'.

Early Latin   Classical Latin   Anglo-Saxon

Carolingian   Italian (italic)   Italian (Roman)

X, x (ĕks) (pl. **X's, x's** or **Xs, xs**). 1. Twenty-fourth letter of modern English and 21st of ancient Roman alphabet, adopted from the Greek alphabet introduced into Italy, with the value (ks, as in lyn*x*) that it usually has in modern English except when occurring initially in words chiefly of Greek origin, when it is pronounced z. 2. Roman numeral symbol for ten; **X**, (slang) ten-dollar bill. 3. (alg. etc.) Symbol for (esp. first) unknown or variable quantity; hence, incalculable or unknown factor or influence. 4. **X**, symbol for Christ, representing the chi in Greek *XPIΣTOΣ*, used in abbreviations, e.g. *Xmas* (= Christmas). 5. Symbol to mark position (*X marks the spot*) or incorrectness or to symbolize a kiss or vote or as signature by illiterate person. 6. **X**, designation of motion picture for showing only to persons over 18 years. 7. **x-height**, height of an x, height of body of letter. 8. Object etc. shaped like X.

x (ĕks) *v.t.* (**x-ed** or **x'd, x-ing**). Mark with x; (also **x out**) delete, cross out.

xan·thate (zăn´thāt) *n.* (chem.) Salt of xanthic acid.

xan·the·in (zăn´thēĭn) *n.* (chem.) Yellow coloring matter found in plants.

xan·thic (zăn´thĭk) *adj.* (chem. etc.) Yellow; of xanthin; ~ **acid**, complex acid ($C_3H_6OS_2$), many of whose salts are yellow.

xan·thine (zăn´thēn, -thĭn) *n.* (chem.) Substance ($C_5H_4N_4O_2$) related to uric acid and found in animal secretions.

Xan·thip·pe, Xan·tip·pe (zăntĭp´ē). Wife of Socrates, reputed to be a shrew; hence, shrewish woman or wife.

xan·tho·phyll (zăn´thofĭl) *n.* Dark brown crystalline compound found in plants, usu. associated with chlorophyll, and forming yellow coloring matter of autumn leaves.

xan·thous (zăn´thus) *adj.* (of a people) Having yellow(ish) or red(dish) hair; having yellow skin.

Xa·vi·er (zā´vēer, zăv´ē-, zāv´yer), **St. Francis** (1506–52).

Spanish Jesuit, one of the founders of the Society of Jesus, and a missionary in the Far East, commemorated Dec. 3.

x-ax·is (ĕks´ăksĭs) *n.* (pl. **x-ax·es** pr. ĕks´ăksēz). (math.) Horizontal axis in two-dimensional coordinate system.

X chromosome: see CHROMOSOME.

Xe *symbol.* Xenon.

xeno- *comb. form.* Foreign(er), other, as *xenolith, xenophobe.*

xen·o·lith (zĕn´olĭth) *n.* (geol.) Stone or rock occurring in a system to which it does not belong. **xen·o·lith·ic** (zĕnolĭth´ĭk) *adj.*

xe·non (zē´nŏn, zĕn´ŏn) *n.* (chem.) Heavy inert gaseous element present in minute quantity in the atmosphere; symbol Xe, at. no. 54, at. wt. 131.30. [Gk. *xenos* strange]

xen·o·pho·bi·a (zĕnofō´bēa) *n.* Morbid dislike or fear of foreigners, foreign customs, etc. **xen·o·phobe** (zĕn´ofōb) *n.* Person showing xenophobia. **xen·o·pho´bic** *adj.*

Xen·o·phon (zĕn´ofon, -fŏn) (*c*428–354 B.C.). Athenian historian and philosopher; pupil of Socrates, about whom he wrote in the *Memorabilia* and the *Symposium*; he described in the *Anabasis* the expedition of Cyrus against Artaxerxes (401–399 B.C.) in which he led Greek mercenaries in their retreat to the Black Sea after they had been left in a dangerous situation between the Tigris and Euphrates.

Xe·res (*Sp.* hĕ´rĕs). Old spelling of JEREZ.

xe·rog·ra·phy (zĭrŏg´rafē) *n.* Dry printing process in which colored resin adheres to those areas of the surface of paper that have been sensitized with a charge of static electricity. **xe·ro·graph·ic** (zērogrăf´ĭk) *adj.*

xe·roph·a·gy (zĭrŏf´ajē) *n.* (pl. **-gies**). Strictest form of fast, practiced in Eastern Church esp. during Lent or Holy Week, and forbidding meat, fish, cheese, milk, butter, oil, wine, and all seasonings except salt.

xe·roph·i·lous (zĭrŏf´ilus) *adj.*

(bot.) Adapted to extremely dry conditions.

xe·roph·thal·mi·a (zērŏfthăl´mēa) *n.* (path.) Inflammation of the conjunctiva with abnormal dryness and corrugation.

xe·ro·phyte (zēr´ofīt) *n.* Plant adapted to very dry conditions, desert plant.

Xer·ox (zēr´ŏks) *n.* (trademark) Process of reproduction by xerography. **x~** *v.t.* Reproduce by Xerox.

Xerx·es (zērk´sēz). King of Persia 486–465 B.C., son of Darius; invaded Greece and overcame the resistance of Leonidas and the Spartans at Thermopylae, but was defeated at Salamis 480 B.C.

xi (zī, sī; *Gk.* ksē) *n.* (pl. **xis**). Fifteenth (later 14th) letter of Greek alphabet (Ξ, ξ), corresponding to *x*.

xiph·i·ster·num (zĭfīstēr´num) *n.* (pl. **-na** pr. -na). Xiphoid process.

xiph·oid (zĭf´oid) *adj.* Swordshaped; ~ **process**, cartilaginous or bony process at lower or posterior end of sternum in man and other animals.

Xi·zang (shē´zahng´) = TIBET.

Xmas *abbrev.* Christmas (see X, x sense 4).

xo·a·non (zō´anŏn) *n.* (pl. **-na** pr. -na). (Gk. antiq.) Primitive usu. wooden image of deity, supposed to have fallen from heaven.

X-ra·di·a·tion (ĕks´rādēa´shon) *n.* Radiation composed of x-rays; treatment with or exposure to this.

x-ray, x ray (ĕks´rā) *ns.* Electromagnetic radiation of very short wavelength emitted by electrons whose velocity is suddenly reduced, capable of passing through opaque bodies, of acting on photographic plates, and of ionizing gases; (also ~ **photograph**) photograph, esp. showing position of bones etc., made with x-rays. **x-ray** *v.t.* Photograph, examine, with x-rays; treat (disease, patient) with x-rays. [Ger. *X-strahlen*, name given by their discoverer, ROENTGEN, to indicate that their essential nature was unknown]

xy·lem (zī´lem, -lĕm) *n.* (bot.) Woody tissue including vessels and fibers forming harder part of fibrovascular tissues of plant (opp. PHLOEM).

xy·lene (zī′lēn) *n.* (chem.) One of three colorless, oily, isomeric hydrocarbons, derivatives of benzene, obtained from wood, tar, etc.

xy·li·tol (zī′litōl, -tawl, -tŏl) *n.* Sugar substitute derived from wood.

xy·lo·graph (zī′logrăf, -grahf) *n.* Woodcut, esp. of early period.

xy·loph·a·gous (zīlŏf′agus) *adj.* (of insects) Feeding on, boring into, wood.

xy·lo·phone (zī′lofōn) *n.* Musical instrument consisting of a series of flat wooden bars, graduated in length to sound the musical scale, resting on strips of straw or felt, and played by striking with small wooden hammer(s).

*Right: Rock tombs at Persepolis in southern Iran which were excavated for such kings as Darius and **Xerxes** between 550 and 331 B.C. The bas relief between is Roman.*

*A modern **X-ray** generator used for medical work. A beam of electrons from the cathode is directed at an anode which rotates at speeds up to 10,000 r.p.m. This prevents over-heating and extends the working life of the equipment.*

anode cable

cathode cable

electrons

rotating anode

hot filament cathode

motor coils

lead shield

rotor

X-ray beam

mirror

light bulb

glass envelope

lead screens

beam of X-rays and light

photographic film holder

The original Roman alphabet ended with X but when the Romans conquered the Greeks, they needed **Y, y** as a letter to be equivalent of upsilon for those words that they had adopted from the Greek. This, in turn, had been adopted from a Phoenician symbol and sounded like a U.

Phoenician   Early Etruscan   Classical Latin

Cursive Majuscule   Cursive Miniscule   Italian (italic)

Y, y (wī) *n.* (pl. **Y's, y's** or **Ys, ys**). 1. Twenty-fifth letter of modern English and 23rd of ancient Roman alphabet, representing ultimately Y, *Y*, of Greek alphabet, a differentiated form of primitive V (see U, V), first adopted in Latin alphabet as V, and later readopted in form Y to represent Y of borrowed Greek works; as a vowel, representing in English all the sounds (except ē) commonly spelled with *i*, and used as the normal spelling (*a*) for final *i*-sounds, (*b*) in words of Greek origin, representing upsilon, (*c*) before *i* in inflectional forms of verbs ending in -*y* or -*ie*, (*d*) in plural of nouns ending in -*y* preceded by another vowel; as a consonant, representing a voiced palatal spirant. 2. (alg. etc.) Symbol of second of series of unknown or variable quantities (cf. x). 3. Object etc. shaped like Y; **Y-branch**, piece of piping with branch at acute angle to main.

Y *symbol.* Yttrium.

Y, Y. *abbrevs.* YMCA, YMHA, YWCA, YWHA.

y. *abbrev.* Year(s).

y- *prefix.* Used esp. with past participles, still found in a few archaic forms, as *yclad* clad, *yclept* called, *ywis* surely.

-y¹ *suffix.* Forming nouns denoting (1) state, condition, or quality (*courtesy, fury, glory*); (2) action or its result (*remedy, subsidy*); (3) activity, shop or goods specified, place of business (*bakery, company, library*).

-y² *suffix.* Forming adjectives with sense full of or containing, having the quality of, addicted to (*gluey, horsy, messy, slangy, thorny*).

-y³ *suffix.* Forming diminutive nouns, pet names, etc. (*granny, Sally*).

yacht (yŏt) *n.* Light sailing vessel kept, and usu. specially built, for racing; vessel propelled by sails, steam, or any motive power other than oars, and used for private pleasure excursions, cruising, travel, etc.; ~ **club**, club esp. for yacht racing; **yachts'man**, person who yachts. **yacht** *v.i.* Race or cruise in yacht. [early mod. Du. *jaght(e)*, = *jaghtschip* (*jagen* to hunt); named f. its speed]

yah (yah) *int.* Exclamation of disgust, defiance, or derision.

ya·hoo (yah′hōō, yā′-, yahhōō′) *n.* In Swift's *Gulliver's Travels*, race of brutes in human shape; hence, degraded or bestial human being.

Yah·weh, Yah·we (yah′wě), **Yah·veh** (yah′vě). Name of God in Old Testament, transliteration of the Tetragrammaton that is rendered JEHOVAH in the Authorized Version etc.

Yah·wist (yah′wĭst) *n.* Author(s) of those parts of the Hexateuch where God is referred to as *Yahweh* rather than *Elohim*. **Yah′wism** *n.* **Yah·wis·tic** (yahwĭs′tĭk) *adj.*

yak¹ (yăk) *n.* Large humped bovine mammal (*Bos grunniens*) with long silky hair on sides, tail, etc., found wild and domesticated in Tibet and other high regions of central Asia; used as a beast of burden. [Tibetan *gyag*]

yak² (yăk) *n. & v.* (**yakked, yak·king**). (Utter) steady senseless chatter.

Yale¹ (yāl) *n.* **Yale′lock**, (trademark) type of cylinder lock for doors etc. [f. Linus *Yale* (1821–68), Amer. locksmith]

Yale² (yāl). University at New Haven, Conn., originally called Yale College in consequence of benefactions received from Elihu Yale (1648–1721).

Yal·ta (yawl′ta). Seaport in S. Ukraine on the Black Sea, scene of wartime conference (Feb. 1945) of Churchill, Roosevelt, and Stalin, at which they made final plans to defeat Germany, and also decided to set up the United Nations Organization.

Ya·lu (yah′lōō). River in North Korea flowing 300 mi. (480 km), along Manchurian border to Yellow Sea.

yam (yăm) *n.* Starchy tuberous root, serving as a staple food in many tropical and subtropical countries; of various species of *Dioscorea*, twining herbs or shrubs with spikes of small inconspicuous flowers; any of these plants; sweet potato.

Ya·ma (yŭm′a). (Hinduism) Ruler of the world of the dead.

Yang (yăng) *n.* (Chin. philos.) Active male principle of universe (opp. YIN).

Yang·tze (yăng′sē; *Chin.* yahng′-tsě′). (also ~ **Kiang**) Principal river of China; rises in Tibet and flows through central China 3,602 mi. (5,797 km) to E. China Sea.

A wild bull **yak** *may have a shoulder height of 6 ft. 8 ins. and may weigh more than 1100 lb. Domesticated yaks are smaller but are useful providers of milk, meat, and even dung for fuel.*

The veiling of a woman with a **yashmak** was not introduced by Muhammad but was a continuation of an existing custom among the Arabs. Today, it has been dropped in some places.

The Yellowstone River drops more than 300 ft. over the Lower Falls—one of the most impressive sights in the **Yellowstone National Park**—to enter the Grand Canyon.

Yank (yăngk) *n. & adj.* (colloq.) Yankee.

yank (yăngk) *n. & v.* (slang) (Pull with) sudden sharp tug or jerk.

Yan·kee (yăng′kē) *n.* Native or inhabitant of New England or of northern states of U.S. generally; (applied by other peoples to) any inhabitant of U.S.; (attrib.) of Yankees, that is a Yankee. [perh. f. Du. *Janke* dim. of *Jan* John used derisively; or f. *Jengees* Indian pronunciation of *English*]

Ya·oun·dé (yahōōndā′). Capital of Cameroon in W. central Africa.

yap (yăp) *n. & v.i.* (**yapped, yap·ping**). (Utter) shrill or fussy bark, yelp. **yap′per** *n.* **yap′-ping·ly** *adv.* [imit.]

yard[1] (yärd) *n.* Piece of enclosed ground, esp. one surrounded by or attached to building(s) or used for manufacturing or other purpose; prison yard, shipyard, dockyard, stockyard, etc.; garden; ground near railroad station where rolling stock is kept, trains are made up, etc.; **the Y ~**, SCOTLAND YARD; **yard′-man**, man who works in railroad or lumber yard; gardener or man doing various outdoor jobs; **yard′-master**, manager of railroad yard. **yard** *v.t.* Enclose (cattle etc.) in yard.

yard[2] (yärd) *n.* 1. Unit of long measure, equal to 3 feet or 36 inches (0.9144 m); measure of area (**square ~**); measure of solidity (**cubic ~**), as in *yard of gravel, lime*, etc.; yard length of material; **~ measure**, rod, tape, etc., one yard long, usu. marked in feet and inches; **yard′stick**, stick as yard measure; (fig.) standard, criterion. 2. (naut.) Long usu. cylindrical spar, tapering to each end, slung (usu. at its center for square sail) from mast, to support and extend sail; **yard′arm**, either end of yard of square-rigged vessel. **yard′age** *n.* Number of yards of material etc.; (football) yards gained in offensive play.

yar·mul·ke (yär′mulke) *n.* Skullcap worn by Jewish men.

yarn (yärn) *n.* 1. Fiber, as of cotton, wool, silk, flax, spun and prepared for use in weaving, knitting, etc. 2. (colloq., orig. naut.) Story, tale; **spin a ~**, tell (usu. long) tale. **yarn** *v.i.* (colloq.) Tell yarn(s).

yar·row (yăr′ō) *n.* Plant of genus *Achillea*, esp. *A. millefolium*, common on roadsides, dry meadows, and waste ground, with tough grayish stem, finely divided bipinnate leaves, and dull white or pinkish flower heads in close flat clusters.

yash·mak (yahsh′mahk, yăsh′-măk) *n.* Double veil concealing face below eyes, worn in public by Muslim women of some countries.

yat·a·ghan (yăt′agăn, -gan; *Turk.* yahtahgahn′) *n.* Short sword of Muslim countries with slight reverse curve.

yaw (yaw) *v.i. & n.* (naut., aeron.) (Make) deviation from straight course owing to action of heavy sea or strong winds.

yawl (yawl) *n.* Ship's boat with four or six oars; two-masted fore-and-aft sailboat with after mast much smaller than mainmast and placed abaft the rudder.

yawn (yawn) *v.* Breathe in involuntarily with mouth wide open, as from drowsiness, fatigue, boredom, etc.; utter or say with yawn; (of chasm etc.) gape, have wide opening. **~ n.** Act of Yawning.

yaws (yawz) *n.pl.* (usu. considered sing.) Skin disease of tropical countries with raspberry-like tubercles or excrescences on skin, having many analogies with syphilis.

y-ax·is (wī′ăksĭs) *n.* (pl. **y-ax·es** pr. wī′ăksēz). (math.) Vertical axis in two-dimensional coordinate system.

Yaz·oo (yăz′ōō). River in Mississippi flowing 190 mi. (305 km), to Mississippi near Vicksburg.

Yb *symbol.* Ytterbium.

Y chromosome: see CHROMOSOME.

y·clept, y·cleped (ēklĕpt′) *adjs.* (archaic or joc.) Called (so-and-so).

yd. *abbrev.* Yard.

ye (yē) *pron.* Second person pl. (archaic, dial. or poet.) = YOU.

yea (yā) *adv. & n.* (archaic) Yes.

year (yēr) *n.* 1. Time occupied by Earth in one revolution around the sun (also **astronomical, equinoctial, natural, solar, tropical, ~** = 365 days, 5 hours, 48 minutes, 46 seconds) or by the sun in recovering its previous apparent relation to the fixed stars (**astral** or **sidereal ~**, longer by 20 minutes, 23 seconds). 2. Period of days (esp. **common ~** of 365 days reckoned from Jan. 1 or **leap** or **bissextile ~** of 366) used by community for dating or other purposes commencing on a certain day, usu. divided into 12 months, and corresponding more or less exactly in length to the astronomical year (also called **calendar, civil,** or **legal** ~). 3. Such space of time with limits not necessarily co-inciding with those of civil year, used in reckoning age, period of office, occupation, etc., or for special purpose, as taxation, payment of dividends, etc. 4. (pl.) Age (of person); (pl.) period, times, a very long time. 5. ~ **in,** ~ **out,** successive through the years, con-tinuously; **year'book,** annual publication containing information for the year. **year'long'** *adj.* Lasting a year. **year-round** *adj.* Existing throughout the year, through all seasons.

year·ling (yēr'lĭng) *n. & adj.* (Animal, esp. lamb, calf, or foal) a year old; (racing) colt one year old from Jan. 1 of year of foaling.

year·ly (yēr'lē) *adj. & adv.* (Occurring, observed, done, etc.) once a year or every year; annual(ly).

yearn (yērn) *v.i.* Long; be moved with compassion or tender feelings. **yearn'ing** *n.*

yeast (yēst) *n.* Minute uni-cellular fungus esp. of family Saccharomycetaceae; grayish-yellow substance produced as froth or sediment during alcoholic fermentation of malt brews and other saccharine fluids, consisting of aggregations of minute fungi and used in manufacture of beer, to leaven bread, etc.; dried form of this substance prepared in cakes or granules. **yeast'y** *adj.* (**yeast·i·er, yeast·i·est**). Frothy like yeast; in a ferment, working like yeast; made with yeast. **yeast'i·ness** *n.*

Yeats (yāts), **William Butler** (1865–1939). Irish lyric poet and dramatist; assisted in the creation of an Irish national theater; received Nobel Prize for literature, 1923.

yegg (yĕg) *n.* (slang) (also **yegg'-man,** pl. **-men**). Burglar, esp. one who breaks open safes. [said to be name of Amer. safe-cracker]

yell (yĕl) *n.* Sharp loud outcry of strong and sudden emotion, as rage, horror, agony; set of words or syllables shouted as an organized cheer, as by college students. ~ *v.* Make, utter with, yell.

yel·low (yĕl'ō) *adj.* Of the color of buttercup or lemon or sulfur or gold, most luminous of the primary colors, occurring in spectrum between green and orange; having a yellow skin or complexion, as the Mongolian peoples; (of newspaper etc.) recklessly or unscrupulously sensational; (slang) cowardly; craven; **yel'lowbelly,** (slang) coward; **yellow fever,** acute, often fatal febrile disease of hot climates, characterized by jaundice, vomiting, hemorrhages, etc., and

transmitted by a mosquito; **yellow jack,** yellow fever; quarantine flag; **yellow jacket,** any of several small wasps (family Vespidae) having black and yellow markings; **yel'-lowlegs,** either of two N. Amer. wading birds (*Totanus melanoleucus* and *T. flavipes*) with long bill and bright yellow legs; **yellow ocher**: see OCHER; **yellow pages,** section of telephone directory on yellow paper listing business subscribers accord-ing to goods or services they offer; **Yellow River,** most northerly of China's great rivers, 2,900 mi. (4,640 km) long, known as "China's Sorrow" because of its uncontrol-lable floods; **Yellow Sea,** arm of Pacific between China and Korea, into which the Yellow River formerly flowed; **Yel'lowstone National Park,** area of about 3,458 sq. miles (8,956 sq. km), chiefly in Wyoming, reserved since 1872 for public uses, named after the **Yellowstone River,** a tributary of the Missouri, which rises there; **yel'lowthroat,** any of several small Amer. birds of the genus *Geothlypis,* esp. *G. trichas,* having yellow breast and throat, and, in the male, a distinctive black mask on the face; **yellow-throated warbler,** wood warbler (*Dendroica dominica*) of southeastern U.S., having gray back, yellow breast, and black, gray, and white striped sides. **yellow** *n.* Yellow color, pigment, fabric, etc.; yellow species or variety of bird, butterfly, moth, flower, etc. **yellow**

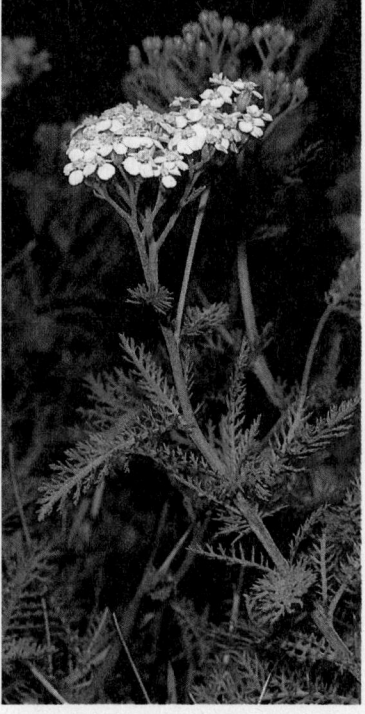

Found primarily through the northern temperate zone, the **yarrow** *comprises about 80 species; some are used to induce sneezing.*

v. Turn yellow. **yel'low·ish** *adj.*

yelp (yĕlp) *n. & v.i.* (Utter) sharp shrill bark or cry (as) of dog in pain, excitement, etc. **yelp'er** *n.*

Yem·en (yĕm'en). Name of two republics in the Arabian peninsula: ~ **Arab Republic,** a republic since 1962 (kingdom 1934–62) of SW. Arabia, the *Arabia Felix* of the ancients, freed from Turkish rule in 1918; capital, Sana'a; **People's Democratic Republic of** ~, a republic since 1967 in S. Arabia bordering on the Yemen Arab Republic; capital, Aden; ad-ministrative capital, Madinat al Shaab; **Yem·en·ite** (yĕm'enīt), **Yem·e·ni** (yĕm'enē) *adjs. & ns.*

yen[1] (yĕn) *n.* (pl. **yen**). Monetary unit of Japan. [Jap., f. Chin. *yüan* round, dollar]

yen[2] (yĕn) *n.* (colloq.) Passionate or impelling desire or longing. [Chin. *yen* smoke, opium]

yeo·man (yō'man) *n.* (pl. **-men**). 1. (hist.) British small landowner, person of middle class engaged in agriculture (esp. attrib., as ~ **farmer**). 2. (hist.) Servant and attendant in British royal or noble household of rank between sergeant and groom or squire and page. 3. (U.S. Navy) Petty officer perform-ing clerical duties on board ship. 4. Member of yeomanry force; ~**('s) service,** help in need; efficient service. **yeo'man·ly** *adj.* Of, befitting, a yeoman or yeomen.

yeo·man·ry (yō'manrē) *n.* 1. Yeomen collectively. 2. (hist.) Volunteer cavalry force in British Army, orig. formed in 18th c. for home defense, merged in the Territorial Force in 1907.

yep (yĕp) *adv.* (dial.) = YES.

yer·ba ma·té (yēr'ba mahtā', mätā'): see MATÉ.

yes (yĕs) *adv.* Particle express-ing affirmative reply to request, question, etc. ~ *n.* (pl. **yes·es**). Word, answer, "yes"; ~ **man,** (colloq.) person who agrees un-critically with everything that is said to him by a superior.

ye·shi·va (yeshē'va) *n.* (pl. **-vahs** pr. -*vaz,* **-voth** pr. -*vawt*). 1. School or college for Talmudic study, esp. seminary for training orthodox rabbis. 2. Jewish day school pro-viding religious and secular education.

yes·ter·day (yĕs'terdā, -dē) *n. & adv.* (On) the day immediately pre-ceding today; (in) time not long past.

yes·ter·year (yĕs'teryēr) *n.* Last year, the past (poet.). [coined by D. G. Rossetti to translate Fr. *antan,* f. L. *ante annum*]

yet (yĕt) *adv.* 1. In addition or continuation, besides, also (archaic); (with comparative) even, still; **nor** ~, and also not. 2. Up to this or that time, till now, till then; at some time in the future, hereafter (though not hitherto), henceforth, even now (though not till now); **not** ~, still not, not by this (or that) time; **as** ~, hitherto. **yet** *adj.* That is still such, still continuing. **yet** *conj.* In spite of that, nevertheless, notwithstanding.

yet·i, Yet·i (yĕt´ē) *ns.* (pl. **yet·i, Yet·i**). (pop. the "Abominable Snowman") Either of two unidentified animals occas. seen on high slopes of Himalayas, the one being prob. the red bear (*Ursus arctos isabellinus*) and the other possibly the langur monkey (*Presbytis entellus achilles*). [Tibetan *yeh* rocky area, *teh* animal]

yew (ū) *n.* Tree of coniferous genus *Taxus*, widely distributed in north temperate zone, esp. common European *T. baccata*, with heavy elastic wood and dense dark green foliage, freq. planted in cemeteries and regarded as symbol of sadness; wood of this, formerly used for making bows.

Y·gerne (ēgĕrn´) = IGRAINE.

Yid·dish (yĭd´ĭsh) *adj. & n.* (Of) the language used by Jews in Europe and America, a German dialect (orig. from Middle Rhine area) written in Hebrew letters, with an admixture of Hebrew elements and of words borrowed from several modern languages. [Ger. *jüdisch* Jewish]

yield (yēld) *v.* 1. Produce or return as fruit, profit, or result. 2. Surrender or make submission (*to*); concede; give way *to* persuasion, entreaty, etc., give consent; be inferior *to*; (of vehicle or traffic) give right of way (*to*); ~ **to**, give way under, be affected by, physical action or agent, as pressure, heat, etc. **yield** *n.* Amount yielded or produced, output, return.

Yin (yĭn) *n.* (Chin. philos.) Passive female principle of universe (opp. YANG).

yip (yĭp) *v.* (**yipped, yip·ping**) & *n.* = YELP.

yip·pee (yĭp´ē) *int.* Expression of delight or excitement.

yip·pie (yĭp´ē) *n.* Politically active student in late 1960s. [Y(outh) I(nternational) P(arty), after HIPPIE]

y·lang-y·lang (ē´lahng ē´lahng) *n.* Tree (*Cananga odorata*) of Malaya, Philippines, etc., with fragrant greenish-yellow flowers; perfume distilled from these.

YMCA, Y.M.C.A. *abbrevs.* YOUNG Men's Christian Association.

YMHA, Y.M.H.A. *abbrevs.* YOUNG Men's Hebrew Association.

yo·del (yō´del) *v.* (**-deled, -del·ing**, Brit. **-delled, -del·ling**). Sing or warble with interchange of ordinary and falsetto voice in manner of Swiss and Tyrolese mountaineers. ~ *n.* Yodeling cry; yodeling match. **yo´del·er** *n.*

yo·ga (yō´ga) *n.* Hindu system of ascetic practice, abstract meditation, and mental concentration as means of attaining union with Supreme Spirit. [Sansk. *yoga* union]

yo·gi (yō´gē) *n.* (pl. **-gis** pr. -gēz). (also **yo·gin** pr. yō´gĭn). Devotee of YOGA.

yo·gurt, yo·ghurt (yō´gert) *ns.* Semisolid junketlike or curdlike food prepared from milk fermented by addition of *Lactobacillus bulgaricus.* [Turk. *yoğurt*]

yoiks (yoiks), **hoiks** (hoiks) *ints.* Exclamation used in fox hunting to urge on hounds.

yoke (yōk) *n.* (pl. **yokes** for senses 1, 3–6; **yoke** for sense 2). 1. Contrivance, usu. curved or hollowed piece of wood over animals' necks, fastened at center to chain or trace by which plow or vehicle is drawn, used from ancient times for coupling two animals, esp. oxen, for drawing vehicle etc. 2. Pair *of* oxen etc. 3. Piece of wood shaped to fit person's shoulders and support pail etc. at each end. 4. (Rom. hist.) Uplifted yoke, or arch of three spears symbolizing it, under which defeated enemy was made to march; (fig.) sway, dominion, servitude; (fig.) bond of union, esp. marriage tie. 5. Upper part of bodice; upper part of garment, from which the rest hangs. 6. Object resembling a yoke in shape, esp. crossbar on which bell swings; crossbar of rudder to whose ends steering lines are fastened; coupling piece of two pipes discharging into one; kinds of coupling or controlling piece in machinery. ~ *v.t.* (**yoked, yok·ing**). Put yoke upon; harness (ox etc.) *to* vehicle or plow; (fig.) couple, unite, join, link (*together*). **yoke´less** *adj.*

yo·kel (yō´kel) *n.* (contempt.) Country bumpkin.

Yo·ko·ha·ma (yōkohah´ma). City and seaport on Tokyo Bay in E. central Honshu Island, Japan.

yolk (yōk) *n.* Yellow(ish) internal part of egg, containing vitellin and other proteins, surrounded by white and serving as nourishment for young before hatching; (biol.) corresponding part in any animal ovum; substance from which embryo is developed.

Yom Kip·pur (yŏm kĭp´er; *Heb.* yawm´ kēpoor´). (Jewish religion) The Day of Atonement, falling on the 10th day of the month Tishri (approx. October) and observed as a solemn fast day acc. to the rites described in Lev. 16.

yon (yŏn) *adj. & adv.* (also **yon·der** pr. yŏn´der). (archaic or dial.) (Situated) over there, at some distance (but within sight).

yore (yōr, yôr) *n.* **of** ~, in or of time long past, former(ly).

York¹ (yôrk). Name of English royal dynasty, descending from Edmund of Langley (1341–1402), fifth son of Edward III and (from 1385) first Duke of York; included Edward IV, Edward V, and Richard III; party of the white rose in the Wars of the Roses (see ROSE sense 2); united with the House of Lancaster when Henry VII married the eldest daughter of Edward IV (1486).

York² (yôrk), **Alvin Collum** (1887–1964). Known as Sgt. York, U.S. soldier and celebrated hero of World War I, who single-handedly captured 132 German soldiers and two machine gun nests.

Yorkshire (yôrk´shēr, -sher). Former county of northeast England; ~ **pudding**, baked batter, usu. eaten with meat, esp. roast beef; ~ **terrier**, small, long-haired terrier.

York·town (yôrk´town). Town on the shore of Chesapeake Bay, where, in 1781, the British army under Lord Cornwallis was blockaded by the American army and the French fleet.

Yo·ru·ba (yär´ōoba, -bah, yôr´) *n.* (pl. **-bas**, collect. **-ba**). Member, language, of a black people of the West African coast.

Yo·sem·i·te (yōsĕm´ĭtē). U.S.

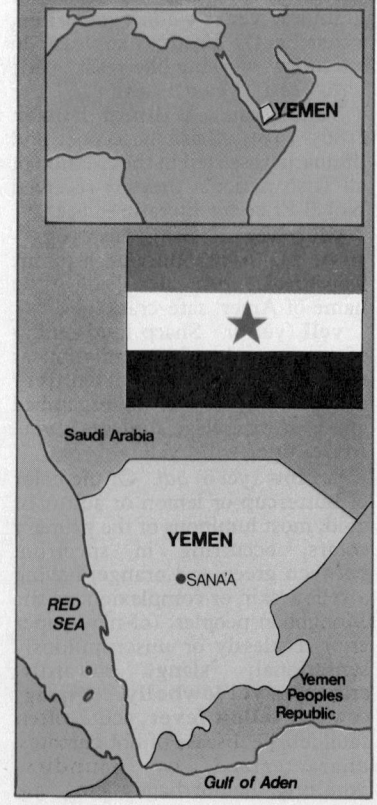

Facing: Elaborate decoration on houses in Sana'a, capital of the **Yemen Arab Republic.** *Together with the adjoining State (which was formerly the British colony of Aden), this is a barren region with few natural resources.*

YEMEN

Saudi Arabia

YEMEN

●SANA'A

RED SEA

Yemen Peoples Republic

Gulf of Aden

national park in E. California, named after the Yosemite River, which traverses it.

you (ū) *pron.* Second person sing. and pl. pronoun denoting person(s) or thing(s) addressed; (in general statements freq. =) one, anyone, everyone, a person.

you'd (ūd) *contr.* You had; you would.

you'll (ūl) *contr.* You will; you shall.

young (yŭng) *adj.* That has lived, existed, etc., a relatively short time; lately begun, formed, introduced, etc., recent, new; of young person(s) or youth; youthful, esp. having freshness or vigor of youth; ~ **blood**, young people; new vigorous ideas and action; **Y~ Chevalier, Y~ Pretender**: see PRETENDER; **Y~ Men's Christian Association** (YMCA), **Y~ Men's Hebrew Association** (YMHA), **Y~ Women's Christian Association** (YWCA), **Y~ Women's Hebrew Association** (YWHA), organizations for promoting spiritual, intellectual, and physical welfare of young people; **young turk**, member of any established political party or group who aggressively advocates reform: **Young Turks**, Turkish party that, in 1908, forced Sultan Abdul Hamid II to proclaim liberal constitution, and in 1909 deposed him in favor of his brother, Muhammad V. **young** *n.* Young people; young ones, offspring, of animals; **with** ~, pregnant. **young'ish** *adj.*

Young (yŭng), **Brigham** (1801–1877). MORMON leader; headed the Mormon migration to Utah (1847),

founded Salt Lake City, and was appointed governor of Utah (1851).

young·ling (yŭng′lĭng) *n.* Young person, animal, or plant.

young·ster (yŭng′ster) *n.* Young person, esp. young man; child, esp. boy.

youn·ker (yŭng′ker) *n.* (archaic) Young gentleman or nobleman; youngster.

your (ūr, yōr, yôr) *poss. pron.* Possessive case of YOU used as attributive adjective, belonging to, affecting, you; (archaic, now usu. derog.) that you know of, familiar.

you're (ūr) *contr.* You are.

yours (ūrz, yōrz, yôrz) *poss. pron.* Abs. and pred. form of YOUR; used in conventional ending to letter (~ **sincerely, truly**, etc.); ~ **truly**, (also, joc.) I; **what's ~?**, what will you drink?

your·self (ūrsĕlf′, yōr-, yôr-) *pron.* (pl. **-selves** pr. -sĕlvz′). Emphatic and reflexive form corresponding to YOU.

youth (ūth) *n.* (pl. **youths** pr. ūths, ūdhz). 1. Being young; early part of life, esp. adolescence; quality or condition characteristic of the young. 2. Young people collectively; ~ **hostel**, cheap lodging, usu. provided by an association, where young travelers put up for the night. 3. Young person, esp. young man between boyhood and maturity. **youth'ful** *adj.* **youth'ful·ly** *adv.* **youth'ful·ness** *n.*

yowl (yowl) *n. & v.* (Utter)

Below: Cattle market at Jajce, in the Bosnian region of Yugoslavia. Despite considerable diversity among its peoples, the country has remained united and independent.

loud wailing cry (as) of dog in distress, pain, etc., howl.

yo-yo (yō′yō) *n.* (pl. **yo-yos**) Kind of toy, small roughly spherical object with string attached to and wound around a deep central groove, made to fall and rise as its weight causes the string to unroll rapidly and roll up again. [orig. a trademark]

yr., yrs. *abbrevs.* Year(s); your(s).

Y'seult (ĭsōolt′) = ISEULT.

yt·ter·bi·um (ĭtēr′bēum) *n.* (chem.) Metallic element of rare-earth group; symbol Yb, at. no. 70, at. wt. 173.04. [f. *Ytterby* in Sweden]

yt·tri·um (ĭ′trēum) *n.* (chem.) Metallic element closely resembling ytterbium and found with it in gadolinite and other minerals; symbol Y, at. no. 39, at. wt. 88.9059.

Yü·an (ū′ahn′). Name of dynasty that ruled in China 1260–1368.

yu·an (ūahn′) *n.* (pl. **yu·an**) Principal monetary unit of China.

Yu·ca·tan (ūkatăn′). Peninsula in SE. Mexico between the Gulf of Mexico and the Gulf of Honduras.

yuc·ca (yŭk′a) *n.* Liliaceous plant of genus *Y* ~, native to Central America, Mexico, etc., with woody stem, a crown of usu. rigid narrow pointed leaves, and upright cluster of white bell-shaped flowers.

Yu·go·slav (ū′gōslahv) *n. & adj.* 1. (Native, inhabitant) of Yugoslavia. 2. (Member) of the southern group of Slavic peoples, comprising Serbs, Croats, and Slovenes. 3. (Branch) of the Slavonic languages spoken in Yugoslavia, Serbo-Croatian. **Yu·go·sla·vi·an** (ūgōslah′vēan) *adj.*

Yu·go·sla·vi·a (ūgōslah′vēa). State in the Balkans; formed under a monarchy in Dec., 1918, by the union of Bosnia, Croatia, Dalmatia, Montenegro, Serbia, and Slovenia, proclaimed a republic in Nov., 1945; capital, Belgrade. [f. Serbian = "South Slav"]

Yu·kon (ū′kŏn). 1. Territory of NW. Canada, constituted a separate political unit in 1898 with its capital at Dawson. 2. River of Canada flowing 1,770 mi. (2,848 km) through Alaska to the Bering Sea.

yule (ūl) *n.* (also **yule'tide**) Christmas season or festival; ~ **log**, large log burned on hearth at Christmas.

yum·my (yŭm′ē) *adj.* (**-mi·er, -mi·est**). (colloq.) Tasty, delicious.

yurt (ūrt) *n.* Mongolian nomads' circular skin- or felt-covered tent with collapsible frame.

YWCA, Y.W.C.A. *abbrevs.* Young Women's Christian Association.

YWHA, Y.W.H.A. *abbrevs.* Young Women's Hebrew Association.

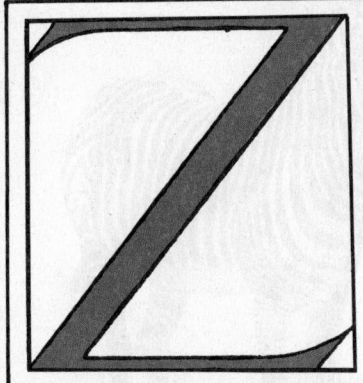

In Semitic and Greek, **Z, z** was represented in the alphabet but fell to the sixth or seventh position. Although at first incorporated into Latin, it was dropped for several centuries there was no use for this letter until the Romans needed to transcribe Greek words. Nevertheless, it was introduced to western European languages by the Romans.

Early Canaanite   Phoenician   Early Greek

Early Etruscan   Anglo-Saxon   Classical Latin

Z, z (zē; *Brit.* zĕd) (pl. **Z's, z's** or **Zs, zs**). 1. Twenty-sixth and last letter of modern English and 23rd of later Roman alphabet, derived through Latin and Greek from Phoenician and ancient Hebrew, I, Z, Z, and representing the voiced form of *s*, especially in loan words; referred to by Shakespeare in *King Lear* as "Thou whoreson zed; thou unnecessary letter"; **from A to Z**, from beginning to end, all through. 2. (alg. etc.) Symbol of third of series of unknown or variable quantities (cf. *x, y*). 3. Object etc. shaped like Z.

za·ba·glio·ne (zahbalyō'nē) *n.* Dessert consisting of a mixture of egg yolks, sugar, and Marsala. [It.]

Za·ire, Za·ïre (zah ēr'). Republic of W. central Africa; formerly Belgian Congo; independent since 1960; capital, Kinshasa; river in central Africa flowing 2,716 mi. (4,371 km), through Zaire to Atlantic Ocean. **Za·ir'e·an** *adj.* & *n.*

Zam·bi·a (zăm'bēa, zahm'-). Republic of central Africa; formerly Northern Rhodesia; member of the British Commonwealth, independent since 1964; capital, Lusaka.

za·ny (zā'nē) *n.* (pl. **-nies**). Buffoon, simpleton; comically crazy or bizarre person; (hist.) attendant on clown or acrobat awkwardly imitating his master's acts. ~ *adj.* (**-ni·er, -ni·est**). **za'ni·ly** *adv.* **za'ni·ness** *n.* [Fr. or It. *zani* servants acting as clowns in Commedia dell' Arte (Venetian form of *Gianni* = *Giovanni* John)]

Zan·zi·bar (zăn'zi·bär). Island off east coast of Africa, formerly (with Pemba and some adjacent islets) a sultanate and British protectorate; since 1963 forming, with Tanganyika, the republic of TANZANIA. **Zan·zi·ba·ri** (zăn-zi·bär'ē) *n.* Native, inhabitant, of Zanzibar.

zap (zăp) *v.t.* (**zapped, zap·ping**). (slang) Kill, destroy, with gun, electric shock, etc.

Za·pa·ta (zahpah'tah),

Emiliano (1877–1919). Mexican revolutionist; advocate of agrarian reforms.

Zar·a·thus·tra (zărathoo'stra). Old Iranian form of ZOROASTER.

zeal (zēl) *n.* Ardor, eagerness, enthusiasm, in pursuit of some end or in favor of person or cause. **zeal·ous** (zĕl'us) *adj.* **zeal'ous·ly** *adv.* **zeal'ous·ness** *n.*

Zea·land (zē'land). (Dan. *Sjoelland*) Group of islands in E. Denmark; largest island of this group, on which Copenhagen is situated.

zeal·ot (zĕl'ot) *n.* 1. Zealous person, fanatical enthusiast. 2. **Z ~**, (hist.) member of Jewish sect that aimed at Jewish theocracy over the world and fiercely resisted Romans until fall of Jerusalem in 70 A.D. **zeal'ot·ry** *n.*

ze·bra (zē'bra) *n.* (pl. **-bras**, collect. **-bra**). African equine mammal of genus *Equus*, related to horse and ass, covered with black or brownish stripes on whitish or buff ground; **ze'brawood**, (ornamentally striped wood of) any of various trees and shrubs, esp. *Connarus guianensis* of tropical Amer., used in cabinetmaking.

ze·bu (zē'bū) *n.* (pl. **-bus**,

A major world copper producer, and with reserves of other minerals, Zambia also exports tobacco grown on the high plateau. Zambia has one of the highest per capita incomes in Africa.

collect. **-bu**). Humped species of ox (*Bos indicus*), domesticated in India, China, Japan, and parts of Africa.

Zech. *abbrev.* Zechariah (Old Testament).

Zech·a·ri·ah (zĕkerī'a). Hebrew minor prophet; book of Old Testament containing his prophecies.

zed (zĕd) *n.* (Brit.) Letter Z, z.

Zed·e·ki·ah (zĕdekī'a). Son of Josiah, and the last king of Judah; he rebelled against Nebuchadnezzar and was carried off to Babylon into captivity (2 Kings 24–25, 2 Chron. 26).

zee (zē) *n.* (pl. **zees**). Letter Z, z.

Zeit·geist (tsīt'gīst) *n.* Spirit of the times; characteristic trend of thought, culture, etc., of period. [Ger. *Zeit* time, *Geist* spirit]

Zen (zĕn) *n.* Form of Buddhism emphasizing value of meditation and intuition.

Zend (zĕnd) *n.* 1. Pahlavi translation and exposition of the Avesta. 2. (archaic, erron.) Avestan. [f. ZEND-AVESTA, because Zend was erron. thought to denote the language of the books]

Zend-A·ves·ta (zĕndavĕs'ta) *n.* Avesta together with the Zend. [properly *Avestava-Zend*, text with interpretation]

Zen·ger (zĕng'ger), **John Peter** (1697–1746). German-born printer and publisher in Amer.; central

Believed to have originated in India, but to have dispersed through China and Africa, the **zebu** *has recently proved ideal for crossing with European cattle breeds for tropical conditions.*

Although a true member of the horse family, the **zebra** *has never proved suitable for domestication. It is found throughout Africa south of the Sahara and there are three species.*

figure in trial for seditious libel resulting from his attacks on British colonial administration; his acquittal established precedent for freedom of the press in America.

ze·nith (zē′nĭth; *Brit.* also zĕn′ĭth) *n.* Point of sky directly overhead (fig.) highest point or state, culmination, acme. **ze′-nith·al** *adj.* ~ **projection**, projection of a portion of the globe upon a plane tangent to it at its center, ensuring that all points have their true compass directions from the center of the map. [Arab. *samt* (*ar-rās*) way (over the head)]

Ze·no (zē′nō) (335–263 B.C.). Greek philosopher born at Citium, Cyprus, founder of STOIC School.

Zeph. *abbrev.* Zephaniah (Old Testament).

Zeph·a·ni·ah (zĕfanī′a) (7th c. B.C.). Hebrew minor prophet; book of Old Testament containing his prophecies.

zeph·yr (zĕf′er) *n.* 1. West wind, esp. personified; soft mild gentle wind or breeze. 2. Fine very thin woolen material; garment made from this.

zep·pe·lin (zĕp′elĭn) *n.* Cigar-shaped rigid dirigible airship of the type constructed by Count Ferdinand von Zeppelin in 1900.

ze·ro (zēr′ō) *n.* (pl. **-ros, -roes**). Figure 0, cipher; nothing, no quantity or number; point or line marked 0 on graduated scale, esp. in thermometer or other measuring instrument; temperature corresponding to zero of thermometer, degree of heat reckoned as 0° (in Celsius and Réaumur scales, freezing point of water; in Fahrenheit scale, 32° below this); (fig.) lowest point, bottom of scale, nullity, nonentity; zero hour; **absolute** ~, lowest possible temperature; temperature (approx. −273.1 °C) at which all substances have lost their heat and can be cooled no further; ~**-base**

budgeting, evaluation of all items in proposed budget each fiscal year to determine their usefulness without consideration of any prior budget; ~ **gravity**, (phys.) state in which gravitational attraction equals zero; weightlessness; ~ **hour**, hour at which any planned military operation is timed to begin; any crucial time; ~ **population growth**, condition in which a nation's population remains constant because birth and death rates are equal. **zero** *adj.* 1. Of, concerning, or being zero. 2. Lacking measurable value. 3. (aeron.) Of or pertaining to a cloud ceiling at or close to the ground and restricting vertical visibility; of or pertaining to visibility along the ground of less than a few feet. ~ *v.t.* (**-roed, -ro·ing**). Adjust (instrument etc.) to a zero point; ~ **in on**, take aim at (target etc.), focus attention on. [Arab. *çifr* cipher]

zest (zĕst) *n.* Piquancy, stimulating flavor; keen enjoyment or interest, relish, gusto. **zest′ful** *adj.* **zest′ful·ly** *adv.* **zest′ful·-ness** *n.* [Fr. *zeste* orange or lemon peel]

ze·ta (zā′ta, zē′-) *n.* Seventh (later sixth) letter of Greek alphabet (Z, ζ), corresponding to *z*.

zeug·ma (zōōg′ma) *n.* Figure of speech in which single word is made to apply to two or more words in sentence while failing to make sense with one of these, e.g. *with weeping eyes and hearts* (where sense requires *grieving hearts*). [Gk., = "yoking"]

Zeus (zōōs). (Gk. myth.) Supreme god, son of Cronus, whom he overthrew and succeeded; Zeus and his brothers divided the

universe by casting lots, Zeus obtaining heaven, Poseidon the sea, and Pluto the underworld; Zeus was regarded as the king and father of gods and men, with powers over all other deities save the Fates, as the dispenser of good and evil, giver of laws and defender of house and hearth; identified by the Romans with Jupiter.

zig·gu·rat (zĭg′ŏŏrăt) *n.* Pyramidal tower in Ancient Mesopotamia, surmounted by a temple and with stages or a continuous ramp to the summit.

zig·zag (zĭg′zăg) *n.* Series of short lines inclined at angles in alternate directions; something having such lines or sharp turns. ~ *adj.* Having form of zigzag; with abrupt alternate left and right turns. ~ *adv.* In zigzag manner or course. ~ *v.i.* (**-zagged, -zag·ging**). Move in zigzag course.

zilch (zĭlch) *n.* (slang) Nothing or zero.

zil·lion (zĭl′yon) *n.* (colloq.) Indefinite large number.

Zim·ba·bwe (zĭmbah′bwā). Formerly Rhodesia; country in central Africa bordered by Zambia, Botswana, the Transvaal, and Mozambique; territory colonized chiefly by British settlers; declared independence from Great Britain in 1965; republic established, 1970; name changed from Rhodesia in 1980; capital, Salisbury.

zinc (zĭngk) *n.* (chem.) Hard bluish-white metallic element, brittle at subnormal temperatures and above 200°C. but malleable between 100° and 150°C., used for roofing, galvanizing sheet iron, to make alloys, esp. brass, and in voltaic cells etc.; symbol Zn, at. no. 30, at. wt. 65.37; ~ **ointment**, white salve made from zinc oxide; **~ oxide**, antiseptic astringent powder used for skin irritations. **zinc** *v.t.* (**zincked, zinck·ing** or **zinced, zinc·ing**). Treat, coat, with zinc.

zing (zĭng) *n.* (colloq.) Vigor, energy. **~** *v.i.* (colloq.) Move swiftly and energetically.

zin·ni·a (zĭn′ēa) *n.* Tropical American composite plant with showy flowers, esp. *Z ~ elegans*, the common garden species. [J. G. *Zinn* (1727–59), German professor of medicine]

Zin·zen·dorf (tsĭn′tsendôrf), **Count Nicholas Ludwig von** (1700–60). German religious leader; founder of Moravian Church.

Zi·on (zī′on). Hill in Jerusalem, on which the city of David was built, and which became the center of Jewish life and worship; hence, the house of God, the Jewish religion, the Christian Church, the Heavenly Jerusalem or kingdom of God, a Christian (esp. Protestant) place of worship. **Zi·on·ism** (zī′onĭzem) *n.* Movement among modern Jews, founded 1897 by Theodor HERZL, that resulted in the reestablishment of Israel. **Zi′on·ist** *adj. & n.* (Adherent) of Zionism. [Heb. *Tsīyón* hill]

zip[1] (zĭp) *n.* (Movement accompanied by) light sharp sound as of tearing canvas, flying bullet, etc.; (fig.) energy, force, impetus; **~** (also **Z ~**) **code**, system of five-figure numbers used to identify postal delivery areas [*z*one *i*mprovement *p*lan]; **~ gun**, crude improvised pistol, usu. made from toy pistol or piece of pipe and having a firing pin activated by an elastic band. **zip** *v.* (**zipped, zip·ping**). 1. Move or go with sound of zip or with great force or rapidity. 2. Close or fasten (up) with zipper. **zip′py** *adj.* (**-pi·er, -pi·est**). (colloq.) Full of energy and vigor.

zip[2] (zĭp) *n.* (sports slang) Zero. **~** *v.t.* (**zipped, zip·ping**). (sports slang) Shut out, defeat, (opponent) by keeping him from scoring.

zip·per (zĭp′er) *n.* Fastening device consisting of two flexible strips with interlocking metal or plastic projections that can be closed or opened by a sliding clip pulled along them, also called slide fastener.

zir·ca·loy (zĕr′kaloi) *n.* Zirconium alloy used in water-cooled nuclear reactors as cladding for fuel rods.

zir·con (zĕr′kŏn) *n.* (min.) Zirconium silicate, occurring usu. in variously colored tetragonal crystals, of which translucent varieties are used as gems, esp. red or brownish kinds called HYACINTH. [Arab. *zarqŭn*]

Introduced to Europe from Mexico in 1796, the zinnia was rapidly adopted by gardeners because of its easy cultivation. There are now dwarf and tall varieties.

zir·co·ni·um (zerkō′nēum) *n.* (chem.) Metallic element obtained from zircon etc. as black powder or grayish crystalline substance; symbol Zr, at. no. 40, at. wt. 91.22.

zith·er (zĭth′er) *n.* Musical instrument somewhat like dulcimer with flat soundbox and numerous strings (up to 40), held horizontally and played with fingers and plectrum. **zith′er·ist** *n.*

zlo·ty (zlaw′tē) *n.* (pl. **-tys**).

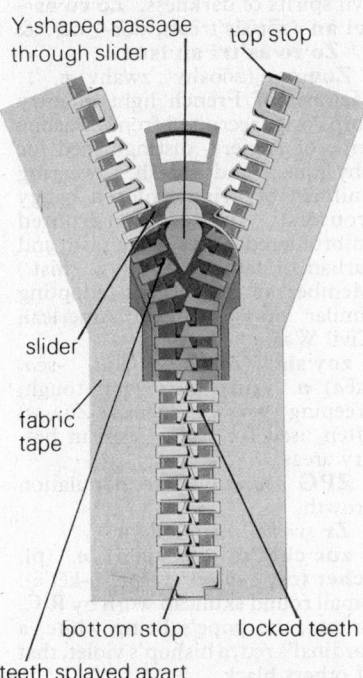

Y-shaped passage through slider

top stop

slider

fabric tape

bottom stop   locked teeth

teeth splayed apart

Principal monetary unit of Poland. [Pol., = "golden"]

Zn *symbol.* Zinc.

zo·di·ac (zō′dēăk) *n.* Belt of the heavens limited by lines about 8° from the ecliptic on each side, including all apparent positions of the sun and planets as known to the ancient astronomers, and divided into 12 equal parts (**signs of the ~**: ARIES, TAURUS, GEMINI, CANCER, LEO[1], VIRGO, LIBRA, SCORPIO, SAGITTARIUS, CAPRICORN, AQUARIUS, PISCES) each formerly containing the similarly named constellation but now by precession of equinoxes coinciding with the constellation that bears the name of the preceding sign (e.g. the constellation Aries is now in Taurus). [Gk. *zodiakos* (*kuklos*) (circle) of figures, f. *zōdion* dim. of *zōon* animal]

zo·di·a·cal (zōdī′akal) *adj.* Of, in, the zodiac; **~ light**, luminous tract of sky shaped like tall triangle occas. seen in east before sunrise or in west after sunset, esp. in tropics.

Zo·la (zō′la; *Fr.* zawlă′), **Émile** (1840–1902). French naturalistic novelist, author of *Germinal, The Earth, Nana*, etc.

Zöll·ner (tsawl′ner), **Johann Karl Friedrich** (1834–82). German physicist; **~ 's lines**, parallel lines made to appear to converge or diverge by series of short lines parallel to each other and intersecting each of them obliquely.

Zoll·ver·ein (tsawl′ferīn) *n.* Union of nations having common customs tariff against outsiders and usu. free trade with one another, specif., customs union formed (1834) among the German States under the leadership of Prussia. [Ger.]

zom·bie (pl. **-bies**), **zom·bi** (pl. **-bis**) (zŏm′bē) *ns.* 1. (in voodoo) Supernatural force or spirit reanimating and controlling corpse; corpse so reanimated. 2. Person thought to resemble zombie; mindless or will-less automaton.

zone (zōn) *n.* 1. (archaic) Girdle or belt; band or ring, esp. one of series of concentric or alternate stripes of color, light or shade, etc. 2. Each of five encircling regions, distinguished by differences of climate, into which surface of Earth is divided by tropics of Cancer and Capricorn and arctic circles. 3. Area enclosed between two concentric circles; any well-defined tract or region of more

*Although the **zip fastener** was conceived by a Chicago engineer in 1893, it took Dr Gideon Sundback, a Swede, to make it reliable. It was first used on U.S. army uniforms, but Schiaparelli convinced the public of its value in 1930.*

or less beltlike form; ~ **time**, standard time in a TIME zone. 4. (geol.) = HORIZON sense 2. 5. Any part of a town or region thought of as divided off from other parts for a particular purpose (esp. in town and country planning). 6. (math.) Part of surface of sphere enclosed between two parallel planes, or of surface of any solid of revolution contained between two planes perpendicular to the axis. 7. (cryst.) Series of faces in crystal having their lines of intersection parallel. **zoned, zon′al, zon·a·ry** (zō′nerē) *adjs.* **zon′al·ly** *adv.* **zone** *v.t.* (**zoned, zon·ing**). Mark, encircle, with a zone, divide into, assign to, zones (esp. in town and country planning). **zo·na·tion** (zōnā′shon) *n.* [f. L. *zona*, f. Gr. *zōnē* girdle]

zoo (zōō) *n.* (pl. **zoos**). Zoological gardens; see ZOOLOGY.

zoo- *comb. form.* Pertaining to animals.

zo·o·ge·og·ra·phy (zōōjēŏg′rafē) *n.* (Study of) the geographical distribution of animals. **zo·o·ge·og′ra·pher** *n.* **zo·o·ge·o·graph·i·cal** (zōōjēogrăf′ĭkal) *adj.*

zo·og·ra·phy (zōōg′rafē) *n.* Descriptive zoology. **zo·og′ra·pher** *n.* **zo·o·graph·i·cal** (zōōgrăf′ĭkal) *adj.*

zo·oid (zō′oid) *n.* Individual member of a colony of animals joined together.

zo·ol·o·gy (zōōl′ojē) *n.* (pl. **-gies**). Branch of biology dealing with the animal kingdom and the physiology, classification, habits, etc., of its members. **zo·o·l·o·gist** *n.* **zo·o·log·i·cal** (zōōlŏj′ĭkal) *adj.* **Z~ Gardens**, orig. gardens of London Zoological Society, housing the society's collection of wild animals; any garden or park in which wild animals are kept for public exhibition. **zo·o·log·ic** *adj.* **zo·o·log·i·cal·ly** *adv.*

zoom (zōōm) *v.* 1. Make loud low-pitched buzzing sound. 2. (of aircraft) Climb for short time at high speed and very steep angle; make (aircraft) climb thus. 3. (cinemat.) Cause (image) to seem to approach or recede from viewer. ~ *n.* Act of zooming; ~ **lens**, (photog.) lens that, by variation of focal length, enables continuous alteration from long shot to close-up. [imit.]

zo·o·mor·phic (zōōmôr′fĭk) *adj.* Representing or imitating animal forms; having form of an animal; attributing form or nature of animal to something, esp. deity.

zo·o·phyte (zō′ofīt) *n.* Any of various animals of low organization, usu. fixed, and freq. resembling plants or flowers in having branched or radiating structure, as crinoids, sea anemones, corals, sponges, etc. **zo·o·phyt·ic**

Originally designed more for public entertainment than for an animal's comfort, zoos today are trying to strike a balance between the two.

(zōōfĭt′ĭk) *adj.*

zo·o·spore (zō′ospōr, -spor) *n.* Spore occurring in certain algae, fungi, etc., having power of locomotion.

Zo·ro·as·ter (zōrōăs′ter, zōr-). (also **Zarathustra**) Persian believed to have lived in the 6th c. B.C., founder of the dualistic religious system of the Magi and ancient Persia, which survives among the Parsees; its scriptures, the ZEND-AVESTA, teach that Ormazd, lord of goodness and light and creator of mankind, is ceaselessly at war with Ahriman and the evil spirits of darkness. **Zo·ro·as·tri·an** (zōrōăs′trēan, zōr-) *adj.* & *n.* **Zo·ro·as′tri·an·ism** *n.*

Zou·ave (zōōahv′, zwahv) *n.* 1. Member of French light infantry corps orig. recruited from Zouaoua tribe of Algiers, distinguished for physique and dash, wearing uniform of bright-colored baggy trousers, short open-fronted embroidered jacket, wide sash, and turban or tasseled cap. 2. (hist.) Member of any corps adopting similar dress, esp. in American Civil War.

zoy·sia (zoi′sha, -zha, -sēa, -zēa) *n.* Any of several tough, creeping grasses (genus *Zoysia*) often used for lawns, esp. in hot, dry areas.

ZPG *abbrev.* Zero population growth.

Zr *symbol.* Zirconium.

zuc·chet·to (zōōkĕt′ō) *n.* (pl. **-chet·tos, -chet·ti** pr. -kĕt′ē). Small round skullcap worn by R.C. priests, the pope's being white, a cardinal's red, a bishop's violet, that of others black.

zuc·chi·ni (zōōkē′nē) *n.* (pl. **-ni,**

-nis). Summer squash that resembles a cucumber.

Zui·der Zee, Zuy·der Zee (zī′der zē′; *Du.* zöï′der zā′). Large shallow inlet of the North Sea in the Netherlands, the reclamation of which was begun in 1924 for the purpose of forming a new province. [Du., = "southern sea"]

Zu·lu (zōō′lōō) *n.* (pl. **-lus**, collect. **-lu**) & *adj.* (Member, language) of a South African Bantu people inhabiting NE. part of Natal; **Zu·lu·land** (zōō′lōōlănd), region inhabited by Zulus, annexed to Natal in 1897.

Zu·ñi (zōō′nyē, -nē, sōō′-) *n.* (pl. **-ñis**, collect. **-ñi**). (Member, language) of a New Mexico tribe of Pueblo Indians. **Zu′ñi·an** *adj.*

zwie·back (zwī′băk, -bahk, zwē′-, swī′-) *n.* Kind of biscuit or sweet cake toasted in slices.

Zwing·li (zwĭng′lē), **Ulrich** or **Huldreich** (1484–1531). Swiss religious reformer; his doctrines contain elements of Reformed as distinguished from Lutheran doctrine. **Zwing′li·an** *adj.* & *n.* (Follower) of Zwingli. **Zwing′li·an·ism** *n.*

zwit·ter·i·on (tsvĭt′erīon) *n.* Molecule or ion having separate positively and negatively charged groups.

zy·go·dac·tyl (zīgodăk′tĭl, zīgo-) *adj.* & *n.* (Bird) with toes arranged in pairs, two before and two behind, e.g. parrot.

zy·go·ma (zīgō′ma, zī-) *n.* (pl. **-ma·ta** pr. -m*ata*). Bony arch on each side of skull of vertebrates, joining cranial and facial bones, and consisting of cheekbone and its connections. **zy·go·mat·ic** (zīgomăt′ĭk, zīgo-) *adj.*

zy·go·spore (zī′gospōr, -spor, zīg′o-) *n.* (in some algae and fungi) Spore or germ cell arising from fusion of two similar cells.

zy·gote (zī′gōt, zĭg′ot) *n.* (biol.) Cell arising from union of two reproductive cells or gametes, fertilized ovum. **zy·got·ic** (zīgŏt′ĭk, zī-) *adj.*

zy·mase (zī′mās) *n.* (biochem.) Any of a group of enzymes converting glucose and a few other carbohydrates, in the presence of oxygen, into carbon dioxide and water, or, in the absence of oxygen, into alcohol and carbon dioxide, or into lactic acid.

zy·mol·y·sis (zīmŏl′ĭsĭs) *n.* Action of enzymes, changes produced by this. **zy·mo·lyt·ic** (zīm*o*lĭt′ĭk) *adj.*

zy·mo·sis (zīmō′sĭs) *n.* (pl. **-ses**). Fermentation; zymotic disease. **zy·mot·ic** (zīmŏt′ĭk) *adj.* Of fermentation.

zy·mur·gy (zī′mĕrjē) *n.* Branch of applied chemistry dealing with science of wine making, brewing, and distilling.

APPENDIX I

Presidents of the United States of America

1.	George Washington	1789
2.	John Adams	1797
3.	Thomas Jefferson	1801
4.	James Madison	1809
5.	James Monroe	1817
6.	John Quincy Adams	1825
7.	Andrew Jackson	1829
8.	Martin Van Buren	1837
9.	William H. Harrison	1841
10.	John Tyler	1841
11.	James K. Polk	1845
12.	Zachary Taylor	1849
13.	Millard Fillmore	1850
14.	Franklin Pierce	1853
15.	James Buchanan	1857
16.	Abraham Lincoln	1861
17.	Andrew Johnson	1865
18.	Ulysses S. Grant	1869
19.	Rutherford B. Hayes	1877
20.	James A. Garfield	1881
21.	Chester A. Arthur	1881
22.	Grover Cleveland	1885
23.	Benjamin Harrison	1889
24.	Grover Cleveland	1893
25.	William McKinley	1897
26.	Theodore Roosevelt	1901
27.	William H. Taft	1909
28.	T. Woodrow Wilson	1913
29.	Warren G. Harding	1921
30.	Calvin Coolidge	1923
31.	Herbert C. Hoover	1929
32.	Franklin D. Roosevelt	1933
33.	Harry S. Truman	1945
34.	Dwight D. Eisenhower	1953
35.	John F. Kennedy	1961
36.	Lyndon B. Johnson	1963
37.	Richard M. Nixon	1969
38.	Gerald Ford	1974
39.	James Carter	1977
40.	Ronald Reagan	1980–

APPENDIX II

Prime Ministers of Canada since 1867

1.	Sir John A. Macdonald	1867–1873
2.	Alexander Mackenzie	1873–1878
3.	Sir John A. Macdonald	1878–1891
4.	Sir John J. Abbott	1891–1892
5.	Sir John S. D. Thompson	1892–1894
6.	Sir Mackenzie Bowell	1894–1896
7.	Sir Charles Tupper	1896
8.	Sir Wilfrid Laurier	1896–1911
9.	Sir Robert L. Borden	1911–1917
10.	Sir Robert L. Borden	1917–1920
11.	Arthur Meighen	1920–1921
12.	William Lyon Mackenzie King	1921–1926
13.	Arthur Meighen	1926
14.	William Lyon Mackenzie King	1926–1930
15.	Richard Bedford Bennett	1930–1935
16.	William Lyon Mackenzie King	1935–1948
17.	Louis Stephen St. Laurent	1948–1957
18.	John G. Diefenbaker	1957–1963
19.	Lester Bowles Pearson	1963–1968
20.	Pierre Elliott Trudeau	1968–1979
21.	Charles Joseph Clark	1979–1980
22.	Pierre Elliott Trudeau	1980–1984
23.	John Napier Turner	1984
24.	Martin Brian Mulroney	1984–

APPENDIX III

Rulers of England and the United Kingdom

House of Normandy

William I (the Conqueror)	1066–1087
William II	1087–1100
Henry I	1100–1135
Stephen	1135–1154

House of Plantagenet

Henry II	1154–1189
Richard I	1189–1199
John	1199–1216
Henry III	1216–1272
Edward I	1272–1307
Edward II	1307–1327
Edward III	1327–1377
Richard II	1377–1399

House of Lancaster

Henry IV	1399–1413
Henry V	1413–1422
Henry VI	1422–1461

House of York

Edward IV	1461–1483
Edward V	1483
Richard III	1483–1485

House of Tudor

Henry VII	1485–1509
Henry VIII	1509–1547
Edward VI	1547–1553
Mary I	1553–1558
Elizabeth I	1558–1603

House of Stuart

James I of England and VI of Scotland	1603–1625
Charles I	1625–1649

Commonwealth (declared 1649)

Oliver Cromwell, Lord Protector	1653–1658
Richard Cromwell	1658–1659

House of Stuart

Charles II	1660–1685
James II	1685–1688
William III and Mary II (Mary d. 1694)	1689–1702
Anne	1702–1714

House of Hanover

George I	1714–1727
George II	1727–1760
George III	1760–1820
George IV	1820–1830
William IV	1830–1837
Victoria	1837–1901

House of Saxe-Coburg-Gotha

Edward VII	1901–1910

House of Windsor

George V	1910–1936
Edward VIII	1936
George VI	1936–1952
Elizabeth II	1952–

APPENDIX IV

Prime Ministers of Great Britain

Sir Robert Walpole	1730–1741
Earl of Wilmington	1741–1743
Henry Pelham	1743–1754
Duke of Newcastle	1754–1756
Duke of Devonshire	1756–1757
Duke of Newcastle	1757–1762
Earl of Bute	1762–1763
George Grenville	1763–1765
Marquis of Rockingham	1765–1766
Earl of Chatham	1766–1768
Duke of Grafton	1768–1770
Lord North	1770–1782
Marquis of Rockingham	1782
Earl of Shelburne	1782–1783
Duke of Portland	1783
William Pitt	1783–1801
Henry Addington	1801–1804
William Pitt	1804–1806
Lord William Grenville	1806–1807
Duke of Portland	1807–1809
Spencer Perceval	1809–1812
Earl of Liverpool	1812–1827
George Canning	1827
Viscount Goderich	1827–1828
Duke of Wellington	1828–1830
Earl Grey	1830–1834
Viscount Melbourne	1834
Duke of Wellington	1834
Sir Robert Peel	1834–1835
Viscount Melbourne	1835–1841
Sir Robert Peel	1841–1846
Lord John Russell	1846–1852
Earl of Derby	1852
Earl of Aberdeen	1852–1855
Viscount Palmerston	1855–1858
Earl of Derby	1858–1859
Viscount Palmerston	1859–1865
Earl Russell	1865–1866
Earl of Derby	1866–1868
Benjamin Disraeli	1868
William Ewart Gladstone	1868–1874
Benjamin Disraeli Earl of Beaconsfield	1874–1880
William Ewart Gladstone	1880–1885
Marquis of Salisbury	1885–1886
William Ewart Gladstone	1886
Marquis of Salisbury	1886–1892
William Ewart Gladstone	1892–1894
Earl of Rosebery	1894–1895
Marquis of Salisbury	1895–1902
Arthur James Balfour	1902–1905
Sir Henry Campbell -Bannerman	1905–1908
Herbert Henry Asquith	1908–1916
David Lloyd George	1916–1922
Andrew Bonar Law	1922–1923
Stanley Baldwin	1923–1924
James Ramsay MacDonald	1924
Stanley Baldwin	1924–1929
James Ramsay MacDonald	1929–1935
Stanley Baldwin	1935–1937
Neville Chamberlain	1937–1940
Winston Spencer Churchill	1940–1945
Clement Richard Attlee	1945–1951
Sir Winston Spencer Churchill	1951–1955
Sir Anthony Eden	1955–1957
Harold Macmillan	1957–1963
Sir Alexander Douglas-Home	1963–1964
Harold Wilson	1964–1970
Edward Heath	1970–1974
Harold Wilson	1974–1976
James Callaghan	1976–1979
Margaret Thatcher	1979–

APPENDIX V
WEIGHTS AND MEASURES
MEASURES OF WEIGHT

In scientific usage the units of weight are units of mass

Avoirdupois weight

	grain	0·0648 gramme
16 drams	dram	1·772 grammes
16 ounces or 7000 grains	ounce (oz)	28·35 grammes
14 pounds	pound (lb)	0·454 kilogramme
28 pounds	stone	6·35 kilogrammes
25 pounds	quarter	12·7 kilogrammes
4 quarters or 112 pounds	U.S. quarter	11·34 kilogrammes
4 quarters or 100 pounds	hundredweight (cwt)	50·80 kilogrammes
20 hundredweight or 2240 pounds	U.S. hundredweight (cwt)	45·36 kilogrammes
20 hundredweight or 2000 pounds	long ton	1016·05 kilogrammes
	U.S. short ton	907·19 kilogrammes

Troy weight

	grain	0·0648 gramme
24 grains	pennyweight (dwt)	1·555 grammes
20 pennyweights or 480 grains	ounce	31·1035 grammes
12 ounces or 5760 grains	pound (not a legal measure but used for convenience)	373·27 grammes

Apothecaries' weight

	grain	0·0648 gramme
20 grains	scruple	1·296 grammes
3 scruples or 60 grains	drachm or (U.S.) dram	3·888 grammes
8 drachms or 480 grains	ounce (= troy ounce)	31·1035 grammes

Apothecaries' fluid measure

	minim	0·0059 centilitre
60 minims	fluid drachm	0·355 centilitre
8 fluid drachms	fluid ounce	0·284 decilitre
20 fluid ounces	pint	0·568 litre
8 pints	gallon	4·546 litres

BRITISH MEASURES OF CAPACITY

	fluid ounce	0·284 decilitre
	gill	1·42 decilitres
4 gills or 20 fluid ounces	pint	0·568 litre
2 pints	quart	1·136 litres
4 quarts	gallon (imperial gallon, 277·274 cubic inches)	4·546 litres
2 gallons	peck	9·092 litres
4 pecks or 8 gallons	bushel	0·364 hectolitre
8 bushels	quarter	2·909 hectolitres

AMERICAN MEASURES OF CAPACITY

Liquid measure

	minim	0·059 millilitre
60 minims	fluid dram	3·6966 millilitres
8 fluid drams	fluid ounce	0·296 decilitre
16 fluid ounces	pint	0·473 litre
2 pints	quart	0·946 litre
4 quarts	gallon (Winchester or wine gallon, 231 cubic inches)	3·785 litres

Dry measure

	pint	0·551 litre
2 pints	quart	1·101 litres
8 quarts	peck	8·809 litres
4 pecks	bushel	35·328 litres

LINEAR MEASURES

	inch	2·54 centimetres (4 in = approx. 10 cm)
7·92 inches	link	0·201 metre
12 inches	foot	0·3048 metre
3 feet	yard	0·9144 metre
6 feet	fathom	1·8288 metres
5½ yards	rod, pole, or perch	5·0292 metres
22 yards or 4 rods or 100 links	chain	20·11678 metres
10 chains or 220 yards	furlong	201·1678 metres
8 furlongs or 1760 yards or 5280 feet	statute mile	1·60934 kilometres (5 miles = approx. 8 km.)
6080 feet	nautical mile	1·8533 kilometres

SQUARE MEASURES

144 square inches	square inch	6·452 square centimetres
9 square feet	square foot	0·0929 square metre
30¼ square yards	square yard	0·8361 square metre
40 square rods	square rod, pole, or perch	25·29 square metres
4 roods or 10 square chains or 4 840 square yards	rood	0·101 hectare
	acre	0·405 hectare
640 acres or 3 097 600 square yards	square mile	2·59 square kilometres

CUBIC MEASURES

1728 cubic inches	cubic inch	16·387 cubic centimetres
27 cubic feet	cubic foot	0·0283 cubic metre
100 cubic feet	cubic yard	0·765 cubic metre
	register ton	2·832 cubic metres

METRIC SYSTEM

Measures of length

1000 microns	millimetre	0·039 inch
10 millimetres	centimetre	0·3937 inch
10 centimetres	decimetre	3·397 inches
10 decimetres	metre	39·37 inches
10 metres	decametre	32 feet 10 inches (nearly 11 yards)
10 decametres	hectometre	328 feet 1 inch (about 1/16 mile)
10 hectometres or 1000 metres	kilometre	0·621 mile (roughly ⅝), or 3280 feet 10 inches

Square measures

100 square millimetres	square centimetre	0·155 square inch
100 square centimetres	square decimetre	15·50 square inches
100 square decimetres	square metre or centiare	1·196 square yards or 1550 square inches
100 square metres	are	119·6 square yards
100 acres	hectare	2·4711 acres

Cubic measures

1000 cubic millimetres	cubic centimetre	0·061 cubic inch
1000 cubic centimetres	cubic decimetre	61·024 cubic inches
1000 cubic decimetres	cubic metre or stere	35·31 cubic feet or 1·308 cubic yards
100 cubic metres	hectostere	130·8 cubic yards

Measures of capacity

	millilitre	16·894 minims
10 millilitres	centilitre	2 fluid drachms 49 minims
10 centilitres	decilitre	3 fluid ounces, 4 drachms, 10·4 minims (about 3½ fluid ounces)
10 decilitres	litre	1·7598 pints or about 35 fluid ounces
10 litres	decalitre	2·2 imperial gallons
10 decalitres	hectolitre	22 imperial gallons

Measures of weight

	milligramme	0·015 grain
10 milligrammes	centigramme	0·154 grain (about 1/7)
10 centigrammes	decigramme	1·543 grains
10 decigrammes	gramme	15·432 grains or 0·035 ounce
10 grammes	decagramme	0·353 ounce (about ⅓)
10 decagrammes	hectogramme	3·527 ounces
10 hectogrammes or 1000 grammes	kilogramme	2·205 pounds (5 kilogrammes = approx. 11 pounds)
100 kilogrammes	quintal	220·46 pounds or 1·968 hundredweights
1000 kilogrammes	tonne	2204·6 pounds

ANGULAR MEASURES

60 seconds	second (″)
60 minutes	minute (′)
90 degrees	degree (°)
4 quadrants or	right angle or quadrant
360 degrees	circle

TEMPERATURES

CENTIGRADE FAHRENHEIT

Centigrade	Fahrenheit
—17·8°	0°
—10°	14°
0°	32°
10°	50°
20°	68°
30°	86°
40°	104°
50°	122°
60°	140°
70°	158°
80°	176°
90°	194°
100°	212°

To convert Centigrade into Fahrenheit: multiply by 9, divide by 5, and add 32.

To convert Fahrenheit into Centigrade: subtract 32, multiply by 5, and divide by 9.

APPENDIX VI

THE CHEMICAL ELEMENTS

Atomic number		Atomic weight	Symbol
1	Hydrogen	1·0080	H
2	Helium	4·00260	He
3	Lithium	6·941	Li
4	Beryllium	9·01218	Be
5	Boron	10·811	B
6	Carbon	12·011	C
7	Nitrogen	14·0067	N
8	Oxygen	15·9994	O
9	Fluorine	18·9984	F
10	Neon	20·179	Ne
11	Sodium	22·9898	Na
12	Magnesium	24·305	Mg
13	Aluminium	26·9815	Al
14	Silicon	28·086	Si
15	Phosphorus	30·9738	P
16	Sulphur	32·06	S
17	Chlorine	35·453	Cl
18	Argon	39·948	Ar
19	Potassium	39·102	K
20	Calcium	40·98	Ca
21	Scandium	44·9559	Sc
22	Titanium	47·90	Ti
23	Vanadium	50·941	V
24	Chromium	51·996	Cr
25	Manganese	54·9380	Mn
26	Iron	55·847	Fe
27	Cobalt	58·9332	Co
28	Nickel	58·71	Ni
29	Copper	63·546	Cu
30	Zinc	65·37	Zn
31	Gallium	69·72	Ga
32	Germanium	72·59	Ge
33	Arsenic	74·9216	As
34	Selenium	78·96	Se
35	Bromine	79·904	Br

36	Krypton	83·80	Kr
37	Rubidium	85·678	Rb
38	Strontium	87·62	Sr
39	Yttrium	88·9059	Y
40	Zirconium	91·22	Zr
41	Niobium	92·9064	Nb
42	Molybdenum	95·94	Mo
43	Technetium	98·9062	Tc
44	Ruthenium	101·07	Ru
45	Rhodium	102·9055	Rh
46	Palladium	106·4	Pd
47	Silver	107·868	Ag
48	Cadmium	112·40	Cd
49	Indium	114·82	In
50	Tin	118·69	Sn
51	Antimony	121·75	Sb
52	Tellurium	127·60	Te
53	Iodine	126·9045	I
54	Xenon	131·30	Xe
55	Caesium	132·9054	Cs
56	Barium	137·34	Ba
57	Lanthanum	138·9055	La
58	Cerium	140·12	Ce
59	Praesodymium	140·9077	Pr
60	Neodymium	144·24	Nd
61	Promethium	147*	Pm
62	Samarium	150·4	Sm
63	Europium	151·96	Eu
64	Gadolinium	157·25	Gd
65	Terbium	158·9254	Tb
66	Dysprosium	162·50	Dy
67	Holmium	164·9340	Ho
68	Erbium	167·26	Er
69	Thulium	168·9342	Tm
70	Ytterbium	173·04	Yb

71	Lutetium	174·97	Lu
72	Hafnium	178·49	Hf
73	Tantalum	180·9479	Ta
74	Tungsten	183·85	W
75	Rhenium	186·2	Re
76	Osmium	190·2	Os
77	Iridium	192·2	Ir
78	Platinum	195·09	Pt
79	Gold	196·9665	Au
80	Mercury	200·59	Hg
81	Thallium	204·371	Tl
82	Lead	207·12	Pb
83	Bismuth	208·9806	Bi
84	Polonium	210*	Po
85	Astatine	211*	At
86	Radon	222*	Rn
87	Francium	223*	Fr
88	Radium	226·0254	Ra
89	Actinium	227*	Ac
90	Thorium	232·0381	Th
91	Protactinium	231·0359	Pa
92	Uranium	238·029	U
93	Neptunium	237·0482	Np
94	Plutonium	239*	Pu
95	Americium	241*	Am
96	Curium	242*	Cm
97	Berkelium	243*	Bk
98	Californium	244*	Cf
99	Einsteinium	253*	E
100	Fermium	256*	Fn
101	Mendelevium†		Me
102	Nobelium†		No
103	Lawrencium†		Lw

† Isotopic weight not yet known.

* Principal isotope.